The New Partridge Dictionary of Slang and Unconventional English

First published in 1937, Eric Partridge's brilliant magnum opus, *The Dictionary of Slang and Unconventional English*, set new standards in the spirited and intelligent appraisal of slang.

This two-volume *The New Partridge Dictionary of Slang and Unconventional English* takes on the mantle to present a definitive record of the slang of the last sixty years. Containing over 65,000 entries, the slang and unconventional English of the English-speaking world since 1945 is detailed with the same thorough, intense and lively scholarship that characterised Partridge's own work.

Editors **Tom Dalzell** and **Terry Victor** have worked to continue the Partridge tradition in an evolutionary and accessible way. American and British English slang are given equal prominence and the dictionary also boasts entries from Australia, New Zealand, Canada, India, South Africa, Ireland, the Caribbean and other countries where English is spoken. Entries are given a published source and, where possible, an early or significant example of the term's use in print.

Like its forebear, *The New Partridge Dictionary of Slang and Unconventional English* is a monumental piece of work infused with humour and learning – a prize for anyone with a love of, and a fascination with, language.

The New Partridge Dictionary of Slang and Unconventional English

Volume I: A – I

Tom Dalzell (Senior Editor)
and
Terry Victor (Editor)

Routledge
Taylor & Francis Group
LONDON AND NEW YORK

First published 2006
by Routledge
2 Park Square, Milton Park, Abingdon, Oxon OX14 4RN

Simultaneously published in the USA and Canada
by Routledge
270 Madison Ave, New York, NY 10016

Routledge is an imprint of the Taylor & Francis Group

Typeset in Parisine-Regular by the Alden Group, Oxford
Printed in the UK by Bell and Bain Ltd, Glasgow

British Library Cataloguing in Publication Data
A catalogue record for this book is available from the British Library

Library of Congress Cataloging in Publication Data
A catalog record has been requested

ISBN10: 0-415-21258-8 ISBN13: 978-0-415-21258-8 (2 volume set)
ISBN10: 0-415-25937-1 ISBN13: 978-0-415-25937-8 (volume I)
ISBN10: 0-415-25938-X ISBN13: 978-0-415-25938-5 (volume II)

CONTENTS

Volume I

CONTRIBUTORS

Dr Richard Allsopp, a native of Guyana, is Director of the Caribbean Lexicography Project and former Reader in English Language and Linguistics, University of the West Indies, Cave Hill, Barbados. He edited the *Dictionary of Caribbean English Usage*.

Dr Dianne Bardsley is Manager of the New Zealand Dictionary Centre at Victoria University of Wellington. Her PhD involved the compilation and analysis of a rural New Zealand English lexicon from the years 1842–2002. She was contributing editor for the *New Zealand Oxford Dictionary* and is currently leading several New Zealand lexicography research projects.

James Lambert has worked primarily in Australian English, specialising in slang in general and Australian slang in particular. He was assistant editor of *The Macquarie Dictionary of New Words* and general editor of *The Macquarie Book of Slang* and *The Macquarie Slang Dictionary*.

John Loftus manages the online archive at www.hiberno-english.com. He was a senior research assistant on *A Dictionary of Hiberno-English*.

Lewis Poteet is a leading Canadian authority on slang and dialect. He has written extensively about language in Canada's maritime provinces and edited *Car & Motorcycle Slang, Hockey Talk, Plane Talk, Car Talk* and *Cop Talk*.

John Williams served as a consulting lexicographer on this project. He has been contributing to general language dictionaries, both monolingual and bilingual, for more than 20 years. He is the author of three children's dictionaries, as well as several articles on the practice of lexicography.

Structure of the entries

ash *noun*
marijuana *UK, 1990s*
The dropped 'h' of the London accent causes a punning variant on **HASH**.

ash *verb*
to drop cigarette ash *AUSTRALIA, 1930*
- I carefully ashed my cigarette on the bed post, wondering what to say.—Frank Moorhouse, *Futility and other animals*, p. 19, 1969
- Women whose clothes are obviously Works of Art – Heaven help you if you laugh hysterically when someone ashes on them and they catch fire.—Ignatius Jones, *True Hip*, p. 127, 1990

ashcan *noun*
1 a depth charge *US, 1918*
- We had ashcans on the stern of the vessel.—*New York Times*, p. 29, 1st January 1987
- —J.E. Lighter, *Historical Dictionary of American Slang*, p. 36, 1994

2 a small, powerful, cylindrical firecracker *US, 1970*
- —Frederic G. Cassidy, *Dicitonary of American Regional English, Volume 1*, p. 95, 1985

3 in the television and film industries, an arc light roughly shaped like a rubbish bin *US, 1942*
- —Wilfred Granville, *The Theater Dictionary*, p. 8, 1952

Ashcan City *nickname*
during the Korean war, a US Army processing centre eight miles from Inchon *US*
From ASCOM (*A*rmy *S*ervice *Com*mand) to 'Ascom City' to 'Ashcan City'.
- —Paul Dickson, *War Slang*, p. 236, 1994

as he has to be *adverb*
used as an intensifier *US*
Follows an adjective, such as 'fine as he has to be'.
- —Anna Scotti and Paul Young, *Buzzwords*, p. 50, 1997

ashes *noun*
marijuana *US, 1977*
- —Richard A. Spears, *The Slang and Jargon of Drugs and Drink*, p. 15, 1986
- —Mike Haskins, *Drugs*, p. 286, 2003

▸ **get your ashes hauled**
to be brought to ejaculation *US, 1906*
- Then he said, "Kimberly, it's very plain to me what you need. You need to get your ashes hauled. This morning. If you went out and got your ashes hauled right now, it'd do wonders for you."—Frederic Wakeman, *The Hucksters*, p. 88, 1946
- They ain't been in my place yet to get their ashes hauled[.]—Chester Himes, *A Rage in Harlem*, p. 47, 1957
- I repeat this one bit of smut only to show what sort of fellows I've been forced to live with – they're going to get their ashes hauled!—Robert Gover, *One Hundred Dollar Misunderstanding*, p. 10, 1961
- "Get the old ashes hauled." Billy and Mule look at each other. "Ashes hauled?" "That's an expression, kinda like, that means, you know, to do it, get it done." —Darryl Ponicsan, *The Last Detail*, p. 119, 1970
- Even the company shitsack got his ashes hauled while we were there. —Larry Heinemann, *Paco's Story*, p. 126, 1986
- This one was set up by Lorrie, her ditzy pal from The Fabric Barn, who knew a guy who had a friend who'd been 'out of circulation for a while' (whatever that means – prison if you ask me) and wanted his ashes hauled in the worst kind of way.—Armistead Maupin, *Maybe the Moon*, p. 222, 1992

ashtray *noun*
the desert *US*
Gulf war usage.
- —*American Speech*, p. 383, Winter 1991: 'Among the new words'

Asian two-step *noun*
any highly venomous snake encountered in the jungles of Southeast Asia *US, 1966*
From the belief that the venom will kill the victim within two steps of the bite.
- —J.E. Lighter, *Historical Dictionary of American Slang*, p. 37, 1994

as if!
used as a humorous expression of extreme skepticism *US*
- —Connie Eble (Editor), *UNC-CH Campus Slang*, p. 1, March 1981
- BEJAMIN: Did you really think I wouldn't end up with the girl. GARTH: As if. —*Wayne's World*, 1992
- "That Stig from Club Wicked is really getting on my nerves." "Why?" "All that backs to the wall crap. I mean, as if? I'm gay, not blind."—Colin Butts, *Is Harry Still on the Boat?*, p. 206, 2003

---

cross-reference: a headword used in a gloss is shown in small bold caps

headword and part of speech: uses indigenous spelling; lists the most common variants (ignoring hyphenation and compounds)

numbered senses: listed under a headword and particular part of speech, generally ordered by frequency of meaning, from central to peripheral

definition: uses conventional English wherever possible, and identifies domain or geographic location of usage if needed

country of origin: notes the origin of the earliest citation found

date: indicates a known citation that is earlier than the earliest citation given here

phrase: placed under its first significant word (to avoid long entries starting with prepositions or common verbs)

citation: printed example of headword use, with a brief source: the date given here is the copyright for the edition used

gloss: editorial comment on the main users, as well as etymology (and false etymologies) and degree of stigmatisation or taboo

invariant phrase: syntactically self-contained unit, listed alphabetically as a headword

PREFACE

Eric Partridge made a deep and enduring contribution to the study and understanding of slang. In the eight editions of *The Dictionary of Slang and Unconventional English* published between 1937 and 1984, Partridge recorded and defined the slang and unconventional English of Great Britain, and to a lesser extent her dominions, from the 1600s to the 1970s. For the years up to 1890, Partridge was by his own admission quite reliant on Farmer and Henley's *Slang and its Analogues*, which he used as an 'expansible framework'. When it came to the slang for the years 1890 to 1945, Partridge was original and brilliant, especially in his treatment of underworld and military slang. His attitude towards language was scholarly and fun-loving, scientific and idiosyncratic. His body of work, scholarship and dignity of approach led the way and set the standard for every other English-language slang lexicographer of the 20th century.

Our respect for Partridge has not blinded us to the features of his work that have drawn criticism over the years. His protocol for alphabetising was quirky. His dating was often problematic. His etymologies at times strayed from the plausible to the fanciful. His classification by register (slang, cant, jocular, vulgar, coarse, high, low, etc.) was intensely subjective and not particularly useful. Furthermore, his early decision to exclude American slang created increasingly difficult problems for him as the years passed and the influence of American slang grew. Lastly, Partridge grew to lose the ability to relate to the vocabulary he was recording. In 1937, Partridge was a man of his time: but the same could no longer be said in 1960. There is a profound relationship between language and culture, and neither Partridge nor Paul Beale, editor of the 8th edition, seem to have assimilated the cultural changes that began at the end of World War 2. This left them without the cultural knowledge needed to understand the language that they were recording. Their lack of cultural understanding accelerated with time, and this is sadly reflected in the later entries. Beatniks and drug addicts, and their slang, baffled Partridge and Beale, who lacked either the personal experience or historical perspective needed to understand underlying countercultures.

Partridge himself observed, 'More than almost any other kind of book, a dictionary constantly needs to be revised; especially, of course, if it deals with the current form of a language and therefore has to be kept up to date'. With *The New Partridge Dictionary of Slang and Unconventional English* we have tried to do just that. We picked up where Partridge left off, recording the slang and unconventional English of the English-speaking world since World War 2 with the same scholarship and joy in language that characterised Partridge's work. We are not, and cannot be, Partridge: but we can strive to be proud heirs of Partridge and to speak with a voice that Partridge would recognise as an echo of his own. We have worked hard to continue the Partridge tradition, observing high standards of lexicography while producing an accessible work informed by, and infused with, the humour, mischief and energy that are endemic to slang.

Criteria for inclusion in *The New Partridge*

We use three criteria for including a term or phrase in this dictionary. We include (1) slang and unconventional English, (2) used anywhere in the English-speaking world and (3) after 1945.

Rather than focus too intently on a precise definition of slang or on whether a given entry is slang, jargon or colloquial English, we take full advantage of the wide net cast by Partridge when he chose to record 'slang and unconventional English' instead of just slang, which is, after all, without any settled test of purity. We have considered for inclusion all unconventional English that has been used with the purpose or effect of either lowering the formality of communication and reducing solemnity and/or identifying status or group and putting oneself in tune with one's company. A term recorded here might be slang, slangy jargon, a colloquialism, an acronym, an initialism, a vulgarism or a catchphrase. In all instances, an entry imparts a message beyond the text and literal meaning. This approach is especially useful when dealing with world slang and unconventional English. A broader range has permitted inclusion of many Caribbean entries, for instance, which merit inclusion but might not meet a stringent pure-slang-only test. Our only real deviation from Partridge's inclusion criteria is a much diminished body of nicknames. The regiment nicknames that populate Partridge's work no longer fulfill the language function that they did in the United Kingdom of Partridge's day.

If there was a question as to whether a potential entry fell within the target register, we erred on the side of inclusion. We generally chose to include poorly attested words, presenting the entry and our evidence of usage to the reader who is free to determine if a candidate passes probation.

Partridge limited his dictionary to Great Britain and her dominions. We elected the broader universe of the English-speaking world. Globalisation has affected many facets of life, not the least of which is our language. There are words that are uniquely Australian, American or British, but it is impossible to ignore or deny the extent of cross-pollination that exists between cultures as regards slang. We were aided in our global gathering by indigenous contributors from Australia, Canada, the Caribbean, Ireland and New Zealand. We also include pidgin, Creolised English and borrowed foreign terms used by English-speakers in primarily English-language conversation.

We include slang and unconventional English heard and used at any time after 1945. We chose the end of the war in 1945 as our starting point primarily because it marked the beginning of a series of profound cultural changes that produced the lexicon of modern and contemporary slang. The cultural transformations since 1945 are mind-boggling. Television, computers, drugs, music, unpopular wars, youth movements, changing racial sensitivities and attitudes towards sex and sexuality are all substantial factors that have shaped culture and language.

No term is excluded on the grounds that it might be considered offensive as a racial, ethnic, religious, sexual or any kind of slur. This dictionary contains many entries and citations that will, and should, offend. To exclude a term or citation because it is offensive is to deny the fact that it is used: we are not prescriptivists and this is simply not our job. At the same time, we try to avoid definitions or editorial comment that might offend.

We were tempted, but finally chose not to include an appendix of gestures, although many serve the same function as slang. Examples include the impudent middle finger, Ralph Cramden's Raccoon greeting and handshake, the elaborate mimes that signal 'jerk-off' or 'dickhead', Johnny Carson's golf swing, Vic Reeve's lascivious thigh rubbing and Arsenio Hall's finger-tip-touch greeting. Neither did we include an appendix of computer language such as emoticons or leet speak, although we have included throughout several of the more prominent examples of Internet and text messaging shorthand that have become known outside the small circle of initial users.

We tried but in the end decided not to include the word/word phenomenon ('Is she your *friend* friend or friend friend?') or the word/word/word construction ('The most important three things in real estate are location, location, location'). We could not include the obvious pregnant silence that suggests 'fuck' ('What the **** do you think you're doing?'). We shied away from the lexicalised animal noises that often work their way into informal conversation, such as a cat noise when someone is behaving nastily. We similarly did not include musical phrases that have become part of our spoken vocabulary, such as the four-note theme of *The Twilight Zone* which is used to imply an uncanny weirdness in any coincidence, or melodramatic hummed violin music that serves as vocal commentary on any piteous tale.

Using *The New Partridge*

We hope that our presentation is self-evident and that it requires little explanation. We use only a few abbreviations and none of the stylistic conceits near and dear to the hearts of lexicographers.

Headwords

We use indigenous spelling for headwords. This is especially relevant in the case of the UK **arse** and US **ass**. For Yiddish words, we use Leo Rosten's spelling, which favours 'sh-' over 'sch-'. An initialism is shown in upper case without full stops (for example, **BLT**), except that acronyms (pronounced like individual lexical items) are lower case (for example, **snafu**).

Including every variant spelling of a headword seemed neither practical nor helpful to the reader. For the spelling of headwords, we chose the form found in standard dictionaries or the most common forms, ignoring uncommon variants as well as common hyphenation variants of compounds and words ending in 'ie' or 'y'. For this reason, citations may show variant spellings not found in the headword.

Placement of phrases

As a general rule, phrases are placed under their first significant word. However, some invariant phrases are listed as headwords. For example, a stock greeting, stock reply or catchphrase.

Terms that involve a single concept are grouped together as phrases under the common headword. For example, **burn rubber**, **lay rubber** and **peel rubber** are all listed as phrases under the headword **rubber**.

Definition

In dealing with slang from all seven continents, we encountered more than a few culture-specific terms. For such terms, we identify the domain or geographic location of the term's usage. We use conventional English in the definitions, turning to slang only when it is both substantially more economical than the use of conventional English and is readily understood by the average reader.

Gloss and citation

The voice and tone of *The New Partridge Dictionary of Slang and Unconventional English* is most obvious in the gloss: the brief explanations that Partridge used for 'editorial comment' or 'further elucidation'. Partridge warned against using the gloss to show what clever and learned fellows we are – a warning that we heed to the very limited extent it could apply to us. We chose to discontinue Partridge's classification by register.

Included in the gloss are attestations of the headword's usage, either in the form of simple citations (usually to a glossary, proving the simple existence of the word) or quotations with citations. We try to include quotations that do more than simply illustrate usage of the word. There are shortcomings of published citations in a slang dictionary, given the lag between the oral origins of most slang and its appearance in print. Yet published citations do shed significant light on a term's origins and use, and are, in our opinion, preferable to sample usages drafted by dictionary editors.

As we drew from written sources, we were also mindful of the possibility of hoax or intentional coinings without widespread usage. An example of hoax is the 15th November, 1992, article in the *New York Times* on the grunge youth movement in Seattle. The article included a sidebar on the 'Lexicon of Grunge'. The lexicon had an authentic ring, but turned out to be a hoax perpetrated by a record company employee in Seattle. An example of deliberate coining is the word 'santorum', purported to mean 'a frothy mixture of lube and fecal matter that is sometimes the byproduct of anal sex'. In point of fact, the term is the child of a one-man campaign by syndicated sex columnist Dan Savage to place the term in wide usage. From its appearance in print and especially on the Internet, one would assume, incorrectly, that the term has gained wide usage.

We created this dictionary in the dawn of electronic literary databases. Most of our citations are culled from reading, although late in the project we augmented some glosses with citations from electronic databases such as Lexis-Nexis and Amazon.com's 'Search Inside the Book' feature. Future editions of *The New Partridge Dictionary of Slang and Unconventional English* will benefit from further use of databases, but we cannot imagine that the art and importance of reading for citations will be lost altogether.

We have not normalised or corrected either the spelling or punctuation in citations. We acknowledge an author's idiosyncratic or aberrant spelling only in extreme cases, such as phonetic representations of regional accents, when the sense may be lost to the average reader.

A source is included in the bibliography if it is cited at least five times. The date of the edition we used is given in the bibliography.

Country of origin

As is the case with dating, further research will undoubtedly produce a shift in the country of origin for a number of entries. We resolutely avoided guesswork and informed opinion.

Dating

Even Beale, who as editor of the 8th edition was the direct inheritor of Partridge's trust, noted that Partridge's dating 'must be treated with caution'. We recognise that the accurate dating of slang is far more difficult than dating conventional language. Virtually every word in our lexicon is spoken before it is written, and this is especially true of unconventional terms. The recent proliferation of electronic databases and powerful search engines will undoubtedly permit the antedating of many of the entries. Individualised dating research, such as Allen Walker's hunt for the origin of 'OK' or Barry Popik's exhaustive work on terms such as 'hot dog', produces dramatic antedatings: we could not undertake this level of detailed research for every entry.

Conclusion

In the preface to his 1755 *Dictionary of the English Language*, Samuel Johnson noted that 'A large work is difficult because it is large,' and that 'Every writer of a long work commits errors'. In addition to improvements in our dating of terms and identification of the country of origin, it is inevitable that some of our definitions are incorrect or misleading, especially where the sense is subtle and fleeting, defying paraphrasing, or where kindred senses are interwoven. It is also inevitable that some quotations are included in a mistaken sense. For these errors, we apologise in advance.

We carry the flame for words that are usually judged only by the ill-regarded company they keep. Just as Partridge did for the 16th century beggars and rakes, for whores of the 18th century, and for the armed services of the two world wars, we try to do for the slang users of the last 60 years. We embrace the language of beats, hipsters, Teddy Boys, mods and rockers, hippies, pimps, druggies, whores, punks, skinheads, ravers, surfers, Valley Girls, dudes, pill-popping truck drivers, hackers, rappers and more. We have tried to do what Partridge saw as necessary, which was simply to keep up to date.

Tom Dalzell, Berkeley, California
Terry Victor, Caerwent, South Wales
Spring 2005

ACKNOWLEDGEMENTS

Our debt to Sophie Oliver defies description. With good humour and a saintly tolerance for our so-called wit and attempts to corrupt, she herded this project through from a glimmer in the eye to print on the page.

We bow to and thank the following who helped along the way: Mary Ann Kernan, who was charged with putting this project together in 1999 and 2000; John Williams, who must be credited for all that is right about our lexicography and excused for anything that is not; Robert Hay and Mike Tarry of Alden for their unending work on the database and cheerful handling of every problem we could throw at them; Claire L'Enfant; James Folan for rescuing us in the content edit phase; Louise Hake for her cheerful determination in the editing and production phases; our fine copy editors Sandra Anderson, Howard Sargeant and Laura Wedgeworth; and Aine Duffy for her enthusiastically scurrilous vision of the whole project as it developed.

Finally, we thank Oxford University Press for providing us with access to the 'Oxford English Dictionary Online', a brilliant online presentation of the *Oxford English Dictionary*, one of the leading sources for dating.

Tom Dalzell and Terry Victor

This dictionary would never have seen the light of day without the time and support given to me by my family – Cathy most notably, also Jake, Julia, Rosalie and Charlotte. I thank and owe you big-time, major league and humongously. Who knew it would take so much? In their own ways, and from a distance, my parents guided. Audrey, Emily and Reggae started the project with me but did not stay for the end.

I also thank: my slang mentors Paul Dickson and Madeline Kripke (and better mentors you could not hope for); Archie Green, who saved Peter Tamony's work for posterity and encouraged me throughout this project; Jesse Sheidlower, Jonathon Green and Susan Ford, slang lexicographers, friends and comrades in words; Dr Lisa Winer for her voluminous and fine work on the slang of Trinidad and Tobago; Jan Tent for his excellent collection of Fijian slang; Dr Jerry Zientara, the learned and helpful librarian at the Institute for Advanced Study of Human Sexuality in San Francisco, which kindly opened its incomparable library to me; Tom Miller, Bill Stolz, John Konzal and Patricia Walker, archivists at the Western Historical Manuscript Collection, University of Missouri at Columbia, for their help and insights during my work with the Peter Tamony archives; the Hon. Sir Colville Young for leading me to Richard Allsopp; Jim Holliday for his help on the slang of pornography; Jennifer Goldstein for her help on the slang of sex dancers; Richard Perlman for his patient and Zen-like technological help; Angela Jacobson, Elizabeth McInnis and Caitlan Perlman, who helped as readers; Mr Baldwin, Mr Muir, Mr Lee, Dr Robert Regan and Dr Gordon Kelly for the English and popular culture they taught me.

I thank my fellow language writers and lexicographers who were generous in their encouragement, advice and assistance: Reinhold Aman, a brave and brilliant pioneer, the late Robert Chapman, Gerald Cohen, Trevor Cralle, Jim Crotty, Connie Eble, Jonathan Lighter, Edward MacNeal, Geoffrey Nunberg, Judi Sanders, Leslie Savan and Oliver Trager.

Our Australian contributor, James Lambert, was given recourse to the various databases of the Macquarie Library Pty Ltd, who publish synchronic dictionaries for the Australian and Asian markets, and for these vast resources we are grateful.

Lastly, I acknowledge Terry Victor. The demands of this project have only strengthened our friendship.

Tom Dalzell

My wife, Liz, deserves a dictionary entry of her own as a definition of tolerance, patience and encouragement way beyond conventional expectations. In the wider world, my sister and family added to both my library and vocabulary; and my other family, now in Spain, even went so far as to put a christening on hold until a deadline had been met, as well as allowing me access to the playground language of our time. I must also thank Gerri Smith for her tolerant understanding that I could not be in two places at once.

Serendipity brought me to Tom Dalzell and through him I have had the advantage and benefit of all of the influences and providers of expertise that he names above, especially Jonathon Green. In addition to those named I am grateful for the knowledgeable encouragement of Michael Quinion and David Crystal; and, in matters polari, Paul Baker.

For particular contributions I would like to thank: Flight Lieutenant Andrew Resoli; Lisa and Tim Hale; David Morrison; some of the inmates at HMP High Down in the summer of 2002; Antonio Lillo for his work on rhyming slang; various magazine editors and journalists who addressed so many of my queries of modern usage; and, for a splendid collection of cocaine-related slang, a certain group of musicians (whose management would prefer that they remain anonymous). I also enjoyed the advantage of the correspondence that the Partridge and Beale 8th edition still attracts: I am grateful to all who wrote in, and I look forward to seeing more contributions at *www.partridge-slang.com*.

Above all, I must make mention of two people: Eric Partridge, who is my hero, and Tom Dalzell, who is my friend.

Terry Victor

OBSERVATIONS ON SLANG AND UNCONVENTIONAL ENGLISH

Some notes on the challenges of lexicography, drawn entirely from the writings of Eric Partridge (1894–1979)

Partridge wrote widely on matters concerning the English language. He did not, by any means, restrict his interest to matters slang and unconventional; however, it is his work in this area that had, and continues to have, the greatest impact, and on which his reputation is most celebrated. He wrote more than forty books in his lifetime, considering such diverse topics as abbreviations, American tramp and underworld slang, British and American English since 1900, comic alphabets, English and American Christian names, Shakespeare's bawdy, usage and abusage, and he contributed to many, many more. It is so substantial a body of work that any list short of a full bibliography will inevitably do his great achievement a disservice. He was a philologist, etymologist, lexicographer, essayist and dictionary-maker; he is a legend and an inspiration.

The flavour, and wisdom, of Partridge's work is gathered in the quotations that follow, loosely grouped by subject, and presented under sub-headings that make new use of a selection of his book and article titles.

Slang Today and Yesterday

From about 1850, slang has been the accepted term for 'illegitimate' colloquial speech: but since then, especially among the lower classes, 'lingo' has been a synonym, and so also, chiefly among the cultured and the pretentious, has 'argot'. Now 'argot', being merely the French for 'slang', has no business to be used thus – it can rightly be applied only to French slang of French cant: and 'lingo' properly means a simplified language that, like Beach-la-Mar and Pidgin-English, represents a distortion of (say) English by coloured peoples speaking English indeed but adapting it to their own phonetics and grammar. 'Jargon' – originally as in Chaucer, used of the warbling of birds – has long been employed loosely and synonymously for slang, but it should be reserved for the technicalities of science, the professions and the trades: though, for such technicalities, 'shop' is an equally good word.[1]

[S]lang is much rather a spoken than a literary language. It originates, nearly always, in speech.[1]

Slang is easy enough to use, but very hard to write about with the facile convincingness that a subject apparently so simple would, at first sight, seem to demand. But the simplest things are the hardest to define, certainly the hardest to discuss, for it is usually at first sight only that their simplicity is what strikes one the most forcibly. And slang, after all, is a peculiar kind of vagabond language, always hanging on the outskirts of legitimate speech, but continually straying or forcing its way into the most respectable company.[2]

Language in general and every kind of language belongs to everyone who wishes to use it.[3]

Slang, being the quintessence of colloquial speech, must always be related to convenience rather than scientific laws, grammatical rules and philosophical ideals. As it originates, so it flourishes best, in colloquial speech.[1]

Slang may and often does fill a gap in accepted language.[1]

Words, Words, Words!

Every group or association, from a pair of lovers to a secret society however large, feels, at some time or other, the need to defend itself against outsiders, and therefore creates a slang designed to conceal its thoughts: and the greater the need for secrecy, the more extensive and complete is the slang[.][1]

The specialization that characterizes every vocation leads naturally to a specialized vocabulary, to the invention of new words or the re-charging of old words. Such special words and phrases become slang only when they are used outside their vocational group and then only if they change their meaning or are applied in other ways [...] But, whatever the source, personality and one's surroundings (social or occupational) are the two co-efficients, the two chief factors, the determining causes of the nature of slang, as they are of language in general and of style.[1]

One kind of *eyewash*, the army's innumerable 'states' and 'returns' was known as *bumf*, short for *bum-fodder*: the abbreviation was common in English public schools from before 1900; the full term for toilet-paper dates back to the seventeenth century, when it was coined by Urquhart, the translator of Rabelais; Urquhart is one of the most prolific originators of the obscenities and vulgarities of our language, and with him rank Shakespeare and Burns.[4]

In English, the ideas most fertile in synonyms are those of drinking, drunkenness, money, and the sexual organs and act.[1]

Many slang words, indeed, are drawn from pleasurable activities (games, sports, entertainments), from the joy of life, from a gay abandon: for this reason it has been wittily called 'language on a picnic'.[1]

Common to – indeed, very common in – the jazzman's and the Beatnik's vocabulary is the noun pad, whence the entirely Beatnik pad me, a cat's invitation to a chick to share his room and bed. [...] The Beatniks got it from the jazzmen who got it from the American underworld who got it from the British underworld (pad, a bed) who got it from Standard English of the sixteenth–eighteenth centuries (pad, a bundle of straw to lie on).[5]

The metaphors and allusions [in slang] are generally connected with some temporary phase, some ephemeral vogue, some unimportant incident; if the origin is not nailed down at the time, it is rarely recoverable.[1]

[B]orrowings from foreign languages produce slang; and every language borrows. Borrowings, indeed, have a way of seeming slangy or of being welcomed by slang before standard speech takes them into its sanctum.[1]

War always produces a rich crop of slang.[6]

[W]ar (much as we may hate to admit the fact), because, in all wars, both soldiers and sailors and, since 1914, airmen and civilians as well, have imported or adopted or invented hundreds of words, terms, phrases, this linguistic aspect ranking as, if we except the unexceptable 'climate of courage,' the only good result of war.[7]

Human characteristics, such as a love of mystery and a confidential air (a lazy freemasonry), vanity, the imp of perversity that lurks in every heart, the impulse to rebellion, and that irrepressible spirit of adventure which, when deprived of its proper outlook in action, perforce contents itself with verbal audacity (the adventure of speech): these and others are at the root of slang[.][1]

Here, There and Everywhere

When we come to slang and familiar speech generally, we come to that department of the vocabulary in which British and American differences are naturally greater than anywhere else, just as they are greater in the colloquial language generally than in the literary.[8]

American slang is more volatile than English and it tends, also, to have more synonyms, but a greater number of those synonyms are butterflies of a day; English synonyms are used more for variety than from weariness or a desire to startle. American slang is apt to be more brutal than English[.][1]

Canada also has an extensive and picturesque objective slang, but that slang is 80 per cent American, with the remainder rather more English than native-Canadian [...] it is linguistically unfair to condemn it for being so much indebted to its near and 'pushing' neighbour[.][1]

Australian speech and writing have, from the outset, tended to be unconventional [...] The unconventionality is linguistic.[9]

The truth is that South African slang, as distinct from indispensable Africanderisms, is not intrinsically so vivid, humorous, witty, or divinely earthy as Canadian and Australian slang, nor is it nearly so extensive, nor has it, except during the Boer War, succeeded in imposing itself upon English slang, much less upon Standard English[.][1]

New Zealand is like South Africa in that its population is too small to have much influenced the language of the mother country whether in Standard or in unconventional English.[1]

Usage and Abusage

Some of the upstart qualities [of slang] and part of the aesthetic (as opposed to the moral) impropriety spring from the four features present in all slang, whatever the period and whatever the country: the search for novelty; volatility and light-headedness as well as light-heartedness; ephemerality; the sway of fashion. In the standard speech and still more in slang we note that the motive behind figurative expressions and all neologisms is the desire to escape from the old accepted phrase: the desire for novelty operates more freely, audaciously, and rapidly in slang – that is the only difference. [...O]f the numerous slang words taken up by the masses and the classes, most have only a short life, and that when they die, unhonoured and unsung, they are almost immediately replaced by novelties equally transitory: the word is dead, long live the word! [...S]lang, as to the greater part of its vocabulary and especially as to its cuckoo-calling phrases and it's parrot-sayings, is evanescent; it is the residuum that, racy and expressive, makes the study of slang revelatory of the pulsing life of the language.[1]

[S]lang is indicative not only of man's earthiness but of his indomitable spirit: it sets him in his proper place: relates a man to his fellows, to his world and the world, and to the universe.[10]

And slang is employed for one (or two or more) of thirteen reasons:

1 In sheer high spirits; 'just for the fun of the thing'.
2 As an exercise in wit or humour.
3 To be 'different' – to be novel.
4 To be picturesque.
5 To be startling; to startle.
6 To escape from clichés and long-windedness.
7 To enrich the language.
8 To give solidity and concreteness to the abstract and the idealistic, and nearness to the distant scene or object.
9 To reduce solemnity, pain, tragedy.

10 To put oneself in tune with one's company.
11 To induce friendliness or intimacy.
12 To show that one belongs to a certain school, trade or profession, intellectual set or social class. In short to be in the fashion – or to prove that someone else isn't.
13 To be secret – not understood by those around one.[11]

But no real stylist, no-one capable of good speaking or good writing, is likely to be harmed by the occasional employment of slang; provided that he is conscious of the fact, he can employ it both frequently and freely without stultifying his mind, impoverishing his vocabulary, or vitiating the taste and the skill that he brings to the using of that vocabulary. Except in formal and dignified writing and in professional speaking, a vivid and extensive slang is perhaps preferable to a jejune and meagre vocabulary of standard English; on the other hand, it will hardly be denied that, whether in writing or speech, a sound though restricted vocabulary of standard English is preferable to an equally small vocabulary of slang, however vivid may be that slang.[1]

The Gentle Art of Lexicography

I began early in life: and it is the course of my life which, allied to a natural propensity to original sin, has made a lexicographer out of me.[12]

For most of us, a dictionary is hardly a book to read; a good dictionary, however, is a book to browse in. Some dictionaries are so well written that one just goes on and on. To write such a dictionary has always been my ambition.[12]

Slang [etymology/lexicography] demands a mind constantly on the *qui vive*; an ear constantly keyed to the nuances of everyday speech, whether among scholars or professional men or craftsmen or labourers; a very wide reading of all kinds of books.[13]

I have read much that is hopelessly inferior, hopelessly mediocre; and much that, although interesting, is yet devoid of literary value. But ever since my taste acquired a standard, I have been able to extract some profit from even the most trashy book.[14]

There is far more imagination and enthusiasm in the making of a good dictionary than in the average novel.[15]

Words at War: Words at Peace

For over a century, there have been protests against the use of slang and controversies on the relation of slang to the literary language or, as it is now usually called, Standard English. Purists have risen in their wrath and conservatives in their dignity to defend the Bastille of linguistic purity against the revolutionary rabble. The very vehemence of the attack and the very sturdiness of the defence have ensured that only the fittest survive to gain entrance to the citadel, there establish themselves, and then become conservatives and purists in their turn.[16]

Any term that prevents us from thinking, any term that we employ to spare us from searching for the right word, is a verbal narcotic. As though there weren't too many narcotics already...[17]

Words are very important things; at the lowest estimate, they are indispensable counters of communication.[18]

Notes/bibliography

1 *Slang Today and Yesterday*, 1933: George Routledge & Sons, London
2 *Slang Today and Yesterday*, 1933, quoting Greenough and Kittredge, *Words and their Ways in English Speech*, 1902: George Routledge & Sons, London
3 'The Lexicography of Cant', *American Speech*, Volume 26, Issue 2, May 1951: The American Dialect Society, Durham, North Carolina
4 'Byways of Soldier Slang' in *A Martial Medley*, 1931: Scholartis Press, London
5 'A Square Digs Beatnik', August 1959. Originally published for private circulation Christmas 1959/New Year 1960. Collected in *A Charm of Words*, 1960: Hamish Hamilton, London
6 'Words Get Their Wings', originally published in *Chamber's Journal*, July–August 1945. Collected in *Words at War: Words at Peace*, 1948: Frederick Muller, London
7 'Introduction' in *Dictionary of New Words*, Mary Reifer, 1957: Peter Owen, London
8 *British and American English Since 1900*, co-authored with John W. Clark, 1951: Andrew Dakers, London
9 'Australian English' in *A Charm of Words*, 1960: Hamish Hamilton, London
10 *Usage & Abusage*, 1947: Hamish Hamilton, London [originally published in the US in 1942]
11 *The World of Words*, 2nd edition, 1939: Hamish Hamilton, London [reduced by Eric Partridge from a fuller consideration in *Slang Today and Yesterday*, 1933, and based on the work of M. Alfredo Niceforo, *Le Génie de l'Argot*, 1912]
12 *The Gentle Art of Lexicography*, 1963: André Deutsch, London
13 *Adventuring Among Words*, 1961: André Deutsch, London
14 *Journey to the Edge of Morning*, ©1946, reprinted 1969: Books for Libraries Press, New York
15 As Corrie Denison, a pseudonymous epigraph to *A Classical Dictionary of the Vulgar Tongue* by Captain Francis Grose (3rd edition, 1796), edited by Eric Partridge, 1931: Scholartis Press, London
16 *Here, There and Everywhere*, 1950: Hamish Hamilton, London
17 'Verbal Narcotics', originally published in *Good Housekeeping* magazine, June 1949. Collected in *From Sanskrit to Brazil*, 1952: Hamish Hamilton, London
18 'Words in Vogue: Words of Power', 1942: collected in *Words at War: Words at Peace*, 1948: Frederick Muller, London

Aa

A *noun*

1 amphetamine *US*

- "A" is considered very bad news, "it rots your teeth and your mind." —Ruth Bronsteen, *The Hippy's Handbook*, p. 12, 1967
- —*Look*, p. 13, 8th August 1967
- —Burton H. Wolfe, *The Hippies*, p. 203, 1968
- [T]hat would come later, when he kicked A in terror after his toenails dropped off. —Ed Sanders, *Tales of Beatnik Glory*, p. 59, 1975
- —Angela Devlin, *Prison Patter*, p. 21, 1996

2 LSD *US*

An abbreviation of **ACID**.

- —Walter Way, *The Drug Scene*, p. 105, 1977
- Street names [:] A, acid, blotter[.] —James Kay and Julian Cohen, *The Parents' Complete Guide to Young People and Drugs*, p. 141, 1998

3 in a deck of playing cards, an ace *US*

- —George Percy, *The Language of Poker*, p. 4, 1988

▸ **get A into G; get your A into G**

to stop idling; to apply yourself to an activity; to start doing something useful *NEW ZEALAND*

Euphemistic for **GET YOUR ARSE IN GEAR**.

- So thanks for motivating me to get A into G and spend 2 minutes on the computer which will hopefully get many hours of coverage of our horsey sports. —*The Horse Magazine (Australia)*, April 2002

A *adjective*

1 reserved for the best; the best *US*

- He went through what Hollywood calls Treatment A, i.e. the works for top visitors, without a mistake. —*Fortune*, p. 225, October 1945
- And part of the magic at Malibu was that Mickey's dinner was unseated which, as any "A" hostess knows, can be hazardous. —*San Francisco Chronicle*, 18th August 1975
- Oh my God Michele, look at the A group. —*Romy and Michele's High School Reunion*, 1997
- You know, if you do go out with Bianca, you'd be set. You'd outrank everyone. Strictly A-list. —*Ten Things I Hate About You*, 1999

2 anal *US*

- Now every scene I do is pretty much an 'A' scene. (Quoting Nici Sterling). —Anthony Petkovich, *The X Factory*, p. 33, 1997

A-1 *adjective*

▹ **see:** **A-ONE**

a2m *noun*

a scene in a pornographic film in which an object or body part is withdrawn from a rectum and taken into a mouth without either washing or editing *US*

Shorthand for 'ass-to-mouth'. Recorded in interview of Jim Holliday, 12th June 1997.

A3

anytime, anyplace, anywhere *UK, 2003*

An abbreviation used in text messaging.

- —*Collins English Dictionary*, 2003

AAA *noun*

an amphetamine tablet *US*

In the US, the AAA is the national automobile club, which, like an amphetamine tablet, helps you get from one place to another.

- —Peter Johnson, *Dictionary of Street Alcohol and Drug Terms*, p. 1, 1993

A and A *noun*

in the military, a leave for rest and recreation *US, 1966*

A jocular abbreviation of 'ass and alcohol'.

- —J.E. Lighter, *Historical Dictionary of American Slang, Vol 1*, p. 1, 1994

A and B *noun*

assault and battery *US*

- You wanna file A-and-B on the sonofabitch? —Carl Hiaasen, *Tourist Season*, p. 55, 1986

aap; arp *noun*

a marijuana cigarette *SOUTH AFRICA, 1946*

From Afrikaans for 'monkey'.

aardvark *noun*

an F-111 combat aircraft or any aircraft that is awkward-looking or difficult to fly *US, 1963*

Vietnam war usage.

- —Linda Reinberg, *In the Field*, p. 1, 1991

ab *noun*

an abcess, especially as a result of injecting drugs *US*

- —*American Speech*, p. 24, February 1952: 'Teen-age hophead jargon'
- —Eugene Landy, *The Underground Dictionary*, p. 21, 1971
- —Angela Devlin, *Prison Patter*, p. 21, 1996

AB *noun*

1 the Aryan Brotherhood, a white prison gang in the US *US*

- "But I'm aces with the A.B. here at Coldwater," Joe objected. —Seth Morgan, *Homeboy*, p. 369, 1990
- The AB began to structure as a whites-only prison gang and formed its own specific rules. —Bill Valentine, *Gangs and Their Tattoos*, p. 4, 2000

2 the bleed period of the menstrual cycle *NEW ZEALAND*

An abbreviation of 'Annie Brown'.

- —David McGill, *David McGill's Complete Kiwi Slang Dictionary*, p. 9, 1998

ABA *noun*

a traveller's cheque *US*

- The most common solution is to purchase traveler's checks, called ABA's, and to further thwart the effort to determine a true income, the ABA's are purchased in the phony name on the always available fake driver's license. —Gene Sorrows, *All About Carnivals*, p. 5, 1985

abb *adjective*

abnormal *US*

- —Trevor Cralle, *The Surfin'ary*, p. 1, 1991

abba-dabba *noun*

chatter, gossip *US, 1961*

Undoubtedly originated with the song 'The Aba-Daba Honey-moon', written in 1913 and re-released with great success by Larry Clinton and His Orchestra in March, 1948, in which 'abba-dabba' is the chatter of monkeys.

- The Abba Dabba Scanties! —*San Francisco Examiner*, 14th June 1963
- Abba-dabba: In and out of our town in a hurry this week was Guy Lewis. —*San Francisco Chronicle*, p. 50, 12th May 1967

abba-dabba *adjective*

dark-skinned, especially Arabic *US*

- This black ass, abba dabba motherfucker looked like he was gonna rabbit, so I drew down and zonked him across the gourd with my roscoe. —Joseph Wambaugh, *The Choirboys*, p. 31, 1975

abbed *adjective*

having well-defined abdominal muscles *UK*

- 12 fabulously abbed, weedy-voiced muppets will be trained to sing and dance in the style of all the other boy and girl bands of recent years[.] —*The Guardian*, 4th October 2002

abbey *noun*

a swindler who impersonates a priest *US*

- —Hyman E. Goldin et al., *Dictionary of American Underworld Lingo*, p. 17, 1950

▸ **on the abbey**

engaged in a swindle involving clergy impersonation *US*

- —Jay Robert Nash, *Dictionary of Crime*, p. 1, 1992

abbott *noun*

a capsule of pentobarbital sodium (trade name Nembutal™), a central nervous system depressant *US*

From the name of the manufacturer.

- —Eugene Landy, *The Underground Dictionary*, p. 21, 1971
- —Donald Wesson and David Smith, *Barbiturates*, p. 121, 1977

Abby Singer *noun*

in television and film making, the next-to-last shot of the day *US*

Singer was active in US television from the early 1950s until the late 1980s; his name became an eponym when he was an Assistant Director in the 1950s.

- —Ralph S. Singleton, *Filmaker's Dictionary*, p. 1, 1990

ABC *noun*

1 an American-born Chinese *US, 1984*

- —Judi Sanders, *Faced and Faded, Hanging to Hurl*, p. 1, 1993
- "Yellow outside, White inside. Like ABC, American Born Chinese." "Jim's not marrying a gwailu (=foreign devil) or a banana. He's marrying a real Chinese."—Howard Marks, *Mr Nice*, p. 230, 1997

2 in poker, the ace, two and three *US*

- —George Percy, *The Language of Poker*, p. 4, 1988

ABC *adjective*

of a piece of chewing gum, *a*lready *b*een *c*hewed *US*

Childish.

- —Jonathan Blyth, *The Law of the Playground*, p. 3, 2004

ABC ad *noun*

a newspaper advertisement listing shows in alphabetical order *US*

- —Sherman Louis Sergel, *The Language of Show Biz*, p. 2, 1973

ABC class *noun*

the entry grade in a primary school *TRINIDAD AND TOBAGO*

- —Lise Winer, *Dictionary of the English/Creole of Trinidad & Tobago*, 2003

ABCing you

used as a farewell *US*

Intended as a clever variant of 'I'll be seeing you'.

- —*San Francisco Examiner*, p. 19, 5th January 1947

ABC's *noun*

underwear *US*

- I took off the a b c's and her stockings.—Hal Ellson, *Duke*, p. 11, 1949

ABC-ya

used as a farewell *US*

Intended as a clever variant of 'I'll be seeing you'.

- —Alonzo Westbrook, *Hip Hoptionary*, p. 1, 2002

abdabs; habdabs; screaming abdabs *noun*

a condition of anxiety, uneasiness, nervousness; also, but rarely, *delirium tremens* or a state of enraged frustration *UK, 1946*

Always following 'the', usually now phrased 'to give you (the screaming abdabs)'. In 1964–65, an early line-up of the band that became Pink Floyd was named 'The Screaming Abdabs', later 'The Abdabs'.

- The thought of disgruntled punters [...] demanding satisfaction of the readies [cash] variety gave me the screaming abdabs[.]—Andrew Nickolds, *Back to Basics*, p. 33, 1994

abdicate *verb*

to vacate a public toilet upon orders of a homosexual-rousting attendant *US, 1941*

The royal imagery derived from the homosexual as **QUEEN**.

Abdul *noun*

1 used as a term of address for any Turkish soldier *UK, 1925*

World War 1 coinage.

- During the Korean War the ordinary enlisted Turkish soldier responded in friendly fashion when he was addressed as "Abdul." —Frank Hailey, *Soldier Talk*, p. 1, 1982

2 any male Arab *US*

Gulf war usage.

- —*American Speech*, p. 382, Winter 1991: 'Among the new words'

Abe *noun*

1 a five-dollar note *US, 1945*

An abbreviation of **ABE LINCOLN**.

- —Ralph de Sola, *Crime Dictionary*, p. 1, 1982

2 any Jewish male *US, 1914*

Also variant 'Abie'. From the archetypal Jewish name: Abraham.

- —Helen Dahlskog (Editor), *A Dictionary of Contemporary and Colloquial Usage*, p. 3, 1972

A bean *noun*

a capsule of MDMA, the recreational drug best known as ecstasy *UK*

- —Mike Haskins, *Drugs*, p. 289, 2003

Abe Lincoln *noun*

a five-dollar note *US, 1966*

The note bears an engraving of President Lincoln.

- If these good people have no objection we'll call it an off the record sidebet. One Abe Lincoln it is.—Robert Edmond Alter, *Carny Kill*, p. 36, 1966

Aber *nickname*

Aberdare, Abergavenny, Aberystwyth or any town so constructed *UK: WALES*

From Welsh for 'where two waters meet'.

- [H]omeless down-a fuckin road in Aber an Mach.—Niall Griffiths, *Sheepshagger*, p. 78, 2001

abercrombie *noun*

someone who strives at creating the impression of knowing all *US*

- —Lou Shelly, *Hepcats Jive Talk Dictionary*, p. 7, 1945

abfab *adjective*

*ab*solutely *fab*ulous *AUSTRALIA, 1965*

By elision. Originally the slang of Australian teenagers. From early 1990s in the UK it has been the widely familiar short-form of popular television situation comedy *Absolutely Fabulous*.

Abie Lincoln *adjective*

▷ see: **ABRAHAM LINCOLN**

Abigail *noun*

a staid, traditional, middle-aged homosexual man *US*

- —Bruce Rodgers, *The Queens' Vernacular*, p. 17, 1972
- —*Maledicta*, p. 222, 1979: 'Kinks and queens: linguistic and cultural aspects of the terminology for gays'

able *adjective*

strong, capable, courageous *CANADA*

In general speech, this word is usually followed by 'to do [something]', but the Canadian use tends to follow the otherwise obsolete pattern of letting it stand alone or with an intensifier.

- A fellow beat up three Mounties in Prince Edward Island. He was some Jesus able, you!—*Atlantic Insight*, June 1980

▸ **can't spell able**

be unable to do what you are told to do *BARBADOS*

- —Richard Allsopp, *Dictionary of Caribbean English Usage*, p. 6, 1996

Able Dog *noun*

the propellor-driven Douglas AD Skyraider *US, 1961*

Based on the phonetic alphabet. The Skyraider was manufactured between 1946 and 1957; it saw service in Korea and Vietnam.

- —J.E. Lighter, *Historical Dictionary of American Slang, Volume 1*, p. 1, 1994

able Grable *noun*

a sexually attractive girl *US*

- —*Yank*, p. 18, 24th March 1945

abo *noun*

an Australian Aboriginal *AUSTRALIA, 1906*

An abbreviation of 'aborigine' blended with the '-o' suffix. Now a strongly taboo word, formerly in frequent use by white people, and viewed by them as less marked than other terms such as 'boong' or 'coon'. It was even used in names for products, businesses, etc.

- Abos in this country are still pretty wild, and when a tracker is wanted most times they're away out beyond, on walkabout.—Arthur Upfield, *Bony and the Mouse*, p. 38, 1959
- Funny how the booze gets them abos.—Jean Brooks, *The Opal Witch*, p. 16, 1967
- Known as Aboriginals (paternally), Abos (patronisingly), boongs (contemptuously), but in white Foolgarah never as people[.]—Frank Hardy, *The Outcasts of Foolgarah*, p. 50, 1971
- They were not pleased when I informed them I was going to marry an abo.—Robert Campbell, *The Cat's Meow*, p. 88, 1988
- You think these abos have got the legs for another story?—Harrison Biscuit, *The Search for Savage Henry*, p. 67, 1995
- 'You a dago or an Abo?' the gang's leading intellectual shouted. —Shane Maloney, *Nice Try*, p. 98, 1998

abo *adjective*

Australian Aboriginal; of, or pertaining to, Australian Aboriginals *AUSTRALIA, 1911*

- The youngster will pick up the abo language faster than his own. — Ion L. Idriess, *Over the Range*, p. 210, 1947
- All pom-named towns should have Abo names. — Michael Peters, *Pommie Bastard*, p. 108, 1969
- But the boy and the girl and the Abo kid and the old man stay here. — Max Fatchen, *Chase through the Night*, p. 28, 1976
- Kiss my ass, Abo shit. — *Passing Show*, p. 10, 2002

aboard *adverb*

present, part of an enterprise *US*

- McDougal led off the tenth. He turned around at the plate and shook hands with the kid. Gil said: "I'm from San Francisco, Commerce High. Glad to have you aboard." — *San Francisco Chronicle*, 11th July 1957
- They met for a couple of days in the plush Lake Tahoe layout of Henry Kaiser – deliberately without any party organization officials or other statewide Democratic candidates aboard. — *San Francisco Call-Bulletin*, p. 13, 15th August 1958

▸ **go aboard of someone**

to act vigorously and aggressively, to attack, or scold vigorously *CANADA*

- I'll fly aboard o'ye and dance a jig on yer palate! — *Nova Scotia Historical Quarterly*, p. 273, December 1980: 'Why did you say that?'

A-bomb; atom bomb *noun*

marijuana combined in a cigarette with cocaine, heroin or opium *US, 1969*

The addition of narcotic enhancements to a **BOMB** (a marijuana cigarette) is signified by the 'A-'.

- — Richard A. Spears, *The Slang and Jargon of Drugs and Drink*, p. 1, 1986
- — Robert Ashton, *This is Heroin*, p. 208, 2002
- — Mike Haskins, *Drugs*, p. 286, 2003

A-bombed *adjective*

under the influence of amphetamines *US*

- There were further speculations that the generals who met in the Pentagon War Room every day planning atomic snuffs were a bit A-bombed themselves. — Ed Sanders, *Tales of Beatnik Glory*, p. 192, 1975

A-bone *noun*

a Model A Ford car, first built in 1927 *US, 1951*

- Those who aren't lucky enough to find an old Model A Fordy body can still buy a fiberglass copy. That adds up to a fiberglass A-bone. — Ed Radlauer, *Drag Racing Pix Dix*, p. 3, 1970
- — John Blair, *The Illustrated Discography of Surf Music 1961 – 1965*, p. 123, 1985

aboot *preposition*

used as a humorous attempt to duplicate a Canadian saying 'about' *US*

- This is not aboot deals. This is aboot dignity. This is aboot freedom. This is aboot respect. — *South Park*, 1995

abort *verb*

to defecate after being the passive partner in anal sex *US*

- — Bruce Rodgers, *The Queens' Vernacular*, p. 17, 1972

abortion *noun*

a misfortune; an ugly person or thing *US, 1943*

- He scanned around his workshop, dropped the plane, reached for an old beaten-up thing with a lot of notches in it and lifted it up with one hand. "What about this abortion?" — Frederick Kohner, *Gidget*, p. 18, 1957
- — Collin Baker et al., *College Undergraduate Slang Study Conducted at Brown University*, p. 69, 1968

about-face *noun*

a 180-degree turn executed while driving fast *US*

- It was Junior Johnson specifically, however, who was famous for the "bootleg turn" or "about face." — Tom Wolfe, *The Kandy-Kolored Tangerine-Flake Streamlined Baby*, p. 128, 1965

about it; 'bout it *adjective*

in favour of something *US*

- — Don R. McCreary (Editor), *Dawg Speak*, 2001

about right *adjective*

correct, adequate *UK, 1850*

above board *adjective*

entirely honest *UK, 1616*

From card playing.

- [N]ot all of the materials I handle are strictly above board, some of them are not VAT registered, some of them may have even fallen off the back of a lorry. — Danny King, *The Burglar Diaries*, p. 30, 2001

above par *adjective*

1 in excellent health or spirits *UK, 1937*

Directly from describing stocks and shares as above face value.

2 mildly drunk *UK, 1984*

By extension from the previous sense.

abracadabra, please and thank you

used as a humorous embellishment of 'please' *US*

A signature line from the *Captain Kangaroo* children's television show (CBS, 1944–84). Repeated with referential humour.

Abraham Lincoln; Abie Lincoln *adjective*

disgusting, contemptible *UK*

Glasgow rhyming slang for **STINKING**.

- Your plates [feet] are Abraham Lincoln! — Michael Munro, *The Patter, Another Blast*, 1988

Abrahampstead *nickname*

Hampstead, an area of north London with a large Jewish population *UK, 1981*

A combination with the archetypal Jewish name Abraham.

abs *noun*

the abdominal muscles *US, 1956*

- Danny and the man begin talking about the relative merits of "frog kicks" for the "abs" as opposed to regular situps[.] — John Rechy, *Numbers*, p. 66, 1967
- The Language of Bodybuilding — *American Speech*, p. 198, Fall 1984
- His abs looked solid but he wasn't shoving them in your face[.] — Diran Abedayo, *My Once Upon A Time*, p. 6, 2000
- Morelli had washboard [flat and rippled] abs. Morelli could actually do sit-ups. — Janet Evanovich, *Seven Up*, p. 208, 2001

absobloodylutely *adverb*

absolutely, utterly *UK, 1914*

First recorded as 'absoballylutely'.

absofuckinglutely *adverb*

absolutely *UK, 1921*

- Principle interpolations used are *bloody*, *f- - -g*, and their euphemisms – e.g. *transconti-bloody-nental*, *abso-f- -g-lutely*, *inde-bloody-pendent*. — Sidney J. Baker, *The Australian Language*, p. 258, 1945
- We would like to thank every single body who has made this years' Recorder so absofuckinglutely brilliant. — *Union Recorder*, 4th November 1991

absolutely!

used for registering complete agreement *UK, 1937*

Absolutely, Mr Gallagher. Positively, Mr Shean.

used for a humorous assent *US*

From the Vaudeville team of Gallagher and Shean.

absotively; absitively *adverb*

certainly *US, 1926*

A jocular blend of 'positively' and 'absolutely'.

- — Joseph Weingarten, *American Dictionary of Slang*, p. 1, 1954
- — Bill Davis, *Jawjacking*, p. 9, 1977

Abyssinian polo *noun*

a game of dice *US*

- — Frank Garcia, *Marked Cards and Loaded Dice*, p. 250, 1962

Abyssinian tea *noun*

khat, a natural stimulant grown in Kenya, Ethiopa and Somalia *UK*

- — Harry Shapiro, *Recreational Drugs*, p. 240, 2004

Ac *noun*

an Acura car *US*

- — Alonzo Westbrook, *Hip Hoptionary*, p. 1, 2002

AC\DC; AC-DC *noun*

in gay society, a couple *UK*

- — Paul Baker, *Polari*, p. 162, 2002

AC\DC; AC-DC *adjective*

bisexual *US, 1960*

A pun on electricity's AC (alternating current) and DC (direct current).

- — Frank Prewitt and Francis K. Schaeffer, *Vocabulary of Inmates' Usages*, 1963
- A Lexicon of Homosexual Slang — Donald Webster Cory and John P. LeRoy, *The Homosexual and His Society*, p. 261, 1963
- I don't trust any of those AC-DC guys. — Mickey Spillane, *Return of the Hood*, p. 124, 1964
- He'd proven that he wasn't as much of a fag as he thought he was! Maybe he was AC/DC, but he wasn't pure fag. — Robert Leslie, *Confessions of a Lesbian Prostitute*, p. 55, 1965
- "There are getting to be more AC-DCs, which is gay language for men who switch back and forth," he explained sardonically. — Johnny Shearer, *The Male Hustler*, p. 168, 1966
- But, all AC-DC folk welcome. — *Screw*, p. 7, 7th March 1969
- The AC-DC chick – the girl who goes both ways sexually, is an affectionate female who likes everybody, boys and girls, men and women. — *Adult Entertainment for Swingers*, 1975
- The sad part of the story is that his family will also suffer. What will "Mr. A.C.-D.C. Dignified Businessman" do then." — *San Francisco Examiner*, 22nd August 1975
- She started out in one of his de-luxe AC-DC cathouses in the suburbs of Havana. — Edwin Torres, *After Hours*, p. 325, 1979
- I said I was AC/DC[.] — Kitty Churchill, *Thinking of England*, p. 113, 1995

ACAB

*a*ll *c*oppers *a*re *b*astards *UK*

An initialism, a philosophy, a tattoo.

- — Angela Devlin, *Prison Patter*, p. 21, 1996

academy *noun*

a jail or prison *US*

- — Vincent J. Monteleone, *Criminal Slang*, p. 9, 1949
- — Marlene Freedman, *Alcatraz*, 1983

Academy Award *noun*

recognition of excelling in a field *US*

- Tuohy became a jailbird early in life and got his academy award, so to speak, when the FBI rated him Public Enemy No. 1 in 1934. — *San Francisco Call-Bulletin*, p. 10, 18th April 1958
- "We won't win any academy awards with our showing in Baltimore," he said disgustedly today. — *San Francisco Call-Bulletin*, p. 45, 17th September 1968

Academy Award *adjective*

1 excellent *US*

- But with the club averaging 7 1/2 runs a game, Academy award pitching may not be necessary. — *San Francisco Call-Bulletin*, p. 19, 21st April 1958

2 histrionic *AUSTRALIA*

- [A]n Academy Award job, overacting by a player to receive a free kick. — Sidney J. Baker, *The Australian Language*, p. 249, 1966
- — Joe Andersen, *Winners Can Laugh*, p. 41, 1982
- Lendl's shoulders slumped and his frown was a study in anguish. He could have won an Academy Award but he settled for another first serve as the umpire fell victim to the 'sting'. — *Sunday Sun*, p. 28, 1st October 1989
- I told them that it was an academy award act from the jockey on the second horse and they agreed. — *Sunday Sun*, p. 90, 1st October 1989

Academy Award winning *adjective*

histrionic *AUSTRALIA*

- That was why I didn't notice what was going on until Mouche started making Academy Award winning noises. — Kathy Lette, *Girls' Night Out*, p. 88, 1987

Acapulco *noun*

marijuana from southwest Mexico *US*

A shortened form of **ACAPULCO GOLD**.

Acapulco gold *noun*

golden-leafed marijuana from southwest Mexico *US, 1965*

A popular, well-known strain of cannabis. The song 'Acapulco Gold' by the Rainy Daze was released in 1967 and had just begun its climb on the pop charts when programme directors figured out what it was about and pulled it off play lists.

- "Gold. It's Acapulco Gold," White Rabbit corrected the doctor, who was mixing up the slang names for different kinds of marijuana. — Nicholas Von Hoffman, *We Are The People Our Parents Warned Us Against*, p. 23, 1967
- The kilo of high grade (poetically named Acapulco Gold) sells for $500 and upward, depending on who's selling and who's buying. — *San Francisco Examiner*, p. 35, 13th March 1967
- We are free to go, but have to be very sneaky and ditch Bruce somewhere inside the Pentagon maze so he won't find the Acapulco Gold in the car. — Abbie Hoffman, *Revolution for the Hell of It*, p. 44, 1968
- I don't know how he finds out these things, but Chase Webb discovers that the term "Acapulco Gold" has been registered in Washington – in anticipation of the day marijuana is legalized. — *San Francisco Chronicle*, p. 25, 25th April 1968
- But he did find several ounces of Acapulco gold, a smokable delicacy for which Plucky had acquired a taste while south of the border. — Tom Robbins, *Another Roadside Attraction*, p. 54–55, 1971
- About midnite she came to me and asked would I like some Acupulco gold, I said yes. — Babs Gonzales, *Movin' On Down De Line*, p. 115, 1975

acca; acker *noun*

an academic whose work serves the market place rather than the intellect; hence a particularly sterile piece of academic writing *AUSTRALIA, 1977*

An abbreviation punning **OCKER** (a coarse Australian).

accelerator *noun*

1 an amphetamine tablet *US*

- — Peter Johnson, *Dictionary of Street Alcohol and Drug Terms*, p. 1, 1993

2 an arsonist *US*

- — William K. Bentley and James M. Corbett, *Prison Slang*, p. 34, 1992

accessory *noun*

a boyfriend or girlfriend *US*

- — Lady Kier Kirby, *The 376 Deee-liteful Words*, 1992

accibounce *noun*

a minor collision or accident *TRINIDAD AND TOBAGO*

- — Lise Winer, *Dictionary of the English/Creole of Trinidad & Tobago*, 2003

accident *noun*

a murder that cannot be proved as such *US*

- — R. Frederick West, *God's Gambler*, p. 222, 1964

accidentally on purpose *adverb*

apparently accidental yet deliberately done, especially with hidden malicious purpose *US, 1887*

- — Joseph Weingarten, *American Dictionary of Slang*, p. 1, 1954

accommodation arrest *noun*

a pre-arranged, consensual raid of an illegal gambling operation, designed to give the appearance of strict enforcement of laws *US, 1961*

- — Thomas L. Clark, *The Dictionary of Gambling and Gaming*, p. 1, 1987

according to Hoyle *adverb*

in keeping with established rules and norms *US, 1904*

After Edmond Hoyle (1672–1769), who codified the rules for many games.

- — Joseph A. Weingarten, *An American Dictionary of Slang*, p. 1, 1954

accordion act *noun*

collapsing under pressure *US*

- Unlike their previous two games against the Rangers, the Devils didn't do an accordion act after allowing an early goal, and scored the next three goals of the first period. — *Record (Bergen County, New Jersey)*, p. E1, 10th January 1989
- — Paul Dickson, *The New Dickson Baseball Dictionary*, p. 1, 1999
- If Tech doesn't get things figured out in a hurry, a possible repeat of the 1997 club's late-season accordion act looms. — *Roanoke (Virginia) Times & World News*, p. C1, 9th November 2001

accordion war *noun*

US tactics during the Korean war: accordion-like movements up and down Korea by land forces *US*

- So MacArthur began sniping at Ridgway and his "accordion war." — Joseph C. Goulden, *Korea*, p. 478, 1982

account executive *noun*

a pimp who procures and profits from high-price prostitutes *US*

- — Robert A. Wilson, *Playboy's Book of Forbidden Words*, p. 13, 1972

accrue *verb*

▸ **accrue chocolate**

to behave towards officers in an obsequious, sycophantic manner *UK, 1929*

Royal Navy usage; a play on **BROWN-NOSE** (to behave obsequiously, etc.)

accumulator *noun*

a type of bet where the amount won on one event becomes the stake for the next event; a bettor who operates in such a manner *UK, 1889*

- While accumulators increase the potential payout, the chance of success, naturally enough, is correspondingly much diminished[.] — David Bennet, *Know Your Bets*, p. 9, 2001

ace *noun*

1 a very close friend *US, 1932*

- One day after we became aces, we had our first fight in over a year[.] —Claude Brown, *Manchild in the Promised Land*, p. 79–80, 1965
- "You're pals with Tommy Dunphy, right, Carlito?" "Yeah, we're aces." —Edwin Torres, *Carlito's Way*, p. 47, 1975
- "But I'm aces with the A.B. here at Coldwater," Joe objected. —Seth Morgan, *Homeboy*, p. 369, 1990
- —Richard Allsopp, *Dictionary of Caribbean English Usage*, p. 8, 1996

2 used as a form of address *UK, 1919*

- George is unable to raise his voice, and when he does he pays heavily for it. CHRISSIE: Alright ace. GEORGE: What a great day Chrissie. —Alan Bleasdale, *Boys From the Blackstuff*, 1982

3 a good and reliable friend *US, 1941*

- It really bugged me when the paddies call us Puerto Ricans the same names they called our colored aces. —Piri Thomas, *Down These Mean Streets*, p. 120, 1967
- —Lois Stavsky et al., *A2Z*, p. 1, 1995

4 one dollar *US, 1900*

- —Robert S. Gould, *A Jazz Lexicon*, p. 3, 1964
- I want to play the nine ball for five dollars, but we decide on a fucking ace. —Jim Carroll, *Forced Entries*, p. 65, 1987

5 one hundred dollars *US, 1974*

- —J.E. Lighter, *Historical Dictionary of American Slang, Volume 1*, p. 4, 1994

6 one-eighth of an ounce of a drug *US*

- —Geoffrey Froner, *Digging for Diamonds*, p. 70, 1989

7 phencyclidine, the recreational drug known as PCP or angel dust *US*

- —Ronald Linder, *PCP*, p. 9, 1981

8 in dice games, a rolled one *US*

- Three crap three, ace-deuce, no use. —Chris Fagans and David Guzman, *A Guide to Craps Lingo*, p. 12, 1999

9 an important or notable CB user *US*
Citizens' band radio slang.

- —*Complete CB Slang Dictionary*, 1976
- —Peter Chippindale, *The British CB Book*, p. 151, 1981

10 a prison sentence of one year *US, 1927*

- —Hyman E. Goldin et al., *Dictionary of American Underworld Lingo*, p. 17, 1950

11 in the theatre, a one-night engagement *US*

- —Don Wilmeth, *The Language of American Popular Entertainment*, p. 3, 1981

12 in pool, the number one ball *US, 1878*

- Fifteen in the corner. Ace in the side. —*The Hustler*, 1961
- —Mike Shamos, *The Illustrated Encyclopedia of Billiards*, p. 1, 1993

13 a table for one at a restaurant *US, 1961*

- —Harold Wentworth and Stuart Berg Flexner, *Dictionary of American Slang*, p. 671, 1975

14 a single rotten fruit *UK*

- One bad peach – we call it an "ace" – turns the whole lot bad. We say, "Get that bleedin' ace out." —*Daily Mail*, 24th July 1963

15 in lunch counter usage, a grilled cheese sandwich *US*

- —Harold Wentworth and Stuart Berg Flexner, *Dictionary of American Slang*, p. 671, 1975

16 the grade 'A' *US, 1964*

- —Collin Baker et al., *College Undergraduate Slang Study Conducted at Brown University*, p. 69, 1968

▸ace in the hole
an undisclosed resource *US, 1908*

- Lapham Has 'Ace In Hole' on UNO —*San Francisco Call-Bulletin*, p. 2, 21st November 1945
- Colonel Calls Gems His 'Ace in Hole' —*San Francisco Examiner*, p. 3, 7th February 1947
- One of the first things I did was borrow $800 from Lillian, my rich ace in the hole. —Dick Gregory, *Nigger*, p. 112, 1964

▸ace up your sleeve
a resource that is yet to be revealed *US, 1927*
From the popular belief that card cheats hide cards up their sleeves.

- I still had a few aces up my sleeve. —Max Shulman, *The Many Loves of Dobie Gillis*, p. 115, 1951

▸on your ace
alone; by yourself *AUSTRALIA, 1904*

- He would rather pen and ink on his ace until some of his Chinas lobbed. —Ryan Aven-Bray, *Ridgey Didge Oz Jack Lang*, p. 11, 1983

ace *verb*

1 to outsmart someone *US, 1929*

- But there was something personal about it if the guy was driving down Telegraph grinning, thinking he'd aced him. —Elmore Leonard, *Swag*, p. 2, 1976

2 to work your way somewhere, to engineer something *US, 1929*

- The scheme is said to have originated among one or more influential groups in San Francisco's Chinatown, one of which for several years has been acing itself into a favored position with the Nationalist China regime. —*San Francisco Call-Bulletin*, p. 1, 2nd September 1953

3 to do well in an examination *US, 1957*

- —Collin Baker et al., *College Undergraduate Slang Study Conducted at Brown University*, p. 69, 1968

4 to kill someone *US, 1975*

- Then Amalia told her about the woman's husband ripping off the Casino Latino with Louis Palo and how Charley had to ace the husband[.] —Richard Condon, *Prizzi's Honor*, p. 88, 1982
- —Linda Reinberg, *In the Field*, p. 1, 1991

ace *adjective*
exceptional, expert, excellent *US, 1930*

- I am glad that the newspaper boys, who later liked to refer to me as an ace narcotic inspector, never heard the story of my first big pinch. —William J. Spillard and Pence James, *Needle in a Haystack*, p. 7, 1945
- Sy Oliver on trumpet (now Tommy Dorsey's ace arranger, who was then playing and arranging with Jimmy Lun ceford's band[.] —Mezz Mezzrow, *Really the Blues*, p. 285–286, 1946
- I became an ace young reporter for the Cincinnati Post and Times-Star. —Jerry Rubin, *Do It!*, p. 12, 1970
- Here he clowns for the camera with an ace Melbourne sporting identity. —Barry Humphries, *Les Patterson's Australia*, p. 24, 1978
- As a shag she might score zero, but she's ace at washing, ironing and keeping a man's tucker warm. —Barry Humphries, *The Traveller's Tool*, p. 25, 1985
- One of my ace informants tells me to see a guy at Charity in there with a gunshot wound he says was from a hunting accident. —Elmore Leonard, *Bandits*, p. 139, 1987
- The feel uv her arse squashin on me legs is ace an starts me knob stirrin in me jeans. —Niall Griffiths, *Grits*, p. 11, 2000
- Most of the coppers I worked with at street level are ace guys[.] —Duncan MacLaughlin, *The Filth*, p. 11, 2002

ace boon coon; ace boon poon *noun*
a very close friend *US, 1958*

- I knew K.B. about a year before we became ace boon coons. —Claude Brown, *Manchild in the Promised Land*, p. 79, 1965
- —Hermese E. Roberts, *The Third Ear*, 1971
- Now my ace-boon-poon / was a young boy named Spoon. —Lightnin' Rod, *Hustlers Convention*, p. 10, 1973
- Margo got up to greet him. 'Lobo. How's my ace boon coon?' —Robert Deane Pharr, *Giveadamn Brown*, p. 14, 1978

ace boy *noun*
a very good male friend *BERMUDA*

- —Peter A. Smith and Fred M. Barritt, *Bermewjan Vurds*, 1985

ace cool *noun*
a very close and trusted friend *US, 1988*

- Your client seemed to be indicating to me over the phone last night that his 'Ace Cool,' which means best friend, told him that he was part of the killing at Trenton Towers and that some Italian mobsters did the work. —Stephen Cannell, *King Con*, p. 66, 1997

ace-deuce *noun*

1 a fellow prisoner upon whom you rely without question *US*

- —James Harris, *A Convict's Dictionary*, p. 28, 1989

2 your best friend *BELIZE*

- —Richard Allsopp, *Dictionary of Caribbean English Usage*, p. 6, 1996
- —Alonzo Westbrook, *Hip Hoptionary*, p. 1, 2002

ace-deuce *verb*
in craps, to sustain a heavy loss *US*

- —Thomas L. Clark, *The Dictionary of Gambling and Gaming*, p. 2, 1987

ace-deuce *adjective*

1 cross-eyed *US*

- They had eleven bowledgged children whose glims[eyes] were ace-deuce and won bingo games on strangers' cards. —*San Francisco Examiner*, p. 6, 20th March 1955

2 riding a racehorse with the right stirrup higher than the left *US*

- Acaro uses what is called the "ace deuce" technique in which the right stirrup is about two inches higher than the left. —*Time*, p. 82, 17th May 1948

ace-deuce *adverb*
on an angle, with one side higher than the other *US, 1948*
- There's vomit all over the bed, all in my hat, and that's sittin' ace-deuce on my head! —Henry Williamson, *Hustler!*, p. 62, 1965
- He broke the stingy brim down and set the hat ace-deuce across his head. —Donald Goines, *Dopefiend*, p. 182, 1971
- Sweet Peter D. cocks his lid ace-deuce, sticks his face three inches from Idella's and, after a quick count of the wages, begins to nibble on her buns, fiercely. —Odie Hawkins, *Ghetto Sketches*, p. 17, 1972

ace-douche *noun*
in craps, a first roll of three *US*
'Douche' is an intentional corruption of 'deuce'; a come-out roll of three loses.
- —Chris Fagans and David Guzman, *A Guide to Craps Lingo*, p. 13, 1999

aceeed!
▷ see: ACIEEED!

ace high; aces high *adjective*
the very best *US, 1896*
From poker.
- I said, "You're aces high with me, Duke." —Dan Jenkins, *Semi-Tough*, p. 177, 1972
- —*Washington Post Magazine*, p. 7, 20th September 1987

ace in *verb*
1 to manipulate someone or something into a situation *US*
- —Eugene Landy, *The Underground Dictionary*, p. 21, 1971

2 to become associated with a group and work your way into it *US*
- —Jay Robert Nash, *Dictionary of Crime*, p. 3, 1992

acelerante *noun*
an amphetamine or central nervous system stimulant *US*
Borrowed Spanish used by English-speakers.
- —Jay Robert Nash, *Dictionary of Crime*, p. 3, 1992

ace man *noun*
a youth gang's top fighter *US*
- —Dale Kramer and Madeline Karr, *Teen-Age Gangs*, p. 174, 1953

ace note *noun*
a one-dollar note *US, 1929*
- —Joe McKennon, *Circus Lingo*, p. 11, 1980

ace of spades *noun*
the vulva *US*
- —Harold Wentworth and Stuart Berg Flexner, *Dictionary of American Slang*, p. 2, 1960

ace on *adjective*
skilled at *BAHAMAS*
- —John A. Holm, *Dictionary of Bahamian English*, p. 1, 1982

ace out *verb*
1 to fool someone; to swindle someone *US, 1933*
- —Kenn "Naz" Young, *Naz's Underground Dictionary*, p. 12, 1973

2 to exclude someone *US*
- —J. R. Friss, *A Dictionary of Teenage Slang*, 1964

3 in poker, to win a hand by bluffing while holding a relatively low-value hand *US, 1983*
- —Thomas L. Clark, *The Dictionary of Gambling and Gaming*, p. 2, 1987

ace over apex *adverb*
head over heels *US, 1960*
- —Frederic G. Cassidy, *Dicitonary of American Regional English, Volume 1*, p. 7, 1985

aces *noun*
in poker, a hand with a pair of aces *US*
- —Thomas L. Clark, *The Dictionary of Gambling and Gaming*, p. 2, 1987

▸ **aces in both places**
in craps, a roll of two *US*
- —Chris Fagans and David Guzman, *A Guide to Craps Lingo*, p. 9, 1999

aces *adjective*
excellent *US, 1901*
- I said it in this very sincere voice. "You're aces, Ackley kid," I said. —J.D. Salinger, *Catcher in the Rye*, p. 50, 1951
- Paddy, why he's aces, a real saint, like; you know? —George Mandel, *Flee the Angry Strangers*, p. 56, 1952

acey-deucey *noun*
1 in backgammon, a variant rule under which the game is started in positions other than the standard layout *US, 1944*
- —Thomas L. Clark, *The Dictionary of Gambling and Gaming*, p. 2, 1987

2 a bisexual *US*
A probable elaboration of **AC/DC**.
- —Joe McKennon, *Circus Lingo*, p. 11, 1980

acey-deucey *verb*
(used of a jockey) to ride with the inside stirrup lower than the outside stirrup *US*
A riding style popularised by legendary jockey Eddie Acaro.
- —*Time*, 17th May 1948
- —Don Voorhees and Bob Benoit, *Railbird Handbook*, p. 44, 1968

acey-deucy *noun*
in craps, a roll of a one and a two *US*
- —John Savage, *The Winner's Guide to Dice*, p. 89, 1974

acey-deucy *adjective*
bisexual *US*
A probable elaboration of **AC/DC**.
- —Bruce Rodgers, *The Queens' Vernacular*, p. 32, 1972
- —Alonzo Westbrook, *Hip Hoptionary*, p. 1, 2002

acher *noun*
▷ see: ACRE

achiever *noun*
a devoted fan of the film *The Big Lebowski* *US*
In the film, the rich Lebowski sponsors a programme named the 'Little Lebowski Urban Achievers'.
- Many of the faithful – who call themselves Achievers after "The Little Lebowski Urban Achievers" in the movie- showed up dressed as their favoriate characters. —*Tallahassee (Florida) Democrat*, p. D1, 11th April 2004

Achnard *noun*
a taxi driver *US*
New York police slang, corrupting 'Ahmed' as an allusion to the preponderance of immigrants among New York's taxi-driving workforce.
- —Samuel M. Katz, *Anytime Anywhere*, p. 386, 1997

acid *noun*
1 LSD *US*
- [T]hen got up late that night, got loaded on acid & went bar-hopping to hear some great Rock & Roll. —Neal Cassady, *The First Third*, p. 218, 1965
- Last night as I left the U.C. theater on University Avenue, a guy walking behind me said to his friend: "That was better than acid, man." —*The Berkeley Barb*, p. 2, 17th December 1965
- Contrary to all expectations, most of the Angels became oddly peaceful on acid. —Hunter S. Thompson, *Hell's Angels*, p. 238, 1966
- She did not want to be left out and requested the acid. —Richard Alpert and Sidney Cohen, *LSD*, p. 42, 1966
- —J. L. Simmons and Barry Winograd, *It's Happening*, p. 167, 1966
- I was on a trip and haven't stopped tripping ... without acid! —*East Village Other*, 20th August 1969
- Acid, booze and ass / Needles, guns and grass / Lots of laughs, lots of laughs. —Joni Mitchell, *Blue*, 1971
- I can't really recommend acid because acid has become an almost meaningful chemical. —*The Last Supplement to the Whole Earth Catalog*, p. 83, March 1971
- So we were not greatly surprised when Eldrige Cleaver announced in Algeria last year that he had placed Dr. Leary under Black Panther arrest for his continued use of "acid." —Christina and Richard Milner, *Black Players*, p. 168, 1972
- Well, Donny's in a coma. He had a very bad acid experience. —*Manhattan*, 1979
- They approved of acid and pot and generally most of the hallucinogens[.] —Herbert Huncke, *Guilty of Everything*, p. 167, 1990
- Writer Ken Kesey and his Merry Pranksters – a travelling caravan which included Neal Cassady [...] and houseband the Grateful Dead, not to mention a bus called Furthur – gave acid a fresh boost as a mind-expanding panacea. —Simon Warner, *Rockspeak!*, p. 272, 1996
- At the first rush I'm waiting for the acid to reach the E and lift it higher. —Melanie McGrath, *Hard, Soft & Wet*, p. 90, 1998

2 rum *BARBADOS*
- —Frank A. Collymore, *Barbadian Dialect*, p. 10, 1965

3 by extension, any alcoholic beverage *TRINIDAD AND TOBAGO*
- —Lise Winer, *Dictionary of the English/Creole of Trinidad & Tobago*, 2003

4 impudence, heavy sarcasm *UK, 1962*
Especially in the phrase 'come the old acid'.

- I didn't altogether take to Raymond... too much of the old acid. —Martin Waddell, *Otley*, p. 101, 1966

▶ put the acid on

1 to pressure someone; to put someone to the test *AUSTRALIA, 1906*

From 'acid test'.

- The day gangs have been ordered to the Port. Eight o'clock. They want to shift the ship at seven. That puts acid on us. We're in the biggest hatch; from all accounts the others will be finished at six. —John Morrison, *Stories of the Waterfront*, p. 53, 1945
- Macauley, who knew the ropes, took the initiative and got busy with the yardman, putting the acid on him to help them to clean up a bit. —D'Arcy Niland, *The Shiralee*, p. 76, 1955
- With young Cynthia growing up and no poppa, Edna evidently had a pang of conscience but she wasn't going to lower herself to put the acid on me. —John Wynnum, *Jiggin' in the Riggin'*, p. 59, 1965

2 to pressure someone sexually *AUSTRALIA, 1939*

- And if you were thinking of putting the acid on that beaut short-haired bird in the leather gear at the office, think again. —Suzy Jarratt, *Permissive Australia*, p. 54, 1970

acid freak *noun*

a habitual user of LSD *US, 1966*

- —Eugene Landy, *The Underground Dictionary*, p. 21, 1971
- In a town full of bedrock crazies, nobody even notices an acid freak. —Hunter S. Thompson, *Fear and Loathing in Las Vegas*, p. 24, 1971

acid funk *noun*

a depression brought on by LSD use *US*

- —Eugene Landy, *The Underground Dictionary*, p. 21, 1971

acid head *noun*

a habitual user of LSD *US*

- For some in the group, it was a weekend party. For others, it was their first trip and several were true "acidheads." —Richard Alpert and Sidney Cohen, *LSD*, p. 100, 1966
- What they'll do is arrest the blacks, the acid heads, and the vagrants. —*Berkeley Barb*, p. 5, 30th December 1966
- Glossary of Hippie Terms —Joe David Brown (Editor), *The Hippies*, p. 217, 1967
- So many acidheads give the impression of having been reared by parents who read the Freudian books carefully and tried to see that baby could be anal and oral and genital and gooey[.] —Nicholas Von Hoffman, *We Are The People Our Parents Warned Us Against*, p. 64, 1967
- —Eugene Landy, *The Underground Dictionary*, p. 22, 1971
- Steve gave a talk at Santa Monica Civic Auditorium, tickets were sold in the Free Press office and I met acid heads galore. —Eve Babitz, *Eve's Hollywood*, p. 192, 1974
- [t]he visual effects by Peter Gardiner made the film [The Trip] a favourite of apprentice acidheads the world over. —Barney Hoskyns, *Waiting For The Sun*, p. 133, 1996

acid house *noun*

a mesmeric dance music genre characterised by electronic 'squelching' sounds *US, 1988*

An artistic and lexicographic extension of **HOUSE (MUSIC)**.

- After the ecstasy-fueled summer of 1987 on the Spanish holiday island of Ibiza, several influential British DJ's used acid house as a jumping-off point for a new ecelcticism. —Steven Daly and Nalthaniel Wice, *alt.culture*, p. 2, 1995
- Acid house became a household name that autumn [1987], when the tabloids ran headlines like "Evil of Ecstasy"; "The Acid House Horror"; "Hell of Acid House Kids". —Sarah Champion, *Disco Biscuits*, p. xiii, 1997
- Although the acid title originally had no reference to drugs, the media in the UK quickly, and wrongly, associated the drug -induced mayhem of acid house parties with LSD and popularised the acid house tag to describe the scene taking off at clubs. —Ben Osborne, *The A-Z of Club Culture*, p. 4, 1999
- Then Acid House and ecstasy came along[.] —Dave Courtney, *Raving Lunacy*, p. 73, 2000

acid jazz *noun*

a dance music genre *UK*

- The acid jazz crowd have their own style[.] —Alon Shulman, *The Style Bible*, p. 2, 1999

acid mung *noun*

the sensation while under the influence of LSD of having an oily face *US*

- —Eugene Landy, *The Underground Dictionary*, p. 22, 1971

acido *noun*

LSD *US*

Spanish used for effect.

- —Eugene Landy, *The Underground Dictionary*, p. 22, 1971

acid rock *noun*

a genre of rock music *US, 1966*

Folk etymology claims the music to be inspired by the altered states of conciousness induced by **ACID** (the hallucinogenic drug LSD); certainly this was a commercial style of music being marketed to the mass-audience when high-profile musicians were experimenting with LSD.

- [A] new sort of music showed us "Strawberry Fields forever" – it was nicknamed acid rock [...] instantly internationalised with the release of The Beatles' "Sergeant Pepper". Acid rock was flower power's jingle. —Richard Neville, *Play Power*, p. 99, 1970

acid test *noun*

an event organised to maximise the hallucinatory experiences of LSD *US*

Ken Kesey and the Merry Pranksters organised acid tests in Palo Alto, Portland (Oregon), Los Angeles and Mexico in 1966.

- Several members of the "Acid Test" dance beneath a flashing stroboscope light which heightens the effects of LSD. —Richard Alpert and Sidney Cohen, *LSD*, p. 97, 1966
- Curiously, after the first rush at the Acid Test, there would be long intervals of the most exquisite boredom. —Tom Wolfe, *The Electric Kool-Aid Acid Test*, p. 218, 1968

acidy *adjective*

psychedelic *UK*

From **ACID** (LSD).

- The music was like – hard House I guess, slow ploddy stuff with a few bits of acidy turns on top. —Ben Malbon, *Cool Places*, p. 274, 1998

acieeed!; aceeed!

called out to register a delight in, and identification with, club dance music *UK*

Three 'e's seem to be a constant in the various spellings that attempt to capture the fervour generated by early acid house culture.

- [A]cross the dance floors of 1987–8, aceeed! became the calling card of acid house and heralded the birth of the dance revolution[.] —Ben Osborne, *The A-Z of Club Culture*, p. 2, 1999
- The music was banging out and everyone started shouting "Acceeid!!" —Dave Courtney, *Stop the Ride I Want to Get Off*, p. 144, 1999
- Aciiiieeed! Free CD! —*The Face*, cover, June 2001
- [J]ust 'cause we all take the piss out of hairdressers doesn't mean we should diss the pre-Aceeeeed audience. —Tony Wilson, *24 Hour Party People*, p. 163, 2002

ack *noun*

a pimple *US*

- —Collin Baker et al., *College Undergraduate Slang Study Conducted at Brown University*, p. 70, 1968

ack *verb*

to acknowledge a letter, etc *UK, 1984*

Clerical, originally Civil Service.

ack-ack *noun*

anti-aircraft artillery *US, 1926*

An initialism, using the phonetic alphabet that was current until 1941. Usage survived the new alphabet rather than amend to 'able able'.

- I had a cross-eyed cousin, an organizer for the farmworker's union, who had been with an ack-ack battery in the defense of Madrid[.] —Clancy Sigal, *Going Away*, p. 119, 1961

ack-ack *verb*

to shoot someone or something *US*

- They barge in, ack-ack the wolf an' Ridinghood is in the groove forever after! —Haenigsen, *Jive's Like That*, 1947

ackamarackus; ackamaracka *noun*

fanciful speech intended to deceive *US, 1933*

- Don't give me the old ackamaraka. —Paul Tempest, *Lag's Lexicon*, p. 1, 1950

ack emma *noun*

the morning *UK, 1890*

Military origins, from the phonetic alphabet: ack (A) current 1904–41, emma (M) 1904–27.

- He'd call for me at six ack emma, in the hired drag [car][.] —Charles Raven, *Underworld Nights*, p. 55, 1956

acker; akka; ackers *noun*
money in any form *UK, 1937*
Originally military for one (Egyptian) piastre or piastres, probably from Arabic *fakka* (small change).
- [T]he Old Lady volunteered to look after the ackers till they came back[.] — Andrew Nickolds, *Back to Basics*, p. 52, 1994

▷ see: ACCA

Acker Bilk *noun*
milk *UK, 1992*
Rhyming slang, based on West Country jazz musician Acker Bilk (b.1929).
- Acker (Bilk=milk) is also West country dialect for friend. — *Antiquarian Book Review*, p. 18, June 2002

ackle *verb*
to fit or function properly *UK, 1961*
- It won't ackle. — *Partridge*, 1961
- Can you ackle it? — *Beale*, 1984

ack Willy; ack Willie *adjective*
absent without leave *AUSTRALIA, 1942*
In World War 2 military use; signalese for *AWOL*, the official abbreviation.
- We go 'ack willy' to the pub, and curse them over our beer. — J.M. Hosking, *Australia First and Last*, p. 120, 1957

acme wringer *noun*
the finger *UK*
Glasgow rhyming slang.
- — Michael Munro, *The Patter, Another Blast*, 1988

acne *noun*
a rough road-surface *US*
- — *Complete CB Slang Dictionary*, 1976
- — Peter Chippindale, *The British CB Book*, p. 151, 1981

acorn *noun*
in a casino, a generous tipper *US, 1984*
- — Thomas L. Clark, *The Dictionary of Gambling and Gaming*, p. 3, 1987

acorns *noun*
the testicles *US*
- "I loaned you part of the down payment!" reminded Harold and shrieked as the spray hit him in the acorns[.] — Joseph Wambaugh, *The Choirboys*, p. 213, 1975

acorn shell *noun*
a condom *UK, 1990s*
- — David Rowan, *A Glossary for the 90s*, 1998

acqua *noun*
▷ see: AQUA

acquire *verb*
to steal something *UK, 1937*
Ironic use of the conventional sense.

acre; acher *noun*
the backside *AUSTRALIA, 1938*
- I'll give you a free kick up the acher if you're not careful. — Frank Hardy, *The Outcasts of Foolgarah*, p. 94, 1971
- [S]ix (two, three etc.) axehandles across the acre: pertaining to a person with a very large backside, or one who is fat, obese. — Lenie Johansen, *The Dinkum Dictionary*, p. 372, 1984
- — Harry Orsman, *A Dictionary of Modern New Zealand Slang*, p. 1, 1999

across *preposition*
▸ **across the bridge to Dartmouth**
mentally ill, institutionalised *CANADA*
In the twin cities of Halifax and Dartmouth, Nova Scotia, the Nova Scotia Hospital, the institution for the mentally unstable, is in the latter.

across the board *noun*
in horse racing, a bet that a horse will win, place (finish second), or show (finish third) *US*
- — Nate Perlmutter, *How to Win Money at the Races*, p. 117, 1964

across the ditch *noun*
Australia *NEW ZEALAND*
- — David McGill, *David McGill's Complete Kiwi Slang Dictionary*, p. 6, 1998

across the pavement *adverb*
(of criminal activity) in a street situation *UK*
- Let's do one across the pavement[.] — David Powis, *The Signs of Crime*, 1977
- Fingers and Joycie were across the pavement, I was in the wheels. — Terry Victor, *A Family Affair*, 1991
- Why get blown away by the Sweeney going across the pavement for ten grand's worth of stolen Tom [jewellery]? — Garry Bushell, *The Face*, p. 24, 2001

act *noun*
the disguise and staged personality assumed by an expert card counter playing blackjack in a casino in the hope of avoiding detection and ejection *US*
- — Michael Dalton, *Blackjack*, p. 25, 1991

▸ **get in on the act; be in on the act**
to become, or be, involved in another's activity *US, 1947*
- But if it takes off, expect the operators to get in on the act quickly[.] — *The Guardian*, 5th June 2003

▸ **get into the act**
to take part *US*
If not coined by, popularised as part of the catchphrase 'everybody wants to get into the act' by comedian Jimmy Durante on the radio in the 1940s.
- Lincoln was such a success that everybody wanted to get into the act. — *Time*, p. 66, 4th March 1946
- School Superintendent Robert F. Savitt said, "It's not possible to say how many just wanted to get into the act." — *San Francisco News*, p. 1, 17th January 1953
- I should have known that you can't escape the frantic desire now possessed by seemingly everyone to, as it were, "get into the act." — *San Francisco New Call-Bulletin*, p. 14, 5th September 1961

▸ **get your act together; get it together**
to take control of your personal condition; to get your mind and emotions under control; to become organised *US, 1973*
A variation of 'pull yourself together'.
- [M]an, we were both sort of really spaced out [drug-intoxicated] [...] but I got it together to clean up the sick. — Paul E Willis, *Profane Culture*, p. 142, 1978
- — Gretchen Cryer, *I'm Getting My Act Together And Taking It On The Road*, 1978

▸ **hard act to follow; tough act to follow**
something or someone who cannot be easily outdone *US*
- With his own yacht and his own island and his own particular brand of charm, Ari is a hard act to follow. — *San Francisco Examiner*, p. 16, 14th December 1963
- When Lombardi left, Bengtson was chosen. What an act to follow. — *San Francisco Chronicle*, p. 50, 28th August 1970

▸ **put on an act**
to give an exaggerated performance; to indulge in histrionics *AUSTRALIA, 1944*
- 'Listen, mate,' he said, 'I'm just hopin' ya'll put on an act, that's all. Just put on an act.' — Lawson Glassop, *We Were the Rats*, p. 176, 1944
- Don't tell me *I* was mean, you were putting on a bigger act that mine! — Willie Fennell, *Dexter Gets The Point*, p. 98, 1961
- They'd all been through her – no worries – but the only reason she'd stacked on an act was because the young idiots had left her out in the bush for a joke because they new her husband was due home from night shift. — David Williamson, *The Removalists*, p. 36, 1972
- I decided to rough him up a bit. I put on the real fierce act and rushed at him. — Sam Weller, *Old Bastards I Have Met*, p. 106, 1979
- I put on a big act and I told the bloke who answered the phone I was gonna complain to the minister. — Frank Hardy, *Hardy's People*, p. 41, 1986

act *verb*
▸ **act as if**
in twelve-step recovery programmes such as Alcoholics Anonymous, used as a slogan for new participants in the programme *US*
- They're told to act as if they were sane, or not wanting to use, because all you can really change for the moment is your actions, not your feelings[.] — Christopher Cavanaugh, *AA to Z*, p. 43, 1998

▸ **act cute**
to behave in an annoyingly adorable fashion *SINGAPORE*
- — Paik Choo, *The Coxford Singlish Dictionary*, p. 1, 2002

▸ **act the angora**
to play the fool *AUSTRALIA, 1942*
The angora goat supplies this variation of ACT THE GOAT.

▸ **act the goat**
to play the fool *AUSTRALIA, 1940*
- Kimiko took me by the hand again and led me back to the Blackbird, and we went on drinking and talking and acting the goat.—Les Such, *A Yen for Yokohama*, p. 56, 1963
- The boys were hoppo-bumping each other, acting the goat, while the girls maintained an air of superior indifference.—Shane Maloney, *Nice Try*, p. 263, 1998

▸ **act the maggot**
to play the fool *IRELAND*
- —Susie Dent, *The Language Report*, p. 83, 2003

▸ **act your age not your shoesize**
to behave in a manner appropriate to your years *US*
A humorous extension of 'act your age'.
- Act your age, mama, not your shoe size, maybe we could do the twirl.—Prince, *Kiss*, 1986

act-ass *noun*
a show-off; a braggart *US, 1970*
- —Frederic G. Cassidy, *Dicitonary of American Regional English, Volume 1*, p. 9, 1985

acting Jack *noun*
1 a lance sergeant *US, 1917*
Korean war usage.
- I took my "acting jack" job most seriously, and was thought to be a shoo-in for the "best trainee" (an honor that included a promotion to PFC on completetion of the course until a week before basic was over[.]—David H. Hackworth, *About Face*, p. 41, 1989

2 a soldier temporarily appointed to higher rank, especially to serve as a platoon leader in basic training *US, 1942*
- —Carl Fleischhauer, *A Glossary of Army Slang*, p. 1, 1968

action *noun*
1 sexual activity *US, 1956*
- Dark and jazzy, the man approaches Johnny. "Lookin for action, babe?"—John Rechy, *Numbers*, p. 136, 1967
- As far as I'm concerned there ain't no difference. Action's action[.] —Malcolm Braly, *On the Yard*, p. 88, 1967
- I'm goin' to the dance to get some action.—Frank Zappa, *Flower Punk*, 1968
- I therefore denounced the idea of conjugal vists as inherently unfair; single prisoners needed and deserved action just as married prisoners did.—Eldridge Cleaver, *Soul on Ice*, p. 7, 1968
- Where did he go to study when he saw the tie placed on the doorknob of our room (the traditional signal for "action within")?—Erich Segal, *Love Story*, p. 36, 1970
- Did you get any action? Did you slam it to her? Did you stick her? Did you hump her? Did you run it down her throat? Did you jam it up her ass? Did you shoot your wad?—*Screw*, p. 6, 29th May 1972
- Excuse me, baby, but if I don't get some action tonight, I'm gonna bust. You interested?—*48 Hours*, 1982

2 activity, especially of the kind to arouse interest or excitement *US*
Often in the greetings 'where's the action?' and 'what's the action?'.
- Man, that chick is puttin' down some action!—William "Lord" Buckley, *Nero*, 1951
- —Richard McAlister, *Rapper's Handbook*, p. 1, 1990

3 betting, gambling *US, 1885*
- You looking for action?—*The Hustler*, 1961
- The sina qua non is that he is a good "money player," can play his best when heavy action is riding on the game (as many non-hustlers can't).—Ned Polsky, *Hustlers, Beats, and Others*, p. 55, 1967
- And I'll take all the action I can get.—*Diner*, 1982

4 the amount that a gambler is willing to bet *US*
- For example, one hundred bets of $5 each is $500 in action.—Michael Dalton, *Blackjack*, p. 25, 1991

5 in pool, a game played with wagers *US*
- —Steve Rushin, *Pool Cool*, p. 5, 1990

6 in pool, spin imparted on the cue ball to affect the course of the object ball or the cue ball after striking the object ball *US, 1913*
- —Mike Shamos, *The Illustrated Encyclopedia of Billiards*, p. 2, 1993

7 a political act, often confrontational or violent *US*
- On that same point, I'd like to say first of all, as Billy mentioned, letters are going to be going to the men whose [draft] files were destroyed, and this in itself is, I think, an action, because it is giving these men a chance to make their own choice.—*The Last Supplement to the Whole Earth Catalog*, p. 18, March 1971

▸ **piece of the action; share of the action**
an involvement in an activity; a share in the profits of something *US, 1957*
- Triads never helped anyone out without a promise of a piece of the action.—Lung Cheng, *I Am Jackie Chan*, p. 261, 1998

action *suffix*
used for emphasis of the noun to which it is suffixed, without change in meaning *US*
- I'm ready for some Chinese food action for lunch[.]—Connie Eble (Editor), *UNC-CH Campus Slang*, p. 1, Spring 1982

action beaver *noun*
a film featuring full nudity and sexual activity short of intercourse *US*
- The action beaver, the next logical cinematic step, featured increasingly explicit sexual activity along with complete nudity. —Kenneth Turan and Stephen E. Zito, *Sinema*, p. 78, 1974

action faction *noun*
a subset of the political left that advocated forceful, confrontational tactics *US*
- The Labor Committee is sometimes referred to as the thought faction, as opposed to the action faction, of SDS.—James Simon Kunen, *The Strawberry Statement*, p. 102, 1968

action player *noun*
a gambler who bets heavily, frequently and flamboyantly *US*
- —Victor H. Royer, *Casino Gamble Talk*, p. 5, 2003

action room *noun*
a poolhall where betting is common *US, 1967*
- —Mike Shams, *The Illustrated Encyclopedia of Billiards*, p. 2, 1993

active citizens *noun*
fleas, bedbugs or body lice *US*
- —Vincent J. Monteleone, *Criminal Slang*, p. 9, 1949

actor *noun*
1 a liar, a bluffer *UK, 1950*
Criminal usage.

2 a troublemaker *US*
- —R. Frederick West, *God's Gambler*, p. 222, 1964

actor-proof *adjective*
denoting a part in a play or performance so well written that no amount of bad acting can ruin it *US*
- —Sherman Louis Sergel, *The Language of Show Biz*, p. 4, 1973

actor's Bible *noun*
Variety magazine *US*
- —Don Wilmeth, *The Language of American Popular Entertainment*, p. 4, 1981

actor's reach *noun*
a seemingly sincere effort to pay for your meal when eating in a group at a restaurant, masking a secret hope that someone else will pay *US*
Based on the stereotype of the actor as starving artist, timing his reach for his wallet to produce a demur from someone else at the table who has already reached for their wallet to pay. Collected in Los Angeles, 1999.

actual *noun*
in the Vietnam war, a unit commander *US*
- —Linda Reinberg, *In the Field*, p. 2, 1991

actuary *noun*
in an illegal betting operation, an oddsmaker *US, 1971*
- —Thomas L. Clark, *The Dictionary of Gambling and Gaming*, p. 3, 1987

AD *noun*
a drug addict *US, 1970*
Either a straightforward abbreviation of 'addict' or, as has been seriously suggested, an initialism of 'drug addict' reversed to avoid confusion with a District Attorney.
- —Eugene Landy, *The Underground Dictionary*, p. 22, 1971
- —Richard A. Spears, *The Slang and Jargon of Drugs and Drink*, p. 4, 1986
- —Mike Haskins, *Drugs*, p. 292, 2003

adafookman!
used as an all-purpose protestation of innocence, e.g. 'have I?', 'I didn't!' *UK*
A phonetic slovening of 'have I fuck, man!'. Current in black criminal society, August 2002.

Ada from Decatur; Ada Ross, the Stable Hoss *noun*
in a game of dice, a roll of eight *US, 1918*
A homophonic evolution of 'eighter'.
- —Sidney H. Radner, *Radner on Dice*, p. 10, 1957
- —Frank Garcia, *Marked Cards and Loaded Dice*, p. 250, 1962

Ad Alley *nickname*
the advertising industry, especially that located in New York and commonly known in the US as 'Madison Avenue' after the New York street where many advertising agencies had their offices *US*
- Ulcers now run second (along Ad Alley) to crackups among ad agency execs—*San Francisco Call-Bulletin*, p. 8G, 3rd October 1952
- The urgently felt need to "stimulate" people brought new power, glory, and prosperity to the professional stimulators or persuaders of American industry, particularly the skilled gray-flanneled suiters of New York's Madison Avenue, known as "ad alley."—Vance Packard, *The Hidden Persuaders*, p. 21, 1957

Adam *noun*
1 MDMA, the recreational drug best known as ecstasy *US, 1985*
An anagram.
- —Bruce Eisner, *Ecstasy*, p. 1, 1989
- —Angela Devlin, *Prison Patter*, p. 22, 1996
- CALL IT... Adam, brownies, burgers, disco biscuits, doves, eckies, tulips, X[.] JUST DON'T CALL IT... MDMA – too scientific—*Drugs An Adult Guide*, p. 34, December 2001
- —Mike Haskins, *Drugs*, p. 289, 2003

2 a partner in a criminal enterprise *UK, 1797*
- —*American Speech*, p. 97, May 1956: 'Smugglers' argot in the southwest'

3 a homosexual's first sexual partner *US*
The first man.
- —Bruce Rodgers, *The Queens' Vernacular*, p. 18, 1972

▸ not know someone from Adam
to be ignorant about an identification *UK, 1784*
- Keep away from the prisoner if you please. We don't know you from Adam—John Wynnum, *Jiggin' in the Riggin'*, p. 95, 1965

Adam and Eve *noun*
a pill of MDEA and MDMA, the recreational drugs best known as ecstasy *UK*
A combination of **ADAM** (MDMA) and the obvious partner; note **MADMAN** and **MADWOMAN** as synonyms for MDMA and MDEA repectively.
- —Angela Devlin, *Prison Patter*, p. 22, 1996
- —Gareth Thomas, *This Is Ecstasy*, p. 54, 2002

Adam and Eve; adam *verb*
1 to believe *UK*
Rhyming slang. Franklyn suggests it ante-dates 1914; the *Oxford English Dictionary* finds the earliest citation at 1925.
- You wouldn't Adam and Eve it.—*The Sweeney*, p. 6, 1976
- You won't adam wot I sees.—Viv Stanshall, *Ginger Geezer*, 1981
- Can you adam and eve it? Eh?—Donald Gorgon, *Cop Killer*, p. 109, 1994

2 to leave, especially in a hurried manner *UK*
- When it's time to go, it's time you were "Adam and Eveing".—Ray Puxley, *Fresh Rabbit*, p. 1, 1998

Adam and Eve on a raft *noun*
two eggs on toast *US, 1909*
Restaurant slang.
- "I'd like two scrambled eggs on toast, and a cup of tea with lemon, please." "Adam and Eve on a raft, wreck'em, and a spot with a twist."—Alexandra Day, *Frank and Ernest*, 1988

Adam Ants *noun*
pants *UK*
Rhyming slang for UK underwear not US trousers; formed on Adam Ant, the stage name of singer and actor Stuart Goddard (b.1954).
- —Bodmin Dark, *Dirty Cockney Rhyming Slang*, 2003

adamatical *adjective*
naked *UK, 1961*
Without a conventional fig leaf.

Adam's off-ox *noun*
a complete stranger *US*
Used in the expression 'he wouldn't know me from Adam's off-ox'.
- The first time I stepped in, he was behind the counter and didn't know me from Adam's off ox.—*Christian Science Monitor*, p. 20, 29th April 1983
- You don't know me from Adam's off ox—*USA Today*, p. 6D, 24th February 2004

Ada Ross, the Stable Hoss *noun*
▷ see: **ADA FROM DECATUR**

adbuster *noun*
in anticorporate activism, the non-specific description for those involved in cultural subversion *CANADA, 1989*
- Nowhere is the adbuster's ear for the pitch used to fuller effect than in the promotion of adbusting itself.—Naomi Klein, *No Logo*, p. 295, 2001

adbusting *noun*
in anticorporate activism, the act of subverting brand advertising, usually by parody or mockery *US*
- Her solutions to the problem includes "adbusting" – parody ads, defacing existing ads – and "take back the street" gatherings.—*News Journal (Wilimington, Delaware)*, p. 7, 5th March 2000
- He believes that adbusting will eventually spark a "paradigm shift" in public conciousness.—Naomi Klein, *No Logo*, p. 286, 2001

addick *noun*
an addict *US*
A misspelling that reflects phonetic use.
- No, he said, you found out how to be a drug addick and a murderer.—Joel Rose, *Kill Kill Faster Faster*, p. 120, 1997

addict *noun*
a victim of a confidence swindle who repeatedly invests in the crooked enterprise, hoping that his investment will pay off *US*
- —M. Allen Henderson, *How Con Games Work*, p. 217, 1985

▸ addict waiting to happen
in twelve-step recovery programmes such as Alcoholics Anonymous, used for describing the childhood of addicts of the future *US*
- —Christopher Cavanaugh, *AA to Z*, p. 45, 1998

additood *noun*
a confrontational manner *UK, 1990s*
The English version of Americanised pronunciation, adopting the US slang sense of an otherwise conventional 'attitude'.
- "Ah, brilliant! Our first outbreak of additood! Hecor's got additood! Brilliant!" "Hector's always had additood," muttered Keva.—Kevin Sampson, *Powder*, p. 227, 1999

addy *noun*
an address *US*
- —Alonzo Westbrook, *Hip Hoptionary*, p. 1, 2002
- [H]is e-mail addy disappeared due to the overwhelming flood of support against the global giant.—*Idaho Statesman*, p. 36, 27th January 2004

A-deck *noun*
a prison cell used for solitary confinement *US*
- —Inez Cardozo-Freeman, *The Joint*, p. 479, 1984

adger *verb*
in computing, to make an avoidable mistake *US*
- —Eric S. Raymond, *The New Hacker's Dictionary*, p. 31, 1991

adidas *noun*
a prison training instructor *UK*
From the similarity between the stripes on an instructor's uniform and the logo-styling on Adidas™ sports equipment.
- —Angela Devlin, *Prison Patter*, p. 22, 1996

adios amoebas
used as a humorous farewell *US*
The 'amoebas' is an intentional butchering of *amigos*.
- —Connie Eble (Editor), *UNC-CH Campus Slang*, p. 1, Spring 1988

adios motherfucker
used as a farewell *US*
Jocular or defiant; sometimes abbreviated to **AMF**.
- Ten days from now I am adios, motherfucker, so till then I'm playing catch-up.—James Ellroy, *Suicide Hill*, p. 585, 1986

Adirondack steak; Adirondack goat *noun*
game, especially venison, killed out of season *US, 1954*
- —Frederic G. Cassidy, *Dicitonary of American Regional English, Volume 1*, p. 13, 1985

adjectival *adjective*
used as a euphemistic substitute for any intensifying adjective that may be considered unsuitable *UK, 1910*
- [S]o the wheels of adjectival justice continue, albeit creakily, to turn. —David Foster Wallace, *Infinite Jest*, back matter, 1996

adjuster *noun*
a hammer *US*
- —Elena Garcia, *A Beginner's Guide to Zen and the Art of Snowboarding*, p. 121, 1990

adjust the stick!
used as a humorous admonition to casino employees at a craps table when the players are losing *US, 1983*
- —Thomas L. Clark, *The Dictionary of Gambling and Gaming*, p. 3, 1987

ad-lib *verb*
to date indiscriminately *US*
- —*San Francisco Examiner*, p. III-2, 22nd March 1960

ad man *noun*
1 a prisoner who is friendly or aligned with the prison administration *US*
- —John R. Armore and Joseph D. Wolfe, *Dictionary of Desperation*, p. 19, 1976

2 a swindler who sells advertising space in a non-existent publication or a publication with whom he has no association *US*
- —Jay Robert Nash, *Dictionary of Crime*, p. 4, 1992

Admiral Browning *noun*
in the navy, human excrement *UK, 1961*
An elaborate promotion of the appropriate colour.

admiral's mate *noun*
in the Royal Navy, a boasting know-all rating *UK, 1962*
- —John W. Mussell, *The Token Book of Militarisms*, p. 6, 1995

admiral's watch *noun*
a good night's sleep *US*
- —Vincent J. Monteleone, *Criminal Slang*, p. 9, 1949

admiralty brown *noun*
toilet paper *AUSTRALIA, 1961*
Originally Royal Australian Navy.

admish *noun*
the admission price of a performance *US*
- —Don Wilmeth, *The Language of American Popular Entertainment*, p. 5, 1981

a-double-scribble *noun*
used as a euphemism for 'ass' in any of its senses *US*
- —Claudio R. Salvucci, *The Philadelphia Dialect Dictionary*, p. 27, 1996

Adrian Quist *adjective*
drunk *AUSTRALIA, 1978*
Rhyming slang for **PISSED**; formed on the name of the Australian tennis player, 1913–91.

adrift *adjective*
1 absent without leave; missing *US, 1841*
Originally nautical.
- If there's anything adrift it'll come off your slop chit[.] —Colin Evans, *The Heart of Standing*, 1962

2 confused *UK*
- Just pay attention to what I say and then we'll have nobody adrift[.] —Colin Evans, *The Heart of Standing*, 1962

adult baby *noun*
a person, often a prostitute's client, whose sexual needs are manifested in a desire to be dressed and treated as an infant *UK*
- Ben refused to see anything wrong with being an adult baby. —Kitty Churchill, *Thinking of England*, p. 17, 1995
- —Caroline Archer, *Tart Cards*, 2003

advance *verb*
▸ **advance the spark**
to prepare *US*
- —Lou Shelly, *Hepcats Jive Talk Dictionary*, p. 21, 1945

advertise *verb*
1 to signal your intentions unwittingly but plainly *US, 1931*
- Relax. Please. This is just another day. Stop advertising. —Horace McCoy, *Kiss Tomorrow Good-bye*, p. 8, 1948

2 to dress or behave in a sexually provocative manner; to pluck and pencil the eyebrows *US, 1972*
Gay use, on the premise that it pays to advertise.

3 in poker, to bluff in a manner that is intended to be caught, all in anticipation of a later bluff *US, 1949*
- —Albert H. Morehead, *The Complete Guide to Winning Poker*, p. 255, 1967

4 in gin, to discard in a manner that is designed to lure a desired card from an opponent *US*
- —Irwin Steig, *Play Gin to Win*, p. 138, 1971

5 to activate the siren and/or flashing lights of a police car *US*
- —Wayne Floyd, *Jason's Authentic Dictionary of CB Slang*, p. 6, 1976

advertised *noun*
▸ **on the advertised**
on the railways, on time *US*
- —J. Herbert Lund, *Herb's Hot Box of Railraod Slang*, p. 176, 1975

adzine *noun*
a single-interest fan magazine containing only advertising *US*
- —*American Speech*, p. 23, Spring 1982: 'The langage of science fiction fan magazines'

a-end *noun*
▷ see: ARSE END

aerated; aeriated *adjective*
excited, angry *UK, 1984*

aerial *adjective*
used as a modifier for any sexual position where at least one participant is off the ground *US*
- —*Adult Video News*, p. 40, August 1995

aeroplane blonde *noun*
▷ see: AIRPLANE BLONDE

Aesop *noun*
in poker, any player who tells stories while playing *US*
- —John Vorhaus, *The Big Book of Poker Slang*, p. 3, 1996

af; aff *noun*
an African *SOUTH AFRICA, 1976*
Derogatory.

A-factor *noun*
the 'Antarctic factor', which explains any and all unexpected and added difficulties encountered *ANTARCTICA, 1988*
- —Bernadette Hince, *The Antarctic Dictionary*, p. 14, 2000
- —*Cool Antartica*, 2003: 'Antarctic slang'

AFAIC
used as shorthand in Internet discussion groups and text message to mean '*as far as I'm concerned*' *US*
- —Gabrielle Mander, *WAN2TLK?*, p. 42, 2002

AFF *noun*
an attraction to South Asian females *US*
An abbreviation of 'Asian female fetish'.
- —Pamela Munro, *U.C.L.A. Slang*, p. 20, 1997

affirmative
yes *US*
Used with irony, mocking a military response.
- —Connie Eble (Editor), *UNC-CH Campus Slang*, November 1976

affy bud *noun*
a type of marijuana that originates in Afghanistan *UK*
- —Steven Wishnia, *The Cannabis Companion*, p. 150, 2004

afgay *noun*
a homosexual *US*
Formed by a pig Latin-like construction called 'Anyway'.
- —Robert A. Wilson, *Playboy's Book of Forbidden Words*, p. 15, 1972

Afghan *noun*
any Afghani, Pakistani or other central Asian who immigrated to Australia in the C19 to work as camel-drivers in desert regions *AUSTRALIA, 1869*
Formerly generally regarded with suspicion and contempt by white Australians, which accounts for the fossilisation of the term in various derogatory phrases; the occupation has long since disappeared.

- You might have thought, if a Royal Oak supporter, that his brown-skinned close-shaven head justified Darky's contention that he had a head on him like an Afghan camel-driver[.] — Frank Hardy, *Legend's from Benson's Valley*, p. 62, 1963
- Any way, not a bad place, is it? Smells a bit like an Afghan's armpit – but the beer goes down well! — Barry Humphries, *The Wonderful World of Barry McKenzie*, p. 32, 1968
- The pub across the road shuts at six o'clock – and I'm thirsty enough to drink a whisky through an Afghan camel-driver's jockstrap. — Frank Hardy, *Hardy's People*, p. 150, 1986

Afghani *noun*
hashish oil from Afghanistan *US*
Although Afghanistan is best known for its heroin, hashish is a second important export.
- — Jay Robert Nash, *Dictionary of Crime*, p. 5, 1992

Afghani black; Afghani pollen *noun*
varieties of hashish from Afghanistan *UK*
- Afghani pollen produces a slightly lighter and crumblier hash than traditional Afghani black. — Nick Jones, *Spliffs*, p. 81, 2003

AFK
used as shorthand in Internet discussion groups and text message to mean '*a*way *f*rom *k*eyboard' *US*
- — Gabrielle Mander, *WAN2TLK?*, p. 42, 2002

Afkansastan *noun*
Afghan marijuana grown in Kansas *US*
- — Simon Worman, *Joint Smoking Rules*, 2001

afloat *adjective*
drunk *US, 1809*
- — J.E. Lighter, *Historical Dictionary of American Slang, Volume 1*, p. 11, 1994

AFO *nickname*
the Arellano-Felix Organization, a criminal enterprise that functioned as a transportation subcontractor for the heroin trade into the US *US*
- Blancornelas' bodyguard was killed, as was David Barron-Corona, who recruited security and hitmen for the AFO[.] — *Newsday (New York)*, p. 40, 15th February 1998
- The drug trade, too, has its courier services, outfits such as "Nigeria Express" or Mexico's notorious A.F.O. — *New York Times*, p. SM29, 23 June 2002

afoot or ahossback *adjective*
unsure of the direction you are going to take *US, 1895*
- — Charles F. Haywood, *Yankee Dictionary*, p. 2, 1963

A for effort *noun*
praise for the work involved, if not for the result of the work *US*
From a trend in US schools to grade children both on the basis of achievement and on the basis of effort expended. Faint praise as often as not.
- If the rest of the movie were up to Miss Bergman, it could be rated very close to excellent. As it is, it rates A for effort. — *Time*, p. 102, 15th November 1948
- If President Johnson is handing our report cards today, he almost certainly is giving Secretary of State Dean Rusk and Gen Maxwell D. Taylor an "A" for effort. — *San Francisco Examiner*, p. 1, 18th February 1966

Africa hot *adjective*
extremely hot *US*
- It ain't hot, it's Africa hot. — Judi Sanders, *Kickin' like Chicken with the Couch Commander*, p. 1, 1992

African *noun*
1 a manufactured cigarette (not hand-rolled) *AUSTRALIA*
- — Sidney J. Baker, *The Drum*, 1959

2 a type of marijuana claimed to have been grown in Africa *UK*
- — Mike Haskins, *Drugs*, p. 286, 2003

3 in American casinos, a black betting chip worth $100 *US, 1983*
- — Thomas L. Clark, *The Dictionary of Gambling and Gaming*, p. 4, 1987

African black *noun*
a potent type of marijuana, presumed to be from Africa, possibly Morocco *US, 1970*
- — Richard A. Spears, *The Slang and Jargon of Drugs and Drink*, p. 5, 1986
- — Mike Haskins, *Drugs*, p. 286, 2003

African bush *noun*
marijuana *US, 1979*
- — Richard A. Spears, *The Slang and Jargon of Drugs and Drink*, p. 5, 1986
- Grass ... Mary Jane, Aunt Hazel, African bush, bambalacha. You pic the cool name. — Stephen J. Cannell, *The Tin Collectors*, p. 60, 2001
- — Mike Haskins, *Drugs*, p. 286, 2003

African dominoes *noun*
dice *US, 1919*
- — Joseph Weingarten, *American Dictionary of Slang*, p. 3, 1954
- Then the colored gamblers set in to pleading with the African dominoes[.] — Guy Owen, *The Flim-Flam Man and the Apprentice Grifter*, p. 117, 1972
- — John Scarne, *Scarne on Dice*, p. 459, 1974

African golf *noun*
the game of craps *US, 1919*
- — Joseph Weingarten, *American Dictionary of Slang*, p. 3, 1954
- — Thomas L. Clark, *The Dictionary of Gambling and Gaming*, p. 4, 1987

African grape *noun*
a watermelon *US*
Based on the stereotypical association between rural black people and a love of watermelon.
- — Edith A. Folb, *runnin' down some lines*, p. 227, 1980

African guff-guff *noun*
a non-existent disease suffered by soldiers *US*
- — *American Speech*, p. 305, December 1947: 'Imaginary diseases in army and navy parlance'

African plum *noun*
a watermelon *US*
- — Malachi Andrews and Paul T. Owens, *Black Language*, p. 96, 1973

African queen *noun*
a white homosexual man who finds black men attractive *US*
Punning on the Bogart film.
- — *Maledicta*, p. 236, 1979: 'Kinks and queens: linguistic and cultural aspects of the terminology for gays'

African salad *noun*
khat, a natural stimulant grown in Kenya, Ethiopa and Somalia *UK*
- — Harry Shapiro, *Recreational Drugs*, p. 240, 2004

African toothache *noun*
any sexually transmitted infection *US*
- — Roger Blake, *The American Dictionary of Sexual Terms*, p. 2, 1964

African Woodbine *noun*
a marijuana cigarette *UK, 1975*
Woodbine™ was a well-known brand of cheaper cigarette.
- — Richard A. Spears, *The Slang and Jargon of Drugs and Drink*, p. 5, 1986
- — Mike Haskins, *Drugs*, p. 286, 2003

Afro *noun*
a bushy, frizzy hairstyle embraced by black people as a gesture of resistance in the 1960s *US, 1966*
- — *Current Slang*, p. 1, Spring 1967
- But real Afros, not the ones that have been shaped and trimmed like a topiary hedge, and sprayed until they have a sheen like acrylic wall-to-wall – but like funky, natural, scraggly. — Tom Wolfe, *Radical Chic & Mau-Mauing the Flak Catchers*, p. 7, 1970
- I knew everything about O.J. from reading that 90-page book that third graders could order from the Weekly Reader. I remember knowing that he had a fine wife and an Afro. — Chris Rock, *Rock This!*, p. 206, 1997

afromobile *noun*
a wicker pedicab *US, 1939*
- — Frederic G. Cassidy, *Dicitonary of American Regional English, Volume 1*, p. 17, 1985

Afro pick *noun*
a gap-toothed comb used for an Afro hairstyle *US*
- Two black guys are about to tear into each other with Afro picks[.] — Josh Alan Friedman, *Tales of Times Square*, p. 64, 1986

afterbirth *noun*
rhubarb *AUSTRALIA, 1943*
- — John W. Mussell, *The Token Book of Militarisms*, p. 6, 1995

afterburner *noun*
a linear amplifier for a citizens' band radio *US*
- — Lawrence Teeman, *Consumer Guide Good Buddy's CB Dictionary*, p. 23, 1976

afterclaps *noun*
consequences *BELIZE*
- — Richard Allsopp, *Dictionary of Caribbean English Usage*, p. 14, 1996

after-hours *adjective*

open after bars and nightclubs close at 2am *US, 1947*

- [T]hose highways which in their time have known throngs of sightseers, which in the heyday of Harlem hotspots housed cabarets and after-hour joints known around the world[.] — Jack Lait and Lee Mortimer, *New York Confidential*, p. 96, 1948
- There are, too, a few after-hours spots left in Harlem[.] — Robert Sylvester, *No Cover Charge*, p. 67, 1956
- So lovely, in fact, that at least three After Hours Sports are serving booze after hours. Good booze, too. — *San Francisco Chronicle*, p. 34, 9th July 1957
- I had always stayed away from after-hours joints because I was afraid they would be busted by the police[.] — Dick Gregory, *Nigger*, p. 139, 1964
- Some of them had little nightclubs, after-hours places. — Claude Brown, *Manchild in the Promised Land*, p. 166, 1965
- Around this time the greatest "after hours" spot ever, opened in "Harlem". — Babs Gonzales, *I Paid My Dues*, p. 98, 1967
- His place, and all the other after-hours joints, wouldn't begin to swing until the bars closed, then they'd come alive. — Nathan Heard, *Howard Street*, p. 85, 1968
- One night, me and Reggie closed up my joint and then went over to this after-hours joint downtown Manhattan. — Edwin Torres, *Carlito's Way*, p. 81, 1975
- What about after hours? VIncent asked him ... After hours what, gambling? Twenty hours you don't get enough? You can find it. — Elmore Leonard, *Glitz*, p. 106, 1985
- In the early morning hours, before the city has washed her face, people stream out of after-hours clubs like Jump-Offs along Seventh Avenue[.] — Terry Williams, *The Cocaine Kids*, p. 97, 1989

afterlater *adverb*

later *US*

- I can't go witcha now, how about afterlater? — Amy and Denise McFadden, *CoalSpeak*, p. 1, 1997

after-nine *noun*

a black male homosexual who pretends to be heterosexual during working hours *SOUTH AFRICA*

- As a homosexual he is only to be found 'after nine' in the evening. — Bart Luirink (translated by Loes Nas), *Moffies*, p. 150, 2000

afternoon *noun*

the buttocks, especially large female buttocks *BARBADOS*

- — Richard Allsopp, *Dictionary of Caribbean English Usage*, p. 15, 1996

afternoon farmer *noun*

a lazy and unsuccessful farmer *CANADA*

- He was what is known as an afternoon farmer. He could never get out into the fields till about half-past eleven in the morning and he never seemed to be able to grow much of anything except buckwheat which as everyone knows is the lazy farmer's crop. — Mavis Gallant, *"The Bully," in Canadian Short Stories*, p. 371, 1960

afters *noun*

1 the dessert course of a meal *UK, 1909*

Originally military; because it comes *after* the rest of the meal. At the end of an adult meal there is a sexual implication when a man asks 'what's for afters?'.

- She got the kids their afters[.] — John Williams, *Cardiff Dead*, p. 105, 2000

2 drinks, or a session of drinking, served in a public house after licensing hours *UK*

- The guv'nor served us afters, and seemed to like having us around. — Jimmy Stockin, *On The Cobbles*, p. 129, 2000

3 the after-effects of too much alcohol *IRELAND*

- I was glad I was jarred. Then, you're always glad you're jarred when you're jarred. The hassle is the afters. — Eamonn Sweeney, *Waiting for the Healer*, p. 70, 1997

after tears *noun*

a post-funeral celebration *SOUTH AFRICA*

Scamto youth street slang (South African townships).

- — *The Times*, 12th February 2005

afterthought *noun*

an unplanned pregnancy; the child of an unplanned pregnancy *UK, 1914*

- [S]he got into her little car and drove to her parents' house [...] She had been an afterthought even for them. — Tim Gautreaux, *The Next Step in the Dance*, p. 29, 1998

after you, Claude – no, after you, Cecil

used to depict a lack of aggression or unnecessary good manners *UK*

A catchphrase regularly delivered by Jack Train and Horace Percival in the BBC radio comedy *ITMA*, 1939–49. Contemporary usage has been widely applied to sports such as cricket, hockey, football and motor-racing, and also to first-past-the-post electoral systems.

- The trouble with English cricket is that the whole debate has been too milky, too "after you, Claude, no after you, Cecil." — *The Electronic Telegraph*, 13th July 1998
- [H]e was more or less saying to opponents who were trying to clear the ball out of defence, "After you, Cecil." — Chris Moore, *www.soccernet.com*, 9th September 2000

after you with the trough!

used in response to someone's belching *UK, 1977*

A unsubtle implication that the belcher is a pig who has eaten too much. Mainly northern England.

ag; agg *noun*

trouble; problems; a nuisance *UK*

A further reduction of **AGGRO** (aggravation).

- — Angela Devlin, *Prison Patter*, p. 23, 1996
- I wouldn't worry about it. He's had a lot of agg recently. — Greg Williams, *Diamond Geezers*, p. 139, 1997
- Perhaps it was just the ag of the divorce[.] — Garry Bushell, *The Face*, p. 64, 2001

ag *adjective*

angry *US*

An abbreviation of 'aggravated'.

- — *Ebony Magazine*, p. 156, August 2000: 'How to talk to the new generation'

AG *adjective*

all good *US*

- — Jim Crotty, *How to Talk American*, p. 220, 1997

ag

used as an all-purpose intensifier *SOUTH AFRICA, 1833*

Pronounced like the German *ach*. Can precede any sentence for various effects, such as the more neutral, 'Ag, I don't know'. Used by some people as a stand-alone expletive.

again!

used for expressing strong approval *ANTIGUA AND BARBUDA*

- — Richard Allsopp, *Dictionary of Caribbean English Usage*, p. 15, 1996

against the law *adjective*

(used of a woman) extraordinarily beautiful *US*

- — Jim Crotty, *How to Talk American*, p. 168, 1997

against the wall *adjective*

said of a confidence swindle which is perpetrated without a fake office, extras, props, etc *US, 1940*

- We're gonna do the play-off somehewre else. The play-off is against the wall. — Stephen Cannell, *Big Con*, p. 341, 1997

A-game *noun*

in a casino or cardroom, the poker game with the highest stakes *US, 1949*

- — George Percy, *The Language of Poker*, p. 5, 1988

Aga saga *noun*

a genre of popular novel-writing, plotting comfortable, domestic and emotional middle-class lives *UK, 1992*

Based on Aga stoves which are recognised as an appropriate social symbol or aspiration.

- Queens of the bonkbuster and Aga saga defend the art – and heart – of their fiction. — *The Guardian*, p. 115, 30th may 2003

agate *noun*

1 a marble in the slang sense of sanity *US*

- He didn't have all his agates and eventually went nuts. — *San Francisco News*, p. 22, 19th December 1951

2 a small penis *US*

- — Dale Gordon, *The Dominion Sex Dictionary*, p. 17, 1967

agates *noun*

the testicles *US, 1941*

- — J.E. Lighter, *Historical Dictionary of American Slang, Volume 1*, p. 12, 1994

A-gay *noun*

a prominent, sought-after homosexual man *US*

- Chuck Lord's addiction to Negroes was a matter of common knowledge among the A-Gays in San Francisco. — Armistead Maupin, *Further Tales of the City*, p. 9, 1982

age *noun*

1 length of service for an employer; seniority *US*

- —Norman Carlisle, *The Modern Wonder Book of Trains and Railroading*, p. 258, 1946

2 in poker and other card games, the person to the immediate left of the dealer *US*

- —Irwin Steig, *Common Sense in Poker*, p. 181, 1963

-age *suffix*

used as an embellishment without meaning at the end of nouns *US*

The suffix got a second wind with the US television series *Buffy The Vampire Slayer*. Buffy lexicographer Michael Adams notes that 'Slayer slang's *-age* is impressive, not only for the number of words it contributes to the lexicon, but for the way in which it helps to bind members of the Buffyverse to one another'.

- —Connie Eble (Editor), *UNC-CH Campus Slang*, p. 4, March 1981
- —Lady Kier Kirby, *The 376 Deee-liteful Words*, 1992

ageable *adjective*

very old *TRINIDAD AND TOBAGO*

- —Lise Winer, *Dictionary of the English/Creole of Trinidad & Tobago*, 2003

age before beauty

used as a mock courtesy when allowing someone to precede you *UK, 1977*

age card *noun*

proof of legal age *US*

- New girl, Jane, she fresh up from Alabama an still funky – she ain't got no age card, can't buy herself a drink t'nurse[.]—Robert Gover, *JC Saves*, p. 17, 1968

agent *noun*

1 the operator of a rigged carnival game *US*

- A good Agent can be listed among the elite super salesmen to be found in any field. Cars, vacuum cleaners, or wheeling land dealers, I'll put a Carny Agent against them anytime.—Gene Sorrows, *All About Carnivals*, p. 6, 1985

2 in casino gambling, a confederate of a cheat *US*

- —Frank Scoblete, *Best Blackjack*, p. 252, 1996

Agent Scully *noun*

oral sex *US*

A reference to the name of the female lead in the *X-Files* television series, punning on her name and **SKULL** (oral sex).

- Brooks and his colleagues also provide police with glossaries of street slang – "Agent Scully" = "oral sex," "getting my cake" = "dating my girl."—*Washington Post*, p. A1, 20th August 2001

agfay *noun*

a homosexual man *US, 1942*

Pig Latin for **FAG**.

- — *Maledicta*, p. 248, 1979: 'Kinks and queens: linguistic and cultural aspects of the terminology for gays'

agg *noun*

▷ see: **AG**

agged *adjective*

angry, aggravated *US*

- —Ethan Hilderbrant, *Prison Slang*, p. 6, 1998

aggie *noun*

1 an aggressive, domineering male *US*

From the conventional 'aggressive'.

- —Collin Baker et al., *College Undergraduate Slang Study Conducted at Brown University*, p. 70, 1968

2 during the Korean war, any young Korean *US, 1951*

- —Paul Dickson, *War Slang*, p. 235, 1994

3 agoraphobia *UK*

- — *Community Care*, 12th June 1980

4 a farm tool, especially a hoe *US*

- —Bruce Jackson, *Outside the Law*, p. 55, 1972

aggie *adjective*

angry, agitated *US*

- —Alonzo Westbrook, *Hip Hoptionary*, p. 2, 2002

aggie overdrive *noun*

in trucking, coasting in neutral gear *US*

- —Wayne Floyd, *Jason's Authentic Dictionary of CB Slang*, p. 8, 1976

Aggie Weston's; Aggie's *nickname*

a hostel for sailors provided by the charity RSR (Dame Agnes Weston's Royal Sailors Rests) *UK*

Co-founded in 1876 by Agnes Weston (1840–1918) to try and save sailors from 'booze and brothels' and still trying. Grateful sailors used to call Weston-Super-Mare in the southwest of England 'Aggie-on-horseback'.

aggravation *noun*

(of police or criminals) an act of harrassment *UK*

Metropolitan Police slang.

- —Peter Laurie, *Scotland Yard*, p. 320, 1970

aggressive *adjective*

used as a coded euphemism for 'dominant' in sadomasochistic sex *US*

- — *Maledicta*, p. 164, Summer/Winter 1986–1987: 'Sexual slang: prostitutes, pedophiles, flagellators, transvestites, and necrophiles'

aggro *noun*

1 trouble, strife; problems; a nuisance *UK, 1969*

Abbreviated from 'aggravation'.

- 'I've said before in this publication that my wife is as Good as Gold and she's never given me much aggro in all our married life.—Barry Humphries, *The Traveller's Tool*, p. 45, 1985
- —Angela Devlin, *Prison Patter*, p. 23, 1996
- [S]pectator aggro at football has been an integral part of working-class youth and adult life for decades.—Irvine Welsh, *The Naughty Nineties*, p. 11, 1999
- How much aggro can stoned hippies, pissed students and off-their-cake new age travellers cause anyway?—Dave Courtney, *Raving Lunacy*, p. 189, 2000

2 aggression *AUSTRALIA*

- There's no 'aggro', just good-natured banter, but it makes you think afterwards.—Roy Higgins and Tom Prior, *The Jockey Who Laughed*, p. 18, 1982
- Their faces were still full of aggro, which seemed to intensify at the sight of Davo bobbing up in front of them[.]—Robert G. Barrett, *Davo's Little Something*, p. 278, 1992

aggro *adjective*

aggressively angry *AUSTRALIA, 1986*

- He come around a few nights later and got real aggro.—Kathy Lette, *Girls' Night Out*, p. 26, 1987
- 'The Cockies' music was aggro and tortured.—Kathy Lette, *Girls' Night Out*, p. 95, 1987
- If you want to get aggro, man, this stick can handle your best rage. —*Point Break*, 1991
- —Connie Eble (Editor), *UNC-CH Campus Slang*, p. 1, Spring 1993
- Sorry for getting aggro before.—Christos Tsiolkas, *Loaded*, p. 123, 1995
- You mob of snakes! God's very aggro with you!—Kel Richards, *The Aussie Bible*, p. 20, 2003

aginner *noun*

a person morally opposed to carnivals and the circus *US*

- —Don Wilmeth, *The Language of American Popular Entertainment*, p. 7, 1981

agitate *verb*

▸ **agitate the gravel**

to leave *US*

Teen slang.

- — *San Francisco News*, p. 6, 25th March 1958

agitprop *noun*

agitation and propaganda as an unfocused political tactic; a fashionable genre of theatre arts with a (usually) left-wing political agenda *UK, 1934*

Adopted from the name given to a department of the Central Committee of the Russian Communist Party responsible for agitation and propaganda on behalf of communist ideals; a conflation of *agitatsiya* and *propaganda*.

- [T]heatre was going through that ghastly depressing agitprop phase: lots of ugly girls with hairy armpits and Dr Martens boots.—Jenny Eclair, *Camberwell Beauty*, p. 95, 2000
- Fighting inertia with agitprop could be exhausting and time-consuming.—Mick Farren, *Give the Anarchist a Cigarette*, p. 142, 2001

aglish *adjective*

nauseated; sick to one's stomach *CANADA*

Used around the Lunenburg area in Nova Scotia, where many German settlers still adapt old expressions.

-a go-go *suffix*

all over the place, in a mess; on the go *UK*

In the manner of **GO-GO** (a disco), hence dancing applied figuratively.

• [W]hat happened when the greatest party poopers since Charles Manson went into overdrive.— *Pogo A Go Go!*, 1986
• Mrs Slocombe staggered from the lift, yellow hair a go-go, legs akimbo[.]—Stuart Jeffries, *Mrs Slocombe's Pussy*, p. 102, 2000
• —Joe Strummer & The Mescaleros, *Global a Go-Go*, 2001

agonies *noun*
the physical and psychological pain suffered when withdrawing from drug addiction *US*
• —Jay Robert Nash, *Dictionary of Crime*, p. 6, 1992

agonised button *noun*
of military uniforms, an anodised aluminium (Staybrite) button *UK, 1984*
Anodised (electro-plated) aluminium replaced brass and white metal as the main metal for British Other Ranks military insignia from about 1950 onwards.

agony *noun*
▸ **pile on the agony; pile up the agony; put on the agony**
to exaggerate, to show-off *US, 1837*
Originally theatrical.
• Ah, [Joseph] Fiennes is piling on the agony again.— *The Guardian*, 24th July 1996

agony aunt; agony auntie *noun*
a newspaper or magazine columnist who advises readers on questions of a personal nature; hence an adviser or counsellor on intimate problems *UK, 1975*
• Mo Mowlam's first outing as an agony aunt for the lads' mag 'Zoo' reveals a frankness previously reserved for politicians.— *The Independent*, 11th July 2004

agony column *noun*
a newspaper or magazine feature of readers' letters seeking help for personal problems with replies from a columnist or agony aunt *UK, 1975*
• Ann Widdecombe's agony column for the Guardian has bitten the dust, and not a moment too soon for most readers.—*New Satesman*, 19th July 2004

a good crafstman never blames his tools
used for dismissing an attempt by someone to blame a mistake on a piece of equipment or something within their control *US*
• —Keith Olberman and Dan Patrick, *The Big Show*, p. 11, 1997

agricultural *adjective*
in cricket, describes a simple, slogging shot off a sweeping bat *UK, 1982*
• —Simon Hughes, *Cricket 4*, 2001

A-head *noun*
1 an amphetamine abuser *US*
• —Edward R. Bloomquist, *Marijuana*, p. 331, 1971
• There's A-heads and there's speedfreaks[.]—Lester Bangs, *Psychotic Reactions and Carburetor Dung*, p. 178, 1975
• She was a bit of an A-head and was a familiar figure at the fountian in her uniform after work.—Ed Sanders, *Tales of Beatnik Glory*, p. 121, 1975

2 a frequent user of LSD *US*
• —Eugene Landy, *The Underground Dictionary*, p. 22, 1971

ahhh, Rooshan
used as a youth-to-youth greeting *US*
A short-lived fad greeting associated with bebop jazz.
• — *Time*, 3rd October 1949

a-hole *noun*
1 the anus *US, 1942*
'A' as in **ASS** or **ARSE**. A euphemism that calls more attention to that which is being skirted than would a direct reference.
• —Dale Gordon, *The Dominion Sex Dictionary*, p. 17, 1967
• —Bruce Rodgers, *The Queens' Vernacular*, p. 18, 1972
• "I'll stick that dang pecker-bat up his lard-ass A-hole!"—Terry Southern, *Texas Summer*, p. 110, 1991
• Cum dribbles down her crack, ultimately resting upon her a-hole. —Anthony Petkovich, *The X Factory*, p. 193, 1997

2 by extension, a despised person *US, 1942*
• Free us (the rock 'n' roll fans) from Nancy Spungen-fixated heroin a-holes who cling to our greatest rock groups and suck out their brains.—Julian Cope, *Advertisement in the music press*, 1993
• You know Jackie is an Aye Hole.—Howard Stern, *Miss America*, p. 192, 1995

-aholic; -oholic; -holic *suffix*
an addict of, or addiction to, the pre-fixed thing or activity *US, 1964*
Usage may be literal or figurative. From 'alco*holic*' (a person addicted to alcohol); the first widely recognised usage was 'workaholic' (1968).
• World is full of chocoholics, as you can see at See's.— *San Francisco Examiner*, p. 3, 15th May 1976
• Therapy for Spendaholics.— *San Francisco Chronicle*, p. A1, 9th April 1980
• A self-confessed shopaholic, Rachel is also a real romantic[.]— *CD:UK*, p. 9, 2000
• [T]he epitome of shambolic, shirkaholic ineptitude[.]—Will Birch, *No Sleep Till Canvey Island*, p. 282, 2003

ai!; aiii!
yes! *UK*
Popularised in the UK in the late 1990s by Ali G (comedian Sacha Baron-Cohen).
• — Susie Dent, *The Language Report*, p. 144, 2003

AIF *adjective*
deaf *AUSTRALIA*
Rhyming slang, from *A*ustralian *I*mperial *F*orces.
• we was talk in to yer, me and Joss was...and you must be a bit AIF, like, 'Cos yerjust was't participatin' with us.—Jim McNeil, *The Chocolate Frog*, p. 21, 1973

a-ight
used for expressing agreement or affirmation *US*
• —Lois Stavsky et al., *A2Z*, p. 1, 1995

aim *verb*
▸ **aim Archie at the armitage**
(of a male) to urinate *AUSTRALIA*
Armitage Shanks are manufacturers of toilet furniture.
• —Barry Humphries, *Bazza Pulls It Off!*, 1971

aimie *noun*
an amphetamine *UK*
• —Mike Haskins, *Drugs*, p. 279, 2003

ain't; aint *verb*
replaces am not, are not, is not, has not, have not *UK, 1710*
A widely used solecism.
• I ain't an effing thicky—Ian Dury, *Billericay Dickie*, 1977
• No reason for me to. His daddy say. You here, aint you? He say this nasty.—Alice Walker, *The Color Purple*, p. 27, 1982
• —Simon Hughes, *Cricket 4*, 2001

ain't buyin' it!
I don't believe you *US*
• —Richard McAlister, *Rapper's Handbook*, p. 1, 1990

ain't havin' it!
it is not allowed *US*
• —Richard McAlister, *Rapper's Handbook*, p. 1, 1990

ain't love grand!
used for registering the pleasure of being in love or, ironically, the opposite *US, 1977*
• If I had this chip outta my head I'da killed you long ago. (REPLACES CORK) Ain't love grand?—Marti Noxon, *Buffy the Vampire Slayer*, 19th December 2000

ain't no joke!
I am serious! *US*
• —Richard McAlister, *Rapper's Handbook*, p. 1, 1990

ain't no shame in my game
used for expressing a lack of shame when engaged in an activity that might shame others *US*
• —Alonzo Westbrook, *Hip Hoptionary*, p. 2, 2002

ain't no thang; ain't no big thang
used for dismissing something as not problematic *US*
• —Conne Eble (Editor), *UNC-CH Campus Slang*, Fall 1985
• —Richard McAlister, *Rapper's Handbook*, p. 1, 1990
• O-Dog: How's the shoulder, nigga? Caine: Fucked up, but it ain't no thang.— *Menace II Society*, 1993
• —Kenn "Naz" Young, *Naz's Dictionary of Teen Slang*, p. 2, 1993

ain't that a bite!
isn't that too bad! *US*
Teen slang.
• — *Newsweek*, p. 28, 8th October 1951

ain't the beer cold!
used for conveying that all is well in the world *US*
According to Paul Dickson, popularised by baseball radio announcer Chuck Thompson, who used the phrase as the title of his autobiography. Repeated with referential humour.
- Thompson is the kind of announcer you listen to while wearing your slippers. He's homey and conversational. An Oriole hits a homer and he says, "Hmmm! Aint the beer cold." — *Washington Post*, p. E12, 27th June 1982
- — Paul Dickson, *The New Dickson Baseball Dictionary*, p. 3, 1999
- When your first two opponents lose their starting quarterbacks in August, well, ain't the beer cold? — *Washingotn Times*, p. F5, 3rd September 2003

ain't with that
I do not agree or consent *US*
- — Richard McAlister, *Rapper's Handbook*, p. 1, 1990

ain't you got no couf?
where are your manners, dress sense, etc? *UK, 1984*
Military; a pun on 'uncouth'.

AIO *noun*
a college student who does not belong to a fraternity *US*
- AIO , Ain't In One, is the way non-Greeks refer to themsleves. — Fred Hester, *Slang on the 40 Acres*, p. 16, 1968

AIP *noun*
heroin from Afghanistan, Iran and/or Pakistan *US, 1982*
- — Robert Ashton, *This Is Heroin*, p. 208, 2002

air *noun*
1 a jump while snowboarding *US*
- — Mike Fabbro, *Snowboarding*, p. 93, 1996

2 in foot-propelled scootering, a jump *UK*
- Any time you jump or Ollie, you are getting some air. Good scoot riders get big air! — Ben Sharpe, *Scooter Crazy*, 2000

3 air support, air power, bombing *US*
Vietnam war usage.
- — Linda Reinberg, *In the Field*, p. 5, 1991

4 in the pornography industry, an ejaculation that cannot be seen leaving the penis and travelling through the air *US*
In a situation which calls for visual proof of the ejaculation, air is not good.
- — *Adult Video News*, p. 40, August 1995

5 air brakes on a truck or railway carriage *US, 1897*
- — J.E. Lighter, *Historical Dictionary of American Slang, Volume 1*, p. 13, 1994

6 the mood created by a person or persons *US*
There is 'good air' and there is 'bad air'.
- — Michael V. Anderson, *The Bad, Rad, Not to Forget Way Cool Beach and Surf Discriptionary*, p. 2, 1988

▸ **in the air**
(used of the flank of an army) unprotected by natural or man-man obstacles *US*
- In Marine parlance, their flanks were "hanging in the air" with no contact save an occasional patrol. — Joseph C. Goulden, *Korea*, p. 348, 1982

▸ **leave in the air**
to abandon someone without support *UK, 1948*

▸ **turn the air blue; make the air turn blue**
to use obscene or blasphemous language *UK, 1890*
- Halfway down a red run, the air turned blue with expletives as I refused to move. — *The Guardian*, 18th March 2004

▸ **up in the air**
(used of a pair in a game of poker) formed with help from the communal face-up cards *US*
- — Edwin Silberstang, *Winning Poker for the Serious Player*, p. 221, 1992

air *verb*
▸ **air your belly**
to vomit *US*
- — Connie Eble (Editor), *UNC-CH Campus Slang*, p. 1, Spring 2000

air artist *noun*
a railway engineer skilled at the use of air brakes *US*
- — Ramon Adams, *The Language of the Railroader*, p. 3, 1977

airbag *noun*
a person who talks too much *US*
- To think. When I got out of the joint, I thought an airbag was Paulie Walnuts. — *The Sopranos (Episode 60)*, 2004

airbags *noun*
the lungs *US*
- — Lou Shelly, *Hepcats Jive Talk Dictionary*, p. 7, 1945

air ball *noun*
1 in pinball, a ball that is lost out of play without having been flipped *US*
- — Bobbye Claire Natkin and Steve Kirk, *All About Pinball*, 1977

2 in pool, a shot in which the cue ball does not hit any other ball *US*
- — Mike Shamos, *The Illustrated Encyclopedia of Billiards*, p. 3, 1993

air bandit *noun*
a gambling cheat *US, 1969*
- — Thomas L. Clark, *The Dictionary of Gambling and Gaming*, p. 4, 1987

air barrel *noun*
in pool, that which backs a bet made without money to back the bet *US*
A **BARREL** is a betting unit; an 'air barrel' is thus an illusory betting unit.
- — Steve Rushin, *Pool Cool*, p. 5, 1990

air biscuit *noun*
a fart *US*
- — Pamela Munro, *U.C.L.A. Slang*, p. 31, 2001
- [I]t's a little early to say whether the tentatively titled No More Lies will, indeed, be directing air biscuits in the direction of its predecessors[.] — Andrew Holmes, *Sleb*, p. 103, 2002
- — *The A-Z of Rude Health*, 18th January 2002

air-conditioned *adjective*
sexually frigid *UK*
- — Tom Hibbert, *Rockspeak!*, p. 9, 1983

air dance *noun*
capital punishment by hanging *US*
A specific dance name is sometimes substituted for 'dance', such as 'air polka'.
- — Ralph de Sola, *Crime Dictionary*, p. 5, 1982

air-dash *verb*
to travel in an aircraft (a degree of urgency is implied)
- [T]hey do not fly to conferences but air-dash to meets. Headlinese has entered everyday [Indian] language[.] — John Simpson, *A Mad World, My Masters*, p. 168, 2001

airedale *noun*
1 a Wall Street gentleman *US, 1925*
An extension of the symbol of the Airedale as an aristocratic dog.
- — *New York Times Magazine*, p. 76, 13th March 1955

2 a navy pilot *US, 1942*
- The pilots are in fact a pleasant, easy-going, affable lot known affectionately to surface sailors as "Airedales" or "birdmen." — *Life*, p. 85, 26th March 1945
- Despite a Navy directive to cut it out, Navy pilots remain "Airedales" and Marines are still "Gyrenes." — *New York Times Magazine*, p. 76, 13th March 1955
- Looks like you Airedale guys aren't gonna take no for an answer today, are you? — Gerry Carroll, *North S*A*R*, p. 88, 1991

3 a plane handler on an aircraft carrier *US, 1943*
- The battle-scarred hangar deck of the carrier Enterprise, cleared of planes and shouting airedales (airplane handlers), has been converted into this gigantic bunk room. — *Time*, p. 24, 10th December 1945
- The air officers, plane handlers who shift and push and manhandle the planes a dozen times a day around the deck. These are ordinarily known as "airedales," but the term isn't much used on our ship. — *San Francisco News*, p. 10, 19th March 1945

air giver *noun*
a railway brakeman *US*
- — Ramon Adams, *The Language of the Railroader*, p. 4, 1977

air guitar *noun*
an imagined guitar used to mimic a rock guitar player *US, 1982*
- The three Figures look at each other, do a ferocious AIR GUITAR, and run OUT OF FRAME. — *Bill and Ted's Excellent Adventure*, p. 91, 1989
- He got up [...] and walked out, playing air guitar. "Arsehole," said Keva. — Kevin Sampson, *Powder*, p. 49, 1999

airhead *noun*
a person who is not inclined to think, not equipped to think, or both *US, 1972*
- —Connie Eble (Editor), *UNC-CH Campus Slang*, April 1977
- [T]here's a good proportion of air heads and space cadets in those courses, too.—*Wesleyan Alumnus*, p. 29, Spring 1981
- ABC could be called the Airhead Broadcasting Network or the Adult Broadcasting Network, depending on what you're watching.—*San Francisco Examiner*, p. 89, 9th July 1984
- I'm sorry about your friend. I thought she was your usual airhead bitch.—*Heathers*, 1988
- Cyra McFadden's return to the land of the airheads: California Revisited.—*San Francisco Examiner*, p. B9, 9th July 1988
- —Ellen C. Bellone (Editor), *Dictionary of Slang*, p. 1, 1989
- Airhead: Term is an objectionable description, generally aimed at women.—Multicultural Management Program Fellows, *Dictionary of Cautionary Words and Phrases*, 1989
- Look at all these airheads!—*Airheads*, 1994
- What am I, some sort of mentally challenged airhead?—*Clueless*, 1995
- [A] woman's right to wear lippy and always be on a diet, yet not be called an airhead[.]—*The Guardian*, p. 38, 1st June 2002

air hog *noun*
in the language of hang gliding, the flier in a group who stays in the air longest *US*
- —Erik Fair, *California Thrill Sports*, p. 328, 1992

airie *noun*
an aeroplane *UK: SCOTLAND*
In Glasgow, a shortening of the local pronuciation 'airieplane'.
- Ur we gaun [going] up in a big airie Da?—Michael Munro, *The Original Patter*, 1985

airish *adjective*
1 cold *US*
- —Connie Eble (Editor), *UNC-CH Campus Slang*, p. 1, Fall 1985

2 arrogant, showing off *US, 1943*
- —Frederic G. Cassidy, *Dicitonary of American Regional English, Volume 1*, p. 29, 1985
- —Richard Allsopp, *Dictionary of Caribbean English Usage*, p. 19, 1996

air jammer *noun*
a railway worker who connects airhoses and air signals on a train *US*
- —Ramon Adams, *The Language of the Railroader*, p. 4, 1977

Air Jesus; Air Hebrews *noun*
sandals *US*
Alluding to Nike Air Jordan™ sports shoes.
- —Connie Eble (Editor), *UNC-CH Campus Slang*, p. 1, Spring 1992

air junkie *noun*
in the language of hang gliding, a devoted, obsessed flier *US*
- —Erik Fair, *California Thrill Sports*, p. 328, 1992

air-kiss *verb*
to go through the motions of kissing but deliberately fail to make contact with the person who would normally be kissed *UK, 1985*
- [M]ultimedia yuppies air kissing, swapping Web addresses and bragging about their kit[.]—Melanie McGrath, *Hard, Soft & Wet*, p. 166, 1998

airlock *verb*
speaking *UK: NORTHERN IRELAND*
C. I. Macafee glosses as 'from the cut-out in a diesel engine if air enters the fuel system' in *A Concise Ulster Dictionary*, 1996.

airlocked *adjective*
extremely drunk *UK: NORTHERN IRELAND*
- —C. I. Macafee, *A Concise Ulster Dictionary*, p. 4, 1996

airmail *noun*
1 rubbish thrown from the upper windows of a building to the courtyard below *US, 1952*
- Throwing garbage out of windows is referred to as AIRMAIL.—Hubert Selby Jr, *Last Exit to Brooklyn*, p. 253, 1957

2 objects thrown by prisoners down onto guards or other prisoners below *US*
- —William K. Bentley and James M. Corbett, *Prison Slang*, p. 99, 1992

airmail *verb*
to throw rubbish from the upper windows of a building to the courtyard below *US*
- [F]rom the back windows of the tenements beyond several people were busy "airmailing," throwing garbage out of the window, into the rubble, beer cans, red shreds, the No-Money-Down Eames roller stand for a TV set, all flying through the air into the scagg—Tom Wolfe, *The Pump House Gang*, p. 240, 1968

air monkey *noun*
a railway air-brake repairman *US*
- —Norman Carlisle, *The Modern Wonder Book of Trains and Railroading*, p. 258, 1946

air off *verb*
to talk loudly *TRINIDAD AND TOBAGO, 1960*
- —Lise Winer, *Dictionary of the English/Creole of Trinidad & Tobago*, 2003

airplane *noun*
1 a device used for holding a marijuana cigarette that has burnt down to the stub *US*
An abbreviation of the fuller **JEFFERSON AIRPLANE**.
- —William D. Alsever, *Glossary for the Establishment and Other Uptight People*, p. 20, December 1970

2 marijuana *UK, 1998*
- —Mike Haskins, *Drugs*, p. 286, 2003

airplane *verb*
to inhale through the nose the smoke of the stub of a marijuana cigarette *US*
- —*Current Slang*, p. 12, Spring 1970

airplane blonde; aeroplane blonde *noun*
a brunette, usually a woman, with dyed blonde hair *UK*
Jocular; punchlined as 'blonde up top but you know there's a black box somewhere'.
- —*Roger's Profanisuarus*, p. 3, October 1999

airplane driver *noun*
a fighter pilot *US*
Gulf war usage.
- —*American Speech*, p. 86, Spirng 1992: 'Gulf War words supplement'

airplane rule *noun*
in computing, the belief that simplicity is a virtue *US*
- Complexity increases the possibility of failure; a twin-engine airplane has twice as many engine problems as a single-engine airplane.—Eric S. Raymond, *The New Hacker's Dictionary*, p. 34, 1991

air ride *noun*
a car with pneumatic shock absorbers *US*
- —*American Speech*, p. 311, Autumn-Winter 1975: 'The jargon of car salesmen'

airs *noun*
a pair of Nike Air Jordan™ trainers (sneakers) *(US)*
- —Richard McAlister, *Rapper's Handbook*, p. 1, 1990

airs and graces *noun*
braces; suspenders *UK, 1960*
Rhyming slang, surviving earlier senses 'Epsom Races' and 'faces'.

air shot *noun*
an act of sexual intercourse that stops short of orgasm *UK, 1979*
Royal Navy slang, from 'torpedo drill'.

air sucker *noun*
a jet aeroplane *US*
- —*American Speech*, p. 118, May 1963: 'Air refueling words'

air-to-mud *adjective*
(used of shots fired or bombs dropped) from the air to the ground *US*
- —Linda Reinberg, *In the Field*, p. 6, 1991
- The CF-5 hasn't got the range it needs for the air-to-mud role.—Tom Langeste, *Words on the Wing*, p. 8, 1995

air tragic *noun*
air traffic control *UK*
In Royal Air Force use, 2002.

airy *adjective*
marijuana-intoxicated *US*
- I just got a little high and airy with the sticks and they made me feel better[.]—Hal Ellson, *Duke*, p. 3, 1949

airy a
none *CANADA*
As used in Nova Scotia's South Shore, this expression is a form of the archaic 'ne'er a' or a short form of 'never a'.

airy-fairy *noun*
a member of the RNAS (Royal Naval Air Service) later the Fleet Air Arm *UK, 1979*
- —John W. Mussell, *The Token Book of Militarisms*, p. 6, 1995

airy-fairy *adjective*
delicate, fanciful; insubstantial, trivial *UK, 1869*
- [T]his was just the airy-fairy, "don't we all live in a wonderful white-bread Christian world" stuff. The hard-core material was, appro-propriately, on the higher shelves. —Christopher Brookmyre, *Not the End of the World*, p. 251, 1998
- Moguls in Hofstadter's day considered intellectualism vaguely feminine and airy-fairy. —David Brooks, *Bobos in Paradise*, p. 114, 2000

aitch *noun*
1 hell *US*
A euphemism.
- As he told his president who wanted to know why the aitch Fresno State wasn't good enough for the track coach's son, it broke his heart to lose a kid who had already thrown the javelin— *Fortnight*, p. 17, 6th January 1950
- "It was boring as aitch," says Hewitt, who does not use profanity, liquor, tobacco or coffee but has a weakness for candy bars. — *Life*, p. 144, 12th April 1954

2 heroin *US*
- The price of pure heroin ("aitch") has gone up from $60 an ounce to $500. — *Time*, p. 48, 16th April 1945

ai te guacho
I'll see you later *US*
'Guacho' prounounced 'watch-o', a pure invention. Border Spanish used in English conversation by Mexican-Americans.
- —George Carpenter Baker, *Pachuco*, p. 40, January 1950
- "Ay te watcho, man.' "Easy." —Thurston Scott, *Cure it with Honey*, p. 14, 1951
- Cruz shook his head and said, "Ahi te huacho," which is anglicized slang meaning I'll be seeing, or rather, watching for you. —Joseph Wambaugh, *The Blue Knight*, p. 61, 1973

AJ *noun*
an 'acting jack', or an acting noncommissioned officer *US*
- —Linda Reinberg, *In the Field*, p. 6, 1991

ajax *noun*
1 in hold 'em poker, an ace and a jack as the first two cards dealt to a particular player *US, 1981*
Punning on the branded name of a cleaning agent.
- —Thomas L. Clark, *The Dictionary of Gambling and Gaming*, p. 5, 1987

2 any youth gang member under the age of 16 *US*
A borrowing from the slogan for Ajax™ cleaner – 'comes out clean' – and the fact that a juvenile offender will be treated far less harshly than an adult.
- —Kenn "Naz" Young, *Naz's Dictionary of Teen Slang*, p. 2, 1993

ajax *adjective*
1 nearby *UK*
Possibly derived from 'adjacent'.
- —Paul Baker, *Polari*, p. 162, 2002

2 clean *US*
An allusion to the branded cleaning product.
- —Alonzo Westbrook, *Hip Hoptionary*, p. 2, 2002

AK *noun*
1 a sycophant *US, 1939*
- —Robert A. Wilson, *Playboy's Book of Forbidden Words*, p. 15, 1972

2 a mean and nasty old man *US, 1942*
An abbreviation of the Yiddish **ALTER KOCKER**.
- Two A.K.'s had sat in silence on their favorite park bench for hours, lost in thought. Finally, one gave a long and languid "Oy!" The other replied, "You're telling me?" —Leo Rosten, *The Joys of Yiddish*, p. 14, 1968

3 an AK-47 semi-automatic rifle *US*
- —Richard McAlister, *Rapper's Handbook*, p. 1, 1990
- —Bill Valentine, *Gang Intelligence Manual*, p. 74, 1995

AK *verb*
to curry favour by obsequious behaviour *US, 1939*
An abbreviation of '*a*ss-*k*iss'.
- — *American Speech*, p. 154, May 1959: 'Gator (University of Florida) slang'

AK47 *noun*
a variety of marijuana
From the automatic weapon designed by Mikhail Kalashnikov.
- Which of the following has no sativa in its genetic make up? A) Warlock Haze B) AK47 C) Top44 D) Kali Mist —Brian Preston, *Pot Planet*, p. 245, 2002

AKA *noun*
an alias *US, 1955*
An acronym of '*a*lso *k*nown *as*'; from police jargon.
- —Angela Devlin, *Prison Patter*, p. 23, 1996
- Reggie Jackson, Reggie Miller – I think 'cause he was given a movie star name at birth he has to pick celebrity names as his a.k.a.s, like they his peers. —Elmore Leonard, *Be Cool*, p. 247, 1999
- Why he's called Kinky don't ask cos i don't fuckin know but that's his AKA. —J.J. Connolly, *Layer Cake*, p. 62, 2000

▸ **go AKA**
to assume an alias *US*
- "The moral of the story," Chucky said, "the punto, any time you go a.k.a. you better be sure everybody with you does too." —Elmore Leonard, *Stick*, p. 121, 1983

AK amp *noun*
an amputation at the knee *US*
Vietnam war medic usage.
- —Gregory Clark, *Words of the Vietnam War*, p. 18, 1990

akey-okey *adjective*
satisfactory *US*
- —Harold Wentworth and Stuart Berg Flexner, *Dictionary of American Slang*, p. 3, 1960

akka *noun*
▷ **see: ACKER**

AL *adjective*
not to be believed *US*
An abbreviation of '*a*lways *l*ying'.
- —Lois Stavsky et al., *A2Z*, p. 2, 1995

ala-ala's *noun*
the testicles *US*
Hawaiian youth usage.
- Wow, da guy when keeck mah ala-alas! Ah t'ought da buggah goin bus'! —Douglas Simonson, *Pidgin to da Max*, 1981

Alabama wool *noun*
cotton *US, 1958*
- —Frederic G. Cassidy, *Dicitonary of American Regional English, Volume 1*, p. 31, 1985

a-la-beff *noun*
vaginal intercourse, the woman on hands and knees and the man entering her from behind *TRINIDAD AND TOBAGO, 1980*
An allusion to the mating of cattle and the French *boeuf*.
- —Lise Winer, *Dictionary of the English/Creole of Trinidad & Tobago*, 2003

Aladdin's cave *noun*
the location of a successful thief's ill-gotten gains *UK*
Metropolitan Police slang. After the tale of Aladdin in *The Arabian Nights*.
- —Peter Laurie, *Scotland Yard*, p. 320, 1970

alambrista *noun*
a Mexican illegally present in the US *US*
Border Spanish used in English conversation by Mexican-Americans; from the Spanish for 'wire'.
- —Dagoberto Fuentes and Jose Lopez, *Barrio Language Dictionary*, 1974

Alameda *noun*
in bar dice games, a roll that produces no points for the player *US*
Alameda is an island city just west of Oakland. In Alameda, a worthless hand is called a 'Milpitas', alluding to a small and relatively poor city just north of San Jose.
- —Jester Smith, *Games They Play in San Francisco*, p. 103, 1971

alamo
used for registering a strong sexual interest in someone *UK*
Derives from an acronym for 'lick me out'.
- —Paul Baker, *Polari*, p. 162, 2002
- — *Attitude*, July 2003: 'Old palare lexicon'

Alamo Hilton *nickname*
a heavily fortified bunker beneath the Khe Sanh base in South Vietnam during the Vietnam war *US*
- —Gregory Clark, *Words of the Vietnam War*, p. 18, 1990

Alan Whickers; Alans *noun*
knickers *UK*
Rhyming slang, formed from reporter, broadcaster and television personality Alan Whicker (b.1925), who first came to prominence in the late 1950s.
- Don't get your Alans in a twist. I'll be home after this pint.—Bodmin Dark, *Dirty Cockney Rhyming Slang*, 2003

Alaska hand *noun*
in hold 'em poker, a king and a three as the first two cards dealt to a particular player *US, 1981*
Built from the synonymous **KING CRAB**, which is found in Alaska.
- —Thomas L. Clark, *The Dictionary of Gambling and Gaming*, p. 5, 1987

Alaskamo *noun*
an American Indian from Alaska *US*
- —*American Speech*, p. 271, December 1963: 'American Indian student slang'

Alaska strawberries *noun*
beans *US*
- —Russell Tabbert, *Dictionary of Alaskan English*, p. 82, 1991

Alaska time *noun*
used for explaining tardiness *US, 1976*
- —Frederic G. Cassidy, *Dicitonary of American Regional English, Volume 1*, p. 32, 1985

Alaska turkey *noun*
salmon *US, 1948*
- —Frederic G. Cassidy, *Dicitonary of American Regional English, Volume 1*, p. 32, 1985

Alaska tuxedo *noun*
a wool work suit *US*
- The Alaskan tuxedo is an ideal jacket in the woods and is commonly worn as a dress-up jacket.—Robert O. Bowen, *An Alaskan Dictionary*, p. 7, 1965
- —Mike Doogan, *How to Speak Alaskan*, p. 6, 1993

Alb *noun*
an Albanian *UK, 1945*

albatross *noun*
1 a very sick, incurable hospital patient, lingering near death *US*
- —*Maledicta*, p. 117, 1984–1985

2 a Grumman HU-16 amphibian aircraft, best known as a rescue aircraft during the Korean and Vietnam wars *US*
- —Linda Reinberg, *In the Field*, p. 6, 1991

3 cooked chicken *UK*
Royal Navy use; presumably inspired by Coleridge's 'The Rime of the Ancient Mariner'.
- —John W. Mussell, *The Token Book of Militarisms*, p. 7, 1995

Albert, Alberts *nouns*
▷ see: PRINCE ALBERT, PRINCE ALBERTS

Alberta Clipper *noun*
a cold weather system that blows from the Canadian Rocky Mountains eastward *CANADA*
A winter phenomenon, with wind and usually snow.

Albert County tartan; Albert County dress tartan *noun*
a plaid wool shirt, as used by woodsmen *CANADA*
Albert County is in the Moncton, New Brunswick, area.
- —David Mazerolle, *Avant tu take off, please close the lights*, 1993

albino *noun*
in pool, the white cue ball *US, 1988*
- —Mike Shamos, *The Illustrated Encyclopedia of Billiards*, p. 4, 1993

albino grass *noun*
snow fallen on a Vancouver, British Columbia, lawn *CANADA*
- —Bill Casselman, *Canadian Sayings*, p. 20, 2002

Alcan *nickname*
the Alaska-Canada Highway *US, 1075*
- As for the third competitor, a route following the Alcan highway, it was a late comer[.]—*Washington Post*, p. A12, 5th February 1977
- —Mike Doogan, *How to Speak Alaskan*, p. 6, 1993

Al Capone *noun*
heroin *UK*
- —Robert Ashton, *This Is Heroin*, p. 205, 2002
- —Mike Haskins, *Drugs*, p. 283, 2003

alcho *noun*
an alcoholic *UK*
- I started because of what my step-dad used to do to me, and he was an alcho.—Macfarlane, Macfarlane and Robson, *The User*, p. 105, 1996

alco; alko *noun*
an alcoholic *AUSTRALIA*
- See that old alco over there. They call him Sputnik – always going around the Globe.—Frank Hardy, *The Yarns of Billy Borker*, p. 39, 1965

alcoholiday *noun*
a holiday or festive period that is spent drinking alcohol *GUYANA*
- Whatever the explanation, this is not time to have a two-day alcohohliday and becoming as high as a kite.—*Sunday Chronicle*, p. 7, 18th April 1975

alcohol rub *noun*
a cocktail party *US*
- Bryn Hemming, that delightful English import, gave an alcohol rub last night for Princess Ibrahim Fazil.—*San Francisco Examiner*, p. 21, 29th October 1968

alderman *noun*
1 in the circus and carnival, an office worker who informs on his fellow workers *US*
- —Don Wilmeth, *The Language of American Popular Entertainment*, p. 7, 1981

2 a big paunch *US, 1933*
Not exactly respectful of local elected officials.
- —Bill Reilly, *Big Al's Official Guide to Chicagoese*, p. 13, 1982

al desko *adverb*
(used of a meal) consumed at your desk at work *US*
A play on *al fresco*.
- But there is grit with the glamor: Lunches usually consist of cold sandwiches consumed al desko.—*Washington Post*, 30th January 1981

alec; aleck; alick *noun*
an idiot *AUSTRALIA, 1919*
Shortening of **SMART ALEC**.
- Boy, I'm going to look awfully silly wandering around waiting for some alec to bite a dog.—Willie Fennell, *Dexter Gets The Point*, p. 21, 1961

aled up *adjective*
under the influence of beer *UK*
- Roberto once said to me – when he was aled up – that he wouldn't mind a bit of bull-fighting with her[.]—Kevin Williamson, *Heart of the Bass (Disco Biscuits)*, p. 113, 1996

aletank *noun*
a heavy drinker *UK*
Compares with earlier, now obsolete 'alecan' (a heavy drinker).
- [T]wo of them must be fucking doorman seagulls, throwing this bit of an aletank seagull out the club.—Kevin Sampson, *Clubland*, p. 189, 2002

a-levels *noun*
anal sex, especially when advertised as a service offered by a prostitute *UK*
A play on the name given to 'advanced-level' examinations in the British education system.
- —Caroline Archer, *Tart Cards*, 2003

Alexander *noun*
a telephone *UK*
From Alexander Graham Bell, 1847–1922, Scottish-born inventor of the telephone.
- She was off running for the Alexander getting Reception hasty. —Jeremy Cameron, *Brown Bread in Wengen*, p. 167, 1999

Alf *noun*
an ordinary uneducated, unsophisticated Australian male *AUSTRALIA, 1960*
Counterpart of the **ROY**.
- When they [the Gods] get a weed on they grab a fistful of thunderbolts and work off a temper that way, hurling them down on the nits and Alfs who scurry about like ants below[.]—Geoff Wyatt, *Saltwater Saints*, p. 103, 1969

alfalfa *noun*

1 money *US, 1917*
Circus and carnival usage.
- —Don Wilmeth, *The Language of American Popular Entertainment*, p. 7, 1981

2 marijuana *US*
- —Lois Stavsky et al., *A2Z*, p. 2, 1995

alias man *noun*
a confidence swindler *JAMAICA, 1961*
- —F.G. Cassidy and R.B. LePage, *Dictionary of Jamaican English*, p. 7, 1967

alibi *noun*

1 in a rigged carnival game, the reason given by the game operator to disqualify a legitimate win *US*
- The most common alibi is to tell the player he went over the foul line. —Gene Sorrows, *All About Carnivals*, p. 8, 1985

2 in sports, an excuse for not performing well *US, 1914*
In 1914, sports writer Ring Lardner created the character Alibi Ike, who always had an excuse for not playing well. The alibi held up.
- —Richard Scholl, *Running Press Glossary of Baseball Language*, p. 8, 1977
- But if injuries are an alibi, which had the biggest impact? —*St Petersburg (Florida) Times*, p. 13C, 16th November 2003

3 a weak excuse *US, 1899*
A watered-down version of the conventional use.

alibi day *noun*
payday *US, 1958*
Used in logging camps, suggesting that loggers suddenly develop illnesses and injuries that prevent them from working when they have cash in hand.
- —Frederic G. Cassidy, *Dicitonary of American Regional English, Volume 1*, p. 35, 1985

alibi ghee *noun*
a person who can be counted upon to provide an alibi for a criminal *US*
- —Hyman E. Goldin et al., *Dictionary of American Underworld Lingo*, p. 17, 1950

alibi Ike *noun*
any criminal who regularly asserts alibis when questioned about a crime *US, 1915*
- —Ralph de Sola, *Crime Dictionary*, p. 6, 1982

Alice *noun*

1 LSD *US, 1972*
A phonetic pun on the first two letters of LSD, influenced by Lewis Carroll's *Alice's Adventures in Wonderland*, 1865, and *Through the Looking-Glass and What Alice Found There*, 1871, which were considered inspirational works by the hippy subculture of the late 1960s. The obvious reference, but not a citation of usage, is Jefferson Airplane's 'White Rabbit', 1969.
- —Mike Haskins, *Drugs*, p. 285, 2003

2 a military backpack *US*
- The only things the men had were their individual weapons and ALICE packs, rucksacks that held the bare bones necessities[.] —Harold Coyle, *Sword Point*, p. 177, 1988
- I hit the ground and grabbed my alice [backpack], then crawled to my humvee [military vehicle]. —*Washington Post*, p. A1, 1st February 1991
- —*American Speech*, p. 383, Winter 1991: 'Among the new words'

▸ **to have Alice**
to experience the bleed period of the menstrual cycle *US*
- —Collin Baker et al., *College Undergraduate Slang Study Conducted at Brown University*, p. 70, 1968

Alice *nickname*
Alice Springs *AUSTRALIA, 1901*
Early use is always prefixed with 'the'.
- [M]ost of them go straight up the main road to Katharine from Alice. —*The Guardian*, 29th May 2001

Alice B. Toklas brownies *noun*
chocolate brownies laced with marijuana or hashish *US, 1969*
Toklas' original 1954 recipe, which was for fudge, not brownies, carried the caution: 'Should be eaten with care. Two pieces are quite sufficient'.
- Mrs. Madrigal had come to her table with a basket of Alice B. Toklas brownies. "I made too many," she had said. "Take two, but save one for later. They'll knock you on your ass." —Armistead Maupin, *Tales of the City*, p. 183, 1978

alick *noun*
▷ **see: ALEC**

alickadoo *noun*
a rugby club official or committee member *IRELAND*
Possibly from a book by Alec Kadoo.
- Not all the rugby action will be taking place on the pitch today – top London restaurant Motcombs is planning a lineout of English and Irish alickadoos at their traditional pre match brunch in the Hibemian United Service Club. —*Irish Times*, 15th February 1997

alien *noun*
in casino gambling, a betting chip from another casino *US, 1983*
- —Thomas L. Clark, *The Dictionary of Gambling and Gaming*, p. 5, 1987

Alimony Gallery *noun*
ex-wives of players at an exhibition game by celebrity filmmakers *CANADA*
- Jake felt there were too many wives, children, and kibitzers about. The Filmmakers' First Wives Club or, as Ziggy Alter put it, the Alimony Gallery, was forming, seemingly relaxed but actually fulminating, on the grass behind home plate. —Mordecai Richler, *from Jake and the Kid in Dispatches from the Sporting Life*, p. 279, 2002

A-list *noun*
used for denoting all that is associated with the greatest contemporary fame and celebrity *US, 1984*
In conventional media jargon the A-list is a notional social elite of those who are considered prestigious enough to add top-value to a guest list.
- [M]any celebrity assistants enjoy at least a few of the perks of an A-list lifestyle. — *The Times Magazine*, p. 43, 13th October 2001

alive *adjective*

1 said of a multiple-race bet in horse racing in which the first or early legs of the bet have been won *AUSTRALIA*
- —Ned Wallish, *The Truth Dictionary of Racing Slang*, p. 1, 1989

2 in horse racing, said of a horse subject to heavy betting *US*
- —Robert V. Rowe, *How to Win at Horse-Racing*, p. 1990, 1990

alize *noun*
any alcoholic beverage *US*
- —Alonzo Westbrook, *Hip Hoptionary*, p. 2, 2002

alko *noun*
▷ **see: ALCO**

alky; alkie *noun*

1 an alcoholic *US*
- I get high drunk, drop money on floor, am panhandled, play Ruth Brown wildjump records among drunken alky whores. —Jack Kerouac, *Letter to John Clellon Holmes*, p. 338, 8th February 1952
- If these boys don't play it just right they're liable to finish their training up in Portland at the alky hospital. —Ken Kesey, *One Flew Over the Cuckoo's Nest*, p. 145, 1962
- Jesus, you think we'd miss your wedding? This bunch of alky's? —*The Deer Hunter*, 1978
- I guess with wormwood in your drink you'd have to be a closet alky. —Barry Humphries, *The Traveller's Tool*, p. 75, 1985
- Juicemen are too smart to lend money to people with habits like booze and skag, though sometimes an alkie or a gow-head in a three-piece suit puts one over on them. —Robert Campbell, *Juice*, p. 21, 1988
- Awwwww, that dude ain't no alky. He's fucked up, but he ain't no real alky. —Odie Hawkins, *Amazing Grace*, p. 71, 1993
- You were never an alky, you were a cokehead. —*Something About Mary*, 1998
- He asks every recovering alkie for money, but hardly anyone gives him any. —Stuart Browne, *Dangerous Parking*, p. 45, 2000

2 alcohol, especially methyl alcohol *US, 1844*
- Alky Orgy Kills One, Fells 8 —*San Francisco Examiner*, p. 5, 13th May 1946
- Maybe he put alky in the radiator and the chassis is snozzled[.] —James T. Farrell, *Saturday Night*, p. 37, 1947
- Long before midnight its habitues have already made sleeping arrangements or are snoring in the alleys, cheap overnight lodgings or hallways, paralyzed by alky or cheap domestic red wine. —Jack Lait and Lee Mortimer, *Washington Confidential*, p. 31, 1951
- I dug him up for Big Al, to protect our trucks and the alky we peddled to the coloreds. —Iceberg Slim (Robert Beck), *Death Wish*, p. 222, 1977

3 methanol used as fuel for racing cars *US*
- Why doesn't everyone use alky? Because it evaporates very fast. If you parked your car in the sun for a few hours, you would be out of fuel! Besides, alky costs twice as much as gasoline. —Ed Radlauer, *Drag Racing Pix Dix*, p. 5, 1970

alkyed *adjective*
drunk *US*
- It was big, loud and rough and there must have been a dozen cops getting alkyed. —Red Rudensky, *The Gonif*, p. 88, 1970

alky tank *noun*
a holding cell in a jail reserved for drunk prisoners *US*
- I insist on a transfer – neurology bin, the alky tank, pediatrics, I just don't care! —Ken Kesey, *One Flew Over the Cuckoo's Nest*, p. 27, 1962

all *adverb*
1 very
- Dante: What? What's with that look? I wasn't talking to anyone, especially her! Look at you, being all sort of, I don't know, stand-offfish. —*Clerks*, 1994
- He's all pissy these days. Won't give me nothin' hardly. —Joseph Wambaugh, *Floaters*, p. 7, 1996

2 so *US*
- Don't walk all slow – we have to go to class. —Pamela Munro, *U.C.L.A. Slang*, p. 20, 1997

▸ **be all**
used as a quotative device to report a conversation *US*
- —Connie Eble (Editor), *UNC-CH Campus Slang*, p. 1, Spring 1992
- So I was all, "What's your problem?" And he was all, "Nothing." —*Boogie Nights*, 1997

all about *adjective*
1 alert, efficient *UK, 1946*
Mostly Royal Navy use.
- —John W. Mussell, *The Token Book of Militarisms*, p. 7, 1995

2 interested in *US*
- I'm all about some basketball. —Connie Eble (Editor), *UNC-CH Campus Slang*, p. 1, Fall 1999

all alone *adjective*
in horse racing, leading a race by several lengths *US*
- —David W. Maurer, *Argot of the Racetrack*, p. 10, 1951

All-American *nickname*
the 82nd Airborne Division *US*
Taken from the two A's on the division's patch. There were many double-A variants, such as 'All-African', 'Alcoholics Anonymous', and 'Almost Airborne', but 'All-American' was the most common.
- —Linda Reinberg, *In the Field*, p. 6, 1991

all-American drug *noun*
cocaine *US, 1998*
- —Mike Haskins, *Drugs*, p. 280, 2003

all and everyone *noun*
every single person *TRINIDAD AND TOBAGO*
- Electrcity problems on the other hand affect all and everyone of us. —*Expresss*, p. 4, 26th May 1973

all a penny *adjective*
inexpensive and plentiful *BARBADOS*
- In the days of my childhood flying fish was considered cheap at ten for the bit. When it reached 'all a penny' often they were not counted. —*Nation*, p. 5, 5th May 1978

all black *nickname*
a member of the New Zealand international men's rugby team *NEW ZEALAND*
- You don't have to be an All Black to know when you're offside. —Dan Davin, *The Salamander and the Fire*, p. 81, 1986
- The All Blacks had worn black jerseys since 1894. —*Dominion*, p. 56, 17th April 1999

all chiefs and no Indians; too many chiefs and not enough Indians
a situation in which too many people are giving orders and too few are available to obey; a top-heavy command structure *US*
Military coinage, meaning all officers not other ranks. Senator William Proxmire was quoted in the *New York Times*, as saying that the US was 'nearing the point where we have all chiefs and no Indians'.
- —*New York Times*, p. 31, 17th June 1972
- [A]t this meeting were some of the most senior officers of the Met [Metropolitan police]. superintendents and chiefs. In fact it was all chiefs and no Indians. —Dave Courtney, *Stop the Ride I Want to Get Off*, p. 295, 1999

all-clear *noun*
authorisation, official approval *UK, 1936*
From the earlier and continuing use as a signal that a danger has passed.
- [T]he advice finally giving the all-clear came on 15 March, only five days before fighting began. —*The Observer*, 7th March 2004

all coppers are bastards; all coppers are cunts
serves as a catchphrase among certain sections of society *UK*
From, or possibly the inspiration for, a chanted jingle: 'I'll sing you a song / And it wont take long (or: It's not very long) / All coppers are bastards.' The original phrase has certainly been in circulation since about 1945.

all dat *noun*
everything *UK*
Popularised in the UK in the late 1990s by Ali G (comedian Sacha Baron-Cohen).
- —Susie Dent, *The Language Report*, p. 144, 2003

all day *adjective*
1 in bar dice games involving up to three rolls, taking all three rolls to make the player's hand *US*
- —Gil Jacobs, *The World's Best Dice Games*, p. 191, 1976

2 in craps, said of a bet that is in effect until the shooter rolls his point or a seven *US, 1983*
- When you tell the dealer you're making an all day bet, that means it's a standard hardway bet rather than a one-roll proposition bet. —Thomas L. Clark, *The Dictionary of Gambling and Gaming*, p. 5, 1987

all day and night *noun*
a life prison sentence *US*
- —John R. Armore and Joseph D. Wolfe, *Dictionary of Desperation*, p. 19, 1976
- He's in the big house for all day and night, a new fish jammed into a drum with a cribman, who acts like a gazoonie." —*San Francisco Examiner*, p. 26, 17th August 1976

all day from a quarter *noun*
a jail sentence of 25 years to life *US*
- —William K. Bentley and James M. Corbett, *Prison Slang*, p. 24, 1992

all-day sucker *noun*
a large lollipop that takes a long time to consume *AUSTRALIA, 1939*
- She could detect better than a geiger counter when Arnie was on the weight-reducing pills, eating laxatives like they were all-day suckers. —Wilda Moxham, *The Apprentice*, p. 84, 1969

all down the line *adverb*
in every way, completely, at every opportunity *UK*
- They'd been seen off [out witted] all down the line. —J Wingate, *Oil Strike*, 1976

allergic *adjective*
having a dislike for someone or something *UK, 1937*
Generally jocular.
- —John Ayto, *The Oxford Dictionary of Slang*, p. 209, 1998

alley *noun*
1 a fictional place characterised by the preceding thing or activity *US*
- Today our readers are getting a preview of a case before it comes up in Alimony Alley, as the divorce courts sometimes are called. —*San Francisco News*, p. 2, 9th September 1954
- Ulcer Alley, the big time in Ad Row, is quivering at all the firings at one big agency. —*San Francisco Examiner*, p. 29, 26th January 1962

2 in horse racing, a stall in the starting barrier *AUSTRALIA, 1982*
- The filly is certain to lead from another good alley today but Pallamallawa will be parked right on her hindquarters. —*Sydney Morning Herald*, p. 2, 25th June 1994

3 on the railways, the track visible ahead of a train *US*
- So down "The Alley" one can't steam / Until the green light is agleam. —J. Herbert Lund, *Herb's Hot Box of Railraod Slang*, p. 2, 1975

4 a walkway between rows of prison cells *US*
- —Jay Robert Nash, *Dictionary of Crime*, p. 7, 1992

5 a playing marble *AUSTRALIA, 1934*
- 'Give yer a game of alleys, glassies up,' challenged Pigeon. —Norman Lindsay, *Saturdee*, p. 124, 1934
- He never could have played marbles in the country where he'd been born, on the other side of the world; he'd have known an ally pitched right could put out an eye. —Wilda Moxham, *The Apprentice*, p. 20, 1969

▸ **make your alley good**
to improve your situation; to redeem yourself in the eyes of others *AUSTRALIA, 1924*
- 'Soon's I've made my alley good with Howie, this is what happens to Jake.' He drew a long pale finger across his throat. — Wilda Moxham, *The Apprentice*, p. 31, 1969

▸ **up your alley**
apt to your style or taste *US, 1924*
- If the whole Big Brother circus has left you cold, on the other hand, perhaps Pig Brother is up your alley. — *The Guardian*, 27th July 2001

alley apple *noun*
1 a brick or cobblestone *US, 1927*
- — Bill Reilly, *Big Al's Official Guide to Chicagoese*, p. 13, 1982
- [W]hen the wine and beer bottles evaded easy reach, we threw half house bricks and roughed out cobblestones, "alley apples." — Odie Hawkins, *Men Friends*, p. 13, 1989

2 horse manure; a piece of faeces; excrement *US, 1960*
- — *Gayness Explained*, p. 142, June 2003

alley bourbon *noun*
strong, illegally manufactured whisky *US*
- — *Star Tribune (Minneapolis)*, p. 19F, 31st January 1999

alley cat *noun*
1 a sexually promiscuous person, especially a woman *UK, 1926*
- He goes on the prowl each night / Like an alley cat / Looking for some new delight / Like an alley cat / She can't trust him out of sight[.] — Jack Harlen, *The Alley Cat Song*, 1963

2 a young person who idles on a street corner *US*
- — Lou Shelly, *Hepcats Jive Talk Dictionary*, p. 21, 1945

3 a person who survives on begged or stolen pickings *GUYANA*
- — Richard Allsopp, *Dictionary of Caribbean English Usage*, p. 24, 1996

alley cleaner *noun*
a handgun *US*
- — *American Speech*, p. 192, October 1957: 'Some colloquialisms of the handgunner'

alley craps *noun*
a spontaneous, loosely organised, private game of craps, rarely played in an alley *US, 1977*
- — Thomas L. Clark, *The Dictionary of Gambling and Gaming*, p. 5, 1987

alley juice *noun*
denatured alcohol (ethyl alcohol) to which a poisonous substance has been added to make it unfit for consumption) *US*
- — Jay Robert Nash, *Dictionary of Crime*, p. 7, 1992

alley-oop *noun*
in snowboarding, a 360-degree turn in the direction of the back of the board *CANADA*
- — Mike Fabbro, *Snowboarding*, p. 93, 1996

alley-scoring *noun*
the recyling of food, furniture or anything else left in the rubbish *US*
- — Vann Wesson, *Generation X Field Guide and Lexicon*, p. 4, 1997

alley up *verb*
to pay off a debt *NEW ZEALAND*
- — Sonya Plowman, *Great Kiwi Slang*, p. 12, 2002

alley-wise *adjective*
sophisticated in the ways of the world *US*
- One way or another, he has been a gambler all his life. Alley-wise. Street-smart. — Edward Lin, *Big Julie of Vegas*, p. 12, 1974

allez-oop!
used to accompany the action when lifting a child, or boosting someone over or onto something *UK, 1931*
Originally used by circus acrobats. A combination of French *allez* (to go) with a Franglais version of 'up'. Douglas Leechman, a correspondent of Partridge, wrote that he remembered it from his childhood, around 1895, however the earliest recorded use is by Joseph Weingarten, *American Dictionary of Slang*, p. 4, 1954.

all fall down
used for describing a catastrophe or chaos *GRENADA*
- — Richard Allsopp, *Dictionary of Caribbean English Usage*, p. 21, 1996

all fart and no shit *adjective*
said of a person who makes empty promises *UK*
- — Rick Jolly, *Jackspeak*, p. A-4, 1989
- — Paik Choo, *The Coxford Singlish Dictionary*, p. 6, 2002

all-fired *adjective*
used as an intensifier *US, 1845*
Perhaps a euphemism for 'hell-fired', as are **INFERNAL**, **DAMNED**, etc.
- Why are people so all-fired concerned about doing things the right way, anyway? — Dick Clark, *To Goof or Not to Goof*, p. 12, 1963
- Well, how come you know so all-fired much about it?" Harold asked. — Terry Southern, *Texas Summer*, p. 45, 1991

all gas and gaiters *adjective*
used as a derisory description of bishops and other church dignitaries; pompous nonsense *UK*
Originally 'All is gas and gaiters', Charles Dickens, *Nicholas Nickleby*, 1838–9. Repopularised as a useful catchphrase by the BBC situation comedy *All Gas and Gaiters*, 1967–71.

all get-out *noun*
a high degree of something *US, 1884*
- It's a simple and enduring principle: make yourself as ugly as all get-out, and life will be just beautiful. — *The Guardian*, 24th August 2002

all gong and no dinner *adjective*
all talk and no action *UK*
- — *The Archers*, 13th October 1981

all hands *adjective*
sexually aggressive *US*
- — *American Speech*, p. 273, December 1963: 'American Indian student slang'

all het up *adjective*
▷ see: **HET UP**

alligation *noun*
the charring of burnt wood *US*
- The point of origin of a fire is determined by depth of charring and what the arson squad calls "alligation" – roughness and cracking of charred wood resembling the hie of an alligator. — *San Francisco Call-Bulletin*, p. 8, 31st January 1955

alligator *noun*
1 an enthusiastic fan of swing jazz *US, 1936*
- Bernie could well remember the "alligators" of the late swing period, those serious types, self-styled students of American jazz, who used to edge up to the orchestra shell and remain there all night, indefatigably listening. — Ross Russell, *The Sound*, p. 81, 1961
- — Robert S. Gould, *A Jazz Lexicon*, p. 6, 1964

2 any unpleasant and difficult task *US*
- — Charles Shafer, *Folk Speech in Texas Prisons*, p. 197, 1990

3 a circus performer's wife *US*
- — Don Wilmeth, *The Language of American Popular Entertainment*, p. 8, 1981

4 in electric line work, an insulated line tool known formally as a 'tie stick' *US*
- — A.B. Chance Co., *Lineman's Slang Dictionary*, p. 1, 1980

5 in television and film making, a clamp used to attach lighting *US*
- — Ira Konigsberg, *The Complete Film Dictionary*, p. 9, 1987

alligator *verb*
(of a painting) to crack *US*
- "Alligatoring" is the word for cracks that develop in paint. — *San Francisco Examiner*, p. 5, 22nd May 1955

alligator
see you later *UK, 1960*
Rhyming slang, inspired or influenced by 'See you later, alligator / In a while, crocodile.' (Bill Haley & the Comets, 'See you later, Alligator', 1956.)

Alligator Alley *nickname*
Interstate Highway 75, which connects Naples and Fort Lauderdale, Florida *US, 1966*
So named because it crosses the heart of what had been an impenetrable wilderness, the Florida Everglades. The name is thought to have been coined by the American Automobile Association in 1966 to express supreme disdain for what it considered to be an unsafe toll road.

- —Wayne Floyd, *Jason's Authentic Dictionary of CB Slang*, p. 8, 1976
- Authorities closed a 20-mile stretch of "Alligator Alley," south Florida's primary cross-state connector, and detonated a package early Friday after stopping three suspects who they believe may have been plotting a terror attack in Miami. — *CNN News*, 13th September 2002

alligator bait *noun*

1 a black person *US, 1901*
- —Harold Wentworth and Stuart Berg Flexner, *Dictionary of American Slang*, p. 4, 1960

2 bad food, especially fried liver *US, 1926*
- —Joseph E. Ragen and Charles Finston, *Inside the World's Toughest Prison*, p. 789, 1962

alligator boot *noun*

a railwayman's work-boot damaged by diesel oil so that the uppers parted from the sides *UK*
From the appearance of the flapping leather.
- —Frank McKenna, *A Glossary of Railwaymen's Talk*, 1970

alligator burns *noun*

charrings on burnt wood in the form of scales that resemble an alligator's hide *US*
- If he'd gone in there he wouldn've known right off, the way those charrings, alligator burns, showed, he would've known you torched it. — George V. Higgins, *The Rat on Fire*, p. 22, 1981

alligator mouth *noun*

a braggart; a verbal bully *US, 1961*
- —J.E. Lighter, *Historical Dictionary of American Slang, Volume 1*, p. 19, 1994

alligator skins *noun*

paper money *US*
- I pulled the score by myself. I was gone about an hour and when I came back I got fistfuls of alligator skins. — Hal Ellson, *Duke*, p. 68, 1949

all in *adjective*

1 exhausted, tired out *UK, 1903*
A term coined in the Stock Exchange where it was used to describe a depressed market.

2 said of a poker player who has bet their entire remaining bankroll *US*
- —John Scarne, *Scarne's Guide to Modern Poker*, p. 272, 1979

all jam and Jerusalem *adjective*

applied derisorily to the Women's Institute *UK*
A catchphrase, probably dating from the 1920s, that targets the two widely-known details of WI lore: jam-making and the anthemic use of William Blake's hymn 'Jerusalem'.
- —Simon Goodenough, *Jam and Jerusalem*, 1977

all jokes and no tokes *adjective*

used by casino employees to describe poor tipping by gamblers *US, 1983*
- When I hear all jokes and no tokes, I know that everybody is having a good time but the dealers. — Thomas L. Clark, *The Dictionary of Gambling and Gaming*, p. 6, 1987

all like

▸ **be all like**

used as a quotative device, combining two other devices for 'to say' *US*
- So then I was all like, "What are you gonna do?" Y' know? And he was all, like acting tough, y' know, with his friends around and stuff. — *Boogie Nights*, 1997

all man jack *noun*

everybody who is involved *TRINIDAD AND TOBAGO, 1973*
- —Lise Winer, *Dictionary of the English/Creole of Trinidad & Tobago*, 2003

all mouth *adjective*

boastful; unable to back up words with deeds *BARBADOS*
- —Richard Allsopp, *Dictionary of Caribbean English Usage*, p. 25, 1996

all mouth and no trousers *adjective*

all talk and no substance *UK*
- He's all mouth and no trousers. — David Powis, *The Signs of Crime*, 1977

all-nighter *noun*

1 an engagement between a prostitute and customer that lasts all night; a prostitute's client who pays to stay all night *UK*
Also known as an 'all-night'.
- Prostitutes still classify their clients as "short-timers" and "all-nighters". — John Gosling and Douglas Warner, *The Shame of a City*, 1960
- I can't be takin no all night fer one fast fiver, so I start in playin roun wiff his lil ol pecker. — Robert Gover, *One Hundred Dollar Misunderstanding*, p. 21, 1961
- Three hundred and fifty scoots for an all-nighter. — James Ellroy, *Brown's Requiem*, p. 236, 1981
- He didn't know if they tricked during the evening and then took an all-nighter. — Robert Campbell, *Alice in La-La Land*, p. 263, 1987

2 any task worked on all night long, especially to meet a deadline for the following day *AUSTRALIA, 1966*
- She did this every time I had a deadline. I'd be in my room pulling an all-nighter, the walls would be shaking and pounding, the baboons bellowing. — John Birmingham, *He Died With a Felafel in his Hand*, p. 94, 1994

3 a person who stays in jail all night after being arrested *US*
- He was isued a pallet to sleep on and locked up with twenty other all-nighters. — Richard Price, *Clockers*, p. 97, 1992

all-night money *noun*

a prostitute's charge for spending the night with a customer *US*
- —Jay Robert Nash, *Dictionary of Crime*, p. 7, 1992

all of a doodah *adjective*

nervous, dithering with excitement *UK, 1952*

all of a tiswas; all of a tizwas; all of a tizzy *adjective*

in a state of panic or excited confusion *UK, 1984*
Probably a Royal Air Force coinage; from TIZZ; TIZZY (a state of panic), contriving what appears to be an etymology by amending the source-word to 'tiswas', a combination of 'it is' and 'was', suggesting a play on the earlier colloquial phrase 'not know whether you are coming or going' (to be in a state of confusion).

all on *adjective*

prepared for violence *NEW ZEALAND*
- The man who approached Mr. Prebble was clearly angry and when he went to the back of the hall she thought, "Oh God, she's all on"[.] — *Evening Post*, p. 2, 17th November 1999

all on top!

that's untrue! *UK, 1984*
Criminal use, probably from the 1920s or 30s; what's 'on top' is in addition to the truth.

all-out *adjective*

very drunk *GUYANA*
- She had drank so excessively, that she had to be taken away by ambulance. After the prosecutor had related how she was found 'all out' and the ambulance had to be summoned, Helga gave her explanation. — *Daily Chronicle*, p. 3, 22nd August 1952

all over bar the shouting *adjective*

finished for all intents and purposes *UK, 1842*
- I always played fair, but if they ever mucked me about, biff! Send for the cleaners. All over bar the shouting. — Alexander Buzo, *Norm and Ahmed*, p. 12, 1969
- It was all over bar the shouting, but they wrangled on until late afternoon. — Frank Hardy, *The Outcasts of Foolgarah*, p. 166, 1971

all over it *adjective*

in complete control *US*
- —Alonzo Westbrook, *Hip Hoptionary*, p. 3, 2002

all over the place like a madwoman's knitting *adjective*

in chaos, in utter disarray *AUSTRALIA, 1953*
Several variants including 'all over the place like a madwoman's custard / lunch-box / shit'. An elaboration of conventional and unconventional senses of 'all over the place'.
- I floored this bloody Kraut. Really laid him out. He was all over the place like a mad woman's lunch box. — Alexander Buzo, *Norm and Ahmed*, p. 10, 1969
- [T]he old bastard's been all over the place like a madwoman's shit! — Barry Humphries, *Bazza Pulls It Off!*, 1971
- —G.A. Wilkes, *A Dictionary of Australian Colloquialisms*, p. 210, 1978

all over the shop *adjective*

confused, in disarray; everywhere *UK, 1874*
- The greenhouse effect he said...but it makes it get colder as well. It makes the weather go all over the shop. — Roddy Doyle, *The Van*, p. 90, 1991
- First of all I personally believe that setting goals are essential to all aspects of our lives as I have the habit of being "all over the shop at times". — *Limerick Leader*, 29th April 2000

all over you like a rash *adjective*
making determined advances of an intimate or personal nature *UK*
- "You should have seen her yesterday," she said to me, "all over him like a rash she was." —Mary Hooper, *(megan)2*, p. 36, 1999
- The copper was all over us like a rash, and we're there with coke, booze, puff and four drunk passengers on board! —Wayne Anthony, *Spanish Highs*, p. 20, 1999
- In London MoPic was all over me like a rash, like an epidemic about to explode. —Lanre Fehintola, *Charlie Says...*, p. 55, 2000

allow *verb*
to be lenient towards someone, to let someone off lightly *UK*
Predominantly black usage.
- Rude: "Why did you lie to me?" (Silly question.) Me: (Incoherent mumble.) Rude's friend: "Allow him, man." —*The Guardian*, p. 9, 27th February 2002

all piss and wind *adjective*
prone to boasting *NEW ZEALAND*
- —Sonya Plowman, *Great Kiwi Slang*, p. 13, 2002

all pissed-up and nothing to show *adjective*
used of someone who has spent or, more precisely, drunk all his wages or winnings *UK, 1961*
A variation, probably from the 1920s, in the manner of 'all dressed up and nowhere to go'.

all quiet on the Western Front *adjective*
used to describe a situation in which not much is happening *UK*
From a World War 1 communiqué that became a satirical catchphrase; now generalised, probably influenced by the 1929 novel by Erich Remarque and the 1930 film so titled. In the US, the phrase replaced the Civil War-era 'all quiet on the Potomoc'.
- When Jerry Shcmier says it's all quiet on the western front of America's first national park, he has a different interpretation from most. —*Christian Science Monitor*, p. 2, 19th December 2003

all reet *adjective*
good; all right *US, 1946*
- —Joseph Weingarten, *American Dictionary of Slang*, p. 6, 1954
- Well, all reet then, tell your story, man. —Ross Russell, *The Sound*, p. 10, 1961

all right *adjective*
in possession of drugs *US*
- "You all right?" one of the dopefiends yelled out of the back window. "I'll be back with some scag in less than an hour," Snake replied. —Donald Goines, *Dopefiend*, p. 174, 1971

all right
used as a greeting among prisoners *US*
- —William K. Bentley and James M. Corbett, *Prison Slang*, p. 45, 1992

all right for some!
used for registering envy of another's advantages or luck *UK, 1969*

all rooters and no shooters
used at casino craps tables for encouraging a player to take a turn as a shooter *US, 1983*
- —Thomas L. Clark, *The Dictionary of Gambling and Gaming*, p. 6, 1987

all rootie
used as an expression of agreement or satisfaction *US*
Especially popular after Little Richard's 1955 hit song 'Tutti Fruity'.
- "All rootie," she said aggreably. —Max Shulman, *Rally Round the Flag, Boys!*, p. 47, 1957

all round the option *adverb*
all over the place, everywhere *UK*
- [T]he old man was still phoning all round the option. —Alan Hunter, *Gently Down the Stream*, 1957

all show and no go *adjective*
used for describing someone who cannot back appearances with action *US*
- He's all show and no go. When he tried to act tough with us, no matter what happened, Hunter THompson got scared. —Ralph "Sonny" Barger, *Hell's Angel*, p. 125, 2000

all singing all dancing *adjective*
configured or equipped with all possible enhancements *US*
Especially of financial and IT products, but originally from the advertising matter for *Broadway Melody*, 1929, the first Hollywood musical.

all star *noun*
a drug user who abuses many different drugs *US*
- —Jay Robert Nash, *Dictionary of Crime*, p. 7, 1992

all systems go *noun*
a state of readiness *US, 1974*
Often humorous; adopted from the jargon of space exploration.

all that *noun*
sexual activity *UK*
A shortening of the conventional, already partially euphemistic 'all that sort of thing'.
- [S]he knew nothing about "all that", so the honeymoon was a revolting experience, ruined by "all that", and since then she has never been able to do with "all that". —Margaret Powell, *The Treasure Upstairs*, 1970

all that *adjective*
superlative, very good *US, 1991*
- —Lady Kier Kirby, *The 376 Deee-liteful Words*, 1992
- —Connie Eble (Editor), *UNC-CH Campus Slang*, p. 1, Spring 1993
- He thinks he's all that, Tai. —*Clueless*, 1995

all that and a bag of chips! *noun*
used for expressing strong approval *US*
- —Connie Eble (Editor), *UNC-CH Campus Slang*, p. 1, Fall 1997

all that and then some *noun*
everything *US*
- —Ethan Hilderbrant, *Prison Slang*, p. 142, 1998

all the best
good bye *UK*
By ellipsis from conventional 'all the best of luck/fortune', etc.
- Outside we said all the best and went off in different directions. —Philip Callow, *Going to the Moon*, 1968

all the better for seeing you
used as a 'witty' riposte to the greeting: 'How are you?' *UK, 1977*
A catchphrase.

all the eighths *noun*
a seven-eighths point movement in a stock price *US*
- —Kathleen Odean, *High Steppers, Fallen Angels, and Lollipops*, p. 96, 1988

all the fives *noun*
fifty-five *UK*
In Bingo, House or Tombola, the formula 'all the' announces a double number. Varies numerically, from 'all the twos' (22) to 'all the eights' (88). Recorded by Laurie Atkinson around 1950.
- [D]ouble numbers such "fifty-five" are called thus: "all the fives". —Michael Harrison, *Reported Safe Arrival*, 1943

all the go *adjective*
in the height of fashion *UK, 1793*
- [O]ne-inch candy-stripes were all the go then, and those shirts made us look like a gang of barber poles topped with slickum. —Mezz Mezzrow, *Really the Blues*, p. 22, 1946
- Now that juvenile delinquency is all the go, and respectable screwsmen [thieves] daren't walk home from their gaffs at night[.] —Charles Raven, *Underworld Nights*, p. 41, 1956

all there *adjective*
1 sane *UK, 1864*
2 alert, aware, sharp *UK, 1880*
- He doesn't like to talk in public, because of the Parkinson's, but he can talk. He's all there. —*The Observer*, 3rd February 2002

all the same khaki pants
used for expressing the sentiment that there is no difference between the matters in question *TRINIDAD AND TOBAGO*
Khaki trousers are the regular schoholboy uniform, eliminating personal, social or class difference.

all the way *adjective*
in the military, destined for leadership *US*
• At the time of the Ia Drang fight, Hal Moore was already being described as an "all the way" man, meaning four stars and probably Chief of Staff one day. — David H. Hackworth, *About Face*, p. 487, 1982

all the way *adverb*
to a championship *US*
• — *San Francisco News*, p. 31, 30th June 1959: 'Dodgers can go all the way'

all the way live *adjective*
excellent, superlative *US*
• So like Andrea's sweet sixteen party was like all the way live! — Mary Corey and Victoria Westermark, *Fer Shurr! How to be a Valley Girl*, 1982
• He has a beautiful girl, a brand new car, and a college degree. That brother is defiintely all the way live. — Fab 5 Freddy, *Fresh Fly Favor*, p. 6, 1992

all the world and his dog *noun*
everybody *AUSTRALIA, 1984*
A humorous variation of ALL THE WORLD AND HIS WIFE.

all the world and his wife *noun*
everybody *UK, 1738*
Generally with a sense of hyperbole.

all-time *adjective*
excellent *US*
• — John Severson, *Modern Surfing Around the World*, p. 162, 1964

all-timer's disease *noun*
used by surfers humorously to describe a person's proclivity to exaggerate when recounting surf conditions or their accomplishments *US*
• — Trevor Cralle, *The Surfin'ary*, p. 2, 1991

all tits and teeth *adjective*
used for describing a woman who makes the most of a distracting smile and breasts *UK, 1967*

all to buggery *adjective*
awry, bungled, utterly confused, unsatisfactory, mixed-up *UK*

all to cock *adjective*
awry, bungled, utterly confused, unsatisfactory, mixed-up *UK, 1948*
• It's wrong is this. It's all-to-fuckin'-cock. — *The Full Monty*, 1997

all to hell *adjective*
utterly ruined *US, 1968*
• The schedules are all to hell, the crews are in the wrong places and the planes are in the wrong countries. — *The Guardian*, 24th July 2003

all two *adjective*
both *BARBADOS*
Collected by Richard Allsopp in 1975.

all up *adjective*
1 (of things) exhausted, fruitless, ruined; (of people) bankrupt, defeated, doomed to die *UK, 1818*
Especially in the phrase 'all up with'.
• [S]cience is telling politicians something they are desperate not to hear: that it's all up with our current model of gung-ho globalisation. — *The Guardian*, 17th July 2002

2 (of betting) with the winnings of one bet forming the stake of the next *AUSTRALIA, 1933*
• Old John has got two horses starting there and they both look a good chance. See him out there and if he says ok stick it on the first one and all up the second. — Sam Weller, *Old Bastards I Have Met*, p. 134, 1979
• Before I pay out, let me say that one of the initiatives, all-up betting for a win or place, is not a bad idea and overdue. — *Sunday Tasmanian*, p. 39, 29th May 1988

allus *adverb*
always *UK, 1852*
• Ooh, I've allus wanted a nosey in men's bogs. — *The Full Monty*, 1997

all vanilla *noun*
in poker, a spade flush *US*
Collected from William E. Rippe by Peter Tamony in March 1948.

all wind and piss; all wind and water *adjective*
boastful; not backing up words with action *UK, 1961*

all wool and a yard wide *adjective*
excellent, reliable *US, 1882*
• — Frederic G. Cassidy, *Dicitonary of American Regional English, Volume 1*, p. 50, 1985

alma mater *noun*
a prison where a criminal has served time *US*
From Latin for 'fostering mother'; adopted with obvious irony from its English use, first recorded in 1718 in school or university use.
• — Vincent J. Monteleone, *Criminal Slang*, p. 11, 1949

almighty *adjective*
great; impressive *UK, 1824*
• Just blast down the road giving it almighty stick, and fucking that's it. — Paul E. Willis, *Profane Culture*, p. 17, 1978

almond rock *noun*
1 a frock, a dress *UK*
Rhyming slang.
• She then began removing / Her full-length almond rock[.] — Ronnie Barker, *Fletcher's Book of Rhyming Slang*, p. 21, 1979

2 the penis *UK*
Rhyming slang for COCK. Recorded as C19 and obsolete by Julian Franklyn in 1969. Also shortened to 'almond'.
• — Sydney (Steak) T. Kendall, *Up the Frog*, p. 63, 1969
• — Chris Donald, *Roger's Profanisaurus*, p. 5, 1998

almond rocks; almonds; rocks *noun*
socks *UK*
Rhyming slang, based on a confection popular from the mid-C19, can be presumed therefore to be late C19 in origin. In the mid-C20 it was popularly abbreviated to 'almonds'; later use seems to favour 'rocks', i.e. 'cotton rocks'. A specialised military variation arising during World War 1 was 'army rocks'.
• And he would put on his almonds rocks, and his Dicky Dirt [shirt]. — Ronnie Barker, *Fletcher's Book of Rhyming Slang*, p. 25, 1979
• — Angela Devlin, *Prison Patter*, p. 23, 1996

Aloha Airlines *nickname*
an aviation unit attached to the 25th Infantry Division during the Vietnam war *US*
• — Linda Reinberg, *In the Field*, p. 7, 1991

alone player *noun*
a card cheat who works alone *US, 1961*
• — Thomas L. Clark, *The Dictionary of Gambling and Gaming*, p. 6, 1987

Al Pacino *noun*
a cappuccino coffee *UK*
Rhyming slang, formed from the name of the US film actor (b.1940).
• — Susie Dent, *The Language Report*, p. 98, 2003

alphabet city *nickname*
an imprecisely defined area on the lower east side of Manhattan, near Avenues A, B, C and D *US, 1980*
• — Carsten Stroud, *Close Pursuit*, p. 269, 1987
• A lot of poet friends have abandoned the squalor of Alphabet City and the Lower East Side for the bovine whines of this little coastal town outside San Francisco. — Jim Carroll, *Forced Entries*, p. 116, 1987

Alphonse *noun*
1 a pimp *UK, 1943*
Rhyming slang for PONCE.
• — Angela Devlin, *Prison Patter*, p. 23, 1996

2 a homosexual *UK*
Rhyming slang for PONCE (an effeminate male).
• Don't be such an Alphonse – have your dinner and come out. — Bodmin Dark, *Dirty Cockney Rhyming Slang*, 2003

alpine snow *noun*
cocaine ingested off a woman's breasts *UK*
• — *Q Magazine*, p. 75, February 2001

alpine stick *noun*
an oversized frankfurter *NEW ZEALAND*
• — Louis S. Leland, *A Personal Kiwi-Yankee Dictionary*, p. 8, 1984

Alpo *noun*
sausage topping for a pizza *US*
An allusion to a branded dog food.
• — *Maledicta*, p. 7, 1996: 'Domino's pizza jargon'

alrightnik *noun*
a person who has succeeded in material terms *US*
- An alrightnik, drowning, was pulled out of the water, and an excited crowd gathered, crying, "Stand back!" "Call a doctor!" "Give him artificial respiration!" "Never!" cried the alrightnik's wife "Real respiration or nothing!" —Leo Rosten, *The Joys of Yiddish*, p. 12–13, 1968

alrighty!
used for expressing agreement or satisfaction *AUSTRALIA*
- 'Alrighty,' said the Decoy, taking the number and climbing out the back door. —John Birmingham, *The Tasmanian Babes Fiasco*, p. 70, 1997

also-ran *noun*
anyone not performing very well *US, 1896*
Originally applied in horse racing to any horse placed fourth or worse and thus not winning any money on the race.
- Veteran Milers Now 'Also Rans' (Headline) —*San Francisco News*, p. 17, 15th January 1947
- 'Also-Ran' Bags Net Upset Win (Headline) —*San Francisco Call-Bulletin*, p. 8G, 1st August 1953
- Newcomers Named for Academy Awards; Past Winners Are Among Also-Rans (Headline) —*San Francisco News*, p. 1, 16th February 1954
- 'Also-Rans' Lead Miami Beach Golf (Headline) —*San Francisco News*, 23rd March 1956
- —Mel Heimer, *Inside Racing*, p. 209, 1962

altar *noun*
a toilet *US*
- —Joseph E. Ragen and Charles Finston, *Inside the World's Toughest Prison*, p. 789, 1962

altered *adjective*
very drunk *US*
A suggestion of a completely altered state of perception.
- —Judi Sanders, *Don't Dog by Do, Dude!*, p. 1, 1991

alter ego *noun*
a false identification card that permits a minor to be served alcohol *US*
- —Connie Eble (Editor), *UNC-CH Campus Slang*, p. 1, November 1990

alter kocker; alte kaker *noun*
a mean and nasty old man *US, 1968*
Yiddish for German for 'old shitter'.
- I'm doing it for Arnie Green, an alte kaker with hair in his ears. —Armistead Maupin, *Maybe the Moon*, p. 46, 1992

altogether *noun*
▸ **the altogether**
complete nudity *UK, 1894*
- It was then that Marcia leaped out of bed, forgetting in her excitement that she was in the "altogether," as the folks on Broadway say. —*San Francisco Call-Bulletin*, 2nd May 1946
- She would sooner have cake-walked out on the Radio City Music Hall stage in the altogether, with a red gardenia in her belly button, than put those crippled thumbs of hers on exhibit over a canasta table or anywhere. —Bernard Wolfe, *The Late Risers*, p. 93, 1954
- Strip teaser Lili St. Cyr made movieland history this week when she appeared in a scene for a new picture in the altogether – that is, absolutely nude. —*San Francisco News*, 16th August 1958
- Male & Female In the Altogether – Free Coffee! —*San Francisco Examiner*, 4th July 1968

alum; alumn *noun*
an alumni or alumna *US, 1934*
- Mary Ann Berger, an Independent Freshman, says, "Stick around Alums – for the football game." —*Life*, p. 21, 20th December 1954
- The university [Princeton] is under growing pressure from the "alums." —*The Oregonian*, p. 15, 22nd April 1956
- Dr. Taylor queried all "alums," got 1,500 answers, about 65 percent of the total. —*San Francisco Call-Bulletin*, 20th March 1957
- Like most chancellors, Dr. Edgar had no doubt been promised by his well-to-do alums that he could scare up more endowment in the end zone than he could at all of the Christian fellowship dinners he attended. —Dan Jenkins, *Life Its Ownself*, p. 83, 1984

aluminium cookie *noun*
a compact disc (CD) *UK*
- [T]his first volume of Kerrang!'s "Hometaping" series has seen us digging through our various collections of dog-eared vinyl and assorted aluminium cookies[.] —Nick Arson (of the Hives), *Hometaping Vol 1*, April 2002

aluminium crow *nickname*
a CF-100 Canuck jet fighter aircraft *CANADA*
The aircraft first flew in 1950, and is also known as **LEAD SLED** and **THE CLUNK**.

aluminum *noun*
▸ **the aluminum**
in horse racing, the inside rail *AUSTRALIA*
- —Ned Wallish, *The Truth Dictionary of Racing Slang*, p. 1, 1989

aluminum overcast *noun*
any very large military aircraft *US, 1961*
- Gansz never served in a command that had jet fighters, and he flew as a copilot on a C-124 – a large propeller-driven troop and cargo carrier nicknamed "The Aluminum Overcast" because of its size and relatively low normal cruising speed of 272 miles per hour —*Chicago Tribune*, p. C6, 28th December 1987
- —J.E. Lighter, *Historical Dictionary of American Slang, Volume 1*, p. 20, 1994
- The B-17 was the bomber workhorse of World War II. When production ended in 1945, 12,726 had been built. The 'Aluminum Overcast' carries the colors of the 398th Bomb Group and commemorates one shot down over France. —*Florida Times-Union*, p. B1, 14th November 2003

Alvin *noun*
a naive, easily-cheated person *US, 1949*
Circus and carnival usage.
- —Harold Wentworth and Stuart Berg Flexner, *Dictionary of American Slang*, p. 5, 1960
- —Don Wilmeth, *The Language of American Popular Entertainment*, p. 8, 1981

always late in take off, always late in arrival *nickname*
the Italian airline Alitalia
Most airlines seem to attract jocular nicknames. This is one of the more memorable.
- —*The Tribune (India)*, 31st August 2002

Alzeihmer's avenue *noun*
an area in a hospital or nursing home frequented by senile patients *AUSTRALIA*
- —*Maledicta*, p. 92, 1986–1987

am *noun*
an *am*ateur *UK*
- —Ben Sharpe, *Scooter Crazy*, p. 39, 2000

amateur half-hour; amateur hour *noun*
a poorly organised event *US, 1939*
- Channel 4's amateur half-hour-one-hour talk show, *Loose Talk*. —Tony Wilson, *24 Hour Party People*, p. 107, 2002

amateur night *noun*
1 New Year's Eve *US*
Just as amateur Christians attend church only twice a year, or amateur Jews attend services only twice a year, amateur drunks only drink to oblivion once a year.
- I was a third-rate amateur. Do you know what alcoholics call New Year's Eve? Amateur night. —Elmore Leonard, *Touch*, p. 168, 1977

2 a night when the tips left by a restaurant's customers are low *US*
- —*Maledicta*, p. 47, 1995: 'Door whore and other New Mexico restaurant slang'

3 sex with a chance acquaintance who is not a prostitute *US*
- —Harold Wentworth and Stuart Berg Flexner, *Dictionary of American Slang*, p. 5, 1960

amazer machine; amazer *noun*
in trucking, a police radar unit used for measuring vehicle speed *US*
- —Elementary Electronics, *Dictionary of CB Lingo*, p. 46, 1976

Amazon *noun*
a tall, strong, sexually attractive woman *US, 1954*
- —J.E. Lighter, *Historical Dictionary of American Slang, Volume 1*, p. 21, 1994

Amazon Annie *nickname*
a cannon designed to fire atomic shells *US*
- The Army's 280-millimeter cannon, nicknamed "Amazon Annie," gave field artillerymen their biggest thrill last week since the first caisson was rolled into place in the Fourteenth Century. —*San Francisco Chronicle, This World*, p. 2, 31 May 1958

ambassador *noun*
a representative of a drug dealer *US*
- —Anna Scotti and Paul Young, *Buzzwords*, p. 127, 1997

amber *noun*
beer *NEW ZEALAND*
In constructions such as 'quaff an amber'.
- —*American Speech*, p. 156, May 1959: 'Gator (University of Florida) slang'
- After a few 'ambers' and many yarns, my mate Bill asked to be handed a sandwich.—Bob Staines, *Wot a Whopper*, p. 9, 1982

amber fluid *noun*
beer *AUSTRALIA, 1906*
- OK, if that's how it is I reckon I'll get stuck into the old amber fluid. —Barry Humphries, *The Wonderful World of Barry McKenzie*, p. 59, 1968
- —Frank Hardy, *The Outcasts of Foolgarah*, p. 35, 1971
- We are regarded as common, large consumers of the amber fluid, and coarse lovers who regard the King's Head pub in Earl's Court as part of our sovereign right.—Bill Hornadge, *The Ugly Australian*, p. 47, 1973
- —Lance Peters, *The Dirty Half-Mile*, p. 202, 1979
- Frothing amber fluid dripped from each bag as it was picked up.—Bob Staines, *Wot a Whopper*, p. 31, 1982
- My room mate, Staff Sergeant Sid who enjoyed a drop of amber fluid came home late after curfew looking for something to eat.—Martin Cameron, *A Look at the Bright Side*, 1988
- —David McGill, *David McGill's Complete Kiwi Slang Dictionary*, p. 7, 1998

amber gambler *noun*
a motorist who speeds up through a yellow light *NEW ZEALAND*
- Amber gamblers go scot free.—*(Christchurch) Star*, p. 6, 2nd February 1979

ambidextrous *adjective*
bisexual *US, 1966*
A pun on the ability to use either hand.

ambisextrous *adjective*
bisexual *US, 1926*
A pun that puts sex in 'ambidextrous'.
- —Donald Webster Cory and John P. LeRoy, *The Homosexual and His Society*, p. 261, 1963

Ambitious City *nickname*
Hamilton, Ontario *CANADA*
Hamilton has thrived through steel and car assembly, benefiting by the Auto Pact between the US and Canada.
- It's hard to be poor in the Ambitious City.—*Toronto Globe and Mail*, p. B5–B8, 21st April 1965

ambo *noun*
1 an ambulance *AUSTRALIA*
- [B]y the end of play an ambo crew is giving happy juice to a girl with a shattered elbow.—*Lesbians on the Loose*, p. 20, 1996

2 an ambulance driver *AUSTRALIA*
Commonly heard in New Zealand.
- He had sustained injuries, the ambos estimated, quite some time before.—Shane Maloney, *Nice Try*, p. 174, 1998
- —William Dodson, *The Sharp End*, p. 187, 2001

ambov *noun*
in prison use, the *A*ssociation of *M*embers of *B*oards *of V*isitors; a member of the association *UK*
An initialism.
- —Angela Devlin, *Prison Patter*, p. 23, 1996

ambulance *noun*
a brakevan (caboose) *US*
- —Ramon Adams, *The Language of the Railroader*, p. 6, 1977

ambulance chaser *noun*
a disreputable solicitor, especially one who arrives or has an agent arrive at the scene of a disaster to seek clients from among the victims; in the UK since the 1990s, solicitors who advertise on television for 'no-win no-fee' clients *US, 1896*
From the image of following an ambulance to an accident; used in variant forms.
- —Vincent J. Monteleone, *Criminal Slang*, p. 11, 1949
- You're a used car salesman, Daniel. You're an ambulance chaser with a rank.—*A Few Good Men*, 1992

ambush academy *noun*
during the Vietnam war, training in jungle warfare, especially of the unconventional sort *US*
- —Linda Reinberg, *In the Field*, p. 7, 1991

ambush alley *nickname*
the section of Route 19 between An Keh and the base of the Mang Giang Pass, South Vietnam *US, 1965*
So named by truckers after countless Vietcong ambushes, borrowed from the Korean war (1952) where the term was used for any dangerous road.
- —Linda Reinberg, *In the Field*, p. 7, 1991

am dram *adjective*
*am*ateur *dram*atic; hence, exaggerated, unsubtle, histrionic *UK, 1985*
- She breaks down in very am. dram. fashion.—Jack Allen, *When the Whistle Blows*, p. 237, 2000

amebiate *verb*
to get drunk *US*
- —*Current Slang*, p. 1, Summer 1966

ameche *noun*
a telephone *US, 1941*
From actor Don Ameche's performance as Alexander Graham Bell in a 1939 film.
- You're wanted on the Ameche, June!—*San Francisco News*, p. 13, 7 July 1945
- The Ameche approach – Friday night and you're waiting for that all important call.—*San Francisco Examiner*, p. 7, 16th November 1947

amen!
used for expressing strong approval *US, 1934*
- —Joseph A. Weingarten, *An American Dictionary of Slang*, p. 7, 1954

amen corner *noun*
the front rows of pews in a church where the most devout sit, approving the words of the preacher with shouts of 'Amen!' *US, 1860*
- —Frederic G. Cassidy, *Dicitonary of American Regional English, Volume 1*, p. 56, 1985

Americalley *nickname*
in Vietnam, the 23rd Infantry Division, which played a key role in the massacre of Vietnamese civilians at My Lai *US*
The 23rd was formally named the Americal Division. The 'calley' variant referred to a key participant in My Lai.
- —Linda Reinberg, *In the Field*, p. 8, 1991

American Airlines *noun*
in hold 'em poker, the ace of diamonds and ace of hearts as the first two cards dealt to a player *US, 1981*
From the initials AA.
- —Thomas L. Clark, *The Dictionary of Gambling and Gaming*, p. 7, 1987

American taxpayer *noun*
any violator of routine traffic laws *US*
From the vociferous indignation voiced when stopped by a police officer.
- —*American Speech*, p. 266, December 1962: 'The language of traffic policemen'

American tweezers *noun*
any specialty tool used by a burglar *US*
- —Ralph de Sola, *Crime Dictionary*, p. 7, 1982

American Wake *noun*
a farewell party for those emigrating to America in the late C19 and early C20 *IRELAND*
- They used to have parties in the old days when anyone would go to America, which was so far away the parties were called American wakes because the family never expected to see the departing one[.] —Frank McCourt, *Angela's Ashes*, p. 418, 1997

American way *noun*
relatively peaceful co-existence by rival organised crime families *US*
- —Jay Robert Nash, *Dictionary of Crime*, p. 8, 1992

Amerika; Amerikkka *noun*
the United States *US, 1969*
A spelling favoured by the political counterculture in the late 1960s and early 1970s; in the second form, 'kkk' signifies the white supremacist Ku Klux Klan. Rap artist Ice Cube's 1990 album 'AmeriKKKa's Most Wanted' gave the KKK spelling high-profile exposure.
- It wasn't until after the slave trade ended that Amerika, England, France, and the Netherlands invaded and settled in on Afro-Asian soil in earnest.—George Jackson, *Soledad Brother*, p. 236, April 1970
- The New York bombers identified themselves afterward as "revolutionary force 9" in a message to "Amerika" (a current fad in radical literature is to spell it with a German "k" to denote facism).—*San Francisco Examiner & Chronicle Datebook*, p. 18, 5th April 1970

- A number of slogans were sprayed in black paint on the walls of the long shopping center, of which the bank branch occupied a portion. The included "Bank of Amerikka." — *San Francisco Chronicle*, p. 1, 27th October 1970
- They put us on trial; we denounced "Amerika," with its teutonic look, or "Amerikkka." — Todd Gitlin, *The Sixties*, p. 288, 1987

Amerikan *adjective*

American *US*

- Berkeley Cop Conspiracy: All-Ameikan Fascism (Headline) — *The Berkeley Tribe*, p. 11, 2nd August–4th September 1969

Amerikill *nickname*

the 23rd Infantry Division *US*

Derisory.

- — Linda Reinberg, *In the Field*, p. 8, 1991

AMF

used as a farewell *US*

From **ADIOS MOTHERFUCKER**.

- An abbreviated form of the phrase adios mother fucker which simply means good-bye friend. — Sedley H. Martin, *College Lore*, 1963

amidships *adjective*

(used of a blow to the abdomen) across the central area of the body *UK, 1937*

From the naval term for the middle of a ship.

- He was cutting across the road, heading for the telephone box, when the lorry caught him amidships. — Charles Raven, *Underworld Nights*, p. 89, 1956

amie *noun*

▷ see: AMY

a mighty roar went up from the crowd

used as a humorous comment on a lack of response to a joke or comment *US*

Coined by Keith Olberman on ESPN 'to describe players or fans who do not seem to be as happy as they should be following a home run, touchdown, or victory'.

- — Keith Olberman and Dan Patrick, *The Big Show*, p. 11, 1997

amigo *noun*

used as a term of address *US*

Spanish for 'friend'.

- "Let me lay it on you again, amigo," the short Mexican had whispered into Benson's ear. — Donald Goines, *Cry Revenge*, p. 80, 1974

Amish golf *noun*

croquet *US, 1969*

An allusion to the perceived joy that the Amish people take in playing croquet.

- — Frederic G. Cassidy, *Dicitonary of American Regional English, Volume 1*, p. 57, 1985

Amityville; 'Ville *nickname*

Detroit, Michigan, US *US*

Coinage is claimed by rap-artist Eminem, after the 1979 film *The Amityville Horror*.

- [W]e don't call it Detroit, we call it Amityville ('Ville)[.] — Eminem (Marshall Mathers), *Amityville*, 2000

ammo *noun*

1 ammunition *US, 1911*

Actual or figurative.

- They put the ammo clips in their jumper pockets and put their coats on the rack above them. — Darryl Ponicsan, *The Last Detail*, p. 26, 1970
- JOHN: Who's got the ammo? AXEL: Ammo! Get the ammo! — *The Deer Hunter*, 1978
- [T]hey've emptied a skip ... they've got plenty of ammo. — Martin King and Martin Knight, *The Naughty Nineties*, p. 38, 1999

2 cash *US*

- Candy, markers, ammo, liners, stocking stuffer, sweetener, garnish, and pledges are all terms for cash. — Henry Hill and Byron Schreckengost, *A Good Fella's Guide to New York*, p. 123, 2003

ammunition *noun*

1 a gambler's bankroll *US, 1983*

- — Mike Shamos, *The Illustrated Encyclopedia of Billiards*, p. 7, 1993

2 a tampon or sanitary towel; tampons or sanitary towels *UK, 1984*

amoeba *noun*

1 phencyclidine, the recreational drug known as PCP or angel dust *US*

- — US Department of Justice, *Street Terms*, October 1994

2 a Commodore Amiga™ personal computer *US*

- — Eric S. Raymond, *The New Hacker's Dictionary*, p. 35, 1991

amonia *noun*

pneumonia *BAHAMAS*

- — John A. Holm, *Dictionary of Bahamian English*, p. 4, 1982

Amos and Andy *noun*

brandy; shandy *UK, 1974*

Rhyming slang, based on a US radio comedy that ran from 1928–43.

amp *noun*

1 an *amp*oule (a glass vessel of drugs intended for hypodermic injection) *UK, 1968*

- — Angela Devlin, *Prison Patter*, p. 23, 1996

2 an *amp*oule of methadone, used to break a heroin addiction *UK*

- — Liz Cutland, *Kick Heroin*, p. 104, 1985

3 *amp*hetamine

- — *www.addictions.org*, 2004

4 an *amp*lifier, especially one for electric instruments *US, 1967*

- Ray, we're here to buy stuff. We need pianos, amps, mikes, the works. — *The Blues Brothers*, 1980
- They were bringing their amps and instrument cases out through the load-in door, a giant illuminated martini glass on the wall above it. — Elmore Leonard, *Be Cool*, p. 61–62, 1999

5 an *amp*utation; an *amp*utee *US, 1942*

Medical slang.

amped *adjective*

1 under the influence of a central nervous system stimulant, usually amphetamines or methamphetamine *US, 1972*

- — Walter L. Way, *The Drug Scene*, p. 105, 1977
- "Too much caffeine," Nell said. "I'm so amped I could jump-start Frankenstein's monster." — Joseph Wambaugh, *Finnegan's Week*, p. 160, 1993
- — Angela Devlin, *Prison Patter*, p. 23, 1996
- Man, we were amped up to the max on those Glaxo Wellcome beanies. — Steve Beard, *The Last Good War [britpulp]*, p. 348, 1999

2 ready for anything, very excited, psyched up *US, 1986*

- It's near midnight on 125th and the hip-hop boutique ... is amped. — Nelson George (writing in 1990), *Hip Hop America*, p. 159, 1998

3 (used of a music system) equipped with powerful amplifiers *US*

- — Lois Stavsky et al., *A2Z*, p. 2, 1995

4 silent *US*

- — Kenn "Naz" Young, *Naz's Dictionary of Teen Slang*, p. 2, 1993

amper *noun*

an ampersand (&) *US*

- — Eric S. Raymond, *The New Hacker's Dictionary*, p. 35, 1991

amphet *noun*

amphetamine *US*

- — Ralph de Sola, *Crime Dictionary*, p. 7, 1982
- Street names[:] Amphet, speed, sulph[.] — James Kay and Julian Cohen, *The Parents' Complete Guide to Young People and Drugs*, p. 129, 1998
- When it comes to Class B, cannabis, amphets, and the like, I'm not interested[.] — Duncan MacLaughlin, *The Filth*, p. 188, 2002

amphoterrible *nickname*

the antifungal drug Amphotericin B *US*

A nickname based on the drug's severe side effects.

- — Sally Williams, *"Strong" Words*, p. 133, 1994

amp joint *noun*

marijuana and *amp*hetamine (or possibly another drug) mixed and rolled for smoking in a cigarette *UK, 1998*

- — Mike Haskins, *Drugs*, p. 286, 2003

ampstids *noun*

▷ see: HAMPSTEAD HEATH

Am Sam *nickname*
American Samoa *US*
- —Ralph de Sola, *Crime Dictionary*, p. 197, 1982

amscray *verb*
to leave *US, 1934*
Pig Latin formation of 'scram'.
- Tab Hunter coughing up a grand 50 grand to amscray out of his Warner Bros. Contract.—*San Francisco Progress*, p. 13, 3rd May 1961
- That's right, it's a free country, so amscray.—Eugene Boe (Editor), *The Wit & Wisdom of Archie Bunker*, p. 35, 1971
- Amscray! Get out of here!—James Ellroy, *Hollywood Nocturnes*, p. 95, 1994

-amundo *suffix*
used as a humorous mechanism to form a slang equivalent *US*
Popularised by Fonz (Henry Winkler) on the US television programme *Happy Days*, set in the 1950s, which aired from 1974 until 1984.
- JACK: Fake blood, fake fight, fake bullets, it was perfect. It was perfectamundo, perfect. JENNIFER: Well, it wasn't exactly perfectamundo.—*Days of Our Lives*, February 1992
- JULES: Correct-amundo! And that's what we're gonna be, we're gonna be cool.—*Pulp Fiction*, 1994
- —Vann Wesson, *Generation X Field Guide and Lexicon*, p. 36, 1997

AMW *noun*
a vacuous female celebrity or hanger-on *US*
An abbreviation of '*a*ctress, *m*odel, *w*hatever'.
- Tommy and Shelby Chong; biker-artists; music video hangers-on; assorted AMWs (actress, model, whatever).—*Los Angeles Times*, p. 2 (Part 5), 24th October 1988
- —Alon Shulman, *The Style Bible*, p. 11, 1999
- Larry devoted his entire program to Anna Nicole Smith, a pneumatically-enhanced AMW (actress/model/whatever) best known for appearing in Playboy and marrying a Texas oil billionaire more than 60 years her senior.—*Toronto Globe and Mail*, p. R2, 31st May 2002

amy; amie *noun*
amyl nitrite; an ampoule of amyl nitrite *US, 1966*
- And have "amies" on hand too: poppers, banana splits, whatever you call them.—Angelo d'Arcangelo, *The Homosexual Handbook*, p. 115, 1968
- —Eugene Landy, *The Underground Dictionary*, p. 25, 1971
- "Amy" is a nickname for amyl nitrate (sic). Better known as "poppers." Sometimes called "snappers."—*San Francisco Examiner*, p. 27, 15th December 1976
- "The place was full of 'amies' (amyl nitrite) and Locker Room (butyl nitrite). People were popping them all over the place," the officer said.—*San Francisco Chronicle*, p. 2, 9th September 1977

amyl *noun*
amyl nitrate or butyl nitrate, when taken recreationally or to enhance sexual arousal *US*
Legal in the UK, but not in the US.
- [N]o more grass, the coke bottle was empty, one acid blotter, a nice brown lump of opium hash and six loose amyls.—Hunter S. Thompson, *Fear and Loathing in Las Vegas*, p. 100, 1971
- The sexual odor of amyl permeates the misty air.—John Rechy, *The Sexual Outlaw*, p. 81, 1977
- [W]e've got amyl and we are filthy and the streetlights join up with each other.—Mike Benson, *Room full of Angels (Disco Biscuits)*, p. 25, 1996
- [M]ade me tip a whole bottle of amyl up my fucking nose. All at once. It set my nose alight.—Dave Courtney, *Raving Lunacy*, p. 135, 2000
- Hunter Thompson probably put it best when he described Humphrey's campaign personality as akin to "a hen on amyls."—*New York Observer*, p. 1, 22nd December 2003

amyl house *noun*
a dance music genre *UK, 1990s*
- A close cousin of trip hop, Amyl House was pioneered by the UK's Chemical Brothers and scores of clubbers on amyl nitrate.—Alon Shulman, *The Style Bible*, p. 11, 1999

anal *noun*
anal sex *US*
A brief search of the Internet reveals an overwhelming and mainly heterosexual use of 'anal' in this sense.
- Anal is a relatively new thing in porn films. It didn't become hugely popular among filmmakers and consumers alike until the mid-80s[.]—Ana Loria, *1 2 3 Be A Porn Star!*, p. 100, 2000
- Extra-strength johnnies [condoms], in hope of anal (unused) £7.—*The FHM Little Book of Bloke*, p. 69, June 2003

anal amigo *noun*
a male homosexual *UK*
- —Chris Lewis, *The Dictionary of Playground Slang*, p. 10, 2003

anal & oral *noun*
anal sex and oral sex, when advertised as services offered by a prostitute *UK*
- —Caroline Archer, *Tart Cards*, 2003

anal groundsman *noun*
a homosexual man *UK*
- —Tom Hibbert, *Rockspeak!*, p. 12, 1983

analog *adjective*
in computing, pertaining to the world outside the Internet *US*
A figurative extension of a technical term.
- —Andy Ihnatko, *Cyberspeak*, p. 7, 1997

anchor *noun*
1 a brake *UK, 1936*
Originally truck driver usage, and then widespread.
- Coming down the Spit Hill he had to hit the anchors hard in order to avoid connecting with a woman and a child crossing the road.—Len Riley, *The Kings Cross Racket*, p. 13, 1967
- —Montie Tak, *Truck Talk*, p. 4, 1971

2 a younger brother or sister *UK*
A younger sibling is likely to hold you back or prevent you from going out with your friends.
- — Susie Dent, *The Language Report*, p. 75, 2003

3 an examination that has been postponed *US*
- —*American Speech*, p. 299, December 1955: 'Wayne University slang'

4 a parachutist who hesitates before jumping *UK, 1943*
- —John W. Mussell, *The Token Book of Militarisms*, p. 7, 1995

5 a brakevan (caboose) *US*
- —Ramon Adams, *The Language of the Railroader*, p. 6, 1977

6 a pick-axe *UK, 1863*
- —Harold Wentworth and Stuart Berg Flexner, *Dictionary of American Slang*, p. 6, 1960

anchor *verb*
1 to stay put, to remain *US, 1906*
- What has a guy gotta do to anchor here in Sing Sing like you did? —A.S. Jackson, *Gentleman Pimp*, p. 130, 1973

2 to wait *US*
- —Charles Shafer, *Folk Speech in Texas Prisons*, p. 197, 1990

3 to the apply the brakes of a car or truck *US*
- —Norman Carlisle, *The Modern Wonder Book of Trains and Railroading*, p. 258, 1946
- —Montie Tak, *Truck Talk*, p. 4, 1971

anchored *adjective*
married *US*
- —Vincent J. Monteleone, *Criminal Slang*, p. 11, 1949

anchor ice *noun*
ice formed along the bottom of bodies of water *CANADA*
This northern phenomenon is also known as 'ground ice'.
- —Thomas Raddall, *Tambour and Other Stories*, 1945

anchor man *noun*
in casino blackjack, the gambler immediately to the dealer's right *US*
- —Steve Kuriscak, *Casino Talk*, p. 56, 1985

ancient *adjective*
unfashionable, out of style *US*
- Your fit is ancient.—Rick Ayers (Editor), *Berkeley High Slang Dictionary*, p. 11, 2004

ancient Mary *noun*
an AM radio *US*
- — Elementary Electronics, *Dictionary of CB Lingo*, p. 46, 1976

and a half
used for intensifying the preceding noun *UK, 1832*
- BLAST and a half – Good party. PANIC and a half – Very funny joke.—*San Francisco News*, p. 6, 25th March 1958
- [F]luckin tosspot-and-a-half. Hope he breaks his fuckin neck on that bastard mountain.—Niall Griffiths, *Sheepshagger*, p. 85, 2001

and all that
1 used for intensifying *US*
- — Fab 5 Freddy, *Fresh Fly Favor*, p. 6, 1992

2 et cetera *UK*
- Ta an all that like but, really, were too bloody tired.—Niall Griffiths, *Sheepshagger*, p. 183, 2001

and all that caper *adverb*
et cetera *UK*
• [T]he coppers take us up the court for driving without insurance and all that caper. — John Peter Jones, *Feather Pluckers*, p. 38, 1964

and all that jazz *adverb*
and so on *US*
From **JAZZ** (nonsense).
• She's so happily married and all that jazz. It must be true love[.] — Peter Nichols, *Promenade [Six Granada Plays]*, p. 54, 1959

and a merry Christmas to you too!
used ironically in response to a disparagement or an insult *UK, 1976*

and and and
and so on, etc *UK*
• [T]he car's on the blink, and we can't find a baby-sitter, and and and. — *Beale*, 1984

and away we go!
used as a humorous signal that something has just started *US*
A signature line of comedien Jackie Gleason; variants conjured the humour of Gleason.
• — Jackie Gleason, *And Awaay We Go!*, 1954
• And away you go! — *San Francisco Examiner*, p. II-7, 5th October 1956
• A tiny foreign car died like a dawg on the Hyde St. cable tracks nr. Vallejo – whereupon the cable's gripman and conductor got out, picked up the car, carried it over to the curb and awaaay they went! — *San Francisco Examiner*, p. II-1, 18th November 1957

and co
and the rest of them (of people or things with something in common) *UK, 1757*
• Seaman and co complete Spanish campaign for spiked Gunners. — *The Guardian*, 10th March 2000

Anderson cart *noun*
a cart made from a cut-down car and pulled by horses, during the 1930s depression; later, any car that ran out of petrol or broke down *CANADA*
• Named after Premier Anderson of Albert, it originated during the depression, as did the Bennett Buggy. [It] was made from a car chassis with much of the body and often the front two wheels removed. The expression blamed politicians for hard times. — Chris Thain, *Cold as a Bay Street Banker's Heart*, p. 3, 1987

Andes candy *noun*
cocaine *US*
A near reduplication based on the cocoa grown in the Andes Mountains; not a common term.
• "What you puttin in my cooker?" "Lil Andes candy ... " "I hate coke," Rooski whimpered. — Seth Morgan, *Homeboy*, p. 77, 1990

and everything
used for completing a list or a thought *UK*
If anything less sincere than synonymous *et cetera*.
• I'm saying good luck and everything. But[.] — Anthony Masters, *Minder*, p. 74, 1984

and like it!
used in anticipation of a grousing reponse to an order *UK, 1943*
Naval use.

and like that
et cetera; and so on *US*
• Interestingly, American slang now includes *and like that* with the same meaning [as **AND THAT**]. I think a parallel development, since *and that* was never in use here. — Robert Claiborne, New York, 1977

and monkeys might fly out of my butt
used as a reflection of the high unlikelihood of something happening *US*
• What I'd really love, is to do "Wayne's World" for a living. It might happen – and monkeys might fly out of my butt! — *Wayne's World*, 1992

andro *adjective*
androgynous *US*
• She chooses from a diverse bunch of African American masculinities, from a super-fly Isaac Hayes to a badass rapper to the andro king himself, The Artist (Prince). — *The Village Voice*, 5th October 1999

android *noun*
a patient with no normal laboratory values *US*
• — Sally Williams, *"Strong" Words*, p. 133, 1994

and so it goes
used as an ironic affirmation *US*
The signature sign-off of television journalist Linda Ellerbee, with homage to Kurt Vonnegut's use of 'so it goes'. Repeated with referential humour.

and that
et cetera; and that sort of thing *UK, 1821*
Also widely used in Australia.
• There was a lot of things I wanted you to be able to do – ride an' that. — Alan Marshall, *I Can Jump Puddles*, p. 2, 1955
• They past [passed] the time of day and that. — Frank Norman, *Bang To Rights*, p. 123, 1958
• No offence and that. — Martin Waddell, *Otley*, p. 9, 1966
• I remember how we used to sit in the dugouts yarning away about tucker and tobacco and home and that. — Barry Humphries, *A Nice Night's Entertainment*, p. 196, 1968
• 'You was only usin' me. Youse feminists are fucked. For me body and that,' he spat. — Kathy Lette, *Girls' Night Out*, p. 61, 1987
• Little pricks in souped-up E-Reg Polos and that, divvy hatchbacks and that[.] — Kevin Sampson, *Outlaws*, p. 2, 2001
• Wonder if Mr Opodopolas knows she's been skiving off the laundrette to do singing and that. — *Sky Magazine*, p. 10, July 2001

and that ain't hay
used for humorous assertion that the topic of discussion is no small thing *US*
Both Abbot and Costello in the film *It Ain't Hay* and Mickey Rooney in *Girl Crazy* used the phrase in high-profile ways in 1943. It stayed popular for most of the decade.

and that's the truth!
used as a humorous affirmation of what you have just said *US*
A signature line of the Edith Ann character played by Lily Tomlin on the television comedy programme *Rowan and Martin's Laugh-In* (NBC, 1968–73). Repeated with referential humour.

and that's the way it is!
used as a humorous affirmation *US*
The signature sign-off of television newsman Walter Cronkite, who ended his nightly newscast thus from 1962 until 1981. Repeated with referential humour, often imitating the lilt and bass of Cronkite's voice.

and then some
and more; and much more *US, 1908*
Probably an elaboration of C18 Scots 'and some'.
• They're proper fucking meatballs these and then some. — Kevin Sampson, *Outlaws*, p. 242, 2001

and there was much rejoicing
used as a humorous comment on a favourable reaction *US*
Popularised in the US by Keith Olberman of ESPN, borrowed from *Monty Python and the Holy Grail*.

and will!
used for expressing a commitment to do something *US*
• — Marcus Hanna Boulware, *Jive and Slang of Students in Negro Colleges*, 1947

Andy Capp's Commandos *nickname*
the Army Catering Corps, the ACC *UK*
A humorous elaboration of the official military abbreviation. Andy Capp is the workshy hero of a long-running cartoon strip.
• — John W. Mussell, *The Token Book of Militarisms*, p. 7–8, 1995

Andy Gump *noun*
the surgical removal of the mandible in the treatment of jaw cancer *US*
The post-operative patient looks like they have no chin, resembling the comic strip character.
• — *Maledicta*, p. 55, Summer 1980: 'Not sticks and stones, but names: more medical pejoratives'

Andy Gump chin *noun*
a receding chin *US, 1970*
• — Frederic G. Cassidy, *Dicitonary of American Regional English, Volume 1*, p. 61, 1985

and you know that!
used for expressing approval or praise *US*
• Yo, last night you had it going on, girls were treating you like a king. And you know that! — Fab 5 Freddy, *Fresh Fly Favor*, p. 6, 1992

and you too!; and you!
used as a sharp rejoinder to an insult *UK, 1961*

Andy Pandy *noun*
1 an effeminate man, heterosexual or homosexual *UK*
From a BBC television puppet who first appeared in 1950.
• — Tom Hibbert, *Rockspeak!*, p. 12, 1983
2 a brandy *UK*
Rhyming slang.
• The old boy wouldn't take any money for the Andy Pandy, simply waved away my fiver[.] — J.J. Connolly, *Layer Cake*, p. 18, 2000

Andy Rooney *noun*
in poker, any player, usually short, who is inclined to complain *US*
An allusion to the US television journalist's stature.
• — John Vorhaus, *The Big Book of Poker Slang*, p. 4, 1996

ANFO *noun*
*a*ny *n*uisance of *f*oreign *o*rigin *UK*
Acronym in use during the 1970s by British Army in Northern Ireland, borrowing the initials from *A*mmonium *N*itrate *F*uel *O*il, a type of explosive.

angel *noun*
1 an outside investor, especially one who backs a theatrical production *US, 1891*
Theatrical origins.
• A committee to save the 96-year-old Humphreys house at Hyde and Chestnut streets from the wrecker's ax today was seeking an "angel" – a group or society willing to make a large cash pledge to start the drive for funds to save the ancient structure. — *The San Francisco Call-Bulletin*, p. 7, 31st August 1948
• Farrell quickly became THE "angel " of the season when it was learned he was the sole backer of a musical called "Hold It!" — *The San Francisco News*, p. 11, 13th July 1948
• Frederick Vanderbilt Field, financial "angel" of left-wing groups, was called today to tell a Senate committee about the bail raised for four missing Communist leaders. — *The San Francisco Examiner*, p. 31, 11th July 1951
2 a male homosexual *US, 1927*
Originally referred to the passive partner, but later to any homosexual.
• — Joseph E. Ragen and Charles Finston, *Inside the World's Toughest Prison*, p. 789, 1962
• Angel, to some, mends the crumpled wings and pride of the denigrated fairy. — Bruce Rodgers, *The Queens' Vernacular*, p. 21, 1972
3 a nurse *US*
In the UK *Angels* was a BBC television drama series about nurses broadcast 1975–83; and later, still focused on nurses and their lives, *No Angels*, Channel 4 television, 2004.
• — Linda Reinberg, *In the Field*, p. 8, 1991
4 cocaine *AUSTRALIA, 1942*
• — Richard A. Spears, *The Slang and Jargon of Drugs and Drink*, p. 11, 1986
5 in aviation, a 1000-foot increment of altitude *UK, 1943*
• Thus, "angels two zero" is 20,000 feet. — Linda Reinberg, *In the Field*, p. 8, 1991
• A former Marine, Bellisario insists on authenticity in aircraft and protocol, and accurate use of military vocabulary, from Angels (altitude in thousands of feet) to Zulu (Greenwich Mean Time). — *The Stuart (Florida) News*, p. 4 (TV Pastime), 29th December 1996
6 in air combat, a misleading image or blind spot *US*
• Did I know any pilots victimized by "angels"; what? Hadn't I heard of an angel incident? — Clarence Major, *All-Night Visitors*, p. 174, 1998

Angel *noun*
a member of the Hells Angels motorcyle gang *US*
• These are the thoughts – anxieties – of anxious marchers / That the Angels will attack them. — *The Berkeley Barb*, p. 1, 5th November 1965
• Angels sing, leather wings / Jeans of blue, Harley Davidsons too[.] — Eric Burdon & The Animals, *San Francisco Nights*, 1967
• "No, don't call the fuzz. Call the Angels," the messenger from the confusion on the sidewalks below puts in. — Nicholas Von Hoffman, *We Are The People Our Parents Warned Us Against*, p. 101, 1967
• So the Angels just shrug and say, 'our thing's violence.' How can the V.D.C. guy answer that? — Joan Didion, *Slouching Toward Bethlehem*, p. 62, 1968
• Fighting broke out all over between Angels and monitors. Panic. — Jerry Rubin, *Do It!*, p. 43, 1970

angel cake *noun*
an attractive girl *US*
• — Dobie Gillis, *Teenage Slanguage Dictionary*, 1962

angel dust *noun*
1 phencyclidine, the recreational drug also it known as PCP *US, 1970*
PCP, a veterinary anaesthetic which became a popular recreational drug that may be inhaled, smoked, ingested or injected; regarded as a cheap(er) substitute for other illicit drugs.
• — Eugene Landy, *The Underground Dictionary*, p. 146, 1971
• — *Drummer*, p. 77, 1977
• "Ain't it some bad shit, baby? It's spiked with angel dust," she slurred as she dropped her head to his naked lap[.] — Iceberg Slim (Robert Beck), *Airtight Willie and Me*, p. 182, 1979
• All you guys do is drop ludes and then, then take Percodans and angel dust. — *Manhattan*, 1979
• We're dealing with killers here, not Barrio punks with switchblades and a snootful of angel dust. — James Ellroy, *Brown's Requiem*, p. 129, 1981
• The Technicolor plant, in an industrial area on Roseville Road not far from McClellan Air Force Base, was hit two weeks ago by robbers looking for drugs that could be used in the manufacture of an illegal drug known as angel dust. — *San Francisco Examiner*, p. A26, 22nd September 1983
• Angel dust is, in effect, a lethal form of Ghetto LSD[.] — Nelson George, *Hip Hop America*, p. 39, 1998
2 money borrowed informally from a friend *US*
• — "Slingo", *The Official CB Slang Dictionary Handbook*, p. 3, 1976

angel face *noun*
an effeminate man *US*
• — Vincent J. Monteleone, *Criminal Slang*, p. 11, 1949

angel food *noun*
a member of the US Air Force as an object of homosexual desire *US*
• — H. Max, *Gay (S)language*, p. 2, 1988

angel gear *noun*
neutral gear while coasting down a hill *NEW ZEALAND*
• — *Dominion*, p. 7, 30th September 1989
• They call it their 'angel gear' because they can disable the dead man brake and 'have a rest'. — *Daily Telegraph*, p. 2, 2nd July 2003
• Another secret of the Tangaras was revealed at the Waterfall inquiry yesterday – the "angel gear", which allows drivers in need of a rest to put the train into neutral, release pressure on the deadman mechanism and let the train coast. — *Sydney Morning Herald*, 2nd July 2003

angel hair *noun*
phencyclidine, the recreational drug known as PCP or angel dust *US*
• — US Department of Justice, *Street Terms*, October 1994

angelina sorority *noun*
the world of the young homosexual male *US*
• — Bruce Rodgers, *The Queens' Vernacular*, p. 21, 1972

angel kiss *noun*
a freckle *US*
• Ain't you ever seen somebody with angel kisses on his face before? — Emmett Grogan, *Ringolevio*, p. 80, 1972

angel mist *noun*
phencyclidine, the recreational drug known as PCP or angel dust *US*
• — US Department of Justice, *Street Terms*, October 1994

angel puss *noun*
used as an endearing term of address *US, 1936*
• — Joseph A. Weingarten, *An American Dictionary of Slang*, p. 8, 1954

Angel's bible *noun*
a Harley-Davidson motorcyle manual *US*
• — Paladin Press, *Inside Look at Outlaw Motorcycle Gangs*, p. 33, 1992

angels in a sky *noun*
LSD *UK*
• — Mike Haskins, *Drugs*, p. 285, 2003

angel's kiss *noun*
a night breeze *US*
Korean war usage.
• The night breeze we called "Angel's Kiss" was in off Macquitti Bay, but it stayed high up in the palm fronds and scarcely moved the ten ropes. —Russell Davis, *Marine at War*, p. 121, 1961

angel's seat *noun*
the cupola on top of a brakevan (caboose) *US, 1946*
• While way up in the Angel's Seat / Conductors rest their weary feet. —J. Herbert Lund, *Herb's Hot Box of Railraod Slang*, p. 4, 1975

angel teat *noun*
a whisky with a rich bouquet *US, 1945*
• —Harold Wentworth and Stuart Berg Flexner, *Dictionary of American Slang*, p. 6, 1960

angel track *noun*
an armoured personnel carrier used as an aid station *US*
• —Ronald J. Glasser, *365 Days*, p. 242, 1971

angel with a dirty face *noun*
a male homosexual who due to caution or fear has yet to act upon his desire *US, 1941*
After the 1938 Warner Brothers film *Angels With Dirty Faces*.
• —Dale Gordon, *The Dominion Sex Dictionary*, p. 20, 1967

Angie *noun*
cocaine *US*
• — US Department of Justice, *Street Terms*, August 1994
• —Nick Constable, *This is Cocaine*, p. 181, 2002

angishore *noun*
▷ see: HANGASHORE

angle *noun*
a scheme, especially an illegal one *US, 1920*
• —J.E. Lighter, *Historical Dictionary of American Slang, Volume 1*, p. 25, 1994

angle shooter *noun*
a poker player who exploits other players by bending the rules of the game *US*
• —David M. Hayano, *Poker Faces*, p. 185, 1982

Anglo *noun*
1 a white person *US, 1943*
Brought to the mainstream by Mexican-Americans in the south-western US.
• Anglo: white, non-Mexican-American. Though normally used simply in a neutral, descriptive manner, the term sometimes has perjorative overtones. It has to some extent replaced gringo. — *Time*, p. 18, 4th July 1969
• This is a firm protest against calling whites "Anglos," as in your articles on the mission district. There is no greater insult than "Anglo" as far as the Welsh, Irish and Scots and other Celt-Americans are concerned and it is more offensive to most whites than the word "nigger" is to blacks. — *San Francisco Examiner*, p. 20, 26th June 1972
• An anglo with a last name for a first name is automatically a prick. —Edwin Torres, *Carlito's Way*, p. 117, 1975
• — Multicultural Management Program Fellows, *Dictionary of Cautionary Words and Phrases*, 1989

2 an Anglo-Australian *AUSTRALIA*
Used as a derogatory term by people from a Mediterranean or Middle Eastern background, opposing the term 'wog'.
• No one seemed to notice the bulk exodus of Australian Anglos. —Gerald Sweeney, *Invasion*, p. 139, 1982
• To be equal to or better than the Anglos. —Alma Aldrette, *Joseph's Coat*, p. 21, 1985

Anglo *adjective*
of or pertaining to Anglo-Australians *AUSTRALIA, 1982*
• Mrs Castellanos thought that these Anglo girls were young and cheap. —Alma Aldrette, *Joseph's Coat*, p. 34, 1985
• There are some Anglo women who hate wog men, can't stand the sight of us[.] —Christos Tsiolkas, *Loaded*, p. 34, 1995

Anglo-Banglo *adjective*
of Anglo-Indian birth *UK, 1984*
• Under a Tin-Grey Sari [a novel by Wayne Ashton set in 1967] tells the story of Khalid, a young cook in the employ of an "Anglo-Banglo" or "Paklish" household. — *The Post, Perth, Western Australia*, 4th January 2003

Angola black; Angola *noun*
a potent marijuana from East Africa *US, 1982*
• —Richard A. Spears, *The Slang and Jargon of Drugs and Drink*, p. 12, 1986
• —Mike Haskins, *Drugs*, p. 286, 2003

angora *noun*
in horse racing, the totalisator *AUSTRALIA*
Rhyming slang, from 'tote' to 'angora goat' to 'angora'.
• —Ned Wallish, *The Truth Dictionary of Racing Slang*, p. 1, 1989

angry *adjective*
(used of a penis) sexually aroused, erect *US*
• Ah'd purely love to see it angry. — *M*A*S*H*, 1970
• Poor little Heather! She's never seen one angry before. But it made quite an impression on her. — *Body Heat*, 1980

angry nine *nickname*
during the Korean war, an AN/GRC-9 radio *US*
• —Paul Dickson, *War Slang*, p. 235, 1994

angryphone *noun*
an anglophone (a native English speaker in Quebec) *CANADA*
• But what people do care about is their tax dollars being wasted by a bunch of has-been angryphones who claim to represent them, but don't. — *Montreal Gazette*, p. A6, 29th April 2002

animal *noun*
1 a person displaying vulgar manners, attitudes, etc; a despicable human being; a brute *AUSTRALIA, 1892*
• 'I bet you roasted the poor bastard, you pot-gutted animal,' grinned Tully. —Eric Lambert, *The Veterans*, p. 99, 1954
• At school he'd been this full-on aggro animal. —Kathy Lette, *Girls' Night Out*, p. 191, 1987
• Look, there's Con and Gavin, pissed out of their brains. They're animals. —Jenny Pausacker, *What are ya?*, p. 10, 1987

2 in American football, an extremely physical player *US*
• —Bill Shefski, *Running Press Glossary of Football Language*, p. 11, 1978

3 used among musicians as a nickname for a drummer *UK*
From the character/puppet/musician 'Animal' (legendarily, based on Keith Moon, 1946–78, the original drummer with The Who) who appeared in *The Muppet Show*, from 1976, and in subsequent film and television Muppet projects.

4 an aggresive approach to surfing *AUSTRALIA*
• —Nat Young, *Surfing Fundamentals*, p. 3, 1985

5 in prison, a sex offender *UK*
Contemptuous.
• —Angela Devlin, *Prison Patter*, p. 23, 1996

6 a thing of a given sort *UK, 1922*
• And yet, in the strict present there are no fundamental problems-for there is no time. No such animal as a present problem exists[.] —Ken Wilbur, *No Boundary*, p. 59, 2001

7 LSD *US*
• —US Department Justice, *Street Terms*, October 1994

8 amyl nitrate *UK*
• [T]hey tended to be more into speed and "animal". —Gareth Thomas, *This Is Ecstasy*, p. 32, 2002

9 in the Vietnam war, a gang-rigged set of claymore mines *US*
• [T]he men opened up with devastating force – first with an "animal," twenty claymores jury-rigged to go off all at once and loose a hailstorm of 14,000 flying steel balls[.] —Peter Goldman and Tony Fuller, *Charlie Company*, p. 114, 1983

10 a furpiece *US*
• — *Swinging Syllables*, 1959

▸ **go animal**
to act wildly, without inhibition *US*
• —Collin Baker et al., *College Undergraduate Slang Study Conducted at Brown University*, p. 71, 1968

animal!
used for expressing approval *UK*
• — Susie Dent, *The Language Report*, p. 75, 2003

animal car *noun*
a brakevan (caboose) *US, 1938*
• —Ramon Adams, *The Language of the Railroader*, p. 6, 1977

animal run *noun*
the wild behaviour of some military personal on shore leave *UK*
• —Nigel Foster, *The Making of a Royal Marine Commando*, 1987

Animals of the Army *nickname*
during the Vietnam war, used as a name for the Airborne Rangers *US*

- He was a LRRP (pronounced "lurp" – for Long-Range Reconnaissance Patrol") with the Airborne Rangers, called by some the "Animals of the Army" due to their ferocity in combat. — Myra McPherson, *Long Time Passing*, p. 597, 1984

animal trainer *noun*
a person who engages in sexual activity with animals *US*
- — Anon., *King Smut's Wet Dreams Interpreted*, 1978

animal zoo *noun*
a rowdy college fraternity *US*
- — *American Speech*, p. 227, October 1967: 'Some special terms used in a University of Connecticut men's dormitory'

anime *noun*
a type of Japanese animation, often adapted to sexual themes *JAPAN*
- Central Park Media's O'donneell expects video retailers that stock offbeat and "cutting edge' foreign films to venture first into the "anime" market. — *Los Angeles Times*, p. F1, 29th August 1991
- Aficianados of Japanese animation, known as "anime," say that the high school uniforms and childlike faces are a standard convention of the genre, a cultural fetish long established as merely fantasy. — *Los Angeles Times*, p. 1 (Part 5), 13th June 2003

ankle *noun*
a woman *US, 1942*
- — Vincent J. Monteleone, *Criminal Slang*, p. 12, 1949

ankle *verb*
1 to walk; to travel *US, 1926*
- In the Fall of 1927, when I ankled back to Chicago from my barnstorming and barn-burning tour of the West, we were still living in a fool's paradise. — Mezz Mezzrow, *Really the Blues*, p. 140, 1946
- Well, Tell ankles past and ganders the beret. — Haenigsen, *Jive's Like That*, 1947
- I ankled over to the club early, about one A.M. — Edwin Torres, *After Hours*, p. 263, 1979

2 in television and film making, to disassociate yourself from a project *US*
- — Ralph S. Singleton, *Filmaker's Dictionary*, p. 8, 1990

▸ **ankle a show**
to walk out of a performance *US*
- — Sherman Louis Sergel, *The Language of Show Biz*, p. 8, 1973
- — Don Wilmeth, *The Language of American Popular Entertainment*, p. 9, 1981

ankle-biter *noun*
1 a petty, narrow-minded bureacrat *US*
- Lieut. Gen Andrew J. Goodpaster, as West Point Superintendent, was described by James Faron in The New York Times in 1981 as "able to make the changes because he had enough prestige to 'keep the ankle-biters away,' according to an aide on the administrative staff. — *The New York Times*, p. 6–8, 12th December 1990
- Ankle biters take the joy and creativity out of computing. They are negative people who spend their workday hours in a deathwatch over new initiatives. — *Computerworld*, p. 39, 20th March 1995

2 a child *US, 1963*
Also 'knee biter'. Humorous, not particularly kind to children.
- — *Complete CB Slang Dictionary*, 1976
- The rank and file have quite rightly pulled the plug on the airline dispute leaving Maureen and the ankle-biters stranded up the Gold Coast[.] — Barry Humphries, *A Nice Night's Entertainment*, p. 188, 1981
- I gotta catch up with my wife. The settlement. The final decree. The property. Our four little ankle-biters! — Joseph Wambaugh, *Fugitive Nights*, p. 27, 1990

ankle bracelets *noun*
the < and > characters on a computer keyboard *US*
- — Eric S. Raymond, *The New Hacker's Dictionary*, p. 36, 1991

ankled *adjective*
drunk *UK*
A Bristol usage.
- — *e-cyclopaedia*, 20th March 2002

ankle express *noun*
walking *US, 1919*
- — *Current Slang*, p. 1, Spring 1969
- The same trip via ankle express took him and his Chinese mercenaries a full day to complete. — Robert Mason, *Chickenhawk*, p. 408, 1983

ankle-slapper *noun*
a small wave *US*
- — Trevor Cralle, *The Surfin'ary*, p. 3, 1991

anklets *noun*
leg irons *US*
- — Hyman E. Goldin et al., *Dictionary of American Underworld Lingo*, p. 19, 1950

Annabel Giles; annabels *noun*
haemorrhoids *UK*
Rhyming slang for 'piles', formed from the UK television presenter (b.1960).
- — Bodmin Dark, *Dirty Cockney Rhyming Slang*, 2003

annex *verb*
to steal *US, 1845*
- — Vincent J. Monteleone, *Criminal Slang*, p. 12, 1949

Annie from Arkansas *noun*
in craps, an eight *US*
- — Frank Scoblete, *Guerrilla Gambling*, p. 294, 1993

Annie Rooney *noun*
an outburst of bad temper *UK*
- If she finds out you broke that clock she'll have an Annie Rooney. — Michael Munro, *The Patter, Another Blast*, 1988

Annie's alley *noun*
the vagina *US*
Peter Tamony's sister Katherine Tamony collected this term from a police matron at the San Francisco Women's Detention Center in April 1949; a woman prisoner was thought to be concealing $13.00 'in Annie's Alley'.

annihilated *adjective*
drunk *US, 1975*
- — *Rutgers Alumni Magazine*, p. 21, February 1986
- [B]attered s**tfaced f**cked messed up annihilated[.] — Stuart Walton, *Out of It*, cover, 2001

annish *noun*
an anniversary issue of a single-interest fan magazine *US*
- — *American Speech*, p. 23, Spring 1982: 'The langage of science fiction fan magazines'

anoint *verb*
to whip someone *US*
- — Joseph E. Ragen and Charles Finston, *Inside the World's Toughest Prison*, p. 789, 1962

anorak *noun*
1 a studious and obsessive hobbyist widely characterised as boring and unfashionable *UK, 1991*
From the stereotypical wardrobe of certain groups of hobbyists such as trainspotters.
- Anorak fact: ten times as much chardonnay is harvested. — *The Sunday Times*, 18th April 2004

2 by extension, a person who is socially inept and therefore unable to be, or not interested in becoming, part of a peer group *UK*
- The City fans under escort were women, children and anoraks. — Martin King and Martin Knight, *The Naughty Nineties*, p. 71, 1999

anoraky *adjective*
studious and obsessive *UK*
- I was just the anoraky bloke that fixed the computers. — Chris Ryan, *The Watchman*, p. 362, 2001

A N Other *noun*
used in speech as an all-purpose formula for an unknown identity *UK*
A written convention that has taken a life of its own.

another country heard from
used for humorously acknowledging that someone who had previously been silent has spoken up *US*
- Mule finally speaks up. "We respectfully request to see the executive officer, sir." "Another country heard from," says the OOD. — Darryl Ponicsan, *The Last Detail*, p. 142, 1970
- Another day, another country heard from in the quest to serve as the summer home for the Washington Redskins. — *The Richmond Times Dispatch*, p. D1, 10th February 2001

another day, another dollar
a humorous expression of a day-by-day philosophy of life *US*
- KAFFEE: How's it going, Luther? LUTHER: Another day, another dollar, captain. — *A Few Good Men*, 1992

anothery *noun*
another, especially another drink of beer *AUSTRALIA, 1963*
- 'I'll get it for you,' offered Fat. 'No,' ordered Squid. 'Better wait till he's thrown anothery.'—D.E. Charlwood, *All the Green Year*, p. 122, 1965
- 'Have anothery.' 'No!' 'Arr, c'mon.'—Geoff Wyatt, *Saltwater Saints*, p. 52, 1969

answer *noun*
a rap artist's response to another's song *US*
- —Lois Stavsky et al., *A2Z*, p. 2, 1995

answer *verb*
to score soon after an opponent has scored *US, 1979*
- —*American Speech*, Winter 1981

answer record *noun*
a rap song released in response to another song *US*
- "Answer records" between feuding rappers, once frequent, are today only sporadic.—Steven Daly and Nalthaniel Wice, *alt.culture*, p. 229, 1995

Antarctica monster *noun*
fire *ANTARCTICA, 1977*
- —Bernadette Hince, *The Antarctic Dictionary*, p. 19, 2000

Antartic 10 *noun*
any moderately good looking person of the sex that attracts you *ANTARCTICA, 1991*
The humour lies in the fact that a 'ten' in Antarctica would be a 'five' anywhere else.
- —Carnegie Mellon Astrophysics Peterson Group, *Antarctic Vocabulary*, 19th September 1997

ante *noun*
the money required to begin a project *US, 1895*
- Yes dear readers, as soon as I have raised the necessary ante I am departing these shores for greener and more promising fields.—Sue Rhodes, *Now you'll think I'm awful*, p. 23, 1967
- The ante on this thing's going up all the time.—Peter Corris, *Pokerface*, p. 138, 1985

anteater *noun*
1 in trucking, a short-nosed C-model Mack tractor *US*
- —Montie Tak, *Truck Talk*, p. 4, 1971

2 an uncircumcised penis *US*
- You get bored you might amuse yourselves by betting quarters whether the next guy in will be a helmet or an anteater.—Joseph Wambaugh, *The New Centurions*, p. 262, 1970

antenna platoon *noun*
during the Vietnam war, a platoon with an unusually large number of radios assigned to it *US*
- I wasn't wearing brass, but with an "antenna platoon" of at least five PRC-25 radios with me, it was kind of obvious[.]—David H. Hackworth, *About Face*, p. 539, 1989

ante up *verb*
to provide money for a project *US, 1865*
- The allies so far have contributed more than $46 billion in cash and in-kind contributions and are expected to ante up another $18.4 billion, the report by the Bush Administration said.—*The Mercury*, p. 6, 1st May 1991

anthem *noun*
in contemporary dance music and club culture of the 1980s, 90s and on, any song that fills the dance floor and gets clubbers singing along *UK*
- —*The Sunday Times Magazine*, p. 48, 1st June 2003

anti-frantic *adjective*
calm, collected *US*
- Yes, above all, anti-frantic. Stay cool. Hang loose.—*Esquire*, p. 180, June 1983

antifreeze *noun*
1 alcohol *US, 1953*
- [S]pent the evening knocking back the anti-freeze[.]—Andrew Nickolds, *Back to Basics*, p. 53, 1994

2 heroin *US*
- —US Department of Justice, *Street Terms*, October 1994

anti-proliferation device *noun*
a condom *UK*
- —David Rowan, *A Glossary for the 90s*, 1998

antique HP *noun*
an old homosexual man *UK*
HP is an abbreviation of 'homee palone' (a man).
- —Paul Baker, *Polari*, p. 163, 2002

antsy *adjective*
agitated, anxious *US, 1950*
- Golf duds and all, Bud Schwartz was antsy about being back on the premises so soon after the ratnapping[.]—Carl Hiaasen, *Native Tongue*, p. 133, 1991
- [E]ven the fashionistas get antsy when Fischerspooner are an hour late.—*The Guardian*, p. 23, 1st June 2002

antwacky *adjective*
old-fashioned, especially of clothes *UK*
Liverpool use; possibly from 'antiquey'.
- She looked like a fucking orphan. Antwacky clothes, bunches, white socks – proper virgin, she were.—Kevin Sampson, *Clubland*, p. 60, 2002

anus bandit *noun*
a predatory male homosexual *US*
- —Joseph E. Ragen and Charles Finston, *Inside the World's Toughest Prison*, p. 789, 1962

anxious *adjective*
good *US, 1944*
- —Lou Shelly, *Hepcats Jive Talk Dictionary*, p. 7, 1945

anybody in there
do you have any intelligence? *AUSTRALIA*
- I made a fist and rapped it hard on his forehead. 'Hello? Hello? Is anybody in there?'—Harrison Biscuit, *The Search for Savage Henry*, p. 103, 1995

anyhoo *adverb*
anyhow *US, 1946*
A deliberate mispronunciation.
- What wall were those Tulls coming off anyhoo? No comprende. —Lester Bangs, *Psychotic Reactions and Carburetor Dung*, p. 132, 1971

any kine *noun*
anything *US*
Hawaiian youth usage.
- She tell any kine fo' get her way.—Douglas Simonson, *Pidgin to da Max*, 1981

any more for any more?
does anyone want more food?; also used to announce a final opportunity to purchase something *UK, 1977*

any old how *adverb*
1 in an untidy or disordered state *UK, 1933*
- [H]is sister already sat in the car, her jersey and shorts just tossed any old how across the back seat.—*Listener [New Zealand]*, 9th January 2004

2 in any case, anyway *UK*
- There is a chap in the death cell waiting to get topped, and it comes to the morning when he is going to get the drop. Any old how the chief comes in and askes [sic] him if he has got a last request.—Frank Norman, *Bang To Rights*, p. 31, 1958

anyone can cook *nickname*
the Army Catering Corps, the ACC *UK*
A humorous elaboration of the official military abbreviation.
- —John W. Mussel, *The Token Book of Militarisms*, 1995

anyone for tennis?
used for humorously suggesting an activity *US*
Seen as quintessentially British and enormously witty in its many variant forms.
- Anyone for tennis? Or lacrosse?—*Marion (Ohio) Daily Star*, p. 24, 19th December 1951
- Having slept that off, you wander recklessly onto the play deck with gay cries of "Anyone for shuffleboard?"—*San Francisco Examiner*, p. 21, 27th August 1952
- Anyone for gold?—*San Francisco Call-Bulletin*, p. 12, 9th July 1953

anyroad
anyway *UK, 1896*
Also used as an adverb. Northern dialect, widely familiar from television programmes such as *Coronation Street*.
- Shut up, will you, Divvo. What the fuck do you know about welding, anyroad?—*The Full Monty*, 1997

anything for a laugh
serves as a justification for doing something because you have no choice in the matter *UK, 1969*
Often rueful.

nything for a quiet wife
a catchphrase that means exactly what it says *UK, 1977*
A jocular perversion of the proverbial saying 'anything for a quiet life'.

ny-to-come *noun*
in gambling, a type of conditional bet in which all or part of a winning is returned on another bet *UK*
May be abbreviated as ATC.
- —David Bennet, *Know Your Bets*, p. 15, 2001

Anytown USA; Anytown *noun*
a notional American town that represents the appearance or values of stereotypical small-town America *UK*
- The scene is set in Anytown USA. In a strange laboratory next to an abandoned cemetery two scientists are about to discover the secrets of life... and death. —Terry Victor, *Return of the Menu Monster*, 1992
- —Susie Dent, *The Language Report*, p. 41, 2003

anywhere *adverb*
in possession of drugs *US*
- Hey, there, Poppa Mezz, is you anywhere? —Mezz Mezzrow, *Really the Blues*, p. 216, 1946

▸ **not get anywhere**
to fail to reach your goal, to not succeed in achieving your object *US, 1932*

Anzac *noun*
a soldier of the Australian and New Zealand Army Corps who served in the Gallipoli campaign; any Australian or New Zealand soldier *AUSTRALIA, 1915*
This acronym was originally used as a telegraphic code, but quickly moved into colloquial use amongst soldiers and thence civilians at home; technically referring only to the Gallipoli soldiers or veterans of that campaign, it has been generalised to any World War 1 veteran, and thence later to any Australian and New Zealand soldier of World War 2. Anzacs have been traditionally held in high reverence in both countries, and the virtues ascribed to them, such as bravery, pride, honesty, hardiness, disregard for military authority and sense of humour, have become generalised as positive notions of national character.
- They're considered hard to handle, and they moan about the stew – / But it's 'SEND IN THE BLOOMING ANZACS' when there's dirty work to do! —Tip Kelaher, *The Digger Hat and other verses*, p. 18, 1942
- Tully wore a brand new set of sergeant's stripes and even Lasher's hat looked less like an apple-turnover than usual. 'The bronze Anzacs!' I hailed them. 'The sheilas were mad about you.' —Eric Lambert, *The Veterans*, p. 12, 1954
- Australia need not fear that the lofty spirit of Anzac is dead! —D.E. Charlwood, *All the Green Year*, p. 125, 1965
- He was in the Gallipoli campaign – one of the original Anzacs. —Alexander Buzo, *Norm and Ahmed*, p. 10, 1969
- Mr Currie who was a very proud traditionalist Anzac but unfortunately had no sense of humour, flung the poker at a hundred miles and hour, just missing his head embedding the iron in a portrait of the Holy Father. —Martin Cameron, *A Look at the Bright Side*, 1988

Anzac *adjective*
of or relating to the Anzacs; characteristic of the Anzacs *AUSTRALIA, 1915*
- And for ever in our track, / Down the years to come, will pace / Pilgrims of our Anzac race. —Lance Corporal Cobber, *The Anzac Pilgrim's Progress*, p. 99, 1916
- If they weren't langing-lights I saw, then I'll drop 'em in Martin Place the first Anzac Day after we get back to Aussie. —W.R. Bennett, *Night Intruder*, p. 112, 1961
- Moss had told him to say it again and the apostles of Anzac mateship had sent for the police and had them thrown out. —Frank Hardy, *The Outcasts of Foolgarah*, p. 182, 1971
- The body might falter but the ANZAC spirit will survive. —Martin Cameron, *A Look or the Bright Side*, 1988

Anzac biscuit; Anzac *noun*
a popular biscuit made with oats, sugar, flour and golden syrup *AUSTRALIA, 1923*
- They were pumpkin scones, and there were anzac biscuits as well. —Hesba Brinsmead, *Longtime Dreaming*, p. 113, 1982
- My Auntie Bess used to make Anzacs. She's dead now, but the Anzacs still remain. Her Anzacs were mostly made of treacle and wheatgerm. Beaut, they were. —Barry Dickins, *What the Dickins*, p. 41, 1985
- Her mother was part-time at Qantas catering at Tullamarine, putting individually wrapped Anzacs on in-flight meal trays. —Shane Maloney, *Nice Try*, p. 196, 1998

A-OK *adjective*
completely acceptable *US, 1959*
US Navy Captain Alan G. Shepard was widely credited for introducing the term to the general public during the first US space flight. Shepard later denied ever having said 'A-OK', insisting that he had been spelling out awkward – 'AWK'.
- That's why George Romney enlisted and secured the support of all our [Rambler's] employees in the new "A-OK Quality Workmanship" program. —*San Francisco Chronicle*, p. 34, 8th August 1961
- —*San Francisco Chronicle*, p. 6, 23rd July 1961
- At Aragon [High School] the right word is "bo." They also say "A-OK" at Aragon occasionally. —*San Francisco Examiner*, p. 8, 27th October 1963
- Big Ed said, "Uh, honey, these boys and your daughter have promised me that their behavior in the future will be A-OK." —Dan Jenkins, *Semi-Tough*, p. 60, 1972
- He winked obscenely as he made a lopsided circle of A-OK with pudgy fingers shiny greasy with bar-be-que he was gnawing. —Iceberg Slim (Robert Beck), *Airtight Willie and Me*, p. 32, 1979

A-one; A-1 *adjective*
excellent, first-class *US, 1846*
Originally of ships, then of persons and things.
- His embassy bespoke the American authorities to give him the A-1 treatment, the best. —Jack Lait and Lee Mortimer, *Washington Confidential*, p. 149, 1951
- Just you and me and thirty grand, maybe five or ten more if it's an A-1 job. —Jim Thompson, *Savage Night*, p. 73, 1953
- I think while you were out on bond, according to my source, which is A-one reliable – you took out the jigs. —Elmore Leonard, *Stick*, p. 128, 1983
- It's fucking A1 dismal. – Fine, said I. —James Hawes, *Dead Long Enough*, p. 72, 2000

AOS
used for suggesting that there are no good options in a particular situation *US*
An abbreviation of '*a*ll *o*ptions *s*uck' or '*a*ll *o*ptions *s*tink'.
- "It's called AOS," they say, using a barracks abbreviation for "all options stink." Another senior military official said there was "no good option that wouldn't make us look useless." —*Deseret News (Salt Lake City)*, p. A2, 30th September 2001
- Add it all up for Martha Stewart it's what they call in the military an "AOS" situation (as in "all options suck") – and the hour is now at hand. —*New York Post*, 23rd February 2004

a over k *adverb*
knocked upside down *NEW ZEALAND*
An abbreviation of '*a*rse *over k*ite'.
- —David McGill, *David McGill's Complete Kiwi Slang Dictionary*, p. 10, 1998

a over t *adverb*
head over heels *UK, 1984*
An abbreviation of **ARSE OVER TIT**.
- [A]ll four blokes ahead fall a over t, and – as stunned as a mullet – Bradbury crossed the line first. —*The Guardian*, 21st February 2002

Apache *noun*
Fentanyl, a synthetic narcotic analgesic that is used as a recreational drug *UK*
- —Harry Shapiro, *Recreational Drugs*, p. 154, 2004

Apache land *noun*
a rough or dangerous urban area *UK: SCOTLAND*
- —Michael Munro, *The Patter, Another Blast*, 1988

apartment *noun*
a prison cell *US*
- —Vincent J. Monteleone, *Criminal Slang*, p. 12, 1949

apartment girl *noun*
a prostitute who works out of her own apartment or comes to a customer's apartment *US*
- —Jay Robert Nash, *Dictionary of Crime*, p. 10, 1992

apartment house *noun*
in bar dice games, a roll from the cup in which some dice are stacked on top of others, invalidating the roll *US*
- —Jester Smith, *Games They Play in San Francisco*, p. 103, 1971

APB *noun*
in police work, an all points bulletin, broadcast to all who are listening *US*
- Guess you've often seen policemen working like this on TV or in the movies. They're sending out an APB. That's an All Points Bulletin. It's

information they send to hundreds of their fellow law enforcement men to help break a case. — Pacific Telephone, *Talk*, p. 1, August 1957
- The police, pleased to have captured major game on a routine trapline, put out APB's on Caterpillar and Chilly. — Malcolm Braly, *On the Yard*, p. 236, 1967
- Your wife will give the police your truck plate number for an A.P.B. They will arrest you here, arrest me on charges of harboring a fugitive. — Iceberg Slim (Robert Beck), *Doom Fox*, p. 117, 1978

apcray *noun*
nonsense; rubbish *US, 1937*
A pig Latin formation of **CRAP**.
- — Joseph A. Weingarten, *An American Dictionary of Slang*, p. 9, 1954

ape *noun*
in the entertainment industry, a technical member of a film crew *US*
- You're gonna put up the actors and the apes in the same hotel?!? Are you outta your nut!?! — Terry Southern, *Blue Movie*, p. 66, 1970

ape *adjective*
crazed, frenzied, demonstrating rage or delight *US, 1955*
Based on the behaviour of apes in films – not in real life.
- I drive you ape, and you just don't trust yourself with me, that's what it is. — Max Shulman, *Rally Round the Flag, Boys!*, p. 58, 1957
- That's why they go ape in Viet Nam. — Darryl Ponicsan, *The Last Detail*, p. 34, 1970
- Promise you won't go spreading it about, or the Tourist Board'll go ape. — James Hawes, *Dead Long Enough*, p. 229, 2000

▸ **go ape**
to lose control; to react unrestrainedly *AUSTRALIA*
- Parents are people who always try and boss you around, and who can't stand it when you have fun, and they go ape all the time for no reason. — Kylie Mole (Maryanne Fahey), *My Diary*, p. 4, 1988

ape bars *noun*
high handlebars on a customised motorcycle *US*
- Across the flats of Southern California hustles a big mean hog. Ape bars, twin exhausts, chrome on everything except the rubber, this Harley is doing a ton and still hot to trot. — *Time*, p. 103, 9th September 1966

ape drape *noun*
a hair style in which the hair is worn short at the front and long at the back *US*
Most commonly known as a 'mullet'.
- — Steven Daly and Nalthaniel Wice, *alt.culture*, p. 158, 1995

ape hangers *noun*
high handlebars on a customised motorcyle *US, 1965*
A term based on the visual, with the handlebars forcing an ape-like pose.
- Tagged for particular critical attention were high handlebars or "ape hangers;" the removal of the front wheel brake and the ornamental "sissy bar," a tubular metal backrest rising from the rear of the passenger's section of the seat. — *San Francisco Examiner*, p. 9, 20th February 1970

apeshit *adjective*
▸ **go apeshit**
to lose control; to go crazy *US, 1951*
- The ceremony was conducted by a lanky preacher who also was an ex-G.I., a former Marine chaplain gone apeshit. — Clancy Sigal, *Going Away*, p. 238, 1961
- The crowd went apeshit and the band went oompa-oomp. — Edwin Torres, *After Hours*, p. 198, 1979
- I turn around and all these cops are outside. You're right, it was like, bam! I blink my eyes and they're there. Everybody starts going apeshit. — *Reservoir Dogs*, 1992
- And then she went apeshit, screaming, 'Don't you know what you're doing is wrong?' — John Birmingham, *He Died With a Felafel in his Hand*, 1994
- Mark Arks really had won the McRae Medal. The whole place went apeshit. — Phillip Gwynne, *Deadly Unna?*, 1998
- The kids are going apeshit. Jammed into a hall, 5,000 rock fans are freaking out to one bloke and a pile of electronic gear. — John Robb, *The Nineties*, p. 212, 1999
- Nice to see Kiddo hasn't gone completley apeshit. [Screenplay, not in final cut] — *Kill Bill*, 2003

apeth *noun*
▹ **see: HA'P'ORTH**

ape wagon *noun*
a brakevan (caboose) *US*
- — Ramon Adams, *The Language of the Railroader*, p. 7, 1977

aphrodite *noun*
a nightgown *NEW ZEALAND, 1875*
Rhyming slang for 'nightie'.

A-pie *noun*
apple pie *US*
- — *American Speech*, p. 61, February 1967: 'Soda-fountain, restaurant and tavern calls'

A-plug *noun*
a plug inserted in the rectum as part of a sadomasochistic encounter *US*
An abbreviation for *'ass-plug'*.
- My world of s/m is full of pleasure and is full of toys and goodies – hand-crafted leather dildoes, A-plugs[.] — *What Color is Your Handkerchief*, p. 17, 1979

apoplectic *adjective*
behaving in a violently temperamental manner *UK*
From the symptoms of apoplexy.

apostles *noun*
▸ **the apostles**
in craps, a roll of twelve *US*
- — Chris Fagans and David Guzman, *A Guide to Craps Lingo*, p. 38, 1999

app *noun*
an application *UK*
- [G]overnor's app. — Angela Devlin, *Prison Patter*, p. 58, 1996
- Tilden: Pined to be NYPD. Three force apps in ten years. — *Copland*, 1997

appalling *adjective*
objectionable, ugly, etc *UK, 1937*
An example of overused society and middle-class hyperbole.

apparatchik *noun*
an office worker in a support role *US*
- The businessmen and apparatchiks at Young & Rubicon have all the formats – checks and balances at their disposal. — Robert Kirk Mueller, *Buzzwords*, p. 42, 1974

appie *noun*
an appendectomy patient *US*
- — *Maledicta*, p. 15, 1984–1985: 'A medical Christmas song'

applause *noun*
a sexually transmitted infection, especially gonnorhea *US*
An excruciating pun on **CLAP**.
- — Richard McAlister, *Rapper's Handbook*, p. 1, 1990

apple *noun*
1 a person *US, 1887*
Usually heard with a qualifying adjective such as 'bad' or 'rotten'.
- I got a nephew. A brainy apple and a good kid. — Philip Wylie, *Opus 21*, p. 114, 1949
- You may be a rough apple, but I can make your face look like it's been run through a grinder[.] — Mickey Spillane, *My Gun is Quick*, p. 20, 1950
- Anyhow, he knew the good kids from the bad apples. — *San Francisco News*, p. 11, 17th January 1950
- In removing what few "bad apples" there may be, the union would be serving two good purposes." — *San Francisco Call-Bulletin*, p. 6G, 14th January 1953
- [T]he hearing should not be interpreted as an indictment of all auto dealers because of the activities of a few "bad apples." — *San Francisco Examiner*, 4th August 1960

2 the gullible victim of a confidence swindle *US*
- — Jay Robert Nash, *Dictionary of Crime*, p. 10, 1992

3 a native American Indian who curries favour with the white establishment by embracing white cultural values *US, 1980*
A variation on a theme – red on the outside, white on the inside.
- — *Maledicta*, p. 124, Summer 1980: 'Racial and ethnic slurs: regional awareness and variations'

4 a particular type of MDMA, the recreational drug best known as ecstasy *UK*
Sometimes embellished to 'apple E' or 'green apple'.
- — Angela Devlin, *Prison Patter*, p. 23, 1996
- Wha' y'after? Special K. Es... Apples. Got some killer Doves. — Nick Barlay, *Curvy Lovebox*, p. 187, 1997
- [A]ll that happened when the adverts came out saying that Apple Es killed Leah Betts was that you couldn't buy one for love nor money cos every raver wanted one. There was a lot of shit pills out there and those ads were just saying to people that apples were pukka — Dave Courtney, *Raving Lunacy*, p. 72, 2000

5 a capsule of secobarbital sodium (trade name Seconal™), a central nervous system depressant *US*
- —Edith A. Folb, *runnin' down some lines*, p. 228, 1980
- —Richard A. Spears, *The Slang and Jargon of Drugs and Drink*, p. 13, 1986

6 a self-propelled barracks barge *US*
From the ship's official designation as an 'APL'.
- The men climbed out, walked over the metal roofing of the tango boats and up the ladders to the LST's and "apples." —Ronald J. Glasser, *365 Days*, p. 28–29, 1971

7 the vagina *US*
- —Edith A. Folb, *runnin' down some lines*, p. 228, 1980

8 a one-hundred dollar note *NEW ZEALAND*
- —David McGill, *David McGill's Complete Kiwi Slang Dictionary*, p. 7, 1998

9 the heart *NEW ZEALAND, 1989*
An abbreviation of 'apple tart', and by rhyming slang to 'heart'.
- —Harry Orsman, *A Dictionary of Modern New Zealand Slang*, p. 2, 1999

10 a citizens' band radio enthusiast of unlimited zeal *US*
- — Radio Shack, *CBer's Handy Atlas/Dictionary*, p. 8, 1976

Apple *noun*
▸ The Apple
New York City *US, 1938*
- There was a giant black pimp from the "Apple." —Iceberg Slim (Robert Beck), *Pimp*, p. 168, 1969
- When I reached the Apple I got off the train at the 125th Street station[.] —A.S. Jackson, *Gentleman Pimp*, p. 133, 1973

apple and pip *verb*
1 to sip *UK*
Rhyming slang.
- —*Daily Telegraph*, 17th December 1972

2 to urinate *UK, 1960*
Rhyming slang, formed on back-slang 'sip'/**PISS**. Also used in a noun sense.
- —Ray Puxley, *Cockney Rabbit*, p. 3, 1992

apple box *noun*
in the television and film industries, any device used to raise an actor or object to the desired height *US*
- —Tony Miller and Patricia George, *Cut! Print!*, p. 34, 1977

apple-catchers *noun*
a type of roomy underpants *AUSTRALIA*
- During 1928 I had worn apple-catchers, but my main Christmas present had been a pair of long 'uns. —D.E. Charlwood, *All the Green Year*, p. 1, 1965

apple core; apple *noun*
twenty pounds; in betting, odds of 20–1 *UK, 1974*
Rhyming slang for **SCORE**.
- —John McCririck, *John McCririck's World of Betting*, p. 112, 1991
- —Ray Puxley, *Cockney Rabbit*, p. 4, 1992

apple fritter; apple *noun*
bitter (beer) *UK*
Rhyming slang.
- Apple (fritter) seems to be the new word for bitter, while the plural remains the word for stairs. —*Antiquarian Book Review*, p. 18, June 2002

applehead *noun*
a dull, stupid person *US, 1951*
- She's not married; I don't believe that applehead. —George Mandel, *Flee the Angry Strangers*, p. 103, 1952
- Why, those apple heads! Who are they supposed to be kidding? —Mickey Spillane, *Kiss Me Deadly*, p. 109, 1952

Apple Isle; Apple Island *noun*
Tasmania *AUSTRALIA, 1906*
The island state is noted for its apple-growing industry.
- Jamie Cox, son of former Tasmanian representative David, will lead the Apple Isle. —*Herald*, p. 21, 1st May 1988

apple jacks *noun*
pieces of crack cocaine *US*
From a resemblance to a popular breakfast cereal.
- —US Department of Justice, *Street Terms*, October 1994

apple-knocker *noun*
1 a rustic, especially a naive one *US, 1919*
- "I'm an apple-knocker," he [Casey Stengel] likes to say, "and I'm against all city slickers." —*Time*, p. 81, 25th October 1948
- He [Arthur Godrfrey] always sounds like the apple-knocker who's in the big town for the very first time. —*San Francisco Examiner*, p. II-1, 6th July 1956
- There are those who think the President sups too heavily on (and with) captains of industry, publishers, and high-placed apple-knockers. —*San Francisco Chronicle*, p. 20, 23rd December 1965
- He was an open apple knocker from the West Side wearing plain Monkey Ward jeans rather than Levi's and high-top horsehide shit kickers. —Earl Thompson, *Tattoo*, p. 55, 1974

2 an outdoor toilet *US*
From the image of apples dropping onto the outhouse roof.
- —John Gould, *Maine Lingo*, p. 36, 1975

apple orchard *noun*
a location where police wait parked, certain that they will soon witness a driving infraction *US*
- "Do you knonw a good spot to sit? Some good spot where we could get a sure ticket?" "An apple orchard, huh?" —Joseph Wambaugh, *The New Centurions*, p. 293, 1970

apple pie order *noun*
complete and perfect order *US*
- —John Gould, *Maine Lingo*, p. 36, 1975

apple pips *noun*
the lips *UK, 1960*
Rhyming slang.
- Who can resist nice rosy "apples". —Ray Puxley, *Cockney Rabbit*, p. 4, 1992

apple-polisher *noun*
a person who shamelessly curries favour from those above him *US, 1927*
Several variant forms.
- Attention apple-polishers! A new Washington crop, bursting with flavor and health, is on the way to you. —*Time*, p. 95, 2nd November 1959
- What's Your Opinion of Office Apple Polishers? (Headline) —*San Francisco Chronicle*, p. 36, 20th July 1966

apples *noun*
the female breasts *US, 1942*
- —Vincent J. Monteleone, *Criminal Slang*, p. 12, 1949

apples *adjective*
1 satisfactory, good *AUSTRALIA, 1943*
Possibly rhyming slang for 'apples and rice', 'nice'.
- Old Kev's apples. He's got Jesus and Cherylene on his side. —Barry Humphries, *Bazza Pulls It Off!*, 1971

2 in good shape or condition *NEW ZEALAND*
- —David McGill, *David McGill's Complete Kiwi Slang Dictionary*, p. 10, 1998

apples and pears; apples *noun*
stairs *UK, 1857*
Rhyming slang.
- The Doctor had shot up the apples like a V2[.] —Charles Raven, *Underworld Nights*, p. 56, 1956
- I dived for the apples[.] —Derek Raymond (Robin Cook), *The Crust on its Uppers*, p. 60, 1962

apple tart; apple *noun*
a fart *UK*
Rhyming slang.
- Have you dropped an apple tart or has a rat died up your Khyber pass [arse]? —Bodmin Dark, *Dirty Cockney Rhyming Slang*, 2003

apple up *verb*
to become frightened *US*
- —John D. Bell et al., *Loosely Speaking*, p. 1, 1966

apple z *verb*
to undo something *US*
A figurative use of the 'undo last command' function on an Apple Macintosh™ computer.
- —Susie Dent, *The Language Report*, p. 10, 2003

application *noun*
▸ take an application
(used of a pimp) to probe the psyche of a woman who is a candidate to come to work for you *US*
- I take an application on a broad when I talk to her that is worse than if she was going to go out and get a job in the Pentagon. I get a mental makeup on her[.] —Christina and Richard Milner, *Black Players*, p. 88, 1972

apprentice *noun*
in horse racing, a jockey who has ridden for less than a year *US*
- —Dan Parker, *The ABC of Horse Racing*, 1947

appro *noun*

▸ **on appro**

on approval *UK, 1874*

- Be an angel and ring up Sydney and tell them to send up a dozen frocs on appro. —Dymphna Cusack, *Picnic Races*, p. 236, 1962

appropriate *verb*

to steal something *US*

Ironic; military use.

- —Harold Wentworth and Stuart Berg Flexner, *Dictionary of American Slang*, p. 8, 1960

appy *noun*

an appendectomy *US*

- —Sally Williams, *"Strong" Words*, p. 133, 1994

apricots *noun*

the testicles *UK*

- Corgh! Look at the apricots on that one! —Henry Sloane, *Sloane's Inside Guide to Sex & Drugs & Rock 'n' Roll*, p. 37, 1985

April fool *noun*

1 a tool *UK*

Rhyming slang, originally of a burglar's tool then, with singular exceptions, in more general use as a workman's tool.

- —Julian Franklyn, *A Dictionary of Rhyming Slang*, p. 33, 1960
- —Ray Puxley, *Cockney Rabbit*, p. 4, 1992

2 a weapon such as a handgun, knife, etc *UK*

Rhyming slang; a narrower sense of the much earlier 'tool'.

3 a stool, usually a bar stool *UK*

Rhyming slang.

- —Julian Franklyn, *A Dictionary of Rhyming Slang*, p. 33, 1960
- —Ray Puxley, *Cockney Rabbit*, p. 4, 1992

April in Paris; April *noun*

the backside, the buttocks *UK, 1998*

Rhyming slang, extending the sequence **ARIS** – **ARISTOTLE** – **BOTTLE; BOTTLE AND GLASS** – **ARSE**.

- —Ray Puxley, *Fresh Rabbit*, 1998

April shower *noun*

a flower *UK, 1960*

Rhyming slang.

April showers *noun*

beer by Flower & Sons, 'Flower's' *UK, 1992*

Rhyming slang.

apron *noun*

1 a woman or wife *US*

- —Clarence Major, *Dictionary of Afro-American Slang*, p. 20, 1970

2 the gross daily receipts from a carnival concession *US*

- —Lindsay E. Smith and Bruce A. Walstad, *Keeping Carnies Honest*, p. 42–43, 1990

▸ **out of the apron**

(used of gambling in a casino) on money borrowed from the casino *US*

- —David M. Hayano, *Poker Faces*, p. 187, 1982

aqua; acqua *noun*

water *UK*

From and synonymous with Latin *aqua* via Italian *acqua*.

- —Paul Baker, *Polari*, p. 163, 2002

aqua boot *noun*

to vomit into the ocean *US*

- —Trevor Cralle, *The Surfin'ary*, p. 3, 1991

A-rab *noun*

an Arab *US*

Not flattering, but more oafish than derogatory. The slang sense of the word is gained strictly through pronunciation – a long first 'A', two drawn out syllables, and a light twang with the second. In his 1962 rock/novelty record 'Ahab the Arab', Ray Stevens gave a loud public voice to this pronunciation.

- You know yourself that a sumbitch who don't block or tackle is nothing but a nigger hebe spick with a little A-rab thrown in. By the way. We got any A-rabs around here? —Dan Jenkins, *Semi-Tough*, p. 5–6, 1972
- One look at your guinea puss and this fuckin' A-rab of yours and he'll bolt like a rabbit. —Edwin Torres, *Carlito's Way*, p. 77, 1975
- Except I can't show you no Arabs on account of I do not know to many A-rabs. —George V. Higgins, *The Rat on Fire*, p. 27, 1981

Arab *noun*

1 used as a term of mild abuse *UK: SCOTLAND*

There is no racist intent in this term, deriving as it does from 'street Arab' an obsolete term for a homeless child.

- In Glasgow, this has been a term of abuse since even before the rise of the oil sheikhs: "Get lost ya Arab ye!" —Michael Munro, *The Original Patter*, 1985

2 a dolt *BERMUDA*

- —Peter A. Smith and Fred M. Barritt, *Bermewjan Vurds*, 1985

3 a street peddler selling fruit or vegetables *US, 1935*

A fixture and term from Baltimore.

- —Frederic G. Cassidy, *Dicitonary of American Regional English, Volume 1*, p. 82, 1985

Arab lover *noun*

a driver who obeys the fifty-five miles an hour speed limit *US*

A term coined during the Arab oil embargo of the early 1970s.

- The boss is an Arab lover so I do a double nickel. —Warren Smith, *Warren's Smith's Authentic Dictionary of CB*, p. 18, 1976

arbitrary *adjective*

insignificant, unimportant *US*

Nowhere near as popular as its conventional cousin **RANDOM**.

- —Connie Eble (Editor), *UNC-CH Campus Slang*, p. 1, Fall 1986

arc *verb*

in computing, to archive something *US*

- I arced all of the code libraries and netted them over to you this morning. —Andy Ihnatko, *Cyberspeak*, p. 12, 1997

arc around *verb*

to engage in enthusiastic and energetic, if meaningless and aimless, activity *US*

US naval aviator usage.

- —*United States Naval Institute Proceedings*, p. 108, October 1986

ARC girl *noun*

a female representative of the American Red Cross *US*

Vietnam war usage.

- —Carl Fleischhauer, *A Glossary of Army Slang*, p. 1, 1968

Archbish *noun*

an Archbishop *UK*

- [S]unday trading and the Archbish of Canterbury having a go at the government[.] —Andrew Nickolds, *Back to Basics*, p. 163, 1994

Archie *noun*

1 the notional cause of confusion *TRINIDAD AND TOBAGO*

As in 'Archie buck them up' or 'Archie fuck them up'; from the late 1960s Jamaican hit record 'Archie Buck Them Up' by Lord Creator.

- —Lise Winer, *Dictionary of the English/Creole of Trinidad & Tobago*, 2003

2 a young and untrained farm hand *NEW ZEALAND*

- —Leopold Acland, *Early Canterbury Runs*, p. 360, 1946
- It is salmost standard practice to set a new and innocent archie walking about asking all and sundry where the snowrake was put away at the end of last winter. —Robert Loughnan, *Glossary*, p. 75, 1981

architect *noun*

in poker, a player who bets heavily *US*

So called because his betting builds the pool of bets.

- —George Percy, *The Language of Poker*, p. 6, 1988

arctic *adjective*

1 cold *US*

- —Pamela Munro, *U.C.L.A. Slang*, p. 15, 1989

2 in poker, said of a very poor hand or series of very poor hands *US*

- —John Vorhaus, *The Big Book of Poker Slang*, p. 4, 1996

Arctic explorer *noun*

a user of heroin and/or cocaine *US*

- —J.E. Schmidt, *Narcotics Lingo and Lore*, p. 7, 1959

arena rat *noun*

1 a young person who hangs around a skating arena *CANADA*

- Most of the 3564 fans had wended their ways homeward before a disgraceful episode occurred with Belleville's players opposing Jim McCormick's youthful "arena rats" in a free-for-all. —*Kingston Whig-Standard*, p. 11, 25th February 1957

2 a woman who invites sexual relations with professional wrestlers *US*

- They are called "Arena Rats" by the boys, though I think this is a harsh name for most of them. There are some who deserve it. They come in all shapes, sizes, ages and social backgrounds. The one thing they have in common is the love of wrestlers. —Pat Barrett, *Everybody Down There Hates Me*, p. 225, 1990

are you for real?
used for humorously questioning a person's sincerity *US*

- While [Dean] Martin sings, [Jerry] Lewis flaps around wild as a keyed-up freshman, breaking his sentences and throwing away the ends, asking the catch phrase, "Are you for real?" — *Vanity Fair*, p. 78, July 1949

are you kidding?
you must be joking!; are you serious? *US*
Derisive, ironic and more of an exclamation than a question. Beale reports a (perhaps mainly Services) riposte of the 1960s – 70s, that punned kidding with a state of pregnancy, as: 'No – it's just the way me coat hangs'.

are you looking at me?
used as a beligerent challenge to a stranger *US*

- —Arnold Brown, *Are You Looking at Me, Jimmy*, 1994

are you ready to throw down?
used as a call soliciting a response ('yes, we are') at a party *US*

- —Alonzo Westbrook, *Hip Hoptionary*, p. 3, 2002

are you stupid or French?
used for expressing a dim opinion of someone's intellectual firepower *CANADA*

- —Bill Casselman, *Canadian Sayings*, p. 3, 2002

arf *noun*
half *UK, 1854*
Written as it's said.

- GRANDPA: He didn't arf look a mess. —Clive Exton, *No Fixed Abode [Six Granada Plays]*, p. 135, 1959

arg *noun*
in computing, an argument *US*

- — *CoEvolution Quarterly*, p. 27, Spring 1981

Argentina *noun*
▸ **do an Argentina**
to go missing presumed dead *UK*

- I would be disappeared in a phoney escape bid. Crooks call it doing an Argentina, from the methods of disappearing undesirables over there. —Jonathan Gash, *The Ten Word Game*, p. 75, 2003

Argie *noun*
an Argentinian *UK, 1982*
This abbreviation is not recorded until the Anglo-Argentine conflict for the Falklands/Malvinos in 1982.

- [D]ebates raged about the best way to smash the Argies[.] —Mark Steel, *Reasons to be Cheerful*, p. 127, 2001
- "A little Argentinian steakhouse five minutes down the road from the Bulldog, they do the best steaks in Holland." "Argies?" said Lesley with disgust. "The war's a long time over," said Johnny Too. —Garry Bushell, *The Face*, p. 218, 2001

argle-bargle *noun*
the sound made by seabirds *CANADA, 1988*
This Nova Scotia expression seems to imitate the sound it describes.

- The argle-bargle of gulls and ravens came from far away, and I wished I were a boy again so I could believe in myself as a pirate. —Harry Bruce, *Down Home*, p. 125, 1988

argue *verb*
▸ **argue the toss**
to argue over something already decided *UK, 1925*

- We were arguing the toss round the bar of Sammy's Spieler[.] —Charles Raven, *Underworld Nights*, p. 188, 1956
- No good argueing the toss with me, Fred. There's Harmon. Ask him. He's the john, not me —Arthur Upfield, *Bony and the Mouse*, p. 157, 1959
- —Arthur Chipper, *The Aussie Swearer's Guide*, p. 76, 1972
- —Jim Ramsay, *Cop It Sweet!*, p. 8, 1977
- —Rex Hunt, *Tall Tales – and True*, p. 24, 1994
- —Shane Maloney, *Nice Try*, p. 152, 1998

argy-bargy *noun*
an argument, quarrelling *UK, 1887*
Also sometimes known as 'argle-bargle'.

argy-bargy *verb*
to argue *UK, 1888*
From the noun.

Aries *noun*
heroin *US*

- —US Department of Justice, *Street Terms*, October 1994
- —Robert Ashton, *This Is Heroin*, p. 205, 2002

aris *noun*
1 the backside, the buttocks; the anus *UK, 1979*
Rhyming slang from **ARISTOTLE – BOTTLE; BOTTLE AND GLASS – ARSE**. Also variants 'arris' and 'harris'.

- "Have you got any snout on you?" Asked the screw with a smile. The Bastard, what did he think I had some stuffed [up] my harris. —Frank Norman, *Bang To Rights*, p. 11, 1958
- JULIAN: Ooh! Look, he's got a baggy old aris! SANDY: I'll say he has. —Barry Took and Marty Feldman, *Round the Horne*, 17th March 1968
- I walk into a well-known bird-bandit's lair and find a comely Richard [woman] flaunting her Arris [buttocks] around the gaff[.] —Anthony Masters, *Minder*, p. 37, 1984
- Recently he author was conversing with one skilled 'linguist' who used 'aris' for 'arse'. Asked to justify its usage, he replied: 'Well, Aristotle is a bottle; bottle-and-glass is an arse, Aris is short for Aristotle, so therefore an Aris is an Arse!' —John Meredith, *Learn to Talk Old Jack Lang*, p. 11, 1984
- I heard a good one the other day – 'arris for bum. Know it? —Peter Corris, *Make Me Rich*, p. 7, 1985
- Dougie keeps banging on about wanting to try it up the aris. —Garry Bushell, *The Face*, p. 140, 2001

2 a bottle *AUSTRALIA*
Also variant form 'aras'.

- —Sidney J. Baker, *The Australian Language*, p. 360, 1966

ari-stock-rat *noun*
a Canadian person of mixed Indian and French ancestry *CANADA*
The pride behind the insult in 'aristocrat' has been justified by the honoring of Louis Riel, who led a Metis rebellion during the settling of the Canadian West.

- "Ari-stock-rats," sometimes "mocassin aristocracy," is a term used to designate the half breeds (or Metis, which they prefer being called). — *Alberta Historical Review*, p. 13, Autumn 1962

Aristotle *noun*
a bottle *AUSTRALIA, 1897*
Rhyming slang.

Aristotle's lantern *noun*
a sea urchin *CANADA, 1990*

- —T. K. Pratt, *Dictionary of Prince Edward Island English*, p. 5, 1988

Arizona *noun*
buttermilk *US, 1946*
Because a waitress thinks any man drinking buttermillk ought to be in Arizona for his health.

- — *American Speech*, p. 87, April 1946: 'The language of West Coast culinary workers'

Arizona stop *noun*
a rolling stop at a traffic signal or stop sign *US*

- — *American Speech*, p. 266, December 1962: 'The language of traffic policemen'
- —Jeffrey McQuain, *Never Enough Words*, p. 54, 1999

Arizona Territory *noun*
an area southwest of Da Nang, South Vietnam, with imprecise boundaries and a strong Vietcong presence *US*

- —Linda Reinberg, *In the Field*, p. 10, 1991

arji *noun*
marijuana *US, 2001*

- —Simon Worman, *Joint Smoking Rules*, 2001

ark *noun*
a dance hall *US*

- —Lavada Durst, *The Jives of Dr. Hepcat*, p. 11, 1953

Arkansas credit card *noun*
a hose used to syphon petrol from another car *US, 1976*

- —Bill Davis, *Jawjacking*, p. 11, 1977

Arkansas fire extinguisher *noun*
a chamberpot *US*
Peter Tamony recorded this term on a visit with folklorist John Greenway in July 1958.

Arkansas flush *noun*
in poker, a worthless hand consisting of four cards in one suit and a fifth in another *US, 1950*
- —*American Speech*, p. 97, May 1951: 'The vocabulary of poker'
- —Albert H. Morehead, *The Complete Guide to Winning Poker*, p. 256, 1967

Arkansas gravel; Arkansas pavement *noun*
small trees used as a makeshift bridge over a mud hole *US*
- —Jerry Robertson, *Oil Slanguage*, p. 23, 1954

Arkansas toad stabber *noun*
a sharp knife *US*
- [A]rkansas toad stabbers drawn and pointed square at my middle[.] —James Ellroy, *Hollywood Nocturnes*, p. 283, 1994

Arkansas toothpick *noun*
a hunting knife *US, 1836*
- Beale Street (Memphis) Negroes could damage each other by exercising some ingenuity. Crump's cops shook them down nightly for pistols, Arkansas toothpicks, brass knucks, razors and ice picks. —*Time*, p. 20, 27th May 1946
- —Joseph Weingarten, *American Dictionary of Slang*, p. 10, 1954

Arkansas traveler; Arkansas special *noun*
any unimportant railway line *US, 1950*
- —Frederic G. Cassidy, *Dicitonary of American Regional English, Volume 1*, p. 86, 1985

Arkansas wedding cake *noun*
cornbread *US, 1958*
- —Frederic G. Cassidy, *Dicitonary of American Regional English, Volume 1*, p. 87, 1985

Arky; Arkie *noun*
a resident of Arkansas; an unsophisticated rustic from the south central US *US, 1927*
Often used with contempt.
- "Did you hear that, chief?" the scurvy Arkie said.—Oscar Zeta Acosta, *The Autobiography of a Brown Buffalo*, p. 119, 1972
- —*Maledicta*, p. 151, Summer/Winter 1978: 'How to hate thy neighbor: a guide to racist maledicta'
- Along about dawn, this Arkie bonhunk named Hutchinson actually got up and went back there[.]—Seth Morgan, *Homeboy*, p. 152, 1990

arm *noun*
1 a police officer *US*
- —*American Speech*, p. 99, May 1956: 'Smugglers' argot in the southwest'

2 the penis *US*
- —Christina and Richard Milner, *Black Players*, p. 296, 1972

▸ **off the arm**
in food and beverage servers' argot, served without a tray *US*
- In truth, it was once very stylish to have a sweetheart who served it "off the arm".—Jack Lait and Lee Mortimer, *Chicago Confidential*, p. 105, 1950

▸ **on the arm**
without charge *US, 1926*
- You can eat at the deli. They're good on the arm.—Peter Maas, *Serpico*, p. 60, 1973
- It was all bar bills and seven-course dinners on the arm.—Vincent Patrick, *The Pope of Greenwich Village*, p. 110, 1979
- But that's cool, 'cause Dave is workin' mostly on the arm now, since at the present time I am in a financial state of insoluble.—Edwin Torres, *After Hours*, p. 161, 1979
- They had a pizza that tasted even better because it was on the arm, and then drove to Hamilton House.—William J. Cavnitz, *One Police Plaza*, p. 238, 1984

▸ **put the arm on**
to pressurise with criminal intent, to extort, to blackmail, to threaten; to arrest *US, 1943*
- Get out before I put the arm on you for interfering with an officer in the performance of his duties.—Raymond Chandler, *Playback*, p. 192, 1958
- "What a forked-tongued phoney you are," I told him, "coming here and trying to put the arm on me for the Mafia.—Harry J. Anslinger, *The Murderers*, p. 238, 1961

▸ **under the arm**
no good, inferior; loathsome *UK*
- [S]ome people go potty, but I read no matter how bad the book and some are right under the arm—Frank Norman, *Bang To Rights*, p. 25, 1958

▸ **up the arm**
in betting, odds of 11–8 *UK*
From the TICK-TACK signal used by bookmakers.
- —John McCririck, *John McCririck's World of Betting*, p. 61, 1991

arm and a leg *noun*
1 a high cost *UK, 1956*
- I imagine it would cost me an arm and a leg.—Elmore Leonard, *Pronto*, p. 100, 1993
- Anglers are paying an arm and a leg for the right to fish depleted stocks[.]—*The Daily Telegraph*, 13th June 2004

2 a prison sentence of five to ten years *US*
- —Lee McNelis, *30 + And a Wake-Up*, p. 6, 1991

arm candy *noun*
1 someone good-looking enough for you to be seen out with *US*
- [Marilyn Monroe] already had mini-roles in eight movies when she turned up as Geroge Sanders' arm candy in the party scenes of this film.—*Chicago Tribune*, 21st August 1992
- Our heroine Carrie walks off into the sunset not as a spinster, or as the arm candy of a suave Russian artist, but hand-in-hand with the guy who has always been in her heart.—*Chicago Daily Herald*, p. 1, 23rd February 2004

2 recreational drugs that are injected into the arm *UK*
- What's more that arm candy you liked so much is gotta get paid for too and that costs plenty.—Ben Elton, *High Society*, p. 60, 2002

armchair *adjective*
removed from the action; said of an observer who acts as if he is a participant *US*
- Coach Pappy Waldorf and his Golden Bears, in the opinion of local Cal's AA – Armchair Alumni in this case.—*San Francisco Call-Bulletin*, p. 29, 28th October 1955
- Town Hall Lists Speakers for 'Arm Chair Cruises' (Headline)—*San Francisco Examiner*, p. 26, 17th June 1956
- Don't miss this armchair safari! Colorful Pictorial Map of Africa only 25 cents and the front from any Lipton Soup Mix envelope.—*New York Times Magazine*, p. 59, 20th October 1957
- Tom Bolan, boxing promoter, called the National Boxing Association a "bunch of armchair schemers" today and suggested the body "drop out of existence along with its assinine ratings."—*San Francisco Examiner*, p. 53, 11th July 1961

armchair general *noun*
a person whose opinions are entirely unsupported by experience *US*
- —Harold Wentworth and Stuart Berg Flexner, *Dictionary of American Slang*, p. 8, 1960

armchair ride *noun*
in horse racing, an easy victory *US*
- —Tom Ainslie, *Ainslie's Complete Guide to Thoroughbred Racing*, p. 327, 1976

Armenian chrome *noun*
aluminium paint *US*
- —*American Speech*, p. 272, December 1961: 'Northwest truck drivers' language'

arm hole *noun*
the armpit *BAHAMAS*
- —John A. Holm, *Dictionary of Bahamian English*, p. 5, 1982

armo *noun*
armed robbery *NEW ZEALAND*
Prison slang.
- —*NZWords*, p. 2, 2nd October 1999

armor *noun*
a female's figure *US*
- —Judi Sanders, *Da Bomb*, p. 1, 1997

▸ **in the armor**
(used of beer) in a can *US*
- —*American Speech*, p. 62, February 1967: 'Soda-fountain, restaurant and tavern calls'

armpiece *noun*
an attractive woman chosen as a social companion for the impression she makes on others *US, 1983*
- —J.E. Lighter, *Historical Dictionary of American Slang*, p. 34, 1994

armpit *noun*
1 a highly undesirable town or place *US, 1968*
- —Connie Eble (Editor), *UNC-CH Campus Slang*, October 2002

2 an obnoxious, unfriendly person *US*
- —Collin Baker et al., *College Undergraduate Slang Study Conducted at Brown University*, p. 71, 1968

armpit of the world; armpit of the universe *noun*
the worst place *US, 1968*
- [L]ike the absolute armpit of the world[.]—James Patterson, *The Midnight Club*, p. 158, 1989
- I been to Asia and it's the armpit of the universe.—Bharati Mukherjee, *Jasmine*, p. 112, 1989

arms *noun*
▸ **get your arms around**
to grasp the meaning of *US*
- In 1984, IBM decided it needed to gets its arms around education. — *Development Journal*, p. 34, January 1989
- Technology that a small company could get its arms around, leads engineer to leave steady job at Hewlett Packard to set up a new firm. — *The Straights Times (Singapore)*, p. 30, 24th May 1999

arm-stretcher *noun*
a heavy suitcase *US*
- As best I could with my two heavy arm stretchers, fighting my way through a mob that kept congratulating me for ending the war, I arrived at the Ambassador Hotel. — Larry Rivers, *What Did I Do?*, p. 23, 1992

armstrong *adjective*
done by hand, necessitating arm strength rather than mechanical leverage *CANADA*
- Hoisting the spoil with old-fashioned windlasses which were facetiously called "Armstrong Hoists" was another tedious chore. — *Western Miner*, p. 20/1, May 1963

armstrong method *noun*
the technique of using hand and arm strength to get a job done *CANADA, 1987*
- Armstrong method: anything done by manual labour as opposed to using powered assistance. — Tom Parkin, *WetCoast Words*, p. 11, 1989

arm trophy *noun*
a stunning and sexually appealing companion, valued for the prestige attached to their presence *US*
- Another girl said, "They want an arm trophy who will be their personal slave." — Anka Radakovich, *The Wild Girls Club*, p. 168, 1994

army *noun*
a large bankroll *US*
Alluding to the green of currency and military uniforms.
- A player backed by an army can do battle all day. — Steve Rushin, *Pool Cool*, p. 7, 1990

Army banjo *noun*
a shovel or other entrenching tool *US*
- — Linda Reinberg, *In the Field*, p. 11, 1991

army brat *noun*
a person who grew up the child of a career member of the army *US, 1931*
- — Lou Shelly, *Hepcats Jive Talk Dictionary*, p. 43, 1945
- I was an army brat, born in Chunking, China, where my parents, both Chinese-Americans, were stationed. — Kathryn Leigh Scott, *The Bunny Years*, p. 154, 1998

army craps *noun*
a game of craps in which the shooter serves as the banker *US, 1984*
- — Thomas L. Clark, *The Dictionary of Gambling and Gaming*, p. 8, 1987

army criminal corps *nickname*
the Army Catering Corps, the ACC *US*
An elaboration of the official military abbreviation

army game *noun*
any game of chance played in an aggressive and/or dishonest fashion *US, 1890*
- — J.E. Lighter, *Historical Dictionary of American Slang*, p. 35, 1994

army marbles *noun*
dice *US, 1963*
From the view that soldiers are fond of dice games.
- — Thomas L. Clark, *The Dictionary of Gambling and Gaming*, p. 8, 1987

Army odds *noun*
in a dice game, the true odds, not approximate odds often used in street games *US*
- — Frank Garcia, *Marked Cards and Loaded Dice*, p. 250, 1962

Army Peace Corps *noun*
the US Army Special Forces *US*
Highly trained killers, so an ironic term.
- — Gregory Clark, *Words of the Vietnam War*, p. 473, 1990

army roll *noun*
a controlled roll of the dice by a skilled cheat in a game of craps *US, 1963*
- — Thomas L. Clark, *The Dictionary of Gambling and Gaming*, p. 8, 1987

army tank *noun*
an American serviceman *AUSTRALIA, 1945*
Rhyming slang for **YANK**. Recorded among Australian prisoners-of-war in the Far East.

Arnold *noun*
pork *JAMAICA, 1988*
- — Velma Pollard, *Dread Talk*, p. 41, 2000

aroha job *noun*
a job done out of friendship without charge or at reduced rates *NEW ZEALAND*
From the Maori word for 'love'.
- That set's too expensive to be just another 'aroha job'. — Barry Mitcalfe, *Hey Hey Hey*, p. 84, 1985

'arold *noun*
▷ **see: HAROLD MACMILLAN, HAROLD PINTER**

aroma *noun*
amyl nitrite or butyl nitrite *US*
- — *Maledicta*, p. 227, Winter 1980: '"Lovely, blooming, fresh and gay": the onomastics of camp'

aroma of man *noun*
an ampoule of amyl nitrite *US*
Originally a brand name; later used generically.
- — Jay Robert Nash, *Dictionary of Crime*, p. 11, 1992

-aroo *suffix*
used as a festive if meaningless embellishment of a noun *US, 1941*
- Nino and his Cash Money Monkeys are dealin' with those spicaroos upon Broadway and 171st. — *New Jack City*, 1990

-arooni *suffix*
used as a meaningless embellishment of a word *US*
A highly affected style of speaking invented and marketed with limited success by jazz musician Slim Gaillard.
- To a word that's already jazz slang like "voot," he adds the sound "arooni" or something like that. — Capitol Records, *The Capitol*, p. 13, March 1946
- Slim Gaillard is a tall, thin Negro with big sad eyes who's always saying "Right-orooni" and "How 'bout a little bourbon-orooni." — Jack Kerouac, *On the Road*, p. 175–176, 1957

around the bend *adjective*
▷ **see: ROUND THE BEND**

around the world *noun*
1 the oral stimulation of all parts of a partner's body *US, 1951*
- — Anon., *The Gay Girl's Guide*, p. 15, 1949
- I say, Yoo-hoo, pitty baby, you wanna lil french? Haff an haff? How about jes a straight? I say, Twenty berries an you alla roun the mothahfuggin worl'. — Robert Gover, *One Hundred Dollar Misunderstanding*, p. 21, 1961
- A Lexicon of Homosexual Slang — Donald Webster Cory and John P. LeRoy, *The Homosexual and His Society*, p. 261, 1963
- [T]hey say she gives a super around the world and also knows about massage[.] — Gore Vidal, *Myra Breckinridge*, p. 56, 1968
- A 'trip around the world' can mean anything at all. — John Warren Wells, *Tricks of the Trade*, p. 26, 1970
- She probably went around the world tonight, he thought, cringing in horror. — Joseph Wambaugh, *The New Centurions*, p. 236, 1970
- I should have been suspicious the first time I as asked if my going price was still $30 for "an around the world." — Gwyneth A. "Dandalion" Seese, *Tijuana Bear in a Smoke 'Um Up Taxi*, p. 23, 1977
- The priest asked for around-the-world service and enjoyed every minute of it. — John Sayles, *Union Dues*, p. 188, 1977

2 in Keno, a bet made on the numbers found in the eight corners of a Keno ticket – 1, 10, 31, 40, 41, 50, 71 and 80 *US, 1969*
- — Thomas L. Clark, *The Dictionary of Gambling and Gaming*, p. 8, 1987

arp *noun*
▷ **see: AAP**

arrest-me-red *noun*
a bright red paint on a car, bound to attract the attention and interest of law enforcement *US*
- — Lewis Poteet, *Car & Motorcyle Slang*, p. 18–19, 1992

arrow *noun*
an amphetamine tablet *US*
- — Peter Johnson, *Dictionary of Street Alcohol and Drug Terms*, p. 11, 1993

▸ **bust an arrow; blow an arrow**

in a carnival or small circus, to become lost when travelling from one town to another *US*

In the past, advance men would paste arrows along the roadside to show the way to the next stop; if you missed an arrow, you got lost.

- —Sherman Louis Sergel, *The Language of Show Biz*, p. 36, 1973

▸ **like an arrow**

in poker, said of a sequence of five cards conventionally known as a 'straight' *US*

- —George Percy, *The Language of Poker*, p. 52, 1988

arrow *verb*

to assign a task to someone *SINGAPORE*

- —Paik Choo, *The Coxford Singlish Dictionary*, p. 8, 2002

arrow of desire *noun*

the penis *UK*

A poetic image drawn from William Blake's 'Jerusalem', 1808.

- —Richard Herring, *Talking Cock*, p. 30, 2003

'Arry's gators

Thank you *AUSTRALIA, 1958*

A play on Japanese *arrigato* (thank you).

arse *noun*

1 the posterior, the buttocks *UK*

In conventional usage from Old English until early C18, at which time it was deemed impolite language and began a celebrated existence in slang, rarely appearing in print with all four letters in place. B.E.'s *Dictionary of the Canting Crew*, probably 1698–9, gives 'ar-'; Francis Grose's *Dictionary of the Vulgar Tongue*, five editions from 1785–1823 omits the 'r'. It was not until 1860 that the American **ASS** appeared. The spelling in Australia is 'arse', but pronounced with a long 'a' and no 'r'. Since the 1980s there has been some encroachment of 'ass', but this is still strongly associated with the US.

- If he does, I'll toss him out – right on his all-American arse!—Eric Lambert, *The Veterans*, p. 25, 1954
- [S]lag birds used to go trotting upstairs with him [...] arses wagging and bristols [breasts] going[.]—Derek Raymond (Robin Cook), *The Crust on its Uppers*, p. 30, 1962
- I'll kick your arse right up through your guts until it's hangin' out of your mouth.—John O'Grady, *It's Your Shout Mate!*, p. 32, 1972
- It was rare that he encountered anything like this, then he cocked his pistol and aimed it at the swagman's arse.—Bob Ellis and Anne Brooksbank, *Mad Dog Morgan*, p. 93, 1976
- I could see Tony whipping the arse off it.—Robert English, *Toxic Kisses*, p. 59, 1979
- We would have to go in and hold the prisoner down while the nurses pumped a syringe full of Largactil into his arse to sedate him.—William Dodson, *The Sharp End*, p. 42, 2001

2 the base, the bottom; the tail end; the seat of a pair of trousers *AUSTRALIA*

- Here was a ship under fair weather canvas, on the starboard tack with a barometer falling as if the arse had dropped out of it.—Robert S. Close, *Love Me Sailor*, p. 173, 1945
- Like most freelance writers in Australia, Henry Lawson often walked around with the arse out of his trousers.—Frank Hardy, *Hardy's People*, p. 16, 1986

3 yourself; your body or person *UK*

- I just kicked a bloke's arse out of my office.—Sam Weller, *Old Bastards I Have Met*, p. 79, 1979
- They wanted me, they wanted my sweet little junkie arse.—Peter Corris, *Pokerface*, p. 159, 1985
- I give them plenty of time before I drag my sorry arse up the cliff face.—Dirk Flinthart, *Brotherly Love*, p. 75, 1995

4 a fool; a despicable person *AUSTRALIA, 1944*

- Ray also felt like an arse for putting Tony down like he had[.]—Clive Galea, *Slipper*, p. 105, 1988
- Let's face it, you've got to be a bit of an arse to go line dancing. —*Attitude*, p. 35, October 2003

5 boldness, gall, gumption, impudence; hence, luck as a result of this *AUSTRALIA, 1958*

- I said 'Are you going to skite about that?' and he said 'My bloody oath I am.' I said 'You shouldn't, you know, because it was sheer arse.' —Sam Weller, *Old Bastards I Have Met*, p. 51, 1979

6 dismissal, especially from a job; rejection *AUSTRALIA, 1955*

Generally with verbs 'give' and 'get'.

- I'll tell you what, if I don't start getting a few free ones for the lounge, he'll be getting the arse out of this pub very shortly.—Sam Weller, *Old Bastards I Have Met*, p. 20, 1979
- The word spread, 'The Doc's been given the arse.'—Kerry Cue, *Crooks, Chooks and Bloody Ratbags*, p. 196, 1983
- If I confessed, Mouche would give me the arse.—Kathy Lette, *Girls' Night Out*, p. 107, 1987
- September 19: Juan Peron given the arse by the Argies.—Ignatius Jones, *The 1992 True Hip Manual*, p. 165, 1992
- He gave me the arse yesterday morning, and I lost him this afternoon.—Dirk Flinthart, *Brotherly Love*, p. 79, 1995

▸ **ask me arse**

used when refusing to cooperate or when withholding information *IRELAND*

Other variations used are: 'ask me bollix', 'ask me sack', 'ask me left one'. 'Me' is a common Hiberno-English pronunciation for 'my'.

- Which one of yis [you] is Bimbo? he said. – Ask me arse, said Jimmy Sr.—Roddy Doyle, *The Van*, p. 213, 1991

▸ **get off your arse; get off your ass**

to start doing something *UK*

Often in the imperative.

- [T]his is the big one, so we've got to get up off our arses and stop just talking about it!—Monty Python, *Life of Brian*, 1979

▸ **get your arse in gear**

to start making an effort *UK*

- [W]ashing it off in my en suite business and getting my arse in gear[.]—Diran Abedayo, *My Once Upon A Time*, p. 325, 2000
- Right! Come ed. Arses in gear. Wales, here we come.—Niall Griffiths, *Kelly + Victor*, p. 45, 2002

▸ **make an arse of**

to make a mess of something; to botch something *UK: SCOTLAND*

- —Michael Munro, *The Complete Patter*, 1996

▸ **not know your arse from a hole in the ground**

to be completely ignorant (of a given subject) *UK*

- [Y]ou don't know anything about anything. You don't know y'arse from a hole in the ground – you – you think that life's like the inside of a Wendy House.—Alan Bleasdale, *Boys From the Blackstuff*, 1982

▸ **not know your arse from your elbow**

to be ignorant *UK, 1930*

- "Ben Hendy clearly doesn't know his arse from his elbow," claims Chris Tall.—*The Guardian*, 20th February 2003

▸ **on your arse**

in dire straits, especially financial *US, 1917*

- [W]here was Liverpool? On its arse with Gizzzza Job as its strap-line. —Tony Wilson, *24 Hour Party People*, p. 164, 2002

▸ **out on your arse**

ejected, evicted, expelled *UK*

A variation of 'out on your ear'.

- What will you be when you're out on your arse?—Ian Dury, *Jack Shit George*, 1998

▸ **put on the arse bit**

to indignantly tell someone what you think of him or her *AUSTRALIA*

- —*The (Sydney) Bulletin*, 26th April 1975

▸ **take it up the arse**

to submit to a more powerful force *UK*

- The government will be told the terms and conditions of the carve-up by their paymasters, the money men, and being joes who take it up the arse from the City cartels anyway they'll go along with the swindle[.]—J.J. Connolly, *Layer Cake*, p. 94, 2000

▸ **the arse drops out of; the arse falls out of**

(of a financial venture) to fail dismally *AUSTRALIA*

- What has the arse dropped out of the market in a bloody week? —D'Arcy Niland, *Dead Men Running*, p. 73, 1969
- Unfortunately, thanks to a few snooping accountants and the odd ten million dollar Oz epic that was so shithouse it never copped a release, the arse has dropped out of the Australian film industry.—Barry Humphries, *The Traveller's Tool*, p. 19, 1985

▸ **up your arse**

very close behind, in close proximity *UK*

- So we turned up and the bizzies are right up our arse.—Shaun Ryder, *Shaun Ryder... in His Own Words*, 1997

▸ up your own arse
very self-involved *UK*
- She looked serious as fuck. I don't mean serious as in solemn or depressed or up her own arse or whatever. —James Hawes, *Dead Long Enough*, p. 137, 2000
- [A]utobiographers are so up their own arses that they think anything to do with them is totally fucking fascinating[.] —Frank Skinner, *Frank Skinner*, p. 193, 2001

▸ you couldn't find your arse with both hands
you are stupid *UK*
- [H]e was a gormless get him, he couldn't find his arse with both hands. —Caroline Aherne and Craig Cash, *The Royle Family*, 1999

▸ your arse is nippin buttons
you are nervous, you are full of trepidation *UK: SCOTLAND*
- —Michael Munro, *The Patter, Another Blast*, 1988

▸ your arse off
to a great degree; vigorously *UK*
Used to intensify verb meanings, thus 'to work your arse off' means 'to work hard'; very common with the verb 'work' and the verb 'fuck' and its synonyms.
- I think it is only emotional, because at other times he becomes the complete dominant male, fucks the arse off me, for weeks on end until he does a switch back. — *Uni Sex*, p. 119, 1972
- [I was] working my arse off for Australia, sometimes a twenty-four, a twenty-five, twenty-six, even a twenty-seven hour week! —Barry Humphries, *A Nice Night's Entertainment*, p. 180, 1978
- Well, me and the other sheilas had been rootin' our arses off for weeks, rakin' in the dough for the old cow see. —Lance Peters, *The Dirty Half-Mile*, p. 94, 1979
- —Barry Humphries, *The Traveller's Tool*, p. 21, 1985
- Some dim, distant spark of rationality tried to get him to give up, to let them in, to shower and change and then lie his arse off for the cameras. —Harrison Biscuit, *The Search for Savage Henry*, p. 84, 1995

arse *verb*
1 to make a mess of something, to botch something *UK: SCOTLAND*
- He had a great chance in front of goal but the wee diddy arsed it. —Michael Munro, *The Complete Patter*, 1996

2 to eat something greedily, to consume something quickly *UK: SCOTLAND*
- Don't leave that gannet wi the carry-oot. He'll arse the whole lot while we're away. —Michael Munro, *The Complete Patter*, 1996

3 of a vehicle, to reverse *UK*
- One of the blokes said, "Arse her [a lorry] up her." I backed her up[.] —John Gosling, *The Ghost Squad*, 1959

arse *adjective*
inferior, shoddy, valueless, unpleasant, disliked for whatever reason *UK*
- [A] life-sapping display that confirms their frequent comparisons with Sham 69, who were arse, too. — *X-Ray*, p. 86, November 2002

arse about; arse around *verb*
to idle, to fool about *UK, 1664*
- Arsing around with him, boy, you're asking for trouble. Take my tip. —D'Arcy Niland, *Dead Men Running*, p. 86, 1969
- [I]t was raining so we were just arsing about, you know, drinking tea and stuff. —David Peace, *Nineteen Seventy-Four*, p. 153, 1999
- When I was a 14 year-old at boarding school, lights out in the dorm was the cue for a whole bunch of arsing around. —*FHM*, p. 250, June 2003

arse about *adjective*
back to front *AUSTRALIA*
- After you left that afternoon I got two drums of kero and rolled them up the petrol ramp arse about. —Sam Weller, *Old Bastards I Have Met*, p. 89, 1979

arse about face *adjective*
back to front *UK, 1984*
- [His] [Tony Blair's] credibility takes a further hammering when Bush's PR goes so spectacularly arse about face. — *The Guardian*, 1st August 2003

arse all *noun*
nothing, nothing at all *UK*
On the model of **FUCK ALL** (nothing).
- It's a new fuckin millennium. Which probly [sic] means arse all in the wider scheme of things. —Niall Griffiths, *Kelly + Victor*, p. 27, 2002

arse bandido *noun*
a male homosexual, especially the active partner in anal sex *UK*
Derogatory.
- "You, sir!" he brayed. "Are you – by any chance – an arse-bandido?" —Chris Ryan, *The Watchman*, p. 155, 2001

arse bandit *noun*
▷ see: **ASS BANDIT**

arse biscuit *noun*
a fart *UK*
A variation of **AIR BISCUIT**.
- He suffered from really bad wind on set and didn't get on with any of the others. Not just because of the arse biscuits. —*X-Ray*, p. 120, June 2003

arse cleavage; arsehole cleavage *noun*
the cleft between the buttocks when partially displayed above an (accidentally) slipped-down trouser waistband *UK*
- Big artics out the back, loads of blokes with ponytails an' arsehole cleavages humpin' gear around. —Ben Elton, *High Society*, p. 214, 2002

arse crawler *noun*
a sycophant *UK, 1937*
Often reduced to **CRAWLER**.

arse cress *noun*
the hair surrounding the anus *UK*
- [E]xcrement clinging to the arse-cress around an inefficiently wiped ringpiece. —Chris Donald, *Rogers Profanisaurus*, p. 54, 2002

arsed *adjective*
bothered; worried *UK*
Popularised since the mid-1990s by television situation comedy *The Royle Family*.
- If they couldn't or wouldn't be arsed to cut it, they were out —Wayne Anthony, *Spanish Highs*, p. 54, 1999
- He's more arsed about fucking Fun Runs and that[.] —Kevin Sampson, *Outlaws*, p. 4, 2001
- Too big and too much of an effort to be arsed with. —Danny King, *The Burglar Diaries*, p. 2, 2001
- Apathy. Can't-be-fuckin-arsed-ness. That's what's wrong with this fuckin country, mun[.] —Niall Griffiths, *Sheepshagger*, p. 74, 2001

-arsed; -arse *suffix*
used to intensify a characteristic *UK*
- [H]appy, bouncy little ravers and not uptight, straight-arsed divs like you[.] —Dave Courtney, *Raving Lunacy*, p. 33, 2000
- Secretly I know she's right but worse still is that smug-arse look she adopts when she knows she's right[.] —Lanre Fehintola, *Charlie Says...*, p. 115, 2000

arse end; a-end *noun*
1 the back or tail end *AUSTRALIA, 1955*
- There's nothing peculiar, or is there, about all those little lads who spend most of their waking hours a-end up on a footy field. —Sue Rhodes, *Now you'll think I'm awful*, p. 106, 1967
- Look, Joe, you know as well as me that as far as the underworld goes, phizgigs are the arse end of the shit heap[.] —Lance Peters, *The Dirty Half-Mile*, p. 151, 1979

2 the end, the final part *UK, 1942*
- Age-wise, I saw the arse-end of punk. — *The Times Magazine*, p. 3, 2nd March 2002

arse-first *adverb*
back-to-front *AUSTRALIA, 1962*
- I hope you all fall down a manhole arse-first onto a nice iron spike! —Colleen McCullough, *Tim*, p. 18, 1975

arsefuck *verb*
to engage in anal sex *AUSTRALIA*
- You gotta write about sweet, tender little girlies getting arsefucked like cheap little whores!! — *Sick Puppy Comix*, p. 21, 1998

arse fucker *noun*
a male who takes the active role in anal sex *AUSTRALIA*
- Seeks one or more horny, well hung arse fuckers. —*Capital Q Weekly*, p. 33, 29th March 1996

arse grapes *noun*
haemorrhoids *UK*
- You got piles or something? Arse grapes? —Greg Williams, *Diamond Geezers*, p. 45, 1997

arsehole *noun*
1 the anus *UK, 1400*
Literally the hole in the **ARSE** (buttocks, posterior); use ranges from the anatomically correct e.g. 'itchy arsehole' to the barely feasible or figurative suggestions associated with 'stick it up your arsehole'.

- You talk to your average lesbian about two men shoving their engorged pricks up each other's sweating arse-holes and they will practically vomit on you. — *Kink*, p. 89, 1993
- He sucks on my fingers, then I push them into his arsehole. — Christos Tsiolkas, *Loaded*, p. 105, 1995

2 by extension, a despised person *UK*
Widely used in the UK and Australia, it is a stronger term than **ASSHOLE**, the US equivalent from which it derives.

- Arseholes, bastards, fucking cunts and pricks — Ian Dury, *Plaistow Patricia*, 1977
- However, with the proliferation of US culture it can now also be virtually synonymous with the milder variant. "Fifty dollars? Oh, you poor arsehole! Let me buy you a drink. — Robert English, *Toxic Kisses*, p. 59, 1979
- The most self-righteous, pompous arsehole on the public payroll. — Terry Lane, *Hectic*, p. 244, 1993
- Hello, my name is Noah. I'm an alcoholic, drug-crazy arsehole." [...] "Would that be a... r... s... e, or a... s... s...hole, Noah? — Stuart Browne, *Dangerous Parking*, p. 80, 2000
- Mr Van der Meer said, "I shouldn't call people arseholes, but stupid fool didn't come to mind at the time. — *Code*, p. 9, January 2002

3 courage, nerve *UK*

- Besides, who's got the arsehole to tell any of you that you were shit? — Dave Courtney, *Dodgy Dave's Little Black Book*, p. 126, 2001

▸ get the arsehole with; have the arsehole with
to become, or be, annoyed with someone *UK*

- Vince clearly had the arsehole with me because he lit up a fag without offering me one. — Danny King, *The Bank Robber Diaries*, p. 159, 2002

arsehole *verb*

1 to dismiss someone, especially from employment; to reject someone *AUSTRALIA, 1950*

- Chairmen of Directors do not get arseholed from their jobs; they are sacked. — Richard Beckett, *The Dinkum Aussie Dictionary*, p. 5, 1986

2 to go, to leave *UK*

- Where are you arse-holing off to? — *New Society*, p. 313, 19th August 1982

arsehole cleavage *noun*
▹ see: **ARSE CLEAVAGE**

arsehole crawler *noun*
a sycophant *UK, 1961*
An extension of **ARSE CRAWLER**, often reduced to **CRAWLER**.

arsehole creeper *noun*
a sycophant *UK, 1984*
A variation of **ARSEHOLE CRAWLER**.

arseholed *adjective*
very drunk *UK, 1984*

- CHRISSIE: How much money have we got? LOGGO: Enough. CHRISSIE: Good. 'Cos I'm gonna get arseholed. — Alan Bleasdale, *Boys From the Blackstuff*, 1982
- [O]ut with boys arseholed ratarsed fucked up[.] — Patrick Jones, *Unprotected Sex*, p. 255, 1999
- "[P]iss artists" are "boozy", "fluffy", "well-gone", "legless", "crocked", "wrecked", "paralytic", "rat-arsed", "shit-faced" and "arse-holed". — Peter Ackroyd, *London The Biography*, p. 359, 2000
- [H]e might as well go to the pub and get arseholed. — Frank Skinner, *Frank Skinner*, p. 52, 2001

arsehole lucky *adjective*
extremely lucky *UK*

- You were arsehole lucky[.] — Martin King and Martin Knight, *The Naughty Nineties*, p. 145, 1999

arsehole of the world *noun*
▹ see: **ASSHOLE OF THE WORLD**

arseholes *noun*
▸ give someone arseholes
to attack someone with vigor *NEW ZEALAND*

- And the only pep talk [the coach] ever gave them, all he ever said every Saturday was go out there and give them arseholes. — Gordon Slatter, *Pagan Games*, p. 174, 1968

arseholes!
used as a general exclamation of rejection, frustration or criticism *UK, 1937*
Occasionally extended as 'arseholes to you!'.

arsehole street *noun*
an unpleasant place to be; serious trouble *UK, 1984*
You can be 'in' or 'up' arsehole street.

arse-holing *adjective*
used as an intensifier *UK*

- Them arse-holing sods [the police] have had Pee[.] — Geoffrey Fletcher, *Down Among the Meths Men*, p. 88, 1966

arse in a sling *noun*
a state of defeat or depression *UK, 1967*
Usually phrased 'have (get) your arse in a sling' or 'your arse is in a sling'. From the obsolete 'eye in a sling'.

arse-kisser *noun*
▹ see: **ASS-KISSER**

arse-lick *verb*
to behave in a sycophantic manner *UK, 1968*

- People here [Mexico] say the English are arse-licking, but it seems more personal. — *The Guardian*, 1st April 2003

arse-licker *noun*
a sycophant *UK, 1938*

- Yes, because I trust you. But not that arse-licker. — D'Arcy Niland, *Dead Men Running*, p. 74, 1969
- [Labor "bad boy" Mark Latham] describes John Howard as an "arse-licker" in the US, and himself as a political "hater". — *Sydney Morning Herald*, 27th June 2002

arse-licking; ass-licking *adjective*
obsequious *UK, 1912*

- There is, after all, nothing more demoralising than coming fourth in an arse-licking competition. — Shane Maloney, *Nice Try*, p. 306, 1998
- You're an asslicking, ball sucking unclefucka! — *South Park*, 1999

arse like a wizard's sleeve *noun*
an unusually loose rectum and anus *UK*

- Fackin' slag. Cunt like a Grimsby welly, arse like a wizard's sleeve. — Andrew Holmes, *Sleb*, p. 151, 2002

arse luck *noun*
very bad luck indeed *SINGAPORE*

- — Paik Choo, *The Coxford Singlish Dictionary*, p. 8, 2002

arse man *noun*
▹ see: **ASS MAN**

Arsenal *noun*
▸ Arsenal are playing at home; Arsenal are at home
the bleed period of the menstrual cycle *UK*
A euphemism based on the colour of blood. Arsenal, a London football team, play in red shirts; as other teams also play in red this is probably also a pun on 'arsenal' (the genitals).

- I rung her one afternoon to ask her if it's all right to pop over. "It's okay but I've got the painters in," she says. "Well, that's okay, they go home at what? Four of five? They got to take their boots off sometime," I say. "No. Arsenal are at home," she says. — J.J. Connolly, *Layer Cake*, p. 291, 2000
- People fink dat you can't have sex when your lady has "arsenal playin at home'. Dis iz not true – you can, but just not wiv her — Sacha Baron-Cohen, *Da Gospel According to Ali G*, 2001

arseness *noun*
annoying stupidity *TRINIDAD AND TOBAGO, 1979*

- — Richard Allsopp, *Dictionary of Caribbean English Usage*, p. 42, 1996

arsenut *noun*
a small, hardened lump of excrement that clings to the hair around the anus *UK*

- — Chris Lewis, *The Dictionary of Playground Slang*, p. 14, 2003

arse over bollocks *adverb*
head over heels *UK*
A variation of **ARSE OVER TIT**.

- Everybody's going arse over bollocks as he sprawls over the first and second row. — Lenny McLean, *The Guv'nor*, p. 105, 1998

arse over head *adverb*
head over heels *AUSTRALIA, 1962*

- [B]y this time we've got ropes on him and all and he's still fighting and he slipped arse over head. — Sam Weller, *Old Bastards I Have Met*, p. 145, 1979

arse over tit *adverb*
head over heels *UK, 1922*

- So piss off or I'll have you flung arse over tit over the side! — Lance Peters, *The Dirty Half-Mile*, p. 314, 1979
- — Ryan Aven-Bray, *Ridgey Didge Oz Jack Lang*, p. 17, 1983

arse over turtle *adverb*
head over heels *AUSTRALIA*

- We turned her arse over turtle down the bank. — Mary Durack, *Keep Him My Country*, p. 212, 1955

arse paper *noun*
any person or thing of limited use *NEW ZEALAND*
- —David McGill, *David McGill's Complete Kiwi Slang Dictionary*, 1998
- —Sonya Plowman, *Great Kiwi Slang*, p. 15, 2002

arse-polishing *noun*
any office job *UK, 1949*
In military use.

arsetronaut *noun*
a male homosexual *NEW ZEALAND, 2002*
An allusion to anal sex.

arse up *verb*
to bungle something, to make a mess of something *UK*
First recorded in adjectival or adverbial form as 'arse up with care' in 1937.

arse-up *adjective*
dead, finished, out of operation *UK*
- [T]he job went arse-up or whatever[.] —Chris Ryan, *The Watchman*, p. 259, 2001

arse-up *adverb*
upside down *AUSTRALIA*
- At last, flat-out he raced towards the built-up area of the railway line – and arse-up went both horse and rider. —Herb Wharton, *Cattle Camp*, p. 73, 1994

arse upwards *adverb*
back to front; upside down *UK, 1984*

arseways *adverb*
incorrectly done, wrongly positioned *IRELAND*
- [N]o matter how I tried it I always got it arseways. It didn't sound like John Wayne at all. —Patrick McCabe, *The Butcher Boy*, p. 116, 1992
- "An Irish cop. Well, fuck me... the Garda Chikini." "Siochna." "You what?" "The pronunciation, you have it arseways." —Ken Bruen, *The Killing of the Tinkers*, p. 37, 2002

arsewipe *noun*
▷ see: **ASSWIPE**

arsewise *adjective*
absurd, foolish, mistaken, wrong *UK, 1962*
- [S]top me if I'm utterly bloody arsewise on this: but would you be that Harry Mac-Donald off the telly? —James Hawes, *Dead Long Enough*, p. 231, 2000

arsey *adjective*
1 lucky *AUSTRALIA, 1950*
From **TIN ARSE**.
- If he is lucky he is tinny, arsy (both of them from tin-arse, a lucky person.) —Sidney J. Baker, *The Australian Language*, p. 113, 1966
- —Jim Ramsay, *Cop It Sweet!*, p. 8, 1977
- —Ryan Aven-Bray, *Ridgey Didge Oz Jack Lang*, p. 17, 1983

2 moody *UK*
Also variant 'arsy'.
- phoning him and then getting all arsey —Greg Williams, *Diamond Geezers*, p. 13, 1997
- I'm sure she was arsy with him and it put him off. —Mary Hooper, *(megan)2*, p. 144, 1999
- "Don't get arsey with me!" she came back. "Ever since we stepped out of the car you've been looking so mean at everyone." —Diran Abedayo, *My Once Upon A Time*, p. 71, 2000
- I was sorry for being so arsey with her. —Frank Skinner, *Frank Skinner*, p. 51, 2001

arsey boo *adjective*
chaotic, unorganised *NEW ZEALAND*
- —David McGill, *David McGill's Complete Kiwi Slang Dictionary*, p. 10, 1998

arsy-varsy; arsy-versy *adverb*
back-to-front; upside-down; perversely *UK, 1539*
- You've got everything arsy-versy. —Saul Bellow, *Humboldt's Gift*, p. 457, 1973
- "Everything here is arsy-varsy." "No. Where you are is arsy-varsy." —Angela Carter, *'The Quilt Maker' in Burning Your Boats*, p. 451, 1995

arsy-versy *adjective*
homosexual *UK*
From **ARSY-VARSY** (perversely) playing on **ARSE** (the bottom) as a stereotypical object of homosexual attraction. *The Sunday Times*, 22nd August 1976, published a letter that preferred the use of **GAY** to 'arsy-versy'.

Artful Dodger *noun*
the penis *UK*
Rhyming slang for **TODGER**, formed from a light-fingered character in Charles Dickens' *Oliver Twist*.
- My "Artful Dodger" has been getting me into some dodgy scrapes[.] —Bodmin Dark, *Dirty Cockney Rhyming Slang*, 2003

Artful Dodger *nickname*
Roger Staubach (b 1942), a dominant quarterback at the college and professional levels in the 1960s and 70s *US*
A two-for-one nickname, rhyming 'Dodger' with 'Roger' and alluding to the Dickens character.

Arthur *noun*
arthritis *UK, 1974*
Used by North Sea trawlermen.

Arthur Ashe; Arthur *noun*
cash *UK, 1992*
Rhyming slang, based on the name of tennis champion Arthur Ashe, 1943–93.
- —*Antiquarian Book Review*, p. 18, June 2002

Arthur Bliss *noun*
an act of urination *UK*
Rhyming slang for **PISS**, formed from classical composer Sir Arthur Bliss, 1891–1975.
- I'm dying for an Arthur Bliss. —Bodmin Dark, *Dirty Cockney Rhyming Slang*, 2003

Arthur Duffy *noun*
▸ **take it on the Arthur Duffy**
to leave quickly *US, 1905*
A sprinter, in 1902 Duffy was the first to run the 100 yard dash in 9.6 seconds; he later wrote a sports column for the *Boston Post*.
- The court there sort of had a hunch that Alfonso might take it on the Arthur Duffy, so it slapped a $50,000 don't-go-away bond on him. —*San Francisco Examiner*, 5th June 1947
- The children took it on the Arthur Duffy. They went next door to watch TV. —*San Francisco Chronicle*, p. 33, 16 February 1971

Arthur Fowler *noun*
a fart *UK*
Rhyming slang for **GROWLER**; formed from a character who appeared in BBC television soap opera *EastEnders*.
- [S]omeone did an Arthur Fowler so bad that the whole carriage empties[.] —Bodmin Dark, *Dirty Cockney Rhyming Slang*, 2003

Arthur Lowe; Arthur *noun*
no *UK: SCOTLAND*
Glasgow rhyming slang, formed from the English actor, 1915–82, who is fondly remembered for *Dad's Army*, BBC, 1968–77 and still repeating.
- —Michael Munro, *The Patter, Another Blast*, 1988

artic *noun*
an articulated lorry *UK, 1951*
- Big artics out the back, loads of blokes with ponytails an' arsehole cleavages humpin' gear around. —Ben Elton, *High Society*, p. 214, 2002

artichoke *noun*
LSD *US*
From the code name for the drug devised by the Central Intelligence Agency during its early experimentation with the drug.
- —*Q Magazine*, p. 75, February 2001

article *noun*
a person, usually of a type denoted *UK, 1811*
Jocular, derogatory.
- Examples heard by me during the 1950s: nosey article, inquisitive; sloppy article; toffee-nosed article. —*Patridge*, 1961
- (DAVE FARTS AGAIN) MAM: (TO DAVE) You dirty article. —Caroline Aherne and Craig Cash, *The Royle Family*, 1999

artificial *noun*
an object the name of which escapes the speaker at the moment *BARBADOS*
- —*Barbadian Dialect*, p. 12, 1965
- —Frank A. Collymore, *Barbadian Dialect*, p. 12, 1965

artillery *noun*

1 guns *US, 1822*

- "Why all the artillery?" I asked him. —Mickey Spillane, *I, The Jury*, p. 34, 1947
- I told my cats to get their artillery. I sent Frenchy back with the car and I went for my pistol. —Hal Ellson, *Duke*, p. 165, 1949
- If you do that, we can stow these damn cannons and arm bands in a locker. Because it's no fun having to eat with artillery on your hip and all. —Darryl Ponicsan, *The Last Detail*, p. 37, 1970
- Only there was no audience, just the guards and their artillery. —Red Rudensky, *The Gonif*, p. 13, 1970
- I ran downstairs and hid all the artillery again. —Edwin Torres, *Carlito's Way*, p. 109, 1975
- This cat was real serious about his artillery. —*48 Hours*, 1982
- COP 1: What kind of artillery? SECRET 1: Perp's brandishing a shotgun. —*Mallrats*, 1995

2 in boxing, heavy blows *US*

- When he was ready to cut loose with his heavy artillery, Carter had no trouble scoring with sharp, hurting blows. —*San Francisco Examiner*, p. 28, 19th November 1954
- Rocky was tossing those artillery shells of his all night at Archie, who weathered them for nine rounds. —*San Francisco Call-Bulletin*, p. 12, 1st December 1956

3 in other sports, something accomplished from a distance *US*

- Dodgers Use Long-Ball Artillery to Clip Bucs 3-0 (Headline)— *San Francisco Chronicle*, 11th August 1957
- St. Mary's long range artillery, led by chief fire control officer LaRay Doss, shelled Santa Clara's zone defense into ruins last night. —*San Francisco Chronicle*, p. 1H, 17th January 1958

4 the equipment needed to inject a drug *US, 1915*

- A cabinet was filled with other "artillery" – the legal connotation addicts give shooting gadgets. —*San Francisco News*, p. 1, 5th December 1951
- —Charles Siragusa, *The Trail of the Poppy*, p. 223, 1966

5 strict discipline; a greater power *US*

- But, before you bring in the heavy artillery, try a more gentle persuasion. —*San Francisco Examiner*, p. 6, 13th June 1954

6 baked beans, or any food producing flatulence *US, 1916*

- —Vincent J. Monteleone, *Criminal Slang*, p. 12, 1949

artillery ears *noun*

partial deafness caused by exposure to the loud noise of the artillery *US*

- After nine years without any improvement, I realized that my "artillery ears" (as they were known by military tradition) were never going to get any better. —David H. Hackworth, *About Face*, p. 349, 1982

artish *noun*

an issue of a single-interest fan magazine containing mostly illustrations *US*

- —*American Speech*, p. 23, Spring 1982: 'The langage of science fiction fan magazines'

artist *noun*

1 a person who is proficient at the activity that precedes *AUSTRALIA, 1889*

- Conkey Tonks, lightning change artist, now emerged in vivacious mood. —Norman Lindsay, *The Cousin from Fiji*, p. 190, 1945
- I wasn't convinced, but this guy was such a gab-artist, damn if he didn't talk me into it. —Mezz Mezzrow, *Really the Blues*, p. 335, 1946
- Michael Kerrigan, a 63 year old bogus check artist who offered to buy the liner Matsonia for $3,500,000, unconcernedly heard himself sentenced to a one to ten year term for forgery yesterday. —*San Francisco Examiner*, p. 28, 2nd July 1948
- He was a tool dresser in the oil field, and I guess a fairly good bad-check artist. —Dan Jenkins, *Semi-Tough*, p. 50, 1972
- It wasn't the kind of place a holdup artist would hit. —Mickey Spillane, *Last Cop Out*, p. 34, 1972
- Guy used to be the super in Roger's building. Cornhole artist. —Edwin Torres, *Q & A*, p. 88, 1977
- The hangers on, the rip-off artists, that is. —*Drugstore Cowboy*, 1988
- "Call up North," Shad said. "Get a real torch artist." —Carl Hiaasen, *Strip Tease*, p. 277, 1993
- "You saying I'm a bullshit artist?" "One of the best." —Elmore Leonard, *Be Cool*, p. 10–11, 1999

2 a person who is devoted to, or especially proficient in, a reprehensible activity *US, 1890*

- I hope no-one's seriously suggesting we've more than one artist bucketing about with a knife in one hand and his cock-robin in the other. —Michael Kenyon, *The Rapist*, 1977

artist for the government *noun*

a person who receives unemployment insurance payments *CANADA*

- "I'm an Artist for the Government" is what you say [around Moncton NB] when you're drawing pogie. —David Mazerolle, *Avant tu take off, please close the lights*, p. n.p., 1993

arts *noun*

▸ **the arts**

martial arts *BERMUDA*

- My boy studies the arts, don't mess wif him! —Peter A. Smith and Fred M. Barritt, *Bermewjan Vurds*, 1985

artsy *adjective*

artistic in a pretentious, vulgar way *UK*

- [Princess Superstar's] reach goes beyond the artsy raparazzi to the record-buying masses[.] —*The Times Magazine*, p. 45, 16th February 2002

artsy-craftsy *adjective*

pretentiously artistic but not notably useful or comfortable *UK, 1902*

- For one, he has never moved his business out of the artsy-craftsy atmosphere of Greenwich Village. —Robert Sylvester, *No Cover Charge*, p. 243, 1956
- —*Current Slang*, p. 1, Summer 1968
- Doctrinaire and elitist. Artsy-craftsy. —Joan Didion, *The White Album*, p. 77, 1970
- Don't go back, it's all artsy-craftsy over there now. Hurley Brothers Funeral Home, they change the name of Death 'n Things. —Elmore Leonard, *Glitz*, p. 119–120, 1985

artsy-fartsy *adjective*

excessively arty *US*

Not exactly praise.

- [A]n artsy-fartsy director had shot a Western with such low-key lighting that it looked as though the wranglers were herding cattle inside a shoe[.] —Max Shulman, *Anyone Got a Match?*, p. 106, 1964
- "United Pictures, Ltd." was one of those mid-sized movie studios that pushed a bunch of now famous actors through, specialized in "small" pictures (nothing arsy fartsy) that made money... —Odie Hawkins, *Lost Angeles*, p. 61, 1994

arty *noun*

artillery *US, 1864*

- Lootenant, they're kicking our ass, they know we're gonna bring heavy shit on 'em pretty soon so they're gonna get in tight under the arty. —*Platoon*, 1986
- They've got fists of iron and nerves of steel / If the "quick" don't get you, then the Arties will. —Sandee Shaffer Johnson, *Cadences*, p. 76, 1986
- —Gregory Clark, *Words of the Vietnam War*, p. 35, 1990

arty-farty *adjective*

pretentious, artificially cultural *US*

- Look for the Gangsters of the New Freedom at the arty-farty and big-business cocktail parties[.] —G. Legman, *The Fake Revolt*, p. 13, 1967
- [T]here are too many "arty farty" films and too much "heritage movie-making". —*The Guardian*, 1st November 2002

arty roller *noun*

a collar *AUSTRALIA, 1945*

Rhyming slang.

arva; harva *noun*

sexual intercourse *UK*

Derives from Romany *charva* (to interfere with). Anal intercourse is the **FULL HARVA**.

- [T]o have the arva. —Paul Baker, *Polari*, p. 163, 2002

Arvin *noun*

any South Vietnamese soldier *US*

The South Vietnamese Army was known as the ARVN (*A*rmy of the *R*epublic of *V*iet *N*am); it took one vowel and very little imagination to get to Arvin.

- Sace and Handson, and a Vietnamese soldier, an Arvin, are already in the rear. —William Wilson, *The LBJ Brigade*, p. 33, 1966
- —Linda Reinberg, *In the Field*, p. 11, 1991

ARVN attitude *noun*

cowardice *US*

Not particularly kind to the South Vietnamese Army (ARVN).

- —Linda Reinberg, *In the Field*, p. 12, 1991

arvo *noun*

afternoon *AUSTRALIA, 1927*

From the first syllable of 'afternoon' (with voicing of the 'f') and -o suffix. Extremely common colloquially, usually in the phrase 'this arvo', giving rise to the common reanalysis 'the sarvo'. Other forms, rare in print, are 'afto', the simple 'arve' and also 'aftie' and 'arvie'.

- I'll try an' drop back this arvo an' see how yer goin'. —Nino Culotta (John O'Grady), *They're A Weird Mob*, p. 34, 1957
- It's a nice arvo and we'll trot back. —J.E. MacDonnell, *Don't Gimme the Ships*, p. 145, 1960
- Jeez, what a snidger time we had on them bygone arvoes! —Barry Humphries, *The Wonderful World of Barry McKenzie*, p. 15, 1968
- [H]e screamed and said if there wasn't thirty quid in the mail by this arvo he'd come and strip the joint – TV, 'fridge, washing machine, the ruddy lot. —Geoff Wyatt, *Saltwater Saints*, p. 20, 1969
- JJJeez, I could do with one this arve. Bugger it, I'll have a go. —Sam Weller, *Old Bastards I Have Met*, p. 10, 1979
- Well young man, I'm going to put you into surgery this arvo and give you a good hard probe. —Paul Vautin, *Turn It Up!*, p. 61, 1995
- Late in the arvo his team came to him[.] —Kel Richards, *The Aussie Bible*, p. 41, 2003
- I have never seen this written before and always thought it was 'this arvey'. — *Wordmap (www.abc.net.au/wordmap)*, 2003
- In South Australia the term "this arftie" is used instead of arvo. — *Wordmap (www.abc.net.au/wordmap)*, 2003

as

as can be *AUSTRALIA*

- 'Thought you boys could learn a lesson.' *'Boys?'* Tristram objected, offended. 'What did *I* do? Unfair as.' —Linda Jaivin, *Rock n Roll Babes from Outer Space*, p. 65, 1996

as all get out

as can be *AUSTRALIA, 1964*

- It was then that he met up with Pancho: big as a bus, arrogant as all get out by the set of his head and the fire in his eye. —Wilda Moxham, *The Apprentice*, p. 79, 1969

asap; ASAP

1 *as* soon *as* possible *US, 1955*

Originally military; either spoken as an acronym spelt out and stressed or vocalised as 'A-sap' in the US, 'assap' in the UK.

- Let's finish this thing off A-sap. —Christopher Brookmyre, *Not the End of the World*, p. 245, 1998
- Mr Hadden wants you back at base, Scoop. Like pronto. Asap. Etc. —David Peace, *Nineteen Seventy-Four*, p. 78, 1999
- You wanted to get down to doing the in-bed, on-the-floor, in-the-bath stuff a.s.a.p. —John Williams, *Cardiff Dead*, p. 31, 2000

2 *as* slowly *as* possible *CANADA*

Facetious, bitter variant on 'as soon as possible'.

- I am working ASAP – as slowly as possible. I got the pink slip yesterday. — *Toronto Globe and Mail*, p. D12, 3rd August 2002

asbestos pants *noun*

in poker, used for describing what a player on a very good streak of luck needs *US*

- —George Percy, *The Language of Poker*, p. 59, 1988

A-sex *noun*

sex experienced while under the influence of amphetamine *US*

- Others joined them writing in insatiable A-sex. —Ed Sanders, *Tales of Beatnik Glory*, p. 210, 1975

ash *noun*

marijuana *UK, 1990s*

The dropped 'h' of the London accent causes a punning variant on HASH.

ash *verb*

to drop cigarette ash *AUSTRALIA, 1930*

- I carefully ashed my cigarette on the bed post, wondering what to say. —Frank Moorhouse, *Futility and other animals*, p. 19, 1969
- Women whose clothes are obviously Works of Art – Heaven help you if you laugh hysterically when someone ashes on them and they catch fire. —Ignatius Jones, *True Hip*, p. 127, 1990

ashcan *noun*

1 a depth charge *US, 1918*

- We had ashcans on the stern of the vessel. — *New York Times*, p. 29, 1st January 1987
- —J.E. Lighter, *Historical Dictionary of American Slang*, p. 36, 1994

2 a small, powerful, cylindrical firecracker *US, 1970*

- —Frederic G. Cassidy, *Dicitonary of American Regional English, Volume 1*, p. 95, 1985

3 in the television and film industries, an arc light roughly shaped like a rubbish bin *US, 1942*

- —Wilfred Granville, *The Theater Dictionary*, p. 8, 1952

Ashcan City *nickname*

during the Korean war, a US Army processing centre eight miles from Inchon *US*

From ASCOM (*A*rmy *S*ervice *Com*mand) to 'Ascom City' to 'Ashcan City'.

- —Paul Dickson, *War Slang*, p. 236, 1994

ash cash *noun*

a fee paid to doctors for signing a cremation form *UK*

Medical slang.

- The hon. Member for Woodspring (Dr. Fox) mentioned the discredited "ash cash" arrangement, whereby, basically, a doctor countersigns the reputation of a colleague without actually doing much in the way of work. —Dr. Brand, *UK Parliament Hansard*, 23rd January 2001
- —Adam T. Fox, St Mary's Hospital, London, 10th October 2002

as he has to be *adverb*

used as an intensifier *US*

Follows an adjective, such as 'fine as he has to be'.

- —Anna Scotti and Paul Young, *Buzzwords*, p. 50, 1997

ashes *noun*

marijuana *US, 1977*

- —Richard A. Spears, *The Slang and Jargon of Drugs and Drink*, p. 15, 1986
- —Mike Haskins, *Drugs*, p. 286, 2003

▸ **get your ashes hauled**

to be brought to ejaculation *US, 1906*

- Then he said, "Kimberly, it's very plain to me what you need. You need to get your ashes hauled. This morning. If you went out and got your ashes hauled right now, it'd do wonders for you." —Frederic Wakeman, *The Hucksters*, p. 88, 1946
- They ain't been in my place yet to get their ashes hauled —Chester Himes, *A Rage in Harlem*, p. 47, 1957
- I repeat this one bit of smut only to show what sort of fellows I've been forced to live with – they're going to get their ashes hauled! —Robert Gover, *One Hundred Dollar Misunderstanding*, p. 10, 1961
- I'm just from behind those gray prison walls / so you can see I'm got to get my ashes hauled. —Bruce Jackson, *Get Your Ass in the Water and Swim Like Me*, p. 125, 1965
- I still get beautiful ladies to haul my ashes when my old balls get heavy. —Iceberg Slim (Robert Beck), *Mama Black Widow*, p. 293, 1969
- "Get the old ashes hauled." Billy and Mule look at each other. "Ashes hauled?" "That's an expression, kinda like, that means, you know, to do it, get it done." —Darryl Ponicsan, *The Last Detail*, p. 119, 1970
- Even the company shitsack got his ashes hauled while we were there. —Larry Heinemann, *Paco's Story*, p. 126, 1986
- This one was set up by Lorrie, her ditzy pal from The Fabric Barn, who knew a guy who had a friend who'd been 'out of circulation for a while' (whatever that means – prison if you ask me) and wanted his ashes hauled in the worst kind of way. —Armistead Maupin, *Maybe the Moon*, p. 222, 1992

ashtray *noun*

the desert *US*

Gulf war usage.

- — *American Speech*, p. 383, Winter 1991: 'Among the new words'

Asian moll *noun*

a prostitute with an Asian customer base *US, 1982*

- —Harry Orsman, *A Dictionary of Modern New Zealand Slang*, p. 67, 1999

Asian two-step *noun*

any highly venomous snake encountered in the jungles of Southeast Asia *US, 1966*

From the belief that the venom will kill the victim within two steps of the bite.

- —J.E. Lighter, *Historical Dictionary of American Slang*, p. 37, 1994

Asiatic *adjective*

deranged *US*

- — *American Speech*, p. 302, December 1955: 'Wayne University slang'

Asia West *nickname*

Richmond, a town in British Columbia *CANADA*

- Throughout Richmond, there are shopping centres and supermarkets that evoke today's Asia so strongly it's no wonder they call it Asia West. — *Montreal Gazette*, p. F2, 22nd May 2002

as if!

used as a humorous expression of extreme skepticism *US*

- —Connie Eble (Editor), *UNC-CH Campus Slang*, p. 1, March 1981
- BEJAMIN: Did you really think I wouldn't end up with the girl. GARTH: As if. — *Wayne's World*, 1992

- He said my debates were unresearched, unstructured, and unconvincing. As if! — *Clueless*, 1995
- "Then we'd get in our sleeping bags and hump our stuffed animals until we came." "As if." — Amy Sohn, *Run Catch Kiss*, p. 116, 1999
- I think they were worried about putting me too near the wedding presents. As if? — Danny King, *The Burglar Diaries*, p. 49, 2001
- "That Stig from Club Wicked is really getting on my nerves." "Why?" "All that backs to the wall crap. I mean, as if? I'm gay, not blind." — Colin Butts, *Is Harry Still on the Boat?*, p. 206, 2003

ask *noun*

1 a request *AUSTRALIA, 1994*
Generally in the collocation 'big ask'.
- That's a hard ask, Min, but I guess I'll promise. — *Sun-Herald (Super Scene)*, p. 1, 13th April 1997

2 the asking price for a racehorse *AUSTRALIA*
A horse with a 'big ask' is deemed by the speaker to be over-priced.
- — Ned Wallish, *The Truth Dictionary of Racing Slang*, p. 2, 1989

ask *verb*

▸ **ask for six and go airborne**
to request the rotation travel allowance of six cents a mile in order to fly home *US*
- — Linda Reinberg, *In the Field*, p. 12, 1991

▸ **ask the question**
to ask someone to have sex *GUYANA*
- — Richard Allsopp, *Dictionary of Caribbean English Usage*, p. 45, 1996

▸ **ask what you have to sell**
to invite sex *BARBADOS*
- — Richard Allsopp, *Dictionary of Caribbean English Usage*, p. 45, 1996

ask yourself!
be reasonable! *AUSTRALIA, 1942*

as like as not *adverb*
▹ see: LIKE AS NOT

as my pappy would say...
used as a humorous introduction or segue *US*
A signature line from *Maverick*, an early and popular television Western (ABC, 1957–62). Repeated with referential humour.

asparagus *noun*

1 a boy's penis *US*
From the language of child pornography.
- In court Monday, Schopp said his computer had inadvertently downloaded some of the images as he searched the Internet for asparagus recipes. Wilken noted that asparagus is apparently a slang term for boys' genitalia. — *San Francisco Chronicle*, p. A17, 28th October 2003

2 in horse racing, a bettor who arrives at the track with an armful of racing forms *AUSTRALIA*
From the observation that the bettor 'has more tips than a tin of asparagus'.
- — Ned Wallish, *The Truth Dictionary of Racing Slang*, p. 2, 1989

aspendicitis *noun*
a notional medical condition of a symptomatic need to spend money *US*
A humorous diagnosis, playing on 'spend' and 'appendicitis'. The earliest use is as the title of a 1961 jazz composition by Peter Shickele.

asphalt eater *noun*
a drag racer who performs well *US*
- — John Lawlor, *How to Talk Car*, p. 16, 1964

asphalt jungle *noun*
a large city *US, 1920*
The title of a 1949 book by W. R. Burnett as well as an ABC television series starring Jack Warden in 1961.
- Shall we take a new stance toward the City and its mass culture – a tougher stance, a more nervy one – so that we may learn to live more gracefully and meaningfully in this Asphalt Jungle we have constructed around us? (Letter to Editor) — *San Francisco Chronicle*, p. 2, 28th December 1952
- "I'm not anxious. I've been waiting too long," her owner and skipper Bradford Simmons said. "I'm free of the asphalt jungle." — *San Francisco Examiner*, p. 17, 19th November 1964

asphalt pilot *noun*
a truck driver *US*
- — Wayne Floyd, *Jason's Authentic Dictionary of CB Slang*, p. 8, 1976

aspirin smoke *noun*
a cigarette adulterated with crushed aspirin, providing a drug-like effect *US*
- — Jay Robert Nash, *Dictionary of Crime*, p. 12, 1992

aspro *noun*
▹ see: ASS PRO

ass *noun*

1 the buttocks, the posterior *US, 1853*
- Samuel slapped Joe's ass lightly. "Like this?" he squeaked, and spanked Joe again. — Dennis Cooper, *Frisk*, p. 49, 1991

2 the vagina *UK, 1684*
- Why, the day he was dropped from his mammy's ass / he slapped his pappy's face. — Bruce Jackson, *Get Your Ass in the Water and Swim Like Me*, p. 58, 1970
- I had saved my hankie that I wiped Ruth's ass out with after we had had our taste of sex, because I had a real freak of a nigger that I was gonna sell a smell of it to after I got back in the joint. — A.S. Jackson, *Gentleman Pimp*, p. 66, 1973
- Why same day he dropped from his mammy's ass / Dolomite rear up slap his pappy's face. — Seth Morgan, *Homeboy*, p. 95, 1990

3 sex; a person as a sexual object *US, 1910*
- The other numerous downtown clubs would not serve us, nor would the white prostitutes sell black G.I.s any ass. — Bobby Seale, *A Lonely Rage*, p. 106, 1978
- And here's what I want you to do: I want you to sell your ass. I'll be in the car waiting. — Chris Rock, *Rock This!*, p. 186, 1997

4 the self; a person *US, 1945*
- Not a living ass in that band could read a note except Elmer Schobel. — Mezz Mezzrow, *Really the Blues*, p. 51, 1946
- Gramma said you better get your filthy ass out of this garden. — Cecil Brown, *The Life & Loves of Mr. Jiveass Nigger*, p. 6, 1969
- Now that's a hard motherfuckin' fact of life, but it's a fact of life your ass is gonna hafta git realistic about. — *Pulp Fiction*, 1994
- My first thought is, "Hey, thanks a lot, man. Thanks for taking her ugly ass off our hands, because we didn't know what we were going to do about her." — Chris Rock, *Rock This!*, p. 129, 1997

5 a fool *UK, 1578*
From the level of intelligence stereotypically credited to the animal.
- Why Tony Benn is an ass[.] — *The Guardian*, 6th February 2003

▸ **ass on fire**
said of a person who is either angry or rushed *US*
- — Terrence M. Steele, *Streettalk Thesaurus*, p. 23

▸ **bring ass to kick ass**
to have the courage needed to fight someone *US*
- You gotta bring ass to kick ass, so come on wid it. — *New Jack City*, 1990

▸ **bust your ass**
to hurry, to exert yourself; to work extremely hard *US, 1941*
- I bust my ass all day to take home a hundred and seventy bucks a week and I just can't swing the kind of money it costs. — George V. Higgins, *The Friends of Eddie Doyle*, p. 33, 1971
- He had always believed Hispanic girls would bust their ass to go out with a white man. — Elmore Leonard, *Maximum Bob*, p. 250, 1991
- One morning I heard my bell ring at dawn. I figured it was the UPS man with a package. I busted my ass down the stairs, trembling, because I couldn't wait to get my hands on that bubble wrap. — Chris Rock, *Rock This!*, p. 67, 1997

▸ **case of the ass**
anger; frustration *US*
Vietnam war usage.
- — Carl Fleischhauer, *A Glossary of Army Slang*, p. 8, 1968

▸ **eat your ass out**
to berate someone *US*
- The magistrate, a lovely, intelligent woman, dismissed the charge and ate the ass out of the assistant U.S. attorney for being overzealous. — Elmore Leonard, *Out of Sight*, p. 64, 1996

▸ **in ass**
in trouble *TRINIDAD AND TOBAGO, 1980*
- — Lise Winer, *Dictionary of the English/Creole of Trinidad & Tobago*, 2003

▸ **take it up the ass**
to take the passive role in anal intercourse *US*
- "There's a lady lawyer at the end of the bar that likes to take it in the ass," he said. — Gerald Petievich, *To Die in Beverly Hills*, p. 93, 1983
- As long as you done your time nice, you didn't rat anybody out, and you never took it in the ass. — Vincent Patrick, *Family Business*, p. 55, 1985
- Padraig Byrne took it up the arse. — Chris Ryan, *The Watchman*, p. 13, 2001

▸ up your ass!; up your arse!
an expression of contempt, rejection or derision *US, 1956*

▸ your ass is grass
used for conveying the state of being in great trouble *US, 1956*
- I never heard the man so pissed. They ass is grass, whoever it is. —Vernon E. Smith, *The Jones Men*, p. 40, 1974
- Else my ass would be grass by now. —Edwin Torres, *Carlito's Way*, p. 74, 1975
- Yo' ass was grass, but he saved you. —Edwin Torres, *Q & A*, p. 39, 1977
- If it all comes down, your ass is new-mown grass. —*48 Hours*, 1982

▸ your ass off
greatly intensifies the effort made in doing something *US, 1946*
- Now you see it poppin off, got you in the club dancing your ass off[.] —Petey Pablo, *I Told Y'All*, 2001
- Nikosi [Johnson] who is slowly succumbing to the disease [AIDS] is being propped up with an expensive cocktail of drugs so that he can "continue working his ass off", as foster mother Gail Johnson puts it. —*The Hindu*, 9th December 2001

ass *verb*
to engage in prostitution *US*
- —William T. Vollman, *Whores for Gloria*, p. 139, 1991

ass *adjective*
terrible, bad *US*
- [T]he cha ("very cool") worlds include: "winded" for hung over; "craftsman" for a complete idiot; and "ass" for awful. —*Washington Times*, p. C3, 26th August 1992

-ass; -assed *suffix*
used as an intensifier for the preceding adjective or adverb *US, 1903*
- "Get up the stairs, you sassy-assed bitch," yelled Agent No. 3. —Tom Robbins, *Another Roadside Attraction*, p. 110, 1971
- A punk-ass kid I was, but I looked it over. —Edwin Torres, *Carlito's Way*, p. 10, 1975
- Shit, it was only about seven miles long, I don't know what we needed it for, little piss-ass island. —Elmore Leonard, *Bandits*, p. 272, 1987
- Plus we're gonna send for a free specialist so you're not at the mercy of those sorry-ass state sawbones. —Seth Morgan, *Homeboy*, p. 288, 1990
- I've seen a lot of crazy-ass shit in my time —*Pulp Fiction*, 1994
- Big ass – huge, enormous. —Connie Eble (Editor), *UNC-CH Campus Slang*, p. 1, March 1996
- Do you know how depressing it is to sit in the same room you two sat in when you were both 14? There's the little-ass dresser, the little-ass bed, and the poster of Tony Doreset on the wall. —Chris Rock, *Rock This!*, p. 93, 1997
- Why are we listening to this whiny-ass music? —*American Beauty*, 1999
- Jeff was in the studio playin' with this old-ass piano. —Eminem (Marshall Mathers), *Angry Blonde*, 2001

ass-and-trash *noun*
during the Vietnam war, people and cargo to be transported by aeroplane *US*
- We flew three missions of local ass-and-trash, single-ship stuff. —Robert Mason, *Chickenhawk*, p. 394, 1983
- The first thing that happened to helicopter pilots when they arrived in Vietnam was assignment to a platoon that flew "slicks," the Hueys used for troop and and cargo transport, or "Ash and Trash" missions. —Dennis Marvicsin and Jerold Greenfield, *Maverick*, p. 36, 1990

ass-ass *verb*
to humiliate yourself *US*
- —Connie Eble (Editor), *UNC-CH Campus Slang*, p. 1, November 2002

ass backwards *adverb*
in reverse order *US, 1942*
- With this joker, the more he lapped it up, the more he got his words ass backwards. —Bernard Wolfe, *The Late Risers*, p. 42, 1954
- "I think you got it ass-backwards," Majestyk said, returning the keys to his pocket. "I'm not going with you, you're going with me." —Elmore Leonard, *Mr. Majestyk*, p. 52, 1974
- All of my information on the Army indicated that they did things so ass backwards that if you were on the west coast they'd send you to the east (France or Italy or somewhere) and vice versa. —Odie Hawkins, *Scars and Memories*, p. 73, 1987

ass bandit; arse bandit; asshole bandit *noun*
a male homosexual, especially the active partner in anal sex *US*
Usually derogatory; combines **ASS** with 'bandit' – or 'brigand', conventionally a generally romantic image of a villain who will take what he wants.
- Which is, dear reader, the true story of this particular asshole bandit[.] —Angelo d'Arcangelo, *The Homosexual Handbook*, p. 78, 1968
- —*Maledicta*, p. 222, 1979: 'Kinks and queens: linguistic and cultural aspects of the terminology for gays'
- Neither of them fell for the 'arse bandit' routine, being both ugly enough and tough enough to not have to worry about any hocks fancying them. —Clive Galea, *Slipper*, p. 86, 1988
- You filthy little arse-bandits should all be nailed to a tree. —John Birmingham, *He Died With a Felafel in his Hand*, p. 15, 1994
- He was strident, self-assured and overtly gay. "Ah, fuck off, you, you arsebandit!" —Kevin Sampson, *Powder*, p. 338, 1999
- The guy was an arse-bandit. Not as good as him being a paedophile or having shares in McDonalds, but it would do. —Christopher Brookmyre, *Boiling a Frog*, p. 119, 2000
- Thinks he's running the show, by the way – fucking arse bandit! —Kevin Sampson, *Clubland*, p. 153, 2002

ass bite *noun*
harsh criticism *US*
- I felt like he was lots older and a damn sight wiser and took the assbite without looking at him. —Joseph Wambaugh, *The Blue Knight*, p. 77, 1973

ass-blow *verb*
to lick, suck and tongue another's anus *US, 1941*
- —Dale Gordon, *The Dominion Sex Dictionary*, p. 23, 1967

ass bucket *noun*
a despised person *US, 1953*
- —J.E. Lighter, *Historical Dictionary of American Slang*, p. 45, 1994

ass burglar *noun*
the active partner in anal sex; more generally, a male homosexual *US*
- —*Maledicta*, p. 231, 1979: 'Kinks and queens: linguistic and cultural aspects of the terminology for gays'

ass cache *noun*
a supply of drugs hidden in the rectum *US*
- —Jay Robert Nash, *Dictionary of Crime*, p. 12, 1992

ass chewing *noun*
a harsh reprimand or scold *US, 1954*
- A vice president of manufacturing once quit the day Paul Allegretto took over as president of his division, complaining that he was not going to put up with Allegretto's "long hours, harsh demands and ass chewing." —*American Metal Market*, p. S5, 2nd January 1984
- "When accolades were coming, he'd give them to you," Martinez added. "And when an ass-chewing was coming, he'd give them, too, and I always appreciated that about him." —*Star Tribune (Minneapolis)*, p. 1B, 7th November 2003

ass cunt *noun*
the anus *US*
Analogised to a vagina.
- Wowee, will you look at that little white kid's ass-cunt. That's a cherry if I ever saw one. —Piri Thomas, *Seven Long Times*, p. 67, 1974

assed out *adjective*
in severe trouble *US*
- Now if you ain't got none, you just assed out. —*Menace II Society*, 1993
- —Lois Stavsky et al., *A2Z*, p. 2, 1995

ass end *noun*
the least desirable part of anything *US*
- —*American Speech*, p. 54, February 1947: 'Pacific War language'
- [T]heir plight caught the ass end of a brief burst of black unity. —Jess Mowry, *Way Past Cool*, p. 29, 1992

ass ends *noun*
the differentials of a truck tractor *US*
- —*American Speech*, p. 273, December 1961: 'Northwest truck drivers' language'

ass English *noun*
the body movements and incantations of a dice shooter who believes that he can control the roll of the dice *US*
- —*The Annals of the American Academy of Political and Social Sciences*, p. 120, May 1950

assets *noun*
the genitals, especially the male genitals *UK*
- I swung one into his derby and he woofed like a dog. I followed it with a really low one, right in the assets. —Lenny McLean, *The Guv'nor*, p. 82, 1998

ass fuck *noun*
1 anal sex *US, 1940*
- It seems like they were having more fun back then. Now it's like, um, you want to do an ass fuck for $250 real quick? —*LA Weekly*, p. 31, 19th November 1999

2 a despicable person *US*
- He'd call her a "stupid ass-fuck" and throw her against the wall, she says. — *Cleveland Scene*, 8th November 2001

ass-fuck *verb*
to engage in anal sex, especially in the active role *US, 1940*
- He denies saying he wanted to "ass fuck" the man, but agrees he was out of line. — *Cleveland Scene*, 2nd August 2001
- Whereas she won't even touch herself when you're around, say she invites him to ass-fuck her and howls like a banshee? — *Seattle Weekly*, 4th October 2001

ass fucker *noun*
the active partner in anal sex *US*
- — *Maledicta*, p. 230, 1979: 'Kinks and queens: linguistic and cultural aspects of the terminology for gays'

ass fucking *noun*
anal sex *US*
- Ass-fucking in general, never so much as crossed my mind until about two years ago[.] — *Screw*, p. 15, 15th March 1970

ass gasket *noun*
a disposable paper toilet seat cover *US*
- — Michael Dalton Johnson, *Talking Trash with Redd Foxx*, p. 129, 1994

ass hammer *noun*
a motorcyle *US*
- — *American Speech*, p. 55, Spring-Summer 1975: 'Razorback slang'

asshole *noun*
1 the anus *US, 1935*
- He put his hands under my ass and then he plunged his cock into my asshole. — Augusten Burroughs, *Running with Scissors*, p. 159, 2002

2 a fool; a person held in contempt *US, 1933*
- The phone rang, Benny O. Bliss answered. "Mort Robell? That asshole. Well, put him on." — Bernard Wolfe, *The Late Risers*, p. 26, 1954
- "Then let the asshole beef," said Matthews, and Gus realized that they used 'asshole" as much here in the divisions as the instructors did in the academy and he guessed it was the favorite epithet of policemen[.] — Joseph Wambaugh, *The New Centurions*, p. 55, 1970
- You're an asshole. You're a fucking asshole. — George V. Higgins, *The Digger's Game*, p. 11, 1973
- Asshole is the going insult this year. Everybody's an asshole. Immediately! Without a moment's notice! Never mind the preliminaries! — Tom Wolfe, *Mauve Gloves & Madmen, Clutter and Vine*, p. 235, 1976
- You ain't nothing but an old stupid God damn fool, motherfucking asshole! — Bobby Seale, *A Lonely Rage*, p. 24–25, 1978
- I was switching gears ... forget about being a conceited asshole. — Jim Carroll, *Forced Entries*, p. 52, 1987
- My job requires mostly masking my contempt for the assholes in charge. — *American Beauty*, 1999

3 in logging and power line work, a kink in a cable *US, 1959*
- — Frederic G. Cassidy, *Dicitonary of American Regional English, Volume 1*, p. 99, 1985

▸ **from asshole to appetite**
all over *US*
- Covers me from asshole t'appetite. — Robert Gover, *Here Goes Kitten*, p. 114, 1964
- — Bill Casselman, *Canadian Sayings*, p. 17, 2002

▸ **your asshole's sucking wind**
you are talking nonsense *US, 1961*

asshole bandit *noun*
▷ **see:** ASS BANDIT

asshole buddy *noun*
a very close friend *US, 1945*
- — *American Speech*, p. 319, October/December 1948: 'Slang of the American paratrooper'
- I recall during the war at the Jockey Club in Cairo, me and my asshole buddy, Lud, both gentlemen by act of Congress. — William Burroughs, *Naked Lunch*, p. 92, 1957
- Meridian, you know that Mister Parnell ain't going to let them arrest his ass-hole buddy — James Baldwin, *Blues for Mister Charlie*, 1964
- — Carl Fleischhauer, *A Glossary of Army Slang*, p. 2, 1968
- I just hope I can keep playing good enough to make it a contest for our ass-hole buddy here. — Dan Jenkins, *Dead Solid Perfect*, p. 107, 1986
- "I mean you're calling this shyster Al, like he's an old friend." "Like he's your asshole buddy," Pat chimed in. — Robert Campbell, *Juice*, p. 155, 1988

asshole naked *adjective*
completely naked *US*
- I came in that hot summer day, took a shower and went to my bedroom asshole naked and layed down. — *Screw*, p. 5, 7th March 1969

asshole of creation *noun*
a remote, desolate place *US*
- Ain't it logical that I should appear here in Potts County, which is just about as close to the asshole of creation as you can get without havin' a finger snapped off? — Jim Thompson, *Pop. 1280*, p. 209, 1964

asshole of the world; arsehole of the world *noun*
the most despised place, area or location *US*
Other embelishments include 'areshole of the universe' or 'of the nation'.
- But you can't vote until you get your citizenship. Not here, not in this Dutch-infested ass-hole of the nation. — John O'Hara, *A Rage to Live*, p. 118, 1949
- Way down here in the ass-hole of the world, the deep, black, funky South. — James Baldwin, *Blues for Mister Charlie*, p. 31, 1964
- All pommies are bastards, bastards or worse. / And England is the arsehole of the universe. — *The Adventures of Barry McKenzie*, 1972
- When I'd last known him, Greg had been enormopusly wealthy, and here he was in the arsehole of the universe[.] — Robert English, *Toxic Kisses*, p. 49, 1979
- Besides, it had hit me about dawn, Australia was not the arsehole of the world. — Kathy Lette, *Girls' Night Out*, p. 115, 1987
- If the Amazon's the arsehole of the world, I reckon we're about 5,000 ks up it. — Chris Ryan, *Stand By, Stand By*, p. 191, 1996

assholes *noun*
▸ **assholes and elbows**
said of a chaotic situation *US*
- Quickly, ladies! Assholes and elbows! — *Full Metal Jacket*, 1987
- I mean, you should've seen it. All asses and elbows flying all over the goddam place. — Robert Campbell, *Juice*, p. 29, 1988

asshole to belly button *adjective*
said of people pressed close together, one behind the other *US*
- I remember when the slime-balls used to be packed in there solid, asshole to belly button, waiting to look at the skin show in the viewer. — Joseph Wambaugh, *The Blue Knight*, p. 26–27, 1973

ass hound *noun*
a man who obsessively engages in the pursuit of women for sex *US, 1952*
- — J.E. Lighter, *Historical Dictionary of American Slang*, p. 48, 1994

assified *adjective*
1 foolish *BARBADOS*
- — Frank A. Collymore, *Barbadian Dialect*, p. 12, 1965

2 pompous *GUYANA*
- — Richard Allsopp, *Dictionary of Caribbean English Usage*, p. 45, 1996

ass in a sling
in deep trouble *US*
- [I]f I made too many wrong moves, my ass was gon' be in another sling, so I had to proceed quietly. — Odie Hawkins, *Great Lawd Buddha*, p. 44, 1990

ass-in-the-grass test *noun*
a rough approximation of the percentage of troops actually in combat at a given moment *US*
Used in the Vietnam war.
- — Gregory Clark, *Words of the Vietnam War*, p. 37, 1990

assishness *noun*
pure stupidity *TRINIDAD AND TOBAGO*
- — Lise Winer, *Dictionary of the English/Creole of Trinidad & Tobago*, 2003

ass kickers *noun*
heavy work shoes or boots *US*
- — Connie Eble (Editor), *UNC-CH Campus Slang*, p. 1, March 1996

ass-kiss *verb*
to behave in an ingratiatingly sycophantic manner *US, 1961*
- Sure, I was ass-kissing the boss, but that's what employees do. — Walter Yetnikoff, *Howling at the Moon*, p. 192, 2004

ass-kisser; arse-kisser *noun*
a sycophant *US, 1766*
Combines **ARSE/ASS** (the buttocks) with conventional 'kisser'. As a demonstration of subservience the image is much older than the term; it can be seen in C16 woodcuts of devil-worshippers lifting the goat's tale to plant their kisses.
- "This guy is an ass-kisser for the company," Johnny whispered. — Piri Thomas, *Stories from El Barrio*, p. 11, 1978

• There had seldom been much danger of the Cardinal experiencing such a perspective, not as long as he moved in such exclusively Catholic circles and was permanently attended by arse-kissers like Toale. —Christopher Brookmyre, *Boiling a Frog*, p. 139, 2000

ass-kissing *noun*
sycophantic or ingratiating behaviour *US, 1942*
• My lips are permanently damaged from the amount of ass-kissing I did today. —Megan McCafferty, *Second Helpings*, p. 155, 2003

ass-kissing *adjective*
sycophantic *US, 1942*
• You ass-kissing little snitch! —John Waters, *Deperate Living*, p. 166, 1099
• Nicky looked him up after doing his time and that was how he got to meet Jimmy Cap and went to work for him: picking up Chinese takeout, lighting his cigars, getting him young girls, generally serving on an ass-kissing basis at first. —Elmore Leonard, *Pronto*, p. 218, 1993

ass-licking *adjective*
▷ see: ARSE-LICKING

ass man; arse man *noun*
a man who considers that the (suggestive) appearance of a woman's posterior provides the supreme initial sexual attraction; a man who so categorises himself *US*
• —Helen Dahlskog (Editor), *A Dictionary of Contemporary and Colloquial Usage*, p. 4, 1972
• [A]n ageing pornographer who specialised in videos devoted to anal sex – "the arse man of the millennium". —*The Guardian*, 8th May 2000

ass munch *noun*
a person who is easily despised *US*
• —Connie Eble (Editor), *UNC-CH Campus Slang*, p. 1, March 1996

assmuncher *noun*
a despised person *US*
• —Chris Lewis, *The Dictionary of Playground Slang*, p. 11, 2003

as soon as *adverb*
as soon as possible *UK*
A shortening of the conventional phrase.
• I'd like to see them as soon as. —J.J. Connolly, *Layer Cake*, p. 90, 2000

ass out *verb*
to make a fool of yourself *CANADA*
• —Bill Casselman, *Canadian Sayings*, p. 125, 2002

ass-out *adverb*
extremely *US*
• —Lois Stavsky et al., *A2Z*, p. 2, 1995

ass over tea kettle; ass over tea cups *adverb*
head over heels *US, 1948*
• They drop four head of cattle and blow two papa-sans ass over teakettle with the fifites. —Larry Heinemann, *Close Quarters*, p. 106, 1977
• Ass over teakettle onto the concrete, right on my wrist. —Robert Campbell, *Juice*, p. 29, 1988

ass peddler *noun*
a male prostitute *US*
• —*Maledicta*, p. 231, 1979: 'Kinks and queens: linguistic and cultural aspects of the terminology for gays'

ass pro; asspro; aspro *noun*
a male homosexual prostitute *AUSTRALIA, 1955*
A combination of **ASS** and 'pro(stitute)', but note Aspro™ the branded analgesic.
• —*Maledicta*, p. 145, Summer/Winter 1986–1987: 'Sexual slang: prostitutes, pedophiles, flagellators, transvestites, and necrophiles'

ass queen *noun*
a homosexual man who is particularly attracted to other men's buttocks *US*
• —Anon., *King Smut's Wet Dreams Interpreted*, 1978

ass ripper *noun*
a difficult course or test *US*
• —Collin Baker et al., *College Undergraduate Slang Study Conducted at Brown University*, p. 71, 1968

ass's gallop *noun*
a brief period of time *IRELAND*
• Mr. Wise had certainly perked up a lot in the initial months of his working in the shop, this had been as short and sweet as an ass's gallop. —Bernard Share, *Slanguage*, p. 7, 2003

ass time *noun*
time wasted sitting around *US*
• —Sally Williams, *"Strong" Words*, p. 133, 1994

assume *verb*
▸ **assume the angle; assume the position**
to kneel for punishment doled out as part of a hazing ritual *US, 1940*
• Next they told her to assume the angle – kneeling with her head down on her arms, which were flat on the floor. Her buttocks were up and her legs apart. —*Time*, p. 80, 13th January 1947
• "Assume the position." While the boy knelt and held his genitals, Roy went for the fraternity paddle —Geoffrey Wadiner, *The Asphalt Campus*, p. 83, 1963

asswipe; arsewipe *noun*
1 toilet paper *US, 1958*
• —Carl Fleischhauer, *A Glossary of Army Slang*, p. 2, 1968
• "Well, the old thief's got enough asswipe stashed to last a week," said Simeone in a loud voice. —Joseph Wambaugh, *The New Centurions*, p. 191, 1970
• —Helen Dahlskog (Editor), *A Dictionary of Contemporary and Colloquial Usage*, p. 4, 1972

2 by extension, a despicable or offensive person *US, 1952*
• Hey! You asswipes, scumbags! —*Saturday Night Fever*, 1977
• —Connie Eble (Editor), *UNC-CH Campus Slang*, p. 1, Fall 1986
• —Pamela Munro, *U.C.L.A. Slang*, p. 16, 1989
• (Sneezing) Ass-wipe! Ass-wipe! —*Wayne's World 2*, 1993
• FRANK: Is this the kind of language your employees use on duty? JOE: Well, Corey's usually very courteous. COREY: Asswipe. —*Empire Records*, 1995
• Hey, Puffy tried to warn you about that Steve guy you was seeing – he was a fucking asswipe – but you had to find out for yourself, didn't you. —*Something About Mary*, 1998
• Same little asswipe motherfuckers everywhere. —*Ten Things I Hate About You*, 1999
• Gotter stick up to some of these arse-wipes, ain't we? —Chris Baker and Andrew Day, *Lock, Stock... & One Big Bullock*, p. 374, 2000
• "Ray was the real deal, asswipe" Drucker hissed. —Stephen J. Cannell, *The Tin Collectors*, p. 30, 2001
• Those sneering, toffee-nosed, modern-novel-reading arse-wipes[.] —Frank Skinner, *Frank Skinner*, p. 72, 2001

A-state *nickname*
Arkansas *US*
• —Alonzo Westbrook, *Hip Hoptionary*, p. 4, 2002

asterisks *noun*
used as an all-purpose euphemism for any noun, singular or plural *UK*
From the publishers' convention of replacing offensive words or parts of words with an * for each missing letter.
• Decathlon is a mecca for us sad asterisks, the sporting equivalent of air guitarists. —*The Times Magazine*, 25th October 2003

as the feller says
used for introducing a statement which the speaker does not necessarily accept *US*
• —John Gould, *Maine Lingo*, p. 37, 1975

as the skua flies
in a straight line *ANTARCTICA, 1936*
Antarctica's adaption of the common 'as the crow flies', using instead the South Pole's predatory gull as the bird in question.
• —Bernadette Hince, *The Antarctic Dictionary*, p. 32, 2000

Astor's pet horse *noun*
used in comparisons with a person, especially a woman, who is over-dressed *US, 1950*
• —Frederic G. Cassidy, *Dicitonary of American Regional English, Volume 1*, p. 101, 1985
• In the 1700s up pops John (Johannes) Jakob Astor (Asdour), who now has hotels, Astor Place, Astoria, the phrase "dressed up like Astor's pet horse" and lots of stuff named for him. —*New York Post*, p. 14, 27th June 2003

astronaut *noun*
the buttocks or anus *US*
• —Chris Lewis, *The Dictionary of Playground Slang*, p. 11, 2003

astro turf *noun*
marijuana *UK*
• —Mike Haskins, *Drugs*, p. 286, 2003

as you do

as you do (but perhaps shouldn't) *AUSTRALIA*

A conversational interjection used to make a comic admission of some odd behaviour.

- They were entirely innocent. They felt guilty anyway. As you do. —Linda Jaivin, *Rock n Roll Babes from Outer Space*, p. 148, 1996

as you were

used for the retraction of a preceding statement *UK, 1864*

From the military drill command.

atari *noun*

crack cocaine *US*

- —Peter Johnson, *Dictionary of Street Alcohol and Drug Terms*, p. 11, 1993

A-Team *noun*

the basic functional unit of the US Special Forces in Vietnam, consisting of 10 to 12 trained commandos *US*

- —Gregory Clark, *Words of the Vietnam War*, p. 2–3, 1990

ate out *adjective*

(of trousers) worn, baggy, saggy *US*

- —Alonzo Westbrook, *Hip Hoptionary*, p. 4, 2002

ate up *adjective*

1 in the US Air Force, dedicated to service *US*

- —*Seattle Times*, p. A9, 12th April 1998

2 in the US Army, confused, dim *US*

- —*Seattle Times*, p. A9, 12th April 1998

Athenian *noun*

in homosexual usage, an anal sex enthusiast *US*

- —*Maledicta*, p. 56, 1986–1987: 'A continuation of a glossary of ethnic slurs in American English'

-athon *suffix*

used to create a word suggesting the root word activity carried on for a long period of time *US, 1934*

From 'marathon'.

- Another year of sitting on the platform at mass meetings in Madison Square Garden, of soirees in Greenwich Village and all-night talkathons at Sixth Avenue cafeterias[.]—Clancy Sigal, *Going Away*, p. 279, 1961
- Why the brother should be renting a room in a fuckathon motel is something that only he could answer, and I'm sure he could.—Odie Hawkins, *Black Casanova*, p. 158, 1984
- The finale of this sepia strokeathon pasri all the participants in a single room, where they're unleashed and let loose.—*Adult Video*, p. 32, August/September 1986
- There's something about all these modern walkathons and bikeathons that recalls the early middle ages, when you could acquire indulgences by paying other people to say masses or make pilgrimages on your behalf.—Geoff Nunberg, *Fresh Air (National Public Radio)*, 2nd November 1999
- [B]ackslapathon, hiphopathon, orgasmathon, thinkathon, blubathon, slimathon[.]—Susie Dent, *The Language Report*, p. 17, 2003

at it *adjective*

1 engaged in criminal activity *UK*

- —G.F. Newman, *Sir, You Bastard*, 1970
- For working-class people to get a living in those days, you had to be involved in some sort of villainy or be "at it", so everybody was breaking the law just to put bread on the table.—Lenny McLean, *The Guv'nor*, p. 2, 1998

2 engaged in sexual intercourse *AUSTRALIA*

- She's got another one now. She's at it again.—Dorothy Hewett, *The Chapel Perilous*, p. 22, 1972

ATL *nickname*

Atlanta, Georgia *US*

- —Alonzo Westbrook, *Hip Hoptionary*, p. 4, 2002

ATM *noun*

a generous person *US*

From the most common US name for a bank's *a*utomatic *t*eller *m*achine.

- —Anna Scotti and Paul Young, *Buzzwords*, p. 49, 1997

a toda madre!

excellent! *US*

Border Spanish used in English conversation by Mexican-Americans.

- —Dagoberto Fuentes and Jose Lopez, *Barrio Language Dictionary*, p. 10, 1974

atom bomb *noun*

▷ see: A-BOMB

atom-bombo *noun*

a cheap but very potent wine *AUSTRALIA, 1953*

A play on the power of the atom bomb, intensifying **BOMBO** (a fortified wine).

atomic *noun*

a cigar-sized marijuana cigarette *US*

- Marijuana (we hear) is now peddled in the form of phony cigars. Called "atomics." A box (less conspicious than ciggies) sells at $35. —*San Francisco Call-Bulletin*, p. 8G, 11th March 1953

atomic *adjective*

(of a drug) very-powerful *US*

- [I]t was an ace bomber of absolutely atomic North African marihooch[.]—Lester Bangs, *Psychotic Reactions and Carburetor Dung*, p. 80, 1971

A-town *nickname*

Atlanta, Georgia *US*

- —Lois Stavsky et al., *A2Z*, p. 2, 1995
- —Don R. McCreary (Editor), *Dawg Speak*, 2001

atrocious *adjective*

very bad, execrable *UK*

An exaggeration in everyday use.

atshitshi *noun*

marijuana *SOUTH AFRICA, 1977*

SHIT disguised by using a variant of 'secret language' pig Latin.

- —Richard A. Spears, *The Slang and Jargon of Drugs and Drink*, p. 16, 1986

attaboy *noun*

praise, especially from a boss *US*

- [H]e likes a little 'at-a-boy' once in a while just like the rest of us, despite his bitching.—Joseph Wambaugh, *The New Centurions*, p. 57, 1970
- They do not volunteer for medals or glory or attaboys.—Richard Marcinko and John Weisman, *Rogue Warrior*, p. 231, 1992

attack *noun*

▸ **attack of the slows**

in horse racing, an imaginary illness that plagues a horse midway through a race *US*

- —David W. Maurer, *Argot of the Racetrack*, p. 11, 1951

attagirl!

used for encouraging a female *US, 1924*

- —Joseph A. Weingarten, *An American Dictionary of Slang*, p. 11, 1954
- "You denied it, though?" "Of course." "Attagirl."—Armistead Maupin, *Back to Barbary Lane*, p. 622, 1991

attention *noun*

▸ **jump to attention; spring to attention**

to achieve an erection *UK, 1984*

From military drill, in use after World War 2.

attic *noun*

a drug addict *US*

A phonetic corruption.

- —Jay Robert Nash, *Dictionary of Crime*, p. 13, 1992

attic hand *noun*

in oil drilling, the worker who handles the drill pipe *US*

- —Jerry Robertson, *Oil Slanguage*, p. 97, 1954

attitude *noun*

an air of detached superiority *US*

- The White Party was hot, but the attitude in the room was a bit much.—Kevin Dillalo, *The Unofficial Gay Manual*, p. 237, 1994

attitude adjustment *noun*

a change in outlook produced by alcohol, threats or other inducements *US*

- —Connie Eble (Editor), *UNC-CH Campus Slang*, p. 1, Fall 1984

attitude arrest *noun*

an arrest motivated by the subject's lack of respect towards the arresting police officer *US*

- —Jay Robert Nash, *Dictionary of Crime*, p. 13, 1992

attitude test *noun*

the extremely subjective criteria used by a traffic police officer in deciding whether to issue a traffic ticket or let the offending driver off with a warning *US*

- He found that the car's left taillight was out and he ebegan writing him a ticket, for failing the attitude test, as they say.—Joseph Wambaugh, *Lines and Shadows*, p. 114, 1984

atto- *prefix*
used as a diminishing intensifier *US*
Literally meaning 'ten to the power of negative eighteen'.
- I will devote nine attointerest units to your proposal.—Andy Ihnatko, *Cyberspeak*, p. 17, 1997

au contraire *adverb*
to the contrary *US*
French used by those who speak no French; adds a camp tone.
- I [Blanche Purka] am not 'renouncing' the theatre, certainly not in any moody bitterness. Au contraire, I shall very probably be busier than ever before.—*New York Times*, p. 2, 6th November 1955
- No more do you prepare lavish meals with his tastes in mind. Au contraire. Now it is for the women you slave and work and cook.—*San Francisco Chronicle*, p. 13, 22nd June 1961
- "How do you talk to someone who keeps saying 'Au contraire?'—*San Francisco Chronicle*, p. 59, 18th October 1972

auction gale *noun*
an equinoctial gale *CANADA*
'Auction' echoes the sound of 'equinoctial'.
- An "auction gale," in Nova Scotia, is an equinoctial gale (at the time of the solstice), often very fierce and sometimes so bad that "you may as well sell up and move out."—Lewis Poteet, *The South Shore Phrase Book*, p. 16, 1999

audi *noun*
▸ **to be audi**
to leave *US*
- —Lady Kier Kirby, *The 376 Deee-liteful Words*, 1992
- Let's just talk when we've mellowed, alright? I'm audi.—*Clueless*, 1995

Audi 5000 *adjective*
already gone *US*
- It means "out of here", as in the line from the phat rap film, Fear Of A Black Hat: "She'll be Audi 5000."—David Rowan, *A Glossary for the 90s*, p. 199, 1998

Audi 5000!
goodbye *US*
Playing on 'Audi' and 'out of here'.
- —Connie Eble (Editor), *UNC-CH Campus Slang*, p. 7, Fall 1991

Audie *nickname*
the voice that announced the time on telephone time services *US*
- The Pacific Telephone and Telegraph Co. will adjust its Audichron (Audie), an electronic timekeeper, which keeps time for most Northern and Central California telephone exchanges. The Audie is the "girl who gives the time" when you dial Rochester 7–8900.—*San Francisco News*, 22nd April 1955

auger in *verb*
to crash an aeroplane *US*
- For a fellow down to his last fuel, it's "bingo." If he "clanks," he's nervous and if he "augers in" he crashed.—*San Francisco Examiner*, p. 10 (II), 2nd June 1957
- There are no black pilots or white pilots, only pilots that make it and pilots that auger in.—Walter J. Boyne and Steven L. Thompson, *The Wild Blue*, 1986

augustus *noun*
a male homosexual *UK*
A roundabout allusion to anal intercourse; Augustus Gloop is a character in *Charlie and the Chocolate Factory*, Roald Dahl, filmed as *Willie Wonka and the Chocolate Factory*, 1971. At the climax of the story Augustus is sucked up a chocolate pipe.
- He's an augustus.—*Does Doug Know*, 15th March 2002

auld lang syne *noun*
mutual, simultaneous oral sex between two people *UK*
Rhyming slang for **69**; formed from the song that people enjoy once a year.
- I'm lucky if my wife gives me a hand job, let alone join me in Auld Lang Syne.—Bodmin Dark, *Dirty Cockney Rhyming Slang*, 2003

auld wan *noun*
▷ see: OUL ONE

au naturel *adjective*
naked *US*
French used by those who speak no French; informal, jocular, affected.
- No frustrating plots, mysteries or symbolism. Just simple, unrestricted, unrestrained action! Men & Women Au-Naturel!—*San Francisco Chronicle*, p. 45, 19th June 1967

aunt *noun*
the manager of a brothel *UK, 1606*
- —Vincent J. Monteleone, *Criminal Slang*, p. 13, 1949

Aunt Bettie *noun*
an overly cautious person *US*
- And so it is shocking to hear some of the old male Aunt Bettys lift their skirts in scat fashion against this one-time Andy Smith quarterback on the pretense that there are several indiscreet chapters in his past life.—*San Francisco News*, p. 16, 10th January 1945
- Prep's 'Aunt Betties' Dawdle Over Age Limit Rule Change (Headline)—*San Francisco News*, p. 13, 23rd January 1951

Aunt Ella *noun*
an umbrella *UK, 1960*
Rhyming slang.
- You'd better take your game of nap [cap] and Aunt Ella.—*The Sweeney*, p. 9, 1976

Aunt Emma *noun*
1 used as a personification of a matronly aunt *US*
- Into this situation comes Waldorf, whose record is nothing to write your Aunt Emma about.—*San Francisco News*, p. 15, 21st February 1947
- Your Aunt Emma could win with a team like that. (Cartoon caption)—*San Francisco News*, p. 17, 24th May 1956

2 in croquet, a cautious, conservative, dull player *US*
- —James Charlton and William Thompson, *Croquet*, p. 155, 1977

Aunt Fanny *nickname*
the Federal Communications Commission *US*
- —Elementary Electronics, *Dictionary of CB Lingo*, p. 46, 1976

Aunt Flo *noun*
the bleed period of the menstrual cycle *US*
- —*American Speech*, p. 298, December 1954: 'The vernacular of menstruation'
- —Pamela Munro, *U.C.L.A. Slang*, p. 16, 1989
- Aunt Flo is visiting.—Karen Houppert, *The Curse*, 1999

Aunt Flo from Red River *noun*
the bleed period of the menstrual cycle *CANADA*
- I asked why and she said, 'Aunt Flo from Red River was visiting.' —a correspondent, *The Museum of Menstruation and Women's Health*, June 2001

Aunt Haggie's children *noun*
any stupid, lazy, despised people *BERMUDA*
- —Peter A. Smith and Fred M. Barritt, *Bermewjan Vurds*, 1985

Aunt Hazel *noun*
marijuana *US*
- "Grass ... Mary Jane, Aunt Hazel, African bush, bambalacha. You pick the cool name."—Stephen J. Cannell, *The Tin Collectors*, p. 60, 2001

auntie *noun*
1 an older, effeminate male homosexual *US, 1930*
A tad cruel, if not derogatory.
- A Lexicon of Homosexual Slang—Donald Webster Cory and John P. LeRoy, *The Homosexual and His Society*, p. 261, 1963
- Later, when I went to the director's house with the auntie – several weeks later – the director would be redecorating his house.—John Rechy, *City of Night*, p. 174, 1963
- I had an address book a mile long, packed with tricks from 'drag queens' to rough trade, old aunties, little nellie queens, queens that stayed home with mother.—Antony James, *America's Homosexual Underground*, p. 78, 1965
- The folklore of the hustler's world has legendary stories of hustlers who supposedly made the scene with a big-time producer, satisfied the old auntie and ended up as a big star.—Johnny Shearer, *The Male Hustler*, p. 141, 1966
- Is this the way to treat another gay person with whom they disagree – calling him "auntie"?—*Screw*, p. 8, 24th January 1969
- Now when they get older, they switch to what the homosexuals call 'aunties.' Now these aunties are 35, 40 and older. (Quoting John B. Williams).—*The Advocate*, p. 2, 7th-20th July 1971
- To the younger homosexual, an auntie often translates as anything over thirty having lived too long with nothing to show for his age. Youth is the premium in the real world, but it is the criterion in the gay world.—Bruce Rodgers, *The Queens' Vernacular*, p. 25, 1972
- —Paul Baker, *Polari*, p. 163, 2002

2 a disoriented unlambed ewe that thinks she has lambed and steals the lamb of another *NEW ZEALAND*
- —Eugene Nelson, *Glossary*, p. 1, 1999

3 the bleed period of the menstrual cycle *NORFOLK ISLAND*
Also variant 'aunty'.
- —Beryl Nobbs Palmer, *A Dictionary of Norfolk Words and Usages*, p. 1, 1992

Auntie; Aunty *nickname*

the British Broadcasting Corporation *UK, 1962*

- Auntie's digital revelation[.] The BBC's director-general announced plans this week to embrace Napster-style file sharing to make its archives free for licence payers. — *The Guardian*, 28th August 2003

Auntie Ena *noun*

a cleaner *UK*

Rhyming slang.

- Have you seen my Auntie Ena / In an office she's a cleaner — Ray Puxley, *Cockney Rabbit*, p. 5, 1992

Auntie Lily *adjective*

silly *UK, 1945*

Rhyming slang.

- Don't be so auntie. — Ray Puxley, *Cockney Rabbit*, p. 5, 1992

auntie man *noun*

1 a man who is completely dominated by his wife *TRINIDAD AND TOBAGO*

- — Lise Winer, *Dictionary of the English/Creole of Trinidad & Tobago*, 2003

2 an effeminate man, especially a homosexual *GUYANA*

- — Richard Allsopp, *Dictionary of Caribbean English Usage*, p. 48, 1996

Auntie Nellie; Aunty Nelly *noun*

the belly *UK, 1961*

Rhyming slang; sometimes shortened to 'aunty'.

- I've got a bit of trouble with my Auntie Nellie. — Ray Puxley, *Cockney Rabbit*, p. 6, 1992
- — Bodmin Dark, *Dirty Cockney Rhyming Slang*, 2003

Auntie Wicky *nickname*

Queen Victoria *BAHAMAS*

- — John A. Holm, *Dictionary of Bahamian English*, p. 6, 1982

Aunt Jane's room *noun*

an outdoor toilet *US, 1939*

- — Frederic G. Cassidy, *Dicitonary of American Regional English, Volume 1*, p. 106, 1985

Aunt Jemima *noun*

a black woman who seeks approval from white people by obsequious behaviour *US*

Ironically, singer/actor Ethel Ernestine Harper, who portrayed Aunt Jemima in pancake commercials from 1948 until 1966, was by all accounts anything but the stereotypical subservient black woman.

- What I [Adam Clayton Powell] cannot abide are the black 'Aunt Jemimas' who snuggle up to the white power structure for approbation by denouncing 'black power' and telling Mr. Charlie what he wants to hear. — *San Francisco Examiner*, 18th August 1966
- Nothing but Aunt Jemimas and Uncle Toms doing the white man's bidding. — *San Francisco Chronicle*, p. 8, 28th October 1967
- You have got to eat lunch anyway, you know, just like aunt Jemima said. — George V. Higgins, *Penance for Jerry Kennedy*, p. 170, 1985

Aunt Julia *noun*

communist propaganda *US*

Peter Tamony collected the following from a radio commentary by Fulton Lewis Jr on April 13, 1953: 'Aunt Julia is here – code word passed to Communist stevedores on waterfronts to indicate the shipment of communist printed material is aboard ship'.

Aunt Maggie *noun*

▸ **out Aunt Maggie's window**

(used of a homerun) out of the ballpark *US*

- — *San Francisco Examiner*, p. 42, 21st July 1962

Aunt Mary *noun*

marijuana *US, 1959*

MARY is a familiar pun on '*mari*juana'.

- — Richard A. Spears, *The Slang and Jargon of Drugs and Drink*, p. 16, 1986
- — Mike Haskins, *Drugs*, p. 286, 2003

Aunt Nell *noun*

the ear *UK*

Usually as a plural.

- — Paul Baker, *Polari*, p. 163, 2002

Aunt Nell *verb*

to listen *UK*

Often an imperative.

- [S]he was Aunt Nelling our chat[.] — the cast of 'Aspects of Love', Prince of Wales Theatre, *Palare (Boy Dancer Talk) for Beginners*, 1989–92
- — Paul Baker, *Polari*, p. 163, 2002

Aunt Nelly fake *noun*

an earring *UK*

A combination of **AUNT NELL** (the ear) and 'fake' (an artificial thing); usually as a plural.

- There goes another aunt nelly fake. — James Gardiner, *Who's a Pretty Boy Then?*, p. 123, 1997
- — Paul Baker, *Polari*, p. 163, 2002

Aunt Nora *noun*

cocaine

- — US Department of Justice, *Street Terms*, August 1994
- — Nick Constable, *This is Cocaine*, p. 181, 2002

Aunt Ruby *noun*

the bleed period of the menstrual cycle *US*

- We call it Aunt Ruby; lots of people say their aunt is visiting, and we added Ruby after a character on General Hospital [a US television programme] back in the 1980s. We always used to laugh at her name and say it sounded like a period. — a contributor, *The Museum of Menstruation and Women's Health*, April 2002

Aunt Thomasina *noun*

1 a black woman who curries favour with white people by obsequious behaviour *US, 1963*

An echo of the much more commonly heard **UNCLE TOM**.

- On the other side are New York activisits led by Al Sharpton and Alton Maddox Jr. They savage their opponents, calling them "Uncles Toms" and "Aunt Thomasinas." — *Record (Bergen County, New Jersey)*, p. B7, 25th April 1990
- "I ain't nobody's Uncle Tom or Aunt Thomasina," said Ada Fisher, a Republican from Salisbury[.] — *Winston-Salem (North Carolina) Journal*, p. 1, 6th May 2003

2 a woman who does not support feminism *US, 1970*

- — Frederic G. Cassidy, *Dicitonary of American Regional English, Volume 1*, p. 107, 1985

Aunt Tillie; Aunt Tilly *noun*

1 used as the personification of a fussy old maid *US*

- They are determined that Aunt Tillie, a symbol of their most tempermental customer, shall love their parking. — *San Francisco News Call-Bulletin*, p. 49, 22nd June 1960

2 the bleed period of the menstrual cycle *US*

- Aunt Tilly is here. — Karen Houppert, *The Curse*, 1999

Aunt Tom *noun*

a woman who does not support the goals of feminism *US, 1968*

An attempt to link semantically the struggle of women with the struggle of black slaves by borrowing from the well-known **UNCLE TOM**.

- — Harold Wentworth and Stuart Berg Flexner, *Dictionary of American Slang*, p. 673, 1975
- In fact, a distaste for Helen is something feminists tend to share. In 1969, Redstockings named her an "Aunt Tom of the Month" in its premier broadsheet. — *Manifesta*, p. 159, 2000

Aunty *and variants*

▷ **see: AUNTIE**

aurora borealis *noun*

phencyclidine, the recreational drug known as PCP or angel dust *US*

- — *Drummer*, p. 77, 1977
- — Jay Robert Nash, *Dictionary of Crime*, p. 14, 1992

Aussie *noun*

1 Australia *AUSTRALIA, 1915*

From *Aus*tralia and '-ie' suffix. Pronounced 'ozzie', not 'ossie', the common mistake made by north Americans. Generally used positively with a sense of national pride in all meanings.

- For it has an air of Aussie, / Of 'Come and have a drink?' — Tip Kelaher, *The Digger Hat and other verses*, p. 10, 1942
- Home! Home to Mum! Good old Aussie! — Eric Lambert, *The Veterans*, p. 183, 1954
- I was over in this dump last year, but I had to shoot through back to Aussie unexpectedly when me auntie took crook. — Barry Humphries, *The Wonderful World of Barry McKenzie*, p. 38, 1968

2 an Australian *AUSTRALIA, 1918*

Originally used of Australian soldiers in World War 1.

- The Aussies' bad temper evaporated and they began to chaff and even invite the Chums into the hole. — Leonard Mann, *Flesh in Armour*, p. 131, 1932
- 'An' our side's the Aussies an' them crowd's the dirty Turks,' said Ponkey. — Norman Lindsay, *Saturdee*, p. 13, 1934

- 'I can take you somewhere,' I urged. 'Better not Aussie,' he told me sadly. 'Only get us in trouble.'—Eric Lambert, *The Veterans*, p. 38, 1954
- Won't find many Aussies interested in butterfly collecting.—John Wynnum, *Tar Dust*, p. 51, 1962
- For some strange reason, known only to South Aussies, a pint of beer is fifteen ounces.—John O'Grady, *It's Your Shout, Mate!*, p. 30, 1972
- True, your average Aussie still relishes a bit of mockery, derision or deflating.—Arthur Chipper, *The Aussie Swearer's Guide*, p. 10, 1972

3 Australian English *AUSTRALIA, 1945*

- Our racy Aussie is a language fruitful and challenging to every extempore swearer.—Arthur Chipper, *The Aussie Swearer's Guide*, p. 91, 1972

4 the Australian dollar *AUSTRALIA*

- —Barry Humphries, *A Nice Night's Entertainment*, p. 9, 1956
- Some of the larger banks decide to dump the Aussie.—*Sydney Morning Herald*, 17th November 1988

Aussie *adjective*

Australian *AUSTRALIA, 1915*

- —Dominic Healy, *A Voyage to Venus*, p. 24, 1943
- I just can't figure this Aussie slang at all.—John Wynnum, *Jiggin' in the Riggin'*, p. 40, 1965
- There's nothing on this earth to beat Aussie beer.—Jean Brooks, *The Opal Witch*, p. 82, 1967
- The Rabbitohs have made one change for Sunday's clash with the Bulldogs at Aussie Stadium.—*Daily Telegraph*, p. 76, 30th July 2003

Aussie haka *noun*

a gesture showing that you have no money to pay for the next round of drinks at a pub *NEW ZEALAND*

- —Sonya Plowman, *Great Kiwi Slang*, p. 17, 2002

Aussie kiss *noun*

oral-genital stimulation *UK*

Described as 'similar to a French Kiss, but given down under'.

- —Chris Donald, *Roger's Profanisaurus*, p. 5, 2002

Aussie steak *noun*

mutton *US*

- —*American Speech*, p. 54, February 1947: 'Pacific War language'
- —*Maledicta*, p. 155, 1979: 'A glossary of ethnic slurs in American English'

Australia *noun*

an ounce of marijuana or other drug *UK*

Punning the abbreviation 'oz' (ounce) with the familiar diminutive 'Oz' (Australia).

- —Nick Jones, *Spliffs*, p. 250, 2003

Australian *noun*

1 Australian English *AUSTRALIA, 1902*

Jocularly seen as a separate language from British English, or other varieties of English.

- —Josef Holman, *As I See Them*, p. 35, 1954
- I think Australian is a bastard of a language.—Nino Culotta (John O'Grady), *They're A Weird Mob*, p. 26, 1957
- [S]ome of them spoke Australian.—Wilda Moxham, *The Apprentice*, p. 23, 1969
- I could not understand her. She [Princess Anne] speaks English and I speak Australian.—Bill Hornadge, *The Ugly Australian*, p. 107, 1974

2 a practitioner of mouth-to-anus sex *US*

From a somewhat forced 'down under' joke.

- —*Maledicta*, p. 218, 1979: 'Kinks and queens: linguistic and cultural aspects of the terminology for gays'

Australian days *noun*

night-work *UK*

- —Frank McKenna, *A Glossary of Railwaymen's Talk*, p. 31, 1970

Australian haka *noun*

an easily detected attempt to evade paying your share of something *NEW ZEALAND*

- —David McGill, *David McGill's Complete Kiwi Slang Dictionary*, p. 9, 1998

Australian salute *noun*

a hand-movement brushing flies away from the face *AUSTRALIA, 1972*

- As you constantly brush away flies from around your face, you are doing the great Australian salute.—John Blackman, *The Aussie Slang Dictionary*, p. 84, 1990

Australian yo *noun*

in craps, a roll of three *US*

A roll of three is rarely a good thing, and is usually best face-down; if a three is face-down, an eleven is face-up. Eleven is 'yo', with the three thus 'down-under the yo'.

- —Chris Fagans and David Guzman, *A Guide to Craps Lingo*, p. 11, 1999

Austrian Oak *nickname*

▷ see: OAK

auto *adjective*

automatic *US*

A colloquial abbreviation.

- Louis was convicted on felony firearms charges when he took part in the drive-by of a dwelling with MAC 10's converted to full auto.—Elmore Leonard, *Riding the Rap*, p. 54, 1995

autocutie *noun*

an attractive but incompetent television presenter *UK*

A compound of 'autocue' and CUTIE (an attractive young woman).

- Kick-boxing Kate becomes the latest autocutie to front the execrable slot[.]—Wyndham King, *www.megastar.co.uk*, April 2003

auto-getem *noun*

automatic weapons fire *US, 1972*

Broken down – 'automatic fire gets 'em'.

- —Linda Reinberg, *In the Field*, p. 13, 1991

automagically *adverb*

in computing, in an automatic but explanation-defying complicated fashion *US*

- —*CoEvolution Quarterly*, p. 27, Spring 1981
- Files that have a name ending in 'TMF' are automagically deleted when you log out.—Guy L. Steele et al., *The Hacker's Dictionary*, p. 28, 1983

automatic tongue-wiper *noun*

a sycophant or toady *US*

- —*Maledicta*, p. 16, Summer 1977: 'A word for it!'

automation *noun*

in poker, a player who bets and plays in an extremely predictable manner *US*

- —John Vorhaus, *The Big Book of Poker Slang*, p. 5, 1996

autumn leaves *noun*

in horse racing, a steeplechase jockey who has suffered a series of falls *AUSTRALIA*

A shameless pun.

- —Ned Wallish, *The Truth Dictionary of Racing Slang*, p. 3, 1989

Av *nickname*

Telegraph Avenue, Berkeley, California *US*

- "Things are really getting rougher," nearly every hippy on the Av will tell you.—*The Berkeley Barb*, p. 1, 2nd September 1966

Ava Gardner *adjective*

avante-garde *UK*

- —Tom Hibbert, *Rockspeak!*, p. 4, 1983

Avenue *noun*

▸ **the Avenue**

1 Fifth Avenue in New York *US, 1940s to 50s*

In gay use. Fifth Avenue was, in the 1940s and 50s, favoured by homosexual prostitutes.

2 Telegraph Avenue, Berkeley, Calfiornia *US*

- Headline: Peace-Rock OK, But Not On "Avenue" / Will Rock "Off-Telly"—*The Berkeley Barb*, p. 1, 5th August 1966

average *adjective*

mediocre; not the best; just plain dreadful *AUSTRALIA, 1981*

- 'How ya feelin'?' he said. 'Pretty average,' I said.—Phillip Gwynne, *Deadly Unna?*, p. 114, 1998

avgas *noun*

jet fuel *US*

- —Gregory Clark, *Words of the Vietnam War*, p. 254, 1990

aviator *noun*

in trucking, a driver who drives very fast *US*

- —Montie Tak, *Truck Talk*, p. 5, 1971

awake *adjective*

sexually aroused *US*

- —Connie Eble (Editor), *UNC-CH Campus Slang*, p. 1, April 1985

awake to

aware of a secret plan, trick, deception or the like; aware of a person's deceitful character or hidden agenda *AUSTRALIA*

Now generally **A WAKE-UP TO**.

- 'Aren't you awake to the Skull yet?' asked Lasher with a cynical leer. —Eric Lambert, *The Veterans*, p. 136, 1954
- Nobody would be awake to it's value. — Bluey, *Bush Contractors*, 1975

a wake-up *adjective*

alert; knowing; wise to *AUSTRALIA, 1916*

There is some confusion about whether this idiom should be construed nominally with 'a' being the article and 'wake-up' being a noun, meaning 'an alert person, a person who knows what's what', or adjectivally as defined here. The earliest evidence (from 1916) supports the noun theory, but since the 1940s it has become impossible to definitely determine the part of speech in print as it is found spelt variously as 'a wake-up', 'a wakeup', 'awake up' and 'awake-up'. The fact that the plural form 'wake-ups' is only attested by a solitary citation from 1943 suggests that it is now conceived of as an adjectival phrase however it may be spelt.

- 'So you're in this, too,' snarled Jim. 'I'm a wake-up now.' —Lawson Glassop, *We were the Rats*, p. 176, 1944
- If Mo can't understand it, how do you expect the mugs to be a wake-up? — *People*, p. 35, 15th March 1950
- They'll be waking up to me soon, sergeant. I think some of them are a wake-up already. —Vince Kelly, *The Bogeyman*, p. 19, 1956
- He said, 'I'm a wake-up to you fellows. I know the full strength of you.' —Vince Kelly, *The Bogeyman*, p. 174, 1956
- Course they're awake up, but they don't seem to mind. Fact, I think Roo likes it. —Ray Lawler, *Summer of the Seventeenth Doll*, 1957
- But be warned – or as we Ordinary Australians say, be a wake-up. —Cyril Pearl, *So, you want to be an Australian*, p. 24, 1959
- Any other guy would have been a wake-up long since. —Robert S. Close, *With Hooves of Brass*, p. 40, 1961
- My only purpose in writing is to advise I am a 'wake up' and that is the only satisfaction I derive. — *Flame*, p. 22, 1972
- His father would have said he ought to be a 'wake-up', whatever that meant, but he hadn't been a wake-up, he had happily eaten a sausage sandwich that hadn't been a sausage sandwich. A piece of shit, they said it was, but how could he know what a piece of shit tasted like, when he had never eaten it before? —Colleen McCullough, *Tim*, p. 18, 1975
- Then I ended up doing it three or four times a week because the older announcers were a wake-up that it interfered with their time off. —Bert Newton, *Bert!*, p. 66, 1977
- I got the message. He was a wake up. —Sam Weller, *Old Bastards I Have Met*, p. 144, 1979
- But Zeca was a wakeup. —B. Selkie, *Lime Juice*, p. 38, 1995

a wake-up to

aware of a secret plan, trick, deception or the like; aware of a person's deceitful character of hidden agenda *AUSTRALIA, 1944*

- This joker reckons he was in Tobruk, but I'm a wake-up to him. —Lawson Glassop, *We were the Rats*, p. 273, 1944
- Of course, they had only been having him on – he was a wake-up to that. —Robert S. Close, *With Hooves of Brass*, p. 113, 1961
- She's a wake-up to Squid, too – keeps him in if he's late. —D.E. Charlwood, *All the Green Year*, p. 90, 1965
- Helen wasn't awake up to what they'd been doing, she was asking Con all the damn fool questions. — Bluey, *Bush Contractors*, p. 153, 1975
- They don't know I'm a bloody wake-up to it all. Nobody fools me. —Derek Maitland, *Breaking Out*, p. 312, 1979
- Robbo was awake-up to Davo's form over the years and his naturally cynical nature told him it wouldn't be beyond him to pull a bit of a scam. —Robert G. Barrett, *Davo's Little Something*, p. 162, 1992

away *adjective*

1 in prison *UK, 1909*

Euphemistic.

- Why I'd not recently seen him, is that he'd been away inside. —Colin MacInnes, *Absolute Beginners*, 1959
- —Angela Devlin, *Prison Patter*, p. 23, 1996
- Where've you been? You "been away" or something? —Diran Abedayo, *My Once Upon A Time*, p. 118, 2000

2 overseas *BARBADOS*

- —Frank A. Collymore, *Barbadian Dialect*, p. 13, 1965

3 crazy *UK: SCOTLAND*

- The guy's no right in the heid, pal, he's away. —Michael Munro, *The Patter, Another Blast*, 1988

4 in bar dice games, counting for nothing *US*

A call of 'aces away' would mean that rolls of one have no point value.

- —Gil Jacobs, *The World's Best Dice Games*, p. 191, 1976

away laughing *adjective*

in a good position, especially when embarking on a new venture *NEW ZEALAND*

- Wait until the insurance for the truck comes through. Then we're away laughing. —Jean Watson, *Stand in the Rain*, p. 14, 1965

awesome *adjective*

great, excellent *US, 1975*

An informal variation of the conventional sense.

- —Connie Eble (Editor), *UNC-CH Campus Slang*, p. 1, March 1979
- Like, OK, so I saw this totally awesome dude at the bonerama checkout, right, like I totally thought it was Rick Springfield. —Mary Corey and Victoria Westermark, *Fer Shurr! How to be a Valley Girl*, 1982
- But NO BIGGIE / It's so AWESOME / It's like TUBULAR, y'know. —Moon Unit and Frank Zappa, *Valley Girl*, 1982
- —Bradley Elfman, *Breakdancing*, p. 40, 1984
- Awesome party! Good tunes! Good brew! Good buddies! — *Wayne's World 2*, 1993
- "Wow, you'd do that for the Mooner? That is so awesome." Mooner gave me a hug. —Janet Evanovich, *Seven Up*, p. 72, 2001

awfuck disease *noun*

the sense of dread that you feel the morning after doing something that you, upon reflection, wished you had not done *US*

Used in jokes more than in real life, with the punch-line a variation on 'Aw fuck, why did I do that?'.

- —Connie Eble (Editor), *UNC-CH Campus Slang*, p. 1, Spring 2001

awful *adverb*

very *UK, 1818*

- He had a nice smile and an awful big heart / Yes he did, Jesse did —Roy Zimmerman, *That Jesse Helms Song*, 1993

awkward squad *noun*

collectively, people who do not, or will not, conform; a notional grouping of people who are 'difficult' *UK*

- Normal people had a lawyer. Maureen was a fully-paid-up member of the awkward squad, she had to do it herself —John Milne, *Alive and Kicking*, p. 186, 1998

AWOL; awol *adjective*

missing *UK, 1920*

Military coinage, from '*a*bsent *w*ithout *l*eave'; now widely applied, both as initialism or acronym, to most circumstances where permission for absence would be required.

- I was AWOL from home. —Diran Abedayo, *My Once Upon A Time*, p. 169, 2000
- Fascinatingly, 12 cut-out Jordans have gone awol from Yates's Wine Lodges. Keep your eyes peeled, ladies. — *The Guardian*, 5th September 2003

AWOL bag *noun*

in the Korea and Vietnam wars, an overnight bag *US, 1956*

- —Carl Fleischhauer, *A Glossary of Army Slang*, p. 2, 1968
- They leave the MAA's office together and return separately, each carrying his AWOL bag. —Darryl Ponicsan, *The Last Detail*, p. 19, 1970
- After a moment of glad-handing and stowing my AWOL bag and settling in, Stepik arrived. —Larry Heinemann, *Close Quarters*, p. 123, 1977
- "A-tent hut!" I yelled. AWOL (overnight) bags and laundry sacks hit the dirt as the mob dropped everything to come to attention for the general. —Robert Mason, *Chickenhawk*, p. 322, 1983
- A moment later Paco stands on the bottom of the coach steps with his AWOL bag in one hand and his black hickoery cane in the other[.] —Larry Heinemann, *Paco's Story*, 1986
- With that, he put on his hat, picked up his gear (one tiny AWOL bag, when most senior officers had two or three footlockers), got into his jeep, and drove away – without looking back even once. —David H. Hackworth, *About Face*, p. 267, 1989

ax; axe *noun*

1 a musical instrument, especially an electric guitar *US, 1955*

Originally used in jazz circles for any instrument, particularly a saxophone or trumpet, instruments on which 'chops' (musical figures) are played; surely 'axe' was coined as a pun. The word itself suggests a chopper, a tool that you can carry over your shoulder – to many jazz and, subsequently, rock musicians, their instrument is exactly that.

- Now these cats were blowing their horns, their axes, whatever they had. —Claude Brown, *Manchild in the Promised Land*, p. 229, 1965
- OK man, we'll take these axes. — *The Blues Brothers*, 1980
- I'd heard an instrument called an "axe" before – that was an old time hipster's term[.] —Sean Hutchinson, *Crying Out Loud*, p. 176, 1988
- [H]e [Jimi Hendrix] just got right up in my face with that axe, and I didn't want to pick up a guitar for the next year. —Mike Bloomfield (1943–81), *quoted in Jabberrock*, p. 100, 1997

2 any sharp-edged weapon *US*

- —Hyman E. Goldin et al., *Dictionary of American Underworld Lingo*, p. 20, 1950

3 a knife used or intended for use as a weapon *US*

- —David Claerbaut, *Black Jargon in White America*, p. 57, 1972

4 dismissal from employment *US, 1883*

Usually heard in the phrases 'get the axe' or 'give the axe'.

- Gordon Explains Why He Got Axe (Headline)—*San Francisco Call-Bulletin*, p. 45, 28th June 1961
- You would have the inside story of my geting the ax.—Mary McCarthy, *The Group*, p. 88, 1963
- Mr. Shapian, please help me before I get the ax. I'm a married man with kids.—Max Shulman, *Anyone Got a Match?*, p. 25, 1964
- They could only give him the axe.—Wilda Moxham, *The Apprentice*, p. 39, 1969
- 'Suspension?' Huck said. 'The axe.' 'Jesus!'—Peter Corris, *Pokerface*, p. 28, 1985

5 in a gambling operation, the house's cut of the bets *US*

- —John Scarne, *Scarne on Dice*, p. 459, 1974

6 the lip of a wave *US*

- —Trevor Cralle, *The Surfin'ary*, p. 4, 1991

▸ get the axe

in surfing, to be knocked off your board by a wave *US*

- I looked around. Only two other guys had made it. The others had got the axe.—Frederick Kohner, *Gidget*, p. 16, 1957
- —Grant W. Kuhns, *On Surfing*, p. 123, 1963

axe god *noun*

a popular electric-guitar player who inspires hero-worship with his musical tecnique *UK*

Based on **AXE** (a guitar). The graffito 'Clapton is God', deifying the popular guitarist Eric Clapton (b.1945), was widespread in the late 1960s.

- The more he indulged in this womanising, axe-god fantasy [...] the more the band loved to bring him back to reality.—Kevin Sampson, *Powder*, p. 21, 1999

axe handle *noun*

an imprecise unit of measurement, especially when applied to the breadth of a man's shoulders or woman's buttocks *US, 1947*

- —Frederic G. Cassidy, *Dicitonary of American Regional English, Volume 1*, p. 109, 1985
- If you're a couple of axehandles across the shoulders with legs like tree trunks and can hand out a good 'shirt-fronter', then, as far as football is concerned, you're 'built like a brick shithouse'.—Ivor Limb, *Footy's No Joke!*, p. 12, 1986
- His wife was short and three axe-handles across the arse.—Herb Wharton, *Cattle Camp*, p. 95, 1994
- —Harry Orsman, *A Dictionary of Modern New Zealand Slang*, p. 3, 1999

axe handle party *noun*

a riot or brawl *US, 110*

- —Frederic G. Cassidy, *Dicitonary of American Regional English, Volume 1*, p. 110, 1985

axe hero *noun*

a popular electric-guitar player who inspires hero-worship with his musical tecnique *UK*

Based on **AXE** (a guitar).

- UK band Bebop Deluxe, fronted by guitarist [axe-hero] Bill Nelson, wittily, if rather gruesomely, titled their 1974 album Axe Victim. —Simon Warner, *Rockspeak!*, p. 274, 1996

axe man *noun*

1 an electric guitarist; rarely, any musician *UK*

Based on **AXE** (a guitar or any instrument).

- Boo Boo's Birthday (Thelonius] Monk) became a vehicle for everything in the leader's axe-man repertoire – from fluent be-bopping to dissonant guitar heroics.—*The Guardian*, 7th March 2001

2 a person who decides when a company will discharge an employee *TRINIDAD AND TOBAGO, 1975*

- —Richard Allsopp, *Dictionary of Caribbean English Usage*, p. 51, 1996

axe-wound *noun*

the vagina *UK*

- —Chris Lewis, *The Dictionary of Playground Slang*, p. 15, 2003

axle grease *noun*

1 money *AUSTRALIA, 1943*

Probably because 'it makes the wheels go round'.

2 any particularly thick and sticky hair pomade *AUSTRALIA, 1943*

Known and used in the UK, US and Australia.

- —Clarence Major, *Dictionary of Afro-American Slang*, p. 21, 1970

aye, doogie aye

used for expressing disbelief in whatever you have just been told *UK: SCOTLAND*

An elaboration of 'aye' (yes) spoken with irony heavy enough to mean 'no'. Several variations including: 'aye, Hawkeye'; 'aye, hooch-aye'; 'aye, Popeye' and 'aye, that eye'.

- —Michael Munro, *The Patter, Another Blast*, 1988

ayemer *noun*

(from television) a morning show *CANADA*

This term has been imported into Canada, according to John Allemang of the *Globe and Mail*, from the US *Variety* magazine.

- "Ayemer" not what a sailor says to his mum when he returns from the sea; it's actually a TV term. The key is to pronounce it as a.m.-er: a show that's on in the morning.—*Toronto Globe and Mail*, p. R2, 28th August 2002

ayo

used as a greeting *US*

- —Lois Stavsky et al., *A2Z*, p. 3, 1995

Ayrton Senna *noun*

a ten pound note *UK*

Rhyming slang for 'tenner'; formed from Brazilian Formula-One racing driver Ayrton Senna da Silva, 1963–1994.

- You take this hundred quid in used Ayrton Sennas and I'll be off in the old Camilla Parker-Bowles [Rolls-Royce car].—Mervyn Stutter, *Getting Nowhere Fast*, 2004

Aztec hop; Aztec revenge; Aztec two-step *noun*

diarrhoea suffered by tourists in Mexico *US, 1953*

- With his luck he'd die of Aztec Revenge anyway, first time he had a Bibb lettuce salad.—Joseph Wambaugh, *The Black Marble*, p. 152, 1978
- Like a thief, traveler's diarrhoea has many aliases. It is euphemistically known as "Turista," Montezuma's Revenge," The Aztec Two Step," "Turkey Trots," and scores more.—*The Patriot Ledger (Quincy, Massachusetts)*, p. 16, 3rd June 1997

azz *noun*

the buttocks *US*

A variation of **ASS**.

- —Alonzo Westbrook, *Hip Hoptionary*, p. 5, 2002

Bb

B *noun*

1 Benzedrine™ (amphetamine sulphate), a central nervous system stimulant *US*

- —Richard A.Spears, *The Slang and Jargon of Drugs and Drink*, p. 18, 1986
- —Angela Devlin, *Prison Patter*, p. 23, 1996

2 a matchbox full of marijuana *US*

- —Eugene Landy, *The Underground Dictionary*, p. 27, 1971
- —Jay Robert Nash, *Dictionary of Crime*, p. 15, 1992

3 a *b*uddy, a *b*rother; used as an address for a fellow black man; used as an address for a fellow of either sex *US*
Initialism.

- Yo, B, ya ready to do your song?—Lois Stavsky et al., *A2Z [quoting Muggs, 1993]*, p. 4, 1995
- I put my name on the line with the parole board, bro [...] I'm in your corner, b.—Joel Rose, *Kill Kill Faster Faster*, p. 141, 1997

4 a bastard *AUSTRALIA, 1921*

- Next time he broke it down and said "B's I Have Met"[.]—Sam Weller, *Old Bastards I Have Met*, p. 121, 1979

5 a Cadillac Brougham car *US*

- —Edith A. Folb, *runnin' down some lines*, p. 228, 1980

▸ **put the B on**
to ask for money for sex after giving the appearance of being seduced *US*

- You goddam tramp! Gettin' me up here, then puttin' the B on me! Twenty bucks!—Dev Collans with Stewart Sterling, *I was a House Detective*, p. 33, 1954

B *adjective*

1 used as an intensifier *UK, 1926*
A euphemistic abbreviation of **BLOODY** or **BASTARD**, sometimes shown in print with leader dots or asterisks representing the missing letters.

- The tactical deployment of the vehicles went to the wall; with all lights on (hazzards [sic], Sgt Cornell's Zippo) and crys of "You b... idiot", "left hand down, left", Get out!".—*London Scottish Regimental Gazette*, p. 80, Winter 1990

2 (used of a film) second-tier in terms of actors and budget *US*

- Being both profitable and meritorious, Lewton's productions are ideal B films.—*Life*, p. 123, 25th February 1946
- A falsehood has been circulating in Hollywood and across the country that B pictures are no longer being made.—*San Francisco Examiner*, p. 34, 30th August 1966

3 in the written shorthand of the Internet and text message, fulfilling the masculine role in a homosexual (male or female) relationship *UK*
Short for **BUTCH**.

- —Michelle Baker and Steven Tropiano, *Queer Facts*, p. 13, 2004

B1 *noun*

▸ **do a B1; do a bee wan**
to go somewhere else, to change direction *UK: SCOTLAND*
This derives from the bureaucracy that governs unemployment benefit; if you are in need of immediate support when you first register unemployed you will be issued with a form B1 (an application for Income Support) which is administered at a different location.

- When Ah seen the big moocher shufflin alang Vicky Road Ah done a Bee Wan up Torrisdale Street.—Michael Munro, *The Patter, Another Blast*, 1988

B2B *adjective*
(used of a business transaction) between two businesses *US*

- Business-to-business transactions – that B2B thing – have grown to $109 billion.—*New York Times*, 20th December 1999

B-40 *noun*
a cigar laced with marijuana and dipped in malt liquor *US, 1998*
Possibly named for the appearance and/or effects of the B-40 grenade launcher used by the Viet Cong during the Vietnam war.

- —Mike Haskins, *Drugs*, p. 292, 2003

B-52 *noun*
a powerful amphetamine tablet *US*

- —Peter Johnson, *Dictionary of Street Alcohol and Drug Terms*, p. 12, 1993

BA *noun*

1 nothing whatsoever *UK, 1961*
A euphemistic abbreviation of **BUGGER ALL**, often elaborated as **SWEET BA**.

2 a *b*are *a*ss *US*
Usually in the context of exposing the buttocks to shock or amuse.

- —*Current Slang*, p. 20, Summer 1970

▸ **hang a BA**

1 to expose your *b*are *a*ss *US, 1970*

- Butt-Head turns around, drops his pants and hangs a "B.A." at the guy.—Mike Judge and Joe Stillman, *Beavis and Butt-Head Do America*, p. 20, 1997

2 naked, nude *US, 1933*
An abbreviation of '*b*are *a*ssed'.

- —Anon, *King Smut's Wet Dreams Interpreted*, 1978

baadass; baaadasss *adjective*
very bad, very dangerous *US*

- —Melvin Van Peebles, *Sweet Sweetback's Baadass Song*, 1971
- —Rapido *Baadass TV*, 1990s
- [A] major attempt to re-brand the legendary Scottish Bard [Rabbie Burns] as an 18th-century baaaadaasss muthafucka, the Johnny Rotten of his time.—*Uncut*, July 2003

babbler *noun*
a sheep camp cook *NEW ZEALAND*
An abbreviation of the rhyming slang **BABBLING BROOK**.

- We worked it out that old babbler made 112,000 rock cakes during those four months.—Peter Newton, *Straggle Muster*, p. 86, 1964

babbling *noun*
cooking *US, 1962*
After **BABBLING BROOK** (a cook). There is no record of 'babble' (to cook) but its existence is surely implied.

babbling brook *noun*

1 a gossip, a chatty person *US, 1913*

- —Harold Wentworth and Stuart Berg Flexner, *Dictionary of American Slang*, p. 11, 1960

2 a cook *AUSTRALIA, 1904*
Rhyming slang. In early use very common among shearers, stockmen and soldiers.

- No doubt about it, my Mary is a bottling babbling brook.—Duke Tritton, *Learn to talk Old Jack Lang*, p. 15, 1905
- 'They reckon the babbling brook's done some rissoles,' said Happy. —Lawson Glassop, *We Were The Rats*, p. 114, 1944
- He always referred to me as the Babbling Brook instead of cook. —Irene Staples, *Cooks & Shepherds Come Away*, p. 22, 1964

3 a criminal *AUSTRALIA, 1919*
Rhyming slang for 'crook'. Can be shortened to 'babbler'.

- —Angela Devlin, *Prison Patter*, p. 24, 1996

babbo *noun*
a naive, law-abiding citizen *US*

- —Jay Robert Nash, *Dictionary of Crime*, p. 15, 1992

babe *noun*

1 an attractive young woman *US, 1905*

- Tonight I got a date with a Sigma, a keen babe, for a hop at the Shoreland Hotel.—James T. Farrell, *Saturday Night*, p. 35, 1947

- For three and a half hours they sat in the Paramount balcony with the two high school babes who were also on the hook. —Irving Shulman, *The Amboy Dukes*, p. 29, 1947
- Bare Babes – Where to find 'em. Or where to keep away from 'em, which is harder. —Jack Lait and Lee Mortimer, *Washington Confidential*, p. 301, 1951
- [T]hree days in New York – three days of babes and booze while I waited to see The Man – hadn't helped it any. —Jim Thompson, *Savage Night*, p. 1, 1953
- Oh you beautiful babes from England, for whom we have traveled through time. —*Bill and Ted's Excellent Adventure*, 1989
- HARP: You think the taxpayers would like it, Utah, if they knew they were paying a federal agent to surf and pick up girls. UTAH: Babes. HARP: What? UTAH: The correct term is babes, sir. —*Point Break*, 1991
- "I'll show you where the No-Cal babes hang," Chuck said. —Francesca Lia Block, *Witch Baby*, p. 104, 1991
- She does have a little gambling problem, she plays the football cards a bit too much, but she's a babe, a surgeon babe. —*Something About Mary*, 1998
- Sexy babes talking to scarred, scary-faced hardnuts. —Dave Courtney, *Raving Lunacy*, p. 99, 2000

2 an attractive young male *US, 1973*

- Well, he is a babe. —Francesca Lia Block, *I Was a Teenage Fairy*, p. 80, 1998

3 used as a term of address *US, 1906*

- Thanks, no, babe. Idon't wanna take hjr time —Edwin Tarres, *Q.&A*, 1977
- "How are you, babes?" —Bret Easton Ellis, *Less Than Zero*, p. 13, 1985
- Now, now, Babe. Not while I'm in uniform. —*Boys on the Side*, 1995

babe alert *noun*

a notification that there are attractive people nearby *AUSTRALIA*

- Whoa. Marty, hold on for a sec. Babe alert. —Linda Jaivin, *Rock n Roll Babes from Outer Space*, p. 89, 1996

babelicious *adjective*

extremely sexually attractive *US*

Coined by Mike Myers on the US television programme *Saturday Night Live*, and popularised by the film *Wayne's World*, 1992.

- She's magically bablicious. —*Wayne's World*, 1992
- Having a babelicious best friend can cause you countless problems. —*Girlfriend*, p. 40, 1995
- Does Sadie, his seeing-eye dog, tell him? Three barks for "that one is babelicious!" —*The Guardian*, 12th November 2003

Babe Ruth *noun*

the truth *NEW ZEALAND*

Prison rhyming slang.

- —Harry Orsman, *A Dictionary of Modern New Zealand Slang*, p. 4, 1999

babes *noun*

used as a term of singular address, both general and affectionate

- Runnin' well late. Well fuckin' late babes. Cos o' you. —Nick Barlay, *Curvy Lovebox*, p. 27, 1997
- Oh, just leave it, babes. —Lanre Fehintola, *Charlie Says...*, p. 22, 2000
- "I love you, babes," he managed to call, but she never looked back. —*The Guardian*, 3rd August 2000: 'A life inside'

▸ **the babes; the wee babes**

used as an expression of appreciation: excellent, good, exactly as required *UK: SCOTLAND*

Glasqow slang. Michael Munro suggests that this may well a product of ryming slang formed on 'Babes in the Wood' (good).

- That soup's the babes, Mammy! —Michael Munro, *The Patter, Another Blast*, 1988

babes, parties, tunes

used as a humorous assessment of what is important in life *US*

The 'Wayne's World' skits on *Saturday Night Live* in the 1990s used the mock-Latin motto 'babum, partium, tuneum'. The English 'translation' is repeated with referential humour.

babiche *noun*

leather laces, strips or thongs made from moose and caribou hide *CANADA*

'Babiche' is adapted from a Micmac word, *apapish* meaning 'cord'.

- Another important product of caribou skin is babiche, made from the dehaired hide. The skin is spread out flat and a long thong produced by cutting in a spiral. —*Beaver*, p. 16/2, 16th March 1948
- Indians still look for babish, the moose hide thongs for sewing. —*Camsell Arrow*, p. 25, January-March 1960

babies *noun*

dice *US, 1974*

- —Thomas L. Clark, *The Dictionary of Gambling and Gaming*, p. 9, 1987

babo *noun*

nalorphine, a morphine derivative that acts to reverse the effects of morphine and other narcotics *US*

- —John B. Williams, *Narcotics and Hallucinogenics*, p. 109, 1967

baboo *noun*

an Indian man *TRINIDAD AND TOBAGO, 1914*

A term of respect within the culture; a term of disrespect when used by outsiders.

- —Lise Winer, *Dictionary of the English/Creole of Trinidad & Tobago*, 2003

baboon butt *noun*

the red, sore buttocks of someone riding as a passenger on a motorcyle *US*

- For the doubters among you, there are pictures, one of which shows Brooke hanging on tight and grimacing, an expression described in the caption as "a serious sign of baboon butt"- the rawness that afflicts first-time chopper riders. —*Washington Post*, p. W5, 3rd January 1988

babu *noun*

an East Indian *JAMAICA, 1921*

Also recorded in the Fiji Islands.

- —F.G. Cassidy and R.B. LePage, *Dictionary of Jamaican English*, 1967

baby *noun*

1 used as a friendly term of address *US, 1921*

- "Look, baby," I said, "if you want to cut out of this joint so bad, I'll take you to Detroit." —Mezz Mezzrow, *Really the Blues*, p. 89, 1946
- The first time I heard the expression "baby" used by one cat to address another was up at Warwick in 1951. Gus Jackson used it. The term had a hip ring to it, a real colored ring. —Claude Brown, *Manchild in the Promised Land*, p. 171, 1965
- "What's happening, baby?" said the clerk, a small, wiry Negro with a goatee. —Nat Hentoff, *Jazz Country*, p. 74, 1965
- This is my generation, baby / My generation. —Peter Townsend (performed by The Who), *My Generation*, 1965
- "Hey, baby, you're my main man," Davis said. —Jim Bouton, *Ball Four*, p. 86, 1970

2 a sweetheart, a girlfriend *US, 1839*

- Lord, I really miss my baby / She's in some far off land. —Bob Dylan, *Down the Highway*, 1963

3 a prostitute's customer *US*

- Still and all, she had a small minute of indecision when he brought the first hundred-dollar baby to his apartment to meet her. —John M. Murtagh and Sara Harris, *Cast the First Stone*, p. 32, 1957

4 a young, inexperienced male homosexual *US*

- The biggest crime against the "babies," who come in through the sewer, is there is usually no other route. —*One: The Homosexual Magazine*, p. 18, February 1954

5 a young performer new to the pornography industry who looks even younger than he or she is *US*

- —*Adult Video News*, p. 40, August 1995

6 in horse racing, a two-year-old horse *US*

- —Tom Ainslie, *Ainslie's Complete Guide to Thoroughbred Racing*, p. 327, 1976

7 in professional wrestling, a wrestler or other participant designed to be an audience favourite *US*

A shortened **BABYFACE**.

- I really wish I could leave this place as a baby," I said, before adding, "This angle's going to change all that. —Mick Foley, *Mankind*, p. 280, 1999

8 in the film industry, a screenplay *US*

- How can someone who is creating a "baby" (screenplay) be given an "assignment?" —Odie Hawkins, *Lost Angeles*, p. 64, 1994

9 an impressive, large object *US, 1907*

- —J. E. Lighter, *Historical Dictionary of American Slang, Volume 1*, p. 57, 1994

10 marijuana *US, 1960*

- "He say, 'Man, don't forgit the baby now!' He mean bring a few sticks of it out to the field, you see, that's what he mean by that. He call it 'charge,' too. Sho'. Them's slang names. —Terry Southern, *Texas Summer*, p. 82, 1991
- —Mike Haskins, *Drugs*, p. 286, 2003

11 a puma or cougar *US, 1946*

Circus and hunting usage.

- —Don Wilmeth, *The Language of American Popular Entertainment*, p. 12, 1981

12 in the television and film industries, a focused 500 watt light source *US*

- —Oswald Skilbeck, *ABC of Film and TV Working Terms*, p. 14, 1960

13 in poker, a 2, 3, 4 or 5 *US*

- —John Scarne, *Scarne's Guide to Modern Poker*, p. 272, 1979

▸ **in baby**

pregnant *TRINIDAD AND TOBAGO, 1942*

- —Lise Winer, *Dictionary of the English/Creole of Trinidad & Tobago*, 2003

baby 007 *noun*

in the Vietnam war, an investigative agent from the Army Criminal Investigation Division, most likely working under-cover to identify drug users *US*

- —Linda Reinberg, *In the Field*, p. 15, 1991

baby ass *noun*

someone who is babyish *US*

Teen slang.

- — Susie Dent, *The Language Report*, p. 75, 2003

baby batter *noun*

semen *US*

- —Vann Wesson, *Generation X Field Guide and Lexicon*, p. 10, 1997
- [I]t's becuase you ain't got the baby batter in your brain any more. —*Something About Mary*, 1998
- [W]e provide the baby batter in the fishy fry-up that creates life. —Richard Herring, *Talking Cock*, p. 56, 2003

baby Benz *noun*

a Mercedes 190 *US*

- I wanted the big Benz because a lot of my friends have the baby Benz but the big one is what the big time is all about. —Terry Williams, *The Cocaine Kids*, p. 31, 1989
- At other times, it is wonderfully descriptive, such as when dealers talk about making "crazy dollars" with which to buy a "baby Benz," a Mercedes 190. — *Washington Post*, p. 9, 12th September 1989

baby bhang *noun*

marijuana *US, 1979*

- —Richard A. Spears, *The Slang and Jargon of Drugs and Drink*, p. 18, 1986
- —Mike Haskins, *Drugs*, p. 286, 2003

baby blue *noun*

a tablet of Viagra, an erection-inducing drug taken recreationally for performance enhancement *US*

- —Amy Sohn, *Sex and the City*, p. 154, 2002

baby blues *noun*

1 capsules of the synthetic opiate oxycodone used recreationally *US*

- Extracts reproduced in the tabloid show Limbaugh referring to "small blue babies" and "the little blues." — *Broward Business Revie*, p. 1, 18th November 2003
- Prosecutors in Florida, where Limbaugh has a $24 million estate, are now investigating whether he used one of his housekeepers to obtain OxyContin painkillers, known on the street as "Baby Blues." — *The Record (Bergen County, New Jersey)*, p. 1, 23rd November 2003

2 blue eyes *US*

- Play it big with the baby blues. —Stephen Sondheim, *West Side Story*, 1957

3 post-natal depression *UK*

- — *New Society*, 5th April 1979

baby bonus *noun*

the Canadian family allowance *CANADA*

Also used in Australia.

- 'Tis all very well, de baby bonus and de like o' dat, and very nice for de wife to buy a bar or soap or a bit of beef, fer ye can't live solid on fish and keep up her stren'th. —Bruce Hutchison, *Canada*, p. 17, 1957
- I would sooner see my baby bonus taken away and given to someone who needed it. — *Calgary Herald*, p. 17/3, 29th April 1964

baby boomer *noun*

a person born roughly between 1945 and 1955 *US, 1974*

After World War 2, the US saw a boom in the birthrate.

- A baby boomer of the Bill Clinton / Al Gore generation, he had three older sisters, the youngest of whom was ten years older than himself. —Joseph Wambaugh, *Finnegan's Week*, p. 72, 1993

baby buggy *noun*

1 a Mini Metro car *UK*

Citizens' band radio slang.

- —Peter Chippindale, *The British CB Book*, p. 161, 1981

2 a convertible Volkswagen Beetle *US*

- —Lewis Poteet, *Car & Motorcyle Slang*, p. 20, 1992

baby bumper *noun*

a child molester *US*

- You know, usually there's nothing up there but snitches, bab bumpers, but then there was this other guy? —Richard Price, *Clockers*, p. 542, 1992

baby burglar *noun*

a young thief *UK*

- —Angela Devlin, *Prison Patter*, p. 24, 1996

babycakes *noun*

used as a term of endearment *US, 1967*

- —J. E. Lighter, *Historical Dictionary of American Slang, Volume 1*, p. 57, 1994

baby catcher *noun*

an obstetrician *US, 1970*

From an earlier (1937) sense of 'midwife'.

- — *Maledicta*, p. 57, Summer 1980: 'Not sticks and stones, but names: more medical pejoratives'

baby discovers!

used as a melodramatic reaction to another's surprise *US*

- A new kind of pill? Baby discovers! —Bruce Rodgers, *The Queens' Vernacular*, p. 26, 1972

baby doll *noun*

any central nervous system stimulant *US*

- — *American Speech*, p. 86, May 1955: 'Narcotic argot along the mexican border'

baby dolls *noun*

pyjamas for girls consisting of a baggy top and a short trouser bottom *UK, 1957*

- She is in a black baby doll, a black laced gown to her belly. —Oscar Zeta Acosta, *The Revolt of the Cockroach People*, p. 193, 1973
- Since the bathroom was down the hall, Taggarty (now clothed provocatively in pale green babydolls) stood guard outside the door as Vijay and I leaned over the grungy sinks and brushed our pearlies. —C.D. Payne, *Youth in Revolt*, p. 193, 1993

babydyke *noun*

a young or inexperienced lesbian *US*

- An innocent babydyke in college, I first heard of female ejacuation when Debi Sundahl came to campus to show her instructional video[.] — *The Village Voice*, 7th September 1999

babyface *noun*

1 in professional wrestling, the wrestler designed by the promoters to be the audience favourite in a match *US*

- In fact, even if people heard us talking above the clamor, they weren't able to understand what we were talking about. For example: wrestle is "work"; fall is "going over"; "finish" is the routine just before the deciding fall; hero is "baby face." —Pappy Boyinton, *Baa Baa Black Sheep*, 1958
- When asked what image he wanted to present, Renda didn't hesitate. "I said, 'I don't want to be a babyface. I want to be a nasty guy.'" — *Associated Press*, 31st August 1984
- Last fall Backlund signed on with Pro Wrestling USA, which has allowed him to perform on his own bland terms, as the ultimate babyface. — *Sports Illustrated*, p. 66, 29th April 1985
- I'd been a babyface for all of his fourteen months back with the company. —Mick Foley, *Mankind*, p. 2, 1999
- — *Washington Post*, p. N36, 10th March 2000
- As one of the leading babyface groups around, chances are they will win this match, unless their opponents are awarded the bout by trickery. — *Rampage*, p. 44, September 2000

2 by extension, any figure in the professional wrestling industry designed to be cheered or liked by the fans *US*

- Paul Bearer is a chubby individual who for years was a babyface manager for The Undertaker. —Jeff Archer, *Theatre in the Square*, p. 28, 1999
- Finally, Vince McMahon, then a babyface announcer, asked Lawler, "What is wrong with people from Alabama?" —Jeff Archer, *Theater in the Square*, p. 137, 1999

3 an attractive young woman *JAMAICA*

Reported by a Jamaican inmate in a UK prison, August 2002.

baby father; baby daddy *noun*

a woman's boyfriend, live-in lover or unmarried partner, especially when the father of her child *JAMAICA, 1987*

- [S]hould baby fathers take more responsibility for dem pickney? —Donald Gorgon, *Cop Killer*, p. 89, 1994
- Four men are about to have their lives turned upside down... Babyfather, a BBC2 drama. — *www.bbc.co.uk*, 2001
- —Peter L. Patrick, *Some Recent Jamaican Creole Words*, 2003

baby femme *adjective*

(used of a fashion style) suggesting both youthful innocence and sexual abandon *US*

- Hair clips worn with middle-parted hair or with pig-tails as part of the "baby femme" style, with color-rimmed tight baby T-shorts or baby-doll dresses and Mary Jane shoesl. — Steven Daly and Nalthaniel Wice, *alt.culture*, p. 17, 1995

babyflot *noun*

a Russian airline created by the breakup of Aeroflot in 1991 *CANADA*

- Russian aviation expert Paul Duffy said that while some of the babyflots have questionable track records, Bashkirian Airlines is not among them. — *Toronto Globe and Mail*, p. A4, 3rd July 2002

baby food *noun*

semen *US*

- — Robert A. Wilson, *Playboy's Book of Forbidden Words*, p. 23, 1972

baby fucker *noun*

a child molestor *US*

- The third was a child molestor who perhaps was not the best choice that the Colebrook Unified School District might have made as the driver of its bus for junior high school students. "The baby-fucker," I said." — George V. Higgins, *Penance for Jerry Kennedy*, p. 85, 1985

baby gangster *noun*

a young member of a youth gang *US*

- In Los Angeles, where Blood and Crip membership totals about 25,000, "baby-gangsters" as young as 9 are regularly recruited and some gangs include even younger "tiny gangsters," the report said. — *UPI*, 4th August 1989
- — Mark S. Fleisher, *Beggars & Thieves*, p. 287, 1995

baby grand *noun*

five hundred dollars *US, 1963*

Punning on the piano size and a 'grand' as $1000.

- — Troy Harris, *A Booklet of Criminal Argot, Cant and Jargon*, p. 4, 1976
- — Thomas L. Clark, *The Dictionary of Gambling and Gaming*, p. 9, 1987

baby gun *noun*

a short, bullet-shaped surf board designed for big-wave conditions *US*

- — Jim Allen, *Locked in Surfing for Life*, p. 193, 1970

baby habit *noun*

the irregular, unaddicted use of a drug *US*

- — Jay Robert Nash, *Dictionary of Crime*, p. 15, 1992

baby hero *noun*

in the Vietnam war, a brave soldier *US*

- — Linda Reinberg, *In the Field*, p. 15, 1991

Baby Huey *noun*

a military helicopter *US, 1969*

An embellishment of the more common and simpler **HUEY**, alluding here to a comic strip character.

- The U.S. government, in the midst of downsizing its military-equipment stockpile, sold the $1 million "Baby Huey" helicopter to the county for $3,000. — *Seattle Times*, p. B2, 15th June 1994

baby legs *noun*

in television and film making, a low-legged tripod for supporting lights *US*

- — Ira Konigsberg, *The Complete Film Dictionary*, p. 23, 1987

baby life *noun*

a prison sentence of at least ten years *US*

- — Gary K. Farlow, *Prison-ese*, p. 1, 2002

baby lifter *noun*

a brakeman on a passenger train *US*

- — Norman Carlisle, *The Modern Wonder Book of Trains and Railroading*, p. 258, 1946

Babylon *noun*

1 the white establishment; a symbol of all that is corrupt and evil *JAMAICA, 1943*

From the mystical 'Babylon of the Apocalypse'.

- — F.G. Cassidy and R.B. LePage, *Dictionary of Jamaican English*, p. 17, 1967
- The capitalistic, imperialistic, doggish pimping of the People must cease by this wanton, sadistic country or perish like Babylon. — *The Black Panther*, 6th April 1969
- Babylon cyaan [cannot] keep a good man down. — Donald Gorgon, *Cop Killer*, p. 23, 1994
- — Judi Sanders, *Da Bomb!*, p. 2, 1997
- "Babylon! Get the fucker!" I was casually dressed and generally of unkempt appearance, but they could smell a copper a mile away. — Duncan MacLaughlin, *The Filth*, p. 165, 2002

2 by extension, the United States *US*

- — David Claerbaut, *Black Jargon in White America*, p. 57, 1972

3 the police *JAMAICA*

- — Richard Allsopp, *Dictionary of Caribbean English Usage*, p. 55, 1996

Babylonian *noun*

a white person *US*

- — Rick Ayers (Editor), *Berkeley High Slang Dictionary*, p. 11, 2004

babylons *noun*

the female breasts *UK*

- BEING FIT DONT JUST MEAN HAVIN GREAT BABYLONS AND A NICE PUNANI. — Sacha Baron-Cohen, *Da Gospel According to Ali G*, 2001
- Babylons the size of Birmingham [...] but where's your Spaghetti Junction? — *Loose Women*, 15th May 2003

baby mix *noun*

short kava drinking sessions, especially on a night before work *FIJI*

Kava is a tranquilising herbal beverage. Recorded by Jan Tent.

baby moon *noun*

in hot rodding, a small, chrome convex wheel cover *US*

- Although the name does describe their shape, it actually comes from the name of the pioneering hot rodder who developed them, Dean Moon. — John Edwards, *Auto Dictionary*, p. 10, 1993

baby mother *noun*

an unmarried mother *JAMAICA, 1989*

- She was a "baby mother", a Caribbean term for women who go through the degrading experience of being one of several girlfriends of a single West Indian — Duncan MacLaughlin, *The Filth*, p. 172, 2002
- — Peter L. Patrick, *Some Recent Jamaican Creole Words*, 2003

baby needs a pair of shoes!

used for summoning good luck while rolling the dice in craps *US*

- — Victor H. Royer, *Casino Gamble Talk*, p. 8, 2003

baby pro *noun*

a very, very young prostitute *US, 1961*

- — Burgess Laughlin, *Job Opportunities in the Black Market*, p. 1, 1978
- — Ralph de Sola, *Crime Dictionary*, p. 13, 1982

baby race *noun*

in horse racing, a relatively short race for two-year-old horses *US*

- — Tom Ainslie, *Ainslie's Complete Guide to Thoroughbred Racing*, p. 327, 1976

baby raper *noun*

a child molestor *US, 1961*

- Even the Baby Raper appeared to believe he could be forgiven. Baby raping didn't necessarily make him a bad fellow. He just forgot to ask for ID. — Malcolm Braly, *On the Yard*, p. 13, 1967
- "Baby rapers" [child molestors], snitches, whites assocating with blacks and other undesirables could no longer live in general population. — Bill Valentine, *Gangs and Their Tattoos*, p. 10, 2000

baby rip *noun*

a small current travelling seaward from shore *US*

An abbreviation of 'rip tide' or 'rip current'.

- He bitched about missing some rad tubes and said that old dorks shouldn't be anywhere near a rip, even a baby rip. — Joseph Wambaugh, *The Golden Orange*, p. 33, 1990

baby-san *noun*

1 an East Asian child; a young woman *US, 1954*

Coined during the US occupation of Japan, used frequently in Vietnam.

- Hey, baby-san, you boum-boum G.I.? — *Screw*, p. 5, 15th February 1971
- — Linda Reinberg, *In the Field*, p. 15, 1991

2 by extension, used by Vietnamese prostitutes to refer to a virgin and by US troops to refer to an inexperienced, untested soldier *US*

- — Gregory Clark, *Words of the Vietnam War*, p. 44, 1990

baby scratch *noun*
the most basic technique of manipulating a vinyl record to create new music *US*
• —J. Hoggarth, *How To Be a DJ*, p. 88, 2002

baby shit *noun*
mustard *US, 1972*
A Vietnam contribution to the time-honoured and considerable lexicon of derogatory references to food in the armed forces.
• —Linda Reinberg, *In the Field*, p. 15, 1991

babysit *verb*
1 to guide a person through an LSD or other hallucinatory drug experience *US*
• —Edward R. Bloomquist, *Marijuana*, p. 155, 1968
2 to act as a mentor or protector for newly arrived prisoners *US*
• —Ines Cardozo-Freeman, *The Joint*, p. 480, 1984
3 to date someone who is substantially younger than you *US*
• —Judi Sanders, *Cal Poly Slang*, p. 1, 1990

babysitter *noun*
in a fleet, a destroyer accompanying an aircraft carrier *US, 1965*
• —Harold Wentworth and Stuart Berg Flexner, *Dictionary of American Slang*, p. 672, 1976

baby's leg *noun*
any food, sweet or savoury, that is presented as a pastry roll *UK, 1935*
School and services use; from the appearance and, surely, a reflection on institutional catering.

baby slit *noun*
a tablet of MDMA, the recreational drug best known as ecstasy *UK*
Possibly, a euphemistic rendering of 'little cunt' (a small thing).
• —Mike Haskins, *Drugs*, p. 289, 2003

baby snatcher *noun*
an adult who is sexually attracted to children or adolescents *UK, 1927*
• — *Maledicta*, p. 221, 1979: 'Kinks and queens: linguistic and cultural aspects of the terminology for gays'

baby stealer *noun*
a male or female lover of a much younger or very young person; an older person who prefers such relationships *UK, 1937*

baby strainer *noun*
a condom *UK*
• —David Rowan, *A Glossary for the 90s*, 1998

baby T *noun*
crack cocaine *US*
• —US Department of Justice, *Street Terms*, 2nd October 1994

baca *noun*
tobacco *NORFOLK ISLAND*
• —Beryl Nobbs Palmer, *A Dictionary of Norfolk Words and Usages*, p. 2, 1992

bacalao *noun*
the unwashed vagina *JAMAICA*
From the Spanish for 'codfish'.
• —Richard Allsopp, *Dictionary of Caribbean English Usage*, p. 56, 1996

baccy; bacco; bacca *noun*
tobacco *UK, 1792*
• Have ye managed to sneak me a pinch of the old man's baccy yet? —Robert S.Close, *Love Me Sailor*, p. 94, 1945
• [H]e left on the mail-truck at Omana, taking with him their gifts like the four-gallon tin of 'bacca that boss Channon had promised him. —Wal Watkins, *Race the Lazy River*, p. 158, 1963
• —Angela Devlin, *Prison Patter*, p. 25, 1996
• [T]he first of many requests for "a fag [cigarette] mate, or a bit of baccy, ay, or a fag, I say have you got a fag, or a bit of baccy". —Mark Steel, *Reasons to be Cheerful*, p. 70, 2001

bach *noun*
a vacation cottage *NEW ZEALAND*
• —Louis S. Leland, *A Personal Kiwi-Yankee Dictionary*, p. 10, 1984

bach *verb*
▷ see: BATCH

bachelor *noun*
in police work, an officer who works best alone *US*
• He was known as a bachelor, a cop who didn't work well harnessed to another cop, keeping everything to himself, going off and investigating angles on his own and sharing what he learned only when he got damned good and ready. —Robert Campbell, *Boneyards*, p. 10, 1992

bachelor pad *noun*
the apartment of a young, single, urbane, sophisticated man *US, 1976*
• For the Club's bachelor-pad look, it had been a simple matter to turn to the pages of Playboy for interior design and furnishing ideas. —Kathryn Leigh Scott, *The Bunny Years*, p. 54, 1998

bachelors' hall *noun*
a residence of unmarried men, originally from a Hudson's Bay trading post building for clerks *UK, 1746*
• The building on the right is Bachelors' Hall where R.M. Ballantine lived. It was worthy of its name, being a place that would have killed any woman, so full was it of smoke, noise, and confusion. — *Beaver*, p. 40/1, Winter 1957

bachy; batchy *noun*
1 a room where a man lives alone or brings women for sex *GUYANA*
• —Richard Allsopp, *Dictionary of Caribbean English Usage*, p. 57, 1996
2 a small house occupied by a single man *TRINIDAD AND TOBAGO*
• —Lise Winer, *Dictionary of the English/Creole of Trinidad & Tobago*, 2003

back *noun*
1 an illegal gambling operation *US*
An abbreviation of '*back* office'.
• We hear Red Scalotta's back offices gross from one to two million a year. And he probably has at least three backs going." —Joseph Wambaugh, *The Blue Knight*, p. 144, 1973
2 a drink taken immediately after another, a 'chaser' *US, 1982*
• Next morning he went to a bar meeting, as in lawyers, and I went to my own, as in bocoo bourbon and beer backs. —Seth Morgan, *Homeboy*, p. 9, 1990
3 the musical accompaniment which a jazz band gives a soloist *US*
• —Clarence Major, *Dictionary of Afro-American Slang*, p. 22, 1970
4 support, help *US*
• He told me to go to this spot with him. He said he needed some back [backup or help] and he didn't have anybody." —Terry Williams, *The Cocaine Kids*, p. 19, 1989
5 the buttocks *US*
• —Connie Eble (Editor), *UNC-CH Campus Slang*, p. 1, Fall 1993
6 potency; virility *GUYANA*
• —Richard Allsopp, *Dictionary of Caribbean English Usage*, p. 57, 1996
• —Lise Winer, *Dictionary of the English/Creole of Trinidad & Tobago*, 2003

▸ **get off your back**
to cease annoying, aggravating, nagging or criticising you *UK, 1961*
Often in the exasperated imperative 'Get off my back!'.

▸ **get on your back**
to annoy, aggravate, nag or criticise you *AUSTRALIA, 1959*

▸ **get someone's back; have someone's back**
to defend or protect someone *US*
• I got your back. — *New Jack City*, 1990
• Do you get my back when she bashes me? Because I know she does. — *Chasing Amy*, 1997

▸ **it's got a back to it**
used of an article that is being lent, stressing that the loaned article must be returned *UK, 1961*
A catchphrase mainly in London use.

▸ **like the back of a bus; like the back end of a bus**
ugly, unattractive *UK, 1959*
• Shit, fix yourself up, you look like the back end of a bus. —Buddy Giovinazzo, *Life Is Hot in Cracktown*, p. 60, 1993

▸ **on your back**

1 (of a woman) working as a prostitute *AUSTRALIA*

• So what with fines, taxation assessments and rent for a room she hardly spends any time in at all, a girl could never get ahead. On her back, I mean. —Sue Rhodes, *And when she was bad she was popular*, p. 10, 1968

2 (of a woman) engaged in sexual intercourse *AUSTRALIA*

• Christ, where was she? On her back probably. She always liked a fuck before the game. —Robert English, *Toxic Kisses*, p. 1, 1979

3 penniless *UK, 1937*

An Australian variant, 'on the back of your arse', is first recorded in 1961.

back *verb*

to carry something on your back *BAHAMAS*

• —John A. Holm, *Dictionary of Bahamian English*, p. 7, 1982

▸ **back and fill**

to vacillate *US*

Nautical imagery, from the term for handling sails to catch and then spill the wind.

• —John Gould, *Maine Lingo*, p. 1, 1975

▸ **back a tail**

to engage in anal sex *AUSTRALIA, 1973*

▸ **back off the course**

to bet a large amount on something *AUSTRALIA*

• 'It's an SP job,' I tells him, 'they'll back it off the course.' —Frank Hardy, *The Yarns of Billy Borker*, p. 107, 1965

▸ **back off the map**

to bet a large amount on something *AUSTRALIA*

• A horse called Coffee was backed off the map. —Frank Hardy and Athol George Mulley, *The Needy and the Greedy*, p. 16, 1975
• They waited a fortnight and at Canterbury in a far stronger field, they backed the beaten horse off the map. —Clive Galea, *Slipper*, p. 66, 1988

back-ah-yard *noun*

in the Caribbean, the West Indies, used for expressing the general concept of home *UK, 1977*

West Indian and UK black; literally 'back [at] our **YARD**'.

backanahan *adjective*

untrustworthy, underhanded *BELIZE*

• —Richard Allsopp, *Dictionary of Caribbean English Usage*, p. 58, 1996

back and belly *noun*

a very thin person, especially a woman *GUYANA*

• —Richard Allsopp, *Dictionary of Caribbean English Usage*, p. 58, 1996

back and belly *adverb*

entirely, completely *TRINIDAD AND TOBAGO*

• —Lise Winer, *Dictionary of the English/Creole of Trinidad & Tobago*, 2003

back-and-forth *noun*

conversation *US*

• —*Complete CB Slang Dictionary*, p. 3, 1976

backasswards *adverb*

in the wrong order *US*

• "You always do everything backasswards." He looked at me. "No wonder you're fluncking the hell out of here," he said. —J.D. Salinger, *Catcher in the Rye*, p. 41, 1951
• "I was born backasswards," she liked to explain, referring to her breech birth. —Seth Morgan, *Homeboy*, p. 4, 1990

backblocker *noun*

a resident of a remote area, especially the area beyond the river gorges in Canterbury and Otago, New Zealand *NEW ZEALAND, 1910*

backblocks *noun*

remote and sparsely populated land beyond the outskirts of a town or city *AUSTRALIA, 1879*

• [H]e knows as much about commanding Police as Captain Standish does about mustering mosquitoes and boiling them down for their fat on the back blocks of the Lachlan[.] —Ned Kelly, *The Jerilderie Letter*, p. 100, 1879
• 'Out in the sticks', 'out in the backblock', 'out in the bush, 'out in the booay', 'out in the cactus', all have the same basic meaning of 'fifty miles from nowhere.' —R.L. Bacon, *In the Sticks*, p. 184, 1963
• Buchanan was originally from Wilcannia or Walgett, one of those shit-awful racist dumps in the backblocks of New South Wales. —Shane Maloney, *Nice Try*, p. 36, 1998

back bottom *noun*

the rump or posterior *AUSTRALIA*

Used as a counterpart to 'front bottom'.

• [I]f you don't wear something to cover your back bottom you could very easily get piles. —Gretel Killeen, *Hot Buns and Ophelia get shipwrecked*, p. 51, 2001

backbreaker *noun*

LSD combined with strychnine *UK, 1998*

• —Mike Haskins, *Drugs*, p. 292, 2003

backcap *noun*

an answer *US*

• —Lou Shelly, *Hepcats Jive Talk Dictionary*, p. 7, 1945

backchat *noun*

1 impudent replies; answering back in an insolent manner *UK, 1901*

Originally military.

• But I wasn't going to let the bastard bait me into giving him backchat. —Robert S. Close, *Love Me Sailor*, p. 4, 1945

2 sexual badinage; verbal flirting *AUSTRALIA*

• It was so simple and direct a statement and so devoid of any sexual import that I made none of the usual coquettish back-chat. —Criena Rohan, *Down by the Dockside*, p. 74, 1963

backchat *verb*

to answer back in an insolent manner *AUSTRALIA, 1919*

• —Norman Lindsay, *Halfway to Anywhere*, p. 87, 1947
• Don't backchat me, girl, or I'll give you one. —Tim Winton, *Cloudstreet*, p. 162, 1991

back dex *noun*

amphetamines *UK*

• —Mike Haskins, *Drugs*, p. 279, 2003

back door; backdoor *noun*

1 the anus and rectum *UK, 1694*

• The other replied, "Lawd have mercy brother, I'd go in the back door! —Phyllis and Eberhand Kronhausen, *Sex Histories of American College Men*, 1960
• I was forced to violate everything he has been taught to regard as sacred, including the sanctity of his tiny back door. —Gore Vidal, *Myra Breckinridge*, p. 231, 1968
• It is very tight, the back door, very tight. —Roger Blake, *The Stimulators*, p. 160, 1968
• She says, "Sweetie, I ain't gonna go three way with you for no sawbuck. You gotta gimme fifteen." He says, "I'll spring for that if you can guarantee a tight back door and quim." —Iceberg Slim (Robert Beck), *Doom Fox*, p. 6, 1978
• There is a lot of "back door" action and some quasi-rape sequences that become passionate embraces. —Kent Smith et al., *Adult Movies*, p. 190, 1982
• For a start the cast will have back doors buffed and, if the rehearsal diet works, blowing off all the time. —Roy Slaven (John Doyle), *Five South Coast Seasons*, p. 66, 1992
• So let her explore your back door, then you can do hers. —*The Village Voice*, 24th August 1999

2 in sports, the advancement of a team in a playoff situation as a result of the actions of another team *US*

• We're lucky. That seven-point underdog stuff is steak on the platter for us," said Mr. Williamson. "They're saying we aren't up to Michigan State and only got here through the back door. —*San Francisco News*, p. 11, 30th December 1952

3 in a group motorcyle ride, the last rider in the group; the final citizens' band radio user in a convoy *US*

Usually the most experienced motorcycle-rider in the group.

• —*Complete CB Slang Dictionary*, 1976
• —Peter Chippindale, *The British CB Book*, p. 151, 1981

4 in computing, a secret password buried in a system that permits a programmer to enter the system surreptitiously *US*

• —Karla Jennings, *The Devouring Fungus*, p. 218, 1990

▸ **go out the back door**

to back down from a confrontation *US*

• —*Maledicta*, p. 266, Summer/Winter 1981: 'By its slang, ye shall know it: the pessimism of prison life'

back-door; backdoor *verb*

1 to commit adultery *US*

• The bawdiest story concerns a merchant who "back-doors" his partner's wife by promisng to tell her his secret of turning a woman to a mare and back to a woman again. —Kent Smith et al., *Adult Movies*, p. 70, 1982

2 in surfing, to start a ride behind the peak of a wave *US*
- —John Grissim, *Pure Stoke*, p. 156, 1980

3 to bypass something; to exclude something *CANADA*
- —Jack Chambers (Editor), *Slang Bag 93 (University of Toronto)*, p. 1, Winter 1993

back-door; backdoor *adjective*

1 adulterous *US*
- He was your mother's back-door man, I thought.—Ralph Ellison, *Invisible Man*, p. 242, 1947
- I was getting back-door stuff from my man's rib.—A.S. Jackson, *Gentleman Pimp*, p. 45, 1973

2 in poker, describing an unexpected hand produced drawing *US*
- —John Scarne, *Scarne's Guide to Modern Poker*, p. 272, 1979

back-door alcoholic *noun*
an alcoholic who admits his alcoholism and joins a twelve-step recovery programme for addicts after initially characterising himself as an enabler of another alcohlic *US*
- —Christopher Cavanaugh, *AA to Z*, p. 53, 1998

backdoor artist *noun*
a swindler, especially a drug user who deceives other drug users *US*
- —Jay Robert Nash, *Dictionary of Crime*, p. 15, 1992

backdoor Betty *noun*
a woman who enjoys anal sex *US*
- The people who've volunteered to get done are always self-proclaimed backdoor betties, but when push comes to penetration, they get shy.—*The Village Voice*, 8th August 2000

back-door bust *noun*
an arrest for one crime, usually major, after a detention or arrest for another, usually minor *US*
- JODIE: He didn't get busted against until he was thirty-two. And then it was a backdoor bust. A routine vice squad roust. They roust this bar, our buddy Lawrence is in there knocking down a few.—*Reservoir Dogs*, 1992

back door closed *adjective*
describes a convoy when the final vehicle is looking out for any police interest *US*
Citizens' band radio slang.
- —*Complete CB Slang Dictionary*, 1976
- —Peter Chippindale, *The British CB Book*, p. 151, 1981

backdooring *noun*
anal intercourse *UK*
- ["]Bradley is referring to the rusty bullet-hole," said Mikey. "The what?" Mario was still struggling. "The chocolate starfish." "Back-dooring." "Uphill gardening." [...] What, you mean shoving it up their arse?" exclaimed Mario.—Colin Butts, *Is Harry on the Boat?*, p. 21, 1997

backdoor parole; backgate parole *noun*
death while serving a prison sentence *US, 1929*
A black joke.
- —Vincent J. Monteleone, *Criminal Slang*, p. 14, 1949
- —Angela Devlin, *Prison Patter*, p. 25, 1996

backdoor pensioner *noun*
a sheep dog who is past his working days *NEW ZEALAND*
The term implies an honourable retirement. A dog of similar years but just a 'bit of an old pooch' would be more likely referred to as a 'pot-licker'.
- —Robert Loughnan, *Glossary*, p. 2, 1981

back door trots *noun*
diarrhoea *UK, 1801*
- —Jim Crotty, *How to Talk American*, p. 171, 1997

back-double *noun*
a back street, a side road *UK, 1932*

back down *verb*
in betting on horse racing, to force the odds on a horse lower through heavy betting *US*
- —David W. Maurer, *Argot of the Racetrack*, p. 11, 1951

back 'em down *verb*
in trucking, to reduce speed *US*
- —*Complete CB Slang Dictionary*, p. 3, 1976

backer *noun*
a person who is a frequent participant in anal sex *TRINIDAD AND TOBAGO*
- —Lise Winer, *Dictionary of the English/Creole of Trinidad & Tobago*, 2003

backfield *noun*
the supporting members of a criminal group *US*
- What he didn't know about wires wasn't invented yet, so now we had the whole backfield.—Red Rudensky, *The Gonif*, p. 93, 1970

backfire *verb*
to fart *UK*
- Somebody just backfired.—Peter Furze, *Tailwinds*, p. 25, 1998

backflash *noun*
in pinball, the painted glass panel at the front of the machine *US*
Conventionally known as the 'backglass'.
- —Bobbye Claire Natkin and Steve Kirk, *All About Pinball*, p. 110, 1977

back flip *verb*
in pinball, to flip the ball to the same side of the playing field as the flipper *US*
- —Bobbye Claire Natkin and Steve Kirk, *All About Pinball*, p. 110, 1977

back forty *noun*
a large, remote piece of land; a backyard *US, 1950*
Originally a reference to a farmer's most distant 40-acre parcel; the usage generalised and then became humorous.
- Of course, finding firewood might be a problem unless you own a "back 40" yourself.—*Christian Science Monitor*, p. 18, 24th September 1980
- —Frederic G. Cassidy, *Dictionary of American Regional English*, p. 120, 1985

back-forty accent *noun*
country speech *CANADA*
- Whether he was cracking jokes in his best "back forty" accent, or singing, he gave the audience what it wanted.—*Ottawa Citizen*, p. 9/3, 25th August 1958

back gate exit *noun*
death while in prison *US*
- —William K. Bentley and James M. Corbett, *Prison Slang*, p. 104, 1992

backhand *adjective*
in surfing, with your back to the wave *AUSTRALIA*
- —Nat Young, *Surfing Fundamentals*, p. 126, 1985

backhander *noun*
a bribe; a gratuity given surreptitiously *UK, 1971*
- [M]ost of them copped a backhander from the manufacturers.—Frank Hardy, *The Outcasts of Foolgarah*, p. 9, 1971
- —Angela Devlin, *Prison Patter*, p. 25, 1996
- Greg, do you think she's taking backhanders?—Colin Butts, *Is Harry on the Boat?*, p. 107, 1997
- Backhanders got be better than they let on[.]—Jeremy Cameron, *Brown Bread in Wengen*, p. 54, 1999
- [A] little "drink" as they called it – or "backhander" as anyone else would call it.—Dave Courtney, *Raving Lunacy*, p. 30, 2000

back haul *noun*
on the railways, a return trip *US*
- —Ramon Adams, *The Language of the Railroader*, p. 9, 1977

backhouse *noun*
an outside toilet, especially without plumbing *US, 1984*

backhouse flush *noun*
in poker, a very poor hand *US, 1984*
From 'backhouse' (an outside toilet).

backie *noun*

1 an act of using someone's bent back as a platform to climb a wall or get over an obstacle *UK: SCOTLAND*
- —Michael Munro, *The Original Patter*, 1985

2 a ride, as passenger, on the back of a bicycle *UK: SCOTLAND, 1985*
- Ah'll gie ye a backie up the road.—Michael Munro, *The Complete Patter*, 1996

backings *noun*
in the illegal production of alcohol, low-proof distillate not potent enough to be considered whisky *US*
- —David W. Maurer, *Kentucky Moonshine*, p. 113, 1974

back in the day *adverb*
at a time in the past that evokes a feel of nostalgia, real or conjured *US, 1988*
- —Connie Eble (Editor), *UNC-CH Campus Slang*, p. 1, March 1996
- Hip Hop America starts "back in the day" – the late '70s[.]—Nelson George, *Hip Hop America*, p. xi, 1998
- When I first used to go down the City back in the day, seventy-seven, seventy-eight, Jason and Jimmy were two of the top faces.—John Williams, *Cardiff Dead*, p. 146–147, 2000
- Back in the day, they say you had anti-freez in them veins.—*Gone in 60 Seconds*, 2000

back in the saddle; back in the saddle again *adjective*
experiencing the bleed period of the menstrual cycle *US, 1954*
- —Frederic G. Cassidy, *Dictionary of American Regional English*, p. 120, 1985
- When I was a teen and the common protection consisted of the elastic sanitary belt and pad, we referred to being "Back in the saddle again."—a contributor *The Museum of Menstruation and Women's Health*, April 2001

back in the teapot, doormouse!
used as an admonition to a child to be quiet *CANADA*
- —Bill Casselman, *Canadian Sayings*, p. 30, 2002

backjunk *noun*
a big piece of wood at the back of a fire *CANADA*
Better known in the US as a 'backlog', the name of the 'back junk' comes from the pronunciation of 'chunk' as 'junk'.
- On Christmas Eve, therefore, the "backjunk" blazed higher and brighter than usual in the big, open fireplaces.—Michael Harrington, *Sea Stories from Newfoundland*, p. 117, 1958
- Huge fire places are filled wi "back Junk" – usually the largest tree in the forest that will burn through the 12th days of Christmas—Kingston *Whig-Standard*, 17th December 1958

back light *noun*
the rear window of a car *US*
- — Chrysler Corporation, *Of Anchors, Bezels, Pots and Scorchers*, September 1959

back line *noun*
the wall of amplifiers and speakers behind a rock band in concert *ANGOLA*
- The 'back line' of amplifiers and speaker cabinets used by the band on stage and originally costing thousands of pounds which is immediated devalued by artistically inclined roadies (see Crew) who insist on covering every square inch of it with spray paint and gaffa tape—Bob Young and Micky Moody, *The Language of Rock 'n' Roll*, p. 16, 1985

backline *verb*
in casino blackjack, to place a bet in another player's square *US*
- —Frank Scoblete, *Best Blackjack*, p. 252, 1996

backlip *noun*
impertinence, talking back *US, 1959*
- Little Jeff give you sass, Big Jeff look around like he ain't even listening, but if you gave backlip – wap! – Big Jeff laid you out. —Edwin Torres, *Carlito's Way*, p. 17, 1975

back-me-up *noun*
a friend who can be counted on for support in a confrontation *US*
- —Inez Cardozo-Freeman, *The Joint*, p. 480, 1984

back number *noun*
a person who is hopelessly out of date *US*
- —Harold Wentworth and Stuart Berg Flexner, *Dictionary of American Slang*, p. 13, 1960
- —Kenn "Naz" Young, *Naz's Dictionary of Teen Slang*, p. 5, 1993

back of beyond *noun*
a remote area *AUSTRALIA, 1879*
- This time again the blacks are away in the back of beyond, and Harmon got two up from Kalgoorlie.—Arthur Upfield, *Bony and the Mouse*, p. 63, 1959
- —Patsy Adam-Smith, *Folklore of the Australian Railwaymen*, p. 107, 1969

back of Bourke *noun*
a remote area *AUSTRALIA, 1896*
Bourke is a county centre in central New South Wales.
- 'You're liable to end up back o'Bourke, as they say.'—Michael Peters, *Pommie Bastard*, p. 72, 1969
- 'Every ratbag club from here to back o'Bourke runs their annual Cup on New Year's Day', he told the Comittee.—Gerald Sweeney, *The Plunge*, p. 100, 1981

back of the yards *noun*
a neighbourhood in Chicago around and behind the now defunct Union Stockyards *US*
- —Bill Reilly, *Big Al's Official Guide to Chicagoese*, p. 13, 1982
- Another settled Back of the Yards and worked in the packing plants. —Robert Campbell, *In a Pig's Eye*, p. 143, 1991

back-o-wall *noun*
any slum *JAMAICA, 1978*
Originally applied to the slums of west Kingston, Jamaica.

back pack *noun*
a gang insignia tattooed on a gang member's back *US*
- —Paladin Press, *Inside Look at Outlaw Motorcyle Gangs*, p. 33, 1992

back passage *noun*
the rectum *UK, 1960*
Euphemistic.
- [T]hong knickers, which move around, can transfer bacteria from the back passage, leading to infections such as cystitis.—*The Guardian*, 5th August 2003

back-pasture hauler *noun*
in trucking, a driver who prefers back roads and smaller motorways *US*
- —Montie Tak, *Truck Talk*, p. 7, 1971

back porch *noun*
a late position in a hand of poker *US*
- —John Vorhaus, *The Big Book of Poker Slang*, p. 5, 1996

back-porch nigger *noun*
an obsequious, fawning black person *US*
- [H]e bowed and scraped and grinned apologetically like some creaky old back-porch nigger.—Tom Robbins, *Another Roadside Attraction*, p. 61, 1971

back rack *noun*
in pinball, the part of the machine that rises as a panel at the front of the machine *US*
Conventionally known as a 'lightbox'.
- —Bobbye Claire Natkin and Steve Kirk, *All About Pinball*, p. 110, 1977

backra fire *noun*
electricity *GUYANA*
- —Richard Allsopp, *Dictionary of Caribbean English Usage*, p. 61, 1996

backra-Johnny *noun*
a poor white person *BARBADOS*
- —Richard Allsopp, *Dictionary of Caribbean English Usage*, p. 61, 1996

backroom boy *noun*
a scientific technician, especially if engaged in research that may be secret *UK, 1943*
Usually used as a plural.

backroom job *noun*
a tattoo on a part of the body that is usually clothed *US*
- —*Los Angeles Times Magazine*, p. 7, 13th July 1997

back row *noun*
a prison cell used for solitary confinement *US*
- —Inez Cardozo-Freeman, *The Joint*, p. 480, 1984

backs *noun*
money, especially counterfeit money *US*
Probably an abbreviation of **GREENBACK**.
- —Lou Shelly, *Hepcats Jive Talk Dictionary*, p. 7, 1945

back-sack-and-crack-wax *noun*
a male depilatory treatment *UK*
'Sack' is sometimes spelt, more correctly, 'sac'; and 'n' is occasionally used for 'and'.
- "I'm excited," replied A.J. in monotone, and looking about as excited as Suzanne did when she learned she'd be doing a back, sack and crack wax.—*The Salon*, 12th March 2003
- —Jonathan Ross, *They Think it's All Over*, 28th October 2003
- —Kate Lawler, *RI:SE*, 29th October 2003

back-sass *noun*
impudent talking back to an elder *US, 1968*
- —Frederic G. Cassidy, *Dictionary of American Regional English*, p. 121, 1985

back-sass *verb*
to talk back impudently *US, 1950*
• —Frederic G. Cassidy, *Dictionary of American Regional English*, p. 121, 1985

back-scratch *verb*
to remove from a tank enemy soldiers who have climbed onto it, usually by directing light-weapon fire onto the tank *US*
• —Linda Reinberg, *In the Field*, p. 15, 1991

back-scuttle *verb*
to play the active role in sex, anal or vaginal, from behind *US, 1885*
• —Dale Gordon, *The Dominion Sex Dictionary*, p. 25, 1967
• —Lise Winer, *Dictionary of the English/Creole of Trinidad & Tobago*, 2003

back seat *noun*
in poker, any of the positions farther from the dealer than the third player to his left *US, 1973*
• —Thomas L. Clark, *The Dictionary of Gambling and Gaming*, p. 11, 1987

▸ **in the back seat**
ignored, forgotten *US*
Building on the **CAR** (clique) metaphor.
• —Ethan Hilderbrant, *Prison Slang*, p. 9, 1998

▸ **take a back seat**
to be or become less important than someone or something else *US, 1902*
• The sulphate had taken a back seat by now, and we were into getting pissed. —John King, *Human Punk*, p. 180, 2000

backshow *noun*
in gambling on broadcast racing, any betting before the current show price *UK*
• —David Bennet, *Know Your Bets*, p. 15, 2001

backside *noun*
▸ **while your backside points to the ground**
while you are alive *AUSTRALIA*
• [H]e wouldn't even get within striking distance of their ability as long as his backside pointed to the ground. —Robert G. Barrett, *Davo's Little Something*, p. 101, 1992

backside!
used for expressing strong scepticism *AUSTRALIA*
• "Mr, Wrorter is an experienced arbitration advocate," Settlum reminded Chilla, "and the secretary of your union." "We always conduct our own cases," Chilla persisted, thinking secretary backside[.] —Frank Hardy, *The Outcasts of Foolgarah*, p. 68, 1971

backside furrit; backside forward *adverb*
thoroughly, inside out *UK: SCOTLAND*
• Never mind whit he says. Ah'm tellin ye Ah know this joab [job] backside furrit. —Michael Munro, *The Patter, Another Blast*, 1988

back-slack *verb*
to talk back *NEW ZEALAND, 1929*

backslap *noun*
a celebratory event of mutual congratulation *AUSTRALIA*
From conventional 'backslapping'.
• [O]ne veteran of the annual backslap. — *The Times Magazine*, p. 12, 23rd march 2002

backslide *noun*
in trucking, a return trip *US*
• —Lanie Dills, *The Official CB Slanguage Language Dictionary*, p. 14, 1976
• [W]e'll catch you on the backslide. —Peter Chippindale, *The British CB Book*, p. 151, 1981

backspace and overstrike!
in computing, used for expressing alarm about a mistake that has just been made *US*
• —Eric S. Raymond, *The New Hacker's Dictionary*, p. 45, 1991

back stairs *noun*
the anus and rectum considered as a sexual passage *UK*
Euphemistic or humorous simile for 'the back way up'.
• [B]ecause women can, and do, let men take the back stairs[.] — *GQ*, p. 117, July 2001

backstop *noun*
1 in baseball, the catcher *US, 1887*
2 by extension, a person who provides a second line of defence in a venture *AUSTRALIA, 1944*
• You wanted me as a backstop. —Edwin Torres, *After Hours*, p. 392, 1979
• He only went along with me as a backstop. —Clive Galea, *Slipper*, p. 111, 1988

backstop *verb*
to act as a backstop *AUSTRALIA, 1955*

backstory *noun*
history, previous experience *UK*
Adopted into wider usage from screen-acting jargon where it is used to describe what has happened before the story starts.
• No one gives a fuck about the backstory, so long as what is going on is worth doing[.] —James Hawes, *Dead Long Enough*, p. 146, 2000
• What's the back story? Born in California, raised in Michigan, son of a professional golfer. — *Uncut*, p. 14, January 2002

backs to the wall!
used as a humorous catchphrase to acknowledge the presence of a male homosexual *UK*
Homophobic; suggesting a fear of anal sex/rape.
• "That Stig from Club Wicked is really getting on my nerves." "Why?" "All that backs to the wall crap. I mean, as if? I'm gay, not blind." —Colin Butts, *Is Harry Still on the Boat?*, p. 206, 2003

backstreet boy *noun*
a young man dressed in the trendiest of clothes with the trendiest of haircuts *US*
Not a compliment; an allusion to a talent-free band of the late 1990s that valued style to the exclusion of substance.
• —Don R. McCreary (Editor), *Dawg Speak*, 2001

backstroke *noun*
in trucking, a return trip *US*
• —Wayne Floyd, *Jason's Authentic Dictionary of CB Slang*, p. 8, 1976

back-talk *noun*
insolent answering back *AUSTRALIA*
• Squalled at me that she owned the business and that she wouldn't take any back talk from me and that the piece wasn't for sale. —Norman Lindsay, *Dust or Polish?*, p. 156, 1950

back-talk *verb*
to answer back with impudence *UK, 1887*
• You going to let that mongrel back-talk you like that? —D'Arcy Niland, *Dead Men Running*, p. 74, 1969
• —John A. Holm, *Dictionary of Bahamian English*, p. 8, 1982
• I didn't want to spend my years back-talking Officer Dibble[.] —Stuart Jeffries, *Mrs Slocombe's Pussy*, p. 27, 2000

back teeth *noun*
▸ **to the back teeth**
to capacity; totally; completely *AUSTRALIA, 1933*
• 'Inked, blithered, full up to the back teeth,' chanted Waldo. —Norman Lindsay, *Halfway to Anywhere*, p. 202, 1947
• 'No,' said Byrne, not hard enough to smart though, 'it was that Hearn had us bewitched to the back-teeth.' —Thomas Keneally, *Bring Larks and Heroes*, p. 238, 1967
• Thanks mate, you always played the game the way it ought to be played – competitive to the back teeth, but more importantly, like a gentleman. —Max Walker, *How To Tame Lions*, p. 49, 1988

back teeth are floating
used for describing an extreme need to urinate *US, 1923*
• I was dehydrated, my back teeth were floating. — *Pittsburgh Post-Gazette*, p. S-13, 13th September 2000

back the card
to bet on every race at a meeting *AUSTRALIA*
• [O]ld Sam drew out his pile of form guides, thinking if only I had a bank I could back the card tomorrow. —Frank Hardy, *The Outcasts of Foolgarah*, p. 78, 1971

back time *noun*
1 in the Vietnam war, rear-area or non-combat duty *US*
• —Linda Reinberg, *In the Field*, p. 15, 1991
2 the portion of a prison sentence not served at the time of parole, which must be served if parole is violated *US*
• —Jay Robert Nash, *Dictionary of Crime*, p. 15, 1992
3 all time spent incarcerated before sentencing *US*
• —William K. Bentley and James M. Corbett, *Prison Slang*, p. 17, 1992

back to *preposition*
used in the names of reunion parties *AUSTRALIA, 1925*
• [A]ll the Smith boys were born with a broad axe in their hands' the old man at the 'Back to Neerim South' had said. — Patsy Adam-Smith, *The ANZACS*, p. 324, 1978

back-to-back *noun*
heroin then crack used in sequence *US*
• — US Department of Justice, *Street Terms*, October 1994
• — Robert Ashton, *This Is Heroin*, p. 208, 2002

back-to-back *adjective*
consecutive *US, 1952*
Usually used in a sports context. If there is a third consecutive event, the term is simply expanded to 'back-to-back-to-back'.
• — *American Speech*, December 1955

back to hacking
used as a farewell, by computer enthusiast to computer enthusiast *US*
• — Guy L. Steele et al., *The Hacker's Dictionary*, p. 76, 1983

back to the drawing board!
used after the failure of an endeavour *US, 1965*

back to the salt mines!; back to the mines!
back to work! *US, 1933*
An ironic reference to hard labour in the Siberian salt mines.

back track *verb*
when injecting a drug, to draw blood up into the syringe to mix with the drug that is being injected *US*
• — Jay Robert Nash, *Dictionary of Crime*, p. 15, 1992

back-up *noun*
1 a person supporting another in a fight *AUSTRALIA*
• — *The (Sydney) Bulletin*, 26th April 1975
• 'Any time, pal, any time.' Hogan turned to go. ''N don't forget t' bring all yer back-ups,' shouted a happy Redford after Hogan. — Bob Jewson, *Stir*, p. 46, 1980

2 a second helping of food *AUSTRALIA, 1929*
• — Tom Ronan, *Only a Short Walk*, 1961
• And we know you appreciate it because you always have a back up of everything, Right. — Frank Hardy, *The Outcasts of Foolgarah*, p. 19, 1971

3 serial sex between one person and many others, usually consensual *AUSTRALIA, 1965*
• The club just had a backup with the new ginch. — Robert A. Wilson, *Playboy's Book of Forbidden Words*, p. 23, 1972

4 the path from the death cell to the death chamber in prison *US*
• — Jay Robert Nash, *Dictionary of Crime*, p. 15, 1992

backups *noun*
extremely bright lights on the rear of a car used to blind would-be kidnappers or terrorists *US*
• — Jay Robert Nash, *Dictionary of Crime*, p. 16, 1992

backward in coming forward *adjective*
reluctant to do something, modest, shy *UK, 1830*
More often phrased as 'not backward in coming forward'.

backwards *noun*
any central nervous system depressant *US*
• — J. L. Simmons and Barry Winograd, *It's Happening*, p. 167, 1966
• — Edward R. Bloomquist, *Marijuana*, p. 155, 1968
• — Mike Haskins, *Drugs*, p. 282, 2003

back-warmer *noun*
a female motorcyle passenger *US*
Biker (motorcyle) usage.

backwash *noun*
answering back in an insolent manner *AUSTRALIA*
• Don't give me any of your dirty backwash. — Wilda Moxham, *The Apprentice*, p. 58, 1969

backwashing *noun*
after injecting a drug, the drawing of blood back into the syringe, with the intention of collecting any drug residue, and reinjecting the resultant mix *UK*
• — Mike Haskins, *Drugs*, p. 271, 2003

backwater *noun*
in trucking, back roads or small motorways *US*
• — Elementary Electronics, *Dictionary of CB Lingo*, p. 4647, 1976

backwhack *noun*
the back-slash key (\) on a computer keyboard *US*
• — Eric S. Raymond, *The New Hacker's Dictionary*, p. 40, 1991

back wheel *noun*
in horse racing, the second bet in a two-part bet *US*
• — Igor Kushyshyn et al., *The Gambling Times Guide to Harness Racing*, p. 211, 1994

back wheels *noun*
the testicles *UK, 1998*
• Right up to the back wheels[.] — *www.LondonSlang.com*, 26th June 2002

backyard *noun*
1 the buttocks *US*
• — Robert A. Wilson, *Playboy's Book of Forbidden Words*, p. 23, 1972
• — John A. Holm, *Dictionary of Bahamian English*, p. 8, 1982

2 the anus *US*
• — Dale Gordon, *The Dominion Sex Dictionary*, p. 25, 1967

3 in a circus, the performers as a group distinguished from the administrative and support staff *US*
• — Harold Wentworth and Stuart Berg Flexner, *Dictionary of American Slang*, p. 13, 1960

4 the road visible behind you *US*
• — *Complete CB Slang Dictionary*, p. 3, 1976

backyard butchery *noun*
an amateur's modification of a surfboard, obviating the design features of the manufacturer *AUSTRALIA*
• — *surfresearch.com.au*

backyarder *noun*
a surfboard built by or modified by an amateur *AUSTRALIA*
• — *surfresearch.com.au*

bacon *noun*
1 the police; a police officer *US, 1974*
From **PIG** (a policeman). During the late 1960s and early 70s, a favoured chant of the radical left youth movement in the US was 'Today's pig, tomorrow's bacon!'.
• Publishers and stuff wouldn't even know "bacon burning" was "pigs" or "cops" coming. — Beatrice Sparks (writing as 'Anonymous'), *Jay's Journal*, p. 60, 1979
• Later, bacon. — *Airheads*, 1994
• — Judi Sanders, *Da Bomb*, p. 1, 1997

2 money *US*
• The boss catered mostly to Indians who had struck oil on the reservation, beefy cattlemen who were sure to be milked, sugar-daddies with their sable-sporting chicken dinners, and butter-and-egg men with plenty of bacon. — Mezz Mezzrow, *Really the Blues*, p. 84, 1946
• We'll save your bacon for you. — Max Shulman, *Rally Round the Flag, Boys!*, p. 115, 1957

3 the buttocks *BAHAMAS*
• — John A. Holm, *Dictionary of Bahamian English*, p. 8, 1982

▸ **bring home the bacon**
to succeed as a wage earner, supporting one's family; to achieve success; to succeed in a given undertaking *US, 1909*
Generally thought to echo the ancient tradition in Dunmow, England, of presenting a flitch of bacon to a happily married couple but originates in the US country-fair 'sport' of catching a greased pig. The phrase was popularised, if not invented, by the mother of Joe Gans, a black lightweight boxer.
• Anyhow, what I'm sayin, everybody dependin on this new gig I got t'bring home the bacon[.] — Robert Gover, *Here Goes Kitten*, p. 53, 1964
• He is fanatical about his job. He always brings home the bacon. — Howard Stern, *Miss America*, p. 448, 1995
• He was marching to work doing his duty, bringing home the bacon. — John King, *Human Punk*, p. 111, 2000

▸ **save your bacon**
to rescue someone financially *UK, 1654*
• I'm just a kid compared to him, so it bothers him that I've saved his bacon more than once. — Robert Campbell, *Nibbled to Death by Ducks*, p. 5, 1989
• You ain't gotta be a genius: Memphis come back to save our bacon. — *Gone in 60 Seconds*, 2000

bacon and eggs *noun*

1 the legs *AUSTRALIA, 1942*
Rhyming slang.
- Wot smashin' bacons. — Jack Jones, *Rhyming Cockney Slang*, 1971
- The best place for yer plates of meat [feet] is at the end of yer bacon and eggs! — *The Sweeney*, p. 8, 1976

2 a black person who is partly or completely albino *TRINIDAD AND TOBAGO*
- — Lise Winer, *Dictionary of the English/Creole of Trinidad & Tobago*, 2003

bacon assegai *noun*

the penis and testicles *UK*
- — Tom Hibbert, *Rockspeak!*, p. 15, 1983

bacon bits *noun*

the breasts *UK*
Rhyming slang for **TIT(S)**.
- She showed me her bacon bits so I covered them in my special sauce. — Bodmin Dark, *Dirty Cockney Rhyming Slang*, 2003

bacon bonce *noun*

1 a slow-witted person *UK*
- — *Daily Telegraph*, 4th June 1958

2 a sex offender *UK*
Rhyming slang for **NONCE**.
- — Angela Devlin, *Prison Patter*, p. 23, 1996

3 a bald or balding man *UK, 1984*

bacon getter *noun*

a handgun, especially a single-action revolver *US*
- — *American Speech*, p. 192, October 1957: 'Some colloquialisms of the handgunner'

bacon rashers *noun*

the vagina *UK*
- However, the category edibility glosses over the variablity within it, which, for FGTs [female genital terms] included frequent reference to meat (e.g., bacon rashers, kebab, meat curtains); fish/seafood (e.g., tuna waterfall; fish, clam); and "sweet tidbits" (e.g. love muffin, fudge, cake-hole). — *Journal of Sex Research*, p. 146, 2001

bad *noun*

1 fault *US*
- "Who's in the den?" "It's me and Kelly!" "My bad, (sorry) let's try another room" — Eminem (Marshall Mathers), *My Fault*, 1999

2 crack cocaine *US*
- — US Department of Justice, *Street Terms*, October 1994

▸ **get in bad with**
to get in trouble or disfavour with someone or some agency of authority *UK, 1928*

bad *adjective*

1 good; tough *US, 1897*
- The latest bop talk requires you to say, if you like a musician, "Man, he's real bad." Or, "he blows bad." This critical pronouncement is delivered in a monotone, with the "b-a-a-d" dragged out for emphasis. Means the exact opposite of what it says. — *Philadelphia Evening Bulletin*, 11th October 1955
- I've mentioned him before – one of Harlem's really bad Negroes. — Malcolm X and Alex Haley, *The Autobiography of Malcolm X*, p. 117, 1964
- In this day when somebody would say something a bad cat, they meant that he was good. Somebody would say, "That was some bad pot," meaning it was good. — Claude Brown, *Manchild in the Promised Land*, p. 292, 1965
- Kocomo was about five times bigger than Egan, but the way Egan was carrying himself had everybody thinking he was bad too. — Cecil Brown, *The Life & Loves of Mr. Jiveass Nigger*, p. 64, 1969
- Some folks say that Willie Green / was the baddest motherfucker the world ever seen. — Bruce Jackson, *Get Your Ass in the Water and Swim Like Me*, p. 57, 1970
- The Copiens, the Socialistics, the Bachelors, the Comanches – all bad motherfuckers – these were the gangs that started using hard-ware. — Edwin Torres, *Carlito's Way*, p. 8, 1975
- It's gonna be bad, like Rex's full-on Thor tattoo. — *Airheads*, 1994
- She's a MC, a girl rapper and she's bad at it too. — Karline Smith, *Letters to Andy Cole*, p. 139, 1998

2 in computing, broken *as designed* *US*
- — Eric S. Raymond, *The New Hacker's Dictionary*, p. 46, 1991

bada-bing; ba-da-bing

▷ **see:** BADDA BING

bad ass *noun*

a tough, fearless person *US, 1956*
- Now Dolomite went on down to Kansas City / kickin' asses till both shoes were shitty. / Hoboed into Chi / Who did he run into but that badass Two-Gun Pete. — Bruce Jackson, *Get Your Ass in the Water and Swim Like Me*, p. 59, 1970
- Buddusky became Bad-Ass, which in navy tolerance means a very tough customer. — Darryl Ponicsan, *The Last Detail*, p. 7, 1970
- [A]lla them badasses've carved outa hunka turf in this town. — Lester Bangs, *Psychotic Reactions and Carburetor Dung*, p. 53, 1971
- A lot of people don't realize – especially from up East – that Texans are thought of pretty highly as badasses. — Bruce Jackson, *Outside the Law*, p. 89, 1972
- So like I'm shooting dice on 105th Street off Madison Avenue on a Saturday afternoon when this bad-ass named Chago grabs all the money on the ground and says, "These dice are loaded." — Edwin Torres, *Carlito's Way*, p. 20, 1975
- I'm a killer and I've got a platoon of the baddest badasses in the Nam. We're bad, baaaad fuckin' killers. — Philip Caputo, *A Rumor of War*, p. 245, 1977
- You wear this to a business meeting, you're the bad-ass in the room. — *Jackie Brown*, 1997

bad-ass *adjective*

excellent; worthy of respect, tough *US, 1955*
Originally black usage but now more widely known.
- I told him about hanging out with those bad-ass boys. — Claude Brown, *Manchild in the Promised Land*, p. 10, 1965
- A truly badass movie! — *San Francisco Examiner*, p. 27, 19th July 1974
- Now down on the ground in a great big ring / Lived a bad-ass lion who knew he was king. — Dennis Wepman et al., *The Life*, p. 22, 1976
- [b]ut they were baaaaad-ass cops. Way too macho to talk about it. — Joseph Wambaugh, *Lines and Shadows*, p. 103, 1984
- You bad-ass little spick. How are you, honey? — *Boogie Nights*, 1997
- Ditched testosterone powered riffs for emotion driven songs. Badass stuff. — *Metal Hammer*, p. 5, May 2001

Bad-Ass Billy *nickname*

Brigadeer General William R. Bond of the 199th Light Infantry Brigade, killed by a sniper's bullet about 70 miles northeast of Saigon on 1st April 1980 *US*
- — Linda Reinberg, *In the Field*, p. 15, 1999

bad-bad *adjective*

very bad *BAHAMAS*
- — John A. Holm, *Dictionary of Bahamian English*, p. 8, 1982

bad beat *noun*

in poker, a disappointing loss, either with a good hand or a big bet *US*
- — David M. Hayano, *Poker Faces*, p. 185, 1982

bad belly *noun*

an upset stomach *BAHAMAS*
- — John A. Holm, *Dictionary of Bahamian English*, p. 8, 1982

bad boy *noun*

1 something that is impressive *US*
- I finally got this bad boy together bout six, seven months. Got the whole place furnished top to bottom. — Vernon E. Smith, *The Jones Men*, p. 139, 1974
- I say, "thanks" for the pills, pop the bad little pink boys and instantly awake. — Odie Hawkins, *Scars and Memories*, p. 56, 1987
- Well, I want two of them bad boys. Two large orders of chili fries. Two large Diet Cokes. — *True Romance*, 1993
- PIP: It's a card thing door opener. REX: I know how to handle these bad boys. — *Airheads*, 1994
- But put that bad boy in a flick, every motherfucker out there want one. — *Jackie Brown*, 1997

2 a rascal, a misfit *US*
- Cincy Trades 'Bad Boy' Eddie Miller to Phillies (Headline) — *San Francisco Examiner*, p. 20, 11th February 1948
- Strange Things Are Happening to Hollywood's 'Bad Boy' — *San Francisco Examiner's Pictorial Review*, p. 13, 27th December 1953

3 a violent, tough young criminal *BARBADOS*
- It is not secret that they do not have enough vehicless and their Divisions are understaffed. But they have still been able to put the crunch on the 'bad boys' and reduce the crime rate for 1975. — *Sunday Chronicle*, p. 17, 15th July 1976

bad bundle *noun*

inferior quality heroin *US, 1971*
- — Robert Ashton, *This Is Heroin*, p. 208, 2002

bad butch *noun*

an aggressive, 'mannish' lesbian *US*

- Known variously as a bull, a stomper, a bad butch, a hard dresser, a truck driver, a diesel dyke, a bull dagger and a half dozen other soubriquets, she is the one who, according to most homosexual girls, gives lesbians a bad name. —Ruth Allison, *Lesbianism*, p. 125, 1967

bad buzz *noun*

an unpleasant event *CANADA*

- —Jack Chambers (Editor), *Slang Bag 93 (University of Toronto)*, p. 1, Winter 1993

bad cop *noun*

in a pair of police, the partner who plays the aggressive and hard-nosed role during an interrogation *US*

- The one that growled is O'Shea who always looks like he's got a bad case of indigestion and plays the bad cop. —Robert Campbell, *In a Pig's Eye*, p. 23, 1991

badda bing; bada-bing; ba-da-bing

used as an embellishing intensifier *US*

The variations are nearly endless.

- You've gotta get up close like this and bada-bing! you blow their brains all over your nice Ivy League suit. —Mario Puzo and Francis Ford Coppola, *The Godfather*, 1972
- And on this farm he shot some guys. Ba-da-bip, ba-da-bing, ba-da-boom. —*The Usual Suspects*, 1995
- Badda-bing, Badda-bang. —Ira Steven Behr and Hans Beimler, *Star Trek*, 1999
- It was cake – 8 cars. Badda-bing. —*Gone in 60 Seconds*, 2000
- [T]hey were drinking shorts and, of course, they were surrounded by fawning, gorgeous young women. As Tony might say: "It's been that way since time immemorial." Ba-da-bing indeed! —*The Guardian*, 16th September 2002

bad dad *noun*

a person whose opinion of his own toughness exceeds the rest of the world's estimation *US*

- —Kenn "Naz" Young, *Naz's Underground Dictionary*, p. 13, 1973

baddap! *verb*

to be shot *UK*

Echoic of gun fire.

- [W]hen a innocent man like Fluxy can just get "baddap!" when he's just goin' about his business not troublin' anyone, it's dread. —Karline Smith, *Moss Side Massive*, p. 60, 1994

badden *verb*

to become intoxicated on drugs or alcohol *TRINIDAD AND TOBAGO*

- —Lise Winer, *Dictionary of the English/Creole of Trinidad & Tobago*, 2003

baddest *adjective*

toughest; most admired *US, 1938*

The unconventional superlative of 'bad' in the 'bad-as-good' sense of the word.

- "Eric [Clapton] is one of the baddest guitarists who ever lived," [Quincy] Jones concluded. —*San Francisco Chronicle*, 8th September 1971
- The baddest one-chick hit squad that ever hit town! —*San Francisco Chronicle*, p. 58, 15th June 1973
- "I'm a killer and I've got a platoon full of the baddest badasses in the Nam. We're bad, baaaad fuckin' killers." —Philip Caputo, *A Rumor of War*, p. 245, 1977
- —Edith A. Folb, *runnin' down some lines*, p. 228, 1980
- Then [presidential spokesman Jody] Powell turned to the statement in Tanzania, where Ali said, "There are two bad white men in the world, the Russian white man and the American white man. They are the two baddest men in the history of the world." —*San Francisco Chronicle*, p. 10, 6th February 1980
- He was employed because he was one of the baddest geezers out there. He'd go into the nastiest situations with ease. —Dave Courtney, *Raving Lunacy*, p. 177, 2000

baddie *noun*

1 a villain, especially in works of fiction *US, 1937*

A childish epithet for a staple character of popular mass-entertainment, also used 'ironically' in law-enforcement. Also variant 'baddy'.

- The question uppermost in my mind was whether Tam and her monsters were baddies or goodies [...] Their behavious suited the baddy routine[.] —Martin Waddell, *Otley*, p. 29, 1966
- India One. If the baddies follow you in, drive straight through, out the other end and back on the highway. —Chris Ryan, *Stand By, Stand By*, p. 84, 1996
- "Mr X"! I sounded like a fucking baddie in a Bond film. —Dave Courtney, *Raving Lunacy*, p. 34, 2000

2 an unwell feeling *UK: SCOTLAND*

- —Michael Munro, *The Patter, Another Blast*, 1988

3 a slight wound, such as a graze or cut *UK*

Nursery and childish.

bad dog *noun*

an unpaid debt *AUSTRALIA, 1953*

bad eye *noun*

a spell or curse caused by looking with envy or insincere goodwill *TRINIDAD AND TOBAGO*

- If you have a well kept flower or kitchen garden you must protect it from persons with 'bad eye'. —*Express*, p. 26, 6th September 1972

badeye *verb*

to glare, to stare with menace *US*

- —Charles Shafer, *Folk Speech in Texas Prisons*, p. 197, 1990

bad food *noun*

food or drink made with ingredients believed to instill sexual fidelity or attraction *BARBADOS*

- —Richard Allsopp, *Dictionary of Caribbean English Usage*, p. 65, 1996

badge *noun*

1 a police officer *US, 1925*

- About that time along come two badges patrolling their beat / arrested this whore for prostituting on the street. —Bruce Jackson, *Get Your Ass in the Water and Swim Like Me*, p. 80,
- —Jack Webb, *The Badge*, p. 220, 1958
- —Don R. McCreary (Editor), *Dawg Speak*, 2001

2 a prison guard *US*

- —William K. Bentley and James M. Corbett, *Prison Slang*, p. 95, 1992

3 a small amount of a drug relative to the amount paid *US*

- —Eugene Landy, *The Underground Dictionary*, p. 28, 1971

badge *verb*

to show a police badge, especially as part of a psychological ploy to elicit information *US*

- She thought he was a PO-lice impersonator when he finally badged her." —Joseph Wambaugh, *The New Centurions*, p. 214, 1970
- "Which one of us is gonna badge him?" Letch asked. —Joseph Wambaugh, *Floaters*, p. 231, 1996

badge bandit *noun*

a police officer, especially a motorcyle police officer *US*

- —Harold Wentworth and Stuart Berg Flexner, *Dictionary of American Slang*, p. 13, 1960

badger *noun*

in horse racing, an inexpensive horse that qualifies its owner for race track privileges *US*

- —Tom Ainslie, *Ainslie's Complete Guide to Thoroughbred Racing*, p. 327, 1976

badger game *noun*

a swindle in which a prostitute lures a customer or victim to a room where he is robbed by a confederate of the prostitute, often posing to be her husband *US, 1909*

- But cases of "badger" workers are everyday occurences[.] —Jack Lait and Lee Mortimer, *New York Confidential*, p. 98, 1948
- [T]he street-level warrens decayed into strip tease clip joints and worthless sucker traps with carnival barkers, broads hustling tables, finger men on the prowl, lookouts for blackmail mobs on steady duty, badger game veterans[.] —Robert Sylvester, *No Cover Charge*, p. 89, 1956
- Blackmail Trap Laid to Clerk, Wife; Contractor Charges Badger Game (Headline) —*San Francisco Examiner*, p. 12, 8th February 1956
- There he met Phillipa, an orphaned teenage whiz at the badger game played with a Baton Rouge based pimp and con man on johns during Mardi Gras. —Iceberg Slim (Robert Beck), *Doom Fox*, p. 46, 1978

badger-gassing *noun*

an act or instance of farting, or its malodorous after-effect *UK*

After a controversial means of exterminating badgers.

- —Chris Lewis, *The Dictionary of Playground Slang*, p. 18, 2003

badger scratching *noun*

the act of fondling a woman's vagina *UK*

- I wouldn't mind doin' a bit of badger scratching with her. —*www.LondonSlang.com*, 26th June 2002

badger's nadgers *noun*

anything considered to be the finest, the most excellent, the best *UK*

Formed on **NADGERS** (the testicles), this is further variation on the **DOG'S BOLLOCKS** and **MUTT'S NUTS** theme; usage noted, most significantly, on a greeting card being sold by a high street chain, January 2004.

bad go *noun*
a small amount of a drug relative to the price paid *US*
• —Eugene Landy, *The Underground Dictionary*, p. 27, 1971

bad guy *noun*
a criminal *US*
Originally children's vocabulary from watching Western films. Perhaps orginating in the mid-1960s.
• "Maybe he didn't," Raylan said. "Maybe he was abducted." They hadn't thought of that, both of them turning to look at each other. "By who," Jerry said, "the bad guys?"—Elmore Leonard, *Pronto*, p. 71, 1977

bad hair day *noun*
a day on which your hair is especially unruly; hence, a day on which nothing goes to plan *US*
• They said I told them I was having a bad hair day. They didn't even talk to me. (Quoting Gary Shandling)—*Seattle Times*, p. 10, 25th January 1991
• Ah, the bad hair day – where would chick lit or chauvinist revenge humour be without this contemporary cultural platitude?—*The Times Magazine*, p. 49, 31st May 2003

bad hat *noun*
1 someone who can be counted on to misbehave *US, 1914*
• He was a thoroughly bad hat, then, but that was the kind, of course, that nice women broke their hearts over.—Mary McCarthy, *The Group*, p. 175, 1963

2 a pimp *US*
• —Anna Scotti and Paul Young, *Buzzwords*, p. 13, 1997

bad head *noun*
a violent, tough young criminal *BELIZE*
• —Richard Allsopp, *Dictionary of Caribbean English Usage*, p. 66, 1996

bad idea jeans *noun*
the notional clothing worn by someone who has displayed an utter lack of common sense *US*
From a skit on *Saturday Night Live*.
• And whoever thought mild-mannered milquetoast Jimmy Buffet was up for a no-holds-barred tag-team match on "Mack the Knife" should be given a pair of "Bad Idea" jeans and maybe a dose or two of electro-shock therapy.—*Philadelphia Daily News*, p. 25, 16th November 1994
• —Ben Applebaum and Derrick Pittman, *Turd Ferguson & The Sausage Party*, p. 4, 2004

bad John *noun*
any man who is violence-prone *TRINIDAD AND TOBAGO, 1935*
An allusion to John 'Bad John' Archer, a criminal who figured prominently in early C20 life.
• —Lise Winer, *Dictionary of the English/Creole of Trinidad & Tobago*, 2003

bad looker *noun*
an ugly person *AUSTRALIA*
Used with a negative.
• She wasn't a bad-looker.—Arthur Upfield, *Bony and the Mouse*, p. 62, 1959
• She wasn't a bad looker either, was Mad Mavis.—Lance Peters, *The Dirty Half-Mile*, p. 90, 1979
• She's not even a bad looker when she smiles.— Edna Everage (Barry Humphries), *My Gorgeous Life*, p. 115, 1989

badly *adverb*
wonderfully, excellently; very *UK*
• [H]is sister is badly fit.—Colin Butts, *A Bus Could Run You Over*, p. 310, 2004

badly packed kebab *noun*
the vagina *UK, 2002*
A visual similarity to the dish eaten late at night, when half-drunk.
• —*www.LondonSlang.com*, 26th June 2002
• —Chris Lewis, *The Dictionary of Playground Slang*, p. 18, 2003

bad medicine *noun*
a person or thing that promises trouble *US, 1920*
An imitation of the speech of native American Indians.
• —Joseph Weingarten, *American Dictionary of Slang*, p. 14, 1954

bad mind *noun*
malice *TRINIDAD AND TOBAGO*
• Dr. Williams's closest friends should advise him that the politics of bad-mind will not do[.]—*Express*, p. 4, 1st December 1979

bad motherfucker *noun*
a fearless, tough person *US*
• [H]e was a very mean and impatient man who had no respect for free enterprise, especially when some cocksucker was freely enterprising in his territory. He was a bad motherfucker[.]—Emmett Grogan, *Ringolevio*, p. 112, 1972

bad mouth *noun*
a curse, a put-down *US*
• Rudy wondered how the bad mouth about him had started, although he'd arrived at the point where he didn't much care.—Clarence Cooper Jr, *The Scene*, p. 12, 1960
• I said, "Mama, look, don't be puttin the bad mouth on him."—Claude Brown, *Manchild in the Promised Land*, p. 287, 1965
• Just that they ken pu the bad-mouth on you, that's all.—Steve Cannon, *Groove, Bang, and Jive Around*, p. 128, 1969

badmouth *verb*
to insult someone, to disparage someone *US, 1941*
• "I had to beat the bitch's ass for bad mouthing you, Mollie," he said.—Dick Gregory, *Nigger*, p. 22, 1964
• Bobby Bodega Pogats, the society stock market operator, has retained Atty. Jim MacInnis to file a slanger suit against the Stock Exchange hotshot who has been badmouthing him.—*San Francisco Chronicle*, p. 29, 2nd July 1969
• "[W]hen you threatened him and bad-mouthed him and everything, you were no better than he was."—Darryl Ponicsan, *The Last Detail*, p. 43–44, 1970
• Taylor said, "They were bad mouthing our ball players when we were on the way into the locker room. It's bush."—*San Francisco Examiner*, p. 50, 26th January 1972

badness *noun*
something that is very good *US*
• "The party was great – we're talking BADNESS."—Connie Eble (Editor), *UNC-CH Campus Slang*, p. 1, Fall 1986

bad news *noun*
1 a person who is better avoided *UK, 1946*
• When Booth arrives on the street where he lived, the pavements suddenly teem with besotted matrons in aprons and girls brimming with oestrogen. He's bad news, that lad.—*The Guardian*, 7th December 2001

2 something, abstract or actual, that is unpleasant or contemptible *US, 1917*
• —*American Speech*, p. 55, Spring-Summer 1975: 'Razorback slang'

3 the M-48 'Patton' tank, designed for combat in Europe against Soviet tanks, then the mainstay of the US Army and Marines in Vietnam *US*
• —Linda Reinberg, *In the Field*, p. 15, 1991

4 in drag racing, a car that performs very well *US*
• —John Lawlor, *How to Talk Car*, p. 17, 1965

bad nigger *noun*
a tough, fearless, respect-commanding black person *US, 1965*
A term of praise.
• —Frederic G. Cassidy, *Dictionary of American Regional English*, p. 121, 1985

bad-o *adjective*
excellent *US*
• —Trevor Cralle, *The Surfin'ary*, p. 5, 1991

badonkadonk *noun*
large, shapely buttocks *US*
From the Comedy Central television programme *Crankyankers*.
• —Connie Eble (Editor), *UNC-CH Campus Slang*, p. 1, April 2004

bad on you!
shame on you! *FIJI*
Recorded by Jan Tent in 1997.

bad paper *noun*
1 a discharge from the military other than an honourable discharge, such as the UD (undesirable discharge) or resignations for the good of the service *US, 1971*
• I've met the bitter veterans with "bad-paper" discharges who hate themselves and everybody else, too.—*The Los Angeles Times*, 20th April 1980
• "Bad paper," that childish-sounding phrase, is loaded with all the negative connotations of leaving the military with anything less than an honorable discharge.—Myra MacPherson, *Long Time Passing*, p. 679, 1984
• —Linda Reinberg, *In the Field*, p. 15, 1991

2 counterfeit money or securities *US*
• If told my partner, if the dude was into bad paper, you'd know who he was.—Gerald Petievich, *Money Men*, p. 13, 1981

bad-pay *adjective*
slow in paying a debt or obligation *GRENADA*
Collected in 1976.

bad penny *noun*

an unreliable or untrustworthy person; someone of little or no worth *UK, 1937*

A figurative sense from debased coinage; orginally 'bad ha'penny' before inflation.

bad rack *noun*

at a casino, a list of customers who are poor credit risks *US, 1974*

- —Thomas L. Clark, *The Dictionary of Gambling and Gaming*, p. 11, 1987

bad rock *noun*

cocaine; crack cocaine *UK*

- —Mike Haskins, *Drugs*, p. 280, 2003

bads *noun*

the depression following the use of hallucinogens or amphetamines *US*

- —William D. Alsever, *Glossary for the Establishment and Other Uptight People*, p. 2, December 1970

bad scene *noun*

an unpleasant situation; a depressing experience *US*

- —J. L. Simmons and Barry Winograd, *It's Happening*, p. 167, 1966
- —Eugene Landy, *The Underground Dictionary*, p. 27, 1971

bad scran *noun*

bad luck *IRELAND*

- 'The coward wouldn't stand his ground,' he said to my mother that evening. 'But he heard me right enough, bad scran to him,'[.]—Hugh Leonard, *Out After Dark*, p. 31, 1989

bad seed *noun*

1 peyote; heroin *US, 1969*

- —Richard A. Spears, *The Slang and Jargon of Drugs and Drink*, p. 20, 1986
- —Mike Haskins, *Drugs*, p. 283, 2003

2 mescaline, the hallucinogenic alkaloid of peyote *US*

3 marijuana *UK, 1998*

- —Mike Haskins, *Drugs*, p. 286, 2003

bad shit *noun*

high quality drugs, especially marijuana

- —Angela Devlin, *Prison Patter*, p. 25, 1996

bad sick *noun*

any sexually transmitted infection *ANTIGUA AND BARBUDA*

- —Richard Allsopp, *Dictionary of Caribbean English Usage*, p. 68, 1996

bad-talk *verb*

to disparage someone or something *BAHAMAS*

- —John A. Holm, *Dictionary of Bahamian English*, p. 9, 1982

bad thing *noun*

an inherently bad idea *US*

From *1066 and All That*, the history parody in which Sellar and Yeatman created the 'bad thing' device: 'Indeed, he had begun badly as a Bad Prince, having attempted to answer the Irish Question by pulling the beards of the aged Irish chiefs, which was a Bad Thing and the wrong answer'.

- "Replacing all of the 9600-baud modems with bicycle courier would be a Bad Thing."—Eric S. Raymond, *The New Hacker's Dictionary*, p. 46, 1991

bad time *noun*

1 time served in prison that does not count towards the overall sentence; time served in a military stockade that does not count towards the overall period of service *US*

- —Carl Fleischhauer, *A Glossary of Army Slang*, p. 2, 1968
- Quinn, your young ass is gonna do some bad time for this.—Larry Heinemann, *Close Quarters*, p. 164, 1977
- The penalty of being derelict on duty was slyly unexplained but understood, the stockade, bad time, serve six months, come out and start over where you left off.—Odie Hawkins, *Scars and Memories*, p. 90, 1987

2 a jail or prison sentence for a petty, avoidable offence *US*

- He had enough to think about, the last thing he needed was the clammy friendship of a dumb sap doing bad time on an alimony beef.—Odie Hawkins, *Chicago Hustle*, p. 102, 1977

3 the bleed period of the menstrual cycle *US*

- —*American Speech*, p. 298, December 1954: 'The vernacular of menstruation'

bad trip *noun*

an unpleasant, frightening or unnerving experience with LSD *US*

- Such precautions are thought to be insurance against bad trips. —Hunter S. Thompson, *Hell's Angels*, p. 236, 1966
- Psychedelic adventurers in San Francisco who are on a bad trip can call in a friendly pilot to bring them down safely.—*Berkeley Barb*, p. 6, 9th December 1966
- —Joe David Brown (Editor), *The Hippies*, p. 217, 1967: 'Glossary of hippie terms'
- There isn't much sense in trying to explain what a "bad trip" is . You simply lose your marbles. You go crazy. There is no bottom, no top. —Oscar Zeta Acosta, *The Autobiography of a Brown Buffalo*, p. 183, 1972
- [H]ow the C.I.A. initiated the "bad trip" propaganda; how it was all a lie, etc., etc.—Cleo Odzer, *Goa Freaks*, p. 62, 1995

bad trot *noun*

a losing streak; a period of heavy or sustained losses *AUSTRALIA*

- —Tom Ellis, *The Science of Turf Investment*, p. 60, 1936
- However, late O'Neill was to suffer one of these bad trots that come to everyone[.]—Richie Benaud, *Spin me a Spinner*, p. 28, 1963
- When the 1904 Melbourne Cup came round he was having 'a bad trot' and he was reported to be down to his last few thousands.—James Holledge, *The Great Australian Gamble*, p. 88, 1966
- A Sydney punter decided to try his luck in the U.S. but he had a bad trot.—Frank Hardy and Athol George Mulley, *The Needy and the Greedy*, p. 120, 1975

bafan *noun*

a clumsy person *JAMAICA, 1956*

From 'baff-hand' (a cripple).

- —Paul Sullivan, *Sullivan's Music Trivia*, p. 35, 2003

baff *verb*

to vomit *US*

- —Collin Baker et al., *College Undergraduate Slang Study Conducted at Brown University*, p. 74, 1968

bafflegab *noun*

verbose language that is difficult to penetrate and impossible to understand *US*

The term, by all accounts, was coined by Milton A. Smith of the United States Chamber of Commerce. Smith defined the term as 'Multiloquence characterized by consummate interfusion of circumlocution or periphrasis, inscrutability, incognizability, and other familiar manifestations of abstruse expatiation commonly utilized for promulgations implementing procrustean determinations by governmental bodies'.

- — *Word Study*, p. 5, May 1952
- Mutual funds are diversifying to the point where you can completely lose your way in this financial industry without a bafflegab guide. — *San Francisco Chronicle*, p. 52, 7th January 1970
- Connoisseurs of bureaucratic bafflegab may salivate over this May 12 memo from Robertio Alioto.— *San Francisco Chronicle*, 15th May 1980
- The crackdown on bafflegab was sought by Councillors Howard Moscoe (North York Spadina) and Chris Stockwell (Lakeshore-Queensway).— *Toronto Star*, p. A1, 21st November 1989
- Bafflegab is still an official language for Parliament Hill and provincial capitals – even city halls – despite a federal anti-babble policy and recent efforts to simplify the written word.— *Toronto Star*, p. A12, 17th January 1994

bag *noun*

1 an interest *US, 1964*

- Anyway you can also be a part-time new American head. That's going to be my bag.—Nat Hentoff, *I'm really dragged but nothing gets me down*, p. 19, 1968
- I mean, what the hell's the matter with you guys? You into some kind of fag bag awready?—Terry Southern, *Blue Movie*, p. 166, 1970
- Bulls ain't never been my bag – but here's to you, anyway, Big Jeff. —Edwin Torres, *Carlito's Way*, p. 17, 1975
- He was a painter and singer but his main bag was hustlin in de Paris streets.—Babs Gonzales, *Movin' On Down De Line*, p. 17, 1975
- We realized that that was his bag, being revolting, and he got off when folks thought he was revolting.—Stephen Gaskin, *Amazing Dope Tales*, p. 225, 1980
- My own personal bag is meditation – no don't laugh.—Macfarlane, Macfarlane and Robson, *The User*, p. 13, 1996
- I don't even know what this [a penis-enlarger] is. This sort of this ain't my bag, baby.— *Austin Powers*, 1997

2 a way of doing things *US, 1962*

- It was clear to me that we were in two different bags; I had it "made" because I had occupied my niche from the age of five, definitely by the time I was eight.—Odie Hawkins, *Lost Angeles*, p. 89, 1994

3 an unattractive young woman *AUSTRALIA*
- Ah, not like the bags here in Woolloomooloo who are either too fat or too thin, too tall or too short. —Frank Hardy, *The Yarns of Billy Borker*, p. 26, 1965
- I found a girl, a friend of a friend, who looked like a refugee from the roller game. She was the worst bag you could find – and as unpleasant in manner as only a true bag could be. —Sue Rhodes, *Now you'll think I'm awful*, p. 151, 1967
- She might be fat and untidy – or a real bag. I might end up being sorry I had to look at her. —Ward McNally, *Supper at Happy Harry's*, p. 84, 1982
- As Bag of the Ball I was presented with a sash suited to the occasion. —Joe Brown, *Just for the Record*, p. 52, 1984

4 a police uniform *US, 1944*
- — *New York Times Magazine*, p. 87, 16th March 1958
- I'd hate to be back in the bag, believe me. —Charles Whited, *Chiodo*, p. 54, 1973
- I tell you, it's a whole different thing when you wear a nice suit to work instead of that damn bag. —Leonard Shecter and William Phillips, *On the Pad*, p. 166–167, 1973

5 duty as a uniformed police officer *US*
- [H]e suddenly declared that maybe he would get out of the pad somebday, that if necessary he would go back to the "bag" – police slang for uniformed duty. —Peter Maas, *Serpico*, p. 187, 1973

6 a breathalyser *UK*
By ellipsis from 'breathalyser bag'.
- — *Bournemouth Echo*, 16th November 1967

7 the scrotum *US, 1938*
- — Anon., *King Smut's Wet Dreams Interpreted*, 1978

8 a sexually promiscuous woman or a prostitute *US, 1893*

9 a condom *US, 1922*
- —Dale Gordon, *The Dominion Sex Dictionary*, p. 25, 1967
- She was on the pill, but I used to use a bag with her anyway. —*Screw*, p. 9, 12th April 1971

10 a diaphragm *US*
- —Roger Blake, *The American Dictionary of Sexual Terms*, p. 11, 1964

11 a collection raised in a single effort *UK, 1900*
Figurative application of the game-bag in which hunters gather their kill.
- This "bag" on a single ship and a single voyage indicated the extent of Communist efforts to get a honeycomb of agents into the United States. —Harry J. Anslinger, *The Murderers*, p. 27, 1961

12 a large score made by a player *AUSTRALIA*
- 'How many did the big fella get?' 'He killed 'em...he kicked a bag.' —Ivor Limb, *Footy's No Joke!*, p. 8, 1986

13 a package of drugs *US, 1952*
- A bag is his supply of drugs. —Clarence Cooper Jr, *The Scene*, p. 54, 1960
- Now you know it's a draf; I copped a bad bag. —Dennis Wepman et al., *The Life*, p. 78, 1976
- Jimmy went and leaned up against a building with them and watched the whores go by and a pusher said you want a bag? —William T. Vollman, *Whores for Gloria*, p. 115, 1991

14 a small paper packet or plastic bag containing heroin; thus a standardised measure of heroin, either by cost or volume *US, 1952*
Also variant 'bagel'.

15 heroin *UK*
Adopted by drug-users from the sense of 'bag' meaning 'an interest or way of doing things'.
- Bit of crack to make them high, bit of bag to lull the comedown. —Kevin Sampson, *Outlaws*, p. 77, 2001

16 a parachute *UK, 1943*
Originally Royal Air Force, then the army also.

17 a fuel tank on an aeroplane *US*
- We're loading you up with Rockeyes and giving you a full bag of gas. —Gerry Carroll, *North S*A*R*, p. 61, 1991

18 a member of a college fraternity *US*
An abbreviation of **BAGGER**, itself an abbreviation of **FRATTY BAGGER**.

19 bed *US*
- —John D. Bell et al., *Loosely Speaking*, p. 2, 1969

▸ bag of snakes
a business acquisition full of bad surprises *US*
- —David Olive, *Business Babble*, p. 12, 1991

▸ get a bag!
learn how to catch! *AUSTRALIA*
In cricket used as a derisive retort to a fielder who drops an easy catch.
- —Richard Beckett, *The Dinkum Aussie Dictionary*, p. 26, 1986

▸ in the bag

1 drunk *US, 1940*
- You know. Drunk stewed, clobbered, gone, liquored up, oiled, stoned, in the bag. —Max Shulman, *Guided Tour of Campus Humor*, p. 106, 1955
- [T]he next night when he came in she was half in the bag[.] —George V. Higgins, *The Rat on Fire*, p. 94–95, 1981
- It took him three hours and forty minutes to hike it half in the bag, from Thebes to the bridge, not seeing one goddman car on the road. —Elmore Leonard, *Killshot*, p. 287, 1989

2 as good as done *US, 1921*
- Israel-Egyptian Peace Pact Believed Virtuallly 'in the Bag' (Headline) — *San Francisco News*, p. 2, 21st February 1949
- The butler said it was in the bag. —Charles Raven, *Underworld Nights*, p. 16, 1956

3 corrupted, bribed, beholden to someone else *US, 1926*
- I'm not asking was the fight put in the bag. —Rocky Garciano (with Rowland Barber), *Somebody Up There Likes Me*, p. 307, 1955
- As far as he's concerned, I'm in the bag. He gave me until the weekend to contact him. —Edwin Torres, *Q & A*, p. 175, 1977

4 (of a horse) not being run on its merits; being run to lose; (of a jockey) not riding to win *AUSTRALIA, 1903*
Literally, the money that has been bet on the horse will stay in the bookmaker's bag.
- The owner of the horse was an undertaker by trade and very light with the sling so the jockey decided to put the horse 'in the bag'. —Frank Hardy and Athol George Mulley, *The Needy and the Greedy*, p. 75, 1975
- During his career, Sam rejected many offers from the smart bookmakers to put him in the bag[.] —Joe Andersen, *Winners Can Laugh*, p. 148, 1982

▸ on someone's bag
in golf, working as a caddie *US*
- Angelo was on Jack's bag for years, but he eventually retired and opened a restaurant in Miami. —Hubert Pedroli and Mary Tiegreen, *Let the Big Dog Eat! A Dictionary of the Secret Language of Golf*, p. 13, 2000

▸ out of the bag
unexpectedly good *AUSTRALIA, 1954*
- She spoke good English and sat down and looked through all the drawings carefully and intelligently, asking questions all the time. Yumi was something out of the bag. —Les Such, *A Yen for Yokohama*, p. 59, 1963

bag *verb*

1 to arrest someone *UK, 1824*
- He wasn't taking no chances on getting bagged. —Hal Ellson, *Duke*, p. 127, 1949
- Tito and Turk said they would get bagged and sent to Warwick by the time I got there. —Claude Brown, *Manchild in the Promised Land*, p. 16, 1965
- I says pal, put that in your pocket before I bag you for bribery. —Leonard Shecter and William Phillips, *On the Pad*, p. 190, 1973
- "Bag him," said the chief, meaning "have him arrested." —Richard Hamilton and Charles Barnard, *20,000 Alarms*, p. 97, 1975
- Our only chance to bag him is if he tries it again. —Gerald Petievich, *Money Men*, p. 17, 1981

2 to catch, capture or obtain something for yourself *US, 1861*
- [B]y midsummer he managed to bag 135 teachers, every one of them with impeccable credentials. —Max Shulman, *Anyone Got a Match?*, p. 66, 1964
- So, Ted, any ideas on who should we bag? Ted? —*Bill and Ted's Excellent Adventure*, 1989
- Yeah, I hear you bagged Martin Weir for Mr. Lovejoy. —*Get Shorty*, 1995

3 to shoot down a plane *UK, 1943*
A hunting allusion in Royal Air Force use.

4 in sport, to score a specified number of goals or points *AUSTRALIA*
- He bagged ten. —June Factor, *Kidspeak*, 2000

5 to disregard, dismiss or stop something *US*
Figurative use of throwing rubbish in a rubbish bag.
- MRS CHANDLER: We are leaving for your grandmother's. If you'd care to join us... HEATHER CHANDLER: Bag that. MRS CHANDLER: Is that a "No" in your lingo? —*Heathers*, 1988

6 to cancel a social engagement *CANADA*
The *Dictionary of American Regional English* lists a related meaning: 'to feign illness in order to avoid one's responsibilities' from 1967.

- "When you want something from someone, you don't bag. Bagging won't get you laid. It won't make you money. It certainly won't make you friends." — *Toronto Globe and Mail*, p. L3, 20 April 2002

7 to abandon or leave a place or thing *US, 1962*
- Let's bag the mall. It's boring. — *American Beauty*, 1999

8 to criticise or denigrate someone or something *AUSTRALIA, 1969*
- She did bag her father, call John Cain 'an ill-bred little cur' and announce impetuously her family members were not fools where money was concerned. — *Sun-Herald*, p. 116, 13th May 1990

9 to dismiss from employment *UK: SCOTLAND*
A variation of **SACK**.
- — Michael Munro, *The Patter, Another Blast*, 1988

10 to bribe someone; to arrange an outcome *US*
- Bagging of a baseball game down in the Carolina League came as a shock to fans and officials throughout the country. — *San Francisco Examiner*, p. 27, 3rd June 1948
- We wink and laugh at wrestling. We go for the bagged fight. — *San Francisco News*, p. 17, 28th February 1951

11 to impregnate *US*
- — Vincent J. Monteleone, *Criminal Slang*, p. 15, 1949

12 to hang in loose folds *UK, 1824*
Especially applied to trousers out of shape at the knees.
- "That's what mob guys do," Chili said, "they sit down they take time to arrange the creases in their pants, so the knees don't bag, then check it every few minutes." — Elmore Leonard, *Be Cool*, p. 181, 1999

13 to use a resuscitation bag *UK*
Medical use.
- We've bronched him, tubed him, bagged him, [and] cathed him. — Diane Johnson, *Doctor Talk*, 1980

14 to sleep, to doze *US*
- — Judi Sanders, *Mashing and Munching in Ames*, p. 1, 1994

15 to leave *US*
Hawaiian youth usage.
- — Douglas Simonson, *Pidgin to da Max*, 1981

▸ **bag and tag**

1 to place a dead soldier in a body bag and identify the soldier with a tag on the outside of the body bag *US*
- — Linda Reinberg, *In the Field*, p. 15, 1991

2 (used of a prison guard) to count and account for prisoners during scheduled count times *US*
- — Gary K. Farlow, *Prison-ese*, p. 2, 2002

3 to apprehend someone and take them into police custody *AUSTRALIA*
- It was certainly a high to lead an entry team in and come out the other end in one piece, with the offender bagged and tagged. — William Dodson, *The Sharp End*, p. 124, 2001

▸ **bag ass**
to leave, especially in a hurry *US*
- — Helen Dahlskog (Editor), *A Dictionary of Contemporary and Colloquial Usage*, p. 5, 1972

▸ **bag beaver**
to have sex with a woman *US*
Combining hunting and sexual metaphors.
- — Michael Dalton Johnson, *Talking Trash with Redd Foxx*, p. 72, 1994

▸ **bag your head**
to stop talking *US*
- — Joseph E. Ragen and Charles Finston, *Inside the World's Toughest Prison*, p. 789, 1962

-bag *suffix*
when in combination with an undesirable thing, used to label a person who epitomises the unpleasant quality *UK*
Michael Munro in *The Patter, Another Blast* (1988), offers the examples 'crap-bag' (a coward), **GROTBAG** (a dirty person) and 'stum-bag' (an idiot).

bagaga; bagadga *noun*
the penis *US, 1963*
Probably from Italian *bagagli* (luggage).
- — Paul Baker, *Polari*, p. 164, 2002

bag and baggage
used for conveying to a prisoner that he is to be released from jail *US*
- He had been told, "Bag and baggage." A little later, Larry found himself outside the jail, still not believing it was all true. — Donald Goines, *Black Gangster*, p. 189, 1977

bag biter *noun*
in computing, something or someone that does not work well *US*
- — *CoEvolution Quarterly*, p. 26, Spring 1981
- This text editor won't let me make a file with a line longer than eighty characters! What a bagbiter! — Guy L. Steele et al., *The Hacker's Dictionary*, p. 28, 1983

bag boy *noun*
a bookmaker *AUSTRALIA, 1945*
- The bag-boys knobbed the Moth's quote at 20/1 but at that price the knobologists bet only peanuts. — Cyril Pearl, *So, you want to be an Australian*, p. 12, 1959
- — James Holledge, *The Great Australian Gamble*, p. 16, 1966
- [A] greater feat than Peter Pan's victory was that of Betting Billy in 'putting the cleaner through the bag boys' to the tune of a cool £200,000. — James Holledge, *The Great Australian Gamble*, p. 38, 1966

bag case *noun*
a fatally injured motorist, especially one with gruesome injuries *US*
- — *American Speech*, p. 266, December 1962: 'The language of traffic policemen'

bag-chaser *noun*
a drug user who is obsessed with getting drugs *US*
- — Geoffrey Froner, *Digging for Diamonds*, p. 7, 1989

bag drag *noun*
in Antarctica, the act of dragging your luggage for a pre-flight weigh-in *ANTARCTICA*
- Due to weather conditions a bagdrag is not always followed by a flight and in any case will rarely take place at a convenient time for the dragger of the bag. — Ethan Dicks, *English, as She is Spoke at McMurdo*, 1996
- — Bernadette Hince, *The Antarctic Dictionary*, p. 39, 2000
- — *Cool Antartica*, 2003: 'Antarctic slang'

bagel *noun*

1 a Jewish person *US, 1955*
Usually playful rather than derogatory.
- — Connie Eble (Editor), *UNC-CH Campus Slang*, p. 1, Spring 1994

2 a tyre *US*
- — Bill Davis, *Jawjacking*, p. 13, 1977

3 a fool *UK*
- — Angela Devlin, *Prison Patter*, p. 25, 1996

bagel *verb*
in a sporting event, to defeat your opponent without letting your opponent score *US, 1976*
It is claimed that the usage was coined by tennis player Eddie Dibbs and popularised by tennis writer and broadcaster Bud Collins.
- — *American Speech*, p. 292–295, Fall-Winter 1976: 'Tennis slang'
- — Peter Schwed, *How to Talk Tennis*, p. 20, 1988

bagel bumper *noun*
a lesbian *UK*
Based on a visual similarity between the vagina and a bagel.
- — Chris Lewis, *The Dictionary of Playground Slang*, p. 18, 2003

bagel face *noun*
a Jewish person *US*
Derogatory.
- He punches some Hebe – Murray something or other. The biggest bagel face in the precinct, and Lawlor belts him. — Vincent Patrick, *The Pope of Greenwich Village*, p. 112, 1979

bag-follower *noun*
an attractive woman who carries packets of heroin for a heroin dealer while bestowing status upon him with her good looks *US*
- — Burgess Laughlin, *Job Opportunities in the Black Market*, p. 1, 1978

bag full of shit *noun*
an utterly contemptible person *UK*
- Candice is a bag full of shit but Shona is scared to tell her that. — Karline Smith, *Letters to Andy Cole*, p. 142, 1998

bagful of busted arseholes *noun*
the epitome of ugliness or feeling poorly *NEW ZEALAND*
- — David McGill, *David McGill's Complete Kiwi Slang Dictionary*, p. 12, 1998

baggage *noun*

1 a boyfriend, agent or other male who accompanies a female pornography performer to the set *US*
Not flattering.
- — *Adult Video News*, p. 50, October 1995

2 a non-playing observer of a card or dice game *US*

- — *The Annals of the American Academy of Political and Social Sciences*, p. 120, May 1950

baggage smasher *noun*

a baggage handler *US*

- — *American Speech*, p. 285, December 1968: 'Addenda to the vocabulary of railroading'

bagged *adjective*

1 fixed, corrupted, bribed *US, 1942*

- —J. E. Lighter, *Historical Dictionary of American Slang, Volume 1*, p. 69, 1994

2 drunk *US, 1953*

- Sure, Gleason is consistently "bagged" throughout, by which is he such an angry drunk? — *Times Union (Albany, New York)*, p. S2, 13th October 2002

bagger *noun*

1 a poker player who does not bet aggressively when holding a good hand until late in the hand *US*

- —John D. Bell et al., *Loosely Speaking*, p. 2, 1966

2 a boy who wears his trousers so low that his boxer shorts hang out above his belt line *US*

- —Connie Eble (Editor), *UNC-CH Campus Slang*, p. 1, March 1986

3 someone who talks, dresses and projects an East Coast, prep-school persona; a member of a college fraternity *US*

- —Connie Eble (Editor), *UNC-CH Campus Slang*, p. 1, Fall 1980

4 someone who plays footbag *US*

- —Jim Crotty, *How to Talk American*, p. 122, 1997

baggers *noun*

baggy shorts or swimming trunks *AUSTRALIA*

- —Jack Pollard, *The Australian Surfrider*, p. 16, 1963

baggie *noun*

1 a plastic bag filled with a variable amount of loose marijuana *US*

From the tradmarked name of a brand of plastic sandwich bags.

- There wasn't any grass in the apartment anyway. Down to seeds and stems. She'd have to stop at the store on the way and pick up a baggie. —Elmore Leonard, *City Primeval*, p. 54, 1980
- [A] form of euphoria that came to me in convenient little plastic Baggies, in eighth or quarter ounces. —Brian Preston, *Pot Planet*, p. 1, 2002

2 a condom *US, 1971*

- [I]f you ever run into sluts like The Rump Humpers be sure and wear a baggie. Anal sex has been linked to several serious diseases[.] — *Adult Video*, p. 66, August/September 1986

baggies *noun*

loose trousers or shorts, especially loose-fitting shorts or swimming trunks popularised by surfers *US*

Trousers have been called **BAGS** on and off since the mid-C19; 'baggies' derives from the baggy fit.

- You'd see 'em wearing their baggies / Huarachi sandals too. —Chuck Berry (Brian Wilson, uncredited lyricist), *Surfin' U.S.A.*, 1963
- — *Paradise of the Pacific*, p. 27, October 1963
- —J. R. Friss, *A Dictionary of Teenage Slang (Mt. Diablo High)*, 1964
- —John Severson, *Modern Surfing Around the World*, p. 162, 1964
- —Collin Baker et al., *College Undergraduate Slang Study Conducted at Brown University*, p. 76, 1968
- [B]aggies, snorkel anoraks and burdensome gold crucifixes[.] — *The Observer*, p. 19, 18th March 2001

bagging *noun*

denigration *AUSTRALIA*

- Naturally it is accepted that umpires and all opposing players and supporters can expect a 'bagging'. —Ivor Limb, *Footy's No Joke!*, p. 65, 1986

bag guy *noun*

a toy balloon vendor *US*

- —Vincent J. Monteleone, *Criminal Slang*, p. 15, 1949

baggy *adjective*

a loose fashion briefly popular with ravers; the baggy trouser style continued to be popular with UK skateboarders *UK*

- [W]e had all these baggy type bands. —Shaun Ryder, *Shaun Ryder... in His Own Words*, 1993
- Baggy started innocently with the holiday-wear simplicity of acid house. —Ben Osbourne, *The A-Z of Club Culture*, p. 18, 1999
- [O]ld-school, baggy ravers really having it[.] —Dave Courtney, *Raving Lunacy*, p. 92, 2000

baggy arse *noun*

an inexperienced, naive prison guard *AUSTRALIA*

- — *Maledicta*, p. 92, 1986–1987: 'Australian maledicta'

baggy-arse; baggy-arsed *adjective*

(of a soldier) substandard, second-rate, shoddy *AUSTRALIA, 1953*

- 'Private Russell you really make a slack baggy-arse soldier.' Russell replied, 'Yes sir, but I would make a grouse civilian.' —Martin Cameron, *A Look at the Bright Side*, 1988

baggy green cap *noun*

the cap worn by Australian test cricketers *AUSTRALIA*

Also simply the 'baggy green', and hence, 'to wear the baggy green' – meaning 'to represent Australia in test cricket'.

- But on one day in November 1975 my hopes and aspirations of wearing the baggy green cap vanished. —Paul Vautin, *Turn It Up!*, p. 7, 1995

Baghdad Betty *nickname*

during the US war against Iraq in 1991, a female Iraqi disc jockey who broadcast propaganda to US troops *US*

- — *Army*, p. 47, November 1991

Baghdad Boys *noun*

during the Gulf war, reporters from the Cable News Network *US*

- — *American Speech*, p. 385, Winter 1991: 'Among the new words'

baghead *noun*

a habitual cocaine or heroin user *UK*

From **BAG** (drugs) combined with **HEAD** (a user).

- —Angela Devlin, *Prison Patter*, p. 25, 1996
- I hate smack. I fucking hate fucking bagheads even worse[.] —Kevin Sampson, *Outlaws*, p. 56, 2001
- [T]hey just stand here, mumbling, twitching, sipping alcopops. Probly [sic] bagheads. —Niall Griffiths, *Kelly + Victor*, p. 12, 2002

bag job *noun*

1 a cheating scheme involving a casino employee as a confederate *US*

- — *The Annals of the American Academy of Political and Social Sciences*, p. 120, May 1950

2 a burglary, especially when committed by law enforcement or intelligence agents looking for information *US, 1971*

- The bag job on his car was a waste of time —Gerald Petievich, *Shakedown*, p. 119, 1988

bag lady *noun*

1 a destitute woman who wanders the streets with her possessions in shopping bags *US, 1972*

- —Harold Wentworth and Stuart Berg Flexner, *Dictionary of American Slang*, p. 674, 1976
- He's like the bag ladies on the Common, or some other shit like that. —George V. Higgins, *Penance for Jerry Kennedy*, p. 234, 1985
- He spent hours upon hours in the old public library at Bayfront Park, amid the snoring winos and bag ladies[.] —Carl Hiaasen, *Tourist Season*, p. 57, 1986
- An old bag lady with an anti-abortion poster has it grabbed and ripped up by man-hating dykes. —Josh Alan Friedman, *Tales of Times Square*, p. 166, 1986

2 a condom *UK*

- —David Rowan, *A Glossary for the 90s*, 1998

bagman *noun*

1 a person who collects, makes or holds illegal payments *US, 1935*

- Tom ("Sailor") Burke had been the sheriff's "bag man," had delivered $36,000 in payoff money to the sheriff's wife and had gotten signed receipts for the boodle. — *Time*, p. 18, 24th July 1950
- The defendant was described by the court as a "bagman" or collector for "higher-ups" in the (police) department. — *New York Times*, p. 1, 3rd September 1952
- The "pad" refers to regular weekly, biweekly, or monthly payments, usually picked up by a police bagman and divided among fellow officers. — *The Knapp Commission Report on Police Corruption*, p. 66, 1972
- I'll bring you to a guy in the Fourth who is the division bagman. —Leonard Shecter and William Phillips, *On the Pad*, p. 261, 1973
- They'd say you were the bag man for the whole fucking borough. —Edwin Torres, *Q & A*, p. 119, 1977
- Turns out the cop was the biggest bagman ever. —Vincent Patrick, *The Pope of Greenwich Village*, p. 247, 1979
- —Richard Condon, *Prizzi's Honor*, 1982
- In front of them were the bag men from the chief inspector's squad, the borough squads, and the PC's squad of the New York police Department. All in plain clothes. —Richard Condon, *Prizzi's Honor*, p. 3, 1982
- Once a day, the policy man handed over his slips and his cash to a runner or "bag man," who took them to the headquarters. —Kim Rich, *Johnny's Girl*, p. 140, 1993
- It's tougher to buy the cheapest bagman than it is to buy a cop. — *The Usual Suspects*, 1995

2 a bookmaker *AUSTRALIA*

- They had worked up a good connection with punters, who were enticed by the offer generally of a point above the odds being shouted by in the ring by the registered bagmen. —Vince Kelly, *The Bogeyman*, p. 182, 1956
- At the end of the day Mr. Wilson, who had kept betting and doubling up, had accumulated liabilities of £2,000 with the bagmen. —James Holledge, *The Great Australian Gamble*, p. 140, 1966
- With exaggerated nonchalance, Harry tossed the roll of fifties to the bagman. —Gerald Sweeney, *The Plunge*, p. 29, 1981
- No names no pack drill but one prominent old-time bookie insists that a flag he sponsors at Tatts be flown at half-mast whenever another bagman is in the Club. —Clive Galea, *Slipper*, p. 213, 1988

3 a bookmaker's clerk *AUSTRALIA, 1973*

- Ray became an expert on the front bag which was an education in itself. The bag man was the first on which all the tricks and shifty dodges were tried. —Clive Galea, *Slipper!*, p. 26, 1988

4 in the circus or carnival, a person who makes change for customers, often cheating them *US*

- —Joe McKennon, *Circus Lingo*, p. 13, 1980

5 a member of a shoplifting team who carries away the stolen goods *AUSTRALIA*

- — *The (Sydney) Bulletin*, 26th April 1975

6 a drug dealer; a person in possession of drugs *US*

- —Richard E. Haorman and Allan M. Fox, *Drug Awareness*, p. 463, 1970
- —William D. Alsever, *Glossary for the Establishment and Other Uptight People*, p. 26, December 1970
- —Angela Devlin, *Prison Patter*, p. 25, 1996

7 an itinerant man carrying his possessions in a bag; a swagman *AUSTRALIA, 1866*

- There was poor old Lasher, the ex-bagman, the drifter, with a lot of beer to be drunk, a lot more brawls to start, and Masie, perhaps. —Eric Lambert, *The Veterans*, p. 199, 1954
- We were working a train from Alpha to Bega and were just out in traffic when we found a bagman riding the buffers. —Patsy Adam-Smith, *Folklore of the Australian Railwaymen*, p. 182, 1969

Bagman's Gazette *noun*

an imaginary publication that is cited as a source of rumours *AUSTRALIA, 1959*

Bagmen's Union *noun*

a fictitious union to which itinerant travellers belonged during the Depression *AUSTRALIA, 1954*

- What? Sundowners never pay fares. It's against the rules of the Bagman's Union. —Frank Hardy, *The Yarns of Billy Borker*, p. 48, 1965

bag of arse *noun*

anything inferior *UK*

- "Yellow" was a big wet bag of arse. — *Uncut*, p. 7, October 2002

bag of bones *noun*

1 a skinny person or animal *AUSTRALIA, 1903*

- Anyone will tell you what that bag of bones is like to handle. —Wilda Moxham, *The Apprentice*, p. 122, 1969

2 a 'bush pilot' aeroplane *CANADA, 1984*

bag of coke *noun*

a man *AUSTRALIA*

Rhyming slang for a **BLOKE**; variation of **BUSHEL OF COKE**.

- I don't know how you bags of coke wear those platform shoes. — *The Sweeney*, p. 6, 1976

bag off *verb*

to form an intitial liaison with someone sexually attractive, especially with a view to greater intimacy *UK*

- Craig an Quockie have bagged off, it looks like. —Niall Griffiths, *Kelly + Victor*, p. 238, 2002

bag of flour *noun*

a bathroom shower *UK, 1980*

Rhyming slang.

- —Ray Puxley, *Cockney Rabbit*, p. 7, 1992

bag of fruit *noun*

a suit *AUSTRALIA, 1924*

Rhyming slang.

- I had to wear this bag of fruit to get into the member's. —Rex Hunt, *Tall Tales – and True*, p. 94, 1994

bag of nails *noun*

a state of confusion *AUSTRALIA, 1942*

bag of shit *noun*

1 a despicable person *AUSTRALIA*

- The slick haired one mutters bag of shit and into the car I go. —Kevin Mackey, *The Cure*, p. 64, 1970

2 anything of poor quality *UK*

- "I see," I said, still only a quarter of the way through building my ricketty bag of shit. —Andy McNab, *Immediate Action*, p. 92, 1995

bag of shit tied up with string *noun*

a clumsy, shapeless or scruffy person *UK, 1984*

Probably military in origin; usually in phrases such as 'looks like a bag of shit tied up with string'.

bag of snakes *noun*

a lively young woman *AUSTRALIA, 1984*

bag of tricks *noun*

▷ **see: BOX OF TRICKS**

bag of yeast *noun*

a priest *AUSTRALIA*

Rhyming slang.

- Yes, and the bag of yeast, old Father Flynn, thought the Red Dean[.] —Frank Hardy, *The Outcasts of Foolgarah*, p. 89, 1971

bag on; bag *verb*

to insult someone in a competitive, quasi-friendly spirit *US*

- Hanging out, shooting craps, playing domino's, bagging on each other, and just plain kickin' it. — *Menace II Society*, 1993
- There are many different terms for playing the dozens, including "bagging, capping, cracking, dissing, hiking, joning, ranking, ribbing, serving, signifying, slipping, sounding and snapping". —James Haskins, *The Story of Hip-Hop*, p. 54, 2000

bag-o-wire *noun*

an informer or betrayer *JAMAICA, 1982*

- —Thomas H. Slone, *Rasta is Cuss*, p. 24, 2003

bagpipe *verb*

to stimulate the penis to orgasm under the armpit of a lover *UK, 1904*

Homosexual use.

- He's a real case for bagpiping guys with big hairy arms. —Bruce Rodgers, *The Queens' Vernacular*, p. 26, 1972
- — *The FHM Little Book of Bloke*, p. 142, June 2003

bags *noun*

1 a great amount of *UK, 1931*

- Great racer, that Juan Pablo Montoya. Terrific chap, bags of talent, no complexes, likes to take a risk and put on a good show. — *The Guardian*, 7th August 2002

2 loose fitting trousers *UK*

There have been 'bum-bags', 1860, 'howling bags' (a loud pattern), 1850–90, and 'go-to-meeting bags' (best clothes), 1870–1910. 'Oxford bags', a very wide-legged cut, were introduced in the early 1920s and are still known.

3 a mess; a botched enterprise *IRELAND*

- The hairdresser made a right bags of me perm. —Colin Murphy and Donal O'Dea, *The Book of Feckin' Irish Slang*, p. 7, 2004

▸ **make a bags of**

make a mess of something *IRELAND*

- Has he asked the Revenue Commissioners how it managed to make a bags of defending an open and shut case before the appeals commissioner? —Mr. Rabbitte, *Houses of the Oireachtas Parlimentary Debates*, 16th December 1998

bags *verb*

to claim rights to something; to reserve something *AUSTRALIA, 1944*

- 'Didn't think you was coming,' said Dumby. 'But I bagsed you this chair just in case.' —Phillip Gwynne, *Deadly Unna?*, p. 114, 1998
- In our house, whoever got a chair first could keep it for the whole night provided they said 'I bags this' if they went to the toilet or answered the door. — *Sydney Morning Herald*, p. 13, 15th March 2003

bags!; bagsy!; bagsey!

used to claim possession or authority *UK, 1897*

Mainly juvenile; may be structured as a verb.

- BILL: What about a game of Monopoly? TONY: Yes. Bags me be the boot. —Ray Galton and Alan Simpson, *Hancock's Half Hour*, 1958
- MAM: I think I'll do chicken. ANTONY: Bagsey me breast. —Caroline Aherne and Craig Cash, *The Royle Family*, 1999

- I bagsy first go and the others think about it for a minute. —John King, *Human Punk*, p. 11, 2000
- —Lise Winer, *Dictionary of the English/Creole of Trinidad & Tobago*, 2003

bag-shanty *noun*
a brothel *UK, 1890*
Royal Navy use; a combination of **BAG** (a promiscuous woman) and conventional 'shanty' (a hut).

bagsing *noun*
the act of claiming priority rights to something; reserving something *AUSTRALIA*
- All households that have more children than comfortable chairs have a bagsing system, and I'm surprised you don't know of it. —*Sydney Morning Herald*, p. 13, 15th March 2003

bagswinger *noun*
a bookmaker's clerk *AUSTRALIA*
- —Jim Ramsay, *Cop It Sweet!*, p. 9, 1977

bag up *verb*
1 to put a condom on a penis *UK*
Also variant construction of 'bag it up'.
- Ah couldn't'a found a fellah's dick, let alone discreetly bagged it up. —Ben Elton, *High Society*, p. 158, 2002

2 to divide a powdered drug into bags preparatory to selling it *US*
- —Geoffrey Froner, *Digging for Diamonds*, p. 7, 1989

3 of a fizzy drink, to fill the stomach with gas *UK: SCOTLAND*
- That Canadian beer fair bags ye up. —Michael Munro, *The Patter, Another Blast*, 1988

4 to laugh *US*
- —Ellen C. Bellone (Editor), *Dictionary of Slang*, p. 2, 1989

Bahama ham *noun*
the conch *BAHAMAS*
- —John A. Holm, *Dictionary of Bahamian English*, p. 9, 1982

Bahama hooter *noun*
a marijuana cigarette *US*
- —Connie Eble (Editor), *UNC-CH Campus Slang*, p. 1, Spring 1992

bahookie *noun*
the buttocks; the anus *UK, 1985*
- Come on, get up off your bahookey! —Ian Pattison, *Rab C. Nesbitt*, 1988
- [A] member of the Scottish executive having a dildo jammed up his bahookie by a piece of telegenic jail-bait[.] —Christopher Brookmyre, *Boiling a Frog*, p. 161, 2000

bail *verb*
1 to leave a relationship or situation *US, 1977*
- "Maybe I just bail myself on home an watch TV or somethin." —Jess Mowry, *Way Past Cool*, p. 10, 1992
- I don't know how I can bail now, he's going to be here any minute. —*Something About Mary*, 1998
- And she bails out on the guy at the end? —Elmore Leonard, *Be Cool*, p. 355, 1999
- We were good when you bailed, weren't we? —*Gone in 60 Seconds*, 2000
- [T]he funniest shit happens when I'm about to bail. —Eminem (Marshall Mathers), *Angry Blonde*, p. 67, 2001

2 to fall while skateboarding *US*
- —*San Francisco Sunday Examiner & Chronicle*, p. 20, 2nd September 1984

3 in mountain biking, to jump off a bicycle in order to avoid an accident *US*
- A few who were born rad go too fast for their skill level – when they need to bail they won't be able to. —*Mountain Bike Magazine's Complete Guide To Mountain Biking Skills*, p. 79, 1996

4 in foot-propelled scootering, to abandon a scooter in mid-jump *UK*
- When you're in the air, and the trick has gone pear-shaped, you bail – leaping away from the scoot to try for a pain-free landing. —Ben Sharpe, *Scooter Crazy*, p. 39, 2000

5 to land inelegantly or badly when completing a snowboarding jump *US*
- —Jim Humes and Sean Wagstaff, *Boarderlands*, p. 220, 1995

bail bandit *noun*
a person who commits a crime while out on bail *UK*
- [Home Secretary] David Blunkett was using very emotive language about crime – using words like hooligan, thug and bail bandit. —*BBC News*, 18th June 2002

bailing-wire artist *noun*
on the railways, a creative but incompetent mechanic *US*
- —Ramon Adams, *The Language of the Railroader*, p. 10, 1977

bail out *verb*
1 to jump off a surfboard when you are about to be knocked off the board by a wave *US*
- —John Severson, *Modern Surfing Around the World*, p. 162, 1964

2 in skateboarding, to fall badly *UK*
- Skateboarding has its camaraderie, especially if someone "bails out". —*The Times*, p. 16, 26th April 2003

bail up *verb*
1 to hold someone up; to rob someone by holding up *AUSTRALIA, 1838*
In common use by bushrangers during the colonial period. Transferred sense from 'bail up' (to place a dairy cow into a bail for milking), from 'bail' (a frame for securing a cow's head). It could also be used intransitively to mean 'to submit to being held up and robbed'. Now only used in historical novels.
- They began with a prosperous station manager, bailed him up, took his money, his watch and his horse with conspicuous ease. —Bob Ellis and Anne Brooksbank, *Mad Dog Morgan*, p. 65, 1976

2 to hold someone at bay; to corner someone *AUSTRALIA, 1841*
- Hey that mate of yours, Roy – a mob of dagoes got him all bailed up outside the police station! —Herb Wharton, *Cattle Camp*, p. 163, 1994

3 to stop someone for a conversation *AUSTRALIA, 1998*

bail up!
stand and deliver! *AUSTRALIA, 1842*
- Stop there, man. Bail up or I'll blow you apart. —Bob Ellis and Anne Brooksbank, *Mad Dog Morgan*, p. 67, 1976

bait *noun*
1 in poker, a small bet that is hoped will lure another player into a larger bet *US*
- —Albert H. Morehead, *The Complete Guide to Winning Poker*, p. 256, 1967

2 in shuffleboard, a shot made to entice the opponent to try to go after the disc *US*
- —Omero C. Catan, *Secrets of Shuffleboard Strategy*, p. 64, 1967

3 a person who attracts a specified type or category of attention *US, 1942*
- But when you look at me, all's you see is prison bait and junkie, someone you gonna get for slingin powder, snortin, shootin, and skin poppin. —Suzanne Kingsbury, *The Gospel According to Gracey*, 2004

4 a small meal *US*
- —*American Speech*, p. 268, December 1958: 'Ranching terms from eastern Washington'

5 in prison, credit, especially on the purchase of drink, drugs or tobacco *UK*
- —Angela Devlin, *Prison Patter*, p. 25, 1996

bait *verb*
in gin, to discard a card in a manner that is designed to lure a desired card from an opponent *US*
- —Irwin Steig, *Play Gin to Win*, p. 138, 1971

▸ **bait the hole**
in American football, to feign a running play in order to draw defenders towards the line and block them there *US*
- —John Riggins and Jack Winter, *Gameplan*, p. 196, 1984

bait can *noun*
a worker's lunch box *US*
- —Frederic G. Cassidy, *Dictionary of American Regional English*, p. 132, 1985

bait money *noun*
cash with pre-recorded serial numbers set aside by a bank to be included in money given to a robber *US*
- —Jay Robert Nash, *Dictionary of Crime*, p. 16, 1992
- Nothing with bank straps or rubber bands, I don't want any dyke packs, I don't want any bait money. —Elmore Leonard, *Out of Sight*, p. 87, 1996

Baja bug *noun*
a Volkswagen Beetle modified for surfer use *US*
'Baja' is a reference to Baja California, the Mexican state immediately south of California.
- —Trevor Cralle, *The Surfin'ary*, p. 6, 1991

ake *noun*

1 a verbal assault, a roasting *AUSTRALIA*

- He [a prisoner] went on to say that the jacks [i.e. the police] gave him the best bake in history[.] — *The (Sydney) Bulletin*, 26th April 1975

2 a complete and hopeless outcast *US*

An abbreviation of Bakersfield, a city at the south end of California's San Joaquin Valley, 'the other side of nowhere' to the surfers who use this term.

- — Trevor Cralle, *The Surfin'ary*, p. 6, 1991

3 illegal drugs manufactured in an illegal laboratory *NEW ZEALAND*

- It takes about two hours to complete a bake excluding 'shelling time.' — *Evening Post*, p. 19, 5th April 1986

bake *verb*

to manufacture illegal drugs in a laboratory *NEW ZEALAND*

- Then he met someone who knew how to bake. — *Evening Post*, p. 19, 5th April 1986

▸ **bake biscuits**

to record and produce a phonograph record *US*

- — *Look*, p. 49, 24th November 1959

baked *adjective*

drug-intoxicated, especially by marijuana *US, 1978*

- I'm still baked. — *Clueless*, 1995
- Now Vita was lighting a joint, needing to get baked before she could turn herself into an International Chick. — Elmore Leonard, *Be Cool*, p. 48, 1999
- I can just sit here on my ass, get baked on fine weed, and let the story come to me[.] — Brian Preston, *Pot Planet*, p. 93, 2002
- Lewis Carroll was baked out of his mind on some amazing Victorian drugs[.] — *Uncut*, p. 76, July 2003

baked-bean *noun*

a sexual interlude *UK*

Rhyming slang for **SCENE**.

- I'm about to press the little green button to connect me to her number, to arrange a little baked bean, my old gent's getting twitchy at the very thought[.] — J.J. Connolly, *Layer Cake*, p. 107, 2000

baked beans *noun*

jeans *UK, 2001*

Prisoners' rhyming slang.

baked potato *noun*

a drug-user who watches television while intoxicated *US*

A play on **COUCH POTATO** (a habitual idler/television watcher) formed on **BAKED** (intoxicated).

- — John Hulme, *Baked Potatoes*, 1996

baked wind pills *noun*

beans *CANADA*

- "Baked wind pills" is a cowboy slang phrase for the staple food, beans. — Bill Casselman, *Canadian Food Words*, p. 232, 1998

baker *noun*

1 the electric chair *US*

- — Hyman E. Goldin et al., *Dictionary of American Underworld Lingo*, p. 21, 1950

2 a marijuana smoker *US*

- — Jim Emerson-Cobb, *Scratching the Dragon*, 1997

3 a grade of 'B' in academic work *US*

- — Collin Baker et al., *College Undergraduate Slang Study Conducted at Brown University*, p. 76, 1968

Baker flying *adjective*

experiencing the bleed period of the menstrual cycle *US*

In the navy, a red Quartermaster B (phonetic Baker) flag is flown to signify 'Danger' and 'Keep out', providing several theories for application to menstruation.

- — Harold Wentworth and Stuart Berg Flexner, *Dictionary of American Slang*, p. 13, 1960

Bakerloo *noun*

in cricket, a batsman who is playing down the wrong line *UK*

A jocular reference to the Bakerloo line on London's underground system.

- — Simon Hughes, *Cricket 4*, 18th June 2003

baker's fog *noun*

in the Maritime Provinces, regular sliced white bread *CANADA*

- "Baker's fog" is a comic label for the spongy, glutinous commercial baked loves of bread sold in Maritime supermarkets. Also called "cotton bread," "ghost bread," and "puff." — Bill Casselman, *Canadian Food Words*, p. 15–16, 1998

bakey; bakie *noun*

a baked potato *UK, 1943*

bakkie *noun*

a utility vehicle used in South Africa *SOUTH AFRICA*

- The "company" – nothing more than a bakkie stuffed with food that travels up and down the freeway – belongs to both of them. — Bart Luirink (translated by Loes Nas), *Moffies*, p. 94, 2000

baksis *noun*

a small extra added to a purchase by a vendor in the hope of encouraging return business *GUYANA*

- — Richard Allsopp, *Dictionary of Caribbean English Usage*, p. 73, 1996

balance *verb*

▸ **balance the books**

in an illegal betting operation, to place bets with other operations when betting is too heavy on one proposition *US, 1979*

- You have to balance the books so you don't get caught too heavy on one side. — Thomas L. Clark, *The Dictionary of Gambling and Gaming*, p. 11, 1987

Balconville *nickname*

the Point St Charles area of Montreal *CANADA, 1980*

One of two nicknames for this neighborhood (the other is 'The Pointe') because most dwellings have a balcony on which people sit a lot. Bilingual and harmonious, its mixture of French and English is noted in the word itself, which is partly from each language. It is the title of a 1980 play by David Fennario.

balcony *noun*

the female breasts *US*

- Polly's balcony might not be something to inflame the pimjple-faced readers of Playboy, but it had exactly what a grown man wanted[.] — Max Shulman, *Anyone Got a Match?*, p. 248, 1964
- — Collin Baker et al., *College Undergraduate Slang Study Conducted at Brown University*, p. 76, 1968

bald head *noun*

to a Rastafarian, any non-Rastafarian *JAMAICA*

- Them crazy, them crazy / We gonna chase those crazy baldheads out of town[.] — Bob Marley, *Crazy Baldhead*, 1976
- Yuh fucking bawl head pussyclaat, yuh[.] — Donald Gorgon, *Cop Killer*, p. 114, 1994
- — Velma Pollard, *Dread Talk*, p. 41, 2000

bald-headed *adjective*

(used of a rotary bit in oil drilling) worn out *US*

- — Jerry Robertson, *Oil Slanguage*, p. 24, 1954

bald-headed mouse *noun*

the penis *UK*

- — Richard Herring, *Talking Cock*, p. 30, 2003

bald-headed prairie *noun*

treeless and shrubless plains *CANADA*

- It was just bald-headed prairie; every waking moment was spent out there. — Colleen Janzen, *Praiaire Post (www.mysouthernalberta.com)*, 17th May 2002

baldheaded row *noun*

the front row of a burlesque or strip show *US, 1887*

- Forth Worth had a number of burlesque houses at that time, and we were able to obtain choice seats on the front or "baldhead" row. — Jim Thompson, *Bad Boy*, p. 329, 1953
- — Sherman Louis Sergel, *The Language of Show Biz*, p. 15, 1973

bald-tyre bandit *noun*

a police officer detailed to traffic duty *UK, 1977*

- — David Powis, *The Signs of Crime*, 1977

Baldwin *noun*

a handsome man *US*

From the family of handsome actor brothers.

- OK, OK, so he's kind of a Baldwin, but what would he want with Tai. — *Clueless*, 1995
- — Judi Sanders, *Da Bomb!*, p. 2, 1997

baldy *noun*

1 a worn tyre; in the US, especially in hot rodding and drag racing *US*

- — Fred Horsley, *The Hot Rod Handbook*, p. 209, 1965

2 a Hereford cow *AUSTRALIA, 1887*
This breed of cattle has a white face or head.
- A big horny baldy would have a go to bust through and finish up with his horns all tangled up in the pipe rails. — Sam Weller, *Old Bastards I Have Met*, p. 52, 1979

3 the white-headed pigeon, endemic to Australia *AUSTRALIA, 1969*
- There was a big flock of baldies in the orchard. — *Wordmap (www.abc.net.au/wordmap)*, 2003

4 an artist's model denuded of pubic hair *UK, 1984*

baldy *adjective*
(of a tyre) with a worn tread *AUSTRALIA*
- Look at this. Baldy tyres – bullshit – there's plenty left on those tyres yet. — Sam Weller, *Old Bastards I Have Met*, p. 116, 1979

baldy!
I refuse! *NEW ZEALAND, 1942*
A children's catchword.

baldy lad *noun*
the penis *UK*
- Is there a famous person who looks like your baldy lad, would you say? Who'd yew say yewer knob looks like, if anyone? — Niall Griffiths, *Sheepshagger*, p. 105, 2001

bale *noun*
1 marijuana compressed into a large bale similar to a bale of hay *US*
- — Eugene Landy, *The Underground Dictionary*, p. 28, 1971

2 any quantity of marijuana *US*
- He exploded away from the wall and made a grab for the Baggie. "Hey, what you be doing with my bale, man?" — Stephen J. Cannell, *The Tin Collectors*, p. 35, 2001

bale *verb*
▸ **bale the kale**
to win a lot of money gambling *US*
From **KALE** (money).
- — Frank Garcia, *Marked Cards and Loaded Dice*, p. 250, 1962

bale of hay *noun*
a male homosexual *UK*
Rhyming slang for **GAY**.
- He's a right bale of hay. — Bodmin Dark, *Dirty Cockney Rhyming Slang*, 2003

bale of straw *noun*
a blonde white woman *US, 1928*
- — Clarence Major, *Dictionary of Afro-American Slang*, p. 23, 1970
- — Don Wilmeth, *The Language of American Popular Entertainment*, p. 14, 1981

Bali belly *noun*
any gastro-intestinal infection obtained when holidaying in Bali, Indonesia or other areas of Southeast Asia *AUSTRALIA*
- There are no canny locals out to get your hard-earned dollars, no souvenirs to tempt you, no pictures to take, no Delhi Belly, Bali Belly or Montezuma's Revenge to contend with. — *Sydney Morning Herald*, p. 15, 28th May 1984

balk *verb*
1 to cover up *AUSTRALIA*
- "[B]alk with a molly" to use a girl as a cover or shield. — *The (Sydney) Bulletin*, 26th April 1975

2 in poker, to hesitate when it is your turn to bet in the hope of seeing whether players who follow you are prepared to call the bet *US*
- — John Vorhaus, *The Big Book of Poker Slang*, p. 5, 1996

ball *noun*
1 a thoroughly good time *US, 1932*
- I had no time now for thoughts like that and promised myself a ball in Denver. — Jack Kerouac, *On the Road*, p. 17–18, 1957
- [T]he other who had eyes for Phil and had been wooing him by stealing morphine styrettes from the life boats, presenting them to him and beseeching him to have a ball[.] — Herbert Huncke, *The Evening Sun Turned Crimson*, p. 101, 1980
- Honest to God, I've had a ball. — *Uncut*, p. 6, February 2002

2 an act of sexual intercourse *US*
- Ball: The accepted word for the sex act. — *Screw*, p. 7, 12th October 1970
- Yeah, she's a good ball, get with it already yet. — Babs Gonzales, *Movin' On Down De Line*, p. 37, 1975

3 a single scoop of ice-cream *US*
- — Harold Wentworth and Stuart Berg Flexner, *Dictionary of American Slang*, p. 16, 1960

4 crack cocaine *US*
- — US Department of Justice, *Street Terms*, October 1994

5 black-tar heroin *UK*
- — Robert Ashton, *This Is Heroin*, p. 208, 2002

6 one dollar *US, 1895*
Mainly prison slang.
- — Gary K. Farlow, *Prison-ese*, p. 2, 2002

▸ **on the ball**
alert to any opportunity *UK, 1967*
- And when Caleb was done [taking cocaine] he felt fucking brilliant Much more alive and on the ball. — Jack Allen, *When the Whistle Blows*, p. 157 2000

▸ **out on a ball; be riding a ball**
(used of a customer trading in a car) believing that your old car is worth more than it is *US*
- — *American Speech*, p. 309–310, Winter 1980: 'More jargon of car salesmen'

▸ **that's the way the ball bounces**
that's how things turn out *US*
- The soldiers coined "That's the way the ball bounces," meaning what was fordained to be. — *East Liverpool (Ohio) Review*, 28th December 1952
- This week's "Spectator" will raise much hell, I'm sure – but that's just the way the ball bounces." — Hunter S. Thompson, *Letter to Jack Thompson*, 24th October 1956
- "General Hanrahan doesn't like to be kept waiting." "Few people do," Oliver said. "But sometimes that's the way the ball bounces." — W.E.B. Griffin, *The Aviators*, p. 379, 1988
- With 10 weeks until the election, it's an instructive reminder that in news and punditry, as in sports, that's now often just the way the ball bounces. — *Variety*, p. 4, 25th August 2004

▸ **the ball is in your court**
it is your turn; it is is your decision *UK, 1963*
A variation of the conventional phrase 'the ball is with you'.

ball *verb*
1 to have sex *US*
- "Well' have time, baby, we'll have all the balling we can hold." — George Mandel, *Flee the Angry Strangers*, p. 304, 1952
- In that time, Dean is balling Marylou at the hotel and gives me time to change and dress. — Jack Kerouac, *On the Road*, p. 43, 1957
- I heard once how in chicago Red shut himself up in a hotel suite with a supply of Horse and five women, and just balled for three days and nights! — Ross Russell, *The Sound*, p. 205, 1961
- I don't mess around in public – too dangerous cause of the vice cops – but if you wanna come to my pad, I'll ball you. — John Rechy, *Numbers*, p. 195, 1967
- [T]hose two kids are definitely balling and I don't like that sort of thing to be too visible on the campus[.] — Gore Vidal, *Myra Breckinridge*, p. 24, 1968
- Work little, eat well, ball like crazy, and use all their energy to perfect their own beings, and to help the perfection of others. — *The Digger Papers*, p. 8, August 1968
- Many a night we spent on dark and lonely roads, balling to hard rock beat. — Jerry Rubin, *Do It!*, p. 19, 1970
- And so when D.R. and Estelle had finished balling, had dressed, and folded the serape and walked back through the darkening campground to their own scene, they found the Lone Outdoorsman leaning against Urge's front, waiting for them. — Gurney Norman, *Divine Right's Trip (Last Whole Earth Catalog)*, p. 45, 1971
- He was there on the acid trip scene, but he wasn't there when we actually balled. — Jefferson Poland and Valerie Alison, *The Records of the San Francisco Sexual Freedom League*, p. 30, 1971
- Eventually, she approached him with her fears, which he dispelled somewhat by balling her on the spot (dust rags beneath her bottom, her head on a mop). — Tom Robbins, *Another Roadside Attraction*, p. 52, 1971
- I know you thought I was cherry, your number-one size / But I was balling Tony, and you weren't wise. — Dennis Wepman et al., *The Life*, p. 142, 1976
- [A] friend or a chick and we would would sit around and ball[.] — Herbert Huncke, *The Evening Sun Turned Crimson*, p. 54, 1980
- Butler puts his buddy up to balling the joyfully slutty Ms. Foxx[.] — *Adult Video*, p. 64, August/September 1986

2 to fondle a man's penis *US*
- — Burton H. Wolfe, *The Hippies*, p. 203, 1968

3 to thoroughly enjoy yourself *US, 1942*
- He's the kind of a cat that balled every big swingin' main day breeze, all the time every day. — William "Lord" Buckley, *Nero*, 1951

4 to go or take something somewhere very quickly *US, 1939*
- But come on, let's ball up there and take a look in that little box of yourn! — John Clellon Holmes, *Go*, p. 105, 1952
- And he balled that thing clear to Iowa City and yelled me the funniest stories[.] — Jack Kerouac, *On the Road*, p. 16, 1957

5 to insert amphetamine or methamphetamine in the vagina before sexual intercourse *US*

- —Eugene Landy, *The Underground Dictionary*, p. 28, 1971
- —Jay Robert Nash, *Dictionary of Crime*, p. 17, 1992

6 to secrete and smuggle cocaine in the vagina *UK*

- —Nick Constable, *This is Cocaine*, p. 182, 2002

▸ **ball the jack**

to travel very quickly *US, 1913*

- [N]o sooner were we out of town than Eddie started to ball that jack ninety miles an hour out of sheer exuberance. —Jack Kerouac, *On the Road*, p. 20, 1957
- —Ramon Adams, *The Language of the Railroader*, p. 11, 1977

-ball *suffix*

combines with an unpleasant substance to create a contemptible person *UK*

balla *noun*

a man with a lot of money *US*

- —Connie Eble (Editor), *UNC-CH Campus Slang*, p. 1, Fall 1999

ballad *noun*

a love letter *US*

- —*San Francisco Examiner*, p. III-2, 22nd March 1960

ballahoo and all the crew *noun*

everybody *TRINIDAD AND TOBAGO*

- —Richard Allsopp, *Dictionary of Caribbean English Usage*, p. 74, 1996

ball and chain *noun*

a man's wife *US, 1921*

- —Lou Shelly, *Hepcats Jive Talk Dictionary*, p. 21, 1945
- —*Complete CB Slang Dictionary*, 1976
- —Peter Chippindale, *The British CB Book*, p. 151, 1981
- —Multicultural Management Program Fellows, *Dictionary of Cautionary Words and Phrases*, 1989
- [G]ot to make some calls. Check on the ball and chain[.] —Greg Williams, *Diamond Geezers*, p. 53, 1997

ballast scorcher *noun*

a fast-riding railway engineer *US*

- —Norman Carlisle, *The Modern Wonder Book of Trains and Railroading*, p. 258, 1946

ballbag *noun*

1 the scrotum *AUSTRALIA*

- —Thommo, *The Dictionary of Australian Swearing and Sex Sayings*, p. 14, 1985
- When we get 'old of Moon, I'm gunner [going to] nail 'im to the ceiling by 'is ballbag. —Chris Baker and Andrew Day, *Lock, Stock... & Spaghetti Sauce*, p. 270, 2000

2 an athletic supporter *US, 1968*

- —J. E. Lighter, *Historical Dictionary of American Slang, Volume 1*, p. 76, 1994

ball blinder *noun*

a condom *UK*

An image of something that debilitates **BALLS** (the testicles).

- —David Rowan, *A Glossary for the 90s*, 1998

ballbreaker *noun*

1 a difficult task, a boring situation; any circumstance that saps your spirit *US, 1942*

The prosaic etymology leads to any task that strains the testicles; more likely that 'balls' represent power or spirit in this context.

- So it was the usual day – ballbreaker? —Richard Price, *Clockers*, p. 284, 1992

2 a powerful, assertive woman; someone who demands or actively exacts a difficult requirement *US, 1944*

Taking 'balls' to mean 'power and spirit', this extends from the previous sense.

- See, at that time the Anglican Church were really ballbreakers. That was one of the words they used then, ballbreakers. Ballbreakers means backbreakers. —Lenny Bruce, *The Essential Lenny Bruce*, p. 210, 1967
- At least she's not a ballbreaker. Christ, if she were a ballbreaker there'd be no way. —*Diner*, 1982
- He prided himself on being as tough, as cruel, as unforgiving as any pimp, macgimper, child stealer, cutthroat, or ball breaker on the street. —Robert Campbell, *Sweet La-La Land*, p. 183, 1990
- For fuck's sake lady don't be a fuckin' ball-breaker on me now, don't fuck me about. —J.J. Connolly, *Know Your Enemy [britpulp]*, p. 156, 1999

ball-busting *adjective*

harassing, dominating, controlling *US*

- —Joseph Weingarten, *American Dictionary of Slang*, p. 54, 1954
- Fuckin' nigger gets Doris Day as a parole office. But a good fella like you gets stuck with a ball-bustin' prick. —*Reservoir Dogs*, 1992
- You're just jealous, because unlike a certain ball-busting, dried-up career woman I might mention, we're all happily married. —*Romy and Michele's High School Reunion*, 1997

ball-cutter *noun*

a person who belittles and demeans others *US*

- [W]hat she is is a ball-cutter. I've seen a thousand of em, old and young, men and women. Seen 'em all over the country and in the homes – people who try to make you weak so they can get you to toe the line, to follow their rules, to live like they want you to. —Ken Kesey, *One Flew Over the Cuckoo's Nest*, p. 58, 1962

baller *noun*

1 a drug dealer, usually of crack cocaine *US*

- She tells me that when she was actively gangbanging, her father's brother, Uncle Darryl (whom she describes as a "baller," a successful drug dealer), supplied her with drugs to sell for him. —*Rolling Stone*, p. 86, 12th April 2001

2 an attractive male *US*

- —Connie Eble (Editor), *UNC-CH Campus Slang*, Fall 2002

3 a member of a youth gang who is prospering financially *US*

- —Bill Valentine, *Gang Intelligence Manual*, p. 74, 1995

ballet master *noun*

on the railways, the supervisor of track crews *US*

An extension of the track worker as a **GANDY DANCER**.

- —Ramon Adams, *The Language of the Railroader*, p. 11, 1977

balley *noun*

a free show outside a carnival attraction, intended to create interest in paying to see the act inside *US*

- —Gene Sorrows, *All About Carnivals*, p. 8, 1985

ballgame *noun*

1 a state of affairs, especially if challenging *US, 1930*

Sporting imagery.

2 during the Vietnam war, an exhange of fire or firefight with the enemy *US*

- —Linda Reinberg, *In the Field*, p. 16, 1991

▸ **a whole new ballgame**

a completely different set of circumstances *US, 1968*

ballhead *noun*

a white New Zealander *NEW ZEALAND*

- —*Press*, p. 19, 14th February 1989

ball hop *noun*

a deliberate fabrication, an unsupported rumour *IRELAND*

Gaelic.

- And then the lads told him. It was all a ball-hop. "Maurice O'Doherty" was in fact a mimic – and friend of the late and great broadcaster – who worked in the next office to Billy. —*Limerick Leader*, 5th May 2001

ballhuggers *noun*

1 very tight trousers *US*

Hawaiian youth usage.

- Whaty, Aaron, you t'ink you macho when you wear dose ball huggahs? —Douglas Simonson, *Pidgin to da Max Hana Hou*, 1982

2 a pair of men's close-fitting and revealing nylon swimming trunks *AUSTRALIA*

- My children grew up in WA in the 80's but speedos were always referred to as 'ballhuggers'. —*Wordmap (www.abc.net.au/wordmap)*, 2003

ballie *noun*

any old person, especially your parent *SOUTH AFRICA*

From the Afrikaans *ou bal*.

ball in hand *noun*

in pool, the right to shoot from anywhere behind the headstring after another player has hit the cue ball into a pocket *UK, 1807*

- —Mike Shamos, *The Illustrated Encyclopedia of Billiards*, p. 18, 1993

ballistic *adjective*

extremely angry; out of control *US, 1985*

Originally applied to an out-of-control missile.

- Officer Nelson Hareem went ballistic and put the hot flogger in a neck brace for three weeks. —Seth Morgan, *Fugitive Nights*, p. 32, 1990

- "Your dad was pissed, huh?" "Totally ballistic."—C.D. Payne, *Youth in Revolt*, p. 302, 1993
- I totally choked. My father is going to go ballistic on me.—*Clueless*, 1995
- [H]e takes one big hit [of cocaine] up one nostril and one up the other one, one straight after the other. He immediately goes fuckin' ballistic. He's twitching and clapping his hands.—J.J. Connolly, *Know Your Enemy [britpulp]*, p. 141, 1999
- Mommy goes ballistic and ends their relationship.—*Cruel Intentions*, 1999
- It's hard being a bloke, because you've nobody to call on if things go ballistic[.]—Jonathan Gash, *The Ten Word Game*, p. 15–16, 2003
- Both the Beckhams went ballistic.—*The Guardian*, p. 4, 12th June 2003

ballistics *noun*
graphic, aggressive rap lyrics *US, 1991*
- —J. E. Lighter, *Historical Dictionary of American Slang, Volume 1*, p. 77, 1994

ballock *and variants*
▷ **see:** BOLLOCK

ballocky; bollocky; bollicky *adjective*
naked *UK, 1961*
Often combined with 'naked', compare with **BOLLOCK NAKED** and **STARK BOLLOCK NAKED**.

ball of chalk *noun*
a walk *UK, 1936*
Rhyming slang, sometimes condensed to a simple 'ball'.
- He was taking a ball of chalk in the Bayswater direction.—Charles Raven, *Underworld Nights*, p. 189, 1956
- I will take a ball of chalk into the town[.]—Ronnie Barker, *Fletcher's Book of Rhyming Slang*, p. 25, 1979

ball-off *noun*
an act of male masturbation *UK, 1961*

ball-off *verb*
(of a male) to masturbate *UK, 1961*

ball of fire *noun*
a dynamic and energetic person *US, 1900*
- He is a ball of fire with the women – the sultry, slow-urning kind, of course.—Max Shulman, *Guided Tour of Campus Humor*, p. 2, 1955
- To listen to you guys tell it, my old man is one ball of fire.—Donald Goines, *El Dorado Red*, p. 32, 1974

ball of malt *noun*
a large glass of whiskey *IRELAND*
- Interested in sport of nearly every variety but particular in the hurling and football games, Pat also kept very informed from reading and engaged with young and old in conversation while enjoying a ball of malt.—*Munster Express*, 20th April 2001

ball of muscle *noun*
1 a powerfully built, fit and healthy person or animal *AUSTRALIA, 1914*
- He was, though, a real ball of muscle, what the Scots call a 'worrrraker'.—Bernard Hesling, *The Dinkumization and Depommification of an artful English Immigrant*, p. 91, 1963
- Well, you tell him that the next time she hoses me down in me own yard I'll knock 'er bloody 'ead off', spat the irate ball of muscle.—Kerry Cue, *Crooks, Chooks and Bloody Ratbags*, p. 106, 1983

2 a person with a great deal of energy *NEW ZEALAND*
- —Louis S. Leland, *A Personal Kiwi-Yankee Dictionary*, p. 11, 1984

ball of wax *noun*
a complete set of facts or situation *US, 1953*
- After 13 years of dinner plates that sports Jackie's face in colors, after writing as many as 100 letters a night in search of a rare Kennedy piece, after "lots and lots" of dollars, Steinberg is trying to sell the whole ball of wax.—*Washington Post, Potomoc Journal*, p. 1, 29th September 1979

balloon *noun*
1 a lieutenant *US, 1951*
Coined in Korea.
- Gasping, I told him that "Combat" was now a first lieutenant, and though I made it a rule not to speak to second balloons, since he'd been instrumental in my development I would make an exception.—David H. Hackworth, *About Face*, p. 211, 1989

2 used as a humorous synonym of 'platoon' *US, 1967*
- —Carl Fleischhauer, *A Glossary of Army Slang*, p. 3, 1968

3 a woman's breast *US, 1962*
Usually in the plural.
- Incidentally, whilst Betty appeals greatly, the balloons on the girlfriend of R.S. are, to me, almost revolting.—*Flame*, p. 12, 1972

4 a condom *US, 1966*
- Box of balloons with the fetherlite touch.—Madness, *House of Fun*, 1982

5 a small amount of heroin, whether or not it is actually in a balloon *US, 1967*
- —Richard Horman and Alan Fox, *Drug Awareness*, p. 463, 1970
- —Robert Ashton, *This Is Heroin*, p. 208, 2002

6 a heroin dealer *UK*
- —Robert Ashton, *This Is Heroin*, p. 208, 2002

7 a foolish, talkative person *UK: NORTHERN IRELAND*
Because they are 'full of hot air'.
- —C. I. Macafee, *A Concise Ulster Dictionary*, p. 14, 1996

8 a dollar *US, 1973*
- —J. E. Lighter, *Historical Dictionary of American Slang, Volume 1*, p. 78, 1994

▸ **the balloon goes up**
something happens *UK, 1924*
Used especially in the past tense in phrases like 'when did the balloon go up?' and 'the balloon went up at 6 o'clock'. Often when the event referred to was in some kind of trouble. Military in origin, probably World War 1, from the raising of an observation balloon just before an attack.

balloon *verb*
to dramatically and constantly change your shape in order not to present a predictable target *UK*
Military.
- I was "ballooning" – hunching down, then standing up, making sure I didn't present a static target.—Andy McNab, *Immediate Action*, p. 25, 1995

balloon car; balloon *noun*
a *saloon* bar *UK, 1960*
Rhyming slang.
- —Ray Puxley, *Cockney Rabbit*, p. 8, 1992

balloon foot *noun*
a slow driver *US*
- —John Edwards, *Auto Dictionary*, p. 11, 1993

balloon head *noun*
an empty-headed, dim-witted dolt *US, 1931*
Sometimes contracted to 'balloon'.
- What a fuckin' balloon head.—*Casino*, 1995
- —Angela Devlin, *Prison Patter*, p. 25, 1996
- I see that friggin balloon-head Darren Taylor an a few of his divvy mates[.]—Niall Griffiths, *Kelly + Victor*, p. 167, 2002

balloon juice *noun*
1 empty talk *US, 1900*
A play on the 'hot air' typically found inside balloons.
- Tonight would have been balloon juice without a big backlog of thinking.—Bernard Wolfe, *The Late Risers*, p. 183, 1954
- —Joseph E. Ragen and Charles Finston, *Inside the World's Toughest Prison*, p. 790, 1962

2 a sweet, bright coloured fruit-based drink *BARBADOS*
- —Frank A. Collymore, *Barbadian Dialect*, p. 15, 1965

balloon knot *noun*
the anus *UK*
Visual imagery.
- —Chris Donald, *Roger's Profanisaurus*, 1998
- One point for a wank, two points for a blow job, three points for a shag, four points if it goes up the balloon knot, eight points for a threesome and bonus points at the discretion of the Shag Master General[.]—Colin Butts, *Is Harry Still on the Boat?*, p. 88, 2003

balloon tyres *noun*
dark bags beneath an actor's eyes *UK*
- —Wilfred Granville, *The Theater Dictionary*, p. 14, 1952

ballot *noun*
▷ **see:** BALOT

ball out *verb*
▷ **see:** BAWL OUT

ballpark *noun*
an approximate range *US, 1957*
- —*American Speech*, Spring-Summer 1976
- Yes, someone older. Yeah, I mean, you know, you know, old, not as old as I am, but in the same general ball park as me.—*Manhattan*, 1979

- Can you give me a ballpark on the time? — Robert Crais, *L.A. Requiem*, p. 42, 1999

ballroom *noun*

a singles bar with a reputation for easy sexual conquests *US*

- — *American Speech*, p. 18, Spring 1985: 'The language of singles bars'

ballroom blitz *noun*

the breasts *UK*

Rhyming slang for **TIT(S)**, formed from the title of a 1973 song that was successful for The Sweet.

- — Bodmin Dark, *Dirty Cockney Rhyming Slang*, 2003

balls *noun*

1 the testicles *UK, 1325*

From the shape.

- I joined the university karate class (not because I wanted a code of honour but so I could kick anyone in the balls who attacked me when I walked home late at night). — *The Guardian*, 20th January 2004

2 courage, daring *UK, 1893*

- He's a smart pitcher too, knows what he's doing out there, and as Jim Owens says, "He has the balls of a burglar." — Jim Bouton, *Ball Four*, p. 324, 1970
- You didn't hit it, but it was a big balls bet. — *Hard Eight*, 1996
- If you think something's going on, have the balls to ask someone instead of just sneaking around. — Robert Crais, *L.A. Requiem*, p. 124, 1999
- [Y]ou need one other vital ingredient for your criminal idea – balls, big balls. And that makes all the difference. — Danny King, *The Burglar Diaries*, p. 33, 2001

3 strength, substance *UK*

- I could bring a bit of balls to programmes like that[.] — Gary Glitter, *Ask*, p. 35, 7th March 1981

4 nonsense *UK, 1857*

- I don't know if that's a spiritual thing beyond my ken – I might be talking balls – but I do think sometimes: 'I shouldn't be here now'. — *The Observer*, 29th September 2002

▸ **all balls**

nonsense *UK, 1937*

An elaboration of **BALLS**.

▸ **as balls**

used as an intensifier *US*

- That test was hard as balls. — Connie Eble (Editor), *UNC-CH Campus Slang*, p. 1,

▸ **balls in a vice**

at an extreme disadvantage, overpowered *US*

- I'm up front with ya, Tilley. I've got my balls in a vice. — *Tin Men*, 1987

▸ **balls like a Scoutmaster**

great courage or sexual prowess *NEW ZEALAND*

Based on the image of a Boy Scout leader as a paedophile.

- — Harry Orsman, *A Dictionary of Modern New Zealand Slang*, p. 5, 1999

▸ **by the twenty-four swinging balls of the twelve apostles!**

used as a register of anger and despair *US*

- "By the twenty-four swinging balls of the twelve apostles!" is the most colourful expression I ever heard uttered during my years on the road. — Howard Bone, *Side Show*, p. 89, 2001

▸ **don't get your balls in a knot**

do not become agitated *AUSTRALIA*

- 'We've been in a funny place called civilisation. You know how to spell that, cowgirl?' 'Don't get your balls in a knot.' — Robert English, *Toxic Kisses*, p. 81, 1979

▸ **get your balls in an uproar**

to become unduly excited *CANADA*

Of military origin.

▸ **have your balls for a necktie**

to punish someone severely *UK, 1973*

Generally in a future tense; an unpleasant if imaginative simile that is no more comprehensive than the actual fate that is threatened.

▸ **have your balls torn off**

to be severely reprimanded *UK, 1977*

▸ **lay your balls on the chopping-block**

to take responsibility (for an action or opinion) and thereby risk humiliation or rejection *UK*

- [T]hen we really had to lay our balls on the chopping-block. — Frank Skinner, *Frank Skinner*, p. 166, 2001

▸ **make a balls of**

to spoil something, to make a mess of something *UK, 1889*

From **BALLS** (nonsense).

- [Y]ou're very aware that the more England are in pole position the more they're likely to make a balls of it. — *The Observer*, 28th January 2001

▸ **to have someone by the balls**

to exert complete control over someone; to have complete power over someone *US, 1918*

- [E]ven though he's got me by the balls out here, Dan knows that in a courtroom, he loses this case. — *A Few Good Men*, 1992

balls *verb*

to secrete objects in a man's underpants, nestling whatever you wish to keep hidden around the testicles (balls) *UK*

- Forget i' man, says Nood ballsin' gear [drugs] an' bills. — Nick Barlay, *Curvy Lovebox*, p. 39, 1997

▸ **bust your balls; break your balls**

to work to your fullest capability; to try your hardest *US, 1944*

- I busted my balls all night for that fuckin' Spencer, even pushing his stuff before my own. — Lanre Fehintola, *Charlie Says...*, p. 161, 2000

balls!

used as an all-purpose expletive *UK*

A figurative use of 'testicles'.

- 'What's the best brand?' 'Log Cabin fine cut,' said Pat and Dennis together. 'Balls,' said Joe. 'That stuff'll kill yer.' — Nino Culotta (John O'Grady), *They're A Weird Mob*, p. 86, 1957
- The heavies are following Greasy John, who drops his torch, which smashes. The noise echoes. GREASY JOHN: Balls. — Bernard Demspey and Kevin McNally, *Lock, Stock... & Two Sips*, p. 324, 2000

balls-achingly *adverb*

tediously *UK, 1972*

- [B]alls-achingly awful Russian ballad singers[.] — Robert Young Pelton, *The World's Most Dangerous Places*, p. 881, 2003

ballsack *noun*

a skimpy bathing suit for a man *US*

- — Anna Scotti and Paul Young, *Buzzwords*, p. 103, 1997

balls-and-all *adjective*

with complete commitment *AUSTRALIA*

- The trick is to try to minimise your risk factors, but in situations like this it comes down to a balls-and-all assault option[.] — William Dodson, *The Sharp End*, p. 261, 2001

balls-ass naked *adjective*

completely naked *US, 1958*

- The two of us were balls-ass naked whhen they carried us to Bellevue. — Herbert Huncke, *Guilty of Everything*, p. 197, 1990

ballsed-up *adjective*

ruined, wrecked, messed up *AUSTRALIA*

- And that's when I reckon men got their ballsed-up ideas about women. — Frank Hardy, *Hardy's People*, p. 126, 1986

balls-out *adverb*

at full speed *US, 1945*

balls-to-the-walls *adjective*

unrestrained, full-out *US, 1967*

- J.L. says that motorcyle of his only has two speeds: dead still and balls to the walls. — Ken Weaver, *Texas Crude*, p. 102, 1984
- There was no glib "yes" to this question [...] it was balls-to-the-wall for real. — Christopher Brookmyre, *The Sacred Art of Stealing*, p. 242, 2002

balls to you!

registers an impatient dismissal of anything specified *UK, 1923*

Variants include 'balls to that', and 'balls to X'.

balls-up *noun*

a mess, a muddle, a mistake *UK, 1934*

- Had they ever made a mistake somewhere, a balls-up? — J.E. MacDonnell, *Big Bill the Bastard*, p. 73, 1976
- — Peter Corris, *Pokerface*, p. 182, 1985
- Tony Kelly made a balls of things, he freely admits it. — *Farmers Journal (Ireland)*, 3rd October 1998
- Another fuckin' balls up... I've lost my stash [of drugs] again! — Lanre Fehintola, *Charlie Says...*, p. 14, 2000

balls up *verb*

to make a mistake; to err; to mess something up *AUSTRALIA, 1969*

- — Wilda Moxham, *The Apprentice*, p. 92, 1969

• Most people get to some point like this and most of them balls it up. —Peter Corris, *Pokerface*, p. 157, 1985

ballsy *adjective*

gutsy, courageous *US, 1935*

• The minesweep guys are a real ballsy bunch. —Darryl Ponicsan, *The Last Detail*, p. 123, 1970
• That Scal, he's a ballsy guy, you know. —George V. Higgins, *The Friends of Eddie Doyle*, p. 203, 1971
• —Eugene Landy, *The Underground Dictionary*, p. 28, 1971
• RANDAL: I've got to tell you, my friend: this is one of the ballsiest moves I've ever been privy to. I never would have thought you capable of such blatant disregard of store policy. —*Clerks*, 1994

ball team; baseball team *noun*

a group of gambling cheats who work in casinos *US*

• —Thomas L. Clark, *The Dictionary of Gambling and Gaming*, p. 12, 1987

ball tearer *noun*

1 something extraordinary *AUSTRALIA*

• This Leonard French is a little balltearer. It's got luxury built in, not tacked on[.] —Barry Humphries, *A Nice Night's Entertainment*, p. 146, 1974
• —Barry Humphries, *A Nice Night's Entertainment*, p. 173, 1978
• To play a 'ball tearer' is another way of describing a brilliant performance[.] —Ivor Limb, *Footy's No Joke!*, p. 10, 1986

2 a violent person *AUSTRALIA*

• —James McNeil, *The Chocolate Frog and The Old Familiatr Juice*, 1973

3 a difficult, physically-demanding task *AUSTRALIA, 1984*

A military variation of **BALLBREAKER**.

ball up *verb*

to ruin something *AUSTRALIA*

• Look, you could ball up a good story. You haven't the experience to tackle something like this. —Ward McNally, *Supper at Happy Harry's*, p. 145, 1982

bally; bally act; ballyhoo *noun*

any method used to draw a crowd; a small, free performance given outside a place of entertainment in the hope of drawing customers inside *US, 1901*

Circus and carnival usage.

• Bally is used by sideshows, girlie shows, and the like to give the tip an idea of the show to be seen inside (the bally is located immediately outside the structure or tent. —
• —Don Wilmeth, *The Language of American Popular Entertainment*, p. 15, 1981

bally *adjective*

1 used as a euphemism for 'bloody' *UK, 1885*

• Men do not take tips because they are bally asses[.] —Edwin Lefevre, *Reminiscences of a Stock Operator*, p. 207, 1993

2 very angry *UK*

Probably by ellipsis from 'bally mad'.

• I'd been seeing some bird so, of course, Oriole goes bally! —Shaun Ryder, *Shaun Ryder... in His Own Words*, 1997

ballyhoo *verb*

to draw a crowd *US*

• Said, "I've ballyhooed in a smalltown circus / throughout the middle west." —Bruce Jackson, *Get Your Ass in the Water and Swim Like Me*, p. 75, 1965

balm *verb*

to embalm a body *BAHAMAS, 1980*

• —John A. Holm, *Dictionary of Bahamian English*, p. 11, 1982

Balmain basket weaver *noun*

a trendy, leftist member of the middle class *AUSTRALIA*

Derogatory; after the affluent Sydney suburb of Balmain.

• Basketweaver from Bailmain: A trendy, basically middle class, upwardly mobile, socially conscious, left-wing member of the Australian Labor Party and one who has no intention of manning the barricades for any cause whatsoever. Derisory. —Richard Beckett, *The Dinkum Aussie Dictionary*, p. 7, 1986
• As someone who's been a republican since long before the Balmain Basket Weavers took up the cause, I don't give much thought to the question of honesty among the Monarchists. —*www.roadtosurfdom.com/surfdomarchives*, 2003

Balmain basket-weaving *adjective*

characteristic of a Balmain basket weaver *AUSTRALIA*

• Jesus, who'd want to try and rape these two? King Kong? They'd be safe working topless on a Greek freighter. Bloody Balmain basket-weaving molls with their hairy legs and army shorts. —Robert G. Barrett, *Davo's Little Something*, p. 281, 1992

Balmaniac *noun*

a person from the affluent Sydney suburb of Balmain *AUSTRALIA*

Recorded as 'Balmain footballers' by Baker, 1943.

• Because there were Balmanians (as distinct from Balmaniacs) afoo and on bicycles in the street, these ladies Doris and Deidre were obliged to display utmost decorum[.] —Geoff Wyatt, *Saltwater Saints*, p. 44, 1969

balmy *adjective*

drunk *US, 1850*

• —Harold Wentworth and Stuart Berg Flexner, *Dictionary of American Slang*, p. 17, 196o

balmy breeze; breeze *noun*

cheese *UK, 1961*

Rhyming slang.

baloney *noun*

1 utter nonsense *US, 1922*

• I met Bob's brother Hank, who says he fell in love with me, which is a bunch of baloney 'cause he fell in love with anything in skirts that would pay any attention to him. —James Mills, *The Panic in Needle Park*, p. 93, 1966
• It might be a load of balloney, but I have always really liked that image. —*Varsity*, p. 6, 14th June 2002

2 the penis *US, 1928*

• Man, wouldn't I love to play hide the baloney with that. —Charles Whited, *Chiodo*, p. 224, 1973
• —J. E. Lighter, *Historical Dictionary of American Slang, Volume 1*, p. 82, 1994

3 a die that has been flattened on several edges to favour one surface *US*

• You watch these dice for so many years and years and years, square dice, that when you throw a pair of baloneys in, it looks like a flat tire. —Edward Lin, *Big Julie of Vegas*, p. 217, 1974

4 electric cable *US*

Electric line industry usage.

• —A.B. Chance Co., *Lineman's Slang Dictionary*, p. 1, 1980

baloney pony *noun*

the penis *US*

• DUANE: How big is your johnson? RAMU: Johnson? DUANE: Your wand, your pork sword, your baloney pony. —*The Guru*, 2002

▸ **ride the baloney pony**

to have sex *US*

• Another way to say "intercourse" [...] Riding the baloney pony[.] —Erica Orloff and JoAnn Baker, *Dirty Little Secrets*, p. 88, 2001

baloobas *noun*

the breasts *AUSTRALIA*

• —James McDonald, *A Dictionary of Obscenity, Taboo and Euphemism*, p. 9, 1988

balot; ballot *noun*

opium; heroin *US*

• —Richard A. Spears, *The Slang and Jargon of Drugs and Drink*, p. 22, 1986
• —Robert Ashton, *This Is Heroin*, p. 205, 2002
• —Mike Haskins, *Drugs*, p. 283, 2003

balsa boy *noun*

a male pornography performer who has trouble maintaining an erection *US*

One of many **WOOD** images.

• —*Adult Video News*, p. 42, August 1995

Balt *noun*

an immigrant of Eastern European extraction; any European immigrant to Australia during the immediate post-World War 2 period *AUSTRALIA, 1963*

Derogatory; common in the 1940–50s when it was often applied indiscriminately to any European migrant.

• [T]here's quite a few wogs, dagos, yids, refugees, spades, Balts, boongs, Huns, Abos and other foreigners amongst the lily white, Anglo-Saxon dinkum Australians who have foregathered for the only ritual practised in Foolgarah[.] —Frank Hardy, *The Outcasts of Foolgarah*, p. 46, 1971
• The Australian mentality of superiority that caused all displaced persons to be labelled 'bloody Balts' and produced euphemisms such as 'new Australians', is hopefully now anachronistic. —Bruce Ford, *The Elderly Australian*, p. 67, 1984

alti belt *noun*
any area with a conglomeration of Indian restaurants; especially Birmingham's Sparkhill and Sparkbrook districts *UK*
Named for the area's preponderence of restaurants and take-aways offering Indian and Pakistani cuisine. (Balti is a kind of curry cooked and served in the pot after which it is named).
- Reporter Nikita Gulhane goes to Birmingham's balti belt to meet Mohammed Ajaib, his son Omar, and some of the customers at the Royal Al Faisal restaurant. —*The Food Programme*, BBC Radio 4, 31st August 2003
- There is a tumbledown house just off Brick Lane – where the balti belt of London's old East End is studded still with the odd surviving bagel bar, pie and mash shop, and Irish lock-in bar[.] —*The Guardian*, 9th June 2003

3alto *nickname*
Baltimore, Maryland *US*
- —Don Wilmeth, *The Language of American Popular Entertainment*, p. 16, 1981

bam *noun*
1 a pill or capsule of amphetamines *US*
An abbreviation of 'bambita'.
- —Clarence Major, *Dictionary of Afro-American Slang*, p. 23, 1970
- [A]rrested 71 persons trying to buy Preludin – known as "bam" in street slang – and Dilaudid. Both are diet pills used as heroin boosters or heroin substitutes. —*Washington Post*, p. A1, 22nd July 1981
- I am steeped in thoughts about "angel dust" and "wacky weed" and "bam" and "speed," not to mention plain old marijuana, cocaine, and heroin because I have spent weeks doing a television special on drug abuse. —*San Francisco Examiner*, p. C10, 28th March 1981

2 a pill containing both a barbiturate and an amphetamine *UK*
- —Tom Hibbert, *Rockspeak!*, p. 16, 1983

3 a central nervous system depressant *UK*
- —Mike Haskins, *Drugs*, p. 282, 2003

4 a cigarette made with poor quality marijuana *US, 1952*

5 a violent individual *UK*
- If you think the bloke in front of you is a bam, but he turns out to be a nugget, for instance, then your tea could be well and truly out. —Christopher Brookmyre, *Boiling a Frog*, p. 55, 2000

6 a female member of the US Marine Corps *US*
A '*b*road-*a*ssed *m*arine'. Gulf war usage.
- —*American Speech*, p. 383, Winter 1991: 'Among the new words'

▷ **see:** BAMPOT; BAMSTICK

bama *noun*
a conventional person, profoundly out of touch with current trends *US*
- —*Current Slang*, p. 1, Fall 1970

bama chukker *noun*
a poor southern white *US*
- —*Current Slang*, p. 1, Fall 1966

bamalacha rambler *noun*
a marijuana smoker *US, 1959*
- —Ernest L. Abel, *A Marijuana Dictionary*, p. 10, 1982

bamalam *noun*
marijuana *US*
Variation of **BAMALACHA**.
- [D]iggin' sounds after hours and smokin' your bamalam and walking down the street stark noble savage naked to the world! —Lester Bangs, *Psychotic Reactions and Carburetor Dung*, p. 117, 1973

bambalacha; bamba; bammy *noun*
marijuana *US, 1938*
- Marijuana is also known as loco weed, love weed, giggle weed, bambalacha and Indian hay. —*San Francisco Examiner*, p. 15, 19th October 1948
- Grass ... Mary Jane, Aunt Hazel, African bush, bambalacha. You pick the cool name. —Stephen J. Cannell, *The Tin Collectors*, p. 60, 2001
- —Mike Haskins, *Drugs*, p. 286, 2003

bambalacha rancher *noun*
a marijuana user, possibly a grower *US*

bam-bam *noun*
the buttocks *TRINIDAD AND TOBAGO*
- —Lise Winer, *Dictionary of the English/Creole of Trinidad & Tobago*, 2003

bamb'clat *noun*
▷ **see:** BUMBOCLOT

bambino *noun*
1 a child *ITALY*
Italian used by English-speakers with no knowledge of Italian.
- Watch your language, your bambinos are coming! —*Boys on the Side*, 1995

2 an amphetamine or other central nervous system stimulant *US*
- —Jay Robert Nash, *Dictionary of Crime*, p. 18, 1992

bambi-sexual *noun*
a homosexual whose sexual activity is characterised by kisses, caresses and emotion *US*
Punning on the gentle deer Bambi, hero of the novel by Felix Salten and the film by Disney.
- —Wayne Dynes, *Homolexis*, p. 147, 1985

bamboo *noun*
▸ **in the bamboo**
neglected, forgotten *TRINIDAD AND TOBAGO, 1987*
- —Lise Winer, *Dictionary of the English/Creole of Trinidad & Tobago*, 2003

bamboo manicure *noun*
torture using bamboo splinters forced under the fingernails *US*
Korean and then Vietnam war usage.
- —Frank Hailey, *Soldier Talk*, p. 3, 1982

bamboo telegraph *noun*
the spreading of gossip or rumours in a jungle *US, 1929*
Vietnam war usage.
- —Linda Reinberg, *In the Field*, p. 16, 1991

bamboo wedding *noun*
a marriage with Hindu rites *GUYANA*
- —Richard Allsopp, *Dictionary of Caribbean English Usage*, p. 76, 1996

bamboozle *verb*
to deceive someone, to swindle someone *UK, 1703*
Arguably conventional English but with a slangy ring nevertheless.
- At this point it was a toss up as to whether the Angels were bamboozling the press or vice-versa. —Hunter S. Thompson, *Hell's Angels*, p. 56, 1966
- I guess she felt that leaving the building with me would bamboozle any spy that Lock Jaw might have had about. —Iceberg Slim (Robert Beck), *Mama Black Widow*, p. 168, 1969
- Back in the Fifties and early Sixties it was simple shit to bamboozle a chick into dropping her step-ins and spreading her legs[.] —*Screw*, p. 9, 29th May 1972
- You think you got the highway cops bamboozled, Billy Ray? —Robert Campbell, *Juice*, p. 199, 1988

bambs *noun*
central nervous system depressants *UK, 1998*
- —Mike Haskins, *Drugs*, p. 282, 2003

Bambu *noun*
any cigarette rolling papers *US*
The brand name of the rolling papers favoured by marijuana-smoking Beats of the 1950s, often used in a generic, eponymous sense.

bamf!
1 in computing, a notional sound during a magical transformation in a multi-user dungeon *US*
Also an acronym produced from '*b*ad-*a*ss *m*other*f*ucker'.
- —Eric S. Raymond, *The New Hacker's Dictionary*, p. 47, 1991

2 used as Internet shorthand to mean 'I am leaving this discussion' *US*
A sound effect from the *X-Men* comic books.
- —Andy Ihnatko, *Cyberspeak*, p. 21, 1997

bammer *noun*
1 weak, low grade marijuana *US*
- —Pamela Munro, *U.C.L.A. Slang*, p. 30, 1997

2 not genuine or of poor quality *US*
Derives, perhaps, from **BUMMER** (a disappointing or depressing event).

bammnie *noun*
a commerically manufactured cigarette adulterated with marijuana *UK*
- —Tom Hibbert, *Rockspeak!*, p. 15, 1983

bammy *noun*
▷ **see:** BAMBALACHA

bampot; bamstick; bam *noun*
a fool; an eccentric; a madman *UK, 1911*
- See the bam that said that? —Ian Pattison, *Rab C. Nesbitt*, 1988
- What it did achieve, though, was to make him extremely resolute in dealing with religious bampots. —Christopher Brookmyre, *Not the End of the World*, p. 376, 1998

bamsie *noun*
the buttocks *BARBADOS*
- —Richard Allsopp, *Dictionary of Caribbean English Usage*, p. 77, 1996

bamsie fly *noun*
a pest, a nuisance *TRINIDAD AND TOBAGO*
- —Richard Allsopp, *Dictionary of Caribbean English Usage*, p. 77, 1996

bamsie man *noun*
a male homosexual *TRINIDAD AND TOBAGO*
- —Richard Allsopp, *Dictionary of Caribbean English Usage*, p. 77, 1996

ban *noun*
a banana *UK, 1984*
Greengrocer's familiar abbreviation, usually in the plural.

banana *noun*

1 an Asian-American who rejects his Asian heritage and seeks to blend into the dominant white culture *US, 1970*
A variation on the most well-known **OREO**. Like a banana, the person described is yellow on the outside, white on the inside.
- —Douglas Simonson, *Pidgin to da Max*, 1981
- — Multicultural Management Program Fellows, *Dictionary of Cautionary Words and Phrases*, 1989

2 a Hong Kong Chinese of European or American parentage or aspirations *HONG KONG*
- "Is he marrying a gwailu (foreign devil) or banana?" "What's a banana?" "Yellow outside, White inside." —Howard Marks, *Mr Nice*, p. 230, 1997

3 a New Zealand-born Chinese person *NEW ZEALAND*
- —David McGill, *David McGill's Complete Kiwi Slang Dictionary*, p. 10, 1998

4 a person of mixed race, with both black and white ancestors *US*
- —Lou Shelly, *Hepcats Jive Talk Dictionary*, p. 7, 1945

5 a hospital patient suffering from jaundice *US*
- — *Maledicta*, p. 38, 1983: 'More common patient-directed pejoratives used by medical personnel'
- —Sally Williams, *"Strong" Words*, p. 133, 1994

6 in American casinos, a $20 chip *US*
From the yellow colour.
- —Steve Kuriscak, *Casino Talk*, p. 2, 1985

7 the penis *US, 1916*
- — Anon., *King Smut's Wet Dreams Interpreted*, 1978

8 a parenthesis sign (or) on a computer keyboard *US*
- —Eric S. Raymond, *The New Hacker's Dictionary*, p. 39, 1991

9 the convex curvature of the bottom of a surfboard *US*
- —D.S. Halacy, *Surfer!*, p. 216, 1965

10 a comic in a burlesque show *US, 1953*
- Why do you think she went out and bought this army cot? Leave it to me: I'm always top banana in the shock department. —Truman Capote, *Breakfast at Tiffany's*, p. 61, 1958
- —Harold Wentworth and Stuart Berg Flexner, *Dictionary of American Slang*, p. 18, 1960
- For years one of the most formidable second bananas in the comedy spectrum, Louis Nye comes into his own and attains premium solo status in his current nitery act. — *Variety*, p. 10, 23rd May 1962
- Lenny had his mother, Sally Marr – a top banana when they all worked in burlesque – fitted out with a recorder[.] —Albert Goldman, *Freak Show*, p. 211–212, 1968

11 a crazy or foolish person *US, 1919*
- The kid was a banana! Bonzo. Loonier than his old man. —Joseph Wambaugh, *Lines and Shadows*, p. 108, 1984

12 a dollar *US*
- I can't help thinking about Billy the Bad-Ass, what a goodnigger, and that kid Meadows and his eight years for a lousy forty fucking bananas. —Darryl Ponicsan, *The Last Detail*, p. 182, 1970

13 a £1 Australian note *AUSTRALIA, 1953*

▸ **off your banana**
mentally unstable, crazy *UK*
- Here I was: off my banana in a nightclub[.] —Wayne Anthony, *Spanish Hig* p. 70, 1999

banana *verb*
in television and film making, to walk in a slight curve in fro of the camera to preserve focus *US*
- —Ralph S. Singleton, *Filmaker's Dictionary*, p. 15, 1990

banana-balancer *noun*
an officer's steward or cabin-hand *AUSTRALIA*
- 'Commander's banana-balancer?' 'Cabin-hand?' Windy interprete incredulously. 'That's what I said. Make sure you tuck his sheets in.' —J.E. MacDonnell, *Don't Gimme the Ships*, p. 149, 1960

banana belt *nickname*

1 southeastern Alaska *US, 1937*
- —Russell Tabbert, *Dictionary of Alaskan English*, p. 47, 1991

2 the South Orkney Islands and South Georgia, warm only in comparison with the harsh cold of Antarctica *ANTARCTICA, 195*
The term has been applied to a relatively less cold area in a cold region since 1898.
- —Bernadette Hince, *The Antarctic Dictionary*, p. 41, 2000
- — *Cool Antartica*, 2003: 'Antarctic slang'

bananabender *noun*
a person from Queensland *AUSTRALIA, 1964*
The Australian state of Queensland has a large banana industry.
- —Frank Hardy, *Hardy's People*, p. 179, 1986
- Why has no enterprising bananabender opened a museum devoted to the cane toad, with startled little critters costumed as leading Queenslanders? — *Australian Magazine*, p. 6, 6th July 1996

banana boy *noun*
a young white man brought up in the Anglo-Saxon tradition of Natal, later KwaZulu-Natal; hence a sportsman who is resident in KwaZulu-Natal *SOUTH AFRICA, 1956*
- —Penny Silva, *A Dictionary of South African English*, 1996

banana clip *noun*
the curved magazine or clip for a US Army carbine *US*
- —Carl Fleischhauer, *A Glossary of Army Slang*, p. 3, 1968

banana farm *noun*
an asylum for the insane *UK*
Used among Britons in tropical or semi-tropical countries.
- —William Marshall, *Hatchet Man*, 1976

banana hammock *noun*
a brief male bikini *US*
- —Vann Wesson, *Generation X Field Guide and Lexicon*, p. 12, 1997

banana jockey *noun*
any person who hangs on to the side of a truck driving a load of bananas to town *GRENADA*
- —Richard Allsopp, *Dictionary of Caribbean English Usage*, p. 77, 1996

Bananaland *nickname*
the state of Queensland *AUSTRALIA, 1880*
Named after the banana industry there.
- It's your first bit of genuine Bananaland food. I tell you, there's no place like Queensland. —Colleen McCullough, *The Thorn Birds*, p. 244, 1977

Bananalander *noun*
a person from Queensland *AUSTRALIA, 1887*

banana oil *noun*
nonsense; persuasive talk *US, 1924*
- —Jerry Robertson, *Oil Slanguage*, p. 24, 1954
- —Helen Dahlskog (Editor), *A Dictionary of Contemporary and Colloquial Usage*, p. 5, 1972

banana peels *noun*
surplus military tyres that are worn smooth and hence useless *US*
- —Lewis Poteet, *Car & Motorcyle Slang*, p. 23, 1992

banana race *noun*
a fixed horse race *US*
- New England tracks are famous throughout the United States for their so-called "banana-races," in which the winner is known in advance to a select few. — *Saturday Evening Post*, p. 29, 18th November 1967

bananas *adjective*
madly excited; mad; behaving oddly *US*
Derives from **BANANA OIL** (nonsense), which abbreviates as 'bananas'; 'to become mad' is 'to go bananas'.
- We heard the police broadcast! They say you're bananas! — *L'il Abner in San Francisco News*, p. 11, 20 March 1957
- If this dude in a pinstripe suit thinks he's going to keep her off The All Weather Panther Committee, he's bananas. — Tom Wolfe, *Radical Chic & Mau-Mauing the Flak Catchers*, p. 63, 1970
- Was Richard Nixon mentally unstable at any time of his Presidency? Did he flip his lid, go bananas? — *San Francisco Chronicle*, p. 7, 14 May 1975
- — *American Speech*, Fall-Winter 1976
- He went totally bananas, cussin' me out instead of thanin' me for savin' his raggedy ass. — Edwin Torres, *After Hours*, p. 264, 1979
- Moscow at the end of the century. Sim City [a computer game] gone bananas. — Melanie McGrath, *Hard, Soft & Wet*, p. 262, 1998
- I'm so bananas I'm showin' up to your open casket / To fill it full of explosive gases / And close it back with a lit match in it[.] — Eminem (Marshall Mathers), *Fuck the Planet (Freestyle)*, 2000
- [I]n the spooky world of hip hop he [Ol' Dirty Bastard]'s revered as something of a genius. The second is that he's bananas. — *Uncut*, p. 20, October 2003

banana shot *noun*
in pool, a shot at an object ball near a cushion, with spin imparted such that the cue ball follows through after striking the object ball and comes to rest after bouncing off the cushion *US, 1983*
- — Mike Shamos, *The Illustrated Encyclopedia of Billiards*, p. 20, 1993

banana skin *noun*
a potential if trivial danger that is easily avoided when not overlooked *UK, 1907*
- The cabinet minister appointed to avoid government banana skins was yesterday corrected by the prime minister, chancellor and a foreign office minister after he slipped up over the single currency. — *The Guardian*, 3rd December 2001

bananas on bananas *noun*
too much of something, even a good something *US*
- — Tony Miller and Patricia George, *Cut! Print! The Language and Structure of Filmmaking*, p. 39, 1977

banana split *noun*
1 amyl nitrite; an ampoule of amyl nitrite *US*
A reference to the banana-like smell of the drug vapours.
- And have "amies" on hand too: poppers, banana splits, whatever you call them. — Angelo d'Arcangelo, *The Homosexual Handbook*, p. 115, 1968

2 a variety of MDMA, the recreational drug best known as ecstasy *UK*
From the logo pressed into the pill; after the cult children's television programme *The Banana Splits* (originally broadcast 1968–70).
- — Gareth Thomas, *This Is Ecstasy*, p. 56, 2002

banana splits *noun*
diarrhoea *UK*
Rhyming slang for **THE SHITS**.
- — Tom Nind, *Rude Rhyming Slang*, p. 8, 2003

banana tree *noun*
the penis *UK*
- I shall keep my word, and you shall keep your banana tree. — Petra Christian, *The Sexploiters*, p. 100, 1973

banana van *noun*
a flatbed railway carriage that sags in the middle *UK*
- — Harvey Shepherd, *Dictionary of Railway Slang*, 1966

banana wagon *noun*
a low handcart used for transporting aeroplane parts *US*
- — *American Speech*, p. 225, October 1955: 'An aircraft production dispatcher's vocabulary'

banana wing *noun*
in motor racing, an aerodynamic wing shape *US*
- — Don Alexander, *The Racer's Dictionary*, p. 9, 1908

banana with cheese *noun*
marijuana and freebase cocaine combined for smoking *US*
- A marijuana-and-base combo is referred to as "banana with cheese"' banana is the rolling paper, usually wheat straw or yellow paper, and cheese is the base, white and crumbly like feta. — *Hi Life*, p. 78, 1979

banano *noun*
marijuana *UK*
- — Mike Haskins, *Drugs*, p. 286, 2003

band *noun*
in prison, a riot squad *US*
- — John R. Armore and Joseph D. Wolfe, *Dictionary of Desperation*, p. 19, 1976

bandaged up *adjective*
in trucking, said of a truck with any improvised winter front *US*
- — Montie Tak, *Truck Talk*, p. 7, 1971

bandage factory *noun*
a hospital *US, 1941*
- — Peter Chippindale, *The British CB Book*, p. 151, 1981

band-aid *noun*
1 in trucking, an improvised winter fronting for a truck *US*
- — Montie Tak, *Truck Talk*, p. 7, 1971

2 a medic *US*
During the Vietnam war, a radio call for a 'band-aid' was a call for a medic.
- — Linda Reinberg, *In the Field*, p. 16, 1991

B and B gang *noun*
on the railways, a *b*uilding and *b*ridge crew *US*
- — Ramon Adams, *The Language of the Railroader*, p. 11, 1977

band box *noun*
a county jail *US*
- — William K. Bentley and James M. Corbett, *Prison Slang*, p. 3, 1992

band chick *noun*
a woman who is attracted to, and makes herself available to, musicians *US*
An early term for what would come to be known as a 'groupie'.
- Although Miriam had known enough musicians and enough Negroes to judge each one on his own, there were "band chicks" at the Savoy, as at nearly every club where jazz is played. — Nat Hentoff, *The Jazz Life*, p. 20, 1961

B and D; B/D *noun*
*b*ondage and *d*omination (or *d*iscipline) as sexual activites *US*
- The term b & d as an abbreviation for bondage and discipline is gaining currency, certainly in the underground press, for s-m. — Gerald and Caroline Greene, *S-M*, p. 205, 1974
- Real-life S/M activity, unlike the cliches of S/M ficiton, rarely is bizarre or extreme; most of it involves biting, hitting, slapping and the like, rather tha heavy B and D (bondage and discipline). — *Playboy*, p. 183, March 1974
- Mild B&D/S&M [sado-masochism]? Well, both were tired. — Lester Bangs, *Psychotic Reactions and Carburetor Dung*, p. 348, 1981
- Look out for terms like dominant, submissive, B/D, and S and M. — Lawrence Paros, *The Erotic Tongue*, p. 148, 1984

B and D *adjective*
*b*ad and *d*angerous *US*
- — Kenn "Naz" Young, *Naz's Dictionary of Teen Slang*, p. 5, 1993

B and E *noun*
burglary *US, 1965*
From the initials for '*b*reaking *and* *e*ntering'.
- "For car theft?" "Robbery." "What kind? From a building? Little B and E?" "Armed." — Elmore Leonard, *Stick*, p. 78, 1983
- He said, "Mom, there's no way anybody could bust in here, even jigs I met who spent their lives doing B and Ees, pros." — Elmore Leonard, *Glitz*, p. 98, 1985
- The one where you do all your B-and-E's? — Carl Hiaasen, *Tourist Season*, p. 15, 1986

bander *noun*
▷ see: **BAND OF HOPE**

Band House *nickname*
the Chicago House of Corrections *US*
- Off I went to Chicago's city prison at 26th and California, the Bridewell, known as "The Band House" in the underworld. — Mezz Mezzrow, *Really the Blues*, p. 33, 1946

bandicoot *noun*
▸ **as a bandicoot**
completely as specified; extremely so *AUSTRALIA, 1845*
- He's been as miserable as a bandicoot stuck down here and wondering miserably how things are going on the place, but he

couldn't bring himself to leave you. —Nourma Handford, *Carcoola Holiday*, p. 217, 1953
- You're lousy as a bandicoot. —Alan Marshall, *I Can Jump Puddles*, p. 101, 1955
- This elegant little creature is the subject of unkind expressions such as: "Miserable as a bandicoot!" "Poor as a bandicoot!" —Lyla Stevens, *Animals of Australia in colour*, p. 50, 1956
- Bold as brass, tongue swung in the middle, no scruples, no conscience and as cunning as a bandicoot. —Dymphna Cusack, *Picnic Races*, p. 219, 1962

▸ **like a bandicoot on a burnt ridge**
lonely and forlorn *AUSTRALIA, 1901*
- [H]e lived out in the bush – all alone like a bandicoot on a burnt ridge – until it was time for him to start spreading the news. —Kel Richards, *The Aussie Bible*, p. 13, 2003

bandicoot *verb*
to dig out a subsoil crop, especially potatoes, without disturbing the plant *in situ*, usually surreptitiously *AUSTRALIA, 1896*
- Well, the abos "bandicooted" his peanuts. —Ion L. Idriess, *Over the Range*, p. 290, 1947

band in the box *noun*
pox *UK*
Rhyming slang.
- —Jack Jones, *Cockney Rhyming Slang*, 1971

bandit *noun*
1 a petty-thief, usually in conjunction with the object of the crime *UK*
Ironic.
- "[O]ne of a gang of international milk bandits" – near-vagrant labourers, who steal milk outside dwellings[.] —David Powis, *The Signs of Crime*, p. 172, 1977

2 an obvious homosexual *UK*
An abbreviation of **ARSE/ASS BANDIT**.
- [T]his pure fucking bandit comes mincing in[.] —Kevin Sampson, *Outlaws*, p. 239, 2001
- Johnny was discussing celebrity "bandits" with Marco the chef[.] —Garry Bushell, *The Face*, p. 136, 2001

3 a hostile aircraft *US, 1942*
- Two friendly aircraft closing on the bandit to intercept, Sir! —Milton Caniff, *Steve Canyon in San Francisco Examiner*, p. 40, 15th December 1954
- I had a SAM come so close I could almost read the tail markings. You get bandit calls all the time. —*San Francisco Chronicle*, p. 10, 30th December 1971
- —Linda Reinberg, *In the Field*, p. 16, 1991

4 an unsolved construction problem *US*
- Today at Inglewood the term applies to unsolved construction problems. Every bandit that appears is handed to one of Estes' colonels. —*Time*, p. 18, 25th August 1961

bandit odds *noun*
betting odds that strongly, if secretly, favour one betting position *US*
- He was fleecing rich sportsmen out of a fortune by betting ringer Upshaw could beat their favorite boxers, usually at bandit odds. —Iceberg Slim (Robert Beck), *Long White Con*, p. 189, 1977

bandit territory *noun*
in Metropolitan Police slang, the Home Counties areas fringing London that are policed by other forces *UK*
- —Martin Fido and Keith Skinner, *The Official Encyclopaedia of New Scotland Yard*, 1999

band moll *noun*
a woman who makes herself sexually available to the members of a rock group; a groupie *AUSTRALIA, 1969*
- A few minutes to myself and then I've got to talk to that silly bird from Scream magazine. An interview with the star. One of those society band molls. —Kevin Mackey, *The Cure*, p. 114, 1970
- Band Moll – A young female who fucks the arses off the members of a rock group. —Thommo *The Dictionary of Australian Swearing and Sex Sayings*, p. 14, 1985

band of hope; bander *noun*
soap *UK, 1938*
Rhyming slang, based on the name of a temperance organisation founded in Leeds in 1847. The truncated variation is recorded in Australia by Sidney J. Baker in 1943.

B and S *noun*
brandy and soda *UK, 1868*
A popular drinker's abbreviation.

bandwidth *noun*
attention span *US*
A borrowing of a technical term with a technical meaning (the volume of information that can be handled within a time unit) fo a humorous, broader usage.
- —Eric S. Raymond, *The New Hacker's Dictionary*, p. 47, 1991

bandy *noun*
a bandicoot *AUSTRALIA, 1953*

Bandywallop *noun*
an imaginary remote town *AUSTRALIA*
- He's the beltman of the Bandywallop Beach Brigade. —J.E. Macdonnell, *Alarm – E-boats!*, p. 39, 1958

b and z *verb*
▷ **see: BOOM AND ZOOM**

bang *noun*
1 an instance of sexual intercourse *UK, 1691*
- You haven't heard about our passenger, Miss Miller? No, and you are not likely to...And that's where the real story starts, young feller – and with a bang. —Robert S. Close, *Love Me Sailor*, p. 230, 1945
- Bob had his bang; he came out and called Big Lug; Big Lug went down and got his bang[.] —Jack Kerouac, *Letter to Neal Cassady*, p. 300, 10 January 1951
- Well is your husband gonna be a good bang? —Jack Kerouac, *The Dharma Bums*, p. 145, 1958
- I figured, what the hell, I'll give her a bang, just for laughs. —Leonard Shecter and William Phillips, *On the Pad*, p. 156, 1973

2 pleasure, enjoyment *US, 1929*
- Many of the younger social and diplomatic sets get a bang out of hot licks. —Jack Lait and Lee Mortimer, *Washington Confidential*, p. 17, 1951
- I got a little bang out of it because I could still recognize them. —James T. Farrell, *The Ain't the Men They Used to Be*, p. 85, 1955
- Boy, did I get a bang out of watching him. —Frederick Kohner, *Gidget*, p. 29, 1957
- The surfers also get a hell of a bang out of slot racing for some reason[.] —Tom Wolfe, *The Kandy-Kolored Tangerine-Flake Streamline Baby*, p. 81, 1965
- Also, I could tell these dudes got a real bang out of playing and winning at cards[.] —Bobby Seale, *A Lonely Rage*, p. 267, 1978

3 a person judged on their sexual performance *UK, 1937*
- I hear she makes an even better bang in the park! —Ward McNally, *Supper at Happy Harry's*, p. 101, 1982

4 a popular schoolgirl *UK*
- If you do what I say you will be a BANG. —Mallory Wober quoting a 13-year-old girl, *English Girls' Boarding Schools*, 1971

5 an injection of a narcotic *US, 1922*
- I found him in such a state of collapse that I had to give him a bang before he could pull himself together and locate the junk in the place where he'd hidden it. —Ethel Water, *His Eye is on the Sparrow*, p. 148, 1952
- [M]ixing his blood with the drug, drawing it from his arm, shooting it and drawing back – till the final bang. —Hal Ellson, *The Golden Spike*, p. 228, 1952
- The physician would take care of her with a "bang" in the arm, employing a strong narcotic drug. —Harry J. Anslinger, *The Murderers*, p. 185, 1961
- —Angela Devlin, *Prison Patter*, p. 25, 1996

6 the sudden effect of a drug *US*
- [T]he top grade, the gungeon, which produces a voluptuous "bang," bringing as high as a dollar. —Jack Lait and Lee Mortimer, *New York Confidential*, p. 102–103, 1948

7 marijuana *US*
- —Kenn "Naz" Young, *Naz's Dictionary of Teen Slang*, p. 6, 1993
- "We could light up, toke some bang?" the teenager said hopefully. —Stephen J. Cannell, *The Tin Collectors*, p. 136, 2001

8 a swallow of alcohol *UK*
- Eeyar, avver bang on tha. Colm offers the wine up to Ianto and he takes it and tips it to his lips. —Niall Griffiths, *Sheepshagger*, p. 50, 2001

9 an attempt *UK, 1948*
Usually in the form 'to have a bang (at)'.
- —Eric Partridge, Wilfred Granville and Frank Roberts, *A Dictionary of Forces' Slang*, 1948

10 an exclamation point (!) *US, 1931*
From the slang of printers to the slang of computer enthusiasts.
- —Guy L. Steele et al., *The Hacker's Dictionary*, p. 28, 1983

bang *verb*

1 to have sex *UK, 1720*

- There was a young man in Havana / Banged a girl on an old player piano. — *Eros*, p. 63, Winter 162
- Because I haven't banged anybody, not anybody, since we picked up Dinah, except her, of course, and this Margo is real cute. — John Clellon Holmes, *Go*, p. 137, 1952
- At one sharp he rushes from Marylou to Camille – of course neither one of them knows that's going on – and bangs her once, giving me time to arrive at one thirty. — Jack Kerouac, *On the Road*, p. 42–43, 1957
- But how long did it take for those guys to bang off a quick one, in the middle of the afternoon, in their inviolable offices? — James Baldwin, *Another Country*, p. 273, 1962
- That's what makes you so goofy, banging her so much. — Jim Thompson, *Pop. 1280*, p. 191, 1964
- I suppose she's a real gunner; bangs away, huh? — John Nichols, *The Sterile Cuckoo*, p. 88, 1965
- [T]his other woman he was banging regular[.] — Johnny Speight, *It Stands to Reason*, p. 53, 1973
- JAKE: You know, like bang her or anything? JOEY: Ah, no, no. I didn't bang her. — *Raging Bull*, 1980
- I get enough just banging crazily away on the set. — *Adult Video*, p. 9, August/September 1986
- The only way he could bang regular chicks is with a Cryptoninte condom, but that would kill him. — *Mallrats*, 1995
- Shep! What the hell are you dong? I'm banging that girl! — *Fargo*, 1996
- Guys banged in her any position they so desired. — Anthony Petkovich, *The X Factory*, p. 183, 1997
- Little matter to me that this woman chose to pursue a career in pornography, nor that she has been "banging" Jackie Treehorn, to use the parlance of our times. — *The Big Lebowski*, 1998
- Even Dave Dummings, a fiftysomething ex-Army colonel, has marketed himself as the sexy older man who doesn't need Viagra and gets to bang beautiful young chicks half his age. — Ana Loria, *1 2 3 Be A Porn Star!*, p. 110, 2000

2 to stimulate a woman's vagina by introducing and withdrawing a finger in rapid order *US*

- — Eugene Landy, *The Underground Dictionary*, p. 28, 1971

3 to inhale or to inject a drug intraveneously *US, 1926*

- If he'd taken an overdose of cocaine, I'd have to bang him with heroin to counteract it. — Ethel Water, *His Eye is on the Sparrow*, p. 148, 1952
- Angel nodded off immediately, hitting himself and banging it all in at once[.] — Hal Ellson, *The Golden Spike*, p. 95, 1952
- He groaned as he banged himself in the arm while the mixture was still warm. — Chester Himes, *A Rage in Harlem*, p. 38, 1957
- My habit screwed my mind up. All I wanted to do was bang 'H' and 'coast.' — Iceberg Slim (Robert Beck), *Pimp*, p. 99, 1969

4 to swallow a tablet *UK*

- I've done 12 [ecstasy tablets] in one night. You bang one, you go out, you have a good night. — *Drugs An Adult Guide [quoting Brian Harvey of pop group East 17]*, p. 8, December 2001

5 to engage in youth gang criminal activity *US*

- In most of Los Angeles, gang members contend that for all the publicity about the killings, the gangs themselves are pretty quiet. "Ain't nobody banging no more," they insist. — *Los Angeles Times*, p. 1, 26th June 1986
- OLDER SHERIFF: Are you a Crip or a Blood? CAINE: I don't bang. — *Menace II Society*, 1993
- Curiously, the 18th Street gangsters, who have definite roots in the I.A. area, nevertheless claim norte while bangin' in EPA. — Bill Valentine, *Gangs and Their Tattoos*, p. 112, 2000

6 (of dance music) to have a danceable beat *AUSTRALIA*

- Flow is essential. It's not enough to just keep it banging. It's important to remember someone is always listening. — *Sydney Scope Magazine*, p. 44, 2001

7 to make a turn *US*

- — *Current Slang*, p. 1, Summer 1969

▸ **bang balls**

to have a plan backfire *SINGAPORE*

- — Paik Choo, *The Coxford Singlish Dictionary*, p. 11, 2002

▸ **bang goes that**

used for suggesting that something has come to an end *NEW ZEALAND*

- — David McGill, *David McGill's Complete Kiwi Slang Dictionary*, p. 13, 1998

▸ **bang heads**

to fight *US*

- — Hy Lit, *Hy Lit's Unbelievable Dictionary of Hip Words for Groovy People*, p. 3, 1968

▸ **bang like a dunny door; bang like a hammer on a nail**

to be an exceptional sexual partner *AUSTRALIA*

Many variations, including 'bang like a rattlesnake', 'bang like a shithouse door in a gale' and 'bang like a shithouse rat'.

- I thought, kiss my bum if that sheila wouldn't bang like a dunny door. — Barry Humphries, *The Wonderful World of Barry McKenzie*, p. 44, 1968
- I'm just an ordinary bloke lookin' for a nice simple homely sheilah with blue eyes and yellow hair who bangs like a shithouse door in a gale. — Barry Humphries, *Bazza Pulls It Off!*, 1971
- [T]he other side of coinages like 'sink the sausage' and 'bangs like a dunny door in a gale' is spurious and pays out despair and disaster to many women and children. — Nancy Keesing, *Lily on the Dustbin*, p. 53, 1982
- I said we were banging away like a shit-house door in a gale, and tried hard to make this dream a reality. — Frank Skinner, *Frank Skinner*, p. 225, 2001

▸ **bang the crap out of**

of a male, to exhaust a sex-partner by vigorous sexual activity *UK*

An intensification of **BANG** (to have sex) on the model of 'beat the crap out of' (to thrash).

- Their favourite [porn film] star is Rocco, a Brazilian guy who bangs the crap out of girls[.] — *Mixmag*, p. 5, April 2003

bang *adverb*

very much, extremely *UK*

- The police still think I'm bang at the old villainy lark[.] — Dave Courtney, *Raving Lunacy*, p. 3, 2000

bangarang; banggarang *noun*

an uproar, a riot *JAMAICA, 1943*

- — Paul Sullivan, *Sullivan's Music Trivia*, p. 35, 2003

bang-bang *noun*

the penis *BAHAMAS*

- — John A. Holm, *Dictionary of Bahamian English*, p. 11, 1982

bang belly *noun*

1 a Newfoundland boiled pudding made of flour, molasses, soda and seal-fat or suet *CANADA*

- And his bullseyes were plastered all over his face / Like the whorts in a bang-belly pie. — John Burke, *Burke's Ballads*, p. 41, 1960

2 the protuding stomach of a child *JAMAICA*

- — Richard Allsopp, *Dictionary of Caribbean English Usage*, p. 79, 1996

bang bottle *noun*

a condom *UK, 1990s*

- — Dand Rowan, *A Glossary for the 90s*, 1998

Bang-clap *nickname*

Bangkok, Thailand *US*

During the Vietnam war, Bangkok was a rest and recreation destination, with plenty of sex and almost as much venereal disease.

- — Linda Einberg, *In the Field*, p. 16, 1991

banged *adjective*

intoxicated on a drug, especially marijuana *US*

- He had me take a long, strong take, and then squat down and blow on my thumb. After a few of those, he had me floating and really banged. — Stephen Gaskin, *Amazing Dope Tales*, p. 7, 1980
- He said he should've held the meeting in here, get everybody zonked and decadent on a strong stone, get them good and banged – using all the words he knew – then present the movie deal. — Elmore Leoanrd, *Stick*, p. 241, 1983
- Two teenage shiteheads both of them banged up[.] — Nick Barlay, *Curvy Lovebox*, p. 20, 1997
- [S]o banged on ups and cocaine she fell out on the floor[.] — Clarence Major, *All-Night Visitors*, p. 201, 1998

banged up *adjective*

1 specifically, being locked in a police or prison cell; generally, imprisoned *UK*

The image of a cell door having been *banged* shut. Closely following the verb sense which is first recorded in 1950.

- [A]lways getting banged up or fucked over [cheated]. — Shaun Ryder, *Shaun Ryder... in His Own Words*, 1990
- Na, that ain't Icky. He's banged up, he is. — Martin King and Martin Knight, *The Naughty Nineties*, p. 54, 1999
- [A]nybody who's banged up is, by definition, not half as fucking successful as they should be. — Val McDermid, *Keeping on the Right Side of the Law*, p. 178, 1999
- I couldn't handle prison again, banged up on one their stinking blocks[.] — John King, *Human Punk*, p. 340, 2000

2 pregnant *NEW ZEALAND*

- — Sonya Plowman, *Great Kiwi Slang*, p. 21, 2002

banger *noun*

1 a sausage *UK, 1919*
Perhaps from the resemblance to a bludgeon.
- Andrew arrives and sits beside her. He shows her two sausages. ANDREW: Banger? RHONDA: No, thanks, Andrew. — Peter Nichols, *Promenade [Six Granada Plays]*, p. 62, 1959
- 'Train smash and bangers,' Splinter advised, and pushed towards him a plate on which two sausages wallowed in a sea of red stewed tomatoes. — J.E. MacDonnell, *Don't Gimme the Ships*, p. 69, 1960

2 a firework producing a loud bang *UK, 1959*
- [H]e was a vicious sort of kid, pulled off frogs' legs for fun, tied cans with bangers in them to cats tails – that sort of caper. — Wilda Moxham, *The Apprentice*, p. 94, 1969

3 a detonator *UK*
- — Harvey Shepherd, *Dictionary of Railway Slang*, 1966

4 a near-derelict motor vehicle, usually a car or van *UK, 1962*
From the back-firing of a worn-out or poorly-maintained engine.
- It's a crappy old banger. Mid-green. Could be a Cortina, but I'm not sure. — Chris Ryan, *Stand By, Stand By*, p. 82, 1996
- I took out all the seats and away I went / It's a right old banger and the chassis' bent — Ian Dury, *Itinerant Child*, 1998

5 a cylinder in a car engine *US*
Usually prefaced with a numeral.
- Does four banger mean four men with hammers or one man with four hammers? Neither. It means a car with four cylinders. — Ed Radlauer, *Drag Racing Pix Dix*, p. 23, 1970

6 a fender, especially a front fender *US*
- — Elementary Electronics, *Dictionary of CB Lingo*, p. 48, 1976

7 a boxer who relies on brute strength and aggressive tactics *US*
- The Big Banger From Parks (Headline) — *San Francisco Chronicle*, p. 42, 21st September 1968
- Robertson is a "banger," a converted southpaw whose left hook has produce 18 KO's. — *San Francisco Chronicle*, p. 46, 28th July 1973

8 in hot rodding and motor racing, a collision *US*
- — John Edwards, *Auto Dictionary*, p. 11, 1993

9 a gang member *US, 1985*
Shortened form of **GANGBANGER**.
- Two of the bangers had shaved heads, two others wore knit caps; all wore black high-top sneakers, half unlaced. — Joseph Wambaugh, *Floaters*, p. 26, 1996
- [T]he Border Brothers, who outnumber both the MRU and the Sur Califas in Nevada's prisons, are aligning with the Sur Califas bangers. — Bill Valentine, *Gangs and Their Tattoos*, p. 32, 2000

10 a heavy metal music enthusiast who dances with zeal *US*
- — Don R. McCreary (Editor), *Dawg Speak*, 2001

11 a hypodermic needle and syringe *US*
- — Richard A. Spears, *The Slang and Jargon of Drugs and Drink*, p. 24, 1986

12 a kiss, especially one that is forcefully delivered *UK, 1898*

13 in pool, an unskilled if forceful player *US*
- — Steve Rushin, *Pool Cool*, p. 7, 1990

14 a billiard ball *UK, 1984*
Usually in the plural, extended from the sense as 'testicle'.

15 in the casino game Keno, the punch tool used to make holes in tickets showing the numbers bet on *US, 1978*
- — Thomas L. Clark, *The Dictionary of Gambling and Gaming*, p. 12, 1987

bangers *noun*
the testicles *UK, 1961*

Bangers *nickname*
Bangkok *AUSTRALIA*
- Would you believe the Lady Patterson once accompanied me on a government mission to Bangers back in the rock'n'rolling 60's? — Barry Humphries, *The Traveller's Tool*, p. 104, 1985

bangers and mash *noun*
an act of urination *UK*
Rhyming slang for **SLASH**, formed from one of the great dishes of British cuisine.
- — Bodmin Dark, *Dirty Cockney Rhyming Slang*, 2003

banggarang *noun*
▷ **see: BANGARANG**

bang gotcher *noun*
any film of the Western genre *AUSTRALIA, 1953*
From children's recreation of the cowboy action in such films: firing toy (or pretend) guns, crying 'Bang! Got you!' so their play-enemies don't miss the point.
- — Jill Morris and Mary Lancaster, *Adventures at Bangotcher Junction*, 1985

banging *adjective*

1 drug-intoxicated
- — Mike Haskins, *Drugs*, p. 291, 2003

2 wonderful, great, excellent *UK*
Originally recorded by Francis Grose in 1788 and possibly anticipated two centuries earlier; in the 1990s 'banging' enjoyed the wide-popularity of a new coinage. Also variant 'bangin'.
- If he's sayin' they was bangin' they was bangin' an' we's blindin'[.] — Nick Barlay, *Curvy Lovebox*, p. 13, 1997
- Came out to one here last summer I did, but it wasnt anywhere near as good as this one. Bangin tonight. — Niall Griffiths, *Sheepshagger*, p. 72, 2001

banging-off *noun*
sexual intercourse *UK, 1984*
Royal Navy use.

Bangla *noun*
a Bangladashi *SINGAPORE*
- — Paik Choo, *The Coxford Singlish Dictionary*, p. 11, 2002

bang on *verb*

1 to talk lengthily and repetitiously about a particular topic *UK, 1959*
- [P]oor Dawn French banging on about chocolate. — *The Guardian*, 17th February 2001

2 in computing, to subject a piece of equipment or a new program to a stress test *US*
- I banged on the new version of the simulator all day yesterday and it didn't crash once. — Eric S. Raymond, *The New Hacker's Dictionary*, p. 48, 1991

bang on *adverb*
exactly, correct *UK, 1943*
Coined by World War 2 Royal Air Force bomber crews for 'bang on the target'; adopted into civilian usage as soon as the war was over.
- I'm here to tell you that that's true, it's absolutely bang on. — Dave Courtney, *Stop the Ride I Want to Get Off*, p. 79, 1999

bang on it *adjective*
drunk or drug-intoxicated *UK*
- Trev had been looking forward to getting bang on the booze and Charlie [cocaine], but he did not want to do it on his own[.] — Colin Butts, *Is Harry Still on the Boat?*, p. 185, 2003
- He had left work and decided to get bang on it. He'd taken two and a half pills and got pissed in Eden[.] — Colin Butts, *Is Harry Still on the Boat?*, p. 211, 2003

bang on the latch *noun*
a last drink after closing time *IRELAND*
- [A] long suffering publican asked them if they had no homes to go to and refused their pleas for "a bang on the latch". — Bernard Share, *Slanguage*, p. 14, 2003

bang on the money *adjective*
absolutely correct, exact *UK*
- And you would be bang on the money to ask[.] — Andrew Nickolds, *Back to Basics*, p. 74, 1994

bang out *verb*

1 to manufacture or produce something, especially without care; to distribute something *UK*
- The hard-won struggle to master "spontaneous prose" both enabled [Jack] Kerouac to write a great book and condemned him, for the rest of his life, to banging out pretty terrible ones. — *The Guardian*, 15th April 2000

2 to eject from a fighter plane *UK*
- — *American Speech*, p. 383, Winter 1991: 'Among the new words'

3 when freefalling from a plane, to spread your body into a wide shape *UK*
- If we got unstable, we "banged ourselves out", stretching our limbs out into a big star. Like the concave surface of a saucer falling towards the earth, you instantly level out. — Andy McNab, *Immediate Action*, p. 146, 1995

bang out of order *adjective*
▷ see: OUT OF ORDER

bang shift *noun*
a quick, forceful gear shift while racing *US*
• —John Lawlor, *How to Talk Car*, p. 17, 1965

bang-shoot *noun*
any thing, matter or business at issue at the moment *UK, 1984*
A playful variation of **SHEBANG** and **SHOOTING MATCH**; usually heard as 'the whole bang-shoot'.

bangster *noun*
a needle-using drug addict *US*
• —Hyman E. Goldin et al., *Dictionary of American Underworld Lingo*, p. 23, 1950

bang stick *noun*
a firearm *UK, 1961*

bangtail *noun*
1 one of several inferior kinds of horse; a racehorse *US, 1921*
From the practice of bobbing the horse's tail.
• —David W. Maurer, *Argot of the Racetrack*, p. 12, 1951
• Most cowboy's horses are sorry-looking beasts, bang-tails, hammer-heads, scruffy animals with questionable parentage. Then there is that black she is riding.—George Bowering, *Caprice*, p. 195, 1987

2 a return-address envelope sent with a bill, containing a product offer on a detachable portion of the envelope flap *US*
• —Rachel S. Epstein and Nina Liebman, *Biz Speak*, p. 16, 1986

bang to rights *adjective*
1 denoting an absolute certainty that fully justifies arrest on a criminal charge, as when caught red-handed *UK, 1904*
Intensifies 'to rights' (fairly, legally).
• I expected the screw who sat in front of me to turn round and capture us bang to rights.—Frank Norman, *Bang To Rights*, p. 49, 1958
• [Y]ou're here with the goods with the intent to supply. You're bang to rights as we say in our end of the business.—J.J. Connolly, *Know Your Enemy [britpulp]*, p. 158, 1999

2 by extension, describing a satisfactory state of affairs *UK*
• Now we've got everything bang to rights, we can lay off for a bit and have a smoke.—Julian Franklyn, 1962

bang-up *noun*
a period during which a prisoner is locked in a cell *UK*
From the verb.
• I was buffing the floor on my spur one day, over the teatime bang-up.—*The Guardian*, p. 7, 17th October 2002

bang up *verb*
1 to inject a drug *UK, 1982*
• Tie it up shoot it up bang it up blow it up[.]—Johnny Thunders, *Too Much Junkie Business*, 1977
• Boaby... ya daft cunt, yir no still bangin up ur ye?—Irvine Welsh, *The State of the Party (Disco Biscuits)*, p. 32, 1995
• —Angela Devlin, *Prison Patter*, p. 25, 1996

2 to prepare marijuana as a cigarette *UK*
• "Hey, groovy, Ken – why not bang up a neat little one-skinner?" And that's what I did.—Ken Lukowiak, *Marijuana Time*, p. 110, 2000

3 in prison, to lock someone or be locked into a cell *UK*
• Moments later the landing officer arrived and banged me up.—*The Guardian*, 26th October 2000

4 to end a poker game *US*
• —John Scarne, *Scarne's Guide to Modern Poker*, p. 272, 1979

bang-up *adjective*
excellent; first-rate *IRELAND, 1821*
• The opening was a bang-up success.—Mezz Mezzrow, *Really the Blues*, p. 288, 1946
• I never forget the night we give him a bang-up send-off.—Kylie Tennant, *Lost Haven*, p. 171, 1946
• Gee, thanks, Dave. Bang-up job so far.—*The Usual Suspects*, 1995

banjax *verb*
to batter, to beat, to destroy someone or something *IRELAND, 1939*
• Any number of things could banjax this whiz kid's operation and all its glamor.—John Brady, *Stone of the Heart*, p. 70, 2001

banjaxed *adjective*
1 not in working order *IRELAND, 1939*
Given fresh impetus in the UK in the 1970s by popular broadcaster Terry Wogan, possibly from the phonetic similarity to the then unacceptable **BOLLOCKSED**.
• I couldn't believe my banjaxed ears.—Ardal O'Hanlon, *The Talk of the Town*, p. 114, 1998
• In recent days, when I hear the Minister for Transport talking about public-private partnerships to finance the Metro and talking heads on the radio and television telling me how banjaxed the French and continentals are, it is hard to square reality with the rhetoric.—*Sunday Business Post*, 22nd January 2004

2 drunk *UK*
Playing on the sense 'not in working order', **SMASHED**.
• —*e-cyclopaedia*, 20th March 2002

banjo *noun*
1 a generously proportioned sandwich or filled roll *UK, 1961*
In military use in forms such as an 'egg banjo' or a 'chip banjo'.
• [A] large, thick slice of bread topped with a thick slice of cheese. —W. Mitford, *Lovely She Goes*, 1969
• I could smell the odour of egg banjos (fried egg sandwiches) and chips coming from the cookhouse.—Andy McNab, *Immediate Action*, p. 22, 1995

2 in prison, any food that has been acquired by illicit means *UK*
• —Paul Tempest, *Lag's Lexicon*, p. 9, 1950

3 a shovel *UK, 1918*
• Well, the only kind of music you'll make around here'll be with a pick and banjo.—Mezz Mezzrow, *Really the Blues*, p. 35, 1946
• —*American Speech*, p. 273, December 1954: 'Fire terms: additional words and definitions'
• —Harvey Shepherd, *Dictionary of Railway Slang*, 1964

4 the rear end of a car or truck *US, 1971*
• —Lewis Poteet, *Car & Motorcyle Slang*, p. 23, 1992

5 in rugby, a head-high tackle *NEW ZEALAND*
• —David McGill, *David McGill's Complete Kiwi Slang Dictionary*, p. 11, 1998

banjo *verb*
1 to beat someone *UK*
From **BANJAX** (to batter).
• —*Listener*, p. 16, 1st July 1982
• —Nigel Foster, *The Making of a Royal Marine Commando*, 1987

2 to murder someone *UK*
• [Y]ou say it was never the family banjo'd your Oliver.—Jeremy Cameron, *Brown Bread in Wengen*, p. 125, 1999

3 to force open a door or window *UK, 1981*
• [S]omeone banjoed [...] my locker and pinched the lot[.]—Duncan MacLaughlin, *The Filth*, p. 105, 2002

banjoed *adjective*
broken down, battered *UK*
From **BANJO** (to beat), ultimately from **BANJAX** (to destroy).
• —Nigel Foster, *The Making of a Royal Marine Commando*, 1987
• But that was before the Edinburgh Executive was banjoed by a sex scandal so odious, even New Labour couldn't spin their way out of it.—Christopher Brookmyre, *Boiling a Frog*, p. Back jacket, 2000

banjo player *noun*
a born-and-(in-)bred country-dweller *UK*
Probably inspired by 'Duelling Banjos', a musical sequence in the film *Deliverance*, 1972, in which the guitar symbolises urban America and the banjo represents an impoverished rural existence.
• Something fuckin weird about you sheepshaggers [Welsh], I'm tellin yer. Fuckin banjo-players round here.—Niall Griffiths, *Sheepshagger*, p. 87, 2001

bank *noun*
1 money; wealth *US*
• —Connie Eble (Editor), *UNC-CH Campus Slang*, p. 1, Spring 1991
• Doing this, we make mad bank.—*Gone in 60 Seconds*, 2000
• Because if the buzz is any indication, the movie's gonna make some huge bank.—Kevin Smith, *Jay and Silent Bob Strike Back*, p. 18, 2001

2 a sum of money ready for immediate use, especially for gambling *AUSTRALIA, 1919*
• Joe Frisco shared a room with his mate, Needles. They had got a 'Bank' together to back a horse at Santa Anita races.—Frank Hardy and Athol George Mulley, *The Needy and the Greedy*, p. 114, 1975
• Rather than waste any of his precious 'bank' on admission, he hid in the boot of a mate's car and got into the course that way.—Roy Higgins and Tom Prior, *The Jockey Who Laughed*, p. 38, 1982

3 a person who finances a gambling enterprise *US*
- —R. Frederick West, *God's Gambler*, p. 222, 1964

4 a prison cell for solitary confinement *US*
- —Joseph E. Ragen and Charles Finston, *Inside the World's Toughest Prison*, p. 790, 1962

5 a toilet *US*
- —Lou Shelly, *Hepcats Jive Talk Dictionary*, p. 7, 1945

▸ **on the bank**
subsisting on bank loans *AUSTRALIA*
- Chris Cotter came over to Jingiddy on train days and saw the farmers who were "on the bank"[.]—F.B. Vickers, *First Place to the Stranger*, 1955

▸ **take it to the bank; put it in the bank**
to be very sure of a fact *US, 1977*
- "One thing you can take to the bank is a white Christmas," a National Weather Service spokesman said of western Illinois and eastern Iowa.— *Washingotn Post*, p. A2, 22nd December 1983
- —J. E. Lighter, *Historical Dictionary of American Slang, Volume 1*, p. 89, 1994
- "I will never forget where I come from, and you can take that to the bank." (Quoting Senator John Edwards).— *Chicago Tribune*, p. C1, 20th February 2004

bank *verb*

1 to enjoy yourself on an outing on a bank holiday *BARBADOS*
- —Frank A. Collymore, *Barbadian Dialect*, p. 15, 1965

2 to prove someone guilty of a crime *US*
- —William K. Bentley and James M. Corbett, *Prison Slang*, p. 18, 1992

3 to surround someone to beat them *US*
- —Anna Scotti and Paul Young, *Buzzwords*, p. 127, 1997

bank bandit *noun*
a barbiturate capsule or other central nervous system depressant *US*
Possibly from the calming effect that enables criminals to overcome nerves.
- —Jay Robert Nash, *Dictionary of Crime*, p. 19, 1992
- —Mike Haskins, *Drugs*, p. 282, 2003

banked out *adjective*
rich *US*
- —Connie Eble (Editor), *UNC-CH Campus Slang*, p. 1, October 2002

banker *noun*

1 a usurer, an illegal lender of money *US*
- How can I figure Bill Ray – he knows the streets like I know the streets – gets a case of the stupids and brags to Pachoulo that he's got a new banker?—Robert Campbell, *Juice*, p. 73, 1988

2 a criminal who controls a stock of forged currency notes *UK, 1966*

3 a person with a large sum of gambling money *AUSTRALIA*
- I've brought two hundred myself – and I'm small bikkies compared to these bankers.—Robert English, *Toxic Kisses*, p. 82, 1979

4 the operator of an illegal numbers racket or lottery *US*
- A numbers banker?—Chester Himes, *The Real Cool Killers*, p. 102, 1959
- They couldn't be trusted by numbers bankers any more.—Claude Brown, *Manchild in the Promised Land*, p. 191, 1965
- There was no problem getting the free-lance Negro bankers out of business.—Mario Puzo, *The Godfather*, p. 252, 1969
- The bankers pay them [the police] off.—Louise Meriwether, *Daddy Was a Number Runner*, p. 116, 1970
- Around Harlem, he'd feed off the policy bankers.—Edwin Torres, *Carlito's Way*, p. 17, 1975

5 in a functionally compartmentalised illegal drug operation, the person who receives payment for drugs bought *US*
- —Carsten Stroud, *Close Pursuit*, p. 269, 1987

6 a creek, river, etc, full to overflowing *AUSTRALIA, 1848*
- If this keeps up she'll be running a banker this afternoon and the river will come down as well. She'll be in flood, for sure.—Allan Skerman, *Beyond Indigo*, p. 424, 1989

▷ **see:** MERCHANT BANKER

banker's bit *noun*
a prison sentence of five to ten years *US*
A common sentence for bankers caught commiting fraud.
- —Hyman E. Goldin et al., *Dictionary of American Underworld Lingo*, p. 23, 1950

banker's row *noun*
a line of side-by-side high-yield gold seams *CANADA*
- My five claims in Dauversiere Township were right in "banker's Row" and might prove to be of considerable worth later on.—L. Wilson, *Chibougamau Venture*, p. 137, 1952

banker's set *noun*
in dominoes, the 3–2 piece *US*
So named because opponents cannot score on it.
- —Dominic Armanino, *Dominoes*, p. 15, 1959

banking *noun*
masturbation *UK*
From **BARCLAY'S BANK** for **WANK**.
- —Tom Hibbert, *Rockspeak!*, p. 17, 1983

bank off *verb*
to place a prisoner in a punishment cell *US*
- —*Maledicta*, p. 266, Summer/Winter 1981: 'By its slang, ye shall know it: the pessimism of prison life'

bank repairs *noun*
a lack of financing *US*
- —Jerry Robertson, *Oil Slanguage*, p. 112, 1954

bankroll *verb*
to finance a project *US, 1928*
The image of a roll of banknotes.
- It means fuck all if you can't bankroll it.—Kevin Sampson, *Outlaws*, p. 71–72, 2001

bank shot *noun*
a delayed fuse shell fired by a tank in such a manner as to bounce off an object and around a corner to explode at or near the target *US*
Borrowed from any number of sports and games. Vietnam war usage.
- —Gregory Clark, *Words of the Vietnam War*, p. 47, 1990

bank teller job *noun*
in horse racing, a bet on the surest of sure things *AUSTRALIA*
So certain is the bettor of winning that he could safely borrow money from a bank one day, bet it that afternoon, and pay it back the next day.
- —Ned Wallish, *The Truth Dictionary of Racing Slang*, p. 3, 1989

bank up *verb*
to save money *BAHAMAS*
- —John A. Holm, *Dictionary of Bahamian English*, p. 11, 1982

banter *noun*
slang *UK*
By extension from its conventional senses.
- "[P]ineapple" might be the brigadier's combat-soldier banter for a hand grenade.—Ken Lukowiak, *Marijuana Time*, p. 41, 2000

banyan *noun*
a picnic on a beach, when organised from a naval vessel *UK*
- —Nigel Foster, *The Making of a Royal Marine Commando*, 1987

banzai *noun*
in drag racing, a complete effort *US*
- A competitor who pushes his car to the absolute limit during a drag race is making an banzai run.—John Lawlor, *How to Talk Car*, p. 17, 1965

banzai!
used as an expression of joy and excitement *US*
- —John Blair, *The Illustrated Discography of Surf Music 1961–1965*, p. 123, 1985

bap *noun*
a sophisticated and privileged black American woman *US*
An acronym, on the model of **JAP** (a *J*ewish-*A*merican *p*rincess).
- The poor Bap has been a subject of satire and ridicule[.]—Nelson George, *Buppies, B-Boys, Baps & Bohos (first published 1992)*, p. xvi, 2001

bap *verb*
to shoot someone or something *US*
- Then I bapped at the first little rabbit and turned him aboutface on his pivot.—Robert Edmond Alter, *Carny Kill*, p. 2, 1966

baparazzi *noun*
press photographers who specialise in catching their subjects topless *UK*
A play on **BAPS** (the breasts) and 'paparazzi'.
- Can you name the naughty snorkellers here in our "baparazzi" shots?— *The FHM Little Book of Bloke*, p. 100, June 2003

bap head *noun*
a fool *UK, 2001*
- — Susie Dent, *The Language Report*, p. 75, 2003

bappo *noun*

a baptist *AUSTRALIA*

- —Sidney J. Baker, *Australia Speaks*, 1953

baps *noun*

the female breasts *AUSTRALIA*

After the small soft bread rolls.

- Another survey – this time by British bra makers – found that Pommy sheilas' baps are getting bigger and bigger and that soon the average girlie will sport enormous 38D-sized noras.—*Picture*, p. 9, 5th February 1992
- Just flashed me baps as the bouncers, like[.]—Niall Griffiths, *Kelly + Victor*, p. 304, 2002

baptism of fire *noun*

an inexperienced soldier's first combat experience *US*

- —Gregory Clark, *Words of the Vietnam War*, p. 74–75, 1990

Baptist bag *noun*

a brown paper bag in which a bottle of beer can be concealed *US*

- You want a Baptist bag with that beer, buddy?—Lewis Poteet, *Car & Motorcyle Slang*, p. 23, 1992

bar *noun*

1 a pound *UK, 1911*

Directly from Romany *bar*, ultimately Romany *bauro* (heavy or big); usually in the phrase 'half a bar' (until decimalisation in 1971: ten shillings; post-decimalisation: 50p) although inflation seems to have had an effect.

- I follow his pound [bet] and raise him half a bar[.]—Derek Raymond (Robin Cook), *The Crust on its Uppers*, p. 40, 1962
- "Well, we had a syndicate see," Smedley said, "Half a bar each on Scottish Tartan at Haydock[.]—Troy Kennedy Martin, *Z Cars*, p. 77, 1962
- I owed Henry half a bar, which left me with thirty bob[.]—John Peter Jones, *Feather Pluckers*, p. 29, 1964
- Chrismiss hamper worth a hundred bar. Pound a ticket likes.—Irvine Welsh, *The State of the Party (Disco Biscuits)*, p. 38, 1995

2 one million dollars *US*

- —Jim Crotty, *How to Talk American*, p. 380, 1997

3 a package of heroin *US*

- All I want is the stuff. Hey, wait a minute, momma, I ain't no petty nigger. Naw, baby, if I was goin' rip off something, it would be a hell of a lot bigger than a twenty-five dollar bar.—Donald Goines, *Crime Partners*, p. 43, 1978

4 a block of cannabis resin weighing approximately a kilogram *US*

Originally so called for a bar-shaped brick.

5 used as a the name for any variable object *US*

- The second metasyntatctic variable, after FOO. If a hacker needs to invent exactly two names for things, he almost always picks the names "foo" and "bar."—Guy L. Steele et al., *The Hacker's Dictionary*, p. 29, 1983

6 an erection *UK, 1961*

Especially used in the form 'have a bar'.

▸ **not stand a bar of; not have a bar of**

to detest, deny or reject someone or something, to be unable to tolerate someone or something *AUSTRALIA, 1945*

- —G.A. Wilkes, *Dictionary of Australian Colloquialisms*, p. 16, 1978

▸ **not to have a bar of**

to refuse to have anything to do with someone or something *AUSTRALIA, 1933*

- —Frank Hardy, *The Yarns of Billy Borker*, p. 39, 1965
- But the old Octopus wouldn't have a bar of it[.]—Frank Hardy, *The Yarns of Billy Borker*, p. 39, 1965
- And I'm sure the Australian battler will not have a bar of the bleatings of "McCarthyism" in a situation which is its very opposite.—Frank Hardy, *Hardy's People*, p. 47, 1986

bar *verb*

1 (especially in Queensland) to claim something as your right; to reserve something *AUSTRALIA*

- T-hat was B-bloody Brown Tongue there with 'em. I bar first shot at him.—Frank Hardy, *The Outcasts of Foolgarah*, p. 226, 1971

2 to give somebody a ride on the bars or your bicycle *NEW ZEALAND*

- Mr. McCormick used to bar Fergus to his school boy matches.—*Star*, p. 19, 5th August 1959

bar *adjective*

a 'minus' attached to a grade *US*

- —Collin Baker et al., *College Undergraduate Slang Study Conducted at Brown University*, p. 76, 1968

bar *preposition*

in betting, used for indicating the number of horses excluded from the offered odds *UK, 1860*

- [Y]ou might hear a bookie calling out "six bar one", to indicate the shortest price of the rest of the field (i.e., bar the favourite) is 6–1.—John McCririck, *John McCririck's World of Betting*, p. 59, 1991

bar!

used as a call in children's games, chiefly in Queensland and New South Wales *AUSTRALIA*

Used in children's games to indicate that one is safe from being caught or tagged.

- I grew up in Brisbane in the 1960s. We always used bar to show the pursuer that we were safe and could not be touched.—*Wordmap (www.abc.net.au/wordmap)*, 2003

barb *noun*

1 a *barb*iturate *US, 1966*

- —John B. Williams, *Narcotics and Hallucinogenics*, p. 109, 1967
- [H]e only lets me come over when he restocks my acid supply and gives me enough grass and barbs to lasts me until I see him again.—Anonymous, *Go Ask Alice*, p. 59, 1971
- —Angela Devlin, *Prison Patter*, p. 25, 1996
- Barbiturates are also known as BARBS, BLUES, REDS, and SEKKIES.—Macfarlane, Macfarlane and Robson, *The User*, p. 97, 1996
- Some kids raid their mother's bathroom cabinets for Valium, barbs or Tuinol.—Wayne Anthony, *Spanish Highs*, p. 65, 1999

2 a college student who is not a fraternity member *US, 1900*

The fraternity system is known as the 'Greek society', and in Greek a 'barbarian' was any non-Greek.

- —J. E. Lighter, *Historical Dictionary of American Slang, Volume 1*, p. 90, 1994

Barbara Hutton *noun*

in hold 'em poker, a five and ten as the first two cards dealt to a player *US, 1981*

Hutton (1913–1979) was heiress to the Woolworth fortune; Woolworth was the foremost five and ten cent store in America.

- —Thomas L. Clark, *The Dictionary of Gambling and Gaming*, p. 13, 1987

barbecue *noun*

1 a self-immolation *US*

The term enjoyed a brief and gruesome popularity in the early 1960s.

- I am not saying that we should accept Mme. Nhu's statements at face value. Nor that we should forgive her for using that unfortunate language. If she had not referred to the Buddhist suicides as "monk barbecues," Americans would surely have greeted her—*San Francisco News Call-Bulletin*, p. 6, 12th October 1963

2 the burning of a prisoner locked in a cell *US*

- —William K. Bentley and James M. Corbett, *Prison Slang*, p. 89, 1992

3 a napalm bombing *US, 1968*

- —J. E. Lighter, *Historical Dictionary of American Slang, Volume 1*, p. 91, 1994

4 radiation treatment *US*

Medical slang.

- —Sally Williams, *"Strong" Words*, p. 134, 1994

5 a fatal overdose of narcotics *US*

- —Jay Robert Nash, *Dictionary of Crime*, p. 19, 1992

6 an attractive girl or woman *US, 1938*

- —Lou Shelly, *Hepcats Jive Talk Dictionary*, p. 7, 1945
- —Jack Lait and Lee Mortimer, *New York Confidential*, p. 235, 1948: 'A glossary of Harlemisms'

barbecue *verb*

to put someone to death by electrocution *US*

- —Charles Shafer, *Folk Speech in Texas Prisons*, p. 197, 1990

barbed wire *nickname*

Castlemaine XXXX beer *AUSTRALIA, 1983*

From the resemblance of the four X's.

- He was on the barbed wire last night.—*Wordmap (www.abc.net.au/wordmap)*, 2003

barbed wire city *noun*

a military stockade *US, 1964*

- —Carl Fleischhauer, *A Glossary of Army Slang*, p. 3, 1968

barber *noun*

1 a thief who operates by stealth *AUSTRALIA, 1938*
Derives from the thief's ability to 'cut and trim'.

2 in pool, a close miss, usually made intentionally to avoid a scratch *US*
- —Mike Shamos, *The Illustrated Encyclopedia of Billiards*, p. 21, 1993

Barber *noun*

▸ **the Barber**
the Greymouth wind coming across and off the Mawhera River *NEW ZEALAND*
- —David McGill, *David McGill's Complete Kiwi Slang Dictionary*, p. 13, 1998

barber *verb*

1 to rob hotel rooms *AUSTRALIA, 1950*
- Second to 'Barney', Smith's rated 'Art the Barber', an Adelaide-born operator who specialized in 'barbering' hotels – he hopped into rooms when guests were absent and pinched things.—George Blaikie, *Remember Smith's Weekly?*, p. 197, 1966

2 to talk; to gossip *US, 1938*
Derives from a stereotypical barber's inconsequential but incessant chatter with a chair-bound customer.

barber chair *noun*
in logging, the stump left from a poorly cut tree, which in falling leaves an upright large splinter *US, 1941*
- It is poor cutting if "barber chairs" are made and butts are very irregular.—A. Koroleff, *Woodcutter's Handbook*, p. 7/2, 1944

barber pole *noun*
in casino gambling, a bet comprised of various coloured chips *US*
- Barber poles are to be broken down and paid color for color.—Lee Solkey, *Dummy Up and Deal*, p. 107, 1980

barber shop *noun*
in trucking, a bridge with a low clearance *US*
Citizens' band radio slang.
- —Bill Davis, *Jawjacking*, p. 13, 1977

barbidex *noun*
a combination of central nervous system stimulants and depressants *US*
- —Jay Robert Nash, *Dictionary of Crime*, p. 20, 1992

barbie *noun*

1 a barbecue *AUSTRALIA, 1976*
- The barbie was out the back. Sizzling on the hotplate were rows of plump sausages and a mass of fatty chops.—Phillip Gwynne, *Deadly Unna?*, p. 115, 1998

2 an outdoor party centred around food cooked on a barbecue *AUSTRALIA, 1981*
- John wouldn't go to your barbies or crack a tinnie with you, so you said: 'He's got a devil of a spirit in him – he's mad.'—Kel Richards, *The Aussie Bible*, p. 37, 2003

Barbie; Barbie Doll *noun*

1 an idealised woman, one who conforms to the role-model of the blonde-haired, blue-eyed plastic doll *US*
A generally derisory usage; from Barbie™, a manufactured doll originally intended for young girls, which has become a cultural symbol. Also variant 'Barbie Girl'.
- —Harold Wentworth and Stuart Berg Flexner, *Dictionary of American Slang*, p. 675, 1976
- Mattel charged that the band's hit song "Barbie Girl" – which contains lyrics like "Kiss me here, touch there, hanky panky" – wrongfully sexualises its wholesome blonde.—Naomi Klein, *No Logo*, p. 180, 2001

2 a barbiturate capsule *US*
- —Joel Homer, *Jargon*, p. 193, 1979
- —Sally Williams, *"Strong" Words*, p. 134, 1994
- —Mike Haskins, *Drugs*, p. 282, 2003

barbied *adjective*
used of a woman who has become subservient to a man *UK*
From **BARBIE DOLL**, an idealised concept of womanhood manufactured and marketed by Mattel.
- —Angela Devlin, *Prison Patter*, p. 25, 1996

Barclaycard *noun*
a sawn-off shotgun used to shoot doors off their hinges *UK*
From the credit card's advertising slogan 'A Barclaycard gets you anywhere'.
- "Barclaycard", a sawn-off, pump-action shotgun with the butt taken off[.]—Andy McNab (writing of the late 1970s/early 80s), *Immediate Action*, p. 251, 1995

Barclay's Bank; barclay *noun*
of a male, an act of masturbation *UK*
Rhyming slang for **WANK** (masturbation); probably, according to most authorities, since the 1930s.
- —*Maledicta*, p. 225, Winter 1980: 'Lovely, blooming, fresh and gay: the onomastics of camp'
- I popped to the bogs for a Barclays Bank three times.—Bodmin Dark, *Dirty Cockney Rhyming Slang*, 2003

Barcoo buster *noun*
a westerly gale in mid- or south Queensland *AUSTRALIA, 1943*
The Barcoo Shire is one of the most isolated areas in Australia.
- —Sidney J. Baker, *The Drum*, p. 87, 1959

Barcoo rot *noun*
a type of scurvy caused by a lack of fresh food *AUSTRALIA, 1870*
- 'James the Second is dead!' 'Naw. What of?' 'Barcoo rot!' I announced, and left him cutting up his sheep.—Bill Wannan, *Bullockies, Beauts and Bandicoots*, p. 72, 1960

Barcoo spews *noun*
a gastric disorder characterised by vomiting *AUSTRALIA, 1901*
Named after a river in Queensland.
- You couldn't keep the food away from the flies so you'd get the Barcoo Spews too.—Wendy Lowenstein and Morag Loh, *The Immigrants*, p. 27, 1977

bare-ass; bare-assed *adjective*
naked *UK, 1562*
- That's what I thought, no gloves. I heard about you. The Digger goes in bare-ass.—George V. Higgins, *The Digger's Game*, p. 4, 1973
- [T]he Zorros marched off, leaving Dougie and Scottie bare-assed and shivering on the bridge.—Richard Price, *The Wanderers*, p. 23, 1974

bareback *verb*

1 to engage in sex without a condom *US*
- —*Current Slang*, p. 12, Spring 1970
- —Judi Sanders, *Faced and Faded, Hanging to Hurl*, p. 2, 1993
- The study by researchers at the CDC and San Francisco's Department of Public Health is the first serious analysis of the practice of "barebacking," in which gay or bisexual men intentionally engage in sex without a condom with someone other than their primary partner[.]—*San Francisco Chronicle*, p. A2, 4th April 2002
- But that [HIV] is the price to pay for bare backing in a male sex club. —Richard Herring, *Talking Cock*, p. 202, 2003

2 to surf without a wetsuit *US*
- —Trevor Cralle, *The Surfin'ary*, p. 6, 1991

bareback *adjective*
in trucking, said of a tractor without a trailer *US, 1942*
- —Mary Elting, *Trucks at Work*, 1946

bareback *adverb*
(used of sex) without a condom *US*
- —Harold Wentworth and Stuart Berg Flexner, *Dictionary of American Slang*, p. 20, 1960
- —Roger Blake, *The American Dictionary of Sexual Terms*, p. 12, 1964
- —Robert A. Wilson, *Playboy's Book of Forbidden Words*, p. 27, 1972
- I always ride bareback myself. Take a chance my way, though.—Joseph Wambaugh, *The Glitter Dome*, p. 165, 1981
- What can I tell you, she let this jockey ride bareback.—James Ellroy, *White Jazz*, p. 113, 1992

bareback rider *noun*
a man who has sex without using a condom *US*
- —Harold Wentworth and Stuart Berg Flexner, *Dictionary of American Slang*, p. 20, 1960

barefoot *adjective*

1 (of sex) without a condom *US, 1963*
- —J. E. Lighter, *Historical Dictionary of American Slang, Volume 1*, p. 92, 1994

2 (of a car or truck) lacking one or more tyres *US, 1941*
- —Montie Tak, *Truck Talk*, p. 8, 1971

3 (of a citizens' band radio) operating without a power booster *US*
- —Wayne Floyd, *Jason's Authentic Dictionary of CB Slang*, p. 9, 1976

4 in craps, said of a bet on the pass line without odds taken *US, 1983*
- —Thomas L. Clark, *The Dictionary of Gambling and Gaming*, p. 13, 1987

barefooted *adjective*
(of a drink) undiluted *US, 1847*
- —Frederic G. Cassidy, *Dictionary of American Regional English*, p. 153, 1985

barefoot pilgrim *noun*

in the used car business, a naive, trusting, unsophisticated customer *US*

- — *Esquire*, p. 118, March 1968

barefoot rice *noun*

plain rice *BAHAMAS*

- —John A. Holm, *Dictionary of Bahamian English*, p. 12, 1982

bare metal *noun*

a new computer which is not equipped with even an operating system *US*

- —Eric S. Raymond, *The New Hacker's Dictionary*, p. 49, 1991

bare-pole *adjective*

naked *CANADA*

- Caught swimming bare pole. —T. K. Pratt, *oral citation from Dictionary of Prince Edward Island English*, p. 12, 1988

bares *noun*

the bare fists *US*

- —Helen Dahlskog (Editor), *A Dictionary of Contemporary and Colloquial Usage*, p. 5, 1972

barf *noun*

beef *US*

- — *Maledicta*, p. 8, 1996: 'Domino's pizza jargon'

barf *verb*

1 to vomit *US, 1958*

- — *American Speech*, p. 228, October 1967: 'Some special terms used in a University of Connecticut men's dormitory'
- LaDonna said, "You want me to barf all over the car?" —Elmore Leonard, *Glitz*, p. 235, 1985
- If you think you're going to barf, walk out and get some air. —Robert Crais, *L.A. Requiem*, p. 97, 1999

2 in computing, to fail to operate *US*

- The division operation barfs if you try to divide by zero. —Guy L. Steele et al., *The Hacker's Dictionary*, p. 29, 1983

3 in hot rodding and drag racing, to damage something completely or partially, leaving parts scattered *US*

- —John Edwards, *Auto Dictionary*, p. 11, 1993

barfbag *noun*

1 a bag provided for airsick air passengers, to use for vomiting *US, 1966*

- Unfortunately, the description of the gal fits just about every stewardess who ever handed out a barf bag. —Gerald Petievich, *One-Shot Deal*, p. 180, 1981
- She took the airsick bag out of the seat pocket in front of her. "Have you ever heard of a barf bag?" she said, holding it so Mab could see. —Francesca Lia Block, *I Was a Teenage Fairy*, p. 118, 1998

2 by extension, a despicable person *US*

- I'd always tried to teach him and other young cops that you can't be a varsity letterman when you deal with these barfbags. —Joseph Wambaugh, *The Blue Knight*, p. 56, 1973

barf, beer and a cigar *noun*

a fighter pilot's breakfast *US*

- — *United States Naval Institute Proceedings*, p. 108, October 1986

barf buddy *noun*

a drinking companion *US*

- [S]ometimes longed for the uncomplicated life of lacrosse and rugby and hou-bro beevo parties, of happily hugging the toilet all night long with your barf buddies after draining a half-keg for no special occasion? —John Sayles, *Union Dues*, p. 279, 1977

barfic *noun*

an unartistic computer graphic created with keyboard characters *US*

- —Christian Crumlish, *The Internet Dictionary*, p. 19, 1995

bar-fly *noun*

a too-frequent frequenter of bars and saloons *US, 1906*

- In the dingy half-light, in the thick, stale miasma of tobacco smoke and alcoholic fumes which are the atmosphere of the innumerable cocktail bars of our cities, a new character has entered the American scene. It is the female bar fly. — *San Francisco Examiner*, p. 14, 10th December 1947
- Barfly Mother Gone; Baby Happy [Headline] — *San Francisco Examiner*, p. 15, 8th January 1948
- Me, now, the first impression I'd had of her was that she wasn't much to look at – just a female barfly with money. —Jim Thompson, *After Dark, My Sweet*, p. 7, 1955
- Janie wouldn't be in a joint like this, she wouldn't be hanging around with bar-flies. —Jim Thompson, *The Kill-Off*, p. 24, 1957
- The kid had still another beer, pulled the cheek of a middle-aged woman bar fly and bought her a drink. —Willard Motley, *Let No Man Write My Epitaph*, p. 73, 1958
- A Los Angeles judge said that alimony laws were making "barflies" out of divorced women. — *San Francisco News Call-Bulletin*, p. 3, 18th May 1965
- She couldn't bear the thought of sitting in a gin mill like a daytime barfly, avoiding the moves of local lotharios so old they were moldering. —Joseph Wambaugh, *Fugitive Nights*, p. 107, 1992
- I listened to a local barfly mutter ominously[.] —Brian Preston, *Pot Planet*, p. 91, 2002

barf me out!

used for expressing disgust *US*

- Sheryl's mom, like she's a total space cadet, like barf me out, she like made Sheryl throw her dead beta fish down the garbage disposal, right? —Mary Corey and Victoria Westermark, *Fer Shurr! How to be a Valley Girl*, 1982
- He like sits there and like plays with all his rings / And he like flirts with all the guys in the class / It's like totally disgusting / I'm like so sure / It's like BARF ME OUT / Gag me with a spoon! —Moon Unit and Frank Zappa, *Valley Girl*, 1982

barfola

used as a general-purpose, all-around expression of disgust *US*

- —Connie Eble (Editor), *UNC-CH Campus Slang*, p. 1, April 1985

barf whiff *noun*

the odour of vomit *US*

- —Connie Eble (Editor), *UNC-CH Campus Slang*, p. 1, Spring 1991

barfy *adjective*

unpleasant, disgusting *US*

- That's what my English-comp teacher says – Mr. Glicksberg that barfy-looking character who's practically invented halitosis. —Frederick Kohner, *Gidget*, p. 3, 1957

bargain *noun*

a stroke of good luck *US*

- —Connie Eble (Editor), *UNC-CH Campus Slang*, p. 1, November 1990

bargain day *noun*

in a criminal proceeding, the final day before trial when the prosecuting attorney will accept a lesser guilty plea *US*

- —Jay Robert Nash, *Dictionary of Crime*, p. 20, 1992

barge *noun*

1 any large car *US*

A nautical comparison similar to the more generic **BOAT**.

- — *Current Slang*, p. 9, Fall 1968

2 a large, unweildly surfboard *US*

- —Grant W. Kuhns, *On Surfing*, p. 113, 1963

3 a large vagina *US*

- —Robert A. Wilson, *Playboy's Book of Forbidden Words*, p. 28, 1972

barge *verb*

to come; to go; to leave; to arrive; to move *US, 1929*

- "Let's barge out of here," Dopey said suddenly. —James T. Farrell, *Saturday Night*, p. 23, 1947

barge in *verb*

to intrude, to interfere, especially if rudely or clumsily *UK, 1923*

- They mumbled something about wanting to buy crack and barged in. — *Sunday Telegraph*, 24th October 2004

barge pole *noun*

a large penis *US*

- —Dale Gordon, *The Dominion Sex Dictionary*, p. 26, 1967

bar girl *noun*

a female prostitute who works in a bar *AUSTRALIA*

- A certain machine-gunner from 'C' company 7RAR was doing a line on a young French/Vietnamese bar girl in the Jade massage parlour in Vung Tau. —Martin Cameron, *A Look at the Bright Side*, 1988

bargoo *noun*

a mixture of meat and vegetables cooked together in a boiling kettle *CANADA*

- —Art Campbell, *Words and Expressions of the Gaspe*, 1986

bargoon *adjective*
cheap; at an unusually low price *CANADA*
- Sometimes normal girls such as self shop there. Especially when there are bargoon (or slash) prices. — *Underwire Chronicles,* 14th July 2002
- Seats that are unsold by Wednesday for travel commencing Thursday at 7 p.m. go up for sale at bargoon prices. — *Air Canada Web Saver,* 14th July 2002

bar-hop *verb*
to move in a group from one bar to another, stopping at each for a drink or two *US*
- For the still missing mother, 18 year old Joyce Swinhart, her bar-hopping appeared to have been a giddy one-way, dead-end road. — *San Francisco Examiner,* p. 15, 8th January 1948
- The few who stayed, and the tourists, kept to the Gay White Way as they used to name it, clubbing, bar hopping or taking in a show. — Mickey Spillane, *Return of the Hood,* p. 60, 1964
- [T]hen they went out to bar-hop the beach bars, avoiding only the gay bars on the crossroads where the main road from the freeway joins the Coast Highway. — Roger Gordon, *Hollywood's Sexual Underground,* p. 145, 1966
- I was barhopping ... I must have hit every place on the West Side of town. — Gerald Petievich, *To Die in Beverly Hills,* p. 205, 1983
- — Connie Eble (Editor), *UNC-CH Campus Slang,* p. 1, November 1983

bari *noun*
a baritone saxophone *US, 1955*
- — Robert S. Gould, *A Jazz Lexicon,* p. 12, 1964

baries *noun*
bare feet *UK: SCOTLAND*
- I hate walkin on lino in my baries. — Michael Munro, *The Original Patter,* 1985

bark *noun*
1 the skin *UK, 1758*
- — Lou Shelly, *Hepcats Jive Talk Dictionary,* p. 7, 1945

2 money *US*
- — Kenn "Naz" Young, *Naz's Underground Dictionary,* p. 14, 1973

3 a cough *UK, 1937*
- Whereupon a distinguished-looking gray-haired man, whose spine was straighter than a T-square, straightened it a little more and gave a short-bark cough for attention. — John McPhee, *Coming into the Country,* p. 137, 1977

bark *verb*
1 to cough *UK, 1937*
- George barks a cough. — DBC Pierre, *Vernon God Little,* p. 36, 2003

2 to brag *US*
- — Hy Lit, *Hy Lit's Unbelievable Dictionary of Hip Words for Groovy People,* p. 3, 1968

3 to tell a lie *US*
- — Judi Sanders, *Da Bomb!,* p. 2, 1997

▸ **bark the tires**
to produce a chirping sound from the tyres on the road while shifting gears *US*
- — Lewis Poteet, *Car & Motorcyle Slang,* p. 24, 1992

barker *noun*
1 a person who stands at the door of a business calling out to people passing by, trying to lure them into the business *UK, 1699*
- The spiel of the leather lunged barker, a Barbary Coast fixture who continued on when Pacific St. became the International Settlement, is to be silenced. — *San Francisco Examiner,* p. 3, 9th January 1957
- Behind him, blazing lights promote a "Male and Female Love Act," topless singers, topless stewardesses, topless wrestlers. To top it off, The Colonel, a Broadway barker, wears a derby. — *San Francisco Examiner,* p. 21, 9th March 1976
- — Joe McKennon, *Circus Lingo,* p. 16, 1980

2 an unsophisticated master of ceremonies *US*
- The barker comes out and says that Hester Prime will now take off her clothes, which is what she does best. — Robert Campbell, *Junkyard Dog,* p. 132, 1986

3 an antique dealer's assistant *UK*
- Tinker is my barker. A barker is a fetch-and-carry bloke who helps an antique dealer. I pay him when I can. — Jonathan Gash, *The Ten Word Game,* p. 81, 2003

4 in craps played in a casino, the stickman *US, 1983*
The stickman controls the pace of the game and engages in steady banter with the players.
- — Thomas L. Clark, *The Dictionary of Gambling and Gaming,* p. 14, 1987

5 a dog *UK*
- — Joe McKennon, *Circus Lingo,* p. 16, 1980

6 a person with a nasty cough *UK, 1937*
From the verb **BARK**.

7 a singer *US*
- — Kenn "Naz" Young, *Naz's Underground Dictionary,* p. 14, 1973

8 a handgun *US, 1814*
- Then, holding his roscoe or barker on Mr. Mach, the policeman moseyed back to the truck and peered inside. — *San Francisco News,* p. 1, 25th August 1950

barkers *noun*
shoes *US, 1929*
An extension of the much more commonly used **DOGS** (shoes).
- — Lou Shelly, *Hepcats Jive Talk Dictionary,* p. 7, 1945

barker's egg *noun*
a piece of dog excrement *AUSTRALIA*
- You just have to tread in one of the ever-popular Barker's Eggs which litter the British pavements and it could throw your sense of smell to buggery. — Barry Humphries, *The Traveller's Tool,* p. 70, 1985

barkey; barkie; barky *noun*
a sailor *UK*
The term appears to derive from Italian *barca* (a boat), perhaps from 'barque'.
- — Paul Baker, *Polari,* p. 164, 2002

barking *adjective*
raving mad *UK, 1968*
Derives, in some way, from the behaviour of a mad, rabid or over-excited dog.
- [T]here's plenty who tell me I'm already totally barking! — Wayne Anthony, *Spanish Highs,* p. 12, 1999

barking cockroach *noun*
the notional creature blamed when someone in a crowd farts *BERMUDA*
- — Peter A. Smith and Fred M. Barritt, *Bermewjan Vurds,* 1985

barking dogs *noun*
tired feet *US*
- — Harold Wentworth and Stuart Berg Flexner, *Dictionary of American Slang,* p. 20, 1960

barking spider *noun*
the notional creature blamed when someone in a crowd farts *US*
- — Pamela Munro, *U.C.L.A. Slang,* p. 17, 1989

Bar-L *noun*
▸ **the Bar-L**
HM Prison Barlinnie in the East End of Glasgow *UK: SCOTLAND*
- — Michael Munro, *The Original Patter,* 1985
- Tom Shields and photographer Arthur Kinlock investigate the new regime at the Bar-L – or Barlinnnie prison, to give it its Sunday name. — *The Herald (Glasgow),* p. 12, 15th August 1992
- I'm less at peace with the thought of never seeing you again, or only seeing you in the Bar-L visiting area. — Christopher Brookmyre, *The Sacred Art of Stealing,* p. 341, 2002

barley *noun*
beer *US*
- — David Claerbaut, *Black Jargon in White America,* p. 57, 1972

barley!
used as a call in children's games, chiefly in Victoria *AUSTRALIA*
Perhaps from French *parlez* (to parley). Used in children's games to indicate that one is safe from being caught or tagged. Some jocular use by adults.
- "Hey, barley!" the Red Dean cautioned[.] — Frank Hardy, *The Outcasts of Foolgarah,* p. 91, 1971
- Apart from claiming immunity during chasey type games, barley was also used to mean "Stop that, I won't stand for it" when someone blatantly cheated at a card game, or went to eat a cake baked for a later special occasion; or even to indicate strong disagreement with the line of the argument being pursued. — *Wordmap (www.abc.net.au/wordmap),* 2002

barley pop *noun*
beer *US*
- — *Complete CB Slang Dictionary,* 1976
- — Peter Chippindale, *The British CB Book,* p. 151, 1981
- — Connie Eble (Editor), *UNC-CH Campus Slang,* p. 1, Spring 1992

barley water *noun*
beer *US*
- — *Current Slang*, p. 1, Summer 1966

Barlinnie drumstick *noun*
a weapon improvised from a length of lead pipe and a few nails *UK: SCOTLAND, 1976*
Barlinnie is a Glasgow prison.

barmpot *noun*
a person who is deranged, crazy or eccentric *UK, 1951*
A fusion of **BARMY** and **POTTY**, ultimately from *barm* (a dialect term for 'yeast').
- It's seven to two he's run to Manchester. He's a barmpot. He killed a policeman. —Troy Kennedy Martin, *Z Cars*, p. 12, 1962
- — *Sunday Times*, 14th July 1963

barmy *noun*
a mad or eccentric person *UK*
Derives from *barm*, a dialect term for 'yeast'. *The English Dialect Dictionary*, 1905, remarks 'frothing like barm hence, full of ferment, flighty, empty-headed'. It is probably relevant to note also the lunatic asylum built in 1828 at Barming Heath, Kent (now the site of Maidstone Hospital).
- [T]he insomniacs and speed freaks, the hypermanics, night prowlers and other barmies[.] —John King, *White Trash*, p. 18, 2001

barmy *adjective*
mad; eccentric *UK, 1851*
- I was drunk. I must have been barmy. It wasn't me talking, it was the beer. —Graeme Kent, *The Queen's Corporal [Six Granada Plays]*, p. 105, 1959
- You're round the bloody bend. That's your trouble. You're barmy. —Geoff Brown, *I Want What I Want*, p. 71, 1966
- Sometimes in Ibiza it's easy to lose yourself in the island's barmy lifestyle. —Wayne Anthony, *Spanish Highs*, p. 77, 1999

Barmy Army *nickname*
fans of the England cricket team *UK*
- [Marcus] Trescothick advanced down the pitch and biffed him for six into the Barmy Army[.] — *The Guardian*, 9th November 2002

barmy wagon *noun*
an ambulance used for the secure transport of the insane *UK*
From **BARMY** (a mad or eccentric person).
- A nut case. They should get the barmy wagon. —Derek Bickerton, *Payroll*, p. 44, 1959

barn *noun*
1 in trucking, a truck garage *US*
- —Wayne Floyd, *Jason's Authentic Dictionary of CB Slang*, p. 9, 1976

2 in poker, a hand consisting of three cards of the same suit and a pair *US*
Conventionally known as a 'full house'.
- —George Percy, *The Language of Poker*, p. 7, 1988

Barnaby Rudge; barnaby *noun*
a judge *UK*
Rhyming slang, formed on the title of the Dicken's novel, first published as a weekly serial in 1841. Recorded as current by Julian Franklyn in 1960, and in *Up the Frog* by Sydney T. Kendall, 1969.

barnburner *noun*
1 an exciting idea, event or thing *US, 1934*
- All the Dub Hotchkisses looked at him with admiration bordering on awe. "A barn-burner!' said one. —Max Shulman, *Rally Round the Flag, Boys!*, p. 185, 1957

2 a member of the Royal Canadian Mounted Police *CANADA*
From an unfortunate miscalculation of force in the 1970s that led to the burning of a barn where separatists met with American Black Panthers.
- — *Maledicta*, p. 182, 1979: 'Canadian slurs, ethnic and other'

barnburner wizard *noun*
a high-achieving salesman *US*
- —Robert Kirk Mueller, *Buzzwords*, p. 44, 1974

Barn dance *noun*
the chaotic movement of pedestrians as soon as traffic signals permit *AUSTRALIA, 1984*
From the name of Henry Barnes, New York's traffic commissioner in the 1960s.

barndance card *noun*
a debriefing after combat *US*
- Sure, I'd handled Barrett's paperwork during my time at UDT-21 and UDT-22, and written "barn-dance cards" (after-action reports), fitreps, and commendation citations for my squads and platoon in Vietnam. —Richard Marcinko and John Weisman, *Rogue Warrior*, p. 147, 1992

barn disease *noun*
the many woes found in a motorcyle that has been left idle for several years *US*
Biker (motorcycle) usage.

barn door *noun*
1 the fly on a pair of trousers *US, 1950*
Used in the euphemistic warning: 'Your barn door is open'.
- —Don R. McCreary (Editor), *Dawg Speak*, 2001

2 any target that is too large to miss *UK, 1679*
- [S]everal thousand Japanese peasants who couldn't hit a barn door at three paces. — *The Times*, 8th January 2004

3 an extremely large halibut *CANADA*
Alaskan and Canadian usage.
- The name came from the East Coast term for the huge barndoor skate, raja laevis. —Tom Parkin, *WetCoast Words*, p. 13, 1989
- —Jim Crotty, *How to Talk American*, p. 5, 1997

4 in stage lighting, and the television and film industries, blinders used to focus a studio lamp *US*
Conventionally known as a 'variable mask'.
- —Oswald Skilbeck, *ABC of Film and TV Working Terms*, p. 16, 1960

5 a type of fuel injection system *US*
- —John Lawlor, *How to Talk Car*, p. 17, 1965

barnet *noun*
the head *UK*
From **BARNET FAIR** (the hair).
- [T]hat was just off the top of my barnet. —Andrew Nickolds, *Back to Basics*, p. 122, 1994

barnet fair; barnet *noun*
the hair *UK, 1857*
Rhyming slang, usually compressed to 'barnet'. Barnet Fair, itself, had ceased be a major event at least 50 years before this slang was coined.
- I wouldn't worry, Fred. You've enough Barnet to protect yer [from the sun]. — *The Sweeney*, p. 6, 1976
- That was a sight – Lenny trying to pull a twenty-stone geezer through the ropes by his barnet. —Dave Courtney, *Stop the Ride I Want to Get Off*, p. 195, 1999
- [T]hat kite [face] with that fucking barnet. He's got a full fringe like a monk's tonsure[.] —Kevin Sampson, *Outlaws*, p. 164, 2001

barney *noun*
1 a fight or argument *AUSTRALIA, 1858*
From British dialect.
- The boss and that homie have been having a proper barney over the prad [a horse]. —Butch Reynolds, *Broken Hearted Clown*, p. 28, 1953
- 'Can anyone buy into this barney?' —Eric Lambert, *The Veterans*, p. 89, 1954
- We had a barney and you stopped us settling it, that's all. —Graeme Kent, *The Queen's Corporal [Six Granda Plays]*, p. 95, 1959
- [C]an you think of any qualities these fellers have, apart from their ability to look afer themselves in a barney? —Troy Kennedy Martin, *Z Cars*, p. 36, 1962
- —Michael Peters, *Pommie Bastard*, p. 175, 1969
- I'm not in the mood for a barney. —Kevin Sampson, *Outlaws*, p. 81, 2001

2 a police officer *US*
- —Lanie Dills, *The Official CB Slanguage Language Dictionary*, p. 14, 1976

3 an unattractive, unpopular young man *US*
- —Mitch McKissick, *Surf Lingo*, 1987
- —Pamela Munro, *U.C.L.A. Slang*, p. 17, 1989
- I don't know where she meets these Barnies. — *Clueless*, 1995

4 a new Internet user whose interest will soon lapse *US*
- Different from a newbie in that newbies become plain decent folk through time and effort; a barney is for good once their ten free hours of AOL time are up[.] —Andy Ihnatko, *Cyberspeak*, p. 23, 1997

5 in the television and film industries, a noise-reducing pad placed over a camera *US*
- —Tony Miller and Patricia George, *Cut! Print!*, p. 40, 1977

barney *verb*

1 to argue about something *AUSTRALIA, 1942*

- I don't recollect owt. Billy Black and Les Stott were barneying about whippets[.] —Peter Robinson, *Hanging Valley*, p. 255, 1989

2 to travel in high style *US*

- —Vincent J. Monteleone, *Criminal Slang*, p. 17, 1949

Barneyano *noun*

speech or writing in a mode of satirical truth, without avoiding anything *CANADA*

- The book [Mordecai Richler's last, "Barney's Version"] even spawned some hip argot – "Barneyano," or "speaking truth without euphemisms." — *Toronto Globe and Mail*, p. D3, 29th June 2002

Barney moke *noun*

an act of sexual intercourse *UK, 1984*

Rhyming slang for **POKE**; a suggestive contrast with **BARNEY** (an argument). Sometimes shortened to 'Barney'. From an earlier pickpockets' use of the rhyme for 'poke' (a bag or pocket).

Barney's brig *noun*

the essence of disorder *US*

The full expression includes 'both main tacks over the foreyard', showing the nautical origins if not explaining who Barney was.

- —John Gould, *Maine Lingo*, p. 6, 1975

Barney's bull *noun*

a condition, especially a worthless or negative state *UK, 1908*

Originally 'to be like Barney's bull' meant 'extremely fatigued or distressed'; Partridge noted the range extended as: 'bitched, buggered, and bewildered like Barney's bull'; 'well fucked and far from home like Barney's bull' and 'all behind like Barney's bull'. In 2003 a quick search of the Internet revealed: 'buggered like Barney's bull' from the northeast UK; 'more mixed up than Barney's Bull' from western Canada, of Scots-Irish descent; 'get into more trouble than Barney's bull' from Australia; and 'mad as Barney's bull'.

barnie *noun*

a big fight or punch-up *SOUTH AFRICA*

barn money *noun*

in horse racing, money bet by purportedly informed track insiders *US*

- —Igor Kushyshyn et al., *The Gambling Times Guide to Harness Racing*, p. 211, 1994

barnstorm *verb*

to travel from town to town, performing, competing or campaigning *US, 1888*

- Murph had joined a circus band after his release and was barnstorming around the country some place. —Mezz Mezzrow, *Really the Blues*, p. 20, 1946
- After observing "Archie" I decided my troubles were small so I joined up with them barnstorming for a month. —Babs Gonzales, *I Paid My Dues*, p. 64, 1967

barnyard expression; barnyard language *noun*

profanity *US, 1968*

- What's amazing is that viewers are making it one of the higest rated shows on TV this season, so people obviously don't find the barnyard language the debutantes use distasteful. — *Daily News Leader (Staunton, Virginia)*, p. 11A, 18th December 2003
- Although Hatch draws chuckles in Washington for uttering Utah-approved epithets like "Bullcorn!" his book gives readers uncensored expletives by the second page and sprinkles what the Denver Post called "barnyard expressions" throughout the narrative. — *Salt Lake Tribune*, p. A1, 16th February 2003

barnyard golf *noun*

the game of horseshoe pitching *US, 1925*

- Eight-one contestants, who don't like to be called "barnyard golfers," gathered under the poplar trees at the county fairgrounds in Murray for the National Horshoe Pitchers Association of America's Ningth World's Championship tourney. — *Time*, p. 15, 21st August 1950
- Barnyard Golf This Week End [Headline]— *San Francisco Chronicle*, p. 1H, 30th August 1957

barnyard hen *noun*

a prostitute not favoured by her pimp *US*

- [T]hey are their "head chicks" instead of just one or another of their "barnyard hens." —John M. Murtagh and Sara Harris, *Cast the First Stone*, p. 10, 1957

barnyard polka *noun*

the elaborate, careful walk of a person trying not to step in cow manure *CANADA*

- The barnyard polka is the fancy footwork employed by those moving about the barnyard to ensure that they arrive back at the farmhouse without boots that require careful scraping before entering the house. —Chris Thain, *Cold as a Bay Street Banker's Heart*, p. 8, 1987

bar of chocolate *noun*

praise, especially when given by senior officers *UK*

Royal Navy, usually phrased as 'get a bar of chocolate'.

- —Wilfred Granville, *A Dictionary of Sailors' Slang*, 1962

bar of soap *noun*

1 marijuana *US, 1940*

Rhyming slang for **DOPE**; a bar of cannabis may coincidentally resemble a bar of soap (see: **SOAP BAR**), but the usage is simply a convenient rhyme. Rhyming slang often clips, here giving **BAR** an alternate etymology.

- —Ray Puxley, *Cockney Rabbit*, p. 9, 1992

2 in dominoes, the double blank *US*

- —Dominic Armanino, *Dominoes*, p. 15, 1959

baron *noun*

in prison, a powerful criminal whose influence is built on illegal trading in drugs, tobacco, phone cards or money *UK, 1950*

From the conventional sense of 'baron' (a man of power and influence).

- The Gum Boot was always in debt to the Barons. —Frank Norman, *Bang To Rights*, p. 102, 1958
- —Angela Devlin, *Prison Patter*, p. 25, 1996
- Being battered with slopping out buckets by barons on the landing. —Mark Powell, *Snap*, p. 95, 2001

▸ on the baron

free *UK*

Royal Navy usage.

- —Wilfred Granville, *A Dictionary of Sailors' Slang*, 1962

barossa *noun*

a girl *AUSTRALIA*

Rhyming slang for Barossa Pearl (a popular white wine).

- —Bill Hornadge, *The Australian Slanguage*, p. 197, 1980

barouche; cabouche *noun*

a car; a taxi *UK*

- Still at least she lent me the slotties [money] to pay for the barouche, bless her. —the cast of 'Aspects of Love', Prince of Wales Theatre, *Palare (Boy Dancer Talk) for Beginners*, 1989–92
- —Paul Baker, *Polari*, p. 167, 2002

bar pit *noun*

▷ see: **BORROW PIT**

barra *noun*

a barrumundi *AUSTRALIA, 1900*

- The old barra might have to be hauled out of a cave; and how many caves might there be down there? —Xavier Herbert, *Poor Fellow My Country*, p. 709, 1975

barrack *verb*

1 to ridicule someone; to jeer at someone *AUSTRALIA, 1878*

Probably from Northern Ireland dialect sense 'to brag or boast'.

- [Those were the] days in which the candidate was barracked by a crowd which knew what he was talking about. —Dymphna Cusack, *Picnic Races*, p. 17, 1962

2 in sport, to cheer for a team; to support a person or team; hence, to cheer on a person *AUSTRALIA, 1890*

The usual meaning since 1945.

- There was the time North Sydney, for whom we always barracked, beat Randwick[.] —Eric Lambert, *The Veterans*, p. 27, 1954
- [H]e pointed to some men in black and red – 'Who ya gonna barrack for?' —Sue Rhodes, *Now you'll think I'm awful*, p. 82, 1967
- He even comes to the games. Barracks like a loon. —Clive Galea, *Slipper*, p. 18, 1988
- As Jesus rode into Jerusalem the mob was barracking and cheering. —Kel Richards, *The Aussie Bible*, p. 52, 2003

barracker *noun*

in sport, a person who 'barracks' for a team; a supporter *AUSTRALIA, 1889*

- Moving in closer, crazy, I have seen that look on barrackers' faces, screaming at you through the wire of the race.—Barry Oakley, *A Salute to the Great McCarthy*, p. 169, 1970
- —Frank Hardy, *Hardy's People*, p. 87, 1986

barrack-room lawyer; barrack-lawyer *noun*

anyone unqualified who argues knowledge of rules, regulations or law, especially in a petty confrontation with authority; hence a generally argumentative person of the 'I know better than you'-type *UK, 1943*

Originally military.

- —Paul Tempest, *Lag's Lexicon*, p. 11, 1950
- "Bit of a troublemaker in that respect." "Barrack-room lawyer?" "That sort of thing, yes."—Terry Pratchett, *Night Watch*, p. 157, 2002

barracouter *noun*

a Tasmanian *AUSTRALIA, 1966*

- —Maureen Brooks and Joan Ritchies, *Tassie Terms*, p. 11, 1995

barracuda *noun*

an aggressive, unprincipled person *US, 1957*

- "My God," he whispered, "get a load of the barracuda with Tompkins."—Jimmy Snyder, *Jimmy the Greek*, p. 211, 1975
- —Multicultural Management Program Fellows, *Dictionary of Cautionary Words and Phrases*, 1989

barrel *noun*

1 a tablet of LSD *US, 1971*

Usually in the plural.

- —Richard A. Spears, *The Slang and Jargon of Drugs and Drink*, p. 28, 1986
- Acid pills roughly the shape and size of asprin tablets are called "barrels" because of their cylindrical shape.—Cam Cloud, *The Little Book of Acid*, p. 37, 1999
- —Mike Haskins, *Drugs*, p. 285, 2003

2 a perfect wave breaking *US*

- —Trevor Cralle, *The Surfin'ary*, p. 7, 1991

3 a cylinder in an car engine *US*

- —*Hot Rod Magazine*, p. 13, November 1948

4 in pool, a betting unit *US*

- If you have $1000 and you're playing for $100 a game, you're packing ten barrels.—Steve Rushin, *Pool Cool*, p. 6, 1990

▸ **have someone over a barrel**

to have someone at a disadvantage *US, 1939*

- How America held the IRA over a barrel.—*The Observer*, 28th October 2001

▸ **in the barrel**

in prison, especially in solitary confinement *US*

- —Jay Robert Nash, *Dictionary of Crime*, p. 20, 1992

▸ **right into your barrel; right up your barrel**

decidedly your concern, interest, business *AUSTRALIA, 1942*

barrel *verb*

1 to knock someone over; to flatten someone; also, to beat up someone, to punch someone, to deliver a blow *AUSTRALIA*

- Hey, remember the last football match, the grand final when Davo got barrelled?—Alexander Buzo, *Rooted*, p. 84, 1969
- That muscular loudmouth who is always barrelling cats and poofters is quite likely to be a screaming drag queen himself—Suzy Jarratt, *Permissive Australia*, p. 54, 1970
- Some mug [...] barrelled a king [a hard and unexpected punch] at him—*The (Sydney) Bulletin*, 26th April 1975
- He was playing for Berry at the time and he was barrelled off in the final minute of the game—Roy Staven(John Doyle), *Five South Coast Seasons*, p. 35, 1992

2 to scold someone *NEW ZEALAND*

Prison usage.

- —Harry Orsman, *A Dictionary of Modern New Zealand Slang*, p. 7, 1999

3 to hold someone at bay; to corner someone *AUSTRALIA*

- Poor old John Waters, the delegate from the Northern Territory, had just arrived and was checking in at the reception desk when we barrelled him and said, 'We want to talk to you.'—Blanche d'Alpuget, *Robert J. Hawke*, p. 320, 1982

4 to drive at great speed *AUSTRALIA*

- We didn't speak but simply barrelled along the freeway, full of our own troublesome thoughts.—Helen Garner, *Monkey Grip*, p. 46, 1977

barrel-ass; barrel *verb*

to move rapidly, generally oblivious to any obstacles *US, 1930*

- Barrel-assing toward Buddhahood.—Tom Robbins, *Another Roadside Attraction*, p. 245, 1971
- "Dagos, eh, drivin' a big Cadillac from the big city – where yo all barrel-assing to?"—Edwin Torres, *Carlito's Way*, p. 33, 1975
- I barreled through the living room, back to the kitchen[.]—Janet Evanovich, *Seven Up*, p. 82, 2001

barrel-back with barn doors *noun*

a 1946 Ford Monarch *US*

The 'barn doors' refer to the car's wood trim.

- —Lewis Poteet, *Car & Motorcyle Slang*, p. 24, 1992

barreled out *adjective*

in pool, depleted of money to bet *US*

- —Steve Rushin, *Pool Cool*, p. 6, 1990

barrel fever *noun*

delirium tremens suffered by an alcoholic *US*

- —Vincent J. Monteleone, *Criminal Slang*, p. 17, 1949

barrelhouse *noun*

some combination of brothel, bar and rooming house *US, 1883*

- I've played the music in a lot of places these last thirty years, from Al Capone's roadhouses to swing joints along 52nd Street in New York, Paris nightclubs, Harvard University, dicty Washington embassies and Park Aven ue salons, not to mention all the barrel house dives—Mezz Mezzrow, *Really the Blues*, p. 4, 1946

barrel roll *noun*

the US air campaign conducted over northern Laos in support of the Royal Lao Government, against the Pathet Lao and North Vietnamese forces *US*

- —Linda Reinberg, *In the Field*, p. 17, 1991

barrier rogue *noun*

a racehorse that is agitated by the starting barrier *AUSTRALIA, 1982*

- —Joe Andersen, *Winners Can Laugh*, p. 163, 1982
- Blue Boss, which has a reputation as a barrier rogue, drew gate 12 on Thursday.—*Sydney Morning Herald*, p. 12, 26th February 1994

barrier-to-box *noun*

in horse racing, the entire length of the race *AUSTRALIA*

- —Ned Wallish, *The Truth Dictionary of Racing Slang*, p. 3, 1989

barrio *noun*

a disadvantaged neighbourhood *UK*

Liverpool usage; adopted from conventional 'barrio' (a Spanish speaking neighbourhood in a US city) to give a romantic identity to an urban locality.

- Girl must think I'm a fucking clown by the way. I've come from the same barrio as her, I've been through the same thingio.—Kevin Sampson, *Clubland*, p. 224, 2002

barrow *noun*

▸ **on my barrow**

giving me trouble *UK*

- —Alan Hunter, *Gently by the Shore*, 1956

▷ **see:** BORROW PIT

barrow wheel *noun*

a cast-metal spoked wheel *UK, 1984*

- —Douglas Dunford, *Motorcycle Department, Beaulieu Motor Museum*, 1979

barry *noun*

1 a youth who drives up and down a Fenland village street with very loud music blaring from the car's sound-system and, apparently, a hoe sticking out of the boot *UK: ENGLAND*

Local teen slang, probably originally mocking an actual boy called Barry; a pun on the detailed **HO/HOE** (a woman) is tempting.

- Ben, a sixth-form college student [...] was incredulous that [government minister, Ivan] Lewis didn't know what a "barry" was [...] But don't be surprised if before long we get a "Don't be a Barry" campaign from the DfES.—*The Guardian*, 29th June 2004

2 something shockingly bad *AUSTRALIA, 1997*

- A Barry could be used to describe a particularly bad day or happening/event.—*Wordmap (www.abc.net.au/wordmap)*, 2003

barry *adjective*

good, excellent, wonderful *UK: SCOTLAND*

Edinburgh slang, widely used in Irvine Welsh, *Trainspotting*, 1993, but not in the film.

Barry Crocker *noun*
something shockingly bad *AUSTRALIA, 1997*
Rhyming slang for **SHOCKER**. After Barry Crocker, born 1935, Australian singer and actor who, amongst other things, starred in the title role of the Barry McKenzie films of the 1970s, based on the cartoon script by Barry Humphries originally published in *Private Eye* in the 1960s.
- — *Sydney Morning Herald*, p. 1, 2002

Barry McGuigan; Barry *noun*
a notable defecation *UK*
Rhyming slang for 'big 'un', formed from the name of the bantamweight/featherweight boxer from Northern Ireland (b.1961).
- I wouldn't go in there if Ii was you, I've just done a Barry. — Bodmin Dark, *Dirty Cockney Rhyming Slang*, 2003

Barry White; Barry *noun*
1 excrement; hence rubbish *UK, 2002*
Contemporary rhyming slang for **SHITE**, based on the name of soul singer Barry White, 1944–2003.
- Just nipping out for a Barry! — *www.LondonSlang.com*, 26th June 2002
- — Bodmin Dark, *Dirty Cockney Rhyming Slang*, 2003

2 a fright *UK, 2001*
Popney rhyming slang, based on the name of soul singer Barry White, 1944–2003. Popney was contrived for *www.music365.co.uk*, an Internet music site.

Barry White; Barry *adjective*
inferior; shoddy *UK*
- — Bodmin Dark, *Dirty Cocknney Ryming Slang*, 2003

Barry-Whiter *noun*
an event that lasts all night, especially a drinking spree or a rave *UK*
Rhyming slang for 'all-nighter'; based on the name of US singer Barry White, 1944–2003. Remembered by Jonathan Telfer, *Writers News*, 2003.

barse-ackwards *adjective*
end-first *US*
- — John Gould, *Maine Lingo*, p. 7, 1975

bar steward *noun*
a bastard *UK, 1961*
A jocular euphemism; although well known previously, widely popularised in the late 1990s as an advertising strapline for Heineken Export lager: 'From your smooth-talking bar steward'.

bar stool *noun*
1 a vehicle which is never or rarely driven *US*
- "I'm gonna sell the Lambretta and use the money to go to Belize. I love it, but it's just a barstool, really." — Lewis Poteet, *Car & Motorcyle Slang*, p. 24, 1992

2 used as a euphemism for 'bastard' *UK*
Jocular.
- Gilman gave me a hard nudge and a wink. "You lucky bar stool." — David Peace, *Nineteen Seventy-Four*, p. 177, 1999

bart *noun*
a criminally-inclined youth, especially a youth gang member *US*
- What a "Z"! The astonishing private language of Bay Area teenagers — *San Francisco Examiner*, p. 8, 27th October 1963

barter *verb*
(among young women in Montreal) to trade sexual favours for desired gifts *CANADA*
- Unlike street kids who sometimes [have sex] to secure shelter or other basic needs, the 14- to 17-year old girls are in it for luxury items like clothes and jewellery. Sinclair and Nguyen call it "bartering." Just don't call them "hos." — *Hour*, p. 46, 27th June 2002

Bart's *nickname*
St Bartholomew's Hospital, London *UK, 1937*

Bart Simpson *noun*
1 a type of LSD identified by an icon of the cartoon hero *UK*
Bart Simpson, an animated character, was created by Matt Groening in 1987.
- — Angela Devlin, *Prison Patter*, p. 25, 1996
- — Mike Haskins, *Drugs*, p. 285, 2003

2 a variety of MDMA, the recreational drug best known as ecstasy, identified by the embossed motif *UK*
- — Gareth Thomas, *This Is Ecstasy*, p. 56, 2002

3 heroin
- — Robert Ashton, *This Is Heroin*, p. 205, 2002

bar up *verb*
1 to get an erection *AUSTRALIA*
- — Ryan Aven-Bray, *Ridgey Didge Oz Jack Lang*, p. 20, 1983

2 to become excited *US*
- — John Vorhaus, *The Big Book of Poker Slang*, p. 6, 1996

bas *noun*
a *bas*tard, generally in its slang sense *UK*
Pronounced, and occasionally written 'bahss' or 'bass' in accordance with the full pronuncation of 'bastard'.
- — G.F. Newman, *The Guvnor*, 1977

Basco *noun*
a person of Basque extraction *CANADA*
- The men who are the backbone of the range sheep industry [are] the sheepherders, as we call the Scottish, Mexican, or Basco (Basque) shepherds. — R.D. Symons, *Many Trails*, p. 58, 1963

base *noun*
1 freebase cocaine; basic cocaine from which the hydrochloride has been removed *US, 1982*
- After some of the fellas would step away form the blackjack table, and the bar, and get ready to buy a fiddy or a hundred dollars' worth of sniff, I would set them up with a hit of base in the back room. — *New Jack City*, 1990
- — Terry Williams, *Crackhouse*, p. 146, 1992
- "They look around, find ten keys of base in the garage, actually in a Mercedes that happens to have my prints on the steering wheel and partials on the door handle." — Elmore Leonard, *Out of Sight*, p. 63, 1996
- — Nick Constable, *This is Cocaine*, p. 181, 2002

2 an amphetamine
- CALL IT... Sulphate, wake-ups, whizz, whites, base JUST DON'T CALL IT... Ice — *Drugs An Adult Guide*, p. 35, December 2001

base *verb*
1 to smoke freebase cocaine *US, 1987*
- — Ellen C. Bellone (Editor), *Dictionary of Slang*, p. 2, 1989
- "At about five a.m. they wanted to base and shit and I knew Max didn't base either." — Terry Williams, *The Cocaine Kids*, p. 33, 1989
- — Terry Williams, *Crackhouse*, p. 146, 1992
- i tried basing a few times but thought it a waste. — Cleo Odzer, *Goa Freaks*, p. 261, 1995

2 to argue *US*
- For home boys and zimmers; This dictionary is def! — *Frederick (Maryland) Post*, p. B2, 24th May 1990

3 to verbally attack someone using sarcasm to convey an accurate if cruel appraisal of them *US*
An abbreviation of 'de*base*'.
- — Vann Wesson, *Generation X Field Guide and Lexicon*, p. 14, 1997

baseball *noun*
1 homosexual activity *US*
Back formation from the use of **PITCH** and **CATCH** as terms meaning 'to have the active and passive roles in homosexual sex'.
- — James Harris, *A Convict's Dictionary*, p. 28, 1989

2 a defensive fragmentation hand grenade that explodes on impact, used in Vietnam *US*
Shaped and sized like a baseball.
- — Linda Reinberg, *In the Field*, p. 17, 1991

3 in horse racing, a bet on one horse in one race and all horses in another *US*
- — Tom Ainslie, *Ainslie's Complete Guide to Thoroughbred Racing*, p. 328, 1976

4 crack cocaine *UK, 1998*
- — Mike Haskins, *Drugs*, p. 281, 2003

Baseball Annie *noun*
a woman who makes herself available sexually to professional baseball players *US, 1949*
- It is permissible, in the scheme of things, to promise a Baseball Annie dinner and a show in return for certain quick services for a pair of roommates. — Jim Bouton, *Ball Four*, p. 204, 1970
- — Richard Scholl, *Running Press Glossary of Baseball Language*, p. 13, 1977

• Roberts' agent, Seth Levinson, was at the ballpark and came out swinging against the woman, described as a "Baseball Annie" living near the Mets' minor-league affiliate in Binghamton. — *New York Post*, p. 51, 21st September 2002

baseball bat *noun*
the penis *AUSTRALIA*
• Sure, I held his circumcised baseball bat so he could pee but, when he'd finished, I tugged it and stroked it too! — *People*, p. 59, 5th July 1999

baseball bum *noun*
in craps, the number nine *US, 1949*
• — Thomas L. Clark, *The Dictionary of Gambling and Gaming*, p. 14, 1987

baseballer *noun*
a drug user who smokes freebase cocaine *US*
• — Jay Robert Nash, *Dictionary of Crime*, p. 20, 1992

baseball team *noun*
▷ see: BALL TEAM

baseball whiskers *noun*
a sparsely bearded face *US*
• "He said I had baseball whiskers," I said, blushing. "Nine on each side." It was a stale joke. — Chester Himes, *Cast the First Stone*, p. 37, 1952

base bludger *noun*
a service personel who is stationed at the base *AUSTRALIA*
Derogatory.
• They're only flamin base bludgers. Gee, you oughta hear them talk. — Sumner Locke Elliott, *Rusty Bugles*, p. 14, 1948
• You're a dirty, thieving base-bludger! — Eric Lambert, *The Veterans*, p. 51, 1954

base camp commando; base camp desk jockey *noun*
somebody with bellicose opinions about the way the war should be conducted but no intention of leaving their post away from combat to do it *US, 1986*
Vietnam war usage.
• — Glory Cclark, *Worries of the Vietnam WAr*, 1990

base crazies *noun*
obsessive searching behaviour experienced by crack cocaine users *US*
• [A] kind of hallucination that leads an indivdiual to search for the smallest particle of cocaine or crack in mistaken belief that they have lost some of the residue. — Terry Williams, *The Cocaine Kids*, p. 135, 1989

base crazy *noun*
a drug user who searches on hands and knees for cocaine or crack cocaine
• — Nick Constable, *This is Cocaine*, p. 182, 2002

base dealer *noun*
a card cheat who deals from the bottom of a deck *US*
• — Frank Scoblete, *Guerrilla Gambling*, p. 296, 1993

based out *adjective*
used of a crack or freebase addict who is unable to control usage
• — Nick Constable, *This is Cocaine*, p. 182, 2002

base gallery *noun*
a room or building where freebase cocaine users pay to enter and then buy and smoke freebase cocaine *US*
An extension of 'shooting gallery'.
• — Terry Williams, *Crackhouse*, p. 146, 1992

base head *noun*
a regular smoker of freebase cocaine *US, 1986*
• — Public Enemy, *Night of the Living Baseheads*, 1988
• — Ellen C. Bellone (Editor), *Dictionary of Slang*, p. 2, 1989
• After a month or two, the place was full of just baseheads who would stay there all day or night, day after day, spending their money. — Terry Williams, *The Cocaine Kids*, p. 108, 1989
• First you wanna be a stick-up kid, but you got shot. Now youse a basehead. You all fucked up, Pookie. — *New Jack City*, 1990
• — Terry Williams, *Crackhouse*, p. 146, 1992
• He was a little part-time basehead though. — *Menace II Society*, 1993

base house *noun*
a house or apartment where freebase cocaine is sold *US*
A term and concept that all but vanished with the advent of crack cocaine in the mid-1980s.
• — Terry Williams, *Crackhouse*, p. 146, 1992

baseman *noun*
a drug user who smokes freebase cocaine *US*
• — Jay Robert Nash, *Dictionary of Crime*, p. 21, 1992

basement *noun*
channel one on a citizens' band radio *US*
• — Wayne Floyd, *Jason's Authentic Dictionary of CB Slang*, p. 9, 1976

▸ in the basement
in stud poker, dealt facing down *US*
• — George Percy, *The Language of Poker*, p. 7, 1988

base out *verb*
to idle *BELIZE*
• — Richard Allsopp, *Dictionary of Caribbean English Usage*, p. 82, 1996

baser *noun*
a user of freebase cocaine *US*
• Most of this thing about rock is really just because basers want more for their money, and regular sniffers do, too. — Terry Williams, *The Cocaine Kids*, p. 41, 1989

bases loaded *noun*
in craps, bets placed on every possible combination *US*
• There's no bigger thrill than when he's got the bases loaded and they hit the numbers[.] — Edward Lin, *Big Julie of Vegas*, p. 112, 1974

base wallah *noun*
a service personel who is stationed at the base *AUSTRALIA, 1919*
Derogatory.
• How would they know, the base wallahs! — Ray Slattery, *Mobbs' Mob*, p. 78, 1966
• — Frank Hardy, *The Outcasts of Foolgarah*, p. 214, 1971

base walloper *noun*
a military officer serving at a rear echelong base *NEW ZEALAND*
• — Sonya Plowman, *Great Kiwi Slang*, p. 22, 2002

basey *noun*
▷ see: BASIE

bash *noun*
1 an attempt, try, go *UK, 1939*
• Heard about this Italian cookin'. Wouldn' mind 'avin' a bash at ut. — Nino Culotta (John O'Grady), *They're A Weird Mob*, p. 126, 1957
• — Barry Humphries, *A Nice Night's Entertainment*, p. 71, 1962
• SIMON: I mean lines, ducky, can you handle lines? GEORGE: I'll have a bash. — *A Hard Day's Night*, 1964
• — Alexander Buzo, *Rooted*, p. 54, 1969
• They'd had all day to get used to the fact of a drunkard on board, and as they themselves gave it a pretty good bash ashore Big Bill found himself less of a cause celebre than he had expected to be. — J.E. MacDonnell, *Big Bill the Bastard*, p. 61, 1976
• [T]hey've all had a bash at taking him off [Elvis Presley], so it must be good[.] — Paul E Willis, *Profane Culture*, p. 63–64, 1978
• Sir Darius-drunk, opium-addled, filled with self-hatred-ordered the tail-coated musicians to "have a bash" at the movie tune "We're Off to See the Wizard. — Salman Rushdie, *The Ground Beneath Her Feet*, p. 48, 2000
• [T]hey had resolved to "give it a bash" when they got back to the house[.] — Frank Skinner, *Frank Skinner*, p. 6, 2001

2 a party *UK, 1901*
• — Collin Baker et al., *College Undergraduate Slang Study Conducted at Brown University*, p. 77, 1968
• Last night in town, you guys gonna have a little bash before you leave? — *American Graffiti*, 1973
• ... you're coming to the bash, of course ... — Kevin sampson, *Powder*, p. 18, 1999

3 a drag racing event *US, 1960s to 70s*
• Sometimes someone plans a bash and no one comes. Then it's not a bash. If there is a huge crowd that has a great time, then you can be sure it's a bash. — Ed Radlauer, *Drag Racing Pix Dix*, p. 7, 1970
• — Phantom Surfers, *The Exciting Sounds of Model Road Racing (Album cover)*, 1997

4 a long cycle ride, especially if fast and arduous *UK, 1961*
'The Brighton Bash' is from London to Brighton and back.

5 a route march, as '5-mile-bash', etc *UK, 1984*
Military usage.

6 an act of sexual intercourse *UK*
• And then you can whip her up top for a quick bash! — Lance Peters, *The Dirty Half-Mile*, p. 318, 1979

7 a person judged on their sexual performance *AUSTRALIA*
• When pressed, one of them admitted that he'd heard on good and personal authority from you-know-who that I was quite the quickest

and the best bash in town. —Sue Rhodes, *Now you'll think I'm awful*, p. 17, 1967

8 marijuana *US, 1971*
A possible pun on **BANG** (marijuana) or misspelling of **BUSH** (marijuana).
- —Richard A. Spears, *The Slang and Jargon of Drugs and Drink*, p. 29, 1986
- —Mike Haskins, *Drugs*, p. 286, 2003

9 a dent put into a felt hat to make it look better, especially an Australian Army slouch hat *AUSTRALIA*
- And while I'm on the subject, get rid of that white puggaree on your hat like all other blokes have. Also, Mr. Bruce told you to straighten out that lairy bash in it. —Eric Lambert, *The Veterans*, p. 100, 1954

▸ **on the bash**
to be working as a prostitute *UK, 1936*
- From the hours you keep [...] I'd say you were on the bash. —Anonymous *Streetwalker*, p. 58, 1959
- —*Maledicta*, p. 144, Summer/Winter 1986–1987: 'Sexual slang: prostitutes, pedophiles, flagellators, transvestites, and necrophiles'

bash *verb*

1 to criticise someone or something *UK, 1963*
Often combined as a suffix with the object of criticism.
- Eurobashing is back in fashion in the United States. —*The Guardian*, p. 3, 26th February 2002

2 to hit someone *UK, 1790*
- Same MO. Somebody bashed in her head. —Janet Evanovitch, *Full Blast*, p. 307, 2004

3 while surfing, to slam into a wave *US*
- —Trevor Cralle, *The Surfin'ary*, p. 7, 1991

4 to work as a prostitute *UK, 1961*
- —James Norton, *Lowspeak*, p. 21, 1989

5 to eat with great fervor *US*
- —Lou Shelly, *Hepcats Jive Talk Dictionary*, p. 7, 1945

6 to indulge in heavy drinking *AUSTRALIA*
- A man's gotta drink [...] but you can't bash it all the time, the way he does[.] —Gavin Casey, *The Wits Are Out*, 1947

▸ **bash ears**
to talk on the telephone *US*
Teen slang.
- —*Newsweek*, p. 28, 8 October 1951

▸ **bash one out**
(of a male) to masturbate *UK*
- I didn't like the thought of him just doing it so cheap, so routine – just bashing one out like that. —Kevin Sampson, *Clubland*, p. 160, 2002

▸ **bash the bishop**
(of a male) to masturbate *UK*
Based on a perceived resemblance between the erect penis and a conventional chess piece or, possibly, the helmet and an episcopal mitre; bishops may also be 'banged', 'battered', 'beaten', 'buffed', 'captured', 'flipped', 'flogged' and 'murdered'; notwithstanding, the bishop has also inspired punning variants: 'cardinal', 'obsolete jesuits', 'pope', 'priests' and 'one-eyed monk'.
- [M]y left hand Bashing the Bishop. —Stuart Browne, *Dangerous Parking*, p. 117, 2000

▸ **bash the bottle**
to drink alcohol to excess *AUSTRALIA*
- —Frank Hardy, *The Outcasts of Foolgarah*, p. 108, 1971
- Funny thing, Philpot thought, still bashing the bottle, I had a feeling there for a moment that I've seen him somewhere before. —Frank Hardy, *The Outcasts of Foolgarah*, p. 167, 1971

▸ **bash the spine**
to sleep *AUSTRALIA, 1945*
- When you've gone, I'll bash me spine for a bit. —Jean Brooks, *The Opal Witch*, p. 131, 1967

▸ **bash wheels**
in the usage of youthful model road racers (slot car racers), to race *US*
- — Phantom Surfers, *The Exciting Sounds of Model Road Racing (Album cover)*, 1997

▸ **bash your ear**
to talk to someone at length *AUSTRALIA*
- Used to get on his mates' nerves down at the club – always bashing their ear about how much money he was making[.] —Frank Hardy, *The Yarns of Billy Borker*, p. 56, 1965
- —Bill Wannan, *Folklore of the Australian Pub*, p. 34, 1972
- —Frank Hardy, *Hardy's People*, p. 78, 1986

basha; basher *noun*
a makeshift temporary shelter *UK, 1961*
Originally Assamese for a 'bamboo hut'; acquired by the military and now in use among the UK homeless.
- [S]leeping in self-built shelters, or "bashas", of birch boughs and snow. —John Winton, *Sunday Telegraph*, 8th April 1979
- [A]t last light, around your own basha (shelter) area. —Andy McNab, *Immediate Action*, p. 93, 1995

bash artist *noun*
a person prone to fighting *NEW ZEALAND*
- —David McGill, *David McGill's Complete Kiwi Slang Dictionary*, p. 13, 1998

bash down *verb*
to record a song in one take *UK*
- —Tom Hibbert, *Rockspeak!*, p. 18, 1983

bashed *adjective*
drunk *US*
- —Connie Eble (Editor), *UNC-CH Campus Slang*, p. 1, Fall 1982

basher *noun*

1 in trainspotting, an enthusiast who will travel for as far as is possible in the train behind a specific locomotive *UK*
- [T]here are scores of specialists – such as bashers. From Joseph [Porter]'s description these seemed to be malodorous, hard-drinking, obsessives, who travel as far as they can behind certain types of locomotive, preferably on the way to a beer festival. —Iain Aitch, *A Fête Worse Than Death*, p. 55, 2003

2 a prize-fighter; a thug *UK, 1937*
- When there was a football game in town or a full moon Mort stuck a couple of bashers in the lolly pops [shops][.] —J.J. Connolly, *Layer Cake*, p. 25, 2000

3 a physical training instructor *UK, 1943*
Military.
- —John W. Mussell, *The Token Book of Militarisms*, p. 10, 1995

4 a fast, reckless skier *US*
- —*American Speech*, p. 205, October 1963: 'The language of skiers'

5 in the television and film industries, a simple 500 watt flood light *US*
- —Oswald Skilbeck, *ABC of Film and TV Working Terms*, p. 16, 1960

bashie *noun*
an impromptu party *GRENADA*
- —Richard Allsopp, *Dictionary of Caribbean English Usage*, p. 82, 1996

bashing *noun*

1 heavy losses *UK, 1948*
Usually as 'get a bashing' or 'take a bashing'.
- Booze culture gets a bashing[.] —*The Guardian*, 27th August 2003

2 a beating-up; a beating *UK, 1958*
- [H]is literary credentials have taken something of a bashing[.] —*The Guardian*, 23rd February 2002

-bashing *suffix*
vigorous compulsory activity *UK, C20*
Military, in combination with an appropriate noun: **SPUD-BASHING** (potato peeling) and **SQUARE-BASHING** (military parade-drill).

bash it up you!
go away! stop bothering me! *AUSTRALIA*
- —Sidney J. Baker, *Australia Speaks*, 1953

bashment *noun*
a dance party; a form of reggae music *BARBADOS*
- —Richard Allsopp, *Dictionary of Caribbean English Usage*, p. 82, 1996
- She's brought her boom box on the bus and it's pumping out the latest bashment beats from Jamaica, a new reggae dancehall style. —Karline Smith, *Letters to Andy Cole*, p. 138, 1998

bash up *verb*

1 to thrash someone, to beat up someone *UK, 1954*
- [T]hat night I went to the pub where I knew he would be and bashed him up. —Jimmy Stockin, *On The Cobbles*, p. 63–64, 2000

2 to construct something with haste and a lack of care *NEW ZEALAND*
- —Harry Orsman, *A Dictionary of Modern New Zealand Slang*, p. 7, 1999

basie; basey *noun*

1 **a person living on a military base** *US*

- Like the adults, they developed their own social hierarchy, carving up the town into a variety of cliques: greasers, soshes, basies, and those who feel somewhere inbetween. —Kim Rich, *Johnny's Girl*, p. 154, 1993

2 **an Antarctica expeditioner** *ANTARCTICA, 1964*

A South African contribution to South Pole slang.

- —Bernadette Hince, *The Antarctic Dictionary*, p. 45, 2000

Basil Boli; Basil *noun*

excrement,; an act of excretion *UK: SCOTLAND*

Modern rhyming slang for **TOLEY** (a turd), based on French footballer Basil Boli who played for Glasgow Rangers and was not highly regarded by the fans.

- I'm just nipping out for a Basil! —*www.LondonSlang.com*, 26th June 2002

Basil Brush *noun*

1 **marijuana** *UK*

From the herb 'basil', thus punning on **WEED** (marijuana), elaborated as the name of a television puppet; at times shortened to a simple 'basil'.

- —Angela Devlin, *Prison Patter*, p. 26, 1996

2 **the vaginal infection** ***Candida albicans*****, commonly called thrush** *UK, 2002*

Contemporary rhyming slang, based on a puppet fox with a distinctive laugh (Boom! Boom!), popular on children's television in the 1960s and 70s.

- —*www.LondonSlang.com*, 26th June 2002
- —Bodmin Dark, *Dirty Cockney Rhyming Slang*, 2003

Basil Fawlty *noun*

a balti (a type of curried dish) *UK*

Rhyming slang.

- — Susie Dent, *The Language Report*, p. 98, 2003

basinful *noun*

as much as you can tolerate *UK, 1935*

- "I've had a basinful" meant "I've had all I can take." —Jim Wolveridge, *He Don't know "A" from a Bull's Foot*, 1978

basing gallery *noun*

a room, apartment or house where cocaine is smoked in freebase form *US*

- —Steven Daly and Nalthaniel Wice, *alt.culture*, p. 50, 1995

basin of gravy; basin *noun*

a baby *UK, 1961*

Imperfectly-formed rhyming slang.

baskervilles *noun*

a police-informer or someone who has assisted the police in some other way in the making of an arrest *AUSTRALIA*

A play on **DOG**, hence *The Hound of the Baskervilles* by Arthur Conan Doyle, 1902.

- —Jim McNeil, *The Chocolate Frog & The Old Familiar Juice*, 1973

basket *noun*

1 **a despicable person; used as a euphemism for 'bastard'** *UK, 1936*

- Until some smart basket got the idea of having a push-button Navy', growled the Chief. —John Wynnum, *Tar Dust*, p. 11, 1962
- Stingy convict basket. Just as well I nicked his transitor and camera! — Barry Humphries, *The Wonderful World of Barry*, p. 1, 1968

2 **the male genitals as seen through tight trousers** *US, 1941*

- A young fellow in a very tight-fitting pair of faded blue jeans walks in. Eyes follow him. "Oh my God! What a basket!" a young man shrills in feminine-like voice. —Willard Motely, *Let No Man Write My Epitaph*, p. 246, 1958
- A Lexicon of Homosexual Slang —Donald Webster Cory and John P. LeRoy, *The Homosexual and His Society*, p. 261, 1963
- —Dale Gordon, *The Dominion Sex Dictionary*, p. 26, 1967
- What a low-cut gown to a faggot must be is like tight Levis with a padded basket. —Lenny Bruce, *The Essential Lenny Bruce*, p. 161, 1967
- [I]t is fashionable to be able to show your legs, your "basket," and your arse. —Angelo d'Arcangelo, *The Homosexual Handbook*, p. 65, 1968
- So underplay your baskets, which is the fashion of the season among the Too-Beautiful People. Sic transit big cocks on display. —*Screw*, p. 15, 22nd December 1969
- Basket Bazaar [Advertisement for Film] —*San Francisco Chronicle*, p. 44, 12th August 1970
- Sure, you lock eyes while you're pounding the pavement, looking for a lay or love or both, but let's face it, the focal point is the crotch. In gay parlance, the basket. —John Francis Hunter, *The Gay Insider*, p. 119, 1971
- Did he have a basket it was like walking into safeway —Bruce Rodgers, *The Queen's Vernocular*, 1972
- "Oh ... " He laughed, hopping back into the stall. "I'm wire-brushing my basket. See?" —Armistead Maupin, *Tales of the City*, p. 123, 1978
- And don't think I didn't see you checkin' out that man's basket!. — *Boys on the Side*, 1995
- — *Attitude*, July 2003: 'Old palare lexicon'

3 **a woman's labia** *US*

- —Vincent J. Monteleone, *Criminal Slang*, p. 17, 1949

4 **an elderly woman** *UK, 1984*

Disrespectful; possibly deriving from a play on **OLD BAG**.

5 **in roulette, a bet on zero, double zero and two** *US, 1983*

Sometimes expanded to 'basket bet'.

- —Thomas L. Clark, *The Dictionary of Gambling and Gaming*, p. 14, 1987

basket!

used for expressing great frustration *SINGAPORE*

- —Paik Choo, *The Coxford Singlish Dictionary*, p. 12, 2002

basketball *noun*

1 **in Vietnam, an aircraft mission to illuminate the terrain below** *US*

- —Linda Reinberg, *In the Field: The Language of the Vietnam War*, p. 17, 1991

2 **a 250 mg capsule of Placidyl™ (ethchlorvynol), a hypnotic drug** *US*

- —Jay Robert Nash, *Dictionary of Crime*, p. 21, 1992

basket case *noun*

1 **a person who is emotionally debilitated** *US, 1952*

- After forcing himself (and his "eccentricity") upon a six-year-old basket case (a victim of pregnancy tranquilizers) he is found out[.] —Terry Southern, *Now Dig This*, p. 195, 1961
- [T]he whole thing was making a young girl who wasn't too bright to being with into some kind of a daffy basekt case. —George V. Higgins, *The Rat on Fire*, p. 149, 1981
- But what we found out is that each one of us is a brain and an athlete and a basket case, a princess and a criminal. — *The Breakfast Club*, 1985
- I don't know about you, but I'm gonna be a basket case just sitting home waiting to hear what happened. —*Avalon*, 1990
- You're a basket case. —*Sleepless in Seattle*, 1993

2 **any dysfunctional organisation or entity** *UK, 1973*

- "Madagascar is the basket case of the Indian Ocean," said a senior Western banker[.] —*New York Times*, p. D11, 28th December 1981
- Romania, the East bloc's basket case No. 2, recently asked Western bankers to reschedule 25 percent of its outstanding debt. —*Christian Science Monitor*, p. 5, 16th November 1981
- —J. E. Lighter, *Historical Dictionary of American Slang, Volume 1*, p. 100, 1994

basket days *noun*

days of good weather *US*

- Basket days – A period of mild weather that permits men to wear garments light enough to reveal the contours of their baskets. —*Fact*, p. 25, January-February 1965

basketful of meat *noun*

a large penis *US, 1941*

From **BASKET**.

basket head *noun*

a Vietnamese peasant *US*

Alluding to the straw hats worn by many.

- —Linda Reinberg, *In the Field*, p. 17, 1991

basket of snakes *noun*

in a car, an exhaust system with individual headers that intertwine *US*

- —John Lawlor, *How to Talk Car*, p. 17, 1965

baskets *noun*

the female breasts *US*

- —Fred Hester, *Slang on the 40 Acres*, p. 3, 1968

basket shopping *noun*

the practice of observing the crotch of a clothed male to gauge the size of his penis *US*

Also known as 'basket watcing'.

- —Roger Blake, *The American Dictionary of Sexual Terms*, p. 13, 1964
- —Dale Gordon, *The Dominion Sex Dictionary*, p. 26, 1967

basketweave *nickname*
Highway 401 (the Trans-Canada) across Toronto *CANADA*
- — *Canada, eh?*, 11th July 2002

basket weaver *noun*
1 a homosexual male who wears tight trousers, thus displaying the countour of his genitals *US, 1960s*
2 an advocate of simple values and an unsophisticated lifestyle *AUSTRALIA, 2003*
Derogatory.

basking shark *noun*
a Citroen DS or Citroen ID car *UK*
Car dealers' slang; from the shape and appearance.
- — *Sunday Times*, 8th August 1981

Basra belly *noun*
diarrhoea experienced by travellers in the Middle East *US*
- — Harold Wentworth and Stuart Berg Flexner, *Dictionary of American Slang*, p. 676, 1976

bass *noun*
1 one fifth of a gallon of alcohol *US*
- — *American Speech*, p. 56, Spring-Summer 1975: 'Razorback slang'

2 a defiant, tough person *US*
An abbreviation of **BAD ASS**.
- — Connie Eble (Editor), *UNC-CH Campus Slang*, p. 1, November 2002

bassackwards *adjective*
in the wrong order *US, 1865*
An intentionally jumbled **ASS BACKWARDS**. US quotation expert Fred Shapiro recently found the term used by Abraham Lincoln in 1865, a substantial antedating.
- By God, I reckon across the river the dogs would have to train the men, they're so bass-ackward and ignorant. — Guy Owen, *The Flim-Flam Man and the Apprentice Grifter*, p. 53, 1972
- I was pissed at him, putting the case in bass-ackwards because that way e can start with me[.] — George V. Higgins, *The Judgment of Deke Hunter*, p. 199, 1976
- It seems bassackwards that the supported Oakland team (the Raiders) is leaving and the team that isn't supported cannot leave. (Letter to the Editor) — *San Francisco Chronicle*, p. 42, 26th January 1980
- My mother came downstaris the way things usually got done in my family, culo avanti – or in regular English, bass ackwards. — Rita Ciresi, *Pink Slip*, p. 4, 1999
- "It's kinda bassackwards from the way people normally do it," he laughs. — *New Times Broward-Palm Beach (Florida)*, 25th December 2003

bastard *noun*
1 a despised or disrespected person; a derogatory insult or challenging form of address to someone considered objectionable *UK, 1598*
Originally, 'a person born out of wedlock', the value of the insult has survived since C16 and ignored the current social acceptance of illegitimate status.
- The Australian will endure an incredible amount of abuse from his friends, and none at all from anybody else. So don't call him a bastard just because you hear somebody else do so. — Nino Culotta (John O'Grady), *They're A Weird Mob*, p. 158, 1957
- You've been a proper bastard all day. — Jean Brooks, *The Opal Witch*, p. 40, 1967
- I always though he was a bit of a bastard.. — *Janie Stagestruck*, p. 50, 1972
- All pommies are bastards, bastards or worse. / And England is the arsehole of the universe. — *The Adventures of Barry McKenzie*, 1972
- The sense of illegitimacy of birth is not present. 'Run the bastards over. – Advice by Sir Robert Askin (Premier of NSW) to President Lyndon Johnston when students laid down before his motorcade.' 1966 quoted in. — Bill Hornadge, *The Ugly Australian*, p. 236, 1975
- Arseholes, bastards, fucking cunts and pricks — Ian Dury, *Plaistow Patricia*, 1977
- There are consequences to breaking ethheart of a murdering bastard. You experienced some of them. — *Kill Bill*, 2003

2 a fellow, a man *US, 1861*
With reduction, from partial to almost full, of the negative sense.
- There's no bastard been near this joint for days. — Eric Lambert, *The Veterans*, p. 126, 1954
- You will be called a bastard because you are a good bloke, but if you are called a bludger you probably are one. — Nino Culotta (John O'Grady), *They're A Weird Mob*, p. 203, 1957
- That's why I've always admired you, you bastard, respected you, because you've always been like a rock[.] — W.R. Bennett, *Target Turin*, p. 65, 1962
- "Yer a silly bastard" may be taken as kindly, meaning that you've done something vaguely foolish but nobody is going to worry about it. "You stupid bastard", on the other hand, may be accompanied by a flying fist. — Sue Rhodes, *Now you'll think I'm awful*, p. 104, 1967
- Cripes, I feel like all me birthdays have come at once! What a decent bunch of bastards! — Barry Humphries, *The Wonderful World of Barry McKenzie*, p. 9, 1968
- The trouble with you bastards from the East, you always want big beers. — John O'Grady, *It's Your Shout, Mate!*, p. 15, 1972
- You're that writer bastard, ain't yer? — Sam Weller, *Old Bastards I Have Met*, p. 22, 1979

3 used as a term of endearment *AUSTRALIA, 1882*
Affectionate usage with no pejorative connotation; whilst by no means exclusive to Australia in this sense, it is almost the defining Australian cliché; on a par with 'G'day'. Recorded in New Zealand: 'You are a right bastard, aren't you?'.
- Bazza you old bastard! Jeez it's good to see youse! — Barry Humphries, *Bazza Pulls It Off!*, 1971
- — Louis S. Leland, *A Personal Kiwi-Yankee Dictionary*, p. 11, 1984

4 a thing, especially one causing problems or distress *AUSTRALIA, 1915*
- It'll be a bastard if we 'as to turn to and bend some 'eavy canvass on 'er. — Robert S. Close, *Loe Me Sailor*, p. 180–1945,
- Nicks: the good, the bad and the bastard – i.e., the merits and demerits of Her Majesty's Prisons. — Charles Raven, *Underworld Nights*, p. 197, 1956
- I think Australian is a bastard of a language." Nino Culotta (John O'Grady). — Nino Culotta(John O'Grady), *They're A Weird Mob*, p. 26, 1957
- 'And how did they come to build a city in a swamp?' 'Drained the bastard, that's how.' — John O'Grady, *It's Your Shout, Mate!*, p. 74, 1972
- This last trip has been a bastard, what with the rain and the older tunnels, so dilapidated that they could collapse at any moment[.] — Petru Popescu, *The Last Wave*, p. 8, 1977
- He went crook. He said, 'You can eat them bastards [goannas] out in the bush, but not in my bloody camp!' — Herb Wharton, *Cattle Camp*, p. 97, 1994

▶ **as a bastard**
used to intensify a personal quality or condition *UK*
- I'm horny as a bastard but not for just anyone only that Victor. — Niall Griffiths, *Kelly + Victor*, p. 178, 2002

▶ **happy as a bastard on Father's Day**
extremely unhappy *AUSTRALIA*
The idea is that a bastard does not knows their father and so cannot celebrate on Father's Day. (Note that 'basket' used below is a euphemism).
- 'What's wrong with him?' rasped Kate. 'Happy as a basket on Father's Day,' came the useless reply from the P.O. — John Wynnum, *Tar Dust*, p. 46, 1962
- We are in more trouble than a bastard on Father's Day[.]. — Frank Hardy, *The Outcasts of Foolgarah*, p. 127, 1971

▶ **like a bastard**
used to intensify a personal quality or condition *AUSTRALIA*
- Rainin' like a bastard, she was. — Nino Culotta (John O'Grady), *Gone Fishin'*, p. 104, 1962
- — John Birmingham, *He Died With a Felafel in his Hand*, p. 11, 1994
- It hurt like a bastard but Henry was already falling backwards[.] — Harrison Biscuit, *The Search for Savage Henry*, p. 102, 1995
- This fuckin bangin [excellent] E [MDMA]. Already ad an arf, shared one with that Scouse twat Colm like, an I'm comin up like a bastard. — Niall Griffiths, *Sheepshagger*, p. 161, 2001

▶ **lonely as a bastard on father's day**
extremely lonely *AUSTRALIA*
- I'm as lonely as a bastard on father's day. — Barry Humphries, *A Nice Night's Entertainment*, p. 205, 1981

bastard *adjective*
bad, unpleasant; used to intensify *UK*
- No one else's bastard problems. — Alan Bleasdale, *Boys From the Blackstuff*, 1982
- 'Yup, Thai body sliding is the most fun a bloke can have in Queensland without breaking the law, wearing a franger or worrying about the bastard AIDS virus. — *Picture*, p. 5, 5th February 1992
- [B]lot out however many miles of be-bungalowed bastard reality it takes[.] — James Hawes, *Dead Long Enough*, p. 84, 2000
- Michael fuckin Bolton. Or Bryan bastard Adams, some wank power-ballad singer. — Niall Griffiths, *Kelly + Victor*, p. 128, 2002
- A book usually takes about three years to write, but this one was particularly difficult, because bastard real estate agents just shifted us from one house to another. — *Sydney Morning Herald*, 15th March 2003

-bastard- *infix*

used as an intensifier *UK*

- That's the pill-fucking-popping, line-bastard-snorting, behind-the-bike-sheds party we never wanted to leave. —James Hawes, *Dead Long Enough*, p. 127, 2000
- Afan Taff road Blackwood South bastard Wales UcuntingK the fucking world[.] —Patrick Jones, *Everything Must Go*, p. 162, 2000
- Left right and bastard centre [...] New fuckin Labour's no bastard better, either. —Niall Griffiths, *Sheepshagger*, p. 1, 2001

bastard amber *noun*

a colour of lighting gel for the theatre *CANADA*

- At least one year, my mother used the [quince] to make a clear jelly with a beautiful colour somewhere between pink and yellow, very close to the theatrical lighting gel that used to be called bastard amber. —David Helwig, *Living Here*, p. 25–26, 2001

bastard from the bush *noun*

a person from the country who comes to the city and behaves in an unmannerly way *AUSTRALIA*

From a bawdy ballad so titled, based on the poem 'The Captain of the Push' (1892) by Henry Lawson.

- Then the stranger made this answer to the Captain of the Push, 'Why, fuck you dead, I'm Foreskin Fred, the bastard from the bush. 'I've been in every two-up school from Darwin to the 'Loo, 'I've ridden colts and black gins – what more can a bastard do. —S. Hogbotel and S. ffuckes, *Snatches and Lays*, p. 82, 1962
- —Sidney J.Baker, *The Australian Language*, 1966
- 'It's you're the bastard.' Again that neigh: 'The Bastard from the Bush. Get back where you belong!' —Xavier Herbert, *Poor Fellow My Country*, p. 1079, 1975
- The bastard from the bush is one of life's great swine and, because of this, tolerated with great affection by Australian males. —Richard Beckett, *The Dinkum Aussie Dictionary*, p. 7, 1986

bastardisation *noun*

debasing and cruel initiation rights; hazing *AUSTRALIA, 1964*

- To the uninitiated, this type of training may appear to fall into the bastardisation category. —William Dodson, *The Sharp End*, p. 65, 2001

bastardise *verb*

to create a single motor vehicle from two others, especially with criminal intent *UK*

- —Angela Devlin, *Prison Patter*, p. 25, 1996

bastardry *noun*

despicable behaviour; cruel punishment *AUSTRALIA, 1945*

- —Sumner Locke Elliott, *Rusty Bugles*, p. 78, 1948

bastardy *adjective*

used as an intensifier *UK*

Elaboration of **BASTARD**.

- Fucky dingnuts and bastardy cunt-holes. —Jenny Eclair, *Camberwell Beauty*, p. 208, 2000

bastartin *adjective*

used as an intensifier *UK: SCOTLAND*

Glasgow slang, probably formed on **BASTARD**.

- Ach, chuck the bastartin thing in the bin! —Michael Munro, *The Patter, Another Blast*, 1988

basted *adjective*

drunk *US, 1928*

- —Joseph Weingarten, *American Dictionary of Slang*, p. 18, 1954
- —Connie Eble (Editor), *UNC-CH Campus Slang*, p. 1, Fall 1988

Bastille *noun*

1 the local police station *AUSTRALIA*

- At the Bastille the lollipop said the fare had to pay the price showing on the meter. —Frank Hardy, *The Yarns of Billy Borker*, p. 96, 1965

2 HMP Strangeways during the prison riot of April 1990 *UK*

Earlier, generalised sense as 'a prison' has given way to this specific, often nostalgic use.

- He was on duty at the Bastille. —Angela Devlin, *Prison Patter*, p. 26, 1996

basuco; bazuko *noun*

coca paste, the basic ingredient in the manufacturing process of cocaine; hence, cocaine *US, 1984*

- CALL IT... Basuco, gianluca, blow, percy, lady, toot, white[.] JUST DON'T CALL IT... Charlie – too Eighties —*Drugs An Adult Guide*, p. 34, December 2001

bat *noun*

1 a foolish or eccentric person *US, 1894*

- A bat can't go it. Bat? You mean a dingbat? [fool, incompetent]. yeah. —Bruce Jackson, *In the Life*, p. 162, 1972
- The old bat on the door who rode shotgun on the money box – really a cigar box – never did act like she was going to give me the chance to take it. —A.S. Jackson, *Gentleman Pimp*, p. 12, 1973

2 an ugly woman *US*

- —David Claerbaut, *Black Jargon in White America*, p. 57, 1972

3 an extended period of drunkenness *CANADA*

- "Lil's still drinkin, if that's what you mean, Goldy," Syd told her. "She's been on an awful bat for the past week." —Hugh Garner, *The Intruders*, p. 304, 1977

4 a drinking binge *US, 1846*

- One sip and I'll go on a nine-week bat. —John D.McDonald, *The Nean Jungle*, p. 21, 1953
- —Eugene Landy, *The Underground Dictionary*, p. 29, 1971
- —Jack Chambers (Editor), *Slang Bag 93 (University of Toronto)*, p. 5, Winter 1993

5 a fat marijuana cigarette *US, 1975*

Puns on 'baseball *bat*' as **STICK**.

- —Richard A. Spears, *The Slang and Jargon of Drugs and Drink*, p. 30, 1986
- —Mike Haskins, *Drugs*, p. 286, 2003

6 a shoe; a slipper *UK*

Variant spellings are 'batt' and 'bate'.

- [B]ats of death but bona maquillage [good make-up], I must say. —the cast of 'Aspects of Love', Prince of Wales Theatre, *Palare (Boy Dancer Talk) for Beginners*, 1989–92
- [She] orderlied over as fast as she could manage in those bats[.] —James Gardiner, *Who's a Pretty Boy Then?*, p. 123, 1997
- —Paul Baker, *Polari*, p. 164, 2002
- —*Attitude*, July 2003: 'Old palare lexicon'

7 male mastubation *AUSTRALIA*

- — Thommo, *The Dictionary of Australian Swearing and Sex Sayings*, p. 15, 1985

8 in horse racing, the whip used by the jockey *US*

- —David W. Maurer, *Argot of the Racetrack*, p. 12, 1951

▸ at bat

said of an appearance before a judge, magistrate or parole board *US*

- You're first a bat, Henry. Take off your cap and come along. —Malcolm Braly, *On the Yard*, p. 17, 1967

▸ like a bat out of hell

at great speed *US, 1909*

- Like a bat out of hell / I'll be gone gone gone. —Jim Steinman, *Bat Out of Hell*, 1977

▸ off the bat

immediately, swiftly *US, 1907*

From the speed that a ball moves when struck by a bat.

- They are not going for a primitive capability, they're basically aiming for a Soyuz or Apollo capability straight off the bat[.] —*New Scientist*, 12th November 2002

▸ off your own bat

without assistance, independently *UK, 1845*

Inspired by cricket.

- Do you suppose he can have decided to go back to England off his own bat? —Douglas Rutherford, *The Creeping Flesh*, p. 74, 1963

▸ on the bat

to be working as a prostitute *UK*

Extended from an obsolete use of 'bat' (a prostitute).

bat *verb*

to dance on a stage *UK*

Also spelled 'batt' or 'bate'.

- —Paul Baker, *Polari*, p. 164, 2002

▸ bat on a sticky wicket

1 to contend with great difficulties *UK*

From the game of cricket; the ball bounces unpredictably on a pitch that is drying out.

2 to have sex with a woman who has recently had sex with another man or other men *AUSTRALIA*

- — Thommo, *The Dictionary of Australian Swearing and Sex Sayings*, p. 15, 1985

▸ bat the breeze

to talk, chat or gossip *US, 1941*

- Jenkins, you've been around the Hall long enough to know a murder isn't something we bat the breeze about. —Thurston Scott, *Cure it with Honey*, p. 23, 1951
- A klatsch of kids was batting the breeze about five or six cars away from his own[.] —Morton Cooper, *High School Confidential*, p. 32, 1958
- Buchanan would introduce them and I'd buy another drink, bat the breeze. —Shane Maloney, *Nice Try*, p. 241, 1998

bat and balls *noun*

the male genitals with the penis erect *UK*

- She [...] took off her glasses and went straight to work with that long tongue of hers licking my bat and balls. — *The Sucker's Kiss (excerpted in 'The Guardian' under the headline 'The Bad Sex award shortlisted passages')*, 4th December 2003

bat and wicket *noun*

a ticket *UK, 1931*

Rhyming slang, sometimes shortened to 'bat'.

bat away *verb*

in a carnival, to operate swindles aggressively and without fear of arrest *US*

A term borrowed from the game of baseball.

- The only time the order to bat away is given is when the police have been paid off. — Gene Sorrows, *All About Carnivals*, p. 9, 1985

bat-bat *noun*

the buttocks *ANTIGUA AND BARBUDA*

batch *noun*

an ejaculation's worth of semen *US*

- The sounds this bitch was making damn near had me ready to unload this batch right in her hand[.] — A.S. Jackson, *Gentleman Pimp*, p. 166, 1973

batch; bach *verb*

to live as a bachelor *US, 1862*

- 'I've been batching,' he mentioned. — Kylie Tennant, *The Honey Flow*, p. 64, 1956
- It came from the boys' cabin – they were batching together to save money. — Jim Thompson, *The Kill-Off*, p. 29, 1957
- He's 'Batching' It In Style! [Headline] — *San Francisco Chronicle*, p. 15, 15th January 1958
- Huck surmised that Crawley was 'baching'. — Peter Corris, *Pokerface*, p. 44, 1985
- I batched up next to a mountain ribbonwood, closse to the headwaters[.] — Wayne Blake, *Trappers, Dogs 'n' Deer*, p. 100, 1999

batcher *noun*

someone who lives alone *AUSTRALIA, 1943*

From earlier 'bach; batch' (to live alone); ultimately from 'bachelor'.

batch kick *noun*

in the usage of pickpockets, the hip pocket *US*

- — Vincent J. Monteleone, *Criminal Slang*, p. 18, 1949

batchy *noun*

▷ **see:** BACHY

Bates; John Bates; Mr Bates *noun*

a gullible victim of a swindle *US, 1908*

- — J. E. Lighter, *Historical Dictionary of American Slang, Volume 1*, p. 103, 1994

bath *noun*

1 a heavy loss in a business or betting proposition *US, 1936*

- — *Cars*, p. 40, December 1953
- — John Scarne, *Scarne's Guide to Modern Poker*, p. 292, 1979
- — Kathleen Odean, *High Steppers, Fallen Angels, and Lollipops*, p. 94, 1988

2 in television and film making, any of the chemical mixtures used to develop film *US*

- — Ira Konigsberg, *The Complete Film Dictionary*, p. 26, 1987

▸ **be in anything except a bath**

to not wash oneself very often; to have poor personal hygiene *AUSTRALIA*

- — Leonard Mann, *Flesh in Armour*, p. 93, 1932
- Concealed as well as possible in the middle of the front rank was Able Seaman Dingo Hancock. Be in anything except a bath, as the saying goes and generally preferred fighting to other activities. — John Wynnum, *Tar Dust*, p. 22, 1962

bath dodger *noun*

an English person *AUSTRALIA*

In Australian folklore the English are noted as stinting on personal hygiene.

- Compared to masturbation or a meat injection, even a Pommy bath-dodger can seem pretty exotic. — Kathy Lette, *Girls' Night Out*, p. 199, 1987

bathers *noun*

a swimming suit *AUSTRALIA, 1930*

- She plastered our faces with zinc cream and made us wear T-shirts tucked into our bathers. — Kerry Cue, *Crooks, Chooks and Bloody Ratbags*, p. 1, 1983
- — Sonya Plowman, *Great Kiwi Slang*, p. 23, 2002

bat house *noun*

1 a brothel *AUSTRALIA, 1941*

A combination of **CATHOUSE** (a brothel) and **ON THE BAT** (to be working as a prostitute).

2 a mental hospital *US*

- — Joseph E. Ragen and Charles Finston, *Inside the World's Toughest Prison*, p. 790, 1962

bathroom locks *noun*

long, combed, styled, braided dreadlocks *JAMAICA, 1979*

- — Thomas H. Slone, *Rasta is Cuss: A Dictionary of Rastafarian Cursing*, p. 25, 2003

baths *noun*

Turkish baths where the main attraction is sex between homosexual men *US*

- You'll never learn to stay out of the baths, will you. — Mart Crowley, *The Boys in the Band*, p. 59, 1968
- Baths can be found in any large city. — *Screw*, p. 2, 29th September 1969
- Some of the New Free gays believe the new culture will grow out of the baths side-by-side with the community centers[.] — John Francis Hunter, *The Gay Insider*, p. 150, 1971
- Often the baths endeavor to compete for the trade with novel decors, a bigger orgy room [pig room] or other gimmicks to attract the gay clientele. — Bruce Rodgers, *The Queens' Vernacular*, p. 28, 1972
- Essentially, the baths are where gay men go for sex. — *The Village Voice*, 27 September 1976
- Man's Country is the largest, the best-equipped, and the most packed baths in the city. — *Drummer*, p. 55, 1980
- You betcha. None o' that nasty heterosexual role-playing for us. Lots of buddy nights at the baths. — Armistead Maupin, *Further Tales of the City*, p. 33, 1982

bathtub *noun*

1 a sedan convertible with two cross seats *US*

Conventionally known as a 'touring car'.

- — *American Speech*, p. 93, May 1954

2 a motorcyle sidecar *US*

- — by Harold Wentworth and Stuart Berg Flexner, *Dictionary of American Slang*, p. 22, 1960

bathtub curve *noun*

in computing, used as a description of a notional graph of the predicted failure rate of a piece of electronic equipment *US*

Evoking a cross-section of a bathtub as the graph – briefly high, long low, high again at the end.

- — Eric S. Raymond, *The New Hacker's Dictionary*, p. 51, 1991

bathtub gin *noun*

homemade alcohol, perhaps approximating gin *US*

- [H]e had been a cab driver in Chicago during the Roaring Twenties but had left town fast due to some trouble with the police over transporting bath tub gin in his cab. — Piri Thomas, *Seven Long Times*, p. 216, 1974

bathtub speed *noun*

methcathinone *US, 1998*

- — Office of National Drug Control Policy *Drug Facts*, February 2003

bati-man *noun*

a homosexual *UK, 1955*

- — F.G. Cassidy & R.B. Le Page, *Dictionary of Jamaican English*, p. 32, 1967

Batman *noun*

1 a variety of MDMA, the recreational drug best known as ecstasy, identified by the embossed Batman motif *UK*

- — Gareth Thomas, *This Is Ecstasy*, p. 56, 2002
- — Mike Haskins, *Drugs*, p. 289, 2003

2 a variety of LSD identified by the printed bat-logo *UK*

- — Angela Devlin, *Prison Patter*, p. 26, 1996

3 cocaine *UK*

- — Nick Constable, *This is Cocaine*, p. 181, 2002

4 heroin *UK*

- — Nick Constable, *This is Cocaine*, p. 181, 2002

bato, bato loco *nouns*

▷ **see:** VATO, VATO LOCO

bat out *verb*
on the railways, to switch cars quickly and expertly *US*
- —Ramon Adams, *The Language of the Railroader*, p. 11, 1977

bat pad *noun*
in cricket, a fielder positioned close to the facing bat *AUSTRALIA*
- —Max Walker, *Hooked on Cricket*, p. 114, 1989

batphone *noun*
a police radio; the police personal radio system *UK*
Acquired from comic book crimefighter Batman's utility belt.
- —David Powis, *The Signs of Crime*, 1977
- —Angela Devlin, *Prison Patter*, p. 26, 1996
- —Martin Fido and Keith Skinner, *The Official Encyclopaedia of New Scotland Yard*, 1999

bats *noun*
a deck-landing officer on an aircraft-carrier *UK*
From the signalling 'bats' the officer carries.
- —Wilfred Granville, *A Dictionary of Sailors' Slang*, 1962

▸ **have bats in the belfry**
to be mad or eccentric *UK, 1911*
- Foot and mouth and now bats in the belfry.— *The Guardian*, 27th March 2001

bats *adjective*
crazy; very eccentric; mad, to any degree *UK, 1911*
From the phrase **HAVE BATS IN THE BELFRY**.
- You're bats. Somebody'll bust in. You can't leave it here.—Harry J. Anslinger, *The Murderers*, p. 72, 1961
- You think I'm nuts because I sew. It's to keep me from going bats. —Antony James, *America's Homosexual Underground*, p. 137, 1965
- I'm not bats, but I got to try this track.— *Pimp*, p. 102, 1969

batsh *noun*
in caving and pot-holing, bat excreta *UK*
A shortening of 'bat shit'.
- —David Morrison of Wessex Cave Club, 29th February 2004

batshit *adjective*
crazy, out of control, angry *US, 1970*
- [H]e just wanted to know whether the private standing in front of hihm was trying to punk out of that war, or was truly bat-shit.—Emmett Grogan, *Ringolevio*, p. 227, 1972
- — *Maledicta*, p. 170, Winter 1980: 'A brief survey of some unofficial prosigns used by the United States armed forces'
- Nothing's working anymore, everything's changing and it's driving me fucking batshit.—James Ellroy, *Brown's Requiem*, p. 105, 1981
- At twilight, just when the long stint of surveillance was starting to drive him batshit, his survivor walked up to the guiar shop window[.]—James Ellroy, *Suicide Hill*, p. 840, 1986
- These things are more likely to fuck up a shoot than trying to stick a needle [S-M piercing] through someone on camera who goes batshit.—Robert Stoller and I.S. Levine, *Coming Attractions*, p. 93, 1991

batten *verb*
(of a man) to live off the earnings of a prostitute *AUSTRALIA*
In the structure 'batten on someone'.
- In the following account of it the names of the girl in question, the man who was battening on her, his wife and his friend have been altered[.]—James Holledge, *The Call-girl in Australia*, p. 93, 1964

batter *noun*
a board used to cover a window before a hurricane or storm *BAHAMAS*
- —John A. Holm, *Dictionary of Bahamian English*, p. 12, 1982

▸ **on the batter**
1 engaging in a self-indulgent variety of drinks, drugs and other recreational excesses *UK, 1839*
- [I]f you cannot hack your life [...] after just one pathetic little old-fashioned night on the batter, you should not be doing it at all[.] —James Hawes, *Dead Long Enough*, p. 13, 2000

2 on the run from the police *UK, 1984*

3 to be working as a prostitute *UK, 1890*
Variation of **ON THE BAT**.
- "Aunt Polly" the lodger, who, I afterward discovered, was on the batter.—Charles Raven, *Underworld Nights*, p. 164, 1956
- [H]avin' to go on the batter day in an' day out and havin' to open up for 'em all[.]—Derek Raymond (Robin Cook), *The Crust on its Uppers*, p. 58, 1962
- May be he was hurrying to his girlfriend and was on the batter.—John Peter Jones, *Feather Pluckers*, p. 39, 1964

- — *Maledicta*, p. 147, Summer/Winter 1986–1987: 'Sexual slang: prostitutes, pedophiles, flagellators, transvestites, and necrophiles'

batter *verb*
to beg on the street *US*
- —Hyman E. Goldin et al., *Dictionary of American Underworld Lingo*, p. 24, 1950

battered *adjective*
drunk *UK*
From an earlier sense as 'debauched'.
- — *e-cyclopaedia*, 20th March 2002

battery *noun*
a concealed device for giving an electric shock to a horse in a race *AUSTRALIA, 1936*
- Once just when a trainer was asking Huck to hit a horse with a battery on the track a DC3 aeroplane flew over.—Frank Hardy and Athol George Mulley, *The Needy and the Greedy*, p. 97, 1975
- If a horse runs unplaced in three consecutive races its jockey should be permitted to use a battery.—Frank Hardy and Athol George Mulley, *The Needy and the Greedy*, p. 123, 1975

▸ **get your battery charged**
to have sex *US, 1935*
- — *American Speech*, p. 56, February 1947: 'Pacific War language'

battery *verb*
to knock; to hit; to knock down *UK*
From Italian *battere*.
- —Paul Baker, *Polari*, p. 164, 2002

battery acid *noun*
1 coffee *US, 1941*
Originally military.
- —Lou Shelly, *Hepcats Jive Talk Dictionary*, p. 21, 1945
- —Wayne Floyd, *Jason's Authentic Dictionary of CB Slang*, p. 9, 1976
- —Peter Chippindale, *The British CB Book*, p. 151, 1981
- He put down the pot, picked up the mug, and took a swallow. "Battery acid," he said.—Robert Campbell, *Sweet La-La Land*, p. 8, 1990

2 grapefruit juice or sour lemonade *US, 1945*
- —J. E. Lighter, *Historical Dictionary of American Slang, Volume 1*, p. 105, 1994

3 LSD *UK, 1998*
An elaboration of **ACID** (LSD).
- —Mike Haskins, *Drugs*, p. 285, 2003

battery girl *noun*
a prostitute who is subject to a controlling supply of drugs, etc, and consequently is managed and kept in a similar way to a battery hen *UK*
- —Stephen Barclay, *Sex Slavery*, 1968

batting and bowling *noun*
bisexual sexual activity *UK, 1984*

battle *noun*
1 in a betting operation, the eternal plus-and-minus relationship between bettors and the betting operation *AUSTRALIA*
- One might ask a colleague, "How's the battle?" The answer might be, "Surviving – just."—Ned Wallish, *The Truth Dictionary of Racing Slang*, p. 5, 1989

2 an unattractive woman *US*
- —Jack Lait and Lee Mortimer, *New York Confidential*, p. 235, 1948

▸ **on the battle**
working as a prostitute *AUSTRALIA, 1944*
- She tells me how she useter be on the battle, and then she seen the light.—Lawson Glassop, *We Were The Rats*, p. 146, 1944

battle *verb*
1 to breakdance competitively with the object of demonstrating the most individual style *US*
Conventional 'battle' (a violent struggle) adopted for this non-violent clash.
- So when you're practising for that whole week, your goal is to hit the jam and battle.—Alex Ogg, *The Hip Hop Years [quoting 'Crazy Legs' Richie Colon]*, p. 32, 1999

2 to compete in a public demonstration of DJ skills or to establish a sound-system's superiority; to compete in rap performance; to compete in graffiti skills *US*
- Confrontation has always been a part of rap music [...] a verbal war for supremacy: battle rap.—James Haskins, *The Story of Hip-Hop*, p. 81, 2000
- But how did battling come about? Well, DJs had always battled with their sound systems in New York.—J. Hoggarth, *How To Be a DJ*, p. 82, 2002

3 to attack someone verbally *US*

- —Ethan Hilderbrant, *Prison Slang*, p. 10, 1998

4 to struggle for a living; to work hard despite troubles and exhibit courage in doing so *AUSTRALIA, 1895*

- The old day. Battling together. If he gave you ten bob you could bet it was half of all he had in the world.—Eric Lambert, *The Veterans*, p. 27, 1954
- We saw the things our parents put up with, we saw them battle, I mean, to get a house, to get any house was their dream[.]—Sandra Jobson, *Blokes*, p. 194, 1984
- —Frank Hardy, *Hardy's People*, p. 34, 1986

5 to have sex; to impregnate someone *NEW ZEALAND*

- —David McGill, *David McGill's Complete Kiwi Slang Dictionary*, p. 11, 1998

6 to work as a prostitute *AUSTRALIA, 1898*

- I've got six other girls all keeping me now. They are all battling from different hotel round the Cross.—James Holledge, *The Call-girl in Australia*, p. 88, 1964

7 to attempt to make a living at the racecourse, either by running or gambling on horses *AUSTRALIA, 1895*

▸ **battle the iron men**

in horse racing, to bet using pari-mutuel machines *US*

- —David W. Maurer, *Argot of the Racetrack*, p. 12, 1951

battleaxe; battleax *noun*

an old or elderly woman who is variously characterised as resentful, vociferous, thoroughly unpleasant, usually arrogant and no beauty *US, 1896*

- Hey, Estelle, ain't that that old battle ax that owns the place next door?—Helen P. Branson, *Gay Bar*, p. 57, 1957
- It's old battleaxes like this that cause all the trouble for everyone[.] —Danny King, *The Bank Robber Diaries*, p. 11, 2002

battle cruiser; battle *noun*

1 a public house *UK, 1960*

Rhyming slang for **BOOZER**, sometimes expanded to 'battle and cruiser'.

- I'd just come out the battle / And was looking for a dog [a telephone]—Ronnie Barker, *Fletcher's Book of Rhyming Slang*, p. 21, 1979

2 an aggressive, 'mannish' lesbian *US*

- —*Maledicta*, p. 134, Summer/Winter 1982

3 a formidable older woman *UK*

As with **BATTLESHIP** this seems to play on **OLD BAT**, but possibly with a rhyming slang influence: 'battle-cruiser' from **BRUISER** (a rugged physical specimen).

Battle of Hastings *adjective*

history, in the past *UK*

The one historical date that most of the UK remembers.

- It was used in the context of a relationshiip – "No mate, she's Battle of Hastings".—*www.LondonSlang.com*, 26th June 2002

battle of the bulge *noun*

an effort to lose weight *US*

- They won their battle of the bulge, according to a male post commander and three foreign correspondents, also eminently male.—*San Francisco Examiner*, p. 17, 13th October 1956
- The inside story of Elvis Presley's battle of the bulge is that Presley tipped the scales at 253 pounds only a few weeks ago.—*San Francisco Chronicle*, p. 43, 27th May 1975

battler *noun*

1 a person who struggles to make a living; a person who 'battles' *AUSTRALIA, 1896*

- Now if a mortar cops me when the shells are falling thick / I hope I'll go where battlers go and meet old Ginger Mick.—Tip Kelaher, *The Digger Hat and other verses*, p. 17, 1942
- [L]ike most young jockeys, he was a battler. He would go anywhere and ride anything to make a dollar.—Roy Higgins and Tom Prior, *The Jockey Who Laughed*, p. 78, 1982
- Anyway, the Australian battler is the same everywhere, ironic, sceptical – and a loyal friend.—Frank Hardy, *Hardy's People*, p. 64, 1986
- Ned Kelly was the first Australian battler.—Frank Hardy, *Hardy's People*, p. 111, 1986
- Fearsome pious, she was. Pope on te wall, Mass at Saint Joey's every Sunday. But a real battler.—Shane Maloney, *Nice Try*, p. 109, 1998

2 a gambler who tries to make a living by gambling; a habitual punter who is always struggling; also, a struggling horse owner-trainer *AUSTRALIA, 1895*

- The only difference between a top trainer and a battler is a good horse.—James Holledge, *The Great Australian Gamble*, p. 25, 1966
- At a place called Dederang ... there was an annual race meeting, th main event being the Dederang Handicap. One year a horse traine by a battler Andy Simpson won it.—Frank Hardy and Athol George Mulley, *Th Needy and the Greedy*, p. 27, 1975

3 a prostitute, especially a self-managed prostitute *AUSTRALIA, 1898*

- —Sidney J. Baker, *Australia Speaks*, 1953

4 in horse racing, someone who is just barely making a a livin from the sport or from betting on the sport *AUSTRALIA*

- —Ned Wallish, *The Truth Dictionary of Racing Slang*, p. 5, 1989

battle scar *noun*

a bruise on the skin caused by sucking *US*

Hawaiian youth usage.

- —Douglas Simonson, *Pidgin to da Max Hana Hou*, 1982

battleship *noun*

1 a powerful and domineering woman *US, 1931*

An extension of **OLD BAT**, playing on the physical similarities between an ironclad and a formidable woman.

2 a railway coal tender *US*

- —Norman Carlisle, *The Modern Wonder Book of Trains and Railroading*, p. 259, 1946

battle wagon *noun*

1 a battleship *UK, 1943*

Royal Navy origins, then Royal Air Force.

2 an expensive car *UK, 1943*

Army usage.

battle weapon *noun*

a specially produced vinyl recording of hip-hop samples, used to 'scratch' (manipulate the sounds into an overall soundscape) and to 'battle' (compete with other another DJ) *US*

DJ and hip-hop use.

- Most of the Dirt Star's label battle weapons are good.—J. Hoggarth, *How To Be a DJ*, p. 86, 2002

battling *noun*

struggling to eke out a living; going through hard times *AUSTRALIA, 1895*

- We felt sorry for the old pioneer, after a life-time of hard battling.—Ion L. Idriess, *Over the Range*, p. 47, 1947
- It [the dog] was a plaything, a distracter that switched the mind from tough battling for a moment, a topic for conversation, and above all a companion.—Patsy Adam-Smith, *Folklore of the Australian Railwaymen*, p. 154, 1969

batty *noun*

1 homosexuality *UK*

Reduced from **BATTY BOY** (a homosexual); ultimately 'batty' (a bottom) is West Indian, hence UK black.

- We talk about law: batty law and ganja [marijuana] law. How can batty be legal and ganga illegal, enh?—Diran Abedayo, *My Once Upon A Time*, p. 24, 2000

2 the buttocks *JAMAICA, 1935*

Also variant 'bati'.

- —John A. Holm, *Dictionary of Bahamian English*, p. 12, 1982
- If yuh touch me batty again, me gwan chop off yuh han'.—Donald Gorgon, *Cop Killer*, p. 56, 1994
- It was the same with the other skirts and dresses she hurriedly tried on. None made proper provision for high-slung batties and calves, for legs curved rather than straight.—Diran Abedayo, *My Once Upon A Time*, p. 66, 2000
- —Lise Winer, *Dictionary of the English/Creole of Trinidad & Tobago*, 2003

batty *adjective*

eccentric, odd, insane *US, 1903*

- "Look," Coyle said, "they're all batty."—George V. Higgins, *The Friends of Eddie Doyle*, p. 132, 1971
- She's been driving me batty lately.—*Body Heat*, 1980

batty boy; batty bwai; batty bwoy *noun*

a homosexual *UK*

Combines **BATTY** (the buttocks) with 'a youth'; from West Indies into wider UK usage popularised in the 1990s by comedian Ali G (Sacha Baron-Cohen).

- An dat goes for any man from Grange an' the rest of dem batty bwai deh [there].—Karline Smith, *Moss Side Massive*, p. 16, 1994
- [T]he usual cross section of late-night London life. Trendy white dance funksters, rude bwoys, soul boys, batty bwoys, ragga gals, slack gals, the drunk and insomniac[.]—Donald Gorgon, *Cop Killer*, p. 88, 1994
- —Angela Devlin, *Prison Patter*, p. 26, 1996

attyfang *verb*
to hit, beat, bite or maul someone *UK*
From earlier conventional 'batterfang' (to batter).
- —J. Redding Ware, *Passing Slang of the Victorian Era*, 1909
- —Paul Baker, *Polari*, p. 164, 2002

atty hole *noun*
the anus *BAHAMAS*
- —John A. Holm, *Dictionary of Bahamian English*, p. 12, 1982

batty man *noun*
a male homosexual *ANTIGUA AND BARBUDA*
- —David Powis, *The Signs of Crime*, 1977
- —Bill Valentine, *Gang Intelligence Manual*, p. 109, 1995
- —Richard Allsopp, *Dictionary of Caribbean English Usage*, p. 84, 1996
- Being gay or lesbain – a "chi-chi" man'gal or a "battyman," is the ultimate sin in Jamaica.—*San Diego Union-Tribune*, p. F8, 26th August 2001

batty rider(s) *noun*
a very short and skimpy skirt or fashion shorts worn to expose as much as they conceal *JAMAICA*
From **BATTY** (the buttocks).
- By this time she had started to peel off her top and was unzipping her batty riders [...] He slipped his hand under her batty rider and felt around.—Donald Gorgon, *Cop Killer*, p. 45, 1994

batty wash *noun*
the act of licking an anus with your tongue *UK*
West Indies origins.
- Tunde made him give him a batty wash [...] And he had to suck out Tunde's arsehole.—*Dog Eat Dog*, 2000

batwank *noun*
nonsense *UK*
- I don't do house calls for a loada batwank.—Nick Barlay, *Curvy Lovebox*, p. 71, 1997

batwings *noun*
in the language of parachuting, surfaces applied to the arms and body to slow the rate of descent *US*
- —Dan Poynter, *Parachuting*, p. 165, 1978

baw *noun*
a ball *UK: SCOTLAND*
A Glasgow word, spelt as the local pronunciation.
- Ma baw! is a cry in football uttered by a player who wants to take responsibility for playing the ball: "If ye hear that big nutjob shoutin 'Ma Baw' just dive oot his road."—Michael Munro, *The Complete Patter*, 1996

bawbag *noun*
a despicable man *UK: SCOTLAND*
A Glasgow variation of **BALLBAG** (the scrotum), hence **SCROAT** (a despicable man).
- Bawbags the lot o' them. You're the one keepin' them in a job[.] —Christopher Brookmyre, *The Sacred Art of Stealing*, p. 195, 2002

bawdy basket *noun*
a woman with a sexually transmitted infection *US*
- —Ruth Todasco et al., *The Intelligent Woman's Guide to Dirty Words*, p. 24, 1973

baw hair *noun*
a pubic hair used as the narrowest possible measurement *UK: SCOTLAND*
Derives from **BAWS** (the testicles).
- That [hammer] wis a baw-hair aff stovin in ma skull!—Michael Munro, *The Patter – Another Blast*, 1988

bawl *verb*
to speak with enthusiasm, especially if complaining *GRENADA, 1977*
- —Richard Allsopp, *Dictionary of Caribbean English Usage*, p. 85, 1996

bawl out; ball out *verb*
to reprimand someone *US, 1899*
- [S]he gave him hell, she bawled him out and cursed him[.]—Salman Rushdie, *The Satanic Verses*, p. 27, 1988

baws *noun*
the testicles *UK: SCOTLAND*
Glasgow slang, extended from **BAW** (a ball).
- —Michael Munro, *The Patter, Another Blast*, 1988

bay *noun*
▸ **over the bay**
drunk *US, 1787*
- —John Gould, *Maine Lingo*, p. 8, 1975

▸ **the bay**
Long Bay Gaol, Sydney *AUSTRALIA, 1942*

bay and a gray *noun*
in poker, a bet involving a red chip (the bay) and a white chip (the gray) *US*
- —*American Speech*, p. 97, May 1951: 'The vocabulary of poker'
- —Albert H. Morehead, *The Complete Guide to Winning Poker*, p. 256, 1967

bayonet *noun*
a hypodermic needle *US*
- —Sacramento Municipal Utility District, *A Glossary of Drugs and Drug Language*, 1986

▸ **take the bayonet course**
to participate in bismuth subcarbonate and neoarsphenamine therapy for syphilis *US*
- —*Maledicta*, p. 227, Summer/Winter 1981: 'Sex and the single soldier'

bayonet drill *noun*
sexual intercourse *US*
- —Roger Blake, *The American Dictionary of Sexual Terms*, p. 14, 1964

Bay State *noun*
any standard medical syringe *US*
Drug addict usage.
- —David Maurer and Victor Vogel, *Narcotics and Narcotic Addiction*, p. 387, 1973

Bay Street barber *noun*
a greedy investment broker who skims large amounts off every transaction as a management fee *CANADA*
- —Bill Casselman, *Canadian Sayings*, p. 21, 2002

Bay Street boys *noun*
the class of politically powerful white Nassau merchants *BAHAMAS*
- —John A. Holm, *Dictionary of Bahamian English*, p. 12, 1982

bay window *noun*
a protruding stomach *US, 1889*
- —Vincent J. Monteleone, *Criminal Slang*, p. 18, 1949

baywop *noun*
an outport Newfoundlander *CANADA*
'Wop' in this use is a Newfoundland pronunciation of 'wasp'.
- 'Baywops' [in Jane's House of Hate] are generally seen as semi-retarded and contemptible.—Patrick O'Flaherty, *The Rock Observed*, p. 175, 1979

bazillion *noun*
a mythical very large number *US*
- —Pamela Munro, *U.C.L.A. Slang*, p. 35, 2001

bazongas; bazoongas; bazonkas *noun*
the female breasts *US, 1972*
Probably a variation of **BAZOOKAS**.

bazoo *noun*
1 the mouth *US, 1877*
- —Hyman E. Goldin et al., *Dictionary of American Underworld Lingo*, p. 24, 1950

2 an old car, usually treasured regardless of its condition *CANADA*
French-Canadian, adapted by English-speakers.
- —Lewis Poteet, *Car & Motorcyle Slang*, p. 24, 1992

bazooka *noun*
1 the penis *US*
The penis as a weapon imagery, here based on the 'bazooker' anti-tank rocket launcher; sometimes embellished to 'bazooka shooter'.
- —Brigid McConville and John Shearlaw, *The Slanguage of Sex*, p. 29, 1984

2 a high-powered car *US*
- —Chrysler Corporation, *Of Anchors, Bezels, Pots and Scorchers*, September 1959
- —*San Francisco Examiner*, p. III-2, 22nd March 1960

3 an extra-large, potent marijuana cigarette laced with cocaine *US, 1984*
Either from the similarity in physical shape and figurative power to the type of artillery shell used by a bazooka anti-tank weapon,

or from (Colombian Spanish) *bazuco*, a cocaine derivative made from coca paste.

- —Kenn "Naz" Young, *Naz's Dictionary of Teen Slang*, p. 7, 1993

4 cocaine; crack cocaine *UK*
The metaphor of a portable rocket-launcher, possibly a variation of **BASUCO**.

- —Mike Haskins, *Drugs*, p. 280, 2003

5 in television and film making, a light support used on a catwalk *US*

- —Ralph S. Singleton, *Filmaker's Dictionary*, p. 16, 1990

bazooka'd *adjective*
drunk *UK: SCOTLAND*

- —Michael Munro, *The Patter, Another Blast*, 1988

bazookas *noun*
the female breasts *UK, 1963*
Usually in the plural; perhaps from the shape of the shell fired by a bazooka anti-tank weapon, probably influenced by conventional 'bosom'.

- — *Doctor in the House*, 1973

bazoomas; bazoombas *noun*
the female breasts *UK*
An elaboration of **BAZOOMS** that echoes the shape of **BAZOOKAS**.

- —Brigid McConville and John Shearlaw, *The Slanguage of Sex*, p. 29, 1984
- Do you wish you played drums so you could peek at her bazoomas on stage?— *FHM*, p. 222, June 2003

bazooms *noun*
the female breasts *US, 1936*
Originally a corruption of 'bosom' with the same sense, then evolved to mean 'breasts'; almost always phrased in the plural.

- How many out-of-town buyers' hands had paraded over those bazooms? How much in fees had each of these bazooms raked in per annum?—Bernard Wolfe, *The Late Risers*, p. 73, 1954
- Mondo Bazooms: From Mountains to Mole Hills [Advertisement for Film]— *San Francisco Chronicle*, 12th May 1967
- —Collin Baker et al., *College Undergraduate Slang Study Conducted at Brown University*, p. 77, 1968
- Their secondary sex characteristics are simply too conspicuous to pass without insult, and we were unmerciful towards them: tits, boobs, knockers, jugs, bubbies, bazooms, lungs, flaps and hooters we called them, and there was no way to be polite about it. — *Screw*, p. 6, 3rd January 1972
- Yeahh, but howdja like them bazooms on that P.R. chick?—Richard Price, *The Wanderers*, p. 27, 1974
- Why shouldn't strippers have a hall of fame?" asks Jennie Lee, known on the indoor runways of America as the Bazoom Girl.— *San Francisco Examiner and Chronicle Sunday Punch*, p. 2, 1st April 1979
- Daddy says tits. Daddy says knockers and jugs and bazooms and dingleberries and jujubes. And then he laughs and goes "wuff! wuff!".— *Journal of British Photography*, 9th May 1980
- Raven does her act barefoot, and never wears heels onstage, since falling and injuring her left bazoom.—Josh Alan Friedman, *Tales of Times Square*, p. 25, 1986
- Bermuda's barometric bazooms were a standing joke on the Strip to all but her.—Seth Morgan, *Homeboy*, p. 16, 1990
- "Scope those bazooms!" the older bosun said, as Bobbie cycled past.—Joseph Wambaugh, *Finnegan's Week*, p. 34, 1993
- I mean, I notice when they're dressed well or when they're fat or ugly or have mongo bazooms-—Rita Ciresi, *Pink Slip*, p. 52, 1999

bazooties *noun*
the female breasts *US*

- —Anna Scotti and Paul Young, *Buzzwords*, p. 16, 1997

bazoo wagon *noun*
a brakevan (caboose) *US*

- —Ramon Adams, *The Language of the Railroader*, p. 12, 1977

bazuca *noun*
the residue of smoked freebase cocaine, itself mixed with tobacco and smoked *US, 1984*

- [O]thers prefer a bazuca, in which the drug is sprinkled on cigarettes or joints and smoked.—Terry Williams, *The Cocaine Kids*, p. 110, 1989
- —Terry Williams, *Crackhouse*, p. 146, 1992

bazuko *noun*
▷ **see: BASUCO**

bazulco *noun*
cocaine *UK*

- —Nick Constable, *This is Cocaine*, p. 181, 2002

bazz *noun*
pubic hair *IRELAND*

- —Terence Dolan, *A Dictionary of Hiberno-English*, p. 21, 1999

Bazza; Bazzer *noun*
used as a common nickname for people named Barry *AUSTRALIA*

- —Barry Humphries, *Bazza Pulls It Off!*, 1971
- —Louis S. Leland, *A Personal Kiwi-Yankee Dictionary*, 1984

Bazzaland *nickname*
Australia *AUSTRALIA, 1973*
A tribute to the cultural influence of Barry (Bazza) McKenzie, a cartoon character created by Barry Humphries (b.1934).

bazzer *noun*
1 an exciting event or situation *UK*

- —Tom Hibbert, *Rockspeak!*, p. 18, 1983

2 a haircut *IRELAND*

- I got a bazzer yesterday.—Sean Beecher, *A Dictionary of Cork Slang*, 1983

bazz-off *noun*
a respite from doing something *IRELAND*

- After 29 years, you can have a 'bazz-off' now, but be back on 23rd May to get a kick in the pants.—Mr. Ryan, *House of the Oireachtas Parliamentary Debates*, 19th May 1960

BB *noun*
1 in baseball, a fastball *US*
A pitch thrown so fast that it seems as small as a BB pellet to the batter.

- But after visiting the clubhouse he came out throwing BBs.—Jim Bouton, *Ball Four*, p. 326, 1970
- Most mortals haven't the foggiest notion what it takes to walk to the plate in the bottom of the 12th inning with the fate of the National League pennant in their hands and some mountainous Baby Huey character from Knobnoster, Mo., throwing BB's at them from the mound.— *Record (Bergen County, New Jersey)*, p. D1, 15th October 1986
- —Mike Whiteford, *How to Talk Baseball*, p. 80, 1987
- Oakland rookie phenom Rich Harden, who came to start the 11th, was doing what he usually does when he's on the mound – throwing BB's.— *Boston Herald*, p. B4, 5th October 2003

2 any smart person, especially a professor *US*
An abbreviation of '*b*ig *b*rains'.

- —Marcus Hanna Boulware, *Jive and Slang of Students in Negro Colleges*, 1947

3 a male homosexual *UK, 1961*
An abbreviation of ***BUM BOY***.

BB *adjective*
in sports betting, said of consecutive wagers *US, 1973*
An initialising of '*b*ack-to-*b*ack'.

- —Thomas L. Clark, *The Dictionary of Gambling and Gaming*, p. 15, 1987

BBA *noun*
a woman with large buttocks *US*
An abbreviation of '*b*roads with *b*ig *a*sses'.

- —Fred Hester, *Slang on the 40 Acres*, p. 3, 1968

BBC *noun*
*B*ritish *b*orn *C*hinese *UK*

- Since 1989 several hundred British born Chinese people (known to each other as 'BBCs') in their early and mid-twenties have left Britain for Hong Kong.—David Parker, *Cool Places*, p. 72, 1998

BBFN
used as shorthand in Internet discussion groups and text message to mean '*b*ye-*b*ye *f*or *n*ow' *US*

- —Gabrielle Mander, *WAN2TLK? ltl bk of txt msgs*, p. 43, 2002

BBL
used in computer message shorthand to mean '*b*e *b*ack *l*ater' *US*

- —Eric S. Raymond, *The New Hacker's Dictionary*, p. 342, 1991

B board *noun*
an electronic newsgroup *US*
A contraction of 'bulletin board'.

- —Eric S. Raymond, *The New Hacker's Dictionary*, p. 52, 1991

B bomb *noun*

an amphetamine inhaler *US*

Withdrawn from the market by Smith Kline & French in 1949 after widespread abuse. A wad of Benzedrine-soaked cotton found in an asthma inhaler would be removed, immersed in a drink until drug and drink form a single intoxicating solution, reputedly 100 times stronger than a single Benzedrine tablet.

- —Richard Lingeman, *Drugs from A to Z*, p. 21, 1969
- —William D. Alsever, *Glossary for the Establishment and Other Uptight People*, p. 2, December 1970
- —Eugene Landy, *The Underground Dictionary*, p. 30, 1971
- For aspiring rock 'n' roll stars, bursting open a B-bomb was hardly glamorous[.]—Simon Napier-Bell, *Black Vinyl White Powder*, p. 25, 2001

B-boy *noun*

1 a breakdancer; later, anyone involved in hip-hop culture *US*

- The "breakers," or "B boys," for rival crews at the playgrounds, discos and skating rinks where they gather.— *New York Times*, p. C1, 14th August 1981
- The B-Boy, a phrase originally applied to break dancers, was, by the time I used it [1992], a catchall phrase among hip hop fans for anyone deeply involved with or influenced by hip hop culture.—Nelson George, *Buppies, B-Boys, Baps & Bohos*, p. xv, 2001

2 a streetwise young black man *US*

By extension from the previous sense.

- Most athletes are all B-boys and homeboys from the block.—Lois Stavsky et al., *A2Z [quoting Run-DMC, 1992]*, p. 4, 1995

3 a *b*uddy, a *b*rother; used as a form of address *US, 1992*

The initialism 'b' muddled with 'B-boy' (a young streetwise black male).

- —Lois Stavsky et al., *A2Z*, p. 4, 1995

BBW *noun*

a fat woman *US*

An abbreviation of '*b*ig, *b*eautiful *w*oman'; a fetish with a large male following.

- "Ninety-five percent of the men are averaged-sized but attracted to BBW" (Big Beautiful Women).— *Newsday (New York)*, p. 2 (Part II), 13th February 1988

BC *noun*

contraception; *b*irth *c*ontrol *US*

- — *American Speech*, p. 19, Spring 1985: 'The language of singles bars'

B cat *noun*

an ostentatiously homosexual male prisoner *US*

From the official categorisation by California prison authorities.

- —James Harris, *A Convict's Dictionary*, p. 28, 1989

BC bud *noun*

high grade marijuana from British Columbia *CANADA*

- —Mike Haskins, *Drugs*, p. 286, 2003

BCD *noun*

military eyeglasses *US*

Because they are so unattractive, they are deemed '*b*irth *c*ontrol *d*evices'. Also variant BCG (*b*irth *c*ontrol *g*oggles).

- —E.M. Flangan Jr, *Army*, November 1991
- — *American Speech*, p. 383, Winter 1991: 'Among the new words'

BC Kush *noun*

a local variety of marijuana in British Columbia *CANADA*

- Surrounded by super-enlarged photo posters of richly resinous buds from strains like B.C. Kush, the store's staff dispensed advice.—Brian Preston, *Pot Planet*, p. 2, 2002

BC Lounge *noun*

a Burger Chef fast-food franchise restaurant *US*

- — *Detroit Free Press*, 4th November 1979

BCNU

used in computer message shorthand to mean 'be seeing you' *US*

- —Eric S. Raymond, *The New Hacker's Dictionary*, p. 342, 1991

BCSD

▷ **see:** BIG CAR, SMALL DICK

BD *noun*

a syringe *US*

An allusion to Becton-Dickison, a medical supplies manufacturer.

- —Ralph de Sola, *Crime Dictionary*, p. 14, 1982

BDF *noun*

a big, strong, dumb brute *US*

New York police slang; an abbreviation of '*b*ig *d*umb *f*uck'.

- —Samuel M. Katz, *Anytime Anywhere*, p. 386, 1997

B dog *noun*

used as a term of address between members of the Bloods gang *US*

- —Ethan Hilderbrant, *Prison Slang*, p. 11, 1998

BDSM; BD/SM *noun*

*b*ondage, *d*omination, *s*adism and *s*asochism or sado-*m*asochism, unified as a sexual subculture *US, 1969*

- —Harold Wentworth and Stuart Berg Flexner, *Dictionary of American Slang*, p. 675, 1976
- I decided to make a pilgrimage to 10a Dryden Street, where the modern age of British BDSM began with the opening of John Sutcliffe's Atomage.—Claire Mansfield and John Mendelssohn, *Dominatrix*, p. 192, 2002
- Even fashion is taking a lead from the BDSM scene. Black leather, chokers, spikes and high heels have all graced the catwalks over the last year or so.— *Code*, p. 62, January 2002

be *verb*

are *UK*

Generally dialect but recorded here as an urban black use.

- "Especially for boys," Cleo continues, "because they're the ones who go out there and chat girls up. Girls be, like, what are you doing with a piece of paper asking for my number?"— *The Times Magazine*, 21st June 2003

▸ be in it

to take part in something *AUSTRALIA, 1928*

- You name it, he's been in it.—John Wynnum, *Jiggin' in the Riggin'*, p. 93, 1965
- Yeah, be in it Doc. You haven't lived until you've chundered on with these lovely shower of bastards!—Barry Humphries, *The Wonderful World of Barry McKenzie*, p. 29, 1968
- You've got to be in it, you blokes.—Ward McNally, *Supper at Happy Harry's*, p. 142, 1982

▸ be on

to watch something; to observe something *AUSTRALIA*

- The barman [...] pointed to us. "Be on 'im," Joe said.—Nino Culotta, *Cop This Lot*, 1960

beach *noun*

in prison, a shower room *US*

- —Jay Robert Nash, *Dictionary of Crime*, p. 22, 1992

▸ on the beach

1 in a fishing community, where people who do not fish are *CANADA*

Though cynical, this division of maritime humans describes the division in most fishing villages in Nova Scotia: people are divided between those who go fishing and those who work at fish plants, are housewives or farmers.

- There are lots of fools at sea, but lots more on the beach.— *Shelburne (NS) Coast Guard*, 1975

2 out of work *US, 1899*

- —Harold Wentworth and Stuart Berg Flexner, *Dictionary of American Slang*, p. 23, 1960

▸ the beach

Saudi Arabia *US*

Gulf war usage.

- "Desert cherries" in "Kevlars" fly the "Sand Box Express" to the "beach" and soon are complaining about "Meals Rejected by Ethiopians" if they can't find a "roach coach" run by "Bedouin Bob."— *Houston Chronicle*, p. 15, 24th January 1991
- — *American Speech*, p. 384, Winter 1991: 'Among the new words'

Beach *noun*

▸ the Beach

Miami Beach, Florida *US*

- "You from somewhere on the East coast. New York?" "Miami. The Beach most of my life."—Elmore Leonard, *Pronto*, p. 120, 1993

beach *verb*

1 to kick a ball very high *BARBADOS*

- —Frank A. Collymore, *Barbadian Dialect*, p. 16, 1965

2 in trucking, to bring a truck to a stop in a parking place *US*

- —Montie Tak, *Truck Talk*, p. 8, 1971

beach-bash *verb*
to lie on the sand, especially when exercised in romantic manoeuvres *AUSTRALIA, 1953*
Jocular variation on **SQUARE-BASHING** (military drill).
- —Sidney J. Baker, *Australia Speaks*, 1953

beach bomber *noun*
a bicycle modified for riding on the sand *US*
- —Trevor Cralle, *The Surfin'ary*, p. 7, 1991

beach boy *noun*
1 a young male who spends a great deal of time at the beach *US*
- —John M. Kelly, *Surf and Sea*, p. 279, 1965

2 a handsome, young black man who takes white female tourists as lovers *BARBADOS*
- —Richard Allsopp, *Dictionary of Caribbean English Usage*, p. 86, 1996

beach bum *noun*
someone whose devotion to spending a lifetime at the beach has left them destitute and an outcast *US*
- —John M. Kelly, *Surf and Sea*, p. 279, 1965

beach bunny *noun*
a young female who spends a great deal of time at the beach, surfing or associating with surfers *US*
- — *Paradise of the Pacific*, p. 27, October 1963
- —John M. Kelly, *Surf and Sea*, p. 279, 1965
- What to other people is a "pad" is called a "hutch" in surfing circles – most properly if it is the beach bunny's own apartment[.] —Roger Gordon, *Hollywood's Sexual Underground*, p. 144, 1966

beach chick *noun*
a young woman living a Bohemian lifestyle near the beach in the 1950s *US*
Peter Tamony described the term as follows: 'Originally applied to girls who lived at Stinson Beach [north of San Francisco] who were bisexual. By those unfamiliar with its background, and both ways implication, it has been extended to any girl who associated with the so-called Beat Generation inhabitants of North Beach in San Francisco'.
- It's [being Beat] shacking up for weeks at a time with a Beach chick, or picking up homosexuals in gay bars. — *San Francisco Chronicle, This World*, p. 4, 15th June 1958
- Nude 'Beach Chick' Strangled Here [Headline] — *San Francisco Call-Bulletin*, p. 10, 18th June 1958

beached whale *noun*
an obese hospital patient *US*
- —Sally Williams, *"Strong" Words*, p. 134, 1994

beach head *noun*
a person who spends a great deal of time at the beach *US*
- —Trevor Cralle, *The Surfin'ary*, p. 9, 1991

beach pig *noun*
a police officer assigned to a beach patrol *US*
- —Judi Sanders, *Don't Dog by Do, Dude!*, p. 2, 1991

beach rat *noun*
a person who spends a great deal of time at the beach *US*
- "I'll certainly point out that a pensioned fifteen-year veteran of the Newport Beach police Department is not just some ordinary unemployed beach rat," Chip addeed. —Joseph Wambaugh, *The Golden Orange*, p. 10, 1990

bead counter *noun*
a Roman Catholic; a worshipper in any religion that uses strung beads (the rosary, 'worry beads', the Nenju, the mala, etc) within its practice *UK, 1809*
- [F]aith firmly puts you on the nerdy team, playing alongside fundamentalist loonies, hysterically joyous born-agains with mad hair, home-made jumpers and no sex life, bearded vicars on motorbikes, jam makers, angel spotters, cross burners, bead counters and the Archbishop of Canterbury— *Sunday Times*, 26th March 2000

beadi *noun*
▷ see: **BEEDI**

bead jiggler *noun*
a Roman Catholic *US, 1966*
After rosary beads.
- —J. E. Lighter, *Historical Dictionary of American Slang, Volume 1*, p. 109, 1994

bead rattler *noun*
a Roman Catholic *UK*
After rosary beads.
- [S]ome bunch of bead-rattlers with their heads in the clouds[.] —Christopher Brookmyre, *Boiling a Frog*, p. 250, 2000

beady *noun*
the eye *US, 1978*
From the conventional cliché, 'beady eye'.
- You know I've had my beadies on these strides [trousers] for, oh, God knows, probably a month now. —Greg Williams, *Diamond Geezers*, p. 134, 1997
- When she got mean that Noreen she got a nasty habit closing her little beadies up. Eyelash job. —Jeremy Cameron, *Brown Bread in Wengen*, p. 9, 1999

beagle *noun*
1 a sausage *US, 1927*
- —Joseph E. Ragen and Charles Finston, *Inside the World's Toughest Prison*, p. 790, 1962

2 a racehorse *US, 1923*
- —David W. Maurer, *Argot of the Racetrack*, p. 12, 1951

be a good bunny
used as a farewell *US*
A catchphrase television sign-off on *The Wendy Barrie Show* (1949–1950), a celebrity-based programme. Repeated with referential humour.

beak *noun*
1 the nose *UK, 1715*
- We called this kid O'Brien because his beak was so big and hooked it kept the sun out of his face and got caught on clothes lines. —Mezz Mezzrow, *Really the Blues*, p. 7, 1946
- You've been snorting coke. You been snuffling that crap up your beak again after you promised – after you swore on your mother's grave[.] —Robert Campbell, *Juice*, p. 130, 1988

2 cocaine *UK*
From the previous sense; a reference to the manner in which the drug is taken.
- See them knobs [fools] hauling beak around the city? —Kevin Sampson, *Outlaws*, p. 18, 2001
- Some of the best beak I've had in a long time. —Niall Griffiths, *Kelly + Victor*, p. 78, 2002

3 in horse racing, a bet that a horse will win *US*
Extended from the sense as a 'nose', suggesting that the horse will win 'by a nose'.
- Give me two tickets right on the beak. —David W. Maurer, *Argot of the Racetrack*, p. 12, 1951

4 a magistrate *UK, 1749*
Widely used by those who have occasion to be 'up before the beak'.
- —Angela Devlin, *Prison Patter*, p. 26, 1996
- —Paul Baker, *Polari*, p. 164, 2002

5 a schoolteacher *UK, 1888*
A dated usage that has survived thanks to Billy Bunter and other schoolboy literature.

beak baby *noun*
a cocaine-user, especially female *UK*
An alliterative extension of **BEAK** (cocaine).
- She's a beak-baby, plain and simple. —Kevin Sampson, *Outlaws*, p. 112, 2001

beaked *adjective*
cocaine-intoxicated *UK*
From **BEAK** (cocaine).
- He's beaked out of his brains. —Niall Griffiths, *Kelly + Victor*, p. 289, 2002

beaker *noun*
a scientist *ANTARCTICA, 1990*
According to Hince, 'presumably after the character Beaker on the television programme *The Muppets*.
- —Bernadette Hince, *The Antarctic Dictionary*, p. 45, 2000
- — *Cool Antartica*, 2003: 'Antarctic slang'

beakerdom *noun*
the world of science and scientists *ANTARCTICA, 1996*
Extends from **BEAKER** (a scientist).
- —Bernadette Hince, *The Antarctic Dictionary*, p. 46, 2000

beak lunch *noun*

cocaine used around the middle of the day *UK*

- Anyone care for a spot of Beak Lunch? [...] just to see us through the afternoon. — *Uncut*, p. 170, October 2002

beak up *verb*

to use cocaine *US*

From **BEAK** (the nose).

- — Connie Eble (Editor), *UNC-CH Campus Slang*, p. 1, Fall 1991

be-all and end-all *noun*

the most important thing *UK, 1854*

- His "be-all and end-all" dream is to meet Steven Spielberg[.] — *The Guardian*, 26th October 2002

beam *noun*

1 the backside, rump *AUSTRALIA*

- A bit narrow in the beam by what I saw of her. — Robert S. Close, *Love Me Sailor*, p. 20, 1945
- She was wide in the beam and wore a tight skirt[.] — Peter Corris, *Make Me Rich*, p. 45, 1985

2 a good person *US*

- — Lou Shelly, *Hepcats Jive Talk Dictionary*, p. 7, 1945

3 cocaine *UK*

- — Mike Haskins, *Drugs*, p. 280, 2003

▸ **off the beam**

incorrect *US*

- — Lou Shelly, *Hepcats Jive Talk Dictionary*, p. 47, 1945

▸ **on the beam**

1 good; to the point; balanced *US, 1941*

- — Lou Shelly, *Hepcats Jive Talk Dictionary*, p. 31, 1945
- And you can get Ann for Benny? That's on the beam. — Irving Shulman, *The Amboy Dukes*, p. 87, 1947
- I lost the argument – the part of me that was on-the-beam lost it – and I went back. — Jim Thompson, *After Dark, My Sweet*, p. 3, 1955
- The signal beam, high over the tracks, could be seen for miles from the engine cab. Three colored lights kept the engineer informed of track conditions ahead. Being on the beam really meant being well-informed. — J. Herbert Lund, *Herb's Hot Box of Railraod Slang*, p. 20, 1975

2 intoxicated on marijuana *US, 1970*

Later to take on a far greater place in the lexicon of crack cocaine.

- — Jay Robert Nash, *Dictionary of Crime*, p. 22, 1992

'Beam *noun*

a Sunbeam motorcycle (in production from 1912 – 57) *UK, 1979*

beam *verb*

1 in computing, to transfer a file electronically *US*

From the terminology of the original *Star Trek* television series.

- — Eric S. Raymond, *The New Hacker's Dictionary*, p. 53, 1991

2 (used of a female) to experience erect nipples *US*

Related to describing such a female as having her **HIGH BEAMS** on.

- — Chris Lewis, *The Dictionary of Playground Slang*, p. 24, 2003

beamer *noun*

1 a smile *UK*

From conventional 'beam' (to smile broadly).

- I locks up and strolls over towards the pub, giving the boys a nice big beamer back[.] — Kevin Sampson, *Outlaws*, p. 12, 2001
- He gets a bit of a beamer an goes back to his mates[.] — Niall Griffiths, *Kelly + Victor*, p. 319, 2002

2 a deep blush *UK: SCOTLAND*

- You should've seen her face – what a beamer! — Michael Munro, *The Original Patter*, 1985
- In times past, he would have gone radge [mad] at such a slur. Or as radge as a shy, soft-spoken, beamer-prone guy like him can ever get. — *Scotland on Sunday*, 24th August 2003

3 in cricket, a fast ball that is bowled at the batsman's head *UK, 1961*

- Bowling beamers constitutes "unfair play"[.] — Michael Rundell, *The Dictionary of Cricket*, p. 22, 1985

4 a crack cocaine user *US*

From **BEAM UP (TO SCOTTY)** (to smoke crack cocaine).

- — Terry Williams, *Crackhouse*, p. 146, 1992

Beamer; Beamie *noun*

▷ see: **BEEMER**

beamers; beemers *noun*

crack cocaine *US*

After **BEAMER** (a crack cocaine user).

- "They say 'Beam Me Up, Scotty.' They say, 'I Need a Beam-Me-Up Scotty. You got some? You got some?' And the rock star say, "Looky here. Lookyhere. I got a dollar beamer. Dollar Beamer. Three dollar Beamer." — *St. Petersburg (Florida) Times*, p. 1F, 28th February 1988
- — Mike Haskins, *Drugs*, p. 281, 2003

beam me up, Scotty

used for a humorous suggestion that one would be better off somewhere else due to the lack of intelligent life here *US*

From the short-lived *Star Trek* television series (1966 – 1969) which has enjoyed an eternal after-life.

- Gary Shaw closed his eyes to keep his composure. Beam me up, Scotty, he thought. — Garry Bushell, *The Face*, p. 77, 2001

beams *noun*

the eyes *UK*

- Look at yer grid. Can't take yer friggin beams away from her, lar. — Niall Griffiths, *Kelly + Victor*, p. 147, 2002

beam up to Scotty; beam up; beam *verb*

to smoke crack cocaine and become cocaine-intoxicated *US, 1986*

From the pop phrase 'Beam me up, Scotty' used repeatedly on the first generation of *Star Trek* television programmes from 1966 to 69.

- — Terry Williams, *The Cocaine Kids*, p. 135, 1989
- On the street, they say when you're smoking crack, that you're beamin' up to Scotty, you're goin' to another world. — *New Jack City*, 1990
- "To buy crack and beam up," Kathy said. — Elmore Leonard, *Maximum Bob*, p. 232, 1991
- — Terry Williams, *Crackhouse*, p. 146, 1992
- [H]ospital personnel struggling to subdue someone "beaming up to Scotty". — Nelson George, *Hip Hop America*, p. 39, 1998

beamy *adjective*

wide *US*

Originally 'broad in the beam', then shortened and applied to a ship's width, and then by extension to other objects and to people, especially those wide in the seat.

- You couldn't possibly be a tadpole – your tail's too beamy. — Willie Fennell, *Dexter Gets The Point*, p. 86, 1961
- — John Gould, *Maine Lingo*, p. 9, 1975

bean *noun*

1 anything at all; very little *US, 1833*

- And another thing – the race made me feel inferior, started me thinking that maybe I wasn't worth beans as a musician or any kind of artist, in spite of all my big ideas. — Mezz Mezzrow, *Really the Blues*, p. 239, 1946
- — *Raging Bull*, 1980
- He's makin' beans compared to what he should be makin'. — *Raging Bull*, 1980
- I had nothing. Not a fuckin' bean[.] — Shaun Ryder, *Shaun Ryder... in His Own Words*, 1996

2 a dollar *US, 1902*

- And I want four hundred beans for the Dinch and I want it soon. — George Mandel, *Flee the Angry Strangers*, p. 269, 1952
- In three weeks after they showed I got my vines out of hock and was doing about fifteen beans a day. — Babs Gonzales, *Movin' On Down De Line*, p. 6, 1975
- Pals of mine at the Ventura courthouse said he logged twenty-one hundred sixty-six beans of the ransom money into the evidence locker. — James Ellroy, *Hollywood Nocturnes*, p. 187, 1994

3 a coin *UK, 1799*

- — Lou Shelly, *Hepcats Jive Talk Dictionary*, p. 7, 1945

4 in American casinos, a $1 betting chip *US*

- — Albert H. Morehead, *The Complete Guide to Winning Poker*, p. 256, 1967
- — Steve Kuriscak, *Casino Talk*, p. 3, 1985

5 a man, a fellow, especially as a form of address *UK, 1917*

Often embellished to 'old bean'.

- Donny old bean! What a nite. Michelle J gave me a gobble. Details later. — Christopher Brookmyre, *The Sacred Art of Stealing*, p. 121, 2002

6 a Mexican, Mexican-American or Latin American *US, 1949*

- — *Maledicta*, p. 151, Summer and Winter 1978: 'How to hate thy neighbor: a guide to racist maledicta'

7 a capsule or tablet of Benzedrine™ (amphetamine sulphate), a central nervous system stimulant *US, 1967*

- After a particularly lackluster effort, I asked a friend of the Cal team what happened. "Oh, it was simple. We just ran out of beans (amphetamines)." — *San Francisco Chronicle*, p. 57, 23rd September 1971
- I ran down the pill man and bought out his supply of beans. — Donald Goines, *Whoreson*, p. 200, 1972

- One game owner I knew goes through a daily ritual of passing out a BEAN to each of his agents before they start work[.] —Gene Sorrows, *All About Carnivals*, p. 10, 1985

8 a capsule of a central nervous system depressant *UK*
- —Mike Haskins, *Drugs*, p. 282, 2003

9 a capsule of MDMA, the recreational drug best known as ecstasy *US*
- —Connie Eble (Editor), *UNC-CH Campus Slang*, p. 1, Spring 2000
- —Don R. McCreary (Editor), *Dawg Speak*, 2001
- Baldness and E[.] Are beans to blame for losing your barnet [hair]? —*Mixmag*, p. 3, April 2003

10 the head *US, 1905*
- [T]heir well-educated little beans[.] —Lester Bangs, *Psychotic Reactions and Carburetor Dung*, p. 42, 1970

11 the hymen *US*
- —Hyman E. Goldin et al., *Dictionary of American Underworld Lingo*, p. 24, 1950

12 the penis *US*
- —Dale Gordon, *The Dominion Sex Dictionary*, p. 27, 1967

13 the clitoris *UK*
- The scenes with her flicking her bean [masturbating] are fucking good. —Kevin Sampson, *Outlaws*, p. 228, 2001

Bean *nickname*

Coleman Hawkins, jazz tenor saxophonist (1901–69) *US*
A signature tune of the Coleman Hawkins Orchestra was his 1940 composition 'Bouncing With Bean'.
- — Coleman Hawkins Orchestra, *Bouncing With Bean*, 1940

bean *verb*

to hit someone on the head *US, 1910*
- I have always felt confident that a [Ronald] Searle girl might bean you with an axe, but never with the back of a hockey stick. —Siriol Hugh-Jones, *The St. Trinian's Story*, p. 23, 1959

bean book *noun*

a worker's book of meal coupons *US*
- —Jerry Robertson, *Oil Slanguage*, p. 96, 1954

bean-choker *noun*

a Mexican or Mexican-American *US*
- —Edith A. Folb, *runnin' down some lines*, p. 229, 1980

bean chute; bean slot *noun*

the opening in a solid prison cell door through which food is passed to the prisoner within *US*
- —Ethan Hilderbrant, *Prison Slang*, p. 11, 1998

bean-counter *noun*

an accountant *US, 1975*
- Bennett calls the culprits accountants. Some call them numbers crunchers. I call them bean counters. —*USA Today*, p. 11A, 5th January 1990
- SEAL TEam Six trained harder than any unit had ever trained before, waiting for the opportunity to show the skeptical bureaucrat-sailors and dip-dunk bean-counters prevalent in Washington that it was possible for the U.S. Navy to fight back effectively against terrorists. —Richard Marcinko with John Weisman, *Rogue Warrior*, p. 5, 1992

bean-eater *noun*

1 a Mexican, Mexican-American or Latin-American *US, 1919*
- —*Maledicta*, p. 151, Summer and Winter 1978: 'How to hate thy neighbor: a guide to racist maledicta'

2 an Argentinian *UK*
- "Argies" and "bean-eaters" have been derisive nicknames for the enemy [Argentinians], on the long voyage south. —*The Guardian*, 2nd July 1982

beaned up *adjective*

under the influence of Benzedrine™ (amphetamine sulphate), a central nervous system stimulant *US*
- —Montie Tak, *Truck Talk*, p. 8, 1971

beaner *noun*

1 a Mexican or Mexican-American *US, 1965*
Derogatory, from the association of beans with the Mexican diet.
- Shit, it's not beaner junk? —Donald Goines, *Kenyatta's Last Hit*, p. 105, 1975
- —*Maledicta*, p. 151, Summer and Winter 1978: 'How to hate thy neighbor: a guide to racist maledicta'
- I mean, here you go around apologizing to everybody cause you got a name like a beaner, and cause you're dark enough to pass for one. —Joseph Wambaugh, *The Delta Star*, p. 25, 1983
- When he made the canteen cart, the beaners ripped off his zuuzuus and whamwhams. —Seth Morgan, *Homeboy*, p. 152, 1990
- "Joey, accidents happen," Tommy pleaded. "People get hit by fallin[g] safes ... a car fulla beaners runs a light and whammo, you got avocad[o] salad." —Stephen Cannell, *King Con*, p. 94, 1997
- She believed he looked for things that would piss him off so he coul[d] pick a fight. Like being called a "beaner" when they were in high school. —Elmore Leonard, *Be Cool*, p. 79, 1999

2 in the universe created by the Firesign Theatre (and accepte[d] by the late 1960s popular culture), one of the five lifestyles o[f] man, characterised by an obsession with colour televisions and rubbish piled up outside homes *US*
Described in Firesign Theater's 'Big Book of Plays'.

beanery *noun*

a low-cost, low-quality restaurant *US, 1887*
- Worked as a waitress in a beanery to keep body and soul together. —Mezz Mezzrow, *Really the Blues*, p. 88, 1946
- When he got his discharge papers he made tracks for Laguna Beach, where he landed a job as a carhop in a drive-in beanery. —Bernard Wolfe, *The Late Risers*, p. 159, 1954

bean feast *noun*

any form of festive occasion or jollification *UK, 1805*
Originally an annual feast given by employers.

bean-flicker *noun*

a lesbian *UK*
A reference to clitoral stimulation.
- —Simon Gage, *Queer*, p. 61, 2002

bean head *noun*

an amphetamine addict *US*
- —Jay Robert Nash, *Dictionary of Crime*, p. 22, 1992

bean house bull *noun*

gossip or tall tales told at a truck stop *US*
- — "Slingo", *The Official CB Slang Dictionary Handbook*, p. 5, 1976

beanie *noun*

1 in Vietnam, a member of the US Special Forces *US*
A shortened form of 'Green Beanies', itself word play based on 'Green Berets'.
- —Linda Reinberg, *In the Field*, p. 19, 1991

2 a police nightstick *US, 1952*
- —J. E. Lighter, *Historical Dictionary of American Slang, Volume 1*, p. 113, 1994

3 breaking and entering *CANADA*
A pronunciation of the common **B AND E**.
- —Lewis Poteet, *Cop Talk*, p. 9, 2000

4 an attractive girl *UK*
Perhaps as an allusion to Beanie Babies™ dolls.
- —Susie Dent, *Larpers and Shroomers*, p. 71, 2004

beanie light *noun*

a flashing, rotating light on an emergency vehicle *US*
- —*American Speech*, p. 202, Fall 1969: 'Truck driver's jargon'

beanies *noun*

tablets of any prescription drug taken recreationally, especially when the appearance resembles a kind of bean *UK*
- Man, we were amped to the max on those Glaxo Wellcome beanies. —Steve Beard, *The Last Good War [britpulp]*, p. 348, 1999

beanies and weenies *noun*

c-rations of hot dogs with beans *US*
Vietnam war usage.
- —Gregory Clark, *Words of the Vietnam War*, p. 52, 1990

bean juice *noun*

tomato sauce that canned baked beans are preserved in, and served with *UK*
- I've got bean juice on my chop now. You've got bean juice on your beard. —Caroline Aherne and Craig Cash, *The Royle Family*, 1999

beanmobile *noun*

a car embellished with bright colours, chrome and other accessories associated with Mexican-American car enthusiasts *US*
- I ditched the bean-mobile at the Ford lot and dropped the keys and repo order with the sales manger. —James Ellroy, *Brown's Requiem*, p. 16, 1981

beano *noun*

1 a Mexican, Mexican-American or Latin American *US*
- —*Maledicta*, p. 151, Summer and Winter 1978: 'How to hate thy neighbor: a guide to racist maledicta'

2 a meal; a feast *UK, 1914*

- —Lance Corporal Cobber, *The Anzac Pilgrim's Progress*, p. 83, 1915
- —Gavin Casey, *It's Harder for Girls*, p. 168, 1941
- You wouldn't have any doubts about an opinion if you'd seen the mess I had to clean up here after Sadie's beano. —Norman Lindsay, *Dust or Polish?*, p. 140, 1950
- [A] coach beano to Southend. —Brian McDonald, *Elephant Boys*, p. 224, 2000

bean oil *noun*

in motor racing, Castrol R^{TM} oil *US*

Castrol R^{TM} is made from castor bean oil.

- —Lewis Poteet, *Car & Motorcyle Slang*, p. 25, 1992

bean patch *nickname*

during the Korean war, an assembly area on the northern outskirts of Masan, a seaport about 40 miles west of Pusan *US*

- The 1st Marine Brigade moved its headquarters to a new bivouac area near Masan that came to be known in marine lore as the Bean Patch. The area in calmer times had been exactly that. —Joseph C. Goulden, *Korea*, p. 182, 1982

beanpole *noun*

a tall, thin person *US, 1837*

- Which is more beautiful, this expert asks – a bean pole or a woman? —*San Francisco Chronicle, This Week*, p. 12, 4th January 1953
- Pat Marichal – dark-skinned Paraguayan beanpole with a stark resemblance to the morgue pic of Chief Joe Running Car. —James Ellroy, *Hollywood Nocturnes*, p. 100, 1994
- One of the two men, a great tall beanpole, looked as if a giant had pressed his face flat with his thumb. —Cornelia Funke (translated by Anthea Bell), *Inkheart*, p. 154, 2003

bean queen *noun*

a homosexual who prefers Latin Americans as sexual partners but is not Latin American themselves *US*

- —H. Max, *Gay (S)language*, p. 4, 1988

bean rag *noun*

a red flag raised on a ship during mealtime *US*

- —Harold Wentworth and Stuart Berg Flexner, *Dictionary of American Slang*, p. 24, 1960

beans *noun*

1 sexual satisfaction *UK*

A meal that 'fills you up'.

- I told him I's givin' her beans before him so he calls me a cunt an' we had a scrap. —Nick Barlay, *Curvy Lovebox*, p. 118, 1997

2 a meal *US, 1942*

Coined in World War 2, still popular in Vietnam.

- —Linda Reinberg, *In the Field*, p. 19, 1991

3 the lunch break during a working day *US*

- —Norman Carlisle, *The Modern Wonder Book of Trains and Railroading*, p. 259, 1946

4 crack cocaine *UK*

- —Mike Haskins, *Drugs*, p. 281, 2003

5 horsepower *US*

- —John Lawlor, *How to Talk Car*, p. 17, 1965

6 a small amount of money; money *UK, 1893*

From earlier values of specific coins.

beans and baby dicks *noun*

in the Vietnam war, beans and hot dogs *US*

- —Linda Reinberg, *In the Field*, p. 19, 1991

beans and motherfuckers *noun*

in the Vietnam war, lima beans and ham, one of the least popular c-rations *US, 1990*

- —Linda Reinberg, *In the Field*, p. 19, 1991

bean sheet *noun*

on the railways, a time card or time sheet *US*

- —Ramon Adams, *The Language of the Railroader*, p. 12, 1977

bean slot *noun*

▷ **see: BEAN CHUTE**

bean-stealer *noun*

in the Royal Air Force, a married man who lives in the mess *UK, 1984*

bean store *noun*

a roadside restaurant or motorway truck stop restaurant *US*

- — "Slingo", *The Official CB Slang Dictionary Handbook*, p. 5, 1976

bean time *noun*

time for a meal *US*

- I had a young kid working with me a couple of years back, and the first day out we'd put in a pretty good mornin', so along about bean time we found us a shade tree to sit under while we had lunch. —Ken Weaver, *Texas Crude*, p. 103, 1984

Beantown; Bean Town *nickname*

Boston, Massachusetts *US, 1901*

Because Boston is known for its baked beans.

- Beantown's No. 1 bachelor, youthful, handsome Nathaniel Saltonstall, has all of Boston society buzzing over the attention he's showering on Bobo Rockefeller. —*San Francisco Examiner*, p. 14, 24 November 1954
- —Montie Tak, *Truck Talk*, p. 9, 1971
- You think this is Bean Town? You think this is New York? You make a mness in Chicago, you clean it up with your tongue. —Robert Campbell, *Junkyard Dog*, p. 49, 1986
- Beantowns premier black-owned 24 hour hip-hop station, WBOT[.] —*The Source*, p. 243, March 2002

bean up *verb*

to take amphetamines *US*

- —*Verbatim*, p. 280, May 1976

bean wagon *noun*

a no-frills lunch counter *US*

- —Harold Wentworth and Stuart Berg Flexner, *Dictionary of American Slang*, p. 24, 1960

beany *noun*

a green polyster baseball cap issued to US soldiers since 1962, known officially as the Army Utility Cap *US*

- —Gregory Clark, *Words of the Vietnam War*, p. 48, 1990

bear *noun*

1 in the US, a motorway patrol officer or state trooper; a police officer in the UK *US, 1975*

Shortened from **SMOKEY THE BEAR**.

- But they's a roadblock up on the cloverleaf / And them bears is wall-to-wall[.] —C.W. McCall, *Convoy*, 1976
- —Connie Eble (Editor), *UNC-CH Campus Slang*, April 1977
- —Peter Chippindale, *The British CB Book*, p. 151, 1981
- No cops around. No bears in the woods from One-twenty-eight all the way the terminal. —George V. Higgins, *The Rat on Fire*, p. 105, 1981

2 a hairy and stocky man, of a type beloved by some homosexuals *US*

- —Kevin Dilallo, *The Unofficial Gay Manual*, p. 237, 1994
- For gay men, the Bear represents the next wave of gay masculinity after the Clone, one of queerdom's most enduring trends. —*Sydney Star Observer*, p. 44, 11th March 1994
- The bears are sweating in a huddle down by the Rembrandt, the chi-chi camp boys are flouncing petulantly up and down[.] —*Attitude*, p. 34, October 2003

3 a boisterous, rowdy or aggressive young man, especially in the context of heavy drinking *UK: SCOTLAND, 1985*

- He's no a bad guy, just a bit of a bear. —Michael Munro, *The Complete Patter*, 1996

4 a building-site or oil-rig worker *UK: SCOTLAND*

- Hes the kind of a manager that enjoys a crack with the bears after work. —Michael Munro, *The Complete Patter*, 1996

5 an unattractive woman *US*

- —Arnold Shaw, *Dictionary of American Pop/Rock*, p. 30, 1982

6 a cautious and conservative poker player *US*

- —George Percy, *The Language of Poker*, p. 8, 1988

7 a difficult task or situation *US*

- —Andy Anonymous, *A Basic Guide to Campusology*, p. 2, 1966

Bear *nickname*

US General H. Norman Schwarzkopf (b.1934), commander of the US forces during the Gulf war *US*

- —*American Speech*, p. 384, Winter 1991: 'Among the new words'

bear cage *noun*

a police station *US*

A logical extension of **BEAR** (the police).

- —*Complete CB Slang Dictionary*, 1976
- —Peter Chippindale, *The British CB Book*, p. 151, 1981

bear cat *noun*

on the railways, a demanding and disliked foreman *US*

- —Ramon Adams, *The Language of the Railroader*, p. 12, 1977

beard *noun*

1 a person used to mask the identity of the actual controlling agent; a person who escorts another to a social function in order to mask the identity of one or the other's lover or sexual orientation *US, 1956*
Originally from gambling, referring to a front for betting.
- "It's supposed to look like the girls are for the clients' entertainment, not his." "Who believes that?" "Not many. He also has a respectable friend he uses as a beard."—Robert Campell, *Junkyard Dog*, p. 147, 1986
- Use him as a beard is what Donny thought he'd do.—Dan Jenkins, *Dead Solid Perfect*, p. 101, 1986
- Maya, did you hear the latest medical report on Clinton's laryngitis? They say it's just an excuse to let Hillary make all the speeches, since all he is, is her beard anyway.—Joseph Wambaugh, *Finnegan's Week*, p. 110, 1993

2 in gambling, a person who bets for someone else, especially for a cheat *US*
- —Frank Garcia, *Marked Cards and Loaded Dice*, p. 250, 1962
- —Thomas L. Clark, *The Dictionary of Gambling and Gaming*, p. 15, 1987
- —Frank Scoblete, *Guerrilla Gambling*, p. 296, 1993

3 a broker who buys up stock quietly and secretly for bidders in a corporate takeover who hope to disguise their intentions *US*
- As one colleague explained about Ivan Boesky, the most closely watched of the arbitrageurs, "He likes a beard when he trades."—Kathleen Odean, *High Steppers, Fallen Angels, and Lollipops*, p. 107, 1988

4 an intellectual or academic *US, 1927*
Unkind if not derisive.
- Man, Dig This Jazz—*Washington Post*, 23rd April 1961
- —Clarence Major, *Dictionary of Afro-American Slang*, p. 24, 1970
- [H]e fills in his nice, right-on applications to get his few poxy grand from the queers and beards and Euro-commies.—James Hawes, *White Powder, Green Light*, p. 152, 2002

5 a male member of an Orthodox Jewish group *US, 1967*
- The beards are picketing the Russian Mission.—Charles Whited, *Chiodo*, p. 154, 1973

6 an 'older' surfer *US*
In the youth culture of surfing, 'old' is a relative term.
- —Trevor Cralle, *The Surfin'ary*, p. 9, 1991

beard *verb*

to serve as a beard for someone *US*
- Bloomquist writes like somebody who once bearded Tim Leary in a campus cocktail lounge and paid for all the drinks.—Hunter S. Thompson, *Fear and Loathing in Las Vegas*, p. 139, 1971

bearded clam *noun*

the vulva *US, 1965*
Combines **FISH** with visual imagery.
- —Dale Gordon, *The Dominion Sex Dictionary*, p. 27, 1967
- He gobbles one beaver and gets promoted. I've ate close to three hundred bearded clams in my time and never even got a commendation.—Joseph Wambaugh, *The Choirboys*, p. 22, 1975
- Our stylish lifesavers would head the queue in any gang-bang on the planet. They certainly notch up more than their fair share of bearded clams[.]— Barry Humphries, *The Traveller's Tool*, p. 13, 1985
- Another way to say "vagina" [...] Bearded clam[.]—Erica Orloff and JoAnn Baker, *Dirty Little Secrets*, p. 71, 2001
- You can't get no bearded clam with your oysters, no way!—Ben Elton, *High Society*, p. 119, 2002

bearded lady *noun*

the vulva *US*
- —Dale Gordon, *The Dominion Sex Dictionary*, p. 27, 1967

beardie; beardy *noun*

1 an act of rubbing a stubbly face against a smooth one *UK*
- —Michael Munro, *The Original Patter*, 1985

2 a bearded person *UK, 1941*

beardie-wierdie *noun*

a bearded person *UK: SCOTLAND*
Disparaging.
- The beardie-wierdie tapped the card laid out beside the board.—Ian Rankin, *The Falls*, p. 110, 2001

beard jammer *noun*

the manager of a brothel *US*
- —Joseph E. Ragen and Charles Finston, *Inside the World's Toughest Prison*, p. 790, 1962

beard man *noun*

a Rastafarian *JAMAICA, 1952*
- —F.G. Cassidy and R.B. LePage, *Dictionary of Jamaican English*, p. 33, 1967
- —Peter L. Patrick, *Some Recent Jamaican Creole Words*, 2003

beardsman *noun*

a Rastafarian with shaved or trimmed hair *JAMAICA, 1985*
- —Thomas H. Slone, *Rasta is Cuss*, p. 25, 2003

beard-stroking *noun*

serious consideration of something, deep thought *UK*
- No mean feat considering the amount of beard stroking involved.—Jeremy Blake, *kultureflash*, 12th March 2003

beard-stroking *adjective*

intellectual or boring or both *UK*
- Otherwise known as IDM or Intelligent Dance Music, which means that the usual audience is beard stroking rather than booty shaking.—*BBCi*, 6th July 2003

bear grease *noun*

in electric line work, any gel used as an electric contact aid *US*
- —A.B. Chance Co., *Lineman's Slang Dictionary*, p. 1, 1980

bearings *noun*

the stomach *AUSTRALIA, 1943*
Suggested derivations all seem based on the body as a machine. However, it is possible that this is from a sense of disorientation after vomiting, thus confusing the losing of the contents of your stomach with a loss of bearings.

▸ **too many bearings on it**

a situation too complicated to explain *CANADA*
This phrase uses a nautical term for location-finding, 'bearings' (i.e. from a compass), metaphorically.
- Why can't I help you shear the sheep this weekend? There are too many bearings on it to tell you about it.—Lewis Poteet, *oral citation from The South Shore Phrase Book*, p. 118, 1999

bearing up

used in response to a personal enquiry such as 'how are you?' or 'how's things?' *UK, 1984*

bear insurance *noun*

a gun, the bigger the better the insurance *US*
- —Robert O. Bowen, *An Alaskan Dictionary*, p. 8, 1965

bear in the air *noun*

a police helicopter *US*
This travelled from citizens' band radio slang into a still-surviving, wider usage.
- Yeah, them smokey's thick as a bugs on a bumper / They even had a bear in the air[.]—C.W. McCall, *Convoy*, 1976

bearish *adjective*

(of a man) large and hairy *AUSTRALIA*
- Hay recalls that he first noticed the emerging popularity of his bearish brothers 'in the early '80s, when gay men took out the hankies from their pockets and put little bears in.'—*Sydney Star Observer*, p. 44, 11th March 1994

bear joint *noun*

in a carnival, a game in which stuffed teddy bears are the prize *US*
- —*American Speech*, p. 308–309, December 1960: 'Carnival talk'

bear meat *noun*

a speeding vehicle without the benefit of citizens' band radio communications *US*
Easy prey for **BEAR** (the police).
- —*Complete CB Slang Dictionary*, 1976
- —Peter Chippindale, *The British CB Book*, p. 151, 1981

bear paw *noun*

1 round-footed snowshoes worn while doing chores *US*
- —Mike Doogan, *How to Speak Alaskan*, p. 7, 1993

2 the badge necessary to get into the inner area of the 2002 G8 summit meeting in Alberta *CANADA*
- The cryptic badge to get into the "red red zone" has been dubbed the Bear Paw. That's because it has three sketches of paw prints on it (one made out of tacky maple leaves, the others resembling real paws. But the [four-toed] prints look like coyotes'.—*Toronto Globe and Mail*, p. A4, 26th June 2002

bear pit *noun*

an auditorium, or other arena, peopled with a rowdy, challenging, even confrontational audience *UK*
From the late night audiences at the Edinburgh Festival's Fringe Club.

• Ah wid gie that place a bye on a Friday night if ye're no inty bearpits. —Michael Munro, *The Complete Patter*, 1996

bear's paw *noun*
a saw *UK, 1934*
Rhyming slang. Noted by Ray Puxley in 1992 as 'a seldom heard term for a carpenter's tool'.

bear trap *noun*
1 in the Canadian Navy, a helicopter haul-down and securing device *CANADA*
• "Beartrap" is a device that enables a helicopter to land safely on a warship's small flight deck, even in heavy seas. It was first installed when the Royal Canadian Navy acquired the Sea King helicopter in 1962–63. —Tom Langeste, *Words on the Wing*, p. 23, 1995
2 the clutch on a Laverda motorcyle *US*
Named after the amount of effort required to pull the clutch lever in.
• —Lewis Poteet, *Car & Motorcyle Slang*, 1992
3 in television and film making, a strong clamp used for attaching lights to rigging *US*
• —Ira Konigsberg, *The Complete Film Dictionary*, p. 26, 1987
4 a police radar-trap for speeding motorists *US*
• —*Complete CB Slang Dictionary*, 1976
• —Peter Chippindale, *The British CB Book*, p. 151, 1981

Bear Whiz Beer *noun*
an inferior beer *US*
A popular beverage in Firesign Theater skits; its motto is the stunning 'It's in the water! That's why it's yellow!'.

beast *noun*
1 a very unattractive woman, especially if sexually proactive *US, 1942*
• Give us the fucking beasts, la, give us the dogs any fucking time. —Kevin Sampson, *Clubland*, p. 85, 2002
2 a sexually available female *US*
• —*American Speech*, p. 302, December 1955: 'Wayne University slang'
3 in prison, a sex offender, a convicted paedophile *UK*
• —Angela Devlin, *Prison Patter*, p. 23, 1996
4 anything excellent *UK*
• [I]'m say that that was the fuckin' best best beast of a monster party[.] —Mike Benson, *Room full of Angels (Disco Biscuits)*, p. 25, 1996
• —Vann Wesson, *Generation X Field Guide and Lexicon*, p. 16, 1997
5 the penis *UK*
• [H]e iz very mesculin [masculine] and iz got a beast dat iz well in hadvance of hiz age. —Sacha Baron-Cohen, *Da Gospel According to Ali G*, 2001
6 a white person; a white US soldier in Vietnam *US*
Used by US soldiers of colour in Vietnam.
• —Linda Reinberg, *In the Field*, p. 19, 1991
7 heroin; heroin addiction *US, 1958*
• —Edward R. Bloomquist, *Marijuana*, p. 332, 1971
• As long as Mable his whore was able / To satisfy his beast. —Dennis Wepman et al., *The Life*, p. 98, 1976
• —Angela Devlin, *Prison Patter*, p. 26, 1996
• —Robert Ashton, *This Is Heroin*, p. 205, 2002
8 LSD *US, 1967*
• —Richard A. Spears, *The Slang and Jargon of Drugs and Drink*, p. 32, 1986
• —Mike Haskins, *Drugs*, p. 285, 2003
9 Milwaukee's Best™, an inexpensive beer favoured by cash-strapped youth *US*
Appropriately, Milwaukee's Best Light is simply 'Beast Light'.
• —Connie Eble (Editor), *UNC-CH Campus Slang*, p. 1, Fall 1987
10 a large, fast car *US, 1951*
• —Edd Byrnes, *Way Out with Kookie*, 1959
• —John Lawlor, *How to Talk Car*, p. 17, 1965
11 a car with a raised front end *US*
• —Edith A. Folb, *runnin' down some lines*, p. 254, 1980
12 an expensive and powerful citizens' band radio *US*
• —Elementary Electronics, *Dictionary of CB Lingo*, p. 49, 1976

▸ **as a beast**
used as an intensifier *US*
• —Connie Eble (Editor), *UNC-CH Campus Slang*, p. 1, November 2003

▸ **the beast**
the police; any figure of authority or oppression *UK*
West Indian, hence UK black.
• Wooh wooh, that's sound of da police / Wooh wooh, that's sound o' the beast —KRS-One *Sound of Da Police*, 1993
• [T]he beast had come knocking[.] —Diran Adebayo, *My Once Upon A Time*, p. 45, 2000

beast *verb*
to have anal sex *UK*
• "What you been up to then, Lisa?" "Well, you know, getting beasted by Jason. What with him being inside for so long, one of the problems is they always want to do it up the arse." —Jeff Pope and Terry Winsor, *Essex Boys*, 1999

▸ **get beasted in**
to eat with great enthusiasm *UK: SCOTLAND, 1985*
• Nothing wrong wi her appetite anyway, by the way she got beasted inty that lasagne. —Michael Munro, *The Complete Patter*, 1996

beast about *verb*
to treat someone with a harsh physicality *UK*
• They'd beast about in the gym but I found it enjoyable[.] —Andy McNab, *Immediate Action*, p. 85, 1995

beastbwai; beast boy *noun*
the police; any figure of authority or oppression *UK*
Combines **THE BEAST** (the police, etc.) with **BWAI** (boy, a youth in UK black/West Indian gang culture).
• Not even beastbwai can test my man. 'Cause my man's coming like the Moss Side Ninja – dem cyaan catch him! —Karline Smith, *Moss Side Massive*, p. 12, 1994

beastie *noun*
1 used as an endearing form of 'beast'; also, in a jocular sense, of an insect *UK, 1864*
From Scottish.
• We weren't acclimatized yet, and were covered in lumps and bumps where the beasties had got in. —Andy McNab, *Immediate Action*, p. 93, 1995
2 an attractive woman *UK*
Objectifying a woman as an animal, much the same as 'filly'.
• A petty officer of my acquaintance, gazing admiringly at a retreating beauty, could be heard muttering "Oh, you gorgeous, long-leggedy beastie!" —*Beale*, 1984

beasting *noun*
from a male perspective, an act of sexual intercourse *UK*
Possibly inspired by the **BEAST WITH TWO BACKS**.
• [T]onight I'm planning to give her a beasting she won't forget. —Colin Butts, *Is Harry Still on the Boat?*, p. 157, 2003

beastly *adjective*
1 bad (to whatever degree), unpleasant, horrid *UK*
Usage considered to be dated, childish or upper-class; summoning images of the iconic public schoolboy and 'fat owl of the remove', Billy Bunter, written by Frank Richards (a nom de plume of Charles Hamilton and at least three other writers), who first appeared in *The Magnet* in 1908, continuing until World War 2, then reappearing in new comic titles and on television through the 1950s into the 60s and is still in print and on talking book; for which reasons, if no other, 'beastly' remains in ironic currency.
• Tell me, sergeant, is it Oxford or Cambridge you're going to when you've finally discharged your beastly National Service obligations? —Graeme Kent, *The Queen's Corporal [Six Granada Plays]*, p. 87, 1959
2 excellent *US*
• —Lavada Durst, *The Jives of Dr. Hepcat*, p. 11, 1953
3 excessive *US*
• —Connie Eble (Editor), *UNC-CH Campus Slang*, p. 1, Spring 2000

beastly *adverb*
badly, unpleasantly, very, excessively *UK, 1844*
Stereotypically upper-class.

beast with two backs *noun*
vaginal, face-to-face sexual intercourse between a heterosexual couple; sex between two people *UK, 1604*
From Shakespeare.
• Hey you!! Did you make the beast with two backs with my little ewe? —Barry Humphries, *The Wonderful World of Barry McKenzie*, p. 13, 1968
• Again the beast with two backs is attempted, this time with her in the ascendant. —Barry Oakley, *A Salute to the Great McCarthy*, p. 151, 1970

- But here, Janet will be dating Sue who's romanced Cathy who's had a fling with Trish who's had a grope with Janet who's done the beast with two backs with Cathy[.] — *Kink*, p. 56, 1993
- I figured they weren't on for a threesome so I climbed up to Scarey Bill's room but could hear the beast with two backs at work in there too. — John Birmingham, *He Died With a Felafel in his Hand*, p. 163, 1994

beasty *noun*

a repulsive, disgusting person *US*

- "Oh, Clay, you're such a beasty," she giggles. — Bret Easton Ellis, *Less Than Zero*, p. 16, 1985

beasty *adjective*

repulsive, disgusting *US*

- Like we went to Dupars and there were all these beasty seventh grade nerds with nine million zits apiece. — Mary Corey and Victoria Westermark, *Fer Shurr! How to be a Valley Girl*, 1982

beat *noun*

1 a regular route or locale (of a prostitute or police officer) *UK, 1721*

- All right. Kill each other! But not on my beat. — Stephen Sondheim, *West Side Story*, p. 2, 1957
- — Peter Laurie, *Scotland Yard*, p. 320, 1970
- Then later, on the beat, he said it was Colin who did it. — Lanre Fehintola, *Charlie Says...*, p. 48, 2000

2 a member of the 1950s youth counterculture *US*

- But insofar as they speak of themselves generically and are forced to choose among evils, they prefer the word "beat." — *Dissent*, p. 339, Summer 1961
- Beats avoid work. — Ned Polsky, *Hustlers, Beats, and Others*, p. 159, 1967

3 in horse racing, an unfortunate defeat *US*

- As when a horse is caught in the last stride and a losing bettor moans, "What a tough beat!" — Tom Ainslie, *Ainslie's Complete Guide to Thoroughbred Racing*, p. 328, 1976

4 a crime which has not been solved *US*

- What the fuck do I care if this goes in as a solve or a beat? — Richard Price, *Clockers*, p. 449, 1992

5 in television and film making, the main storyline *US*

- — Ralph S. Singleton, *Filmaker's Dictionary*, p. 16, 1990

6 a car *US*

- — Marcus Hanna Boulware, *Jive and Slang of Students in Negro Colleges*, 1947

beat *verb*

1 to cheat, to swindle, to steal *US, 1849*

- It was early one morning / the temperature read about twenty below / I was on my way to the Union Station to beat some sucker for his dough. — Bruce Jackson, *Get Your Ass in the Water and Swim Like Me*, p. 66, 1964
- I didn't want to put my money in his hand and then get beat for it[.] — James Mills, *The Panic in Needle Park*, p. 28, 1966
- I knew the cab driver had beat me for my bread but there was no use crying, it was gone. — Babs Gonzales, *I Paid My Dues*, p. 24, 1967
- He beat me for two-and-a-half points of gross, that's what he did! — Terry Southern, *Blue Movie*, p. 72, 1970
- I also looked for righteous spots where I could beat a car. — A.S. Jackson, *Gentleman Pimp*, 1973
- He's still going around checking to see if they beat him out of anything. — Edwin Torres, *Carlito's Way*, p. 52, 1975
- They also beat me for a ten dollar bill. — Herbert Huncke, *The Evening Sun Turned Crimson*, p. 177, 1980
- We was over in New York and we got beat on some dope. — Richard Price, *Clockers*, p. 461, 1992

2 to defy your understanding *UK, 1882*

- It beats me why only an Olympic Games can rejuvenate school sports, fitness, slums, London transport etcetera. — *The Guardian*, 28th May 2004

▸ **beat about the bush; beat around the bush**

1 (of a female) to masturbate *UK*

Wordplay on 'beat' (used in many terms of male masturbation) and **BUSH** (the pubic hair), in some way reversing the familiar meaning of 'beat around the bush' (to avoid coming to a point).

- Forgive me. I probably don't have time to beat about your bush. — Terry Victor, *Return of the Menu Monster*, 1991
- Another way to say "the girl is masturbating" [...] Beating around the bush[.] — Erica Orloff and JoAnn Baker, *Dirty Little Secrets*, p. 67, 2001

2 to avoid coming to the point of a discussion *UK*

A term that has its origin in the hunting of birds.

- I gave it to him straight. No fucking beating about the bush. — Dean Cavanagh, *Mile High Meltdown (Disco Biscuits)*, p. 207, 1996

▸ **beat feet**

to leave *US, 1944*

- So he snags his blunderbuss, calls his bonecruncher, blows the barracks and beats feet for the timber. — Haenigsen, *Jive's Like That*, 1947
- — Collin Baker et al., *College Undergraduate Slang Study Conducted at Brown University*, p. 78, 1968
- — Gregory Newbold, *The Big Huey*, p. 244, 1982
- Well, shit, fella, you might as well keep fuckin' beatin' feet, as they say. — Larry Heinemann, *Paco's Story*, p. 64, 1986
- "I'll be glad when all these sailboat tourists beat feet," Fortney said. — Joseph Wambaugh, *Floaters*, p. 178, 1996

▸ **beat hollow**

to outdo someone utterly and completely *BARBADOS*

- — Richard Allsopp, *Dictionary of Caribbean English Usage*, p. 88, 1996

▸ **beat it**

1 to leave quickly *US, 1878*

- I sneaked into the house and stole my sister's Hudson-seal fur coat out of the closet, then I beat it down to a whorehouse and sold it to a madam for $150. — Mezz Mezzrow, *Really the Blues*, p. 54, 1946
- He forgot all about the money, and beat it. — Jim Thompson, *The Kill-Off*, p. 132, 1957

2 (of a male) to masturbate *US*

- The plane started spinning around, going out of control. So my cousin decides it's all over, and he whips it out and starts beating it right there. — *Mallrats*, 1995

▸ **beat off with a stick**

to get more than enough sexual offers *AUSTRALIA*

- Chances of pulling a root: James Bond has to beat them off with a shitty stick, so we reckon there'll be no worries in that department. — *People*, p. 14, 5th July 1999

▸ **beat the band**

to surpass everything *US, 1897*

▸ **beat the board**

in poker, to hold the best hand showing *US*

- — Irwin Steig, *Common Sense in Poker*, p. 181, 1963

▸ **beat the bushes**

1 in horse racing, to race a horse in minor circuits, where the horse can be a big fish in a little pond *US*

- — David W. Maurer, *Argot of the Racetrack*, p. 13, 1951

2 to drive in the lead position of a group of trucks travelling together on a motorway *US*

- — "Slingo", *The Official CB Slang Dictionary Handbook*, p. 6, 1976

▸ **beat the clock**

1 to finish a task before the prescribed time *UK, 1961*

In the UK orginally military, perhaps from an American parlour game. From the late 1950s–60s, it was used as the title of a gameshow segment in the television variety programme *Saturday Night at the London Palladium*.

2 to return alive from an SAS mission *UK*

- The names of those [SAS men] killed in action are incsribed on the clock tower at the SAS barracks in Hereford. [They] talk of coming back alive from a particular mission as "beating the clock". — *Harper & Queens*, November 1980

▸ **beat the cotton**

to soak and then pound used cottons, used to strain drug doses, in an attempt to leach out enough heroin for another dose *US*

- — Geoffrey Froner, *Digging for Diamonds*, p. 8, 1989

▸ **beat the Dutch**

to astonish or frustrate someone *US, 1775*

- — Frederic G. Cassidy, *Dictionary of American Regional English*, p. 192, 1985

▸ **beat the eightball**

to use heroin *US*

- — Eugene Landy, *The Underground Dictionary*, p. 31, 1971

▸ **beat the favorite**

in horse racing, to place a small bet on a horse with long odds to win rather than betting on the horse favoured to win *US*

- — David W. Maurer, *Argot of the Racetrack*, p. 13, 1951

▸ **beat the gun**

(of an engaged couple) to have sex, especially if the fiancée falls pregnant *AUSTRALIA, 1984*

The sporting imagery of being under starter's orders.

▸ **beat the man**
to sleep *US*
Prison usage suggesting that in sleep one escapes domination by prison authorities.
• —Charles Shafer, *Folk Speech in Texas Prisons*, p. 197, 1990

▸ **beat the priest and take his gown; beat the priest**
to do that which you should not do in an open, notorious and brazen fashion *GRENADA, 1978*
• —Richard Allsopp, *Dictionary of Caribbean English Usage*, p. 88, 1996

▸ **beat the pup**
(of a male) to masturbate *US*
• —Hyman E. Goldin et al., *Dictionary of American Underworld Lingo*, p. 25, 1950

▸ **beat the rap**
to withstand harsh interrogation *UK*
• —Angela Devlin, *Prison Patter*, p. 26, 1996

▸ **beat the snot out of**
to thrash someone soundly, to beat someone up *US*
• [W]e will get together and beat the snot out of that guy over there. —Frank Zappa, *The Real Frank Zappa Book*, p. 230, 1989

▸ **beat the starter**
(of an engaged couple) to have sex, especially if the fiancée falls pregnant *UK, 1984*
Sporting imagery, racing ahead while still under starter's orders.

▸ **beat your baloney**
(of a male) to masturbate *US*
• One maverick among those polled got his kicks beating his baloney during TV commercials. —*Screw*, 10th November 1969

▸ **beat your bishop**
(of a male) to masturbate *US, 1916*
• In fact you can sit here and rest or beat your bishop while I go ramblin around there, I like to ramble by myself. —Jack Kerouac, *The Dharma Bums*, p. 53, 1958

▸ **beat your chops; beat up your chops**
to talk *US*
• Herbie was beating up his chops about Lend-Lease to Russian when I walked up. —Chester Himes, *If He Hollers Let Him Go*, p. 112, 1945
• When I stood around outside the Pekin, beating up my chops with Big Buster, and he put his arm around my shoulder in a friendly way[.] —Mezz Mezzrow, *Really the Blues*, p. 48, 1946
• —Sherman Louis Sergel, *The Language of Show Biz*, p. 19, 1973

▸ **beat your face**
to perform push-ups *US*
• —*Seattle Times*, p. A9, 12th April 1998

▸ **beat your gums; beat up your gums**
to talk without purpose or without effect *US, 1945*
• "Never mind, I am who I am. Just don't beat up your gums at me," I said, throwing him a newly acquired phrase. —Ralph Ellison, *Invisible Man*, p. 269, 1947
• On the way to Biff's, Betsy, dressed in a knocked-out strapless, bloobers more out than in, kept beating her gums. —Bernard Wolfe, *The Late Risers*, p. 157, 1954

▸ **beat your meat; beat the meat**
(of a male) to masturbate *US, 1936*
• Suppose you just sit down and beat your meat if you're getting anxious. —Norman Mailer, *The Naked and the Dead*, p. 124, 1948
• The young man held his fist up and agitated it meaningfully, yet with such a disinterested air that his gesture – ordinarily such a smutty one – seemed quite abstract and inoffensive. "You know – onanism – 'beating your meat,'" he explained. —Terry Southern, *Candy*, p. 74, 1958
• —Donald Webster Cory and John P. LeRoy, *The Homosexual and His Society*, p. 261, 1963: 'A lexicon of homosexual slang'
• I have affairs, Arn, and I beat my meat. —Philip Roth, *Portnoy's Complaint*, p. 197, 1969
• Beating your meat is not a substitute for fucking. —*Screw*, p. 11, 1st September 1969
• You talking like I lost something real sweet / But I got more kick out of beating my meat. —Dennis Wepman et al., *The Life*, p. 143, 1976
• I'm beating my meat with one hand and writing with the other. —Anka Radakovich, *The Wild Girls Club*, p. 223, 1994
• [S]tanding over the toilet bowl and beating my meat. —Howard Stern, *Miss America*, p. 154, 1995
• I think Leroy thinks about fay chicks too, when he beats his meat. —Clarence Major, *All-Night Visitors*, p. 25, 1998
• You've basically been in the bushes beating your meat your whole life. —*The Guru*, 2002

▸ **beat yourself up**
to be harshly self-critical, to struggle with your conscience *UK*
• Greg had been beating himself up about it more than he thought he would. —Colin Butts, *Is Harry Still on the Boat?*, p. 243, 2003

▸ **can't beat it in the Navy**
used for expressing admiration of a boat-handling job *CANADA*
Among Canadian east coast fishermen, with the tradition of navy techniques very strong, this term expresses high praise.
• You couldn't have beaten it in the Navy. He did a neat job of manoeuvering and docking the boat. —Joshua Slocum, *Sailing Alone Around the World*, 1908

beat *adjective*
1 world-weary, spiritual, jaded, intellectual *US, 1947*
• You know, everyone I know is kind of furtive, kind of beat. —John Clellon Holmes, *Go*, p. 38, 1952
• The beatest characters in the country swarmed on the sidewalk[.] —Jack Kerouac, *On the Road*, p. 85, 1957
• If while living in the Honor Unit you get into a "beef" which results in action against you by the disciplinary committee, one of the certain penalties is that you are immediately kickied out of No. 5 Building. —Eldridge Cleaver, *Soul on Ice*, p. 52, 1968
• If all the unemployed had followed the lead of the beatniks, Moloch would gladly have legalized the use of euphoric drugs and marijuana, passed out free jazz albums and sleeping bags, to all those willing to sign affidavits promising to remain "beat." —Eldridge Cleaver, *Soul on Ice*, p. 72, 1968

2 utterly tired *UK, 1821*
• Mother heard you were feeling pretty beat. —Steve Allen, *Bop Fables*, p. 42, 1955

beat artist *noun*
a swindler *US*
• One response to freebase buyers' increasing demand for purer and purer cocaine was a proliferation of dealers and con men ("beat artists") purporting to sell the real thing. —Terry Williams, *The Cocaine Kids*, p. 40, 1989

beat bag *noun*
a bag of drugs that is heavily adulterated or is completely counterfeit *US*
• —*Washington Post*, p. C5, 7th November 1993

beatdown *noun*
a physical beating; hence figuratively, a defeat *US*
• The stupid punk got himself a beat down. —*A2Z*, p. 6, 1995
• And the competition has come and caught beatdowns[.] —*The Source*, p. 36, March 2002

beater *noun*
1 an older car, usually not in good condition, used for day-to-day driving *US*
• Paco hears them getting into Marty-boy's rusted-out beater of a Mustang[.] —Larry Heinemann, *Paco's Story*, p. 187, 1990
• —Judi Sanders, *Don't Dog by Do, Dude!*, p. 2, 1991
• —John Edwards, *Auto Dictionary*, p. 13, 1993
• Beano would mail the picture to the geezer next week with an inscription from Testaverde saying how much Vinnie missed his rusted-out beater, which had really been owned by an airport yellow cab company before Bob's paint shop had sprayed it green. —Stephen Cannell, *Big Con*, p. 31, 1997

2 a drumstick *BAHAMAS, 1975*
• —John A. Holm, *Dictionary of Bahamian English*, p. 14, 1982

beat for *adjective*
lacking *US*
• —Kenn "Naz" Young, *Naz's Underground Dictionary*, p. 14, 1973

beat generation *noun*
the alienated class of young Americans who came of age in the mid-1940s and then embraced an alternative lifestyle and values in the 1950s *US*
• It's time we thought about our material. Call them hipsters, the 'beat generation,' 'postwar kids,' or our own displaced person whatever you will. —John Clellon Holmes, *Letter to Jack Kerouac*, 28th April 1950

beating *noun*
a violent ache *BARBADOS*
• —Frank A. Collymore, *Barbadian Dialect*, p. 17, 1965

beat loot *noun*
a pittance; a small amount of money *US*
• —Kenn "Naz" Young, *Naz's Underground Dictionary*, p. 14, 1973

beatnik *noun*

a follower of the beat generation (avante garde 'visionaries, rebels and hipsters') derided and defined by stereotypical appearance (black beret for men, black tights for women) and lifestyle choices (Charlie Parker's jazz, marijuana, performance poetry, etc) *US*

Coined in 1958 (the first popular, non-Russian use of the suffix **-NIK**) by San Francisco newspaper columnist Herb Caen, extended from **BEAT** (a member of the 1950s youth counterculture), and a pun on the **FAR OUT** example of 'sputnik' (a Russian satellite launched in 1959).

- Beatniks happened elsewhere – even in Australia [...] The Beats showed it was possible, even glamorous, to throw the gauntlet at the lifestyle of IBM. —Richard Neville, *Play Power*, p. 23–24, 1970

beat off *verb*

(of a male) to masturbate *US, 1962*

- [T]hen there was only emptiness and the same sort of something-wasted feeling he'd had when he was his little brother's age and beat off in the bathroom. —Jess Mowry, *Way Past Cool*, p. 33, 1992
- He's still beating off. Still working it. —Peter Sotos, *Index*, p. 11, 1996
- Just as he'd begun to beat off, there was a knock on the bedroom door, which had no lock. —John Irving, *A Widow for a Year*, p. 50, 1998

beat out *verb*

to strip someone of their membership in a youth gang, accomplished by a ritualistic beating *US*

- —Mark S. Fleisher, *Beggars & Thieves*, p. 287, 1995

beat pad *noun*

an establishment where poor quality marijuana is sold *US*

- —Harold Wentworth and Stuart Berg Flexner, *Dictionary of American Slang*, p. 26, 1960

Beatrix Potter; Beatrix *noun*

an ugly woman *UK*

Possibly rhyming slang for **ROTTER** based on the name of author and illustrator Beatrix Potter (1866–1943).

- A bit of a Beatrix! —*www.LondonSlang.com*, June 2002

beat sheet *noun*

1 in television and film making, a short summary of a story *US*

- —Ralph S. Singleton, *Filmaker's Dictionary*, p. 16, 1990

2 a pornographic magazine *US*

- —Anna Scotti and Paul Young, *Buzzwords*, p. 14, 1997

Beattie and Babs *noun*

pubic lice, crab-lice *UK, 1960*

Rhyming slang for **CRABS** based on an early C20 music hall act who are, unfortunately, best remembered by this term.

beat-up *adjective*

shoddy, shabby, worn out *US*

- He'd light up and get real high and when he was groovy as a ten-cent movie he'd begin to play the blues on a beat-up guitar. —Mezz Mezzrow, *Really the Blues*, p. 51–52, 1946

beau *noun*

used as a term of address between young males *US*

- —*This Week Magazine, New York Herald Tribune*, p. 47, 28th February 1954

beaut *noun*

1 a beauty, an impressive person or thing *US, 1895*

- Interior Secretary Harold L. Ickes, who previously had been denying applications for federal tidelands oil leases on the ground that the submerged territory clearly was the property of the States, wise-cracked, "When I make a mistake, it's a beaut." —*San Francisco Examiner*, 15th April 1946
- Jimmy Kelly's, a beaut of a room specializing in fan wielders and dancing gals, is patronized chiefly by merchants and Wall Streeters. —Jack Lait and Lee Mortimer, *New York Confidential*, p. 67, 1948
- A few minutes later he was back in an entirely different car, a brand-new convertible. "This one is a beaut!" he whispered in my ear. —Jack Kerouac, *On the Road*, p. 211, 1957
- He said Patrolman Salvatore Polani's attempts to make the jury believe the mastermind of the plot was Robert K. Worthington "is a beaut" no one would believe. —*San Francisco Examiner*, p. 15, 22nd October 1965
- Hang on to them drinks for a couple of jiffs Faye, there's a little beaut. —Barry Humphries, *Bazza Pulls It Off!*, 1971
- BB: You know, I hear the new Cadillac's gonna be out in a couple of months. TILLEY: You're kidding? BB: Yeah, they're changing the body. I hear it's a beaut. —*Tin Men*, 1987
- Fisher recovers and nuts [headbutts] the driver who's out of the car now, a real beaut right between the eyes. —John King, *Human Punk*, p. 61, 2000
- He's even got Prada trainies, the beaut. —Kevin Sampson, *Outlaws*, p. 13, 2001

2 a potent amphetamine capsule *US*

An abbreviation of **BLACK BEAUTY**.

- —Jay Robert Nash, *Dictionary of Crime*, p. 23, 1992

beaut *adjective*

excellent, terrific, wonderful, splendid *AUSTRALIA, 1918*

- 'Have you seen Ingrid Bergman? I think she's beaut.' —Nevil Shute, *The Far Country*, p. 139, 1952
- Everything was wrong with Rick. And yet, he was still the most beaut bloke Rob had ever known, and the next most beaut bloke was Hughie. —Randolph Stow, *The Merry-Go-Round in the Sea*, p. 195, 1965
- Jeez, what a flamin' colossal bunch of fellers! What a fan-bloody-tastically beaut pack of bastards! —Barry Humphries, *The Wonderful World of Barry McKenzie*, p. 10, 1968
- 'Mum was beaut about the baby,' Carol said. 'She even stayed here for the first month to help out.' —Suzy Jarratt, *Permissive Australia*, p. 20, 1970
- 'Beaut sheilas wandering round – real friendly – we help them inot the carts you know – remember when young Joe got lost in the crinoline!' —*Kings Cross Venus*, p. 13, 1st November 1972
- I've heard it said to Paul Hogan, 'It's all rather beaut, Paul, that TV hasn't changed you.' —Bert Newton, *Bert!*, p. 182, 1977
- Her Anzacs were mostly made of treacle and wheatgerm. Beaut, they were. —Barry Dickins, *What the Dickins*, p. 41, 1984

beaut *adverb*

excellently, splendidly *AUSTRALIA*

- She danced real beaut, as Danny said, and had a certain flair for challenging looks, which are there to be challenged. —Geoff Wyatt, *Saltwater Saints*, p. 105, 1969

beaut

used for expressing strong admiration *AUSTRALIA*

- Beaut. You'll like it. —Nourma Handford, *Carcoola Holiday*, p. 146, 1953
- Beaut, Florrie, you always were handy with the pen. —Frank Hardy, *The Outcasts of Foolgarah*, p. 105, 1971

beauteous maximus *noun*

something that is excellent *US*

Mock Latin.

- — *Merriam-Webster's Hot Words on Campus Marketing Survey '93*, p. 2, 13th October 1993

beautiful *adjective*

in the counterculture of the 1960s and 70s, used as an all-purpose adjective of approval *US*

A vague but central word of the hippie era, suggesting a passivity, appreciation for nature, kindness, etc.

- —Francis J. Rigney and L. Douglas Smith, *The Real Bohemia*, p. xiii, 1961
- The following program is dedicated to the city and people of San Francisco, who may not know it but they are beautiful, and so is their city. —Eric Burdon and Victor Briggs et al., *San Franciscan Nights (performed by Eric Burdon and the Animals)*, 1967
- —Joe David Brown (Editor), *The Hippies*, p. 217, 1967
- I hear it's a very good scene there. Not much heat, beautiful people, no speed freaks, and righteous dope. —Nicholas Von Hoffman, *We Are The People Our Parents Warned Us Against*, p. 47, 1967
- I met a lot of verey heavy beautiful people in jail. —Leonard Wolfe (Editor), *Voices from the Love Generation*, p. 3, 1968
- For a few days, we were all in a beuatiful place. Can we do it again? —*East Village Other*, 20th August 1969
- Oh, it's groovy. He's a beautiful guy. —Fred Baker, *Events*, p. 30, 1970

beautiful and; lovely and

satisfactory; nice *UK, 1939*

Always followed by another adjective for which this serves as an intensifier. Examples: 'I hit it beautiful and hard'; 'The water was lovely and hot'.

beautiful!

1 used for expressing enthusiastic agreement *US*

- "Yes, Elliot, I'll be waiting." "Beautiful, beautiful." —Donald Goines, *Inner City Hoodlum*, p. 88, 1975

2 used, with heavy irony, as a register of disappointment *UK*

An ironic reversal.

beautiful boulders *noun*

crack cocaine

- —Mike Haskins, *Drugs*, p. 281, 2003

beautiful people *noun*
the cream of society's crop; the wealthy, fashionable people of high society and the arts, especially those celebrated as trendsetters *US, 1964*
- Two of the Beautiful (and famous) People, actress-model Suzy Parker and her husband Brad Dillman of film, TV and stage game, flew into San Francisco airport last evening. — *San Francisco Chronicle*, p. 9, 27th February 1965
- How does it feel to be / One of the beautiful people? — Lennon & McCartney, *Baby You're a Rich Man*, 1967

beautifuls; boofuls *noun*
beautiful, as a form of address; the latter is addressed to babies or those behaving so and thus characterised as babies *UK, 1984*

beauty *noun*
1 something excellent; a splendid example of something *AUSTRALIA, 1852*
- 'I copped one!' he exulted. 'I copped a beauty.' — Eric Lambert, *The Veterans*, p. 182, 1954
- Anyway, we got Amanda back a beauty[.] — Kylie Mole (Maryanne Fahey), *My Diary*, p. 115, 1988
- I hit off and drove a beauty 230 metres down the middle[.] — Paul Vautin, *Turn It Up!*, p. 124, 1995

2 used as an affectionate form of address *UK: WALES*
- "All right, Treez," she said to the Italian girl. "How's it going, beauty?" she said to the blonde girl. — John Williams, *Cardiff Dead*, p. 15, 2000

3 an amphetamine *US*
A shortened **BLACK BEAUTY**.
- He popped three more beauties, and stepped on the pedal. — Carl Hiaasen, *Strip Tease*, p. 177–178, 1993

beauty *adjective*
excellent *NEW ZEALAND, 1963*
- — Harry Orsman, *A Dictionary of Modern New Zealand Slang*, p. 8, 1999

beauty!
1 used for registering great approval *AUSTRALIA*
Also spelt 'bewdy' to represent Australian pronunciation.
- Beauty, Beauty! Bring 'em around! — T.A.G. Hungerford, *The Ridge and the River*, p. 88, 1952
- When asked, you should say, 'Aw, beauty, mate. I'm honoured. — John O'Grady, *Aussie Etiket*, p. 13, 1971
- A pause and then that word of special Aussie approbation. "Beauty!" – but the Chief [Engineer] pronounced it in three distict syllables, "Be-yew-ty!" — Wilbur Smith, *Hungry as the Sea*, 1978
- You caught the crippled old coot for me, didja?' she asked the priates. 'Bloody beauty!' — Lance Peters, *The Dirty Half-Mile*, p. 328, 1979
- Bewdy! Me grog money's gone in! — Sick Puppy, p. 10, 1998

2 thank you! *AUSTRALIA, 1968*

beauty bolt *noun*
in the used car business, a new and shiny bolt intended to give the impression of a complete engine rebuild *US*
- They screwed beauty bolts onto the engine block and coaxed the tired, mashed-potato transmission back to life. — Stephen Cannell, *King Con*, p. 29, 1997

beauty farm *noun*
a resort with a focus on improving appearances *US*
- Her old lady's at the beauty farm[.] — John Rechy, *The Fourth Angel*, p. 76, 1972

beauty parlor *noun*
a brothel *US*
- — Vincent J. Monteleone, *Criminal Slang*, p. 19, 1949

beaver *noun*
1 a woman's pubic region; a woman as a sex object; sex with a woman *US, 1927*
Although recorded at least as early as 1927, 'beaver' did not come into its own until the mid-1960s, with an explosion of films featuring full frontal female nudity but no sexual activity and titles punning on 'beaver' – 'Bald Beaver', 'Beaver Works in the Bush Country', 'Hair Raising Beaver', 'Fine Feathered Beavers', 'Leave it to Beavers', and so on. As published sexual material got more graphic, so did the association of the term. Despite the highly sexual origin of the term, it was used by truck drivers with a slightly naughty innocence, emphasis on the innocence, to refer to women.
- Hey, you know what the cryptic term "Beaver" refers to in those nudie movie ads? Then you're sharper than a Gillette. — *San Francisco Chronicle*, p. 31, 27th September 1967
- — Collin Baker et al., *College Undergraduate Slang Study Conducted at Brown University*, p. 78, 1968
- It, the famous Beaver, is literally right before your eyes, ten feet high, eight feet wide and in full color. — *Adam Film Quarterly*, p. 75, February 1969
- While "The Star-Spangled Banner" was played you could run under the stands and look up at all kinds of beaver. — Jim Bouton, *Ball Four*, p. 37, 1970
- No front shots of girls, though beavers were all right. — Elmore Leonard, *52 Pick-up*, p. 144, 1974
- Truckers expanded the existing slang term of "beaver" into their own vocabulary and "sweet thing" and "mini skirt," two previous names used for females were discarded. Beaver became the national word for a female[.] — Gwyneth A. "Dandalion" Seese, *Tijuana Bear in a Smoke 'Um Up Taxi*, p. 45, 1977
- For girls, we [truck drivers] use the word "beavers." — *San Francisco Chronicle*, p. 2, 22nd April 1977
- Anyone who would drink Jack Daniels on the rocks would eat raw beaver. — *Maledicta*, p. 170, Winter 1980
- [W]hy that fuckin' drunk from San Francisco is gonna cop the beaver! — Bill Cardoso, *The Maltese Sangweech*, p. 151, 1984
- Lots of high-class beaver up in New York, huh? — Dan Jenkins, *Life Its Ownself*, p. 105, 1984
- I 'magine he's in town hunting beaver. Get himself some of the real thing 'fore he goes away. — Elmore Leonard, *Maximum Bob*, p. 121, 1991
- And unlike men, who seem to get excited by looking at close-up shots of beavers-only, most women say that a man with a bulge in his Calvins is sexier than one who's nude. — Anka Radakovich, *The Wild Girls Club*, p. 13, 1994
- Beaver? You mean vagina? — *The Big Lebowski*, 1998
- Perhaps you're daring enough to make your beaver completely bare. — *The Village Voice*, 8th-14th November 2000
- Her slippery silk gown parts at the waist and for the briefest of moments while she readjusts it, I see her dark furry beaver[.] — Danny King, *The Burglar Diaries*, p. 221–222, 2001
- [A] Latino-looking girl who trimmed her beaver down to one little strip[.] — Kevin Sampson, *Outlaws*, p. 38, 2001

2 a pornographic film *US*
- The first two beavers were disappointing for a unique reason. The girls were splendidly proportioned creatures with saliva-inducing propensities for any males' libido, but they didn't do anything. — *Screw*, p. 5, 24th January 1969

3 a beard *US, 1871*
- — Lou Shelly, *Hepcats Jive Talk Dictionary*, p. 7, 1945
- She plunged her hands into the beaver, and I decided I'd better go home and think, becuase I was in very big trouble. — Max Shulman, *I was a Teen-Age Dwarf*, p. 104, 1959
- "When did this all happen?" says Parker. "The beaver. When did you grow the beaver?" — Tom Wolfe, *The Kandy-Kolored Tangerine-Flake Streamline Baby*, p. 279, 1965

4 a top hat *BARBADOS*
- — Frank A. Collymore, *Barbadian Dialect*, p. 17, 1965
- — John A. Holm, *Dictionary of Bahamian English*, p. 14, 1982

5 a white police helmet *BARBADOS*
- — John A. Holm, *Dictionary of Bahamian English*, p. 14, 1982

6 a police officer *US*
- When the information came over the station ticker type that the Missouri state police had captured the right man, these local beavers knocked me around all the way to the edge of town[.] — Clancy Sigal, *Going Away*, p. 138, 1961

beaver away *verb*
to work industriously *UK, 1946*
From the characteristic behaviour of the beaver.
- I am at work, head down, busily beavering away on my next script. — Jane Green, *Straight Talking*, p. 205, 2003

beaver bait *noun*
money *US*
- — "Slingo", *The Official CB Slang Dictionary Handbook*, p. 7, 1976

beaver bear *noun*
a policewoman *US*
Combines **BEAVER** (a woman) with **BEAR** (the police).
- — *Complete CB Slang Dictionary*, 1976

beaver biscuits!
used for expressing disapproval *US*
A signature line of Colonel Sherman Potter on *M*A*S*H* (CBS, 1972–83). Repeated with referential humour.

beaver cleaver *noun*
a womaniser; the penis *UK*
It opens or splits the **BEAVER** (a woman or the vagina).

- —Peter Chippindale, *The British CB Book*, p. 152, 1981
- Do black men truly have such burdensome Beaver Cleavers? —Richard Herring, *Talking Cock*, p. 247, 2003

beaver creek *noun*

▸ **have a bite at beaver creek**

to perform oral sex on a woman *US*

- Another way to say "cunnilingus" [...] Having a bite at beaver creek[.] —Erica Orloff and JoAnn Baker, *Dirty Little Secrets*, p. 86, 2001

beaver-eater *noun*

a person who performs oral sex on a woman *US*

In a brilliant sexually charged pun, Vladamir Nabokov in *Lolita* wrote of 'the Palace Sentries, or Scarlet Guards, or Beaver Eaters, or whatever they are called', creating misdirected confusion with 'Beef Eaters' but leaving no doubt as to the sexual nature of his malapropism.

beaver fever *noun*

an obsession with women and sex *US*

- —Anna Scotti and Paul Young, *Buzzwords*, p. 14, 1997

beaver film *noun*

a mildly pornographic film, featuring full frontal nudity *US*

- If the beaver film is not something like that, then what? —*Adam Film Quarterly*, p. 75, February 1969
- The original Avon was the first in New York to screen "beaver" films, i.e., those showing pubic hair, five or six years ago. —Joseph Slade, *The Sexual Scene*, p. 269, December 1971
- For a time, this genre of "beaver" film was the most explicit pornographic entertainment available. —George Paul Csicsery (Editor), *The Sex Industry*, p. 166, 1973
- The simple beaver film soon developed two significant variations. —Kenneth Turan and Stephen E. Zito, *Sinema*, p. 77, 1974

beaver flick *noun*

a pornographic film *US*

- Shortly after this, the first genuine beaver flick was shown in another dingy house on 50th Street near 8th Avenue. —*Screw*, p. 14, 27th April 1970
- "We know we've got a long way to go but we're trying not to make just beaver flicks." (Quoting Jim Mitchell). —*The Berkeley Tribe*, p. 9, 22nd-28th August 1970

beaver leaver *noun*

a male homosexual *US*

Rhymed on **BEAVER** (the vagina) to suggest no interest in the female sex.

- —Chris Lewis, *The Dictionary of Playground Slang*, p. 25, 2003

beaver loop *noun*

a repeating video featuring female frontal nudity *US*

- During my career, I've probably seen close to 500 beaver loops and maybe 200 hard-core shorts[.] —*Screw*, p. 18, 2nd August 1971

beaver magazine *noun*

a magazine featuring photographs of nude women, focused on their genitals, usually not engaged in sex *US, 1967*

- Guys from around the league wrote to him regularly and sent him CARE packages – cakes, cookies, video cassettes, beaver magazines – because he refused to name any of his customers. —Dan Jenkins, *Life Its Ownself*, p. 28, 1982

beaver movie *noun*

a film featuring at the least female frontal nudity *US*

- Do you think that for many of the girls the decision to work in a beaver movie – besides just being an economic decision – is a way of saying – "Why should I be afraid of this?" —Jefferson Poland and Valerie Alison, *The Records of the San Francisco Sexual Freedom League*, p. 75, 1971
- [S]he was back down on Main Street competing with beaver movies between reels, and taxi dancing part-time down the street at the ballroom. —Joseph Wambaugh, *The Blue Knight*, p. 21, 1973
- The first beaver movies – whose main attraction was the visible pubic region of the women (and later men) who posed for them – were nothing more than short loops, several loops making up a show[.] —Kenneth Turan and Stephen E. Zito, *Sinema*, p. 77, 1974

beaver patrol *noun*

girl-watching *US*

- —*Current Slang*, p. 1, Summer 1967

beaver picture *noun*

a film, the main attraction of which is a number of shots of women's genitals; a photograph of a woman's genitals *US*

- For those interested in semantics, the pictures with the legs in normal position showing only the pubic bush are called "beaver pictures" but if the legs are spread apart and the camera angle shows the vaginal aperture or clitoris, then it is called "spread." —*Screw*, p. 16, 18th August 1969
- Sells, I figure he sells beaver pictures. —George V. Higgins, *The Friends of Eddie Doyle*, p. 171, 1971
- Her "co-star" in the beaver picture? —*The Big Lebowski*, 1998

beaver pie *noun*

the female genitals, especially as the object of sucking and licking *UK*

- —Tom Hibbert, *Rockspeak!*, p. 19, 1983

beaver-shooting *noun*

a concerted voyeuristic effort to find women whose genitals or pubic hair can be seen *US*

- I better explain about beaver-shooting. A beaver-shooter is, at bottom, a Peeping Tom. It can be anything from peering over the top of the dugout to look up dresses to hanging from the fire escape on the twentieth floor of some hotel to look into a window. —Jim Bouton, *Ball Four*, p. 36, 1970
- —Helen Dahlskog (Editor), *A Dictionary of Contemporary and Colloquial Usage*, p. 6, 1972

beaver shot *noun*

a photograph or filming of a woman's genitals *US*

In the early 1960s LA-based band The Periscopes recorded a rock'n'roll tune called 'Beaver Shot' which was banned from the radio after two plays.

- In commercial film prior to this, other than documentaries on nudism, a view of the pubic region – the "beaver shot" it was called – occurred only as a brief glimpse[.] —Terry Southern, *Blue Movie*, p. 24, 1970
- —Eugene Landy, *The Underground Dictionary*, p. 31, 1971
- A beaver shot taken with a 60-second camera takes very little artistic ability. —Stephen Ziplow, *The Film Maker's Guide to Pornography*, p. 142, 1977
- The Plumber slept, when he wasn't driving, in the driver's bunk, which within two days he had decorated with nude beaver shots from the national magazines. —Richard Condon, *Prizzi's Honor*, p. 271, 1982
- What's there to steal? Two bucks and a beaver shot. —*The Breakfast Club*, 1985
- Yeah, I think we'll give it the old beaver shot this time. —*Drugstore Cowboy*, 1988

beaver tail *noun*

1 a quick-baked or quick-fried sweet bread *CANADA*

- A swatch of sweet, whole-wheat pastry dough, rolled and stretched out to a vaguely beavertail-like shape, fried, buttered, and topped with cinnamon and sugar – a favourite of every winter carnival in Canada's capital city. —Bill Casselman, *Canadian Food Words*, p. 177, 1998

2 a design configuration on a shotgun *US*

- He pulled the beaver tail back, noted that a twelve-gauge round was chambered and ready to fire. —Gerald Petievich, *Money Men*, p. 150, 1981

beaver-with-stick *noun*

full frontal male nudity *US*

- Back in the good old days, like the middle '60s, when female "beaver" films were all the rage, the industry catered primarily to the heterosexual trade. Oh, sure, there was the occasional male "beaver-with-stick" flick, but these were the exception. —*San Francisco Chronicle*, 24th January 1977

be-back *noun*

in the used car business, a potential customer who has visited the car lot, inspected the cars for sale, left, and then returned to negotiate *US*

- —Chrysler Corporation, *Of Anchors, Bezels, Pots and Scorchers*, September 1959
- —Peter Mann, *How to Buy a Used Car Without Getting Gypped*, p. 188, 1975
- It had been a slow morning ... mostly tire-kickers and be-backs. —Stephen Cannell, *Big Con*, p. 27, 1997

bebe *noun*

crack cocaine *US*

Possibly an initialism of **BEAUTIFUL BOULDERS**.

- —US Department of Justice, *Street Terms*, October 1994
- —Mike Haskins, *Drugs*, p. 281, 2003

bebop *verb*

to take part in gang fights *US*

- This was one way of putting down bebopping. When you were on horse, you didn't have time for it. —Claude Brown, *Manchild in the Promised Land*, p. 153, 1965

be careful, Matt!

used as a humorous caution *US*

A signature line of Miss Kitty Russell (portrayed by Amanda Blake) to Marshall Matt Dillon on the television Western *Gunsmoke* (CBS, 1955–75). Repeated with referential humour.

Becks and Posh *noun*
food *UK*
Rhyming slang for **NOSH**, formed from the nicknames of footballer David Beckham and his wife, singer Victoria Beckham.
- —Susie Dent, *The Language Report*, p. 98, 2003

becky *noun*
in electric line work, a cable sling *US*
- —A.B. Chance Co., *Lineman's Slang Dictionary*, p. 1, 1980

be cool
used as a farewell *US*
- —Connie Eble (Editor), *UNC-CH Campus Slang*, p. 1, Fall 1984

bed *noun*
the playing surface of a pool table *US*
- —Steve Rushin, *Pool Cool*, p. 6, 1990

▸ **get into bed with**
in business or politics, to merge with, to become a partner of, to start a venture with *UK, 1977*
- —Sir Edward Playfair, 1977
- [T]he opposition Socialists, who have been implacably opposed to the war, have got into bed with the communists.— *The Guardian*, 7th April 2003

bed *verb*
to have sex with someone *UK, 1548*
- [T]hree years earlier he'd taken one look and wedded and bedded her, not necessarily in that order.—Dana Stabenow, *A Grave Denied*, p. 50, 2003

bed and breakfast *noun*
a very short prison sentence *UK*
- —Angela Devlin, *Prison Patter*, p. 26, 1996

bedbait *noun*
a sexually alluring young woman or young man *UK*
- — *Sunday Times*, 8th September 1963

bed blocker *noun*
a patient who has an extended stay in hospital *CANADA, 1986*
- Older people are now routinely described and referred to as "bed blockers". However, this euphemistic term carries with it a very powerful negative connotation[.]— *Memorandum by the National Pensioners Convention to the UK Parliament, Select Committee on Health*, July 2002

bedbug *noun*
1 a Pullman porter *US, 1940*
- —Jack Lait and Lee Mortimer, *Chicago Confidential*, p. 301, 1950
- —Clarence Major, *Dictionary of Afro-American Slang*, p. 25, 1970
- —Ramon Adams, *The Language of the Railroader*, p. 12, 1977

2 a person who is somewhere between amusingly eccentric and alarmingly disturbed *US, 1832*
- "Agh, Clancy is a bedbug," Solly said.—Evan Hunter, *The Blackboard Jungle*, p. 149, 1954

3 a Volkswagen camper van *UK*
- —Peter Chippindale, *The British CB Book*, p. 161, 1981

bedbug hauler *noun*
a moving van driver *US*
- —Montie Tak, *Truck Talk*, p. 9, 1971

bedbug row; bedbug alley *noun*
a poor, crime-ridden area in a city *US, 1969*
- —Frederic G. Cassidy, *Dictionary of American Regional English*, p. 196, 1985
- [T]he central business area and the red-light districs, variously known as the Levee, Hair-Trigger Block, Little Cheyenee, Gamblers' Alley, Bad Lands, Bedbug Row and Hell's Half Acre.—*Chicago Tribune*, p. 7C, 25th January 1987

bed-check Charlie *noun*
a pilot flying night air raids against US troops *US*
Korean war usage.
- Although these night raids did no major damage, they did affect the morale of the ground troops, who called the raiders "Bed Check Charlies."—Don Lawson, *The United States in the Korean War*, p. 66, 1964

bedden *verb*

▸ **bedden your head**
to become drunk or drug-intoxicated *TRINIDAD AND TOBAGO*
- In order to compensate for this disorder, he develops a dislike for good manners, a hatred for clean surroundings, plaits his hair in dread-locks, shoots pool the whole day long, and if he isn't beddening his head with a colombie, is either rolling dice, squeezing eards or guzzling cendless grog.— *Express*, p. 8, 2nd December 1979

beddie-weddie *noun*
bed *US, 1945*
Children's vocabulary borrowed by adults.
- —Harold Wentworth and Stuart Berg Flexner, *Dictionary of American Slang*, p. 27, 1960

beddy *noun*
1 in circus and carnival usage, the place where a person spends the winter or off-season *US*
- —Don Wilmeth, *The Language of American Popular Entertainment*, p. 19, 1981

2 a promiscuous girl *US*
- —Pamela Munro, *U.C.L.A. Slang*, p. 20, 1989

beddy-bye; beddy byes; beddie-byes *noun*
sleep or bed *UK, 1906*
A nursery term, used for effect elsewhere.
- [I]t's two o'clock in the afternoon by golly, and he, for one, is going to take his little chicks home to beddy-by.—John M. Murtagh and Sara Harris, *Cast the First Stone*, p. 13, 1957
- Come on Milly, beddy byes. You've had a skinful tonight.—Graeme Kent, *The Queen's Corporal [Six Granada Plays]*, p. 97, 1959
- Mr. Cherry said he had a hard day's driving to Spokane tomorrow to pruchase some varnish wholesale and he would have to go beddy-bye now. He said beddy-bye. We said goodnight to him[.]—Clancy Sigal, *Going Away*, p. 95, 1961
- Well, I better get my ass beddy-by. I'll see you in the morning.—Elmore Leonard, *Gold Coast*, p. 71, 1980
- And she's wearing her Frederick's of Hollywood silkies for beddy-bye.—Joseph Wambaugh, *Fugitive Nights*, p. 82, 1992
- We would normally leave the main meal of the pack until last thing in the day. It helped warm us up for beddie-byes.—Ken Lukowiak, *A Soldier's Song*, p. 26, 1993

bed flute *noun*
the penis *AUSTRALIA*
- [T]hey reckon one night when William Shakespeare, Dazza Braithwaite and Ted Mulry had had a skinful, they stripped off and had a jam session playing their bed flutes.—Roy Slaven (John Doyle), *Five South Coast Seasons*, p. 155, 1992

Bedfordshire *noun*
a bed; bed *UK, 1665*
A humorous location from the name of an English county.

bed-hop *verb*
to habitually have casual sex *US*
- HI! GREAT WEEK! Mine was really great – back bed-hopping again. — *Screw*, p. 2, 4th March 1974

bed-hopper *noun*
a person who lives a sexually promiscuous life *AUSTRALIA*
- You won't want a piece of advice from a seasoned bed-hopper, but here it is anyway, in two words and some. Forget him.— *Janie Stagestruck*, p. 85, 1972

bed house *noun*
1 a brothel *US*
- —Ruth Todasco et al., *The Intelligent Woman's Guide to Dirty Words*, p. 2, 1973

2 a brakevan (caboose) *US*
- —Ramon Adams, *The Language of the Railroader*, p. 12, 1977

bedlamer *noun*
in Newfoundland, a young seal; also a young boy *CANADA*
The term comes either from the noise they make, or, according to some sources, the French *bête de la mer* (beast of the sea).
- He, as a "bedlammer" boy, entertained the notion of going to St. John's.—Solomon Samson, *A Glimpse of Newfoundland*, p. vii, 1959
- A bedlamer is a juvenile harp seal from about 1 to 5 years of age which has a spotted coat.— *Decks Awash*, p. vii, 1978

Bedouin Bob *noun*
any Saudi; any desert nomad *US*
Gulf war usage.
- — *American Speech*, p. 384, Winter 1991: 'Among the new words'

Bedourie shower *noun*
a dust storm *AUSTRALIA, 1945*
Bedourie is an inland town in Queensland. The name Bedourie is taken from an Aborigine word for 'dust storm'. Other locations similarly used by nature, weather and irony: Bourke, Bogan, Cobar, Darling, Wilcannia and Wimmera.

bedpan commando *noun*
a medic in the Medical Corps in Vietnam *US*
- —Linda Reinberg, *In the Field*, p. 19, 1991

Bedrock *noun*
a common name for US armed forces camps during the Persian Gulf war *US*
An allusion to the prehistoric town on the cartoon television series *The Flinstones* (ABC, 1960–66), home to quarry worker Fred Flintstone and his wife Wilma.
- They live in a tent city nicknamed "Bedrock," for Fred Flintstone's home town, and eat two hot meals a day and packaged rations for the third in a mess tent dubbed "Dino's Diner." — *Washington Post*, p. A20, 1st October 1990

bed rock *verb*
in low riding, to rock the bed of a truck from side to side using hydraulic pumps *US*
- — Lewis Poteet, *Car & Motorcyle Slang*, p. 27, 1992

bedroom *noun*
any place where homosexual men can have sex *UK*
- — Paul Baker, *Polari*, p. 164, 2002

bedroom eyes *noun*
a sensual face and eyes that convey desire *US, 1947*
- Pretty, blonde Mrs. Acaro sees beyond the end of his nose, thinks the most striking thing about his face are his "big, brown bedroom eyes." — *Time*, p. 78, 17th May 1948
- They all have to have bedroom eyes. — Raymond Chandler, *The Little Sister*, p. 42, 1949
- The "bedroom eyes" of Italian film star Sophia Loren stole the show from a star Swiss girl skier at the Winter Olympics. — *San Francisco News*, p. 4, 13th February 1956
- She ran the tip of her red tongue slowly across her full, cushiony, sensuous lips, making them wet-red, and looked him straight in the eys with her own glassy, speckled bedroom-eyes. — Chester Himes, *A Rage in Harlem*, p. 139, 1957
- "Why not stay here?" Nancy said and added, looking up at him with the bedroom brown eyes, "No one's home." — Elmore Leonard, *The Big Bounce*, p. 41, 1969
- When she smiled and looked up at me with her big bedroom eyes, I couldn't refrain from taking her in my arms and kissing those tender lips. — Donald Goines, *Whoreson*, p. 133–134, 1972
- Nick: Six-two, big shoulders, soft blue bedroom eyes. — C.D. Payne, *Youth in Revolt*, p. 224, 1993
- I was still sweating from my recent flirtation in the Casino Royale where I made bedroom eyes with a sexy black-haired, blue-eyed croupier. — Anka Radakovich, *The Wild Girls Club*, p. 73, 1994

Beds *noun*
Bedfordshire *UK, 1937*
A spoken form of the conventional written abbreviation, considered colloquial when used in speech as a genuine equivalent of the original name.

bed-sit jungle *noun*
an urban area where a bed-sitter is usually available as rented accommodation; the generality of life in rented bedsit accommodation *UK*
- West Eleven, the Bed-Sit Jungle. — Jake Arnott, *He Kills Coppers*, p. 69, 2001

bed-sitter; bedsit *noun*
a single-room combining bedroom and living accommodation; a bed-stting room *UK, 1927*
- Move in with me in a ratty bedsit. — Greg Williams, *Diamond Geezers*, p. 179, 1997

bed-sitter-land *noun*
an urban area where a bed-sitter is commonly available as rented accommodation; the generality of life in rented bedsit accommodation *UK, 1968*

Bed-Stuy *nickname*
the Bedford-Stuyvesant neighbourhood of New York City *US*
The area is the epitome of urban American poverty.
- G.B. ran back up to his neighborhood (Bed-Sty New Yawk) for a bag of bad smoke[.] — Odie Hawkins, *Men Friends*, p. 51, 1989
- It's one of the original ghettos. I grew up there. Bed-Stuy is such a ghetto that in Billy Joel's song, "You May Be Right," he brags about walking through Bedford-Stuyvesant by himself: "I walked through a combat zone." — Chris Rock, *Rock This*, p. 40, 1997

bedworthy *adjective*
sexually desirable *UK, 1936*
- — John Trimble, *5000 Adult Sex Words & Phrases*, 1966

bee *noun*
1 a drug addiction *US*
Also known as 'a bee that stings'.
- A bee is what he calls his habit; it's always stinging him to get a fix. — Clarence Cooper Jr, *The Scene*, p. 54, 1960
- — David Maurer and Victor Vogel, *The Slang and Jargon of Drugs and Drinks*, p. 387, 1973

2 a barbiturate or other central nervous system depressant, especially Nembutal *US*
A Nembutal capsule is commonly known as a **YELLOW JACKET**, hence the 'bee'.
- I have a fine connection here, baby, and we'll get tanked on bees and pods and then I'll really show you a sex-scene. — John Rechy, *City of Night*, p. 184, 1963

3 in a deck of playing cards, a joker, especially when the deck is made by the playing card manufacturer Bee *US*
- — George Percy, *The Language of Poker*, p. 8, 1988

▸ **get a bee up your arse; have a bee up your arse**
to be in a restless or anxious condition; to be obsessed by a notion *UK, 1990s→*
A variation on 'a bee in the bonnet'.
- And in the 70s everyone got a bee up their arse over punk rock. — Dave Courtney, *Raving Lunacy*, p. 38, 2000

▸ **put the bee on**
to swindle someone *US*
- — Vincent J. Monteleone, *Criminal Slang*, p. 186, 1949

bee *verb*
to beg *US*
- — Joseph E. Ragen and Charles Finston, *Inside the World's Toughest Prison*, p. 790, 1962

bee *adjective*
bloody (an intensifier) *UK, 1926*
A rendering of the initial letter for euphemism's sake.

bee aitch
▷ see: **BLOODY HELL!**

be easy!
relax! *US*
- — Connie Eble (Editor), *UNC-CH Campus Slang*, p. 1, Spring 2003

Beeb *nickname*
the BBC (British Broadcasting Corporation) *UK, 1967*
- [N]ot too keen on the old media. Thinks the dear old Beeb is stuffed the gills with pinko poofters[.] — Mike Stott, *Soldiers Talking, Cleanly*, 1978

bee-bee *noun*
crack cocaine *US*
- — Peter Johnson, *Dictionary of Street Alcohol and Drug Terms*, p. 17, 1993

bee-bopper *noun*
a person who is trying too hard to be something that they are not – fashionable, trendy, up-to-date *US*
- — Connie Eble (Editor), *UNC-CH Campus Slang*, p. 1, Fall 1987

beech *verb*
during the period 1963–5, to permanently close down a section of railway or a railway station *UK*
After Richard Beeching, 1913–85, chairman of the British Rail Board 1963–5, at the end of which time he was made a Life Peer, author of the 'Beeching Report' that prescribed a substantial contraction of the UK's rail networks.
- A railway (or station) marked down for closure is aid to be "due for beeching"; and axed personnel are described as "on the beech". — Sean Fielding, February 1964

beechams *noun*
▸ **the beechams**
the police *UK*
Rhyming slang from Beecham's Pill™, a branded medication, to **THE BILL** (the police).
- — Ray Puxley, *Cockney Rabbit*, p. 11, 1992

Beecham's pill *noun*
1 a fool, an idiot *AUSTRALIA, 1950*
Rhyming slang for **DILL** (a fool). From the proprietary name of a laxative formerly popular as a cure-all.
- The Beecham Pill had them pegged as dope fiends. — Ryan Aven-Bray, *Ridgey Didge Oz Jack Lang*, p. 11, 1983

2 a photographic still *UK, 1971*
Rhyming slang.

3 a theatrical bill; an advertising poster *UK*
Rhyming slang.
- —Ray Puxley, *Cockney Rabbit*, p. 11, 1992

Beecham's pills *noun*
the testicles *UK*
Rhyming slang.
- — *Maledicta*, p. 196, Winter 1980: 'A new erotic vocabulary'

bee cocky *noun*
a bee farmer; an apiarist *AUSTRALIA*
- Certainly he thought I was a bit of a joke, but a man with a sore leg is welcome to any light entertainment he might find in the thought of me as a bee cocky.' —Kylie Tennant, *The Honey Flow*, p. 17, 1956

beedi; beadi; bidi; biri *noun*
a small, high nicotine-content, cigarette made of tobacco dust poured into a small tube of rolled leaf tied with a cotton thread, often flavoured with strawberry, vanilla, mint, chocolate, mango, pineapple, grape, licorice, cherry, etc *UK*
From Hindi. Popular brands are Mangalore, Kailas, Shiv Sagar and Irie.
- — Bangalore Ganesh Beedies product label, 2003

beedler *noun*
a hard-driving work foreman or supervisor *US*
- —Norman Carlisle, *The Modern Wonder Book of Trains and Railroading*, p. 259, 1946

bee eff *noun*
▷ see: BF

beef *noun*

1 a complaint, an argument, a fight *US, 1899*
- These fellers have a beef, boss. —Chester Gould, *Dick Tracy Meets the Night Crawler*, p. 61–62, 1945
- I can't go myself this time, I had a beef with him. —William Burroughs, *Junkie*, p. 36, 1953
- Man, I tell you we had some real beefs. —Hunter S. Thompson, *Hell's Angels*, p. 40, 1966
- Naturally, this pimp put up a beef, but not knowing Ralph was an ex-pug, he wound up with a broken jaw and a warning to leave town. —Babs Gonazles, *I Paid My Dues*, p. 104, 1967
- If while living in the Honor Unit you get into a "beef" which results in action against you by the disciplinary committee, one of the certain penalties is that you are immediately kicked out of No. 5 Building. —Eldridge Cleaver, *Soul on Ice*, p. 52, 1968
- She had tested me with her beef. —Iceberg Slim (Robert Beck), *Pimp*, p. 273, 1969
- Regan listened to some of their beefs... "We want our money back!" — *The Sweeney*, p. 11, 1976
- Mr. Wilson apparently has a beef against society. A serious beef. —Carl Hiaasen, *Tourist Season*, p. 195, 1986
- And remember, there's no need to shoot unless you get beef. —Donald Gorgon, *Cop Killer*, p. 5, 1994
- I don't want him bringin' beefs backhome 'cause that could be a problem. — *Casino*, 1995
- I've been involved in a few street beefs. — *The Times Magazine*, p. 44, 23rd February 2002

2 conflict, feuding *US*
A wider use of the previous sense.
- Their deaths [Tupac Shakur and Notorious B.I.G] forever alter the way we look at beef, death – and life – in hip-hop. — *The Source*, p. 133, March 2002

3 an arrest or criminal charge *US, 1928*
- Satin picked up three beefs in six months, and since the High One was still an undercvoer bondsman he raised her each time. —A.S. Jackson, *Gentleman Pimp*, p. 121, 1973
- [P]risoners with felony beefs outranked the other prisoners. —Bobby Seale, *A Lonely Rage*, p. 268, 1978
- He's got all these drunk-driving beefs. —James Ellroy, *White Jazz*, p. 33, 1992

4 in prison, a written reprimand *US*
- They should have given you a medal instead of a beef. —Malcolm Braly, *On the Yard*, p. 183, 1967
- —Paul Glover, *Words from the House of the Dead*, 1974

5 the vagina; an attractive and sexual woman *BARBADOS*
- —John A. Holm, *Dictionary of Bahamian English*, p. 15, 1982
- —Richard Allsopp, *Dictionary of Caribbean English Usage*, 1996

6 the penis *US*
- —Edith A. Folb, *runnin' down some lines*, p. 229, 1980
- The boy is masturbating" [...] Beef Strokin' off[.] —Erica Orloff and JoAnn Baker, *Dirty Little Secrets*, p. 89, 2001

7 in homosexual society, a masculine man or a member of the armed forces whatever his gender-preference *US*
- So he married a real girl, huh? Well, I guess he preferred fish to beef. —Bruce Rodgers, *The Queens' Vernacular*, p. 30, 1972

8 in the navy, a male homosexual *UK, 1962*

9 a dramatic and unintended ending of a surf ride *US*
- Dude, check out these hot beefs. —Trevor Cralle, *The Surfin'ary*, p. 9, 1991

10 a backwards fall off a skateboard *US*
- —Vann Wesson, *Generation X Field Guide and Lexicon*, p. 18, 1997

▸ **put some beef into it**
to try hard, to work hard, to make an effort *UK, 1961*

beef *verb*

1 to complain *US, 1866*
From an earlier sense (to shout).
- Johnson had started beefing about the job, and now they all had it. —Chester Himes, *If He Hollers Let Him Go*, p. 11, 1945
- He was always beefing how he couldn't clear anything, he had to put out so much for hotel rooms, and the law kept him on the move. —William Burroughs, *Junkie*, p. 76, 1953
- Some bitch in Newton Division beefed a policeman last week. Says he took her in a park and tried to lay her. —Joseph Wambaugh, *The New Centurions*, p. 54, 1970
- "Have you been beefed before?" "When I was on the police department a prisoner spit in my face. I was accused of punching him in the stomach so hard it knocked him out." —Gerald Petievich, *To Live and Die in L.A.*, p. 64, 1983
- Safe [OK], man. You're cool. I ain't beefin'. —Diran Adebayo, *My Once Upon A Time*, p. 47, 2000

2 to have sex *US*
- — *American Speech*, p. 56, Spring-Summer 1975: 'Razorback slang'
- There were sounds from Connel's bedroom [...] Connell was beefing her. —G.F. Newman, *The Gurnor*, 1997

3 in prison, to issue a disciplinary reprimand *US*
- [O]n such nights he would literally beef you because he didn't like your looks. —Malcolm Braly, *On the Yard*, p. 70, 1967

beef *adjective*

1 aggressive, violent, hostile *US*
- That guy got beef with me because I talked with his girl. —Connie Eble (Editor), *UNC-CH Campus Slang*, p. 1, November 2002

2 homosexual *UK, 1962*
Navy usage.

beef!
in the youth trend for 'souped-up' motor-scootering, used for registering approval of the achievements of a daring, risk-taking rider *UK*
- At the next set of lights, the daredevil tricks which had horrified the commuters are rewarded with shouts of "Beef!" and "Sick, man!" from his mates. — *The Independent Magazine*, p. 17, 28th August 2004

Beefa *nickname*
the Balearic island of Ibiza *UK*
- Beefa: was it any cop this year? — *Ministry*, p. 7, October 2002

beef and shrapnel *noun*
in the Vietnam war, a meal of beef and potatoes *US*
- —Linda Reinberg, *In the Field*, p. 19, 1991

beef-a-roni *noun*
a muscular, handsome male *US*
Punning with the name of a food product and the many meat images involved in sexual slang.
- —Connie Eble (Editor), *UNC-CH Campus Slang*, p. 1, April 1985

beef bayonet *noun*
the penis *AUSTRALIA*
- I know you don't like it plain and simple, but you're not goin' to see my beef bayonet in action!!! —Barry Humphries, *Bazza Pulls It Off!*, p. [22], 1971

beef bugle *noun*
the penis, especially as an object of oral sex *AUSTRALIA*
- Have youse tried blowin' the old beef bugle? —Barry Humphries, *Bazza Pulls It Off!*, 1971

beefcake *noun*

1 artistic or photographic depictions of nude or partially nude muscular men *US, 1949*
The sexual reciprocal of CHEESECAKE.
- —Roger Blake, *The American Dictionary of Sexual Terms*, p. 14, 1964

- — *The Guild Dictionary of Homosexual Terms*, p. 3, 1965
- Doubleday Book Shops have run smirking ads for The Gay Cookbook and newsstands make room for "beefcake" magazines of male nudes. —Joe David Brown, *Sex in the '60s*, p. 66, 1968
- Lesbian periodicals, male "beefcake," pamphlets, cards, buttons, and a host of fine fiction on the homosexual theme adorm the shelves of Craig's bookstore. — *Screw*, 21st February 1969
- True, the beefcake cowboy murals struck a somewhat citified note in the overall scheme of things, but Michael didn't mind. —Armistead Maupin, *Further Tales of the City*, p. 31, 1982

2 a muscular man *US, 1949*

- —Roger Blake, *The American Dictionary of Sexual Terms*, p. 14, 1964
- I really don't feel the need to be a great macho beefcake. — *Ask*, p. 75, 8th May 1981

beef curtains *noun*

the labia *US, 1998*

- —Paul Baker, *Polari*, p. 164, 2002
- — *www.LondonSlang.com*, June 2002

beefer *noun*

1 a constant and tiresome complainer *US*

- — *The Annals of the American Academy of Political and Social Sciences*, p. 120, May 1950
- Most of the guests were pretty good about the blizzard, like they lent each other newspsapers and so on, but the other people, the beefers, just hung around the lobby and stared out at the snow going up higher and higher, and made trouble. —Richard Condon, *Prizzi's Honor*, p. 24, 1982
- —George Percy, *The Language of Poker*, p. 8, 1988

2 a male homosexual *UK*

Royal Navy use.

- You got a crush on that beefer in the N.A.A.F.I., that's what it is. — *Heart*, p. 87, 1982

beef-heart; beef *verb*

to fart *UK, 1960*

Also used as a noun. Rhyming slang; perhaps related to obsolete non-rhyming sense: a 'bean'.

- There's farting, tooting, breaking wind, beefing, queefing [probably a nonce-term] and cutting cheese. —Peter Furze quoting L. Collingwood, *Tailwinds*, p. 28, 1998

beef injection; hot beef injection *noun*

sexual intercourse *US*

- [W]hat Rollo really needs is love, affection, understanding, etc., etc. In other words, a beef injection. —Angelo d'Arcangelo, *The Homosexual Handbook*, p. 229, 1968
- —Robert A. Wilson, *Playboy's Book of Forbidden Words*, p. 33, 1972
- —Pamela Munro, *U.C.L.A. Slang*, p. 77, 1989
- —Michael Dalton Johnson, *Talking Trash with Redd Foxx*, p. 70, 1994

beef it *verb*

in motorcyle racing, to fall to the ground and suffer a severe scrape *US*

- —Lewis Poteet, *Car & Motorcyle Slang*, p. 27, 1992

beef of the sea *noun*

the loggerhead turtle *BARBADOS*

- —John A. Holm, *Dictionary of Bahamian English*, p. 15, 1982

beef squad *noun*

a group of thugs hired by management to help break a strike *US, 1956*

- —Harold Wentworth and Stuart Berg Flexner, *Dictionary of American Slang*, p. 28, 1960

beefsteak eye *noun*

a black eye *US, 1950*

From the folk remedy of covering the blackened eye with a raw steak.

- —Frederic G. Cassidy, *Dictionary of American Regional English*, p. 201, 1985

beef torpedo *noun*

the penis *UK*

- —Tom Hibbert, *Rockspeak!*, p. 19, 1983

beef trust *noun*

1 in sports, a group of large athletes *US, 1928*

- Defensively the 49ers came up with a beef trust on the line that really held the vaunted Browns in check. — *San Francisco News*, p. 11, 29th August 1958
- Lincoln Line More Like Beef Trust [Headline]— *San Francisco Examiner*, p. 61, 17th September 1970

2 a chorus of large women who entertain men *US, 1931*

- The beef trust was out in full force – these ladies were all shaped like barrels, wherever there wasn't a crease in their meat there was a dimple. —Mezz Mezzrow, *Really the Blues*, p. 91, 1946
- Beef Trust Chorus: Heavy Duty! Screamlined! Four tons of furious fun! [Advertisement]— *San Francisco Examiner*, 7th June 1947
- 5 More Girls WANTED FOR Beef Trust Chorus. Weight from 175 lbs. Up [Advertisement]— *San Francisco Chronicle*, p. 1, 4th May 1947
- Now touring the burlesque houses is a troupe known as "The Beef Trust." The women in this aggregation weight 250 pounds or over. — *San Francisco Examiner*, 21st June 1948

beef up *verb*

to enhance someone or something, to strengthen someone or something *US, 1944*

- I got all beefed up – and then got sick in Poland – and the beef evaporated. —Philip Wylie, *Opus 21*, p. 280, 1949
- Say I got an idea for the recording, I want to lay in some more tracks, beef it up. —Elmore Leonard, *Be Cool*, p. 8, 1999

beefy *adjective*

(used of a shot in croquet) long and hard *US*

- —James Charlton and William Thompson, *Croquet*, p. 155, 1977

beehive *noun*

1 a five pound note *UK*

Rhyming slang, playing on **BEES AND HONEY** (money).

- I used to pull out a couple of ton in beehives[.]—Derek Raymond (Robin Cook), *The Crust on its Uppers*, p. 29, 1962

2 in trucking, any large truck stop offering a full range of services *US*

- — Elementary Electronics, *Dictionary of CB Lingo*, p. 49, 1976

3 an office in a railway yard *US*

- —Norman Carlisle, *The Modern Wonder Book of Trains and Railroading*, p. 259, 1946

Beehive *noun*

▸ **the Beehive**

New Zealand's Parliament buildings *NEW ZEALAND*

Designed by Sir Basil Spence, the building's domes are evocative of a beehive.

- I had an hour with [the Prime Minister] in his office in the Beehive. —John Kennedy, *Straight from the Shoulder*, p. 94, 1981

beehive burner *noun*

a combustion chamber to burn waste wood from sawmills *CANADA, 1989*

- —Tom Parkin, *WetCoast Words*, p. 15, 1989

beehive it *verb*

to leave hurriedly *US*

Vietnam war use.

- —Linda Reinberg, *In the Field*, p. 19, 1991

beehive round *noun*

an artillery shell that scatters small nails with fins instead of shrapnel, first used in Vietnam in 1964 *US*

- —Linda Reinberg, *In the Field*, p. 19, 1991

beeitch *noun*

used as a synonym of 'bitch', especially as a term for a woman *US*

- Beeitch, if you ain't got no kinda chronic, yo punk ass gots to go! —Snoop Doggy Dogg, *A Day in the Life of Snoop Doogy Dog [Cover art]*, 1993

beekie *noun*

during a labour dispute or organising drive, a company spy *US, 1949*

- —Harold Wentworth and Stuart Berg Flexner, *Dictionary of American Slang*, p. 28, 1960

beel *noun*

a car *VIRGIN ISLANDS, US*

- —Richard Allsopp, *Dictionary of Caribbean English Usage*, p. 89, 1996

Beemer; Beamer; Beamie *noun*

a BMW car *US, 1982*

- —Connie Eble (Editor), *UNC-CH Campus Slang*, p. 1, Spring 1890
- "I think you oughtta tell patrol to watch for a blue Beemer convertible," Letch said. —Joseph Wambaugh, *Floaters*, p. 213, 1996
- We're movin' down Green Lanes the land of triple-parked beemers where parkin' law don't count[.]—Nick Barlay, *Curvy Lovebox*, p. 53, 1997
- He took the Beamie ten yards down the track and killed the lights. —Christopher Brookmyre, *Boiling a Frog*, p. 362, 2000

- I upgraded my wheels at Sammy's rental to a crimson nine series Beemer. —Diran Adebayo, *My Once Upon A Time*, p. 27, 2000

beemers *noun*
▷ see: BEAMERS

Bee More *nickname*
Baltimore, Maryland *US*
- —Ellen C. Bellone (Editor), *Dictionary of Slang*, p. 2, 1989

been *verb*
▸ **been around**
sexually experienced *US*
- Brad and Dell both told me "for my own good" that Deb "has been around." —Beatrice Sparks (writing as 'Anonymous'), *Jay's Journal*, p. 19, 1979

▸ **been there**
said of a person with whom the speaker has had sex *FIJI*
- She's a fuck-around man. Lotsa fellas been there. —Jan Tent, 1996

▸ **been there, doing that**
experiencing the bleed period of the menstrual cycle *US*
The 'been there' part offers consolation to those who recently were on it or had cramps previously, while the 'doing that' part refers to the fact that you are on your period currently.
- —a contributor, *The Museum of Menstruation and Women's Health*, June 2001

▸ **been there, done that**
used as a laconic, world-weary dismissal of another's suggestion *AUSTRALIA*
- Money is only an object. I'll get it. Got it, been there. —Edwin Torres, *Carlito's Way*, p. 30, 1975
- —*American Speech*, p. 389, Winter 1995: 'Among the new words'
- "Been there, done that," Blaze said. "I've already met Auckland and Wllington." —Joseph Wambaugh, *Floaters*, p. 65, 1996

▸ **been there, done that, bought the tee-shirt**
used as a laconic, world-weary dismissal of another's suggestion *UK*
An elaboration of BEEN THERE, DONE THAT.
- MOON: Are we nearly there yet? BACON: Bin there, done it, bought the fuckin' tee-shirt, son. —Bernard Dempsey and Kevin McNally, *Lock, Stock ... & Two Hundred Smoking Kalashnikovs*, p. 122, 2000

been-there medal *noun*
the Vietnam Campaign Service Medal *US*
- —Linda Reinberg, *In the Field*, p. 19, 1991

been-to *noun*
a west African, especially a Ghanaian or Nigerian, who has 'been to' England, usually for study, and whose social status has thereby been enhanced; a British academic who has 'been to' any one of the more prestigeous US universities *UK*
- [Y]oung lecturers self-conciously emphasising their "been-to" status on return from Stanford or Berkeley. —*The Guardian*, November 1982

beep *noun*
an effeminate man, especially a homosexual *JAMAICA, 1995*
- —Peter L. Patrick, *Some Recent Jamaican Creole Words*, 2003

beep beep
pay attention! *US*
- [U]sed in the expression 'beep beep to X'. —*San Francisco Examiner*, p. 21, 12th December 1961

beeper *noun*
1 the telephone *US*
- "Here's why I'm on the beeper, Ron," said the telephone voice on the all-night radio show. —Joan Didion, *Slouching Toward Bethlehem*, p. 220, 1968

2 an electronic paging device *US, 1970*
- He had an answering service and an electronic beeper that fit onto his belt. The beeper didn't make Keyes feel particularly important; every shyster lawyer, dope dealer, and undercover agent in Dade County wore one. —Carl Hiassen, *Tourist Season*, p. 33, 1986
- Max prefers to be called on the tiny beeper attached to his belt. —Terry Williams, *The Cocaine Kids*, p. 31, 1989
- Besides, everybody had a beeper these days. —Richard Price, *Clockers*, p. 6, 1992
- They [call girls] drive Porsches, live in condos, have stockbrokers, carry beepers, you know, like Nancy Allen in Dressed to Kill. —*True Romance*, 1993
- In 1993 alone, the number of beeprs (more officially, "pagers") in use in the US increased by nearly 50 percent. —Steven Daly and Nalthaniel Wice, *alt.culture*, p. 20, 1995
- There's a card in there with my beeper number. —*American Beauty*, 1999

beer *noun*
1 in the illegal production of alcohol, fermented grain or sugar mash *US, 1887*
- —David W. Maurer, *Kentucky Moonshine*, p. 114, 1974

2 the chest *UK*
Rhyming slang, from the slogan 'beer is best'.
- That'll put some barnet [hair] on your beer. —Red Daniells, 1980

▸ **on the beer**
engaged in a drinking session *UK, 1909*

beer barn *noun*
a tavern *NEW ZEALAND*
- But the suburban travern is frequently a 'beer-barn', continuing the old mass-consumption methods. —R.J. Johnston, *New Zealanders*, p. 147, 1976

beer belly *noun*
the protruding stomach of an excessive beer drinker *US, 1960*
- [A] large, brawny man about the shade of a chestnut with a crop of snow-white hair, a white billygoat goatee and a beer belly that hung out over his belt. —Robert Gover, *Poorboy at the Party*, p. 37, 1966

beer blast *noun*
a party organised around the consumption of beer *US*
- Not like the Socs, who jump greasers and wreck houses and throw beer blasts for kicks[.] —S.E. Hinton, *The Outsiders*, p. 5, 1967
- —Collin Baker et al., *College Undergraduate Slang Study Conducted at Brown University*, p. 78, 1968

beer bottle glasses *noun*
thick eye glasses *US*

beer bummer *noun*
a person who cadges drinks from others *NEW ZEALAND, 1906*

beer bust *noun*
a party organised around the consumption of beer *US, 1913*
- Police said they were called to the picnic grounds of Enrico Rosotti, favorite "beer bust" locale of Stanford students, and there found the sextette hilariously dancing about the flaming tables. —*San Francisco Examiner*, p. 32, 2nd March 1948
- Have a real beer bust, like we used to in the old days, and make a tour of the burly houses. —Jim Thompson, *Roughneck*, p. 119, 1954
- Beer Bust Crashed – 3 Hurt [Headline] —*San Francisco Call-Bulletin*, p. 3, 13th April 1957
- Dirty Remark Turns Beer Bust Into a Brawl [Headline] —*San Francisco Chronicle*, p. 3, 15th May 1966
- —Collin Baker et al., *College Undergraduate Slang Study Conducted at Brown University*, p. 78, 1968
- He was the only one of them who didn't like to join the beer busts after work. —Joseph Wambaugh, *Lines and Shadows*, p. 41, 1984
- DON: Hey, I've got an idea. PINK: What? Don: A beer bust later on. —*Dazed and Confused*, 1993

beer can *noun*
any small car that would easily get crushed in a significant accident *US*
- —Lewis Poteet, *Car & Motorcyle Slang*, p. 27, 1992

beer can grenade *noun*
a crude hand grenade fashioned by the Viet Cong, packed inside a beer can *US*
- —Gregory Clark, *Words of the Vietnam War*, p. 53, 1990

beer chit *noun*
money *UK*
In Royal Air Force use, 2002.

beer coat *noun*
a warm feeling, or one of imperviousness to weather conditions, that prevails after drinking *NEW ZEALAND*
From private correspondence, 2002.

beer compass *noun*
the homing instinct that remains active when drunk *UK*
- —*Roger's Profanisaurus*, , p. 14, 2002

beer cozy *noun*
a styrofoam or plastic cylinder that slips over a beer can, serving as insulation *US*
- —Connie Eble (Editor), *UNC-CH Campus Slang*, p. 5, Fall 2000

beered; beered out *adjective*
drunk on beer *US, 1930*
- Lasher remained, raucously beered, back-slapping and issuing to the bar a violent manifesto of friendship.—Eric Lambert, *The Veterans*, p. 68, 1954
- [The cocktail was] designed to get the sheilas tanked enough to spread 'em for their barbaric, beered-out boyfriends.—Ignatius Jones, *The 1992 True Hip Manual*, p. 64, 1992

beer flat *noun*
an apartment where beer is sold privately and illegally *US*
- It was shortly prior to the repeal of prohibition and beer flats were popular.—Herbert Huncke, *The Evening Sun Turned Crimson*, p. 27, 1980

beer goggles *noun*
a drink-induced clouding of visual perception that enhances the sexual allure of previously unappealing companions *US*
- —Connie Eble (Editor), *UNC-CH Campus Slang*, p. 1, Fall 1987
- Aside from inappropriate vomiting and public urination, one of the most puzzling effects are the "beer goggles" that accompany the latter stages of a bender.—*Drugs An Adult Guide*, p. 32, December 2001

beer goitre *noun*
the protruding stomach of a serious beer drinker *NEW ZEALAND*
- —David McGill, *David McGill's Complete Kiwi Slang Dictionary*, p. 14, 1998

beer gut *noun*
the protruding stomach of an excessive beer drinker *AUSTRALIA*
- You wait till you've got six chins and a beer gut[.]—*Janie Stagestruck*, p. 88, 1972
- "What's he look like? Regular old beer-gut dick?" "No, he's skinny almost."—Elmore Leonard, *City Primeval*, p. 54, 1980
- His pants hang perfectly flat, while out front his angry red beer gut balloons out like the front end of a '51 Studebaker.—C.D. Payne, *Youth in Revolt*, p. 10, 1993

beer-gutted *adjective*
(of men) having a protruding stomach from drinking beer excessively *AUSTRALIA*
- Billy homed in on the beer-gutted billionaires by the far side of the pool.—Kathy Lette, *Girls' Night Out*, p. 178, 1987

beer high grade *noun*
cash from rich gold-prospecting seams *CANADA*
- There is hardly a miner in the camp who hasn't at one time or another high-graded enough [gold] to pay for a round or two at his favorite neighborhood taproom. In fact, "beer high-grade" is a common term for money spent in the hotels.—*Maclean's*, p. 30/1, 4th May 1963

beer me!
please give me another beer! *US*
- —Connie Eble (Editor), *UNC-CH Campus Slang*, p. 1, March 1986

beernoculars *noun*
your vision and judgment after drinking too many beers *US*
- —Connie Eble (Editor), *UNC-CH Campus Slang*, p. 1, March 1986

beer o'clock *noun*
quitting time on a job *NEW ZEALAND*
- It's beer o'clock for some now, it's finished.—*Country Calendar*, 4th May 2000

beer parlour *noun*
a room in a hotel licensed to sell beer *CANADA*
Originally named to distinguish them from taverns, they have been more recently licensed to serve men and women.
- In Saskatchewan today–hold your breath–women hustle the suds in men's beer parlors.—*Toronto Globe and Mail*, p. 6/5, 13th October 1965

beer run *noun*
a trip to a store to buy beer for a party *US*
- —*Current Slang*, p. 8, Spring 1971

beer sandwich *noun*
a lunch consisting of beer, beer and more beer *NEW ZEALAND*
- —David McGill, *David McGill's Complete Kiwi Slang Dictionary*, p. 12, 1998

beer scooter *noun*
the ability to return home when too drunk to, afterwards, remember the journey *UK*
- —*Roger's Profanisaurus*, p. 4, 3rd October 1999

beer spanner *noun*
a bottle opener *UK, 1984*
Royal Air Force use.
- —John W. Mussell FRNS, *Militarisms*, 1995

beer-thirty *noun*
a fictional time of day, suggesting that a beer is overdue *US*
- —Don Alexander, *The Racer's Dictionary*, p. 10, 1980

beer-up *noun*
a session of beer drinking *AUSTRALIA, 1919*
- I'm telling you Alec, sometimes I feel like a good old beer-up in some city pub.—Jean Brooks, *The Opal Witch*, p. 84, 1967

beer up *verb*
to drink a great deal of beer *US*
- —Harold Wentworth and Stuart Berg Flexner, *Dictionary of American Slang*, p. 28, 1960

beer vouchers *noun*
money *UK*
- Andy busked on Buchanan Street, near the corner of Gordon Street, as a means of generating some extra beer vouchers[.]—Christopher Brookmyre, *The Sacred Art of Stealing*, p. 59, 2002

bees and honey *noun*
money *UK, 1892*
Rhyming slang.
- I'll be getting me greengages [wages] today. Reckon I'll have enough bees and honey for a bit of a blowout.—*The Sweeney*, p. 6, 1976
- [B]eing very short of bees and honey, and unable to pay the Burton-on-Trent[.]—Ronnie Barker, *Fletcher's Book of Rhyming Slang*, p. 25, 1979
- It's not my money and the bloke who I put it on for is going to be very angry when I arrive without the bees and honey.—Clive Galea, *Slipper*, p. 183, 1988

bee shit *noun*
honey *US*
From the mistaken belief that bees defecate honey.
- She calls me "beeshit," 'cause I'm so sweet.—Ken Weaver, *Texas Crude*, p. 103, 1984

bee's knees *noun*
the acme of perfection, the best *AUSTRALIA, 1905*
Always configured with 'the'; a favourite construction of the flapper of the 1920s.
- Not exactly the bee's knees in romance.—Peter Cook, *Not Only But Also*, 1970
- I thought Vo Rogue was the bees-knees until today[.]—*Sunday Herald*, p. 51, 1st October 1989
- I thought I was the bee's knees because there was a police car outside the house.—Andy McNab, *Immediate Action*, p. 8, 1995

bee stings *noun*
small female breasts *US*
- —Roger Blake, *The American Dictionary of Sexual Terms*, p. 15, 1964
- —Michael Dalton Johnson, *Talking Trash with Redd Foxx*, p. 62, 1994
- —Chris Donald, *Roger's Profanisuarus*, p. 10, 1998

beeswax *noun*
1 business, in the senses 'mind your own business' and 'none of your beeswax' *US, 1934*
- "I can't tell you everything." "Why not?" "Because it's none of your beeswax, Laura!"—Ben Elton, *High Society*, p. 122, 2002
- Jordan's response? Mind your own beeswax, I've got a baby to bring up.—*The Observer*, 18th August 2002

2 income tax; betting tax *UK*
Rhyming slang, cleverly punning 'bees' (**BEES AND HONEY**, 'money') and, possibly, 'whack(s)' for the taxman's portion.
- —Ned Wallish, *The Truth Dictionary of Racing Slang*, p. 6, 1989
- —John McCririck, *John McCririck's World of Betting*, p. 59, 1991

bees wingers *noun*
the fingers *UK*
Rhyming slang.
- —Red Daniells, 1980

beetle *noun*
1 in horse racing, a poorly performing horse *US, 1915*
- —David W. Maurer, *Argot of the Racetrack*, p. 13, 1951

2 a female *US, 1931*
Circus and carnival usage
- —Don Wilmeth, *The Language of American Popular Entertainment*, p. 20, 1981

Beetle *nickname*
the original Volkwagen car and later models of a similar shape *US*
Derives from the shape of the car; first imported to the US in 1949, by 1960 the nickname was in worldwide usage and by Volkswagen's advertisers by the 1970s. In 1998 the manufacturers unveiled the 'New Beetle'.

beetle-crusher; beetle-stomper *noun*
a soldier in the infantry *UK, 1889*
- —J. E. Lighter, *Historical Dictionary of American Slang, Volume 1*, p. 128, 1994

beetle-crushers *noun*
heavy boots, especially 'Doc Martens' *UK*
In *The Lore and Language of Schoolchildren*, 1959, Iona and Peter Opie record 'beetle-crushers' as 'big-feet or the nickname for someone so-blessed'.
- Drape jackets, velvet collars, DA haircuts, luminous socks and beetle crushers is the gear that's go'. —Amy De La Haye (quoting Lesley Ebbetts, Daily Mirror, 23rd December, 1976), *Surfers Soulies Skinheads & Skaters*, p. 24, 1996
- Troy heard the thick, black beetle-crusher boots clump on the floorboards. —John Lawton, *Old Flames*, p. 12, 2003

beevo *noun*
an alcoholic beverage *US*
- [S]ometimes longed for the uncomplicated life of lacrosse and rugby and hou-bro beevo parties, of happily hugging the toilet allnight long with your barf buddies after draining a half-keg for no special occasion? —John Sayles, *Union Dues*, p. 279, 1977

Bee Wee *nickname*
British West Indian Airways *TRINIDAD AND TOBAGO, 1980*
- "After all, external carriers come and go," said Bertrand. "At Bee Wee, we are the Caribbean.' —*Air Transport World*, p. 90, February 1991

beeyatch *noun*
used as an emphatic variation of 'bitch', especially when used to a woman or as an exclamation *US*
- One time for your mind, beeyatch[.] —Too $hort, *Tell the Feds*, 2001
- Cuz you ask the questions I got answers, beeyatch[.] —Ja Rule, *Survival of the Illest 2*, 2004

beeze *noun*
the penis *UK*
- —Martin Page, *For Gawdsake Don't Take Me (a World War 2 collection)*, 1976

beezer *noun*
1 excellent; most attractive *UK, 1961*
Children's comic *The Beezer* was first published in 1957.
- Ben has to choose between landing a beezer job in New York City or attending his kid's school play in New Jersey[.] —*The Observer*, 20th June 2004

2 the nose *US, 1908*
- How many ways can you wrinkle your beezer? Do you show your teeth when you say the letter S? —Bruce Brooks, *The Moves Make the Man*, p. 62, 1984

3 in horse racing, a horse's nose *US*
- —David W. Maurer, *Argot of the Racetrack*, p. 13, 1951

4 a pedigree Ibizan hound *US*
- "Beezers" are good with other dogs, but likely to pursue (and catch!) smaller pets. —Michele Welton, *Your Purebred Puppy*, p. 150, 2000

Beezer; Beeza *noun*
a BSA motorcyle, in production since 1909; also a BSA car *UK, 1961*
The company name is actually an initialism of *B*irmingham *S*mall *A*rms. BSA owners claim that the initials in fact stand for '*B*astard *S*talled *A*gain' or '*B*olts *S*catted *A*ll Over'.
- In Oakland he wore a blue suit to work and drove a white Thunderbird, but when the Angels went out on a run he joined them on his old Beezer. —Hunter S. Thompson, *Hell's Angels*, p. 132, 1966

befok *adjective*
crazy, angry, lacking emotional control *SOUTH AFRICA, 1979*
From the Afrikaans for 'fucked up'.
- —Penny Silva, *A Dictionary of South African English*, 1996

before-days *adverb*
in the past *BARBADOS*
- —John A. Holm, *Dictionary of Bahamian English*, p. 15, 1982

before time *adverb*
long ago *US*
Hawaiian youth usage.
- "Befo' time I had real popolo kine hair, you know!" —Douglas Simonson, *Pidgin to da Max Hana Hou*, 1982

befuggered *adjective*
drunk *UK*
A conflation of **BUGGERED** and **FUCKED**.
- —*e-cyclopaedia*, 20th March 2002

beg *noun*
in a telephone solicitation, the actual plea to purchase that which is being sold *US*
- —*American Speech*, p. 150–151, May 1959: 'Notes on the cant of the telephone confidence man'

▸ on the beg
begging, scrounging *UK*
- —Michael Munro, *The Patter, Another Blast*, 1988

beg *verb*
▸ go begging
to be spare and available *UK*
- There's one [sausage] going begging. —Helen Simpson, *Bed and Breakfast*, 17th August 2004

begerk *noun*
male masturbation *AUSTRALIA*
Oil rig workers use the term to refer to a 'big jerk'.
- —Thommo, *The Dictionary of Australian Swearing and Sex Sayings*, p. 15, 1985

beggar *noun*
1 a person, usually a man or boy *UK, 1833*
Euphemistic for **BUGGER**; sometimes spelt 'begger'.
- [T]he car happened to stop at the traffic lights and the little beggar recognised me. —Charles Raven, *Underworld Nights*, p. 129, 1956
- LOMPER: Told you, he went out. I saw him go. DAVE: There's the begger. —*The Full Monty*, 1997

2 an unpleasant, very dangerous or difficult thing, project, episode or circumstance; a nuisance *UK, 1937*
Euphemistic for **BUGGER**.
- My computer is playing silly beggars[.] —*The Guardian*, 7th March 2003

beggar
used as a euphemistic replacement for 'bugger' in all expletive phrases and exclamations *UK, 1937*

beggar boy's arse; beggar boy's ass *noun*
money *UK, 1960*
Rhyming slang for **BRASS** (money).

beggar my neighbour *noun*
the dole *UK, 1960*
Rhyming slang for the **LABOUR** (Exchange); usually follows 'on the' as in 'on the labour' (to be drawing unemployment benefit). Sometimes shortened to 'beggar'.

beggar's lagging; tramp's lagging *noun*
a prison sentence of 90 days *UK, 1950*
- —Angela Devlin, *Prison Patter*, p. 26, 1996

beggered *adjective*
tired *NEW ZEALAND*
A euphemism for **BUGGERED UP**.
- I've been fencing with Sam all day and that bastard works so hard I'm beggared. —Louis S. Leland, *A Personal Kiwi-Yankee Dictionary*, p. 13, 1984

be good to yourself
used with humour as a farewell *US*
A catchphrase television sign-off on *The Don McNeil TV Club* (ABC, 1950–51). Repeated with referential humour.

begorrah!; begorah!; begor!
by God! *IRELAND*
Originally a genuine euphemism, latterly a cliché ascribed to stereotypical Irish.

beg your pardon *noun*

a garden *UK, 1961*

Rhyming slang. Ray Puxley argues that this is a post-World War 2 coinage on the grounds that pre-war Cockneys had 'yards' not 'gardens'.

- —Ray Puxley, *Cockney Rabbit*, p. 13, 1992

behavior report *noun*

a letter home from a military recruit to his girlfriend *US*

- —Lou Shelly, *Hepcats Jive Talk Dictionary*, p. 43, 1945

behind *noun*

the buttocks *UK, 1786*

behind *adjective*

1 imprisoned *US*

- Before I left Chicago he had been "behind" twice, once for car stealing and once, of all things, for bond forgery or something complicated like that.—Clancy Sigal, *Going Away*, p. 355, 1961

2 committed, dedicated *US*

- —Lewis Yablonsky, *The Hippie Trip*, p. 367, 1968

behind *preposition*

1 (of a drug) under the influence of *US*

- I could write behind STP, but not behind acid.—Joan Didion, *Slouching Toward Bethlehem*, p. 109, 1967
- —Edward R. Bloomquist, *Marijuana*, p. 333, 1971
- —Peter Johnson, *Dictionary of Street Alcohol and Drug Terms*, p. 17, 1993
- Simone de Beauvoir, whom I knew during her Nelson Algren period, worked very well behind absinthe, or its substitute, Pernod[.]—Terry Southern, *Now Dig This*, p. 206, 2001

2 as a result of *US, 1957*

- —Anthony Romeo, *The Language of Gangs*, p. 16, 4th December 1962
- Went to Q behind armed robbery.—Joseph Wambaugh, *The Blue Knight*, p. 27, 1973

behind-the-behind *noun*

anal sex *US*

- —Dale Gordon, *The Dominion Sex Dictionary*, p. 27, 1967

behind the bridge *adverb*

in any ghetto or slum *TRINIDAD AND TOBAGO*

Originally a reference to the slums of Port of Spain at the back of the East Dry River.

behind the door *adverb*

locked in a prison cell *UK*

- —Angela Devlin, *Prison Patter*, p. 26, 1996
- He'd just done 11 months behind the door and he was belting shit out of me for getting myself nicked.—Lenny McLean, *The Guv'nor*, p. 25, 1998
- Well, out of 25 years in prison I have spent 22 years in isolation. In solitary confinement; behind the door.—Dave Courtney [quoting Charlie Bronson], *Dodgy Dave's Little Black Book*, p. 57, 2001

behind the door when brains were given out

stupid *AUSTRALIA*

- I though you'd ask that, dimwit. You sure were behind the door when the brains were given out.—Wilda Moxham, *The Apprentice*, p. 26, 1969
- Dolly, you've just got to try harder with your lessons! I'm sure you can do them. You weren't behind the door when brains were given out! —Ellen Bosworth, *Shelley and the bushfire mystery*, p. 67, 1972

behind with the rent *adjective*

homosexual *UK*

Extended from a pun on 'buttocks' and 'behind'.

- "You're not a homosexual, are you?" "No, I'm not. Definitely not." "Not behind with the rent?" "No way."—J.J. Connolly, *Layer Cake*, p. 48, 2000

beige *noun*

a light-skinned black person *US*

Sometimes spelled unconventionally, as in the Gover citation.

- —Lou Shelly, *Hepcats Jive Talk Dictionary*, p. 7, 1945
- Sweetheart, yo's as baij as they come.—Robert Gover, *JC Saves*, p. 68, 1968

beige *verb*

to chemically darken cocaine to give it the appearance of a purity that it does not possess *US*

- —Terry Williams, *The Cocaine Kids*, p. 135, 1989

beige *adjective*

bland, boring *US, 1982*

- —J. E. Lighter, *Historical Dictionary of American Slang, Volume 1*, p. 129, 1994

beige frame *noun*

a light-skinned black woman *US*

- —Lavada Durst, *The Jives of Dr. Hepcat*, p. 11, 1953

beiging *noun*

a chemical process to change the colour of cocaine and enhance its commercial possibilities

- —Nick Constable, *This is Cocaine*, p. 182, 2002

be-in *noun*

an organised gathering for the celebration of counterculture lifestyles and values *US*

Originally applied to an event in San Francisco in January 1967, and then to similar events elsewhere. Organisers ('inspirers') of that event wrote: 'When the Berkeley political activists and the love generation of the Haigh Ashbury and thousands of young men and women from every state in the nation embrace at the gathering of the tribes for a Human Be-In at polo field in Golden Gate Park the spiritual revolution will be manifest and proven'.

- THE BEGINNING IS THE HUMAN BE IN [Headline]—*Berkeley Barb*, p. 1, 6th January 1967
- Be-In. A kind of instant hippie evangelism. Park grass, open skies and trees is the usual church architecture.—Sidney Bernard, *This Way to the Apocalypse*, p. 58, 1968
- Like a super be-in, a live-in, real freedom. Wow!—*East Village Other*, 20th August 1969
- [Allen Ginsberg] helped to launch yet another cataclysmic voyage of human discovery – the world's first Human Be-in.—Richard Neville, *Play Power*, p. 33, 1970
- Of course not everyone at the Be-in belonged to a specific tribe.—Ann Fettamen, *Trashing*, p. 23, 1970
- As I came up to the Human Be-In, walking from my apartment on Broderick Street, I got several blocks away from the polo field and the energy and vibrations were so strong that I trembled and my knees shook[.]—Stephen Gaskin, *Amazing Dope Tales*, p. 46, 1980
- The Be-In was conceived by San Francisco Oracle editor Allen Cohen as an "ecstatic union of love and activism" between Berkeley antiwar activists and the pyschedlic revolutionaries of the Haight-Ashbury. —David Shenk and Steve Silberman, *Skeleton Key*, p. 20, 1994

bejabbers; bejabers *noun*

used as a jocular euphemism for 'bejesus' *US, 1959*

- They arrived in time to be scared by a group of drunken townies beating the bejabbers out of three or four hippy boys they'd caught in the lot.—Nicholas Von Hoffman, *We Are The People Our Parents Warned Us Against*, p. 67, 1967
- Does he want, bejabers, to get me sacked for nothing?—Murphy Tom, *A Crucial Week in the Life of a Grocer's Assistant*, p. 155, 1989

bejesus; bejasus *noun*

used as a mild expletive *US, 1908*

An ameliorated 'Jesus', originally recorded in 1908 but not widely used until the 1930s.

- Becoss by this time there's the carptender and he's by this time got a kind of crowbar and he tearing the bejeezus out of the back of the newstand.—John McNulty, *Third Avenue, New York*, p. 39, 1946
- But stories about dykes bore the bejesus out of me. I just can't put myself in their shoes.—Truman Capote, *Breakfast at Tiffany's*, p. 21, 1958
- Did you know he got four purple hearts in Vietnam? Did he? Bejesus.—Doug Lang, *Freaks*, p. 21, 1973
- There we were, Tom, in the pool in Leisureland, down in your part of the world, playing, you know, trying to drown the bejayzus out of each other...—Joseph O'Connor, *Red Roses and Petrol*, p. 70, 1995
- That Saturday morning, April Fool's Day, one of the lifeguards was impressing the bejesus out of a ride-along female citizen by whipping his boat into 180s on Fiesta Bay...—Joseph Wambaugh, *Floaters*, p. 22, 1996

bejiminy *noun*

used as a mild expletive *US*

- I like Rocky Graziano's way of belting the bejiminy out of his opponents without any shilly-shallying.—*San Francisco Examiner*, p. 14, 9th April 1946

bejonkers *noun*

the female breasts *AUSTRALIA*

- —James McDonald, *A Dictionary of Obscenity, Taboo and Euphemism*, p. 9, 1988

Bela and Boris *noun*

in hold 'em poker, the two of clubs and the two of spades *US*

An allusion to Bela Lugosi and Boris Korloff of horror film fame, with a nod to the horror that they visit upon a hand in hold 'em poker.

- —John Vorhaus, *The Big Book of Poker Slang*, p. 6, 1996

belasian *noun*
a drunk, *bel*ligerent *Asian* *US*
• —Connie Eble (Editor), *UNC-CH Campus Slang*, p. 1, Spring 2003

belch *noun*
a complaint *US*
Circus and carnival usage.
• —Don Wilmeth, *The Language of American Popular Entertainment*, p. 20, 1981

belch *verb*
to act as a police informer *US, 1901*
• —Vincent J. Monteleone, *Criminal Slang*, p. 20, 1949
• —Hyman E. Goldin et al., *Dictionary of American Underworld Lingo*, p. 25, 1950
• —J. E. Lighter, *Historical Dictionary of American Slang, Volume 1*, p. 129, 1994

belcher *noun*
1 the mouth *US*
• —Hyman E. Goldin et al., *Dictionary of American Underworld Lingo*, p. 25, 1950

2 a police informer *US*
• —*American Speech*, p. 99, May 1956: 'Smugglers' argot in the southwest'

Belgian lace *noun*
a pattern of white foam from the frothing head of beer that remains in an empty glass *UK*
• —Nick Brownlee, *This Is Alcohol*, p. 161, 2002

believe
used as an assertion of sincerity *UK*
A shortening of phrases like 'you can believe me', 'you must believe what I say', etc. Recorded in use among young, urban blacks.
• I had a cris' pair ah Versace jeans dat got bun [burnt] up. I'm screwin' about dat, believe.—Courttia Newland, *Society Within*, p. 11, 1999

believer *noun*
1 in trucking, a driver who follows all laws and company rules *US*
• —Montie Tak, *Truck Talk*, p. 10, 1971

2 a dead enemy soldier *US*
Vietnam war use.
• —Linda Reinberg, *In the Field*, p. 19, 1991

be like
used as a meaningless response to a greeting *US*
• —Connie Eble (Editor), *UNC-CH Campus Slang*, p. 1, Fall 1980

Belinda Carlisles *noun*
haemorrhoids *UK*
Rhyming slang for 'piles', formed from the name of US singer Belinda Carlisle (b.1958).
• —Bodmin Dark, *Dirty Cockney Rhyming Slang*, 2003

bell *noun*
1 the head of the penis *UK*
From the shape; very popular since the 1990s.
• The whole package. The shaft and that right up to his bell. Hairy as fuck. Not the actual bell-end itself, to be fair, but the rest of it[.]—Kevin Sampson, *Outlaws*, p. 12, 2001

2 the clitoris *AUSTRALIA*
• —James McDonald, *A Dictionary of Obscenity, Taboo and Euphemism*, p. 10, 1988

3 a telephone call *US*
Teen slang.
• —*Newsweek*, p. 28, 8th October 1951
• I think you better give him a bell on Monday, Dad.—Barry Humphries, *A Nice Night's Entertainment*, p. 122, 1968

▸**give a bell**
to telephone someone *UK, 1982*
From the ringing bell of original telephones.
• Alright. Give us a tanner and I'll give him a bell.—Bruce Robinson, *Withnail and I*, 1987

▸**on a bell**
in television and film making, shooting a scene *US*
From the bell used on location to signal that shooting is about to begin.
• —Ralph S. Singleton, *Filmaker's Dictionary*, p. 115, 1990

bell *verb*
to telephone someone *US*
An allusion to Alexander Graham Bell, telephone pioneer, and/or to the bell that rang on early telephones.
• —Kenn "Naz" Young, *Naz's Underground Dictionary*, p. 14, 1973
• [W]ithout much further ado I belled our local Ombudsperson. —Andrew Nickolds, *Back to Basics*, p. 40, 1994
• It seemed to Zaffir that she only ever belled him for a whinge.—Greg Williams, *Diamond Geezers*, p. 13, 1997
• [T]he publican will be belling the boys in blue[.]—Martin King and Martin Knight, *The Naughty Nineties*, p. 35, 1999

belladonna *noun*
an extremely potent hybrid marijuana *UK*
Bella donna is Italian for 'beautiful woman'. This plant, a hybrid of SUPERSKUNK, shares its name with *Atropa belladonna*, the poisonous deadly nightshade.
• —*Seedbank*, 2001

bell cow *noun*
in marketing, a popular, high-profit item *US*
• —Rachel S. Epstein and Nina Liebman, *Biz Speak*, p. 18, 1986

belle *noun*
a young and effeminate male homosexual *US, 1940*
• —Florida Legislative Investigation Committee (Johns Committee), *Homosexuality and Citizenship in Florida*, 1964: 'Glossary of homosexual terms and deviate acts'
• —*Maledicta*, p. 164, Summer/Winter 1986–1987: 'Sexual slang: prostitutes, pedophiles, flagellators, transvestites, and necrophiles'

bell end *noun*
the head of the penis *UK*
From the shape.
• [H] brushed his bell end up and down her lips before ramming himself inside her—Colin Butts, *Is Harry on the Boot?*, 1997
• —*Roger's Profanisaurus*, December 1997
• [C]aught that poor horse right on its bell-end.—Lenny McLean, *The Guv'nor*, 1998
• [O]ne thing a do remember clearly – mine was a full bell-end bigger[.]—Niall Griffiths, *Grits*, p. 38, 2000
• Belinda or "Bell-end-her" as he likes to call her[.]—Danny King, *The Burglar Diaries*, 2001
• Tattoo of smiley face on bell end.—Richard Herring, *Talking Cock*, 2003

bellhop *noun*
a member of the US Marine Corps *US, 1929*
An abbreviated form of the longer SEAGOING BELL HOP, which teases the marines for their uniforms.
• —J. E. Lighter, *Historical Dictionary of American Slang, Volume 1*, p. 131, 1994

bellied *adjective*
drunk *UK*
• —Pete Brown, *Man Walks into a Pub*, 2003

bellows *noun*
the lungs *US, 1843*
• —Joseph Weingarten, *American Dictionary of Slang*, p. 23, 1954

bell-ringer *noun*
any door-to-door salesman or canvasser *US*
• —Harold Wentworth and Stuart Berg Flexner, *Dictionary of American Slang*, p. 29, 1960

bell rope *noun*
the penis *US, 1969*
• —Eugene Landy, *The Underground Dictionary*, p. 31, 1971

bells *noun*
bell-bottomed trousers *UK, 1948*
Naval origins.
• —*Current Slang*, p. 13, Spring 1970

bells!
used for expressing approval *US, 1948*
• —Robert S. Gould, *A Jazz Lexicon*, p. 17, 1964

bells and whistles *noun*
1 entertaining features that are not necessary to a computer program *US*
• "Now that we've got the basic program working, let's go back and add some bells and whistles."—Guy L. Steele et al., *The Hacker's Dictionary*, p. 29, 1983

2 extra features designed by underwriters to attract investors in a bond issue *US*
• —Kathleen Odean, *High Steppers, Fallen Angels, and Lollipops*, p. 20, 1988

Bell Telephone hour *noun*
a session of torture in which US soldiers use the electricity from field telephones to shock suspected Viet Cong *US*
The term suggests a television programme, not genital-oriented electric torture.
- —Linda Reinberg, *In the Field*, p. 19, 1991

belly *noun*
1 a fat person *US*
- The labels were cruel: Gimp, Limpy–go-fetch, Crip, Lift-one-drag one, etc. Pint, Half-a-man, Peewee, Shorty, Lardass, Pork, Blubber, Belly, Blimp. Nuke-knob, Skinhead, Baldy. Four-eyes, Specs, Coke bottles.—*San Francisco Examiner*, p. A15, 28th July 1997

2 the swell in a thicker-than-normal surfboard *US*
- —Grant W. Kuhns, *On Surfing*, p. 113, 1963

3 a stomach ache *BARBADOS*
- —Frank A. Collymore, *Barbadian Dialect*, p. 18, 1965

4 pregnancy *BARBADOS*
- Dat girl get belly again.—John A. Holm, *Dictionary of Bahamian English*, p. 16, 1982

belly *verb*
▸ **belly the wall**
to stand facing a wall for inspection by prison guards *US*
- —Hyman E. Goldin et al., *Dictionary of American Underworld Lingo*, p. 26, 1950

bellyache *noun*
any small-town newspaper *US*
- Anything in the Bellache this week?—John Gould, *Maine Lingo*, p. 11, 1975

bellyache *verb*
to complain *US, 1881*
- They get that idea in their heads, all they can do is stand there and bellyache Gosepl at you[.]—George V. Higgins, *The Friends of Eddie Doyle*, p. 39, 1971
- Okay, hogs, I've listened to you bellyache about moving to this new town. This said bellyaching will end as of 0859 hours[.]—Lewis John Carlino, *The Great Santini*, 1979
- Now he's bellyaching in Paris and L.A. and Honolulu about the ropes and the canvas and a short count.—Bill Cardoso, *The Maltese Sangweech*, p. 304, 1984
- Quit your bellyaching, Hawkings.—*Gone in 60 Seconds*, 1992

bellyacher *noun*
a complainer *US, 1930*
- My dad wasn't a bellyacher[.]—*St. Petersburg Times*, 6th March 2004

belly and back *adverb*
completely; without mercy *GUYANA*
- —Richard Allsopp, *Dictionary of Caribbean English Usage*, p. 92, 1996

belly board *noun*
in television and film making, a low camera platform *US*
- —Ralph S. Singleton, *Filmaker's Dictionary*, p. 16, 1990

bellybump *verb*
1 to jostle; to shove; to rough up *US*
- Most of the time, Slim said, all he did was write and mimeograph leaflets, though once or twice he was called ujpon to "belly bump" in the picket lines.—Clancy Sigal, *Going Away*, p. 83, 1961

2 to ride a sled face-down *US, 1912*
- —Charles F. Haywood, *Yankee Dictionary*, p. 10, 1963
- —Claudio R. Salvucci, *The Philadelphia Dialect Dictionary*, p. 30, 1996

bellybuster *noun*
1 a stomach-first dive into the water *AUSTRALIA, 1941*
- —Louis S. Leland, *A Personal Kiwi-Yankee Dictionary*, p. 13, 1984

2 a greasy hamburger or other food likely to provoke indigestion *US*
- So I get myself one of Danny's bellybusters there, that a self-respecting do would not eat, and I ate it all[.]—George V. Higgins, *The Rat on Fire*, p. 102, 1981

belly button *noun*
1 the navel *US, 1877*
More naïve than childish; derives from the appearance of an umbilical knot.
- Well. I'm up here in this womb / I'm looking all around / Well, I'm looking out my belly button window[.]—Jimi Hendrix, *Belly Button Window*, 1970
- "You're [sic] bellybutton birthday's on March thirtieth, right?" "Yes is." Bellybutton birthday!—Stuart Browne, *Dangerous Parking*, p. 119, 2000

2 a bullet hole *UK*
- —Dave Courtney, *Dodgy Dave's Little Black Book*, p. 7, 2001

belly fiddle *noun*
a guitar *US*
- —Clarence Major, *Dictionary of Afro-American Slang*, p. 25, 1970

belly flop *noun*
a dive into the water stomach first, intentionally or not *US, 1895*
- California's greatest exponent of the calculated belly-flop [comic diver Norman Hanley] had forgotten to eat breakfast.—*San Francisco Examiner*, p. 20, 1st September 1957
- Biggest splash in the world, according to the judges in Vancouver, B.C., where the fifth annual World Belly-Flop Championships were held, is made by Robin Gentile.—*San Francisco Examiner and Chronicle, This World*, p. 25, 12th August 1979
- Could I do her a favour? Cathy, I wanted to say, all you have to do is ask. A belly flop from the lighthouse? Of course.—Phillip Gwynne, *Deadly Unna?*, p. 180, 1998

belly flopper *noun*
1 a poorly executed dive resulting in a painful impact on the water surface with the belly *AUSTRALIA, 1941*
- Tony hunched his big Father-Bear shoulders, then spread his arms as he did when he was going to take a belly-flopper in the lake just to make the kids laugh.—Paul Radley, *Jack Rivers and Me*, p. 94, 1981

2 a rifleman shooting from a prone position *US*
- —*American Speech*, p. 192, October 1957: 'Some colloquialisms of the handgunner'

bellyful *noun*
as much as you can tolerate; more than enough *UK, 1687*
- I'd had a bellyful of those swindlers and their dirty politics.—Wally Lamb, *I Know This Much Is True*, p. 834, 1998

belly full and behind drunk *adjective*
too full with food and drink to act *BARBADOS*
- —Richard Allsopp, *Dictionary of Caribbean English Usage*, p. 93, 1996

belly fummux *noun*
stomach pains *IRELAND*
- —C. I. Macafee, *A Concise Ulster Dictionary*, p. 22, 1996

belly gas *noun*
air injected into the abdominal cavity to raise the diaphragm *US*
- —*American Speech*, p. 145–148, May 1961: 'The spoken language of medicine; argot, slang, cant'

belly gun *noun*
a handgun *US, 1926*
- —Vincent J. Monteleone, *Criminal Slang*, p. 20, 1949

belly habit *noun*
1 severe stomach cramping suffered during withdrawal from a drug addiction *US*
- —Clarence Major, *Dictionary of Afro-American Slang*, p. 25, 1970

2 a drug addiction, especially to an opiate *US*
- —Jay Robert Nash, *Dictionary of Crime*, p. 24, 1992

belly hit *noun*
in poker, a card drawn that completes an inside straight *US*
- —*American Speech*, p. 97, May 1951: 'The vocabulary of poker'
- —Albert H. Morehead, *The Complete Guide to Winning Poker*, p. 256, 1967

bellyologist *noun*
a person who eats too much *BARBADOS*
- —Frank A. Collymore, *Barbadian Dialect*, p. 18, 1965

belly pad *noun*
a pancake *US, 1958*
- —Frederic G. Cassidy, *Dictionary of American Regional English*, p. 215, 1985

belly queen *noun*
a male homosexual who prefers face-to-face intercourse *US, 1965*
- —Robert A. Wilson, *Playboy's Book of Forbidden Words*, p. 33, 1972

belly ride *noun*
sexual intercourse *US*
- —Kenn "Naz" Young, *Naz's Dictionary of Teen Slang*, p. 7, 1993

ellyrubber *noun*
a slow song in which partners dance close to each other *US*
- The blast of the music ended for a few counts before going on to a slower piece, a bona fide Chicago belly rubber. —Odie Hawkins, *Black Chicago*, p. 138, 1992

elly rubbing *noun*
dancing *UK*
- —David Powis, *The Signs of Crime*, 1977

elly-stick; stick *noun*
in a confidence swindle involving fixed gambling, a confederate who appears to win consistently *US, 1940*
- I said, "I'll learn fast. I'll be the best stick you ever saw." —Iceberg Slim (Robert Beck), *Trick Baby*, p. 91, 1969
- "Kid, there isn't a helluva lot a belly-stick has to know. All you do is keep your belly against the joint cointer and let me make lucky on the wheel." —Iceberg Slim (Robert Beck), *Trick Baby*, p. 92, 1969

belly tanker *noun*
in drag racing, a car made out of salvaged aeroplane fuel tanks for lake bed racing *US*
- —Lewis Poteet, *Car & Motorcyle Slang*, p. 199, 1992

belly up *verb*
to approach and stand against something, usually a bar *US, 1907*
- [B]y the time they hit the doorway I bellied up to the bar, put a foot on the rail, one hand casually resting on the back of Susie's chair. —Larry Heinemann, *Close Quarters*, p. 175, 1977
- The road crews belly up to the bar, swilling mugs of Pabst Blue Ribbon on tap[.] —Larry Heinemann, *Paco's Story*, p. 62, 1990

belly-up *adjective*
bankrupt, out of business; dead *US, 1920*
- Air Control Union Goes Belly Up [Headline] —*San Francisco Chronicle*, p. 10, 3rd July 1982
- Your Uncle Milton lost all his money in a Puerto Rican condominium that went belly up. —*Sleepless in Seattle*, 1993
- The other Master Lee dropped the business in his lap just before he was about to go belly up. —Odie Hawkins, *Lost Angeles*, p. 25, 1994

bellywash *noun*
a soft drink, soda *US, 1926*
Originally applied to a weak drink, and then to soda.
- It's hotter than the hubs of hell today! Whatd'ya say we stop off over here and get us a bellywash? —Ken Weaver, *Texas Crude*, p. 103, 1984

belly whacker *noun*
a poorly executed dive resulting in a painful impact on the water surface with the belly *AUSTRALIA*
- "Belly whacker" was used on the Mornington Peninsula, Victoria in the 50s and 60s. —*Wordmap (www.abc.net.au/wordmap)*, 2003

belly-whop *verb*
in sledding, to dive stomach-first onto the sled *US*
- There is always plenty of ice and snow for "belly-whopping." —*San Francisco Call-Bulletin*, 17th March 1955
- Belly whopping while under the influence, Sarge. —*New Yorker*, p. 53, 28th February 1968

belly woman *noun*
a pregnant woman *JAMAICA, 1834*
- —F.G. Cassidy and R.B. LePage, *Dictionary of Jamaican English*, p. 38, 1967
- —John A. Holm, *Dictionary of Bahamian English*, p. 16, 1982

belly works *noun*
diarrhoea *GUYANA*
- —Richard Allsopp, *Dictionary of Caribbean English Usage*, p. 93, 1996

below par *adjective*
in poor health or spirits *UK, 1937*
Directly from describing stocks and shares as below face value.

below the radar *adverb*
keeping a low profile; unperceived *US*
- Susan Howell says because of GoPer David Duke's "racist background," "people are reluctant to say they're for Duke. The saying is, 'he flies below the radar" – he's difficult to pick up." —*USA Today*, 26th February 1990

below the zone *adverb*
(used of a military promotion) unexpectedly early *US*
Vietnam war usage.
- All of my guys from the 1/327 – Peeping Tom Hancock, Ben Willis, Wayne Dill, Don Chapman, Glynn Mallory – had made it "below the zone" to major. —David H. Hackworth, *About Face*, p. 606, 1989

belt *noun*

1 a hit, a punch *UK, 1937*

2 a gulp, especially of strong alcohol *US, 1922*
- Mrs. Larkin cried a little too and took Guido out in the garage and gave him a belt form a pint bottle of Schenley hidden behind the skid chains. —Max Shulman, *Rally Round the Flag, Boys!*, p. 14, 1957
- After a frustrating day at the office a couple of belts lift me out of the dumps. —Lenny Bruce, *How to Talk Dirty and Influence People*, p. 46, 1965
- Give me a drink, fella. Gimme a belt of Scotch. —Edwin Torres, *Q & A*, p. 51, 1977
- Hard day at the job, no lunch maybe, get so fuckin' pissed off you don't want any dinner, only thing on your mind's a good couple of belts, huh? —George V. Higgins, *The Rat on Fire*, p. 74, 1981

3 the first, strong effect of a drug *US*
- [W]hite women learned where they could get a "belt," a "jolt," or "gow." —Jack Lait and Lee Mortimer, *New York Confidential*, p. 103–104, 1948

4 a prostitute; any woman regarded as a sex-object *AUSTRALIA*
The earlier sense of 'prostitute' seems to have been spread from the Australian to the British forces during World War 2 and, in so doing, broadened its intention.
- —Sidney J Baker, *The Australian Language*, p. 123, 1945

▸ **below the belt**
unfair, unsportsmanlike *UK, 1890*
From the language of boxing, where a blow below the belt is prohibited.
- Jacobs attacked the prosecution for a secret grand jury session last week. He said that the defense had been refused a transcript of the testimony. He said, "This move was below the belt." —*San Francisco Call-Bulletin*, 26th May 1947
- The press at first made me [Liberace] angry. I'm used to being kidded, but I didn't expect that below-the-belt stuff. —*San Francisco News*, p. 23, 15th November 1956
- Hitting Ike Below The Belt [Headline] —*San Francisco Call-Bulletin*, p. 24, 22nd March 1957

▸ **under your belt**
personal experience of something *UK, 1958*
From an earlier use, of food in your stomach.
- Get a couple of languages under your belt in this Corps and you can't go wrong. —*Beale*, 1984

belt *verb*
to hit someone or something *UK, 1838*
From earlier sense (to hit with a belt).

belta *adjective*
good, excellent *UK*
- Typical slang words that Charvas use are "belta", "mint" and "waxa" all meaning good or great[.] —Chris Lewis, *The Dictionary of Playground Slang*, p. 53, 2003

belt along; belt *verb*
to move at great speed *UK, 1890*
Originally Gloucestershire dialect.

belt buckle polisher *noun*
a song suited for slow dancing *US*
- Now here's a belt buckle polisher, so all you lovers can dance cheeck to cheeck ... to cheek ... to cheek... —Ken Weaver, *Texas Crude*, p. 103, 1984

belt down; belt *verb*
to rain heavily *UK, 1984*

belted *adjective*
drunk or drug-intoxciated *US*
- —William D. Alsever, *Glossary for the Establishment and Other Uptight People*, p. 15, December 1970

belter *noun*

1 a thrilling event; a wonderful thing *UK*
- —Tom Hibbert, *Rockspeak!*, p. 20, 1983
- NANA: Get lost...I've not got my hat on yet. DAD: Uh, that'll be a belter... have you borrowed Cilla's? —Caroline Aherne and Craig Cash, *The Royle Family*, 1999
- This [darts match] is a belter and it could be incredibly tight[.] —Stuart Jeffries, *Mrs Slocombe's Pussy [quoting Sid Waddell]*, p. 75, 2000
- The three-test New Zealand v. Australia cricket series was an absolute belter, even if each match was drawn. —*Listener*, p. 36, 29th December 2001

2 a song that can be sung with great vigour; a type of singer that has a vigorous approach to a song *UK, 1984*

belting *noun*
a beating whether punitive or pugilistic *UK, 1825*
- [I]nstead of putting him on a charge, he gave him a private belting. —Charles Raven, *Underworld Nights*, p. 43, 1956
- "It's a pity you're Gerald's wife," I tell her. She doesn't answer. "Because that means I can't give you a belting without him seeing the marks." —Ted Lewis, *Jack Carter's Law*, p. 63, 1974

belting *adjective*
excellent *UK*
- You'll have a belting time. —*Staines Guardian*, 5th June 2002

belt out *verb*
to sing or play a musical instrument with great vigour *UK, 1953*
- The best advice is not to try and go in with the intention of turning the amp up to 11à la Spinal Tap and belting out the solo from Stairway to Heaven. —*The Guardian*, 11th June 2002

belts and boards *noun*
accoutrements for a Royal Canadian Air Force officer's uniform on formal ceremonial occasions *CANADA*
- Belts and Boards comprised stiff epaulettes in blue and gold, and a gold ceremonial cloth belt. —Tom Langeste, *Words on the Wing*, p. 26, 1995

belt up!
be quiet! *UK, 1949*
- "Ow, do belt up and leave off," growled the Archbubble. —Derek Raymond (Robin Cook), *The Crust on its Uppers*, p. 60, 1962
- I gets sort of irritable and says, "For Chrissake belt up and take it." —John Peter Jones, *Feather Pluckers*, p. 108, 1964

Beltway commando *noun*
any military bureaucrat working in Washington D.C. *US*
Gulf war usage.
- —*American Speech*, p. 384, Winter 1991: 'Among the new words'

be lucky
goodbye *UK*
Cockney, maybe **MOCKNEY**.
- "I'll let you know, Tel." "Be lucky." —P.B. Yuill (pen name of Gordon Williams and Terry Venables), *Hazell Plays Solomon*, 1974

Belushi *noun*
a combination of cocaine and heroin *US, 1998*
In memory of the **SPEEDBALL** mix that killed film actor John Belushi, 1949–82.
- —Robert Ashton, *This Is Heroin*, p. 208, 2002
- —Mike Haskins, *Drugs*, p. 292, 2003

Belyando spruce; Belyando sprue *noun*
marijuana from the Belyando area of Queensland *AUSTRALIA, 1977*
- —Richard A. Spears, *The Slang and Jargon of Drugs and Drink*, p. 39, 1986
- —Mike Haskins, *Drugs*, p. 286, 2003

be my guest!
do as you wish; you are welcome to have whatever has been asked for *US, 1955*
- [After making love] "Goodnight, Ty." "Goodnight, honey." "Thanks for everything." "Be my guest." —Dick Francis, *Forfeit*, 1968

ben *noun*
1 a lavatory *UK*
Rhyming slang for 'Benghazi', **KARZY** (a lavatory); from the Libyan seaport and probably originating in the desert campaign of World War 2.
- —Ray Puxley, *Cockney Rabbit*, p. 13, 1992

2 *benzodiazepine*, an antidepressant, especially Valium™
Also referred to as 'benzo'.
- Bens are commonly found in medicine cabinets[.] —Macfarlane, Macfarlane and Robson, *The User*, p. 99, 1996
- Seventeen million people were legally prescribed benzos in 1999[.] —*Drugs An Adult Guide*, p. 22, December 2001

Ben; Bennie; Benjamin *noun*
Benzedrine™ (amphetamine sulphate), or another central nervous system stimulant *US*
Truckers often personify stimulants, referring to 'my good friend Benjamin' or saying 'better let Bennie drive'.
- —Montie Tak, *Truck Talk*, p. 11, 1971

ben *adjective*
▷ see: **BENE**

benar *adjective*
better *UK*
Originally C16, conjugated as **BENE** (good), 'benar/benat' (best); the 'best' sense is now obsolete but 'good' and 'better' survived the affected surroundings of polari.
- —Paul Baker, *Polari*, p. 164, 2002

bench *noun*
1 an athletic's team coaching staff and reserve players, collectively *US*
- —Howard B. Bonham, *Football Lingo*, p. 3, 1962

2 a youth gang *US*
- —*American Speech*, p. 194, October 1951: 'A study of reformatory argot'

▸ **ride the bench**
to sit on the sidelines of an athletic competition as a substitute player *US, 1911*
- Neither did his coaches or fellow players notice when Joe Connors tired of bench-riding in the second half, walked to the dressing room changed clothes and disappeared. —*San Francisco Examiner*, p. 43, 30th September 1955

▸ **warm the bench**
to sit on the sidelines of an athletic contest as a substitute player *US, 1911*
- The most unplayed, but not unpaid, athlete of his time, Charlie [Silvera], as Yogi Berra's stand-in with the Yankees, collected over $50,000 in bonus pelf for six World Series, during which he did nothing but practice the gentle art of bench-warming. —*San Francisco News Call-Bulletin*, p. 30, 23rd September 1960

bench *verb*
1 to remove someone from competition *US, 1917*
Originally a sports term – the player literally returned to the bench during a game. Later applied to a variety of situations.
- Zippy Sheree North will come to bat for the benched Marilyn Monroe in "How to Be Very, Very Popular" next month. —*San Francisco News*, p. 13, 25th January 1955
- If you believed Sen. Hubert Horatio Humphrey really benched himself after that Presidential primary in West Virginia, take another look. —*San Francisco News Call-Bulletin*, p. 18, 9th June 1960

2 to reprimand someone *US*
- —Vann Wesson, *Generation X Field Guide and Lexicon*, p. 18, 1997

bench boy *noun*
an athlete who never makes the starting lineup and thus spends most of the time during games sitting on the team bench *US*
- —Connie Eble (Editor), *UNC-CH Campus Slang*, p. 1, Fall 1999

bench jockey *noun*
in a team sport, a substitute player, especially one who makes his opinion known from the bench *US, 1939*
- —Parke Cummings, *Dictionary of Baseball*, p. 5, 1950
- What I can't understand is why professional baseball players are highly praised as bench jockeys, but professional football players are considered ding-a-ling for doing the same thing. —*San Francisco Chronicle*, p. 1H, 19th April 1959
- —*American Speech*, p. 158–159, May 1960: 'The burgeoning of 'jockey''
- In the end, the bench jockeys and the bullpen carried the Cubs home in their first NLCS game on the road. —*Baltimore Sun*, p. 1C, 11th October 2003

bench race *verb*
to talk about drag racing without actually doing it *US, 1960s to 70s*
- —Lyle K. Engel, *The Complete Book of Fuel and Gas Dragsters*, p. 149, 1968

benchwarmer *noun*
a substitute player on a sports team *US, 1905*
- Presidential Campaigner Estes Kefauver explained to Drake University students in Des Moines how he achieved fame: "I was just a benchwarmer on the University of Tennessee football team." —*Time*, p. 39, 17th March 1952
- "When the team is so far ahead that it doesn't matter, you let the poor little bench-warmers come in for an inning or two." —Max Shulman, *Rally Round the Flag, Boys!*, p. 223, 1957

bend *noun*
1 a spree, especially involving hard drinking; hence, a drug-induced hallucinogenic experience *UK, 1979*
Perhaps playing on **TRIP**.

2 money *US*
- —Kenn "Naz" Young, *Naz's Underground Dictionary*, p. 14, 1973

bend *verb*

1 to deliberately slur or distort a musical note *US*
• —Harold Wentworth and Stuart Berg Flexner, *Dictionary of American Slang*, p. 31, 1960

2 to fraudulently affect the outcome of a sporting event; to bribe or by other means corrupt authority *UK, 1864*
• —John Ayto, *The Oxford Dictionary of Slang*, 1998

3 to take part in a gang fight *US*
• —Kenn "Naz" Young, *Naz's Dictionary of Teen Slang*, p. 7, 1993

bend the elbow
to enjoy a few drinks *NEW ZEALAND*
• —Harry Orsman and Des Hurley, *The Beaut Little Book of New Zealand Slang*, 1994

bend the iron; bend the rust; bend the rail
to change the position of a railway point *US*
• —Norman Carlisle, *The Modern Wonder Book of Trains and Railroading*, p. 259, 1946

bended knees *noun*
cheese *UK, 1960*
Rhyming slang, sometimes shortened to 'bended'; noted in use amongst tramps.

bender *noun*

1 a prolonged session of hard drinking *US, 1845*
• Frisco Kate, who was en route to New York on a bender, came in there accompanied by a young pug she had picked up.—Jack Lait and Lee Mortimer, *Chicago Confidential*, p. 30–31, 1950
• You go on a bender after all those years, it's like all that sober time never was.—Richard Price, *Clockers*, p. 274, 1992
• [H]is Mom was alcoholic really abusive [...] he was big enough that he could beat the crap out of her if she went on a bender.—Susan Ruddick, *Cool Places*, p. 348, 1998
• They are "up the monument" or "half seas over"; they are "on a bender", "out of it" or "off their tits".—Peter Ackroyd, *London The Biography*, p. 359, 2000

2 a male homosexual who plays the passive role in anal sex; a homosexual *US*
• —*The Guild Dictionary of Homosexual Terms*, p. 3, 1965
• —Dale Gordon, *The Dominion Sex Dictionary*, p. 28, 1967
• "Women only..." Cheeky benders. It's a bloody working men's club, ta for asking.—*The Full Monty*, 1997
• [H]e'd been worried that the pig hormones might arouse benders as well as grannies.—Stewart Home, *Sex Kick [britpulp]*, p. 230, 1999
• He tenses, but the bender [a homosexual] doesn't seem to notice, his bum chum smiling at Dave.—John King, *Human Punk*, p. 79, 2000
• [A]ll kinds of knocking shops [brothels] and bars for benders and cokeheads and all sorts.—Kevin Sampson, *Clubland*, p. 64, 2002

3 a stolen car *US*
• —Jay Robert Nash, *Dictionary of Crime*, p. 25, 1992

4 any bending joint in the body, such as the elbow or knee *US*
• —Kenn "Naz" Young, *Naz's Underground Dictionary*, p. 14, 1973

5 a Roman Catholic *NEW ZEALAND*
• —David McGill, *David McGill's Complete Kiwi Slang Dictionary*, p. 13, 1998

6 a suspended prison sentence *UK*
• —Angela Devlin, *Prison Patter*, p. 26, 1996

7 a hammer *US*
• —A.B. Chance Co., *Lineman's Slang Dictionary*, p. 1, 1980

bender mender *noun*
a hangover cure, especially a stiff drink *UK: SCOTLAND*
Elaborated on **BENDER** (a prolonged session of hard drinking).
• —Michael Munro, *The Patter, Another Blast*, 1988

bending drill *noun*
an act of defecation in the open-air *UK*
Military use, originating with the British army in North Africa during World War 2.

bend over *verb*
to submit; to give in to someone *US, 1960s*
An image that suggests bending over is 'to be buggered'.
• Fuck this! I'm not going to get bent over by some deranged American union extortionist!—Frank Zappa, *The Real Frank Zappa Book*, p. 151, 1989
• They're bendin' over for it[.]—Nick Barlay, *Curvy Lovebox*, p. 9, 1997

bend over, brown eyes
used as a humorous instruction to a patient about to undergo a rectal examination *US*
• —*Maledicta*, p. 31, 1988–1989: 'Medical maledicta from San Francisco'

bends and motherfuckers *noun*
the squat-thrust exercise drill *US*
Vietnam war usage. In gentler times, known as a 'burpee'.
• —Linda Reinberg, *In the Field*, p. 20, 1991

bend up *verb*
to encourage or enable another's intoxication *UK*
• The Yardies guzzle down bottles of this toxic waste [100% proof rum), bend up a few women and then take them home for a full session. —Wayne Anthony, *Spanish Highs*, p. 110, 1999

bene; ben; bien *adjective*
good *UK*
Originally C16, adapted from Italian *bene*, possibly Latin *bonus* (good).
• —Paul Baker, *Polari*, p. 164, 2002

benefit *noun*
any hardship or unpleasant feature of army life *US*
Used with obvious irony.
• —Carl Fleischhauer, *A Glossary of Army Slang*, p. 3, 1968

Ben Franklin *noun*
a $100 note *US*
From the engraving on the note.
• Winnie looked up sharply when Buster, still staring at the pile of money, said, "That's a lot of Ben Franklins."—Joseph Wambaugh, *The Golden Orange*, p. 108, 1990

Bengal lancer *noun*
an opportunist, especially one who takes risks in pursuit of criminal gain *UK*
Glasgow rhyming slang for **CHANCER**.

be nice!
used by US troops in Vietnam when caught by surprise or provoked by another *US*
• —*Maledicta*, p. 257, Summer/Winter 1982: 'Viet-speak'
• —Linda Reinberg, *In the Field*, p. 18, 1991

benies *noun*
benefits *US*
• There sure are the benies if you don't have an education. —Darryl Ponicsan, *The Last Detail*, p. 33, 1970

Benjamin *noun*
▷ see: **BEN**

Benjie; Benji *noun*
a $100 note *US, 1985*
From the portrait of Benjamin Franklin on the note.
• Just go blow five benjies and stop chewing on me.—Stephen Cannell, *Big Con*, p. 208, 1997
• —Puff Daddy and the Family, *It's All About the Benjamins*, 1997
• [H]avin' a Benz and a fat knot of Benji's definitely helps.—*The Source*, p. 218, March 2002

benjo *noun*
a toilet *AUSTRALIA*
From Japanese.
• I went to another bar where I started to pay dearly for U.S. beer and the dreaded 'Saigon Tea', after a few beers my bladder guided me to the benjo or place of piss-piss – what a hygiene officer's nightmare it was!—Martin Cameron, *A Look at the Bright Side*, 1988

Bennett buggy *noun*
a car converted to a four-wheel, horse-drawn carriage by removal of the engine, drive train and windshield (in depression times); later, any broken-down car *CANADA*
• —Chris Thain, *Cold as a Bay Street Banker's Heart*, p. 11, 1987

Ben Nevis *noun*
a long prison sentence *UK*
Prison slang, reported in private correspondence by a serving prisoner in January 2002. Ben Nevis is the highest mountain in Britain.

bennie *noun*
a female prostitute's customer who prefers to perform oral sex on the prostitute *US*
• —Roger Blake, *The American Dictionary of Sexual Terms*, p. 16, 1964
• —Robert A. Wilson, *Playboy's Book of Forbidden Words*, p. 34, 1972

Bennie *noun*
▷ see: BEN

bennie God *noun*
the sun *US*
- I learned, with the advent of the "Bennie God" to make an acceptable "bennie machine" out of aluminum foil, and use it on the flat back porch every afternoon during the spring semester to "catch a few rays" while downing some frosties. —John Nichols, *The Sterile Cuckoo*, p. 60, 1965

bennie machine *noun*
a reflector used while sunbathing *US*
- I learned, with the advent of the "Bennie God" to make an acceptable "bennie machine" out of aluminum foil, and use it on the flat back porch every afternoon during the spring semester to "catch a few rays" while downing some frosties. —John Nichols, *The Sterile Cuckoo*, p. 60, 1965

bennies *noun*
1 sun rays *US*
A shortened form of 'beneficial'.
- Nothing to do but laze around, drink beer on the back porch roof, and soak up the bennies. —John Nichols, *The Sterile Cuckoo*, p. 137, 1965
- —Collin Baker et al., *College Undergraduate Slang Study Conducted at Brown University*, p. 79, 1968

2 during the Vietnam war, basic comforts *US*
A shortened form of 'benefits'.
- On top of all those bennies they had ice cream and ice-cold beer! —Charles Anderson, *The Grunts*, p. 29, 1976
- The troops were always talking about service "bennies," the little perks like the BX and the commissary, as if they made much difference. —Walter Boyne and Steven Thompson, *The Wild Blue*, p. 241, 1986
- —Linda Reinberg, *In the Field*, p. 20, 1991

benny *noun*
1 an amphetamine, especially Benzedrine™ (amphetamine sulphate), a central nervous system stimulant *US*
- I feel an incredible need to talk to you ... Not because I'm high on Benny, and lone in the cursed kitchen, but as a matter of mood. —Jack Kerouac, *Letter to Allen Ginsberg*, p. 99–100, 13th November 1945
- "Don't panic," the girls tell each other as pre-exam work piles up. But some do panic, and a few secretly resort to "bennies" (Benzedrine). —*Time*, p. 78, 10th October 1949
- Oh, I've been trying benny but its peeds everything up, it's all wrong and besides it makes you talk. —John Clellon Holmes, *John Clellon*, p. 47, 1952
- Or take two strips of benny and two goof balls. They get down there and have a fight. —William Burroughs, *Junkie*, p. 28, 1953
- With each week of work, bombed and sapped and charged and stoned with lush, with pot, with benny[.]—Norman Mailer, *Advertisements for Myself*, p. 243, 1955
- [W]hat do I really know about it except you've got to stick to it with the energy of a benny addict. —Jack Kerouac, *On the Road*, p. 6, 1957
- I was carrying some bennies, but I wasn't worried about my vulnerability. —Alexander Trocchi, *Cain's Book*, p. 155, 1960
- Tarbush had been nailed twice for pushing Bennies on the teenage set[.]—Mickey Spillane, *Return of the Hood*, p. 122, 1964
- At Bass Lake he tended the fire with the single-minded zeal of a man who's been eating bennies like popcorn. —Hunter S. Thompson, *Hell's Angels*, p. 185, 1966
- "Top" was back in town, so I stopped on the way home and copped cocaine, yellows, and bennies. —Iceberg Slim (Robert Beck), *Pimp*, p. 206, 1969
- We gotta couple poppers, three bennies, two joints, half a fifth of vodka. —*Saturday Night Fever*, 1977
- I had lost no time in locating a drugstore – following my arrival in the city – that supplied me with bennies first[.]—Herbert Huncke, *The Evening Sun Turned Crimson*, p. 46, 1980
- Since you're wired on bennies you get to stay up and stare at the building. I'm tired, so I'm going to sleep. —*48 Hours*, 1982
- —Angela Devlin, *Prison Patter*, p. 21, 1996
- Guy high on bennies looked at the guy with no teeth, then looked away, at me. —Joel Rose, *Kill Kill Faster Faster*, p. 197, 1997

2 a Benzedrine™ inhaler *US*
- —Clarence Major, *Dictionary of Afro-American Slang*, p. 25, 1970

3 a Benson & Hedges cigarette *UK*
- Or who's going to get some Rizla and ten Bennies[.]—Macfarlane, Macfarlane and Robson, *The User*, p. 78, 1996

4 in Vancouver Island, an order of Eggs Benedict *CANADA*
- Not only are they all healthy on the island, they even have suntans. The people are so casual they call eggs Benedict "Benny." —*Montreal Gazette*, p. F2, 22nd May 2002

5 an overcoat *UK, 1812*
- He lay on the hard boards, his feet cramping in the soft leather of his shoes, the hundred and twenty-five dollars Benny rolled beneath his head as a cushion[.]—Clarence Cooper Jr, *The Scene*, p. 218, 1960
- What size 'benny' and 'vine' you wear? —Iceberg Slim (Robert Beck), *Pim*[p], p. 92, 1969
- 'Pon her arm she had my six-button benny / Said, "Here you a[re] MacDaddy, here's your coat." —Roger Abrahams, *Positively Black*, p. 79, 197[0]
- He had a camel-hair benny with the belt in the back / Had a pair [of] nice shoes, and a pair of blue slacks. —Anonymous ("Arthur"), *Shine and t[he] Titanic; The Signifying Monkey; Stackolee*, p. 1, 1971
- He wore a herringbone jacket with Hollywood slacks / And a ragla[n] benny with slits in the back. —Dennis Wepman et al., *The Life*, p. 31, 1976

6 a Ben Sherman shirt, a fashion item given iconic status by skinheads *UK*
- [T]hese older lads, skins they were, Bennies, Comos [Fred Perr[y] shirts], Flemmings [brand-name], full kit, come ambling over. —Kevi[n] Sampson, *Outlaws*, p. 245, 2001

7 a sports fan who looks back at a basketball game and analyse[s] what might have been *US*
A note in the archives of Peter Tamony explains: 'The boys who gather in a hotel room of an evening and mull over things that happened. Synonymous with "Monday Morning Quarterback" except basketball people like to call them "Bennys".' Probably from the image of men in overcoats.
- There was nothing mysterious about the performance of Jimmy Pollard, the gangly Oakland sensation many of the tournament "Bennys" have been calling the "all-time great." —*San Francisco Examiner*, p. 18, 22nd March 1946

8 a person who looks and talks the part of a surfer but does not actually surf *US*
- —Trevor Cralle, *The Surfin'ary*, p. 9, 1991

▸ **get a benny on**
to lose your temper *UK*
- DAVE: "Not-so-bad"? "Not-so-bad"? Not much of a fuckin' SOS, that, is it? GAZ: Alright, alright, don't get a benny on[.]—*The Full Monty*, 1997

Benny *noun*
a Falkland Islander *UK, 1982*
- —Bernadette Hince, *The Antarctic Dictionary*, p. 46, 2000
- When the British soldiers arrived to liberate the islands, they nicknamed the islanders 'Bennies' after Benny, the simple soul on Crossroads. —*The Guardian Weekly*, 17th March 2002

benny blue *noun*
in craps, a roll of seven when shooting for your point *US*
From the call, 'Benny blue, you're all through!'.
- —Steve Kuriscak, *Casino Talk*, p. 3, 1985

benny boost *noun*
a shoplifting technique involving the use of an oversized, especially equipped overcoat *US*
- —Jay Robert Nash, *Dictionary of Crime*, p. 25, 1992

Benny boy *noun*
a young transvestite prostitute found in Manila and other Southeast Asian cities *PHILIPPINES, 1967*
- The Benny Boy is a man who is dressed as a woman and uses adhesive tape to keep his genitals flat against his abdomen. —Charles Winick and Paul Kinsie, *The Lively Commerce*, p. 260, 1972

benny chaser *noun*
coffee consumed with Benzedrine™ (amphetamine sulphate), a central nervous system stimulant *US*
Used with humour by truckers who rely on different forms of stimulation to stay awake for long periods.
- —Montie Tak, *Truck Talk*, p. 11, 1971

benny house *noun*
a primarily heterosexual brothel that will upon request procure a male sexual partner for a male client *US*
- —*The Guild Dictionary of Homosexual Terms*, p. 4, 1965

Benny Mason; Mr Mason *noun*
marijuana that is so potent that it must be stored in a pot or mason jar (a glass jar for preserving food) to contain the smell *US*
- —Connie Eble (Editor), *UNC-CH Campus Slang*, p. 5, Spring 1992

benny suggs *noun*
good ideas *UK*
Military; from '*bene*ficial *sugg*estions'.
- —John W. Mussell, *Militarisms*, p. 12, 1995

benny worker *noun*
a thief who uses an overcoat to hide his movements or goods *US*
• —Vincent J. Monteleone, *Criminal Slang*, p. 20, 1949

beno *adjective*
used as a humorous description of a woman's condition while experiencing the bleed period of the menstrual cycle *US*
From the pronouncement – 'There will *be no* fun tonight'.
• —*American Speech*, p. 298, December 1954: 'The vernacular of menstruation'

benson *noun*
a toady, a sycophant *UK: SCOTLAND*
Apparently derived from the name of the butler character in US television situation comedy *Soap*, 1978–82, and its concurrent spin-off *Benson*, 1979–86.
• You're alwaya sookin up tae the teachers, ya wee benson.—Michael Munro, *The Complete Patter*, 1996
• When [At school in the mid-1980s] somebody did you a favour you could easily piss them off by saying "Cheers Benson" instead of saying "Thanks", to imply that they were some sort of servant or slave.—Chris Lewis, *The Dictionary of Playground Slang*, p. 28, 2003

bent *noun*
a homosexual *UK, 1957*
• —Angela Devlin, *Prison Patter*, p. 26, 1996

bent *adjective*
1 stolen *US, 1930*
• —Vincent J. Monteleone, *Criminal Slang*, p. 21, 1949
• —Hyman E. Goldin et al., *Dictionary of American Underworld Lingo*, p. 26, 1950

2 corrupt, crooked, criminal *UK, 1914*
The opposite of **STRAIGHT** (honest/conventional).
• [M]uch thought is given to the causes of crime: i.e: why blokes go bent.—Charles Raven, *Underworld Nights*, p. 41, 1956
• One of the worst things in the nick are the bent screws—Frank Norman, *Bang To Rights*, p. 63, 1958
• —Angela Devlin, *Prison Patter*, p. 27, 1996
• [A]ll I get offered is fifty kinds of bent gear.—Val McDermid, *Keeping on the Right Side of the Law*, p. 184, 1999

3 unfaithful *UK*
• My bird's gone bent.—Frank Norman, *Bang To Rights*, p. 58, 1958

4 sexually deviant *UK, 1957*
• Being tall I could pass for a foreign soldier, albeit a slightly bent one.—Fiona Pitt-Kethley, *Red Light Districts of the World*, p. 53, 2000

5 homosexual *UK, 1959*
• —Eugene Landy, *The Underground Dictionary*, p. 32, 1971
• —Anon., *Ring Smut's Wet Dreams Interpreted*, 1978
• —*Maledicta*, p. 229, 1979: 'Kinks and queens: linguistic and cultural aspects of the terminology for gays'
• Does your family know you're bent?—Armistead Maupin, *Babycakes*, p. 214, 1984

6 drunk or drug-intoxicated *US, 1833*
• —Eugene Landy, *The Underground Dictionary*, p. 32, 1971
• CAMERON: Will Bogey get bent? MICHAEL: Are you kidding? He'll piss himself with joy.—*Ten Things I Hate About You*, 1999

7 ill-humoured; grouchy *US*
• —Miss Cone, *The Slang Dictionary (Hawthorne High School)*, 1965

8 spoiled, broken, out-of-order *UK, 1930*

9 suffering from decompression sickness *UK, 1984*

▸ **bent as a butcher's hook**
very corrupt, incontrovertibly criminal *UK*
• —David Powis, *The Signs of Crime*, 1977

▸ **bent as a nine-bob note**
1 corrupt, crooked *UK*
In pre-decimalisation currency, ten-bob (ten shillings) was the only currency note for less than a pound value; a nine-bob note would have been an obvious forgery.
• [H]e was a shrewd copper [policeman], bent as a nine-bob note, who made enough for a luxurious retirement.—Brian McDonald, *Elephant Boys*, p. 81, 2000

2 ostentatiously homosexual *UK*
A sterling elaboration of **BENT**.
• "Bent as a nine-bob note. Rampant homosexual," announces Gene, rolling the "r" with glee.—J.J. Connolly, *Layer Cake*, p. 194, 2000

▸ **bent as arseholes**
corrupt, crooked *UK*
• Somebody said coppers could be trusted in those days and they were right – trusted to be bent as arseholes.—Lenny McLean, *The Guv'nor*, p. 72, 1998

bent and greased *adjective*
prepared to be taken advantage of *US*
The sexual allusion is difficult to miss.
• —Michael Dalton Johnson, *Talking Trash with Redd Foxx*, p. 107, 1994

bent eight *noun*
an eight-cylinder V engine *US*
• Racing Jargon—*Hot Rod Magazine*, p. 13, November 1948
• You've sacrificed many dollars on your "bent-eight" block, bringing it beautiful gifts in the form of special equipment.—Oscar J. Gude, *Hot Rod Comics*, June 1952
• Shimmering heat waves danced along the tops of Beamers and Bent Eights, parked in shiny rows, dressed in cheap new fifty-dollar paint jobs.—Stephen Cannell, *Big Con*, p. 27, 1997

bent stovebolt *noun*
in drag racing and hot rodding, a Chevrolet V-8 engine *US*

Bent Whore *nickname*
Bien Hoa, South Vietnam, site of an American air base during the Vietnam war *US*
• —Linda Reinberg, *In the Field*, p. 20, 1991

benz *noun*
a tablet of Benzedrine™ (amphetamine sulphate), a central nervous system stimulant *US*
• —Richard Lingeman, *Drugs from A to Z*, p. 22, 1969
• —Eugene Landy, *The Underground Dictionary*, p. 32, 1971
• —Angela Devlin, *Prison Patter*, p. 21, 1996

Benz *nickname*
a Mercedes-Benz car *US*
• One day he paid me $100 to stand in line and get him some fish and chips, 'cause he didn't want to get out of his Benz.—*New Jack City*, 1990
• [H]avin' a Benz and a fat knot of Benji's [$100 bills] definitely helps. —*The Source*, p. 218, March 2002

Benzedrina *noun*
in homosexual usage, a personification of Benzedrine™ (amphetamine sulphate), a central nervous system stimulant *US*
• —*Maledicta*, p. 227, Winter 1980: '"Lovely, blooming, fresh and gay": the onomastics of camp'

Benzo *noun*
a Mercedes-Benz car *US, 1986*
• That Benzo missed her ass by a red pussy hair.—Robert Campbell, *Alice in La-La Land*, p. 11, 1987
• You'd rather see, me in the pen / than me and Lorenzo rollin in a Benz-o—NWA, *Fuck Tha Police*, 1988
• Who's Benzo was that I saw you rolling in yesterday?—*Boyz N The Hood*, 1990
• —Connie Eble (Editor), *UNC-CH Campus Slang*, p. 1, Spring 1993
• [H]avin' a Benz and a fat knot of Benji's [$100 bills] definitely helps. —*The Source*, p. 218, March 2002

beone *noun*
▷ see: **BIANC**

bequeenum *adjective*
homosexual *UK*
• —*Attitude*, p. 60, July 2003: 'New palare lexicon'

Berb *noun*
a social outcast *US*
• —*Merriam-Webster's Hot Words on Campus Marketing Survey '93*, p. 2, 13th October 1993

Berdoo; San Berdoo; San Berdu *nickname*
San Bernadino, California, east of Los Angeles *US, 1914*
• —Joseph E. Ragen and Charles Finston, *Inside the World's Toughest Prison*, p. 816, 1962
• Anything less would forfeit the spritiual leadership back to southern California, to the San Bernadino (or Berdoo) chapter[.]—Hunter S. Thompson, *Hell's Angels*, p. 11, 1966
• [T]he next thing I knew we're headed toward the mountains above San Berdoo.—Odie Hawkins, *Black Casanova*, p. 92, 1984
• I heard about you from some cops in San Berdoo.—Joseph Wambaugh, *Fugitive Nights*, p. 94, 1992
• According to Vic, the first Hell's Angels motorcyle club was formed around 1948 in Berdoo[.]—Ralph "Sonny" Barger, *Hell's Angel*, p. 30, 2000

bergwind *noun*
a warm offshore land breeze *SOUTH AFRICA*

bergy bit *noun*
a small iceberg *UK, 1906*
• —Bernadette Hince, *The Antarctic Dictionary*, p. 161, 2000

bergy seltzer *noun*
a fizzing produced in an iceberg when trapped air is released *ANTARCTICA*
• —Bernadette Hince, *The Antarctic Dictionary*, p. 47, 2000

berk; birk; burk; burke *noun*
a fool *UK, 1936*
Almost certainly a reduction of the rhyming slang **BERKSHIRE HUNT** or **BERKELEY HUNT** (a **CUNT**) so widely used that the original sense has almost been lost; there is a suggestion that 'berk' may be a diminution of **BERKELEYS** (the female breasts), thus **TIT** (a fool).
• The boss was a "birk" (pain in the neck) who kept "rousting" (bawling out) the tentmen[.] —Butch Reynolds, *Broken Hearted Clown*, p. 31, 1953
• I reckoned that the chinless berk was still safely tucked up in the bog. —John Peter Jones, *Feather Pluckers*, p. 37, 1964
• "Bastard" and "bloody" are commonplace, but a lot of obscenity is slipped in with phrases like "stupid berk." —Suzy Jarratt, *Permissive Australia*, p. 79, 1970
• Barry you silly old burke, where are you scarpering off to. —Barry Humphries, *Bazza Pulls It Off!*, 1971
• A man's been a proper Burke all his life. —Frank Hardy, *The Outcasts of Foolgarah*, p. 136, 1971
• Kenny walked all over that racketland looking for a gun he could buy to shoot the elbows and kneecaps off of the berk who paid to have Matt done. —Emmett Grogan, *Ringolevio*, p. 203, 1972
• [T]he berk should have got the hell out of there right away. —Johnny Speight, *It Stands to Reason*, p. 60, 1973
• "[H]ow could you trust a man who's stupid enough to trust these ponces, you could see it coming." and Gerald says "Too fucking true, he was a berk." —Ted Lewis, *Jack Carter's Law*, p. 10, 1974
• How come you're involved with a burk like Altman? —Anthony Masters, *Minder*, p. 79, 1984
• Is there any tea left, berk? —Caroline Aherne and Craig Cash, *The Royle Family*, 1999
• Burkes, I thought, and went to see the dancers rehearsing[.] —Jonathan Gash, *The Ten Word Game*, p. 226, 2003

Berkeley Quality Software *noun*
any computer program that is incomplete or incorrect *US*
• —Eric S. Raymond, *The New Hacker's Dictionary*, p. 53, 1991

berkeleys *noun*
the female breasts *UK*
From Romany *berk* (a breast).

berkers *adjective*
angry, emotionally unstable *NEW ZEALAND*
From 'beserk'.
• —David McGill, *David McGill's Complete Kiwi Slang Dictionary*, p. 13, 1998

berko *adjective*
berserk; crazy *AUSTRALIA*
• He's okay when he's sober but when he's got a few in he goes berko. —Barry Crump, *Hang on a Minute Mate*, p. 163, 1961
• 'You went what is commonly called berko,' Mr. Ross said when remanding the defendant for sentence. —*Otago Daily Times*, p. 4, 4th April 1972
• If you've gone a bit berko when plucking you eyebrows and they've stopped growing back, don't go mental – now you can have a transplant! —*Girlfriend*, p. 10, 1995
• As if Woeful didn't have enough on his plate without a berko nephew. —Shane Maloney, *Nice Try*, p. 179, 1998

Berks *noun*
Berkshire *UK, 1937*
A spoken form of the conventional written abbreviation, considered colloquial when used in speech as a genuine equivalent of the original name.

Berkshire hunt; Berkeley hunt *noun*
1 a fool *UK, 1937*
Rhyming slang for **CUNT**, generally in the reduced form **BERK**. Also variant 'Birchington hunt'.

2 the vagina *UK*
Rhyming slang for **CUNT**. Also variant 'Birchington hunt'.

berky *noun*
a complete loss of temper and emotional stability *NEW ZEALAND*
• 'Suppose you boys tell me exactly what happened yesterday.' "Joe did a 'berky.' Reckoned we wrecked his machines!' —Barry Mitcalfe, *Hey Hey Hey*, p. 102, 1985

berley *noun*
in fishing, any material added to water in order to attract fish *AUSTRALIA, 1874*
Origin unknown.
• —Roy Slaven (John Doyle), *Five South Coast Seasons*, p. 79, 1992
• [W]e had to scrimp on every cent, even to the extent of making our own berley and packaging our own bait. —Rex Hunt, *Tall Tales – and True*, p. 2, 1994

berley *verb*
to place berley in the water to attract fish *AUSTRALIA, 1852*
• The hippie musicians had been using LSD, wrapped in dough to keep the water out, to berley the snapper. —Bob Staines, *Wot a Whopper*, p. 29, 1982

Berlin Wall *noun*
a testicle *UK*
Rhyming slang for 'ball', generally in the plural (**BALLS**).
• She's always having a go at me, banging on my Berlin Walls. —Bodmin Dark, *Dirty Cockney Rhyming Slang*, 2003

Bermuda crescent *noun*
a semi-circle of dance floor in front of a stage that remains empty when a band is playing *UK*
A joke on the Bermuda Triangle, a vast three-sided area of the Atlantic with angles at Bermuda, Puerto Rico and Fort Lauderdale, Florida, where ships and planes apparently disappear.
• [T]hey were too few to penetrate the Bermuda Crescent and they settled, instead, for earnest head-nodding in the shadows of the bar[.] —Kevin Sampson, *Powder*, p. 7, 1999

Bermuda time *adverb*
late *BERMUDA*
• —Peter A. Smith and Fred M. Barritt, *Bermewjan Vurds*, 1985

Bermuda triangle *noun*
the vagina *UK*
• The female genitalia represented as places from which people/things never return (e.g., the Bermuda triangle) or get sucked into (e.g., the black hole, electrolux), hidden dangers (e.g., squirrel trap) and warnings of danger (e.g., hairy growler, bomb doors). —*Journal of Sex Research*, p. 146, 2001

Bernard Langered *adjective*
drunk *UK*
An elaboration of **LANGERED** (drunk), playing on the name of German golfer Bernard Langer (b.1957), possibly as an ironic swipe at his 'born-again' Christianity.
• —*e-cyclopaedia*, 20th March 2002

Berni; Bernice; Bernie *noun*
cocaine *US, 1933*
• —Richard A. Spears, *The Slang and Jargon of Drugs and Drink*, p. 41, 1986
• —Mike Haskins, *Drugs*, p. 280, 2003

Bernie *noun*
one million pounds *UK*
A jibe at Formula One motor racing tycoon Bernie Ecclestone who had his £1,000,000 donation to the Labour Party returned for reasons of political expediency; reported by David Davies, a Conservative member of the Welsh Assembly, September 2002.

Bernie's flakes; Bernie's gold dust *noun*
cocaine
• —Nick Constable, *This is Cocaine*, p. 181, 2002

berries *noun*
1 crystalised cocaine *US*
• —Vincent J. Monteleone, *Criminal Slang*, p. 21, 1949

2 anything considered to be the finest, the most excellent, the best *UK: SCOTLAND*
Probably a figurative use of **THE BERRIES** (testicles) in the same way that **BOLLOCKS** carries both senses. Also variant 'the berrs'.
• "Oh, yes," he says. "The fucking berries, that's what this is. The fucking berries." —Ted Lewis, *Jack Carter's Law*, p. 200, 1974
• This lasagne's the berrs! —Michael Munro, *The Patter, Another Blast*, 1988
• This hot weather's the berries. —Michael Munro, *The Complete Patter*, 1996

▸ the berries
the testicles *UK, 1984*
The image of hanging fruit.

berry *noun*
1 a dollar *US, 1916*
- —Lou Shelly, *Hepcats Jive Talk Dictionary*, p. 7, 1945
- Hand two hundred berries in my billfold and I couldn't afford to lose it.—Mickey Spillane, *I, The Jury*, p. 113, 1947
- "It's the berries, Phil," Dopey said.—James T. Farrell, *Saturday Night*, p. 22, 1947
- The mayor says he'll pay a thousand berries if the Pied Piper will disc his jig.—Haenigsen, *Jive's Like That*, 1947
- Twenty berries an you alla roun the mothahfuggin worl'.—Robert Gover, *One Hundred Dollar Misunderstanding*, p. 21, 1961

2 crack cocaine *US*
- —Peter Johnson, *Dictionary of Street Alcohol and Drug Terms*, p. 17, 1993

berry *verb*
to communicate via instant wireless messaging *CANADA*
- In three short years it has become both a status symbol and a verb (as in "Berry me the answer.") The Blackberry [from Waterloo ONT] is an instant-messaging device that lets you get and send wireless email anywhere.—*Toronto Globe and Mail*, p. A17, 21st June 2002

berry sugar *noun*
extra fine granulated sugar *CANADA*
- Pudding: 1 cup (250 ml) unsalted butter 1 cup (250 ml) Rogers Berry Sugar 4 large eggs, beaten 1/2 teaspoon (2 ml) vanilla essence —*banner.com*, 14th July 2002

Bert *nickname*
▹ see: FAT ALBERT

berth *noun*
a job working on a fishing boat *CANADA*
Originally, when fishing was done from dories, a 'berth' was a specific spot on one side of the dory where a fisherman was to row and work lines. It has come to mean any job on a fishing boat.
- He's found his berth – now he can work the fishing season and draw pogie all winter.—Lewis Poteet, *The South Shore Phrase Book*, p. 20, 1999

Bertie *noun*
▸ do a Bertie
to become an important informer *UK*
Police slang; after Bertie Smalls, a notorious or legendary (depending on your point of view) small-time robber turned police informer who, in 1973, became the original SUPERGRASS.
- —Martin Fido and Keith Skinner, *The Official Encyclopaedia of New Scotland Yard*, 1999

be seeing you
goodbye *UK, 1937*
'Be seeing you' gained a sinister, threatening edge in 1967 when used in cult television series *The Prisoner*.
- "Hooray, Buck. Be seeing you."—Kylie Tennant, *Lost Haven*, p. 232, 1946
- —Nino Culotta (John O'Grady), *They're A Weird Mob*, p. 24, 1957

Bess *noun*
used as a term of address among male homosexuals *US*
- —*Fact*, p. 25, January-February 1965

bessie *noun*
1 the penis *US*
- And then I'm suddenly staring at the biggest bessie I ever seen in my life.—Richard Frank, *A Study of Sex in Prison*, p. 28, 1973

2 a best-friend *UK*
Pronounced 'bezzie', used by teenagers.
- — Susie Dent, *The Language Report*, p. 75, 2003

best *noun*
a stroke of a cane, or 'the slipper' applied as corporal punishment *UK, 1912*
For some reason six was always the most popular number of deliveries ('six of the best') but the term varies to account for the punisher's preference. Corporal punishment has not been permitted in UK schools since the later C20.

▸ give (a number) of the best
to give (so many) belts with a cane *AUSTRALIA*
- If I get caught it'll be six of the best on the behind for sure.—Colin Johnson, *Wild Cat Falling*, p. 64, 1965
- I was carrying a note inscribed with the numeral 6, meaning that I was to be given six of the best.—Clive James, *Unreliable Memoirs*, p. 106, 1980
- I gave myself a dozen of my very best.—Paul Vautin, *Turn It Up!*, p. 109, 1995

▸ one of the best
a good man, a good companion *UK, 1937*

best *verb*
should *US*
- You BEST move on up.—Malachi Andrews and Paul T. Owens, *Black Language*, p. 98, 1973

best-best *adjective*
the very best *BARBADOS*
- —John A. Holm, *Dictionary of Bahamian English*, p. 16, 1982

best bet *noun*
the most advantageous option *UK, 1941*
- He has no ambitions, except to, somehow, successfully assimilate to an American way of life. His best bet, he believes, is to love and be loved by American women, and become American via a kind of amorous osmosis.—*The Guardian*, 14th June 2003

best bib and tucker *noun*
your best clothes *UK, 1747*
Originally of an article worn by women and girls, in more generalised use by mid-C19.

best blue; best BD *noun*
the better of an airman's or a soldier's two issued uniforms *UK*
BD is '*b*attle*d*ress'. In use throughout World War 2 and National Service, 1939–62.

best boy *noun*
in television and film making, the electrician's assistant *US*
- —Ira Konigsberg, *The Complete Film Dictionary*, p. 27, 1987

bestest *adjective*
best *UK, 1905*
A solecism; childish, occasionally jocular or as an endearment.
- The world's greatest, bestest super-ultimate inside story[.] —*The Observer*, 6th October 2002
- Dear Deidre, should I succumb to temptation and sell the story of my very bestest friends?—*The Guardian*, 17th September 2003

best friend *noun*
your penis *AUSTRALIA*
- So I wrapped a $50 note around my best friend (*he means his DICK readers*) and fastened it on with a rubber band. I woke up next morning with my Morning Glory being choked.—*Picture*, p. 45, 5th February 1992

best girl *noun*
a fiancée, a wife or a special girlfriend *US, 1887*
- Leaping from tree to tree! As they float down the mighty rivers of British Columbia! With my best girl by my side!—Monty Python, *The Lumberjack Song*, 1971

be's that way
used as a world-weary but wise acknowledgement that what is, is *US*
- —Hy Lit, *Hy Lit's Unbelievable Dictionary of Hip Words for Groovy People*, p. 4, 1968

best of British luck!; best of British!
used as an offer of good wishes, sometimes sincerely but generally with such heavy irony that the opposite is intended and inferred *UK, 1940s→*
Military coinage, in general use by 1960.
- STRAW: Want me to deal with it? DRUMMOND: No, it's my job. STRAW: Well, all I can say is the best of British luck.—Graeme Kent, *The Queen's Corporal [Six Granada Plays]*, p. 95, 1959
- —Louis S. Leland, *A Personal Kiwi-Yankee Dictionary*, p. 14, 1984

best piece *noun*
a girlfriend or wife *US*
- —Eugene Landy, *The Underground Dictionary*, p. 32, 1971

best seller *noun*
a Ford Cortina car *UK*
Citizens' band radio slang, presumably inspired by Ford's sales figures at the time of coinage.
- —Peter Chippindale, *The British CB Book*, p. 161, 1981

bet *verb*
▸ bet a pound to a piece of shit
used as a statement of absolute certainly *UK, 1937*
Usually construed positively as 'I will' or 'would bet'; occasional and earlier use may be negative.

▸ **bet like the Watsons**
to bet heavily on horses *AUSTRALIA*
After legendary Australian gamblers.
• —Lawson Glossop, *Lucky Palmer*, 1949

▸ **bet London to a brick**
used as a statement of absolute certainty *AUSTRALIA, 1945*

▸ **bet on a horse**
to be addicted to heroin or morphine *US*
• —Jay Robert Nash, *Dictionary of Crime*, p. 26, 1992

▸ **bet on the blue**
to gamble on credit *AUSTRALIA*
• —Lawson Glossop, *Lucky Palmer*, 1949

▸ **bet on the coat**
to place a dummy bet with a bookmaker to encourage genuine interest in a bet *AUSTRALIA*
• —Lawson Glossop, *Lucky Palmer*, 1949

▸ **bet the dog**
in bar dice games, to bet the total amount of the pot *US*
• —Jester Smith, *Games They Play in San Francisco*, p. 103, 1971

▸ **bet the ranch; bet the farm**
to be absolutely certain about something *US*
• "I'm not a betting man, but if I was, I would bet the fuckin' ranch you don't know where the complaints are." —George V. Higgins, *The Rat on Fire*, p. 124, 1981
• But if I had a place be make a wager, I'd bet the farm on Erin's Boy in the seventh. —Robert Campbell, *Juice*, 1988

▸ **bet until your nose bleeds**
in horse racing, to bet all of your resources on a sure thing *AUSTRALIA*
• —Ned Wallish, *The Truth Dictionary of Racing Slang*, p. 6, 1989

▸ **bet your ass**
used as a statement of absolute certainty *US, 1928*

▸ **bet your boots**
used as a statement of absolute certainty *US, 1856*

▸ **bet your bottom dollar**
used as a statement of absolute certainty *US, 1935*

▸ **bet your hat**
used as a statement of absolute certainty *US, 1879*

▸ **bet your life**
used as a statement of absolute certainty *US, 1852*

▸ **want to bet on it?**
a catchphrase used, with *bet* emphasised, as a challenging expression of doubt *UK*
• He was good, but not that damned good, I told him. "Does the sahib ever value his house, his cattle and his wife?" which is the Pathan way of saying, "You want to bet on it?" —Berkeley Mather, *The Terminators*, 1971

bet!
used for expressing approval *US*
• —*Washington Post Magazine*, p. 17, 28th June 1987
• —Connie Eble (Editor), *UNC-CH Campus Slang*, p. 1, Fall 1995

beta *noun*
1 a test or probationary stage *US*
Borrowed from the technical process of external testing of a product.
• "His girlfriend is in beta" means that he is still testing for compatibility and reserving judgment. —Eric S. Raymond, *The New Hacker's Dictionary*, p. 55, 1991

2 the grade 'B' in academic work *US*
• —Collin Baker et al., *College Undergraduate Slang Study Conducted at Brown University*, p. 79, 1968

betcha!
used as a statement of certainty *UK*
A phonetic blending of 'bet you' or an elision of **BET YOUR ASS/BOOTS/LIFE**, etc.
• He kept twisting my collar so it was hard to breathe and saying, "Betcha don't feel so cocky now, do you, dirty little yobs?["] —John Peter Jones, *Feather Pluckers*, p. 8, 1964
• Betcha by golly, wow / You're the one that I've been waiting for forever. — The Stylistics, *Betcha By Golly Wow*, 1971
• You'll be thrilled by them. You betcha. —Brian Preston, *Pot Planet*, p. 232, 2002

bet-down *adjective*
very ugly *IRELAND*
• [A]nd four birds, three of them are bet-down, the other I'd file under 'Ugly But Rideable'. —Paul Howard, *The Teenage Dirtbag Years*, p. 77, 2001

be the ...
used as a command *US*
• Mockingly from Zen philosophy. Expression used to tell another to do something: Driver, be the fast lane! = Switch into the fast lane. —Connie Eble (Editor), *UNC-CH Campus Slang*, p. 1, Spring 1984

be there, aloha
used as a farewell *US*
Repopularised by ESPN's Keith Olberman, borrowed from Jack Lord's comment to Steve McGarrett when he would narrate the highlights of the next episode of *Hawaii 5-0*.
• —Connie Eble (Editor), *UNC-CH Campus Slang*, April 1978
• —Keith Olberman and Dan Patrickp, *The Big Show*, p. 12, 1997

be there or be square
if you do not attend an event thus advertised you will risk being thought unfashionable *UK*
A popular catchphrase slogan.
• Among the Deviants and everyone we knew, the attitude was: be there or be square. —Mick Farren [writing of the late 1960s and early 70s], *Give the Anarchist a Cigarette*, p. 191, 2001

betise *noun*
an ill-timed remark *CANADA*
The term comes from French.
• Meanwhile the National Movement against Terrorism has poured choler on the business tycoons and viewed the call as a betise. —*isleditr.htm*, 17th July 2002

bet on top *noun*
a bogus bet laid by a bookmaker's confederate to encourage genuine interest in a particular gamble *UK, 1961*
The bookmaker's clerk will place the bet 'on top' (not in the body) of the betting book.

Bette *noun*
a person who looks better from a distance *UK*
After singer Bette Midler who recorded the song 'From a Distance', 1990.
• —*Popbitch*, 19th February 2004

better half *noun*
a wife *UK, 1580*
A jocular usage that, over time, has also referred to 'a husband', 'a close friend' and 'a man's soul'.

better idea *noun*
in car repair shops, used to describe any of several ill-advised equipment developments by Ford *US*
Derived from a Ford advertising slogan – 'Ford has a better idea'.
• —Lewis Poteet, *Car & Motorcyle Slang*, p. 29, 1992

better living through chemistry
used as a humorous endorsement of mind-altering recreational drug use *US*
Borrowed from an advertising slogan of DuPont Chemicals.
• Abbie Hoffman encouraged students at Bolumbia University to experiment further with such "better living through chemistry." —J. Anthony Lukas, *The Barnyard Epithet and Other Obscenities*, p. 10, 1970

better than a poke in the eye with a sharp stick
describes an event or circumstance that is of minimal desirability *AUSTRALIA, 1974*
A 'burnt stick' or a 'blunt stick' allow further variation of the basic formula.

betting ring *noun*
the area at a racecourse devoted to betting *AUSTRALIA*
• The red flag was hoisted and in the betting ring Grafter's aides collected all their bets[.] —James Holledge, *The Great Australian Gamble*, p. 142, 1966

betting shop *noun*
an illegal establishment for betting *AUSTRALIA*
• Their betting-shops were crowded with desks of clerks and could have passed for the offices of busy stockbrokers. —Vince Kelly, *The Bogeyman*, p. 128, 1956
• —James Holledge, *The Great Australian Gamble*, p. 82, 1966

betting tool *noun*

in horse racing, a horse that consistently wins *US*

- —Robert Saunders Dowst and Jay Craig, *Playing the Races*, p. 160, 1960

Betty *noun*

1 an attractive female *US*

- —Surf Punks, *Oh No! Not Them Again! (liner notes)*, 1988
- —Connie Eble (Editor), *UNC-CH Campus Slang*, p. 1, Spring 1993
- Not a total Betty, but a vast improvement.—*Clueless*, 1995

2 an old woman *UK*

Probably named for Betty Hoskins (b.1922), well known to audiences of Graham Norton's television programmes since 1998.

- The aeroplane is full of awayday passengers, mostly over 50. Although a guided tour is on offer for part of the day, the girls make a mental note not to get stuck with the "Bettys".—*The Times*, 8th April 2003

betty bracelets *noun*

police *UK*

- Take it easy will you. We don't want any trouble with betty bracelets.—Emma Hindley, *Storm in a Teacup*, 1993
- —Paul Baker, *Polari*, p. 164, 2002

Betty Coed *noun*

the stereotypical female high school or college student *US, 1961*

- Betty Coed and her football hero – he's the coach – will be married in Richmond a week from tomorrow.—*San Francisco News Call-Bulletin*, p. 9, 6th May 1960
- Betty Coed passesd by outside, unmindful of the drizzle and the heart that skipped a beat behind windows.—Bill Cardoso, *The Maltese Sangweech*, p. 91, 1984

Betty Crocker *noun*

used by combat troops in Vietnam to describe their peers not in combat, especially those in Saigon *US, 1969*

Betty Crocker is the mythical yet trademarked American homemaker created in 1921 by the Washburn Crosby Company, forerunner to General Mills Incorporated. One of many terms coined in Vietnam.

- —Linda Reinberg, *In the Field*, p. 20, 1991

Betty Grable *noun*

1 sable *UK*

Rhyming slang in criminal use, based on the name of film actress Betty Grable (1916–73).

- [T]here's a pen-and-ink (mink) and Betty Grable (sable) in -'s window in – Street, off Bond Street[.]—Charles Raven, *Underworld Nights*, p. 36, 1956

2 a table *UK, 1992*

Rhyming slang, based on the name of film actress Betty Grable (1916–73). Also shortened to 'betty'.

- —Ray Puxley, *Cockney Rabbit*, p. 14, 1992

between pictures *adjective*

out of work, unemployed *US*

A euphemism, true in the entertainment industry, jocular elsewhere.

- "I'm between pictures" is a popular Hollywood phrase. But for the "Barefoot Girl with Coat of Mink" – sultry Ava Gardner – a more appropriate line is "I'm between headlines."—*San Francisco News*, p. s, 30th August 1954

between you and me and the gate-post; between you and me and the bedpost

between ourselves *UK, 1832*

Conjuring the image of a confidence passed over a garden gate. The 'bedpost', a still-used variation, allows for more intimate intercourse.

- "This is just between you and me." "And the gatepost. I gotcha."—Elmore Leonard, *Glite*, p. 104, 1985

Beulah land *noun*

heaven *US, 1939*

From the book of Isaiah, 62:4.

- There ain't nothin' up there. If you would read that Bible, you would know. There is no Beulah land.—*Los Angeles Times*, p. L7, 8th January 2004

bevels *noun*

dice that have been altered by rounding off the sides slightly so as to produce a desired point *US*

- —John S. Salak, *Dictionary of Gambling*, p. 20, 1963

beverada; bevois *noun*

1 a drink, especially beer *UK*

Affected variations of **BEVVY**.

- —Paul Baker, *Polari*, p. 164, 2002

2 a public house *UK*

An affected variation of **BEVVY CASEY**.

- —Paul Baker, *Polari*, p. 164, 2002

Beverley Pills *noun*

the prescription drug Vicodin™ when taken recreationally *US*

- In Beverly Pills March 29, 8 p.m. BBC World's reporters speak to Hollywood stars about their battle with the drug[.]—*The Sunday Tribune (India)*, 10th March 2002

bevie homie *noun*

a heavy drinker *UK*

- Anyone known to be a heavy drinker is a "bevie homie" and anyone having an occasional blind is "on the bevie".—Butch Reynolds, *Broken Hearted Clown*, p. 29, 1953

Bevin *noun*

in the mining industry, a shift spent at home as a result of mechanical breakdown *UK*

Named for Ernest Bevin, 1881–1951, statesman and creator of the Transport and General Workers Union. This term, like most of the UK's mining industry, has not survived the intervening years.

- —W. Foster (Editor), *Pit Talk*, 1970

bevo *noun*

any alcoholic beverage *US*

- —Connie Eble (Editor), *UNC-CH Campus Slang*, p. 1, Spring 2003

bevvied; bevvied up *adjective*

drunk *UK, 1960*

From **BEVVY** (an alcoholic drink).

- Once we got well bevvied up Marchmare let go.—Derek Raymond (Robin Cook), *The Crust on its Uppers*, p. 23, 1962
- [We] get bevvied up and generally go ahead.—Derek Raymond (Robin Cook), *The Crust on its Uppers*, p. 55, 1962
- [A]s she's getting more bevvied, I'm tipping mine in the plant pot.—Kevin Sampson, *Outlaws*, p. 102, 2001

bevvy; bevie; bevv *noun*

1 an alcoholic drink, especially beer *UK, 1889*

Possibly from the circus term 'bevie' (a public house), or an abbreviation of 'beverage'; both derive from C15 'bever' (drink), and ultimately from Latin *bibere*.

- Any alcoholic drink is a "bevie" in circus language and to bevie is to drink.—Butch Reynolds, *Broken Hearted Clown*, p. 29, 1953
- [W]e nipped smartly off for a bevvy.—Derek Raymond (Robin Cook), *The Crust on its Uppers*, p. 23, 1962
- You come out the pub late, you've had a few bevvies[.]—Paul E Willis, *Profane Culture*, p. 123, 1978
- Plus all the rides, performers, food and bevvies, prizes and markets you could possibly handle!—*Beat*, p. 17, 1996
- TW met up with a few other top British DJs for a few bevvs.—Wayne Anthony, *Spanish Highs*, p. 157, 1999
- He's in Liverpool, it's, like, 1963, yeah – and he's about to sit down for a bev with John fucking Lennon.—Kevin Sampson, *Powder*, p. 129, 1999
- [H]e's walking away and he's half thinking about having a bet or a bevvy or going home to give his missus stick.—Kevin Sampson, *Outlaws*, p. 91, 2001
- [Y]ou were the first bod in the queue waiting to buy him a bevvy down the pub.—Mark Powell, *Snap*, p. 186, 2001
- —Paul Baker, *Polari*, p. 164, 2002

2 a public house *UK*

A shortening of **BEVVY CASEY**.

▸ **on the bevvy; on the bevie**

to be drinking, especially for a period of time dedicated to drunkenness *UK*

- Anyone known to be a heavy drinker is a "bevie homie" and anyone having an occasional blind is then "on the bevie".—Butch Reynolds, *Broken Hearted Clown*, p. 29, 1953

bevvy *verb*

to drink alcohol *UK, 1934*

bevvy casey; bevie casey *noun*

a public house *UK*

A combination of **BEVVY** (an alcoholic drink) and, ultimately, Italian *casa* (house).

- —Paul Baker, *Polari*, p. 164, 2002

bevvy omee *noun*
a drunkard *UK, 1937*
A combination of **BEVVY** (an alcoholic drink) and **OMEE** (a man).
• —Paul Baker, *Polari*, p. 164, 2002

bevvy-up *noun*
a drinking session *UK*
• [A] right old bevvy-up at Aristov's in Greek Street[.]—Derek Raymond (Robin Cook), *The Crust on its Uppers*, p. 53, 1962

bevvy up *verb*
to drink alcohol *UK*
An elaboration of **BEVVY**.
• —Bill Naughton, *Alfie Darling*, 1970

bewitched, bothered and bewildered *adjective*
confused *US*
The title of a song from the 1940 show *Pal Joey*, lyrics by Lorenz Hart, music by Richard Rodgers.
• [T]he bewitched, bothered and bewildered fathers and mothers of these expensively educated lads and lassies.—*San Francisco Chronicle*, p. 17, 21st May 1950
• The 49ers are bewitched, bothered, and bewildered. Plain confused too.— *San Francisco Examiner*, p. II-5, 3rd October 1955
• Bewitched, Bothered, Bewildered [Headline]— *San Francisco Examiner*, p. 23, 1st November 1967
• Bewitched, Bothered, and Bewildered [Episode Title]—Marti Noxon, *Buffy the Vampire Slayer*, 10th February 1998

Bexley Heath; bexleys *noun*
the teeth *UK*
Rhyming slang, based on a convenient area of Greater London.
• —Ray Puxley, *Cockney Rabbit*, p. 14, 1992
• —Paul Baker, *Polari*, p. 165, 2002

beyond *adjective*
1 outstanding, amazing, extraordinary *US*
• Gigglepuss was so beyond.— *Ten Things I Hate About You*, 1999
• I mean murder! For fuck's sakes! How they could ever have thought they'd be able to get us on that one, mun... fucking beyond, mun, aye[.]—Niall Griffiths, *Sheepshagger*, p. 238, 2001
2 in England *IRELAND*
• You can't be that busy. Just because you're doing well beyond. And we're all proud of you.—Eamonn Sweeney, *Waiting for the Healer*, p. 14, 1997

beyonek; beyong *noun*
▷ see: **BIANC**

bezazz; bizzazz *noun*
glamour, sparkle, energy, excitement *US, 1970*
A variation, if not a misspelling, of **PIZZAZZ**.
• Hats off to British technical wizards who are responsible for the glitter, bezazz and stylishness of this British studio production.— *The Listener*, 18th December 1980

bezel *noun*
any car part *US*
• — Chrysler Corporation, *Of Anchors, Bezels, Pots and Scorchers*, September 1959

be-ziffed *adjective*
▷ see: **ZIFFED**

bezzie *adjective*
best *UK*
• [W]ell ahead of their Scottish peers, or bezzie mates Kaiser Chiefs. — *Mojo*, p. 96, July 2005

BF; bee eff *noun*
a *b*loody *f*ool *UK, 1960*
A euphemistic abbreviation.

BFD *noun*
a *b*ig *f*ucking *d*eal *US*
Sometimes euphemised from 'fucking' to 'fat'.
• —J. W. Mays, *A Basic Guide to Campusology*, p. 2, 1966
• — *Current Slang*, p. 5, Fall 1967
• —Helen Dahlskog (Editor), *A Dictionary of Contemporary and Colloquial Usage*, p. 7, 1972
• —Connie Eble (Editor), *UNC-CH Campus Slang*, p. 1, Spring 1982
• "BFD! By one stupid little minute!"—Jess Mowry, *Way Past Cool*, 1992

BFE *noun*
any remote location *US*
An abbreviation of **BUMFUCK, EGYPT**.
• —Pamela Munro, *U.C.L.A. Slang*, p. 20, 1989

BFI *noun*
1 in computer technology, an approach relying on *b*rute *f*orce and *i*gnorance rather than elegant analysis *US*
• —Rachel S. Epstein and Nina Liebman, *Biz Speak*, p. 19, 1986
2 a massive heart attack or stroke; a *b*ig *f*ucking *i*nfarct *US*
• —Sally Williams, *"Strong" Words*, p. 133, 1994

B flat *adjective*
fat *UK*
Rhyming slang.
• B-flat omee [man]—Paul Baker, *Polari*, p. 163, 2002

BFN *noun*
an extremely remote place *US*
An abbreviation of **BUTT FUCKING NOWHERE**.
• —Connie Eble (Editor), *UNC-CH Campus Slang*, p. 1, November 2002

BFU *adjective*
*b*ig, *f*at and *u*gly *US*
• —Connie Eble (Editor), *UNC-CH Campus Slang*, p. 1, March 1996

BG *noun*
a young member of a youth gang *US*
An abbreviation of **BABY GANGSTER**.
• —Mark S. Fleisher, *Beggars & Thieves*, p. 287, 1995
• —James Haskins, *The Story of Hip-Hop*, p. 135, 2000

B game *noun*
in a gambling establishment or cardroom, the table with the second highest betting limit *US*
• —George Percy, *The Language of Poker*, p. 9, 1988

BGF
the *B*lack *G*uerilla *F*amily, a black prison gang *US*
• The BGF, a radical prison security threat group, got its start in San Quentin in 1966.—Bill Valentine, *Gangs and Their Tattoos*, p. 17, 2000

B girl *noun*
1 a woman who works in a bar, encouraging customers through flirtation to buy drinks, both for themselves and for her *US, 1936*
• New York's cafes and clubs are forbidden by law to employ hostesses or "B" girls[—Jack Lait and Lee Mortimer, *New York Confidential*, p. 127, 1948
• —Jack Leit and Lee Mortimer, *Chicago Confidential*, 1950
• Told the management they'd have to stop those B -girls from tricking the tourists so badly if they wanted to retain an artist of my caliber. —Dick Gregory, *Nigger*, p. 130, 1964
• In the more posh coktail lounges such as the Continental Hotel, undated B girls sit quietly nursing a Metaxa or Pernod[.]—Roger Gordon, *Hollywood's Sexual Underground*, p. 115, 1966
• Despite her propriety and abject sanctity, Mama still spoke English like a bordertown B-girl.—Seth Morgan, *Homeboy*, p. 305, 1990
• Ginger was my mother's nightclub name, to match here new career worked as a part-time stripteaser and "B-girl" in Tenderloin "B-joints."—Kim Rich, *Johnny's Girl*, p. 48, 1993
• You've got to pay $5 to the B-girl [who serves drinks to customers], $10 to the deejay.—James Ridgeway, *Red Light: Inside the Sex Industry*, p. 169, 1996
• A bunny sitting near me was more succinct. "They don't want us to look like B girls hustling drinks."—Kathryn Leigh Scott, *The Bunny Years*, p. 24, 1998
2 a young woman involved in early hip-hop *US*
From 'break girl'.
• —James Haskins, *The Story of Hip-Hop*, p. 135, 2000

BH!
used in anger, astonishment, disappointment and frustration *UK, 1928*
A euphemistic abbreviation of **BLOODY HELL!**.

bhang *noun*
1 marijuana, usually presumed to be from India *INDIA*
Urdu for *cannabis indica* (Indian hemp), also used for a marijuana tea. Known in various forms since 1598, modern usage and variant spelling, 'bang', probably begins with hippies.
• In India, it is known as hashish, and is either smoked or drunk as an infusion with the colorful name of bhang.— *Fortnight*, p. 12, 24th September 1948
2 a mixture of marijuana pollen and ghee for smoking *UK*
• —Nick Brownlee, *This Is Cannabis*, p. 151, 2002

bhang lassi *noun*
yoghurt and marijuana combined in a drink *INDIA*
• —Mike Haskins, *Drugs*, p. 292, 2003

B head *noun*
a barbiturate user or addict *US*
• —Joel Homer, *Jargon*, p. 193, 1979

bhong *noun*
▷ see: BONG

bhoy *noun*
an Irishman involved in crime or political violence, especially as 'the Bhoys' *UK: NORTHERN IRELAND*
Irish pronunciation of 'boy'.
• Almost all of my [drug] trade comes via the Bhoys, the Dubliners, the Irish connection. —Kevin Sampson, *Outlaws*, p. 52, 2001

bi *noun*
a *bi*sexual person *US, 1956*
• If he were a "bi" he'd want to get into the act and maybe hump his buddy while ol' buddy is humping you. — *Screw*, p. 16, 16th May 1969
• Though the hanky code was originated by gay men, it has been adopted by cruising lesbians and bi's. — *Taste of Latex*, p. 24, Winter 1990–1991

bi *adjective*
*bi*sexual *US, 1956*
• Met this quietly sensual "bi" friend of Martin's, wearing a clerical collar. —Jefferson Poland and Valerie Alison, *The Records of the San Francisco Sexual Freedom League*, p. 45, 1971
• This is a pretty sensual group of girls, mostly bi. —Robert Stoller and I.S. Levine, *Coming Attractions*, p. 148, 1991
• We ticked off everything – Bi, Sub, Dom, Leather, Rubber, PVC, Bondage, Water Sports[.] —Kitty Churchill, *Thinking of England*, p. 100, 1995
• [Y]ou have to be gay-friendly to be successful in certain businesses cos a lot of people in that world [fetish clubs], and music and entertainment, are gay or bi. —Dave Courtney, *Raving Lunacy*, p. 113, 2000
• But me is not bi. —Ali G (Sacha Baron Cohen), *Ali G Indahouse*, p. 16, 23rd March 2002

bianc; beone; beyonek; beyong *noun*
a shilling *UK*
From Italian *bianco* (white) for the silver of the coin; these variations survived in theatrical and gay society from mid-C19 until UK decimalisation in 1971.
• —Paul Baker, *Polari*, p. 164, 2002

Bianca blast *noun*
oral sex performed with a mouth full of Bianca mouth wash *US*
• —J.R. Schwartz, *The Official Guide to the Best Cat Houses in Nevada*, p. 163, 1993

bib *noun*
1 in horse racing, a horse's nose or head as a measure of a close finish *AUSTRALIA*
• —Ned Wallish, *The Truth Dictionary of Racing Slang*, p. 6, 1989

2 a tablet of MDMA, the recreational drug best known as ecstasy *UK*
• —Mike Haskins, *Drugs*, p. 289, 2003

▸ **push your bib in; put your bib in; stick your bib in**
to interfere *AUSTRALIA, 1959*

bib *verb*
to sound a horn *UK*
A variation of conventional 'beep'.
• — *The Chris Moyles Show*, 2nd August 2004

bibby *noun*
1 a native woman or girl *UK*
A new spelling for obsolete Anglo-Indian 'bebee'.
• —Charles Allen (Editor), *Plain Tales from the Raj*, 1975

2 mucus *BARBADOS*
• —John A. Holm, *Dictionary of Bahamian English*, p. 16, 1982

bibby-dibby *adjective*
petty, trivial, worthless *JAMAICA*
• —Peter L. Patrick, *Some Recent Jamaican Creole Words*, 2003

bibi *adjective*
bisexual *UK*
• —Paul Baker, *Polari*, p. 165, 2002

Bible *noun*
1 the truth *US*
• —Jack Lait and Lee Mortimer, *New York Confidential*, p. 235, 1948
• —John A. Holm, *Dictionary of Bahamian English*, p. 17, 1982

2 a fundamental source book, if not the most authoritative reference book in a given field *US, 1893*
• —Eric S. Raymond, *The New Hacker's Dictionary*, p. 56, 1991
• I'll offer up my bible for a small fee. — *Gone in 60 Seconds*, 2000

3 on the railways, the book of company rules *US*
• —Norman Carlisle, *The Modern Wonder Book of Trains and Railroading*, p. 261, 1946

4 in trucking, the Interstate Commerce Commission's book of regulations governing trucking *US*
• —Montie Tak, *Truck Talk*, p. 11, 1971

5 the Harley-Davidson repair manual *US*
Biker (motorcyle) usage.

6 in a unionised work environment, the union contract *US*
• — *American Speech*, p. 42, February 1963: 'Trucker's language in Rhode Island'

7 in circus and carnival usage, a programme or souvenir magazine *US*
• —Don Wilmeth, *The Language of American Popular Entertainment*, p. 21, 1981

8 in the circus or carnival, *The Billboard*, a business newspaper *US*
• —Joe McKennon, *Circus Lingo*, p. 15, 1980

▸ **the Bible**
Glass's Guide to Used Car Prices, first published in 1933 *UK*
A specialist use for the motor trade.
• Glass's Guide to Used Car Prices, the motor dealers' bible. — *Sunday Times*, 9th August 1981

bibleback *noun*
1 a prisoner who has turned to religion, sincerely or not *US*
• There is the Bibleback, a particularly disgusting type of sycophant, who attends all the religious functions, wails the loudest, sings, prays and performs all the external functions required to become known as a Christian. —Bruce Jackson, *Outside the Law*, p. 178, 1972

2 in the circus or carnival, a folding plank used for grandstands *US*
• —Joe McKennon, *Circus Lingo*, p. 15, 1980

Bible-basher; Bible-thumper *noun*
an evangelical Christian *US, 1885*
• —Jerry Robertson, *Oil Slanguage*, p. 28, 1954
• I could have told you for free that people think cigarettes are the road to perdition. Ain't you never heard one of them Bible-thumpers? —Max Shulman, *Anyone Got a Match?*, p. 43, 1964
• Any cheap Bible thumper on the outside has all the qualifications of a navy chaplain. —Darryl Ponicsan, *The Last Detail*, p. 46, 1970
• 'Drunken louts disrupting the work of Her Majesty's Council in a Christian community.' Chilla determined to go out with the colours flying: 'Shut up, you old bible basher.' —Frank Hardy, *The Outcasts of Foolgarah*, p. 31, 1971
• —Connie Eble (Editor), *UNC-CH Campus Slang*, March 1973
• —Louis S. Leland, *A Personal Kiwi-Yankee Dictionary*, p. 14, 1984
• [W]ondering who's come knocking this late, Bible-bashers or locked out neighbours[.] —John King, *Human Punk*, p. 217, 2000
• The bible bashers were showmen in their own right[.] —Jimmy Stockin, *On The Cobbles*, p. 75, 2000

bible-bashing *adjective*
Christian, especially zealously so *AUSTRALIA*
• What makes it all the more nauseating, of course, is that Mr Bjelke-Petersen is such a Bible-bashing bastard. —Gough Whitlam, *The Ugly Australian*, p. 114, 1975

Bible belt *noun*
1 rural America, especially in the south, where fundamentalist Christians dominate the culture *US, 1924*
• Coming under the influence of the green-covered American Mercury, he looked back on home as the uncivilized "Bible belt." —James T. Farrell, *Ruth and Bertram*, p. 91, 1955
• Pity Terpsichore in the Bible Belt. —Angelo d'Arcangelo, *The Homosexual Handbook*, p. 155, 1968
• Gay Liberation Comes To Missouri Bible belt! [Headline] — *The Advocate*, p. 7, March 31st-April 13th 1971
• Gonna let it rock / Let it roll / Let the Bible Belt come down / And save my soul. —John Cougar Mellencamp, *Jack and Diane*, 1982
• — Multicultural Management Program Fellows, *Dictionary of Cautionary Words and Phrases*, 1989

2 the political interests and constituency of the (Christian) religious right *UK*
• Author angers the Bible Belt[:] Philip Pullman's humanist tales of good and evil are a far cry from CS Lewis and A A Milne. But to the horror of the religious Right, they are a runaway hit. — *The Observer*, 26th August 2001

3 any area with a fundamentalist Christian majority *UK*
- Church attendance is high in Ballymena, the buckle on Ian Paisley's North Antrim Bible belt constituency. — *The Guardian*, 17th February 2001

Bible belter *noun*
a person from the rural mid-western or southern US *US*
Implies ignorance, gullibility and backwardness.
- — *Maledicta*, p. 151, Summer/Winter 1978: 'How to hate thy neighbor: a guide to racist maledicta'

Bible bunny *noun*
a Christian who is filled with spiritual joy *US*
- Suddenly you're ansty about a parking lot full of Bible-bunnies. Jeez. — Christopher Brookmyre, *Not the End of the World*, p. 33, 1998
- "Who was it?" he asked. "Another Bible bunny," I said. — Julie Anne Peters, *A Snitch in the Snob Squad*, p. 82, 2001

Bible puncher *noun*
in the armed services, a chaplain *UK*
Not recorded until 1961 but suggested by BIBLE-PUNCHING, 1937.
- — John W. Mussell, *Militarisms*, p. 12, 1995

Bible-punching *noun*
a sermon, a religious talk *UK, 1937*
Also, now more usually, used as an adjective.
- Ron Cephas Jones, who made a big impact as a bible-punching serial killer in 'Jesus Hopped the A Train'. — *The Guardian*, 15th October 2003

Bible run *noun*
in television and film making, a weekly print-out of all production expenses *US*
- — Ralph S. Singleton, *Filmaker's Dictionary*, p. 17, 1990

Biblical neckline; Biblical top *noun*
a low-cut neckline on an item of ladies-wear that reveals generous amounts of cleavage, or more *UK*
A pun on 'Lo and behold!'. Possibly Australian in origin and, when noted in 1984, was thought to have slipped into disuse by the mid-1960s. It is currently alive and well in the UK in comedian's patter: 'I see you're wearing your biblical top tonight ... Lo and behold! And, yea, I can see the promised land. And, hallelujah! – there is milk and honey! One on each tap'.

bic *verb*
to understand *US*
Vietnam war usage; a corrupted *biet*, Vietnamese for 'understand'.
- — Linda Reinberg, *In the Field*, p. 21, 1991

bicarb *noun*
bicarbonate of soda *US, 1922*
- Sid was pacing up and down with a glass of bicarb in one hand and a fag in the other[.] — Jake Arnott, *He Kills Coppers*, p. 100, 2001

bice; byce *noun*
two, especially £2 *UK, 1937*
From French *bis* (twice).

bice and a roht; bice and a half *noun*
in betting, odds of 5–2 *UK, 1937*
The literal sense is 'two and a half'; in betting odds the '–1' is usually implied. From BICE (two).

bicho *noun*
the penis *US*
- — Harold Wentworth and Stuart Berg Flexner, *Dictionary of American Slang*, p. 677, 1976

bicky; bikky *noun*
a biscuit *UK, 1886*
- Nood's tuckin' in to them biccies just eatin' one while checkin' out the next. — Nick Barlay, *Curvy Lovebox*, p. 73, 1997
- Fancy a bicky? He took a biscuit and dipped in his tea. — John King, *White Trash*, p. 185–186, 2001

bicoastal *adjective*
pertaining to the west and east coasts of the US *US*
Almost always used with a sense of mocking, hyper-formality.
- To one side of us in the bleachers, as part of the audience, were the bicoastal network executives[.] — Dan Jenkins, *Life Its Ownself*, p. 174, 1984
- HBS, Stanford Forge a Bicoastal e-Alliance. — *Harvard Magazine*, p. 67, March-April 2001

bi-curious *adjective*
interested in experimenting with bisexuality
- [T]o check if I have missed this week's edition of Bi-Curious Girls. — *The Guardian*, 28th October 2002

bicycle *noun*
1 a sexually promiscuous female *UK*
- A fellow might easily marry a girl whose oul' one had been getting her oats morning, noon and night, tongue hanging out for it, the town bicycle, like, only she never got caught. — Hugh Leonard, *Out After Dark*, p. 104, 1989

2 a bisexual *US*
- Only those in the know understood the reference in the 1978 Top 10 hit recording by Queen, "I want to Ride My Bicycle.
- — Arnold Shaw, *Dictionary of American Pop/Rock*, p. 35, 1982

3 in lowball poker, the lowest possible straight *US*
- — Jim Glenn, *Programmed Poker*, p. 155, 1981

4 in electric line work, a chain drill used for drilling holes *US*
- — A.B. Chance Co., *Lineman's Slang Dictionary*, p. 1, 1980

▸ **on your bicycle**
in boxing, staying away from the opponent's punches by back pedalling *US, 1936*
- Bolden, strictly a defensive fighter, got on his bicycle in the first session and back pedaled through the entire fight. — *San Francisco Examiner*, p. 19, 13th November 1945
- Fusari rode his bicycle all night. The 6 to 1 underdog escaped the knockout that was predicted, but that's about all he did. — *San Francisco Examiner*, p. 26, 10th August 1950
- It takes two to make a fight and it's no easy trick to capitalize on your superiority if the other fellow spends too much time on his bicycle. — *San Francisco News*, p. 7, 3rd April 1954
- So he kept me away with left hooks and got on his bicycle where I charged him. — Rocky Garciano (with Rowland Barber), *Somebody Up There Likes Me*, p. 275, 1955

bicycle *verb*
1 in television and film making, to work on mutliple projects simultaneously *US*
In the days of silent films, to show a film at several different theatres required transporting it from one theatre to another, often by bicycle.
- — Tony Miller and Patricia George, *Cut! Print!*, p. 40, 1977
- — Ira Konigsberg, *The Complete Film Dictionary*, p. 27, 1987
- — Ralph S. Singleton, *Filmaker's Dictionary*, p. 17, 1990

2 to ride a surfboard with a wide stance *US*
- — Gary Fairmont R. Filosa II, *The Surfer's Almanac*, p. 182, 1977

bicycle pump *noun*
a large syringe *US*
Korean war usage.
- The bicycle pump was the giant, legendary needle that Navy medics used to scare noisy Marines. When threatened with the "bicycle pump," the Marine would pretend to scorn such a story. — Russell Davis, *Marine at War*, p. 167, 1961

bid *noun*
an old woman, especially one who complains or fusses *UK, 1984*
A shortening of BIDDY.

biddims *noun*
trousers that are too short and narrow *BARBADOS*
- — Richard Allsopp, *Dictionary of Caribbean English Usage*, p. 98, 1996

biddle move *noun*
a manoeuvre by a cheat or a conjuror that moves a selected playing card to the bottom of the deck *UK*
- — *Card Trick Central*, 2003

biddy *noun*
an old woman, usually one prone to complain and fuss *US, 1938*
The dominant sense of the term in the US, with the older sense of a 'young woman' unknown.
- Now then ... bring a biddy up to date on your personal life. — *San Francisco Examiner*, p. 14, 8th January 1946
- "Those old welfare biddies will find her a fine family to live with." — Chester Himes, *The Real Cool Killers*, p. 45, 1959
- The captain whispered in my ear: "Don't make any dramatic gestures to those biddies or I'll crease your head with this club." — Lenny Bruce, *How to Talk Dirty and Influence People*, p. 70, 1965
- Have you seen the way those old biddies look at you when we walk into the dining room? — Armistead Maupin, *Further Tales of the City*, p. 195, 1982

- But when his wife returned and heard about this bet from the biddies at the bridge club, she would kill him. —Jimmy Buffett, *Tales from Margaritaville*, p. 120, 1989
- When Bobbie questioned Fin about the age of all the fun-loving fogies, coots, geezers, codgers, duffers and biddies she'd met in the saloon, he didn't know how to tell her that the oldest fossil in the joint wasn't fifteen years his senior. —Joseph Wambaugh, *Finnegan's Week*, p. 230, 1993

bidi *noun*
▷ see: BEEDI

bidness *noun*
business *US*
A Texas corrupted pronunciation of a Texas activity.
- He blessed Bid Ed's oil bidness, said young people were the hope of the world, acknowledged the talented tap-dance team of Jesus and Mary, forgave the Catholics and Jews, and pronounced us man and wife. —Dan Jenkins, *Life Its Ownself*, p. 65, 1984
- Doing Bidness With Roger Clinton —*Washington Post*, p. A25, 21st June 2001

bien *adjective*
▷ see: BENE

biff *noun*
1 a blow, a hit, a whack *US, 1847*
- [G]et your kicks and biffs. It's your night! —Lester Bangs, *Psychotic Reactions and Carburetor Dung*, p. 38, 1970
- Then a biff from an idea that blowled him over. —Neal Cassady, *The First Third*, p. 168, 1971

2 fighting, especially fighting on a sporting field *AUSTRALIA*
- [W]e don't hold a bit of biff against a player who turns in a blinder. —Alexander Buzo, *The Roy Murphy Show*, p. 111, 1970
- [He was a] Manly Rugby League player who didn't mind a bit of biff. —Roy Slaven (John Doyle), *Five South Coast Seasons*, p. 170, 1992
- The Australians are too big, fast, mobile and too well-drilled to be beaten. Great Britain's only hope may be to resort to the biff. —Paul Vautin, *Turn It Up!*, p. 200, 1995

3 in mountain biking, a crash *US*
- We've grimaced and chuckled simultaneously at face plants [a face-first encounter with the gound], endos [an accident in which the cyclist flies over the handlebars], biffs and crash-landings. —*Mountain Bike Magazine's Complete Guide To Mountain Biking Skills*, p. 32, 1996

4 in pinball, a forceful hit with the flipper *US*
- —Bobbye Claire Natkin and Steve Kirk, *All About Pinball*, p. 110, 1977

5 the vagina, the vulva *UK*
- Rayon reckons that their biffs are shaved differently. —Colin Butts, *Is Harry on the Boat?*, p. 91, 1997
- —*Journal of Sex Research*, p. 146, 2001

6 a person deformed to some degree by spina bifida *UK*
An offensive term used by schoolchildren.
- —Chris Lewis, *The Dictionary of Playground Slang*, p. 30, 2003

7 a toilet *US, 1942*
- —*The Guild Dictionary of Homosexual Terms*, p. 4, 1965
- —Collin Baker et al., *College Undergraduate Slang Study Conducted at Brown University*, p. 79, 1968

biff *verb*
1 to hit someone or something *UK, 1888*
- [England cricketer, Marcus] Trescothick advanced down the pitch and biffed him for six[.] —*The Guardian*, 9th November 2002

2 to throw something *NEW ZEALAND*
- 'All I can do is biff.' 'Then just biff – as hard as you can.' —*Listener*, p. 4, 1st May 1964

3 in computing, to inform someone of incoming mail *US*
- —Eric S. Raymond, *The New Hacker's Dictionary*, p. 56, 1991

4 to fail *US*
- —Vann Wesson, *Generation X Field Guide and Lexicon*, p. 18, 1997

biffa *adjective*
very ugly *UK*
Probably derives from US **BIFFER** (an unattractive woman), however UK theories abound, including: 'Biffo the Bear' in the *Beano* comic from 1948, simply known as 'Biffo' by the 1990s; 'Biffa Bacon' in the later *Viz* comic; and the familiar company name, 'Biffa Waste Services'.
- —Chris Lewis, *The Dictionary of Playground Slang*, p. 30, 2003

biffer *noun*
1 someone with a reputation as a hard hitter, especially in sports *UK*
- The big biffer [Ian Blackwell] can begin to rebuild his reputation not just with some hefty leg-side blows —*The Guardian*, 13th June 2003

2 any implement used for hitting, whether designed for such a purpose or improvised *UK, 2003*
- —*Collins English Dictionary*, 2003

3 an unattractive woman *US, 1932*
- —Robert George Reisner, *The Jazz Titans*, p. 150, 1957

biffoe *noun*
a rude and obnoxious person *UK*
- —Tom Hibbert, *Rockspeak!*, p. 20, 1983

biffy *noun*
a toilet *US, 1942*
- New! Handy "biffy brush"! [Advertisement] —*San Francisco Examinaer*, p. 29, 25th July 1954
- [A]t a recent cocktail party Chief Justice Earl Warren, cocktail hand, was backed up against the door leading to the biffy reserved for the children in the house[.] —*San Francisco Call-Bulletin*, p. 11, 25th March 1954
- There's a towel in the biffy. —Elmore Leonard, *The Big Bounce*, p. 92, 1969

biffy *adjective*
drunk *UK, 1961*

bifta *noun*
1 a marijuana cigarette; sufficient marijuana to make a cigarette *UK*
Also variant spellings 'biftah' or 'bifter'.
- —Angela Devlin, *Prison Patter*, p. 27, 1996
- [S]it back, skin up a bifta[.] —Sacha Baron-Cohen, *Da Gospel According to Ali G*, 2001
- —Nick Brownlee, *This Is Cannabis*, p. 151, 2002

2 a cigarette *UK*
Sometimes shortened to 'bif'.
- —Angela Devlin, *Prison Patter*, p. 27, 1996

big *verb*
to impregnate someone *US, 1917*
- He tu blame fuh biggin yu. —Iceberg Slim (Robert Beck), *Mama Black Widow*, p. 184, 1969
- Damn near every man likes a girl when she's bigged and young at the same time; this makes it a double treat. —A.S. Jackson, *Gentleman Pimp*, p. 47, 1973
- —History of Medicine Society, *A Folk Medical Lexicon of South Central Appalachia*, 1990

big *adjective*
1 generous *US, 1934*
Often ironic, especially in the phrase 'that's big of you'.
- JOE: Funny listening to him saying it all the same. And he's leaving you and Sarah the upper fields and the bog and the two boats and any other stuff there is about the place. PHILLY: That's big of him – I made the boats myself. —Brian Friel, *The Gentle Island*, 1971

2 in darts, the larger of two sections of a number on the dartboard *US*
For example, the larger 6 section would be 'big six'.
- —Keith Turner, *Darts*, p. 129, 1980

▸ **like a big dog**
to an extreme *US*
- —*Washington Post Magazine*, p. 9, 6th September 1987

▸ **the big dish**
a big win *AUSTRALIA*
Australian gambling slang.
- —Lawson Glossop, *Lucky Palmer*, 1949

▸ **too big for your boots**
conceited, self-important *UK, 1879*
- Mkoll regularly gets too big for his boots. I'll reprimand him when this is done. —Dan Abnett, *Honour Guard*, p. 11, 2001

big *adverb*
very successfully; to a great degree *US, 1893*
Especially in the phrase **GO OVER BIG**.

▸ **go over big**
to achieve great success *US, 1962*

big 4's, big 8's
▷ see: BIG FOURS, BIG EIGHTS

Big A *noun*
1 AIDS *US*
- —Terry William, *Crackhouse*, p. 146, 1992
- —Sally Williams, *"Strong" Words*, p. 134, 1994
- —Angela Devlin, *Prison Patter*, p. 27, 1996

2 in poker, an ace, especially when it is the deciding card in a hand *US*

- —George Percy, *The Language of Poker*, p. 10, 1988

▸give the Big A

to dismiss, reject or sack someone *AUSTRALIA*

The 'big A' is a euphemism for 'arse'.

- Normally if I smell a No in the air I give the bird the big A. No risk. —David Ireland, *The Glass Canoe*, p. 20, 1976
- So remember, big is a big word in football. And should you be a 'big G' for the Croweaters then nothing will give you more pleasure than to give the 'big girls' from the 'big V' the 'big A'. —Ivor Limb, *Footy's No Joke!*, p. 9, 1986
- Show the customers a bit more respect or you'll get the big 'A' yourself[.] —Clive Galea, *Slipper*, p. 165, 1988

Big A *nickname*

1 Eddie Arcaro (1916–1917), dominant jockey in American horse racing from 1933 until 1962, one of only two jockeys to win the Kentucky Derby five times *US*

The 'Big' sobriquet supplied a dose of irony when applied to a man who stood 5' 2" and weighed 114 pounds.

2 the Aqueduct Race Track in Westbury, New York *US*

- Everything about the new Aqueduct is so big that it is referred to as the Big A. —*New York Times*, p. 21, 9th September 1959

3 the US federal penitentiary in Atlanta, Georgia *US*

- —Ralph de Sola, *Crime Dictionary*, p. 15, 1982

big air *noun*

an impressive distance between a snowboarder and the snow *US*

big an heavies *noun*

Benson & Hedges™ cigarettes *UK: SCOTLAND*

- Ah'll take wan a yer big an heavies if ye're offerin. —Michael Munro, *The Patter, Another Blast*, 1988

big apple *noun*

a cap with a big visor *US*

In vogue during the 'Superfly' era of the early 1970s.

- —*Current Slang*, p. 5, Fall 1970

Big Apple *nickname*

New York *US, 1921*

Slang etymologists Gerald Cohen and Barry Popik have researched the origins of the term extensively, destroying along the way a number of popular yet false etymologies. Cohen and Popik trace the first printed use of the term to New York sportswriter John J. Fitzgerald, who heard the term used by black racetrack stable hands.

- Why the Big Apple was ripe for [Arthur] Miller's return. —*The Guardian*, 16th March 2002

big-arsed *adjective*

big *UK*

- Boy, what a big-arsed mess[.] —Diran Adebayo, *My Once Upon A Time*, p. 109, 2000

big-ass *adjective*

very large *US*

- He left the house and didnt stop till he opened the door of his bigass Cadillac. —Hubert Selby Jr, *Last Exit to Brooklyn*, p. 304, 1957
- —Connie Eble (Editor), *UNC-CH Campus Slang*, p. 1, March 1996

big-ass bird *noun*

the Boeing B-17 military aircraft *US, 1961*

- —J. E. Lighter, *Historical Dictionary of American Slang, Volume 1*, p. 143, 1994

big-assed *adjective*

large *US, 1945*

- If he could think of some way not to – he's bird-brained and chicken-hearted and big-assed. —James Baldwin, *Blues for Mister Charlie*, p. 25, 1964

Big B *nickname*

Berlin *US, 1944*

- —J. E. Lighter, *Historical Dictionary of American Slang, Volume 1*, p. 143, 1994
- The crew couldn't make their original target in Berlin – "Big B," as they called it. —*Seattle Post-Intelligencer*, p. B2, 20th May 2003

big bag *noun*

a large bag of heroin; heroin *US, 1969*

- —Richard A. Spears, *The Slang and Jargon of Drugs and Drink*, p. 42, 1986
- —Robert Ashton, *This Is Heroin*, p. 205, 2002
- —Mike Haskins, *Drugs*, p. 283, 2003

big ball *noun*

1 in pool, an object ball that can be hit either directly or on the rebound off a cushion *US, 1913*

Because there are two ways to hit it, it is a bigger target, hence a 'big ball'.

- —Mike Shamos, *The Illustrated Encyclopedia of Billiards*, p. 25, 1993

2 in bowling, a roll that forcefully hooks into the standing pins *US*

- —Frank Bryan, *Tackle Tenpin Bowling This Way*, 1962

big baller *noun*

a big spender *US*

- Saturday's "Evening in Paradise" at the Hotel Inter-Continental in Miami, at $250 per person, is a big-baller special. —*Sun-Sentinel (Fort Lauderdale, Florida)*, p. 1E, 11th July 2001

big banger *noun*

a motorcyle with a large one-cylinder engine *US*

- —John Lawlor, *How to Talk Car*, p. 18, 1965

big beast *noun*

an important, powerful person *UK*

- [Michael Heseltine] is regularly referred to as one of the "big beasts" on the Tory benches. —Nick Assinder, *BBC World Service*, 27th April 2000

big belly *noun*

a B-52 bomber *US*

- A stream of bomb trailers rolled under them, stuffing their Big Bellys with eight-four bombs. —Walter J. Boyne and Steven L. Thompson, *The Wild Blue*, p. 464, 1986

Big Ben *noun*

1 ten; ten pounds *UK, 1960*

Rhyming slang.

- —Julian Franklyn, *A Dictionary of Rhyming Slang*, p. 39, 1960

2 the new, large design hundred-dollar note minted in the late 1990s *US*

The 'Ben' is an allusion to Benjamin Franklin, the C18 slang lexicographer whose portrait graces the note.

- —John Vorhaus, *The Big Book of Poker Slang*, p. 6, 1996

3 Benzedrine™ (amphetamine sulphate), a central nervous system stimulant *US*

- —*Mr*, p. 8, April 1966: 'The hippie's lexicon'

4 in craps, a roll of ten *US*

Rhyming slang.

- —Chris Fagans and David Guzman, *A Guide to Craps Lingo*, p. 33, 1999

5 a prison siren that announces an escape or riot *US*

- —Hyman E. Goldin et al., *Dictionary of American Underworld Lingo*, p. 26, 1950

6 the penis *UK*

A visual pun from the London landmark.

- —*Sky Magazine*, July 2001

Big Ben *nickname*

the USS Franklin (heavily damaged off Japan on 19th March 1945, repaired and mothballed); the USS Bennington (commissioned in 1944, decommissioned in 1970) *US*

The Bennington was featured in the opening scene of the CBS television programme *Navy Log* in 1956 and 1957.

- To me and many other World War II sailors, there is only one "Big Ben" and that is the U.S.S. Franklin. [Letter to Editor] —*Life*, p. 5, 28th June 1954
- The Big Blast in 'Big Ben' [Headline] —*Life*, p. 36, 7th June 1954

Big Bertha *noun*

an over-sized slot machine used as a promotion for hotel guests and to lure prospective gamblers into a casino *US*

- —J. Edward Allen, *The Basics of Winning Slots*, p. 57, 1984
- Berthas, as in "Big Bertha," are giant, oversized machines sprinkled here and there around the casino. —Jim Regan, *Winning at Slot Machine*, p. 49, 1985

Big Bertha *nickname*

the Ringling Brothers, Barnum and Bailey Circus *US*

- —Sherman Louis Sergel, *The Language of Show Biz*, p. 20, 1973
- —Don Wilmeth, *The Language of American Popular Entertainment*, p. 22, 1981

big bikkies *noun*

a large amount of money *NEW ZEALAND, 1980*

From **BICKY**, a diminuitive form of 'biscuit'.

- —Ned Wallish, *The Truth Dictionary of Racing Slang*, p. 6, 1989
- Answering critics who say even more thermal generation should have been committed late last year, Dr. Deane says that costs 'big bikkies'. — *Evening Post*, p. 14, 25th July 1992

big bill *noun*

a $100 note *US*

- "Here's a big bill as a binder." Vann took a new one-hundred-dollar bill from his wallet, folded it the long way and poked it into Red's breast pocket. —Ross Russell, *The Sound*, p. 62, 1961

big bird *noun*

a long prison sentence *UK*

A play on **BIRD** (**LIME**) (time served in prison) and 'Big Bird' a large puppet featured on *Sesame Street*, a children's television programme since 1969.

- [T]here were a few good people "doing big bird" (long sentences) because of him. — *The Guardian*, 28th September 2000: 'A life inside'
- [Erwin] James describe[s] life in the slammer with the authenticity of an inmate doing "Big Bird" (more than 19 years so far)[.] — *The Guardian*, p. 4, 13th May 2003

Big Bird *noun*

in homosexual usage, a man with a large penis *US*

An allusion to a character on the children's television programme *Sesame Street*.

- — *Maledicta*, p. 236, Winter 1980: '"Lovely, blooming, fresh and gay": the onomastics of camp'

big bitch *noun*

the prison sentence given to habitual criminals *US*

- —Frank Prewitt and Francis Schaeffer, *Vacaville Vocabulary*, 1961–1962
- "If Chilly wasn't doing the big bitch," Nunn told Manning, "he'd own half this state." —Malcolm Braly, *On the Yard*, p. 38, 1967

big bloke *noun*

cocaine *US*

- —J.E. Schmindt, *Narcotics Lingo and Lore*, p. 16, 1959
- —Nick Constable, *This is Cocaine*, p. 181, 2002

big blow *noun*

a hurricane *AUSTRALIA, 1944*

Used by Australian fishermen and sailors.

Big Blue 82 *noun*

a 12,540-pound BLU-82 bomb *US*

A vicious anti-personnel weapon, developed for vegetation clearing in Vietnam, used again in the Persian Gulf war and Afghanistan.

- A unique bomb which also provides tremendous blast overpressures and was reported to have been used in the Mideast ("a favorite of the Marine Corps," according to one anonymous Pentagon spokesman) is the BLUE-82, otherwise known as "Big Blue 82." — *Boston Globe*, 16th April 1991
- The type depicted in the leaflets, and also used in Afghanistan, is the BLU-82B Commando Vault or Big Blue 82, also known as the Daisy Cutter. — *BBC News*, 6th November 2001

big blue bin *noun*

the outdoors, when surplus grain is stored there *CANADA*

- Grain stored in the big blue bin is stored in the biggest bin available, i.e., on the ground under the sky. In years of bumper crops, when all other storage has been exhausted, there have been cases where the main street of the local town has been used. —Chris Thain, *Cold as a Bay Street Banker's Heart*, p. 13, 1987

big-boobed *adjective*

of a female, having generously proportioned breasts *UK*

- A whopping one in 20 big-boobed women in Northern Ireland own more than 20 bras[.] — *Belfast Telegraph*, 28th July 2004

big book *noun*

in twelve-step recovery programmes such as Alcoholics Anonymous, the book *Alcohlic Anonymous*, first published in 1939 and still the central document of the recovery movement *US*

- —Christopher Cavanaugh, *AA to Z*, p. 54, 1998

Big Bopper *nickname*

J. P. Richardson (1930–59), a Texas disc jockey in the early years of rock and roll whose hit recording of 'Chantilly Lace' propelled him into performing stardom, which in turn placed him on the small aeroplane 'American Pie' that carried Buddy Holly and him to death *UK*

- —Arnold Shaw, *Dictionary of American Pop/Rock*, p. 37, 1982

big boss *noun*

heroin *US*

- Having been an addict I know something about it, one of the narcotics especially; heroin. Some people call it "the Big Boss; Horse". —Bruce Jackson, *In the Life*, p. 210, 1972

big box *noun*

a large chain of shops featuring a single type of merchandise *US, 1993*

- — *American Speech*, p. 302, Fall 1996: 'Among the new words'

big boy *noun*

1 a tank *US*

Vietnam war usage. The bigger the tank and the more weapons mounted on the tank, the more likely it was to be called a 'big boy'.

- —Carl Fleischhauer, *A Glossary of Army Slang*, p. 4, 1968
- I want the two big boys leading the first and third platoons. —Ronald J. Glasser, *365 Days*, p. 113–114, 1971
- —Linda Reinberg, *In the Field*, p. 21, 1991

2 a marijuana cigarette *UK*

- I held up a pre-rolled big boy, with the minimum tobacco and maximum Jamaican Sensee. —Wayne Anthony, *Spanish Highs*, p. 72, 1999

big boys' toy *noun*

▷ see: **BOYS' TOY**

big brother *noun*

1 the penis, especially a large penis *US*

- — *The Guild Dictionary of Homosexual Terms*, p. 4, 1965
- —Dale Gordon, *The Dominion Sex Dictionary*, p. 28, 1967

2 the erect penis *US*

- —Dale Gordon, *The Dominion Sex Dictionary*, p. 28, 1967
- —Robert A. Wilson, *Playboy's Book of Forbidden Words*, p. 34, 1972

Big Brother *noun*

used as the personification of all-encompassing government authority *UK, 1949*

From George Orwell's 1949 novel *1984*.

- At midnight Sunday, 30 hours after our arrival, a mechnical Big Brother voice boomed from the Pentagon that all who stayed would be arrested. —Jerry Rubin, *Do It!*, p. 80, 1970
- Consequently, the manufacture of "conspiracy theories" may be the most recession-proof industry in America today. Big Brother is being seen in more places than Elvis. — *St. Petersburg Florida Times*, p. 2, 8th January 1992

big brown eye *noun*

the female breast *US*

- —Eugene Landy, *The Underground Dictionary*, p. 32, 1971

big brownies *noun*

MDMA, the recreational drug best known as ecstasy *UK*

A variation of **BROWNIE** (amphetamine or MDMA) that distinguishes **SPEED** from **ECSTASY**.

- Street names[:] Adam, big brownies, California sunrise[.] —James Kay and Julian Cohen, *The Parents' Complete Guide to Young People and Drugs*, p. 136, 1998

big bud *noun*

a very popular variety of marijuana with heavy buds *UK*

Big C *noun*

1 cancer *US, 1964*

- Walt Disney, who was killed by the big C, was a very heavy ciggie smoker. — *San Francisco Examiner and Chronicle*, p. II-1, 15th January 1967
- The Washington Whispers have it that Jack Ruby doesn't stand a chance of beating the Big C. — *San Francisco Examiner and Chronicle*, p. 19, 1st January 1967
- 'Big C' Finally Beats John Wayne [Headline] — *San Francisco Examiner and Chronicle*, p. 14, 17th June 1979
- I've been sick. The big C...cancer. —Ward McNally, *Supper at Happy Harry's*, p. 153, 1982
- They don't think it's anything silly do they? Like ... Big C ... or any of his pals? —Dan Jenkins, *Dead Solid Perfect*, p. 26, 1986
- Mo held his own against the Big C. —James Ellroy, *Hollywood Nocturnes*, p. 226, 1994
- His wife's in the hospital, has been for a couple months. The big C. — *Fargo*, 1996
- That's when I decided I was going to beat this monster, the Big C. —Ralph "Sonny" Barger, *Hell's Angel*, p. 243, 2000

2 cocaine *US*

- —J.E. Schmindt, *Narcotics Lingo and Lore*, p. 16, 1959

- —William D. Alsever, *Glossary for the Establishment and Other Uptight People*, p. 6, December 1970
- —Donald Louria, *The Drug Scene*, p. 189, 1971
- —Nick Constable, *This is Cocaine*, p. 181, 2002

3 commitment to a relationship seen as something to be feared or avoided *UK*
- [T]he commitment they represented, the Big C, had caused him to completely forget the night[.]—Colin Butts, *Is Harry Still on the Boat?*, p. 354, 2003

4 in citizens' band radio slang, applied to many UK towns beginning with C, specifically Caernarfon, Carlisle, Chichester or Chippenham *UK*
This logic is continued throughout the alphabet, e.g. 'big B by the sea' (Brighton), 'big D' (Dorchester), 'big W' (Worthing); also, villages beginning with C become 'little C' or, in Scotland, 'wee C'.
- —Peter Chippindale, *The British CB Book*, p. 168, 1981

5 a female as an sexual object *US*
A hint of **CUNT**.
- —*American Speech*, p. 273, December 1963: 'American Indian student slang'

6 a railway conductor *US*
- —*American Speech*, p. 285, December 1968: 'Addenda to the vocabulary of railroading'

big cage *noun*
a prison *US, 1949*
- —Jay Robert Nash, *Dictionary of Crime*, p. 27, 1992

big car, small dick; BCSD
used for insulting someone who has a large or expensive car *UK*
Used proverbially: a car is a phallic symbol.
- There is a saying about people with big cars: BCSD. I don't know whether that applies to motorbikes, but I can assure the committee I only have a small car.—Gyles Brandreth (quoting Phillip Oppenheim), *Breaking the Code*, p. 470, 1999

big casino *noun*
1 the best that you can do; your greatest resource *US, 1922*
- Jimmy had written a $2,500,000 life insurance policy on Hill. Ask your insurance agent whether that would be peanuts or the big casino in the insurance.—*San Francisco Call-Bulletin*, p. 10, 17th March 1950
- The big casino in Nixon's over-all program is the next stage of the Vietnam troop withdrawals.—*San Francisco Examiner and Chronicle*, p. A-2, 14th September 1969
- Jerry Brown should go for the Big Casino [Headline]—*San Francisco Examiner*, p. 31, 16th March 1976

2 cancer *US, 1951*
- His grin was forced. He knows he's got Big Casino – cancer. —*San Francisco Examiner and Chronicle*, p. III-6, 7th May 1967
- Wee Willie Wilkin, former St. Mary's College tackle (so named because at 270 he was considered the largest item in football during the '30s) is fighting the Big Casino.—*San Francisco Chronicle*, p. 48, 14th December 1971
- "It's true, Billy," he said, gazing bleakly at his glass. "Big casino. It's hopeless."—*San Francisco Examiner and Chronicle*, p. 5, 27th February 1983

3 any sexually transmitted infection *US*
- Nitti, like Capone, had picked up in his travels the occupational malady of the underworld, euphemistically known as the capital prize, or big casino.—*San Francisco Call-Bulletin*, p. 14, 23rd February 1948
- It was hinted that poor, departed Will had once acquired a case of what the boys call big casino, which ended in the same paresis that finished Al Capone.—*San Francisco News*, p. 11, 8th October 1951

4 capital punishment, the death penalty *US*
- Will "Call Me Bernie" for Big Casino. Yes, say the results of an informal poll of the Nation's press covering the sensational Finch murder trial here.—*San Francisco Examiner*, p. 12, 22nd January 1960

big cat *noun*
1 a Jaguar car *UK*
- —Peter Chippindale, *The British CB Book*, p. 161, 1981

2 in poker, a hand comprised of five cards between eight and king and no pairs among them *US*
Also known as 'big tiger'.
- —Irwin Steig, *Common Sense in Poker*, p. 182, 1963

big Charlie *noun*
1 a CH-3C helicopter used during the Vietnam war for counterinsurgency airlifts *US*
- —Ian Padden, *U.S. Air Commando*, p. 104, 1985

2 an important white man *US*
- I knows they's nothin but overseers on the big plantation, jes doin like Big Charlie tell 'em to.—Robert Gover, *JC Saves*, p. 112, 1968

big cheese *noun*
the most important person in a given organisation or enterprise *US, 1914*
- Reggie Jackson: the big cheese of the holey AL West. [Caption] —*Washington Post*, p. F8, 3rd April 1983
- ex-ITV soccer big cheese Jeff Foulser—John McCririck, *John McCririck's World of Betting*, p. 16, 1991
- Ito-san was the head honcho, the big cheese, the number-one Tomodachi ... or to put it another way, the overall manager of the SPN group.—Rhiannon Paine, *Too Late for the Festival*, p. 27, 1999
- It's getting a bit close to three o'clock and one of the big cheeses might catch us[.]—Colin Butts, *Is Harry Still on the Boat?*, p. 85, 2003

big chicken dinner *noun*
a bad conduct discharge *US*
Playing with initials: armed forces usage.
- —Linda Reinberg, *In the Field*, p. 21, 1991

big chief *noun*
the hallucinogenic drug, mescaline *US*
- —Edward R. Bloomquist, *Marijuana*, p. 332, 1971

big conk, big cock
used as a summary of the folk wisdom that there is correlation between the size of a man's nose and the size of his penis *UK, 1961*
- —Robert A. Wilson, *Playboy's Book of Forbidden Words*, p. 35, 1972

Big D *noun*
1 death *US, 1977*
- —J. E. Lighter, *Historical Dictionary of American Slang, Volume 1*, p. 146, 1994

2 LSD *US*
- —Donald Louria, *Nightmare Drugs*, p. 45, 1966
- —John B. Williams, *Narcotics and Hallucinogenics*, p. 109, 1967
- —Eugene Landy, *The Underground Dictionary*, p. 33, 1971

3 the penis *US*
D as in **DICK**.
- —Ethan Hilderbrant, *Prison Slang*, p. 12, 1998

big D *nickname*
1 Dallas, Texas *US, 1930*
- In Big D, do as the heteros do.—Phil Andros (Samuel M. Steward), *Stud*, p. 89, 1966
- Well, you probably have certain opinions about the security arrangements they had that bad Friday down in Big D – inadequate, I suppose.—Terry Southern, *Now Dig This*, p. 137, 2001

2 Detoit, Michigan *US, 1961*
- It ain't like the Big D, where so many brothers is startin' to snitch on each other.—Donald Goines, *El Dorado Red*, p. 92, 1974
- After a short run he settled in Detroit. During the early fifties, every jazz artist who played the big D, usually ran into him.—Babs Gonzales, *Movin' On Down De Line*, p. 56, 1975

3 Denver, Colorado *US*
- —*Current Slang*, p. 5, Fall 1967

big dad *noun*
a senior drill instructor *US*
Vietnam war usage.
- —Linda Reinberg, *In the Field*, p. 21, 1991

big daddy *noun*
1 an immense wave *US*
- —Gary Fairmont R. Filosa II, *The Surfer's Almanac*, p. 182, 1977

2 an important and influential man *US, 1948*
- —J. E. Lighter, *Historical Dictionary of American Slang, Volume 1*, p. 146, 1994

Big Daddy *nickname*
1 Jesse Unruh (1922–1987), a Democratic politican of great influence in California *US*
- One day in the heat of legislative battle in Sacramento, an assemblyman suddenly switched his vote to back one of Boss Unruh's bills. Asked why, he answered in the voice of a man who had just been put through the wringer, "Big Daddy put the muscle on me."—*Look*, p. 78, 25th September 1962

2 Ed Roth (1932–2001), the hot rod artist most famous for creating the Rat Fink character in the early 1960s *US*
- Ed "Big Daddy" Roth was flat on his back underneath a yellow dragster he has, "Yellow Fang," and he twisted his head out from under the side of the thing and stuck his beard out and stared at me.—Tom Wolfe, *The Pump House Gang*, p. 97, 1968

3 Don Garlits (b.1932), the dominant drag racing driver in the US from the early 1960s to 70s *US*

4 the Federal Communications Commission *US*
- — Radio Shack, *CBer's Handy Atlas/Dictionary*, p. 11, 1976

big dago *noun*
a sandwich made on Italian bread *US*
- "You know the signs all over for what we call in New York 'submarines," hero sandwich on sliced Italian bread? On the coast, they advertise 'Don's big Dagos, Red Hot Dagos!"—*Esquire*, p. 153, 1st November 1960

big dance in Newark *noun*
in circus and carnival usage, a jocular explanation for a small audience *US*
- —Don Wilmeth, *The Language of American Popular Entertainment*, p. 21, 1981

big day *noun*
visiting day in prison *US*
- —Vincent J. Monteleone, *Criminal Slang*, p. 21, 1949
- —*American Speech*, p. 194, October 1951: 'A study of reformatory argot'
- —Troy Harris, *A Booklet of Criminal Argot, Cant and Jargon*, p. 5, 1976

big dead one *nickname*
later in the Vietnam war, the First Infantry Division *US*
A sad play on **BIG RED ONE** after heavy attrition through casualties.
- —Linda Reinberg, *In the Field*, p. 21, 1991

big deal *noun*
a major issue; often ironic, occasionally as an exclamation, used to dismiss such an issue as of little or no importance *US, 1943*
- Rozzers in his pocket? Big deal.—John Milne, *Alive and Kicking*, p. 36, 1998

big Dick *noun*
1 in craps, a roll of ten *US, 1904*
Often embellished to 'big Dick from Boston', 'big Dick from Battle Creek', and 'big Dick the ladies' friend'. Gambling slang authority, the late Thomas Clark, theorised that 'dick' came from the French *dix*. Another popular folk etymology is that the original Big Dick was Boston dice cheater Richard Mantell who was shot to death as he switched dice while trying to shoot a ten. The addition of 'the ladies' friend' leaves little doubt as to the most probable etymology – ten inches would indeed be big.
- —*The Annals of the American Academy of Political and Social Sciences*, p. 121, May 1950
- —Frank Garcia, *Marked Cards and Loaded Dice*, p. 250, 1962

2 a 14-inch rocket *US*
- Here from 300 safe yards away we watched naval technicians fire a free-launched 14-inch rocket known to the men developing it as "Big Dick." That's to distinguish it from the older, smaller 11.75 inch "Tiny Tim."—*San Francisco News*, p. 1, 27th December 1946

Big Dig *noun*
a massive public works project in Boston, Massachusetts, replacing an existing six-lane central arterial motorway with an eight-to-ten lane underground expressway directly beneath the existing road *US*
- Harold Hestnes, 51, of Boston's Hale and Dorr; in his second year as chairman of the Greater Boston Chamber of Commerce, he is deeply involved in helping private enterprise get ready for Boston's $10 billion "Big Dig."—*The National Law Journal*, p. 51, 2nd May 1988

big ditch *nickname*
the Atlantic Ocean *US, 1909*
A refinement of **DITCH**.

big dog *noun*
in poker, a hand comprised of five cards between nine and ace and no pairs among them *US*
- —Irwin Steig, *Common Sense in Poker*, p. 182, 1963

big dollar *noun*
a great deal of money in any currency *UK*
- Why have big dollar if you can't let people know you got big dollar?—J.J. Connolly, *Layer Cake*, p. 4, 2000

big drink *noun*
an ocean, especially the Atlantic Ocean *US, 1883*
The term was first used to mean the Mississippi River; by the time it was applied to the ocean, the river sense had receded.
- —J. E. Lighter, *Historical Dictionary of American Slang, Volume 1*, p. 147, 1994

big drive *noun*
a powerful injection of a drug *US, 1949*
- —Harold Wentworth and Stuart Berg Flexner, *Dictionary of American Slang*, p. 34, 1960

big duck *noun*
in trucking, a Republic moving van *US*
- —Wayne Floyd, *Jason's Authentic Dictionary of CB Slang*, p. 9, 1976

big duke *noun*
in poker, especially hold 'em poker, a strong hand *US, 1981*
- —Thomas L. Clark, *The Dictionary of Gambling and Gaming*, p. 18, 1987

Big E *noun*
1 a dismissal, a rejection *UK*
The first letter of **ELBOW** (a dismissal).
- She gave me the big E.—Ann Barr and Peter York, *The Official Sloane Ranger Handbook*, p. 158, 1982
- So... why d'y'get the sack then? she asks like it just popped into her head. – 'Spute with the chief. – And... – And nothin'. Big E.—Nick Barlay, *Curvy Lovebox*, p. 114, 1997

2 a railway engineer *US*
- —Ramon Adams, *The Language of the Railroader*, p. 13, 1977

Big E *nickname*
the USS Enterprise *US, 1942*
Two aircraft carriers carried the name Enterprise and the nickname 'Big E', the first commissioned in 1936 and the second in 1961.
- 'Big E' Plays Cat and Mouse with Russ Sub [Headline]—*San Francisco Examiner and Chronicle*, p. A-2, 15th September 1968
- Battleflat of'B ig E' to new Enterprise [Headline]—*San Francisco Examiner*, p. 48, 18th April 1974

big ears *noun*
in the language of paragliding, an intentional collapsing of both tips of the wing to increase speed *US*
- —Erik Fair, *California Thrill Sports*, p. 335, 1992

Big Easy *nickname*
New Orleans, Louisiana *US, 1970*
- The Big Easy, as New Orelans calls itself, regards progress with a skeptical eye.—*New York Times*, p. 10, 4th January 1981

big eat; big heaps *noun*
a feast; a great meal *TRISTAN DA CUNHA, 1964*
- —Bernadette Hince, *The Antarctic Dictionary*, p. 49, 2000

big eight *noun*
in poker, four twos *US*
A borrowing from the game of craps.
- —George Percy, *The Language of Poker*, p. 10, 1988

big eights; big 8's
good wishes *US*
- —*Complete CB Slang Dictionary*, 1976
- —Peter Chippindale, *The British CB Book*, p. 152, 1981

big enchilada *noun*
the supreme leader *US, 1973*
A term coined and popularised by the Nixon White House during the Watergate scandal.
- —Harold Wentworth and Stuart Berg Flexner, *Dictionary of American Slang*, p. 677, 1976

big end *noun*
1 in drag racing, the end of the quarter-mile race course where highest speeds are attained *US, 1960s to 70s*

2 top speed *US*
Biker (motorcyle) usage.

big-endian *adjective*
in computing, denoting computer architecture in which the most significant byte is found in the lowest address *US*
- —Eric S. Raymond, *The New Hacker's Dictionary*, p. 57, 1991

big eye *noun*

1 a high-powered telescope, especially the one located on Palomar Mountain, California *US*

- Palomar's "Big Eye" – already the apple of astronomers' eyes – is going to be even better than expected after a final polishing.— *San Francisco Call-Bulletin*, p. 11, 6th May 1949
- California's second "Big Eye," the 120 inch mirror for the new telescope at Mt. Hamilton, near San Jose, is ready to probe the heavens.— *San Francisco News*, p. 11, 26th June 1959
- Flying low over the Gulf of Mexico, pilots approaching the Florida panhandle can see the Big Eye staring at them like some baleful guardian of the coast.— *Los Angeles Times*, p. I-3, 22nd February 1968

2 a Lockheed EC-121 Warning Star aircraft *US*

Deployed in Vietnam to provide early warning and communication relay; later redesignated the **COLLEGE EYE**.

- —Linda Reinberg, *In the Field*, p. 21, 1991

3 insomnia *ANTARCTICA, 1959*

A common condition in Antarctica because of the wild swings in daylight hours.

- —Bernadette Hince, *The Antarctic Dictionary*, p. 49, 2000
- — *Cool Antartica*, 2003: 'Antarctic slang'

4 avarice *BAHAMAS*

- —John A. Holm, *Dictionary of Bahamian English*, p. 17, 1982

big F

the word 'fuck', in all uses *INDIA*

- In the ultimate style sheet – the dictionary of road rage, however, where signs and gestures do most of the talking, the popular ice cream stick shaken at the end of the conversation, the big F generally has the last word.— *The Times of India*, 30th September 2002

big fat *noun*

a large marijuana cigarette *UK*

- —Simon Worman, *Joint Smoking Rules*, 2001

big fat one *noun*

a large marijuana cigarette *UK*

- —Simon Worman, *Joint Smoking Rules*, 2001

big fat zero *noun*

▷ see: **FAT ZERO**

big-feeling *adjective*

inordinately proud *CANADA*

- When a student from Campbellton said a student from Yarmouth was "too big-feeling for me," I could taste the contempt in his voice. [It is] a pungent expression of the scorn Maritimers feel for all those who dare to put on airs.—Harry Bruce, *Down Home*, p. 102, 1988
- I can't get involved; you're so big-feeling.—Lewis Poteet, *The South Shore Phrase Book*, p. 20, 1999

big fella *noun*

the penis *UK, 2001*

An obvious, perhaps boastful, variation of **OLD FELLOW**.

- — *Sky Magazine*, July 2001

big fellow *noun*

a law enforcement official of the US federal government *US*

- We best pull out. The big fellows was by here today.—David W. Maurer, *Kentucky Moonshine*, p. 114, 1974

big fish *noun*

a very important person or thing *US, 1836*

- They spared most of the big fish. Congress must face up to social security costs.— *Christian Science Monitor*, p. 1, 25th November 1981
- "I was a big fish in a little pond, but it was nice for my ego and I learned how to win," he said. [Quoting Patrick Horgan]— *Los Angeles Times*, p. C2, 1st February 1992
- Martha was a little fish when it comes to these crimes. We're still waiting for the big fish at Enron, WorldCom, Tyco and Harken to pay for their crimes.— *Post-Crescent (Appleton, Wisconsin)*, p. 7C, 11th March 2004
- Over the next few months, that same informant helped apprehend or implicate several "big fish," such as 17 corrupt state police officers.— *Dallas Morning News*, 14th March 2004

big fish, little fish, cardboard box *noun*

the hand movements that characterised techno-style dancing in the early 1990s *UK*

big flake *noun*

cocaine *UK, 1998*

- —Mike Haskins, *Drugs*, p. 280, 2003

big foot *noun*

1 a prominent, highly visible journalist or columnist, especially one covering politics *US, 1980*

- Aside from being a Canadian journalism legend, Peter [Worthington] remains year in and year out one of our most popular and best-read columnists, a true "Big Foot" of our business. That means he's a journalist who's done it all.— *Toronto Sun*, p. C3, 8th October 2000

2 an inflammation of the foot *JAMAICA*

- —Peter L. Patrick, *Some Recent Jamaican Creole Words*, 2003

big foot country *noun*

the deep, rural south of the US *US*

- I heard you had went down to the big foot country and decided to stay there for your health.—Donald Goines, *Never Die Alone*, p. 20, 1974
- You're a champ chump from the Big Foot Country (deep South) and you're creaming to get laid.—Iceberg Slim (Robert Beck), *Airtight Willie and Me*, p. 6, 1979

big fours; big 4's

yes, emphatically *US*

Citizens' band radio slang.

- — *Complete CB Slang Dictionary*, 1976
- —Peter Chippindale, *The British CB Book*, p. 152, 1981

big friend *noun*

a bomber aircraft *US*

- — *American Speech*, p. 310, December 1946: 'More air force slang'

big fucking deal *noun*

a major issue *US*

An elaboration of **BIG DEAL**. Often used to dismiss something as not being a major issue.

- Lawyer, huh? Big fuckin' deal.—Edwin Torres, *Q & A*, p. 121, 1977
- What's the big fucking deal?— *South Park*, 1999

big full *noun*

in poker, a hand consisting of three aces and two kings *US, 1978*

This hand represents the best possible variation of the hand conventionally known as a 'full house'.

- —Thomas L. Clark, *The Dictionary of Gambling and Gaming*, p. 18, 1987

big G *noun*

God *US*

- —Peter Chippindale, *The British CB Book*, p. 152, 1981
- — *Washington Post*, p. B1, 17th January 1985

big general *noun*

in a bar dice game, a first roll showing five dice of the same denomination *US, 1974*

- —Thomas L. Clark, *The Dictionary of Gambling and Gaming*, p. 18, 1987

Big George *noun*

a twenty-five cent piece *US*

- —Kenn "Naz" Young, *Naz's Underground Dictionary*, p. 15, 1973

biggie *noun*

1 a big deal; something of consequence or difficulty *US, 1970*

Often in the negative: 'no biggie'.

- —Connie Eble (Editor), *UNC-CH Campus Slang*, p. 5, Fall 1989
- FABIAN: You're hurt? BUTCH: I might've broke my nose, no biggie. — *Pulp Fiction*, 1994
- Just the one [drugs] drop today, but it's a biggie.—Kevin Sampson, *Outlaws*, p. 56, 2001

2 an important person *US, 1926*

- She will dance till she's dippy at the Sunset Strip cabarets, meeting the biggies[.]—Jack Lait and Lee Mortimer, *New York Confidential*, p. 145, 1948
- A big argument is going on among the prosecutors as to the "advisability" of calling to the stand a political biggie "who can collaborate large hunks of [Whitaker] Chambers' story.— *San Francisco Call-Bulletin*, p. 5, 23rd November 1948
- When Banker Belford Brown and other Cancer Society biggies here heard THAT (they're trying to raise $175,000 locally) they hit the roof with a woof.— *San Francisco Examiner*, p. 25, 19th April 1951
- He was in with all those biggies.—Edwin Torres, *After Hours*, p. 185, 1979
- So you got a biggie, Brian.—Carl Hiaasen, *Tourist Season*, p. 19, 1986

3 a big-name actor who can be counted on to draw a large audience *US, 1926*

- —Wilfred Granville, *The Theater Dictionary*, p. 18, 1952

4 an act of defecation *NEW ZEALAND, 1994*

Children's vocabulary.

- —Harry Orsman, *A Dictionary of Modern New Zealand Slang*, p. 9, 1999

5 marijuana *UK*
- —Mike Haskins, *Drugs*, p. 286, 2003

6 a 26-ounce bottle of rum *GUYANA, 1978*

big girl *noun*
an effeminate, weak and/or cowardly male *AUSTRALIA*
- You'll often hear supporters of one team describing a player on the opposite team as a 'big girl'. —Ivor Limb, *Footy's No Joke!*, p. 35, 1986
- I've watched the show before, I've always said the ones who turn down the dares are big girls. —*Australian Magazine*, p. 12, 6th July 1996

big girl's blouse *noun*
an effeminate, weak and/or cowardly male *AUSTRALIA*
- For a start, despite what the big girl's blouses at the Ponds Institute say, you already look great. —*Good Weekend*, p. 16, 23rd September 1995
- —Sonya Plowman, *Great Kiwi Slang*, p. 26, 2002

big girls' board *noun*
the London variety of dartboard *UK*
Used with derision by Manchester board players.
- —Keith Turner, *Darts*, p. 129, 1980

biggity *adverb*
in a haughty, arrogant or conceited way *US, 1880*
- We had a yen, every time we got away from home and school, to strut and act biggity and shoot the works, live our whole lives out before the sun went down. —Mezz Mezzrow, *Really the Blues*, p. 5, 1946
- Our captive's getting biggety since we saved him from the cops. —Chester Himes, *The Real Cool Killers*, p. 93, 1959
- Mama never acted biggety in court, but she would bow her head only so low. —Claude Brown, *Manchild in the Promised Land*, p. 95, 1965
- These rotten hearted workers act biggity like it's their money the poor people get. —Iceberg Slim (Robert Beck), *Mama Black Widow*, p. 103, 1969
- —John A. Holm, *Dictionary of Bahamian English*, p. 17, 1982

big green *noun*
in sporting and music events, corporate sponsors *US*
- —Lewis Poteet, *Car & Motorcyle Slang*, p. 30, 1992

biggums *adjective*
overweight *US*
- —*Evening Sun (Baltimore)*, p. 12A, 19th January 1994

big gun *noun*
a large surfboard designed for big-wave conditions *AUSTRALIA*
- —Jack Pollard, *The Australian Surfrider*, p. 18, 1963
- —D.S. Halacy, *Surfer!*, p. 215, 1965

biggun *noun*
anything big *UK*
A shortening of 'big one'; either deliberately jocular or matter-of-factly.
- —Ivor Biggun, *The Winker's Song (Misprint)*, 1978
- It was one thing giving it the biggun up north but we had the best mob in the country[.] —Martin King and Martin Knight, *The Naughty Nineties*, p. 46, 1999

Big H *noun*
heroin *US*
- You ever hear of dope? Snow? Junk? Big H? Horse? —John D. McDonald, *The Neon Jungle*, p. 61, 1953
- —*Bournemouth Echo*, 3rd October 1967
- —Helen Dahlskog (Editor), *A Dictionary of Contemporary and Colloquial Usage*, p. 29, 1972
- —Angela Devlin, *Prison Patter*, p. 27, 1996
- We black boys had ganja [marijuana] and cocaine whilst the Asians peddled the big "H". —Lanre Fehintola, *Charlie Says...*, p. 129, 2000
- —Robert Ashton, *This Is Heroin*, p. 205, 2002

big hair *noun*
an extravagant, large-sized hairdo *US*
- I think I'm more like a cartoon character, this big hair flapping all over, big hips, big bosom. It's a gimmick." [Quoting Dolly Parton] —*Washington Post*, p. B1, 8th May 1978
- —Connie Eble (Editor), *UNC-CH Campus Slang*, p. 1, Fall 1990
- I went out and bought a fall and did 'big hair' for about six months – and looked horrid! —Kathryn Leigh Scott, *The Bunny Years*, p. 265–266, 1998
- [M]y daughter Airel subsequently changed her middle name to Lowell in an attempt to blend into the "big-hari" girls and the Texas landscape of her university[.] —Peter Coyote, *Sleeping Where I Fall*, p. 185, 1998
- Together Hot Buns and Ophelia endured their teens and their twenties, survivng white mascara, leg warmers, ugg boots, big hair, the Stair Master and lilca halter-neck jumpsuits. —Gretel Killeen, *Hot Buns and Ophelia get shipwrecked*, p. i, 2001
- Lash the Big Hair spray on. —Kevin Sampson, *Clubland*, p. 119, 2002

Big Harry *noun*
heroin *US, 1975*
An elaboration of **HARRY** (heroin) on the model of **BIG H** (heroin).
- —Richard A. Spears, *The Slang and Jargon of Drugs and Drink*, p. 43, 1986
- —Robert Ashton, *This Is Heroin*, p. 205, 2002

big hat *noun*
a local state trooper *US, 1967*
From the wide-brimmed hats formerly worn by many state troopers.
- —Montie Tak, *Truck Talk*, p. 12, 1971

big hat, no cattle
used for describing someone who appears the part but has no substance *US*
- Mr. Davis is not like a lot of Texans, big hat, no cattle. —*Lima (Ohio) News*, 15th December 1977

big head *noun*
1 a conceited, arrogant or haughty person *US, 1846*
- And goodnight to you too. Bighead. —Ray Galton and Alan Simpson, *Hancock's Half Hour*, 14th June 1955
- "Well,"said Ron. "In you go, bighead." —Joe Morgan, *Eastenders Don't Cry*, p. 21, 1994

2 arrogance, excessive pride *US*
- —Connie Eble (Editor), *UNC-CH Campus Slang*, p. 1, Spring 1992

big-headed *adjective*
conceited, arrogant, haughty *US*
- The great thing about him is with all his talent he never became big-headed. —Babs Gonzales, *I Paid My Dues*, p. 140, 1967

big heaps *noun*
a large meal *ANTARCTICA, 1964*
- —Bernadette Hince, *The Antarctic Dictionary*, p. 49, 2000

big hit *verb*
to defecate *AUSTRALIA, 1960*
Rhyming slang for **SHIT**.

big hitter *noun*
1 an important, influential or powerful person *UK*
From the sporting sense.
- She was widely regarded as one of the big hitters among Westminster lobby correspondents. —*The Guardian*, 3rd September 2002

2 a sportsperson who strikes a ball especially hard with a bat, club or racket, etc *UK*
- I'm just starting out, not very experienced with a driver, and am not and never will be a big hitter. —*The Guardian*, 20th December 2002

big hole *noun*
1 the emergency stop position on a railway air brake *US, 1931*
- —Norman Carlisle, *The Modern Wonder Book of Trains and Railroading*, p. 259, 1946

2 in trucking, the position of the gear shift with the most gear combinations *US, 1942*
- —Montie Tak, *Truck Talk*, p. 12, 1971

big hook *noun*
a wrecking crane *US, 1929*
- —Norman Carlisle, *The Modern Wonder Book of Trains and Railroading*, p. 259, 1946

big house *noun*
1 a prison *US, 1913*
Usually follows 'the'.
- "You won't get to Pontiac this time," one guy said. "Hell no, he'll make the Big House with this one." —Mezz Mezzrow, *Really the Blues*, p. 88, 1946
- "Strebhouse and Stevens spent a stretch in the big house," I said. —Mickey Spillane, *I, The Jury*, p. 111, 1947
- [M]any honest people with whom he mingled socially – came out of the Big House, the top mobsters called a huddle with him and advised him to retire. —Jack Lait and Lee Mortimer, *Chicago Confidential*, p. 172, 1950
- "Don't worry, Judge," he said. "The minute we got outside, one of the kids shook hands with the other and said, 'Hey, we finally made it – the Big House!'" —*San Francisco Examiner*, 22nd February 1956
- In fact, their fate was often worse. Suicide. Dope addiction and the d.t.'s. The big house and the nuthouse. —Jim Thompson, *The Grifters*, p. 24, 1963
- A California nabber took me, white slavery was my charge / convicted me and in twenty-four hours in the bighouse I did lodge. —Bruce Jackson, *Get Your Ass in the Water and Swim Like Me*, p. 151, 1965

- As the gates of the Atlanta big house swung open, I flippantly remarked to the guard on duty: "So long, Jim." — Red Rudensky, *The Gonif*, p. 137, 1970
- "Sock both of the bastards in the Hole!" the warden growled, looking at Buddha as though he were a fellow warden, someone who understood the problems of managing the Big House. — Odie Hawkins, *The Busting Out of an Ordinary Man*, p. 167, 1985
- Chazz, I don't want to go to the Big House! — *Airheads*, 1994
- Zeke gave me a quick matchbook education on how to live and exist in the big house. — Ralph "Sonny" Barger, *Hell's Angel*, p. 197, 2000
- I should [...] ask him in every tiny detail all about his adventures in the big house. But I did that the last time he came out[.] — Danny King, *The Burglar Diaries*, p. 39, 2001

2 a crown court *UK*

- I was weighed off (sentenced) at the big house[.] — Angela Devlin, *Prison Patter*, p. 27, 1996

3 a mental hospital; any large, impersonal, threatening institution *UK, 1984*

Extended from an earlier usage (a workhouse).

Big House *noun*

▸ **the Big House**

New Scotland Yard *UK*

- He never felt quite at ease in the Big House. To him, it was the place senior officers went to hide from real police work. — Garry Bushell, *The Face*, p. 94, 2001

big Huey; big Huey Long *noun*

a long prison sentence *NEW ZEALAND*

An allusion to Huey Long, former governor of Louisiana reputed to have advocated harsh prison sentences.

- A long sentence may be called the big Huey (Long) in reference to Governor Huey Long of Louisiana[.] — *NZWords*, p. 2, 2nd October 1999

big idea *noun*

a bad idea *US*

- — Harold Wentworth and Stuart Berg Flexner, *Dictionary of American Slang*, p. 35, 1960

Big Inch *nickname*

a pipeline from east Texas to the northeast states, built 1942–43 *US*

The success of the project – and its naughty-sounding nickname – gave birth to the 'Little Big Inch' (Texas to New Jersey, 1943–44) and 'Big Inch-by-Inch' (Edmonton to British Columbia, 1951–53).

- It marked the end of a two-year $70 million pipline project, bigger than the "Big Inch," that stretches for 1200 miles. — *Fortnight*, p. 13, 21st November 1947

big iron *noun*

1 a large car *US*

- — *American Speech*, p. 312, Autumn-Winter 1975: 'The jargon of car salesmen'

2 a large, powerful, fast, expensive computer *US*

- — Eric S. Raymond, *The New Hacker's Dictionary*, p. 56, 1991

Big J *nickname*

Juarez, Mexico *US*

- — *Current Slang*, p. 13, Spring 1970

big jobs *noun*

an act of defecation; excrement *UK*

Thus 'to do big jobs'; childish.

- Nick in the dunnee [toilet] and do big jobs[.] — Barry Humphries, *Bazza Pulls It Off!*, 1971

Big Joe *noun*

a novice, especially a military recruit *US*

- — *American Speech*, p. 54, February 1947: 'Pacific War language'

Big Joe from Boston *noun*

in craps, a ten *US*

- — Sidney H. Radner, *Radner on Dice*, p. 10, 1957

big John *noun*

used mainly by black teenagers, a police officer; the police *US*

- — Edith A. Folb, *runnin' down some lines*, p. 229, 1980

Big John *nickname*

the John Hancock Center, Chicago, Illinois *US*

- — Jim Crotty, *How to Talk American*, p. 43, 1997

big juicer *noun*

a powerful, all-night AM radio station *US*

- — Porter Bibb, *CB Bible*, p. 87, 1976

Big K *nickname*

Korea *US, 1970*

- — J.E. Lighter, *Historical Dictionary of American Slang, Volume 1*, p. 150, 1994

big kahuna *noun*

a top leader *US*

From a Hawaiian term for 'priest' or 'wiseman'.

- This might be the big kahuna, gentlemen. — *New Jack City*, 1990

Big L *noun*

1 love *US, 1987*

- It's love, baby. And Whatcom County residents found it at the Northwest Washington Fair in Lynden. From horse barn to the grandstand, they tell how they walked through the gates and into the big "L." — *Bellingham (Washington) Herald*, p. 1C, 13th August 2002

2 a loser *US*

- — Connie Eble (Editor), *UNC-CH Campus Slang*, p. 1, Fall 1984

Big L *nickname*

1 Lubbock, Texas *US*

- — Wayne Floyd, *Jason's Authentic Dictionary of CB Slang*, p. 47, 1976

2 the federal penitentiary in Leavenworth, Kansas *US*

- I was broke, back in stir, and the Big L was surrounding me. — Red Rudensky, *The Gonif*, p. 6, 1970

3 the offshore 'pirate' radio station, Radio London, that broadcast off the Essex coast from 1964 until it was forced off the air on 14th August 1967 *UK*

- We Love the Pirates: Charting the Big 'L' Fab 40 CD[.] — *The Guardian*, 2nd January 2004

big-league *verb*

to associate with important, influential, connected or rich people *US*

- — Connie Eble (Editor), *UNC-CH Campus Slang*, p. 1, Fall 1999

big-league *adjective*

powerful, influential, important *US, 1919*

- CLARENCE: Is he big league? DICK: He's nothing. — *True Romance*, 1993

big leagues *noun*

a high level in any field *US, 1941*

Also used in the singular.

- Relax. This is the big league... — Horace McCoy, *Kiss Tomorrow Good-bye*, p. 293, 1948
- A dazzling crowd. The names escaped Reilly, but the titles and affiliations were awesome: bank trustees, Senior Wall Street lawyers, jurists, legislators. Al Reilly was in the big leagues. — Edwin Torres, *Q & A*, p. 139, 1977

big legs *noun*

a generous spender *US*

- — *Maledicta*, p. 149, Summer/Winter 1986–1987: 'Sexual slang: Prostitutes, pedophiles, flagellators, transvestites, and necrophiles'

Big M *noun*

1 morphine *US, 1959*

- Les, quite disheveled, still wearing his gray nut-house bathrobe, and totally strung-out in coming off the big M, had been trying to brief them as to the true nature of the movie they were producing. — Terry Southern, *Blue Movie*, p. 219, 1970

2 a million pounds *UK*

Dates from a time in the C20 when a million pounds was less commonplace.

- — Wilbur Smith, *Hungry as the Sea*, 1978

3 marriage *US*

- — *Current Slang*, p. 1, Winter 1966

Big M *nickname*

Memphis, Tennessee *US*

- — Wayne Floyd, *Jason's Authentic Dictionary of CB Slang*, p. 47, 1976

Big Mac *noun*

a large area of grazed skin *UK*

Skateboarders' slang; from the similarity of appearance to a branded hamburger.

- — David Rowan, *A Glossary for the 90s*, 1998

big mama *noun*

the ocean *US*

- — Trevor Cralle, *The Surfin'ary*, p. 10, 1991

Big Man *noun*
God *UK*
- [H]e discovered the Big Man in the Big Hoose [prison] and started his own bampot [lunatic] Christian pressure group. —Christopher Brookmyre, *The Sacred Art of Stealing*, p. 367, 2002

big man on campus *noun*
a socially prominent student *US, 1930s to 70s*
Initially used with respect, but often in later years with irony, if not scorn.
- "All the Big Men on Campus are wearing them. Where've you been?" "In the library," I said, naming a place not frequented by Big Men on Campus." —Max Shulman, *The Many Loves of Dobie Gillis*, p. 40, 1951

big meeting in the sky *noun*
heaven as characterised by those who are part of twelve-step recovery programmes such as Alcoholics Anonymous *US*
- —Christopher Cavanaugh, *AA to Z*, p. 54, 1998

Big Mo *nickname*
the USS Missouri *US, 1945*
- But she [Maureen Connolly] was a dynamo called Little Mo, the nickname an admiring comparison to Big Mo, the US Navy battleship Missouri famed at the time for World War II exploits. —*Boston Globe*, p. E7, 17th January 2003

big mother *noun*
a Sikorsky SH-3 helicopter used by the US Navy in Vietnam for search and rescue missions *US*
- The Sea Kings were affectionately known as "Big-Mothers" to those who flew and depended on them for rescue. —Gregory Clark, *Words of the Vietnam War*, p. 462, 1990

big mouth *noun*
an indiscreet, boastful or overly verbose person; a quality of indiscreet talkativeness *US, 1889*
- —Tony Parsons, *Big Mouth Strikes Again*, 2004
- She's got a big mouth, but I tell her if she gives me any lip, I'll wheel her out in front of the traffic. —*The Observer*, 12th December 2004

big mover *noun*
a person who is, either consistently or on a specific occasion, highly successful *AUSTRALIA*
- GARY: So you're a big mover with Diane, are you? BENTLEY: Practically home and hosed. —Alexander Buzo, *Rooted*, 1969

Big Muddy *nickname*
1 the Mississippi River *US, 1846*
- Not only is the "Big Muddy" a long, long river, it is filled with majestic dams that create monstrous lakes. —*Mansfield (Ohio) News Journal*, p. 1B, 7th March 2004

2 the Missouri River *US, 1825*
- Uncertain about the depth of the Missouri River over the summer, the two barge companies that move grain and fertilizer on the Big Muddy have shut down their operations, at least through 2004. —*St. Louis Post-Dispatch*, p. C1, 15th January 2004

big nickel *noun*
five hundred dollars *US, 1961*
- —John Scarne, *Scarne's Guide to Modern Poker*, p. 273, 1979

big noise *noun*
1 an important and influential person *US, 1906*
- "We want an exciting campaign, we want you to be a big noise in this campaign." [Quoting Chris Matthews]— *New York Observer*, p. 1, 2nd February 2004

2 in poker, the alpha player at a table *US*
- —John Vorhaus, *The Big Book of Poker Slang*, p. 7, 1996

big-note *verb*
in betting, to exaggerate your status or bankroll *AUSTRALIA*
- —Ned Wallish, *The Truth Dictionary of Racing Slang*, p. 7, 1989

big-noter *noun*
a zealous horse racing fan *AUSTRALIA, 1967*
- —Roy Higgins and Tom Prior, *The Jockey Who Laughed*, p. 48, 1982
- People in the nearby seats, who had been listening, burst into laughter and the big-noter turned scarlet and hurried off with his mate.' —Roy Higgins and Tom Prior, *The Jockey Who Laughed*, p. 49, 1982
- Kulchad did earn a bag of chaff booby award at Eisdvold so she left the course as satisfied as any of the big noters. —*Sydney Morning Herald*, p. 12, 25th June 1994

big-note yourself *verb*
to overstate your importance *AUSTRALIA, 1953*
- At the top of the stairs the Red Dean met Abe Larons himself, just back from Moscow, where he had big-noted himself in the capitalist press by refusing to endorse the documents of the world meeting[.] —Frank Hardy, *The Outcasts of Foolgarah*, p. 155, 1971

bignum *noun*
any very large number, especially if greater than 2,147,483,648 *US*
- —Guy L. Steele et al., *The Hacker's Dictionary*, p. 30, 1983

big number *noun*
in drag racing, 200 miles per hour, first officially recorded on 12th July 1964 *US*
- But the quest for the "big number" was on, the race to see who would first officially break the 200-mile-per-hour barrier which had been considered impossible just a few months before. —Ross Olney, *Kings of the Drag Strip*, p. 176, 1968

big NUMBER-oh *noun*
a birthday ending with a zero, especially 30, 40 and 50 *US, 1980*
- Some women get depressed when they hit the big five-oh. Others get motivated. —*Atlanta Journal-Constitution*, p. 21JA, 27th November 2003
- Helping her ring in the big three-oh were Sean Patrick Thomas, Alanna Ubach, Tiffany Limos... —*Hollywood Reporter*, 13th October 2003
- Brett Hawthorne hits the big "4-oh" today. —*Herald-Dispatch (Huntington, West Virginia)*, p. 9A, 28th February 2004

Big O *noun*
1 an orgasm *US*
- Then, just as I was about to reach the big O, shrieking with pleasure, he hurled me down the stairs[.] —Gore Vidal, *Myra Breckinridge*, p. 270, 1968
- One of them is the wedge-shaped "Snap-On Stimulator" which again is aimed at the Clirotal big "O." —Angelo d'Arcangelo, *The Homosexual Handbook*, p. 223, 1968
- He's got spine, but he's not the type who can't wait to leave after the big O. —Anka Radakovich, *The Wild Girls Club*, p. 21, 1994
- He'd been active in one of the drive-in cars and had, unfortunately, got his head stuck through the sun roof during the Big O. —Kitty Churchill, *Thinking of England*, p. 114, 1995
- On the subject of the Big O, the Newsweek article gets even more infuriating. —*The Village Voice*, 13th June 2000
- Mutual masturbation during these encounters allows each party to reach the big O. —Erica Orloff and JoAnn Baker, *Dirty Little Secrets*, p. 21, 2001

2 opium; heroin *US, 1957*
- —Richard A. Spears, *The Slang and Jargon of Drugs and Drink*, p. 43, 1986
- —Mike Haskins, *Drugs*, p. 283, 2003

3 a railway conductor *US, 1930*
From the labour organisation name 'Order of Railroad Conductors'.
- —Norman Carlisle, *The Modern Wonder Book of Trains and Railroading*, p. 259, 1946

Big O *nickname*
1 Okinawa, Japan *US, 1972*
- —J. E. Lighter, *Historical Dictionary of American Slang, Volume 1*, p. 151, 1994

2 Omaha, Nebraska *US*
- —Wayne Floyd, *Jason's Authentic Dictionary of CB Slang*, p. 48, 1976
- —Jim Crotty, *How to Talk American*, p. 193, 1997

big on *adjective*
especially enthusiastic about something; considering something to be particularly important *US, 1864*
- [W]e were big on positivity at the Jillian Jackson Show. —Lauren Henderson (Editors: Stella Duffy and Lauren Henderson), *Talk Show [Tart Noir]*, p. 175, 2002

big one *noun*
1 one hundred dollars *US*
- "How much?" "I said, three big ones." —Ross Russell, *The Sound*, p. 135, 1961

2 one million dollars *US, 1967*
- "Three big ones, baby! And final cut!" "Three million? You're kidding." —Terry Southern, *Blue Movie*, p. 47, 1970

3 one thousand dollars *US, 1863*
- He could tell a bitch he needed – not wanted – five or six big ones without her saying "Whatta you need that kinda money for?" —A.S. Jackson, *Gentleman Pimp*, p. 59, 1973
- I pay you a thousand dollars a week. That's fifty two big ones a year. —Charles W. Moore, *A Brick for Mister Jones*, p. 64, 1975

- We're sitting on fifty big ones apiece, Charlie.—Vincent Patrick, *The Pope of Greenwich Village*, p. 103, 1979
- But twenty big ones each?—George V. Higgins, *Penance for Jerry Kennedy*, p. 76, 1985
- "That's eighteen big ones," Chip said, giving the collector a thoughtful look.—Elmore Leonard, *Riding the Rap*, p. 20, 1995
- Fifteen for the vig plus the ten, that's twenty-five big ones you go for a whole year, buddy! You hear me?—*Get Shorty*, 1995

4 in prison, one pound (£1) *UK*

- He asked if I'd manged to "bring anything in" off my visit, and when I said that I had and that it was twenty big ones, he offered me some tobacco and/or hash for it.—Ken Lukowiak, *Marijuana Time*, p. 272, 2000

5 World War 2 *US*

- Well, I was in Italy, fighting the Big One, one-hundred fifty-six missions over Europe, my group.—Eugene Boe (Compiler), *The Wit & Wisdom of Archie Bunker*, p. 39, 1971

6 in horse racing, the race on a given day with the highest prize money *AUSTRALIA*

- —Ned Wallish, *The Truth Dictionary of Racing Slang*, p. 7, 1989

7 the Ringling Brothers, Barnum and Bailey circus *US*

- —Sherman Louis Sergel, *The Language of Show Biz*, p. 20, 1973

8 a substantial lie *UK, 1984*

big orange pill *noun*

during the war in Vietnam, the anti-malarial pill taken once a week in addition to the daily medication *US*

Chloroquine-primaquine was taken weekly in the form of a large, orange-coloured pill.

- —Linda Reinberg, *In the Field*, p. 21, 1991

bigot *noun*

in computing, a person who is irrationally attached to a particular operating system or computer language *US*

- True bigots can be distinguished from mere partisans or zealots by the fact that they refuse to learn alternatives even when the march of time and/or technology is threatening to obsolete the favored tool. —Eric S. Raymond, *The New Hacker's Dictionary*, p. 59, 1991
- —Christian Crumlish, *The Internet Dictionary*, p. 21, 1995

big ouch *noun*

a serious injury *US*

- —*American Speech*, p. 271, December 1962: 'The language of traffic policemen'

big outpatient department in the sky *noun*

death *US*

- —*Maledicta*, p. 35, 1988–1989: 'More Milawukee medical maledicta'

Big Owe *nickname*

the Olympic Stadium in Montreal, built for the 1976 Games *CANADA*

- The ugly Olympic Stadium, more properly known in Montreal as the Big Owe, cost $650 million to build in 1976, more than the combined cost of all the domed stadiums constructed in North America up to that time. And the roof wouldn't retract, and leaked.—Mordecai Richler, *Dispatches from the Sporting Life*, p. 124–125, 2002

big ox *noun*

on the railways, a freight train conductor *US*

- —Ramon Adams, *The Language of the Railroader*, p. 13, 1977

big pond *noun*

1 the Atlantic Ocean *US, 1833*

An ironic understatement of the distance between the UK and the US; 'great pond', an earlier variation, is recorded from 1641.

2 during the Vietnam war, the Pacific Ocean *US*

Playing on the use of the term since the 1830s to refer to the Atlantic Ocean.

- —Linda Reinberg, *In the Field*, p. 21, 1991

big PX in the sky *noun*

death *US*

Vietnam war usage, grim humour based on many cheerful euphemisms for death as a 'big [fill in the blank] in the sky'.

- —Linda Reinberg, *In the Field*, p. 21, 1991

Big Q *nickname*

the San Quentin State Prison, California *US, 1961*

Just north of San Francisco, San Quentin houses California's death chamber.

- Simpkins was convicted of five counts of robbery one with aggravated assault, for give-to-life at Big Q[.]—James Ellroy, *Hollywood Nocturnes*, p. 129, 1994

big quid *noun*

a great deal of money *AUSTRALIA*

Pre-1966, a 'quid' was a one-pound note; its usage did not change with the change to Australian dollars, referring to money in general.

- —Ned Wallish, *The Truth Dictionary of Racing Slang*, p. 66, 1989

Big R *noun*

1 during the Korean war, rotation home *US*

Distinguished from the conventional **R AND R** (rest and recreation).

- —*American Speech*, p. 121, May 1960: 'Korean bamboo English'

2 in trucking, a Roadway Express truck *US*

- —Wayne Floyd, *Jason's Authentic Dictionary of CB Slang*, p. 9, 1976

big red *noun*

1 secobarbitol, a sedative-hypnotic drug marketed under the brand name Seconal™ *US*

- He'd also legally scored far more interesting dope called secobarbital and sold as "Big Reds". These actually produced a slice of long-lasting silent giggles.—Howard Marks, *The Howard Marks Book of Dope Stories*, p. 113, 2001

2 adriamycin, an extremely toxic agent used in chemotherapy *US*

- —Sally Williams, *"Strong" Words*, p. 134, 1994

3 in craps, a one-roll bet on a seven *US*

If the shooter rolls a seven, he loses; 'big red' thus serves as a diplomatic way to bet that the shooter will lose on the next roll.

- —N. B. Winkless, *The Gambling Times Guide to Craps*, p. 91, 1981

4 the desert sun *US*

- —*Army*, p. 47, November 1991

Big Red One *nickname*

the First Infantry Division, US Army *US, 1970*

The Division's patch is a big red number one.

- He had led a battalion, originally in the renowned 1st Infantry Division, "the Big Red One," and then a regiment flawlessly for more than two years[.]—Neil Sheehan, *A Bright Shining Lie*, p. 272, 1988

big red wrench *noun*

in hot rodding and motor racing, an oxyacetylene cutting torch *US*

- —John Edwards, *Auto Dictionary*, p. 14, 1993

big rig *noun*

a large tractor trailer with eighteen or more wheels *US*

- —Ed and Ruth Radlauer, *Truck Tech Talk*, p. 10, 1986

Big Rock *nickname*

the US federal penitentiary on Alcatraz Island, San Francisco Bay *US*

- "Is there a blast, or are you going to the Big Rock?" He meant Alcatraz Island that we all used to joke about[.]—Red Rudensky, *The Gonif*, p. 60, 1970

big rush *noun*

cocaine *UK, 1998*

- —Mike Haskins, *Drugs*, p. 280, 2003

bigs *noun*

1 in pool, the striped balls numbered 9 to 15 *US*

- —Steve Rushin, *Pool Cool*, p. 6, 1990

2 cigarettes *US*

- —Anna Scotti and Paul Young, *Buzzwords*, p. 52, 1997

bigs-and-littles *noun*

in hot rodding, the combination of large rear tyres and small front tyres *US*

- —John Edwards, *Auto Dictionary*, p. 14, 1993

big shit *noun*

1 an important person, if only in their own eyes *US, 1934*

- "Tommy's trying to act big shit and order Italian dishes like he knows what he's doing." [Quoting James Lee Burke]—*USA Today*, p. 8D, 2nd August 1994

2 an important event or thing *US, 1960*

- We going down the road, smoking, talking cash trash, in laymen's terms, we talking big shit, right? — *Washington Post*, p. F1, 11th October 1992

big shot *noun*

an important and influential person *US, 1927*

- The cry to cut the big shots' pay or tie it to performance displays a deep misunderstanding of what today's executive does to earn his daily crust [.] — *The Guardian*, 6th June 1999

big shotgun *noun*

a 106 mm recoilless rifle, developed during the Korean war and used extensively by the US Marines in Vietnam *US*

- — Linda Reinberg, *In the Field*, p. 22, 1991

big-six talk *noun*

talk unsupported by action *US*

- — Charles Shafer, *Folk Speech in Texas Prisons*, p. 198, 1990

big sleep *noun*

death; capital punishment *US*

- He told me he was going to get some one guy, even if he had to do the big sleep for it. — Thurston Scott, *Cure it with Honey*, p. 13, 1951

big slick *noun*

in hold 'em poker, an ace and a king as the first two cards dealt to a player *US, 1981*

- An ace and a king are a Santa Barbara. The older term for that is big slick, but a few years ago there was an oil spill off the coast and the California players started called it Santa Barbara. — Thomas L. Clark, *The Dictionary of Gambling and Gaming*, p. 18–19, 1987

Big Smoke *noun*

1 any large city or town *AUSTRALIA, 1848*

Originally Australian Aboriginal pidgin.

- Only got down to the big smoke last night from Bathurst. — Vince Kelly, *The Bogeyman*, p. 10, 1956
- — Louis S. Leland, *A Personal Kiwi-Yankee Dictionary*, p. 12, 1984
- When none of their friends, and none of their rels, had seen him, they headed back to the Big Smoke. — Kel Richards, *The Aussie Bible*, p. 19, 2003

2 any city in British Columbia *CANADA, 1989*

- — Tom Parkin, *WetCoast Words*, p. 16, 1989

Big Smoke *nickname*

1 the city of Sydney *AUSTRALIA*

- — D'Arcy Niland, *The Big Smoke*, 1959

2 Pittsburgh, Pennsylvania *US, 1930*

- Today, Pittsburgh is ranked among the cleanest cities in the world and often listed as one of the five most livable cities by several national magazines. Old "Big Smoke" has finally left its cloudy legacy behind. — *Times Union (Albany, New York)*, p. J1, 2nd June 2002

big snip *noun*

a vastectomy *CANADA*

- There's no scar and, without a mark, I join the abundant ranks of those who have opted for the Big Snip. — *Montreal Gazette*, p. B10, 15th July 2002

big spark *noun*

an electric shock administered in a hospital to a patient whose heart has failed in an attempt to revive the heart *US*

- — Sally Williams, *"Strong" Words*, p. 143, 1994

big spit; long spit *noun*

the act of vomiting; vomit *AUSTRALIA*

- Calling for Herb, see, that's one of the many euphemisms for vomit, others include spue, burp, hurl, the big spit, the long spit, throw, the whip o'will, the technicolour laugh and, in Queensland, the chuckle. — Frank Hardy, *Billy Borker Rides Again*, 1967
- You can keep the cider thanks all the same Erica – it always makes me go the big spit! — Barry Humphries, *Bazza Pulls It Off!*, 1971
- — David McGill, *David McGill's Complete Kiwi Slang Dictionary*, p. 14, 1998

▸ go for the big spit

to vomit *AUSTRALIA, 1964*

- — Barry Humphries, *A Nice Night's Entertainment*, p. 78, 1964
- The bastard barely swallowed it / When he went for the big spit / And I chundered in the old Pacific Sea. — Barry Humphries, *The Wonderful World of Barry McKenzie*, p. 15, 1968
- Remember the time he got sick at Davo's twenty-first and went for the big spit? — Alexander Buzo, *Rooted*, p. 43, 1969
- — Barry Humphries, *The Traveller's Tool*, p. 119, 1985

big stick *noun*

the large aerial ladder used by firefighters *US*

- Rolling up to a burning building, the big stick is raised in seconds, the extension reaches out, the turntable moves the ladder to the exact point where needed, and firemen go monkeying up to rescue whoever may be trapped by the fire. — Charles F. Haywood, *Yankee Dictionary*, p. 11, 1963

big stuff *noun*

1 any very important or influential person *US, 1911*

- — John W. Mussell, *Militarisms*, 1995

2 artillery, artillery fire *US*

Vietnam war usage.

- — Linda Reinberg, *In the Field*, p. 22, 1991

big-style *adverb*

very much; completely, absolutely *UK*

- I got my own back, though, big-style. — Dave Courtney, *Stop the Ride I Want to Get Off*, p. 165, 1999
- NANA: Looking forward to the wedding, Dave? DAVE: Oh aye, big style. I can't wait. — Caroline Aherne and Craig Cash, *The Royle Family*, 1999

big tender *noun*

a scene in a pornographic film when the participants hug each other *US*

- Now, this [on screen] is what we call "the big tender," only the dialogue is a little different[.] — Robert Stoller and I.S. Levine, *Coming Attractions*, p. 88, 1991
- — *Adult Video News*, p. 42, August 1995

big-ticket *adjective*

expensive; representing a major purchase *US, 1945*

- Dick Nichols said, "Now you're talking about a big-ticket item." — Elmore Leonard, *Bandits*, p. 192, 1987

big time *noun*

1 the highest level of achievement in a field *US, 1910*

Originally theatrical.

- "I been away." She said, "Uh-oh. You mean you were in jail?" "Jail, shit, the big time." — Elmore Leonard, *Maximum Bob*, p. 149, 1991
- They started off robbing 7/11 type stores and gas stations and later graduated to banks and the big time. — *Natural Born Killers*, 1994

2 a long sentence to state prison *US, 1939*

- — Eugene Landy, *The Underground Dictionary*, p. 33, 1971

3 heroin *US*

- — Eugene Landy, *The Underground Dictionary*, p. 33, 1971
- — Richard A. Spears, *The Slang and Jargon of Drugs and Drink*, p. 44, 1986

▸ get big time

to put on airs, to assume a 'posh' accent *UK*

Used by a Midlands professional man, in a BBC Radio 4 programme on class distinction, 4th February 1980.

big-time *verb*

to show off *US*

- That was the way jokers in Harlem carried their money when they wanted to big-time. — Chester Himes, *A Rage in Harlem*, p. 76, 1957

big time *adverb*

very much, entirely, utterly *US, 1957*

The term got a big boost in the US during the 2000 presidential election when Republican vice-presidential candidate Dick Cheney concurred with candidate Bush's assessment of a *New York Times* reporter as a 'major-league asshole' by mumbling 'Yeah, big time' at a campaign stop in Naperville, Illinois, on 4th September. A live microphone picked up the insults, giving 'big-time' its fifteen minutes of fame.

- — Connie Eble (Editor), *UNC-CH Campus Slang*, p. 1, Spring 1987
- He was the Kiddie. I owe him big time. I owe him everything. — Kevin Sampson, *Outlaws*, p. 1, 2001
- But fuck that big time! — Danny King, *The Burglar Diaries*, p. 90, 2001
- "I feel certain that you and I share the same agenda on drugs, Tommy." "Yeah, def', big time." — Ben Elton, *High Society*, p. 69, 2002

Big Tom *noun*

in a carnival ball-throwing game, a big stuffed cat target that has been weighted and is thus hard to knock down *US*

- — Don Wilmeth, *The Language of American Popular Entertainment*, p. 22, 1981

big top *noun*
a prison, especially a maximum-security state prison *US*
- He went straight to the big top, Rikers Island. —Rocky Garciano (with Rowland Barber), *Somebody Up There Likes Me*, p. 76, 1955
- Fixer, I'm going to send those dirty bastards to the big-top for murder-one. —Iceberg Slim (Robert Beck), *Trick Baby*, p. 306, 1969
- This killing was witnessed by twelve hundred cons during the noon meal at the Big Top's messhal[.] —Red Rudensky, *The Gonif*, p. 21, 1970
- —John R. Armore and Joseph D. Wolfe, *Dictionary of Desperation*, p. 20, 1976

Big T-Owe *nickname*
the sports stadium in downtown Toronto, which loses money *CANADA*
- Now all the crazy stuff happens in Toronto, where they have a wacky Montreal-style mayor and a SkyDome that's losing so much money it's become the "Big T-Owe." —*Montreal Gazette*, p. A2, 6th July 2002

big train *noun*
in horse racing, a great racehorse *US*
- —David W. Maurer, *Argot of the Racetrack*, p. 14, 1951

big trip *noun*
a holiday to Britain and Europe *AUSTRALIA*
For many Australians such a holiday is only taken once in a lifetime.
- His wife was on and on at him to take the big trip[.] —Barry Humphries, *A Nice Night's Entertainment*, p. 161, 1978
- —Barry Humphries, *The Traveller's Tool*, p. 30, 1985

big truck *adjective*
of lesbians, 'manly', masculine *UK*
Probably inspired by DIESEL (a 'manly' lesbian).
- This is break-dancing for bears [hairy men] and big truck lezzers who'd need an industrial winch to get them off the floor. —*Attitude*, p. 34, October 2003

big Turk *noun*
an ostrich *US*
Circus and carnival usage.
- —Don Wilmeth, *The Language of American Popular Entertainment*, p. 22, 1981

big twenty *noun*
a 20-year career in the armed forces *US*
- —Linda Reinberg, *In the Field*, p. 22, 1991

big twist *noun*
an occasion for celebration; an outstanding success *AUSTRALIA*
- —Sidney J. Baker, *The Drum*, p. 149, 1959

Big Two *nickname*
World War 2 *US, 1961*
- He'd been in the Big Two and had come out a war hero, having been among those who'd fought their way up the boot of Italy and past the slaughterhouse known as Monte Cassino. —Robert Campbell, *Boneyards*, p. 10, 1992
- —J. E. Lighter, *Historical Dictionary of American Slang, Volume 1*, p. 156, 1994

big up *noun*
1 very positive agreement *UK*
- Well yeah, for sure. Yeah, big up to that. I mean, like, we've got to get the kids off drugs[.] —Ben Elton, *High Society*, p. 69, 2002

2 a socially prominent person *BARBADOS*
- —Richard Allsopp, *Dictionary of Caribbean English Usage*, p. 100, 1996

big up *verb*
to boost, to promote something, to show off; to praise something *UK*
- [T]his tune really did big up the ghetto people's side of things[.] —Donald Gorgon, *Cop Killer*, p. 28, 1994
- Everyone's joshin' an' posin' in the limelight biggin' up their lives like they was auditionin' for cockrocker of the year. —Nick Barlay, *Curvy Lovebox*, p. 122, 1997
- When's someone going to say "Big up" on the big night? Big up our own movie people[.] —Tony Wilson, *24 Hour Party People*, p. 5–6, 2002

big-up *adjective*
pregnant *BAHAMAS*
- —Patricia Clinton-Meicholas, *More Talkin' Bahamian*, p. 21, 1995

Big V *noun*
a vasectomy *CANADA*
- The Big V: for such a small cut, it is remarkable just how big and broad a difference it has made [to my sex life]. —*Ottawa Citizen quoted in Montreal Gazette*, p. B10, 15th July 2002

Big V *nickname*
Vietnam *US, 1972*
- However, it was not ABOUT our time, was it? Director Steven Spielberg steered clear of the big "V." Vietnam. —*Austin American-Statesman*, p. A15, 30th July 1998

big wheel *noun*
a prominent, powerful and important person *US, 1942*
- Heretofore I thought Kalecki was the big wheel behind the syndicate, but now I could see that he was only a small part of it. —Mickey Spillane, *I, The Jury*, p. 157, 1947
- Every one of us is a big wheel, and I don't mind telling you I'm one of the biggest. —Hal Ellson, *Tomboy*, p. 90, 1950
- He [Teamsters president Dave Beck] may be a big wheel, but to me [Fred Loomis] he's only a hub cap. —*San Francisco Examiner*, p. 2, 10th May 1957
- The athletes and the rich boys and the brains were the big wheels at Summer High School. —Dick Gregory, *Nigger*, p. 47, 1964
- Big hara put the cuffs on me in the car, just in case a big wheel was present when they brought me in. —Piri Thomas, *Down These Mean Streets*, p. 314, 1967

big white chief; great white chief *noun*
your boss; a person of importance in a superior or most superior position *UK, 1937*
A casually racist, supposedly jocular usage, modelled on Native American Indian speech.

big white telephone *noun*
the toilet bowl when vomitting into it *AUSTRALIA*
- [Y]ou'll spend the next few days on your knees putting a long distance call on the big white telephone. —Barry Humphries, *The Traveller's Tool*, p. 81, 1985
- I ran back to the squat, hung my head over the toilet and talked to God on the big white telephone. —Kathy Lette, *Girls' Night Out*, p. 98, 1987

big whoop!
used to mock the importance of what has just been said *US, 1981*
- I'll never drive your precious Mercedes again. Big whoop. —*American Beauty*, 1999

bigwig *noun*
a person of high rank or position or money *UK, 1731*
- [I]f it means I buck every bigwig in the record industry you'll pay for this gimmick, son. —*The Sweeney*, p. 15, 1976
- [Christopher Nolan]'s been picked by industry bigwigs Castle Rock to write and direct a forthcoming Howard Hughes biopic[.] —*The Times Magazine*, p. 10, 2nd March 2002

big win *noun*
complete luck *US*
- "Yes, those two physicists discovered high-temperature superconductivity in a batch of ceramic that had been prepared incorrectly according to their experimental schedule. Small mistake; big win!" —Eric S. Raymond, *The New Hacker's Dictionary*, p. 56, 1991

big yard *noun*
the main yard in a prison where the general population mingles for recreation *US*
- Jack gave him the Big Yard stare, cold and hard, set his tone low, and asked, "What did you say?" —Elmore Leonard, *Bandits*, p. 104, 1987

bijou *adjective*
small, as a positive characteristic *UK, 1860*
Adopted from French *bijou* (small); used widely of houses and other buildings, and with greater variation in homosexual society.
- —Barry Took and Marty Feldman, *Bona Bijou Tourettes*, 7th May 1967
- I've got a bona [good] bijou flatette just up the road from Shepherd's Bush —Paul Baker, *Polari*, 2002

bijoux *noun*
jewels *UK*
Directly from French *bijoux*.
- I wanted a new scheitl [wig] to match the bona bijoux[.] —the cast of 'Aspects of Love', Prince of Wales Theatre, *Palare (Boy Dancer Talk) for Beginners*, 1989–92

bike *noun*

1 a promiscuous woman *AUSTRALIA, 1945*

Suggests 'easy availability for a ride'. Often in compound as 'office bike', 'school bike', 'town bike', 'village bike', etc.; occasionally, if reputation demands, 'the bike'.

- What an ugly old bike. I wouldn't ride her for practice!!! —Barry Humphries, *Bazza Pulls It Off!*, 1971
- She's the University bike —Dorothy Hewett, *The Chapel Perilous*, p. 33, 1972
- Village bike[:] accomodating local lady —Peter Chippindale, *The British CB Book*, p. 160, 1981

2 a motorcyle police officer *US*

- —*New York Times Magazine*, p. 87, 16th March 1958

3 in harness racing, a two-wheeled horse drawn vehicle for one person, used for training or for racing *US*

- —Igor Kushyshyn et al., *The Gambling Times Guide to Harness Racing*, p. 112, 1994

4 in lowball poker, a sequence from five down to ace *US, 1978*

- —Thomas L. Clark, *The Dictionary of Gambling and Gaming*, p. 19, 1987

bike chemist *noun*

a person who uses his knowledge of chemistry to manufacture illegal drugs *US*

- —Jay Robert Nash, *Dictionary of Crime*, p. 28, 1992

bike doc *noun*

in mountain biking, a bicycle mechanic *US*

- —William Nealy, *Mountain Bike!*, p. 162, 1992

biker *noun*

a person who rides a motorbike *AUSTRALIA*

In Australia generally used as distinct from 'bikie' (a member of a motorcycle gang).

- He [the tattooist] was working on the very large forearm of a biker who was watching the work, with his lips moving. —Peter Corris, *Make Me Rich*, p. 57, 1985

bike space *noun*

the vagina *UK, 2001*

From the phrase 'I know **WHERE I'D LIKE TO PARK MY BIKE**', said by a man considering a woman as a sexual object.

- —*Sky Magazine*, July 2001

bikie *noun*

a member of a motorcyle gang *AUSTRALIA, 1967*

- He's a nice, clean-cut gun dealer, is what he is, and if he wanted to, he could purobably make half the hoods and forty percent of the bikies in this district. —George V. Higgins, *The Friends of Eddie Doyle*, p. 215, 1971
- [S]he found a young freckle-faced boy in a weather-beaten leather jacket which looked snatched off the back of a bikie leader. —Petru Popescu, *The Last Wave*, p. 171, 1977
- —Louis S. Leland, *A Personal Kiwi-Yankee Dictionary*, p. 14, 1984

bikie chick *noun*

a female member, or associate of a member, of a motorcycle gang *AUSTRALIA*

- He was coming out of a doomed relationship with a bikie chick and knocking back two or three bottles of overproof rum every day. —John Birmingham, *He Died With a Felafel in his Hand*, p. 59, 1994

bikini bar *noun*

a sex club where the dancer strips down to her bikini *US*

- Those exercises and her three-our shifts as an exotic dancer in bikini bars would one day give her the physical strength to hoist people twice her weight over her head. —*Los Angeles Times*, p. 1 (Part 5), 18th January 1988
- "I just want a bikini bar. Girls are going to wear beach bikinis, not tiny little strings," she said. —*Riveride (California) Press Enterprise*, p. B1, 2nd September 1994
- A Scottsdale cabaret owner is currently working on turning the property around the corner from Majerle's into a "bikini bar" (translation: topless, but with panties). —*Phoenix New Times*, 11th December 2003

bikini wax *noun*

an application of hot wax to remove a woman's pubic hair *US*

- —Mary Corey and Victoria Westermark, *Fer Shurr! How to be a Valley Girl*, 1982
- Cosmo may mention where to get a good bikini wax for that trip to the Bahamas, but what about the girl who wants to go beyond the bathing-suit line? —*The Village Voice*, 8th-14th November 2000

bilged *adjective*

worn out, tired *US*

- —Fred Hester, *Slang on the 40 Acres*, p. 15, 1968

bilingual *adjective*

bisexual *US*

- —Roger Blake, *The American Dictionary of Sexual Terms*, p. 17, 1964
- —Dale Gordon, *The Dominion Sex Dictionary*, p. 29, 1967
- —Anon., *King Smut's Wet Dreams Interpreted*, 1978

bill *noun*

1 a dollar *US, 1915*

- He'd raised one hundred sixty-five bills to buy an anti-war ad in the school paper, and then the principal, who is widely held to be a bad person, refused to let the ad run. —James Simon Kunen, *The Strawberry Statement*, p. 80, 1968
- Like I was saying about the hundred bills: the suit and shoes would run about eight bill, right? —Nathan Heard, *Howard Street*, p. 160, 1968
- They must have won eighty dollars between them last night at poker (and spent considerable time letting us be reminded of the fact on the way over here), and they walk after being shot down for a measly five bills. —Jim Carroll, *Forced Entries*, p. 65, 1987

2 one hundred dollars *US, 1929*

- Scat Man Crothers, as zany as they come, plucks his gitbox and hums like a hummingbird. He too just recorded in Hollywood for Capitol. Crothers is grabbing five bills a week as a nitery comic. —*Capitol News*, p. 15, March 1949
- Five bills to find out where she lived and not who she was. —Mickey Spillane, *My Gun is Quick*, p. 66–67, 1950
- Do you realize I lost nearly three bills when my connect got busted? —Clarence Cooper Jr, *The Scene*, p. 88, 1960
- I'll sound Jimmy on a stronger advance, say a bill and a half, but I can't guarantee anything. —Ross Russell, *The Sound*, p. 189, 1961
- So I gave him a half a bill, fifty dollars. —Claude Brown, *Manchild in the Promised Land*, p. 163, 1965
- You're getting almost six bills a month, Mike. —Joseph Wambaugh, *The New Centurions*, p. 57, 1970
- He's pulling down six bills a week. —*The Blues Brothers*, 1980
- You pull down four bills a week which is damn good. —*48 Hours*, 1982
- Two bills a week, room and board. All you can eat – got a great cook. But, no fucking the maids, they're nice girls. —Elmore Leonard, *Stick*, p. 83–84, 1983
- Hey, Ernie, wanna buy this baby for two bills? —Carl Hiaasen, *Tourist Season*, p. 15, 1986
- If this stuff is worth twenty-five bills then I probably won't have to sell all of it. —Kenneth Lonergan, *This is Our Youth*, p. 94, 2000

3 the nose *US, 1952*

- —Harold Wentworth and Stuart Berg Flexner, *Dictionary of American Slang*, p. 37, 1960

▷ **see:** **BILL WYMAN, BILLY WHIZZ**

▸ do a bill

to spend one hundred dollars *US*

- —Stewart L. Tubbs and Sylvia Moss, *Human Communication*, p. 120, 1974

▸ the bill

the police *UK, 1969*

Abbreviated from **OLD BILL**; can also be used of a single police-officer in the sense of representing the whole organisation. Widespread usage popularised since 1985 by UK television police drama *The Bill*.

- —Angela Devlin, *Prison Patter*, p. 27, 1996

Bill!

used as a warning that police are near *US*

- "Now, when they see me, they yell '5-0' or "Bill! Bill!'" street slang for police. —*Record (Bergen County, New Jersey)*, p. L1, 24th February 1998

billabong *noun*

▸ on the billabong

unemployed and camped by a waterhole, especially in Western Australia and the Northern Territories *AUSTRALIA*

- —G.A. Wilkes, *A Dictionary of Australian Colloquialisms*, 1978

billabonger *noun*

an unemployed, homeless person who camps by a waterhole, especially in Western Australia and the Northern Territories *AUSTRALIA*

- —G.A. Wilkes, *A Dictionary of Australian Colloquialisms*, 1978

billards *noun*

the testicles *AUSTRALIA*

- —James McDonald, *A Dictionary of Obscenity, Taboo and Euphemism*, p. 7, 1988

Bill Blass *noun*

crack cocaine *US, 1998*

Quite why the name of American fashion designer Bill Blass (1920–99) should be used for this drug is uncertain.

- —Mike Haskins, *Drugs*, p. 281, 2003

Bill Clinton *noun*

an act of oral sex on a man *US*

In the late 1990s the US Presidency of William Jefferson Clinton (b.1946) was nearly brought down by a sex scandal that involved the President with Whitehouse intern Monica Lewinsky. Bill Clinton denied 'sexual relations with that woman' but eventually admitted that fellatio had occurred and 'a relationship with Miss Lewinsky that was not appropriate'.

- They walked down a back alley and into a punter getting a Bill Clinton from a hooker. —Stewart Home, *Sex Kick [britpulp]*, p. 214, 1999

Bill Daley *noun*

▸ on the Bill Daley

in horse racing, having taken the lead at the start of the race and held it for the entire race *US, 1932*

- Tod [Sloan] got his horses away from the post fast and put them out in front. He was "off on a Bill Daly." —*San Francisco Examiner*, p. 17, 28th June 1949
- —David W. Maurer, *Argot of the Racetrack*, p. 46, 1951
- He would, as the saying goes, "be off on a Bill Daly" and get so far out in front that the foreign jockeys employed the "come from behind" technique couldn't catch him. —*San Francisco Examiner*, p. 21, 15th January 1952
- Claude was a wire-to-wire winner and as a result the phrase "on the Bill Daley" was coined and today it is uttered hundreds of times daily by racetrackers. —*San Francisco News Call-Bulletin*, p. 51, 14th April 1965

billfold biopsy *noun*

a hospital's analysis of the ability of a patient seeking admission to pay their bill *US*

- —Rachel S. Epstein and Nina Liebman, *Biz Speak*, p. 20, 1986

Bill from the Hill *nickname*

the Notting Hill police *UK*

An elaboration of **THE BILL** (the police).

- —Angela Devlin, *Prison Patter*, p. 27, 1996

Billie Hoke *noun*

cocaine *US*

A personification based on **COKE**.

- —J.E. Schmidt, *Narcotics Lingo and Lore*, p. 16, 1959

billies; billys *noun*

money *US*

- I saw the kill mini, but like I totally don't have the billys to buy it[.] —Mary Corey and Victoria Westermark, *Fer Shurr! How to be a Valley Girl*, 1982

bills *noun*

1 money *US*

- Those without bills have spare change. —Vann Wesson, *Generation X Field Guide and Lexicon*, p. 18, 1997

2 the game of pool *US*

- —Mike Shamos, *The Illustrated Encyclopedia of Billiards*, p. 29, 1993

bill shop *noun*

a police station *UK, 1977*

From **THE BILL** (the police).

- —Angela Devlin, *Prison Patter*, p. 27, 1996

bill stickers *noun*

underpants *UK, 1992*

Rhyming slang for 'knickers', sometimes shortened to 'bills'.

- —Angela Devlin, *Prison Patter*, p. 27, 1996

Bill Wyman; bill; wyman *noun*

the hymen *UK*

Rhyming slang, based on the name of Rolling Stone bassist Bill Wyman (b.1936).

- The allusion to Wyman (meaning hymen) the Rolling Stone is really rather clever given his acknowledged penchant for young girls. —*Antiquarian Book Review*, p. 18, June 2002

billy *noun*

1 a metal pail with a handle used for boiling water, making tea, cooking, etc, over a fire when camping or in the bush *AUSTRALIA, 1849*

A quintessential item of the Australian bush. Scottish English had (c.1828 *Scottish National Dictionary*) 'billy-pot' as 'a cooking utensil' and this is probably the origin. Not, as variously conjectured, from French *bouilli* 'boiled', nor Wiradjuri (an eastern Australian Aboriginal language) *billa* 'water', nor the proper name Billy.

- Would you mind lending us your billy to get a drink of water? —Norma Lindsay, *Comic Art of Norman Lindsay*, p. 165, 1911
- Sheep and horses were soon feeding quietly and the billy hangin over the fire. —Charles Melaun, *The Squatter's Daughter*, p. 2, 1933
- For he's gone away and left us / Here, marooned on foreign soil, Where 'round our spitting primuses / We watch our billies boil. —T Kelaher, *The Digger Hat and other verses*, p. 50, 1942
- Florrie said at last, 'Time we got some water for washing up,' an picked up the billy. —Norman Lindsay, *The Cousin from Fiji*, p. 117, 1945
- By the fire the billies were boiling, the tucker of both camps sprea out on tarpaulins. —Ion L. Idriess, *Over the Range*, p. 10, 1947
- Outside I could hear the milkman dipping milk into grandmother' billy[.] —D.E. Charlwood, *All the Green Year*, p. 112, 1965
- The billy – a battered and blackened old container with a wire handl on it, or on big jobs a four-gallon kero-tin in similar condition – is filled with water and boiled by the Peggy. —John O'Grady, *Aussie Etiket*, p. 5 1971
- The billy's boiling – you could at least make the tea. —Jenny Pausacker *What are ya?*, p. 102, 1987

2 a police officer's blackjack or club, a truncheon *US, 1850*

- I clung desperately to the back of the seat until one of the cops hit me on the arm with a billy. —Hunter S. Thompson, *Songs of the Doomed*, p. 86, 1962
- The cop came down. He had his billy out. —Nat Hentoff, *Jazz Country*, p. 129, 1965
- Back at school I eat in a restaurant full of police. As audibly as possible I compose a poem entitled "Ode to the TPF." It extolls the beauty of rich wood billies, the sheen of handcuffs, the feel of a boot on your face. —James Simon Kunen, *The Strawberry Statement*, p. 45, 1968

3 a warning signal *IRELAND*

- The billy (warning) would go from street to street and road to road – 'Look out, Missus, here's the Glimmer Man' —Eamonn MacThomas, *Gur Cake and Coal Blocks*, p. 120, 1976

4 a bong (a water-pipe) for smoking marijuana *AUSTRALIA*

A play on 'billabong' (a water hole).

- —Lenie Johansen, *The Dinkum Dictionary*, 1988
- —James Lambert, *The Macquarie Book of Slang*, 1996

▷ **see:** **BILLY WHIZZ**

▸ boil the billy

to stop for a break and make tea in a billy *AUSTRALIA, 1867*

Occasionally used to mean to make tea not in a billy but an electric kettle or the like.

- —Ion L. Idriess, *Over the Range*, p. 72, 1947
- 'Joe will be boiling the billy somewhere this side of Lacey's Crossing,' Blaze prophesised. —Kylie Tennant, *The Honey Flow*, p. 51, 1956

Billy Bowleg *noun*

the personification of a Seminole Indian *US*

- —John A. Holm, *Dictionary of Bahamian English*, p. 18, 1982

Billy-boy; billy *nickname*

a Protestant, especially a supporter of Glasgow Rangers football club *UK: SCOTLAND*

This goes back to William of Orange, and is now most familiar from the song (to the tune of 'Marching Through Georgia') which is used as a football battle-hymn: 'Hurrah! Hurrah! We are the Billy Boys; / Hurrah! Hurrah! We make a lot of noise; / We're up to here, we never fear – we all are Billy's sons, / We are the Glasgow Billy Boys. / We belong to Glasgow, we're Orange and we're true / Scotland is our country, our colours white and blue, / We're Protestants and proud of it , we're known near and far, / Glasgow Billy Boys they call us.'

- Are you a Billy or a Tim? —Michael Munro, *The Original Patter*, 1985

Billy Bragg; billy *noun*

1 an act of sexual intercourse *UK*

Rhyming slang for **SHAG**, formed from the name of the UK singer and political activist (b.1957).

- Did you get a Billy of that girl last night? —Bodmin Dark, *Dirty Cockney Rhyming Slang*, 2003

2 stolen goods *UK*

Rhyming slang for **SWAG**, formed from the name of the UK singer and political activist (b.1957).

- Hand over the Billy Bragg. —Mervyn Stutter, *Getting Nowhere Fast*, 2004

Billy Bunter; billy *noun*

1 a customer, especially of discreet or illegal services *UK, 1992*

Rhyming slang for **PUNTER**; from the fictional schoolboy created by Frank Richards (Charles Hamilton 1876–1961).

- She tells the Billy Bunter to take it home[.] —J.J. Connolly, *Layer Cake*, p. 26, 2000

- In fact, our regular Billies know full well that we are nothing other than the dearest firm around. —Kevin Sampson, *Outlaws*, p. 64, 2001

2 a shunter *UK*
Hauliers' rhyming slang.
- —*British Road Services Magazine*, December 1951

Billy Button *noun*
any foolish person who works without assurances that he will be paid for his work *VIRGIN ISLANDS, U.S.*
- —Richard Allsopp, *Dictionary of Caribbean English Usage*, p. 101, 1996

billy can *noun*
1 a can used for making coffee *AUSTRALIA, 1885*
- Bob came back to the tent carrying a blackened can for boiling coffee over an open fire. The old men who had been in Australia called it a "billy can." —Russell Davis, *Marine at War*, p. 118, 1961

2 a metal pail with a handle used for boiling water, making tea, cooking etc, over a fire when camping or in the bush *AUSTRALIA, 1870*
- [B]ony brought water, billycan and quart pot, tea and sugar, and a simple first-aid kit. —Arthur Upfield, *Bony and the Mouse*, p. 13, 1959
- [T]here was a large billy-can by the side of the fire, with hot water for tea and coffee. —Herb Wharton, *Cattle Camp*, p. 99, 1994

billy cart *noun*
a child's toy racing cart *AUSTRALIA, 1923*
From 'billy' as 'a male goat', originally billycarts were hitched to goats and raced.
- You could have a success story like that, you know. Start off with a billy-cart and finish up with a fleet of Boeing 727s. —Alexander Buzo, *Norm and Ahmed*, p. 22, 1969

Billy Fury *noun*
a jury *UK*
Rhyming slang, formed from the name of the popular UK singer, 1940–83.
- It's into court in front of the old vanilla fudge [judge] and Billy Fury. —Mervyn Stutter, *Getting Nowhere Fast*, 2004

billy goat *noun*
1 a tufted beard *UK, 1882*
From the similarity between the wearer's facial hair and that of a male goat.

2 in horse racing, the totalisator *AUSTRALIA*
Rhyming slang for 'tote'.
- —Ned Wallish, *The Truth Dictionary of Racing Slang*, p. 1, 1989

3 in trucking, the 318 horsepower Detroit diesel engine *US*
- —Montie Tak, *Truck Talk*, p. 13, 1971

Billy Guyatt *noun*
a diet *AUSTRALIA*
Rhyming slang, sometimes shortened to 'Billy'.
- —Ned Wallish, *The Truth Dictionary of Racing Slang*, p. 7, 1989

billy lid *noun*
a kid *AUSTRALIA*
Rhyming slang.
- Love to your cheese and kisses and the billy lids. —Clive Galea, *Slipper*, p. 187, 1988

Billy No-Bird *noun*
a man who is characteristically without a girlfriend *UK*
- I just feel a bit like a Billy No-Bird. —Frank Skinner, *Frank Skinner*, p. 307, 2001

Billy No-Mates *noun*
a friendless person *UK*
Chris Donald, in *Roger's Profanisaurus*, 2002, adds this subsequent sense: 'A lonely little buoyant turd that remains hanging around in the pan after all the others have gone to the beach.'
- [D]esperately trying to engage anyone in conversation so as not to appear a Billy-no-mates saddo[.] —Colin Butts, *Is Harry Still on the Boat?*, p. 5–6, 2003
- For the anxious parent who is convinced their child is a social outcast at school, a Billy No-Mates doomed to lonely lunch hours, head lice are living proof that close contact has been achieved. —*The Guardian*, 9th April 2003
- But, as Mike Carter finds out, being Billy No Mates can have its advantages. — *The Observer*, 27th July 2003

billyo *noun*
▸ **like billyo**
at great speed *UK, 1885*
- You run like billio. —Michael Holt, *Doctor Who*, p. § 58, 1986
- I ran all the way home, like the billyo. —Kathy Lette, *Girls' Night Out*, p. 107, 1987
- Pete Philpott, Stan Jurd, Ash and Marcia and Daz Braithwaite with their bots hanging out the window going to town like billyo. —Roy Slaven (John Doyle), *Five South Coast Seasons*, p. 7, 1992
- We'd work like billyo to get it right. —Roy Slaven (John Doyle), *Five South Coast Seasons*, p. 81, 1992
- Helmut and Eva grabbed a nipple apiece and tugged away like billy-o. —Kitty Churchill, *Thinking of England*, p. 139, 1995
- —Sonya Plowman, *Great Kiwi Slang*, p. 27, 2002

▸ **to billyo**
to hell; to blazes *AUSTRALIA, 1939*
- I said let's call it a day when lo and behold a gust of wind blew a piece of Beryl's greaseproof paper way off to billyo. —Barry Humphries, *A Nice Night's Entertainment*, p. 112, 1968

Billy Ocean *noun*
suntan lotion *UK*
Rhyming slang, formed from the name of popular Trinidad-born singer (b.1950).
- —Susie Dent, *The Language Report*, p. 98, 2003

billys *noun*
▹ see: BILLIES

Billy's Slough *nickname*
a town named Williams Lake in British Columbia *CANADA, 1989*
- —Tom Parkin, *WetCoast Words*, p. 16, 1898

billy tea *noun*
tea made in a billy *AUSTRALIA, 1890*
- —Charles Melaun, *The Squatter's Daughter*, p. 15, 1933
- Now, sweating after the hot billy tea and rather dry sandwiches, she lay back on a shaded rock[.] —Robert S. Close, *With Hooves of Brass*, p. 84, 1961
- —John O'Grady, *Aussie Etiket*, p. 58, 1971
- —Sam Weller, *Old Bastards I Have Met*, p. 38, 1979

Billy Whizz; Billy Whiz; billy; bill *noun*
an amphetamine *UK*
WHIZZ (amphetamine) disguised as cartoon strip character Billy Whizz, whose adventures started in the *Beano* in 1964.
- —Liz Cutland, *Kick Heroin*, p. 104, 1985
- [H]e'd marked the outsides with a letter so he wouldn't get mixed up. BW stood for Billy Whizz. —Nicholas Blincoe, *Ardwick Green (Disco Biscuits)*, p. 12, 1996
- [A]mphetamine sulphate, aslo known as SPEED, UPPERS, SULPHATE, SULPH, WHIZZ, LEAPERS, and BILLY. —Macfarlane, Macfarlane and Robson, *The User*, p. 95, 1996
- All that bleedin billy he was using, aye. Sent im off is trolley. It would anyone, that amount. Billy for fuckin breakfast, like. —Niall Griffiths, *Sheepshagger*, p. 55, 2001
- Charlie [cocaine] cut with bill. It's not bad. —Niall Griffiths, *Kelly + Victor*, p. 77, 2002
- Well, it's got a coke base. Wee bit of billy thrown in, wee bit of smack. Plus me own secret ingredient. —Niall Griffiths, *Kelly + Victor*, p. 316, 2002
- —Suroosh Alvi et al., *The Vice Guide*, p. b, 2002

billy willy *noun*
a symptomatic reduction in the size of a penis caused by amphetamine use *UK*
A combination of **BILLY** (**WHIZZ**) (amphetamine) and **WILLY** (the penis).
- —Mike Haskins, *Drugs*, p. 271, 2003

bim *noun*
1 a shortened form of 'bimbo' *US, 1925*
- —Lou Shelly, *Hepcats Jive Talk Dictionary*, p. 7, 1945
- I date the best-looking bims in Sigma at school, and I'm a Kapp, the best frat there. —James T. Farrell, *Saturday Night*, p. 34, 1947
- The table is so situated that the town's aging and more prosperous squab-hunters who congregate at it nightly can case the door and ogle the bims brought in by younger and more energetic men. —Jack Lait and Lee Mortimer, *New York Confidential*, p. 166, 1948
- But a bim that won't bolt while you doin' a little jolt / is just one out of a thousand my friend. —Bruce Jackson, *Get Your Ass in the Water and Swim Like Me*, p. 116, 1964

2 a police officer *US*
- The bims went bam and took me to the slams. —Eugene Landy, *The Underground Dictionary*, p. 33, 1971

Bim and Bam *noun*
two inseperable friends *TRINIDAD AND TOBAGO, 1987*
• —Lise Winer, *Dictionary of the English/Creole of Trinidad & Tobago*, 2003

bimbette *noun*
a young, mindless, attractive woman *US, 1982*
A diminuitive of the more widely known **BIMBO**.
• Shannon and the other blonde bimbettes gasp in delight as they bring this ballbusting orgy to its only possible conclusion.—*Adult Video*, p. 32, August/September 1986
• I don't need these bimbettes you got me chasing.— *Something About Mary*, 1998

bimble *verb*
to wander without purpose *UK*
A variation of 'bumble' (to idle), perhaps with reference to **BIMBO** ('a dupe', hence 'mindless').
• —Nigel Foster, *The Making of a Royal Marine Commando*, p. 184, 1987

bimbo *noun*
1 a well-built, attractive, somewhat dim woman *US, 1920*
An offensive term.
• New York has the most beautiful bimbos on earth and it will amuse you to learn that few of them come from New York.—Jack Lait and Lee Mortimer, *New York Confidential*, p. 130, 1948
• When Biff gets there with the bimbo he finds 94 of my baby turtles crawling in the bed[.]—Bernard Wolfe, *The Late Risers*, p. 13, 1954
• I gloated on the moral perfection of a high-ranking L.A.P.D. bimbo being brought to justice by a former L.A.P.D. minion out of moral limbo.—James Ellroy, *Brown's Requiem*, p. 166–167, 1981
• Sparky rents himself a bimbo, dresses up in this goofy outfit —Carl Hiaasen, *Tourist Season*, p. 10, 1986
• Then the bimbo gets kidnapped by some Zombies[.]—Joe Bob Briggs, *Joe Bob Goes to the Drive-In*, p. 156, 1987
• He had a typical Frenchman's attitude toward women – i.e., that they were all bimbos.—Terry Southern, *Now Dig This*, p. 174, 1991
• Nobody blinks an eye if an older man goes out with a young girl bimbo. But what's really sick is when a non-bimbo girl marries a really old man.—Jennifer Saunders, *Absolutely Fabulous*, p. 35, 1992

2 a dupe *UK*
• —Paul Baker, *Polari*, p. 165, 2002

bimph *noun*
toilet paper *UK*
A variation on 'bumph' (paperwork) which is derived from **BUM FODDER**.
• —Paul Baker, *Polari*, p. 165, 2002

bin *noun*
1 a pocket *UK, 1936*
• taken it out of his bin—Frank Norman, *Bang To Rights*, p. 123, 1958
• So, from being dead skint at getting-up time, I've now got ninety-five quid in the bin.—Derek Raymond (Robin Cook), *The Crust on its Uppers*, p. 41, 1962
• You see – apart from that – you've got twenty notes of folding green in the bin [pocket].—Anthony Masters, *Minder*, p. 113, 1984
• They won't scoff at the extra half-mill in my back bin and all. —Kevin Sampson, *Outlaws*, p. 235, 2001

2 a hospital or other institution for the treatment of psychiatric problems and mental illness *UK, 1938*
Abbrevation of **LOONY BIN**.
• —Evelyn Waugh, *Mr Loveday's Little Outing*, 1936
• —Ann Barr and Peter York, *The Official Sloane Ranger Handbook*, p. 158, 1982
• [T]he psychiatric staff at the local bin continued to investigate the uninvestigable[.]—Tony Wilson, *24 Hour Party People*, p. 76, 2002

3 a cell in a prison or a police station *UK*
• —David Powis, *The Signs of Crime*, 1977

bin *verb*
1 to throw something away *UK, 1991*
Reduced from the sense 'to throw in the rubbish bin'.
• [H]e binned the mag.—Kevin Sampson, *Powder*, p. 3, 1999
• a woman's glossy that she'll skim through... then bin.— *The FHM Little Book of Bloke*, p. 69, June 2003

2 to finish with a friend or a lover *UK*
From the sense 'to throw away'.
• "I thought you were married, Andy," murmured Alex. "Separated. Wendy binned me when the squadron got back from Kosovo."—Chris Ryan, *The Watchman*, p. 184, 2001
• [W]hen I'm up there, these'll have to be binned.—Kevin Sampson, *Clubland*, p. 247, 2002

3 to dismiss someone or something; to abandon someone or something *UK*
• There were still people binning it and getting binned after these runs.—Andy McNab, *Immediate Action*, p. 59, 1995

bind *noun*
a bore, a nuisance *UK, 1930*
Originally Royal Air Force use.

binders *noun*
brakes *UK, 1942*
Used in many contexts, from military transport to trains to dra racing.
• —Norman Carlisle, *The Modern Wonder Book of Trains and Railroading*, p. 259, 1946
• Racing Jargon— *Hot Rod Magazine*, p. 13, November 1948
• —Montie Tak, *Truck Talk*, p. 13, 1971
• Just then a wino lurched across Main Street against the red light and Lincoln jammed on the binders almost creaming him. —Joseph Wambaugh, *The Blue Knight*, p. 9, 1973

bindi-eye; bindii *noun*
any of various native spiny Australian plants; also, the introduced South American plant, *Solvia sessilis*, a common lawn weed having sharp prickles; hence, one of these prickles *AUSTRALIA, 1896*
The word comes from the Australian Aboriginal languages Kamilaroi and Yuwaalaraay.
• In those days rodeo riders used little saddles and there were no sof landings – the arena was hard, slatey ground full of bindi-eye. —Herb Wharton, *Cattle Camp*, p. 160, 1994
• Then, in the corner under the Hills Hoist, she plucked twelve prickly bindi-eyes from her left foot[.]—Gretel Killeen, *Hot Buns and Ophelia get shipwrecked*, p. 37, 2001

bindle *noun*
1 heroin *UK*
From an earlier sense (a portion of drugs).
• —Mike Haskins, *Drugs*, p. 283, 2003

2 a portion or packet of drugs *US, 1934*
After an obsolete term for 'a vagrant's bundle'.
• —Richard A. Spears, *The Slang and Jargon of Drugs and Drink*, p. 44, 1986

bindle stiff *noun*
a migratory worker; a tramp *US, 1897*
• Every bindle stiff on the street lifted his lids, and eyed this group of black kids coming along the Bowery.—Emmett Grogan, *Ringolevio*, p. 9, 1972

bine *noun*
a cigarette; an act of smoking a cigarette *UK*
Shortened from the brand name Woodbine™ but used generically.
• —Warren Tute, *The Rock*, 1975

bing *noun*
1 jail, especially solitary confinement in jail *US, 1932*
• Mrs. McDonnell one day passes the bing (cramped little cell where guys are stuck in solitary confinement, as punishment), finds somebody locked up there and runs to Big John screaming[.] —Mezz Mezzrow, *Really the Blues*, p. 315, 1946
• Later on, Collier made the bing again on a battery charge. —*San Francisco Examiner*, p. 16, 13th November 1947
• Boys sent to the bing (the solitary confinement cell, the punishment chamber – without mattress, light, or reading matter, an inmate must stand silently for five days and sleep on the cement floor), sent there for fighting, talking, dressing improperly, or getting seconds on food.—Jack C. Shottler, *Evergreen*, p. 46, April 1970

2 an injection with a hypodermic needle and syringe *US, 1918*
• —J.E. Schmidt, *Narcotics Lingo and Lore*, p. 16, 1959

3 crack cocaine; a piece of crack cocaine *US*
• —US Department of Justice, *Street Terms*, October 1994

bing!
used as a sound effect for something that happens instantly *UK*
Probably echoic of a bell.
• [E]verything he touched turned to cack [shit]. – Not only touched, either; all he had to do was fuckin look at something, mum, an that's be it, bing, brown and mingin.—Niall Griffiths, *Sheepshagger*, p. 12–13, 2001

binge *noun*
a period of heavy drinking or drug-taking; a drinking spree *UK, 1854*
From dialect sense 'to soak'.
• One thing I'd never done though, even in the wake of a mammoth post-binge lowie, was take it out on myself.—*The Guardian*, 12th June 2003

binge *verb*

1 to eat or drink to excess *UK, 1854*

2 to use crack cocaine heavily *UK*
From the sense 'to drink heavily'.
- —Jonathon Green, *The Cassel Dictionary of Contemporary Slang*, p. 92, 1998

binger *noun*

1 a deep inhalation of marijuana smoke filtered through a water-pipe *US*
- —Connie Eble (Editor), *UNC-CH Campus Slang*, p. 1, Spring 1998

2 a drug addict, especially of crack cocaine *UK, 1998*
Extended from **BINGE** (to heavily use crack cocaine).
- —Mike Haskins, *Drugs*, p. 292, 2003

3 a losing bet *UK: SCOTLAND*
Glasgow slang.
- Ah've had nothing but bingers aw day.—Michael Munro, *The Original Patter*, 1985

bingey; bingy; binghi; binjey *noun*

the stomach, the belly *AUSTRALIA, 1926*
Of Aboriginal origin.

bingle *noun*

1 a motor accident causing only minor damage and not resulting in injury *AUSTRALIA, 1970*
- Mum's a very good driver. She hasn't had any bingles has she? —Kerry Cue, *Crooks, Chooks and Bloody Ratbags*, p. 149, 1983

2 a dent or crack in a surfboard *AUSTRALIA, 1966*

bingo *noun*

1 a cheap wine *CANADA*
The exclamation 'bingo' alludes to the sudden effect of the drink.
- And the two boys [stood] amid a litter of paper and bingo bottles in a lane near River Street.—*Maclean's*, p. 44/1, 6th July 1963

2 a prison riot *US*
- —William K. Bentley and James M. Corbett, *Prison Slang*, p. 100, 1992

bingo *verb*

to inject a drug intravenously *US*
- —Jay Robert Nash, *Dictionary of Crime*, p. 29, 1992
- —Mike Haskins, *Drugs*, p. 290, 2003

bingo *adjective*

(of a plane's fuel tank) just enough fuel to reach home base *US, 1956*
- For a fellow down to his last fuel, it's "bingo."—*San Francisco Examiner*, p. 10 (II), 2nd June 1957
- I've got bingo fuel, boss.—T.E. Cruise, *Wings of Gold III*, p. 197, 1989
- "Us too, almost bingo." Bingo – the low fuel level that would force them to return to the KC-135 for an inflight refueling.—Richard Herman, *Force of Eagles*, p. 384, 1990

bingo!

used for emphasis or for registering pleasurable surprise, success, excitement *UK, 1927*
- They take a bit here and a bit there until the picture is complete and bingo, they have something we're trying to keep under the hat. —Mickey Spillane, *One Lonely Night*, p. 94, 1951
- CHARLIE: Now the Land Rover is in the piazza... ARFUR: Right behind our target. CHARLIE: That's it... Bingo!—Troy Kennedy Martin, *The Italian Job [uncut script]*, 1969
- Then you heard Billy had been fished out and you thought – bingo – it's Christmas!—Anthony Masters, *Minder*, p. 81, 1984
- Some Beach cop nails the guy for running a traffic light and, bingo, there's Mr. Spark Harper's missing automobile.—Carl Hiaasen, *Tourist Season*, p. 20, 1986
- No way, Jose, the cop said. Bingo: nine months in the laundry at Wayside.—James Ellroy, *Suicide Hill*, p. 597, 1986
- I put my mouth to his ear and gave him a thumbs up. "Bingo!" —Andy McNab, *Immediate Action*, p. 336, 1995
- HITCHHIKER: "You see Eight-Minute Abs and right next to it you see Seven-Minute Abs – which you you gonna spring for? TED: I'd go with the seven. HITCHHIKER: Bingo.—*Something About Mary*, 1998
- Before I worked up the bottle to make a move, bingo, they were married.—Val McDermid, *Keeping on the Right Side of the Law*, p. 182, 1999
- ELLE: Bill? BUDD: Wrong brother, you hateful bitch. ELLE: Budd? BUDD: Bingo.—*Kill Bill*, 2003

bingo boy *noun*

a young alcoholic *US, 1946*
- —Harold Wentworth and Stuart Berg Flexner, *Dictionary of American Slang*, p. 38, 1960

bingo wing *noun*

a pendulous spread of flabby upper arm that is characteristic of some older women *UK, 2002*
- Gone are the days of "bingo wings", those flaps of upper-arm flesh that plague the mature gambler.—*The Times Magazine*, p. 7, 21st June 2003

bings *noun*

crack cocaine *UK, 1998*
- —Mike Haskins, *Drugs*, p. 281, 2003

binky *noun*

1 a baby's dummy (pacifier) that a heroin user has converted into a squeeze bulb for injecting a dose of heroin through an eye dropper and needle into the vein *US*
From the common childrens' nickname for a dummy.
- —Geoffrey Froner, *Digging for Diamonds*, p. 9, 1989

2 marijuana; a marijuana cigarette *UK*
- —Mike Haskins, *Drugs*, p. 286, 2003

binocs *noun*

binoculars *US, 1943*
- —Fiona Murray, *Invitation to Danger*, 1965

bin off *verb*

to set something aside, to discard something *UK, 2002*
Teen slang.
- —Susie Dent, *The Language Report*, p. 75, 2003

binos *noun*

binoculars *US*
- The platoon commanders went up on top for one last look through the binos and to hear the Captain's plan.—Charles Anderson, *The Grunts*, p. 58, 1976
- Just pick up the bino's and do a quick sweep.—Martin Cameron, *A Look at the Bright Side*, 1988

bin rat *noun*

a supply clerk in the Royal Canadian Air Force *CANADA*
- "Bin rat" was coined because supply personnel spend much of their time around the bins containing equipment and materiel, in a supply depot.—Tom Langeste, *Words on the Wing*, p. 27, 1995

bins *noun*

a pair of spectacles, glasses; binoculars; hence, the eyes *UK*
Abbreviated from 'binoculars'; also variant 'binns'.
- The whole time this was being said the governor was clocking me over the top of his bins with more than a little distaste.—Frank Norman, *Bang To Rights*, p. 24, 1958

▸ **the bins**

a Goodwill Industry's used clothing store, where used clothing is sold by the pound *US*
- —Jim Crotty, *How to Talk American*, p. 261, 1997

bint *noun*

1 a girlfriend, a young woman *UK, 1855*
From Arabic *bint* (a daughter), often combined with a critcal adjective to derogatory effect.
- [W]e couldn't think what to do, until Henry remembers that those three bints up at the Lido had promised to meet us over Clapham Common.—John Peter Jones, *Feather Pluckers*, p. 19, 1964
- I'll be Donald Ducked if I'm gonny yodel [sing] for any bint. —Ian Pattison, *Rab C. Nesbitt*, 1988
- I like ropy bints, they're the ones.—Kevin Sampson, *Clubland*, p. 85, 2002
- Daft friggin bint.—Niall Griffiths, *Kelly + Victor*, p. 285, 2002

2 a promiscuous woman *UK, 1855*
Derogatory.
- Roger takes a great swig of his lager and says, quietly: – slags. Ianto sniggers and agrees. – Bints.—Niall Griffiths, *Sheepshagger*, p. 183, 2001

bio *noun*

a biography *US, 1947*
- There was a bio to be written. Also one on his famous father. Oh boy!—Lionel Davidson, *The Chelsea Murders*, 1978

bio *adjective*

excellent *US*
- —Jonathan Roberts, *How to California*, p. 166, 1984

bio break *noun*

a visit to the toilet
A euphemism popular with the more jargon-friendly computer-users.
- —David Rowan, *A Glossary for the 90s*, p. 71, 1998

biog *noun*
a biography *US, 1942*

biologist *noun*
a person whose interest in companionship is primarily sexual *US*
- —Kenn "Naz" Young, *Naz's Underground Dictionary*, p. 15, 1973

biopic *noun*
a biographical film *US, 1951*
- a forthcoming Howard Hughes biopic starring Jim Carrey—*The Times Magazine*, p. 10, 2nd March 2002

bip *noun*
the head; the brain *US*
- At first the good citizens say he's off his bip.—Haenigsen, *Jive's Like That*, 1947

bip *verb*
1 to break into a house while the housewife is outside hanging laundry on the line to dry *US*
An abbreviation of **SCALLYBIP**.
- Around Christmas of that year me and a friend was going to go up through Oklahoma bipping – scallybipping [burglarizing a home when they saw the wife out back hanging clothes], you know. —Bruce Jackson, *In the Life*, p. 82, 1972

2 to simultaneously take heroin and cocaine into the body through the nose
- —Nick Constable, *This is Cocaine*, p. 182, 2002

bipe *verb*
to break and enter the dwelling of another while they sleep, with the intent of stealing *US*
- —Charles Shafer, *Folk Speech in Texas Prisons*, p. 198, 1990

bippy *noun*
used as a jocular euphemism for 'ass' *US, 1967*
Coined and popularised by Rowan and Martin on the television programme *Laugh-In* (NBC,1968–73); a wildly popular word for several years, the key word in the title of the 1969 Rowan and Martin film *The Maltese Bippy*, and then abandoned on the junk heap of slang.
- You bet your sweet bippy I did. [Quoting Apollo 10 crew member Tom Satfford)—*San Francisco Examiner*, p. 1, 26th May 1969
- —Helen Dahlskog (Editor), *A Dictionary of Contemporary and Colloquial Usage*, p. 7, 1972

bird *noun*
1 a young woman; a sweetheart *UK, 1838*
First used in C14; not considered a slang term until C19 when it also meant 'a prostitute' (obsolete by 1920). Primarily a British term, but briefly popular in the US in the late 1960s.
- My bird's gone bent.—Frank Norman, *Bang To Rights*, p. 58, 1958
- The ratio is about ten guys to every bird. [Letter to Ann Landers] —*San Francisco Examiner*, p. 36, 12th December 1968
- This is the same bloke that I've seen headbutt someone for looking at his bird's drink[.]—Dave Courtney, *Raving Lunacy*, p. 73, 2000

2 the vagina *US, 1963*
- —J. E. Lighter, *Historical Dictionary of American Slang, Volume 1*, p. 163, 1994

3 an ordinary fellow *US, 1839*
Also known as an 'old bird'.
- This is an inside job, pulled by one of the company or some bird working for them.—Chester Gould, *Dick Tracy Meets the Night Crawler*, p. 28, 1945
- You birds say that knowledge is power – yet all your knowledge turns into impotence when you want it used for human harmony and peace.—Philip Wylie, *Opus 21*, p. 58, 1949
- We pay my bird five because he isn't doing this for love. —Derek Bickerton, *Payrool*, p. 15, 1959

4 the penis *US*
- —John D. Bell et al., *Loosely Speaking*, p. Addenda, 1969
- "Bird" – the male organ. Used in jovial greeting, as in "How's your bird?"—*Washington Post*, p. B1, 17th January 1985

5 a homosexual man *US*
- The muggers and the sluggers who in recent years have made it unsafe for almost anyone to walk the public streets late at night, learned about the Birds long ago.—Robert Sylvester, *No Cover Charge*, p. 268, 1956

6 a 25-cent piece *US*
- —Vincent J. Monteleone, *Criminal Slang*, p. 23, 1949

7 a surfer who uses any bird or wings as his surfboard logo *US*
- —Michael V. Anderson, *The Bad, Rad, Not to Forget Way Cool Beach and Surf Discriptionary*, p. 3, 1988

8 a police informer *CANADA*
From the sense of **STOOL PIGEON** and **SING**.
- According to prison lore, only birds (i.e., stool pigeons) whistle. —Suroosh Alvi et al., *The Vice Guide*, p. 224, 2002

9 a certainty *AUSTRALIA, 1941*
A shortening of **DEAD BIRD**.
- Follow me to the three if you want to make a bird of it.—Wilda Moxham, *The Apprentice*, p. 66, 1969
- I play it all up in the second; / And when it came to the third, / They told me the filly by Show-Down, / Was the next best thing to a bird. —Roy Higgins and Tom Prior, *The Jockey Who Laughed*, p. 41, 1982

10 in horse racing, a horse that as seen as likely to win a race *AUSTRALIA*
- —Ned Wallish, *The Truth Dictionary of Racing Slang*, p. 7, 1989

11 a twenty-five cent betting token *US, 1974*
- —Thomas L. Clark, *The Dictionary of Gambling and Gaming*, p. 19, 1987

12 a gesture of the middle finger, meaning 'fuck you' *US*
- It was Red's way of giving him the bird.—Ross Russell, *The Sound*, p. 177, 1961
- —Frank Prewitt and Francis Schaeffer, *Vacaville Vocabulary*, 1961–1962
- —Collin Baker et al., *College Undergraduate Slang Study Conducted at Brown University*, p. 79, 1968
- He got up the juice to give me a feeble middle-finger farewell, and when the bird was in midair I stepped on his heart and pushed down[.]—James Ellroy, *Hollywood Nocturnes*, p. 141, 1994

13 an amphetamine tablet *US*
- —Jay Robert Nash, *Dictionary of Crime*, p. 29, 1992
- —Peter Johnson, *Dictionary of Street Alcohol and Drug Terms*, p. 19, 1993

14 a kilogram of cocaine *US*
- 'In the past two or three years around here, a brick, kilo of coke – 1,000 grams of the drug, they'd call a 'bird,'" Hagedorn said. —*Milwaukee Journal Sentinel*, p. 1B, 9th February 2002

15 Wild Turkey™ whisky *US*
- "I've never seen anybody that loved that ol' Bird as much as Jim Ed. When he buys a bottle, he just throws the cap away."—Ken Weaver, *Texas Crude*, p. 64, 1984
- We just chillin' out, drinking a little Bird, that's all. You want a taste?—Odie Hawkins, *Great Lawd Buddha*, p. 11, 1990

16 an aeroplane *US, 1918*
- Turn this crazy bird around / I shouldn't have got on this flight tonight.—Joni Mitchell, *This Flight Tonight*, 1971
- He assists Brooks in establishing unit-to-bird contact.—John M. Del Vecchio, *The 13th Valley*, p. 632, 1982

17 a helicopter *US*
- But we got special permission tonight for this big shot, 'cause we had to land the bird in the middle of the street[.]—Stephen J. Cannell, *The Tin Collectors*, p. 239, 2001

18 a Ford Thunderbird car *US*
- —Lanie Dills, *The Official CB Slanguage Language Dictionary*, p. 17, 1976

19 a Pontiac Firebird car *US*
- —Porter Bibb, *CB Bible*, p. 88, 1976

▷ see: **BIRD LIME**

▸ **out of your bird**
insane *UK*
- Dennis [Hopper] was out of his bird, totally gone.—*Uncut*, May 2001

▸ **the bird**
1 negative criticism *UK, 1884*
Originally theatrical; now usually phrased 'get the bird' or 'give the bird'.

2 a vocal demonstration of complete disapproval *UK*
- —Wilfred Granville, *The Theater Dictionary*, p. 19, 1952

Bird *nickname*
Charlie Parker (1920–1955), the jazz legend credited as an originator of bebop, the jazz style that followed the big band swing era *US, 1946*
- [N]ow it was the beginning – returning to the Red Drum for sets, to hear Bird[.]—Jack Kerouac, *The Subterraneans*, p. 14, 1958
- Ah, yes, the Bird – and ole Diz – then here's Miss Sarah herself. —Ross Russell, *The Sound*, p. 24, 1961
- Gus gave me a whole album of 78's by Bird called Charlie Parker with Strings.—Claude Brown, *Manchild in the Promised Land*, p. 148, 1965

• Fifteen years ago I knew a raggedly kid out of Chicago who used to come uptown to a place where me, Dizzy, and Bird jammed. —Nat Hentoff, *Jazz Country*, p. 127, 1965
• Some skinny joker with scald burns on his face was fronting a combo. He tried to ape the "Birds" phrasing and tone. —Iceberg Slim (Robert Beck), *Pimp*, p. 95, 1969
• In that atmosphere, with the spiraled hints of Bird, Prez, Diz or Miles cuttin' up on somebody's box, we'd have orgies. —Odie Hawkins, *Black Casanova*, p. 163, 1984
• All the great black musicians – Bird, Diz, Thelonius, Bud Powell, Miles, Kenny Clarke, etc., etc. were first appreciated there. —Terry Southern, *Now Dig This*, p. 4, 1986

bird bandit *noun*
a womaniser *UK*
• I walk into a well-known bird-bandit's lair and find a comely Richard [woman] flaunting her Arris [buttocks] around the gaff[.] —Anthony Masters, *Minder*, p. 37, 1984

birdbath *noun*
1 a cursory washing of the body using little water *US, 1953*
• [A]fter I've finished my calisthenics and the hot water has arrived, I take me a bird (jailbird) bath in the little sink. —Eldridge Cleaver, *Soul on Ice*, p. 43, 1968
• —Frederic G. Cassidy, *Dictionary of American Regional English*, p. 241, 1985
2 the area in a military motor pool where vehicles are washed *US*
Coined in Vietnam.
• —Linda Reinberg, *In the Field*, p. 22, 1991

birdbrain *noun*
a human who gives the impression of possessing a bird-size brain; a fool *US, 1933*
• Leo wasn't there – probably out chasing missing persons, the birdbrain[.] —Bernard Wolfe, *The Late Risers*, p. 4, 1954
• In spite of his father's reputation as the family intellectual, Billy, at about age twelve, considered him something of a birdbrain[.] —Darryl Ponicsan, *The Last Detail*, p. 11, 1970

bird-brained *adjective*
foolish; not-clever-enough; stupid *UK, 1922*
• We bird-brained humans are also forever coming a cropper by bumping into obstacles we really ought to have spotted. —*The Guardian*, 17th March 2004

birdcage *noun*
1 the anus *US*
• —Bruce Rodgers, *The Queens' Vernacular*, p. 18, 1972
2 a used car lot, especially one surrounded by chicken wire *NEW ZEALAND*
• —David McGill, *David McGill's Complete Kiwi Slang Dictionary*, p. 15, 1998
3 a mounting enclosure at a racecourse *AUSTRALIA, 1893*
So named as it is often surrounded by a wire mesh fence.
• Is there movement, life and laughter from the 'birdcage' to the tote / As the old friends congregate from near and far? —Tip Kelaher, *The Digger Hat and other verses*, p. 34, 1942
• The bird cage was surrounded by a 200 by 100 feet picket fence[.] —Joe Andersen, *Winners Can Laugh*, p. 94, 1982
• When the trainer and jockey joined them in the birdcage it was the Wagga publican who spoke out[.] —Clive Galea, *Slipper*, p. 122, 1988
4 in harness racing, the enclosure where horses are paraded before events *US*
5 an air control tower *US, 1965*
• —J. E. Lighter, *Historical Dictionary of American Slang, Volume 1*, p. 165, 1994
6 a railway lantern *US, 1945*
• —Norman Carlisle, *The Modern Wonder Book of Trains and Railroading*, p. 259, 1946
7 a Volvo car *UK*
• —Peter Chippindale, *The British CB Book*, p. 161, 1981
8 in motor racing, a chassis made of many small pieces of tubing or a tubular roll bar structure *US*
• —John Lawlor, *How to Talk Car*, p. 19, 1965
9 a box used for storing dice *US*
• —Frank Garcia, *Marked Cards and Loaded Dice*, p. 250, 1962

Birdcages *noun*
▸ **the Birdcages**
the first legislative buildings in Victoria, British Columbia *CANADA*
[B]ecause of their gimcrack architectural elaboration; now all obliterated. Leechman, 1968.

bird circuit *noun*
a prolonged group tour of gay bars; the bars themselves *US*
• The Bird Circuit – a network of saloons and small night clubs catering exclusively to the homosexuals – and what are generally known as Broad Joints. —Robert Sylvester, *No Cover Charge*, p. 265, 1956
• — *The Guild Dictionary of Homosexual Terms*, p. 4, 1965
• — *Maledicta*, p. 236, Winter 1980: 'Lovely, blooming, fresh and gay: the onomastics of camp'

bird colonel; full-bird colonel *noun*
in the US Army, a full colonel *US, 1946*
From the eagle insignia.
• This bald-headed, wrinkle-necked, full-bird colonel from the Officer's Candidate School stood at the tag end[.] —Larry Heinemann, *Close Quarters*, p. 145, 1977
• One fine day this full-bird colonel pulled up in a deuce-and-a-half and volunteered a bunch of us. —Larry Heinemann, *Paco's Story*, p. 130, 1986
• Had NCO's all around his desk / And a full Bird Colonel in the leanin' rest. —Sandee Shaffer Johnson, *Cadences*, p. 66, 1986
• He [Oliver North] is a lieutenant colonel in the United States Marine Corps, although his chances of making bird colonel seem dim this week. —Hunter S. Thompson, *Generation of Swine*, p. 184, 1988
• —Linda Reinberg, *In the Field*, p. 22, 1991

bird course *noun*
an easy course in university *CANADA*
• So I guess you could say [Sexual Ethics 260] was a bird course. —*McGill Tribune*, 16th July 2002

bird dog *noun*
1 a scout *US, 1929*
• The boys had instructed their courtroom bird dogs to call that number as soon as the verdict was in. —Robert Sylvester, *No Cover Charge*, p. 205, 1956
• —R. Frederick West, *God's Gambler*, p. 223, 1964
• Art says Mansell used him as a bird dog. Mr. Sweety would go in a dope house – very friendly type of guy – sit around and chat a while, pass out some angel dusty, tell a few jokes – that's the way they worked. Get 'em laid back on the dusty, then Clement comes in and takes 'em off eassy...' —Elmore Leonard, *City Primeval*, p. 100, 1980
2 in professional sports, a talent scout or a scout's associates who let him know about players who may be prospects for professional play *US, 1950*
• —Richard Scholl, *Running Press Glossary of Baseball Language*, p. 16, 1977
• —Bill Shefski, *Running Press Glossary of Football Language*, p. 15, 1978
• Paul's scouts also found Vada Pinson, Jim Maloney, Tony Perez and – after much cajoling from Bbbbbuddy Bloebaum, a bird-dog scout who was the kid's uncle – Pete Rose. —*Cincinnati Enquirer*, p. 4D, 28th October 2003
3 a person who provides information about potential victims to a thief or group of thieves *US*
• —Robert C. Prus and C.R.D. Sharper, *Road Hustler*, p. 169, 1977
4 a navigational device in planes that points in the direction of a radio signal *US*
• —*American Speech*, p. 227, October 1956: 'More united states air force slang'
• —*American Speech*, p. 118, May 1963: 'Air refueling words'
5 a person who solicits players for gambling, whether in a casino or a private poker game *US, 1949*
• —Thomas L. Clark, *The Dictionary of Gambling and Gaming*, p. 19, 1987
• —George Percy, *The Language of Poker*, p. 10, 1988
6 in the used car business, either a customer who has been referred to a salesman or the person doing the referring *US*
• —Peter Mann, *How to Buy a Used Car Without Getting Gypped*, p. 188, 1975
7 in a two-car police speed-monitoring unit, the car that chases down speeding cars or trucks based on radar readings in the second car *US*
• —Montie Tak, *Truck Talk*, p. 13, 1971

bird-dog *verb*
1 to flirt with another's date *US, 1941*
• You oughta be out running around in a convertible, bird-dogging girls. —Ken Kesey, *One Flew Over the Cuckoo's Nest*, p. 184, 1962
• —*American Speech*, p. 193, October 1965: 'Notes on campus vocabulary, 1964'
2 to look for, find and return with someone or something *US, 1948*
• Old Preston was back out there bird-dogging suckers. —Iceberg Slim (Robert Beck), *Pimp*, p. 98, 1969
• [T]he pilot-mogul had me out bird-dogging quiff: prowling bus depots and train stations for buxom young girls who'd fall prey to RKO contracts in exchnage for frequent nightime visits. —James Ellroy, *Hollywood Nocturnes*, p. 199, 1994

bird egg *noun*
an amphetamine tablet *US*
• —Peter Johnson, *Dictionary of Street Alcohol and Drug Terms*, p. 18, 1993

bird feeder *noun*
in trucking, the air-intake pipe *US*
• —Montie Tak, *Truck Talk*, p. 13, 1971

bird food *noun*
inferior quality marijuana *US*
• "Bet he didn't sell you this crummy bag a' bird food," Shane said, holding up the bag of thin, seed-ridden grass."—Stephen J. Cannell, *The Tin Collectors*, p. 98, 2001

bird head *noun*
a type of LSD *UK*
• —Mike Haskins, *Drugs*, p. 285, 2003

bird house *noun*
a jail or prison *US*
• —Vincent J. Monteleone, *Criminal Slang*, p. 23, 1949

birdie *noun*
1 a passive, effeminate male homosexual *US, 1921*
• —Vincent J. Monteleone, *Criminal Slang*, p. 23, 1949
• He didn't turn around even when he heard the crunch of boots on the gravel, or felt the heavy body of the bulldog creature filling the space at his back, or even when the sodomite spoke. "You're a birdie and I'm going to have your ass."—Robert Campbell, *Alice in La-La Land*, p. 6–7, 1987

2 a bird, especially a small bird *UK, 1792*
Childish.
• Oh, there's a birdie! See the little birdie? See the birdie up in the tree?—Linda Acredolo, *Baby Signs*, p. 44, 2002

3 an aircraft *AUSTRALIA*
Used by the Australian Army in Korea, 1951–53.
• —A.M. Harris, *The Tall Man*, 1958

birdie powder *noun*
any powdered drug, such as heroin or cocaine *US*
• —Jay Robert Nash, *Dictionary of Crime*, p. 29, 1992
• —Robert Ashton, *This Is Heroin*, p. 205, 2002
• —Mike Haskins, *Drugs*, p. 280, 2003

bird in a cage *noun*
the rank of Specialist 5 in the US Army *US*
From the eagle under a curved stripe on the chevron.
• —Carl Fleischhauer, *A Glossary of Army Slang*, p. 4, 1968

bird lime; bird *noun*
1 a sentence of imprisonment *UK, 1857*
Rhyming slang for **TIME**. The abbreviation is used especially in 'do bird' (to serve a prison sentence).
• I've never actually worked out the exact total of bird I've done in my time.—Charles Raven, *Underworld Nights*, p. 111, 1956
• The reason for this was so that they could diside [decide] where they were going to send me to do my bird.—Frank Norman, *Bang To Rights*, p. 28, 1958
• Never done bird, our Marchmare, but sus [suspicion] clings to him like an aura.—Derek Raymond (Robin Cook), *The Crust on its Uppers*, p. 23, 1962
• [T]he landlord of the rub-a-dub called bird lime.—Ronnie Barker, *Fletcher's Book of Rhyming Slang*, p. 26, 1979
• —William K. Bentley and James M. Corbett, *Prison Slang*, p. 25, 1992
• —Angela Devlin, *Prison Patter*, p. 27, 1996
• I could earn almost as much doing something which would get me much less bird.—Dave Courtney, *Raving Lunacy*, p. 247, 2000

2 by extension, a personal history of imprisonment *UK, 1857*
Rhyming slang for **TIME**.

birdman *noun*
a prisoner *UK*
A combination of **BIRD (LIME)** (a prison sentence) and 'man', playing on famous convict 'the Birdman of Alcatraz'.
• —Angela Devlin, *Prison Patter*, p. 27, 1996

bird nest *noun*
a person's room, apartment or house *US*
• Dickie held the sting, and I split back to the bird next to get what I left.—A.S. Jackson, *Gentleman Pimp*, p. 23, 1973

bird of paradise *noun*
the US armed forces insignia designating honourable discharge *US*
• —*American Speech*, p. 153, April 1946: 'GI words from the separation center and proctology ward'

birds *noun*
▸ **for the birds**
1 no good, shoddy *US, 1944*
• —Arnold Shaw, *Lingo of Tin-Pan Alley*, p. 7, 1950

2 trivial; not worthy of intelligent interest *US, 1951*
• All talk of a leadership contest now is strictly for the birds[.] —*Daily Telegraph*, 21st September 2003

bird sanctuary *noun*
any institution where traffic violators who are under pursuit are free from further pursuit once they pass the gates *US*
• —*American Speech*, p. 267, December 1962: 'The language of traffic policemen'

birdseed *noun*
1 nonsense *US, 1909*
• —J. E. Lighter, *Historical Dictionary of American Slang, Volume 1*, p. 166, 1994

2 a small amount of money *US*
• —Ralph de Sola, *Crime Dictionary*, p. 15, 1982

bird's eye *noun*
a small dose of heroin *US*
• A bird's eye is generally what a junker takes in his first bang after being on vacation for a while.—David Maurer and Victor Vogel, *The Slang and Jargon of Drugs and Drinks*, p. 388, 1973
• —Angela Devlin, *Prison Patter*, p. 27, 1996

bird shit *noun*
a paratrooper *US*
From the jocular tease that only two things fall from the sky, paratroopers and bird shit.
• —Linda Reinberg, *In the Field*, p. 22, 1991

bird's nest *noun*
1 pubic hair that can be seen to extend from the crotch to the navel; pubic hair *US*
Homosexual use; tangled imagery.
• —Bruce Rodgers, *The Queens' Vernacular*, 1972

2 in the Royal Navy, a WRNS' cabin *UK*
A member of the *W*omen's *R*oyal *N*aval *S*ervice is popularly known as a Wren, hence this pun; remembered from World War 2 but not recorded until 1984.
• —John W. Mussell, *Militarisms*, 1995

3 the chest, especially (of a man) if hairy *UK, 1970*
Rhyming slang, but also partly from the imagery. Coincidentally adjacent to the following sense.
• She's got a nice boat race [face] but a really tiny bird's nest. —Bodmin Dark, *Dirty Cockney Rhyming Slang*, 2003

4 a hole in the upholstery of the driver's seat of a car from long use and too much weight *US*
• —Lewis Poteet, *Car & Motorcyle Slang*, p. 30, 1992

bird speed *adverb*
extremely fast *BARBADOS*
• —Frank A. Collymore, *Barbadian Dialect*, p. 19, 1965

bird-turd *verb*
to disparage someone or something; to speak with a lack of sincerity *US, 1947*
A close relation of **CHICKENSHIT**.
• —J. E. Lighter, *Historical Dictionary of American Slang, Volume 1*, p. 167, 1994

bird watcher *noun*
a man given to the practice of watching girls go by *UK, 1984*
A pun on **BIRD** (a young woman).

bird watching *noun*
(used of young males) looking sensually and whistling at passing young women *TRINIDAD AND TOBAGO*
Collected in 1995.

birdwood *noun*
a cigarette *US, 1944*
• —Lou Shelly, *Hepcats Jive Talk Dictionary*, p. 7, 1945

birdyback *noun*
containers or trailers shipped by air *US*
A poor borrowing from **PIGGYBACK**.

birk *noun*
a mentally slow person *US*
- —Harold Wentworth and Stuart Berg Flexner, *Dictionary of American Slang*, p. 677, 1976

▷ see: **BERK**

biri *noun*
▷ see: **BEEDI**

birling *adjective*
drunk *UK: SCOTLAND*
From Scottish dialect *birl* (to spin).
- —Michael Munro, *The Patter, Another Blast*, 1988

biro *noun*
a ballpoint pen used as an improvised means of injecting drugs *UK*
From the conventional generic sense of 'biro' as 'a ballpoint pen'.
- —Angela Devlin, *Prison Patter*, p. 27, 1996

birth control engine *noun*
a large locomotive which could burn up to five tons of coal per shift *UK*
Firing them up in the early morning was said to make a man impotent for weeks.
- —Frank McKenna, *A Glossary of Railwaymen's Talk*, 1970

birthday card *noun*
in poker, the one card needed and drawn to complete an unlikely good hand *US*
- —John Vorhaus, *The Big Book of Poker Slang*, p. 7, 1996

birthday present *noun*
in tiddlywinks, a stroke of good luck *US*
- — *Verbatim*, p. 525, December 1977

birthdays *noun*
▸ **think all your birthdays have come at once**
to be overjoyed or overwhelmed, especially from something unexpected *AUSTRALIA*
- Gees I got a shock when I landed on 'im. Thought all me birthdays had come at once.—Nino Culotta (John O'Grady), *They're A Weird Mob*, p. 116, 1957
- She sat on his knee and pulled his white whiskers and ruffled his white hair, and the Fourth mate thought all his birthdays had come at once.—Les Such, *A Yen for Yokohama*, p. 58, 1963
- Once you've wrapped yourself around a few ice colds you'll feel as though all your birthdays have come at once!—Barry Humphries, *The Wonderful World of Barry McKenzie*, p. 28, 1968

birthday suit *noun*
a state of nudity *UK, 1771*
- "Why don't you go back to your place and change into something comfortable? "My birthday suit?"—Robert Gover, *The Maniac Responsible*, p. 115, 1963
- It's a flamin' stiff!!! In his birthday suit too, the dirty bastard!!! —Barry Humphries, *Bazza Pulls It Off!*, 1971

biscuit *noun*
1 a good-looking member of whatever sex attracts you *US*
- My brother was seeing this biscuit out here and she almost got him shot.—*Boyz N The Hood*, 1990
- But even the grunge-wear could not dull the brilliant polished-mineral black of his eyes or lessen the effect of his lavish eyelashes, pouting lips, or leanly muscled babe-of-life body. A biscuit, as Mab would say.—Francesca Lia Block, *I Was a Teenage Fairy*, p. 73, 1998
- —Connie Eble (Editor), *UNC-CH Campus Slang*, p. 1, Spring 1998

2 a promiscuous woman *US*
- —Kenn "Naz" Young, *Naz's Dictionary of Teen Slang*, p. 10, 1993

3 the buttocks *US*
- —Hyman E. Goldin et al., *Dictionary of American Underworld Lingo*, p. 28, 1950

4 the head *US, 1934*
- —Lou Shelly, *Hepcats Jive Talk Dictionary*, p. 7, 1945

5 a watch *US, 1905*
- Think our nut will show to take his biscuit out of hock?—Iceberg Slim (Robert Beck), *Doom Fox*, p. 175, 1978

6 a phonograph record *US*
- —Arnold Shaw, *Lingo of Tin-Pan Alley*, p. 7, 1950

7 in the context of live rock and roll, a deep bass note when it is felt as well as heard *US*
A term especially but not exclusively applied to the bass playing of Phil Lesh of the Grateful Dead.
- —Judi Sanders, *Da Bomb*, p. 2, 1997

8 a white tablet of methadone, a synthetic narcotic used to treat heroin addicts *US, 1972*
- —Richard A. Spears, *The Slang and Jargon of Drugs and Drink*, p. 46, 1986

9 fifty rocks of crack cocaine *US*
- —Mike Haskins, *Drugs*, p. 281, 2003
- —Office of National Drug Control Policy, *Drug Facts*, February 2003

10 a tablet of MDMA, the recreational drug best known as ecstasy *UK*
- Biscuits – Big, flat and granular. None to date includes a cream filling.—Gareth Thomas, *This Is Ecstasy*, p. 55, 2002

11 the hallucinogenic drug, peyote *US*
- —Jay Robert Nash, *Dictionary of Crime*, p. 30, 1992

12 a handgun *US*
- —Joseph E. Ragen and Charles Finston, *Inside the World's Toughest Prison*, p. 791, 1962
- "You have the biscuit?" Godineaux asked, using street slang for a gun.— *New York Post*, p. 4, 28th May 2000

13 a black prisoner *US*
- —John R. Armore and Joseph D. Wolfe, *Dictionary of Desperation*, p. 20, 1976

14 a can of c-rations *US*
Vietnam war usage.
- —Linda Reinberg, *In the Field*, p. 22, 1991

15 used as a euphemism for 'bitch' *US*
- Drop the biscuit. (I will!)—Eminem (Marshall Mathers), *Guilty Conscience*, 1999

16 a fool, an idiot *SOUTH AFRICA*
- John, you biscuit!— *Surfrikan Slang*, 2004

biscuit *adjective*
easy *US*
- —Vann Wesson, *Generation X Field Guide and Lexicon*, p. 20, 1997

biscuit bitch *noun*
a female Red Cross volunteer *US, 1983*
Vietnam war usage; less common than the more popular **DOUGHNUT DOLLY**.
- —Linda Reinberg, *In the Field*, p. 22, 1991

biscuit box *noun*
a Ford Transit van, or other vehicle of similar style *UK*
When struck, an unladen van has a similar tonal quality to an empty biscuit tin.
- —Peter Chippindale, *The British CB Book*, p. 161, 1981

biscuit class *noun*
economy class air travel on a small route *NEW ZEALAND, 1987*
A playful allusion to 'business class' travel and the biscuits given to economy class passengers.
- —Harry Orsman, *A Dictionary of Modern New Zealand Slang*, p. 10, 1999

Biscuit Foot McKinnon *nickname*
used as a nickname for a stereotypical Cape Bretoner *CANADA*
Because of the large Scottish settlement of this part of Nova Scotia, many people have the same last name: MacDonald, McKinnon, and so forth. Nicknames are common to distinguish family members with the same first name, too. 'When a group of strikers raided the Company Store in 1925, a man named McKinnon was injured when a box of biscuits fell from a top shelf and crushed his foot' (Mellor, 1983).
- —Richard MacKinnon, *The Use of English in Nova Scotia*, p. 71, 1999: 'Use of nicknames in Cape Breton'

biscuits *noun*
1 money *US*
- —Bill Davis, *Jawjacking*, p. 18, 1977

2 crack cocaine *UK*
From **BISCUIT** (a measure of crack).
- —Mike Haskins, *Drugs*, p. 281, 2003

biscuits and cheese *noun*
the knees *UK, 1960*
Rhyming slang, remembered in use during World War 2, sometimes shortened to 'biscuits'.

biscuit snatcher *noun*
the hand; a finger *US*
- —Lavada Durst, *The Jives of Dr. Hepcat*, p. 11, 1953

bi-sex *noun*
bisexual sex *UK, 2003*

bish *noun*
a *bishop* *UK, 1937*
- First the Bish, now this. What a day for insolence.—*The Guardian*, 26th July 2002

bish, bash, bosh; bish-bash-bosh *adjective*
rough and ready; also used in a semi-exclamatory sense as an echoic representation of anything swiftly expedited *UK*
- [M]y pals are learnin about "this is how the old canister [the head] works, bish, bash, bosh," and I guess there is a lot of truth in that old voodoo[.]—J.J. Connolly, *Layer Cake*, p. 40, 2000
- What they do well is to trade on the stereotypical bish, bash, bosh culture of wideboys[.]—*The Guardian*, 11th November 2000
- The bish-bash-bosh streets are cruised angrily by villainous-looking cars driven by villainous-looking types.—*The Guardian*, 30th April 2001
- He's the chirpy chippy chappy whose 'bish bash bosh' style of cooking made him a celebrity in his own lunchtime.—*The Observer*, 14th April 2002

bishop *noun*
1 the penis *US, 1916*
Used in a variety of expressions that refer to male masturbation.
- —Collin Baker et al., *College Undergraduate Slang Study Conducted at Brown University*, p. 80, 1968
- [B]anging his bishop[.]—Ann Barr and Peter York, *The Official Sloane Ranger Handbook*, p. 158, 1982
- I banged the bishop over this one more times than I care to count. —Armistead Maupin, *Babycakes*, p. 75, 1984

2 a private investigator *UK*
- —Peter McCabe, *Apple to the Core*, 1972

bissom; besom *noun*
a slovely woman *UK: SCOTLAND, 1911*
Dialect.
- Och, I'm sorry to be such a moaning-faced bissom[.]—Ian Pattison, *Rab C. Nesbitt*, 1988

bisto *noun*
a fart *UK*
From the advertising slogan 'Aaah Bisto...' savouring the aroma of a branded gravy.
- —Jonathan Blyth, *The Law of the Playground*, p. 16, 2004

bit *noun*
1 a prison sentence *US, 1866*
- Now that I was in the money and had done two bits in the pen, I got more respect from the gang.—Mezz Mezzrow, *Really the Blues*, p. 44, 1946
- He was sent up for his first real bit when he was 16.—Hubert Selby Jr, *Last Exit to Brooklyn*, p. 42, 1957
- Everybody wants to know your bit, big or small, maybe to measure his hope by it.—Piri Thomas, *Down These Mean Streets*, p. 247, 1967
- By the time he was twenty-three he had done four bits in the joint. —Iceberg Slim (Robert Beck), *Pimp*, p. 33, 1969
- Yeah, it was the summer of 1967 and I was once again awaiting transfer to the world's largest walled prison for a new bit - eighteen months to two years.—A.S. Jackson, *Gentleman Pimp*, p. 7, 1973
- Thirty-six month bit I did.—Edwin Torres, *Carlito's Way*, p. 20, 1975
- By this time his looks had coarsened some as a result of his bit in San Quentin at the end of the '50s.—Herbert Huncke, *Guilty of Everything*, p. 95, 1990
- Jack Hardy, he worked for a safe company after he did a six-year bit. —*Casino*, 1995
- —Angela Devlin, *Prison Patter*, p. 27, 1996

2 an interest; an affected mannerism; a role *US*
- "What a drag!" said Red. "What's the bit?" "Hangoversville, for all I know," said her mother.—Steve Allen, *Bop Fables*, p. 37, 1955
- She had done the champagne-and-stout bit, the Westhampton bit, the French poodle bit.—Max Shulman, *Rally Round the Flag, Boys!*, p. 71, 1957
- Aly's been calling her long-distance ever since he left, and doing the flowers-and-jewels bit.—*San Francisco Call-Bulletin*, p. 18, 16th December 1957
- One of the changes of our times is this Prom bit.—*San Francisco Call-Bulletin*, p. 22, 19 June 1957
- Kim Novak is doing the intellectual bit. Reading scads of books. —*San Francisco Call-Bulletin*, p. 24, 21st November 1957

3 a woman, especially when regarded sexually *UK, 1923*
- [T]hat tidy bit off the telly (and what a dirty little bitch she must be, eh? Phwoaaar)..—Christopher Brookmyre, *Boiling a Frog*, p. 105, 2000

4 sexual intercourse *AUSTRALIA*
- Don't those society dames have a bit when they get that way? —Robert S. Close, *Love Me Sailor*, p. 21, 1945
- He just lived it up. Booze, bits. A simple soul.—A. Hunter, *Gently Coloured*, 1969
- And what's more, if she is going to have a bit off on the side, she's more likely to keep it that way, on the side.—*Flame*, p. 11, 1972
- Like a bit, Sal?—Dorothy Hewett, *The Chapel Perilous*, p. 66, 1972
- —Lance Peters, *The Dirty Half-Mile*, p. 92, 1979

5 an activity *US*
- —Burton H. Wolfe, *The Hippies*, p. 203, 1968

6 used as a meaningless embellishment of the preceding noun *US*
- In the white-collar canyons of Manhattan, the smart-talk boys are almost constantly "doing" some kind of "bit." If they want to propose going to lunch, they say: "Let's do the lunch bit." If they see a motion picture, they "do the movie bit."—*Philadelphia Evening Bulletin*, 11th October 1955

7 twelve and a half cents *US, 1821*
- "Two bits!" he yelled to the boy who took the hat.—Irving Shulman, *The Amboy Dukes*, p. 228, 1947
- It is customary to give her four bits for the pro in the powder-room. —Jack Lait and Lee Mortimer, *New York Confidential*, p. 221, 1948
- I had to panhandle two bits for the bus. I finally hit a Greek minister who was standing around the corner. He gave me the quarter with a nervous lookaway.—Jack Kerouac, *On the Road*, p. 107, 1957

8 twelve dollars and fifty cents *US, 1929*
- Sweet meat, you wouldn't be happy, respect me, couldn't love me if say I became a funky tire changer for six bits a week to support us and whatsit's name?—Iceberg Slim (Robert Beck), *Doom Fox*, p. 75, 1978

9 your home or home area *UK: SCOTLAND*
- —Michael Munro, *The Patter, Another Blast*, 1988

10 a bullet *UK*
- —Dave Courtney, *Dodgy Dave's Little Black Book*, p. 7, 2001

▸ **champ at the bit; chomp at the bit**
to be enthusiastically eager *UK, 1645*
From a horse's characteristic behaviour.
- [D]on't think for a minute the overlords aren't champing at the bit it could become a nation of triads.—Robert Ludlum, *The Bourne Supremacy*, p. 556, 1986
- Ariel Sharon, a bellicose man who seemed to be chomping at the bit to start a war[.]—Ronald Reagan, *Ronald Reagan*, p. 418, 1990

▸ **pull a bit**
to serve a prison sentence *US*
- I thought about Oscar and wondered if he could pull his bit or if he would go back to his parents in a pine box, or worse to the crazy farm.—Iceberg Slim (Robert Beck), *Pimp*, p. 51, 1969

▸ **take the bit out of**
to exhaust someone *UK: SCOTLAND*
- Those stairs of yours fair take the bit out of me.—Michael Munro, *The Patter, Another Blast*, 1988

▸ **wee red bit**
the glowing end of a cigarette, especially when used as a means of lighting another cigarette *UK: SCOTLAND*
- Ah've no goat any matches, but Ah'll gie ye a wee red bit.—Michael Munro, *The Patter, Another Blast*, 1988

bita *noun*
a bit of *UK*
Phonetic laziness.
- [W]e're out to collect a nice bita wedginald from snake face. —J.J. Connolly, *Know Your Enemy [britpulp]*, p. 151, 1999

bitaine *noun*
a prostitute *UK*
- —Paul Baker, *Polari*, p. 165, 2002
- —*Attitude*, July 2003

bit bashing *noun*
low level, tedious computer programming *US*
- —Eric S. Raymond, *The New Hacker's Dictionary*, p. 60, 1991

bit bucket *noun*

in computing, the mythical place where lost information goes *US*

- —Guy L. Steele et al., *The Hacker's Dictionary*, p. 33, 1983

bitch *noun*

1 a woman *UK, 1713*

Although Grose considered it 'the most offensive appellation that can be given to an English woman,' it is used in this sense with no derogatory intent; it is dismissive or patronising, based on gender rather than the unpleasant and lewd characteristics of earlier and concurrent usages. Comedian Richard Blackwood (b.1972) used 'bitch' in this sense, referring to Queen Elizabeth II, during an edition of BBC television's *Have I Got News For You* in October 2000. Six viewers complained to the Broadcasting Standards Commission. The BBC argued 'Richard Blackwood was using the term as it is currently used, for example, in British and American Rap Music simply to mean "woman", and not as a term of abuse'. The complaints were not upheld.

- Johnny was always telling us about bitches. To Johnny, every chick was a bitch. Even mothers were bitches. Of course, there were some nice bitches, but they were still bitches.—Claude Brown, *Manchild in the Promised Land*, p. 113, 1965
- I know you been traveling a lot of Europe and used to 'dem harems' and things so I brought you four bitches. They're going to do anything you ask them to[.]—Babs Gonzales, *I Paid My Dues*, p. 84, 1967
- [W]e voted to split to a strip bar and spent the evening boozing and picking up bitches.—Jamie Mandelkau, *Buttons*, p. 89, 1971
- Bitch involves many connotations. It is, of course, allied to White middle-class usage, buit is far from synonymous with it. Sometimes it is used insultingly or as a curse, but often it is used casually and without malice[.]—Christina and Richard Milner, *Black Players*, p. 32, 1972
- Hey baby, how many times do I have to tell you that bitch is a term of endearment? It depends on the tone of voice the person used. —Donald Goines, *El Dorado Red*, p. 21, 1974
- And if you bitches talk shit I'll have to put the smack down[.]—Dr Dre, *Nuthin' But a 'G' Thang*, 1992

2 a despicable woman *UK, 1400*

- Don't get me wrong; I never reacted to her queen-hell-bitch persona in ways that would encourage the behavior.—Daniel Jones, *The Bastard on the Couch*, p. 142, 2004

3 the person taking the passive role in a male homosexual relationship; a feminine or weak man *US, 1923*

- He was neither a wolf nor a wolverine but just a pleasant bitch who had a crush on me.—Chester Himes, *Cast the First Stone*, p. 72, 1952
- —Donald Webster Cory and John P. LeRoy, *The Homosexual and His Society*, p. 261, 1963: 'A lexicon of homosexual slang'
- — Florida Legislative Investigation Committee (Johns Committee), *Homosexuality and Citizenship in Florida*, 1964: 'Glossary of homosexual terms and deviate acts'
- The boyfriend is some kind of vague engineer. Awful-looking little bitch.—William Burroughs, *Queer*, p. 23, 1985
- I ain't nobody's bitch, you a bitch, Bitch. You a bitch, your daddy's a bitch and your momma's a bitch!—*Boyz N The Hood*, 1990
- Archie was the bitch and Jughead was the butch.—*Chasing Amy*, 1997
- You want to be my bitch or you want to be someone else's bitch, bitch?—Joel Rose, *Kill Kill Faster Faster*, p. 118, 1997
- TYRONE: You know that I love you. COLONEL: I like hearing you say it. TYRONE: You're my bitch. You always will be.—*Boogie Nights*, 1997
- And he said you're the bitch and you're the butch.—Kevin Smith, *Jay and Silent Bob Strike Back*, p. 11, 2001
- —Paul Baker, *Polari*, p. 165, 2002

4 a sexual submissive of either gender in a sado-masochistic relationship *UK*

Generally attached to a possessive pronoun.

- The sound of a voice I barely recognize as mine, moaning, "I'm your bitch, fuck me harder."—Val McDermid (Editors: Stella Duffy and Lauren Henderson), *Metamorphosis [Tart Noir]*, p. 19, 2002

5 a remarkable person or thing *US, 1943*

- Jack, I finally made it,I I was a musician. If you'll pardon my beat-up English, ain't that a bitch.—Mezz Mezzrow, *Really the Blues*, p. 56, 1946

6 something that is difficult or unpleasant *UK, 1814*

- "That's a bitch," Robell said sympathetically.—Bernard Wolfe, *The Late Risers*, p. 263, 1954
- And a kid like this they give eight years to for nothing. Ain't that a bitch.—Darryl Ponicsan, *The Last Detail*, p. 34, 1970
- The Moore School was known for misfits, and I could tell from one look at the niggers that went there that this school was a bitch. —A.S. Jackson, *Gentleman Pimp*, p. 17, 1973
- I heard Prohibition was a btich, but the dope rumbles sure has buried a lot of people in my time.—Edwin Torres, *Carlito's Way*, p. 93, 1975
- You can bet that Texas boy, Charles Whitman, the fella who shot all them guys from that tower, I'll bet you green money that the first little black dot that he took a bead on, was the bitch of the bunch.—*True Romance*, 1993
- If I can't fly anymore, I'm gonna have a bitch of a time gettin' my brand.—*Jackie Brown*, 1997
- The traffic was a bitch.—Greg Williams, *Diamond Geezers*, p. 99, 1997

7 in the youth trend for 'souped-up' motor-scootering, a driver's scooter *UK*

- [I]t's no surprise to hear one young rider referring to his bike as his "bitch".—*The Independent Magazine*, p. 17, 28th August 2004

8 in a deck of playing cards, any queen; in the game of hearts, the queen of spades *US, 1900*

- —Joseph Weingarten, *American Dictionary of Slang*, p. 29, 1954

9 in chess, the queen *US*

- Checkschmuck! The Slang of the Chess Player—*American Speech*, p. 232, Autumn-Winter 1971

10 a complaint; an extended period of complaining *US, 1945*

- Have a bitch about the bosses[.]—*The Guardian*, 13th April 2001

11 a crude candle *CANADA*

- During the long winter evenings "office" work was done by candle-light and sometimes by nothing better than a "bitch" – a wick in a shallow tin of tallow.—*Canadian Geographical Journal*, p. 14/2, January 1961

12 a u-turn *US*

- —Connie Eble (Editor), *UNC-CH Campus Slang*, p. 3, Fall 2000

13 the middle position of the back seat of a car *US*

- —Pamela Munro, *U.C.L.A. Slang*, p. 62, 1989

▸ **put the bitch on you**

to file criminal charges accusing someone of being a habitual criminal *US*

- —Bruce Jackson, *Outside the Law*, p. 59, 1972

bitch *verb*

1 to complain *US, 1918*

- He's like... Oh shit... I don't wanna bitch about my old man. —Lanre Fehintola, *Charlie Says...*, p. 22, 2000

2 to inform *UK*

- Probably even TK didn't think I had bitched; he just seized a rumour.—Diran Adebayo, *My Once Upon A Time*, p. 109, 2000

3 to identify and punish someone as a habitual criminal *US, 1976*

- "While you wuz on Sick Bay I got bitched," Smoothbore cried over the crashing water.—Seth Morgan, *Homeboy*, p. 122, 1990

4 to ruin something *UK, 1823*

- —John Ayto, *The Oxford Dictionary of Slang*, p. 413, 1998

bitch about *verb*

to be unreliable and troublesome; to change or renegotiate arrangements *UK*

- "You wouldn't bitch me about, would you?" "We've got to discuss things."—Derek Bickerton, *Payroll*, p. 7, 1959

bitch-ass *adjective*

weak, effeminate *US*

- Are you sayin' you want me to play Queensberry Rules with that bitch-ass motherfucker?—Christopher Brookmyre, *The Sacred Art of Stealing*, p. 350, 2002

bitch-ass nigga *noun*

a weak or effeminate black male *US*

- [H]arrass them bitch-ass niggas[.]—Big L *Da Graveyard*, 1995

bitch bar *noun*

anything that serves as a hand grip for a motorcyle passenger *US*

Biker (motorcyle) usage, alluding to a female passenger.

- It became a style and look: a bitch bar (sissy bar) so your chick could lay back.—Ralph "Sonny" Barger, *Hell's Angel*, p. 61, 2000

bitch basket *noun*

a Volkswagen Cariolet *US*

- —Vann Wesson, *Generation X Field Guide and Lexicon*, p. 20, 1997

bitch bath *noun*

a cleaning of the body using little water, powder or other odour-masking agents *US, 1953*

- —Frederic G. Cassidy, *Dictionary of American Regional English*, p. 248, 1985

bitch blow *noun*

a violent blow *BAHAMAS*

- —John A. Holm, *Dictionary of Bahamian English*, p. 19, 1982

bitch box *noun*
a public address loudspeaker system *US, 1945*
- — *American Speech*, p. 54, February 1947: 'Pacific war language'
- The Karp punched the general alarm and got on the bitch box to all the towers on the perimeter. — Malcolm Braly, *On the Yard*, p. 198, 1967
- — Bobby Seale, *A Lonely Rage*, 1978
- I was awakened by a loud banging on the locked door coupled with the noise coming from the loudspeaker – the bitch box, we called it, from dispatch. — Bobby Seale, *A Lonely Rage*, p. 126, 1978
- — Gregory Clark, *Words of the Vietnam War*, p. 58, 1990
- Welch called down to the ship's bridge, using the "bitch box," the intercom system that connected important parts of the ship with each other. — Gerry Carroll, *North S*A*R*, p. 56, 1991

bitchcakes *adjective*
aggressive *US*
- — Connie Eble (Editor), *UNC-CH Campus Slang*, p. 3, April 2004

bitchen; bitching *adjective*
excellent *US*
- It was a bitchen day, too. — Frederick Kohner, *Gidget*, p. 4, 1957
- — Miss Cone, *The Slang Dictionary (Hawthorne High School)*, 1965
- — John M. Kelly, *Surf and Sea*, p. 280, 1965
- — *Current Slang*, p. 1, Summer 1966
- "Wouldn 't that be bitchen?" says Tom Coman. Bitchen is a surfer's term that means "great," usually. — Tom Wolfe, *The Pump House Gang*, p. 19, 1968
- I add 20 points to my average if I know I look bitchin' out there. — Jim Bouton, *Ball Four*, p. 27, 1970
- It was so bitchin' mon. Everybody is talking about it. — *Fast Times at Ridgemont High*, 1982
- Encino is like SO BITCHEN! — Moon Unit and Frank Zappa, *Valley Girl*, 1982
- Our royalty was sixty or seventy cents per double LP, which wasn't so bitchen either. On paper, at least, we had a flop. — Frank Zappa, *The Real Frank Zappa Book*, p. 82, 1989
- Gone were the leotards and the tank tops and the bitchin' black jumpsuit that made me look like a paratrooper. — Rita Ciresi, *Pink Slip*, p. 109, 1999

bitchen twitchen *adjective*
excellent *US*
- — Mimi Pond, *The Valley Girl's Guide to Life*, p. 52, 1982

bitcher *noun*
a habitual criminal *US*
- — Marlena Kay Nelson, *Rookies to Roaches*, p. 7, 1963

bitches' Christmas *noun*
Halloween *US*
A glorious homosexual holiday, erotic and exotic.
- — Guy Strait, *The Lavendar Lexicon*, 1 June 1964
- — *The Guild Dictionary of Homosexual Terms*, p. 4, 1965
- — Dale Gordon, *The Dominion Sex Dictionary*, p. 29, 1967
- They were singing 'Don us now our gay apparel' on Bitches' Christmas. — Bruce Rodgers, *Queens' Vernacular*, p. 32, 1972
- — Robert Wilson, *Playboy's Book of Forbidden Words*, p. 38, 1972
- In some homosexual newspapers it's called Bitches' Christmas. — *San Francisco Examiner*, p. 3, 1st November 1976

bitch fight *noun*
a quarrel between ostentatiously effeminate male homosexuals *US*
- — Guy Strait, *The Lavendar Lexicon*, 1964

bitch fit *noun*
a temper tantrum *US*
- Carey-Lee, secure in his knowledge that he is loved, does not throw a "bitch fit" when his nellie neighbor, Tommy (Edward Dunn) intimates that something more than a simple "visit" may have taken place while he was away. — *Screw*, p. 20, 27th October 1969

bitch hook *noun*
an all-purpose quick-release hook for use with a tractor and chain *CANADA*
- The name "bitch hook" comes from a hole at one end of a slot in the long, flat central part of the device. A chain may be pulled through the hole, slide down and catch. When it is pulled back up to the hole, it releases quickly. — Lewis Poteet, *Talking Country*, p. 23, 1992

Bitchin' Betty *noun*
in the Canadian Air Force, an automatic audible vocal warning system of danger *CANADA*
- The pre-recorded voice [to give warnings] is female, because the higher-pitched female voice is more easily distinguished from background noises. Therefore, the term Bitchin' Betty. — Tom Langeste, *Words on the Wing*, p. 28–29, 1995

bitching *noun*
the act of complaining about or disparaging someone or something *US*
From the verb **BITCH** (to complain).
- I'm afraid the others will notice – the bitching, the gossip, they'd have a field day. — Jane Rogers, *Lucky*, p. 15, 1999

bitching *adjective*
used as a negative intensifier *US, 1928*
An abbreviation of 'son-of-a-bitching'.
- But he'd manage it somehow. He bichin' well had to. — Tom Ronan, *Moleskin Midas*, 1956
- — J. E. Lighter, *Historical Dictionary of American Slang, Volume 1*, p. 171, 1994

bitching week *noun*
on an Atlantic weather ship, the third week of a four week tour of station
Derives from **BITCH** (to complain) as this is the time when tempers are shortest.
- — J.G. Drummond, *Gap of Danger*, 1963

bitch kitty *noun*
an excellent instance of, or example of, something *US, 1944*
- I was havinng one bitch kitty of a time tunning out the interracial sewer mouth shucking and jiving[.] — Iceberg Slim (Robert Beck), *Airtight Willie and Me*, p. 3, 1979

bitch lamp *noun*
an improvised lamp *US*
- — Harold Wentworth and Stuart Berg Flexner, *Dictionary of American Slang*, p. 40, 1960

bitch money *noun*
earnings from prostitution and pimping *UK*
- — Joanna Traynor, *Bitch Money*, cover, 2001

bitch off *verb*
to irritate someone *US*
- — *American Speech*, p. 56, Spring-Summer 1975: 'Razorback slang'

bitch on wheels *noun*
a person, especially a woman, with a truly nasty disposition *US*
- — John D. Bell et al., *Loosely Speaking*, p. 2, 1966

bitch out *verb*
to criticise someone harshly *US*
- — Connie Eble (Editor), *UNC-CH Campus Slang*, p. 1, Fall 1986

bitch pad *noun*
a small seat mounted behind the regular seat on a motorcycle *US*
- — Lewis Poteet, *Car & Motorcyle Slang*, p. 30, 1992

bitch pie *noun*
a pizza with pepperoni, mushroom and sausage *US*
The initials of the toppings – PMS – suggest a cranky woman.
- — *Maledicta*, p. 8, 1996: 'Domino's pizza jargon'

bitch piss *noun*
bottled alcopop (branded alcoholic beverage with the characteristics of a soft drink) or other alcoholic drinks deemed to be for feminine consumption *UK*
- What's that bitch piss you're drinking, get a pint dahn yer. — *www.LondonSlang.com*, June 2002

bitch session *noun*
a group airing of complaints *US*
- — Harold Wentworth and Stuart Berg Flexner, *Dictionary of American Slang*, p. 40, 1960

bitch slap *verb*
1 to slap someone full across the face *US*
- Kint's lawyer comes in and five minutes later the D.A. comes out looking like he'd been bitch-slapped by the boogey man. — *The Usual Suspects*, 1995
- — Pamela Munro, *U.C.L.A. Slang*, p. 30, 1997
- Dr. Evil charges at Klansman and starts to bitch slap him. — *Austin Powers*, 1999
- His old lady was screaming, so one of the Misfits bitch-slapped her, making her lay down on the floor. — Ralph "Sonny" Barger, *Hell's Angel*, p. 85, 2000

- But we bitch-slapped that little fuck and sent him packing, so it's smooth sailing. —Kevin Smith, *Jay and Silent Bob Strike Back*, p. 44, 2001

2 by extension, to soundly defeat or better someone or something *US*

- An announcer in Vancouver said the Seattle Mariners baseball team had "bitch-slapped" its opponent. The Canadian Broadcast Standards Committee says, "Broadcasters shall not telecast programming which promotes any aspect of violence against women." — *Toronto Globe and Mail*, p. R2, 18th April 2002
- A couple of weeks after I did the show, I was stopped by a TV news producer (not from CBS) who said, "Man, you really bitch-slapped Bernie Goldberg." —Al Franken, *Lies*, p. 28, 2003

bitchsplitter *noun*

the penis *US*

Used on-air in the telling of a joke by syndicated US broadcaster Mancow Muller, adopted as a name by a Canadian death metal band.

- —Chris Lewis, *The Dictionary of Playground Slang*, p. 32, 2003

bitch up *verb*

to spoil or ruin something *BARBADOS*

- —Frank A. Collymore, *Barbadian Dialect*, p. 19, 1965
- —John A. Holm, *Dictionary of Bahamian English*, p. 19, 1982

bitch with a capital C *noun*

a truly hideous person *US*

A suggestion of **CUNT**.

- I was a total bitch with a capital C. — *Stuck on You*, 2003

bitchy *adjective*

malicious, spiteful *US, 1925*

bite *noun*

1 a small meal or a snack *US, 1899*

- Think I'll go get a bite to eat, then. —Jim Thompson, *A Swell-Looking Babe*, p. 44, 1954
- I had seen them before, when Brenda and I had gone out for a bite in the afternoon[.] —Philip Roth, *Goodbye, Columbus*, p. 68, 1959
- "You're going to have some lunch before you go, aren't you?" "I'll get a bite donwtown.' —J.D. Salinger, *Franny and Zooey*, p. 117, 1961
- While I grabbed a bite, I called the Naples Cafe, got a number for me to call Art and dialed it. —Mickey Spillane, *Me, Hood!*, p. 44, 1963
- You wanna grab a bite or something like that? — *Manhattan*, 1979
- You guys go on inside, get yourselves a bite. — *The Blues Brothers*, 1980

2 the portion of the money bet by gamblers taken as the share for the establishment sponsoring the gambling *US*

- —George Percy, *The Language of Poker*, p. 10, 1988

3 a price *US, 1958*

- You want the blue too? The bite is two for fifty slats. —Iceberg Slim (Robert Beck), *Pimp*, p. 92, 1969
- —Kenn "Naz" Young, *Naz's Underground Dictionary*, p. 15, 1973

4 in motor racing, traction between the tyres and track *US*

- When tires grab the ground, we can say they have bite, too. —Ed Radlauer, *Drag Racing Pix Dix*, p. 7, 1970

5 something that is very disagreeable *US*

- If they can't get the car, that's the way the ball bounces (tough luck) or ain't that a bite? (too bad). — *Newsweek*, 8th October 1951

▸ put the bite on

to extort *AUSTRALIA, 1919*

- They put the bite on guys who are afraid to talk or who can't talk. —Mickey Spillane, *Kiss Me Deadly*, p. 43, 1952
- And in Denver, in front of the Brown Palace Hotel, I'd put the bite on a big flashy-looking guy for coffee money. —Jim Thompson, *Savage Night*, p. 25, 1953
- He'll pop in any minute and put the bite on you, as soon as he has his gymnasts climbing ropes or playing basketball or pulling their dummies. —Evan Hunter, *The Blackboard Jungle*, 1954
- And don't get the idea that I'm trying to put a bite on you – Like Goble. —Raymond Chandler, *Playback*, p. 89, 1958
- I thought I'd pop down to her studio one evening with a view to putting the bite on for some reddy [cash]. —Derek Raymond (Robin Cook), *The Crust on its Uppers*, p. 31, 1962
- His car had broken down, and he left it in Nygan, and put the bite on me for a lift. —John O'Grady, *It's Your Shout, Mate!*, p. 31, 1972
- "Now, if some of you out there are worried about us puttin' the bite to you, forget it, don't cost but twenty-five cents to join, and I might add," he added for emphasis, "if you think of yourself as a black brother, you'll join." —Donald Goines, *Black Gangster*, p. 94, 1977
- I'm not putting in the bite for a lousy quid. —Roy Higgins and Tom Prior, *The Jockey Who Laughed*, p. 82, 1982

bite *verb*

1 to copy or steal another person's style, especially to copy a breakdancing move, or to plagiarise a rap lyric *US, 1979*

- Biting moves is really wack, but everyone does it. —Bradley Elfman, *Breakdancing*, p. 40, 1984
- —Connie Eble (Editor), *UNC-CH Campus Slang*, p. 9, October 1986
- —Terry Williams, *The Cocaine Kids*, p. 135, 1989
- You wacker than the motherfucker you bit your style from —Eminem (Marshall Mathers), *Just Don't Give a Fuck*, 1999
- Even if you bit someone's move from the week before, you took that move and you made it your own. —Alex Ogg, *The Hip Hop Years [quoting Jorge 'Fabel' Pabn]*, p. 32, 1999
- In spite of unabashed bitin' – Big Bank Hank uses a rap from Grandmaster Caz – the song [Rapper's Delight] is a megahit[.] — *The Source She fell*, p. 136, March 2002

2 to ask someone for a loan of money *AUSTRALIA, 1912*

- —Patsy Adam-Smith, *Folklore of the Australian Railwaymen*, p. 119, 1969
- She'd put it on a horse on Sunday and the horse had run up a lane, and she wasn't game to bite hubby for another lot. —Sam Weller, *Old Bastards I Have Met*, p. 63, 1979

3 to be taken in, to be duped *UK*

A figurative use of the literal 'take the bait'.

- —Nigel Foster, *The Making of a Royal Marine Commando*, 1987

4 to be unfair or extremely distasteful *US*

- —John D. Bell et al., *Loosely Speaking*, p. 2, 1966
- You know what really bites; when people watch that cafeteria stuff on TV and see all those Geeks and Metalheads jumping around, they're going to think UnCool is the Rule at Westerburg. — *Heathers*, 1988

5 to itch *BARBADOS*

- My toes biting me too bad. —Frank A. Collymore, *Barbadian Dialect*, p. 19, 1965

6 to flex, and thus contract, the sphincter during anal sex *US*

- —Bruce Rodgers, *The Queens' Vernacular*, p. 32, 1972

▸ bite feathers

to lie on your stomach, especially in anticipation of anal sex *US*

- —Guy Strait, *The Lavendar Lexicon*, 1964

▸ bite it

to die *US, 1977*

- She bit it. — *Drugstore Cowboy*, 1988

▸ bite off more than you can chew

to be unable to complete any task that is too great for your ambitions *US, 1878*

- Hitler had bitten off more than he could chew by provoking the hostility of Britain and France[.] —John F. Pollard, *The Fascist Experience in Italy*, p. 5, 1998

▸ bite the bag

in computing, to fail, especially in a dramatic fashion *US*

- —Guy L. Steele et al., *The Hacker's Dictionary*, p. 28, 1983

▸ bite the big one

to die *US, 1979*

- Most people think of the Chateau as the place where Belushi bit the big one, but it's got a lot more going for it than that. —Armistead Maupin, *Maybe the Moon*, p. 142, 1992

▸ bite the brown

to perform mouth-to-anus sex *US*

- —Robert A. Wilson, *Playboy's Book of Forbidden Words*, p. 38, 1972

▸ bite the dust

to go down in defeat *US*

- —Connie Eble (Editor), *UNC-CH Campus Slang*, p. 1, Fall 1982

▸ bite the pillow

to take the recipient role in anal sex *AUSTRALIA*

- 'He bites pillows,' she whimpers. —Kathy Lette, *Girls' Night Out*, p. 222, 1987

▸ bite to the bone

to punish someone with all the severity allowed under the law *US*

- — *American Speech*, p. 267, December 1962: 'the language of traffic policemen'.

▸ bite your lips

to smoke a marijuana cigarette *US, 1959*

- Bite your lip and take a trip. —Curtis Mayfield, *Move On Up*, 1970
- —Richard A. Spears, *The Slang and Jargon of Drugs and Drink*, p. 217, 1986
- —Mike Haskins, *Drugs*, p. 290, 2003

bite and a button *noun*
a negligible price *UK*
- She probably bought them from some old dear "for a bite and a button" as the antique trade says enviously of anything cheaply got. —Jonathan Gash, *The Ten Word Game*, p. 32, 2003

bite in the britches *noun*
in trucking, a speeding ticket *US*
- —Elementary Electronics, *Dictionary of CB Lingo*, p. 51, 1976

biter *noun*
1 a copier of breakdance moves; a plagiarist of rap lyrics *US*
- Back in the days you could get booed out of the circle [...] if you looked too much like the next man. They'll tell right off you're a biter and you're wack [inferior]. —Alex Ogg, *The Hip Hop Years [quoting Jorge 'Fabel' Pabon]*, p. 32–33, 1999

2 the vagina *US*
- a out on the floor, after a long sexy masturbatory dance, her miniskirt around her hips; her rosy biter winking its hairy eye at me where I sat[.] —Clarence Major, *All-Night Visitors*, p. 201, 1998

3 a tooth *US*
- During this period I sat in on a recording date with the Pollack band, just a couple hours after I'd had a gang of teeth yanked, because my biters were going bad along with all my other parts. —Mezz Mezzrow, *Really the Blues*, p. 188, 1946

bit hurt *noun*
the agony of withdrawal from a drug addiction *US*
- Then the Big Hurt pushed aside all thinking and Joe could only lie hugging his cramped middle[.] —Seth Morgan, *Homeboy*, p. 96, 1990

bit much *noun*
used to describe, or in response to, anything that is excessive, too demanding, arrogant, objectionable, etc *UK, 1974*

bit 'na half people *noun*
a family that is just above the poverty line *GUYANA*
In collonial British Guyana currency, a 'bit' was a silver coin valued at 8 cents; 12 cents was a popular retail food-price marker for items of poor fare in markets.
- —Richard Allsopp, *Dictionary of Caribbean English Usage*, p. 103, 1996

bit of *noun*
used to stress an affection or sympathy for the noun it describes *UK, 1808*
- [A]s for this: two bits of kids bringing up a baby with no money and no prospects! —Mary Hooper, *(megan)2*, p. 38, 1999

bit of a bugger *noun*
a nuisance; a difficulty *UK*
- [I]t was just a bit of a bugger to get going in the morning. —Iain Aitch, *A Fête Worse Than Death*, p. 213, 2003

bit of alright; bit of all right *noun*
1 a sexually attractive person *UK, 1898*
- There's always room for a bit of skirt! Is she a bit of alright? —Barry Humphries, *The Wonderful World of Barry McKenzie*, p. 29, 1968
- [T]he manager's wife I think she was and a bit of alright to boot. —Danny King, *The Bank Robber Diaries*, p. 65, 2002

2 something excellent, especially an unexpected treat or a stroke of good luck *UK, 1907*
Sometimes also a 'little bit of all right'.
- "That's a bit of all right," said the guard, cutting off a piece of the stem and putting it into his mouth. —Alexander Macdonald, *In the Land of Pearl and Gold*, 1907

bit of black *noun*
a black person objectified sexually *UK*
- I'd like to see how you'd handle a bit of black. Or vice versa. —Ted Lewis, *Jack Carter's Law*, p. 62, 1974

bit of bod *noun*
the body as an object of sexual interest *UK*
- Hey, Willie, do you want a bit of bod? —Margaret Powell, *The Treasure Upstairs*, 1970

bit of Braille *noun*
1 sexual fondling and groping *AUSTRALIA*
The Braille alphabet is read with fingertips – hence the image of feeling and touching.

2 a racing tip *AUSTRALIA*
Designed for the blind, the Braille alphabet is read by feeling; in horse racing gamblers mainly decide on bets by 'reading' form or because they have 'a feeling'.

bit of brush *noun*
a woman regarded and categorised as a sexual object; the act of sex *AUSTRALIA*
- —William Dick, *A Bunch of Ratbags*, 1965

bit of bum *noun*
from a male perspective, sex with another person; the person so desired objectified in a purely sexual context *UK, 1984*

bit of crackling *noun*
a woman regarded as a sexual object *UK, 1949*

bit of cunt *noun*
a woman regarded and categorised as a sex object; an act of sexual intercourse *UK, 1984*
- It's all a Macc Lad wants / Beer 'n' sex 'n' chips 'n' gravy / Tasty bit of cunt. —The Macc Lads, *Beer 'n' Sex 'n' Chips 'n' Gravy*, 1985

bit of dirt *noun*
a farm *NEW ZEALAND*
- To get your own bit of dirt has always been the aim of those get involved in farming. —John Gordon, *People, Places & Paddocks*, p. 81, 1987

bit of ebony *noun*
a black woman regarded as a sexual category *UK, 1984*
- A bit of Ebony and Ivory as they both take turns proving that it's all pink inside[.] —Internet pornography advertising at *Best Adult Content*, 2005

bit of elastic *noun*
the penis *UK*
- For me though, you can reserve your nice bit of elastic down there Nicky, do the trick just nicely. —Jeremy Cameron, *Brown Bread in Wengen*, p. 11, 1999

bit of fluff *noun*
a woman, especially when regarded sexually *UK, 1847*
- Was I simply a bit of fluff you found amusing to tease [?] —Cheryl Holt, *Deeper than Desire*, p. 92, 2004

bit of hard *noun*
1 an erection *UK*
- [G]ive a bit of hard for a bit of soft [of a man, to have sex]. —Laurie Atkinson, 1978

2 in homosexual sexual relations, a male partner *UK*
- —Paul Baker, *Polari*, p. 165, 2002

bit of hod *noun*
a promiscuous, or potentially promiscuous, girl *UK*
- At a rave, blast or orgy – all synonyms for party – a guy (never a boy) meets a bit of hod, or tart (whether or not she is). —*Sunday Times*, 8th September 1963

bit of kit *noun*
an item of equipment, especially mechanical or electrical *UK*
- They're real state of the art as well, laser sights, six hundred rounds a minute delivery, same bit of kit as the Yard's Diplomatic Protection Unit have got. —J.J. Connolly, *Layer Cake*, p. 80, 2000

bit of mess *noun*
a prostitute's lover who is neither ponce nor client *UK*
- —David Powis, *The Signs of Crime*, 1977

bit of nonsense *noun*
an easily achieved criminal act *UK*
- "A nice bit of nonsense," commented Louis, meaning a piece of villainy that had all the makings of a walk-over. —James Barlow, *The Burden of Proof*, 1968

bit of posh *noun*
an upper-class or socially superior young woman regarded as a sexual object *UK*
- Come and lie on the couch / With a nice bit of posh / from Burnham-On-Crouch —Ian Dury, *Billericay Dickie*, 1977

bit of rough *noun*
a male lover, categorised as of a lower social status, or a rougher background than the partner *UK*
The relationship defined may be homo- or heterosexual. Original usage described a female but from the mid-C20 the male predominates.
- I haven't had a bit of rough for too long. —Henry Sloane, *Sloane's Inside Guide to Sex & Drugs & Rock 'n' Roll*, p. 41, 1985
- They're howling for a bit of rough, this lot! —Kevin Sampson, *Powder*, p. 20, 1999
- She was that well bred and posh that she still acted like she was the top dog in the relationship and I was just some jolly bit of rough. —Ben Elton, *High Society*, p. 22, 2002

bit of skin *noun*
a woman viewed as a sex object *AUSTRALIA*
- Isn't that the loveliest bit of skin you've clapped eyes on? —John Wynnum, *Tar Dust*, p. 28, 1962

bit of skirt *noun*
a woman viewed as a sex object *AUSTRALIA, 1904*
- [Y]ou never chased a bit of skirt like some. —Wilda Moxham, *The Apprentice*, p. 81, 1969
- Fancy a flirt with a bit of skirt? —Stella Duffy, *The Guardian*, 11th March 1999

bit of slap and tickle *noun*
1 kissing and cuddling; sexual petting which may be considered as foreplay by one participant *UK*
- [M]aking sure my sister was still drawing the line between a bit of slap-and-tickle, and the unthinkable. — *The Guardian*, 11th November 2000

2 sexual intercourse *UK, 1984*
An extension of the previous sense.

bit of spare *noun*
anyone providing sexual favours, even on a short-term or occasional basis; an unattached woman, especially at a club, party or any place where men may be expected to look for a sexual companion or conquest *UK*
'Bit of' plus conventional use of 'spare' (available).
- I always got the impression that Maurice was down her on the look out for a bit of spare. —Roger Busley, *Garvey's Code*, 1978

bit of stray *noun*
a casual sexual acquaintance, usually female *UK*
- She was posh, too, and a lot brighter than his usual bits of stray. —Garry Bushell, *The Face*, p. 42, 2001

bit of tail *noun*
1 a woman regarded as a sexual object *UK, 1984*
2 an act of anal intercourse; an act of sexual intercourse where the male partner enters the female from behind *UK, 1984*

bit of the other *noun*
sexual intercourse *UK, 1984*
- Life is, after all, a bit of this, a bit of that and a bit of the other. — *The Observer*, 29th June 2003

bit of tickle *noun*
a woman regarded as a sexual object; sexual intercourse *UK*

bit of tit *noun*
a woman regarded as a sexual object; sex with a woman *UK*
- "I fancy a bit of tit tonight." "Lovely bit of tit, she was." — Beale, 1984

bit of work *noun*
a crime; a robbery *UK*
- —Angela Devlin, *Prison Patter*, p. 27, 1996
- [A]t some stage in their careers [they] have been involved in the same "bits of work"[.] — *The Guardian*, 28th September 2000

bit on the side *noun*
a secret lover in addition to your regular partner; a love affair; extra-marital sex *UK*
- —David Powis, *The Signs of Crime*, 1977
- —Louis S.Leland, *A Personal Kiwi Yankee Dictonary*, 1984
- [A] ladies' man who regarded a bit-on-the-side as harmless[.] —Mark Powell, *Snap*, p. 7–8, 2001

bits *noun*
1 the male genitals *UK*
Sympathetically of a baby boy, jocularly of a man.
- "Got all his bits, has he?" she asked the two doctors doubtfully. —Roy Lewis, *Witness My Death*, 1976

2 in betting, odds of 11–10 *UK*
- —John McCririck, *John McCririck's World of Betting*, p. 112, 1991

▸ **in bits**
emotionally distraught; tearful *UK*
- ["]You wanna see it! You wanna see it! Keva was in bits!" Keva nodded. "It's ... it's everything we hoped it'd be. It's beautiful." —Kevin Sampson, *Powder*, p. 234, 1999
- I looked at her, thinking she'd be in bits, but she wasn't. —Dave Courtney, *Stop the Ride I Want to Get Off*, p. 274, 1999
- All upset about Roger was he? – In bits, yeh. —Niall Griffiths, *Sheepshagger*, p. 191, 2001

▸ **to bits**
(of a specified emotion) extremely *UK, 1964*
- He's just gorgeous and I love him to bits. —Mary Hooper, *(megan)2*, p. 20, 1999

bits and bats *noun*
knick-knacks *UK, 1961*

bits and bobs *noun*
miscellaneous small articles *UK, 1896*
- [W]e've managed to offload a few bits and bobs ourselves but that's a lot of hassle[.] —Danny King, *The Burglar Diaries*, p. 61, 2001

bits and tits *noun*
the controls *AUSTRALIA*
- The fact that you were handling the bits and tits made just that difference. —W.R. Bennett, *Night Intruder*, p. 13, 1962

bits of kids *noun*
youngsters *UK*
- They were the kind who could afford it: they were older people not bits of kids[.] —Dave Courtney, *Stop the Ride I Want to Get Off*, p. 157, 1999

bits on the ear'ole *noun*
in betting, odds of 13–8 *UK*
From the **TICK-TACK** signal used by bookmakers, an elaboration of **EAR'OLE** (6–4).
- —John McCririck, *John McCririck's World of Betting*, p. 59, 1991

bit spit *noun*
any electronic communication *US*
- —Vann Wesson, *Generation X Field Guide and Lexicon*, p. 20, 1997

bitsy *adjective*
small, tiny *US, 1905*
- Always dressed to the hilt, white gloves and hats, bitsy waists just like their mother. —James Dodson, *Ben Hogan*, p. 71, 2004

bitter-mouth *verb*
to speak harshly *US*
- —Marcus Hanna Boulware, *Jive and Slang of Students in Negro Colleges*, 1947

bit twiddler *noun*
a computer operator *US*
- —Robert Kirk Mueller, *Buzzwords*, p. 46, 1974

bitty *noun*
a girl *US*
- —Anthony Romeo, *The Language of Gangs*, p. 16, 4th December 1962

bitty *adjective*
tiny *US, 1905*
A corruption and shortening of **ITSY-BITSY**.
- [H]e was sorta convinced already that there was something odd about this little-bitty nigger who tink he can beat somebody five times his size. —Cecil Brown, *The Life & Loves of Mr. Jiveass Nigger*, p. 64, 1969
- There never was a man who could stand up to Kokomo, and he started to wonder where this little-bitty nigger could get such confidence. —Christina and Richard Milner, *Black Players*, p. 175, 1972
- Little itty-bitty things accumulate. —Susan Hall, *Gentleman of Leisure*, p. 6, 1972
- Darrol Woods was saying "Two larceny from a person reduced from larceny not armed and a little bitty assault thing..." And Hunter was saying, "Little bitty ... little bitty fucking tire iron you used on the guy." —Elmore Leonard, *City Primeval*, p. 58, 1980

bitty box *noun*
a small computer, especially a single-tasking-only machine *US*
- —Eric S. Raymond, *The New Hacker's Dictionary*, p. 64, 1991

bitumen blonde *noun*
an Aboriginal woman *AUSTRALIA*
- — Thommo, *The Dictionary of Australian Swearing and Sex Sayings*, p. 17, 1985

bitzer; bitser; bitza *noun*
a dog of mixed breed *AUSTRALIA, 1936*
A shortening of the phrase 'bits of this and bits of that'.

- [T]his young navvy began to sool their 'bitza' on with a stick. —Patsy Adam-Smith, *Folklore of the Australian Railwaymen*, p. 154, 1969
- The two other regular companions on these trips were Bill's mare Les Thorogood and Bill's dog Tiger, a real Heinz 57 varieties bitser if ever I saw one. —Rex Hunt, *Tall Tales – and True*, p. 126, 1994

biz; bizz *noun*

1 business *US, 1861*

- I remember we were doing some biz near Munich last summer[.] —Derek Raymond (Robin Cook), *The Crust on its Uppers*, p. 23, 1962
- Rumor had it that there were quite a few pinks in the publishing biz. —Mary McCarthy, *The Group*, p. 185, 1963
- Lead you to draw bad conclusions (or "bad vibes" as they say in the rock biz) about what happened. —Abbie Hoffman, *Woodstock Nation*, p. 4, 1969
- [H]e had to stay in L.A. for the music biz, and if he stayed in L.A., Bobby would find him[.] —James Ellroy, *Suicide Hill*, p. 673, 1986
- The rockbiz presence was more than evidenced by Tony Secunda, the Move's outrageously extreme manager[.] —Mick Farren, *Give the Anarchist a Cigarette*, p. 119, 2001

2 the syringe and other equipment used by intravenous drug users *US*

- —Vincent J. Monteleone, *Criminal Slang*, p. 24, 1949
- —William D. Alsever, *Glossary for the Establishment and Other Uptight People*, p. 19, December 1970

3 a small amount of a drug *US*

- —Eugene Landy, *The Underground Dictionary*, p. 34, 1971

▸ do the bizz

to engage in sexual activity *IRELAND*

- Sure he's a face like an arse, Ma. Even Annie Murphy wouldn't do the bizz with Father Morton. —Joseph O'Connor, *Red Roses and Petrol*, p. 10, 1995

▸ in the biz bag

in trouble with police management *US*

- —*Los Angeles Times*, p. B8, 19th December 1994

▸ the biz

the 'profession', loosely the entertainment, theatre or film making business *UK, 1961*

An industry coinage that lends dignity to the least secure of employment paths.

bizarro *noun*

a bizarre person *US, 1980*

Influenced by, if not directly descended from, 'Bizarro' a comic-book villain who first challenged Superman in the late 1950s.

- [T]he reclusive bizarro I've been goofing on for the past year wants to come on my radio show. —Howard Stern, *Miss America*, p. 60, 1995

bizarro *adjective*

bizarre *US, 1971*

- Out here in the bizarro city by the bay, things are different. —Jim Carroll, *Forced Entries*, p. 130, 1987
- Hey, this question wouldn't be that bizarro thing you were blabbing about over the phone[.] —*Heathers*, 1988

biznatch; biznitch *noun*

used as a euphemism for 'bitch' in any sense *US*

From rapper JayZ.

- —Connie Eble (Editor), *UNC-CH Campus Slang*, p. 1, October 2002

bizotic *adjective*

unexpected, out of the ordinary *US*

- —*San Francisco Sunday Examiner & Chronicle*, p. 20, 2nd September 1984
- —Vann Wesson, *Generation X Field Guide and Lexicon*, p. 20, 1997

bizzazz *noun*

▷ see: BEZAZZ

bizzies; busies *noun*

the police *UK*

From the plural of **BUSY** (a detective, a CID officer), but all distiction of rank is lost.

- —Angela Devlin, *Prison Patter*, p. 27, 1996
- So we turned up and the bizzies are right up our arse. —Shaun Ryder, *Shaun Ryder... in His Own Words*, 1997
- Subjects are: the weather forecast and the bizzies —Melanie McGrath, *Hard, Soft & Wet*, p. 88, 1998

bizzing *noun*

sliding on an icy road while hanging onto the rear bumper of a car *US, 1969*

A verbal noun with no recorded use of 'bizz' as a verb.

- —Frederic G. Cassidy, *Dictionary of American Regional English*, p. 252, 1985
- Not to mention bizzingin the Northwest and bum-riding in Utah; all these denote the action of daring, often foolish, children who grab a ride on the back end of a moving vehicle. —*New York Times Magazine*, p. 18, 13th March 1994

bizzle *noun*

a brother, in the sense as male companion, especially in the phrase 'fa' shizzle my bizzle' (emphatically yes) *US*

A hip-hop, urban black coinage, formed as a rhyming reduplication of **SHIZZLE** (sure, yes), after 'fa' shizzle my nizzle' (yes my nigger).

bizzo *noun*

1 business *AUSTRALIA, 1969*

- And just so there's no funny bizzo, the kid and Kermie go with me! —Glyn Parry, *Mosh*, p. 102, 1996
- —Harry Orsman, *A Dictionary of Modern New Zealand Slang*, p. 11, 1999

2 an ill-tempered woman *US*

A corruption or evolution of 'bitch'.

- —Don R. McCreary (Editor), *Dawg Speak*, 2001

bizzurd *adjective*

bizarre and *absurd* *UK*

Derived by ellipsis. Hip-hop, urban slang; noted in connection with a legal dispute over rap lyrics by *BBC News*, 6th June 2003.

bizzy *noun*

▷ see: BUSY

BJ; bj *noun*

an act of oral sex, a blow job *US*

- —Anon., *The Gay Girl's Guide*, p. 3, 1949
- "B.J." – "Blowjob". —Richard Price, *The Wanderers*, p. 101, 1974
- And what should be this film's finest sex scene, the finale between Ashlyn and Jamie, turns out to be mainly a simple b.j. ending in a facia. —*Adult Video News*, p. 48, February 1993
- BJ's the name, bjs the game[.] —David Peace, *Nineteen Seventy-Four*, p. 104, 1999
- How about a BJ? – Why can't Janey do it? —Mark Powell, *Snap*, p. 58, 2001

B joint *noun*

a bar where women coax customers to buy drinks *US*

- Ginger was my mother's nightclub name, to match her new career working as a part-time stripteaser and "B-girl" in Tenderloin "B-joints." —Kim Rich, *Johnny's Girl*, p. 48, 1993

BJs *noun*

crack cocaine *UK*

- —Mike Haskins, *Drugs*, p. 281, 2003

BK Lounge *noun*

a Burger King™ fast-food restaurant *US*

Mocking attribution of class.

- —Connie Eble (Editor), *UNC-CH Campus Slang*, p. 1, April 1985

BK's *noun*

British Knight™ shoes *US*

Favoured by members of the Crips youth gang, for whom the initials also stand for 'Blood Killer'.

- —Bill Valentine, *Gangs and Their Tattoos*, p. 77, 2000

blab *verb*

to inform on someone, to reveal something while speaking *UK, 1583*

- —Angela Devlin, *Prison Patter*, p. 27, 1996

blabber *noun*

a very talkative hospital patient *US*

- —Sally Williams, *"Strong" Words*, p. 134, 1994

black *noun*

1 hashish *US, 1975*

An all-purpose abbreviation for strains of dark-coloured cannabis resin, e.g. **PAKISTANI BLACK**.

- "Want a smoke?" she asked, flicking the video off. "Smoke what?" "Anything, coke, black, sensi." —Karline Smith, *Moss Side Massive*, p. 52, 1994
- —Mike Haskins, *Drugs*, p. 286, 2003

2 a black amphetamine capsule *UK*

- —Mike Haskins, *Drugs*, p. 279, 2003

3 night *US*

- —*Time Magazine*, p. 92, 20 January 1947
- About a deuce of long black and whites ago, a stud from the low lands came to the Apple. —Babs Gonzales, *"A Manhattan Fable" in Movin' On Down De Line*, p. 89, 1975

4 in American casinos, a $100 chip *US*
- I've never dealt to blacks before. —Lee Solkey, *Dummy Up and Deal*, p. 107, 1980

▸ in the black
financially solvent *US, 1928*
From the pre-computer practice of recording credit items in black ink.

▸ on the black
engaged in black-market activities *UK, 1961*

▸ the black
1 *black*mail; the information held by a blackmailer *UK*
Hence, 'put the black on' (to blackmail).
- —Peter Laurie, *Scotland Yard*, p. 321, 1970
- I'll put the black on you. —Ian Dury, *Blackmail Man*, 1977
- —Angela Devlin, *Prison Patter*, p. 27, 1996

2 the black market *UK, 1961*
During the war in Vietnam, the term referred specifically to the black market which flourished on Le Loi Street, Saigon.
- —Gregory Clark, *Words of the Vietnam War*, p. 59, 1990

black *verb*
to *black*mail someone *UK, 1928*
An abbreviation of the conventional activity.
- Georgie Taylor, doing life for blacking a clergyman[.] —Charles Raven, *Underworld Nights*, p. 157, 1956
- —Angela Devlin, *Prison Patter*, p. 27, 1996

black *adjective*
1 secret *US, 1965*
- He dubbed the group his little "black box" ("black" for secret) and promised them carte blanche. —Frank Snepp, *Decent Interval*, p. 218, 1977
- When completed it filled a large spiral notebook nicknamed "the Black Book," and it covered all of Delta's skills. —Charlie A. Beckwith and Donald Knox, *Delta Force*, p. 168, 1983

2 extremely crowded *IRELAND*
- The Mirage was black. You couldn't move. There must have been over five thousand people there. —Ardal O'Hanlon, *The Talk of the Town*, p. 49, 1998

▸ it's a black thing; it's a black thang
used for identifying a behaviour or sensibility that is associated with black people *US*
- —Kenn "Naz" Young, *Naz's Dictionary of Teen Slang*, p. 1, 1993

black acid *noun*
LSD *US, 1970*
- —Richard A. Spears, *The Slang and Jargon of Drugs and Drink*, p. 47, 1986
- —Mike Haskins, *Drugs*, p. 285, 2003

black action *noun*
casino betting in $100 increments *US*
- —Michael Dalton, *Blackjack*, p. 31, 1991

blackamoor *noun*
a black Angus or Friesian cow *NEW ZEALAND*
- At least she's a Jersey, not like those blackamoors. —Nancy H. Ellison, *Whirinaki Valley*, p. 134, 1956

Black and Decker *noun*
the penis *UK*
Rhyming slang for **PECKER** (the penis). In its many slang manifestations the penis appears as all kind of tools, here it is formed on a manufacturer of power tools.
- —Ray Puxley, *Fresh Rabbit*, 1998

black and tan *noun*
1 a drink of porter or stout mixed equally with ale (pale or brown) *UK, 1889*

2 a capsule of Durophet™, trade name for a combination of central nervous system stimulants and depressants *UK*
- —Home Office, *Glossary of Terms and Slang Common in Penal Establishments*, 1978

black and tan *adjective*
catering to both black and white customers *US, 1887*
- Many of these small clubs have become, for all practical purposes, "black and tan" spots where whites and Negroes (of opposite sexes) mix, not furtively. —Jack Lait and Lee Mortimer, *New York Confidential*, p. 45, 1948
- In some places – like Georgia – the Populists "fused" with the lily-white wing of the Republican Party, not with the so-called black-and-tan wing. —Stokely Carmichael and Charles V. Hamilton, *Black Power*, p. 68, 1967
- As one old queen – who had the apartment next to Spencer's – told me – "My dear – it was really too much. It was a regular black and tan fantasy." —Herbert Huncke, *The Evening Sun Turned Crimson*, p. 43, 1980
- My father was a regular at the Oasis as well as at the other all-black nightclubs, including bars that catered to all races, called "black and tan" bars. —Kim Rich, *Johnny's Girl*, p. 81, 1993

black and white *noun*
1 a police car *US, 1958*
From the traditional colours of police cars in the US.
- Officer Breslin and I took cover behind our, uh, black and white, and ordered the suspects to, uh, halt. —Darryl Ponicsan, *The Last Detail*, p. 153, 1970
- The policia drive black and whites, 'ey? Most towns in the States I think our policia drive black and whites too. —Elmore Leonard, *Glitz*, p. 7, 1985
- Jimmy said shit because he saw the black-and-white rolling up. —William T. Vollman, *Whores for Gloria*, p. 130, 1991
- A shitlaod of Hollywood division black-and-whites showed up[.] —James Ellroy, *Hollywood Nocturnes*, p. 191, 1994
- —Angela Devlin, *Prison Patter*, p. 27, 1996

2 an amphetamine capsule, especially Durophet™ *UK*
From the colours of the capsule.
- —Home Office, *Glossary of Terms and Slang Common in Penal Establishments*, 1978
- —Mike Haskins, *Drugs*, p. 279, 2003

3 a capsule containing both a central nervous system stimulant and a barbiturate *US*
- —Eugene Landy, *The Underground Dictionary*, p. 34, 1971

4 a soda fountain drink made with chocolate syrup, seltzer and vanilla ice-cream *US*
- "You want black and whites?" Benny asked the boys at the table. —Irving Shulman, *The Amboy Dukes*, p. 192, 1947
- —Harold Wentworth and Stuart Berg Flexner, *Dictionary of American Slang*, p. 41, 1960

5 night *UK, 1937*
Rhyming slang, always spoken in full.
- —Ray Puxley, *Cockney Rabbit*, p. 17, 1992

black and white fever *noun*
an aversion to police *US*
- Funny, how many people get black and white fever and start moving fast in the opposite direction. —Joseph Wambaugh, *The New Centurions*, p. 127, 1970

black and white minstrel *noun*
an amphetamine tablet (Durophet™) *UK*
An elaboration of **BLACK AND WHITE**, used especially in the plural, based on *The Black and White Minstrel Show*, a 1960s television programme.
- —Home Office, *Glossary of Terms and Slang Common in Penal Establishments*, 1978
- —Angela Devlin, *Prison Patter*, p. 21, 1996

black and whites *noun*
the black trousers or skirt and white shirt worn by American casino dealers *US, 1961*
- —Thomas L. Clark, *The Dictionary of Gambling and Gaming*, p. 19, 1987

black and white taxi *noun*
a police car *US*
- —*American Speech*, p. 267, December 1962: 'The language of traffic policemen'

black art *noun*
in computing, an array of techniques developed and discovered for a particular system or application *US*
- The huge proliferation of formal and informal channels for spreading around new computer-related technologies during the last twenty years has made both the term black art and what it describes less common than formerly. —Eric S. Raymond, *The New Hacker's Dictionary*, p. 65, 1991

black ash *noun*
marijuana *UK*
London pronunciation of 'black hash'.
- —*Last of the Whole Earth Policemen*, BBC Radio 4, 9th May 1991

black ass *noun*
a car without working rear lights *US*
- —*American Speech*, p. 267, December 1962: 'The language of traffic policemen'

black as the ace of spades *adjective*
utterly black or, of skin, deeply black *US, 1882*
- [N]owadays, I think, applied more often to Negroes and other dark-skinned people than to, say, weather conditions[.] —Beale, 1976

black bag *noun*
a brown-haired prostitute *US*
- The telegraphic doe is "black bag" for brunettes and "tan valise" for blondes. —Lee Mortimer, *Women Confidential*, p. 141, 1960

black bag job *noun*
a burglary, especially one committed by law enforcement or intelligence agents *US, 1966*
- —Ralph de Sola, *Crime Dictionary*, p. 16, 1982

black Bart *noun*
dark hashish *UK, 1998*
A generic for 'marijuana'; connotes a romantic view of the drug's ilegal status by association with the C19 US outlaw.
- —Mike Haskins, *Drugs*, p. 286, 2003

black beauty *noun*
1 a black amphetamine capsule *US, 1969*
- They are known as "black mollies" or "black widows" or "black beauties," because they were put in black capsules.—*San Francisco Chronicle*, p. 24, 19th January 1972
- "Processed any speed lately?" "Black beauties?" "Music to my ears."—James Ellroy, *Suicide Hill*, p. 836, 1986
- —Ellen C. Bellone (Editor), *Dictionary of Slang*, p. 3, 1989
- also black beauties, pink hearts, et cetera, advertised ion the back of magazines like Creem, High Times, Hustler—Editors of Ben is Dead, *Retrohell*, p. 50, 1997

2 a capsule containing both barbiturate and amphetamine *US*
- —David Maurer and Victor Vogel, *Narcotics and Narcotic Addiction*, p. 389, 1973

black belt *noun*
1 a neighbourhood of black families that circles a city or area *US*
- But Washington's Black Belt is no belt at all. It is sprawled all over[.] —Jack Lait and Lee Mortimer, *Washington Confidential*, p. 37, 1951
- He had got on the subway – there had been no subway in Chicago in the old days – and then had ridden out on the El, shooting along the express tracks, looking out at the same old deteriorating buildings of the Black Belt[.]—James T. Farrell, *Kilroy was Here*, p. 63, 1954
- Once they had gone together to a chicken shack in the black belt, hot-fried chicken-in-the-basket.—Chester Himes, *The Primitive*, p. 61, 1955
- The Black Belt is there.—Willard Motley, *Let No Man Write My Epitaph*, p. 167, 1958
- Unlike other areas in the black belt, Macon County remained relatively free of overt acts of violence and intimidation during the forties and fifties.—Stokely Carmichael and Charles V. Hamilton, *Black Power*, p. 129, 1967
- Growing up in Hyde Park, the University of Chicago's stockade on the edge of the Black Belt, Paul led a quietly schizzy life.—Albert Goldman, *Freak Show*, p. 105, 1968
- There are more people starving in the U.S., in the Black Belt of southeastern U.S. in all the large cities, in the Appalachian Mountains and grape fields of California than in any other country on earth with the possible exception of India.—George Jackson, *Soledad Brother*, p. 261, April 1970
- To be able to go over into the black belt in the South Side of Chicago; there wasn't anything then that knocked me out more.—Herbert Huncke, *Guilty of Everything*, p. 36, 1990

2 in the US Army, a senior drill instructor *US*
Not a reference to martial arts, simply to the uniform. Vietnam war usage.
- —Linda Reinberg, *In the Field*, p. 23, 1991

black bess
yes *UK*
Rhyming slang.
- A definite affirmative is "a big black bess".—Ray Puxley, *Cockney Rabbit*, p. 17, 1992

black Betty *noun*
a van for transporting prisoners *US*
- 'Cause one day on Main she caught a convict chain / and rode Black Betty to her new pad.—Bruce Jackson, *Get Your Ass in the Water and Swim Like Me*, p. 155, 1965

blackbird *noun*
1 a black person *US, 1832*
A US mass murderer believed that among the secret messages hidden in the music of the Beatles were references to a coming black uprising in the song 'Blackbird'.
- —J. E. Lighter, *Historical Dictionary of American Slang, Volume 1*, p. 176, 1994

2 an unmarked military aircraft, such as a C-123 or C-130 *US*
Used by the Studies and Observations Group (SOG) in Vietnam, the highly secret, elite, unconventional warfare component of the US military presence in Southeast Asia.
- —Linda Reinberg, *In the Field*, p. 23, 1991

3 an amphetamine capsule *US*
- —Carl Chambers and richard Heckman, *Employee Drug Abuse*, p. 201, 1972

4 LSD *UK*
- —Mike Haskins, *Drugs*, p. 285, 2003

black blizzard *noun*
a black prairie soil dust storm *CANADA*
- Having no roots to hold it together, the soil turned to dust, and the hot winds carried it off in a "black blizzard."—Donalda Dickie, *Great Golden Plain*, p. 275, 1962

black Bombay *noun*
hashish, potent and dark in colour *US*

black bomber; bomber *noun*
any central nervous system stimulant, especially a capsule of diethylpropion (Durophet^{TM}), an amphetamine-like stimulant *UK, 1963*
- —Home Office, *Glossary of Terms and Slang Common in Penal Establishments*, 1978
- in less time than it takes to get a buzz from a Block Bomber. —Tony Parsons, *Limelight Blues*, 1983
- "I'm going to make a connection. I'll be right back." "Get Durophet. Bombers!" shouted Kay happily.—Tony Parsons, *Limelight Blues*, 1983
- —Liz cutland, *Kick Heroin*, p. 104, 1985
- —Angela Devlin, *Prison Patter*, p. 21, 1996

black book *noun*
1 a corporation's plan for battling a hostile takeover *US*
- —Kathleen Odean, *High Steppers, Fallen Angels, and Lollipops*, p. 111, 1988

2 in a casino, a list of persons to be excluded from the casino *US*
- —Michael Dalton, *Blackjack*, p. 32, 1991

3 a graffiti artist's notebook containing ideas, outlines, sketches and plans for future graffiti pieces *US*
- —Jim Crotty, *How to Talk American*, p. 140, 1997
- If you live, breathe, piss, and shit hip-hop culture, you'll feel at home hanging out at Oaklandish, checking out its weeking series and live music happenings – ot maybe just collecting wildstyle hieroglyphs from local graf-heads in your black book.—*East Bay Express (Oakland, California)*, 5th May 2004

black bottom *noun*
a neighbourhood where most of the population are poor black people *US, 1915*
- —Frederic G. Cassidy, *Dictionary of American Regional English, Volume 1*, p. 256, 1985
- Eatonville has been described as a place neither ghetto, nor slum, nor black bottom[.]—*Pittsburgh Post-Gazette*, p. F1, 14th October 2001

black box *noun*
1 in an aeroplane, the container and equipment used for the automatic recording of all flight data and cockpit conversation *UK, 1964*
A specialised use of Royal Air Force slang.
- —Lewis Poteet and Martin Stone, *Plane Talk*, p. 31, 1997

2 the notional container in which proprietary technical information is secured in dealings over industrial property rights *US*
- In dealing with the sale or purchase of industrial property rights, classified technical information can be often dealt with as proprietary knowledge without revealing the confidential know-how of what is n the black box.—Robert Kirk Mueller, *B uzzwords*, p. 47, 1974

3 any high technical piece of electronics equipment *US, 1945*
- I think now of our first celestial computer, known commonly as the Black Box. It was a gadget with counters on it, and cranks which you turned.—Curtis E. LeMay with MacKinlay Knator, *Mission with LeMay*, p. 98, 1965

4 a hearse *UK*
- —Peter Chippindale, *The British CB Book*, p. 152, 1981

5 a linear amplifier for a citizens' band radio *US*
Sometimes embellished as 'little black box.'
- —Porter Bibb, *CB Bible*, p. 98, 1976

black Cadillac *noun*
an amphetamine capsule *US*
- —National Institute on Drug Abuse, *What do they call it again?*, 1980

black cap *nickname*
a member of the New Zealand international men's cricket team *NEW ZEALAND*
- Why are the Black Caps, as the marketing boffins want them called, now finally playing so well?—*Evening Post*, p. 18, 13th February 2000

black Christmas *noun*
a snow-free Christmas *US, 1938*
A forced allusion to the famous 'White Christmas'.
- —Frederic G. Cassidy, *Dictionary of American Regional English, Volume 1*, p. 257, 1985

black-coated worker; black-coated workman; little black worker *noun*

a prune *UK*

From the appearance and the work done during the digestive process. Remembered, in 1970, as being used by Lord Hill 'The Radio Doctor' during World War 2. Noted in Manchester in *Daltonian*, December 1946, then generally in the Midlands and London.

black crow *noun*

during the Vietnam war, a long-range ignition detector *US*

Highly effective from the air in locating enemy convoys; used in conjunction with a beacon tracking system.

- —Linda Reinberg, *In the Field*, p. 23, 1991

black-dog *adjective*

melancholic, depressed *UK, 1826*

- [H]e had bad attacks of class-traitor guilt, which [...] would precipitate black-dog whiskey drunks and trigger unspeakable incidents[.] —Mick Farren, *Give the Anarchist a Cigarette*, p. 351, 2001

black domina *noun*

dark hashish *UK, 2002*

An allusion to the sexual domination of a black mistress.

black dot *noun*

a type of LSD *UK*

From the appearance.

- The girls on the other hand have swallowed a black dot each that they scored from one of the DJs. —Kevin Williamson, *Heart of the Bass (Disco Biscuits)*, p. 114, 1996

black eagle *noun*

heroin *UK*

- —Mike Haskins, *Drugs*, p. 283, 2003

black-enamelled *adjective*

dark-skinned *UK*

Military, intended as jocular.

- C'm'ere, Ali, you black enamelled bastard[.] —Beale *(remembering the Middle East, 1945–55)*, 1984

blacketeer *noun*

a black market racketeer *AUSTRALIA*

A World War 2 coinage, possibly journalistic.

- —Sidney J. Baker, *The Australian Language*, p. 185, 1953

blackfellow's delight *noun*

rum *AUSTRALIA*

A disparaging view of Aboriginal Australians' drinking habits

- Rum is variously known as blackfellow's delight, cocky's joy and whip. —Sidney J. Baker, *The Australian Language*, p. 227, 1953

black fever *noun*

sexual attraction felt by a white person for black people *US*

- Black Fever is when a girl, awhite girl she gets ths thing in herhead she's got to have a black guy. —John Sayles, *Union Dues*, p. 147, 1977

black forest *noun*

the female genitals *UK*

This pet name for a vagina describes its location in a straightforward simile for the pubic hair, ostensibly punning on the *Schwarzwald* region of southwest Germany. Derived possibly as a reference to Black Forest gateaux (sticky, chocolatey, cherry-laden cakes; a cultural-icon in the UK since the 1970s), the cake imagery suggesting an oral-sex dimension to the usage. Also note 'A Walk In The Black Forest' by Horst Jankowski, a popular instrumental recording in the 1960s; a satisfying metaphor for sexual activity.

- — *Sky Magazine*, July 2001

black Friday *noun*

the day after Thanksgiving *US*

- Philadelphia police and bus drivers call it "Black Friday" – that day each year between Thanksgiving and the Army-Navy game. It is the busiest shopping and traffic day of the year in the Bicentennial City[.[— *New York Times*, p. 21, 29th November 1975

black gang *noun*

1 collectively, a ship's engineer's department *US, 1895*

- —J. E. Lighter, *Historical Dictionary of American Slang, Volume 1*, p. 177, 1992

2 an aviation mechanics team *CANADA*

The source of the term is likely to be their black overalls.

- "Black gang," for airplane mechanics, seems to have been coined by Alan Bill, Winnipeg Tribune, reporting on the search and rescue of the MacApline Expedition in the Canadian Arctic. —Lewis Poteet, *Plane Talk*, p. 31, 1997

black ganja *noun*

hashish, dark in colour *US, 1978*

The term is heard and seen with all the possible variant spellings of **GANJA** found at that entry.

- —Richard A. Spears, *The Slang and Jargon of Drugs and Drink*, p. 48, 1986
- —Mike Haskins, *Drugs*, p. 286, 2003

black gold *noun*

1 oil *US*

An outsiders' term, not used by those in the business.

- I'm headed south to Louisiana where Pete's already contracted to prospect a field. Ought to yield enough black gold to retire to a life of plenty. —Seth Morgan, *Homeboy*, p. 298, 1990

2 highly potent marijuana *US, 1946*

Derived from the previous sense, punning on the richness and the colour of the hashish.

- —Richard A. Spears, *The Slang and Jargon of Drugs and Drink*, p. 48, 1986

3 distilled, concentrated heroin *US*

- —Carsten Stroud, *Close Pursuit*, p. 269, 1987

Black Hand *noun*

a secret criminal organisation composed of first-generation Italian immigrants to the US *US, 1898*

- The Mafia and the dread Black Hand are the same thing. The black hand was the sign over which the Mafia's threats were delivered. —Jack Lait and Lee Mortimer, *Washington Confidential*, p. 180, 1951
- The Black Hand? You think you can laugh it off? —Mickey Spillane, *Kiss Me Deadly*, p. 38, 1952

black hash *noun*

hashish mixed and darkened with opium *US, 1975*

- —Richard A. Spears, *The Slang and Jargon of Drugs and Drink*, p. 48, 1986

black hat *noun*

1 in a drama, or in life viewed as a drama, the villain *US*

- Why are we talking about Alfred North Whitehead when we ought to be out looking for a black hat? —Max Shulman, *Anyone Got a Match?*, p. 41, 1964
- Well, from where this peace monger sits, I'd say the black hats are succeeding. —William C. Anderson, *Bat 21*, p. 161, 1980

2 a computer hacker with no honourable purpose *US*

Sometimes embellished to 'black hat hacker'.

- Max's pet project centered on clearly establishing the difference between "white hat" and "black hat" hackers. He said white hats used their computer skills to understand and secure systems, but black hats used their abilities to break into systems for profit or glory. —Michelle Delio, *Wired News*, 22nd May 2001

3 a member of Pathfinder platoon, dropped behind enemy lines to make deep reconnaissance patrols and to establish landing zones for the initial helpicopter waves *US*

- " You know how to operate that thang?" asked the Black Hat, a staff sergeant member of SERTS' cadre. —John Del Vecchio, *The 13th Valley*, p. 9, 1982
- —Linda Reinberg, *In the Field*, p. 23, 1991

4 a US Army drill instructor *US*

- Look to your left and what did you see? / A mean old black hat lookin' at me. —Sandee Shaffer Johnson, *Cadences*, p. 24, 1986
- The Black Hats are looking for any lack of motivation, and they jump, quickly and hard, on anybody they think is suspect. —Hans Halberstadt, *Airborne*, p. 34, 1988

blackhead *noun*

a black person *UK*

Derogatory, unless ironically self-descriptive. Otherwise a 'blackhead' is a skin blemish.

- Rah! Who'd have freakin' thought it? I was a blackhead with connections. —Diran Adebayo, *My Once Upon A Time*, p. 183, 2000

black heart *noun*

depression *UK*

- —Angela Devlin, *Prison Patter*, p. 27, 1996

black hole *noun*

1 the vagina *UK*

Originally a reference to 'the black pit of hell'. Now a 'black hole' is widely known to be a celestial phenomena into which anything may be sucked to disappear without trace.

- The female genitalia were represented as places from which people/things never return (e.g., the Bermuda triangle) or get sucked into (e.g., the black hole, electrolux), hidden dangers (e.g., squirrel trap), and warnings of danger (e.g., hairy growler, bomb doors). — *Journal of Sex Research*, p. 146, 2001

2 in computing, the notional place where e-mail that is sent but not received disappears *US*

- "I think there's a black hole at foovax!" conveys suspicion that site foovax has been dropping a lot of stuff on the floor lately[.] — Eric S. Raymond, *The New Hacker's Dictionary*, p. 65, 1991

black horse *nickname*

the US Army's 11th Armored Cavalry Regiment *US*

So named because of the Regiment's insignia.

- — Linda Reinberg, *In the Field*, p. 23, 1991

blackie, blackie-white *nouns*

▷ **see:** BLACKY, BLACKY-WHITE

black-is-white *adverb*

completely, thoroughly *TRINIDAD AND TOBAGO*

Collected by Richard Allsopp.

black jack *noun*

1 the penis of a black man *US*

Homosexual usage.

- — *The Guild Dictionary of Homosexual Terms*, p. 4, 1965

2 a fifty-ton Santa Fe Railroad coal hopper *US*

- — Ramon Adams, *The Language of the Railroader*, p. 14, 1977

Black Jack *nickname*

1 black-labelled Jack Daniels™ whisky *US*

- — Connie Eble (Editor), *UNC-CH Campus Slang*, p. 2, Spring 1982

2 US General John J. Pershing (1860–1948) *US*

- Mrs. Brooks, after after divorce from her first husband, met "black Jack" Pershing abroad. — Jack Lait and Lee Mortimer, *Washington Confidential*, p. 143, 1951

blackjack mission *noun*

during the war in Vietnam, an operation carried out by a mobile strike force *US*

The mobile strike forces were light infantry battalions equipped and trained to operate in remote areas without any significant logistical requirements or support.

- — Linda Reinberg, *In the Field*, p. 23, 1991

Black Jeff *noun*

a wasp *BAHAMAS*

- — John A. Holm, *Dictionary of Bahamian English*, p. 20, 1982

black light *noun*

an ultraviolet light, under which flourescent paint glows *US*

- — Eugene Landy, *The Underground Dictionary*, p. 34, 1971

Black Lions *nickname*

a navy fighter squadron formally identified as VF-213, commissioned in 1955 *US*

- Nash was one of those rare Phanton pilots who, against the trend, had been dogfighting int he F-4 since his squadron, the V-213, nicknamed "The Black Lions," had transitioned to it in 1964. — Robert K. Wilcox, *The Scream of Eagles*, p. 45, 1990

black magic *noun*

1 the M-16 rifle, the standard rifle used by US troops in Vietnam after 1966 *US*

- — Linda Reinberg, *In the Field*, p. 23, 1991

2 in computing, a technique that works without any apparent reason for its success *US*

- — Eric S. Raymond, *The New Hacker's Dictionary*, p. 65, 1991

Black Magic box *noun*

a police van *UK*

Plays on **BLACK MARIA** (a police van) and Black Magic™ chocolates.

- — Peter Chippindale, *The British CB Book*, p. 152, 1981

black man kissed her *noun*

a sister *UK*

Rhyming slang from the early part of C20 which appears to have all but died out by 1948 when Carribean immigration began in earnest and revived usage. Noted as coming back into currency by 1960 when Julian Franklyn's *Dictionary of Rhyming Slang* was published. Recorded as obsolete in 1992 by Ray Puxley's *Cockney Rabbit*.

black man's wheels *noun*

a BMW car *UK*

- TT got a BMW. Reckoned he was a black geezer maybe, Black Man's Wheels. — Jeremy Cameron, *Brown Bread in Wengen*, p. 54, 1999

Black Maria *noun*

1 a police wagon or van for transporting those who have been arrested *US, 1843*

The etymology is uncertain beyond the colour black.

- — Paul Tempest, *Lag's Lexicon*, p. 18, 1949
- Along with about 65 others he was conveyed by Black Maria to Darlinghurst Police Station. — James Holledge, *The Great Australian Gamble*, p. 106, 1966
- Po-lice thought it was really funny . . . two niggers fightin' over some bags of coffee on their way to the Black Maria. — Odie Hawkins, *Ghetto Sketches*, p. 123, 1972

2 in a deck of cards, the queen of spades *US*

- — George Percy, *The Language of Poker*, p. 10, 1988

3 highly potent marijuana *UK*

black marketeer *noun*

an unlicensed bookmaker quoting his own prices and odds *AUSTRALIA*

- — Sidney J. Baker, *The Australian Language*, p. 185, 1953

black micro *noun*

a variety of LSD in tablet form *UK*

- — Angela Devlin, *Prison Patter*, p. 28, 1996

black mo; black moat; black mote *noun*

highly potent, dark coloured marijuana resin *US, 1972*

- — Richard A. Spears, *The Slang and Jargon of Drugs and Drink*, p. 48, 1986
- — Mike Haskins, *Drugs*, p. 286, 2003

black molly *noun*

1 a black amphetamine capsule *US, 1970*

- There are known as "black mollies" or "black widows" or "black beauties," because they were put in black capsules. — *San Francisco Chronicle*, p. 24, 19th January 1972

2 a barbiturate capsule *US*

- — David W. Maurer and Victor Vogel, *Narcotics and Narcotic Addiction*, p. 389, 1973

Black Monday *noun*

1 28th May 1962 *US*

The date of a dramatic stock market crash.

- Was it the "little woman" who panicked on Black Monday, May 28, in Wall Street, then in unreasoning terror dumped off her stocks in skyrocketing volume and thereby set off one of the worst stock market slumps of this century? — *San Francisco Chronicle*, p. 54, 18th June 1962
- Will 1968 see another "Black Monday" in the stock market? — *San Francisco Chronicle*, p. 58, 1 April 1968

2 19th October 1987 *US*

The date of the greatest single-day stock market crash in the US since the Depression.

- By 4 p.m., after the market bell clanged, economics reporter Mike Jensen would appear with Brokaw to intone that "today will be known as Black Monday" and NBC News consultant Donald Regan would bid "goodbye to the bull market." — *Washington Post*, p. D6, 20th October 1987
- — Kathleen Odean, *High Steppers, Fallen Angels, and Lollipops*, p. 165, 1988
- — *American Speech*, Fall 1988

black money *noun*

cash that is not accounted for in the financial records of a business *US*

- Attorney General Robert F. Kennedy is concerned about "black money" – also known as "hot money." — Ed Reid and Ovid Demaris, *The Green Felt Jungle*, p. 212, 1963

black oil *noun*
hashish oil *US, 1977*
- —Richard A. Spears, *The Slang and Jargon of Drugs and Drink*, p. 49, 1986

black on black *noun*
a car with a black exterior and black upholstery *US*
Black teen slang.
- —Edith A. Folb, *runnin' down some lines*, p. 229, 1980

black-out *noun*
a very dark-skinned black person *US*
- —Marcus Hanna Boulware, *Jive and Slang of Students in Negro Colleges*, 1947

black pearl *noun*
herion *US*
- —US Department of Justice, *Street Terms*, October 1994
- —Robert Ashton, *This Is Heroin*, p. 205, 2002

black pen *noun*
a parole report *UK*
- —Angela Devlin, *Prison Patter*, p. 28, 1996

black peter *noun*
in prison, a punishment cell *AUSTRALIA, 1953*
An elaboration of 'peter' (a cell).
- —Kylie Tennant, *The Joyful Condemned*, 1953

black pill *noun*
a pill of opium; heroin *US, 1969*
- —Richard A. Spears, *The Slang and Jargon of Drugs and Drink*, p. 49, 1986
- —Mike Haskins, *Drugs*, p. 283, 2003

Blackpool rock *noun*
the penis *UK*
Rhyming slang for **COCK**; a visual pun on a long pink sweet that is made to be sucked. Similarly sweet references to the male anatomy can be found at **ALMOND ROCK**, **BRIGHTON ROCK** and **STICK OF ROCK**. Probably inspired by the innuendo-laden song 'With My Little Stick of Blackpool Rock' by George Formby, 1937.
- —Ray Puxley, *Cockney Rabbit*, p. 17, 1992

black powder *noun*
ground hashish and opium *US*
An explosive mixture named as an early form of gunpowder.
- —*www.addictions.org*, 2001

black power *nickname*
a Maori gang or member of the gang *NEW ZEALAND*
- The Black Power boys will block you if you struggle.—*Truth*, p. 3, 14th February 1978
- At one end members of the Black Power gang stood about in bandanas and black T-shirts and tattoos and attitudes of lethal ease.—*Listener*, p. 15, 23rd March 1985

black Protestant *noun*
1 used as a term of contempt for Protestants in Ireland *IRELAND*
This term appears to have become diluted over the years.
- As a black Protestant, I fully endorse what Senator Manning said. The Roman Catholic Church has behaved very well and with immense dignity in this controversy and has been put in great political difficulty.—*Irish Times*, 18th May 2001

2 a non-observant Protestant or one prejudiced against Roman Catholics *US, 1969*
- —Frederic G. Cassidy, *Dictionary of American Regional English, Volume 1*, p. 269, 1985

black rain *noun*
rain that has been contaminated by smoke from oil field fires *US*
Gulf war usage.
- —*American Speech*, p. 384, Winter 1991: 'Among the new words'

Black Rats *nickname*
the Traffic Division of the Metropolitan Police based at New Scotland Yard *UK*
- The sleek but at times ungainly uniform led to their acquiring the in-force nickname "Black Rats".—Martin Fido and Keith Skinner, *The Official Encyclopedia of Scotland Yard*, p. 266, 1999
- I always had a healthy respect for the Black Rats[.]—Duncan MacLaughlin, *The Filth*, p. 52, 2002

black rock *noun*
crack cocaine
An elaboration of **ROCK** (crack cocaine) which has more to do with the drug's reputation than colour.
- —Mike Haskins, *Drugs*, p. 281, 2003

black rover *noun*
a Metropolitan Police warrant card *UK*
This card authorises free travel throughout the London Transport system and thus plays on a London Transport Red Rover ticket which allowed the purchaser unlimited travel.
- It was the day we were issued with a black Rover apiece – sadly, not a car, but police-speak for warrant cards[.]—Duncan MacLaughlin, *The Filth*, p. 76, 2002

black Russian *noun*
1 blackened opium *US, 1969*
- —Jay Robert Nash, *Dictionary of Crime*, p. 32, 1992

2 dark hashish *US*
- —Jay Robert Nash, *Dictionary of Crime*, p. 32, 1992

3 marijuana resin mixed with opium *US*
- —*www.addictions.org*, 2001

black shoe *noun*
an officer in the US Navy other than an aviator *US, 1950*
Aviation officers wore brown shoes.
- —Linda Reinberg, *In the Field*, p. 23, 1991

blacksmith *noun*
an incompetent sheep station cook *NEW ZEALAND, 1941*
- They called a crook cook a 'blacksmith', perhaps because he used his stove like a forge and welded all the food to the pot.—*New Zealand Journal of Agriculoture*, 19th March 1986

black snake *noun*
a freight train composed entirely of coal tenders *US, 1938*
- —Norman Carlisle, *The Modern Wonder Book of Trains and Railroading*, p. 259, 1946
- —Harold Wentworth and Stuart Berg Flexner, *Dictionary of American SLang*, p. 41, 1960

Black Sox *nickname*
the New Zealand international men's softball team *NEW ZEALAND*
- Our men's softball team, the Black Sox, created history by being the first country to have won back-to-back world series.—*Listener*, p. 10, 5th August 2000

black star *noun*
a type of LSD *UK, 1998*
- —Mike Haskins, *Drugs*, p. 285, 2003

blackstick *noun*
a clarinet *US, 1937*
- —Robert S. Gould, *A Jazz Lexicon*, p. 21, 1964

black stranger *noun*
a complete stranger *IRELAND*
- You're expectin' too much of me. Man I'm nearly a black stranger to you.—John B. Keane, *The Man from Clare*, p. 43, 1962

Black Street *noun*
the notional location of a clinic treating those with sexually transmitted infections *UK: SCOTLAND*
Euphemistic.
- —Michael Munro, *The Patter, Another Blast*, 1988

black stuff *noun*
opium; heroin *US, 1936*
- —Robert Ashton, *This Is Heroin*, p. 205, 2002
- —Mike Haskins, *Drugs*, p. 283, 2003

blackstuff *noun*
tarmacadam *UK*
- MRS MALONE: He was blacklisted in '58 and went to work on the blackstuff. DOCTOR: The blackstuff? MRS MALONE: The tarmac. —Alan Bleasdale, *Boys From the Blackstuff*, 1982

black stuff *nickname*
Guinness *IRELAND*
- Research on Guinness in the UK has found that an estimated 162,719 pints of the drink each year are caught in moustaches, costing

drinkers an annual £423,070 in wasted alcohol...Unfortunately, we have no figures for Ireland. This is strange. After all, it was here that the black stuff was invented. — *Irish Times*, 25th February 2000

Black Stump *noun*
used as an imaginary marker for a remote place *AUSTRALIA*
Often used in phrases such as 'this side of the Black Stump', 'out near the Black Stump', 'the other side of the Black Stump' or 'beyond the Black Stump'. From a fire-blackened tree stump used as a marker for navigation in the country.
- I'm just the greatest little worker this side of the black stump. — Nino Culotta (John O'Grady), *They're A Weird Mob*, p. 89, 1957
- I was at the races with the greatest pessimist this side of the black stump. — Frank Hardy, *The Yarns of Billy Borker*, p. 106, 1965
- Clarrie, I would be the last one to deny or deride the tenacious veracity of these boys from the Black Stump and points west[.] — Alexander Buzo, *The Roy Murphy Show*, p. 119, 1970
- He plays hard and there's no bigger bastard this side or that of the black stump. — *Janie Stagestruck*, p. 85, 1972
- Janie Sommers from out near the black stump had come to town to make the big time. — *Janie Stagestruck*, p. 102, 1972
- — Sonya Plowman, *Great Kiwi Slang*, p. 28, 2002

black sunshine *noun*
LSD *UK, 1998*
- — Mike Haskins, *Drugs*, p. 285, 2003

black tabs *noun*
a type of LSD *US, 1982*
- — Richard A. Spears, *The Slang and Jargon of Drugs and Drink*, p. 49, 1986
- — Mike Haskins, *Drugs*, p. 285, 2003

black tar *noun*
crude, impure, potent heroin from Mexico *US, 1986*
- — Peter Johnson, *Dictionary of Street Alcohol and Drug Terms*, p. 20, 1993
- [I]t brushes up against the competition, including Mexican-produced Black Tar, known derisively as Mexican Mud because of its poor quality; the more superior Mexican Brown in powder form; and especially high-grade Colombian White, its biggest rival. — *New York Times*, p. SM29, 23rd June 2002

black tar blanco *noun*
heroin *UK*
- — Robert Ashton, *This Is Heroin*, p. 205, 2002

black tide *noun*
an oil slick on the ocean surface *US*
- — Trevor Cralle, *The Surfin'ary*, p. 11, 1991

black-tie *adjective*
1 calling for formal dress *UK*
- "I know that if I wore a suit and tie, unless I'm going to a funeral or it's a black-tie function ... I take that back. Even when it's black tie you don't wear a tie anymore." — Elmore Leonard, *Be Cool*, p. 8, 1999

2 said of an event in Antarctica in which those in attendance are not wearing red clothes issued by the US National Science Foundation *ANTARCTICA, 1991*
- — Carnegie Mellon Astrophysics Peterson Group, *Antarctic Vocabulary*, 19th September 1997

black type *noun*
in horse racing, a horse that has won or been placed in a stakes race *US*
Bold face type is used in a sales catalogue to identify horses that have won or been placed.

Blackus *noun*
used as a term of address for a dark-skinned person *BAHAMAS*
- — John A. Holm, *Dictionary of Bahamian English*, p. 21, 1982

black velvet *noun*
1 sexual relations with Aboriginal or other dark-skinned women *AUSTRALIA, 1899*
- 'You're in the land of Black Velvet now,' one of the loungers remarked. 'Unless you go round to Darwin you'll not find a white woman in the north between Burketown and Broome.' — Mary Durack, *Kings in Grass Castles*, p. 261, 1959

2 a black woman's vagina *US*
- — Dale Gordon, *The Dominion Sex Dictionary*, p. 30, 1967
- — Robert A. Wilson, *Playboy's Book of Forbidden Words*, p. 40, 1972

3 a drink of stout mixed with champagne *UK, 1937*
From the colour and texture. An economic variation is **POOR MAN'S VELVET** (stout and cider); sometimes shortened to 'blackers'.

black water *noun*
1 coffee, especially when weak *US, 1850*
- — *Complete CB Slang Dictionary*, 1976
- — Peter Chippindale, *The British CB Book*, p. 152, 1981

2 sewage *US*
Euphemism used in recreational vehicle camping.
- — John Edwards, *Auto Dictionary*, p. 15, 1993

black whack *noun*
phencyclidine, the recreational drug known as PCP or angel dust *US*
- — US Department of Justice, *Street Terms*, October 1994

black widow *noun*
1 a black amphetamine capsule; Benzedrine™ (amphetamine sulphate), a central nervous system stimulant *US*
- They are known as "black mollies" or "black widows" or "black beauties," because they were put in black capsules. — *San Francisco Chronicle*, p. 24, 19th January 1972
- — *American Speech*, p. 56, Spring-Summer 1975: 'Razorback slang'
- — Angela Devlin, *Prison Patter*, p. 23, 1996

2 a capsule containing both barbiturate and amphetamine *US*
- — David Maurer and Victor Vogel, *Narcotics and Narcotic Addiction*, p. 389, 1973

3 an M-16 rifle equipped with a night scope *US*
- — Linda Reinberg, *In the Field*, p. 23, 1991

4 a limited edition, fuel-injected 1957 Chevrolet 150 sedan, built strictly for racing but then banned from stock car racing *US*
- — Lewis Poteet, *Car & Motorcyle Slang*, p. 32, 1992

black wings *noun*
oral sex with a black woman *US*
- You got your Red Wings by eating a girl on her period and your Black Wings by eating a black girl. — Ralph "Sonny" Barger, *Hell's Angel*, p. 99, 2000

blacky; blackie *noun*
a black person *UK, 1815*
Derogatory, but not necessarily deliberately so.
- Look at the Blackies; we're getting over colour prejudice aren't we? — Troy Kennedy Martin, *Z Cars*, p. 73, 1962
- LOMPER: A sprinter? GAZ: No, a blackie. Every lass's fantasy, is that. — *The Full Monty*, 1997

blacky carbon *noun*
in drag racing, petrol *US*
- — John Lawlor, *How to Talk Car*, p. 19, 1965

blacky-white; blackie-white *noun*
an Anglo-Indian half-caste *INDIA*
- I'm an Anglo-Indian – a half-chat, a chillicracker, a blackie-white – the first is the polite term – the other's are what they [the full-whites] call us behind our backs. — Berkely Mather, *The Memsahib*, 1977

bladder *noun*
1 a balloon *US*
Circus and carnival usage.
- — Don Wilmeth, *The Language of American Popular Entertainment*, p. 26, 1981

2 a collapsible drum for holding liquids *US*
- — Linda Reinberg, *In the Field*, p. 23, 1991

3 a local newspaper *UK*
Derives from a less-than-favourable description of its contents.
- — Frank McKenna, *A Glossary of Railwaymen's Talk*, 1970

bladder bird *noun*
a tanker aircraft used for aerial bulk fuel delivery *US*
Vietnam war usage.
- — Linda Reinberg, *In the Field*, p. 23, 1991

bladder boat *noun*
an inflatable rubber boat *US*
Vietnam war usage.
- — Linda Reinberg, *In the Field*, p. 23, 1991

bladder-buster *noun*

a very large beverage container *US*

- —Connie Eble (Editor), *UNC-CH Campus Slang*, p. 1, April 1997

bladdered *adjective*

very drunk *UK*

- Six pints of it. Enough to get you bladdered, if it was strong lager. —Greg Williams, *Diamond Geezers*, p. 70, 1997
- I was coming out of the Brat Awards, totally fookin' bladdered[.] —Shaun Ryder, *Shaun Ryder... in His Own Words*, 1997
- You look as if you could do with a top up 'n' all. Unlike some people I could mention. Bladdered ain't the word. —Diran Adebayo, *My Once Upon A Time*, p. 52, 2000

blade *noun*

1 a knife *US, 1896*

- He came back, pulling a blade[.] —Malcolm X and Alex Haley, *The Autobiography of Malcolm X*, p. 131, 1964
- And I pointing to my pocket making believe they a blade in it[.] —Sara Harris, *The Lords of Hell*, p. 22, 1967
- Hip little kiddies never carry a BLADE; it's a bad scene if you meet up with your equalizer or John Law. —Hy Lit, *Hy Lit's Unbelievable Dictionary of Hip Words for Groovy People*, p. 5, 1968
- [S]ince she knew Carri wouldn't work without having her blade on her she knew it was wise to get off my ass. —A.S. Jackson, *Gentleman Pimp*, p. 83, 1973
- I thought only PRs went to the blades over a broad. —Edwin Torres, *Q & A*, p. 45, 1977
- Bama, you got your blade? — *True Romance*, 1993
- Aw, my blade! — *Airheads*, 1994
- Wonder why O.J. used a blade? Why not a gun with a silencer? A guy like him could get any weapon he wanted. Why a blade? —Joseph Wambaugh, *Floaters*, p. 128, 1996

2 a surgeon *US, 1974*

- — *Journal of American Folklore*, p. 568–581, January–March 1978: 'The gomer'

3 a man *US*

- Vice does not thrive here, becuase the young blades seek it elsewhere. —Jack Lait and Lee Mortimer, *New York Confidential*, p. 83, 1948

4 a Cadillac car, especially a Coupe de Ville or Fleetwood *US*

Black teen slang.

- —Edith A. Folb, *runnin' down some lines*, p. 229, 1980

5 a type of expensive chrome car wheel rim *US*

- —Ethan Hilderbrant, *Prison Slang*, p. 13, 1998
- —Don R. McCreary (Editor), *Dawg Speak*, 2001
- Dubs, blades, shoes, sneakers, twinkies – street slang for custom wheels – are status symbols, made popular by athletes and rap stars. — *Cincinnati Enquirer*, p. 1B, 29th August 2003

6 a moped *BERMUDA*

- —Peter A. Smith and Fred M. Barritt, *Bermewjan Vurds*, 1985

7 a dollar *US*

- —Gary K. Farlow, *Prison-ese*, p. 4, 2002

blade *verb*

to skate on rollerblades *US*

- —Pamela Munro, *U.C.L.A. Slang*, p. 31, 1997

blader *noun*

a rollerblader *US*

- The most common injury to a blader is a sprained or broken wrist. — *New York Times*, p. C12, 17th April 1989
- —Pamela Munro, *U.C.L.A. Slang*, p. 44, 2001
- The bladers have abandoned their coats in a high pile and wear skater attire from around the world, baggy trousers and huge T-shirts. — *Listener*, p. 46, 25th January 2003

blade-runner *noun*

someone who transports stolen goods or contraband *UK*

Taken from the science-fiction film *Blade Runner*, 1982, based on Philip K. Dick's cyberpunk novel *Do Androids Dream of Electric Sheep?*, 1968.

- [T]he Church – the Customs and Excise – had seized a substantial quantity of wines and spirits from a Brummie blade-runner. —Garry Bushell, *The Face*, p. 115, 2001

blading *noun*

the act of using rollerblades *US*

- Blading exploded in the late '80s and early '90s, appealing both to ex-joggers looking for low-impact workouts and death-defying speed freaks[.] —Steven Daly and Nalthaniel Wice, *alt.culture*, p. 211, 1995

blag *noun*

1 a robbery, especially an armed robbery; a bank or post-office robbery *UK, 1885*

Probably an abbreviation of 'blackguard'.

- First offenders or not, you do a blag like that one and that [Dartmoor]'s where you'll end up. —Derek Bickerton, *Payroll*, p. 32, 1959
- —Peter Laurie, *Scotland Yard*, p. 320, 1970
- "What's it about, guv?" "A blag!" — *The Sweeney*, p. 16, 1976

2 a piece of persuasive bluff *UK*

- —Robin Cook, *The Crust on its Uppers*, 1962
- Blagging a year abroad when you're an English student is quite a result [...] What a blag, as they say in Austria. — *The Guardian*, 4th April 2003

3 used as a term of abuse *UK*

Usage appears restricted to northern grammar schools deriving, perhaps, from a shortening of 'blaggard' (a blackguard).

- — *New Society*, 22nd August 1963

blag *verb*

1 to hoax or deceive someone; to bluff someone; to persuade someone; to wheedle something; to scrounge something *UK*

From French *blaguer* (to joke), possibly informed by conventional English 'blaggard'.

- This time I went the guntz (the whole way) and blag[g]ed her for a grand (£1,000) —Frank Norman, *Bang To Rights*, p. 113, 1958
- —Bob Young and Micky Moody, *The Language of Rock 'n' Roll*, p. 17, 1985
- Are we gonna go and blag some whizz [amphetamine] or what? —Ben Graham, *Weekday Service (Disco Biscuits)*, p. 163, 1996
- I've always told him it's Tom we're bringing in, always blagged it that it's only a little VAT [value added tax] sting. —Kevin Sampson, *Outlaws*, p. 100, 2001
- Blag. Use your bloody gob. —Chris Ryan, *The Watchman*, p. 2, 2001
- In one programme [Donna Air] blags a limo for herself for a day. — *The Face*, p. 14, June 2001

2 to successfully persuade another person into having sex with you *UK*

- —Paul Baker, *Polari*, p. 165, 2002

3 to rob something, especially with violence *UK, 1933*

- —Angela Devlin, *Prison Patter*, p. 28, 1996

blagard *verb*

to talk profanely or obscenely *CANADA*

According to Joseph Ross, *History of Cape Negro and Blanche* (2nd edition, 1988), this term is in use with this meaning in Nova Scotia's South Shore. It derives from the French *blague* (chaff, humbug, hoax, fib) but may also derive from an English gang of blacking boys and torch-carriers in London known for their scurrilous language. In the form 'blackguarding', it is in use in parts of the US with the same meaning as in Nova Scotia.

blagger *noun*

1 a robber who will use violence as necessary *UK*

In *The Lag's Lexicon*, 1950, Paul Tempest noted the term was 'used very occasionally'; during the 1970s usage proliferated through the agency of television programmes like *The Sweeney*.

2 a persuasive person who is employed to attract customers *UK*

- It is the job of the Blagger to invite, persuade or trap into the [Bingo] parlour. — *Sunday Telegraph*, 18th August 1963

3 a persuasive criminal, a confidence trickster *UK*

- — *The Bournemouth Evening Echo*, 20th April 1966

blagging *noun*

a robbery, especially with violence *UK, 1933*

Derives, possibly, from 'blackguard'.

- One of his best performances was a pay-roll blagging job from a factory out Stamford Hill way. —Charles Raven, *Underworld Nights*, p. 48, 1956
- —Peter Laurie, *Scotland Yard*, p. 321, 1970

blag merchant *noun*

a pay-roll bandit, an armed robber *UK*

Combines **BLAG** (a robbery with violence) with the colloquial use of 'merchant' (a man).

- MIAMI: You've 'eard of Toothless. LEE: Yeah. Top blag merchant. MIAMI: Blag merchant. Dunno if I would go so far as to say 'top'. —Chris Baker and Andrew Day, *Lock, Stock... & One Big Bullock*, p. 402, 2000

blah; blah blah; blah blah blah *noun*

empty and meaningless talk; so on and so forth; used for implying that what is being said is not worth the saying or has been said too often already *UK, 1918*

Echoic of nonsense speech, possibly German *blech* (nonsense); synonymous with **RHUBARB** (nonsense) which may also be repeated two or three times for emphasis.

- "You can give me a whole rationof shit and this and that, and blah, blah, blah." — George V. Higgins, *The Friends of Eddie Doyle*, p. 75, 1971
- — Eugene Landy, *The Underground Dictionary*, p. 35, 1971
- So the guy goes to the doctor for a physical. They do all those tests, all that stuff, blah blah blah. — *Tin Men*, 1987
- We all decided to chuck the idea because I'd have trouble making friends, blah-blah-blah. — *Heathers*, 1988
- His secretary's on vacation, everything's backed up, he's got a big case in Newark, blah blah blah. — *When Harry Met Sally*, 1989
- This country is just one big global village with everyone out there going blah blah blah. — *Sleepless in Seattle*, 1993
- [The employers] can say "Oh yes and then you'd be wanting more leave blah blah blah and then you'll be having kids, we know what you Asian women are like". — S. Bowlby, S. Lloyd Evans and R. Mohammad, *Cool Places*, p. 237–238, 1998
- No can do, old boy. Not that simple, sorry. Procedure blah-blah. — Kevin Sampson, *Powder*, p. 41, 1999
- [E]xperienced [Tony] Blair-watchers, who've long known that his claims to techno know-how are mostly blah. — *The Guardian*, p. 6, 12th June 2003

blah *verb*

to say empty and meaningless things, to talk without saying anything worth saying *UK*

- [T]hese folk (who would doubtless blah on about how "free-spirited" they are) always revert to their predictable uniform. — *The Guardian*, p. 16, 28th June 2004

blah *adjective*

without energy, without spark, unmotivated *US, 1922*

- Part of the problem is a blah role: Steve is not a protagonist of many words, or even many revealing looks. — *Washington Post*, p. E7, 6th May 1981

blahs *noun*

a minor illness; a feeling of ennui *US*

- — Collin Baker et al., *College Undergraduate Slang Study Conducted at Brown University*, p. 81, 1968

blair; blare *verb*

to criticise, humiliate or mock someone or something *UK*

Possibly from conventional 'blare' (to shout); probably predates Tony Blair's rise to politcal and media prominence, although current usage is certainly informed by his Prime Ministership.

- — David Rowan, *A Glossary for the 90s*, p. 46, 1998

blak *noun*

black *UK*

Fashionable misspelling.

- Radio 1 prides itself on new spelling: def, lite, blak, tekno, dreem and teem. — *The Sunday Times*, p. 13, 23rd June 2002

blam *verb*

to slam loudly *BARBADOS*

- — Frank A. Collymore, *Barbadian Dialect*, p. 20, 1965

blamed; blame *adjective*

used as a euphemistic intensifier replacing 'damned' *US*

An equivalent to **BLINKING**.

- Music was different in New Orleans because many were too blamed ignorant to read — R.M. Jones, *quoted in Chicago Documentary by Frederic Ramsay Junior*, p. 10, 1944

blancas *noun*

amphetamines or other central nervous system stimulants *US*

Border Spanish used in English conversation by Mexican-Americans; from the Spanish for 'white'.

- It's something like bennies – blancas – only not as good. — Malcolm Braly, *On the Yard*, p. 281, 1967
- — Dagoberto Fuentes and Jose Lopez, *Barrio Language Dictionary*, p. 17, 1974

blanco *noun*

heroin; cocaine *US, 1973*

Spanish for 'white'.

- — US Department of Justice, *Street Terms*, October 1994
- — Mike Haskins, *Drugs*, p. 280, 2003

blank *noun*

1 a packet of non-narcotic white powder sold as narcotics *US*

- Heroin itself has a bitter taste and if a junkie tastes some stuff before he uses it and it's real sweet he figures he's bought a blank and gets upset. — James Mills, *The Panic in Needle Park*, p. 72, 1966
- — Richard Lingeman, *Drugs from A to Z*, p. 25, 1969
- — Angela Devlin, *Prison Patter*, p. 28, 1996

2 a worthless person or thing *US*

- — Hyman E. Goldin et al., *Dictionary of American Underworld Lingo*, p. 29, 1950

3 in a carnival, a bad day, a bad engagement or a bad customer *US*

- What a BLANK that bum was. He looked like he had money, but all he had was three lousy bucks. — Gene Sorrows, *All About Carnivals*, p. 10, 1985

4 in poker, a useless card in the dealt hand *US*

- — Edwin Silberstang, *Winning Poker for the Serious Player*, p. 217, 1992

5 the top of a skateboard *US*

- — Laura Torbet, *The Complete Book of Skateboarding*, p. 105, 1976

6 a refusal of parole *UK*

- — Angela Devlin, *Prison Patter*, p. 28, 1996

7 a tablet of Aspirin *US*

- — Charles Shafer, *Folk Speech in Texas Prisons*, p. 198, 1990

▸ **give someone the blank**

to ignore someone *UK*

- [H]e gives me the blank! — Martin King and Martin Knight, *The Naughty Nineties*, p. 45, 1999

blank *verb*

1 to ignore someone *UK, 1977*

Any response is 'blanked out'.

- — Angela Devlin, *Prison Patter*, p. 28, 1996
- Aussie blanks me and leaves. — Pete McCarthy, *McCarthy's Bar*, p. 131, 2000
- Nina blanks him – fucking class. Now that is a lady. Blanking the likes of Randall is nothing bar quality. — Kevin Sampson, *Outlaws*, p. 110, 2001
- Blanking someone in prison as you pass them on a landing can have dire consequences [...] getting blanked, even by a stranger, is tantamount to receiving a threat[.] — *The Guardian*, 5th September 2002

2 to forget something *UK*

- I just blanked it. — Angela Devlin, *Prison Patter*, p. 28, 1996

3 to erase something *UK*

An abbreviated variation of the conventional 'blank out'.

- — Jonathon Green, *Dictionary of Slang*, 1998

blank; blankety; blankety-blank

used as a self-censored deletion of an expletive, regardless of part of speech *UK, 1854*

Written more often than spoken, but not without uses in speech.

- Two Judges Wish Two Thieves A Blankety-Blank Christmas [Headline] — *San Francisco News*, p. 8, 20th December 1945
- "This blanking weather," he growled. "Blanking out-of-town blanks brought it with 'em, probably." — *San Francisco Chronicle, This World*, p. 9, 20th June 1948
- "Throw that blank blank out!" ordered Dressen angrily. "Throw him out!" — *San Francisco Examiner*, p. 33, 7th August 1953
- — Joseph A. Weingarten, *An American Dictionary of Slang*, p. 30, 1954
- It seems that Bond (who is lustily and very affectionately described by Ford as that "low-down blankety-blank") had so pestered the director (known to Bond simply as "The Old Man" or, more sentimentally, "that phony old Irish blank of a blank") that Ford was forced to perform this unconscionable act in order to get Bond off his back. — *TV Guide*, p. 6, 19th November 1960
- Oh, go ahead and inject your blankety-blank personal note, you old geezer. — *Washington Post*, p. B1, 4th July 1977
- It would have been cool if I was up against some other heavy hitters and beat them. And then said, 'In your face, Blankety Blank!' [Quoting Jack Black] — *Variety*, p. A4, 23rd March 2004

blank canvas *noun*

the body of a person who is about to get their first tattoo *US*

- — *Los Angeles Times Magazine*, p. 7, 13th July 1997

blanket *noun*

1 a cigarette paper *US, 1925*

- — Hyman E. Goldin et al., *Dictionary of American Underworld Lingo*, p. 29, 1950

2 a marijuana cigarette *US, 1935*

Perhaps because it is shaped as a *blanket* roll.

- — Richard A. Spears, *The Slang and Jargon of Drugs and Drink*, p. 50, 1986
- — Mike Haskins, *Drugs*, p. 286, 2003

3 any sandwich *US*

- — *San Francisco Examiner*, p. III-2, 22nd March 1960

4 an overcoat; a top coat *US, 1925*

- —H. Craig Collins, *Street Gangs*, p. 221, 1979

5 in the US military, a beret *US*

- He'd always refused to wear the blanket, the green beret.—Richard Marcinko and John Weisman, *The Rogue Warrior*, p. 238, 1992

6 in trucking, a parking lot *US*

- —Wayne Floyd, *Jason's Authentic Dictionary of CB Slang*, p. 10, 1976

▸ on the blanket

1 used of prisoners who refuse to wear a uniform as a means of protest and are thereby wrapped in a blanket *UK*
Originating with republican prisoners making a political protest in the Maze Prison in Belfast in the mid-1970s.

2 (of an Indian) used for describing someone who has been aggressive but has stopped *CANADA*

- He made a flat motion with his two hands against the ground. "But I'm on the blanket." "What's that mean?" she asked. "It's what an Indian says when he's through fighting, running around, raising hell.—Ernest Haycox, *Earthbreakers*, p. 44, 1959
- The younger generation of Indians speaks contemptuously of the old Indian ways and sneers at returning "to the blanket."—*Native Voice*, p. 1, 4th January 1959

blanket-ass *noun*
a native American Indian *US, 1973*
Derogatory.

- The Native American Student Council says it will not sit by idly while slurs such as "mucket," "blanket ass," "dirty skin" and "lazy" are hurled at the school's 138 American Indians[.]—*Salt Lake Tribune*, p. D1, 10th October 1994
- "I've been called 'blanket ass' and 'prairie nigger' more times than I can count," he said.—*Philadelphia Inquirer*, 7th November 1999

blanket craps *noun*
an informal game of craps with the shooter acting as banker *US, 1977*

- —Thomas L. Clark, *The Dictionary of Gambling and Gaming*, p. 20, 1987

blanket drill *noun*
sex in bed *US*

- —Roger Blake, *The American Dictionary of Sexual Terms*, p. 19, 1964

blanket finish *noun*
in horse racing, a close finish between several horses *US*
So called because the horses contending for the lead could all be covered by a single figurative blanket.

- —David W. Maurer, *Argot of the Racetrack*, p. 14, 1951

blanket game *noun*
in the circus or carnival, a private gambling game for employees only, played on a blanket *UK*

- —Joe McKennon, *Circus Lingo*, p. 17, 1980

blanket harbour *noun*
bed *CANADA*

- —T.K. Pratt, *oral informant in Prince Edward Island Sayings*, p. 92, 1998

blanket party *noun*
a ritual in which the offending person is covered with a blanket, which prevents identification of the wrong-doers, and then beaten *US, 1969*

- —John R. Armore and Joseph D. Wolfe, *Dictionary of Desperation*, p. 20, 1976
- —Linda Reinberg, *In the Field*, p. 24, 1991

blanket roll *noun*
a controlled roll of the dice by a skilled cheat, best made on a blanket spread on the ground *US*

- —*The Annals of the American Academy of Political and Social Sciences*, p. 128, May 1950

blankety; blankety-blank
▷ **see:** BLANK

blare *verb*
▷ **see:** BLAIR

blarney *noun*

1 honeyed flattery, pleasant talk that seeks to deceive; hence plausible nonsense *IRELAND, 1766*
A fine example can be found at *www.blarneycastle.ie* in the gentle assertion that 'the term "Blarney" was introduced into the English language by Elizabeth 1 of England[.]'.

2 an Irish accent *UK*
The Blarney stone is incorporated into the battlements of Blarney Castle – eight miles north of Cork city in southern Ireland. Familiar legend holds the promise that whoever kisses this stone will receive the gift of eloquence, hence 'blarney' (pleasant talk), here considered to be speech with an Irish lilt.

- [H]e still had that ridiculous twang in his TV accent, that helpful suggestion of blarney[.]—James Hawes, *Dead Long Enough*, p. 85, 2000

blarney *verb*
to talk flatteringly or persuasively *UK, 1803*

- [W]ithin a minute, after out-blarneying the Irish, she handed me the receiver silently—Dick Francis, *Break In*, p. 147, 1986
- [They] had blarneyed their way past the library-attendant[.] —David Foster Wallace, *Infinite Jest*, p. 653, 1996

blarneying *adjective*
of a manner of speech, persuasive, flattering *US, 1869*

- [T]his careful reliable person who wrote such blarneying letters[.] —Ivan Doig, p. 136, 1980

blarry *adjective*
▷ **see:** BLERRY

blart *verb*
to talk compulsively, especially about emotional upheaval *UK*
A combination of conventional 'blurt' and **BLAB** (to talk) or 'blub' (to cry).

- I remember explaining to her that I was still upset but I wasn't crying anymore. I called it my post-blart stage.—Frank Skinner, *Frank Skinner*, p. 342, 2001

blase blase
and so on and so on *US*
An embellishment of the more expected **BLAH BLAH BLAH**.

- —Gary K. Farlow, *Prison-ese*, p. 4, 2002

blasé queen *noun*
a characteristically up-market homosexual male *UK*

- —Paul Baker, *Polari*, p. 165, 2002

blast *noun*

1 an extremeley enjoyable time *US, 1950*

- [B]efore you know it she's going tandem with you and that's the end of the whole blast.—Frederick Kohner, *Gidget*, p. 39, 1957
- "The cops saw us so we had to ditch," she wrote, adding, "Everyone was the party... what a blast ... everyone was drunk."—*San Francisco Chronicle*, p. 3, 15th March 1958
- It would be such a blast for you guys to reach a half-million houses. —*Wayne's World*, 1992
- [I]t should sound like I'm having a blast[.]—Howard Stern, *Miss America*, p. 138, 1995

2 a party, especially a loud and raucous one *UK, 1959*

- I said yes, she could have a party here – now she's inviting all her friends to come to a blast. [The Neighbors comic strip]—*San Francisco News Call-Bulletin*, p. 13, 20th June 1960
- Patrolman Charles Roberts called it "a real blast" in the usually quiet Westerview residential section on the San Mateo coast.—*San Francisco News Call-Bulletin*, p. 3, 25th September 1964

3 an injection of a drug *US*

- I want it main line for one blast.—George Mandel, *Flee the Angry Strangers*, p. 378–379, 1952

4 cocaine; any drug with a powerful effect *US, 1992*

- —Mike Haskins, *Drugs*, p. 280, 2003

5 a taste or a portion, especially of alcohic drink *UK*

- See's another blast a that malt[.]—Michael Munro, *The Patter, Another Blast*, 1988

6 a parachute jump *US*
Vietnam war usage.

- —Linda Reinberg, *In the Field*, p. 24, 1991

7 an escape *US*

- Red, we need some hooks and need them quick. We've got a blast going in two weeks[.]—Red Rudensky, *The Gonif*, p. 47, 1970

8 a stern admonishment; a severe rebuke *US, 1874*

blast *verb*

1 to use a drug, especially to smoke marijuana *US, 1943*

- Sure, we'll be seeing you over the weekend, and we'll blast some of this tea, okay?—John Clellon Holmes, *John Clellon*, p. 106, 1952

- We were at a crazy pad before going and were blasting like crazy and were up so high that I just didn't give a shit for anyone[.] — Hubert Selby Jr, *Last Exit to Brooklyn*, p. 39–40, 1957
- Do you want to blast? I have two in my purse. — Morton Cooper, *High School Confidential*, p. 69, 1958
- — Francis J. Rigney and L. Douglas Smith, *The Real Bohemia*, p. xiii, 1961
- I didn't know this bit coot blasted any? — Mickey Spillane, *Return of the Hood*, p. 88, 1964
- Nay, dad, I've been blasting yerba. I have a going high. — Piri Thomas, *Down These Mean Streets*, p. 110, 1967
- Here you'd be with a joint in your hand, and you'd be blasting before you knew what had happened. — Herbert Huncke, *Guilty of Everything*, p. 1–2, 1990
- — Angela Devlin, *Prison Patter*, p. 28, 1996

2 to criticise someone or something severely *UK, 1953*
Mainly journalistic.
- Critics Blast N.Y. School for Gay Pupils[.] — *Minneapolis-St. Paul Pioneer Press*, 25th August 2003

3 to reprimand someone *UK, 1984*

blast!
used for expressing disgust or dismay *UK, 1634*
- Blast! Out of ammo! — *Austin Powers*, 1997

blasted *adjective*
1 cursed, damned; often used as a euphemism for 'bloody' *UK, 1750*
- I'm up with the lark again (before the blasted lark) so I'm writing back straight away[.] — Mary Hooper, *(megan)2*, p. 99, 1999

2 highly intoxicated on any drug or alcohol *US, 1928*
- Everyone would leave the Strip at 2 when the clubs closed and go to Cantor's en masse so blasted out of their heads that if you asked someone what time it was they backed away, wide-eyed, as though you'd presented them with a philosophical impossibility. — Eve Babitz, *Eve's Hollywood*, p. 234, 1974
- Cause like this one time with Eric, when we got blasted at his house. — *Kids*, 1995
- The only things to do in an airport are shop, drink, drink, shop, and then get completely blasted. — Wayne Anthony, *Spanish Highs*, p. 89, 1999
- — Mike Haskins, *Drugs*, p. 291, 2003

blaster *noun*
1 a gun, especially a pistol *US*
- [N]either of them had the guts to go for a rod because they knew I had a blaster in my belt and would chop them down the second they moved. — Mickey Spillane, *Return of the Hood*, p. 106, 1964

2 a powerful, hard-breaking wave *US*
- — John Severson, *Modern Surfing Around the World*, p. 165, 1964

blast from the past *noun*
a song that was popular in the past and is still popular with those who were young when the song was popular *US, 1965*
- Speedy went with a blast from the past: cold-storaged Kate Smith, a known quantity once, of uncertain mornings of late[.] — Bill Cardoso, *The Maltese Sangweech*, p. 127–128, 1984

blasting oil *noun*
nitroglycerin, used by criminals to blast open safes *US*
- — Vincent J. Monteleone, *Criminal Slang*, p. 25, 1949

blast off *verb*
1 to leave *US, 1954*
Borrowed with great fervour from the language of space travel.
- — J. E. Lighter, *Historical Dictionary of American Slang, Volume 1*, p. 182, 1994

2 to use and become intoxicated by a drug *US, 1961*
- She immediately broke it in two and blasted off one half right there[.] — Lanre Fehintola, *Charlie Says...*, p. 33, 2000

3 of a car, especially a racing car, to drive off at speed *AUSTRALIA, 1984*
Uses a rocket launch as a metaphor.

blast party *noun*
a gathering of marijuana smokers *US*
- — *New York Times Magazine*, p. 87, 16th March 1958

blasty *adjective*
in Newfoundland, used of a dead, dry branch, good for kindling *CANADA*
- The branches would make perfect "blasty boughs" - dry tree parts which create a crackling noise when burned. — Clyde Rose, *The Blasty Bough*, p. 47, 1980

blat *noun*
a short journey, usually for pleasure *UK*
Used by late 1980s – early 90s counterculture travellers.
- — Martin Roach, *Dr. Marten's Air Wair*, 1999: 'Glossary of travellers' terms'

blat *verb*
to fire a gun *UK*
Probably derived from a comic strip representation of a weapon in action: 'Blat! Blat! Blat!'.
- His weapon was already cocked, so he just started blatting like an idiot. I blatted back, getting the rounds down at him[.] — Andy McNab, *Immediate Action*, p. 40, 1995

blatant *adjective*
excellent *UK*
Recorded in use among young urban blacks.
- Mind you, Elisha thought, I'd be gigglin' if I was dealin' wid summick like him. Blatant. — Courttia Newland, *Society Within*, p. 4, 1999

blathered *adjective*
drunk *UK*
From the dialect word *blather* (to talk nonsense).
- — *e-cyclopaedia*, 20th March 2002

blatherskite; bletherskite; bletherskate *noun*
a person who talks too much or too offensively *US, 1791*
Originally Scottish dialect.
- Gloves or no gloves, Arsene Wenger's Arsenal are more likely to warm the hands than did George Graham's team during its bleaker periods. Yet, the old blatherskite did win two league championships[.] — *Irish Times*, 30th December 1996

blats *noun*
cash, money *UK*
In Royal Air Force use, 2002.

blatted *adjective*
drunk *UK, 2003*

blaxploitation *noun*
the exploitation of black culture and imagery for commercial gain, especially in films *US, 1971*
- THE VERY BEST OF BLAXPLOITATION 70'S MOVIE THEMES & FUNK SOUL CLASSICS — *SUPERBAD*, 2004

blaze *noun*
1 in a card game with five cards per hand, a hand with five face cards *US*
- — Frank Garcia, *Marked Cards and Loaded Dice*, p. 250, 1962
- — Irwin Steig, *Common Sense in Poker*, p. 182, 1963

2 in a deck of playing cards, a face card *US*
- — Thomas L. Clark, *The Dictionary of Gambling and Gaming*, p. 20, 1987

3 marijuana *US*

blaze *verb*
1 to leave *US, 1983*
- — *Washingnton Post*, 14th October 1993

2 to move quickly *US*
- — Connie Eble (Editor), *UNC-CH Campus Slang*, p. 1, Fall 1996

3 to have sex *US*
- — Judi Sanders, *Da Bomb*, p. 2, 1997

4 to light a marijuana cigarette or other drug-smoking conveyance *US*
Also expressed as to 'blaze up'.
- Yo wastoid – you're not gonna blaze up in here! — *The Breakfast Club*, 1985
- Go behind tha curtains while my fanz they point / You know what Loc's doin', I'm blazin a joint — Tone Loc, *Cheeba Cheeba*, 1989
- So I'm blazing with my friends man. — *Dazed and Confused*, 1993
- She was in the living room stripping off her clothes and blazing the other half. — Lanre Fehintola, *Charlie Says...*, p. 33, 2000
- — Mike Haskins, *Drugs*, p. 290, 2003

blazed *adjective*
drug-intoxicated
- — Nick Brownlee, *This Is Cannabis*, p. 151, 2002

blaze full *noun*
in poker, a hand consisting of three cards of one face card rank and a pair of another *US, 1968*

The 'full' is drawn from the conventional name for the hand, a 'full house'.

• —Thomas L. Clark, *The Dictionary of Gambling and Gaming*, p. 20, 1987

blazer *noun*

a big diamond *US*

• —Vincent J. Monteleone, *Criminal Slang*, p. 25, 1949

blazes *noun*

the flames of hell *UK, 1818*

Used in comparisons and as a euphemism for 'hell'.

• There's a might big crop out there and we sure as blazes could use a couple of extry hands. —Mezz Mezzrow, *Really the Blues*, p. 133, 1946
• We're going to scare the blazes out of some people, I think. —Mickey Spillane, *My Gun is Quick*, p. 120, 1950

blazing *adjective*

exceptionally attractive *UK, 1864*

• — *Ebony Magazine*, p. 156, August 2000

blazing *adverb*

used as an intensifier *US, 1855*

Generally euphemistic for **BLOODY**.

bleach *verb*

1 to spend an extended period of days and nights in night-clubs *UK*

• "Bleaching" they call it. When you're out for so long and you don't see the sun for so long that your skin goes white. —Dave Courtney, *Raving Lunacy*, p. 78, 2000

2 to soak and flush a hypodermic needle and syringe with bleach to prevent transmission of HIV *US*

• —Geoffrey Froner, *Digging for Diamonds*, p. 10, 1989

3 to lie awake at night with a sense of impending doom *JAMAICA*

• —Peter L. Patrick, *Some Recent Jamaican Creole Words*, 2003

bleacher bum *noun*

1 a loud, rowdy sports fan who favours the inexpensive bleacher seats *US*

• Giant's centerfielder Bill North recieved an afternoon of heckling from the Wrigley Field bleacher bums. [Caption] —*San Francisco Chronicle*, p. 53, 25th June 1981
• In a booming bleacher bum voice C.C. ordered coffee from a trusty passing his open office door. —Seth Morgan, *Homeboy*, p. 106, 1990

2 a fan of the Chicago Cubs professional baseball team *US*

• —Louis Phillips and Burnham Holmes, *The Complete Book of Sports Nicknames*, p. 204, 1998

bleach tabs *noun*

sterilising tablets issued to drug addicts *UK*

• —Angela Devlin, *Prison Patter*, p. 28, 1996

bleat *noun*

1 in prison, a petition to the Home Secretary *UK*

• The new geezer put in a bleat the day he arrived. —Paul Tempest, *Lag's Lexicon*, p. 18, 1950

2 a feeble complaint *UK, 1916*

bleat *verb*

1 to complain *US*

• —M. Allen Henderson, *How Con Games Work*, p. 217, 1985

2 to repeatedly deny guilt *UK*

• —Angela Devlin, *Prison Patter*, p. 28, 1996

bleed *noun*

in pinball, a ball that leaves play having scored few points *US*

• —Edward Trapunski, *Special When Lit*, p. 152, 1979

bleed *verb*

1 to extort money from someone *UK, 1680*

• —Vincent J. Monteleone, *Criminal Slang*, p. 25, 1949

2 to dilute a drug *US*

• Buy four, bleed in a ounce of cut, make it five. —Richard Price, *Clockers*, p. 185, 1992

3 to be showing lipstick on your face or clothes *US*

• Sandy sat up and grinned, and said,"You're bleeding, Peter," meaning I had lipstick on my face[.] —Evan Hunter, *Last Summer*, p. 187, 1968

▸ **bleed someone dry; bleed someone white**

to drain a person or other resource of all money or value *UK, 1982*

The image of draining a life's blood.

bleeder *noun*

1 a person *UK, 1887*

• The aunt was a proper aunt and what a busy bleeder she was. —Bill Naughton, *Alfie Darling*, 1970
• There aint half been some clever bastards / Lucky bleeders. lucky bleeders[.] —Ian Dury, *There Aint Half Been Some Clever Bastards*, 1977

2 a contemptible person *UK, 1887*

• [A]s for this bugger, you only have to clock the bleeder, looks like the very devil[.] —Salman Rushdie, *The Satanic verses*, p. 169, 1988

3 a casino employee or executive who worries extensively about money being lost to gamblers *US, 1974*

• He will try to avoid picking "bleeders" or "sweaters." That is executives who so hate to see the player win they may cheat the customer without the permission of the hotel, just out of sheer competitiveness. —Mario Puzo, *Inside Las Vegas*, p. 182, 1977
• —Thomas L. Clark, *The Dictionary of Gambling and Gaming*, p. 20, 1987

4 in poker, a player who methodically if undramatically drains money from the game by conservative, steady play *US*

• —George Percy, *The Language of Poker*, p. 10, 1988

5 a boxer who is prone to bleeding *US*

• [H]e was not a good defnesive fighter and to cap it, a bleeder. —Edwin Torres, *Carlito's Way*, p. 135, 1975

bleeding *adjective*

used as an intensifier *UK, 1858*

Originally replaced **BLOODY**, then used in its own right or as a substitute for less acceptable intensifiers; not necessarily intended as euphemistic.

• I wish it was as bleeding easy as that. —Frank Norman, *Bang To Rights*, p. 31, 1958
• What was his fucking problem? Bleedin' snob. —Dave Courtney, *Raving Lunacy*, p. 65, 2000

bleeding *adverb*

used as an intensifier *UK, 1884*

After the adjective.

• 'Will you bleeding well shut up?' – the horrid soundtrack to so much British life. — *The Guardian*, 1st May 2004

bleeding deacon *noun*

a person with an over-inflated sense of self-importance to an organisation *US*

Usually used in the context of self-help recover groups such as Alcoholics Anonymous.

• It will be what I call the 'tradition lawyers.' They find it easier to live with black and white than they do with gray. These 'bleeding deacons' – these fundamentalists – are afraid of and fight any change. — *New York Times*, p. 40 (Section 6), 21st February 1988
• People who behave in this manner in the A.A. program – those who abandon self in the effort to help others – are called "bleeding deacons." —Terence T. Gorski, *Understanding the Twelve Steps*, p. 123, 1989
• He was just one very dry and very angry alcoholic – often called a "bleeding deacon" (as contrasted to an "elder statesman") in earlier A.A. parlance. —Dick B., *That Amazing Grace*, p. 109, 1996
• Most will do the right thing and accept discussion of drugs. Those that don't will be populated mostly by "bleeding deacons" masquerading as elder statesmen, as members vote with their feet. (Letter to the editor). — *Village Voice*, p. 42, 5th June 2001

bleeding edge *noun*

the absolute forefront of technology *US, 2000*

A punning combination of 'leading edge' and 'cutting edge'.

• — Susie Dent, *The Language Report*, p. 30, 2003

bleeding heart *adjective*

sensitive to the plight of others, anguished *UK*

Disparaging, often as 'bleeding heart liberal'.

• Oh, she's a peace marcher. One of those bleeding-heart types. —Elmore Leonard, *Bandist*, 1987
• [A]ll those bleeding-heart lefty liberal idiots who thought the working classes invented football[.] —Tony Wilson, *24 Hour Party People*, 2002

bleeding obvious *noun*

anything that really shouldn't need saying *AUSTRALIA*

In 2003 the British satirical website 'University of the Bleeding Obvious' was one of the most popular comedy sites on the Internet.

- Another from the Department of the Bleeding Obvious: [...] What To Do is: Do not use them. — *Sydney Morning Herald*, 12th September 1996
- Pedlars of the bleeding obvious. — *Sydney Morning Herald*, 10th June 2003

bleeding spot *noun*

an oil leak on an asphalt road *US*

- — *American Speech*, p. 267, December 1962: 'The language of traffic policemen'

bleeding well *adverb*

certainly, definitely *UK, 1884*

- SHOPKEEPER: You don't need a license for your cat. CUSTOMER: I bleeding well do and I got one. — *Monty Python's Flying Circus*, 1970

bleep *verb*

to superimpose an electronic noise over expletives in a television or radio broadcast *US, 1966*

- — *American Speech*, Fall-Winter 1976
- Just bleep out the fucks and shit shits. — *Natural Born Killers*, 1994
- Stern has made the same kind of threat dozens of times in the past, often in response to the way his flagship station, WXRK-FM in New York, bleeps out extreme sexual content. — *Los Angeles Times*, p. F1, 22nd March 2004

bleep

used as a euphemistic replacement for an expletive, regardless of part of speech *US, 1968*

- You could hardly hear Columnist Sheilah Graham for the "bleeps" on KPIX's "Hot Line" Wednesday morning. Once she started discussing "Portnoy's Compalint," it was bleepers' creepers all the way. — *San Francisco Chronicle*, p. 29, 7th March 1969
- When you're having trouble stopping them and you're not moving the ball, it's going to be a bleeping long day. [Quoting John Madden] — *San Francisco Chronicle*, p. 44, 4th September 1972
- — *American Speech*, Fall-Winter 1976
- I'm a bleep," Howard said, "because if you say what I think you're going to say, that's the way it'll come out. — Elmore Leonard, *Touch*, p. 220, 1977

bleezin *adjective*

drunk *UK*

- — *e-cyclopaedia*, 20th March 2002

blem *noun*

a pimple *US*

A shortened form of the conventional English 'blemish'.

- — Collin Baker et al., *College Undergraduate Slang Study Conducted at Brown University*, p. 82, 1968

blench *adjective*

used approvingly to describe a muscular person *UK*

- Usher was looking extremely blench on Richard and Judy this afternoon. — *The Guardian*, 12th January 2005

Blenheimers *noun*

memory loss due to wine consumption *NEW ZEALAND*

Named after a wine brand.

- — David McGill, *David McGill's Complete Kiwi Slang Dictionary*, p. 15, 1998

blerry; blarry; blirry *adjective*

used as an intensifier *SOUTH AFRICA, 1920*

A variation of **BLOODY** reflecting Afrikaans pronunciation.

- "Come on, gel!" bellowed the sturdy farmer as he hauled me through a vicious, biting thicket. "Not so blerry Miss World anymore, hey! Miss blerry Worzel Gummidge now, ha!" — *The Observer*, 2nd June 2002

blert *noun*

a fool *UK*

Liverpool usage.

- You BLERT! You fucking soft cunt! — Kevin Sampson, *Clubland*, p. 118, 2002
- Play fuckin football, O'Brien. Defend. Yer blert. — Niall Griffiths, *Kelly + Victor*, p. 103, 2002

bless *verb*

to approve the forwarding of a proposed action *US*

Military usage.

- — Department of the Army, *Staff Officer's Guidebook*, p. 56, 1986

bless

used ironically, as if patronising a child *UK*

An abbreviation of the prayer: 'God bless', often preceded with a cod-sympathetic 'aah!'.

- Before we set off Marcus got out, bent a lamp-post in two and tied it in a knot. His little, harmless way of getting rid of pent-up aggression, bless. — Dave Courtney, *Stop the Ride I Want to Get Off*, p. 185, 1999
- But you had to be back in your room by 10.30 p.m. And we always were. Bless. — Alan Titchmarsh, *Trowell and Error*, p. 126, 2002

blessed sacrament *noun*

marijuana *US*

- — Rick Ayers (Editor), *Slang Dictionary*, p. 5, 2001

blessing *noun*

a harsh rebuke *BAHAMAS*

- — John A. Holm, *Dictionary of Bahamian English*, p. 21, 1982

bless your cotton socks; bless your little cotton socks

used for registering gratitude or affection *UK, 1961*

A catchphrase favoured by the middle-classes. Considered to be archaic when first recorded however the phrase has survived into C21.

- Tony Benn, for instance, God bless him and his cotton socks[.] — Stuart Jeffries, *Mrs Slocombe's Pussy*, p. 201, 2000

bless your pea-pickin' hearts

used for expressing thanks *US*

A catchphrase television sign-off on *The Ernie Ford Show* (NBC, 1956–61), a music variety programme. Repeated with referential humour.

bletch!

used as an all-purpose, potent expression of disgust *US*

From the German *brechen* (to vomit).

- — *CoEvolution Quarterly*, p. 26, Spring 1981
- — Guy L. Steele et al., *The Hacker's Dictionary*, p. 33, 1983

bletcherous *adjective*

in computing, poorly designed, dysfunctional *US*

- — *CoEvolution Quarterly*, p. 26, Spring 1981
- — Guy L. Steele et al., *The Hacker's Dictionary*, p. 33, 1983

bletherskite; bletherskate *noun*

▷ **see:** BLATHERSKITE

blew-it *noun*

a Buick car *US*

- — Anna Scotti and Paul Young, *Buzzwords*, p. 35, 1997

blighter *noun*

1 a despicable male *UK, 1896*

- Billy had had a good start, and he was a mad little blighter. — John Burke and Stuart Douglass, *The Boys*, p. 104, 1962
- The blighter has put me in a damn' tricky spot. — Douglas Rutherford, *The Creeping Flesh*, p. 74, 1963

2 a man *UK, 1904*

From jocular use of the previous sense.

Blighty *nickname*

Britain; England *UK, 1915*

Originally military, from Hindustani *bilayati* and Arabic *wilayati* (foreign, especially European).

- [W]e end up back in Blighty because some dumb bitch hasn't filled in the right forms. — Colin Butts, *Is Harry on the Boat?*, p. 57, 1997
- Those are quite popular back home in Blighty[.] — Christopher Brookmyre, *Not the End of the World*, p. 79, 1998

bliksem *noun*

a despicable person, a contemptible fool *SOUTH AFRICA, 1950*

From Afrikaans *bliksem* (lightning).

- — Jean Branford, *A Dictionary of South African English*, p. 21–22, 1978

bliksem *verb*

to smack, punch or beat up someone *SOUTH AFRICA*

Probably a reduction of the earlier South African 'to donner the bliksem out of' (to beat the lights out of).

- I'm going to bliksem that doos! — *Surfrikan Slang*, 2004

blim *noun*

a small crumb of cannabis resin *UK*

- I'd pick up blims which I would then stick down cigarettes to smoke[.] — Macfarlane, Macfarlane and Robson, *The User*, p. 116, 1996

blim burn *noun*

a scorch mark or a tiny burn-hole as a result, when smoking hashish, of burning particles; a small burning cinder of cannabis resin *UK*

- —Nick Jones, *Spliffs*, p. 250, 2003
- I sparked up a fat spliff of fucking soapbar / a blim-burn burnt right down to my dick[.]—Goldie Looking Chain *Soap Bar*, 2004

blim burn *verb*

to mark or burn something with a blim burn *UK*

- Well anyway, I think it's better myself to lean forward when smoking the soapbar, coz, er, you're less likely to, er, blim burn yourself, know what I mean.—Goldie Looking Chain *Soap Bar*, 2004

blimey!; blime!

used for registering surprise or shock *UK, 1889*

An abbreviation of **COR BLIMEY!** (God blind me!).

- Oh, blimey, another student prince.—Graeme Kent, *The Queen's Corporal [Six Granada Plays]*, p. 87, 1959
- "Blimey!" laughed Tony—Kevin Sampson, *Powder*, p. 21, 1999
- "Blimey," Josie said. "What brought this on?"—Mary Hooper, *(megan)2*, p. 36, 1999

blimey O'Riley!; blimey O'Reilly!

used for registering surprise *UK*

- That'll do. That'll do. THAT'LL DO! They stop. A silence. Blimey O'Reilly. It's like the bloody Borgias' bathroom in here. —Alan Ayckbourn, *A Small Family Business*, 1987
- —Robert Wyatt and Hugh Hopper, *Blimey O'Riley*, 2003
- "It's the onset of a new Nazism for the 21st century." Blimey O'Reilly.—*The Guardian*, 23rd December 2003

blimmin'; blimmin' well *adjective*

used as a euphemistic intensifier *UK*

Possibly derived from **BLIMEY!** or **BLOOMING**.

- If British Rail want fifty pounds they can blimmin' well go out and become a prostitute.—*The Young Ones*, 8th May 1984
- In fact, they're offering everything that you're blimmin' well not! —Virgin Mobile *advertising leaflet*, June 2001

blimp *noun*

1 in necrophile usage, a corpse with a distended abdomen *US*

- —*Maledicta*, p. 180, Summer/Winter 1986–1987: 'Sexual slang: prostitutes, pedophiles, flagellators, transvestites, and necrophiles'

2 an obese person *US, 1934*

- —*Maledicta*, p. 38, 1983: 'More common patient-directed pejoratives used by medical personnel'

3 in the television and film industries, a camera's sound-proofing housing *US*

- —Tony Miller and Patricia George, *Cut! Print!*, p. 41, 1977

4 a bus *US*

- —Charles Shafer, *Folk Speech in Texas Prisons*, p. 198, 1990

5 a private inter-personal signal *UK*

- She was sendin over blimps, you know, she had the hots for me big time.—J.J. Connolly, *Layer Cake*, p. 89, 2000

blimpish *adjective*

very conservative or reactionary *UK, 1938*

After Colonel Blimp, a reactionary man.

- I realized I was in serious danger of turning into one of the Colonel Blimp types who sat around me in considerable numbers, eating cornflakes or porridge with their blimpish wives[.]—Bill Bryson, *Notes from a Small Island*, p. 249, 1995

blimp out; blimp up *verb*

to put on weight, especially if such growth is rapid or dramatic *US, 1979*

From the shape of a conventional 'blimp'.

blind *noun*

1 a legitimate business used to conceal an illegal one *US, 1929*

- Why didn't you tell us Carlito was using the office as a blind? We could have all been embarrassed.—Edwin Torres, *After Hours*, p. 369, 1979
- A sports news wire, set up in a back room that displayed the latest results from thee region's horse tracks, was the shop's reason for existing. My grandfather called the shop a "blind": a front for an off track betting operation.—Kim Rich, *Johnny's Girl*, p. 33, 1993

2 an area in prison where guards cannot easily see what is going on *US*

- Allright, you lame bastard, let's go to the blind.—James Harris, *A Convict's Dictionary*, p. 34, 1989

3 a baggage carriage, usually immediately behind the engine of a passenger train *US, 1893*

- I started to buzz fast in Louis' ear, telling him that A-Number-One was the greatest hobo who ever lived, hoboes ride the rods, blinds, and tops of trains[.]—Mezz Mezzrow, *Really the Blues*, p. 256, 1946

4 a wallet or purse *UK*

Pickpocket use.

- —*New Society*, 7th July 1977

▸ make the blind see

to perform oral sex on an uncircumcised man *US*

- —*Male Swinger Number 3*, p. 48, 1981: 'The complete gay dictionary'

blind *verb*

to curse, to swear *UK, 1943*

The meaning survives in **EFF AND BLIND**.

▸ blind by science

to defeat brawn with brains *AUSTRALIA, 1937*

According to Julian Franklyn 'it arose when the scientific boxers began, ca. 1880, to defeat the old bruisers'.

▸ blind with science

to confuse or convince someone by superior, inventive or nonsensical argument, explanation or vocabulary *UK, 1948*

Synonymous variation of earlier 'dazzle with science'.

- —*Time Out*, 20th October 1978

blind *adjective*

1 an intensifier, a euphemism for 'bloody' or 'bleeding' *UK*

- If you don't watch it, Monty, he said to himself, you'll be stone blind raving paralytic drunk.—Derek Bickerton, *Payroll*, p. 120, 1959

2 very drunk *UK, 1630*

- Many a night we put on the whole floor show, chorus and all, for a party of six or eight, and they were usually too blind to see it. —Mezz Mezzrow, *Really the Blues*, p. 84, 1946
- But you – being a man – don't care if the boys get blind.—Philip Wylie, *Opus 21*, p. 101, 1949
- [W]e were m ore than pretty well loopoed – we were blind. —John Nichols, *The Sterile Cuckoo*, p. 190, 1965

3 highly drug-intoxicated *US*

From an earlier alcohol sense.

- Later, they entered the movie house blind and sat down upstairs. —Hal Ellson, *The Golden Spike*, p. 234, 1952

4 (used of a car) stripped of headlights *US*

- They are all, as Tom Wolfe has written, "nude and blind," because they've been stripped of chrome and their headlights are gone. —*San Francisco Chronicle (from New York Times)*, p. 70, 2nd September 1977

5 (used of a bet) placed before seeing the cards being bet on *US*

- —Irwin Steig, *Common Sense in Poker*, p. 181, 1963

6 uncirmcumcised *US, 1925*

7 nasty, cruel *SOUTH AFRICA*

- Bru, that's a blind move. You scaled [stole] Jay's Britney Spears poster.—*Surfrikan Slang*, 2004

▸ like blind cobbler's thumbs

describes thickly swollen nipples *UK*

- Her nipples were huge and pierced, genuinely like the "blind cobbler's thumbs" to which stag comics always referred. —Garry Bushell, *The Face*, p. 104, 2001

▸ not take a blind bit of notice

to utterly ignore or disregard someone or something, to be oblivious to someone or something *UK, 1961*

blind bat *noun*

an AC-130 aircraft used for night flare missions in Vietnam between 1964 and 1970 *US*

Bats are not, of course, blind; they see at night.

- —Linda Reinberg, *In the Field*, p. 24, 1991

blind blast *noun*

a parachute jump at night in enemy territory *US*

Vietnam war usage.

- —Linda Reinberg, *In the Field*, p. 24, 1991

blind country *noun*

closed-in country of the colourless type and of little worth *AUSTRALIA*

- —Sidney J. Baker, *The Drum*, p. 91, 1959

blind drunk *adjective*

very drunk *UK*

- Sergeant Reed, so the story goes, got blind drunk, split his skull open, and remained unconscious until his death an hour and a half ago. —Graeme Kent, *The Queen's Corporal [Six Granada Plays]*, p. 106, 1959

blinded *adjective*
drunk *US*
• —Connie Eble (Editor), *UNC-CH Campus Slang*, p. 1, Spring 1984

blinder *noun*
anything excellent, or something excellently well-performed *UK, 1950*
From the 'dazzling' nature of anything so-called.
• —Bob Young and Micky Moody, *The Language of Rock 'n' Roll*, p. 17, 1985
• I think they all used to get together in the screws' tearoom and work out what shitty job to give me the next day. Then they came up with a blinder. —Lenny McLean, *The Guv'nor*, p. 43, 1998

blind fence *noun*
a person who unknowingly buys stolen goods *US*
• —Vincent J. Monteleone, *Criminal Slang*, p. 26, 1949

Blind Freddy; Blind Freddie *noun*
an imaginary blind man *AUSTRALIA, 1946*
Used as a type for an inability to see the obvious. The existence of a real person nicknamed 'Blind Freddy' has not been confirmed.
• —Sidney J. Baker, *The Australian Language*, p. 269, 1953
• Blind Freddie could see her frock had been practically ripped from her back. —John Wynnum, *Jiggin' in the Riggin'*, p. 89, 1965

blinding *adjective*
great, excellent, terrific, etc *UK*
Conventional brilliance can be 'blinding', literally.
• —Bob Young and Micky Moody, *The Language of Rock 'n' Roll*, p. 17, 1985
• Fucking blinding mate, fucking blinding! Happy as fuck! —Gavin Hills, *White Burger Danny*, p. 65, 1996
• He was a blinding geezer[.] —Dave Courtney, *Raving Lunacy*, p. 105, 2000
• Should be a blinding night out. — *Metro*, p. 23, 17th May 2002

blindingly *adverb*
excellently, wonderfully, stupendously *UK*
From **BLINDING** (excellent).
• No matter how blindingly I did a bit of work there was only so many people I could tell. —Dave Courtney, *Stop the Ride I Want to Get Off*, p. 399, 1999

blindjaret *noun*
a cigarette *JAMAICA, 1985*
• —Thomas H. Slone, *Rasta is Cuss*, p. 28, 2003

blind link *noun*
on the Internet, a link that is misleading or false, taking you somewhere other than where you expect to go *US*
Common on pornography websites.
• Detracting from the site are a few "blind links," notably under "Contact us," which lead to annoying error messsages. — *Legal Times*, p. 20, 19th June 2000

blindman's buff *noun*
snuff *UK*
Rhyming slang, noted by Red Daniells, 1980.

blindman's snow *noun*
a late spring snowfall, supposed to have curative properties for the eyes and feet *CANADA*
• A snow in May (Mary's month) when put in the eyes, will cure blindness. —T. K. Pratt, *oral citation in The Dictionary of Prince Edward Island English*, p. 18, 1988

blind mullet *noun*
a piece of excrement floating in the water *AUSTRALIA*
• Squid heaved his board sideways to avoid a nasty looking clump of toilet paper and turd. 'Blind mullets' he warned and the boys lifted up their legs. —Kathy Lette, *Girls' Night Out*, p. 192, 1987

blind pig *noun*
1 a speakeasy, where alcohol is served illegally *US, 1886*
• Of the 50-odd blind pigs in 52nd Street, between Fifth and sixth, only two remained. —Jack Lait and Lee Mortimer, *New York Confidential*, p. 43, 1948
• They hadn't been able to locate him in any of the blind pigs or whorehouses where he usually holed up, but he could have found a new place. —Jim Thompson, *The Nothing Man*, p. 142, 1954
• There is no way of estimating how many night clubs, speakeasies and blind pigs existed in the Broadway sector then. —Robert Sylvester, *No Cover Charge*, p. 138, 1956
• I found out from arguments between Mama and Pap that cousin Bunny had been a fast twenty five year old hustler who was operating a blind pig and poker trap in Vicksburg's sin district that night that Mama saw Papa for the first time. —Iceberg Slim (Robert Beck), *Mama Black Widow*, p. 56, 1969
• Prohibition closed down every bar in the city. Blind pigs sprouted like crocuses in April. "We had about four bootleg joints right around here," Alex Nickerson told me, "and there were dozens and dozens all around the city." —Harry Bruce, *Down Home*, p. 262, 1988

2 in poker, an unskilled but lucky player *US*
From the addage that even a blind pig will find an acorn over time.
• —John Vorhaus, *The Big Book of Poker Slang*, p. 7, 1996

blind pigeon *noun*
stuffed cabbage *US*
• —Amy and Denise McFadden, *CoalSpeak*, p. 2, 1997

blinds *noun*
1 dark glasses *BERMUDA*
• —Peter A. Smith and Fred M. Barritt, *Bermewjan Vurds*, 1985

2 among bus-spotters, a bus' roller display of desinations *UK*
• The bit that tells you where the bus is going – the "blinds" if you are an enthusiast – said that the bus was a rail replacement service. —Iain Aitch, *A Feete Worse Than Death*, p. 91, 2003

blindside *verb*
to hit or attack someone without warning *US, 1968*
Originally a term from American football, and then extended as a metaphor.
• "He got past me Rog. He blindsided me," Walter Pulaski said. —Robert Campbell, *Alice in La-La Land*, p. 45, 1987
• And next thing I knew the little bastard had blindsided the lot of us, got the contract for himself. —John Williams, *Cardiff Dead*, p. 234, 2000

blind tiger *noun*
an illegal drinking establishment *US, 1909*
• —Jack Lait and Lee Mortimer, *Washington Confidential*, p. 130, 1951
• Washington is loaded with bootleggers and blind tigers. —Jack Lait and Lee Mortimer, *Washington Confidential*, p. 130, 1951

blindza *noun*
money *BARBADOS, 1984*
• —Thomas H. Slone, *Rasta is Cuss:*, p. 28, 2003

bling *noun*
a vulgar or ludicrously ostentatious display of wealth *US*
• Leave the bling and attitude at home. Abstract Rude's on the microphone. — *Anchorage (Alaska) Daily News*, p. H5, 25th April 2003
• [Jennifer] Lopez' erstwhile boyfriend [Puff Daddy/P Diddy] was "bling" personified. — *The Guardian*, p. 23, 21st May 2003

bling-bling *noun*
1 wealth, especially as manifested in expensive, if tasteless, jewellery *US*
Coined by hip-hop rapper B.G. and appearing in his 1999 'Chopper City in the Ghetto'.
• Like B.G.'s hit song says, it's about "Bling! Bling!" Li'l Wayne calls it "braggin' rights." A teenager whose gold teeth say "CASH MONEY," Wayne says he lives with Baby in English Turn just so he can say he does. — *Atlanta Journal and Constitution*, p. 1C, 28th November 1999
• —Connie Eble (Editor), *UNC-CH Campus Slang*, p. 1, Fall 2000
• She [Aaliyah] didn't traffic in Glocks, didn't indulge in big pimpin', didn't court the bling-bling life. — *Washington Post*, p. C1, 28th August 2001
• [G]angster UK hard men, bling-bling bitch ho' slappin' bad boys So Solid Crew. — *Hip-Hop Connection*, p. 9, July 2002
• [T]he modern-day "bling-bling" era of hip-hop has emerged. Gold has taken a back seat to the new metal of choice – platinum. — *The Source*, p. 64, March 2002
• "Bling bling" is vulgarity beyong parody. — *The Guardian*, p. 23, 21st May 2003

2 ostentation *UK*
A generalised sense that derives from the previous sense.
• Now there is even anti-bling bling. Before his London tour in February, the rapper Nas announced that his show would be "stripped of over-the-top bling bling trappings". — *The Guardian*, p. 23, 21st May 2003

bling-bling *verb*
to be successful, especially in hip-hop; hence, to be ostentatious; to make money *US*
• Lyrix, Reggie, Akino and even Hank are bling-blinging it all the way to the bank. —Patrick Neate, *Where You're At*, p. 14, 2003

bling-blinger *noun*
a successful or established member of the hip-hop community *US*
From the **BLING-BLING** worn as an ostentatious symbol of status.

blinged; blinged out *adjective*
ostentatious; expensively bejewelled, especially if a tasteless display *US*
From **BLING-BLING** (ostentatious jewellery).
- The Honda's driver cuts the gas, his jaw working a wad of gum as he checks out what Avila and his friends bring to the table: two Integras, a '93 and a '98, and a moderately blinged-up Benz sedan. — *Los Angeles Times*, p. B1, 9th December 2000
- [T]he Sugababes were "blinged out with diamonds" at the Mobo Awards ceremony. — *The Guardian*, p. 23, 21st May 2003

blinging *adjective*
ostentatious and expensive *UK*
Derives from **BLING-BLING** (ostentatious jewellery).
- You can have a "blinging" lifestyle. You can "bling it up" in the West End. — *The Guardian*, p. 23, 21st May 2003

bling it up *verb*
to have an ostentatiously expensive lifestyle; to temporarily lead such a life *UK*
Extended from **BLING-BLING** (wealth, tasteless ostentation).
- You can have a "blinging" lifestyle. You can "bling it up" in the West End. — *The Guardian*, p. 23, 21st May 2003

bling-tastic *adjective*
extravagantly ostentatious *UK*
- — *The Daily Telegraph*, 25th October 2002

blink *noun*
a hiding place *US*
- —Vincent J. Monteleone, *Criminal Slang*, p. 26, 1949

▸ **on the blink**
1 broken, not functioning *US, 1899*
- "Our car's on the blink," she said. "I took a bus." —Robert Campbell, *Juice*, p. 104, 1988
- Although Keb' Mo', in his Monday night performance at the Birchmore, showed hints of ownership, it appeared as if his mojo was on the blink. — *Washington Post*, p. C2, 24th March 2004

2 without funds *US*
- —Vincent J. Monteleone, *Criminal Slang*, p. 166, 1949

blink *verb*
to miss seeing a fight, attack or other cause of excitement *US*
- —John R. Armore and Joseph D. Wolfe, *Dictionary of Desperation*, p. 20, 1976

blinkenlights *noun*
diagnostic lights on the front panel of a computer *US*
- —Eric S. Raymond, *The New Hacker's Dictionary*, p. 66, 1991

blinker *noun*
1 a quadriplegic *US, 1980*
Vietnam war gallows humour, suggesting that a quadriplegic is capable only of blinking his eyes.
- —Gregory Clark, *Words of the Vietnam War*, p. 61, 1990

2 an eye *UK, 1809*
- —J. E. Lighter, *Historical Dictionary of American Slang, Volume 1*, p. 185, 1994

3 a police helicopter *US*
- —Edith A. Folb, *runnin' down some lines*, p. 229, 1980
- —Angela Devlin, *Prison Patter*, p. 28, 1996

blinkey *noun*
1 a vehicle with one headlight not working *US*
- — Elementary Electronics, *Dictionary of CB Lingo*, p. 51, 1976

2 a timing light at the finish line of a drag strip *US*
- —Lyle K. Engel, *The Complete Book of Fuel and Gas Dragsters*, p. 149, 1968

blink-eyed *adjective*
cross-eyed *US, 1969*
- —Frederic G. Cassidy, *Dictionary of American Regional English, Volume 1*, p. 285, 1985

blinking *adjective*
used as a mild intensifier; a euphemisim for 'bleeding' *UK*
The term probably derives from 'blank', an obsolete euphemism for **DAMNED** which stresses the fact of euphemism – the blank space – as much as the object of intensification.
- I'm not a blinking thicky[.] —Ian Dury, *Billericay Dickie*, 1977
- [Y]ou would never have agreed to the blinking gig in the first place[.] —Kevin Sampson, *Powder*, p. 26, 1999

blinkus of the thinkus *noun*
a momentary loss of concentration *US*
- —Dick Squires, *The Other Racquet Sports*, p. 219, 1971

blinky *noun*
1 a person with poor or no eyesight *US, 1922*
- —Joseph E. Ragen and Charles Finston, *Inside the World's Toughest Prison*, p. 791, 1962

2 freebase cocaine *US*
- —Jay Robert Nash, *Dictionary of Crime*, p. 33, 1992

blinky *adjective*
agitated, upset *US*
- And she gets all blinky on me. 'What you say!' —Richard Price, *Clockers*, p. 366, 1992

blip *noun*
1 a temporary effect, especially one that is unwanted *UK, 1975*
- But the loss was a just a blip, and a 151-run stand for the second wicket took Pakistan to within two runs of victory[.] — *BBC Sport*, 30th November 2002
- Rise in CO2 is 'blip' says minister [...] The environment minister, Elliot Morley, said: "This blip, although disappointing, was expected and does not knock us off the downward trend on emissions." — *The Guardian*, 26th March 2004

2 a minor fluctuation, usually upward, in the stock market or other measures of corporate fortunes *US*
- —Kathleen Odean, *High Steppers, Fallen Angels, and Lollipops*, p. 97, 1988
- The rise of Reese [Witherspoon] is explicable both as a blip (she's a perky, funny, charming freak of nature) and as a trend: chick flicks are performing better than ever before. — *The Times*, 2nd August 2003

3 a source of surprise *US*
- You young New York Negroes is a blip! I swear you is! —Ralph Ellison, *Invisible Man*, p. 330, 1947
- I lit the stick of pot. Damn, that whole scene was a blip. —Piri Thomas, *Down These Mean Streets*, p. 62, 1967

4 a nickel (five-cent piece) *US, 1935*
- —Lou Shelly, *Hepcats Jive Talk Dictionary*, p. 7, 1945
- Even before I was in the money I togged like a fashion plate, so I could run with the hip cats who hung around the poolroom. I was always as ready as they were, although sometimes I never had a blip in my poke. —Mezz Mezzrow, *Really the Blues*, p. 22, 1946

blip *verb*
1 to send a message by e-mail *UK*
- What happens when ICM try to blip you a script from LA and you're jammed up because you were too fucking cheapskate to go broadband? —James Hawes, *White Powder, Green Light*, p. 139, 2002

2 in hot rodding or drag racing, to throttle up quickly and then release, momentarily increasing the revolutions per minute *US*
- —John Lawlor, *How to Talk Car*, p. 19, 1965

blip *adjective*
classy *US*
- —Jack Lait and Lee Mortimer, *New York Confidential*, p. 235, 1948

blip jockey *noun*
a person who monitors electronic equipment *US*
- —Harold Wentworth and Stuart Berg Flexner, *Dictionary of American SLang*, p. 43, 1960

blippy *adjective*
used as a euphemism roughly meaning 'damned' *US*
- How many times have I stood on my street corner, looking out at your blippy world full of pros? —Piri Thomas, *Seven Long Times*, p. 4, 1974

blirry *adjective*
▹ **see: BLERRY**

bliss *noun*
any drug that is smoked, especially a mixture of heroin, methamphetamine and MDMA, the recreational drug best known as ecstasy *US*
- Bell had some of this shit called bliss. Sort of a cross between smack, E and ice. You've got to smoke it in a little pipe [...] "Hey, Todd, wanna come back to my place and do some bliss?" —Will Self, *The Sweet Smell of Psychosis*, p. 39, 1996

bliss cup *noun*
in the usage of counterculturalists associated with the Rainbow Nation gatherings, a homemade cup or bowl for eating and drinking *US*
- —Jim Crotty, *How to Talk American*, p. 288, 1997

bliss out *verb*
to become ecstatic *US*
Used in a derogatory fashion, usually when applied to religious or cult zealots.
- —Connie Eble (Editor), *UNC-CH Campus Slang*, November 1973
- The trumpet fanfares in ["It's All Too Much" by The Beatles]... completely blissed-out, over the top.—*Uncut*, p. 34, July 2001

B list; C list *noun*
used for denoting all that is associated with a level of fame and celebrity that is not quite paramount *US*
In conventional media jargon the **A-LIST** is a notional social elite of those who are considered prestigious enough to add top-value to a guest list. The B-list and C-list are the lesser ranks of the well-known and media-friendly who nevertheless get invited to events by those who market the cult of celebrity.

blisted *adjective*
intoxicated by drug smoking *US*

blister *noun*
1 a bump placed on a playing card by pressing it against a small sharp object, used by card cheats to identify the value of the card *US*
- —Michael Dalton, *Blackjack*, p. 33, 1991

2 a fine attached to a window of a vehicle for a parking infringment *AUSTRALIA*
- Their activities provoke car owners to describe them as a 'pack o' bastards', or to say, 'Gor strike, a bloody blister for a lousy extra ten minutes.'—John O'Grady, *Aussie Etiket*, p. 20, 1971
- I just stuck a bodgie blister on his windscreen.—Sam Weller, *Old Bastards I Have Met*, p. 116, 1979

3 an unpleasant, obnoxious person *UK, 1806*
- —*Current Slang*, p. 3, Spring 1967
- Yeah. And is he ever an asshole. A blister, that one.—Stephen J. Cannell, *The Tin Collectors*, p. 167, 2001

4 a prostitute *US, 1905*
- —Dale Gordon, *The Dominion Sex Dictionary*, p. 30, 1967

blister *verb*
to attack someone; to attack someone verbally *AUSTRALIA*
- When he rang to apologize she blistered him soundly.—Sue Rhodes, *And when she was bad she was popular*, p. 112, 1968

blisterfoot *noun*
an infantry soldier *US*
- —Lou Shelly, *Hepcats Jive Talk Dictionary*, p. 43, 1945

blister work *noun*
extortion *US*
- When we pipe, it's a hard lay we do a little blister work.—*The New American Mercury*, p. 708, 1950

blisty *adjective*
windy, cold, not suitable for surfing *US*
- —Trevor Cralle, *The Surfin'ary*, p. 11, 1991

blithering *adjective*
contemptible; used as an negative intensifier *UK, 1889*
- [T]his blithering drunken dolt hasn't even the excuse of being in the Army[.]—Mike Stott, *Soldiers Talking, Cleanly*, 1978

blitz *noun*
an intensive campaign; a concentrated effort *US, 1940*
After German *blitz* (understood in English as 'all-out offensive warfare').
- The Utah Highway Patrol's recent speeding-enforcement blitz betwen Lehi and Provo showed there are a significant number of drivers who exceed the posted 65 mph limit along tha stretch of I-15.—*Desert Utah Morning News*, 1st April 2004

blitz *verb*
1 to intensively campaign for and achieve maximum public awareness *UK*
From German *blitzkrieg* (a lightning war).
- Beatlemania, having blitzed the UK, swept the world.—*Uncut*, p. 44, February 2002

2 to defeat someone soundly *US, 1940*
- The Mountaineers led 14–9 before being blitzed 74–53.—*Charleston (West Virginia) Daily Mail*, p. B1, 22nd March 2004

3 in horse racing, to win convincingly *AUSTRALIA*
- The filly fair dinkum blitzed them.—Ned Wallish, *The Truth Dictionary of Racing Slang*, p. 8, 1989

4 in tiddlywinks, to pot all six winks of one colour before the 20-minute time-limit has elapsed and thus score an easy victory *US*
- —C.W.Edwards, sometime Secretary of the English Tiddlywinks Association, *Glossary*, 1980

5 in gin, to win and leave an opponent scoreless *US*
- —Irwin Steig, *Play Gin to Win*, p. 138, 1971

6 in bar dice games, to bet the total amount of the pot *US*
- —Jester Smith, *Games They Play in San Francisco*, p. 103, 1971

blitz buggy *noun*
a car *US, 1941*
Teen slang, reported by a Toronto newspaper in 1946, and reported as 'obsolescent or obsolete' by Douglas Leechman, 1959.

blitzed *adjective*
drunk or drug-intoxicated *US, 1966*
- [E]very time we got together we wound up blitzed out of our skulls on booze or speed or both[.]—Lester Bangs, *Psychotic Reactions and Carburetor Dung*, p. 218, 1977
- —Connie Eble (Editor), *UNC-CH Campus Slang*, April 1977
- DANTE: I get blitzed and pass out in his bedroom. Caitlan comes in and dives all over me.—*Clerks*, 1994
- We lay down the rhythm tracks and then we get blitzed on weed. —Shaun Ryder, *Shaun Ryder... in His Own Words*, 1995
- hammered, blitzed, mashed, off-your-tits—Stuart Walton, *Out of It*, cover, 2001
- My head's addled, too blitzed to think[.]—Niall Griffiths, *Kelly + Victor*, p. 172, 2002

blitzkrieged *adjective*
suddenly drunk *US*
- —Connie Eble (Editor), *UNC-CH Campus Slang*, Fall 1974

blivet *noun*
1 an obnoxious person, especially with bad hygiene *US, 1949*
- —Sally Williams, *"Strong" Words*, p. 134, 1994

2 in computing, a problem which cannot be solved or any impossibility *US*
- —Eric S. Raymond, *The New Hacker's Dictionary*, p. 67, 1991

blizz *noun*
a blizzard *ANTARCTICA, 1911*
- —Bernadette Hince, *The Antarctic Dictionary*, p. 58, 2000

blizz *verb*
to blow a blizzard *ANTARCTICA, 1911*
- —Bernadette Hince, *The Antarctic Dictionary*, p. 58, 2000

blizzard *noun*
1 poor television reception characterised by flickering white dots *US*
- Life in this great pretzel center is distinguished by the worst television reception enjoyed by any metropolitan American city – not even barring blast-furnacy Pittsburgh, runner-up for ghosts, blizzards, fade-outs and other visual blah.—*San Francisco News*, p. 21, 22nd May 1952

2 the cloud of thick, white smoke produced when smoking freebase cocaine *US*
- —Terry Williams, *Crackhouse*, p. 147, 1992

3 cocaine *UK*
A play on **SNOW** (cocaine).
- —Mike Haskins, *Drugs*, p. 280, 2003

blizzard head *noun*
in the early days of black and white television, a blonde *US*
So called because a blonde's hair takes up all the light in the picture.
- —*Time*, p. 76, 24th May 1948

blizzed in *adjective*
confined indoors by harsh weather conditions *ANTARCTICA, 1951*
- —Bernadette Hince, *The Antarctic Dictionary*, p. 59, 2000

blizzy *adjective*
snowy *ANTARCTICA, 1996*
- —Bernadette Hince, *The Antarctic Dictionary*, p. 59, 2000

blo *noun*
cocaine *US*
- —Peter Johnson, *Dictionary of Street Alcohol and Drug Terms*, p. 22, 1993

bloater *noun*
1 a fat person *UK*
From 'bloat' (to swell), influenced by the 'bloater fish'. There is some evidence of a similar usage in the late C19, and, again, in mid-C20 in South Africa where the sense is 'gross and ugly'.
- [U]nwilling to tolerate the public insults to his sister, unwilling to endure taunts of "Bloater", of "Fat Jam"[.] —Mark Powell, *Snap*, p. 99, 2001

2 a dead sheep or cow *NEW ZEALAND*
- Shall I get a truck and cart those bloaters away, Dick? —W. V. and John Kerr, *High Times in the High Country*, p. 188, 2000

blob *noun*
1 in cricket, a batsman's innings score of no runs *UK, 1889*
From the image of a zero shown beneath the batsman's name on the scoresheet.

2 a mistake *UK, 1903*
From the previous sense.
- —John Ayto, *The Oxford Dictionary of Slang*, p. 409, 1998

3 a fool *AUSTRALIA, 1916*
- —Sidney J. Baker, *The Australian Language*, p. 135, 1953

4 the bleed period of the menstrual cycle *UK*
- Friends of mine call it the "blob." They say, "I am on the blob" or "I have got the blob". —*The Museum of Menstruation and Women's Health*, December 2000

5 a gonorrhoeal ulcer *UK, 1961*

▸ **on blob; on the blob**
in the bleed-period of the menstrual cycle *US*
The image of blobs of blood.
- Friends of mine call it the "blob." They say, "I am on the blob" or "I have got the blob". —*The Museum of Menstruation and Women's Health*, December 2000
- [A]dverts on the telly [...] makes out dat women on da blob is all happy and smilin and doin sports and stuff[.] —Sacha Baron-Cohen, *Da Gospel According to Ali G*, 2001

blob *verb*
1 to suffer from a sexually transmitted infection *UK, 1984*
Literally, 'to drip', but after **BLOB** (a gonorrhoeal ulcer).

2 to make a mistake *UK*
- DAD: Come on quick he's winding up. I'm saying two thousand, four hundred pounds. DAVE: You've blobbed it this time Jim, it's double that. —Caroline Aherne and Craig Cash, *The Royle Family*, 1999

blobby *adjective*
used for describing uneven stage lighting *UK*
- —Wilfred Granville, *The Theater Dictionary*, p. 20, 1952

blob hammock *noun*
a sanitary towel *UK*
Combines **BLOB** (the bleed period of the menstrual cycle) with the image of a hammock, also seen in **WEE HAMMOCK**.
- — *www.LondonSlang.com*, June 2002

blob out *verb*
to relax completely *NEW ZEALAND*
Commonly used in conversation since the 1980s.

block *noun*
1 a prison segregation unit *UK*
- —Angela Devlin, *Prison Patter*, p. 28, 1996

2 prison *US*
- He paused. Stick was looking at him now. Cornell said, "You from the block, aren't you?" —Elmore Leonard, *Stick*, p. 98, 1983

3 marijuana or hashish compressed in a block *UK*
- "Mmm," replied Sundays distractedly, still breaking down, measuring and bagging his blocks. —Diran Abedayo, *My Once Upon A Time*, p. 21, 2000

4 a measured quantity of morphine *UK*
- —Jay Robert Nash, *Dictionary of Crime*, p. 33, 1992

5 a ban, an embargo *UK*
Used in phrases like **PUT A BLOCK ON** and **PUT THE BLOCK ON**.
- —Peter Laurie, *Scotland Yard*, p. 321, 1970

6 used as a retort after being insulted *US*
- —Judi Sanders, *Kickin' like Chicken with the Couch Commander*, p. 3, 1992

7 a watch *US*
Circus and carnival usage.
- He had an old dollar block [watch] and a few picks and he'd lay around the yard and every fish [new convict] that come in, if the fish had anything he'd con him out of it if he could. —Bruce Jackson, *In the Life*, p. 285, 1972
- —Don Wilmeth, *The Language of American Popular Entertainment*, p. 26, 1981

▸ **do your block; do the block**
to lose control; to lose your temper *AUSTRALIA, 1907*
- Cripes, I just about done me block that time I nearly king hit that greasy drongo! —Barry Humphries, *The Wonderful World of Barry McKenzie*, p. 39, 1968
- [H]e said a few things about my Valda back in Oz that really made me do my block!!! —Barry Humphries, *Bazza Pulls It Off!*, 1971

▸ **knock your block off**
used as a threat of personal violence *UK, 1984*
- DENISE: He don't look at other girls when I'm with him. MAM: Don't he? DENISE: No, I'd knock his bloody block off. —Caroline Aherne and Craig Cash, *The Royle Family*, 1999

▸ **on the block**
1 engaged in prostitution on the street *US, 1941*
- Have all the players and working girls smiling on her, lapping up the news that Inez been put out on the block again, handed over her little black book and gone back in harness. —John Sayles, *Union Dues*, p. 182, 1977

2 subjected to serial rape *NEW ZEALAND*
- Home had told the girl: 'You've got between now and the time I finish this cigarette until you go into the bedroom and go on the block.' — *Truth*, p. 5, 4th December 1973

▸ **put a block on; put the block on**
1 to veto, ban or embargo something *UK*
Literally, to apply 'a block' (a ban).

2 in prison, to reinforce the regulations *UK*
- —Angela Devlin, *Prison Patter*, p. 93, 1996

▸ **use your block**
to act wisely *AUSTRALIA*
- 'Good enough, if he uses his block, to get a long way,' asserted Joyce, now gathering glasses, which Bony proceeded to wash and polish. —Arthur Upfield, *Bony and the Mouse*, p. 102, 1959

block *verb*
1 to sodomise someone or subject them to serial rape *NEW ZEALAND*
- The Black Power boys will block you if you struggle. — *Truth*, p. 3, 14th February 1978
- When a sheila came she knew what was going to happen, she was going to be blocked, gang raped. —Bill Payne, *Staunch*, p. 109, 1991

2 to fool someone *AUSTRALIA*
- Take this boy Job – look at his features, and smart – you can't block him! —Mary Durack, *Keep Him My Country*, 1955

block!
used as the riposte to 'face!', thus preventing notional embarrassment *US*
Youth slang.
- You held your arm in front of your face and ostensibly halted getting faced, all the while exclaiming "Block!" Then you would fight over whether you blocked the face in time or not. —Editors of Ben is Dead, *Retrohell*, p. 71, 1997

blockaides *noun*
condoms *UK*
Coined in response to AIDS.
- —David Rowan, *A Glossary for the 90s*, 1998

block and tackle *noun*
illegally manufactured whisky *US, 1974*
- —Burgess Laughlin, *Job Opportunities in the Black Market*, p. 4, 1978
- — *Star Tribune (Minneapolis)*, p. 19F, 31st January 1999

block boy *noun*
a youth who spends his abundant free time idling on a street corner, looking or hoping for trouble *US*
- — *Current Slang*, p. 5, Fall 1970

blockbuster *noun*

1 a capsule of pentobarbital sodium (trade name Nembutal™), a central nervous system depressant *US*
Sometimes shortened to 'buster'.
- —Clarence Major, *Dictionary of Afro-American Slang*, p. 27, 1970
- —Mike Haskins, *Drugs*, p. 282, 2003

2 a heavy bomb powerful enough to flatten a city block; hence anything that makes a considerable impact *US, 1942*
Initially used by the Royal Air Force; since the 1960s generally applied as journalistic or marketing terms for films, novels, etc.
- When I was a child in the London blitz, a blockbuster was a massive bomb that could knock out a neighbourhood. The blockbuster movie, now utterly dominant and crushing better films, is set to destroy the Hollywood studios; the monster is turning on its makers. The blockbuster now costs so much to make and market that no one can afford them ann more. — *The Guardian*, 6th September 2003

3 a .357 Magnum bullet *US*
- — *American Speech*, p. 267, December 1962: 'The language of traffic policemen'

blocked *adjective*

drunk or drug-intoxicated, especially by amphetamine, barbiturate or marijuana *US, 1956*
The experiencing of real life is *blocked* out.
- Jack and me are starting to feel a bit blocked as well so, out with the chewing gum and onto the floor. —Ian Hebditch, *Weekend, The Sharper Word*, p. 134, 1969
- —Eugene Landy, *The Underground Dictionary*, p. 35, 1971
- Blowsers [glue-sniffers] often use the 1960s pillhead word "blocked" to describe being high on glue – and that is literally its effect: it blocks out everything. — *Time Out*, 8th January 1982
- [T]heir main obsession was pills. Getting "blocked" at the weekend was what separated "them from us". —Simon Napier-Bell, *Black Vinyl White Powder*, p. 43, 2001

blocker *noun*

1 a confederate who shields a casino cheat from being seen as he robs a slot machine *US, 1984*
- —Thomas L. Clark, *The Dictionary of Gambling and Gaming*, p. 22, 1987

2 a member of a shoplifting team who distracts attention and blocks pursuit *UK*
- —Angela Devlin, *Prison Patter*, p. 28, 1996

blockhead *noun*

1 a stupid fool, an idiot *UK, 1549*
Originally, 'a wooden base for hats or wigs', hence 'wooden-*head*ed'.
- I can never be satisfied with anyone who would be blockhead enough to have me. —Abraham Lincoln,

2 a drunken yob *UK, 1977*
This usage was coined by Ian Dury in the song 'Blockheads', which offered the lyrical definition: '"pissed up" gangs of lads'.
- You must have seen parties of Blockheads / With blotched and lagered skin / Blockheads with food particles in their teeth / What a horrible state they're in[.] —Ian Dury, *Blockheads*, 1977

3 a marijuana user *UK*
A combination of **BLOCK** (marijuana) and **HEAD** (a user).

4 a railway brakeman *US*
- —Ramon Adams, *The Language of the Railroader*, p. 16, 1977

block hustle *noun*

a small-scale swindle *US*
- I prosecuted a few bunco cases, but they were just block hustles, street scams. —Stephen Cannell, *Big Con*, p. 152, 1997

blockie *noun*

1 a farmer on a small block of land *AUSTRALIA, 1944*
Sometimes heard as 'blocker'.
- These latter-day pioneers [were] known as 'blockies' in the districts where they had settled[.] — *Weekend Australian*, p. 7, 14th January 1995

2 in Queensland, Victoria and Tasmania, a circuit of a street block in a vehicle done, especially repeatedly, for entertainment *AUSTRALIA*
- There's someone on the street doing blockies again. I'd better call the cops. — *Wordmap (www.abc.net.au/wordmap)*, 2003

blocking *noun*

serial sex between one person and multiple partners, consensual or not, heterosexual or homosexual *NEW ZEALAND*
- —David McGill, *David McGill's Complete Kiwi Slang Dictionary*, p. 16, 1998

block-rockin' *adjective*

expressive of greatness with regard to hip-hop and club culture *US*
Extends 'rockin' as a general term of approval with the punning suggestion that whatever is so described has the power to rock a city block.
- And while it took a long time to accept the mixed race and relationship thing, that ten-year block-rockin' period of raving force-fucking-fed acceptance. Until nearly every white kid knew a black kid. —Dave Courtney, *Raving Lunacy*, p. 266, 2000
- Block-rockin' beats abound, but there are gentler moments too. — *Uncut*, p. 16, January 2002

blocks *noun*

dice *US*
- —Frank Garcia, *Marked Cards and Loaded Dice*, p. 262, 1962

▸ put the blocks to

to have sex with someone *US, 1888*
- —Joseph E. Ragen and Charles Finston, *Inside the World's Toughest Prison*, p. 814, 1962
- Guys who spoke of "putting the blocks to" a chick were bound to be assholes too[.] — *Screw*, p. 7, 3rd January 1972

▸ up on blocks

in the bleed period of the menstrual cycle *UK*
A mechanical image of an out of service car being up on blocks for repair.
- I don't think I'll be in luck tonight lads, the missus is up on blocks. — unknown sorce quoted in private correspondence, 13th March 2002

block-up *adjective*

marijuana-intoxicated *UK*
- I'm totally block-up[.] —Nick Brownlee, *This Is Cannabis*, p. 151, 2002

blog *noun*

a regularly updated Internet webpage of links to interesting news stories or websites annotated with personal commentary *US, 1999*
An abbreviation of 'we*blog*'.
- They other people who have blogs – they are known as bloggers – read your blog, and if they like it they blog your blog on their own blog. — *The New Yorker*, p. 102, 13th November 2000

blog *verb*

to create or update a weblog *US*
- They other people who have blogs – they are known as bloggers – read your blog, and if they like it they blog your blog on their own blog. — *The New Yorker*, p. 102, 13th November 2000
- [P]articipants at a PC Forum conference began heckling a speaker, after members of the audience live-blogged unflattering comments about him that were picked up by others listening to the speech[.] — *The Guardian*, 12th December 2002

blogger *noun*

a person who maintains a weblog *US*
- They other people who have blogs – they are known as bloggers – read your blog, and if they like it they blog your blog on their own blog. — *The New Yorker*, p. 102, 13th November 2000

bloke *noun*

1 a man; a fellow *UK, 1829*
Generally used in a neutral sense, but also commonly in a positive sense connoting a 'decent, down-to-earth, unpretentious man', especially in the phrase 'good bloke'. There has been a recent trend, since the 1990s, to also use 'bloke' negatively to mean a 'male chauvinist'.
- I know I'll mix with all these blokes; they'll speak my language too; / They'll talk of beer and fights and fun the way they used to do. —Tip Kelaher, *The Digger Hat and other verses*, p. 17, 1942
- You know, come to think of it, Murk's not a bad sort of bloke! —Willie Fennell, *Dexter Gets The Point*, p. 40, 1961
- Therefore we are not permitted to love the missus of the bloke next door. —John O'Grady, *Aussie Etiket*, p. 49, 1971
- The typical bloke does a good day's work, but he likes to go to the pub in the night time. He's pretty genuine, and if he borrows a quid off you he'll pay you back. —Sandra Jobson, *Blokes*, p. 37, 1984

2 a boyfriend *AUSTRALIA, 1908*
- Wot yer doin' about that bloke o' yours, Millie? —Norman Lindsay, *Comic Art of Norman Lindsay*, p. 141, 1908

- That's 'im, Eddie, me mother's new bloke! — Ward McNally, *Supper at Happy Harry's*, p. 22, 1982

3 a homosexual man's boyfriend or partner *UK, 1937*
Originally recorded as a navy usage.

4 a male animal *AUSTRALIA*
- They quickly revised their opinion of the 'hairy goat' [poor racehorse]. This bloke was something special. — Joe Andersen, *Winners Can Laugh*, p. 81, 1982

5 a person of any gender *AUSTRALIA*
A rare usage.
- Despite his adoption by the cafe society, Kurt was a simple man, dividing the world into shit men, good blokes (of both sexes) and people he hadn't met. — Clive Galea, *Slipper*, p. 150, 1988

bloke car *noun*
a sports car on the downslope of its career sold to American pilots stationed in the United Kingdom *UK*
- "I'd like to have a Porsche or BMW," he confides to me, "after I get out, but for here, this bloke car is a hell of a lot of fun to drive, and it was fairly cheap to buy." — Lewis Poteet, *Car & Motorcyle Slang*, p. 32, 1992

bloker *noun*
a cocaine user *US*
- — Jay Robert Nash, *Dictionary of Crime*, p. 34, 1992

blokey *noun*
a man *UK*
An elaboration of **BLOKE**.
- Blokey finishes speakin with an apologetic cough[.] — Niall Griffiths, *Grits*, p. 27, 2000

blokey *adjective*
(of a man) chauvinistic; masculine in a negative way *AUSTRALIA*
- It's still a huge mystery to all quim quacks and dick doctors why so many otherwise normal blokey-blokes get so turned on by wearing women's clothing. — *Picture*, p. 28, 5th February 1992
- I'm sort of blokey and I like to spend the weekends in front of the telly watching the footy[.] — John Birmingham, *He Died With a Felafel in his Hand*, p. 138, 1994

blokeyness; blokiness *noun*
the state of being blokey *AUSTRALIA*
- That was the aspect of my blokiness that just wasn't going to work in a gay house. — John Birmingham, *He Died With a Felafel in his Hand*, p. 138, 1994
- [T]hey're ranged along a ten-point-scale of blokeyness from extreme-hairy-yobbo to spotty scientist — *Sydney Star Observer*, p. 27, 20th June 1996

blokish; blokeish *adjective*
describes men's behaviour that is straightforwardly, perhaps stereotypically, 'masculine' *UK, 1957*
- Sandy masked his jealous anxiety in a show of blokish insensitivity[.] — Patrick Gale, *Rough Music*, p. 38, 2000
- Andrea is everything I dread. She's more "blokeish" than most of the blokes I know. — Jane Green, *Straight Talking*, p. 4, 2003

blonde *noun*
1 coffee with cream *US*
- — *American Speech*, p. 232, October 1952: 'The argot of soda jerks'

2 golden-leafed marijuana *UK*
- — *www.addictions.org*, 2003

blonde *adjective*
foolish, daft, silly *UK*
Teen slang, from the stereotypical attributes ascribed to blondes.
- — Susie Dent, *The Language Report*, p. 75, 2003

blonde and sweet *adjective*
(used of coffee) with cream and sugar *US, 1945*
- — *American Speech*, p. 37, February 1948: 'Talking under water: speech in submarines'
- — Helen Dahlskog (Editor), *A Dictionary of Contemporary and Colloquial Usage*, p. 8, 1972
- — "Slingo", *The Official CB Slang Dictionary Handbook*, p. 9, 1976

blonde from the coast *noun*
a pale, light-coloured marijuana with claims by sellers that it comes from Colombia *US, 1976*
- — *American Speech*, Winter 1982

blondie; blondy *noun*
a blonde-haired person; when spelt with a capital B, a nickname for such a person *US*
Famously in the cartoon strip *Blondie* by Chic Young, from 1930, although unlikely to have been coined by him. Adopted in 1974 by the pop group Blondie.

blonk *noun*
an incompetent, inept, boring person *AUSTRALIA*
- — Thommo, *The Dictionary of Australian Swearing and Sex Sayings*, p. 16, 1985

bloober *noun*
a female breast *US*
- On the way to Biff's, Betsy, dressed in a knocked-out strapless, bloobers more out than in, kept beating her gums. — Bernard Wolfe, *The Late Risers*, p. 157, 1954

bloochie *noun*
any cumbersome object *US*
From Polish immigrants.
- Bloochie – Any awkward, unwieldy object. Something without handles, making it difficult to pick up or steal. — Bill Reilly, *Big Al's Official Guide to Chicagoese*, p. 16, 1982

blood *noun*
1 a black person *US, 1965*
- — J. L. Simmons and Barry Winograd, *It's Happening*, p. 167, 1966
- Annette downtown going for broke, while Chicanos and bloods outside the bars beat the nightlight out of po' trash from across the way, driving them out their territory. — Steve Cannon, *Groove, Bang, and Jive Around*, p. 24, 1969
- They never inquired if the bloods they were giving the jobs to were the same ones who were causing the trouble. — Tom Wolfe, *Radical Chic & Mau-Mauing the Flak Catchers*, p. 98–99, 1970
- A young blood stops him, gives him his address. — Ken Kesey, *Last Whole Earth Catalog*, p. 234, 1971

2 used as a general form of address regardless of race, signalling friendliness *UK*
From the previous sense; sometimes spelt 'blud'.
- Oi blud, wanna buy a draw? — *The Guardian*, p. 9, 27th February 2002
- — Julian Johnson, *Urban Survival*, p. 258, 2003

3 wine *US, 1959*
- — Robert George Reisner, *The Jazz Titans*, p. 151, 1960
- 'Ever try blood?' Joe Richards snickered across the room. 'The kind distilled from grapes, I mean.' — Clarence Cooper Jr, *Black*, p. 12, 1963
- I told him like I did every stud / that it wasn't shit for me to drink two or three fifths a some real good blood. — Bruce Jackson, *Get Your Ass in the Water and Swim Like Me*, p. 89, 1964

4 pizza sauce *US*
- — *Maledicta*, p. 12, 1996: 'Domino's pizza jargon'

5 tomato juice *US, 1936*
- — Lou Shelly, *Hepcats Jive Talk Dictionary*, p. 7, 1945

▸ make your blood boil
to infuriate you *UK, 1848*
- The thought that such a woman would mock him made his blood boil. — Aron Appelfeld (translated by Jeffrey M Green), *The Conversion*, p. 35, 1998

▸ your blood is worth bottling
you are wonderful *AUSTRALIA*
- To Nino Culotta, therefore, in thanks for this book, I say: "Thanks, mate. Yer blood's worth bottling". — Russell Braddon, *They're a Wierd Mob*, 1958
- When we rode into Busselton the S.M. said our blood was worth bottling. — Patsy Adam-Smith, *Folklore of the Australian Railwaymen*, p. 69, 1969

blood!
used for expressing strong disapproval *JAMAICA, 1978*
- — Thomas H. Slone, *Rasta is Cuss*, p. 29, 2003

blood alley *noun*
an unsafe stretch of a road *US*
- 'Blood Alley' Claims Victim — *San Francisco Examiner*, p. 54, 9th March 1978
- The site of the crash was a desolate desert stretch of Highway 86, a two-lane highway known as "Bloody Alley" and "killer Highway" becaues of the hundreds of collisions there each year. — *New York Times*, p. A12, 11th August 1983
- How many injuries or deaths are required on the 74 to increase CHP and local police enforcement to improve conditions on this highway which is fast becoming Blood Alley? [Letter to Editor] — *Press Enterprise (Riverside, California)*, p. B2, 26th January 2004

blood bank *noun*

1 a hospital *UK*

- —Peter Chippindale, *The British CB Book*, p. 152, 1981

2 a finance company *US*

- —*American Speech*, p. 312, Autumn-Winter 1975: 'The jargon of car salesmen'

blood box *noun*

an ambulance *US*

- —Wayne Floyd, *Jason's Authentic Dictionary of CB Slang*, p. 10, 1976

blood bread *noun*

payment for donating blood *US*

- —Eugene Landy, *The Underground Dictionary*, p. 35, 1971

blood chit *noun*

a written notice in several languages, carried by members of the American armed forces, identifying the person as American and promising a reward for help in evading the enemy *US, 1941*

The US Department of Defense Policy on Blood Chits states that the chits 'are a tool used by an evader or escapee after all other measures of independent evasion and escape have failed and the evader(s) considers assistance vital to survival. Upon receiving assistance, the evader or escapee provides the assistor with the blood chit number. The blood chit represents an obligation of the U.S. Government to compensate the claimant, or his immediate family if the claimant is deceased, for services rendered to DoD personnel.' The version used in the Vietnam war had the plea for 'assistance in obtaining food, shelter and protection' in English, Burmese, Chinese, Thai, Laotian, Cambodian, Vietnamese, Malayan, Indonesian, Tagalog, Visayan, French and Dutch.

- —Linda Reinberg, *In the Field*, p. 24, 1991

bloodclaat; bloodclot; blood clot *noun*

a contemptible person *JAMAICA*

West Indian, hence UK black patois; literally a 'sanitary towel', applied figuratively.

- Dem bloodclaat babylon lick down nuff yout' a'ready.—Donald Gorgon, *Cop Killer*, p. 111, 1994
- Me bus' up your bloodclaat!—Diran Adebayo, *My Once Upon A Time*, p. 39, 2000
- Ja want amends, ja say low down de peace pipes, Bloodclot. —Bernard Dempsey and Kevin McNally, *Lock, Stock ... & Two Hundred Smoking Kalashnikovs*, p. 112, 2000
- No blood clot clot But-But using my tools man! No way!—Jack Allen, *When the Whistle Blows*, p. 172, 2000

blood cloth *noun*

an improvised sanitary towel *ANTIGUA AND BARBUDA*

- —Richard Allsopp, *Dictionary of Caribbean English Usage*, p. 107, 1996

blood factory *noun*

a hospital *UK*

- [A] couple of them went to the blood factory.—J.J. Connolly, *Layer Cake*, p. 101, 2000

bloodhound *verb*

to track someone down *US*

- That hundred and a quarter was in my fist almost, and I went bloodhoundin after you.—Clarence Cooper Jr, *Black*, p. 190, 1963

blood house *noun*

a tavern with a reputation for brawling *NEW ZEALAND*

- —Harry Orsman, *A Dictionary of Modern New Zealand Slang*, p. 12, 1999

bloodhouse *noun*

a public hotel, especially a rough one *AUSTRALIA, 1952*

- It was a man-to-man, middy-to-middy bloodhouse.—Peter Corris, *Make Me Rich*, p. 103, 1985
- —Shane Maloney, *Nice Try*, p. 86, 1998

blood in *verb*

in prison, to establish your credentials for toughness by slashing another prisoner *US*

- Rikers inmates had to "blood in," or slash someone across the face. —*Village Voice*, p. 54, 19th December 2000

blood in, blood out

used for expressing the rules for entering (to kill) and leaving (to be killed) a prison gang *US*

- —William K. Bentley and James M. Corbett, *Prison Slang*, p. 41, 1992
- A "blood-in, blood-out" entry requirement is absolute.—Bill Valentine, *Gangs and Their Tattoos*, p. 8, 2000

bloodman *noun*

a person who is at any moment capable of physical violence *US*

- —Gary K. Farlow, *Prison-ese*, p. 5, 2002

blood money *noun*

in gambling, money that is won after long, hard work *US*

- —John Scarne, *Scarne's Guide to Modern Poker*, p. 273, 1979

blood nose *noun*

a nose that is bleeding, as from a punch *AUSTRALIA*

- —S.H. Courtier, *Gently Dust the Corpse*, 1960
- By the time I got there and found a decent possie with a view of the beach Wayne got one of his blood noses and the car radio packed up.—Barry Humphries, *A Nice Night's Entertainment*, p. 54, 1961
- —Kevin Mackey, *The Cure*, p. 81, 1970
- —Kerry Cue, *Crooks, Chooks and Bloody Ratbags*, p. 11, 1983

bloodnut *noun*

a red-haired person *AUSTRALIA*

- 'What are youse looking at?' said a red-haired kid with heaps of freckles. 'What's it to you, bloodnut?' said Prickles.—Phillip Gwynne, *Deadly Unna?*, p. 27, 1998

blood poker *noun*

poker played as business with no social trappings *US*

- —George Percy, *The Language of Poker*, p. 11, 1988

blood simple *adjective*

crazed by violence *US*

- But the caper went blood simple: guard snuffed, stray bullets flying.—James Ellroy, *Hollywood Nocturnes*, p. 286, 1994

blood stripe *noun*

a military promotion that is made possible only by the demotion of another unit member *US*

- —Carl Fleischhauer, *A Glossary of Army Slang*, p. 4, 1968

bloodwagon *noun*

an ambulance *UK, 1922*

- There are guides. Even 'bloodwagons,' as the English call them, to bring down anyone who has an accident.—William F. Buckley Jr, *Stained Glass*, p. 183, 1978

blood weapon *noun*

a weapon captured from an enemy soldier, especially a soldier killed by the man taking the weapon *US*

- —Gregory Clark, *Words of the Vietnam War*, p. 62, 1990

blood wings *noun*

the first set of parachute insignia that a paratrooper receives upon qualification at different levels of expertise *US*

- His master-blaster "blood wings" were on his hat and he desperately wanted them back.—David H. Hackworth, *About Face*, p. 449, 1989

Bloody *noun*

a Bloody Mary drink, made with vodka and tomato juice *US, 1978*

- "You want another Bloody? I think I'm ready."—Elmore Leonard, *Glitz*, p. 162, 1985

bloody *adjective*

1 used as an intensifier; damned *UK, 1676*

After the adverbial use. Popular belief holds 'bloody' to be blasphemous and derives it as a contraction of 'by our lady', however there are no grounds to support this contention. Life's blood itself must be the significant source. In the UK the most famous use is probably 'Not bloody likely!' in the play *Pygmalion* by George Bernard Shaw, which shocked London audiences when first performed in 1916. The high frequency with which this term was used in Australia, especially in colonial times, has led to the appellation 'the Great Australian Adjective'. In 1847, a commentator noted that a bullock-driver (proverbially great swearers) used the term 25 times in a quarter-hour period, and thus calculated that he would have said 'this disgusting word' no less than 18,200,000 times in the course of 50 years (*Australian National Dictionary*). Though formerly ranked amongst the strongest taboo terms among polite speakers, and not permitted in print, it was evidently part of daily speech for many working class people. Now still commonly used in informal contexts. Taboo-wise its place has been taken by the synonymous **FUCKING**. Writing in 1942, Rohan D. Rivett observed 'that "bloody" was no longer the main

Australian adjective' and recounts overhearing the following gem involving its successor: 'I'm -ed if a -er can -ing well find out where the -ing hell he's -ing well expected to eat his -ing dinner' (*Behind Bamboo*, p.184).

- The word bloody is so common in modern parlance that it is not regarded as swearing. — Halse Rogers, *The Ugly Australian*, p. 111, 1942
- — Dymphna Cusack, *Picnic Races*, p. 60, 1962
- Suit yourself! Win or lose you'll still be a bloody parasite to me! — Wal Watkins, *Race the Lazy River*, p. 19, 1963
- — Patsy Adam-Smith, *Folklore of the Australian Railwaymen*, p. 218, 1969
- 'I don't know bloody well what you're so bloody upset about,' he shouted at her. 'Since every bloody cove I ever bloody met says bloody anytime he bloody feels like it.' — Bob Ellis and Anne Brooksbank, *Mad Dog Morgan*, p. 125, 1976
- Like bloody hell, I'll go in my land rover. — Sam Weller, *Old Bastards I Have Met*, p. 57, 1979
- He looked me straight in the eye and said "I'd like to punch you on the bloody jaw, for what you're doing to the English language." — Simon Napier-Bell, *Black Vinyl White Power*, p. 35, 2001

2 unpleasant; unpleasantly difficult *UK, 1934*

- — John Ayto, *The Oxford Dictionary of Slang*, p. 222, 1998

bloody *adverb*

exceedingly *UK, 1676*

- It was bloody good of the Maitlands to have me there at all. — Martin Boyd, *Lucinda Brayford*, p. 238, 1946
- Why did my parents have to be such a bloody bad selection? — Len Riley, *The Kings Cross Racket*, p. 74, 1967
- He asked how the bees were doing and was told they were in bloody poor shape. — Kylie Tennant, *The Man on the Headland*, p. 25, 1971
- Constable Ross was only doing his duty and you bloody went berserk. — David Williamson, *The Removalists*, p. 72, 1972
- I told him I thought he was bloody mad. — Blanche d'Alpuget, *Robert J. Hawke*, p. 68, 1982
- My friend, an old chap called Dusty, he was bloody good at that. — B. Wongar, *Walg*, p. 33, 1983

-bloody- *infix*

damned *AUSTRALIA, 1945*

- — John Wynnum, *Tar Dust*, p. 87, 1962
- That's fan-bloody-tastic! Lead me to 'em! — Barry Humphries, *The Wonderful World of Barry McKenzie*, p. 8, 1968
- Anyway, I reckon one sip's more than e-bloody-nough. — John O'Grady, *It's Your Shout, Mate!*, p. 61, 1972
- I had dinner on the table at eight o'bloody clock. — Danny King, *The Burglar Diaries*, p. 23, 2001
- Hoo-bloody-rah. — James Hawes, *White Powder, Green Light*, p. 25, 2002

bloody cunt hat *noun*

a narrow green cap worn by English Army officers *UK*

- Robert Th., a former member of the New Mexico National Guard (1948 to 1955), reports the use of cunt hat for oversea hat and bloody cunt hat for the oversea hat of English officers (it had a red stripe). — *Maledicta*, p. 222, Winter 1980

bloody hell!; bee aitch; BH

used for registering shock, surprise, exasperation, etc *UK*

Combines **BLOODY** (an intensifier) with **HELL** (used in oaths) to create an expletive so familiar that it is often pronounced as one word. Occasionally abbreviated to euphemistic initials.

- FREDA: Go 'way. Please go away. MARIE: ... Bloody hell, Freda. — Alan Bleasdale, *Boys From the Blackstuff*, 1982
- Lee is having no luck. LEE: Bloody hell. — Guy Ritchie et al., *Lock, Stock... & Four Stolen Hooves*, p. 57, 2000

Bloody Mary *noun*

1 a drink made of vodka and tomato juice, and, optionally, Tabasco or Worcester Sauce *UK, 1956*

From the colour; ultimately a pun on the nickname of Queen Mary, 1516–1558.

2 the bleed period of a woman's menstrual cycle *US, 1968*

- — Karen Houppert, *The Curse*, 1999

bloody oath!

used to register (enthusiastic) agreement *AUSTRALIA, 1848*

- 'Hell, we'll have a binge when we get home! Just the four of us!' 'Bloody oath!' — Eric Lambert, *The Veterans*, p. 193, 1954
- 'We all thought we'd come and have a yarn and a beer with you.' 'My bloody oath,' roared Tom. 'Come on in.' — Geoff Wyatt, *Saltwater Saints*, p. 14, 1969
- 'Could you do a cold stubbie?' John said 'Bloody oath.' — Sam Weller, *Old Bastards I Have Met*, p. 22, 1979
- Bloody oath, I can't wait. — Robert G. Barrett, *Davo's Little Something*, p. 48, 1992

bloody well *adverb*

definitely, certainly *AUSTRALIA, 1904*

A British slang expression used in English parts of its former colonies; extended from the adverbial sense of **BLOODY**.

- [T]hey reckon it serves him bloody well right. — Dymphna Cusack, *Picnic Races*, p. 146, 1962
- 'Well, bloodywell wait,' he threatened, while extracting a shirt button from the frilly lampshade. — Geoff Wyatt, *Saltwater Saints*, p. 46, 1969
- I don't bloodywell swear and any fucking cunt who says I do is a bloody liar. — Barry Prentice, 22nd May 1969
- Since you invited him," said Christine, "you can bloody well stick around and help me entertain him. — Margaret Atwoood, *Dancing Girls*, p. 21, 1977

blooey *adjective*

▸ **go blooey**

to go out of business; to break down completely *US, 1910*

- One More American Tradition Goes Blooey [Headline] — *San Francisco News*, p. 15, 12th June 1950
- Because fish fall in love with other fish, a wartime dream of a Sunnyvale industrial plant's employee went blooey today. — *San Francisco news*, p. 1, 18th July 1952
- Oblivious shitbird – he didn't know the whole scheme had gone blooey. — James Ellroy, *Hollywood Nocturnes*, p. 115, 1994

blooker *noun*

an M79 grenade launcher *US, 1973*

Vietnam war usage. It is a single-shot, break-open, breech-loading, shoulder-fired weapon.

- — *Maledicta*, p. 259, Summer/Winter 1982: 'Viet-speak'
- — Peter Kokalis, *Solider of Fortune*, p. 57, July 1992

bloomer *noun*

1 a mistake *UK, 1889*

- The budget bloomer. Undoubtedly the biggest mistake made by hard-pressed heads who either do not have the skills, or the time, to mount a serious strategic review of their costs. — *Education Guardian*, 11th November 2003

2 in the circus or carnival, a complete lack of business *UK, 1904*

- — Joe McKennon, *Circus Lingo*, p. 70, 1980

3 in horse racing, a horse that performs well early in the morning during the workout but not in a race later in the day *US*

- — David W. Maurer, *Argot of the Racetrack*, p. 14, 1951

4 an empty wallet, purse or safe *US*

- — Vincent J. Monteleone, *Criminal Slang*, p. 26, 1949

bloomer boy *noun*

a paratrooper *US*

- — *American Speech*, p. 319, October/December 1948: 'Slang of the American paratrooper'

Bloomie's *nickname*

the Bloomingdale's department store, especially the original store located on Third Avenue between 59th and 60th Streets, New York *US*

- Pitstopping on her way to Paris, where she will shoot pix of Raquel, our heroine hit Bloomie's New York where with credit card in hand racked up a $240 bill in 15 minutes. — *New York Times*, p. B1, 22nd April 1977
- Even with the Bloomie's job, I carefully rationed myself to one 23-cent can of tuna fish a day. — Kathryn Leigh Scott, *The Bunny Years*, p. 13, 1998
- The limited-edition tees are available at all Bloomie's locations. — *Atlanta Journal-Constitution*, p. 18NE, 18th March 2004

blooming *adjective*

a mild intensifier, a euphemism for 'bleeding' *UK, 1879*

Usage popularised in the 1880s by music hall singer Alfred 'The Great' Vance.

- A rotten little flat in a big old block, with galleries, what makes it look look like a bloomin' prison. — John Peter Jones, *Feather Pluckers*, p. 9, 1964
- Stop – you're breaking me bloomin' heart! — *The Sweeney*, p. 17, 1976
- [I]f I have to keep checking every decision back with you then it makes for a bloomin' long day. — Kevin Sampson, *Powder*, p. 26, 1999

blooming well *adverb*

used as an intensifier *UK*

- If you ask me we're all blooming well redundant. — Graeme Kent, *The Queen's Corporal [Six Granada Plays]*, p. 92, 1959

bloop *noun*

in the television and film industries, a device used on the junction of a photographic sound track to eliminate any audio cue that there is a splice in the film *US*

- — Oswald Skilbeck, *ABC of Film and TV Working Terms*, p. 19, 1960

blooper *noun*

1 an error, especially a humiliating and/or humorous one *US, 1947*

- —Helen Dahlskog (Editor), *A Dictionary of Contemporary and Colloquial Usage*, p. 8, 1972

2 in television, radio or film making, an unintentionally funny misspoken line *US, 1926*

- —Ira Konigsberg, *The Complete Film Dictionary*, p. 32, 1987

3 an M79 grenade launcher *US, 1978*

Vietnam war usage. It is a single-shot, break-open, breech-loading, shoulder-fired weapon.

- —*Maledicta*, p. 259, Summer/Winter 1982: 'Viet-speak'
- —Peter Kokalis, *Solider of Fortnue*, p. 57, July 1992

blooper ball *noun*

1 slow-pitch softball *US*

- [T]hey'd come in after a softball game, CYO League or Catholic War Vets – fast pitch, none of this blooper-ball shit – and drink Stroh's and play the juke box and argue about American League batting averages and ERAs.—Elmore Leonard, *Split Images*, p. 253, 1981

2 a grenade used in an M-79 grenade launcher *US*

- —*Maledicta*, p. 259, Summer/Winter 1982: 'Viet-speak'
- —Linda Reinberg, *In the Field*, p. 24, 1991

bloop tube; bloop gun *noun*

an M79 grenade launcher *US, 1971*

Vietnam war usage. It is a single-shot, break-open, breech-loading, shoulder-fired weapon.

- —Peter Kokalis, *Solider of Fortnue*, p. 57, July 1992

blooter *noun*

a task that is quickly and sloppily performed *UK: SCOTLAND*

- Look at the runs in this paintwork; this's been a blooter of a job. —Michael Munro, *The Patter, Another Blast*, 1988

blooter *verb*

1 to incapacitate someone with a violent blow *UK: SCOTLAND*

- There they are, the cavalry, charging down in waves, heads like battering rams in the oncoming chests. Whoomph! "You can run at someone and blooter them," enthuses Scotland's most capped [rugby] winger, Kenny Logan. "You can smash them out of the road."—*Scotland on Sunday*, 14th December 2003

2 to do something to excess *UK: SCOTLAND*

- For example, if you quickly spend a sum of money you may be said to have "blootered the whole lot".—Michael Munro, *The Patter, Another Blast*, 1988

3 to drink heavily *UK: SCOTLAND*

- —Michael Munro, *The Patter, Another Blast*, 1988

blootered *adjective*

drunk *UK, 1911*

Possibly from Scottish *bluiter* (to talk foolishly), or a corruption of PLOOTERED (drunk).

- ANDRA. (RAISING GLASS.) I'm for getting blootered!—Ian Pattison, *Rab C. Nesbitt*, 1988
- Everyone was blissfully blootered[.]—Kevin Sampson, *Powder*, p. 439, 1999

bloozer *noun*

an utter sentimentalist *UK*

- —Bob Young and Micky Moody, *The Language of Rock 'n' Roll*, p. 18, 1985

blossom *noun*

a facial blemish *US, 1942*

- —Frederic G. Cassidy, *Dictionary of American Regional English, Volume 1*, p. 291, 1985

blot *noun*

the anus or backside *AUSTRALIA, 1945*

From conventional 'blot' (a dark patch).

- Sorry if I made that climb a bit sudden, but I wanted to get as much ozone under the blot as I could, just in case some smart bastard down there was tracking us on radar.—W.R. Bennett, *Night Intruder*, p. 19, 1962
- He gave me a kick up the blot.—William Dick, *A Bunch of Ratbags*, 1965
- "Well, we just thought we'd ask your advice," Tich said, disappointed but still respectful. "Get out of his blot," Chilla said.—Frank Hardy, *The Outcasts of Foolgarah*, p. 57, 1971

blot *verb*

▸ **blot the copybook**

in horse racing, to fail dramatically and completely *AUSTRALIA*

- —Ned Wallish, *The Truth Dictionary of Racing Slang*, p. 8, 1989

▸ **blot your copy book**

to make a mistake, or to make a bad impression, or to spoil your record *UK, 1937*

A figurative use of school-imagery.

blotch *noun*

food

Anglo-Irish.

- Let's all go out and eat. You know even the smell of a cork makes me woozy and I must have blotch.—Nigel Fitzgerald, *The Student Body*, 1958

blotch *verb*

to stain your underwear when what had seemed like flatulence was something more *US*

- —Pamela Munro, *U.C.L.A. Slang*, p. 21, 1989

blotter *noun*

1 a tiny piece of absorbent paper impregnated with LSD and ingested as such *US*

- He was rummaging around in the kit bag. "I think it's about time to chew up a blotter," he said.—Hunter S. Thompson, *Fear and Loathing in Las Vegas*, p. 20–21, 1971
- 'What kind is it?" "Blotter. Has a little numeral one on it." —Elmore Leonard, *Freaky Deaky*, p. 20, 1988
- [H]e sticks half a blotter in my half-open mouth and we are fuckin' flying man[.]—Mike Benson, *Room full of Angels (Disco Biscuits)*, p. 25, 1996
- —Angela Devlin, *Prison Patter*, p. 28, 1996
- This plan ended up with us walking up and down Haight Street in S.F. trying to sell blotter to amused and disinterested ex-hippies. —Jennifer Blowdryer, *White Trash Debutante*, p. 37, 1997
- An E-pink, with a bird stamped on it, so a dove, I suppose – one blotter and a little grass.—Melanie McGrath, *Hard, Soft & Wet*, p. 89, 1998
- She did some blotter when she started with the Chicks and made the mistake of telling him one time, on the phone.—Elmore Leonard, *Be Cool*, p. 79, 1999
- Blotter acid is paper which has been soaked in a liquid solution of LSD.—Cam Cloud, *The Little Book of Acid*, p. 31, 1999

2 cocaine *UK*

- —Mike Haskins, *Drugs*, p. 280, 2003

3 the record of arrests held at a police station *US*

- [T]he first issue was widely regarded as "a police blotter". —Richard Neville, *Play Power*, p. 165, 1970

blotter cube *noun*

a type of LSD *UK*

- —Mike Haskins, *Drugs*, p. 285, 2003

blotting paper *noun*

food eaten to mollify the effects of alcohol when on a binge *AUSTRALIA*

- Com on, the old blotting paper's starting to work. I'm dry. —J.E. MacDonnell, *Don't Gimme the Ships*, p. 112, 1960

blotto *adjective*

very drunk; in a drunken stupor *UK, 1917*

Possibly from the absorbent quality of blotting paper, or from a conventional mid-C19 usage of 'blotted' as 'blurred', hence 'blotto' as 'very blurred'.

- "You can sit up and drink with me until I go blotto," I said. —Chester Himes, *If He Hollers Let Him Go*, p. 95, 1945
- One blotto bird in a narrow night club foyer, yelling for his coat and insisting he never got a check, can hold up 300.—Jack Lait and Lee Mortimer, *New York Confidential*, p. 221, 1948
- One of the men [...] fell forward, suddenly, head first on to the muddy pavement. He was quite blotto. The bottle he was holding fell without breaking and rolled down the alley.—Geoffrey Fletcher, *Down Among the Meths Men*, p. 24, 1966
- And the Barfers got blotto and fell in love with everything about these movie guys[.]—Joseph Wambaugh, *Lines and Shadows*, p. 336, 1984
- [H]is M.O. for the evening, I soon began to disern, was to get Donleavy so totally blotto that he could have his way with him, in terms of contracts[.]—Terry Southern, *Now Dig This*, p. 174, 1991
- The elevator's broke so Frog sends me up alone, he ain't gonna jog up six stories, he's blotto anyhow.—Richard Price, *Clockers*, p. 102, 1992
- What the bloody hell could be happening in your bloody mind to find it necessary to get blotto before noon?—Odie Hawkins, *Amazing Grace*, p. 17, 1993

blottoed *adjective*

drunk *UK*

- —*e-cyclopaedia*, 20th March 2002

blouse *noun*

1 a woman, especially a business woman *UK*

- [S]ome dippy [foolish] blouse in a Volvo.—Nick Barlay, *Curvy Lovebox*, p. 53, 1997

2 an overly effeminate male; a weak man *AUSTRALIA*
- [Do you] understand why it's important to moisturise but still think Saxon from *Big Brother* is a 'blouse'. — *SLM*, p. 7, 23th July 2003

3 in card playing, a singleton *UK, 1961*
Sometimes embellished to 'blousey suit'.

bloused *adjective*
in card playing, to have been dealt a singleton *AUSTRALIA*
From **BLOUSE**.
- "I had only the king (or any other card) bloused" = I had only a singleton king. — J.W. Sutherland, 1941

blow *noun*
1 cocaine *US, 1971*
- "I think I'll have a little blow before we begin," he said as he produced the folded hundred-dollar bill in which he carries his cocaine. — Christina and Richard Milner, *Black Players*, p. 177, 1972
- ten dollars worth of fine blow while Alan was talking out of his cut mouth — Elmore Leonard, *52 Pick-up*, p. 120, 1974
- DEALER: Hey, man. You wanna cop some blow? / JUNKIE: Sure, watcha got? Dust, flakes or rocks? / DEALER: I got China White, Mother of Pearl...I reflect what you need. — Grandmaster Flash & The Furious Five featuring Melle Mel, *White Lines*, 1983
- He says he owes you for blow and he just got some product himself. — *Heathers*, 1988
- He got a job dealing blow with Max, but he fucked that up. — Terry Williams, *The Cocaine Kids*, p. 128, 1989
- You got some blow? — *Boyz N The Hood*, 1990
- You got some good blow, right? — *The Bad Lieutenant*, 1992
- [S]uperb Bolivian blow. Brought it over myself[.] — Cleo Odzer, *Goa Freaks*, p. 110, 1995
- You feel bad you tested positive? Quit doing blow! — *Jerry Maguire*, 1996
- Yeah, well when you quit blow, you gotta quit the booze, too. — *Something About Mary*, 1998
- The two of us liked to get high a lot around the house, and we used more than our share of blow during the early 1970s. — Ralph "Sonny" Barger, *Hell's Angel*, p. 113, 2000

2 heroin *US*
- "We've been sitting out here for the last couple hours and haven't heard anyone shouting about 'rocks' and 'blows,'" said Talley, 65, referring to the street slang for crack and heroin. — *Chicago Tribune*, p. C1, 3rd August 2003

3 a dose of a drug, especially a dose of cocaine to be snorted *US, 1953*
- "You goin' give me a blow, ain't you Terry?" she asked in a pleading voice. — Donald Goines, *Dopefiend*, p. 197, 1971
- I felt it getting a bit heated so I ordered another blow of cocaine and a round of drinks and I split. — A.S. Jackson, *Gentleman Pimp*, p. 58, 1973
- I'm dying, baby. If I don't get a blow I'm goin to die. — Charles W. Moore, *A Brick for Mister Jones*, p. 26–27, 1975
- After a while Lalin said, "Carlito where can we go for a blow?" I wasn't too much into candy anymore since I came out. — Edwin Torres, *After Hours*, p. 241, 1979

4 marijuana *UK*
- — Angela Devlin, *Prison Patter*, p. 28, 1996
- Evenings spent on the steps, smoking blow, listening to the pirates[.] — Mark Powell, *Snap*, p. 21, 2001
- [H]e set up a small-scale business selling pills and blow[.] — Chris Ryan, *The Watchman*, p. 4, 2001

5 a cigarette; a smoke *UK, 1936*

6 a rest from work *AUSTRALIA, 1910*
From the sense as 'smoking tobacco', traditionally done on a break.
- Stay with us as long as yer can. Then sing out an' I'll give y'a blow. — Nino Culotta (John O'Grady), *They're A Weird Mob*, p. 79, 1957
- — Sam Weller, *Old Bastards I Have Met*, p. 18, 1979

7 a breath of fresh air, a 'breather', especially in the phrase 'get a blow' *UK, 1849*

8 an act of oral sex performed on a man *US, 1946*
A contraction of **BLOW JOB**.
- Oh J-A-N-E-T *I want a blow* I love you so. — Sal Piro and Michael Hess, *The Official 'Rocky Horror Picture Show' Audience Participation Guide*, p. 9, 1991

9 a high wind; a strong storm; a cyclone *AUSTRALIA, 1935*
- I told you it's nothing, bit of a blow, that's all. — Phillip Gwynne, *Deadly Unna?*, p. 72, 1998

10 in horse racing, a lengthening of the odds being offered *AUSTRALIA*
- The track was a bog and with a big weight of 9 stone 7lbs to carry, the old Button went for a giant blow in the betting. Five-to-one out to twenty-five's and no one wanted to back him. — Clive Galea, *Slipper!*, p. 6, 1988

11 a confidence swindle involving the claimed ability to change the denomination on currency *US*
- It didn't surprise Goldy that Jackson had been trimmed on The Blow. — Chester Himes, *A Rage in Harlem*, p. 40, 1957

▸ have a blow
1 to sniff glue *NEW ZEALAND*
- — David McGill, *David McGill's Complete Kiwi Slang Dictionary*, p. 16, 1998

2 of musicians, to make music *UK*
- Whilst she was waiting they were having a blow and producing some excellent rock and jazz. — Anthony Masters, *Minder*, p. 74, 1984

blow *verb*
1 to smoke, especially to smoke marijuana *US, 1772*
Originally 'to smoke a pipe or cigar', now drugs use only. Usage often specifies marijuana thus 'blow **SHIT**', 'blow a **STICK**', etc.
- "I just needs some pot to steady my nerves." "Okay, we're going to blow two now." — Chester Himes, *The Real Cool Killers*, p. 48, 1959
- At times, after we had fixed and blown some pot, with a sleek thrust of my own soul, a thrust of empathy, I used to find myself identifying with him. — Alexander Trocchi, *Cain's Book*, p. 75, 1960
- "Yes, indeed-y!" He grinned at Bernie. "Man blow pot, hey?" — Ross Russell, *The Sound*, p. 20, 1961
- Shorty would take me to groovy, frantic scenes in different chicks' and cats' pads, where with the lights and juke down mellow, everybody blew gage and juiced back and jumped. — Malcolm X and Alex Haley, *The Autobiography of Malcolm X*, p. 56, 1964
- I played stickball, marbles and Johnny-on-the-Poney, copped girls' drawers and blew pot. — Piri Thomas, *Down These Mean Streets*, p. 13, 1967
- Sho', I bet he done blow a lot of it too, aint he? — Terry Southern, *Red-Dirt Marijuana and Other Tastes*, 1967
- I could not see how they were more justified in drinking than I was in blowing the gage. — Eldridge Cleaver, *Soul on Ice*, p. 4, 1968
- But the trouble began when I ranked my hand / And stopped blowing and started to hit. — Dennis Wepman et al., *The Life*, p. 84, 1976
- — Home Office, *Glossary of Terms and Slang Common in Penal Establishments*, 1978
- Did I ask if they're tooting cocaine, maybe blowing a little weed? No, I didn't ask him that either. — Elmore Leonard, *Split Images*, p. 16, 1981

2 to register on a blood alcohol breath testing device *US*
- Someone at the club that evening had said that anybody coming from Deep Run after a Saturday night party, anybody at all, would blow at least a twenty on the breathalizer. — Elmore Leonard, *Switch*, p. 1, 1978

3 to perform oral sex *US, 1930*
- I, anticipating even more pleasure, wouldn't allow her to blow me on the bus[.] — Neal Cassady, *The First Third*, p. 190, 1947
- One of the boys talked about a girl who was in our mathematics class whom he was going to take out that same night, and who had promised to "blow him." — Phyllis and Eberhard Kronhausen, *Sex Histories of American College Men*, p. 55, 1960
- — Donald Webster Cory and John P. LeRoy, *The Homosexual and His Society*, p. 262, 1963: 'A lexicon of homosexual slang'
- Here, man. Blow me here! — John Rechy, *Numbers*, p. 106, 1967
- [I]t was Crane's kick to blow those sailors he encountered along the squalid waterfronts of that vivid never-to-be-recaptured prewar world[.] — Gore Vidal, *Myra Breckinridge*, p. 97, 1968
- Larry and Judy were sprawled out on the floor, her big white thighs around his neck, red-lipped black-haired cunt in his mouth, she working his balls and joint while he blew her cunt. — Steve Cannon, *Groove, Bang, and Jive Around*, p. 87, 1969
- Girls will blow girls, girl will blow boys, boys will blow girls, and boys will blow boys. — *Screw*, p. 11, 5th January 1970
- Well, that's the last time I blow him behind your back. — *Something About Mary*, 1998
- Oh, if you think I'm gonna blow this guy for your sick purposes, you are sadly mistaken. — *The Sopranos (Episode 57)*, 2004

4 to masturbate *UK*
- — Home Office, *Glossary of Terms and Slang Common in Penal Establishments*, 1978

5 to orgasm; to ejaculate *AUSTRALIA, 1952*
- Jackson's like...well, he's alright in bed. He's not brilliant. You know, when he blows he pretends he hasn't. — Kathy Lette, *Girls' Night Out*, p. 22, 1987
- — Kathy Lette, *Girls' Night Out*, p. 30, 1987

6 to open something with explosives *US*
- I prefer blowing one. I blowed quite a few. — Bruce Jackson, *In the Life*, p. 96, 1972
- Convicts, they'd sit around talking about jobs, banks they'd held up, argue about how to blow a safe. — Elmore Leonard, *Maximum Bob*, p. 107–108, 1991

7 to inform, to betray someone; to tell tales *UK, 1575*
Originally a conventional usage but progressed in status to slang in the mid-C17.

- He blew the local C.I.D. and they, having been alerted about hot [stolen] pussies [furs] of all descriptions, blew the Yard. —Charles Raven, *Underworld Nights*, p. 194, 1956

8 to boast *AUSTRALIA, 1858*
- Men strut and blow about themselves all the time without shame. —Miles Franklin, *My Career Goes Bung*, p. 129, 1946

9 to spoil something, to destroy something *US, 1899*
- I was in it ['Quadrophenia'] just long enough to create a big impression and not long enough to blow it. —Sting (Gordon Sumner), *Ask*, p. 111, 12th April 1980

10 to waste an opportunity, to bungle *US, 1907*
- I had the market on the good pot uptown sewed up; I didn't want to blow that. —Claude Brown, *Manchild in the Promised Land*, p. 161, 1965
- Anyway, she blew her whole weekend looking for someone for me to debate. —James Simon Kunen, *The Strawberry Statement*, p. 63, 1968
- You know, Billy, we blew it. —*Easy Rider*, 1969
- You blew it, asshole. —*Fast Times at Ridgemont High*, 1982
- You've blown it, man. You've fucked up the Mondays. —Shaun Ryder, *Shaun Ryder... in His Own Words*, 1994

11 to dismiss something as of no importance; to damn something *UK, 1835*
Semi-exclamatory; euphemistic.
- MOLLY: Being so hot mightn't be so good for the tummy, though. ALF: Oh, blow the tummy! —John O'Toole, *The Bush and the Tree [Six Granada Plays]*, p. 29, 1960
- We thought our troubles were behind us and blow us if Windsor Castle doesn't go and burn down. —Andrew Nickolds, *Back to Basics*, p. 19, 1994

12 to be useless, unpopular, distasteful *US*
Often in the context of an exclamation such as 'That blows!'.
- —Anna Scotti and Paul Young, *Buzzwords*, p. 53, 1997
- —Connie Eble (Editor), *UNC-CH Campus Slang*, p. 2, Fall 1999

13 to spend money, especially in a lavish or wasteful manner *UK, 1874*
- Just jacked me job in at the time, like, an was blowin me last wages. —Niall Griffiths, *Kelly + Victor*, p. 112, 2002

14 to leave *US, 1898*
- And did she put on an act when I blew town! —*It Happened One Night*, 1934
- I picked up my battered hat from the desk and stretched. "Got to blow, pal." —Mickey Spillane, *I, The Jury*, p. 24, 1947
- Two bucks would have paid him eight; five, two hundred; and he could have blown town for New Orelans[.] —James T. Farrell, *Saturday Night*, p. 9, 1947
- "Go ahead," he said to her. "You can blow." —Irving Shulman, *The Amboy Dukes*, p. 43, 1947
- As far as Roamer is concerned, they blew with the dough. —Horace McCoy, *Kiss Tomorrow Good-bye*, p. 264, 1948
- Dave also blew town, for reasons of his own, the new government cracked down on pushers. —Jack Kerouac, *Letter to Neal and Carolyn Cassady*, p. 386, 9th December 1952
- —J. L. Simmons and Barry Winograd, *It's Happening*, p. 168, 1966
- But if I begin to sense that she won't, because she's flaky or immature, then I try to get as much money as I can before she blows. —Susan Hall, *Gentleman of Leisure*, p. 8, 1972
- You're gonna blow town, but you'll give him an hour to get here and bring you some money. —Edwin Torres, *Q & A*, p. 179, 1977
- Lemme get my old lady and blow this joint. —Edwin Torres, *After Hours*, p. 354, 1979
- Why don't you just tell al to go blow? —Rita Cirtesi, *Pink Slip*, p. 3, 1999

15 to play a musical instrument *US, 1949*
Used with all instruments, not just those requiring wind.
- And the gate that rocked at the eighty-eight was blowin' "How High the Moon." —William "Lord" Buckley, *The Ballad of Dan McGroo*, 1960
- You blew piano with Jimmy Vann, huh? —Ross Russell, *The Sound*, p. 108, 1961
- This gave me a stronger urge to blow piano, or blow a box, as they used to say. —Claude Brown, *Manchild in the Promised Land*, p. 229, 1965
- [O]ne whom he intended looking up at the Capitol Theater where he was blowing with a name band (Glenn Miller's old band). —Herbert Huncke, *The Evening Sun Turned Crimson*, p. 75, 1980

16 used as a mild replacement for 'damn' *UK, 1781*
- I'm blowed if I can remember. —Mary Hooper, *(megan)2*, p. 106, 1999

17 to lengthen the odds offered on a horse or greyhound; to have its odds lengthen *AUSTRALIA*
- A smart bookmaker from the south took a horse he owned to the Darwin races. It was odds-on with the other bookies in a four-horse race. He decided to lay it. He told the jockey to pull it up, then blew the price to 2–1 against. —Frank Hardy and Athol George Mulley, *The Needy and the Greedy*, p. 61, 1975
- He's just blown from sixes to thirty-threes. —Joe Andersen, *Winners Can Laugh*, p. 198, 1982
- The other bookies followed his lead and blew the horse in the betting. —Clive Galea, *Slipper*, p. 120, 1988

▸ **blow a gasket**
to lose your temper completely *US, 1949*
- Watching it one day I saw the normally mild mannered Stuart almost blow a gasket on the air. —Sue Rhodes, *Now you'll think I'm awful*, p. 100, 1967
- —Helen Dahlskog (Editor), *A Dictionary of Contemporary and Colloquial Usage*, p. 8, 1972

▸ **blow a hype**
to become overexcited *US*
- —Gary Goshgarian (Editor), *Exploring Language*, p. 302, 1986

▸ **blow a load**
to ejaculate *US*
- Lois could never have Superman's baby. Do you think her fallopian tubes could handle his sperm? I guarantee he blows a load like a shotgun. —*Mallrats*, 1995

▸ **blow and go**
to vent air before an ascent to the surface while outside a submarine *US*
- —Linda Reinberg, *In the Field*, p. 24, 1991

▸ **blow a nut**
to ejaculate *US*
- JAY: So I blow a nut on her belly, and I get out of there, just as my uncle walks in. —*Clerks*, 1994

▸ **blow a shot**
while trying to inject a drug, to miss the vein or otherwise waste the drug *US*
- You keep blowing shots like that and all you'll have for an arm is abcesses. —James Mills, *The Panic in Needle Park*, p. 80, 1966
- —David Maurer and Victor Vogel, *Narcotics and Narcotic Addiction*, p. 390, 1973

▸ **blow a tank**
to use an explosive charge to open a safe *NEW ZEALAND*
- —David McGill, *David McGill's Complete Kiwi Slang Dictionary*, p. 16, 1998

▸ **blow a vein**
while injecting a drug, to cause a vein to collapse *US*
- —Stewart L. Tubbs and Sylvia Moss, *Human Communication*, p. 119, 1974
- —Geoffrey Froner, *Digging for Diamonds*, p. 11, 1989
- —Sally Williams, *"Strong" Words*, p. 134, 1994

▸ **blow beets**
to vomit *US*
- —Collin Baker et al., *College Undergraduate Slang Study Conducted at Brown University*, p. 82, 1968
- —Lewis Poteet, *Car and Motorcyle Slang*, p. 32, 1992

▸ **blow chow**
to vomit *US*
- —Michael V. Anderson, *The Bad, Rad, Not to Forget Way Cool Beach and Surf Discriptionary*, p. 3, 1988
- I gagged a couple of times, but I didn't blow chow so I was pretty pleased. —Janet Evanovich, *Seven Up*, p. 201, 2001

▸ **blow chunks**
to vomit *US*
- I think he's gonna blow chunks. —*Wayne's World*, 1992
- If some disco freak popped out of a trunk and blew chuncks all over the hood of my car, I'd be hopping mad. —Elissa Stein and Kevin Leslie, *Chunks*, p. 3, 1997

▸ **blow dinner**
to vomit *US*
- —Collin Baker et al., *College Undergraduate Slang Study Conducted at Brown University*, p. 82, 1968

▸ **blow down your ear**
to whisper to you *UK, 1938*
- —David Powis, *The Signs of Crime*, 1977

▸ **blow dust**
to shoot a gun *US*
- At one point, a woman overheard one of Mendrell's friends tell Miguel's security guard they would "blow dust also, if they have to," which is street slang for shooting a gun, police said. —*Intelligencer Journal (Lancaster, Pennsylvania)*, p. B1, 10th March 2001

▸ **blow grits**
to vomit *US*
- —Connie Eble (Editor), *UNC-CH Campus Slang*, p. 1, March 1979

▸ **blow its poke**
(of a fish) to regurgitate its stomach *CANADA*
The word 'poke' is a very old English word for 'bag'.

- I've seen a pollock coming up on the line and there'd be herring and small fish coming out of its mouth. Then it would blow its poke-out would come the poke. — *Paper Clip*, September 1982

▸ blow lunch
to vomit *US*
- I ate the porridge with onions and salt in it that had a raw egg tinted with blue vegetable coloring on top, blew my lunch, and ate some more. —John Nichols, *The Sterile Cuckoo*, p. 55, 1965
- —Collin Baker et al., *College Undergraduate Slang Study Conducted at Brown University*, p. 82, 1968

▸ blow pies
to vomit *US*
- —Chris Lewis, *The Dictionary of Playground Slang*, p. 36, 2003

▸ blow smoke
1 to brag *US*
- —Norman Carlisle, *The Modern Wonder Book of Trains and Railroading*, p. 259, 1946

2 to inhale crack cocaine smoke *UK, 1998*
- —Mike Haskins, *Drugs*, p. 291, 2003

▸ blow the brains out
to install a sun roof on a car *US*
- —Jim Crotty, *How to Talk American*, p. 35, 1997

▸ blow the cobwebs away
to take some fresh air or exercise and so become revivified *UK*
- Blow the cobwebs away – at the top of a mountain. — *The Guardian*, 4th January 2003

▸ blow the gaff
to reveal a secret, to inform *UK, 1812*

▸ blow the lid off
(of a secret plan or a hidden state-of-affairs) to publicly reveal something, especially to expose it in a spectacular way *US, 1928*

▸ blow the rag
to deploy a reserve parachute when the main parachute fails to deploy *US*
- —Linda Reinberg, *In the Field*, p. 25, 1971

▸ blow the whistle
to inform against an activity or crime and by so-doing cause the subject of such complaint to cease *UK, 1934*
- So I tell him Coyle blew the whistle, he gets mad and tells me what he was doing wiht Coyle. —George V. Higgins, *The Friends of Eddie Doyle*, p. 139, 1971
- I'm blowing the whistle on a sicko bastard[.] —Danny King, *The Burglar Diaries*, p. 169, 2001
- An accountant blew the whistle on his managing director who had run up more than £300,000 in unsubstantiated expenses and cash advances. — *The Observer*, 9th December 2001

▸ blow this cookie stand
to leave *US*
- Let's blow this cookie stand and get ourselves some breakfast. —John Sayles, *Union Dues*, p. 373, 1977

▸ blow this disco
to leave *US*
- —Connie Eble (Editor), *UNC-CH Campus Slang*, p. 2, Spring 1994

▸ blow this popsicle stand
to leave *US*
- —Connie Eble (Editor), *UNC-CH Campus Slang*, p. 6, Fall 1986

▸ blow this taco stand
to leave *US*
- —Connie Eble (Editor), *UNC-CH Campus Slang*, p. 1, Fall 1988

▸ blow this trap
to leave *US*
- Why don't we all blow this trap and have us some laughs? —Morton Cooper, *High School Confidential*, p. 19, 1958

▸ blow tubes
to smoke marijuana filtered through glass tubes *US*
- —Connie Eble (Editor), *UNC-CH Campus Slang*, p. 1, Spring 1991

▸ blow your bags
to boast *AUSTRALIA*
Possibly from 'bagpipes', in a similar way to the conventional 'blow your own trumpet'.
- —Tom Ronan, *Only a Short Walk*, 1961

▸ blow your beans
to ejaculate *AUSTRALIA*
- — Thommo, *The Dictionary of Australian Swearing and Sex Sayings*, p. 17, 1985

▸ blow your bowel bugle
to fart *UK*
- I've blown my bowel bugle, / I've been eating peas, / I've broken wind[.] —Ivor Biggun, *I've Parted (Misprint)*, 1978

▸ blow your cap
to become uncontrollable with anger or excitement *UK, 1984*
Beatniks' variations on **BLOW YOUR TOP**.

▸ blow your cookies
to ejaculate *UK*
- I got a coachload of Japanese booked in [to a massage parlour] for the weekend. Don't want 'em to blow their cookies in the first five minutes and refuse to pay for the whole hour. —Chris Baker and Andrew Day, *Lock, Stock... & a Fist Full of Jack and Jills*, p. 158, 2000

▸ blow your cool
to become very angry, excited, nervous, etc *US, 1961*
Since the mid-1950s it has been uncool in youth and counter-culture to demonstrate too much emotion.

▸ blow your dust
to ejaculate *UK, 1978*

▸ blow your jets
to become angry *US*
- — *San Francisco Examiner*, p. III-2, 22nd March 1960

▸ blow your lid
to lose your control emotionally; to become angry *US, 1935*
- We were in my room, Mrs. Winroy had come in a couple of minutes behind him, and she'd blown her lid so high we'd had to come upstairs. —Jim Thompson, *Savage Night*, p. 24, 1953

▸ blow your lump
to completley lose your emotional composure *US*
- — *American Speech*, p. 194, October 1951: 'A study of reformatory argot'

▸ blow your mind
1 to have a hallucinogenic experience; to experience a pyschotic break as a result of drug use *US, 1965*
- What's it like to blow you mind? [Advertisement for Look Magazine's "Hippie issue"] — *San Francisco Examiner*, p. 26, 12th September 1967
- Freak-Out With Peter Fonda as he Blows his mind [Advertisement for film, The Trip] — *San Francisco Chronicle*, p. 45, 20th September 1967
- Since that time I've had a few friends that have blown their minds on acid[.] —Leonard Wolfe (Editor), *Voices from the Love Generation*, p. 70, 1968

2 to amaze someone; to surprise someone; to shock someone *US, 1965*
A figurative sense, extended from the sense as a 'hallucinogenic experience'.
- "People are already down on us because we're Hell's Angels," Zorro explained. "This is why we like to blow their minds." —Hunter S. Thompson, *Hell's Angels*, p. 117, 1966
- —J. L. Simmons and Barry Winograd, *It's Happening*, p. 168, 1966
- Because when the Red Sox rallied to beat the Minnesota Twins, 5–3, and clinch at least a tie for the title, Boston fans blew their minds. — *San Francisco Chronicle*, p. 49, 2nd October 1967
- Who was the passenger? You guess it – Peter Fonda. It blew my mind. I couldn't believe it. —Darryl Ponicsan, *The Last Detail*, p. 83, 1970
- Van Dyke blew Brian's mind and I hadn't seen anyone else do that. —David Anderle, *quoted in Waiting For The Sun*, p. 128, 1996
- That she knew my name blew my mind. Some of my best friends didn't know my name. — *Something About Mary*, 1998

3 to lose your mind, to go crazy, to render unable to comprehend *US, 1965*
- He blew his mind out in a car. —The Beatles, *A Day in the Life*, 1967
- There's a man in the line / And she's blowing his mind / Thinking that he's already made her —Arlo Guthrie, *Coming into Los Angeles*, 1969
- [A] big fat woman threw me out, she blew her mind when she seen that room[.] —Richard Neville [quoting Otis Cook], *Play Power*, p. 244, 1970
- Guaranteed to blow your mind. —Queen, *Killer Queen*, 1974
- I'd never seen fresh tomatoes, mushrooms, garlic, olives ... dinner blew my mind! —Sally Cline, *Couples*, p. 127, 1998

▸ blow your roof
to smoke marijuana *US, 1950*
- —Richard A. Spears, *The Slang and Jargon of Drugs and Drink*, p. 56, 1986
- —Mike Haskins, *Drugs*, p. 290, 2003

▸ blow your stack
to lose your temper *US, 1947*
- He waited to see what would happen and when nothing did, said, "you go blowing off your stack like you been doing and you'll be wearing a D.O.A. tag on your toe." —Mickey Spillane, *Kiss Me Deadly*, p. 65, 1952

- I want to say something to you without you blowing your stack. —*Raging Bull*, 1980
- [T]he day that Nigel looked at the meter and blew his stack. —Mick Farren, *Give the Anarchist a Cigarette*, p. 160, 2001

▶ blow your top

1 to explode with anger *UK, 1928*
- When she blew her top she would draw a pistol. Sometimes she shot some of her workers[.] —*The Observer*, 8th February 2004

2 to lose your mind, to go crazy, to render unable to comprehend *US*
- In her condition she may blow her top at any time. —Harry J. Anslinger, *The Murderers*, p. 185–186, 1961

3 to lose emotional control, to induce pyschosis *US*
- It left me so shaky I almost blew my top and got sicker than a hog with the colic. —Mezz Mezzrow, *Really the Blues*, p. 4, 1946
- The weed available in the U.S. is evidently not strong enough to blow your top and weed psychosis is rare in the States. —William Burroughs, *Junkie*, p. 32, 1953

4 to engage in inconsequential conversation *US*
- —Marcus Hanna Boulware, *Jive and Slang of Students in Negro Colleges*, 1947

▶ blow your wheels

to act without restraint *US*
- You feel like you want ot blow your wheels right now? —*Rebel Without a Cause*, 1955

▶ blow your wig

to lose emotional control; to become angry *US*
- She'll probably blow her wig when she sees me —George Mandel, *Flee the Angry Strangers*, p. 133, 1952
- The Chick, you may dig, may blow her wig if a lad is sad and when he visits her pad and can't talk trash and has no cash. —Dan Burley, *Diggeth Thou?*, p. 5, 1959

▶ blow z's

to sleep *US*

Vietnam war usage.
- —Linda Reinberg, *In the Field*, p. 25, 1991

blow!; blow it!; blow you!

used as a non-profane oath *UK, 1823*

blow away *verb*

1 to kill someone, usually with a gun *US, 1913*
- —H. Craig Collins, *Street Gangs*, p. 222, 1979
- He should have just taken a dollar out of the wallet, given it to Joe the Grinder, and walked out, instead of blowing her away like he did. —Gerald Petievich, *Money Men*, p. 120, 1981
- That's what he has workers for, to blow people away for nothing. —Richard Condon, *Prizzi's Honor*, p. 223, 1982
- I said, 'Okay, I'll give you three seconds.' By the time he started to reach in his pocket I was at three and it was too late. So I blew him away. —Elmore Leonard, *Killshot*, p. 22, 1989
- not only blow you away, but suffer absolutely no come-back for it whatsoever —Danny King, *The Burglar Diaries*, p. 206, 2001

2 to impress or astonish someone; hence, to be impressed or astonished *US, 1975*
- [James] Brown blew me away. The footwork, the precision, the beat ... and all that screaming. —Jay Saporita [quoting Billy Joel], *Pourin' It All Out*, p. 25, 1980
- blown away by the guitar/bass/organ combination —Barney Hoskyns, *Waiting For The Sun*, p. 191, 1996

blowback *noun*

a method of smoking marijuana that requires two people: one takes the lit end of a joint into the mouth and blows, thus forcing the smoke into the lungs of the inhaler at the usual end; hence, any improvised method of forcing marijuana smoke for another to inhale; an act of inhaling exhaled marijuana smoke by simply placing your lips close to the exhaler's *UK*
- If we didn't have a bong, we used to get my brother's motor-cycle helmet, put it on, and get blowbacks into it through a crack in the visor. —Macfarlane, Macfarlane and Robson, *The User*, p. 79, 1996
- —Mike Haskins, *Drugs*, p. 271, 2003

blow back *verb*

in gambling, to lose all or most of your winnings *US*
- —Anthony Holden, *Big Deal*, p. 298, 1990

blow bath *noun*

during the war in Vietnam, a bath, massage and sex *US*
- —Linda Reinberg, *In the Field*, p. 24, 1991

blow blue *verb*

to inhale powdered cocaine *UK, 1998*
- —Mike Haskins, *Drugs*, p. 291, 2003

blowboy *noun*

a male homosexual *US, 1935*
- —Michael Dalton Johnson, *Talking Trash with Redd Foxx*, p. 66, 1994

blowby *noun*

in a car or truck, exhaust gases and carbon particles that enter the crankcase instead of being diverted into the exhaust system *US*

So named because the particles and gases 'blow by' the piston rings.
- —Tom MacPherson, *Dragging and Driving*, p. 136, 1960

blow dart *noun*

a hypodermic needle used to inject drugs *US*
- —Edward R. Bloomquist, *Marijuana*, p. 334, 1971

blow down *verb*

to shoot and kill someone *US, 1871*
- —J. E. Lighter, *Historical Dictionary of American Slang, Volume 1*, p. 201, 1994

blower *noun*

1 a telephone *UK, 1922*

Carried over from the 'speaking tube' which was blown through to alert the receiver; has also been applied to the telegraph system when used for the transmission of racing results. During World War 2, and for some time after, applied to a public address system.
- [T]he bent bogey [corrupt policeman] was on the blower to Charley. —Charles Raven, *Underworld Nights*, p. 62, 1956
- This geezer on the blower was so roundabout that he sounded deadly sus [suspicious][.] —Derek Raymond (Robin Cook), *The Crust on its Uppers*, p. 37, 1962
- Regan wished he hadn't been duty officer when the blower gave him details of a pop show's bust-up. —*The Sweeney*, p. 11, 1976
- Love getting on the blower and mouthing off to other mobs. —Martin King and Martin Knight, *The Naughty Nineties*, p. 174, 1999
- Get on the blower to those lads of yours. —Chris Baker and Andrew Day, *Lock, Stock... & Spaghetti Sauce*, p. 228, 2000

2 someone who succeeds at failing most of what they attempt *US*

A noun formation from **BLOW** as a verb (to be useless).
- —Judi Sanders, *Faced and Faded, Hanging to Hurl*, p. 4, 1993

3 a respirator *US*
- —Sally Williams, *"Strong" Words*, p. 135, 1994

4 in a jazz band, a soloist *US, 1960*
- —Robert S. Gould, *A Jazz Lexicon*, p. 26, 1964

5 a handkerchief *US*
- —Harold Wentworth and Stuart Berg Flexner, *Dictionary of American SLang*, p. 45, 1960

6 a marijuana smoker *US*
- —Vincent J. Monteleone, *Criminal Slang*, p. 27, 1949

7 a party *US*
- —Don R. McCreary (Editor), *Dawg Speak*, 2001

8 a pistol *US*
- —Porter Bibb, *CB Bible*, p. 94, 1976

9 in hot rodding and drag racing, a supercharger *US*
- —*Hot Rod Magazine*, p. 13, November 1948

blowhard *noun*

a boaster, a braggart *US, 1857*
- "[A] braggart and a blowhard of the type who may climb up on a sopabox and shout for a following, the way we've all seen Mr. Ceswick do, then back down the moment there is any real danger to him personally.' —Ken Kesey, *One Flew Over the Cuckoo's Nest*, p. 149, 1962
- I don't have to listen long before another empurpled, rightwing blowhard starts pontificating[.] —*The Guardian*, 25th July 2003

blowhole *noun*

1 the mouth *US*
- "You shut your blowhole," Tomboy said, turning to Liz. —Hal Ellson, *Tomboy*, p. 85, 1950

2 the anus *US, 1947*
- —J. E. Lighter, *Historical Dictionary of American Slang, Volume 1*, p. 201, 1994

blowie *noun*

1 an act of oral sex on a man *AUSTRALIA*

An abbreviated **BLOW JOB**.
- Chances of pulling a root: No root for legal reasons, but heaps of blowies. —*People*, p. 13, 5th July 1999

- [She] had also promised her cabby a 'blowie' if he waited like a getaway car outside Ophelia's house[.] — Gretel Killeen, *Hot Buns and Ophelia get a Bloke*, p. 3, 2000
- Adultery meanz shaggin someone elses bitch. Hobviously it don't refer to receivin a blowie or shake 'n vac. — Sacha Baron-Cohen, *Da Gospel According to Ali G*, 2001

2 a blowfly *AUSTRALIA, 1916*
- There's beer all over the floor and blowies all over the bar. — Bill Hornadge, *The Australian Slanguage*, p. 68, 1980
- I started this lot off on meat, nice bucket of pig guts I got offa Porky Fraser. Let the blowies strike that. — Phillip Gwynne, *Deadly Unna?*, p. 167, 1998

blow-in *noun*

1 the arrival in prison of a new prisoner *US*
- — Vincent J. Monteleone, *Criminal Slang*, p. 27, 1949

2 a new arrival; a person who has dropped in *AUSTRALIA, 1937*
- — Hyman E. Goldin et al., *Dictionary of American Underworld Lingo*, p. 30, 1950
- Mosta you blow-ins are queers. — Nino Culotta (John O'Grady), *They're A Weird Mob*, p. 60, 1957
- Him and his blow-ins trying to pervert our anniversary for their own ends! — Dymphna Cusack, *Picnic Races*, p. 9, 1962

blow in *verb*

to arrive *US, 1882*
- About that time Sid Barry blew in from New York[.] — Milton Mezzrow, *Really the Blues*, p. 21, 1946
- Well, children, the big bad wolf blew into town as advertised[.] — Steve Allen, *Bop Fables*, p. 21, 1955
- Sapphire waited until 2.30. Then he blew in by the kitchen window round at the back[.] — Charles Raven, *Underworld Nights*, p. 11, 1956
- Always had him up for a ding-dong yarn when he blew in. — Dymphna Cusack, *Picnic Races*, p. 218, 1962
- He had blown into town with no 'ho. — Iceberg Slim (Robert Beck), *Airtight Willie and Me*, p. 21, 1979
- According to Lairdy, some terrific birds blow in up there. — Roy Slaven (John Doyle), *Five South Coast Seasons*, p. 56, 1992

blow it!

▷ see: BLOW!

blowing smoke *noun*

marijuana *UK, 1998*
- — Mike Haskins, *Drugs*, p. 286, 2003

blow job *noun*

1 an act of oral sex performed on a man, or, occasionally, a woman *US, 1942*
- That white chick – Jane – of yours – she ever give you a blow job? — James Baldwin, *Another Country*, p. 69, 1962
- — Donald Webster Cory and John P. LeRoy, *The Homosexual and His Society*, p. 262, 1963: 'A lexicon of homosexual slang'
- — Florida Legislative Investigation Committee (Johns Committee), *Homosexuality and Citizenship in Florida*, 1964: 'Glossary of homosexual terms and deviate acts'
- "I made $650." "All blow jobs?" I nodded yes. He handed me a Scotch. — Sara Harris, *The Lords of Hell*, p. 100, 1967
- Blowjob to orgasm? They call it "full French" here. — Gerald Paine, *A Bachelor's Guide to the Brothels of Nevada*, p. 15, 1978
- Well, the last you could do is give me a blow job. — *Repo Man*, 1984
- "You've written the definite blow-job!" he kept shouting. "The definite blow-job!" — Terry Southern, *Now Dig This*, p. 13, 1986
- [T]he proposed site was a mecca for homos who wanted to get quick blowjobs. — Howard Stern, *Miss America*, p. 460, 1995
- Mario and Greg emerged triumphant from the same toilet, having received a wank and a blow-job respectively from a girl called Geraldine. — Colin Butts, *Is Harry on the Boat?*, p. 263, 1997
- The current popularity of blow jobs is clearly the result of a feminist conspiracy to suck out our vital forces. — Howard Marks, *The Howard Marks Book of Dope Stories*, p. 153, 2001
- [P]articularly useful for women when they're giving a blow job. — *GQ*, p. 117, July 2001
- The fluffer on the perfect blowjob: "The first two inches are the most sensitive part of the penis – use gentle suction[.] — *Sky Magazine*, p. 88, July 2001
- After all, if you're the kind of guy who'll pay for blowjobs from a black chick on the Sunset Strip, it's humiliating to have to keep saying "Oh, bugger" as if it were the most adorable thing in the world. — *LA Weekly*, p. 15, 31st May 2002

2 a favourable film review *US*
- — Anna Scotti and Paul Young, *Buzzwords*, p. 5, 1997

3 a safe robbery in which explosives are used to gain access to the safe *US*
- There's also the old-fashioned blow job, which nobody uses anymore. You blow the whole goddamn safe. — Leonard Shecter and William Phillips, *On the Pad*, p. 179, 1973

4 a jet aircraft *UK, 1984*

Royal Air Force use. A jocular application of the sexual sense (oral sex) but also in comparison to a piston-driven engine.

blowman *noun*

a member of a youth gang designated as a shooter *US*
- — H. Craig Collins, *Street Gangs*, p. 222, 1979

blow me down!

used as an expression of surprise *UK, 1928*
- Well blow me down, says Daniel, I've barely worked the gel into a suitable consistency and suddenly all these car horns start honking in the streets. — *The Guardian*, 23rd October 2003

blow monkey *noun*

a person with a strong interest in performing oral sex and/or using cocaine *US*
- — Anna Scotti and Paul Young, *Buzzwords*, p. 15, 1997

blown *adjective*

1 drunk or drug-intoxicated *US*
- On the way over to the band's house, I saw that I was still pretty seriously blown. — Stephen Gaskin, *Amazing Dope Tales*, p. 135, 1980
- — Mike Haskins, *Drugs*, p. 291, 2003

2 of a blood vein, collapsed *US*
- A vein is said to be "blown" when it can no longer be used because it has collapsed. — Geoffrey Froner, *Digging for Diamonds*, p. 11, 1989

3 in hot rodding and drag racing, using a supercharger; of any car, but especially a racing car, supercharged *US*
- — *Hot Rod Magazine*, p. 13, November 1948
- — Fremont Drag Strip, *Guide to Drag Racing*, 1960
- — Capitol Records, *Hot Rod Jargon*, 1963

blown away *adjective*

drunk or drug-intoxicated *US*
- I checked out an unmarked car, drove to the apartment of an informant and got blown away on hash[.] — James Ellroy, *Brown's Requiem*, p. 220, 1981

blown in *adjective*

of a car, partially resprayed *UK*

Used by the motor trade.
- — *Woman's Own*, 28th February 1968

blown out *adjective*

1 said of choppy ocean conditions unfavourable for surfing *US*
- — Grant W. Kuhns, *On Surfing*, p. 114, 1963
- [H]e took first place in the U.S. Surfing Championship on a "blown-out" (rotten) day when he got one of the few decent waves. — Eve Babitz, *Eve's Hollywood*, p. 204, 1974

2 among London taxi drivers, having failed to get a final fare-paying passenger *UK, 1939*

3 drug-intoxicated *US*
- — Helen Dahlskog (Editor), *A Dictionary of Contemporary and Colloquial Usage*, p. 8, 1972

blow-off *noun*

1 the end of a circus performance; the final performance in a circus engagement *US, 1913*
- — J. E. Lighter, *Historical Dictionary of American Slang, Volume 1*, p. 203, 1994

2 in the circus or carnival, the crowd leaving a performance *US*
- — Joe McKennon, *Circus Lingo*, p. 18, 1980

3 oral sex performed on a man *US*
- Through Oregon and Washington we were cut down quite a bit; we couldn't give the blow-off and we couldn't strip all the way and things like that. — Bruce Jackson, *In the Life*, p. 390, 1972

4 the moment in a confidence swindle when the victim is left to discover his loss *US*
- White grifters call it the blowoff. — Iceberg Slim (Robert Beck), *Trick Baby*, p. 124, 1969

blow off *verb*

1 to fart *UK, 1984*
- For a start the cast will have back doors buffed and, hopefully, if the rehearsal diet works, be blowing off all the time. — Roy Slaven (John Doyle), *Five South Coast Seasons*, p. 66, 1992

2 (of a male) to orgasm, ejaculate *AUSTRALIA*
- Hold the Commo bastard, Gomorrah, for crissake or I'll blow orf. — Frank Hardy, *The Outcasts of Foolgarah*, p. 171, 1971

3 to scold someone *AUSTRALIA*
- Old man's been blowing off at me ever since I woke up. — Norman Lindsay, *Halfway to Anywhere*, p. 199, 1947

4 to ignore, to dismiss someone *US, 1965*
- Well then blow him off when he gets here. — *Something About Mary*, 1998

5 to fail to attend *US*
- — *Rutgers Alumni Magazine*, p. 21, February 1986

6 in hot rodding, to win a race *US*
- — Fred Horsley, *The Hot Rod Handbook*, p. 209, 1965

blow-off number *noun*
a wrong telephone number deliberately given to an unwanted suitor *US*
From **BLOW OFF** (to dismiss). Coined for US television comedy *Seinfeld*, 1993–98.
- — Susie Dent, *The Language Report*, p. 146, 2003

blow out *noun*
1 a heavy meal *UK, 1924*
- "I usually cater to the very rich," he said. "They work in their offices all month and then they want a blow-out." — *The Daily Telegraph*, 18th January 2003

2 a party or meal unlimited by normal rules of conduct *US, 1815*
- Two summers ago he decided to throw a blowout reunion party at the China Club[.] — Elissa Stein and Kevin Leslie, *Chunks*, p. 8, 1997

3 in horse racing, a short but intense workout several days before a race *US*
- — Don Voorhees and Bob Benoit, *Railbird Handbook*, p. 44, 1968

4 crack cocaine *UK, 1998*
- — Mike Haskins, *Drugs*, p. 281, 2003

5 an utter failure *US, 1938*
- Blowouts, both times, wiped me clean. — Elmore Leonard, *Bandits*, p. 66, 1987

▸ **give the blowout**
to rid yourself of someone *US*
- — Patrick O'Shaughnessy, *Market Traders' Slang*, 1979

blow out *verb*
1 (of a police case) to fail *UK*
Metropolitan Police slang. Figurative use of 'blow out' (a pneumatic tyre puncturing suddenly).
- — Peter Laurie, *Scotland Yard*, p. 321, 1970
- — Angela Devlin, *Prison Patter*, p. 28, 1996

2 to reject an agreement or responsibility *UK*
More often elaborated as **BLOW OUT OF THE WATER**.

3 to manufacture drugs *UK*
- I should have blew out a kilogram or so [of E] then quit. — Eleusis *Lightning on the Sun*, p. 331, 2001

4 to lengthen the odds offered on a horse or greyhound; to have its odds lengthen *AUSTRALIA, 1911*
- My situation became hopeless when Greg, to my utter amazement, blew out the local to sixes. — Robert English, *Toxic Kisses*, p. 158, 1979
- He could smell trouble before a bet was laid in the shape of a big plunge or a favourite about to blow out the backdoor. — Clive Galea, *Slipper!*, p. 25, 1988
- It was a win not without controversy, as a whisper went around the track said Keltrice was suffering an injury and the colt's price blew out in the betting ring, but he showed no ill effects in recording a powerful win. — *Sydney Morning Herald*, p. 1, 26th February 1994
- I was firming in the market, he was blowing out and when he's about a hundred to one, he decideds to play his party trick. — Paul Vautin, *Turn It Up!*, p. 136, 1995

▸ **blow out of the water**
to reject something absolutely, especially when applied to an agreement or responsibility *UK*
- Having seen his softly-softly, "try not to offend" policy blown out of the water by Israel's offensive of the past two weeks[.] — *New Statesman*, 15th April 2002
- Republicans say that if they were edging toward any rapprochement over joining the policing board, that has been blown out of the water. — *The Guardian*, 7th October 2002

blows *noun*
heroin *UK*
- — Robert Ashton, *This Is Heroin*, p. 205, 2002
- — Mike Haskins, *Drugs*, p. 283, 2003

blowsing *noun*
the sniffing of glue or other industrial solvents *UK*
- Black youth, comfortable with it's spliffs, disdains glue-sniffing ... or blowsing as it is often called by the glue-sniffers themselves. — *Time Out*, 8th January 1982

blow that for a joke!
used for a complete rejection *NEW ZEALAND*
- — David McGill, *David McGill's Complete Kiwi Slang Dictionary*, p. 16, 1998

blow through *verb*
1 to leave *AUSTRALIA, 1950*
- It's six o'clock. I'll blow through. — William Dick, *A Bunch of Ratbags*, 1965
- Two blokes there said they were ok so I just blew through. — Sam Weller, *Old Bastards I Have Met*, p. 16, 1979
- They waltzed inside, determined to eat, dress, and blow through posthaste[.] — Kerry Cue, *Crooks, Chooks and Bloody Ratbags*, p. 143, 1983

2 to give information over the telephone *UK*
To use the **BLOWER** (a telephone).
- — Peter Laurie, *Scotland Yard*, p. 321, 1970
- — Angela Devlin, *Prison Patter*, p. 28, 1996

blow torch *noun*
1 in military aviation, a jet fighter *US, 1950*
- — Harold Wentworth and Stuart Berg Flexner, *Dictionary of American Slang*, p. 47, 1960

2 in drag racing, a car powered by a jet engine *US*
- — John Lawlor, *How to Talk Car*, p. 20, 1965

Blowtorch Bob; Blowtorch *nickname*
Robert William Komer, a Lieutenant Colonel in the US Army and a CIA operative in Vietnam from 1967 to 70 *US*
It is said that the nickname was coined by US Ambassador to Vietnam Henry Cabot Lodge, who likened arguing with Komer to having a blowtorch aimed at the seat of your trousers.
- — Linda Reinberg, *In the Field*, p. 25, 1991

blow-up *noun*
1 an emotionally intense quarrel that soon blows over *UK, 1809*
From the explosive quality of such conflicts.
- There was a big blow-up when I'd been with Pete and other family members for a whole week's vacation. — Sally Cline, *Couples*, p. 290, 1998

2 a corpse that has exploded from a build-up of internal gas *US*
- — *American Speech*, p. 267, December 1962: 'The language of traffic policemen'

blow up *verb*
1 to lose your temper *UK, 1871*
- '[W]ell, Gary, maybe that's beyond your control.' At this point Gary blew up. 'Those sons of bitches, those sons of bitches,' he kept saying. — Norman Mailer, *The Executioner's Song*, p. 652, 1979

2 in an endurance sport, especially cycling, to reach a point of utter exhaustion *US*
- The athlete may "bonk," "hit the wall"or "blow up," as the terminology goes. — *Washington Post*, p. A1, 11th June 2001

3 to quit a job without notice *US*
- — Norman Carlisle, *The Modern Wonder Book of Trains and Railroading*, p. 259, 1946

4 to inform against someone *UK*
A variation of **BLOW THE WHISTLE**.
- DIXIE: Someone's blown you up, Freda. FREDA: But who'd do a thing like that? — Alan Bleasdale, *Boys From the Blackstuff*, 1982

5 (used of a telephone, especially a mobile phone) to ring *US*
- — Connie Eble (Editor), *UNC-CH Campus Slang*, p. 2, Fall 2002

6 to receive repeated electronic pages *US*
- — Rick Ayers (Editor), *Slang Dictionary*, p. 5, 2001

7 (used of a racehorse) to breath hard after a race *US*

blow you!
▹ see: **BLOW!**

blow-your-mind roulette *noun*
a drug activity in which a variety of pills are mixed together and individuals take a random selection of pills from the mix *US*
- — Clarence Major, *Dictionary of Afro-American Slang*, p. 29, 1970

BLT *noun*
1 a *b*acon, *l*ettuce and *t*omato sandwich *US, 1952*
- — Harold Wentworth and Stuart Berg Flexner, *Dictionary of American Slang*, p. 679, 1976

2 a police officer *l*ooking for *t*rouble *CANADA*
From **BACON** (a police officer). Punning on the common usage as a 'bacon, lettuce and tomato sandwich'.
- — Bill Casselman, *Canadian Sayings*, p. 66, 2002

blubber *noun*

1 a fat person *US*

- The labels were cruel: Gimp, Limpy-go-fetch, Crip, Lift-one-drag one, etc. Pint, Half-a-man, Peewee, Shorty, Lardass, Pork, Blubber, Belly, Blimp. Nuke-knob, Skinhead, Baldy. Four-eyes, Specs, Coke bottles. —*San Francisco Examiner*, p. A15, 28th July 1997

2 the act of using the thumb and forefinger to pinch another's cheeck *US*

- —Hyman E. Goldin et al., *Dictionary of American Underworld Lingo*, p. 31, 1950

blubberbag *noun*

a rubber petrol or fuel-oil transport tank *CANADA*

- At Thule five collapsible neoprene rubber tanks are installed in each Hercules, permitting 4500 gallons of fuel to be airlifted. Nicknamed blubberbags, five were [later] used to airlift 192260 gallons of fuel-oil to the Canadian Arctic weather stations. —*North*, p. 8/1, November-December 1964

blubberbutt *noun*

an obese person *US, 1952*

- And watch: if Gore wins, America's blubberbutts will file a class action suit against the beer companies. —*New York Post*, p. 20, 30th July 2000

blubbers *noun*

the female breasts *US*

- —Vincent J. Monteleone, *Criminal Slang*, p. 28, 1949

bludge *noun*

1 an easy job, requiring little work *AUSTRALIA, 1943*

- He was happy in his job, it was a good bludge. —John Cleary, *The Long Shadow*, 1949
- 'You're mad!' the medical corporal remarked to me as I climbed into the jeep that was to take me to the second village. 'Wanting to leave a bludge like this and go back up the ridge.' —Eric Lambert, *The Veterans*, p. 185, 1954

2 a respite from work or duty *AUSTRALIA*

- Then yer swing 'er over ter Pat again, an' 'ave a bludge while 'e's fillin' 'er up. —Nino Culotta (John O'Grady), *They're A Weird Mob*, p. 79, 1957
- Tomorrow morning will see you ashore for a quiet bludge in Brisbane. —John Wynnum, *Tar Dust*, p. 115, 1962

3 an instance of taking it easy on a job *AUSTRALIA*

- Dennis said, 'Looks like you an' me havin' a good bludge ter-morrer, Nino. Away from the boss.' —Nino Culotta (John O'Grady), *They're A Weird Mob*, p. 85, 1957

4 an act of borrowing or sponging *NEW ZEALAND*

- I suppose you're on the bludge again? Why don't you earn it this time? —Ronald Morrieson, *Predicament*, p. 202, 1974

bludge *verb*

1 to live off another's hospitality *AUSTRALIA, 1899*

A backformation from **BLUDGER**. Usually with 'on', though since the 1960s also with 'off'.

- You come out here bludging on Uncle Matt when he gave Mum a home. —Kylie Tennant, *The Honey Flow*, p. 133, 1956
- 'Bludge off me then,' Kestrel said coldly. 'Not off your mates. I'll make sure you work for it.' —Randolph Stow, *Tourmaline*, p. 44, 1963
- She was bludging off an Austudy house full of dishwashers and mop jockeys. —John Birmingham, *He Died With a Felafel in his Hand*, p. 119, 1994

2 to borrow something; to cadge something *NEW ZEALAND, 1945*

- He's over there wingeing because he can't bludge a drink[.] —Barry Humphries, *Bazza Pulls It Off!*, 1971
- And they spent every living minute trying to get into her and her girlfriends' pants while bludging money from them at the same time. —Robert G. Barrett, *Davo's Little Something*, p. 27, 1992
- [I]'ve seen them bludging meals from the Krishnas. —John Birmingham, *He Died With a Felafel in his Hand*, p. 6, 1994
- —Harry Orsman, *A Dictionary of Modern New Zealand Slang*, p. 13, 1999

3 to relax, especially when there is work to be done *AUSTRALIA, 1942*

- All you have is a king size hangover and you are lucky as a chow you aren't in the hoosegow instead of bludging in comfort in a hospital. —John Wynnum, *Jiggin' in the Riggin'*, p. 55, 1965

bludger *noun*

1 a pimp; a man who lives off the earnings of a prostitute *AUSTRALIA, 1898*

This is the earliest sense of this word and derives from the obsolete British and early Australian slang 'bludgeoner' (a pimp who uses a bludgeon to rob people visiting his prostitute). From 1856 in the UK, c.1882 in Australia (*Sydney Slang Dictionary*). They were also called 'stick slingers'. By 1900 the sense 'pimp' was well established. The strongly negative sense of sponging off others derives from the fundamental nature of the pimp.

- Wot you got is a couple of big fat bludgers who will knock me on the 'ead an' take me money. —Robert S. Close, *Love Me Sailor*, p. 70, 1945
- He sees himself not as a lowly pimp or 'bludger', but as a big-time operator[.] —James Holledge, *The Call-girl in Australia*, p. 107, 1964
- Drunks, petty crims, bludgers and a few alcoholic or amphet pill addicted musicians. —Kevin Mackey, *The Cure*, p. 74, 1970

2 a lazy person who does not do their fair share of work; a person who lives off another's hospitality *AUSTRALIA, 1900*

- But if you are ever told you are a 'bludger', go home. A bludger is the worst thing you can be in Australia. It means that you are criminally lazy, that you 'pole on yer mates', that you are a 'piker' – a mean, contemptible, miserable individual —Nino Culotta (John O'Grady), *They're A Weird Mob*, p. 203, 1957
- Geddup, you skulkin' bludger. —John Wynnum, *Tar Dust*, p. 76, 1961
- 'Weren't you scared you still mightn't get a job?' 'Not me, baby, I'm not one of those bludgers'. —Jenny Pausacker, *What are ya?*, p. 45, 1987
- "If ya got off ya lardarse an' got a job, Lardarse, you'd be denying a young person a job." "Yeah, long-harired, lay-about bludgers! Ha! Ha ha! Ha!" —Carter and Rydyr, *Sick Puppy*, p. 10, 1998
- He told me a bludger is a lazy cunt who does fuck-all. —Brian Preston, *Pot Planet*, p. 90, 2002

3 a despicable person *AUSTRALIA, 1906*

- 'The bludgers!' Windy expostulated. 'A whole week! Sure they can spare it?' —J.E. MacDonnell, *Don't Gimme the Ships*, p. 45, 1960
- I don't suppose it's easy to put up with an old bludger like me. —Alexander Buzo, *Norm and Ahmed*, p. 23, 1969
- I'll get square with you bludgers, if it's the last thing I ever do. —Roy Higgins and Tom Prior, *The Jockey Who Laughed*, p. 82, 1982
- To make matters worse, he was laughing his head off, the little bludger. —Rex Hunt Tall Tales – and True, p. 40, 1994

4 a stingy person who borrows rather than buys *AUSTRALIA*

- The great Australian cadger, the Bludger is out for anything he can get – and never return. —Arthur Chipper, *The Aussie Swearer's Guide*, p. 30, 1972

5 any person *AUSTRALIA*

Often in the phrase 'poor bludger' (a sorry individual).

- Now suppose a man here in this country found himself as hard up as some of those poor bludgers in Pakistan. —Geoff Wyatt, *Saltwater Saints*, p. 86, 1969
- —Paul Vautin, *Turn It Up!*, p. 39, 1995
- Well, by the time I got the shopping upstairs, the useless bludger had fallen off onto the roof of the alcove, smashed thirty or forty tiles, pulled the guttering off as well, and hit the terracotta tiles on the ground – breaking a dozen of them as well. —Paul Vautin, *Turn It Up!*, p. 134, 1995

6 used jocularly or affectionately as a term of address to friends *AUSTRALIA*

- 'There you are, you old bludger,' he greeted amicably. —J.E. MacDonnell, *Don't Gimme the Ships*, p. 21, 1960

7 something which causes aggravation *AUSTRALIA*

- [He] was too interested in landing his fish to take a great deal of notice. 'Yeah, hold on a second,' he grunted. 'I've nearly got this bludger.' —Robert G. Barrett, *Davo's Little Something*, p. 321, 1992
- In the end I found five of the bludgers [funnel-web spiders] in there, including two in the skimmer box. —Paul Vautin, *Turn It Up!*, p. 163, 1995

bludging *noun*

used as the verbal noun of bludge *AUSTRALIA, 1984*

bludging *adjective*

lazy *AUSTRALIA, 1948*

- —Nino Culotta (John O'Grady), *They're A Weird Mob*, p. 203, 1957
- Okay, you bludgin' old bag of bones, get up orf your spine and give me a hand to cart your rocking chair out to the truck. —Geoff Wyatt, *Saltwater Saints*, p. 71, 1969
- —Clive Galea, *Slipper*, p. 132, 1988

blue *noun*

1 methylated spirits as an alcoholic drink *UK*

From the colour of the fluid.

- The usual practice is to extend it [metal polish] with lemonade or a shot of blue. —Geoffrey Fletcher, *Down Among the Meths Men*, p. 17, 1966
- [O]n a cold night, if you lie down, take a drink of the blue, and then pull the collar of your coat up over your head, "it keeps you warm". —Robin Page, *Down Among the Dossers*, p. 122, 1973
- They [vagrant alcoholics] subsist on a diet of methylated spirits (jake or the blue), surgical spirit (surge or the white) and other forms of crude alcohol. —Peter Ackroyd, *London The Biography*, p. 359, 2000

2 an amphetamine tablet *UK*
From the colour of the tablet.
- You spent all night at the Scene, you took blues, you went home in the morning. —Maldwyn Thomas, *The Sharper Word*, p. 50, 1992
- I'd had a couple of blues and I was proper on it. —Dave Courtney, *Raving Lunacy*, p. 117, 2000
- [T]he most popular pills were either Purple Hearts (legally made and lilac-coloured), or blues (home-made, or imported from France). —Simon Napier-Bell, *Black Vinyl White Powder*, p. 42, 2001

3 a barbiturate capsule *US*
- —Norman W. Houser, *Drugs*, p. 13, 1969
- I laughed to myself as I pictured blues or dilaudid in such great amounts that the spoon would literally be overflowing. —*Drugstore Cowboy*, 1988
- Barbiturates are also known as BARBS, BLUES, REDS, and SEKKIES. —Macfarlane, Macfarlane and Robson, *The User*, p. 97, 1996

4 a capsule of Drinamyl™, a combination of dexamphetamine sulphate and amylobarbitone *UK*
A favourite drug of abuse for mid-1960s Mods.
- —Liz Cutland, *Kick Heroin*, p. 104, 1985

5 crack cocaine *UK*
- —Mike Haskins, *Drugs*, p. 281, 2003

6 cocaine *US*
- They ordered cocaine or morphine by the pieces (ounces) and used the dope peddler's slang or code terms, red or blue identifying morphine or cocaine. —William J. Spillard and Pence James, *Needle in a Haystack*, p. 147, 1945

7 Foster's beer *AUSTRALIA*
- The basic requirements of a good 'happening' were: an ample supply of 'Blue' or 'Green' (Vic. or Foster's beer), the sappers, and someone fool enough to let it happen in his tent[.] —Martin Cameron, *A Look at the Bright Side*, 1988

8 an argument, dispute *AUSTRALIA*
- —Willie Fennell, *Dexter Gets The Point*, p. 24, 1961
- Listen, this strike isn't over me and Tich here getting our walking tickets, or about the blue at the meetin' or sortin' bottles, nor nothin' like that. —Frank Hardy, *The Outcasts of Foolgarah*, p. 62, 1971

9 a fight, a brawl *AUSTRALIA, 1943*
- Grab him. He's trying to turn on a blue. —Nino Culotta (John O'Grady), *They're A Weird Mob*, p. 69, 1957
- Then some more came, and there was a proper blue. —Arthur Upfield, *Bony and the Mouse*, p. 50, 1959
- I had a commercial licence before the blue started over here. —W.R. Bennett, *Target Turin*, p. 103, 1962
- However, we received a call saying that there was a 'blue' at a locake hotel. —Rex Hunt, *Tall Tales – and True*, p. 64, 1994

10 an error, a mistake *AUSTRALIA, 1941*
- And so they left the immensely complex city of Sydney to its own devices, including Balmain – which could have been a bad blue on their parts. —Geoff Wyatt, *Saltwater Saints*, p. 81, 1969
- —Herb Wharton, *Cattle Camp*, p. 190, 1994

11 a police officer *UK, 1844*
- Couple of years ago, I just missed getting locked up myself, or maybe getting shot by a "blue." It happened on a Mardi Gras. I was walking along and looked at a "fay bitch," just a little too long. —Robert deCoy, *The Nigger Bible*, p. 234, 1967
- Let's shoot through [go] before this dag [eccentric] yells for the blues. —Barry Humphries, *Bazza Pulls It Off!*, 1971
- If you want to be a copy, if you want to do for law and order," Schoonover said sarcastically, "why don't you put in your application? Be a blue? —Robert Campbell, *In La-La Land We Trust*, p. 26–27, 1986
- I'll have one of the blues park it for you in the underground garage[.] —Stephen J. Cannell, *The Tin Collectors*, p. 16, 2001

12 a trusted prisoner with special privileges and responsibilies *NEW ZEALAND*
- Most inmates still wore brown or white moleskins but trusties, known as 'Blues,' wore blue denim trousers. —Greg Newbold, *Punishment and Politics*, p. 76, 1989

13 boy, as an affectionate or possessive form of address; a young male homosexual *UK*
Gay slang, current in UK prisons February 2002; possibly from the nursery rhyme 'Little Boy Blue come blow on your horn', punning on **HORN** (an erection).

14 a black man *US*
A shortened **BLUE BOY**.
- —*New York Times Magazine*, p. 62, 23rd August 1964
- If Mathis wasn't a blue, he'd be a big movie star. —*Diner*, 1982

15 a work protest *NEW ZEALAND*
- In many homes, all the men were involved in the blue, locked out or on strike in support of those locked out. —*Listener*, p. 33, 17th February 2001

▸ **on the blue**
(used of a bet) on credit *AUSTRALIA*
- —Ned Wallish, *The Truth Dictionary of Racing Slang*, p. 59, 1989

▸ **out of the blue**
unexpectedly, suddenly and surprisingly *US, 1910*
- "The call from Nasa came out of the blue," [David] Harrington [of the Kronos Quartet] says. "I didn't even know they had an arts programme." —*The Guardian*, 6th December 2002

▸ **under the blue**
said of a rigged carnival game being operated with police protection *US*
- —Gene Sorrows, *All About Carnivals*, p. 27, 1985

blue *verb*

1 to squander money *UK, 1846*
A possible variant of **BLOW**.
- Johnnie, instead of blueing his crinkle [money] on the dogs, ought Frankie four art-silk frocks[.] —Charles Raven, *Underworld Nights*, p. 122, 1956

2 of a bookmaker, to lose on a race *UK, 1937*

3 to fight *AUSTRALIA, 1962*
- They all burst out in a cold sweat and Neil grabbed a fistful of jacket to jerk him back if he looked like bluing again[.] —Sam Weller, *Old Bastards I Have Met*, p. 65, 1979

4 to arrest someone *UK*
To be taken in by the **BOYS IN BLUE** (the police).
- He was going to be blued in, and all the fuss ensured that he was going to get a good kicking[.] —Greg Williams, *Diamond Geezers*, p. 187, 1997

5 in horse racing, to commit an error of judgment *AUSTRALIA*
- —Ned Wallish, *The Truth Dictionary of Racing Slang*, p. 8, 1989

blue *adjective*

1 depressed, sad *UK, 1821*
- —Gram Parsons, *Still Feeling Blue*, 1973
- Sometimes I feel blue, sometimes I see red, sometimes I'm green with envy.... I'm Amber Brown[.] —Paula Danziger, *Amber Brown is Feeling Blue*, p. back matter, 1998
- [A] difficulty in maintaining erections during a two week period when he was feeling blue. —David D. Burns, *Feeling Good*, p. 58, 1999

2 sexually explicit, pornographic *UK, 1864*
- Angela Hoffa hung up her pink telephone and muttered a blue word. —Max Shulman, *Rally Round the Flag, Boys!*, p. 70, 1957
- [B]ut then one night he took us to a blue movie, and what do you suppose? There he was on the screen—Truman Capote, *Breakfast at Tiffany's*, p. 61, 1958
- [H]is material was blue and old, but after a while I was laughing too[.] —Dick Gregory, *Nigger*, p. 101, 1964
- I've always enjoyed the various "blue" French 16mm I've come across. —*Screw*, p. 2, 4th July 1969
- Assuming it would be a reverse version of the stag parties our dad had routinely attended when we were young – which probably involved a lot of cigar smoke and blue movies and G-strings dangling over empty shot glasses – I had not attended. —Rita Ciresi, *Pink Slip*, p. 12, 1999

▸ **all blue**
in poker, a flush consisting of clubs or spades *US*
- —Albert H. Morehead, *The Complete Guide to Winning Poker*, p. 255, 1967

blue acid *noun*
LSD *US, 1969*
Named because of its colour when dripped onto sugar or blotting paper, or from the colour of a hallucination.
- —Richard A. Spears, *The Slang and Jargon of Drugs and Drink*, p. 57, 1986
- —Mike Haskins, *Drugs*, p. 285, 2003

blue almonds *noun*
a recreational drug cocktail of Viagra™, an erection inducing drug taken recreationally for performance enhancement, and MDMA, the recreational drug best known as ecstasy *AUSTRALIA*
Apparently in popular use amongst lesbians in Sydney.
- —*Popbitch*, 3rd December 2003

blue and clear *noun*
an amphetamine tablet *US*
- —Peter Johnson, *Dictionary of Street Alcohol and Drug Terms*, p. 191, 1993

blue and white *noun*
a police car *US, 1974*
A variation on **BLACK AND WHITE**.
- There were three blue and whites in front of it, blocking the north side of the boulevard.—Robert Campbell, *Boneyards*, p. 36, 1992

blue angel *noun*
a tablet of Amytal™, a central nervous system depressant *US, 1967*
- —Norman W. Houser, *Drugs*, p. 13, 1969
- —Angela Devlin, *Prison Patter*, p. 28, 1996
- Barbies, downers; for nembutal, nebbies, abbots; for amytal, amies, blue angel[.]—*Providence (Rhode Island) Journal-Bulletin*, p. 6B, 4th August 1997

blue-arsed fly *noun*
used as an example of something in a state of agitation or frenzied activity *AUSTRALIA, 1955*
- The MOB here have been running around like blue-arsed flies, making straight the way.—Shane Maloney, *Nice Try*, p. 32, 1998

blue baby *noun*
a capsule of the synthetic opiate oxycodone used recreationally *US*
- Extracts reproduced in the tabloid show Limbaugh referring to "small blue babies" and "the little blues."—*Broward Business Review*, p. 1, 18th November 2003

blue bag *noun*
1 a police uniform *US*
- You miss the blue bag.—Charles Whited, *Chiodo*, p. 143, 1973

2 heroin *UK*
- —Robert Ashton, *This Is Heroin*, p. 205, 2002
- —Mike Haskins, *Drugs*, p. 283, 2003

blue balls *noun*
1 a pain in the testicles caused by long periods of sexual arousal without release *US, 1916*
Also South African variant 'blou balles'.
- Know what the cure for blueballs is? Scratch them until they're red! —Bruce Rodgers, *The Queens' Vernacular*, p. 34, 1972
- —Helen Dahlskog (Editor), *A Dictionary of Contemporary and Colloquial Usage*, p. 8, 1972
- She's taken their blood pressures on a wild-goose chase, and abandoned them with blueballs.—Josh Alan Friedman, *Tales of Times Square*, p. 9, 1986
- Ho Chi Minh is a son of a bitch / Got the blueballs, crabs and the seven-year itch.—*Full Metal Jacket*, 1987
- I went at it anyway, and just as I was about to blast a hole through the ceiling, Jerry kicked the wall and yelled, "Hey, kid, you want beat your meat, go outside!" I told him I was scratching my foot. Just wait 'til that jerk wants some privacy. I'm going to stick to him like glue, Meanwhile, I hope I don't get terminal blue balls.—C.D. Payne, *Youth in Revolt*, p. 22, 1993
- Men worry about having blue balls for life, while women fear that all the men they meet will either be in love with themselves or each other.—Anka Radakovich, *The Wild Girls Club*, p. 40, 1994
- My balls were bluer than the tip of Walt Disney's frozen nose.—Howard Stern, *Miss America*, p. 36, 1995
- First of all, long periods of arousal and the accompanying genital congestion can cause discomfort in both sexes. There just isn't any female vernacular for 'blue balls'.—*Sydney City Hub*, p. 15, 4th April 1996

2 any sexually transmitted infection *US, 1912*
- —Roger Blake, *The American Dictionary of Sexual Terms*, p. 19, 1964

blue band *noun*
a capsule of Carbitral™, a central nervous system depressant *US*
On 27th August 1967, Brian Epstein, manager of the Beatles, was found dead from an overdose of Carbitral.
- —Edward R. Bloomquist, *Marijuana*, p. 334, 1971

blue bark *noun*
a pass for a military person travelling home for a family member's funeral *CANADA*
- "Blue Bark" is a term describing the travel entitlement given to persons travelling home because of a death in the family. The origins of the term are obscure, though it has been suggested that the word "Bark" derives from "embark."—Tom Langeste, *Words on the Wing*, p. 32, 1995

blue barrel *noun*
a blue, barrel-shaped tablet of LSD *US*
- —Eugene Landy, *The Underground Dictionary*, p. 36, 1971
- "I met her on the plane and I had all that acid." He shrugged. "You know, those little blue barrels."—Hunter S. Thompson, *Fear and Loathing in Las Vegas*, p. 114, 1971

blueberry *noun*
1 marijuana with blue-coloured buds and a 'fruity' flavour; especially a locally grown variety in British Coumbia *CANADA*
- Blueberry comes out of various crossings and recrossings of three strains: Highland Thai, also called Juicy Fruit when it was first bred in the 1970s in the American Pacific Northwest; Purple Thai, which was a cross between Chocolate Thai and Oaxacan—Brian Preston, *Pot Planet*, p. 5, 2002
- —Nick Jones, *Spliffs*, p. 66, 2003

2 a resident of the Lac-St-Jean area, Quebec *CANADA*
The most famous and widespread use of this word (which comes from the large blueberry crop grown in the area) was the nickname of Howie Morenz, Canadiens hockey player, known as the 'Bionic Blueberry'.
- And in the Lac-St-Jean area, the local "blueberries" (as they are known) speak with an almost comical inflection.—Will Ferguson, *How to be a Canadian*, p. 71, 2001

blueberry grunt *noun*
in Nova Scotia, a deep-dish blueberry pie *CANADA*
- Fungy or fungee is deep-dish blueberry pie in Nova Scotia, also called blueberry grunt. Grunt is the plurping sound made as baking drives pockets of heated air out of the gelatinous mass of the cooking blueberries.—Bill Casselman, *Canadian Words*, p. 71, 1995

bluebird *noun*
a capsule of amobarbital sodium (trade name Amytal™), a central nervous system depresssant *US, 1953*
- Her equipment is a small bottle of knockout drops (chloral dydrate) or "blue-birds," (sodium amytol).—Lee Mortimer, *Women Confidential*, p. 301, 1960
- —John B. Williams, *Narcotics and Hallucinogenics*, p. 109, 1967

bluebirds *noun*
waves on the horizon, seen from near the shore *US*
- —John Severson, *Modern Surfing Around the World*, p. 165, 1964

blue blazes *noun*
used as a euphemism for 'the hell' *AUSTRALIA*
- —Leonard Mann, *Flesh in Armour*, p. 196, 1932
- 'What the blue blazes is happening?' he was asked as he came in. —Hugh Atkinson, *Grey's Valley*, p. 63, 1986

blue bloater *noun*
1 a hospital patient suffering from chronic bronchitis *US*
The blue colouring is from lack of oxygen; the bloating is from the lungs as they retain water.
- —Sally Williams, *"Strong" Words*, p. 135, 1994

2 an overweight patient suffering from emphysema *US*
- —*American Speech*, p. 202, Fall-Winter 1973: 'The language of nursing'

blue bomber *noun*
a central nervous system stimulant *UK*
- Geordie the Pill, who makes no charge for delivering the blue bombers and petrifying liquid he peddles on the Row. —Geoffrey Fletcher, *Down Among the Meths Men*, p. 11, 1966

blue book *noun*
1 in horse racing, a sheet showing the contenders in a day's races, the odds on the horses and the handicapping *US*
- —David W. Maurer, *Argot of the Racetrack*, p. 15, 1951

2 a test in school or university *US, 1951*
From the examination booklets bound in light blue paper used in many US schools and universities.
- —Harold Wentworth and Stuart Berg Flexner, *Dictionary of American Slang*, p. 47, 1960

bluebottle *noun*
1 a police officer *UK, 1846*
A singular occurence in Shakespeare's *Henry IV Part 1*, 1597, then unrecorded until 1846.
- "You watch it, you bluebottle," he said.—Troy Kennedy Martin, *Z Cars*, p. 37, 1962
- —Angela Devlin, *Prison Patter*, p. 28, 1996
- [S]ix bluebottles, all restlessly eager for action[.]—Christopher Brookmyre, *The Sacred Art of Stealing*, p. 351, 2002

2 a Ministry of Defence uniformed warden *UK, 1969*

3 a Portugese man-of-war *US*
- —Trevor Cralle, *The Surfin'ary*, p. 12, 1991

blue box *noun*

1 a homemade electronic tone generator used for manipulating and defrauding telephone networks *US, 1974*

Generic, possibly after the colour of the first model.

- —Harold Wentworth and Stuart Berg Flexner, *Dictionary of American Slang*, p. 679, 1976
- This one-off film reveals how [...] "blue box" technology pioneered by people such as John Draper, the legendary Captain Crunch, [...] passed directly to one of the pioneers of personal computers[.] — *Radio Times*, p. 77, 22nd July 2001

2 a police van used for transporting prisoners *US*

- — *Complete CB Slang Dictionary*, 1976
- —Peter Chippindale, *The British CB Book*, p. 152, 1981

blue boy *noun*

1 an amphetamine tablet *US*

- [T]aken two or three at one time with coffee, they gave a wonderful jag. The capsules were blue so we called them blue boys. After we got jagged we found no one would know what we were talking about when we said blue boys.—Chester Himes, *Cast the First Stone*, p. 247, 1952

2 a black man *US*

- BLUE BOY – Synonym for a Nigger male.—Robert deCoy, *The Nigger Bible*, p. 29, 1967

3 a police officer *UK, 1883*

From the traditional blue uniform.

- In one minute there were seventeen blue boys out there.— *Reservoir Dogs*, 1992
- Lotta blue boys are out there.— *Airheads*, 1994

blue bullet *noun*

a capsule of amobarbital sodium (trade name Amytal™), a central nervous system depressant *US*

- —Walter L. Way, *The Drug Scene*, p. 106, 1977

blue can *noun*

a can of Foster's beer *AUSTRALIA*

- — *Wordmap (www.abc.net.au/wordmap)*, 2003

blue cap *noun*

a military prison staff member *UK, 1979*

From the blue-topped cap worn as a part of the uniform.

- —John W. Mussell, *Militarisms*, p. 13, 1995

blue chair *noun*

LSD *US, 1975*

Possibly a variation of **BLUE CHEER** (LSD).

- —Richard A. Spears, *The Slang and Jargon of Drugs and Drink*, p. 57, 1986
- —Mike Haskins, *Drugs*, p. 285, 2003

blue cheer *noun*

a type of LSD (usually mixed with Methedrine™) supplied in blue pills or capsules *US*

From Blue Cheer™, a branded detergent.

- In the package, 250 caps of Blue Cheer, so I thought I would give a party.—Richard Neville, *Play Power*, p. 240, 1970
- Blue Cheer [formed in 1966] appeared in the summer of 1968 [...] the group was named for an especially high-quality strain of LSD. — *The Rolling Stone Encyclopaedia of Rock & Roll*, p. 52, 1983

blue cheese *noun*

hashish *US*

- —Jay Robert Nash, *Dictionary of Crime*, p. 36, 1992

blue-chip *adjective*

of the highest quality *US, 1904*

A term that spread from poker (the blue chip is the highest value) to stocks to general usage.

- T.J. soon discovered that the blue-chip athletes coming out of Texas high schools rarely chose to become Horned Frogs.—Dan Jenkins, *Life Its Ownself*, p. 21, 1984

blue-chipper *noun*

an excellent student athlete with potential for playing professionally *US*

- —Arthur Pincus, *How to Talk Football*, p. 16, 1984
- —Don R. McCreary (Editor), *Dawg Speak*, 2001

blue-clue caper *noun*

a scheme by one police officer to cause harm to another police officer *US*

- "You're talking about a blue-clue caper," Higgins said. "You're talking about going against another cop."—Gerald Petievich, *To Die in Beverly Hills*, p. 66, 1983

bluecoat *noun*

a police officer *US*

- About the weather being bad and the business being slow / And the bluecoat on the beat taking all her dough.—Dennis Wepman et al., *The Life*, p. 165, 1976

blue collar *adjective*

belonging to or characteristic of the working class *US, 1950*

- — *American Speech*, December 1960

blue de Hue *noun*

marijuana from Vietnam *US, 1982*

Misspelt and mispronounced, 'blue' sounds like the past tense of **BLOW** (marijuana) and the Vietnamese city of 'Hue' does not rhyme with 'blue', except in this instance.

blue devil *noun*

a capsule of amobarbital sodium (trade name Amytal™), a central nervous system depressant *US*

- —John B. Williams, *Narcotics and Hallucinogenics*, p. 109, 1967
- —Helen Dahlskog (Editor), *A Dictionary of Contemporary and Colloquial Usage*, p. 8, 1972

blue doll *noun*

a capsule of amobarbital sodium (trade name Amytal™), a central nervous system depressant *US*

- —Walter L. Way, *The Drug Scene*, p. 106, 1977

blue duck *noun*

1 a failure, a flop *AUSTRALIA, 1895*

- It may prove to be another blue duck, of course, but if there's to be another rush it means an immediate local market for the cattle. —Mary Durack, *Kings in Grass Castles*, p. 284, 1959

2 rain or fog *NEW ZEALAND*

- Another expression for a hopeless day when rain or fog prevents any chance of mustering is a blue duck.—David McLeod, *New Zealand High Country*, p. 43, 1951

blue duppy *noun*

a bruise, especially one produced by a cricket ball *BARBADOS*

- —Frank A. Collymore, *Barbadian Dialect*, p. 20, 1965

blue-eyed boy *noun*

a person who is unreasonably favoured *UK, 1924*

Derogatory.

- That was well received by all. He was the blue-eyed boy for a day or two after you left.—Evelyn Waugh, *Brideshead Revisited*, p. 173, 1945

blue-eyed devil *noun*

a white person *US*

- I'm tellin' you I know what that blue-eyed devil was hooked you up on.—Odie Hawkins, *Ghetto Sketches*, p. 210, 1972
- Don't thank me, Home ... thank that blue-eyed devil. He's the one who made it mean somethin' to you.—Odie Hawkins, *Chicago Hustle*, p. 80, 1977

blue-eyed Indian *noun*

in trucking, a truck owned by the Navajo Freight Lines *US*

- —Wayne Floyd, *Jason's Authentic Dictionary of CB Slang*, p. 10, 1976

blue eyes *noun*

a pupil favoured by a teacher *UK, 1974*

From conventional **BLUE-EYED BOY**.

blue fever *noun*

any sexually transmitted infection *UK, 1961*

Navy 'lower decks' usage.

blue fit *noun*

a state of shock *NEW ZEALAND*

- He was a regular hard case to talk to, his aunt would have a blue fit if she found out.—Frank Sargeson, *That Summer*, p. 139, 1946

blue flags *noun*

LSD *US*

- —Harold Wentworth and Stuart Berg Flexner, *Dictionary of American Slang*, p. 679, 1976

blue-flame *verb*

to ignite a fart *AUSTRALIA*

- The photos included] Boyd relieving himself, Boyd dressed as an Arab, Boyd dancing on tables, Boyd blue-flaming, Boyd asleep[.] —Roy Slaven (John Doyle), *Five South Coast Seasons*, p. 87, 1992

blue flamer *noun*
a zealot *US*
- Added to which indignity, I got three months left to retirement and they saddle me with some blue-flamer fresh out of Quantico for a partner. — *Point Break*, 1991

blue flat *noun*
▷ see: FLAT BLUE

blue flu *noun*
an organised work stoppage in which all the affected workers call in sick the same day *US, 1967*
- More than 1,200 of Cleveland's 1,500 police officers called in sick with "blue flu" yesterday in a contract dispute and Mayor Dennis J. Kucinich sent his new police chief, Richard Hongisto, out to help patrol the streets. — *Washington Post*, p. A15, 16th December 1977
- Christchurch police say they are threatening to take blue flu. — *Dominion*, p. 3, 16th February 1990
- Too, docents at the center voted two weeks ago to take sick leave, in reaction to Bolton's termination. In the world of the public employee, that's called blue flu. — *Rocky Mountain News (Denver)*, p. 4D, 13th March 2004

blue flue boat *noun*
a ship of the Blue Funnel Line ('Blue Flue Line') *UK*
Recorded as a 'Blue-Funneller' in 1929 and not recorded in this form until 1984; the shipping line ceased to exist in 1986.

blue foot *noun*
1 a prostitute *UK*
David Powis suggests that this is possibly of West Indian origin. In 1940s Jamaica 'a bluefoot man' is an 'outsider'.
- — David Powis, *The Signs of Crime*, 1977

2 a white prisoner *UK*
Used by black prisoners.
- — Angela Devlin, *Prison Patter*, p. 29, 1996

blue funk *noun*
a state of extreme fear *UK, 1861*

bluegill *noun*
the penis *US*
- — Charles Shafer, *Folk Speech in Texas Prisons*, p. 198, 1990

bluegrass *verb*
to commit someone to the Lexington (Kentucky) Federal Narcotics Hospital *US, 1953*
Kentucky's nickname is 'the Bluegrass State'.
- — *American Speech*, p. 86, May 1955: 'Narcotic argot along the Mexican border'
- "They blue-grassed me to Lex, and all that shit," Red said sullenly. — Ross Russell, *The Sound*, p. 155, 1961

blue hair *noun*
an older person, especially an older woman *US*
- This joint is where you find busloads a blue-hairs when they get off the freaking cruise ships. — Joseph Wambaugh, *The Glitter Dome*, p. 85, 1981
- — Multicultural Management Program Fellows, *Dictionary of Cautionary Words and Phrases*, 1989
- — Connie Eble (Editor), *UNC-CH Campus Slang*, p. 7, Fall 1991

blue happiness *noun*
liquid morphine *US*
- — *Maledicta*, p. 31, 1988–1989: 'Medical maledicta from San Francisco'

blue haze *noun*
the sense of euphoria and distance produced by a large dose of alprazolam (trade name Xanax™), a benzodiazepine used for short term relief of symptoms of anxiety *US*
- — Peter Johnson, *Dictionary of Street Alcohol and Drug Terms*, p. 227, 1993

blue heaven *noun*
1 sodium amytal, a barbiturate *US, 1954*
- They also take Amytal ("blue heaven"), Nembutal ("yellow jackets") and Tuinal. — Hunter S. Thompson, *Hell's Angels*, p. 216, 1966
- — Donald Louria, *Nightmare Drugs*, p. 25, 1966
- — *Current Slang*, p. 10, Fall 1968

2 LSD *US, 1977*
Named because of the colour of the drug when dripped onto sugar or blotting paper, or possibly from the colour of a hallucination.
- — Richard A. Spears, *The Slang and Jargon of Drugs and Drink*, p. 58, 1986
- — Mike Haskins, *Drugs*, p. 285, 2003

blue hero *noun*
heroin *UK*
- — Mike Haskins, *Drugs*, p. 283, 2003

blue ice *noun*
frozen toilet waste from an aircraft which melts off and falls *US*
- A 30-pound chunk of ice that fell from the sky over Tecumseh, Okla., was not the world's largest hailstone but probably "blue ice" from an airliner's leaky lavatory, officials say. — *United Press International*, 15th March 1982
- A block of what is known in the aircraft industry as "blue ice" crashed through the bedroom ceiling of a home in Toronto on Canadian Thanksgiving Day, 1994. Aircraft's frozen dropping terrifies Toronto householder. — *Toronto Globe and Mail*, p. A3, 13th October 1994
- 48. Blue ice falling on houses. [List of 100 things that wouldn't have occurred without development of the airplane]. — *Newsday (New York)*, p. B10, 8th December 2003

blue in the armor *noun*
a can of Pabst Blue Ribbon beer *US*
- — *American Speech*, p. 61, February 1967: 'Soda-fountain, restaurant and tavern calls'

bluejack *verb*
to send an anonymous one-way message to a mobile phone enabled with 'Bluetooth' radio technology *UK*
- [I]f for example, on a crowded train, the message "fancy it?" appears on your phone, you've been Bluejacked. By whom? You'll probably never know. — *The Times*, p. 5, 12th June 2004

blue jay *noun*
a capsule of sodium amytal, a compound used as a sedative and hypnotic *US*
- [W]e have a pretty complete exhibit of the little pills downtown. Bluejays, redbirds, yellow jackets, goofballs, and all the rest of the list. — Raymond Chandler, *The Long Goodbye*, p. 230, 1953

blue job *noun*
any member of an official service that wears a blue uniform (police, Royal Navy, Royal Air Force, etc) *UK, 1943*
- — John W. Mussell, *Militarisms*, p. 13, 1995

blue John *noun*
strong, homemade whisky *US*
- Masters of moonshine prided themselves in their ancient, father-to-son receipes and the white lightning, blue John, red eye, happy Sally, and stumphole whiskey they made, Smith said. — *Chicago Tribune*, p. C-1, 15th January 1986
- — *Star Tribune (Minneapolis)*, p. 19F, 31st January 1999

blue juice *noun*
a powerful wave *US*
- — Trevor Cralle, *The Surfin'ary*, p. 12, 1991

blue lady *noun*
methylated spirits *NEW ZEALAND*
- Meths is blue or white lady, and steam is a mixture of meths and sherry. — *Dominion Sunday Times*, p. 19, 14th February 1988

blue lamp disco *noun*
a police car with flashing lights *UK*
- — Peter Chippindale, *The British CB Book*, p. 152, 1981

blue light *noun*
a marked police car *US*
- — Lanie Dills, *The Official CB Slanguage Language Dictionary*, p. 18, 1976

blue line *noun*
a river *US*
From the designation of a river on a map.
- This is Six! Tell your people they can stop at this here blue line, but to fill only two canteens. — Charles Anderson, *The Grunts*, p. 41, 1976

blue line sweep *noun*
a military operation on a river or stream *US*
In Vietnam military jargon, a 'blue feature' was a body of water and a 'blue line' was a stream or river as depicted on a map.
- — Linda Reinberg, *In the Field*, p. 25, 1991

Blue Max *nickname*
1 the Congressional Medal of Honor *US, 1988*
- — J. E. Lighter, *Historical Dictionary of American Slang, Volume 1*, p. 210, 1994

2 a gunship of the First Air Cavalary Division, one of only two aerial rocket artillery battalions in the US Army's history *US*
Vietnam war usage.

- —Linda Reinberg, *In the Field*, p. 25, 1991

blue meanie *noun*
Copelandia cyancens or *Panaeolus cyanescens*: a mushroom with potent psychactive properties *NEW ZEALAND*

- Invercargill police said there had been an upsurge in the number of people out looking for the mushrooms, colloquially known as blue meanies and gold tops.—*Dominion*, 13th May 1991
- Since touching down they'd been taking nothing but Blue Meanies, the notorious South American mushrooms believed to contain mysterious powers, and used by the Incas for thousands of years. —Wayne Anthony, *Spanish Highs*, p. 66, 1999

blue meanies *noun*
the police or other enforcement authorities; a section of society with an anti-freedom point of view *US, 1969*
From so-named predatory characters in the 1968 Beatles' cartoon film *The Yellow Submarine*.

- Alas, the Blue Meanies and politicians in the area did not see Our People as separate and distinct human beings at all[.]—Raymond Mungo, *Famous Long Ago*, p. 52, 1970
- —Angela Devlin, *Prison Patter*, p. 29, 1996

blue microdot *noun*
a type of LSD *UK, 1998*

- —Mike Haskins, *Drugs*, p. 285, 2003

blue mist *noun*
LSD *US, 1974*
Named because of the colour of the drug when dripped onto sugar or blotting paper, or possibly from the colour of a hallucination.

- —Richard A. Spears, *The Slang and Jargon of Drugs and Drink*, p. 59, 1986
- —Mike Haskins, *Drugs*, p. 285, 2003

blue molly *noun*
an amphetamine capsule *UK*

- —Mike Haskins, *Drugs*, p. 279, 2003

blue moons *noun*
1 a type of LSD *UK*
Identified by blue moon pictures on blotting paper **TAB(S)** (tablets) of **ACID**, a boastful comparison to the rare quality of a 'blue moon'.

- —Mike Haskins, *Drugs*, p. 285, 2003

2 marijuana with a blue-coloured leaf *UK*

blue movie *noun*
a sexually themed or pornographic film *US*

- Cunts, pricks, fence straddlers, tonight I give you – that international-known impressario of blue movies[.]—William Burroughs, *Naked Lunch*, p. 88, 1957

blue murder *noun*
cries of terror or alarm; a great noise *UK, 1859*
Generally in combination, e.g. 'cry blue murder', 'howl', 'scream', 'yell', etc.

- He was ready to shout blue murder about the rent[.]—John Williams, *Cardiff Dead*, p. 131, 2000

blue mystic *noun*
a powerful psychedelic drug in pill or powder form *UK*

blue nitro *noun*
the recreational drug GHB *US*

- Three young people were treated at Southwest Washington Medical Center on Thanksgiving and released apparently after taking a drug called GHB or "Blue Nitro."—*The Columbian (Vancouver, Washington)*, p. B4, 27th November 1998

bluenose *noun*
a Nova Scotian *CANADA, 1785*
This persistent nickname for residents of the province has several suggested origins, starting of course with the colour the nose turns in cold weather on a fishing boat, as well as an attribution by Canadian author Charles G. D. Roberts to the fame of a privateer from the province which had a blue cannon in the prow.

- The Loyalists who were mostly called "blues" from the names of their regiments, such as Royal Blues, Jersey Blues, etc, together with the former inhabitants who remained loyal to the Crown, met to count noses and see who could be relied upon: a Bluenose. —*Yarmouth Vanguard*, 16th July 1980

blue-nosed *adjective*
excessively moral, puritanical, repressed *US, 1890*

- The Mann Act was invented by a Chicago blue-nosed representative named Mann, after a hophead parlor-whore in melodramatic mood threw a note out of the window of the late Harry Guzik's cathouse on which she had written "I am a white slave."—Jack Lait and Lee Mortimer, *Washington Confidential*, p. 86, 1951

blue-on-blue *noun*
1 in battle, fire unintentionally directed at friendly forces *US*

- On the night of 17 February, we had the first blue-on-blue (what some call fratricide, or so -called friendly fire) in the lst Infantry Division[.] —Tom Clancy, *Into the Storm*, p. 248, 1991
- —*American Speech*, p. 384, Winter 1991: 'Among the new words'
- [T]hey would not move forward in case of a blue-on-blue.—Andy McNab (writing of the late 1970s/early 80s), *Immediate Action*, p. 177, 1995
- Blue-on-blue – the new euphemism for "friendly fire".—*The Times*, p. 18, 5th April 2003
- Blue on blue, which made its debut yesterday after the downing of an RAF Tornado by an American Patriot missile, comes from wargaming exercises where the goodies are blue and – in a hangover from cold war days – the baddies are red.—*The Guardian*, 24th March 2003

2 clear blue sky and a calm blue sea *US*

- —*American Speech*, p. 122, Summer 1986: 'The language of naval fighter pilots'

blue one *noun*
in carnival usage, poor location or slow business for a concession stand *US*

- —Don Wilmeth, *The Language of American Popular Entertainment*, p. 28, 1981

blue pages *noun*
in television and film making, additions to a script after production has started *US*

- —Ralph S. Singleton, *Filmaker's Dictionary*, p. 19, 1990

blue-pencil *verb*
to censor something *US, 1888*
From the traditional colour of an editor's pencil.

blue pill *noun*
a very powerful handgun *US*

- —*American Speech*, p. 192, October 1957: 'Some colloquialisms of the handgunner'

blueprint *verb*
in drag racing, to bring an engine precisely to its tolerance for racing *US*

blue room *noun*
1 a toilet *US*
Usually applied to a portable toilet on a construction site.

- Federal Aviation Agency official had locked himself in the "blue room." He emerged on his own when the stewardess informed him the captain was coming back with an ax.—*San Francisco Examiner*, p. 13, 10th September 1965

2 a cell used for solitary confinement *US*

- —John R. Armore and Joseph D. Wolfe, *Dictionary of Desperation*, p. 21, 1976

3 any room in a police station or jail where rough interrogations take place *US*

- —Jay Robert Nash, *Dictionary of Crime*, p. 37, 1992

blues *noun*
1 a deeply felt sense of sadness, rejection or depression *UK, 1741*
Shortened from the 'blue devils'.

- They taught me the blues in Pontiac – I mean the blues, blues that I felt from my head to my shoes, really the blues.—Mezz Mezzrow, *Really the Blues*, p. 4, 1946
- Beating the baby blues[.] Worried about giving your child antidepressants?—*The Observer*, 16th May 2004

2 methylated spirits as an alcoholic drink *UK*
From its colour.

- All he wanted was a cigarette. Cigarettes are all they ever want – except for the blues and money.—Geoffrey Fletcher, *Down Among the Meths Men*, p. 15, 1966

3 an illegal drinking house, especially one where music is also provided *UK*

- —David Powis, *The Signs of Crime*, 1977

4 in the army, a dress uniform; in the navy, a walking out uniform *UK, 1948*

- —Carl Fleischhauer, *A Glossary of Army Slang*, p. 4, 1968
- —John W. Mussell, *Militarisms*, p. 13, 1995

5 a formal blue dress uniform of the US Marines *US*
- —Linda Reinberg, *In the Field*, p. 25, 1991

6 jeans worn by convicts *UK*
- —Angela Devlin, *Prison Patter*, p. 29, 1996

7 unreserved bleacher seats in a circus *US*
- —Joe McKennon, *Circus Lingo*, p. 18, 1980

8 money *US*
From blue gambling chips.
- Playing blackjack, short on blues / A game all bad motherfuckers were booked to lose. —Dennis Wepman et al., *The Life*, p. 125, 1976

blue sage; blue saze *noun*
a variety of marijuana with a blue tint *US, 1943*
It is likely that 'saze' is a misspelling or mispronunciation. Also known as **BLUE MOONS**.

blues and twos *noun*
police emergency response vehicles *UK*
UK police cars have *blue* flashing lights and *two*-tone sirens, thus when a police vehicle is attending an emergency with all its alarms blazing and wailing it is said to be using 'blues and twos', and hence the derivation of this term.
- [H]e would've cleaned out the place first then phoned the Blues and Twos[.] —Danny King, *The Burglar Diaries*, p. 80, 2001

blue shirt *noun*
an active firefighter, as distinguished from an officer *US*
- — *American Speech*, p. 272, December 1954: 'Fire terms: additional words and definitions'

blue sky *noun*
1 worthless securities; a pleasant appearance with difficulties ignored *US, 1906*
- Although fakers, known as blue sky promoters, promise to fulfill all the aspirations of the average man for a comfortable nest egg, prudent analysts know that Ponzi and his ilk were not public benefactors. — *San Francisco Examiner*, p. 16, 26th November 1945
- Henry A. Wallace: Apostle of Political Blue Sky [Headline] —*San Francisco Examiner*, p. 10, 14th January 1948
- It violates the blue-sky laws. —Jim Thompson, *Bad Boy*, p. 294, 1953
- I'm not selling blue sky, Gypsy! I can place you tonight! [Gordon comic strip] — *San Francisco Chronicle*, p. 14, 26th March 1958

2 heroin *US*
- —Carsten Stroud, *Close Pursuit*, p. 269, 1987

blue sky blonde *noun*
highly potent marijuana from Columbia *US*

blues man *noun*
a methylated spirits drinker *UK*
- In fact, the real gone blues man has created a new dimension in which to live – way out there in the environs of Skid Row. —Geoffrey Fletcher, *Down Among the Meths Men*, p. 22, 1966

bluesnarf *verb*
to steal personal information from a mobile phone enabled with Bluetooth™ radio technology *UK*
A compound of the *Blue*tooth brand and **SNARF** (to take, to grab).
- Bluesnarfing is when someone breaks the codes for your Bluetooth with a laptop to steal personal details from your mobile. — *The Times*, p. 5, 12th June 2004

Blue Spader *nickname*
a soldier of the 1st Battalion, 26th Infantry, 2nd Brigade, 1st Infantry Division *US*
From the blue spade on the insiginia. Served in World War 2, Berlin, Vietnam from 1965 until 1970, Bosnia, Macedonia and Kosovo.
- —Linda Reinberg, *In the Field*, p. 25, 1991

blue spot *noun*
a spotlight with a blue filter, sometimes required by law during strip tease shows *US*
- When Hester shows every inch she can show and struts off the floor in a blue spot, Choo-Choo gets up and hurries over towards the men's room. —Robert Campbell, *Junkyard Dog*, p. 133, 1986

blue star *noun*
a type of LSD identified by a printed blue star *UK, 1998*
- —Mike Haskins, *Drugs*, p. 285, 2003

blue steeler *noun*
a particularly erect erection *US*
- —Vann Wesson, *Generation X Field Guide and Lexicon*, p. 22, 1997

blue streak *noun*
an emphatic and vigorous degree *US, 1830*
Used to modify 'talk' or variations on talking.
- INDIGO: I'll curse up a blue streak if my heat so desires. Motherfucker – Shit – Bastard – Cocksucker – Bastard. — *Mo' Better Blues*, 1990

bluesuit *noun*
a uniformed police officer *US*
- Sheee-it, man, when the bluesuits stops me, I always gets nervous. —Joseph Wambaugh, *The New Centurions*, p. 73, 1970

bluesuiter *noun*
a member of the US Air Force *US, 1963*
- [I]t was wrong for the Air Force to fire civil service workers and replace them with former blue-suiters. — *San Antonio (Texas) Express-News*, p. 3B, 11th September 2003

blue swimmer *noun*
a ten dollar note *AUSTRALIA*
From the resemblance of the colour of the note to the 'blue swimmer' crab.
- Blue swimmer: also means a 10 dollar note (it's blue). — *Wordmap (www.abc.net.au/wordmap)*, 2003

blue ticket *noun*
1 a one-way train or bus ticket given by the police to criminals whose presence in town is no longer deemed acceptable *US*
- If your past did catch up with you, the police were more than happy to buy you a "blue ticket," the term used to describe the one way passages they'd purchase to send shady characters back to wherever they'd come from. —Kim Rich, *Johnny's Girl*, p. 53, 1993

2 a discharge from the US armed services as 'unsuitable for military service' *US*
- —Linda Reinberg, *In the Field*, p. 25, 1991

3 a one-way ticket out of Alaska *US*
- —Mike Doogan, *How to Speak Alaskan*, p. 14, 1993

blue tip *noun*
a capsule of amobarbital sodium (trade name Amytal™), a central nervous system depressant *US*
- —Donald Wesson and David Smith, *Barbiturates*, p. 121, 1977

blue tongue *noun*
an unskilled worker *AUSTRALIA, 1943*
After the blue-tongued lizard.

blue veiner *noun*
a rigid erection *US*
- During his one month convalescence Rosco was unable to raise what Harold Bloomguard called a "diamond cutter" or even a "blue veiner" due to the shooting pains in his groin. —Joseph Wambaugh, *The Choirboys*, p. 45, 1975
- —Michael Dalton Johnson, *Talking Trash with Redd Foxx*, p. 58, 1994
- —Sonya Plowman, *Great Kiwi Slang*, p. 30, 2002

blue velvet *noun*
a combination of cough syrups, especially codeine-based syrups, used as a weak heroin substitute *US*
- — US Department of Justice, *Street Terms*, October 1994
- —Angela Devlin, *Prison Patter*, p. 29, 1996

blue vex *adjective*
extremely angry *BARBADOS, 1990*
- —Richard Allsopp, *Dictionary of Caribbean English Usage*, p. 108, 1996

blue vials *noun*
LSD *UK, 1998*
- —Mike Haskins, *Drugs*, p. 285, 2003

blue-water man *noun*
a sailor experienced in ocean sailing *US*
- —John Gould, *Maine Lingo*, p. 17, 1975

blue water Navy *noun*
during the war in Vietnam, a ship that was part of the US Navy presence off the coast of Vietnam *US*
- —Linda Reinberg, *In the Field*, p. 25, 1991

bluey *noun*

1 a capsule of Drinamyl™, a combination of amphetamine and barbiturate *UK*

- The demand for the minor drugs: Pot (marijuana), Purple Hearts and Blueies (Drinamyl), Black Bombers, Prels (Preludin), Bennies and Dexies (Benzedrine and Dexedrine) is almost unlimited. — *Sunday Telegraph*, 20th October 1963

2 a methylated spirit drinker *UK, 1961*
From the colour of the spirit

3 a five pound note (£5) *UK, 1982*
From the colour.

- "Drop him a bluey," he said... a fiver changed hands. — *Sunday Express*, 31st January 1982
- It costs me a bluey every time I come across him. — Jake Arnott, *He Kills Coppers*, p. 221, 2001

4 an airmail letter *UK*
Gulf war usage.

- — *American Speech*, p. 384, Winter 1991: 'Among the new words'

5 a blue blanket as used by itinerants for carrying possessions; a swag *AUSTRALIA, 1878*

- Mum, helping patients out from a boat when it reached Kooweeup platform, found Dad's bluey round an old lady who had only a thin nightdress beneath it. — Patsy Adam-Smith, *Folklore of the Australian Railwaymen*, p. 111, 1969
- Wake up, Col, the dogs are pissing on your bluey. — Alexander Buzo, *The Roy Murphy Show*, p. 103, 1970

6 a summons *AUSTRALIA, 1909*
In late C19 called 'a piece of blue paper'.

- The object of the sport was, therefore, to spring a 'bluey' on the victim when he least expected it. — Kerry Cue, *Crooks, Chooks and Bloody Ratbags*, p. 53, 1983
- — Frank Hardy, *Hardy's People*, p. 52, 1986

7 a portable gas stove used by Royal Marines in Northern Ireland *UK, 1984*

8 a pornographic film *AUSTRALIA*

- — Thommo, *The Dictionary of Australian Swearing and Sex Sayings*, p. 18, 1985

Bluey *noun*

used as a nickname for a red-haired person *AUSTRALIA, 1906*
Ironic in origin.

- Remember that robbery in Bondi, you know the one where Bluey give it to those jacks, six of them there were? — Kevin Mackey, *The Cure*, p. 100, 1970
- — Joe Andersen, *Winners Can Laugh*, p. 67, 1982
- Cut it out, Chook, you'll get us in trouble,' I squirmed to him. 'No worries Bluey, they'll never know who's doin' it. — Paul Vautin, *Turn It Up!*, p. 22, 1995

blueys *noun*

denim trousers, jeans *AUSTRALIA, 1917*

bluff *noun*

a lesbian who enjoys both the active and passive role in sex *US*

- — *American Speech*, p. 56, Spring-Summer 1970: 'Homosexual slang'

blunderturd *noun*

a Triumph 'Thunderbird' motorcycle *UK, 1984*

blunjie; blunjy *adjective*

yielding, squashy *UK*
Given some currency in the 1950s by surreal radio comedy *The Goons*.

blunk *adjective*

in a state of intoxication that is the result of drink and drugs *UK, 1984*
An elision of any word for 'intoxicated' that begins 'bl' and 'drunk'.

blunt *noun*

1 marijuana rolled and smoked in a hollowed out cigar *US, 1988*
Generic usage but originally made with a Phillies Blunt™.

- Purchase a Philly, not the city of Philly / Silly punk, I'm talking 'bout the shit called the Philly blunt / Lick the blunt and then the Philly blunt middle you split[.] — Redman, *How To Roll A Blunt*, 1992
- We don't smoke blunts, strictly Zigzags — *The Source*, p. 64, September 1993
- TELLY: What do you want? CASPER: Get another forty. Smoke a blunt. — *Kids*, 1995
- — Connie Eble (Editor), *UNC-CH Campus Slang*, p. 1, April 1995
- Drinking beers, beers, beers, rolling fatties, smoking blunts! — Kevin Smith, *Jay and Silent Bob Strike Back*, p. 9, 2001

2 a mixture of marijuana and cocaine *UK*

- — Mike Haskins, *Drugs*, p. 292, 2003

3 a capsule of Seconal™ or other barbiturate in a black capsule *US*

- — Edith A. Folb, *runnin' down some lines*, p. 230, 1980

4 cocaine *UK*

- — Mike Haskins, *Drugs*, p. 280, 2003

5 a hypodermic syringe *US*

- — Edith A. Folb, *runnin' down some lines*, p. 230, 1980

6 a knife *US*

- — Eugene Landy, *The Underground Dictionary*, p. 37, 1971

7 a coin *UK, 1708*
Circus and carnival usage.

- — Don Wilmeth, *The Language of American Popular Entertainment*, p. 29, 1981

blunted *adjective*

marijuana-intoxicated *US*

- Being a little blunted at the time, the first thing that came to mind was women[.] — *The Source*, p. 54, May 1993
- — Connie Eble (Editor), *UNC-CH Campus Slang*, p. 2, Spring 1998
- I get too blunted off funny homegrown[.] — Eminem (Marshall Mathers), *Role Model*, 1999

blunted up *adjective*

marijuana-intoxicated *UK*

- They're gonna get so blunted-up out there that their eyes will go bright red and they'll be talking about UFOs up in the sky and shit[.] — *Mixmag, The Drugs Issue*, February 2001

blunt end *noun*

the stern of a ship *UK, 1961*
Used by 'landlubbers', often jocular.

bluntie *noun*

marijuana rolled and smoked in a hollowed out cigar *US*

- Rucker proudly holds up a bluntie and bag of pot. — James Mangold, *Copland*, p. 91, 1997

blunt nib; blunt *noun*

a reporter *UK*
Press photographers' slang.

- — *Word of Mouth*, 6th August 2004

blur *noun*

someone who is lost in his own world *SINGAPORE*
Intensified at times as 'blur like fuck'.

- — Paik Choo, *The Coxford Singlish Dictionary*, p. 14, 2002

blurt *noun*

the vagina *UK*
In conventional English 'blurt' (to puff with scorn) involves compressing and opening lips. The imagery, perhaps, explains the etymology.

- — *Sky Magazine*, July 2001

blurter *noun*

the anus *NEW ZEALAND*

- — David McGill, *David McGill's Complete Kiwi Slang Dictionary*, p. 17, 1998

blute *noun*

newspapers cut and folded to look like currency *US*

- — Jay Robert Nash, *Dictionary of Crime*, p. 37, 1992

bluttered *adjective*

drunk *UK*
Possibly a variation of **BLOOTERED**.

- — *e-cyclopaedia*, 20th March 2002

bly *noun*

an oxy-acetylene blow torch *UK*
Criminal use.

- — Angela Devlin, *Prison Patter*, p. 29, 1996

BM *noun*

a *BMW* car *UK*
Further abbreviated from **BEEMER** rather than directly from the BMW brand name; the car is a status-symbol, and seeking to sound evermore casual about its name is simple snobbery.

- Roy used to play the music in his motor up real loud cos he was so fuckin' para about being bugged in the BM. — J.J. Connolly, *Know Your Enemy [britpulp]*, p. 150, 1999

BMO *noun*

used by US troops in the war against Iraq to describe Saudi women *US*

Initialism of '*b*lack *m*oving *o*bjects'.

- — *Newsweek*, 21st January 1991
- — *Army*, p. 47, November 1991

BMOC *noun*

a popular and visible college boy *US, 1934*

A '*b*ig *m*an *o*n *c*ampus'.

- — Marcus Hanna Boulware, *Jive and Slang of Students in Negro Colleges*, 1947
- "This is the most important event of the year, and if you should come up with a winning idea for us, you'd be a B.M.O.C." "A what?" "A Big Man on Campus." — Max Shulman, *I was a Teen-Age Dwarf*, p. 131, 1959
- — Collin Baker et al., *College Undergraduate Slang Study Conducted at Brown University*, p. 73, 1968

BMQ *noun*

a homosexual male who hides his sexuality *UK*

A '*b*lack *m*arket *q*ueen'.

- — Paul Baker, *Polari*, p. 165, 2002

BMT *noun*

habitual lateness *UK*

Initialism of '*b*lack *m*an's (or *m*en's) *t*ime', based on a stereotypical characteristic.

- "And don't give me none of that b.m.t.!" [...] I surmised from her crack about black men's time, that she was probably a frustrated intimate. — Diran Abedayo, *My Once Upon A Time*, p. 93, 2000

BNF *noun*

a science fiction fan well known by other fans *US*

A '*b*ig-*n*ame *f*an'.

- — *American Speech*, p. 24, Spring 1982: 'The langage of science fiction fan magazines'

bo *noun*

1 a man, a companion; often used as a form of address *UK, 1729*

From the nickname Beau, or abbreviated from 'boy'. Originally English but now US. UK cryptic crosswords often rely on the clue 'an American' to signal the letters 'bo'.

2 a hobo *US, 1899*

A reality and term that only barely lingered into the 1950s.

- I reclined on a flatcar reading the Sunday funnies with the other [ho]bos, and the brakemen smiled at us and waved cheerfully. — Jack Kerouac, *Letter to Allen Ginsberg*, p. 151, 18th May 1948
- Mr. Davis informs me there are no more hoboes riding the rails any more – "only a few bums and tramps passing themselves off as boes. The real boes all quit to go work during the war." — *San Francisco News*, p. 21, 16th June 1949

3 marijuana *US, 1975*

- — J. E. Lighter, *Historical Dictionary of American Slang, Volume 1*, p. 214, 1994

BO *noun*

body odour *US, 1931*

An initialism coined for soap advertisements; made even more infamous by the comic strip villain B.O. Plenty in *Dick Tracy*.

- — Lou Shelly, *Hepcats Jive Talk Dictionary*, p. 21, 1945
- with bright almond-shaped eyes and a mishapen, pear-shaped head, with tremendous b.o., and endowed, through his stupidity, with a certain curious thrusting intelligence — Clancy Sigal, *Going Away*, p. 476, 1961
- The Angels' old ladies are generally opposed to B.O. — Hunter S. Thompson, *Hell's Angels*, p. 47 (note), 1966
- That don't mean I gotta die of B.O. — Darryl Ponicsan, *The Last Detail*, p. 91, 1970
- Give the big pig with the B.O. to Healy, right? — *Something About Mary*, 1998
- He was coming this way now as Speedy was telling Chili this girl had b.o. so bad he was sorry he ever sat next to her; he had to breathe with his mouth open. — Elmore Leonard, *Be Cool*, p. 222–223, 1999
- [H]e didn't wash or clean his teath so he had bad breath and BO that could bubble paint. — Dave Courtney, *Stop the Ride I Want to Get Off*, p. 261, 1999
- I sniffed at it this morning an was surprised at how much it ponged. Stale BO an that. — Niall Griffiths, *Kelly + Victor*, p. 277, 2002

bo *adjective*

excellent, fashionable, trendy *US*

- — *San Francisco Examiner: People*, p. 8, 27th October 1963

bo!; boh!

used as an expression of approval *UK*

As in the phrase 'Bo Yashaka!' used by cult comic figure Ali G (Sacha Baron-Cohen).

- Tell me, whatcha gonna do / Re-rewind, when the crowd say Bo Selecta / Re-rewind, when the crowd say Bo Selecta — Artful Dodger, *Rewind*, 2000
- — Susie Dent, *The Language Report*, p. 75, 2003

BO!

go away! *UK, 1984*

A euphemistic abbreviation of **BUGGER OFF**.

boak *noun*

▷ **see: BOKE**

board *noun*

1 a surfboard *US*

- — Grant W. Kuhns, *On Surfing*, p. 114, 1963
- — Ross Olney, *The Young Sportsman's Guide to Surfing*, p. 88, 1965

2 in a game of poker in which some cards are dealt face-up, all face-up cards collectively *US*

- — Edwin Silberstang, *Winning Poker for the Serious Player*, p. 217, 1992

▸ **off the board**

in horse racing, said of odds greater than 99 – 1 *US*

- — Tom Ainslie, *Ainslie's Complete Guide to Thoroughbred Racing*, p. 335, 1976

▸ **on board**

on the railways, on duty, at work *US*

- — Ramon Adams, *The Language of the Railroader*, p. 107, 1977

▸ **take off the board**

in sports betting, to fail to establish a pointspread on a game or event *US*

- I didn't establish a line – a point spread – on the Kansas City Chiefs. In betting parlance, they were "taken off the board." — Jimmy Snyder, *Jimmy the Greek*, p. 145, 1975

board *verb*

▸ **board with Aunt Polly**

to draw disability insurance *US, 1931*

A logging term.

- — Frederic G. Cassidy, *Dictionary of American Regional English, Volume 1*, p. 315, 1985

board cord *noun*

a line attached at one end to a surfer and at the other to the surfboard *US*

- — Gary Fairmont R. Filosa II, *The Surfer's Almanac*, p. 183, 1977

boarded up *adjective*

in prison, wearing an improvised armour, such as magazines inserted under clothing to protect yourself from attack by other prisoners *UK*

- — Angela Devlin, *Prison Patter*, p. 29, 1996

boardie *noun*

a surfer *NEW ZEALAND*

- Boardies riding high as cash splashes in [Headline] — *Sunday Star-Times*, p. D4, 8th August 1999

boardies *noun*

baggy surfing shorts *AUSTRALIA, 1979*

- — Trevor Cralle, *The Surfin'ary*, p. 12, 1991
- Well, you're finally gonna meet him, Jay, ol' mate. The big fella upstairs. Gotcha Mambo baordies on? — Glyn Parry, *Mosh*, p. 28, 1996
- Adding insult to injury are those gorgeous girls who insist on wearing boardies despite believing cellulite is a technical cinematic term. — *Sunday Star-Times*, p. D4, 14th January 2001

boarding house *noun*

a jail *US, 1942*

- — Frederic G. Cassidy, *Dictionary of American Regional English, Volume 1*, p. 314, 1985

boarding house reach *noun*

an effort by a diner to reach for a serving plate rather than ask for it to be passed *US, 1906*

- — Joseph A. Weingarten, *An American Dictionary of Slang*, p. 35, 1954
- Well, my old ma always said you had to have a boarding house reach if you were ever going to get your share off the table. — Robert Campbell, *Alice in La-La Land*, p. 104, 1987
- Yes, we are responsible for our own actions, our own boarding-house reach at the table, our own failure to get any exercise more strenuous than fumbling for the remote. — *Salt Lake Tribune*, p. A12, 13th November 2003

board jock; board sock *noun*
a protective surfboard cover *US*
• —Gary Fairmont R. Filosa II, *The Surfer's Almanac*, p. 183, 1977

board knees *noun*
lumps on a surfer's knees from prolonged hours kneeling on a surfboard *AUSTRALIA*
• —Jack Pollard, *The Australian Surfrider*, p. 16, 1963

Board of Trade duff *noun*
tinned pudding *UK*
Merchant Navy use.
• —John Malin, 1979

boards *noun*
1 the stage; live theatre *UK, 1768*
Always after the denifite article.
• There's still a lot of tradition in The Police; we're still on the boards and we go through a lot of showbizzy things. —Sting (Gordon Sumner), *Ask*, p. 112, 12th April 1980
• De Niro! Pacino! Only the serious artists work on the boards! —Joseph Wambaugh, *Fugitive Nights*, p. 92, 1992
2 skis *CANADA*
Probably from the fact that early homemade skis were sometimes shaped from planks.
• —Tom Parkin, *WetCoast Words*, p. 17, 1989

▸ **on the boards**
in solitary confinement *US*
• —John R. Armore and Joseph D. Wolfe, *Dictionary of Desperation*, p. 42, 1976

board shorts *noun*
almost knee-length shorts favoured by surfboarders *AUSTRALIA*
• —*(Sydney) Bulletin*, 30th March 1963

boardwalk oyster *noun*
a used condom *UK*
From the appearance and location of discovery.
• —David Rowan, *A Glossary for the 90s*, 1998

boar's nest *noun*
in oil drilling, any poorly planned, makeshift arrangement of equipment *US*
• —Jerry Robertson, *Oil Slanguage*, p. 29, 1954

boast *verb*
1 to brag as a part of a rap performance *US*
• Big Daddy is "boasting", a tradition in rap music derived from reggae. —James Haskins, *The Story of Hip-Hop*, p. 3–4, 2000
2 to smoke marijuana *US*

boasty *adjective*
arrogant *BAHAMAS*
• —John A. Holm, *Dictionary of Bahamian English*, p. 23, 1982

boat *noun*
1 a car, especially a large car *US, 1914*
• With a mean boat like the one you got, you'll be a menace to public safety. When you get snozzled, it'll be even worse. —James T. Farrell, *Saturday Night*, p. 23, 1947
2 a prison transfer; a group of prisoners being transferred; the bus used to transfer them *US, 1956*
• —Frank Prewitt and Francis Schaeffer, *Vacaville Vocabulary*, 1961–1962
• When I heard I was on a boat to Comstock, I knew you'd be here. —Piri Thomas, *Down These Mean Streets*, p. 265, 1967
• Have you anything to say before we send you away / On the next Sing Sing boat? —Dennis Wepman et al., *The Life*, p. 59, 1976
3 a non-prostitute who flaunts her sexual availability to hotel customers *UK*
• "There's a kind of girl who comes in dressed to the nines," says a West End hotel manager. "We call them 'Boats' – Bordering On A Tart". —*The Times*, 16th April 2005
4 phencyclidine, the recreational drug known as PCP or angel dust *US*
A shortened form of **LOVE BOAT**.
• With a police officer on every corner directly traffic, dealers simply lined the curbs along 11th Street and silently formed the word "boat," street slang for PCP, with lips pursued like a fish. —*Washington Post*, p. B1, 29th July 1984
• —Peter Johnson, *Dictionary of Street Alcohol and Drug Terms*, p. 24, 1993
5 heroin *US*
• —Peter Johnson, *Dictionary of Street Alcohol and Drug Terms*, p. 24, 1993
6 a combination of marijuana and phencyclidine, the recreational drug known as PCP or angel dust *UK*
• —Mike Haskins, *Drugs*, p. 293, 2003
7 in poker, a hand consisting of three of a kind and a pair *US*
Conventionally known as a 'full house'.
• —Jim Glenn, *Programmed Poker*, p. 155, 1981

▸ **off the boat**
said of immigrants, especially black people *UK*
• Alphonse isn't from the South End, I think he's off the boat. —Kevin Sampson, *Outlaws*, p. 39, 2001

boat anchor *noun*
a crippled or useless piece of computer equipment; by extension, a useless person *US*
• That was a working motherboard once. One lightning strike later, instant boat anchor! —Eric S. Raymond, *The New Hacker's Dictionary*, p. 71, 1991

boat and oar *noun*
a whore *UK*
Rhyming slang.
• Don't listen to her – she's a lying boat and oar! —Bodmin Dark, *Dirty Cockney Rhyming Slang*, 2003

boat girl *noun*
a prostitute plying her trade on the docks *NEW ZEALAND, 1978*
• —Harry Orsman, *A Dictionary of Modern New Zealand Slang*, p. 14, 1999

boatie *noun*
the operator of a small motorboat *NEW ZEALAND*
• Skippers and boaties have to be very careful when using the channel. Some boaties take little notice of the markers and navigation aids. —*Marlborough Express*, p. 6, 29th September 1972

boat in a moat *noun*
a casino that must, as a result of gambling laws, float *US*
• —Victor H. Royer, *Casino Gamble Talk*, p. 16, 2003

boatload *noun*
a large amount *UK*
• A whole boatload of Ecstasy had obviously been consumed[.] —Dave Courtney, *Stop the Ride I Want to Get Off*, p. 144, 1999

boat people *noun*
people who arrive at casinos on bus excursion trips *US*
• We are the boat people. That is casino workers' slang for the millions of Americans now arriving at their portals in smelly diesel waves. We come by bus – "motorcoach," if you want to get la-di-da about it. —*New York Times*, p. 36, 17th July 1994

boat race *noun*
1 a fixed horse race or other competition *US, 1917*
• —Walter Steigleman, *Horseracing*, p. 271, 1947
• I bet crooked horse races – 'boat races' we called them. My two detectives at the track would hear of a fix. They'd telephone me. I'd say get down a hundred for me. I made about $50,000 on 'boat races' when I was chief of detectives. —*San Francisco News*, p. 40, 16 November 1950
• It was claimed then, reported United Press, that Berry engineered two "boat races" on Feb. 7–8. —*San Francisco News*, 26th November 1952
• —*Current Slang*, p. 4, Summer 1969
2 the face *UK, 1958*
Rhyming slang, probably in use from the late 1940s. Often shortened to 'boat'.
• A big bandage round his thumb and a big smile on his boat race. —Frank Norman, *Bang To Rights*, p. 29, 1958
• [A] gemini same as me, with a boat-race that can slip straight from looking like an angel's to a snake's. —Derek Raymond (Robin Cook), *The Crust on its Uppers*, p. 23, 1962
• Meanwhile take a butcher's at this lot and keep a penny a mile on your boat race! —*The Sweeney*, p. 7, 1976
• ["]Was she as dirty as she looked?" "Can't really remember. Plenty of Harry [semen] on the boat, though. —Colin Butts, *Is Harry on the Boat?*, p. 89, 1997

boats *noun*
shoes or feet, especially large ones *US*
• Too small for your fat fuckin' boats. —Richard Price, *Clockers*, p. 97, 1992

boat tail *noun*
an Alfa Romeo Spyder convertible *US*
The rear end comes to a point, not unlike a boat.
• —Lewis Poteet, *Car & Motorcyle Slang*, p. 34, 1992

bob *noun*

1 a shilling; a non-specific amount of money *UK, 1789*
Obsolete since decimalisation in 1971, except in phrases like **QUEER AS A NINE BOB NOTE** and abstract representations of money such as 'a few bob' (an undefined sum of money).
- Are yer gunna pay me the three bob or ain't yer?—Nino Culotta (John O'Grady), *They're A Weird Mob*, p. 16, 1957
- [F]our gets a free card and last card down. "Bob ante," says Marchmare.—Derek Raymond (Robin Cook), *The Crust on its Uppers*, p. 40, 1962
- All seems to add up to a pretty fair reason for making a few bob.—John Wynnum, *Tar Dust*, p. 30, 1962
- I owed Henry half a bar [ten shillings], which left me with thirty bob.—John Peter Jones Feather Pluckers, p. 29, 1964
- Your King and Sam and Matilda need you – bob a day keeps the Gooks away.—Michael Peters, *Pommie Bastard*, p. 7, 1969
- Your young Miss Ring was charging two bob a fling in the back seat.—Kerry Cue, *Crooks, Chooks and Bloody Ratbags*, p. 168, 1983
- [T]hey was all getting thirty bob a week.—Herb Wharton, *Cattle Camp*, p. 5, 1994
- I had a few bob on me that day and, with the weather being very hot, I had my eyes out for the ice-cream boy.—Rex Hunt, *Tall Tales – and True*, p. 66, 1994

2 a dollar *US, 1930*
- —Harold Wentworth and Stuart Berg Flexner, *Dictionary of American Slang*, p. 49, 1960

3 marijuana *US*
Very likely derived from Bob Marley, a highly visible marijuana lover. A long list of derivatives play with the term – 'see bob', 'talk with bob', 'bob's on the phone' – serve as a code for discussing marijuana and its use.
- —Jim Emerson-Cobb, *Scratching the Dragon*, April 1997

4 a marijuana cigarette *US, 1998*
Probably abbreviated from Bob Marley or **BOB HOPE**, possibly from **BOBO BUSH**.
- —Mike Haskins, *Drugs*, p. 291, 2003

5 crack cocaine *UK*
An abbreviation of **BOBO**.

6 in hot rodding and drag racing, to cut or shorten a fender *US*
- Other modifications include a half-size, custom-designed gas tank, no front fender and a shortened or "bobbed" rear fender that ends at the top of the wheel[.]—Hunter S. Thompson, *Hell's Angels*, p. 98, 1966

7 a shoplifter *US*
- —Joseph E. Ragen and Charles Finston, *Inside the World's Toughest Prison*, p. 791, 1962

bob *verb*

to perform oral sex on a man *US*
- How much more can I bob here?—*Kids*, 1995

▸ **bob for apples**

to remove impacted faeces by hand *US*
- —*Maledicta*, p. 31, 1988–1989: 'Medical maledicta from San Francisco'

bob *adjective*

pleasant *UK, 1721*
Survives in the phrase 'all is bob' and the variant 'on bob'.

Bob *adjective*

used by US troops in the war against Iraq as an adjective for all things Saudi *US*
- Bob car, Bob clothes, and the like.—*Army*, p. 47, November 1991

Bob and Dick *noun*

the penis *UK, 1974*
Rhyming slang for **PRICK** (the penis).

Bob and Dick; Bob, Harry and Dick *adjective*

sick *UK, 1868*
Rhyming slang; from the people who brought you **TOM AND DICK; TOM, HARRY AND DICK**.

bobber *noun*

a person who has died by drowning or has fallen into the water *US*
- —*Maledicta*, p. 180, Summer/Winter 1986–1987: 'Sexual slang: prostitutes, pedophiles, flagellators, transvestites, and necrophiles'

bobbers *noun*

1 the female breasts *UK*
- —John Wainwright, *Edge of Destruction*, 1968

2 pieces of cork hung as a fringe around a hat's brim to keep flies away *AUSTRALIA, 1942*

bobble *verb*

(used of a racehorse) to stumble or break stride in a clumsy manner *US*
- —Tom Ainslie, *Ainslie's Complete Guide to Thoroughbred Racing*, p. 328, 1976

bobble bumper *noun*

in pinball, a bumper that scores and kicks the ball on contact *US*
- —Bobbye Claire Natkin and Steve Kirk, *All About Pinball*, p. 111, 1977

bobble twanger *noun*

a lesbian *UK*
In Royal Air Force use, 2002.

Bobbsey Twins *noun*

1 used as a representation of either innocence or a strong resemblance *US*
From a popular series of children's books created by Edward Stratemeyer and written under the name of Laura Lee Hope by writers under contract to Stratemeyer.
- The backlot scuttle is that Mike Frankovich's "Doctors' Wives" will make the Kinsey Report look like Bobbsey Twins research.—*San Francisco Examiner*, p. 37, 3rd November 1969
- One of the questions show folks often discuss is, "Which of the Britishn Bobbsey Twins, Tom Jones or Engelbert Humperdinck, will be around longer?"—*San Francisco Examiner*, p. 33, 2nd August 1971

2 two girls who regularly double-date *US*
An allusion to a 72-book juvenile series created by Edward Stratemeyer, writing under the name Laura Lee Hope, in 1904.
- —Mary Swift, *Campus Slang (University of Texas)*, 1968

bobby *noun*

1 a police officer *UK, 1844*
A familiar abbreviation of the name Robert honouring Mr, later Sir, Robert Peel, who is credited with the founding of the Metropolitan Police in 1928.
- [T]he Bobbies aren't carrying guns and clubs and the [Hell's] Angels respect that.—Jamie Mandelkau quoting Ken Kesey, *Buttons*, p. 117, 1969
- —Angela Devlin, *Prison Patter*, p. 29, 1996

2 during the Korean war, the Soviet BA-64 light armored car used by North Korea *US*

bobby *verb*

to serve as a police officer *UK*
- —John Wainwright, *The Worms Must Wait*, 1967

bobby dangler *noun*

the penis *CANADA, 1971*
A play on **BOBBY-DAZZLER**.

bobby-dazzler *noun*

something or someone wonderful, exciting, magnificent *UK, 1866*
- I could have kissed Dale when he came across with that field goal. Right from half-way, too. A bobby dazzler, no kidding.—F.J. Thwaites, *The Melody Lingers*, p. 85, 1935
- You little bobby dazzler!—Barry Humphries, *The Wonderful World of Barry McKenzie*, p. 29, 1968
- —Wilda Moxham, *The Apprentice*, p. 189, 1969
- Evidently Fred, or more precisely John Savident, used to be a bit of a bobby dazzler. By 'eck, Fred, what 'appened?—*The Guardian*, 20th May 2004

Bobby Moore; bobby *noun*

1 a door *UK, 1998*
Rhyming slang, based on the name of the footballer who was England's 1966 World Cup winning captain, 1942–93.

2 the state of affairs, the current situation *UK*
Rhyming slang for **THE SCORE** (the current situation) based on the name of England's 1966 football World Cup winning captain, 1942–93.
- —Angela Devlin, *Prison Patter*, p. 29, 1996
- What's happenin, kidder? What's the Bobby?—Niall Griffiths, *Kelly + Victor*, p. 145, 2002

bobbysoxer *noun*

a teenage girl *US, 1944*

'Bobby socks' (ankle-high white socks, first recorded in 1927) as a generational trademark for American teenagers arrived on the national scene in June 1937, with a cover photograph in *Life* magazine. After 'the socks' came 'the soxer'. The 'bobby' is most likely constructed on 'to cut or shorten' (to bob).

- Champion of the Bobby Soxers [Headline]—*San Francisco Chronicle*, p. 10, 18 February 1946
- "Occasional" prostitutes work some of the bars, and bobby soxers flirt at Washington Square.—Jack Lait and Lee Mortimer, *New York Confidential*, p. 69, 1948
- Gregory Peck, or some of the new boy friends of the bobby-soxers I'm too old to remember the names of?"—Philip Wylie, *Opus 21*, p. 83, 1949
- America's Favorite Bobby-Soxer [Headline]— *Life*, p. 23, 14th November 1949
- She's been around, she knows what the score is, she ain't some punk bobby-soxer with the mood in her eyes.—Jim Thompson, *A Swell-Looking Babe*, p. 80, 1954

bobette *noun*

a London Metropolitan Woman Police Officer *UK*

A feminised variation of **BOBBY** (a policeman).

- —Martin Fido and Keith Skinner, *The Official Encyclopaedia of New Scotland Yard*, 1999

bobfoc *noun*

a girl with a beautiful body but an ugly face *NEW ZEALAND*

Reported in private correspondence from New Zealand in March 2002. Acronym formed from *Body Off Baywatch, Face Off Crimewatch*, two television programmes – one fiction, one factual – which represent (apparently) the extremes of human appearance.

- Eighteen is this bird, a real BOBFOC job – Body Off 'Baywatch', Face Off 'Crimewatch' – don't know her name and don't want to, she kisses me like she's kissing a focking [fucking] corpse.—Paul Howard, *Ross O'Carroll-Kelly*, p. 64, 2003

Bob, Harry and Dick *adjective*

▷ **see:** BOB AND DICK

Bob Hope *noun*

marijuana *UK, 1992*

Abbreviates to **BOB**. British born American entertainer Bob Hope (1903–2003) is not associated with drugs except as a rhyme for **DOPE**.

- —Suroosh Alvi et al., *The Vice Guide*, p. b, 2002
- Don't ask me – I've been smoking Bob all afternoon.—Bodmin Dark, *Dirty Cockney Rhyming Slang*, 2003

bob job *noun*

a reduction in size achieved by cutting *US*

- Just today the papers were saying how Louis B. Mayer was all set to build up Thomas as a big romantic lead if only he would have a bob-job on his meandering Syrian nose.—Bernard Wolfe, *The Late Risers*, p. 187, 1954

Bob Marley *noun*

cocaine *UK*

Rhyming slang for **CHARLIE** (cocaine); after reggae musician Bob Marley (1945–1981), a Rastafarian.

- Got any Bob Marley? Sorted.— *Mixmag*, p. 138, September 2001

bobo *noun*

1 a person who enjoys the trappings of success but nevertheless espouses countercultural values *US*

From '*bo*urgeois *bo*hemian', but surely too close to a clown's name to be a coincidence.

- —David Brooks, *Bobos in Paradise*, 2000
- We've had Hippies, Yuppies, Buppies and Dinkies. Now it's time for the Bobos. Melinda Wittstock in New York reports on the rise of the new urban upper class[.]— *The Observer*, 28th May 2000
- Prague in the 21st century seems no more prey than any other great city to sex tourism, galumphing Germans, loonies out on licence or American trust-fund BoBos[.]— *The Guardian*, 2nd August 2003

2 a fool *JAMAICA, 1943*

- —Paul Sullivan, *Sullivan's Music Trivia*, p. 35, 2003

3 the vagina *BAHAMAS*

- —John A. Holm, *Dictionary of Bahamian English*, p. 23, 1982

4 the buttocks *US*

- —Connie Eble (Editor), *UNC-CH Campus Slang*, March 1974

5 crack cocaine *UK, 1998*

Possibly playing on **BEBE**.

- —Mike Haskins, *Drugs*, p. 281, 2003

6 prison-issued canvas shoes *US*

- —Gary K. Farlow, *Prison-ese*, p. 5, 2002

bobo bush *noun*

marijuana *US, 1936*

- —Vincent J. Monteleone, *Criminal Slang*, p. 28, 1949
- —Richard A. Spears, *The Slang and Jargon of Drugs and Drink*, p. 60, 1986

Bobo Johnny *noun*

any naive, gullible person *SAINT KITTS AND NEVIS, 1969*

- —Richard Allsopp, *Dictionary of Caribbean English Usage*, p. 108, 1996

Bob Squash *noun*

an area of a public lavatory where hands are washed *UK, 1961*

Rhyming slang for 'wash'; originally, during the World War 1, 'to wash'; thereafter used by pickpockets as 'on the bob' (stealing from the jackets of people washing their hands).

bobsy-die *noun*

a commotion or fuss *NEW ZEALAND, 1935*

A variation on the British dialect *bob-a-dying*.

- —Harry Orsman, *A Dictionary of Modern New Zealand Slang*, p. 15, 1999

Bob's your uncle

everything is all right *UK, 1937*

Most commentators offer the relationship between Prime Minister Robert Gasgoine-Cecil, 3rd Marquis of Salisbury (1830–1903) and his nephew Arthur Balfour (1848–1930) as the source of the phrase; the former (Uncle Bob), in 1887, controversially (allegedly nepotistically) appointed the latter as secretary for Ireland. This idiom, very familiar in the UK, is all but unknown in the US so that when Jann Turner-Lord published *A Dictionary of Slang for British Mystery Fans* in 1992 it was entitled *Bob's Your Uncle*.

- All I need is a return ticket to Bombay and a couple of pounds for food and hotel and Bob's your uncle.—Anthony Masters, *Minder*, p. 123, 1984

bobtail *noun*

1 in poker, four fifths of a straight that can be completed at either end *US, 1865*

- —Oswald Jacoby, *Oswald Jacoby on Poker*, p. 141, 1947
- —Thomas L. Clark, *The Dictionary of Gambling and Gaming*, p. 23, 1987

2 on the railways, a switching engine *US*

- —Ramon Adams, *The Language of the Railroader*, p. 17, 1977

bobtail *verb*

in trucking, to drive a tractor without a trailer *US*

- —Mary Elting, *Trucks at Work*, 1946

Bob White *noun*

in trucking, a flap valve on the smokestack *US*

- —Montie Tak, *Truck Talk*, p. 15, 1971

bod *noun*

1 person *UK, 1935*

An abbreviation of 'body'.

- All the bods in our little complex were to my taste.—Johnny Speight, *It Stands to Reason*, p. 66, 1973
- I'm Gillian. This is Edward. Legal bods in the city[.]—Nick Barlay, *Curvy Lovebox*, p. 69, 1997
- Only the bods who thought they knew the score took E[.] —Wayne Anthony, *Spanish Highs*, p. 2, 1999
- coupla bods I did some work for—Diran Adebayo, *My Once Upon A Time*, p. 46, 2000

2 the body, as in physique *UK, 1933*

- "I'm not gonna have this dude write anything on my bod," says Billy.—Darryl Ponicsan, *The Last Detail*, p. 115, 1970
- Life's True Goal must be enoblement of the mind and bod! [Gordo comic strip]—*San Francisco Examiner and Crhonicle*, p. 2, Comics II, 21 March 1971
- Hi, cousin. How's your bod—*American Graffiti*, 1973
- Park your bod in the bed by the window.—Cleo Odzer, *Goa Freaks*, p. 184, 1995
- "Yeah, nice healthy chest," Letch said, leering. "She was hot for my bod."—Joseph Wambaugh, *Floaters*, p. 154, 1996

3 an aeroplane passenger *UK*

Flight crew use.

- I didn't know the [orange juice] was so concentrated that the bods were going to use all my fresh water.—Patrick Campbell, *Come Here Till I Tell You*, 1960

bodacious *adjective*

amazing, impressive *US, 1843*

A C19 word from the American frontier, rediscovered by the late C20 young. The term 'bodacious tatas' as descriptive of 'magnificent breasts' was made widely popular by the 1982 film *Officer and a Gentleman*. In Australia, popularised by radio announcer Doug Mulray.

- —Helen Dahlskog (Editor), *A Dictionary of Contemporary and Colloquial Usage*, p. 8, 1972
- —Connie Eble (Editor), *UNC-CH Campus Slang*, p. 1, November 1983
- Ted, you and I have witnessed many things, but nothing as bodacious as what just happened.—*Bill and Ted's Excellent Adventure*, 1989
- Long haired surfing goose blue blood shot left eye Testosterone fixated fool and gratuitous user of the word sperm wants blonde haired blue/green eyed surfing chick. Boadcious tatars a must, slab carrying (silent) mute preferred. Must own VCR.—*City Hub*, p. 33, 13th November 1997

bo-deen *noun*

a police officer *US*

- While kids in Northwest refer to police as "one-time," Northeast teenagers call them"bo-deen" or "hot dog," and in Southeast they're "po-pos" or good old "feds."—*Washington Post*, p. A1, 20th August 2001

bodega *noun*

a shop *UK*

An affected acquisition, directly from Spanish.

- —Paul Baker, *Polari*, p. 165, 2002

bodewash *noun*

dry buffalo dung *CANADA*

The word is an adaptation of the French *bois de vache* (cow wood).

- If I hadn't heard that crack, we'd all be dead right now! Mashed flatter than a bodewash chip!—William Mowery, *Tales of the Mounted Police*, p. 76, 1953
- In the pre-railway days every traveller on the plains used bois des vaches (buffalo droppings) as fuel, filling it into sacks whenever they found it.—*B.C. Digest*, p. 51/1, November-December 1963

bodger *noun*

in the building trade, any inferior tradesman (such as a builder, electrician, mechanic or plumber) who is able to patch and mend, and is, perhaps, unqualified; on a building site, the jack-of-all-trades worker who fixes minor problems *UK*

A dialect word first recorded in 1552.

- The day after the [Hutton] report was published, a letter appeared in the Guardian. "As any inept DIY bodger could tell you, whitewash applied carefully and thinly will last years", said the writer.—*The Guardian*, 6th February 2004

bodger *adjective*

fake; false *AUSTRALIA*

Also recorded as a noun, 1945. Rare.

- This entailed the addition of as many more bodger votes as possible.—Frank Hardy, *Power Without Glory*, 1950

bodgie *noun*

1 anything worthless *AUSTRALIA*

Also variant 'bodgey'.

- —Sydney J. Baker, *Australia Speaks*, 1953

2 a male member of an urban youth subculture of the 1950s *AUSTRALIA*

Now only historical use. 'Bodgies' were noted for a peculiar style of dress (shocking for its day) that was in conscious imitation of American youth, including tight trousers, jackets, no ties and having slicked back hair with large sideburns. Their female counterparts were 'widgies'. This group was the subject of numerous alarmist media reports about youth deliquency. In origin the term must be related to other senses of 'bodgie/bodger', but exactly how is unclear. The notion put forward in the *Australian National Dictionary* (1988) that it is a nominal use of 'bodgie' as 'counterfeit', referring to clothing made from poor quality cloth passed off as American material, is unsubstantiated by any early evidence.

- —Josef Holman, *As I See Them*, p. 53, 1954
- For one evening when they were having a few quiet beers in a park a bunch of bodgies decided to break up the party.—*Weekend*, p. 3, 1st June 1957
- For this article shows that the hard central core of all these cults – whether they call themselves 'Teddy Boys', 'Zoot-Suit Boys', or 'Bodgies' – lies in a deliberate international criminal conspiracy that also runs the international dope traffic.—*Weekend*, p. 10, 1st June 1957
- But most young chaps who wear red shirts and call themselves bodgies are not bodgies – in this criminal sense – at all.—*Weekend*, p. 10, 1st June 1957
- There were Japanese bodgies, perverts, negros, five deaf and dumb call girls sitting at the bar in a row[.]—Les Such, *A Yen for Yokohama*, p. 114, 1963
- The performance of bodgies and widgies should make anyone look twice at these so innocent thirteen-year-olds.—James Holledge, *The Call-girl in Australia*, p. 133, 1964
- So far there's been nothing but a steady stream of bodgies calling in at Billy's, sitting around hurling spent beer cans at the local cats and swearing at anyone who happens to walk by.—Roy Slaven (John Doyle), *Five South Coast Seasons*, p. 121, 1992
- [T]hey reminded him of something from outer space or his old man's wedding photos, when dad was a bodgie and the old girl was a widgie.—Robert G. Barrett, *Davo's Little Something*, p. 18, 1992

3 a young swing jazz enthusiast *US, 1952*

- —Harold Wentworth and Stuart Berg Flexner, *Dictionary of American Slang*, p. 49, 1960

bodgied up *adjective*

dressed up in a pretentious manner *AUSTRALIA*

- This is a handy malicious adjective, especially useful in deflating the egos of people wearing new clothes. As in: 'In he lobs, bodgied up and smelling like dead horse gully.'—Arthur Chipper, *The Aussie Swearer's Guide*, p. 31, 1972

bodgy; bodgie *verb*

to conceal someone or something *AUSTRALIA*

- I'll bet old Gorty's got a few thirst quenching tubes bodgied away in this den of his!—Barry Humphries, *The Wonderful World of Barry McKenzie*, p. 7, 1968

bodgy; bodgie *adjective*

1 false, counterfeit, phoney, sham *AUSTRALIA, 1944*

Appearing simultaneously with the synonymous 'bodger', these terms must derive from British dialect *bodge* (to make or mend clumsily or poorly), a variant of 'botch'. Recorded earliest in prison and underworld use it perhaps referred originally to a poorly done quota of work that prisoners had to submit daily. Ted Hartley, writing in 1944, notes that wide use of the term is 'resulting in its becoming a general term to denote "bad"'.

- I just stuck a bodgie blister on his windscreen.—Sam Weller, *Old Bastards I Have Met*, p. 116, 1979
- On one occasion a Sydney horse called Simba was taken to Melbourne and entered under a 'bodgie' name.—Joe Andersen, *Winners Can Laugh*, p. 175, 1982
- [T]he trainer followed the storyline by claiming him for a bodgy bet.—Clive Galea, *Slipper*, p. 65, 1988

2 poorly made or executed; worthless, hopeless *AUSTRALIA, 1944*

- [H]is head already felt like a bodgy lab experiment.—Linda Jaivin, *Rock n Roll Babes from Outer Space*, p. 144, 1996

bodice-ripper *noun*

a sexually themed romantic/historical novel aimed at an adult female audience *US*

- Miss Faust reminds us thatwomen, too, are a little bit beastly, that they too have their pornography: Harlequin romances, novels of "sweet savagery," bodice-rippers.—*New York Times*, p. 7-4, 28th December 1980
- A steamy bodice-ripper to help while away the hours in an airport lounge?—*Opera News*, p. 48, October 1998
- Diana Lindsay admits that Marshal's journalism is as romantic as a Harlequin bodice-ripper.—*San Diego Union-Tribune*, p. E1, 14th March 2004

bodied *adjective*

(used of a female) well built *US*

- —Marcus Hanna Boulware, *Jive and Slang of Students in Negro Colleges*, 1947

bodilicious *noun*

an attractive physique *UK*

A compounding of 'body' and 'delicious', perhaps intended as a gentle pun on **BODACIOUS**. Recorded in contemporary gay culture as an 'edible body'.

- —*Attitude*, p. 60, July 2003

body *noun*

1 a person, especially if under suspicion or arrest; a person to be framed for a crime *UK*

Police and criminal usage.

- —Peter Laurie, *Scotland Yard*, p. 321, 1970
- —G.F. Newman, *Sir, You Bastard*, p. 253, 1970
- I'd never take bribes or anything. Do deals for information or bodies, for sure. But never the bung.—Jake Arnott, *He Kills Coppers*, p. 15, 2001

2 a prisoner *UK*
Prison officers' use.
- Let's get those bodies moved from upstairs! —Angela Devlin, *Prison Patter*, p. 29, 1996

3 a person you have killed *US*
- Vega allegedly bragged to the undercover cops that he had "bodies" on his criminal resume[.] — *Daily News (New York)*, p. 1, 9th May 2001

4 in the usage of showgirls, a man *US*
- —Don Wilmeth, *The Language of American Popular Entertainment*, p. 29, 1981

body *verb*
to kill someone *US*
- Investigators went on to learn from several other people that Parker bragged that "I bodied him for his drugs." — *Hartford (Connecticut) Courant*, p. B1, 15th October 1999

body armour *noun*
a condom *UK*
- —David Rowan, *A Glossary for the 90s*, 1998

body by Fisher *noun*
a woman with an attractive body *US*
An allusion to an advertising slogan of the General Motors Corporation, boasting of the superiority of a car 'body by Fisher'.
- —Vincent J. Monteleone, *Criminal Slang*, p. 29, 1949

body cheese *noun*
any buildup of body cells such as ear wax or eye secretions *US*
- — Eble (Editor), *UNC-CH Campus Slang*, p. 2, Spring 1988

body contact squad *noun*
Korean soldiers who acted as suicide bombers *US*
- Without out knowledge, they prepared charges designed to strap around the waist of a soldier and formed some "body contact squads." Members of these squads were to move into the side of a tank, pull a fuze lighter on a two-second fuze, perhaps disable the tank and certainly join their honored aucestors. —Joseph C. Goulden, *Korea*, p. 128, 1982

body knocker *noun*
a person who works in a car body repair shop *US*
- —John Edwards, *Auto Dictionary*, p. 16, 1993

body lotion *noun*
a drink *UK*
Citizens' band radio slang.
- —Peter Chippindale, *The British CB Book*, p. 152, 1981

body packer *noun*
a person who smuggles drugs inside their bodies *US*
- —Jim Crotty, *How to Talk American*, p. 89, 1997
- —Nick Constable, *This is Cocaine*, p. 182, 2002

body popping *noun*
an urban dance-style incorporating robotic movements *US*
- [B]ody-popping (developed on the west coast by Boogaloo Sam). —Alex Ogg, *The Hip Hop Years*, p. 15, 1999

body queen *noun*
a homosexual man attracted to men with muscular bodies *US*
- — *American Speech*, p. 56, Spring-Summer 1970: 'Homosexual slang'

body rain *noun*
corporate executives in search of employment after a takeover, merger or business failure *US*
A macabre image harkening the suicides by jumping associated with the market crash of 1929.
- —Kathleen Odean, *High Steppers, Fallen Angels, and Lollipops*, p. 119, 1988

body shop *noun*
a bar catering to an unmarried clientele with sexual agendas *US*
- Pete Rozelle was in town this weekend. He popped into one of those body shops on Union Street Friday night, squeezing past the sweet young things and the hot-to-trot hustlers. — *San Francisco Examiner*, p. 63, 24th September 1970
- San Francisco's cocktail body shops are the only saloons that are really doing a business today. — *San Francisco Examiner*, p. 3, 24th September 1970
- But its [Union Street's] detractors are confusing its present nature with its image of half a decade ago – when it surely was home of Dark-Glass-in-the-Rain, every girl a stewardess, and fast bucks to be picked up by operating body shops. — *San Francisco Examiner and Chronicle*, p. 10, 4th March 1973

body shot *noun*
a ritual in which a person licks salt off someone else, drinks a shot of tequila and then sucks on a lemon in the other's mouth *US*
- —Don R. McCreary (Editor), *Dawg Speak*, 2001

body snatcher *noun*
1 a morgue employee who retrieves and transports corpses to the morgue *US*
- After talking to the body snatcher, Nell wasn't sure whether she'd be better off trying to upchuck or work. —Joseph Wambaugh, *Finnegan's Week*, p. 161, 1993

2 someone who steals another's date *US*
- — *American Speech*, p. 302, December 1955: 'Wayne University slang'

3 a person who selects prime farm stock for butchering *NEW ZEALAND*
- — *Dominion Post*, p. C6, 22nd November 2002

body swerve *noun*
any deliberate act of avoiding someone or something *UK: SCOTLAND*
From football terminology into general parlance.
- I'm meant to be goin to my old dear's but I think I'll give it a body swerve. —Michael Munro, *The Original Patter*, 1985

body-swerve *verb*
to avoid something *UK: SCOTLAND, 1992*
- spits his fury at those who bodyswerve the decision between support or protest at the concept of deterrents. — *The Herald (Glasgow)*, p. 15, 23rd June 1993
- Fancy body-swervin the union meetin an nickin oot for a pint? — MichaelMunro, *The Complete Patter*, 1996
- Billy Bragg bodyswerved his own reputation as political-commentator-in-chief to reinvent himself as Woody Guthrie's voice on earth[.] —Simon Broughton, *Rough Guide to World Music*, p. 65, 1999

body time *noun*
in casinos, the amount of time a player, whose playing time is being tracked, spends gambling *US*
- —Frank Scoblete, *Best Blackjack*, p. 254, 1996

body-to-body *noun*
a sexual service offered in some massage parlours in which a girl will massage her client with her body *UK*
- [T]wo-way body-to-body: the girl will massage her client with her body and vice versa. —Caroline Archer, *Tart Cards*, 2003

body womping *noun*
body surfing *US*
- —Mitch McKissick, *Surf Lingo*, 1987

boerewors curtain *noun*
the invisible line marking the beginning of South African suburbs where Afrikaans people dwell *SOUTH AFRICA*
- —Penny Silva, *A Dictionary of South African English*, 1996

boerie *noun*
the penis *SOUTH AFRICA*
From the Afrikaans for 'farm sausage'.
- [P]laying with my boerie[.] — *Surfrikan Slang*, 2005

bo-excuse-me *noun*
▷ see: EXCUSE-ME

bof *noun*
a record album consisting of the 'best of' the artist's previous recordings *US*
- —Arnold Shaw, *Dictionary of American Pop/Rock*, p. 47, 1982

boff *noun*
1 a hearty laugh *US, 1945*
- More to be desired, though, is the boff, which is the Homeric response to an elementary comic situation. — *Atlantic Monthly*, p. 136, April 1946
- Boff: a full, hearty burst of laughter that comes from the bottom of the stomach. — *Everybody's Digest*, p. 21, September 1951
- The producer orders a gross of assorted yaks and boffs, and sprinkles the whole sound track with a lacing of simpering snorts. —Vance Packard, *The Hidden Persuaders*, p. 204, 1957

2 sex; an act of sexual intercourse *US, 1956*
- Ladies flock to kiss him, pay respects, and, in some cases, hope for a little boff. —Josh Alan Friedman, *Tales of Times Square*, p. 108, 1986

boff *verb*

1 to have sex *US, 1937*
- Don't give me that innocent bit. I know you were boffing Virgil Tatum this afternoon. — Max Shulman, *Anyone Got a Match?*, p. 253, 1964
- Why, just the thought of boffing some hairy boy makes me sick all over. — Gore Vidal, *Myra Breckinridge*, p. 158, 1968
- And yet, go understand people – it is her pleasure while being boffed to have one or the other of my forefingers lodged snugly up her anus. — Philip Roth, *Portnoy's Complaint*, p. 116, 1969
- This torrid tribute to the joys of dark meat features a chorus line of ebony beauties bouncing and boffing through a series of raunchy, relentlessly racist, and often unbearably funny skits that mine just about every sick cliche[.] — *Adult Video*, p. 16, August/September 1986
- Then I asked him if it was true he was boffing Kate Cruikshank. — C.D. Payne, *Youth in Revolt*, p. 71, 1993
- the astounding split between boffing and babies — Erica Orloff and JoAnn Baker, *Dirty Little Secrets*, p. 18, 2001

2 to kiss and caress *US*
- — Collin Baker et al., *College Undergraduate Slang Study Conducted at Brown University*, p. 84, 1968

3 to make a mistake, to do something wrong *UK*
Possibly euphemistic; sometimes 'boff up'. Recorded in use at Loughborough Grammar School by Phillip Reed, 1977.

4 to vomit *US*
- — Kenn "Naz" Young, *Naz's Dictionary of Teen Slang*, p. 12, 1993

boffed *adjective*

drunk *US*
- — Connie Eble (Editor), *UNC-CH Campus Slang*, p. 1, Spring 1984

boffin *noun*

a scientist; a forensic expert *UK, 1945*
- — Angela Devlin, *Prison Patter*, p. 30, 1996
- Was he serious? Or was this a cunning plan devised by prison-service boffins to test my reaction? — *The Guardian*, 7th December 2000

boffo *noun*

1 a great joke *US*
- Billy Wilder's One, Two, Three was a boffo (cf. Variety) spoof of international relations. — Joan Didion, *Slouching Toward Bethlehem*, p. 157, 1968

2 a one-year prison sentence *US, 1930*
- — Frank *Vacaville Vocabulary*, 1961 – 1962

boffo *adjective*

very impressive, popular, successful *US, 1949*
Originally theatrical when it was often used of a comedic success, and in which sense it probably derives from 'buffo' (a comic actor; comic).
- [A] film sale to boffo book-buyer Robert Redford. — *Maclean's (magazine)*, August 1976
- They had tried in vain to convince one another and the brass that they had been boffo in the canyon. — Joseph Wambaugh, *Lines and Shadows*, p. 100, 1984
- [Barry] Humphries launches into the boffo opening, a hymn to frivolity's refusal to suffer. — John Lahr, *Dame Edna Everage and the Rise of Western Civilisation*, p. 17, 1991

boffola *noun*

1 a hearty laugh; a joke that produces a hearty laugh *US*
- It'll sound all right. Good jokes, laughs, I'll pack the script with boffolas. — Frederick Wakeman, *The Hucksters*, p. 47, 1946

2 a smash hit, a success *US*
- Working with Dirty Eddie, Cassard thought he could make a big boffola* of Will You Marry Me? *Variant of the Hollywood term, "Boffo Terrific," big box-office smash. — *Time*, p. 86, 1st September 1947
- The new boffola of the Soviet Screen is Meeting on the Elbe, and it has everything. — *Time*, p. 30, 23rd May 1949

bog *noun*

1 a lavatory *UK, 1789*
Abbreviated from obsolete 'bog house'. Often follows 'the' and often in the plural.
- He crept off to the bog and got a grip on himself. — Alexander Buzo, *Rooted*, p. 85, 1969
- Wait till she comes back from the bog and we'll make a move. — Robert G. Barrett, *Davo's Little Something*, p. 258, 1992
- I said to direct it into the bogs and try and block some of the smell[.] — Dave Courtney, *Raving Lunacy*, p. 28, 2000
- On the way back from the bog I sees these couple of lads from Kirkby[.] — Kevin Sampson, *Outlaws*, p. 165, 2001
- [A]ll these pints an the bugle [cocaine] in the bogs[.] — Niall Griffiths, *Kelly + Victor*, p. 116, 2002

2 an act of defecation *AUSTRALIA, 1932*
- 'Where's the sergeant, corporal?' he demanded. 'Outside somewhere, sir.' 'Gone for a bog,' said someone. — Leonard Mann, *Flesh in Armour*, p. 189, 1932
- If that phone rings get hold of me. It doesn't matter if I'm on stage or having a bog. — Murray Bail, *Holden's Performance*, p. 177, 1988

3 a police station *UK*
- The Office, Barlow called it. Home, John Watt called it. The Stir,Clink, Bog, Nick, depending on what your are, and where you come from. — Troy Kennedy Martin, *Z Cars*, p. 21, 1962

4 in Western Australia, an unrefined and loutish person from a lower socio-economic area *AUSTRALIA, 1997*
- Bogan is also used in Western Australia, sometimes shortened to 'bog' (rhymes with log). — *Wordmap (www.abc.net.au/wordmap)*, 2003

5 a type of putty used to fill dents in the bodywork of vehicles *AUSTRALIA*
- Best quality bog and paint used. — Ken Maynard, *Ettamogah Pub Mob*, 1989

bog *verb*

1 to defecate *UK*
- "If Robert De Niro walked into this room now," Adam warns me, "you would bog yourself. I swear." — *Ask*, p. 45, 16th January 1982

2 (used of a motorcyle engine) to lose power and slow down *US*
- — Ed Radlauer, *Motorcylopedia*, p. 6, 1973

bogan *noun*

an unrefined and loutish person from a lower socio-economic area *AUSTRALIA*
The term gives rise to any number of derivatives, such as 'boganhood', 'boganism', 'boganity' and 'Bogansville' (the notional home of bogans).
- BOGAN: A Westie – one who wears tight jeans, flannel shirts, ugh boots, smokes Winfield Reds or drives a car with a huge engine and a very loud exhaust. Bogans are not usually popular and tend to inhabit Queanbeyan. — Bill Cowham, *Legolingo*, p. 3, 1987
- Only bogans play the piano. At least I'm crummy at it. — Kylie Mole (Maryanne Fahey), *My Diary*, p. 58, 1988
- Reformed Otorohanga bogan Rohan Max, now of Hamilton, says a bogan is working class, talks about loud music, fights, dogs, women they've never met and cars. — *Waikato Times*, p. 3, 2nd April 2000
- It just happens that a lot of our characters are chockos, but we also touch on the bumkins, the bogans. — *Sydney Morning Herald*, p. Metro 5, 11th April 2003
- We're not bogans who wear moccasins and are really scungy of anything. — *TV Week*, p. 41, 1st November 2003

bogan *adjective*

of or relating to a bogan *AUSTRALIA*
- It's so hard to be trendy knowing you've got bogan undies on. — Kylie Mole (Maryanne Fahey), *My Diary*, p. 3, 1988
- The first mistake of the day was leaving the safety of that sand dune back there where some bogan kid stood watching him. — Tim Winton, *Lockie Leonard*, p. 3, 1993

Bogan shower *noun*

a dust storm *AUSTRALIA, 1945*
Bogan is an inland town in New South Wales. Other locations similarly used by nature, weather and irony: Bedourie, Bourke, Cobar, Darling, Wilcannia and Wimmera.

bogart *noun*

a bully *US*
From the verb 'to bogart'; a critical view of out-of-fashion film 'tough guy' behaviour personified by 1950s film actor Humphrey Bogart.

bogart *verb*

1 to bully *US*
As 'tough guy' films and the forceful characters portrayed by actors like Humphrey Bogart went out fashion, so the usage moved from admiring to critical. Also variant 'bogard'.
- — *Current Slang*, p. 1, Fall 1966
- Cool Breeze jus' bogarts his way in. — Malcolm Braly, *On the Yard*, p. 195, 1967
- "Then I'm going to Bogart some pussy," Green spouted. — Bobby Seale, *A Lonely Rage*, p. 118, 1978
- Pookie, walking with a Ratzo Rizzo limp, pushes and shoves people out of the way who are waiting to get a turkey; he "bogarts" his way to the front, facing Nino and his crew. — *New Jack City*, p. 27, 1990
- DREXL: Next time you Bogart your way into a nigger's crib, an' get all in his face, make sure you do it on white boy day. — *True Romance*, 1993
- The one where you bogarted nine grand and flew to Vegas. — *Empire Records*, 1995

2 to selfishly keep possession of something that you are expected to return or forward, especially drugs *US*
After the alleged meanness of film actor Humphrey Bogart (1899–1957), or, perhaps, from the way he would keep a cigarette dangling from his lips. Sometimes spelt 'bogard' or 'bogarde'.
- You've been holding on to it and I sure would like a hit/Don't bogart that joint my friend, pass it over to me — Fraternity Of Man, *Don't bogart me*, 1969
- — Connie Eble (Editor), *UNC-CH Campus Slang*, October 1972
- Motherfuckers try to come up and bogard your weed at the club, and they don't wanna share theirs[.] — Cypress Hill, *Can I get a hit?*, 1999
- Mazz not being one to bogart his drugs he passed the wrap round to a couple of acquaintances[.] — John Williams, *Cardiff Dead*, p. 196, 2000

3 to overdose on drugs *UK*
- — Angela Devlin, *Prison Patter*, p. 30, 1996

bog bird *noun*
a woman who is willing to have sex in a public lavatory *UK*
- Just a dirty old bog-bird. — Colin Butts, *Is Harry Still on the Boat?*, p. 386, 2003

bogey *noun*
1 a uniformed police officer; a police detective *UK, 1924*
From 'bogey-man' (a terrifying creature), ultimately from 'old bogey' (the devil); alternatively spelt 'bogie' or 'bogy'.
- To make things worse, he said, one "diddy" [gypsy] was a "tealeaf" who "scarpered Joh Orderley [left in a hurry] when the "bogeys" [police] came round.. — Butch Reynolds, *Broken Hearted Clown*, p. 30, 1953
- [T]he bogies were about to search him on some very hot sus[.] — Charles Raven, *Underworld Nights*, p. 9, 1956
- [T]hey were two bogies of his own manor[.] — Frank Norman, *Bang To Rights*, p. 122, 1958
- "Don't be daft, if it is the bogeys how can they touch us?" "With two hot motors round the back? Who are you kidding?" — Derek Bickerton, *Payroll*, p. 43, 1959
- — Angela Devlin, *Prison Patter*, p. 30, 1996

2 an unidentified aircraft, presumed to be hostile until identified as friendly *US, 1943*
Coined in World War 2 and used since.
- — Linda Reinberg, *In the Field*, p. 26, 1991

3 in betting, the outstanding loser in any book *UK*
- [H]e could have had the bogey back at 40–1[.] — John McCririck, *John McCririck's World of Betting*, p. 131, 1991

4 a small lump of dried nasal mucus *UK, 1937*
Variant spellings include 'bogy' and 'bogie'.
- Everyone was at it: bogies, fag ash, great oysters of phlegm, and this was a posh place too. — Jenny Eclair, *Camberwell Beauty*, p. 97, 2000

5 a wash taken in a creek, dam, etc, especially after a day's work *AUSTRALIA, 1874*
- He was a dog worth looking at. Except that he was dusty from a day's work – and a shake and a bogey would remove that – he was dusty in name only. — Frank Dalby Davison, *Dusty*, p. 93, 1946
- So you hit yourself with a rozener of rum in an enamel panniken, go for a bogey in the creek, put on clean gear and have another rum. — Sam Weller, *Old Bastards I Have Met*, p. 38, 1979

6 a child's steerable cart constructed from pram wheels and odds and ends of wood *UK: SCOTLAND*
- — Michael Munro, *The Original Patter*, 1985

7 in trucking, a set of two axles *US*
- — Ed and Ruth Radlauer, *Truck Tech Talk*, p. 10, 1986

8 a stalemate, a deadlock *UK: SCOTLAND*
- The game's a bogey. — Michael Munro, *The Original Patter*, 1985

bogey *verb*
to swim and wash in a creek, damn, etc, especially after a day's work; (of working dogs) to take a dip in a body of water to cool down and as a break from work *AUSTRALIA, 1788*
From Dharug, the extinct Australian Aboriginal language of the Sydney region.
- Savitra wanted at once to bogey in the big hole they made camp on, despite Prindy's saying he wanted to fish it first, and stripped off. — Xavier Herbert, *Poor Fellow My Country*, p. 1314, 1975

bogey *adjective*
fraudulent, bogus *US*
- "I got a great-uncle lives over to Kentucky, he's in one of them bogey locals. Bunch of old miners drawin from the retirement fund but somehow they still got a vote." — John Sayles, *Union Dues*, p. 41, 1977

Bogey *nickname*
Humphrey Bogart (1899–1957), American actor *US*
- So I figured I'd better wait it out like Bogey had done in Casablanca. — Oscar Zeta Acosta, *The Autobiography of a Brown Buffalo*, p. 116, 1972

bog-eyed *adjective*
bleary-eyed as the result of too much drink or too little sleep, or both *UK*
- [B]og-eyed schizos asking to be taken to heaven. — Simon Lewis, *In The Box [britpulp]*, p. 131, 1999

bogger *noun*
a person from or living in a rural part of Ireland especially anyone not living in Dublin *IRELAND*
This term makes use of the suffix **-ER**, especially common in Dublin Hiberno-English.
- The state of him, he's a total bogger, I mean, who dressed him – Stevie Wonder? — Paul Howard, *Ross O'Carroll-Kelly*, p. 157,
- Rathbawn town of high renown. What was the rhyme the boggers used have? — Eamonn Sweeney, *Waiting for the Healer*, p. 24, 1997

boggie *noun*
a hippy who is resistant to change, or too drug-intoxicated to be a part of any activity *UK*
Coinage credited to counterculture artist Edward Barker, 1970.
- The super-hippies had retaliated by referring to these early-to-arrive nomads as the "boggies". — Mick Farren, *Give the Anarchist a Cigarette*, p. 269, 2001

boggie bear *noun*
an ugly person *US*
- — Marcus Hanna Boulware, *Jive and Slang of Students in Negro Colleges*, 1947

boggie board *noun*
a small, foam board surfed in a prone position *AUSTRALIA*
- — Nat Young, *Surfing Fundamentals*, p. 126, 1985

bogging *adjective*
filthy *UK: SCOTLAND*
- Sumdy's feet are boggin. — Michael Munro, *The Original Patter*, 1985
- It's absolutely bogging. — Television trailer *How Clean is Your House?*, 21st May 2003

bogie man *noun*
a worker who repairs railway rolling stock *UK*
A pun on a devilish creature and a conventional piece of under-carriage.
- The bogie men were men who worked in the carriage repair shop. — Frank McKenna, *A Glossary of Railwaymen's Talk*, 1970

bog-in *noun*
a hearty meal *AUSTRALIA*
After the verb sense.
- — John Cleary, *The Climate of Courage*, 1954

bog in *verb*
to eat voraciously *AUSTRALIA, 1917*
- 'Bog in Nino,' he said, and took a piece of fish in his hand. — Nino Culotta (John O'Grady), *They're A Weird Mob*, p. 109, 1957
- — Jim Ramsay, *Cop It Sweet!*, p. 14, 1977
- [W]e felt it necessary to express our positive revulsion just as Mother was about to bog in. — Kerry Cue, *Crooks, Chooks and Bloody Ratbags*, p. 165, 1983

bog lap *noun*
in Western Australia, a circuit of a street block in a vehicle done, especially repeatedly, for entertainment *AUSTRALIA*
- Talk about bog laps. — Glyn Parry, *Mosh*, p. 109, 1996

bogman *noun*
anyone who does not live in a city or a town *IRELAND*
- By God Father that's a cold one I said rubbing the hands real bogman style. — Patrick McCabe, *The Butcher Boy*, p. 16, 1992

Bogners *noun*
blue jeans worn when skiing *US*
Alluding to the stylish stretch trousers manufactured by the German Bogner firm.
- — *American Speech*, p. 205, October 1963: 'The language of skiers'

bogof *noun*
a retail special offer: *Buy One Get One Free* *UK*
- It is lined with the weekly offers, most of which are Bogofs, as in Buy One Get One Free. — *The Times Magazine*, p. 18, 31st May 2003

bog off *verb*
to go, to depart; generally used as a euphemistic imperative *UK*
Originally Royal Air Force, possibly from 'take-off' (in an aircraft), to 'leave the earth (bog) behind'.
- What's the matter with you? Bog off, before you get hurt. —Chris Ryan, *Stand By, Stand By*, p. 59, 1996

bogosity *noun*
the degree to which anything can be described as wrong or in error *US*
Computer hacker slang from **BOGUS** (wrong).
- —*CoEvolution Quarterly*, p. 27, Spring 1981
- This leads to a hacker's response to someone who has just said something so outrageously bogus that it has slid off the bogosity scale: "You just pinged my bogometer." —David Rowan, *A Glossary for the 90s*, p. 72, 1998

bog out *verb*
to become intoxicated on drugs *US*
- —Ethan Hilderbrant, *Prison Slang*, p. 14, 1998

bog-standard *adjective*
ordinary, normal, usual *AUSTRALIA, 1983*

bog-trotter *noun*
an Irish person *UK, 1682*
From the nature of Eire's terrain.

bog-trotting *adjective*
Irish *UK*
From **BOG-TROTTER** (an Irish person).
- I'm sending my bogtrotting mates over to see you. —Greg Williams, *Diamond Geezers*, p. 50, 1997

bogue *noun*
a cigarette *US*
- —Judi Sanders, *Mashing and Munching in Ames*, p. 2, 1994

bogue *verb*
1 to smoke a cigarette *US*
A part-of-speech slight of hand from Humphrey Bogart, cigarette-smoking icon.
- —*Concord (New Hampshire) Monitor*, 23rd August 1983
- —Vann Wesson, *Generation X Field Guide and Lexicon*, p. 24, 1997

2 to depress someone *US*
- That fire alarm really bogued my high. —Connie Eble (Editor), *UNC-CH Campus Slang*, p. 2, Fall 1986

bogue *adjective*
wrong; sick *US*
From **BOGUS**; sometimes seen spelt as 'boag'.
- I'm bogue, but I ain't gonna indulge. I'm tryin' to kick. —Clarence Cooper Jr, *The Scene*, p. 13, 1960
- Whenever a kid did something that was boag, you were never told to get under the desk[.] —A.S. Jackson, *Gentleman Pimp*, p. 17, 1973
- Man, I'm as boguie a a Hong Kong coolie with his piles hangin out! —Charles W. Moore, *A Brick for Mister Jones*, p. 32, 1975
- —Connie Eble (Editor), *UNC-CH Campus Slang*, p. 1, October 1986

bogue out *verb*
in computing, to become non-functional suddenly and without warning *US*
- —Guy L. Steele et al., *The Hacker's Dictionary*, p. 35, 1983

bog up *verb*
to make a mess of something, to do something incompetently *UK, 1948*
Originally military; likely to derive from **BOG** (a lavatory) and all that implies, but at the same time euphemistic and tending towards **BUGGER UP**.

bogus *noun*
counterfeit money *US, 1798*
- There's a hell of a lot of bogus flying around in tens and twenties. —George V. Higgins, *The Friends of Eddie Doyle*, p. 87, 1971
- He was sitting in a motel room on Hollywood Boulevard waiting for the money man, and two hippies kicked in the door, tied him up, and took the bogus. —Gerald Petievich, *One-Shot Deal*, p. 218, 1981

bogus *adjective*
1 disagreeable, offensive; wrong *US, 1876*
- So, like when Jefferson went before the people what he was saying was 'Hey, we left this place in England because it was bogus, and if we don't come up with some cool rules ourself, we'll be bogus, too!' —*Fast Times at Ridgemont High*, 1982
- "Heard you dropped out of U.S.C.' "Oh yeah. Couldn't deal with it. It's so totally bogus." —Bret Easton Ellis, *Less Than Zero*, p. 48, 1985
- Bogus. My dad's home. —*Bill and Ted's Excellent Adventure*, 1989
- I still live with my parents, which I admit is both bogus and sad. —*Wayne's World*, 1992
- The scene – the kids, the two big men, the shotgun wary while the black cop holstered his pistol but left the snap undone – would have looked bogus on network TV, like a parody of something from a long time ago. —Jess Mowry, *Way Past Cool*, p. 17, 1992

2 in computing, non-functional, useless, false or incorrect *US*
- —*CoEvolution Quarterly*, p. 27, Spring 1981
- —Guy L. Steele et al., *The Hacker's Dictionary*, p. 34, 1983

bogus beef *noun*
idle, insincere conversation *US*
- —Marcus Hanna Boulware, *Jive and Slang of Students in Negro Colleges*, 1947

bogwash *verb*
to force a person's head into the toilet bowl, and flush *UK*
From **BOG** (a lavatory).
- —Angela Devlin, *Prison Patter*, p. 30, 1996

bogwoppit *noun*
an ugly woman *UK*
In Royal Air Force use, 2002

bohawk *noun*
a member of the Bohemian counterculture *US*
- "She's only a bohawk anyway," Dincher complained. "Like – one of them screwy artists." —George Mandel, *Flee the Angry Strangers*, p. 249, 1952

bohd *noun*
1 marijuana *UK, 1998*
- —Mike Haskins, *Drugs*, p. 286, 2003

2 phencyclidine, the recreational drug known as PCP or angel dust *UK*
Possibly a mispronunciation of **BOAT**.
- —*www.addictions.org*, 2001

boho *noun*
a Bohemian, in the sense of an unconventional person *US, 1958*
- A few local bohos saw it and came out, but mainly it was the Pranksters and their friends who showed up at the Spread that night, including a lot of the Berkeley crowd that had been coming to La Honda. —Tom Wolfe, *The Electric Kool-Aid Acid Test*, p. 209,
- —*Current Slang*, p. 2, Winter 1971
- [A] happily modern mix of [Jeffrey] Bernard-era boho remnants – Britain's rock'n'roll class, before there was rock'n'roll[.] —*Uncut*, p. 171, July 2001

boho *adjective*
unconventional, bohemian *US, 1958*
- I can't say I gave her costume an honor grade, however; it was a bit too Boho for my taste. I especially loathed the Indian thing she carried for a handbag. —Erich Segal, *Love Story*, p. 3, 1970
- [A] big creative boho scene of dropouts from London, Brighton is the perfect place for something to kick off. —John Robb, *The Nineties*, p. 260, 1999
- We lacked expertise, a guitar player and any coherent definition beyond that of a ragged, slap-back boho band[.] —Mick Farren, *Give the Anarchist a Cigarette*, p. 48, 2001
- [Elvis] Presley plays a successful photographer grappling with a succession of boho babes. —*Q*, p. 62, May 2002

bohunk *noun*
1 a Czechoslavakian immigrant *US, 1903*
- Generally Czechs, or "Bonhunks," as they once were called, are law-abiding people[.] —Jack Lait and Lee Mortimer, *Chicago Confidential*, p. 72, 1950
- Hell, when I was a kid I knew guys who were real Bohemians, I mean in the blood – Bohunks. —Darryl Ponicsan, *The Last Detail*, p. 75, 1970

2 a ill-mannered, loutish person *US, 1919*
- Hey, who the hell's this bohunk, anyhow? —Robert Gover, *The Maniac Responsible*, p. 22, 1963
- Along about dawn, this Arkie bohunk named Hutchinson actually got up and went back there[.] —Seth Morgan, *Homeboy*, p. 152, 1990

boil *noun*
in surfing, a turbulence or disturbance on a developing wave *US*
- —John Grissim, *Pure Stoke*, p. 156, 1980

▸ **off the boil**
having lost your form and luck *AUSTRALIA*
- —Ned Wallish, *The Truth Dictionary of Racing Slang*, p. 58, 1989

boil *verb*
▸ **boil it till it assholes**
to continue to heat maple sap until it forms vortexes, indicating that it is nearing the candy stage *CANADA*
- "Boil it till it assholes" is a vivid [Quebec Eastern Townships], visual direction for cooking maple syrup to make candy. —Lewis Poteet, *Talking Country*, p. 21, 1992

▸ **boil the hides**
in drag racing, to smoke a car's tyres *US*
- —John Lawlor, *How to Talk Car*, p. 20, 1965

boil down *verb*
to reduce something to its essence *UK, 1880*
A figurative use of the conventional sense.
- It boils down to intolerance[.] —*The Guardian*, 2nd July 2004

boiled *noun*
a boiling hot solution of sugar and water used as an offensive weapon *UK*
- —Angela Devlin, *Prison Patter*, p. 30, 1996

boiled *adjective*
1 very drunk *US, 1884*
- —Collin Baker et al., *College Undergraduate Slang Study Conducted at Brown University*, p. 84, 1968
- Ken Kelly got boiled on vodka for courage[.] —Joseph Wambaugh, *Lines and Shadows*, p. 254, 1984

2 angry *US, 1929*
- —J. E. Lighter, *Historical Dictionary of American Slang, Volume 1*, p. 221, 1994

boiled owl *noun*
1 used as a representation of the ultimate drunkard *US, 1864*
- —Lou Shelly, *Hepcats Jive Talk Dictionary*, p. 21, 1945

2 the last thing in the world that you would want to eat *US*
- —John Gould, *Maine Lingo*, p. 17, 1975

boiler *noun*
1 a woman considered by most to be devoid of, or past the age of, sexual appeal *UK*
Flesh considered as chicken meat: a 'boiler' is no longer a fresh and tasty chick but a tough old bird.
- [A] well-used woman of forty or over...Daisy was a right old boiler[.] —Derek Raymond (Robin Cook), *The Crust on its Uppers*, 1962
- I certainly haven't started knocking over sixty year old boilers yet. —Ted Lewis, *Jack Carter's Law*, p. 119, 1974
- The rest of us are happy enough going down Rocket's to pull a pig, happy to fuck some old boiler in the car park[.] —John King, *Human Punk*, p. 232, 2000

2 an unskilled cook *US*
Proficient only at boiling meals.
- —John Gould, *Maine Lingo*, p. 256, 1975

3 the stomach *US, 1886*
- Boiler, as in "he's got the bad boiler," or upset stomach. —Jim Bouton, *Ball Four*, p. 252, 1970

4 the vagina *UK*
- —Bob Young and Micky Moody, *The Language of Rock 'n' Roll*, p. 18, 1985

boilermaker *noun*
1 a shot of whisky followed by a glass of beer; a beer and whisky combined *US, 1942*
- They are hard workers and good citizens who seldom get into trouble except on Saturday nights after too many boilermakers – whiskey and beer. —Jack Lait and Lee Mortimer, *Chicago Confidential*, p. 78, 1950
- —Oscar A. Mendlesohn, *The Dictionary of Drink and Drinking*, 1966
- They go to a bar and order boilermakers. —Darryl Ponicsan, *The Last Detail*, p. 149, 1970
- At four in the afternoon, two old men were huddled over boilermakers at the far end of the bar[.] —Walter Tevis, *The Color of Money*, p. 69, 1984
- While he's having his first boilermaker, he asks me what's new in my precinct. —Robert Campbell, *Junkyard Dog*, p. 17, 1986

2 a pint of beer that is an equal mixture of draught mild and bottled brown ale; a salted beer *UK, 1961*

boiler room *noun*
an office used in an elaborate swindle *US, 1931*
- —*American Speech*, May 1959: 'Notes on the cant of the telephone confidence man'
- —Joe McKennon, *Circus Lingo*, p. 18, 1980
- "An office, a sedcretary, a car, juice money for the real estate people, tehe boiler room, bleepety, bleepety bleep." —Gerald Petievich, *Money Men*, p. 78, 1981
- —M. Allen Henderson, *How Con Games Work*, p. 218, 1985
- Those boiler-room scams can get a guy chucked into a single room with three roommates. For about five years. —Joseph Wambaugh, *The Golden Orange*, p. 251, 1990
- He ran boiler rooms and bucket shops. —Stephen Cannell, *King Con*, p. 35, 1997

boiler water *noun*
whisky *US*
- —Ramon Adams, *The Language of the Railroader*, p. 17, 1977

boiling *adjective*
extremely hot *UK, 1930*
A familiar exaggeration.
- [Y]ou haven't put the heating on 'ave you – it's boiling in yer [here][.] —Patrick Jones, *Unprotected Sex*, p. 227, 1999

boilover *noun*
in horse racing, an unexpected win by a long shot; a loss by the favourite *AUSTRALIA, 1871*
- The biggest postwar sensation at Stawell occurred in 1947 with a 'boilover'. —James Holledge, *The Great Australian Gamble*, p. 117, 1966
- —Wilda Moxham, *The Apprentice*, p. 71, 1969

boil-up *noun*
a trail stop for tea and rest *CANADA*
- On northern trails, the term is used as noun and verb: "We paused for a boil-up just past seven in the evening," and "We'll boil up at the next ridge." —Bill Casselman, *Canadian Food Words*, p. 251, 1998

boing *verb*
while snowboarding, to bounce off something *US*
- —Elena Garcia, *A Beginner's Guide to Zen and the Art of Snowboarding*, p. 121, 1990: 'Glossary'

bo-ing!
used for humorously expressing approval or delight *US*
Teen slang.
- —*American Weekly*, p. 2, 14 August 1955

boing!
used as a jocular catchphrase that indicates a sexual interest or readiness *US, 1948*
Sometimes embellished to 'Boing! said Zebedee'. Coincidental to the original US catchphrase, this began with the UK translation/adaptation, by Eric Thomson, 1929–84, of French animated children's television programme *Le Manege Enchanté* into *The Magic Roundabout*, BBC 1963–71 and 1974–77. Zebedee was a spring-mounted character, best remembered as making his entrances and exits to a narrated 'Boing!' and signalling the end of each episode by announcing that it was time for bed. Popularised in the UK with the recording of a stand-up comedy routine by Jasper Carrott.
- —Harold Wentworth and Stuart Berg Flexner, *Dictionary of American Slang*, p. 50–51, 1960
- 'You know I've fancied you for a long time' said Florence. 'I've fancied you too' said Dillon. 'Where do we go from here?' said Florence. 'Booinngg!!!'. —Jasper Carrott, *Magic Roundabout*, 1975

boink *noun*
an in-person meeting of participants in an Internet discussion group *US*
- —Christian Crumlish, *The Internet Dictionary*, p. 24, 1995

boink *verb*
to have sex with someone *US, 1897*
- —Connie Eble (Editor), *UNC-CH Campus Slang*, p. 1, Spring 1987
- Thing was, Marty never got down to doing it. You know, it. Boinking. —Seth Morgan, *Homeboy*, p. 84, 1990
- Real pedophiles try and convince everyone it's OK to boink pre-pub kids. —Nancy Tamosaitis, *net.sex*, p. 113, 1995
- On one call-out Anne had told the pathologist that she wouldn't have had any problem at all with a first-date boinking of the actor who'd played Hari. —Joseph Wambaugh, *Floaters*, p. 136, 1996
- You didn't mind so much that your boyfriend was boinking a skank [slut]. —Janet Evanovitch, *High Five*, 1999

- Was there any greater sin than this? Fantasizing about embracing – or boinking – a priest?—Rita Ciresi, *Pink Slip*, p. 64, 1999

Bo Jimmy *noun*
marijuana *US*
- —Jay Robert Nash, *Dictionary of Crime*, p. 38, 1992

bok *noun*
an eager person *SOUTH AFRICA*
- —Jean Branford, *A Dictionary of South African English*, p. 29, 1978

Bok *noun*
a sportsman or woman in a team that represents South Africa in international competition, a 'Spring*bok*' *SOUTH AFRICA, 1972*
- Could the Boks be all black?—*The Observer*, 5th October 2003

bok *adjective*
keen for something interesting *SOUTH AFRICA, 1975*
- —Jean Branford, *A Dictionary of South African English*, p. 29, 1978

boke; boak *noun*
nausea; a need to vomit; vomiting *UK, 1911*
- Got a wee touch of the boak, eh doll?—Ian Pattison, *Rab C. Nesbitt*, 1988
- Follow the trail of bars an beak (cocaine). – An boak. – You know it, Roz.—Niall Griffiths, *Kelly + Victor*, p. 308, 2002

boke; boak *verb*
to vomit; to induce vomiting *UK, 1911*
- —Michael Munro, *The Original Patter*, p. 12, 1985

boker *noun*
an unsophisticated rustic *US*
- —Mary Swift, *Campus Slang (University of Texas)*, 1968

bokkie; bok *noun*
a lover, especially as an endearment *SOUTH AFRICA, 1959*
- —Jean Branford, *A Dictionary of South African English*, p. 29, 1978

boko *noun*
the nose *US, 1859*
- I timed that punch to a second – bing on the boko.—Norman Lindsay, *Halfway to Anywhere*, p. 106, 1947

bold *adjective*
1 used to suggest homosexuality or of the stereotypical characteristics associated with gay men *UK*
This usage was originated and made familiar by the BBC radio comedy *Round The Horne*, 1965–86.
- KENNETH: Oh bold! Very bold! KEN W: I wonder where he spends his evenings?—Barry Took and Marty Feldman, *Round The Horne*, 16th April 1967
- Even to use the word bold is to be linked with homosexuality, as it shows an understanding of the subtext that would not be available otherwise.—Paul Baker, *Polari*, p. 165, 2002

2 successful, excellent *US*
- —Carol Covington, *A Glossary of Teenage Terms*, 1965

bold-as-brass; as bold as brass *adjective*
audacious, extremely impudent *UK, 1789*
- Iraq's bold-as-brass information minister, Mohammed Saeed al-Sahaf, is a man suffering a severe case of denial.—*The Guardian*, 8th April 2003

Bolivian marching powder *noun*
cocaine *US*
- All might come clear if you could just slip into the bathroom and do a little more Bolivian Marching Powder.—Jay McInerney, *Bright Lights, Big City*, p. 1, 1984
- "Because," he screams over the music, grabbing me by the collar, "we need some Bolivian Marching Powder..."—Bret Easton Ellis, *American Psycho*, p. 54, 1991
- —Vann Wesson, *Generation X Field Guide and Lexicon*, p. 26, 1997
- For £50 you could snort up the finest mixture of baby laxative (interspersed with the odd grain of Bolivian marching powder) in the land.—Tim Southwell, *Getting Away with It*, p. 254, 2001
- —Nick Constable, *This is Cocaine*, p. 181, 2002

bollards *noun*
the testicles *UK*
A play on **BOLLOCKS**.
- —Richard Herring, *Talking Cock*, p. 30, 2003

bollicky; bollocky *adjective*
(of either sex) totally naked *AUSTRALIA, 1950*
Literally, 'with the bollocks exposed'.
- Chilla heard because he had turned the shower off and came out bollicky.—Frank Hardy, *The Outcasts of Foolgarah*, p. 18, 1971

bollix *noun*
1 nonsense talk *IRELAND*
The spelling reflects Hiberno-English pronunciation of **BOLLOCKS**.
- If people in here didn't talk so much bollix, then there'd be a lot less trouble.—Paul Howard, *The Joy*, p. 40, 1996

2 a contemptible person *IRELAND*
Variant spelling of **BOLLOCKS**.
- Taxi! Taxi, ya bollix!—James Hawes, *Dead Long Enough*, p. 100, 2000

bollix *verb*
to bungle something, to ruin something *US, 1937*
- One of the three commissioners is noted for his ability to bollix everything up after a big, bad night – which is almost every night.—Jack Lait and Lee Mortimer, *Washington Confidential*, p. 235, 1951
- Write to me. The mail gets bollixed up at Xmastime.—James Ellroy, *White Jazz*, p. 167, 1992

bollixing *adjective*
used as a negative intensifier *US*
- On top of everything else I got those bollixing poems.—Jim Thompson, *The Nothing Man*, p. 242, 1954

bollo *noun*
nonsense *UK*
A shortening of **BOLLOCKS**.
- 1981 was the [International] Year of the Disabled, which meant that in 1982 everybody was going to be all right. I thought that's a load of bollo[.]—Jim Dury [quoting Ian Dury, 1999], *Ian Dury and the Blockheads – Song by Song*, p. 130–131, 2003

bollock *noun*
1 a ball (a society dance) *UK*
A pun on **BALL(S)** (a testicle/testicles).
- [A]s in hunt bollock, charity bollock (even Caroline says this).—Ann Barr and Peter York, *The Official Sloane Ranger Handbook*, p. 158, 1982

2 a chronic failure, a mess *UK*
- I don't want another bollock. No fuck-ups.—Mark Powell, *Snap*, p. 91, 2001

bollock; ballock *verb*
to reprimand someone, to admonish someone, to scold someone *UK, 1938*
- I could hear Dave M bollocking Dave P.—Brian McDonald, *Elephant Boys*, p. 213, 2000
- They were sources of information to be bullied, cajoled, praised and bollocked as the occasion demanded.—Duncan MacLaughlin, *The Filth*, p. 196, 2002
- Like all females, they delightedly seized the chance of ballocking a man for being ill in the first place[.]—Jonathan Gash, *The Ten Word Game*, p. 257, 2003
- By a real stroke of bad luck my mum caught me smoking outside the local off-licence and I was grounded for a few days. We hadn't embraced the language of Neighbours and Buffy the Vampire Slayer then though. We called it getting bollocked.—Stuart Maconie, *Cider with Roadies*, p. 109, 2003

bollockache *noun*
an unnecessary or annoying cause of weariness *UK*
- [O]ne who has suffered the bollockache of public transport.—Ray Puxley, *Fresh Rabbit*, p. 110, 1998

bollockchops *noun*
a stupid person, an idiot; used as a ribald form of address *UK*
- Come here you, Bollockchops, said Billy. They roared [with laughter] What's happened your long throw, pal? Billy wanted to know. -My mother's cat could throw the fuckin' ball further than you did today.—Roddy Doyle, *The Van*, p. 25, 1991
- Oi, bollockchops. Yew gunner av a shot then or ar yew just gunner stand yer gawpin all fuckin day?—Niall Griffiths, *Sheepshagger*, p. 165, 2001

bollocking; ballocking *noun*
a telling-off, a scolding *UK, 1938*
From **BOLLOCK** (to reprimand, to scold).

bollocking *adjective*
used as an intensifier, especially in a negative context *UK*
- I get the subway map and spend bollocking hours taking the Z train all the way through Brooklyn[.]—John Williams, *Cardiff Dead*, p. 120, 2000
- He can't bollocking sing, can he? He said he could but he can't.—Stuart Maconie, *Cider with Roadies*, p. 119, 2003

bollockless *adjective*
cowardly, lacking in courage *UK*
A lack of **BOLLOCKS** (the testicles, hence 'manly' qualities).
- [L]ike a bollockless twat.—James Hawes, *Dead Long Enough*, p. 194, 2000

bollock naked *adjective*

totally naked *UK, 1922*

- Bollock naked with his socks still on? — Mike Hodges, *Get Carter*, p. 3, 1971
- It wasn't until I was a few hundred yards down the street that I realised what a ridiculous picture I must have looked, stark bollock naked with all my clothes tucked under my arm. — *Alvin Purple*, p. 67, 1974
- — Barry Humphries, *The Traveller's Tool*, p. 33, 1985
- But being spied on by a group of bollock-naked Chelsea Pensioners? — Kitty Churchill, *Thinking of England*, p. 203, 1995

bollocko *adjective*

naked *UK*

Abbreviated from **STARK BOLLOCK NAKED**.

- Paul, who's just been standing there bollocko, wanking himself off. — Kevin Sampson, *Outlaws*, p. 135, 2001
- Ianto was near fuckin bollocko wrapped in a blanket before a blazin fire. — Niall Griffiths, *Sheepshagger*, p. 93, 2001

bollocks; ballocks *noun*

1 the testicles *UK, 1744*

Rarely singular.

- I've got fuckin' massive bollocks. Let me show you how big my bollocks are. — Guy Ritchie et al., *Lock, Stock ... & Four Stolen Hooves*, p. 92, 2000
- He grabs at my bollocks. I try to get away[.] — John King, *Human Punk*, p. 81, 2000

2 nonsense *UK, 1919*

The 1977 album 'Never Mind The Bollocks Here's The Sex Pistols' brought 'bollocks' to shop windows across the UK. At the time there was outrage but a quarter of a century later the word is now commonplace.

- "Mmmm... a fruity little number with a surprising bite," like some kind of wine tasting-type bollocks. — Dave Courtney, *Raving Lunacy*, p. 10, 2000
- "That silver piece was made by the hand of one of the greatest -" "Ballocks, miss." — Jonathan Gash, *The Ten Word Game*, p. 115, 2003

3 anything considered to be the finest, the most excellent, the best *UK*

An abbreviated form of **DOG'S BOLLOCKS**; usually after 'the'.

- Vinoo was, and is, the absolute bollocks — Dave Courtney, *Raving Lunacy*, p. 10, 2000

4 nerve, courage *UK*

An international conceit: **BOLLOCKS** (testicles) and bravery are both symbols of masculinity, one must therefore equal the other.

- I saw him walking into the dead end of the estate. That took a lot of bollocks: he didn't know what he walking into. — Andy McNab, *Immediate Action*, p. 282, 1995
- [H]e shouts above the din, seemingly oblivious to the fact that World War III has broken out around him. He's got some bollocks[.] — Martin King and Martin Knight, *The Naughty Nineties*, p. 94, 1999
- I just think you need a bit more fire, you know? A bit of bollocks. — David Bowker, *The Joy of Sexism*, p. 46, 1999
- I reckon you're full of shit. Firebug Doug wouldn't have the bollocks. — Guy Ritchie et al., *Lock, Stock ... & Four Stolen Hooves*, p. 92, 2000

5 trouble, conflict *UK*

- D'you want to say something to myself? D'you want bollocks? Little cunt. — Kevin Sampson, *Outlaws*, p. 3, 2001

6 a despicable, contemptible person *UK*

- Ask that bollocks. — *Ultimate Force*, 25th June 2003

▷ **see:** DOG'S BOLLOCKS

▸ **do your bollocks**

1 to become enraged, to lose your temper *UK*

- [H]er fella found out she'd been redistributing his stock [...] he'd have done his bollocks. — Wayne Anthony, *Spanish Highs*, p. 170, 1999

2 to lose all your money gambling *UK*

- [T]hey must hold back $10 each to ensure they could get a cab back to Epsom should they do their bollocks. — Jimmy Stockin, *On The Cobbles*, p. 143, 2000

▸ **go to bollocks**

to be forgotten *UK*

- The teaching went to bollocks now. — Andy McNab, *Immediate Action*, p. 338, 1995

bollocks *adjective*

nonsensical *UK*

- Anything's got to be better than listening to his bollocks tale of drugs and shagging. — Kevin Williamson, *Heart of the Bass (Disco Biscuits)*, p. 113, 1996

bollocks!

used as an all purpose expletive *UK, 1969*

Figurative use of 'testicles'.

- Gerald stands up and begins to turn bright red. "Bollocks!" he says. "Bloody bollocks." — Ted Lewis, *Jack Carter's Law*, p. 16, 1974

bollocks

used rhetorically to register doubt and disbelief *UK*

- LEE: That'll keep you awake. MOON: Will it bollocks. — Chris Baker and Andrew Day, *Lock, Stock... & a Fist Full of Jack and Jills*, p. 190, 2000

bollocks about; ballocks about *verb*

to play the fool *UK, 1961*

bollocksed; ballocks'd *adjective*

1 ruined, thwarted *UK, 1961*

2 damned *UK*

- Babies be bollocksed. Nowadays it's a quick hand-shandy in a test-tube and you're out the door, mate. — *The Full Monty*, 1997

3 drunk *UK*

- — Pete Brown, *Man Walks into a Pub*, 2003

bollocks on *verb*

to talk nonsense *UK*

From **BOLLOCKS** (nonsense).

- All these years they'd been bollocksing on about hoow the IRA were just a bunch of nutters with no support. — John Williams, *Cardiff Dead*, p. 132, 2000

bollocky *adjective*

used as an intensifier *UK*

On the model of **BLOODY**.

- [T]he bollocky halls of residence[.]. — Jennifer Saunders, *Absolutely Fabulous*, p. 16, 1992

▷ **see:** BALLOCKY, BOLLICKY

bolloxed *adjective*

1 unwell *UK*

- I was feeling a bit unwell, and it looked like we hadn't started yet. I said to my mate, "I wish the law would hurry up and give us a raid because I'm absolutely bolloxed." — Lenny McLean, *The Guv'nor*, p. 65, 1998

2 drunk *US*

A variation of **BOLLOCKSED**.

- — *Rutgers Alumni Magazine*, p. 21, February 1986
- [M]angled caned w**nkered bolloxed[.] — Stuart Walton, *Out of It*, cover, 2001

boll weevil *noun*

1 in oil drilling, an inexperienced worker *US*

- — Jerry Robertson, *Oil Slanguage*, p. 29, 1954

2 a novice trucker *US*

- — Montie Tak, *Truck Talk*, p. 15, 1971

Bolly *nickname*

*Bolli*nger, a branded champagne *UK*

- Ab Fab made the Bolly-Stolly combo famous[.] — *Sky Magazine*, p. 88, May 2001

Bollywood *nickname*

the film industry in Bombay *INDIA*

- Indian film buffs are agreed that Bollywood – as the film industry is popularly known – is in the throes of a crisis. — *South Magazine*, p. 71, September 1989
- India's theaters are filled with the commercial froth of Bombay's huge movie studios, what they call Bollywood, which churn out saccharine and predictable stories of love and violence, all liberally lathered withsong and dance. — *New York Times*, p. 2-13, 16th February 1992
- Indians are passionate about films from Bollywood – as Bombay's version of Hollywood is known – and celebrities have participated in earlier elections. — Anjana Pasricha, *Voice of America Radio News*, 2nd April 2004

bolo *noun*

1 in boxing, an uppercut *US, 1950*

- Gavilan, a hustling bolo-swinger, fought in flurries and piled up an early lead on points. — *Time*, p. 91, 10th September 1951
- Kid Gavilan, whose famed bolo punches made him world welterweight champion in the 1950s, has arrived from his native Cuba to live in exile. — *San Francisco Examiner*, p. 47, 17th September 1968
- Kid Gavilan's 'Bolo Punch' Renamed ALI'S GHETTO WHOPPER [Headline] — *San Francisco Chronicle*, 16th May 1974

2 a directive to be on the look-out for something *US*

- I'm sorry, old man, but he cops put a BOLO out on the Caddy so I had Tommy get rid of the darn thing. —Carl Hiaasen, *Tourist Season*, p. 231, 1986
- Struggling frantically through traffic to get back behind the fleeing car, they radioed the dispatcher for what Fort Lauderdale police call a Bolo – "be on the lookout." —James Mills, *The Underground Empire*, p. 157, 1986

3 a friend *UK*
Described as a 'hippy term'.

- —David Powis, *The Signs of Crime*, 1977

4 a traveller to Antarctica who is jaded and exhausted from having been there too long *ANTARCTICA*

- —*Cool Antartica*, 2003: 'Antarctic slang'

5 crack cocaine *US*
Spanish.

- —US Department of Justice, *Street Terms*, October 1994

6 an unknown, sinister male *US*

- —Connie Eble (Editor), *UNC-CH Campus Slang*, p. 2, October 2002

bolo badge *noun*
a Purple Heart military decoration for battle wounds, especially those suffered in a foolish action *US, 1968*

- —*New York Newsday*, 14th February 1991
- —*American Speech*, p. 384, Winter 1991: 'among the new world'

bolohead *noun*
a bald person *US*

- —Douglas Simonson, *Pidgin to da Max*, 1981

bolo shot *noun*
in handball, any shot hit with the fist *US*

- —George J. Zafferano, *Handball Basics*, p. 169, 1977

bolshie; bolshy *noun*
a Bolshevik *US, 1919*

- —Joseph A. Weingarten, *An American Dictionary of Slang*, p. 36, 1954
- Her coverage of Iraqi weapons of mass destruction (WMDs) has been quite properly thumped by both CounterPunch Bolshie Alexander Cockburn and Slate's Jack Shafer[.] —*LA Weekly*, p. 14, 6th June 2003

bolshie; bolshy *adjective*
obstructive, unco-operative, deliberately difficult *UK, 1918*
From 'Bolshevik', but without political significance.

- [W]henever he got too bolshie they'd give him a tug. —Lanre Fehintola, *Charlie Says...*, p. 125, 2000

bolt *noun*

1 an escape, a flight *AUSTRALIA*

- —Lance Corporal Cobber, *The Anzac Pilgrim's Progress*, p. 53, 1915
- I'll do a bolt ter Sydney an' enlist there. —Barbara Baynton, *Trooper Jim Tasman*, p. 91, 1917
- I prove it by Randal's slavey, Millie Sanders, seeing old man Randall doing a bolt out of that piece's bedroom in his shirt[.] —Norman Lindsay, *Halfway to Anywhere*, p. 42, 1947
- He's gone tits up for about thirty million and taken the bolt, reckons the Japanese Mafia are going to kill him[.] —Harrison Biscuit, *The Search for Savage Henry*, p. 22, 1995

2 phencyclidine, the recreational drug known as PCP or angel dust *US, 1986*

- —J. E. Lighter, *Historical Dictionary of American Slang, Volume 1*, p. 223, 1994

3 a blemish; a pimple *US, 1969*

- —Richard Scholl, *Running Press Glossary of Baseball Language*, p. 17, 1977

bolt *verb*

1 to leave *US, 1845*

- —*USA Today*, 29th September 1983

2 to escape from prison or custody *UK, 1811*

- If he bolts, it's gunna be your fault, missy. —Kathy Lette, *Girls' Night Out*, p. 167, 1987

3 in poker, to withdraw from a hand *US*

- —George Percy, *The Language of Poker*, p. 11, 1988

bolter *noun*

1 a landing on an aircraft carrier in which the plane misses the arresting mechanisms *US*

- After the day's operations, pilots who have made sloppy approaches or too many bolters (missing the arresting gear) are sharply criticized by their squadron commanders. —*San Francisco Chronicle*, p. 7, 28th September 1958

2 an unexpected selection for a sports team, a board or political team *NEW ZEALAND*

- Several bolters making their way into the New Zealand XV from outside the two summer World Cup squads. —*Sunday Star-Times*, p. B1, 9th April 1995

3 in horse racing, a winning horse with long odds *AUSTRALIA*

- —Ned Wallish, *The Truth Dictionary of Racing Slang*, p. 8, 1989

bolts *noun*
a tattooed depiction of lightning bolts, symbolising a prisoner's association with a white pride prison gang *US*

- —James Harris, *A Convict's Dictionary*, 1989

bolts and jolts *noun*
a combination of central nervous system stimulants and depressants *US*

- Dr. Freireich's discovery was anticipated by bored Boradwayites, who had made a pastime of "bolts and jolts" – mixtures of barbiturates and Benzedrine which knock them for a loop, then slap them to. —*Time*, p. 67, 1st July 1946

bolts and nuts *adjective*
mentally unstable; crazy *US*

- —Inez Cardozo-Freeman, *The Joint*, p. 483, 1984

bomb *noun*

1 a great deal of money *UK, 1958*

- There are not many bent screws the reason being that most of them are to[o] honest or scared to do any traffic[k]ing, but the ones that do make a bomb. —Frank Norman, *Bang To Rights*, p. 64, 1958
- [He] had made a bomb out of most of them[.] —Derek Raymond (Robin Cook), *The Crust on its Uppers*, p. 30, 1962
- Now that you mention it, I don't know why I haven't sold this shirt. It's probably worth a bomb. —*Sydney Morning Herald*, 15th March 2003

2 a marijuana cigarette, especially a large one *US, 1951*

- By the way, boy, I am of course indulging in a perfect orgy of Miss Green & can hardly see straight right at this minute, whoo! 3 bombs a day. —Jack Kerouac, *Letter to Neal and Carolyn Cassady*, p. 358, 10th May 1952
- I paid 75 cents a stick, or a dollar for a bomb. A bomb is about as big as a Pall Mall and as fat as a Pall Mall. Like a regular cigarette. —Jeremy Larner and Rlaph Tetterteller, *The Addict in the Street*, p. 33, 1964
- When my buddy told me, we smoked around five bombs[.] —Bruce Jackson, *Get Your Ass in the Water and Swim Like Me*, p. 133, 1964
- —*Mr*, p. 8, April 1966: 'The hippie's lexicon'
- [T]ake a head of this Skunk / Twist up a big bomb of this serious dope / Smoke it down to the dub or roach tip[.] —Tone Loc, *Cheeba Cheeba*, 1989

3 high potency, relatively pure heroin *US, 1960*

- "You know," Curtis began, "if you say the stuff will take a five, then I put a four on it. That way, I always have the bomb." —Donald Goines, *Cry Revenge*, p. 107, 1974

4 crack cocaine *US*

- —US Department of Justice, *Street Terms*, October 1994

5 potent heroin *US, 1969*

- Lee here says he knows where to cop the bomb at. —Donald Goines, *Dopefiend*, p. 104, 1971

6 a dose of sedative, especially one administered to dope a racehorse; a sedative pill *AUSTRALIA, 1950*

- The doctor gave me these bombs that kept me asleep nearly twenty-four hours a day. —Robert G. Barrett, *Davo's Little Something*, p. 136, 1992

7 in horse race, a winning horse that ran with very high odds *US*

8 a forceful blow with the fist *US*

- From Challenge Jake La Motta's corner, he heard the entreaties of La Motta's handlers above the buzz of 22,183 spectators: "'At's it, Jackson. 'Atta go, Jackson ... put the bomb in." —*Time*, p. 53, 27th June 1949
- Johnny Summerlin planned today to "stay out of the way of the bombs" and let youth carry him to victory tonight. —*San Francisco News*, p. 27, 20th June 1956
- Moore moved quickly and threw another overhand bomb flush to the chin. —*San Francisco Chronicle*, p. 39, 9th April 1961
- Rush Bomb Decks Johnson [Headline] —*San Francisco Examiner*, p. 47, 22nd February 1967

9 in tiddlywinks, a long-distance shot *US*

- —*Verbatim*, p. 525, December 1977

10 a skateboarding manoeuvre in which the rider crouches and holds the sides of the board as the board leaves the ground *US*

- —Laura Torbet, *The Complete Book of Skateboarding*, p. 105, 1976

11 a fast car *US, 1953*
Teen slang.

- —*American Weekly*, p. 2, 14th August 1955

12 a dilapidated motor vehicle *AUSTRALIA, 1950*
- It's a wonder you haven't got a defect notice for that old bomb of yours. —Alexander Buzo, *Rooted*, p. 44, 1969
- Good lord. Is that your bomb outside? —Barry Oakley, *A Salute to the Great McCarthy*, p. 154, 1970
- —Frank Hardy, *The Outcasts of Foolgarah*, p. 62, 1971
- —Peter Corris, *Make Me Rich*, p. 152, 1985

13 an improvised water-heating device in prison *NEW ZEALAND*
- Every night Junk used to pull out his water-boiling gadget, called a tea bomb, and make up a brew of illegal tea or Milo. —Greg Newbold, *The Big Huey*, p. 77, 1982

14 a dismal failure, especially in show business *US, 1952*
- The 10 biggest bombs [Headline] — *San Francisco Examiner and Chronicle, Sunday Scene*, p. 12, 13th January 1974
- The title of the book was How to Talk Dirty and Influence People, and, oddly enough, it was a bomb. —Mort Sahl, *Heartland*, p. 25, 1976

15 an unexpected bass drum accent *US*
- He taught me how to turn on what the kids now call "dropping bombs." —Nat Shapiro and Nat Hentoff, *Hear Me Talkin to Ya*, p. 289, 1955
- He [Kenny Clarke] uses his bass drum, but only to "drop an occasional bomb," that is, he "boots" the soloist forward with an infrequent and unerringly timed explosion. —Hugh Panassie and Madeline Gautier, *Guide to Jazz*, p. 41, 1956
- Hassan dropped bombs, flailed tom-toms, rapped the snare, stirred his cymbals. —Ross Russell, *The Sound*, p. 32, 1961

▸ go like a bomb; go down a bomb
to be very successful and exciting *UK*
- Seeing the world and brushing up my Arabic [...] Oh, it all went like a bomb. —Mary Stewart, *The Gabriel Hounds*, 1967

▸ make a bomb
to become rich, to make a large profit *UK*
From **BOMB** (a great deal of money).
- —Frank Norman, *Bang to Rights*, 1958
- They worked hard, played hard, made a bomb. — *The Observer*, 14th July 2002

▸ the bomb; da bomb
the very best, something that is very good *US*
- The crescent was the bomb. —A.S. Jackson, *Gentleman Pimp*, p. 13, 1973
- Smoking a spliff of high-octaine chronic (street talk for pot) in the back room, he explains his bond to Dre. "He's the bomb," says Snoop. — *People*, p. 77, 23rd May 1994
- It's the bomb! — *Clueless*, 1995
- —Connie Eble (Editor), *UNC-CH Campus Slang*, p. 1, Fall 1995
- I just did a movie about teen moeling with Todd and Griffin Tyler. Itt's the bomb. —Francesca Lia Block, *I Was a Teenage Fairy*, p. 72, 1998
- Yeah, I'm not too big a fan either. Though Affleck was the bomb in Phantoms. —Kevin Smith, *Jay and Silent Bob Strike Back*, p. 19, 2001
- [Fred Durst] is, after all, the man who appeared in infamous rock porn vid Backstage Sluts [...] opening a tired-looking groupie's labia and declaring it "the bomb". — *Loaded*, p. 63, June 2003

bomb *verb*

1 to place graffiti with an emphasis on quantity, not quality *US*
- [A]erosol artists find a place to bomb in peace[.] — *The Source*, April 2000
- When I started off I was like that-bombing everything, windows, whatever, you name it. But what is the point? Two weeks from now 8 other guys are going to go over it with the same color. —Alroy *Cultural Identity and Identity Performance among Latin American Youths in Toronto*, p. 122, 2001
- "Bombing," trying to put your name up in as many challenging and highly visible places as possible, was how a graffiti writer maintained his reputation among peers. — *Plain Dealer (Cleveland, Ohio)*, p. L1, 29th July 2001
- Graffiti artists don't work. They bomb. And graffiti artist Banksy is one of the most explosive in the graf-writing squadron. — *The Face*, p. 146, June 2001

2 to swallow a quantity of a powdered drug and its cigarette-paper wrapping *UK*
- Christ, ee bombed abaht a gram av crystal meth yesterday, ee'l be aht av it fa days[.] —Niall Griffiths, *Grits*, p. 51, 2000

3 in horse-racing, to dope a horse *AUSTRALIA*
- —Sydney J. Baker, *Australia Speaks*, 1953

4 to run or drive at speed *UK*
- [Y]ou're bombing down the road. —Paul E Willis, *Profane Culture*, p. 73, 1978

5 in mountain biking, to travel fast downhill *US*
- —William Nealy, *Mountain Bike!*, p. 160, 1992

6 to train intensely, alternating heavy weights with light weights *US*
- — *American Speech*, p. 198, Fall 1984: 'The language of bodybuilding'

7 in tiddlywinks, to play a wink at a pile of winks with destructive intent *UK*
- —C.W. Edwards, *Glossary*, 1980

8 to fail dramatically; to flop *US, 1958*
Originally theatrical.
- "They bomb and I serve their time," was Lenny's view of the situation. —Albert Goldman, *Freak Show*, p. 211, 1968
- "Are you saying we're the Dambusters of the movie world?" [...] "Your films always bomb and your cheques always bounce." —Stewart Home, *Sex Kick [britpulp]*, p. 245, 1999

9 in computing, to cease to function completely and suddenly *US*
- Don't run Empire with less than 32K stack, it'll bomb. —Eric S. Raymond, *The New Hacker's Dictionary*, p. 73, 1991

▸ get bombed
to be overcome by a wave while surfing *US*
- —Duke Kahanamoku with Joe Brennan, *Duke Kahanamoku's World of Surfing*, p. 172, 1965

bomb *adjective*
dilapidated *AUSTRALIA*
- For instance, if some old bomb shack is in the road of progress, stick the dozer in. —Sam Weller, *Old Bastards I Have Met*, p. 36, 1979

bomba *noun*
a vintage car that has been restored *US*
- —Steven Daly and Nalthaniel Wice, *alt.culture*, p. 138, 1995

Bombay bloomers *noun*
baggy, loose-fitting shorts *US*
- —Sonya Plowman, *Great Kiwi Slang*, p. 32, 2002

Bombay Welsh *noun*
English as spoken by Indians and Anglo-Indians *UK, 1984*
From the similarity in lilting cadences of speech between the broadest Indian and Welsh accents. It is interesting to note that an English person attempting a Welsh accent often sounds Indian, particularly to Welsh ears. Remembered by Beale as of military origins in the 1940s and thought to be obsolete by the late 1970s.

bomb doors *noun*
the vagina *UK*
- The female genitalia were represented as places from which people/things never return (e.g., the Bermuda triangle) or get sucked into (e.g., the black hole, electrolux), hidden dangers (e.g., squirrel trap), and warnings of danger (e.g., hairy growler, bomb doors). — *Journal of Sex Research*, p. 146, 2001

bombed *adjective*
extremely drunk or drug-intoxicated *US, 1956*
- With each week of work, bombed and sapped and charged and stoned with lush, with pot, with benny[.] —Norman Mailer, *Advertisements for Myself*, p. 243, 1955
- Last weekend the men got so bombed they couldn't make the stairs. [Letter to Ann Landers] — *San Francisco Examiner*, p. 24, 27th May 1966
- Beam's Choice Is Too Good To Get "Bombed" On [Advertisement] — *San Francisco Examiner*, p. 57, 10th November 1967
- —Collin Baker et al., *College Undergraduate Slang Study Conducted at Brown University*, p. 84, 1968
- She gets totally bombed anyway, but having him around makes it worse. —Bret Easton Ellis, *Less Than Zero*, p. 16, 1985
- Afterward Bellamy and his pals got bombad and sneaked out to the Place Pigalle to watch a 325-pound woman do a strip-tease —Cart Miassen, *Tourist Season*, 1986
- —Angela Devlin, *Prison Patter*, p. 30, 1996
- [T]rolleyed, mullered, bombed[.] —Stuart Walton, *Out of It*, cover, 2001

bombed out *adjective*

1 extremely marijuana-intoxicated *US*
- We were only on our first joints and everyone in the room showed visible signs of being bombed out. —Wayne Anthony, *Spanish Highs*, p. 111, 1999

2 crazy *UK*
- —Nigel Foster, *The Making of a Royal Marine Commando*, 1987

3 (of a motor) worn out *UK*
The result when a car is made to **BOMB** (to drive flat-out) too often.
- Can still hear his bombed-out fucking engine now[.] —Kevin Sampson, *Outlaws*, p. 275, 2001

bomber *noun*

1 a graffiti artist *US*
- —Jim Crotty, *How to Talk American*, p. 140, 1997
- [Pat DeLillo] created a safe haven for the same young bombers he once pursued. — *The Source*, p. 86, March 2002

2 an extra large, thick or potent marijuana cigarette *US*
Named as an allusion to size and shape.
- I was only carrying the bombers. The bombers are big. They're just like regular cigarettes, the same size[.] —Hal Ellson, *Duke*, p. 3, 1949
- I felt its size. It was king-sized, a bomber. —Piri Thomas, *Down These Mean Streets*, p. 58, 1967
- —*Current Slang*, p. 11, Fall 1968
- I'm gonna roll you up a bomber. —Iceberg Slim (Robert Beck), *Pimp*, p. 181, 1969
- [T]here's a eight-year-old kid in there twisting up hash-bombers big as cigars. —Terry Southern, *Blue Movie*, p. 149, 1970
- [I]t was an ace bomber of absolutely atomic North African marihooch[.] —Lester Bangs, *Psychotic Reactions and Carburetor Dung*, p. 80, 1971
- —Simon Worman, *Joint Smoking Rules*, 2001
- —Mike Haskins, *Drugs*, p. 286, 2003

3 a tablet or capsule of amphetamine or barbiturate, hence a generic name for amphetamine or barbiturate in any form *US, 1950*
- —Jay Robert Nash, *Dictionary of Crime*, p. 39, 1992

4 a hard-hitting, aggressive boxer *US, 1937*
- —J. E. Lighter, *Historical Dictionary of American Slang, Volume 1*, p. 226, 1994

5 a powerful, hard-breaking wave *US*
- —John Severson, *Modern Surfing Around the World*, p. 165, 1964

6 an old, battered car, especially one used in a demolition derby contest *US*
- They're running modifieds, late models, bombers, and the front-and-back demotion derby. —*San Francisco Chronicle (from the New York Times)*, p. 70, 2nd September 1977
- Take a '63 Ford Fairlane, rip out the torn upholstery, weld in a roll cage, paint a number on its dented sides and what do yo have? A bomber. —*San Francisco Examinaer and Chronicle*, p. 6, 1st July 1979

7 a person with poor fashion sense *US*
- —Anna Scotti and Paul Young, *Buzzwords*, p. 15, 1997

8 a sixteen ton oil carrying wagon *UK*
- —Frank McKenna, *A Glossary of Railwaymen's Talk*, 1970

▷ see: BLACK BOMBER

bomb farm *noun*
an area on a military base where bombs are stored *US*
- He made his way through the "Bomb Farm," the area were the weapons readied for loading were kept handy. —Gerry Carroll, *North S*A*R*, p. 172, 1991

bomb-happy *adjective*
with nerves gone through exposure to bombing *UK, 1944*

bombida *noun*
a mixture of heroin and cocaine *US, 1975*
From the Spanish, literal translation 'little bomb'.
- "I need you to fire a bombida, Rooski," Joe said softly. —Seth Morgan, *Homeboy*, p. 77, 1990

bombido *noun*
1 injectable Benzedrine™ (amphetamine sulphate), a central nervous system stimulant *US*
- —Ralph de Sola, *Crime Dictionary*, p. 18, 1982

2 heroin *UK*
- —Robert Ashton, *This Is Heroin*, p. 205, 2002
- —Mike Haskins, *Drugs*, p. 283, 2003

bombie; bommie *noun*
a hazardous submerged off-shore reef over which waves break *AUSTRALIA, 1949*
From *bombora*, from an Australian Aboriginal language.

bombilla *noun*
an ampoule filled with a drug *US*
- "Absolutely!" he said emphatically and opened the second refrigerator, which was filled to overflowing with row upon row of small bombillas (glass ampules) filled with methedrine[.] —Peter Coyote, *Sleeping Where I Fall*, p. 162, 1998

bombing *adjective*
in foot-propelled scootering, at great speed *UK*
- —Ben Sharpe, *Scooter Crazy*, p. 39, 2000

bombita; bombito *noun*
a tablet of amphetamine sulphate (Dexedrine™), a central nervous system stimulant *US*
- —Donald Louria, *Nightmare Drugs*, p. 28, 1966
- He was on amphetamines, stimulants, and had been shooting bombitas, small glass ampules of a drug called Desoxyn. —James Mills, *The Panic in Needle Park*, p. 34, 1966
- One outstanding defensive back was officially known as the Gulper. He would stand there swallowing a gaudy assortment of bombitos. —*San Francisco Examiner*, p. 46, 30th March 1970

bomb line *noun*
during the Korean war, the line beyond which bombing was deemed safe *US*
- Jim called back, past "the bomb line," the arbitrary division beyond which it was safe to bomb with assurance of not hitting any United Nations patrol. —Steven L. Thompson, *The Wild Blue*, p. 137, 1986

bombo *noun*
cheap and poor quality wine or stronger alcoholic drink *AUSTRALIA, 1942*
- They might have a stoush over cards if they've been stuck into the bombo. —Robert S. Close, *With Hooves of Brass*, p. 16, 1961

bomboara *noun*
a large wave that breaks seaward of the normal surf line *AUSTRALIA*
- —Peter L. Dixon, *The Complete Book of Surfing*, p. 212, 1965

bombosity *noun*
the buttocks *US, 1932*
- —Frederic G. Cassidy, *Dictionary of American Regional English, Volume 1*, p. 327, 1985

bomb-out *noun*
in competitive surfing, early elimination *US*
- —Brian and Margaret Lowdon, *Competitive Surfing*, 1988

bomb out *verb*
1 to fail to appear as expected *UK*
- "I gather [the minister]'s bombed out." "Not at all [...] The Cabinet's simply not over yet." —*Sunday Times*, 9th December 1979

2 to reject someone *UK, 1985*
- SECOND GIRL. (To First Girl.) No, don't bomb them out yet. The waiters might be pigs. —Ian Pattison, *Rab C. Nesbitt*, 1988

3 to knock a surfer off a surfboard *US*
- —John Severson, *Modern Surfing Around the World*, p. 165, 1964

bomb-proof *adjective*
having an impregnable excuse to avoid selection or responsibility for a (unpleasant) task; invulnerable *UK, 1984*
Military use; remembered as 1950s, but possibly earlier.

bombs *noun*
the female breasts *US*
- —Collin Baker et al., *College Undergraduate Slang Study Conducted at Brown University*, p. 85, 1968

bombs away *noun*
heroin *UK*
- —Robert Ashton, *This Is Heroin*, p. 205, 2002
- [S]lang [names for heroin] draws on words associated with death [...] or its methods ("bombs away"). —Robert Ashton, *This Is Heroin*, p. 55, 2002
- —Mike Haskins, *Drugs*, p. 283, 2003

bombshell *noun*
1 a sudden or great surprise *UK, 1860*
Often in the phrase 'drop a bombshell'.
- A bombshell, then oblivion for Alun Michael [...] In a stunning move he formally submitted his resignation to the assembly's presiding officer Dafydd Elis Thomas[.] —*The Guardian*, 10th February 2000

2 a woman who is astonishingly attractive *US, 1933*
- Kaye Stratford, "The Blond Bombshell," an international favorite, in person 3 shows nitely at Spanish Village, 54 Mason, near Market. —*San Francisco Call-Bulletin*, p. 21, 10th April 1951
- Italian Bombshell Silvana Mangano Jolts America [Headline] —*Quick Magazine*, p. 55, 13th November 1951
- I never know what she is trying to be, except noisy. Miss Tanguay is billed as a "bombshell." —*San Francisco Call-Bulletin*, p. 11, 9th January 1956

bomb up *verb*
while hunting, to fire a flurry of loosely aimed shots at a herd *NEW ZEALAND, 1984*
- —Harry Orsman, *A Dictionary of Modern New Zealand Slang*, p. 16, 1999

Bom-de-Bom *noun*
Ba Muoi Ba beer, a staple in Saigon during the Vietnam war *US*
- Nobody in Maverick's platoon could pronounce the name, so they just called it Bom-de-Bom. —Dennis J. Marvicsin and Jerold A. Greenfield, *Maverick*, p. 45, 1990

bomfog *noun*
dense and verbose language *US, 1965*
When Governor Nelson Rockefeller campaigned for the Republican nomination for president in 1964, he tended to end speeches with a reference to the 'brotherhood of man under the fatherhood of God', a phrase which compacts into the acronym BOMFOG. Reporters covering the campaign began to refer to the end of his speeches as BOMFOG. The term survived and eventually took on a more general, less flattering meaning.
- "Do you remember Nelson Rockefeller's 'bomfog?'" asked the American. — *New York Times*, p. 1-1, 9th June 1984
- BOMFOG has now acquired a meaning along the lines of highfalutin verbiage. — *Time*, 26th April 1999

bommie *noun*
a huge wave *AUSTRALIA*
An abbreviation of *bombara*, from an Australian Aboriginal language.
- — Trevor Cralle, *The Surfin'ary*, p. 13, 1991

▷ **see: BOMBIE**

bona; bonar *adjective*
good, pleasant, agreeable *UK, 1875*
Theatrical origins from Latin *bonum* and Italian *buono* (good).
- Met 2 marines – very charming. Bonar Shamshes [good looking men]. — *Kenneth Williams' Diary*, 24th October 1947
- We had had a few "burster" houses lately and he thought the "bunce" must be "bona"[.] — Butch Reynolds, *Broken Hearted Clown*, p. 29, 1953
- Yes, we've got some bona curtain material. — Marty Feldman and Barry Took, *Round the Horne*, 1965–8
- — Morrissey, *Bona Drag*, 1990

bonafide *noun*
the significant other in your emotional life *UK*
Latin for 'good faith'. Black usage.
- As far as he was concerned, Lalah was now his "bonafide". — Karline Smith, *Moss Side Massive*, p. 6, 1994

bonaroo *adjective*
▷ **see: BONNEROO**

bona vardering *adjective*
attractive *UK*
A combination of 'bona' (good) and 'varda' (to look) thus 'good looking'.
- Shame really, as she's quite bona vardering[.] — James Gardiner, *Who's a Pretty Boy Then?*, p. 123, 1997
- — Paul Baker, *Polari*, p. 166, 2002

bonce *noun*
the head *UK, 1889*
Originally adopted by schoolboys from the name given to a large marble, in a jocular reference to the shape.
- [I]t was good to feel the sun on the back of my bonce again. — Kevin Sampson, *Outlaws*, p. 3-4, 2001
- [A] spark of curiosity is ignited in my bonce. — Danny King, *The Burglar Diaries*, p. 185, 2001

bondage *noun*
indebtedness *US*
- — Lou Shelly, *Hepcats JiveTalk Dictionary*, p. 7, 1945

bondage pie *noun*
a pizza with sausage and mushroom topping *US*
The initials of the toppings – S and M – suggest bondage as a recreational sport.
- — *Maledicta*, p. 8, 1996: 'Domino's pizza jargon'

Bondi cigar *noun*
in Sydney, a piece of excrement floating in the surf *AUSTRALIA, 1996*
So-named from the notoriety of a sewerage outlet near Bondi beach.
- Don't surf at the point there are Bondi cigars everywhere. — *Wordmap (www.abc.net.au/wordmap)*, 2003

Bondi tram; Bondi bus *noun*
used as an example of something that moves quickly *AUSTRALIA, 1959*
According to Sydney J. Baker, writing in 1966, the actual tram went out of business in 1960.

Bondo mechanic *noun*
a body shop worker who relies too heavily upon large amounts of body putty and too little upon finesse or craft *U*
- — Lewis Poteet, *Car & Motorcyle Slang*, p. 35, 1992

bondook *noun*
a weapon *UK*
Gulf war usage.
- — *American Speech*, p. 385, Winter 1991: 'Among the new words'

bone *noun*

1 the penis, especially when erect *US, 1916*
- "Why, if you mean do I think I could get a bone up over that old buzzard, no, I don't believe I could..." — Ken Kesey, *One Flew Over the Cuckoo's Nest*, p. 69, 1962
- And when you fall down on your good gal and lower your bone / you got to make that pussy call your dick "Bad Mr. Al Capone." — Bruce Jackson, *Get Your Ass in the Water and Swim Like Me*, p. 135, 1964
- Torn or nicked cocks are common casualties as one endeavors to stuff a full bone into his pants and zip up. — John Francis Hunter, *The Gay Insider*, p. 191, 1971
- Let her suck me up good, till I've got a fresh bone / And then I'll come in like the sword in the stone. — *Screw*, p. 7, 15th May 1972
- Every time she'd move her big ass, my bone would ache and throb. — A.S. Jackson, *Gentleman Pimp*, p. 15, 1973
- Jessica Wylde is excellent as the chorus girl with a heart of gold, a head for business, and a body for balling, which she uses on financial backers when not getting the bone from Bert. — *Adult Video*, p. 80, August/September 1986

2 the active participant in homosexual sex *US*
- — AFSCME Local 3963, *The Correctional Officer's Guide to Prison Slang*, 2001

3 the middle finger raised in a gesture meaning, roughly, 'fuck you!' *US*
- [A]ll Jeff did was flip the bone at his old man which is a very dirty way of telling somebody where to get off. — Frederick Kohner, *Gidget*, p. 48, 1957
- — Collin Baker et al., *College Undergraduate Slang Study Conducted at Brown University*, p. 85, 1968
- — Eugene Landy, *The Underground Dictionary*, p. 38, 1971

4 a marijuana cigarette; hence, marijuana *US, 1978*
A visual pun.
- — Richard A. Spears, *The Slang and Jargon of Drugs and Drink*, p. 62, 1986
- Take a big bone hit/Cause after tha bud, My rhymes start flowin — Tone Loc, *Cheeba cheeba*, 1989
- I used to go out wid him, but he's a e-dyat [idiot] man, smokes too much bone. — Courttia Newland, *Society Within*, p. 13, 1999
- — Mike Haskins, *Drugs*, p. 286, 2003

5 a tobacco cigarette *US*
A visual pun.
- — Jay Robert Nash, *Dictionary of Crime*, p. 39, 1992

6 a measurement of crack cocaine sold for $50 dollars *US*
- We got Rocks, we got Bones, we got Brown, we got Stones. — Julian Johnson, *Urban Survival*, p. 170, 2003

7 heroin *US*
- — Peter Johnson, *Dictionary of Street Alcohol and Drug Terms*, p. 25, 1993

8 a dollar *US, 1889*
- Man, I had twelve bones on two twenty-seven and two thirty-seven came out. — Chester Himes, *A Rage in Harlem*, p. 48, 1957
- I never heard of anybody offering a twenty-bone bounty for bagging a ball-cutter. — Ken Kesey, *One Flew Over the Cuckoo's Nest*, p. 69, 1962
- "I'll give you five dollars for it," Mr. Goodman said. "Five bones!" Uncle Bud exclaimed indignantly. — Chester Himes, *Cotton Comes to Harlem*, p. 64, 1965
- I sent you two dollars of it, but don't spend it fast / 'cause those two bones will be your first and last. — Dennis Wepman et al., *The Life*, p. 141, 1976
- Gimme twenty bones for both of 'em and take 'em on home! — Odie Hawkins, *Chicago Hustle*, p. 85, 1977
- — Connie Eble (Editor), *UNC-CH Campus Slang*, p. 1, Fall 1996
- Thousand, yes, bones or clams or whatever you call them. — *The Big Lebowski*, 1998

9 one thousand dollars *US*
- They lend you a thousand and call it a bone. — Robert Campbell, *Juice*, p. 20, 1988

10 a trombone *US, 1918*
- Ross frequently lays aside his "bone" to take over the mike as Benny's vocalist. — *The Capitol*, p. 6, July 1946
- Many of the performers belonged to a San Francisco trombone choir called the Bay Bones. — *Time*, p. 73, 5th March 1979

11 an irritation; an annoyance; an aggravation *US, 1944*
A figurative extension of a 'bone in the throat'.

- Three Feet angrily sweeps some glasses off the bar crashing them noisily to the floor. The bar falls silent. The barman saunters back to Three Feet. BARMAN (CONT'D) Tut. T'ain't no need for dat bone, man. — Bernard Dempsey and Kevin McNally, *Lock, Stock ... & Two Hundred Smoking Kalashnikovs*, p. 112, 2000

12 a domino *US, 1959*
Usually in the plural.
- Joe played dominoes with Smoothbore and Clovis. The thwacking of the bones punctuated desultory conversation. — Seth Morgan, *Homeboy*, p. 90, 1990

13 in private poker games or other private gambling, a white betting chip *US, 1866*
- — George Percy, *The Language of Poker*, p. 12, 1988

14 a black person *US*
- — William K. Bentley and James M. Corbett, *Prison Slang*, p. 54, 1992

15 in baseball, an error in judgment *US, 1915*
An abbreviation of 'bonehead play' or **BONER**.
- — Parke Cummings, *Dictionary of Baseball*, p. 9, 1950

bone *verb*

1 to have sex from the male point of view *US, 1971*
- You kin change the engine on your bike, you kin paint the kitchen, you kin bone your old lady twice. — Joseph Wambaugh, *The Secrets of Harry Bright*, p. 191, 1985
- It's a lot more interesting than just flinging off your clothes and boning away on the neighbor's swing set. — *Heathers*, 1988
- — Connie Eble (Editor), *UNC-CH Campus Slang*, p. 1, Fall 1989
- CLARK: It's definitely not making love! BLEEK: Boning! CLARK: You've been a lot more imaginative. — *Mo' Better Blues*, 1990
- That's bullshit, they all wanna bone, its human, they just don't like admitting it to nobody except they girlfriends and all. — *Boyz N The Hood*, 1990
- That girl you boned last year. Remember? — *Kids*, 1995
- Been bonin' the bitch three years man: she knows the score[.] — Nick Barlay, *Curvy Lovebox*, p. 54, 1997
- When we bone these gutter-sluts [...] we don't respect them or even think of them as proper people with mums and dads and feelings and shit. — Colin Butts, *Is Harry Still on the Boat?*, p. 257, 2003
- [H]ow in God's name did he manage to bone so many women? — *X-Ray*, August 2003

2 to interrogate a suspect *UK*
Police and criminal use; probably from earlier sense (to seize, to arrest).
- — *Bournemouth Evening Echo*, 20th April 1966

3 in mountain biking, to strike the nose of your seat with your buttocks *US*
- — William Nealy, *Mountain Bike!*, p. 160, 1992: 'Bikespeak'

4 to study intensely *US, 1859*
- I was back at State again, boning for my finals[.] — Chester Himes, *Cast the First Stone*, p. 55, 1952

bone *adjective*

tasteless, unfortunate, inferior *UK*
- I threw myself into all the bone bravado[.] — Andy McNab, *Immediate Action*, p. 46, 1995
- — Jim Crotty, *How to Talk American*, p. 352, 1997

bone banger; bone crusher *noun*

an orthopaedist *US*
- — Sally Williams, *"Strong" Words*, p. 135, 1994

bone blanket; bone bonnet *noun*

a condom *UK*
Contrived to wrap the **BONE** (an erection).
- — David Rowan, *A Glossary for the 90s*, 1998

bone box *noun*

the mouth *CANADA*
Teen slang, reported by a Toronto newspaper in 1946, and reported as 'obsolescent or obsolete' by Douglas Leechman, 1959.

bonecrusher *noun*

1 in trucking, a truck that rides very roughly *US*
- — Montie Tak, *Truck Talk: The Language of the Open Road*, p. 16, 1971

2 crack cocaine *UK, 1998*
- — Mike Haskins, *Drugs*, p. 281, 2003

bonecrushers *noun*

the very painful symptoms of withdrawl from drug addiction *US*
- I've held off the bonecrushers two days, rationing that stuff up my nose – horned the last just an hour ago. — Seth Morgan, *Homeboy*, p. 49, 1990

boned *adjective*

1 tipsy *UK*
- — Mary Fitt, *The Banquet Ceases*, 1949

2 having been hit hard on the head *UK*
- — David Powis, *The Signs of Crime*, 1977

bone dance *noun*

sex *US*
- — Connie Eble (Editor), *UNC-CH Campus Slang*, p. 2, Fall 1988

bone dome *noun*

a protective helmet; a crash helmet *UK*
Originally aviators' usage (1930s), subsequently used by motorcyclists (1950s) and cyclists (1980s).
- Where is de rave? says Marcello takin' off his dayglo green bone dome. — Nick Barlay, *Curvy Lovebox*, p. 141, 1997

bonehead *noun*

1 an idiot *US, 1908*
- I don't know which bonehead dreamed up this business of splitting up teams that have been working together for years. — Robert Campbell, *Juice*, p. 216, 1988
- Look a' them muggy boneheads. — Nick Barlay, *Curvy Lovebox*, p. 51, 1997

2 a bald headed person; a skinhead; hence an extreme skinhead haircut *UK*
- East End skinheads – mods call them "boneheads" – coming down [to Brighton][.] — *New Society*, 3rd September 1981
- — Jim Crotty, *How to Talk American*, p. 144, 1997
- [T]he whole of the Shed [a stand at Chelsea FC's Stamford Bridge ground] is moon-stomping. Boneheads, number one clipper shorn, some with shaved in parting. — Jake Arnott, *He Kills Coppers*, p. 214, 2001

bone hog *noun*

a sexually active female, especially one who enjoys performing oral sex on men *US*
- — Chris Lewis, *The Dictionary of Playground Slang*, p. 39, 2003

bone-on *noun*

an erection *US, 1927*
- I swear to Christ, B., I never got such a terrific bone-on in my life! Like a fucking rock[.] — Terry Southern, *Blue Movie*, p. 206, 1970
- I got a bone-on would slow a racehorse on a hard track. — Bill Casselman, *Canadian Sayings*, p. 109, 2002

bone orchard *noun*

a cemetery *UK*
- I hang around dying to be tortured / You'll never be alone in the bone orchard. — Elvis Costello, *Beyond Belief*, 1982

bone out *verb*

1 to back down from a confrontation; to run away from danger *US*
- — *People Magazine*, p. 72, 19th July 1993
- — Bill Valentine, *Gang Intelligence Manual*, p. 75, 1995

2 to leave quickly *US*
- I know if I had some money I'd bone the fuck out. — *Menace II Society*, 1993
- Blood, I can't go back to the Valley. I snatched the blood up out of the car and I pulled out the strap on him, and when I busted, I just jumped in the —— and boned out. — *Los Angeles Times*, p. B5, 10th September 1994

3 while snowboarding, to hold your leg straight during a manoeuvre in the air *US*
- — Elena Garcia, *A Beginner's Guide to Zen and the Art of Snowboarding*, p. 121, 1990

bone queen *noun*

a male homosexual who favours performing oral sex *US*
- — Roger Blake, *The American Dictionary of Sexual Terms*, p. 21, 1964

boner *noun*

1 a blunder *US, 1912*
- Right here is where we pulled a boner. I didn't know at the time I was being followed, but my leaving the bandstand out of a clear sky and taking Frank's car called for a tail. — Mezz Mezzrow, *Really the Blues*, p. 66, 1946
- Merkle's "boner" wasn't baseball's dumbest. — *San Francisco Examiner*, 1st May 1947

- A mental lapse by Detroit Catcher Aaaron Robinson, which goes into the books as one of baseball's costliest boners, gave the Cleveland Indians a breahtaking 2–1 victory over the Tigers today. — *San Francisco Examiner*, 25th September 1950
- He had a pretty good idea that he'd pulled a boner. — Jim Thompson, *Savage Night*, p. 61, 1953
- Like every Secretary of State since the war, John Foster Dulles has pulled some loverly boners. — *New York Times*, p. 10, 15th January 1956
- As for Japhy he was quite pleased with anything I did provided I didn't pull any boners like making the kerosene lamp smoke from turning the wick too far up[.] — Jack Kerouac, *The Dharma Bums*, p. 147, 1958
- This, indeed, is a spectacular boner, an irreversible boo-boo, a typical San Franciscan slow-motion scandal. — *San Francisco Examiner*, p. 37, 7th February 1966
- "Now remember you get a roust out here, crack my name. Don't repeat your boner." — Iceberg Slim (Robert Beck), *Pimp*, p. 192, 1969

2 an erection *US*

The supposed bone-like quality of an erect penis, with which you **BONE** (have sex).

- The little dog used to raise a boner every time it walked into a room where Rickie was present[.] — Clancy Sigal, *Going Away*, p. 68, 1961
- In the classroom I sometimes set myself consciously to thinking about DEATH and HOSPITALS and HORRIBLE AUTOMOBILE ACCIDENTS in the hope that such grave thoughts will cause my "boner" to recede before the bell rings and I have to stand. — Philip Roth, *Portnoy's Complaint*, p. 200, 1969
- I graduated into the "talking mood" – a group of neighborhood kids who met behind the garage to tell the same warn-out dirty jokes and recount when they (the boys) had last had a "boner." — Jefferson Poland and Valerie Alison, *The Records of the San Francisco Sexual Freedom League*, p. 111, 1971
- Don't like to look like I'm hustling, and there I am, sitting next to you with a boner. — *Diner*, 1982
- The oral action by Tash Voux (not only sucking, but also her raspy, sexy voice) and Susan Nero (who really puts a boner in your pocket) is well worth the price of admission. — *Adult Video*, p. 13, August/September 1986
- ORGY! I already had a boner. — Howard Stern, *Miss America*, p. 7, 1995
- You can get a boner, I bet. I know you can. — *Boogie Nights*, 1997
- [D]eep inside of me still burned the soul of a stupid and simple girl, who wanted nothing more out of life than to induce in every man she met a good hard boner. — Rita Ciresi, *Pink Slip*, p. 12, 1999
- Vinnie looked down. "Jesus," he said, "I've got a boner." — Janet Evanovich, *Seven Up*, p. 249, 2001

3 an old or poor-quality steer, slaughtered for mince or sausage *NEW ZEALAND*

- A lot of them had to go to the freezing works as boners. — R. Casey, *As Short a Spring*, p. 159, 1963

boneroo *noun*

high quality drugs *US*

- — Jay Robert Nash, *Dictionary of Crime*, p. 39, 1992

bones *noun*

1 dice *UK, 1400*

The term has journeyed from colloquial to standard English and now to slang.

- And I'd take some loaded craps down there, some bones, and I would beat the paddy boys out of all their money. They were the only ones who were dumb enough to shoot craps with bones. — Claude Brown, *Manchild in the Promised Land*, p. 151, 1965
- How come they marked like bones then? — Guy Owen, *The Flim-Flam Man and the Apprentice Grifter*, p. 116, 1972
- We now had five yards to spend / so I made the same bet again / as I watched the bones fly from Spoon's hand. — Lightnin' Rod, *Hustlers Convention*, p. 52, 1973
- "The Price is Right," Duffy trumpeted. "My lucky dice. Harry wants them bones." — Stephen Cannell, *Big Con*, p. 229, 1997
- How bout it new kid, you wanna handle my bones, or do you just like to watch. [Screenplay, not in final cut]. — *Kill Bill*, 2003

2 heroin *US*

- Heroin is called either "bones," referring to a high level of purity, or "scramble," meaning a much less pure version, which is much cheaper. — *Washington Post*, p. B1, 29th July 1984

3 crack cocaine *UK*

- — Mike Haskins, *Drugs*, p. 281, 2003

4 the basic facts of something *UK*

- [T]old her to go by her mum till I checked her there. Gave her the bones, give her the rest later. — Jeremy Cameron, *Brown Bread in Wengen*, p. 4, 1999

5 an orthopaedist *US, 1892*

- — Sally Williams, *"Strong" Words*, p. 135, 1994

6 spare ribs *US*

- — Charles Shafer, *Folk Speech in Texas Prisons*, p. 198, 1990

▸ make your bones

1 to establish yourself as a fully fledged member of a crime organisation, usually by carrying out an execution-style murder *US*

- Only a few weeks before he had made his bones, a double kill of Herm and Sal Perigino[.] — Mickey Spillane, *Last Cop Out*, p. 8, 1972
- Mr. Bellini wants you to join the Family. He told me to see that you make your bones. I have the guy you need in mind already. — Iceberg Slim (Robert Beck), *Death Wish*, p. 65, 1977
- When he was thirteen he had made his bones on the Gun Hill Road in the Bronx, where he had never been before that afternoon. — Richard Condon, *Prizzi's Honor*, p. 4, 1982

2 by extension, to establish yourself as an equal in a group setting *US*

- She'd made her bones back in the days when there were still a lot of dinosaurs left on thejob, guys who wanted women to fail. — Joseph Wambaugh, *Floaters*, p. 139, 1996

▸ on your bones

destitute or almost so *UK, 1924*

An image of emaciation.

- one winter, in the desperate group and on the bones of my backside — *Guardian Weekly*, 27th March 1971

▸ the bones

the boyfriend *UK*

- — Paul Baker, *Polari*, p. 166, 2002

bone shack *noun*

any place where a couple have sex *US*

- — Pamela Munro, *U.C.L.A. Slang*, p. 42, 1997

boneshaker *noun*

1 a bicycle *US, 1871*

Coined as a literal description of early bicycles, and remains in use despite technological advances.

- I've rode round the whole peninsula on that bike [...] I drive as far as the Green Lodge, parks up and gets the boneshaker out the back. — Kevin Sampson, *Outlaws*, p. 271, 2001

2 a rigid-frame motorcyle, especially a rigid-frame Harley-Davidson *US*

- — *American Speech*, p. 267, December 1962: 'The language of traffic policemen'

bone up *verb*

to study, especially at the last minute *US, 1918*

An American outgrowth of the C18 'bone' with the same meaning.

- Then we started boning up on the dog-ass Jets, who had dusted off Oakland thirty-five to ten for the American Conference title. — Dan Jenkins, *Semi-Tough*, p. 91, 1972

bone works *noun*

rough treatment *US*

- I wasn't leaned on too much, but I got the bone works when it came to security. They stayed on me like hawks for six months. — Red Rudensky, *The Gonif*, p. 50, 1970

boney *adjective*

genuine, satisfactory *UK*

An alteration of '*bona*fide'.

- — Angela Devlin, *Prison Patter*, p. 30, 1996

boneyard *noun*

1 a cemetery *US, 1866*

- — Bill Davis, *Jawjacking*, p. 20, 1977
- So if he did the work on the plumber he would be sending the only woman he had ever really loved to a boneyard. — Richard Condon, *Prizzi's Money*, p. 90, 1994
- [W]ith that gear you can indulge yourself into the boneyard. — J.J. Connolly, *Layer Cake*, p. 61, 2000

2 in various industrial settings, the site for dumping broken vehicles and equipment which can be cannibalised for parts *US, 1913*

- — Ramon Adams, *The Language of the Railroader*, p. 18, 1977

3 in dominoes, the pile of unusued tiles *US, 1897*

- — Dominic Armanino, *Dominoes*, p. 16, 1959
- Never mind the sun, Homer – help yourself to the boneyard – you're 5 pegs from a skunking. [Homer comic strip] — *San Francisco Examiner*, p. 48, 2nd April 1963

4 the area off a beach where waves break *US*

- [O]n Malibu Mac's how to get out of a "boneyard" when you're caught in the middle of a set of breakers – and on Scooterboy Miller's hot rod I learned how to avoid a pearl dive. — Frederick Kohner, *Gidget*, p. a, 1957
- — John M. Kelly, *Surf and Sea*, p. 280, 1965

5 a conjugal visit in prison *US*
- —James Harris, *A Convict's Dictionary*, p. 28, 1989

boneyize *verb*
to lay claim to something *CANADA*
- A kids' expression from the late 1940s meaning "first dibs." The person who first stated "I boneyize that" gained rights of possession. On the prairies, it has been reported as an expression of covetousness. —Tom Parkin, *WetCoast Words*, p. 17, 1989

boney maroney *noun*
a very thin person *US*
In various spellings, but surely originating in the following rock'n'roll lyric.
- I've got a girl named Bony Maroney / She's as twiggy as a stick of macaroni. —Larry Williams, *Bony Maronie*, 1957
- —Kenn "Naz" Young, *Naz's Underground Dictionary*, p. 16, 1973

bone you! bone ya!
used as an all-purpose, defiant insult *US*
- —*American Speech*, p. 276, December 1963: 'American Indian student slang'

bonfire *noun*
1 in firefighter usage, a multiple-alarm fire *US*
- — *American Speech*, p. 274, December 1954: 'Fire terms: additional words and definitions'

2 a burning cigarette stub *US*
- —Lou Shelly, *Hepcats Jive Talk Dictionary*, p. 8, 1945

bong; bhong *noun*
1 a pipe with a water-filled bowl through which marijuana or crack cocaine smoke is drawn for inhalation *US, 1971*
- I like a blunt or a big fat coal / But my double-barrel bong is gettin me stoned / I'm skill it, There's water inside don't spill it—Cypress Hill, *Hits from the Bong*, 1993
- "Come smoke a few bhongs with the sheriff." A bhong was a vertical bamboo pipe containing water. —Cleo Odzer, *Goa Freaks*, p. 75, 1995
- If we didn't have a bong, we used to get my brother's motor-cycle helmet[.]—Macfarlane, Macfarlane and Robson, *The User*, p. 79, 1996
- She wondered what misshapen bong or other embarassment was drawn on him. —Francesca Lia Block, *I Was a Teenage Fairy*, p. 90, 1998
- [T]his is an essential soundtrack for a spliffed-out nation. Now where did I put that bong[.]—*Ministry*, May 2002

2 a bong's worth of marijuana *AUSTRALIA*
- They guys inside were either asleep in the back or pulling a morning bong[.]—Kathy Lette, *Girls' Night Out*, p. 188, 1987

3 a Maori or Pacific Islander *NEW ZEALAND*
- —Louis S. Leland, *A Personal Kiwi-Yankee Dictionary*, p. 16, 1984

bong *verb*
to drink beer directly from a keg, using a hose and funnel *US*
- —Mary Corey and Victoria Westermark, *Fer Shurr! How to be a Valley Girl*, 1982

bong; bung *adjective*
dead *AUSTRALIA, 1857*
From Aborigine *bong* (dead).

bong brain *noun*
a marijuana addict *AUSTRALIA*
- —Kathy Lette, *Girls' Night Out*, p. 13, 1987
- 'Bong brains' or 'Cone heads' derive their names from inhaling vast amounts of marijuana smoke. —*Sydney Morning Herald*, p. 7, 3rd January 1987

bong land *noun*
a state of marijuana intoxication *UK*
Extended from **BONG** (a water-pipe, used for smoking marijuana).
- [T]he thumping bass and rolling acidline will make the walls veritably crawl after a visit to bong-land. Tread carefully! —*Ministry*, May 2002

bongo *noun*
1 a marijuana cigarette *UK*
- —Tom Hibbert, *Rockspeak!*, p. 27, 1983

2 in skateboarding, a fall or the wounds resulting from a fall *US*
- —Laura Torbet, *The Complete Book of Skateboarding*, p. 105, 1976

bongo mag *noun*
a pornographic magazine *UK*
- He now works as the editor of top-shelf bongo mag Mayfair[.] —Danny King, *The Bank Robber Diaries*, 2002
- — *Roger's Profanisaurus*, p. 24, 2002

bong on *verb*
to smoke marijuana *AUSTRALIA*
Often seen as a graffiti'd credo.
- —Lenie Johansen, *The Dinkum Dictionary*, 1988

bong up *verb*
to become intoxicated by inhaling marijuana through a water-filled pipe *UK*
- We used to bong up on oil after that[.]—Macfarlane, Macfarlane and Robson, *The User*, p. 88, 1996

bonhunkus *noun*
the buttocks *US, 1941*
- If surfing isn't vigorous enough, you can go zipping down the Sun Streaker water slide, a 220-foot nearly straight shot that you take from four stories high, sitting only on your bohunkus. — *Washington Post*, p. 5 (Weekend), 1st April 1983

boning tool *noun*
the penis *US*
Combines 'boning' (sexual intercourse) with a pun on 'tool' (an implement suited to a given task/the penis).
- —Erica Orloff and JoAnn Baker, *Dirty Little Secrets*, p. 90, 2001

bonish *adjective*
covetous *CANADA*
- It apparently means to covet, to wish you had, or to want to borrow, as in, "I'm bonish about (or boneyize) your new snowmobile, so don't leave it around unguarded. —Chris Thain, *Cold as a Bay Street Banker's Heart*, p. 17, 1987

bonita *noun*
1 heroin
- —Robert Ashton, *This Is Heroin*, p. 205, 2002
- —Mike Haskins, *Drugs*, p. 283, 2003

2 milk sugar (lactose) used to dilute heroin *US*
Mexican Spanish.
- —David Maurer and Victor Vogel, *Narcotics and Narcotic Addiction*, p. 390, 1973

bonk *noun*
sexual intercourse *UK*
A light-hearted, almost euphemistic term; probably from 'bonk' (a noise) playing on **BANG**.
- I had a really funny bonk in Tenerife once. Or was it twice, No, I only did her once but it was a good one. —Dave Courtney, *Raving Lunacy*, p. 237, 2000

bonk *verb*
1 to hit someone or something with, or against, something hard *UK, 1931*
- "He was going to shoot me," I said. "But I threw the lamp at him and then I thumped him and then he ran away and Jean bonked him." —Martin Waddell, *Otley*, p. 136, 1966

2 to have sex *UK, 1975*
- His plan was to shack up with some fat girlfriend of his, piping [smoking crack cocaine] and bonking the night away[.] —Lanre Fehintola, *Charlie Says...*, p. 160, 2000
- [T]hose caught bonking livestock were quickly put to death. —Erica Orloff and JoAnn Baker, *Dirty Little Secrets*, p. 9, 2001
- [Y]ou can hear us bonking but you're not getting a look at our record collection. —Mark Steel, *Reasons to be Cheerful*, p. 176, 2001

3 in an endurance sport, especially cycling, to reach a point of utter exhaustion *US, 1979*
- The challenge is to fuel ourbodies to meet enormous energy needs, spare glycogen stores so we don't "bonk"[.]— *Baltimore Sun*, p. 7D, 2nd August 1994
- The athlete may "bonk," "hit the wall" or "blow up," as the terminology goes. — *Washington Post*, p. A1, 11th June 2001

4 to bounce a snowboard off a non-snow platform *US*
From the noise of the contact between board and **DEATH BOX**.
- —Jim Humes and Sean Wagstaff, *Boarderlands*, p. 220, 1995

bonkbuster *noun*
a type of popular novel containing frequent, explicit sexual encounters *UK, 1988*
- We have these high-toned sex journals in the finest bookstores, but old-fashioned Harold Robbins-style bonkbusters are declasse. —David Books, *Bobos in Paradise*, 2000
- Much of her bonkbuster is set in South Africa— *The Observer*, p. 13, 18th March 2001

bonker board *noun*
a large, cumbersome, old-fashioned surfboard *AUSTRALIA*
- — *surfresearch.com.au*,

bonkers *noun*
the female breasts *US*
An elision of **BAZONKAS**.
- If I were to ask about your chest and I called them zonkers or bonkers or watermelons or boobs – how would you react? —Howard Stern, *Miss America*, p. 441, 1995

bonkers *adjective*
crazy *UK, 1957*
- All you lot oughta be in the nut-house, you're bonkers, stone raving bonkers. —John Peter Jones, *Feather Pluckers*, p. 34, 1964
- North rim? Man, are you bonkers! They'll shoot you. —Bill Cardoso, *The Maltese Sangweech*, p. 247, 1984

bonkers *adverb*
crazy *UK, 1957*
- You going bonkers or something? —Graeme Kent, *The Queen's Corporal [Six Granada Plays]*, p. 83, 1959
- If it wasn't for you bringing my boiled egg in the morning I'd go bonkers. —Ray Galton and Alan Simpson, *Hancock's Half Hour*, 28th June 1959
- That's incredible! Richard Marks will go bonkers. —Dan Jenkins, *Life Its Ownself*, p. 198, 1984
- That's when Letch devised the scheme to pee on the tree and drive the little bowwow bonkers. —Joseph Wambaugh, *Floaters*, p. 11, 1996
- It's all gone bonkers! —Kevin Sampson, *Powder*, p. 4, 1999
- This she could deal with: a woman going bonkers over a man. —Rita Ciresi, *Pink Slip*, p. 340, 1999

bonkers as conkers *adjective*
crazy, mad, very eccentric *UK*
An elaboration of **BONKERS**.
- [Ol' Dirty Bastard]'s revered as something of a genius. The second [thing to know] is that he's bananas. Screwy. Poco loco. Bonkers as conkers. — *Uncut*, p. 20, October 2003

bonneroo; bonaroo *adjective*
good, smart, sharp *US, 1926*
Largely, if not exclusively, prison slang.
- The uniform of the 10-piece ensemble was "boneroo" – that's lingo on the inside for "cool" on the outside. —*San Francisco Examiner*, p. 19, 13th June 1960
- —Board of Corrections, State of California, *A Dictionary of Criminal Language For Official Law Enforclement Use Only*, 1962
- These are boneroo free-world shoes. —Malcolm Braly, *On the Yard*, p. 140, 1967
- —Paul Glover, *Words from the House of the Dead*, 1974
- If you weren't a Mexican, I'd call it a bonaroo taco wagon. —James Ellroy, *Suicide Hill*, p. 611, 1986

bonnet *noun*
in motor racing, a safety helmet *US*
- —John Edwards, *Auto Dictionary*, p. 17, 1993

bonnie *noun*
a Triumph Bonneville motorcyle *US*
- — "Slingo", *The Official CB Slang Dictionary Handbook*, p. 9, 1976
- [Y]ou're fucking pissing away on an export bonnie or sommat [something] —Paul E Willis, *Profane Culture*, p. 15, 1978

Bonnie Dick *nickname*
the USS Bonhomme Richard *US*
An aircraft carrier named after Capt. John Paul Jones' famous ship in the American Revolution.
- Bonnie Dick Rejoins Fleet [Headline]— *San Francisco News*, p. 12, 7th September 1955

Bonny Prince *noun*
cocaine *UK*
A disguising of **CHARLIE** (cocaine) using the name of 'Bonny (or Bonnie) Prince Charlie', Charles Edward Stuart, 1720–88.
- Oh and, any sign of the Bonny Prince today? —James Hawes, *White Powder, Green Light*, p. 289, 2002

bonspiel *noun*
a curling tournament *CANADA*
- Bonspiel: a word meaning "big tournament" or "big drunk." In some bonspiels the prize is a bottle of Canadian whisky. —Will Ferguson, *How to be a Canadian*, p. 99, 2001

bontoger; bontogeriro; bontoser *adjective*
excellent, admirable *AUSTRALIA, 1904*
Elaborations of **BONZER** (excellent).
- —G.A. Wilkes, *A Dictionary of Australian Colloquialisms*, 1978

bonus!
used for expressing delight and/or approval *US*
- —Anna Scotti and Paul Young, *Buzzwords*, p. 53, 1997

bonus baby *noun*
an amateur athlete who signs a professional contract with a large signing bonus *US*
- —Howard B. Bonham, *Football Lingo*, p. 4, 1962
- —Richard Scholl, *Running Press Glossary of Baseball Language*, p. 17, 1977
- Better find our bonus baby, eh? — *Bull Durham*, 1988
- He's an overaged (25) former baseball bonus baby who doesn't have a big-time arm but can beat you on scrambles, draws and smarts. — *Richmond (Virginia) Times Dispatch*, p. C3, 4th January 2004

bony-bony *adjective*
very thin *NORFOLK ISLAND*
- —Beryl Nobbs Palmer, *A Dictionary of Norfolk Words and Usages*, p. 4, 1992

bonzer; bonza *noun*
someone or something that is excellent *AUSTRALIA, 1904*
- —Norman Lindsay, *Saturdee*, p. 40, 1934
- It's a bonzer, says Fish, taking the business right down to Lester's habitual finishing words. —Tim Winton, *Cloudstreet*, p. 191, 1991

bonzer; bonza *adjective*
excellent, terrific, wonderful, fabulous, good *AUSTRALIA, 1904*
This word is the only survivng member of a set of synonymous terms that all appeared in the first decade of C20, the others being 'bontosher', 'boshter' and 'bosker'. *The Bulletin*, in 1904, claimed that these were all corruptions of an original term that was a compound of the French words *bon* (good) and *toujours* (always).
- Ah, but what a bonzer pair of youngsters they were! —Barry Humphries, *A Nice Night's Entertainment*, p. 50, 1961
- And aren't they a bonzer shape? —John Wynnum, *Tar Dust*, p. 31, 1962
- That's a bonzer sheila! —Dymphna Cusack, *Picnic Races*, p. 173, 1962
- [T]heir men gather in a solid mass around the bar, there to sing smutty songs, tell dirty jokes, guzzle beer and discuss, in lurid details, the bonzer naughty they had last night, last week or whenever. —Sue Rhodes, *Now you'll think I'm awful*, p. 56, 1967
- Easy peasy innit. Bonza. —Jeremy Cameron, *Brown Bread in Wengen*, p. 195, 1999
- Hope you're feelin' top notch, 'cos have I got a bonza plan for you. — *Australian Ultimate*, p. 7, 2003

bonzer; bonza *adverb*
excellently; brilliantly; well *AUSTRALIA, 1914*
- 'And a bonzer looking girl,' added Waldo. 'Bonzerest looking girl in town,' chanted Bill. —Norman Lindsay, *Halfway to Anywhere*, p. 87, 1947
- Strike, listen to that mob! I reckon the old song went over real bonzer! —Barry Humphries, *The Wonderful World of Barry McKenzie*, p. 21, 1968

bonzo *noun*
a chance *UK*
- "Not a fuckin' bonzo," I went to TT [...] "You tell your own porkies [lies] TT, I ain't doing it for you. [...] No fuckin' bonzo." —Jeremy Cameron, *Brown Bread in Wengen*, p. 25, 1999

bonzo *adjective*
crazy *US, 1979*
- The kid was a banana! Bonzo. Loonier than his old man. —Joseph Wambaugh, *Lines and Shadows*, p. 108, 1984

boo *noun*
1 marijuana *US, 1959*
- 'Boo is a crutch fo you,' Lee snorted. —Clarence Cooper Jr, *Black*, p. 104, 1963
- Smoking marijuana – also called pot, tea, grass, stuff, boo, hemp and Mary Jane – seems to be this year's way among students of preserving the perennial illusion that the younger generation is going to hell. — *Time*, 12th March 1965
- Hey, really, you know my manic thing with boo. If I start seeing spiders, you can always slip me a little niacin. —Richard Farina, *Been Down So Long*, p. 66, 1966
- Other brands seeking trademarks include "Weed," "Hemp," "Giggle Grass," "Tea Brand Sticks," Tijuana Boo," "Loco Weed" – all slang for Marijuana. — *San Francisco Examiner*, p. 1, 27th October 1967
- I stopped by my man's room and picked up a zulu stick of boo and then I stepped out in front of the hotel to smoke and ready myself up to peck. —A.S. Jackson, *Gentleman Pimp*, p. 76, 1973
- His father had been unable to figure out any other way to ice Little Phil Terrone, the heaviest shit and boo dealer in the North Bronx. —Richard Condon, *Prizzi's Honor*, p. 4, 1982
- —Mike Haskins, *Drugs*, p. 286, 2003

2 a sexual partner or lover *US*
- —Connie Eble (Editor), *UNC-CH Campus Slang*, p. 2, 1997
- — *Milwaukee Journal-Sentinel*, 5th March 2001
- —Gary K. Farlow, *Prison-ese*, p. 5, 2002

3 an attractive young person *US*

- —Collin Baker et al., *College Undergraduate Slang Study Conducted at Brown University*, p. 84, 1968

4 used as a term of endearment *US*

- —Rick Ayers (Editor), *Berkeley High Slang Dictionary*, p. 13, 2004

5 an unlexicalised verbalisation of disapproval *UK, 1801*

- There are boos from the back.—James Mangold, *Copland*, p. 53, 1997

6 a sulk *UK*

Adapted from **BOOHOO** (a childish vocalisation of sobbing).

- I saw Terry storm off in a boo after none of the lads would ever back him up with anything[.]—Danny King, *The Burglar Diaries*, p. 112, 2001

7 bird or lizard droppings *BARBADOS*

Collected by Richard Allsopp.

8 anything at all *US, 1883*

Usually heard in the warning – 'don't say boo'.

- —Joseph A. Weingarten, *An American Dictionary of Slang*, p. 38, 1954

9 nasal mucus *BAHAMAS*

- —John A. Holm, *Dictionary of Bahamian English*, p. 24, 1982

boo *verb*

in contemporary dance culture, to give an unlexicalised verbalisation of approval *UK*

A deliberate reversal of the negative sense.

- These London crowds take no prisoners. You have to kill it out there. And remember – if they boo you, that's good!—Julian Johnson, *Urban Survival*, p. 301, 2003

boo *adjective*

excellent *US, 1952*

Youth usage.

- —Harold Wentworth and Stuart Berg Flexner, *Dictionary of American Slang*, p. 53, 1960

boo!

used for frightening someone after sneaking up on them *US*

- In dangerous situations, he acted like he wasn't afraid of anything but he always looked like he was about to fall down in a faint if anybody said boo.—Robert Campbell, *Juice*, p. 69, 1988

booay; boohai *noun*

a remote area *NEW ZEALAND*

Probably a corruption of the Marori placename, Puhoi.

- 'Out in the sticks', 'out in the backblock', 'out in the bush, 'out in the booay', 'out in the cactus', all have the same basic meaning of 'fifty miles from nowhere.'—R.L. Bacon, *In the Sticks*, p. 184, 1963

boob *noun*

1 a fool *US, 1907*

Almost certainly from C16 'booby', meaning a 'stupid fellow'.

- There's another buddyship of boobs who think the earth is hollow and we live inside.—Philip Wylie, *Opus 21*, p. 85, 1949
- When Mr. Money arrived at the airport, the grifter had him paged, then introduced himself with a bunk story, such as being a friend of the hotel manager, who had asked him to pick up the boob.—Jack Lait and Lee Mortimer, *Washington Confidential*, p. 277, 1951
- In the majority of cases, it was a sloppily managed dive controlled by hoodlums (at its worst) or amateurs and arrogant boobs (at its best) for years before the paying popular became awake.—Robert Sylvester, *No Cover Charge*, p. 298, 1956
- But wouldn't it be funny if he suddenly turned to him and said, "Phil Latham, you're a boob."—John Knowles, *A Separate Peace*, p. 175, 1959
- [T]his poor girl is stuck with a boob!—Hunter S. Thompson, *Songs of the Doomed*, p. 49, 1959
- New York Billie dug that Willie was from Lame Junction so he figured he'd take this boob for the New York pig.—Babs Gonzales, *"A Manhatten Fable" in Movin' On Down De Line*, p. 89, 1975

2 the female breast *US, 1931*

From synonymous 'bub', generally used in the plural.

- She had a nice pair of boobs and hed like ta catch her sometime, —Hubert Selby Jr, *Last Exit to Brooklyn*, p. 268, 1957
- Someone would sit up and point at some sex display, "Look at those boobs!"—Frederick Kohner, *Gidget*, p. 49, 1957
- You know, Lynda Robb – Johnson – came to my last party and here were all these girls in the crocheted see-through dresses with their boobs sticking out.—*San Francisco Examiner*, p. 51, 23rd July 1970
- Her breasts weren't especially big, or little, or round, or pointy or any of those magazine-writer tit fetish cliches. They were just nice boobs on a nice woman.—Gurney Norman, *Divine Right's Trip (Last Whole Earth Catalog)*, p. 41, 1971
- "Oh, I wish you wouldn't use that expression [flat]," retorted Miss Andrews in her precise British voice. "Everyone including Carol Burnett knows I have bigger boobs than she does."—*San Francisco Chronicle*, p. 58, 15th December 1971
- I was the east coast rep for one of the biggest distributors of girlie magazines in the country, and as I sold magazines to wholesalers I began to notice that big boob material was always a consistant seller[.]—*Adult Video*, p. 47, August/September 1986
- Are you a boob guy or a butt guy?—*Sky Magazine*, p. 51, July 2001

3 jail *US, 1908*

Hartley (1944) claims that an old prisoner he knew remembered the term from as far back as the 1880s, which is feasible since 'booby hatch', from which 'boob' is ultimately derived, dates back as far 1859 in the US.

- He'll probably put a stone through a window to get back into boob. —Kevin Mackey, *The Cure*, p. 70, 1970
- —Shane Maloney, *Nice Try*, p. 290, 1998
- —David McGill, *David McGill's Complete Kiwi Slang Dictionary*, p. 19, 1998
- [H]er old man's out of the boob now and he's one fuckin' mean mother.—Garry Bushell, *The Face*, p. 15, 2001

4 a blunder, a *faux pas* *US, 1934*

- A generation of young people out there will never ever forgive us if we make a boob this time.—Mr Savage, *Northern Ireland Assemby [Hansard]*, 16th February 1999

boob *verb*

1 to blunder *UK, 1935*

- So, OK, they boobed – four times in successive decisions[.]—*Daily Telegraph*, 8th June 2001

2 to perform poorly, to botch something *US, 1919*

- —J. E. Lighter, *Historical Dictionary of American Slang, Volume 1*, p. 226, 1994
- The growing consensus, says the pro-American Economist, is "that American intelligence boobed."—*Tampa (Florida) Tribune*, p. 6, 9th September 1998
- "I just completely boobed three 5-irons and plunked two or three woods," Wessels said of her morning qualifying round in the Illinois Women's State Amateur.—*Rockford (Illinois) Star*, p. 1D, 8th June 1999

boob box *noun*

a television; television *US*

- [G]lomming the presidential conventions from the boob box[.] —Sidney Bernard, *This Way to the Apocalypse*, p. 72, 1968

boob gear *noun*

prison clothing *NEW ZEALAND*

- —*NZWords*, p. 2, 2nd October 1999

boob gun *noun*

an improvised tattoo machine *NEW ZEALAND*

- —*NZWords*, p. 2, 2nd October 1999

boob happy *adjective*

mentally unbalanced as the result of being imprisoned *AUSTRALIA, 1968*

Derives from **BOOB** (a jail) and the suffix **-HAPPY** (mentally unbalanced).

boob head *noun*

a prisoner *NEW ZEALAND*

- —Harry Orsman and Des Hurley, *The Beaut Little Book of New Zealand Slang*, 1994

boobie *noun*

used as an endearing term of address *US*

Popularised by comic Jerry Lewis in the mid-1950s; mock Yiddish.

- —Harold Wentworth and Stuart Berg Flexner, *Dictionary of American Slang*, p. 53, 1960

▷ **see: BOOBY**

boo-bird *noun*

a sports fan who constantly and loudly boos during a game *US*

- Cleveland Boo-Birds Backed by Veeck [Headline]—*Sporting News*, p. 1, 14th July 1948
- General Manager Hank Greenberg of the Cleveland Indians sounded a warning today to the incessant boo-birds: "Shut up or you may get thrown out of the park."—*San Francisco Examiner*, 21st February 1950
- "Boobirds" are fans who boo an umpire when things go wrong.—*Look*, p. 94, 311 March 1959
- Philadelphia is reputed to be the biggest sports boobird city int he U.S.—*San Francisco Examiner*, p. 50, 17th November 1966
- Enraged boo birds, many fueled by beer, took over the game for about 20 minutes Sunday, making so much noise play had to be held up because the Eagles couldn't hear Garbril's signals.—*San Francisco Chronicle*, p. 46, 29th October 1974

boobitas; boobititas *noun*

small female breasts *US*

A borrowed use of the Spanish diminutive.

- —Carol Ann Preusse, *Jargon Used by University of Texas Co-Eds*, 1963

boob job *noun*

surgery to alter a woman's breast size *US*

- Half the girls get boob jobs and butt tucks. — Carl Hiaasen, *Tourist Season*, p. 259, 1986
- Cop Don Fernando, who's been trying to find Spankenstein for five years, discovers pint-sized Nasty Natasha (Courtney plus a boob job). — *Adult Video News*, p. 56, February 1993
- The picture here was taken before my boob job. — Anthony Petkovich, *The X Factory*, p. 58, 1997
- "How she was gonna pay pay for the voice lessons." Elaine said, "And the boob job." — Elmore Leonard, *Be Cool*, p. 225, 1999
- I've got almost three thousand dollars. I was saving it for a boob job. — *American Beauty*, 1999
- Kelly wants a boob job. I tell her she'd be better off with a brain job. — Cath Staincliffe, *Trainers*, p. 59, 1999
- Dodie Carmine got a boob job. — Janet Evanovich, *Seven Up*, p. 56, 2001
- [B]rutal bouncer boyfriends, boob jobs gone wrong[.] — Kevin Sampson, *Clubland*, p. 25, 2002

boo-boo *noun*

1 an error *US*

Children's vocabulary.

- The other day, Mr. B. made a lamentable boo-boo. — *San Francisco Examiner*, p. 29, 24th January 1953
- But then when said pal makes a boo-boo then, oboy, watch how fast it fades away. [There Ought to Be a Law comic strip] — *San Francisco News*, 29th June 1953
- How could she have made such a thundering booboo as to cut Oscar loose before she had Harry properly hooked? — Max Shulman, *Rally Round the Flag, Boys!*, p. 233, 1957
- A Big $400 Million Booboo in a Bank [Headline] — *Life*, p. 135, 7th December 1959
- I lay and listened to Junior pitching himself hoarse convincing Mama that Rajah's Soutside execution was the result of some private boo boo[.] — Iceberg Slim (Robert Beck), *Mama Black Widow*, p. 157, 1969
- This is a male institution. Someone's made a ... booboo. — Seth Morgan, *Homeboy*, p. 251, 1990

2 a bruise or scrape *US*

- But in Springfield, Mass., you say "I fell down and got a boo-boo on my elbow" (a bruise). This boo-boo may come from a French slang word, bo-bo, any small bruise or hurt. — *Junior Parade Magazine*, p. 22, 20th June 1954
- Has the poor little girl got a Booboo? — Hubert Selby Jr, *Last Exit to Brooklyn*, p. 47, 1957
- He says, "Well, whaddaya know – Champ Pimp's got himself a boo-boo." — *Raging Bull*, 1980
- [D]on't worry about that little boo-boo on her throat / It's just a little scratch[.] — Eminem (Marshall Mathers), *'97 Bonnie and Clyde*, 1999

3 the human posterior *UK*

A childish reduplication of 'bottom'.

- No use sitting around on your boo-boo, brooding. — Nicholas Blake, *The Sad Variety*, 1964
- Kiss my boo-boo. — Sal Piro and Michael Hess, *The Official 'Rocky Horror Picture Show' Audience Participation Guide*, p. 38, 1991

4 any vexatious flying insect *BAHAMAS*

- — John A. Holm, *Dictionary of Bahamian English*, p. 24, 1982

boo boo bama *noun*

marijuana *UK*

- — Mike Haskins, *Drugs*, p. 286, 2003

boo-boos *noun*

the testicles *US, 1951*

- — Harold Wentworth and Stuart Berg Flexner, *Dictionary of American Slang*, p. 53, 1960
- — Dale Gordon, *The Dominion Sex Dictionary*, p. 31, 1967

boob rat *noun*

a prisoner who is always returning to prison *AUSTRALIA, 1967*

Derives from **BOOB** (a jail).

boobs *noun*

in poker, a pair of queens *US*

- — George Percy, *The Language of Poker*, p. 12, 1988

boob sling *noun*

a brassiere *US*

- — Collin Baker et al., *College Undergraduate Slang Study Conducted at Brown University*, p. 85, 1968

boob talk *noun*

any secret or coded language used in prison *AUSTRALIA, 1993*

Derives from **BOOB** (a jail).

boob tat *noun*

a tattoo acquired in prison *US*

- — David McGill, *David McGill's Complete Kiwi Slang Dictionary*, p. 19, 1998

boob tube *noun*

1 television *US*

First came **THE TUBE**, and then the obvious reduplication.

- Maybe you do a few things which irritate her and she retaliates via the boob tube. — *San Francisco News Call Bulletin*, p. 11, 21st January 1963
- Then comes his two weeks off and how does he spend it? On the prone watching the boob tube. [They'll Do It Every Time comic strip] — *San Francisco News Call-Bulletin*, p. 50, 2nd October 1963
- One interesting development as the primary progresses is a certain shakiness among Democrats the more they see Ronnie [Reagan] on the boob tube. — *San Francisco Examiner and Chronicle*, p. II-3, 6th February 1966
- Hi-fi comes to the boob tube [Headline] — *Life*, p. 22, 15th May 1970
- Parked in front of the boob tube, Carol and I used to gawk and hoot at those hunks[.] — Rita Ciresi, *Pink Slip*, p. 163, 1999

2 in women's fashion, a strapless top made of stretchable material *UK, 1978*

Sometimes also called a 'booby tubey'.

- "There is no function you go to without seeing ladies wearing the top," says Amaka Eligie, boob tube lover. — *Daily Sun (Nigeria)*, 3rd June 2005

boob weed; boob tobacco *noun*

prison-issue tobacco *AUSTRALIA, 1967*

Derives from **BOOB** (a jail) and **WEED** (tobacco).

booby; boobie *noun*

1 a female breast *US, 1916*

- Sitting in the back seat with the pudgy girl was his date – big boobies, he remembered, they jiggled. — Bernard Wolfe, *The Late Risers*, p. 46, 1954
- Bib boobies, straight backs, with behinds as round as watermelons. And tight, too. — Charles Angoff, *H.L. Mencken*, p. 21, 1956
- She's going to do the strip tease absolutely different. She calls it 'Bounce Your Boobies'. — Dorothy Hewett, *The Chapel Perilous*, p. 60, 1972
- He would have ripped the blouse off Nina Foch's boobies himself given the opportunity. — Earl Thompson, *Tattoo*, p. 4, 1974
- 'So what's your best part?' 'My boobies, 'cos they're a handful.' — *People*, p. 74, 5th July 1999

2 nasal mucus *BAHAMAS*

- — John A. Holm, *Dictionary of Bahamian English*, p. 24, 1982

booby *adjective*

foolish *US*

- [W]e'll poetize the lot and make a fat book of icy bombs for the booby public. — Jack Kerouac, *The Dharma Bums*, p. 158, 1958

booby hatch *noun*

a mental hospital *US, 1896*

- If I was, they'd drive me into the booby hatch. — James T. Farrell, *Saturday Night*, p. 20, 1947
- like something someone dreamt up in the booby hatch — William Rose, *The Ladykillers*, 1955
- Now they are going to send me to the Boobie Hatch which is probably where I belong. — Anonymous, *Go Ask Alice*, p. 153, 1971
- Frank had to content himself wiht getting her committed to the booby hatch for life, innocent by reason of insanity. — George V. Higgins, *Penance for Jerry Kennedy*, p. 37, 1985

booby prize *noun*

a reward for stupidity, often given humorously to whoever comes last in a contest *US, 1889*

Elaborated on **BOOBY** (foolish).

- Monica treated me like the booby prize, while her mate Sybil looked dead chuffed. — John Peter Jones, *Feather Pluckers*, p. 32, 1964

booby trap *noun*

a dishonest carnival game *US*

- — *American Speech*, p. 235, October 1950: 'The argot of outdoor boob traps'

boochie *noun*

a Japanese person *US*

- Chicago Japs refer to those from the old country and Hawaii as "Buddha heads" or "Boochies." — Jack Lait and Lee Mortimer, *Chicago Confidential*, p. 88, 1950

boo-coo; boo koo *noun*

a large number; a lot *US, 1918*

- Bama said, "Yeah, he'll be there. So what has that to do with boo koos of fine foxes?" — Iceberg Slim (Robert Beck), *Death Wish*, p. 130, 1977
- I can't remember boo koos of kilometers 'bfore we bean to reallly hear theh mortar shells singing in the curves they take, the perfection of U.S. electric magic! — Clarence Major, *All-Night Visitors*, p. 36, 1998

boo-coo; boo koo *adverb*
a large number of; a lot of *US*
- We got boo-coo movement. 3rd Battallion just got hit 15 kliks north of here. — *Platoon*, 1986
- He's book-koo koo-koo. — *Gone in 60 Seconds*, 2000

boodle *noun*
1 profits appropriated quietly, and usually illegally *US, 1858*
- Tom ("Sailor") Burke had been the sheriff's "bag man," had delivered $36,000 in payoff money to the sheriff's wife, and had gotten signed receipts for the boodle. — *Time*, p. 18, 24th July 1950
- Of the boodle with which she had skipped St. Louis, she still had several thousand dollars, plus, of course, such readily negotiable items as her car, jewelry, and furs. — Jim Thompson, *The Grifters*, p. 87, 1963
- Sister Heavenly reckoned that Gus was carrying the boodle on him. — Chester Himes, *Come Back Charleston Blue*, p. 48, 1966
- We gotta go and score for decent bennys and bread to make up a playing boodle. — Iceberg Slim (Robert Beck), *Airtight Willie and Me*, p. 5, 1979
- All the same, I just trousered the boodle. — Viv Stanshall, *Ginger Geezer*, 1981

2 a fake bankroll used in confidence swindles *US*
- — M. Allen Henderson, *How Con Games Work*, p. 218, 1985

3 a package of snacks *US, 1900*
- Those with friends or family in the military are sure to find the online Gift Shop an easy way to send "boodle," as soldiers often refer to much-anticipated packages from home. — *PR Newswire*, 17th June 2003

booed and hissed *adjective*
drunk *UK*
Rhyming slang for **PISSED** (drunk).
- — *The Guardian*, 7th January 1980

boof *verb*
to hide prison contraband in your rectum *US*
- Like prisoners everywhere, Rikers inmates use their rectums as a sort of suitcase for weapons, concealing one or two razor blades – or sometimes even 20 or 30 – by "slamming" or "boofing" them. — *Village Voice*, p. 45, 19th December 2000

boofhead *noun*
a person with an oversized head; hence, a fool, idiot, dimwit *AUSTRALIA*
In his 1950 prison glossary Thirty-five states that one prisoner 'was known as "Boof" or "Boofhead" for over 20 years at Goulburn [jail] for the size and thickness of his head', thus dating the term back to the 1930s. It first appears in print in 1941. Popularised by Boofhead, a cartoon character appearing in the Sydney *Mirror* in the 1940s. Probably a contraction of earlier British and Australian 'bufflehead'. The suggestion that it is from British dialect *boof* (stupid) is chronologically improbable.
- Listen, boofhead, you know who I am, but I haven't got a clue as to who you are! — Rex Hunt, *Tall Tales – and True*, p. 32, 1994
- The lawyers sneered. 'This boofhead thinks he's God! Only God can forgive sins!' — Kel Richards, *The Aussie Bible*, p. 27, 2003

boof-headed *adjective*
fat-headed; stupid *AUSTRALIA, 1965*
- When we hit the bar, the boss pointed at Charles and said 'Out you boof-headed bastard' (Charles takes about a 7 1/2 hat). — Sam Weller, *Old Bastards I Have Met*, p. 122, 1979
- She had to hand it to the boof-headed yahoo. He knew his door technique. — Harrison Biscuit, *The Search for Savage Henry*, p. 83, 1995

boofuls *noun*
▷ **see: BEAUTIFULS**

boofy *adjective*
(of a male) brawny, overtly masculine and a bit stupid *AUSTRALIA*
- A big boofy bloke who played footie for Wests and was much admired and loved for doing so. — Roy Slaven (John Doyle), *Five South Coast Seasons*, p. 170, 1992
- The problem was that I was a bit boofy, you know. I'm sort of blokey and I like to spend the weekends in front of the telly watching footy[.] — John Birmingham, *He Died With a Felafel in his Hand*, p. 138, 1994

boog *noun*
a black person *US, 1937*
Offensive.
- Christ, let's take all of them – the fucking boogs may turn cannibal any minute! — Terry Southern, *Blue Movie*, p. 182, 1970
- Everybody is doing okay, Irish, Poles, the ghinnies even, paddling along, all except the boogs. Right to the bottom. — John Sayles, *Union Dues*, p. 22–23, 1977

boogaloo *noun*
1 basic rock 'n' roll music; in a broader sense, the spirit of rock 'n' roll *US*
Originally 1965, and conventionally, 'a dance performed to rock 'n' roll music'.
- New album, Fiends of Dope Island [by the Cramps], their 12th, continues the raw, vampiric boogaloo. — *X-Ray*, p. 39, June 2003

2 a black person *US*
- — Clarence Major, *Dictionary of Afro-American Slang*, p. 29, 1970

boogaloo *adjective*
drunk *UK*
- — *e-cyclopaedia*, 20th March 2002

booger *noun*
1 a glob of nasal mucus *US, 1891*
- Eeeeuwww! You got a booger on your shirt! — Richard Price, *The Wanderers*, p. 76, 1974
- She peered at me with fierce suspicion, so I crossed my eyes and probed for a booger. — C.D. Payne, *Youth in Revolt*, p. 36, 1993

2 cocaine *US*
- — Jim Crotty, *How to Talk American*, p. 114, 1997

3 a fellow; a rascal *UK, 1708*
- I couldn't help wondering where the old booger was and what he was up to, now that we were separated and our pardnership busted. — Guy Owen, *The Flim-Flam Man and the Apprentice Grifter*, p. 19, 1972

4 the vagina; and so, woman as sexual object *US, 1959*
- I bet LaNelle got some sweet booger up top of them nice long legs. — Ken Weaver, *Texas Crude*, p. 105, 1984

5 a technician in avionics *CANADA*
- — Tom Langeste, *Words on the Wing*, p. 36, 1995

booger drag *noun*
a man dressed as a woman, but revealing his masculinity by not shaving his face, arms and/or legs *US*
- — Jim Crotty, *How to Talk American*, p. 138, 1997

booger-picker *noun*
a long shafted tool used to remove oil seals and install windshields *US*
- — Lewis Poteet, *Car & Motorcyle Slang*, p. 36, 1992

booger wire *noun*
in electric line work, a neutral wire *US*
- — A.B. Chance Co., *Lineman's Slang Dictionary*, p. 2, 1980

boogie *noun*
1 a black person *US, 1923*
Offensive.
- Strike a match, the boogy's nuts. — Ralph Ellison, *Invisible Man*, p. 566, 1947
- She was with some boogey and then some other boogey came in and shot them both in the head. How do you like that? Fucking for boogies. — Philip Roth, *Portnoy's Complaint*, p. 197, 1969
- Let the boogies and wops kill each other, Cockroach once told him. — Gilbert Sorrentino, *Steelwork*, p. 15, 1970
- Make our job a lot easier, keep the boogies inside. — John Sayles, *Union Dues*, p. 22, 1977

2 the vagina *US, 1969*
- — J. E. Lighter, *Historical Dictionary of American Slang, Volume 1*, p. 235, 1994

3 syphilis, especially in its second stage *US*
- — Ralph de Sola, *Crime Dictionary*, p. 19, 1982

boogie *verb*
1 to dance, especially with abandon *US, 1947*
- He could hear the hi-fi going next door, Lesley boogying around the apartment to the Bee-Gees, ignoring her aunt, who was a little deaf. — Elmore Leonard, *Gold Coast*, p. 58, 1980
- And I'm boogieing away when I clock some undercover Old Bill [police] watching me. — Dave Courtney, *Raving Lunacy*, p. 195, 2000

2 to go, especially in a hurry *US*
- If you were lonely you could always boogie on down to the Vietnam Day Committee house and find somebody to talk to. — Jerry Rubin, *Do It!*, p. 37, 1970
- Let's boogie. — *The Blues Brothers*, 1980
- Gazing into the mirror he used an actor's trick and conjured images of middle-aged sociopaths: Fat Tony Salerno, Saddam Hussein, Ted Kennedy. Nothing worked. The killer had boogied. — Joseph Wambaugh, *Finnegan's Week*, p. 2, 1993

3 to have sex *US, 1960*

- — *The Sunday Telegraph Magazine*, 11th March 1979
- — J. E. Lighter, *Historical Dictionary of American Slang, Volume 1*, p. 235, 1994

boogie box *noun*

a large portable stereo system associated, stereotypically, with black youth culture *US*

- — Connie Eble (Editor), *UNC-CH Campus Slang*, p. 4, Fall 1987

boogie-joogie *verb*

to fool around *US*

- Hadn't he messed up his own chances at life by boogy-joogying with them? — Nathan Heard, *Howard Street*, p. 53, 1968

boogie man; boogy man *noun*

a mythical demon, used to frighten children *US, 1905*

- Television, the early boogie-man of all forms of show business, has had a definite effect on night clubbing, Walters thinks. — Robert Sylvester, *No Cover Charge*, p. 36, 1956
- Betty, John, and I believed there was a boogie man in the church at night[.] — Bobby Seale, *A Lonely Rage*, p. 5, 1978
- Damn, you daddy mean. He worse than the boogy man himself. — *Boyz N The Hood*, 1990
- I couldn't tie my shoes until I was 9, I wet the bed until I was 13, and I still can't go to sleep without Mommy making sure the Boogie Man isn't under the bed. — Chris Rock, *Rock This!*, p. 57, 1997

boogie pack *noun*

a pocket-sized portable cassette-player with lightweight headphones *UK*

- — *The Observer*, 1st August 1982

boogie party *noun*

a party held to raise money to pay the rent *US*

- — Arnold Shaw, *Dictionary of American Pop/Rock*, p. 159, 1982

boohai *noun*

▷ see: BOOAY

boo-hiss!

used as an expression of disappointment *US*

- Oh, boohiss! I got an F on my final exam. — Connie Eble (Editor), *UNC-CH Campus Slang*, p. 1, Spring 2000

boohonged *adjective*

drunk *UK*

- — Pete Brown, *Man Walks into a Pub*, 2003

boohoo *verb*

to cry loudly *UK, 1840*

- [W]hen it was all over he said give me my ten dollars back and started shaking her and hurting her until she went to boohooing and gave him the money back and then he pulled over and let her out. — William T. Vollman, *Whores for Gloria*, p. 54, 1991

boo hoo

used ironically for pretending sorrow *UK*

Echoic of genuine weeping.

- She'll be along later, so she made me her deputy; only she didn'y give me a star – boo hoo! — Malcolm Pryce, *Aberystwyth Mon Amour*, p. 22, 2001
- Coro-fucking-nation Street wasn't on until 10 o'clock. Oh boo-hoo. — Danny King, *The Burglar Diaries*, p. 122, 2001

boojie *noun*

a middle-class person *US, 1970*

A refinement of 'bourgeois' and not used with kindness.

- "We know those Boojies (bourgeois Negroes) don't want to hear about us," was their reaction, "but that's too bad: we exist!" — Christina and Richard Milner, *Black Players*, p. 11, 1972

book *noun*

1 in horse racing, the schedule of a jockey's riding assignments *US*

- — Tom Ainslie, *Ainslie's Complete Guide to Thoroughbred Racing*, p. 328, 1976

2 a betting operation *US, 1917*

- One of my rules, forty years in the business – going back to the syndicate days – twenty years running my own book, you have to always know who you're doing business with. — Elmore Leonard, *Riding the Rap*, p. 16, 1995

3 in sports, the collective, conventional wisdom in a given situation *US*

- Williams went against the book, and sent pitching coach Galen Cisco to the mound with instructions. — *Los Angeles Times*, p. 1 (Part 3), 10th April 1985
- In sports, it is always referred to as "the Book." It doesn't exist, not in any tangible form at least, but it is referenced by coaches on every level, from little league to the NFL. — *Atlanta Journal-Constitution*, p. 7F, 2nd January 2004

4 collectively, the mares bred with a single stallion in a year *US*

- The stallion's dream is a full book. — *www.equineonline.com*

5 ten thousand doses of LSD soaked into paper *US*

- Ten pages – ten thousand hits – constitute a "book," which is a common wholesale unit. — Cam Cloud, *The Little Book of Acid*, p. 34, 1999

6 one pound of drugs *US*

- — Robert Sabbag, *Snowblind*, p. 271, 1976

7 half a kilogram of drugs *US*

- — Robert Sabbag, *Snowblind*, 1976

8 a hard-working, focused, serious student *US*

- — Collin Baker et al., *College Undergraduate Slang Study Conducted at Brown University*, p. 85, 1968

▸ do the book

to serve a life sentence *US*

- — John R Armore and Joseph D. Wolfe, *Dictionary of Desperation*, 1976

▸ do the book and cover

to serve a life sentence in prison *US*

- — Jay Robert Nash, *Dictionary of Crime*, p. 40, 1992

▸ get the book

1 in prison, to be reprimanded *UK*

- — Angela Devlin, *Prison Patter*, p. 56, 1996

2 to become religious *UK*

The book is the *Bible* but other works could apply equally well.

- — Angela Devlin, *Prison Patter*, p. 30, 1996

▸ make book

to bet *US*

- [H]e was shrugging it off like water, makin' book with the technicians on how long he could keep his eyes open after the poles touched. — Ken Kesey, *One Flew Over the Cuckoo's Nest*, p. 277, 1962

▸ on the book

1 used of a high-security prisoner who must constantly be identified by a small official book and photograph *UK*

- — Angela Devlin, *Prison Patter*, p. 30, 1996
- Donny was "on the book" (a Category A prisoner) and was known for his short temper. — *The Guardian*, 15th February 2001

2 in the theatre, working as a prompter *UK*

The book in question is a play's text.

- — Dulcie Gray, *No Quarter for a Star*, 1964

3 on credit *UK, 1984*

▸ the book

the unwritten code of style and conduct observed by pimps *US*

- During the study we only met three White pimps, and all of them mimicked the Black style in their speech, dress, and in their adherence to "The Book," the unwritten pimp's code. — Christina and Richard Milner, *Black Players*, p. 12, 1972

▸ throw the book at; give the book

to sentence someone to a maximum penalty allowed by law *US, 1908*

- That's what they do, give you the book. That's supposed to scare the other guys. — Chester Himes, *Cast the First Stone*, p. 12, 1952
- The assistant U.S. attorney argued that the defendant had been involved in criminal endeavors for over four decades and wanted an upward departure. Which Raylan understood to mean throw the book at him. — Elmore Leonard, *Riding the Rap*, p. 280, 1995

book *verb*

1 to study *US*

- — Collin Baker et al., *College Undergraduate Slang Study Conducted at Brown University*, p. 86, 1968

2 to realise; to see and understand *UK*

- [T]he man immediately booked who they [detectives] were. — G.F. Newman, *Sir, You Bastard*, 1970

3 to assume something *UK*

- They've got Roy booked as the Mister Big[.] — J.J. Connolly, *Know Your Enemy [britpulp]*, p. 159, 1999

4 to depart, usually hurriedly *US, 1974*

- Belly sprang to her feet. "We gotta book – fast." — Seth Morgan, *Homeboy*, p. 66, 1990
- Marsellus: Whatch got? English Dave: He booked. — *Pulp Fiction*, 1994
- We gotta book it if we're going ot make it to P.E. — *Clueless*, 1995
- We gotta book. We're catching a bus to Chi-town. — *Chasing Amy*, 1997
- Hey, sorry, but we gotta book. You coming? — *200 Cigarettes*, 1999

▸ **book a party of two**
to arrange for oral sex to be performed on two male prisoners *US*
• —James Harris, *A Convict's Dictionary*, 1989

▸ **book the action**
to accept a bet *US*
• If a player puts down a roll of dimes, you book the action.—Lee Solkey, *Dummy Up and Deal*, p. 108, 1980

▸ **book your seat**
to pad the seat of your trousers with newspaper or a book before going to be caned *UK, 1961*
Schoolboy usage, post World War 2 until the 1970s when corporal punishment was outlawed.

book-beater *noun*
a serious, hard-working student *US*
• — *Yank*, p. 18, 24th March 1945

book 'em, Danno
used for humorous suggestion that somebody has been caught in an improper act *US*
From the US television series *Hawaii Five-O* (1968–1980), in which Detective Steve McGarrett would order Detective 'Danno' Williams to arrest a suspect.

bookend *verb*
in twelve-step recovery programmes such as Alcoholics Anonymous, to speak with a fellow recovering addict both before and after confronting a difficult situation *US*
• —Christopher Cavanaugh, *AA to Z*, p. 58, 1998

booket *noun*
a woman who receives a cunnilinguist's attention *UK*
West Indian patois for 'bucket', recorded August 2002.

book gook *noun*
a diligent, socially inept student *US*
Teen slang.
• — *Newsweek*, p. 28, 8th October 1951

bookie *noun*
a bookmaker *UK, 1885*
Sometimes spelt 'booky'.
• He spotted the young Duke of Salamanca drawing stacks of white from the bookies[.]—Charles Raven, *Underworld Nights*, p. 174, 1956
• The Pope is the world's biggest bookie. Makes people bet on their own salvation.— *The Bad Lieutenant*, 1992
• [H]e just hung around with a bunch of fellow deadbeats doing the pub, bookie's, Spar [a grocery store] shuffle.—John Williams, *Cardiff Dead*, p. 78, 2000

bookie's chance *noun*
in horse racing, a horse with high odds (12–1 or higher) that bookmakers deem the favourite *AUSTRALIA*
• —Ned Wallish, *The Truth Dictionary of Racing Slang*, p. 9, 1989

bookman *noun*
a prisoner serving a life sentence *US*
• —Vincent J. Monteleone, *Criminal Slang*, p. 30, 1949

boo koo *noun*
▷ see: BOO-COO

books *noun*
1 used as a figurative description of membership in a criminal organisation *US*
• — *American Speech*, p. 305, December 1964: 'Lingua cosa nostra'
• The bosses are sitting on millions and they say, you no do-a this, you no do-a that – meanwhile they close the books and the soldiers have to drive trucks on the side to live.—Edwin Torres, *Carlito's Way*, p. 41, 1975
2 employment documents that are returned to a dismissed worker *UK: SCOTLAND*
• [T]o get your books means to get the sack.—Michael Munro, *The Patter, Another Blast*, 1988

▸ **do books**
to steal or forge official benefit books, such as child benefit *UK*
• —Angela Devlin, *Prison Patter*, p. 46, 1996

▸ **in your bad books**
in disfavour *UK, 1861*
• I was in her bad books for a longer time than ever.—Saul Bellow, *The Adventures of Augie March*, p. 31, 1953

▸ **in your good books**
in favour *UK, 1839*
• After paying more than 50 times the face value of each ticket, he said: "I don't care if she is mad for Vin Diesel, these put me in her good books for life."— *The Scotsman*, 7th November 2003

book up *verb*
to study *US*
• — *American Speech*, p. 56, Spring-Summer 1975: 'Razorback slang'

boola-boola *adjective*
characterised by extreme boosterism and spirited support of an institution *US, 1900*
The song 'Boola Boola' has been one of Yale University's football fight songs since 1901 when it was written by Allan M. Hirsh, who explained the meaning of the word as follows: 'It is interesting to note that many people have asked us what the word "Boola" meant, and we said it was Hawaiian and meant a joy cry. We stuck to this for several years until someone came along and pointed out to us that there was no B in the Hawaiian language and therefore Boola could not possibly be Hawaiian. So the fact remains that we do not know what it means, except that it was euphonious and easy to sing and to our young ears sounded good'. The song was an 'adaptation' of an 1898 'La Hoola Boola' performed by Bob Cole and Billy Johnson.
• It was a real boola-boola reunion.—Edwin Torres, *After Hours*, p. 294, 1979
• — *Yale Alumni Magazine*, October 2000

boolhipper *noun*
a black leather jacket with a belt in the back *US*
• —Roger D. Abrahams, *Deep Down in the Jungle*, p. 258, 1970

boolum *noun*
a boaster or an intimidating braggart *IRELAND*
From the Irish *buaileam sciath*.
• Don't be acting the boolum.—Irwin Liam, *North Munster Antiquarian Journal*, p. 84, 2000

boom *noun*
1 potent marijuana *US, 1946*
• Stoned Raider, in the Temple of Boom— Cypress Hill, *Stoned Raider*, 1995
• Yo, Cass, you got any boom?— *Kids*, 1995
• Look: you was after the boom poly [Polynesian marijuana] an' I got two kees.—Nick Barlay, *Curvy Lovebox*, p. 33, 1997
2 fake crack cocaine *US*
• One of the officers patted him down and felt a "rock-like substance," said Sgt. Clifford Gatlin. Smith told the officer it was "boom," street slang for fake crack cocaine.— *Daily Town Talk (Alexandria, Louisiana)*, p. 3A, 25th April 2001
3 the erect penis *US, 1958*
• —J. E. Lighter, *Historical Dictionary of American Slang, Volume 1*, p. 237, 1994

boom *adjective*
fashionable, pleasing *CANADA*
• You look boom in that new dress.—Jack Chambers (Editor), *Slang Bag 93 (University of Toronto)*, p. 1, Winter 1993

boom!
used for expressing enthusiasm *US*
• How many times have the Tar Heels beat Kentucky in basketball? The answer is 16. Boom!—Connie Eble (Editor), *UNC-CH Campus Slang*, p. 2, October 2002

boom and zoom; b and z *verb*
in air combat, to use a relative altitude advantage to attack an opponent (to boom) and then return to a superior position out of danger (to zoom) *US*
• But that bunch of good old boys, big-shot lawyers, ex-Marine Corps heroes, ring-knocking fighter jocks who can't get enough of that boom' and zoomin'[.]—Larry Heinemann, *Paco's Story*, p. 157, 1986

boombastic *adjective*
excellent; also (of music) resounding *CANADA*
Elaboration of conventional 'boom' (a booming sound) or BOOM (pleasing), informed by BOOM (marijuana).
• [Y]ou're smothered and covered up in the sound / you stand strong as you pump your fist / I'm talkin' all that jazz / now what's my definition[.]—Dream Warriors, *My Definition of a Boombastic Jazz Style*, 1991
• What you want is some boombastic romantic fantastic love. —Shaggy *Mr Boombastic*, 1995
• [O]ld-fashioned, boombastic deep house party[.]— *Mixmag*, p. 138, December 2001

boom-boom *noun*

1 sex *US, 1964*

From Asian pidgin. Major use in Vietnam during the war.

- —Carl Fleischhauer, *A Glossary of Army Slang*, p. 5, 1968
- [A]nd I get to wondering what the fuck am I doing sleeping on the couch in my own house instead of in there doing boom-boom with the little woman[.]—Robert Campbell, *Juice*, p. 201, 1988
- —Linda Reinberg, *In the Field*, p. 26, 1991
- —Connie Eble (Editor), *UNC-CH Campus Slang*, p. 1, Fall 1997
- She love you good. Boom-boom long time. Ten dolla.—*Full Metal Jacket*, 67

2 the buttocks *BAHAMAS*

- —John A. Holm, *Dictionary of Bahamian English*, p. 25, 1982

3 an act of defecation *US*

Children's bathroom vocabulary.

- —Harold Wentworth and Stuart Berg Flexner, *Dictionary of American Slang*, p. 54, 1960

4 live music *US*

- Quirky alt-rockers The Anarcy Orchesetra will provide the boom boom[.]—*The Record (Bergen County, New Jersey)*, p. 37, 24th October 2003

5 a pistol *US*

- —Lou Shelly, *Hepcats Jive Talk Dictionary*, p. 22, 1945

6 a cowboy or Western film *US*

- —Marcus Hanna Boulware, *Jive and Slang of Students in Negro Colleges*, 1947

boom-boom *verb*

to copulate *US*

- Hey, baby-san, you boum-boum G.I.?—*Screw*, p. 5, 15th February 1971

boom boom!

used for signalling or accompanying the punch-line of a joke, especially a bad or corny joke *UK*

Coined as a catchphrase for children's television puppet Basil Brush, first seen in 1963.

boom-boom girl *noun*

a prostitute *US, 1966*

Vietnam usage.

- The rest of the day was spent in finding a boom-boom girl. —Charles Anderson, *The Grunts*, p. 159, 1976
- —Linda Reinberg, *In the Field*, p. 26, 1991

boom-boom house; boom-boom parlor *noun*

a brothel *US, 1966*

- —*American-Statesman (Austin, Texas)*, p. A7, 9th January 1966
- —Carl Fleischhauer, *A Glossary of Army Slang*, p. 5, 1968

boom-booms-a-gogo *noun*

a unit of quad-fifty machine guns *US*

Korean war usage.

- —Frank Hailey, *Soldier Talk*, p. 7, 1982

boom box *noun*

a large, portable radio and tape player *US, 1981*

- —Ellen C. Bellone (Editor), *Dictionary of Slang*, p. 3, 1989
- They measured their warrior cakewalk to a boombox beat as deadly and mechanical as automatic fire.—Seth Morgan, *Homeboy*, p. 18, 1990
- I could hear sirens and boom boxes and Valley kids howling at the moon as if they owned the night.—Armistead Maupin, *Maybe the Moon*, p. 138, 1992
- And there were a lot of young people on the streets, leaning into cars, chatting, listening to boom boxes.—Joseph Wambaugh, *Finnegan's Week*, p. 59, 1993
- The normal noises of the Cabrinin-Taylor projects continued to accompany their weekly sexual get together: doors slamming, boom boxes blaring raps, screams, yells, car horns blasting[.]—Odie Hawkins, *Amazing Grace*, p. 9, 1993
- She's brought her boom box on the bus[.]—Karline Smith, *Letters to Andy Cole*, p. 138, 1998
- My boom box, which I strapped into the passenger seat with the safety belt, could hardly project over the constant sound of traffic. —Rita Ciresi, *Pink Slip*, p. 191, 1999
- No children playing on the sidewalk. No metal blaring out of a second-story boombox. A bastion of repectability and decorum. —Janet Evanovich, *Seven Up*, p. 113, 2001

boom boy *noun*

a marijuana user *US*

- —Jay Robert Nash, *Dictionary of Crime*, p. 40, 1992

boom bye; boom bwoy *noun*

a homosexual male *JAMAICA, 2002*

Jamaican patois rendering of **BUM BOY**.

boomer *noun*

1 a large example of something *AUSTRALIA, 1843*

- The opposite of 'cow' in this usage is not 'bull' but often 'boomer' or 'bottler' as in 'a boomer of a day.'—Arthur Chipper, *The Aussie Swearer's Guide*, p. 34, 1972
- We were there to cover the boat race – big off-shore boomers like Cigarettes and Scarabs and Panteras, ninety miles an hour on the open sea.—Hunter S. Thompson, *Songs of the Doomed*, p. 215, 1980
- —Louis S. Leland, *A Personal Kiwi-Yankee Dictionary*, p. 16, 1984
- Mooney Valley Racing Club secretary Ian McEwen described Melbourne's second Sunday race meeting as a tremendous success. "It was an absolute boomer," he said last night.—*Sun-News Pictorial*, p. 4, 1987

2 a large kangaroo *AUSTRALIA, 1830*

- One big boomer came towards us when the dogs were after the others.—A.B. Facey, *A Fortunate Life*, p. 79, 1981

3 a powerful, hard-breaking wave *AUSTRALIA, 1942*

- I've seen those boomers in a movie and I'm telling you they'd damn near kill you just seeing them on the screen.—Frederick Kohner, *Gidget*, p. 4–5, 1957
- —John Severson, *Modern Surfing Around the World*, p. 165, 1964
- Bells: A beach on the Victorian west coast famous for its boomers, its Easter surfing carnival and its lack of nightlife.—Phil Jarratt, *Surfing Dictionary*, p. 10, 1985

4 a nuclear submarine armed with missiles *US, 1976*

- On the other question, no, they've never recalled all their boomers at once, but they do occasionally reshuffle all their positions at once. —Tom Clancy, *The Hunt for Red October*, p. 88, 1984

5 a member of the baby boom generation, born between roughly 1945 and 1955 *US, 1982*

- The boomers have failed to provide or protect or prepare us for any kind of hopeful life.—*Empire Records*, 1995
- It was all so depressing. Boomers weren't supposed to get old. It sucked.—Joseph Wambaugh, *Floaters*, p. 138, 1996

6 a worker who travels from job to job *US, 1893*

- Uncle Bill Balloon is a boomer and I have a few railroad things written that'll give you a laugh.—Jack Kerouac, *Letter to Neal and Carolyn Cassady*, p. 396, 10th January 1953
- I was surprised there were no hitchhikers or boomers on the road; it was still picking season.—Clancy Sigal, *Going Away*, p. 82, 1961
- Tell her I've become a boomer, gone down to Missouri to work on permit, they got this two-story structure they're putting up. —Elmore Leoanrd, *Killshot*, p. 161, 1989

7 during aerial refuelling, the boom operator on the fuelling plane *US*

- The bomber pilot's task was then simply to formate within a prescribed envelope while the boomer, the refueling operator, actually flew the patented Boeing boom into the receptacle. —Walter J. Boyne and Steven L. Thompson, *The Wild Blue*, p. 442, 1986

8 in trucking, a binder used to tie down a load *US*

- —Montie Tak, *Truck Talk*, p. 16, 1971

boomer!

excellent! *AUSTRALIA*

- "The race track! Boomer! What a sweet gig!" "We'll be able ta bet an' booze all day long."—*Sick Puppy*, p. 10, 1998

boomerang *noun*

1 a young person who moves back in with their parents after moving out *US*

- —Vann Wesson, *Generation X Field Guide and Lexicon*, p. 26, 1997

2 a repeated offender, a recidivist *US*

- —Gary K. Farlow, *Prison-ese*, p. 5, 2002

3 a plane flight that returns without reaching its destination because of poor weather *ANTARCTICA, 1994*

- —Bernadette Hince, *The Antarctic Dictionary*, p. 66, 2000
- —*Cool Antartica*, 2003: 'Antarctic slang'

4 a man with more than one girlfriend *UK*

In West Indian and UK black use, August 2002.

5 in television and film making, a device that holds a filter in front of a light *US*

- —Ira Konigsberg, *The Complete Film Dictionary*, p. 33, 1987

boomerang *verb*

to return to prison shortly after being released *US*

- —William K. Bentley and James M. Corbett, *Prison Slang*, 1992

boomers *noun*
LSD *UK*
- —Harry Shapiro, *Recreational Drugs*, p. 266, 2004

booming *adjective*
excellent *US*
- Baby was fine, body was boomin', like right outta Jet centerfold o somethin.—*Boyz N The Hood*, 1990
- —Kenn "Naz" Young, *Naz's Dictionary of Teen Slang*, p. 13, 1993

boom out *verb*
to go to the US to work *CANADA*
- Mohawks from Kahnawake, near Montreal, and Akwesasne, near Cornwall, Ont., have come to New York, seeking dangerous and well-paid work at the top of construction sites. They called [it] "booming out" for work. They worked in Texas, Arizona, Florida.—*Toronto Globe and Mail*, p. R3, 29th April 2002

boomps-a-daisy!
used as a childish catchphrase or light-hearted response to trivialise a minor physical accident *UK*
Blending **WHOOPS-A-DAISY!** with 'bump'. 'Hands, Knees and Boomps-a-Daisy!' was a popular song and 'The Boomps-a-Daisy' a popular dance in the 1930s.

booms *noun*
drums *US*
- —Harold Wentworth and Stuart Berg Flexner, *Dictionary of American Slang*, p. 54, 1960

boom squad *noun*
the group of prison guards who are used to quell disturbances *US*
- Depending on whom you ask, the ESU, or "boom squad," is a group of dedicated officers with the toughest job on the island or a bunch of testosterone-fueled thugs who get a rush from brawling with the inmates.—*Village Voice*, p. 62, 19th December 2000

boom wagon *noun*
in trucking, a truck hauling dynamite *US, 1942*
- —Mary Elting, *Trucks at Work*, 1946

boomy *adjective*
emphasising low frequencies, producing poorly defined sound *US*
Used in television and film making.
- —Ira Konigsberg, *The Complete Film Dictionary*, p. 33, 1987

boon *noun*
a black person *US, 1967*
Possibly reduced from **BOON COON** (a good friend) or as outlined in the following citation.
- ["A]ll these boons just sat there laughing at me." "Boons?" I said. "What's boons?" "You know," she said. "Black guys." "Why do you call them that?" "I dunno. From 'baboons,' I guess." I didn't say anything.—Lester Bangs, *Psychotic Reactions and Carburetor Dung*, p. 272, 1978

boon *adjective*
close, intimate *US*
- They pounded each other on the back. They looked like boon buddies.—Iceberg Slim (Robert Beck), *Pimp*, p. 123, 1969

boona *noun*
▸ **give it the full boona**
to hold nothing back *UK: SCOTLAND*
From *boona*, an Indian dish which, when served in some Glasgow Indian restaurants, is available as a 'half boona' or a 'full boona'.
- Are ye for the off after this pint or are we gaunny gie it the full boona the night?—Michael Munro, *The Patter, Another Blast*, 1988

boon coon *noun*
a very close friend *US, 1958*
- He said, "About a month ago, your 'boon coon' 'Party' caught sixty in the county."—Iceberg Slim (Robert Beck), *Pimp*, p. 79, 1969
- That's cool for you. You his boon-coon.—Edwin Torres, *Q & A*, p. 187, 1977

boondagger *noun*
a lesbian with overtly masculine mannerisms and affectations *US, 1972*
- —Harold Wentworth and Stuart Berg Flexner, *Dictionary of American Slang*, p. 680, 1976

boondie *noun*
1 in Western Australia, a rock *AUSTRALIA*
Probably from an Australian Aboriginal language.

2 in Western Australia, a piece of conglomerated sand used by children to throw at one another in play *AUSTRALIA*
- Well – they horse around and chiack each other, and – there, see that bastard, practising grenade-throwing with bits of boondies? I done that many a time!—T.A.G. Hungerford, *The Ridge and the River*, p. 94, 1952
- That autumn the street seemed full. There were always Pickles kids and Lamb kids up one end of the street throwing boondies or chasing someone's dog.—Tim Winton, *Cloudstreet*, p. 51, 1991
- In Western Australia we called boondies the clumps of sand at the beach and on building sites, there was a competition of throwing boondies at a wall and seeing whose boon[d]ie left the most sand on the wall.—*Wordmap (www.abc.net.au/wordmap)*, 2003

boondock *verb*
1 in trucking, to drive on back roads, avoiding major motorways *US*
- —Montie Tak, *Truck Talk*, p. 16, 1971

2 to drive off-road through a remote area *US*
- —John Edwards, *Auto Dictionary*, p. 17, 1993

3 in tiddlywinks, to send an opponent's wink a long way away, especially out of the playing area *UK*
After US **BOONDOCKS** (an isolated region).
- —C.W.Edwards *Glossary*, 1980

4 in tiddlywinks, to shoot from a position far from the action *US*
- —*Verbatim*, p. 525, December 1977

boondocker *noun*
a party held in the country *US*
- —*Current Slang*, p. 1, Winter 1966

boondockers *noun*
marine-issued combat boots *US, 1942*
- In preparation for disembarking I'm wearing the following articles: scivvie shirt and drawers, long johns, flannel shirt, utility trousers, cold-weather trousers, pile-lined vest, park w/hood, gloves and inserts, flannel cap, socks, boondockers[.]—Martin Russ, *The Last Parallel*, p. 58, 1957
- I could sure use those size-twelve boondockers of yours. —Joseph Wambaugh, *The Blue Knight*, p. 137, 1973
- Kavanaugh lay next to MacCauley, his face dead white, his boondockers smelling of vomit.—Alfred Coppel, *The Burning Mountain*, p. 211, 1983
- The first thing he saw was the man's shoes, black boondockers, then bell-bottom jeans, then the gym bag and the Uzi.—Stephen Coonts, *Final FLight*, p. 338, 1988

boondocks *noun*
the remote end of nowhere *US, 1909*
- Schauer told me he saw the accident but it is so far out in the boondocks people were afraid to stop.—*San Francisco Examiner*, p. 125, 21st June 1964
- [H]e had this thing for a P.R. chick, which in those days was unheard of, so like his uncle kept him in the boondocks.—Edwin Torres, *Carlito's Way*, p. 22, 1975

boondoggle *noun*
a business trip or venture designed for the enjoyment of those involved, not for its stated purpose *US, 1935*
- It's just a big boondoggle for the Army; they're trying to get the guided missile program away from the Air Force.—Max Shulman, *Rally Round the Flag, Boys!*, p. 95, 1957

booner *noun*
1 a talent scout *US*
An allusion to American frontier pioneer Daniel Boone.
- —Don Wilmeth, *The Language of American Popular Entertainment*, p. 30, 1981

2 an unrefined and loutish person from a lower socio-economic area *AUSTRALIA*
- Crossing through a small park, they found themselves in the heart of the Cross, a magnet for sleazebags and booners of every description.—Linda Jaivin, *Rock n Roll Babes from Outer Space*, p. 82, 1996
- While 50% of Canberra's surface area is wood, leaves and pornography, the other 50% is taken up by the suburb of Kambah. Named after Sir Doug Shane Gary 'Giz a VB' Kambah, Kambah is the largest manufacturer of panel vans with loud booners in them screaming incoherent swear words out the window whilst trying to steer.—Ben Hutchings, *www.effect.net.au/geeen/geeenc.htm*, 2000

boong *noun*

an Aboriginal person; hence, any other dark-skinned person *AUSTRALIA, 1924*

From the Australian Aboriginal language Wemba, meaning 'person'. Used disparagingly by white people. Now strongly taboo.

- All the boongs'll reckon yer off your onion. —John Wynnum, *Tar Dust*, p. 24, 1962
- I'd rather a boong any day. —Wal Watkins, *Race the Lazy River*, p. 64, 1963
- You have orders that Miss Zelmara and I should go and live with the boongs in the hills? —Ray Slattery, *Mobbs' Mob*, p. 107, 1966
- The boongs from the Catalina Base have got their airflow matresses laid out all over the Uni lawns. —Dorothy Hewett, *The Chapel Perilous*, p. 29, 1972
- Bloke? He's someone who's male and Australian. Even a boong could be a bloke—Sandra Jobson, *Blokes*, p. 34, 1984
- Don't shake hands with no boongs—Phillip Gwynne, *Deadly Unna?*, p. 29, 1998

boonga *noun*

a Pacific Islander or any other dark-skinned person *NEW ZEALAND*

- Aucklanders called Maoris niggers, blacks and 'boshees', a long-forgotten mid-century forerunner of such terms as wog, goo, boonga, and hun. —*(Aukland) Star*, p. 4, 29th November 1957

boong moll *noun*

a prostitute who serves dark-skinned men *AUSTRALIA*

A combination of **BOONG** (an Aboriginal or dark-skinned man) and **MOLL** (a prostitute)

- —Sydney J. Baker, *Australia Speaks*, 1953

boongy *noun*

the buttocks *BAHAMAS*

- —Patricia Clinton-Meicholas, *More Talkin' Bahamian*, p. 22, 1995

boonie hat *noun*

a fatigue hat, made of cotton canvas with a brim around, that kept the sun and rain off the heads of American soldiers in Vietnam *US, 1972*

- [C]amouflage T-shirts for the kids, stiff-brim drill instructor hats, Ranger boonie hats and combat caps, holsters, binoculars, canteens, knives, and bayonets with sawtooth blades[.]—Elmore Leonard, *Bandits*, p. 266, 1987
- —Linda Reinberg, *In the Field*, p. 26, 1991

boonie rat *noun*

a soldier serving in the jungle or other remote area *US, 1967*

- Everyone has always portrayed infantryman, boonierat, as dumb. Everyone, except anyone who has ever been a boonierat. —John M. Del Vecchio, *The 13th Valley*, p. 121, 1982
- From this point on, with the possible exception of a seven-day rest-and-recuperation (R&R) leave (probably spent somewhere else in Asia), he would live each day of the next year in the surreal, virtually indescribable existence of the "boonie rat." —James L. Estep, *Company Commander, Vietnam*, p. 22, 1996

boonies *noun*

a remote rural area *US, 1956*

An abbreviation of **BOONDOCKS**.

- —Carl Fleischhauer, *A Glossary of Army Slang*, p. 5, 1968
- Life in the boonies: SF's Jim Schoettler, now teaching first graders in Oroville, wrote "love and peace" on his chalkboard – as a writing exercise for his pupils – and was promptly ordered to remove the phrase by a superior. —*San Francisco Chronicle*, 10th February 1969
- In the boonies the whole time? —Ronald J. Glasser, *365 Days*, p. 130, 1971
- "Anything more than six blocks from Hollywood and Vine is to you the boonies," Pachoulo said. —Robert Campbell, *Juice*, p. 168, 1988
- The place was deep in the boonies, but after a few wrong turns on backcountry roads, we came to a tiny, run-down shack perched on stilts over a steep hillside. —C.D. Payne, *Youth in Revolt*, p. 37, 1993

booooo!

an exclamation of approval *UK*

The difference with 'boo' (an unlexicalised verbalisation of disapproval) is essentially one of intention; explained by Cleo Soazandry, co-editor of *Live* magazine: 'If you make it sound a bit cheery – kind of like a firework – then it's a good thing'.

- We're talking BOOOOO! Which may or may not have been "boom", before the "m" got knocked off, but which you do want to hear as a roar of appreciation. —*The Guardian*, 12th January 2005

booorrring *adjective*

very boring *US*

Slang by drawn out pronunciation. From popular entertainment.

- Would you want to drive a truck all day? Boorrring! —C.D. Payne, *Youth in Revolt*, p. 217, 1993
- Back in the early part of my career, I think Cleveland was the most boring city to go in and play. But now it's one of the hottest cities to go in and play. But when I came into the league, it was boooring. —*Denver Post*, p. C4, 27th July 2003

boo out *verb*

to leave *US*

- —*American Speech*, p. 154, May 1959: 'Gator (University of Florida) slang'

boops *noun*

a man who supports a woman with whom he lives without the benefit of marriage *JAMAICA*

- —Peter L. Patrick, *Some Recent Jamaican Creole Words*, 2003

boopsie *noun*

a woman supported by a man with whom she lives without the benefit of marriage *JAMAICA*

- —Richard Allsopp, *Dictionary of Caribbean English Usage*, p. 111, 1996

boo-reefer *noun*

marijuana *US*

- —David Claerbaut, *Black Jargon in White America*, p. 58, 1972

booshway *noun*

the boss *CANADA*

A slurring of the French *bourgeois*.

- When it was all over the booshway–the leader of the party–came into the tent and gave Kimmel hell. —Ernest Haycox, *Earthbreakers*, p. 172, 1952

boost *noun*

1 a theft, especially a car theft *US*

- You down with the boost? —*Kids*, 1995
- MEMPHIS: What kind of job? ATLEY JACKSON: A boost. A big boost. —*Gone in 60 Seconds*, 2000

2 in poker, an increased or raised bet *US*

- —George Percy, *The Language of Poker*, p. 12, 1988

3 a background player in a large confidence swindle *US*

- —M. Allen Henderson, *How Con Games Work*, p. 218, 1985

4 crack cocaine *UK*

- —Mike Haskins, *Drugs*, p. 281, 2003

▸ **on the boost**

engaged in shoplifting *US*

- —Joseph E. Ragen and Charles Finston, *Inside the World's Toughest Prison*, p. 810, 1962

boost *verb*

1 to steal, especially (in the US) to steal a car or to shoplift *US, 1928*

- Lie detector tests were given today to two bank employes (sic) who reported that their car was "boosted" last week of $27,000 in currency. —*San Francisco Call-Bulletin*, p. 7, 7th February 1955
- A boosting girl made twice as much money in an hour as a whore made in a week. —Clarence Cooper Jr, *The Scene*, p. 31, 1960
- I'm going uptown tomorrow, boost a good coat. —Alexander Trocchi, *Cain's Book*, p. 37, 1960
- "Pinched. Jobbed. Swiped. Stole," he says, happily. "You know, man, like somebody boosted my threads." —Ken Kesey, *One Flew Over the Cuckoo's Nest*, p. 94, 1962
- Then there was boostin' in department stores – and there was dice, cards, writin' numbers (single action) for Jakie Cooperman[.] —Edwin Torres, *Carlito's Way*, p. 14, 1975
- [B]oosting the plane had been a snap. —Jack W. Thomas, *Heavy Number*, p. 107, 1976
- But he was not into the boostin' and thievin' with us. —Edwin Torres, *Q & A*, p. 162, 1977
- "In my youth, Louis said, "I boosted cars, sent them over to Nassau, Freeport, Eleuthera..." —Elmore Leonard, *Riding the Rap*, p. 65, 1995
- Hell no, I boosted a 'Vette. —*Gone in 60 Seconds*, 2000
- When "boosting" declined as an industry at the onset of the First World War other activities had to be found to supplant thieving traditions. —Brian McDonald, *Elephant Boys*, p. 9, 2000

2 to illegally open a lock using force, skill or technology *UK*

From the sense 'to steal'.

- "Then our man takes a quick trot to the front door, boosts the lock and..." He shrugged. "That's the how of it, anyway[."]—Chris Ryan, *The Watchman*, p. 93, 2001

3 in poker, to increase the amount bet on a hand *US*

- —Albert H. Morehead, *The Complete Guide to Winning Poker*, p. 257, 1967

4 to inject a drug intravenously *US, 1998*

- —Mike Haskins, *Drugs*, p. 290, 2003

▸ **boost one**

to defecate *US*

- — *Surfer Magazine*, p. 30, February 1992

booster *noun*

1 a thief, especially a shoplifter or car thief *US, 1908*

- "Boosters," Inspector Smith explained, "pick on out-of-state cars because they know the people are traveling and have a lot of stuff with 'em."— *San Francisco Call-Bulletin*, 28th June 1949
- Martha had not been a booster when she worked for me[.]—Polly Adler, *A House is Not a Home*, p. 121, 1953
- —Jack Webb, *The Badge*, p. 220, 1958
- He would have a booster someday. He had made up his mind to that.—Clarence Cooper Jr, *The Scene*, p. 31, 1960
- Most male addicts are eventually pimps, boosters, or pushers. —Alexander Trocchi, *Cain's Book*, p. 158, 1960
- That was the gang of organized boosters, who would deliver to order, in one day, C.O.D., any kind of garment you desired.—Malcolm X and Alex Haley, *The Autobiography of Malcolm X*, p. 66, 1964
- [H]e was always copping her furs, jewelry, etc., from the "Boosters" (junkie thieves) for practically nothing.—Babs Gonzales, *I Paid My Dues*, p. 97, 1967
- Then you ready for high school. She might decide that she wants to be a booster [thief].—Christina and Richard Milner, *Black Players*, p. 96, 1972
- "Now I ain't flat," said the beat-up cat / "We're traveling boosters, you know."—Dennis Wepman et al., *The Life*, p. 55, 1976
- Two cops blown away by a credit card booster – that don't figure. — *48 Hours*, 1982

2 a full-time, career thief *US*

- —Robert C. Prus and C.R.D. Sharper, *Road Hustler*, p. 169, 1977

3 a criminal who specialises in selling stolen goods *US*

- Some Boosters specialize in such wares as jewelry, cars, dope, etc. —Gene Sorrows, *All About Carnivals*, p. 11, 1985

4 a confederate of a cheat who lures players to a card game, carnival concession or other game of chance *US, 1906*

- —Don Wilmeth, *The Language of American Popular Entertainment*, p. 30, 1981
- —Thomas L. Clark, *The Dictionary of Gambling and Gaming*, p. 24, 1987

5 an additional dose of a drug taken to prolong intoxication *US*

- —William D. Alsever, *Glossary for the Establishment and Other Uptight People*, p. 4, 1970

booster fold *noun*

a special inside jacket pocket used by shoplifters *US*

- With both suits tucked under my armpits in a booster fold, I scanned the moving traffic until I saw an empty cab.—Donald Goines, *Whoreson*, p. 88, 1972

booster pill *noun*

a central nervous system stimulant *US*

- —Eugene Landy, *The Underground Dictionary*, p. 38, 1971

booster stick *noun*

a tobacco cigarette that has been enhanced with marijuana or marijuana extract *US, 1973*

- —Jay Robert Nash, *Dictionary of Crime*, p. 40, 1992

boosting ben *noun*

a special overcoat used by shoplifters *US*

- —Hyman E. Goldin et al., *Dictionary of American Underworld Lingo*, p. 32, 1950

boosting bloomers; booster bloomers *noun*

underwear designed for concealing merchandise that has been shoplifted *US*

- Boots was able to go back to work, so I stopped her from doing any more boosting. Her boosting bloomers were packed away for later use.—Donald Goines, *Whoreson*, p. 134, 1972
- Booster Bloomers – a large pair of underclothing worn under the outer pants or dress – can be used to "steal hundreds of dollars worth of goods in a matter of a few seconds."— *San Francisco Examiner*, p. 6, 22nd February 1974

boot *noun*

1 dismissal from employment or other engagement *UK, 1881*

The image of being kicked away.

- So we both gets the boot from this job[.]—John Peter Jones, *Feather Pluckers*, p. 38, 1964
- WAYNE[:] Aw... but I got a new bird now. WAYNETTA[:] Well giver her the boot!—Harry Enfield, *Harry Enfield and His Humorous Chums*, p. 15, 1997

2 a black person *US, 1954*

- My Dad has taught me that in England some foolish man may call me sambo, darkie, boot or munt or nigger, even.—Colin McInnes, *City of Spades*, 1957
- —Robert George Reisner, *The Jazz Titans*, p. 151, 1960
- What's wrong with a white broad helping two spades? She's a 'boot.' She looks like what she is.—Iceberg Slim (Robert Beck), *Pimp*, p. 207, 1969
- One boot got the tom-tom and the other grabbed a flute. —Steve Cannon, *Groove, Bang, and Jive Around*, p. 187, 1969

3 a newly enlisted or drafted recruit in the armed services, especially the marines *US, 1911*

- For a good many years, as long as many an older salt can remember, the word "boot" has been synonymous with the younger and less experienced men of the Navy and Marine Corps.— *Leatherneck*, p. 7, September 1946
- A former Marine "boot" told the courtmartial of S/Sgt. Matthew McKeon that the drill instructor warned his platoon non-winners would drown while sharks would devour the rest before they plunged into the waters of Ribbon Creek.— *San Francisco News*, p. 1, 21st July 1956
- I've never seen a more disgusting, disreputable bunch of boots in my life.—Earl Thompson, *Tattoo*, p. 141, 1974
- At 21, Laing, a quiet, dark, and handsome man from Waterloo, Iowa, just a few years out of undergraduate school in engineering at Dubuque's Catholic Loras University, was just a "boot ensign." —Robert K. Wilcox, *Scream of Eagles*, p. 50, 1990

4 in the US Army, a second lieutenant *US*

- — *True*, p. 4, July 1966
- —Carl Fleischhauer, *A Glossary of Army Slang*, p. 5, 1968

5 amusement or pleasure *US, 1979*

- Down Atherton way, the peasants are getting a big boot out of the guy who's having a home built on Valparaiso Ave.— *San Francisco Examiner*, p. 25, 2nd January 1952
- He got such a boot out of being a big-dog fight manager, he never found out why I coudln't lose weight except in a steam bath. —Rocky Garciano (with Rowland Barber), *Somebody Up There Likes Me*, p. 261, 1955
- You'll Get a Real Boot out of this Beauty [Advertisement]— *San Francisco Examiner*, p. I-13, 30th March 1956
- I told her I packed the pipe by mistake and she said she wanted to give it to you anyway since you seemed to get a boot out of it[.] —Darryl Ponicsan, *The Last Detail*, p. 112, 1970

6 a bootleg product *US*

- He'd copy hits, big ones, Madonna, Elton John, the Spice Girls, and sell the boots down in South America at a discount.—Elmore Leonard, *Be Cool*, p. 205, 1999

7 while injecting a drug intravenously, the drawing of blood into the syringe to mix with the drug *US*

- I was just finishing up, the needle still in the vein for one last boot down the old line[.]—Jim Carroll, *Forced Entries*, p. 47, 1987

8 any central nervous system depressant *US*

- —Jay Robert Nash, *Dictionary of Crime*, p. 41, 1992

9 a bag of heroin *UK*

- —Angela Devlin, *Prison Patter*, p. 30, 1996

10 a cigarette *US*

- —John Fahs, *Cigarette Confidential*, p. 301, 1996

11 a woman, especially an unattractive woman *UK*

- —Tom Hibbert, *Rockspeak!*, p. 28, 1983
- Youse fucin boots say anthing aboot this n yis ur deid!—Irvine Welsh, *The State of the Party (Disco Biscuits)*, p. 53, 1995

12 an error, especially in sports *US, 1913*

- —Lou Shelly, *Hepcats Jive Talk Dictionary*, p. 8, 1945

13 a cash incentive designed to improve a business deal *US*

- —Jim Crotty, *How to Talk American*, p. 380, 1997

14 a linear amplifier for a citizens' band radio *US*

- —Lawrence Teeman, *Consumer Guide Good Buddy's CB Dictionary*, p. 32, 1976

15 a condom *US*

- —John D. Bell et al., *Loosely Speaking*, p. 3, 1966

16 in television and film making, a tripod cover *US*

- —Ira Konigsberg, *The Complete Film Dictionary*, p. 33, 1987

▷ **see:** OLD BOOT

▸ **stick the boot in; put the boot in**

to kick a prostrate foe, hence, figurative usage 'to kick someone when they're down'; (political and commercial) to take an unnecessary advantage, to betray someone *UK, 1916*

In widespread usage since mid-C20; the figurative sense has been known from the mid-1960s.

- And, worst of all, hadn't heard from Mark again. Mum had definitely put the boot in for me there. — Mary Hooper, *(megan)2*, p. 146–147, 1999

▸ **the boot is on the other foot; the boot is on the other leg**
the balance of power or responsibility has shifted to the opposing party *UK, 1866*

boot *verb*

1 while injecting a drug, to draw blood into the syringe, diluting the drug dose so as to prolong the effect of the injection *US*
- Just look at me boot it and you will. — Hal Ellson, *The Golden Spike*, p. 139, 1952
- — Dale Kramer and Madeline Karr, *Teen-Age Gangs*, p. 174, 1953
- "Lou'll turn on next if Fay ever stops booting it." Fay's thick, dark, purplish-red blood rose and fell in the eye-dropper like a column of gory mercury in a barometer. — Alexander Trocchi, *Cain's Book*, p. 166, 1960
- The technique, known as "booting," is believed to prolong the drug's initial effect. — James Mills, *The Panic in Needle Park*, p. 78, 1966
- — Geoffrey Froner, *Digging for Diamonds*, p. 12, 1989
- On the wall alongside Randy's head was a starburst of rust-brown dots where someone had booted the blood from their hypes. — Richard Price, *Clockers*, p. 232, 1992

2 to kick something, literally or in the slang sense of 'breaking a habit' *US, 1877*
- — Francis J. Rigney and L. Douglas Smith, *The Real Bohemia*, p. xiii, 1961
- You think the white folks booted you in the butt? — Iceberg Slim (Robert Beck), *The Naked Soul of Iceberg Slim*, p. 203, 1971
- My girlfriend kicked me out of the apartment, I got booted out of Capitol Records, and somebody wrote "Fag-Mobile" on my gas tank. — *Airheads*, 1994

3 to dismiss someone from employment *UK*
- Did ah no tell ye ye're booted? — Michael Munro, *The Patter, Another Blast*, 1988

4 to walk; to patrol on foot *US, 1905*
Vietnam war usage.
- — Linda Reinberg, *In the Field*, p. 27, 1991

5 in horse racing, to spur or kick a horse during a race *US*
- — David W. Maurer, *Argot of the Racetrack*, p. 15, 1951

6 in a game, to misplay a ball *US*
- I think I booted one that should've been a double play[.] — George V. Higgins, *The Judgment of Deke Hunter*, p. 86, 1976

7 to vomit *US, 1971*
- Booted his insides all over my God damn shoes and my last pair of dry socks. — John Sayles, *Union Dues*, p. 57–58, 1977
- — Connie Eble (Editor), *UNC-CH Campus Slang*, p. 2, Spring 1988
- Looking uncomfortable and defeated, he turned to his left, meaning to burp, and instead booted all over the back of a brunette we had just been talking to. — Elissa Stein and Kevin Leslie, *Chunks*, p. 37, 1997

8 in Alberta, to purchase alcohol or tobacco illegally for a minor *CANADA*
- — Emily *An American's Guide to Canada*, p. 9, 2001

▸ **boot and rally**
to continue drinking after vomiting *US*
- — Connie Eble (Editor), *UNC-CH Campus Slang*, p. 1, Spring 1989

▸ **boot the gong**
to smoke marijuana *UK, 1998*
A play on **KICK THE GONG** where **GONG** is 'opium'.
- — Mike Haskins, *Drugs*, p. 290, 2003

boot *adjective*
inexperienced and untested *US*
Vietnam war usage.
- — Linda Reinberg, *In the Field*, p. 27, 1991

bootalize *verb*
to have sex *BAHAMAS*
- — John A. Holm, *Dictionary of Bahamian English*, p. 25, 1982

boot-and-shoe *adjective*
(used of a drug addict) desperately addicted *US, 1936*
- He said she was "just a boot-and-shoe hype" with a $60-a-day heroin habit. — *San Francisco Examiner*, p. 12, 9th March 1962

bootboy *noun*
a member of the youth fashion and gang movement that was synonymous with and then succeeded the skinheads *UK*
Characterised by heavy lace-up boots (Doc Martens), tidy hair and smart utilitarian wear; as a group, boot boys are associated with aggressive behaviour, especially football hooliganism.
- [S]kinheads, suedeheads, bootboys and now smooths[.] — Richard Allen (James Moffat), *Author's Notes [britpulp]*, p. 63, 1972
- [T]he fighting between mods, rockers, skinheads, Pakistanis, suedeheads, Hell's angels, boot boys, greasers, Teds, punks, soulboys, rockabillies, rude boys, casuals and every other shade of herbert going[.] — John King, *Human Punk*, p. 295, 2000

booted *adjective*
intoxicated by marijuana, or another narcotic drug *US*
- We was too booted to see the cops comin'. — Lois Stavsky et al., *A2Z*, p. 11, 1995
- — Mike Haskins, *Drugs*, p. 291, 2003

booter *noun*
a jockey with an inclination to spur his mount incessantly *US*
- The number of riders in America who will give a horse of any age a chance to settle into stride is pitifully few, the great majority being strictly "whoop-de-do" booters who might have been developed by the late Bill Daly. — *Daily Racing Form*, p. 4, 27th November 1959

booth *noun*
a room, especially a bedroom *UK*
- — Paul Baker, *Polari*, p. 166, 2002

booth bimbo; booth bunny *noun*
an attractive, well-built, sometimes scantily clad woman hired to work in a company's booth during a trade show *US*
- Booth bunnies, flashy video displays and tacky giveaways ("Register Here To Win a Free Ounce of Gold") notwithstanding, this is indeed gold's darkest hour. — *Boston Globe*, p. 73, 31st May 1989
- Did it ever occur to you that the booth bimbos are just as proud of their work as you are proud of being a member of the plasics industry – whatever that is? [Letter to editor] — *Plastic News*, p. 7, 3rd January 1994
- Women are underrepresented among the professional-managerial types who frequent Comidex and overrepresented among the "booth bunnies," the working girls who hawk wares by looking pretty. — *San Francisco Bay Guardian*, 29th November 2000

bootie *noun*
▷ see: **BOOTNECK, BOOTY**

booties *noun*

1 rubber surf boots *US*
- — Mitch McKissick, *Surf Lingo*, 1987

2 in electric line work, meter clip insulators *US*
- — A.B. Chance Co., *Lineman's Slang Dictionary*, p. 2, 1980

3 boots, especially knitted boots for a baby *US*
- Who cares? You can buy booties. — John Nichols, *The Sterile Cuckoo*, p. 186, 1965

boot it!; boot it baby!
used as an exhortation to continue *US*
- — My Lit, *My Lit's Unbelievable Dictionary of Hip Words for Groovy People*, p. 6, 1968

bootlace *noun*

▸ **not be someone's bootlace**
to not come close to equalling another's achievements *AUSTRALIA*
- [T]he instructor at the barracks said I'd never be a policeman's bootlace. — Arthur Upfield, *Bony and the Mouse*, p. 83, 1959
- — Frank Hardy, *The Outcasts of Foolgarah*, p. 82, 1971
- Why in the hell should I listen to a mug like you? You weren't a jockey's bootlace! — Roy Higgins and Tom Prior, *The Jockey Who Laughed*, p. 23, 1982
- — William Dodson, *The Sharp End*, p. 87, 2001

bootleg *noun*

1 a pirated and illegally marketed recording *UK, 1951*
In the 1960s and 70s only dedicated music fans were really aware of such product. The bootlegs of Bob Dylan's music easily outnumbered his official releases so, in 1991, his record company began to release 'The Bootleg Series'. As ever, other artists followed where Dylan led. Alas many use it as an excuse to release material that may otherwise not be of sufficient quality. 'Bootleg' has always implied a lesser quality of recording, now it's official.

2 illegally manufactured alcohol *US, 1898*
- It used to be a bootleg spot during prohibition[.] — Mickey Spillane, *I, The Jury*, p. 43, 1947
- We would buy five-gallon containers of bootleg, funnel it into the bottles, then deliver, according to Hymie's instructions, this or that many cartes back to the bars. — Malcolm X and Alex Haley, *The Autobiography of Malcolm X*, p. 124, 1964
- I got Temple of Doom bootleg. Cost me four hundred dollars. — Bret Easton Ellis, *Less Than Zero*, p. 34, 1985

bootleg *verb*

1 to manufacture or provide something illegally *US, 1928*

- We finally found a guy bootlegging rides and he took us to the project where my sister Dolores lived with her three kids. —Dick Gregory, *Nigger*, p. 116, 1964

2 to manufacture or distribute illegal alcohol *US, 1922*

- He used to bootleg whiskey from the mountains[.] —Jack Kerouac, *On the Road*, p. 215, 1957

3 in roller derby, to deviate from the scripted game plan *US*

- A skater who bootlegs is viewed with disfavor, usually accused of showboating. —Keith Coppage, *Roller Derby to Roller Jam*, p. 126, 1999

bootleg *adjective*

1 smuggled; illegally copied; unofficial; counterfeit *US, 1889*
Derives from the practice of carrying a flat bottle of alcohol hidden in a boot leg.

- Another Negro industry is the sale of bootleg booze. —Jack Lait and Lee Mortimer, *Washington Confidential*, p. 55, 1951
- A group of gangster made me their distributor for booting whiskey. —Jim Thompson, *Roughneck*, 1954
- He got tagged smuggling a truckload of bootleg cigarettes up from Virginia[.] —Janet Evanovich, *Seven Up*, p. 3, 2001

2 imitation *US, 1893*

- Half of the Black "militans" ain't nothing but a bunch of potheads, bootleg preachers and coffeehouse intellectuals. —H. Rap Brown, *Die Nigger Die!*, p. 104, 1969

3 inferior, shoddy *US*

- —Connie Eble (Editor), *UNC-CH Campus Slang*, p. 1, November 2002

4 (used of an action paper) unofficial, advance *US*

- — Department of the Army, *Staff Officer's Guidebook*, p. 56, 1986

bootlegger *noun*

a manufacturer or a dealer in illegally manufactured alcohol *US, 1890*

- The bootlegger's product had to be good, and his prices reasonable. —Jim Thompson, *Bad Boy*, p. 391, 1953

bootlegger turn *noun*

a 180-degree turn executed while driving fast accomplished by a combination of spinning the wheel, shifting down the gears and accelerating *US, 1955*

- — *American Speech*, p. 98, May 1956: 'Smugglers' argot in the southwest'
- It was Junior Johnson specifically, however, who was famous for the "bootleg turn" or "about face." —Tom Wolfe, *The Kandy-Kolored Tangerine-Flake Streamlined Baby*, p. 128, 1965

bootleg tool *noun*

a tool that is used by workers despite the fact that it has not been approved by tooling inspectors *US*

- — *American Speech*, p. 225, October 1955: 'An aircraft production dispatcher's vocabulary'

bootlick *verb*

to seek favour through obsequious behaviour *US, 1845*

- [A]nd allows the television networks to recover some of the dignity they lose every time they bootlick Lewis until their tongues grow raw and grisly. — *Pittsburgh Post-Gazette*, p. B2, 9th January 2004

bootlicker *noun*

a person who seeks favour through obsequious behaviour *US, 1848*

- Seale had come ambivalently, having okayed King's being called a "bootlicker" in Panther newspapers. — *Washington Post*, p. D1, 10th March 1978
- Of course, he doesn't say the number of listeners Limbaugh has and that they're coast to coast; he just refers to them as bootlickers. [Letter to Editor] — *Tampa (Florida) Tribune*, p. 10, 8th October 2003

boot mooch *noun*

a person who is always asking others for a cigarette *US*

- —John Fahs, *Cigarette Confidential*, p. 301, 1996

bootneck; bootie *noun*

a Royal Marine *UK, 1925*

- [T]he ordinary bootneck, in his boots, in the field[.] — *Sunday Telegraph*, 8th April 1979
- —Nigel Foster, *The Making of a Royal Marine Commando*, 1987
- 200 bootnecks would run past and give their marks out of ten. —Andy McNab (writing of the late 1970s/early 80s), *Immediate Action*, p. 214, 1995
- More than one bootneck [marine] filled a pillowcase with sand and slung it out of the window three floors up. —Duncan MacLaughlin, *The Filth*, p. 17, 2002

boot party *noun*

a senseless beating, initiated for the sheer joy of the beating *CANADA*

- —Bill Casselman, *Canadian Sayings*, p. 39, 2002

boot pie *noun*

a series of kicks delivered in a scuffle *UK*

- —Tom Hibbert, *Rockspeak!*, p. 28, 1983

boot rest *noun*

an accelerator pedal *US*

- — "Slingo", *The Official CB Slang Dictionary Handbook*, p. 9, 1976

boots *noun*

a tyre *US*

- — *Hot Rod Magazine*, p. 13, November 1948
- — *Current Slang*, p. 1, Fall 1966
- She [a car]'s had a new set of boots. — *Sunday Times*, 9th August 1981

▸ **put the boots to**

1 to have sex with someone *US, 1933*

- I'd rather put the boots to Mrs. A. than Mrs. S. — *Screw*, p. 9, 18th July 1969

2 to kick someone, especially when they are on the ground *US, 1894*

- —Hyman E. Goldin et al., *Dictionary of American Underworld Lingo*, p. 169, 1950

-boots *suffix*

a person, when combined with a trait *UK, 1599*
Found in terms such as **BOSSY-BOOTS**, 'lazy-boots', **SLY-BOOTS** and 'smooth-boots'.

boots and all *adverb*

enthusiastically, in a totally committed way *AUSTRALIA*

- When you do a thing you go into it boots and all. —Dymphna Cusack, *Sothern Steel*, 1953
- —Sonya Plowman, *Great Kiwi Slang*, p. 33, 2002

boots and socks *noun*

syphilis; hence any sexually transmitted infection *UK*
Rhyming slang for **POX**.

- I went to Amsterdam and all I came back with was boots and socks. —Bodmin Dark, *Dirty Cockney Rhyming Slang*, 2003

boot scoot *verb*

to dance side-by-side in a line to country and western music *US, 1991*

- — *American Speech*, p. 177, Summer 1994: 'Among the new words'

bootstraps *noun*

▸ **pull yourself up by your bootstraps; raise yourself by your own bootstraps**

to try harder, to improve yourself within a given area *UK, 1936*

- [T]he compliant masses should be happy to be sacrificed so that we can pull ourselves up by our bootstraps[.] — *The Guardian*, 27th March 2004
- Through sacrifice, we raise ourselves above our mortal condition – by our own bootstraps, so to speak. — *The Guardian*, 1st May 2004

boot suppository *noun*

any strong measure taken to encourage an obnoxious patient to leave a hospital *US*
An image based on a 'kick in the ass'.

- —Sally Williams, *"Strong" Words*, p. 135, 1994

bootsy *noun*

in a small hotel, a boots (the servant who was employed to clean guest shoes) also working as a porter *UK, 1966*
In 1957, *The Army Game*, a television situation comedy, introduced a character called Bootsy; this workshy character, played by Alfie Bass (1921–87), proved so popular that *Bootsy and Snudge*, a spin-off, was aired. The elaboration of conventional 'boots' was not a great leap.

bootsy *adjective*

bad, unpleasant *US*

- — *San Francisco Chronicle*, p. E5, 10th August 2003
- —Rick Ayers (Editor), *Berkeley High Slang Dictionary*, p. 14, 2004

boot up *verb*

to prepare for a fight *US*

- —Ethan Hilderbrant, *Prison Slang*, p. 15, 1998

booty; bootie *noun*

1 the buttocks *US, 1928*

- Wine-and-whisky-taster, downtown money-waster / back-binder, booty-grinder, sweetspot-finder. —Dennis Wepman et al., *The Life*, p. 148, 1976
- He's Cyndia Lauper's boyfriend, so no skin search; Cyndi wouldn't want us looking up his boodie. —James Ellroy, *Suicide Hill*, p. 574, 1986
- Big country bootie, big country titties. — *Boyz N The Hood*, 1990
- Breda knew he'd scope out the woman's booty before closing the door, and he did. —Joseph Wambaugh, *Fugitive Nights*, p. 45, 1992
- —Connie Eble (Editor), *UNC-CH Campus Slang*, p. 2, Spring 1994

2 the vagina *US, 1925*

The first citation here may equally apply to the earlier sense as 'buttocks' but the context is absolutely sexual.

- I've got a body as well as a booty. — Parlet, *Booty Snatchers*, 1979
- —Edith A. Folb, *runnin' down some lines*, p. 230, 1980

booty *adjective*

unpleasant; unattractive *US*

- — *Maybeck High School Yearbook (Berkeley, California)*, 1997
- — *San Francisco Chronicle*, p. E5, 10th August 2003

booty bandit *noun*

an aggressive, predatory male homosexual *US, 1962*

- Inmates subject to rape ("punks") face threats and violence perpetrated by stronger inmates ("daddies,' "jockers," or "booty bandits") who initiate unwanted sexual acts. — *Corrections Today*, p. 100, December 1996

booty bump *verb*

to ingest drugs, usually methamphetamine, diluted in an enema *US*

booty call *noun*

a date made for the sole purpose of engaging in sex *US*

- —Judi Sanders, *Da Bomb!*, p. 4, 1997
- —All Saints *Bootie Call*, 1998
- He cruises the streets of L.A. in one long booty call. —Ana Loria, *1 2 3 Be A Porn Star!*, p. 111, 2000
- —Susie Dent, *The Language Report*, p. 75, 2003

booty cheddar *noun*

nonsense *US*

- —Chris Lewis, *The Dictionary of Playground Slang*, p. 40, 2003

booty-dance *verb*

to shake the buttocks *US*

- [R]ude DJs played music faster and faster to make girls "booty-dance", and went on about G-strings and girls "getting nekkid". — *The Sunday Times Magazine*, p. 50, 1st June 2003

booty drought *noun*

a sustained lack of sex *US*

- —Pamela Munro, *U.C.L.A. Slang*, p. 23, 1989

booty juice *noun*

the drug MDMA, the recreational drug best known as ecstasy, dissolved in any liquid *US*

- —Jim Crotty, *How to Talk American*, p. 87, 1997
- —Mike Haskins, *Drugs*, p. 289, 2003

bootylicious *adjective*

sexually attractive, especially with reference to the buttocks *US*

A compound of **BOOTY** (the buttocks) and 'delicious'.

- I don't think you / Ready for this / 'Cause my body too / Bootylicious for ya babe—Destiny's Child *Bootylicious*, 2001

boo-yah!; booyaka!; boo-yakka!

used for registering delight *UK*

Echoic of gun use. West Indian and UK black.

- "Zukie!" Chico called, grinning from ear to ear, "Boo-yah! What happen, Blood?" —Karline Smith, *Moss Side Massive*, p. 20, 1994
- Lloyd made his right hand into the shape of a gun and aimed it at the car. "Boo-yakka! Every dog has his day," he said out loud, a grin stretched across his face. —Donald Gorgon, *Cop Killer*, p. 40, 1994

booyakasha!; boyakasha!

used for registering delight *UK*

An elaboration of **BOO-YAKKA!**; similarly echoic of gun use. Popularised in the UK in the late 1990s by Ali G (comedian Sacha Baron-Cohen).

- Boyakasha! breathed Ricky Sutton to his left and opened up with a long stream of tracer at the guards. —Chris Ryan, *The Watchman*, p. 52, 2001

boo-yakka *verb*

to shoot *UK*

Onomatopoeic.

- With Segeant Summers boo-yakkad and now Inspector Reid eradicated, even a half-wit cop would suspect the connection[.] —Donald Gorgon, *Cop Killer*, p. 179, 1994

booze *noun*

1 alcoholic drink of any kind *UK, 1859*

In Australia generally referring to beer.

- —A.B. Paterson, *Rio Grande and Other Verses*, p. 117, 1902
- —Eric Lambert, *The Veterans*, p. 18, 1954
- 'Funny how the booze gets them abos. —Jean Brooks, *The Opal Witch*, p. 16, 1967
- I heard you'd given up the booze but I see my information was inaccurate. —Kevin Mackey, *The Cure*, p. 74, 1970
- —Sam Weller, *Old Bastards I Have Met*, p. 126, 1979
- Reggy can't make it tomorrow. He's back on the booze. —Phillip Gwynne, *Deadly Unna?*, p. 212, 1998
- Betty [Ford] herself was America's First Lady when booze got a grip on her[.] — *Drugs An Adult Guide*, p. 31, December 2001

2 a drinking-bout; drinking *UK, 1864*

- Come on, let's go and have a quick booze. —Petra Christian, *The Sexploiters*, p. 46, 1973

▸ **on the booze**

engaged in a period of hard drinking *NEW ZEALAND, 1850*

- They turn up every morning on the dot, are not out on the booze every night and do their job well. — *The Guardian*, 5th March 2003

booze *verb*

to drink alcohol, especially immoderately *UK, 1325*

- [A]ll members of the Griggs family served shop while old Griggs boozed his days away at the Bull and Mouth next door[.] —Norman Lindsay, *Halfway to Anywhere*, p. 38, 1947
- The dregs of society hang out here, and hustlers of both sexes intermingle with short-con men, narcotics pushers, junkies, and plain bottle babies who booze their way through life. —Johnny Shearer, *The Male Hustler*, p. 55, 1966
- [T]hey were boozing their army pay away and were pretty noisy and a couple had been scrapping. —Patsy Adam-Smith, *Folklore of the Australian Railwaymen*, p. 55, 1969
- 'You come here, yes, to booze and go mad.' —Barry Oakley, *A Salute to the Great McCarthy*, p. 103, 1970
- We'll be able ta bet an' booze all day long. — *Sick Puppy*, p. 10, 1998

booze artist *noun*

a habitual drinker; an alcoholic *AUSTRALIA, 1940*

- This is the land of what they call the booze artist. —Xavier Herbert, *Poor Fellow My Country*, p. 146, 1975
- —Jim Ramsay, *Cop It Sweet!*, p. 15, 1977

booze bag *noun*

a blood alcohol measuring device of the early-type that required a suspected drinker to blow into a bag *UK, 1969*

booze balloon *noun*

a heavy drinker's protruding stomach *US*

- That's a booze balloon around his middle region, and his shoulders slope a bit. —Robert J. Williams, *Skin Deep*, p. 17, 1979

booze belly *noun*

the protruding stomach of a drunkard *US, 1970*

- —Frederic G. Cassidy, *Dictionary of American Regional English, Volume 1*, p. 340, 1985

booze cruise *noun*

1 a return Channel-crossing from England to France for the purpose of buying and importing cheaper (less heavily taxed) alcohol *UK*

- —Tom Hickman, *Drink*, p. 291, 2003

2 in Scotland, a pleasure cruise on the Clyde, or on a loch or canal, during which the main pleasure and purpose is heavy drinking *UK: SCOTLAND*

- —Michael Munro, *The Complete Patter*, 1996

3 a drive while drinking *US*

- —Judi Sanders, *Kickin' like Chicken with the Couch Commander*, p. 1, 1992

boozed; boozed up *adjective*

drunk *US, 1737*

First recorded by amateur slang lexicographer Benjamin Franklin in 1737; obsolete, perhaps, but not forgotten.

- I know you've been cutting down, but you can't be boozed up or have a hangover on this job. —Jim Thompson, *After Dark, My Sweet*, p. 42, 1955

- It's kind of hard to tell with him – he acts boozed up sometimes even when he's sober. —S.E. Hinton, *The Outsiders*, p. 27, 1967
- If she's snuffed it I'll never forgive that boozed old bastard. —Barry Humphries, *The Wonderful World of Barry McKenzie*, p. 34, 1968
- At that same moment, in the bedroom of Erica's flat, boozed Baptiste has the problem of dressing for a grocery shopping trip with Erica. —Iceberg Slim (Robert Beck), *Doom Fox*, p. 102, 1978
- I was getting a young piece boozed in an old pub over in South Townsville, preparatory to taking her home to my flat for a bit of nonsense. —Bettina Arndt, *The Australian Way of Sex*, p. 38, 1985

boozehound *noun*

an alcoholic *US, 1911*

- Her mother was married again to some booze hound. —J.D. Salinger, *Catcher in the Rye*, p. 32, 1951
- The booze hounds just make a man a lot of trouble for no fun. —Raymond Chandler, *The Long Goodbye*, p. 3, 1953
- Irish playwright Brendan Behan, ace booze hound of the Western World, received the press yesterday in Toronto's Sunnyside Hospital, where he is recovering from a series of alcoholic seizures that nearly killed him. —*San Francisco Chronicle*, 4th April 1961
- I can't read a list of my academic credentials to every booze-hound that comes in the place. —*48 Hours*, 1982

boozer *noun*

1 a drinker of alcohol; a habitual drinker; an alcoholic *UK, 1606*

- That was the only way to bring back to life the shodden, shaky boozers. —Jack Lait and Lee Mortimer, *Chicago Confidential*, p. 53, 1950
- These are the boozers who still have entree to the better clubs but no credit whatever. —Robert Sylvester, *No Cover Charge*, p. 231, 1956
- Seated in a railway train, I have heard myself described as a boozer of the first magnitude. —Norman Lindsay, *Bohemians at the Bulletin*, p. 7, 1965
- 'Jus' never bin a midday boozer.' —Jean Brooks, *The Opal Witch*, p. 132, 1967
- You hit the liver and it doesn't give, you know the guy was a boozer, had cirrhosis. —Elmore Leonard, *Bandits*, p. 13, 1987
- Sounded like it ought to be Dean Martin or one of those big-name boozers[.] —John Williams, *Cardiff Dead*, p. 6, 2000

2 a place where alcohol is served; a public house or bar *UK, 1895*

- You had a drink in a boozer down the Nile —Frank Norman, *Bang To Rights*, p. 122, 1958
- —Louis S. Leland, *A Personal Kiwi-Yankee Dictionary*, p. 17, 1984
- Clad in Australian flying suits we found a U.S. boozer and settled in for a session. —Martin Cameron, *A Look at the Bright Side*, 1988

boozeroo *noun*

1 a drinking spree or party *NEW ZEALAND, 1908*

- 'Meeting!' retorted Mother witheringly. 'Boozeroo you mean!' —Jean Boswell, p. 106, 1960
- —Harry Orsman, *A Dictionary of Modern New Zealand Slang*, p. 17, 1999

2 a pub *NEW ZEALAND*

- Till any Scotsman with the stakes / Can pile on your head his mistakes. / And petrify a boozaroo / Reciting Tam O'Shanter through. —James K. Baxter, *Collected Poems*, p. 290, 1963

booze-rooster *noun*

a heavy drinker *US*

- The way she talks, you'd think I was a regular booze-rooster. —M.K. Joseph, *Pound of Saffron*, p. 253, 1962

booze snooze *noun*

a nap taken in anticipation of a night of drinking *US*

- —Ben Applebaum and Derrick Pittman, *Turd Ferguson & The Sausage Party*, p. 9, 2004

booze-up *noun*

a drinking bout *UK*

- [S]o Bill filched a half-bottle of cooking sherry from the panrty for a reckless booze-up with Waldo. —Norman Lindsay, *Halfway to Anywhere*, p. 74, 1947
- —Norman Lindsay, *Halfway to Anywhere*, p. 183, 1947
- Look at them, the miserable bunch of teetotallers. Come on, let's be having a booze-up. —Graeme Kent, *The Queen's Corporal [Six Granada Plays]*, p. 88, 1959
- —Gerald Sweeney, *The Plunge*, p. 56, 1981

boozle *noun*

sexual intercourse *UK*

- —Noel Coward, *Pomp and Circumstance*, 1960

boozorium *noun*

a bar-room, especially in a hotel *CANADA*

- —H. Dempsey, *Bob Edwards*, 1975

boozy *noun*

a drunkard *IRELAND*

- —Michael Kenyon, *The Rapist*, 1977

boozy *adjective*

mildly drunk *UK, 1536*

- "[P]iss artists" are "boozy", "fluffy", "well-gone", "legless", "crocked"[.] —Peter Ackroyd, *London The Biography*, p. 359, 2000

bop *noun*

1 a dance; any dance to popular music *UK*

Derives from bebop (a jazz genre first recorded in 1945).

- like an Old Testament prophet having a bop at a disco —*The Guardian*, 17th November 2001
- Lady Helen promised she would be "having a bit of a bop". —*Daily Telegraph*, 5th March 2002

2 a dance party *US*

- —Kenn "Naz" Young, *Naz's Underground Dictionary*, p. 16, 1973

3 liveliness, spirit, rhythm *US*

- My father also didn't want any of us to be cool. "I noticed when you walked in here you had a little bop in your walk. No bopping around here." —Chris Rock, *Rock This!*, p. 45, 1997

4 a member of a youth gang *US*

- Heart, as the bop defines it, is audacity, devil-may-care disregard for self and consequences. —Harrison E. Salisbury, *The Shook-up Generation*, p. 25, 1958

5 a blow; a punch *US, 1932*

- —Nino Culotta, *Cop This Lot*, 1960

6 phencyclidine, the recreational drug known as PCP or angel dust *US*

- —Maria Hinojas, *Crews*, p. 166, 1995

7 nonsense *US, 1973*

- "Yeah, you talk all that off the wall bop," Roger stammered. —Joseph Nazel, *Black Cop*, p. 104, 1974

bop *verb*

1 to dance to popular or rock music *UK*

Abbreviated and adapted from bebop (a jazz genre first recorded in 1945).

- Oh, yes, you can bop to it, any record I can bop to, I like it, that's it. —Paul E Willis, *Profane Culture*, p. 69, 1978

2 to move with rhythm *US, 1959*

- Hobie put the box in and slammed the trunk lid down and the two bopped away. —John Sayles, *Union Dues*, p. 11105, 1977
- Glenn would listen to the two morons and watch Maurice bopping around from table to table giving brothers the brother handshake, touch fists in their ritual ways, Maurice the hipster, a dude black felt cap set on his head, just right, and shades. —Elmore Leonard, *Out of Sight*, p. 287, 1996

3 to have sex with someone *US, 1974*

- Your dick been limp for a year, 'cept when you're bopping your buddy Tony up there. —*Platoon*, 1986
- It's all that accountant-meets-cowboy, muscle-beach-bop-in-the-surf shit that they churn out on the West Coast at the rate of four miles of celluloid a day. —Jim Carroll, *Forced Entries*, p. 39, 1987

4 to engage in gang fighting *US*

- What were you doing, bopping it up? —Hal Ellson, *Tomboy*, p. 122, 1950
- The Cobras are an active "bopping" or street-fighting club which has its base in one of the older Brooklyn housing projects. —Harrison E. Salisbury, *The Shook-up Generation*, p. 19, 1958
- She's the head guy's deb. You stick your nose in there any more, the Mau Maus'll slice it off. My information is they're all set up to go bopping. —*Man's Magazine*, p. 12, February 1960

5 to hit someone, to beat someone *UK, 1928*

- [I] hung around with a crew up there setting fire to mansions early in the morning and bopping skinheads. —Jamie Mandelkau, *Buttons*, p. 30, 1971

6 to murder someone *UK*

- She reckoned they never bopped their bro. —Jeremy Cameron, *Brown Bread in Wengen*, p. 117, 1999

7 in team gambling, to move to a card table identified by a confederate counting cards there to be primed for better-than-average odds *US*

- —Steve Kuriscak, *Casino Talk*, p. 5, 1985

▶ **bop the baloney**

(of a male) to masturbate *US*

- Do you ever bop your baloney? —*National Lampoon's Vacation*, 1983

bo peep *noun*

a look or polite search *AUSTRALIA, 1941*

- I'd seen a smart-looking piece of goods drying her face and having a bo-peep out of the bathroom window. —Frank Sargeson, *That Summer*, p. 61, 1946

- Talk about laugh. Did yous get a bo peep at them Pom's faces. Ten to one I nearly had a snakes in me strides.—Barry Humphries, *The Wonderful World of Barry McKenzie*, p. 19, 1968

Bo Peep; Little Bo Peep *noun*
sleep; a sleep *UK*
Rhyming slang, formed from the name of a nursery rhyme character (who should have been counting sheep).
- —Julian Franklyn, *A Dictionary of Rhyming Slang*, 1960

bop glasses *noun*
horn-rimmed eye glasses *US, 1958*
From the style favoured by bop jazz musicians.
- —Harold Wentworth and Stuart Berg Flexner, *Dictionary of American Slang*, p. 56, 1960

bop 'n slop *verb*
to lose your inhibitions and enjoy yourself at a party *US*
- —Collin Baker et al., *College Undergraduate Slang Study Conducted at Brown University*, p. 87, 1968

bop off *verb*
to leave *US*
- —*American Speech*, p. 154, May 1959: 'Gator (University of Florida) slang'

bopper *noun*
1 a fighter, especially a gang fighter *US*
- You're not only expected to talk like a boppere, but to think like one, too.—Morton Cooper, *High School Confidential*, p. 13, 1958
- I owed them nine more years, which they'd probably make me do if I joined up with the boppers.—Piri Thomas, *Down These Mean Streets*, p. 282, 1967
- Annette smiled and turned to face the crowd: high-school and college dropouts, ex-Muslims, cons, boppers and bullshit hustlers with their dates[.]—Steve Cannon, *Groove, Bang, and Jive Around*, p. 4, 1969

2 a song in the style of bebop jazz *US*
- Fifteen years ago he got caught with very little of what Charlie Parker and Dizzy were doing, and until he began recording boppers fast, he lost some bread as modern jazz became moderately popular. —Nat Hentoff, *Jazz Country*, p. 110, 1965

boppers *noun*
shoes *US*
- —*American Speech*, p. 56, Spring-Summer 1975: 'Razorback slang'

boppy *adjective*
affected gang mannerisms *US*
- You did people watching you an' walk a little more boppy. —Piri Thomas, *Down These Mean Streets*, p. 58–59, 1967

boracic *noun*
smooth, insincere talk *UK*
- —Paul Tempest, *Lag's Lexicon*, 1950

boracic lint; boracic; brassic; brassick *adjective*
having little or no money, penniless *UK, 1959*
Rhyming slang for **SKINT** (penniless).
- When boys have money they think they're men. But when they're brassic they're boys again.—Ray Puxley, *Cockney Rabbit*, p. 19, 1992
- —Angela Devlin, *Prison Patter*, p. 30, 1996
- So he never came up Howard Road brassick. And like as not he was carrying pennies.—Jeremy Cameron, *Brown Bread in Wengen*, p. 5, 1999
- The guy was skint – "borracic, H, some cunt knocked me"[.] —Garry Bushell, *The Face*, p. 107, 2001

Borax *noun*
any low quality retail merchandise that is impressive on first glance *US, 1929*
- —Rachel S. Epstein and Nina Liebman, *Biz Speak*, p. 25, 1986

border *noun*
1 a capsule of a noncommercial barbiturate compound *US*
- —Eugene Landy, *The Underground Dictionary*, p. 39, 1971
- —Edith A. Folb, *runnin' down some lines*, p. 230, 1980

2 a woman's pubic hair *UK*
A cultivated variation of the **GARDEN** theme.
- I love the way the girls in Nirvana do their borders. It's like they're having a little contest to see who can shave their minge in the most eye-catching way.—Kevin Sampson, *Outlaws*, p. 38, 2001

border work *noun*
subtle markings on the printed edge of the back of a playing card for identification of the card by a cheat *US*
- —George Percy, *The Language of Poker*, p. 12, 1988

bore *verb*
▸ **bore the pants off**
to bore someone utterly *UK*
- —P.G. Wodehouse, *Jeeves and the Feudal Spirit*, 1954

▸ **bore the twat off**
to bore someone utterly *UK*
- Music business. It bores the twat off me.—Shaun Ryder, *Shaun Ryder... in His Own Words*, 1993

bore it up *verb*
to attack someone; to harrangue or verbally abuse someone *AUSTRALIA, 1951*
- Good on you, Tich, bore it up 'em.—Frank Hardy, *The Outcasts of Foolgarah*, p. 70, 1971
- —Frank Hardy, *Hardy's People*, p. 15, 1986
- I'm going to really bore it up Edwardian society.—Roy Slaven (John Doyle), *Five South Coast Seasons*, p. 66, 1992

borer *noun*
a knife *UK*
- He'll mention he's got a "borer" – a folding knife. Nine times out of 10 they [phone-jackers] don't, but you don't want to find out.—*The Guardian*, p. 9, 27th February 2002

boress *noun*
a practical joke *US, 1958*
- —J. E. Lighter, *Historical Dictionary of American Slang, Volume 1*, p. 249, 1994

Boris Becker *noun*
the penis *UK*
Rhyming slang for **PECKER**, formed from the name of the German tennis player (b.1967).
- —Bodmin Dark, *Dirty Cockney Rhyming Slang*, 2003

born-again *noun*
a devout, conservative Christian who professes to have been born again in a religious sense *US*
Often uttered without sympathy.
- Sergeants and lieutenants, all born-agains and all ambitious. —James Ellroy, *Suicide Hill*, p. 635, 1986

born-again *adjective*
used derisively to describe anyone who expediently and enthusiastically adopts, or is re-associated with, an earlier belief or stance *US, 1977*
A satirical adoption of a fundamental Christian tenet.
- They started to notice the dirty looks they were getting from all the born-again Welsh patriots around them[.]—John Williams, *Cardiff Dead*, p. 56, 2000

born in a trunk *adjective*
born into a family in show business *US*
- —Don Wilmeth, *The Language of American Popular Entertainment*, p. 31, 1981

Boro *noun*
a Marlboro™ cigarette *US*
- —John Fahs, *Cigarette Confidential*, p. 301, 1996

boro-boros *noun*
old clothes worn for dirty tasks *US*
Hawaiian youth usage.
- —Douglas Simonson, *Pidgin to da Max*, 1981

borrow *noun*
an act of borrowing *UK*
Especially in the phrase 'can I have a borrow?'.
- Dad, can you do us a borrow?—Caroline Aherne and Craig Cash, *The Royle Family*, 1999

▸ **on the borrow**
on the scrounge, cadging *UK, 1937*

borrow *verb*
1 to steal *US, 1821*
- —Vincent J. Monteleone, *Criminal Slang*, p. 31, 1949
- —Terry Williams, *The Cocaine Kids*, p. 135, 1989

2 to arrest someone *UK*
Metropolitan Police slang; a narrow sense of conventional 'borrow' (to take temporary possession).
- —Peter Laurie, *Scotland Yard*, p. 321, 1970

Borrowers *noun*

▶ **the Borrowers**

the UK armed forces *US*

This nickname, used by the US armed forces of their UK allies, mocks the paucity of basic supplies such as toilet paper that force the UK troops to beg from their American neighbours. Probably influenced by *The Borrowers*, Mary Norton, 1952, and the 1998 Hollywood film version.

- The Americans call them The Borrowers. She says "they have burger bars, pizza huts and shops. We have nothing." — *Evening Standard*, p. 6, 7th March 2003

borrow pit; barrow; bar pit *noun*

in rural western Canada, the pit from which earth is being removed for construction purposes *CANADA*

- In some cases it is, in fact, only borrowed and returned later as would be the case when building temporary dikes during spring flooding. However, it is still the borrow pit (or barrow, or bar pit) when the earth is gone for good. Often the road ditch. — Chris Thain, *Cold as a Bay Street Banker's Heart*, p. 9–17, 1987

borsch!

used for expressing disgust *US*

- — Fred Hester, *Slang on the 40 Acres*, p. 10, 1968

Borsch circuit *noun*

the Borsch belt *US, 1936*

- Great for a couple of lads who, when we first knew them owned one Catskills' Borscht Circuit hotel. — *San Francisco Examniner*, p. 35, 21st June 1966

Borscht Belt *noun*

a group of resort hotels in the Catskill Mountains of the eastern US with a primarily Jewish clientelle *US, 1941*

Alluding to the cold beet soup 'borscht' because of the eastern European heritage of many of the Jewish guests.

- — *American Speech*, December 1949
- It is hard to believe that anybody is unfamiliar with New York's Borscht Belt. Books, movies, plays and TV skits have centered around this vacationland in Sullivan County, about 100 miles north of New York City. — *San Francisco News Call-Bulletin*, p. 6, 22nd December 1962
- Damon Runyon described it [Grossinger's] as Linday's with trees. It has also been called the ancestral home of the bagel, the pride of the "Borscht Belt," the Waldorf of the Catskills. — *San Francisco Examiner and Chronicle*, p. 11 (Travel), 25th February 1973
- The Emcee was a slimy, bald exile from the Borscht Belt. — Seth Morgan, *Homeboy*, p. 313, 1990

bory *adjective*

1 big, large *UK*

English gypsy use, from Romany *bawro*.

- [A] strong, bory chavvy [man] who was known as a rugby-playing, hard-drinking man[.] — Jimmy Stockin, *On The Cobbles*, p. 146, 2000

2 pregnant *UK*

English gypsy use, from the previous sense.

- — Jimmy Stockin, *On The Cobbles*, p. 9, 2000

bo selecta!

used in approval of a dance music DJ's performance or technique *UK*

Bo Selecta! was used as the title of a Channel 4 television comedy programme first broadcast in 2002.

- Re-rewind, when the crowd say Bo Selecta / Re-rewind / This goes out to all the DJ's. — Artful Dodger featuring Craig David, *Re-Rewind (The Crowd Say Bo Selecta)*, 1999

bosh *noun*

nonsense *UK, 1834*

bosh *verb*

1 to swallow drugs, especially in tablet-form; to inhale drug-smoke *UK*

- We boshed two grams each of the beast 10 [a nickname for a water-filled pipe used for smoking marijuana] [...] We would bosh a few Es, take some amyl, and then go to raves. — Macfarlane, Macfarlane and Robson, *The User*, p. 88–89, 1996
- [W]hen odd-balls like your gran's favourite, Michael Barrymore, get discovered boshing eccies [E] and hoovering gak [snorting cocaine], you know things have turned weird. — *Ministry*, p. 39, January 2002

2 to put an end to something *US*

An extension of 'put the **KIBOSH** to'.

- — Anna Scotti and Paul Young, *Buzzwords*, p. 53, 1997

bosh *adjective*

performed quickly and without great thought *UK*

- Do a bosh job, bosh, bosh, bosh, write a novella, fulfil your contract. — *The Guardian*, 11th June 2000

bosh!

used for registering a humorous victory or triumphant action *UK*

Echoic of a comedy sound effect.

- I could give that one. I really could [...] bosh, just like that, across the kitchen table — John Milne, *Alive and Kicking*, p. 48, 1998
- Oh yes! Bosh! We just killed ourselves laughing. — Dave Courtney, *Stop the Ride I Want to Get Off*, p. 83, 1999

bosker *adjective*

splendid *AUSTRALIA, 1904*

- 'By crikey!' we said. "What a bosker cop!' — Stewart Kinross, *Please to Remember*, p. 85, 1963
- Here, wrap your laughing gear around this curry. It's bosker. — John Wynnum, *Tar Dust*, p. 34, 1962

boso *noun*

used as a term of address to a male whom the speaker deems socially superior *FIJI*

- Boso, you got the time, please? — Jan Tent, 1993

boson *noun*

in computing, an imaginary concept, the smallest possible unit measuring the bogus content of something *US*

- — Andy Ihnatko, *Cyberspeak*, p. 29, 1997

boss *noun*

1 used as an informal address or reference to the officer in command *UK*

- — Nigel Foster, *The Making of a Royal Marine Commando*, 1987
- Uniformed sergeants are "Skip" or "Sarge", or it's first name terms. A senior officer would be "Boss". — Duncan MacLaughlin, *The Filth*, p. 82, 2002

2 the commanding officer *AUSTRALIA*

- I had been there and done that myself and so justice was tempered with mercy; 'Will you front the Boss? or would you perhaps volunteer for some extra duty time in which you can repent of your sinfulness.' — Martin Cameron, *A Look at the Bright Side*, 1988

3 a marine drill instructor *US*

- — Linda Reinberg, *In the Field*, p. 27, 1991

4 a prison guard or official *US*

- Pace up and down, pace up and down you, you're gonna get through a lot of paces before you get out of here. Yes boss. Always yes boss. — Kevin Mackey, *The Cure*, p. 101, 1970
- — Bruce Jackson, *Outside the Law*, p. 55, 1972
- — David Powis, *The Signs of Crime*, 1977
- When they were in a good mood they called us 'screws', 'four-by-twos' or 'boss'; but when they were pissed off it degenerated to 'fuckin' cunts' and 'fuckin' dogs. — William Dodson, *The Sharp End*, p. 11, 2001

5 the owner or man in charge of a large rural property *AUSTRALIA, 1902*

- But, Boss, you'd better not fight with me – it wouldn't be fair nor right. — A.B. Paterson, *Rio Grande and Other Verses*, p. 84, 1902
- The sky and plain still drowsed dreamily, and neither the sick Boss's home, not Nungi the half-caste's hut on the other side of the river-split plain, showed a sign of smoke. — Barbara Baynton, *Human Toll*, p. 117, 1907
- So I pipes up and asks if the boss is at 'ome. — Erle Cox, *Out of the Silence*, p. 253, 1925
- Above all, she must not tell the boss of any little irregularity she may see. — Ion L. Idriess, *Over the Range*, p. 5, 1947
- Look, the boss is all right. — Arthur Upfield, *Bony and the Mouse*, p. 50, 1959
- The boss was away, and his missus, who recognised Jimmy, wasn't one of the giving sort. — Bill Wannan, *Bullockies, Beauts and Bandicoots*, p. 47, 1960

6 the best *US, 1878*

- Angel laughed. "Horse is the boss," he said. — Hal Ellson, *The Golden Spike*, p. 51, 1952

7 in poker, the best hand at a given moment *US*

- — Anthony Holden, *Big Deal*, p. 298, 1990

8 pure heroin *US*

- — Francis J. Rigney and L. Douglas Smith, *The Real Bohemia*, p. xiii, 1961

9 the penis *US*

Either a male coinage or heavily ironic.

- — Erica Orloff and JoAnn Baker, *Dirty Little Secrets*, p. 69, 2001

10 in carnival usage, a person whom thieves use to estimate the value of articles that they have stolen *US*

- —Don Wilmeth, *The Language of American Popular Entertainment*, p. 31, 1981

▸ **the boss**

your wife *AUSTRALIA, 1984*

Jocular, probably.

Boss *noun*

▸ **the Boss**

songwriter and musician Bruce Springsteen (b.1949) *US*

boss *adjective*

very good, excellent *US, 1873*

The word was around for 70 years before taking off; it was popular beyond description in 1965 and 1966.

- —Francis J. Rigney and L. Douglas Smith, *The Real Bohemia*, p. xiii, 1961
- Even the kids who aren't full-time car nuts themselves will be influenced by which car is considered "boss." They use that word a lot, "boss."—Tom Wolfe, *The Kandy-Kolored Tangerine Falke Streamline Baby*, p. 80, 1964
- He said he had a real boss feeling.—Claude Brown, *Manchild in the Promised Land*, p. 112, 1965
- In the past few months, "good" has been replaced by "neat," "sane," "tough," "boss," "kicky," "gear," "wild," "crazy" and "herman" to name but a few.—*San Francisco Chronicle*, p. 23, 17th August 1965
- Of all the people I have spoken to, only one person really thought they (beach movies) were "boss" (great) and that was my 10-year-old kid sister. [Letter to the Editor]—*Life*, p. 59, 6th August 1965
- They left the joint and "Willie" knew that he'd scored, when she ushered him into a chauffeur driven limosine and to a boss pad in the East Seventies.—Babs Gonzales, *I Paid My Dues*, p. 101, 1967
- —Hy Lit, *Hy Lit's Unbelievable Dictionary of Hip Words for Groovy People*, p. 6, 1968
- It would be a boss honor to buy you a taste.—Iceberg Slim (Robert Beck), *Pimp*, p. 126, 1969
- Don't you think the Beach Boys are boss?—*American Graffiti*, 1973
- He thought it was boss when he shot that horse / He thought he was being hip.—Dennis Wepman et al., *The Life*, p. 97, 1976
- What's with the boss threads?—*Empire Records*, 1995
- Considering that it's nearly Christmas and that, it's a boss fucking day. You could almost get a bronzie off've that sun.—Kevin Sampson, *Outlaws*, p. 3, 2001

boss

used as a sentence-ending intensifier *SINGAPORE*

- Did you see the shirt Ah Beng was wearing? Can go blind, boss. —Paik Choo, *The Coxford Singlish Dictionary*, p. 18, 2002

boss Charley *noun*

a white person or white people collectively *US*

- It doesn't matter, the end result, as long as trick Whitey, fuck up Boss Charley.—Lenny Bruce, *The Essential Lenny Bruce*, p. 12, 1967

boss cocky *noun*

1 an owner of a rural property who employs labour *AUSTRALIA, 1879*

- So he decided he wanted to be the boss cocky, the man who strolled up and down the lines of stooping shearers to watch the fleeces he owned being stripped away by that smooth, flawless motion. —Colleen McCullough, *The Thorn Birds*, p. 230, 1977

2 a self-important person in authority; one who lords it over others *AUSTRALIA, 1902*

- But let me make it very clear indeed to you, Mrs Jacquard. I am the boss cocky here. I set high standards and they have to be met. —Keith Hetherington, *Patrick*, p. 15, 1978

boss-eyed *adjective*

1 having only one eye; having only one good eye; having a squint, cross-eyed *UK, 1860*

- Birmingham's boss-eyed Mike Skinner has been plastered on the pages of hip-hop bible XXL[.]—*The Guardian*, 3rd July 2004

2 lopsided, skewed; wrong *UK, 1898*

- It went boss-eyed for a number of reasons.—Dave Courtney, *Dodgy Dave's Little Black Book*, p. 92, 2001

boss game *noun*

a highly developed, status-conscious sense of style *US*

- Rembrandt, Remington, ai't no difference, man. It all mounts to the same thing – boss game.—Charles W. Moore, *A Brick for Mister Jones*, p. 113, 1975

boss (her) *verb*

in trucking, to back a tractor and trailer into position *US*

- —Montie Tak, *Truck Talk*, p. 17, 1971

boss hoss *noun*

an admired, popular man *US*

- —Hy Lit, *Hy Lit's Unbelievable Dictionary of Hip Words for Groovy People*, p. 6, 1968

bossin' *adjective*

excellent *UK*

Youth slang.

- And the cool thing is, folks are making up bossin' new phrases all the time, so there's nothing to stop you adding your own faves. —Ben Sharpe, *Scooter Crazy*, p. 42, 2000

bossman *noun*

a male leader *US, 1934*

Elaboration of **BOSS**.

- [T]he biggest band of the decade [Oasis] learnt their chops under the eye of bossman Noel.—John Robb, *The Nineties*, p. 124, 1999

Bosstown *nickname*

Boston, Massachusetts *US*

The nickname and the presumed rock and roll genre of the 'Bosstown Sound' were largely the artificial engineerings of a record company executive trying to convince the record-buying world that groups such as Ultimate Spinach, Bagatelle, Beacon Street Union and Earth Opera were worth their record-buying dollars.

- —Arnold Shaw, *Dictionary of American Pop/Rock*, p. 53, 1982

bossy-boots *noun*

a domineering person *UK, 1983*

- [S]he first wormed her way into the nation's affections as the archetypal suburban bossy-boots.—*The Daily Telegraph*, 18th July 2002

Boston coffee *noun*

1 tea *US*

A historical allusion to the Boston Tea Party.

- —Harold Wentworth and Stuart Berg Flexner, *Dictionary of American Slang*, p. 57, 1960

2 coffee with a lot of cream or milk *US*

- 'Do you like Boston Coffee?' she asked the young man brightly. 'You mean coffee with a lot of cream?' "Half cream, half coffee,' she informed him.—Terry Southern, *Flash and Filigree*, p. 109, 1958

Boston Glob *nickname*

the *Boston Globe* newspaper *US*

- —*CoEvolution Quarterly*, p. 27, Spring 1981

Boston marriage *noun*

an arrangement in which two women live together in an outwardly platonic relationship *US*

- So-called "Boston marriages," intense but ostensibly non-sexual relationships between two women, were well recognised, and in fact, self-consciously survive.—Jeffrey Weeks, *Same Sex Intimacies*, p. 54, 2001
- To fulfill this longing, many of us have created a version of the "Boston marriage," making romantic friendships where we daily experience true love.—Bell Hooks, *Communion*, p. 212, 2002

Boston quarter *noun*

a tip of five or ten cents *US, 1942*

A jab at the parsimony of New Englanders.

- —Ramon Adams, *The Language of the Railroader*, p. 18, 1977

Boston screwdriver *noun*

a hammer *US, 1969*

- —Frederic G. Cassidy, *Dictionary of American Regional English*, *Volume 1*, p. 346, 1985

Boston States *noun*

New England, from the Maritime Provinces perspective *CANADA*

- And she would tell of her correspondence, although no one ever saw a letter, with the young bloods of her day, now residing in the Boston States.—Neal MacNeil, *The Highland Heart in Nova Scotia*, p. 71, 1948
- As soon as they are able to work for wages, young people leave the Shore. A few do remain, but the best go to Toronto or further west, while the remainder find work in the "Boston States."—*New Maritimes*, p. 23, March-April 1990

Boston tea party *noun*

a sexual fetish in which the sadist defecates or urinates on the masochist *US*

- —Dale Gordon, *The Dominion Sex Dictionary*, p. 31, 1967
- —Robert A. Wilson, *Playboy's Book of Forbidden Words*, p. 46–47, 1972
- —Thomas Murray and Thomas Murrell, *The Language of Sadomasochism*, p. 43, 1989

bot *noun*

1 the buttocks, the *bot*tom *UK, 1961*
Also spelt 'bott'.

2 an on-line software agent that performs a specified task *US*
Short for 'ro*bot*'.
- While the master or mistress is brewing coffee, the bot is retrieving Web documents[.] —Constance Hale, *Wired Style*, 1996
- [B]ots can be malicious, cloning themselves (clonebots) or flooding the IRC channel with garbage (floodbots). There are hundreds of different types of bots: cancelbots, chatterbots, softbots, userbots, taskbots, slothbots, and Xbots. —Gareth Branwyn, *Jargon Watch*, 1997

3 a habitual cadger *AUSTRALIA, 1916*
From the sense as 'a parasitic worm, a maggot'.
- When you're on the bot, you're generally down on your luck and asking someone for money or a cigarette. —John Blackman, *The Aussie Slang Dictionary*, p. 15, 1990

bot *verb*

to cadge something *AUSTRALIA, 1921*
- A four-a-day smoker does not stand in a draughty vestibule, tossing off a quick puff. Botting from strangers. —Shane Maloney, *Nice Try*, p. 63, 1998

-bot *suffix*

used in combination with a noun or abbreviated noun to create a robotic entity or creature with mechanical characteristics *US, 1978*
From 'ro*bot*'.
- Mary Daly imagined a visionary women's spiritiual circle that would 'spark' and 'spin' its way free of masculinist thinking, leaving the masses of 'fem-bot' and 'token' women behind. —Andrea Nye, *Feminist Theory and the Philosophies of Man*, p. 101, 1988
- [T]hat moronic culture of macho lunkheads and pap music fem-bots[.] —Jessica Berens and Kerri Sharp, *Prada sucks!*, p. ix, 2002

botanist *noun*

a physician who views his patients as having plant-level intelligence *US*
- —*Maledicta*, p. 68, Summer/Winter 1978: 'Common patient-directed pejoratives used by medical personnel'

Botany Bay *verb*

to run away *AUSTRALIA*
Rhyming slang. Botany Bay was the name given to the original penal settlement in Australia.

Botch *nickname*

the Canadian Basic Officer Training Course *CANADA*
- "Botch", the occasional nickname, from its abbreviation BOTC. —Tom Langueste, *Words on the Wing*, p. 36, 1995

bother *noun*

trouble *UK, 1834*
- [T]hey can cause trouble. Bother. —Mike Stott, *Soldiers Talking, Cleanly*, 1978

bother *verb*

▸ **bother your arse; bother your shirt; bother your bunnit; bother your puff**
to make an effort *UK: SCOTLAND*
Glasgow slang.
- Ah telt ye tae go afore if got busy but naw, ye never bothered yer shirt. —Michael Munro, *The Original Patter*, 1985

bother!; bother it!

used for registering annoyance *UK, 1840*

botheration *noun*

annoyance; nuisance *UK, 1797*
Often used as an exclamation of annoyance.

bothered!

used sarcastically for expressing a lack of care or interest in something that has just been spoken of *UK, 1937*
- So she hates me. Bothered! —Susie Dent, *The Language Report*, p. 75, 2003

both-eye principle *noun*

the careful surveillance of company operations, in a large family business *CANADA*
- "It's the both-eye principle; not the one-eye principle, we use." – The Bata (shoe) family of Toronto, articulating their supervision policy over their family-owned business. — *The Bata Story on Canadian Broadcasting Company's Life and Times*, 11th May 2002

both ways *noun*

1 a wager that a selected horse, dog, etc will finish a race in the first three *UK, 1869*
Also heard as 'each way'.

2 a bet in craps both that the shooter will win and that the shooter will lose *US*
In craps, gamblers can bet that the shooter will win, that he will lose, or both.
- — *The Annals of the American Academy of Political and Social Sciences*, p. 120, May 1950

both ways *adverb*

1 willing to play both the active and passive role in homosexual sex *US*
- All the punks go both ways, the queens don't. —Bruce Jackson, *In the Life*, p. 400, 1972

2 to be bisexual *US*
- You trying to tell me if I don't like spiders it means I go both ways? —Elmore Leonard, *Freaky Deaky*, p. 30, 1988

botray *noun*

crack cocaine *UK, 1998*
- —Mike Haskins, *Drugs*, p. 281, 2003

bottie *noun*

▷ see: BOTTY

Botties; Botanicals *nickname*

the Royal Botanical Gardens in Sydney, Australia *AUSTRALIA*
- —Barry Humphries, *A Nice Night's Entertainment*, 1981

bottle *noun*

1 courage, nerve, spirits *UK, 1958*
A figurative sense of the rhyming slang **BOTTLE AND GLASS** (**ARSE**). If you lose your nerve you are said to 'lose your bottle' (to lose control of your arse), literally 'to defecate uncontrollably as a result of fear'.
- What's the matter, Frank? Your bottle fallen out? —Frank Norman, *Bang To Rights*, p. 50, 1958
- It's the worst that can be said about you, that you'd lost your bottle[.] —Tony Park, *The Plough Boy*, 1965
- The cunt's bottle had gone, no doubt about it. —Greg Williams, *Diamond Geezers*, p. 141, 1997
- [B]efore I worked up the bottle to make a move, bingo, they were married. —Val McDermid, *Keeping on the Right Side of the Law*, p. 182, 1999

2 a dose of crack cocaine, whether or not it is actually in a small bottle *US*
- In Tunnely, crack came in tinfoil because it was easier to hide and cheaper to package, but out of habit everybody still called it bottles. —Richard Price, *Clockers*, p. 190, 1992

3 a small container of amphetamine or methamphetamine in liquid form *US*
- — National Institute on Drug Abuse, *What do they call it again?*, 1980

4 in electric and telephone line work, any glass insulator *US*
- —A.B. Chance Co., *Lineman's Slang Dictionary*, p. 2, 1980

5 in betting, odds of 2 – 1 *UK*
- —John McCririck, *John McCririck's World of Betting*, p. 59, 1991

▸ **on the bottle**
engaged as a pickpocket *UK*
From rhyming slang **BOTTLE OF FIZZ** for **THE WHIZ**, and thus a direct translation from **ON THE WHIZ**.

▸ **the bottle, big house, or box**
in twelve-step recovery programmes such as Alcoholics Anonymous, used as a description of the three options for an addict who does not recover from their addiction – a return to drinking, prison and death *US*
- —Christopher Cavanaugh, *AA to Z*, p. 59, 1998

bottle *verb*

1 to attack someone with a bottle, especially in face *UK, 1984*
- He's had threats saying one of them will bottle him or stab him. — *Wimbledon Guardian*, 24th January 2002

2 to lose your nerve, to back down *UK*
A 1980s contraction of **BOTTLE OUT**; a contradiction of **BOTTLE** (nerve). Often in the expression 'bottle it'.
- [H]is firm were not bottling this time around. — Martin King and Martin Knight, *The Naughty Nineties*, p. 158, 1999

- [T]hey are just about to get to TOOTHLESS'S cell [...] LEE: Still clear? BACON: Yeah. Don't bottle it. — Chris Baker and Andrew Day, *Lock, Stock... & A Good Slopping Out*, p. 410, 2000
- Did he think I was going to bottle it? — Jimmy Stockin, *On The Cobbles*, p. 34, 2000
- Two blondes grabbed me and tried to take me into the bathroom [...] I bottled it and shat myself. — *The Guardian*, p. 4, 28th June 2004

3 to have anal sex, especially with a woman *UK, 1961*
From rhyming slang **BOTTLE AND GLASS** (**ARSE**).

4 of a man, to have sex with a woman; to impregnate a woman *UK, 1961*

5 to lick someone's anus *UK, 1984*
Homosexual use; from rhyming slang **BOTTLE AND GLASS** (**ARSE**).

6 to smell badly, to stink *UK*
- — Patrick O'Shaughnessy, *Market Traders' Slang*, 1979

7 in prison, to conceal articles such as drugs or money in the rectum *UK*
From rhyming slang **BOTTLE AND GLASS** (**ARSE**).
- — Angela Devlin, *Prison Patter*, p. 30, 1996

bottle and a half *noun*
in betting, odds of 5–2 *UK*
In bookmaker slang **BOTTLE** is 2–1, here the addition of a half increases the odds to 2½–1 or 5–2.
- — John McCririck, *John McCririck's World of Betting*, p. 112, 1991

bottle and glass *noun*
1 quality; elegant behaviour *UK*
Rhyming slang for **CLASS**, usually as a negative.
- [N]o bottle and glass. — John Gosling, *The Ghost Squad*, 1959

2 the backside; the anus *UK*
Can be shortened to 'bottle'. Rhyming slang for **ARSE**. First recorded in *Songs and Slang of the British Soldier*, John Brophy and Eric Partridge, 1930. This rhyme extends to **APRIL IN PARIS**.
- I have more than enough to cover my bottle and glass. — Ronnie Barker, *Fletcher's Book of Rhyming Slang*, p. 27, 1979
- Just because a geezer takes it up the bottle doesn't mean he hasn't got any bottle (nerve). — Dave Courtney, *Raving Lunacy*, p. 45, 2000
- Meanwhile, Sid's going waffling on in my ear'ole about some old bollocks but really the canister [the head]'s gonski.[S]pin her over and bite her firm little bottle. — J.J. Connolly, *Layer Cake*, p. 77, 2000

bottle and stopper *noun*
a police officer *US, 1928*
Rhyming slang for **COPPER**. Sometimes shortened to 'bottle'.
- Every other stud you meet on the streets belongs to the bottles. They got four snitches on each block. — Malcolm Braly, *On the Yard*, p. 159, 1967

bottle baby *noun*
an alcoholic *US, 1925*
- We were on another plane in another sphere compared to the musicians who were bottle babies, always hitting the jug and then coming up brawling after they got loaded. — Mezz Mezzrow, *Really the Blues*, p. 94, 1946
- — *New York Times Magazine*, p. 87, 16th March 1958
- The dregs of society hang out here, and hustlers of both sexes intermingle with short-con men, narcotics pushers, junkies, and plain bottle babies who booze their way through life. — Johnny Shearer, *The Male Hustler*, p. 55, 1966

bottle blonde *noun*
a person whose blonde hair is the result of bleach, not nature *US*
- — Helen Dahlskog (Editor), *A Dictionary of Contemporary and Colloquial Usage*, p. 9, 1972
- He brings in this bottle-blond sissy, it was like getting a righteous college degree in fruitness. — James Ellroy, *White Jazz*, p. 52, 1992
- Bawdy bottle-blonde rapper Princess Superstar[.] — *The Times Magazine*, p. 43, 16th February 2002

bottle-cap colonel *noun*
a lieutenant colonel in the US Army *US*
Vietnam war usage. From the insignia.
- I don't have time to tell you about it; I've got a bottle-cap colonel named Homer Kisling coming over to brief you. — Walter Boyne and Steven Thompson, *The Wild Blue*, p. 450, 1986

bottle club *noun*
a business disguised as a club in an attempt to circumvent alcohol laws *US*
- A bottle club is a resort which gets around the law which provides that all liquor dispensaries shall close at 2 A.M. — Jack Lait and Lee Mortimer, *Washington Confidential*, p. 11, 1951

bottle dealer *noun*
a drug dealer who sells pills in large quantities *US*
- — Edward R. Bloomquist, *Marijuana*, p. 334, 1971

bottle-fed *adjective*
said of a car engine that is being tested with petrol fed from a bottle through a rubber hose *US*
- — Lewis Poteet, *Car & Motorcyle Slang*, p. 37, 1992

bottle man *noun*
a drunkard *US, 1944*
- — Harold Wentworth and Stuart Berg Flexner, *Dictionary of American Slang*, p. 57, 1960

bottle merchant; bottler *noun*
a coward, someone who loses nerve *UK*
From **BOTTLE** (nerve) and **BOTTLE OUT** (to lose your nerve).
- You're a bottle merchant, turning your back on your mates[.] — John King, *Human Punk*, p. 223, 2000
- I have to do this and he fucking knows it, otherwise I get called a bottler for the rest of my life[.] — Danny King, *The Burglar Diaries*, p. 139, 2001

bottleneck *noun*
1 a style of guitar playing in which a smooth piece of metal or glass is moved smoothly up and down the fretboard creating a glissando effect *US, 1973*
The original device was, in fact, the neck of a bottle worn over the a finger.
- [Elmore] James learned his familiar bottleneck style at twelve by running a broken bottle along wire fastened to the wall of the family shack. — Nick Logan and Rob Finnis, *The NME Book of Rock*, p. 195, 1975

2 a marijuana pipe made from the neck of a beer or soft drink bottle *SOUTH AFRICA*
- — *Surfrikan Slang*, 2004

bottle of beer *noun*
the ear *UK, 1961*
Rhyming slang. Ray Puxley noted in *Cockney Rabbit*, 1992, that it is always used in full.

bottle of fizz *verb*
to work as a pickpocket; to steal something quickly as an opportunity arises *UK, 1938*
Rhyming slang for **THE WHIZ** (pickpocketing).

bottle of scent *noun*
a male homosexual *UK*
Rhyming slang for **BENT**.
- [Y]ou great big bottle of scent. — Bodmin Dark, *Dirty Cockney Rhyming Slang*, 2003

bottle of water *noun*
a daughter *UK, 1961*
Rhyming slang.

bottle-oh *noun*
a person who collects and sells used bottles *AUSTRALIA, 1898*
- It was an approach as familiar as the postmen with their whistles, and the cockatoos glanced idly at the sweating pony and the two bottle-os in their grubby trousers and singlets. — Vince Kelly, *The Bogeyman*, p. 186, 1956

bottle out *verb*
to lose your nerve *UK*
From **BOTTLE** (nerve), a contraction of 'bottle fallen out'.
- If they don't have the courage to do a crime. They, as they say, "bottle out"[.] — *The Listener*, 8th March 1979

bottler *noun*
1 a man who takes the active role in anal sex *UK, 1961*
Extended from the verb **BOTTLE** (to have anal sex).

2 someone or something that is excellent *AUSTRALIA, 1855*
Origin unknown.
- Cripes it's a little beauty bottler though I say so meself! — Barry Humphries, *The Wonderful World of Barry McKenzie*, p. 56, 1968

3 a collector of money for a street-entertainer *UK, 1935*
Used by showmen and buskers.

bottler; bottling *adjective*
superlatively good, excellent *AUSTRALIA*
- — Sydney J. Baker, *The Drum*, p. 93, 1959

bottletop *noun*
something gained; a thing of some value *UK*
Rhyming slang on **COP** (to obtain) but used as a noun; sometimes abbreviated to 'bottle'.
- To say something/someone is "not much bottle (or bottle top)" means not much cop which implies it/he/she is a doubtful or useless asset. — Hillman, 15th November 1974

bottle top *verb*
to catch, gain or understand something *UK*
Rhyming slang on various senses of the verb **COP**. Sometimes heard as an abbreviated 'bottle'.
- 'E's gorn an' bottled (or bottle topped) the 'oppin' pot! — Hillman, 15th November 1974

bottle to the field *noun*
in racing, bookmaker's odds of 2–1 *UK*
- — *Sunday Telegraph*, 7th May 1967

bottle up *verb*
to repress or contain your feelings *UK, 1853*
- I'm not saying you have to be a fount of perpetually-spewing emotion, but if you keep everything bottled up, it's hard for people to feel close to you. — Rhiannon Paine, *Too Late for the Festival*, p. 129, 1999

bottle up and go *verb*
to leave *US*
- — Marcus Hanna Boulware, *Jive and Slang of Students in Negro Colleges*, 1947

bottley *adjective*
nervous *UK*
From **BOTTLE** (courage, nerve, spirits).
- He's off the phone already. Sounded a bit bottley, not like Cody at all. — J.J. Connolly, *Layer Cake*, p. 170, 2000

bottom *noun*
1 the buttocks *UK, 1699*
A colloquial usage, delightfully defined in the *Oxford English Dictionary* as follows: 'The sitting part of a man, the posteriors, the seat'.
2 the submissive partner in a homosexual or sado-masochistic relationship *US*
- If he is said to be "tops," it means that he will assume only the active partnership in sodomy, whlie if he is called "tops or bottoms," he will assume either the so-called male or female role in sodomy. — *New York Mattachine Newsletter*, p. 6, June 1961
- Boots could take either the top or the bottom, without the least show of emotion. — Donald Goines, *Whoreson*, p. 265, 1972
- He always played the bottom role and, and he did this without question or hesitation. — *The Leatherman's Handbook*, p. 30, 1972

Bottom *nickname*
Miami, Florida *US*
- Police say the Miami Boys had such a leader in Atlanta in Theophilus Lujuan "Big Wheel" Roker, 28, a Miami native who is suspected of recruiting personnel, drugs and weapons form "The Bottom" – street slang for Miami. — *Atlanta (Georgia) Journal and Constitution*, p. D1, 4th March 1991

bottom bitch *noun*
the pimp's favourite of the prostitutes working for him; the leader of the prostitutes *US, 1967*
- Oliver had assured her that she was his top bitch but demanded to know why she couldn't catch as many dates as Alice, his bottom bitch. — Joseph Wambaugh, *Floaters*, p. 67, 1996

bottom burp; botty burp; burp; botty banger *noun*
a fart *UK*
- The World's Stupidest Bottom-Burp: Vyvyan, Britain — Ben Elton and Rik Mayall, *The Young Ones*, 8th May 1984
- — Peter Furze, *Tailwinds*, p. 36, 1998
- DIY botty-burp bombs and glow-in-the-dark alien farts. — *Sunday Herald*, 28th July 2002

bottom dollar *noun*
your last dollar *US*
Heard in the context of betting your 'bottom dollar'.
- — Joseph A. Weingarten, *An American Dictionary of Slang*, p. 40, 1954

bottom end *noun*
in drag racing, the portion of the track just after the starting line *US*
- — Fremont Drag Strip, *Guide to Drag Racing*, 1960

bottom feeder *noun*
1 a despised person of low-status who grasps any opportunity or means of survival *US*
An allusion to the underwater lifestyle of certain fish.
- All those people we knew at Andover with more money and better families than God – where are they? Why aren't they running the country instead of a bunch of bottom-feeders? — Jamake Highwater, *The Sun, He Dies*, 1980
- Brought low by a bottom feeder. — *The Observer*, 26th September 2004

2 in poker, a low-betting player who tries to eke out meager winnings against unskilled players *US*
- — John Vorhaus, *The Big Book of Poker Slang*, p. 7, 1996

bottom fisher *noun*
a stock investor looking for stocks with a poor recent showing *US*
- — Kathleen Odean, *High Steppers, Fallen Angels, and Lollipops*, p. 86, 1988

bottom girl *noun*
the pimp's favourite of the prostitutes working for him; the leader of the prostitutes *US*
- It would just keep me too busy, and I wouldn't have the time to be free. That is, unless I had a top-notch bottom girl to check the traps for me. — A.S. Jackson, *Gentleman Pimp*, p. 82, 1973

bottom line *noun*
the final analysis *US, 1967*
- Bottom line? Elyse turns into Iceland and Eddie's not the type to look elsewhere. — *Diner*, 1982

bottom man *noun*
the passive partner in a homosexual relationship *US*
- — Bruce Rodgers, *The Queens' Vernacular*, p. 36, 1972
- — *Maledicta*, p. 231, 1979: 'Kinks and queens: linguistic and cultural aspects of the terminology for gays'
- Bottom man is the masochist in an S/M relationship (antonym: top man). The term refers exclusively to the hierarchial contrast of the two partners, one subject to the other, and need not correspond to the actual physical position — Wayne Dynes, *Homolexis*, p. 25, 1985

bottoms *noun*
1 dice that have been marked to have two identical faces *US*
- — Frank Garcia, *Marked Cards and Loaded Dice*, p. 265, 1962

2 the worst *US*
- I've had it. This is bottoms. I'm really locked. — Max Shulman, *Guided Tour of Campus Humor*, p. 105, 1955

bottom's up *noun*
a common position for anal and/or vaginal sex, in which the passive partner lies on their stomach *US, 1960*
- — Dale Gordon, *The Dominion Sex Dictionary*, p. 31, 1967
- — Bruce Rodgers, *The Queens' Vernacular*, p. 90, 1972

bottoms up!
used as a toast *UK, 1917*
From drinking by upturning a glass or a bottle.
- Jamie said, "Oh, well, bottoms up." He took a big bite of the candy, chewed and swallowed. — E.L. Konigsburg, *From the Mixed-Up Files of Mrs. Basil E. Frankweiler*, p. 76, 1967

bottom weight *Crust*
a minimum amount *UK*
- [I]f their little plan worked they could put us away for a three [years] bottom weight and round up the slush [counterfeit money][.] — Derek Raymond (Robin Cook), *The Crust on its Uppers*, p. 152, 1962

bottom woman *noun*
the pimp's favourite of the prostitutes working for him; the leader of the prostitutes *US*
- There ain't more than three or four good bottom women promised a pimp in his lifetime. — Iceberg Slim (Robert Beck), *Pimp*, p. 215, 1969
- My bottom woman, Sandy – she's been with me the longest – takes care of most of my business and helps me make decisions. — Susan Hall, *Gentleman of Leisure*, p. 10, 1972
- — Ruth Todasco et al., *The Intelligent Woman's Guide to Dirty Words*, p. 2, 1973

Botts' dots *noun*
small bumps delineating lanes on motorways *US*
- — Montie Tak, *Truck Talk*, p. 17, 1971
- Those things that everybody calls Botts Dots are actually, in highway parlance, raised pavement markers. Elbert D. Botts was just the guy who, in the 1950's, invented a certain kind of dot and found a way to stick it to the surface of the road. — California Department of Transportation, *Fact Sheet*, 2001

botty; bottie *noun*
the human bottom *UK, 1874*
Originally of a baby's or child's posterior; now less specific but usage is generally childish.
- When me nose gets snotty / An me cannot feel me botty. —Benjamin Zephaniah, *The Cold War*, p. 26, 1992

botty burp; botty banger *noun*
▷ see: BOTTOM BURP

botzelbaum pie *noun*
an upside-down pie *CANADA*
Used in Mennonite Waterloo County, Ontario.

boubou *noun*
crack cocaine *UK, 1998*
A possible play on **BEBE**, ***BOULYA*** or ***BOULDER*** (crack cocaine).
- —Mike Haskins, *Drugs*, p. 281, 2003

boucher *noun*
in Franco-Ontario, a fiddle player *CANADA*
Boucher is French for 'butcher', and is applied to fiddle playing from the fact that the player 'saws and saws' to make music.
- I'm the best damn boutcher from Calibogie to Kalindar! —*Calibogie Fiddler*, 1969

boudoir *noun*
an army tent *US*
- —Lou Shelly, *Hepcats Jive Talk Dictionary*, p. 43, 1945

bougie; bouji *adjective*
bourgeois *US*
- I pay you a thousand dollars a week and you can't even get one bougie nigga! —Charles W. Moore, *A Brick for Mister Jones*, p. 62, 1975
- —Edith A. Folb, *runnin' down some lines*, p. 230, 1980
- —Connie Eble (Editor), *UNC-CH Campus Slang*, p. 2, Spring 1991

boulder; boulders *noun*
crack cocaine; a piece of crack cocaine *US*
Built on the **ROCK** metaphor.
- —Ethan Hilderbrant, *Prison Slang*, p. 15, 1998

boulder baby *noun*
a crack cocaine addict *US*
From the **ROCK** metaphor.
- —Gary K. Farlow, *Prison-ese*, p. 6, 2002

boulder-holder; over-the-shoulder boulder-holder *noun*
a brassière *UK, 1970*
- "What's the definition of a bra?" "An over-the-shoulder boulder-holder." —*The World According to Garp*, 1982

boulevard *noun*
1 a long, straight hallway *US*
- They'd take us downstairs in the boulevard and strip us naked! —Henry Williamson, *Hustler!*, 1965

2 in trucking, a major motorway *US*
- —Ed and Ruth Radlauer, *Truck Tech Talk*, p. 10, 1986

boulevard boy *noun*
a young male prostitute in an urban setting *US*
- —*Maledicta*, p. 145, Summer/Winter 1986–1987: 'Sexual slang: prostitutes, pedophiles, flagellators, transvestites, and necrophiles'

boulya *noun*
crack cocaine *UK, 1998*
A possible play on ***BOULDER*** (crack cocaine).
- —Mike Haskins, *Drugs*, p. 281, 2003

bounce *noun*
1 a brainstorming session *US*
- Bounce, she thought with a weak smile, that's what they call it. Bounce is cop vernacular for a brainstorm session. —Michael Slade, *Headhunter*, p. 313, 1984

2 a jail or prison sentence *US, 1957*
- With their priors, they're looking at a serious bounce. —*Gone in 60 Seconds*, 2000

3 in horse racing, a poorly run race followed by a well-run race *US*

4 an air-to-air attack *US, 1943*
- —J. E. Lighter, *Historical Dictionary of American Slang, Volume 1*, p. 251, 1994

▸ **on the bounce**
consecutively, one after the other *UK*
- I remember coming here to summer camp. I loved it. Three years on the bounce we come. —Kevin Sampson, *Outlaws*, p. 269, 2001

▸ **the bounce**
bouncers, door-security, collectively *UK*

bounce *verb*
1 to maintain order in a bar or nightclub, ejecting people from the premises if necessary *US, 1874*
- [T]here's nothing much can be done about it, because the muddled situation of District law and law enforcement makes it impossible to bounce that sort of undesirables[.] —Jack Lait and Lee Mortimer, *Washington Confidential*, p. 14, 1951
- He cut her off with the wave of a hand. "A bouncer's job is to bounce. I pay that asshole good money." —Carl Hiaasen, *Strip Tease*, p. 22, 1993

2 to leave *US*
- —Connie Eble (Editor), *UNC-CH Campus Slang*, p. 1, March 1996
- —*Newsday*, p. B2, 11th October 1997

3 (of a cheque) to be returned as worthless by the bank with which it has been drawn *US, 1936*
- [Y]our cheques always bounce. —Stewart Home, *Sex Kick [britpulp]*, p. 245, 1999

4 (used of a message sent electronically) to return to the sender, undeliverable as addressed *US*
- —Eric S. Raymond, *The New Hacker's Dictionary*, p. 75, 1991

5 to pay; to provide without charge *US*
- I think she'd bounce for a free meal if the boss isn't there. —Joseph Wambaugh, *The New Centurions*, p. 245, 1970

6 to activate a car's suspension system so as to cause the car to bounce up and down *US*
- —Edith A. Folb, *runnin' down some lines*, p. 230, 1980

bounce back *noun*
the return of an overdraft *US*
- —Vincent J. Monteleone, *Criminal Slang*, p. 31, 1949

bounce back *verb*
to recover or return from a setback *UK, 1950*
- The basket case of British opera has bounced back with a 3m sponsorship deal[.] —*The Guardian*, 10th October 2003

bouncer *noun*
1 a person, usually a strong man, employed to maintain and restore order in a bar, restaurant, club or performance *US, 1883*
In the UK, 'bouncers' collectively are **THE BOUNCE**. John Godber's all-male cast play about UK nightlife *Bouncers* (1984) is a classic of the contemporary British theatre and one of the most performed plays in the English language.
- [W]hen your friends come around asking for you they don't get thrown out by the bouncer for not spending enough loot[.] —Mezz Mezzrow, *Really the Blues*, p. 198, 1946
- As the years gather on him, his personal temper seems to be cooling, but when he was younger and even more nervous he never needed a bouncer in any of his cafes. —Robert Sylvester, *No Cover Charge*, p. 104, 1956
- The bouncers took care of them in a hurry and a few were hustled out lengthwise. —Mickey Spillane, *Me, Hood!*, p. 63, 1963
- In the meantime a bouncer name Eddie come along. —Sara Harris, *The Lords of Hell*, p. 22, 1967
- I used to be the head bouncer here back in the 70s. —*The Blues Brothers*, 1980
- The go-go whore starts yelling I owe her five bucks and this bouncer come running over. —Elmore Leonard, *Maximum Bob*, p. 1, 1991
- [T]he bouncers are really chilled out – I don't think some of them actually realise that they are supposed to be on the door. —Ben Malbon, *Cool Places*, p. 270, 1998

2 the female breast *UK, 1972*
Obvious imagery and, equally obvious, usually in the plural.

3 a brakevan (caboose) *US*
- —Norman Carlisle, *The Modern Wonder Book of Trains and Railroading*, p. 259, 1946
- —Ramon Adams, *The Language of the Railroader*, p. 18, 1977

bounce shot *noun*
in a dice game, a type of controlled shot by a skilled cheat *US*
- —*The Annals of the American Academy of Political and Social Sciences*, p. 121, May 1950

bouncing Betty *noun*
a land-mine first used in World War 2, prevalent in Vietnam, that bounches waist-high and then sprays shrapnel when triggered *US, 1943*
- Kurt gritted his teeth, but kept on talking about a trooper who'd frozen on a pull-release bouncing betty. —Ronald J. Glasser, *365 Days*, p. 14, 1971

- He was going to take a patrol out in the morning and said he hoped they did not trip any Bouncing Betties. His last company commander had been hit by one. —Philip Caputo, *A Rumor of War*, p. 229, 1977

bouncing powder *noun*
cocaine *US*
- —Eugene Landy, *The Underground Dictionary*, p. 39, 1971
- —Nick Constable, *This is Cocaine*, p. 181, 2002
- —Mike Haskins, *Drugs*, p. 280, 2003

bouncy-bouncy *noun*
sexual intercourse *US*
- —Harold Wentworth and Stuart Berg Flexner, *Dictionary of American Slang*, p. 58, 1960
- —Kenn "Naz" Young, *Naz's Dictionary of Teen Slang*, p. 13, 1993

bounder *noun*
someone whose manners or company are unacceptable; hence a vulgar and unwelcome pretender to polite society; a nuisance *UK, 1889*
Survives in ironic usage, often applied to inanimate objects.
- Aha! Gotcha you boundah! —Kevin Sampson, *Powder*, 1999

boungy; bungy *noun*
the anus *BAHAMAS*
- —John A. Holm, *Dictionary of Bahamian English*, 1982

bounty *noun*
a black person who sides with the white authorities *UK*
Derives from 'Bounty', a chocolate and coconut confection that is brown on the outside and white on the inside.
- —Angela Devlin, *Prison Patter*, p. 30, 1996

bouquet straight *noun*
in poker, a sequenced hand comprised of all red or all black suits, but not a flush *US*
It looks impressive, but is worth no more than any non-flush straight.
- —John Vorhaus, *The Big Book of Poker Slang*, p. 8, 1996

bourbon bibber *noun*
an oil worker from Kentucky *US*
- —Jerry Robertson, *Oil Slanguage*, 1954

Bourke shower *noun*
a dust storm *AUSTRALIA, 1945*
Bourke is an inland town in New South Wales. Other locations similarly used by nature, weather and irony: Bedourie, Bogan, Cobar, Darling, Wilcannia and Wimmera.

Bournville Boulevard *noun*
the anus, the rectum *UK*
Cadbury's chocolate is made in Bournville, in Birmingham; a UK version of **HERSHEY HIGHWAY**.
- Used to denote homosexuality, as in: "I believe he strolls down the Bourneville Boulevard." — *Roger's Profanisaurus*, p. 5, December 1997

'bout it *adjective*
▷ see: **ABOUT IT**

Boutros Boutros Ghali; boutros *noun*
cocaine *UK*
Rhyming slang for **CHARLIE** (cocaine), formed on the name of the Secretary General of the United Nations, 1992–1996.
- —Mike Haskins, *Drugs*, p. 272, 2003
- I've had a couple of lines of Boutros and my Boris Becker (penis) is the size of a Tic Tac. —Bodmin Dark, *Dirty Cockney Rhyming Slang*, 2003

bovina *noun*
in homosexual usage, a woman, especially one with large breasts *US*
- — *Maledicta*, p. 227, Winter 1980: 'Lovely, blooming, fresh and gay": the onomastics of camp'

bovver *noun*
trouble, fighting, violent behaviour, especially when associated with skinhead culture *UK, 1969*
From a London pronunciation of 'bother'.

bovver boot *noun*
a heavy-duty boot used as a kicking-weapon, stereotypically worn by a skinhead *UK, 1969*

bovver boy *noun*
a member of a hooligan gang, generally characterised as a skinhead, and therefore associated with extreme right-wing, racist violence *UK, 1970*
Extended from **BOVVER** (trouble) and very rarely seen in the singular.
- They weren't really calling it football hooliganism yet; it was all "bovver boys" and "aggro" and was still very much tied up with the skinhead cult. — Martin King and Martin Knight, *The Naughty Nineties*, p. 166, 1999
- Steven Mackintosh (above centre) plays Ray, a reform bovver boy who is tempted back into Jazi ways by his daughter's heroin addiction and by his inability to rehouse his family[.] — *The Independent*, p. 22, 5th April 2004

bow *noun*
the elbow *US*
Elbows used to establish position are a key part of the anatomy in basketball.
- —Chuck Wielgus and Alexander Wolff, *The In-Your-Face Basketball Book*, p. 30, 1980

▸ **on the bow**
gratis; scrounging *UK, 1938*
From an earlier, related sense (without paying).
- —David Powis, *The Signs of Crime*, 1977

bow *verb*
to perform an act of oral sex *JAMAICA, 1995*
From the conventional sense (bending at the waist).

bow and arrow *noun*
1 a native American Indian; Indian ancestry *US, 1930*
- —Frederic G. Cassidy, *Dictionary of American Regional English, Volume 1*, p. 353, 1985
- —Chris Thain, *Cold as a Bay Street Banker's Heart*, p. 18, 1987

2 a sparrow *UK, 1931*
Cockney rhyming slang.

bow-and-arrow *adjective*
not armed with a pistol *US*
- Keenan was currently assigned to the "bow-and-arrow squad," which meant that he would not be allowed to carry a gun until such time as his attitude improved. —Thomas Larry Adcock, *Precinct 19*, p. 38, 1984

bow and quiver *noun*
the liver, especially in contexts of irritability or liverishness *UK, 1961*
Rhyming slang.

bow-cat *noun*
a man who fellates *JAMAICA, 1995*
A combination of **BOW** (oral sex) and **CAT** (a man).

bower bird *noun*
an avid collector of many and various things *AUSTRALIA, 1926*
From the mating habit of certain male bower birds which collect coloured items to make a display for females.
- All fettlers are bower birds, the most notorious in railways. —Patsy Adam-Smith, *Folklore of the Australian Railwaymen*, p. 27, 1969
- My father had just the right thing, thanks to his bower-bird habits. —Rex Hunt, *Tall Tales – and True*, p. 76, 1994

bowl *noun*
1 a pipe for smoking marijuana, hashish or crack cocaine *US, 1974*
- Jeff and I smoked a couple of bowls and then went to a screening of the new Friday the 13th movie. —Bret Easton Ellis, *Less Than Zero*, p. 130, 1985
- I'm at my best after some methical or a bowl of sense[.] —Tone Loc, *Cheeba Cheeba*, 1989
- And every day George would come home from work, she'd have a big fat bowl waiting for him, man, when'd come in the door, man. — *Dazed and Confused*, 1993
- —Pamela Munro, *U.C.L.A. Slang*, p. 44, 1997

2 an approximate measure of marijuana, between one thirty-second and one sixteenth of an ounce *US, 1972*
The amount needed to fill a pipe.

3 in cricket, a period of bowling *UK, 1961*
- —Keith Foley, *A Dictionary of Cricketing Terminology*, p. 48, 1998

bowl along *verb*
to move easily *UK*
- For as long as I could remember, before then, it seemed that I'd been forever on the move, bowling along from one disaster to another. —Erwin James, *A Life Inside*, p. xi, 2003

bowl basher *noun*
the active male in anal sex *AUSTRALIA*
- — Thommo, *The Dictionary of Australian Swearing and Sex Sayings*, p. 18, 1985

bowl brandy *noun*
faeces, excrement *UK*
- —Paul Baker, *Polari*, p. 166, 2002

bowlegged *adjective*

(of prison sentences) concurrent *US*

- Ring's public defender argued till he was blue in the face, and the judge relented just a little, running the deuces [two-year sentences] bowlegged instead, as in concurrent.—Seth Morgan, *Homeboy*, p. 85, 1990

bowler *noun*

an ugly girl *IRELAND*

Uncertain origin, possibly from 'bow', abbreviated from BOW-WOW, with the suffix -ER.

- Daisy, roysh [right], she's this bird from Lillies, a bit of a bowler if the truth be told, but she has the total hots for yours truly.—Paul Howard, *Ross O'Carroll-Kelly*, p. 83, 2003

bowling green *noun*

a fast stretch of railway line *UK*

- —Harvey Sheppard, *Dictionary of Railway Slang*, 1970

bowl it around *verb*

to strut and posture in an unsubtly masculine way *UK*

Teen slang.

- — Susie Dent, *The Language Report*, p. 76, 2003

bowlodrome *noun*

a blowling alley *US*

- —Lester V. Berrey and Melvin Van den Bark, *The American Thesaurus of Slang*, p. 633, 1953

bowl of fruit *noun*

▷ see: BOX OF FRUIT

bowlster *noun*

a bowler *US*

- —Lester V. Berrey and Melvin Van den Bark, *The American Thesaurus of Slang*, p. 633, 1953

bows *noun*

▸ **take bows**

to falsely take credit for something *US*

- —Anna Scotti and Paul Young, *Buzzwords*, p. 10, 1997

bowser *noun*

1 a dog *US, 1965*

- Letch thought about slipping the bowser some barbiturates but was afraid it might croak. He didn't want an OD'd Scottie on his conscience.—Joseph Wambaugh, *Floaters*, p. 10, 1996

2 by extension, an ugly person *US, 1978*

- —Connie Eble (Editor), *UNC-CH Campus Slang*, p. 2, Fall 1980

3 a petrol pump *AUSTRALIA, 1918*

- We were over at the workshop and when we dipped the bowser we're about sixty gallons up.—Sam Weller, *Old Bastards I Have Met*, p. 88, 1979
- —Louis S. Leland, *A Personal Kiwi-Yankee Dictionary*, p. 17, 1984

bowser bag *noun*

a container used by restaurants to package unfinished meals to be taken home by diners *US, 1965*

A variation on the more common DOGGY BAG.

- Whereupon the child asked, "Father, if you were in a whorehouse and you couldn't finish, would it be permissible to ask for a bowser bag to take the leftovers home?"—Tom Robbins, *Another Roadside Attraction*, p. 47, 1971

bowsie *noun*

a disreputable drunkard, a lout, a quarrelsome drunkard *IRELAND*

- Behan . . . had been an inmate . . . of both Borstal in England and Mountjoy in Dublin. Such credentials defined him as a 'character', which is usually a Dublin synonym for a bowsie or a gurrier (q.v.). —Hugh Leonard, *Out After Dark*, p. 166, 1990

bowsprit *noun*

an erect penis *UK, 1741*

It does not take much imagination to see the comparison.

- — *The Guild Dictionary of Homosexual Terms*, p. 5, 1965
- —Dale Gordon, *The Dominion Sex Dictionary*, p. 32, 1967

bow tie *noun*

1 a married woman's lover *NEW ZEALAND*

- Come off it. You wouldn't like your sister-in-law to park her ears to all I know about you. You and your bow-tie.—David Ballantyne, *The Cuninghams*, p. 125, 1948

2 a Chevrolet car *US*

- —John Edwards, *Auto Dictionary*, p. 18, 1993

bow-wow *noun*

a 'dog', literally and in its slang senses *US, 1935*

- [T]he network wants to burn off as soon as possible a series it considers to be a real bow-wow[.]—*Washington Post*, p. C14, 18th August 1983
- "A bow-wow," Purdue said. "Thirty to one on the morning line." —Robert Campbell, *Juice*, p. 2, 1988
- That's when Letch devised the scheme to pee on the tree and drive the little bowwow bonkers.—Joseph Wambaugh, *Floaters*, p. 11, 1996
- Judge Reinhold, whose career has spiraled downhill ever since "home Alone," stars in the direct-to-video installment of the St. Bernard series. It's a real bow-wow.—*Boston Globe*, p. N9, 23rd July 2003

box *noun*

1 the vagina; a woman *UK, 1605*

- I grabbed her by the shoulders, kissed her, and right quick from some instinctive sense shoved my hand right up her dress and came up with her box shining golden in the golden sun.—Jack Kerouac, *Letter to Neal Cassady*, p. 298, 10th January 1951
- And do you know that the same thing happened to that dumb little box?—Jack Kerouac, *On the Road*, p. 184, 1957
- She has no cherry, but she thinks it's no sin / for she still has the box that the cherry came in.—Bruce Jackson, *Get Your Ass in the Water and Swim Like Me*, p. 229, 1964
- He said, "All I have to do is scarf her a few times and I get anything I want." Nuttee asked Diehl to explain the word "scarf." "To eat her box, in other words."—Richard Honeycutt, *Candy Mossler*, p. 80, 1966
- Max was still down on the floor with his nose up V's smelly box.—Steve Cannon, *Groove, Bang, and Jive Around*, p. 146, 1969
- The broad was there in a short skirt with no drawers; when the guard wasn't looking – zip – she flashed her box, now you see it, now you don't – like the guy in the raincoat on the subway.—Edwin Torres, *Carlito's Way*, p. 123, 1975
- Are the billboards around town promoting Kook cigarettes' flip-top box in poor taste, pornographic – or neither? The ones that show a young woman in bathing attire floating in an inner tube under the caption: "Coolest box around."—*San Francisco Examiner*, p. 37, 15th September 1976
- Wanting to test the mettle of Dave's 42nd Street schlong, she bit off more than her little box could chew.—Josh Alan Friedman, *Tales of Times Square*, p. 117, 1986

2 the posterior, the buttocks *US, 1965*

Originally black, then gay usage.

- —Paul Baker, *Polari*, p. 166, 2002

3 a jail or prison *US*

Usually heard as 'the box'.

- —Bill Valentine, *Gang Intelligence Manual*, p. 130, 1995

4 a secure prison cubicle for a one-to-one visit *UK*

- —Home Office, *Glossary of Terms and Slang Common in Penal Establishments*, July 1978
- —Angela Devlin, *Prison Patter*, p. 30, 1996

5 a cell used for solitary confinement *US*

- —John R. Armore and Joseph D. Wolfe, *Dictionary of Desperation*, p. 21, 1976

6 a safe *US, 1902*

- Can you bust a box, if you have to?—Robert Edmond Alter, *Carny Kill*, p. 102, 1966
- I was supposed to be the best box-man in the country and as I look back, I must have busted four hundred boxes and lifted more than a million.—Red Rudensky, *The Gonif*, p. 6, 1970
- What they weigh depends on the box you're going after. —Bruce Jackson, *Outside the Law*, p. 91, 1972
- I'm thinking about my own place, Nicky. Would you be able to put a box in?—Vincent Patrick, *The Pope of Greenwich Village*, p. 9, 1979

7 in a court of law, the witness box *AUSTRALIA*

- Jump in the box [give Queen's evidence].—Jim McNeil, *The Chocolate Frog' and 'The Old Familiar Juice'*, 1973

8 approximately 20 one-kilogram plates of pressed hashish *CANADA*

- The plates are bundled into "boxes" of approximately twenty kilos, wrapped in burlap and buried until they can be shipped. —Suroosh Alvi et al., *The Vice Guide*, p. 113, 2002

9 a small amount of marijuana, approximately enough to fill a matchbox *US, 1967*

10 a guitar *US, 1911*

May also refer to a banjo.

- —Robert S. Gold, *A Jazz Lexicon*, p. 35, 1964
- —David Powis, *The Signs of Crime*, 1977

11 a piano *US, 1908*

- —Arnold Shaw, *Lingo of Tin-Pan Alley*, p. 8, 1950
- This gave me a stronger urge to blow piano, or blow a box, as they used to say.—Claude Brown, *Manchild in the Promised Land*, p. 229, 1965

12 a record player *UK, 1924*

- [A] record player is a "box"[.]—Harrison E. Salisbury, *The Shook-up Generation*, p. 161, 1958

- [W]hy did Lester [Bangs] mention tha El Cajon means "The Box"? Was it because "box" is old hipster slang for record player[?] —Greil Marcus, *Psychotic Reactions and Carburetor Dung*, 1986

13 a large, portable radio and tape player *US*
A shortened **GHETTO BOX**.
- He was no legal scholar but even he knew the kids call a ghetto blaster a box. —Andrew Vachss, *Flood*, p. 342, 1985

14 television *US, 1950*
Usually after 'the'.
- He came on the box early, drummed home the law and order theme, honored his cops and firemen. —Sidney Bernard, *This Way to the Apocalypse*, p. 72, 1968
- Nice to see a West Country babe on the box instead of those mingin' birds with fake knockers. —Chris Baker and Andrew Day, *Lock, Stock... & Spaghetti Sauce*, p. 260, 2000

15 a polygraph machine *US*
- She was taken to the next room and connected to "the Box." —Stephen Cannell, *Big Con*, p. 325, 1997

16 an old and inferior car *US*
- —Hal Higdon, *Finding the Groove*, p. 296, 1973
- No matter how much money we made, he always drove a shit box; in December, he'd be in a convertible with no top. —Leonard Shecter and William Phillips, *On the Pad*, p. 187, 1973

17 a new car showroom *US*
- —*Doctor's Review*, August 1989

18 a coffin *UK, 1864*
- I pity him in the box, coz it's not a patch on a Slumberland[.] —Ian Pattison, *Rab C. Nesbitt*, 1988
- There's only one way I'm getting out of here, and that's in a box. —Joel Rose, *Kill Kill Faster Faster*, p. 14, 1997

19 in bar dice games, a leather or vinyl cup used to shake dice before spilling them out *US*
- —Gil Jacobs, *The World's Best Dice Games*, p. 194, 1976

20 in horse racing, a combination bet that covers many different possible outcomes *US*

21 in horse racing, a horse stall *AUSTRALIA*
- —Ned Wallish, *The Truth Dictionary of Racing Slang*, p. 9, 1989

22 a pool table, especially a large one *US*
- —Steve Rushin, *Pool Cool*, p. 6, 1990

23 in the sport of fencing, an electric recording apparatus *UK*
- —E.D. Morton, *Martini A-Z of Fencing*, 1988

24 a reinforced item of underwear designed to protect a sportsman's genitals *UK, 1961*

25 a person who is profoundly out of touch with current trends *US*
A three-dimensional **SQUARE**.
- —Harold Wentworth and Stuart Berg Flexner, *Dictionary of American Slang*, p. 681, 1976

26 in the Royal Air Force, an aircraft cockpit simulator *UK, 1984*

27 in the Vietnam war, an aerial target zone approximately 5/8 of a mile wide by 2 miles long *US*
- Every three hours around the clock, six B-52s from the Strategic Air Command bases in Guam and Thailand obliterated a "box" with 162 ons of boms. —Neil Sheehan, *A Bright Shining Lie*, p. 706, 1988

28 a submarine's main battery *UK*
Reported by John Malin, 1979.

▸ **in the box**

1 engaged in vaginal sex *US*
- —Helen Dahlskog (Editor), *A Dictionary of Contemporary and Colloquial Usage*, p. 9, 1972

2 dealing drugs *US*
- —Jim Crotty, *How to Talk American*, p. 86, 1997

▸ **off your box; out of your box**

1 drunk or drug-intoxicated *UK*
- I did everything I wanted to. Went to Thailand, get out of my box, meditated, get into yoga. —*Ask*, 7th March 1981
- We were just off our boxes, just daft lads. —Shaun Ryder, *Shaun Ryder... in His Own Words*, 1993
- a biker who kept screaming like a wolf because he was out of his box on magic mushrooms —Maik Steel, *Reasons to be cheerful*, 2001

2 mentally disturbed; behaving erratically *UK*
Perhaps an allusion to the Greek myth of Pandora's box and the evils it contained.
- I now know this guy is tripping off his box. —Dave Courtney, *Raving Lunacy*, p. 10, 2000

▸ **out of the box**
in motor racing, exactly as produced by the manufacturer, without any modifications *US*
- —John Edwards, *Auto Dictionary*, p. 119, 1993

▸ **put in the box**
to kill someone *US*
- There are three reasons a familiano can be put in the box [killed]: cowardice, treason, or desertion. —Bill Valentine, *Gangs and Their Tattoos*, p. 36, 2000

▸ **take a box**
to defecate *IRELAND*
- To slash (to piss), to take a box (to crap), to spoon (to court), to sow (to love), to sigh, to sin-o. —Aidan Higgins, *Donkey's Years*, p. 146, 1995

▸ **take out of the box**
to kill someone *US*
- —Bill Valentine, *Gang Intelligence Manual*, p. 78, 1995: 'Black street gang terminology'

box *verb*

1 to confirm the death of a hospital patient *US*
- —*Philadelphia Magazine*, p. 145-151, November 1977

2 to die *US*
- —Sally Williams, *"Strong" Words*, p. 135, 1994

3 in an illegal lottery, to bet on a group of related numbers rather than a single number *US*
- I guess you just gotta do like the Reverend I Doo Little tell the people: If you must play 'em, brothers and sisters, box 'em. —Vernon E. Smith, *The Jones Men*, p. 92, 1974

4 to make a mistake; to muddle things *AUSTRALIA, 1873*
Originally of mixing flocks of sheep.

▸ **box clever**
to use your wits; to behave shrewdly *UK, 1936*
- [H]e decided it was his turn to box clever. —Charles Raven, *Underworld Nights*, p. 62, 1956

▸ **box the fox**
to steal apples *IRELAND*
Origin obscure.
- Now the only time I saw apples was when we boxed the fox or collected them door-to-door on Hallowe'en evening. —Eamonn MacThomais, *Gur Cake and Coal Blocks*, p. 21, 1976

▸ **couldn't box chocolates; couldn't box kippers**
to be a poor quality boxer *UK, 1936*
Punning on conventional senses of 'box'.
- I was no longer young, strong and fit [...] I was probably incapable of boxing chocolates. —Vernon Scannell, *A Proper Gentleman*, 1977

Box *nickname*
▷ **see: BOX FIVE**

Box 100 *noun*
the notional repository for information given to police by informants *US*
- It's the rattingest fucking neighborhood in the city. Half the mail into box 100 must come from the Village. —Vincent Patrick, *The Pope of Greenwich Village*, p. 183, 1979

box bag *noun*
the amount of marijuana (the bag) which can be bought for a carton of cigarettes (the box) *US*
- —William K. Bentley and James M. Corbett, *Prison Slang*, p. 74, 1992

box boy *noun*
a DJ's assistant who has the responsibility for the DJ's boxes of records *UK*
- I'm carrying one of Sasha's record boxes. Tonight I am Sasha's box boy. —Dave Haslam, *Adventures of the Wheels of Steel*, p. xi, 2001

boxcar *noun*

1 any four-engine bomber *US*
- —*American Speech*, p. 310, December 1946: 'More Air Force slang'
- Yeah. He was my buddy on the boxcar. —Kurt Vonnegut, *SlaughterhouseFive*, p. 141, 1969

2 a prison cell *US*
- —Ralph de Sola, *Crime Dictionary*, p. 20, 1982

3 an amphetamine or central nervous system stimulant *US*
- —Jay Robert Nash, *Dictionary of Crime*, p. 42, 1992

boxcar numbers *noun*

a lot of money *US*

- He's OK for a short tab but make sure you don't let him go into box-car numbers. — *The Annals of the American Academy of Political and Social Sciences*, p. 121, May 1950

boxcars *noun*

1 in horse racing, high odds *US, 1934*

From the high numbers used to identify railway carriages.

- — *San Francisco Examiner*, p. 25, 3rd April 1953
- — Robert Saunders Dowst and Jay Craig, *Playing the Races*, p. 160, 1960

2 in a game of dice, a roll of two sixes *US, 1949*

- Abie the Jew bet the dice to win or lose, barring box cars and snake-eyes. — Chester Himes, *A Rage in Harlem*, p. 26, 1957
- — Frank Garcia, *Marked Cards and Loaded Dice*, p. 250, 1962
- I learned about percentage dice that are shaved to favor an ace-six – and a plentitude of snake eyes and boxcars. — Jimmy Snyder, *Jimmy the Greek*, p. 15, 1975
- — Thomas L. Clark, *The Dictionary of Gambling and Gaming*, p. 25, 1987

3 in poker, a pair of sixes or three sixes *US*

A borrowing from the game of craps.

- — George Percy, *The Language of Poker*, p. 12, 1988

4 any large number; a long prison sentence *US*

- — Hyman E. Goldin et al., *Dictionary of American Underworld Lingo*, p. 41, 1950

boxcar tourist *noun*

a hobo travelling by freight train *US*

- — Norman Carlisle, *The Modern Wonder Book of Trains and Railroading*, p. 259, 1946

boxed *adjective*

1 marijuana-intoxicated *US, 1958*

- — Robert George Reisner, *The Jazz Titans*, p. 151, 1960
- — Robert S. Gold, *A Jazz Lexicon*, p. 36, 1964
- — William D. Alsever, *Glossary for the Establishment and Other Uptight People*, p. 15, December 1970

2 muscular, well-toned *US*

- — Anna Scotti and Paul Young, *Buzzwords*, p. 107, 1997

3 incarcerated *US*

- — William D. Alsever, *Glossary for the Establishment and Other Uptight People*, p. 16, December 1970

boxer *noun*

1 an urban youth with a large and loud portable radio and tape player *UK*

- — Tom Hibbert, *Rockspeak!*, p. 29, 1983

2 a person running a game of two-up *AUSTRALIA, 1911*

- The expense to Thompson was enormous, but it was more than covered by the two shillings in the pound collected by his boxer from each spinner who 'headed 'em'. — Vince Kelly, *The Bogeyman*, p. 167, 1956
- — James Holledge, *The Great Australian Gamble*, p. 100, 1966

3 a railway boxcar *US*

- — Ramon Adams, *The Language of the Railroader*, p. 19, 1977

boxes *noun*

in craps, a roll of two fours *US, 1983*

- — Thomas L. Clark, *The Dictionary of Gambling and Gaming*, p. 25, 1987

Box Five; Box Six; Box *nickname*

the UK secret intelligence services *UK*

- Box Five and Box Six are how the police refer to MI5 and MI6. The derogatory term for MI5, incidentally, is MFI, as I would later learn when I had to work with them. — Duncan MacLaughlin, *The Filth*, p. 137, 2002

boxfresh *adjective*

of shoes, especially trainers, unworn *UK*

- [T]he multi-million-pound, state-of-the-art sportswear facility, show-casing the latest in hi-tech imported "boxfresh" minty joints[.] — Julian Johnson, *Urban Survival*, p. 67, 2003

boxie *noun*

a person with bleached blond hair *US*

- — *Washington Post*, p. 18, 8th November 1987

boxies *noun*

men's boxer shorts

- [T]hey ends up getting chased through the club in their boxies, with half their clobber still in the lockers. — Kevin Sampson, *Outlaws*, p. 167, 2001

boxing glove *noun*

a condom *UK*

Playing on **BOX** (the vagina; the male genitals; sexual intercourse), with **GLOVE** (a condom).

- — David Rowan, *A Glossary for the 90s*, 1998

boxing Josh *noun*

masturbation *BAHAMAS*

- — John A. Holm, *Dictionary of Bahamian English*, p. 26, 1982

box-it *noun*

a mixture of cheap wine and cider *UK*

- Drinking schools mix wine and cider to make a cheap heady drink called box-it. — *New Society*, 2nd September 1982

box-kicker *noun*

a supply clerk in the US Marines *US*

- — *Seattle Times*, p. A9, 12th April 1998

boxla *noun*

box lacrosse *CANADA*

Lacrosse, an Indian game, was played practically without side boundaries and with goals as much as a half mile apart. Box lacrosse introduced side boards and a playing surface the size of a hockey rink.

- The 'Pics knocked the front running Drewrys from the playoff picture in one of the biggest upsets in local boxla history. — *Winnipeg Free Press*, p. 25/3, 4th June 1958

box lunch; box lunch at the Y *noun*

oral sex on a woman *US*

The character Y resembles a woman's groin; plays on **BOX** (the vagina).

- — Roger Blake, *The American Dictionary of Sexual Terms*, p. 21, 1964
- [C]omments such as "likes to make," "frigid," "the picture does her too much justice, "box lunch," "a real roller," "gete laid," ad infinitum. — John Nichols, *The Sterile Cuckoo*, p. 7, 1965
- — Dale Gordon, *The Dominion Sex Dictionary*, p. 32, 1967
- 'Some special terms used in a University of Connecticut men's Dormitory' — *American Speech*, p. 228, October 1967
- Another way to say "cunnilingus" [...] Having a boxed lunch at the Y[.] — Erica Orloff and JoAnn Baker, *Dirty Little Secrets*, p. 86, 2001

box man *noun*

a criminal who specialises in breaking into safes *US, 1902*

- "I don't know, for godsake," I said. "I'm no box man." — Robert Edmond Alter, *Carny Kill*, p. 103, 1966
- I was supposed to be the best box-man in the country and as I look back, I must have busted four hundred boxes and lifted more than a million. — Red Rudensky, *The Gonif*, p. 6, 1970
- The old boxmen [safecrackers] they was not dope fiends. — Bruce Jackson, *In the Life*, p. 68, 1972

box of birds; box of fluffly ducks *noun*

a state of great contentment *NEW ZEALAND, 1943*

- I had always been confident it would be a box of birds. — *Sunday Telegraph*, 6th May 1979
- — Louis S. Leland, *A Personal Kiwi-Yankee Dictionary*, p. 17, 1984

box of fruit; bowl of fruit *noun*

a suit *NEW ZEALAND, 1963*

Rhyming slang.

- I decked myself out in a box of fruit, with knife-creased terrace of houses [trousers]. — Harry Orsman, *Modern New Zealand Slang*, 1999

box of L *noun*

a box of 100 ampoules containing methamphetamine hydrochloride (trade name Methedrine™), a central nervous system stimulant *US*

- — David Maurer and Victor Vogel, *Narcotics and Narcotic Addiction*, p. 391, 1973

box of sharks *noun*

used for expressing great surprise, in phrases such as: 'she nearly gave birth to a box of sharks' *CANADA, 1984*

box of tricks; bag of tricks *noun*

a tool box, or any similar receptacle; a notional repertoire of tools and skills needed for any purpose *UK, 1953*

In September 1941, London taxi drivers were recorded as using 'box of tricks' for Euston Station. It is more than likely that this 'tool box' sense preceded the cabbies' sense.

box-on *noun*
a fight, a struggle *AUSTRALIA, 1919*

box on *verb*
to continue fighting; to persevere with anything important or strenuous *AUSTRALIA, 1919*

box on wheels *noun*
a hearse *US*
- — *Complete CB Slang Dictionary*, 1976
- — Peter Chippindale, *The British CB Book*, p. 152, 1981

box screw *noun*
a bank guard *US*
- — Vincent J. Monteleone, *Criminal Slang*, p. 32, 1949

box seat *noun*
the most advantageous area off a beach for a surfer to catch a wave *AUSTRALIA*
- — John M. Kelly, *Surf and Sea*, p. 281, 1965

box shot *noun*
in a dice game in which the dice are rolled from a cup, a controlled shot *US, 1950*
- — Thomas L. Clark, *The Dictionary of Gambling and Gaming*, p. 26, 1987

Box Six *nickname*
▷ see: BOX FIVE

box slugger *noun*
a criminal specialising in breaking into safes *US*
- Later, I heard that they had picked up a tip that two major outfits outside were in dire need of a box slugger and would collaborate to break me out. — Red Rudensky, *The Gonif*, p. 49, 1970

box tool *noun*
any tool used for breaking into a safe *US*
- [T]hey'd go in there with nothing but regular old box tools. — Bruce Jackson, *Outside the Law*, p. 96, 1972

box-up *noun*
a mix-up, a confusion *AUSTRALIA, 1945*
Also used a verb and, as 'boxed-up', an adjective.

box your ears *verb*
to hit you round the head *UK, 1601*
- [T]he elders boxed the ears of a young child to make sure he remembered[.] — William Strauss and Neil Howe, *The Fourth Turning*, p. 15, 1997

boy *noun*

1 heroin *US, 1953*
- But now he had the boy; he could lie around up in his crib, twisted, drugged to the verge of insensibility. — Clarence Cooper Jr, *The Scene*, p. 12, 1960
- Since I had the boy in a balloon I wasn't worried about it. — A.S. Jackson, *Gentleman Pimp*, p. 66, 1973
- Dig my man, how about dropping off two spoons of boy, and a hundred dollar bag of girl. — Donald Goines, *El Dorado Red*, p. 69, 1974
- — Angela Devlin, *Prison Patter*, p. 30, 1996
- — Robert Ashton, *This Is Heroin*, p. 205, 2002

2 the penis *IRELAND*
- I'm the man would slip the boy in there double quick! — Patrick McCabe, *The Butcher Boy*, p. 138, 1992

3 a male friend *US*
Connotes affection and loyalty.
- A man gets off work, he's got to go somewhere. He's got to drink something. He's got to smoke something. He's got to watch a game. He's got to hang out with his boys. — Chris Rock, *Rock This!*, p. 169, 1997

4 a homosexual male prostitute *US*
- The boys – who are called boys and not hookers or hustlers – generally go to the john's apartment, usually staying until the john has his mind-blowing climax and not lingering for the night. — John Francis Hunter, *The Gay Insider*, p. 213, 1971

5 a lesbian *US*
- Gay or straight – ugly's still ugly. And most of those boys are scary. — *Chasing Amy*, 1997

6 a boxer or wrestler *US*
- A specialist, in Berlin, told me last year to retire Upshaw after he was knocked out in the last of three boys in three days. — Iceberg Slim (Robert Beck), *Long White Con*, p. 189, 1977

7 in a deck of playing cards, a jack or knave *US*
- — Albert H. Morehead, *The Complete Guide to Winning Poker*, p. 258, 1967

8 in horse racing, a jockey *US*
- — David W. Maurer, *Argot of the Racetrack*, p. 15, 1951

9 a dollar; money *UK, 1780*
- I say, Ain you got no skins, no kale? No bread? No bones, no berries, no boys? — Robert Gover, *One Hundred Dollar Misunderstanding*, p. 22, 1961

boy! oh boy!
used for registering shock, surprise, satisfaction, etc; also used to emphasise or draw attention to the statement that follows *US, 1917*
- MARK ANTHONY: Puer! O puer! O puer! VO: Which, as any schoolboy knows, means "Boy! Oh boy! Oh boy! — Talbot Rothwell, *Carry On Cleo*, 1964
- — David Peace, *Nineteen Seventy-Four*, p. 287, 1999

boyakasha!
▷ see: BOOYAKASHA!

boy beaver *noun*
the male sex organs and pubic hair *US*
- The job: co-manager (with Gerry Malanga) of a boy-beaver movie house operating under Andy's name. — Jim Carroll, *Forced Entries*, p. 39, 1987

boychik *noun*
a boy or young man *US*
Also variant 'boychick'. As is the case with most diminuitives, used with affection; coined by Yiddish speakers in America.
- You see, boychick, I can spike any script with yaks, but the thing I can't do is heartbreak. — Norman Mailer, *Advertisements for Myself*, p. 159, 1951
- "Where you been, boychi?" chirped Joel. — Clancy Sigal, *Going Away*, p. 10, 1961
- Mama would say that she only hoped I would only turn into a good boychik — Red Rudensky, *The Gonif*, p. 39, 1970

boyf *noun*
a boyfriend *UK*
Used by homosexuals.
- [I]ntroducing your boyf to your parents[.] — *Attitude*, p. 12, October 2003

boy-gal *noun*
a male homosexual *US*
- — Charles Shafer, *Folk Speech in Texas Prisons*, p. 199, 1990

boy-girl *noun*
a young, effeminate, male homosexual *US, 1952*
- [I]t was in that bar that I first saw flagrantly painted men congregate and where a queen boy-girl camped opened with a cop. — John Rechy, *City of Night*, p. 62, 1963

boy-hole *noun*
a young and passive homosexual male *US*
Sexual objectification.
- Now would chime in the litany of abuse: naughty sissy, baby-boy, not-really-a-boy-but-a-pussy, little faggot, secret cocksucking toy, queer-bait, boy-hole, powder-puff. — Terence Sellers, *Dungeon Evidence*, p. 58, 1997

boy in the boat *noun*
the clitoris *US, 1916*
- [T]hose who felt that the ladies should have big bursts but could have them only in that highly localized surface nodule known in the trade as the vestigal phallus, or button, or boy in the boat. — Bernard Wolfe, *The Magic of Their Singing*, p. 93, 1961

boykie; boytjie *noun*
a boy, a youth; used as an admiring from of adress to a man *SOUTH AFRICA, 1974*
An Anglo-Afrikaans diminutive of 'boy'.
- To cries of "dit's my boytjie" (that's my man) he [Nelson Mandela] said the people of the province had proven the National Party Wrong. — *ANC Daily News Briefing*, 27th May 1995
- When a man's [rugby] team members are impressed, you will hear "what a boykie!" — *Surfrikan Slang*, 2003

boyno
hello *UK*
- — Paul Baker, *Polari*, p. 166, 2002

boyo *noun*

1 used as a good-humoured form of address to a man *IRELAND, 1898*
An elaboration of 'boy' stereotypically Irish or Welsh.
- We haven't got an overt act, Terrence me boyo. — George V. Higgins, *The Rat on Fire*, p. 32, 1981
- [N]o five day week and off to the Leisure Centre then, boyo. — Alan Bleasdale, *Boys From the Blackstuff*, 1982
- You don't mind, do you, boyo? — Joel Rose, *Kill Kill Faster Faster*, p. 34, 1997

2 a Welsh man *UK*
Somewhat patronising; after what is thought to be a stereotypically Welsh form of address.
- We want him [Ron Davies, Shadow Secretary of State for Wales] to hang around as long as possible: we can have a lot more fun with this boyo before we're through. —Gyles Brandreth, *Breaking the Code*, p. 286, 1999

boyo *adjective*
mildly pornographic, featuring naked men *US*
- [A] tawdry grocery store where every known Girlie and Boyo magzine is sold; and a colorful assortment of pimps, hustlers, prostitutes, petty thieves, and alcoholics. —Raymond Mungo, *Famous Long Ago*, p. 25, 1970

boys *noun*
1 the male genitals *US*
From *Seinfeld* (NBC, 1990–98). Both Seinfeld and his wacky neighbour Karmer (Michael Richards) referred to their genitals as 'my boys'. Repeated with referential humour.

2 a group of homosexual male friends; collectively, the male homosexual community *US*
- You've been seeing a real woman – what will the boys think? —Bruce Rodgers, *The Queens' Vernacular*, p. 36, 1972
- They have everything for young men to enjoy/You can hang out with all the boys. — Village People, *Y.M.C.A.*, 1978

3 racketeers *US*
- The boys financed this Poker game. —John Scarne, *Scarne's Guide to Modern Poker*, p. 273, 1979

4 used by professional wrestlers to refer to other professional wrestlers *US*
- They were nasty affairs and could go on for long periods of time with the wrestlers, or "boys" as is the common term used in the business, capitalizing on the situation. A "boy" could be any age, from sixteen to sixty, as long a she wore wrestling trunks. —Pat Barrett, *Everybody Down There Hates Me*, p. 72, 1990
- A lot of AWA people live there when they move to town. Many of the boys live there now. —Larry Nelson and James Jones, *Stranglehold*, p. 55, 1999
- The last was the one that angered the boys the most. Nikita Koloff questioned this commandment at a meeting a short time later. Bill addressed the boys and asked if there were any questions. —Mick Foley, *Mankind*, p. 221, 1999

5 sledge dogs *ANTARCTICA, 1966*
- —Bernadette Hince, *The Antarctic Dictionary*, p. 68, 2000

▸ **do the boys**
to engage in homosexual activity *US*
- —Gary K. Farlow, *Prison-ese*, p. 17, 2002

boys and girls *noun*
heroin and cocaine, mixed and injected together *US*
- —Peter Johnson, *Dictionary of Street Alcohol and Drug Terms*, p. 27, 1993

boy scout *noun*
1 a state trooper *US*
- —Kenn "Naz" Young, *Naz's Underground Dictionary*, p. 16, 1973
- —Wayne Floyd, *Jason's Authentic Dictionary of CB Slang*, p. 10, 1976

2 a person who is extremely, and usually distressingly, sincere *US*
- He's got a whole troop of Boy Scout lawyers ready to swear for him. —Stephen Cannell, *King Con*, p. 47, 1997

boyshape *noun*
a boyfriend *UK*
Teen slang
- — Susie Dent, *The Language Report*, p. 76, 2003

boysie *noun*
used as a term of address to a boy or man *AUSTRALIA, 1929*
- —Dave Courtney, *Dodgy Dave's Little Black Book*, p. 7, 2001

boys in blue *noun*
the police; sailors; US Federal troops *UK, 1851*
Rarely, if ever, occurs in the singular. Derives from the colour of the uniform; sometimes heard as 'men in blue' or 'gentlemen in blue'.
- One or two of the boys in blue will dull this lull with well-whipped heads needing white-togged meds. —Dan Burley, *Diggeth Thou?*, p. 18, 1959
- Some time around ten or ten thirty we'll get a visit from the boys in blue. —Donald Goines, *White Man's Justice, Black Man's Grief*, p. 81, 1973
- [T]he publican will be belling the boys in blue[.] — Martin King and Martin Knight, *The Naughty Nineties*, p. 35, 1999
- As one of the boys in blue, I would stumble on an unexpected perk[.] —Duncan MacLaughlin, *The Filth*, p. 69, 2002

boys of Baghdad *noun*
during the Gulf war, reporters for the Cable News Network *US*
- — *American Speech*, p. 385, Winter 1991: 'Among the new words'

boys on the hill *noun*
the members of New Zealand's parliament *NEW ZEALAND*
- —Louis S. Leland, *A Personal Kiwi-Yankee Dictionary*, p. 18, 1984

Boy's Town *noun*
a city neighbourhood dominated by homosexual men *US*
A play on Father Flanagan's Boys Home, a home for delinquent and homeless boys in Omaha, Nebraska.
- Officer Pig was, of course, corruption incarnate – an up-for-grabs cop who took bribes from the male prostitutes of Boy's Town, allowing them to ply their wicked craft while he and his sleazy cop buddies looked the other way. —James Ellroy, *Blood on the Moon*, p. 58, 1984
- —Anna Scotti and Paul Young, *Buzzwords*, p. 43, 1997

boys' toy; big boys' toy *noun*
any automotive, mechanical or electronic piece of technology designed to appeal to men, especially an unecessary one; a gadget *UK*
- Boys' toys spin out of control[.] — *The Guardian*, 14th September 2000

boytjie *noun*
▷ **see:** BOYKIE

boy toy *noun*
a young, attractive woman or man who is the object of sexual desire of their elders, homosexual or heterosexual *US, 1989*
- They're soon joined by a wealthy local widow (Tanya Berezin) and her new "boy toy" of a lover (Brian Tarantina), an aspiring tennis star. — *New York Times*, p. C15, 18th October 1982
- — *American Speech*, Winter 1990
- Boy toy – young (18–22 years old) club kid, often seen wearing go-go outfits. —Kevin Dilallo, *The Unofficial Gay Manual*, p. 237–238, 1994
- After two months he started complaining about being used as a boy toy – in bed he had no objection to being a sex object, but afterward he wanted me to respect him for his mind. —Anka Radakovich, *The Wild Girls Club*, p. 157, 1994
- Sounds like a storm best-frienship, especially if Hope knows you hate it when she plays boy-toy to all your crush objects but does it anyway. — *Seventenn*, p. 52, July 1994
- our glitzy diva French-kissing a boy toy in a tongue-wrestling match that would make Madonna salivate— *Miami New Times*, 8th April 2004

boy wonder *noun*
a man not held in high esteem *AUSTRALIA*
An ironic usage.
- 'I heard you bastards got lost last night,' he began. 'Yair,' said Lasher. 'Thanks to the Boy Wonder.' —Eric Lambert, *The Veterans*, p. 99, 1954
- And tell me, how long have you known the boy wonder? [referring to her despised husband] —Alexander Buzo, *Rooted*, p. 49, 1969

bozack *noun*
1 sex *US*
Usually heard as 'do the bozack'.
- —Terry Williams, *The Cocaine Kids*, p. 138, 1989

2 the penis; the entire male genitalia *US*
Sometimes shortened to 'zack'.
- And the bitches? They'll do anything for it. I got my bozack done every day last week. Several times a time. — *New Jack City*, 1990
- I put the starter cap on the bozack, can't get with no kid rap[.] —Kwest Tha Madd Lad *Lubrication*, 1996
- a knack for grabbin' the bozack— *The Source*, p. 181, March 2002

bozo *noun*
1 a buffoon *US, 1916*
In the US, the older sense of 'bozo' as 'a fellow' was supplanted by the figure Bozo the Clown, who first appeared on record in 1946 and then became a fixture on local television programmes throughout the US beginning in 1949.
- It's the horn-goggled bozos who sit in swivel chairs that make wars. [Quoting Dr Leo Eloesser] — *San Francisco Chronicle*, p. 21, 3rd December 1950
- C'mon now, Blondie, what you want to mess with these bozos for? —Ken Kesey, *One Flew Over the Cuckoo's Nest*, p. 231, 1962
- Eric Burdon is [...] infinitely entertaining for precisely the bozo he is. —Lester Bangs, *Psychotic Reactions and Carburetor Dung*, p. 99, 1972
- The unflattering moniker of Bozo the President bestowed on him by a New York, writer, has become so common that a standing White House joke has the Secret Service adopting it as Ford's code identification. — *San Francisco Examiner and Chronicle (from the Chicago Tribune)*, p. A2, 21st December 1975
- "These bozos mean business." "Bozos?" the chairman said tentatively, glancing around the table. "The bad guys, " Keyes explained. —Carl Hiaasen, *Tourist Season*, p. 194, 1986

- Hey, Murtaugh, tell these bozos to lay off. — *Lethal Weapon*, 1987
- And this bozo looks me up and down, giving me this oily smile, and tells me I got any complaints I should go talk to the owner. — Robert Campbell, *In a Pig's Eye*, p. 169, 1991
- I had bozos operating this. — Robert Stoller and I.S. Levine, *Coming Attraction*, p. 31, 1991
- The guy's a Bozo deluxe. — *Airheads*, 1994

2 heroin *UK, 1998*
- — Robert Ashton, *This Is Heroin*, p. 205, 2002
- — Mike Haskins, *Drugs*, p. 283, 2003

3 an ounce of heroin *US*
- — Jay Robert Nash, *Dictionary of Crime*, p. 43, 1992

bozotic *adjective*

in computing, ridiculous *US*
- — Eric S. Raymond, *The New Hacker's Dictionary*, p. 77, 1991

BP *noun*

1 in blackjack counting teams, the player who places the large bets based on cues from other members of the team who have been counting cards at a particular table *US*
An initialism for '*b*ig *p*layer'.
- — Michael Dalton, *Blackjack*, p. 31, 1991

2 in American casinos, a serious gambler *US*
The initials stand for '*b*ig *p*layer'.
- — Steve Kuriscak, *Casino Talk*, p. 6, 1985

3 a young prostitute *US*
An abbreviation of '*b*aby *p*ro'.
- So the next day she registered in school as the woman's niece and began living as a high class BP. — Anonymous, *Go Ask Alice*, p. 161, 1971

BPOM *noun*

in homosexual shorthand usage, a man with a large penis, a *b*ig *p*iece *o*f *m*eat *US*
- — *Maledicta*, p. 220, 1979: 'Kinks and queens: linguistic and cultural aspects of the terminology for gays'

BPS *noun*

a wooden stick used by police for probing a corpse *US*
New York police slang; an abbreviation of '*b*rain-*p*icking *s*tick'.
- — Samuel M. Katz, *Anytime Anywhere*, p. 386, 1997

BQ *noun*

a male homosexual who favours anal sex *US*
An abbreviation of **BROWNIE QUEEN**.
- — Roger Blake, *The American Dictionary of Sexual Terms*, p. 22, 1964

BR *noun*

1 a bankroll *US, 1915*
- After finding the fat BR, I removed a few pound-notes from the center and placed it back in the same way it was when I found it. — A.S. Jackson, *Gentleman Pimp*, p. 12, 973

2 money *US, 1915*
From the term 'bankroll'.
- I'm broke as Lazarus, with no B.R. for the free world when I hit it. — Iceberg Slim (Robert Beck), *Doom Fox*, p. 214, 1978

3 in carnival usage, any hyperbolic story *US*
An extension of the sense as 'bankroll', the roll of money used by the operator of a rigged game to distract and divert the attention of a player from how the game is rigged.
- — Gene Sorrows, *All About Carnivals*, p. 11, 1985

4 Banana Republic™, a chain of shops selling casual clothing *US*
- — Pamela Munro, *U.C.L.A. Slang*, p. 44, 1997

bra *noun*

used for addressing a friend *UK*
Phonetic abbreviation of **BROTHER** (a fellow).
- Obladi oblada life goes on bra / Lala how the life goes on[.] — Lennon/McCartney *Ob-La-Di, Ob-La-Da*, 1968
- "So what's happening, bra?" said Col once they were sat in a corner with a couple of pints of Guinness. — John Williams, *Cardiff Dead*, p. 28, 2000

brace *verb*

to apprehend someone; to arrest someone; to accost someone *US, 1889*
- Then I thought: brace him at his pad? — James Ellroy, *Brown's Requiem*, p. 209, 1981
- We're going to brace a suspected gun dealer. — James Ellroy, *Suicide Hill*, p. 701, 1986
- They haven't braced Girod's killer. — Seth Morgan, *Homeboy*, p. 239, 1990

brace and bit; brace *noun*

1 the equipment needed to prepare and inject a drug *NEW ZEALAND*
Rhyming slang, from **OUTFIT**.
- — Harry Orsman, *A Dictionary of Modern New Zealand Slang*, p. 19, 1999

2 the female breast *US, 1928*
Rhyming slang for **TIT**; usually in the plural. Sometimes shortened to 'brace'.

3 an act of defecation *UK*
Rhyming slang for **SHIT**. Sometimes shortened to 'brace'.
- I'm dying for a brace. — Bodmin Dark, *Dirty Cockney Rhyming Slang*, 2003

brace face *noun*

any person wearing an orthodontic brace *US*
- "Fewer people make fun of me; they want to see them," Shawn said. "And they don't call me as many names as they used to, like 'brace face' and 'metal mouth.'" — *St. Petersburg (Florida) Times*, p. 2D, 9th September 1991
- — Chris Lewis, *The Dictionary of Playground Slang*, p. 41, 2003
- For boomers, taunts like "brace-face," tin grin" and "metal mouth" have made way for more sophisticated teasing. — *Washington Post*, p. F1, 13th January 2004

bracelet play *noun*

in poker, an exceptionally crafty play *US*
An allusion to the 'bracelet prize' in the World Series of Poker.
- — John Vorhaus, *The Big Book of Poker Slang*, p. 8, 1996

bracelets *noun*

handcuffs *UK, 1661*
- I was cold, stiff, sore all over, and if I had any hands left behind me they could have been stone for all they felt the bite of the bracelets. — Thurston Scott, *Cure it with Honey*, p. 175, 1951
- I can also see us in bracelets pictured on page three of the Daily News the next day too. — Emmett Grogan, *Final Score*, p. 70, 1976
- Take off the bracelets or no deal. — *48 Hours*, 1982
- — Angela Devlin, *Prison Patter*, p. 30, 1996
- I clapped the bracelets on her and she sat down. — Janet Evanovich, *Seven Up*, p. 94, 2001

bracer *noun*

any strong alcoholic drink *US, 1830*
- These first are merely "bracers," to protect them from the morning chill. — Robert deCoy, *The Nigger Bible*, p. 248, 1967

brace-up *noun*

a prison- or police-cell *UK*
- Jimmy was never happy in a brace-up. — Ted Lewis, *Jack Carter's Law*, p. 18, 1974

brace work *noun*

poorly executed markings on the back of cards by card cheats *US, 1961*
- — Thomas L. Clark, *The Dictionary of Gambling and Gaming*, p. 26, 1987

bra chute *noun*

a type of parachute malfunction *US, 1982*
- The bra chute or semi-inverted chute resulted when the rigging lines were routed incorrectly causing the lines to split the chute canopy into two sections. — Gregory Clark, *Words of the Vietnam War*, p. 498, 1990

bracket *noun*

an unspecified part of the body *UK*
Usually as part of a threat; 'a punch up the bracket'; probably coined by scriptwriters Ray Galton and Alan Simpson.
- I shall feel the benefit of his weighted sock up me bracket. Very nasty. — Galton and Simpson, *'The New Shoes', Hancock's Half Hour*, mid-1950s

Bradman pills *noun*

in horse racing, diuretic pills used by jockeys to lose weight *AUSTRALIA*
An allusion to cricket legend Donald Bradman; if you take enough diuretics, you will make a hundred runs before lunch.
- — Ned Wallish, *The Truth Dictionary of Racing Slang*, p. 9, 1989

Brad Pitt; brad *noun*

an act of defecation *UK*
Rhyming slang for **SHIT** formed on the name of American film actor Brad Pitt (b.1963).
- — Ray Puxley, *Fresh Rabbit*, 1998

brads *noun*
money *UK, 1812*
• —Paul Baker, *Polari*, p. 166, 2002

Brady *noun*
a theatre seat reserved for a friend of the theatre management *US*
An allusion to William Brady (1863–1950), American impressario.
• —Don Wilmeth, *The Language of American Popular Entertainment*, p. 33, 1981

braggadocious; bragadocious *adjective*
boastful *US, 1956*
• The black who caused more nightmares for white America than any other was bullet-headed, braggadocious heavyweight boxing champion Jack Johnson. —Mary Frances Berry and John W. Blassingame, *Long Memory*, p. 131, 1982
• —John A. Holm, *Dictionary of Bahamian English*, p. 27, 1982
• I don't mean to sound braggadocious, but it does not strap me or hurt me to do it. —*Washington Post*, p. A1, 26th April 1983
• —Frederic G. Cassidy, *Dictionary of American Regional English, Volume 1*, p. 361, 1985
• —Peter L. Patrick, *Some Recent Jamaican Creole Words*, 2003
• We're full of it. We're vain, we're braggadocious. At Passover, we try to come down to a normal level[.] —*Ledger (Lakeland, Florida)*, p. D1, 3rd April 2004

brag-rag *noun*
a military decoration in the form of a ribbon *US*
• —Harold Wentworth and Stuart Berg Flexner, *Dictionary of American Slang*, p. 60, 1960

brah *noun*
used as a term of address, young surfing male to young surfing male *US*
A surfer's 'brother'.
• —Douglas Simonson, *Pidgin to da Max*, 1981
• Chill, brah. —*Point Break*, 1991

brahma; Brahma *noun*
a pleasing thing *UK*
From Hindu mythology *Brahmâ*, the creator.
• Noel Coward was a charmer / As a writer he was a Brahma[.] —Ian Dury, *There Aint Half Been Some Clever Bastards*, 1977

Brahms and Liszt; Brahms *adjective*
drunk *UK, 1978*
Rhyming slang for **PISSED** (drunk).
• You must've been Brahms that night. —Anthony Masters, *Minder*, p. 122, 1984

braid *noun*
a prison warden or other official *US*
• —Hyman E. Goldin et al., *Dictionary of American Underworld Lingo*, p. 33, 1950

brain *noun*
1 oral sex performed on a male *US, 1998*
An extension of **HEAD**.
• Kids say "get brain" does not mean smarts. It's slang for oral sex. —*Daily News (New York)*, 5th November 2004
2 a smart person *UK, 1914*
• The athletes and the rich boys and the brains were the big wheels at Summer High School. —Dick Gregory, *Nigger*, p. 47, 1964
3 a dumb person *US*
• —Connie Eble (Editor), *UNC-CH Campus Slang*, p. 2, March 1981
4 the penis *US*
Derisory.
• —Erica Orloff and JoAnn Baker, *Dirty Little Secrets*, p. 69, 2001

▸ **get something or someone on the brain**
to become obsessed by something or someone *UK, 1989*
• man with money on the brain —*The Guardian*, 20th May 2003

▸ **out of your brain**
drunk or drug-intoxicated *UK*
• Where have I been? / Out of my brain on the five fifteen. —The Who *5.15*, 1973
• —Michael Munro, *The Original Patter*, 1985

brain *verb*
to hit someone on the head *US, 1938*
• Do you know when they're fulfilled? When you tell them not to go any further or you'll brain them. —Mort Sahl, *Heartland*, p. 60, 1976
• He wanted to brain Lefty and drag Millie Filbert into the bushes. —C.D. Payne, *Youth in Revolt*, p. 131, 1993
• Schmalowtiz picked a kid up in a gay bar, took him home, and the kid brained him. —Richard Condon, *Prizzi's Money*, p. 146, 1994

brain bag *noun*
in trucking, anything used by a trucker to store maps, permits and other paperwork *US*
• —Montie Tak, *Truck Talk*, p. 17, 1971

brain bender *noun*
a strenuous, rowdy party *US*
• At least twice a year outlaws from all parts of the state gather somewhere in California for a king-size brain-bender. —Hunter S. Thompson, *Hell's Angels*, p. 116, 1966

brain bleach *noun*
LSD *UK*
A variation on the conventional 'brainwash': advertising for a proprietory brand of bleach claims to 'clean round the bend' and 'round the bend' means 'madness'.

brain-boshing *adjective*
intoxicating *UK*
Extending from **BOSH** (to take pills).
• [H]igh velocity, brain-boshing techno [music][.] —*Ministry*, May 2002

brain box *noun*
1 the head; the mind *UK, 1823*
• [T]he A's portable brain-box of manager Ken Macha and general manager Bill Meane decided it would behoove them to push Ted Lilly back three days to help align the rotation for the postseason. —*San Francisco Chronicle*, p. B1, 21st September 2003
2 a person of above average intelligence *UK*
• Carol Vorderman, the woman doomed to be billed by the tabloids as "TV brainbox" —Stuart Jeffries, *Mrs Slocombe's Pussy*, p. 92, 2000

brain boy *noun*
in oil drilling, an engineer *US*
• —Jerry Robertson, *Oil Slanguage*, p. 31, 1954

brain bucket *noun*
a safety helmet *US, 1955*
Coined in the US Air Force, adapted to drag racing and then to a variety of sports.
• For a fellow down to his last fuel, it's "bingo." If he "clanks," he's nervous and if he "augers in" he crashed. Preferably he ought to have his crash helment, or "brain bucket" on. —*San Francisco Examiner*, p. 10 (II), 2nd June 1957
• —*Current Slang*, p. 1, Winter 1966
• —*Complete CB Slang Dictionary*, 1976
• —Peter Chippindale, *The British CB Book*, p. 152, 1981
• Brainbucket, skid lid, melon gear, crash hat. It doesn't matter what you call it, just as long as you have one – a helmet for hitting the slopes, trails, skating rinks and half-pipes. —*Times Union (Albany, New York)*, p. D1, 23rd December 2003

brain burner *noun*
an intravenous injection of amphetamine or methamphetamine *US*
• —Jay Robert Nash, *Dictionary of Crime*, p. 44, 1992

brain candy *noun*
an insignificant entertainment or diversion as opposed to something that requires thought *US*
• I was writing in a medium – the Sunday supplement – that tended to be ignored, treated like brain candy. [Quoting Tom Wolfe] —*New York Times*, p. 6–46, 20th December 1981
• One of [Po] Bronson's more provocative insights is that "the conclusion that brain candy is not enough is probably the most threatening to our generation's belief system". —*The Guardian*, 8th March 2003

brain cramp *noun*
a mental error *US*
• Utah coach Jerry Pimm said his team seemed victimized by "brain cramps." —*United Press International*, 7th February 1982
• —Paul Dickson, *The New Dickson Baseball Dictionary*, p. 82, 1999

brain damage *noun*
heroin *UK, 1998*
• —Robert Ashton, *This Is Heroin*, p. 205, 2002

brain-damaged *adjective*
in computing, clearly wrong *US, 1983*
• —*CoEvolution Quarterly*, p. 27, Spring 1981
• Calling someting brain-damaged is really bad; it also implies it is unsuable, and that its failure to work is due to poor design rather than some accident. —Eric S. Raymond, *The New Hacker's Dictionary*, p. 77, 1991

brain derby *noun*
a test or examination *US*
- — *San Francisco Examiner*, p. 21, 12th December 1961

brain donor *noun*
an idiot *UK*
The image of an empty head.
- — Peter Chippindale, *The British CB Book*, p. 152, 1981

brain drain *noun*
1 the large-scale migration of talented and intelligent people from and/or to somewhere *UK*
According to William Safire, probably coined in 1963 to describe the exodus of British scientists to the US.
- Speaking in the House of Lords debate on what has come to be called Britain's "brain drain," Hailsham charge the U.S. business, universities and government have embarked on a systematic drive "often initiated by talent scouts specially sent over here." — *San Francisco Examiner*, p. 19, 28th February 1963
- — *American Speech*, May 1965
- A "brain-drain" robbing Japan of some of its most promising scientists and teachers is beginning to alarm responsible officials here. — *San Francisco Chronicle*, p. 16, 5th August 1966
- 'The bloody brain-drain to London is over,' Julia exclaims. — Kathy Lette, *Girls' Night Out*, p. 201, 1987
- The Fraser Institute is holding a conference Friday, November 13 to discuss the "brain drain" and its economic implications for Canada. — *Canadian Corporate Newsire*, 6th November 1998

2 forensic scientists; a forensic science department *UK*
Police term, used ironically.
- — John Wainwright, *Dig His Grave and Let Him Lie*, 1971

brain fade *noun*
a momentary mental lapse *US*
- — Don Alexander, *The Racer's Dictionary*, p. 11, 1980

brain fart; mind fart *noun*
a temporary mental lapse *US, 1983*
Probably a jocular derivation from **BRAINSTORM**.
- — Rick Jolly, *Jackspeak*, p. 40, 1989
- — Connie Eble (Editor), *UNC-CH Campus Slang*, p. 2, Spring 1992
- [T]hey painted the den "grape" the first time, an embarrassing goof. "It was some kind of brain fart," said the always-blunt Peterson. — *Atlanta Journal and Constitution*, p. G5, 26th August 1994
- — Peter Furze, *Tailwinds*, p. 37, 1998
- Did retired General Anthony Zinni really call George W. Bush's war in Iraq a "brain fart"? That seems to be the case. — *The Nation*, 26th September 2003

brain freeze *noun*
a searing headache experienced when eating frozen food or drinks *US*
- Though onimous-sounding, brain freeze is nothing more than the fleeting headache that befalls most of us after consuming too much ice cream too quickly. — *Columbus (Ohio) Dispatch*, p. 1C, 3rd May 1993
- Why do you get brainfreeze if you eat ice cream too fast? — *Chicago Daily Herald*, 9th July 1998
- The culprit, in most cases, isn't an ice pick, but rather an icy drink or ice cream that spawns the cold frontal lobotomy known as "brainfreeze." — *The Orlando Sentinel*, p. E1, 26th June 2001

brainfucker *noun*
an idea that is difficult to comprehend *UK*
- And the Gillian thing wasn't the only heads-up [clever] brainfucker that Gretton came up with. — Tony Wilson, *24 Hour Party People*, p. 108, 2002

brainiac *noun*
a very intelligent person *US, 1986*
- — Ellen C. Bellone (Editor), *Dictionary of Slang*, p. 4, 1989
- — Jack Chambers (Editor), *Slang Bag 93 (University of Toronto)*, p. 2, Winter 1993
- Hey, brainiac. — *Clueless*, 1995

brainless *adjective*
1 very drunk *UK: SCOTLAND*
- — Michael Munro, *The Original Patter*, 1985

2 good, excellent *UK*
- — Paul Baker, *Polari*, p. 166, 2002

brain pill *noun*
an amphetamine tablet *UK*
- — Mike Haskins, *Drugs*, p. 279, 2003

brain plate *noun*
on the railways, a conductor's cap badge *US*
- — J. Herbert Lund, *Herb's Hot Box of Railraod Slang*, p. 28, 1975

brains *noun*
1 oral sex *US*
In the progression of **HEAD** to 'skull' to 'brains'.
- — Connie Eble (Editor), *UNC-CH Campus Slang*, p. 2, Spring 2000

2 a railway conductor *US*
Often after 'the'.
- — Norman Carlisle, *The Modern Wonder Book of Trains and Railroading*, p. 259, 1946

brain screw *noun*
a prison psychological counsellor *US*
- Cheer up, brain screw. — Thurston Scott, *Cure it with Honey*, p. 20, 1951

brainstorm *noun*
a sudden, good idea *US, 1925*
- — Lou Shelly, *Hepcats Jive Talk Dictionary*, p. 8, 1945

brain surgeon *noun*
a poker player who over-analyses every situation *US*
- — David M. Hayano, *Poker Faces*, p. 185, 1982

brain surgery *noun*
any difficult, demanding work *US*
Used in contrast to the job at hand.
- "I think this so-called intelligence factor is being a bit overrated," said Healy. "Let's face it, this isn't brain surgery." — *Washington Post*, p. E1, 27th July 1980
- — Anna Scotti and Paul Young, *Buzzwords*, p. 54, 1997
- As a coach, you have one basic tool and that is playing time. This isn't brain surgery. — *Milwaukee Journal Sentinel*, p. 7C, 21st March 2004

brain tickler *noun*
a tablet or capsule of amphetamine *UK, 1998*
- — Mike Haskins, *Drugs*, p. 279, 2003

brain train *noun*
a school bus *US*
- — "Slingo", *The Official CB Slang Dictionary Handbook*, p. 10, 1976

brain trust *noun*
a group of expert advisors *US, 1910*
Although found at least as early as 1910, not popularised until 1933 in association with US President Franklin Roosevelt's advisors.
- Oakland's new "brain trust" includes Manager Chuck Dressen, left, and Long George Kelly, former major league baseball luminaries. — *San Francisco News*, 19th January 1949
- But the strategy of the Democratic brain-trust miscarried. — Jack Lait and Lee Mortimer, *Washington Confidential*, p. 200, 1951
- It is not altogether strange that President Kenney's brain trust should find itself under heavy fire from the Republican side of the fence. — *San Francisco Chronicle*, p. 1, 1st July 1962
- Well, he ain't popl'lar neither. He ain't no brain trust. He ain't even good-lookin'. — C.D. Payne, *Youth in Revolt*, p. 409, 1993

brainwash *verb*
to convince someone systematically and in a manipulative manner that something they do not believe is true *US, 1951*
Although the term was coined to describe the actions of authoritarian, Soviet-bloc regimes, probably the most famous use of 'brainwash' in the US was by George Romney, candidate for the Republican presidential nomination in 1968, who claimed that he had been brainwashed to support the US war against Vietnam.
- — *American Speech*, February 1952

brainy *adjective*
intelligent, clever *UK, 1845*
- [A] wacky-yet-sexy waitress with long hair who acquires an uptight brainy boyfriend after his marriage fails[.] — *The Guardian*, 27th February 2004

brake fluid *noun*
any medication used to sedate an unruly prisoner *US*
- — Lee McNelis, *30 + And a Wake-Up*, p. 6, 1991

brake pads *noun*
the condition that exists when a tight-fitting pair of trousers, shorts, bathing suit or other garment forms a wedge between a woman's labia, accentuating their shape *US*
A visual image.

braker *noun*

a railway brakeman *US*

- —Ramon Adams, *The Language of the Railroader*, p. 21, 1977

brakie *noun*

a brakeman on a freight train *US, 1887*

- [I]s brakie job still open by then?—Jack Kerouac, *Letter to Neal Cassady*, p. 326, 1 October 1951
- [H]is world became a world of brakies, reefers, redballs, railroad dicks in hard-up midwest towns[.]—John Clellon Holmes, *The Horn*, p. 159, 1958
- —Ramon Adams, *The Language of the Railroader*, p. 21, 1977

bram *noun*

a small party with dancing *BARBADOS*

- —Frank A. Collymore, *Barbadian Dialect*, p. 21, 1965

Brambladesh; Bramistan *nickname*

the Brampton region of Toronto *CANADA*

- The term "Brambladesh" comes from the predominant population of Indian and Bengladesh immigrants in the Brampton area.—Chris Coyle, 10th June 2002

brammer *adjective*

excellent, outstandingly good *UK*

Derives from **BRAHMA** (something good).

- —Nigel Foster, *The Making of a Royal Marine Commando*, 1987

branch *noun*

a match *US*

- —Kenn "Naz" Young, *Naz's Underground Dictionary*, p. 16, 1973

Brancher *nickname*

a member of the Special Branch of the Irish police force *IRELAND*

- I'm Special Branch. Do you know what that means?...It means you get called a Brancher bastard by little fuckers...when you arrest them for selling Easter lilies without a permit.—Eamonn Sweeney, *Waiting for the Healer*, p. 242, 1997

branch out *verb*

to become fat *AUSTRALIA*

- —Ruth Park, *A Power of Roses*, 1953

brand new *adjective*

good, excellent *UK*

From the condition of new goods.

- DODIE. Have you ever been shackled, Rab? NESBITT: No. DODIE: I have. It's pure brand new so it is.—Ian Pattison, *Rab C. Nesbitt*, 1988

Brandon Block *noun*

the penis; a fool *UK*

Rhyming slang for **COCK**; formed from the name of a London-born dance music DJ.

- Don't be a Brandon Block – let's go while you can still walk straight.—Bodmin Dark, *Dirty Cockney Rhyming Slang*, 2003

brand X *noun*

1 marijuana *US*

- —Edith A. Folb, *runnin' down some lines*, p. 230, 1980

2 a marijuana cigarette *US*

- —Jay Robert Nash, *Dictionary of Crime*, p. 43, 1992

3 in trucking, a small and unknown trucking company *US*

- —Wayne Floyd, *Jason's Authentic Dictionary of CB Slang*, p. 10, 1976

brandy *noun*

lubricant applied to the anus in preparation for anal sex *UK*

- —Paul Baker, *Polari*, p. 186, 2002

brandy and rum; brandy *noun*

the buttocks, the posterior *UK*

Rhyming slang for **BUM**.

- B: You don't fancy him do you? A: Well, I'm not sure. Bona brandy on it. Dolly [nice/attractive] drag [clothes] too.—Emma Hindley, *Storm in a Teacup*, 1993
- —Paul Baker, *Polari*, p. 166, 2002

brandy latch *noun*

a toilet *UK*

A combination of **BRANDY (AND RUM)** (the posterior) and 'latch' (a lock).

- —Paul Baker, *Polari*, p. 166, 2002

brandy snap *noun*

a slap *UK*

Rhyming slang.

- Shut up before I give you a brandy snap.—Bodmin Dark, *Dirty Cockney Rhyming Slang*, 2003

brannigan *noun*

a brawl, literal or figurative *US, 1940*

- But no matter how great the whoop-de-do, nothing in Chicago is likely to approach the heroic brannigan of 1920, when an earlier and perhaps more stalwart Democratic generation convened for the first and only time in San Francisco.—*San Francisco Chronicle*, p. 19, 20th July 1952
- Another brannigan is expected to break out for control of the Democratic party on the San Francisco county level.—*San Francisco News*, p. 3, 9th June 1956
- Next came the brannigan.—*San Francisco Examiner*, p. 7, 11th August 1960

branzy *noun*

▷ **see: BRONZIE**

brasco *noun*

a toilet *AUSTRALIA, 1955*

Origin unknown. Baker, 1966, gives 'brasker'. The suggestion that it is from Brass Co., a company that made brass toilet cisterns, lacks evidence, as does the notion that it is from a clipping of Nebraska.

- [S]he spends rather a lot of time in the ladies' brasco moaning loudly and vigorously manipulating herself to orgasm.—*Sydney Morning Herald*, 4th March 2002

brass *noun*

1 in the military, high-ranking officers as a collective entity *US, 1864*

- As perspiring VIPs, government guides, Navy brass and reporters stood by, the President came out, shook hands with Guzick, his wife and three children, then patted his pockets for the check.—*Washington Post*, p. B2, 19th May 1979
- [I]t is by considerations largely beyond the control of the air crews or even the Air Force Brass.—*Washington Post*, p. E7, 9th August 1981
- Secretary of Defense Donald Rumsfeld won the first argument, about the size of the invasion force; it was far smaller than Army brass wanted.—*Chicago Tribune*, p. C24, 8th April 2004

2 money, cash *UK, 1598*

- I'm trying to get some brass together so as you and me can keep seeing each other.—*The Full Monty*, 1997

3 in carnival usage, fake jewellery *US*

- —Don Wilmeth, *The Language of American Popular Entertainment*, p. 33, 1981

4 brass knuckles *US*

- —Edith A. Folb, *runnin' down some lines*, p. 231, 1980

▷ **see: BRASS NAIL, TOP BRASS**

brass *verb*

to rob a person of their money by deception; to con someone *AUSTRALIA, 1939*

- John explained that he had got a wine flagon full in return for a favour he did for those idyllic pair of swingers Mindless and Mainline who had it seemed been brassed for a few grains of coke by Speedy Bill[.]—Kevin Mackey, *The Cure*, p. 103, 1970

▸ **brass it out**

to brazen it out *UK*

From the conventional use of 'brass' (effrontery or impudence).

- —*Z Cars*, 10th February 1969

brass *adjective*

fashionable, smart *UK*

- Some of them were speaking French because it was the brass thing to do.—James Barlow, *The Burden of Proof*, 1968

brass band *noun*

1 the hand *UK, 1952*

Rhyming slang.

2 a back-up military unit sent to help a small, outnumbered unit *US*

- —Linda Reinberg, *In the Field*, p. 27, 1991

brass buttons *noun*

a police officer; the police in general *US*

- —John Scarne, *Scarne on Dice*, p. 462, 1974

brass collar *noun*

railway management *US*

- —Ramon Adams, *The Language of the Railroader*, p. 21, 1977

brassed off; brassed *adjective*

disgruntled *UK, 1942*

Originally military.

brasser; brazzer *noun*

a female of dubious sexual morals *IRELAND*

- Don't misunderstand me, compadre, he said. Not just women. All men are brassers as well. —Roddy Doyle, *The Van*, 1991
- Absolute brazzers. Mid-twenties, bet into their Ilac Centre clothes – thought they were only gorgeous. —Donal Ruane, *Tales in a rear view mirror*, p. 17, 2003

brass fart *noun*

a thing of negligible value *UK*

Probably a convenient shortening of **BRASS FARTHING**.

- Starling: What have you taken? Jig: Not a brass fart. We'll be here from arsehole to breakfast-time at this rate. —Rod Wooden, *Smoke and Moby Dick*, 1996

brass farthing *noun*

a trivial sum of money, or less *UK, 1642*

- Wales was not getting a "brass farthing" from the treasury[.]— *The Guardian*, 2nd February 2000

brass-happy *adjective*

extremely anxious to be promoted within the officer corps *US*

- —*American Speech*, p. 238, October 1946: 'World War II slang of maladjustment'

brass house *noun*

a brothel, a whorehouse *UK*

Where a **BRASS** (**NAIL**) (a prostitute) works.

- Always getting off without paying at some brasshouse[.] —Kevin Sampson, *Outlaws*, p. 165–166, 2001

brassic; brassick *adjective*

▷ **see:** BORACIC LINT

brassies *noun*

brass knuckles *US*

- —Vincent J. Monteleone, *Criminal Slang*, p. 33, 1949

brass man *noun*

a confidence trickster *AUSTRALIA, 1953*

From earlier 'brass' (a horse-racing confidence trick).

brass monkey *noun*

used in a number of figures of speech, especially as a basis for comparison *US, 1857*

- It would take what Kipling called the nerve of a brass monkey to talk about democracy versus totalitarianism or about fighting the anti-Christ. —Geroge N. Crocker, *Roosevelt's Road to Russia*, p. 85, 1959
- "It's cold enough to breeze the balls off a brass monkey" (which has nothing to do with a monkey or its private parts, but rather the brass rings that held cannonballs on ships. — *St. Petersburg (Florida) Times*, p. 1, 19th January 2003
- Clem Dubose can talk the ears off a brass monkey. — *Orlando (Florida) Sentinel Tribune*, p. K1, 29th February 2004

brass-monkey *adjective*

(of weather) bitterly cold *UK, 1857*

May be of nautical origin but the popular etymology involving powder monkeys and cannon balls remains unproven. Usually as 'brass-monkey weather'; from the phrase 'cold enough to freeze the balls off a brass monkey'.

- It was a beautiful night – but brass-monkey time out there. —Duncan MacLaughlin, *The Filth*, p. 234, 2002

brass nail; brass *noun*

a prostitute *UK, 1933*

Rhyming slang for **TAIL** (a woman sexually objectified), also punning on something you buy 'to bang'.

- [H]is old woman who a brass on the game down the Baze[.] —Frank Norman, *Bang To Rights*, p. 8, 1958
- You're nothing but a blasted brass. I wouldn't touch you with a bloody bargepole, let alone pay for you. —Anonymous *Streetwalker*, p. 43, 1959
- He would definitely get value for money. The brasses were very skillful, he shortly realised that. —G.F. Newman, *Three Professional Ladies*, p. 282, 1979
- "Take him to a hotel – George's gaff – he'll let anybody in; all the brasses use it." ""Don't you call me a bloody brass," said Rita indignantly. —Anthony Masters, *Minder*, p. 161, 1984
- Richard didn't want the man on the corner to go up and fuck one of the brasses. —Will Self, *The Sweet Smell of Psychosis*, p. 2, 1996
- I'd just bunk off and walk the length of Mill Street and up to round by the Proddie [Protestant] cathedral just to look at the brasses. —Kevin Sampson, *Outlaws*, p. 102, 2001

brass razoo *noun*

a small amount of money *AUSTRALIA, 1941*

- Could it be that you failed to copyright the name Carringbush and never got a brass razoo for all these places called after it? —Frank Hardy, *Hardy's People*, p. 79, 1986
- —David McGill, *David McGill's Complete Kiwi Slang Dictionary*, p. 20–21, 1998

brass ring *noun*

an elusive but valuable prize *US, early 1950s*

- There are plenty of women who see me as the brass ring. — *Sleepless in Seattle*, 1993

brass tacks *noun*

the basic facts; the basic reality *US, 1895*

Rhyming slang for 'facts', but not accepted as such by authorities who combine 'brass tacks' with its variation 'brass nails'.

- Let's get down to brass tacks here. We've got a sweetheart of a deal to do. —Vincent Patrick, *Family Business*, p. 53, 1985

brass up *verb*

1 to pay money *UK, 1898*

- Trevor said that he was going to ask him to offer his word that he'd brass up. —Greg Williams, *Diamond Geezers*, p. 12, 1997

2 to rebuke someone *BARBADOS*

- —Frank A. Collymore, *Barbadian Dialect*, p. 21, 1965

brassy *adjective*

(of a woman) ostentatious, cheap but flashy; prostitute-like *UK, 1937*

A variation of an earlier, obsolete sense (impudent and shameless); probably from **BRASS** (**NAIL**) (a prostitute), but note the bright appearance of polished brass, a relatively cheap metal.

- It's funny how when you get two skirts going together one of them is always sorta shy and twisted like and the other is always dead brassy. —John Peter Jones, *Feather Pluckers*, p. 40, 1964
- A girl was walking past us; eighteen-going-on-fifty, with already a brassy look to her, badly-dyed blonde hair, a tight skirt, a wiggle-wiggle walk. —John Milne, *Alive and Kicking*, p. 44, 1998

brat *noun*

1 a child, especially a troublesome junior; a baby *UK, 1505*

Possibly from Scottish dialect *bratchart*.

- We are thinking of calling the brat James[.] —Ann Barr and Peter York, *The Official Sloane Ranger Handbook*, p. 78, 1982
- And I was grateful for all the kudos he give us and the times when he directly bailed us out when I was half being a brat and things was getting thingy on us. —Kevin Sampson, *Outlaws*, p. 105, 2001

2 a young and/or weak man used as a passive homosexual partner, especially in prison *US*

- Punks and brats are those prisoners who take the passive role in sodomy; there is no chronological age limit. — *New York Mattachine Newsletter*, p. 6, June 1961
- —Joseph E. Ragen and Charles Finston, *Inside the World's Toughest Prison*, p. 792, 1962

brat pack *nickname*

a group of young film actors who played roles in John Hughes films of the 1980s *US*

Frequently mentioned as members of the group included Anthony Michale Hall, Emilio Estevez, Charlie Sheen, Judd Nelson, Molly Ringold, Rob Lowe and Ally Sheedy. A play on the Sinatra-centric Rat Pack of the 1950s and 60s.

- No, he insists, the Brat Pack (the name given Estevez and some of his young actor pals) is not a tightly knit group of friends[.]— *Chicago Tribune*, p. 7C, 31st October 1985
- "Went to the movies?" "Any good?" "Tedious. Brat-pack stuff." —Joseph Wambaugh, *The Golden Orange*, p. 54, 1990
- — Editors of Ben is Dead, *Retrohell*, p. 24, 1997

bravo *noun*

a soldier in the US infantry *US, 1980*

Vietnam war coinage and usage.

- —Linda Reinberg, *In the Field*, p. 27, 1991

bravo delta *noun*

a nonfunctioning piece of hardware *US*

A phonetic-alphabet euphemism for '*b*roke *d*ick'.

- —Hans Halberstadt, *Airborne*, p. 130, 1988

brawl *noun*

a rowdy party *US, 1927*

- —Collin Baker et al., *College Undergraduate Slang Study Conducted at Brown University*, p. 88, 1968
- —Kenn "Naz" Young, *Naz's Underground Dictionary*, p. 17, 1973

brazil *verb*

to decline to pay interest on an existing loan *CANADA*

- I listened to your financial analysts discuss the announcement that Brazil would no longer pay out the interest charges on that country's loans. The new term "braziling" was mentioned. That is to say, we take out a loan to pay off interest charges—Debbie Koppel, *in The Latest Morningside Papers*, p. 34, 1989

Brazilian landing strip; Brazilian *noun*

the trimming of a woman's pubic hair such that only a narrow strip remains; the result thereof *US*

- Maybe one percent of my clients have stuck to the old conservative bikini line wax – the rest have converted to Brazlians.—*Nerve*, p. 20, December 2000 -January 2001
- Brazilian landing strip or 70s-style unclipped?—*Sky Magazine*, p. 83, July 2001
- "I got mugged. She took everything I've got." Carrie Bradshaw in Sex and the City after a Brazilian bikini wax.—*Real Simple*, p. 65, May 2001
- The Brazilian[:] Leaves a vertical stripe in front, two or three fingers in width.—*Loaded*, p. 5, June 2002

Brazil water *noun*

coffee *US, 1949*

- —Harold Wentworth and Stuart Berg Flexner, *Dictionary of American Slang*, p. 61, 1960

brazzer *noun*

▷ see: BRASSER

BRB

used in computer message shorthand to mean '*b*e *r*ight *b*ack' *US*

- —Eric S. Raymond, *The New Hacker's Dictionary*, p. 342, 1991

brea *noun*

heroin *UK*

- —Mike Haskins, *Drugs*, p. 283, 2003

breach *noun*

▸ in the breach

in poker, first to act in a given situation *US*

- —George Percy, *The Language of Poker*, p. 47, 1988

bread *noun*

1 money *US, 1935*

The term was used at least as early as the 1930s, but it did not gain wide acceptance until the 1960s.

- Without bread a stud can't even rule an anthill.—William "Lord" Buckley, *Marc Anthony's Funeral Oration*, 1955
- We spent two hours in Testament waiting for Hyman Solomon to show up; he was hustling forhis bread somewhere in town, but we couldn't see him.—Jack Kerouac, *On the Road*, p. 137, 1957
- I'm gettin' some bread tomorrow, honest!—Alexander Trocchi, *Cain's Book*, p. 172, 1960
- "There's a lot of bread to be made gigging right around here in Roxbury," Shorty explained to me.—Malcolm X and Alex Haley, *The Autobiography of Malcolm X*, p. 45, 1964
- I knew the cab driver had beat me for my bread but there was no use crying, it was gone.—Babs Gonzales, *I Paid My Dues*, p. 24, 1967
- Whenever time you is down and out – busted – haven't got any bread – you call yourself an Israelite.—Desmond Dekker, 1969
- Black Panther Platform and Program No. 10: We want land, bread, housing, education, clothing, justice and peace.—*The Black Panther*, p. 18, 25 January 1969
- No artists ever did it for the bread. If money motivates you, you're not an artist.—Jerry Rubin, *Do It!*, p. 121, 1970
- "Bread? Osca, you want bread?" Maria, the Jewish switchhitter screamed in Billie Holiday tones.—Oscar Zeta Acosta, *The Autobiography of a Brown Buffalo*, p. 44, 1972
- They are moochers [beggars]. "Hey, man, got any bread?"—Rhiannon Paine, *Too Late for the Festival*, p. 207, 1999

2 ship's biscuits *TRISTAN DA CUNHA, 1910*

- —Bernadette Hince, *The Antarctic Dictionary*, p. 68, 2000

bread and bread *noun*

a homosexual couple; more generally, any dull combination of two similar things *UK, 1984*

bread and butter *noun*

1 a livelihood, the means of living; a basic, motivating interest *UK, 1837*

- This is my bread and butter. This is where I come in.—*The Guardian*, 12th March 2003

2 used by bookmakers to describe bets by inexperienced, unskilled bettors *AUSTRALIA*

- —Ned Wallish, *The Truth Dictionary of Racing Slang*, p. 10, 1989

3 a crazy person *UK*

Rhyming slang for **NUTTER**.

- —Ray Puxley, *Cockney Rabbit*, p. 22, 1992
- I bet he's a total bread and butter in the John-Wayne-style straightener.—J.J. Connolly, *Layer Cake*, p. 101, 2000

bread and butter!

used as a charm when two people who are walking side-by-side are momentarily separated by a person or object *US, 1939*

- —Frederic G. Cassidy, *Dictionary of American Regional English, Volume 1*, p. 368, 1985

bread and cheese *verb*

to sneeze *UK, 1938*

Rhyming slang; also used as a noun.

- Me cherry [dog] bread and cheesed.—Viv Stanshall, *Ginger Geezer*, 1981

bread and jam *noun*

a tram *AUSTRALIA, 1902*

bread and lard *adjective*

hard *UK*

- Gor blimey! ain't that bread an' lard, eh?—Julian Franklyn, *A Dictionary of Rhyming Slang*, 1961

bread and point *noun*

a meagre meal, mainly bread *CANADA*

Another surviving, related expression is 'bread and pullet' or 'pull-it'.

- During the lean years of the depression there was usually some homemade bread at mealtime, but often little or no butter. You were told just to point the knife at the butter dish. To this day some prairie parents will refer to dry bread as bread-n-point.—Chris Thain, *Cold as a Bay Street Banker's Heart*, p. 20, 1987

breadbasket *noun*

the stomach *UK, 1785*

- I had to stand on top of the pile trying to catch four or five bricks at a time when the man below heaved them at me. The first batch caught me right in the breadbasket and bounced square on my toe.—Mezz Mezzrow, *Really the Blues*, p. 36, 1946
- I pivoted like a soldier doing an aboutface and planted my right in Pansy-face's bread basket[.]—Robert Edmond Alter, *Carny Kill*, p. 110, 1966
- Come on, you pup, you're up against Gerry O'Byrne!' and laid the fellow out with an almighty haymaker in the breadbasket.—Aidan Higgins, *Donkey's Years*, p. 149, 1995

bread box *noun*

1 the stomach *US, 1919*

A lesser-known cousin of **BREADBASKET**.

- Also, he needed more cash – ought to see a doctor about this bum breadbox.—Bernard Wolfe, *The Late Risers*, p. 170, 1954

2 a safe that is easily broken into *US*

- —Vincent J. Monteleone, *Criminal Slang*, p. 33, 1949

breadfruit swopper *noun*

a conventional if cheap person *BARBADOS*

- —Frank A. Collymore, *Barbadian Dialect*, p. 22, 1965

bread hooks *noun*

the fingers, the hands *CANADA*

- [H]e won't take any action until he gets his money "in his bread hooks".—*The Daily Colonist*, 1st July 1973

bread knife *noun*

a wife *UK*

Rhyming slang.

- —Bodmin Dark, *Dirty Cockney Rhyming Slang*, 2003

breads *noun*

money *BAHAMAS*

- —John A. Holm, *Dictionary of Bahamian English*, p. 27, 1982

breadwinner *noun*

the person responsible for supporting a family *UK, 1821*

Drawn from **BREAD** (money).

- "I don't blame you, dear Kay," he said gravely, "for comparing yourself to me as a breadwinner."—Mary McCarthy, *The Group*, p. 87, 1963
- MICKEY: Because it's expected . He's – KAY: The breadwinner. —Elmore Leonard, *Switch*, p. 34, 1978

break *noun*

1 in hip-hop culture, an instrumental section from any recorded source that is mixed with other similar selections to make a new piece of music *US*

- [H]e plays the instrumental breakdown section – or the breaks – of his favourite funk, soul and reggae songs, sending partygoers to the dancefloor in droves.—*The Source*, p. 137, March 2002

2 a piece of luck, good unless otherwise qualified, e.g. 'bad break' *US, 1926*
- One day he got a break. — *The Guardian*, 29th August 2001

3 a break-in, or illicit entry, into a building *UK*
- — Frank Norman, *Screwsman's Lament*, 1959

break *verb*

1 to escape from prison *UK*
- — Angela Devlin, *Prison Patter*, p. 30, 1996

2 in blackjack, to exceed 21 points, losing the hand *US*
- — Avery Cardoza, *Winning Casino Blackjack for the Non-Counter*, p. 73, 1991

3 to run away *US*
- We gon' have to get out and break. — *Menace II Society*, 1993
- — Ann Lawson, *Kids & Gangs*, p. 56, 1994

4 in theatrical use, to stop work during or at the end of rehearsal, e.g. 'the cast broke for tea' *UK, 1984*

5 of money, to change a coin or a note into coins or notes of smaller denominations *UK, 1844*

6 to steal something *US*
- — *San Francisco Chronicle*, p. E5, 10th August 2003

7 to do something to excess *US*
- — Terry Williams, *The Cocaine Kids*, p. 135, 1989

▸ **break bad**
to act in a threatening, menacing manner *US*
- — Anna Scotti and Paul Young, *Buzzwords*, p. 54, 1997

▸ **break camp**
to leave *US*
Military or Western overtones.
- — Connie Eble (Editor), *UNC-CH Campus Slang*, p. 2, March 1986

▸ **break fives**
to shake hands *BARBADOS*
- — Frank A. Collymore, *Barbadian Dialect*, p. 22, 1965

▸ **break his (or her) cherry**
(used of a racehorse) to win the first race in a racing career *US*
- — David W. Maurer, *Argot of the Racetrack*, p. 17, 1951

▸ **break ill**
to make a mistake, to blunder *US*
- — Connie Eble (Editor), *UNC-CH Campus Slang*, p. 1, Spring 1989

▸ **break it big**
to win a great deal of money *AUSTRALIA*
- — Tom Ronan, *Vision Splendid*, 1954

▸ **break it down**
to stop, to cease; as an imperative, stop talking! *AUSTRALIA*
- — Lawson Glossop, *We Were the Rats*, 1944
- — Jon Cleary, *The Sundowners*, 1952

▸ **break luck**
(of a prostitute) to have sex with the first customer of the day or night *US*
- The runt was gone. She was breaking her luck with Chuck. — Iceberg Slim (Robert Beck), *Pimp*, p. 154, 1969
- A ho breaks her luck when she turns the first trick of her work day. — Christina and Richard Milner, *Black Players*, p. 297, 1972
- Even if Satin didn't break luck I could pay for another few nights. — A.S. Jackson, *Gentleman Pimp*, p. 99, 1973
- Several of her stable prosses were chatting over too hot cups of coffee, eager to break luck, anxious for Leila to tell them where to turn the first trick of their workday. — Emmett Grogan, *Final Score*, p. 68, 1976
- Out on the rack nearly an hour and half and she still hadn't broke luck. — John Sayles, *Union Dues*, p. 182, 1977

▸ **break out into assholes**
to become deeply frightened *US*
- — Arnold Shaw, *Dictionary of American Pop/Rock*, p. 54, 1982

▸ **break out the rag**
to lose your temper after losing a game *US*
- — *American Speech*, p. 232, Autumn-Winter 1971: 'Checkschmuck! the slang of the chess player'

▸ **break starch**
to put on a fresh uniform *US*
- — Carl Fleischhauer, *A Glossary of Army Slang*, p. 5, 1968
- Every day in the Airborne began in a freshly washed and starched pair of cut-down fatigues, and both officer and NCO "broke starch" – put on a fresh pair – once or twice throughout the day. — David H. Hackworth, *About Face*, p. 442, 1989

▸ **break stick in ears**
to ignore advice or counel *GRENADA*

▸ **break tape**
to fire your weapon *US*
Vietnam war usage.
- — Linda Reinberg, *In the Field*, p. 27, 1991

▸ **break the bank**
to divide the winnings up among members of a blackjack counting team *US*
- — Michael Dalton, *Blackjack*, p. 34, 1991

▸ **break the house**
in gambling, especially an illegal gambling enterprise, to win a great deal of money from the house *US*
- I will never forget watching him stroll across Washburne Avenue after breaking the house. — Odie Hawkins, *Men Friends*, p. 130, 1989

▸ **break the night**
to stay up all night *US*
- Then Thursday he tried to "break the night," street slang for staying up until sunrise – in search of a good time. — *Newsday (New York)*, p. 20, 14th May 1989

▸ **break the seal**
to urinate for the first time in a serious bout of drinking *UK*
Subsequent visits to the toilet will occur with urgent regularity after 'breaking the seal'.
- — *Roger's Profanisaurus*, p. 26, 2002

▸ **break the sound barrier**
to fart *CANADA, 1984*
Probably dating to the late 1960s when the test-flights of supersonic airliner Concorde first made the potential simile widely-known.

▸ **break watches**
(of a racehorse) to run very fast during a morning workout *US*
- — David W. Maurer, *Argot of the Racetrack*, p. 16, 1951

▸ **break weak**
to back down from a confrontation *US*
- — William K. Bentley and James M. Corbett, *Prison Slang*, p. 31, 1992

▸ **break wide**
to leave *US*
- — William K. Bentley and James M. Corbett, *Prison Slang*, p. 48, 1992

▸ **break wind**

1 to fart *UK, 1606*
- The only problem in their relationship was the husband's bad habit of breaking wind every morning[.] — Alec Bromcie, *The Complete Book of Farting*, p. 141, 1999

2 to drive in the lead position in a group of trucks travelling along a motorway together *US*
Citizens' band radio usage.
- — Bill Davis, *Jawjacking*, p. 22, 1977

▸ **break your balls**
to harrass, to nag someone *US*
- C'mon, man, don't break my balls, I'm just trying to get along. — Darryl Ponicsan, *The Last Detail*, p. 3, 1970

▸ **break your chops**
to give someone a hard time, to harass someone *US, 1953*
- We don't get those bullshit complaints and they won't break our chops on the paper work. — Peter Maas, *Serpico*, p. 175, 1973
- Kids used to call me a "hallelujah" – break my chops. — Edwin Torres, *Carlito's Way*, p. 7, 1975

▸ **break your duck**
to do something for the first time *UK*
A figurative application of the cricketing term (to score at least one run).
- I've never had a ginger bird. And I think this one is just about gorgeous enough to make me break my duck. — John Milne, *Alive and Kicking*, 1998

breakage *noun*
in horse racing pari-mutuel betting, the change left over after paying off bets to the nearest nickel, dime or dollar *US*
- — Dan Parker, *The ABC of Horse Racing*, p. 144, 1947

break a leg!
to an actor, good luck! *US, 1973*
Theatrical superstition considers a wish of good luck to be tempting fate. Folk-etymology offers the example of American actor John Wilkes Booth who assassinated President Abraham Lincoln. The assassin jumped on stage and broke his leg. Unlikely.

It is remembered in use in the 1930s, and is suspected to be of English origin; it is certainly widely used in the UK.

breakaway *noun*

1 any piece of equipment or clothing that will tear free from a police officer's body during a fight *US*

- — *American Speech*, p. 267, December 1962: 'The language of traffic policemen'

2 in television and film making, a prop designed to break easily upon impact *US*

- — Ralph S. Singleton, *Filmaker's Dictionary*, p. 22, 1990

breakbeat *noun*

in contemporary dance culture, a sampled beat that is looped to create a rhythmic pattern; hence, a musical style *US*

- The best-stocked is the Music Factory (1476 Broadway, between 42nd and 43rd), which is jammed with the latest New York-based label rap hits, breakbeat collections (which feature hit songs with extended breaks for rap deejays or record producers)[.] — *Los Angeles Times*, p. 92, 13th March 1988
- intense breakbeat sessions — Alon Shulman, *The Style Bible*, p. 42, 1999
- — Gareth Thomas, *This Is Ecstasy*, p. 43, 2002
- Became popular when dance producers who couldn't play drums themselves sampled so-called "breakbeats" from old soul and funk records, and repeated these on backing tracks for their new productions. — *The Sunday Times Magazine*, p. 49, 1st June 2003

breakdancer; breaker *noun*

a dancer who finds expression in the rhythms of hip-hop music *US*

- Breakdancers, according to Crazy Legs [Richie Colon], were simply partygoers who would wait on Herc [DJ Kool Herc]'s "breaks" before going into action. — Alex Ogg, *The Hip Hop Years*, p. 15, 1999

breakdancing *noun*

an energetic dance improvised to the rhythms of hip-hop; often danced competitively *US*

The origin of hip-hop is credited to New York DJ Kool Herc who mixed in rhythmic '*break*down parts' which dancers then interpreted.

- Breakdancing, also perofrmed during a Nike fashion show and at the Hyde booth, is a stylized movement form, straight from New York City sidewalks, characterized by fast, robotic movements and synchronized acrobatics. — *Footwear News*, p. 1, 10th October 1983
- Breakdancing went with rap, the way graffiti went up on the subway trains and schoolyard walls. — Bonnie Nadell and John Small, *Breakdance*, p. 8, 1984
- The discipline of breakdancing/B-boying was one of four separate styles that converged throughthe late 70s. Up-rocking [...] pop-locking [...] and body-popping[.] — Alex Ogg, *The Hip Hop Years*, p. 14, 1999

breakdown *noun*

1 a shotgun *US*

- — Ann Lawson, *Kids & Gangs*, p. 56, 1994: 'Common african-american gang slang/phrases'
- — Bill Valentine, *Gang Inteligence Manual*, 1995

2 a noisy, rowdy party *JAMAICA*

- — Richard Allsopp, *Dictionary of Caribbean English Usage*, p. 115, 1996

break down *verb*

to explain something *US, 1965*

- So I clean out Margo's refrigerator of all its food and drive back over to the Communication Company where is lovely Sam and Cassandra and Claude and Helene who I break it down to. — *The Digger Papers*, p. 10, August 1968

breaker *noun*

1 a citizens' band radio user *US*

Directly from the announcement of a citizens' band radio user's presence on a waveband.

- Ah, breaker, Pigpen, this here's the Duck[.] — C.W. McCall, *Convoy*, 1976
- On the air you are just another breaker. — Peter Chippindale, *The British CB Book*, p. 15, 1981

2 in horse racing, a horse that starts a race with a great burst of speed *US*

- — Bob and Barbara Freeman, *Wanta Bet?*, p. 288, 1982

breaker!; break!

used for announcing your presence on citizens' band radio *US*

Literally announcing someone who wishes to 'break-in' to the airwaves, often formulated with information on direction, radio channel, road number or type of contact sought.

- Ah, breaker one-nine, this here's the Rubber Duck. — C.W. McCall, *Convoy*, 1976
- Break one nine for a copy. — Peter Chippindale, *The British CB Book*, p. 44, 1981

breakers *noun*

in certain games of poker, cards that qualify a player to open betting *US*

- — George Percy, *The Language of Poker*, p. 13, 1988

breakers ahead!

used as a general purpose warning of impending problems *US*

Of obvious nautrical origin, from the cry of the masthead lookout.

- — Charles F. Haywood, *Yankee Dictionary*, p. 15, 1963

breakfast burrito *noun*

the penis *UK*

- — Richard Herring, *Talking Cock*, p. 30, 2003

breakfast club *noun*

a nightclub operating after other clubs close at 2am, staying open until the early morning when breakfast is served *US*

- Wilbur Stump, the noted pianist, opened a "breakfast club" (one of those bring-your-own bottle joints, opening at 2 a.m.) on the second floor at 207 Powell. — *San Francisco Examiner*, p. 19, 4th September 1954
- But since she began operating Guys and Dolls as a breakfast club last October, the alliances arranged there have been somewhat less permanent, Sgt. Robert Davis of the vice squad charged. — *San Francisco News Call-Bulletin*, p. 2, 20th February 1965
- Joint police-health department action has dealt almost a knockout blow to San Francisco's after-hours "breakfast" clubs, reducing their number from 14 to only two. — *San Francisco Examiner*, p. 3, 24th April 1970

breakfast of champions *noun*

1 simultaneous, mutual oral sex *AUSTRALIA*

- — Thommo, *The Dictionary of Australian Swearing and Sex Sayings*, p. 20, 1985

2 crack cocaine *UK, 1998*

A new, ironic application for the slogan used by Wheaties™ since the 1930s; adopted as the title of a 1973 novel by Kurt Vonnegut Jr, and released as a film in 1999.

- — Mike Haskins, *Drugs*, p. 281, 2003

3 beer *US*

- She handed one to Steve, then took a long drink from her own. "Breakfast of Champions" she proclaimed, holding up the can in a mock toast until Steve had taken a drink. — Jack W. Thomas, *Heavy Number*, p. 53, 1976

breakfast of losers *noun*

methaqualone, the recreational drug best known as Quaaludes™ *US*

Punning on the slogan of a popular cereal brand – 'breakfast of champions'.

- — Carsten Stroud, *Close Pursuit*, 1987

breakfast time *noun*

▸ **to breakfast time**

to eternity *AUSTRALIA*

- Everyone from Alice Springs to breakfast time. — Alexander Buzo, *Norm and Ahmed*, p. 25, 1969
- I'd kick his arse from here to breakfast time. — Derek Maitland, *Breaking Out*, p. 85, 1979

breaking *noun*

the gymnastic and acrobatic aspect of breakdancing *US*

- — Bradley Elfman, *Breakdancing*, p. 11, 1984

break in the weather *noun*

in betting on horse racing, a change of luck *AUSTRALIA*

- — Ned Wallish, *The Truth Dictionary of Racing Slang*, p. 10, 1989

break into *verb*

to achieve an entrance into an occupation or activity *US, 1899*

break it off!

give me your money! *US*

- Just about a year ago, when Deon Jones was 17, he pulled a green Halloween mask over his face and put a gun to the head of a Fairywood neighbor. "Break it off," Jones said – street slang for "Hand over your money." — *Pittsburgh Post-Gazette*, p. A1, 7th August 1997

break loose *verb*

in drag racing, to lose traction and spin the wheels without moving *US*

- Sometimes a car has so much power that the wheels lose their bite and spin or break loose without moving the car forward much. — Ed Radlauer, *Drag Racing Pix Dix*, p. 9, 1970

break-luck *noun*
a prostitute's first customer of the day *US*
- — *Washington Post*, p. C5, 7th November 1993

break man *noun*
a prison guard who orchestrates the opening of cells in the morning *US*
- Voices were raised in harsh humor, as over four hundred men joked and argued back and forth. "Break three!" the break man screamed as he reached the third gallery. — Donald Goines, *Black Gangster*, p. 7, 1977

break out *verb*
to leave *US*
- — Vann Wesson, *Generation X Field Guide and Lexicon*, p. 28, 1997

breakup *noun*
in Alaska, the season between winter and summer *US, 1904*
- Break-up is a term that refers to the melting and eventual break-up of ice in the rivers of the north. — Mark Wheeler, *Half Baked Alaska*, p. 31, 1972
- Breakup is what happens when a lot of ice and snow melts in a short time. River ice breaks up, causing floods. Frozen streets break up, causing potholes. and various things that were better off frozen thaw out, causing an indescribable odor. — Mike Doogan, *How to Speak Alaskan*, p. 15, 1993

break up *verb*
to cause someone to laugh uproariously *US, 1895*
- [S]he [Carol Burnett] ad-libbed outrageously, and it always broke me up. — *Good Housekeeping*, January 1972

breast check *noun*
a walk through a crowd in search of attractive female breasts *US*
- — *Maledicta*, p. 47, 1995: 'Door whore and other New Mexico restaurant slang'

breast job *noun*
surgery to alter a woman's breast size *US*
- [T]he city sat as pert and bright as a socialite's breast job[.] — Chris Niles, *Revenge is the Best Revenge [Tart Noir]*, p. 13, 2002

breathe *noun*
in poker, to pass without betting *US*
- — George Percy, *The Language of Poker*, p. 13, 1988

breather *noun*
1 in sports, a game against a weak opponent *US*
From the conventional sense (a rest).
- The coaches used to talk about breathers. That's a sad excuse. There are no breathers today anyway. — *San Francisco News*, p. 18, 15th November 1945
- Da Grosa also assailed the scheduling of "breathers" as unfair to the paying public. — *San Francisco Cann-Bulletin*, p. 16, 26th December 1950
- The UCLA Bruins, toppled from No. 1 last week amid the mud and might of Maryland, drew their "breather" tomorrow and are figured to beat Washington State by three or four touchdowns. — *San Francisco Chronicle*, p. 3H, 1st October 1955
- Women Look to Get on Track With Nonconference Breather [Headline] — *Daily Tar Heel (Chapel Hill, North Carolina)*, 10th February 1995

2 the nose *US*
- — Kenn "Naz" Young, *Naz's Underground Dictionary*, p. 17, 1973
- — Charles Shafer, *Folk Speech in Texas Prisons*, p. 199, 1990

3 a person who derives sexual pleasure from telephoning someone and breathing heavily when they answer the phone *US*
- When I lift up the receiver, at first I think I got a breather. Then a voice says, "Check it out. There was a bullet in Helen Caplet." — Robert Campbell, *Junkyard Dog*, p. 75, 1986

4 in trucking, the air intake pipe *US*
- — Montie Tak, *Truck Talk*, p. 18, 1971

breather crimp *noun*
a virtually undetectable bend or crease put onto a playing card by a cheat or a conjuror
- The breather crimp is an undetectable crimp that can be put on a card at a moment's notice[.] — *Card Trick Central*, 2003

Breather U *noun*
any college with a poor sports programme *US*
Humourous to those who attach importance to a college's sports programme.
- — Connie Eble (Editor), *UNC-CH Campus Slang*, p. 2, Spring 1988

breath of God *noun*
crack cocaine *US*
- — Anna Scotti and Paul Young, *Buzzwords*, p. 131, 1997

breck *noun*
breakfast *US*
- — *Concord (New Hampshire) Monitor*, p. 17, 23rd August 1983

brecko *noun*
breakfast *AUSTRALIA*
- — Tom Hibbert, *Rockspeak!*, p. 30, 1983

bredda *noun*
1 a brother, a fellow black person
Phonetic spelling of West Indian pronunciation. West Indian and UK black.
- An de Bredda feels betta dan dis Bredda next door / Cause did Bredda's got money, but de Bredda's got more / And de Bredda tinks dis Bredda not a Bredda cause he's poor[.] — Benjamin Zephaniah, *Money*, p. 20, 1992
- Wha'ever 'appen tu trus? Bredda don't treat me like dat. — Q, *The Sparrow (Disco Biscuits)*, p. 262, 1996

2 a boy *JAMAICA*
- — Velma Pollard, *Dread Talk*, p. 41, 2000

bredgie *noun*
a friend *UK, 2002*
Originally black usage, now youth slang.

bredren; bredrin *noun*
a man's friend; friends; a fellow youth gang member *UK*
Conventional 'brethren' ('brothers', with religious and political overtones) adopted for everyday use by the West Indian and UK black communities.
- Chico and Hair Oil were his bredrin, culture-wise and otherwise, he didn't mind sharing a joke with them. — Karline Smith, *Moss Side Massive*, p. 21, 1994
- Sometimes to hail up a bredrin but more likely to chivvy the buspass people across the road. — Diran Adebayo, *My Once Upon A Time*, p. 14, 2000
- looking out for our bredren, sistren still. — Diran Adebayo, *My Once Upon A Time*, p. 21, 2000

bree *noun*
a young woman *US*
- — Jack Lait and Lee Mortimer, *New York Confidential*, p. 235, 1992: 'A glossary of Harlemisms'

breed *noun*
1 a person of mixed ancestry, Indian and non-Indian *CANADA*
- There are in this area, besides the Indians and whites, a considerable percentage of people with both white and Indian blood, referred to as metis, half-breeds, or 'breeds'. — Charles Crate, *We Speak for the Silent!*, p. 1, 1956
- [They] referred to them [Metis] as the "breds" and the "coyote French." — George Stanley, *Louis Riel*, p. 242, 1963

2 a person who is not white *US*
- — William K. Bentley and James M. Corbett, *Prison Slang*, p. 54, 1992

breed *verb*
▸ **breed a scab**
to create trouble *US, 1941*
- — Frederic G. Cassidy, *Dictionary of American Regional English, Volume 1*, p. 376, 1985

breeder *noun*
1 from the homosexual point of view, a heterosexual *US, 1979*
Usually used as an insult.
- — *Maledicta*, p. 243, Winter 1980: 'Lovely, blooming, fresh and gay': the onomastics of camp'
- "Hey, what does a breeder know?" Michael grinned. "Where did you learn that word?" The light changed. They proceeded with graceless caution across the pebbly asphalt. "One of the guys at Perry's," replied Brian. "He said that's what the faggots call us." — Armistead Maupin, *Further Tales of the City*, p. 167, 1982
- — Pamela Munro, *U.C.L.A. Slang*, p. 24, 1989
- — Jeff Fessler, *When Drag Is Not a Car Race*, p. 34, 1997
- She seems like such a breeder. It's hard to believe she's bisexual. — Amy Sohn, *Run Catch Kiss*, p. 162, 1999
- Butt-banging breeders may even throw their own pride parade. — *The Village Voice*, 7th March 2000

2 any food that is believed to render a man potent and fecund *JAMAICA*
- — Peter L. Patrick, *Some Recent Jamaican Creole Words*, 2003

breeze *noun*

1 something that is achieved easily and quickly *US, 1928*
- [T]he boosts are a breeze. — *Gone in 60 Seconds*, 2000

2 in horse racing, an easy pace during a workout or race *US*
- — David W. Maurer, *Argot of the Racetrack*, p. 16, 1951

3 an escape from prison *US, 1948*
- — Harold Wentworth and Stuart Berg Flexner, *Dictionary of American Slang*, p. 62, 1960

4 a prison sentence that is nearly completed *US*
- — Joseph E. Ragen and Charles Finston, *Inside the World's Toughest Prison*, p. 806, 1962

5 a calm, collected person *US*
- — K. Bentley and James M. Corbett, *Prison Slang*, p. 48, 1992

6 the air used in air brakes *US, 1939*
- — Norman Carlisle, *The Modern Wonder Book of Trains and Railroading*, p. 260, 1946

7 (of a car) power *US*
- Clean as a whistle. They both got plenty breeze. — *Rebel Without a Cause*, 1955

8 used as a term of address *US*
- — *Current Slang*, p. 2, Fall 1966

▷ **see:** BALMY BREEZE

breeze *verb*

1 to move or go quickly; to move or go casually or without effort *US, 1907*
Generally before 'along', 'in', 'off', 'through', etc.
- Evo from the association executive breezed in for a beer. — *The Guardian*, 6th April 2002

2 to succeed in achieving something without making a great effort *UK*
- They may have breezed their way to victory in Jamaica[.] — *The Guardian*, 20th March 2004

3 to escape; to go *US, 1913*
- Any time I breezed down the street, cats would flash me friendly grins and hands would wave at me from all sides, and I felt like I was king of the tribe. — Mezz Mezzrow, *Really the Blues*, p. 48, 1946
- Soon as I got the angle on that I breezed. — Hal Ellson, *Duke*, p. 124, 1949
- Take the dough and breeze. — Raymond Chandler, *The Little Sister*, p. 62, 1949
- He kept breezing and getting caught and brought back into the detail building. — Claude Brown, *Manchild in the Promised Land*, p. 142, 1965

4 in pool, to only barely glance the object ball with the cue ball *US*
- — Steve Rushin, *Pool Cool*, p. 6, 1990

breeze off *verb*
to stop working and relax in the shade *BELIZE*
- — Richard Allsopp, *Dictionary of Caribbean English Usage*, p. 115, 1996

breezer *noun*

1 a fart *AUSTRALIA, 1973*
- Julius Caesar blew a breezer on the coast of France[.] — Peter Furze, *Tailwinds*, p. 39, 1998

2 a despised person *UK*
- — Connie Eble (Editor), *UNC-CH Campus Slang*, p. 2, November 2003

breezeway *noun*
the area in a prison where the most derelict of the convicts gather *US*
- — Inez Cardozo-Freeman, *The Joint*, p. 484, 1984

breezy *noun*
a young woman *US*
- What's up with you and that breezy. — Rick Ayers (Editor), *Berkeley High Slang Dictionary*, p. 14, 2004

breid and watter *noun*
talk, speechifying *UK*
Glasgow rhyming slang for **PATTER**, on the Scottish pronunciation of 'bread and water'.
- He's the wee boy fur the breid an watter. Wait tae ye hear um. — Michael Munro, *The Patter, Another Blast*, 1988

brekker; brekkers *noun*
breakfast *UK, 1889*
- Ah! Miss Lockhart! Come and have some brekker. There's porridge and toast and there's some tea in the pot[.] — Philip Pullman, *The Tiger in the Well*, p. 192, 1990
- That Mammee gave me a whack on the paw with a ladle when I mentioned brekkers this mornin', flippin' spiky old tyrant! — Brian Jacques, *Triss*, p. 181, 2002

brekkie; brekky *noun*
breakfast *UK, 1904*
Childish.
- I don't reckon I feel like brekkie. — Barry Humphries, *Bazza Pulls It Off!*, 1971
- Dools for brekky on Wednesday, right? — Kevin Sampson, *Outlaws*, p. 194, 2001
- If you have to catch an early ferry, they'll provide brekkie for you to take away. — *Lonely Planet Italy*, p. 728, 2002

Brenda Bracelets; Brenda *noun*
a police officer; the police *UK*
An example of **CAMP** trans-gender assignment, in this case as an assonant play on **BRACELETS** (handcuffs) as stereotypical police equipment.
- It's funny, looking at the bats [boots] on that Brenda, you wouldn't think she was light on her feet [gay], but she is. — the cast of 'Aspects of Love', Prince of Wales Theatre, *Palare (Boy Dancer Talk) for Beginners*, 1989–92

Brenda Frickers *noun*
knickers *UK*
Rhyming slang, formed on the name of the Irish actress (b.1945), best known for her film work.
- — Bodmin Dark, *Dirty Cockney Rhyming Slang*, 2003

Brenda skunk; Brenda *noun*
a hybrid variety of potent marijuana
- "Brenda Skunk. Brenda." "No, they'd be mostly indica." — Brian Preston, *Pot Planet*, p. 232, 2002

brer *noun*
a fellow black man *UK*
Old contraction of 'brother'.
- I've got nothing against him. I love the brer[.] — Diran Abedayo, *My Once Upon A Time*, p. 144, 2000
- Young brers now they didn't know who he was, didn't give a fuck either. — John Williams, *Cardiff Dead*, p. 49, 2000

bressles *noun*
pubic hair *NORFOLK ISLAND*
- — Beryl Nobbs Palmer, *A Dictionary of Norfolk Words and Usages*, p. 5, 1992

brew *noun*

1 beer; a glass, bottle or can of beer *US, 1907*
- I shook hands with the guy and ordered a brew. — Mickey Spillane, *I, The Jury*, p. 43, 1947
- [W]ith a few brews my fingers flail and less than fly as usual. — Jack Kerouac, *Letter to Neal Cassady*, p. 318, 10th June 1951
- It was a stripped-down Ford, loaded with road workers, and they were loaded with home brew. — Jim Thompson, *Roughneck*, p. 6, 1954
- Americans are always drinking in crossroads saloons on Sunday afternoon; they bring their kids; they gabbl eand brawl over brews[.] — Jack Kerouac, *On the Road*, p. 92, 1957
- And I'll bet you're smart enough to get us some brew. — *American Graffiti*, 1973
- He might sip a brew if the peer pressure got to be too much[.] — Joseph Wambaugh, *Lines and Shadows*, p. 41, 1984
- Went into the store just to get a brew, came out the muthafucka an accessory to murder and armed robbery. — *Menace II Society*, 1993
- Awesome party! Good tunes! Good brew! Good buddies! — *Wayne's World 2*, 1993
- And whether it's brew or skag you do become that sort of bloke. — Shaun Ryder, *Shaun Ryder... in His Own Words*, 1997
- MAFADA: Would you like a glass of tea or something? HEALY: You got a brew? — *Something About Mary*, 1998

2 a cup, mug or pot of tea *AUSTRALIA, 1905*
Tea is *brewed* by immersing tea leaves (loose or bagged) in boiling water.
- We harboured in the relative cool of a bamboo thicket and relaxed over a brew. — Martin Cameron, *A Look at the Bright Side*, 1988
- it was safe to have the occasional brew. — Chris Ryan, *Stand By, Stand By*, p. 103, 1996
- "Just made a brew," said Skin. — Greg Williams, *Diamond Geezers*, p. 17, 1997
- Will you be stopping for a brew, Mary? — Caroline Aherne and Craig Cash, *The Royle Family*, 1999

3 an illicitly made alcoholic beverage *AUSTRALIA, 1950*
- During cell searches we would often find gaol brews and bongs hidden inside the toilet cisterns. — William Dodson, *The Sharp End*, p. 35, 2001

4 a stew *AUSTRALIA*
- 'Ever tasted rabbit stew before, Nino?' 'No, Joe.' 'Got a treat comin' ter yer, matey. She's an extra good brew.' — Nino Culotta (John O'Grady), *They're A Weird Mob*, p. 152, 1957

5 used as a male-to-male term of address *BERMUDA*
- — Peter A. Smith and Fred M. Barritt, *Bermewjan Vurds*, 1985

6 a Jewish person *US*
An abbreviation of 'Hebrew'.
- —Pamela Munro, *U.C.L.A. Slang*, p. 45, 1997

▷ **see:** BURROO

brew *verb*
to make and heat an injectable solution of heroin and water *UK*
- —Angela Devlin, *Prison Patter*, p. 30, 1996

brewdog *noun*
a can of beer *US*
- —Connie Eble (Editor), *UNC-CH Campus Slang*, p. 2, Fall 1988

brewed *adjective*
drunk *US*
- —Connie Eble (Editor), *UNC-CH Campus Slang*, p. 2, Fall 1986

brewer *noun*
a prostitute who will allow sexual intercourse without a condom *UK*
- He leered at Russell "Knowotlmean? One of them is even a brewer," he whispered[.] —Greg Williams, *Diamond Geezers*, p. 112, 1997

brewer's droop *noun*
a temporary inability to achieve an erect penis caused by drinking too much alcohol, especially beer *AUSTRALIA, 1970*
- I know you've had a few but don't tell me you've copped a brewer's droop. —Barry Humphries, *Bazza Pulls It Off!*, 1971
- ANYA: [O]ne guy's dick stayed up for hours and it really annoyed him. LOADED: The opposite to brewer's droop. Does that happen to you often, ladies? —*Loaded*, p. 59, June 2003

brewha *noun*
a glass, bottle or can of beer *US*
- —Pamela Munro, *U.C.L.A. Slang*, p. 47, 2001

brewski; brewsky *noun*
beer; a serving of beer *US, 1978*
Mock Polish.
- —*Wesleyan Alumnus*, p. 29, Spring 1981
- —Connie Eble (Editor), *UNC-CH Campus Slang*, p. 2, Spring 1982
- JD: This is Ohio. If you don't have a brewsky in your hand you might as well be wearing a dress. —*Heathers*, 1988
- Did this. They're charging for brewskies. —*Clueless*, 1995

brewster *noun*
a beer *US*
- —Connie Eble (Editor), *UNC-CH Campus Slang*, p. 2, Fall 1986

Brewster's *noun*
a great deal of money; a fortune *UK*
A reference to *Brewster's Millions*, 1945, remade 1985, a comedy film about huge amounts of money.
- Costing us Brewster's, by the way. —Kevin Sampson, *Outlaws*, p. 84, 2001

brew up *verb*
to make tea *UK, 1916*
- Brew up. Then take a swim in the fjord and dry off on a rock in the sun. —*The Observer*, 20th April 2003

briar *noun*
a hacksaw blade *US*
- —Hyman E. Goldin et al., *Dictionary of American Underworld Lingo*, p. 34, 1950

briar patch *noun*
a female's pubic hair *US*
- —Dale Gordon, *The Dominion Sex Dictionary*, p. 32, 1967

bribe *noun*
in marketing, the initial, attractive offer to join a book or music club *US*
- —Rachel S. Epstein and Nina Liebman, *Biz Speak*, p. 27, 1986

brick *noun*

1 a good man *UK, 1840*
A term of approval.

2 someone with exceptionally good credit *US*
Collected in San Rafael, California, at a car dealership, in March 2001.

3 a person lacking social skills *US*
- —Collin Baker et al., *College Undergraduate Slang Study Conducted at Brown University*, p. 88, 1968

4 a profit made fraudulently *UK*
- "Making brick" is slang for the various ways in which some [bus-] drivers and conductors defraud the Passenger Transport Executive. —*The Guardian*, 10th December 1979

5 a sentence of ten years in jail *AUSTRALIA, 1944*

6 a street tough person *AUSTRALIA, 1840*
- —Maureen Brooks and Joan Ritchie, *Tassie Terms*, p. 20, 1995

7 a die that has been shaved on one face *US, 1950*
- —Thomas L. Clark, *The Dictionary of Gambling and Gaming*, p. 27, 1987

8 in poker, a drawn card that fails to improve the hand *US*
- —John Vorhaus, *The Big Book of Poker Slang*, p. 8, 1996

9 ten cartons of stolen cigarettes *US*
- —Bill Reilly, *Big Al's Official Guide to Chicagoese*, p. 17, 1982

10 a carton of cigarettes *US*
- —Reinhold Aman, *Hillary Clinton's Pen Pal*, p. 22, 1906
- —*Maledicta*, p. 266–267, Summer/Winter 1981: 'By its slang, ye shall know it: the pessimism of prison life'

11 a kilogram of, usually compressed, marijuana, or, less commonly, another drug *US*
- —*Current Slang*, p. 2, Summer 1967
- FREDDY: She had a brick of weed she was sellin', and she didn't want to go to the buy alone. —*Reservoir Dogs*, 1992
- CRASKY: Oh yeah? How much blow you do tonight? I heard they had a fuckin' brick. —*Copland*, 1997
- Here was some dude, not even a chemistry major, coming on to you with mikes [microdots], grams, bricks, kilos and hundredweights. —Robert Sabbag, *A Way with the Spoon [The Howard Marks Book of Dope Stories]*, p. 351, 2001
- —Nick Brownlee, *This Is Cannabis*, p. 151, 2002

12 marijuana *UK*
From the sense as a measurement of the drug.
- —Angela Devlin, *Prison Patter*, p. 31, 1996

13 crack cocaine
- —Mike Haskins, *Drugs*, p. 281, 2003

14 a ten pound note; the sum of ten pounds *AUSTRALIA, 1914*
From the colour of the note. After the introduction of decimal currency in 1966 the meaning changed to either 'twenty dollars' (an equivalent value) or, most commonly, 'ten dollars' (numerically the same). Neither of the new notes were brick coloured and the term has all but died out.
- One race-dat at Flemington, a well-dressed stranger approached Porter and asked him, without any preamble, for 'a brick' ($10). —Roy Higgins and Tom Prior, *The Jockey Who Laughed*, p. 82, 1982

15 a pound sterling (£1) *UK: SCOTLAND*
- —Michael Munro, *The Patter, Another Blast*, 1988

16 an Australian twenty-pound note *AUSTRALIA*
Because of its reddish colour.
- —Ned Wallish, *The Truth Dictionary of Racing Slang*, p. 10, 1989

17 a four-man infantry patrol *UK*
Used by the British Army in Northern Ireland.
- There was a fellow in the brick at the time who was a right pain in the arse. —Andy McNab, *Immediate Action*, p. 26, 1995

18 an abandoned, partially consumed can or bottle of beer *US*
- —Connie Eble (Editor), *UNC-CH Campus Slang*, p. 2, October 2002

brick *verb*

1 to have sex leaning against a brick wall for balance and purchase *UK*
- [D]escribe a sex act (eg: "bricking" means shagging against a brick wall)[.] —*Sky Magazine*, p. 55, May 2001

2 to cheat or defraud someone *UK*
- He was bricking me, so I gave him the bellows [got rid of him]. —Patrick O'Shaughnessy, *Market Traders' Slang*, 1979

3 to fail to deliver as promised *US*
- The delivery guy bricked. —*Dazed and Confused*, 1993

4 to hurl bricks, rocks or other hard objects *US*
A word commonly used in the 1960s in American cities during events called 'riots' by the dominant power and 'uprisings' by leftists.
- —David Claerbaut, *Black Jargon in White America*, p. 59, 1972

5 to miss a shot; to fail *US*
- She threw th' fuckin' case, went in the tank, intentionally bricked it. —Stephen J. Cannell, *The Tin Collectors*, p. 156, 2001

brick *nickname*
the British Columbia Resources Investment Corporation *CANADA, 1979*
A near-abbreviation.
- —Tom Parkin, *WetCoast Words*, p. 20, 1989

bricked *adjective*
1 drug-intoxicated *US*
- —Jay Robert Nash, *Dictionary of Crime*, p. 45, 1992

2 in a court of law, having an unsigned police statement used against you *AUSTRALIA*
- —Ian Grindley, Governor of Pentridge Gaol, Melbourne, 1977

bricker *verb*
to steal; to shoplift *UK*
- [Y]ou can always bricker a dress from a shop if you need one.—Adrian Reid, *The Confessions of a Hitch-Hiker*, 1970

brick gum *noun*
heroin *UK, 1998*
- —Robert Ashton, *This Is Heroin*, p. 205, 2002
- —Mike Haskins, *Drugs*, p. 283, 2003

brickhouse *noun*
in poker, a full house that is not the best hand *US*
An allusion built on 'brick' as a 'useless card'.
- —John Vorhaus, *The Big Book of Poker Slang*, p. 8, 1996

brick it *verb*
to be very nervous or worried; to be thoroughly frightened *UK*
Variation of **SHIT IT**.
- —Angela Devlin, *Prison Patter*, p. 31, 1996
- —Vann Wesson, *Generation X Field Guide and Lexicon*, p. 28, 1997
- "I swear to God, knobhead, I'll fucking kill you..." James trembled his lower lip with his three middle fingers. "Ooh, ay – I'm bricking it..."—Kevin Sampson, *Powder*, p. 489, 1999
- Now it's their turn to brick it as the knife falls on the ground[.]—John King, *Human Punk*, p. 7, 2000

bricks *noun*
in prison, the world outside the prison walls *US*
- —John R. Armore and Joseph D. Wolfe, *Dictionary of Desperation*, p. 21, 1976

▸ **hit the bricks**
1 to leave, especially to leave prison *US, 1931*
- Maybe I could fly one of my magnetized copping kites (high voltage letters) when I hit the bricks, and steal a 'ho!—Iceberg Slim (Robert Beck), *Airtight Willie and Me*, p. 3, 1979
- Just say goodbye once, and then hit the bricks, you big-bottomed freaks, you.—Stuart Jeffries, *Mrs Slocombe's Pussy*, p. 10, 2000

2 to go on strike; to be on strike *US, 1938*
Also variants 'on the bricks' or 'pound the bricks'.
- So I voted to strike – and now I'm pounding the bricks in front of the Mission Street Store. [Advertisement in support of striking Sears workers]—*San Francisco Examiner*, p. 26, 14th September 1947
- The grocer down at the corner has been giving me credit, but how long can he keep it up? He's got maybe 10 or 15 guys on the bricks like me to take care of.—*San Francisco Chronicle, This World*, p. 2, 24th April 1949
- This nightmare mood helps explain why the members of the International Longshoremen's Association have voted down a contract that promised them greater gains than any group of martime workers this year and why they are clamoring to "hit the bricks" in a new port-wide shutdown.—*New York Times*, p. 8, 19th December 1954

▸ **to the bricks**
extremeley, utterly, completely *US, 1928*
- You sure are getting togged to the bricks, pal. [Freckles and His Friends comic strip]—*San Francisco News*, 23rd May 1946
- —Clarence Major, *Dictionary of Afro-American Slang*, p. 115, 1970

bricks and clicks *noun*
a business that combines trading from traditonal business premises with e-commerce and Internet-only custom *UK*
- Forty four of the companies were dot.com start-ups and the rest were "bricks and clicks" retailers – high street names with a web presence.—*The Guardian*, 1st November 2000

bricks and mortar *noun*
1 a house; houses, property *UK, 1855*
Usually in phrases like 'his money's in bricks and mortar'.

2 a daughter *UK, 1960*
Rhyming slang.
- [H]e lived with his bricks and mortar, Mary.—Ronnie Barker, *Fletcher's Book of Rhyming Slang*, p. 25, 1979

brick shithouse *noun*
a woman, or rarely a homosexual man, with a curvaceous figure; a powerfully built man *US, 1928*
Sometimes euphemised to a simple 'house'.
- Must say I like the look of old Claudie. Big bloke. Built like a brick shithouse.—Barry Humphries, *The Wonderful World of Barry McKenzie*, p. 41, 1968
- The other great legs belong to Jabby Morse Hess, who is built like the proverbial brick bleephouse.—*San Francisco Chronicle*, p. 27, 7th July 1971
- Janet is something to write home about. Blonde with a shape like a brick shit house.—Donald Goines, *Never Die Alone*, p. 107, 1974
- She's a brick – house / The lady's stacked and that's a fact.—The Commodores, *Brick House*, 1977
- The girl is underage but built like a brick shit-house, and there's no corroboration.—Edwin Torres, *Q & A*, p. 63, 1977
- This guy was built like a brick shithouse, with an elephantine mustache and smoldering brown eyes.—Armistead Maupin, *Further Tales of the City*, p. 150, 1982
- You with some fine bitch, I mean a brick shithouse bitch – you're with Jayne Kennedy.—*True Romance*, 1993
- He relayed the story and added untruthfully that the "brick shithouse" of a husband was arriving on Wednesday.—Colin Butts, *Is Harry on the Boat?*, p. 226, 1997
- I mean if your son is a sensitive sort of a soul who isn't exactly built like a brick shithouse and doesn't appear to have much luck with girls, you could be forgiven for thinking he might turn out to be a nancy-boy.—Alan Titchmarsh, *Trowell and Error*, p. 92, 2002

bricktop *noun*
a red-haired person *US, 1856*
- Greer, in common with all bricktops, especially those of Irish origin can be a little difficult to handle at times.—*San Francisco Examiner*, p. II-3, 21st June 1957

Bricktop *nickname*
Ada Smith de Conge, a singer, actress and Paris nightclub hostess (died 1984) *US*
- Real name of "Bricktop," whose nickname was inspired by her orange colored hair, is Ada Smith de Conge.—*San Francisco Examiner*, p. 33, 9th June 1952

brickweed *noun*
marijuana that has been compressed into a brick for transportation *UK*
- —Steven Wishnia, *The Cannabis Companion*, p. 150, 2004

bricky; brickie *noun*
a bricklayer *UK, 1880*
- Dennis was a brickie's labourer.—Nino Culotta (John O'Grady), *They're A Weird Mob*, p. 45, 1957
- So, you ask Joyce and Vicky / Who's their favourite brickie—Ian Dury, *Billericay Dickie*, 1977
- It might be a matter of giving the foreman a smack in front of the brickies, just to show them he's not as smart as what he's told them.—Kevin Sampson, *Outlaws*, p. 211–212, 2001

Brickyard *nickname*
the Indianapolis speedway *US*
The speedway was once faced with bricks.
- Introducing Tony Hulman/The Man Who Runs the Brickyard [Cover Headline]—*Sports Illustrated*, 26th May 1958
- —John Lawlor, *How to Talk Car*, p. 24, 1965
- It's called the "Brickyard." Two and half miles of track in a lop-sided circle.—*San Francisco Examiner and Chronicle, California Living*, p. 13, 14th May 1967
- Foyt 2–1 favorite to win again at Indy's brickyard [Headline]—*San Francisco Examiner and Chronicle*, p. B3, 25th May 1975

bridal suite *noun*
1 a two-man prison cell *NEW ZEALAND*
A frank allusion to homosexual sex in prison.
- —Harry Orsman, *A Dictionary of Modern New Zealand Slang*, p. 19, 1999

2 a room where police assigned the late night shift can sleep *US*
- —*Los Angeles Times*, p. B8, 19th December 1994

bride *noun*
1 a model of good behaviour *BARBADOS*
- —Frank A. Collymore, *Barbadian Dialect*, p. 22, 1965

2 a prostitute *UK*
- —R. Samuel, *East End Underworld*, 1981

bride's nightie *noun*

▸ **like a bride's nightie**

very quickly *AUSTRALIA*

- — *Weekend Australian*, p. 10, 1984
- However, you know as well as I do the economy is up and down like a bride's nightie. — Humphries, *The Traveller's Tool*, p. 36, 1985
- He took off like a bride's nightie. — *The Dinkum Dictionary Of Australian English*, p. 12, 1990
- Come out [of solitary confinement] after two days, fight again, more chokey. I was up and down like a bride's nightie until we were ghosted off to the seaside. — Lenny McLean, *The Guv'nor*, p. 42, 1998

bride's slide *noun*

in backgammon, the customary play with a first roll of 6–5: moving a back man 11 points *US*

- — Dave Thompson, *Play Backgammon Tonight*, p. 58, 1976

bridge *noun*

1 a holder for a marijuana cigarette *US*

A common term in the 1950s, largely supplanted by **ROACH CLIP** in the 1960s.

- — *American Speech*, p. 86, May 1955: 'Narcotic argot along the mexican border'
- — Jay Robert Nash, *Dictionary of Crime*, p. 45, 1992

2 a slightly curved playing card, altered by a cheat to manipulate the cutting of a deck *US*

- — Michael Dalton, *Blackjack*, p. 34, 1991

3 a pickpocket who reaches around the victim to pick their pocket *US*

- — Vincent J. Monteleone, *Criminal Slang*, p. 34, 1949

4 a group of four in a restaurant or soda fountain *US*

An allusion to a bridge party.

- — *American Speech*, p. 61, February 1967: 'Soda-fountain, restaurant and tavern calls'

▸ **under the bridge**

in a smuggling operation, across a border *US*

- — *American Speech*, p. 98, May 1956: 'Smugglers' argot in the southwest'

bridge and tunnel *adjective*

said of a resident of New Jersey who commutes to New York *US*

Disparaging.

- I said to the team, "We can't go to New Jersey. What would they call us, the Bridge and Tunnels?" — Dan Jenkins, *Life Its Ownself*, p. 18, 1984
- Eww! Not a bridge-and-tunnel Jersey dyke! — *Chasing Amy*, 1997

bridge bender *noun*

a motor vehicle manufactured by Vauxhall *UK*

- — Peter Chippindale, *The British CB Book*, p. 161, 1981

bridge jumper *noun*

in horse racing, a person who regularly bets on favourites and is distraught if the favourite does not win *US*

- — David W. Maurer, *Argot of the Racetrack*, p. 16, 1951

bridge monkey; bridge stiff *noun*

on the railways, a bridge construction worker *US*

- — Ramon Adams, *The Language of the Railroader*, p. 22, 1977

Bridge of Sighs *nickname*

an overpass connecting the New York City jail with the criminal court building *US*

A borrowing from Venice's Ponte de Sospiri, romanticised by Lord Byron.

- He walked me down this long dark corridor and then into a narrower corridor. Now I knew were I was. This was the Bridge of Sighs that led from the court building high up over the street into the old Tombs. — Rocky Garciano (with Rowland Barber), *Somebody Up There Likes Me*, p. 105, 1955
- Few lawyers alive today remember the old court house or the grey granite, twin-peaked Tombs and the famous "Bridge of Sighs" that rose over Franklin Street to connect the two buildings. — *New York Law Journal*, p. S-14, 6th May 1991

bridges *noun*

bridge tolls for which a truck driver is paid in advance or reimbursed *US*

- — *American Speech*, p. 42, February 1963: 'Trucker's language in Rhode Island'

brief *noun*

1 a solicitor, a barrister or other legal representative of an accused person *UK*

From an earlier sense (the legal case presented to a barrister).

- My brief'll have me out in hours. Nobody'll grass on me, Regan. — *The Sweeney*, p. 44, 1976
- — Angela Devlin, *Prison Patter*, p. 31, 1996
- I've always had a brief sitting beside me[.] — Val McDermid, *Keeping on the Right Side of the Law*, p. 177, 1999

2 a warrant to search or arrest someone; a Metropolitan Police warrant-card *UK*

- — Peter Laurie, *Scotland Yard*, p. 321, 1970
- — Angela Devlin, *Prison Patter*, p. 31, 1996

3 a ticket for any purpose *UK, 1937*

- A couple of "briefs" for your local custodians of law and order might be a nice idea. — Anthony Masters, *Minder*, p. 23, 1984

4 a playing card that has been trimmed slightly so that a cheat can locate it within a deck by feel *US*

- — George Percy, *The Language of Poker*, p. 13, 1988

brig *noun*

a Brigadier; also, until the rank was abolished, a Brigadier General *UK, 1899*

Military.

- I put the brig's mind at rest by confirming that no pineapples had left my postroom. — Ken Lukowiak, *Marijuana Time*, p. 41, 2000

briggity *adjective*

arrogant, vain, stubborn *US, 1884*

- Come to think of it, you never hear briggity anymore either. Briggity-britches was one of the insults we used to hurl at one another when we were kids. — *Charleston (West Virginia) Gazette*, p. 4C, 15th August 2003

bright *noun*

1 morning *US, 1941*

- Many was the night we sniffed and philosophized, philosophized and sniffed, until the early bright was upon us. — Mezz Mezzrow, *Really the Blues*, p. 170, 1946
- — *Time Magazine*, p. 92, 20th January 1947
- With a pocketful of green I was digging the scene the other bright[.] — Dan Burley, *Diggeth Thou?*, p. 36, 1959
- Bitch, one of these 'brights' you're going to shoot your 'jib' [mouth] off, I'll curtsy and call you Runt the corpse. — Iceberg Slim (Robert Beck), *Pimp*, p. 136, 1969

2 a light-complexioned black person *US, 1976*

- "Break it down, yuou even got one set for brights and – " "Brights?" "-another for bloods. She looked at her hands before she answered the question. "Light-skinned niggers." — Robert Campbell, *Boneyards*, p. 268, 1992

bright *adjective*

(of skin) light-coloured *BAHAMAS*

- — John A. Holm, *Dictionary of Bahamian English*, p. 28, 1982

bright and frisky; bright 'n' frisky; Brighton *noun*

whisky *UK*

Rhyming slang, probably as a deliberate variation of the earlier 'gay and frisky' reflecting the shift in the meaning of 'gay'; it is interesting to note therefore that the contraction 'Brighton' also has rhyming slang noun and adjective senses (homosexual), and that Brighton is regarded as one of the UK's centres of homosexual culture.

- — Sydney (Steak) T. Kendall, *Up the Frog*, p. 26, 1969

bright disease *noun*

the condition of knowing too much for your own good *US*

- — Lavada Durst, *The Jives of Dr. Hepcat*, p. 11, 1953

bright-eyed and bushy-tailed *adjective*

alert and enthusiastic, lively *US, 1942*

- I'm telling you, he's bright-eyed and bushy-tailed, none of that sulking, suspicious nature. — *Washington Post*, p. D1, 28th January 1979
- Good morning, everybody! Are we all bright-eyed and bushy-tailed? — Ian Pattison, *Rab C. Nesbitt*, 1988
- Alex Rodriguez was the first Yankee at the stadium. He showed up for work ahead of every other ballplayer Thursday morning, although not exactly bright-eyed and bushy-tailed, as his droopy lids betrayed. — *Chicago Tribune*, p. C2, 9th April 2004

bright eyes *noun*

1 a lookout during a criminal venture *US*

- Smugglers' Argot in the Southwest — *American Speech*, p. 96, May 1956
- — Joseph E. Ragen and Charles Finston, *Inside the World's Toughest Prison*, p. 792, 1962: 'Penitentiary and underworld glossary'

2 the high beam setting on headlights *US*

- — Bill Davis, *Jawjacking*, p. 23, 1977

brightlight team *noun*
in Vietnam, a small group from the special forces sent to rescue American prisoners of war *US*
- —Linda Reinberg, *In the Field*, p. 28, 1991

Brighton bucket *noun*
▸ **like a Brighton bucket**
without recognising someone when you pass them in the street *TRINIDAD AND TOBAGO, 1987*
An image of the pitch buckets on a conveyor system at the Brighton pier, passing each other on belts.
- —Lise Winer, *Dictionary of the English/Creole of Trinidad & Tobago*, 2003

Brighton pier *verb*
to disappear *UK, 1998*
Rhyming slang.

Brighton pier; brighton *adjective*
(especially of a man) homosexual *UK, 1960*
Rhyming slang for **QUEER** (homosexual). Recorded by Ray Puxley, 1992. Earlier use of the same rhyme meant 'unwell' or 'peculiar', the meaning shifting with the sense of 'queer'; possibly also influenced by the reputation of Brighton as a centre for gay society and culture.
- I wouldn't go into that bar if I was you; it's full of Brightons.—Bodmin Dark, *Dirty Cockney Rhyming Slang*, 2003

Brighton rock *noun*
the penis *UK*
Rhyming slang for **COCK**, and a visual pun on a long pink sweet that is made to be sucked. Noted by Ray Puxley, 1992. Similarly sweet references to the male anatomy can be found at **ALMOND ROCK**, **BLACKPOOL ROCK** and **STICK OF ROCK**.

brights *noun*
white socks *US*
- —*Current Slang*, p. 5, Summer 1969

Bright's Disease *nickname*
Bright's Wine™, a brand of cheap wine, grown and processed in Niagara, Ontario *CANADA*
- They make fine wines there now, but in my day there were only wines that were given nicknames like Bright's Disease.—David Helwig, *Living Here*, p. 26, 2001

bright spark *noun*
a cheerful, energetic person *NEW ZEALAND*
- —Sonya Plowman, *Great Kiwi Slang*, p. 37, 2002

bright spot *noun*
in oil drilling, an area that has indications of a productive field *US*
- I we get what is known as a 'hot spot' or a 'bright spot' on our computer graphs, we notify the company and then they spend a lot of money to develop the potential field, put in pipes and cisterns. —Stephen Cannell, *Big Con*, p. 263, 1997

bright, white and dead white *adjective*
▷ see: **LIGHT, BRIGHT, DAMN NEAR WHITE**

brighty *adjective*
very smart *US*
- —Lou Shelly, *Hepcats Jive talk Dictionary*, p. 8, 1945

brig rat *noun*
a prisoner *US, 1942*
- [H]e could imagine Red in the Navy, a brig rat of course, an old white hat, shipping over until the sailors' home claimed him.—Malcolm Braly, *On the Yard*, p. 211, 1967

brill; brills *adjective*
excellent, marvellous *UK, 1979*
An abbreviation of '*brill*ant'; also used as exclamation. Nigel Foster in *The Making of a Royal Marine Commando*, 1987, claims military usage pre-dates modern slang by several decades.
- Oh, fucking brill, said Harry[.]—James Hawes, *Dead Long Enough*, p. 281, 2000
- Anne and Lisa playing such brill choons.—*Mixmag*, p. 11, February 2002

brilliant *adjective*
wonderful, excellent *UK, 1979*
- The baby is brilliant, by the way.—Mary Hooper, *(megan)2*, p. 32, 1999

brim *noun*
1 any hat *US, 1965*
- —David Claerbaut, *Black Jargon in White America*, p. 59, 1972

2 a straw hat *BAHAMAS*
- —John A. Holm, *Dictionary of Bahamian English*, p. 28, 1982

brims *noun*
identical hats worn by members of a youth gang *US*
- —Ralph de Sola, *Crime Dictionary*, p. 20, 1982

brimson *noun*
a braggart; a fantasist *UK*
English gypsy use.
- —Jimmy Stockin, *On The Cobbles*, p. 9, 2000

bring *verb*
to compel someone to do something. *US*
- —Bruce Jackson, *Outside the Law*, p. 55, 1972

▸ **bring it in**
in poker, to make the first bet of a hand *US*
- —Anthony Holden, *Big Deal*, p. 298, 1990

▸ **bring it on**
used for challenging an opponent to begin a competition *US*
- VICTOR: Game point, cousin, game point. JUNIOR POLATKIN: Bring it on, Victor, bring it on.—*Smoke Signals*, 1998
- Bring it on, Mum, bring it on!—Dave Haslam, *Adventures of the Wheels of Steel*, p. 117, 2001

▸ **bring pee**
to frighten someone severely *US*
Vietnam war usage.
- —*Post (New York)*, p. 42, 16th July 1966
- —Carl Fleischhauer, *A Glossary of Army Slang*, p. 5, 1968

▸ **bring smoke**
1 to call for an artillery barrage *US*
- —Gregory Clark, *Words of the Vietnam War*, p. 69, 1990

2 by extension, to reprimand someone in harsh, profane tones *US*
- —Carl Fleischhauer, *A Glossary of Army Slang*, p. 6, 1968

bring-a-plate *adjective*
(of a party or the like) partially self-catered *AUSTRALIA, 1979*
- At parties when other girls more nervous than she spilt claret cup or trifle on the hostess's carpet at those endless bring-a-plate kitchen teas she seemed always to be attending, she would say offhandedly, 'Don't worry[.]'—Thea Astley, *Hunting the Wild Pineapple*, p. 85, 1979
- He made most of the supper break as supper, a bring-a-plate affair, was undoubtedly the highlight of the bush dance.—Kerry Cue, *Crooks, Chooks and Bloody Ratbags*, p. 199, 1983

bringdown *noun*
an event or person that discourages or depresses you *US, 1939*
- "You'll have to go home, son," the doc said. "You've got a slight murmur in your heart." That was a bringdown.—Milton Mezzrow, *Really the Blues*, p. 19, 1946
- If you come right to the point, they say you are a "bring down." —William Burroughs, *Junkie*, p. 31, 1953
- And that coming right after a big bug-sized bringdown from the Naxi's put on him.—William Lord Buckley, *Hip Einie*, 1955
- We sophisticate our tases in order to tap dance by hassles and shove the poignancy of 'bring downs' into impersonal shadows.—*Berkeley Barb*, p. 6, 18th November 1966
- To be honest, there is an element of the bring-down about the whole affair and I was feeling a bit melancholy about it all that morning[.] —*The Last Supplement to the Whole Earth Catalog*, p. 111, 1971

bring down *verb*
to depress someone, to deflate someone *US, 1935*
- What brings you down in a tale like that is not that it's phony but that it's so ture.—Mezz Mezzrow, *Really the Blues*, p. 88, 1946
- What really brought him down was the way Danny Atlas, owner of the Broadway novelty shop called Fun, Inc., gave him the big slough-off.—Bernard Wolfe, *The Late Risers*, p. 5, 1954
- The Hare Krishna boys got up and chanted, bringing most everyone down from the super-high place we had been.—*East Village Other*, 20th August 1969
- Don't let it bring you down, it's only castles burning.—Neil Young, *Don't Let It Bring You Down*, 1970
- —Eugene Landy, *The Underground Dictionary*, p. 39, 1971
- All those news reports, and the bullshit they're dragging up now. It's bringing me down.—*Airheads*, 1994
- That even seeing you in that chair can't bring me down!—*South Park*, 1999

bring it away *verb*
to effect an abortion *UK, 1984*
The 'it' in question is the foetus.

bring it, don't sing it!
used to invite action instead of words *US*
- — Ethan Hilderbant, *Prison Slang*, p. 144, 1998

bring off *verb*
1 to achieve an intended outcome, to be successful in making something happen *UK, 1928*
- I still think that, although he never really brought it off, Somerset Maugham was the most polished narrative stylist of his period. — *The Observer*, 17th December 2000

2 to induce and achieve an orgasm *UK, 1984*
- "Bring me off," I'm saying. "Finger me. Fuck me." — Kevin Sampson, *Clubland*, p. 243, 2002

bring on *verb*
to excite someone sexually *UK, 1961*

bring on the dancing girls!
a facetious call for exciting spectacle that is used as a register of boredom *UK, 1984*

bring out *verb*
to introduce someone to homosexuality, to awaken in someone their homosexuality *US, 1941*
- — Anon., *The Gay Girl's Guide*, p. 4, 1949
- — Donald Webster Cory and John P. LeRoy, *The Homosexual and His Society*, p. 262, 1963

bring to book *verb*
to bring someone to account; to cause someone to face authority, investigation or judgement *UK, 1804*

bring up *verb*
1 to vomit *UK, 1719*

2 to try someone on a criminal charge *US, 1823*
- He's dirty, for one thing. Twice brought up on assault, the people he beat up failed to show. — Elmore Leonard, *Be Cool*, p. 179, 1999

brinny *noun*
a stone, especially a small stone or pebble that is used for throwing *AUSTRALIA, 1943*
Probably from an Australian Aboriginal language.
- Brinnie: A stone a bit smaller than a yonnie, as used in brinnie fights. — Phillip Adams, *The Unspeakable Adams*, p. 50, 1977

Bris; Brissie; Brizzie *noun*
*Bris*bane *AUSTRALIA, 1945*

Brish *adjective*
British *AUSTRALIA*
From a drunken slurring; especially in Sydney. Noted by Elizabeth Lambert, 1951.

brisket *noun*
the female breast *UK*
A butcher's pun describing the cut of breast meat next to the ribs.
- — Patrick O'Shaughnessy, *Market Traders' Slang*, 1979

bristol *noun*
in tiddlywinks, a shot that moves both the player's wink and an opponent's, the manoeuvre starting and finishing with the player's wink sitting on the opponent's *UK*
The manoeuvre, dating from the 1960s, is credited eponymously to Bristol University Tiddlywinks Society.
- Most recent derivatives include 'a John O'Groats' – a disastrous attempt at a Bristol shot that closes the opponent's wink. — C.W. Edwards, *Glossary*, 1980

Bristol City; bristol *noun*
the female breast *UK, 1960*
Rhyming slang: *Bristol City* Football Club and **TITTY** (a breast); supported by an assonant connection between 'breast' and 'brist'; usually in the plural.
- [A]rses wagging and bristols going[.] — Derek Raymond (Robin Cook), *The Crust on its Uppers*, p. 30, 1962
- Her bristols pointed at me / Through a dicky [shirt] crisp and white[.] — Ronnie Barker, *Fletcher's Book of Rhyming Slang*, p. 21, 1979
- — Bob Young and Micky Moody, *The Language of Rock 'n' Roll*, p. 20, 1985
- Five-ten, nicely-sized medium-to-large bristols, hips crying out to have your hands round them[.] — John Milne, *Alive and Kicking*, p. 53, 1998

Bris-vegas *nickname*
Brisbane *AUSTRALIA*
- Getting out of the Canberra-cold for a holiday in Bris-vegas was made all the more fun by the welcome received from all players and administrators we caught up with. — *Australian Ultimate*, p. 3, 2003

Brit *noun*
a *Brit*on *UK, 1901*
- And that change from the almost affectionate poms to the dismissive Brits tells the whole story. — Bill Hornadge, *The Ugly Australian*, p. 96, 1975
- 'While I was Australian Cultural Attaché to the Court of St James in London, England, I got to suss out the Brits pretty well. — Barry Humphries, *The Traveller's Tool*, p. 7, 1985
- I'm sure the Brit always won. — Brian McDonald, *Elephant Boys*, p. 25, 2000
- The Brit who had the most success [in the US] was Mickie Most, the sharpest commercial British record producer of the sixties. — Simon Napier-Bell, *Black Vinyl White Powder*, p. 65, 2001

Brit *adjective*
*Brit*ish *AUSTRALIA*
An abbreviation, usually as a prefix. Usages include: Britflick (a UK film), Britlit (new UK writing) and *britpulp!* (an anthology of short-stories).
- [S]ex-starved Brit sheilahs[.] — Barry Humphries, *Bazz Pulls It Off!*, 1971
- The British music press love labels. When they thought up Britpop they were delighted with themselves. — Simon Napier-Bell, *Black Vinyl White Powder*, p. 313, 2001

britch *noun*
a side trouser pocket *US*
- — Hyman E. Goldin et al., *Dictionary of American Underworld Lingo*, p. 35, 1950

britches *noun*
in Newfoundland, the sac of codfish eggs found in the pregnant female *CANADA*
- "Britches" consist of the egg sacks of the female cod, and are named for their resemblance to a pair of baggy trousers. — *The Rounder*, p. 12, September 1975

Brit hop *noun*
British hip-hop *UK*
- — Alon Shulman, *The Style Bible*, p. 43, 1999

British disease *noun*
a strike or work stoppage *NEW ZEALAND*
- — Louis S. Leland, *A Personal Kiwi-Yankee Dictionary*, p. 18, 1984

British Standard Handful *noun*
the average female breast *UK, 1977*
A play on standards established by the British Standards Institute.
- — *The Independent*, p. 6, 29th October 1995
- A third nurse complained that Dr. Galea, a married man, squeezed one of her breasts and told her:"You are the three British standard handfuls." — *The Mirror*, p. 8, 25th May 1999

Britland *nickname*
Britain *UK*
- I love London! The undisputed capital of Northern Europe, my God, how can anyone live in Britland and not want to live here? — James Hawes, *White Powder, Green Light*, p. 189, 2002

Britney Spear; britney *noun*
a year *UK*
Rhyming slang, formed on the name of popular US entertainer Britney Spears.
- It's into court in front of the old vanilla fudge [judge] and Billy Fury [jury] where he gets a couple of britneys and JJ Cale [jail]. — *Getting Nowhere Fast*, 21st May 2004

Britney Spears; Britneys *noun*
beers *UK, 2001*
Popney rhyming slang, based on the name of popular entertainer Britney Spears (born 1981). Popney was contrived for *www.music365.co.uk*, an Internet music site.
- [Y]ou might want a couple of Britneys[.] — *Antiquarian Book Review*, p. 18, June 2002
- Couple of Britneys please, Peggy. — *private correspondence*, 13th March 2002

Britpop *noun*
a loose categorisation of contemporary *Brit*ish *pop*ular music *UK*
- Britpop! It may have been a naff term but it was a hell of a launching pad for a whole gamut pf British guitar pop action. — John Robb, *The Nineties*, p. 141, 1999

brittle *adjective*

(used of a computer program) functional, but easily rendered dysfunctional by changes or external stimuli which should not have the effect they have *US*

- —Eric S. Raymond, *The New Hacker's Dictionary*, p. 78, 1991

Brixton briefcase *noun*

a large portable stereo system associated, stereotypically, with black youth culture *UK, 1990*

- —Angela Devlin, *Prison Patter*, p. 31, 1996

Brizzie *noun*

▷ see: BRIS

bro *noun*

a *bro*ther, in the sense of a fellow in a given situation or condition; especially of a fellow black; also of a fellow student in UK public school usage *US, 1957*

- Crazy, bro. I gotcha.—Nathan Heard, *Howard Street*, p. 88, 1968
- "What's the tab, bro?"—Piri Thomas, *Stories from El Barrio*, p. 57, 1978
- Goodnight, bro – good dreams.—Herbert Huncke, *The Evening Sun Turned Crimson*, p. 205, 1980
- Bro? You in the "Mod Squad?"—*Copland*, 1997
- If they don't feel good about me, bro, where I'm coming from, they're not gonna listen.—Elmore Leonard, *Be Cool*, p. 8, 1999
- What are you doin' to her, dude? Oh my God, bro, dude.—*American Pie*, 1999
- A chilled-out Yardie Bro[.]—Dave Courtney, *Raving Lunacy*, p. 79, 2000
- I've got to get out of here, bro, East says[.]—Mark Powell, *Snap*, p. 19, 2001

broach *verb*

to inject an illegal drug *US*

- —Jay Robert Nash, *Dictionary of Crime*, p. 45, 1992

broad *noun*

1 a woman *US, 1911*

Somewhere between derogatory and so old-fashioned as to be charming in a hopeless way.

- "I smell Arpege," said the mama bear to her mate. "Gus, you've had a broad here."—Steve Allen, *Bop Fables*, p. 8, 1955
- During the Cal-Baylor football game, a topflight senior student and Marine veteran (last initial H.) grabbed the mike and made a fight speech to the rooting section – in the course of which he referred to women as "broads." This, UC officialdom decided,was "likely to incite to riot" – ehhhh? – and the student has been suspended for six months.'—*San Francisco Examiner*, 7th October 1956
- The only time I went out for TV was to dig the broads on Shindig and Hollywood-A-Go-Go[.]—Eldridge Cleaver, *Soul on Ice*, p. 44, 1968
- Local Women's Libbers may have been right to equate the tacky term "broad" with "nigger," and I was wrong to act snappish about it earlier this week. Let's be friends again, people – and people again, friends.—*San Francisco Chronicle*, p. 35, 21st April 1972
- Do you know one that says "faggot" also says "nigger", "broad," "chink," "kike," "spic"?—John Rechy, *The Sexual Outlaw*, p. 232, 1977
- This is the end result of all the bright lights and the comped tripus, of all the campagne and free hotel suites, and all the broads and all the booze.—*Casino*, 1995

2 a male homosexual who plays the passive sexual role *US*

- —Inez Cardozo-Freeman, *The Joint*, p. 484, 1984

3 in a deck of playing cards, a queen *UK, 1781*

- —Thomas L. Clark, *The Dictionary of Gambling and Gaming*, p. 29, 1987

4 an identity card; any paper of identification, insurance book, etc *UK*

- —Paul Tempest, *Lag's Lexicon*, 1950

5 a credit card *UK*

Extended from the previous sense.

- —David Powis, *The Signs of Crime*, 1977

broadcast *verb*

to engage in conversation *US*

- —*Swinging Syllables*, 1959

broadie *noun*

1 a woman *US, 1932*

A slightly embellished **BROAD**.

- She don't bother no one at all. Not even little broadies going by. —George Mandel, *Flee the Angry Strangers*, p. 386, 1952
- One of the broadies (as the driver referred to the madams and girls) had a couple of sixteen-year-olds in her place.—Monroe Fry, *Sex, Vice and Business*, p. 10, 1959

2 the movement of a surfer across the face of a wave *SOUTH AFRICA*

- —John M. Kelly, *Surf and Sea*, p. 281, 1965

broad joint *noun*

a bar where prostitutes are available along with the drinks *US*

- A Broad Joint can furnish you a cooperative-type girl if you'll make proper financial arrangements.—Robert Sylvester, *No Cover Charge*, p. 265, 1956

broads *noun*

playing cards *UK, 1781*

- Then we got the broads out. "Your deal, morrie."—Derek Raymond (Robin Cook), *The Crust on its Uppers*, p. 157, 1962

broadski *noun*

a woman *US*

- I hear you latched on to a broadski.—Malcolm Braly, *On the Yard*, p. 250, 1967

broad squad *noun*

in prison, a group of homosexual men *US*

- —Charles Shafer, *Folk Speech in Texas Prisons*, p. 199, 1990

broad tosser *noun*

the operator of a three-card monte game swindle *US*

- —Joe McKennon, *Circus Lingo*, p. 21, 1980

Broadway *noun*

in poker, a five-card sequence ending with an ace as the highest card of the sequence *US*

- —George Percy, *The Language of Poker*, p. 13, 1988

Broadway Arab *noun*

a Jewish person *US*

- The Pavilion catered mostly to Gentiles, and when the manager found out that three of us musicians were Broadway arabs from the tribe of Israel he wouldn't let us blow note one.—Mezz Mezzrow, *Really the Blues*, p. 86, 1946

broccoli *noun*

marijuana *US, 1969*

- —Richard A. Spears, *The Slang and Jargon of Drugs and Drink*, p. 79, 1986
- —Mike Haskins, *Drugs*, p. 286, 2003

brockly *adjective*

muscular *US*

A vegetable pun, alluding to professional wrestler Brock Lesnar.

- —Connie Eble (Editor), *UNC-CH Campus Slang*, p. 2, November 2003

Brodie; Brody *noun*

1 a fall or leap from a great height *US, 1899*

An allusion to Steve Brodie, a New York bookmaker who in 1886 claimed to have survived a leap from the Brooklyn Bridge and then opened a tavern which succeeded as a result of the publicity surrounding his claimed leap.

- I wondered if the undertaker had been born yet who was slick enough to paste a sucker's ass together after a "Brodie" fifteen-stories down.—Iceberg Slim (Robert Beck), *Pimp*, p. 165, 1969

2 a feigned drug withdrawal spasm *US, 1936*

- A drug addict's life is dedicated to cheating, lying, conniving, and 'conning' to obtain illegal drugs. It's an obsession. And they'll go to any length to achieve their purpose. They'll pull a 'Brody' or 'Cartwheel' (feigned spasms) to elicit sympathy.—*San Francisco News*, p. 1, 5th December 1951
- —David Maurer and Victor Vogel, *Narcotics and Narcotic Addiction*, p. 392, 1973

3 a failure to perform as expected *CANADA, 1976*

- Now, Gogerty, you do handy with those chicks, hear? You pull a brodie and it's your ass, right?—Hugh Garner, *The Intruders*, p. 34, 1976

4 a play that is a complete failure *US*

- —Sherman Louis Sergel, *The Language of Show Biz*, p. 29, 1973

5 a skid, usually controlled *US, 1953*

- —John Lawlor, *How to Talk Car*, p. 24, 1965
- He swung the car out into the stream of traffic, punching the gas, doing a deft brody that set off a chain of honks from cut-off motorists.—James Ellroy, *Suicide Hill*, p. 598, 1986

broform *noun*

a retail discount given to friends *US*

Snowboarder's slang; conflates **BRO** (a friend) with 'proform' (a discount given to professionals).

- —Jim Humes and Sean Wagstaff, *Boarderlands*, p. 220, 1995

brogans *noun*
heavy work shoes *US, 1835*
From the Gaelic. During the US Civil War, the sturdy and durable leather shoes issued to infantrymen were nicknamed Brogans or Jefferson Booties.
- They took one of the opened bottles with them from which Agatson drank continually, brazenly, as he stumbled along in his oversize G.I. brogans.—John Clellon Holmes, *Go*, p. 219, 1952
- Vice President Nixon will put his shoes under Ike's bed before the voters decide whether he can fill the presidential brogans.—*San Francisco News Call-Bulletin*, p. 19, 6th September 1960
- He let her up to put her skirt and shoes on while he finished lacing his brogans.—Nathan Heard, *Howard Street*, 1968
- [M]any of us bought him a beer and a Polish sausage when he came in with his paint-splattered cords and brown brogans, broke as ever.—Oscar Zeta Acosta, *The Autobiography of a Brown Buffalo*, p. 47, 1972
- The very next evening, Daddy came home with shoes for Betty, John and me – three pairs of black, sturdy, strong, steel-toed brogans.—Bobby Seale, *A Lonely Rage*, p. 37, 1978

broges *noun*
work shoes *US*
An abbreviation of **BROGANS**.
- —Charles Shafer, *Folk Speech in Texas Prisons*, p. 199, 1990

bro-ing *noun*
in market research, the testing of fashion prototypes in inner-city, predominantly black neighbourhoods *US*
From **BRO** (a fellow black) in a sense that categorises a target customer.
- So focused is Nike on borrowing style, attitude and imagery from black urban youth that the company has its own word for the practice: bro-ing—Naomi Klein, *No Logo*, p. 75, 2001

broja *noun*
heroin
- —Robert Ashton, *This Is Heroin*, p. 205, 2002
- —Mike Haskins, *Drugs*, p. 283, 2003

broke *adjective*
having little or no money, bankrupt *UK, 1661*
A variant of conventional 'broken' used in this sense from C16.
- [H]ave a look at Britain's great new upper class – broke[.]—Derek Raymond (Robin Cook), *The Crust on its Uppers*, p. 26, 1962
- I was dead skint and it's bleedin' awful being broke[.]—John Peter Jones, *Feather Pluckers*, p. 85, 1964

▸ **go for broke**
to make the utmost effort to achieve a desired end *US, 1951*
- Rather than going for broke, Sangakkara is watchful. Perhaps this will be a slow death after all[.]—*The Guardian*, 10th March 2003

broke dick *noun*
a nonfunctioning piece of hardware *US*
- —Hans Halberstadt, *Airborne*, p. 130, 1988

broke-down *noun*
a brawl *BAHAMAS*
- —Patricia Clinton-Meicholas, *More Talkin' Bahamian*, p. 24, 1995

broke money *noun*
a small amount of money given to a gambler who has lost his entire bankroll *US*
- —*The Annals of the American Academy of Political and Social Science*, p. 122, May 1950

broken *adjective*
1 in the bleed period of the menstrual cycle *US*
- My husband says I'm "broken" when I try to persuade him to have sex during my period.—a contributor *The Museum of Menstruation and Women's Health*, January 2001

2 depressed, acting oddly *US*
- —*CoEvolution Quarterly*, p. 27, Spring 1981

broken arrow *noun*
1 an accident involving nuclear weapons *US*
- Mr. Affeldt said that he learned of the incident when he received a telephone call from a regional office saying that personnel monitoring radio traffic had overheard a message containing the code word "broken arrow," which he said indicated "a major accident with a nuclear weapon aboard—*New York Times*, p. A13, 17th September 1980
- —Eric S. Raymond, *The New Hacker's Dictionary*, p. 79, 1991
- It might not have been a "broken arrow" nuclear missile accident, but a mishap that damaged a Bangor Trident submarine ballistic missiple and was kept under wraps by the Navy until this week threatens broken trust on an international scale.—*Seattle Post-Intelligencer*, p. B1, 13th March 2004

2 in computing, an error code on line 25 of a 3270 terminal *US*
- —Eric S. Raymond, *The New Hacker's Dictionary*, p. 79, 1991

broken arse *noun*
a person who has been completley subjugated *NEW ZEALAND*
Prison usage.
- —Harry Orsman, *A Dictionary of Modern New Zealand Slang*, p. 19, 1999

broken knuckles *noun*
sleeping quarters on a train *US*
- —Norman Carlisle, *The Modern Wonder Book of Trains and Railroading*, p. 260, 1946

broken rail *noun*
an older, physically run-down railway worker *US*
- —Ramon Adams, *The Language of the Railroader*, p. 22, 1977

broken wrist *noun*
an effeminate male homosexual *US*
- —Mary Swift, *Campus Slang (University of Texas)*, 1968

broker *noun*
a drug dealer *US*
- —Joseph E. Ragen and Charles Finston, *Inside the World's Toughest Prison*, p. 792, 1962
- —William D. Alsever, *Glossary for the Establishment and Other Uptight People*, p. 26, December 1970

broket *noun*
on a computer keyboard, the characters < and > *US*
A contraction of 'broken bracket'.
- —Guy L. Steele et al., *The Hacker's Dictionary*, p. 36, 1983

brolly *noun*
an umbrella *UK, 1874*
- —Louis S. Leland, *A Personal Kiwi-Yankee Dictionary*, p. 18, 1984

broly *adjective*
conforming to surfer etiquette *US*
- —Trevor Cralle, *The Surfin'ary*, p. 15, 1991

bro-man *noun*
used as a male-to-male term of address *BAHAMAS*
- —John A. Holm, *Dictionary of Bahamian English*, p. 29, 1982

bronc *noun*
in oil drilling, an inexperienced driller *US*
- —Jerry Robertson, *Oil Slanguage*, p. 32, 1954

bronch *verb*
to use a bronchoscope *UK*
Medical use.
- We've bronched him, tubed him, bagged him, [and] cathed him.—Diane Johnson, *Doctor Talk, The State of the Language*, 1980

bronco *noun*
a young male recently initiated into homosexual sex *US*
- —Dale Gordon, *The Dominion Sex Dictionary*, p. 33, 1967
- —Robert A. Wilson, *Playboy's Book of Forbidden Words*, p. 50, 1972

bronc stomper *noun*
a cowboy who specialises in the breaking of horses, i.e. getting them to accept bridle, bit and saddle *CANADA*
- His two listeners [were] watching the ranch's bronc stomper working a green colt.—E.F. Hagell, *When the Grass Was Free*, p. 48, 1954
- I shook my head, doubting that I'd ever be a bronc stomper.—Alan Fry, *Ranch on the Cariboo*, p. 122, 1962

bronski *verb*
to sandwich a face between female breasts *US*
- Ludwig Vogel managed to get bronskied by that night's headliner, Colt 45.—Howard Stern, *Miss America*, p. 336, 1995

Bronson *noun*
cocaine *UK*
From the infamous UK criminal Charlie Bronson (b.1952), with **CHARLIE** leading to 'cocaine'.

Bronx Bull *nickname*
Jake LaMotta (b.1921), a middleweight boxer who fiercely made his presence felt in the ring in the 1940s and 1950s *US*

Bronx cheer *noun*
a combination of booing and a derisory farting noise, expressing disgust *US, 1922*
- —Lou Shelly, *Hepcats Jive Talk Dictionary*, p. 22, 1945

- Bronx Cheer Hits Di Maggio At Failure to Clout Ball [Headline] — *San Francisco News*, p. 13, 13th May 1946
- I mentioned that maybe he ought to save it – meaning the Bronx cheer – till he started using his title regularly. — J.D. Salinger, *Nine Stories*, p. 98, 1953
- I kept giving "p-r-rt" Bronx cheers thru the blanket[.] — Jack Kerouac, *Letter to John Clellon Holmes*, p. 407, 19th February 1953
- [T]he hogs trained to give the Bronx cheer when the pilgrims show. — William Burroughs, *Naked Lunch*, p. 159, 1957
- [A] nation of peep freaks who prefer the bikini to the naked body, the white lie to the black truth, Hollywood smiles and canned laughter to a soulful Bronx cheer. — Eldridge Cleaver, *Soul on Ice*, p. 84, 1968
- [T]hat Bronx cheer still leads us to questions as to the critic's motivations. — Lester Bangs, *Psychotic Reactions and Carburetor Dung*, p. 75, 1971

bronze; bronza; bronzer; bronzo *noun*
the anus; the buttocks *AUSTRALIA, 1953*
Probably derives as a shade of brown.
- — D'Arcy Niland, *The Big Smoke*, 1959

bronze John *noun*
the sun *US*
- — Jerry Robertson, *Oil Slanguage*, p. 33, 1954

Bronzeville *noun*
a city neighbourhood with a largely black population *US*
- This one concerns chiefly the South Side major settlement, which its residents euphmistically call "Bronzeville." — Jack Lait and Lee Mortimer, *Chicago Confidential*, p. 32, 1950

bronze-wing *noun*
a person of part-Aboriginal and part white descent *AUSTRALIA, 1956*
From the colour of a bronze-wing pigeon.

bronzie; branzy *noun*
a sun tan; bronzed skin *UK*
- — Nigel Foster, *The Making of a Royal Marine Commando*, 1987
- You could almost get a bronzie off've that sun. — Kevin Sampson, *Outlaws*, p. 3, 2001

bronzie machine *noun*
a tanning machine *UK*
- This is fucking state of the fucking art by the way, as far as bronzie machines goes. — Kevin Sampson, *Clubland*, p. 170, 2002

broo *noun*
the employment exchange; unemployment benefit *UK*
The Scots shortened form of 'bureau'.
- If what they say is true, there could be 1,000 people to get jobs for. That would be some amount of people signing on the broo," she says. — *Irish Times*, 28th November 1998

Brookolino *nickname*
Brooklyn, New York *US*
- — Ralph de Sola, *Crime Dictionary*, p. 198, 1982

broom *noun*

1 the person who is assigned to or takes it upon himself to keep a workplace neat *US*
Sometimes embellished to 'broom man'.
- The only person he ever saw making up the bunks, however, was the "broom man," an elderly cop who served as the station-house janitor and sometimes cooked hot meals for the clerical staff on a stove in the basement. — Peter Maas, *Serpico*, p. 68, 1973
- Sweeping the steps was the precinct "broom", an old-timer no longer eager for street duty and working out retirement doing station-house chores. — Charles Whited, *Chiodo*, p. 129, 1973
- The stationhouse broom – a thirty-year hairbag who in addition to keeping the stationhouse clean was the precinct's gofer – saw his plight and shouted to him. — William J. Cavnitz, *One Police Plaza*, p. 359, 1984

2 a hat *US*
- — Robert George Reisner, *The Jazz Titans*, p. 151, 1960

broom *verb*

1 to travel *UK, 1921*
- No, no, he broomed in from the Apple, but no eyes to make it with these peasants. — Ross Russell, *The Sound*, p. 32, 1961

2 to run away, to leave *UK, 1821*
- So, what's your story, Miss Morning Glory, hip me before I broom[.] — Dan Burley, *Diggeth Thou?*, p. 48, 1959
- — John R. Armore and Joseph D. Wolfe, *Dictionary of Desperation*, p. 21, 1976

broomie *noun*
in sheep-shearing, a person employed to keep the shearing floor swept clean *AUSTRALIA, 1895*
Extended from a conventional 'broom'; also known and used by New Zealand sheep-shearers.

broom stack *noun*
a truck exhaust stack that is flaming or smoking *US*
- — *American Speech*, p. 273, December 1961: 'Northwest truck drivers' language'

broomstick *noun*
in electric line work, a phase spacer used for keeping phases from contacting each other midspan *US*
- — A.B. Chance Co., *Lineman's Slang Dictionary*, p. 2, 1980

broosted *adjective*
rich; having achieved great wealth *UK*
Extended from **BREWSTER'S** (a great deal of money).
- We are going to be broosted. — Kevin Sampson, *Clubland*, p. 119, 2002

bros before hoes
used as a rallying cry for the precedence of male friendship over relationships with females *US*
Sometimes seen as the abbreviatoin BBH.
- — Ben Applebaum and Derrick Pittman, *Turd Ferguson & The Sausage Party*, p. 6, 2004

broski; browski *noun*
used as a male-to-male term of address *US*
Doing to **BRO** what was done to **BREW**.
- — Judi Sanders, *Da Bomb*, p. 2, 1997

brothel creeper *noun*
a patron of brothels *US*
- — *Maledicta*, p. 9, Summer 1977: 'A word for it!'

brothel creepers *noun*
suede-topped, crepe-soled shoes, either of the style also known as desert boots or the thick-soled variety favoured by Teddy Boys *UK*
Originally military, from World War 2; the etymology appears to be obvious, certainly the early types of these shoes allowed for silent movement.

brothel spout *noun*
a prostitute who is physically and emotionally worn out by her work *US*
- — J.R. Schwartz, *The Official Guide to the Best Cat Houses in Nevada*, p. 164, 1993

brother *noun*

1 a black man *US, 1910*
- Everywhere he looked he saw cats in their sharp vines, chicks looking just like the ads he'd seen in the colored magazines and at every red light a "brother in his sharp wheels (car) and an ofay girl. — Babs Gonzales, *I Paid My Dues*, p. 94, 1967
- The brothers who had gathered around the table burst out laughing. — Cecil Brown, *The Life & Loves of Mr. Jiveass Nigger*, p. 60, 1969
- Young bloods wanted to be like these brothers. — H. Rap Brown, *Die Nigger Die!*, p. 15, 1969
- Both of these brothers were shot in the head. Both Brothers were members of the Central Staff of the revolutionary party. — *The Black Panther*, p. 14, 19th May 1969
- And if we got some righteous work to do for black liberation, whether it's with guns or if it's just recruiting brothers who are interested, then let's get it on[!] — Bobby Seale, *A Lonely Rage*, p. 170, 1978
- This place don't seem real popular with the brothers. — *48 Hours*, 1982
- I wouldn't go so far as to call the brother fat. He's got a weight problem. What's the nigger gonna do, he's Samoan. — *Pulp Fiction*, 1994
- Have you ever been to Montana? Not a lot of brothers there. Not too many black people in Minnesota, aside from Prince and Kirby Puckett. — Chris Rock, *Rock This!*, p. 9, 1997
- Because I know all you white folks are pissed off that the studio'd entrust a multi-million-dollar movie to a brother. — Kevin Smith, *Jay and Silent Bob Strike Back*, p. 112, 2001

2 a fellow member of a countercultural or underground political movement *US*
- Each service should be performed by a tight gang of brothers and sisters whose commitment should enable them to handle an overload of work with ability and enthusiasm. — *The Digger Papers*, p. 15, August 1968

3 in carnival usage, a woman's husband or lover *US*
- — Don Wilmeth, *The Language of American Popular Entertainment*, p. 35, 1981

4 heroin *US*
A rare variant on the common **BOY**.
- — Gilda and Melvin Berger, *Drug Abuse A-Z*, p. 38, 1990

Brother Andre's Last Erection *nickname*
the Oratory near the top of the mountain in Montreal *CANADA, 1990*
Brother Andre was a poor priest, whose charisma made him widely known in Quebec as a healer; he raised funds to build the mammoth St Joseph's Oratory, and slept in an anteroom as caretaker.

brother Ben *noun*
Benzedrine™ (amphetamine sulphate), a central nervous system stimulant, or another central nervous system stimulant *US*
- —Montie Tak, *Truck Talk*, p. 11, 1971

Brother Jonathan *nickname*
the United States *CANADA*
- Big-Brother Jonathan is no longer friendly Uncle Sam to us, but our landlord, adviser and stern disciplinarian.—*Vancouver Press*, p. 10, October 1962

brother man *noun*
used as a term of address to establish solidarity, among black men *US*
- I understand your problem, brother man, but don't come in here comin' down on me.—Vernon E. Smith, *The Jones Men*, p. 127, 1974
- Uhhh, say, look, borther man, I know the pussy is exquisite 'n all that but I got a family down in L.A. and they're missing me. Know what I mean?—Odie Hawkins, *Lost Angeles*, p. 44, 1994

broth of a boy *noun*
a boy or man who represents the absolute quintessence of what a boy or man should be *UK*
The earliest recorded instance is in Byron's *Don Juan*, 1822, however modern usage is mainly Irish and dismissed by Bernard Share as a 'Paddyism'.

brought down *adjective*
in a sad or suddenly depressed state of mind, especially after drug use *US, 1946*
- I see you've met my faithful handyman. / He's a little brought down / Because when you knocked / He thought you were the candyman. —Richard O'Brien, *The Rocky Horror Show*, 1973
- —Home Office, *Glossary of Terms and Slang Common in Penal Establishments*, July 1978

brown *noun*
1 the anus and/or rectum *US, 1916*
- —Joseph E. Ragen and Charles Finston, *Inside the World's Toughest Prison*, p. 792, 1962
- Up your brown with a Roto-Rooter – and spin it!—*Maledicta*, p. 15, Summer 1977
- Then, I'll wanna pinky you and put it in your friend's brown.—Kevin Smith, *Jay and Silent Bob Strike Back*, p. 90, 2001

2 faeces *IRELAND*
- Do none of yis [you] go up to the Hikers at all? I do, said Kenny. Yeh do in your brown, said Anto.—Roddy Doyle, *The Van*, p. 22, 1991

3 anal sex; an act of anal intercourse *UK, 1894*

4 heroin, especially if only partially refined *US*
- He explained that what addicts refer to as "The Brown" is opium which has been incompletely refined into heroin. Usually, he said, it comes from Mexico.—*San Francisco Examiner*, p. 4, 6th March 1962
- Problem is, you feel like the brown you got that enough for making a fuckin' sandwich.—Jeremy Cameron, *Brown Bread in Wengen*, p. 112, 1999
- [H]e's bringing all kinds of brown into the city[.]—Kevin Sampson, *Clubland*, p. 2, 2002
- Feels nice and still / Good thing about brown is it always will.—The Streets *Stay Positive*, 2002
- Martin had the same affinity for mind alteration as the band. That is to say total. Utter. And in particular, the brown.—Tony Wilson, *24 Hour Party People*, p. 191, 2002
- We got Rocks, we got Bones, we got Brown, we got Stones.—Julian Johnson, *Urban Survival*, p. 170, 2003

5 darker coloured hashish *US, 1981*
- —Richard A. Spears, *The Slang and Jargon of Drugs and Drink*, p. 80, 1986
- —Mike Haskins, *Drugs*, p. 286, 2003

6 an amphetamine tablet *US*
- —Carl Chambers and Richard Heckman, *Employee Drug Abuse*, p. 202, 1972

brown *verb*
1 to perform anal sex upon someone *US, 1933*
- —Donald Webster Cory and John P. LeRoy, *The Homosexual and His Society*, p. 262, 1963: 'A lexicon of homosexual slang'
- Let's just say a little friendly browning, OK?—Angelo d'Arcangelo, *The Homosexual Handbook*, p. 173, 1968

2 to force others to behave in an obsequious, sycophantic manner *UK*
- So you're the tough guy who's browning all the little ones in Amby. —Lenny McLean, *The Guv'nor*, p. 31, 1998

brown *adjective*
1 (of behaviour) obsequious, sycophantic *UK: SCOTLAND*
As in **BROWN NOSE** (a sycophant); extends from an image of submissive homage to another's backside.
- BURNEY. (To Nesbitt.) Who's the creep with the brown mooth [mouth]? NESBITT. [...] He's gawn to be the next MP for the area.—Ian Pattison, *Rab C. Nesbitt*, 1988

2 used for describing sexual activities involving excrement *UK*
- I leans back in my chair thinking about my brown adventures and the way we was both fucking covered in shite.—Kevin Sampson, *Clubland*, p. 155, 2002

3 (of a person's skin colour) white *JAMAICA*
- —Peter L. Patrick, *Some Recent Jamaican Creole Words*, 2003

brown Abe *noun*
a US penny *US*
From the engraving of President Abraham Lincoln on the coin.
- —Lou Shelly, *Hepcats Jive Talk Dictionary*, p. 22, 1945

brown acid *noun*
a type of LSD *US, 1969*
At the Woodstock festival in August 1969, there were several public address announcements recording the 'brown acid' that was 'not specifically good'.
- —Richard A. Spears, *The Slang and Jargon of Drugs and Drink*, p. 80, 1986

brown ankles *noun*
an utter sycophant *NEW ZEALAND, 1976*
An ordinary sycophant is a **BROWN NOSE**; the toady here is even further ensonced in the nether regions.
- The Prisoner's Code: I can't crawl to screws (cops, prison officers, etc) anyone who does is a 'Nark' .... or has 'brown ankles'.—*Salient*, p. 6, 12 July 1976
- —Harry Orsman, *A Dictionary of Modern New Zealand Slang*, p. 20, 1999

brown-back *noun*
a ten-shilling note *UK*
From the colour of the note; such currency was in use between 1928–40 and again from 1948–70 and withdrawn from circulation with the onset of decimalisation in 1971.

brown bag *noun*
an unmarked police car *US*
- —Radio Shack, *CBer's Handy Atlas/Dictionary*, p. 12, 1976

brown-bag *verb*
to carry lunch to work, especially in a brown paper lunch bag *US, 1968*
- He used to brown-bag down from the Bronx in the subway.—Edwin Torres, *After Hours*, p. 187, 1979

brown bagger *noun*
a married person *US, 1947*
From the image of bringing lunch packed in a brown bag to work; originally military usage.
- —*American Speech*, p. 227, October 1956: 'More United States Air Force slang'
- —*American Speech*, p. 153–154, May 1961

brown bar *noun*
in the US Army, a second lietenant *US*
The single brass bar worn by the second lieutenant was camouflaged in the field and became a single brown bar.
- I was alliteratively known as the "boot brown-bar," slang for a raw second lieutenant.—Philip Caputo, *A Rumor of War*, p. 31, 1977
- Except that the lieutenant, that fucking brown-bar ROTC idiot no more than three days in-country, had to tag along for the ride.—John Skipp and Craig Spector, *The Scream*, p. 98, 1988
- —Linda Reinberg, *In the Field*, p. 29, 1991

brown bomb *noun*
a laxative *US*
- —Charles Shafer, *Folk Speech in Texas Prisons*, p. 199, 1990

brown bomber *noun*

1 a large laxative pill, favoured by military medics since World War 2 *US, 1941*

- —Linda Reinberg, *In the Field*, p. 29, 1991

2 a type of LSD *UK, 1998*

From the colour of the capsule.

- —Mike Haskins, *Drugs*, p. 285, 2003

brown boot Army *noun*

the army as it once was *US*

- —Carl Fleischhauer, *A Glossary of Army Slang*, p. 6, 1968

Brown Bothers *noun*

the black community *UK*

- "I reckon this is down to the Brown Brothers, don't you, John." "Who?" "The Shades" I have noticed before that you have to be very current to keep up with young London coppers' slang. —John Milne, *Alive and Kicking*, p. 92, 1998

brown bottle *noun*

beer *US*

- — *Complete CB Slang Dictionary*, 1976
- Good golly, ya wouldn't consider takin' the night off havin' a few brown bottles and takin' a chance on my Indian blanket? —Gwyneth A. "Dandalion" Seese, *Tijuana Bear in a Smoke 'Um Up Taxi*, p. 30, 1977

brown bottled *adjective*

drunk on beer *UK*

- —Peter Chippindale, *The British CB Book*, p. 152, 1981

brown bottle shop *noun*

a pub *UK*

- —Peter Chippindale, *The British CB Book*, p. 152, 1981

brown boy *noun*

a male who derives sexual pleasure from eating the faeces of others *US*

- —Eugene Landy, *The Underground Dictionary*, p. 40, 1971

brown bread *adjective*

dead *UK, 1979*

Rhyming slang.

- Of course it's very easy to have a go at him now that Mr [Robert] Maxwell is brown bread[.] —Andrew Nickolds, *Back to Basics*, p. 61–62, 1994
- —Angela Devlin, *Prison Patter*, p. 31, 1996
- You could be fucking brown bread. —Greg Williams, *Diamond Geezers*, p. 17, 1997
- Never fancy getting a kicking round them cells just on account of some geezer got brown bread on my stairs. —Jeremy Cameron, *Brown Bread in Wengen*, p. 3, 1999

brown bucket *noun*

the rectum and/or anus *US*

- —Vincent J. Monteleone, *Criminal Slang*, p. 34, 1949

brown coat *noun*

in prison or borstal, a prisoner on remand or awaiting deportation *UK*

From the colour of the uniform which differentiates this type of prisoner from the majority of inmates who were, at the time of use, dressed in grey.

- —Paul Tempest, *Lag's Lexicon*, 1950

brown cow *noun*

an alcoholic drink made from coffee liqueur and cream or milk *CANADA*

It is identified in Tom Dalzell's *The Slang of Sin* as a 'barrel of beer'.

- A brown cow, in Canada, is a cocktail of coffee liqueur and milk or cream. — *Toronto Globe and Mail*, p. C6, 30th May 1998

brown crown *noun*

a notional sign of one who has failed miserably *US*

- —John D. Bell et al., *Loosely Speaking*, p. 3, 1966

brown crystal *noun*

heroin *UK, 1998*

- —Robert Ashton, *This Is Heroin*, p. 205, 2002
- —Mike Haskins, *Drugs*, p. 283, 2003

brown derby *noun*

during the Vietnam war, a hot meal that was flown to the troops in the field *US*

- —Linda Reinberg, *In the Field*, p. 29, 1991

brown dots *noun*

a type of LSD *US, 1975*

- —Richard A. Spears, *The Slang and Jargon of Drugs and Drink*, p. 80, 1986
- —Mike Haskins, *Drugs*, p. 285, 2003

brown downtown *noun*

brown heroin *US*

- — *The Bad Lieutenant*, 1992

browned off *adjective*

1 bored or fed-up with something or something *UK, 1938*

- Losing that amount [£25,000 from the value of a house] through something beyond our control does leave one feeling more than a little browned off[.] — *The Observer*, 25th May 2003

2 depressed, angry *US*

- They tell us good ol' Hap Chandler is plenty browned off at the Hollywood STars for coming out in those above-the-knee baseball panties. — *San Francisco Call-Bulletin*, p. 15, 3rd April 1950
- Do you wonder, Charlie, that I get a bit browned off? —Charles Raven, *Underworld Nights*, p. 56, 1956
- She'd been browned off at him ever since he dug up her tulip bulbs for kicks last spring. —Max Shulman, *I was a Teen-Age Dwarf*, p. 61, 1959
- — *American Speech*, p. 235, October 1964: 'Student slang in Hays, Kansas'
- —Robert J. Glessing, *The Underground Press in America*, p. 175, 1970
- I am genuinely browned off. That's why I called you here. —John Milne, *Alive and Kicking*, p. 133–134, 1998

brown eye *noun*

the anus *US, 1954*

- The video continues as Stag fucks Trinity's brown eye while she finishes reaming North. — *Adult Video*, August/September 1986
- — *Adult Video News*, p. 42, August 1995
- I stick these little pieces of paper over my brown-eye, and bam – no shit stains in my undies. —Kevin Smith, *Jay and Silent Bob Strike Back*, p. 13, 2001

brown-eyed cyclops *noun*

the anus *UK*

In Greek mythology the Cyclops were one-eyed giants; the imagery employed here is clear.

- [She] gets on her knees on the bed and suddenly I'm staring at the brown-eyed Cyclops. —Ben Elton, *High Society*, p. 215, 2002

brown eyes *noun*

the female breasts, especially the nipples *US, 1932*

- —Collin Baker et al., *College Undergraduate Slang Study Conducted at Brown University*, p. 89, 1968
- — *Maledicta*, p. 131, Summer/Winter 1982: 'Dyke diction: the language of lesbians'

Brown family *noun*

collectively, all passive participants in anal sex *US*

- —Hyman E. Goldin et al., *Dictionary of American Underworld Lingo*, p. 149, 1950

brown-hatter *noun*

a homosexual man *UK, 1950*

- —Walter Baxter, *Look Down in Mercy*, 1951

brown helmet

a notional sign of one who has been rejected in romance *US*

- —Fred Hester, *Slang on the 40 Acres*, p. 17, 1968

brownie *noun*

1 the anus *US, 1927*

- She bends over to pick up the suit. Look at that. Taking my picture with her brownie. —Elmore Leonard, *Split Images*, p. 193, 1981

2 a sycophant *US*

An abbreviation of **BROWN NOSER**.

- —Kenn "Naz" Young, *Naz's Dictionary of Teen Slang*, p. 15, 1993

3 a homosexual, especially one of wealth or position *US, 1916*

- —David Powis, *The Signs of Crime*, 1977

4 a notation of bad conduct or poor work performance; a demerit *US, 1910*

- On some roads, merit marks given for exceptional service offset the brownies. Named after man who invented the system, reputedly a Superintendent Brown on the New Haven. —Norman Carlisle, *The Modern Wonder Book of Trains and Railroading*, p. 260, 1946

5 a black person *UK*

Coincidental to the US sense (a brown-skinned Asian).

- Brownies are fast runners aren't they? — *an 8 year old girl, South Wales*, 14th July 2002

6 a traffic police officer *US*

- —Carsten Stroud, *Close Pursuit*, p. 269, 1987

7 a police radar unit used for measuring vehicle speed *US*
An allusion to the camera brand, a metaphor for radar.
- — "Slingo", *The Official CB Slang Dictionary Handbook*, p. 11, 1976

8 in trucking, a three-speed auxiliary gearbox *US*
Originally manufactured by the Brownolite Transmission Company, hence the diminutive.
- — Montie Tak, *Truck Talk*, p. 19, 1971

9 marijuana *US*
- The man at the door was the old dope peddler with his bag of brownie, also known as pot, shit, cannabis, or to the staid, marihuana. — Roger Gordon, *Hollywood's Sexual Underground*, p. 150, 1966

10 any amphetamine; MDMA, the recreational drug best known as ecstasy *UK*
Originally 'amphetamines', from the colour; hence, via confused recreational drug-users, 'ecstasy'.
- CALL IT... Adam, brownies, burgers, disco biscuits, doves, eckies, tulips, X[.] JUST DON'T CALL IT... MDMA – too scientific — *Drugs An Adult Guide*, p. 34, December 2001

11 an empty beer bottle *NEW ZEALAND*
- You return your empties. You know they've sunk as many as you have and it's a fair bet their own garden sheds are bursting with brownies. — *Star*, p. 2, 3rd January 1979

brownie point *noun*
an imaginary award or credit for a good deed *US, 1953*
- He was tryin' to make brownie points with some of the boys. — *Raising Arizona*, 1987
- Give yourself a Brownie point for everyone you recognise[.] — Dave Courtney, *Stop the Ride I Want to Get Off*, p. 365, 1999
- More brownie points for me[.] — Duncan MacLaughlin, *The Filth*, p. 113, 2002

brownie queen *noun*
a male homosexual who enjoys the passive role in anal sex *US*
- A 'brownie queen' is a homosexual male interested primarily in being the passive partner in anal intercourse. — James Harper, *Homo Laws in all 50 States*, p. 147, 1968
- We call that a brownie queen. In prison they call it under-yonder and round-brown. — Bruce Jackson, *In the Life*, p. 397, 1972

brownies *noun*
1 the female breasts, especially the nipples *US*
- — *Maledicta*, p. 131, Summer/Winter 1982: 'Dyke diction: the language of lesbians'

2 dice that have had their spots altered for cheating *US*
More commonly known as 'busters', which leads to the cartoon character 'Buster Brown', which leads to 'Brown'.
- — *The Annals of the American Academy of Political and Social Sciences*, p. 122, May 1950

Browning Sister *noun*
a male homosexual *US, 1941*
From **BROWN** (anal sex). A term used in the 1940s.

brown job *noun*
1 a soldier *UK, 1943*
From the khaki uniform.
- — John W. Mussell, *Militarisms*, p. 15, 1995

2 oral-anal sex *US*
- — Eugene Landy, *The Underground Dictionary*, p. 40, 1971

brown list *noun*
an imagined list of those in disfavour *UK*
A euphemistic **SHIT LIST**.
- Then when they are finally forced to let you go the police will keep you on their brown list for the rest of your life. — John Milne, *Alive and Kicking*, p. 86, 1998

brown lover *noun*
a person with a fetishistic love of excrement *US*
- This series was started by some brown lovers like yourself[.] — Peter Sotos, *Index*, p. 61, 1996

brownmouth *noun*
a talkative fool *IRELAND*
- — *Great Tuam Annual*, p. 87, 1991

brown nose; brown noser *noun*
a toady; a sycophant *US, 1938*
Originally military.
- You are such a brown-noser. — *Clueless*, 1995
- I'm sorry you've got to eat shit from a hack brownnoser like Krantz[.] — Robert Crais, *L.A. Requiem*, p. 97, 1999

brown-nose *verb*
to curry favour in a sycophantic fashion *US, 1938*
- — *American Speech*, p. 54, February 1947: 'Pacific War language'
- Don't try and brownnose me Mike. — Hubert Selby Jr, *Last Exit to Brooklyn*, p. 143, 1957
- No wonder the world was going to hell when a grown man pranced around in a monkey suit, brown-nosing dames who made a big deal out of ordering a belt of booze! — Jim Thompson, *The Grifters*, p. 78, 1963
- "Nick," she said when I had finished, "six months ago you were just another brownnosing honor student. What happened?" — C.D. Payne, *Youth in Revolt*, p. 334, 1993
- Now you're gonna brown nose me? Don't be doing me any more favors, Pancho. — *Airheads*, 1994
- [J]ust do your music and leave it to a bit of mystiqure and charisma, rather than trying to brown nose every individual member of an audience. — *X-Ray*, p. 20, April 2003

Brown Nurses *nickname*
Our Lady's Nurses (for the Poor), a Catholic organisation founded in 1913 *AUSTRALIA*
From the brown uniform.

brown one; brown 'un *noun*
on the railways, a distant signal *UK*
- — Harvey Sheppard, *Dictionary of Railway Slang*, 1970

brownout *noun*
a near but not complete loss of consciousness *US*
Not quite a 'blackout'.
- An occasional brownout on a couch where I accidentally sat on a hypodermic needle full of heroin took time too. — Larry Rivers, *What Did I Do?*, p. 47, 1992

brown paper *noun*
1 a sycophant *US, 1968*
A logical extension of **ASSWIPE**.
- — Frederic G. Cassidy, *Dictionary of American Regional English, Volume 1*, p. 396, 1985

2 a caper in the sense of an occupation or racket *UK, 1974*
Rhyming slang.
- What's your bown paper then? — Ray Puxley, *Cockney Rabbit*, p. 24, 1992

brown-paper roll *noun*
a cigarette hand-rolled in brown paper *BAHAMAS*
- — John A. Holm, *Dictionary of Bahamian English*, p. 29, 1982

brown rhine; brown rine *noun*
heroin *US, 1953*
From the colour and a pronunciation of 'heroin'.
- — Richard A. Spears, *The Slang and Jargon of Drugs and Drink*, p. 80, 1986
- — Robert Ashton, *This Is Heroin*, p. 205, 2002
- — Mike Haskins, *Drugs*, p. 283, 2003

browns *noun*
the uniform issued to a prisoner on remand or awaiting deportation in borstals and detention centres *UK*
From the colour.
- — Home Office, *Glossary of Terms and Slang Common in Penal Establishments*, July 1978

brown shoes *noun*
a person who does not use drugs *US*
- — William D. Alsever, *Glossary for the Establishment and Other Uptight People*, p. 23, December 1970

brown shower *noun*
an act of defecation as part of sadomasochistic sex play *UK*
- — Caroline Archer, *Tart Cards*, 2003

brown slime *noun*
a mixture of cola syrup and nutmeg, used as a substitute for drugs by the truly desperate *US*
- — Jay Robert Nash, *Dictionary of Crime*, p. 46, 1992

brown stuff *noun*
opium *US, 1950*
- — Angela Devlin, *Prison Patter*, p. 31, 1996

brown sugar *noun*
1 grainy, poor quality heroin *US*
- But now something new and more deadly has been added to the bazaar's wares – "brown sugar," an opium derivative close to heroin. — *Washington Post*, p. A22, 26th March 1981
- — Richard A. Spears, *The Slang and Jargon of Drugs and Drink*, p. 80, 1986

- [W]ith "Brown Sugar" [a record released in 1971], which compared the taste of unrefined heroin to a black dancer's pussy, [the Rolling Stones] let the public know they had jumped the divide between soft and hard drugs. — *Black Vinyl White Powder*, p. 124, 2001
- — Robert Ashton, *This Is Heroin*, p. 205, 2002
- Chinese-made ammonium chloride, which transforms the morphine into the lower-grade No. 3 heroin, or "brown sugar," as it is popularly known — *New York Times*, p. SM27, 23rd June 2002

2 a black woman, especially a beautiful one *US*
Originally black use only, from the skin colour and a suggestion of sweetness.
- Brown sugar; how come you taste so good / Brown sugar; just like a young girl should[.] — The Rolling Stones *Brown Sugar*, 1971

3 by extension, a sexually desirable black man *US*
Adopted by black women.
- And what about D'Angelo? / I want some of that brown sugar / And watch this rap bitch bust all over ya nuts[.] — Lil' Kim *Dreams*, 1996

4 a coarse, unrefined person *AUSTRALIA*
Shameless and clever.
- — Ned Wallish, *The Truth Dictionary of Racing Slang*, p. 10, 1989

brown tape *noun*
heroin *UK*
- — Robert Ashton, *This Is Heroin*, p. 205, 2002

brown tongue *noun*
an informer *UK*
The disdainful image of an informer licking the anus of authority.
- — Angela Devlin, *Prison Patter*, p. 31, 1996

brown trout *noun*
faeces, when thrown by prisoners from their cells onto guards *US*
- — William K. Bentley and James M. Corbett, *Prison Slang*, p. 89, 1992

brown 'un *noun*
▷ see: **BROWN ONE**

brown underpants *noun*
used as a symbol of extreme fear or cowardice *UK*
An image of soiled underwear.
- She figures, he'll spot me and have an attack of the brown underpants[.] — John Milne, *Alive and Kicking*, p. 217, 1998

brown water navy *noun*
during the Vietnam war, the US Navy presence on rivers and deltas *US*
- — Linda Reinberg, *In the Field*, p. 29, 1991

brown windsor *noun*
▷ see: **WINDSOR CASTLE**

brown wings *noun*
experience of anal intercourse, or anal-oral sexual contact, considered as an achievement *US*
Originally Hell's Angel usage; 'brown' (the colour associated with the anus) plus 'wings' (badge of honour).
- Most of the Frisco chapter earned their brown wings on this occasion. It was some shindig! The queen never had it so good! — Jamie Mandelkau, *Buttons*, p. 101, 1971
- But if you're the proud owner of an enormous penis and you still want to get your brown wings, the way is not to ask, it's to do. — *GQ*, p. 117, July 2001

browski *noun*
▷ see: **BROSKI**

Bruce *noun*
used as a stereotype of an effeminate male homosexual *US*
- Too Many 'Bruce' Jokes [Headline] — *San Francisco Examiner*, p. 27, 28th May 1973

Bruce Lee *noun*
an erect nipple *UK*
Clever but misinformed pun on San Francisco-born martial arts film actor Bruce Lee as a **HARD** (muscular) **NIP** (a Japanese person); in fact Bruce Lee (1940–73) was a native of Hong Kong not Japan. From private correspondence, March 2002.

bruck *noun*
in western Canada, a combination bus and truck *CANADA*
- Last year a bruck was used to cross the ice as long as possible. According to one official, the brucks carry everything from "soup to nuts." — *Edmonton Journal*, p. 3/3, 1st August 1961

bruckins *noun*
a noisy, rowdy party *JAMAICA*
- — Richard Allsopp, *Dictionary of Caribbean English Usage*, p. 118, 1996

brud *noun*
used as a friendly term of address *NORFOLK ISLAND*
- — Beryl Nobbs Palmer, *A Dictionary of Norfolk Words and Usages*, p. 5, 1992

bruiser *noun*
1 a rugged physical specimen; a thug *UK, 1742*
- If you fell behind with your rent the prince sent a couple of bruisers round to punch seven bells out of you. — John Peter Jones, *Feather Pluckers*, p. 17, 1964
- — Collin Baker et al., *College Undergraduate Slang Study Conducted at Brown University*, p. 89, 1968
- "Christ, he'll be an incredible bruiser," I continued. — Erich Segal, *Love Story*, p. 102, 1970

2 a club *BAHAMAS*
Used for beating sediment out of sponges.
- — John A. Holm, *Dictionary of Bahamian English*, p. 30, 1982

brukdown *noun*
a noisy, rowdy party *BELIZE*
- — Richard Allsopp, *Dictionary of Caribbean English Usage*, p. 118, 1996

bruk up *verb*
to thrash someone, to beat up someone *UK*
Early C21 black youth usage; an elision of 'break up' and **FUCK UP** (to destroy).
- [T]he kid said: "I'm jacking [mugging] you. I'm not your friend. I'll bruk you up." (Luckily he didn't.) — *The Guardian*, p. 9, 27th February 2002

brumby *noun*
a feral horse *AUSTRALIA, 1880*
Origin unknown. Various conjectures, such as an eponymous Major Brumby, or that an Aboriginal language is the source, are based on no solid evidence.
- Alice said I was once knocked out by a brumby mare that bucked and threw me. — Herb Wharton, *Cattle Camp*, p. 120, 1994

brummy; brummie *adjective*
from Birmingham, England *UK, 1941*
Both the city of Birmingham and its inhabitants can be called 'Brum'. From Brummagem; the local spelling was a phonetic reflection of the local pronunciation: 'Brummagem' = Bromwichham (after Bromwich), in turn a corruption of Brimidgeham, the old form of Birmingham. Brummagem has an obsolete sense as 'counterfeit, inferior or fake' (of coins, antiques, etc.) as Birmingham was a centre of manufacture for such articles in the C17 and C18.
- One has to concede, however, that he had something of a problem when initial research for the promotion threw up only two names that the target market – "well-informed businessmen" – associated with the city: Janice ("Oi'l give it fove" of pop jury fame and Marlene (the lady with the big earings and thick Brummy accent played by actress Beryl Reid) — *Financial Times*, p. 31, 21st October 1983
- I remember a fellow recruit, a man from Birmingham, exclaiming, in a very Brummy accent, 1952, "Ooh! A letter from tart! I'm off to the lats for a wank!"' — *Beale*, 1984
- [We] were sent to this car show at the NEC, up in Brum, for the weekend. — Danny King, *The Burglar Diaries*, p. 107, 2001
- Now Julie Walters wants to follow in their footsteps by playing Lady Macbeth with her native Birmingham accent. "I did it first about 17 years ago, with Bernard Hill as the King," she says. "This time, however, I want to do it with a Brummy accent. Shakespeare makes a lot more sense when you do him in Brummy. — *The Express*, p. 39, 23rd October 2003

brush *noun*
1 female pubic hair *AUSTRALIA, 1941*
- — Eugene Landy, *The Underground Dictionary*, p. 40, 1971
- — David McGill, *David McGill's Complete Kiwi Slang Dictionary*, p. 22, 1998

2 a moustache *US, 1824*
- — J. E. Lighter, *Historical Dictionary of American Slang, Volume 1*, p. 278, 1994

3 an intravenous injection of an illegal drug *US*
- — Jay Robert Nash, *Dictionary of Crime*, p. 47, 1992

4 a person who organises the seating for card players *UK*
- In small cardrooms the brush, chip runner, and floorperson positions are often filled be [sic] a single person. — Dave Scharf, *Winning at Poker*, p. 233, 2003

5 a technique for introducing altered dice into a game as the dice are passed from player to shooter *US*
Also known as a 'brush-off'.
- — *The Annals of the American Academy of Political and Social Sciences*, p. 122, May 1950

brush *verb*
to introduce marked cards or loaded dice into a game *US*
- — Frank Scoblete, *Guerrilla Gambling*, p. 299, 1993

▶ **brush your teeth and comb your hair**
in trucking, to slow down to the legal speed limit because of the presence of police ahead *US*
- — Elementary Electronics, *Dictionary of CB Lingo*, p. 54, 1976

brush ape *noun*
an unsophisticated rustic *US, 1920*
- — Joseph A. Weingarten, *An American Dictionary of Slang*, p. 45, 1954

brusher; brushman *noun*
a casino employee who tries to lure casino visitors into playing poker *US*
- — George Percy, *The Language of Poker*, p. 13, 1988

brush-off *noun*
a rejection *US, 1938*
- [S]he reminded him of Lindy whom he'd given the brush-off. — Wilda Moxham, *The Apprentice*, p. 174, 1969
- [H]e got negative responses, distinguished only by hostile looks and shakes of the head from low-rider types who made him for fuzz and annoyed brush-offs from young women who didn't like his style. — James Ellroy, *Because the Night*, p. 312, 1984
- Give councillor the brush off. — *Wanstead and Woodford Guardian*, 22nd August 2003

Brussels sprout; brussel *noun*
1 a Boy Scout, a Scout *UK*
Rhyming slang, since about 1910.

2 a tout, either of the ticket or racing tipster variety *UK*
Rhyming slang.
- — Ray Puxley, *Cockney Rabbit*, p. 24, 1992

brutal *adjective*
1 extremely good, intense *US, 1964*
- — *Time*, p. 56, 1st January 1965
- — Connie Eble (Editor), *UNC-CH Campus Slang*, p. 2, Fall 1987

2 terrible, very bad *US, 1983*
- Your show is fucking brutal, man. Get off the air. — Howard Paul, *The Joy*, p. 42, 1996
- Howaraya, God, Maggie, sorry I'm dead late, but the traffic was only brutal around town. — *Sunday Tribune*, 1st December 1996
- Have ye had da [the] curry sauce over here? Fookin [fucking] brutal, man. — Paul Howard, *Ross O'Carroll-Kelly*, p. 119, 2003

brutally *adverb*
very *US*
- Christian is brutally hot, and I am going to remember tonight forever. — *Clueless*, 1995

brute *noun*
1 any large vehicle or vessel that is difficult to handle *US, 1860*
- — J. E. Lighter, *Historical Dictionary of American Slang, Volume 1*, p. 279, 1994

2 in the television and film industries, a large spotlight used to simulate sunlight *US*
- — Oswald Skilbeck, *ABC of Film and TV Working Terms*, p. 21, 1960
- — Tony Miller and Patricia George, *Cut! Print!*, p. 44, 1977

brute force *noun*
in computing, a simplistic and unsophisticated programming style *US*
- — Eric S. Raymond, *The New Hacker's Dictionary*, p. 80, 1991

brute force and ignorance *noun*
physicality applied without thought; also, a deliberate disregard for tact or delicacy *UK, 1930*
A catchphrase that means exactly what it says, usually jocular.

bruv *noun*
a brother; a friend; used as a friendly form of address from one man to another *UK*
A phonetic abbreviation.
- You should get to hospital, bruv[.] — Jimmy Stockin, *On The Cobbles*, p. 38, 2000
- — Julian Johnson, *Urban Survival*, p. 258, 2003

bruz *noun*
used as a term of address, man to man *US, 1958*
- — Robert S. Gold, *A Jazz Lexicon*, p. 42, 1964

BS *noun*
bullshit, in all its senses *US, 1900*
A euphemism accepted in polite society.
- Elijah shared the indulgent smiles of the men who had graciously granted Monkeydude some b.s. time. — Odie Hawkins, *Chicago Hustle*, p. 7, 1977
- What a bunch of B.S. — Beatrice Sparks (writing as 'Anonymous'), *Jay's Journal*, p. 146, 1979
- We have more lesbians working there, or they are bisexual. That's because they have to put up with men all night long and listen to all that BS. — Marilyn Suriani Futterman, *Dancing Naked in the Material World*, p. 57, 1992
- No B.S. Where do you work out? — *Boogie Nights*, 1997
- She's way too smart to fall for your line of b.s. — *Cruel Intentions*, 1999

BS and bells *noun*
in firefighter usage, a long period with activity *US*
- — *American Speech*, p. 274, December 1954: 'Fire terms: Additional words and definitions'

BSH *noun*
the average female breast *UK, 1977*
An abbreviation of **BRITISH STANDARD HANDFUL**, a play on BSI standards set by the British Standards Institute.
- — *The Independent*, p. 6, 29th October 1995

B-squared *noun*
a brassiere *UK*
Schoolgirl slang, presumably also written B^2.
- — Mallory Wober, *English Girls' Boarding Schools*, 1971

BT *noun*
1 the posterior, the buttocks *UK: SCOTLAND*
By elision, a euphemism for 'bottom'.
- Usually she'd hit him on the BT or the legs[.] — Christopher Brookmyre, *Not the End of the World*, p. 170, 1998

2 an inhalation of marijauna smoke filtered through a water-pipe *US*
An abbreviation of '**BONG** toke'.
- — Pamela Munro, *U.C.L.A. Slang*, p. 113, 1997

BT Baracus *noun*
a child who lives in a house without a phone; subsequently a child without a mobile phone *UK*
Derives from a reliance on BT (British Telecom) and a play on the character BA Baracus played by Mr T in the television adventure series *The A Team*, 1984–88.
- — Jonathan Blyth, *The Law of the Playground*, p. 20, 2004

BTI *noun*
television interference with a citizens' band signal *US*
An abbreviation of '*b*oob *t*ube *i*nterference'.
- — "Slingo", *The Official CB Slang Dictionary Handbook*, p. 12, 1976

BTM *noun*
the posterior, the buttocks *UK, 1937*
A domestic euphemism for 'bottom'.

BTO *noun*
an influential and admired person *US, 1944*
A '*b*ig-*t*ime *o*perator' – not without overtones of swarminess.
- — *Cosmopolitan*, p. 76, October 1949
- We'd raced tanks down hills, chased big-time operators (BTOs) who tried to screw us in our small-time forays into the black market, fought in the TRUST 15th Tank Company smokers[.] — David H. Hackworth, *About Face*, p. 219, 1989

BTW
used in computer message shorthand to mean '*b*y *t*he *w*ay' *US*
- — Eric S. Raymond, *The New Hacker's Dictionary*, p. 342, 1991
- Orient Road looks like a fucking resort, btw[.] — Eleusis *Lightning on the Sun [The Howard Marks Book of Dope Stories]*, p. 325, 2001

BU *noun*
sexual attraction *US, 1934*
An abbreviation of '*b*iological *u*rge'.
- — Joseph A. Weingarten, *An American Dictionary of Slang*, p. 45, 1954

Bu; the Bu; Mother Bu *nickname*
Malibu, California *US*
• —*The Surfin'ary*, p. 16, 1991

BUAG *noun*
a simple drawing made with computer characters *US*
A 'big ugly ASCII graphic'.
• —Christian Crumlish, *The Internet Dictionary*, p. 27, 1995

bub *noun*
1 used as a term of address, usually to a stranger and usually in a condescending tone *US, 1839*
• "Having trouble, bub?" I grinned at him.—Mickey Spillane, *I, The Jury*, p. 90, 1947
• "Call it a dollar for the shirt and pants," he said. "What size you wear, bub?"—Jim Thompson, *Bad Boy*, p. 382, 1953
• "Looks like you've got a ticket, bub!" said a voice somewhere behind him.—Terry Southern, *The Magic Christian*, p. 14, 1959
2 the female breast *UK, 1826*
• A flask that fits over her bubs.—Irving Shulman, *The Amboy Dukes*, p. 99, 1947
• —Dale Gordon, *The Dominion Sex Dictionary*, p. 33, 1967
3 a baby *AUSTRALIA*
• Too many bubs were going the squeal after sitting with Ed.—Roy Slaven (John Doyle), *Five South Coast Seasons*, p. 59, 1992
• But with the bub due on September 10, the middle of the finals season, their timing is a little unfortunate.—*Daily Telegraph*, p. 14, 22nd April 2002
• —Kel Richards, *The Aussie Bible*, p. 15, 2003
4 a blue flashing police car light *US*
• The blue flashers, called bubbles or bubs by the troopers, on top of the cruiser were dead and dark.—Stephen King, *The Tommyknockers*, p. 675, 1987

bubba *noun*
1 a stereotypical white, southern male *US, 1982*
• —*American Speech*, p. 100, Spring 1993: 'Among the new words'
2 a friend, especially as a term of address *US*
A variation of **BROTHER**.
• Fuckin' A, bubba.—*The Right Stuff*, 1983
3 marijuana *US*
• —Jim Emerson-Cobb, *Scratching the Dragon*, April 1997

bubbie circus *noun*
a chorus line or other display of multiple women with large breasts *US*
• —Dale Gordon, *The Dominion Sex Dictionary*, p. 33, 1967

bubbies and cunt *noun*
a poor woman's dowry *US*
• —Dale Gordon, *The Dominion Sex Dictionary*, p. 33, 1967

bubblate *verb*
to idle, to pass time with friends *US*
• We weren't causing any problem. We were just bubblatin'.—Rick Ayers (Editor), *Berkeley High Slang Dictionary*, p. 14, 2004

bubble *noun*
1 an informer *UK*
From rhyming slang **BUBBLE AND SQUEAK** (to inform).
• —Angela Devlin, *Prison Patter*, p. 31, 1996
2 a glass-enclosed control panel on a vehicle of any sort *US*
• [T]hey had chest protectors up to their eyeballs. So many, in fact, that they kept the extras up in the chin bubbles.—Robert Mason, *Chickenhawk*, p. 402, 1983
• The tour of the ship began in the waist catapult control cab, known as the waist bubble. A similar control cab was on the bow, situated between the cats. Here on the waist the bubble sat on the catwalk outboard of Cat Four.—Stephen Coonts, *Final Flight*, p. 130, 1988
3 an aeroplane cockpit *US*
• —*American Speech*, p. 122, Summer 1986: 'The language of naval fighter pilots'
4 in motor racing, a clear plastic dome that covers the driver *US*
• —John Lawlor, *How to Talk Car*, p. 24, 1965
5 in the television and film industries, an incandescent electric light bulb *US*
• —Oswald Skilbeck, *ABC of Film and TV Working Terms*, p. 21, 1960
6 a specialisation *US*
• Don't laugh it off, buddy. Sweetheart scams are my bubble.—Stephen Cannell, *Big Con*, p. 298, 1997
7 an instance of weeping *UK: SCOTLAND*
• I had a wee bubble.—Michael Munro, *The Original Patter*, 1985

▸**on the bubble**
1 engaged in swindling as a career *US*
• Stuart Bates, like Carol Sesnick, was one of the few Bates family members who wasn't on the bubble.—Stephen Cannell, *Big Con*, p. 357, 1997
2 in motor racing, in one of the lower spots in the qualifying stage of an event, subject to being displaced by a better performance of another car *US*
• —John Edwards, *Auto Dictionary*, p. 117, 1993
3 in motor racing, the most favourable starting position (the pole position) *US*
• —*Hot Rod Magazine*, p. 13, November 1948

bubble *verb*
1 to weep *UK: SCOTLAND*
• What are you bubblin for?—Michael Munro, *The Original Patter*, 1985
2 to kill someone by injecting air into their veins *US*
• —Ralph de Sola, *Crime Dictionary*, p. 21, 1982

bubble and squeak *noun*
1 an act of urination *AUSTRALIA*
Rhyming slang for **LEAK**.
• —John Ayto, *The Oxford Dictionary of Rhyming Slang*, p. 42, 2002
2 a week *UK*
Rhyming slang.
• —Ronnie Barker, *Fletcher's Book of Rhyming Slang*, p. 29, 1979
3 a Greek *UK, 1938*
Rhyming slang; derogatory. Can be shortened to 'bubble', or used in the plural form 'bubbles and squeaks' to refer to Greeks and Cypriots, collectively.
• —*The Observer*, 1st March 1959
• [M]alts [Maltese], spades [black people], bubbles and the queens [homosexuals].—Derek Raymond (Robin Cook), *The Crust on its Uppers*, p. 58, 1962
• the local greasy spoon cafe run by a family of bubbles—Duncan MacLaughlin, *The Filth*, p. 93, 2002

bubble and squeak; bubble; bubble up *verb*
to inform on someone *UK, 1961*
The original rhyming slang meaning was 'to speak'; hence 'to speak about', 'to inform'.
• "They told me to keep dog. Then they came running out and I ran with them." And I kept on bubbling.—Andy McNab, *Immediate Action*, p. 10, 1995
• It wasn't defiance, misplaced loyalty, fear of what Roy would do if he found out I bubbled him up, or anything like that made me keep quiet.—J.J. Connolly, *Know Your Enemy [britpulp]*, p. 159, 1999
• If I scorned Gloria she might bubble me to Benjo, and that would be that.—Jonathan Gash, *The Ten Word Game*, p. 15, 2003

Bubbleberry *noun*
in British Columbia, a hybrid variety of marijuana *CANADA*
• Shishkaberry, like the currently popular Bubbleberry, is a hybrid developed from a strain called Blueberry.—Brian Preston, *Pot Planet*, p. 5, 2002

bubble brain *noun*
a distracted, unfocused person *US*
• —*Wesleyan Alumnus*, p. 29, Spring 1981
• [O]r maybe a blond bubble-brain to show the poor niggers that drug bucks could buy what you couldn't score with a high school diploma or a hard-muscled bod.—Jess Mowry, *Way Past Cool*, p. 25, 1992

bubble-burner *noun*
in trucking, an engine run on propane gas *US*
• —Montie Tak, *Truck Talk*, p. 20, 1971

bubble chaser *noun*
a bombadier on a bomber aircraft *US, 1945*
A reference to the bubbles in the levelling device used.
• —*American Speech*, p. 310, December 1946: 'More Air Force slang'

bubble dance *verb*
to wash dishes *US*
• —Marcus Hanna Boulware, *Jive and Slang of Students in Negro Colleges*, 1947

bubble-dancer *noun*
a person employed as a dishwasher *US*
• —Harold Wentworth and Stuart Berg Flexner, *Dictionary of American Slang*, p. 66, 1960

bubblegum *noun*

1 the posterior, the buttocks, especially of a curvaceous woman *UK*
Rhyming slang for **BUM**.
- —Ray Puxley, *Fresh Rabbit*, p. 14, 1998

2 cocaine; crack cocaine *UK, 1998*
Probably a play on Bazooka™, a branded bubble-gum, and **BAZOOKA** (cocaine; crack).
- —Mike Haskins, *Drugs*, p. 281, 2003

3 a hybrid marijuana with a sweet 'pink' taste *UK*
- —Nick Jones, *Spliffs*, p. 67, 2002

bubblegum *adjective*

unimaginative, highly commercial, insincere *US, 1963*
Usually used to describe music.
- We had an hysterical call from Buddah Records complaining about the way I insulted their bubblegum music.—*Screw*, p. 17, 4th July 1969
- A coke-jerking rhythm, a Woody Woodpecker voice, a scoopful of cliches from a bin labeled "sweet talk" and you've got – bubble-gum music.—*Life*, p. 13, 30th January 1970
- —Connie Eble (Editor), *UNC-CH Campus Slang*, October 1972

bubble gum machine *noun*

1 a vehicle with flashing lights especially a police car *US, 1968*
Sometimes shortened to 'bubble machine'.
- —*Dictionary of American Regional English*, 1966–68
- —*Complete CB Slang Dictionary*, 1976
- [D]id you know there was a Texas Bubblegum Machine on your back door?—*Smokey and the Bandit*, 1977
- —Peter Chippindale, *The British CB Book*, p. 153, 1981

2 the H-13 army helicopter *US*
Vietnam war usage.
- —Carl Fleischhauer, *A Glossary of Army Slang*, p. 7, 1968

bubblegummer *noun*

a pre-teenager or young teenager *US*
- —William D. Alsever, *Glossary for the Establishment and Other Uptight People*, p. 32, December 1970
- She was the force behind subversive club chapters starting on her high school campus when she was still a bubblegummer.—Joseph Wambaugh, *The Blue Knight*, p. 78, 1973

bubblehead *noun*

1 a person whose thinking is not grounded in reality *US*
- By now it is obvious even to the bubbleheads that we exorcised one set of devils from the earth in 1945 only to make room for another equally evil horde.—Daniel V. Gallery, *Clear the Decks*, p. 221, 1945

2 a submariner *US*
- I live in a submarine. I'm a bubblehead, and that gives me a certain point of view.—Mark Joseph, *To Kill the Potemkin*, p. 81, 1986
- —*Seattle Times*, p. A9, 12th April 1998

bubbler *noun*

a water tank or cooler *US*
Korean war usage. Also heard in New South Wales and Queensland.
- Buck must have carried a filled canteen all the way from Pavuvu. It was brackish. "Why didn't you fill it from the bubblers on the transport?" I asked him.—Russell Davis, *Marine at War*, p. 50, 1961
- Dryness gripped my throat; I went to a stone drinking fountain and drank from the bubbler.—Frank Hardy, *But The Dead Are Many*, p. 312, 1975

bubble team *noun*

a sports team that might or might not make a play-off or be invited to a tournament *US*
- I hope we could be a bubble team for the NCAA.—*Newsday (New York)*, p. 105, 7th March 1989
- —*Morning Edition (National Public Radio)*, 12th March 2001
- Other than enhancing their status as an NCAA tournament "bubble team," the victory didn't mean much for the Golden Eagles.—*Chicago Tribune*, p. C1, 24th March 2004

bubble-top *noun*

an OH-13 Sioux helicopter, used for observation, reconnaissance, and medical evacuation in the Korean war and the early years of the war in Vietnam *US*
So named because of the distinctive plexiglas canopy.
- When the sheriff's helicopter, which looked like the old military bubble-tops, finally got landed on suitable ground, Manny Lopez was ministering to the bandit[.]—Joseph Wambaugh, *Lines and Shadows*, p. 183, 1984
- —Linda Reinberg, *In the Field*, p. 29, 1991

bubble trouble *noun*

a flat tyre or other tyre problem *US*
- —Lanie Dills, *The Official CB Slanguage Language Dictionary*, p. 20, 1976
- —Peter Chippindale, *The British CB Book*, p. 153, 1981

bubble up *verb*

▷ see: **BUBBLE AND SQUEAK**

bubbling *adjective*

(of an event) beginning to get exciting *US*
- —*Johnny Vaughan Tonight*, 13th February 2002

bubbling bundle of barometric brilliance *noun*

used as the introduction for Bobbie the weather girl on AFVN television, Saigon, during the Vietnam war *US*
Officially she served as a secretary for the US Agency for International Aid in Saigon from 1967 to 1969. Her unpaid weather broadcasts, which always ended with the benediction of wishing 'everyone a pleasant evening weather-wise and good wishes for other-wise,' were greatly appreciated by the men in the field.
- —Gregory Clark, *Words of the Vietnam War*, p. 63, 1990
- As "Bobbie the Weather Girl" for Armed Forces Television Vietnam in Saigon, she was a "bubbling bundle of barometric brilliance" with her lighthearted nightly broadcasts to tens of thousands of Americans in Vietnam.—*USA Today*, p. 11A, 11th November 1993
- When a friend teased Bobbie unmercifully, she decided to go for the audition, and she became the weather girl, the "bubbling bundle of barometric brilliance."—Olga Gruhzit-Hoty, *A Time Remembered*, p. 238, 1999

bubbly *noun*

champagne *UK, 1920*
- The lush was a complete stranger, having been delivered by a cabdriver who steered for various joints, and Tappy had just gotten around to selling him the first bottle of bubbly.—Robert Sylvester, *No Cover Charge*, p. 213, 1956
- In the red-lit murk, there was the counterpoint bedlam of profane ribaldry as they loaded their skulls with cocaine and bubbly.—Iceberg Slim (Robert Beck), *Airtight Willie and Me*, p. 26, 1979
- Nabokov only got two-fifty. You're getting top dollar! Break out the bubbly!—Terry Southern, *Now Dig This*, p. 155, 1991
- Instead, Lefty handed her a cup and poured her some bubbly.—C.D. Payne, *Youth in Revolt*, p. 132, 1993
- Get Rex some bubbly, whatever.—*Empire Records*, 1995

bubbly *adjective*

1 cheerful, full of spirit *US, 1939*
- For weeks he lay in his hospital bed and cursed steadily, cheered only slightly by the bubbly letter which arrived every three days from Maggie.—Max Shulman, *Rally Round the Flag, Boys!*, p. 17, 1957

2 tearful, sulky *UK: SCOTLAND*
- Are you comin or no? Ach well stick, bubbly!—Michael Munro, *The Original Patter*, 1985

3 (used of the ocean) rough *TRISTAN DA CUNHA, 1993*
- —Bernadette Hince, *The Antarctic Dictionary*, p. 73, 2000

bubby *noun*

the female breast *UK, 1655*
Usually in the plural.
- —Dale Gordon, *The Dominion Sex Dictionary*, p. 33, 1967
- Their secondary sex characteristics are simply too conspicuous to pass without insult, and we were unmerciful towards them: tits, boobs, knockers, jugs, bubbies, bazooms, lungs, flaps and hooters we called them, and there was no way to be polite about it.—*Screw*, p. 6, 3rd January 1972
- —Patricia Clinton-Meicholas, *More Talkin' Bahamian*, p. 26, 1995

bubonic *noun*

potent marijuana *US*
- —Pamela Munro, *U.C.L.A. Slang*, p. 48, 2001

bubonic *adjective*

potent, extreme, intense *US*
- [A] fat ass J, of some bubonic chronic that made me choke[.]—Snoop Doggy Dogg, *Gin and Juice*, 1993

bucanneer *noun*

a homosexual *UK*
Rhyming slang for **QUEER**.
- —Ray Puxley, *Fresh Rabbit*, 1998

buccaneer *adjective*

homosexual *UK*
Rhyming slang for **QUEER**.
- —Ray Puxley, *Fresh Rabbit*, 1998

buck *noun*

1 a dollar *US, 1856*
Originally US but applied in Hong Kong and other countries where dollars are the unit of currency.
- There was no mention of a full or partial refund of my two-hundred-buck fee for said license to said state. —Mickey Spillane, *Kiss Me Deadly*, p. 33, 1952
- She was here last night. All night. For two lousey bucks. —Harry J. Anslinger, *The Murderers*, p. 54, 1961

2 one hundred dollars; a bet of one hundred dollars *US*
- He'd go a buck and a half apiece for as many as I could get. —George V. Higgins, *Friends of Eddie Coyle*, p. 10, 1973
- —Don R. McCreary (Editor), *Dawg Speak*, 2001

3 in motor racing, 100 miles per hour *US*
- —John Edwards, *Auto Dictionary*, p. 20, 1993

4 a young black man *US, 1835*
Overtly racist; an unfortunate favourite term of US President Ronald Reagan when speaking unscripted.
- We saw one buck pull a razor on his sugar in front of Gamby's. —Jack Lait and Lee Mortimer, *Washington Confidential*, p. 272, 1951
- —*Maledicta*, p. 152, Summer/Winter 1978: 'How to hate thy neighbor: a guide to racist maledicta'

5 used as a term of address *BAHAMAS*
The racist implications of the word from the US are not present in the Bahamas.
- —John A. Holm, *Dictionary of Bahamian English*, p. 30, 1982

6 a male Australian Aboriginal *AUSTRALIA, 1870*
Now only in racist or historical use.
- A couple of the Old Men wanted that young lubra and they've spurred on the bucks to chase Possum and cut his liver out. —Ion L. Idriess, *Over the Range*, p. 44, 1947

7 a male homosexual *US*
- —Inez Cardozo-Freeman, *The Joint*, p. 485, 1984

8 a criminal; a hoodlum; a young ruffian *UK*
Originally Liverpool use, where it survives.
- I used to think I was a bit of a buck back in them days[.] —Kevin Sampson, *Outlaws*, p. 124, 2001

9 a type of homemade alcoholic drink *US*
- Some pretty good shine we call buck, made of rice or orange juice with some yeast and sugar. We'd have some poor asshole keep it in his cell while it set up. —Elmore Leonard, *Maximum Bob*, p. 108, 1991
- —Gary K. Farlow, *Prison-ese*, p. 7, 2002

10 an attempt *NEW ZEALAND, 1941*

11 in prison, a sit-down strike by the prisoners *US*
- —Bruce Jackson, *Outside the Law*, p. 55, 1972

12 a used car that is in very poor condition *US*
- —*American Speech*, p. 309–310, Winter 1980: 'More jargon of car salesmen'

▸ **pass the buck**
to avoid responsibility by shifting the onus to someone else *US, 1912*
Deriving from the game of poker.

▸ **the buck stops here**
the ultimate responsibility for whatever may be avoided by others is accepted here, or by me, or by this office *US*
A popular catchphrase, originally coined in 1952 by US president Harry S. Truman who had it as a personal motto and displayed on his desk, just in case he forgot.

buck *verb*

1 to fight your way through a difficult surfing situation *US*
- —John M. Kelly, *Surf and Sea*, p. 281, 1965

2 in electric line work, to lower voltage *US*
- —A.B. Chance Co., *Lineman's Slang Dictionary*, p. 2, 1980

▷ see: BUCK IT

▸ **buck the clock; buck the calendar**
in oil drilling, to work hard in the hope of finishing a job by quitting time *US*
- —Jerry Robertson, *Oil Slanguage*, p. 32, 1954

▸ **buck the tiger**
to play faro, a game of chance that was extremely popular in the C19 and only rarely seen in modern times *US, 1849*
- She's right here in Atlantic City. She's been bucking the tiger in clubs off the Boardwalk. —Stephen Cannell, *King Con*, p. 120, 1997

buck *adjective*
newly promoted, inexperienced *US, 1917*
Military; a back-formation from now conventional 'buck private', also ranked in such company as 'buck sergeant' and 'buck general'.

buck and doe *noun*
snow *UK*
Rhyming slang, generally as a complete rhyme on 'fuckin' snow'.
- —Ray Puxley, *Cockney Rabbit*, p. 25, 1992

buckaroo; buckeroo *noun*
a proud, manly man, of the Western sort, likely a cowboy *US, 1827*
- I ain't the kind of buckeroo to disappoint a lady. —George Bowering, *Caprice*, p. 127, 1987

buck cop *noun*
a new constable in the Royal Canadian Mounted Police *CANADA*
- Holman was a green buck cop then, just out of the Awkward Squad. —William Mowery, *Tales of the Mounted Police*, p. 90, 1953

bucker *noun*
a lumberman who works on felled trees *CANADA, 1989*
- —Tom Parkin, *WetCoast Words*, p. 21, 1989

buckeroo *noun*
one dollar *US, 1942*
An embellishment of BUCK.
- Thirty-five thousand buckaroos, lady. —Gerald Petievich, *Shakedown*, p. 79, 1988

bucket *noun*

1 a jail *US, 1894*
- If anybody is found carrying a gun or blackjack, he will be tossed in the bucket. —*San Francisco Examiner*, p. 1, 30th August 1946
- A poor book can't make a buck without making the bucket. —*San Francisco Chronicle*, p. 16, 30th October 1957
- —*Los Angeles Times*, p. B1, 19th December 1994

2 a cell used for solitary confinement *US*
- —James Harris, *A Convict's Dictionary*, p. 28, 1989

3 the vagina *UK*
- Women's genitalia were represented as (potential) containers (e.g., bucket, box, hair goblet), places to put things in (e.g., furry letterbox, disk drive, socket, slot), containers for semen (e.g., gism pot, spunk bin, honey pot), and containers for the penis/sex (e.g., willy warmer, wank shaft, shagbox). —*Journal of Sex Research*, p. 146, 2001

4 the buttocks; the anus *US, 1938*
- —Ellen C. Bellone (Editor), *Dictionary of Slang*, p. 5, 1989

5 a car *US, 1939*
- —Marcus Hanna Boulware, *Jive and Slang of Students in Negro Colleges*, 1947
- —Connie Eble (Editor), *UNC-CH Campus Slang*, p. 2, Spring 1992

6 a small car *US*
- There's even street slang for stealing cars such as "new buckets are being splacked." Buckets refer to small cars, susch as Dodge neons, and to splack is to steal a car using a screwdriver to break into the steering column and start it. —*Tampa (Flordia) Tribune*, p. 1, 6th May 2000

7 a truck with a non-roofed container *UK*
- —Peter Chippindale, *The British CB Book*, p. 153, 1981

8 in hot rodding, the body of a roadster, especially one from the 1920s *US*
- —John Lawlor, *How to Talk Car*, p. 24, 1965

9 an engine cylinder *US*
- —Montie Tak, *Truck Talk*, p. 20, 1971

10 in pool, a pocket that appears receptive to balls dropping *US, 1988*
- —Mike Shamos, *The Illustrated Encyclopedia of Billiards*, p. 36, 1993

11 a impressive quantity of alcoholic drinks *UK, 1985*
From the original sense (a single glass of spirits).
- If it wisnae [was not] for the prospect of a good bucket, I'd have no reason to get up in the morning! —Ian Pattison, *Rab C. Nesbitt*, 1988

- [S]tart running off at the mouth once they've had a bucket[.] —J.J. Connolly, *Layer Cake*, p. 31, 2000

bucket *verb*

1 to denigrate someone or something *AUSTRALIA, 1974*

- Now I'm no bloody saint for Christ's sake, but I yield to none in my abhorrence of elitist Uni-types bucketing the Good Book. —Barry Humphries, *The Traveller's Tool*, p. 125, 1985

2 to throw something out, to throw something in the bin *UK: SCOTLAND*

- Ah knocked ma pan in gettin that report ready an aw he can say is "Bucket that". —Michael Munro, *The Patter, Another Blast*, 1988

bucket-a-drop *adverb*

(of rain) falling heavily *GRENADA*

- —Richard Allsopp, *Dictionary of Caribbean English Usage*, p. 119, 1996

bucket and pail; bucket *noun*

a jail *US, 1894*

Rhyming slang.

- Those goddamn girls were gigglin, righteously laughin ... you know, 'Ha, ha, that's one of em.' So off I went to the bucket, for rape. —Hunter S. Thompson, *Hell's Angels*, p. 17, 1966
- For a shorter sentence say "in the bucket". —Ray Puxley, *Cockney Rabbit*, p. 25, 1992
- —Angela Devlin, *Prison Patter*, p. 32, 1996

bucket bong; bucket *noun*

a water-pipe improvised using a bucket of water and a plastic bottle used for smoking marijuana *AUSTRALIA*

A combination of conventional 'bucket' and **BONG** (a water-pipe).

- But their lifestyle hasn't changed. Smoke before work. Beers at lunch. Buckets after dinner. —John Birmingham, *He Died With a Felafel in his Hand*, p. 209, 1994
- [H]e couldn't help but round up those few pathetic motes of marijuana and pack them into the bucket bong. —Harrison Biscuit, *The Search for Savage Henry*, p. 60, 1995
- [A] proper session will be in a small room – bit of music, bucket bong, couple of beers. —Macfarlane, Macfarlane and Robson, *The User*, p. 142, 1996
- Then one of the boys got a "bucket" [...] sorted and we each had one. — *The Guardian*, p. 10, 15th January 2003

bucketfull *noun*

▸ have a bucketfull

said of a racehorse that has been fed heavily before a race to decrease its chances of winning *US*

- —David W. Maurer, *Argot of the Racetrack*, p. 34, 1951

bucket gunner *noun*

in carnival usage, a person who from a hidden location operates the mechanisms that determine a game's outcome *US*

- —Don Wilmeth, *The Language of American Popular Entertainment*, p. 35, 1981

bucket head *noun*

a socially inept person *US, 1906*

- — *Detroit Free Press*, 4th November 1979

bucket job *noun*

an intentional loss in an athletic contest *US*

- The Olson-Maxim bout was one of the top bucket jobs since the Carnera trail of hoaxes. — *San Francisco News*, p. 14, 24th February 1955

bucketload *noun*

a great amount *UK*

- [T]he Britsh Navy started building a bucketload of tracks, thus for the first and last time in our history creating full employment. —Andrew Nickolds, *Back to Basics*, p. 158, 1994

bucket mouth *noun*

in trucking, a trucker who monopolises conversation on the citizens' band radio *US*

- —Wayne Floyd, *Jason's Authentic Dictionary of CB Slang*, p. 11, 1976

bucket of blood *noun*

a bar or dance hall where hard drinking and hard fighting go hand in hand *US, 1915*

- My place, before I bought it, was referred to as a bucket of blood. —Helen P. Branson, *Gay Bar*, p. 52, 1957
- You walk into a nigger bucket-of-blood bar on the wooliest corner in the state and spout stupid insults. —Iceberg Slim (Robert Beck), *Trick Baby*, p. 276, 1969
- This dislike gave the sstore a bucket-of-blood reputation which warned anyone who wasn't already known by, or friendly with, someone in the establishment, to stay away unless his head was made of concrete. —Emmett Grogan, *Ringolevio*, p. 99, 1972
- Peeking into the "430" club, a bucket of blood type establishment with sawdust and ground up bones on the floor[.] —Odie Hawkins, *Black Casanova*, p. 184, 1984

bucket of bolts *noun*

a dilapidated car, truck, boat or plane *US, 1942*

- —Montie Tak, *Truck Talk*, p. 20, 1971
- If the French had felt so threatened by the Rainbow Warrior (a "bucket of bolts," according to a New Zealand national security official), disabling the ship at sea with a low-charge explosive on the propeller shaft – or even tangled wire – would have been enough covert action to deter its further passage. —*American Journal of International Law*, p. 15, 1992
- The Marines got me airborne in this piece of *** that looked ragged and was shaking like a bucket of bolts. —Stephen K. Scroggs, *Army Relations with Congress*, p. 92, 2000
- Many charities can arrange to have that bucket of bolts towed right out of your driveway. — *Alameda (California) Times-Star*, 12th March 2004

bucket of steam *noun*

a mythical task for a newly hired helper on a job *US*

- —Charles F. Haywood, *Yankee Dictionary*, p. 19–20, 1963
- The usual leg-pulling was inflicted on new starters; the more gullible were sent to the stores for a bucket of steam, a packet of big ends or side rods[.] —Frank McKenna, *Railway Workers 1840–1970*, p. 114, 1980

bucket shop *noun*

an investment office that swindles its clients *US, 1879*

- He ran boiler rooms and bucket shops. —Stephen Cannell, *King Con*, p. 35, 1997

bucket worker *noun*

a swindler *US*

- —Vincent J. Monteleone, *Criminal Slang*, p. 35, 1949

buck fever *noun*

in shuffleboard, the anxiety often experienced on the last shot *US*

- —Omero C. Catan, *Secrets of Shuffleboard Strategy*, p. 64, 1967

buck for *verb*

to energetically strive towards promotion, honours or some other target of personal ambition or recognition *UK*

- In Who's Who are you?! Be bucking for your KBE next, I suppose! — *The Guardian*, 18th June 1979

buck general *noun*

a brigadier general *US*

- — *American Speech*, p. 54, February 1947: 'Pacific War language'

buck it; buck *verb*

in craps, to roll a number that has previously been rolled *US*

- —John Scarne, *Scarne on Dice*, p. 462, 1974

buckle *verb*

▸ buckle for your dust

in the Vietnam war, to fight with spirit and determination, thus winning the respect of fellow soldiers *US*

- —Linda Reinberg, *In the Field*, p. 29, 1991

buckle bunny *noun*

a woman who seeks short-term sexual liaisons with rodeo cowboys *US, 1978*

- Baseball players call them "Annies." To riders on the rodeo circuit, they are "buckle bunnies." To most other athletes, they are just "the wannabes" or "the girls". — *Time Magazine*, p. 77, 25th November 1991
- Poem, poem on the range / Where the dudes and buckle bunnies all play. — *Denver Westword*, 26th August 2004

bucklebuster *noun*

a line in a performance that is guaranteed to produce loud laughter *US*

- —Sherman Louis Sergel, *The Language of Show Biz*, p. 30, 1973

buckled *adjective*

1 ugly *US*

- — *People Magazine*, p. 73, 19th July 1993

2 drunk *UK*

- — *e-cyclopaedia*, 20th March 2002

buckle my shoe *noun*

a Jewish person *UK*

Most rhyming slang for 'Jew' uses 'two'; this term takes a traditional nursery-rhyme: 'one, two / buckle my shoe'.

- [A] raspberry ripple, a buckle my shoe[.] — Ian Dury, *Blackmail Man*, 1977

Buckley's chance; Buckley's hope; Buckley's *noun*

no chance at all *AUSTRALIA, 1895*

Thought to be named after William Buckley, an escaped convict, but the fact that he evaded capture by living with Aboriginals for 32 years would rather imply that Buckley's chance should be very good. The ironic phrase 'You've got two chances: Buckley's and none!' is perhaps punningly connected with the name of a former Melbourne firm 'Buckley and Nunn'.

- That blasted squirt's capable of doing almost five hundred and twenty, straight and level, we wouldn't have Buckley's chance. — W.R. Bennett, *Night Intruder*, p. 26, 1962
- — Dymphna Cusack, *Picnic Races*, p. 19, 1962
- She had Buckley's — Alexander Buzo, *Rooted*, p. 66, 1969
- Still a man of ambition, he had his eye on the Chief Judgeship of the High Court itself, but Buckley's hope, if he only realised it[.] — Frank Hardy, *The Outcasts of Foolgarah*, 1971
- — John O'Grady, *It's Your Shout, Mate!*, p. 35, 1972

bucko *noun*

1 a man, especially an unrefined or crude man *US, 1883*

- But when it came to the belligerent buckos, there'd be a house officer call. — Dev Collans with Stewart Sterling, *I was a House Detective*, p. 66, 1954

2 used as a term of address to a man *UK, 1890*

Slightly derisive, or at least kidding. From the C19 sense (a blustering bully).

- "I'm in good shape for any age, bucko!" she said, truculently. — Joseph Wambaugh, *Finnegan's Week*, p. 156, 1993

buck-passer *noun*

anyone who avoids a personal responsibilty by shifting the onus onto someone else *US, 1933*

From **PASS THE BUCK**.

buck-passing *noun*

an avoidance of responsibility by shifting the onus to someone else *US, 1933*

From **PASS THE BUCK**.

buckra *noun*

a white person *US, 1787*

- "Buckra? What's that?" "The kind of white folks ain't got time for nuthen but kicken niggers and ass-kisen rich folks," the driver said. — Robert Penn Warren, *Wilderness*, p. 84, 1961
- — John A. Holm, *Dictionary of Bahamian English*, p. 30, 1982
- — Frederic G. Cassidy, *Dictionary of American Regional English, Volume 1*, p. 421, 1985

buck rat *noun*

the eptiome of physical fitness *NEW ZEALAND*

- Everybody thought, 'I'm as fit as buck rat, good as gold.' — Winston McCarthy, *Rugby in my Time*, p. 48, 1958

Buck Rogers gun *noun*

an M-3 Tommy gun *US*

- — *American Speech*, p. 54, February 1947: 'Pacific War language'

bucks *noun*

▸ **the bucks**

a lot of money *US*

- — Judi Sanders, *Kickin' like Chicken with the Couch Commander*, p. 3, 1992

Bucks *noun*

Buckinghamshire *UK, 1937*

A spoken form of the conventional written abbreviation, considered colloquial when used in speech as a genuine equivalent of the original name.

buckshee *noun*

something above a usual amount that is given for free *UK, 1916*

Originally from the British Army in Egypt and India, ultimately from Persian. Occasionally used in the plural. Variant spellings include 'bucksheesh', 'buckshish', 'backsheesh', 'backshish', 'bakshee', 'baksheesh' and 'bakshish'.

- "Can I have a spot of that bumf?" – "Sure, it's buckshees – be my guest." — *Beale*, 1974

buckshee *adjective*

1 free, spare, extra *UK, 1916*

- Don't tell me – you came for a buckshee dinner. I still owe you that favor, after all. — Elizabeth Young, *Asking for Trouble*, p. 354, 2001

2 worthless *CANADA*

- To a Canadian airman or air woman, "buckshee" is an adjective meaning nothing or worthless. From backsheesh, a gift or a bribe. "We speak of a buckshee repair, or a buckshee plan". — Tom Langeste, *Words on the Wing*, p. 40, 1995

3 of a local non-commissioned officer, with rank but no additional pay *AUSTRALIA*

From **BUCKSHEE** (free).

- [Y]ou should have gone in for a commission but you were too idle. If you'd done that they would have made you a buckshee one-pipper [a second lieutenant][.] — Graeme Kent, *The Queen's Corporal [Six Granada Plays]*, p. 85, 1959

buck slip *noun*

a form used for intra-office handwritten communications; officially a Routing and Transmittal Slip, Optional Form 41 *US*

- — Department of the Army, *Staff Officer's Guidebook*, p. 56, 1986

buck's party *noun*

a party or outing that is exclusively male; now especially an all-male pre-wedding party thrown for the groom *AUSTRALIA, 1918*

- 'What is a buck's party, Joe?' 'Bucks only. No women.' — Nino Culotta (John O'Grady), *They're A Weird Mob*, p. 89, 1957
- — Kathy Lette, *Girls' Night Out*, p. 29, 1987

bucks up *adjective*

in drag racing, winning and making money *US*

- — Lyle K. Engel, *The Complete Book of Fuel and Gas Dragsters*, p. 149, 1968

buck up *verb*

1 to improve *UK*

- I should "mend my ways" and "buck up my ideas" and that kinda crap. — Dave Courtney, *Stop the Ride I Want to Get Off*, p. 40, 1999

2 to enjoy good luck *JAMAICA*

- — Peter L. Patrick, *Some Recent Jamaican Creole Words*, 2003

buckwheat *noun*

1 an unsophisticated rustic *US, 1866*

- — Frederic G. Cassidy, *Dictionary of American Regional English, Volume 1*, p. 423, 1985

2 a black male *US*

- — *Maledicta*, p. 153, Summer/Winter 1978: 'How to hate thy neighbor: a guide to racist maledicta'

buckwheat farmer *noun*

an unsuccessful, incompetent farmer *CANADA*

- It was his settled habit to be late and incompetent; a "buckwheat farmer" who had watched his farm going back. — Angus Mowat, *Carrying Place*, p. 90, 1944

buckwheats *noun*

1 abuse, persecution *US, 1942*

- — Hyman E. Goldin et al., *Dictionary of American Underworld Lingo*, p. 98, 1950
- He gave me the buckwheats, this sergeant. — Rocky Garciano (with Rowland Barber), *Somebody Up There Likes Me*, p. 202, 1955

2 diminution of power or standing in an organised crime enterprise *US*

- — *American Speech*, p. 306, December 1964: 'Lingua cosa nostra'

buck willy *adjective*

uninhibited, rowdy, drunk *US*

- — Connie Eble (Editor), *UNC-CH Campus Slang*, p. 2, November 2002

bucky *noun*

1 a shotgun *US*

- — Bill Valentine, *Gang Intelligence Manual*, p. 110, 1995

2 a home-made gun *JAMAICA*

- I pulled my bottom drawer out slightly, so my bucky and my blade were to hand[.] — Diran Adebayo, *My Once Upon A Time*, p. 6, 2000

bud *noun*

1 the flower of the marijuana plant; hence marijuana *US, 1978*

- — Mary Corey and Victoria Westermark, *Fer Shurrl*, 1982
- Take a big bone hit/Cause after tha bud, My rhymes start flowin' — Tone Loc, *Cheeba Cheeba*, 1989
- But nothin's worse when someone's askin for some weed/What do I look like a tree where the bud grows?/Here pick my left nut and smoke it in the bowl — Cypress Hill, *Can I get a hit?*, 2000
- — Stephen J. Cannell, *The Tin Collectors*, p. b, 2001
- Chooch rolled a bud, fat and short. — Stephen J. Cannell, *The Tin Collectors*, p. 62, 2001
- [T]he soothing vocals and blissful sunshine harmonies make it something of a top bud accompaniment. — *Ministry*, p. 12, October 2002

2 a girl *US*

- Elsewhere, Las Vegas' beautiful little high-school buds in their buttocks-decolletage stretch pants are back on the foam-rubber upholstery of luxury broughams peeling off the entire chick ensemble[.] —Tom Wolfe, *The Kandy-Kolored Tangerine-Flake Streamline Baby*, p. 12, 1965

3 the female nipple *US*

- Your buds is as hard as two frozen huckleberries. —Robert Campbell, *Sweet La-La Land*, p. 175, 1990

4 a friend, a buddy *US, 1935*

- I'm sorry about the show. Buds? —*Wayne's World*, 1992
- Aw, be a bud, let me in. I was having a blast. —*Airheads*, 1994

5 used as a term of address, usually male-to-male *UK, 1614*

- Hey, bud. What's your problem[?] —*Fast Times at Ridgemont High*, 1982

6 the penis *BAHAMAS*

- —John A. Holm, *Dictionary of Bahamian English*, p. 30, 1982

Bud *noun*

*Bud*weiser™ beer; a *Bud*weiser™ beer *US*

- [S]he stood there pointedly drinking nothing while he choked down a Bud, that great Satan of beers. —John Williams, *Cardiff Dead*, p. 187, 2000

bud *verb*

to subject a boy to his first homosexual experience *UK*

- —*Maledicta*, p. 155, Summer/Winter 1986–1987: 'Sexual slang: prostitutes, pedophiles, flagellators, transvestites, and necrophiles'

budded; budded out *adjective*

intoxicated on marijuana *US*

- —Judi Sanders, *Da Bomb*, p. 3, 1997
- —Vann Wesson, *Generation X Field Guide and Lexicon*, p. 30, 1997

buddha *noun*

1 a type of LSD identified by a representation of Buddha *UK*

- —Harry Shapiro, *Recreational Drugs*, p. 266, 2004

2 a marijuana cigarette embellished with crack cocaine *US*

- —Terry Williams, *The Cocaine Kids*, p. 135, 1989

3 potent marijuana, usually of Asian origin *US, 1988*

Also spelt 'buddah' or 'buda'.

- I hit they' ass like the buddah thats stinkey[.] —Cypress Hill, *Stoned is the Way of the Walk*, 1991
- —Connie Eble (Editor), *UNC-CH Campus Slang*, p. 2, Spring 2000
- —Mike Haskins, *Drugs*, p. 286, 2003

buddhaed *adjective*

intoxicated on marijuana *US*

Buddha grass *noun*

marijuana *US*

Vietnam war usage.

- In 1968, when heroin found its way into those Buddha grass "Marlboro" joints (eventually turning some 20 to 30 percent of the U.S. military in Vietnam into junkies before you could say "Far out, man"), it would be too late to turn the tide. —David H. Hackworth, *About Face*, p. 574, 1982

Buddhahead *noun*

a Japanese person *US, 1945*

Offensive.

- Chicago Japs refer to those from the old country and Hawaii as "Buddha heads" or "Boochies." —Jack Lait and Lee Mortimer, *Chicago Confidential*, p. 88, 1950
- —Eugene Landy, *The Underground Dictionary*, p. 41, 1971
- "So now if I wanna get somewhere in the department I gotta be a Buddhahead," Francis moaned to his partner. —Joseph Wambaugh, *The Choirboys*, p. 91, 1975
- —Edith A. Folb, *runnin' down some lines*, p. 231, 1980
- —Douglas Simonson, *Pidgin to da Max*, 1981

Buddha stick *noun*

marijuana from Thailand packaged for transport and sale on a small stick *US, 1982*

- [They] went into the business of picking up drops of Thai sticks, also known as Buddha sticks, dried and compressed cannabis from the Golden Triangle of South-East Asia —*Guardian*, p. 14, 14th July 1981
- —Nick Brownlee, *This Is Cannabis*, p. 151, 2002

Buddha zone *noun*

death; the afterlife *US*

Vietnam war usage; just a bit cynical.

- —Linda Reinberg, *In the Field*, p. 29, 1991

Buddhist priest!

used as a mock profanity to express surprise, disgust or annoyance during the war in Vietnam *US*

A region-appropriate evolution of **JUDAS PRIEST!**.

- —Linda Reinberg, *In the Field*, p. 30, 1991

buddy *noun*

1 a companion, a friend *US, 1850*

A colloquial usage that is probably derived from 'brother'.

2 a fellow citizens' band radio user *US*

Citizens' band radio slang, adopted from the more general sense as 'a fellow, a man'; often used as 'good buddy'.

- Well, mercy's sakes, good buddy, we gonna back on outta here[.] —C.W. McCall, *Convoy*, 1976
- [W]ish your good buddies all the best when you sign off. —Peter Chippindale, *The British CB Book*, p. 226, 1981

3 in homosexual culture, a good friend who may or may not be a lover *US, 1972*

- "And how does he feel about you?" "He thinks of me as a fuck buddy. Period." —Armistead Maupin, *Further Tales of the City*, p. 190, 1982
- "Lots of buddy nights at the baths. I can't even count the number of times I rolled over in bed and told some hot stranger: 'You'd like my lover.'" —Armistead Maupin, *Further Tales of the City*, p. 22, 1982

4 a volunteer companion to a person with AIDS *US, 1984*

- There also exist buddy programs that team a recently diagnosed person with an HIV-positive person who is more experienced in dealing with the issues. —Darrell Ward, *The Amfar AIDS Handbook*, p. 15, 1999

5 a marijuana cigarette *US*

- —Judi Sanders, *Don't Dog by Do, Dude!*, p. 4, 1991

6 a beer *US*

- —Judi Sanders, *Mashing and Munching in Ames*, p. 3, 1994

buddy-buddy *adjective*

friendly *US, 1944*

- A friendly, laconic man – but definitley not the back-slaping, buddy-buddy type – Mr. Cadell politely declined to discuss these episodes. —*San Francisco News*, p. 2, 26th February 1946
- Joan and my woman probation officer real buddy buddy shaking hands[.] —Jack Kerouac, *Letter to Allen Ginsberg*, p. 459, 1st January 1955
- I have no respect for a duck who runs up to me on the yard all buddy-buddy, and then feels obliged not to sit down with me. —Eldridge Cleaver, *Soul on Ice*, p. 47, 1968
- So he tried to be buddy-buddy with me, but I wans't buying that either. —H. Rap Brown, *Die Nigger Die!*, p. 44, 1969

buddy check *noun*

a last-minute inspection of a parachutist's gear by his jump partner *US*

- —Murry A. Taylor, *Jumping Fire*, p. 455, 2000

buddy-fuck *verb*

(of a male) to steal a friend's date *US, 1966*

- —Collin Baker et al., *College Undergraduate Slang Study Conducted at Brown University*, p. 89, 1968

buddy gee *noun*

a close friend *US*

- —Kenn "Naz" Young, *Naz's Underground Dictionary*, p. 17, 1973

Buddy Holly *noun*

money *UK*

Rhyming slang for **LOLLY**, formed from the name of the US singer, 1936–59.

- He then gives him a right Ronan Keating [beating] and nicks all his Buddy Holly. —Mervyn Stutter, *Getting Nowhere Fast*, 2004

buddy poker *noun*

a game of poker in which two friends are playing as partners, but not in collusion *US, 1968*

- —Thomas L. Clark, *The Dictionary of Gambling and Gaming*, p. 30, 1987

buddyro; buddyroo *noun*

a pal; used as a term of address for a friend *US*

- Be a buddy. Be a buddyroo. Okay? —J.D. Salinger, *Catcher in the Rye*, p. 28, 1951

buddy system *noun*

during the Korean war, a plan teaming American and Korean soldiers in the hope of providing one-on-one mentoring and training *US*

- This was the much-vaunted "buddy system" under which the Koreans were paired off with Americans who were supposed to give them on-the-job training in the soldier's craft. —Robert Leckie, *The Wars of America, Volume II*, p. 353, 1968

buddy window *noun*
a hole between private video booths in a pornography arcade designed for sexual contact where none is officially permitted *US*
• The peep show has lost its popularity. The buddy window, glory hole. — James Ridgeway, *Red Light*, p. 212, 1996

budge *noun*
in the language of pickpockets, the front trouser pocket *US*
• — Vincent J. Monteleone, *Criminal Slang*, p. 35, 1949

budget *adjective*
below expectations, disappointing *US*
• — Connie Eble (Editor), *UNC-CH Campus Slang*, p. 2, Fall 1986

budgie *noun*
1 a budgerigar, a small parrot native to inland Australia and a common cage bird *AUSTRALIA, 1935*
2 a talkative man, especially one of small stature; a small-time police-informer *UK*
From a passing similarity to a budgerigar's characteristics. The television drama *Budgie*, 1971 – 72, starred Adam Faith as the epitome of all of the above definition. It is difficult to tell whether the television programme created or popularised this usage.
• — David Powis, *The Signs of Crime*, 1977
3 the time *UK*
Used by miners, usually in the form of a question.
• [U]sed only since the introduction of Pakistani labour. "Budgie" is a corruption of "Baje", a transliteration from the Urdu. — W. Forster, *Pit Talk*, AROUND 1970
4 a hippie who moved back to the land in Slocan Valley, British Columbia *CANADA*
• — Tom Parkin, *WetCoast Words*, p. 21, 1989

budgie-smugglers *noun*
a pair of men's close-fitting and revealing nylon swimming trunks *AUSTRALIA*
• I don't think men should be allowed to wear budgie-smugglers in public. — *Wordmap (www.abc.net.au/wordmap)*, 2002

budgie's tongue *noun*
the clitoris, especially when erect *UK*
From the visual similarity.
• [Y]ou find the budgie's tongue and bingo! — *www.LondonSlang.com*, June 2002

budgy *adjective*
chubby *US*
• — Eugene Landy, *The Underground Dictionary*, p. 41, 1971

bud head *noun*
1 a beer drinker *US*
Not confined to drinkers of Budweiser™ beer.
• — David Claerbaut, *Black Jargon in White America*, p. 59, 1972
2 a frequent marijuana user *US*
• — Pamela Munro, *U.C.L.A. Slang*, p. 45, 1997

budli-budli *noun*
1 anal sex *INDIA, 1961*
From Urdu *badli* (to change).
2 a homosexual man *UK, 1998*

bud mud *noun*
diarrhoea from drinking too much beer *US*
An allusion to Budweiser™ beer.
• — Judi Sanders, *Da Bomb!*, p. 5, 1997

buds *noun*
1 small female breasts *US*
• — Dale Gordon, *The Dominion Sex Dictionary*, p. 34, 1967
2 marijuana, especially the most psychoactive part of the plant *US*
Also spelled 'budz'.
• — Jim Emerson-Cobb, *Scratching the Dragon*, April 1997

bud sesh *noun*
an informal gathering for the social consumption of marijuana *US*
Punning on BUDDY/BUD plus 'session'.

budsky *noun*
used as a term of address *US*
A meaninglessly decorative 'buddy'.
• Maybe he's looking for a job? Huh budsky? — *Repo Man*, 1984

Budweiser crest; Budweiser label *noun*
the emblem of the Navy SEALS (the sea, air and land team) *US*
• Even when I was full commander, wet-behind-the-ears ensigns straight out of the Academy would look at the Budweiser cresty – the eagle, anchor, and trident emblem all SEALS wear – on my uniform blouse and snear. — Richard Marcinko and John Weisman, *Rogue Warrior*, p. 147, 1992

buf; buff *noun*
any large military aircraft like a Grumman A-6, a Boeing B-52, and a Sikorsky CH-33, especially the B-52 Stratofortress *US, 1968*
An abbreviation of '*b*ig *u*gly *f*at *f*ucker' or, in polite company, '*f*ellow'.
• — Linda Reinberg, *In the Field*, p. 30, 1991
• — John Horton, *The Grub Street Dictionary of International Aircraft Nicknames*, p. 25, 1994
• When a B-52 takes off, Flinn cocks her head to listen. "There goes a Buf," she announces. She knows not only the nickname of this plane, but its classified secrets[.] — *Washington Post*, p. D1, 29th April 1997
• Boeing and the Air Force have elicited almost half a century of widely varied service form the Buf by masterful planning. — Walter J. Boyne, *The B-52 Story*, 2001

BUFE; buffy *noun*
a ceramic elephant, ubiquitous in souvenir shops in Vietnam during the war *US, 1973*
An initialism and acronym created from '*b*ig *u*gly *f*ucking *e*lephant'.
• — Linda Reinberg, *In the Field*, p. 30, 1991***

buff *noun*
1 an enthusiast, especially a knowledgable enthusiast, a specialist *US, 1903*
Originally 'an enthusiast about going to fires', Webster, 1934, from the buff uniform of New York's volunteer firemen. The sense has gradually generalised until the field of interest has, in all cases, to be specified.
2 a fart *UK, 1965*
Echoic.
3 a workout with weights *US*
• — James Harris, *A Convict's Dictionary*, p. 28, 1989
4 a water buffalo *US*
• He called Quinn and told him to put the buff out of its misery and take the farmer's name so the Army could pay him back. — Larry Heinemann, *Close Quarters*, p. 97, 1977
• The Vietnamese used the buffs for pulling plows and carts. — Gregory Clark, *Words of the Vietnam War*, p. 555, 1990

▸ **in the buff**
naked *UK, 1602*
• He thought about what was bothering him. And it wasn't that some gazoony had snapped his picture in the buff or that somebody had taken a couple of shots at Nell. — Robert Campbell, *Alice in La-La Land*, p. 247, 1987
• Garry, my friend, no bugger robs pipes in the buff. — *The Full Monty*, 1997

buff *verb*
1 to erase graffiti *US*
• He buffed my piece so he could write his stupid name all over the wall. — *A2Z*, p. 14, 1995
• By 1988 the graf gallery scene began to phase out and the trains were gradually "buffed". — *The Source*, p. 85, March 2002
2 in hospital usage, to make notations in a patient's chart that makes the patient look better than they are and ready for the next stage of their care *US*
• — Sally Williams, *"Strong" Words*, p. 135, 1994

▸ **buff the banana**
(of a male) to masturbate *US*
• Another way to say "the boy is masturbating" [...] Buffing the banana[.] — Erica Orloff and JoAnn Baker, *Dirty Little Secrets*, p. 65, 2001

buff *adjective*
1 handsome, excellent *US*
• — Lillian Glass with Richard Liebmann-Smith, *How to Deprogram Your Valley Girl*, p. 29, 1982

- Buff – means the bollocks "Them jeans are buff". — prison inmate, 5th August 2002

2 (of a young woman) sexually attractive *UK*
Current in south London according to *Johnny Vaughan Tonight*, 13th February 2002.
- Where you from? / Hot stuff (Buff ting) / I really hope you're not grim[.] — Dizzee Rascal, *Jezebel*, 2003

3 (used of a body) well-toned, well-exercised *US, 1982*
- — *National Education Association Today*, April 1985: 'A glossary for rents and other squids'
- I'm gonna get buff, dude. — *Kids*, 1995
- Gorgeous, buff, volleyball player's legs? — Joseph Wambaugh, *Floaters*, p. 149, 1996

buffalo *noun*

1 an American Indian male with especially long hair *US*
- — *American Speech*, p. 272, December 1963: 'American Indian student slang'

2 a five-cent piece *US*
From the engraving on the coin.
- — Lou Shelly, *Hepcats Jive Talk Dictionary*, p. 8, 1945

3 the CV-7, a military transport aircraft built by DeHavilland Aircraft of Canada *US*
- — Linda Reinerg, *In the Field*, p. 30, 1991

buffalo *verb*
to confuse someone, to intimidate someone *US*
- They're Champs at Hockey But – Russians Buffaloed by Banquets. — *Vancouver Sun*, p. 1, 26th January 1960
- I never saw nobody buffalo Bill the way she buffaloed Bill. — *Kill Bill*, 2003

buffalo bagels!
used for expressing disapproval *US*
A signature line of Colonel Sherman Potter on *M*A*S*H* (CBS, 1972–83). Repeated with referential humour.

buffalo gun *noun*
a large calibre gun *US*
Korean war usage.
- Then two more enemy soldiers appeared out of the smoke and confusion dragging a .57 caliber antitank "buffalo gun." — David H. Hackworth, *About Face*, p. 27, 1989

buffarilla *noun*
an ugly girl *US*
A blend of 'buffalo' and 'gorilla'.
- — Collin Baker et al., *College Undergraduate Slang Study Conducted at Brown University*, p. 89, 1968

buff book *noun*
a magazine catering to enthusiasts of a particular hobby or pastime *US*
- — John Edwards, *Auto Dictionary*, p. 20, 1993

buffed; buffed up *adjective*
muscular; in very good physical condition *US*
- They can tell, just from looking at you all buffed up, that you just got outta jail. — Odie Hawkins, *Midnight*, p. 20, 1995
- — Connie Eble (Editor), *UNC-CH Campus Slang*, p. 1, Fall 1996

buffer *noun*

1 a pleasant, foolish old man; a man *UK*
From French *bouffon* (a jester). As 'buffer' since 1749 but in the latter-half of C20 it seems to survive only as 'old buffer'. Modern usage implies a tolerant attitude to the subject.

2 in the world of crack cocaine users, a woman who will perform oral sex in exchange for crack cocaine or the money to buy it *US*
- — Terry Williams, *Crackhouse*, p. 147, 1992

buffers *noun*
the female breasts *US*
- — Roger Blake, *The American Dictionary of Sexual Terms*, p. 23, 1964

buffet flat *noun*
a party held to raise rent money *US*
- — Arnold Shaw, *Dictionary of American Pop/Rock*, p. 179, 1982

buff up *verb*
to engage in strenuous exercise with a goal of body conditioning *US*
- They had to buff up and get mean. — Bill Valentine, *Gangs and Their Tattoos*, p. 10, 2000

bufu *noun*
a male homosexual *US*
An abbreviation of **BUTTFUCKER**.
- — Mary Corey and Victoria Westermark, *Fer Shurr!*, 1982
- He's like Mr. BU-FU (Valley Girl) / We're talking Lord God King BU-FU (Valley Girl). — Moon Unit and Frank Zappa, *Valley Girl*, 1982

bug *noun*

1 a hidden microphone or listening device *US*
- — *American Speech*, December 1956
- This was a world of bugs, lumps [tracking devices], phone taps, both landline and mobile, both legal and illegal. — Duncan MacLaughlin, *The Filth*, p. 192, 2002

2 in the television and film industries, a small earphone used by a sound mixer *US*
- — Tony Miller and Patricia George, *Cut! Print!*, p. 184, 1977

3 any unspecified virus *UK, 1919*
- You better call the school and tell them we've all got the bug and the children'll be absent. — George V. Higgins, *The Friends of Eddie Doyle*, p. 59, 1971

4 a malfunction in design, especially of a computer or computer software *US, 1878*
- — *CoEvolution Quarterly*, p. 27, Spring 1981
- — Eric S. Raymond, *The New Hacker's Dictionary*, p. 82, 1991

5 a sociopathic criminal *US*
- — Carsten Stroud, *Close Pursuit*, p. 269, 1987

6 a burglar alarm *US, 1926*
- — John R. Armore and Joseph D. Wolfe, *Dictionary of Desperation*, p. 22, 1976

7 an illegal numbers lottery *US*
- The numbers game, or, to use the regional term, "the bug," remains the most lucrative racket. — *Saturday Evening Post*, p. 72, 9th March 1963

8 in poker, a joker played as an ace or a wild card to complete a flush or straight *US*
- — Albert H. Morehead, *The Complete Guide to Winning Poker*, p. 258, 1967

9 an enthusiastic interest; a popular craze *UK, 1902*
- [Y]ou've already been bitten by the collecting bug. — Ron Guth, *Coin Collecting for Dummies*, p. 3, 2001
- And Alex again – yes, he's got the [dance] bug. — *The Guardian*, 16th June 2004

10 a Bugatti sports car *US*
- — John Lawlor, *How to Talk Car*, p. 26, 1965

11 a Volkswagen car *US*
A VW **BEETLE** is the eponymous hero of the Disney film *The Love Bug*, 1969.
- She'd heard that when the "bugs" were originally sold in the States, their prime attraction was not gas mileage but their airtightness. — Jack W. Thomas, *Heavy Number*, p. 1, 1976

12 a chameleon *US*
Circus and carnival slang.
- — Sherman Louis Sergel, *The Language of Show Biz*, p. 33, 1973

13 in horse racing, a weight handicap *US, 1941*
- They've got Imarazzo on her. He gets the five-pound bug and she's running against stiffs, except for Green Grip. — Vincent Patrick, *The Pope of Greenwich Village*, p. 82, 1979

14 in electric line work, a transformer *US*
- — A.B. Chance Co., *Lineman's Slang Dictionary*, p. 2, 1980

15 a torch *US*
Circus and carnival usage.
- — Joe McKennon, *Circus Lingo*, p. 21, 1980

▸ **have a bug up your ass**
to be annoyed or angry *US, 1949*
- "Beeker's got a bug in his ass," he said. — Clarence Cooper Jr, *The Scene*, p. 25, 1960
- Sometimes Moran the cop would get a bug up his ass and grab me or Colorado on the street and put us back in the Home. — Edwin Torres, *Carlito's Way*, p. 16, 1975
- Castlebeck's got a bug up his ass over this guy. — *Gone in 60 Seconds*, 2000

▸ **put a bug in someone's ear**
to hint at something *US, 1905*
- I'm just saying maybe you should put a bug in her ear all the same. You never know. — Robert Campbell, *In a Pig's Eye*, p. 56, 1991

▸ **the bug**
malaria *US*
- — *American Speech*, p. 54, February 1947: 'Pacific War language'

bug *verb*

1 to bother someone, to annoy someone *US*

- You must start reading Balzac, incidentally, but don't let me rush you and bug you. —Jack Kerouac, *Letter to Neal Cassady*, p. 126, 13th September 1947
- Don't bug me with them Christian cats, let them goof off anyway they want to. —William "Lord" Buckley, *Nero*, 1951
- Goldilocks rolled over and mumbled sleepily, "Jack, don't bug me." —Steve Allen, *Bop Fables*, p. 12, 1955
- You want to bug us till we have to lock you up. —*Rebel Without a Cause*, 1955
- Man, don't bug me. —Jack Kerouac, *The Subterraneans*, p. 77, 1958
- What really bugs him is when I say that there are many blacks who, if they were in the position, would do a little rounding up of the Eichmann types in America. —Eldridge Cleaver, *Soul on Ice*, p. 47, 1968
- CARTER: What was bugging Frank? —Mike Hodges, *Get Carter*, p. 49, 1971
- She didn't even bother to pick up hihs clothes or belongings. Naturally, I was very bugged by that. —Herbert Huncke, *Guilty of Everything*, p. 156, 1990
- Nothing bugs me 'cause everything is super. —*South Park*, 1999

2 to panic, to be anxious *US, 1988*

- But people came that like, did not R.S.V.P., so I was like, totally buggin.' —*Clueless*, 1995

3 to watch something *US*

- He sat forward to bug the picture – and again lost himself in fantasy. —Hal Ellson, *The Golden Spike*, p. 196, 1952

4 to talk and act in a disassociated, irrational way while under the influence of crack cocaine *US*

- —Terry Williams, *Crackhouse*, p. 147, 1992

5 to confine someone in a psychiatric ward *US*

- —Jay Robert Nash, *Dictionary of Crime*, p. 48, 1992

6 to arm something with an alarm *US, 1919*

- The question is whether they got this door bugged or not. —Vincent Patrick, *Family Business*, p. 209, 1985

7 to attach or install a listening device *US, 1919*

- [T]hey are even bugging her telephone and just now sent over this tape[.] —Gore Vidal, *Myra Breckinridge*, p. 133, 1968

8 among vagrant alcoholics, to attack someone with bricks, bottles and boots *UK*

- An alcoholic will be robbed of even a few pence he may have about him immediately he has been bugged. —Geoffrey Fletcher, *Down Among the Meths Men*, p. 51, 1966

9 to dance *US*

- —Joan Fontaine et al., *Dictionary of Black Slang*, 1968

Bug *nickname*

the Green Hornet Tavern in Pointe Claire, Quebec *CANADA*

- Customers come from all different walks of life, as the sunshine dances [in front of the Green Hornet Tavern] on Lake St. Louis, to drink "the best draft in the west. The Dorval ball-hockey league players affectionately call this place "The Bug." —*Pointe Claire Chronicle*, p. B4, 17th July 2002

bugaboo *noun*

an imagined object of terror *UK, 1740*

- Selling apples on the streets became the great national bugaboo, a coast-to-coast phobia. —Max Shulman, *The Zebra Derby*, p. 109, 1946
- [W]e are having fish for supper this Friday nite because I mentioned Iwas Catholic – their bugaboo. —Neal Cassady, *The First Third*, p. 219, 1965

bugaboos *noun*

nasal mucous *BARBADOS*

- —Frank A. Collymore, *Barbadian Dialect*, p. 23, 1965

bugas *noun*

a pair of trainers (sneakers) *JAMAICA*

Collected by Richard Allsopp.

bug bag *noun*

a sleeping bag *CANADA*

- I've just been up to where he left his sleeping bag–that bug-bag of his. It's gone, and his rifle too. It's all gone. —Howard O'Hagan, *Tay John*, p. 141, 1957

bug boy *noun*

in horse racing, a jockey who has not yet won a race and who is given a five-pound weight allowance *US*

Because of the 'bug' or asterisk denoting the jockey's status in the racing programme.

- —Don Voorhees and Bob Benoit, *Railbird Handbook*, p. 44, 1968

bug buster *noun*

a physician specialising in infectious diseases *US*

- —*Maledicta*, p. 117, 1984–1985: 'Milwaukee medical maledicta'

bug catcher *noun*

in drag racing, an air scoop that forces air into the carburettor *US*

- The name, bug catcher, was not made up by a bug caught by a dragster going 230 miles per hour. —Ed Radlauer, *Drag Racing Pix Dix*, p. 9, 1970

bug collectors *noun*

in motorcyle racing, unbreakable goggles *US*

- —Ed Radlauer, *Motorcyclopedia*, p. 7, 1973

bug doctor *noun*

a pyschiatrist *US*

- —*American Speech*, p. 194, October 1951: 'A study of reformatory argot'
- —Gary K. Farlow, *Prison-ese*, p. 7, 2002

bug dope *noun*

insect repellant *US*

- —Mike Doogan, *How to Speak Alaskan*, p. 16, 1993

bug eye *noun*

1 in television and film making, a fisheye lens *US*

- —Ira Konigsberg, *The Complete Film Dictionary*, p. 36, 1987

2 an Austin-Healy Sprite *US*

- —Lewis Poteet, *Car & Motorcyle Slang*, p. 40, 1992

bug flea *noun*

an epidemiologist specialising in infectious diseases *US*

- —Sally Williams, *"Strong" Words*, p. 135, 1994

bugfuck *adjective*

deranged, out of control *US*

- When he saw the cat, that old bulldog went bugfuck. —Michael Dalton Johnson, *Talking Trash with Redd Foxx*, p. 110, 1994

buggalugs *noun*

used as a term of address *NEW ZEALAND*

A variation of **BUGGERLUGS**.

- G'day buggalugs, how ya goin? —Sonya Plowman, *Great Kiwi Slang*, p. 38, 2002

bugged *adjective*

1 angry *US, 1956*

- I guess he was bugged also, and when two bugged convics meet head on, pressure gotta come out. —Piri Thomas, *Down These Mean Streets*, p. 259, 1967
- What's the point of being bugged if you don't have any power to change anything? —Nat Hentoff, *I'm really dragged but nothing gets me down*, p. 9, 1968

2 mentally unbalanced, crazy *UK*

Often used as 'bugged-out'.

- I didn't want to write a corny love song. It had to be some bugged-out shit. —Eminem (Marshall Mathers), *Angry Blonde*, p. 78, 2001

3 covered with sores and abcesses from sceptic injection of a narcotic *UK*

Drug addicts' use.

- —Home Office, *Glossary of Terms and Slang Common in Penal Establishments*, July 1978

bugged up *adjective*

anxious, nervous *US*

- I wasn't more than two blocks away from Juan's place when I started getting bugged up again. —Hal Ellson, *Duke*, p. 164, 1949

bugger *noun*

1 a person who takes part in anal sex *UK, 1555*

A perfectly correct usage in legalese, otherwise considered vulgar.

2 a disagreeable person; often used as a term of abuse *UK, 1719*

- If the buggers get him, they'll make me look like his favorite uncle. —Orson Scott Card, *Ender's Game*, p. 1, 1991

3 a person, a regular fellow *UK, 1830*

- Did you manage anything, you craft old bugger? —Geoffrey Fletcher, *Down Among the Meths Men*, p. 32, 1966
- Serious little bugger with their old-timey ideas about honor, the omerta – no talking, man, keep you mouth shut – all that brotherhood bullshit. —Elmore Leonard, *Gold Coast*, p. 19, 1980
- This doctor was a shifty booger though. —Elmore Leonard, *Maximum Bob*, p. 110, 1991

4 an unpleasant, very difficult or dangerous thing, project, episode, circumstance; a nuisance *UK, 1918*
- "That solo is a bugger to play," Red said.—Ross Russell, *The Sound*, p. 91, 1961
- Well, I just swallowed the bugger ... soon it will take hold; I have no idea what to expect.—Hunter S. Thompson, *Songs of the Doomed*, p. 119, 18/19 February 1969
- The windshield's cracked, it's a bugger to drive / It starts making smoke over thirty-five—Ian Dury, *Itinerant Child*, 1998

▶ **give a bugger**
to care, generally in a negative context *UK, 1922*
- Just go off their heads and don't give a bugger at that Cash and Carry[.]—Andrew O'Hagan, *Personality*, p. 43, 2003

bugger *verb*
1 to play the active role in anal sex *UK, 1598*
- His tool was so long / And so pointed and strong / He could bugger six Greeks en brochette.—*Eros*, p. 62, Winter 162
- Don't try to analyze it. The quarterback buggering the linebacker. What a waste.—*Heathers*, 1988

2 to bungle something, to ruin something *US, 1847*
- The way to handle it is to pass the word to some crabby dumb mick of a DA, and he'll bugger it up fast enough.—George V. Higgins, *The Friends of Eddie Doyle*, p. 65, 1971

▶ **be buggered**
used for dismissing the sense of a word repeated from a preceding statement *UK*
- Squirrels, just fuckin vermin ey are, mun, cute be buggered. —Niall Griffiths, *Sheepshagger*, p. 34, 2001

bugger!
used as an expletive *UK, 1923*
- [They] bounced over a speed-bump and turned erratically into Abbey Road. "Bugger." Mo's [hot] dog had gone all over the place. —Michael Moorcock, *The Spencer Inheritance [britpulp]*, p. 3, 1998

bugger about; bugger around *verb*
1 to waste time *UK, 1923*
- —*Hansard, The Growth of Democracy*, 7th April 1968

2 to meander, to wander pointlessly around *UK, 1923*

3 to inconvenience or make difficulties for someone *UK, 1957*
- Maybe Henman was not pressurised and simply was not buggered about enough as a child – didn't suffer sufficient adversity – to have the kind of hunger that an Agassi has.—*The Guardian*, 21st January 2002

4 to be unfaithful to your wife, or husband, etc *CANADA, 1980*
Whilst the act may well remain the same the sense here is not to commit adultery with someone but, rather, is defined in terms of the person spurned.

5 to fiddle with something or someone; to caress or interfere with someone *UK, 1937*

bugger all; sweet bugger all *noun*
nothing whatsoever *UK, 1918*
- [A] big yawn-yawn expose of bugger all[.]—Dick Francis, *Whip Hand*, p. 13, 1979
- Like what guys do you know have fathers only seventeen years older than them? Sweet bugger all is what.—William Taylor, *Jerome*, p. 23, 1999
- [H]e'd give them absolution until the cows came home and sweet bugger all penance into the bargain.—Larry Kirwan, *Liverpool Fantasy*, p. 49, 2003
- One may be freer to do as one pleases sans enfants but for many doing exactly what one pleases adds up to doing bugger-all.—*Sunday Star-Times*, p. 4, 17th August 2003

buggerama!
used for expressing self-deprecating distress *NEW ZEALAND*
- —David McGill, *David McGill's Complete Kiwi Slang Dictionary*, p. 22, 1998

buggeration!
used as an expletive *UK*
An elaboration of **BUGGER!**.
- [T]he brigadier's having kittens and Bogge is running around like a fart in a colander – where in buggeration are you, sir?—Ken Follett, *The Key to Rebecca*, p. 359, 1988

buggeration factor *noun*
any unforseen hazard that complicates a proposed course of action *UK*
Originally military.
- —Strong and Hart-Davis, *Fighter Pilot*, 1981

bugger-bafflers *noun*
side-vents at the bottom rear of a man's jacket *UK*
Tailors' usage.
- —Nik Cohn, *Today There Are No Gentlemen*, 1971

buggered *adjective*
1 damned *UK, 1937*
- FAYE: He was rather attractive in a rugged colonial way... BARRY: Rugged be buggered!!! Pigs arse he was attractive!!!—Barry Humphries, *Bazza Pulls It Off!*, 1971
- I was buggered if I was going to stand there all night long. —James Hawes, *Dead Long Enough*, p. 236, 2000

2 very drunk *UK*
- —*www.collegestories.com*, 2005
- —*www.bollixed.net*, 2005

buggered if I know!
used as a profession of absolute ignorance *UK, 1984*

buggered up; buggered *adjective*
exhausted, broken *UK, 1923*
- Jesus, Ianto mun... I'm buggered... how far now?—Niall Griffiths, *Sheepshagger*, p. 14, 2001

bugger for *noun*
a person who is energetically committed to a subject noun, e.g. 'a bugger for work', 'a bugger for women' *UK*
- Aristotle, Aristotle was a bugger for the bottle / Hobbes was fond of his dram.—Eric Idle (Monty Python), *Bruce's Philosophers Song*, 1970

bugger-grips; bugger's grips *noun*
side-whiskers, especially when generously proportioned *UK*
Originally naval; the image is of a convenient pair of grips for a sodomiser to hold on to during anal sex.
- Tufts of biscuit-coloured hair grew on his cheeks in what were called in the Service "bugger's grips".—John Winton, *H.M.S. Leviathan*, 1967

bugger-in-a-bag *noun*
around Cascapedia Bay, a fruit pudding in an oiled, floured bag to make it waterproof *CANADA*
- —Bill Casselman, *Canadian Food Words*, p. 168, 1998

buggerise about; buggerise around *verb*
to fool about *AUSTRALIA, 1953*
- Look at all the dough an buggerising around he would have saved. —Sam Weller, *Old Bastards I Have Met*, p. 43, 1979

bugger it!
used as an expletive *UK, 1961*
A variation of **BUGGER!**.

buggerlugs *noun*
used as a form of friendly address *UK, 1934*
Originally nautical, used between men.
- DAD [to Denise]: See y'buggerlugs.—Caroline Aherne and Craig Cash, *The Royle Family*, 1999

bugger me!
used as an expletive *UK*
- "Bugger me!" says a lad with a shark's tooth on a chain round his neck.—*New Society*, 8th October 1981

bugger me backwards!
used for registering surprise or exasperation *UK*
An elaboration on **BUGGER ME!**.
- But, bugger me backwards, did we have to tolerate a load of the ballsachingly crap old bollocks as well?—*NME*, April 2000

bugger me dead!
used for registering surprise *AUSTRALIA*
- Bugger me dead!! I'm stoney! Haven't got a zac to me name!—Barry Humphries, *Bazza Pulls It Off!*, 1971

bugger me gently!
used for registering surprise *UK, 1984*
In the late 1980s and early 90s, this exclamation was very much associated with the character Lizzie Birdsworth in the Australian TV drama series *Prisoner Cell Block H*.

bugger off *verb*
to leave, to go *UK, 1922*
- He buggered off sharpish.—Hamish Imlach, *Cod Liver Oil and Orange Juice*, 1966

bugger sideways *verb*
to defeat someone, to confound someone *UK*
Often used as a personal exclamation: 'bugger me sideways!'.
- Tied them up in knots, turned them inside out and skinnned the sods alive. – Alive? – Buggered them sideways. Great days, great days. —James Hawes, *White Powder, Green Light*, p. 54, 2002

bugger sugar *noun*
cocaine *UK*
- —Mike Haskins, *Drugs*, p. 280, 2003

bugger that for a joke!
used as an expression of disbelief *NEW ZEALAND*
- Bugger that for a joke! —Dan Davin, *Roads from Hhomes*, p. 223, 1949

bugger this for a game of soldiers!; bugger that for a game of soldiers!
'no chance'; used as an emphatic dismissal of any activity or notion that you have no wish to subscribe to *UK*
A variation of SOD THIS FOR A GAME OF SOLDIERS!; FUCK THIS FOR A GAME OF SOLDIERS!, etc.

bugger up *verb*
to spoil something; to ruin something; to exhaust something *UK, 1937*
- The bad adjustment in your back has a ricochet effect all down your spine and buggers up your nervous system[.] —*The Guardian*, 24th August 2004

buggery *noun*
hell *UK, 1898*
A substitute for 'hell' in strong phrases of rejection, ruination and disapproval. Used in phrases such as 'like buggery' (vigorously: 1937), 'go to buggery!' (go away!: 1966) or 'is it buggery!' (not likely!: 1984).

▸ **to buggery; all to buggery**
a state of ruination or destruction *UK, 1923*
- I think that our sort – the slow sort – learns from failure (my novel is all to buggery). —Philip Larkin *(in a letter to JB Sutton)*, 26th January 1950

▸ **will I buggery!**
used as an expression of strong disagreement *UK, 1961*
Often applied in the third person: 'will he buggery!', 'will they buggery!'.

buggery *adjective*
used as an intensifier *UK*
On the model of BLOODY.
- [T]he buggery mountain rescue[.] —Jennifer Saunders, *Absolutely Fabulous*, p. 16, 1992

buggery bollocks!
used for registering annoyance *UK*
- EDINA: (Nearly fainting.) Oh, my buggery bollocks. Why the bloody hell didn't you tell me earlier? —Jennifer Saunders, *Absolutely Fabulous*, p. 19, 1992

bugger you!
used for registering anger towards someone *UK, 1887*
- 'I didn't do this to you.' I splutter, resisting the urge to scream 'Bugger you, what about me?!'. —Adele Parks, *Larger Than Life*, 2002

bugging *noun*
an instance of attacking someone with violence *UK*
- Bugging, I may explain, is what one meths man does to another. It is a cruder form of the infighting which goes on in polite society. —Geoffrey Fletcher, *Down Among the Meths Men*, p. 51, 1966

bugging *adjective*
1 disappointed, let down *US*
- —Connie Eble (Editor), *UNC-CH Campus Slang*, p. 2, March 1996

2 crazy *US*
- That cess [marijuana] got me buggin'. —Lois Stavsky et al., *A2Z*, p. 18, 1995

bugg off *verb*
▷ see: BUG OFF

buggy *noun*
1 a car *US, 1926*
Unavoidably, if not deliberately, folksy.
- I climbed into my buggy and turned it over. —Mickey Spillane, *I, The Jury*, p. 21, 1947
- What do you think a buggy like that costs? —Jim Thompson, *The Kill-Off*, p. 32, 1957

2 a brakevan (caboose) *US, 1899*
- —Norman Carlisle, *The Modern Wonder Book of Trains and Railroading*, p. 260, 1946

buggy *adjective*
silly, insane, or inbetween *US, 1902*
- Now, beat it, you baggy old bitch! Take your buggy boy friend and clear out of here before I forget I'm a lady. —Jim Thompson, *Pop. 1280*, p. 201, 1964
- He had no desire to go back up to his cutting room again, get all buggy with his thoughts. —Richard Price, *Clockers*, p. 435, 1992

buggy whip *noun*
a long radio antenna on a car or truck *US*
- —*American Speech*, p. 267, December 1962: 'The language of traffic policemen'

bug hole *noun*
a run-down, disreputable theatre *US*
- —Wilfred Granville, *The Theater Dictionary*, p. 26, 1952

bughouse *noun*
a mental hospital *US, 1899*
- "I told you he was bug-house, didn't I?" Jinx said. —Horace McCoy, *Kiss Tomorrow Good-bye*, p. 108, 1948
- Diane reminds old New Yorkers of the fabulous Broadway Rose, who used to panhandle in front of Lindy's until she was carted to the bug house. —Jack Lait and Lee Mortimer, *Washington Confidential*, p. 26–27, 1951
- You know you're not going to get out of here until you're ready for the bughouse, don't you? —Rocky Garciano (with Rowland Barber), *Somebody Up There Likes Me*, p. 214–215, 1955
- Yeah, what a business. Put a man in the bughouse if he ain't careful. —Robert Gover, *The Maniac Responsible*, p. 25, 1963
- I could snap up and get sent to the federal bughouse in Springfield, Missouri, or I could refuse to come out of my cell. —Edwin Torres, *Carlito's Way*, p. 124, 1975
- "Twelve years in St. Liz's bughouse," Harry said. —Elmore Leonard, *Pronto*, p. 258, 1993

bughouse *adjective*
insane, mad *US, 1894*
- Joe Castillo was, in his words, totally bughouse. —Joseph Wambaugh, *Lines and Shadows*, p. 135, 1984

bug joint *noun*
a premises that is infested with insects *UK*
- You could see as well as hear the fattened lice as they moved up the wallpaper in these bug-joints. Dead men are two a penny here. —Geoffrey Fletcher, *Down Among the Meths Men*, p. 60, 1966

bug juice *noun*
1 an insect repellant *US, 1944*
The term was coined in World War 2 and has been used since. In Vietnam, there was no shortage of bugs or 'bug juice', which was also used to light fires, clean weapons and heat cans of c-rations.
- Neither fire nor water nor bug juice nor anything except burning the bunks could get rid of them. —Chester Himes, *Cast the First Stone*, p. 77, 1952
- —Linda Reinberg, *In the Field*, p. 30, 1991

2 Kool-Aid™ (a fruit drink made from a powder to which you add water), or a sugary, powdered, artificially flavoured Kool-Aid-like drink *US, 1946*
Coined in World War 2, popular in Vietnam, and the title and subject of a rousing Girl Scout song sung to the tune of 'On Top of Old Smokey'.
- —Linda Reinberg, *In the Field*, p. 30, 1991
- He went up to the wardroom and got a glass of "bug juice" before he returned to his room. —Gerry Carroll, *North S*A*R*, p. 255, 1991
- Amazingly, it still tasted vaguely like grape bug juice. —Elissa Stein and Kevin Leslie, *Chunks*, p. 78, 1997

3 medication given those with mental disorders *US*
- —Gary K. Farlow, *Prison-ese*, p. 8, 2002

4 any antibiotic *US*
- —*Maledicta*, p. 117, 1984–1985: 'Milwaukee medical maledicta'
- —Sally Williams, *"Strong" Words*, p. 135, 1994

5 an opiate or other depressant used as knock-out drops *US*
- —Vincent J. Monteleone, *Criminal Slang*, p. 35, 1949

6 cheap alcohol *US, 1863*
Originally just meaning 'whisky' but, over time, less discerning.

7 in aviation, propeller de-icing fluid *US, 1945*
US Air Force use.

8 tear gas *US*
- —Hyman E. Goldin et al., *Dictionary of American Underworld Lingo*, p. 35, 1950
- —Jay Robert Nash, *Dictionary of Crime*, p. 48, 1992

bugle *noun*

1 the nose *US, 1865*

- George Piccolo, "a guy with a tremendous bugle on him," stumbled on some gang kids in Queens who were armed with chains and switchblades. —Leonard Shecter and William Phillips, *On the Pad*, p. 84, 1973
- —Tom Hibbert, *Rockspeak!*, p. 32, 1983
- And how much of my cocaine has gone up that big fat Filth [police] bugle of yourn? —Garry Bushell, *The Face*, p. 88, 2001
- —Paul Baker, *Polari*, p. 167, 2002

2 cocaine *UK*

Adapted from the previous sense, which is the favoured point of entry for most cocaine.

- If I tuck into too much skunk [strong marijuana] or bugle before I get on the decks all sorts of chaos is likely to follow. —Charlie Hall, *The Box [The Howard Marks Book of Dope Stories]*, p. 198, 1997
- They're not even going through the motions of sloping off to the WC for their bugle, these lads. It's right there, racked out in fat lines on the table. —Kevin Sampson, *Outlaws*, p. 162, 2001
- all these pints an the bugle in the bogs —Niall Griffiths, *Kelly + Victor*, p. 116, 2002

3 the erect penis *IRELAND*

- He could'ev given himself a bugle now, out there in the hall, just remembering what she was like and her smile; no problem. —Roddy Doyle, *The Van*, p. 53, 1991

bug off; bugg off *verb*

to go away *UK, 1976*

A broadcastable euphemism for **BUGGER OFF**.

- I could put a sign on the gate telling all BBC spies to bug off, but actually I have nothing to hide. — *The Times*, 29th September 2002

bug-out *noun*

1 any hasty retreat; a dramatic evasive manoeuver used by fighter pilots *US*

- If the feces really hits the fan, there are three points through which a man can run for the hills – rear exits in the trench called "bug-outs." —Martin Russ, *The Last Parallel*, p. 116, 1957
- In these "bug-outs" the men sometimes threw away their weapons without firing a shot. It was this "bug-out" atmosphere that caused General Walker to make his "stand-or-die" order. —Don Lawson, *The United States in the Korean War*, p. 33, 1964
- For those situations in which barrel rolling didn't work, McKeown devised a maneuver called the "bug out." —Robert K. Wilcox, *Scream of Eagles*, p. 140, 1990

2 a lively, wild time *US*

- His parents are away. It's gonna be a bug-out. — *Kids*, 1995

bug out *verb*

1 to flee *US, 1950*

- "Bugging out," a phrase describing unseemly and precipate flight, was already a battlefield cliche, and one regiment had already adopted "the Bug-Out Blues" as its "theme song." —Robert Leckie, *The Wars of America, Volume II*, p. 349, 1968
- Not long before I bugged out, there was violence in St. Peter's Square. —Tom Robbins, *Another Roadside Attraction*, p. 254, 1971
- The all-black 24th Infantry Regeiment had bugged out scandalously in Korea, even adopting the pop song "Bug-Out Blues' as its unofficial regimental theme[.] —Earl Thompson, *Tattoo*, p. 658, 1974
- The troops came up with a better catchword than Vietnamization, pithier, to the point. They were "bugging out." —Walter J. Boyne and Steven L. Thompson, *The Wild Blue*, p. 533, 1986
- There are strategic withdrawals, panicked routs, narrow escapes and many other forms of what mud soldiers call "bugging out." — *New York Times*, p. WK3, 18th November 2001

2 to go insane *US*

- —Francis J. Rigney and L. Douglas Smith, *The Real Bohemia*, p. xiii, 1961
- Dr. Dre admitted that it "tripped me out, bugged me the fuck out" when he discovered white kids were buying his records[.] —Barney Hoskyns, *Waiting For The Sun*, p. 337, 1996

bugout unit *noun*

a military unit with a reputation for running under fire *US*

Korean war usage.

- The 24th Regiment never overcame its reputation as a "bugout" unit – a derisive name GIs gave to troops who broke under fire. —Joseph C. Goulden, *Korea*, p. 169, 1982

bug rake *noun*

a comb *UK*

Juvenile; certainly since the 1950s, probably earlier.

- —Tom Hibbert, *Rockspeak!*, p. 32, 1983

bug roost *noun*

a hotel catering to oil field workers *US*

- —Jerry Robertson, *Oil Slanguage*, p. 32, 1954

bug run *noun*

a parting in the hair *UK, 1948*

- —John Laffin, *Jack Tar*, 1969

bugs *noun*

biology *UK*

School use.

- — *New Society*, 22nd August 1963

bugs *adjective*

crazy *US, 1903*

- "He's nutty." "He's bugs," said another. —Robert Gover, *The Maniac Responsible*, p. 191, 1963

Bugs Bunny; bugs; bugsy *noun*

money *AUSTRALIA*

Rhyming slang, based on the name of the Warner Brothers' animated cartoon character.

- —Ned Wallish, *The Truth Dictionary of Racing Slang*, p. 10, 1989
- —Ray Puxley, *Cockney Rabbit*, p. 26, 1992
- —Angela Devlin, *Prison Patter*, p. 32, 1996

Bugs Bunny *adjective*

funny *NEW ZEALAND, 1997*

Prison rhyming slang.

- —Harry Orsman, *A Dictionary of Modern New Zealand Slang*, p. 21, 1999

bug ship *noun*

during the Vietnam war, a Bell UH-1H Huey helicopter converted to spray the chemical defoliant Agent Orange *US*

- —Linda Reinberg, *In the Field*, p. 30, 1991

bugsmasher *noun*

a Beech C-47 Expeditor, a military transport plane used from World War 2 until early in the Vietnam war *US*

- —Linda Reinberg, *In the Field*, p. 30, 1991

bug splat *noun*

the limited devastation of targeted bombing *US*

- With typical sensitivity the Pentagon has dreamt up this term, with its shades of a blitzkreig-style computer game, to describe the bombing of Iraq. — *The Guardian*, 8th April 2003

bug test *noun*

a psychological fitness test *US*

- —Jay Robert Nash, *Dictionary of Crime*, p. 48, 1992

bug torch *noun*

a railway lantern *US*

- —J. Herbert Lund, *Herb's Hot Box of Railraod Slang*, p. 130, 1975

buh-bye

goodbye *US*

From a *Saturday Night Live* skit teasing the formulaic way in which flight attendants wish farewell to air passengers as they leave the plane.

- —Connie Eble (Editor), *UNC-CH Campus Slang*, p. 2, March 1996

build *verb*

1 to serve time in prison *US*

- You mean you've built two big ones in this jailhouse and you still don't know when to leave your cell partner alone for a few minutes? —Malcolm Braly, *On the Yard*, p. 209, 1967

2 to construct a marijuana cigarette *UK*

A variant is 'build up'.

- Back at his yard [home], he built up a killer spliff and enjoyed it. —Donald Gorgon, *Cop Killer*, p. 34, 1994
- He [...] started to build up with the bumper-sized patchouli skins he'd picked up in Macynlleth. —Kevin Sampson, *Powder*, p. 20, 1999
- She asked if I had any smoke [marijuana] [...] After due deliberation, I built one. —Diran Abedayo, *My Once Upon A Time*, p. 206, 2000
- I pulled up at the kerb and discreetly built myself a spliff. —Lanre Fehintola, *Charlie Says...*, p. 1, 2000

▸ **build a fire**

to operate a diesel truck at top speed *US*

- —Montie Tak, *Truck Talk*, p. 21, 1971

▸ **build that bridge**

to get over something that took place in the past *US*

- Girl, you need to build that bridge and get over it. He doesn't like you anymore. —Connie Eble (Editor), *UNC-CH Campus Slang*, p. 2, April 1995

builder *noun*
a bodybuilder *US*
- —*American Speech*, p. 198, Fall 1984: 'The language of bodybuilding'

building *noun*
▸ **on the building**
in the building trade *UK*
- I had a mate on the building once, he went crooked. —Clive Exton, *No Fixed Abode [Six Granada Plays]*, p. 121, 1959

build-up *noun*
in horse racing, betting at the track designed to increase the odds on a bet made away from the track *US*
- —Robert Saunders Dowst and Jay Craig, *Playing the Races*, p. 161, 1960

bukkake *noun*
a photograph or video depicting multiple men ejaculating onto a single woman *US*
Japanese slang meaning 'splash', used by English-speakers with no further knowledge of Japanese; a popular fetish in the US and UK. The prototype video shows a pretty young girl kneeling at the centre of a room with many men (up to several hundred) masturbating off camera and ejaculating on her with no further sexual contact.
- Bizarre rituals such as bukkake videos, which feature as many as 80 men ejaculating one after another into a woman's face while she holds a bowl underneath her chin, pushed the limits even further. —*LA Weekly*, p. 18, 14th January 2000
- Liquid Gold 5 features women doing number one and (ain't that America!) getting paid for it. —*New Times Los Angeles*, 19th July 2001
- The porn phenomenon known as bukkake shoots homophobia and misogyny right in the face. —*Village Voice*, p. 144, 20th March 2001

bukuso'clock *noun*
in the evening *SOUTH AFRICA*
- —*Sunday Times (South Africa)*, 1st June 2003

bulb *noun*
the core of a capsule of drugs *US*
- —Eugene Landy, *The Underground Dictionary*, p. 41, 1971

bulb snatcher *noun*
an electrician, especially one engaged in bulb replacement *US*
- You're the bulb snatcher. You go from one end of the ship to the other and change any burnt-out bulb you find. —Earl Thompson, *Tattoo*, p. 312, 1974

bulge *noun*
1 the male genitals, especially as may be hinted at or imagined when dressed *UK*
- —Paul Baker, *Polari*, p. 185, 2002

2 a lead *US, 1951*
Sports usage, describing team standings.
- —Harold Wentworth and Stuart Berg Flexner, *Dictionary of American Slang*, p. 71, 1960

bulk *noun*
▸ **in bulk; in baulk; in balk**
unable to do anthing; disabled *UK, 1937*
From 'baulk' (an area of a snooker or billiards table) suggesting 'out of play'.
- We was in bulk, though. Fucking killing ourselves [with laughter], we was. —Kevin Sampson, *Outlaws*, p. 36, 2001
- Fuckin hurts as well. Me back's in bulk. —Niall Griffiths, *Kelly + Victor*, p. 106, 2002

bulk *adjective*
large in amount or quantity *AUSTRALIA, 1977*
- Maybe Leith doesn't want to take on bulk reading, just so we can pretend we're Edwardians. —Jenny Pausacker, *What are ya?*, p. 32, 1987
- After an arm-wrestle with the garlic crusher over the guacamole, you pig out on a bulk bowl of beans. —Kathy Lette, *Girls' Night Out*, p. 12, 1987

bulk *adverb*
many; much
- He musn't be allowed to think that you don't have bulk other things to do. —Kathy Lette, *Girls' Night Out*, p. 15, 1987

bulkhead *verb*
to speak disparagingly in a voice intended to be overheard *US, 1863*
- —J. E. Lighter, *Historical Dictionary of American Slang, Volume 1*, p. 297, 1994

bulkie *noun*
in Boston, a sandwich roll *US*
- —Jim Crotty, *How to Talk American*, p. 24, 1997

bull *noun*
1 nonsense *US, 1902*
An abbreviation of **BULLSHIT**.
- [W]e cook weenies, drink Tokay – I make love to big Swedish student girl Edeltrude. —Jack Kerouac, *Letter to Allen Ginsberg*, p. 384, 8th November 1952
- No use going crook at the Yanks. They're a poor, silly, ignorant mob of bastards, who've been fed on bull from the day they were born. —Eric Lambert, *The Veterans*, p. 159, 1954
- Cut the bull. An' don't call me sir. —Nino Culotta (John O'Grady), *They're A Weird Mob*, p. 15, 1957
- Not the bull they teach you in Sunday school. —John Rechy, *City of Night*, p. 327, 1963
- When you spout that old bull I know you're going to give me good advice. —Jean Brooks, *The Opal Witch*, p. 125, 1967
- You don't bung on bull like a lot of these blokes you see around tha place these days. —Alexander Buzo, *Rooted*, p. 78, 1969
- ''We were just unlucky to strike that one in a thousand.' 'Bloody bull, Mike and you know it.'' —Bettina Arndt, *The Australian Way of Sex*, p. 86, 1985

2 a police officer, especially a detective; a prison guard *US, 1893*
- It's better you tell me than have the bulls drag you to the station. —Mickey Spillane, *I, The Jury*, p. 43, 1947
- Now I know the bulls of the Fifth Street station are really after me. —Rocky Garciano (with Rowland Barber), *Somebody Up There Likes Me*, p. 71, 1955
- Madam alla time sayin how them bulls extorshun her. —Robert Gover, *One Hundred Dollar Misunderstanding*, p. 175, 1961
- "Rucker!" a bull's voice calls. "I comin." —Ken Kesey, *Last Whole Earth Catalog*, p. 234, 1971
- Big Jeff, as usual, was the first bull through the door. Imagine, Augie Robles, cornered, with four, count 'em, four pistols, waiting on you. SHee-it. The bulls killed Augie that night[.] —Edwin Torres, *Carlito's Way*, p. 17, 1972
- We spoke generally of a couple mutual acquaintances, complained a bit about how hot the streets are these days with bulls every-where[.] —Herbert Huncke, *The Evening Sun Turned Crimson*, p. 161, 1980
- "The British Columbia Provincials are a hopeless gang of men," he said. Canadian bulls never bothered me for a minute. —George Bowering, *Caprice*, p. 125, 1987
- The bulls are across the street. They're watching everything we do. —*Goodfellas*, 1990

3 an aggressive, mannish lesbian *US*
- Known variously as a bull, a stomper, a bad butch, a hard dresser, a truck driver, a diesel dyke, a bull dagger and a half dozen other soubriquets, she is the one who, according to most homosexual girls, gives lesbians a bad name. —Ruth Allison, *Lesbianism*, p. 125, 1967

4 in prison, a person who can withstand physical hardship *US*
- —Charles Shafer, *Folk Speech in Texas Prisons*, p. 199, 1990

5 a wharf labourer unfairly favoured for employment *AUSTRALIA, 1957*

6 an aggressive poker bettor *US*
- —George Percy, *The Language of Poker*, p. 14, 1988

7 in the circus, an elephant, male or female *US, 1921*
- [E]lephants are called "bulls" or "pigs". —Butch Reynolds, *Broken Hearted Clown*, p. 32, 1953
- —Joe McKennon, *Circus Lingo*, p. 21, 1980
- —Don Wilmeth, *The Language of American Popular Entertainment*, p. 36, 1981

8 a battle tank *US*
- Get that bull off us, over! —Charles Anderson, *The Grunts*, p. 119, 1976

9 in a deck of playing cards, an ace *US*
- —Irwin Steig, *Common Sense in Poker*, p. 182, 1963

▷ **see: BULLDYKE**

bull *verb*
1 to polish something, especially boots; hence, to clean a uniform, kit or quarters *UK*
A variant is 'bull up'. Services usage since 1950, possibly earlier.

2 to lie; to pretend; to distort the truth or exaggerate; to tell tall stories *AUSTRALIA*
- I suppose that's why he goes on like that, skiting and "bulling". —Eric Lambert, *The Veterans*, p. 129, 1954
- And guess wot? I was bulling! —Kylie Mole (Maryanne Fahey), *My Diary*, p. 6, 1988

3 to take the active role in homosexual anal sex; to be a homosexual *BARBADOS*
- G– said that he heard M– say that C– 'bulled his way through the Gold Coast in St. James'. —*The Advocate (Barbados)*, p. 1, 13th February 1987

4 in poker, to bluff repeatedly, betting in amounts designed to drive other players out of hands simply by virtue of the size of the bet *US*
- —Irwin Steig, *Common Sense in Poker*, p. 182, 1963

bull *adjective*
when describing a military rank, full *US*
Korean war usage.
- He finally made bull colonel: he's deserved it a long time. —Walter J. Sheldon, *Gold Bait*, p. 47, 1973
- The orders came, brawled by a bull sergeant. —Michael Shaara, *The Killer Angels*, p. 326, 1974

bull!
used as an expression of utter disbelief, often surprised or contemptuous disbelief *AUSTRALIA*
A euphemistic shortening of BULLSHIT.
- Foo was here. Bull to that. *We* was there! —J.E. MacDonnell, *Sabotage!*, p. 48, 1964
- 'Bull!' he snorted. 'You can't give a thing the Victoria Cross.' —J.E. MacDonnell, *Sabotage!*, p. 52, 1964
- 'You'll have to watch your step there tonight. They think you pulled a fast one.' 'Bull.' —Wilda Moxham, *The Apprentice*, p. 75, 1969

Bullamakanka *noun*
an imaginary remote place *AUSTRALIA, 1953*

bull and cow *noun*
an argument, a disturbance *UK, 1859*
Rhyming slang for 'row'.

bull and pants *noun*
trousers *AUSTRALIA, 1961*
Rhyming slang for 'pants'.

bull artist *noun*
a person who habitually lies or exaggerates *US, 1918*
- "Oh, brother!" she said. "What a bull artist!!" —Jim Thompson, *Pop. 1280*, p. 209, 1964
- God, you're a bull artist. —Wilda Moxham, *The Apprentice*, p. 144, 1969
- —Alexander Buzo, *Rooted*, p. 78, 1969
- But then when dad woke up Adam reckoned it was me! Adam is such a bull artist. —Kylie Mole (Maryanne Fahey), *My Diary*, p. 34, 1988

bullcrap *noun*
nonsense *US, 1935*
A slightly euphemised BULLSHIT.
- "She's too good for me," Chico admitted. Bull-crap, Angel thought[.] —Hal Ellson, *The Golden Spike*, p. 57, 1952

bulldag *verb*
to perform oral sex on a woman *US, 1954*
- Cause, whore, I'm gonna sleigh-ride you and bulldag you too. —Bruce Jackson, *Get Your Ass in the Water and Swim Like Me*, p. 125, 1965

bulldagger *noun*
a lesbian with masculine affectations and mannerisms *US, 1929*
A variant of BULLDYKE.
- She dresses like a goddamn bull dagger. —James Baldwin, *Another Country*, p. 31, 1962
- Now the hostess of the evenin' was Free-Turn Flor / she brought fifteen bulldaggers to put on the show. —Bruce Jackson, *Get Your Ass in the Water and Swim Like Me*, p. 148, 1964
- I remember once my little sister asked my mother, "Mama, is that a lady or a man?" It wa a stud. Mama just looked at her and said, "That's a bull-dagger, baby." —Claude Brown, *Manchild in the Promised Land*, p. 205, 1965
- Known variously as a bull, a stomper, a bad butch, a hard dresser, a truck driver, a diesel dyke, a bull dagger and a half dozen other soubriquets, she is the one who, according to most homosexual girls, gives lesbians a bad name. —Ruth Allison, *Lesbianism*, p. 125, 1967
- Feeling low and square, bashful as a faggot at a bulldagger's ball, Dip pulled his bill out of his pocket and threw them on the table. —Steve Cannon, *Groove, Bang, and Jive Around*, p. 28, 1969
- [I]t would be terrible to get your ass kicked on the street ... even if it was by a bulldagger ... like, well, after all, she was still a woman. —Odie Hawkins, *Chicago Hustle*, p. 71, 1977
- They'll put you right back in with the bull daggers. —Gerald Petievich, *Money Men*, p. 85, 1981
- "Like old turkey necks," is how they [penises] looked to this bulldagger fitted with boobs bigger than her head. —Seth Morgan, *Homeboy*, p. 16, 1990
- She's so beautiful. I always thought bulldaggers were ugly. —Eve Ensler, *The Vagina Monologues*, p. 81, 1998
- My girlfriend grabs my candy-coated hand and lugs me back to the Lex, where the jukebox is booming Cheapt Trick and the bulldaggers are stalking the pool table. —*Nerve*, p. 17, October-November 2000

bull derm *noun*
any low grade of tobacco issued by the state to prisoners *US*
A corruption of Bull Durham™, an RJ Reynolds tobacco brand.
- —AFSCME Local 3963, *The Correctional Officer's Guide to Prison Slang*, 2001

bulldog *noun*
1 the earliest edition of a morning newspaper *US*
- —Rachel S. Epstein and Nina Liebman, *Biz Speak*, p. 28, 1986

2 a Mack™ truck *US*
From the company's logo.
- —Montie Tak, *Truck Talk*, p. 21, 1971

3 in electric line work, a wire grip used for holding a conductor under tension *US*
- —A.B. Chance Co., *Lineman's Slang Dictionary*, p. 3, 1980

bulldog *verb*
1 to turn a safe upside down and use an explosive to open it from the bottom *US*
- —Vincent J. Monteleone, *Criminal Slang*, p. 36, 1949

2 (used of a professional insider in horse racing) to falsely claim to have given good information in a completed race *US*
- —*San Francisco News*, 14th February 1968

3 in the illegal production of alcohol, to sweat whisky out of used barrel staves *US*
- —David W. Maurer, *Kentucky Moonshine*, p. 114, 1974

4 to intimidate someone verbally and/or physically *US*
- —William K. Bentley and James M. Corbett, *Prison Slang*, p. 91, 1992

bulldog nose *noun*
a severe case of gonorrhea *US*
A truly hideous image.
- —Dale Gordon, *The Dominion Sex Dictionary*, p. 34, 1967

bulldoze *verb*
to coerce, to bully or to intimidate someone, especially to further political ends *US, 1876*
By back-formation from conventional 'bulldozer' (a heavy caterpillar tractor for removing obstacles).

bulldozer *noun*
a poker player whose aggressive betting is not contingent upon holding a good hand *US*
- —George Percy, *The Language of Poker*, p. 14, 1988

bull dust *noun*
nonsense, rubbish *AUSTRALIA, 1951*
A euphemism for BULLSHIT, but based on the Australian English term 'bulldust' (fine powdery dirt or sand as found in a stockyard).
- —John Wynnum, *Tar Dust*, p. 27, 1962
- Sydney papers, Sydney beer. Bulldust an' Pommy piss. Not worth readin', not worth drinkin'. —John O'Grady, *It's Your Shout, Mate!*, p. 68, 1972
- —David McGill, *David McGill's Complete Kiwi Slang Dictionary*, p. 22, 1998

bulldust *verb*
to lie; to pretend; to distort the truth or exaggerate; to tell tall stories *AUSTRALIA, 1967*
- "I'll stick to me mates, like a dinkum Aussie," Little Tich bulldusted on[.] —Frank Hardy, *The Outcasts of Foolgarah*, p. 23, 1971

bulldyke; bulldike; bull *noun*
a lesbian with masculine affectations and mannerisms *US, 1931*
- You lousy bulldike! —George Mandel, *Flee the Angry Strangers*, p. 386, 1952
- He was torn in two by a bull dike. Most terrific vaginal grip I ever experienced. —William Burroughs, *Naked Lunch*, p. 91, 1957
- "Well, really, darling," she said, because I was clearly puzzled, "if it's not about a couple of old bull-dykes, what the hell is it about?" —Truman Capote, *Breakfast at Tiffany's*, p. 21, 1958
- On the dancefloor, too, lesbians – the masculine ones, the bull-dikes – dance with hugely effeminate queens[.] —John Rechy, *City of Night*, p. 184, 1963
- The occasional cigar-smoking leather-jacket bull dyke may bend the regulation. —Roger Gordon, *Hollywood's Sexual Underground*, p. 25, 1966
- Deputy Dot Rothstein, 200 + pounds of bull dyke with the hots for my friend Chris Staples. —James Elroy, *Hollywood Nocturnes*, p. 21, 1994
- I looked like a bull dyke or the trick of one, with handcuffrs, a leather jacket, metal belts, and levi 501's, so I would try to method act. —Jennifer Blowdryer, *White Trash Debutante*, p. 56, 1997
- —Paul Baker, *Polari*, p. 167, 2002

bulldyker; bulldiker *noun*
a lesbian with masculine affectations and mannerisms *US, 1906*
A variant of BULLDYKE.
- The compound bulldiker seems to stem from adjectival use of bull and ram as intensifiers among West Indians. —Peter Tamony, *Dike*, p. 6, 1972

- Last night some bulldiker tried to stab Apeman when he tried to collect.—Donald Goines, *Black Gangster*, p. 213, 1977

buller *noun*
a male homosexual *BARBADOS*
- —Richard Allsopp, *Dictionary of Caribbean English Usage*, p. 120, 1996

bullet *noun*
1 one year of a prison sentence *US, 1967*
- He had served a bullet 'n' a deuce.—Lightnin' Rod, *Hustlers Convention*, p. 10, 1973
- Richard, you're looking at a dime minimum this time. Ten bullets. You think you can handle that?—James Ellroy, *Blood on the Moon*, p. 90, 1984
- What's another bullet, wild or bowlegged . . . Anyways they have to convict first.—Seth Morgan, *Homeboy*, p. 141, 1990

2 in cards, an ace *US, 1807*
- The banker spread his hand. A flush. "Four bullets," Rick said joyously, slapping them down.—John D. McDonald, *The Neon Jungle*, p. 57, 1953
- —Steve Kuriscak, *Casino Talk*, p. 7, 1985

3 a portion of marijuana wrapped in plastic or tinfoil *NEW ZEALAND*
- When a search warrant was executed at the defendant's flat they found 19 cannabis 'bullets'.—*Preess*, p. 19, 21st August 1979
- Dean smoked dope every day. Scoring a bullet (about three joints) on a Thursday was almost a ritual.—*(Aukland) Metro*, p. 122, September 1993

4 a quart bottle of beer, especially of Budweiser™ beer *US*
- —*American Speech*, p. 61, February 1967: 'Soda-fountain, restaurant and tavern calls'

5 a capsule of secobarbital sodium (trade name Seconal™), a central nervous system depressant *US, 1972*
- —Richard A. Spears, *The Slang and Jargon of Drugs and Drink*, p. 83, 1986

6 a device that delivers a measured quantity of powdered drug for inhalation *UK*
- —Alon Shulman, *The Style Bible*, p. 45, 1999

7 a narcotic suppository *US*
- —Inez Cardozo-Freeman, *The Joint*, p. 485, 1984

8 a rivet *US*
- —Harold Wentworth and Stuart Berg Flexner, *Dictionary of American Slang*, p. 72, 1960

9 a short surfboard with a rounded nose *US*
- —Trevor Cralle, *The Surfin'ary*, p. 16, 1991

10 in skateboarding, a riding position: crouching low on the board with arms outstretched *US*
- —Laura Torbet, *The Complete Book of Skateboarding*, p. 105, 1976

11 a single spurt of semen during male ejaculation *US, 1966*
Plays on **SHOOT** (to ejaculate).
- —David Rowan, *A Glossary for the 90s*, 1998

12 dismissal from employment *UK, 1841*
- I got the hoof, man. The sack, the chop, the proverbial bullet.—Doug Lang, *Freaks*, p. 89, 1973

13 a rejection letter *US*
- —Connie Eble (Editor), *UNC-CH Campus Slang*, p. 1, Fall 1982

▸ **put a bullet in Rover**
to stop talking and start listening *US*
- The expression "put a bullet in Rover" is common street slang for "shut up and listen," Mike explained. "It's an everyday expression, but they don't know it because they don't know the streets."—*Orlando (Florida) Sentinel Tribune*, p. E1, 23rd July 1992

▸ **with a bullet**
advancing up the popular music charts *US*
From the typographical symbol that indicates the tune's progress.
- —Jay Saporita, *Pourin' It All Out*, p. 201, 1980

bullet bag *noun*
a condom *UK*
Combines **BULLET** (an ejaculation of semen) with a suitable carrier/container.
- —David Rowan, *A Glossary for the 90s*, 1998

bullet lane *noun*
the passing lane on a motorway *US*
- —Lanie Dills, *The Official CB Slanguage Language Dictionary*, p. 21, 1976

bulletproof *adjective*
1 invulnerable, irrefutable *UK, 1961*
- Mr. Rumsfeld claimed last month that American intelligence had 'bulletproof' evidence of links between al-Qaida and the Iraqi regime. He later added: 'But they're not photographs. They're not beyond a reasonable doubt'.—*The Guardian*, 10th October 2002

2 in computing, able to withstand any change or external stimulus *US*
- —Eric S. Raymond, *The New Hacker's Dictionary*, p. 84, 1991

bullet-stopper *noun*
a soldier in the infantry *US*
- —*Seattle Times*, p. A9, 12th April 1998

bull feathers *noun*
nonsense *US*
A euphemism for **BULLSHIT**.
- The statement left no room for doubt. "Bullfeathers," said Charles O. Finley, owner of the Oakland A's.—*San Francisco Examiner*, p. 45, 15th June 1971
- Bull feathers. That amonts to bureaucratic blackmail.—*San Diego Union-Tribune*, p. NC2, 18th October 2003

bullfighter *noun*
an empty railway carriage *US*
- —Norman Carlisle, *The Modern Wonder Book of Trains and Railroading*, p. 260, 1946
- —Ramon Adams, *The Language of the Railroader*, p. 24, 1977

bull fries *noun*
the cooked testicles of castrated bulls *CANADA*
More commonly known in the US as 'prairie oysters'.
- —Chris Thain, *Cold as a Bay Street Banker's Heart*, p. 27, 1987

bullfrog *verb*
in craps, to make a bet on a single roll of the dice *US, 1983*
- —Thomas L. Clark, *The Dictionary of Gambling and Gaming*, p. 30, 1987

bullfucker *noun*
a liar; used as a friendly form of address to a fellow *US*
Blends **BULLSHITTER** (a liar) and **MOTHERFUCKER** (a person).
- "You promised me that if I did the European tour I wouldn't have to drive with you," claims a grinning Davis. "Bullfucker," retorts Nugent. "You don't mind my driving!"—*Ask*, p. 44, 5th May 1979

bull gang *noun*
a large work crew, especially of unskilled workers *US*
- —Jerry Robertson, *Oil Slanguage*, p. 33, 1954

bull goose *noun*
1 a railway yardmaster *US*
- —Ramon Adams, *The Language of the Railroader*, p. 24, 1977

2 by extension, the person in charge of any situation *US, 1932*
- "Old Foster is the bull goose out at the Army Hospital," meaning that Colonel Foster was the commandant."—Vance Randolph, *Down in the Holler*, p. 231, 1953
- Who's the bull goose loony here?—Ken Kesey, *One Flew Over the Cuckoo's Nest*, p. 18, 1962
- —Frederic G. Cassidy, *Dictionary of American Regional English, Volume 1*, p. 445, 1985
- Tara Redi, 26, who plays a student writing about Van at the behest of campus newspaper editor Tom Everett Scott, 31, when she's not suffering the company of her bull-goose jerk of a boyfriend, Daniel Cosgrove, also 31.—*Cincinnati Enquirer*, p. 9W, 5th April 2002

bullhead *noun*
an extremely large penis *US*
- I told her to make a guy think he has a bullhead for a dick even if it's not as large as her clitoris.—A.S. Jackson, *Gentleman Pimp*, p. 167, 1973

bull horrors *noun*
the terror of the police felt by a drug addicit *US, 1927*
- —Vincent J. Monteleone, *Criminal Slang*, p. 36, 1949
- —Eugene Landy, *The Underground Dictionary*, p. 41, 1971

bullia capital *noun*
crack cocaine *UK, 1998*
- —Mike Haskins, *Drugs*, p. 281, 2003

bulling *adjective*
1 very good *US*
- —Lavada Durst, *The Jives of Dr. Hepcat*, p. 11, 1953

2 enraged *IRELAND*
- It was unfair of Balls to pick on me like that. I was bulling.—Ardal O'Hanlon, *The Talk of the Town*, p. 185, 1998

bullion *noun*
crack cocaine *UK, 1998*
- —Mike Haskins, *Drugs*, p. 281, 2003

bull it through *verb*
to accomplish something by sheer strength rather than by skill and planning, especially of an outdoor task *CANADA, 1961*

bull jive *noun*
1 insincere talk *US*
• —Hermese E. Roberts, *The Third Ear*, 1971

2 marijuana that has been adulterated with catnip or another leaf-like substance *US*
• —David W. Maurer and Victor Vogel, *Narcotics and Narcotics Addiction*, p. 393, 1973

bull juice *noun*
condensed milk *UK*
Mainly nautical use.
• —Robert Harbinson, *Up Spake the Cabin-Boy*, 1961

bull-moose *noun*
a huge, powerful man; hence, a foreman *US, c. 1940*

bull night *noun*
an evening on which recruits and trainees are confined to barracks to prepare for an inspection the following day *UK*
Military, based on **BULL** (to polish, to clean). Remembered by Beale, 1984, from usage during National Service which ended in 1962.

bull nun *noun*
a monk *CANADA*
• I thought of my sins and decided that next year I would enter a monastery. "So you want to be a bull nun, Mr. Crogan?"—J. McNamee, *Florencia Bay*, p. 121, 1960

bullo *noun*
nonsense *AUSTRALIA, 1942*
An elaboration of **BULL**.

bullock *verb*
1 to work tirelessly *AUSTRALIA, 1875*
Adopting the characteristic from the beast.

2 to use an inner-strength and determination in order to get your way or follow your ambition *AUSTRALIA, 1930*
A figurative use of the previous sense.

bullocking *adjective*
strong and aggressive in attack *NEW ZEALAND*
From an earlier sense of the word (hard physical work).
• Now the bullocking forward is king of the field.—Gordon Slatter, *A Gun in my Hand*, p. 80, 1959

bullock's blood *noun*
a drink of rum mixed in strong ale *UK*
• —Michael Gilbert, *The Doors Open*, 1949

bullocky *noun*
beef *AUSTRALIA, 1839*
Pidgin.

bull of the woods *noun*
1 a college official such as a dean *US*
• —Marcus Hanna Boulware, *Jive and Slang of Students in Negro Colleges*, 1947

2 in oil drilling, an important company official *US*
• —Jerry Robertson, *Oil Slanguage*, p. 118, 1954

3 on the railways, a carriage shop foreman *US*
• —*American Speech*, p. 286, December 1968: 'Addenda to the vocabulary of railroading'

bullpen *noun*
1 a holding cell in a courtroom or a jail *US, 1880*
• I stepped into the bull pen, followed him dumbly.—Chester Himes, *If He Hollers Let Him Go*, p. 200, 1945
• From there they were sent to the bullpen to await the wagon[.]—Hal Ellson, *The Golden Spike*, p. 240, 1952
• They come from the bullpen to the Tombs up to their floor.—James Mills, *The Panic in Needle Park*, p. 44, 1966
• I was in what is called the bullpen, waiting to go into court.—Piri Thomas, *Down These Mean Streets*, p. 245, 1967
• The last time I saw Elsie was in the bullpen – sort of cowering in the corner surrounded by a group of young Westside hoods[.]—Herbert Huncke, *The Evening Sun Turned Crimson*, p. 40, 1980
• The bailiff thrust him into the bullpen.—Seth Morgan, *Homeboy*, p. 145, 1990

2 an open area in an office with desks *US*
• The bullpen was a large room in the Field Office which was crammed wiht rows of gray metal desks facing one another.—Gerald Petievich, *To Live and Die in L.A.*, p. 53, 1983
• —Kathleen Odean, *High Steppers, Fallen Angels, and Lollipops*, p. 157, 1988

3 in a nightclub, chairs without tables for patrons who want only to listen to the music *US*
• These bull pens still exist in bop palaces around the country.—Robert Sylvester, *No Cover Charge*, p. 275, 1956

4 a room where a work crew congregates *US*
• —Norman Carlisle, *The Modern Wonder Book of Trains and Railroading*, p. 260, 1946

bull prick *noun*
in oil drilling, an elevator pin *US*
• —Jerry Robertson, *Oil Slanguage*, p. 33, 1954

bullpup *noun*
1 a target pistol, especially one with an elaborate stock *US*
• —*American Speech*, p. 192, October 1957: 'Some colloquialisms of the handgunner'

2 the air-to-ground missile (AGM) carried on fighter jets *US*
• —Linda Reinberg, *In the Field*, p. 20, 1991

bull ring *noun*
1 a strongly-muscled anus; in terms of anal intercourse, a virgin anus *UK*
Homosexual use.
• —*Gayness Explained, The FHM Little Book of Bloke*, p. 142, June 2003

2 in motor racing, an oval track *US*
• —John Lawlor, *How to Talk Car*, p. 26, 1965

3 in horse racing, a small track *US*
• —Tom Ainslie, *Ainslie's Complete Guide to Thoroughbred Racing*, p. 329, 1976

bullring camp *noun*
a homosexual male brothel *UK*
• —*Maledicta*, p. 144, Summer/Winter 1986–1987: 'Sexual slang: prostitutes, pedophiles, flagellators, transvestites, and necrophiles'

bullringer *noun*
on the railways, a yard pointsman *US*
• —Linda Niemann, *Boomer*, p. 247, 1990

bulls *noun*
nonsense *AUSTRALIA*
A shortening of **BULLSHIT**.
• —Alex Buzo, *Rooted*, 1969

bull-scare *verb*
(used of the police) to frighten or intimindate someone without arresting them *US*
• At four a.m. my man the grifter called to report that the gorilla had been bull scared into taking a train back to New York.—Iceberg Slim (Robert Beck), *The Naked Soul of Iceberg Slim*, p. 86, 1971

bull session *noun*
an informal group discussion *US, 1919*
• —Lou Shelly, *Hepcats Jive Talk Dictionary*, p. 22, 1945
• For instance, if you were having a bull session in somebody's room, and somebody wanted to come in, nobody'd let them in if they were some dopey, pimply guy.—J.D. Salinger, *Catcher in the Rye*, p. 167, 1951
• The kids who come from tough families, who have fathers or brothers serving time someplace upstate, are much further advanced than the rest of us, and they learn us all they know in our bull sessions.—Rocky Garciano (with Rowland Barber), *Somebody Up There Likes Me*, p. 36, 1955
• He said that when Kossmeyer came down the three of us ought to get together some night and have us a bull session.—Jim Thompson, *The Kill-Off*, p. 28, 1957
• Once a week, he said, a very few of the other people employed by the university dropped in at one another's houses for a bull session.—Clancy Sigal, *Going Away*, p. 244, 1961
• For instance, the bullsessions: I found that half the things they talked about were over my head[.]—Robert Gover, *Poorboy at the Party*, p. 5, 1966
• As for the college audiences, they listened to me in the early '50's because they were surprised that a comedian could have written term papers and wondered about the meaning of life in bull sessions.—Mort Sahl, *Heartland*, p. 103, 1976

bull's eye *noun*
1 a powerful, focused torch *US*
• —Jay Robert Nash, *Dictionary of Crime*, p. 49, 1992

2 fifty pounds (£50) *UK*
From the score at darts.
- [H]e peeled off twenty second-hand bull's eyes[.] —Greg Williams, *Diamond Geezers*, p. 12, 1997
- Harry offered him a "bulls-eye" to come and watch over him during a trade in his Stratford local. —Garry Bushell, *The Face*, p. 107, 2001

bullsh *noun*
nonsense, rubbish *AUSTRALIA, 1919*
A euphemistic shortening of **BULLSHIT**.
- I can't flamin' wait to get shot of these pommy drongos. I've just about had a Ned-Kelly-full of their line of bullsh! —Barry Humphries, *The Wonderful World of Barry McKenzie*, p. 9, 1968

bullshipper *noun*
an oilfield worker from Oklahoma *US*
- —Jerry Robertson, *Oil Slanguage*, p. 33, 1954

bullshit *noun*
nonsense *US, 1914*
- Let's jus leave all this bullshit and beat it. —George Mandel, *Flee the Angry Strangers*, p. 205, 1952
- Efan was a man who always backed up his bullshit with action, which explains why he was always getting himself in these impossible situations. —Cecil Brown, *The Life & Loves of Mr. Jiveass Nigger*, p. 62, 1969
- Nearly everything I have ever read or been told about why people gamble is just plain bullshit. —Mario Puzo, *Inside Las Vegas*, p. 133, 1977
- Every fucking scientist in the country would get in on the action, every paper would write tons of bullshit[.] —Petru Popescu, *The Last Wave*, p. 120, 1977
- Carter, Reagan and Anderson. It's all bullshit. (Radio commerical for Barry Commoner). —*San Francisco Chronicle*, p. 12, 15th October 1980
- [PRESIDENT RICHARD] NIXON [heard on radio]: I have never been a quitter. *Bullshit.* —Sal Piro and Michael Hess, *The Official 'Rocky Horror Picture Show' Audience Participation Guide*, p. 12, 1991
- This is bullshit. This is a bullshit lead. This is totally bullshit. —*Break Point*, 1991
- You don't want to believe any of that bullshit about these characters all being great mates after stumps are pulled. —Harrison Biscuit, *The Search for Savage Henry*, p. 8, 1995

bullshit *verb*
to deceive someone, to fool someone *US, 1937*
- Through the port...I climbed out on the bodkin...I'm not bullshitting Chris. —Robert S. Close, *Love Me Sailor*, p. 141, 1945
- I was just bull shittin' her all the way down the line anyway to try to make peace before I get out of the house. —Babs Gonzales, *Movin' On Down De Line*, p. 126, 1975
- Elijah leaned in closer, glancing into Toe's eyes, from time to time, checking out the pulse vein on the side of his throat, watching his hands as he talked, paying close attention to all the things that might tell him whether or not the bullshitter was trying to bullshit the bullshitter. —Odie Hawkins, *Chicago Hustle*, p. 126, 1977
- I took the liberty of bullshitting you, okay? —*The Blues Brothers*, 1980
- I knew he was bullshitting. —*Ferris Buehler's Day Off*, 1986
- Lonely John had bullshitted the receivers with his new suit and his dodgy business cards. —Harrison Biscuit, *The Search for Savage Henry*, p. 94, 1995
- I didn't care. I had lost the ability to bullshit. —*Jerry Maguire*, 1996
- The way I see it, bullshitting and lying are completely different [...] When a bullshitter bullshits, it's purely for the sake of bullshitting. —Danny King, *The Burglar Diaries*, p. 111, 2001

bullshit
nonsense!, rubbish! *AUSTRALIA*
- —Barry Humphries, *The Traveller's Tool*, p. 61, 1985
- 'No, wake up. There's been a shooting!' 'Bullshit.' 'Fair dinkum. Down at the pub.' —Phillip Gwynne, *Deadly Unna?*, p. 193, 1998

bullshit artist *noun*
a person who habitually lies or exaggerates *US, 1942*
- And, of course, Borky was a champion bullshit artist[.] —Frank Hardy, *The Outcasts of Foolgarah*, p. 198, 1971
- The next day Vladimir goes to a Cuban-American immigration lawyer, who tells of coming to America to escape Castro, "a Cuban bullshit artist who has been taken in by Russian bullshit artists." —*Perpetuating Patriotric Perceptions*, p. 102, 1993
- —John Birmingham, *He Died With a Felafel in his Hand*, p. 172, 1994
- He knew he was a phoney. He was a total bullshit artist on some levels, and often that makes a great writer. —Nancy Steinbeck, *The Other Side of Eden*, p. 150, 2000
- My wife always thought that he was a bullshit artist, so we just played with him, let him entertain himself. —*New Times Boward-Palm Beach (Florida)*, 25th December 2003

bullshit-ass *adjective*
rubbishy, awful *US*
Combines **BULLSHIT** (nonsense) with **-ASS** (an intensifier for the preceeding adjective).
- After reading that Mobb Deep [hip-hop artists] article and hearing that bullshit-ass album, I don't know what's going on[.] —*The Source*, p. 44, March 2002

bullshit baffles brains
used to describe the defeat of logic by a convincing argument *UK*
Originally military, probably from World War 2, this catchphrase even gave rise to the pig Latin *excrementum vincit cerebellum*.
- I'd finally got to grips with the system of "bullshit baffles brains" – just do what they say, even if you know it's a bag of shit, and it keeps everybody happy. —Andy McNab, *Immediate Action*, p. 15, 1995
- No blood clot clot But-But using my tools man! No way! He was following the golden rule of Senior Management success that bullshit baffles brains. —Jack Allen, *When the Whistle Blows*, p. 200, 2000

bullshit black *noun*
the flat black paint often found on a used car's chassis *US*
- —*American Speech*, p. 267, December 1962: 'The language of traffic policemen'

bullshit bomber *noun*
a plane used in a propaganda-dropping operation *US, 1980*
- —Linda Reinberg, *In the Field*, p. 30, 1991

bullshit rich *adjective*
very rich *US*
A gem from the slang of miners.
- —Michael Dalton Johnson, *Talking Trash with Redd Foxx*, p. 120, 1994

Bullshit Tax *nickname*
the Canadian Blended Sales Tax (BST), as the Goods and Services Tax was known at first in the Maritime Provinces *CANADA, 1990*
The introduction of this national tax in 1990 provoked protests, and the parody of the acronym BST in the Maritimes actually caused the government to change it to the HST (Harmonized Sales Tax).
- "It looks like BS, and it smells like BS, so it is BS." —1990

bullshitter *noun*
a liar, a braggart, a bluffer *US, 1933*
- I'm a bigger bullshitter than any of them. —Jack Kerouac, *Letter to John Clellon Holmes*, p. 200, 24th June 1949
- What a bullshitter, geez, I never – is he a bullshitter! —Jack Kerouac, *Doctor Sax*, p. 40, 1959
- Although he was a great bullshitter, Tony also had a great bullshit detector. —Dick Cluster, *THey Should Have Served That Cup of Coffee*, p. 173, 1979
- He was a real bullshitter, but he was an exciting guy and as long as he wasn't bullshitting me, I didn't mind. —Marilyn G. Haft, *Time without Work*, p. 172, 1983
- A lot of Greek bullshitters read the coffee cups but I reckon my Aunt Tasia is the real thing. —Christos Tsiolkas, *Loaded*, p. 16, 1995
- I admit I'm a top bullshitter. But we all used to act. —Shaun Ryder, *Shaun Ryder... in His Own Words*, 1996
- He won't give us fuck all. He's a bullshitter. He's just into ripping people off. —Lanre Fehintola, *Charlie Says...*, p. 23, 2000
- [A] lot of blokes who give it the large [boast] in pubs [...] turn out to be bullshitters the moment you take them out to the boot of your car[.] —Danny King, *The Burglar Diaries*, p. 61, 2001

Bullshit Towers *noun*
the control tower of an aerodrome *CANADA*
- —Tom Langeste, *Words on the Wing*, p. 42, 1995

bullskate *verb*
to pretend, to deceive someone, to brag *US*
A euphemism for **BULLSHIT**.
- —Marcus Hanna Boulware, *Jive and Slang of Students in Negro Colleges*, 1947
- —John A. Holm, *Dictionary of Bahamian English*, p. 31, 1982

bull's nose *noun*
on the railways, a goods wagon coupler *US*
- —J. Herbert Lund, *Herb's Hot Box of Railraod Slang*, p. 176, 1975

bull's wool *noun*
any stolen goods *US*
- —Lou Shelly, *Hepcats Jive Talk Dictionary*, p. 22, 1945

bullsworth *noun*
in circus usage, a lie *US*
- —Don Wilmeth, *The Language of American Popular Entertainment*, p. 37, 1981

bully *noun*
a bulldozer *NEW ZEALAND*
• Anchor the bully over there and winch her across. — Gordon Johnston, *Fish Factory*, p. 156, 1981

bully *adjective*
excellent *UK, 1599*
• Give me some bully jacks. — Ken Kesey, *Sometimes a Great Notion*, p. 156, 1964

bully beef *noun*
a senior prison-officer; a prison officer *UK*
Rhyming slang for 'chief'.
• "Alright thats all you can go." said the bully-beaf with a wave of his arm[.] — Frank Norman, *Bang To Rights*, p. 156, 1958
• — Angela Devlin, *Prison Patter*, p. 32, 1996

bully beef *adjective*
deaf *UK, 1961*
Rhyming slang, depending on Scottish pronunciation.

bully club *noun*
a police baton *US*
• The beatman held a bully-club in his right hand and used it for short, rapid blows to Dena's head and back[.] — Robert Gover, *The Maniac Responsible*, p. 160, 1963

bully for you!
excellent; good for you! *US, c. 1788*
Originally sincere, now ironic or jocular.

bullyon *noun*
cannabis resin and herbal marijuana *UK*
A misspelling of 'bouillon', a thin clear soup similar in appearance to marijuana tea, commercially available as small cubes which resemble blocks of **HASH**.
• — Mike Haskins, *Drugs*, p. 286, 2003

bully stick *noun*
a police baton *US*
• Police used bully sticks against the protesters, who rained rocks and bottles on the officers. — *USA Today*, 29th October 1990

bullywhack *verb*
to lie or at least exaggerate *CANADA*
• Ah, you're just bullywhackin' the way you was when you tried to tell me about the side-hill gouger. — George Bowering, *Caprice*, p. 159, 1987

bulrush *noun*
a paint brush *UK*
Rhyming slang.
• — Ray Puxley, *Fresh Rabbit*, 1998

buly *noun*
an ambu*lance UK*
• Ye better pull in tae the side an let this buly by. — Michael Munro, *The Patter – Another Blast*, 1988

bum *noun*
1 the buttocks; occasionally and specifically, the anus, the rectum *UK, 1387*
A good Middle English word that survived in conventional usage until the late C18. The etymology is very uncertain; possibly from Italian *bum* (the sound of an explosion), and it is suggested (elsewhere) that 'bum' is echoic of buttocks slapping a flat surface. What is certain is that it is now in semi-conventional currency. It is not an abbreviation of **BOTTOM** which is a much later coinage.
• [S]he infuriated a number of men who thought that they should be able to rub her small breasts and round bum simply because she was an Indian. — Leonard Cohen, *Beautiful Losers*, p. 33, 1966
• Is she with you? he asked, looking at Paula in the background, the other bouncers staring at her bum and licking their lips. — John King, *White Trash*, p. 63, 2001

2 a bag in which classified documents which are to be destroyed are placed *US*
• — Department of the Army, *Staff Officer's Guidebook*, p. 57, 1986

3 a lazy person; a beggar; a vagrant *US, 1864*

4 a boaster, a braggart *UK: SCOTLAND*
• — Michael Munro, *The Original Patter*, p. 14, 1985

▸ **give your bum an airing**
to use the lavatory *UK*
• Shan't be a moment Florrie. Must just go and give me bum an airin'. — *Beale*, 1984

▸ **on the bum**
1 living as a beggar *US, 1907*
2 (of machinery) not working, broken, not operating correctly *CANADA, 1961*

▸ **take it up the bum**
to take the passive role in anal intercourse *UK*
• — Bodmin Dark, *Dirty Cockney Rhyming Slang*, p. 50, 2003

bum *verb*
1 to engage in anal intercourse *UK*
From **BUM** (the buttocks, the bottom); possibly playing on the phrase 'bum a fag' (to scrounge a cigarette) which can be understood to mean 'sodomise a gay man'.
• I thought he was bumming Keva! Honest to God! I hears this mad moaning [...] just mad talking really... Oh my God! You've got your cock up me... fuck my butt, you bastard! — Kevin Sampson, *Powder*, p. 408, 1999
• They're only kids and you want to bum them. — John King, *Human Punk*, p. 81, 2000

2 to beg; to borrow something without the expectation of returning it *US, 1857*
• Sure, I always got cigarettes. Reason is, I'm a bum. I bum them whenever I get the chance is why my pack lasts longer than Harding's here. — Ken Kesey, *One Flew Over the Cuckoo's Nest*, p. 173, 1962
• I bum a cigarette from one. We're all brothers. — Abbie Hoffman, *Revolution for the Hell of It*, p. 19, 1968
• — *Columbia Missourian*, p. 1A, 19 October 1998

3 to feel poorly or depressed *US, 1989*
• There I was, bumming about Cassandra, and out of the blue, I meet Bjergen, Bjergen Kjergen from Knuergen near the Jbergen Fjords. — *Wayne's World 2*, 1993
• Something about having to hear the woman you really like going to the toilet always bummed me. — *Airheads*, 1994

4 to have a bad experience with a hallucinogenic drug *US*
• "He's bumming,' comes Manny's voice. 'We have to get him out,' Shell says. For them, the drug's spell has ended. And they realize that for Jerry the insane world has spilled into reality. — John Rechy, *The Fourth Angel*, p. 130, 1972

5 in computing, to improve something by removing or rearranging it *US*
• "I bummed the program not to write the file if it would be empty." — Guy L. Steele et al., *The Hacker's Dictionary*, p. 39, 1983

6 to wander, to idle, to live as a vagrant *AUSTRALIA, 1933*

7 to boast, to brag *UK, 1937*
Also used as 'bum up'.
• He's always bummin himself up. — Michael Munro, *The Original Patter*, p. 14, 1985

▸ **bum your chaff; bum your chat; bum your load**
to tell a tall story to impress or convince someone *UK, 1937*

bum *adjective*
1 injured, damaged, faulty *US, 1902*
• "That trap door turned out to be a bum lead," Pat said. — Chester Gould, *Dick Tracy Meets the Night Crawler*, p. 138, 1945
• Edgar, her husband, succumbed to "bum kidneys" (his term) on Christmas Eve, 1976. — Armistead Maupin, *Further Tales of the City*, p. 16, 1982
• I got a bum prostate [...] I had to stop to take a leak. — Janet Evanovich, *Seven Up*, p. 9, 2001

2 inferior, bad, of poor-quality *US, 1859*
• [G]one from one bum job to another[.] — Geoffrey Fletcher, *Down Among the Meths Men*, p. 31, 1966

bum about; bum around *verb*
to wander or live idly *US, 1926*
• Laith was "bumming about" in Sapporo for several months, working when he felt like it as a surfing wet-suit salesman. — Josie Dew, *The Sun In My Eyes*, p. 285, 2001

bumba; bumbo *noun*
the anus or vagina *JAMAICA, 1980*
• — Thomas H. Slone, *Rasta is Cuss*, p. 32, 2003

bumbaclaat *noun*
▷ **see: BUMBOCLOT**

bumbai *adverb*
▷ **see: BUMBYE**

bum bandit *noun*

a male homosexual *UK*

- —Tom Hibbert, *Rockspeak!*, p. 33, 1983
- —Angela Devlin, *Prison Patter*, p. 32, 1996

bum-beef *verb*

to frame an innocent person *US*

- —*Current Slang*, p. 12, Fall 1968

bum bend *noun*

an unpleasant experience under the influence of a hallucinogen *US*

- —Eugene Landy, *The Underground Dictionary*, p. 42, 1971

bumbershoot *noun*

an umbrella *US, 1896*

- What is form, in any case, but a bumbershoot held up against the absence of all cloud?—William Gass et al., *On Being Blue*, p. 8, 1976
- While the umbrella – or brolly or bumbershoot or parasol – has protected people from sun or rain for some 4,000 years, there apparently are a few rude umbrella handlers left on the planet —*Chicago Tribune*, 6th April 2003

bumble bee *noun*

1 a motor cycle, especially a two-stroke model *UK*
Citizens' band radio slang, after the US sense (1976) as a 'two-stroke/two-cycle engine'; in both cases an allusion to the sound of the motor.

- —Peter Chippindale, *The British CB Book*, p. 153, 1981

2 any two-cycle engine *US*

- —Montie Tak, *Truck Talk*, p. 22, 1971

3 an amphetamine tablet *US*

- —The National Institute on Drug Abuse, *What do they call it again?*, 1980
- —Mike Haskins, *Drugs*, p. 279, 2003

bumbled up *adjective*

drunk to the point of passing out *US*

- —Collin Baker et al., *College Undergraduate Slang Study Conducted at Brown University*, p. 91, 1968

bumblee *noun*

1 a small car not built in the US *US*
Dismissive, vaguely jingoistic; of the era when American-made cars dominated the market in the US but the influx of foreign-made cars had begun.

- —Lyle K. Engel, *The Complte Book of Fuel and Gas Dragsters*, p. 149, 1968

2 in Passaic, New Jersey, a police officer *US*

- "I know the bumblees are out tonight." "Bumblees" is street slang for the community police officers, whose uniform includes yellow shirts.—*Record (Bergen County, New Jersey)*, p. L3, 15th September 2000

Bumblefuck *noun*

any remote, small town *US*

- —Pamela Munro, *U.C.L.A. Slang*, p. 26, 1989

bumblepuppy *noun*

in poker, an inexperienced and/or unskilled player *UK, 1884*
Originally from the game of whist.

- —George Percy, *The Language of Poker*, p. 14, 1988

bumbo *noun*

whisky *AUSTRALIA, 1942*

▷ **see:** BUMBA

bumboclot; bumboclaat; bamb'clat; bumbaclaat *noun*

1 a sanitary towel; a cloth for wiping faeces *JAMAICA*
West Indian and UK black patois, literally 'bottom-cloth'. There is a, possibly disingenuous, belief amongst some Jamaicans that Bumbo was a king of Africa.

2 used as direct abuse or as an intensifier *UK*
West Indian and UK black patois. Can also be used as an exclamation to register shock, surprise or anger.

- "You stupid bumboclaat eedyat [idiot]!" Easy-Love screamed. "How could you fuck up like that?"—Karline Smith, *Moss Side Massive*, p. 197, 1994
- [He] wondered how she could afford to live there. "Bumbaclaat! Ah your yard dis?—Donald Gorgon, *Cop Killer*, p. 44, 1994
- Me jus' box the girl so and kick him bombaclaat out!—Diran Adebayo, *My Once Upon A Time*, p. 22, 2000
- Right... le's see where this bamb'clat place is den.—Chris Baker and Andrew Day, *Lock, Stock... & One Big Bullock*, p. 342, 2000

bum boy *noun*

1 a homosexual male, especially a youthful, sexually inexperienced male who is the object of an older homosexual's desire *UK, 1929*

- You can find Christians as well as meths men, tear offs, outcasts, bum boys, prostitutes and head breakers on Skid Row.—Geoffrey Fletcher, *Down Among the Meths Men*, p. 11, 1966
- —*Maledicta*, p. 221, 1979: 'Kinks and queens: linguistic and cultural aspects of the terminology for gays'
- —Tom Hibbert, *Rockspeak!*, p. 33, 1983
- They all look at me. Dave laughs. – You fucking bum boy.—John King, *Human Punk*, p. 8, 2000
- "Did you steal 'em [trousers] off your trick?" "I've told you, I in't a fookin' bumboy."—Ben Elton, *High Society*, p. 287, 2002

2 a sycophant *UK, 1929*

- He'd received a phone call yesterday from a Father Grady, Shelley's assistant or bum-boy or whatever[.]—Christopher Brookmyre, *Boiling a Frog*, p. 325, 2000

bumbrella *noun*

an umbrella *US, 1896*

- —Frederic G. Cassidy, *Dictionary of American Regional English, Volume 1*, p. 455, 1985

bum bud *noun*

inferior marijuana *US*

- —Kenn "Naz" Young, *Naz's Dictionary of Teen Slang*, p. 16, 1993

bum-bum *noun*

the buttocks *TRINIDAD AND TOBAGO*

- —Lise Winer, *Dictionary of the English/Creole of Trinidad & Tobago*, 2003

bum-bust *verb*

to arrest someone on false or non-existent charges *US*

- "He doesn't look like a bad kid, be a shame the city put him up for a week, he gets bum-busted by some hod case."—John Sayles, *Union Dues*, p. 29, 1977

bumbye; bumbai *adverb*

sometime soon *US*
Hawaiian youth usage.

- Bumbye we goin ovah Harold's, get radical.—Douglas Simonson, *Pidgin to da Max*, 1981

bum chum *noun*

a passive homosexual male *AUSTRALIA, 1972*

- Or they get a bum chum and go drilling for Vegemite.—Kathy Lette, *Girls' Night Out*, p. 174, 1987
- —David McGill, *David McGill's Complete Kiwi Slang Dictionary*, p. 24, 1998
- [G]et down there to see yer bum chum.—Chris Baker and Andrew Day, *Lock, Stock... & Spaghetti Sauce*, p. 223, 2000
- He tenses, but the bender [a homosexual] doesn't seem to notice, his bum chum smiling at Dave.—John King, *Human Punk*, p. 79, 2000

bum crumb *noun*

a small lump of excrement that clings to the anal hair *UK*

- —Chris Lewis, *The Dictionary of Playground Slang*, p. 46, 2003

bum dough *noun*

counterfeit money *US*

- —Jay Robert Nash, *Dictionary of Crime*, p. 49, 1992

bumf; bumph *noun*

1 paperwork; official papers *UK, 1889*
An abbreviation of BUM FODDER (toilet paper).

- Why does the Ministry have to send out all this bumph?—Ann Barr and Peter York, *The Official Sloane Ranger Handbook*, p. 158, 1982
- [T]hat glossy bumf which comes through the letter-box every morning[.]—Andrew Nickolds, *Back to Basics*, p. 54, 1994
- What's this? Bumf from Charlie about Lloyd's.—Harry Enfield, *Harry Enfield and His Humorous Chums*, p. 51, 1997

2 toilet paper *UK, 1889*
An abbreviation of BUM FODDER. The elaboration, 'bog bumf', not recorded until 1984, is tautological but pleasingly alliterative.

bum-face *noun*

used as a derogatory form of address *UK, 1972*

bum-fluff *noun*

1 the soft facial hair of an adolescent boy *UK, 1949*
The image of sparsely spread hair on a backside.

- Minty [bad] bumfluff muzzy [moustache].—Niall Griffiths, *Kelly + Victor*, p. 256, 2002

2 empty talk; nonsense *AUSTRALIA*

- —Sidney J Baker, *The Australian Language*, p. 128, 1945

3 a contemptible man, especially one who is younger than, or of junior status to, the speaker *UK*

- Listen, bum-fluff, you've taken my cash and what you've come back with has been canteen gossip. — J.J. Connolly, *Layer Cake*, p. 148, 2000

bum-flufferies *noun*

details; the small print *UK*

An extension of **BUMF** (paperwork) but note **BUM-FLUFF** (nonsense).

- You're on two percent. Two and a half. Maybe even three. Depends on the usual bum-flufferies[.] — *Sexy Beast*, 2001

bum fodder *noun*

toilet paper *UK*

Around 1660 an anonymous author, now presumed to be Alexander Brome (1620–66), wrote 'Bumm-foder: or Waste-Paper Proper to Wipe the Nations Rump with'.

- — John D. Bell et al., *Loosely Speaking*, p. 3, 1966

bum freezer *noun*

a short coat *UK, 1932*

- I was buttoning up my handsome short Mod overcoat (that my father called a bum-freezer) and listening to the men debating. — Billy Roche, *Tumbling Down*, p. 16, 1984
- The jacket would ride up at the back, thereby giving the style its nickname the "bum-freezer", and the pants were too short in the ankle[.] — Nik Cohn, *Yellow Socks Are Out*, p. 18–19, 1989
- The day I went into the Bodega in John Street snow was in the air and a sharp wind snapped at the tail of a too short coat – a bum freezer. — *Munster Express*, 17th January 2003

bum fuck *noun*

a digital massage of the prostate via the anus and rectum as a diagnostic and therapeutic procedure *UK, 1961*

bumfuck *verb*

to have anal intercourse, to sodomise someone *US, 1866*

Combines **BUM** (the posterior) with **FUCK** (to have sex).

- I love being fucked up the arse, I just love it! Will you bum fuck me? — Stewart Home, *Sex Kick [britpulp]*, p. 233, 1999

Bumfuck, Egypt *noun*

a mythical town that is the epitome of remoteness *US, 1972*

With variants.

- "This ... ain't ... Bumfuck, Egypt." — Jack Hawkins, *Chopper One #2*, p. 89, 1987
- After that, I went to Aberdeen Proving Grounds, and you went to ... bumfuck Saudi Arabia? — Edward Lee, *Ghouls*, p. 202, 1988
- Well, yes, in a way, but it's better than being stuck somehewere outside of Bhum Fuk Vietnam in the middle of a bomb crater the size of the Superdome under fire by determinedly hostile forces. — Dannie J. Marvicsin and Jerold A. Greenfield, *Maverick*, p. 205, 1990
- — Connie Eble (Editor), *UNC-CH Campus Slang*, p. 1, Fall 1993

bum fun *noun*

an intimate fondling of another's bottom *UK*

- [N]o snogging, lap dancing or bum fun. — Pete McCarthy, *McCarthy's Bar*, p. 308, 2000

bum gravy *noun*

liquid excreta, diarrhoea *UK*

- — *www.LondonSlang.com*, June 2002

bumhole; bum-hole *noun*

the anus *UK*

Logically follows **BUM** (the posterior).

- And with a bit of tissue, he wiped its bum-hole clean[.] — Ian Dury, *This is What We Find*, 1979
- JOE: I don't like the bitter. DAVE: Neither does my bumhole, it's like a chewed orange. — Caroline Aherne and Craig Cash, *The Royle Family*, 1999

bum-hole *adjective*

inferior, bad *UK, 1984*

bum jacket *noun*

a short, everyday jacket *US, 1967*

- — Frederic G. Cassidy, *Dictionary of American Regional English, Volume 1*, p. 457, 1985

bum-kicked *adjective*

depressed *US, 1974*

- Tramp's drug thing spun out of control and he was found dead from an overdose of Seconal. It happened right after the Hell's Angels '69 movie was released. Nobody knows whether he was bum-kicked or was just being his usual reckless self. — Ralph "Sonny" Barger, *Hell's Angel*, p. 74, 2000

bum-knuckle *noun*

the coccyx; hence, also used as a generalised insult *UK*

- Has Julesy ever called you a "bum-knuckle"? — *Muzik*, p. 9, February 2003

bumlicker *noun*

a sycophant, a toady *UK*

Combines **BUM** (the buttocks, the anus) with 'someone who licks'; as a demonstration of subservience this image is far older than the term and can be seen in C16 woodblocks of devil-worshippers pledging their service to the hindquarters of a goat.

- [T]he Cardinal's highly protective secretary, personal assistant and dedicated bum-licker. — Christopher Brookmyre, *Boiling a Frog*, p. 129, 2000

bum lift *noun*

a procedure in cosmetic surgery to firm up the buttocks *UK*

- PASTY: Surgery. Lipo, on the hips and stomach, bum lift, tit lift, lose a rib. — Jennifer Saunders, *Absolutely Fabulous*, p. 34, 1992

bum man *noun*

a man who is especially fond of female buttocks *NEW ZEALAND*

- — David McGill, *David McGill's Complete Kiwi Slang Dictionary*, p. 23, 1998

bummed *adjective*

depressed, irritated *US, 1973*

- That fucking mousse-haired, white-skinned, needlenose scumbag better show up, 'cause I'm getting bummed. — Howard Stern, *Miss America*, p. 74, 1995
- Meg had just broken her wrist, jeopardizing the whole tour that they were holding out for. No wonder he was bummed. — *X-Ray*, p. 52, June 2003

bummer *noun*

1 a male homosexual *UK, 1967*

Also known as a 'bummer boy'.

2 a disappointing or depressing event *US*

- — Miss Cone, *The Slang Dictionary (Hawthorne High School)*, 1965
- But then we came outside and saw all those clippings about us, pasted up like advertisements. Man, it was a bummer, it wasn't right. — Hunter S. Thompson, *Hell's Angels*, p. 89, 1966
- If you consider that the sheer number of beautiful people struggling against the inclement weather, and basic needs of survival, turned the festival into a Nation dedicated to victory, then the bummers get put in quite a different perspective. — Abbie Hoffman, *Woodstock Nation*, p. 4, 1969
- As desperate as she was for someone to help her drive, and generally hassle the whole bummer of a scene on to St. Louis, Estelle wished she was by herself again. — Gurney Norman, *Divine Right's Trip (Last Whole Earth Catalog)*, p. 87, 1971
- I wish I could honestly say that without your gift I would've had one bad bummer of a Christmas[.] — Tom Robbins, *Another Roadside Attraction*, p. 162, 1971
- Man, what a bummer. Ten days and a wakeup and I'm still dealing wid this shit. — *Platoon*, 1986
- He's the one responsible for all those bummers you've had. — Jim Carroll, *Forced Entries*, p. 73, 1987
- It's a bummer about your party, man. — *Dazed and Confused*, 1993
- CHER: I failed. TAI: Oh, bummer. — *Clueless*, 1995
- What a bummer, we'll have to miss the Anal Exciters gig[.] — Stewart Home, *Sex Kick [britpulp]*, p. 238, 1999

3 a bad experience with LSD or another hallucinogen *US, 1966*

- Some of them had terrible bummer – bummer was the Angels' term for a bad trip on a motorcyle and very quickly it became the hip world's term for a bad trip on LSD. — Tom Wolfe, *The Electric Kool-Aid Acid Test*, p. 159, 1968
- Whatever it was, I had a bummer. One of those rare acid trips when everything caves in. I learned enough shit from it, through, that maybe it wasn't such a bummer after all. — Abbie Hoffman, *Woodstock Nation*, p. 5, 1969
- Bummers were when the acid had something in it that didn't agree with you. — Eve Babitz, *Eve's Hollywood*, p. 234, 1974
- He was having a paranoid bummer while driving a rented Mustang with a U-haul trailer full of kilos up from Tijuana on the freeway and was stopped by the cops — Stephen Gaskin, *Amazing Dope Tales*, p. 65, 1980
- — Angela Devlin, *Prison Patter*, p. 32, 1996
- Crisis-level bummers are less likely to happen on low doses of acid – 100 mikes or less – than on high doses of 150 mikes or more. — Cam Cloud, *The Little Book of Acid*, p. 22, 1999

4 a beggar, a tramp, a bum *US, 1855*

- Where do you come off knowing a bummer like Billings? — Mickey Spillane, *Me, Hood!*, p. 29, 1963

bummy *noun*

a transient, penniless, dirty person *US, 1923*

- I was carrying the banner down yonder in Atlanta, but watch out, keep out, stay awake – they throw bummies in for thirty days. — John Clellon Holmes, *The Horn*, p. 160, 1958

bummy *verb*

to intimidate someone *JAMAICA*

Current among UK Yardies and other West Indian communities.

- He went, "You're the only man to bummy me!" which is like patois for "being scared". — Dave Courtney, *Raving Lunacy*, p. 81, 2000

bummy *adjective*

dirty, wretched *US, 1896*

- Young and emaciated girl, dressed in a raggedy trenchcoat, bummy blue prom dress, and bummy Air Joradans – who is also in another world. — *New Jack City*, p. 28, 1990
- Strike liked her because she was clean, not bummy, a working woman with a kid, holding down the world. — Richard Price, *Clockers*, p. 75, 1992

bummy-ass *adjective*

low, disreputable, shoddy *US*

- Gone are the days of sellin' on street corners, in dark alleys, or in the bathroom of some bummy-ass bar. — *New Jack City*, 1990

bum-numbing *adjective*

used to describe any tedious activity that keeps a participant seated until the posterior has lost any sense of feeling *UK, 1976*

- This will take the film's total length to a bum-numbing four hours and 10 minutes. — *The Guardian*, 9th March 2004

bum of the month *noun*

a person identified as a poor performer *US*

A term coined in connection with heavyweight boxer Joe Louis, who fought against a series of unworthy contenders.

- Production picks out the engineer who'll be the "bum of the month." — Gene W. Dalton et al., *Organizational Structure and Design*, p. 78, 1970
- One concern, according to some of those involved, is that an unfriendly prosecutor could make charges of political corruption a priority. "She might start a 'bum of the month' club – you can indict anybody," said Mr. Diamond. — *New York Times*, p. 46, 6th September 1981

bum out *verb*

to depress someone; to disappoint someone *US, 1970*

- Having bummed out almost the entire population of one room, I took my show into another[.] — Lester Bangs, *Psychotic Reactions and Carburetor Dung*, p. 232, 1977
- "Don't look so bummed out," Wiley said. — Carl Hiaasen, *Tourist Season*, p. 101, 1986
- It would truly bum me out if this turned into a commodification of "girl zines". — Marion Leonard, *Cool Places*, p. 108, 1998
- He gets really bummed out a lot though. — Francesca Lia Block, *I Was a Teenage Fairy*, p. 95, 1998

bump *noun*

1 in a striptease or other sexual dance, a forceful pelvic thrust *US, 1931*

- A lot of white vocalists, even some with the big name bands today, are either as stiff as a stuffed owl or else they go through more wringing and twisting than a shake dancer, doing grinds and bumps all over the place[.] — Mezz Mezzrow, *Really the Blues*, p. 27, 1946
- She hummed to herself, trying out words: "I'm out on my cast at last, and rarin' for some darin'..." Bump on "rarin'," grind on "darin'." — Bernard Wolfe, *The Late Risers*, p. 292, 1954
- Surviving from cooch dancing in the stripper's routine are such essential bodily movements as the fishtail – the hip-wiggling part – and the bumps – the forward and backward movement of the abdomen. — William Green, *Strippers and Coochers*, p. 165, 1977
- Traditional stripping involves several dance movements, including the bump, the grind, and the "hootchy-kootchy." — Marilyn Suriani Futterman, *Dancing Naked in the Material World*, p. 126, 1992

2 a dance style, popular during the 1970s and 80s, in which dance partners bump hips on the beat *US*

- In clubland, you're bound to find the yin for your yang, the Greg for your Dharma – but lately it's been as challenging as dancing the Bump with one of the Hiltons. — *Village Voice*, p. 14, 28th October 1997

3 in professional wrestling, a fall to the mat or floor, embellished with grunts, shakes and body spasms that create the impression that the opponent has truly hurt the victim *US*

- Dave Meltzer brought up that wrestling was growing into a stunt man show with crazier and crazier bumps. — Herb Kunze, *Herb's Wrestling Tidbits*, 2000
- As a pro, Morrus took major bumps when he faced off against another super-heavyweight. — *Rampage*, p. 33, September 2000
- Lita spent another three weeks in Mexico, where she got a crash course in taking bumps. — *Raw Magazine*, p. 24, September 2000

4 a dose of cocaine *UK*

- You were literally offered it [cocaine] by everyone, from your accountant to the head of your record company. Everyone was like, "Wanna bump?" — Elliot Roberts, *quoted in Waiting For The Sun*, p. 247, 1996
- Doing another bump of coke when you know you've had enough. — Suroosh Alvi et al., *The Vice Guide*, p. 16, 2002

5 a single dose of the recreational drug ketamine *US*

- It's a tongue-in-cheek reference to a "bump," which is a dose of ketamine, or Special K, a surgical anesthetic snorted by clubgoers to magnify dance floor sensations lights, bass, chaos. — *Daily News (New York)*, p. 42, 8th October 1995

6 a single dose of crystalised methadrine *US, 1985*

- You don't need to do that much. You only have to do bumps with crystal. — *Boogie Nights*, 1997
- In the clubs, men exchnage what are known as "bumps," or snorts, on the dance floor or in rest room stalls. — *San Francisco Chronicle*, p. A1, 4th May 2003

7 crack cocaine; also counterfeit crack cocaine *UK, 1998*

- — Mike Haskins, *Drugs*, p. 281, 2003

8 a fatal overdose of a drug *UK*

A nuance of the sense as 'a single dose of a drug', possibly influenced by the sense 'to kill'

- OD's on meth. Carked it. The prick. – Overdose like. Bump, that's him. — Niall Griffiths, *Sheepshagger*, p. 55, 2001

9 an assassination; a murder *US, 1919*

- '[I]t was Zotta who did the bump — Adam Hall, *The 9th Directive*, 1966
- [T]he death of Primero, and it was Zotta who did the bump. — Adam Hall, *The 9th Directive*, 1966
- — Jay Robert Nash, *Dictionary of Crime*, 1992

10 in poker, an increase in the bet on a hand *US*

- — George Percy, *The Language of Poker*, p. 14, 1988

11 in betting, a doubling of the bet in effect *US*

- — Sam Snead and Jerry Tarde, *Pigeons, Marks, Hustlers and Other Golf Bettors You Can Beat*, p. 110, 1986

12 a promotion in pay or responsibility *US, 1949*

- — Harold Wentorth and Stuart Berg Flexner, *Dictionary of American Slang*, p. 75, 1960

13 in computing, an increment *US*

- — Eric S. Raymond, *The New Hacker's Dictionary*, p. 85, 1991

14 in volleyball, an underhand forearm pass to a team mate *US*

- — Janet Thigpen, *Power Volleyball*, p. 97, 1985

▸ **the bump**

dismissal from employment *UK: SCOTLAND*

- I see wee Doagie got the bump fae his work[.] — Michael Munro, *The Patter, Another Blast*, 1988

bump *verb*

1 to kill someone *US, 1914*

- — Lou Shelly, *Hepcats Jive Talk Dictionary*, p. 8, 1945
- But somebody was afraid of what he knew and bumped him. — Mickey Spillane, *I, The Jury*, p. 24, 1947
- Only six days after they had bumped Bannon they had almost been trapped. — Irving Shulman, *The Amboy Dukes*, p. 169, 1947
- That don't make me know who bumped him. Lots of cats didn't go for him because he was snitchin. — Clarence Cooper Jr, *The Scene*, p. 182, 1960
- Any bumping I don't want done on the premises. — Mickey Spillane, *Me, Hood!*, p. 33, 1963

2 (of a prisoner) to let it be known that a debt owed to another inmate cannot be repaid *UK*

- — Angela Devlin, *Prison Patter*, p. 32, 1996

3 to give an employee a promotion *US, 1957*

- — Harold Wentorth and Stuart Berg Flexner, *Dictionary of American Slang*, p. 75, 1960

4 to slide a large stack of gambling chips up next to a player's bet to size the amount of chips for a payoff *US*

- — Michael Dalton, *Blackjack*, p. 34, 1991

5 in poker, to increase another player's bet *US*

- — Irv Roddy, *Friday Night Poker*, p. 216, 1961

6 to talk a customer into a higher price *US*

- — *American Speech*, p. 309–310, Winter 1980: 'More jargon of car salesmen'

7 to defraud someone, to swindle someone *UK*

- He's lost his job as a pools collector for bumpin the money. — Michael Munro, *The Patter, Another Blast*, 1988

8 in professional wrestling, to fall to the mat in feigned pain *US*

- Bumping is, without a doubt, the most valuable thing a wrestler can learn. — Mick Foley, *Mankind*, p. 65, 1999

9 to boost a state of drug intoxication *UK*

10 in a striptease or other sexual dance, to thrust the hips forward as if copulating *US, 1936*
- Dancing boys strip-tease with intestines, women stick severed genitals in their cunts, grind, bump, and flick it at the man of their choice. —William Burroughs, *Naked Lunch*, p. 37–38, 1957
- You can sacrifice your sacro, workin' in the backrow / Bump in a dump till you're dead. —Stephen Sondheim, *You Gotta Get a Gimmick*, 1960

11 in hot rodding and low riding, to drive slowly in a lowered vehicle, especially one with a hydraulic suspension system that will bounce the car up and down *US*
- —John Edwards, *Auto Dictionary*, p. 21, 1993

12 to develop breasts *BAHAMAS*
- —John A. Holm, *Dictionary of Bahamian English*, p. 31, 1982

13 to play music loudly *US*
- — *Columbia Missourian*, p. 1A, 19th October 1998

▸ **bump fuzz**
(used of a female) to have sex with another woman *US*
- —Pamela Munro, *U.C.L.A. Slang*, p. 46, 1997

▸ **bump gums**
to speak without saying much *US, 1945*
- [T]he religious halfwits had been bumping their gums in protest about the cost[.] —Christopher Brookmyre, *The Sacred Art of Stealing*, p. 336, 2002
- —Connie Eble (Editor), *UNC-CH Campus Slang*, p. 2, October 2002

▸ **bump heads**
to fight *US*
- —Eugene Landy, *The Underground Dictionary*, p. 42, 1971

▸ **bump pussies**
(used of lesbians) to have sex, especially by engaging in vulva-to-vulva friction *US*
- What would we do – bump pussies? —Malcolm Braly, *On the Yard*, p. 296, 1967
- Two girls can, by interlacing themselves like forks, "bump pussies" as we used to say when I was a lad, and enjoy all of the thrills and chills of intercourse without even fingering themselves. —Angelo d'Arcangelo, *The Homosexual Handbook*, p. 208, 1968

▸ **bump the blanket**
to masturbate in bed *UK*
- If you ned a toss [masturbation] you wait till association. We take it in turns, the rest of us go out [of the prison cell]. Don't wanna hear you bumping the blanket in the middle of the night. —Chris Baker and Andrew Day, *Lock, Stock... & A Good Slopping Out*, p. 411, 2000

▸ **bump titties**
to fight *US*
- —Jennifer Blowdryer, *Modern English*, p. 57, 1985
- —Ann Lawson, *Kids & Gangs*, p. 56, 1994

▸ **bump uglies**
to have sex *US*
- And Tango adds a phrase to the popular lexicon when Sly's Tango asks Russell's Cash, "Did you bump uglies with my sister?" — *USA Today*, p. 7D, 22nd December 1989
- —Connie Eble (Editor), *UNC-CH Campus Slang*, p. 2, Spring 1992
- Another way to say "intercourse" – Bumping uglies[.] —Erica Orloff and JoAnn Baker, *Dirty Little Secrets*, p. 63, 2001
- [W]here's the strangest place you lovely girls have ever bumped uglies? — *FHM*, p. 68, June 2003

bump and bore *verb*
(of a racehorse) to veer off course and bump into an opponent *UK*
- — *www.tiptext.com*, 2003

Bump City *nickname*
Oakland, California *US*
The title of a 1972 record album by the group Tower of Power, as well as a 1979 book by John Krich.

bumper *noun*
1 the buttocks *US*
- While I was taking a turn around the floor with Jim Bacon of the Associated Press, the Prince and I felt our bumpers collide, and he promptly marched off the floor. — *San Francisco Chronicle*, p. 24, 18th April 1963
- I'll moor it on the Chicago River and put on a big sign, "Babes with Big Bumpers Wanted. —Red Rudensky, *The Gonif*, p. 102, 1970
- He gets his hands on more bumper than a body shop. — *Airheads*, 1994
- In the old days, people had metaphors for what they wanted to say. Even the nasty songs aspired to a certain level of craftmanship. Remember "Pull Up to the Bumper?" For a song about anal sex, it was pretty tongue-in-cheek. —Chris Rock, *Rock This!*, p. 213, 1997

2 the female breast *US, 1947*
Generally in the plural.
- —J.A. Cuddon, *The Bride of Battersea*, 1067

3 a person who enjoys performing oral sex on women *US*
- —Hyman E. Goldin et al., *Dictionary of American Underworld Lingo*, p. 36, 1950

4 a lesbian *US*
- — *Maledicta*, p. 132, Summer/Winter 1982: 'Dyke diction: the language of lesbians'

5 in pool, the cushion on the side of the table *US*
- —Steve Rushin, *Pool Cool*, p. 6, 1990

6 in horse racing, a (National Hunt) flat race *UK*
- —John Welcome, *Wanted for Killing*, 1965

7 any alcholic beverage *BERMUDA*
- —Peter A. Smith and Fred M. Barritt, *Bermewjan Vurds*, 1985

8 crack cocaine *UK*
- —Mike Haskins, *Drugs*, p. 281, 2003

9 a cigarette butt *AUSTRALIA, 1899*

bumper *verb*
1 to make a whole cigarette from collected butts *AUSTRALIA, 1968*
From **BUMPER** (a cigarette butt).

2 to extinguish a cigarette and save the butt for smoking later *AUSTRALIA, 1978*
From **BUMPER** (a cigarette butt).

bumper *adjective*
especially large or enlarged *UK, 1759*
- —Chris Donald, *Viz Bumper Book of Shite for Boys and Girls*, 1993
- MPs slam insurance chiefs' bumper pay rises. — *The Guardian*, 28th January 2004

bumper jumper *noun*
a vehicle that is too close behind another *UK*
Citizens' band radio slang.
- —Peter Chippindale, *The British CB Book*, p. 153, 1981

bumper kit *noun*
the female buttocks *US*
- —Bill Valentine, *Gang Intelligence Manual*, p. 75, 1995

bumper shine *verb*
▷ **see:** **BUM SHINE**

bumper-shooter *noun*
someone who picks up cigarette ends *AUSTRALIA*
- —Sydney J. Baker, *Australia Speaks*, 1953

bumper tag *noun*
1 a slight collision between cars, especially a rear end collision *US*
- And because the judge was involved in a little bumper tag with a black car that was either a Buick or an Olds. —Elmore Leonard, *City Primeval*, p. 63, 1980
- Once, while biking on a lonely road near Desert Hot Springs, two dirtbag rednecks in a raggedly pickup truck had played bumper tag, forcing her off the road. —Joseph Wambaugh, *Fugitive Nights*, p. 54, 1992

2 in pool, a shot that is made off two cushions on the side of the table *US*
Punning on a term commonly used to describe a traffic jam.
- —Steve Rushin, *Pool Cool*, p. 6, 1990

bumper-to-bumper *adjective*
(used of car traffic) moving slowly and close together *US, 1938*
- They started south on Collins and pretty soon turned west toward Washington, not much traffic yet. By December it would be bumper to bumper down here. —Elmore Leonard, *Pronto*, p. 7–8, 1993

bumper-up; bumper-upper *noun*
a prostitute's handyman *AUSTRALIA*
- —Sydney J. Baker, *Australia Speaks*, 1953

bumph, bumpie *nouns*
▷ **see:** **BUMF, BUPPIE**

bumping *adjective*
excellent *US*
- — *National Education Association Today*, April 1985: 'A glossary for rents and other squids'
- — *The Washington Post*, 15th March 1987
- —Connie Eble (Editor), *UNC-CH Campus Slang*, p. 2, Fall 1988
- —Vann Wesson, *Generation X Field Guide and Lexicon*, p. 30, 1997

bump list *noun*
a list of murder targets *US*
- Who's bump list you on now?—Mickey Spillane, *Me, Hood!*, p. 16, 1963

bumpman *noun*
in a pickpocket team, a confederate who bumps and distracts the targeted victim *US, 1940*
- It is understood by the police that a "bump man" or a "hook" does not operate at the Garden under the code long agreed upon between the stadium and the artistes.—Robert Sylvester, *No Cover Charge*, p. 286, 1956

bump off *verb*
to kill someone *US, 1907*
- [T]hey'll get out of here now, all join up in the Air Corps and become heroes and bump off fifty, a hundred, a thousand Japs[.]—Mezz Mezzrow, *Really the Blues*, p. 314, 1946
- Can I help it if somebody bumps off the teacher?—Irving Shulman, *The Amboy Dukes*, p. 91, 1947
- You can see the processes working in the reuslts: two of the eye witnesses recanted; the third was bumped off.—Jack Lait and Lee Mortimer, *Chicago Confidential*, p. 234, 1950

bumps *noun*
1 cocaine *US*
From **BUMP** (a dose of cocaine).
- —Anna Scotti and Paul Young, *Buzzwords*, 1997

2 loud bass notes as amplified on a stereo *US*
- Did you hear the bumps coming from that car?—Pamela Munro, *U.C.L.A. Slang*, p. 46, 1997

bump shop *noun*
a car body repair shop *US*
- "She's out in Pontiac someplace at a bump shop, getting an estimate," Ordell said.—Elmore Leonard, *Switch*, p. 68, 1978
- Its owner sold it to the owner of the bump shop who sold it to us. — *Detroit News*, p. 2F, 7th April 2004

bump spot *noun*
in drag racing, the elapsed time of the driver in the final spot of the qualifying field, subject to being displaced by a better performance of a car yet to qualify *US*
- —Ross Robert Olney, *Kings of the Drag Strip*, p. 185, 1968
- Glidden's best of the weekend was 7.073, eight-thousandths of a second behind Jerry Eckma (7.065), in the bump spot.— *Richmond (Virginia) Times Dispatch*, p. D2, 5th May 1996

bump stick *noun*
in drag racing, a camshaft *US*
- —Ross Robert Olney, *Kings of the Drag Strip*, p. 185, 1968

bum puncher *noun*
a male taking the active role in anal sex, especially when finesse is not an issue *AUSTRALIA*
- — Thommo, *The Dictionary of Australian Swearing and Sex Sayings*, p. 20, 1985

bump up *verb*
to increase something *UK, 1940*
- [E]lite eateries in the prestigious Michelin guide bumped up their prices when marks, francs and lire were replaced by the single currency in January 2002.— *The Guardian*, 2nd April 2004

bumpy *noun*
the buttocks *BERMUDA*
- —Peter A. Smith and Fred M. Barritt, *Bermewjan Vurds*, 1985

bum rap *noun*
1 an unfair or false accusation or reputation *US, 1952*
- I'm positive neither bartender's so much as pocketing a wrong tip. Your client may be giving these bartenders a bum rap.—Joseph Wambaugh, *Fugitive Nights*, p. 118, 1992
- I think to blame that all on Reagan is unfair. It's a bum rap. [Quoting Richard Rosenbaum]—Natalie Datiof et al., *Ronald Reagan's America, Vol. 2*, p. 634, 1997
- Let me tell you something, doctor. Chicks love a guy with a bum rap.— *Cruel Intentions*, 1999

2 a false criminal accusation; an unfair conviction *US, 1926*
- —Charles Hamilton, *Men of the Underworld*, p. 320, 1952
- During the trial, LaMotta denied having any part in steering the gir into prostitution, insisting that he had never seen her before and that he was being given a "bump rap" becuase he had a "big name." — *Confidential*, p. 29, July 1957
- They demand due process for colleagues beyond all legal necessity because they're so concerned about anyone's getting a bum rap. —Billie Wright Daziech and Linda Weiner, *The Lecherous Professor*, p. 51, 1984

bum-rap *verb*
to arrest someone without proof of guilt *US, 1947*
- I can't ever scream about being bum-rapped.—Bruce Jackson, *In the Life*, p. 160, 1972
- I was in a schoolyard, fer chrissake, maybe five, ten minutes, when these two cops from the 86th precinct bum-rap me!—Terry Southern, *Now Dig This*, p. 146, 2001

bum robber *noun*
a male homosexual *UK, 1972*
An exact synonym of **ASS/ARSE BANDIT**.

bum-rush *verb*
to swarm someone; to attack someone *US*
- Homeboys I don't know but they're part of the pack / In the plan against the man, bum rush attack / For the suckers at the door—Public Enemy *Yo! Bum Rush The Show*, 1987
- It was on a Sunday. Rick and I were kicking it upon Crenshaw. All these females roled up in a Rabbit. Everybody started to bum rush them, trying to get their numbers and all.— *Boyz N The Hood*, 1990
- Should he just bumrush the cunt now?—Donald Gorgon, *Cop Killer*, p. 74, 1994

bumscare *verb*
to drop your trousers, bend over and expose your buttocks *AUSTRALIA*
- — Thommo, *The Dictionary of Australian Swearing and Sex Sayings*, p. 20, 1985

bum shine; bumper shine *verb*
to hang onto the rear bumper of a car and slide behind it in icy weather *CANADA*
- It is, of course, a dangerous practice. It is usually called bum shining even though you can slide on your feet, your back, your bum, or just about any other part of your anatomy.—Chris Thain, *Cold as a Bay Street Banker's Heart*, p. 27, 1987

bumsicle *noun*
a hypothermic alcoholic *US*
- —Sally Williams, *"Strong" Words*, p. 135, 1994

bums-on-seats *noun*
a theatrical audience seen as a source of income *UK, 1982*
- So: is saving the world a good enough motivation to go around doing bad stuff, and I mean really bad, I mean bums-on-seats bad?—James Hawes, *White Powder, Green Light*, p. 10, 2002

bum steer *noun*
a piece of bad advice *US, 1924*
A combination of **BUM** (inferior) and obsolete, except in this connection, 'steer' (direction).

bumsters *noun*
trousers designed to be worn very low on the hips *UK*
A play on the more familiar 'hipsters' and **BUM** (the buttocks).
- [Alexander McQueen] the man who seemed dedicated to playing tricks on women (from those bumsters to Gwyneth Paltrow's see-through evening dress)[.]— *The Guardian*, 6th October 2003

bumsucker *noun*
a sycophant *UK*
- We're all respectable householders – that's to say Tories, yes-men and bumsuckers.—George Orwell, *Coming Up for Air*, p. 15, 1950

bum-sucking *adjective*
sycophantic *UK, 1949*
- Yesterday there was a marked absence of the bum-sucking, bottom-feeding, creepy, oleaginous praise for the prime minister we suffered for the last four years.— *The Guardian*, 28th June 2001

bum tag *noun*
a piece of faecal matter in the hair about the anus *UK, 1961*
- —James McDonald, *A Dictionary of Obscenity, Taboo and Euphemism*, p. 20, 1988

bum trip *noun*
1 a bad experience with LSD or another hallucinogen *US*
- —Richard Alpert and Sidney Cohen, *LSD*, 1966
- —Joe David Brown (Editor), *The Hippies*, p. 217, 1967

- See, if you consider the event [Woodstock] as a festival in the traditional sense of the word... then three people getting killed, a few thousand injuries, lack of food and water and hundreds of bum trips lead you to draw bad conclusions — Abbie Hoffman, *Woodstock Nation*, p. 4, 1969
- Sure, there was some bad shit around and some bum trips were had, but mostly it was ok. — *East Village Other*, 20th August 1969
- — Angela Devlin, *Prison Patter*, p. 32, 1996

2 any bad experience *US*

- — Miss Cone, *The Slang Dictionary (Hawthorne High School)*, 1965
- They had been shunted off to a parched meadow nine or ten thousand feet up in the Sierras and it was obviously a bum trip. — Hunter S. Thompson, *Hell's Angels*, p. 135, 1966
- — J. L. Simmons and Barry Winograd, *It's Happening*, p. 168, 1966
- It was a bum trip all the way to the central police station in Casablanca. — Richard Neville, *Play Power*, p. 245, 1970
- The hippie ethos tended to deny the relevance of political power for liberation, viewing the pursuit of power as ego-tripping and power itself as inevitably oppresive, a bum trip. — Gilbert Zicklin, *Countercultural Communes*, p. 26–27, 1983
- But "You Are Free" is not a relentless bum trip. — *Chicago Tribune*, p. 33, 17th February 2003

bum tripper *noun*

a person experiencing a psychotic break while using a hallucinogenic drug *US*

- In the mornings there would be a sign on the clinic's door: BUM TRIPPERS AND EMERGENCIES ONLY. NO DOCTORS TILL 4 P.M. — Nicholas Von Hoffman, *We Are The People Our Parents Warned Us Against*, p. 12, 1967

bumwad *noun*

toilet paper, or any material used in place of toilet paper *US, 1896*

- — J.E. Lighter, *Historical Dictionary of American Slang, Volume 1*, p. 314, 1994

bum-waggle *verb*

to power-walk *AUSTRALIA*

From the exaggerated motions of those who practice the sport.

bum warmer *noun*

a car coat *US*

- Used to be a time when these jackets, affectionately known as "bum warmers," were for just that! Now they're just status symbols. — *San Francisco Progress*, p. 2, 18th August 1961

bun *noun*

1 the vagina *US*

- [He is] hung like a stud horse, too. If she can't feel what he's throwing her she must have a bun full of novocaine. — Lawrence Block, *No Score [The Affairs of Chip Harrison Omnibus]*, p. 115–116, 1970

2 a woman who has sexual intercourse with multiple male partners *AUSTRALIA*

- 'I don't know what she's complaining about,' said one former club 'bun' or groupie, who used to make herself available for any of one club's players who asked. 'I thought it was a great time.' — *Sydney Morning Herald*, 22nd March 2003

3 marijuana *UK*

- — The New Initiatives Project, *The Grass aint always Greena [a report of a Drug Education Programme]*, p. 9, April 1998

4 the head *NEW ZEALAND*

- — Louis S. Leland, *A Personal Kiwi-Yankee Dictionary*, p. 19, 1984

▸ **do your bun**

to lose your temper *NEW ZEALAND*

- Jock did is bun properly. 'So my money's not good enough, eh mate?' he snarled at the driver. — Barry Crump, *A Good Keen Man*, p. 76, 1960

▸ **have a bun on**

to be drunk *US*

- — Harold Wentorth and Stuart Berg Flexner, *Dictionary of American Slang*, p. 76, 1960

bun *verb*

to take the active role in anal sex *AUSTRALIA*

- 'Some of Wayne's poof mates might've got him and bunned him,' suggested Kathy. — Robert G. Barrett, *Davo's Little Something*, p. 76, 1992

bun bandit *noun*

the active male in male-on-male anal sex *US*

- — Guy Strait, *The Lavendar Lexicon*, 1964

bun-biter *noun*

a sycophant or toady *US*

School usage.

- — *Washington Post*, 23rd April 1961

bun boy *noun*

1 a male homosexual prostitute whose prominent feature is his buttocks *US*

- Though it was early in the day, the usual assortment of street hustlers, whores (they all seemed to be wearing straight skirts slit up the side), bun boys (tight jeans, tennis shoes and tropical shirts) and black pimps[.] — Gerald Petievich, *To Die in Beverly Hills*, p. 82, 1983

2 a sycophantic assistant *US*

- I don't want any of your bun-boys around when you and I talk business. — Gerald Petievich, *Shakedown*, p. 149, 1988

bunce; bunts; bunse *noun*

money; profit; extras *UK, 1812*

Possibly a corruption of 'bonus'.

- We had had a few "burster" houses lately and he thought the "bunce" must be "bona"[.] — Butch Reynolds, *Broken Hearted Clown*, p. 29, 1953
- "Plenty of bunce?" "I'm sorry, sir?" "Fringe benefits?" — Anthony Masters, *Minder*, p. 111, 1984
- [W]e took him out for the evening a week or three later, once we had a bit of bunce. — Danny King, *The Burglar Diaries*, p. 214, 2001

bunce *verb*

to overcharge someone, especially if obviously rich or eager *UK*

- — Patrick O'Shaughnessy, *Market Traders' Slang*, 1979

bunce up *verb*

to pool your financial resources *UK: NORTHERN IRELAND*

- — C. I. Macafee, *A Concise Ulster Dictionary*, p. 47, 1996

bunch *noun*

a non-specific amount of something

- The kind of girl they put a bunch of make-up on and photograph for the cover of Vogue. — Douglas Rushkoff, *The Snow that Killed Manuel Jarrow (Disco Biscuits)*, p. 197, 1996
- When I was a 14 year-old at boarding school, lights out in the dorm was the cue for a whole bunch of arsing around. — *FHM*, p. 250, June 2003

▸ **the bunch**

in a race, the main body of competitors *UK, 1961*

A specialised variation of the conventional sense (a group of people).

bunch *verb*

1 to gather a deck of playing cards to shuffle *US*

- — George Percy, *The Language of Poker*, p. 15, 1988

2 to quit a job *US, 1927*

- — Frederic G. Cassidy, *Dictionary of American Regional English, Volume 1*, p. 459, 1985

bunched *adjective*

physically exhausted *IRELAND*

- And lucky thing for me, the third guy wasn't too anxious 'cause I was bunched. — Murphy Tom, *A Whistle in the Dark*, p. 66, 1989

bunch of bananas *noun*

in a car, an exhaust system with individual headers that intertwine *US*

- — John Lawlor, *How to Talk Car*, p. 26, 1965

bunch of bastards *noun*

a tangled rope *UK, 1961*

Naval origins.

bunch of fives *noun*

the fist; a punch; a series of blows delivered with the fist *UK, 1821*

- — Clarence Major, *Dictionary of Afro-American Slang*, p. 33, 1970
- — Louis S. Leland, *A Personal Kiwi-Yankee Dictionary*, p. 19, 1984

bunch of flowers *noun*

in horse racing, used by jockeys to describe a very small tip, or no tip at all, from an owner after winning a race *AUSTRALIA*

- — Ned Wallish, *The Truth Dictionary of Racing Slang*, p. 11, 1989

bunch of grapes *noun*

a large mess of knots in a fishing line *AUSTRALIA*

- Being the sort of fellow he was he sat down and patiently began to unpick the huge 'bunch of grapes'. — Bob Staines, *Wot a Whopper*, p. 24, 1982

bunch punch *noun*

1 sex involving multiple males and a single female *US*

- — *American Speech*, p. 56, Spring-Summer 1975: 'Razorback slang'

2 by extension, any chaotic situation in which it is not clear who is doing what to whom *US*
- As he described it, the editorial board meeting quickly abandoned crucial judgments regarding the business of publishing The Shriek of Revolution and assumed the form of a bunch-punch.—Ed Sanders, *Tales of Beatnik Glory*, p. 183, 1975

bunco *noun*

1 fraud; an act of fraud, especially a swindle by means of card-trickery; a confidence trick *US, 1914*

2 a squad of police assigned to confidence swindles *US, 1947*
- The graying captain of bunco was sitting behind his orante desk in the well-appointed office, sipping coffee.—Iceberg Slim (Robert Beck), *Long White Con*, p. 68, 1977

bunco *verb*

to swindle someone, to cheat someone *US, 1875*
- "Don't give me that, man – I've been buncoed by experts!" means "Don't try to deceive me!"—David Powis, *The Signs of Crime*, 1977

bunco artist *noun*

a professional swindler *US, 1945*
- —Thomas L. Clark, *The Dictionary of Gambling and Gaming*, p. 31, 1987
- The journal kept up a steady barrage against Cox, making him well known among its readers as a bunco artist.—Dianna Davids Olien et al., *Easy Money*, p. 125, 199
- In simple terms, maskirovka combines concealment and misdirection in a way that would be familiar to bunco artists or stage magicians.—*Providence (Rhode Island) Journal-Bulletin*, p. 8F, 1st March 1998

bunco booter *noun*

an infrequent smoker *US*
- —John Fahs, *Cigarette Confidential*, p. 302, 1996

bundie *noun*

a hamburger bun *IRELAND*
- Jimmy Sr. did a burger for himself and when he bit into it, before his teeth met, he could feel the sand in the bundie.—Roddy Doyle, *The Van*, p. 202, 1991

bundle *noun*

1 a good deal of money *US, 1903*
From an earlier sense (a roll of money).
- Even if the grass had a bundle he would plead poverty. Not that he ever had much in his kick [trouser pocket].—*The Sweeney*, p. 50, 1976
- —George Percy, *The Language of Poker*, p. 15, 1988

2 a long prison sentence *US*
- —Hyman E. Goldin et al., *Dictionary of American Underworld Lingo*, p. 37, 1950

3 a bundle of packets of heroin; heroin *US*
- —Richard A. Spears, *The Slang and Jargon of Drugs and Drink*, p. 84, 1986
- —Robert Ashton, *This Is Heroin*, p. 205, 2002
- —Mike Haskins, *Drugs*, p. 283, 2003

4 a sexually appealing woman *US*
- —Kenn "Naz" Young, *Naz's Dictionary of Teen Slang*, p. 16, 1993

5 a fight *US, 1937*
- —Chris Lewis, *The Dictionary of Playground Slang*, 2003

▸**go a bundle on**

to highly regard someone or something *UK, 1957*
- I don't go a bundle on razzmatazz.—*The Observer*, 3rd September 2000

bundle *verb*

1 to fight *UK*
- "Oh, so you want to bundle, you Irish bastard?" said Hanson. "Come on, then."—Brendan Behan, *Borstal Boy*, 1958

2 to make someone incapable of action *US*
- —John R. Armore and Joseph D. Wolfe, *Dictionary of Desperation*, 1976

bundle buggy *noun*

a small delivery truck *US*
- —Montie Tak, *Truck Talk*, p. 23, 1971

bundle of socks *noun*

the head *AUSTRALIA, 1945*
Rhyming slang for 'thinkbox'.

bundu *noun*

wilderness, desert; the bush, the jungle; the countryside *SOUTH AFRICA, 1939*
Etymology unknown; possibly derived from the Shona word for 'grassland'. Possibly adopted into British military use during the compaign against the Mau-Mau in Kenya in the early 1950s; in 1984, the variant 'bundoo' was recorded in use by the British military in Northern Ireland.
- [O]ut in the frozen "bundu", at surrounding temperatures of 30 below freezing.—*Sunday Telegraph*, 8th April 1979

bunfight *noun*

a tea party *UK*
A 'bun' is a 'sticky cake', and this describes what happens when a children's tea party gets out of hand.
- [T]his bunfight helps [...] for an hour or two at least, anyway. Them kiddies' faces, lar – worth all the thingy of putting a do like this together.—Kevin Sampson, *Outlaws*, p. 222, 2001

bun floss *noun*

a thong-backed bikini bottom *US*
- —Trevor Cralle, *The Surfin'ary*, p. 39, 1991

bung *noun*

1 a bribe *UK, 1950*
- "Alright so how much is the bung?" Asked Solie. "Well let[']s say a fifty and we did'nt [sic] see a thing"—Frank Norman, *Bang To Rights*, p. 122, 1958
- —Angela Devlin, *Prison Patter*, p. 32, 1996
- I'd never take bribes or anything. Do deals for information or bodies, for sure. But never the bung.—Jake Arnott, *He Kills Coppers*, p. 15, 2001

2 a tip, a gratuity *UK*
Glasgow slang
- —Michael Munro, *The Original Patter*, 1985

3 the anus *UK, 1788*
- First, I'll want to tongue your bung while you juggle my balls in one hand and play with my asshole with the other.—Kevin Smith, *Jay and Silent Bob Strike Back*, p. 90, 2001

▸**on the bung**

being in regular receipt of bribes, or receiving benefits in exchange for bribery *UK*
- I've heard a little rumour that he's on the bung.—Jake Arnott, *He Kills Coppers*, p. 44, 2001

bung *verb*

1 to throw; to put; to send, especially with use of force *UK, 1825*
- I can see myself now being bunged off to a twilight home[.]—Barry Humphries, *Bazza Pulls It Off!*, 1971

2 to tip; to pay a financial gratuity *UK*
- I saw the geezer who presses the suits for the geezers who are going out and I bunged him a quarter of an ounce of snout so that he would do a good job of mine—Frank Norman, *Bang To Rights*, p. 149, 1958

3 to bribe someone *UK, 1950*
- —Angela Devlin, *Prison Patter*, p. 32, 1996

4 to pay protection money to someone in authority *UK*
A specialisation of the previous sense.
- Sergeant Connor. He's one of them slime-sniffers [the Vice Squad]. Every girl in Bayswater bungs to him if she wants to stay on the game.—Bill Turner, *Sex Trap*, 1968

5 to hit someone *UK*
- He was getting a bit stroppy so I bunged one him [or I bunged him one on]—*Beale*, 1984

▸**bung on an act**

to give an exaggerated performance; to indulge in histrionics *AUSTRALIA*
- He's only got one fault; he likes to bung on an act. An' 'e's bunging' one on now.—Nino Culotta (John O'Grady), *Gone Fishin'*, p. 212, 1962
- Come on there, quit bunging on an act.—Geoff Wyatt, *Saltwater Saints*, p. 71, 1969
- —John O'Grady, *Aussie Etiket*, p. 70, 1971
- Good umpires can usually 'pick' those players who are playing for an emmy or 'bunging on an act.'—Ivor Limb, *Footy's No Joke!*, p. 27, 1986
- —Kel Richards, *The Aussie Bible*, p. 59, 2003

▸**bung on side**

to behave pretentiously; to give oneself airs and graces *AUSTRALIA*
- Have you ever tried to bung on side with the locals in a country town – I can tell you, from painful experience, that it just doesn't work. —Sue Rhodes, *Now you'll think I'm awful*, p. 133, 1967
- —Alexander Buzo, *Norm and Ahmed*, p. 14, 1969

▸**bung on the bull**

to behave pretentiously *AUSTRALIA*
Reported by Alex Buzo, 1973.

bung *adjective*
broken, ruined, wrecked *AUSTRALIA, 1897*
Originally Aboriginal pidgin English meaning 'dead', from the Australian Aboriginal language Jagara.
- He scrounged old parts from local garages, riding home with a school-bag crammed with bung distributors and defunct generators. —Kerry Cue, *Crooks, Chooks and Bloody Ratbags*, p. 161, 1983
- Happened to me the other day, I was there minding my own business when a trolley hit my bung foot at about Warp Nine speed. —Paul Vautin, *Turn It Up!*, p. 140, 1995

▷ see: BONG

▸ **go bung**
to fail *AUSTRALIA, 1885*
- —Norman Lindsay, *Bohemians at the Bulletin*, p. 99, 1965
- My nose hurts. I'm seeing wonky. My hearing's gone bung. —Glyn Parry, *Mosh*, p. 6, 1996

bungalow *noun*
a dormitory room *US*
- —Judi Sanders, *Kickin' like Chicken with the Couch Commander*, p. 4, 1992

bunged *adjective*
tipsy *SOUTH AFRICA*
- — *Cape Argus*, 4th July 1946

bungee *noun*
▷ see: BUNJEE

bunger *noun*
1 a bruised and discoloured eye *US*
- —Vincent J. Monteleone, *Criminal Slang*, p. 38, 1949

2 an exploding firework *AUSTRALIA, 1929*
- —Jim Ramsay, *Cop It Sweet!*, p. 18, 1977

3 a cigarette *AUSTRALIA*
- I mean the in thing as a 15-year-old was to walk around in front of your mates with a bunger hanging out of your mouth. —Paul Vautin, *Turn It Up!*, p. 26, 1995

bung-full *adjective*
absolutely full, especially as a result of eating and drinking *UK, 1984*
Full up to the point where a stopper should be necessary to contain it all.

bunghole *noun*
1 the anus *UK, 1611*
- The way you were banging the bunghole, you damned near fell in —Jim Thompson, *Pop. 1280*, p. 192, 1964
- Just a lot of screwballs jumping bare-assed over swords and fire, kissing the master's bunghole. —Robert Campbell, *Sweet La-La Land*, p. 247, 1990

2 by extension, a despicable, unlikeable person *US*
- —Collin Baker et al., *College Undergraduate Slang Study Conducted at Brown University*, p. 91, 1968

3 a pastry treat made from leftover pie dough spread with brown sugar, cinnamon and butter *CANADA*
- The Quebec Eastern Townships calls a "bung hole" what is known elsewhere as a "hoedunker" or a "nun's fart." —Lewis Poteet, *Talking Country*, p. 26–27, 1992

4 cheese *AUSTRALIA, 1919*
- Turtle soup, steak, and beautiful cheese – not like the bunghole here in Woolloomooloo[.] —Frank Hardy, *The Yarns of Billy Borker*, p. 25, 1965

bunghole *verb*
to sodomise someone *US, 1939*
From the noun BUNGHOLE (the anus).

bungi *verb*
to have anal sex *CANADA*
- "You don't need a condom," she'll say. "We can bungi" (that's their special word for it), and then that spoiled little boy is ruined forever. —Suroosh Alvi et al., *The Vice Guide*, p. 38, 2002

bungie *noun*
a mildly left-wing white student in South Africa during the struggle against apartheid *SOUTH AFRICA*
- —Penny Silva, *A Dictionary of South African English*, 1996

bungie-hole *verb*
to sodomise someone *US*
A variation of BUNGHOLE.
- [H]e think he slick and he bungie-hole me[.] —Joel Rose, *Kill Kill Faster Faster*, p. 18, 1997

bung it on
to behave pretentiously; to give oneself airs and graces *AUSTRALIA, 1942*
- The Doc's paying, Ikey. So bung it on, mate. —Barry Humphries, *The Wonderful World of Barry McKenzie*, p. 28, 1968
- —Sonya Plowman, *Great Kiwi Slang*, p. 39, 2002

bung navel *noun*
a protruding navel *BARBADOS*

bungo *noun*
a very black, ugly and stupid rustic *JAMAICA, 1979*
- —Thomas H. Slone, *Rasta is Cuss*, p. 33, 2003

bung on *verb*
1 to put on an article of clothing, especially carelessly *UK, 1984*
From BUNG (to throw, to put).

2 to stage a party, event, etc *AUSTRALIA*
- I'm bungin' on a barbecue lunch. Bring the wife. —John O'Grady, *It's Your Shout, Mate!*, p. 91, 1972

bungo-toughy *noun*
a young child who behaves poorly; a little ruffian *GUYANA*
- —Richard Allsopp, *Dictionary of Caribbean English Usage*, p. 121, 1996

bungy *noun*
▷ see: BOUNGY

bunhead *noun*
a dolt; an outcast *US*
- —Michael V. Anderson, *The Bad, Rad, Not to Forget Way Cool Beach and Surf Discriptionary*, p. 4, 1988

bun-huggers *noun*
tight-fitting trousers *US*
- —J. R. Friss, *A Dictionary of Teenage Slang (Mt. Diablo High)*, 1964

bunjee; bunjie; bungee *noun*
an India-rubber eraser; India rubber *UK, 1928*
More familiar in later use as 'elasticated rope' and, since 1979, in an extreme sports context (the practical half of a bungee jumper).

bunk *noun*
1 nonsense *US, 1900*
- All that crap they have in cartoons in the Saturday Evening Post and all, showing guys on street corners looking sore as hell because their dates are late – that's bunk. —J.D. Salinger, *Catcher in the Rye*, p. 124–125, 1951
- When Mr. Money arrived at the airport, the grifter had him paged, then introduced himself with a bunk story, such as being a friend of hotel manager, who had asked him to pick up the boob. —Jack Lait and Lee Mortimer, *Washington Confidential*, p. 277, 1951
- To Johnny, that was bunk from a punk. —Ed Sanders, *Tales of Beatnik Glory*, p. 77, 1975

2 a weak drug, especially heroin *US*
- —Jay Robert Nash, *Dictionary of Crime*, p. 50, 1992
- —Mark S. Fleisher, *Beggars & Thieves*, p. 287, 1995

3 a hiding place *US*
- I don't see how anybody could know they were there. That's a good bunk we have. —Hal Ellson, *Tomboy*, p. 24, 1950

4 a prisoner's cell or the area immediately around his bed in a dormitory setting *US*
- —Ethan Hilderbrant, *Prison Slang*, 1998

▸ **do a bunk; pull a bunk**
to abscond, to run away *UK, 1870*
- —Lou Shelly, *Hepcats Jive Talk Dictionary*, p. 24, 1945
- Just trying to pull a bunk from the country and the place turns into Bosnia. —Greg Williams, *Diamond Geezers*, p. 206, 1997
- He's just done a bunk. Sent a telegram to say he's gone for ever. —Bill Naughton, *The Day My Dad Ran Away*, p. 272, 1999
- Haven't seen him for ages because he did a bunk after rippin off Tommy Maguire[.] —Niall Griffiths, *Kelly + Victor*, p. 47, 2002

bunk *verb*
1 to abscond or play truant, usually from school or work *UK, 1934*
Also to 'bunk off'.
- He [a 12-year-old boy] bunks off full time from education these days. — *Time Out*, p. 15, 8th January 1982
- Shaun and Bez, the working-class bohemians, doing drugs and bunking off around Europe[.] —John Robb, *The Nineties*, p. 62, 1999

- There's still a bit of the 1970s teenager in us: a slaggy, cider-drinking and bunking off school mentality. — *The Times*, 8th April 2003

2 to sleep, to stay the night *US, 1840*
Introduces a military or Western feel.
- Or you can bunk out in the Rumpus Room. It doesn't matter to me. — Odie Hawkins, *Lost Angeles*, p. 203, 1994

3 to travel without a ticket *UK*
- I have to bunk the train up to London[.] — Gavin Hills, *White Burger Danny (Disco Biscuits)*, p. 76, 1996
- bunking the train into Paddington and legging it through the barriers — John King, *Human Punk*, p. 1461, 2000

4 to carry a passenger on the cross-bar of a bicycle *AUSTRALIA*
- — Sydney J. Baker, *The Drum*, 1959

5 to hide something *US*
- "I hope the cigarettes we bunked last night don't get wet," she said, avoiding his eyes. — Hal Ellson, *Tomboy*, p. 12, 1950

bunk *adjective*
worthless *US*
- Noontimes Rooski often hustled bunk hash there and Joe planned to do the same[.] — Seth Morgan, *Homeboy*, p. 59, 1990

bunker *noun*
1 anal sex *US*
- — Vincent J. Monteleone, *Criminal Slang*, p. 38, 1949

2 a premises used by a criminal gang as a base from which to conduct violent robberies *UK*
- — *Review of the Sunday Papers*, 1st August 1982

bunkered *adjective*
in a situation from which it is difficult to escape *UK, 1894*
A figurative application of golfing terminology.

bunk fatigue *noun*
sleep *US, 1915*
- — J.E. Lighter, *Historical Dictionary of American Slang, Volume 1*, p. 317, 1994

bunk fee *noun*
the amount charged to smoke opium in an opium den *US*
- — Jay Robert Nash, *Dictionary of Crime*, p. 50, 1992

bunk flying *noun*
dramatic, on-the-ground discussions of flying exploits *US, 1933*
- — J.E. Lighter, *Historical Dictionary of American Slang, Volume 1*, p. 317, 1994

bunk in *verb*
to sneak into an entertainment venue without paying *UK*
Schoolboy reversal of 'bunk off'.
- [N]ot befitting the description of games was "bunking in". Favourite for this was the Trocette cinema in Tower Bridge Road[.] — Brian McDonald, *Elephant Boys*, p. 39, 2000

bunk patrol *noun*
a nap while off duty *CANADA*
Mounted Police usage.
- [He pulled] off his boots and heavy clothing in anticipation of "bunk patrol" that afternoon. — William Mowery, *Tales of the Mounted Police*, p. 165, 1953

bunkum *noun*
nonsense *US, 1862*
In or around 1820 the Congressman representing Buncombe County in North Carolina, USA, in seeking to impress his constituents, made a pointless speech to Congress; over time 'Buncombe' became 'bunkum'.
- Have you found inner peace and all that bunkum? — *The Guardian*, 12th March 2004

bunk-up *noun*
1 an act of sexual intercourse *UK*
Originally military, post-World War 2.
- I'll have a leavy [levy] at the same time and imagine that I'm having [sic] a bunk up instead of you. — Frank Norman, *Bang To Rights*, p. 153, 1958
- A cheap bunk-up in the sun. — David Robb, *The Nineties*, p. 47, 1999
- fifteen-year-old boot boys with little chance of a bunk-up — John King, *Human Punk*, p. 23, 2000
- You wouldn't fancy a bunk-up, would you? — Mark Steel, *Reasons to be Cheerful*, p. 55, 2001

2 a lifting-up as assistance in climbing or reaching *AUSTRALIA, 1919*

bunky *noun*
in jail or prison, a cellmate *US, 1858*
- — Vincent J. Monteleone, *Criminal Slang*, p. 38, 1949
- — Paul Glover, *Words from the House of the Dead*, 1974
- — James Harris, *A Convict's Dictionary*, p. 28, 1989

bunnit *noun*
▸ **do your bunnit**
to lose your temper *UK*
Glasgow slang.
- — Michael Munro, *The Original Patter*, 1985

bunny *noun*
1 a Playboy Club hostess; a nightclub hostess dressed in a costume that is representative of a rabbit *US, 1960*
A shortening of the official job-description: Bunny Girl.

2 a woman blessed with few if any sexual inhibitions *US*
- — Eugene Landy, *The Underground Dictionary*, p. 42, 1971

3 a female surfer or a male surfer's girlfriend *US, 1936*
- — Rob Burt, *Surf City, Drag City*, 1986

4 a homosexual male prostitute *US*
- — Dale Gordon, *The Dominion Sex Dictionary*, p. 35, 1967

5 the rectum *US*
- — *Maledicta*, p. 15, Summer 1977: 'A word for it!'

6 a conversation *UK*
- One of the chaps came up to me on the exercise yard and we began to have a bunny. — Frank Norman, *Bang To Rights*, p. 57, 1958

7 a person who talks too much, especially stupidly *UK, 1954*
- — *News Chronicle*, 23rd May 1958

8 a fool, a dupe *AUSTRALIA, 1943*
- I'm an awful bunny, aren't I? — John Wynnum, *Jiggin' in the Riggin*, p. 31, 1965
- I discovered what bloody bunnies we buyers of Scratchit tickets really are. — Frank Hardy, *Hardy's People*, p. 124, 1986

9 a pilotman *UK*
- — Harvey Sheppard, *Dictionary of Railway Slang*, 1970

10 in shuffleboard, the disc on a number representing the winning score *US*
- — Omero C. Catan, *Secrets of Shuffleboard Strategy*, p. 64, 1967

11 in the sport of field archery, a 15 cm target face *UK*
Derives from the small face of a 'bunny' (rabbit) which, along with faces of other small creatures, is used as a target.
- — John Kember-Smith, *Archery Today*, 1988

bunny *verb*
to talk, to chat *UK*
The childish word for a 'rabbit' replaces the rhyming slang **RABBIT AND PORK; RABBIT** (to talk).
- Some geeser [geezer] comes up to me and starts bunnying to me about one thing and another[.] — Frank Norman, *Bang To Rights*, p. 31, 1958

bunny boiler *noun*
an obsessive, possessive woman *UK*
From the action in the film *Fatal Attraction*, 1987, in which actress Glenn Close put the fear of God into adulterous men.
- She was an emotional loose cannon and he would have to disengage from her with the utmost delicacy or she would turn into what he had heard called a bunny-boiler. — Ben Elton, *High Society*, p. 201, 2002
- I don't like the look of her mate, could be a bunny-boiler. — *www.LondonSlang.com*, June 2002
- What I actually want, he thought, is to get this bunny-boiler carted off by the men in white coats. She kissed him on the cheek. "See you later." — Colin Butts, *Is Harry Still on the Boat?*, p. 202, 2003

bunny boilery *adjective*
of a woman scorned, unhealthily obsessed with her (ex-) lover *UK*
From **BUNNY BOILER**.
- Rio seems to have gone all bunny boilery on me already. — Colin Butts, *Is Harry Still on the Boat?*, p. 257, 2003

bunny book *noun*
a sexually explicit magazine *US*
From the Playboy bunny.
- — *Current Slang*, p. 7, Fall 1967

bunny boot *noun*
a large white felt boot, now usually made of rubber with an inflatable air layer for insulation *US, 1954*
- Bunny boots are the warmest footgear worn in the Northland excepting the Eskimo mukluk. — Robert O. Bowen, *An Alaskan Dictionary*, p. 10, 1965
- — Bernadette Hince, *The Antarctic Dictionary*, p. 73, 2000

bunny cap *noun*
a fur-lined pile cap *US*
Vietnam war usage.
- — Carl Fleischhauer, *A Glossary of Army Slang*, p. 7, 1968

bunny chow *noun*
a hot Indian or Malay curry served in a hollowed out loaf of bread *SOUTH AFRICA*
Created and coined by Hindi Indians in Durban.
- Then and there I vowed never again to eat something as vile as a bunny chow. — *Sunday Times (South Africa)*, 4th March 2001

bunny dip *noun*
a method of serving bar customers drinks calculated to keep a woman's breasts from spilling out from a low-cut, tight bodice *US*
A technique perfected by and taught to Playboy Bunnies.
- "In a frosted glass with an umbrella," Vincent said, as the girl did the bunny dip to place the drink on the table without losing her breasts. — Elmore Leonard, *Glitz*, p. 112, 1985
- Chief among these [skills] was the Bunny Dip, a manoeuvre performed with a tray in hand and designed to offer drinks and puffed-up Bunny tails to customers at just the right angle. — *Daily Express*, 4th September 1999

bunny fuck *verb*
to have sex quickly, if not frantically *US*
- — Eugene Landy, *The Underground Dictionary*, p. 42, 1971

bunny hole *noun*
an excavation in a fox hole to provide protection from a mortar attack *US*
Korean war usage.
- These caves correspond roughly to our "bunny holes," which are only large enough for one man to huddle in during a mortar barrage. Bunny holes are usually dug so that a man can jump from his fighting-hold into the bunny hole[.] — Martin Russ, *The Last Parallel*, p. 115, 1957

bunny hop *noun*
the act of bouncing both wheels of a bicycle off the ground into the air *US, 1953*
- — William Nealy, *Mountain Bike!*, p. 160, 1992

bunny hug *noun*
a girl's hooded sweatshirt *CANADA*
Especially in Saskatchewan, where it gets very cold in winter, this term is used for a key warm layer of clothing.
- And Saskatchewan province, as Isabel Gibson wrote in last week's Maclean's, goes its neighbors one better: There the hoodie is a "Bunny hug." — *Boston Globe*, p. H3, 14th March 2004

bunny suit *noun*
a thick flight suit worn by an aircrew member over an anti-gravity suit *US, 1966*
- — *The Listener*, 13th July 1978
- Clad in bright-white bunny suits, the Delta engineers and their interpreter stepped into a clean room[.] — *The Oregonian*, p. A1, 9th March 2004

buns *noun*
1 the buttocks *US, 1877*
- Her skirt was a short one, almost reaching the bottom of her buns which tended to hang down into her net stockings. — Jack C. Shottler, *Evergreen*, p. 19, 1968
- It was a drag with all the whiteys looking at a brother getting his buns kicked. — Babs Gonzales, *Movin' On Down De Line*, p. 74, 1975
- Cher, I don't wanna do this any more, and my buns, they don't feel nothin' like steel. — *Clueless*, 1995
- I know she usually does Buns of Steel on Tuesdays. — Greg Williams, *Diamond Geezers*, p. 101, 1997

2 the feet *US*
- — Kenn "Naz" Young, *Naz's Underground Dictionary*, p. 17, 1973

bunse; bunts *noun*
▷ **see:** BUNCE

bunt *noun*
the buttocks *US*
A blend of 'buttocks' and 'cunt'.
- — Dale Gordon, *The Dominion Sex Dictionary*, p. 35, 1967

bunter *noun*
a prostitute *US*
- — Ruth Todasco et al., *The Intelligent Woman's Guide to Dirty Words*, p. 2, 1973

bunty *noun*
1 semen *UK*
- I'd give that a good service I can tell you. Pump a couple of gallons of bunty up it any day of the week. — John King, *Human Punk*, p. 236, 2000

2 an affectionate term for a small person, especially a small middle-aged woman *UK*
From Scottish/Irish dialect.
- — David Powis, *The Signs of Crime*, 1977

buoy *noun*
a surfer who lingers in the water, rarely catching a wave *US*
- — Trevor Cralle, *The Surfin'ary*, p. 16, 1991

bupkes; bupkis *noun*
nothing – used for expressing scorn at something deemed foolish or trivial *US, 1942*
From the Russian for 'beans'.
- I worked on it three hours – and what did he give me? Bubkes! — Leo Rosten, *The Joys of Yiddish*, p. 55, 1968
- Three go-rounds – zero, zilch, buppkis. — James Ellroy, *White Jazz*, p. 53, 1992
- While two volunteers said it "does make your lips appear fuller," the other two noticed "nothing, bupkis, zilch." — *Daily News (New York)*, p. 62, 15th April 2004

bupp *verb*
to strike your head against something *BARBADOS*
- — Frank A. Collymore, *Barbadian Dialect*, p. 23, 1965

buppie; buppy; bumpie *noun*
a (young) *b*lack *u*rban *p*rofessional; a (young) *b*lack *u*pwardly *m*obile *p*rofessional *US, 1986*
A socio-economic acronym on the model of **YUPPIE**; as forced as 'yuppie' seemed natural and only a marginal term in the vernacular.
- — *American Speech*, Summer 1989
- — Nelson George, *Buppies, B-Boys, Baps, & Bohos*, 1992
- [Brixton] now contained a multi-complex cinema, a string of upwardly-mobile buppie shops, and the largest Caribbean-style market for a thousand miles in any direction. — Donald Gorgon, *Cop Killer*, p. 29–30, 1994
- Fort Green [in New York], an area Kenyatta dismisses as "full of buppies and bohemian shit"[.] — Patrick Neate, *Where You're At*, p. 34, 2003

buppies *noun*
bread and butter; a slice of bread and butter *UK*
After earlier variations: 'bupper', 'buppie', 'bups', 'bupsie'; derived by 'infantile reduction' (Ware, 1909).
- — Peter O'Donnell, *Dragon's Claw*, 1978

'burb *noun*
a sub*urb* *US*
- HOLDEN: You're saying you're from the 'burbs! ALYSSA: Middletown, J.J. — *Chasing Amy*, 1997
- East Molesey is a middle-class 'burb. The high street is full of antique shops[.] — Melanie McGrath, *Hard, Soft & Wet*, p. 238, 1998

burble *verb*
in computing, to post an inflammatory message that displays the person's complete ignorance on the subject in question *US*
From Lewis Carroll's 1871 *Through the Looking Glass*, in which the Jabberwock 'burbled' (spoke in a murmuring or rambling manner).
- — Eric S. Raymond, *The New Hacker's Dictionary*, p. 85, 1991
- — Christian Crumlish, *The Internet Dictionary*, p. 28, 1995

'burbs *noun*
the sub*urbs* *US*
- Everybody said we were moving to the 'burbs, and none of my friends wanted us to go where only white people stayed. — Terry Williams, *The Cocaine Kids*, p. 76, 1989

bureau-drawer special *noun*
a small, inexpensive handgun *US*
- —*American Speech*, p. 267, December 1962: 'The language of traffic policemen'

burg *noun*
1 a city or town *US, 1835*
- Young love gets a break in Washington, too, because the burg with its environs is small-town in construction[.]—Jack Lait and Lee Mortimer, *Washington Confidential*, p. 88, 1951
- I've got to get out of this burg.—Jim Thompson, *The Nothing Man*, p. 266, 1954
- There was another cat in the burg that owned all the beer, the Copa, a basketball team and his jazz club.—Babs Gonzales, *Movin' On Down De Line*, p. 33, 1975
- I want you hogs to let this burg know you're here.—Lewis John Carlino, *The Great Santini*, 1979
- That freak who tried to kill me had to have been sent by the Pimp Blimp – who, if he can get at me in the jailhouse, can reach me in this burg.—Seth Morgan, *Homeboy*, p. 115, 1990

2 a burglary *US*
- Sometimes he just sets up burg's. He doesn't do them himself, but farms out the address and steers the stolen property to his own fencing channels.—Gerald Petievich, *To Die in Beverly Hills*, p. 113, 1983

burger *noun*
1 a variety of MDMA, the recreational drug best known as ecstasy *UK*
- —Macfarlane, Macfarlane and Robson, *The User*, p. 74, 1996
- [Y]ou'd give him your twenty quid and he'd give you a plastic burger box with a bun inside, and when you opened the bun there was a special filling – a little E called a Burger.—Dave Courtney, *Raving Lunacy*, p. 41, 2000

2 a shapeless, uneven wave *US*
An abbreviation of **MUSHBURGER**.
- —Trevor Cralle, *The Surfin'ary*, p. 16, 1991

3 a scrape or raw bruise suffered while skateboarding *US*
- —Laura Torbet, *The Complete Book of Skateboarding*, p. 105, 1976

burgher *noun*
a townsperson *US*
- This town hasn't been occupied since the Revolutionary War, and I'd just as soon not make the burghers any shakier than I have to.—Max Shulman, *Rally Round the Flag, Boys!*, p. 197, 1957

burglar *noun*
1 a prison officer doing a surprise cell-search, especially of an officer who is considered an expert in this business *UK*
Heavily ironic.
- —Sean McConville, *The State of the Language*, 1980
- —Angela Devlin, *Prison Patter*, p. 32, 1996
- Without ceremony, the three prison officers from the security department (also responsible for cell searches and endearingly known as "burglars") marched him out of the wing[.]—*The Guardian*, 30th March 2000

2 the operator of a dishonest carnival game *US*
- —*American Speech*, p. 235, October 1950: 'The argot of outdoor boob traps'

buried *adjective*
1 of food, canned *JAMAICA, 1979*
- —Thomas H. Slone, *Rasta is Cuss*, p. 34, 2003

2 in new car sales, owing more on a loan than the car securing the loan is worth *US*
- —*American Speech*, p. 312, Autumn-Winter 1975: 'The jargon of car salesmen'

buried treasure *noun*
in computing, an unexpected and usually poorly written piece of code found in a program *US*
- —Eric S. Raymond, *The New Hacker's Dictionary*, p. 85, 1991

burk; burke *noun*
▷ see: **BERK**

burk *verb*
to vomit *US, 1960*
- —Frederic G. Cassidy, *Dictionary of American Regional English, Volume 1*, p. 459, 1985

burl *noun*
1 an attempt, try or go at anything *AUSTRALIA, 1917*
- Cripes – fair crack of the whip – like no – but I'll give it a burl if you really reckon my song was a bit of all right.—Barry Humphries, *The Wonderful World of Barry McKenzie*, p. 16, 1968
- Is that all? No probs. I'll give it a burl.—*The Adventures of Barry McKenzie*, 1972

2 in horse racing, odds of 5–1 *AUSTRALIA*
Rhyming slang, abbreviated from 'Burl Ives' for 'fives'.
- —Ned Wallish, *The Truth Dictionary of Racing Slang*, p. 10, 1989

burlap *noun*
dismissal from employment *US, 1951*
An elaboration of the more common term, 'getting the **SACK**'.
- —Harold Wentorth and Stuart Berg Flexner, *Dictionary of American Slang*, p. 76, 1960

burley; burly *noun*
burlesque *US, 1934*
- —Harold Wentorth and Stuart Berg Flexner, *Dictionary of American Slang*, p. 76, 1960

burleycue *noun*
burlesque *US, 1923*
- There was also burly burleycue queen Carrie Finnell, who could make the tassels on her breasts swing in multiple directions.—Samuel L. Letter, *The Encyclopedia of the New York Stage, 1940–1950*, p. 589, 1992

burlin *adjective*
drunk *UK*
- —*e-cyclopaedia*, 20th March 2002

Burlington hunt *noun*
1 the vagina *UK*
Rhyming slang for **CUNT**. A lesser known variation of the **BERKSHIRE HUNT** and **BERKELEY HUNT**.
- —Julian Franklyn, *A Dictionary of Rhyming Slang*, p. 45, 1960

2 a fool *UK*
Rhyming slang for **CUNT**.
- —Julian Franklyn, *A Dictionary of Rhyming Slang*, p. 45, 1960

burly *noun*
1 something which is not easily accomplished *US*
- —Kenn "Naz" Young, *Naz's Dictionary of Teen Slang*, p. 16, 1993

2 in foot-propelled scootering, a difficult trick or stunt which has pain or injury as the price of failure; a scooter-rider who specialises in such tricks *UK*
- If you're a scoot sider who gets his thrills from the trickier stunts, you're definitely a Burly[.]—Ben Sharpe, *Scooter Crazy*, p. 39, 2000

burly *adjective*
1 intimidating *US*
A surfer term used to describe a wave, brought into broader youth usage.
- —Judi Sanders, *Faced and Faded, Hanging to Hurl*, p. 6, 1993
- —Connie Eble (Editor), *UNC-CH Campus Slang*, p. 2, Spring 2003

2 very cold *US*
- —Trevor Cralle, *The Surfin'ary*, p. 16, 1991

burly show *noun*
in carnival usage, a burlesque show *US*
- —Don Wilmeth, *The Language of American Popular Entertainment*, p. 38, 1981

BURMA
written on an envelope, or at the foot of a lover's letter as lovers' code for '*be undressed (or upstairs) – and ready my angel*' *UK*
Widely-known, and well-used by servicemen. Now a part of the coded vocabulary of texting.
- —John Winton, *We Saw the Sea*, 1960
- —Andrew John with Stephen Blake, *The Total TxtMsg Dictionary*, p. 62, 2001

Burmese Fuckin' Incredible *noun*
a variety of marijuana seed from British Columbia *CANADA*
- Most orders call for three or four varieties, and one of the choices is invariably the strain called Burmese Fuckin' Incredible, from Vancouver Island Seed Company, because it won the smoking contest I helped judge in the winter.—Brian Preston, *Pot Planet*, p. 231, 2002

burn *noun*
1 tobacco; a cigarette *AUSTRALIA*
- 'Hiya, cobber. Have a burn?' Windy shook his head at the proffered packet.—J.E. MacDonnell, *Don't Gimme the Ships*, p. 132, 1960
- You got a burn there? The thieving tiffies knocked mine off.—John Wynnum, *Jiggin' in the Riggin*, p. 56, 1965
- "Can we smoke, sir?" "One quick burn. Permission from Mr. Goodyear."—*Scum*, 1979
- —Angela Devlin, *Prison Patter*, p. 32, 1996

2 a swindle *US*

- Outside he got in a cab with the Puerto Rican's money and told the driver to take off. The perfect burn, he thought, humming to himself. —Clarence Cooper Jr, *The Scene*, p. 105, 1960
- There are many stories about marihuana being cut with bay leaves, oregano, etc., and about an increase in the number of "burns" (in which someone who claims he can obtain drugs takes money in advance and never returns. —Ned Polsky, *Hustlers, Beats, and Others*, p. 171, 1967
- MR. ORANGE: Look, Eddie, he was pullin' a burn. He was gonna kill the cop and me. And when you guys walked through the door, he was gonna blow you to hell and make off with the diamonds. —*Reservoir Dogs*, 1992
- If I was really pullin' a burn, I'd have take two out, wouldn't I? —*Jackie Brown*, 1997

3 an exhibition, a display *US*

From **BURN** (to spray graffiti).

- [T]o get Yo! MTV Raps some burn in the TV room. —*The Source*, p. 36, March 2002

4 a thrill-seeking act of fast driving *AUSTRALIA*

- We came up by car for a burn. —William Dick, *A Bunch of Ratbags*, 1965

5 the initial flooding of sensations after injecting heroin *US*

- —David Maurer and Victor Vogel, *Narcotics and Narcotic Addiction*, p. 393, 1973

6 a caustic chemical treatment of the skin *US*

- —Anna Scotti and Paul Young, *Buzzwords*, p. 107, 1997

burn *verb*

1 to put someone to death by electrocution *US, 1927*

- [T]hese mouthpieces finally made a deal with the D.A. for Mackey to plead guilty to manslaughter or something like that, and Mackey was ready to do it because at least it meant he wouldn't burn. —Mezz Mezzrow, *Really the Blues*, p. 268, 1946
- "Listen, rat" – Benny's face paled – "one more word like that and I'll plug you too. They can only burn me once, and I'd just as soon knock you off to stay alive as not." —Irving Shulman, *The Amboy Dukes*, p. 85, 1947
- And if I burn for it, here or anywhere, at least I won't burn like a slave. —Thurston Scott, *Cure it with Honey*, p. 37, 1951
- We ain't going to let her die, get me? Not this way. I'm going to see that she burns. —Jim Thompson, *The Killer Inside*, p. 54, 1952
- He said, "Forgive this man, he knows not what he did." / I said, "Can that shit, Father, don't let them burn the kid." —Dennis Wepman et al., *The Life*, p. 120, 1976

2 to kill someone *US, 1933*

- Do you really want to burn this cat, man? —Claude Brown, *Manchild in the Promised Land*, p. 176, 1965

3 to shoot a gun at someone, either just grazing them or making them jump to avoid being hit *US*

- —Dale Kramer and Madeline Karr, *Teen-Age Gangs*, p. 174, 1953

4 to cheat, swindle someone *UK, 1698*

- I drank all day in a wild poolhall-bar-restaurant-saloon two-part joint, also got burned for a fin (Mexican, 5 pesos, 60 cents) by a connection. —Jack Kerouac, *Letter to Neal and Carolyn Cassady*, p. 359, 10th May 1952
- He even cut me into the good drygoods thieves, so that I would never get burned by fences. —Claude Brown, *Manchild in the Promised Land*, p. 167, 1965
- Hawaiian Chuck was handing out hepatitis-infected points to friends who'd burned him. —Nicholas Von Hoffman, *We Are The People Our Parents Warned Us Against*, p. 83, 1967
- It is alright to burn one's victims as long as they can be referred to as marks, but never – never – burn the guy you work with and who is your partner. —Herbert Huncke, *The Evening Sun Turned Crimson*, p. 138, 1980
- He probably got burned trying to make a drug buy and did have to run for his life. —Joseph Wambaugh, *Finnegan's Week*, p. 301, 1993

5 to obligate someone unfairly *UK*

- Kings an' Baba get burned for the whole fee cos of course they wanna look flush in front of everybody. —Nick Barlay, *Curvy Lovebox*, p. 101, 1997

6 to expose the identity of a person or place *US, 1959*

- He didn't want any dopefiends burning up his house, even though he paid off the vice squad monthly to allow him to operate. —Donald Goines, *Dopefiend*, p. 37, 1971
- PARK SWEEP "BURNS" L.A. GAYS —*The Advocate*, 24th October 1973
- He said I burned one of his sources. —Carl Hiaasen, *Tourist Season*, p. 201, 1986

7 to completely cover another graffiti artist's work with your own *US*

- I burn my name up all over the hood. —*A2Z*, p. 15, 1995
- —Jim Crotty, *How to Talk American*, p. 140, 1997

8 in private dice games, to stop the dice while rolling, either as a superstition or to check for cheating *US*

- —*The Annals of the American Academy of Political and Social Sciences*, p. 122, May 1950

9 while playing blackjack, to place an unplayed card into the discard card holder *US*

- —Thomas F. Hughes, *Dealing Casino Blackjack*, p. 71, 1982

10 to smoke marijuana *US, 1964*

- — Home Office, *DSUE8*, 1970s
- Hey, man, Pickford's got a dube we're about to burn. —*Dazed and Confused*, 1993
- I hate standing around when everyone's burning and I ain't got none[.] —Two Fingers, *Puff (Disco Biscuits)*, p. 220, 1996

11 to infect someone with a sexually transmitted disease *US*

- —Dale Gordon, *The Dominion Sex Dictionary*, p. 35, 1967
- —Don R. McCreary (Editor), *Dawg Speak*, 2001

▸ **burn an Indian**

to smoke marijuana *US*

- —Jay Robert Nash, *Dictionary of Crime*, p. 51, 1992

▸ **burn logs**

to smoke marijuana *UK*

▸ **burn paint**

(used of a car or truck) to be engulfed in flames *US*

- —Bill Davis, *Jawjacking*, p. 24, 1977

▸ **burn the breeze**

to drive fast *US*

- —Montie Tak, *Truck Talk*, p. 23, 1971

▸ **burn the lot**

(used of a carnival) to cheat a town so badly that no carnival will be able to come to that town for some time *US*

- —Lindsay E. Smith and Bruce A. Walstad, *Sting Shift*, p. 115, 1989

▸ **burn the main line**

to inject a drug intravenously *UK, 1998*

- —Mike Haskins, *Drugs*, p. 290, 2003

▸ **burn the road up**

to leave *US*

- —Gary K. Farlow, *Prison-ese*, p. 9, 2002

▸ **burn the yellow**

to race through a yellow traffic light *CANADA*

Used in Montreal, translated and borrowed from the French.

- —Lewis Poteet, *Car & Motorcyle Slang*, p. 42, 1992

▸ **burn up the wires**

to spend a great deal of time on the telephone *US*

Originally a term applying to the telegraph. As telephones become increasingly independent of wires, it will be interesting to see if the phrase survives.

- —Joseph A. Weingarten, *An American Dictionary of Slang*, p. 50, 1954

▸ **burn your butt**

to annoy, to irritate you *US*

- I've always sung the praises of lobsters, and it really burns my butt when people drop 'em in a pot of boiling water. —*The Observer*, 9th December 2001

▸ **enough money to burn a wet mule**

a great deal of money *US, 1895*

Slang synonyms for 'money' are found in variants of the phrase.

- I also got enough bread to burn a wet mule. —Babs Gonzales, *Movin' On Down De Line*, p. 27, 1975
- As Mr. Barbour is fond of saying in such circumstances, the GOP had "enough cash to burn a wet mule." —*Washington Times*, 16th January 1997
- "We got enough money to burn a wet mule," Big Bill said. —Bill Fitzhugh, *Fender Benders*, p. 267, 2003

burn and smoulder *noun*

the shoulder *UK*

Rhyming slang, perhaps in reference to a sunburnt shoulder.

- —Ray Puxley, *Cockney Rabbit*, p. 27, 1992

burn artist *noun*

a cheat, a conman, especially in dealings with drugs *US, 1968*

- I received som eheavy complaints regarding burn artists and protection. —Jamie Mandelkau quoting Ken Kesey, *Buttons*, p. 147, 1971
- One of the burn artist's tricks is to take your money, tell you to wait and split with your dough. There are various side show gimmicks each burn artist works. —Abbie Hoffman, *Steal This Books*, p. 96, 1995
- The Barksdale gang murders people for a variety of reasons: to instill fear and respect among prospective rivals, to send a message to residents of the projects to mind their own business and keep their mouths shut, to punish thieves and burn artists. —*Tri-Valley Herald (Pleasanton, California)*, 17th August 2002

burn, bash, bury
used as the rubbish disposal creed of Australian troops in Vietnam *AUSTRALIA*
- —Gregory Clark, *Words of the Vietnam War*, p. 74, 1990

burn cards *noun*
in blackjack played in casinos, a few cards taken from the top of a newly shuffled pack and discarded *US*
- —Lee Solkey, *Dummy Up and Deal*, p. 108, 1980

burn down *verb*
1 to overuse and thus ruin something *US*
- I've about burned down all the pawnshops in New York.—William Burroughs, *Junkie*, p. 60, 1953
- Three junkies say that there have been a sharply increased number of sick junkies unable to support their habits at former levels, trying to taper off on such things as Cocinil, and hitting so often that somes stores have been totally "burned down," i.e. refuse to supply even non-prescription items to known junkies.—Ned Polsky, *Hustlers, Beats, and Others*, p. 168, 1967

2 to shoot and kill someone *US, 1932*
- —Hyman E. Goldin et al., *Dictionary of American Underworld Lingo*, p. 37, 1950

burned out; burnt out *adjective*
1 recovering from drug dependence *UK*
- —Home Office, *Glossary of Terms and Slang Common in Penal Establishments*, July 1978

2 exhausted beyond mental or physical capacity *US*
- I had no emotions on court. I felt burned out and didn't want to play.—*UPI*, 15th December 1980
- [O]ne of Thatcher's City boys, burnt-out at twenty-four.—Jenny Eclair, *Camberwell Beauty*, p. 346, 2000
- "I was kind of burned out playing," Colbert said.—*The Columbian (Vancouver, Washington)*, p. B1, 16th April 2004

burner *noun*
1 a criminal who specialises in breaking into safes using an acetylene torch *US*
- —Hyman E. Goldin et al., *Dictionary of American Underworld Lingo*, p. 37, 1950

2 a handgun *US, 1926*
- Gray got caught up in a beef with a group of about 10 Hispanic men, one of whom was boasting about having a burner – street slang for a handgun – and trying to bait him with taunts of "You want it? You want it?"—*Boston Herald*, p. 14, 23rd June 2002

3 a very fast runner *US*
- —Bill Shefski, *Running Press Glossary of Football Language*, p. 21, 1978
- Can you imagine what it's gonna be like to have them two burners in my backfield?—Dan Jenkins, *Life Its Ownself*, p. 164, 1984

4 an extraordinary person *US*
- "He's a burner, ain't he?" he said.—Chester Himes, *Cast the First Stone*, p. 76, 1952

5 a marijuana smoker *US*
- Only burners like you get high.—*The Breakfast Club*, 1985
- Jay and Silent Bob watch as Dante passes. A small group of burners are poised around the store door.—Kevin Smith, *Clerks*, p. 125, 1994
- —Pamela Munro, *U.C.L.A. Slang*, p. 47, 1997

6 a drug addiction *US*
- —Jay Robert Nash, *Dictionary of Crime*, p. 51, 1992

7 a complete piece of graffiti art *US*
- —Jim Crotty, *How to Talk American*, p. 140, 1997

Burnese; burnie *noun*
cocaine *US, 1933*
A variation on Berni, Bernice or Bernie.
- —Richard A. Spears, *The Slang and Jargon of Drugs and Drink*, p. 86, 1986
- —Mike Haskins, *Drugs*, p. 280, 2003

burn head *noun*
any Rastafarian who defies the norms and shaves *JAMAICA, 1980*
- —Thomas H. Slone, *Rasta is Cuss*, p. 35, 2003

burnie *noun*
a partially smoked marijuana cigarette *US*
- —*American Speech*, p. 24, February 1952: 'Teen-age hophead jargon'
- BURNIE, drug connotation, partially smoked marijuana cigarette.—*Chicago Tribune*, p. C3, 27th December 1998

burning and turning *adjective*
of a helicopter, with engine running and blades rotating *UK*
- The air-sea rescue crew climb in the naval Wessex helicopter [...] soon the engine is running and the huge rotor blades begin to swing round faster and faster – "burning and turning" as they say.—*Illustrated London News*, May 1978

burn off *verb*
to drive very fast, especially if showing off *AUSTRALIA, 1984*

burnout *noun*
1 a person whose mental capacity has been diminished by extended drug or alcohol use *US, 1973*
- —J.E. Lighter, *Historical Dictionary of American Slang, Volume 1*, p. 322, 1994

2 an uninhabitable, ruined tenement, whether it has been burnt or not *US*
- —Carsten Stroud, *Close Pursuit*, p. 270, 1987

3 in drag racing, the pre-race spinning of the car's rear tyres to clean and heat the tyres, producing crowd-pleasing smoke and noise *US*
- Police were abused and pelted with bottles and cans as they tried to break up the crowds cheering drag racing and burnout competitions.—*Herald*, p. 3, 4th April 1988

4 in the youth trend for 'souped-up' motor-scootering, any achievement of a daring, risk-taking rider *UK*
- The boy in front is the stunt guy, pulling wheelies and "burnouts".—*The Independent Magazine*, p. 17, 28th August 2004

burn out *verb*
to make a fire in a prisoner's cell as retaliation for real or perceived cooperation with prison authorities *US*
- —Paul Glover, *Words from the House of the Dead*, 1974

burnout box *noun*
in drag racing, the area where tyres are heated and cleaned before a race *US*
- —John Edwards, *Auto Dictionary*, p. 22, 1993

burn rubber!
leave me alone! *US*
- —Reinhold Aman, *Hillary Clinton's Pen Pal*, p. 23, 1996

burnt *adjective*
exhausted *US*
- "I'm feeling kind of burnt," Dirk said. "You can just drop me off."—Francesca Lia Block, *Baby Be-Bop*, p. 403, 1995

burnt cheese *noun*
a fart *AUSTRALIA*
- —Peter Furze, *Tailwinds*, p. 54, 1998

burnt cinder; burnt *noun*
a window *UK*
Cockney rhyming slang, relying on the accent for an accurate rhyme. Recorded in 1960 by Julian Franklyn as a pre-World War 1 coinage.
- Do you fancy going through the burnt, when we stop at the next traffic lights?—Frank Norman, *Bang To Rights*, p. 49, 1958
- [S]ling the brick through the burnt, grab the loot and scarper.—Ray Puxley, *Cockney Rabbit*, p. 27, 1992

burnt end *noun*
in bowls, a stage of play that has to be replayed when the jack is driven out of bounds *UK*
- —David Bryant, *The Game of Bowls*, p. 38, 1990

burn-through *noun*
the process of cleaning tyres on a dragster with bleach poured on the ground over which the tyres are spun *US*
- During the spinning or burn through, the bleach and dirt on the tires make clouds of smoke.—Ed Radlauer, *Drag Racing Pix Dix*, p. 10, 1970

burnt money *noun*
a bet in a dice game lost because of a rule violation *US*
- —*American Speech*, p. 398, Winter 1997: 'Among the new words'

burnt offering *noun*
overcooked food, especially meat *UK, 1937*
Adopted, ironically, from the conventional religious sense.

burnt out *adjective*
▷ see: BURNED OUT

burn-up *noun*
the act of racing or riding fast on a motorcycle *UK*
To 'burn-up' the tyre-rubber and leave scorch-marks on the road.
- [W]e used to do a round of all the cafes in town every night, with burn-ups to the North Circular.—Jamie Mandelkau, *Buttons*, p. 30, 1971

- If you can't dance anymore, or if the dance is over, you've just got to go for a burn-up. — Paul E Willis, *Profane Culture*, p. 73, 1978
- [H]e was more into burn-ups and punch-ups than kids[.] — John King, *White Trash*, p. 160, 2001

burn up *verb*
to fall silent; to stop talking *AUSTRALIA*
Often as an imperative.
- — James Barlow, *All Good Faith*, 1971

burp *noun*
1 an act of vomiting; vomit *AUSTRALIA*
- Calling for Herb, see, that's one of the many euphemisms for vomit, others include spue, burp, hurl, the big spit, the long spit, throw, the whip o'will, the technicolour laugh and, in Queensland, the chuckle. — Frank Hardy, *Billy Borker Rides Again*, 1967

2 a belch *US, 1932*
Echoic.
- The ship sank. It made a sound like a monstrous metallic burp. — Yann Martel, *Life of Pi*, p. 97, 2001

3 any alcoholic beverage *BERMUDA*
- — Peter A. Smith and Fred M. Barritt, *Bermewjan Vurds*, 1985

▷ **see:** **BOTTOM BURP**

burp *verb*
to belch; to cause a baby to belch *US, 1932*
The variant spelling, 'birp', was recorded in Wolverhampton in 1967.
- [Timothy Spall] has always refused to have lunch with journalists since one reported that he burped and farted during their meal[.] — *The Guardian*, 29th September 2002

▸ **burp the worm**
(of a male) to masturbate *US*
- "The boy is masturbating" Burping the worm[.] — Erica Orloff and JoAnn Baker, *Dirty Little Secrets*, p. 88, 2001

burp gun *noun*
a submachine gun *US*
- In general character, this one developed like the second: the same whistles and roll calling to start with, then heavy and inaccurate fire, involving several machine guns and burp guns which sprayed the hedgerow and the fields beyond. — United States War Department, *Small Unit Actions*, p. 57, 1946
- Next – and it was in this order – we heard the BRRRP! sound of one Chinese pp-S or "burp gun" as it is called. — Martin Russ, *The Last Parallel*, p. 107, 1957

burp 'n' blow *noun*
an act of burping into your cupped hands then blowing the retained air at a chosen victim *UK*
- — Jonathan Blyth, *The Law of the Playground*, p. 23, 2004

burqa *noun*
an out-of-style fashion garment *US*
The conventional 'burqa' is a complete head and body shroud worn by women in the strictest Muslim societies. This teenspeak reflects the end of fundamentalist Taliban rule in Afghanistan.
- Is that a burqa? — *The Washington Post*, 19th March 2002

burr *noun*
the recurring operating expenses in a circus or carnival *US*
- — Joe McKennon, *Circus Lingo*, p. 22, 1980

burrhead *noun*
a black person *US, 1902*
- — Helen Dahlskog (Editor), *A Dictionary of Contemporary and Colloquial Usage*, p. 11, 1972
- — *Maledicta*, p. 153, Summer/Winter 1978: 'How to hate thy neighbor: a guide to racist maledicta'
- [J. Edgar] Hoover was apparently convinced that the content of these tapes would "destroy the burrhead [King]. — Ward Churchill and Jim Vander Wall, *Agents of Repression*, p. 55, 1988

burrito *adjective*
cold *US*
From 'brrrr' as a vocalisation of feeling cold.
- — Pamela Munro, *U.C.L.A. Slang*, p. 47, 1997

burrito bag *noun*
a mesh restraint used by police to contain a violent person *US*
- — Samuel M. Katz, *Anytime Anywhere*, p. 389, 1997

burrito poncho *noun*
a condom *UK*
- — David Rowan, *A Glossary of the 90s*, 1998

burro *noun*
a racehorse that does not perform well *US*
- — *San Francisco Call-Bulletin*, p. 16, 2nd April 1947

burroo; brew; buro *noun*
an unemployment exchange; the Department of Social Security *UK, 1937*
From a Glasgow pronunciation of 'bureau' as in 'Employment Bureau'.
- — Michael Munro, *The Original Patter*, 1985

burrower *noun*
a researcher *UK*
Security service jargon.
- — John Le Carré, *The Honourable Schoolboy*, 1977

burr under your saddle blanket *noun*
an unexplained irritability *CANADA*
- — Chris Thain, *Cold as a Bay Street Banker's Heart*, p. 29, 1987

burr up your ass *noun*
a person with a displeased focus on something *US, 1960*
- I showed up at the rink with a burr up my ass. [Quoting Billy Smith] — *Boston Globe*, p. D1, 3rd November 2003

burst *noun*
1 a period of re-enlistment in the military *US*
A 'burst of six' would thus be re-enlistment for six years.
- — Carl Fleischhauer, *A Glossary of Army Slang*, p. 7, 1968

2 a drinking binge *NEW ZEALAND*
- — David McGill, *David McGill's Complete Kiwi Slang Dictionary*, p. 24, 1998

burst *verb*
1 to strike someone violently *IRELAND*
This usage is common all over Ireland, and is used in a rhetorical sense, rather than literally.
- He'd been going out with Mary for six years and he bursted [sic] anyone who looked crooked at her. — Eamonn Sweeney, *Waiting for the Healer*, p. 100, 1997
- Shut yer bleedin' mouth Trace or I'll burst ye. — Donal Ruane, *Tales in a rearview mirror*, p. 21, 2003

2 to pay for something that costs relatively little with a banknote *UK*
Literally 'to burst the completeness of the banknote'; a variation of conventional 'break'.
- — Michael Munro, *The Patter, Another Blast*, 1988

3 to ejaculate *BAHAMAS, 1971*
- — John A. Holm, *Dictionary of Bahamian English*, p. 32, 1982

▸ **burst out in fairy lights**
to show an expected level of enthusiasm *UK: SCOTLAND*
- Whit d'ye want me tae dae... burst oot in fairy lights? — Michael Munro, *The Complete Patter*, 1996

burster; buster *noun*
anything of superior size or astounding nature *US, 1831*
- We had had a few "burster" houses lately[.] — Butch Reynolds, *Broken Hearted Clown*, p. 29, 1953

bursting at the seams *adjective*
overfull *UK, 1962*
- Jails are bursting at the seams, charity warns[.] — *The Guardian*, 8th October 2003

Burton-on-Trent; Burton *noun*
1 rent *UK, 1932*
Rhyming slang, based on an East Midlands' town.
- [B]eing very short of bees and honey, and unable to pay the Burton-on-Trent[.] — Ronnie Barker, *Fletcher's Book of Rhyming Slang*, p. 25, 1979

2 homosexual *UK*
Rhyming slang for **BENT** (homosexual).
- — Angela Devlin, *Prison Patter*, p. 32, 1996

burwash *noun*
a swindle, for fun or profit *UK*
- — Tom Hibbert, *Rockspeak!*, p. 34, 1983

bury *verb*

1 to sentence a criminal to a long or life term in prison *US, 1904*
- —William K. Bentley and James M. Corbett, *Prison Slang*, p. 18, 1992

2 in casino gambling, to place a card in the middle of a deck or in the discard pile *US*
- —Michael Dalton, *Blackjack*, p. 34, 1991

▸ **bury the stiffy**

from a male perspective, to have sex *US*
- —Michael Dalton Johnson, *Talking Trash with Redd Foxx*, p. 53, 1994

▸ **bury the tach**

to rev an engine up beyond what would be considered a prudent revolutions per minute level *US*

The tachometer measures the revolutions per minute.
- —Lewis Poteet, *Car & Motorcyle Slang*, p. 42, 1992

bus *noun*

1 an ambulance *US*
- —Jay Robert Nash, *Dictionary of Crime*, p. 51, 1992

2 a wheelbarrow *TRISTAN DA CUNHA, 1906*
- —Bernadette Hince, *The Antarctic Dictionary*, p. 74, 2000

3 a plane *UK, 1913*
- —J.E. Lighter, *Historical Dictionary of American Slang, Volume 1*, p. 323, 1994

4 a car *UK, 1921*
- "You bastard, Fredericks!" said Jumbo. "You've smashed my little bus."—Charles Raven, *Underworld Nights*, p. 50, 1956

5 a large touring motorcyle *US*

Biker (motorcycle) usage.

▸ **more bus than Battoo**

big-breasted *TRINIDAD AND TOBAGO*

Battoo is the owner of a bus company.
- —Lise Winer, *Dictionary of the English/Creole of Trinidad & Tobago*, 2003

▸ **on the bus**

part of a countercultural movement *US*

From the language of Ken Kesey, Neal Cassady and the Merry Pranksters.
- —David Shenk and Steve Silberman, *Skeleton Key*, p. 210, 1994

bus *verb*

to shoot a gun at someone *US*
- —Bill Valentine, *Gang Intelligence Manual*, p. 75, 1995

▸ **bus one**

to leave *US*
- — *Washingnton Post*, 14th October 1993

bus and tram *noun*

jam *UK*

Rhyming slang, possibly punning on the constituent parts of a traffic jam. Noted by Laurie Atkinson, 1978.

bus and truck *adjective*

said of a travelling show, with the cast and crew travelling by bus, with the props and wardrobe in a truck *US*
- —Sherman Louis Sergel, *The Language of Show Biz*, p. 34, 1973

bus driver *noun*

1 in poker, the player in a given hand who controls the betting *US*
- —John Vorhaus, *The Big Book of Poker Slang*, p. 9, 1996

2 a pilot, especially the pilot of a military transport aircraft *US, 1944*
- Finding pilots wasn't difficult, as all the USAF "bus drivers" – transport pilots – had to qualify regularly in CARP.—Richard Marcinko and John Weisman, *Rogue Warrior*, p. 47, 1992

buse *verb*

to swear at someone *BARBADOS*

An abbreviation of 'abuse'.
- —Frank A. Collymore, *Barbadian Dialect*, p. 24, 1965

bus face *noun*

the worn-out look gained from sleeping on a bus overnight *US*
- —Jim Crotty, *How to Talk American*, p. 218, 1997

bush *noun*

1 pubic hair, especially a woman's pubic hair *UK, 1650*

A source for endless punning during the US presidential election of 2000; President Bush Jr's lack of *gravitas* opened him up to 'bush' puns to an extent that his father did not have to endure.
- He reached down and pulled her pubic hair. WHATTA BUSH.—Hubert Selby Jr, *Last Exit to Brooklyn*, p. 249, 1957
- The liberated chick up front appears not to be wearing any underwear and the print reveals what might be construed by some as a hairy bush.— *Screw*, p. 8, 4th April 1969
- That's how you tell if a broad dyes her hair, look at her bush.—Elmore Leonard, *Split Image*, p. 191, 1981
- And then Jayne Kennedy says, "First things first, nigger, I ain't suckin' shit till you bring your ass over here an' lick my bush!"— *True Romance*, 1993
- Bob waxed Renee's bush with a giant vibrator that looked like a cross between a minivac and a shoe polisher.—Anka Radakovich, *The Wild Girls Club*, p. 117, 1994
- JACK: What're you doing? We're shooting in twenty minutes. BECKY: I'm shaving my bush.— *Boogie Nights*, 1997
- I always figured that, you know, everyone had a bush. It wasn't specifically female.— *Jabberrock [quoting Gavin Rossdale of the band Bush, 1995]*, p. 187, 1997
- I'm surprised they didn't just explode the moment they glimpsed a bit of bush.—Danny King, *The Burglar Diaries*, p. 29, 2001
- Dude – she had seventies bush.—Kevin Smith, *Jay and Silent Bob Strike Back*, p. 30, 2001
- Know what the biggest change is for me? Broads shavin' their bushes. I went over to Silvio's, it's like the Girl Scouts in there.— *The Sopranos (Episode 53)*, 2004

2 a sexually active female *US*
- —Andy Anonymous, *A Basic Guide to Campusology*, p. 5, 1966

3 a bushy hairstyle, especially on a black person *US*
- —David Claerbaut, *Black Jargon in White America*, p. 59, 1972

4 marijuana *US, 1951*
- As soon as we got some of that Mexican bush we almost blew our tops.—Mezz Mezzrow, *Really the Blues*, p. 215, 1946
- We've caned some bush in our time but nowt like that.—Shaun Ryder, *Shaun Ryder... in His Own Words*, 1991
- —Angela Devlin, *Prison Patter*, p. 32, 1996
- I licked my fingers, and took hold of the bag of bush that Sundays had tossed over to me. The bush was in fine, grainy pieces[.]—Diran Adebayo, *My Once Upon A Time*, p. 20, 2000
- I got stoned on some really good bush[.]—Lanre Fehintola, *Charlie Says...*, p. 52, 2000

5 cocaine *UK, 1998*
- —Mike Haskins, *Drugs*, p. 280, 2003

6 the woods *US*
- "What are yez doin tonight?" "We're gettin some kortz and goin upda bush."—Amy and Denise McFadden, *CoalSpeak*, p. 2–3, 1997

7 the suburbs *AUSTRALIA, 1942*

An urban sneer; from the conventional Australian sense of 'bush' (country in its natural state).

▸ **go bush**

to move to or visit the county *AUSTRALIA, 1916*
- I've decided to go bush and sort myself out.—Alexander Buzo, *Rooted*, p. 76, 1969
- I've heard stories about men who escaped the prisons. Went bush. Went cannibal.—Bob Ellis and Anne Brooksbank, *Mad Dog Morgan*, p. 82, 1976
- He beat the beast to the end of the shed by a short head, shot around the corner, and the beast flew straight past and went bush.—Sam Weller, *Old Bastards I Have Met*, p. 53, 1979
- After that I went bush with my oldest daughter, Pat, and worked around Quilpie for a while[.]—Herb Wharton, *Cattle Camp*, p. 104, 1994

▸ **take the bush; take to the bush**

to escape; to run wild; to leave the town for the country *AUSTRALIA, 1804*

Originally of escaping convicts; but also carrying the sense of an Aborigine returning to traditional life.

bush *verb*

1 to ambush someone *US, 1947*
- You 'bush in this area near that ol' Buddhist temple we passed on the hump in.— *Platoon*, 1986

2 in the used car business, to extract through any of a series of questionably ethical means more from a customer than originally contemplated by the customer *US*
- — *Cars*, p. 40, December 1953
- — *Esquire*, p. 118, March 1968

3 to deceive someone *US*

- Don't bush me," the man said. "Don't hand me that crap[.] —George V. Higgins, *The Friends of Eddie Doyle*, p. 198, 1971

bush *adjective*

1 second-rate, amateurish *US, 1959*

- Taylor said, "They were bad mouthing our ball players when we were on the way into the locker room. It's bush." —*San Francisco Examiner*, p. 50, 26th January 1972
- I'll tell you something, wise-ass, you think you're so fucking clever. You're bush. Homicide lieutenant, all that goes with it, you're still bush. —Elmore Leonard, *Split Images*, p. 65, 1981
- You're showing up my pitcher, bush – get your ass in gear. —*Bull Durham*, 1988

2 rough and ready *AUSTRALIA*

- I could see what he was going to do. Bush surgery. —Patsy Adam-Smith, *Folklore of the Australian Railwaymen*, p. 53, 1969

bush *nickname*

Flatbush, Brooklyn, New York *US*

- —Lois Stavsky et al., *A2Z*, p. 15, 1995

bush Baptist *noun*

a religious zealot lacking formal theological training *US, 1967*

- —Frederic G. Cassidy, *Dictionary of American Regional English, Volume 1*, p. 476, 1985
- —David McGill, *David McGill's Complete Kiwi Slang Dictionary*, p. 25, 1998

bush-bash *verb*

to forge a path through scrubland; to travel through virgin bush *AUSTRALIA, 1967*

- Two Christmases ago I bush-bashed the whole neighbourhood on that thing. —Glyn Parry, *Mosh*, p. 82, 1996

bush basher *noun*

a person who forges a new pathway through scrubland *AUSTRALIA, 1971*

bush blaster *noun*

the penis *US*

- —Erica Orloff and JoAnn Baker, *Dirty Little Secrets*, p. 90, 2001

bush bunny *noun*

a woman from a remote area; a naive, unsophisticated woman *FIJI*

Recorded by Jan Tent.

bush captial *nickname*

Canberra, the capital city of Australia *AUSTRALIA, 1906*

So-called because it was a new city built in the 'bush' (countryside) halfway between the two major cities of Sydney and Melbourne.

- From the bush capital where the town plan radiated stability or instability in strong or weak waves the shock of the killings was digested and recycled in acceptable local form. —Murray Bail, *Holden's Performance*, p. 320, 1988

bush child *noun*

an illegitimate child *CAYMAN ISLANDS*

- —Aarona Booker Kohlman, *Wotcha Say*, p. 25, 1985

bush dance *noun*

an Australian-style country dance *AUSTRALIA*

- He made most of the supper break as supper, a bring-a-plate affair, was undoubtedly the highlight of the bush dance. —Kerry Cue, *Crooks, Chooks and Bloody Ratbags*, p. 199, 1983

bush dinner *noun*

oral sex on a woman *US*

- —Dale Gordon, *The Dominion Sex Dictionary*, p. 35, 1967

bus head *noun*

hair that is in complete disarray after a long bus ride *US*

- —*Washington Post Sunday Magazine*, p. 7, 3rd January 1988

bushed *adjective*

1 very tired *US, 1879*

- He said, "Cecil, I'm bushed. Goodnight." —Iceberg Slim (Robert Beck), *Long White Con*, p. 53, 1977
- You look bushed. What time did you get to bed? —*Clerks*, 1994

2 showing adverse psychological effects from having to live in bad weather *CANADA, 1952*

Confinement and isolation, especially in the north of North America, give this widely used term a special meaning, different from 'going native'.

- Bushed. He knew the country, but he had been away. And then he had returned alone to this place, where for so long every year the winter buried you, snow blinded you, the wind screamed up the hill at night, and the water thundered. —Joyce Marshall, *Canadian Short Stories*, p. 289–290, 1960

3 lost in bushland *AUSTRALIA, 1844*

- —Barbara Baynton, *Human Toll*, p. 293, 1907
- They got bushed in Australia's wildest country. —*Weekend*, p. 14, 1st June 1957
- —Herb Wharton, *Cattle Camp*, p. 13, 1994

4 lost, but not in the bush *AUSTRALIA*

- I couldn't help him with direction – I was always bushed in Japan, night or day. —Les Such, *A Yen for Yokohama*, p. 91, 1963
- —Peter Corris, *Make Me Rich*, p. 155, 1985

bushel *noun*

1 in trucking, a load of half a ton *US*

- —Wayne Floyd, *Jason's Authentic Dictionary of CB Slang*, p. 11, 1976

2 the neck, the throat *UK*

The full form is 'bushel and peck'. Rhyming slang, based on imperial units of volume; first recorded in *Songs and Slang of the British Soldier*, John Brophy and Eric Partridge, 1930.

- [B]eing too poor to purchase any Cape of Good Hope, his bushel and peck [the neck] was extremely two-thirty [dirty]. —Ronnie Barker, *Fletcher's Book of Rhyming Slang*, p. 25, 1979

bushel-cunted *adjective*

possessing a slack and distended vagina *US*

- —*Maledicta*, p. 184, Winter 1980: 'A new erotic vocabulary'

bushel of coke *noun*

a man *UK, 1960*

Rhyming slang for a **BLOKE**.

bushes *noun*

any place where sexual activity takes place, whether or not an actual bush is involved *US*

- To take a girl into the bushes means what it means, but the sense has been generalized. It may be the bushes but it doesn't have to be. —John Gould, *Maine Lingo*, p. 29, 1975

bushfire *noun*

used as a comparison for something that is exceedingly fast *AUSTRALIA*

- [The news] went through the first-class like a bushfire and from then on his shipboard expenses were assured. —Dymphna Cusack, *Picnic Races*, p. 190, 1962

bushfire blonde *noun*

a red-headed woman *AUSTRALIA, 1943*

- —Sidney J. Baker, *The Australian Language*, p. 76, 1966

bush gang *noun*

a prison work gang working without the traditional chains *CANADA*

- The bush gang is a bastardized version of the southern U.S. prison chain gang, only without the chains. It got the name bush because heavily guarded prisoners worked the cedar brush and forests[.] —Thomas Renner and Cecil Kirby, *Mafia Enforcer*, p. 49, 1987

bush herb *noun*

unremarkable marijuana *UK*

- [I]t was now almost impossible to find anything but the basic bush herb. —Donald Gorgon, *Cop Killer*, p. 32, 1994

bushie *noun*

1 a rough, tough, unattractive or otherwise unappealing woman *AUSTRALIA*

From **BUSHPIG**.

- Think ya can surf, ya bushie. —Kathy Lette, *Girls' Night Out*, p. 196, 1987

2 a person who lives in the bush *AUSTRALIA, 1887*

Can be used negatively to mean a 'country bumpkin', or positively to refer to someone skilled at surviving in the harsh conditions of the Australian outback.

- Dave stood on the scales with the saddle over his arm; among the silks of the other jockeys, he did look very much like a bushie just trying his luck. —Anne Brooksbank, *Archer*, p. 72, 1985
- —David McGill, *David McGill's Complete Kiwi Slang Dictionary*, p. 25, 1998

Bushie *noun*

a supporter or a member of the administration of US President George W. Bush *US*

- If you're not a Bushie you're a Taliban. If you don't love us, you hate us. — *The Guardian*, 30th September 2002

Bush is another word for cunt

used as a slogan that registers absolute contempt for US President George W. Bush *US*

Not strictly accurate at the time of coining as **BUSH** (in its punned sense, 'pubic hair'); it cannot be long before the meaning shifts to include **CUNT** (the vagina), punned here with its sense as a 'despicable individual'.

- "Bush is another word for cunt" banners. — *Mixmag*, p. 16, April 2003
- I took the subway into town and ran into a few people headed for the protests. One girl was wearing a shirt that said, "Bush is just another word for cunt." Another had a sign reading, "Regime change in 2004." — Hanah Quare, *A relatively average weblog*, 15th March 2003

bush lawyer *noun*

a person with some knowledge of law but no actual qualifications *AUSTRALIA, 1835*

- Others – in the dock – are confident and even aggressive. Mostly these are the "bush-lawyer" type who confidently hope, in one fell swoop, to annihilate the Crown case with an absolutely unanswerable piece of evidence. — 'Sweeney - ex-crook', *I Confess*, p. 3, 1936
- Integrity Hanson was a bit of a bush lawyer. — Frank Hardy, *The Yarns of Billy Borker*, p. 61, 1965
- At the same time many prisoners became 'bush lawyers' simply for the relief it offered from daily tedium. — Donald Catchlove, *Ray Denning My Life and Time*, p. 57, 1994

bush-league *adjective*

petty, medicore, trivial, inconsequential, second-rate *US, 1908*

- But I now sense that it might be attained without long years of bush-league apprenticeship. — Horace McCoy, *Kiss Tomorrow Good-bye*, p. 90, 1948
- I had lost my taste even for bush league vindictiveness. — Clancy Sigal, *Going Away*, p. 5, 1961
- They were bush-league hoods known only to California cops and a few thousand cycle buffs. — Hunter S. Thompson, *Hell's Angels*, p. 37, 1966

bush light *noun*

in the pornography industry, a light used to illuminate the genitals of the performers *US*

- — *Adult Video News*, p. 50, October 1995

bushline *noun*

▸ put out the bushline on the ice

in Cape Breton, to set out the small evergreen trees on solid ice to mark a trail for skating, skimobiling or a road *CANADA*

The term, by extension, seems to apply to a variety of metaphorical situations, involving fitness.

- Remember Johnny MacPhail, Johnny Nookie we called him? Lord, yes, he put out the bushline on the ice until he was too old to stand. — D.R. MacDonald, *Cape Breton Road*, p. 32, 2000

bush mag *noun*

a magazine featuring photographs of naked women, focusing on their pubic hair and vulvas *US*

- The "tit magazines" of the Fifties and Sixties, which were fit only for the garbage pail, have transformed themselves of late into "bush mags." — *Screw*, p. 4, 3rd July 1972

bushman's breakfast *noun*

a yawn, a stretch, urinating and a look around, or some variation thereof *NEW ZEALAND*

- — David McGill, *David McGill's Complete Kiwi Slang Dictionary*, p. 24, 1998

bushman's clock *noun*

a kookaburra, a native Australian bird with a loud laughing territorial call frequently heard at dawn and dusk *AUSTRALIA, 1846*

- — Jim Ramsay, *Cop It Sweet!*, p. 19, 1977

bushman's hanky *noun*

the act of blowing nasal mucus from one nostril while holding the other closed *AUSTRALIA*

- — James Lambert, *The Macquarie Book of Slang*, 1996

bush mechanic *noun*

a mechanic with no formal training and, often, no special skill *BAHAMAS*

- — John A. Holm, *Dictionary of Bahamian English*, p. 33, 1982

Bush-muncher *noun*

a proponent of US President George W. Bush's points of view *US*

Derogatory; a play on **BUSH** (the pubic hair, hence the vagina) and **CARPET-MUNCHER** (a cunnilinguist), which leads to an obvious parallel with **ARSE/ASS-LICKER** (an obsequious sycophant).

- To hear the Bush-munchers tell it, TV and movies are chocker with advertisements for the feminist "agenda" and the homosexual "lifestyle"[.] — *The Guardian*, 25th July 2003

bush orchestra *noun*

a morning chorus of indigenous New Zealand song birds *NEW ZEALAND*

- (Another good night, no crashes) and I was awakened by my bush orchestra which seemed to play an extra piece for my special benefit. — Arthur Bates, *The Bridge to Nowhere*, p. 50, 1982

bush pad *noun*

a motorcyle's passenger seat *US*

Biker (motorcycle) usage, coarsely identifying a woman passenger in terms of her genitals.

bush parole *noun*

escape from prison *US, 1960*

- — Inez Cardozo-Freeman, *The Joint*, p. 486, 1984

bush patrol *noun*

sex with a woman *US*

The **BUSH** in question here is the woman's pubic hair.

- — Roger Blake, *The American Dictionary of Sexual Terms*, p. 26, 1964
- — Kenn "Naz" Young, *Naz's Dictionary of Teen Slang*, p. 17, 1993

bushpig *noun*

a rough, tough, unattractive or otherwise unappealing woman *AUSTRALIA*

- — Thommo, *The Dictionary of Australian Swearing and Sex Sayings*, p. 24, 1985
- Chicks are nicknamed bush pigs, swamp hogs, maggots, spitters and swallowers. — Kathy Lette, *Girls' Night Out*, p. 187, 1987
- The Real Bush-pig is the female counterpart and proper companion for the Male Hoon. — Ignatius Jones, *True Hip*, p. 124, 1990
- — John Birmingham, *He Died With a Felafel in his Hand*, p. 122, 1994
- That bushpig, Cathy, was looking for ya. — Phillip Gwynne, *Deadly Unna?*, p. 245, 1998

bush-pop *verb*

(of cowboys) to ride in the bush to round up cows *CANADA*

- Last week, with the last fall round-ups underway, cowboys bush-popped cattle out of the forested summer ranges, moved them down to the haystacked meadows for winter feeding. — *Time (Canadian edition)*, p. 18/1, 13th November 1964

bushranger *noun*

a person who commits petty crime; a swindler or cheat *AUSTRALIA, 1855*

Figurative use of the usual sense as 'an escaped convict who lives by highway robbery', common during Australia's colonial era.

- Where can I find something safe from you bushrangers? — John Wynnum, *Tar Dust*, p. 130, 1962
- Even the tax collectors – who were sharks and bushrangers – came along and said, 'What do you want us to do?' — Kel Richards, *The Aussie Bible*, p. 21, 2003

bush shave *noun*

a shave without the benefit of water or shaving cream *US*

- — Gregory Clark, *Words of the Vietnam War*, p. 156, 1990

bush telegraph *noun*

an information network utilising word of mouth; the grape-vine *AUSTRALIA*

- — Dymphna Cusack, *Picnic Races*, p. 192, 1962
- He'd been caught outside Wangaratta counting troopers, which implied he was part of Morgan's bush telegraph. — Bob Ellis and Anne Brooksbank, *Mad Dog Morgan*, p. 117, 1976
- — Kel Richards, *The Aussie Bible*, p. 12, 2003

bush time *noun*

during the Vietnam war, the amount of time spent in combat *US*

- — Gregory Clark, *Words of the Vietnam War*, p. 74, 1990

bush tucker *noun*

food consisting of native Australian flora and fauna *AUSTRALIA, 1895*

Originally used to refer to food making up the diet of Australian Aboriginals, nowadays also for items of restaurant cuisine.

- We had plenty of rice, too, and sometimes goanna and other bush tucker. —Herb Wharton, *Cattle Camp*, p. 3, 1994
- The place was running a special bush-tucker promotion. Fillet of emu with quandong chutney. Wallaby sausages in a lilly-pilly coulis. —Shane Maloney, *Nice Try*, p. 232, 1998

Bush Week *noun*

a putative week during which country folk visit the city and the normal rules of society are laid aside *AUSTRALIA, 1919*
Always in the formulaic rhetorical question 'What do you think this is? Bush Week?'.

- —Lawson Glossop, *Lucky Palmer*, 1949
- What does Jimmy think this is – Bush Week? —John Wynnum, *Tar Dust*, p. 19, 1962

bushwhacker *noun*

1 an outlaw who attacks by ambush *US, 1926*
- But outlawing could be one of the hardest jobs in the old west. Drygulchers, bushwhackers, and hold-up men suffered assaults on their nerves that would send many an ordinary citizen around the bend. —George Bowering, *Caprice*, p. 124, 1987

2 a rapist *US*
Playing on the sexual meaning of **BUSH**.
- —John R. Armore and Joseph D. Wolfe, *Dictionary of Desperation*, p. 22, 1976

3 a man who enjoys sex in park bushes *US*
- We don't tolerate any of those toilet quickies or a job with a bushwhacker. —Johnny Shearer, *The Male Hustler*, p. 20, 1966

4 a person from the country; a country bumpkin *US, 1809*
- The easily-caught 'bush-whacker' is no longer a reality. —'Sweeney ex-crook', *I Confess*, p. 54, 1936
- She had wanted to show Greg as an uncultivated bushwhacker against Ralph's elegant sophistication[.] —Dymphna Cusack, *Picnic Races*, p. 175, 1962
- The bushwhackers have been weakened this year by the loss of Don "Chopper" Pascoe[.] —Alexander Buzo, *The Roy Murphy Show*, p. 126, 1970

bush whiskey *noun*

strong, homemade whisky *US*
- —*Star Tribune (Minneapolis)*, p. 19F, 31st January 1999

Bushy Park *noun*

1 a lark, a spree *UK, 1859*
Rhyming slang, formed on the name of a park close to Hampton Court.

2 a woman's pubic hair *US*
By extension, the shortened form 'bushy' is a pet name for 'the vagina', deriving from **BUSH** (pubic hair); possibly a play on the outer London beauty spot Bushey Park, source of the similar, now obsolete C19 phrase 'take a turn in Bushey Park' (to have sex).
- —*Maledicta*, p. 187, Winter 1980: 'A new erotic vocabulary'

busie, busies *nouns*

▷ see: BUSY, BIZZIES

business *noun*

1 sex with a prostitute; prostitution *UK, 1911*
From a sense, originating in C17, as 'sexual intercourse'; in 1630 the described cost was 'one hundred crownes'.
- He only had £20 in his pocket and wanted to do business but Sadie took him upstairs and robbed him. —Lanre Fehintola, *Charlie Says...*, p. 48, 2000
- "Look," she said, impatiently, "d'you want business?" —Frank Skinner, *Frank Skinner*, p. 214, 2001
- She asked me if I was looking for business, I said no[.] —Niall Griffiths, *Kelly + Victor*, p. 67, 2002

2 the genitals, male or female *US*
- —Vincent J. Monteleone, *Criminal Slang*, p. 39, 1949

3 a syringe employed by intravenous drug users *US*
- —Vincent J. Monteleone, *Criminal Slang*, p. 39, 1949
- —*American Speech*, p. 24, February 1952: 'Teen-age hophead jargon'
- —Home Office, *Glossary of Terms and Slang Common in Penal Establishments*, July 1978

4 the actual cheating move of a card cheat *US, 1973*
- —Thomas L. Clark, *The Dictionary of Gambling and Gaming*, p. 32, 1987

5 used as a deliberately vague reference to any matter that is of concern or under consideration; later use tends to describe the matter (in phrases such as 'a bad business') without being any more specific *UK, 1605*

6 when combined with an indefinite intensifier in phrases such as 'what a business', 'quite a business', etc, something unexpectedly difficult to do or get *UK, 1843*

▸ do business

1 to engage in an illegal activity such as bribery *US*
- Coach, you don't think there's even a remote chance an official would do some business. —Dan Jenkins, *Life Its Ownself*, p. 194, 1984

2 in pool, to intentionally lose a game or other competition *US, 1989*
- —Mike Shamos, *The Illustrated Encyclopedia of Billiards*, p. 38, 1993

3 in horse racing, to cooperate in the fixing of a race *US*
- —David W. Maurer, *Argot of the Racetrack*, p. 24, 1951

▸ do the business

to settle the matter *UK, 1823*

▸ do your business

to defecate *UK, 1645*
- Some dog did his business on my lawn, again. —Janet Evanovich, *Seven Up*, p. 37, 2001

▸ give someone the business; do the business

to have sex *US, 1942*
- Shimmy's buddy is in the back room giving my date the business. —Irving Shulman, *The Amboy Dukes*, p. 204, 1947
- After they've done the business and are having a smoke and a chat[.] —Duncan MacLaughlin, *The Filth*, p. 193, 2002

▸ on the business

engaged in prostitution *UK, 1961*

▸ the business

1 the finest, the most perfect, the most complete; anything particularly good *UK, 1982*
- I think they really suit you. The whole outfit is the business. —Greg Williams, *Diamond Geezers*, p. 134, 1997
- [F]ifteen-year-old boot boys with little chance of a bunk-up even though we know we look the business[.] —John King, *Human Punk*, p. 23, 2000
- Alex addressed his breakfast – black pudding, bubble and squeak, eggs, beans, mushrooms, two fried slices and a mug of tea. The business. —Chris Ryan, *The Watchman*, p. 195, 2001

2 prostitution *US*
- Prostitutes, from the very young beauties to the shabbiest old fleabags, say that you can measure women in the "business" by the kinds of operations in which they engage[.] —John M. Murtagh and Sara Harris, *Cast the First Stone*, p. 1, 1957

business end

the operative part of something, the part that matters *UK, 1878*

business girl *noun*

a prostitute *UK, 1888*

businessman *noun*

1 any official or witness who will accept a bribe *US*
- —Hyman E. Goldin et al., *Dictionary of American Underworld Lingo*, p. 37, 1950

2 in horse racing, a jockey who may be persuaded to lose a race intentionally *US*
- —David W. Maurer, *Argot of the Racetrack*, p. 17, 1951

businessman's special; businessman's lunch *noun*

DMT (dimethyltryptamine), a powerful but short-lasting hallucinogen *US*
An allusion to the fact that it can be taken, experienced and recovered from in short order.
- —John Williams, *The Drug Scene*, p. 111, 1967
- —Eugene Landy, *The Underground Dictionary*, p. 43, 1971
- They call this the Businessman's lunch. This is a twenty minute, half-hour psychedelic trip. —Stephen Gaskin, *Amazing Dope Tales*, p. 174, 1980

bus jockey *noun*

a bus driver *US, 1954*
- —*American Speech*, p. 158–159, May 1960

busk *verb*

to work as a street entertainer *US, 1920*
The earlier sense from which this derives means 'to offer goods and entertainment for sale in bars'.

busker *noun*

an itinerant purveyor of entertainment to passers-by in the street, or on the London Underground, or other informal locations *UK, 1859*

Possibly from 'buskin', a short boot worn by entertainers from C16–19.

bussie *noun*

a bus driver *US, 1967*

Common among professional baseball players in the days when bus travel dominated travel between cities.

- Someone asked the bus driver, "How many miles on this baby?" "Don't know," the bussie said. "Thing's broken." — *Washingotn Post*, p. D1, 26th February 1983
- — Paul Dickson, *The New Dickson Baseball Dictionary*, p. 94, 1999

bust *noun*

1 a police raid, especially for suspected drug offences *US, 1938*
- Release, the London drug-bust organisation[.] — Richard Neville, *Play Power*, p. 15, 1970

2 an arrest *US, 1953*
- I didn't burn you, Joe, honest ... I told you it was a bust, honest. — Alexander Trocchi, *Cain's Book*, p. 150, 1960
- Since a bust does not seem imminent, I climb out the window and go to crew at four. — James Simon Kunen, *The Strawberry Statement*, p. 35, 1968
- Hey you smoking Mother Nature / this is a bust — The Who, *We're Not Gonna Take It*, 1969

3 to reduce someone in rank or standing *US, 1878*
- Word's going around that in addition to losing Ganz for the second time, and in addition to Haden busting you back to Patrolman, some jig beat the crap out of you. — *48 Hours*, 1982

4 a burglary *UK, 1857*
- Omnopon – are sold in ampoules or hypodermic tablets. These are usually obtained from chemist-shop busts. — Kevin Mackey, *The Cure*, p. xv, 1970

5 a complete failure *US, 1842*
- Don't spend much time here himself. He's a bust. — Marvin Wald and Albert Maltz, *The Naked City*, 1947
- Them PRs are the reason my old man's gone bust. — Stephen Sondheim, *West Side Story*, 1957

6 in poker, a worthless hand *US*
- — Irwin Steig, *Common Sense in Poker*, p. 182, 1963
- — George Percy, *The Language of Poker*, p. 15, 1988

bust *verb*

1 to arrest someone *US, 1940*
- "That's because the local pushers probably got busted," Hassan cautioned. — Ross Russell, *The Sound*, p. 86, 1961
- She told the group how she had been busted. — James Mills, *The Panic in Needle Park*, p. 33, 1966
- How I came to be busted at Heathdrow I don't know. — Doug Lang, *Freaks*, p. 15, 1973
- A midnight call from a friend: "I've been busted! – the guy propositioned me! Please get me out!" — John Rechy, *The Sexual Outlaw*, p. 98–99, 1977

2 to catch someone with evidence of guilt; to report on someone *US, 1960*
- Oh, that's just great. Are you busted? — *Ferris Buehler's Day Off*, 1986
- I was sorry for busting you on that. — *As Good As It Gets*, 1997

3 to inform the police; in later use especially, to inform the police about illicit drugs *UK, 1859*
- — Home Office, *Glossary of Terms and Slang Common in Penal Establishments*, July 1978

4 to inform on a fellow prisoner *UK*
- — Sean McConville, *The State of the Language*, 1980

5 to insult someone *US*
- — *National Education Association Today*, April 1985: 'A glossary for rents and other squids'

6 to praise and promote something *US*
- — Anna Scotti and Paul Young, *Buzzwords*, p. 116, 1997

7 to give someone something, to lend someone something *US*
- Tre, bust me a ride to the store. — *Boyz N The Hood*, 1990

8 in pontoon (blackjack, vingt-et-un), to exceed 21 points *UK, 1939*
- — Jerry L. Patterson, *Blackjack*, p. 20, 1978

9 in pool, to break to start a game *US*
- — Steve Rushin, *Pool Cool*, p. 6, 1990

10 when driving, to turn in a new direction *US*
- Bust a left at the light! — *Menace II Society*, 1993
- "Bust a left, Russ," instructed Ron[.] — Greg Williams, *Diamond Geezers*, p. 47, 1997

11 in the used car business, to reduce a car in price *US*
- The salesman will try to bust the customer's trade-in value, and the customer will try to bust the price of the salesman's car. — Peter Mann, *How to Buy a Used Car Without Getting Gypped*, p. 188, 1975

12 to smoke a marijuana cigarette *UK, 1998*

▸ **bust a box**

to break into a safe *US*
- Can you bust a box, if you have to? — Robert Edmond Alter, *Carny Kill*, p. 102, 1966
- I was supposed to be the best box-man in the country and as I look back, I must have busted four hundred boxes and lifted more than a million. — Red Rudensky, *The Gonif*, p. 6, 1970

▸ **bust a cap**

1 to shoot a gun *US*
- The sister ran out and said, "Call the law!" / And I bust two caps right dead in her jaw. Bruce Jackson, *Get Your Ass in the Water and Swim Like Me*, p. 49, 1965
- You better shut up fool! 'N haul ass 'less you want t'get a cap busted in it! — Odie Hawkins, *Ghetto Sketches*, p. 12, 1972
- Them people are going to come to in a minute and we're going to have more damn caps busting, more dogs barking than you ever heard in your life. — Bruce Jackson, *In the Life*, p. 324, 1972
- Awww shit! Niggas is bustin' caps fuck that[.] — DAS-EFX *Hard Like a Criminal*, 1992
- Can't go to a movie the first week it opens. Why? Because niggers are shooting at the screen. "This movie is so good I gotta bust a cap in here." — Chris Rock, *Rock This!*, p. 20, 1997

2 to use drugs *US*
- — Eugene Landy, *The Underground Dictionary*, p. 43, 1971

▸ **bust a few**

to surf *US*
- — Vann Wesson, *Generation X Field Guide and Lexicon*, p. 32, 1997

▸ **bust a grape**

in prison, to commit a foolish act as a result of a sense of intense desperation *US*
- — Charles Shafer, *Folk Speech in Texas Prisons*, p. 199, 1990

▸ **bust a gut**

to make a great effort *UK, 1912*

Originally a dialect term.

▸ **bust a move**

1 to make a move; to take action; to dance *US, 1984*
- Amanda busted her moves[.] — Wayne Anthony, *Spanish Highs*, p. 84, 1999
- — Don R. McCreary (Editor), *Dawg Speak*, 2001

2 to move quickly *US*
- — Judi Sanders, *Don't Dog by Do, Dude!*, p. 5, 1991

▸ **bust a stop sign**

to ignore a stop sign *US*
- Let's see, did I ever tell you about the big dude I stopped for busting a stop sign out front of your place? — Joseph Wambaugh, *The Blue Knight*, p. 156, 1973

▸ **bust a trick**

in foot-propelled scootering, to achieve success in a difficult manoeuvre *UK*
- If you bust a trick, you've got it right! — Ben Sharpe, *Scooter Crazy*, p. 40, 2000

▸ **bust jungle**

to break through a jungle with a tank or armoured carrier *US*

Vietnam war usage
- We mounted up and moved off, and while we busted jungle I kept looking back at Stepik[.] — Larry Heinemann, *Close Quarters*, p. 68, 1977
- — Linda Reinberg, *In the Field*, p. 119, 1991
- They called it "busting jungle,k" where armored vehicles literally made a road through the forest by knocking trees down. — Tom Clancy with Fred Franks Jr, *Into the Storm*, 1991

▸ **bust laugh**

to laugh outloud *US*

Hawaiian youth usage.
- — Douglas Simonson, *Pidgin to da Max Hana Hou*, 1982

▸ **bust someone's balls**

to tease someone relentlessly, provoking their anger *US, 1955*
- Busting his balls? If I was busting your balls, I'd send you home for your shine box. — *Goodfellas*, 1990

- The Sheriff's lookin' to bust your balls. — *Casino*, 1995
- [T]hey just sit in the kitchen playin' chess all day. An' decidin' the universe. An' bustin' everyone's balls. — Nick Barlay, *Curvy Lovebox*, p. 32, 1997

▸ **bust someone's drawers**
to have sex, seen as a conquest *US*
- Yeah, I've bust them draws once. But I just met her. I need time to get to know her. — *New Jack City*, 1990

▸ **bust suds**
to wash dishes *US*
- — Hermese E. Roberts, *The Third Ear*, 1971

▸ **bust the mainline**
to inject a drug into a vein *US, 1938*
- Do you go in the skin or do you bust the mainline? — Douglas Rutherford, *The Creeping Flesh*, p. 104, 1963

▸ **bust the rut; bust a rut**
to blaze a trail *AUSTRALIA*
From the Northern Territory.
- — Ernestine Hill, *The Teritory*, 1951

▸ **bust your boiler**
to over-exert yourself *NEW ZEALAND*
- And there's no need to bust your boiler. — Frank Sargeson, *That Summer*, p. 41, 1946

▸ **bust your buns**
to exert yourself; to try hard *US*
- Don't be afraid to try the newest sport around / (Bust your buns, bust your buns now). — Jan Berry and Dean Torrance, *Sidewalk Surfin'*, 1964

▸ **bust your chops**
to harass or provoke someone *US, 1953*
- Okay, Reggie, start bustin' my chops. Tell me how great you were with that chick. — *48 Hours*, 1982
- Jimm's busting my chops. — *Goodfellas*, 1990
- Dad, have you been busting Ted's chops? — *Something About Mary*, 1998

▸ **bust your conk**
to feel very happy, especially under the influence of a drug *US*
- — Kenn "Naz" Young, *Naz's Underground Dictionary*, p. 18, 1973

▸ **bust your guts out**
to over-exert yourself *NEW ZEALAND*
- He got on to me about smoking in the shed. No sense bustin ya guts out. — Gordon Slatter, *A Gun in my Hand*, p. 23, 1959

▸ **bust your hump**
to work extremely hard *UK*
- This was assuredly not the publication I'd busted my hump to preserve[.] — Mick Farren, *Give the Anarchist a Cigarette*, p. 147, 2001

▸ **bust your nut**
to experience an orgasm *US*
- They say, "Make me hot when a sucker get up on top a me and don't make me bust my nut." — Bruce Jackson, *Get Your Ass in the Water and Swim Like Me*, p. 103, 1964
- She lay with her arms spread, like a female Christ or a woman who has just busted her nuts[.] — Clarence Cooper Jr, *The Farm*, p. 5, 1967
- He busted his nuts, feeling the tongue working around the bottom of his member taking care of his johnson[.] — Steve Cannon, *Groove, Bang, and Jive Around*, p. 137, 1969
- Just then the earth gave a quiver, the ground gave a crut / Everybody in town knew Big Dick had busted his nut. — Anonymous ("Arthur"), *Shine and the Titanic*, p. 14, 1971
- After she had bust her nuts three or four times she wanted me to pop it to her in the ass. — A.S. Jackson, *Gentleman Pimp*, p. 109, 1973
- Back before Slick, when she was chambermaiding at the Malar Inn and putting out for free she used to bust her nut all the time. — John Sayles, *Union Dues*, p. 189, 1977
- I became somewhat self-conscious and proceeded to move my butt around, with the head of my penis doubling her hairy lips back into her vagina. I wanted to bust my nuts now. — Bobby Seale, *A Lonely Rage*, p. 136, 1978
- Which is more important to you: a fortune in diamonds or busting a nut? — Kevin Smith, *Jay and Silent Bob Strike Back*, p. 94, 2001

bust *adjective*
without funds *US*
- Can't play boys, I'm bust. — Steve Rushin, *Pool Cool*, p. 6, 1990

busta *noun*
1 a person who informs on another *US*
- — James Haskins, *The Story of Hip-Hop*, p. 136, 2000

2 a social outcast *US*
- — Connie Eble (Editor), *UNC-CH Campus Slang*, p. 2, Spring 1998
- — James Haskins, *The Story of Hip-Hop*, p. 136, 2000

bust developer *noun*
a singer who performs during a striptease act *US*
- — Don Wilmeth, *The Language of American Popular Entertainment*, p. 40, 1981

busted *adjective*
1 without, or very short of, money; bankrupt, ruined *US, 1837*
- Whenever time you is down and out – busted – haven't got any bread – you call yourself an Israelite — Desmond Dekker, 1969

2 ugly *US*
- — Connie Eble (Editor), *UNC-CH Campus Slang*, p. 2, November 2002

buster *noun*
1 pleasure, especially sexual pleasure *US*
- It's not a thing you rush through, and it's important not to leave a girl hanging. She must reach her busters too. — A.S. Jackson, *Gentleman Pimp*, p. 164, 1973

2 something that is excellent *US*
- — Kenn "Naz" Young, *Naz's Underground Dictionary*, p. 18, 1973

3 used as a term of address *US, 1866*
Lends a self-conscious, old-fashioned tone.
- "You're grounded, buster!" she screamed. — C.D. Payne, *Youth in Revolt*, p. 130, 1993

4 a fool *US*
- In other words, "Man, you're a real buster," is not a compliment. — *Orlando (Florida) Sentinel Tribune*, p. E1, 11th May 1995
- — *Maybeck High School Yearbook (Berkeley, California)*, p. 28, 1997
- — Rick Ayers (Editor), *Berkeley High Slang Dictionary*, p. 15, 2004

5 in circus usage, a bad fall *US*
An allusion to comic actor Joseph 'Buster' Keaton.
- — Don Wilmeth, *The Language of American Popular Entertainment*, p. 40, 1981

6 a heavy fall from a horse *AUSTRALIA, 1878*
- — A.B. Paterson, *Rio Grande and Other Verses*, p. 77, 1902
- Peter told me that in all the years he was on Norley, he never had a buster. — Herb Wharton, *Cattle Camp*, p. 92, 1994

7 a firecracker *US*
- When the months-old buster blew up, it scattered a profusion of filth everywhere. — John Clellon Holmes, *Go*, p. 36, 1952

8 a hard roll of bread *UK*
Trawlermen's term.
- — William Mitford, *Lovely She Goes*, 1969

9 any of several tools used by burglars or as weapons *US*
- — Vincent J. Monteleone, *Criminal Slang*, p. 49, 1949

10 in poker, a card that does not improve a hand *US*
- — Irv Roddy, *Friday Night Poker*, p. 216, 1961

11 a shoplifter *CANADA, 1984*

12 a strong wind from the south *AUSTRALIA, 1873*
A shortening of **SOUTHERLY BUSTER**.

13 on a plane, full power *US*
- — Linda Reinberg, *In the Field*, p. 31, 1991

▷ **see:** **BURSTER**

busters *noun*
dice that have had their spots altered to aid cheating *US*
- — Frank Garcia, *Marked Cards and Loaded Dice*, p. 261, 1962

bust hand *noun*
in bar dice games, a roll that produces no points for the player *US*
- — Jester Smith, *Games They Play in San Francisco*, p. 103, 1971

bust-head *noun*
potent whisky or beer, especially if manufactured illegally *US, 1857*
- I got so drunk I couldn't see. They were using this homemade beer, they used to call it"busthead"in Keokuk [Iowa].. — *Evergreen Review*, p. 137, 1957
- — Ramon Adams, *The Language of the Railroader*, p. 25, 1977

bus therapy *noun*
keeping a problem prisoner in transit in prison transport between prisons *US*
- — Angela Devlin, *Prison Patter*, p. 32, 1996

- When there were problems – race hassles, drugs, violence, whatever – in San Quentin, they'd grab everybody and ship 'em out, keeping their actual location in bureaucratic limbo. "Bus therapy" was another name for moving the problem rather than solving it. — Ralph "Sonny" Barger, *Hell's Angel*, p. 194, 2000

busticate *verb*

1 to break *US, 1916*
- We make fun of learned or formal vocabulary by inventing and using such words as discombobulate, busticate, ruction, rambunctious (and the verb formed on the last-mentioned, rambunct). — Robert A. Hall, *Leave Your Language Alone!*, p. 126, 1950

2 to leave *US*
- — Connie Eble (Editor), *UNC-CH Campus Slang*, p. 2, November 2002

bus ticket *noun*

a transfer from one prison to another *US*
- — James Harris, *A Convict's Dictionary*, p. 29, 1989

bust in *verb*

in a dice cheating scheme, to introduce altered dice into a game *US*
- — John S. Salak, *Dictionary of Gambling*, p. 35, 1963

bustle-punching *noun*

frottage; an act of unwanted intimacy, usually in a crowded place, when a man rubs his penis against the hindquarters of an unsuspecting woman *UK*
- The practice, not uncommon in dense crowds, of a male rubbing his penis against the buttocks of females. The penis may or may not be exposed. — David Powis, *The Signs of Crime*, 1977

bustle rack *noun*

on a tank, welded pipe framework on the turret used as a sort of roof rack, storing food, drinks and supplies *US*
- — Linda Reinberg, *In the Field*, p. 31, 1991

bust off *verb*

to experience orgasm *US*

Derives from **BUST YOUR NUT**.
- And watch this rap bitch bust all over ya nuts[.] — Lil' Kim *Dreams*, 1996
- [W]ant to bust off[.] — Kool Keith *Sex Style*, 1997

bust on *verb*

1 to criticise someone, to tease someone *US*
- — Connie Eble (Editor), *UNC-CH Campus Slang*, p. 2, Fall 1986

2 to shoot someone *US*
- "And then we pull heat and bust on 'em." I interrupt to ask if that means to shoot. "Shoot, yeah. Bust a cap." — *Rolling Stone*, p. 82, 12th April 2001

bust-out *noun*

a bankruptcy forced upon a business by organised crime, usually a lending enterprise owed money by the head of the business *US*
- Forced bankruptcy is the newest golden pot. In some cities it's called scam and in some bust-out. — Robert Campbell, *Juice*, p. 238, 1988

bust out *verb*

1 to take over a legitimate business, exploit its credit to the maximum, and then liquidate all assets *US, 1962*
- And, finally, when there's nothing left, when you can't borrow another buck from the bank or buy another case of booze, you bust the joint out. — *Goodfellas*, 1990

2 in a dice cheating scheme, to remove altered dice from a game and reintroduce the legitimate dice *US*
- — John S. Salak, *Dictionary of Gambling*, p. 35, 1963

bust-out *adjective*

1 in gambling, dishonest or part of a cheating scheme *US, 1937*
- That way I'll know up front if he's switched in bust-out cards of his own. — Iceberg Slim (Robert Beck), *Doom Fox*, p. 48, 1978

2 without money, broke *US*
- If this syllogism holds true, the bust-out junkie will say to his cellmate: "I am a heroin addict. I started smoking marijuana and then naturally I graduated to heroin." — Lenny Bruce, *How to Talk Dirty and Influence People*, p. 129, 1965

bust-out joint *noun*

a casino or gambling establishment that cheats gamblers *US*
- I started in this business behind the bar in bust-out joints on Third Street. Strippers hustling drinks between their numbers. — Vincent Patrick, *The Pope of Greenwich Village*, p. 151, 1979
- — Frank Scoblete, *Guerrilla Gambling*, p. 299, 1993

bust-out man *noun*

in a dice cheating scheme, the confederate whose special skill is the switching of tampered dice with the legitimate dice *US*
- — *The Annals of the American Academy of Political and Social Sciences*, p. 122, May 1950

bust-out mob *noun*

a group of confederates gambling with altered dice *US*
- I do – and this is a divergence with what I just said – work with what they call a "bust-out' mob. Craps in conventions, picnis, things like that. There you work eight- or ten-handed. — Bruce Jackson, *In the Life*, p. 176, 1972

bust-up *noun*

an altercation; a serious argument or disagreement *UK, 1899*

From the earlier sense (an explosion).
- Regan wished he hadn't been duty officer when the blower gave him details of a pop show's bust-up. — *The Sweeney*, p. 11, 1976

busty substances *noun*

the female breasts *UK*

A jocular coinage by comedian Peter Cook.
- PETE: There's a tremendous rushing wind and it blows up against her and it blows the damp dress right up against her and reveals, for all the world to see, her pefectly defined... DUD: Busty substances. PETE: Busty substances. — Peter Cook, *Not Only But Also*, 1966

bus' up *verb*

to wreak havoc *US*

Hawaiian youth usage.
- Junior's face all bus' up form da fight! — Douglas Simonson, *Pidgin to da Max*, 1981

bus-whargus *adjective*

extremely ugly *NORFOLK ISLAND*
- — Beryl Nobbs Palmer, *A Dictionary of Norfolk Words and Usages*, p. 5, 1992

busy; bizzy; busie *noun*

police; a police officer, originally a detective *UK, 1904*

From earlier 'busy fellow' – a suggestion that plain clothes officers are busy while their uniformed colleagues 'plod'.
- "Now what was their names?" says the big fat busie; so me and Henry tells him. — John Peter Jones, *Feather Pluckers*, p. 9, 1964
- That's if the busys don't find yi first! — Ian Pattison, *Rab C. Nesbitt*, 1988
- Mostly, we were off the estate and miles away before the local bizzies even rolled up. — Val McDermid, *Keeping on the Right Side of the Law*, p. 181, 1999
- I'm looking around me all the time. There's a bizzy station just up from here[.] — Kevin Sampson, *Outlaws*, p. 92, 2001

busy *adjective*

1 actively searching for, or engaged in, a sexual liaison *US*

Homosexual usage.
- "I'm busy, dear; talk to you later..." If this latter is said over the phone, it always means, "I'm in the middle of sex ..." (nothing more). — *The Guild Dictionary of Homosexual Terms*, p. 6, 1965

2 (used of a card in poker) producing a pair or otherwise improving a hand *US*
- — George Percy, *The Language of Poker*, p. 15, 1988

▸ get busy

1 to have sex *US*
- — Terry Williams, *The Cocaine Kids*, p. 138, 1989

2 to rob someone *US*
- — Carsten Stroud, *Close Pursuit*, p. 272, 1987

busy as a one-armed paper-hanger in a gale *adjective*

extremely busy *US, 1939*

First recorded in the US and New Zealand, but also known in Canada where it may be lengthened by 'with the itch', and in Australia and UK with the elaboration 'with crabs' or 'with the crabs'.
- [H]e reaches his office where he is "as busy as a one-armed paper-hanger with hives." — John Haverstick, *The Saturday Review Treasury*, p. 135, 1957
- If you want to hit the nail on the head and keep the students as busy as a one-armed paper hanger use idioms to help teach semantic principles. — Bob Bohlken, *Etc.*, p. 1, 1996

- At the time Jesus was busy – as busy as a one-armed paper-hanger in a gale – dealing with every kind of sickness in the medical dictionary. — Kel Richards, *The Aussie Bible*, p. 36, 2003

busy bee *noun*

phencyclidine, the recreational drug known as PCP or angel dust *US*

- — US Department of Justice, *Street Terms*, October 1994

busylickum *noun*

a nosey person *BARBADOS*

- — Frank A. Collymore, *Barbadian Dialect*, p. 24, 1965

but *noun*

a halibut *UK*

Trawlermen's use.

- — D. Butcher, *Trawlermen*, 1980

but *adverb*

though, however *AUSTRALIA*

Used at the end of a statement. This is one feature of Australian English that parents and teachers have long sought to wipe out via the correction of any youth saying it. Typically the argument 'you can't end a sentence with a preposition/conjunction' is put forward, but clearly 'but' is an adverb here, modifying the verb of the statement (not to mention highlighting the grammatical ignorance of the would-be corrector). Speakers of US and British English are often confused when first meeting this regionalism, and will patiently wait for the continuation of the sentence following what they hear as a conjunction – 'it isn't coming, but!'. The *Australian National Dictionary* (1988) proffers early examples, including one from 1853, however it is not entirely definite from the context given that this is how the quotation should be read. The first undeniable example dates to 1938, and it was common by the 1950s. Also heard among Hawaiian youth.

- 'Comes up blue in the face, spittin' sand an' seaweed.' 'I caught a boomer just after, but.' — Nino Culotta (John O'Grady), *They're A Weird Mob*, p. 71, 1957
- Junior nice guy. He get ugly face but. — Douglas Simonson, *Pidgin to da Max*, 1981
- It wasn't his fault, but. — Kathy Lette, *Girls' Night Out*, p. 25, 1987
- We're real sorry about Maureen's wrist but. — Roy Slaven (John Doyle), *Five South Coast Seasons*, p. 56, 1992
- Each set carries its own rock 'n' roll memory: Skyhooks, The Beatles, and loads of oldies I don't even recognise. I recognise Billy Thorpe and the Aztecs but. — Glyn Parry, *Mosh*, p. 13, 1996
- Been here ages, nearly a year. Just come back from six weeks in Queensland, but. — Shane Maloney, *Nice Try*, p. 11, 1998

but

1 used for expressing express surprise or recognition of something unexpected *UK, 1846*

- God, but you're beautiful, aren't you? — Kate Bush, *Feel It*, 1978

2 used for emphasising the following word or words *UK, 1887*

- While it's still early enough in the season that a blowout or two can wreck it but good, let's take a look at team's expected won-loss records as opposed to their actual records. — *The Week in Preview*, 6th May 2003

butch *noun*

1 the person fulfulling the masculine role in a homosexual relationship *US, 1954*

- Billy, the butch, squares off, putting up her fists. — Willard Motely, *Let No Man Write My Epitaph*, p. 248, 1958
- — Donald Webster Cory and John P. LeRoy, *The Homosexual and His Society*, p. 262, 1963: 'A lexicon of homosexual slang'
- The door opened to reveal a full blown 'butch,' even dressed in men's clothing. — John O'Day, *Confessions of a Male Prostitute*, p. 90, 1964
- One often hears a story of a butch who carries a switchblade knife, ready to attack any male who accosts her. — Donald Webster Cory, *The Lesbian in America*, p. 204, 1964
- And most of your strength went in fighting off the butches. — Sara Harris, *The Lords of Hell*, p. 73, 1967
- Del is a thoroughgoing butch and has never taken anything but the aggressive role in her homosexual contacts. — Ruth Allison, *Lesbianism*, p. 20, 1967
- One of the butches, half in real pity for Irene and partly in an attempt to cement a future opportunity, stepped up to breach the custom of noninterference. — Nathan Heard, *Howard Street*, p. 229, 1968
- A stone butch, she had a cute li'l chick, Sarita, she used to abuse for days. — Edwin Torres, *After Hours*, p. 323, 1979
- Archie was the bitch and Jughead was the butch, that's why Jughead wears that crown-looking hat all the time. — *Chasing Amy*, 1997
- After I saw teenagers Tatum O'Neal and Kristy McNichol in LIttle Darlings (the perfect butch-femme dyke couple), I couldn't wait to – not to lose my virginity to Matt Dillon, but to have a sex slumber party with those two cuties. — *The Village Voice*, 17th June 2002

2 a very short haircut *US*

- — Connie Eble (Editor), *UNC-CH Campus Slang*, p. 2, Spring 1982

butch *adjective*

1 overtly masculine *US, 1936*

- "And when we got into bed, that tough butch number – he turned over on his stomach and I – ..." a score had told me about a very masculine young man I had seen on the streets. — John Rechy, *City of Night*, p. 59, 1963
- [V]ada [observe] that great butch lucoddy [body]. — Barry Took and Marty Feldman, *Round The Horne*, 25th June 1967
- I can remember when, years back, they shunted you through the side door, admitting only those who appeared "butch enough." — John Francis Hunter, *The Gay Insider*, p. 74, 1971
- We wore blue jeans, tight T-shirts. We were all so butch, man, and we were proud. — John Rechy, *The Sexual Outlaw*, p. 69, 1977
- [T]hey were much too butch pour moi, sister[.] — the cast of 'Aspects of Love', Prince of Wales Theatre, *Palare (Boy Dancer Talk) for Beginners*, 1989–92
- She used to be quite butch when she first came in here, but that was back in the year blob. — James Gardiner, *Who's a Pretty Boy Then?*, p. 123, 1997

2 fulfilling the masculine role in a male or female homosexual relationship *US, 1941*

Originally applied to male and female homosexuals, but later predominantly to lesbians.

- — Donald Webster Cory and John P. LeRoy, *The Homosexual and His Society*, p. 262, 1963: 'A lexicon of homosexual slang'
- — Florida Legislative Investigation Committee (Johns Committee), *Homosexuality and Citizenship in Florida*, 1964: 'Glossary of homosexual terms and deviate acts'
- — *The Guild Dictionary of Homosexual Terms*, p. 6, 1965
- I had to run out to catch the end of the Sunday-afternoon-Saturday-night recover bout at Julius' – where the oldest college sophojmores in the world gather and everyone still pretends to be so butch that she just dropped in famished for one of those greasy hamburgers — *Screw*, p. 15, 22nd December 1969
- In spite of the fact that butch was not a friendly designation, it was, for the most part, adopted by the lesbian peoples. — Monique Wittig and Sande Zeig, *Lesbian People*, p. 23, 1979
- Darling, there's nothing I love more than knowing some big butch number fancies my arse. Except, perhaps letting him have it. — Simon Napier-Bell, *Black Vinyl White Powder*, p. 302, 2001

3 heterosexual *US*

- — Anon., *The Gay Girl's Guide*, p. 4, 1949

4 unafraid, unabashed *UK*

A nuance of the 'overtly masculine' sense used in contemporary gay society.

- — *Attitude*, p. 60, July 2003: 'New palare lexicon'

butch broad *noun*

an aggressive lesbian with masculine affectations *US, 1966*

- Ordinarily, he wouldn't have gotten away with this behavior among the butch-broads[.] — Nathan Heard, *Howard Street*, p. 229, 1968

butch dike *noun*

a aggressive, mannish lesbian *US*

- Rumors have it that a truly "butch dike" can whip any muscleman with her little finger. — *Screw*, p. 18, 27th June 1969

butcher *noun*

1 a beer glass of 170 ml capacity; also, a serving in one of these glasses *AUSTRALIA, 1889*

Used only in the state of South Australia, the 'butcher' was originally a long thin glass holding over a pint; the size has gradually diminished over the years. Said by some to be derived from the German *becher* (C19 South Australia had a large German migrant community), but this doesn't sound remotely like 'butcher'. Other folk etymologies about butchers requiring a certain type of beer glass abound.

- And as it was my 'shout', I drank the last inch of West End in my 'butcher'[.] — John O'Grady, *It's Your Shout, Mate!*, p. 29, 1972

2 a surgeon *US, 1849*

- — *Maledicta*, p. 57, Summer 1980: 'Not sticks and stones, but names: more medical pejoratives'

3 a medical student *AUSTRALIA, 1984*

Used by undergraduates of the University of Sydney.

4 a prison dentist *UK*

- — Angela Devlin, *Prison Patter*, p. 32, 1996

5 a prison guard captain *US*

- — Marlene Freedman, *Alcatraz*, 1983

6 in a pack of playing cards, a king *UK, 1937*

- —Jay Robert Nash, *Dictionary of Crime*, p. 52, 1992

Butcher Brigade *nickname*

the 11th Infantry Brigade of the Americal Division, US Army *US*

So named after the Brigade's role in the massacre at My Lai became known.

- —Linda Reinberg, *In the Field*, p. 31, 1991

butcher charts *noun*

large pieces of paper used during a briefing or brainstorming session *US*

Named because the paper used is similar to the paper used by butchers to wrap meat.

- — Department of the Army, *Staff Officer's Guidebook*, p. 57, 1986

butcher's apron *nickname*

the ribbon of the United Nations' medal for active service in Korea *UK, 1984*

From the narrow vertical white stripes and washed-out blue background. The nickname was already current in 1954.

butcher's hook; butcher's *noun*

a look *UK, 1936*

Rhyming slang.

- Do you mind if we have a butchers in the boot?—Frank Norman, *Bang To Rights*, p. 122, 1958
- [A] new dance-hall had been opened over at Peckham and we were all dying to have a butchers and lamp all the new bird[.]—Derek Raymond (Robin Cook), *The Crust on its Uppers*, p. 34, 1962
- Save your breath for a Mayday call, skip, and take a quick butcher's hook at what's coming up at our four o'clock!—W.R. Bennett, *Night Intruder*, p. 25, 1962
- Meanwhile take a butcher's at this lot and keep a penny a mile on your boat race!— *The Sweeney*, p. 7, 1976
- [T]ake a butcher's hook at what lies before us[.]—Ronnie Barker, *Fletcher's Book of Rhyming Slang*, p. 39, 1979
- 'I brung you this.' A gold chain slithered down the front of my shirt. 'Take a butchers.'—Kathy Lette, *Girls' Night Out*, p. 174, 1987
- "Shall we swoop down for a quick butcher's?" He stresses the last word, proud of his bit of Cockney.—Stuart Browne, *Dangerous Parking*, p. 261, 2000

butcher's hook; butcher's *adjective*

sick, ill, unwell *AUSTRALIA, 1967*

Rhyming slang for **CROOK**.

- So I padded the hoof along the frog and toad, still feeling butcher's hook.—Duke Tritton, *Learn to talk Old Jack Lang*, p. 12, 1905
- I suppose you're still feeling butchers after your op, are you?—Barry Humphries, *A Nice Night's Entertainment*, p. 186, 1981

▸ **go butcher's hook**

to get angry or upset *AUSTRALIA, 1918*

- No good going butcher's hook is it?—Barry Dickins, *What the Dickins*, p. 67, 1985

butcher shop *noun*

a hospital casualty department or operating room *US, 1918*

- — *American Speech*, p. 267, December 1962: 'The language of traffic policemen'

butcher's overall *noun*

a surgeon's white protective overall *UK*

Royal Navy use.

- —D.M.J. Clark, *Suez Touchdown*, 1964

butch it up *verb*

to act in an aggressive, manly manner *US*

Homosexual usage, male and female.

- —Donald Webster Cory and John P. LeRoy, *The Homosexual and His Society*, p. 262, 1963: 'A lexicon of homosexual slang'
- — *Maledicta*, p. 138, Summer/Winter 1982: 'Dyke diction: the language of lesbians'

butch kick *noun*

in the usage of pickpockets, a hip pocket *US*

- —Vincent J. Monteleone, *Criminal Slang*, p. 40, 1949

butch number *noun*

a manly homosexual man desired by others as a partner in sex *US*

- He is very masculine, and he has been described recurrently in homosexual jargon as "a very butch number"[.]—John Rechy, *Numbers*, p. 16, 1967

butch out *verb*

(used of a woman) to affect a mannish appearance *US*

- I went over to the window and gazed down on a group of girls butched out in buzz cuts and work boots.—Rita Ciresi, *Pink Slip*, p. 11, 1999

butch pad *noun*

an apartment or house where lesbians congregate *US*

- Then you can lay up in those butch pads with a bunch of bull daggers and a pack of smelly houses cats and drop pills and shoot junk[.] —Joseph Wambaugh, *The Blue Knight*, p. 148, 1973

butch queen *noun*

a decidedly masculine male homosexual *US*

- —Kenneth Marlowe, *The Gay World of Kenneth Marlowe*, p. 3, 1966

butch trade *noun*

a seemingly heterosexual man who consents to homosexual sex in the male role, receiving orally or giving anally *US*

- They want their men to be "butch trade."— *Screw*, p. 18, 22nd June 1970

butchy *adjective*

overtly masculine in affectation and mannerisms *US*

- Then she started buying and sending me presents – slacks and jackets, suits cut and tailored like a man's with butchy accessories. —Billie Holiday with William Dufty, *Lady Sings the Blues*, p. 102, 1956
- "The public conception of a lesbian is that she's a butchy kind of person – an aggressive dyke," said Dr. Fort.—*San Francisco Chronicle*, p. 22, 30th June 1969
- No Birkenstocks or butchy buzz cuts here.— *Record (Bergen County, New Jersey)*, p. E1, 18th January 2004

bute *noun*

butazolodin, a pain-killer *UK*

- —David Broom, *Desert Island Discs*, 14th February 1981

but, I digress

used as a humorous end to a wandering thought *US*

A catchphrase attrbitued to author Max Shulman in cigarette advertisements of the 1950s.

- But – like Max Shulman in those clever cigarette advertisements – I digress.—Robert Gover, *One Hundred Dollar Misunderstanding*, p. 12, 1961

butler *noun*

crack cocaine *UK*

- —Mike Haskins, *Drugs*, p. 281, 2003

butler's revenge *noun*

an inaudible fart *UK, 1984*

A public school coinage, commenting on the dignified restraint of senior male servants; *not* an eponym.

but mine is worth...

used as a a bragging description of a BMW car *CANADA*

- BMW–the automobile of choice for braggarts–"But Mine is Worth...."— *Toronto Globe and Mail*, p. D12, 3rd August 2002

butt *noun*

1 the buttocks, the posterior; used in many senses and phrases as a replacement for 'arse' or 'ass' *UK, 1720*

- It's the perils of coaching. You work your butt off, and then get kicked in it.— *Honolulu Advertiser*, 27th April 2003

2 by extension, the tail end of anything *US*

- — *Current Slang*, p. 15, Winter 1970

3 the tail end of a prison sentence *US*

- —Vincent J. Monteleone, *Criminal Slang*, p. 40, 1949
- —William K. Bentley and James M. Corbett, *Prison Slang*, p. 18, 1992

4 a cigarette *US, 1902*

- "Now ya can buy butts, kid," Chirechillo said.—Nathan Heard, *Howard Street*, p. 107, 1968
- I took packs of butts to the coal pile the next day.—Iceberg Slim (Robert Beck), *Pimp*, p. 260, 1969
- We'll give you a slice of pizza and a pack of butts.—Richard Price, *The Wanderers*, p. 20, 1974
- It drove Rocco nuts; guys would buy ten loose cigarettes on ten trips for a dollar fifty when they could have bought a pack – twice as many butts for the same price.—Richard Price, *Clockers*, p. 264, 1992

butt *verb*

in tiddlywinks, to knock a wink off a pile *US*

- — *Verbatim*, p. 525, December 1977

butt *adverb*

very *US*

- I'm going to get butt wild tonight.—Connie Eble (Editor), *UNC-CH Campus Slang*, p. 2, November 1990

butt board *verb*
to ride a skateboard sitting down *US*
• —Anna Scotti and Paul Young, *Buzzwords*, p. 111, 1997

butt boy *noun*
a sycophant; a toady *US*
• [H]e's the only one I can point to and say I'm sure I hate. Him and his butt boys.—Mickey Spillane, *My Gun is Quick*, p. 90, 1950
• He's nothing but a pipe-smoking, draft-dodging, headquarters-carted butt-boy.—Gerald Petievich, *To Die in Beverly Hills*, p. 26, 1983

butt can *noun*
any improvised ashtray *US*
• —Carl Fleischhauer, *A Glossary of Army Slang*, p. 7, 1968

butt-check *verb*
in snowboarding, to maintain balance by making brief contact between buttocks and snow *UK*

butt drop *noun*
a backwards fall while snowboarding *US*
• Are you perfecting your butt drop?—Elena Garcia, *A Beginner's Guide to Zen and the Art of Snowboarding*, p. 120, 1990

butt end *noun*
the discarded end of a cigarette or marijuana cigarette *UK*
• [A]n ashtray complete with the butt ends of several joints, smoked right down to the roach.—John Williams, *Cardiff Dead*, p. 7, 2000

buttendski *noun*
the buttocks *NEW ZEALAND*
• —David McGill, *David McGill's Complete Kiwi Slang Dictionary*, p. 25, 1998

butter *noun*
1 insincerity *US*
• —Lou Shelly, *Hepcats Jive Dictionary*, p. 8, 1945

2 crack cocaine *US*
• Frank Sarubbi, 20, of 106 Prospect St., allegedly walked up to an undercover officer and asked if he was "looking to buy butter," street slang for crack.—*Hartford (Connecticut) Courant*, p. B5, 23rd December 1998

butter; butters *adjective*
ugly, unattractive
Perhaps a play on **BUTT UGLY**. Current in south London according to *Johnny Vaughan Tonight*, 13th February 2002.
• —Susie Dent, *The Language Report*, p. 76, 2003

butter-and-egg man *noun*
a unsophisticated free spender *US, 1924*
Coined by 1920s nightclub performer Texas Guinan for a shy, middle-aged man so flattered by her friendliness that he paid the steep cover charge for every guest in the house and pressed $50 notes on all the entertainers. When he said he was in the dairy business, she introduced him as 'the big butter-and-egg man'.
• He puffed on the big cigar like he always had stuck in his face and posed back like a big butter-and-egg man.—Mezz Mezzrow, *Really the Blues*, p. 69, 1946
• —Rosalie Maggio, *Talking About People*, p. 82, 1997

butter and eggs *noun*
an illegal lottery *US, 1973*
Most commonly known as a **NUMBERS** game.
• —Thomas L. Clark, *The Dictionary of Gambling and Gaming*, p. 32, 1987

butterball *noun*
1 a fat person or animal *US, 1941*
• Anna, sister of Huldah Purdick, was a rolypoly and a butterball, with pink-and-white plump cheeks.—Sinclair Lewis, *The God-Seeker*, p. 137, 1949
• Start your little butterball on her new diet by mixing small amounts of the canned kitten food with her dry.—*Albuquerque (New Mexico) Journal*, p. C3, 29th March 2004

2 an idiot *UK*
• —Peter Chippindale, *The British CB Book*, p. 153, 1981

butterbar *noun*
a second lieutenant in the US Army *US, 1973*
Vietnam coinage, from the gold-bar insignia.
• On April 25, 117 marched out as "butterbars" – Second Lieutenants of Marines.—*Washington Post Magazine*, p. 24, 25th May 1980
• A crusty old Sergeant major is not going to accept the indignity of becoming a "butterbar" second lieutenant.—Christopher Bassford, *The Spint-Shine Syndrome*, p. 141, 1988
• —Linda Reinberg, *In the Field*, p. 31, 1991

butterbox *adjective*
(of a man) effeminate *UK*
From an earlier sense (fop).
• You Aussies are so deliciously butterbox[.]—Barry Humphries, *Bazz Pulls It Off!*, 1971

butter boy *noun*
a very young police officer *UK*
After an earlier sense as 'novice' applied to sailors and taxi drivers.
• —David Powis, *The Signs of Crime*, 1977

buttered bread *adjective*
dead *UK*
Rhyming slang.
• —Ray Puxley, *Fresh Rabbit*, 1998

buttered bun *noun*
a prostitute, or, less specifically any woman, who has already had sex with several customers/men; sex with this woman *UK, 1699*
Also heard in the plural.
• —Dale Gordon, *The Dominion Sex Dictionary*, p. 36, 1967
• —Robert A. Wilson, *Playboy's Book of Forbidden Words*, p. 57, 1972
• She knew that some men were inflamed by a woman who had just been with another man – April had told her the slang term for a woman in that state, a buttered bun – and she knew intuitively that Edward was such a man.—Ken Follett, *A Dangerous Fortune*, p. 175, 1993

butter-face *noun*
a girl or woman with an attractive body and an unprepossessing face *UK*
From the qualifier 'but her face' in the appreciation of such a person.
• —Chris Lewis, *The Dictionary of Playground Slang*, p. 48, 2003
• —Connie Eble (Editor), *UNC-CH Campus Slang*, p. 1, November 2003

butter-fingered *adjective*
prone to dropping things *UK, 1615*

butterfingers *noun*
a clumsy person, prone to dropping things *UK, 1837*
After the adjective.
• Those soggy chunks kept slipping out of my hands before I got them two inches off the ground. Slap my wrist and call me Butterfingers.—Mezz Mezzrow, *Really the Blues*, p. 36, 1946

butterflies in your stomach; butterfiles *noun*
the feeling of queasiness that accompanies fear or nervousness *US, 1940*
The fluttering of butterflies as a metaphor for the unsettled sensations of trepidation.
• [E]very time it gives me the butterflies[.]—Derek Raymond (Robin Cook), *The Crust on its Uppers*, p. 48, 1962

butter flower *noun*
marijuana *US, 1971*
From the appearance of canabis resin.
• —Richard A. Spears, *The Slang and Jargon of Drugs and Drink*, p. 88, 1986
• —Jay Robert Nash, *Dictionary of Crime*, p. 52, 1992
• —Mike Haskins, *Drugs*, p. 286, 2003

butterfly *noun*
1 a person who is romantically fickle *US*
• —*American Speech*, p. 54, February 1947: 'Pacific War language'

2 a note thrown from a train to a repair crew *US*
• —Norman Carlisle, *The Modern Wonder Book of Trains and Railroading*, p. 260, 1946

3 in electric line work, a conductor take-up reel *US*
• —A.B. Chance Co., *Lineman's Slang Dictionary*, p. 3, 1980

4 in television and film making, a large screen used to direct or diffuse light *US*
• —Ira Konigsberg, *The Complete Film Dictionary*, p. 36, 1987
• —Ralph S. Singleton, *Filmaker's Dictionary*, p. 24, 1990

butterfly *verb*
1 to engage in promiscuous sex *US, 1946*
• —*American Speech*, p. 120, May 1960: 'Korean bamboo English'
• —Linda Reinberg, *In the Field*, p. 31, 1991

2 in the gambling game two-up, to toss the coins so that they flutter in the air and appear to be actually spinning *AUSTRALIA, 1949*
The object of butterflying is to make the coins fall the way the tosser wishes and is consequently illegal in the game.
- All school children to be taught from an early age to spin and butterfly pennies. —Frank Hardy and Athol George Mulley, *The Needy and the Greedy*, 1975

3 to leave someone *US*
- —Linda Reinberg, *In the Field*, p. 221, 1991

butterfly kiss *noun*
an intimate caress made by fluttering eyelashes over a partner's skin *UK, 1871*
- I kept thinkin about her an those butterfly kisses she used ta give me – you know. He blinked his eyes rapidly – with her fucking eyes right up against ya cheek. —Gilbert Sorrentino, *Steelwork*, p. 21, 1970

butterfly wheel *noun*
in drag racing, a bifurcated steering wheel shaped like two opposing butterfly wings *US*

butterhead *noun*
a stupid person, especially a stupid black person *US, 1963*
- Other black terms for blacks are implicitly or overtly derogating, such as butterhead for an embarassingly stupid person. —Irving Lewis Allen, *The Language of Ethnic Conflict*, p. 111, 1983

buttering-up *noun*
an act of persuasive flattery *UK, 1819*
- [Y]ou may be afraid that your compliment will be perceived as buttering up or brown nosing. —Michael S. Dobson, *Managing Up*, p. 82, 2000

butter legs *noun*
a promiscuous woman *AUSTRALIA*
Because, like butter, her legs are 'easy to spread'.
- — Thommo, *The Dictionary of Australian Swearing and Sex Sayings*, p. 24, 1985

buttermilk *noun*
beer *US*
- —Bill Davis, *Jawjacking*, p. 25, 1977

butters *adjective*
▷ **see: BUTTER**

butter up *verb*
to flatter someone with an intent to persuade them *UK, 1819*
- Jack was buttering up her mom[.] —Kristen Kemp, *I Will Survive*, p. 3, 2002

butter would not melt in your mouth
an appearance of innocence *UK, 1530*
Usually contemptuous in phrases 'as if butter would not melt in your mouth' and 'seem as if butter would not melt in your mouth', occasionally shortened to 'butter would not melt'.

butt floss *noun*
a thong or string bikini with only a slender piece of fabric passing between the cheeks of the buttocks *US*
- —Trevor Cralle, *The Surfin'ary*, p. 17, 1991
- —Judi Sanders, *Kickin' like Chicken with the Couch Commander*, p. 4, 1992

butt-fuck *verb*
1 to copulate anally *US, 1968*
- I hear when Caroline was living with that Greek bartender he used to butt-fuck her all the time. —Joseph Wambaugh, *The Choirboys*, p. 325, 1975
- He'll be at the Betty Ford Clinic while you and me do twenty-five at Raiford, getting butt-fucked in the showers. —Carl Hiaasen, *Tourist Season*, p. 130, 1986
- Me and Marcus Allen was butt fuckin' Nicole / When we heard a knock at the door[.] —Eminem (Marshall Mathers), *Role Model*, 1999

2 to light one cigarette with the burning butt of another *US*
- —Pamela Munro, *U.C.L.A. Slang*, p. 50, 2001

3 since the Vietnam war, to attack from the rear *US*
- —Linda Reinberg, *In the Field*, p. 31, 1991

buttfucker *noun*
a homosexual male *US*
- I'm watching my ass all the time, and a bunch of these greasy-haired nancy boys, these fucks, these buttfuckers, they come for me. —Joel Rose, *Kill Kill Faster Faster*, p. 17, 1997

butt fucking *noun*
anal sex *US*
- The Back Door Boys go for all the fag subtext of these homoerotic groups, exploring their interpretation of the hit song "I Want It That Way" – it's all about butt fucking. —*The Village Voice*, 5th October 1999

Butt Fucking Nowhere *noun*
any remote place *US*
- —Connie Eble (Editor), *UNC-CH Campus Slang*, p. 1, November 2002

butt hair *noun*
a parting down the centre of the head *US*
- —Connie Eble (Editor), *UNC-CH Campus Slang*, p. 1, Fall 1991

butthead *noun*
a generally unlikeable, disagreeable, dim-witted person *US, 1973*
- MURTAUGH: Tell Martin what you think of crooks. CARRIE: Butt-heads. They're buttheads. —*Lethal Weapon*, 1987
- —Connie Eble (Editor), *UNC-CH Campus Slang*, p. 1, Spring 1989
- 'Why they don't stick around.' "Because they're buttheads.' —Armistead Maupin, *Maybe the Moon*, p. 44, 1992

butthole *noun*
1 the anus *US, 1951*
- We want to be phalluses ramming in the butthole of pop. —*Jabberrock [quoting Gibby Haines of the band Butthole Surfers]*, p. 186, 1997
- We can all experience what it feels like to be a pitcher or catcher on the butthole diamond. —*The Village Voice*, 24th August 1999

2 by extension, a despicable or offensive person *US, 1962*
- —Collin Baker et al., *College Undergraduate Slang Study Conducted at Brown University*, p. 93, 1968
- Dad says you're late again, you butthole! —*Fast Times at Ridgemont High*, 1982
- This sucks more than anything has ever sucked before. We must find this butt-hole that took the TV. —Mike Judge and Joe Stillman, *Beavis and Butt-Head Do America*, p. 2, 1997

buttie *noun*
a walk in the company of a friend *UK: SCOTLAND*
Possibly extended from 'butty/buttie' (a friend).
- Wait a wee minute an Ah'll gie ye a buttie up the road. —Michael Munro, *The Patter, Another Blast*, 1988

butt in *verb*
to intrude into another's business or conversation *US, 1899*
- You can't just drop into a newsgroup and start butting in talking about your brand[.] —*The Guardian*, 9th February 2004

buttinski; buttinsky
a meddler; a person who interferes in the affairs of others *US, 1902*
- Look who's talking about stickin' noses. You're the God-damndest buttinski I ever run into! —Garson Kanin, *Born Yesterday*, p. 131, 1946
- Are you going to let your coach have a free hand or are you going to be a buttinsky and keep trying to make him use your ideas? —*San Francisco Examiner*, p. 19, 20th December 1948
- —Helen Dahlskog (Editor), *A Dictionary of Contemporary and Colloquial Usage*, p. 11, 1972
- You're a buttinsky, a guy who sticks his nose in places he shouldn't stick his nose. —Robert Campbell, *Junkyard Dog*, p. 120, 1986
- To some, Diane Vollmer is a buttinski. To others, she's the Lady Bird Johnson of her north Denver neighborhood. —*The Denver Post*, p. B1, 9th March 1997
- Eddie Love is a "buttinski," someone who interferes when it's none of his business. —*Ventura (California) County Star*, p. A1, 11th April 1998
- In the current issue of Orion, America's finest environmental magazine, Oregon rancher Mike Connelly rakes environmentalists over the coals as a bunch of buttinski tree-huggers. —*The Boston Globe*, p. C2, 4th October 1999
- Unfortunately some well-meaning (or NOT-so-well-meaning) buttinskies report parents who are a little too firm but certainly not abusive. —*Chicago Tribune*, 29th November 2003

buttkiss *noun*
nothing at all *US*
Variation of **BUPKES; BUPKIS**.
- But we did nothing, absolutely buttkiss that day / And I say, what the hell am I doing drinking in L.A. at 26? —Bran Van 3000 *Drinking in LA*, 1997

butt kit *noun*
an ashtray *US, 1958*
- —Montie Tak, *Truck Talk*, p. 24, 1971

buttlegger *noun*
a person who smuggles cigarettes from states with low or no cigarette taxes to states with high cigarette taxes *US*
- —*New York Times*, p. 2-13, 31st December 1976
- —Ralph de Sola, *Crime Dictionary*, p. 22, 1982

buttlegging *noun*
the smuggling of cigarettes from states with low or no cigarette taxes to states with high taxes *US*
- — *Maimi Herald*, p. 1, 4th July 1977

buttload *noun*
a large amount *US*
- — Connie Eble (Editor), *UNC-CH Campus Slang*, p. 2, Spring 1991
- I don't have time to fight. We have to find out what kind of algorithm we need here. I have to write a buttload of code. — Gary Dorsey, *Silicon Sky*, p. 144, 1999

buttly *adjective*
very ugly *US*
A blend of 'butt' and 'ugly'.
- — Pamela Munro, *U.C.L.A. Slang*, p. 27, 1989

buttmunch *noun*
a contemptible person *US*
- He looks irritated and says, "Cut it out butt-munch!" — Mike Judge and Joe Stillman, *Beavis and Butthead Do America*, 1996
- — Judi Sanders, *Da Bomb!*, p. 5, 1997

button *noun*
1 a police badge *US, 1929*
- — Hyman E. Goldin, *Dictionary of American Underworld Lingo*, p. 38, 1950
- He said, "Folks, you got that button? Those Mau Mau are going to maim our damn-fool host." I reached under the seat and got the fake detective badge. — Iceberg Slim (Robert Beck), *Trick Baby*, p. 44–45, 1969

2 by extension, a police officer *US*
- It was pretty obvious that the buttons in the prowl car were about ready to drop the hook on him, so I went over there fast and took hold of his arm. — Raymond Chandler, *The Long Goodbye*, p. 6, 1953

3 a person who acts as lookout *US*
- — William K. Bentley and James M. Corbett, *Prison Slang*, p. 40, 1992

4 in organised crime, a person who kills on the orders from above *US, 1966*
Sometimes expanded as 'button man' or 'button guy'.
- Two apartments were set up in the city and furnished with mattresses for the button men to sleep on. — Mario Puzo, *The Godfather*, p. 253, 1969
- All they saw were the openings because the Big Board had called in the button men from Sal Roma's territory[.] — Mickey Spillane, *Last Cop Out*, p. 98, 1972
- Pete says to this button-guy with him — Edwin Torres, *Carlito's Way*, p. 23, 1975
- The FBI file on Reilly's desk read him as a middle-echelon button. — Edwin Torres, *Q & A*, p. 35, 1977
- Vincent was arrested twice; and his three capi and about two hundred of his button men, as if they were moving through a revolving turnstile. — Richard Condon, *Prizzi's Honor*, p. 233, 1982
- The buttons had driven over from Las Vegas where they worked as freelance muscle. — Stephen Cannell, *Big Con*, p. 251, 1997

5 a small quantity of an item to be smuggled *US*
- — *American Speech*, p. 97, May 1956: 'Smugglers' argot in the southwest'

6 the edible, psychoactive portion of a peyote cactus *US*
- Peyote is a small cactus and only the top part that appears above the ground is eaten. This is called a button. — William Burroughs, *Junkie*, p. 122, 1953

7 opium *UK*
- — Angela Devlin, *Prison Patter*, p. 32, 1996

8 a tablet of Mandrax™, a branded tranquillizer *SOUTH AFRICA*
- — *Surfrikan Slang*, 2002

9 the clitoris *UK, 1900*
- [T]hose who felt that the ladies should have big bursts but could have them only in that highly localized surface nodule known in the trade as the vestigal phallus, or button, or boy in the boat. — Bernard Wolfe, *The Magic of Their Singing*, p. 93, 1961
- — Dale Gordon, *The Dominion Sex Dictionary*, p. 36, 1967
- — Robert A. Wilson, *Playboy's Book of Forbidden Words*, p. 58, 1972
- — *Maledicta*, p. 131, Summer/Winter 1982: 'Dyke diction: the language of lesbians'

10 the chin *US, 1920*
Boxing jargon, usually in the phrase 'on the button', describing a blow right on the chin.
- — Helen Dahlskog (Editor), *A Dictionary of Contemporary and Colloquial Usage*, p. 11, 1972
- [H]is chin was exposed and presented to me on a plate. BOOF! I whacked him smack on the button. I fucking lifted him. — Dave Courtney, *Stop the Ride I Want to Get Off*, p. 246, 1999

11 in poker, a marker on the table that signifies the dealer; the dealer *UK*
- "Paul is the button." The button acts last and is the most desirable seat[.] — Dave Scharf, *Winning at Poker*, p. 233, 2003

12 a Chrysler car equipped with push-button automatic transmission *US*
- — Lyle K. Engel, *The Complete Book of Fuel and Gas Dragsters*, p. 150, 1968

13 in the television industry, a dramatic or funny climax to a scene *US*
- — Ralph S. Singleton, *Filmaker's Dictionary*, p. 24, 1990

▸ **haven't a button**
to have no money *IRELAND*
- Sure I haven't got a button Stapler[.] — Billy Roche, *The Wexford Trilogy (A Handful of Stars)*, p. 8, 1992

▸ **on the button**
exactly; precisely *US*
Possibly from boxing jargon, 'on the **BUTTON**' (on the chin).
- I shot him right in the forehead [...] I thought – Wow! Right on the fucking button. — Dave Courtney, *Stop the Ride I Want to Get Off*, p. 273, 1999

button *verb*
▸ **button your lips**
to stop talking *US*
- — Marcus Hanna Boulware, *Jive and Slang of Students in Negro Colleges*, 1947

button B *adjective*
very short of money *UK*
From the 1920s until the 60s, in a UK telephone box you would press button B to get your money back, hence this pun on 'pressed for money'.

button-dicked *adjective*
possessing a small penis *US*
- — Michael Dalton Johnson, *Talking Trash with Redd Foxx*, p. 63, 1994

buttoned up *adjective*
1 of a reserved or uncommunicative nature *UK, 1936*
A figurative image.

2 silent, refusing to answer questions *UK, 1959*
In line with the injunction to **BUTTON YOUR LIP**.

3 (of persons) alert, well-prepared *UK*
- — *Bournemouth Evening Echo*, 11th August 1967

4 (of a plan or a situation) successfully organised or well-prepared *UK, 1940*
A variant is 'buttoned'.

button-hole *noun*
a *button-hole* flower; a bouquet *UK, 1879*

buttonhole maker *noun*
a person who has only female children *US*
- — Joseph A. Weingarten, *An American Dictionary of Slang*, p. 52, 1954

button mob *noun*
uniformed police officers, especially in large numbers when present at a political demonstration or similar gathering *UK*
Used by those in whom the police seem interested.
- — David Powis, *The Signs of Crime*, 1977

buttons *noun*
1 a page (a domestic servant) *UK, 1848*
Survives mainly as Buttons, a character in the pantomime of *Cinderella*.
- When he left school he was sent to London to be buttons to the old dear's sister[.] — Charles Raven, *Underworld Nights*, p. 42, 1956

2 a messenger *US*
- — Joseph E. Ragen and Charles Finston, *Inside the World's Toughest Prison*, p. 793, 1962

button up *verb*
to close completely *US, 1941*
- Instead, his comrades killed the North Korean who shot him, and with that the rest of the tanks shot the pass, roaring down the road fully buttoned up and firing wildly as they went. — Robert Leckie, *The Wars of America, Volume II*, p. 340, 1968
- — Carl Fleischhauer, *A Glossary of Army Slang*, p. 7, 1968
- Also, he never learned to button up when he gets him, so if you two can get a good shot at him once, you can hurt him. — *M*A*S*H*, 1970

- The crew then "buttons up" – closes the blast doors and switches to emergency air and power. —Peter Pringle and William Arkin, *S.I.O.P.*, p. 166, 1983
- But for now, why not put everyone on full security alert and have NIS button up your house. —Richard Marcinko and John Weisman, *Rogue Warrior*, p. 306, 1992

button your lip; button your face; button it; button up *verb*
to stop talking *US*
Often as an injunction or exclamation. Used since 1836; and 'button it' first recorded in 1980.
- [Y]ou yerd [heard] – button it – i need to talk to you pair[.] —Patrick Jones, *Unprotected Sex*, p. 250, 1999
- TREVOR: Er... Miami... what do we want with a missile? [...] MIAMI: I want a missile and I'm goin' to get a fuckin' missile. So button it. —Bernard Dempsey and Kevin McNally, *Lock, Stock ... & Two Hundred Smoking Kalashnikovs*, p. 129, 2000

butt out *verb*
to extricate yourself from the interference in which you are engaging *US, 1906*
Generally as an imperative.
- "Oscar, butt out!" her voice was a shriek and her eyes were swimming with tears. —Max Shulman, *Rally Round the Flag, Boys!*, p. 191, 1957
- EDINA: Darling, we are you parents having a civilized conversation. Butt out! —Jennifer Saunders, *Absolutely Fabulous*, p. 37, 1992

butt plant *noun*
a backwards fall while snowboarding *US*
- —Doug Werner, *Snowboarders Start-Up*, p. 111, 1993

butt plate *noun*
used as a friendly if derisive term by the marines to describe the army infantry, and by the army infantry to describe the marines *US*
In the literal sense, a 'butt plate' is the metal or rubber covering of the end of the stock on a rifle.
- —Linda Reinberg, *In the Field*, p. 31, 1991

butt plug *noun*
1 a device that is inserted into the anus during sex, sometimes to retain an enema and sometimes simply for the sensation *US, 1989*
- Even today I still get a major hard-on watching Harry Reems (as 'the Teacher') stick a butt plug slowly into Splevin's hot, willing anus. —Anthony Petkovich, *The X Factory*, p. 8, 1997

2 an offensive, unlikeable person *US, 1993*
- TED: But you said she was a sparkplug? HEALY: I said buttplug. She's heinous. —*Something About Mary*, 1998

buttrose *adjective*
very bad *US*
- —Connie Eble (Editor), *UNC-CH Campus Slang*, p. 2, October 2002

butt slut *noun*
a male homosexual who takes a passive sexual role *US*
- —William K. Bentley and James M. Corbett, *Prison Slang*, p. 58, 1992

butt tuck *noun*
cosmetic surgery reducing and lifting the buttocks *US*
- Big Barb was a regal brunette with the Rolls-Royce of face lifts and butt-tucks. —Dan Jenkins, *Life Its Ownself*, p. 92, 1984
- "Half the girls get boob jobs and butt tucks," Kara Lynn said. —Carl Hiaasen, *Tourist Season*, p. 259, 1986

butt-twitcher *adjective*
revealing the shape of the wearer's buttocks *US*
- So we went and after they gave us our skates, they gave Sally this little butt-twitcher of a dress to wear. —J.D. Salinger, *Catcher in the Rye*, p. 129, 1951

butt ugly *adjective*
very ugly *US, 1986*
- If I want to know the latest slang, if I want to talk about "caps" and "marks" and "icy clothes" and "butt-ugly" boys," I'll have to do it with the Other Emma. —*Los Angeles Times*, p. 5-1, 25th May 1988
- Let me tell you something. Diana Ross is butt ugly to me. —Karen A. Callaghan, *Ideals of Feminine Beauty*, p. 150, 1994

buttwipe *noun*
1 toilet paper *US, 1971*
- —Helen Dahlskog (Editor), *A Dictionary of Contemporary and Colloquial Usage*, p. 12, 1972

2 a despicable or offensive person *US, 1991*
- Freeze, butt-wipe! —Mike Judge and Joe Stillman, *Beavis and Butt-Head Do America*, p. 3, 1997
- That was a New Guinea Peaberry, you Folger's-crystals-slurping buttwipe. —*Ten Things I Hate About You*, 1999

butty *noun*
1 a sandwich *UK, 1855*
Also spelt 'buttie'. Originally used in northern England, especially Liverpool, as a dialect elision of 'buttery'; now widespread, especially as 'jam butty', 'chip butty', etc.
- [C]leaner than the hands outside that grip bacon butties, steering wheels, coins in pocket for train[.] —Mark Powell, *Snap*, p. 5, 2001
- [S]omethin to eat. Pasty or butty or somethin. I'm Lee friggin Marvin [starving]. —Niall Griffiths, *Kelly + Victor*, p. 49, 2002

2 a non-powered, towed canal boat that is part of a working pair *UK, 1944*
Also known as a 'butty boat'.
- —D.J. Smith, *Canal Boats and Boaters*, p. 116, 1973

3 a friend, a workmate; also used as a form of address *UK, 1859*
Variants are 'butt' and 'buttie'. Either from mining where 'butty' was 'a middleman', or from Romany *booty-pal* (a fellow workman), or, most probably, Warwickshire dialect *butty* (a fellow servant or labourer). Modern use may be influenced by **BUDDY**.
- My auld butty John McDermott reminded me recently of a college event we had once helped to organise called 'Poets Against Apartheid'. —Joseph O'Connor, *The Irish Male at Home and Abroad*, p. 44, 1996
- Yo, butt, hand me dat hammer. —Amy and Denise McFadden, *CoalSpeak*, p. 3, 1997
- PIP: right ok butt, sorry about tha' – fuck me —Patrick Jones, *Everything Must Go*, p. 143, 2000
- You can tell all your oppo's butty I'm made of stronger stuff. —Jack Allen, *When the Whistle Blows*, p. 15, 2000
- Fuckin' hell, butt. It's been a while. —John Williams, *Cardiff Dead*, p. 9, 2000

buttyboy *noun*
a friend; a workmate; also used as a form of address *UK: WALES*
An elaboration of **BUTTY**.
- Look, just fuck off will you, buttyboy[.] —James Hawes, *White Powder, Green Light*, p. 190, 2002

butu *noun*
heroin *UK, 1998*
- —Robert Ashton, *This Is Heroin*, p. 205, 2002
- —Mike Haskins, *Drugs*, p. 283, 2003

buturakie *verb*
to jump on a person in order to rob them or beat them up *AUSTRALIA, 1958*
From Fijian *buturaka*, the equivalent of and perhaps playing on **STICK/PUT THE BOOT IN**. Picked up from Fijian sailors on the waterfronts of Sydney and Aukland.

but why?
used humorously with varying meanings *US*
For example, a teacher might ask the class to pass in their homework, whereupon at least one member of the class will mutter, 'But why?'.
- —*American Speech*, p. 275, December 1963: 'American Indian student slang'

buvare *noun*
anything drinkable *UK*
Originally C19 theatrical slang.
- —Paul Baker, *Polari*, p. 167, 2002

buy *noun*
1 a purchase of illicit merchandise, especially drugs *US, 1906*
- [O]ur agents made a number of "buys" of opium at Chinese establishments. —Harry J. Anslinger, *The Murderers*, p. 30, 1961

2 a purchase *AUSTRALIA*
- He fingers the rust patches and peers beneath the bonnet. 'Yeah, top buy. It's in good nick.' —Kathy Lette, *Girls' Night Out*, p. 120, 1987

buy *verb*
1 to gamble on a result higher than the bookmaker's favoured spread *UK*
- The "spread" in spread-betting is a pair of values, usually a point or two apart, which represent the bookmaker's favoured outcome. The investor has two choices: to bet higher, known as "buying", or bet lower, known as "selling". —David Bennet, *Know Your Bets*, p. 107, 2001

2 to accept a fiction as truth *UK*
- He made a few subtle hints when we had that meeting and I bought his line. Didn't see what was coming till he stabbed me in the back. —John Williams, *Cardiff Dead*, p. 235, 2000

3 in poker, to draw a card or cards after the initial deal *US*
- —Albert H. Morehead, *The Complete Guide to Winning Poker*, p. 258, 1967

▸ **buy a homestead**
to be thrown from your horse *CANADA*
- The expression is really a bit of a put-down and reveals the rivalry between ranchers and farmers. [It] implies that if you can't [stay] on a horse, maybe you should give up riding and become a farmer now that you have bought a homestead face first.—Chris Thain, *Cold as a Bay Street Banker's Heart*, p. 30, 1987

▸ **buy a pot**
in poker, to win a hand by betting so excessively as to drive all other players from the hand *US*
- —Richard Jessup, *The Cincinnati Kid*, p. 21, 1963

▸ **buy a pup**
to be the victim of a swindle *UK*
- —Angela Devlin, *Prison Patter*, p. 93, 1996

▸ **buy a suit**
to kill someone *US*
Referring to funeral attire.
- Y'see what I'm saying? Now I gotta either watch my back constantly or buy you a fuckin' suit right now.—Stephen Cannell, *King Con*, p. 25, 1997

▸ **buy an orchard**
in trucking, to drive off the road into trees or brush *US*
- —Montie Tak, *Truck Talk*, p. 24, 1971

▸ **buy some new shoes**
to flee while released from custody on bale *US*
- —Vincent J. Monteleone, *Criminal Slang*, p. 40, 1949

▸ **buy the dick**
to die *US*
- —Eugene Landy, *The Underground Dictionary*, p. 43, 1971

▸ **buy the farm**
to die *US, 1958*
- Whooie! Plenty dinks bought the fuken farm last night.—Larry Heinemann, *Close Quarters*, p. 230, 1977
- He was driving forty-five miles an hour and he bought the farm two miles inside the tunnel.—Richard Price, *Clockers*, p. 288, 1992

▸ **buy the rack**
in horse racing, to bet on every possible combination of winners in a Daily Double bet *US*
- —Dan Parker, *The ABC of Horse Racing*, p. 144, 1947

▸ **buy the ranch**
to die *US*
A primary euphemism used by US soldiers in Vietnam.
- How can I hide my girl's pictures so no NVA ever puts his dirty commie gook hands on them if I buy the ranch?—Charles Anderson, *The Grunts*, p. 136, 1976

▸ **buy you a suit**
to bribe someone *US*
- When someone 'wants to buy you a suit' or 'give you a hat' that means there is a payoff waiting for you if you overlook a violation of law, fail to do your job.—William J. Cavnitz, *One Police Plaza*, p. 81, 1984

buy-and-bust *noun*
a police operation in which an undercover officer buys an illegal drug and then immeidately arrests the seller *US*
- An undercover naroctics detective who minutes before had bought $30 worth of heroin in a buy-and-bust operation in Brooklyn yesterday shot and killed a man who tried to rob him, the police said.—*New York Times*, p. B3, 21st October 2000

buy-down *noun*
a bribe paid to a police officer to release a criminal or to reduce the severity of the charges against him *US*
- You think it's some kinda buy-down? Some bullshit collars-for-dollars scheme?—Stephen J. Cannell, *The Tin Collectors*, p. 174, 2001

buyer *noun*
a gambler who bets on a result higher than the bookmaker's favoured spread *UK*
- Brian is optimistic about Arsenal's chances and decides to be a buyer (bets higher) at £10 per point. Sally, on the other hand, is pessimistic. She is a seller (bets lower), also at £10 per point.—David Bennet, *Know Your Bets*, p. 108, 2001

buy-I *noun*
an East Indian *JAMAICA, 1979*
An English adaptation of the Hindi *Niyabingi* (merchant).
- —Thomas H. Slone, *Rasta is Cuss*, p. 35, 2003

buying-and-selling cord *noun*
a rough measure of wood depending on the bargaining skill of the buyer and seller *CANADA*
When you're buying, it's more; when you're selling, it's less.

buy into *verb*
to involve yourself in something, to believe in something *AUSTRALIA, 1943*
Originally a gambling term, 'to buy into a game'.
- [E]verything started to have that nice fuzzy sort of feel, I soon found it quite easy to buy into.—James Hawes, *Dead Long Enough*, p. 111, 2000
- Women buy into the idea that they have to be perfect[.]—Maggie Balistreri, *The Evasion-English Dictionary*, p. 27, 2003

buy it *verb*
1 to accept an answer or punch-line; especially in the catchphrase that signals resignation: I'll buy it *UK, 1937*

2 to die; to become a casualty *UK, 1920*
World War 1 and 2.
- Perry Chops was a long-dead narcotics pusher who bought it in a five-floor fall from a rooftop[.]—Mickey Spillane, *Last Cop Out*, p. 73, 1972
- By the time I gave it to the meat wagon, the ants had bought it! —Joseph Wambaugh, *Finnegan's Week*, p. 133, 1993

buy money *noun*
the money used to buy contraband *US*
- I will show you my ten grand buy money before you show me the funny money.—Gerald Petievich, *Money Men*, p. 5, 1981

buy-up *noun*
in prison, a purchase of groceries, toiletries, etc, made by prisoners *AUSTRALIA, 1944*
'Buy-ups' are restricted to a certain small amount for each prisoner, often consisting of wages earned for prison work.
- Nothing about the fact that I was signing for my buy-up at the exact time the bashing and escape attempt took place, as I have a screw to prove it.—Ray Denning, *Prison Diaries*, p. 52, 1978
- —Donald Catchlove, *Ray Denning My Life and Time*, p. 10, 1994
- The [activities] centre also ran 'buy-ups', which provided them with the opportunity to place orders for and purchase various goods that weren't on issue.—William Dodson, *The Sharp End*, p. 25, 2001

Buzby *noun*
British Post Office Telephones, subsequently British Telecoms, the authorities controlling the use of citizens' band radio in the UK *UK*
Citizens' band radio slang; the name of the cartoon bird created in the late 1970s to market British Post Office Telephones; in turn a play on **BUZZ** (a telephone call).
- —Peter Chippindale, *The British CB Book*, p. 153, 1981

buzz *noun*
1 a rumour; gossip; news *UK, 1821*
- What's the buzz? Tell me what's happening.—Andrew Lloyd Webber, *What's The Buzz?*, 1971
- Ashore, troops were becoming a little excited by a 'buzz' that a breakout from the bridgehead was imminent.—Robert McGowan and Jeremy Hands, *Don't Cry For Me, Sergeant-Major*, p. 144, 1983
- Did the buzz say how he died?—Anthony Masters, *Minder*, p. 67, 1984
- It's out two days here and there, L.A., the Bay Area, San Diego today, and the buzz is better than expected.—Elmore Leonard, *Be Cool*, p. 335, 1999
- The buzz sweeps around the forecourt that the first City firm has been sighted.—Martin King and Martin Knight, *The Naughty Nineties*, p. 65, 1999
- Because if the buzz is any indication, the movie's gonna make some huge bank.—Kevin Smith, *Jay and Silent Bob Strike Back*, p. 18, 2001

2 an immediate sensation of a drug or alcohol *US, 1849*
- Everybody looked like they'd got in a good buzz. There was liquor all over the place and women.—Hal Ellson, *Duke*, p. 111, 1949
- I don't get strung out on any speed; there's no chemical I need. I like the buzz. I like the rush.—Nicholas Von Hoffman, *We are the People Our Parents Warned Us Against*, p. 151, 1967
- neither the pleasure of shooting up, nor the same buzz as a shot of smack—*Bournemouth Echo*, 28th November 1968
- Cold is nice going down, but I've swilled enough warm, now, so that it don't mean much. A buzz is a buzz.—Larry Heinemann, *Close Quarters*, p. 141, 1977
- [T]he only buzz you could get was a 70p tube of gas.—Shaun Ryder, *Shaun Ryder... in His Own Words*, 1990
- Once he got a buzz, he'd start daydreaming about himself as an inventor, or a sports tycoon.—Richard Price, *Clockers*, p. 379, 1992
- See, that almost destroyed my buzz.—*Clueless*, 1995
- That fucked up my little buzz for a second, I can tell you.—Dave Courtney, *Raving Lunacy*, p. 4, 2000

3 a thrilling sensation *US, 1937*

- —Angela Devlin, *Prison Patter*, p. 32, 1996
- "Love Me Do", was released early in October 1962, and when George [Harrison] heard it on the radio for the first time, it "sent me shivery all over. It was the best buzz of all time." — *Uncut*, p. 43, February 2002

4 a telephone call *US, 1930*

- I'll give you a buzz in the morning, Yvonne. — Philip Wylie, *Opus 21*, p. 106, 1949
- I started toying with the idea, while I kept standing there, of giving old Jane a buzz – I mean calling her long distance at B.M., where she went, instead of calling up her mother to find out when she was coming home. — J.D. Salinger, *Catcher in the Rye*, p. 63, 1951

5 to circulate in a crowded place *UK*

- —David Powis, *The Signs of Crime*, 1977

6 a police car *US*

- —Kenn "Naz" Young, *Naz's Underground Dictionary*, p. 18, 1973

7 x-ray therapy *US*

- —Sally Williams, *"Strong" Words*, p. 135, 1994

buzz *verb*

1 to telephone someone; to summon someone by buzzer *US, 1929*

- One night, when we were drinking in a saloon after a crap game, George buzzed the bartender and asked for the key to the piano in the back room. — Milton Mezzrow, *Really the Blues*, p. 24–25, 1946
- That's why you buzzed me so fast. — Mickey Spillane, *I, The Jury*, p. 10, 1947
- I buzz the attendant and he tells me that he notes the license number of every car he parks[.] — Gerald Petievich, *To Die in Beverly Hills*, p. 229, 1983
- When I got there, I buzzed her for at least five minutes. — Sandra Bernhard, *Confessions of a Pretty Lady*, p. 100, 1988
- She buzzes through and tells Mr. Perrea I'm outside[.] — Robert Campbell, *The Cat's Meow*, p. 147, 1988
- A few days later the guy comes back and this time Tommy's there. She buzzes him, says the guy's here who left the photo." — Elmore Leonard, *Be Cool*, p. 183, 1999

2 to call for someone *US*

- For three or four days I lived on fluids, and I got so raving hungry I was ready to chew on the bedclothes. Finally I buzzed Big Buster, a colored boy who worked in the hospital kitchen, and he took pity on me. — Mezz Mezzrow, *Really the Blues*, p. 38, 1946

3 to leave *UK, 1914*

A variant is 'buzz off'.

- As you see, I am off to a shindig. Late already. So if you don't mind, I'll buzz. — John Burke and Stuart Douglass, *The Boys*, p. 58, 1962
- You got the message, buzz off. — Edwin Torres, *Carlito's Way*, p. 128, 1975
- MANDY: Buzz off! — Monty Python, *Life of Brian*, 1979

4 to kiss someone *US*

- —Lou Shelly, *Hepcats Jive Talk Dictionary*, p. 8, 1945

5 to feel pleasurable sensations resulting from drug use *UK*

- —Angela Devlin, *Prison Patter*, p. 32, 1996
- I was proper buzzing[.] — Dave Courtney, *Raving Lunacy*, p. 4, 2000

6 to engage in solvent abuse *UK: SCOTLAND*

- He just started buzzin because there's nothin else to do round here. — Michael Munro, *The Original Patter*, 1985

7 to pick pockets *UK, 1812*

- —David Powis, *The Signs of Crime*, 1977

8 to snatch a woman's purse *US*

- —Hyman E. Goldin et al., *Dictionary of American Underworld Lingo*, p. 38, 1950

9 to fly very close to an object *US, 1944*

- I am told that Soviet fighter planes are buzzing our air lift. — Philip Wylie, *Opus 21*, p. 146, 1949

10 (used of a computer program or operation) to run without any sign of progress *US*

- — *CoEvolution Quarterly*, p. 27, Spring 1981
- —Guy L. Steele et al., *The Hacker's Dictionary*, p. 39, 1983

11 to activate a remote device unlocking a door *US*

From the buzzing sound the device often makes.

- I'm always afraid of those stores where they have to buzz you in. I'm concerned they won't buzz me in. Then I'll just have to stand there feeling like shit. — Chris Rock, *Rock This!*, p. 11, 1997

12 to anger someone; to alienate someone; to annoy *US*

- It's your brother. I don't want to buzz him, you understand. — Hal Ellson, *The Golden Spike*, p. 30, 1952

13 of music, to become lively and energetic *UK*

- The Geils band really began to buzz after their third number. — *Melody Maker*, 8th July 1972

▸ **be buzzing**

to be happening *US, 1941*

A criminal context.

- —Frank Norman, *Encounter*, 1959

▸ **buzz around the barrel**

to eat a snack *US*

- —Harold Wentorth and Stuart Berg Flexner, *Dictionary of American Slang*, p. 82, 1960

buzzard *noun*

the eagle insignia of a full colonel or the Women's Army Corps *US, 1931*

- An eagle for the cap was also designed, less intricate than the Army eagle and later to be familiarly known to Waacs, for reasons connected with its appearance, as "the buzzard." — Mattie E. Treadwell, *The Women's Army Corps*, p. 39, 1954

buzzard's roost *noun*

1 the office in a railway yard *US*

- —Ramon Adams, *The Language of the Railroader*, p. 25, 1977

2 the highest seats in a cinema balcony *US, 1920*

- We sat upstairs in the buzzard's roost 'cause it only costs a dime[.] — Louise Meriwether, *Daddy Was a Number Runner*, p. 94, 1970

buzz bomb *noun*

a person rendered emotionally unstable due to long incarceration *US*

- —John R. Armore and Joseph D. Wolfe, *Dictionary of Desperation*, p. 23, 1976

buzz boy *noun*

a fighter pilot *US, 1944*

- — *American Speech*, p. 310, December 1946: 'More Air Force slang'

buzzcocks *noun*

people, a general term of address *UK*

An extention of **COCK** (a male-to-male term of address). 'Get a buzz, cock', allegedly the final words of a magazine review for 1970s UK television drama series *Rock Follies*, adopted as the name of Manchester punk band The Buzzcocks. In the mid-1990s BBC television screened a new music panel game that should have been called *Never Mind The Bollocks*, after the Sex Pistols' 1977 album. To avoid causing offence the programme makers substituted 'Buzzcocks' for 'Bollocks' and the programme's continuing success inspired this new, heavily ironic usage which, probably by chance, echoes the original sense.

- Yes, buzzcocks, as the sap rises in ye olde sap-making tree, the sap doth rise in us all[.] — *Sky Magazine*, p. 137, May 2001

buzz-crusher *noun*

anything or anyone who dampens your sense of euphoria *US*

- —Connie Eble (Editor), *UNC-CH Campus Slang*, p. 2, Spring 1988

buzz-cut *noun*

a very short haircut; a person with a very short haircut *US, 1977*

Perhaps from the sound of the electric clippers.

- She looked around, sure there would be a government sedan with two buzz-cuts somewhere nearby watching, but she saw nothing. — Stephen Cannell, *Big Con*, p. 339, 1997
- The men went for Ross Kemp buzzcuts, pastel leisurewear and extensive facial scarring. — Chris Ryan, *The Watchman*, p. 271, 2001

buzzed *adjective*

1 drunk *US, 1952*

- —Judi Sanders, *Don't Dog by Do, Dudel*, p. 5, 1991

2 drug-intoxicated *US, 1972*

From the previous sense.

- STACY is getting more buzed by the minute. He takes a drag from a big, fat joint[.] — *Menace II Society*, 1993
- She be buzzed on somethin' most the time. — Lois Stavsky et al., *A2Z*, p. 16, 1995
- —Mike Haskins, *Drugs*, p. 291, 2003

buzzed up *adjective*

drug-intoxicated *UK*

- We milled around in a buzzed-up but aimless fashion[.] — Diran Abedayo, *My Once Upon A Time*, p. 200, 2000

buzzer *noun*

1 a badge *US, 1914*

- Next time ask to see the buzzer. — Raymond Chandler, *The Little Sister*, p. 19, 1949
- I flashed my buzzer. So did Velda. — Mickey Spillane, *One Lonely Night*, p. 91, 1951

- The one who had flashed the buzzer was of medium height, spare built[.] —Robert Edmond Alter, *Carny Kill*, p. 109, 1966
- Grave Digger fished a felt-lined leather folder from his side coat pocket and showed his buzzer. —Chester Himes, *Come Back Charleston Blue*, p. 19, 1966
- The War of Garry's Badge began when Mayor Alioto's new police commissioners, in the first flush of the power and the glory, issued a bunch of golden buzzers to friends of the new regime. —*San Francisco Examiner*, p. 35, 21st January 1970
- I flashed my buzzer, is all. —Joseph Wambaugh, *Fugitive Nights*, p. 206, 1992

2 a burglar alarm *US*

- —Vincent J. Monteleone, *Criminal Slang*, p. 41, 1949

3 a door-bell *US, 1934*

4 in a hospital casualty department, a defibrillator paddle *US*

- —Sally Williams, *"Strong" Words*, p. 135, 1994

5 in horse racing, a battery-powered device used illegally by a jockey to shock a horse during a race *US, 1942*

- Jockey Gets 'Life' for Using Buzzer [Headline] —*San Francisco News*, p. 19, 26th May 1950
- —David W. Maurer, *Argot of the Racetrack*, p. 17, 1951

buzzing *adjective*

1 drunk *US*

- —Connie Eble (Editor), *UNC-CH Campus Slang*, p. 2, November 2003

2 manic, hyperactive *US*

- —Sally Williams, *"Strong" Words*, p. 135, 1994

buzzing your tits off *adjective*

very drug-intoxicated *UK*

- Not long after they left the airport Alison realised that Stan was buzzing his tits off. —Colin Butts, *Is Harry Still on the Boat?*, p. 295, 2003

buzz job *noun*

the flying of an aircraft low to the ground to impress or scare those on the ground *US, 1943*

- Class was interrupted when a Mosquito night fighter gave us a good buzz job. That is a beautiful aircraft. We got quite a thrill out of it. —Calvin L. Christman et al., *Lost in the Victory*, p. 62, 1998

buzz ticket *noun*

a dole card required to sign-on as unemployed in order to receive benefit *UK*

The dole is seen here as money to be spent on drugs to get a 'buzz' (a pleasurable sensation); the whole puns on 'bus ticket'.

- Finally park up round the pissy corner from the pissy dole office. – Righ' where's me buzz ticket? says Nood steppin' out hands in pockets. —Nick Barlay, *Curvy Lovebox*, p. 82, 1997

buzztrack *noun*

in the television and film industries, a sound track without modulations *US*

- —Oswald Skilbeck, *ABC of Film and TV Working Terms*, p. 22, 1960

buzzword; buzz-phrase *noun*

a currently fashionable word or expression, especially a borrowing from jargon or technology that is used to impress rather than inform and is thus rendered essentially meaningless *US, 1946*

BW *noun*

an obese hospital patient *US*

An abbreviation of **BEACHED WHALE**.

- —Sally Williams, *"Strong" Words*, p. 134, 1994

BW *nickname*

the Black Warriors prison gang *US*

- Borrowing from the AWs, the blacks were now organizing under the name the Black Warriors (BWs). —Bill Valentine, *Gangs and Their Tattoos*, p. 11, 2000

bwai *noun*

a black youth involved in gang culture *UK*

West Indian pronunciation of 'boy'.

- As far as Jigsy was concerned, no "bwai" was going to test Piper Mill and get away with it. —Karline Smith, *Moss Side Massive*, p. 4, 1994

BWOC *noun*

a popular and visible college girl; a *b*ig *w*oman *o*n *c*ampus *US*

- —Marcus Hanna Boulware, *Jive and Slang of Students in Negro Colleges*, 1947

BY *adjective*

(of a telphone line) busy *US*

- EMORY: B.Y. MICHAEL: It's busy? EMORY: Lorraine is probably talking to her mother. —Mart Crowley, *The Boys in the Band*, p. 149, 1968

by

▸ **by here; by there**

here; there *UK: WALES*

A south Walian form probably based on the rhythm or sound of the original Welsh *yma* (here) and *yno* (there).

- "Come over by 'ere a minute" and "That's the one youer looking for – over by there". —John Edwards, *Talk Tidy*, p. 14, 1985

by any means necessary; by whatever means necessary

used as a slogan by the radical political left of the 1960s to reflect a belief that the end justifies the means *US*

- We relate to a phrase coined by Malcom X: 'By any means necessary.' —Tom Wolfe, *Radical Chic & Mau-Mauing the Flak Catchers*, p. 23, 1970
- Those who make a life of seeking power, whether they are members of SDS or the Defense Department, must first establish enemies from whom they will wrest control – and then do it, By Any Means Necessary. —Raymond Mungo, *Famous Long Ago*, p. 51, 1970
- "How do you plan to go about doin' all this?" "By whatever means necessary!" Kwendi answers, jaws clenched. —Odie Hawkins, *Ghetto Sketches*, p. 213, 1972

byce *noun*

▹ **see: BICE**

by Christchurch!

used as an oath *UK, 1984*

A euphemistic avoidance of blasphemy, used in New Zealand (by reference to Christchurch, Canterbury Province) and in the UK (Christchurch, Dorset).

by crikey

used as euphemism for 'by Christ!' *AUSTRALIA, 1901*

- Rufe knew one thing he wouldn't make, by crikey. —Wilda Moxham, *The Apprentice*, p. 115, 1969

by cripes!

used as a euphemism for 'by Christ!' *AUSTRALIA, 1902*

- "By cripes," exclaimed Blue, starting up from the grass. "What have you got there?" —Eve Langley, *The Pea-Pickers*, p. 37, 1958
- 'Hang on to that bit of paper, won't you!' 'By cripes I will!' —Bill Wannan, *Bullockies, Beauts and Bandicoots*, p. 38, 1960

bye-bye; bye-byes *noun*

sleep *UK, 1867*

From an earlier use as a soothing sound used to lull a child to sleep, pehaps from a shortening of 'lullaby'.

bye Felicia!

used for inviting someone to leave *US*

From the film *Friday*.

- —Ben Applebaum and Derrick Pittman, *Turd Ferguson & The Sausage Party*, p. 10, 2004

bye now

goodbye *UK, 1967*

- [She] said the things she always said: "How's tricks?" and "Can't complain" and "Bye now." —Jean Potts, *An Affair of the Heart*, 1970

by George!

used as a mild exclamation or oath *UK, 1598*

Derives from St George, the patron saint of England.

- By George, she's got it! By George, she's got it! —Alan Jay Lerner (after George Bernard Shaw, *The Rain in Spain*, 1956

by George, one of these days I gotta straighten up that closet!

used as a humorous commentary on a cluttered mess *US*

A signature line from the comedy *Fibber McGree and Moll* (radio 1935–1957, television 1959–1960). Repeated with referential humour.

by golly!

used as a euphemism for 'by God!' *US, 1833*

- Betcha by golly, wow / You're the one that I've been waiting for forever —The Stylistics, *Betcha By Golly Wow*, 1971
- By golly, it's clean clear to Flagtown. —C.W. McCall, *Convoy*, 1976

by guess and by gosh *adjective*
without planning, relying on serendipity *US, 1914*
- Success in tacical field communications, Tully believed, was apt to be a "by guess and by gosh" proposition, amid the genreal lack of advanced information. —George Raynor Thompson, *The Singal Corps*, p. 384, 1957

by gum!
used euphemistically for 'by God' *UK*
Northern English usage.
- By Gum – it's going to pour down. —John O'Toole, *The Bush and the Tree*, p. 26, 1960

by heck!
used as an exclamation of surprise, indignation, etc; also as a means of stressing what follows *US, 1922*
Northern English usage.
- By heck, Saltaire mill and its surrounding "model" workers' village rank with the Pyramids and Angkor Wat. — *The Guardian*, 13th September 2003

by himself in the box
used as a stock answer to describe a racehorse's lineage if it is either unknown or none of the asker's business *AUSTRALIA*
- —Ned Wallish, *The Truth Dictionary of Racing Slang*, p. 11, 1989

by hokey!
used for expressing great surprise *NEW ZEALAND*
- 'It's good to be back' screamed an enthusiastic Julia Deans, and by hokey it was good to have her back. —*Evening Post*, p. 17, 29th October 2001

by jumbo!
used as a substitute for an oath *US*
- 'You've got to look ahead in this man's game,' he emphasized at the first conference, 'or by jumbo you're up crap creek without a paddle!' —Terry Southern, *The Magic Christian*, p. 50, 1959

by me
in poker, used for expressing a player's decision not to bet *US*
- —George Percy, *The Language of Poker*, p. 16, 1988

BYO
a request that guests '*b*ring *y*our *o*wn' *US*
- — *Current Slang*, p. 13, Fall 1968
- It will commence with a BYO lunch, with gas barbecues available and plenty of off-street parking. — *Messenger*, p. 2, 1st May 1991

BYOB
used in invitations as an admonition to *b*ring *y*our *o*wn *b*ooze or *b*ottle *US*
- —Collin Baker et al., *College Undergraduate Slang Study Conducted at Brown University*, p. 73, 1968

BYOG
an invitation to *b*ring *y*our *o*wn *g*rog to a party *NEW ZEALAND*
- The invitation probaby said BYOG (bring your own grog) and 'Ladies plate.' —Ronald Johnston, *New Zealanders*, p. 150, 1976

byplay *noun*
a device on a dishonest carnival game that can be activated to let players win *US*
- — *American Speech*, p. 235, October 1950: 'The argot of outdoor boob traps'

bysie-bye
goodbye *UK, 1984*
An elaboration of 'bye'.

by the centre!; by the left!
used as an emphatic register of shock, surprise, etc *UK*
Adopted, originally by the military, from military drill commands.
- "By the centre," Bayfield said. "That's an angle, sir." —Alan Hunter, *Gently at a Gallop*, 1971

by the holy old dynamiting Jesus!
used as an extreme oath in Nova Scotia *CANADA*
- These were curse-word combinations I'd never heard before: by the holy old dynamiting Jesus. —Harry Bruce, *Down Home*, p. 106–107, 1988

by the holy old twist
used as an oath *CANADA*
Many Nova Scotia oaths refer to Christ and go back to the Elizabethan style of sacrilegious, elaborate expressions, e.g. the twisted body on the cross echoes 'sblood' (God's blood) and 'sbody' (God's body).
- I might not be sharp enough to tell what county, cove, or valley he'd come from, but by the holy old twist, I'd surely know he was from somewhere Down Home. —Harry Bruce, *Down Home*, p. 106, 1988

by-the-hour hotel; by-the-hour motel *noun*
a motel or hotel used by prostitutes where it is possible to rent a room in short increments *US*
- —Jay Robert Nash, *Dictionary of Crime*, p. 53, 1992

by the lord liftin' Jesus!
one of many elaborate Nova Scotian sacrilegious oaths *CANADA*
- In my freshman year at Mount Allison, the thing that amazed and bewildered me was the rhythm, imagination, and humour of the blasphemy that shot from the lips of certain male students who were not studying theology – e.g. by the lord liftin' Jesus. —Harry Bruce, *Down Home*, p. 106–107, 1988

by the rattly-eyed Jesus!
in Nova Scotia, used as an oath *CANADA*
- "By the rattly-eyed Jesus" is an oath heard in Shelburne County, Nova Scotia. —Lewis Poteet, *The South Shore Phrase Book*, p. 91, 1999

by whatever means necessary
▷ see: BY ANY MEANS NECESSARY

Cc

C *noun*

1 the Viet Cong; a member of the Viet Cong *US*

- Vietnamese Communists, we call then Vietcong, we call them VC and C and Charlie and all the usual names[.] —William Wilson, *The LBJ Brigade*, p. 31, 1966

2 cocaine *US, 1921*

- The guy and the girl are both plenty loaded with C and feeling high. —William J. Spillard and Pence James, *Needle in a Haystack*, p. 74, 1945
- I'd smoke pot, shook H and C, and get a broad and eat her alive. —Hal Ellson, *The Golden Spike*, p. 113, 1952
- He was a junkie for sure. He would know where to cop "C," and probably gangster for the runt. —Iceberg Slim (Robert Beck), *Pimp*, p. 126, 1969
- When the "C" hit us we started to rapping. —A.S. Jackson, *Gentleman Pimp*, p. 162, 1973
- Two hundred of C, hundred of the other. —*Traffic*, 2000

3 amphetamines *UK*

Heard as 'the C'.

- —Mike Haskins, *Drugs*, p. 279, 2003

4 methcathinone *US*

Heard as 'the C'.

- —Office of National Drug Control Policy, *Drug Facts*, February 2003

5 a woman viewed as a sexual object *US*

An abbreviation of **CUNT**.

- —Harold Wentworth and Stuart Berg Flexner, *Dictionary of American Slang*, p. 6, 1976

6 a CBE (Commander of the Order of the British Empire) *UK, 1961*

Civil servant usage; suggestive of a casual familiarity with the honour.

7 contraception *US*

Interview with Jim Holliday, 12th June 1997.

8 one hundred dollars *US, 1839*

- The two C's got him. —Mickey Spillane, *Kiss Me Deadly*, p. 78, 1952
- I rolled her for a C, man —John Rechy, *City of Night*, p. 140, 1963
- A fin for a number-five cap. A sixteenth for a 'C." A piece for a grand. —Iceberg Slim (Robert Beck), *Pimp*, p. 128, 1969

9 in poker, the third player to the left of the dealer *US*

- —George Percy, *The Language of Poker*, p. 16, 1988

10 the commission charged by a bookmaker *US*

- —Harold Wentworth and Stuart Berg Flexner, *Dictionary of American Slang*, p. 83, 1960

C-47 *noun*

a clothes peg *US*

Used by television and film crews, mocking the formality of the official jargon of their craft.

cab *noun*

▸ take a cab

to die *US*

- [H]is character suffers such a vicious beating that, as they say in New York, he took a cab. That is Big Apple street slang for saying that a person has breathed his last. —*San Diego Union-Tribune*, p. E10, 8th September 2000

caballo *noun*

1 heroin *US*

Spanish for 'horse'.

- —Richard Horman and Allan Fox, *Drug Awareness*, p. 464, 1970
- —Robert Ashton, *This Is Heroin*, p. 205, 2002

2 a person who smuggles drugs into a prison *US*

Spanish for 'horse', which is almost a **MULE**.

- —Jay Robert Nash, *Dictionary of Crime*, p. 54, 1992

cabaret *verb*

1 to lie in bed masturbating *US*

- You better knock off reading that hot stuff and going carbareting or you'll wind up bugged —Hyman E. Goldin et al., *Dictionary of American Underworld Lingo*, p. 39, 1950

2 to use an addictive drug in a semi-controlled pattern *US*

- Only he and Extra Black Johnson could cabaret – have their morning and evening fix and then take some whenever they felt like taking off and really getting charged up. —Willard Motley, *Let No Man Write My Epitaph*, p. 119, 1958

cabbage *noun*

1 money *US, 1903*

- Claims he's a human juke box and can lead the rats away if he jives the right tune which he'll do if the top squatters will put up the cabbage. — Haenigsen, *Jive's Like That*, 1947
- [H]e spent the winters in Miami and dropped a wad of cabbage at the tables there. —Mickey Spillane, *Kiss Me Deadly*, p. 114, 1952
- [A] little bit of green cabbage sprinkled delicately from his expensively tailored pocket would do the trick[.] —Morton Cooper, *High School Confidential*, p. 36, 1958
- On seeing me, he had said, Look, kid, ya gotta make the cabbage before you can carry the torch. —Clancy Sigal, *Going Away*, p. 433, 1961
- If we don't draw fans, we're not going to be making the old cabbage. —Jim Bouton, *Ball Four*, p. 267, 1970
- Made a little cabbage on the Tommy Bell fight too. —*Raging Bull*, 1980
- The main one [complaint] was about the squadron sergeant major and something to do with "cabbage". It took me a while to find out that this meant money. —Andy McNab (writing of the late 1970s/early 80s), *Immediate Action*, p. 193, 1995

2 the vagina *US*

Perhaps from the image of leaves peeling back.

- —Dale Gordon, *The Dominion Sex Dictionary*, p. 39, 1967
- —*Maledicta*, p. 131, Summer/Winter 1982: 'Dyke diction: the language of lesbians'

3 low grade marijuana *NEW ZEALAND*

From the quality of the leaves.

4 a coronary artery bypass graft *US*

A loose pronunciation of the acronym CABG.

- —Sally Williams, *"Strong" Words*, p. 136, 1994

cabbage *verb*

1 to become vegetable-like *UK*

- [A]ll the stink of all them miserable, unwashed, unproud bodies cabbaging on smack [heroin] for day after day after day. —Kevin Sampson, *Outlaws*, p. 77, 2001

2 to smoke marijuana, especially low grade marijuana *NEW ZEALAND*

- —David McGill, *David McGill's Complete Kiwi Slang Dictionary*, p. 25, 1998

cabbage *adjective*

poor-quality *NEW ZEALAND*

- The first significant thefts of chemical solvents were reported as growers started processing low-grade bulk 'cabbage' cannabis leaf into cannabis oil. —*New Zealand Green*, p. 1559, 1990

cabbage cutter *noun*

on the railways, a freight engine *US*

- —Ramon Adams, *The Language of the Railroader*, p. 26, 1977

cabbaged *adjective*

1 mentally and physically exhausted *UK*

Punning on 'a vegetative state'.

- Took me three weeks to recover [from an overdose and heart attack]. I couldn't even move the side of me body. Totally cabbaged. —Shaun Ryder, *Shaun Ryder... in His Own Words*, 1992
- Groups of people are ploddin along without words, absolutely cabbaged, or swayin an singin on corners[.] —Niall Griffiths, *Kelly + Victor*, p. 174, 2002

2 under the influence of MDMA, the recreational drug best known as ecstasy *UK*

- A minority get "cabbaged" by taking between three and six tablets – a process known as "stacking." — *The Independent*, p. 5, 28th December 1991
- Ecstasy (a combination of mescaline and amphetamine) and LSD were a big help in reaching hte ultimate state of "getting cabbaged." — *The Commercial Appeal (Memphis)*, p. 1C, 10th June 1994

3 drunk *UK*

- — *e-cyclopaedia*, 20th March 2002

cabbage-eater *noun*

a German or Russian immigrant *US, 1942*
Offensive.

- He did not live there, for the apartment was kept by Israel Amter, the cabbage-eater, and his wife. — Bejamin Gitlow, *The Whole of Their Lives*, p. 111, 1948
- — Irving Lewis Allen, *The Language of Ethnic Conflict*, p. 66, 1983

cabbage hat *noun*

a Royal Marine *UK*
After the uniform green beret.

- — Christopher Hawke, *For Campaign Service*, 1979

cabbage out *verb*

to relax *NEW ZEALAND*

- When Cullen was home 'cabbaging out' he was 'just another guy' in the village. — *Dominion Post*, p. 1, 17th July 2003

cabbage patch *noun*

a remote, insignificant place *US, 1862*

- — Frederic G. Cassidy, *Dictionary of American Regional English, Volume 1*, p. 499, 1985

cabbage patch *nickname*

1 the state of Victoria, Australia *AUSTRALIA, 1882*
Also referred to as 'cabbage garden' and 'the cabbage state'. Hence, a native may be a 'cabbage patcher', 'cabbage gardener' or 'cabbage stater'.

- — Sidney J. Baker, *The Australian Language*, 1966

2 Kingston prison in Portsmouth *UK*

- — Angela Devlin, *Prison Patter*, p. 33, 1996

Cabbagetown *nickname*

a mixed residential and business area near downtown in Toronto *CANADA, 1958*
This term was likely derived from the days when poor people lived downtown and presumably could only afford to eat cabbage.

- In a Cabbage Town tavern brawl, on a Saturday night, speed is important. — *Liberty*, p. 70, 1st January 1958
- Studio execs eventually agreed that the film's credibility and viability would be damaged by shooting Cabbage Town for Brooklyn and Bay Street for Wall Street, so the film will spend its entire shoot in New York City. — *Daily Variety*, p. A1, 12th April 2002

cabby; cabbie *verb*

to drive a motor vehicle; to be driven *UK, 1974*
Army use.

cabello *noun*

cocaine

- — Mike Haskins, *Drugs*, p. 280, 2003

cabez *noun*

intelligence *TRINIDAD AND TOBAGO, 1956*
From the Spanish *cabeza* (head).

- — Lise Winer, *Dictionary of the English/Creole of Trinidad & Tobago*, 2003

cab freight *noun*

an attractive woman passenger in a truck *US*

- — *American Speech*, p. 273, December 1961: 'Northwest truck drivers' language'

cabin car *noun*

a brakevan (caboose) *US*

- — Ramon Adams, *The Language of the Railroader*, p. 26, 1977

cabin stabbing *noun*

(from a male perspective) an act of conventional sexual intercourse *JAMAICA*
As in the title of the 1990 song 'Cabin Stabbing' by Super Cat (William Maraugh).

- Real Rasta man to come / And sprinkle di lawn / And give her di cabin stabbing dem / From evenings to dawn. — Damien Marley, *MiBrenda*, 2001

cab joint *noun*

a brothel whose customers are spotted and transported by taxi drivers *US, 1930*

- — *Maledicta*, p. 149, Summer/Winter 1986–1987: 'Sexual slang: prostitutes, pedophiles flagellators, transvestites, and necrophiles'

cabled *adjective*

(of a vehicle) equipped with a winch *US*
Collected by John Thompson of Hendersonville, North Carolina, 2004.

cábóg *noun*

an ignorant male; a rustic clodhopper *IRELAND*

- He had a right go at the then Minister for Agriculture, Dr Ryan and protested lovelly that he was not going to take being called a cábóg by anyone — *Munster Express*, 5th November 2004

caboodle *noun*

all of something *US, 1848*

- It wasn't the money, mind you – he was dead set against the whole caboodle. — Frederick Kohner, *Gidget*, p. 23, 1957
- I left the whole caboodle under a bench in Washington Square. — Mary McCarthy, *The Group*, p. 174, 1963

caboose *noun*

1 the buttocks *US, 1919*

- He cussed her as he drove his needle-toed shoe into her wide caboose several times. — Icerberg Slim (Robert Beck), *Pimp*, p. 168, 1969
- Kitty bemoaned, "She's got a sexy caboose." — Seth Morgan, *Homeboy*, p. 135, 1990

2 the final participant in serial sex *US*
From the phrase **PULL A TRAIN** used to describe the practice.

- — *Current Slang*, p. 14, Spring 1970

3 the youngest child in a family *US, 1969*

- — Frederic G. Cassidy, *Dictionary of American Regional English, Volume 1*, p. 502, 1985

4 a jail *US, 1865*

- — J.E. Lighter, *Historical Dictoinary of American Slang, Volume 1*, p. 344, 1994

5 a small house or shack *TRINIDAD AND TOBAGO, 1956*

- — Lise Winer, *Dictionary of the English/Creole of Trinidad & Tobago*, 2003

6 a cooking shed *CAYMAN ISLANDS*

- — Aarona Booker Kohlman, *Wotcha Say*, p. 25, 1985

caboose bounce *noun*

a train consisting of nothing more than an engine and a brakevan (caboose) *US, 1929*

- — James Marshall, *Santa Fe, the Railraod that Built an Empire*, p. 363, 1945

cabouche *noun*

▷ **see: BAROUCHE**

cabron *noun*

a guy, especially a brutish or dim-witted one *US*
Border Spanish used in English conversation by Mexican-Americans.

- — Dagoberto Fuentes and Jose Lopez, *Barrio Language Dictionary*, p. 23, 1974

cab sav *noun*

cabernet sauvignon wine *AUSTRALIA*

- The new design is seen on the 1988 Yellow Label cab sav-shiraz blend and the '86 classic Brown Label shiraz. — *News*, p. 90, 3rd July 1990
- Under the circumstances, we'd just as soon take it home and open a bottle of cheap Chilean cab sav, perhaps Santa Rita 120. — *Arkansas Democrat-Gazette*, 21st October 1994

ca-ca *noun*

1 excrement *US, 1952*
Probably from Spanish children's speech; used by non-Spanish speakers. Sometimes seen spelt as 'kaka' or other such variations.

- All right, he made a kahkah, call a policeman. — Lenny Bruce, *How to Talk Dirty and Influence People*, p. 123, 1965
- BLEEK: Midget, you're doing a doo-doo job. You're fucking up. It's shit. Ca-ca. — *Mo' Better Blues*, 1990

2 nonsense *US, 1980*

- It was nothing but pure caca far as I could tell – boring isn't a good enough word. — Arturo Islas, *La Mollie and the King of Tears*, p. 20, 1996

3 marijuana, especially if poor quality, adulterated or fake *US, 1969*

4 heroin, especially low quality heroin *US*

- — Richard A. Spears, *The Slang and Jargon of Drugs and Drink*, p. 90, 1986

- —Gilda and Melvin Berger, *Drug Abuse A-Z*, p. 40, 1990
- —Robert Ashton, *This Is Heroin*, p. 205, 2002

5 drugs, not necessarily heroin *US*
- — *Gang Intelligence Manual*, p. 40, 1995

caca-hole *noun*
the anus *TRINIDAD AND TOBAGO*
- —Lise Winer, *Dictionary of the English/Creole of Trinidad & Tobago*, 2003

cack; cak; kack *noun*
1 excrement *AUSTRALIA*
- Go and dip your left eye in hot cocky cack.— *The Adventures of Barry McKenzie*, 1972
- What happens when this cack gets out of the harbour and onto the beaches?—Tim Winton, *Lockie Leonard*, p. 128, 1993
- I walk across a patch of grass watchin' for dog cak[.]—Nick Barlay, *Curvy Lovebox*, p. 174, 1997

2 rubbish, nonsnese *UK*
- [T]he cack we talk, the daft shit we do.—Shaun Ryder, *Shaun Ryder... in His Own Words*, 1997
- "The shite we throw away is more tuneful than all that sampled cack Helmet's fucking with..." "Maybe people like sampled cack. Maybe Cindy Hogan's a secret cack fanatic..."—Kevin Sampson, *Powder*, p. 122, 1999

3 someone or something extremely funny *AUSTRALIA*
- I was just reading No. 290, Battyman was a cack.— *Mad*, p. 3, 1989

cack; cak; kack *verb*
1 to fall asleep *US, 1959*
- —Robert George Reisner, *The Jazz Titans*, p. 153, 1960
- —Robert S. Gold, *A Jazz Lexicon*, p. 46, 1964

2 to defecate *UK, 1436*
Like many other words for bodily functions, 'cack' was part of everyday conventional speech for many years before slipping into impolite usage in the late C19.
- The cunt's caked his fucking pants. Fucking stinks.—Stephen Fry, *Revenge*, p. 91, 2000

▸cack your dacks
1 to lose control of your bowels *AUSTRALIA*
- If anything it looked as funny as buggery. Fair dinks, I just about kacked my dacks when I saw it.—Roy Slaven (John Doyle), *Five South Coast Seasons*, p. 148, 1992

2 to become scared *AUSTRALIA*
- Naturally enough I thought he was just kacking his dacks a bit because it was me hopping in – being police and whatnot, a lot of people do that[.]—Roy Slaven (John Doyle), *Five South Coast Seasons*, p. 158, 1992

▸cack yourself
1 to be terrified *UK*
Literally 'to shit yourself'; used figuratively (most of the time), often as an exaggeration.
- The bloke, clocking the size of Ally [...], cacks himself. He drops the plank and runs off.— Martin King and Martin Knight, *The Naughty Nineties*, p. 39, 2000

2 to laugh uncontrollably *AUSTRALIA*
A variant is 'cack yourself laughing'.
- On the other hand, these are also the kind of people who don't cack themselves when they see someone slip on dog poo.— *Sydney Morning Herald (Guide)*, p. 13, 18th May 1987
- —Roy Slaven (John Doyle), *Five South Coast Seasons*, p. 148, 1992
- But when I told the class during big lunch they all cacked themselves laughing.—Hugh Lunn, *Fred & Olive's Blessed Lino*, p. 18, 1993

cack; kack *adjective*
contemptible, unpleasant, inferior *UK*
Variant spellings abound – 'cak', 'kak', etc.
- We've had a lot of ketamine victims but that is largely through kak Es.—Macfarlane, Macfarlane and Robson, *The User*, p. 139, 1996
- They wanna know why the take is so cak[.]—Nick Barlay, *Curvy Lovebox*, p. 125, 1997

cackersarnie *noun*
the condition that exists when someone pulls your trousers or underpants forcefully upward, forming a wedge between buttock cheeks; the act of putting someone in that position *UK*
Mainly used by schoolboys. From **CACK** (excrement, faeces) and **SARNIE** (sandwich).
- —Chris Lewis, *The Dictionary of Playground Slang*, p. 49, 2003

cack-handed *adjective*
left-handed; clumsy *UK, 1854*
- That's more than any of you cack-handed bastards could do.—Robert S. Close, *With Hooves of Brass*, p. 117, 1961
- —Sonya Plowman, *Great Kiwi Slang*, p. 43, 2002
- It's a sign that they are frustrated at the cack-handed American occupation and want them to get on with the transition.— *The Independent*, p. 31, 14th April 2004

cackies *noun*
trousers, especially khakis *US*
- So I then go into my Mack Daddy mode cause I'm getting a woodie in my cackies y'know.— *Boyz N The Hood*, 1990

cack it *verb*
to be very nervous or worried; to feel thoroughly frightened *UK*
A variation of **SHIT IT**.
- I mean we were fookin' jibberin' at each other, both absolutely cackin' it.—Ben Elton, *High Society*, p. 313, 2002

cackle *verb*
1 to chatter; to talk inconsequentially *UK, 1530*
- [C]ome on lads, we might as well nip down the pub and leave the cackling to the women.—Mark Steel, *Reasons to be Cheerful*, p. 165, 2001

2 to confess and/or to inform on others *US*
- —Vincent J. Monteleone, *Criminal Slang*, p. 41, 1949

3 as part of a controlled roll of dice, to give them the appearance and sound of being shaken while actually preventing their turning *US*
- —John S. Salak, *Dictionary of Gambling*, p. 37, 1963

cackle crate *noun*
in trucking, a truck hauling chickens *US*
- —Mary Elting, *Trucks at Work*, 1946

cackle factory *noun*
a mental hospital *US, 1950*
- —J.E. Lighter, *Historical Dictoinary of American Slang, Volume 1*, p. 345, 1994

cacky *noun*
1 a yellowish-brown colour *UK, 1984*
From the adjective sense (shitty), giving a joke at the expense of 'khaki'.

2 human excrement *UK, 1961*
Childish.

cacky *adjective*
1 covered with excrement; hence filthy, malodorous *UK, 1937*
- Not bloody likely! Spend my life wiping snotty noses and cacky bums?—Colleen McCullough, *The Thorn Birds*, p. 403, 1977

2 in the language of striptease, overtly if not excessively sexual *US*
- —Don Wilmeth, *The Language of American Popular Entertainment*, p. 41, 1981

cacto *noun*
the moth *Cactoblastis cactorum*, a successful biological control of introduced prickly pear *AUSTRALIA, 1941*

cactus *noun*
in hospital usage, a severely burnt patient *US*
- —Sally Williams, *"Strong" Words*, p. 136, 1994

▸in the cactus
in trouble, especially with one person *NEW ZEALAND*
- Rather funny you being in the cactus at home – I'm in the dog box with my wife too.— *(Wellington) Evening Post*, p. 12, 9th March 1953

▸out in the cactus
in a very remote area *NEW ZEALAND*
- 'Out in the sticks', 'out in the backblock', 'out in the bush, 'out in the booay', 'out in the cactus', all have the same basic meaning of 'fifty miles from nowhere.'—R.L. Bacon, *In the Sticks*, p. 184, 1963

cactus *adjective*
ruined, wrecked *AUSTRALIA, 1945*
- Nine operations later his leg is just about cactus, the bone got infected, and they still haven't got it all.—Paul Vautin, *Turn It Up!*, p. 207, 1995
- —Shane Maloney, *Nice Try*, p. 21, 1998

cactus juice *noun*
tequila; mescal *US, 1971*
- If tequila spin-doctors can transform cactus juice into snob central, why not gin? — *Riverfront Times (St. Louis)*, 21st January 2004

cad *noun*
1 an ill-bred, ill-mannered lout *UK, 1827*
- TRICIA: What happened was pretty obvious, I should have thought. MAURICE: Yessir, you behaved like a cad. — Peter Nichols, *Promenade [Six Granada Plays]*, p. 71, 1959
- [T]hat language! Is it eating Spam for breakfast that makes them sound as though they're trying to clear a huge wad of phlegm from their throats, or is it the immortal tongue of Goethe and Nietzsche? Whatever – what a swine. — *The Guardian*, 22nd September 2001
- — *James Hewitt: Confessions of a Cad*, 24th July 2003

2 *cad*mium *UK*
- — Wilbur Smith, *Hungry as the Sea*, 1978

3 one ounce of marijuana *US*
A confusion with CAN expanded to CADILLAC.

4 a railway conductor *US*
- — Ramon Adams, *The Language of the Railroader*, p. 27, 1977

Cad *noun*
a Cadillac car *US, 1929*
- They got the Cad turned around. — Thurston Scott, *Cure it with Honey*, p. 41, 1951
- I knew the car wasn't a Cadillac. Hell, what would a guy like me do with a Cad? — Jim Thompson, *The Nothing Man*, p. 162, 1953
- Bill Wilson's yellow Cad made the corner at Western and Pacific Coast Highway, below Rolling Hills Estates. — Joseph Nazel, *Black Cop*, p. 51, 1974
- — John Edwards, *Auto Dictionary*, p. 23, 1993

cadaver cadet *noun*
a necrophile *US*
- — *Maledicta*, p. 178, Summer/Winter 1986–1987: 'Sexual slang: prostitutes, pedophiles, flagellators, transvestites, and necrophiles'

cadbury *noun*
a person who gets drunk on very little alcohol *AUSTRALIA, 1996*
Referring to the advertising slogan of Cadbury Dairy Milk chocolate, which has '*a glass and a half* of full cream milk'.
- She is such a Cadbury, she threw up after only 1 drink. — *Wordmap (www.abc.net.au/wordmap)*, 2003

caddie shack *noun*
any small building where gold caddies congregate and wait for work *US*
- Later in the day, when the jobs were being passed out, you would engage in profane and bloody struggle behind the caddie shack. — Jim Thompson, *Bad Boy*, p. 341, 1953

Caddy; Caddie *noun*
a Cadillac car *US, 1929*
- It was a late model Caddy, about a '41. — Mickey Spillane, *I, The Jury*, p. 83, 1947
- Mom needed the stationwagon, having planned for months to attend her annual bridge tournament in Boston, and that left the Caddy[.] — Robert Gover, *One Hundred Dollar Misunderstanding*, p. 8, 1961
- There were two carloads of thugs following Wilson's Caddie. — Joseph Nazel, *Black Cop*, p. 193, 1974
- Viceroy Wilson adjusted his Carrera sunglasses, lit up a joint, jacked up the a/c, and mellowed out behind the Caddy's blue-tinted windows — Carl Hiaasen, *Tourist Season*, p. 58, 1986
- He said, "I had a Caddy myself one time, till I sold it for parts and went to work at Disney's." — Elmore Leonard, *Riding the Rap*, p. 3, 1995

caddy *adjective*
sharp, stylish, fashionable *US*
- — Connie Eble (Editor), *UNC-CH Campus Slang*, p. 2, Fall 1984

caddy blackjack *noun*
a private game of blackjack *US, 1981*
- — Michael Dalton, *Blackjack*, p. 35, 1991

caddy-old-punch *noun*
an improvised, brown-paper kite *GUYANA*
- — Richard Allsopp, *Dictionary of Caribbean English Usage*, p. 129, 1996

cadet *noun*
1 a pimp *US, 1904*
- — Hyman E. Goldin et al., *Dictionary of American Underworld Lingo*, p. 39, 1950

2 a new drug user *US*
- — Vincent J. Monteleone, *Criminal Slang*, p. 41, 1949

cadge *verb*
to beg; to wheedle something from someone *US, 1812*
- Joe told him he only needed to find Rooski this morning, who often cadged Demerols from Hymie's migraine script. — Seth Morgan, *Homeboy*, p. 59, 1990
- I thought better of cadging a go off him in his state. — Dean Cavanagh, *Mile High Meltdown (Disco Biscuits)*, p. 213, 1996

cadger *noun*
a beggar; a scrounger *UK, 1851*

cadie; caddy; caddie *noun*
a hat; originally a bush name for a slouch hat *AUSTRALIA, 1898*
English gypsy use.
- — Jimmy Stockin, *On The Cobbles*, p. 9, 2000

cadillac *noun*
1 cocaine *US, 1953*
- "Are the Marmon and Cadillac working tonight?" "Yeah." "That Marmon's an eight, isn't it? And Cadillac's a twelve?" — William J. Spillard and Pence James, *Needle in a Haystack*, p. 145, 1945
- — Richard A. Spears, *The Slang and Jargon of Drugs and Drink*, p. 91, 1986
- — Mike Haskins, *Drugs*, p. 280, 2003

2 one ounce of a powdered drug *US*
- — Hyman E. Goldin et al., *Dictionary of American Underworld Lingo*, p. 39, 1950

3 phencyclidine, the recreational drug known as PCP or angel dust *US*
- — US Department of Justice, *Street Terms*, October 1994

4 a cup of coffee with cream and sugar *US*
- — James Harris, *A Convict's Dictionary*, p. 29, 1989

5 a note-and-string based method of communication in prison *US*
- [O]r using a cadillac [a line with the attached message and a wieght that is whipped down the tier along the floor from one cell to another.] — Bill Valentine, *Gangs and Their Tattoos*, p. 38, 2000

6 the maximum amount which may be spent at a prison canteen *US*
- — James Harris, *A Convict's Dictionary*, p. 29, 1989

7 in the language of the homeless, a shopping cart *US*
- — Jim Crotty, *How to Talk American*, p. 262, 1997

8 the US Army M-1 tank *US*
- The generic nickname for the Army's M-1 Abrams tank is Cadillac. But most tankers give their own tank a name, too. — *Houston Chronicle*, p. 7A, 20th January 1991

9 a large surfboard used for big-wave conditions *US*
- — D.S. Halacy, *Surfer!*, p. 215, 1965

Cadillac bunk *noun*
a single prison bed in a setting where most beds are two-tiered bunk beds *US*
- — James Harris, *A Convict's Dictionary*, p. 29, 1989

cadillac express *noun*
the drug methcathinone *US, 1998*
- — Office of National Drug Control Policy, *Drug Facts*, February 2003

Cadillac pusher *noun*
a person whose job it is to push carts with garments through the streets *US*
- They used to call us "Cadillac Pushers," street slang for people who pushed those old, wooden box carts loaded down with piece goods through the heavy traffic of Seventh Avenue. — *Newday (New York)*, p. A34, 3rd April 2002

café au lait *noun*
a person of mixed race with skin the shade of milky coffee *UK, 1961*

caff *noun*
a café *UK, 1931*
- [I]ts denizens were followed into their caffs by ardent visitors[.] — Geoffrey Fletcher, *Down Among the Meths Men*, p. 10, 1966
- Henry lunches with the lads, in a resaurant, pub or a specially treasured working-class caff[.] — Ann Barr and Peter York, *The Official Sloane Ranger Handbook*, p. 117, 1982
- You thought it [the Taj Mahal] was a caff in the Commercial Road. — Anthony Masters, *Minder*, p. 117, 1984

• They were quite unconcerned that here [Amsterdam] was a caff peddling marijuana. —Jonathan Gash, *The Ten Word Game*, p. 82, 2003

caffuffle *noun*
chaos, confusion *BARBADOS, 1975*
• —Richard Allsopp, *Dictionary of Caribbean English Usage*, p. 129, 1996

caffuffle *verb*
to confuse someone or something *BARBADOS*
• —Frank A. Collymore, *Barbadian Dialect*, p. 25, 1965

cage *noun*
1 an elevator *US, 1938*
• —J.E. Lighter, *Historical Dictoinary of American Slang, Volume 1*, p. 346, 1994
2 a brakevan (caboose) *US, 1931*
• —Norman Carlisle, *The Modern Wonder Book of Trains and Railroading*, p. 260, 1946
3 an abandoned house *US*
• Jackson considers herself lucky that she never had to resort to sleeping in "cages," the street slang for abandoned houses. —*Clarion-Ledger (Jackson, Mississippi)*, p. 1, 24th January 2000
4 a car *US, 1981*
Biker (motorcyle) usage.
5 the body *US*
• —Kenn "Naz" Young, *Naz's Underground Dictionary*, p. 19, 1973

caged lion *noun*
in horse racing, a racehorse battling back from apparent defeat to win a race *AUSTRALIA*
• —Ned Wallish, *The Truth Dictionary of Racing Slang*, p. 12, 1989

cage girl *noun*
a ticket seller in a theatre *US*
• —Wilfred Granville, *The Theater Dictionary*, p. 28, 1952

cagey *adjective*
wary, non-commital, cautious *US, 1893*
• [T]hey think I'm deaf and dumb. Everybody thinks so. I'm cagey enough to fool them that much. —Ken Kesey, *One Flew Over the Cuckoo's Nest*, p. 10, 1962

caggie; kaggie *noun*
a cagoule or kagool (a weatherproof outer-garment) *UK, 1984*

cahoo-hole *noun*
a pothole in the road *CANADA*
• A cahoo-hole, in Quebec's Eastern Townships, is a hollow worn into the snow of a poorly plowed winter road, or a pothole. Derived from "cahot," the French word for a jerk or jolt of a coach, later also applied to frost heave damage. —Lewis Poteet, *Talking Country*, p. 28, 1992

cahoots *noun*
▸ **in cahoots with**
conspiring or planning with someone *US, 1829*
• O'Connor, however, is the Democratic leader of the Maryland organization, which is in cahoots with one of the tightest and biggest Mafia concentrations in the country. —Jack Lait and Lee Mortimer, *Washington Confidential*, p. 201, 1951
• Was she in cahoots with some Puerto Rican pusher who was about to make his entrance in my life? —Philip Roth, *Portnoy's Complaint*, p. 180, 1969
• [B]ecause when you father finds out you spent that money on drugs, he's gonna think I'm in cahoots with you, and then he's gonna forgive you and kill me. —Kenneth Lonergan, *This is Our Youth*, p. 88, 2000

Cain and Abel; Cain *noun*
a table *UK*
Rhyming slang, based on the sons of Adam and Eve who are remembered as the first murderer and his victim; recorded by Ducange Anglicus in 1857.
• How I wish we could be [...] filling our Darbies [stomachs] round your Cain and Abel. —Ronnie Barker, *Fletcher's Book of Rhyming Slang*, p. 39, 1979

caine; cane *noun*
cocaine, crack cocaine *US, 1983*
• I said, "Listen homeboy, what you talkin about? / You're mistakin my pad for a rockhouse / Well, I know to you we all look the same / But I'm not the one slingin caine —Toddy Tee, *Batterram*, 1985
• He's got a scale on the table, with some cut foil, some 'caine, and a bag full of money. —Terry Williams, *The Cocaine Kids*, p. 106, 1989
• I don't wanna be like my brother and shit, hanging out not doing shit, end up dealing cane just like him. —*Boyz N The Hood*, 1990
• It takes too much caine to make base – ain't no real profit in base – it's too expensive and it's too much trouble. —*New Jack City*, 1990
• What d'ya know. A kilo of 'caine. —*The Bad Lieutenant*, 1992
• "Chester, you do 'cane?" "Coke?" "Same thing." "I have." —Odie Hawkins, *Lost Angeles*, p. 95, 1994
• — US Department of Justice, *Street Terms*, August 1994

Caisse Pop *noun*
in Quebec, a kind of cooperative bank *CANADA*
The term is shortened from *Caisse Populaire* or 'popular bank', a French term universally used by anglophones.
• — *home.istar.ca/~awright/WORDS1.HTM*, p. 1, 10th November 2001

cak *noun*
▷ see: **CACK**

cake *noun*
1 a beautiful girl or young woman *US, 1941*
• What's on your mind, Jim-Jam? Thinkin' 'about that new cake you pulled from Baxter Terrace, huh? —Nathan Heard, *Howard Street*, p. 63, 1968
• —Vann Wesson, *Generation X Field Guide and Lexicon*, p. 34, 1997
2 the female breast *US*
• What they want is shows where one guy kicks another guy in the belly while a dame leans over 'em with her cakes falling out of her negligee. —Max Shulman, *Rally Round the Flag, Boys!*, p. 67, 1957
3 the vagina *US*
• —Dale Gordon, *The Dominion Sex Dictionary*, p. 39, 1967
• —John A. Holm, *Dictionary of Bahamian English*, p. 34, 1982
4 bread *TRISTAN DA CUNHA*
• —Bernadette Hince, *The Antarctic Dictionary*, p. 77, 2000
5 a meal provided as compensation in addition to wages *US*
• —Sherman Louis Sergel, *The Language of Show Biz*, p. 39, 1973
6 money; a good deal of money *US, 1965*
Extends, perhaps, from **BREAD** (money) but 'cake' has traditionally been associated with wealth. *'Qu'il mangent de la brioche'* – 'Let them eat cake', attributed to Queen Marie-Antoinette (1755–93) on being told that her people had no bread.
• —Hermese E. Roberts, *The Third Ear*, 1971
• But you'd go out with her if you had the cake? —*Ten Things I Hate About You*, 1999
7 marijuana resin *UK*
• —V.S. Ganjabhang, *The Little Book of Pot*, p. 8, 2001
8 a round disc of crack cocaine *US*
• — US Department of Justice, *Street Terms*, October 1994
9 a rural person *IRELAND*
Derogatory.
• —*Great Tuam Annual*, p. 87, 1991

▸ **get your cake**
to date your girlfriend *US*
• Brooks and his colleagues also provide police with glossaries of street slang – "Agent Scully" = "oral sex," "getting my cake" = "dating my girl." —*Washington Post*, p. A1, 20th August 2001

▸ **off your cake**
confused, drug-intoxicated *UK*
The latter meaning gained dates from the late C20 and the distinction between the two senses may be blurred.
• I got proper fucking off my cake, I did. —Dave Courtney, *Raving Lunacy*, p. 152, 2000

cake *adjective*
1 easy *US*
• —Collin Baker et al., *College Undergraduate Slang Study Conducted at Brown University*, p. 93, 1968
• — AFSCME Local 3963, *The Correctional Officer's Guide to Prison Slang*, 2001
2 homosexual *UK*
Clipped from **FRUITCAKE** (a homosexual man).
• And Jesus, is he cake! You couldn't get him more cake if he'd been to Dick Emery's Fruit School and eaten all the strawberries. —Kevin Sampson, *Outlaws*, p. 240, 2001

cake boy *noun*
an attractive, usually younger homosexual male *US*
• Are you bitches blind or something? Your man, Christian, is a cake-boy. —*Clueless*, 1995
• —Ethan Hilderbrant, *Prison Slang*, p. 21, 1998

cake-cutting *noun*
short-changing *US*
• On the midway, he learned the art of "cake cutting," or shortchanging customers, using "sticks" – carnies posing as customers pretending

to win a big prize – and "gaffs" – concealed devices such as magnets used to ensure that the house always won. —Kim Rich, *Johnny's Girl*, p. 37, 1993

caked *adjective*

1 to be wealthy, monied *UK, 1940s*
From **CAKE** (money). Variants include 'caked out', 'caked up' and 'cakeholed'.
- It was obvious to me that she was caked up with gilt[.] —Frank Norman, *Bang To Rights*, p. 109, 1958
- And everyone was completely fucking cakeholed, mate! —Dave Courtney, *Raving Lunacy*, p. 98, 2000
- [T]hat off-duty look that the rich kids, the genuinely caked, seem to get without even trying[.] —J.J. Connolly, *Layer Cake*, p. 43, 2000
- —Connie Eble (Editor), *UNC-CH Campus Slang*, p. 2, October 2002

2 drug-intoxicated *US*
- —Judi Sanders, *Mashing and Munching in Ames*, p. 4, 1994

cake-eater *noun*

1 an effeminate young man, who may or may not be homosexual *US, 1916*
An important word of the flapper era, but seldom heard thereafter.
- And Three-Star Hennessey, the lousy little cake-eater who used to rob girls' pocketbooks while he danced with them.. —James T. Farrell, *Saturday Night*, p. 31, 1947

2 a person who enjoys performing oral sex on women *US*
- —Dale Gordon, *The Dominion Sex Dictionary*, p. 39, 1967
- —Robert A. Wilson, *Playboy's Book of Forbidden Words*, p. 58, 1972
- —Helen Dahlskog (Editor), *A Dictionary of Contemporary and Colloquial Usage*, p. 12, 1972

cakehead *noun*

an idiot, a fool *UK*
- I'm running this. You sit back, cakehead. —John Milne, *Alive and Kicking*, p. 48, 1998

cake hole *noun*

1 the vagina *UK*
- However, the category edibility glosses over the variablity within it, which, for FGTs [female genital terms] included frequent reference to meat (e.g., bacon rashers, kebab, meat curtains); fish/seafood (e.g., tuna waterfall; fish, clam); and "sweet tidbits" (e.g. love muffin, fudge, cake-hole) —*Journal of Sex Research*, p. 146, 2001

2 the mouth *UK, 1943*
Also heard as 'cake 'ole'.
- I told you to shut your bloody cake-hole. —Wilda Moxham, *The Apprentice*, p. 144, 1969
- —Barry Humphries, *Bazza Pulls It Off!*, 1971
- Jeremy asks no one in particular, as he jams a slab of lox into his cake hole. —Anthony Petkovich, *The X Factory*, p. 183, 1997
- —Pamela Munro, *U.C.L.A. Slang*, p. 106, 1997
- Shut your cakehole, Tom. —John Milne, *Alive and Kicking*, p. 67, 1998
- —Nick Brownlee, *Everything You Didn't Need To Know About The UK*, p. 46, 2003

cake-o *adjective*

all right, correct, safe, suitable, what is required, comfortable *UK*
Back slang for **OK**.
- The trade-mark Baker brashness had dissolved, he clearly wanted the hold-all away from him. "Cake O?" asked Harry. —Garry Bushell, *The Face*, p. 207, 2001

cakes *noun*

1 the buttocks, especially female buttocks *US*
- —Judi Sanders, *Faced and Faded, Hanging to Hurl*, p. 7, 1993

2 crack cocaine *UK*
- —Mike Haskins, *Drugs*, p. 281, 2003

cake tin *nickname*

the Wellington, New Zealand, sports stadium *NEW ZEALAND*
- On the Friday before the All Blacks played France at the Cake Tin, four South Island farmers ambled into the court room in their jerseys and farm trousers. —*Listener*, p. 23, 14th July 2001

cakewalk *noun*

an easy or overwhelming success *US, 1897*
Originally a boxing term for an easy victory, then expanded to general use.
- They came out of the chute with fire in their eyes and a tiger in their tank and turned this old-fashioned, gut-bustin' sidewinder into a cakewalk! —Dan Jenkins, *Life Its Ownself*, p. 219, 1984
- Solving Iraq will not be easy, and it won't be quick. This is not a cakewalk. —*Baltimore Sun*, p. 16A, 21st April 2004

cakey *adjective*

foolish, daft *UK: SCOTLAND, 1985*
- Did you give him the len [loan him] of a tenner [£10]? You're cakey, so ye are! —Michael Munro, *The Complete Patter*, 1996

calabash cut *noun*

a haircut in which the hair is cut on a line equidistant from the top of the head *TRINIDAD AND TOBAGO, 1990*
A 'calabash' is a squash, and the suggestion is that a hollowed out squash shell was used to guide the scissors.
- —Lise Winer, *Dictionary of the English/Creole of Trinidad & Tobago*, 2003

calaboose *noun*

a jail, especially a local one *US, 1792*
From the Spanish *calabazo* (dungeon).
- [T]hey'll find you and kick you out and you'll wind up in a Mexican calaboose boy. —Jack Kerouac, *The Dharma Bums*, p. 101, 1958
- —John A. Holm, *Dictionary of Bahamian English*, p. 34, 1982
- Jail, man! The fuckin calaboose. —Joseph Wambaugh, *Finnegan's Week*, p. 51, 1993

calamity howler *noun*

a person who predicts disaster *US, 1892*
- All those calamity-howlers who have been taking it for granted that downtown San Francisco is ready to fold up have been given the kind of jolt they deserved. —*San Francisco Examiner*, p. 32, 22nd March 1954

Calamity Jane *noun*

in a deck of playing cards, the queen of spades *US*
Martha Jane 'Calamity Jane' Canary (1852–1903) was a legendary figure in the settling of the western US.
- —George Percy, *The Language of Poker*, p. 16, 1988

calbo *noun*

heroin *UK*
Probably from a confusion of **CABALLO** (heroin).
- —Mike Haskins, *Drugs*, p. 283, 2003

calc out *verb*

to calculate something *US*
- I'll be able to calc it out pretty close. —Robert Crais, *L.A. Requiem*, p. 42, 1999

calculator *noun*

1 in horse racing, a parimutuel clerk who calculates odds *US*
- —Tom Ainslie, *Ainslie's Complete Guide to Thoroughbred Racing*, p. 329, 1976

2 in poker, a player skilled at assessing the hands of other players *US*
- —George Percy, *The Language of Poker*, p. 16, 1988

Calcutta *noun*

1 butter *UK*
Rhyming slang.
- —Ray Puxley, *Fresh Rabbit*, 1998

2 a Calcutta sweep *AUSTRALIA*
- The event of the evening was the Calcutta, when three score men and women thronged the dark, smoke-laden back parlour for the auction of sweep tickets that had won a horse. —George Farwell, *Land of Mirage*, p. 120, 1950
- The promoting of Calcuttas today, on such races as the Melbourne Cup, is quite pointless as the results will have no bearing on the prices offered on the course. —Joe Andersen, *Winners Can Laugh*, p. 116, 1982

Calcutta sweeps; Calcutta sweep *noun*

a type of sweepstake in which contestants' names are auctioned off *AUSTRALIA, 1914*
- A ration of thirty squares was distributed by the storeman every Saturday night, and for purposes of betting, games of chance, "Calcutta sweeps" on the monthly wind-velocity and general barter, chocolate held the premier place. —Douglas Mawson, *The Home of the Blizzard*, 1914
- The Bellbird Gold Cup was run in two divisions and it was decided to run two Calcutta Sweeps on them. —Joe Andersen, *Winners Can Laugh*, p. 115, 1982

caleche *noun*

in Quebec, a one-horse, two-wheeled carriage *CANADA*
- Nearby are the two-wheeled horse-drawn caleches and victorias which provide an amusing means of touring. —*Holiday*, p. 73/2, April 1963

calendar *noun*

a prison sentence of one year *US, 1926*
- —Troy Harris, *A Booklet of Criminal Argot, Cant and Jargon*, p. 5, 1976
- —Angela Devlin, *Prison Patter*, p. 33, 1996

calendar days; calendar time *noun*
the bleed period of a woman's menstrual cycle *US*
- —Lalia Phipps Boone, *American Speech*, December 1954: 'The vernacular of menstruation'
- —Karen Houppert, *The Curse*, 1999

calf *noun*
1 a young teenage girl *US*
- —*Look*, p. 49, 24th November 1959

2 a Cadillac car *US*
- —Edith A. Folb, *runnin' down some lines*, p. 231, 1980

▷ see: COW'S CALF

▸ **have a calf**
to become emotionally overwrought; to lose control *US*
A variation born of **HAVE A COW**.

calf-lick *noun*
a limp quiff, or a tuft of hair on someone's forehead which will not lie smoothly *UK*
Northern dialect in wider use.
- —Bernard Hesling, *Little and Orphan*, 1954

calf slobber *noun*
meringue *US*
- —Harold Wentworth and Stuart Berg Flexner, *Dictionary of American Slang*, p. 85, 1960

calf's tail *noun*
the cord attached to a railway whistle *US*
- —Norman Carlisle, *The Modern Wonder Book of Trains and Railroading*, p. 267, 1946

Calgary Redeye *noun*
a drink made of tomato juice and beer *CANADA*
- —Chris Thain, *Cold as a Bay Street Banker's Heart*, p. 32, 1987

Cali *noun*
1 California *US, 1930*
- We were recording in Cali up to a few days ago— *The Source*, p. 56, July 1993
- —Pamela Munro, *U.C.L.A. Slang*, p. 49, 1997

2 MDMA, the recreational drug best known as ecstasy, originating in California
A shortening of **CALIFORNIA ECSTASY**.
- We all dropped a Cali and hit the dance floor.—Wayne Anthony, *Spanish Highs*, p. 69, 1999

calibrate *verb*
to correct someone's information or opinion *US*
Derives from making minor adjustments to high-tech weaponry.
- The Republican Guard has – calibrate me, Dick [General Richard Myers] – they pulled south in the north and they went north in the southern portion of the country.—*The Guardian*, 1st March 2003

calico cluck *noun*
a female railway worker *US*
- —J. Herbert Lund, *Herb's Hot Box of Railraod Slang*, p. 120, 1975

Cali dreamers *noun*
a variety of MDMA, the recreational drug best known as ecstasy *UK*
The whole plays on the song 'California Dreamin' by The Mamas and Papas, 1966.

Califas *nickname*
California *US*
Border Spanish used in English conversation by Mexican-Americans.
- —Dagoberto Fuentes and Jose Lopez, *Barrio Language Dictionary*, p. 27, 1974
- Some had ended up in Texas and others in Califas[.]—Jim Sagel, *El Santo Queso*, p. 187–188, 1988
- Even Texans are surprised at California's vehemence and, being more experienced, are wooing Mexican business away from Califas.—*Los Angeles Times*, p. B7, 5th May 1995

California bankroll *noun*
a single large-denomination note wrapped around small-denomination notes, giving the impression of a great deal of money *US*
- —Edith A. Folb, *runnin' down some lines*, p. 231, 1980

California bible *noun*
a deck of playing cards *US, 1960*
- —Thomas L. Clark, *The Dictionary of Gambling and Gaming*, p. 34, 1987

California blackjack *noun*
in blackjack, an ace and a nine, which produce a score of 20, not 21 *US, 1982*
- —Thomas L. Clark, *The Dictionary of Gambling and Gaming*, p. 34, 1987

California blankets *noun*
newspaper used as bedding *US, 1926*
- —Vincent J. Monteleone, *Criminal Slang*, p. 42, 1949

California C-note *noun*
a ten-dollar note *US, 1983*
- —Thomas L. Clark, *The Dictionary of Gambling and Gaming*, p. 34, 1987

California coffee *noun*
inexpensive wine *US*
- — Elementary Electronics, *Dictionary of CB Lingo*, p. 55, 1976

California cornflakes *noun*
cocaine *US*
- — Elementary Electronics, *Dictionary of CB Lingo*, p. 55, 1976
- —Nick Constable, *This is Cocaine*, p. 181, 2002

California Crybaby Division *nickname*
in the Korean war, the 40th California National Guard Division *US*
- [A]ll of these had only reinforced the unit's reputation as a sorry, undisciplined, ineffective fighting force. Its nickname – the California "Crybaby" Division – spoke for itself.—David H. Hackworth, *About Face*, p. 225, 1989

California ecstasy *noun*
MDMA, the recreational drug best known as ecstasy, originating in California
- [A] narcotic selection box: top quality Peruvian flake [cocaine], California Ecstasy and Caribbean smoke [marijuana].—Wayne Anthony, *Spanish Highs*, p. 67, 1999

California girl *noun*
a variety of marijuana *US*
- "Heh." "Mighty Mite seeds." "California Girl cross Durban." "Same."—Brian Preston, *Pot Planet*, p. 232, 2002

Californian *noun*
a variety of MDMA, the recreational drug best known as ecstasy *UK*
- —Angela Devlin, *Prison Patter*, p. 33, 1996

Californian northern lights *noun*
a hybrid marijuana grown in California *US*
The northern lights *(aurora borealis)*, a luminous atmospheric display, is a metaphor for potent effects and a romantic simile for the plant's appearance.
- It is sticky, aromatic and almost completely covered in a frosty coating which reflects in the light—Mike Rock, *This Book*, 1999

California pimping *noun*
working as a pimp in a relaxed, low-pressure style *US*
- California pimpin' is the relaxed style of pimping peculiar to the Golden State, also known as the slow track.—Christina and Richard Milner, *Black Players*, p. 48, 1972

California quail *noun*
a tablet of the recreational drug methaqualone, the recreational drug best known as Quaaludes™ *US*
- — *Providence (Rhode Island) Journal-Bulletin*, p. 6B, 4th August 1997

California sunrise *noun*
1 a variety of MDMA, the recreational drug best known as ecstasy; a blend of amphetamine and caffeine marketed as MDMA *UK*
- —Macfarlane, Macfarlane and Robson, *The User*, p. 74, 1996
- Street names[:] Adam, big brownies, California sunrise[.]—James Kay and Julian Cohen, *The Parents' Complete Guide to Young People and Drugs*, p. 136, 1998

2 LSD *UK*
A variation of **CALIFORNIA SUNSHINE**.
- Street names [of Ecstasy:] Adam, big brownies, burgers, California sunrise (also sometimes LSD)[.]—James Kay and Julian Cohen, *The Parents' Complete Guide to Young People and Drugs*, p. 136, 1998

California sunshine *noun*
LSD *US, 1977*
- —Richard A. Spears, *The Slang and Jargon of Drugs and Drink*, p. 91, 1986
- —Mike Haskins, *Drugs*, p. 285, 2003

California tilt *noun*
a car with the bonnet (hood) sloping downward to a front end that is lower than the rear end *US*
• —Harold Wentworth and Stuart Berg Flexner, *Dictionary of American Slang*, p. 683, 1976

California tires *noun*
tyres with little remaining tread *US*
• —Montie Tak, *Truck Talk*, p. 26, 1971

California turnaround *noun*
any powerful central nervous system stimulant *US*
So potent that a trucker who takes one can drive to California and back.
• —Wayne Floyd, *Jason's Authentic Dictionary of CB Slang*, p. 11, 1976

Californicator *noun*
a Californian, especially one who has moved to Oregon or Washington state *US*
• —*Maledicta*, p. 153, Summer/Winter 1978: 'How to hate thy neighbor: a guide to racist maledicta'

calipers *noun*
dice that are true to an extremeley minute tolerance, approximately 1/1000th of a inch *US*
• —*The Annals of the American Academy of Political and Social Sciences*, p. 122, May 1950

Cali red beard *noun*
a distinctive marijuana grown in California *US*
• —Mike Rock, *This Book*, 1999

call *noun*
1 an opinion; a prediction *US*
• "Okay. She changed into her running things and left the other stuff, figuring to change back later." "That's my call."—Robert Crais, *L.A. Requiem*, p. 30, 1999
2 the initial flooding of sensations after injecting heroin *US*
• —David Maurer and Victor Vogel, *Narcotics and Narcotic Addiction*, p. 394, 1973

call *verb*
▶ **call Earl**
to vomit *US*
• —Collin Baker et al., *College Undergraduate Slang Study Conducted at Brown University*, p. 93, 1968

▶ **call for a cab**
(of a jockey) to make jerky arm movements as he battles to remain in the saddle *UK*
• —*Sunday Telegraph*, 13th August 1961
• —Ned Wallish, *The Truth Dictionary of Racing Slang*, p. 12, 1989

▶ **call for Herb**
to vomit *AUSTRALIA, 1984*
An echoic play on the sounds produced by a sudden expulsion of vomit.

▶ **call for Hughie**
to vomit *UK, 1974*
Onomatopoeic play on Hughie as the involuntary sounds of vomiting. A joke current in the 1970s described getting drunk on green *crème de menthe* and calling for television personality Hughie Green (1920–97).
• —Ann Barr and Peter York, *The Official Sloane Ranger Handbook*, p. 158, 1982

▶ **call for the butter**
to have completed a task or arrived at your destination *US*
Fishing skippers who claimed the ability to locate fish by the taste of the bottom mud would smear butter on a lead weight, lower it to the bottom, and then taste the mud brought to the surface on the buttered lead.
• —John Gould, *Maine Lingo*, p. 30, 1975

▶ **call hogs**
to snore *US*
• —Kenn "Naz" Young, *Naz's Underground Dictionary*, p. 19, 1973

▶ **call it on**
to challenge another gang to a gang fight *US*
• —*New York Times*, p. 2, 15th May 1955

▶ **call Ralph**
to vomit *US*
• —Connie Eble (Editor), *UNC-CH Campus Slang*, p. 1, Spring 1983

▶ **call someone full-mouth**
to address your elder without using an honorific Mr or Mrs *GUYANA*
• —Richard Allsopp, *Dictionary of Caribbean English Usage*, p. 131, 1995

▶ **call someone raw**
to address your elder without using an honorific Mr or Mrs *ANGUILLA*
• —Richard Allsopp, *Dictionary of Caribbean English Usage*, p. 131, 1995

▶ **call the shots**
to be in a position of power; to direct the actions of others *US, 1967*
• Sexism: who's calling the shots?—*The Observer*, 29th June 2003

callabo *noun*
a collaboration *US*
• Run-DMC drag Aerosmith back into the spotlight in '86 for their rap/rock collabo "Walk This Way."—*The Source*, p. 135, March 2002

callalloo *noun*
a confused set of circumstances; a mix-up *TRINIDAD AND TOBAGO*
From the name of a popular stew. Recorded by Richard Allsopp.

call book *noun*
a list, formal or highly informal, kept by a pool hustler, of locations where money can be made playing pool *US*
• —Steve Rushin, *Pool Cool*, p. 7, 1990

call boy *noun*
1 a male prostitute whose clients book his services by telephone *US, 1942*
• There are clandestine call boy rings, operated by discreet male madams (often called "misters" in Miami) who supply male prositutes to guests at beach hotels.—Johnny Shearer, *The Male Hustler*, p. 123–124, 1966
• The frequent performance of fellatio on customers raises the question for the call boy of what to do with the fluid at ejaculation.—George Paul Csicsery (Editor), *The Sex Industry*, p. 32, 1973
• Students and middle-class youngmen [...] become callboys (the callboy faction being safer, more "conservative"[.)]—John Rechy, *The Sexual Outlaw*, p. 152, 1977
2 a boy or young man who called railway workers to work *US, 1898*
• Cather found a simple but supple voice for Tom, an orphan (his parents perished in a wagon train) first seen working as a "call boy" – that is, one who summons Santa Fe railroad engineers for early trains – in New Mexico.—*New Criterion*, p. 1, January 2000

calley *noun*
marijuana *JAMAICA*
From **KALI** and **COLLIE**.
• —The Aggrovators *Calley Version*,
• —Horace Andy, *Better Calley (aka Better Collie)*, 1975

call girl *noun*
a prostitute who makes bookings with customers by telephone *US, 1922*
• James Hurley, 26, 340 Grove St., arrested yesterday on charges of soliciting a "call girl," faces loss of his taxi drivers permit and jail sentence if he is convicted.—*San Francisco News*, p. 1, 4th February 1948
• The girl actually was – a professional tart. A call girl.—Philip Wylie, *Opus 21*, p. 62, 1949
• The aristocrats among prostitutes are expensive call-girls who work for fancy fees and keep their pimps in luxury.—John M. Murtagh and Sara Harris, *Cast the First Stone*, p. 1, 1957
• Because a man told me that I would make very, very good money, that I was a lovely girl, and that I could start out as a $100 call girl any time I wanted.—James Mills, *The Panic in Needle Park*, p. 92, 1966
• I worked as an independent and could not imagine why a $100-a-night call girl like myself or Blossom would want or need a pimp.—Sara Harris, *The Lords of Hell*, p. 31, 1967
• One whole floor was a brothel of the most expensive call girls – beauties, all of them.—Herbert Huncke, *Guilty of Everything*, p. 29, 1990
• Coz says he's been beefing up his East Coast staff, in part by hiring Richard Gooding, who broke the 1996 story about Dick Morris's call girl for the rival Star.—*Washington Post*, p. C1, 26th February 2001
• High-priced call girls have come to town for the Super Bowl, but real economists understand that most of the money spent on them – like most of the money spent on inflated rates at top hotels – leaves town.—*Houston Chronicle*, p. A33, 1st February 2004

call house *noun*
a brothel from which prostitutes are procured by telephone *US, 1913*
• It's the telephone number of a call house.—Mickey Spillane, *I, The Jury*, p. 61, 1947

- The call houses that specialize in sixteen-year-old virgins are doing a land-office business. — Raymond Chandler, *The Little Sister*, p. 1, 1949
- Then somebody will suggest the call houses. Address books with lists of cryptic phone numbers will be consulted. — Dev Collans with Stewart Sterling, *I was a House Detective*, p. 152, 1954
- Then Fullenwider asked, "Did you ever conduct a call house there?" Again MacInnis objected: "What is a call house? What does that phrase mean?" — *San Francisco News*, p. 8, 21st October 1955
- — Ruth Todasco et al., *The Intelligent Woman's Guide to Dirty Words*, p. 2, 1973

callibogus *noun*

an alcoholic drink of spruce beer, rum or whisky, and molasses *CANADA*

- Recipes differ for callibogus, a Canadian Maritime drink, but it's usually spruce beer fortified with rum or whisky, sometimes with a dollop of molasses added. — Bill Casselman, *Canadian Words*, p. 14, 1995

calling card *noun*

1 a fingerprint *US*

- — Vincent J. Monteleone, *Criminal Slang*, p. 42, 1949
- Calling cards, in the form of fingerprints left at the scene of East bay holdups, led today to the arrest of two suspected big-shot partners in crime. — *San Francisco News*, p. 1, 21st March 1953

2 needle marks on a drug user's arm *US*

- — Eugene Landy, *The Underground Dictionary*, p. 45, 1971

3 during the Vietnam war, a printed card identifying the unit, left on the bodies of dead enemy soldiers *US*

- — Gregory Clark, *Words of the Vietnam War*, p. 81, 1990

calling station *noun*

in poker, an unskilled player who calls bets prematurely *US*

- — John Scarne, *Scarne's Guide to Modern Poker*, p. 274, 1979

call it *verb*

while working as a prositute, to state the price expected for the service requested *UK*

- — *Maledicta*, p. 144, Summer/Winter 1986 – 1987: 'Sexual slang: prostitutes, pedophiles, flagellators, transvestites, and necrophiles'

Call Me God *noun*

a CMG (Commander of the Order of St Michael and St George) *UK, 1961*

A pun elaborated on the initials; used by civil servants demonstrating a jocular familiarity with the honour.

- BERNARD WOOLLEY: Of course in the service, CMG stands for Call Me God. And KCMG for Kindly Call Me God. JIM HACKER: What does GCMG stand for? BERNARD WOOLLEY: God Calls Me God. — Anthony Jay and Jonathan Lynn, *Yes Minister ('Doing the Honours')*, 2nd March 1981

call money *noun*

a demand for payment of a debt *US*

- Max's friends began to call him to tell him his brother was creating heavy debt, and asking Max for "call money." — Terry Williams, *The Cocaine Kids*, p. 122, 1989

call of the great outdoors *noun*

a need to defecate or urinate *UK*

An elaboration of 'a call of nature' which is the conventional euphemism.

- — Maurice Leitch, *The Liberty Lad*, 1965

call out *verb*

to challenge someone to a fight *US*

- — Edith A. Folb, *runnin' down some lines*, p. 231, 1980

call that George!

used for expressing finality or completion *TRINIDAD AND TOBAGO, 1983*

- — Lise Winer, *Dictionary of the English/Creole of Trinidad & Tobago*, 2003

call-up *noun*

in prison, a summons to a governor's office *UK*

- There were three of us on a governor's call-up on the day I got my first knock-back [rejection of parole, etc]. — *The Guardian*, 15th November 2001

Cally *nickname*

▷ **see:** CARLY

cally dosh *noun*

money *UK*

- — Michael Munro, *The Patter, Another Blast*, 1988

calmer *noun*

a barbiturate or other central nervous system depressant *UK*

- Fuck it. I got a few calmers off Jimmy and steadied down. — Jeremy Cameron, *Brown Bread in Wengen*, p. 105 – 106, 1999

Calumet fever *noun*

(among Ottawa valley lumbermen) fear of riding logs down the slide at Calumet, Quebec *CANADA*

- Most old-time river drivers know what it meant to have Calumet Fever, that sudden sickening fear that you couldn't run the Calumet this time and live. — *Canadian Geographical Journal*, p. 68/3, February 1964

Calvin Klein *noun*

1 wine *UK*

Rhyming slang, formed on the name of American fashion designer Calvin Klein (b.1942). Sometimes shortened to 'Calvin'.

- — Ray Puxley, *Fresh Rabbit*, 1998

2 a fine *UK*

Rhyming slang, formed on the name of fashion designer Calvin Klein (b.1942).

- — Ray Puxley, *Fresh Rabbit*, 1998

Calvin Klein special *noun*

a mixture of cocaine and the recreational drug ketamine *US*

A back formation from the initials.

- Users pay from $20 to $40 per dose, or "bump," usually to be mixed with heroin or cocaine and snorted (the coke/ketamine combo is called CK or the "Calvin Kelin Special")[.] — *The Record [Bergen County, New Jersey]*, p. A1, 5th December 1995

Calvins *noun*

blue jeans or underwear designed by Calvin Klein *US*

- — Connie Eble (Editor), *UNC-CH Campus Slang*, p. 2, Spring 1982
- Rock and Rap Stars Show Their Calvins — *Rolling Stone*, 4th June 1999
- [T]his month's CD is so rude you'll probably wad your Calvins [underpants]. — *Mixmag*, p. 4, April 2003

cam *noun*

1 camouflage *UK*

Military.

- I put more cam cream and mozzie [mosquito] rep on my face and hands. — Andy McNab, *Immediate Action*, p. 93, 1995

2 a camera

- Beat the jams with these traffic cams. — *BBCi Wales*, 29th June 2003

Camberwell carrot *noun*

an exceptionally long and fat marijuana cigarette *UK*

- It's called a Camberwell Carrot because I invented it in Camberwell [in London] and it looks like a carrot. — *Withnail & I*, 1987
- The joint I am about to roll requires a craftsman and can utilise up to twelve skins. It is called a Camberwell carrot. — *Withnail and I*, 1986
- Zaffir dripped saliva on his thumb and forefinger before extinguishing the glowing tip of the Camberwell carrot. — Greg Williams, *Diamond Geezers*, p. 185, 1997
- A proper Camberwell Carrot. — Dave Courtney, *Raving Lunacy*, p. 63, 2000
- — Mike Haskins, *Drugs*, p. 291, 2003

Cambo *adjective*

Cambodian *US*

- — Harold Wentworth and Stuart Berg Flexner, *Dictionary of American Slang*, p. 683, 1976

Cambodian red *noun*

marijuana from Cambodia *US, 1973*

Named for its reddish hue.

- I was literally stunned to see how gorgeous the three sisters were, after everybody got dressed and assembled in the main room for a going-out toke on the Cambodian Red. — Odie Hawkins, *Lost Angeles*, p. 187, 1994
- — Mike Haskins, *Drugs*, p. 287, 2003

Cambodia trip *noun*

a highly potent strain of marijuana from Cambodia *US, 1960s?*

Cambodie *adjective*

Cambodian *US, 1964*

Vietnam war usage.

- [W]e kept smoking our Cambodie smokes and took turns trying to nap and swatted flies. — Larry Heinemann, *Close Quarters*, p. 240, 1977

Camden Lock *noun*

a shock *UK*

Rhyming slang, based on a vibrant area of north London.

- You haven't been to Camden Lock for twenty years? You're in for a Camden Lock then. — Ray Puxley, *Fresh Rabbit*, 1998

Camden rules *noun*
poor table manners *US*
A tribute to Camden, New Jersey.
- —Connie Eble (Editor), *UNC-CH Campus Slang*, p. 2, October 1986

came *noun*
cocaine *UK, 1953*
Probably by misspelling or mishearing of 'cane' (cocaine).
- —Richard A. Spears, *The Slang and Jargon of Drugs and Drink*, p. 92, 1986
- —Mike Haskins, *Drugs*, p. 280, 2003

camel *noun*
1 in twelve-step recovery programmes such as Alcoholics Anonymous, a person who maintains sobriety *US*
From the sense of 'dry as a camel'.
- —Christopher Cavanaugh, *AA to Z*, p. 65, 1998

2 a poor performing racehorse *AUSTRALIA*
- I've got one ride today and it's a fair dinkum camel.—Ned Wallish, *The Truth Dictionary of Racing Slang*, p. 12, 1989

3 a marijuana cigarette *US*
- —John R. Armore and Joseph D. Wolfe, *Dictionary of Desperation*, p. 23, 1976

camel driver *noun*
an Arab *US*
- — *Maledicta*, p. 117, 1984–1985: 'Milwaukee medical maledicta'

camelfucker *noun*
an Arab *US*
Offensive.
- Look at our current situation with that camelfucker in Iraq – pacificism is not something to hide behind.— *The Big Lebowski*, 1998

camel jockey; camel jock *noun*
a Arab; anyone mistaken for an Arab *US*
Used with contempt.
- The Vice President's lenghty preoccupation with that Pakistani camel-jockey, Bashir Ahmed[.]— *Reno (Nevada) Evening Gazette*, p. 4, 11th June 1961
- —Andy Anonymous, *A Basic Guide to Campusology*, p. 5, 1966
- — *Current Slang*, p. 14, Spring 1970
- Clement couldn't picture this skinny camel-jockey-looking guy shooting anybody anyway.—Elmore Leonard, *City Primeval*, p. 145, 1980
- So it must be disconcerting, and scary, for Arab-Americans and Muslims to hear Savage and his kind refer to them as "towel heads" and "camel jockeys."— *Corpus Christi (Texas) Caller-Times*, p. A7, 28th January 2004

camel's hump *noun*
an act of defecation *UK*
Rhyming slang for **DUMP**.
- —Bodmin Dark, *Dirty Cockney Rhyming Slang*, 2003

camel stop *noun*
a taxi stand *US*
New York police slang; an allusion to the preponderance of immigrants in New York's taxi-driving workforce.

camel toe *noun*
the condition that exists when a tight-fitting pair of trousers, shorts, bathing suit or other garment forms a wedge or cleft between a woman's labia, accentuating their shape *US*
- Camel lips, an offensive name from the '50s when women wear their pants too tight. Also known as camel toes. The pants were designed to capitalize on that.— *USA Today*, p. 1D, 12th April 1994
- —Anna Scotti and Paul Young, *Buzzwords*, p. 104, 1997
- When you put them back on you knew they were tight enough if you could see the outline of your pussy, which, with the seam going up the crotch, made it sort bulge on each side, vaguely reminding one of a camel's toe.— Editors of Ben is Dead, *Retrohell*, p. 31, 1997
- —Connie Eble (Editor), *UNC-CH Campus Slang*, p. 2, Spring 2000
- —Pamela Munro, *U.C.L.A. Slang*, p. 51, 2001
- She walked right by, the poor woman didn't know / She had a frontal wedige, a Camel Toe. Oh no, fix yourself girl, you got a Camel Toe. — Fannypack, *Camel Toe*, 2003
- "They're too tight, too revealing, and the souce of both visible panty lines and camel toe" – an unsightly affliction[.]— *New York Post*, p. 12, 9th October 2003

camera *noun*
a police radar unit *US*
- —Wayne Floyd, *Jason's Authentic Dictionary of CB Slang*, p. 11, 1976

Camilla Parker-Bowles *noun*
a Rolls Royce car, usually called a 'rolls' *UK*
Rhyming slang, formed on the mistress (later wife) of Prince Charles, Prince of Wales. Variants are 'Camilla Parker', 'Parker-Bowles' and 'Parker'.
- Park the Parker, Parker.—Ray Puxley, *Fresh Rabbit*, 1998
- You take this hundred quid in used Ayrton Sennas [tenners] and I'll be off in the old Camilla Parker-Bowles.—Mervyn Stutter, *Getting Nowhere Fast*, 2004

Camille *noun*
1 a homosexual man who moves from one unfortunate, failed love affair to another *US*
- —Bruce Rodgers, *The Queens' Vernacular*, p. 40, 1972

2 a melodramatic hospital patient who always feels on the verge of dying *US*
From the novel by Alexandre Dumas.
- —Sally Williams, *"Strong" Words*, p. 136, 1994

camisole *noun*
a strait jacket used to restrain the violent or insane *US*
- —Vincent J. Monteleone, *Criminal Slang*, p. 42, 1949

cammies; camies *noun*
a camouflage uniform *US, 1971*
- Hey you ... you in the camies.—Ronald J. Glasser, *365 Days*, p. 201, 1971
- The uniforms may well be necessary. Even though women are barred from combat jobs, many open specialties require "cammies." — *Insight*, 28th November 1988
- Some "ground pounders" wearing "chocolate chip cookie cammies" even talk of an "Adopt-a-Pilot" campaign and cheer when the jets roar overhead.— *Shreveport (Louisiana) Journal*, p. 4B, 1st February 1991

camo *noun*
camouflage *US, 1984*
- A pair of bearded soldiers armed with matt black machine pistols, and wearing berets and desert camo uniforms, appeared from out of a tent along the side of the road.—T.E. Cruise, *Wings of Gold III*, p. 300, 1989
- Okay. Was the shooter wearing camo gear?—Andrew Vachss, *Blossom*, p. 200, 1990
- Today he wore camo fatigues.—Carl Hiaasen, *Strip Tease*, p. 208, 1993

camouflage *noun*
the disguise and staged personality assumed by an expert card counter playing blackjack in a casino in the hope of avoiding detection and ejection *US*
- —Michael Dalton, *Blackjack*, p. 25, 1991

camp *noun*
1 ostentation, flamboyant behaviour; extravagance of gesture, style etc; also, deliberately overt effeminacy used to signal homosexuality *US*
May be further refined (or otherwise) as **HIGH CAMP** or **LOW CAMP**.
- I love camp. I'm as camp as a row of tent. Pop shouldn't take itself seriously.—John Robb, *The Nineties*, p. 309, 1999

2 a dramatically effeminate homosexual man *US, 1923*
In Australia not necessarily a flagrantly effeminate homosexual.
- Still, when this assistant prop man, crew-cut kid, flit, floppy wrists and pursy lips, what they called rough trade, a real camp, when he'd begun stroking Biff's elbows and saying how gone he was on him, Biff hadn't come down with the immediate kyawkyaws.—Bernard Wolfe, *The Late Risers*, p. 202, 1954
- Since culture means camps, I listened in amazement as everyone from the baritone to the bass player was dubbed a queer.—Sue Rhodes, *Now you'll think I'm awful*, p. 108, 1967
- It is the camps, the crims, the pros, our friends in the counter culture and other anti-authoritarians, who like our paper.—Wendy Bacon, *Uni Sex*, p. 65, 1971
- [Reporting on 'I'm a Celebrity – Get Me Out of Here' TV programme] Apparently, nothing about the camp was real. I don't know, I thought Wayne Sleep looked quite human.—Ian Lea, *Rise*, 16th May 2003

3 a habitual resting place for wild animals *AUSTRALIA*
- 'We must have sat down on a kangaroo camp when we boiled the billy at midday,' I remarked irritably. Laurie laughed while I burned three kangaroo ticks from my legs.—Ion L. Idriess, *Over the Range*, p. 82, 1947

4 a temporary location to stay at *AUSTRALIA*
- I set up camp. Found a table to put my typewriter on.—John Birmingham, *He Died With a Felafel in his Hand*, p. 143, 1994

5 a resting or holding place for stock animals *AUSTRALIA, 1845*
- Affairs often left little part-white boys with their black mothers in the cattle camps on the stations, thinking they could be trained to a useful life as stockmen.—Coralie Rees, *Spinifex Walkabout*, p. 169, 1953

6 a rest *AUSTRALIA, 1899*
- I thought I'd never get across that street. Better go back to Gordon House and have a camp.—Herb Wharton, *Cattle Camp*, p. 35, 1994

7 jail *US*
- —Hy Lit, *Hy Lit's Unbelievable Dictionary of Hip Words for Groovy People*, p. 7, 1968

▸ **in camp**
of a government or military officer, being based away from the regular place of duty *INDIA*
- A senior officer [...], even if staying in a luxury hotel, may describe his location as "in camp" or "Camp" followed by the name of the place.—Nigel Hankin, *Hanklyn-Janklin*, 2003

camp *verb*

1 to exhibit humorously exaggerated, dramatic, effeminate mannerisms (usually but not exclusively of a homosexual male) *US, 1925*
Variants are 'camp around', 'camp about' and 'camp it up'.
- Ooever seen such camping about and going ahead?—Derek Raymond (Robin Cook), *The Crust on its Uppers*, p. 26, 1962
- —Donald Webster Cory and John P. LeRoy, *The Homosexual and His Society*, p. 262, 1963: 'A lexicon of homosexual slang'
- She can neither act, nor even camp the role.—Sidney Bernard, *This Way to the Apocalypse*, p. 147, 1964
- So then years later they meet a fresh bloke like me who's not afraid to camp a bit.—Antony James, *America's Homosexual Underground*, p. 80, 1965
- Goldie can camp it up with the best of the gays[.]—Roger Gordon, *Hollywood's Sexual Underground*, p. 18, 1966
- When Miss Marlowe camps, Honey, she camps!!!—Kenneth Marlowe, *The Gay World of Kenneth Marlowe*, p. 42, 1966
- That's exactly what I'm talking about, Emory. No camping!—Mart Crowley, *Boys in the Band*, p. 51, 1968
- They were camping it up like a couple of kids.—Jamie Mandelkau, *Buttons*, p. 90, 1971

2 to stay at a place temporarily; to have a short rest *AUSTRALIA, 1848*
Originally (1840s) meaning 'to stop travelling or working and set up a quick camp for making refreshments'.
- 'Anyhow,' she said in a pondering, wary fashion, 'are you camping here to-night?'—Eric Lambert, *The Veterans*, p. 25, 1954
- —Kylie Tennant, *The Honey Flow*, p. 101, 1956
- The theatre will be empty. I can camp in the back row.—Wilda Moxham, *The Apprentice*, p. 36, 1969
- In the end I shrugged. There was a patch of carpet beneath my feet. I'd camp there.—John Birmingham, *He Died With a Felafel in his Hand*, p. 163, 1994

3 to sit on a man's face during heterosexual love-making *UK, 2001*
A rare non-gay usage, from the conventional sense 'to take up temporary residence'.

4 (of wild animals) to rest or sleep *AUSTRALIA, 1861*
- These birds seem to camp at midday, for when travelling we saw comparatively few.—Ion L. Idriess, *Over the Range*, p. 75, 1947

camp *adjective*

1 ostentatious, effeminate, affected; usually applied to behaviour or style *UK, 1909*
Possibly French in origin; however it may well be an ironic reversal of 'unkempt' (ungroomed) or, less likely, derive from the acronym KAMP: '*k*nown *a*s *m*ale *p*rostitute'.
- —Paul Baker, *Polari*, p. 168, 2002

2 homosexual *AUSTRALIA, 1941*
In Australia not necessarily flagrantly effeminate.
- When one comes across a camp cop or taxi driver or ditch-digger one doesn't immediately label all and sundry in that profession as queer.—Sue Rhodes, *Now you'll think I'm awful*, p. 109, 1967
- Crapped off with one-night stands, shat off with shallowness, quiet camp guy, twenty-five, would like to meet couple under thirty willing to dally discreetly during daytime.—*Alvin Purple*, p. 96, 1974
- —Jim Ramsay, *Cop It Sweet!*, p. 51, 1977

campaign *noun*

▸ **on a campaign**
drunk *UK*
- —*e-cyclopaedia*, 20th March 2002

campaign *verb*
in horse racing, to run a racing stable as a business *US*
- —David W. Maurer, *Argot of the Racetrack*, p. 18, 1951

camp as a row of tents *adjective*

1 flagrantly homosexual *AUSTRALIA*
- He's really put a bomb under that show and Karen reckons he's world class. Camp as a row of tents as course.—Barry Humphries, *A Nice Night's Entertainment*, p. 91, 1965
- Arr don' gimme that. Them pansies is camp as a row of tents.—Sue Rhodes, *Now you'll think I'm awful*, p. 108, 1967

2 (often, but not exclusively, of homosexual men) ostentatious, effeminate, extravagantly styled *UK*
Elaboration of **CAMP** (ostentatious, etc.), punning on conventional 'camping'. The phase is often ornamented with adjectives that describe the tents as 'frilly', 'pink', etc.
- —John Gardner, *Madrigal*, 1967
- I love camp. I'm as camp as a row of tents. Pop shouldn't take itself too seriously.—John Robb, *The Nineties*, p. 309, 1999

camp as Christmas *adjective*
(often, but not exclusively, of homosexual men) ostentatious, effeminate, extravagantly styled *UK*
- MAM: Is that Russell Grant?... He's very good. DAD: He's as camp as Christmas.—Caroline Aherne and Craig Cash, *The Royle Family*, 1999

camp bitch *noun*
an overtly, extravagently effeminate male homosexual *US*
- —Roger Blake, *The American Dictionary of Sexual Terms*, p. 28, 1964

camper *noun*

1 any person *US, 1987*
Usually described as a 'happy camper' or 'unhappy camper', but sometimes simply as a 'camper'.
- —J.E. Lighter, *Historical Dictoinary of American Slang, Volume 1*, p. 351, 1994

2 a restaurant customer who lingers too long at their table *US*
- —*Maledicta*, p. 47, 1995: 'Door whore and other New Mexico restaurant slang'

campery *noun*
a showing-off of qualities that are considered camp *UK, 1976*
- And in between all the laughter and campery, real anguish.—Gyles Brandreth, *Breaking the Code*, p. 7, 1999

campness *noun*
a tendency towards or, simply, a quality of effeminacy or flamboyance, hence of homosexual behaviour *UK*
- The sensitive [male] lover of the married man (heavy blue eye shadow to establish sensitivity rather than campness, I think).—*The Times*, 24th December 1971

camp thief; camp robber *nickname*
the gray jay or Canada jay *CANADA, 1893*
Also known by these names in the US since 1893, this bird is nicknamed for its habit of scrounging food at outdoor work and play sites.
- Camp robbers will take anything small enough to carry off, particularly if it is bright or edible, and then laugh at you from the trees.—Mike Doogan, *How to Speak Alaskan*, p. 19, 1993

campus *noun*
a prison's grounds *US*
- —Ralph de Sola, *Crime Dictionary*, p. 23, 1982

campy *adjective*
melodramatically and blatantly homosexual *US*
- The rest were largely "campy" homosexuals who enjoyed dressing up in women's clothes and performing dirty sketches and singing off-color songs.—Antony James, *America's Homosexual Underground*, p. 83–84, 1965
- —*Maledicta*, p. 229, 1979: 'Kinks and queens: linguistic and cultural aspects of the terminology for gays'

Cam red *noun*
Cambodian red marijuana *US*
- —Mike Haskins, *Drugs*, p. 287, 2003

cam-stick *noun*
a *stick* of face makeup used for *cam*ouflage *UK*
Military.
- Beneath the frayed rims of their bush-hats their faces were blackened with cam-stick.—Chris Ryan, *The Watchman*, p. 17, 2001

Cam trip *noun*
a highly potent strain of marijuana from Cambodia *UK*
An abbreviated form of **CAMBODIA TRIP**.

can *noun*

1 a jail or prison *US, 1912*

- The day he got out of the can he was in business in Union Station again and still was at this writing, though arrested again and out on bail. —Jack Lait and Lee Mortimer, *Washington Confidential*, p. 130, 1951
- "Give me four caps for this coat," he said. "I've been in the can twenty-four hours." —William Burroughs, *Junkie*, p. 62, 1953
- Once you lose the hatred, then the can's got you. —Piri Thomas, *Down These Mean Streets*, p. 263, 1967
- You're gonna spend eight years in the can – minimum – and for what? —*King of Comedy*, 1976
- Metropolitan Correction Center (in other words, the new federal can on Park Row, lower Manhattan) beat the hell outa their former rat joint[.]. —Edwin Torres, *After Hours*, p. 158, 1979
- So there I am in the can, and not the one that says "gentlemen" on the door. I'm talking about jail. —*Raging Bull*, 1980
- Jeannie's husband went to the can just to get away from her, she's such a pain in the ass. —*Goodfellas*, 1990

2 a toilet; a bathroom or water closet *US, 1914*

- In the corner I spied a bucket coated with two inches of lime inside and out, with no cover; from the tip-off my nose gave me, I figured this was the can. —Mezz Mezzrow, *Really the Blues*, p. 33–34, 1946
- I didn't have anything special to do, so I went down to the can and chewed the rag with him while he was shaving. —J.D. Salinger, *Catcher in the Rye*, p. 26, 1951
- "He sits when he goes to the can, doesn't he?" he asked philosophically. —Evan Hunter, *The Blackboard Jungle*, p. 28, 1954
- You mean if I go into latrine to relieve myself I should take along at least seven buddies to keep me from brooding on the can? —Ken Kesey, *One Flew Over the Cuckoo's Nest*, p. 158, 1962
- Small hara bought me a couple of packs of tailor-mades and asked me if I wanted to go to the can. —Piri Thomas, *Down These Mean Streets*, p. 311, 1967
- Only man in history who ever found fulfillment in the ladies' can of a Boston and Maine Railroad car! —*M*A*S*H*, 1970

3 the buttocks *US, 1914*

- Yeah, sitting on your can. Ever think of working? —Hal Ellson, *The Golden Spike*, p. 22, 1952
- Sat around on our cans all evening, Brownie. —Jim Thompson, *The Nothing Man*, p. 209, 1954
- Hey motherfucker! / All you do is sit on your can / Get out in the streets and prove you're a man[.] —Lester Bangs, *Psychotic Reactions and Carburetor Dung*, p. 103, 1972
- Mr. Preston overheard him ask Miss Pliny how long she'd been "parking her pretty can at Regressive Plywood." —C.D. Payne, *Youth in Revolt*, p. 184, 1993

4 an imprecise amount of marijuana, usually one or two ounces *US, 1967*

Derived from the practice in the 1940s of selling marijuana in Prince Albert tobacco cans.

- We bought three cans of reefer for fifty dollars, and split the rest of the money. —Donald Goines, *Whoreson*, p. 36, 1972
- So frequently when you'd be going to cop a few joitns or a can – a Prince Albert can of the best pot you ever smoked in your life[.] —Herbert Huncke, *Guilty of Everything*, p. 27, 1990
- —Angela Devlin, *Prison Patter*, p. 33, 1996

5 one ounce of marijuana *US, 1959*

Probably from a pipe tobacco container, possibly a shortening of '*can*nabis'.

- —Richard A. Spears, *The Slang and Jargon of Drugs and Drink*, p. 92, 1986

6 marijuana *UK*

Probably a shortening of '*can*nabis' but possibly from 'can' (a measured amount of cannabis).

- —Richard A. Spears, *The Slang and Jargon of Drugs and Drink*, p. 92, 1986
- —Mike Haskins, *Drugs*, p. 287, 2003

7 a Saracen armoured-car *UK*

- The can crews themselves had a pretty shitty job. —Andy McNab, *Immediate Action*, p. 24, 1995

8 a railway tank carriage *US*

- —Norman Carlisle, *The Modern Wonder Book of Trains and Railroading*, p. 260, 1946

9 a car *US*

- —William D. Alsever, *Glossary for the Establishment and Other Uptight People*, p. 5, December 1970

10 a safe *US*

- —Vincent J. Monteleone, *Criminal Slang*, p. 42, 1949

11 in electric line work, an overhead transformer *US*

- —A.B. Chance Co., *Lineman's Slang Dictionary*, p. 3, 1980

12 in drag racing, nitromethane fuel *US*

- —Lyle K. Engel, *The Complete Book of Fuel and Gas Dragsters*, p. 150, 1968

▸ **in the can**

not trying to win *US*

- —David W. Maurer, *Argot of the Racetrack*, p. 37, 1951
- Somebody on the golf tour used to be a hustler who went in the can and intentionally lost a lot of amateur tournaments one time. —Dan Jenkins, *Dead Solid Perfect*, p. 47, 1986

can *verb*

1 to discharge someone from employment *US, 1908*

- Two, almost three years ago, and then the FBI came around and they canned me. —Clancy Sigal, *Going Away*, p. 120, 1961
- I hear Thompson got canned at Bob's this summer. —*Fast Times at Ridgemont High*, 1982
- I'm the only thing those Jamaican yahoos had going for 'em and I get canned. —Elmore Leonard, *Glitz*, p. 125, 1985
- Wonder if the boss'll fire us for letting his rig get ripped off? Not that it matters since we're getting canned anyways. —Joseph Wambaugh, *Finnegan's Week*, p. 54, 1993

2 to stop something, to cease something *US, 1906*

- "Let's just can the comedy and come on, huh?" said Grady. —Max Shulman, *Rally Round the Flag, Boys!*, p. 217, 1957
- Can that Uncle Tom crap. —Chester Himes, *The Real Cool Killers*, p. 99, 1959
- "Can the brochure, daddy," I said, surprising myself by the Fifties jargon that so amused Myron but rather repelled me. —Gore Vidal, *Myra Breckinridge*, p. 52, 1968
- RIGGS: Oh, brother. This is good. I like this. MURTAUGH: Can it, Martin. —*Lethal Weapon*, 1987

canab *noun*

marijuana

Also variant 'canaib'. From the '*canna*bis' plant.

Canada flash *noun*

in the Canadian military, a visible identification badge *CANADA*

- (current: since WWII) A "Canada flash," or shoulder flash, is a cloth shoulder badge used as the national, or service identifier on Canadian military uniforms. —Tom Langeste, *Words on the Wing*, p. 47, 1995

Canada honker *noun*

a Canada goose *US, 1927*

- Flock after flock of these large Canada honkers began to descend from the heavens. —*Kootenaian*, p. 3/3, 20th March 1958

Canada potato *noun*

a Jerusalem artichoke *CANADA*

- This edible tuber of one of the sunflowers was first collected in the wild and sent back to England from Halifax. These "Canada potatoes" are sweeter and crunchier than ordinary potatoes. —Bill Casselman, *Canadian Food Words*, p. 129, 1998

Canadian *noun*

1 a Jewish person *US*

- —Jack Lait and Lee Mortimer, *Chicago Confidential*, p. 301, 1950

2 a multiple bet *UK*

- The Canadian, also known as a Super Yankee, combines five selections in 10 doubles, 10 trebles, five four-horse accumulators and one fivefold. A £1 Canadian costs £26. —John McCririck, *John McCririck's World of Betting*, p. 45, 1991

Canadian bacon *noun*

in homosexual usage, an uncircumcised penis *US*

- —*Maledicta*, p. 53, 1986–1987: 'A continuation of a glossary of ethnic slurs in American English'

Canadian black *noun*

dark marijuana from Canada *US, 1969*

- —Richard A. Spears, *The Slang and Jargon of Drugs and Drink*, p. 92, 1986
- —Simon Worman, *Joint Smoking Rules*, 2001
- —Mike Haskins, *Drugs*, p. 287, 2003

Canadian bouncer *noun*

the central nervous system depressant Seconal™, manufactured in Canada *US*

- —Eugene Landy, *The Underground Dictionary*, p. 46, 1971
- —Jay Robert Nash, *Dictionary of Crime*, p. 55, 1992

Canadian passport *noun*

a hair style in which the hair is worn short at the front and long at the back *US*

Most commonly known as a **MULLET**.

- —Ben Sharpe, *Scooter Crazy*, p. 41, 2000
- —Don R. McCreary (Editor), *Dawg Speak*, 2001

- It's called the ape drape. The Tennessee top hat. The hockey head. The Kentucky waterfall. The Canadian passport. — *New York Times*, p. G11, 8th March 2001
- — Connie Eble (Editor), *UNC-CH Campus Slang*, p. 4, Spring 2001

Can Air *noun*
a putative merged Air Canada/Canadian Airlines conglomeration *CANADA*
- A Montreal commentator suggested Can Air for the proposed merger of Canadian and Air Canada. Punsters quickly converted it to "Tin Can Air." — Gord Sinclair, *CJAD, Montreal*, 15th November 1991

canal boat *noun*
the Horserace Totaliser Board, the Tote *UK, 1984*
Rhyming slang. The Tote was created by an Act of Parliament in 1928. This term (unlike synonymous **NANNY GOAT**) does not appear until after 1972 when the legislation was amended to allow the Tote to operate as an on-course bookmaker.

canal boats *noun*
big shoes *US, 1926*
- — J.E. Lighter, *Historical Dictoinary of American Slang, Volume 1*, p. 354, 1994

canal conch *noun*
a promiscuous woman *TRINIDAD AND TOBAGO, 1985*
The 'conch' at issue is of the vaginal type.
- — Lise Winer, *Dictionary of the English/Creole of Trinidad & Tobago*, 2003

canal wrench *noun*
in oil drilling, a shovel *US*
- — Jerry Robertson, *Oil Slanguage*, p. 34, 1954

canamo *noun*
marijuana *US, 1971*
From the Spanish *cañamo* (hemp) and *cañamo indio* (cannabis).
- — Richard A. Spears, *The Slang and Jargon of Drugs and Drink*, p. 92, 1986
- — Mike Haskins, *Drugs*, p. 287, 2003

can-a-piss *noun*
a can of beer *NEW ZEALAND*
- — David McGill, *David McGill's Complete Kiwi Slang Dictionary*, p. 27, 1998

canappa *noun*
marijuana *US, 1938*
The Italian name given to the *cannabis* plant.
- — Richard A. Spears, *The Slang and Jargon of Drugs and Drink*, p. 92, 1986
- — Mike Haskins, *Drugs*, p. 287, 2003

canary *noun*
1 a female singer *UK, 1886*
- — Arnold Shaw, *Lingo of Tin-Pan Alley*, p. 9, 1950
- But Jan Du Mond, a five-foot-three night club canary, pianist and composer, drives a cab by day. — Jack Lait and Lee Mortimer, *Washington Confidential*, p. 83, 1951
- [A] socially connected, prominently married carpet muncher with a yen for nightclub canaries was prime meat for the four-star Herald. — James Ellroy, *Hollywood Nocturnes*, p. 270, 1994
- At a time when it was hip to be cool and well-tailored, and female singers were still referred to as "songbirds" and "canaries," the Playboy Club became the most popular nighclub in town. — Kathryn Leigh Scott, *The Bunny Years*, p. 58, 1998

2 a police informer *US, 1929*
Canaries sing, as do informers.
- Scott was carrying on like the MC in a lounge act, like here he is, the one and only made-guy canary in captivity. — Edwin Torres, *Carlito's Way*, p. 130, 1975
- [Y]a sang to the fuckin' rozzers. Didn't ya? Sang like a fuckin' canary ya cuntprick. — Nick Barlay, *Curvy Lovebox*, p. 19, 1997

3 a person who is perceived to bring bad luck *US*
- [A]nybody who is a carrier of such disasters is known in Las Vegas as a "canary." The word canary is dervied from the Yiddish word, kinnahora, which means evil eye. — Edward Lin, *Big Julie of Vegas*, p. 255, 1974

4 a capsule of pentobarbital sodium (trade name Nembutal™), a central nervous system depressant *US*
- — David W. Maurer and Victor Vogel, *Narcotics and Narcotic Addiction*, p. 394, 1973

canary *verb*
to inform to the police *US*
- He was going to canary and the pusher went around to jail and told him, 'Don't talk.' — Willard Motely, *Let No Man Write My Epitaph*, p. 381, 1958

can-can *noun*
gossip *TRINIDAD AND TOBAGO, 1956*
- — Lise Winer, *Dictionary of the English/Creole of Trinidad & Tobago*, 2003

cancel *verb*
▶ **cancel someone's ticket**
to kill someone *US*
- If he uses a knife you use a gun and cancel his ticket then and there. — Joseph Wambaugh, *The New Centurions*, p. 11, 1970

Cancel Canada's Freedom *nickname*
the Co-Operative Commonwealth Federation, a leftist political party that evolved into Canada's New Democratic Party *CANADA, 1985*
The parody of the acronym CCF arose from critics feeling that the party was too global in its outlook, and not nationalistic enough.
- The CCF? Study their policies? For other Stanfields, it was enough to know that CCF stood for Cancel Canada's Freedom. — Harry Bruce, *Movin' East*, p. 196, 1985

cancelled stick *noun*
a tobacco cigarette that has been emptied of tobacco and refilled with marijuana *US*
- — *Mr.*, p. 8, April 1966: 'The hippie's lexicon'
- — William D. Alsever, *Glossary for the Establishment and Other Uptight People*, p. 5, December 1970
- — Richard A. Spears, *The Slang and Jargon of Drugs and Drink*, p. 92, 1986
- — Mike Haskins, *Drugs*, p. 287, 2003

cancer *noun*
1 any artificial sweetener *US*
Because of the belief that the sweeteners are carcinogens.
- Do you want sugar in your tea, or CANCER? — Connie Eble (Editor), *UNC-CH Campus Slang*, p. 2, Fall 1986

2 rust or corrosion on a car body *US*
- — *American Speech*, p. 312, Autumn-Winter 1975: 'The jargon of car salesmen'
- — Jim Crotty, *How to Talk American*, p. 36, 1997

Cancer Alley *noun*
any area with high levels of environmental carcinogens *US, 1981*
- Similar threats exist in East St. Louis, in Louisiana's "Cancer Alley," on Navaho lands where uranium is mined, and in farmworker communities where laborers and their families are routinely poisoned by pesticides. — Robert D. Bullard and Benjamin Chavis, *Confronting Environmental Racism*, p. 4, 1993

cancer center *noun*
a tobacco shop *US*
- — *American Speech*, p. 302, December 1955: 'Wayne University slang'

cancer stick *noun*
a cigarette *US, 1958*
- — Andy Anonymous, *A Basic Guide to Campusology*, p. 5, 1966
- Dally searched his pocket for a cigarette, and finding none, said, "You gotta cancer stick, Johnny-cake?" — S.E. Hinton, *The Outsiders*, p. 71, 1967
- Later on she was lighting another cancer stick and I leaned over to get a light. — Babs Gonzales, *Movin' On Down De Line*, p. 67, 1975
- [Y]our pussy's been tampered with / Did you show him that new trick of how you can make it smoke a cancer stick? — Dr Dre, *Fuck You*, 2001

Cancon *noun*
*Can*adian *con*tent, a percentage of which is required in broadcasting *CANADA*
- When I contemplate the Canada Council, our cultural medicare, pumping oxygen into the collapsed lung of Canadian Content, some might foresee a massive dumbing down of the culture – a Cancon confined to Harlequin Romances, greeting-card drivel, and so on. — *Toronto Globe and Mail*, p. R1, 25th June 2002

CanCult *noun*
*Can*adian *Cul*ture *CANADA*
Subsidised by the government, and enjoying a measure of world recognition, this industry is the site of much infighting and jealousy.
- A 19-year-old who pans a CanCult icon in a college review would be well advised in future to write poetry under a pseudonym. — *Toronto Globe and Mail*, p. R1, 18th June 2002

c and b there
used as an invitation to an event *TRINIDAD AND TOBAGO, 1987*
- — Lise Winer, *Dictionary of the English/Creole of Trinidad & Tobago*, 2003

c and d *noun*
cocaine and marijuana *UK, 1997*
- [J]ust see the scene, C and D, coke and dope, don't do nothing about scoring. — Joel Rose, *Kill Kill Faster Faster*, p. 12, 1997

C and E *noun*

1 a member of the church who only goes to services at Christmas and Easter *UK, 1966*

- —Frederic G. Cassidy, *Dictionary of American Regional English*, p. 655, 1985

2 in craps, a bet on any craps and eleven *US*

- —Steve Kuriscak, *Casino Talk*, p. 9, 1985

C and H *noun*

cocaine and heroin *US*

A borrowing of a branded name for sugar; sometimes used with the sugar company's advertising slogan: 'pure cane sugar from Hawaii'.

- —Edith A. Folb, *runnin' down some lines*, p. 231, 1980

can die!

used for expressing despondency *SINGAPORE*

- —Paik Choo, *The Coxford Singlish Dictionary*, p. 22, 2002

candle *noun*

1 a semi-solid stalactite of nasal mucus *UK*

- He would pinch his yellow nostrils and surreptitiously wipe the residue of his "candle" on to anything within his reach[.] —Brian McDonald, *Elephant Boys*, p. 168, 2000

2 an emergency flare *US*

- —Montie Tak, *Truck Talk*, p. 26, 1971

candle money *noun*

a pay-out on fire insurance *UK*

Police and underworld use; derives from a candle left burning in an insured property, perhaps deliberately.

- —Maurice Proctor, *Man in Ambush*, 1958

candlestick *noun*

in electric line work, a fiberglass downlead bracket *US*

- —A.B. Chance Co., *Lineman's Slang Dictionary*, p. 3, 1980

C&M *noun*

▷ **see:** CLICKS AND MORTAR

C and M *noun*

a mixture of cocaine and morphine *US*

- —Hyman E. Goldin et al., *Dictionary of American Underworld Lingo*, p. 39, 1950

can-do *adjective*

confident, optimismtic *US, 1921*

- The Belgian battalion, for example, was attached to the U.S. 15th Infantry Regiment which proudly called itself the "Can Do" outfit. —Don Lawson, *The United States in the Korean War*, p. 24, 1964

candy *noun*

1 any barbiturate capsule *US, 1969*

- —William D. Alsever, *Glossary for the Establishment and Other Uptight People*, p. 2, December 1970
- —Donald Wesson and David Smith, *Barbiturates*, p. 121, 1977

2 cocaine *US, 1931*

- Me he caught with some bad candy at a party years back[.] —Edwin Torres, *Carlito's Way*, p. 53, 1975
- —Angela Devlin, *Prison Patter*, p. 33, 1996

3 a sugar cube treated with LSD *US*

- —Helen Dahlskog (Editor), *A Dictionary of Contemporary and Colloquial Usage*, p. 12, 1972

4 crack cocaine *UK*

- —Mike Haskins, *Drugs*, p. 281, 2003

5 inexpensive plastic or acrylic jewellery *US*

- —Vincent J. Monteleone, *Criminal Slang*, p. 42, 1949
- —*American Speech*, p. 96, May 1956: 'Smugglers' argot in the southwest'
- —Bill Casselman, *Canadian Sayings*, p. 53, 2002

6 cash *US*

- Candy, markers, ammo, liners, stocking stuffer, sweetener, garnish, and pledges are all terms for cash. —Henry Hill and Byron Schreckengost, *A Good Fella's Guide to New York*, p. 123, 2003

7 anything good or enjoyable *US*

- —Inez Cardozo-Freeman, *The Joint*, p. 487, 1984

8 a girl with extremely conservative sexual mores *US*

- —*Washington Post*, 23rd April 1961

candy *verb*

to enhance a marijuana cigarette with another drug *US*

- —Ernest L. Abel, *A Marijuana Dictionary*, p. 21, 1982
- —Jay Robert Nash, *Dictionary of Crime*, p. 56, 1992

candy *adjective*

excellent *US*

- —Connie Eble (Editor), *UNC-CH Campus Slang*, p. 1, Fall 1991

candy apple red *noun*

bright red; in hot rodding, a clear coated metallic red paint *US*

- I take her to the drags, man, and everyone flips / For her big blue eyes and her candy apple lips. —The Beach Boys, *Car Crazy Cutie*, 1963
- Customized: candy-apple red paint, mink interior, rhinestone-studded mud flaps. —James Ellroy, *Hollywood Nocturnes*, p. 53, 1994

candy-armed *adjective*

injured *US*

Used for describing pitchers in the game of baseball.

- Surely you haven't forgotten the year 1938, when Rickey, then heading the St. Louis Cardinals, unloaded candy-armed Dizzy Dean on Wrigley. —*San Francisco Call-Bulletin*, p. 3G, 5th June 1953

candy-ass *noun*

a weak person *US*

- Get yourselves squared away, candy-asses. —Darryl Ponicsan, *The Last Detail*, p. 102, 1970
- He (Nixon) said something to the effect, well, if Schultz thinks he's been put over there to be some sort of candy ass, he is mistaken. —*San Francisco Examiner*, p. 10, 25th July 1974
- There are places you can coach and get by, by being a candy ass (wimp). Buffalo is not one of those places. —*Buffalo (New York) News*, p. B1, 15th January 2004

candy-ass; candy-assed *adjective*

weak, ineffective, timid *US, 1952*

- I just couldn't see myself growing old and telling my children that during the war I'd been a member of such a candy-assed organization. —David H. Hackworth, *About Face*, p. 225, 1989
- —Michael Dalton Johnson, *Talking Trash with Redd Foxx*, p. 98, 1994

candy-bar punk; candy-bar fag *noun*

a male prisoner whose sexual favours are bought with purchases from the prison shop *US*

- There are two classes of homos in here. You have what they call the "original" or 'square' and you have what they call the "candy-bar punk["]. —Bruce Jackson, *In the Life*, p. 359, 1972

candy butcher *noun*

a walking vendor who sells sweets *US*

- —*American Speech*, p. 279, December 1966: 'More carnie talk from the west coast'
- —Joe McKennon, *Circus Lingo*, p. 23, 1980

candy C; candy cee *noun*

cocaine *US, 1953*

An elaboration of CANDY (cocaine) by combination with C (cocaine).

- —Richard A. Spears, *The Slang and Jargon of Drugs and Drink*, p. 92, 1986

candycaine; candycane *noun*

cocaine *US*

Punning on the Christmas hard peppermint 'candy cane' and 'cocaine'.

- —Ellen C. Bellone (Editor), *Dictionary of Slang*, p. 6, 1989

candy flip *noun*

1 a combination of LSD and MDMA, the recreational drug best known as ecstasy, taken at the same time *US*

- —Connie Eble (Editor), *UNC-CH Campus Slang*, p. 2, Spring 1992

2 an LSD-based drug-experience enhanced with a multiplicity of other intoxicants *US*

From CANDY (cocaine).

- Part of the new upsurge in psychedelia, the band's name [Candy Flip] refers to a drug cocktail. —Simon Warner, *Rockspeak!*, p. 21, 1996

candy floss *noun*

the recovered entrails of someone who has been hit by a train *UK*

From the technique employed.

- "Wait till you see the candyfloss..." And by the end of that summer I had indeed seen the candyfloss, and wished I hadn't [...] The only way to get the late Mr Brown together for his trip to the mortuary is by using a pair of sticks that twiddle like noodles on a fork. Or candy floss. —Duncan MacLaughlin, *The Filth*, p. 65, 2002

candy grabbers *noun*

in electric line work, channel lock pliers *US*

- —A.B. Chance Co., *Lineman's Slang Dictionary*, p. 3, 1980

candy kid *noun*
a girl who wears a lot of inexpensive plastic or acrylic jewellery *CANADA*
- —Bill Casselman, *Canadian Sayings*, p. 53, 2002

candy maker *noun*
a male homosexual who masturbates a partner to ejaculation and then licks and swallows the semen *US*
- —Roger Blake, *The American Dictionary of Sexual Terms*, p. 29, 1964
- —Dale Gordon, *The Dominion Sex Dictionary*, p. 40, 1967

candyman *noun*
1 a drug dealer, especially a cocaine dealer; a heavy cocaine user *US, 1969*
- He's a little brought down / Because when you knocked / He thought you were the candyman—Richard O'Brien, *The Rocky Horror Show*, 1973
- Hear they had to bring the coke in a wheelbarrow. He's a real candy man, our boy Bobby Tex.—Edwin Torres, *Q & A*, p. 21, 1977
- —Walter Way, *The Drug Scene*, p. 106, 1977
- Guy was becomin' a regular candy man.—Edwin Torres, *After Hours*, p. 297, 1979
- Also there was Taffy Boyd, Helena's candy man, who'd come early in the day to ask why Pachoulo wouldn't extend Helena any more credit and was still hanging around.—Robert Campbell, *Juice*, p. 203, 1988
- —Angela Devlin, *Prison Patter*, p. 33, 1996

2 a field enforcement official of the Federal Communication Commission *US*
- —Porter Bibb, *CB Bible*, p. 89, 1976

candy pail *noun*
a chamber pot *CANADA*
- The candy pail is another euphemism, along with thunder mug, for the chamber pot – a very common object before indoor plumbing and still in existence in many places. At one time you could buy candy in small tin pails, later used for indoor night relief.—Chris Thain, *Cold as a Bay Street Banker's Heart*, p. 33, 1987

candy stick *noun*
a cigarette with a menthol filter *US*
- Look at that sissy, smokin' a candy stick, just like a woman.—Ken Weaver, *Texas Crude*, p. 106, 1984

candy store *noun*
a casino with rules that favour gamblers *US*
- —Michael Dalton, *Blackjack*, p. 35, 1991

candystore dice *noun*
mass-produced dice that are imperfect even when unaltered by a cheat *US, 1974*
- —Thomas L. Clark, *The Dictionary of Gambling and Gaming*, p. 219, 1987

candy striper *noun*
a teenaged volunteer nursing assistant in a hospital *US, 1963*
From their pink and white uniforms.
- Candy Stripers are not saccaharine youngsters with a Lady Bountiful complex.—*San Francisco Examiner and Chronicle California Living Magazine*, p. 22, 20th November 1966
- A candy striper at 17, Roth helped a doctor, who had artificial arms, rehabilitate a boy who had just lost his foot.—*Washington Post*, p. B7, 22nd April 1979
- I even cleaned up and wore a suit so I wouldn't panic the little candy stripers.—Joseph Wambaugh, *The Secrets of Harry Bright*, p. 195, 1985
- When she was growing up, Furukawa did a lot of volunteer work, including serving as a candy striper.—*Chicago Daily Herald*, p. 1, 11th April 2004

candy wagon *noun*
in trucking, a truck with a light load *US, 1942*
- —Mary Elting, *Trucks at Work*, 1946

candy wrapper *noun*
a hundred-dollar note *US, 1983*
Probably because of its association with the snorting of cocaine, or 'nose candy'.
- —Thomas L. Clark, *The Dictionary of Gambling and Gaming*, p. 3435, 1987

cane *noun*
1 a short crowbar used by criminals for breaking and entering *UK, 1937*
An ironic allusion to a gentleman's cane.
- [Y]ou'll be out and get back to graft put[t]ing the cane about[.]—Frank Norman, *Bang To Rights*, p. 58, 1958
- —Angela Devlin, *Prison Patter*, p. 33, 1996

2 sugar *US*
- —Charles Shafer, *Folk Speech in Texas Prisons*, p. 200, 1990

▷ **see:** CAINE

cane *verb*
1 to defeat someone in a humiliating fashion *UK, 1937*
- —Ivan Bracklin and William Fitzgerald, *All About Darts*, p. 97, 1975
- [S]he was one of the people who had to clean up the mess, the Old Bill [police] were caned, everybody knows that[.]—John King, *White Trash*, p. 7, 2001

2 to have sex *US, 1966*
- Fuck me, was I caning last night.—Colin Butts, *Is Harry on the Boat?*, p. 88, 1997

3 to do something to excess or, at least, to the limit *UK, 2001*
- — Susie Dent, *The Language Report*, p. 76, 2003

▸ **cane the loop**
to play the 9th, 10th and 11th holes at St Andrews golf course, Scotland, in two under par *UK*
- I caned a lot of Dover sole, but I never caned the loop.—Dan Jenkins, *Dead Solid Perfect*, p. 54, 1986

caned *adjective*
drug-intoxicated, drunk *UK*
- "Yeah. Bit pissed, though," replied Brad. "Fuck me, you're not the only one. I'm caned. Those bloody La Mumbas.["]—Colin Butts, *Is Harry on the Boat?*, p. 113, 1997
- Sample too much ketamine and you can "take risks and do things you'd normally never do," [...]. Which is worrying, especially if you're with caned strangers[.]—*Sky Magazine*, p. 76, July 2001

cane it *verb*
1 to drive at speed *UK*
To 'cane' (to punish) a motor.
- Come on man load up load up. Go'a cane i' now. Runnin' well late. —Nick Barlay, *Curvy Lovebox*, p. 27, 1997

2 to react, especially beyond sensible physical limitations, to chemical stimulants taken recreationally *UK*
- The London Chamber of Commerce reckons UK industries lose £2billion a year because of employees caning it and taking time off. — *Mixmag*, p. 97, February 2002

can house *noun*
a brothel *US, 1906*
- The Roamer Inn was like a model of all the canhouses I ever saw around Chicago[.]—Mezz Mezzrow, *Really the Blues*, p. 22, 1946
- —Kenn "Naz" Young, *Naz's Underground Dictionary*, p. 19, 1973

Caniac *noun*
a Montreal Canadiens fan who travels to other cities to see playoff games *CANADA*
The term comes from the combining into one word of shortened forms of '*Can*adiens' and 'man*iacs*'.
- The self-described "Caniacs" wave white towels and pom-poms. They cheer crunching hits, scoring chances, big saves, and penalty kills. — *Montreal Gazette*, p. A7, 4th May 2002

can I do you now, sir?
a catchprase that is usually appropriate to context *UK*
Adopted from the radio comedy *It's That Man Again*, otherwise known as *ITMA*, that was broadcast on the BBC from 1939–49; the catchphrase was spoken by Mrs Mopp, the office char, played by Dorothy Summers. Still heard occasionally.

can I speak to you?
used as the commonest euphemism for 'Are you willing to listen to a corrupt proposal I am about to put to you?' *UK*
- —David Powis, *The Signs of Crime*, 1977

canister *noun*
1 a safe *US*
- —Hyman E. Goldin et al., *Dictionary of American Underworld Lingo*, p. 40, 1950

2 the head *UK*
- It obviously helps if you ain't out of the old canister all the fuckin time.—J.J. Connolly, *Layer Cake*, p. 14, 2000

can it!
be quiet!; stop talking! *US, 1919*

cankle *noun*
a thick ankle *US, 2000*
Possibly, as a compound of 'calf' and 'ankle'.
- "He doesn't have ankles, he has cankles," Lilly said, using a phrase coined by telecast analyst John Madden.—*Charleston West Virginia Daily Mail*, 16th December 2003

CanLit *noun*

*Can*adian *lit*erature *CANADA*

- Richler, unusually for a Canadian novelist, was a satirist and a journalist who aimed his deadly typewriter at any aspect of public life that he felt needed skewering, whether it was Quebecois nationalism or CanLit boosterism. — *Toronto Globe and Mail*, p. R1, 19th June 2002

cannatt *noun*

a mean, insignificant, unpleasant person *IRELAND*

- Come out of it Tony and stop actin' the cannatt. Hey Paddy this lad is cheatin' out there. — Billy Roche, *The Wexford Trilogy (A Handful of Stars)*, p. 5, 1992

canned *adjective*

1 tipsy, drunk *US, 1918*

- And one I'm half-canned, I don't mind admitting it – I'm punyani [women] crazy. — Kevin Sampson, *Outlaws*, p. 36, 2001

2 of music, recorded, especially to serve as background music *UK, 1904*

Derogatory.

- [H]is hatred of canned music. — *The Guardian*, 8th June 2002

3 recorded, repetitive *US, 1903*

- Mom gave him one of her canned high-volume diatribes. — C.D. Payne, *Youth in Revolt*, p. 5, 1993

canned goods *noun*

1 a virgin *US*

- — Dale Gordon, *The Dominion Sex Dictionary*, p. 40, 1967
- — Anon., *King Smut's Wet Dreams Interpreted*, 1978

2 a male who has never experienced passive anal sex *US*

- — Bruce Rodgers, *The Queens' Vernacular*, p. 21, 1972

canned heat *noun*

a gel formed with liquid ethanol and saturated calcium acetate solution; when ignited, the alcohol in the gel burns *US*

Used as a source of fuel in portable cooking stoves and as a source of alcohol by truly desperate derelicts.

- Dope is sold everywhere, as are denatured alcohol, bay rum, canned heat, fermented cider and anything else that will produce a jag. — Jack Lait and Lee Mortimer, *Chicago Confidential*, p. 60, 1950
- I was one of them, a guy who could talk knowingly of Four-Trey Whitey and the Half-a-Half Pint Kid, who knew how to filter canned heat through a handkerchief and rubbing alcohol through dry bread[.] — Jim Thompson, *Roughneck*, p. 65, 1954
- They are drinking Victory Punch, compounded of paregoric, Spanish Fly, heavy black rum, Napoleon brandy and canned heat. — William Burroughs, *Naked Lunch*, p. 135, 1957
- He drank quarts of it a day. Any kind. Gallo, sneaky pete, the distillation of canned heat. — Clancy Sigal, *Going Away*, p. 238, 1961
- And the wino cringes from the canned-heat binges / And finds his grave in the snow. — Dennis Wepman et al., *The Life*, p. 80, 1976
- — Joe McKennon, *Circus Lingo*, p. 23, 1980

canned up *adjective*

drunk on *canned* beer or lager *UK*

- Look, this is just the ale talking, the pair of you are canned up. — Caroline Aherne and Craig Cash, *The Royle Family*, 1999

cannibal *noun*

a person who performs oral sex *US, 1916*

- Head-hunters, cannibals and kid-fruits are fellators[.] — *New York Mattachine Newsletter*, p. 6, June 1961
- Two to one, he is a "Cannibal" who ate her before she ate him. — Robert deCoy, *The Nigger Bible*, p. 128, 1967
- — Clarence Major, *Dictionary of Afro-American Slang*, p. 34, 1970

cannon *noun*

1 a large handgun *US, 1846*

- When Diamond came back he had a pitchfork. But Legs had a cannon. — Jack Lait and Lee Mortimer, *New York Confidential*, p. 161, 1948
- If you do that, we can stow these damn cannons and arm bands in a locker. — Darryl Ponicsan, *The Last Detail*, p. 37, 1970
- About this time, four detectives come out of an unmarked car with their cannons out. — Edwin Torres, *Carlito's Way*, p. 73, 1975
- I'm talking nice to him about Julio Sierra, when all of a sudden he pulls out this cannon[.] — Edwin Torres, *Q & A*, p. 13, 1977
- Listen, you motherfucker, you tried to kill me with a fucking cannon. — *Traffic*, 2000

2 a large surfboard designed for big-wave conditions *US*

- — John M. Kelly, *Surf and Sea*, p. 297, 1965

3 an extra large marijuana cigarette *UK*

- — *www.addictions.org*, 1999

4 a muscular arm *US*

- — Ellen C. Bellone (Editor), *Dictionary of Slang*, p. 6, 1989

5 a pickpocket *US, 1909*

- Jake, a con man, a cannon or a fake of any kind / make a C or so, the day after tomorrow you serving time. — Bruce Jackson, *Get Your Ass in the Water and Swim Like Me*, p. 141, 1965
- A "cannon" with a tired horse face took the vacant stool in my right. — Iceberg Slim (Robert Beck), *Pimp*, p. 91, 1969
- The cannon is the guy who actually goese in the guy's pocket. — Leonard Shecter and William Phillips, *On the Pad*, p. 159, 1973

cannonball *noun*

1 an express train *US, 1894*

- They range from Independence Hall and the Alamo to Indian pueblos, Alaskan totem poles, livery stables, breweries, old time kilns and a section of railroad track where Casey Jones rammed his "cannonball" into a freight train. — *Washington Post*, p. E21, 4th August 1979
- — J.E. Lighter, *Historical Dictionary of American Slang, Volume 1*, p. 357, 1994
- "There are two cannonball high-speed trains leaving Des Moines for Manchester, and we already have a hint (in preliminary polling) that Kerry and Edwards will benefit," said pollster John Zogby. — *Winston-Salem (North Carolina) Journal*, p. A1, 20th January 2004

2 a dive in which the diver grips and tucks their knees against their chest to maximise the splash *US, 1949*

- But a cannonball is neither aeshtetic nor much fun to watch. — Barnaby Conrad, *Fun While It Lasted*, p. 46, 1969

cannonball *adjective*

(used of a road race) unofficial, illegal *US*

- — Lewis Poteet, *Car & Motorcyle Slang*, p. 44, 1992

cannon-cocker *noun*

a member of an artillery unit *US, 1952*

Vietnam war usage.

- The efforts of the cannon cockers were rewarded. — Harold Coyle, *Team Yankee*, p. 94, 1997

cannon fodder *noun*

infantry soldiers *UK*

Used with sympathy or derision by journalists, agitators and, occasionally, the troops.

- — Eric Partridge, Wilfred Granville and Frank Roberts, *A Dictionary of Forces' Slang*, 1948

canny *noun*

a bird; a pheasant *UK*

English gypsy use.

- — Jimmy Stockin, *On The Cobbles*, p. 9, 2000

canoe *noun*

a marijuana cigarette which burns unevenly or is holed

The resemblance to a simple canoe: 'a log with a hole in one side'.

canoe *verb*

1 to have sex *US, 1954*

- — Harold Wentworth and Stuart Berg Flexner, *Dictionary of American Slang*, p. 87–88, 1960

2 (used of a marijuana cigarette) to burn only on the top *US*

- Masterrap, puffing on a cocaine-laced cigarette, complains to Charlie, "Hey, it's canoeing" – burning only on top so the unburnt paper looks like a canoe. — Terry Williams, *The Cocaine Kids*, p. 86, 1989

canoe inspection *noun*

a medical inspection of a woman's genitals for signs of a sexually transmitted disease *US*

- — Roger Blake, *The American Dictionary of Sexual Terms*, p. 30, 1964
- — Robert A. Wilson, *Playboy's Book of Forbidden Words*, p. 60, 1972

canoe licking *noun*

the act of oral sex on a woman *US*

- — Erica Orloff and JoAnn Baker, *Dirty Little Secrets*, p. 87, 2001

canoe-maker *noun*

a forensic pathologist *US*

From the image of the body on the autopsy table, opened up to resemble a canoe.

- [T]he old canoe maker at the autopsy today claimed she punctured the aorta with a three and a half inch blade. — Joseph Wambaugh, *The New Centurions*, p. 58, 1970
- She was a canoemaker with a sense of humor and Anne enjoyed her accent. — Joseph Wambaugh, *Floaters*, p. 136, 1996

Canoe U *nickname*
the US Naval Academy at Anapolis *US, 1963*
The 1998 Naval Academy yearbook included a CD-ROM supplment entitled *Canoe U*, providing a virtual tour of the Naval Academy.
• —Linda Reinberg, *In the Field*, p. 34, 1991

can of coke *noun*
a joke *UK*
Rhyming slang.
• [T]he cheapest 'can of cokes' are usually at someone else's expense.—Ray Puxley, *Fresh Rabbit*, 1998

can off *verb*
to fall off *NEW ZEALAND*
• —Louis S. Leland, *A Personal Kiwi-Yankee Dictionary*, p. 20, 1984

can of gas *noun*
a small butane torch used in the preparation of crack cocaine *US*
• —Terry Williams, *Crackhouse*, p. 147, 1992

can of oil; canov *noun*
a boil *UK, 1961*
Usually reduced.

can of striped paint *noun*
a mythical task assigned to a newly hired helper *US*
• [H]e was likely to be told next day to go draw a can of striped paint or a left handed monkey wrench or a spool of pipe thread.—Charles F. Haywood, *Yankee Dictionary*, p. 20, 1963

can of whip-ass; can of whup-ass *noun*
a notional repository for a physical beating *US*
• She started it back in the days when I, me, Billy Clyde Puckett, your basic all-pro immortal, was expected to go out there every Sunday and crack open a 220-pound can of whipass.—Dan Jenkins, *Life Its Ownself*, p. 15, 1984
• "I remember when we were losing at halftime (Cougar All-America guard Mike) Utley said to get out a can of whip ass," he said.—*Lewiston (Idaho) Morning Tribune*, p. 1C, 7th July 1991
• —Connie Eble (Editor), *UNC-CH Campus Slang*, p. 6, Spring 1994
• So go open a can of whup-ass on that little fuck, and get me his game!—Kevin Smith, *Jay and Silent Bob Strike Back*, p. 25, 2001

can of worms *noun*
1 a complex issue or situation, consideration of which may cause further problems, scandal or unpleasantness *US, 1927*
• Ehrlichman was worried that it could open a can of worms, which could lead prosecutors to Haldeman, Mitchell, himself, and a host of embarrassing and illegal activities that could not stand the light of day.—Michael A. Genovese, *The Watergate Crisis*, p. 29, 1999
• Raise questions? Open up cans of worms? Not me, my friend.—James Hawes, *Dead Long Enough*, p. 154, 2000
2 a can of c-ration spaghetti *US*
• —Linda Reinberg, *In the Field*, p. 35, 1991

canonical *adjective*
in computing, in the usual and accepted form *US*
Literally, 'according to religious law'.
• —*CoEvolution Quarterly*, p. 27, Spring 1981
• —Eric S. Raymond, *The New Hacker's Dictionary*, p. 88, 1991

can opener *noun*
a curbed bar used by criminals to pry open a safe *US*
• —Vincent J. Monteleone, *Criminal Slang*, p. 42, 1949
• —Hyman E. Goldin et al., *Dictionary of American Underworld Lingo*, p. 40, 1950
• —Angela Devlin, *Prison Patter*, p. 34, 1996

can or no can
used for expressing the decision-making process used by a big-wave surfers *US*
• —Trevor Cralle, *The Surfin'ary*, p. 18, 1991

cans *noun*
1 the female breasts *US, 1959*
• —Collin Baker et al., *College Undergraduate Slang Study Conducted at Brown University*, p. 93, 1968
• Cans up to her chin and an ass like a brick shithouse.—Oscar Zeta Acosta, *The Autobiography of a Brown Buffalo*, p. 112, 1972
• What's your breat size? I know it sounds crazy but my grandmother told me as she breathed her last breath: "Only talk to ladies with huge cans."—Howard Stem, *Miss America*, 1995
• —Judi Sanders, *Da Bomb*, p. 3, 1997
2 headphones *CANADA*
• —John Brand, *Hello, Good Evening and Welcome... a Guide to Being Interviewed on Television and Radio*, p. 20, 1977
3 money *UK*
English gypsy use.
• —Jimmy Stockin, *On The Cobbles*, p. 9, 2000

can shooter *noun*
a criminal who specialises in breaking into safes *US*
• —Vincent J. Monteleone, *Criminal Slang*, p. 42, 1949

can spanner *noun*
a tin opener *UK*
Royal Navy use.
• —Christopher Hawke, *For Campaign Service*, 1979

cantaloupe *noun*
a misfit; an outcast *US*
• "Clyde" – a loser, a shmendrick. Also, "a cantaloupe."—*Washington Post*, p. B1, 17th January 1985

cantaloups *noun*
dice weighted by a cheat to show a four, five or six *US, 1983*
• —Thomas L. Clark, *The Dictionary of Gambling and Gaming*, p. 35, 1987

can't be bad!
used as an expression of, sometimes envious, approval or congratulation *UK*
• She said she loves you / And you know that can't be bad—The Beatles *She Loves You*, 1964

canteen *noun*
1 a truck stop *US*
• —"Slingo", *The Official CB Slang Dictionary Handbook*, p. 13, 1976
2 goods purchased against earnings credited, or cash *UK*
Prison use.
• —Home Office, *Glossary of Terms and Slang Common in Penal Establishments*, 1978

canteen boat *noun*
the rear craft in a sea-borne minesweeping formation *UK*
• —John W. Mussell, *Militarisms*, 1995

canteen cowboy *noun*
1 a ladies' man, especially one who loiters is the NAAFI (the armed forces shop or canteen) for the purpose of meeting women *UK, 1943*
Royal Air Force use, still current in the 1970s. Formed on US **DRUGSTORE COWBOY** (a young man who loiters in or around a drugstore for the purpose of meeting women).
2 a railways' employee on an unexpected or extended tea break *UK*
• Canteen cowboys were either maintenance men on shed duties, taking a rest between the shunting of locomotives and trains, or drivers and their mates who had signed on in a spare capacity and were there awaiting foreman's orders.—Frank McKenna quoting Mr Bill Handy, *A Glossary of Railwaymen's Talk*, 1970
3 an orderly corporal on duty in a Royal Airforce Station Institute, NAAFI or Junior Ranks' Club *UK*
Roughly contemporary with the sense as 'ladies' man'; still current in the early 1970s.

canteen letters *noun*
an extra two letters per week if an inmate pays for stamps *UK*
Prison use.
• —Home Office, *Glossary of Terms and Slang Common in Penal Establishments*, 1978

canteen punk *noun*
a prisoner who engages in sexual acts for payment in goods bought at the prison canteen or shop *US*
• —Paul Glover, *Words from the House of the Dead*, 1974

canter *noun*
the speed with which a prisoner believes that his prison sentence will race by *UK: SCOTLAND*
From conventional 'canter' (a horse's easy speed of movement, not quite a gallop), thus a prisoner's boast of an 'easy ride'.
• It was six months, likely to serve three. "Six moon," as they put it in here; or more probably "six moon – canter", in predicting the ease with which they intended to see it out.—Christopher Brookmyre, *Boiling a Frog*, p. 40–41, 2000

can't go swimming
experiencing the bleed period of a woman's menstrual cycle *US*
- —Karen Houppert, *The Curse*, 1999

can't hear you – your mouth's full of shit
used as a refusal to acknowledge what someone else is saying, implying that what is being spoken is nonsense or offensive *UK*
Used by some comedians as a 'heckle put-down'.
- Can't hear 'coz your mouth's full of shit / Can't hear 'coz your mouth's full of shit / Do something about it.—Chumbawumba *Mouthful*, 1994

can't-help-it *noun*
an imagined disease *US, 1970*
From an earlier sense of the term as 'menstruation'.
- —Frederic G. Cassidy, *Dictionary of American Regional English, Volume 1*, p. 535, 1985

can't-miss *noun*
in horse racing, a racehorse that is a sure thing to win a race to the extent that a sure thing is a sure thing *US*
- —David W. Maurer, *Argot of the Racetrack*, p. 18, 1951

can to can't
all day, from early morning (when you can just see) to late evening (when you can't see) *US, 1931*
- His aunt worked from can to can't, and by the time she got home at night she was too tired to bend over the scrub board to wash out some clothes for J.S. to wear every day.—H. Rap Brown, *Die Nigger Die!*, p. 20, 1969

can't-see-um *noun*
any small, annoying insect *US*
- —Frederic G. Cassidy, *Dictionary of American Regional English, Volume 1*, p. 535, 1985

can't take you anywhere!
used as a jocular reprimand to a companion who has just said or done something contrary to the accepted social code; or (replacing *you* with *him* or *her*) to the company at large, as a humorous acknowledgement of such a *faux pas* *UK, 1975*
- That's me dad. I can't take him anywhere.—Jane McDonald, *Follow Your Dreams*, 2000

Canuck *noun*
a Canadian, especially a French-Canadian *US, 1835*
Insulting. Most likely to be heard in portions of the US bordering Canada. During the 1972 campaign for US President, a newspaper in New Hampshire printed an anonymous letter accusing candidate Senator Muskie of having used the term 'Canuck' to describe the state's French-Canadian population. The sound and fury created by the accusation stunned Muskie, and by the time it was learnt that the letter had been a concoction of President Nixon's election campaign the damage had been done.
- I am a Canuck. I could not speak Enlgish till I was 5 or 6[.]—Jack Kerouac, *The Subterraneans*, p. 3, 1958
- At a heated juncture, I made the unfortunate error of referring to their center as a "fucking Canuck."—Erich Segal, *Love Story*, p. 17, 1970
- Fucking Canucks. Worse than guineas.—Robert Campbell, *Juice*, p. 149, 1988

Canuck *adjective*
Canadian *US*
Insulting.
- Reassure Canuck painter too.—Jack Kerouac, *Letter to Allen Ginsberg*, 1st January 1955
- [A]nd then, hunch over, holding the money close to the glove-compartment light, to look at it. "What's this, all Cannuck?" "Most of it." "It's pretty but, shit, what's it worth?"—Elmore Leonard, *Killshot*, p. 31, 1989

can-up *noun*
a particularly bad fall while skiing *US*
- —*American Speech*, p. 205, October 1963: 'The language of skiers'

canvas *noun*
1 a strait jacket *US*
- —Vincent J. Monteleone, *Criminal Slang*, p. 43, 1949

2 a sports shoe, whether or not made from canvas *FIJI*
Recorded by Jan Tent in 1997.

canvasback *noun*
a boxer or fighter whose lack of skills leads him to find himself on his back *US, 1955*
- It's a train hijack, canvasback.—James Ellroy, *Hollywood Nocturnes*, p. 138, 1994

canyon *noun*
the vagina *US*
- —Edith A. Folb, *runnin' down some lines*, p. 231, 1980

canyon-dive *noun*
oral sex performed on a woman *US*
- —Edith A. Folb, *runnin' down some lines*, p. 231, 1980

canyon slicker *noun*
a condom *UK*
Combines **CANYON** (the vagina) with a waterproof outergarment.
- —David Rowan, *A Glossary for the 90s*, 1998

cap *noun*
1 a bullet; a shot *US, 1925*
- But before he got within ten feet of the door / I dropped him with a cap from my Colt .44.—Dennis Wepman et al., *The Life*, p. 42, 1976
- There was no doubt in everyone's mind that he would let off a couple of caps in the next fucker[.]—Dean Cavanagh, *Mile High Meltdown (Disco Biscuits)*, p. 211, 1996

2 a capsule of drugs *US, 1929*
- Local street sales of narcotics are concentrated on Pennsylvania Avenue in the Negro district, where indivdiual caps of heroin, morphine and reefers are available cheap.—Jack Lait and Lee Mortimer, *Washington Confidential*, p. 271, 1951
- Angel watched him begin preparations again, and didn't move until all six caps were in the spoon, ready to be cooked.—Hal Ellson, *The Golden Spike*, p. 7, 1952
- Lots of jive and goofballs, maybe a couple caps of Horse.—George Mandel, *Flee the Angry Strangers*, p. 56, 1952
- The H caps cost three dollars each and you need at least three a day to get by.—William Burroughs, *Junkie*, p. 43, 1953
- Ginny's got some caps. A hell of a lot of them.—John D. McDonald, *The Neon Jungle*, p. 44, 1953
- M-a-a-n, I'm drug by that son of a bitch MacDoud with all his routines about how he ain't got enough money for one cap[.]—Jack Kerouac, *The Subterraneans*, p. 29, 1958
- Why don 't you bust a cap with me? It's choice.—Clarence Cooper Jr, *The Scene*, p. 14–15, 1960
- Red dumped out the contents of the bottle: a ball of cotton wool and a generous handful of capsules containing white powder, which he proceeded to line up like a row of soldiers. "Ten caps, baby!"—Ross Russell, *The Sound*, p. 243, 1961
- I was discovering why heroin caps are so often called "courage pills."—Douglas Rutherford, *The Creeping Flesh*, p. 149, 1963
- I had never seen horse in bags before, and it seemed like a whole lot. All I'd ever seen was caps; that's what eveyrbody was snorting back then. They were buying dollar caps.—Claude Brown, *Manchild in the Promised Land*, p. 109, 1965
- We bought one cap and we split it, y'know. It was a giant cap, it was supposed to be five hundred grams, micrograms or something. —Leonard Wolfe (Editor), *Voices from the Love Generation*, p. 172, 1968
- Late in the evening we cut into Hugh and picked up two more caps. —Herbert Huncke, *The Evening Sun Turned Crimson*, p. 85, 1980
- He fixed two rum-and-Cokes then, emptying a street-lude cap into Iris's – eighty milligrams of Valium to take off her edge – and brought their drinks out to the living room.—Elmore Leonard, *Glitz*, p. 188, 1985
- But now, word! Hey, I be selling thirty-forty caps in a few minutes. —Terry Williams, *The Cocaine Kids*, p. 57, 1989

3 a psychoactive mushroom *US*
Conventionally, the domed upper part of a mushroom; possibly an abbreviation of 'liberty cap', the name given to psilocybin mushrooms.
- I took three, she ate the other twenty-two caps[.]—Eminem (Marshall Mathers), *My Fault*, 1999

4 the amount of marijuana that will fit into the plastic cap of a tube of lip gloss *US*
- —James Harris, *A Convict's Dictionary*, p. 29, 1989

5 crack cocaine *UK, 1998*
Sometimes in the plural.
- —Mike Haskins, *Drugs*, p. 281, 2003

6 used as a term of address for someone whose actions are provoking physical violence *US*
Hawaiian youth usage; an abbreviated form of 'capillary'.
- —Douglas Simonson, *Pidgin to da Max Hana Hou*, 1982

7 captain *US, 1759*
- The cap got all pissed off and had another shit fit, and we didn't get going again until after daybreak.—Larry Heinemann, *Paco's Story*, p. 22, 1990

8 a capital letter *UK, 1937*
Originally used by printers, then publishers and authors.
- Small caps X and O, by the way, are usually made to the same height as the lower case x and o. — *www.microsoft.com/typography/glossary*, 2003

9 a recapped tyre *US*
- — Montie Tak, *Truck Talk*, p. 27, 1971

10 the penis *FIJI*
- You should have seen his cap. Covered in VD. — Jan Tent, 1993

11 in casino gambling, a chip of one denomination on top of a stack of chips of another denomination *US*
- — Michael Dalton, *Blackjack*, p. 35, 1991

cap *verb*

1 to package a drug in capsules *US*
- "We got a little cappin to do," Buster told the Dinch. — George Mandel, *Flee the Angry Strangers*, p. 248, 1952
- They cut it, cap it, and retail it at about a hundred per cent profit. — John D. McDonald, *The Neon Jungle*, p. 61, 1953
- If you're a good capper and cap it yourself and sell part of it and use the rest yourself you can double your money. — Willard Motley, *Let No Man Write My Epitaph*, p. 122, 1958

2 to shoot someone *US, 1970*
- They said he got capped by a junkie; shit, but didn't die. — Elmore Leonard, *Glitz*, p. 57, 1985

3 to insult someone in a competitive, quasi-friendly spirit; to outdo someone *US, 1944*
- "Sing it you sweet cow!" some fellow shouted from the table next to ours. The chick that was with him capped this with "Yeah baby, he can't help it, it's the way you do it." — Mezz Mezzrow, *Really the Blues*, p. 26, 1946
- I would remark to Jessie that I was ready to pimp, but she would only laugh and cap: "You think you know to talk slick, boy, but that ain't the key." — Donald Goines, *Whoreson*, p. 37, 1972
- There are many different terms for playing the dozens, including "bagging, capping, cracking, dissing, hiking, joning, ranking, ribbing, serving, signifying, slipping, sounding and snapping". — James Haskins, *The Story of Hip-Hop*, p. 54, 2000

4 to steer business to someone *US*
- Herb was fired for capping for a bail bondsman and had a nice thing going until they caught him. — Joseph Wambaugh, *The Blue Knight*, p. 123, 1973

5 in casino gambling, to add to an existing bet, usually illegally *US*
- — Lee Solkey, *Dummy Up and Deal*, p. 109, 1980

6 to assist in a fraudulent scheme by fast talk that helps lure the victim into the swindle *UK, 1811*
- — Hyman E. Goldin et al., *Dictionary of American Underworld Lingo*, p. 40, 1950
- Both of us could cap on or build up a sucker who had been caught. — Iceberg Slim (Robert Beck), *Trick Baby*, p. 120, 1969

7 to fly on combat *a*ir *p*atrol (CAP) *UK*
Royal Air Force use.
- — Robert Prest, *F4 Phantom*, 1979

Cape Breton attache case *noun*
a plastic bag *CANADA, 1980*
- He had some books in a plastic bag from the Halifax public library. (I see you've got a Cape Breton attache case," Al Thomson said.) — Harry Bruce, *Movin' East*, p. 8, 1985

Cape Cod turkey *noun*
salt cod *US, 1865*
- Along Cape Cod Bay in Massachusetts cod fish is sometimes called Cape Cod Turkey — George Earlie Shankle, *American Nicknames*, p. 74, 1955
- — Charles F. Haywood, *Yankee Dictionary*, p. 24, 1963

Cape Doctor *noun*
the strong southeasterly trade wind that blows in Cape Town over summer *SOUTH AFRICA, 1861*
- — Penny da Silva, *A Dictionary of South African English*, 1996

cape horn *noun*
a condom *UK, 1990s*
The southernmost tip of the South American continent puns on 'cape' (an outer garment, often waterproof) worn on a **HORN** (the erect penis). A similar pun was behind the C19 sense, now obsolete, as 'the vagina' – the southernmost tip, often subject to stormy weather, where many men have been lost.

capella *noun*
a hat *UK*
An affected elaboration of 'cap'; easily confused with the obsolete sense (a coat) which derives directly from Italian.
- A: Do you think she's on the team [homosexual]? B: Who? A: The omee [man] in the bijou [small] capella. — Emma Hindley, *Storm in a Teacup*, 1993

Cape of Good Hope *noun*

1 soap *UK, 1925*
Rhyming slang, based on the South African headland; sometimes shortened to 'cape'.
- [B]eing too poor to purchase any Cape of Good Hope, his bushel and peck [the neck] was extremely two-thirty [dirty]. — Ronnie Barker, *Fletcher's Book of Rhyming Slang*, p. 25, 1979

2 the Pope *UK*
Rhyming slang.
- [T]he Cape of Good Hope was well pleased with the result. — Andrew Nickolds, *Back to Basics*, p. 163, 1994

caper *noun*

1 a criminal undertaking, especially a swindle or theft *US, 1925*
- It always seems that way when a guy's going on a caper. — Jim Thompson, *A Swell-Looking Babe*, p. 79, 1954
- By the time Oscar had been functioning for a year, the Drake caper had assumed such proportions that scores of donators, after shelling out their own money, were taken on as salesmen. — *San Francisco Examiner, American Weekely*, p. 17, 24th May 1959
- He was always and forever cooking up deals, figuring the angles, plotting a caper, with a mournful, long-faced and unhappy expression as though he knew someone would catch him. — Clancy Sigal, *Going Away*, p. 355, 1961
- The St. Louis jewelry caper was a major operation, but I had the finest possible team. — Red Rudensky, *The Gonif*, p. 63, 1970
- Meanwhile, I've got some capers I want to pull with that Corpse. — Tom Robbins, *Another Roadside Attraction*, p. 234, 1971
- I was going to tell you about one other caper. — Bruce Jackson, *Outside the Law*, p. 225, 1972
- I'm surprised you weren't in on that toilet caper. — *Body Heat*, 1980
- They planned a caper in Washington D.C. and spent much time rushing back and forth between the two cities. — Herbert Huncke, *The Evening Sun Turned Crimson*, p. 57, 1980
- No more chickenshit two- and three-grand capers that cost two or three years. — Gerald Petievich, *Money Men*, p. 85, 1981
- Finally, someone comes up with the idea, wait a minute, while we were planning this caper, all we did was sit around and tell fucking jokes. — *Reservoir Dogs*, 1992

2 that which is going on; business; an undertaking *AUSTRALIA*
- What's the caper? What's Tuttle say? — Eric Lambert, *The Veterans*, p. 177, 1954
- 'Blimey isn't this a ridiculous caper in this day and age of automation,' dipper Dinger. — John Wynnum, *Jiggin' in the Riggin'*, p. 20, 1965
- Next thing, I'll invite you home to my place. That's the caper, isn't it? — Frank Hardy, *The Yarns of Billy Borker*, p. 109, 1965
- Snowy now: he was a vicious sort of kid, pulled off frog's legs for fun, tied tin cans with bangers in them to cats' tails – that sort of caper. — Wilda Moxham, *The Apprentice*, p. 94, 1969
- Yeah, an' I'll kill th' shits if they try this caper on me when I grow up. — Ward McNally, *Supper at Happy Harry's*, p. 39, 1982
- You done much of this martial arts caper have you? — Robert G. Barrett, *Davo's Little Something*, p. 154, 1992

3 the time devoted to pleasure; a hedonistic lifestyle *UK*
Probably from the conventional sense (a dance).
- I'm going to be a better man. I'll sack [give up] the caper – I'll sack snorting the shite, anyway. — Kevin Sampson, *Outlaws*, p. 197, 2001

4 cocaine *UK*
Etymology uncertain; possibly rhyming slang: 'cape of good hope' for 'dope'.
- I've taken fucking massive packages of caper round in the boot, done up like a kid's birthday present. — Kevin Sampson, *Outlaws*, p. 49, 2001

5 a costume worn for erotic effect *UK*
- She's wearing the same caper as what she's got on in the photie. — Kevin Sampson, *Clubland*, p. 131, 2002

caper *verb*
to commit a criminal undertaking, especially a swindle or theft *US*
- During the years of his cruising around the country, Leo would caper and regularly send money through Joanie to his attorney[.] — Emmett Grogan, *Final Score*, p. 22, 1976
- Harold and Joe had capered together on the streets, though petty boosting only[.] — Seth Morgan, *Homeboy*, p. 89, 1990

caper car *noun*
a car used for a crime and then abandoned *US*
• It's a caper car, for sure.—Gerald Petievich, *Money Men*, p. 99, 1981

capey; capie *noun*
a person who is part of the non-white, or 'coloured' population in South Africa's Cape province *SOUTH AFRICA*
A term that has survived apartheid.
• [T]he Cape-coloureds and Malays are known, respectively, as Capeys and Gamats[.]—*Partridge*, 1977

capisce?; capeesh?
do you understand? *US*
Thanks to gangster films and television programmes, almost always a blatant affectation with an organised, Sicilian ring to it.
• Mr. Collucci has got my ass dragging with all our troubles with Tat Taylor's Warriors and other serious trouble I can't talk about. Capisce?—Iceberg Slim (Robert Beck), *Death Wish*, p. 12, 1977
• In this enterprise you do as I say. Obey me, and you'll escape unscathed. Capeesh?—Jonathan Gash, *The Ten Word Game*, p. 74, 2003
• As anyone who's seen the mob melodrama knows, loose lips are likely to result in a major loss of blood, capisce?—*The News-Press (Fort Myers, Florida)*, p. 8E, 6th February 2004

capital *adjective*
attractive, good-looking *US*
• —Don R. McCreary (Editor), *Dawg Speak*, 2001

capital H *noun*
heroin *US, 1975*
An embellishment of **H** (heroin).
• —Richard A. Spears, *The Slang and Jargon of Drugs and Drink*, p. 95, 1986
• —Robert Ashton, *This Is Heroin*, p. 205, 2002
• —Mike Haskins, *Drugs*, p. 283, 2003

capital prize *noun*
a sexually transmitted infection *US*
• Nitti, like Capone, had picked up in his travels the occupational malady of the underworld euphemistically known as the capital prize, or big casino.—*San Francisco Call-Bulletin*, p. 14, 24th February 1948

cap man *noun*
a confederate in a swindle *US*
• Jackson's cap man (confederate) heckled the mark to blow close to a C note to Jackson with such violent enthusiasm that the mark woke up.—Iceberg Slim (Robert Beck), *The Naked Soul of Iceberg Slim*, p. 123, 1971

Cap'n Crunch *nickname*
a captain of a British Columbia provincial ferry who had a spectacular collision *CANADA, 1989*
• The BC ferry captain who so badly smashed the Tsawassen slip that it was out of operation for several weeks. Perhaps the honorary title ought to be passed around to three other crown corporation mariners who ran aground or smashed docks in 1989.—Tom Parkin, *WetCoast Words*, p. 27, 1989

capo *noun*
a leader of a Mafia organisation *US, 1952*
• That was an operation for any local capo, not the boss.—Mickey Spillane, *Last Cop Out*, p. 114, 1972

capon *noun*
an effeminate or homosexual male *US*
• —Lou Shelly, *Hepcats Jive Talk Dictionary*, p. 8, 1945

cap on *verb*
to look at someone or something *US*
• —Eugene Landy, *The Underground Dictionary*, p. 46, 1971

capoonkle *adjective*
confusing, confused *US*
• —John A. Holm, *Dictionary of Bahamian English*, p. 36, 1982

capper *noun*
1 a clincher; something that beats all others *UK, 1960*
• —Robert S. Gold, *A Jazz Lexicon*, p. 48, 1964
• You know, like the capper on a bad fuckin' day.—Richard Price, *Clockers*, p. 381, 1992

2 in a drug-selling enterprise, a person who fills capsules with a drug *US*
• If you're a good capper and cap it yourself and sell part of it and use the rest yourself you can double your money.—Willard Motley, *Let No Man Write My Epitaph*, p. 122, 1958

3 in a confidence swindle, a person who lures the victim into the swindle *US, 1753*
From the verb **CAP**.
• "I understand you guys are looking for a capper to rope a mark," she said as she hugged John, but only looked over at Beano.—Stephen Cannell, *King Con*, p. 138, 1997

4 in an auction, a dummy bidder *US, 1853*
• 14. No person shall at any auction act as a "capper", "booster" or "shill" or offer to make any false bid to buy or pretend to buy any article sold or offered for sale.—*City of Halifax Ordinance Number 146*, 1985

caps *noun*
heroin *UK, 1998*
• —Mike Haskins, *Drugs*, p. 283, 2003

capsula *noun*
crack cocaine *UK*
• —Mike Haskins, *Drugs*, p. 281, 2003

capsule con *noun*
a prisoner convicted on drug charges *US*
• To me, he didn't look like a capsule con.—Red Rudensky, *The Gonif*, p. 17, 1970

captain *noun*
1 a railway conductor *US*
• —Norman Carlisle, *The Modern Wonder Book of Trains and Railroading*, p. 261, 1946

2 the person buying the drinks *AUSTRALIA, 1953*
• —Jim Ramsay, *Cop It Sweet!*, p. 20, 1977
• —Ryan Aven-Bray, *Ridgey Didge Oz Jack Lang*, p. 21, 1983

▸ **out with the captain**
out drinking *CANADA*
Especially in the Maritime Provinces, the Captain is of course Captain Morgan Rum.

Captain Bob *nickname*
corrupt businessman Robert Maxwell (1923–1991) *UK*
• [P]eople not fit to adjust Captain Bob's braces[.]—Andrew Nickolds, *Back to Basics*, p. 60, 1994
• How blue chips failed to tame Captain Bob—*The Guardian*, 31st March 2001

Captain Cook; captain's *noun*
a look *AUSTRALIA, 1960*
Rhyming slang, after Captain James Cook, 1728–79, British sea explorer who 'discovered' the east coast of Australia.
• I think I'll have a Captain Cook at the galley.—John Wynnum, *Tar Dust*, p. 32, 1962
• I can't wait to get me first Captain Cook at London!—Barry Humphries, *The Wonderful World of Barry McKenzie*, p. 2, 1968
• Just have a captain's at em for now, so's you can see what you're gettin'!—Lance Peters, *The Dirty Half-Mile*, 1979

Captain Cook *adjective*
ill *AUSTRALIA*
Rhyming slang for **CROOK** (ill), formed on the name of explorer Captain James Cook (1728–1779).
• —John Ayto, *The Oxford Dictionary of Rhyming Slang*, 2002

Captain Grimes *nickname*
The Times newspaper *UK: ENGLAND*
Rhyming slang.
• —*The Times*, 10th June 1982

Captain Hicks *noun*
in craps, the number six *US, 1941*
• —Vincent J. Monteleone, *Criminal Slang*, p. 44, 1949
• —Thomas L. Clark, *The Dictionary of Gambling and Gaming*, p. 36, 1987

Captain Kirk *noun*
a Turk *UK*
Rhyming slang, based on a famous character of the original television and film science fiction adventure series *Star Trek*, since 1969.
• —Ray Puxley, *Fresh Rabbit*, 1998

captain of the head *noun*
an orderly assigned to latrine duty *US*
• —*American Speech*, p. 54, February 1947: 'Pacific War language'

captain's log *noun*
1 a lavatory *UK*
Rhyming slang for 'bog', based on a famous detail of television and film science fiction adventure series *Star Trek*, since 1969.
• When there are rumblings in the poop deck, an entry in the Captain's Log is warranted.—Ray Puxley, *Fresh Rabbit*, 1998

2 the penis *US*

A *Star Trek* cliché punning on **WOOD** (the erect penis).

- —Erica Orloff and JoAnn Baker, *Dirty Little Secrets*, p. 69, 2001

captain's man *noun*

a police officer designated to pick up bribes from criminals for his superior officers *US*

- Precinct commanders who received graft almost always desiganted a patrolman, "the captain's man," to make their pickups[.]—*The Knapp Commission Report on Police Corruption*, p. 76, 1972

Captain Trips *nickname*

Jerry Garcia (1942–1995), lead guitarist and spiritual bedrock of the Grateful Dead *US*

- —David Shenk and Steve Silberman, *Skeleton Key*, p. 31, 1994

capture *noun*

an arrest and imprisonment *UK*

- [N]o thief and tearaway shows any emotion just because he has got a capture, and has got a lagging to do [.]—Frank Norman, *Bang Too Rights*, p. 8, 1958

capture *verb*

▸ **capture the bishop**

(of a male) to masturbate *UK*

Punning 'capture' with 'to lay hands on'; a variation of **BASH THE BISHOP** (to masturbate).

capun *noun*

capital punishment *US*

- —William K. Bentley and James M. Corbett, *Prison Slang*, p. 104, 1992

caput *adjective*

▷ see: **KAPUT**

cap work *noun*

the alteration of dice for cheating by making them resilient on certain surfaces, which makes them more likely to bounce off the altered sides *US*

- —*The Annals of the American Academy of Political and Social Sciences*, p. 122, May 1950

car *noun*

1 a clique of prisoners *US*

- —James Harris, *A Convict's Dictionary*, p. 29, 1989

2 a radio *US*

- —Gary K. Farlow, *Prison-ese*, p. 10, 2002

3 in lobstering, a slatted box in the water in which lobsters are kept until they are sold *US*

- A small car holds from 1500 to 2000 pounds of lobsters.—Kendall Merriam, *The Illustrated Dictionary of Lobstering*, p. 19, 1978

caramel *noun*

▸ **drop a caramel**

to defecate *UK: SCOTLAND*

- Ah widny go in there fur a wee bit. Ah've jist drapped a caramel. —Michael Munro, *The Patter, Another Blast*, 1988

caramel *adjective*

mixed race *US*

- I noticed a lot of Jungle Fever action, with people describing themselves as "vanilla" or "chocolate" or "caramel."—Anka Radakovich, *The Wild Girls Club*, p. 43, 1994

caramello *noun*

a type of hashish from Morocco *UK*

From the Spanish for 'caramel'.

- —Nick Jones, *Spliffs*, p. 85, 2003

caravan *nickname*

the section of Mountjoy jail where members of the travelling community are incarcerated *IRELAND*

- The poor blokes were trying to explain as diplomatically as they could that the caravan – our name for the cells where the travellers were kept – was full and the screws had told them to move in with him. —Howard Paul, *The Joy*, p. 24–25, 1996

carb *noun*

a carburettor *US, 1942*

- Some cars use two, four, or even six carbs. More carbs mean more air, more fuel, and more power.—Ed Radlauer, *Drag Racing Pix Dix*, p. 11, 1970

car banger *noun*

a criminal who specialises in stealing from cars *US*

- —Ralph de Sola, *Crime Dictionary*, p. 23, 1982

carbie; carby *noun*

a carburettor *NEW ZEALAND, 1956*

- 'Carburettor, matey,' said Joe. 'We'll start on the carby.'—Nino Culotta (John O'Grady), *They're A Weird Mob*, p. 47, 1957
- —Harry Orsman, *A Dictionary of Modern New Zealand Slang*, p. 26, 1999

carbo *noun*

carboyhydrates *US, 1977*

- Three days before the Ironman "I ate carbos. Bread. Spaghetti. Anything."—*Washington Post*, p. E1, 3rd November 1982

carbolic dip *noun*

the bath or shower with carbolic dip given to prisoners when they arrive at a prison *US*

- —Hyman E. Goldin et al., *Dictionary of American Underworld Lingo*, p. 40, 1950

car bra *noun*

a cover placed on the front of a car in the hope or belief that it will foil radar speed-detection *US*

- —*American Speech*, Winter 1990

carburettor *noun*

a tube with holes used for smoking marijuana; a hole that is designed to let air into a pipe used for smoking marijuana *US*

As its automotive namesake forces a mixture of fuel and oxygen into an engine, the marijuana-related carburettor forces a mixture of marijuana smoke and air into the smoker's lungs.

- —*High Times*, May 1976
- —Simon Worman, *Joint Smoking Rules*, 2001
- —Steven Wishnia, *The Cannabis Companion*, p. 151, 2004

carcass *noun*

one's body; oneself *AUSTRALIA*

- [H]e began to curse the shire engineer and the road gang responsible for the upkeep of this by-blow of a road, a set of wool-brained gutless wonders, none of whem worked an ounce of fat off their carcasses in a month.—Kylie Tennant, *The Honey Flow*, p. 58, 1956
- Plant your carcass and prepare for battle.—Frank Hardy, *The Outcasts of Foolgarah*, p. 26, 1971
- Rest your carcass[.]—Frank Hardy, *The Outcasts of Foolgarah*, p. 39, 1971

car catcher *noun*

a rear brakeman on a freight train *US*

- —Norman Carlisle, *The Modern Wonder Book of Trains and Railroading*, p. 260, 1946

car clout *noun*

a thief who breaks into and steals the contents of cars *US*

- —*American Speech*, p. 267, December 1962: 'The language of traffic policemen'

card *noun*

1 a tactic held in reserve and then used to win an advantage *US, 1973*

Usually in the expression 'playing the (fill in the blank) card'.

- —*American Speech*, Winter 1983

2 an eccentric; a lively personality *UK, 1836*

- Mr [Charles] Kennedy has a well perked image because he's a card, who appears on bantering chat shows[.]—*The Guardian*, 12th February 2002

▸ **go through the card**

to have everything on offer; to cover something comprehensively *UK*

Originally, 'to back every winning horse at a race-meeting'.

- —David Powis, *The Signs of Crime*, 1977

▸ **on the card**

on the railways, on time *US*

- —Ramon Adams, *The Language of the Railroader*, p. 108, 1977

card *verb*

1 to ask someone for proof of age before selling or serving them alcohol *US, 1975*

- —Sue Black, *The Totally Awesome Val Guide*, p. 21, 1982
- Whoa, he didn't even card us.—*Bill and Ted's Excellent Adventure*, 1989
- I never get carded either, have to show any proof.—Elmore Leonard, *Maximum Bob*, p. 3, 1991

2 to trade credit card numbers illegally *UK*

- Living one rung higher are the COdeZ KidZ, who specialize in swapping fraudulent credit card numbers, and break authorization codes to the phone company lines. Carding and auth.code boards exist everywhere, but particularly in Eastern Europe.—Melanie McGrath, *Hard, Soft & Wet*, p. 79, 1998

cardboard *noun*
in horse racing, a betting ticket *AUSTRALIA*
• —Ned Wallish, *The Truth Dictionary of Racing Slang*, p. 13, 1989

cardboard box *noun*
any sexually transmitted infection *UK*
Rhyming slang for **POX**.
• —Red Daniells, 1980
• —Bodmin Dark, *Dirty Cockney Rhyming Slang*, 2003

cardboard caver *noun*
in caving and pot-holing, a caver who gives up at the first sign of wetness *UK*
Derogatory.
• —David Morrison of Wessex Cave Club, 29th February 2004

cardboard city *noun*
a prison segregation unit *UK*
Derives from the fact that the furniture in such prison cells is often made from cardboard.
• —Angela Devlin, *Prison Patter*, p. 34, 1996

card-carrying *adjective*
devout, dedicated *US, 1963*
First used in the late 1940s to describe fervent leftists in the US as 'card-carrying Communists', the term was given new life in 1988 when Democratic presidential candidate Michael Dukakis described himself as a 'card-carrying member of the American Civil Liberties Union'.
• Donald, you are a real card-carrying cunt. —Mart Crowley, *The Boys in the Band*, p. 42, 1968
• They are efficient card-carrying members of our tight-knit organisation which is pledged to take over the Government through the ballot box. —Colin Sinclair, *Tall, Bronzed and Handsome*, p. 82, 1968
• Currently, I'm a fully paid-up card-carrying Sniffer from way back[.] —Barry Humphries, *The Traveller's Tool*, p. 70, 1985
• But people in politics remembered the Communist history of the word and were careful not to apply it to a left-leaning noun. A card-carrying hawk offended nobody, but a card-carrying dove was an insult. —*The New York Times Magazine*, p. 20, 18th September 1988
• They pursued liberals, pinkos and others they suspected of being card-carrying commies[.] —*The Chicago Tribune*, p. C3, 30th September 1988
• Miss Lambell took me through all her exercises and shared with me all the secrets of a fully paid-up, card-carrying glamourpuss. —Edna Everage (Barry Humphries), *My Gorgeous Life*, p. 120, 1989
• Only a card-carrying shithead would show his face at a nudie joint in an election year. —Carl Hiaasen, *Strip Tease*, p. 11, 1993
• Yet here we have this card-carrying gibberer coming out and attacking an Olympic gold medallist[.] —*Daily Telegraph*, 2nd July 2003

cardenales *noun*
barbiturates *US*
From the Spanish for 'cardinal' (a red bird).
• —*Providence (Rhode Island) Journal-Bulletin*, p. 6B, 4th August 1997

carder *noun*
a person employed to place prostitutes' advertising cards in telephone boxes and other public places *UK*
• But the 'carders', who can earn up to 350 a day, simply tail the councilmen around the prime phone booth sites and move in once they have been cleaned up. —*Evening Standard (London)*, p. 21, 28th September 1994
• In the London borough of Westminster alone there are approximately 150 carders operating, another 24 covering the Soho area and 59 carders have been prosecuted in Paddington. —Caroline Archer, *Tart Cards*, p. 36, 2003

cardi; cardie; cardy *noun*
a *cardi*gan, a knitted woollen jacket *UK*
Named after James Brudenell, the seventh Earl of Cardigan (1797–1868) whose cavalry troops, during the Crimean War (1853–56), wore a similar garment for warmth.
• If you wear your heart on your sleeve, wear a cardie. —Kathy Lette, *Girls' Night Out*, p. 147, 1987
• Keva examined his manager's [...] suede-and-corduroy zip-up cardi and smiled to himself. —Kevin Sampson, *Powder*, p. 27, 1999
• I had the cardy tied round my waist[.] —Dave Courtney, *Stop the Ride I Want to Get Off*, p. 266, 1999

cardies *noun*
electronic gambling machines that display playing cards *AUSTRALIA*
• On the Great Northern Hotel at the Pacific Highway-Mowbray Road intersection at Chatswood, he says, there's a sign: Pokies and Cardies. —*Sydney Morning Herald*, p. 1, 21st March 1998

cardinal *noun*
▸ **the cardinal is home**
used for conveying that the speaker is experiencing the bleed period of the menstrual cycle *US*
• —*Maledicta*, p. 197, Winter 1980: 'A new erotic vocabulary'

card mob *noun*
two or more card cheats working together *US*
• —John Scarne, *Scarne's Guide to Modern Poker*, p. 274, 1979

cards *noun*
▸ **on the cards**
likely, probable *UK, 1849*
• As Iraq tries to rebuild itself, a struggle over the country's internet identity is on the cards[.] —*The Guardian*, 5th July 2004

cards speak *noun*
in high-low poker, the rule that players need not declare whether they are playing for a low or high hand *US*
• —Peter O. Steiner, *Thursday Night Poker*, p. 409, 1996

card surfing *noun*
1 a moving of custom between credit cards to achieve financial advantage *UK*
• [T]he phenomenon of card surfing, whereby cardholders readily switch debt between cards to minimise repayments and the interest that accrues to outstanding balances[.] —*Minutes of Evidence to the Select Committee on Treasury*, 31st July 2000

2 a criminal act in which a criminal closely observes a person using an automatic cash machine (by looking over his or her shoulder) and notes the personal identity number that is enterered on the keypad; the user's card is subsequently stolen, without making the user aware of the theft, and fraudulent withdrawals of cash are the criminal's reward *US*
Also known as 'shoulder surfing'.
• Mostly it starts with what is called "shoulder surfing." While you're holding your credit card at a pay phone, especially in a large public area, people can stand at your shoulder and get your card number. —*Atlanta Journal and Constitution*, p. H10, 10th May 1992
• In fact, "shoulder surfing" is an outdated, low-tech approach. Thieves no longer need to steal a debit card to gain access to a bank account through an ATM. They simply make the cards themselves. —*Baltimore Sun*, 15th April 2003

care *verb*
▸ **not care less**
to be absolutely unconcerned *US, 1966*
• Politicians couldn't care less about social care[.] —*The Guardian*, 21st May 2001

care bear *noun*
a person working in a prison who is seen to be too sympathetic to the prisoners' needs *UK*
Derogatory; based on cute cartoon characters The Care Bears, originally created in 1981 for US greeting cards, and subsequently animated for television and film.
• —Angela Devlin, *Prison Patter*, p. 34, 1996
• People who viewed them [prisoners] in a more positive light and tried to help were labelled "care bears", and this applied to officers and "civilian " staff like myself. —*The Guardian*, p. 19, 25th September 2002

career girl *noun*
a ewe that refuses to nurse her young *NEW ZEALAND*
• —*Dominion Post*, p. C6, 22nd November 2002

career mangler *noun*
in the Canadian military, a Career Manager *CANADA*
• A "career mangler" is the slang nickname for the person at National Defence Headquarters who controls the personnel within a given military occupation. So it pays to maintain a good relationship with one's career manager. —Tom Langeste, *Words on the Wing*, p. 53, 1995

care factor: zero! *noun*
I don't care about what you just said! *US*
• —Judi Sanders, *Da Bomb!*, p. 6, 1997

CARE package *noun*
1 a box of treats and/or necessities, sent to someone away from home with the hope of cheering them up *US, 1962*
Suggested by CARE packages sent by the United Nations.

- [H]e paid the priest for the funeral, arranged a CARE pacakage for Jack in the Sierra (Hersheys and khaki socks)[.] —Richard Farina, *Been Down So Long*, p. 256, 1966
- If you didn't get a care package and couldn't make a buy, you made sandwiches out of bread and whatever food you got at supper. —Piri Thomas, *Down These Mean Streets*, p. 256–257, 1967
- —*Current Slang*, p. 8, Fall 1967
- I sent him a care package while he was in quarantine and the deputy allowed me to visit him. —A.S. Jackson, *Gentleman Pimp*, p. 61, 1973
- [I]n two or three Care Packages as the couple called them[.] —Ed Sanders, *Tales of Beatnik Glory*, p. 22, 1975

2 a small amount of a drug disguised for safe carrying and later use *UK*

- —Tom Hibbert, *Rockspeak!*, p. 36, 1983

careware *noun*

computer software offered free by its developer, with the request that the user make a contribution to a charity in place of paying a fee for the software *US*

- —Eric S. Raymond, *The New Hacker's Dictionary*, p. 89, 1991

carga *noun*

heroin *US*

Border Spanish used in English conversation by Mexican-Americans.

- Depending on who is listening, heroin can be referred to as carga (heroin), la chiva (the thing), or la madre (the mother). —George R. Alvarez, *Semiotic Dynamics of an Ethnic-American Sub-Cultural Group*, p. 4, 1965
- —*Current Slang*, p. 14, Fall 1968
- [Y]ou take your first the of carga before you get laid. —Oscar Zeta Acosta, *The Revolt of the Cockroach People*, p. 90, 1973
- —Dagoberto Fuentes and Jose Lopez, *Barrio Language Dictionary*, p. 29, 1974
- —Walter Way, *The Drug Scene*, p. 106, 1977

cargo *noun*

ostentatious jewellery worn as a status symbol *UK*

- One of the men in green baggy trousers, matching silk shirt and heavy gold "cargo" around his neck[.] —Donald Gorgon, *Cop Killer*, p. 87, 1994

carhop *noun*

1 an employee in a drive-in restaurant who serves customers in their cars *US, 1939*

- I drove on past the gaudy neons and the false fronts behind them, the sleazy hamburger joints that look like palaces under the colors, the circular drive-ins as gay as circuses with the chipper hard-eyed car-hops[.] —Raymond Chandler, *The Little Sister*, p. 79, 1949
- When he got his discharge papers he made tracks for Laguna Beach, where he landed a job as a carhop in a drive-in beanery. —Bernard Wolfe, *The Late Risers*, p. 159, 1954
- It was a big year for a drive-in restaurant carhop. —Merle Haggard, *The Way It Was in '51*, 1975
- They don't have carhops there, they have a radio speaker into which you call your order. —Mort Sahl, *Heartland*, p. 61, 1976
- Son of a carhop in an all-night dive. —Rodney Crowell, *Ain't Livin' Long Like This*, 1978

2 a girl who chooses partners on the basis of their car *US*

- —Bill Valentine, *Gang Intelligence Manual*, p. 75, 1995

cariole *noun*

a horse-drawn sleigh *CANADA*

- In La Perade [Quebec] fur-coated cariole drivers sing as they drive the fishing parties to and from the fishing huts. —*Star Weekly*, p. 21/2, 2nd January 1965

carjack *verb*

to steal a car from its driver under threat of bodily harm *US, 1991*

An elision of 'car' and 'hijack'.

- Last night I watched two guys carjack a Camero down on the corner of Argyle there. —*Get Shorty*, 1995
- In New York, police have warned drivers to drive on if another car so much as touches theirs: it could be just another carjacker seeking a long-term test drive. —David Rowan, *A Glossary for the 90s*, p. 37, 1998
- Car-jacking is the lazy man's boost. No skill. No finesse. —*Gone in 60 Seconds*, 2000

car jockey *noun*

1 a race car driver *US*

- Doug Nash picked the kind of career that appealed to most of his young Indian friends – an auto mechanic or perhaps, if he got lucky, a stock car jockey. —*Washington Post*, p. A2, 7th February 1977
- The stock car boys usually get on with such high jinks while the high-dollar Indy car jockeys tippy-toe around because they know a second's brashness can mean instant disintegration. —*Washington Post*, p. C1, 31st May 1982

2 a parking attendant *US, 1956*

- Even the car jockeys in Washington have college degrees. —*New York Times*, p. 14 (Section 7), 7th February 1982
- "Me and My White Pal," which deals with an African student in France who must work as a car jockey to pay for his tuition. —*Chicago Tribune*, p. C7, 2nd January 2004

cark; kark *verb*

to die *AUSTRALIA, 1977*

Origin unknown. Suggestions that it is from 'carcass', or from 'cark' (the harsh cry of a crow) are not very convincing.

- If the silly basket-case carks, he carks – but you will have done everything humanly possible to save him with the least possible fuss. —Ignatius Jones, *The 1992 True Hip Manual*, p. 203, 1992

car key *noun*

a screwdriver used for breaking into cars *UK*

- —Angela Devlin, *Prison Patter*, p. 34, 1996

cark it; kark it *verb*

to die *AUSTRALIA, 1982*

- But my fiance says we have to wait until the inherited terrier carks it and we can get ourselves a real "four-wheel-drive dog"...you know, like a terrier. —Gretel Killeen, *Hot Buns and Ophelia get a Bloke*, p. 4, 2000
- I wasn't to know my dad was going to cark it a couple of years later and leave me a shed load of cash. —Jenny Eclair, *Camberwell Beauty*, p. 30, 2000
- Comes out of jail that very fuckin day and to celebrate OD's on meth. Carked it. The prick. —Niall Griffiths, *Sheepshagger*, p. 55, 2001
- Thought I was gunner cark it with laughin so much. —Niall Griffiths, *Kelly + Victor*, p. 227, 2002

Carl Rosa *noun*

a poser, a poseur; hence, as 'the old Carl Rosa', fraud or deceipt *UK*

Rhyming slang, formed on the name of German musician Carl Rosa, 1842–89; in 1873 he founded the Carl Rosa Opera which is now Britain's oldest opera company.

- —David Powis, *The Signs of Crime*, 1977

Carly; Cally *nickname*

lager manufacturers Carlsberg™; lager manufactured by Carlsberg™ *UK: SCOTLAND*

'Carly' may be used for the basic brand lager or Carlsberg Special Brew, or combined with 'extra' for Carlsberg Extra, and 'special' for Carlsberg Special Brew.

- They'd get blootered on Carly specials to dodge listening to your crummy patter. —Ian Pattison, *Rab C. Nesbitt*, 1988
- That's three heavies, two Callies, an a vodka an Irn Bru. —Michael Munro, *The Patter, Another Blast*, 1988

carmabis *noun*

marijuana *US, 1977*

A visual pun on the word 'cannabis' and a quasi-spiritual reference to **KARMA** (fate); possibly an error in spelling or reading.

- —Richard A. Spears, *The Slang and Jargon of Drugs and Drink*, p. 96, 1986
- —Mike Haskins, *Drugs*, p. 287, 2003

carn!

come on! *AUSTRALIA, 1965*

A call of encouragement especially common amongst sports spectators. Eye-dialect rendering of typical Australian pronunciation. Commonly preceding the name of a team beginning with 'the', e.g. 'carn the Blues' (come on the Blues).

- 'Carn' the magpies,' one kid yelled. —Kerry Cue, *Crooks, Chooks and Bloody Ratbags*, p. 52, 1983
- Not that they were a bad team. They were just poor, that's all. They just couldn't seem to be able to afford to win. Anyway, Carn the mighty Roys! —Barry Dickins, *What the Dickins*, p. 99, 1985
- —Ivor Limb, *Footy's No Joke!*, p. 15, 1986
- Carn! he's yelling, Carn, let's go! —Tim Winton, *Cloudstreet*, p. 107, 1991
- —David McGill, *David McGill's Complete Kiwi Slang Dictionary*, p. 25, 1998

carna

used in exortations *AUSTRALIA*

- "Carna Cats," shrieked my escort. "Carna Bombers, you bloody beauties!" yelled the man beside me. —Sue Rhodes, *Now you'll think I'm awful*, p. 82, 1967
- Saints, please stay at Moorabbin. I know about Waverley. I was a member there for 18 years. It's cold, dark, impersonal, and lifeless. Carna Saints. —*Herald Sun*, p. 14, 9th July 1992

carnal *noun*
among Mexican-Americans, a very close male friend *US*
Border Spanish used in English conversation by Mexican-Americans.
- —George Carpenter Baker, *Pachuco*, p. 41, January 1950
- —Dagoberto Fuentes, *Barrio Language Dictionary*, p. 29, 1974
- [T]hey automatically became members of La Eme, the so-called Mexican Mafia, and were now sworn carnales, the Hispanic term for homeboys.—Seth Morgan, *Homeboy*, p. 176, 1990
- A carnal had to be prepared to fight at all times.—Bill Valentine, *Gangs and Their Tattoos*, p. 33, 2000

carnapper *noun*
a person who habitually steals cars *UK, 1984*
On the pattern of 'kidnapper'.

carne *noun*
heroin *US*
From the Spanish for 'meat'.
- —Richard A. Spears, *The Slang and Jargon of Drugs and Drink*, p. 96, 1986
- —Jay Robert Nash, *Dictionary of Crime*, p. 58, 1992
- —Mike Haskins, *Drugs*, p. 283, 2003

carney; carny *noun*
a carnival *US, 1931*

carnie *noun*
1 a young person under the legal age of consent *NEW ZEALAND*
An abbreviated reference to 'carnal knowledge'; sometimes embellished as 'carnie kid'.
- —Louis S. Leland, *A Personal Kiwi-Yankee Dictionary*, p. 22, 1984

2 a carnation *AUSTRALIA*
- Now, most other invalids get glads or carnies so Beryl said Valda must have really put her thinking cap on.—Barry Humphries, *A Nice Night's Entertainment*, p. 110, 1968

3 cocaine *UK*
- —Mike Haskins, *Drugs*, p. 280, 2003

carnival croquet *noun*
the shell game *US*
- Here we are, ladies and gentlemen! Carnival croquet, the preacher's pastime.—Robert Edmond Alter, *Carny Kill*, p. 34, 1966

carnival louse *noun*
a person who follows a carnival from town to town and associates with carnival employees, but is not one himself *US*
- —Don Wilmeth, *The Language of American Popular Entertainment*, p. 44, 1981

carny *noun*
1 any person employed by or associated with a travelling carnival *US, 1939*
- Itinerant short con and carny hyp men have burned down the croakers of Texas.—William Burroughs, *Naked Lunch*, p. 13, 1957
- —*American Speech*, p. 279, December 1966: 'More carnie talk from the West Coast'
- This girl, I think the most important thing in her background was that her family was carnies.—Bruce Jackson, *In the Life*, p. 196, 1972
- —Gene Sorrows, *All About Carnivals*, p. 12, 1985

2 the insider's language used by carnival workers *US, 1948*
- —Harold Wentworth and Stuart Berg Flexner, *Dictionary of American Slang*, p. 89, 1960

carny Bible *noun*
the Amusement Business magazine *US*
- The Amusement Business magazine is such an integral tool to a carny that it is referred to as the "Carny Bible."—Gene Sorrows, *All About Carnivals*, p. 5, 1985

carny divorce *noun*
an arrangement in which a man and woman who are living together without benefit of a wedding end their relationship, often consisting of one ride backwards around on a ferris wheel *US*
- —Gene Sorrows, *All About Carnivals*, p. 12, 1985

carny's Christmas *noun*
Labor Day (the first Monday in September) *US*
- —Don Wilmeth, *The Language of American Popular Entertainment*, p. 45, 1981

carny wedding *noun*
an arrangement in which a man and woman live together without benefit of a wedding, often consisting of one ride around on a ferris wheel *US*
- —Joe McKennon, *Circus Lingo*, p. 23, 1980
- —Gene Sorrows, *All About Carnivals*, p. 12, 1985

Carolina *noun*
1 in craps, a nine *US, 1950*
- —Thomas L. Clark, *The Dictionary of Gambling and Gaming*, p. 37, 1987

2 a friend, a mate *UK*
A Glasgow rhyming slang extension of 'china plate' (mate), a piece of Cockney rhyming slang.
- —Michael Munro, *The Patter, Another Blast*, 1988

Carolina spread *noun*
significant weight gain below the waist *US*
- —Connie Eble (Editor), *UNC-CH Campus Slang*, p. 2, March 1981

Carolina stocker *noun*
in drag racing, a stock car with illegal equipment or with an illegally large engine *US*
- —Lyle K. Engel, *The Complete Book of Fuel and Gas Dragsters*, p. 150, 1968

carp *noun*
1 anchovies as a pizza topping *US*
- —*Maledicta*, p. 99, 1996: 'Domino's pizza jargon'

2 a black prisoner *US*
- —James Harris, *A Convict's Dictionary*, p. 29, 1989

3 a carpenter, especially on a theatre set *US*
- —Wilfred Granville, *The Theater Dictionary*, p. 31, 1952

car park *noun*
an informer *UK, 1992*
Rhyming slang for **NARK** (an informer).
- —*Daily Telegraph*, 17th December 1972
- —Angela Devlin, *Prison Patter*, p. 34, 1996

carped *adjective*
drug-intoxicated *UK*
- —Macfarlane, Macfarlane and Robson, *The User*, p. ix, 1996

carpenter *noun*
an orthopaedist *US*
- —Sally Williams, *"Strong" Words*, p. 136, 1994

carpenter's dream *noun*
a flat-chested woman *US*
From the pun 'flat as a board, and easy to screw'.
- Nanalie Wood, a carpenter's dream." "Flat as a board an' easy to screw.—Richard Price, *The Wanderers*, p. 27, 1974
- —Michael Dalton Johnson, *Talking Trash with Redd Foxx*, p. 79, 1994

carpet *noun*
1 a three month period of imprisonment *UK, 1903*
A shortening of 'carpet bag', rhyming slang for 'drag', an obsolete term for 'a three month sentence'; this origin is now mainly forgotten; therefore it has since been reasoned that 'carpet' is so-called because it is easy to do.
- If I had pleaded guilty, the chances are I would have been sentenced to a carpet[.]—Frank Norman, *Bang To Rights*, p. 125, 1958
- [S]he got nicked for a carpet[.]—Derek Raymond (Robin Cook), *The Crust on its Uppers*, p. 58, 1962
- —Julian Franklyn, *A Dictionary of Rhyming Slang*, 1969
- [L]ong enough to weave a carpet[.]—Angela Devlin, *Prison Patter*, p. 34, 1996

2 a three year sentence of imprisonment *UK*
- Charlie Shorncliffe came in to serve a carpet – three years.—Charles Raven, *Underworld Nights*, p. 124, 1956

3 in betting, odds of 3–1 *UK, 1967*
- —John McCririck, *John McCririck's World of Betting*, p. 59, 1991

4 a sum of £3 *UK*
- —*Picture Post*, January 1954
- —Brian McDonald (writing of 1960s London underground), *Elephant Boys*, p. 203, 2000

5 three hundred pounds, £300 *UK*
Ticket-touting slang, recorded August 2002. Also spelt 'carpits'.

6 an artificial grass playing surface *US*
- —Bill Shefski, *Running Press Glossary of Football Language*, p. 22, 1978
- A kick off the side of the foot will cut in the carpet and spin like a tennis ball.—*Washington Post*, p. D1, 18th August 1980
- —Mike Whiteford, *How to Talk Baseball*, p. 86, 1987
- What the Rams need to do to win: Give QB Marc Bulger enough protection, and ensuing confidence, to exploit a defense that isn't at its best on carpet.—*USA Today*, p. 4C, 9th January 2004

▸ clean the carpet
(of a female) to masturbate *US*
- Another way to say "the girl is masturbating" [...] Cleaning the carpet[.] —Erica Orloff and JoAnn Baker, *Dirty Little Secrets*, p. 67, 2001

▸ matching carpet and drapes; carpet and drapes that match
applied to a person, usually a woman, whose hair is neither bleached nor dyed *US*
A jocular suggestion that the hair on the head is of the same natural shade as the pubic hair.
- Gwen Stefani's wild pink hair. "Does the carpet match the drapes? Heh, heh, heh." —*OC (Orange County, California) Weekly*, p. 6, 22nd October 1999
- "I ended up doing the photoshoot in her bedroom because she has this real nice pink carpet..." And nice pink hair, half the time. "Yeah..." He laughs an utterly filthy laugh. "The carpet matches the drapes." —*Bang*, p. 43, May 2003
- She then described how she and a friend discuss whether another woman's hair color is truly natural. "What do you think: Does the carpet match the drapes?" she said with a cocked eyebrow. —*Marion (Ohio) Star*, p. 1A, 17th November 2003

carpet and a half *noun*
in betting, odds of 7–2 *UK*
In bookmaker slang **CARPET** is 3–1, here the addition of a half increases the odds to 3½–1 or 7–2.
- —John McCririck, *John McCririck's World of Betting*, 1991

carpetbagger *noun*
a person who interferes in local politics without being a true part of the local community *US, 1868*
- A fantastic notion to turn back time, to drive out the carpetbaggers, to reclaim the land by painting it as treacherous and uninhabitable. —Carl Hiaasen, *Tourist Season*, p. 159, 1986

carpet burger *noun*
oral sex performed on a woman *US*
- —Pamela Munro, *U.C.L.A. Slang*, p. 52, 2001

carpet burn *noun*
a rawness of the skin due to frictional contact with a carpet *US*
On the model of 'rope-burn'. Tends to be used mainly of knees and elbows and generally in the context of wounds received in the course of unconventionally located love-making.
- No fight. No shoving. Not so much as a carpet burn. —*Los Angeles Times*, p. 1 (Part 6), 15th August 1986

carpet control *noun*
an obsessive belief, held whilst under the influence of crack cocaine, that there are useable traces of crack cocaine on the floor *UK, 2001*
A variation on **CARPET PATROL**. From a discreet correspondent.

carpet crawler *noun*
a young child *US*
- —*Complete CB Slang Dictionary*, 1976
- —Peter Chippindale, *The British CB Book*, p. 153, 1981

carpet game *noun*
a swindle in which the swindler holds and then steals the wallet of a customer going to see a non-existent prostitute *US*
- He settled back and found himself listening to Henry Jackson describing his arrest for something he called "carpet game." —Malcolm Braly, *On the Yard*, p. 24, 1967

carpet joint *noun*
a fancy, high-class casino *US, 1961*
- —John Scarne, *Scarne on Dice*, p. 463, 1974
- And he saw the "carpet joint" for what it was – an institution designed with neither windows, doors, chairs, nor wall clocks in order to mesmerize the tourists therein trapped into losing track of time and place as they squandered money. —Gerald Petievich, *Shakedown*, p. 64, 1988
- I used ta only work carpet joints 'cause the ritzy casinos didn't float the dice. —Stephen Cannell, *Big Con*, p. 215, 1997

carpet muncher *noun*
a cunnilinguist; hence, and especially, a lesbian *US*
- [A] socially connected, prominently married carpet muncher with a yen for nightclub canaries was prime meat for the four-star Herald. —James Ellroy, *Hollywood Nocturnes*, p. 270, 1994
- Lesbians and straight women are insulted as 'carpet-munchers.' —*New York Post*, p. 18, 13th February 1999

carpeto; carpito *noun*
thirty pounds (£30) *UK*
Ticket-touting slang, recorded August 2002. From **CARPET** (£300).

carpet patrol *noun*
smokers of crack cocaine who search the floor for droppings of crack cocaine *UK*

carpet slashing *noun*
a dance party *US*
From the more common **CUT A RUG**.
- One night at a carpet slashing Romeo got a gander at Julie. —Haenigsen, *Jive's Like That*, 1947

carpet walker *noun*
a drug addict *US*
- —Eugene Landy, *The Underground Dictionary*, p. 46, 1971

car-popping *noun*
car-theft *UK*
From **POP** (to steal).
- [I]t was mainly ram-raiding or car popping to fund the next buzz. —Macfarlane, Macfarlane and Robson, *The User*, p. 106, 1996

Carrie; Carrie Nation; Carry; Carry Nation *noun*
cocaine *US*
- —*American Speech*, p. 86, May 1955: 'Narcotic argot along the Mexican border'
- —R.C. Garrett et al., *The Coke Book*, 1984
- —Peter Johnson, *Dictionary of Street Alcohol and Drug Terms*, 1993
- —Nick Constable, *This is Cocaine*, p. 181, 2002

carrier pigeon *noun*
a messenger or courier *US, 1933*
- We relied on 'carrier pigeons' – other Korean agents who would take messages back and forth. Damnably dangerous work but necessary. —Joseph C. Goulden, *Korea*, p. 470, 1982

carrot *noun*
a marijuana cigarette *US, 2001*
- —Simon Worman, *Joint Smoking Rules*, 2001

carrot cruncher *noun*
(from an urban perspective) a country-dweller *UK*
- —David Powis, *The Signs of Crime*, 1977
- [A] load of fucking carrot crunchers smashed their heads in at a picnic. —Danny King, *The Burglar Diaries*, p. 208, 2001

carrot eater; carrot snapper *noun*
a Mormon *US, 1968*
Offensive.
- In and around the state of Utah, Mormons have been called carrot-eaters or carrot-snappers. —Irving Lewis Allen, *Unkind Words*, p. 50, 1990

carrot-top *noun*
a red-headed person *US, 1889*
- Arthur Godfrey is going to have the whole Buckeye State after his carrot top for what he did to Miss Ohio last night. —*San Francisco News*, p. 12, 6th November 1956
- Another carrot-top had been dead for over a year. —Gerald Petievich, *Money Men*, p. 97, 1981
- If only the carrottop kook were hunkered beside him on the grass. —Seth Morgan, *Homeboy*, p. 190, 1990

carry *noun*
1 any victim of a crime who must be taken from the scene by stretcher *US*
- —*New York Times Magazine*, p. 87, 16th March 1958

2 a consignment or substantial quantity of drugs *UK*
- —Angela Devlin, *Prison Patter*, p. 34, 1996

carry *verb*
1 to carry a firearm *US*
- I'd get three Hail Marys and the priest'd ask me confidentially if I could get him something light he could carry under his coat. —George V. Higgins, *The Friends of Eddie Doyle*, p. 7, 1971
- Turn around a lift your tail. All right, you ain' carryin'. —Robert Campbell, *In La-La Land We Trust*, p. 173, 1986

2 to be in possession of drugs *US, 1961*
- "Are you carrying?" = "Got any drugs?" —Angela Devlin, *Prison Patter*, p. 34, 1996

3 to have surplus money *UK: NORTHERN IRELAND*
- —C. I. Macafee, *A Concise Ulster Dictionary*, p. 56, 1996

4 to lead or be in charge of something *US*
• —Bruce Jackson, *Outside the Law*, p. 56, 1972

▸ **carry a big spoon**
to stir up trouble *AUSTRALIA*
• —Ned Wallish, *The Truth Dictionary of Racing Slang*, p. 7, 1989

▸ **carry a case**
to be out of prison on bail *UK*
A neat play on a basic travel requirement and a 'court case'.
• —Angela Devlin, *Prison Patter*, p. 34, 1996

▸ **carry a torch**
to yearn for an unrequited love or a love affair that is over; to be devoted to someone without having your devotion reciprocated *US, 1927*
• Well, back in New York I carried a torch, as we used to say.—John O'Hara, *Assembly*, p. 83, 1961
• Man I must have been blind / To carry a torch / For most of my life —Starsailor, *Fever*, 2001

▸ **carry it to the door**
to serve all of a prison sentence *US*
• —Gary K. Farlow, *Prison-ese*, p. 11, 2002

▸ **carry news**
to gossip *TRINIDAD AND TOBAGO, 1970*
• —Lise Winer, *Dictionary of the English/Creole of Trinidad & Tobago*, 2003

▸ **carry someone's bags**
to be romantically involved with someone *US*
• —Sherman Louis Sergel, *The Language of Show Biz*, p. 107, 1973

▸ **carry the banner**
to stay up all night *US*
• —Joe McKennon, *Circus Lingo*, p. 23, 1980

▸ **carry the bug**
in circus usage, to work as a night watchman *US*
From **BUG** (a torch).
• —Don Wilmeth, *The Language of American Popular Entertainment*, p. 46, 1981

▸ **carry the can back; carry the can**
to take the blame or punishment on behalf of another; to be made a scapegoat; to do the dirty work while another gets the credit *UK, 1929*
Navy origins.
• He got two years. The others got off, and he carried the can back. —Clive Exton, *No Fixed Abode [Six Granada Plays]*, p. 121, 1959
• Regan raised an eyebrow. "You're the guv'nor – but I take the can!" — *The Sweeney*, p. 75, 1976

▸ **carry the mail**
1 to buy drinks *AUSTRALIA*
• —Sidney J Baker, *The Australian Language*, 1966

2 to commit a murder for hire *US*
• I hear they used to call up from Providence whenever they had a particularly bad piece of work and get ahold of Artie Van to carry the mail.—George V. Higgins, *The Friends of Eddie Doyle*, p. 101, 1971

3 to move quickly *US*
• —Norman Carlisle, *The Modern Wonder Book of Trains and Railroading*, p. 260, 1946

▸ **carry the shit bucket**
to perform the lowliest tasks *AUSTRALIA*
• Somebody has to carry the healing arts shit bucket.—Petru Popescu, *The Last Wave*, 1977

▸ **carry the silks**
in horse racing, to race for a particular owner *US*
• —David W. Maurer, *Argot of the Racetrack*, p. 18, 1951

▸ **carry the stick**
to live without a fixed abode *US*
• Carrying the stick means not having a fixed address.—Burgess Laughlin, *Job Opportunities in the Black Market*, p. 13–2, 1978

▸ **carry the target**
in horse racing, to run in the last position for an entire race *US*
• —Tom Ainslie, *Ainslie's Complete Guide to Thoroughbred Racing*, p. 329, 1976

▸ **carry the wheels**
to accelerate so quickly that the vehicle's front wheels lift off the ground *US*
• —Lyle K. Engel, *The Complete Book of Fuel and Gas Dragsters*, p. 150, 1968

▸ **carry your bat out**
in cricket, to survive your team's innings undismissed *UK, 1934*
• —Michael Rundell, *The Dictionary of Cricket*, 1985

carryall *noun*
a vehicle for transport, either wheeled or on rails for snow *CANADA*
• —*Report of DME Test Team IA*, p. 2, 1949
• Securely laced into the canvas carry-all of the dog sled, Mam [a bitch] screamed monotonously.—R. M. Patterson, *Far Pastures*, p. 67, 1963

carry-away *noun*
a robbery in which a safe is taken and opened at leisure away from the crime scene *US*
• —Jack Webb, *The Badge*, p. 220, 1958

carry day *noun*
in television and film making, a day in which the cast and crew are paid but do not have to work *US*
• —Ralph S. Singleton, *Filmaker's Dictionary*, p. 28, 1990

carry down *verb*
to arrest someone *TRINIDAD AND TOBAGO, 1971*
• —Lise Winer, *Dictionary of the English/Creole of Trinidad & Tobago*, 2003

carrying all before her *adjective*
of a woman, having a generous bust or obviously pregnant *UK, 1984*
Jocular.

carryings-on *noun*
conspicuous behaviour *UK, 1859*
• For those of us who have not really followed EastEnders closely since the days of the Pinteresque Dot and Ethel exchanges, it is a shock to learn of the outrageous 21st-century carryings-on in Walford.—*The Guardian*, 4th November 2002

carrying weight *adjective*
depressed *UK, 1984*
Beatniks' use, late 1950s-60s; from the notion of being under a heavy burden.

Carry Nation *noun*
▷ **see: CARRIE**

carry-on *noun*
1 a fuss; an uproar; an outbreak of excited behaviour *UK, 1890*
• Ooh er missus, what a carry on at the Beeb[.]—*The Guardian*, 22nd July 2002

2 any continuing activity or catalogue of details *UK*
• He's fucking potty about films, by the way [...] Always going on about the plot and that, supporting roles and all of that carry-on.—Kevin Sampson, *Outlaws*, p. 227, 2001

carry on *verb*
1 to behave in a conspicuous way, to make a fuss *UK, 1828*

2 to be involved in a flirtatious or adulterous relationship *UK, 1856*
Generally phrased 'carry on with', specifying the other person.

3 to act in an ostentatiously effeminate manner in public *US*
• —Donald Webster Cory and John P. LeRoy, *The Homosexual and His Society*, p. 262, 1963: 'A lexicon of homosexual slang'

carry tos *noun*
(around Shigawake in the Gaspe) social welfare *CANADA*
The word is pronounced 'carry toss'.
• Carry tos is a bit of franglais or an anglicization of a word in ecclesiastical Latin, "caritas," "Christian love of one's fellow humans, and the origin of the word "charity."—Bill Casselman, *Canadian Food Words*, p. 168, 1998

carry your ass!
go away! *GUYANA*
• —Richard Allsopp, *Dictionary of Caribbean English Usage*, p. 138, 1998

carsey; karsey *noun*
a brothel *UK*
From the Italian *casa* (a house) which is also its original use.
• —Paul Baker, *Polari*, p. 168, 2002

car-shop *verb*
to break into a car to steal its contents *US*
• —Jim Crotty, *How to Talk American*, p. 144, 1997

cart *verb*

1 to carry something somewhere *UK*
From the conventional sense (to transport by cart).
• [T]he manager of a shoe shop up in Wembley who, it seemed, carted the week's takings to the bank every Saturday night. — John Peter Jones, *Feather Pluckers*, p. 30, 1964

2 in cricket, to hit the ball or attack the bowling with unrestrained power *UK, 1903*
• — Michael Rundell, *The Dictionary of Cricket*, 1985

Carter's Little Liver Pills *noun*
any central nervous system stimulant *US*
• — Elementary Electronics, *Dictionary of CB Lingo*, p. 56, 1976

cart-nap *verb*
to steal a shopping trolley *UK*
A jocular combination of 'cart' and 'kidnap'.
• — Angela Devlin, *Prison Patter*, p. 34, 1996

car toad; car tink; car tonk; car whacker *noun*
a railway inspector *US*
Named for the squatting position taken when inspecting the underside of a car.
• — Norman Carlisle, *The Modern Wonder Book of Trains and Railroading*, p. 260, 1946

carton-pusher *noun*
a person who sells cigarettes that have been stolen or smuggled from a state with lower taxes *US*
• The "carton pusher" is the other kind of retailer. He attracts customers by selling below the price for legal cigarettes. — Burgess Laughlin, *Job Opportunities in the Black Market*, p. 10–9, 1978

car trick *noun*
an act of sex between a prostitute and customer in a car *US*
• Sue never let Sadie have another room – to pay her money out finished their relationship. Now most of Sadie's tricks were car tricks. — Nathan Heard, *Howard Street*, 1968

carts; cartz *noun*
a man's genitalia *UK*
• "So sister," I polaried. "Will you take a varder at the cartz on the feely-omi [young man] in the naf [poor taste] strides [trousers][.] — James Gardiner, *Who's a Pretty Boy Then?*, p. 123,
• [L]oads of bona omes [good men] with huge carts[.] — the cast of 'Aspects of Love', Prince of Wales Theatre, *Palare (Boy Dancer Talk) for Beginners*, 1989–92

cartucho *noun*
a package containing marijuana cigarettes, equivalent to a packet of cigarettes *UK*
From 'cartouche' (a roll or case of paper, etc., containing a charge for a firearm).
• — *The Shorter Oxford English Dictionary*, 1986

cartwheel *noun*

1 a feigned drug withdrawal spasm *US, 1936*
• A drug addict's life is dedicated to cheating, lying, conniving, and 'conning' to obtain illicit drugs. It's an obsession. And they'll go to any length to achieve their purpose. They'll pull a 'Brody' or 'Cartwheel' (feigned spasms) to elicit sympathy. — *San Francisco News*, p. 1, 5th December 1951

2 an amphetamine tablet *US*
• I asked what they were and somebody beside me said, "Cartwheels, man. Bennies. Eat some, they'll keep you going." — Hunter S. Thompson, *Hell's Angels*, p. 216, 1966
• — Donald Louria, *The Drug Scene*, p. 189, 1971
• Army officers pass out "cartwheels" – 20-milligram dextroampheta-mine pills – to keep their men alert and moving on patrol duty. — *The San Francisco Chronicle*, p. 12, 24th June 1971

3 a silver dollar piece *US*
• — Vincent J. Monteleone, *Criminal Slang*, p. 44, 1949
• — Steve Kuriscak, *Casino Talk*, p. 10, 1985

cartzo; catso; cartes *noun*
the penis *UK, 1702*
From Italian *cazzo* (to thust).
• — Paul Baker, *Polari*, p. 168, 2002
• — *Attitude*, p. 60, July 2003

carve *verb*

1 in skateboarding, to take a turn sharply *US*
• — Albert Cassorla, *The Skateboarder's Bible*, p. 199, 1976

2 in surfing, to change the course of the surfboard by digging it into the water *US*
• — John Grissim, *Pure Stoke*, p. 156, 1980

3 in mountain biking, to travel at great speed around corners *US*
• I put a lot of weight on it and carve the turn. — *Mountain Bike Magazine's Complete Guide To Mountain Biking Skills*, p. 148, 1996

4 in foot-propelled scootering, to turn sharply while in mid-jump *UK*
Glossed as 'Pulling off a big, fast, aerial scoot-turn'.
• — Ben Sharpe, *Scooter Crazy*, p. 40, 2000

5 to outplay another musician in a competition of solos *US*
• — Clarence Major, *Dictionary of Afro-American Slang*, p. 35, 1970

▸ **carve some beef**
to grant sexual favours; to consent to sex *US*
• "So what's the deal, then? She carving you some beef?" Another gangbang sexual reference. — Stephen J. Cannell, *The Tin Collectors*, p. 34, 2001

▸ **carve up the mob**
to surf recklessly through a crowd of surfers or swimmers *AUSTRALIA*
• — John Severson, *Modern Surfing Around the World*, p. 165, 1964

▸ **carve your knob**
to make you understand *US*
• — Lavada Durst, *The Jives of Dr. Hepcat*, p. 12, 1953

▸ **carve yourself a slice**
from the male point of view, to have sex *UK, 1984*

carved up *adjective*
(used of a bodybuilder) without fat *US*
• — *American Speech*, p. 198, Fall 1984: 'The language of bodybuilding'

carve-up *noun*

1 a fight; a battle; a gang war *UK, 1961*
• There was too much of this sort of carve-up going on. Getting themselves all dolled up and then setting out to start a row – deliberately setting out to start trouble. — John Burke and Stuart Douglass, *The Boys*, p. 45, 1962

2 an act of poor driving in which one vehicle cuts in front of another *UK, 1984*

3 a division of loot, profits or the legacy of a will *UK, 1935*
• [T]he Chair is supposed to be politically neutral. It is not supposed to be part of a carve-up between parties[.] — P. Robinson, *Northern Ireland Assembley*, 15th February 1999

4 a swindle *UK, 1937*
• — Jonathan Coe, *The Winshaw Legacy; or, What a Carve Up!*, 1996

carve up *verb*

1 of a driver, to cut in front of another vehicle and force the driver of that vehicle to brake or take other emergency action *UK, 1984*
• Every day motorists pull out when I have the right of way, carve me up, overtake other cars when I'm travelling in the opposite direction[.] — *The Observer*, 25th January 2004

2 to spoil the chances of another's business *UK, 1961*
• Tenders and contracts are discussed and carved up beyond the democratic gaze of Bristolians. — *The Bristolian*, 16th July 2002

3 to swindle an accomplice out of a share *UK, 1937*

carvie *noun*

1 a fellow-prisoner who shares in a supply of tobacco, perhaps by subscription to a common supply *UK*
• "He's my carvie" = he is my partner in this week's tobacco. — Paul Tempest, *Lag's Lexicon*, p. 32, 1950

2 a prisoner who deals in contraband tobacco; a tobacco baron *UK*
From the earlier sense (a prisoner who shares your tobacco). This sense describes the prisoner who *carves up* the supply.
• — Angela Devlin, *Prison Patter*, p. 35, 1996

carving knife *noun*
a wife *UK*
Rhyming slang.
• Poor sod got cash and carried [married] to a carving knife with a face like a totem. — Bodmin Dark, *Dirty Cockney Rhyming Slang*, 2003

car wash *noun*

during the Vietnam war, an establishment in Vietnam where a man went for a haircut, bath, massage and sex *US*

- And finally the convoy would crank and crash past the strip of car-wash and hand-laundry whorehouses outside the Tay Ninh Base Camp gate, where the housecats got laid. — Larry Heinemann, *Close Quarters*, p. 95, 1977
- Some of us would sneak off to Tu Duc Phuc's #1 Souvenirs and Car Wash in town and get laid. — Larry Heinemann, *Paco's Story*, p. 116, 1990
- — Linda Reinberg, *In the Field*, p. 35, 1991

car whacker *noun*

▷ see: CAR TOAD

casa *noun*

the operator of a gambling establishment or game *TRINIDAD AND TOBAGO, 1952*

Spanish for 'house'.

- — Lise Winer, *Dictionary of the English/Creole of Trinidad & Tobago*, 2003

casabas *noun*

the female breasts *US, 1970*

- What ever happened to comparing breasts to fruit – casabas, melons, peaches? [Letter to Editor] — *New York Times*, p. 20 (Section 6), 19th September 1993

Casablanca *noun*

a wanker (an all-purpose term of abuse) *UK*

Rhyming slang.

- — Tom Nind, *Rude Rhyming Slang*, p. 9, 2003

Casablanca gold *noun*

a variety of hashish produced on the higher slopes of the Rif Mountains *UK*

- [T]he quality of Casablanca gold is a cut above your average. — Nick Jones, *Spliffs*, p. 89, 2003

Cascadia *noun*

an imaginary proposed state or area formed of the states of Washington and Oregon and British Columbia *CANADA*

- Cascadia is the name of the putative area [if Canada broke up] of Washington and Oregon, plus British Columbia. Perhaps named for the Cascade mountain range watershed, it also appeals to Vancouver business, which complains the feds favour the East.. — Bill Casselman, *Canadian Words*, p. 3, 1995

case *noun*

1 a promiscuous woman *AUSTRALIA*

- "Blimey!" said a man just behind me. "That one'd be a case, wouldn't she?" A case, when the word is used in this fashion, is not a funny person, known as a hard case. A case, at least the female variety, has a case of nymphomania. — Sue Rhodes, *Now you'll think I'm awful*, 1967
- — Sue Rhodes, *And when she was bad she was popular*, p. 104, 1968
- — Jim Ramsay, *Cop It Sweet!*, p. 21, 1977
- She was being far too familiar too early. A case, obviously. — Robert English, *Toxic Kisses*, p. 76, 1979

2 a patient with a sexually transmitted infection *US*

- — Sally Williams, *"Strong" Words*, p. 136, 1994

3 a love-affair *UK, 1860*

- — *[South African] Cape Argus*, 4th July 1946

4 to engage in an adulterous relationship *UK*

- — David Powis, *The Signs of Crime*, 1977

▸ **go case**

to have sex with someone *UK*

From 'case' (a love affair).

- "I went case with a tart at the gaff" = I slept with a woman at (my) home. — Paul Tempest, *Lag's Lexicon*, p. 33, 1950
- [S]he went case with some geezer now she's liveing [sic] with him. — Frank Norman, *Bang To Rights*, p. 58, 1958

case *verb*

1 to look over a place or person, especially in anticipation of criminal activity *US, 1914*

- [A]nd probably was frightened either for the idea I'd bust right in and pull a holdup on the spot, or was merely casing for later. — Jack Kerouac, *Letter to Neal Cassady*, p. 277, 3rd January 1951
- [T]hey case the pussy [fur coat]. — Charles Raven, *Underworld Nights*, p. 22, 1956
- Bud, after critically if surreptitiously 'casing' the boy, decided to have a try at examining Sam. — Arthur V. Huffman, *New York Mattachine Newsletter*, p. 6, July 1961
- Another principal need is someone able to "case" these places' physical layouts – to determine means of entry, the best getaway routes, and so forth. — Malcolm X and Alex Haley, *The Autobiography of Malcolm X*, p. 140, 1964
- I went out and cruised around to case the city. — Iceberg Slim (Robert Beck), *Pimp*, p. 91, 1969
- — Angela Devlin, *Prison Patter*, p. 35, 1996

2 to work as a prostitute *UK*

A cynical variation of 'go case' (to have sex with).

- — Angela Devlin, *Prison Patter*, p. 57, 1996

3 to tease someone, to scold someone *US*

- — Hermese E. Roberts, *The Third Ear*, 1971

4 to put a prisoner on report for a breach of regulations *UK, 1950*

- — Angela Devlin, *Prison Patter*, p. 35, 1996

case!

used for asserting that all has gone as planned *TRINIDAD AND TOBAGO, 1966*

- — Lise Winer, *Dictionary of the English/Creole of Trinidad & Tobago*, 2003

case ace *noun*

in card games, the fourth and remaining ace when three have been played *US*

- — Harold Wentworth and Stuart Berg Flexner, *Dictionary of American Slang*, p. 90, 1960

case game *noun*

in pool, a situation in which each player can win with their next shot *US, 1985*

- — Mike Shamos, *The Illustrated Encyclopedia of Billiards*, p. 42, 1993

case note *noun*

1 a one-dollar note *US*

- — Joseph E. Ragen and Charles Finston, *Inside the World's Toughest Prison*, p. 794, 1962

2 a gambler's last money *US*

- — Frank Garcia, *Marked Cards and Loaded Dice*, p. 261, 1962

case out *verb*

to engage in sexual foreplay *US*

- — *American Speech*, p. 273, December 1963: 'American Indian student slang'

caser *noun*

1 a skilled card-counter in blackjack *US, 1983*

- A good caser can track every card played in a six-deck shoe. — Thomas L. Clark, *The Dictionary of Gambling and Gaming*, p. 38, 1987

2 in poker, the last card in a particular rank or suit in a deal *US*

A term borrowed from the card game of faro.

- — Irwin Steig, *Common Sense in Poker*, p. 183, 1963

3 a strict prison officer; one with a reputation for putting prisoners on report *UK, 1950*

- — Angela Devlin, *Prison Patter*, p. 35, 1996

4 a five shilling piece; five shillings *AUSTRALIA, 1825*

Recorded earliest in Australia. Became obsolete after the introduction of decimal currency in 1966.

- CASER – Five shillings. — Gilbert H. Lawson, *A Dictionary of Australian Words and Terms*, 1924
- What I mean is I can dook you a caser if it's any good to you. — D'Arcy Niland, *The Shiralee*, p. 138, 1955
- — Jim Ramsay, *Cop It Sweet!*, p. 21, 1977

5 a sexually aggressive boy *US*

- — *American Speech*, p. 273, December 1963: 'American Indian student slang'

Casey Jones *noun*

1 in poker, a player who draws the last card of a rank, the case card *US*

John Luther 'Casey' Jones (1864–1900) was an American locomotive engineer whose death in a train accident made him a legend celebrated in ballad and song.

- — George Percy, *The Language of Poker*, p. 17, 1988

2 in pool, a case game (one that either player can win with their next shot) *US*

- — Mike Shamos, *The Illustrated Encyclopedia of Billiards*, p. 42, 1993

cash *verb*

to finish consuming something *US*

Usage is in the context of drug or alcohol consumption.

- — Don R. McCreary (Editor), *Dawg Speak*, 2001

cash and carriage *noun*

marriage *UK, 1992*

Rhyming slang. Derives only from CASH AND CARRY (to marry) as the term 'cash and carriage' has no other existence.

cash and carried *adjective*
married *UK, 1961*
Rhyming slang, from **CASH AND CARRY** (to marry); not 'cashed'.
- Poor sod got cash and carried to a carving knife [wife] with a face like a totem. — Bodmin Dark, *Dirty Cockney Rhyming Slang*, 2003

cash and carry *verb*
to marry *UK, 1961*
Rhyming slang.

cash ass *noun*
sex for money *UK*
- — *Maledicta*, p. 144, Summer/Winter 1986–1987: 'Sexual slang: prostitutes, pedophiles, flagellators, transvestites, and necrophiles'

cash cow *noun*
any business or business-sector that provides a steady cash flow *US, 1974*
- The scrap-heaps of business are littered with concepts which went – to use the Boston Group matrix – from being question marks to dogs, without the intervening periods of star and cash cow status. — Fiona Czerniawska, *Corporate-Speak*, p. 224, 1997
- The Scottish secretary, Helen Liddell, last night became the latest member of Tony Blair's cabinet to warn the prime minister against embracing student top-up fees as a "cash cow" to expand the incomes of Britain's universities. — *The Guardian*, 4th December 2002

cashed *adjective*
completely consumed, empty *US*
- — Vann Wesson, *Generation X Field Guide and Lexicon*, p. 34, 1997
- The keg was cashed at 10 o'clock so we decided to go uptown earlier than usual. — Connie Eble (Editor), *UNC-CH Campus Slang*, p. 1, Spring 2001

cashed up *adjective*
with a ready supply of money *AUSTRALIA, 1930*
- — Jim Ramsay, *Cop It Sweet!*, p. 21, 1977
- We walked onto the racecourse like a pair of Wyatt Earps, cashed up and plenty of ammo and we walked off like a pair of Elmer Fudds, out of 'buwwets'. — Paul Vautin, *Turn It Up!*, p. 110, 1995

casher *noun*
a front trouser pocket *UK*
Pickpockets' use, because that is where coins are usually carried.
- — *Sunday Times*, 25th August 1974

cashew *noun*
a psychiatric patient *US*
- — Sally Williams, *"Strong" Words*, p. 136, 1994

cashie *noun*
a cash transaction that is tax-free by virtue of not being reported *NEW ZEALAND, 1995*
- — Harry Orsman, *A Dictionary of Modern New Zealand Slang*, p. 26, 1999

cash-in *noun*
a profitable product or activity that is tied-into – and would not exist without – another product or activity that has a greater presence in the marketplace *UK*
- "It's not a love-in. It's a cash-in. A hot dog is costing 1/9d... We are disgusted." Guest in flowered tunic. Sunday Mirror. [1967] — Richard Neville, *Play Power*, p. 33, 1970

cash in *verb*
1 to die *US, 1891*
A shortened form of 'cash in your chips'.
- She must have died. She must have cashed in. — Harry J. Anslinger, *The Murderers*, p. 175, 1961
- "You got boo-koo [many] years before you cash in," Young Joe whispers. — Iceberg Slim (Robert Beck), *Doom Fox*, p. 135, 1978

2 to take advantage of something and profit thereby *US, 1904*
- Richard supported himself through school by employing a compliance trick that cashed in handsomely on the tendency of most people to miss simple point. — Robert B Cialdini, *Influence*, p. 268, 1993

cashish *noun*
money *UK*
- [W]hen the establishment Mafioso realise how much gilt, paper, cashish, wonga, wedge, corn, cutter, loot, spondos, dollar, readies, shillings, folding, dough, money is on offer — J.J. Connolly, *Layer Cake*, p. 94, 2000

cashmere *noun*
a jumper, whether actually cashmere or not *US*
- — Clarence Major, *Dictionary of Afro-American Slang*, p. 35, 1970

cash money!
used for expressing great joy or pleasure *US*
- — Connie Eble (Editor), *UNC-CH Campus Slang*, p. 3, October 2002

cashola *noun*
money *US, 1977*
- This is just from ticket sales, not concessions, and still you're talking three hundred and forty thousand. Cash-ola. — Carl Hiaasen, *Native Tongue*, p. 394, 1991
- Mickey Cohen is Skidsville, U.S.A, and he needs moolah, gelt, the old cashola. — James Ellroy, *White Jazz*, p. 7, 1992
- I had living quarters, cashola, a job[.] — Paolo Hewitt, *Heaven's Promise*, p. 120, 1999

cash sale *noun*
a US Marine newly arrived in Vietnam and inexperienced in combat *US*
Cash Sales was the name of an outlet found on marine bases in the US; a marine newly arrived in Vietnam looked like and smelled like a Cash Sales outlet.
- — Gregory Clark, *Words of the Vietnam War*, p. 88, 1990

cash talk *noun*
a Canadian male game in which participants aggressively insult each other *CANADA*
- CashTalk involves making fun of everything from a new shirt to premature balding. It's supposed to be an expression of affection. — *The National Post*, p. B10, 24th June 2002

cash up *verb*
1 to get money *AUSTRALIA*
- But I thought the idea would be to work on here for a bit longer [...] Get cashed up a bit, then move. — D'Arcy Niland, *Call Me When the Cross Turns Over*, 1958

2 to pay someone *UK*
- — Tom Hibbert, *Rockspeak!*, p. 36, 1983

casino-hop *verb*
to move from one casino to another *US*
- I tried a white blouse under the blue gown, but concluded I looked like a nun out for an evening of casino-hopping in Las Vegas. — C.D. Payne, *Youth in Revolt*, p. 442, 1993

casino perfects *noun*
high quality dice used in casinos *US*
The dice are almost certain to roll true because they are milled to a very precise tolerance.
- Besides letter 'imperfections,' the Sabre Bay casino perfects probably also have black-light marks or some other identifying device. — Stephen Cannell, *Big Con*, p. 192–193, 1997

casket nail *noun*
a cigarette *US, 369*
Far less common than **COFFIN NAIL**.
- — J.E. Lighter, *Historical Dictionary of American Slang, Volume 1*, p. 366, 1994

casper *noun*
a very pale white person, especially a tourist at the beach *US*
- — Trevor Cralle, *The Surfin'ary*, p. 19, 1991

Casper; Casper the ghost *noun*
crack cocaine *US*
Based on the cartoon-strip character Casper the Friendly Ghost; from the cloud of smoke produced when smoking the product.
- — US Department of Justice, *Street Terms*, October 1994
- — Mike Haskins, *Drugs*, p. 281, 2003

cass-cass *adjective*
messy, slovenely *GUYANA*
- — Richard Allsopp, *Dictionary of Caribbean English Usage*, p. 140, 1998

cast *verb*
▸ **cast an eyeball**
to look *US*
Teen slang.
- — *San Francisco News*, p. 6, 25th March 1958

▸ **cast the runes**
in computing, to operate a program that will not work for anyone else *US*
- — Eric S. Raymond, *The New Hacker's Dictionary*, p. 90, 1991

casters-up mode *adjective*
in computing, broken *US*
• —Eric S. Raymond, *The New Hacker's Dictionary*, p. 90, 1991

cast-eye *noun*
a squint *BELIZE*
• —Richard Allsopp, *Dictionary of Caribbean English Usage*, p. 140, 1998

casting couch *noun*
the notional or real sofa in a director's office, used for sex with an actor hoping for a part *US, 1931*
Based on the commonly held belief that a sexual performance is all the audition required.
• "I don't care if you go over Niagra Falls in a barrel with it," Betsy said. "You and your casting couch."—Bernard Wolfe, *The Late Risers*, p. 7, 1954
• [O]nce he starts making a living he'll be off with the cute young chicks, leaving poor old Letitia to her Scotch and casting couch.—Gore Vidal, *Myra Breckinridge*, p. 219, 1968
• Are you referring to what we in the trade have come to term the casting couch? DONA MASON: No. Oh, it still exists, of course, but I've managed to keep my back off of it so far.—*Flick*, p. 10, February 1970
• Any place where theatrical people cluster is a casting couch.—John Francis Hunter, *The Gay Insider*, p. 107, 1971
• —Bruce Rodgers, *The Queens' Vernacular*, p. 43, 1972
• Both agents profess to being proud family men who never ran casting couches.—Josh Alan Friedman, *Tales of Times Square*, p. 38, 1986
• And he, this purveyor of porn, gets her on a casting couch at first callback in an office in Midtown, the oldest gambit in the business of show.—Jim Carroll, *Forced Entries*, p. 104, 1987

cast-iron *adjective*
irrefutable *UK, 1943*
• [T]he efforts of a certain Guy Fawkes and his gang to blow up Parliament gave future generations a cast-iron excuse to fire off recreational rockets once a year.—*World Wide Words*, January 1998

cast iron college *noun*
a local jail *US*
Carnival usage.
• —E.E. Steck, *A Brief Examination of an Esoteric Folk*, p. 11, 1968

castle *noun*
1 a house or apartment *US*
• —Lavada Durst, *The Jives of Dr. Hepcat*, p. 12, 1953
2 in cricket, the wicket that a batsman is defending *UK, 1959*
• —*The Sunday Times*, 31st May 1959
• —Michael Rundell, *The Dictionary of Cricket*, 1985
• —Keith Foley, *A Dictionary of Cricketing Terminology*, p. 66, 1998

castled *adjective*
in cricket, bowled out *UK*
From **CASTLE** (a wicket that is being defended).
• —Steve James (captain of Glamorgan County Cricket Club), 18th June 2003

castor *noun*
▸ **on the castor**
popular, well-regarded *AUSTRALIA*
Extended from **CASTOR** (excellent).
• —Kylie Tennant, *The Joyful Condemned*, 1953

castor *adjective*
excellent; all right *AUSTRALIA, 1944*
From 'castor' (a hat), which was used in tick-tack.
• [O]n the castor Good oh. Excellent etc. It is derived from the secret signal of tugging the brim of one's hat with the thumb & forefinger to indicate that the coast is clear, that it is safe to proceed. Hence 'It's Castor' – It's excellent. It's top—Hartley, *Prison Glossary*, 1944
• To touch the hat meant 'good'; to touch the nose or the coat meant, 'bad'. The necessity for silence has largely disappeared and the signs remain. CASTOR or HAT or HAT JOB meant good, under control[.] —Thirty-five, *The Argot*, 1950
• Don't worry, skipper, she will be castor.—*Sydney Morning Herald*, p. 6, 3rd January 1980

Castor and Pollux; Caster and Pollux *noun*
the testicles *UK*
The classical twins of the Zodiac provide the source for this rhyming slang for **BOLLOCKS**.
• —Ray Puxley, *Cockney Rabbit*, 1992

Castro *nickname*
a neighbourhood in San Francisco, California, dominated by homosexual men since the early 1970s *US*
Castro Street is the main artery of the neighbourhood.
• —Laurence Urdang, *Names and Nicknames of Places and Things*, p. 53, 1987

Castro clone *noun*
a homosexual who conforms to a clean-cut, fashionable image *US*
The Castro is a predominantly gay neighbourhood in San Francisco.
• If the Castro Clone* look of self-conscious masculinity, for example, seems to be the image of choice among San Francisco gay men, there is still a greater awareness that those gender symbols are assumed not inherent. (*The short hair, trimmed moustache and athletic build currently popular among many gay men in the Castro district of San Francisco.)—Wendy Chapkis, *Beauty Secrets*, p. 136, 1986
• Most of the gay men in S.F., except for my friends, were going through this generic lumberback period, and were called "Castro Clones" because they all lived or hung out in the Castro.—Jennifer Blowdryer, *White Trash Debutante*, p. 58, 1997

cast up *verb*
to vomit *BARBADOS*
• —Frank A. Collymore, *Barbadian Dialect*, p. 26, 1965

casual *noun*
1 a member of a violent faction of football supporters (a firm), aligned to a football team and identified by a uniform of casual-wear *UK*
Since the late 1970s. Examples recorded June 2002: Aberdeen Soccer Casuals, Cambridge Casuals, Celtic Casuals, Darlington Casuals, Fine Young Casuals (Oldham FC), Suburban Casuals (Southampton).
• Casuals were devoted to expensive labels[.]—Sarah Callard and Will Hoon, *Surfers Soulies Skinheads & Skaters*, 1996
2 a youth fashion from the late 1970s, based on designer labels, in the 1980s a working-class trend, in the 1990s a positive symbol of urban chic; a follower of this fashion style *UK*
A variant is 'caj'.
• —Alon Shulman, *The Style Bible*, p. 50, 1999
• [T]he fighting between mods, rockers, skinheads, Pakistanis, suedeheads, Hell's angels, boot boys, greasers, Teds, punks, soulboys, rockabillies, rude boys, casuals and every other shade of herbert going[.]—John King, *Human Punk*, p. 295, 2000
• [P]allid goths, wedge-haired casuals, boys dressed like Madonna and girls dressed like Boy George[.]—Patrick Neate, *Where You're At*, p. 1, 2003

casual *adjective*
excellent, fashionable, trendy *US*
Youth usage.
• —*San Francisco Examiner: People*, p. 8, 27th October 1963

cat *noun*
1 a man *US, 1920*
• The other cats from the corner of Division and Western didn't do so good.—Mezz Mezzrow, *Really the Blues*, p. 3, 1946
• So for the lawyer for these two cats that got twisted found out the cat was a Federal narcotics agent.—William Burroughs, *Junkie*, 1953
• I don't want to sound square or anything, but you don't look like my grandmother at all. You look like some other cat.—Steve Allen, *Bop Fables*, p. 46, 1955
• Man, he'd be blasting with every mad cat he could find.—Jack Kerouac, *On the Road*, p. 158, 1957
• The sharp-dressed young "cats" who hung on the corners and in the poolrooms, bars and restaurants, and who obviously didn't work anywhere, completely entranced me.—Malcolm X and Alex Haley, *The Autobiography of Malcolm X*, p. 43, 1964
• After this, I met a lot of cats I'd known at Wiltwyck, in Youth House, in the streets; cats from Brooklyn, cats K.B. had cut me into; and cats I had only seen passing by.—Claude Brown, *Manchild in the Promised Land*, p. 141, 1965
• Well, this cat is well read and we exchange reading material.—Eldridge Cleaver, *Soul on Ice*, p. 46, 1968
• A strong trio of serious business-oriented cats should develop this liberation of space within the cities[.]—*The Digger Papers*, p. 15, August 1968
• Hippy term for any male within the hippy world or the drug scene. "He's a cool cat" would mean "He is a self-assured, 'knowing' man who is one of us".—David Powis, *The Signs of Crime*, 1977
2 a black person *US*
• Where we grew up, you never came in contact very often with many cats.—Dan Jenkins, *Semi-Tough*, p. 11, 1972
3 a spiteful, gossiping woman *UK*
A back-formation from **CATTY** (spiteful, sly).
• —Angus Wilson, *Such Darling Dodos*, 1950
4 the vagina *UK, 1720*
• That puckered gash looked like she had grown an extra 'cat.'—Iceberg Slim (Robert Beck), *Pimp*, p. 116, 1969

5 a passive homosexual male; any male homosexual *AUSTRALIA, 1950*
Simes (*A Dictionary of Australian Underworld Slang*, 1990) notes that in prison 'cats' are 'young prisoners who, though usually heterosexual prior to incarceration, submit to the passive role in homosexual relations in prison'. But also in prison 'cat' is used to refer to known homosexuals who are often segregated from other inmates. Outside of prison the term is used generally of homosexual men: perhaps an extension of the meaning as 'a woman'. The suggestion that it is a shortening of 'catamite' has no supporting evidence.
- That muscular loudmouth who is always barrelling cats and poofters is quite likely to be a screaming drag queen himself.—Suzy Jarratt, *Permissive Australia*, p. 54, 1970
- 'Well, t' put it bluntly, are you a cat?' 'No, I'm fucken not!' Redford relaxed a little realising that he'd upset him. 'Well, if you are, you've got no worries. I won't lag you – you've go no worries on that score.' 'I don't know what gives you the idea that I might be, er,' Andrew hesitated over the word, 'camp, but you can forget it, I'm not!'—Bob Jewson, *Stir*, p. 108, 1980
- Hocks give it. And Cats take it.—Kathy Lette, *Girls' Night Out*, p. 174, 1987
- He's a fair dinkum cat. They deserve each other those two[.]—Clive Galea, *Slipper*, p. 223, 1988
- Some of the prisoners had decided that if they were going to have to fuck a man then he may as well at least look like a woman, and so they took the cats on as lovers.—William Dodson, *The Sharp End*, p. 40, 2001
- The cat wing was the home of Long Bay's transsexual criminals.—William Dodson, *The Sharp End*, p. 40, 2001

6 a lion; a tiger; a leopard *UK*
Circus; usually in the plural.
- Horses are "prads", lions and tigers "cats", monkeys are "monks" and dogs "buffers".—Butch Reynolds, *Broken Hearted Clown*, p. 32, 1953

7 in circus and carnival usage, a trouble-making southern rustic *US*
- —Don Wilmeth, *The Language of American Popular Entertainment*, p. 47, 1981

8 a poorly performing racing greyhound *AUSTRALIA*
- —Ned Wallish, *The Truth Dictionary of Racing Slang*, p. 13, 1989

9 in poker, a nonstandard hand such as the 'little cat', 'big cat', etc *US*
- —George Percy, *The Language of Poker*, p. 18, 1988

10 heroin *US*
- —Peter Johnson, *Dictionary of Street Alcohol and Drug Terms*, p. 34, 1993

11 meth*cat*hinone *US*
- The recipe for cat, based on (widely available) ephedrine, has been widely disseminated on the Internet.—Steven Daly and Nalthaniel Wice, *alt.culture*, p. 148, 1995
- —Office of National Drug Control Policy, *Drug Facts*, February 2003

12 a *cat*egory *UK, 1984*
- "He's got his Cat D!" [...] "Cat D" meant recategorisation to "suitable for open conditions".—*The Guardian*, 11th January 2001
- They can shove their C Cat and they can shove their D Cat. In a little while I'm gonna be a free Cat!—*The Guardian*, 27th June 2002

13 a Caterpillar™ tractor or other type of heavy equipment *US, 1918*
- I felt a little embarrassed with my silly beret but the cat operators didn't even look and soon we left them behind[.]—Jack Kerouac, *The Dharma Bums*, p. 45, 1958

14 a catalytic converter, an emissions-control device *US*
- —John Edwards, *Auto Dictionary*, p. 26, 1993

15 a hydraulic catapult on an aircraft carrier *US, 1962*
- —John Winton, *HMS Leviathan*, 1967

16 a *cat*amaran *UK, 1984*

17 a boat of any description *UK*
- —F.H. Burgess, *A Dictionary of Sailing*, 1961

▸ let the cat out of the bag
to disclose a secret *UK, 1760*
- Greg Dyke rather let the cat out of the bag at Edinburgh when he said he wasn't quite sure what BBC2 was about.—*The Guardian*, 23rd October 2000

▸ on the cat
staying away from home at night *US*
- When I was on the cat, I knew that I was going to get caught sooner or later, but I just didn't want to get caught before I had stolen a new suit.—Claude Brown, *Manchild in the Promised Land*, p. 69, 1965

▸ on the cat hop
on the railways, on time *US*
- —Norman Carlisle, *The Modern Wonder Book of Trains and Railroading*, p. 266, 1946
- —Ramon Adams, *The Language of the Railroader*, p. 108, 1977

▸ put a cat among the pigeons; set the cat among the pigeons
to stir up trouble *UK, 1976*
- But it might put a cat among the pigeons.—A.S. Byatt, *Possession*, p. 99, 1990
- [H]e whistled up some pal of his to set the cat among the pigeons up here in Chinatown, and then he sat back and waited for the tongs to do what they always do.—Lee Child, *Running Blind*, p. 216, 2000

▸ something the cat dragged in; something the cat has brought in
used as the epitome of someone who is bedraggled *UK, 1928*
- Christ, you look like something the cat dragged in. Don't tell me that's the latest style in London.—Fern Michaels, *Texas Rich*, p. 240, 1985

Cat *noun*
a Cadillac car *US*
- Tia Juana pulled up in his long green Cat, and parked in a No Parking zone.—Chester Himes, *If He Hollers Let Him Go*, p. 42, 1945

cat *verb*
1 to stay away from home overnight, prowling for sin *US*
From the alleycat as a role model for behaviour.
- "But you was away?" "Catting out. I holed up with a rich lady for a while."—Hal Ellson, *Duke*, p. 154, 1949
- The older guys had been doing something called "catting" for years. That catting was staying away from home all night was all I knew about the term.—Claude Brown, *Manchild in the Promised Land*, p. 18, 1965

2 to pursue someone in the hopes of sexual relations *US, 1946*
- She was catting, getting me all bothered.—Hal Ellson, *Duke*, p. 112, 1949
- —Robert S. Gold, *A Jazz Lexicon*, p. 48, 1964

Cat A *noun*
the *cat*egorisation of most secure prisons, thus the *cat*egory for highly dangerous prisoners or those considered most likely to escape *UK*
'Cat B', 'Cat C' and 'Cat D' are also used in decreasing order of required security. These categories have been in force since 1966.
- —Angela Devlin, *Prison Patter*, p. 35, 1996

Cat A *verb*
to *cat*egorise a prisoner as Cat A *UK*
'Cat B', 'Cat C' and 'Cat D' are also used in decreasing order of required security.
- —Angela Devlin, *Prison Patter*, p. 35, 1996

catalog man *noun*
a gambling cheat whose superficial knowledge of cheating is acquired from studying catalogues of cheating devices *US, 1945*
A derisive term when used by cheats who carefully hone their craft.
- —Thomas L. Clark, *The Dictionary of Gambling and Gaming*, p. 40, 1987

cat and class *noun*
cataloguing and classification *UK, 1984*
Librarians' use.

cat and mouse *noun*
a house *UK, 1857*
Rhyming slang.
- [T]he man set off back towards his cat and mouse, reeling all over the frog and toad [road]—Ronnie Barker, *Fletcher's Book of Rhyming Slang*, p. 26, 1979

catapult *noun*
in the language of wind surfing, a high-speed exit from the board assisted by high winds *US*
- —Frank Fox, *A Beginner's Guide to Zen and the Art of Windsurfing*, p. 149, 1985

catatonia *noun*
in computing, the condition that exists when a computer is in suspended operation, unable to proceed *US*
- —*CoEvolution Quarterly*, p. 27, Spring 1981

catatonic *adjective*
(of a computer) caught in an inextricable operation and thus suspended beyond reach or response *US*
- —Eric S. Raymond, *The New Hacker's Dictionary*, p. 91, 1991

catawampus *adjective*

crooked, bent *US, 1851*

- Poor Buster and Sybil's trials and tribulations in building their comically catawampus house and then seeing it tossed about in a twister and finally leveled by a train build to a small masterpiece of slapstick[.] — *Tulsa (Oklahoma) World*, p. H3, 13th July 2003

catbird seat *noun*

an advantageous position *US, 1942*

Coined or at the very least popularised by humourist James Thurber in 1942.

- — *American Speech*, December 1954
- Hell, they were all finished and he was in the catbird seat now. — Mickey Spillane, *Last Cop Out*, p. 154, 1972
- "Gee, that's a shame," Harvey said, "sitting where you are, right there in the catbird seat." — Elmore Leonard, *Stick*, p. 115, 1983
- He is in the catbird seat, with time on his hands and plenty of money and handsome Danny Quayle to take his place, if anything goes wrong. — Hunter S. Thompson, *Songs of the Doomed*, p. 249, October 1988

catbox *noun*

the Middle East *US*

- — *Seattle Times*, p. A9, 12th April 1998

catcall *noun*

a derisive jeer *US, 1839*

- — Joseph A. Weingarten, *A Dictionary of American Slang*, p. 58, 1954
- "There's no comparison to this rivalry," A-Rod had said before the game, while steeling himself for the inevitable booing and catcalls he was to get from the Fenway rabble[.] — *Daily News (New York)*, 17th April 2004

catch *noun*

1 a person who is considered matrimonially or romantically desirable *UK, 1749*

- Andy was very good-looking. He was a catch. That's what we called it in my day. — Eve Ensler, *The Vagina Monologues*, p. 27, 1998

2 a prostitute who has been recruited to work for a pimp *US*

- It was time for me to get another good catch and I found this edge full of fine whores. — A.S. Jackson, *Gentleman Pimp*, p. 74, 1973

3 in Keno, the number of winning numbers that a player has marked *US*

- — John Mechigian, *Encyclopedia of Keno*, p. 111, 1972

4 a hidden condition or consequence *US, 1855*

- What's the catch? — *New Jack City*, 1990
- You're certain there must be a catch, but he [Tony Blair] looks so reassuring[.] — *The Guardian*, 2nd October 2003

catch *verb*

1 (used of a pimp) to recruit a prostitute to work for him; to recruit a woman to work as a prostitute *US*

- I said, "What are you doing down here?," and he said, "I'm trying to catch." I said, "There's lots of women out here." — Christina and Richard Milner, *Black Players*, p. 238, 1972

2 (used of a prostitute) to engage a customer *US*

- Never know it t'find her at the bar in her catchin clothes[.] — Robert Gover, *JC Saves*, p. 112, 1968

3 to play the passive sexual role in a homosexual relationship *US, 1966*

- They say, if you pitch, you'll catch. Any truth in that? — Malcolm Braly, *On the Yard*, p. 250, 1967
- — Eugene Landy, *The Underground Dictionary*, p. 46, 1971
- — *Maledicta*, p. 231, 1979: 'Kinks and queens: linguistic and cultural aspects of the terminology for gays'
- The young man walked over and leaned in through the window. "It's thirty; head only, pitch or catch." — James Ellroy, *Blood on the Moon*, p. 133, 1984
- Elaine caught his slight grin and was sure Chili did too. He said, "You pitch or catch, Elliot?" "Mostly pitch." — Elmore Leonard, *Be Cool*, p. 269, 1999

4 to take calls or complaints called in to a police station; to be assigned a case *US*

- — *New York Times Magazine*, p. 87, 16th March 1958
- Gee, Blackjack's catching that case, and he's off for a couple of days. — Peter Maas, *Serpico*, p. 76, 1973
- You weren't catching, you didn't need me. — Leonard Shecter and William Phillips, *On the Pad*, p. 147, 1973

5 in an illegal number gambling lottery, to win *US*

- — *American Speech*, p. 191, October 1949

6 in gin, to draw a card *US*

- — Irwin Steig, *Play Gin to Win*, p. 138, 1971

▸ **catch a bullet**

to be shot *US*

- But even if that was true, the woman had to be crazy, since any body could catch a bullet. — Richard Price, *Clockers*, p. 209, 1992

▸ **catch a buzz**

to smoke marijuana and become intoxicated *US*

- — Jim Emerson-Cobb, *Scratching the Dragon*, 1997

▸ **catch a crab**

in rowing, to err in a stroke, disrupting the timing and momentum of the rowing *US*

- The famous "crab" which University of Washington oarsmen caught when they lost to California in a driving finish in Seattle is subject of a communication from Don McNary, Cal '46. — *San Francisco Chronicle*, p. 1H, 24th June 1949

▸ **catch a dummy**

in prison, to refuse to speak *US*

- — Charles Shafer, *Folk Speech in Texas Prisons*, p. 200, 1990

▸ **catch a fish**

in poker, after making a small bet with a good hand (the bait), to lure another player into increasing the bet *US*

- — George Percy, *The Language of Poker*, p. 18, 1988

▸ **catch a glad**

to act with spontaneous joy *TRINIDAD AND TOBAGO, 1984*

- — Lise Winer, *Dictionary of the English/Creole of Trinidad & Tobago*, 2003

▸ **catch a hit**

to be scolded or harshly criticised *US*

Marine usage in the Vietnam war.

- — Linda Reinberg, *In the Field*, p. 37, 1991

▸ **catch a horse**

to urinate *AUSTRALIA, 1942*

A euphemism.

▸ **catch air**

to become airborne while skateboarding or surfing *US*

Recorded in surfing by Mitch McKissick and in skateboarding by Dan Maley.

- — Mitch McKissick, *Surf Lingo*, 1987
- — *Macon Telegraph and News*, p. 9A, 18th June 1989

▸ **catch a pay**

to be beaten and robbed *US*

- — Anna Scotti and Paul Young, *Buzzwords*, p. 130, 1997

▸ **catch a run**

to wet one side of a marijuana cigarette to promote even burning *US*

- — Jim Emerson-Cobb, *Scratching the Dragon*, 1997

▸ **catch ass**

to have a hard time *TRINIDAD AND TOBAGO, 1956*

- — Lise Winer, *Dictionary of the English/Creole of Trinidad & Tobago*, 2003

▸ **catch a stack**

to rob someone with a lot of cash *US*

- — Carsten Stroud, *Close Pursuit*, p. 270, 1987

▸ **catch a vaps**

to become suddenly inspired *GRENADA*

- — Richard Allsopp, *Dictionary of Caribbean English Usage*, p. 141, 1998

▸ **catch no ball**

to fail to understand *SINGAPORE*

- — Paik Choo, *The Coxford Singlish Dictionary*, p. 23, 2002

▸ **catch on the flipper; catch on the (old) flip-flop**

to make contact on your return *US, 1976*

- [C]atch you on the flip-flop[.] — Peter Chippindale, *The British CB Book*, p. 153, 1981

▸ **catch on the rebound**

to become emotionally involved with a person who has just been rejected from another relationship *UK, 1864*

Probably the pun from which the emotional condition **ON THE REBOUND** derives.

- For all the wrong reasons you want it all, even now / Caught on the rebound turnin' you inside out — Nazareth, *Cover Your Heart*, 1992

▸ **catch on the reverse; catch on the rebound**

to make contact on a return journey *US, 1976*

Citizens' band radio slang.

- [C]atch you on the rebound[.] — Peter Chippindale, *The British CB Book*, p. 153, 1981

▸ catch some
to engage in heavy sexual caressing *US*
• —Collin Baker et al., *College Undergraduate Slang Study Conducted at Brown University*, p. 94, 1968

▸ catch (some) lead
to be shot *US*
• Smitty apparently caught some lead and headed out of town to recover. —Red Rudensky, *The Gonif*, p. 113, 1970

▸ catch squeals
to take calls or complaints called into a police station *US*
• The detective who picks up the phone (this activity is called "catching squeals") is the man on the case, and will hold this distinction forever. —Martin Meyer, *All You Know is Facts*, p. 107, 1969

▸ catch the bumps
in a striptease act, to synchronise the dancer's pelvic thrusts with the drum and cymbal beat *US*
• —Don Wilmeth, *The Language of American Popular Entertainment*, p. 47, 1981

▸ catch thrills
to engage in an activity that excites or stimulates *US*
Hawaiian youth usage.
• —Douglas Simonson, *Pidgin to da Max Hana Hou*, 1982

▸ catch tricks
(used of a drummer in a performance) to create sound effects on sight *US*
• —Sherman Louis Sergel, *The Language of Show Biz*, p. 44–45, 1973

▸ catch wreck
to achieve respect for your actions *US*
• My sun moon sets and catches wreck, when we be cruisin. — Digable Planets, *The May 4th Movement*, 1995
• "If I get on the stage before the other man, I'm taking all ta tenergy, just to make sure he don't catch wreck." [Quoting Busta Rhymes] — *Daily News (New York)*, p. 35, 7th April 1996
• skilled rhyme animals who stalk the stage ready to "catch wreck" at a moments notice—Nelson George, *Hip Hop America*, p. 113, 1998

▸ catch your death of cold; catch your death
to catch a very bad cold *UK*
Dating is obscure; the traditional Yorkshire folk song 'On Ilkley Moor bah t'at' contains the line 'Then thee will catch thy death of cold' which, while the intent may be literal, means no more than '[If you go out on] Ilkley Moor without a hat [...] you will catch a bad cold'.
• Grandma always said you'd catch your death of cold for going out in the rain without your umbrella[.] — *The Seattle Times*, 11th April 2003

▸ catch yourself on
to recover your common sense *UK, 1984*
Usually in the imperative.
• Fuckin "flower" my arse. Catch yerself on, yer knobhead. —Niall Griffiths, *Kelly + Victor*, p. 129, 2002

catch 22 *noun*
a self-cancelling dilemma *US*
Coined by Joseph Heller for his 1955 novel *Catch 22*, which was originally to be titled 'Catch 18'– until *Mila 18* by Leon Uris was published.
• The law was one of those Catch-22 things that put you in jail. If you complied with the federal law to buy stamps, then the state law got you for being a bookmaker. If you didn't buy the stamps, the feds jugged you. —Mario Puzo, *Inside Las Vegas*, p. 291, 1977
• In other words, it was established that the [Smothers] Brothers could do what they wanted, but so could the network. In other words, grok Catch-22. —Bill Cardoso, *The Maltese Sangweech*, p. 237, 1984
• Catch twenty-two. Let things go like they're going and somebody suffers. Complain to see if you can make things better and somebody suffers more. —Robert Campbell, *Nibbled to Death by Ducks*, p. 105, 1989
• It's such a Catch-22 that I'm not sure it ain't gonna kill me. —Marilyn Suriani Futterman, *Dancing Naked in the Material World*, p. 67, 1992
• It's not gonna happen. This is a Catch-22. — *Boogie Nights*, 1997

catch colt *noun*
an illegitimate child *US, 1901*
• A catch colt is a colt with an unknown sire. The term is applied euphemistically to the human condition. It sounds nicer to say that he is a catch colt than to say that no one, except perhaps his mother (and maybe not even she) knows who his father is. —Chris Thain, *Cold as a Bay Street Banker's Heart*, p. 35, 1987

catch driver *noun*
in harness racing, a driver hired on the day of the race *US*
• —Igor Kushyshyn et al., *The Gambling Times Guide to Harness Racing*, p. 112, 1994

catcher *noun*
1 the passive partner in homosexual sex *US, 1966*
• I've been known to pitch, but I'm no catcher. —Malcolm Braly, *On the Yard*, p. 149, 1967
• — *Maledicta*, p. 231, 1979: 'Kinks and queens: linguistic and cultural aspects of the terminology for gays'
• —H. Max, *Gay (S)language*, p. 7, 1988
• Hey, hey! I'll play your victim, but not your catcher. —*Chasing Amy*, 1997

2 a peripheral member of an illegal drug enterprise hired to retrieve drugs hurriedly thrown out of a window to avoid confiscation and arrest *US*
• Chillie has hired the fourteen-year-old son of the building superintendent as a "catcher" – he is on call to retrieve any cocaine thrown out the window during a bust. —Terry Williams, *The Cocaine Kids*, p. 28, 1989

catcher's mitt *noun*
a dense jungle area with a heavy Viet Cong and North Vietnamese presence northeast of Phu Loi *US*
Based on a vague resemblance between the area and a catcher's mitt on a map.
• —Gregory Clark, *Words of the Vietnam War*, p. 89, 1990

catch hand *noun*
a casual workman who moves from job to job to get more favourable rates and conditions but has no intention of staying with any job until its completion *UK, 1964*
• —Catch Hand, *BBC TV drama scenes*, 1964

catch it *verb*
1 to get it into trouble with an authority, especially to incur a beating or a severe telling off *UK, 1835*
• Maggie Durkin, look at our Billy, I said. You'll catch it. —Livi Michael, *Robinson Street*, p. 26, 1999

2 to be killed *US*
• Ask your people if they ever saw this woman on the night Louis Palo caught it. —Richard Condon, *Prizzi's Honor*, p. 169, 1982

catch on *verb*
1 to understand; to grasp the meaning or significance of something *US, 1884*
• When the director of the London office of the Australian Wine Bureau went to see the head of wine-buying at a leading UK supermarket in 1980, she was told that 'Australian wine will never catch on'. — *The Guardian*, 10th May 2003
• What started off as a good service was subject to abuse. People caught on to how easily it could be manipulated. — *The Guardian*, 29th July 2004

2 to become popular or fashionable *UK, 1887*
• Now, this might work in Manhattan, but could it really catch on here? — *The Guardian*, 7th January 2003

catch one *verb*
to drink or use drugs to the point of mild intoxication *US*
• —Vann Wesson, *Generation X Field Guide and Lexicon*, p. 34, 1997

catchy *adjective*
attractive, appealing, especially if vulgarly so *UK, 1831*
• [British tromobonist, Dennis] Rollins has a knack for catchy, idiomatic hooks, which he uses to good advantage on tunes such as Shake It Down, The Funky Funk and Where It's At[.] — *The Guardian*, 8th June 2001

catch you later
used as a farewell *US*
• —Connie Eble (Editor), *UNC-CH Campus Slang*, p. 2, March 1979
• Catch you men later. Enjoy yourselves. — *Platoon*, 1986

Cat City *nickname*
Cathedral City, California *US*
A resort town just south of Palm Springs in the Coachella Valley.
• I don't know, but he's got a cousin up there, in Cat city. —James Ellroy, *Brown's Requiem*, p. 184, 1981
• Our seniors have never beaten Cat City and we haven't beaten Brawley in six years. — *Desert Sun (Palm Springs, California)*, p. 1C, 25th October 2003

cat daddy *noun*
a male with charm and charisma *US*
• I thought my roommate was going to be a dork, but he's turned out to be a cat daddy. —Connie Eble (Editor), *UNC-CH Campus Slang*, p. 2, November 2002

caterpillar *noun*
during the war in Vietnam, a convoy of non-combat vehicles on a passably secure road *US*
• —Linda Reinberg, *In the Field*, p. 37, 1991

caterpillar *verb*
in mountain biking, to pedal with a fluctuating, inefficient cadence *US*
- —William Nealy, *Mountain Bike!*, p. 160, 1992

catever; kerterver *adjective*
bad *UK*
From Italian *cattivo* (bad) but via earlier senses as 'an odd occurence or person'.
- —Paul Baker, *Polari*, p. 168, 2002

cat-eye *noun*
an irregular work shift *US*
- Won't be long now, Hunt, they got him workin a ten-to-six cat-eye over there. Damn people won't even run a regular shift. —John Sayles, *Union Dues*, p. 64, 1977

cat eyes *noun*
eyes that are anything other than dark brown *US*
- —John A. Holm, *Dictionary of Bahamian English*, p. 38, 1982

catface *noun*
a pucker left in a garment after ironing *US, 1952*
- —Frederic G. Cassidy, *Dictionary of American Regional English, Volume 1*, p. 565, 1985

cat fever *noun*
catarrhal gastroenteritis, suffered by troops in the field in Vietnam *US*
- —Gregory Clark, *Words of the Vietnam War*, p. 89, 1990

cat fight *noun*
a no-holds-barred fight between women *AUSTRALIA*
- Since I didn't want to start a cat-fight in public I decided I'd better avoid the Spag's lustful gaze as much as possible. —Sue Rhodes, *Now you'll think I'm awful*, p. 122, 1967
- —Judi Sanders, *Cal Poly Slang*, p. 2, 1990
- I asked him to film my girlfriend and me as we staged a female boxing match followed by a hair-pulling cat fight. —Anka Radakovich, *The Wild Girls Club*, p. 96, 1994

catfish *noun*
a person who speaks too much and thinks too little *US*
- —Jerry Robertson, *Oil Slanguage*, p. 35, 1954

catfish row *noun*
a black neighbourhood in a southern US city *US*
For the setting of his 1935 folk opera *Porgy and Bess*, George Gershwin used Catfish Row, a fictionalisation of an alleyway named Cabbage Row off Church Street in Charleston, South Carolina.
- It's a night for temptation, the kind of temptation one might see on Catfish Row at the end of the cotton season on the weekend. —Claude Brown, *Manchild in the Promised Land*, p. 315, 1965
- No lights, not even porch lights in this catfish row-alley section of Augusta. —Odie Hawkins, *Men Friends*, p. 60, 1989

cat got your tongue?
'why aren't you talking?'; used for mocking or asking why a temporary speechlessness has struck *UK, 1911*
Elliptical for 'has the cat got your tongue?'; generally addressed to a child but equally patronising when asked of an adult.
- Come here little Queenie... or ah / Has the cat got your tongue? My best shot for a C note baby she said / That's why this Janie's got a gun —Aerosmith, *Black Cherry*, 1973

cath *verb*
to insert a catheter into a patient *UK*
Medical use.
- We've bronched him, tubed him, bagged him, [and] cathed him. —Diane Johnson, *Doctor Talk, The State of the Language*, 1980

cat-haul *verb*
to interrogate someone fiercely *US, 1951*
From a form of punishment used with slaves – a cat was forcibly dragged by the tail down the slave's bare back.
- —Harold Wentworth and Stuart Berg Flexner, *Dictionary of American Slang*, p. 91, 1960

cat head *noun*
a biscuit *US*
- —Frank Prewitt and Francis Schaeffer, *Vacaville Vocabulary*, 1961–1962

Catherine Wheel *noun*
in the youth trend for 'souped-up' motor-scootering, a lifting of the front wheel off the ground due to sudden acceleration performed in conjunction with a flaming trail *UK*
Probably from the Catherine Wheel firework as a fiery elaboration of WHEELIE.
- [A] rider pulls off a Catherine Wheel – pulling a wheelie while a mate puts lighter fluid on the ground and lights it. —*The Independent Magazine*, p. 22, 28th August 2004

Catho *noun*
a member of the Catholic Church *AUSTRALIA*
- —James Lambert, *The Macquarie Book of Slang*, 1996

cat hole *noun*
a one-time, one-man field latrine dug by the user in Vietnam *US, 1978*
- —Gregory Clark, *Words of the Vietnam War*, p. 89, 1990

Catholic *noun*
a pickpocket *US*
- —Vincent J. Monteleone, *Criminal Slang*, p. 45, 1949

Catholic asprin *noun*
a tablet of Benzedrine™ (amphetamine sulphate), a central nervous system stimulant *US*
From the cross scores on the white tablet.
- —David Maurer and Victor Vogel, *Narcotics and Narcotic Addiction*, p. 395, 1973

cathouse *noun*
a brothel *US, 1893*
- She looked as if she might have worked half those years in a cat house. —Chester Himes, *If He Hollers Let Him Go*, p. 19, 1945
- The Mann Act was invented by a Chicago blue-nosed representative named Mann, after a hophead parlor-whore in melodramatic mood threw a note out of the window of the late Harry Guzik's cathouse on which she had written "I am a white slave." —Jack Lait and Lee Mortimer, *Washington Confidential*, p. 86, 1951
- Just a while ago you were as hard as a little boy's peter in a fifty-cent cat house. —Clarence Cooper Jr, *The Scene*, p. 199, 1960
- We got on a high and I asked my newfound amigo if he knew a cathouse, a white cathouse. —Piri Thomas, *Down These Mean Streets*, p. 187, 1967
- We're in transit, the three of us, and we could sure use the services of a decent cathouse that don't hate G.I.'s. —Darryl Ponicsan, *The Last Detail*, p. 121, 1970
- She started out in one of his de-luxe AC-DC cathouses in the suburbs of Havana. —Edwin Torres, *After Hours*, p. 325, 1979

cat in hell's chance *noun*
a very slim chance or possibility *UK*
In 1796, Francis Grose recorded 'No more chance than a cat in hell without claws'. Almost always phrased in the negative: 'not a cat in hell's chance' (no chance whatsoever).
- I don't think there's a cat in hell's chance of reaching the 2004 targets. —David Hart, *BBC News*, 27th February 2003

cat lapper *noun*
a lesbian; someone who enjoys performing oral sex on women *US*
- —Dale Gordon, *The Dominion Sex Dictionary*, p. 41, 1967

cat-lick; cat-licker *noun*
a Roman Catholic *US, 1942*
- I remember in the third grade the kids calling me "cat licker" because I was Catholic and "four eyes" because I wore glasses. —*San Francisco Examiner*, p. 29, 14th Janaury 1974
- He viewed such casual insults as signs of good fellowship, the easy, rude, irrevent ways of family, fellow soldiers, brothers-in-combat, laughing when they called him a harp or a cat-lick. —Robert Campbell, *Boneyards*, p. 10, 1992
- A rich kid whose big house we passed by every day in walking to and from school started calling us "cat lickers, cat lickers" and "sissies" from, he thought the safety of his front lawn. —*Chicago Sun-Times*, p. 5, 19th June 1994

cat-life *noun*
a prison sentence of two or more consecutive life terms *US*
- —Jay Robert Nash, *Dictionary of Crime*, p. 60, 1992

cat man *noun*
a burglar who relies on stealth *US, 1962*
- —J.E. Lighter, *Historical Dictionary of American Slang, Volume 1*, p. 371, 1994

catnip *noun*

1 poor quality, adulterated or entirely fake marijuana *US*
Catmint, the botanical genus *nepeta*, known in the US as 'catnip', may be passed off as marijuana to the unsuspecting, or mixed with genuine marijuana as a make-weight; consequently any impotent marijuana.
- —Anthony Romeo, *The Language of Gangs*, 1962
- —Richard A. Spears, *The Slang and Jargon of Drugs and Drink*, p. 98, 1986
- —Mike Haskins, *Drugs*, p. 287, 2003

2 a marijuana cigarette *UK*
An ironic adoption of the previous sense.
- —Mike Haskins, *Drugs*, p. 291, 2003

cat out *verb*
to sneak away *UK*
- —Tom Hibbert, *Rockspeak!*, p. 36, 1983

cat pack *noun*
a loosely defined group of wealthy, famous and fashionable people *US*
- This kind of kinship between fashion and society that not too many years ago produced the Beautiful People also characterizes the newest social species on the New York scene – the Cat Pack. — *San Francisco Chronicle*, p. 23, 1st December 1971

cat pan *noun*
a bowl used for washing the vagina *TRINIDAD AND TOBAGO*
A play on 'cat' as **PUSSY**.
- —Lise Winer, *Dictionary of the English/Creole of Trinidad & Tobago*, 2003

cat-piss-and-pepper *noun*
a noisy, unrestrained argument *BARBADOS*
Recorded by Richard Allsopp.

cat pisser *noun*
windscreen wipers *US*
- —Lewis Poteet, *Car & Motorcyle Slang*, p. 45–46, 1992

cat plant *noun*
a facility where crude oil is separated by catalysis *US*
- —Harold Wentworth and Stuart Berg Flexner, *Dictionary of American Slang*, p. 91, 1960

cat rack *noun*
a game concession in a carnival in which a player throws balls at stuffed cats on a platform or fence *US*
- —*American Speech*, p. 308–309, December 1960: 'Carnival talk'
- —Don Wilmeth, *The Language of American Popular Entertainment*, p. 47, 1981

cats *noun*

1 trousers *UK*
- —Paul Baker, *Polari*, p. 168, 2002

2 heavy rain *UK, 1976*
From the older (1738) and more familiar adverb form.
- Bex man, it's fucking cats and dogs outside.—Danny King, *The Burglar Diaries*, p. 176, 2001

3 stocks without proven performance *US*
- —Jim Crotty, *How to Talk American*, p. 380, 1997

cat's arse *noun*
anything very good, superlative or exceptional; someone who is considered the best by themselves or others *UK, 1984*

cat's ass *noun*

1 an extraordinarily good or extraordinarily bad example of something *US, 1967*
- After working on the tactical unit of the high-crime Fillmore District, protecting languorous women in bikinis was a nice change of pace. "Believe me, it was the cat's ass," Delaney digresses.—*Chicago Tribune*, p. C12, 6th March 1994
- Chief's vs. Raiders. In football, this one is the cat's ass.—*Sporting News*, p. 6, 22nd September 2003

2 a knot or kink in a wire or rope *US, 1942*
- —Jerry Robertson, *Oil Slanguage*, p. 36, 1954

cat's bar *noun*
a female-only or mixed-sex bar *NEW ZEALAND*
- They could not help being brought into close contact with what some of them coarsely termed the 'cats' bar' or the 'mares' nest.' —*New Zealand Observer*, p. 6, 1st July 1953
- —David McGill, *David McGill's Complete Kiwi Slang Dictionary*, p. 26, 1998

cat's breakfast *noun*
an unpleasant mess *UK, 1984*
A variation of **DOG'S BREAKFAST**.
- JUST WHEN YOU THOUGHT you'd seen every kind of screen ineptitude, All the Queen's Men presents new varieties. As a movie, it's like the cat's breakfast.—*Metro, Silicon Valley's Weekly Newspaper*, 24th-30th October 2002

cat's eyes *noun*
in craps, a roll of three *US*
- —Lou Shelly, *Hepcats Jive Talk Dictionary*, p. 22, 1945

cat shit *noun*
used as a basis for comparison when describing someone who is mean *US, 1970*
- —Frederic G. Cassidy, *Dictionary of American Regional English, Volume 1*, p. 569, 1985

cat shot *noun*
a take-off from an aircraft carrier assisted by a catapult *US*
Vietnam war usage.
- What had it been? A "cold-cat" shot, whatever that was, from a carrier.—Hank Searls, *The Big X*, p. 221, 1959
- Its squadrons of Phantoms and A-6 Intruders practiced "cat shots" (catapulted takeoffs) and landings all day long.—James W. Canan, *The Superwarriors*, p. 36, 1975
- —*American Speech*, p. 385, Winter 1991: 'Among the new words'

cat's meat *noun*
an easily accomplished task *NEW ZEALAND*
- I sure got an ear bashing for being late, but I knew it was only cat's meat to what I would get when I got home.—Hori, *Half-gallon Jar*, p. 84, 1962
- —Harry Orsman, *A Dictionary of Modern New Zealand Slang*, p. 27, 1999

cat's meow; cat's miaow *noun*
anything very good, superlative or exceptional; someone who is considered the best by themselves or others *US, 1921*
- Yeah, she thinks you're the cat's meow, too.—Joel Rose, *Kill Kill Faster Faster*, p. 188, 1997

cat's mother *noun*
▸ **'she' is the cat's mother; 'she' is a cat's mother**
addresed as a catchphrase reproof to a child who fails to show proper respect by referring to the mother, or any other adult woman, as 'she' *UK, 1897*
Occasionally 'she' is 'the cat'; at other times 'she' is 'the cat's grandmother'.

cat's nut *noun*
an extraordinary thing or person *US, 1928*
- If I ever saw a babe who's the cat's nuts, it's you.—James T. Farrell, *Ruth and Bertram*, p. 100, 1955

cat's pajamas; cat's pyjamas *noun*
anything very good, superlative or exceptional; someone who is considered the best by themselves or others *US, 1922*
Coined by, or inspired by, an illustration by New York Journal sports cartoonist Thomas Aloysius 'TAD' Dorgan (1877–1929); in the UK by 1923 but rare by 1939. Still occasionally recorded.
- [H]e was sleeping with a rich, beautiful and highly sexed girl who gave every sign of thinking he was the cat's pyjamas.—Chris Ryan, *The Watchman*, p. 148, 2001

catspraddle *verb*
to beat someone with the fists *TRINIDAD AND TOBAGO*
- —Richard Allsopp, *Dictionary of Caribbean English Usage*, p. 142, 1998

cat's prick *noun*
an elongated ember at the lit end of a cigarette *UK*
- Imagine 5 or 6 lads in the boys' bogs passing round a Benson & Hedges. By the time it's almost finished the burning ember is about an inch long, and someone would always exclaim, "look at the fuckin' cat's prick on that!"—Chris Lewis, *The Dictionary of Playground Slang*, p. 51, 2003

cat's whiskers *noun*
anything very good, superlative or exceptional; someone who is considered the best by themselves or others *UK, 1927*
A variation of **CAT'S PAJAMAS**. From the 1960s on, usage is mainly Australian.
- —Dorothy L. Sayers, *Unnatural Death*, 1927

cattie *noun*
a mail-order catalogue *UK*
- Did ye get that coat oot the cattie? — Michael Munro, *The Patter, Another Blast*, 1988

cattle *noun*
racehorses *AUSTRALIA*
- In November 1987, Jim Cassidy remarked that trainer Brian Mayfield-Smith had some "pretty good cattle" coming along — Ned Wallish, *The Truth Dictionary of Racing Slang*, p. 13, 1989

cattle call *noun*
a mass audition *US, 1952*
- Well, let's say I go to one of those cattle calls, a try out[.] — *Klute*, 1971
- One method used in casting is called the cattle call. Everybody who wants to be in your picture shows up at the specified time, and you see each person on a first-come, first-served basis. — Stephen Ziplow, *The Film Maker's Guide to Pornography*, p. 46, 1977
- I went to one of the early huge cattle calls, although I had never thought of myself as glamorous or particularly pretty. — Kathryn Leigh Scott, *The Bunny Years*, p. 137, 1998
- But the Generals are not cattle calls. Actors are cut off "Time!" only if they surpass their three-minute limit. — *San Francisco Chronicle*, 27th February 2001

cattle dog *noun*
1 a Catholic school student *NEW ZEALAND*
- Cattledogs, cattledogs, stink like dogs and live under logs. — David McGill, *David McGill's Complete Kiwi Slang Dictionary*, p. 28, 1998

2 a catalogue *AUSTRALIA*
Punning on the similarity of the pronunciation.
- — John Meredith, *Learn to talk Old Jack Lang*, p. 21, 1984

cattle truck *noun*
1 any large truck used to transport troops *US*
Vietnam war usage.
- — Carl Fleischhauer, *A Glossary of Army Slang*, p. 8, 1968
- — Gregory Clark, *Words of the Vietnam War*, p. 90, 1990

2 in oil drilling, a bus that transports workers to the oil fields *US*
- — Jerry Robertson, *Oil Slanguage*, p. 36, 1954

3 a driver-operated omnibus *UK, 1973*

cattle truck; cattle *verb*
'fuck', generally in a figurative or expletive sense *UK, 1961*
Rhyming slang.
- Stand in line then watch the time / you're cattled up and weeks behind. — Radar Brothers, *Shifty Lies*, 1999

cattle wagon *noun*
a large car, especially a station wagon *US*
- — Kenn "Naz" Young, *Naz's Underground Dictionary*, p. 20, 1973

cat tranquilizer *noun*
the recreational drug ketamine *CANADA*
- I do identify with 2.5 bumps of cat tranquilizer. — Suroosh Alvi et al., *The Vice Guide*, p. 273, 2002

catty *adjective*
1 sly, spiteful, mean-spirited *UK, 1886*
- He and another prissy lad were in our cocktail lounge one evening, drinking, making catty and audible cracks about other patrons[.] — Dev Collans with Stewart Sterling, *I was a House Detective*, p. 105, 1954

2 nimble and sure-footed in a cat-like manner *CANADA, 1984*
Lumberjacks' use.

catty-cat *noun*
the vagina *US*
- — Edith A. Folb, *runnin' down some lines*, p. 232, 1980

catty-catty *adjective*
promiscuous *TRINIDAD AND TOBAGO*
- — Lise Winer, *Dictionary of the English/Creole of Trinidad & Tobago*, 2003

cat wagon *noun*
a mobile brothel *US, 372*
- — J.E. Lighter, *Historical Dictionary of American Slang, Volume 1*, p. 372, 1994

cat-walk *verb*
on a motorcyle or bicycle, to perform a wheelstand and then ride forward on the rear wheel *US*
- — Paladin Press, *Inside Look at Outlaw Motorcyle Gangs*, p. 33, 1992

cat walker *noun*
a burglar who steals at night *UK*
- — Charles Shafer, *Folk Speech in Texas Prisons*, p. 200, 1990

cat wash *noun*
a quick cleaning of the body using a washcloth but not a full bath or shower *BAHAMAS*
- — John A. Holm, *Dictionary of Bahamian English*, p. 38, 1982

catweed *noun*
marijuana *UK*
- — Angela Devlin, *Prison Patter*, p. 35, 1996

cat work *noun*
criminal employment as a cat-burglar *UK*
- [T]hey had enjoyed a run of luck, screwing country houses in the prosperous Home Counties, with Bunge doing the cat-work[.] — Charles Raven, *Underworld Nights*, p. 15, 1956

caught short *adjective*
1 unprepared, especially with regards to bodily functions *AUSTRALIA, 1964*
- DAWN: Barry feels the call of nature...'Cripe! Caught short again! I wonder where these jokers keep it?' — Barry Humphries, *The Wonderful World of Barry McKenzie*, p. 17, 1968
- "I want to go for a Gerry Riddle and an Edgar Britt," Little Tich whispered, suddenly caught short. — Frank Hardy, *The Outcasts of Foolgarah*, p. 28, 1971
- Bush's troops won't be caught short [...] Defence Secretary Donald Rumsfeld has published new operational requirements for military latrines after a top-to-bottom review concluded that current models are no longer acceptable for all situations[.] — *The Guardian*, 2nd September 2001

2 embarrassed by an untimely lack of whatever is required *UK, 1984*
- Like so many other players in the county system, they are likely to be caught short unless they are toughened physically and mentally in the nursery for Test cricket which ideally should be county cricket. — Justin Langer, *BBC Sports Online*, 9th August 2001

caught using purple *adjective*
apprehended making non-farm use of tax-free farm petrol *CANADA*
To help ease the strain on farm budgets, the prairie provinces allow farmers to buy petrol for farm equipment exempt from certain taxes. The petrol is dyed purple. Police in rural areas check. It also means being caught at some other technical illegality.
- — Chris Thain, *Cold as a Bay Street Banker's Heart*, p. 36, 1987

Cauliflower Alley *noun*
the boxing world *UK, 1961*
Journalists' use. Extending the punning **TIN-EAR ALLEY**.

cauliflower ear; cauliflower *noun*
an ear that has been damaged and deformed by blows *US, 1896*
Originally and still used as a boxing term.
- All he had now were his job as a houseman, his cauliflower ears and broken nose, his precious scrapbook, the bitter memories of his former glory, and an insane temper. — Irving Shulman, *The Amboy Dukes*, p. 53, 1947
- Down the stairs a cauliflower-eared gent played doorman with a nod, a grunt and an open palm. — Mickey Spillane, *My Gun is Quick*, p. 65, 1950
- But it was a while before the hard guys turned their cauliflower ears toward the jazz bandstands[.] — Robert Sylvester, *No Cover Charge*, p. 84, 1956
- There are some people with craggy chins, cauliflower ears, burning eyes under jet-black brows who look like murderers on furlough[.] — Derek Bickerton, *Payroll*, 1959
- Big Tom was quizzical and oblique and had a cauliflower ear from the Peekskill riot. — Clancy Sigal, *Going Away*, p. 66, 1961

caulks *noun*
▸ **put the caulks to**
to stamp with studded boots on someone's face *CANADA*
Lumberjacks' and loggers' use; 'caulks' are the spiked studs on their specialised waterproof boots.

caulk up *verb*
to use spiked working boots to stamp on someone *CANADA, 1939*
Lumberjacks' and loggers' use; 'caulks' are the spiked studs on their specialised waterproof boots.

cause *verb*

▸ **cause a vacancy**

in poker, to win a hand that drives a player from the game *US*

• —George Percy, *The Language of Poker*, p. 18, 1988

'cause; cos; coz; cuz

because *UK*

An accepted and conventional term in C16 that has slipped into dialect and vulgar use.

• Just cos I ain't never had, no, nothing worth having[.] —Ian Dury, *Clevor Trever*, 1977
• Cuz if we don't, my dad's sendin' me to military school. —*Bill and Ted's Excellent Adventure*, 1989
• [H]allelujah hallelujah yah know i do some things more different than i used ta coz i'm a player doing what the players do . —Outkast *Player's Ball*, 1994
• I don't have so many albums 'cuz music's only been a recent influence on my life. —Melanie McGrath, *Hard, Soft & Wet*, p. 121, 1998
• Now I know why you want to hate me / Cuz hate is all the world that's even seen lately[.] —Limp Bizkit *Take A Look Around*, 2000
• I cry hopelessly / Cause I know I'll never breathe your love again[.] —Westlife, *I Cry*, 2001
• If you are that kind of man / 'Cos I'm that kind of girl / I've gotta freaky secret everybody sing / 'Cos we don't give a damn about a thing / Cos I will be a freak until the day[.] —Sugababes, *Freak Like Me*, 2002

cause it *verb*

to cause trouble to, or damage something *UK*

• [D]rilling a hole in the kitchen wall, hitting the cable and putting all the lights out: "O Lor'! That's caused it!" —*Beale*, 1974

cav *adjective*

cavalier *US*

In the pornography industry, an attitude towards sexually transmitted disease.

• —*Adult Video News*, p. 42, August 1995

cavalier *noun*

the uncircumcised penis *UK*

Probably of Royal Navy origin, then juvenile; derives as an antonym of **ROUNDHEAD** (a circumcised penis).

• —Paul Baker, *Polari*, p. 168, 2002

cavalry *noun*

▸ **the cavalry are coming; the cavalry are here**

help is coming; help is here *UK, 1984*

From the literal military sense, probably informed in use by film Westerns.

Cav and Pag *nickname*

the short operas *Cavalleria Rusticana*, by Pietro Mascagni, and *Pagliacci*, by Ruggero Leoncavallo, when paired as a double bill *UK*

Cavalleria Rusticana was first performed in 1890, *Pagliacci* in 1892.

• Though billed under its usual nickname, "Cav and Pag", Raymond Gubbay's latest Albert Hall offering should be retitled "Pag and Cav", since the traditional order of this most familiar of operatic double bills has been reversed. —*The Guardian*, 28th September 2002

cave *noun*

1 a deep sore at the site of repeated drug injections *US*

• —David Maurer and Victor Vogel, *Narcotics and Narcotic Addiction*, p. 395, 1973

2 the vagina *UK*

From the conventional meaning (a large hole or crevice).

• —*Sky Magazine*, July 2001

▸ **keep cave**

to keep a lookout *UK, 1906*

Extends from **CAVE!** pronounced 'kay-vee' (beware!); school slang.

cave *verb*

to have sex with someone *US*

• And Carri with your class and swiftness you can cave the bellboys and save the four outta ten[.] —A.S. Jackson, *Gentleman Pimp*, p. 84, 1973

cave!

beware! *UK, 1868*

School slang, pronounced 'kay-vee', from Latin *cavere* (to beware). Still familiar, but mainly from its convenience as a crossword clue to a generation who read a certain sort of children's fiction.

caveman *adjective*

1 obsolete *US*

• Their computer is caveman. —Robert Kirk Mueller, *Buzzwords*, p. 51, 1974

2 used of any skateboarding manouevre performed in an old-fashioned style *UK*

• —Fabrice le Mao, *Skateboarding*, p. 90, 2004

cave tubing *noun*

a floating exploration of underground river and cave systems on an inflated rubber tube *BELIZE*

• The cave tubing was a big disappointment. ...However, I did get an attractive photo of me in figure-hugging caving outfit. —*The Guardian*, July 2003

caviar *noun*

1 human faecal matter in the context of a sexual fetish *UK*

A euphemism used in pornography.

• I had never seen a "caviar" video before, and was fascinated by the sight of a well-dressed German couple working on their plate of faeces with forks and knives[.] —Anabel Chong, *Life Beyond the Bidet [Inappropriate Behaviour]*, p. 112, 2002

2 residue in whatever utensils are used for manufacturing crack cocaine *US*

• —Peter Johnson, *Dictionary of Street Alcohol and Drug Terms*, p. 36, 1993

3 a mixture of marijuana and crack cocaine prepared for smoking in a cigarette *US*

• —Geoffrey Froner, *Digging for Diamonds*, p. 33, 1989

4 cocaine; crack cocaine *UK*

• —Mike Haskins, *Drugs*, p. 280, 2003

caviar can *noun*

an armoured tank from the former Soviet Union *US, 1952*

• —J.E. Lighter, *Historical Dictionary of American Slang, Volume 1*, p. 373, 1994

Cavite all star *noun*

marijuana, probably from the Philippines *US, 1977*

Cavite was a US military base and is now an 'Export Processing Zone', ninety miles south of Manila.

• —Richard A. Spears, *The Slang and Jargon of Drugs and Drink*, p. 99, 1986
• —Mike Haskins, *Drugs*, p. 287, 2003

cav of the cav *nickname*

the First Squadron of the Ninth US Cavalry *US*

Organised in 1866, the Ninth Cavalry saw action in every war through to Vietnam.

• —Linda Reinberg, *In the Field*, p. 37, 1991

cavvy *noun*

a substitute horse, or person *CANADA*

• A cavvy is a spare horse taken along when working cattle over a long period of time. This [term] can also be used figuratively for a backup, or spare, to the usual object of use. Do not tell your spouse that the person they saw you with was only a cavvy[.] —Chris Thain, *Cold as a Bay Street Banker's Heart*, p. 36–37, 1987

cazh *adjective*

▷ **see:** **KAZH**

cazooled *adjective*

drunk *US*

• —Collin Baker et al., *College Undergraduate Slang Study Conducted at Brown University*, p. 94, 1968

CB *noun*

used as an abbreviation for 'cock block' *US*

• —Edith A. Folb, *runnin' down some lines*, p. 231, 1980

CB *adjective*

could be *US*

Used in tentative diagnoses, such as 'could be lupus'.

• —Sally Williams, *"Strong" Words*, p. 136, 1994

CBC sunshine *noun*

rain after a Canadian Broadcasting Corporation forecast of sun *CANADA*

• CBC sunshine is the rain that pours down an hour or so after a CBC radio weather forecast stating that it will be sunny. —Chris Thain, *Cold as a Bay Street Banker's Heart*, p. 37, 1987

CBT *noun*

in the subculture of consensual sado-masochism, the infliction of discomfort and pain on a male's genitals *UK*

An initialism of **COCK** (the penis), '*b*all' (the testicle) and '*t*orture'.

- She wanted pretty severe CBT, and no, I'm not going to describe what it involved in this case[.] —Claire Mansfield and John Mendelssohn, *Dominatrix*, p. 166, 2002

CC *noun*

1 Canadian Club™ whisky *US*
- You had about two hundred cases of C.C. on that truck[.] —George V. Higgins, *The Friends of Eddie Doyle*, p. 14, 1971
- Canadian Club is a brand of rye. Not to be confused with "hockey stick," another kind of Canadian club. —Will Ferguson, *How to be a Canadian*, p. 63, 2001

2 cocaine offered as a gift by a dealer *US*
- Generally, cocaine dealers come to after-hours clubs withh "C-C," or calling card cocaine, to give out. —Terry Williams, *The Cocaine Kids*, p. 97, 1989

3 a prison segregation unit *UK*
An abbreviation of CARDBOARD CITY.
- —Angela Devlin, *Prison Patter*, p. 34, 1996

CC *verb*
to send someone to a prison segregation unit, or to replace cell-furniture with cardboard items *UK*
From CARDBOARD CITY (the segregation unit).
- —Angela Devlin, *Prison Patter*, p. 34, 1996

CCW *noun*
the criminal charge of carrying a concealed weapon *US*
As the US moved to the right, gun enthusiasts have been successful in enacting legislation in many states that permit – not forbid – carrying concealed weapons, changing the meaning of the acronym to 'concealed-carry weapon'.
- He saw dozens of c-c-w cases come through the courtroom, and he knew that had Chester been white, he'd have been given a small bond or released on his own personal word. —Donald Goines, *White Man's Justice, Black Man's Grief*, p. 30, 1973
- "We have a ton of CCW (carrying concealed weapon) cases with these exact facts," McCarty said. —*Plain Dealer (Cleveland, Ohio)*, p. 4B, 8th May 1994

CD *noun*
a condom *SOUTH AFRICA*
Scamto youth street slang (South African townships).
- —*The Times*, 12th February 2005

C-Day *noun*
the day when new car models were available for civilian purchase after the end of World War 2 *US, 1944*
- —*American Speech*, October 1946

C-duct *noun*
cocaine *US*
- —Richard A. Spears, *The Slang and Jargon of Drugs and Drink*, p. 99, 1986
- —Mike Haskins, *Drugs*, p. 280, 2003

C-dust *noun*
cocaine *US*
- —William D. Alsever, *Glossary for the Establishment and Other Uptight People*, p. 6, December 1970
- —Mike Haskins, *Drugs*, p. 280, 2003

cábóg *noun*
an ignorant male *IRELAND*
- He had a right go at the then Minister for Agriculture, Dr. Ryan, and protested loudly that he was not going to take been called a cábóg by any one. —*Munster Express*, 5th November 2004

cecil *noun*
cocaine *UK*
A disguise like CHARLIE, another man's name.
- —Angela Devlin, *Prison Patter*, p. 35, 1996
- —Nick Constable, *This is Cocaine*, p. 181, 2002

Cecil Gee; cecil *noun*
one thousand pounds *UK*
The high street designer menswear shop Cecil Gee is used for 'dressing up' the common G (£1,000). Noted in use by television presenter Johnny Vaughan.
- —*www.LondonSlang.com*, June 2002

Cecil B. DeMille *noun*
any large job that evolves into a chaotic mess *US*
New York police slang.
- —Samuel M. Katz, *Anytime Anywhere*, p. 387, 1997

ceech *noun*
hashish *US*
- —Jay Robert Nash, *Dictionary of Crime*, p. 60, 1992

ceefa *noun*
a cat *NEW ZEALAND*
A play on 'c for cat'.
- —David McGill, *David McGill's Complete Kiwi Slang Dictionary*, p. 28, 1998

ceiling bet *noun*
the highest bet permitted in a given game or situation *US*
- —George Percy, *The Language of Poker*, p. 18, 1988

ceiling chicken *noun*
an Air Canada baggage handler with a particular assignment *CANADA*
- The "ceiling chicken" is the person who goes up the baggage belt to free something that is jammed in it. —*Horizons*, p. 7, 27th April 1994

ceitful *adjective*
deceitful *GUYANA*
- —Richard Allsopp, *Dictionary of Caribbean English Usage*, p. 144, 1996

celeb *noun*
a celebrity *US, 1916*
- [S]ome juvenile half-wits plant themselves outside the hotels when such celebs are in town. —Jack Lait and Lee Mortimer, *Washington Confidential*, p. 132, 1951
- I don't mean the celebs and the legit high rollers, he's got to take care of them, and he loves it. —Elmore Leonard, *Glitz*, p. 119, 1985
- Messy-haired rock stars are the celeb squeeze of choice[.] —*Sky Magazine*, p. 8, May 2001

celebrity-fucker *noun*
a person who seeks out sexual relationships with famous people *US, 1969*
- She was always such a celebrity fucker. It must be said of Lillian that when the chips were down she'd always go for the guy who had the most clout. —George Plimpton, *Truman Capote*, 1997
- Should I tell them that he deserves the grant because every gifted young artist does, or throw the information request back in their faces, screaming that they're just youth-hungry celebrity-fuckers like the rest of this disgusting country? —*Village Voice*, p. 119, 4th August 1998

celestial discharge *noun*
death in a hospital *US*
- —Sally Williams, *"Strong" Words*, p. 136, 1994

cell *noun*
a wireless telephone that is part of a system in which a geographical area is divided into sections served by a limited-range transmitter *US*
An abbreviation of 'cell phone' a term first heard in the late 1980s as an abbreviation of 'cellular'.
- CARSON: So – on the way home from the strip bar – at 0200 – you get this call on your cell saying something happened to Superboy on the bridge. —*Copland*, 1997
- —Pamela Munro, *U.C.L.A. Slang*, p. 49, 1997
- —Connie Eble (Editor), *UNC-CH Campus Slang*, p. 1, Fall 2001

cell *verb*
to occupy a prison cell *US, 1901*
- I could see the new red-brick chapel building across the yard, and part of the west cell house where I had celled on 5-11. —Chester Himes, *Cast the First Stone*, p. 36, 1952
- It was bad enough trying to cell with someone halfway regular, let alone some knickknacking nut. —Malcolm Braly, *On the Yard*, p. 205, 1967
- But, nine times out of ten, after they cell with the guy a while, after this relationship goes on for a while, they quit it. —Bruce Jackson, *In the Life*, p. 379, 1972

cell 99 *noun*
a prison morgue *US*
- —Vincent J. Monteleone, *Criminal Slang*, p. 46, 1949

cellar *noun*
in a sports league, the last place in team standings *US*
- —Parke Cummings, *Dictionary of Baseball*, p. 12, 1950
- "Thrown out at first base, West was returning to the Boston dugout on the third base line," the account said of a game against the Braves' rival for the NL cellar, the Philadelphia Phillies. —*Boston Globe*, p. B7, 9th January 2004

cellar dealer *noun*
a card cheat who deals from the bottom of a deck *US*
- —George Percy, *The Language of Poker*, p. 18, 1988

cellar flap; cellar *verb*
to borrow something *UK*
Rhyming slang for **TAP** (to borrow). According to Julian Franklyn, the term still had 'a restricted usage' in 1960.
- —Julian Franklyn, *A Dictionary of Rhyming Slang*, 1960

cell block *noun*
1 a condom *UK*
A clever play on words: 'cell' (a basic life-form) representing spermatazoa, combined with 'block' (a barrier); the whole ironically suggesting imprisonment (of the penis).
- —David Rowan, *A Glossary for the 90s*, 1998

2 a school classroom *US*
Teen slang.
- —*San Francisco News*, p. 6, 25th March 1958

cellie; celly *noun*
1 in jail or prison, a cellmate *US, 1966*
- What do yeh got, a bear for a celly?—Paul Glover, *Words from the House of the Dead*, 1974
- —Clement and La Frenais, *A Further Stir of Porridge*, 1977
- He had hurt lots of people, but the Trasbag Man had been his cellie at Attica and the headaches had started about then[.]—James Ellroy, *Because the Night*, p. 329, 1984
- Robert "Robot" Salas, a Sureno from a street gang called Big Hazard, and Hector Padilla, a Norteno, were cellies[.]—Bill Valentine, *Gangs and Their Tattoos*, p. 24, 2000
- "Well cellie what can I say" says en entry inside a card to a member of a central L.A. street gang.—*Los Angeles Times*, p. A1, 5th April 2004

2 a cellular telephone *US*
- [T]he play-by-play via cellie from 7-year-old Patrick's first ball season did it.—*Sporting News*, p. 7, 20th September 1999
- —Connie Eble (Editor), *UNC-CH Campus Slang*, p. 3, October 2002
- Forty-nine percent use a "cellie" to make plans with friends.—*Chicago Daily Herald*, p. 1, 9th September 2003

cell-shocked *adjective*
deranged from life in prison *US*
An obvious, although sharp, play on 'shell-shocked'.
- He's cellshocked. Done so much time he can only concentrate long enough to tie his shoe.—Seth Morgan, *Homeboy*, p. 211, 1990

cell spin *noun*
a surprise search of a cell by prison authorities *UK*
From **SPIN** (to search).
- —Angela Devlin, *Prison Patter*, p. 35, 1996

cell task *noun*
in prison, a pin-up *UK*
A focus on location and inspiration for a prisoner's **TASK** (masturbation).
- —Angela Devlin, *Prison Patter*, p. 35, 1996

cell warrior *noun*
a prisoner whose actions outside his cell do not match his aggressive words uttered in the safety of his cell *US*
- —Jim Goad, *Jim Goad's Glossary of Northwestern Prison Slang*, 2001

cement arm *noun*
an intravenous drug user's arm that is toughened with scar tissue over the veins *US*
- —David Maurer and Victor Vogel, *Narcotics and Narcotic Addiction*, p. 395, 1973

cemented *adjective*
very drunk *UK*
- —Tom Hibbert, *Rockspeak!*, p. 36, 1983

cementhead *noun*
a stupid person *US, 1949*
- For example, throwing office supplies and constantly calling women "assholes," "morons," and "cementheads" probably would not have been considered part of the hostile environment[.]—*Wisconsin Women's Law Journal*, p. 397, Summer 1997

cement mixer *noun*
1 a dancer who rotates her pelvis in a simulation of sexual intercourse *US*
- Belly down she's a cement mixer."—Thurston Scott, *Cure it with Honey*, p. 152, 1951

2 a dance, a ball *UK*
A beatnik term not recorded until 1984.

3 a loud car or truck *US, 1914*
- —Mary Elting, *Trucks at Work*, 1946
- —Judi Sanders, *Da Bomb!*, p. 6, 1997

cement overcoat *noun*
hardened cement in which a murder victim is concealed *US, 1969*
- —Angela Devlin, *Prison Patter*, p. 35, 1996

cement overshoes *noun*
concrete poured around a person's feet, used to weigh them down when their body is disposed of in a body of water *US, 1962*
- For example, a defense lawyer who double-crosses a drug lord during the defense of an underling may end up in cement overshoes.—*Harvard Law Review*, p. 693, January 1992
- Onlookers whisper jokes about bumping into Jimmy Hoffa's cement overshoes.—*USA Today*, p. 6D, 30th June 2003

census office *noun*
in prison, the office where incoming and outgoing mail is checked *UK*
- —Angela Devlin, *Prison Patter*, p. 35, 1996

cent *noun*
a dollar *US, 1957*
- One cent is a dollar.—Willard Motley, *Let No Man Write My Epitaph*, p. 148, 1958
- "I'll be givin you three cents extra – what's wrong with that?"—Clarence Cooper Jr, *The Scene*, p. 43, 1960
- Red came toward Bernie, menacing. "You don't understand, I gotta have twenty cent, like I tell you." Twenty cent meant twenty dollars; Red always spoke of dollars in amounts under one hundred as cents; perhaps it expressed his contempt for money.—Ross Russell, *The Sound*, p. 157, 1961
- Man, like how many times some cat's come up to me with his old man's watch or sister's coat and swap for a three-cent bag.—Piri Thomas, *Down These Mean Streets*, p. 206, 1967

▸ **like a cent worth of shaved ice**
humiliated, belittled *TRINIDAD AND TOBAGO, 1987*
- —Lise Winer, *Dictionary of the English/Creole of Trinidad & Tobago*, 2003

centerfield *noun*
1 in craps, a field bet on the nine *US*
- —Steve Kuriscak, *Casino Talk*, p. 11, 1985

2 in blackjack played in casinos, the seat directly across from the dealer *US*
- —Steve Kuriscak, *Casino Talk*, p. 11, 1985

centre *noun*
in the gambling game two-up, the bets placed with the person spinning the coins *AUSTRALIA, 1911*
- —James Holledge, *The Great Australian Gamble*, p. 100, 1966
- The keeper said, 'Centre set? All set of the side?' Then he nodded to me.—John O'Grady, *It's Your Shout, Mate!*, p. 25, 1972
- —Jim Ramsay, *Cop It Sweet!*, p. 21, 1977

Centre *noun*
▸ **the Centre**
the central parts of the Australian mainland *AUSTRALIA, 1899*
- But Bob Buck and Jimmy Wickham were appreciated as members of the bush fraternity of the Centre, and Walter chuckled as he yarned with Frank about Jimmy's cattleduffing exploits.—R.G. Kimber, *Man from Arltunga*, p. 106, 1986

centurion *noun*
a cricketeer who scores 100 runs *BARBADOS*
- She also compiles those facinating starburst charts of each batsman's innings, on which the direction of every stroke is recorded. (She gives them to centurions).—*The Times*, 15th July 1985
- —Richard Allsopp, *Dictionary of Caribbean English Usage*, p. 144, 1996

century *noun*
1 a $100 note *US, 1859*
- I took them out and riffled them. Ten centuries. All new. All nice. An even thousand dollars.—Raymond Chandler, *The Little Sister*, p. 239, 1949
- The next bag had bigger bills, and the last bag had nothing but centuries – sparkling $100 greens.—Red Rudensky, *The Gonif*, p. 118, 1970

2 one hundred pounds (£100) *UK, 1861*
- [S]old to Dave for the knock-down price of a couple of centuries.—Andrew Nickolds, *Back to Basics*, p. 128, 1994
- [S]igning a century (£100) or even a monkey (£500) away[.]—Duncan MacLaughlin, *The Filth*, p. 117, 2002

3 one hundred yards *US*

- I always ran when I was with Leonard, maybe it had something to do with the fact that he was a natural 440 man and I had the dashes covered up to the century.—Odie Hawkins, *Men Friends*, p. 117, 1989

4 one hundred miles *US*

- Years ago, there used to be bicycle clubs, meeting Sundays, who had what was termed "century" runs.—*San Francisco Progress*, p. 4, 1st August 1956

5 in motor racing, 100 miles per hour *US*

- —John Lawlor, *How to Talk Car*, p. 29, 1965

century *verb*

to save one hundred dollars *US*

- —Clarence Major, *Dictionary of Afro-American Slang*, p. 35, 1970

century note *noun*

a one-hundred dollar note *US, 1908*

- He ended up borrowing a century-note from them.—Jack Lait and Lee Mortimer, *Washington Confidential*, p. 278, 1951

'cept

except *UK, 1851*

- Nothing 'round here I care to try for / 'Cept you, yeah you / Got nothing left to live or die for / 'Cept you, yeah you—Bob Dylan, *Nobody 'Cept You*, 1991
- I'm getting screwed over by some fucker who doesn't care for anything 'cept his own pocket.—John Williiams, *Cardiff Dead*, 2000

cereal *noun*

marijuana, especially when smoked in a bowl

- —*www.addictions.org*, 1999
- —Mike Haskins, *Drugs*, p. 287, 2003

cert *noun*

1 a certainty *UK, 1889*

- If they take up his offer I'm a cert—Gavin Casey, *It's Harder for Girls*, p. 90, 1941
- Nor a word more or it'll be porridge and cocoa for a cert. —Charles Raven, *Underworld Nights*, p. 91, 1956
- —Bill Wannan, *Bullockies, Beauts and Bandicoots*, p. 16, 1960
- Currently, the Pope's a Jew if that daughter of mine isn't a cert for the political spectrum one day.—Barry Humphries, *The Traveller's Tool*, p. 125, 1985
- —Phillip Gwynne, *Deadly Unna?*, p. 132, 1998
- Others will hope the fiendish mess of insurance regulation [...] will ultimately make compensation a cert.—*The Guardian*, 27th June 2003

2 a horse that is considered to be a *cert*ain winner; a likely winner in any contest *UK, 1889*

- The Return of the King is more of a racing cert than Gladiator[.] —*The Guardian*, 24th February 2004

certifiable *adjective*

mentally deranged *UK, 1939*

Carried over from an earlier legal requirement to certify a person as insane.

- In fact, he [Philip K. Dick] was a near certifiable Californian freak who hammered out more than 40 books during his short life, most of them written in fortnight-long, amphetamine-fuelled frenzies —*The Observer*, 23rd June 2002

cess *noun*

marijuana, possibly of inferior quality *US*

- That cess got me buggin'.—Lois Stavsky et al., *A2Z*, p. 18, 1995
- [S]moke a pound of cess a day[.]—Eminem (Marshall Mathers), *Rock Bottom*, 1999
- —Mike Haskins, *Drugs*, p. 287, 2003

cess!; ciss!

used as an expression of contempt or disgust, also used for registering disappointment *SOUTH AFRICA, 1862*

Directly from Afrikaans *sies*. Variants include 'sis!', 'sies!' and 'siss!'.

cest *noun*

marijuana *UK*

- —Mike Haskins, *Drugs*, p. 287, 2003

CFA *noun*

someone not originating from a particular place in the Maritime Provinces *CANADA*

An acronym for '*c*ome *f*rom *a*way', well known to Newfoundlanders and other coastal people.

- That said, [Donna] Morrissey doesn't want to fall into the regional-author trap. "Only CFAs wear rubber boots and Sou'westers," she says. And if you don't know what a CFA is, well, let's just say that if you lived in Newfoundland, you'd be one by now.—*Toronto Globe and Mail*, p. D8–D9, 30th March 2002

CFB *adjective*

very clear indeed *US*

An abbreviation of '*c*lear as a *f*ucking *b*ell'. Vietnam war usage.

- It wouldn't be long now until the visibility was CFB (clear as a frapping bell) and the Jolly Greens would be chattering in.—William C. Anderson, *Bat 21*, p. 77, 1980

CFD *noun*

a chilled 12-ounce can of beer *US*

An abbreviation of '*c*old *f*rothy *d*og'.

- —Connie Eble (Editor), *UNC-CH Campus Slang*, p. 3, October 2002

CFM *adjective*

sexually suggestive *US*

An abbreviation of COME-FUCK-ME.

- —Pamela Munro, *U.C.L.A. Slang*, p. 28, 1989

C-H *noun*

a cheating scheme in poker involving two players; if one player signals that he is holding a good hand, his confederate raises the bet *US*

An abbreviation of '*c*rooked-*h*onest'.

- —George Percy, *The Language of Poker*, p. 18, 1988

cha *noun*

▷ see: CHAR

cha *adjective*

fashionable, trendy, stylish *US*

- [T]he cha ("very cool") words include: "winded" for hung over; "craftsman" for a complete idiot; and "ass" for awful.—*Washington Times*, p. C3, 26th August 1992

cha!, chaa!

▷ see: CHO!

chabobs *noun*

the female breasts *US*

- McMurphy starts. "She's got one hell of a set of chabobs," is all he can think of.—Ken Kesey, *One Flew Over the Cuckoo's Nest*, p. 174, 1962

chach *noun*

the vagina; a despised woman *US*

- —Connie Eble (Editor), *UNC-CH Campus Slang*, p. 2, November 2003

cha-cha *verb*

to have sex *US*

- —Edith A. Folb, *runnin' down some lines*, p. 232, 1980

chaff bandit *noun*

a racehorse that does not win enough to pay its way *AUSTRALIA*

- —Ned Wallish, *The Truth Dictionary of Racing Slang*, p. 13, 1989

chaffy *noun*

a fellow prisoner *UK*

- —Angela Devlin, *Prison Patter*, p. 36, 1996

chain *noun*

a bus or van used to transport prisoners *US*

- —Inez Cardozo-Freeman, *The Joint*, p. 487, 1984

▸ **off the chain**

excellent *US*

- —Don R. McCreary (Editor), *Dawg Speak*, 2001
- —Connie Eble (Editor), *UNC-CH Campus Slang*, p. 7, November 2003

▸ **pull your chain**

1 to tease you; to mislead you *US, 1962*

- He realized after a few weeks that the guy had been pulling his chain about the women, but that was all right.—Elmore Leonard, *The Big Bounce*, p. 111, 1969
- He's pulling your chain. And the fact that you even bought it for a second makes you look like an idiot.—*Chasing Amy*, 1997

2 to control your actions against your will; to treat you with contempt *US, 1962*

The image of a dog on a leash. Variants are 'jerk your chain' and 'yank your chain'.

- "Hey, Dave," Eddie said, "don't jerk my chain."—George V. Higgins, *The Friends of Eddie Doyle*, p. 154, 1971
- [H]er organisation could jerk his chain any bloody time they felt like it.—Chris Ryan, *The Watchman*, p. 100, 2001

Chain *noun*

▸ **The Chain**

the Aleutian Islands *US, 1886*

- Many a ship has been lost in The Chain, and many a man lies there with no gravestone. — Robert O. Bowen, *An Alaskan Dictionary*, p. 11, 1965
- Traveling to the Aleutians is commonly called "going out on The Chain." — Mike Doogan, *How to Speak Alaskan*, p. 20, 1993

chain-drink *verb*

to drink one beverage after another, barely pausing between drinks *US, 1976*

- Fueled by the coffee he chain-drinks, he likes to get going before dawn and often goes with little sleep. — *Washington Post*, p. D1, 22nd December 1982

chain gang *noun*

1 a railway crew assembled from the first available workers *US*

- — Norman Carlisle, *The Modern Wonder Book of Trains and Railroading*, p. 260, 1946

2 the Lord Mayor and Lady Mayoress of London *UK, 1976*

After the chains of office.

chain it *verb*

to chain smoke *UK*

- [M]e and Charlie sit a couple of feet away from him chaining it until the bastard chokes. — Danny King, *The Burglar Diaries*, p. 101, 2001

chains and canes *noun*

restraint and corporal punishment when advertised as services offered by a prostitute *UK*

- — Caroline Archer, *Tart Cards*, 2003

chain-saw *verb*

to exhange positions with someone; to take over; to cut in *UK*

- And as for you, you bastard. Chain-sawing me on Milly like that. — Colin Butts, *Is Harry Still on the Boat?*, p. 268, 2003

chain-smoke *verb*

to smoke cigarettes continuously and addictively *UK, 1934*

- — *American Speech*, October 1956
- Mother and doctor seem to be involved in an activity in which they claim exclusive expertise, and husband is left to chain-smoke in the waiting room. — Thomas Harris, *I'm Ok – You're OK*, p. 180, 1973
- This chain-smoking, slightly stooped lad, took a deep breath[.] — Kevin Sampson, *Powder*, p. 10, 1999

chainsuck *noun*

in mountain biking, a condition that occurs when the bicycle chain doubles back on itself and gets jammed between the frame and the chain rings *US*

- Muddy water washes the lube from the chain, which leads to chainsuck, so lube your chain before and after every ride[.] — *Mountain Bike Magazine's Complete Guide To Mountain Biking Skills*, p. 126, 1996

chair *noun*

1 the electric chair; the death penalty *US, 1895*

- I'm going to get that louse that killed you. He won't sit in the chair. He won't hang. He will die exactly as you died[.] — Mickey Spillane, *I, The Jury*, p. 7, 1947
- Rub out a cop an' you'll really get the chair. — Marvin Wald and Albert Maltz, *The Naked City*, p. 125, 1947
- The whole town knows that if he'd been a little older he'd have gone to the chair instead of reform school. — Jim Thompson, *The Killer Inside 19*, 1952
- If Ready has killed some trick he was steering to Reba's the chair's too good for him. — Chester Himes, *The Real Cool Killers*, p. 64, 1959
- Tell us the truth, Black, and you might beat the chair. — Clarence Cooper Jr, *The Scene*, p. 226, 1960
- If he died, I would get the chair. — Piri Thomas, *Down These Mean Streets*, p. 242, 1967
- I'm not sayin' you won't go to jail, but you sure ain't gotta go to the chair. — Nathan Heard, *Howard Street*, p. 208, 1968
- Maybe one day I'll make you a really proud father – I'll croak [kill] a whore and make the chair. — Iceberg Slim (Robert Beck), *The Naked Soul of Iceberg Slim*, p. 45, 1971

2 a motorcycle sidecar *UK, 1984*

- — Douglas Dunford, *Motorcycle Department, Beaulieu Motor Museum*, 1979

chairbacker *noun*

an unordained, self-taught preacher *US, 1955*

- — Frederic G. Cassidy, *Dictionary of American Regional English*, p. 584, 1985
- "Chairbacker" (a preacher whose pulpit was a common chair in a slave cabin) and "floor preacher" became common appellations[.] — Mechal Sobel, *Trabelin' On*, p. 160, 1988

chairborne *adjective*

in the miliary, assigned to a rear-echelon support job *US, 1943*

A pun on 'airborne', applied to 'chairborne commandos', 'chairborne generals', the 'chairborne infantry', 'chairborne rangers', etc.

- Mission demands led Brig. Gen. John Iffland, 146th Airlift Wing commander, to fly the 36-year-old plane, stepping away from dealing with personnel and paperwork – what GIs call the chairborne division. — *Ventura County (California) Star*, p. A1, 22nd November 1998
- Is it possible that a "chairborne" general was unhappy because he was not qualified to wear the headgear awarded to certain combat troops of the U.S. Army? — *Columbus (Ohio) Dispatch*, p. 6A, 16th January 2001

chairman of the board *noun*

the most important person of a set of people

Probably extended from its use as a nickname for Frank Sinatra, 1915–98.

- You've got your big fook-off minders, your drop-dead gorgeous backin' singers, your wasted, monged-out old musos ... an' then me, right in the middle, the Boss, the Man. The Chairman o' the fookin' board. — Ben Elton, *High Society*, p. 216, 2002

Chairman of the Board *nickname*

actor and entertainer, Frank Sinatra, 1915–1998 *US*

Coined in tribute to his rôle as founder of Reprise Records in 1961.

chairwarmer *noun*

an idler, a loafer *US, 1960*

- — Harold Wentworth and Stuart Berg Flexner, *Dictionary of American Slang*, p. 93, 1960
- He added "do-nothing" and "chairwarmer" to rhetorical blasts at a news conference, even as he urged Sundquist to devote half the campaign to daily debates at towns across the state. — *Knoxville (Tennessee) News-Sentinel*, p. A4, 9th August 1994

chale!

no! never! *US*

Border Spanish used in English conversation by Mexican-Americans.

- — George Carpenter Baker, *Pachuco*, p. 41, January 1950
- "Chale, chalee. Quit being a sergeant," I said. — Joseph Wambaugh, *The Blue Knight*, p. 58, 1973

chalewa *noun*

a marijuana pipe *JAMAICA*

Defined as 'A pipe for smoking herb, usually made from coconut shell and tubing, used ritually by Rastas' by Desmond Johnson.

- — Desmond Johnson, *Patois Terms*, 2001

Chalfont St Giles; chalfonts *noun*

haemorrhoids *UK*

Rhyming slang for 'piles', formed from the name of a village in Buckinghamshire. Noted by Red Daniells, 1980.

- I've been using cream on my Chalfonts all week and my underpass is still killing me. — Bodmin Dark, *Dirty Cockney Rhyming Slang*, 2003

chalice *noun*

a pipe for smoking marijuana *JAMAICA*

A word with wider religious significance adopted into ritual by Rastafarians and hence into more general use. Celebrated in the song 'chalice to chalice' by Tappa Zukie, 1996.

- [H]im puff a serious Planet Zion chalice. — Diran Adebayo, *My Once Upon A Time*, p. 24, 2000
- — Velma Pollard, *Dread Talk*, p. 42, 2000
- It's one of the many reasons Bob Marley remains a paradox, shrouded in myth and trailing smoke screens of collie weed from the ever-present chalice and cutchie which accompanied him all his days. — *Uncut*, p. 46–67, March 2001

chalk *noun*

1 a white person *US, 1945*

Not flattering.

- If it wasn't for Uncle Tom ass dudes like me, niggers like you wouldn't be havin' a chance to eat all the chalk pussy you want, or nothin' else, for that matter! — Odie Hawkins, *Chicago Hustle*, p. 138, 1977

2 methamphetamine or amphetamine *US*

- — J. L. Simmons and Barry Winograd, *It's Happening*, p. 173, 1966
- The most common drugs in use in industry, according to the police sergeant, are amphetamine sulfate compounds and barbiturates, known among workers in the plants as "chalk," "whites," "bennies," "reds," "jackets," "blue heavens" and "rainbows." — *The San Francisco Chronicle*, p. 5, 11th October 1966
- — Edward R. Bloomquist, *Marijuana*, p. 156, 1968

- He was really in a bad way and begged me for some chalk or anything. — Anonymous, *Go Ask Alice*, p. 85, 1971

3 crack cocaine *UK*
From the appearance.
- — Mike Haskins, *Drugs*, p. 281, 2003

4 a potent homemade 'wine' made from yeast, sugar, water and rice or fruit *US*
- — AFSCME Local 3963, *The Correctional Officer's Guide to Prison Slang*, 2001

5 low quality beer *US*
- — Vincent J. Monteleone, *Criminal Slang*, p. 46, 1949

6 in sports betting, the contestant or team favoured to win *US*
- — *Bay Sports Review*, p. 8, November 1991

7 chocolate syrup *US*
- — *American Speech*, p. 88, April 1946: 'The language of West Coast culinary workers'

▸ **by a long chalk**
by much; by a great degree *UK, 1859*
In the later C20 the predominant usage becomes 'not by a long chalk' with the meaning as 'grossly inferior'.

chalk *verb*

1 to prepare cocaine for inhalation *UK*
The image of white chalk lines.
- Nood starts chalkin' a few lines on the desktop includin' a real fat one for Joe. — Nick Barlay, *Curvy Lovebox*, p. 143, 1997

2 to chemically lighten the colour of cocaine for buyers who believe that the white colour reflects purity *US*
- — Terry Williams, *The Cocaine Kids*, p. 136, 1989

3 to observe something or someone *US*
- "Shhhh," Choo-Choo cautioned. "Chalk the walking Jeffs." — Chester Himes, *The Real Cool Killers*, p. 120, 1959

4 to ban a gambler from a table, game or casino *US*
- — *The Annals of the American Academy of Political and Social Sciences*, p. 122, May 1950

5 to steal something *US*
- — Rick Ayers (Editor), *Slang Dictionary*, p. 6, 2001

chalk and talk *noun*
teaching; those methods of teaching which are currently considered old-fashioned *AUSTRALIA, 1942*
Slightly contemptuous.
- Whereas in my day teachers used to stand at the front of the class and lecture "chalk and talk" style every session, the emphasis is now on student activities[.] — *The Guardian*, 18th February 2003

chalk-eater *noun*
in horse racing, a bettor who consistently bets on favourites *US*
From the old custom of a bookmaker chalking odds on a blackboard.
- — David W. Maurer, *Argot of the Racetrack*, p. 18, 1951

chalked up *adjective*
under the influence of cocaine *US*
- — *American Speech*, p. 86, May 1955: 'Narcotic argot along the Mexican border'
- — Richard A. Spears, *The Slang and Jargon of Drugs and Drink*, p. 562, 1986
- — Nick Constable, *This is Cocaine*, p. 182, 2002

chalker *noun*
a very fat person *US*
- — Connie Eble (Editor), *UNC-CH Campus Slang*, p. 1, Fall 1990

chalker and talker *noun*
a teacher *AUSTRALIA, 1942*
Later use is slightly contemptuous.

Chalk Farm; chalk *noun*
the arm *UK, 1857*
Rhyming slang, formed on an area of north London.

chalk hand *noun*
in poker, a hand that is almost certain to win *US*
- — George Percy, *The Language of Poker*, p. 18, 1988

chalk horse *noun*
in horse racing, the favourite in a race *US*
- — David W. Maurer, *Argot of the Racetrack*, p. 18, 1951

chalkie *noun*
a school teacher *AUSTRALIA, 1945*
From the use of chalk on a blackboard.
- — Arthur Chipper, *The Aussie Swearer's Guide*, p. 65, 1972
- At school he'd been this full-on aggro animal. Now he was a chalkie. — Kathy Lette, *Girls' Night Out*, p. 191, 1987

chalk it up *verb*
to claim or give someone the credit for something *UK, 1923*
- [I]t will be a struggle even for Tony Blair to chalk it up as another feather in the cap of his doctrine of international community. — *The Guardian*, 22nd November 2001

chalk it up!
used for drawing attention to a triumph or extraordinary happening, often accompanied by a gesture of chalking a figure 1 on a wall *UK, 1923*

chalk man *noun*
the police employee who chalks the outline of a corpse where it has fallen before the body is removed *US*
- — Lewis Poteet, *Car & Motorcyle Slang*, p. 46, 1992

chalk people *noun*
people who live far from the ocean *US*
- — Trevor Cralle, *The Surfin'ary*, p. 20, 1991

chaloupe *noun*
a wide, heavy, large American car *CANADA*
French used by the English-speaking in Quebec.
- — Lewis Poteet, *Car & Motorcyle Slang*, p. 46, 1992

chambermaid *noun*
a railway machinist working in a roundhouse *US*
- — Norman Carlisle, *The Modern Wonder Book of Trains and Railroading*, p. 260, 1946

chamber of commerce *noun*

1 a toilet *US, 1960*
A pun on 'chamber pot'.
- — Lou Shelly, *Hepcats Jive Talk Dictionary*, p. 22, 1945
- — Clarence Major, *Dictionary of Afro-American Slang*, p. 35, 1970

2 a brothel *US*
- — Vincent J. Monteleone, *Criminal Slang*, p. 47, 1949

chamber pipe *noun*
a type of pipe used to smoke marijuana *US*
- — Jay Robert Nash, *Dictionary of Crime*, p. 61, 1992

champ *noun*

1 a drug addict who does not inform on others when questioned by the police *US*
- A champ is a junkie who won't snitch or inform, although no such animal exists. — Clarence Cooper Jr, *The Scene*, p. 55, 1960
- — Eugene Landy, *The Underground Dictionary*, p. 47, 1971
- — Jay Robert Nash, *Dictionary of Crime*, p. 61, 1992

2 a *champion* *US, 1868*
- Computer humbles chess champ. — *BBCi*, 17th October 2002

3 used between contemporary, unrelated males as a familiar form of address *UK*
- — Dave Courtney, *Dodgy Dave's Little Black Book*, p. 7, 2001

champagne *noun*

1 human urine in the context of a sexual fetish *US, 1987*
- — Thomas E Murray and Thomas R Murrell, *The Language of Sadomasochism*, p. 50, 1989

2 a well-paying customer of a prostitute *US*
- — Jay Robert Nash, *Dictionary of Crime*, p. 61, 1992

champagne blonde *noun*
a woman with pale blonde hair *UK, 1904*
- As these words were being typed, a nineteen-year-old champagne blonde snatched $1500 from a Las Vegas bank and was caught only because she was so beautiful no one could forget her police description. — Lee Mortimer, *Women Confidential*, p. 25, 1960

champagne Charlie *noun*
a man who enjoys a luxurious, if somewhat dissipated, lifestyle *UK, 1868*
After a music hall song about a noted drinker of champagne.

• They are not paid, but they get to enjoy a 'Champagne Charlie' lifestyle, meeting their favourite rap stars, having access to the coolest gear and CDs. — *The Observer*, 26th November 2000

champagne chins *noun*
folds of flesh creating the image of more than one double chin as a result of the good life *UK*
• [A] terrifying lump of a man with his bull's head and champagne chins. — Greg Williams, *Diamond Geezers*, p. 164, 1997

champagne drug *noun*
cocaine *US*
• Cocaine prices dropped dramatically from 1980 onwards as the drug cartels successfully expanded their client base, bringing in many people who previously could not afford to use the "champagne drug." — Richard Rudgley, *The Encyclopedia of Psychoactive Substances*, p. 67, 1998
• After years of decline, prompted by rocketing prices and the fashion for LSD and speed, coke resurfaces and gains a reputation as the "champagne drug". — *Drugs An Adult Guide*, p. 16, December 2001

champagne house *noun*
wealthy clubbers *UK*
Champagne, generally prefixed with a sense of derision or criticism (as **CHAMPAGNE SOCIALISM**), combines with **HOUSE** (**MUSIC**) (the umbrella-genre for contemporary club music).
• [T]he Champagne house set consists of professionals who, having graduated through the rave years, cannot put their old habits to bed but have on the way picked up new habits commensurate with their occupational status (and pay packet). — Ben Osborne, *The A-Z of Club Culture*, p. 47 – 48, 1999

champagne socialism *noun*
a belief in socialist ideals apparently contradicted by an expensively indulgent lifestyle *UK, 1987*
Critical and derisory.
• Top floor of the Ritz Carlton, getting all kinds of perks – and they were going on about the virtues of communism. And that's classic champagne socialism, you know? — Keay Davidson, *Carl Sagan*, p. 395, 1999

champagne socialist *noun*
a person attached to socialist politics who enjoys a luxurious lifestyle *UK, 1987*
• They forgot to ask whether I have communist sympathies, or perhaps they don't care any more. And after today I can only ever be described as a champagne socialist anyway. — *The Guardian*, 6th December 2001

champagne tap *noun*
a bloodless sample from a lumbar puncture *UK*
Glossed as 'traditionally rewarded by a bottle of bubbly from the consultant' by Adam Fox.
• — Adam T. Fox, St Mary's Hospital, London, 10th October 2002

champagne tastes and mauby pockets *noun*
something said to be possessed by those who do not have the money to live the lifestyle that they affect *BARBADOS, 1976*
• — Richard Allsopp, *Dictionary of Caribbean English Usage*, p. 146, 1996

champagne trick *noun*
a wealthy, big-spending customer of a prostitute *US, 1973*
• — Harold Wentworth and Stuart Berg Flexner, *Dictionary of American Slang*, p. 684, 1976

champers *noun*
champagne UK, 1955
The original word is abridged and the suffix '-ers' is added; this process of amendment, credited to students at Oxford University, is discussed by Partridge and Beale in the appendix to the 8th edition of the *Dictionary of Slang and Unconventional English* and called 'Oxford -er(s)'.
• I'll pop another tiny bottle of champers on the ice for our delicious jailbird. — Barry Humphries, *Bazza Pulls It Off!*, 1971
• [W]hat the hell does he think he's doing, sitting sipping champers[?] — Mike Stott, *Soldiers Talking, Cleanly*, 1978
• I was savouring the champers[.] — Wayne Anthony, *Spanish Highs*, p. 82, 1999
• champers mixed with a shot of voddy — *Sky Magazine*, p. 88, May 2001

champion *noun*
a completely inept and unlucky person *SINGAPORE*
• — Paik Choo, *The Coxford Singlish Dictionary*, p. 23, 2002

champion *adjective*
excellent *UK, 1937*
Mainly, or stereotypically from the north of England.

champion *adverb*
excellently *UK, 1937*
Mainly, or stereotypically from the north of England.

chance *verb*
▸ **chance your arm**
to take unnecessary risks *UK*
• That and the doctrine of chancing your arm is the Alpha and Omega of its philosophy. — Geoffrey Fletcher, *Down Among the Meths Men*, p. 10, 1966

chance 'em *verb*
while surfing, to decide to ride a big wave *US*
• — Trevor Cralle, *The Surfin'ary*, p. 20, 1991

chancer *noun*
an opportunist, especially one who takes risks in pursuit of criminal gain; someone who takes or creates *chances UK, 1884*
• I never did like the cunt. He's always been too much of a chancer. — Ted Lewis, *Jack Carter's Law*, p. 87, 1974
• This one's really persistent. You can usually tell the chancers, but this guy says he's been with Keva all night[.] — Kevin Sampson, *Powder*, p. 458, 1999

chance would be a fine thing!; chance is a fine thing!
'I wish I had that opportunity!' or 'You wouldn't know what to do if you got the opportunity!' or 'that is very unlikely!' *UK, 1977*
Each variant has all meanings.
• On the looming prospect that some unions may be tempted to transfer their party donations to the Lib Dems, he [Charles Kennedy] joked: "Chance would be a fine thing." — *The Guardian*, 11th September 2002

chancre mechanic *noun*
a military medic, especially one assigned to diagnose and treat sexually transmitted infections *US, 1944*
• [H]e had been doc of Baker Company, survivor of the Makin Raid, as opposed to your typical natty, run-of-the-mill chancre mechanic. — W.E.B. Griffin, *The Corps Book II*, p. 339, 1987
• — Linda Reinberg, *In the Field*, p. 39, 1991
• "After that first day," says the 1st Battalion surgeon Ben Sullivan, "we were no longer pill rollers or chancre mechanics. We were all beloved." — Gerald Astor, *Battling Buzzards*, p. 130, 1993

chandelier *noun*
1 where non-existent bids in a fraudulent auction are said to come from *UK*
• It's where an auctioneer accepts bids "off the chandelier" or "off the wall", as auctioneers say – meaning phoney non-existent bids – then knocks an antique down to some joker[.] — Jonathan Gash, *The Ten Word Game*, p. 61, 2003

2 a homosexual *UK*
Rhyming slang for **QUEER**. Shortened to 'shandy'.
• — Ray Puxley, *Fresh Rabbit*, 1998

chandelier sign *noun*
a dramatic reaction to being touched in a painful area *US*
It is said that the patient 'hits the ceiling' or 'hits the chandelier'.
• — Sally Williams, *"Strong" Words*, p. 136, 1994

chanel *noun*
cocaine *US*
A slightly forced formation, playing on the name of designer Coco Chanel.
• — Robert Sabbag, *Snowblind*, p. 271, 1976

chang *noun*
cocaine *UK*
• How many times do you sniff a given gram of chang? — James Hawes, *White Powder, Green Light*, p. 7, 2002
• [T]hey've got a huge appetite for chang and don't mind banging you in some horrible old toilet. — *Ministry*, p. 42, 2002

change *noun*
1 money *US*
• — David Claerbaut, *Black Jargon in White America*, p. 60, 1972

2 an approximation or a fraction *US*
• So I did three and change. — Edwin Torres, *Carlito's Way*, p. 52, 1975

▸ **the change**
the menopause *UK, 1934*
Elliptical for **CHANGE OF LIFE**.

change *verb*

▸ **change address**

to leave *TRINIDAD AND TOBAGO*

- —Lise Winer, *Dictionary of the English/Creole of Trinidad & Tobago*, 2003

▸ **change tune**

to retreat *US*

- —Linda Reinberg, *In the Field*, p. 39, 1991

▸ **change water**

to engage in an unproductive activity *US*

From lobstermen, who refer to the hauling and baiting of an empty trap as 'changing water'.

- —John Gould, *Maine Lingo*, p. 47, 1975

▸ **change your luck**

(used of a white person) to have sex with a black person; to have sex with a person of the sex with whom one would not ordinarily have sex *US, 1916*

- The Harlem community accepts – though it despises – these Caucasians who cross the color line, or as it is known above 110th Street, "change their luck" or "deal in coal." —Jack Lait and Lee Mortimer, *New York Confidential*, p. 161, 1948
- Go to bed with a nigger and change your luck. —Willard Motely, *Let No Man Write My Epitaph*, p. 327, 1958
- —Dick Gregory, *Nigger*, 1964
- Hey, Flo, gonna take the little monkey home with you, change your luck? —Dick Gregory, *Nigger*, p. 10, 1964
- She gives me a hug and a kiss on the cheek and says very loud, "Wipe that lipstick off before Mary sees it," making a joke about how we're carrying on behind eveyrbody's back and how, like she says, she'd change her luck if I weren't married. —Robert Campbell, *Cat's Meow*, p. 36, 1988

▸ **change your tune**

to alter your professed opinion or manner of speech *UK, 1578*

- Mr Portillo changed his tune after the downfall of Lord Archer. — *The Guardian*, 24th November 1999

change artist *noun*

a swindler who gives customers too little change *US*

- We will assume that the change artist is behind the cash register, and you are the customer; you hand him a bill and he takes the change from the drawer. —W.M. Tucker, *The Change Raisers*, p. 17, 1960

change machine *noun*

a prostitute who charges very little for sex *US*

- DARLING DOLLY DANE: "Two miserable bucks!" LOLA: "Youve gone for less, dear." "DARLING DOLLY DANE, wiggling: "This aint no change-machine, Mae." —John Rechy, *City of Night*, p. 114, 1963

change of life *noun*

the menopause *UK, 1834*

- Like everyone in their 50s, I went through the change of life[.] — *The Guardian*, 18th July 2002

change of luck *noun*

(used of a white person) sex with a black person *US, 1916*

- I know you, you after a change of luck. —Bernard Wolfe, *The Magic of Their Singing*, p. 103, 1961

change raiser *noun*

a swindler who tricks cashiers into giving him too much change *US*

- Change raisers deliberately confuse the victim by repeatedly handling the change back and forth, then they throw the change out of balance. Then they balance it again, but in the process a good portion of the change sticks to their own fingers. —W.M. Tucker, *The Change Raisers*, p. 7, 1960

changes *noun*

difficulties *US*

- She really worked me over good, she was a credit to her gender/ She put me through some changes Lord, sort of like a Waring blender. —Warren Zevon, *Poor Poor Pitiful Me*, 1973
- —Anna Scotti and Paul Young, *Buzzwords*, p. 56, 1997

changies *noun*

changing rooms *UK*

- The other girls cleared out of the changies – just about big enough to roast a girl it were[.] —Kevin Sampson, *Outlaws*, p. 40, 2001

chank *noun*

a chancre; any sexually transmitted infection *US*

- —Harold Wentworth and Stuart Berg Flexner, *Dictionary of American Slang*, p. 93, 1960

chank *verb*

to eat loudly and rudely *US, 1844*

- —Frederic G. Cassidy, *Dictionary of American Regional English*, p. 589, 1985

channel *noun*

a vein, especially a prominent vein suitable for drug injection *US*

- — US Department of Justice, *Street Terms*, October 1994

channel *verb*

in car customising, to lower the body of the car *US*

- Most of the work he was doing then was modifying Detroit cars – chopping and channeling. Chopping is lowering the top of the car, bringing it nearer to the hood line. Channeling is lowering the body itself down between the wheels. —Tom Wolfe, *The Kandy-Kolored Tangerine-Flake Streamline Baby*, p. 90, 1965
- Leotis McCarver was undoubtedly black, but his car was a full dress taco wagon: chopped and channeled, lowered, with a candy apple, lime-green paint job with orange and yellow flames covering the hood and weeping halfway back over the sides of the vehicle. —James Ellroy, *Brown's Requiem*, p. 13, 1981

Channel Bore *nickname*

UK television Channel 4 *UK*

- You know we make this frightful Underground series for Channel Bore? —Kevin Sampson, *Powder*, p. 224, 1999

channel fever *noun*

a strong desire by someone at sea to be back on land *UK, 1929*

- Most were infected with "channel fever," the giddiness that overcomes crew members in the days before warships return to San Diego Bay. — *Orange County (California) Register*, 3rd June 2003

channel fleet *noun*

a street *IRELAND*

Rhyming slang.

- —Julian Franklyn, *A Dictionary of Rhyming Slang*, 1960

channel-surf *verb*

to browse distractedly through a variety of television programmes, switching from channel to channel *US*

- —Connie Eble (Editor), *UNC-CH Campus Slang*, p. 2, Spring 1994
- The TV was on for 11 hours. She channel-surfed, flicking backwards and forwards never watching anything properly. —Sally Cline, *Couples*, p. 203, 1998

channel swimmer *noun*

a heroin user *US, 1959*

Punning on 'channel' as 'a vein'.

- —Jay Robert Nash, *Dictionary of Crime*, p. 61, 1992
- — US Department of Justice, *Street Terms*, October 1994
- —Robert Ashton, *This Is Heroin*, p. 208, 2002

chant *verb*

to sing *UK, About 1386*

- [S]o I trolled back to my lattie to go over my chanting and walloping for tonight's concert[.] —The cast of 'Aspects of Love', Prince of Wales Theatre, *Palare (Boy Dancer Talk) for Beginners*, 1989–92
- —Paul Baker, *Polari*, p. 168, 2002

chantoosie *noun*

in Montreal, a female nightclub singer *CANADA*

The word is adapted from French *chanteuse* (a woman who sings).

- "We're waiting for a French chantoosie." "She's at the hairdresser's upstairs." —Mordecai Richler, *Dispatches from the Sporting Life*, p. 136, 2002

chap *noun*

1 a man, a fellow *UK, 1704*

- Harold, just bugger off, would you, there's a good chap. — *The Guardian*, 12th December 2002

2 a young fellow who wouldn't yet know about the ways of the world *IRELAND*

- Stapler was always the same though lads yeh know. Even when he was a chap. —Billy Roche, *The Wexford Trilogy (A Handful of Stars)*, p. 37, 1992

3 a juvenile offender or detention centre inmate who is top of the pecking order *UK*

- —Home Office, *Glossary of Terms and Slang Common in Penal Establishments*, 1978

chapel *adjective*

being part of a chapel's congregation *UK, 1946*

- Oh them! They're chapel, so of course they sing much louder. — *Beale*, 1984

chapel hat pegs *noun*
used for comparisons with things that are exaggeratedly conspicuous or obvious when not normally so *UK, 1984*
- Her poor fingers were stiff as chapel hat-pegs already.—Angela Carter, *Nights at the Circus*, p. 222, 1986
- And my nipples have grown enormous. Men stare at them in the street. As Yorkshire folk would say, they stick out like chapel hat pegs.—Peter Godwin and Joanna Coles, *The Three of Us*, p. 113, 2000
- [T]heir eyes weren't out on stalks like chapel hat-pegs, so I began to realize I was doing something wrong.—A Alvarez, *Feeding the Rat*, p. 27, 2001
- Pat's eyes bugged out like chapel hat pegs, but she didn't dare say anything[.]—Sonya Fitzpatrick, *What the Animals Tell Me*, p. 13, 2003

chapess *noun*
a girl; a woman *UK*
A jocular extension of **CHAP** (a man).
- I met, or reacquainted myself with, dozens of chaps and chapesses who were, mostly, only too pleased to spill the beans.—Will Birch, *No Sleep Till Canvey Island*, p. vii, 2003

chapopote *noun*
heroin *UK*
- —Mike Haskins, *Drugs*, p. 283, 2003

chapped *adjective*
1 depressed *US*
- —*Surfing*, p. 43, 14th March 1990

2 irritated, angry *US*
- —*Current Slang*, p. 2, Fall 1966

chapped off *adjective*
very angry *US*
- —Carol Ann Preusse, *Jargon Used by University of Texas Co-Eds*, 1963

chappie; chappy *noun*
a man, a fellow *UK, 1882*
Originally (1820s) a diminutive for **CHAP** (a man), meaning 'a little fellow'; in the current sense and as a form of address by 1880s. Current usage however is often ironic, probably affected by Chappie™, a branded dog food.
- "Open up, chappie!" Dopey said.—James T. Farrell, *Saturday Night*, p. 31, 1947
- [A]nd chappie the way they pull their lay hips our ship that they are from the land of razz ma tazz—Lavada Durst, *The Jives of Dr. Hepcat*, p. 1, 1953
- Room for an ample chappie?—Kevin Sampson, *Powder*, p. 440, 1999

chaps *noun*
▸ **the chaps**
(of men) a grouping of peers; us *UK, 1978*
- Ronnie [Kray] was more of a friend than Reggie, but I've come along today because he was one of the "chaps".—Roy Shaw, *BBC News*, 11th October 2000

chapstick lesbian *noun*
a lesbian who is athletic or has a notable interest in sports *UK*
Formed on the model of **LIPSTICK LESBIAN**.
- —Michelle Baker and Steven Tropiano, *Queer Facts*, p. 200, 2004

chapter and verse *noun*
complete detail; detailed knowledge *US, 1956*
- If the terrorists do not surface, the United States Government will soon be forced to lay out its evidence in chapter and verse.—*New York Times*, p. A31, 10th December 1981

chapter herald *noun*
a Hell's Angels motorcycle gang member *UK, 1984*
A play on 'herald angels' combined with the fact that Hell's Angels are grouped into 'chapters'.
- —Douglas Dunford, *Motorcycle Department, Beaulieu Motor Museum*, 1979

char; cha; chah *noun*
tea *UK, 1919*
From Chinese – Mandarin *ch'a* (tea) used conventionally from C17.
- With showman's hospitality, generally lavish, he invited me to a cup of "char"[.]—Butch Reynolds, *Broken Hearted Clown*, p. 29, 1953
- [T]he only thing he'll get me is a cup of char.—Clive Exton, *No Fixed Abode [Six Granada Plays]*, p. 135, 1959
- "He always invites me into his cubby-hole," he said. "'A nice cup of char, Mr Guyler', he says.—*The Guardian*, 9th October 1999

character *noun*
1 a man; a fellow; a person *UK, 1931*
- Detaining a suspicious character is already unpleasant enough for a policeman[.]—*Daily Telegraph*, 12th March 2002

2 a person with an underworld lifestyle *US, 1958*
- The only pistol you can count on is a revolver. Every real character [criminal] knows that.—Ned Polsky, *Hustlers, Beats, and Others*, p. 136, 1967
- I mean somebody who makes a living without a legitimate job. Their income is not legitimate. He might be a pimp – he's a character.—Bruce Jackson, *Outside the Law*, p. 144, 1972

3 a chilled 12-ounce bottle of beer *US*
- —Connie Eble (Editor), *UNC-CH Campus Slang*, p. 3, October 2002

charas; churus *noun*
hashish from India *INDIA, 1957*
- An increasing number of hippies are being found in possession of "charas".—Richard Neville [quoting 'The Times of India'], *Play Power*, p. 227, 1970
- I am looking for literature on the religious context of charas, ganja or bhang. I have noticed that quite a few sadhus [men dedicated to the quest for spiritual enlightenment] are smoking charas—Heidi Fadum, *message posted on www.hindunet.org*, 25th May 1997
- Charas is the cream of Indian hashes with the pollen being collected for it's [sic] production before the resin is removed from the leaves[.]—Mike Rock, *This Book*, 1999
- —Mike Haskins, *Drugs*, p. 287, 2003

charcoal *adjective*
(used of skin colouring) gray-brown *BAHAMAS*
- —John A. Holm, *Dictionary of Bahamian English*, p. 39, 1982

chardie *noun*
chardonnay *AUSTRALIA*
- Individual taste is, well individual, but I've got a feeling that if you sit down and discuss this with the guys over a nice glass of (good) chardie, you might be surprised by how much you do actually agree on.—*Sydney Morning Herald*, p. 13, 15th March 2003

charge *noun*
1 an intoxicated sensation, emotional or narcotic *UK, 1950*
- She was scarcely out with the needle when the charge set in.—George Mandel, *Flee the Angry Strangers*, p. 379, 1952
- I gets a big charge going in there with these two birds[.]—John Peter Jones, *Feather Pluckers*, p. 42–42, 1964
- —Angela Devlin, *Prison Patter*, p. 36, 1996

2 intense excitement *US*
- Ooh man! This is a great charge—William "Lord" Buckley, *Martin's Horse*, 1960

3 marijuana *US, 1941*
From an earlier sense meaning 'drugs in general'; it contains a charge – produces a **KICK**.
- I got all the charge I wanted, the good stuff, and we had another arrangement.—Hal Ellson, *Duke*, p. 16, 1949
- "Do you have any charge? Do you Diane? Dincher?" as he sat at her sister's elbow. "Do you have any hemp you could leave me?"—George Mandel, *Flee the Angry Strangers*, p. 259, 1952
- She had her charge but no place to take it.—Willard Motley, *Let No Man Write My Epitaph*, p. 147, 1958
- Not least amongst the geezers I met in the nick are the geezers who are doing a bit of bird for smokeing [sic] charge[.]—Frank Norman, *Bang To Rights*, p. 142, 1958
- Some were quietly trying to borrow money from other guests while some became intoxicated as others smoked "charge" or ate pigs feet in the kitchen at $1.10 apiece.—Dan Burley, *Diggeth Thou?*, p. 45–46, 1959
- He mean bring a few sticks of it out to the field, you see, that's what he mean by that. He call it "charge", too.—Terry Southern, *Red-Dirt Marijuana and Other Tastes*, 1967
- —Mike Haskins, *Drugs*, p. 287, 2003

4 an injection of a drug *US, 1925*
- She applied the needle herself, jabbed quickly and gasped, then pumped the charge and drew it back with her blood[.]—George Mandel, *Flee the Angry Strangers*, p. 379, 1952
- If he tried mainlining with the sugar in the capsule he'd find out in a hurry he had nothing going for him and would do a crazy dance to get a charge.—Mickey Spillane, *Return of the Hood*, p. 104, 1964

5 an alcoholic drink *AUSTRALIA, 1963*
- Wait a sec, till we get another charge.—John O'Grady, *It's Your Shout, Mate!*, p. 69, 1972

6 prison contraband secreted in a prisoner's rectum *NEW ZEALAND, 1997*
- —Harry Orsman, *A Dictionary of Modern New Zealand Slang*, p. 27, 1999

7 a person arrested and held in charge *UK*
- —G.F. Newman, *Sir, You Bastard*, 1970

8 a Charge Nurse, the nurse in charge of a ward, especially if male *UK, 1961*
Often after 'the'.

charge *verb*
to go surfing *US*
• Let's charge it bro, the waves are sweet. —Trevor Cralle, *The Surfin'ary*, p. 20, 1991

▸ **charge it to the rain and let the dust settle it**
to pay for something on credit without fully expecting to pay the charge *US, 1946*
• Look. Charge it to the dust and let the rain settle it. —Brian Pera, *Troublemaker*, p. 54, 2000

charge account *noun*
a person who can be counted upon to post bail if you are arrested *US*
• —Harold Wentworth and Stuart Berg Flexner, *Dictionary of American Slang*, p. 684, 1976

charged; charged up *adjective*
drug-intoxicated *US, 1942*
• Half marijuana, half tobacco. And he was always charged up. —Willard Motley, *Let No Man Write My Epitaph*, p. 108, 1958
• —Eugene Landy, *The Underground Dictionary*, p. 48, 1971
• —Peter A. Smith and Fred M. Barritt, *Bermewjan Vurds*, 1985
• —Richard A. Spears, *The Slang and Jargon of Drugs and Drink*, p. 101, 1986
• Now these very same guys do all their shillings on charlie [cocaine], in cold blood, fuck the consequences, grafting all week just to get charged up[.] —J.J. Connolly, *Layer Cake*, p. 10, 2000
• —Mike Haskins, *Drugs*, p. 291, 2003

charge 'em!
used as an exortation to action *US*
Hawaiian youth usage.
• —Douglas Simonson, *Pidgin to da Max Hana Hou*, 1982

charger *noun*
a bullet shaped container for anal concealment and storage of drugs *UK*
• —Angela Devlin, *Prison Patter*, p. 36, 1996

charge up *adjective*
excited; drunk *TRINIDAD AND TOBAGO*
• —Lise Winer, *Dictionary of the English/Creole of Trinidad & Tobago*, 2003

charidee *noun*
charity seen as a self-serving, publicity-seeking enterprise *UK*
Comedians Harry Enfield and Paul Whitehouse captured this heavily ironic mid-Atlantic pronunciation for the comic caricatures Smashie and Nicey.
• He's more arsed [bothered] about fucking Fun Runs and that, playing golf with his Brookie [Brookside, a soap opera] B-list cronies, doing his bit for charidee and that. —Kevin Sampson, *Outlaws*, p. 4, 2001
• Bought a swanky house for your parents and gave a hefty donation to a children's charidee. —*Ministry*, p. 42, January 2002
• [B]uilder, Brian Walker, is to walk from Land's End to John o'Groats carrying a three-stone pine door – for charidee, natch. —*The Guardian*, p. 5, 28th May 2003

Charing *noun*
a horse *UK, 1857*
Rhyming slang, from Charing Cross (considered by traffic-planners to be the absolute centre of London); the rhyme-word was pronounced 'crorse' in C19 Cockney.
• [H]orses are still known as Charings. —Ray Puxley, *Cockney Rabbit*, 1992

chariot *noun*
1 a car *US, 1935*
Ironic, jocular.
• We dove every which way into that green monster of mine (that's what the boys called my chariot)[.] —Mezz Mezzrow, *Really the Blues*, p. 121, 1946
• Maybe he's got a chariot too. —Chester Himes, *The Real Cool Killers*, p. 54, 1959
• [A] glass or two of shampoo before it was off in the chariot up to a grown-ups club in the West End. —Garry Bushell, *The Face*, p. 82, 2001

2 a brakevan (caboose) *US, 1945*
• —Norman Carlisle, *The Modern Wonder Book of Trains and Railroading*, p. 260, 1946

charity dame; charity moll *noun*
an amateur prostitute, or one undercutting the going-rate *AUSTRALIA*
• —Sidney J. Baker, *Australia Speaks*, 1953

charity fuck *noun*
sexual intercourse engaged in by one partner as an act of generosity *US*
• He described the awkward union which he terms "the charity fuck." —John D. Macdonald, *The Empty Copper Sea*, p. 47, 1978
• [A]sk her for an affair, a charity fuck, anything[.] —Joel Rose, *Kill Kill Faster Faster*, p. 106, 1997
• I sort of stumbled into her. I reckon it must have been a charity fuck, to be honest. From Sally's point of view, that is. —Alan Wall, *The School of Night*, p. 268, 2001

charity girl *noun*
an amateur prostitute or promiscuous woman *US, 1916*
• —Dale Gordon, *The Dominion Sex Dictionary*, p. 42, 1967

charity hop *noun*
in baseball, the last long hop taken by a ground ball, making it simple to field *US*
• —Zander Hollander, *Baseball Lingo*, p. 21, 1967
• Gonzalez, a .243 career hitter who lives by the glove, was even the recipient of a waist-high charity hop. —*Washington Times*, p. C1, 16th October 2005

charity stuff *noun*
a woman who, while promiscuous, does not prostitute herself *US*
• —Hyman E. Goldin et al., *Dictionary of American Underworld Lingo*, p. 42, 1950

Charles *noun*
1 cocaine *UK*
More familiarly known as **CHARLIE** (cocaine).
• I wouldn't mind some Charles but I'm a bit skint. What about the fast stuff [amphetamine]? —Colin Butts, *Is Harry on the Boat?*, p. 114, 1997
• BUNNY: Ah, white boy, ya got no style. We goin' take de Russian deal. [Does a line of Charles.] From under Miami nose. —Chris Baker and Andrew Day, *Lock, Stock... & One Big Bullock*, p. 336, 2000

2 a Viet Cong; the Viet Cong *US, 1966*
• —*Apocalypse Now*, 1979
• —Linda Reinberg, *In the Field*, p. 39, 1991

3 a female's underwear *US*
• —Collin Baker et al., *College Undergraduate Slang Study Conducted at Brown University*, p. 95, 1968

Charles Dance *noun*
a chance *UK*
Rhyming slang, formed on the name of the British actor born in 1946.
• —Ray Puxley, *Fresh Rabbit*, 1998

Charley *noun*
1 the penis *US, 1969*
• Also, if you get caught eating at the table after a game with Charley uncovered, that costs a dollar. —Jim Bouton, *Ball Four*, p. 152, 1970

2 heroin
• —Robert Ashton, *This Is Heroin*, p. 205, 2002

▷ **see: CHARLIE** *and variants*

charley horse *noun*
a muscle cramp *US, 1888*
• Sure, I'm fine now, Sugar Tit. Just a bitch-kitty charley horse in the foot. —Iceberg Slim (Robert Beck), *Death Wish*, p. 196, 1977
• He jerked LaVerne up again, his muscles screaming protest, trying to knot into charley horses. —Stephen King, *Skeleton Crew*, p. 300, 1985

Charley Paddock *noun*
used as a personification of a hacksaw *US*
• —Vincent J. Monteleone, *Criminal Slang*, p. 47, 1949

charley price *noun*
a large rat *JAMAICA*
An allusion to Sir Charles Price, member of the Houses of Asssembly of Jamaica for St Mary, 1756–61, and three times speaker, who introduced a large species of rat to Jamaica to kill cane rats.

charleys *noun*
the testicles *US*
• —Roger Blake, *The American Dictionary of Sexual Terms*, p. 33, 1964

Charley's dead
between schoolgirls, used as a warning that a slip or petticoat can be seen below the hem of a skirt *UK, 1974*
• —Partridge, *A Dictionary of Catch Phrases*, p. 33, 1977

Charley Wheeler *noun*
a girl *AUSTRALIA, 1945*
Rhyming slang for **SHEILA** (a girl).

Charlie; charlie *noun*

1 cocaine *US, 1935*
The phonetic alphabet has 'Charlie' for 'C' in use from around the same time that 'charlie' for 'cocaine' first appears. Also spelt 'charley'.
- More specifically, it was classified as M, C, and H – Mary, Charlie, and Harry – which stood for morphine, cocaine, and heroin. —William J. Spillard and Pence James, *Needle in a Haystack*, p. 147–148, 1945
- "When you shoot Henry [heroin] and Charley, you can smell it going in.—William Burroughs, *Junkie*, p. 84, 1953
- Certainly no Charlie snorting here.— Martin King and Martin Knight, *The Naughty Nineties*, p. 107, 1999
- Sixty quid for a gramme of Charlie was a fucking lot of money[.] —Dave Courtney, *Raving Lunacy*, p. 182, 2000
- Next time you're introduced to Charlie, by all means enjoy his company.—Nick Constable, *This is Cocaine*, p. 180, 2002

2 crack cocaine *UK*
- But the drug of choice now was crack cocaine. Coke. Rock. White. Stones. Charlie.—Lanre Fehintola, *Charlie Says...*, p. 129, 2000

3 a member of the Viet Cong *US, 1965*
- So you have to look for it, you have to check every damn hootch, even if its been burned to the ground. Cause maybe Charlie is down in a hole—John Sayles, *Union Dues*, p. 255, 1977
- "Charlie was always a gook? But a gook wasn't always Charlie?" Farley smiled for the first time. "You never knew when a gook was Charlie."—Nelson DeMille, *Word of Honor*, p. 414, 1985
- He wore a string of ears right across his chest / Just to show Charlie he was always the best.—Sandee Shaffer Johnson, *Cadences*, p. 139, 1986
- Wanna kill those Chinese Charlies!—William T. Vollman, *Whores for Gloria*, p. 124, 1991

4 the Viet Cong *US*
- Charlie hit a village. He's gone, but we gotta secure the joint. —William Wilson, *The LBJ Brigade*, p. 20, 1966
- There was a hell of a lot of Charlies (Communists) in here yesterday. — *San Francisco Chronicle*, p. 19, 3rd February 1966
- But once you've hit a village where Charlie's gotten no cooperation you sort of get a different view of things.—Ronald J. Glasser, *365 Days*, p. 13, 1971
- Charlie don't surf.— *Apocolypse Now*, 1979
- —Linda Reinberg, *In the Field*, p. 39, 1991

5 a fool *UK*
Often as 'a right charlie' or 'a proper charlie'. Possibly a reduction of **CHARLIE HUNT** (a **CUNT**) somewhat softened, or simply a jocular nomination, perhaps for a professional fool such as Charlie Chaplin (1889–1977).
- I mean he thinks Bertrand Russell's a bit of a Charlie, you can't blame him for not reckoning you.—Ray Galton and Alan Simpson, *Hancock's Half Hour*, 25th June 1959

6 a white man, or white men in general *US, 1928*
- I am perplexed and hard pressed in finding a solution or reason that will adequately explain why we are so eager to follow Charlie. —George Jackson, *Soledad Brother*, July 1965
- So you going back to Charlie country.—Cecil Brown, *The Life & Loves of Mr. Jiveass Nigger*, p. 206, 1969
- Sapphire is the world's foremost authority on Charlie. She has borne his children, been his servant, his mistress, his confidante, and the recipient of perversion for hundreds of years.—Carolyn Greene, *70 Soul Secrets of Sapphire*, p. 32, 1973

7 a woman *AUSTRALIA, 1942*
Short for **CHARLIE WHEELER** (a woman).
- In some cosy Alpine spot There you're sure to find us, Propelling Charlies to the cot With a queue of blokes behind us.—Barry Humphries, *A Nice Night's Entertainment*, p. 80, 1964
- A young female [is] also called a 'sort', a 'skirt', a 'dame, a 'doll', a 'charlie', a 'fabulous drop', a 'slashin' line', a 'bit o' homework', and many other things.—John O'Grady, *Aussie English*, p. 79, 1965
- —John O'Grady, *Aussie Etiket*, p. 65, 1971

8 a female prostitute *AUSTRALIA, 1950*

9 the bleed period of the menstrual cycle *AUSTRALIA*
- — *The Museum of Menstruation and Women's Health*, May 2002

10 a glass or bottle of Carlsberg™ lager *UK*
Used by the British Army in Germany in the 1950s and 60s. Noted by Beale, 1974.

11 a dollar *US, 1924*
- Hey, man, you got a couple charlies you can lend me?—Piri Thomas, *Down These Mean Streets*, p. 106, 1967
- —Eugene Landy, *The Underground Dictionary*, p. 48, 1971

12 in poker, the third player to the left of the dealer *US*
- —George Percy, *The Language of Poker*, p. 16, 1988

▷ **see:** CHARLIE HUNT

▸ **go to see Uncle Charlie**
to use cocaine, especially to go to a lavatory for discreet ingestion of the drug *UK*
- She was obviously tipsy and had been to see her uncle Charlie during the evening[.]—Garry Bushell, *The Face*, p. 235, 2001

Charlie *verb*
in the circus or carnival, to dump posters or advertising leaflets that have not been distributed or posted *US*
- —Joe McKennon, *Circus Lingo*, p. 25, 1980

charlie *adjective*

1 ostentatious but lacking in quality *UK*
Upper-class; possibly even an attempt at rhyming slang, 'charlie horse' (coarse).
- Cheap attempt at style, flashy, non-U, as in "a bit charlie".—Ann Barr and Peter York, *The Official Sloane Ranger Handbook*, p. 158, 1982

2 scared, afraid *UK*
Probably a shortening of rhyming slang **CHARLIE HOWARD** (a coward).
- I was dead charlie and the fairies were having a right game in my guts[.]—Frank Norman, *Bang To Rights*, p. 49, 1958

charlie bender *noun*
a prolonged session of cocaine abuse *UK*
A new influence, **CHARLIE** (cocaine), for a traditional **BENDER** (a drinking session).
- [H]e flashes his shades on an' off givin' out insane stares like he's on a charlie bender. Which I guess he is.—Nick Barlay, *Curvy Lovebox*, p. 141, 1997

Charlie bird *noun*
during the Vietnam war, a helicopter used by a tactical commander *US*
- —Linda Reinberg, *In the Field*, p. 39, 1991

Charlie boy *noun*
an effeminate man *US, 1896*
Patronising.
- Charlie Boy's attitude was, "You got me, charge me or let me go." —Duncan MacLaughlin, *The Filth*, p. 172, 2002

Charlie Brown *noun*
a citizens' band radio set *UK*
The name of a much-loved cartoon character, created in 1950 by Charles M. Schulz, disguises a conventional initialism.
- —Peter Chippindale, *The British CB Book*, p. 153, 1981

Charlie Chaplin *noun*
a chaplain, especially a prison chaplain *SOUTH AFRICA*
After the famous comedy actor.
- —Angus Hall, *On the Run*, 1974

Charlie Chase *verb*
in horse racing, to finish second *AUSTRALIA*
Rhyming slang, from 'Charlie Chase' (to place).
- —Ned Wallish, *The Truth Dictionary of Racing Slang*, p. 13, 1989

Charlie Chester; charlie *noun*
a paedophile, a child molester; often used as a nickname for a headmaster *UK*
Rhyming slang, used by schoolchildren, formed, for no reason other than a convenient rhyme, from the name of the comedian and broadcaster, 1914–96.
- —Chris Lewis, *The Dictionary of Playground Slang*, p. 52, 2003

Charlie Clore; Charlie *noun*

1 twenty pounds (£20) *UK*
Rhyming slang for **SCORE**. Formed, no doubt with irony, on the name of British financier Charles Clore (1904–79), a 1960s symbol of great wealth.
- —Ray Puxley, *Fresh Rabbit*, 1998

2 a floor, the floor *UK*
Rhyming slang, as above, but without any irony.
- [T]o put an opponent down was to put him on the "Charlie". —Ray Puxley, *Fresh Rabbit*, 1998

charlie cocaine *noun*
cocaine *UK*
- How much of the charlie cocaine was you after?—Nick Barlay, *Curvy Lovebox*, p. 71, 1997

Charlie Cong *noun*
the Viet Cong; a Viet Cong *US, 1970*
- In the iconology of the Vietnam war, drugs occupy as significant a role as B-52s, napalm, free fire zones, and Charlie Cong. — *Washington Post*, p. 3 (Book World), 30th October 1983

Charlie Cooke *noun*
a look *UK*
Rhyming slang, formed on the name of Chelsea and Scotland midfielder Charlie Cooke (b.1942) who was especially well-known from the mid-1960s to the late 70s.
- — Ray Puxley, *Fresh Rabbit*, 1998

charlied; charleyed; charlied up; charleyed-up *adjective*
cocaine-intoxicated *UK*
- My usual, outgoing character sank into a miserable, pathetic, charlied-up introverted maniac who was completely on edge. — Wayne Anthony, *Spanish Highs*, p. 59, 1999
- Let's get charleyed up. — Darren Francis, *The Sprawl [britpulp]*, p. 296, 1999
- Love the way smokin feels when I'm charlie'd, me lungs openin wide, chest swellin. — Niall Griffiths, *Kelly + Victor*, p. 260, 2002

Charlie Drake *noun*
1 a brake *UK*
Rhyming slang, formed on the name of British comedian and recording artist Charlie Drake (b.1925); in the late 1950s and early 60s he was one the UK's most famous entertainers. The plural, unusually, is Charlie Drakes.
- It would be interesting to see a fitter's reaction if a woman drove into his garage and asked to have her Charlies looked at. — Ray Puxley, *Fresh Rabbit*, 1998

2 a break *UK*
Rhyming slang, formed as above.
- — Ray Puxley, *Fresh Rabbit*, 1998

Charlie Howard *noun*
a coward *UK, 1936*
Rhyming slang.

Charlie Hunt; Charlie *noun*
1 the vagina *UK, 1961*
Rhyming slang for **CUNT**. Also variant spelling 'Charley Hunt', shortened to 'Charley'.

2 a fool *UK*
Rhyming slang for **CUNT**.
- — Julian Franklyn, *A Dictionary of Rhyming Slang*, 1961

Charlie is my darling
used as a catchphrase by cocaine-users *UK*
From an old Scottish folk-song celebrating Bonnie Prince Charlie,1720–88, playing on **CHARLIE** (cocaine).
- I don't use pot at all as a rule. Charlie is my darling, as every News of the World reporter knows[.] — Ben Elton, *High Society*, p. 95–96, 2002

Charlie Noble *noun*
an exhaust stack or chimney *US, 1940*
Originally nautical, referring to a ship's smokestack.
- [I]n addition to which they are often to leeward of exhaust pipes and charlie nobles and are slammed mercilessly form side to side when lying ahull to a windless seaway. — Emiliano Marino, *Sailmaker's Apprentice*, p. 99, 2001

Charlie Potatoes *noun*
an important man *UK*
- [E]veryone's a grass, a slag, a muggy-cunt or a wrong'un, or thinks they're Charlie Potatoes cos they've got a few bob. — J.J. Connolly, *Layer Cake*, p. 183, 2000

Charlie Pride *noun*
a ride in or on something *UK*
Rhyming slang, formed on the US country and western musician (b.1938).
- — Bodmin Dark, *Dirty Cockney Rhyming Slang*, 2003

Charlie rats *noun*
US Army c-rations *US*
A combination of the phonetic 'C' and an abbreviation of 'rations'.
- Ham and lima beans. Taste like shit. Worst Charlie Rat there is. — John M. Del Vecchio, *The 13th Valley*, p. 47, 1982
- — *Maledicta*, p. 259, Summer/Winter 1982: 'Viet-speak'
- PFC Eric R. Shimer, a grenadier in third squad, 3d Platoon, dumped the paraphenalia from it and reshouldered it with only his last can of warm beer, a can of charlie rats, and thirty rounds of ammunition. — Keith Nolan, *Death Valley*, p. 140, 1987
- We ate C rations or "charlie Rats," as they were often called. The olive-drab cans contained approximatley eleven ounces of solid food such as frankfurters and beans, ham and lima beans, spaghetti and meat balls, sausage patties, and corned-beef hash. — Robert W. Black, *Rangers in Korea*, p. 131, 1989
- — Linda Reinberg, *In the Field*, p. 39, 1991

Charlie Ridge *noun*
a ridge in the mountainous region west of Da Nang at the base of Ba Na Mountain; during the Vietnam war, also used as a jocular, generic term for any piece of landscape in Vietnam *US*
- — Linda Reinberg, *In the Field*, p. 39, 1991

Charlie rockets *noun*
a marine contraption in Korea, a small cart with 144 tubes that fire 42-pound projectiles over a range of approximately 5,200 yards *US*
- The marines have a unit called "Charlie rockets." — Martin Russ, *The Last Parallel*, p. 280, 1957

Charlie Ronce; Charley Ronce *noun*
a ponce (a man who lives off a prostitute's earnings); hence a derogatory term for any man *UK*
Variants are 'Joe Ronce' and 'Johnnie Ronce'. Rhyming slang, frequently reduced to 'Charlie' but never 'Joe' or 'Johnnie'.
- I'm a tiddly-wink, a Charlie Ronce — Ian Dury, *Blackmail Man*, 1977

charlies *noun*
the female breasts *UK, 1909*
Always in plural; of uncertain derivation.
- — Louis S. Leland, *A Personal Kiwi-Yankee Dictionary*, p. 24, 1984

Charlie's Angels *noun*
police women *US*
From the cult television series about three female detectives that commenced broadcasting in 1976 and is first recorded in this sense in the same year.
- — Peter Chippindale, *The British CB Book*, p. 153, 1981

Charlie Sheard *noun*
a beard *UK*
Rhyming slang. Recorded by Red Daniells, 1980.

Charlie Smirke; Charley Smirke *noun*
a fool *UK*
Rhyming slang for **BERK**, formed from a British champion jockey of the 1930s–50s.
- — Bodmin Dark, *Dirty Cockney Rhyming Slang*, 2003

Charlie Tom *noun*
a communist terrorist *UK*
Military slang, based on early phonetic alphabet.
- [S]et up ambushes against Communist Terrorists. CT. The Charlie Toms. Bandits. Seek out and destroy. — Jake Arnott, *He Kills Coppers*, p. 3, 2001

Charlie Wheeler *noun*
a woman *AUSTRALIA, 1953*
Rhyming slang for **SHEILA**, after Charles Wheeler, the Australian artist of nudes.
- — Lawson Glossop, *Lucky Palmer*, 1949
- "Yes, there are not so many new faces come in here now," the Charlie Wheeler added. — Ryan Aven-Bray, *Ridgey Didge Oz Jack Lang*, p. 11, 1983

charlie willy *noun*
a real or imagined state of sexual arousal as a result of cocaine usage
Combines **CHARLIE** (cocaine) with **WILLY** (the penis).
- — Alon Shulman, *The Style Bible*, p. 51, 1999

charm *verb*
to talk to someone *US*
- All the Kids would rap, charm (talk to), or game to impress girlfriends; hang it up (insult) or fresh (compliment) male friends by using special words. — Terry Williams, *The Cocaine Kids*, p. 90, 1989

Charmin' *noun*

a timid prisoner *US*

From the advertising slogan for Charmin'™ toilet paper – 'Please don't squeeze the Charmin''.

- —John R. Armore and Joseph D. Wolfe, *Dictionary of Desperation*, p. 24, 1976

charming!

used for expressing disapproval *UK*

An ironic variation of the conventional sense, signalled with heavy emphasis on the first syllable.

- PRINCE'S WIFE: You've wronged me for the last time. It is my misfortune that I still love you but no other woman is going to have you. I have this bomb. We shall die together. HANCOCK: Ooh charming. Madam, I'm not your husband, I'm an actor over 'ere doing 'The Student Prince'. —Galton and Simpson, *Hancock's Half Hour*, 18th January 1956
- "Oh, bleeding charmin," Audrey says, her hand over the receiver, "just bleeding charming." —Ted Lewis, *Jack Carter's Law*, p. 9, 1974

charms *noun*

the parts of a woman's body that are imagined in a sexual context or revealed for titillating effect *UK, 1937*

- While Australians are just acquainting themselves with [Maurizia] Cacciatori, the Italians have been admiring her charms and skills for some time. — *Olympics 2000*, 24th September 2000

charm school *noun*

any leadership training course *US, 1971*

Originally applied to officer training in the military.

- Until 1978, women attended a separate OCS, nicknamed the "charm school," at Quantico. — *Washington Post Magazine*, p. 24, 25th May 1980
- The airline picked him to head what we pilots called a charm school – a program of a couple of days that taught how to conduct oneself as an airline captain. — *Atlanta Journal-Constitution*, p. 6B, 23rd March 2004

charper *verb*

to search for something, to seek something *UK*

- —Paul Baker, *Polari*, p. 168, 2002
- —*Attitude*, p. 60, July 2003

charperer; charpering omee; charpering omi *noun*

a police officer *UK, 1893*

From **CHARPER** (to seek) and **OMEE** (a man).

- —Paul Baker, *Polari*, p. 168, 2002
- —*Attitude*, p. 60, July 2003

charpering carsey *noun*

a police station *UK, 1893*

From **CHARPERER** (a policeman) and **CARSEY** (originally, a house).

- —Paul Baker, *Polari*, p. 168, 2002

charra *noun*

a person of Indian descent living in Durban *SOUTH AFRICA, 1970*

A term that is acceptable in Hindu-to-Hindu conversation, but not for outsiders.

- —Penny Silva, *A Dictionary of South African English*, 1986

Chartocracy *nickname*

Canada, in which the Charter of Rights and Freedoms gives courts wide powers *CANADA*

- We live in a Chartocracy in which judges will determine what are the best and most representative means of citizen involvement in the democratic process. — *Toronto Globe and Mail*, p. A13, 3rd July 2002

charver *noun*

1 a woman, especially when objectified sexually; an act of heterosexual intercourse with a woman *UK*

A consequent usage of **CHARVER** (to have sex).

- —Patrick O'Shaughnessy, *Market Traders' Slang*, 1979
- I need a good charver, a bitta freestyle, a good bunk-up. —J.J. Connolly, *Layer Cake*, p. 211, 2000

2 any member of a subcultural urban adolescent group that wears hip-hop dress and jewellery (and acts older than their years) *UK*

- Mason ('Penal Peter' to associates) reports on words such as 'prat', 'musher', 'Judy', 'rap', 'charver', bevvies', bevvyken', 'wirnkiles' and of 'being given a carpet' (handed down a six-month stretch). — *Mail on Sunday (London)*, p. 5, 9th June 1996
- [V]ariations on their type [chav], also known as Neds, Charvers and Townies, can be spotted across the UK. Their icons are Posh and Becks, Daniella Westbrook, singer Charlotte Church's former boyfriend Stephen Johnson and the pop star Brian Harvey. — *The Independent*, 1st February 2004

charver; charva *verb*

to have sex *UK*

From Romany *charvo* (to interfere with).

- Marchmare walloping a strange bird he later charvered —Derek Raymond (Robin Cook), *The Crust on its Uppers*, p. 26, 1962

charvering donna *noun*

a prostitute *UK*

A combination of **CHARVER** (to have sex) and 'donna' (a woman).

- —Paul Baker, *Polari*, p. 168, 2002

Chas *noun*

1 cocaine *UK*

A conventional diminutive of **CHARLIE** (cocaine).

- There'd been some Chas flying about[.] —Wayne Anthony, *Spanish Highs*, p. 12, 1999
- It was far easier for the boys in blue to nick the odd knobhead for possessing a gram of Chas a few miles down the road. —Garry Bushell, *The Face*, p. 34, 2001

2 a Viet Cong; the Viet Cong *US*

Also spelt 'chaz'. One of not a few variants of **CHARLIE**.

- —Linda Reinberg, *In the Field*, p. 39, 1991

Chas and Dave *verb*

to shave *UK*

Rhyming slang, formed (perhaps ironically) on the names of two bearded Cockney musicians, Charles (Chas) Hodges and Dave Peacock, who have been known as a double-act since 1975. Also used as a noun.

- —Ray Puxley, *Cockney Rabbit*, 1992

chase *noun*

in horse racing, a steeplechase race *US*

- —Tom Ainslie, *Ainslie's Complete Guide to Thoroughbred Racing*, p. 329, 1976

chase *verb*

1 to vigorously pursue a person responsible for some matter and who can achieve a specific result, such as the completion of a piece of work or the provision of urgently needed documents *UK, 1958*

A variant is 'chase up'.

- And it means getting administrators from Auckland to Dublin to chase up companies which fail to put the right information on the right documents – or which just don't bother with paperwork at all. — *The Guardian*, 19th September 2001

2 in poker, to play against an opponent's superior hand *US*

- —Irwin Steig, *Common Sense in Poker*, p. 183, 1963

3 to smoke any drug *UK, 1998*

An abbreviation and broadening of the meaning of **CHASE THE DRAGON** (to smoke heroin).

▸ **chase the bag**

to engage yourself in a near constant search for drugs to buy *US*

- —William D. Alsever, *Glossary for the Establishment and Other Uptight People*, p. 5, December 1970
- —Geoffrey Froner, *Digging for Diamonds*, p. 16, 1989

▸ **chase the dog**

to loaf on the job *US*

- —Jerry Robertson, *Oil Slanguage*, p. 37, 1954

▸ **chase the dragon**

to inhale heroin smoke, especially from heroin burnt on a piece of aluminium foil *US, 1961*

- —David Maurer and Victor Vogel, *Narcotics and Narcotic Addiction*, p. 396, 1973
- —Geoffrey Froner, *Digging for Diamonds*, p. 16, 1989
- Two Iranians sat on phallic bolsters, moodily chasing the dragon[.] —Will Self, *The Sweet Smell of Psychosis*, p. 58, 1996
- —Angela Devlin, *Prison Patter*, p. 36, 1996
- It was well known that Binion liked to "chase the dragon" or smoke heroin. —Jeff German, *Murder in Sin City*, p. 120, 2001
- [T]he Central Drugs Squad boasted a Chinese Dragon as its emblem, based on the famous phrase "chasing the dragon", where addicts sniff the swirling smoke of burning heroin[.] —Duncan MacLaughlin, *The Filth*, p. 138, 2002
- Shaun [Ryder] chased the dragon. —Tony Wilson, *24 Hour Party People*, p. 192, 2002

▸ **chase the kettle**

to use drugs *US*

- —Anna Scotti and Paul Young, *Buzzwords*, p. 130, 1997

▸ **chase the nurse; chase the white nurse**
to become addicted to morphine *US*
- —Jay Robert Nash, *Dictionary of Crime*, p. 62, 1992

▸ **chase the tiger**
to smoke heroin *UK*
- —Robert Ashton, *This Is Heroin*, p. 208, 2002

▸ **chase your losses**
when losing at gambling, to bet more and more and with less discretion in an increasingly frustrating attempt to win back what has been lost *US*
- —Christopher Cavanaugh, *AA to Z*, p. 67, 1998

chaser *noun*
1 a drink taken immediately after another *US, 1897*
- After drinking eight Harvey Wallbangers with chasers[.]—Stewart Home, *Sex Kick [britpulp]*, p. 243, 1999
- Boilermaker. This is a shooter followed by a chaser.—Mardee Regan, *The Bartender's Best Friend*, p. 93, 2003

2 a womaniser *US, 1894*
- —J.E. Lighter, *Historical Dictionary of American Slang, Volume 1*, p. 382, 1994

3 a prison guard *US*
- —Ralph de Sola, *Crime Dictionary*, p. 26, 1982

4 a military police officer assigned to escort prisoners in transport *US, 1927*
Short for 'brig chaser'.
- In August of 1969, shortly before coming home, I was made a "brig chaser" and told to escort another 19-year-old to the brig in Da Nang.—*Providence (Rhode Island) Journal-Bulletin*, p. 1E, 20th April 2000

5 a supplementary message that demands to know what action has been taken on a previous message *UK*
A military usage.
- Wavell's signal to Churchill left the strategic directors little or no choice [...] A "chaser", sent off early the following morning, amplified this instruction.—John Connell, *Wavell: Supreme Commander*, 1969

6 a crack cocaine user with obsessive compulsive behaviours *US*
- —Terry Williams, *Crackhouse*, p. 147, 1992

chase-up *noun*
a car chase or informal car race *UK*
- There were ten of us and we each stole a car from a car-park to have a bit of a chase-up.—Peter Crookston, *Villain*, 1967

chasping *adjective*
excellent *UK*
- —Tom Hibbert, *Rockspeak!*, p. 37, 1983

chassis *noun*
1 a human body *US, 1930*
- She had the kind of chassis that gallant men died for, but, despite her terrific good looks and her knockout shape, she was starting to become a hell of a drag.—Morton Cooper, *High School Confidential*, p. 37, 1958

2 the female breasts *US*
- They really had no idea what was coming off – even though Barbara had a couple of fangled chassis that would put Jayne Mansfield to shame.—Frederick Kohner, *Gidget*, p. 39, 1957

3 the skull *US*
- —Sally Williams, *"Strong" Words*, p. 136, 1994

4 a car *US*
- "When I get 'em out in this chassis of mine and step on the gas, their hearts will pop right out of their mouths – they'll cry for more like babies cry for Castoria," Phil said.—James T. Farrell, *Saturday Night*, p. 23, 1947

chastity belt *noun*
in gambling, the loss limit that some players impose on themselves *US*
- —John Vorhaus, *The Big Book of Poker Slang*, p. 9, 1996

chastity rig *noun*
a skin-coloured patch worn over a woman's vulva to give the appearance of nudity *US*
- Feral's hands, gripping her bottom, covered the adhesive strips which secured her chastity rig[.]—Terry Southern, *Blue Movie*, p. 208, 1970

chat *noun*
1 a vocabulary, style or manner of speech or writing *UK*
- "Says he's a nice fellow, likes hurting people, knocks girls about, sticks knives in people. An emotional pauper." "How much?" "That's college chat for a right bastard."—Laurence Henderson, *With Intent*, 1968

2 a talent for glibly persuasive speech; the gift of the gab *UK*
- —James Barlow, *The Burden of Proof*, 1968

3 a thing, an article, an object *UK, 1906*
- If a horse is being held by a groom, you can say "Put that chat in the stable". If you do not want to buy a wagon that a diddy [gypsy] is trying to sell you: "I don't want the chat"; or if a man is telling you he left a show at Reading, he will say: "I left the chat at Reading.—Butch Reynolds, *Broken Hearted Clown*, p. 31, 1953

4 the vagina *UK, 1937*
French *chat* (cat), thus **PUSSY**.

5 an old man, usually a vagrant, deadbeat and alcoholic, or otherwise degraded *AUSTRALIA, 1950*
Especially in prison use.
- —Jim McNeil, *The Chocolate Frog [and] The Old Familiar Juice*, 1973
- The crims had nicknames for most things and they called the filthy ones 'chats'.—William Dodson, *The Sharp End*, p. 23, 2001

6 a louse *AUSTRALIA, 1812*
Prison usage.
- —Leonard Mann, *Flesh in Armour*, p. 108, 1932
- —Jim Ramsay, *Cop It Sweet!*, p. 21, 1977

chat *verb*
1 to talk persuasively to someone as a strategy for seduction; to flirt *UK, 1898*
Also 'chat-up'.

2 to reveal a secret *JAMAICA*
- —Peter L. Patrick, *Some Recent Jamaican Creole Words*, 2003

▸ **chat stupidness; chat foolishness**
to talk nonsense *ANGUILLA*
- —Richard Allsopp, *Dictionary of Caribbean English Usage*, p. 147, 1996

chatarra *noun*
heroin *UK*
- —Mike Haskins, *Drugs*, p. 283, 2003

chat down *verb*
to engage in flirtatious conversation *BARBADOS*
- —Frank A. Collymore, *Barbadian Dialect*, p. 28, 1965

châteaued *adjective*
drunk on wine
Upper-class society pun on the French *château* (origins of good wine) with conventional 'shattered'.
- —Ann Barr and Peter York, *The Official Sloane Ranger Handbook*, p. 158, 1982

chateaux cardboard *noun*
cheap wine that comes contained in a cardboard box *AUSTRALIA, 1996*
- At our home we use Chateau Cardboard for cask wine, especially cheap stuff.—*Wordmap (www.abc.net.au/wordmap)*, 2003

chat room *noun*
a network on the Internet that hosts real-time typed conversations *US*
- Rush Limbuagh makes regular appearances on CompuServe, although acerbic "Rush Rooms" – a Limbaugh-oriented chat room where users can discuss issues in real time – pop up on several online services.—*Boston Globe*, p. 51, 8th July 1993
- Subscribers can talk directly to one another in "chat rooms' – subnetworks in which up to two-dozen people can type comments to one another.—*New York Times*, p. 1, 20th June 1993
- When the Internet first happened, chat rooms were the place to be. —Suroosh Alvi et al., *The Vice Guide*, p. 16, 2002

Chattanooga choo-choo *noun*
a marijuana cigarette made with two or three rolling papers laid longways *US*
- —Jim Emerson-Cobb, *Scratching the Dragon*, 1997

chatter *noun*
the flexing of a surfboard riding over choppy water or the slapping sound created *US*
- —Grant W. Kuhns, *On Surfing*, p. 114, 1963

chatter *verb*

(used of a car) to vibrate as a result of loose parts in the drive line *US*

- — *American Speech*, p. 93, May 1954

chatterati *noun*

a grouping of articulate middle-class people, especially those occupied in academic, artistic or media work *UK*

A variation of **CHATTERING CLASS**, by a combination of 'chatter' and **-ERATI** (a suffix that creates a fashionable grouping).

- [H]e showed no clear way of rescuing Labour from its middle class chatterati leaders. — *The Guardian*, 19th March 2001

chatterbox *noun*

1 a very talkative person *UK, 1774*

Conventionally contemptuous, but often affectionate, especially of children.

2 a typewriter *US*

- — Hyman E. Goldin et al., *Dictionary of American Underworld Lingo*, p. 42, 1950

chattering class; chattering classes *noun*

articulate middle-class people, especially those occupied in academic, artistic or media work *UK*

- Despite all the wailing and gnashing of teeth among the chattering classes, the outlook for British broadcasting is actually rather cheery. — *The Times*, 11th August 1985
- Tories woo Labour's lost chattering class . — *The Observer*, 31st March 2002
- Liberals and Democratic politicans, goes the argument, are treated with kid gloves, but conservatives and Republicans enjoy the barely concealed hostiliy of the chattering classes. — Eric Alterman, *What Liberal Media?*, p. 139, 2003

chatty *adjective*

dirty; worn out; in poor repair *AUSTRALIA, 1944*

- — Jim Ramsay, *Cop It Sweet!*, p. 21, 1977

chatty, catty and scatty *adjective*

of a woman talkative, spiteful and incapable of serious thought *UK, 1969*

Offensive.

chatty-chatty *adjective*

talkative, gossipy *UK*

West Indian and UK black usage.

- If she too chatty-chatty, me nah interested. — Diran Abedayo, *My Once Upon A Time*, p. 21, 2000

chat up *verb*

1 to bluff or to trick someone by the use of convincing speech *UK*

- — Derek Raymond (Robin Cook), *The Crust on its Uppers*, 1962

2 to flatter someone; to flirt with someone *UK, 1963*

- — Lise Winer, *Dictionary of the English/Creole of Trinidad & Tobago*, 2003

chat-up line *noun*

a conversational gambit intended to initiate a seduction *UK*

Extended from **CHAT UP** (to talk flirtatiously).

- [S]he's married with a baby so doesn't get the chat-up lines she deserves. — John King, *Human Punk*, p. 93, 2000

chaud *noun*

the penis *UK*

- — Paul Baker, *Polari*, p. 168, 2002

chav *noun*

any member of a subcultural urban adolescent group that dresses and acts older than their years *UK*

Variants are 'chava', 'charva', 'chavster' and 'charver'. Usually derogatory, even contemptuous; possibly derived from an abbreviation of Chatham, the town in Kent where the genus is reputed to have originated; possibly from, or influenced by, Romany *chavvy* (a child).

- Typical slang words that Charvas use are "belta", "mint" and "waxa" all meaning good or great[.] — Chris Lewis, *The Dictionary of Playground Slang*, p. 53, 2003
- They said "chavs" or "townies," youngsters who wear jeans and smart-casual clothes and "trendies," who wear fashionable clothes, all picked on them. — *The Gloucester Citizen*, p. 2, 30th July 2003
- For some time now, we've all had a bit of a laugh at neds, chaves, or however we choose the describe anti-social, uneducated, trouble-making teenagers with a style bypass. — *Evening News (Edinburgh)*, p. 11, 19th April 2004
- We are appalled when our professional footballers behave like a troop of booze-fuelled, delinquent macaques, biting and shagging their way from chav-infested nightclub to nightclub. — *The Times*, p. 8, 3rd April 2004
- From the tips of their Burberry baseball caps to the toes of their cashmere Calvin Klein socks, Chavs are a walking advertisement for luxury brands, and are helping to maintain sales for many designers. — *The Independent*, 1st February 2004
- Chav or chavster is one of many terms to describe a certain feckless element of society[.] — *Sunday Times*, 8th February 2004

chavtastic *adjective*

unashamedly in the chav style *UK*

- Britain goes Chavtastic — *Sunday Times*, 8th February 2004

chavvy; chavy; chavvie *noun*

a child; occasionally used, in a derogatory sense, for a man *UK, 1860*

English gypsy use; ultimately from Romany *chavi* (child, daughter) and *chavo* (child, son).

- This was such a big success, especially with the chavies, that I decided to keep that bit [of clown business] in for the future[.] — Butch Reynolds, *Broken Hearted Clown*, p. 17, 1953
- We tell 'em you've just split with the missus, miss the chavvise like fuck and all that[.] — J.J. Connolly, *Know Your Enemy [britpulp]*, p. 148, 1999
- I felt that these chavvies might not let it lie. — Jimmy Stockin, *On The Cobbles*, p. 97, 2000
- I thought as a chavvie he was on about some big old three-eyed monster[.] — J.J. Connolly, *Layer Cake*, p. 38, 2000

chaw *verb*

to cut something up, to disfigure something *UK*

A figurative use of an old form of 'chew'.

- [T]hey cut him to his knees with razor or chaw his face with broken bottle[.] — Anonymous, *Streetwalker*, p. 69, 1959

chawbacon *noun*

an unsophisticated country dweller *US, 1834*

- It's a rule in these parts, so black chawbacons don't git took unawares! — George MacDonald Fraser, *Black Ajax*, p. 68, 1997

ChCh; cheech *nickname*

Christchurch, New Zealand *ANTARCTICA*

- — *Cool Antartica*, 2003: 'Antarctic slang'

che

then *ANTARCTICA, 1985*

In phrases such as 'cheers che'.

- — Bernadette Hince, *The Antarctic Dictionary*, p. 83, 2000

C head *noun*

a cocaine user or addict *US, 1982*

- — Jay Robert Nash, *Dictionary of Crime*, p. 63, 1992

cheap *noun*

▸ **do the cheap**

to take a shortcut *CANADA*

- — Marcel Danesi, *Cool*, p. 116, 1994

▸ **on the cheap**

economically, cheaply, and often, too cheaply *UK, 1859*

- [A] British expert in disaster management, who saw pictures of the collapsed school [...] said he believed the school had "been built on the cheap". — *The Guardian*, 2nd November 2002

cheap *adjective*

mean, lacking in generosity *US, 1904*

- My father could not place his mother in an instituion. It was against his religion. Greeks just didn't do things like that. They were too cheap – that's what has always kept their families together[.] — David Sedaris, *Naked*, p. 31, 1997

cheap and cheerful; cheap but cheerful *adjective*

inexpensive but acceptible *UK, 1978*

Deprecatory, but not as harsh as the conventional 'cheap and nasty'.

- A cheap-and-cheerful design sets the tone for this would-be bargain basement electrical dealer. — *Guardian Unlimted*, 2nd June 2003

cheap and nasty *noun*

a pasty (a small pastry turnover that may contain a variety of fillings) *AUSTRALIA, 1937*

Rhyming slang, depending on an Australian accent for intelligent delivery.

cheap as chips *adjective*

very good value; under-priced *UK, 2000*

The catchphrase of television presenter and antique dealer David Dickinson (b.1941).

- Scooters! Get 'em 'ere, cheaps [sic] as chips!! — Julian Johnson, *Urban Survival*, p. 222, 2003

cheap at the half the price!

used for extolling or appreciating a very reasonable price *UK, 1977*

Often ironic. It seems likely that this is a perversion of the more sensible claim: 'cheap at twice the price'.

- We liked this, it was nice, / and frankly cheap at half the price. — *The Guardian*, 10th November 1999

cheap basing *noun*

crack cocaine *UK, 1998*

The drug is cheaper and less pure than **FREEBASE** cocaine.

- — Mike Haskins, *Drugs*, p. 281, 2003

cheap Charlie *noun*

a cheapskate *US*

- You number fucking ten cheap charlie GI cocksucker! — *Maledicta*, p. 257, Summer/Winter 1982
- — Linda Reinberg, *In the Field*, p. 40, 1991
- — David McGill, *David McGill's Complete Kiwi Slang Dictionary*, p. 26, 1998
- — Dave Walker, *"Hello My Big Honey!"*, p. 22, 2000

cheap heart *noun*

a Purple Heart award resulting from a minor combat wound *US*

- A "cheap heart" was a very minor wound, not requiring medical evacuation, hospitalization or any major treatment; any combat wound was grounds for a Purple Heart. — Gregory Clark, *Words of the Vietnam War*, p. 417, 1990

cheapie; cheapy *noun*

something cheap, or that is made available at a cheaper cost *UK, 1898*

- I like to have two types of bubbles to hand at Christmas: a cheapie for Buck's fizz and impromptu parties and a decent Champagne to drink as an aperitif before lunch. — *The Guardian*, 9th December 2001
- [Android, 1982] is a cheapie out of the Roger Corman production factory[.] — *The Guardian*, 9th April 2003

cheapie *adjective*

cheap; of inferior quality *UK, 1898*

Frequently, but not originally, applied to films.

- [A] Prince Charles mug designed by cartoonist Marc Boxer, with an ear as the handle. The mug is one of the few cheapie Royal souvenirs that now fetch high prices. — *The Guardian*, 11th May 2002

cheapies *noun*

cheap thrills *AUSTRALIA*

- If you want your cheapies, look elsewhere[.] — *Drum Media*, p. 66, 8th December 1992

cheap-jack *adjective*

used of goods sold cheaply, or of cheap quality *UK*

An elaboration of 'cheap', but based on a partial misunderstanding of the conventional 'cheapjack' (a travelling hawker with a diminishing scale of 'bargain' prices).

- It was only plain white cotton from the cheap-jack shop in town – mum said it wouldn't last more than one wash[.] — Mary Hooper, *(megan)2*, p. 89, 1999

Cheap John *adjective*

shoddy, inferior *US, 1855*

- "Cheap John" jewelry salesmen gulled naive countrymen with their suavity and faked generosity. — Thomas D. Clark, *The Southern Country Editor*, p. 38, 1948
- — Harold Wentworth and Stuart Berg Flexner, *Dictionary of American Slang*, p. 95, 1960

cheap line *noun*

a person who buys inexpensive merchandise *FIJI*

- Look at her! She's a cheap line alright. — Jan Tent, 1992

cheapo *noun*

1 a cheap, or inferior, thing *US, 1975*

2 in chess, a trick move or a game won because of an opponent's error *US*

- — *American Speech*, p. 233, Autumn-Winter 1971: 'Checkschmuck! The slang of the chess player'

cheapo *adjective*

inexpensive *US, 1972*

- It's a cheapo takeoff on porn flicks and movie musicals that might have been expected to die unheralded of its own terminal ineptitude. — *Washington Post*, p. B4, 5th September 1977
- [W]ith cheapo bullets like these it don't all the time go clear around. — Jess Mowry, *Way Past Cool*, 1992
- Usually I kind of like the Valley, with its mix of uptown sidewalk cafe bars and downtown cheapo sleaze. — Dirk Flinthart, *Brotherly Love*, p. 87, 1995
- Mum comes crying, finds me at my aunt's watching cheapo Greek video. — Christos Tsiolkas, *Loaded*, p. 148, 1995
- [S]hooting speedballs and drinking lethal cocktails of Niquil [a branded sedative] and cheapo bourbon. — Stuart Browne, *Dangerous Parking*, p. 65, 2000
- [George Harrison] was the proud owner of a "real cheapo horrible little guitar"[.] — *Uncut*, p. 40, February 2002
- [Safeway's] beer team has avoided the cheapo policy of some of its competitors and has been both imaginative and innovative[.] — *The Guardian*, 1st March 2003

cheapo-cheapo *adjective*

very cheap; of inferior quality *UK, 1977*

- [T]he dull and irrefutable reckoning of our four-day shopping trip to cheapo cheapo New York[.] — *The Guardian*, 27th November 1999

cheap physical stuff *noun*

sexual activity short of intercourse *US*

- — Collin Baker et al., *College Undergraduate Slang Study Conducted at Brown University*, p. 95, 1968

cheap play *noun*

in dominoes, a move that scores one point *US*

- — Dominic Armanino, *Dominoes*, p. 16, 1959

cheapshit *adjective*

inexpensive and inferior *UK, 2000*

Combines conventional 'cheap' with **SHIT** (rubbish, something of no value).

- Beadie thrusted sufficiently hard for the cheapshit gyproc [a building material] partition to collapse at her back [...] bringing down a section of equally cheapshit ceiling tiles on top. — Christopher Brookmyre, *Boiling a Frog*, p. 124, 2000

cheap shot *noun*

1 a petty, unfair insult *US, 1971*

- I resent his cheap shot at Dan Quayle. Dan Quayle has been viciously smeared by the media and comedians for spelling potato with an "e" at the end. — *Telegraph Herald (Dubuque, Iowa)*, p. A4, 12th March 1999
- She also called the flap on Bush's inability to answer questions on foreign leaders a cheap shot. Bush could not name the leaders of Chechnya, India and Pakistan. — *Lansing (Michigan) State Journal*, p. 1B, 19th November 1999
- What surprised me were the cheap shots, like calling Bennett a bad steward. His gaming has added millions to state treasuries. — *Tulsa (Oklahoma) Wolrd*, p. A14, 3rd June 2003
- Why aren't there more black quarterbacks? The old racist slander was that they weren't smart enough. Having had that lie thrown in their faces, the cheap-shot artists like Limbaugh would now say, Well, maybe they're good, but they're not as good as that — *Baltimore Sun*, p. 1B, 10th October 2003
- Arianna said, "Let me finish. Let me finish. Let me finish. You know this is completley impolite and" – here's the kicker – "we know how you treat women." Okay, Arnie, so it was a cheap shot". — *Washington Post*, p. A25, 27th September 2003

2 in sports, an unnecessary, unprovoked act of violence *US, 1970*

- [I]f anything goes wrong, if there's any cheap shots, I'll be right there for them. — *Sun-Sentinel (Fort Lauderdale, Florida)*, p. 3C, 29th October 2003

cheapskate *noun*

a miserly person *US, 1896*

- "We'd love to take you up on that, we really would, but the bank's already got us on more payment plans than we can handle." "Fucking cheapskates." — David Sedaris, *Naked*, p. 186, 1997

cheapskate *adjective*

miserly *US, 1903*

- What happens when ICM try to blip you a script from LA and you're jammed up because you were too fucking cheapskate to go broadband? — James Hawes, *White Powder, Green Light*, p. 139, 2002

cheapy *noun*

▷ see: **CHEAPIE**

cheat *verb*

1 when bodybuilding, to use muscles other than those designed for use in a particular exercise *US*

- — *American Speech*, p. 198, Fall 1984: 'The language of bodybuilding'

2 in the entertainment industry, to move slightly to create a better camera angle *US*

- The word is cheat: "Cheat your left leg out a little," or "Open to the camera." —Robert Stoller and I.S. Levine, *Coming Attractions*, p. 121, 1991

cheater *noun*

anything that makes a job easier, such as a short length of pipe or anything else that is handy to slip over the handle of a wrench to increase leverage *US, 1941*

- —Jerry Robertson, *Oil Slanguage*, p. 37, 1954
- —Lewis Poteet, *Car & Motorcyle Slang*, p. 47, 1992

cheaterbug *noun*

a person who cheats *SINGAPORE*

- —Paik Choo, *The Coxford Singlish Dictionary*, p. 25, 2002

cheater five *noun*

while surfing, the toes of one foot extended over the nose of the board only because the surfer has stretched his leg far forward *US*

- —Ross Olney, *The Young Sportsman's Guide to Surfing*, p. 88, 1965

cheaters *noun*

1 eye glasses *US, 1908*

- Tesch mumbled in his signifying way, cocking his sorrowful eyes over those hornrimmed cheeters. —Mezz Mezzrow, *Really the Blues*, p. 177, 1946
- The eyes behind the rimlesss cheaters flashed. —Raymond Chandler, *The Little Sister*, p. 5, 1949
- "Take those cheaters off," Sheik said. —Chester Himes, *The Real Cool Killers*, p. 46, 1959

2 dark glasses *US, 1938*

- —Robert S. Gold, *A Jazz Lexicon*, p. 54, 1964

3 the eyes *UK*

- —David Powis, *The Signs of Crime*, 1977

4 padding that enhances the apparent size of a female's breasts *US*

- —Helen Dahlskog (Editor), *A Dictionary of Contemporary and Colloquial Usage*, p. 12, 1972

5 metal skis *US*

- When metal skis were first introduced by racers, they were called chaters because of their easier maneuverability. —*American Speech*, p. 205, October 1963: 'The language of skiers'

6 in electric line work, channel lock pliers *US*

- —A.B. Chance Co., *Lineman's Slang Dictionary*, p. 3, 1980

cheater's bar *noun*

an anti-cheating mechanism in a slot machine *US, 1968*

- —Thomas L. Clark, *The Dictionary of Gambling and Gaming*, p. 41, 1987

cheater slicks *noun*

car tyres that are smooth but not quite treadless *US*

- People use cheater slicks for street driving and for racing in slower classes. —Ed Radlauer, *Drag Racing Pix Dix*, p. 12, 1970
- In all candor, I made that supercharged / dual-quad / cheater-slicked motherfucker FLY. —James Ellroy, *Hollywood Nocturnes*, p. 18, 1994

cheat sheet *noun*

1 a written memory aid, usually but not always clandestine *US, 1957*

- — *Time Magazine*, p. 46, 24th August 1959
- —Collin Baker et al., *College Undergraduate Slang Study Conducted at Brown University*, p. 95, 1968
- He [Socrates] reads from a cheat sheet under his toga. — *Bill and Ted's Excellent Adventure*, p. 93, 1989

2 in casino gambling, a listing of the payoffs for a particular ticket *US*

- —Jim Claussen, *Keno Handbook*, p. 17, 1982

cheat spot *noun*

an establishment that sells alcohol after closing hours *US*

- Few racketeers could afford to operate a cheat spot if every time a liquor-law violation was proven the court imposed the maximum penalties. — *Saturday Evening Post*, p. 72, 9th March 1963

cheat throat *noun*

oral sex performed on a man in which the person doing the performing simulates taking the penis completely into their mouth without actually doing so *US*

A play on **DEEP THROAT**, the real thing.

- — *Adult Video News*, p. 48, August 1995

che-che *noun*

a light-skinned person; an unlikeable person *SAINT KITTS AND NEVIS*

- —Richard Allsopp, *Dictionary of Caribbean English Usage*, p. 147, 1996

check *noun*

a gambling token *US*

- And then a rush for the cage to cash in the chips (which, for whatever this information may be worth, are always called "checks" by the people who work in the casinos and "chips" by everybody else). —Edward Lin, *Big Julie of Vegas*, p. 23, 1974
- Griffin, the quiet Irishman, was fascinated by the way I handled chips – "checks" in dealers' slang. —Jimmy Snyder, *Jimmy the Greek*, p. 16, 1975

check *verb*

1 to murder someone *US*

- —Anna Scotti and Paul Young, *Buzzwords*, p. 130, 1997

2 to forget or ignore something, often deliberately *UK*

A variant is 'check out'.

- —Angela Devlin, *Prison Patter*, p. 36, 1996

3 to have an intimate relationship with someone *UK*

West Indian and UK black youth.

- I hear, whore, that you're checkin' my man. —Karline Smith, *Letters to Andy Cole*, p. 145, 1998

4 as a prank, to pull down a friend's bathing suit from behind *US*

- —Vann Wesson, *Generation X Field Guide and Lexicon*, p. 36, 1997

▸ check hat

to prepare to leave *US*

- — *Current Slang*, p. 2, Fall 1966

▸ check the cheese

to watch girls as they walk by *US*

- — *American Speech*, p. 154, May 1959: 'Gator (University of Florida) slang'

▸ check the dictionary

to confirm vague or confusing orders or directions *US*

Vietnam war usage.

- —Linda Reinberg, *In the Field*, p. 40, 1991

▸ check the oil level

to pentrate a vagina with your finger *CANADA*

- —Chris Lewis, *The Dictionary of Playground Slang*, p. 54, 2003

▸ check the war

to stop arguing *US*

- —Marcus Hanna Boulware, *Jive and Slang of Students in Negro Colleges*, 1947

▸ check your nerves

to stay calm *US*

- —Marcus Hanna Boulware, *Jive and Slang of Students in Negro Colleges*, 1947

▸ check your six

used as a warning to a pilot to check behind his aircraft for enemy planes *US*

Based on the clock configuration, with twelve o'clock being straight ahead and six o'clock straight behind.

- —Linda Reinberg, *In the Field*, p. 40, 1991

checkbook; chequebook *adjective*

characterised by a seemingly unlimited ability and will to pay for something *US, 1975*

Applied most commonly to journalism (paying for news), but also to enterprises such as baseball.

- — *American Speech*, Fall-Winter 1976
- While this was unfolding, Police Chief Charles Gain was hit with accusations of checkbook detective work. —Bill Cardoso, *The Maltese Sangweech*, p. 13, 1984
- The settlement has been hailed by Mr Paddick's solictor as a "nail in the coffin for chequebook journalism". —*The Guardian*, 19th December 2003

check cop *verb*

to use an adhesive placed on a cheater's palm to steal chips while sliding a pile of chips in a poker game to the winner *US*

- —George Percy, *The Language of Poker*, p. 19, 1988

check crew; check gang; check team *noun*

a racially integrated work crew *US*

- —Harold Wentworth and Stuart Berg Flexner, *Dictionary of American Slang*, p. 95, 1960

checkerboard *adjective*

racially integrated *US, 1930*

- —Ramon Adams, *The Language of the Railroader*, p. 31, 1977

check in *verb*

1 to place yourself in protective police custody *US*

- —Don R. McCreary (Editor), *Dawg Speak*, 2001

2 to be intitiated into a youth gang *US*

- —Ann Lawson, *Kids & Gangs*, p. 55, 1994

check out *verb*

1 to leave prison *US*

- —Hyman E. Goldin et al., *Dictionary of American Underworld Lingo*, p. 42, 1950

2 to die *US, 1927*

A euphemism not without its black humour.

- —Sally Williams, *"Strong" Words*, p. 137, 1994

3 to commit suicide while in prison *US*

- —William K. Bentley and James M. Corbett, *Prison Slang*, p. 104, 1992

checkout chick *noun*

a woman who works at a shop checkout *AUSTRALIA, 1983*

- At their centre, a male body in a jockstrap and coconut oil and nothing else, gyrated in a pool of light on a circular stage, mechanically thrusting his groin into the face of an off-duty checkout chick in a sequined cashmere sweater.—Shane Maloney, *Nice Try*, p. 199, 1998

check, please!

used as a humorous suggestion that a conversation is at an end *US*

Popularised by Keith Olberman on ESPN, used by Woody Allen in *Annie Hall* and Catherine Keener in *Being John Malkovich*.

- —Hermese E. Roberts, *The Third Ear*, 1971
- —Keith Olberman and Dan Patrick, *The Big Show*, p. 13, 1997

check this!

listen to this! *US*

- —Ethan Hilderbrant, *Prison Slang*, p. 146, 1998

check writer *noun*

a criminal who passes bad cheques *US*

- And they just do not worry about check writers because they are too numerous.—Bruce Jackson, *Outside the Law*, p. 78, 1972

check you later; check ya later

used as a farewell *US*

- —Connie Eble (Editor), *UNC-CH Campus Slang*, p. 1, Fall 1982
- —*Washington Post Magazine*, p. 17, 2nd August 1988

cheddar *noun*

money *US*

- —*Columbia Missourian*, p. 1A, 19 October 1998
- —Connie Eble (Editor), *UNC-CH Campus Slang*, p. 2, Spring 1998
- C.R.E.A.M. Cash Rules Everything Around Me. It's just an old word for money. After bread and readies, but before corn and cheddar and ducats and collats. About the same time as wonga.—Diran Adebayo, *My Once Upon A Time*, p. 59, 2000

cheeba; cheeb *noun*

a potent marijuana, now a generic term *US*

- Cause when we're together, blazin' tha cheeba / She does things to me that you wouldn't believe—Tone Loc, *Cheeba cheeba*, 1989
- —Judi Sanders, *Mashing and Munching in Ames*, p. 4, 1994
- —Mike Haskins, *Drugs*, p. 287, 2003
- A lot of hip-hoppers puff cheeb, man—*The Source*, p. 56, November 91

cheech *noun*

a leader of an Italian-American criminal organisation *US*

- And the guy belonged to some downtown cheech. There was a hell of a row with the mob and with the department.—Edwin Torres, *Q & A*, p. 157, 1977

cheech *nickname*

▷ see: CHCH

chee-chee; chi-chi *noun*

a person of mixed European and Indian parentage; the English accent of Eurasians in India *INDIA, 1816*

Derives from Hindi *chhi chhi* (dirt, filth).

chee-chee; chi-chi *adjective*

of mixed European and Asian parentage; used for describing the English accent of Eurasians in India *INDIA, 1781*

Derives from Hindi *chhi chhi* (dirt, filth).

cheek *noun*

1 the buttock *UK, c. 1600*

Variants are 'arse-cheek', 'ass-cheek' and 'butt-cheek'. Usually in the plural.

- Say my name baby, Before you nut I'm a dribble down your butt cheek, / make you wiggle and giggle just a little[.]—Lil Kim, *No Time*, 1997
- [A]ss cheeks being breastlike, but not so prominently positioned that is, easily noticed[.]—*The Village Voice*, 24th October 2002
- [C]an they move enough to use a bedpan and do they have some bizarre spreading devices to get their arse cheeks to separate for the big event?—*Bizarre*, June 2003

2 impudence; audacity; effrontery *UK, 1840*

- No tries, then, but plenty of cheek and confidence. Just the ticket. —*The Observer*, 11th November 2001
- They can see the riches in a small section of our society developing and expanding beyond their wildest imagination, and the government have the cheek to tell us that that is a sensible economic strategy.—*The Guardian*, 24th March 2003

3 a sexually loose female *US*

- —*American Speech*, p. 302, December 1955: 'Wayne University slang'

cheek *verb*

to address someone with impudence *UK, 1840*

- Paul Marsden [...] cheeked the prime minister in a commons debate over air strikes on Afghanistan, calling for a parliamentary vote on the use of force.—*The Guardian*, 23rd October 2001

cheekiness *noun*

effrontery; impudence *UK, 1847*

- Former escort to Winona Ryder [Beck] exhibits broken heart rather than customary post-modern cheekiness[.]—*The Guardian*, 17th January 2003

cheek up *verb*

to speak to someone with a decided lack of respect *BAHAMAS*

- —John A. Holm, *Dictionary of Bahamian English*, p. 40, 1982

cheeky *adjective*

impudent, insolent *UK, 1859*

- They're so likable and cheeky, I can feel my blood pressure rising[.] —*The Guardian*, 22nd November 2001

cheeky-arsed *adjective*

impudent, insolent *UK*

- You cheeky-arsed young bugger.—F. Leech, 1972

cheeky monkey *noun*

an impudent person, often as a term of address and semi-exclamatory *UK*

Popularised as a catchphrase by Comedian Al Read (1909–1987) in the late 1950s.

- NURSE: Ah there you are Mr Hancock..TONY: Where did you expect me to be? NURSE: Now now. Cheeky monkey.—Ray Galton and Alan Simpson, *Hancock's Half Hour*, 28th June 1959

cheeky possum *noun*

an impudent fellow, a cheeky boy *AUSTRALIA*

- —Sidney J. Baker, *Australia Speaks*, 1953

cheekywatter *noun*

any alcoholic drink, especially when being dismissive of its intoxicating properties *UK: SCOTLAND*

- The booze is only cheekywatter tae them. They're inty other stuff fur a real buzz.—Michael Munro, *The Complete Patter*, 1996

cheeo *noun*

marijuana seeds for chewing *US, 1973*

Possibly from an exaggerated pronunciation of 'chew'.

- —Richard A. Spears, *The Slang and Jargon of Drugs and Drink*, p. 103, 1986
- —Mike Haskins, *Drugs*, p. 287, 2003

cheep *verb*

to betray someone, to inform upon someone *US, 1903*

- —Frederic G. Cassidy, *Dictionary of American Regional English*, p. 602, 1985

cheeper *noun*

a police informer *US*

- —Vincent J. Monteleone, *Criminal Slang*, p. 48, 1949

cheer *noun*

LSD *UK*

An abbreviation of **BLUE CHEER**.

- Street names[:] A, acid, blotter, cheer, dots[.]—James Kay and Julian Cohen, *The Parents' Complete Guide to Young People and Drugs*, p. 141, 1998

cheerful giver *noun*

the liver *UK*

Recorded as 1930s–40s by Julian Franklyn and as still in contemporary use by Ray Puxley.

- —Julian Franklyn, *A Dictionary of Rhyming Slang*, 1961
- —Ray Puxley, *Fresh Rabbit*, 1998

cheeri

goodbye *NEW ZEALAND*

An abbreviation of **CHEERIO**.

cheeribye

goodbye *UK, 1961*

A blend of **CHEERIO** and 'goodbye'.

cheerio *adjective*

tipsy *SOUTH AFRICA*

- — *Cape Argus*, June 1946

cheerio; cheeri-ho; cheero

goodbye *UK*

- CORP: Well, cheerio then, Lofty. LOFTY: Oh – well, cheerio, Corp. —Clive Exton, *No Fixed Abode [Six Granada Plays]*, p. 140, 1959

cheers!

1 used as a drinking toast *UK*

- ([Staff Officer] Watson has passed a bottle to Vale, who pours it) First time in a small unit, eh? You won't like it. VALE: Why not Staff? Cheers. WATSON: Cheers. —Graeme Kent, *The Queen's Corporal [Six Granada Plays]*, p. 84, 1959

2 thank you *UK, 1976*

From the drinking toast.

- Cheers for the weights, Terry. Later. —Donald Gorgon, *Cop Killer*, p. 67, 1994
- So if there's one figure who is partly responsible [...] for getting me where I am, it's the Queen's old fella, that scheming Duke of Edinburgh. Cheers, Phil. —Dave Courtney, *Stop the Ride I Want to Get Off*, p. 40, 1999

cheer-up *noun*

an anti-depressant tablet; an amphetamine or other central nervous system stimulant *UK*

- Yeah she was on the pills. Not likely she got any bars so she probably had a jar of cheer-ups. —Jeremy Cameron, *Brown Bread in Wengen*, p. 67, 1999

cheerybyes

goodbye *UK: SCOTLAND*

- Right, that's me Joe the toff [off]. Cheerybyes! —Michael Munro, *The Patter, Another Blast*, 1988

cheese *noun*

1 smegma, matter secreted by the sebaceous gland that collects between the glans penis and the foreskin or around the clitoris and labia minora *US, 1927*

G. Legman wrote in his 1941 homosexual glossary that 'The term is derived from the dull whitish color of the smegma'.

- —G. Legman, *The Language of Homsexuality*, p. 1160, 1941
- —Donald Webster Cory and John P. LeRoy, *The Homosexual and His Society*, p. 262, 1963: 'A lexicon of homosexual slang'
- We pushed heavily on the new moral outlook: get a VD test often or face the fact that you're just as dirty as a person who never washes the cheese off his uncircumcised cock[.] — *Screw*, p. 13, 6th November 1972
- "Some places I've worked, some guys will come in real cruddy, you know, their penis hasn't been clean for weeks. They call it 'cheese,'" she says graphically, wriggling up her nose. —George Paul Csicsery (Editor), *The Sex Industry*, p. 8, 1973
- RUBBERBABY: I slide my hand under your balls RUBBERBABY: And between your legs Shit, I hope there's no cheese under there. —Howard Stern, *Miss America*, p. 35, 1995

2 in auto repair, a plastic body filler used to fill in dents on a car body, usually referring to Bondo Body Filler™ *US*

- —Lewis Poteet, *Car & Motorcyle Slang*, p. 48, 1992

3 the wife *AUSTRALIA, 1919*

Short for **CHEESE AND KISSES**.

- Old Spiro reckons he's gonna take us to the Greek Ball tonight. All of us. Even the old cheese. —Angelo Loukakis, *For the Patriarch*, p. 29, 1981

4 an attractive young woman *US, 1959*

- I got into the habit of studying at the Radcliffe libary. Not just to eye the cheese, although I admit that I liked to look. —Erich Segal, *Love Story*, p. 2, 1970

5 a wedge-shaped piece of coloured plastic used in the board game Trivial Pursuits™ *UK*

- [S]tabbing a friend twice during a game of Trivial Pursuit in which his mate committed the unforgivable crime of cheating by adding extra cheeses to his counter —Huw Davies, *Another Wierd Year*, p. 162, 2002
- There's a bizarre rose window whose stained glass recalls the 'cheeses' used in Trivial Pursuit. —Clare Thomson, *Footprint Tallinn*, p. 116, 2004

6 in pool, a situation where a player needs to make only one shot to win *US*

- —Mike Shamos, *The Illustrated Encyclopedia of Billiards*, p. 49, 1993

7 money; a gambler's bankroll *US, 1985*

A locution popularised by Minnesota Fats, as in, 'I never lost when we played for the cheese'.

- —Mike Shamos, *The Illustrated Encyclopedia of Billiards*, p. 49, 1993

8 heroin *UK*

- —Robert Ashton, *This Is Heroin*, p. 205, 2002
- —Mike Haskins, *Drugs*, p. 283, 2003

9 freebase cocaine *US*

- —Jay Robert Nash, *Dictionary of Crime*, p. 63, 1992

10 an amphetamine user *US*

- —Peter Johnson, *Dictionary of Street Alcohol and Drug Terms*, p. 38, 1993

11 money *US*

- —Connie Eble (Editor), *UNC-CH Campus Slang*, p. 2, November 2002

12 nonsense *US*

- Joe Flaherty nailed the essence of TV monster movie cheese without even using a real word from the English language[.] —Frank Zappa, *The Real Frank Zappa Book*, p. 168, 1989

13 luck *US*

- —Steve Rushin, *Pool Cool*, p. 10, 1990

▸ **piece of cheese**

in poker, a truly terrible hand *US*

- —David M. Hayano, *Poker Faces*, p. 186, 1982

cheese *verb*

1 to leave *US*

- He's going to cheese, I tell you. Nobody arrested him! —*Rebel Without a Cause*, 1955
- Cheese it! Here comes the socialite man. —Mart Crowley, *The Boys in the Band*, p. 85, 1968

2 to smile *US*

From the urging by photographers that those having their picture taken say 'cheese' to form a smile.

- —Connie Eble (Editor), *UNC-CH Campus Slang*, p. 2, March 1986

cheese!

spoken by the subject of a photograph in order to shape the lips into a smile *UK, 1930*

Often heard in the photographer's injunction: 'say cheese!'.

- —Viktor E. Frankl, *Man's Search for Meaning*, p. 163, 1997

cheese and crackers *noun*

the testicles *UK*

Rhyming slang for **KNACKERS**.

- —Ray Puxley, *Fresh Rabbit*, 1998

cheese and crackers!

used as a non-profane oath *US, 1924*

A euphemistic 'Jesus Christ!'.

- —Frederic G. Cassidy, *Dictionary of American Regional English*, p. 602, 1985

cheese and kisses *noun*

a wife *AUSTRALIA, 1898*

Rhyming slang for **MISSUS**.

- Keep in touch. Love to your cheese and kisses and the billy lids. —Clive Galea, *Slipper*, p. 187, 1988

cheese and rice!

used for expressing surprise or irritation *TRINIDAD AND TOBAGO, 1950*

- —Lise Winer, *Dictionary of the English/Creole of Trinidad & Tobago*, 2003

cheeseball *noun*

a corny, socially inept person *US, 1990*

- —Connie Eble (Editor), *UNC-CH Campus Slang*, p. 2, Spring 1992
- You don't need to come to a place like Lookout Point and spout off all those cheeseball lines to be romantic. — *American Pie*, 1999

cheesebox *noun*

a telephone device used to transfer calls received by an illegal operation *US*

So named, according to Maas, because the first one was found by police hidden in a cheese box.

- — *Life*, p. 39, 19th May 1952
- Next he would install the cheesebox, an electrical device that connected the lines of the two phones. —Peter Maas, *Serpico*, p. 112, 1973

Cheesebox *nickname*
the Stateville Prison in Joilet, Illinois *US*
- —Jay Robert Nash, *Dictionary of Crime*, p. 63, 1992

cheese bun *noun*
a worker who informs on his fellow workers *US*
- —Harold Wentworth and Stuart Berg Flexner, *Dictionary of American Slang*, p. 96, 1960

cheesecake *noun*
a scantily clad woman as the subject of a photograph or artwork *US, 1934*
- —*Cheesecake*, September 1968
- I had done only cheesecake photos before – never anything nude – but I did the centerfold for December 1959 because I knew it would please him. —Kathryn Leigh Scott, *The Bunny Years*, p. 73, 1998

cheesecutter *noun*
a wedge-shaped hat *UK*
From the shape, and the memory of the vaguely similar late C19/early C20 'cheese-cutter caps'.
- There was a short spell when tearaways wore the "cheesecutter", a cap narrow at the peak and perched forward on the head – very much in the style of Del-boy. —Brian McDonald, *Elephant Boys*, p. 229, 2000

cheesed off; cheesed *adjective*
disgruntled, bored, miserable *UK, 1941*
'Cheese off!' (go away!), a euphemistic exclamation from 1890s Liverpool, may be the origin. On the other hand 'say cheese' is a photographer's formula to create a smile and if you don't feel like smiling you may well be 'cheesed off'.
- I was cheesed off up to the eyebrows. —Frank Norman, *Bang To Rights*, p. 30, 1958
- Another one of my habbits [sic] when I was cheesed was singing to myself[.] —Frank Norman, *Bang To Rights*, p. 91, 1958
- Pat Malone again! Cripes am I cheesed [fed up]! —Barry Humphries, *Bazza Pulls It Off!*, 1971

cheesedog *noun*
a socially inept person who perceives himself in somewhat grandiose terms *US*
- —Vann Wesson, *Generation X Field Guide and Lexicon*, p. 36, 1997

cheese-down *verb*
to laugh uncontrollably *UK*
Military usage; probably extended from **CHEESE** (to smile) but note obsolete naval slang 'cheese down' (to coil rope into neat spirals for a harbour stow).
- —Nigel Foster, *The Making of a Royal Marine Commando*, 1987

cheese eater *noun*
an informer *US, 1886*
Playing on **RAT**.
- —Kenn "Naz" Young, *Naz's Underground Dictionary*, p. 20, 1973
- —John Scarne, *Scarne on Dice*, p. 463, 1974
- —William K. Bentley and James M. Corbett, *Prison Slang*, p. 35, 1992

cheese-eating surrender monkeys *noun*
the French; anyone who does not support American imperialism *US*
Coined on *The Simpsons* television show as a parody of American arrogance; often used by arrogant Americans unaware of the irony of their use. Such is the pervasive presence of this term that it was the subject of a question on *Mastermind* (11th October 2004).
- If these old gasbags really prefer to live in a nation of cheese-eating surrender monkeys (Groundskeeper Willie's delicious phrase from "The Simpsons") because they cannot lower themselves to accept the democratic judgment of their fellow Americans, then bon voyage, jerks. —*New York Post*, p. 4, 7th November 2000
- [S]pare a thought for the French translators, who have struggled for words to convey the full force of the venom. "Cheese-eating surrender monkeys" – a phrase coined by Bart Simpson but made acceptable in official diplomatic channels around the globe by Jonah Goldberg, a columnist for the rightwing weekly National Review (according to Goldberg) – was finally rendered: "Primates capitulards et toujours en quête de fromages". —*The Guardian*, 11th February 2003

cheese-grater *noun*
a waiter *UK*
Rhyming slang.
- —Ray Puxley, *Fresh Rabbit*, 1998

cheese grater *nickname*
the Chateau Champlain Hotel in Montreal *CANADA*
- From the station, cross Peel St. to the Marriott Chateau Champlain, often referred to as "the cheese grater" because of its 36 floors of half-moon windows. The hotel was originally built by Canadian Pacific for Expo 67, and opened in 1965. —Alan Hustak, p. F11, 18th May 2002

cheesehead *noun*
1 a Dutch person *UK*
Derogatory, if not intentionally so. Probably from the shape and preponderence of Edam and Gouda.
- The cheese-heads have one [tug] lying handy. —Wilbur Smith, *Hungry as the Sea*, 1978
- Rude Boy was waggling his little dick in the unaware face of a Dutch tourist who was having her cheese-head cheesily portrayed by an Ethiopian economic migrant. —Will Self, *How The Dead Live – part two*, 2000

2 a resident of the state of Wisconsin *US*
Playful but not particularly kind.

cheesemo *noun*
gossip *US*
A corruption, intentional or not, of the Spanish *chisme* (gossip).
- —Judi Sanders, *Da Bomb!*, p. 7, 1997

cheese off *verb*
to annoy someone *UK*
- —*The Felstedian*, December 1947

cheese off!
go away! *US*
- —*Maledicta*, p. 99, 1996: 'Domino's Pizza jargon'

cheese on!
used for expressing enthusiastic approval *BARBADOS*
- —Frank A. Collymore, *Barbadian Dialect*, p. 29, 1965

cheese-on!; cheese-on and bread!
used as a euphemistic cry in place of 'Jesus Christ!' *BARBADOS*
- —Richard Allsopp, *Dictionary of Caribbean English Usage*, p. 148, 1996

cheeser *noun*
1 a person with smelly feet *UK*
From the malodourous quality of ripe cheese.
- —Jonathan Thomas, 1976

2 a police informer *US*
- —H. Craig Collins, *Street Gangs*, p. 222, 1979

cheese table *noun*
a metal hole-lined table used in sheet metal fabrication *US*
- —*American Speech*, p. 226, October 1955: 'An aircraft production dispatcher's vocabulary'

cheesy *adjective*
1 of poor quality, inexpensive, shoddy *US, 1863*
- The driver asked us whether we had had fun. We said not too much, and pretty cheesy. —Jack Lait and Lee Mortimer, *Chicago Confidential*, p. 63, 1950
- "Then, you mean it's cheesy..." she said hollowly. "It costs me a dollar a stick and it's still cheesy..." 'that's about the best word for it." —Morton Cooper, *High School Confidential*, p. 70, 1958
- Jammed between a grimy-windowed bookstore and a cheesy luncheonette was the marquee of a tiny art theater[.] —Philip Roth, *Goodbye, Columbus*, p. 22, 1959
- I started up the car and cruised along Ogden Boulevard until I found an open bar, a cheesy, small place called John's On. —Clancy Sigal, *Going Away*, p. 358, 1961

2 smelly *UK, 1889*
From the malodourous quality of ripe cheese.

cheesy-feet *noun*
used as a derogatory form of address *UK*
From the malodourous quality of ripe cheese. Noted by F. Leech, 1972.

cheesy-foot *noun*
bad-smelling feet *TRINIDAD AND TOBAGO*
- —Lise Winer, *Dictionary of the English/Creole of Trinidad & Tobago*, 2003

cheesy quaver *noun*
a raver *UK, 2002*
Contemporary rhyming slang, from a cheese-flavoured snack.
- —*www.LondonSlang.com*, June 2002
- He's strictly Old Skool. He's been a cheesy quaver since 1988. —Bodmin Dark, *Dirty Cockney Rhyming Slang*, 2003

cheesy quaver raver *noun*
a member of a social grouping within the hardcore rave-culture, characterised by a fashion for boiler suits, white gloves and paint masks *UK*
After Quavers™, a cheese flavoured snack food, punning on 'cheesy' (unfashionable) and using **RAVER** (a party goer).

chellum *noun*
a clay marijuana pipe *SOUTH AFRICA*

Chelsea bun *noun*
a son; the sun *UK*
Rhyming slang; a variation of **CURRANT BUN**.
• —Ray Puxley, *Fresh Rabbit*, 1998

Chelsea Pier *adjective*
queer, odd *UK*
Rhyming slang, formed on a London landmark; similar to **BRIGHTON PIER** but here 'queer' doesn't lead to 'homosexual'.
• —Bodmin Dark, *Dirty Cockney Rhyming Slang*, 2003

chemical *noun*
1 crack cocaine *US*
• —US Department of Justice, *Street Terms*, October 1994
2 any drug with addictive characteristics *UK*
• — Susie Dent, *The Language Report*, p. 19, 2003

chemical generation *noun*
a section of society identified as the first to have MDMA, the drug best known as ecstasy, as a recreational option, especially those who were actually a part of the attendant dance culture *UK*
The chemical generation began in the late 1980s but was probably not identified by this title until the late 90s; the definitive recreational drug culture was not restricted to MDMA but its wide-use signalled a greater-than-ever-before acceptance of man-made and designer drugs.
• [T]he Edinburgh underworld, replete with gangsters, pushers, alcoholics, Freemasons [...]and the laureate of the chemical generation. Rare are the schoolboys who like their in-jokes as much as Irvine Welsh.— *The Observer*, 9th August 1998
• A government report, called the Chemical Generation, has revealed that nearly half of all young people across the country have tried illegal drugs.— *Derby Evening Telegraph*, 15th November 1999
• [H]e relaxed and enjoyed the experience. An hour later, the Chemical Generation had another new recruit.—Colin Butts, *Is Harry Still on the Boat?*, p. 19, 2003

chemically challenged *adjective*
drunk *US*
'Challenged' is a key word in the lexicon of political correctness, lending an air of humour to this use.
• —Connie Eble (Editor), *UNC-CH Campus Slang*, p. 2, Spring 1994

chemical persuasion *noun*
in caving and pot-holing, explosives *UK*
• —David Morrison of Wessex Cave Club, 29th February 2004

chemise-lifter *noun*
a lesbian; an effeminate homosexual male *AUSTRALIA*
Originally, a play on **SHIRT-LIFTER** (a homosexual man) coined by Barry Humphries who defined it in *A Nice Night's Entertainment*, 1981, as 'a female invert'; subsequently, derived perhaps by a misunderstanding of the original definition, the male variation has gained a little currency.

chemist *noun*
a person who uses a mainframe computer for the academic purposes for which it was designed, depriving the speaker of the chance to use it for more interesting, less academic purposes *US*
• —Eric S. Raymond, *The New Hacker's Dictionary*, p. 93, 1991

chemmie *noun*
a shirt; a blouse *UK*
Probably from 'chemise'.
• —Paul Baker, *Polari*, p. 168, 2002

chemmy; shemmy *noun*
the card-game 'chemin-de-fer' *UK, 1923*
• [N]ightclubs, restaurants, swimming-pools, the South of France, chemmy in Paris[.]—Derek Raymond (Robin Cook), *The Crust on its Uppers*, p. 25, 1962

chemo *noun*
1 *chemo*therapy, a cancer treatment *US*
• Personal memos were returned to him with "chemo" written in, he said.— *Washington Post*, p. B1, 2nd December 1978
• At night the kids play video games in the den and gossip about their doctors and their current regimen of what they call "chemo."
— *New York Times*, p. 27 (Section 2), 9th May 1981
• I took pictures of myself everyday and hoped to chart my demise through the chemo and the recovery out the other side.
— *The Guardian*, 16th February 2004
2 a liquid octane booster that is inhaled for its intoxicating effects *US*

chep *noun*
a kiss, intimate or otherwise; kissing *IRELAND*
• —John Morton, *Skegs and Skangers*, 2001

chequebook *adjective*
▷ see: **CHECKBOOK**

chequed-up *adjective*
having ready money after receiving payment for seasonal work *AUSTRALIA, 1905*
• They was both chequed-up, and they bought a car, paying cash for it.—Herb Wharton, *Cattle Camp*, p. 37, 1994

cheroot *noun*
a large marijuana cigarette *US*
• —N. Peter Johnson, *Dictionary of Sreet Alcohol and Drug Terms*, p. 38, 1993

cherry *noun*
1 the hymen; virginity (male or female); the state of sustained sexual abstinence *US, 1918*
Combines with a variety of verbs (bust, crack, pop) to indicate the ending of a virgin condition.
• And they always wanted to go whoring, and he still had his cherry, even though he pretended that he'd lost it.—James T. Farrell, *Saturday Night*, p. 26, 1947
• Not when he's about the cash in his cherry.—Ken Kesey, *One Flew Over the Cuckoo's Nest*, p. 279, 1962
• My cherry was there, just like it'd been for years, and I wanted the money he'd offered me for it.—John O'Day, *Confessions of a Hollywood Callgirl*, p. 109, 1964
• She has no cherry, but she thinks it's no sin / for she still has the box that the cherry came in.—Bruce Jackson, *Get Your Ass in the Water and Swim Like Me*, p. 229, 1964
• But I felt that bragging to other fellas about how many cherries I'd cracked or how many panties came down on rooftops or backyards was nobody's business but my own[.]—Piri Thomas, *Down These Mean Streets*, p. 15, 1967
• Some "cherries" completely close the cunny hole and have to be opened by surgery.— *Screw*, p. 9, 29th December 1969
• The broads were fantastic and they all tried desperately to get me into bed so they could claim a cherry, but I was waiting for my beloved[.]
—Oscar Zeta Acosta, *The Autobiography of a Brown Buffalo*, p. 108, 1972
• The good girls held on to their cherry. And it was a big deal.—Edwin Torres, *Carlito's Way*, p. 11, 1975
• The sister had an ounce of Mexican grass and called her mama long distance because she said she had promised to call her when she lost her cherry.—Babs Gonzales, *Movin' On Down De Line*, p. 18, 1975
• I drove around the desolate southern perimeter of the city while Willie muledicked her and blew off his jail cherry[.]—Iceberg Slim (Robert Beck), *Airtight Willie and Me*, p. 8, 1979
• "It's blood, you just got my cherry." "Where? Where's it at? Lemme see what it looks like." "You can't see nothin' like that, fool! You just busted my cherry, that's all."—Odie Hawkins, *Black Casanova*, p. 147 - 148, 1984
• [H]e was shy about his errand like a pom-pom girl who's never even had her cherry popped.—William T. Vollman, *Whores for Gloria*, p. 33, 1991
• Joey Dorsey is only after one thing – your cherry. He practically made a public announcement.— *Ten Things I Hate About You*, 1999
• Silent Bob even busted his cherry there.—Kevin Smith, *Jay and Silent Bob Strike Back*, p. 42, 2001
2 a virgin; someone who because of extenuating circumstances has abstained from sex for a long period *US, 1942*
• A no-poot green cherry.—Bernard Wolfe, *The Late Risers*, p. 30, 1954
• The puzzled expectant look on his face excited her. She had a cherry.—Hubert Selby Jr, *Last Exit to Brooklyn*, p. 205, 1957
• "Yeah man, they ain't never had no cherry before, and they think this is a cherry they'll be getting," Prince replied, and laughed.—Donald Goines, *Black Gangster*, p. 23, 1977
• BRIAN: I'm not a cherry. BENDER: When have you ever gotten laid? BRIAN: I've gotten laid lotsa times.— *The Breakfast Club*, 1985

3 by extension, any innocence that can be lost *US, 1956*
- He had no idea he was talking to a young man who cracked his cherry in the thievery business with forty times that at Ludwig's. —Red Rudensky, *The Gonif*, p. 76, 1970
- I've talked about it to other guys who've lost their cherry, and we all agree: You appreciate different things. —James Ellroy, *Blood on the Moon*, p. 33, 1984
- [As Henry leaves court after his first arrest] You broke your cherry! You broke your cherry! —*Goodfellas*, 1990
- Folks do not want to hear about Alpha Company – us grunts – busting jungle and busting cherries from Land Zone Skator-Gator to Scat Man Do (wherever that is). —Larry Heinemann, *Paco's Story*, p. 5, 1990

4 by extension, someone who is completely inexperienced *US, 1946*
- "They shoulda never done it, throwing a cherry in with hardened sailors like us," says Mule. —Darryl Ponicsan, *The Last Detail*, p. 74, 1970
- "Any ever been here before?" "No, all cherries." —Ronald J. Glasser, *365 Days*, p. 29, 1971
- They didn't have time to get acclimated. That's why so many of em had their shit scattered. They weren't comin in as one cherry among one hundred dues with time in-country. —John M. Del Vecchio, *The 13th Valley*, p. 95, 1982
- And nobody wanted to see me because I was a new guy. Nobody wanted a "cherry" out there. —Al Santoli, *To Bear Any Burden*, p. 127, 1985

5 a pretty young woman, a girlfriend *SOUTH AFRICA, 1962*
Also spelt 'cherrie', 'cherie', 'tcherrie' and 'tjerrie'.
- —Penny da Silva, *A Dictionary of South African English*, 1996

6 a young woman regarded as the object or subject of a transitory sexual relationship *SOUTH AFRICA*
Scamto youth street slang (South African townships).
- —*The Times*, 12th February 2005

7 of a male, the 'virginity' of the anus *US*
- MISTRESS: [...] Now let's dress you – let's get you ready for your defloration. DAMEN [a male 'slave']: I'm going to lose my cherry. MISTRESS: You're just a little girl, an innocent thing[.] —Terence Sellers, *Dungeon Evidence*, p. 55, 1997

8 an entry-level youth gang member *US*
- When he was sold enough he hoped to be a cherry, then a cutdown, then finally, after he'd been shot and stabbed ten times and was too old to fight, a veterano. —Joseph Wambaugh, *The Glitter Dome*, p. 109, 1981

9 in pool, an extremely easy shot *US*
- —Mike Shamos, *The Illustrated Encyclopedia of Billiards*, p. 49, 1993

10 in horse racing, a horse that has yet to win a race *US*
- —David W. Maurer, *Argot of the Racetrack*, p. 19, 1951

11 in greyhound racing, the inside starting position *AUSTRALIA*
- —Ned Wallish, *The Truth Dictionary of Racing Slang*, p. 14, 1989

12 the clitoris *AUSTRALIA*
- — Thommo, *The Dictionary of Australian Swearing and Sex Sayings*, p. 25, 1985

13 a female nipple *US*
- —Roger Blake, *The American Dictionary of Sexual Terms*, p. 34, 1964

14 in cricket, a new ball *UK*
- — *The Observer*, 21st June 1953

15 the flashing red light on top of a police car *US*
- —Warren Smith, *Warren's Smith's Authentic Dictionary of CB*, p. 59, 1976

16 a blush; a red face *UK*
From the colour.
- I can still feel myself getting a cherry on [...] The more I think about how red I must be going, the hotter I seem to feel. —Kevin Sampson, *Outlaws*, p. 240–241, 2001

▸ **pick a cherry**
in bowling, to knock over a pin that had been previously missed *US*
- —Lester V. Berrey and Melvin Van den Bark, *The American Thesaurus of Slang*, p. 633, 1953

cherry *adjective*

1 virginal *US, 1933*
- I know a waitress. She ain't cherry. —Willard Motley, *Let No Man Write My Epitaph*, p. 179, 1958
- I know you thought I was cherry, your number-one size / But I was balling Tony, and you weren't wise. —Dennis Wepman et al., *The Life*, p. 142, 1976

2 without a criminal record *US*
- "You lied to me, Darrold," sounding a little hurt – "try to tell me you're cherry and they got a sheet on you, man." —Elmore Leonard, *City Primeval*, p. 58, 1980

3 (used of a car) restored to better than mint condition *US, 1953*
- The wildest short around is my cherry, cherry coupe / It's the sharpest thing in town and the envy of my group. — The Beach Boys, *Cherry Cherry Coupe*, 1963
- You know it's not very cherry, it's an oldie but a goodie. —Jan Berry and Dean Torrance, *Surf City*, 1963
- —J. R. Friss, *A Dictionary of Teenage Slang (Mt. Diablo High)*, 1964
- —John Lawlor, *How to Talk Car*, p. 30–31, 1965
- He then got the Mercedes roadster that is still parked in his basement in the mansion in Chicago. Pretty cherry – about twelve miles on it. —Mort Sahl, *Heartland*, p. 25, 1976
- I'm gonna fix it up and paint it up 'til I make it stone cherry wheels. —Iceberg Slim (Robert Beck), *Doom Fox*, p. 97, 1978

cherryade *noun*
an assistant to Cherie Booth, wife of UK Prime Minister Tony Blair *UK*
Both the drink and the aide may be described as 'red, sweet and fizzing'.
- —David Rowan, *A Glossary for the 90s*, p. 48, 1998

cherryberry *noun*
a uniform red beret of the Parachute Regiment; hence, a soldier of the Parachute Regiment *UK*
- —Christopher Hawke, *For Campaign Service*, 1979

cherry boy *noun*
a male virgin *US, 1974*
- Some are revealed as male models and others as adolescent, self-confessed virgins who have never kissed before. "Cherry boys," the host-comics leer to the squeals of young women in the audience. —*BPI Entertainment News Wire*, 2nd May 2000

Cherry Coke *adjective*
bisexual *UK*
Suggests 'neither one thing nor the other'.

cherry farm *noun*
a prison, or the section of a prison reserved for first-time offenders *US*
- —*Current Slang*, p. 2, Winter 1966
- —Helen Dahlskog (Editor), *A Dictionary of Contemporary and Colloquial Usage*, p. 13, 1972

cherry fine *adjective*
excellent *US*
- —Andy Anonymous, *A Basic Guide to Campusology*, p. 5, 1966

cherry girl *noun*
a virgin *US*
US military usage during the Vietnam war.
- —*Maledicta*, p. 256, Summer/Winter 1982: 'Viet-speak'

Cherry Hill *nickname*
during the Vietnam war, the base camp of the 3rd Battalion, 16th Artillery Regiment, just outside Chu Lai *US*
So named because the Viet Cong and North Vietnamese did not attack the camp during the 1968 Tet Offensive, hence the 'cherry'.

cherry hog; cherry *noun*
a dog, especially a greyhound *UK, 1960*
Rhyming slang, formed on the old name for 'a cherry stone'.
- Me cherry bread and cheesed [sneezed]. —Viv Stanshall, *Ginger Geezer*, 1981
- To go dog racing is to go to "the cherries". —Ray Puxley, *Cockney Rabbit*, 1992
- But then the old cherry-hog started to growl. —Andrew Nickolds, *Back to Basics*, p. 96, 1994

cherry juice *noun*
hydraulic fluid in a tank turret traversing system *US*
Vietnam war usage.
- —Linda Reinberg, *In the Field*, p. 40, 1991

cherry kicks *noun*
the first drug injection enjoyed by someone just released from prison *US*
- —Eugene Landy, *The Underground Dictionary*, p. 48, 1971

cherry menth; cherry meth *noun*
the recreational drug GHB *US*
- Police have identified a substance that left three people unconscious and close to death on a Fillmore sidewalk last month as a legal yet potentially dangerous drug know as "Cherry Meth." —*Los Angeles Times*, p. B2, 4th November 1995

- GHB has been marketed as a liquid or powder and has been sold on the street under names such as Grevious Bodily Harm, Georgia Home Boy, Liquid Ecstasy, Liqiud X, Liquid E, GHB, GBH, Soap, Scoop, Easy Lay, Salty Water, G-Riffick, [and] Cherry Menth. — *Morbidity and Morality Weekly Report*, p. 281, 4th April 1997
- Grieving Mom of GHB Victim Warns Others of Drug Dangers — *Sunday Advocate (Baton Rouge, Louisiana)*, p. 3H, 21st April 2002

cherry orchard *noun*

a woman's college *US*

- — *Current Slang*, p. 2, Winter 1966
- — Helen Dahlskog (Editor), *A Dictionary of Contemporary and Colloquial Usage*, p. 13, 1972

cherry patch *noun*

a poker game being played by a group of poor players, ripe for the taking by a good professisonal *US*

- — David M. Hayano, *Poker Faces*, p. 186, 1982

cherry picker *noun*

1 a boy or youth in a sexual relationship with an older man *UK, 1961*
Royal Navy use.

2 a person who targets virgins for seduction *US, 1960*

- They call me Rap the dicker the ass kicker / The cherry picker the city slicker the titty licker. — H. Rap Brown, *Die Nigger Die!*, p. 28, 1969

3 the penis *UK*
A play on **CHERRY** (virginity).

- — Richard Herring, *Talking Cock*, p. 30, 2003

4 one pound (£1) *UK*
Rhyming slang for **NICKER** (a pound).

- — David Hillman, 1974

5 a machine, mounted on a rail car or caterpillar tractor, for picking up logs dropped from cars or on roadsides *CANADA*

- This fabulous machine for loading the enormous logs from the British Columbia forests onto trailers is nicknamed the "cherry-picker." — *Canada 1962*, p. 158, 1962

6 a crane *US*

- — Ira Konigsberg, *The Complete Film Dictionary*, p. 47, 1987

7 a large bucket on a boom attached to a truck used to raise a worker to work in an elevated position on power lines, telephone lines, etc *US*

- The cherry picker, a crane with a basket that will lift Edna [Everage] fifty feet above the stalls to sing her finale straight into the eyes of her balcony fans[.] — John Lahr, *Dame Edna Everage and the Rise of Western Civilisation*, p. 6, 1991

8 an engine hoist *US*

- — Lewis Poteet, *Car & Motorcyle Slang*, p. 48, 1992

9 a railway pointsman *US*
Named because of the red railway signal lights.

- — Norman Carlisle, *The Modern Wonder Book of Trains and Railroading*, p. 260, 1946

10 a prominent, hooked nose *US, 1968*

- — Frederic G. Cassidy, *Dictionary of American Regional English*, p. 605, 1985

cherry pie *noun*

1 in the entertainment industry, extra money earned for something other than ordinary work *US*

- — *American Speech*, p. 310-311, December 1955: 'Cherry pie'

2 in circus and carnival usage, extra work for extra pay *US*

- — Don Wilmeth, *The Language of American Popular Entertainment*, p. 51, 1981

cherry-popping *noun*

the act of taking someone's virginity *US*

- — Xaviera Hollander, *The Best Part of a Man*, 1975

cherry red *noun*

the head *UK*
Rhyming slang.

- — Ray Puxley, *Fresh Rabbit*, 1998

cherry ripe *noun*

1 a pipe *UK, 1857*
Rhyming slang, propbably influenced by 'cherry-wood pipe'.

- I will take a ball of chalk [walk] into the town and buy some tobacco for my cherry ripe. — Ronnie Barker, *Fletcher's Book of Rhyming Slang*, p. 25, 1979

2 nonsense *UK, 1960*
Rhyming slang for **TRIPE**. Can be shortened to 'cherry'.

- What a load of cherry. — Ray Puxley, *Cockney Rabbit*, 1992

cherrytop *noun*

a police car; a police car's coloured lights *US, 1970*

- Now, finally, Joe heard sirens: across the valley, miles away, cop-car cherrytops were blinking. — John Nichols, *The Nirvana Blues*, p. 492, 1981
- [W]e were as unprepared as we possibly could have been for the piercing white strobe and swirling red cherrytop of the police car tat swooped in from nowhere and pulled up behind us. — Mark Winegardner, *Elvis Presly Boulevard*, p. 31, 1987

Chessex girl *noun*

an upper-class young woman dressed with the down-market trappings of vulgar glamour *UK*
Coined by the *Tatler* magazine, July 2003, as a compound of 'Chelsea' (a traditonally well-off area of London) and **ESSEX GIRL** (a social stereotype of a loud, vulgar, sexually available woman).

- Meet the Chessex girls. — *The Evening Standard*, 2nd June 2003

chest *noun*

a woman's breasts *US*

- Another great chest on parade in Big Bust #5 is that of Barbara Alton, a diminuitive little vixen who obviously loves fondling, squeezing, licking and just generally fiddling with her two tremendous tits[.] — *Adult Video*, p. 54, August/September 1986
- "Yeah, nice, healthy chest," Letch said, leering. — Joseph Wambaugh, *Floaters*, p. 155, 1996

▸ **get it off your chest**

to say something that you have, or may have been expected to have, previously kept private or secret; to confess *UK, 1902*

- The president got it off his chest and France will host the World Cup of 2007. — *The Observer*, 20th April 2003

chestbonz *noun*

the marijuana smoker who takes the greatest inhalation from a shared water-pipe *UK*

- — *www.addictions.org*, 1999

Chester and Esther *noun*

in craps, a bet on any craps and eleven *US*
A back formation from the initials 'c and e'.

- — Steve Kuriscak, *Casino Talk*, p. 67, 1985

chesterfield *noun*

a sofa or couch *CANADA, 1950*
Especially in the western provinces of Canada, this word is the universal term for this common piece of furniture.

- I was lying on the chesterfield (a Canadian word) eating my gourmet pizza and drinking orange pop when I noticed that my feet were cold. — Suroosh Alvi et al., *The Vice Guide*, p. 301, 2002
- We rest in our "Muskoka chairs" when we sit outdoors (at least in summer) and on our steadfast "chesterfields," as opposed to "couches" or "sofas," when we move indoors. — *The Globe and Mail*, p. F3, 5th January 2002

Chester the Molestor; Chester *noun*

a lecherous man *US*

- — Pamela Munro, *U.C.L.A. Slang*, p. 29, 1989

chestily *adverb*

arrogantly, conceitedly *US, 1908*

chestnut *noun*

1 a chestnut horse *UK, 1670*

- [Richard] Guest successfully explained that Red Marauder had hung badly at one stage at the far side and that he had also heard the chestnut gurgle. — *The Guardian*, 25th February 2003

2 a stale story or outworn jest *US, 1880*
Also known as 'an old chestnut'.

- "The Customer Is Always Right" – that pony [rubbishy] old chestnut[.] — Andrew Nickolds, *Back to Basics*, p. 33, 1994
- Mortal Enemies [by Brian Haig] boils down to that very old chestnut, the locked-room mystery, glossed with a contemporary frankness (gay necrophilia). — *The Observer*, 30th November 2002

chestnuts *noun*

1 the testicles *US*

- — Eugene Landy, *The Underground Dictionary*, p. 48, 1971

2 the female breasts *US*

- — Eugene Landy, *The Underground Dictionary*, p. 48, 1971
- — *The Guardian*, 5th April 1976

chesty *adjective*

1 of a woman, having generously proportioned breasts *UK, 1955*

- A lot of men who watch TV have been used to seeing blonde, chesty, leggy women in skimpy clothes. — *Daily Express*, 3rd April 1999

2 used of symptoms (such as a cough) that result from an unhealthiness or weakness in the chest; also used of someone who is inclined to such a condition *UK, 1930*

- [A] one-month-old baby admitted with a chesty cough[.]—*The Guardian*, 29th December 2002

3 arrogant, conceited *US, 1899*

- Mr. Harrison stood there chesty as a peacock[.]—Mezz Mezzrow, *Really the Blues*, p. 310, 1946
- —Kenn "Naz" Young, *Naz's Underground Dictionary*, p. 20, 1973

Chev; Chevy; Chevvy *noun*

a Chevrolet car *US, 1937*

- Drove my Chevy to the levee but the levee was dry.—Don McLean, *American Pie*, 1971

chevoo *noun*

a party *AUSTRALIA, 1963*

A variant of **SHIVOO**.

- Real nice people, having a big chevoo, must invite them up here next Saturday night for a quick beer and a game of Euchre.—Frank Hardy, *The Outcasts of Foolgarah*, p. 195, 1971

Chevy Chase *noun*

the face *UK*

Rhyming slang, originally for the scene of a Scottish and English battle recorded in a famous ballad of 1624. The original slang usage, pronounced 'chivvy', flourished from 1857 but was presumed obsolete by 1960. The revival, recorded by *www.LondonSlang.com* in June 2002, is more likely inspired by a US bank or the comedy actor Chevy Chase (b.1943).

- She had a Chevy Chase like a bulldog licking piss off a nettle. —Bodmin Dark, *Dirty Cockney Rhyming Slang*, 2003

Chevy Chased *adjective*

drunk *UK*

Possibly rhyming slang for **SHITFACED** (drunk) from **CHEVY CHASE** (face), possibly a variant of **OFF YOUR FACE** (very drunk).

- —*e-cyclopaedia*, 20th March 2002

Chevy eleven *noun*

in the used car business, a Chevrolet II *US*

- —Lewis Poteet, *Car & Motorcyle Slang*, p. 48, 1992

chew *noun*

1 chewing tobacco *US*

- The uncles toil good-naturedly in the kitchen ("It beats the shit out of the old country," they'd tell you if they could), singing Caruso and arias and spitting chew on the floor.—Larry Heinemann, *Paco's Story*, p. 105, 1990

2 an act of oral sex *UK*

- When I was pissed I wouldn't refuse anything, slut, beef, chews, anything.—*Heart*, 1962

3 food *SOUTH AFRICA, 1961*

South African school usage.

chew *verb*

▸ chew face

to kiss *US, 1980*

- "Who can tell me what petting means?" asked subsitute teacher Sharon Simon, who has a master's degree in psychology. "You mean chewing face?" queried one student.—*Los Angeles Times*, p. 2–6, 3rd February 1986

▸ chew it

in skateboarding, to fall from the board *US*

- —Albert Cassorla, *The Skateboarder's Bible*, p. 199, 1976

▸ chew pillows

to be the passive partner in anal sex *UK*

- [A] scrounger, parasite, pervert, a worm, a self-confessed player of the pink oboe, a man or woman who by his own admission chews pillows.—Peter Cook, *Entirely a Matter for You*, 1979

▸ chew steel

(of a racehorse) to strain against the bit *AUSTRALIA*

- —Ned Wallish, *The Truth Dictionary of Racing Slang*, p. 14, 1989

▸ chew the cud

to consider something; to be very thoughtful *UK, 1749*

- Adlai Stevenson [...] chewing the cud of his two defeats and talking to no one—*The Guardian*, 21st January 1961

▸ chew the fat

to gossip, to chatter idly *US, 1907*

- The farmers were chewing the fat in feed and hardware stores, the women were chopping their gums in Five-and-tens and department stores[.]—Jack Kerouac, *Letter to Caroline and Paul Blake*, p. 143, 16th March 1948
- [I]n the course of chewing the fat we told each other all about our form.—Charles Raven, *Underworld Nights*, p. 148, 1956
- We stood around the De Soto and chewed the fat a while.—Clancy Sigal, *Going Away*, p. 258, 1961
- So I check the meters, which takes me maybe two hours, what with the fact that I chew the fact with a couple of the engineers, and then Alfie and me drive home.—Robert Campbell, *The Cat's Meow*, p. 44, 1988
- Now I want to create the illusion that this is just Mickey and I chewin' the fat all by ourselves.—*Natural Born Killers*, 1994
- Did ministers not need to get together sometimes just to chew the fat?—*The Guardian*, 5th July 2002

▸ chew the rag

to discuss something; to complain, to moan; hence, to argue *UK, 1885*

- We chewed the rag for quite a while and shot the con for fair / and when it came to spreadin' jive, you could gamble that I was there. —Bruce Jackson, *Get Your Ass in the Water and Swim Like Me*, p. 131, 1965
- "Oi," yelled Eldon. "You still chewing the rag?"—Anthony Masters, *Minder*, p. 8, 1984

▸ chew the scenery

to over-act in a dramatic performance *US*

- —Sherman Louis Sergel, *The Language of Show Biz*, p. 48, 1973
- I see scenery and / chew it, chew it / that's how I do it[.] —Gerard Alessandrini, *Chew It [Forbidden Broadway Volume 3]*, 1993
- Johnny Depp and rival pirate Geoffrey Rush, both chewing the scenery with such abandon it's a wonder their vessels don't spring a leak[.]—*Bang*, p. 64, August 2003
- A surprisingly entertaining high-seas actioner with Perkins chewing the scenery as the leader of a group of terrorists who have taken over a supply ship.—David Beller, *TLA Video & DVD Guide 2004*, p. 206, 2004

▸ chew the sugar cane

to gossip *US*

- The family was in the living room chewing the sugar cane on what was happening in Puerto Rico.—Piri Thomas, *Stories from El Barrio*, p. 118, 1978

▸ chew your tobacco more than once

to repeat yourself *US, 1893*

- —Shirley Brice Heath, *Ways with Words*, back matter, 1983

chew and choke *noun*

a roadside restaurant; a motorway services *US, 1976*

- —*Complete CB Slang Dictionary*, 1976
- —Peter Chippindale, *The British CB Book*, p. 153, 1981

chew and spew; chew 'n' spew *noun*

a fast-food outlet; the food served at such a place, especially if the quality of the food is lower than expectations *AUSTRALIA*

- —*Australian Phrasebook*, 1998

chewed to loon shit *adjective*

ground up; ruined *CANADA*

Reported by Robin Leech, 1974.

chewers *noun*

the teeth *US*

- —Clarence Major, *Dictionary of Afro-American Slang*, p. 36, 1970

chewies *noun*

crack cocaine *US*

- —US Department of Justice, *Street Terms*, October 1994
- —Mike Haskins, *Drugs*, p. 281, 2003

chew out; chewing out *noun*

a rebuke *US*

- Yet instead of forty lashes, or even a thorough chewing out, she had given them her car.—Max Shulman, *Anyone Got a Match?*, p. 55, 1964

chew out *verb*

1 to perform oral sex on a woman *AUSTRALIA*

- —Thommo, *The Dictionary of Australian Swearing and Sex Sayings*, p. 25, 1985

2 to rebuke someone harshly *US, 1929*

- How could I inform her? If she knew she would have chewed me out.—Salman Rushdie, *The Moor's Last Sigh*, p. 135, 1996

chew over *verb*

to consider something, to discuss something *US, 1939*

- Need a little time to chew it over / But every day I grow a little older —10cc, *How'm I Ever Gonna Say Goodbye*, 1980
- Motor mouths chew over industry debates.—*The Observer*, 4th July 2001

chewsday *noun*

Tuesday *US, 1877*

Humourous.

- —Joseph A. Weingarten, *An American Dictoinary of Slang*, p. 63, 1954

chewy *noun*

1 crack cocaine mixed with marijuana for smoking *US*

- —Kenn "Naz" Young, *Naz's Dictionary of Teen Slang*, p. 21, 1993

2 chewing gum *AUSTRALIA, 1924*

Also spelt 'chewie'. Usually as a non-count noun, but can also be used to refer to a single piece of chewing gum. This usage is now restricted to Western Australia.

- "Shut up, mug," Danny said. "Give us a chewie."—William Dick, *A Bunch of Ratbags*, p. 244, 1965
- —Jim Ramsay, *Cop It Sweet!*, p. 22, 1977
- Your lips are so pure, They taste like horses' manure, Your lips are so dewy, They stick to me like chewy.—Wendy Lowenstein, *Improper Play Rhymes*, p. 55, 1988
- [T]he turd at school who's always got chewie on the arse of his kecks[.]—*X-Ray*, p. 20, April 2003

chewy on your boot!

I hope your kick goes astray *AUSTRALIA, 1966*

Used as a cry of discouragement in Australian Rules football.

- —Jim Ramsay, *Cop It Sweet!*, p. 22, 1977
- Chewy on your boot, ya great black and yellow scumbag! —Lawrence Money, *The Footy Fan's Handbook*, p. 12, 1982

Chi *nickname*

Chicago, Illinois *US, 1895*

- That number is a wonderful example of what happened to the blues when they moved out of the gallion, the work-gang and the levee and rode the rods into big towns like New Orleans, Charleston, Memphis and Chi.—Mezz Mezzrow, *Really the Blues*, p. 45, 1946
- The news spread across an amused United States. WRITING IN SKY PANICS CHI—Philip Wylie, *Opus 21*, p. 204, 1949
- The seeker of the unusual will find more than fifty Japanese restaurants all over Chi.—Jack Lait and Lee Mortimer, *Chicago Confidential*, p. 87, 1950
- It's in a bus envelope so he must have taken a bus as far as Chia then switched to rail.—Mickey Spillane, *One Lonely Night*, p. 52, 1951
- I arrived in Chi quite early in the morning[.]—Jack Kerouac, *On the Road*, p. 14, 1957
- Out in Chi . . . We is working the fags in Lincoln Park. —William Burroughs, *Naked Lunch*, p. 2, 1957
- I charged him ten beans and when we got to Chi, we checked in at John Williams hotel on 47th Street.—Babs Gonzales, *Movin' On Down De Line*, p. 63, 1975
- I'm back in Chi! Stole the finest three-way silk bitch in the Apple. —Iceberg Slim (Robert Beck), *Airtight Willie and Me*, p. 47, 1979

chiac; shack *noun*

the dialect of residents of the Shediac, New Brunswick area *CANADA*

- Acadian has its own subvarieties, such as the Chiac dialect of the coast–pronounced "shack" in reference to Shediac, New Brunswick, where they practically speak another language.—Will Ferguson, *How to be a Canadian*, p. 71, 2001

chiack; chiak *noun*

teasing *AUSTRALIA, 1869*

- —Frank Hardy, *The Outcasts of Foolgarah*, p. 2, 1971
- 'Hullo! Hullo!' Chilla said, always a bit too keen on the old chiak, especially when it came to Tich's unsuccessful carryings on with the female of the species.—Frank Hardy, *The Outcasts of Foolgarah*, p. 50, 1971
- —David McGill, *David McGill's Complete Kiwi Slang Dictionary*, p. 29, 1998

chiack; chiak; chyack *verb*

to tease someone *AUSTRALIA, 1853*

From C19 British costermonger's slang 'chi-hike' (a hurrah or friendly commendation).

- —Barbara Baynton, *Trooper Jim Tasman*, p. 91, 1917
- Then the two children plunged in, all hands laughing and chiacking each other as to whose fingers or toes would feel the first bite. —Ion L. Idriess, *Over the Range*, p. 155, 1947
- —W.R. Bennett, *Wingman*, p. 72, 1961
- The crew members who were staying behind lined up at the rail chiaking and hurling mad obscenities at us as we took off[.]—Les Such, *A Yen for Yokohama*, p. 129, 1963
- The holy father comes over to the gang at Zeehan one day and he begins to chiak one of the Irish fettlers for not coming to mass. —Patsy Adam-Smith, *Folklore of the Australian Railwaymen*, p. 222, 1969
- The boys met him next day with bows and extravagant curtsies. They would not stop chyacking him until he had punched up a couple. —Ronald McKie, *The Mango Tree*, p. 99, 1975

chiacking; chiaking *noun*

teasing *AUSTRALIA, 1853*

- As he expected, he had to take some chiacking from his colleagues in the police station.—Vince Kelly, *The Bogeyman*, p. 15, 1956
- —Wilda Moxham, *The Apprentice*, p. 139, 1969

Chiantishire *nickname*

Tuscany, especially the area around Chianti *UK, 1986*

Humorously formed in the manner of an English county; from the popularity of the area with British expatriates and tourists.

- Mike Kiely enjoys the simple pleasures of farmhouse living, a long way from fashionable Chiantishire.—*The Guardian*, 5th July 2003

chib *noun*

a knife or razor used as a weapon *UK: SCOTLAND*

Probably a variation of **CHIV** (a knife).

- I shouted he's got a chib [...] but nobody came to help me[.] —Robin Page, *Down Among the Dossers*, p. 23, 1973
- —*The Observer*, 4th February 1973
- Only a matter of time surely before chib-wielding nerds recreate scenes form West Side Story in Sauchiehall Street of a Friday evening.—*The Herald (Glasgow)*, p. 16, 24th March 2004

chib *verb*

to stab or otherwise cut someone with a knife or a razor *UK: SCOTLAND*

From **CHIB** (a knife).

- Hey doll! My boy's been malkied [stabbed]. Is that the chib unit? —Ian Pattison, *Rab C. Nesbitt*, 1990
- Keith Allison, the cunt that chibbed Mooby—Irvine Welsh, *The State of the Party (Disco Biscuits)*, p. 39, 1995
- [T]here to dwell in perpetual fear of being chibbed and humped by rabid schemies [a Scot who lives in social housing].—Christopher Brookmyer, *Boiling a Frog*, p. 3, 2000
- As Grady had fled, Mo had threatened to "chib" him[.]—*The Guardian*, 23rd November 2000
- If I did, March "The Knife" Dillon might chib me, or worse, big Michelle McManus might come over and SIT on me.—*The Sun*, 27th October 2003

chiba *noun*

1 heroin *UK*

Probably a misspelling or mishearing of **CHIVA** (heroin).

- —Mike Haskins, *Drugs*, p. 283, 2003

2 marijuana *US, 1981*

Spanish slang embraced by English-speakers.

- 11 of 12 tracks are dedicated to the joys of boo, tea, dope, grass, ganga, chiba, the doob – whatever street you're on.—*Riverfront Times (Missouri)*, 21st November 2001

chiba-chiba *noun*

marijuana, especially potent marijuana from Colombia or Brazil *US*

- Over the past few years in New York, the magic moniker has been successively, Chiba-Chiba, wacky, red, red wacky, gold and Santa Marta.—*Hi Life*, p. 15, 1979
- Chiba-Chiba – a Brazilian form of pot, usually compressed into bricks.—Nick Brownlee, *This Is Cannabis*, p. 151, 2002

chibbing *noun*

a deliberate wounding by stabbing or razor-cutting *UK*

- The resulting forty stitches made it look as if he had been flung face first through a car windscreen. It was the worst chibbing I ever saw. —*The Guardian*, 29th January 2001

chibs; chips *noun*

the buttocks *US*

- I had a couple a sweet kids but they didn't have chips like this, patting her again on the ass and looking at the others, smiling, and waiting for them to smile in appreciation of his witticisms.—Hubert Selby Jr, *Last Exit to Brooklyn*, p. 44, 1957
- I ain't a profane cat, but I had to say, "Thank you God, for them fine chibs."—Edwin Torres, *Carlito's Way*, p. 94, 1975

chic *noun*

▷ **see: CHIC MURRAY**

chica *noun*

a girl *US*

Spanish; used largely as a term of address, and largely by those without a working knowledge of Spanish.

- —Connie Eble (Editor), *UNC-CH Campus Slang*, p. 2, Spring 2000

Chicago bankroll *noun*

a single large denomination note wrapped around small denomination notes, giving the impression of a great deal of money *US, 1966*

- —Edith A. Folb, *runnin' down some lines*, p. 232, 1980
- In the right pocket was something known in the trade as a "Chicago bankroll." This consisted of one twenty wrapped around the outside of a roll of sixty ones and secured with a rubber band. —David McCumber, *Playing Off the Rail*, p. 27, 1996

Chicago black *noun*

a dark-leaved variety of marijuana *US, 1971*

Grown in and around Chicago.

- —Richard A. Spears, *The Slang and Jargon of Drugs and Drink*, p. 104, 1986
- —Mike Haskins, *Drugs*, p. 287, 2003

Chicago contract *noun*

a binding oral agreement, secured by honour *US*

- So we make a Chicago contract. Nothing on tape. Nothing on paper. No outside witnesses. We don't ever have to spit on our palms and shake. —Robert Campbell, *Boneyards*, p. 53, 1992

Chicago green *noun*

a green-leafed variety of marijuana *US, 1967*

Grown in and around Chicago.

- —Richard A. Spears, *The Slang and Jargon of Drugs and Drink*, p. 104, 1986
- —Mike Haskins, *Drugs*, p. 287, 2003

Chicago G-string *noun*

a g-string designed to break open, revealing the dancer's completely naked state *US*

- —Don Wilmeth, *The Language of American Popular Entertainment*, p. 51, 1981

Chicago heavy mess *noun*

boiled salt pork *CANADA*

- Lunch consisted of boiled salt pork – very fat Chicago heavy mess – and bread and tea. —Mrs. Carl Price, *Notes on Renfrew County*, p. 48, 1961

Chicago leprosy *noun*

infections, scars and abcesses caused by prolonged intravenous drug use *US*

- —Jay Robert Nash, *Dictionary of Crime*, p. 63, 1992

Chicago piano *noun*

an anti-aircraft gun or other automatic weapon *US, 1941*

- A submachine gun is a Chicago piano. —*Austin (Texas) American-Statesman*, p. A15, 4th December 1999
- Floyd Farragut recalled the South Pacific and the war there, the anti-aircraft guns they called "Chicago pianos". —*Florida Times-Union*, p. B1, 31st May 1999

Chicago pill *noun*

a bullet *US*

- —Vincent J. Monteleone, *Criminal Slang*, p. 48, 1949

Chicago rattlesnake *noun*

salt pork *CANADA*

- Many are the stories told about "Chicago rattlesnake," as the salt pork was affectionately called by the shantymen, whose mainstay it was. —Audrey Saunders, *Algonquin Story*, p. 37, 1947

Chicago typewriter *noun*

a fully automatic weapon *US, 1963*

- His weapon of choice was the "Chicago typewriter," the submachine gun prized by warring Chicago mobs. —*Boston Globe*, p. A29, 24th September 1989

chicamin *noun*

money *CANADA*

The word is adapted from Chinook jargon 'chikamnin' (iron, metal).

- "Mebbeso," Charlie went on, "helo chickamun stop I come back," meaning that he might return broke. —R.D. Symons, *Many Trails*, p. 74, 1963

Chicano *noun*

a Mexican-American *US*

Originally a slur; by the later 1960s a term of self-identification and pride.

- What business has a Chicano got to love a man like you?" —Thurston Scott, *Cure it with Honey*, p. 209, 1951
- A few frames of Chicano heroes highlighted the corners: Cesar Chavez, the father of hte United Farm Workers. —Denise Chavez, *Loving Pedro Infante*, p. 136, 2001

Chicano time *noun*

used for denoting a lack of punctuality *US*

- "He's keeping C.P. time – colored people and Chicano time" one of the postal academy sign carriers cried[.] —*San Francisco Examiner*, p. 6, 24th May 1972
- Sonny knew they were going to be late for the opening pitch. What the hell, it was summer and they were operating on Chicano time. —Rudolfo Anaya, *Zia Summer*, p. 260, 1995
- I got there "Chicano time," late. —Gary Soto, *The Afterlife*, p. 130, 2003

chi-chi *noun*

first aid *US*

- —William Nealy, *Mountain Bike!*, p. 160, 1992

▷ **see:** CHEE-CHEE

chi-chi *adjective*

1 homosexual *UK*

From the conventional usage denoting a fussy style.

- [T]he rest of the gay world migrated to the chi-chi bars of the newly gay Soho[.] —*The Guardian*, p. 15, 14th May 2002
- [T]he chi-chi camp boys are flouncing petulantly up and down like they've got lost on the way to a Pop Idol audltion. —*Attitude*, p. 34, October 2003

2 fashionable; fussy *UK, 1932*

Also spelt 'she-she'.

- Smooth adventurers set up swank apartments on the chi chi North Side gold Coast[.] —Jack Lait and Lee Mortimer, *Chicago Confidential*, p. z, 1950
- In some New Deal left-wing circles it is considered chi-chi to meet socially and even sexually with Negroes[.] —Jack Lait and Lee Mortimer, *Washington Confidential*, p. 39, 1951
- Markie's apartment very she-she. It's all furnished very elegant and everything. —Joel Rose, *Kill Kill Faster Faster*, p. 37, 1997

chi-chi gal *noun*

a lesbian *JAMAICA*

- Another song asks listeners to raise their hands if they agree: "Hang chi-chi gal wid a long piece a rope." —*St. John's Telegram (Newfoundland)*, p. B5, 18th September 2004

chi-chi man *noun*

a male homosexual *JAMAICA, 2000*

- The chorus of one of his [Beenie Man] songs begins "We burn chi-chi man and then we burn sodomite and everybody bawl out, say 'Dat right!'" —*St. John's Telegram (Newfoundland)*, p. B5, 18th September 2004

chi-chis *noun*

a woman's breasts *US, 1961*

- "Oh yeah," I said, seeing only a blur and feeling one of those heavy chi-chis resting on my shoulder. —Joseph Wambaugh, *The Blue Knight*, p. 24, 1973
- This feeling was quickly engulfed by a wave of sweaty lust – directed at Sister Kallie and her big chi-chi's. —James Ellroy, *Brown's Requiem*, p. 143, 1981
- Still astride him after sex in their sixdollar room at the Jupiter Hotel overlooking the Strip, she laughed: "Big ass and chichis is all you love." —Seth Morgan, *Homeboy*, p. 20, 1990
- I, on the other hand, seize the synchornous opportunity to stare at those Monster Chi-Chis for ninety splendid minutes. —Marty Beckerman, *Death to All Cheerleaders*, p. 125, 2000

chick *noun*

1 a young woman *US, 1899*

- It set me up to have a chick like her. It gave me a personal pride to have her for my girl. —Chester Himes, *If He Hollers Let Him Go*, p. 6, 1945
- To give you an idea of what a sweet thing she was, children, I'll just say she was not only a lovely little girl; she was a fine chick. —Steve Allen, *Bop Fables*, p. 36, 1955
- Across the cornfield in back lived a beautiful young chick that Dean had been trying to make ever since he arrived. —Jack Kerouac, p. 218, 1957
- I met chicks who were fine as May wine, and cats who were hip to all happenings. —Malcolm X and Alex Haley, *The Autobiography of Malcolm X*, p. 56, 1964
- Lank-haired chicks, many wearing boots and leather, leafed through copies of Nova Expressa and Naked Lunch. —Sidney Bernard, *This Way to the Apocalypse*, p. 113, 1966
- When we would come out of the stage door, there would be three hundred beautiful chicks, and all we had to do was take one by the hand. —Babs Gonzales, *I Paid My Dues*, p. 68, 1967
- Says that he lived in North Beach and all that, and that he has this chick who writes him who is a member of the DuBois Club in Frisco. —Eldridge Cleaver, *Soul on Ice*, p. 46, 1968
- There's not a chick in the world who's half as hip as she / My swingin' little goddess from Avenue D. —The Fugs, *Slum Goddess*, 1968
- [S]pace should be available for chicks to sew dresses, make pants to order, recut garmets to fit, etc. —*The Digger Papers*, p. 15, August 1968

- I was 22 years of age and shacking with a chick named Julie, I gave her one "joint" which she stashed and later turned over to the cops – a joint that netted me one of the 5-to-life sentences. — *The Berkeley Tribe*, p. 5, 5th-12th September 1969
- Chick: A female (when talked about between males). To be used with greatest caution around chicks. — *Screw*, p. 7, 12th October 1970
- Although I don't usually respond to 'chick thing' or 'Miss Pesky'. — Francesca Lia Block, *I Was a Teenage Fairy*, p. 158, 1998
- You know Nadia the Czechoslovakian chick? — *American Pie*, 1999

2 a male prostitute *UK, 1984*

- — A.D. Peterkin, *Outbursts! A Queer Exotic Thesaurus*, p. 115, 2003

3 a friendly fighter aircraft *US, 1951*

- — *Washington Post Magazine*, p. W8, 3rd February 1991

4 cocaine *US*

One of many variations on the cocaine-as-female theme.

- — Gilda and Melvin Berger, *Drug Abuse A-Z*, p. 43, 1990

chickabiddy *noun*

used as a term of endearment for a child *UK, 1829*

From a C18 childish variation on 'chicken'.

- Hello my little chickabiddies! — Barry Humphries, *Bazza Pulls It Off!*, 1971

chicken *noun*

1 a woman *US*

- Three of the groping, licking, grinding pairs of cops and chickens had managed everything but penetration. — Joseph Wambaugh, *The Glitter Dome*, p. 2, 1981

2 a boy, usually under the age of consent, who is the target of homosexual advances *US, 1914*

- — Vincent J. Monteleone, *Criminal Slang*, p. 49, 1949
- — Donald Webster Cory and John P. LeRoy, *The Homosexual and His Society*, p. 262, 1963: 'A lexicon of homosexual slang'
- — Florida Legislative Investigation Committee (Johns Committee), *Homosexuality and Citizenship in Florida*, 1964: 'Glossary of homosexual terms and deviate acts'
- — Dale Gordon, *The Dominion Sex Dictionary*, p. 43, 1967
- The drug-pitch skells would rather tear off with a wallet than transact an actual exchange, and they make the teenage chicken fags seem like the most discreet commodity on the street. — Josh Alan Friedman, *Tales of Times Square*, p. 51, 1986
- Like seeing a big new car with Ohio plates come driving up in front of that skinny little ten-year-old chicken selling his tender ass for a night's bed and board — Robert Campbell, *Alice in La-La Land*, p. 9, 1987
- And feature – him and that bottle-blond fruitcake are porking in trailers every chance they get, and chasing chicken down at the Fern Dell toilets. — James Ellroy, *White Jazz*, p. 59, 1992
- — Paul Baker, *Polari*, p. 168, 2002

3 a child, a youthful or inexperienced person; often as an affectionate form of address *UK, 1711*

4 a young and inexperienced male prostitute *UK, 1988*

- — John Ayto, *Oxford Dictionary of Slang*, p. 85, 1998

5 someone under the legal drinking age *US*

- — Judi Sanders, *Cal Poly Slang*, p. 2, 1990

6 used as a term of endearment *IRELAND*

- I know chicken, I know, but dat's [that's] all behind ye [you] now, ye're doin' great. — Donal Ruane, *Tales In a Rear View Mirror*, p. 114, 2003

7 a test of wills in which two cars drive directly at each other until one driver – the loser – veers off course *US, 1952*

- — Michael Innes, *Appleby Plays Chicken*, 1956
- I used to play 'chicken' on Miceltorena when I was a kid. Rebel Without A Cause had just come out and chicken was in. — James Ellroy, *Blood on the Moon*, p. 160, 1984

8 a coward *US, 1936*

From the characteristics ascribed to the best of 'chickens'; in an earlier sense, found in Shakespeare, the meaning is 'someone timorous and defenceless'.

9 marijuana *US*

- — Jim Emerson-Cobb, *Scratching the Dragon*, April 1997

10 a small halibut *US*

Alaskan usage.

- — Jim Crotty, *How to Talk American*, p. 5, 1997

▷ see: CHICKEN PERCH

▸ **no chicken; no spring chicken**

no longer young *UK, 1860*

- He's no spring chicken but 33 isn't that old for a defender. — *The Guardian*, 26th April 2002

chicken *adjective*

scared, cowardly, afraid *US, 1933*

- "You're chicken," Sheik said contemptuously, sucking another puff. — Chester Himes, *The Real Cool Killers*, p. 49, 1959
- What are ya, chicken, Charlie? — *The Hustler*, 1961
- It was true that he was becoming afraid, but he was even more afraid of being called "chicken" if he refused to go with them. — Nathan Heard, *Howard Street*, p. 62, 1968
- If you passed it [a joint] on, no-one would call you chicken or anything[.] — Macfarlane, Macfarlane and Robson, *The User*, p. 32, 1996
- GARY: s' do it – wha' – chicken? — Patrick Jones, *Unprotected Sex*, p. 248, 1999

chicken bone *noun*

a chocolate-filled hard sweet confection invented by the Ganong family firm of St Stephen, New Brunswick *CANADA*

- A standard maritime treat, the "chicken bone" was being made–muscular men stretching lumps of sticky pink candy into those inch-long "chicken bones." — *Montreal Gazette*, p. H6, 11th May 2002

chickenbone special *noun*

any small, local railway *US, 1970*

- After all, the Chickenbone Special ran both ways. The Dixie Highway goes south from Ohio as well as north to it. — John Shelton Reed, *My Tears Spoiled my Aim*, p. 108, 1993

chicken burner *noun*

a Pontiac 'Firebird' car *UK*

- — Peter Chippindale, *The British CB Book*, p. 161, 1981

chicken bus *noun*

during the war in Vietnam, a troop transport bus *US*

From the chicken wire that covered the windows in the hope of keeping enemy grenades outside the bus.

- — Gregory Clark, *Words of the Vietnam War*, p. 98, 1990

chicken catcher *noun*

in electric line work, an armsling *US*

- — A.B. Chance Co., *Lineman's Slang Dictionary*, p. 4, 1980

chicken colonel *noun*

in the US Army, a full colonel *US, 1918*

From the eagle insignia of the rank.

- That was the first time anybody ever told me they're proud of me, and it's a full chicken colonel in the U.S. Army! — Rocky Garciano (with Rowland Barber), *Somebody Up There Likes Me*, p. 235, 1955
- But I've seen the Air Force turn out generals and chicken colonels in brigade strength to welcome junketing congressmen. — *San Francisco Examiner*, p. 27, 9th April 1966

chicken cookies *noun*

frozen ground chicken patties *ANTARCTICA, 1991*

- — Carnegie Mellon Astrophysics Peterson Group, *Antarctic Vocabulary*, 19th September 1997

chicken coop *noun*

1 a women's jail or prison *US*

- — Vincent J. Monteleone, *Criminal Slang*, p. 49, 1949

2 an outdoor toilet *US, 1970*

- — Frederic G. Cassidy, *Dictionary of American Regional English*, p. 614, 1985

3 a weight station *US, 1975*

Citizens' band radio and trucking slang.

- Yeah, them chicken coops was full of bears [police] / And choppers filled the skies[.] — C.W. McCall, *Convoy*, 1976

chicken crank *noun*

an amphetamine fed to chickens to accelerate their egg-laying *US*

- — Geoffrey Froner, *Digging for Diamonds*, p. 68, 1989

chicken curry *verb*

to worry *UK*

Rhyming slang.

- The CID tells them not to chicken curry, he's got the perfect solution[.] — Danny King, *The Burglar Diaries*, p. 198, 2001

chicken dinner *noun*

a pretty woman *US*

- When we saw one of buddies blowing his top over some chicken dinner we pitied him for going tangent[.] — Mezz Mezzrow, *Really the Blues*, p. 78, 1946
- — Kenn "Naz" Young, *Naz's Underground Dictionary*, p. 20, 1973

chickenfeed *noun*

1 a less than generous amount of money *US, 1836*

- —Marcus Hanna Boulware, *Jive and Slang of Students in Negro Colleges*, 1947
- He comes from one of the few states where there is no gangsterism except in picayune city and county affairs, and in those the Republicans share the chicken-feed rewards.—Jack Lait and Lee Mortimer, *Washington Confidential*, p. 195, 1951
- Harry would turn up his nose and say: "Chickenfeed. Not interested."—Charles Raven, *Underworld Nights*, p. 101, 1956

2 a task that can be accomplished with ridiculous ease *SINGAPORE*

- —Paik Choo, *The Coxford Singlish Dictionary*, p. 29, 2002

3 methamphetamine *US*

- She believes crystals are a form of Methedrine and that "they're called chicken feed because they're actually given to chickens."—*San Francisco News Call Bulletin*, p. 3, 17th February 1964

chicken fillet *noun*

a gel-filled pad placed into a brassiere cup to uplift and enhance the appearance of a woman's breast; a gel-filled full breast prosthesis *UK*

- [M]astectomy, laughing and joking at wigs and 'chicken fillet' boobs, hair loss, menopause, no more children.—*Breast Cancer Care*, 3rd January 2003

chicken fink *noun*

an unlikeable, disloyal person *US*

- You chicken fink!—*American Graffiti*, 1973

chickenguts *noun*

braided military decorations *US, 1943*

- Resplendent in feathres and loops of gold braid known locally as 'chicken guts', his personal staff included Hungarians and Italians. —*Albuquerque (New Mexico) Journal*, p. 5, 1st September 2000

chickenhawk *noun*

1 during a war, someone who supports the war but avoids military service themselves *US*

Virtually every member of the US government that supported the 2003 invasion of Iraq avoided active military service in Vietnam during their youth.

- Vann had warned Komer that if he arrived with less authority and access, he would be eaten by the chicken hawks.—Neil Sheehan, *A Bright Shining Lie*, p. 656, 1988
- Calling Quayle "chicken hawk" or "yellow bird" is cruel and unfair, but I guess that's politics.—*Newsday (New York)*, p. 85, 2nd September 1988
- What do you get when you cross a chicken and a hawk? A Quayle. —*Maledicta*, p. 256, 1988–1989
- Here's a list of pro-war Republicans who had better things to do than serve in the military: Dick Cheney, Bill Frist, Tom DeLay, Dennis Hastert, Pat Buchanan, Newt Gingrich, George Will, and a couple of talk-show geeks I'll call Rust Lambug and Shame Han[.]—*Leaf-Chronicle (Clarksville, Tennessee)*, p. 13A, 20th April 2003
- Limbaugh is a prime example of what is known as a Chicken Hawk – a noisy, preening master of the martial art of talking who, back when it was a question of getting anywhere near harm's way for the sake of his country, discovered that he had (as Vice President Cheney once put it, explaining his own absence from the fray) "other priorities." —*New York*, p. 39, 27th October 2003

2 a mature homosexual man who seeks much younger men as sexual partners *US, 1965*

- —Dale Gordon, *The Dominion Sex Dictionary*, p. 43, 1967
- Basically the Flamingo Isles was a dive for pimps, chicken hawks, and hookers.—Carl Hiaasen, *Tourist Season*, p. 33, 1986
- [A]nd instead of a chicken hawk flagging him inside with a twenty-dollar bill, his old mother, wrapped in furs and flashing newly capped teeth, comes rushing out.—Robert Campbell, *Alice in La-La Land*, p. 9, 1987
- —Carsten Stroud, *Close Pursuit*, p. 270, 1987
- [W]e three go up there frequently, proud to still elicit, in our post-teen years, the lurid howls of chickenhawks as we pass on by.—Jim Carroll, *Forced Entries*, p. 7, 1987
- The next day Jules was in several adult magazine and book shops in downtown San Diego looking for chickenhawk and pedophile publications.—Joseph Wambaugh, *Finnegan's Week*, p. 18, 1993
- —*Gayness Explained, The FHM Little Book of Bloke*, p. 142, June 2003

3 by extension, a woman who seeks out young male lovers *US*

- "She's a chickenhawk!" Natalie sneered. "These kids come and go hourly through her zoo."—Joseph Wambaugh, *The Black Marble*, p. 306, 1978

chickenhead *noun*

1 a female who pursues a male solely because of the male's success and visibility as a musician, athlete, etc *US*

- —Connie Eble (Editor), *UNC-CH Campus Slang*, p. 2, Spring 1999

2 a person performing oral sex on a man *US*

Also 'chickhead'. From the bobbing motion.

- Thinkin' of this chickenhead I stuck my dick in.—Originoo Gunn Clapazz, *Elite Fleet*, 1996
- Rap made slang aimed at women like "skeezer," "hootchie," "chickhead," and the ubiquitous "bitch"[.]—Nelson George, *Hip Hop America*, p. 186, 1998
- —Chris Lewis, *The Dictionary of Playground Slang*, p. 55, 2003

3 an aggressive or violent woman *US*

- —Edith A. Folb, *runnin' down some lines*, p. 232, 1980

4 a foolish, frivolous person *US, 1906*

- Your reviewer, who never put any chips on [bet on] the old chickenhead anyway[.]—Lester Bangs, *Psychotic Reactions and Carburetor Dung*, p. 162, 1976
- —Don R. McCreary (Editor), *Dawg Speak*, 2001

chicken heart *verb*

to fart *UK*

Rhyming slang, only recorded in the past tense.

- Who chicken hearted?—Ray Puxley, *Cockney Rabbit*, 1992

chicken in a basket *noun*

in the Canadian military, an Air Command badge worn on the tunic until 1992 *CANADA*

- The "chicken in a basket," a small, circular badge, depicts an eagle arising in flight from within a Crown.—Tom Langeste, *Words on the Wing*, p. 57, 1995

chicken jalfrezi *adjective*

crazy *UK, 2002*

Contemporary rhyming slang, inspired by a popular curry dish.

- —*www.LondonSlang.com*, June 2002
- She took too many drugs when she was a teenager and she's been chicken jalfrezi ever since.—Bodmin Dark, *Dirty Cockney Rhyming Slang*, 2003

chickenkiller *noun*

a Cuban or Haitian *US, 1970s*

From the stereotype of Cubans and Haitians as voodoo practioners sacrificing chickens in religious rites; insulting.

- Somebody who thought American but worked for the chickenkillers.—Elmore Leonard, *Stick*, p. 86, 1983

chicken oriental *adjective*

insane, crazy *UK*

Rhyming slang for **MENTAL**.

- —Bodmin Dark, *Dirty Cockney Rhyming Slang*, 2003

chicken out *verb*

to lose courage and retreat from an endeavour *US, 1934*

- I was wondering if he had chickened out again, when he came down the sidewalk and got in the Buick beside me.—Iceberg Slim (Robert Beck), *Trick Baby*, p. 223, 1969
- I don't want to ignore anything. I want to look. I don't want to chicken out.—Douglas Rushkoff, *The Snow that Killed Manuel Jarrow (Disco Biscuits)*, p. 195, 1996

chicken perch; chicken *noun*

a church; church *UK, 1931*

Rhyming slang.

chickenplate *noun*

a steel vest that helicopter and other aircrew wore in the Vietnam war, designed as bulletproof *US, 1971*

- —Linda Reinberg, *In the Field*, p. 41, 1991
- Before we climbed in, Terzala grabbed him. "Major," he said, "today you need to wear your chicken plate. You are not getting on this helo until you put it on." Franks didn't usually wear the chicken plate, but he took Terzala's advice and put it on.—Tom Clancy with Fred Franks Jr, *Into the Storm*, p. 58, 1991

chicken powder *noun*

amphetamine in powdered form, used intravenously *US*

- —Edward R. Bloomquist, *Marijuana*, p. 336, 1971
- —Mike Haskins, *Drugs*, p. 279, 2003

chicken pox *noun*

an obsession of an older homosexual male with young men or boys *US*

- —*Maledicta*, p. 222, 1979: 'Kinks and queens: linguistic and cultural aspects of the terminology for gays'

chicken queen *noun*

a mature male homosexual who is especially attracted to boys or young men *US*

- —Donald Webster Cory and John P. LeRoy, *The Homosexual and His Society*, p. 262, 1963: 'A lexicon of homosexual slang'

- — *The Guild Dictionary of Homosexual Terms*, p. 8, 1965
- I hope you're not a chicken queen. I'm twenty-six. —Armistead Maupin, *Tales of the City*, p. 134, 1978
- — *Maledicta*, p. 220, 1979: 'Kinks and queens: linguistic and cultural aspects of the terminology for gays'
- The Complete Gay Dictionary— *Male Swinger Number 3*, p. 47, 1981
- Natch, he eventually leaves her for girls his own age and poor Lola becomes an anxiety ridden chicken queen. —John Waters, *Crackpot*, p. 113, 1986
- Boy prostitutes are typically referred to on the streets as chickens, while homosexual men that solicit young male prostitutes are known as chicken hawks or chicken queens. —R. Barri Flowers, *Runaway Kids and Teenage Prostitution*, p. 139, 2001

chicken ranch *noun*

a rural brothel *US, 1973*

Originally the name of a brothel in LaGrange, Texas, and then spread to more generic use.

- Hey, you don't make a thousand bucks tax-free by staying in bed unless you're working at one of those chicken ranches in Nevada. —Joseph Wambaugh, *Fugitive Nights*, p. 43, 1992

chicken run *noun*

the exodus of people from Rhodesia (now Zimbabwe) for fear of the future; hence, the exodus of people from South Africa for fear of the future *ZIMBABWE, 1977*

- [T]he newspaper cartoonists are using the image of the chicken run (the phrase for white flight first popularised in Ian Smith's Rhodesia). — *New Statesman*, 13th November 1998

chicken scratch *noun*

cocaine *UK*

Probably from the sense, 'a search for crack cocaine'.

- —Mike Haskins, *Drugs*, p. 280, 2003

chickenshit *noun*

a coward *US, 1929*

- [A]ll the Richard Hells are chickenshits who trash the precious gift too blithely[.] —Lester Bangs, *Psychotic Reactions and Carburetor Dung*, p. 267, 1977
- When did they start hiring chickenshits like you on Robbery-Homicide, Krantz? —Robert Crais, *L.A. Requiem*, p. 44–44, 1999
- Oi, come out you chicken-shits. —Chris Baker and Andrew Day, *Lock, Stock... & Spaghetti Sauce*, p. 249, 2000

chickenshit *adjective*

cowardly *US, 1934*

- They after my job, the chickenshit bastards! —Ralph Ellison, *Invisible Man*, p. 228, 1947
- "They want to destroy religion. They're chickenshit," Marty said. —James T. Farrell, *Saturday Night*, p. 35, 1947
- He got mad at the guys from acting too cagey – too chicken-shit, he called it. —Ken Kesey, *One Flew Over the Cuckoo's Nest*, p. 113, 1962
- They did it chickenshit. They told me in the office when I went to get my paycheck. —Jim Bouton, *Ball Four*, p. 71, 1970
- Then cut to me talking about the two chickenshit pyschiatrists and straight in Dr. Reinghold laughing. — *Natural Born Killers*, 1994

chicken skin *noun*

the sensation and physical manifestation of the chills *US*

Hawaiian youth usage, instead of the more common 'goose bumps'.

- When we wen keess, ah got chicken skin! —Douglas Simonson, *Pidgin to da Max*, 1981

chicken's neck *noun*

a cheque *UK*

Rhyming slang. A variation of **GOOSE'S NECK**.

- —Ray Puxley, *Fresh Rabbit*, 1998

chicken switch *noun*

a switch that will abort a mission; a notional switch that will end a project *US, 1960*

- A quick-thinking sailor hit the "chicken switch" in the control room, which blew the main ballast tanks and brought the Edison to the surface. — *Chicago Tribune*, p. C1, 9th January 1991
- And a switch, the chicken switch. The purpose was that if anything at all went wrong, we could disconnect. — *Providence (Rhode Island) Journal-Bulletin*, p. 1A, 16th July 1995

chicken tracks *noun*

in electric line work, a device formally known as an Epoxirod tri-unit *US*

- —A.B. Chance Co., *Lineman's Slang Dictionary*, p. 4, 1980

chicken wing *noun*

a bowler whose elbow strays outward from the body during the backswing motion of rolling the ball *US*

- —Dawson Taylor, *How to Talk Bowling*, p. 30, 1987

chicken yellow *noun*

the recreational drug PMA *US*

Also known as 'chicken fever' or 'chicken powder'.

- Also known as "Chicken Yellow" or "Chicken Fever", PMA is often contained in a thick white tablet. — *The Guardian*, 14th January 2001
- In 1972 and 1973 several deaths in the USA were thought to be caused by PMA ("Chicken Yellow" and "Chicken Powder") being sold as methylenedioxyamphetamine (MDA) —London Toxicology Group, February 2002

chickey-babe; chicky-babe *noun*

a young woman, especially a good-looking one *AUSTRALIA, 1991*

- We are six girls from sub-camp 5 and we are really sick of being called chickey-babe and whistled at every time we even step out of our tent. — *Nugget*, p. 8, 6th January 1992

chick flick *noun*

a film that is desiged to appeal to a female audience *US, 1993*

- —Connie Eble (Editor), *UNC-CH Campus Slang*, p. 2, Spring 1998
- Boys and young men will simply refuse to see the "chick flicks" their girlfriends and wives want to attend, while females will accommodate their boyfriends and husbands. — *National Review*, 16th June 2001

chickie; chicky *noun*

1 a lookout or decoy *US, 1934*

- Not having anyone to lay chickie for me, I had to do it quicker than most of the time. —Claude Brown, *Manchild in the Promised Land*, p. 31, 1965
- Three of us went in for the bread; Crip stayed behind to play chicky. —Piri Thomas, *Down These Mean Streets*, p. 75, 1967
- They searched for a money belt and ripped his shoes from his feet while Butch and Brother played chickie. —Nathan Heard, *Howard Street*, p. 67, 1968
- This was a two-man operation; one guy on his hands and knees looking at the mirror, the other at the end of the hall laying chicky, as they say. —Jim Bouton, *Ball Four*, p. 37, 1970
- I went in but now I had nobody to lie chicky for me[.] —Herbert Huncke, *Guilty of Everything*, p. 102, 1990
- Victoria had also been assigned the task of getaway driver and "lay chickie," which she found out, to her relief, was a lookout. —Stephen Cannell, *Big Con*, p. 195, 1997

2 a young girl *US, 1919*

Teen slang.

- —William Dick, *A Bunch of Ratbags*, 1965
- Shit never been his pleasure, but as you say, maybe it's for some chickie friend. —Elmore Leonard, *52 Pick-up*, p. 146, 1974

chickie!

used as warning *US, 1934*

- Then, almost before it began, it was over, for a lookout on the corner heard sirens, and yelled, "Chickie, the nabs!" —Hal Ellson, *Tomboy*, p. 110, 1950
- [A]s he was jumping off the fender to Angus' shouted chicky! —Gilbert Sorrentino, *Steelwork*, p. 53, 1970

chickie poo *noun*

a young and beautiful girl *US*

Recorded in the usage of counterculturalists associated with the Rainbow Nation.

- You didn't come home last night. What were you up to, out messing around with all the chickie-poos? —John Nichols, *The Nirvana Blues*, p. 90, 1981
- —Jim Crotty, *How to Talk American*, p. 289, 1997
- If I was a cute young chickie-poo with big boobs, I would be seen as flirtatious, looking for action. — *St. Petersburg (Florida) Times*, p. 1F, 13th April 2003

chickie run *noun*

a test of wills in which two cars drive at high speeds towards a cliff; the driver who jumps from his car first loses *US*

- We're going to have us some real kicks. Little chickie-run. You been on chickie-runs before? — *Rebel Without a Cause*, 1955

chicklet *noun*

a young woman *US, 1922*

Elaboration by conventional diminution of **CHICK** (a young woman).

- [T]he newest of the teenage raves, with beside him his brother, and his composer, and his chicklet, and his Personal Manager[.] —Colin MacInnes, *Absolute Beginners*, 1959

chick lit *noun*

literature directed at young women; literature written by women *US*

- By the way, the very proper sounding "Female Literary Tradition" is known there as "Chick Lit." — *Newsday (New York)*, p. 96, 13th April 1993

- Later in the show colourful debates ensue, drawing a little on Walsh's trademark wit, over the notion of [Edna O'Brien's The Country Girls Trilogy] being a form of "chick lit." — *Toronto Globe and Mail*, p. R1, 24th July 2002
- I would rather write chick-lit than literary fiction that gets lots of reviews but not many readers. — *The Guardian*, p. 8, 26th March 2002
- Ah, the bad hair day – where would chick lit or chauvinist revenge humour be without this contemporary cultural platitude? — *The Times Magazine*, p. 49, 31st May 2003

chick magnet *noun*

a male who is attractive to women *AUSTRALIA*

- So once again I turned to my mates to help me out. In this case it was Johnny Gibbs, Manly footy star at the time, with flowing blond locks and a deadset chick magnet. — Paul Vautin, *Turn It Up!*, p. 83, 1995

chicko; chico *noun*

a child *UK*

Either by elaboration of 'chick' (a child) or adoption of Spanish *chico* (a boy). Remembered in army service in the 1960s – early 70s, by Beale, 1984.

chick with a dick *noun*

a transexual or, rarely, a hermaphrodite *US*

Almost always plural.

- Asserting that neither the "glamorized" movie stars nor the queens are desirable (they are "asexual," despite the evidence of star fan clubs and Chicks-with-Dicks phone sex numbers) Bersani condemns them to/for masturbation. — Diana Fuss, *Inside/Out*, p. 39, 1991
- All right, but your're missing out. Chicks with dicks. — *Clerks*, 1994
- The third floor is live performance with chicks with dicks and dominatrix acts, transvestites, and other such novelties. — James Ridgeway, *Red Light*, p. 136, 1996
- ["]I've always wanted to shag a chick with a dick, just to see what it's like." "You mean, shag a bloke or a bird with a gender crisis?" — Darren Francis, *The Sprawl [britpulp]*, p. 299, 1999

chicky *noun*

a female *US*

Used with an ironic nod towards the outmoded 'chick'.

- — Connie Eble (Editor), *UNC-CH Campus Slang*, p. 2, Spring 1994

▷ see: CHICKIE

chicky-babe *noun*

▷ see: CHICKEY-BABE

chicle *noun*

heroin *US*

Spanish for 'gum', alluding to the gummy nature of heroin that has not been processed to powder form.

- — US Department of Justice, *Street Terms*, October 1994

chiclet keyboard *noun*

a computer keyboard with small plastic keys *US*

A visual allusion to a branded chewing gum.

- Customers rejected the idea with almost equal unanimity, and chiclets are not often seen on anything larger than a digital watch any more. — Eric S. Raymond, *The New Hacker's Dictionary*, p. 94, 1991

Chic Murray; chic *noun*

a curry *UK: SCOTLAND*

Glasgow rhyming slang, formed from the name of the Scottish comedian, 1919–85.

- Ah wish Ah'd went straight hame efter the pub instead a gaun fur that Chic! — Michael Munro, *The Patter, Another Blast*, 1988

Chicom *noun*

a soldier from the People's Republic of China; a Chinese communist *US, 1967*

- On a three-hundred-mile front, countless thousands of Chinese Communists – "Chicoms," as MacArthur's headquarters had begun to call them, had howled down from what the General had previously described as "a rugged spinal mountain range" too precipitous to shelter troops. — William Manchester, *American Caesar*, p. 726, 1978

Chicom *adjective*

Chinese communist *US, 1964*

- The American side wanted the British to support United States political policy on China, while noting that this would "make it easier to meet the British views on some of the trade matters and the alignment of the Cocom and Chicom lists." — Michael A. Guhin, *John Foster Dulles*, p. 296, 1972
- [A] young man or a boy who wore a cap with a short visor and held a Chicom machine gun across his skinny knees[.] — Elmore Leonard, *Mr. Majesty*, p. 146, 1974
- We grabbed the weapons. I gave them a quick once-over. They were Chicom AK-47s. — Richard Marcinko, *Rogue Warrior*, p. 116, 1992

chiddles *noun*

in Newfoundland, cooked cod roe or cod milt *CANADA*

- Chiddles: Chidlins or chitlins. Small, pink or red, edible viscera in the stomach of a codfish, shaped like a pair of pants. — Ronald Noseworthy, *Dialect Survey of Grand Bank, Nfld.*, p. 182, 1971

chief *noun*

1 a Flight Sergeant *UK, 1942*

Royal Air Force use; a hangover from Chief Petty Officer, the corresponding rank in the Royal Naval Air Service (established in 1914, it was a military service that, in 1918, combined with the Royal Flying Corps to form the Royal Air Force). Sometimes personalised to the diminutive 'chiefie'.

2 a Petty Officer *UK, 1929*

Royal Navy use.

3 a Chief Engineer; a Lieutenant Commander; a First Mate *UK, 1894*

Nautical usage.

4 a Chief Inspector *UK, 1961*

Police usage.

5 LSD *US*

- — Donald Louria, *Nightmare Drugs*, p. 45, 1966
- — Steve Salaets, *Ye Olde Hiptionary*, 1970

6 used as a term of address *US, 1935*

Jocular, sometimes suggesting deference.

- "With the money you're paying you'll probably get Muhammad Ali. Tara, chief," said Terry as he headed for the door. — Anthony Masters, *Minder*, p. 58, 1984
- TRAINER: Roll up your sleeve, chief. — *Clerks*, 1994

chief *verb*

in a group smoking marijuana, to hog the cigarette or pipe *US*

- — Jim Emerson-Cobb, *Scratching the Dragon*, April 1997

chief cook and bottle washer *noun*

used as a humorous title for someone with important duties and responsibilities *US, 1840*

Often, not always, used with irony.

- Mother as "chief cook and bottle washer," responsible for all tasks that she cannot effectively delegate. — Howard Becker, *Family, Marriage and Parenthood*, p. 545, 1948
- Suppose you had a father like me – chief cook and bottle-washer at sea, and jack-of-all-trades on land. — S.N. Behrman et al., *Fanny*, p. 127, 1955
- The dads wore aprons that said "Chief Cook and Bottle Washer," and they grilled burgers and hot dogs on backyard barbecues. — Caroline Kettlewell, *Skin Game*, p. 36, 1999

chiefie *noun*

used as a friendly term of address to a man *UK: SCOTLAND*

- Ye finished wi that paper, chiefie? — Michael Munro, *The Complete Patter*, 1996

chief itch and rub *noun*

an organisation's key leader *US*

- — Harold Wentworth and Stuart Berg Flexner, *Dictionary of American Slang*, p. 99, 1960
- Do all successful athletic teams need an on-the-field leader, or leaders? If so, who are UTEP's chief itch and rubs this football season? — *El Paso (Texas) Times*, p. 1C, 22nd August 2001

Chief Nasty-Ass of the No-Wipe-Um Tribe *noun*

anyone completely lacking in personal hygiene *US*

- — Jim Crotty, *How to Talk American*, p. 335, 1997

chief of heat *noun*

a non-commissioned officer commanding an artillery battery *US*

- — Hans Halberstadt, *Airborne*, p. 130, 1988

chief of staff *noun*

a soldier's girlfriend back home *US*

Vietnam war usage.

- Yeah, I believe you numbah one soldier 'cuz you write chief of staff in states alla time. — Tony Zidek, *Choi Oi*, p. 123, 1965

chiefs *noun*

▸ **all chiefs and no Indians; too many chiefs and not enough Indians**

used of a situation where too many people are in command and not enough are doing the work *US*

Imagery from the Old West.

chief tin shoe *noun*
a person who has no money at the moment *US*
A mock native Indian name.
- —Connie Eble (Editor), *UNC-CH Campus Slang*, p. 2, Fall 1984

chieva *noun*
heroin *UK, 1998*
Probably a variation of **CHIVA** (heroin).
- —Robert Ashton, *This Is Heroin*, p. 205, 2002
- —Mike Haskins, *Drugs*, p. 283, 2003

chiff *noun*
▷ see: **CHIV**

chiffy *noun*
in prison, a razorblade fixed to a toothbrush handle as an improvised weapon *UK*
A variation on **CHIV**.
- —Angela Devlin, *Prison Patter*, p. 36, 1996

chigger *noun*
a person with Chinese and black ancestors *US*
Derogatory.
- —Connie Eble (Editor), *UNC-CH Campus Slang*, p. 3, Spring 1992

Chihuahua town *noun*
a neighbourhood where many Mexican immigrants or Mexican-Americans live *US, 2967*
- —Frederic G. Cassidy, *Dictionary of American Regional English*, p. 622, 1985

chikwa *adjective*
▷ see: **CHINKER**

child, please!
used for expressing great surprise or disbelief *BAHAMAS*
- Well, child, please! I even din't know she bin pregnant.—John A. Holm, *Dictionary of Bahamian English*, p. 41, 1982

child-proof lid *noun*
a condom *UK*
A pun on a device designed to 'keep children out'.
- —David Rowan, *A Glossary for the 90s*, 1998

chile pimp *noun*
a pimp, especially a Mexican-American pimp, who has no professional pride and only mediocre success in the field *US*
- Black pimps never solicit for their women if they are "true pimps," and call a man who does a cigarette pimp, popcorn pimp, or chile pimp.—Christina and Richard Milner, *Black Players*, p. 33, 1972
- After Vietnam they had taken up where they'd left off. Bessie working, Free Lee chili pimpin' and trying to be nickel slick[.]—Odie Hawkins, *The Busting Out of an Ordinary Man*, p. 137–138, 1985

chili *adjective*
Mexican *US, 1936*
- "No es un problema, chiquita," he said confidently, flashing a little chili chatter he'd picked up in the tomato fields of the Youth Authority.—Seth Morgan, *Homeboy*, p. 64, 1990

chili bean *noun*
a Mexican or Mexican-American; any Spanish-speaking person *US*
Derogatory.
- —Edith A. Folb, *runnin' down some lines*, p. 232, 1980

chili belly *noun*
a Mexican or Mexican-American *US, 1967*
- Junior snarls, "Lissen to the chili bellies cheer that lucky fart." —Iceberg Slim (Robert Beck), *Doom Fox*, p. 179, 1978

chili bowl; chili-bowl haircut *noun*
an untapered haircut that looks as if the barber simply placed a bowl on the person's head and trimmed around the edge of the bowl *US, 1960*
- A group of boys with mohawks sporting leather and chains would be more likely to be asked to "leave the premises" before a bunch of boys with chili-bowl haircuts and blue jeans.—*Tulsa (Oklahoma) World*, 15th January 1999

chili chaser *noun*
an agent of the US Immigration and Naturalization Service Border Patrol *US, 1956*
- —*Maledicta*, p. 166, 1979: 'A glossary of ethnic slurs in American English'

chili choker *noun*
a Mexican or Mexican-American *US*
Derogatory.
- That same night the niggers and chilichokers dragged that boy back to the showers[.]—Seth Morgan, *Homeboy*, p. 152, 1990

chili chomper *noun*
a Mexican or Mexican-American *US*
Derogatory.
- —*Current Slang*, p. 15, Spring 1970

chili eater *noun*
a Mexican or Mexican-American *US, 1911*
Derogatory.
- Mexican officials accused the Canadian catcher, Alex Andreopoulos, of provoking their players by calling them "chili-eaters."—*Los Angeles Times*, p. C8, 11th August 1991

chill *verb*
1 to kill someone *US*
- —Marcus Hanna Boulware, *Jive and Slang of Students in Negro Colleges*, 1947
- Remember the night Stein got chilled out front?—Raymond Chandler, *The Little Sister*, p. 247, 1949

2 to calm down; to be calm *US, 1979*
- Chill, brah. You know who this is?—*Point Break*, 1991
- "Griff," Todd said, "just chill, man."—Francesca Lia Block, *I Was a Teenage Fairy*, p. 109, 1998

3 to idle *US*
- [E]ver since I first sat chilling and rocking to things like John Coltrane's Africa / Brass[.]—Lester Bangs, *Psychotic Reactions and Carburetor Dung*, p. 104, 1972
- All are talking, drinking and chilling.—*Boyz N The Hood*, p. 67, 1990

4 to suddenly slow down while driving after spotting a police car *US*
- —*American Speech*, p. 267, December 1962: 'The language of traffic policemen'

▸ **chill like a megavillain**
to relax *US*
Especially effective in the participle form – 'chillin'.
- —*Surfer Magazine*, p. 30, February 1992

▸ **chill the beef; chill the rap**
to escape prosecution by bribery or intimidation of witnesses *US*
- —Hyman E. Goldin et al., *Dictionary of American Underworld Lingo*, p. 43, 1950

chill *adjective*
1 calm, unexcited *US*
- —*Washington Post Magazine*, p. 17, 13th September 1987

2 excellent *US*
- We were sniffing all night long. It was chill.—Terry Williams, *The Cocaine Kids*, p. 33, 1989

chillax *verb*
to calm down and relax *US*
- —Judi Sanders, *Faced and Faded, Hanging to Hurl*, p. 8, 1993

chilled *adjective*
calm, relaxed *US*
- He had a big .45 Army pistol and generally just flashing it kept the kids chilled and shit to a minimum.—Jess Mowry, *Way Past Cool*, p. 31, 1992

chilled down *adjective*
calm and relaxed *UK, 1990s*
- Tony fell in love with the chilled-down stasis of the place.—Kevin Sampson, *Powder*, p. 195, 1999

chilled out *adjective*
relaxed, especially after chemically enhanced dancing *UK, 1980s*
- The football boys were all loving it and all, getting right off their nuts and dancing their heads off. So a lot of that violence stopped cos every fucker was too chilled-out.—Dave Courtney, *Raving Lunacy*, p. 57, 2000

chillen *noun*
children *US*
A phonetic slurring.
- But chillen, I'm tellin' ya that it took me many weeks[.]—Lester Bangs, *Psychotic Reactions and Carburetor Dung*, p. 10, 1971

chiller *noun*
in publishing or films, a thriller that 'chills the blood' *UK*
The publisher's blurb for Alistair Maclean's *Night Without End*, 1961, describes it as 'a chiller'.

chillicracker *noun*
an Anglo-Indian *UK*
Derogatory. Derives, presumably, from the use of hot spices in Indian cooking contrasted with the bland, essentially white nature of a cracker.
- I'm an Anglo-Indian – a half-chat, a chillicracker, a blackie-white – the first is the polite term – the other's are what they [the full-whites] call us behind our backs. —Berkely Mather, *The Memsahib*, 1977

chill out *verb*
to calm down, to relax *US, 1983*
- — *Rutgers Alumni Magazine*, p. 21, February 1986
- We just chillin' out, drinkin' a little Bird, that's all. —Odie Hawkins, *Great Lawd Buddha*, p. 11, 1990
- JULES: Tell that bitch to be cool! Say, bitch be cool! Say, bitch be cool! PUMPKIN: Chill out, honey! *Pulp Fiction*, 1994
- Chill out, Phil. Four deputies and you, I can live with that. — *Natural Born Killers*, 1994
- Number one, you need to chill out, nigga. — *Jackie Brown*, 1997

chill pill *noun*
a mythical pill that will induce calm *US*
- —Connie Eble (Editor), *UNC-CH Campus Slang*, p. 8, Spring 1982
- Okay, you got it. Just take a chill pill, for Christ's sake. — *Jackie Brown*, 1997
- —Don R. McCreary (Editor), *Dawg Speak*, 2001
- "Take a chill pill," Kim, who really did watch too many American [...] sitcoms, laughed as we sat down[.] —Claire Mansfield and John Mendelssohn, *Dominatrix*, p. 125, 2002
- I'll take a chill pill. I'll be fine. —*heard in conversation in a UK pub*, 7th September 2002

chillum; chilum *noun*
a pipe for smoking marijuana *JAMAICA*
Originally late C18 Hindi for the bowl (*chilam*) of a 'hookah' (*hugga*) intended for tobacco. More than 150 years later a modified usage rolled up in the West Indies. Widely used in the UK thanks, in part, to **HEAD SHOP(S)**.
- [A]rounda chillum with a Thai girl on her way to a finishing school[.] —Richard Neville, *Play Power*, p. 210, 1970
- An Indian chilum was instantly produced[.] —Richard Neville, *Play Power*, p. 233, 1970
- Most Rastas have no interest in violent action – and with such devotion to consuming vast quantities of the very finest sinsemilla ganja in chalices, chillums or spliffs the size of ice-cream cones , how could it be otherwise? —Harry Shapiro, *Waiting For The Man*, 1999

chill with you later
used as a farewell *US*
- — *Washington Post Magazine*, p. 17, 13th September 1987

chilly *adjective*
1 excellent, fashionable, desirable *US, 1971*
- I was a chilly homeboy, yes / I was down because I came to school just to mess around. — All for Love, *School*, 1985

2 cold-hearted *US, 1971*
- That's awful chilly, I tol' her. —Joseph Nazel, *Black Cop*, p. 144, 1974

chilly bin *noun*
a portable cooler *NEW ZEALAND*
- A chilly-bin is a polystgryrene picnic hamper which will keep ice, cold drinks cold up to ten hours, dependably. —John McDermott, *How to Get Lost and Found in New Zealand*, p. 18, 1976
- —John A. Holm, *Dictionary of Bahamian English*, p. 41, 1982

chilly most *adjective*
calm and collected *US*
- —William K. Bentley and James M. Corbett, *Prison Slang*, p. 48, 1992

chime *noun*
1 an hour *US*
- At the Mexican's we could at least get loaded on good hay and forget our misery for a couple of chimes. —Mezz Mezzrow, *Really the Blues*, p. 164, 1946
- —Jack Lait and Lee Mortimer, *New York Confidential*, p. 235, 1948: 'A glossary of Harlemisms'

2 the even firing of a multi-cylinder motocycle engine *UK*
- —Douglas Dunford, *Motorcycle Department, Beaulieu Motor Museum*, 1979

chimer *noun*
a clock or watch *US*
- I asked him what time was it just to see if my chimer was right[.] —A.S. Jackson, *Gentleman Pimp*, p. 128, 1973

chimney *noun*
1 a person who smokes, especially a heavy smoker *UK, 1937*

2 in trucking, a smokestack on a cab *US*
- —Montie Tak, *Truck Talk*, p. 178, 1971

chimney sweep run *noun*
in trucking, a job that requires the driver to handle the freight and get dirty *US*
- —Montie Tak, *Truck Talk*, p. 30, 1971

chimo!
Let's drink! *CANADA*
- Chimo! is the Engineer greeting or toast, derived from the Inuktitut language, meaning "Are you friendly?" — *Canadian Military Engineers – logau.tripod.ca*, 15th June 2002
- "Chimo" is an Inuit greeting that is now used as a toast before drinking as well. — *cbc4kids.ca*, 15th June 2002

chimping *noun*
in digital photography, the activity of reviewing captured images on a camera's screen *US*
Originally used of White House press-photographers who accompanied pointing at such images with a chorus of *oohs* and *aahs* and were, naturally, compared to chimpanzees.
- — *Word of Mouth*, 6th August 2004

chin *noun*
1 gossip, idle conversation *US, 1862*
- Call me sometime and we'll have a good chin. I'm in the book. —Max Shulman, *Rally Round the Flag, Boys!*, p. 209, 1957

2 on a bomber, the area immediately below and slightly behind the nose of the plane *US*
- They had so many, in fact, that they kept the extras up in the chin bubbles. —Robert Mason, *Chickenhawk*, p. 402, 1983
- The Americans hadn't put a chin like that on a plane in forty years. —Stephen Coonts, *Final Flight*, p. 369, 1988

▸ **keep your chin up**
to maintain your courage or fortitutde; often said as an encouraging injunction *UK, 1938*
- Keep your chin up, Liz, and try not to worry. —Lois Duncan, *Don't Look Behind You*, p. 18, 1989
- [K]eep your group's chin up, even in moments of great adversity. —Jean Lipman-Blumen and Harold J. Leavitt, *Hot Groups*, p. 122, 1999

chin *verb*
1 to punch someone on the chin *UK*
- "I'll chin you," put in Terry menacingly. —Anthony Masters, *Minder*, p. 10, 1984
- —Angela Devlin, *Prison Patter*, p. 36, 1996
- Someone, who shall remain nameless, followed him into the corridor and chinned him. One punch – spark out. —Dave Courtney, *Raving Lunacy*, p. 196, 2000
- [A]s the rapist walked past my cell I jumped out and chinned him with all my might. —Jimmy Stockin, *On The Cobbles*, p. 138, 2000
- My best mate threatens to chin him[.] —Danny King, *The Burglar Diaries*, p. 109, 2001

2 to talk idly *US, 1872*
- They used to spend more time chinning than cheating, around here. —Philip Wylie, *Opus 21*, p. 112, 1949
- One night in Hutton's, Kiefer had started chinning about Leo's interest in missing heirs. —Bernard Wolfe, *The Late Risers*, p. 208, 1954
- I've got nothing to do except sit around chinning with little girls like you. —John M. Murtagh and Sara Harris, *Cast the First Stone*, p. 45, 1957

china *noun*
1 a friend, a mate *UK, 1880*
Rhyming slang for **CHINA PLATE**. Also variant 'chiner'.
- Kevin," he said dully, "come on, china. We'd better get them moving. —T.A.G. Hungerford, *The Ridge and the River*, p. 160, 1952
- Toby was an old china of mine. —Charles Raven, *Underworld Nights*, p. 178, 1956
- Never let it be said we let down our old china. —Ray Slattery, *Mobbs' Mob*, p. 33, 1966
- It's champers on the house, me old china. —Frank Hardy, *The Outcasts of Foolgarah*, p. 18, 1971
- Cor, the currant [sun]'s 'ot today, Oates, me old China. — *The Sweeney*, p. 6, 1976
- So what is it? Chinas? —Kathy Lette, *Girls' Night Out*, p. 174, 1987

- You might have put the wind up Father Shelley and his china, but I'm not quaking. —Christopher Brookmyre, *Boiling a Frog*, p. 161, 2000

2 teeth; false teeth *US, 1942*

- —John R. Armore and Joseph D. Wolfe, *Dictionary of Desperation*, p. 24, 1976

China *noun*

1 the whole world other than Europe and English-speaking lands *UK*

A Cockney view of the world, as defined by Julian Franklyn and quoted in the supplement to the 5th edition of the *Dictionary of Slang and Unconventional English*, 1961: 'The place rich folk go for their holidays. The place any person not wearing European dress comes from. Also distant-local, as in "Yeh sends that boy aht fer a errind an' 'e goes orf teh bleed'n Choina!"'.

2 heroin *UK*

From **CHINA CAT** (heroin) or **CHINA WHITE** (heroin). The lower case variant 'china' is sometimes used.

- —Mike Haskins, *Drugs*, p. 283, 2003

China cat *noun*

strong heroin *US*

- —US Department of Justice, *Street Terms*, October 1994
- —Robert Ashton, *This Is Heroin*, p. 208, 2002

china chin *noun*

(of a boxer or fighter) a vulnerability to blows on the chin *US, 1940*

- "Lennox has a china chin," Dundee said. —*Los Angeles Times*, p. 4 (Sports Section), 21st June 2003

China circuit *noun*

in the language of travelling performances, a circuit of small, unsophisticated towns *US*

Named after the Pennsylvania towns of Pottstown, Pottsville and Chambersburg, all of which were home to chamber pot manufacturing concerns.

- —Sherman Louis Sergel, *The Language of Show Biz*, p. 49, 1973

China clipper *noun*

a dishwasher, human or mechanical *US*

Vietnam war usage.

- —*Columbus (Ohio) Citizen-Journal*, p. 14, 21st July 1966
- —Carl Fleischhauer, *A Glossary of Army Slang*, p. 9, 1968

China girl *noun*

Fentanyl™, a synthetic narcotic analgesic that is used as a recreational drug *UK*

- —Harry Shapiro, *Recreational Drugs*, p. 154, 2004

Chinaman *noun*

1 an addiction to heroin or another opiate *US*

- Is getting that Chinaman off his back, too. —Jack Kerouac, *Letter to Neal Cassady*, p. 175, 8 December 1948
- You know, man, Win's just about got the Chinaman off her back! —John Clellon Holmes, *Go*, p. 81, 1952
- The Chinaman's riding you, huh? —Willard Motley, *Let No Man Write My Epitaph*, p. 91, 1958
- She just kicked, she ain't got to worry about the Chinaman no more. —Donald Goines, *Dopefiend*, p. 130, 1971
- I would fool with stuff a little bit and I'd see a Chinaman coming – that is, I'd see a habit coming on – and I would back away and smoke reefers for a while, then I'd juice a while. —Bruce Jackson, *In the Life*, p. 180, 1972
- The Chinaman spoke, and it wasn't a joke / For I knew this was the end. —Dennis Wepman et al., *The Life*, p. 84, 1976

2 a numbing substance put on the penis to forestall ejaculation *TRINIDAD AND TOBAGO*

- —Lise Winer, *Dictionary of the English/Creole of Trinidad & Tobago*, 2003

3 in politics, a mentor or protector *US, 1973*

A term from Chicago, a major cradle of machine politics in the US.

- Chinaman (Polit.) – Political sponsor. Your personal clout, your man upstairs. —Bill Reilly, *Big Al's Official Guide to Chicagoese*, p. 21, 1982
- Then comes my Chinaman – who is called a rabbi in New York, a mentor in the colleges and a political sponsor elsewhere – Delvin, who has plenty of jobs to give out since the shit has to be kept moving. —Robert Campbell, *Junkyard Dog*, p. 7–8, 1986

4 an Irishman *UK*

- —Brendan Behan, *Borstal Boy*, 1956

5 in cricket, a left-handed bowler's leg-break to a right-handed batsman *UK, 1937*

Homage to Elliss 'Puss' Achong, a 1930s West Indian cricketer of Chinese ancestry.

- People go to cricket and find beauty in many things: the church spire, Holding's unholy run up, the rhododendrons, Gower's timing, Sober's chinaman. —*The Times*, 15th July 1985
- [H]e batted shrewdly and creatively and his left-arm chinaman and googly bowling is improving at a pace. —*The Guardian*, 27th January 2003

6 an unshorn lock on a sheep's rump *NEW ZEALAND*

Thought to resemble a pigtail.

- —*Straight Furrow*, 21st February 1968

▸ **must have killed a Chinaman**

there must be a reason for your bad luck *AUSTRALIA*

Chinese people have been in Australia from the earliest colonial times and there was formerly great superstition attached to them. Joe Andersen explains: 'The sighting of an Oriental person before, during or after placing a bet is always regarded as a sure sign that fortune will smile on you. (A run of bad luck is usually attributed to the killing of one by the unlucky punter)'. Today the word 'Chinaman' is long dead and persists only in this saying.

- —Joe Andersen, *Winners Can Laugh*, p. 58, 1982
- You've heard the expression, 'You must have killed a Chinaman,' well I'm so out of luck that I reckon in a past life I must have been a tank driver in Tiananmen Square or something because I must have got dozen's of 'em. —Paul Vautin, *Turn It Up!*, p. 62, 1995

Chinaman on your back; Chinaman on your neck *noun*

the painful symptoms and craving need for drugs experienced by an addict during withdrawal *US, 1959*

- No one knows what it's like to have a Chinaman on your back. —Douglas Rutherford, *The Creeping Flesh*, p. 84, 1963

Chinaman's chance; Chinaman's *noun*

an absence of luck, no real chance at all *US, 1911*

Reflecting the status of the Chinese population of early C20 US.

- Tell me could there be / A Chinaman's chance for me —Leroy Shield and the Victor Hollywood Orchestra, *Sing Song Girl*, 1930

Chinamat *noun*

an inexpensive Chinese restaurant *US*

- —*Maledicta*, p. 155, 1979: 'A glossary of ethnic slurs in American English'

china plate *noun*

a mate *AUSTRALIA, 1905*

Now generally used as a stock idiom: 'me old china plate'.

- —Jim Ramsay, *Cop It Sweet!*, p. 22, 1977
- —Ryan Aven-Bray, *Ridgey Didge Oz Jack Lang*, p. 22, 1983
- Me ole china plate, I knew you'd come! —Tim Winton, *Lockie Leonard*, p. 121, 1997
- For you, Les, me old china plate, it's a pleasure. —Robert G. Barrett, *The Wind and the Monkey*, p. 4, 1999

chin armour *noun*

a false beard *US*

Theatrical usage.

- —Wilfred Granville, *The Theatre Dictionary*, p. 43, 1952

China white *noun*

1 heroin; less frequently, cocaine *US*

The presumed location of the drug's origin (although it's just as likely to come from Pakistan, Afghanistan or Thailand) plus the colour.

- China White they called it when they had first seen the stuff from New York City. —Donald Goines, *Never Die Alone*, p. 53, 1974
- Its euphoric effect is similar to that of heroin, and is in fact being passed off on the street as China White, the exotic Southeast Asian variety considered to be the Cadillac of heroin. —*San Francisco Chronicle*, p. 1, 31st December 1980
- DEALER: Hey, man. You wanna cop some blow? / JUNKIE: Sure, watcha got? Dust, flakes or rocks? / DEALER: I got China White, Mother of Pearl...I reflect what you need. —Grandmaster Flash & The Furious Five featuring Melle Mel, *White Lines*, 1983
- They're dealing China white out of the place like they had a license. —Gerald Petievich, *The Quality of the Informant*, p. 57, 1985
- We all know the story of the whore, who finding her China white to be less and less reliable a friend no matter how much of it she injected into her arm, recalled in desperation the phrase "shooting the shit", and so filled the needle with her own watery excrement and pumped it in[.] —William T. Vollman, *Whores for Gloria*, p. 1, 1991
- He administered fatal injections of "China White" heroin and lay down to die. —Barney Hoskyns, *Waiting For The Sun*, p. 306, 1996
- Though China White is often packaged by refiners in 700-gram bricks, known as units, the universal measure in the global narcotics business is the 1,000-gram kilo. —*New York Times*, p. SM27, 23rd June 2002

2 a tablet of MDMA, the recreational drug best known as ecstasy *UK*

- —Gareth Thomas, *This Is Ecstasy*, p. 54, 2002

3 Fentanyl^{TM}, a synthetic narcotic analgesic that is used as a recreational drug *UK*

- —Harry Shapiro, *Recreational Drugs*, p. 154, 2004

chinch; chintz *noun*

a bedbug *US*

- I found out then that chinches never die. When they get tired of scuffling for their chow and want to retire, they just go and live happily forever after in the Band House.—Mezz Mezzrow, *Really the Blues*, p. 34, 1946
- One night as I awoke a little wee chintz spoke to me as I raised my head / He said, "Don't you get rough and don't you get tough, for you and I both must share this bed."—Bruce Jackson, *Get Your Ass in the Water and Swim Like Me*, p. 211, 1966

chinche *noun*

heroin *UK*

- —Mike Haskins, *Drugs*, p. 283, 2003

chin-chin

used as a toast *UK, 1909*

Originally used as a salutation to Chinese people.

- Lilli raised her glass. "Chin-chin." "Here's how." We drank.—Douglas Rutherford, *The Creeping Flesh*, p. 43, 1963

chin-chin man *noun*

a male homosexual *US*

- —Charles Shafer, *Folk Speech in Texas Prisons*, p. 200, 1990

chinch pad *noun*

an inexpensive, shoddy boarding house or hotel *US, 1958*

- —Clarence Major, *Dictionary of Afro-American Slang*, p. 36, 1970
- Vermin-infested flops were also called flea houses, flea boxes, flea traps, bug houses, louse traps, louse cages, scratch houses, and chinch pads.—Irving Lewis Allen, *The City in Slang*, p. 156, 1993

chinchy *adjective*

1 cheap; parsimonious, stingy *UK, 1400*

- I guess when you get into the atom-bomb class of brains, you get pretty chinchy everywhere else.—Philip Wylie, *Opus 21*, p. 351, 1949
- "You all are so chinchy," Lowry lectured company officials.—Daniel J. Clark, *Like Night & Day*, p. 60, 1997
- Spending by a few board members does seem high, and billing the state $151.21 for attending the funeral of a legislator's wife seems especially chinchy. [Editorial]—*Charleston (West Virginia) Daily Mail*, p. 4A, 2nd March 2000

2 infested with bedbugs *US*

- What in the world would these important big-time musicians want to hang around a chinchy old uptown joint like this for?—Ross Russell, *The Sound*, p. 216, 1961

chinee *noun*

1 a free ticket to a sporting event *US*

- —Don Wilmeth, *The Language of American Popular Entertainment*, p. 52, 1981

2 a Chinese meal, a Chinese take-away; a Chinese restaurant *UK*

3 a Chinese person *US, 1871*

- [A] little Chinee impression of Judge Ito.—Howard Stern, *Miss America*, p. 138, 1995

chinee *adjective*

of a presumed Chinese origin *US*

▸ **not in a chinee world**

impossible; wholly unacceptable *BARBADOS*

From the notion that Chinese language and culture are beyond comprehension.

- I wun be happy wid dat 'cause de impression it gi' to de public is dat de sentence impose by a judge shun gete tek serious! An' dat cyahn be right – not in a Chinee world'.—*Advocate*, p. 9, 31st January 1992

chinee brush *noun*

a numbing liquid put on the penis to delay ejaculation *TRINIDAD AND TOBAGO*

- —Lise Winer, *Dictionary of the English/Creole of Trinidad & Tobago*, 2003

chinee bump *noun*

a black woman's hair temporarily set in neatly aligned clumps to facilitate drying *JAMAICA*

- —Richard Allsopp, *Dictionary of Caribbean English Usage*, p. 151, 1996

chinee shop *noun*

a small neighbourhood grocery shop, whether owned by Chinese people or not *TRINIDAD AND TOBAGO*

- —Lise Winer, *Dictionary of the English/Creole of Trinidad & Tobago*, 2003

Chinese *noun*

1 in circus and carnival usage, hard work, especially hard work without payment *US*

- —Don Wilmeth, *The Language of American Popular Entertainment*, p. 52, 1981

2 a Chinese meal; a Chinese restaurant *UK*

- [P]ubs, a few pints and a Chinese before home[.]— *Time Out*, 22nd February 1980
- Did I tell you I saw Duckers down the Chinese?—Caroline Aherne and Craig Cash, *The Royle Family*, 1999

3 a small grocery store *BAHAMAS*

- —Patricia Clinton-Meicholas, *More Talkin' Bahamian*, p. 30, 1995

4 adulterated heroin *UK*

- —Angela Devlin, *Prison Patter*, p. 36, 1996

Chinese *verb*

in the circus or carnival, to perform heavy labour *US*

- —Joe McKennon, *Circus Lingo*, p. 25, 1980

Chinese *adjective*

in horse racing, said of blurred numbers on the tote board *US*

- —Dan Parker, *The ABC of Horse Racing*, p. 144, 1947

▷ **see:** CHINESE LACQUERED

Chinese ace *noun*

a pilot who makes a landing with one wing lowered; a pilot who has a reputation for crashing planes on landing *US, 1928*

After CHINESE LANDING.

- —Harold Wentworth and Stuart Berg Flexner, *Dictionary of American Slang*, p. 100, 1960
- —*Maledicta*, p. 156, 1979: 'A glossary of ethnic slurs in American English'
- He called me a "damned Chinese ace" – a term developed from the reputation Chinese pilots had in those days for crashing more of their own planes than they shot down of the enemy's.—Carroll V. Glines, *I Could Never Be So Lucky Again*, p. 51, 1991
- A "Chinese ace" was someone who accidentally managed to destroy five planes belonging to his own air force.—*Winged Victory*, p. 384, 1993

Chinese auction *noun*

a charity auction, in which a buyer is selected at random for each item *US*

- —Amy and Denise McFadden, *CoalSpeak*, p. 4, 1997

Chinese burn *noun*

a torment inflicted by grasping a victim's wrist or forearm in both hands and twisting the skin harshly in opposite directions *UK, 1956*

Children's slang for a juvenile cruelty, known in the UK, Canada and Australia. May also be used as a verb.

Chinese copy *noun*

a reproduction that captures the original's defects as well as its strengths *US*

- —*Maledicta*, p. 156, 1979: 'A glossary of ethnic slurs in American English'

Chinese cure *noun*

an all-natural treatment for the symptoms associated with withdrawal from heroin addiction *US*

- A variation of it is known as the Chinese cure, which is carried out with hop and Wampole's Tonic.—William Burroughs, *Junkie*, p. 63, 1953

Chinese cut *noun*

in cricket, a batting stroke that unintentionally deflects the ball off the inside edge of the bat *UK, 1982*

- —Michael Rundell, *The Dictionary of Cricket*, 1985
- He continued to look tentative after the interval, turning to watch as his Chinese cut sent Flintoff's delivery scudding past his leg stump. —*The Guardian*, 9th August 2002

Chinese cut *verb*

in cricket, to perform a Chinese cut *UK, 1982*

- —Michael Rundell, *The Dictionary of Cricket*, 1985

Chinese dolly *noun*

in the television and film industries, a dolly on slanted tracks *US*

- —Ira Konigsberg, *The Complete Film Dictionary*, p. 47, 1987

Chinese dominoes *noun*
in road haulage, a load of bricks *UK*
- — *British Road Services Magazine*, December 1951

Chinese dragons *noun*
LSD *UK*
- — Mike Haskins, *Drugs*, p. 285, 2003

Chinese eyed *adjective*
squinting through tired eyes following the use of marijuana *US*
Described by racial stereotype.

Chinese fashion *adverb*
sex with both participants lying on their sides, the active male lying behind his partner *US*
- — *Maledicta*, p. 198, Winter 1980: 'A new erotic vocabulary'

Chinese fire drill *noun*
1 any situation in which confusion reigns *US*
Frequent use in the Vietnam war.
- As far as Burton was concerned, everything was fouled up like a Chinese fire drill as Hogan finished with his plus 51 to lead Lloyd Mangrum. — *Coshocton (Ohio) Tribune*, p. 8, 5 June 1946
- — *American Speech*, p. 267, December 1962: 'The language of traffic policemen'
- — *Maledicta*, p. 156, 1979: 'A glossary of ethnic slurs in American English'
- — Gregory Clark, *Words of the Vietnam War*, p. 106, 1990

2 a prank loved by generations of American youth in which a car full of people stops at a red light and the passengers suddenly leap from the car, run around it, and get back in as the light turns green *US, 1972*
- — Hugh Rawson, *Wicked Words*, p. 81, 1989
- — Lewis Poteet, *Car & Motorcyle Slang*, p. 49, 1992
- We had stopped to do Chinese fire drill, trading spots during the long ride. I was trading with Dad, taking his spot in the backseat, while he went up front to drive. — Barbara Camens, *Girls' Night Out*, p. 204, 2002

Chinese flush; Chinese straight *noun*
in poker, a worthless hand approximating but not equalling a flush or straight *US*
- — *Maledicta*, p. 156, 1979: 'A glossary of ethnic slurs in American English'

Chinese gunpowder; gunpowder *noun*
cement *UK*
- — *British Road Services Magazine*, December 1951
- — *Drive*, p. 113, 1968

Chinese lacquered; Chinese *adjective*
extremely tired *UK*
Rhyming slang for **KNACKERED** (extremely tired). Recorded in prison use in August 2002.

Chinese lady *noun*
a multiple-seat toilet *NEW ZEALAND*
- Indicative of low regard held for Chinese miners last century. — David McGill, *David McGill's Complete Kiwi Slang Dictionary*, p. 29, 1998

Chinese landing *noun*
the typical angling of an aeroplane when it lands in Antarctica, with one wing low *US, 1918*
Humour based on the premise that 'one wing low' has a certain Chinese ring to it.
- — *Cool Antartica*, 2003: 'Antarctic slang'

Chinese molasses *noun*
opium; heroin *US, 1953*
From the appearance of opium in an early stage of manufacture.
- — Richard A. Spears, *The Slang and Jargon of Drugs and Drink*, p. 105, 1986
- — Mike Haskins, *Drugs*, p. 283, 2003

Chinese needlework *noun*
intravenous use of narcotics *US, 1942*
- — Vincent J. Monteleone, *Criminal Slang*, p. 49, 1949
- Do you go for Chinese needlework, reindeer dust [powdered drugs], Texas tea [marijuana] – that kind of stuff? — Douglas Rutherford, *The Creeping Flesh*, p. 49, 1963
- — *Maledicta*, p. 156, 1979: 'A glossary of ethnic slurs in American English'
- — Mike Haskins, *Drugs*, p. 273, 2003

Chinese red *noun*
heroin *US, 1977*
- — Richard A. Spears, *The Slang and Jargon of Drugs and Drink*, p. 105, 1986
- — Robert Ashton, *This Is Heroin*, p. 205, 2002
- — Mike Haskins, *Drugs*, p. 283, 2003

Chinese rocks *noun*
1 relatively pure heroin *US*
- Wanna go cop / Wanna go get some Chinese Rock / I'm livin' on Chinese Rocks — Dee Dee Ramone and Richard Hell, *Chinese Rocks*, 1975
- — Harry Orsman, *A Dictionary of Modern New Zealand Slang*, p. 27–28, 1999

2 crack cocaine *UK*
- [H]e turned a couple of blue-rinsed old bints on to the joys of Chinese Rocks[.] — Dean Cavanagh, *Mile High Meltdown (Disco Biscuits)*, p. 213, 1996

Chinese rong *noun*
a non-existent disease suffered by soldiers *US*
- — *American Speech*, p. 305, December 1947: 'Imaginary diseases in army and navy parlance'

Chinese rot *noun*
any unidentified skin disease or sexually transmitted infection *US, 1940*
- Imagine the worst of the fungoid-type skin diseases you have ever encountered – ringworm, Dhobie itch, athlete's foot, Chinese rot, saltwater itch, seven year itch. — *Logic of Empire, (reprinted in The Green Hills of Earth)*, p. 225, 1951
- — J.E. Lighter, *Historical Dictionary of American Slang, Volume 1*, p. 405, 1994

Chinese screwdriver *noun*
a hammer *AUSTRALIA*
- — Barry Prentice, 1974

Chinese speed *noun*
ginseng *UK*
- — Tom Hibbert, *Rockspeak!*, p. 38, 1983

Chinese Texan *noun*
a daring, dangerous driver *CANADA*
Toronto usage.
- How do you make a Chinese driver in Scarborough blind? Put a windshield in front of him. — Chris Coyle, 10th June 2002

Chinese tobacco *noun*
opium *US, 1951*
- — Eugene Landy, *The Underground Dictionary*, p. 49, 1971
- — *Maledicta*, p. 156, 1979: 'A glossary of ethnic slurs in American English'
- — Richard A. Spears, *The Slang and Jargon of Drugs and Drink*, p. 105, 1986
- — Mike Haskins, *Drugs*, p. 283, 2003

ching *noun*
1 in betting, odds of 5 – 1 *UK*
- — John McCririck, *John McCririck's World of Betting*, p. 112, 1991

2 five pounds (£5) *UK*
London slang.
- People were begging to pay three ching to party in a field up by the M25. — J.J. Connolly, *Layer Cake*, p. 14, 2000

ching and a half *noun*
in betting, odds of 11 – 2 *UK*
In bookmaker slang **CHING** is 5 – 1, here the addition of a half increases the odds to $5\frac{1}{2}$ – 1 or 11 – 2.
- — John McCririck, *John McCririck's World of Betting*, p. 112, 1991

chingazos *noun*
fisticuffs; blows *US*
Border Spanish used in English conversation by Mexican-Americans.
- Calo has terms for activities, such as eating (refinar), drinking (pistiar), fighting (chingazos), and dancing (borlotear). — George R. Alvarez, *Semiotic Dynamics of an Ethnic-American Sub-Cultural Group*, p. 10, 1965
- — Dagoberto Fuentes and Jose Lopez, *Barrio Language Dictionary*, p. 47, 1974

ching! ching! ching!
used as a descriptive expression of the speed of a quick succession of events *UK, 1974*
Echoic of bells ringing.

chinger *verb*
to grumble; to complain; to scold; hence, to deter a prospective customer *UK*
Used by market traders.
- — Patrick O'Shaughanessy, *Market Traders' Slang*, 1979

chingon *noun*
an important person; a leader *US*
Border Spanish used in English conversation by Mexican-Americans.
- —Dagoberto Fuentes and Jose Lopez, *Barrio Language Dictionary*, p. 48, 1974

chink *noun*
▸ **another push and you'd have been a chink**
used insultingly as a slur on the morals of the subject's mother, imputing that she would have sex with anyone of any race *UK, 1961*

Chink *noun*
1 a Chinese person *US, 1878*
Derives from 'ching-ching', the phonetic understanding of a Chinese courtesy, adopted as a racist term, now obsolete; this abbreviated, still derogatory, variation is much used in Britain and the US. Variants are 'Chinkie' and 'Chinky'.
- Walking into a den of Chinks as though you owned the place. Wonder you didn't get raped, and serve you right if you were. —Ruth Park, *Poor Man's Orange*, p. 65, 1949
- Liang Shih smokes opium – what Chink doesn't?—Nevil Shute, *In The Wet*, p. 28, 1953
- "Sergeant Milligan", he says, "the chinkies aren't going to bother us ever again[.]"—Graeme Kent, *The Queen's Corporal [Six Granada Plays]*, p. 82, 1959
- "Sometimes a chink or wetback gets into the city with some; it doesn't last long."—Clarence Cooper Jr, *The Scene*, p. 83, 1960
- I'm a Paki, Chink, a half-cocked ponce—Ian Dury, *Blackmail Man*, 1977
- Only junk comin' in is with the chinks and niggers, behind them spook Air Force sergeants from Nam.—Edwin Torres, *After Hours*, p. 169, 1979
- That's no NVA man. That's a chink – look at -im, the cocksucker's six and half feet tall.—*Platoon*, 1986
- Close up he looked like a light-skinned brother with a little Chinese or something in him. Strange-looking dude, Chink with nappy hair. —Elmore Leonard, *Bandits*, p. 199, 1987
- Cheech was the wetback,' I said. 'Chong was the chink.—Shane Maloney, *Nice Try*, p. 245, 1998
- I would've probably been ready to bayonet a couple of Chinks too[.] —Danny King, *The Burglar Diaries*, p. 28, 2001

2 a Vietnamese person *US*
- —*Current Slang*, p. 15, Summer 1970

Chink *adjective*
1 Chinese *US*
- Old Pete men suck the black smoke in the Chink laundry back room[.]—William Burroughs, *Naked Lunch*, p. 6, 1957

2 Vietnamese *US*
- —*Current Slang*, Summer 1970

chinker; chikwa; chinqua *adjective*
five *UK*
From Italian *cinque*, via mid-C19 ligua franca.
- [Y]ou might like to count to ten in Polari: una, duey, trey, quater, chicker, sey, setter, otto, nobber, dacha.—Michael Quinion, *World Wide Words*, 1996
- —Paul Baker, *Polari*, p. 169, 2002

chinki-chonks; chinky-chonks *noun*
the Chinese, or Asian people in general *UK*
A derogatory or patronising term, playing on CHINK and CHINKIE in a fashion which suggests a drunken coinage.
- We could fill the school with candidates with four A-levels if we took all the little chinki-chonks who flood the public schools[.]—*The Guardian*, 18th December 1978

Chinkie; Chinky; Chink *noun*
1 something of Chinese origin; a general description of anything perceived to originate in the Far East *AUSTRALIA*
Sometimes spelt (with contemptuous familiarity) with a lower case 'c'.

2 a Chinese meal; a Chinese take-away *US, 1948*
- Hey, I got an idea. Feel like eating Chink?—Max Shulman, *Anyone Got a Match?*, p. 109, 1964
- What he really fancied was getting a take-away Chinky – sweet and sout pork, beef in oyster sauce[.]—Greg Williams, *Diamond Geezers*, p. 191, 1997

chinkie munchy shop *noun*
a Chinese restaurant or take-away *UK*
- —Peter Chippindale, *The British CB Book*, p. 153, 1981

chink ink *noun*
an indelible ink used by card cheats to mark cards *US*
- —George Percy, *The Language of Poker*, p. 20, 1988

chinks *noun*
a small bit of anything, given up grudgingly *GRENADA*
Collected by Richard Allsopp.

chinky *noun*
1 a shop selling Chinese take-away meals *UK*
- The Takeaway. Or, as the locals called it, "The Chinky"[.]—David Parker, *Cool Places*, p. 70, 1998

2 a small firecracker *US*
- —Amy and Denise McFadden, *CoalSpeak*, p. 4, 1997

chinky *adjective*
1 parsimonious *BARBADOS*
- —Frank A. Collymore, *Barbadian Dialect*, p. 29, 1965
- —*American Speech*, p. 57, Spring-Summer 1975: 'Razorback slang'

2 small *TRINIDAD AND TOBAGO, 1956*
- —Lise Winer, *Dictionary of the English/Creole of Trinidad & Tobago*, 2003

Chinky speed *noun*
ginseng *UK*
- —Tom Hibbert, *Rockspeak!*, p. 38, 1983

chinless wonder *noun*
an upper-class man who is naïve or foolish; or is considered to be foolish by virtue of his privileged circumstances *UK*
While 'chinless' may be an accurate physical description of some, figuratively it is seen to suggest a weakness of character.
- They are all ex-public schoolboys and are different from the others altogether in dress and manner. [...] The mob look at them in disgust. CHARLIE [Michael Caine]: All right. These chinless wonders are going to get you out of Turin [...] Don't be frightened by their posh accents.—Troy Kennedy Martin, *The Italian Job [uncut script]*, 1969
- A couple of years ago I had the onerous job of showing some chinless wonder from England over the Australian outback.—Barry Humphries, *The Traveller's Tool*, p. 132, 1985
- Look at the opposition. One of three chinless wonders.—Shane Maloney, *Nice Try*, p. 125, 1998

chin music *noun*
gossip, idle conversation *UK, 1826*
- "Cut out all that chin music!" he would holler.—Bobby Seale, *A Lonely Rage*, p. 5, 1978

chinois *noun*
▷ **see:** SCHINWHARS

Chinook arch *noun*
in western Canada, an archway of cloud forecasting the arrival of Chinook winds *CANADA*
- This Chinook arch appeared in the western sky Sunday but its usual promise of warm air sweeping in from the west is not expected to come true.—*Calgary Herald*, p. 1/1, 6th January 1964

Chinook fever *noun*
among Calgary newcomers, a sort of ill-ease like spring fever, during warm winter days caused by Chinook winds *CANADA*
- "You're suffering from a typical case of Chinook fever," the doctor said. "People coming here from the coast are particularly vulnerable."—*Calgary Herald*, p. 4–5, 6th December 1963

chin pubes *noun*
sparse facial hair *US*
- You don't want to be the last one at the coffee house without chin pubes.—*Clueless*, 1995

chinqua *adjective*
▷ **see:** CHINKER

chinstrap *noun*
▸ **on your chinstrap**
extremely tired *UK*
Military. Also occasionally, but not military, 'on your nose'.
- I was on my chinstrap one day. We'd probably covered twice the distance we should have done[.]—Andy McNab, *Immediate Action*, p. 99, 1995

chintz *noun*
a cheapskate *US, 1949*
- —*American Weekly*, p. 2, 14th August 1955

▷ **see:** CHINCH

chintzy *adjective*

cheap, miserly, stingy *UK, 1902*

- There are the 1919 Chicago White Sox, infamously known as the Black Sox, who threw the World Series to make some money and to spite their chintzy owner, Charles Comiskey. —Chad Millman, *The Odds*, p. 38, 2001

chinwag *noun*

a chat, a conversation *UK, 1879*

- Suke and I will have a little chin-wag in the other room! —Barry Humphries, *Bazza Pulls It Off!*, 1971
- I shall long remember the former's look of breezy jollity as he recklessly intrudes on an all-girl chinwag[.] — *The Guardian*, 9th April 2002

chinwag *verb*

to chat, to converse *UK, 1920*

- [S]he wanted to adjourn to a club in Soho to chinwag about art with some of her friends. —John Milne, *Alive and Kicking*, p. 60, 1998

chin-whiskered *adjective*

small-time, lacking professionalism *US, 1930*

A logging term.

- —Frederic G. Cassidy, *Dictionary of American Regional English*, p. 636, 1985

chip *noun*

1 heroin, particularly when weakened below the market norm *US, 1974*

- —Richard A. Spears, *The Slang and Jargon of Drugs and Drink*, p. 105, 1986
- —Robert Ashton, *This Is Heroin*, p. 205, 2002
- —Mike Haskins, *Drugs*, p. 283, 2003

2 a shilling *UK*

Hence, **HALF A CHIP** (6d).

- —Paul Tempest, *Lag's Lexicon*, 1950

3 in games of chance, a counter that represents a monetary value *US, 1840*

4 a cash register *US*

- —Hyman E. Goldin et al., *Dictionary of American Underworld Lingo*, p. 43, 1950

5 a *chip*olata sausage *UK*

Usually used in the plural. Noted by Anthony Burgess in a letter to Partridge, 1967.

6 a quarrel *AUSTRALIA*

- We had a bit of a chip over one thing and another. —Kylie Tennant, *Lost Haven*, 1947

7 a small surfboard made from lightweight balsa wood *US*

Also known as a 'potato chip'.

- —John Severson, *Modern Surfing Around the World*, p. 166, 1964

Chip; Chippie; Chippy *noun*

a member of the California Highway Patrol *US*

Thanks to the 1977–1983 television series *CHiPS*.

- "CHIPS" stands for California Highway Patrol. The "i" was added because "CHPs" is hard to pronounce and the guys don't like being called "Chippies." — *The Washington Post*, p. D13, 15th September 1977
- He couldn't understand what the Chippy wanted. Maybe he'd better pull over. Then an extraordinary thing happened. The Chip yelled at him so loudly it hurt. —Joseph Wambaugh, *The Glitter Dome*, p. 11, 1981
- The Chippie, frequently interrupted by Nelson's "Whadhesay?" learned that the husky bald man had stashed the stolen car[.] —Joseph Wambaugh, *Fugitive Nights*, p. 69–70, 1992
- It was the CHiPs versus the Deputies in a turf war as members of the Alameda County Sheriff's Department and the California Highway Patrol landed verbal punches over traffick patrols in unincorporated areas. — *The Argus (Fremont, California)*, 19th March 2003

chip *verb*

1 to use drugs occasionally or irregularly *US*

Applied to all narcotics but especially heroin.

- Well, all the studs I knew was on stuff now, and their habits was a good mile long / but I thought I could chip and never get hooked, for my will was strong. —Bruce Jackson, *Get Your Ass in the Water and Swim Like Me*, p. 91, 1964
- He was only "chipping," using drugs occasionally when they were handy, and had not yet acquired a habit. —James Mills, *The Panic in Needle Park*, p. 29, 1966
- Prince whistled. "He sure ain't chippin' then. That's a goddamn oil-burner." —Donald Goines, *Black Gangster*, p. 128, 1977
- I don't mind chipping when I know I'm chipping – that was what we called just biting off a corner of a tab just for the buzz. —Stephen Gaskin, *Amazing Dope Tales*, p. 20, 1980

2 to depart, to go *UK*

- Well, Lloyd, gotta chip, man. I said I'd meet Sharron at six. —Donald Gorgon, *Cop Killer*, p. 122, 1994
- She hung about tryin to sort him but he weren't havin it so she chipped. —J.J. Connolly, *Layer Cake*, p. 176, 2000

3 to find fault with someone; to reprimand someone *AUSTRALIA, 1915*

- —Robert S. Close, *With Hooves of Brass*, p. 59, 1961
- —Jim Ramsay, *Cop It Sweet!*, p. 22, 1977
- One time, that head stockman, Doug Houghton, chipped this bloke who'd come from another station – he never used to wash[.] —Herb Wharton, *Cattle Camp*, p. 93, 1994

4 in shuffleboard, to barely touch another disc *US*

- —Omero C. Catan, *Secrets of Shuffleboard Strategy*, p. 65, 1967

▸ **chip the ivories**

to take part in casual conversation *US, 1945*

- —Harold Wentworth and Stuart Berg Flexner, *Dictionary of American Slang*, p. 102, 1960

▸ **chip your teeth**

1 to become very angry *US*

- — *American Speech*, p. 268, December 1962: 'The language of traffic policemen'

2 to talk incessantly *US*

- Okay, okay, quit chipping your teeth. You complain more than any kid I ever saw. —Joseph Wambaugh, *The Blue Knight*, p. 252, 1973

chip along; chip in *verb*

in poker, to make the minimum bet required *US*

- —George Percy, *The Language of Poker*, p. 20, 1988

chip back *verb*

to rebate an amount, to discount an amount *UK*

Second-hand car-dealers' use.

- I'd want some change out of that. Can't you chip me a tenner back? — *Sunday Times*, 24th October 1965

chip dip *noun*

an adhesive placed on a cheater's palm, enabling him to steal chips as he helpfully slides a pile of chips in a poker game to the winner *US*

- —George Percy, *The Language of Poker*, p. 19, 1988

chip head *noun*

a computer enthusiast *US*

- — *Merriam-Webster's Hot Words on Campus Marketing Survey '93*, p. 2, 13th October 1993

chip in *verb*

1 to contribute to an undertaking; to make a contribution *US, 1861*

- [P]articipants in the annual Prince William spring golf tournament usually chip in a total of about $30,000 to the campaign fund of their local Democratic politician and host. — *Washington Post*, 20th March 2003

2 to interpose smartly in a converation, discussion or speech; occasionally, by so doing, to interfere *US, c.1870*

- "My Democrat colleague hasn't done his homework on this one, Peter," she chips in cheerfully. — *The Guardian*, 6th May 2000

chip off the old block *noun*

someone with the same character as a parent; someone with inherited characteristics *UK, 1642*

Originally 'a chip of the same (old) block'.

- Far from being a chip off the old block, [George Gilbert] Scott Jr was a kind of revolutionary. — *The Guardian*, 9th December 2002

chip on your shoulder *noun*

a grievance or a sense of inferiority which is often manifested in defiance or ill-humoured behaviour *US, 1855*

Derives, probably, from juvenile conflict: when two boys were determined to fight, a chip of wood was placed on the shoulder of one, and the other challenged to knock it off.

- [T]he teenage [Tom] Cox often plays with a jumbo-sized class-chip on his shoulder, desperate to say: "My clubs aren't as good as your clubs, my clothes don't have labels on, I drink Happy Shopper ginger beer – but I've still beaten the lot of you!" — *The Guardian*, 10th August 2002

chipper *noun*

1 a chip shop *IRELAND*

- 'Let's go inside' he said, just as it was getting dark and the last of the queue filed from the chipper. —Neil Jordon, *Night in Tunisia*, p. 24, 1993

- [T]hen run, feet not touching the ground, farting helium, greeting the early morning crows cleaning up outside the chipper[.] —Ardal O'Hanlon, *The Talk of The Town*, p. 67, 1998
- This development is understandable, and largely due to the arrival of international burger chains, pizza delivery services, Chinese take-aways and kebab joints, but a good chipper can still be judged by the quality of its fish and chips. — *Irish Times*, 12th September 1998

2 an occasional non-habitual drug-user *US, 1938*

- —Macfarlane, Macfarlane and Robson, *The User*, p. ix, 1996
- —Robert Ashton, *This Is Heroin*, p. 208, 2002

3 in prison, an illegal tinder box *UK*

- —Paul Tempest, *Lag's Lexicon*, 1950

chipper *adjective*

well, fit, lively *US, 1840*

- [J]ust a small cup of it turned out to be an antidote that had me feeling chipper enough to order some more. —Calvin Trillin, *The Tummy Trilogy*, p. 122, 1983
- Your apartment burned down last night, so today you've been feeling chipper, you'll just go to tea in Skokie. —Sara Paretsky, *Killing Orders*, p. 211, 1985
- I'm starting to feel quite chipper. —Kevin Sampson, *Outlaws*, p. 20, 2001

chippy; chippie *noun*

1 a fish-and-chip shop *UK, 1961*

- "I think there are very real questions about what the role of head teachers will be. From November 1, do we really have to lose every lunchtime to supervise the chippie down the road?" — *The Guardian*, 29th July 1986
- [A]t the bus stop by the chippie[.] —Patrick Jones, *Unprotected Sex*, p. 210, 1999
- We've got our chippies, the hot-dog van, a Chinese takeaway, an Indian. —John King, *Human Punk*, p. 79, 2000
- To the chippy for a portion, saveloy, gherkin, in salt and vinegar. —Mark Powell, *Snap*, p. 28, 2001

2 a person who uses addictive drugs occasionally without developing a habit *US, 1924*

- She's no chippie, man. —Alexander Trocchi, *Cain's Book*, p. 29, 1960

3 a modest drug addiction *US, 1964*

- At the moment, like Sammy, he had only a chippy, and got most of the heroin he needed by hanging around other addicts who occassionally turned him on with a taste[.] —James Mills, *The Panic in Needle Park*, p. 35, 1966

4 a young woman, usually of loose morals, at times a semi-professional prostitute *US, 1886*

- That was some other quick-trick chippy. —Thurston Scott, *Cure it with Honey*, p. 143, 1951
- I deserve it for acting like a two dollar chippie! —John Clellon Holmes, *Go*, p. 134, 1952
- [W]hy would I fool around with some chippy when I had you? —Jim Thompson, *The Killer Inside*, p. 61, 1952
- A guilty furtiveness in the gray eyes. The cast of weakness across the mouth, with its sullten swollen lips. The look of the chippy. —John D. McDonald, *The Neon Jungle*, p. 26, 1953
- He played the pads on Saturday night and jumped with the chippies till broad daylight. —Dan Burley, *Diggeth Thou?*, p. 22, 1959
- Also, he had gotten into the habit of falling in love with teen-age girls, like this Chippy on the Strip, for whom he had just bought a new cloth coat. —Clancy Sigal, *Going Away*, p. 3, 1961
- A nice-looking chippy, drunk as hell, staggered toward me and tried to put her arms around me[.] —Piri Thomas, *Down These Mean Streets*, p. 232, 1967
- This is what my father used to call "a chippy." Of course! And can I bring home a chippy, Doctor? —Philip Roth, *Portnoy's Complaint*, p. 226, 1969
- "We had a few drinks aftewards." "We? You and some chippie from Ruffles?" —Armistead Maupin, *Tales of the City*, p. 36, 1978
- Pretty Melvin, the fickle humper, the dapper campus god, cruising with Reba plastered against him in his low-riding purple chippie-catcher. —Iceberg Slim (Robert Beck), *Doom Fox*, p. 3, 1978

5 a carpenter *UK, 1916*

Also in the reduced form 'chips'.

- —Oswald Skilbeck, *ABC of Film and TV Working Terms*, p. 28, 1960
- But scores of workers – including dockies, wharfies and chippies – regard the Pacific Hotel in Stephen St as a second home. — *Glebe and Western Weekly*, p. 2, 8th November 1989
- In the heart of Glasgow, a group of women are becoming brickies and chippies, and making that dream come true. — *The Guardian*, 2nd August 1999

6 cocaine *UK, 1998*

- —Mike Haskins, *Drugs*, p. 280, 2003

7 marijuana *UK*

- —Mike Haskins, *Drugs*, p. 287, 2003

8 a person in a gambling casino who tries to hustle or steal chips *US*

- —Victor H. Royer, *Casino Gamble Talk*, p. 32, 2003

9 an inexperienced gambler *US*

- —Steve Kuriscak, *Casino Talk*, p. 12, 1985

chippy; chippie *noun*

▷ see: CHIP

chippy; chippie *verb*

1 to be unfaithful sexually *US, 1930*

- "You ever chippied on your wife?" "Never." Never chippied on your wife one time in eighteen years?" "Never." —Lenny Bruce, *How to Talk Dirty and Influence People*, p. 104, 1965
- But Momma's an alcoholic, chippying on Dad. —Christina and Richard Milner, *Black Players*, p. 264, 1972
- They will avoid bars and restaurants that are patronized by girls who, they feel, have inferior status as professionals or whom they consider amateurs just "chipping around"[.] —Harold Greenwald, *The Call Girl*, p. 18, 1978
- Prince Ranier and Princess Grace couldn't have afforded to get caught chippyinig around, but it's different here. —Joseph Wambaugh, *Fugitive Nights*, p. 8–9, 1992

2 to use drugs occasionally but not habitually *US, 1924*

Applied particularly to heroin.

- "Hoss was his Boss." He had chippied around and gotten hooked. —Iceberg Slim (Robert Beck), *Pimp*, p. 63, 1969

chippy *adjective*

1 impudent *UK, 1888*

- Unlike his jolly, hairy and friendly off-screen self, [Paul] Merton's on-screen persona is surly, disruptive, a bit chippy, dangerous[.] — *The Daily Telegraph*, 21st April 2003

2 quarrelsome, dirty, rough *UK, 1898*

- Spearing is the sort of chippy crime Shack might commit. — *Toronto Globe and Mail*, p. 22/1, 27th December 1965

3 unwell, especially as a result of drinking alcohol; hungover *UK, 1877*

chippy chaser *noun*

a man obsessed with the seduction of women *US*

- — *Maledicta*, p. 10, Summer 1977: 'A word for it!'

chippy joint; chippie joint *noun*

a brothel *US*

- —Jay Robert Nash, *Dictionary of Crime*, p. 63, 1992

chips *noun*

1 money *US, 1840*

- So when the big day rolled around I spent my last chips on a taxi. —Mezz Mezzrow, *Really the Blues*, p. 152, 1946
- Nay, old dude, I don't need chips. —A.S. Jackson, *Gentleman Pimp*, p. 41, 1973

2 the action of looking out or serving as a watchman *SOUTH AFRICA*

If a school boy is smoking a cigarette in the toilet, his friend will 'keep chips' for him.

▷ see: CHIBS

▸ **get your chips**

to be dismissed from employment *UK*

- —Albert E. Petch, 1969

▸ **have had your chips**

to have been beaten; to be finished or utterly defeated; to have been killed *UK, 1959*

Ultimately from gambling symbolism.

- In 1997 Enfield Southgate told Michael Portillo he'd had his chips. — *Vote 2001', BBCi*, 1st June 2001

▸ **have your chips**

to be ruined *UK, 1959*

- Except [Sarel] Burger had made only 5. Oh well, he's had his chips now[.] — *The Guardian*, 19th February 2003

▸ **in the chips**

1 well funded *US, 1842*

- If you're in the chips and Burroughs feels good, all three of you could come out here for kicks sometime. —Jack Kerouac, *Letter to Neal Cassady*, p. 115, 26th August 1947

2 in poker, winning *US*

- —George Percy, *The Language of Poker*, p. 47, 1988

▸ when the chips are down
at the crucial moment *US, 1943*
- When the chips are down you play safe. When the blue chips are down you go to war. — *The Observer*, 16th March 2003

chips and peas; chips *noun*
the knees *UK*
Rhyming slang.
- — Ray Puxley, *Fresh Rabbit*, 1998
- She was down on her chips before I'd got my trousers off. — Bodmin Dark, *Dirty Cockney Rhyming Slang*, 2003

chips and salsa *noun*
a computer's hardware *US*
- — Anna Scotti and Paul Young, *Buzzwords*, p. 116, 1997

chips and whetstones *noun*
odds and ends *US, 1927*
- You're like as not famished, Mr. Birdwell, delivering trees all day and feeding and chips and whetstones. — Jessamym West, *The Friendly Persuasion*, p. 154, 1945

chira *noun*
marijuana, especially shredded marijuana
Originally South American Spanish.
- [T]o prohibit the export of the resin obtained from Indian hemp and the ordinary preparations of which the resin forms the base (such as hashish, esrar, chiras [chira], djamba) to countries which have prohibited their use. — *Second Opium Conference 1924–5, The League of Nations*,
- — Richard A. Spears, *The Slang and Jargon of Drugs and Drink*, p. 106, 1986
- — Mike Haskins, *Drugs*, p. 287, 2003

chiro *noun*
a *chiro*practor *AUSTRALIA*
- — Lenie Johansen, *The Dinkum Dictionary*, 1991

chirp *noun*
1 a female singer *US, 1944*
- — Jack Lait and Lee Mortimer, *New York Confidential*, p. 235, 1948: 'A glossary of Harlemisms'
- — Robert S. Gold, *A Jazz Lexicon*, p. 56, 1964

2 a type of manipulation of a record to create a musical effect *UK*
Derives from the 'chirping' sound that is created.
- With the chirp, you are using the crossfader to cut off the beginning and end of the sample[.] — J. Hoggarth, *How To Be a DJ*, p. 93, 2002

3 a quick use of cocaine *US*
- — Anna Scotti and Paul Young, *Buzzwords*, p. 130, 1997

chirp *verb*
to make an exaggerated kissing sound *US*
- — Hyman E. Goldin et al., *Dictionary of American Underworld Lingo*, p. 43, 1950

chirpiness *noun*
liveliness, cheerfulness, a pleasing pertness *UK, 1867*
The state of being **CHIRPY**.
- [Brenda] Blethyn's performance, combining an outward chirpiness with an inner turmoil, brought her an Oscar nomination. — Andrew Walker, *BBC News*, 18th October 2002

chirps *verb*
to talk persuasively to someone as a strategy for attempted seduction, to flirt *UK*
- P Diddy is STILL trying to chirps J-Lo! — *RWD – UK Underground Urban Music Magazine*, 16th February 2004

chirpy *adjective*
always happy *UK, 1837*
From the cheerful chirping of songbirds.
- Mr. Frank Chapple, the electricians' union leader, is rough, tough and right wing – a sort of chirpy British version of an American trade union leader[.] — *The Economist*, p. 80, 21st January 1978
- During the war these tunnels were lined with bunks and makeshift beds and helped foster that indomitable, "chirpy" spirit which really did exist among Londoners at the time. — Brian McDonald, *Elephant Boys*, p. 27, 2000
- They've already snapped up the rights to her chirpy Oirish [Irish] romance[.] — *The Guardian*, 11th January 2003

chirrupy *adjective*
cheerfully chatty *UK, 1808*
- [Richard] Strauss was a secretive man, and his chirrupy letters to [Hugo von] Hofmannsthal make no mention of the trauma he was going through. — *The Guardian*, 21st March 2003

chisboy *noun*
a pampered youth *SOUTH AFRICA*
Derogatory or disdainful teenage slang from the South African townships.
- [T]eenagers who attend private schools or mixed-race public schools. The township youth often refer to them as "chisboys" – a derogatory term that means "spoiled brat". — *Sunday Times (South Africa)*, 1st June 2003

chisel *noun*
▸ on the chisel
involved in a swindle *US*
- My old man owns the company. He'd be pretty sore if I was on the chisel. — Raymond Chandler, *Playback*, p. 44, 1958

chisel *verb*
1 to cheat *UK, 1808*
- And he was proud of his chiseling. He felt the crisp five-dollar bill in his pocket. — James T. Farrell, *Saturday Night*, p. 18, 1947
- Can you imagine people that can afford to drive thirty- and forty-thousand-dollar cars chiseling an insurance company for five hundred bucks? — Gerald Petievich, *To Die in Beverly Hills*, p. 209, 1983
- Serenity never tried to chisel her girls and wouldn't stand for it in return. — Joseph Wambaugh, *Floaters*, p. 13, 1996

2 to place small, conservative bets *US*
- — *The Annals of the American Academy of Political and Social Sciences*, p. 122, May 1950

chisel charter *noun*
an illegal bush plane charter *CANADA*
- The "chisel charter" is usually done by a private pilot without a charter license. The costs are much lower than those of a legitimate charter operator. — Lewis Poteet, *Plane Talk*, p. 47, 1997

chiseled *adjective*
without fat, well sculpted *US*
- — *American Speech*, p. 198, Fall 1984: 'The language of body building'

chiseler *noun*
1 a cheat, a petty swindler *US, 1918*
- "I don't like competition from amateur chiselers," Dopey said. — James T. Farrell, *Saturday Night*, p. 27, 1947
- "Amboy Dukes are supposed to be regular guys" – she wept and clutched her purse with both hands – "not a bunch of chiselers." — Irving Shulman, *The Amboy Dukes*, p. 43, 1947
- [M]any a fearful anhd repentant chiseler has been fleeced by smart operators who told him they were wonder-workers. — Jack Lait and Lee Mortimer, *Washington Confidential*, p. 161, 1951
- Two of the worst chiselers I ever seen. Why, I'd never seen the characters before, and they tired to put the bite on me! — Jim Thompson, *Roughneck*, p. 144, 1954

2 a gambler who places small, conservative bets *US*
- — *The Annals of the American Academy of Political and Social Sciences*, p. 122, May 1950

chisler *noun*
a hardy child, usually a boy *IRELAND*
- Men, women and chislers tilted askew in the blustery square. — *The Guardian*, p. 26, 6th February 1993
- Corkery recalls that, on the streets of Summerhill, "chislers would play in the sun; fish and chips would scent the air; oul' wans sitting on the windows of the tall old houses taking the sunshine would give and receive the news. — *Irish Times*, 2nd January 1999

chisme *noun*
gossip; rumours *US*
Border Spanish used in English conversation by Mexican-Americans.
- — Dagoberto Fuentes and Jose Lopez, *Barrio Language Dictionary*, p. 48, 1974

chit *noun*
a youthful-looking homosexual male *US*
- — *Maledicta*, p. 155, Summer/Winter 1986–1987: 'Sexual slang: prostitutes, pedophiles, flagellators, transvestites, and necrophiles'

chit *verb*
to sign a chit accepting responsbility for an item or amount of money *US*
- I chitted for the contents of one station. — James Ellroy, *Suicide Hill*, p. 685, 1986

chitari *noun*
marijuana *US, 2001*
- — Simon Worman, *Joint Smoking Rules*, 2001

chit-chat *noun*

small talk *UK, 1605*

- Maybe later, if things cooled out a little, they could manage a little chit-chat[.] —Gurney Norman, *Divine Right's Trip (Last Whole Earth Catalog)*, p. 87, 1971
- Well, enough chitchat. Let's get to work. —Armistead Maupin, *Tales of the City*, p. 52, 1978
- Neither of us is a big one for chit-chat, we just go about our own thing. —Kevin Sampson, *Clubland*, p. 75, 2002

chit-chat *verb*

to engage in small talk *UK, 1821*

- [W]e stand in the chekcout line, chit-chattin'. —Odie Hawkins, *Ghetto Sketches*, p. 126, 1972
- The staff wants to be chit-chatting all the time. —Brian Preston, *Pot Planet*, p. 132, 2002

Chitlin Circuit *noun*

the notional collection of ghetto bars and nightclubs where black musicians perform in the hope of having a hit that will launch them into better venues *US*

A term which Shaw attributes to black singer Lou Rawls.

- He [Rawls] used to sing on what he calls "the chitlin' circuit"- "Places so small you had to dress in the men's room." —*Times Recorder (Zanesville, Ohio)*, p. 2-B, 28th May 1967
- —Arnold Shaw, *Dictionary of American Pop/Rock*, p. 74, 1982

Chitlins 101 *noun*

any black studies course *US*

A derogatory term, drawing from 'chitterlings', a dish made with pork innards.

- "Normally, when people think of a black institution, they think of 'Chitlins 101' – something not very sophisticated," he added. —*Chicago Tribune*, p. CN1, 22nd July 1998

Chi-town *nickname*

Chicago, Illinois *US, 1922*

- By the time we hit that "Chi-town" / Them bears were a-gettin smart[.] —C.W. McCall, *Convoy*, 1976
- We gotta book. We're catching a bus to Chi-town. —*Chasing Amy*, 1997

chiv; chive; chiff *noun*

a knife, a razor or other blade used as a cutting weapon *UK, 1673*

Of Romany origin.

- He is a dark, middle-sized, middle-aged geezer with an ugly, oh but definitely ugly, kisser and a navy blue, chiv-scarred jowl. —Charles Raven, *Underworld Nights*, p. 9, 1956

chiv; chive *verb*

to cut someone with a knife or a razor *UK, 1812*

Multiple variant spellings, including 'shive', 'shiv' and 'shife'. Probably from 'shive' (to slice bread), 1570; originally seen in this sense as 'chive', 1725; 'chiv' is not recorded until 1812; 'shiv' and 'shive' are C20 variations that hark back to the word's origins.

- I always wondered if he had dipped his head and grinned before he started chiving on him. —Chester Himes, *Cast the First Stone*, p. 202, 1952
- [R]espectable screwsmen [thieves] daren't walk home from their gaffs at night for fear being chivved by teddy-boys, and left to bleed to death over the ragwort in a bomb-site[.] —Charles Raven, *Underworld Nights*, p. 41, 1956
- a bit nervous of the ponces who'd shive them without thinking —Derek Raymond (Robin Cook), *The Crust on its Uppers*, p. 33, 1962
- —Angela Devlin, *Prison Patter*, p. 102, 1996

chiva *noun*

heroin *US, 1967*

From the Spanish of Mexican-Americans.

- Depending on who is listening, heroin can be referred to as carga (heroin), la chiva (the thing), or la madre (the mother). —George R. Alvarez, *Semiotic Dynamics of an Ethnic-American Sub-Cultural Group*, p. 4, 1965
- —Dagoberto Fuentes, *Barrio Language Dictionary*, p. 48, 1974
- —Geoffrey Froner, *Digging for Diamonds*, p. 18, 1989
- Next to the highgrade chiva he dealt, La Barba was proudest of his lowrider. —Seth Morgan, *Homeboy*, p. 57, 1990

chix *noun*

a Pacific halibut under 4.5 kg *CANADA, 1989*

- In the days when commercial fishermen caught halibut by handline, they preferred the greater work of catching as many chix as opposed to 45 kg. "barn doors" because the men were paid by the fish. —Tom Parkin, *WetCoast Words*, p. 33, 1989

chiz *noun*

1 in circus and carnival usage, a swindler *US*

An abbreviation of **CHISELER**.

- —Don Wilmeth, *The Language of American Popular Entertainment*, p. 52, 1981

2 an annoying occurrence or circumstance *UK, 1953*

From the verb **CHISEL** (to cheat).

- TIM[:] OH, NO! (Pause) Major chiz, Mrs P. England are 181 for 5. —Harry Enfield, *Harry Enfield and His Humorous Chums*, p. 51, 1997

3 the best *US*

- —Anna Scotti and Paul Young, *Buzzwords*, p. 89, 1997

Chizler *noun*

a Chrysler car or engine *US*

- —Lyle K. Engel, *The Complete Book of Fuel and Gas Dragsters*, p. 150, 1968
- —Robert C. Post, *High Performance*, p. 359, 2001

cho!; cha!; chaa!

used for registering impatience, disdain or disappointment *JAMAICA, 1827*

- Bow-Wow simply kissed his teeth and said "Cho'!" —Karline Smith, *Moss Side Massive*, p. 179, 1994
- Cho' man, this is pure road block. —Donald Gorgon, *Cop Killer*, p. 12, 1994
- Chaa. Ever since he got that motor he ain't had nothing but aggravation, man. —Greg Williams, *Diamond Geezers*, p. 31, 1997
- Cha man, wassup wid you now Orry? I only wanned you to do me a favour. —Courttia Newland, *Society Within*, p. 16, 1999
- —Paul Sullivan, *Sullivan's Music Trivia*, p. 35, 2003

choad *noun*

1 the penis *US, 1968*

- [N]obody to my knowledge spoke of "choad," "rod," stem" or any other more strictly pornographic term. —*Screw*, p. 5, 3rd January 1972
- —Christian Crumlish, *The Internet Dictionary*, p. 34, 1995

2 a person who is easily despised *US*

Sometimes spelt 'chode'.

- —Connie Eble (Editor), *UNC-CH Campus Slang*, p. 2, Spring 1998
- "Break up with that choad," he said. —Megan McCafferty, *Second Helpings*, p. 207, 2003

choc *noun*

1 chocolate, a chocolate *UK, 1896*

Variants are 'choccy' and 'chocky'.

- When it comes to proper choccies and cooking, French converture chocolate is the tops. —*The Observer*, 24th October 1999
- 'I adopted the fire-hose method of management. I stood with my mouth open and they poured into it'. Does he [Todd Stitzer, boss of Cadbury Schweppes] mean the chocs? —*The Daily Telegraph*, 2nd November 2004

2 a non-white, especially an African *SOUTH AFRICA*

A shortening of 'chocolate' that is both derogatory and offensive.

- —Jean Branford, *A Dictionary of South African English*, 1978

3 a person of Mediterranean or Middle Eastern background *AUSTRALIA*

Short for **CHOCOLATE FROG**. Offensive.

- This one's called Petro. He's a big choc, you know really woggy. —Kathy Lette, *Girls' Night Out*, p. 126, 1987

choc beer *noun*

an unfiltered ale, sweeter and fruitier than traditional beer, brewed in Oklahoma *US*

From the Choctaw Indians, who are said to have taught immigrant Italians the recipe for the beer.

- A sign behind the latter fixture announced that choc beer was fifteen cents, whiskey two shots for a quarter. —Jim Thompson, *Roughneck*, p. 90, 1954

choccy *noun*

a cough after chocolate has been in the mouth *UK*

- A choccy produced by a friend of mine was visible on the wall of the gym for over nine months[.] —Chris Lewis, *The Dictionary of Playground Slang*, p. 57, 2003

choccy!

used for expressing approval *UK*

- — Susie Dent, *The Language Report*, p. 75, 2003

chocha *noun*

the vagina *US*

From Spanish.

- It shouldn't be an issue whether you arrive in possession of a Johnson or a chocha as long as you show up with your records —Frank Broughton and Bill Brewster, *How to DJ Right*, p. 247, 2002
- "Show me you don' have some little pistola pushed up your chocha." Belinda dismissed the request with a wave of her hand. —David Cray, *Partners*, p. 271, 2004

chock *noun*

home-fermented, vegetable-based alcohol *US*

- I'll tell you about chock. They used to make it here all the time. —Bruce Jackson, *In the Life*, p. 301, 1972

chockablock; chocka *adjective*
jammed close together, crammed full *UK, 1840*
From C19 nautical slang.
- I know, for example, that he was the creepiest guy in our office (which, believe you me, was choc-a-bloc full). —Terry Southern, *Now Dig This*, p. 31, 1975
- It took me forever to wend my way back south. Traffic was chocka. —Diran Abedayo, *My Once Upon A Time*, p. 93, 2000
- Portland is chockablock with beautiful, historic houses, and on the right day, you can walk right in the front door. —Chuck Palahniuk, *Fugitive and Refugees*, p. 39, 2003

chock-a-block (up) *adjective*
(of a man) with the penis entirely inserted into a sexual partner *AUSTRALIA*
- BENTLEY: How do I know? I walked in on them, mate. RICHARD: And Simmo was... BENTLEY: Chock-a-block. —Alexander Buzo, *Rooted*, p. 85, 1969
- I will admit they caught me at it once on the sofa in the living room, caught me right in the bloody act with a woman who came to do the cleaning; chocker-block up her. —Frank Hardy, *The Outcasts of Foolgarah*, p. 80, 1971
- I should have really shook his hand you know, but seeing him right choc-a-block up Jenny I went off my nut. —Bluey *Bush Contractors*, p. 273, 1975

chocker; chocka *adjective*
1 disgruntled, fed up *UK, 1942*
From 'chock-full' (crammed full) or, more likely, **CHOCKABLOCK** (crammed full), the variant spellings lend credence to the latter.
- Well to tell you the trueth [sic] old chap I'm a little chocker of this place. —Frank Norman, *Bang To Rights*, p. 107, 1958
- I am getting chocker with it all[.] —Kevin Sampson, *Clubland*, p. 4, 2002

2 completely full *NEW ZEALAND, 1980*
- The Cross was chocker with suburban bozos hanging out for some debauchery. —Kathy Lette, *Girls' Night Out*, p. 85, 1987
- —Harry Orsman, *A Dictionary of Modern New Zealand Slang*, p. 28–28, 1999
- Switzerland is full of them Swiss maids. Chocker. —Jeremy Cameron, *Brown Bread in Wengen*, p. 130, 1999

chockers *noun*
feet *UK, 1979*
Market traders' slang.

chockers *adjective*
1 completely full *AUSTRALIA, 1981*
- —Frank Hardy, *The Outcasts of Foolgarah*, p. 123, 1971
- The hall was chockers now. All the seats were taken. —Phillip Gwynne, *Deadly Unna?*, p. 127, 1998
- After the festivities were over, while his Mum and Dad were on their way back home, young Jesus stayed behind in Jerusalem, but because the road was chockers he wasn't missed. —Kel Richards, *The Aussie Bible*, p. 19, 2003

2 (of a man) with the penis entirely inserted into a sexual partner *AUSTRALIA*
- Her brothers sprang me one night when I was chockers outside her house, and they beat the shit out of me. —William Nagel, *The Odd Angry Shot*, p. 61, 1975

chocko; choco *noun*
1 an person of Mediterranean or Middle Eastern background *AUSTRALIA*
An abbreviation of **CHOCOLATE FROG** with the '-o' suffix. Offensive.
- Our ethnic minorities whether they be oil slicks, chockos or slopies have certainly given a new dimension to the Australian business-man's lunch. — Barry Humphries, *The Traveller's Tool*, p. 79, 1985
- chocko: (derog.) a dark-skinned person. —Lenie Johansen, *The Dinkum Dictionary*, p. s.v., 1988
- C'mon, mate: *Ned Kelly* is about a bunch of inbred bumpkins. How's that going to compete with a bunch of chockos? —*Sydney Morning Herald*, p. Metro 5, 11th April 2003

2 a conscripted soldier or militiaman who remained in Australia and did not fight overseas *AUSTRALIA, 1943*
World War 2; from **CHOCOLATE SOLDIER**. In World War 1 the term was simply 'choc'.
- But no doubt they'll find things different: / I've a letter here to hand, / Saying Chockos, Yanks and Refugees / Have overrun the land. —Tip Kelaher, *The Digger Hat and other verses*, p. 51, 1942
- In your great dinger, you rotten crawling chocko. —Sumner Locke Elliott, *Rusty Bugles*, p. 80, 1948
- —Jim Ramsay, *Cop It Sweet!*, p. 22, 1977

chocks away!
let's go!; let's get on with it! *UK, 1943*
From the wooden blocks that were used to stop an aircraft's wheels from rolling; to take the chocks away allowed the plane to take off.

choco-fan *noun*
heroin *UK*
- —Mike Haskins, *Drugs*, p. 283, 2003

chocoholic *noun*
a person who is excessively fond of chocolate *AUSTRALIA*
- He ate the chocolate layer first. You could call him a chocoholic. —Wilda Moxham, *The Apprentice*, p. 25, 1969

chocolate *noun*
1 a black person *US, 1906*
- —Anon., *The Gay Girl's Guide*, 1949

2 amphetamines *UK*
- —Mike Haskins, *Drugs*, p. 279, 2003

3 opium *US*
- —Jay Robert Nash, *Dictionary of Crime*, p. 65, 1992

4 a twenty rand banknote *SOUTH AFRICA, 1984*
Urban, especially township, slang, from the brown colour of the note.

5 a southern European *AUSTRALIA*
- —Ned Wallish, *The Truth Dictionary of Racing Slang*, p. 14, 1989

▷ **see: CHOCOLATE FUDGE, CHOCOLATE THAI**

▸ **in the chocolate**
in considerable trouble *UK*
A euphemism for **IN THE SHIT**.
- If anyone cops our number here Jimmy, and we haven't reported the shooting to the police, we're going to be in the chocolate, know what I mean? —John Milne, *Alive and Kicking*, p. 87, 1998

chocolate *adjective*
of African heritage *US, 1906*
- I noticed a lot of Jungle Fever action, with people describing themselves as "vanilla" or "chocolate" or "caramel. —Anka Radakovich, *The Wild Girls Club*, p. 43, 1994

chocolate bobby *noun*
a community police officer *UK*
Used by lower-ranking police.
- Derisive terms used on several occasions to describe community officers were "hobby-bobbies" and "chocolate bobbies". — *The Times*, 16th July 1981

chocolate box *noun*
in art, a sentimental or romantic style such as you might expect on a chocolate box *UK, 1901*
Generally used with reproach if not with a degree of contempt.
- [A]nybody looking for chocolate box art should look elsewhere. —a reader's review of 'Darkwerks', *Amazon.com*, 14th September 2000

chocolate boxey *adjective*
in the decorative arts, sentimentally romantic *UK, 1894*

chocolate bunny *noun*
a Vietnamese prostitute who favoured black American soldiers over white American soldiers *US*
- —Linda Reinberg, *In the Field*, p. 42, 1991

chocolate button *noun*
an attractive or petite black person *UK*
Patronising and offensive.
- [E]very wee shite who had ever called her 'the Chocolate Button'[.] —Christopher Brookmyre, *The Sacred Art of Stealing*, p. 53, 2002

chocolate canal *noun*
the rectum *NEW ZEALAND*
Collected during an extensive survey of New Zealand prison slang, 1996–2000.

chocolate chip cookies *noun*
MDMA, the recreational drug best known as ecstasy, mixed with heroin or methadone *UK*
- —Robert Ashton, *This Is Heroin*, p. 208, 2002

chocolate chips *noun*

1 desert camouflage uniforms *US*

- Some "ground pounders" wearing "chocolate chip cookie cammies" even talk of an "Adopt-a-Pilot" campaign and cheer when the jets roar overhead. — *Houston Chronicle*, p. 15, 24th January 1991
- — *Army*, p. 48, November 1991

2 a type of LSD marketed in brown capsules *UK, 1998*

- — Mike Haskins, *Drugs*, p. 285, 2003

3 a variety of MDMA, the recreational drug best known as ecstasy *UK*

- — Mike Haskins, *Drugs*, p. 289, 2003

chocolate drop *noun*

1 a black person *US, 1900*
Offensive.

- — Harre, Morgan, O'Neill, *Nicknames*, 1979
- Piss off, chocolate drop. Black get. — Trevor Griffiths, *Oi For England*, p. 2, 1982
- — Frederic G. Cassidy, *Dictionary of American Regional English*, p. 644, 1985

2 a girl below the age of sexual consent who regularly has sex wlth seamen *UK*
Recorded by Frank Peppitt, as occurring in the *Daily Telegraph*, 1971.

chocolate ecstasy *noun*
crack cocaine blended with chocolate milk powder during processing *US*

- — Jim Crotty, *How to Talk American*, p. 90, 1997

chocolate frog *noun*

1 a person of Mediterranean or Middle Eastern background *AUSTRALIA, 1971*
Rhyming slang for **WOG**. Offensive.

- — Ryan Aven-Bray, *Ridgey Didge Oz Jack Lang*, p. 21, 1983
- — Kathy Lette, *Girls' Night Out*, p. 187, 1987
- The badly-maligned 'Wogs' (Dapto dogs/Chocolate frogs) are finally wreaking revenge on Anglo-Saxon kids. 'Aussies' are 'Skips' or 'Joeys'. — *Sydney Morning Herald*, p. 7, 3rd January 1987

2 a police informer *AUSTRALIA, 1971*
Rhyming slang for **DOG**. A chocolate frog is a popular confectionary.

- — Jim McNeil, *The Chocolate Frog*, 1973

chocolate fudge; chocolate *noun*
a judge, especially one who shows leniency *UK*
Rhyming slang, gently punning on the judge's sweet nature or a **SWEET** (excellent) result.

- I thought I'd go down but the Chocolate let me off with a suspended. — Ray Puxley, *Cockney Rabbit*, 1992

chocolate hearts *noun*
a variety of LSD

- LSD (about 300 micrograms in the form of five 'chocolate hearts') with four St. John's Wort tablets ... one of the best drugs 'n' sex combos. — Simon Napier-Bell, *Black Vinyl White Powder*, p. 330, 2001

chocolate highway *noun*
the anus and rectum *US, 1977*

- — J.E. Lighter, *Historical Dictionary of American Slang, Volume 1*, p. 410, 1994

chocolate rock *noun*
a blend of crack cocaine and heroin that is smoked

- — Robert Ashton, *This Is Heroin*, p. 208, 2002

chocolate rocket *noun*
crack cocaine blended with chocolate milk powder during processing *US*

- — Jim Crotty, *How to Talk American*, p. 90, 1997

chocolate soldier *noun*
a member of an Australian militia during World War 2 who did not serve in a theatre of war *AUSTRALIA, 1943*
Derogatory.

- — Sumner Locke Elliott, *Rusty Bugles (glossary)*, p. 91, 1948

chocolate starfish *noun*
the anus *UK*
A visual pun.

- ["]Bradley is referring to the rusty bullet-hole," said Mikey. "The what?" Mario was still struggling. "The chocolate starfish." — Colin Butts, *Is Harry on the Boat?*, p. 21, 1997
- [K]iss my starfish, my chocolate starfish[.] — limp bizkit, *hot dog*, 2000

chocolate Thai; chocolate thi; chocolate *noun*
a variety of marijuana *UK*

- The chocolate thai got me nice in ten minutes. — Lois Stavsky et al., *A2Z*, p. 20, 1995
- Purple Thai, which was itself a cross between Chocolate Thai and Highland Oaxaca Gold[.] — Brian Preston, *Pot Planet*, p. 5, 2002
- — Mike Haskins, *Drugs*, p. 287, 2003

chocolate time *noun*
the bleed period of the menstrual cycle *US*

- — *The Museum of Menstruation and Women's Health*, January 2001

chod *noun*
the penis *UK*

- Nonsense slang referred to vague, inoffensive terms that had little or no means in standard English: terms like biff, foo-foo, minky and winkie in FGTs [female genital terms], and chod, dongce, spondoolies, and winks in MGTs [male genital terms]. — *Journal of Sex Research*, p. 146, 2001

choggy shop *noun*
a shop catering to the needs of servicemen and women *UK*
Military.

- [T]aking them down the choggy shop for a refund of two cents a bottle[.] — Andy McNab (writing of the late 1970s/early 80s), *Immediate Action*, p. 216, 1995

chogi *noun*
a Korean worker *US, 1951*

- — J.E. Lighter, *Historical Dictionary of American Slang, Volume 1*, p. 411, 1994

chogie!
move out of here! *US*
Korean war usage.

- — Frank Hailey, *Soldier Talk*, p. 13, 1982

choice *noun*
in horse racing, the favoured horse in a race *US*

- — Robert Saunders Dowst and Jay Craig, *Playing the Races*, p. 161, 1960

choice *adjective*
excellent *US, 1958*

- — *Washington Post*, 23rd April 1961
- — J. R. Friss, *A Dictionary of Teenage Slang (Mt. Diablo High)*, 1964
- — Miss Cone, *The Slang Dictionary (Hawthorne High School)*, 1965
- — Trevor Cralle, *The Surfin'ary*, p. 21, 1991

choice!
used for expressing strong approval *NEW ZEALAND*

- — David McGill, *David McGill's Complete Kiwi Slang Dictionary*, p. 29, 1998

choiceamundo *adjective*
excellent *US*

- — Trevor Cralle, *The Surfin'ary*, p. 21, 1991
- — Vann Wesson, *Generation X Field Guide and Lexicon*, p. 38, 1997

choirboy *noun*

1 a novice criminal *US*

- — Vincent J. Monteleone, *Criminal Slang*, p. 50, 1949

2 a newly initiated member of a youth gang *US*

- — *American Speech*, p. 99, May 1956: 'Smugglers' argot in the southwest'

3 a newly recruited police officer *UK*

- — Angela Devlin, *Prison Patter*, p. 36, 1996

4 a prisoner who informs on others *NEW ZEALAND*
From the sense of 'to **SING**' (to inform). Collected during an extensive survey of New Zealand prison slang, 1996–2000.

choir practice *noun*
an after-hours gathering of policemen, involving liberal amounts of alcohol and sex, usually in a remote public place *US*

- The first choir practice in MacArthur Park took place in the early spring when the nights became warm enough. — Joseph Wambaugh, *The Choirboys*, p. 25, 1975
- According to Hart, many officers participate in a rite of passage in many police departments – the so-called "choir practice" or heavy after-hours drdinking. — *Boston Globe*, p. 16, 30th October 1991
- I can tell you this much: these cops are having choir practice with first-string girls and two guys from the mayor's staff. — Stephen J. Cannell, *The Tin Collectors*, p. 231, 2001
- They used to call it choir practice when a squad would go out together after their shift. They would hang out, blow off steam, try to pick up

women, whatever. — *The Journal News (Westchester County, New York)*, p. 1A, 2nd September 2001

choke *noun*

1 a swallow or drink of alcohol *US*
- Have a choke, man. Like it might loosen up your right hand so you can really blow. — John Clellon Holmes, *The Horn*, p. 192, 1958

2 an artichoke of either Jerusalem or globe variety *UK*
The punning 'have hearty chokes for breakfast' (to be hanged) dates from 1785; it is difficult to be more accurate with this greengrocers' usage.

3 a Mexican-American *US*
Derogatory. A shortened form of **CHILI CHOKER**.
- That's Flaco de la Oilslick, a Nester General. One evil choke, yeah. — Seth Morgan, *Homeboy*, p. 185, 1990

4 a garotting *AUSTRALIA*
- — Sidney J. Baker, *Australia Speaks*, 1953

5 a nervous shock; something grievous *UK*
- — L.J. Cunliffe, *Having It Away*, 1965

choke *verb*

1 to forget *US*
Especially in the imperative.
- — Joan Fontaine et al., *Dictionary of Black Slang*, 1968

2 to fail to perform under pressure *US*
- A lot of pros in my position would already be thinking about the $130,000 check for winning, and they'd choke quicker on that than they would on their name in a history book. — Dan Jenkins, *Dead Solid Perfect*, p. 75, 1986

3 to prevent a horse from winning a race *UK*
Strictly, and originally, by pulling back on the reins so strongly that the horse is almost choked.
- He said if I wanted a lesson in how to choke a horse I'd better watch him on Bolingbroke. — Dick Francis, *Dead Cert*, 1962

4 in computing, to reject data input *US*
- I tried building an EMACS binary to use X, but cpp(1) choked on all those #defines. — Eric S. Raymond, *The New Hacker's Dictionary*, p. 94, 1991

5 to borrow something; to scrounge something; to beg *FIJI*
- He just sit around this shop and choke paisa from everyone. — Jan Tent, 1993

6 to turn off a light *US*
- — Hyman E. Goldin et al., *Dictionary of American Underworld Lingo*, p. 44, 1950

7 to drink something quickly *UK: SCOTLAND*
- The perr a them were chokin a bottle a whiskey. — Michael Munro, *The Patter, Another Blast*, 1988

▸ **choke a darkie**
to defecate *AUSTRALIA*
Also 'strangle a darkie', and 'sink a darkie' or 'teach a darkie to swim' when on a flush toilet.
- These Pom dogs aren't fussy where they flamin' choke the odd darkie and that's for sure! — Barry Humphries, *The Wonderful World of Barry McKenzie*, p. 57, 1968
- Sink a darkie: go to the toilet. — Jim Ramsay, *Cop It Sweet!*, p. 81, 1977
- He was not even slightly concerned so he stalled out to the brasco on the pretext that he had to give a swimming lesson to a darkie. — Ryan Aven-Bray, *Ridgey Didge Oz Jack Lang*, p. 14–15, 1983
- — Barry Humphries, *The Traveller's Tool*, p. 101, 1985
- '[Y]ou don't have to get undressed in those cramped little airborne dunnies to choke a darkie or give some hostie a quick knee-trembler. — Barry Humphries, *The Traveller's Tool*, p. 117, 1985

▸ **choke the chicken**

1 (of a male) to masturbate *US, 1976*
- He likes killin ... the way you like chokin your chicken. — Seth Morgan, *Homeboy*, p. 124, 1990
- "Guest home" meant "fuck pad" meant Howard Hughes left to choke his own chicken. — James Ellroy, *White Jazz*, p. 57, 1992
- Spanking the monkey. Flogging the bishop. Choking the chicken. Jerking the gherkin. — *American Beauty*, 1999
- Another way to say "the boy is masturbating" [...] Choking the chicken[.] — Erica Orloff and JoAnn Baker, *Dirty Little Secrets*, p. 65, 2001

2 (of a male) to masturbate with the adrenaline-inducing agency of autoerotic strangulation or suffocation *UK*
- Guide to "The Choking of the Chicken"[.] Please note: all the following are extremely hazardous to health[.] — *Loaded*, p. 3, June 2002

▸ **choke the Chihuahua**
(of a male) to masturbate *UK*
- — Richard Herring, *Talking Cock*, p. 113, 2003

▸ **choke your chauncy**
(of a male) to masturbate *US*
- Who's sitting by himself in a room choking his chauncey to a bunch of videotapes, Graham? — *Sex, Lies and Videotape*, 1989

▸ **choke your mule**
(of a male) to masturbate *US*
- I get to choke my mule on the Mighty Man Agency's time. — James Ellroy, *White Jazz*, p. 111, 1992

choke *adjective*
many *US*
Hawaiian youth usage.
- Wow, get choke pakalolo until Green Hahvest! — Douglas Simonson, *Pidgin to da Max Hana Hou*, 1982

choke and chew *noun*
a roadside restaurant *US*
- — Elementary Electronics, *Dictionary of CB Lingo*, p. 57, 1976

choke and puke *noun*
a restaurant with bad food at low prices *US*
- — Connie Eble (Editor), *UNC-CH Campus Slang*, p. 3, Spring 1988

chokecherry farmer *noun*
an unsuccessful farmer *CANADA*
- — Chris Thain, *Cold as a Bay Street Banker's Heart*, p. 41, 1987

choked *adjective*
emotionally upset, annoyed *UK*
The sense of 'a lump in your throat'.
- [H]ow choked they used to get when some little calf or something got took to market and sold. — John Peter Jones, *Feather Pluckers*, p. 49, 1964

choked down *adjective*

1 (of a racehorse) experiencing difficulty breathing during a race *US*
- — Igor Kushyshyn et al., *The Gambling Times Guide to Harness Racing*, p. 114, 1994

2 well-dressed *US*
- — Edith A. Folb, *runnin' down some lines*, p. 232, 1980

choked off *adjective*
disgusted, fed-up *UK*
- I'm frustrated with cars, cheesed off with buses, and choked off in tubes. — *Time Out*, 4th January 1980

choke down *verb*
to force yourself to swallow an alcoholic drink despite any difficulty with taste or capacity *UK*
- — Michael Munro, *The Patter, Another Blast*, 1988

choked up tight *adjective*
dressed up, especially with button-down collars *US*
- He was choked up tight in a white-on-white / And a cocoa front that was down. — Dennis Wepman et al., *The Life*, p. 54, 1976

choke off *verb*
to punish or berate a prisoner *UK*
Prison officer slang, from military origins.
- — L.W. Merrow-Smith and J. Harris, *Prison Screw*, 1962
- — Angela Devlin, *Prison Patter*, p. 36, 1996

choke out *verb*
to render someone unconscious through a choke hold that cuts off cerebral blood flow at the carotid artery in the neck, usually applied with a police officer's baton across the throat *US*
- Don't ... don't never try to choke out a ... a hard-core street cop! — Joseph Wambaugh, *The Secrets of Harry Bright*, p. 199, 1985
- [O]nce, when he'd choked out a San Bernadino County deputy D.A. who'd stopped at a minimarket to buy some nonprespcription sleeping pills[.] — Joseph Wambaugh, *Fugitive Nights*, p. 31, 1990

choker *noun*
a necktie *US*
- — Lou Shelly, *Hepcats Jive Talk Dictionary*, p. 8, 1945
- — Clarence Major, *Dictionary of Afro-American Slang*, p. 37, 1970

choke rag *noun*
a necktie *US, 1944*
- — Frederic G. Cassidy, *Dictionary of American Regional English*, p. 646, 1985

choke up *verb*
to lose your composure; to totter on the verge of tears *US, 1941*
- And the whole damned United States gets choked up and goes into mourning. — Philip Wylie, *Opus 21*, p. 7–8, 1949

chokey; choky *noun*

1 a prison; a detention cell; a segregation unit *UK, 1837*
From Hindustani *chauki* (a four-sided place or building).
- P.O. Ferris was officer in charge of E wing, which contains the chokey or punishment cells[.] —Charles Raven, *Underworld Nights*, p. 106, 1956
- —Angela Devlin, *Prison Patter*, p. 37, 1996
- Our colleague Peter Buck was a stone's (or should that be a yoghurt's) throw from two years in chokey[.] —*Q*, p. 10, May 2002

2 the time spent in a prison segregation unit; the punishment itself *UK*
- —Angela Devlin, *Prison Patter*, p. 37, 1996

3 a prison diet of bread and water, served as punishment *UK*
- It is forbidden to talk whilst at labour, and to do so and get captured, usual[l]y means three days chockey. —Frank Norman, *Bang To Rights*, p. 22, 1958

chokey *adjective*

crowded, tight-fitting *TRINIDAD AND TOBAGO*
- —Lise Winer, *Dictionary of the English/Creole of Trinidad & Tobago*, 2003

Chokie *adjective*

Chinese *UK*
Used of Hong Kong Chinese crew on a Royal Fleet Auxiliary vessel during the Falklands war. The variation 'chogey' is remembered by Beale as in army usage in Hong Kong during the 1960s.
- —*The Guardian*, 2nd July 1982

choking *adjective*

1 extremely thirsty *UK: SCOTLAND*
- Any danger of some service at this end of the bar? There's guys chokin up here. —Michael Munro, *The Patter, Another Blast*, 1988

2 desperate for a cigarette, a drink, sex or whatever may bring relief or satisfaction *UK*

chokkas *noun*

shoes *UK*
From **CHOCKERS** (feet). English gypsy use.
- —Jimmy Stockin, *On The Cobbles*, p. 9, 2000

cholly *noun*

cocaine *US*
- —William D. Alsever, *Glossary for the Establishment and Other Uptight People*, p. 6, December 1970
- —US Department of Justice, *Street Terms*, August 1994
- —Nick Constable, *This is Cocaine*, p. 181, 2002

cholo *noun*

a young, tough Mexican-American *US*
Border Spanish used in English conversation by Mexican-Americans.
- The language of East L.A. is a speedy sort of cholo mixture of Mexican Spanish and California English. —Hunter S. Thompson, *Fear and Loathing in Las Vegas*, p. 230, 1971
- —Dagoberto Fuentes and Jose Lopez, *Barrio Language Dictionary*, p. 49, 1974
- The cholo shaded his eyes squinting into the Mission forenoon. —Seth Morgan, *Homeboy*, p. 57, 1990
- He saw a group of cholos in their oversized white T-shirts and baggy pants making their way through the yard. —Michael Connelly, *The Black Ice (in The Harry Bosch Novels)*, p. 379, 1993

chomeur *noun*

in Quebec, a person receiving unemployment insurance benefits *CANADA*
- "La chomage" is unemployment insurance in Quebec. A chomeur is someone on the dole. In France, the French verb "chomer" from which chomeur and chomage sprang has less pejorative meanings. —Bill Casselman, *Canadian Food Words*, p. 170, 1998

cho-mo *noun*

a child molester *US*
- —William K. Bentley and James M. Corbett, *Prison Slang*, p. 35, 1992

chomo *noun*

a child molester *US, 1997*
- Like the "chomos" (child molesters) and rapists, he [Charles Manson] needed protection. —Edward George, *Taming the Beast*, p. 6, 1998
- Nevada prisons are crawling with punks, J-cats, snitches, and child molesters (called Chomos). —Jimmy A. Lerner, *You Got Nothing Coming*, p. 44, 2002

chomp *verb*

to eat *US*
- —Collin Baker et al., *College Undergraduate Slang Study Conducted at Brown University*, p. 96, 1968

chompers *noun*

1 the teeth; false teeth *US, 1950*
- "Jesus, he had fake teeth,' Julia said, staring at the pink and super-white upper and lower chompers smiling up from the carpet. —Richard Condon, *Prizzi's Money*, p. 111, 1994
- I've heard those horror stories about folks with false teeth who tossed their net and watched their expensive store-bought chompers go sailing into the water with it. —*Tampa Tribune*, p. 11, 6th July 2003

2 a snack or meal *ANTARCTICA, 1963*
- —Bernadette Hince, *The Antarctic Dictionary*, p. 83, 2000

chong *adjective*

good-looking, handsome *UK*
Used by urban black youths.
- My new English lecturer in extremely chong. —*Live*, p. 38, Winter 2004

chonga *noun*

marijuana *UK*
- [W]e adjourn to the van to sample the chonga[.] —Niall Griffiths, *Kelly + Victor*, p. 57, 2002

choo-choo *noun*

a train *US, 1898*
Formed from the child's imitation of a steam whistle.
- "No, the choo-choo comes in, we get mostly appliances," Ordell said. —Elmore Leonard, *Switch*, p. 18, 1978

choof *verb*

1 (of a person) to go; to depart *AUSTRALIA, 1947*
As used of a steam train in stories for children.
- —Frank Hardy, *The Yarns of Billy Borker*, p. 82, 1965
- Soon as my mate give her the house-keeping money, off she choof to the club. —Frank Hardy, *Billy Borker Yarns Again*, 1967
- They climb effortlessly into a Rolls-Royce and choof away to their chalet. —Barry Dickins, *What the Dickins*, p. 61, 1985
- So up they choof to a travel agency and buy two one-way air tickets to the Bahamas. —Frank Hardy, *Hardy's People*, p. 12, 1986

2 to smoke marijuana *AUSTRALIA*
- —James Lambert, *The Macquarie Book of Slang*, 2000

choof off *verb*

to depart, to leave *AUSTRALIA, 1972*
- —Jim Ramsay, *Cop It Sweet!*, p. 22, 1977
- I used to drink beer at home wiv Dad until he choofed off[.] —Kathy Lette, *Girls' Night Out*, p. 25, 1987

chook; chookie; chuckie *noun*

1 an adult domestic chicken, male or female *AUSTRALIA, 1900*
First appearing in Australia in the diminutive form 'chuckey' this word is imitative of the cluck of the hen but also owes something to 'chicken'. In general use in British dialect from C18 as *chuck*, *chuke*, and the diminutive *chookie*, *chucky*, where it was also used as a term of endearment from the C19.
- They shuffled back, like chooks scolded with an old woman's apron. —Robert S. Close, *Love Me Sailor*, p. 150, 1945
- Ever see the poultry at the Royal Show? There's a lot of interest in chooks. —George Blaikie, *Remember Smith's Weekly?*, p. 109, 1950
- The scent lay across the compound to a shed where were kept bags of wheat for Esther Harmon's chooks, and lucerne for her brother's horse. —Arthur Upfield, *Bony and the Mouse*, p. 126, 1959
- He put down the phone and stood cackling like a chook who's sniffed laughing gas. —Willie Fennell, *Dexter Gets The Point*, p. 87, 1961
- At four I had showed a slight aptitude for country living. I would willingly help Father throttle chooks for the dinner table by cleaning the giblets and plucking out the pin-feathers. —Kerry Cue, *Crooks, Chooks and Bloody Ratbags*, p. 16, 1983
- Prime Ministers, their wives, and Ministers start scratching around like chooks for ways to raise taxes. They can think of nothing else but to try to find out how they can get more taxes. —Joh Bjelke-Petersen, *Johspeak*, p. 13, 1988
- I want to say everything, but instead I'm making chook noises I'm swallowing so hard. —Glyn Parry, *Mosh*, p. 41, 1996
- Did I ever tell you about when I was in the RAAF and those chooks got on the runway? —Phillip Gwynne, *Deadly Unna?*, p. 48, 1998

2 a slaughtered chicken dressed for cooking; a cooked chicken *AUSTRALIA*
- You should have come down and had Christmas dinner with us. We had a chook, but it was as hard as a football. —Ruth Park, *The Harp In The South*, p. 72, 1948
- I won a chook at a pub once. —Alexander Buzo, *Rooted*, p. 52, 1969
- You can't go from being a fun-loving, outrageous, independent woman to being the wife of 'some bloke' you've grabbed like a chook

from the freezer at Wollies! —Gretel Killeen, *Hot Buns and Ophelia get a Bloke*, p. 73, 2000

3 cooked chicken meat *AUSTRALIA*

- Well, what do you expect aboard a bloody windjammer, Miss Miller – roast chook? —Robert S. Close, *Love Me Sailor*, p. 160, 1945
- Probably chook for tea tonight. —Patsy Adam-Smith, *Folklore of the Australian Railwaymen*, p. 213, 1969
- Once my father killed four of them and she cooked them for Sunday dinner, but although we liked chook my sisters and I cried all through it, and would only eat the vegetables. —T.A.G. Hungerford, *Stories From Suburban Road*, p. 54, 1983
- 'That means there's chook for dinner tonight,' Mum says with a smile. —Tim Winton, *That eye, the sky*, p. 84, 1986

4 a woman, especially an elderly woman *AUSTRALIA, 1915*

- The old chook here owns the block. We change in the laundry. She makes us a cuppa tea, we bring our own lunch. —Nino Culotta (John O'Grady), *They're A Weird Mob*, p. 35, 1957
- That reminds me, when you see the old chook you might tell her..it's been a hundred-and-bloody-three in the shade here, and there's not all that much call for mittens or balaclavas! —George Johnston, *My Brother Jack*, p. 307, 1964
- First thing he does is knock the hat off an old chook sittin' in front of us. —John O'Grady, *Aussie Etiket*, p. 15, 1971

5 a fool *AUSTRALIA, 1955*

- He wondered why the Navy bred so many 'chooks.' —John Wynnum, *Tar Dust*, p. 48, 1962
- She twitched her head swiftly from side to side and Danny reached out to steady the large label secured round her neck. It read: 'Greetings – From One Prize Chook to Another.' —John Wynnum, *Tar Dust*, p. 64, 1962

6 a coward *AUSTRALIA*

A variation of **CHICKEN**.

- I've recently taken up mountain bike riding, but I'm a bit of a chook when it comes to sitting tall in the saddle. —*Lesbians on the Loose*, p. 46, 1997

▸ **choke the chook; milk the chook**

(of a male) to masturbate *AUSTRALIA*

Variant of **CHOKE THE CHICKEN**.

▸ **like a chook with its head chopped off; like a chook without a head**

without rhyme or reason *AUSTRALIA*

A variant of **HEADLESS CHICKEN**.

- The local coppers had been running around like chooks without their heads for the last few days, looking for an old bloke from the town who had gone missing. —Kerry Cue, *Crooks, Chooks and Bloody Ratbags*, p. 204, 1983
- And Master Egoroff aren't you the lunatic who was running around like a chook with its head chopped off giving away penalties all the time? —Hugh Lunn, *Fred & Olive's Blessed Lino*, p. 90, 1993

chook!

a call made to domestic chickens *AUSTRALIA, 1903*

- 'Chook! Chook! Chook!' she called to the fowls. —Kylie Tennant, *Tiburon*, p. 33, 1935
- 'Chook-chook-chook-chook,' called the children, scattering wheat. —Randolph Stow, *The Merry-Go-Round in the Sea*, p. 51, 1965
- Maddy Rivers...half-chicken half-boy...the midway wheat-eater... chook-chook-chook-chook-chook!' —PaulRadley, *Jack Rivers and Me*, p. 47, 1981

chookas!

used for wishing an actor good luck *AUSTRALIA*

Actors are, by tradition, superstitious, and to actually wish an actor 'good luck' in so many words is thought to be tempting fate; this abstract (derivation unknown) or surreal benediction was used by Evan Dunstan, an Australian theatrical agent in London during the 1980s.

chook chaser *noun*

a small motorcycle or its rider *AUSTRALIA*

A derogatory term used by riders of larger motorcycles.

- —James Lambert, *The Macquarie Book of Slang*, 1996
- All you need is any old chook chaser that can pass scrutineering[.] —*The Weipa Bulletin (Northern Queensland)*, p. 25, 4th April 2003

chookhouse *noun*

an enclosure for domestic chickens *AUSTRALIA, 1938*

- Down the back when he's building the chookhouse, Quick finds a pile of newspapers and magazines someone's tied up and thrown over the fence. —Tim Winton, *Cloudstreet*, p. 61, 1991

chookie *noun*

a fool *AUSTRALIA, 1855*

- Come along, chookies. —Randolph Stow, *The Merry-Go-Round in the Sea*, p. 51, 1965
- "Honestly, what a hopeless lot of chookies you are!" she lectured them severely as she poked in the nests. —Colleen McCullough, *The Thorn Birds*, p. 167, 1977
- Think ye can make me look lik a chookie an get away wi it? —Michael Munro, *The Complete Patter*, 1996

▸ **will you chookie!**

you will not!; used for emphasising a contradiction of a preceding statement *UK: SCOTLAND, 1985*

- "He says he'll take it with him." "Will he chookie!" —Michael Munro, *The Complete Patter*, 1996

chook poop *noun*

chicken manure *AUSTRALIA*

- I know Mum'll ask me anyway, so I shovel out all the chook poop from under the roost and put it into bags for the vegie garden. —Tim Winton, *That eye, the sky*, p. 37, 1986

chook raffle *noun*

a raffle to raise money for charity offering a dressed chicken as a prize *AUSTRALIA, 1979*

- —Sandra Jobson, *Blokes*, p. 47, 1984
- —Frank Hardy, *Hardy's People*, p. 188, 1986
- The simple truth is that a city the size of Melbourne can't support 12 clubs who have all got to find somewhere between $4–6 million just to stay alive. That's a lot of chook raffles, eh? —Max Walker, *How To Tame Lions*, p. 160, 1988
- People who didn't follow the footy, who never bought a ticket in the Friday-night chook raffle. —Phillip Gwynne, *Deadly Unna?*, p. 114, 1998

chooks *noun*

▸ **I hope your chooks turn into emus and kick your dunny down**

I wish you bad luck *AUSTRALIA*

- — *The Adventures of Barry McKenzie*, 1972
- Other expressions in such emergencies include: 'Oh Yeah!', 'Up yours!', 'Get stuffed!', 'In yer boot!' And if all else fails: 'I hope your chooks turn into emus and kick your dunny down!' —John Blackman, *The Aussie Slang Dictionary*, p. 113, 1990

chook wheel *noun*

a spinning wheel with numbered pegs used for a chook raffle *AUSTRALIA*

- Out on the verandah a cricket was chirping like a ratchet on a chook wheel. —Russell Guy, *What's Rangoon to you is Grafton to me*, p. 45, 1991

chookyard *noun*

an enclosed yard for domestic chickens *AUSTRALIA, 1941*

- And if you want to see Venice, Florence and the Old World, then first eat your chooks, or sell them, and then you will know you will have nothing worse to come back to than a chookyard full of rank weed. —Peter Carey, *Oscar and Lucinda*, p. 272, 1988

choom *noun*

an Englishman *AUSTRALIA, 1916*

Representing a toney English pronunciation of **CHUM**. Used jocularly and mildly derisively.

- —Leonard Mann, *Flesh in Armour*, p. 43, 1932
- But what can you do (I tell them) when a New Australian migrant, a Pommy bastard and a Choom to be exact, moves into your house and marries your beautiful sister-in-law. —Frank Hardy, *The Outcasts of Foolgarah*, p. 23, 1971
- Where are you stayin', choom? —John O'Grady, *It's Your Shout, Mate!*, p. 44, 1972
- —Jim Ramsay, *Cop It Sweet!*, p. 22, 1977
- —Frank Hardy, *Hardy's People*, p. 98, 1986

choon *noun*

within house and other contemporary dance styles, a piece of recorded music *UK*

A mispronounced and misspelt 'tune'.

- Anne and Lisa playing such brill choons — *Mixmag*, p. 11, February 2002

choose *verb*

(of a prostitute) to agree to work for a pimp *US*

- This bitch come over talkin' about she gon' choose me. —Christina and Richard Milner, *Black Players*, p. 87, 1972
- I was behind him with my hand in my pocket gripping the gun when Rose looked at him and said, "Ace, I"ve chosen Stonewall for my man." —A.S. Jackson, *Gentleman Pimp*, p. 145, 1973

choosing money *noun*

the money a prostitute pays a pimp to join his fold *US*

- Then get your choosin money ready 'cause I don't chippy around. —Christina and Richard Milner, *Black Players*, p. 42, 1972

chop *noun*

1 dismissal from employment *UK, 1945*

- I got the hoof, man. The sack, the chop, the proverbial bullet. —Doug Lang, *Freaks*, p. 89, 1973
- Two were rumored to be leaving as a result of the report, said Toddy, and he was convinced that the two for the chop were himself and yours truly, young Bert Newton. —Bert Newton, *Bert!*, p. 63, 1977
- On the other hand, if I disobey him, the raid will probably succeed, but well, I'll get the chop —Lance Peters, *The Dirty Half-Mile*, p. 138, 1979
- Senior managers given the chop by intercontinental— *The Guardian*, 25th April 2003

2 approval *US*

- He taught me the intricacies of getting a superior's "chop," or approval on a draft memo that the superior might in fact not like at all. —Richard Marcinko and John Weisman, *Rogue Warrior*, p. 150, 1992

3 a share or division of something *AUSTRALIA, 1919*

- Make sure you get them. Hop in for your chop. —Eric Lambert, *The Veterans*, p. 16, 1954
- But what about the rest of the gang – and Ray down in Bunbury – they were gonna be in the chop? —Bluey, *Bush Contractors*, p. 379, 1975
- —Ned Wallish, *The Truth Dictionary of Racing Slang*, p. 14, 1989
- Might as well get in for your chop. —Shane Maloney, *Nice Try*, p. 27, 1998
- —David McGill, *David McGill's Complete Kiwi Slang Dictionary*, p. 29, 1998

4 a scathing, cutting remark or joke *US, 1957*

- Very funny. What a chop. Ha, ha, ha. —*American Graffiti*, 1973

5 a short and sudden type of scratch (a manipulation of a record to create a musical effect) *UK*

- —J. Hoggarth, *How To Be a DJ*, p. 89, 2002

6 a wood-chopping contest *AUSTRALIA, 1926*

Also known as a 'chops'.

7 food *US*

US military usage during the Vietnam war.

- — *Maledicta*, p. 253, Summer/Winter 1982: 'Viet-speak'

8 a dolt, an idiot, a fool *SOUTH AFRICA*

- Yissus bru, you pulled a blind move dropping that bottle of Tassies. You are such a chop! —*Surfrikan Slang*, 2004

▸ **have had the chop**

to be no good; to be ruined *AUSTRALIA*

- I think my feet have had the chop. Have a look at this —William Nagel, *The Odd Angry Shot*, p. 11, 1975

▸ **no chop**

no good, inferior *AUSTRALIA, 1864*

From the conventional sense of 'chop' as 'class, rank or quality' implied in 'first chop', 'second chop', etc.

▸ **not much chop**

not very good *AUSTRALIA, 1847*

From the British and Anglo-Indian 'chop' (quality).

- Obviously couldn't have been much chop, otherwise he'd have left more of an impression. —W.R. Bennett, *Target Turin*, p. 76, 1962
- —Alexander Buzo, *Norm and Ahmed*, p. 25, 1969
- —Paul Vautin, *Turn It Up!*, p. 156, 1995

chop *verb*

1 in car and motorcyle customising, to lower the upper portion of the car body or motorcyle by shortening the structural supports *US, 1953*

- It's one of its kind and it really looks good / chopped nose and deck with louvers on the hood. — The Beach Boys, *Cherry, Cherry Coupe*, 1963
- Most of the work he was doing then was modifying Detroit cars – chopping and channeling. Chopping is lowering the top of the car, bringing it nearer to the hood line. —Tom Wolfe, *The Kandy-Kolored Tangerine-Flake Streamline Baby*, p. 90, 1965
- The hard core, the outlaw elite, were the Hell's Angels ... wearing the winged death's-head on the back of their sleeveless jackets and packing their "mams" behind them on big "chopped hogs." —Hunter S. Thompson, *Hell's Angels*, p. 5, 1966
- Leotis McCarver was undoubtedly black, but his car was a full dress taco wagon: chopped and channeled, lowered, with a candy apple, lime-green paint job with orange and yellow flames covering the hood and weeping halfway back over the sides of the vehicle —James Ellroy, *Brown's Requiem*, p. 13, 1981
- It seems I've been working on motorcycles all my life, modifying them, chopping them, customizing them to my own taste[.] —Ralph "Sonny" Barger, *Hell's Angel*, p. 51, 2000

2 to cut a car into pieces *US, 1953*

- You're lucky she wasn't chopped, Mr. Lebowski. Must've been a joyride situation. — *The Big Lebowski*, 1998

3 to go into action as a soldier *UK*

Extended from the sense 'to shoot'.

- SAS officers, or "Ruperts" as they were known, were usually directed into planning roles, while the "chopping" was done by the troopers and NCOs. —Chris Ryan, *The Watchman*, p. 17, 2001

4 to kill someone *UK*

- We find him, you chop him – finito, end of story. —Chris Ryan, *The Watchman*, p. 140–141, 2001

5 to execute someone by hanging them *UK*

Prison use, probably dating from the time when the axe was the preferred method of official execution. Capital punishment was abolished in the UK in 1965.

- —Paul Tempest, *Lag's Lexicon*, 1950

6 to shoot someone to death *US, 1933*

- They were taking the two downtown to the D.A.'s and somebody chopped them. —Mickey Spillane, *Kiss Me Deadly*, p. 108, 1952

7 to approve something *US*

- We would scramble to do the research and draft an answer. Our superiors would "chop," or approve, our work and pass it up the ladder. —Richard Marcinko and John Weisman, *Rogue Warrior*, p. 190, 1992

8 to adulterate a powdered drug *US, 1970*

- You buy, you chop, you mix, you measure, then bag and sell. —Lanre Fehintola, *Charlie Says...*, p. 14, 2000

9 in handball, to add spin to the ball when hitting it *US*

- —Paul Haber, *Inside Handball*, p. 65, 1970

10 (of dice in a crap game) to pass once and then not pass *US*

- Don't count on it, they have been chopping. —N. B. Winkless, *The Gambling Times Guide to Craps*, p. 92, 1981

11 in motor racing, to pull sharply in front of another car *US*

- —John Lawlor, *How to Talk Car*, p. 31, 1965

▸ **chop it up**

to talk with enthusiasm and energy *US*

- —Rick Ayers (Editor), *Berkeley High Slang Dictionary*, p. 15, 2004

▸ **chop sin**

to gossip; to talk idly *BERMUDA*

- —Peter A. Smith and Fred M. Barritt, *Bermewjan Vurds*, 1985

▸ **chop ten**

to sit with your legs crossed as others work *JAMAICA*

Recorded by Richard Allsopp.

▸ **chop the clock**

to reset a vehicle's mileometer (odometer) to a reduced measure *US*

- You know chopping the clock is a felony. But maybe in the old days sometimes a mechanic, up in the dasboard anyway, kind of had his screwdriver slip on the odometer. —John Updike, *Rabbit is Rich*, p. 116, 1981
- —Angela Devlin, *Prison Patter*, p. 37, 1996
- Chop the cloc: The illegal practice of setting back a car's odometer. —Robert Genat, *The American Car Dealership*, p. 99, 1999

▸ **chop wood**

to drive off a road or motorway into a tree *US*

- — *American Speech*, p. 268, December 1962: 'The language of traffic policemen'

▸ **chop your gums**

to engage in idle talk *US*

- The farmers were chewing the fat in feed and hardware stores, the women were chopping their gums in Five-and-tens and department stores[.] —Jack Kerouac, *Letter to Caroline and Paul Blake*, p. 143, 16th March 1948

chop-chop *noun*

1 food *US, 1951*

- —J.E. Lighter, *Historical Dictionary of American Slang, Volume 1*, p. 413, 1994

2 a meal

Used by UN troops in the Korean war, 1950–53.

3 oral sex performed on a man *US*

From the vocabulary of Vietnamese prostitutes, taken and used by US soldiers.

- —Gregory Clark, *Words of the Vietnam War*, p. 172, 1990

4 trade union factionalism *US*
- Soon I was indulging in "chop chop," union jargon for factionalism. You couldn't avoid it in those days in Detroit.—Clancy Sigal, *Going Away*, p. 315, 1961

5 loose-leaf tobacco sold illegally *AUSTRALIA*
- [T]hey were the go-betweens in the lucrative trade of 'chop chop ' – or illicit tobacco.— *Weekend Australian (Inquirer)*, p. 19, 2nd February 2001

chop-chop *verb*

during the Korean war, to eat *US*
- Chop-chop in World War II meant hurry up, snap into it, get on the ball, etc. In Korea, chop chop is most natives' term for eat, and many GI's are picking it up.— *The Baltimore Sun*, 24th June 1951

chop-chop *adverb*

immediately; in an instant *UK, 1836*

Pidgin or mock pidgin, sometimes used as an imperative.
- Boy, bring us three Reverend Davidsons. And boy: chop-chop!—Max Shulman, *Anyone Got a Match?*, p. 110, 1964
- At the sound of which word Little Cousin Norman would take off chop-chop at a chubby little scamper for the house.—Robert Gover, *Poorboy at the Party*, p. 102, 1966
- Wilson, take him and brief him. Chop-chop.—*Airheads*, 1994

chop-chop square *nickname*

a large square in Riyadh, Saudi Arabia, that, on a Friday, is the chosen site for public execution by beheading (with a sword) of those the state has sentenced to death
- [T]hey don't go to sleep wondering if they will be taken to 'chop-chop square' for decapitation in front of cheering crowds[.]— *The Guardian*, 9th December 2001
- The locals call it 'chop-chop square'. Chopping people's heads off in public is fine by the man who's going to be the next Saudi ambassador to Britain.— *State of Denial*, 24th November 2002

chop house *noun*

a restaurant *US*
- [H]e conferred with three captains of waiters who were yearning to desert the fabled chophouse of James "Dinty" Moore.—Robert Sylvester, *No Cover Charge*, p. 99, 1956

chop it up *verb*

to engage in enthusiastic group conversation *US*
- —Rick Ayers (Editor), *Slang Dictionary*, p. 7, 2001

chop out *verb*

to separate a dose of powdered cocaine *UK*
- Brandon [Block] chopped out a fat one behind the decks[.]—*Ministry*, p. 22, January 2002

chopped *adjective*

1 marijuana-intoxicated *US*
- —Maria Hinojas, *Crews*, p. 167, 1995

2 ugly *US*
- — *Washingnton Post*, 14th October 1993

chopped and channeled *adjective*

(of a car) modified by cutting larger windows and lowering the body of the chassis frame, producing a sleeker profile that hugs the road *US*
- This was Barris' chopped-and-channeled Mercury period.—Tom Wolfe, *The Kandy-Kolored Tangerine-Flake Streamline Baby*, p. 88, 1965
- Get your big dynaflo Buick off the fuckin road and let my chopped and channeled Merc fly.—Abbie Hoffman, *Woodstock Nation*, p. 26–27, 1969
- I took apart the cars I saw and put them back together in more interesting ways, lowered, louvered, dagoed, chopped-and-channeled.—Tobias Wolff, *This Boy's Life*, p. 122, 1989

chopped liver *noun*

1 the vagina *UK*
- Abjection was invoked in various ways: through reference to dirtiness (e.g., front bum, dirt box), uncooked (bloody?) meat (e.g., meat seat, chopped liver), vaginal secretions of all types (e.g., slushing fuck pit, the snail trail), smell (e.g. smelly hole, stench trench), and wounds (e.g., gash, gaping axe wound)— *Journal of Sex Research*, p. 146, 2001

2 something of no consequence *US, 1954*
- MURTAUGH: Jesus. Maybe I should call for backup. RIGGS: What am I, chopped liver?— *Lethal Weapon*, 1987

chopped off *adjective*

annoyed, angry *US*
- — *American Speech*, p. 276, December 1963: 'American Indian student slang'

chopped rag *noun*

a parachute which has been altered *US*

Vietnam war usage.
- —Linda Reinberg, *In the Field*, p. 43, 1991

chopped top *noun*

a hot rod that has had its roof removed *US, 1960*
- Aguilar stared at the street as a three-window '35 Ford Coupe with a chopped top rolled past.— *Los Angeles Times*, p. 3 (Calendar), 22nd June 1986

chopper *noun*

1 a helicopter *US, 1951*
- There aren't more choppers coming?— *M*A*S*H*, 1970
- Chopper's on the way, Gardner, hang in there, you gonna be okay. — *Platoon*, 1986
- Our choppers can see them from miles away / Those guys at "Reach" will then relay.—Sandee Shaffer Johnson, *Cadences*, p. 147, 1986
- The Vietcong had no helicopters (generally referred to as "choppers," by the way); those were American aircraft that accidentally shot up their own men.— *Natinal Review*, 10th November 1989
- [T]he chopper's tracked her the whole way but is going to lose contact any second[.]—John King, *White Trash*, p. 15, 2001

2 a modified motorcyle with an emphasis on function, not form, usually featuring high handlebars *US*

From CHOP.
- A chopped hog, or "chopper," is little more than a heavy frame, a tiny seat and a massive 1,200-cubic-centimeter (or 74-cubic-inch) engine.—Hunter S. Thompson, *Hell's Angels*, p. 97, 1966
- After twenty minutes of being told how to turn some kind of 1957 motorcyle into a chopper, he turned his back in disgust.—Donald Goines, *Black Gangster*, p. 18, 1977
- FABIAN: Where did you get this motorcyle? BUTCH: It's a chopper, baby, hop on.— *Pulp Fiction*, 1994
- Hell's Angel "choppers" were born when we started taking the front fenders off our bikes, cutting off the back fender, and changing the handlebars.—Ralph "Sonny" Barger, *Hell's Angel*, p. 56, 2000

3 a bicycle modified with an emphasis on function, not form, usually featuring high handlebars *UK*
- —David Powis, *The Signs of Crime*, 1977

4 the penis *UK, 1973*
- Now, guys, brace yourselves, there's no avoiding this, and I'm not talking about my chopper.—Ben Elton and Rik Mayall, *The Young Ones*, 8th May 1984
- That's why they call me Moby – end of the day, I've got a fucking big chopper. Fucking whale of a thing, truth be known.—Kevin Sampson, *Clubland*, p. 31, 2002

5 a machine gun *US, 1929*
- Time was when you stood behind a chopper yourself, now you let a college kid do your blasting.—Mickey Spillane, *I, The Jury*, p. 18, 1947
- [Y]ou did not have to be twenty-one to press the trigger on a chopper.—Paul Gallico, *Trial By Terror*, p. 88, 1951

6 a pistol *US*
- — *American Speech*, p. 193, October 1957: 'Some colloquialisms of the handgunner'

7 a hacksaw; a hacksaw blade *US*
- —Hyman E. Goldin et al., *Dictionary of American Underworld Lingo*, p. 44, 1950

8 a logger or lumberjack *US*
- —John Gould, *Maine Lingo*, p. 49, 1975

9 an elderly sow or boar suitable to be turned into pork sausages *NEW ZEALAND*
- Choppers were in good supply and included a line of 55 from a Hawke's Bay vendor which averaged $160.— *New Zealand Farmer*, p. 42, 1988

10 a cow destined for slaughter rather than a dairy life *AUSTRALIA, 1987*
- —Maureen Brooks and Joan Ritchie, *Tassie Terms*, p. 30, 1995

11 a deer-skin mitten with a wool mitten insert *US*

Michigan Upper Peninsula usage.

12 a car taken in part-exchange *UK*

Second-hand car dealers' slang.
- — *Sunday Times*, 24th October 1965

13 a ticket taker *US*
- —Harold Wentworth and Stuart Berg Flexner, *Dictionary of American Slang*, p. 103, 1960

14 a bad mood *UK*
Used by printers and compositors. No longer in use by 1960.
- A companion is choppery when he is surly and unapproachable and therefore looks hatchet-faced: hence having a chopper on. —G.E. Rowles, *The "Line" Is On*, 1948

chopper *verb*
to transport something by helicopter *US, 1968*
From **CHOPPER** (a helicopter).
- —David Walker, *Devil's Plunge*, 1968

chopper coppers *noun*
the police in helicopters *US*
Quoted as a term used by residents of Berkeley, California.
- —*New York Times*, p. 24, 10th February 1970
- Most of it was growing outside on a porch, clearly visible to anybody at a higher elevation, such as, say, a snooping copper chopper. —Larry "Ratso" Sloman, *Reefer Madness*, p. 420, 1979
- That game's halftime show will include an exhibition by LAPD's Special Weapons and Tactics (SWAT) unit, as well as helicopter-borne officers flying into the stadium and rappelling from the "copper choppers" to a simulated crime scene on the Coliseum floor. —*San Francisco Chronicle*, p. D6, 24th January 1990
- These chopper coppers are zeroing on Ruby[.] —John King, *White Trash*, p. 6, 2001
- There's a new breed of police officer on the hunt for the menacing motorists who make highway travel an unwelcome hell ride: the chopper copper. —*Boston Herald*, p. 5, 9th June 2001

chopper jockey *noun*
a helicopter pilot or crew member *US*
- —*American Speech*, p. 158–159, May 1960: 'The burgeoning of 'jockey''

choppers *noun*
1 the teeth *US, 1944*
- He was smiling, grim through his cheap false choppers and blurred alcoholic face[.] —Gilbert Sorrentino, *Steelwork*, p. 153, 1970
- [A]n avenging old witch whose gorgeous smile and girlish face were courtesies of a five grand set of upper and lower choppers and a New York face lift[.] —Iceberg Slim (Robert Beck), *Doom Fox*, p. 100, 1978

2 the female legs *US*
- —*American Speech*, p. 273, December 1963: 'American Indian student slang'

choppy *noun*
a choppy wave *AUSTRALIA*
Surfers' use, reported by Barry Prentice, 1984.

choppy *adjective*
1 (of railway track) uneven, producing a rough ride *US*
- —J. Herbert Lund, *Herb's Hot Box of Railraod Slang*, p. 78, 1975

2 in autombile racing, describing abrupt movements in vertical wheel displacement *US*
- —Don Alexander, *The Racer's Dictionary*, p. 15, 1980

3 (of a temperature chart) uneven *UK, 1961*
Hospital nurses' use.

chop-ride *noun*
a test-flight to examine a pilot's suitability to continue flying *UK*
To fail the test would result in the **CHOP**.
- —Robert Prest, *F4 Phantom*, 1979

chops *noun*
1 the teeth or mouth *UK, 1589*
- He spit blood on the floor. "Boss, suh, please be careful with my chops – they're tender." —Chester Himes, *The Real Cool Killers*, p. 71, 1959
- A clout in the chops is what they deserved after dropping their Austin-Healey in the drink last night[.] —Max Shulman, *Anyone Got a Match?*, p. 54, 1964
- If I'd been on the outside, not being able to play until my chops healed, I'd probably have brooded the time away. —Nat Hentoff, *Jazz Country*, p. 141, 1965
- [S]mashing the mike in his [Iggy Pop] chops, jumping into the crowd to wallow around a forest of legs[.] —Lester Bangs, *Psychotic Reactions and Carburetor Dung*, p. 31–32, 1970
- Maytbe Mailer punches Vidal in the chops, maybe Vidal kicks Mailer in the cozies. —Robert Campbell, *Alice in La-La Land*, p. 52, 1987

2 musical ability *US, 1968*
- [D]ecades of musicians with their "licks" and "chops"[.] —Sean Hutchinson, *Crying Out Loud*, p. 176, 1988
- Man, your chops must've been really tight —Elmore Leonard, *Be Cool*, p. 108, 1999

3 an ability; a technique *US*
Extends the skilled sense of jazz 'chops'.
- [Kirsten Dunst]'s already been brilliant in so many bad movies (and a few good ones) that she's a by-word for progidous acting chops. —*Uncut*, p. 16, February 2002

4 the female legs *US, 1960*
- —*American Speech*, p. 273, December 1963: 'American Indian student slang'

chops *verb*
to talk *UK*
Adapted from **CHOPS** (the mouth), hence 'to use the mouth'.
- Just another old geezer goes down the bookie's, goes down the pub, chopsing about the old days. —John Williams, *Cardiff Dead*, p. 49, 2000

chop shop *noun*
a car body repair shop where stolen cars are altered or parts are stripped for sale separately *US*
- Jimmie (The Bomber) Catuara, 72, was assassinated yesterday in what police called a continuing chop-shop stolen auto parts vendetta. —*Washington Post*, p. A7, 29th July 1978
- —Bill Reilly, *Big Al's Official Guide to Chicagoese*, p. 21, 1982
- Pachoulo owned a piece of a chop shop on Alameda, near Olive Avenue Park over in Burbank, where stolen cars were dismembered with acetylene torches and the parts parceled out for sale. —Robert Campbell, *Juice*, p. 116, 1988
- The chop shop. Where are the stripped cars? The rolled-back odometers? The part bins? —*Gone in 60 Seconds*, 2000
- After that, it would either be professionally stripped in a chop shop or dismembered by petty thieves. —Robert Ludlum, *The Cassandra Compact*, p. 297, 2001
- The only BMW's you see around here are from the chop shop. —Alisa Valdes-Rodriguez, *The Dirty Girls Social Club*, p. 204, 2003

chopsocky *noun*
oriental martial arts; low-budget martial arts films *US*
Probably a blend of *chop suey* (a popular Chinese dish) and **SOCK** (to hit).
- [Stan Shaw] got to play bone-crushers on TV cop shows, a martial arts maestro in a chopsocky melodrama called 'TNT Jackson'. —*The Washington Post*, 10th February 1978
- Bright spot here is Kriel, a South African star who dressed up the James Ryan chopsocky hit "Kill and Kill Again" a decade ago. —*Daily Variety*, 27th June 1990
- There was a time when merely mentioning this chopsocky skill [Kung Fu] would send men running. —*The FHM Little Book of Bloke*, p. 6, June 2003

chops on *verb*
to talk and talk *UK*
A variation of **CHOPS**.
- Used to chops on a lot about how he did karate[.] —John Williams, *Cardiff Dead*, p. 194, 2000

chopstick *noun*
a South Asian person *US*
Offensive.
- —Edith A. Folb, *runnin' down some lines*, p. 232, 1980

chopsticks *noun*
1 the number six *UK*
Rhyming slang.
- —Leighton Rees, *Leighton Rees on Darts*, p. 19, 1980

2 mutual, simultaneous masturbation *US, 1941*
From the crossing of hands in the piano piece 'Chopsticks'.
- —Robert A. Wilson, *Playboy's Book of Forbidden Words*, p. 197, 1972

chop suey *adjective*
mixed up *US*
Hawaiian youth usage.
- "I get Japanese, Chinese, Filipino, Irish, German, Hawaiian, French-" "Real chop suey, yeah?" —Douglas Simonson, *Pidgin to da Max*, 1981

chopsy *adjective*
loquacious, too talkative *UK*
- Just ignore him, Janey. Chopsy cunt, that's all he is. —Niall Griffiths, *Sheepshagger*, p. 111, 2001

choptop *noun*
a crewcut haircut *US*
- —Edd Byrnes, *Way Out with Kookie*, 1959

chop-up *noun*
a division of plunder *AUSTRALIA*
- —Sidney J. Baker, *The Australian Language*, 1966

chor *noun*

a thief *FIJI*

- I look back at what I could have done if I wanted to be a uniformed crook, chor. — *Sunday Post*, p. 4, 15th June 1997

chorals; corals *noun*

a central nervous system depressant, especially chloral hydrate *US, 1998*

- — Richard A. Spears, *The Slang and Jargon of Drugs and Drink*, p. 122, 1986
- — Mike Haskins, *Drugs*, p. 282, 2003

chorb *noun*

a spot, a pimple *SOUTH AFRICA, 1970*

School slang.

- — Jean Branford, *A Dictionary of South African English*, 1978

chord-ially

used as a humorous closing in letters between singers *US*

- — *American Speech*, p. 296, Autumn-Winter 1975: 'The jargon of barbershop'

chordy *adjective*

stolen *UK*

From Romany *côr* (to steal).

- — Patrick O'Shaughnessy, *Market Traders' Slang*, 1979

chore *verb*

1 to steal something *UK*

English gypsy use; from original Romany *côr*.

- — Patrick O'Shaughnessy, *Market Traders' Slang*, 1979
- He chored that food from the kitchens. — Angela Devlin, *Prison Patter*, p. 37, 1996
- I didn't chore his brother's burger. — Jimmy Stockin, *On The Cobbles*, p. 95, 2000

2 to arrest someone *UK*

- It's like asking to get yourself chored, making yourself conspicuous, putting yourself on offer. — J.J. Connolly, *Layer Cake*, p. 74, 2000

chorer *noun*

a thief *UK*

Derives from **CHORE** (to steal).

- — Patrick O'Shaughnessy, *Market Traders' Slang*, 1979

chore whore *noun*

an assistant *UK*

- Slatter was Bell's right-hand man, his factotum, his chore whore. It was he who ran errands, took messages, bought cocaine[.] — Will Self, *The Sweet Smell of Psychosis*, p. 21, 1996

chorine *noun*

a member of a theatrical chorus *US, 1922*

- Makes a change from those cottage queen chorines[.] — The cast of 'Aspects of Love', Prince of Wales Theatre, *Palare for Beginners*, 1989–92
- It was what looked like twelve Las Vegas chorines crowded in with one old boy who was wearing the biggest cowboy hat and the darkest Foster Grants I'd ever seen. — Stephen King, *Nightmares & Dreamscapes*, p. 41, 1993
- composing his daily letter to Maura Zell, his mistress, who was a chorine in the road company of Pearls of Broadway — Michael Chabon, *The Amazing Adventures of Kavalier & Clay*, p. 81, 2000
- With Steven Tyler, John Entwistle and Joan Jett in attendance, Jimmy Stoma marries a chorine turned professional wrestler in Las Vegas. — Carl Hiaasen, *Basket Case*, p. 3, 2002

choro *verb*

to steal something *FIJI, 1989*

- You see those shoes? He choro-ed them. — Jan Tent, 1995

chorrie; tjorrie *noun*

a near-derelict car *SOUTH AFRICA, 1961*

- [O]nly chewing gum and axle grease is holding that old chorrie together. — Bryce Courtenay, *Power of One*, p. 380, 1989

chorus and verse; chorus *noun*

the posterior, the backside *UK*

Glasgow rhyming slang (reliant on the local accent) for **ARSE**.

- Are ye corned beef [deaf]? I said sit doon on yer chorus and we'll have a wee Salvador [drink]. Mine's a Mick Jagger [lager] by the way. — *The Guardian*, 29th April 2002
- She was no angel, either, the way she worked her chorus. — Bodmin Dark, *Dirty Cockney Rhyming Slang*, 2003

chossel *noun*

a girlfriend *BARBADOS*

- — Richard Allsopp, *Dictionary of Caribbean English Usage*, p. 153, 1996

chota *noun*

the police; a police officer *US*

Border Spanish used in English conversation by Mexican-Americans.

- — Dagoberto Fuentes and Jose Lopez, *Barrio Language Dictionary*, p. 49, 1974

chovies *noun*

anchovies *US*

- — *Maledicta*, p. 9, 1996: 'Domino's Pizza jargon'

chow *noun*

1 food *US, 1856*

- "What the hell, roomy," he said. "Let's go to chow." — Ralph Ellison, *Invisible Man*, p. 106, 1947
- You tried to hurry good chow and you'd screw it up sure as hell. — Jim Thompson, *The Nothing Man*, p. 245, 1954
- Privacy exists because you pretend nothing else is there and in a chow joint you're expected to obey the rules of the game. — Mickey Spillane, *Return of the Hood*, p. 82, 1964

2 a Chinese person *AUSTRALIA, 1864*

Offensive.

- They even inspected an ancient hovel in the diggings, long deserted by other Chows because old Jimmy Ah Wah had pegged out there[.] — Norman Lindsay, *Halfway to Anywhere*, p. 114, 1947
- I just passed his kitchen and there's not a bloody chow in sight out there. — Bert Newton, *Bert!*, p. 131, 1977

chow *verb*

to eat *US, 1900*

- You want something to chow? — *Airheads*, 1994

Chow *adjective*

Chinese *AUSTRALIA, 1903*

Offensive.

- [A] knowledgeable Chow driver is a sheer delight. — Barry Humphries, *The Traveller's Tool*, p. 99, 1985
- — David McGill, *David McGill's Complete Kiwi Slang Dictionary*, p. 29, 1998

chow

used as a greeting and as a farewell *UK*

A variation of **CIAO**. Recorded in this spelling in a 1961 letter to Partridge from Nicholas Bentley noting its popularity as a form of both salutation and goodbye, and particularly at the Royal College of Art.

chowderhead *noun*

a fool *UK, 1819*

- — Helen Dahlskog (Editor), *A Dictionary of Contemporary and Colloquial Usage*, p. 13, 1972
- Does this chowderhead really believe Time magazine wants to hire him? — Carl Hiaasen, *Tourist Season*, p. 200, 1986

chow down *verb*

1 to set to eating *US, 1945*

Originally military, then spread into widespread, if affected, use.

- Most people would chow down on cheese and cold cuts before heading upstairs. — Armistead Maupin, *Tales of the City*, p. 128, 1978

2 to perform oral sex *US*

- — J.E. Lighter, *Historical Dictionary of American Slang, Volume 1*, p. 416, 1994

chow for now

goodbye *US*

An intentional corruption of the Italian *ciao*.

- — Connie Eble (Editor), *UNC-CH Campus Slang*, p. 1, Fall 1991

chow hall *noun*

a school cafeteria *US*

- — *American Speech*, p. 274, December 1963: 'American Indian student slang'

chowhound *noun*

an enthusiastic eater *US, 1917*

- Not to mention such obvious rhymings as the charge-of-quarters' morning wakey-wakey call, "Okay, men. Drop your cocks and grab your socks!," or chowhound or shit list or walkie-talkie or the favorite term for those unhappy in the army, nervous in the service. — Paul Fussell, *Wartime*, p. 256, 1989
- Now you know why Marco Polo – a real chowhound – traveled clear up Rainier Avenue South to discover Aurora Avenue North. — *Seattle Post-Intelligencer*, p. E2, 31st March 2004

chowmeinery *noun*

in circus and carnival usage, a Chinese restaurant *US*

- — Don Wilmeth, *The Language of American Popular Entertainment*, p. 52, 1981

chow miaow *noun*
Chinese food *AUSTRALIA*
Punning **CHOW** as food generally, a Chinese person, and a shortening of *chow mein* (itself a root for the sense as 'food') with a convenient rhyme to suggest catmeat is a staple ingredient.
- —Edward Morrisby, 1958

Chriggy; Chriggie *noun*
Christmas *UK*
A variation of **CHRISSY**, recorded in 1984 but has since disappeared without trace.

Chrimbo; Chrimble; Crimble *noun*
Christmas *UK*
- He's stopped the Chrimbo party and all, too[.]—Kevin Sampson, *Outlaws*, p. 41, 2001
- Just, "Happy Chrimbo", yer know.—Niall Griffiths, *Kelly + Victor*, p. 47, 2002

Chrissake!; chrisake!
Christ's sake! *UK*
- For Chrissake belt up and take it.—John Peter Jones, *Feather Pluckers*, p. 108, 1964
- Here we were knocking ourselves out for chrisake, giving them all we have.—Johnny Speight, *It Stands to Reason*, p. 92, 1973

chrissie *noun*
a chrysanthemum *AUSTRALIA*
- Within the year, people have planted their prissy shrubs and garden gnomes where Grandpa had grown his 'chrissies'.—Phillip Adams, *The Unspeakable Adams*, p. 6, 1977

Chrissy; Chrissie *noun*
Christmas *AUSTRALIA, 1966*
- Of course the older I get it's not hard to work out that Chrissy is mainly for kids[.]—Paul Vautin, *Turn It Up!*, p. 115, 1995
- Christmas morning he said my chrissie present was in the garage[.] —*The Guardian*, 15th January 2001

Christ *adjective*
used as an adjectival intensifier *BAHAMAS*
- Not one Christ t'ing.—John A. Holm, *Dictionary of Bahamian English*, p. 114, 1982

Christ!
used as a register of anger, frustration, wonder, etc *UK, 1748*
Blasphemous by derivation, probably blasphemous in use.

Christ almighty!
used as a register of anger, frustration, wonder, etc *UK*
Blasphemous by derivation, probably blasphemous in use.
- Oh Christ Almighty. Sinew in nicotine base. Keep back, keep back. The entire sink's gone rotten.—Bruce Robinson, *Withnail and I*, 1987

Christ almighty wonder *noun*
a person of remarkable talent; such a person who is very aware of how special he or she is; an asounding event *UK, 1961*
A combination of the exclamation **CHRIST ALMIGHTY!** with 'wonder' (an outstanding thing).

christen *verb*
1 to give a name to something, to call something by a particular name *UK, 1642*
After the Christian tradition.
- The scientists christened the new mouse "obese", later abbreviated to "ob", and pronounced "OB".—*The Guardian*, 11th January 2003

2 to use something for the first time *UK*
- It was the perfect way to christen the new £3m training centre[.] —*BBCi*, 8th June 2003

▸ **christen the queen**
to urinate *AUSTRALIA*
- —Thommo, *The Dictionary of Australian Swearing and Sex Sayings*, p. 26, 1985

christer *noun*
a Christian who proclaims his beliefs to all, whether they wish to hear or not *US, 1921*
- "Why don't you get the hell out of here and go clean up or something?" "What are you – a christer?"—John Nichols, *The Sterile Cuckoo*, p. 219, 1965
- Bush is a Christer. He takes every opportunity to inform the American people that he is in touch with the Lord and therefore that, by deduction, what he does is the Lord's work.—*Chattanooga (Tennessee) Free Press*, p. B9, 10th September 2003

Christian *adjective*
(of a person) decent; (of a thing) civilised, decent, respectable *UK, 1577*
In early use the sense was human as opposed to animal. Contemporary use tends towards irony.

Christians in Action *nickname*
the US Central Intelligence Agency *US*
Back formation from the agency's initials.
- They worked for my brothers-in-arms from the organization we fondly called Christians In Action – the CIA.—Richard Marcinko and John Weisman, *Rogue Warrior*, p. 126, 1992

christina *noun*
▷ see: **CRISTINA**

Christine *noun*
1 in homosexual usage, used as a personification of methamphetamine powder *US*
- —*Maledicta*, p. 227, Winter 1980: '"Lovely, blooming, fresh and gay": the onomastics of camp'

2 cocaine *US*
Another in a long series of personifications of drugs based on the drug's first letter.
- He got up, dressed, we took a few more toots of Christine and Henry (pineapple) and split.—A.S. Jackson, *Gentleman Pimp*, p. 71, 1973

Christ-killer *noun*
a Jewish person *UK, 1861*
Offensive.
- Through the centuries, the Church has, wittingly and unwittingly, helped to nurture hate for the Jew, the "Wandering Jew," the "Christ Killer." [Letter to the editor]—*Life*, p. 13, 14th January 1946
- "No, I'm different. (Pause) I'm Jewish." "(Shocked) Christ-killer!" —Raymond Mungo, *Famous Long Ago*, p. 58, 1970

Christless *adjective*
cursed, damned *US, 1912*
- Talk about a Christless mess. And for what?—*Indianapolis (Indiana) Star*, p. 1B, 28th November 1999

Christmas!
used as a mild expletive *UK, 1909*
A euphemistic evasion of **CHRIST!**.

Christmas card *noun*
1 in trucking, a speeding ticket *US*
- —Wayne Floyd, *Jason's Authentic Dictionary of CB Slang*, p. 12, 1976

2 a guard, especially a train guard *UK*
Rhyming slang.
- —Julian Franklyn, *A Dictionary of Rhyming Slang*, 1960

▸ **off your Christmas card list; not on your Christmas card list**
used as an expression of displeasure towards someone *UK*
A jocular threat, often in verb form: 'to cross someone off your Christmas card list'.
- When my first son was born, a friend who hovered on the fringes of the radical feminist movement whispered poison in my ear. "Poor you," she hissed, "having to raise one of the enemy." I crossed her off my Christmas card list, but the words still rankled.—*The Guardian*, 5th July 2003

Christmas cheer; Christmas *noun*
beer *UK*
- The last time I was sober was eight Christmases [sic] ago.—Ray Puxley, *Cockney Rabbit*, 1992

Christmas crackers *noun*
the testicles *UK*
Rhyming slang for **KNACKERS**. Noted by David Hillman, 1974.

Christmas dinner *noun*
a winner *UK*
Rhyming slang.
- —Ray Puxley, *Cockney Rabbit*, 1992

Christmases *noun*
▸ **like all your Christmasses have come at once**
very happy, delighted *UK*
- Colonel Jones, looking like all his Christmasses have come at once (whilst playing male lead in "Debbie Does Dallas")—Ken Lukowiak, *A Soldier's Song*, 1993

Christmas hold *noun*
a grabbing of another's testicles *AUSTRALIA, 1950*
That is, 'a handful of nuts'.
• The good old 'Christmas hold', otherwise known as the brutal act of grabbing another's testicles, is being outlawed.—*Sydney Morning Herald*, p. 46, 28th February 1997

Christmas kitty *noun*
a holiday bonus cheque *US*
• —Jerry Robertson, *Oil Slanguage*, p. 87, 1954

Christmas log *noun*
a racing greyhound *UK*
Rhyming slang for 'dog'.
• —David Hillman, 1974

Christmas present *noun*
in tiddlywinks, a stroke of good luck *US*
• —*Verbatim*, p. 525, December 1977

Christmas roll *noun*
a multi-coloured assortment of barbiturate capsules *US*
• —David W. Maurer and Victor Vogel, *Narcotics and Narcotic Addiction*, p. 397, 1973

Christmas shopping; Christmas shop; Christmas *noun*
of a male, masturbation *UK*
Rhyming slang for **STROP(PING)**.
• [D]oing your Christmas shopping in the privacy of your own home[.]—Ray Puxley, *Cockney Rabbit*, 1992

Christmas tree *noun*
1 a capsule of amobarbital sodium and secobarbital sodium (trade name Tuinal™), a combination of central nervous system depressants *US*
• —Donald Louria, *The Drug Scene*, p. 189, 1968
• —*Current Slang*, p. 9, Spring 1971
• Tuinal is what I like. Some people call them Christmas Trees. That's the underworld slang for them because they're a kind of a green and kind of a red[.]—Bruce Jackson, *Outside the Law*, p. 110, 1972

2 an assortment of multi-coloured pills *US*
• —Jay Robert Nash, *Dictionary of Crime*, p. 66, 1992

3 marijuana *US*
Draws a parallel between two plants that appear at times of celebration.
• Anyway, he said the shit was garbage ... Christmas tree smoke.—Jim Carroll, *Forced Entries*, p. 70, 1987
• —Mike Haskins, *Drugs*, p. 287, 2003

4 in drag racing, an electronic starting device consisting of a set of lights *US*
• Drivers watch the yellow lights blink one at a time down the tree until the green light goes on. If a driver moves his car before the green light is on, he gets a red light... That's what a Christmas tree is all about. —Ed Radlauer, *Drag Racing Pix Dix*, p. 13, 1970
• The black and white and the shining orange Camaro perch at the starting line, both drivers' eyes glued on the "Christmas tree" – the vertical light stand that signals the start of every race.—*Los Angeles Times*, p. A26, 6th June 2003

5 a bank of red and green-coloured lights that are part of an instrument panel *US, 1945*
• Captain Rogers? I have a a green Christmas tree on board.—Edwin Corley, *The Jesus Factor*, p. 167, 1970
• First, we waited for the "Christmas tree," the bank of indicator lights showing the status of all hull openings, to change from red to green to all green, signaling that they were closed.—Richard O'Kane, *Clear the Bridge*, p. 14, 1977

6 in the car sales business, a car loaded with accessories and gadgets *US*
• —*Cars*, p. 40, December 1953

7 in trucking, a tractor trailer embellished with many extra running lights *US*
• —Montie Tak, *Truck Talk*, p. 30, 1971

8 in oil drilling, the collection of equipment at the top of an oil well *US, 1925*
• —William Haggard, *The Telemann Touch*, 1950
• —Jerry Robertson, *Oil Slanguage*, p. 37, 1954

9 in the television and film industries, a cart used for storing and carrying lighting equipment *US*
• —Tony Miller and Patricia George, *Cut! Print!*, p. 51, 1977

10 in the television and film industries, a stand with more than one light mounted on it *US*
• —Ira Konigsberg, *The Complete Film Dictionary*, p. 47, 1987

11 in railway terminology, a colour light signal *UK*
• —Harvey Sheppard, *Dictionary of Railway Slang*, 1970

12 a woman who over-dresses or over-uses cosmetics *US, 1960*
• —Frederic G. Cassidy, *Dictionary of American Regional English*, p. 656, 1985

13 the knee *UK*
Rhyming slang; the plural is 'Christmas trees'.
• —Ray Puxley, *Fresh Rabbit*, 1998

14 in electric line work, a pole-mounted auxiliary arm used for hoisting a conductor *US*
• —A.B. Chance Co., *Lineman's Slang Dictionary*, p. 4, 1980

15 in Nova Scotia, a piece of fishing gear with many lines, hooks and pegs attached *CANADA*
• As the boat is kept moving, the drale is towed behind it, and the fish bite into the pegs. A drale is known to the fishermen as a Christmas tree, because of all the dangling pieces.—*The Paper Clip*, 1980

▸ **(just) come down off the Christmas tree**
foolish, inexperienced, gullible *UK*
• [Y]ou reckon you got me for a grass. Jesus TT you reckon I came down off the Christmas tree or what?—Jeremy Cameron, *Brown Bread in Wengen*, p. 21, 1999

▸ **lit up like a Christmas tree**
dazzling; resplendent *AUSTRALIA*
• —W.R. Bennett, *Target Turin*, p. 15, 1962
• This is one time when you can hang the lot, light yourself up like a Christmas tree.—Geoffrey Tolhurst, *Flat 4 Kings Cross*, p. 45, 1963
• In the evening, a hospital ship arrived, lit from stem to stern – "like a bloody Christmas tree," said Barney – its great blood-red cross floodlit.—Jack Bennett, *Gallipoli*, p. 198, 1981

Christ on a bike!; Jesus Christ on a bike!
used as a register of shock or amazement *US*
• Brian Keyes removed the rum and dumped the ice cubes over Wiley's naked chest. "Christ on a bike!" Wiley sat up like a bolt.—Carl Hiaasen, *Tourist Season*, p. 163, 1986
• You think grown-up people pay their seven quid to see non violence? To see people being nice? Jesus Christ on a mountain bike!—James Hawes, *White Powder, Green Light*, p. 8, 2002

Christ on a boogie board!
used for registering surprise or disbelief *US*
• "Christ on a Boogie Board," I said. "You never told me there was a cop shop this close[.]"—Kinky Friedman, *Steppin' on a Rainbow*, p. 88, 2001

Christ on a crutch!
used for expressing exasperation *US, 1928*
• But Christ on a crutch, the news that Britney Spears and Fred Durst are hitting it has blown nearly every other coherent thought right out of our little peanut brains.—*Seattle Weekly*, p. 46, 22nd January 2003

Christopher Lee *noun*
urine; urination; an act of urination *UK*
Rhyming slang for **PEE** or **WEE**; formed on the name of British film actor Christopher Lee (b.1922).
• —Ray Puxley, *Fresh Rabbit*, 1998

Chris Wren *noun*
a fifty pound note *UK*
An illustration of Sir Christopher Wren, architect, 1632–1723, featured on Bank of England £50 notes from 1981. Recorded in use in August 2002.

chrome *noun*
1 in computing, software features that attract buyers but add little functionally *US*
• The 3D icons in Motif are juts chrome but they certainly are pretty chrome.—Eric S. Raymond, *The New Hacker's Dictionary*, p. 95, 1991

2 the best, judged in terms of appearance; the shiniest examples *UK*
• They had missed being part of the Easter showcase for the chrome of their generation[.]—Alan Fletcher, *The Blue Millionaire*, 1998

chrome *verb*
in hot rodding, to add chrome features to a car *US*
• If it won't go, chrome it.—*American Speech*, p. 93, May 1954

chrome dome *noun*

1 a bald man; a bald head *US, 1962*

- Hose Nose / Chrome Dome / Mr. Absent Offenhauser. — Ron Padgett, *New and Selected Poems*, p. 78, 1995
- Last month in Dallas, an Associated Press photographer at a political fund-raiser captured Bush grabbing the chrome dome of an unidentified supporter so forcefully you can see identation marks. — *Austin (Texas) American-Statesman*, p. E1, 7th August 2003

2 a fibre helmet used between April and October in Vietnam to protect soldiers from the sun *US*

Aluminum paint gave rise to the 'chrome'.

- — Linda Reinberg, *In the Field*, p. 43, 1991

chrome-plated *adjective*

nicely dressed *US*

High school student usage, borrowing from car vocabulary.

- — *San Francisco Examiner*, p. 21, 12th December 1961

chrome to the dome *noun*

a pistol held to the head *US*

- — Ethan Hilderbrant, *Prison Slang*, p. 146, 1998

chromie *noun*

a chromed wheel, popular with hot rodders *US*

- — Lyle K. Engel, *The Complete Book of Fuel and Gas Dragsters*, p. 150, 1968

chromo *noun*

1 a female prostitute *AUSTRALIA, 1883*

From '*chromo*lithograph', a type of painted lithographic picture, referring to the 'painted' (i.e. made-up) faces of prostitutes.

- "What are you babbling about?" Infuriated, the boy picked the crumbs off his shirt. "About that wop chromo your old man knocks about with, that's all." — Ruth Park, *Poor Man's Orange*, p. 200, 1949
- — Jim Ramsay, *Cop It Sweet!*, p. 22, 1977

2 anything that is inexpensive, shoddy or inferior *US, 1934*

- — Joseph A. Weingarten, *An American Dictoinary of Slang*, p. 67, 1954

chrondo *noun*

potent marijuana *US*

A blend of **CHRONIC** and **INDO**.

- — Pamela Munro, *U.C.L.A. Slang*, p. 51, 1997

chroned out *adjective*

suffering from a hangover *US*

- — Don R. McCreary (Editor), *Dawg Speak*, 2001

chronic *noun*

1 potent marijuana *US*

A word popularised in hip-hop usage. 'The Chronic' by Dr Dre (1992) is one of the biggest-selling rap albums of all time.

- Beeitch, if you ain't got no kinda chronic, yo punk ass gots to go! — Snoop Doggy Dogg, *A Day in the Life of Snoop Doogy Dog [Cover art]*, 1993
- Smoking a spliff of high-octaine chronic (street talk for pot) in the back room, he explains his bond to Dre. "He's the bomb," says Snoop. — *People*, p. 77, 23rd May 1994
- Gimme a taste of the mothafuckin chronic. — *Kids*, 1995
- Look, I'll make amends. How about some chronic shit? — *Clueless*, 1995
- — Connie Eble (Editor), *UNC-CH Campus Slang*, p. 2, April 1995

2 marijuana mixed with crack cocaine *US, 1998*

- [A] fat ass J, of some bubonic chronic that made me choke[.] — Snoop Doggy Dogg, *Gin and Juice*, 1993
- — Mike Haskins, *Drugs*, p. 293, 2003

chronic *adjective*

1 constant; bad, objectionable, severe, unpleasant *UK, 1860*

From the conventional medical sense.

- PFI school scheme hit by chronic delays. — *The Guardian*, 20th November 2002

2 very good *US*

- — Connie Eble (Editor), *UNC-CH Campus Slang*, p. 2, Fall 1998

chronic bubonic *noun*

marijuana that is more potent than simple 'chronic' or simple 'bubonic' *US*

- — Pamela Munro, *U.C.L.A. Slang*, p. 54, 2001

Chryco *nickname*

the Chrysler Corporation, a car manufacturer *US*

- — John Edwards, *Auto Dictionary*, p. 31, 1993

chub *noun*

1 a moderately overweight person *UK, 1838*

- [Y]ou can be sure that plump women such as myself and many of my "chub" friends all over the country, who perhaps are contemplating weight loss, will never enter a Jenny Craig office. [Letter to the editor] — *Virginian-Pilot (Norfolk, Virginia)*, p. J4, 9th January 2000

2 the penis *US*

- — Anna Scotti and Paul Young, *Buzzwords*, p. 16, 1997

chub *verb*

to smuggle items into a prison by secreting the contraband up the anus *UK*

- — Angela Devlin, *Prison Patter*, p. 37, 1996

chub-a-dub *noun*

an act of masturbation *CANADA*

- Eli performs a "chub-a-dub" on his morning erection, still scenting Jezebel's hair on his pillow. — *Toronto Globe and Mail*, p. D23, 27th April 2002

chubb; chubb up *verb*

to lock a prison cell door *UK, 1950*

From the well-known branded lock.

- — Angela Devlin, *Prison Patter*, p. 37, 1996

chubbies *noun*

large female breasts *US*

- — Roger Blake, *The American Dictionary of Sexual Terms*, p. 35, 1964
- — *Current Slang*, p. 3, Winter 1971

chubby *noun*

1 an overweight man as a homosexual object of desire *US*

- Are there any straight bars for chubbies and chubby-chasers? — *Screw*, p. 11, 2 August 1971
- — *Maledicta*, p. 227, Winter 1980: '"Lovely, blooming, fresh and gay": the onomastics of camp'

2 an erection *US*

- — Pamela Munro, *U.C.L.A. Slang*, p. 51, 1997
- — Anna Scotti and Paul Young, *Buzzwords*, p. 16, 1997

chubby *adjective*

(of the penis) erect *UK*

- [T]he sight of her big old arse is getting me chubby. — *Loaded*, p. 57, June 2003

chubby-chaser *noun*

a person who is sexually attracted to overweight people *US, 1976*

- Are there any straight bars for chubbies and chubby-chasers? — *Screw*, p. 11, 2 August 1971
- — *Maledicta*, p. 227, Winter 1980: '"Lovely, blooming, fresh and gay": the onomastics of camp'
- — Wayne Dynes, *Homolexis*, p. 30, 1985
- — *American Speech*, p. 19, Spring 1985: 'The language of singles bars'
- Watching Buffy Davis and Tammy White going at it with a dildo in between them is a chubby-chaser's delight. — *Adult Video*, p. 50, August/September 1986

chubster *noun*

1 a overweight person *UK*

From conventional 'chubby' (overweight/fat).

- [A] balding, pasty-faced chubster[.] — *Q*, p. 24, May 2002

2 the penis *US*

- — Anna Scotti and Paul Young, *Buzzwords*, p. 16, 1997

chuc; chuke *noun*

a Pachuco, or young Mexican-American with a highly stylised sense of fashion and a specialised idiom *US*

The Pachuco was the Mexican zoot-suiter of the 1940s, and his legacy is seen today in Mexican-American culture. The term can be used either as a term of pride or as a term of derision.

- — *San Francisco Examiner: People*, p. 8, 27th October 1963
- They came in Packards, two of them, they dig big white cards; twelve, maybe thirteen chucs in all. — Richard Farina, *Been Down So Long*, p. 63, 1966
- — *Current Slang*, p. 15, Spring 1970

chuck *noun*

1 food *UK, 1850*

- — Joseph E. Ragen and Charles Finston, *Inside the World's Toughest Prison*, p. 794, 1962
- Surely he couldn't really be that upset over me picking up the wrong bit of chuck – even if I did? — Jimmy Stockin, *On The Cobbles*, p. 94, 2000

2 vomit *AUSTRALIA, 1966*
- Like for example if your kid chucks up and you don't notice, and those particles of chuck are sort of just dangling there, then that would also be a dingleberry. — *Wordmap (www.abc.net.au/wordmap)*, 2003

3 a white man *US, 1965*
A diminuitive of Charles or Charlie.
- — Clarence Major, *Dictionary of Afro-American Slang*, p. 37, 1970
- A few years ago, Civil Rights workers took to calling White "Chuck." — Roger Abrahams, *Positively Black*, p. 32, 1970

4 the Viet Cong *US, 1981*
- Chuck, Charlie, Mr. Charles, VC, Viet Cong, Victor Charlie. Whom are we talking about? — Nelson DeMille, *Word of Honor*, p. 131, 1985

5 a throw, a toss; in cricket, a thrown ball, an illegal delivery *UK, 1862*
- — Keith Foley, *A Dictionary of Cricketing Terminology*, p. 74, 1998

6 a shove that leads to a fight *BARBADOS*
- — Frank A. Collymore, *Barbadian Dialect*, p. 30, 1965

▸ give it a chuck
to stop, to desist *UK: SCOTLAND*
Often as an imperative.

chuck *verb*

1 to vomit *AUSTRALIA, 1957*
- His tie might be a little scraggy because the baby chucked all over his only paisley silk one[.] — Sue Rhodes, *And when she was bad she was popular*, p. 35, 1968
- — Alexander Buzo, *Norm and Ahmed*, p. 19, 1969
- — Wilda Moxham, *The Apprentice*, p. 115, 1969
- The green-faced fellow lifted his head and replied, 'What do you mean, not doing too well? I'm chucking as far as anyone else.' — Bob Staines, *Wot a Whopper*, p. 43, 1982
- — David McGill, *David McGill's Complete Kiwi Slang Dictionary*, p. 28, 1998

2 to throw something *UK, 1593*
- Robert Jr. and I got to be tight friends – by chucking rocks at a tin can, the next day in the courtyard. — Bobby Seale, *A Lonely Rage*, p. 25, 1978

3 to throw something away, to discard something *US, 1911*
- We all decided to chuck the idea because I'd have trouble making friends. — *Heathers*, 1988
- Well maybe I should just chuck it all and go sell derby hats to women in Boliva. — Joseph Wambaugh, *Finnegan's Week*, p. 11, 1993

4 to throw a case out of court *UK*
Police slang.
- — G.F. Newman, *Sir, You Bastard*, 1970

5 to dismiss someone, to reject someone; to jilt someone *AUSTRALIA*
- — Leonard Mann, *Flesh in Armour*, p. 155, 1932
- If you chucked me for another woman I wouldn't have much to live for, but you wouldn't find me playing the dying dove for all that. — Norman Lindsay, *The Cousin from Fiji*, p. 229, 1945

6 to eat excessively when being withdrawn from drug dependence *UK*
- — David Powis, *The Signs of Crime*, 1977

7 to forget *US*
Also 'chuck it'.
- — Marcus Hanna Boulware, *Jive and Slang of Students in Negro Colleges*, 1947

▸ chuck a charley; chuck a charlie
to have a fit of temper *AUSTRALIA, 1945*
- 'E was gonna chuck a charlie an' I wanted to shoot through[.] — Kathleen Spaulding, *An Aussie Tale (Tail)*, 1998

▸ chuck a dummy
to feign an illness or injury *US*
- — Jay Robert Nash, *Dictionary of Crime*, p. 66, 1992

▸ chuck a mental
to lose your temper and composure in a manner that suggests emotional instability *NEW ZEALAND*
- — David McGill, *David McGill's Complete Kiwi Slang Dictionary*, p. 30, 1998

▸ chuck a seven

1 to have a fit of temper *AUSTRALIA*
From the langauage of dice-playing.
- — Sidney J. Baker, *The Australian Language*, p. 121, 1945

2 to die *AUSTRALIA*
From the game of craps, in which to throw a seven (except on the first roll) is to lose.

▸ chuck a six; chuck a sixer
to have a fit of temper *AUSTRALIA*
From dice-playing.
- — Sidney J. Baker, *The Australian Language*, p. 121, 1945

▸ chuck a willy
to have a fit of temper *AUSTRALIA*
- — Sidney J. Baker, *The Australian Language*, p. 121, 1945

▸ chuck a wing-ding
to feign a seizure while in prison in the hope of obtaining drugs in treatment *US*
- — Jay Robert Nash, *Dictionary of Crime*, p. 66, 1992

▸ chuck your weight about; chuck your weight around
to behave in an unpleasant, domineering way; to bully someone *UK, 1909*

▸ chuck yourself about; chuck yourself into
to move about energetically *UK, 1984*
- Not sure on his classical abilities but he chucked himself into everything and smiled regardless of how exhausted he must have been at the end. — *Ballet Magazine*, May 2000
- Matt [Rippy] has spent the past three years chucking himself about the stage with the Reduced Shakespeare Company performing "THE COMPLETE WORKS OF WILLIAM SHAKESPEARE (abridged)" — *excert from the biography of an actor at the English Theater, Frankfurt*, 9th June 2003

chuck and jam *adjective*
crowded *TRINIDAD AND TOBAGO*
- — Lise Winer, *Dictionary of the English/Creole of Trinidad & Tobago*, 2003

chucked *adjective*
acquitted *UK*
From **CHUCK** (to throw a case out of court).
- Of three men on trial two were weighed off and one got chucked. — Paul Tempest, *Lag's Lexicon*, 1950

chucker *noun*
in cricket, a bowler who is apt to throw the ball *UK, 1882*
- Being called a chucker is the ultimate cricketing humiliation, bringing into question a player's skill, his honesty, and his achievements. — *BBC Sport*, 11th July 2000

chucker-out *noun*
a man employed to keep out and get rid of unwanted patrons; a bouncer *UK, 1884*
- If a dispute arose, the game was stopped immediately while the ring-keeper and chuckers-out investigated — Tom Hibbert, *Rockspeak!*, p. 38, 1983

chucker-outer *noun*
a bouncer *AUSTRALIA*
- A crowd-control supervisor, an event-management security consultant, a chucker-outer. Professional muscle. — Shane Maloney, *Nice Try*, p. 112, 1998

Chuck Fuck *noun*
a man of no real significance *US*
- "Who are you?" "Joe Schmoe. Chuck Fiuck. Who do you think?" — Christophre Brookmyre, *Country of the Blind*, p. 370, 1997
- [T]hey aren't worried about upsetting Chuck Fuck from Schmuck-film. — Christopher Brookmyre, *Not the End of the World*, p. 25, 1998

chuck horrors *noun*
the painful symptoms of withdrawal from drug addiction *US, 1926*
- So you might as well get yourself set for the steel-and-concrete and the chuck horrors. I had 'em. — *The New American Mercury*, p. 711, 1950
- "You look like you've got the chuck horrors," he commented[.] — Morton Cooper, *High School Confidential*, p. 58, 1958

chuckie *noun*
▷ **see: CHOOK**

chuck-in *noun*
a piece of good fortune; a bonus *AUSTRALIA, 1916*
From an earlier sense (to add to a collection).

chuck in *verb*

1 to get rid of something, to discard something, to quit something *UK, 1944*
- Make sure you have done your homework before you chuck in the day job[.] — *The Observer*, 30th November 2003

2 to contribute something *AUSTRALIA, 1907*

- They had just finished building a house, and they and all who had worked on it had 'chucked in' for a nine-gallon keg. — Nino Culotta (John O'Grady), *Gone Fishin'*, p. 201, 1962

3 to include something as an extra *AUSTRALIA*

- champagne and a chicken dinner chucked in — Frank Hardy, *The Yarns of Billy Borker*, p. 26, 1965
- The government may chuck in a few points about disability into a single equalities bill. — *The Guardian*, 17th July 2002

chucking *noun*

in cricket, an illegal act of throwing, not bowling, a ball *UK*

- Chucking: Why the fuss? — *BBC Sport*, 11th July 2000

chucking-out *noun*

an ejection, especially from a premises *UK, 1881*

chucking-out time *noun*

closing time in a public house or other licensed premises *UK, 1909*

An image of forced ejection.

- Got a situation that could boil over. Chucking-out time, and possible disturbance. — Duncan MacLaughlin, *The Filth*, p. 83, 2002

chuck it down *verb*

to rain, hail or snow, very heavily *UK*

Sometimes elaborated as, for example, 'chuck it down with rain'.

- You'll be on site and it's chucking it down and everyone wants an answer to every question within five minutes. — *The Guardian*, 7th October 2002

chuckle *noun*

an instance of vomiting *AUSTRALIA*

- Why don't y'go an' have a quick chuckle at the dirt, boy-san? — W.R. Bennett, *Wingman*, p. 69, 1961
- Calling for Herb, see, that's one of the many euphemisms for vomit, others include spue, burp, hurl, the big spit, the long spit, throw, the whip o'will, the technicolour laugh and, in Queensland, the chuckle. — Frank Hardy, *Billy Borker Rides Again*, 1967
- I'll hop out for a swift chuckle to make room for the last couple of chug-a-lugs! — Barry Humphries, *The Wonderful World of Barry McKenzie*, p. 18, 1968

chuckle *verb*

to vomit *AUSTRALIA*

- I've never chuckled so much in all my life as I did that night last summer[.] — Barry Humphries, *A Nice Night's Entertainment*, p. 77, 1964
- Now I've had liquid laughs in bars / And I've hurled from moving cars / And I've chuckled where and when it suited me. — Barry Humphries, *The Wonderful World of Barry McKenzie*, p. 15, 1968
- — Jim Ramsay, *Cop It Sweet!*, p. 22, 1977

chucklehead *noun*

a fool *UK, 1731*

- I enjoy a good har-dee-har-har as much as the next chucklehead[.] — *San Francisco Bay Guardian*, 4th December 2002

chuckleheaded *adjective*

simple, dim-witted *UK, 1768*

- A chuckleheaded, no-talent cook shovels food around a burned-out griddle with a warped spatula in one hand and a beat-up barbecue fork in the other, pouring sweat into the food for all to see. — Larry Heinemann, *Paco's Story*, p. 104, 1990

chuck off *verb*

1 to voice abuse; to let fly *AUSTRALIA, 1915*

- First you chuck off at the Wingco for insinuating that you're accident prone – then you turn round and contradict yourself by saying that *you* think you *are*. — W.R. Bennett, *Night Intruder*, p. 19, 1962

2 to throw someone off something *UK, 1841*

A colloquial use.

- It's all Tony Blair's fault that Frederick Forsyth has been chucked off the Today programme. — *The Observer*, 12th May 2002

chuck one up *verb*

to salute *UK*

Military.

- There was the general, so I chucked him one up, but he never saw me. — *Beale*, 1984
- — Nigel Foster, *The Making of a Royal Marine Commando*, 1987

chuck out *verb*

to eject someone forcibly; to get rid of someone *UK, 1869*

Usage may be actual, figurative or jocular.

- There used to be this competition between him [Brian Eno] and Bryan Ferry to get the most cheers, and when Eno won Ferry chucked him out. — *The Guardian*, 22nd February 2002

chucks *noun*

1 a powerful craving for food associated with withdrawal from heroin addiction *US*

Also 'chuckers'.

- After eight days I got the "chucks" and developed a tremendous appetite for cream puffs and macaroons. — William Burroughs, *Junkie*, p. 40, 1953
- This excessive desire for sweets is the beginning of what is known as the chucks, an enormous hunger which addicts experience in the last stages of withdrawal[.] — Emmett Grogan, *Ringolevio*, p. 63, 1972
- The chucks is a state of being so damn hungry from the meals you've missed 'til you feel like you could eat a wet mop. — A.S. Jackson, *Gentleman Pimp*, p. 127, 1973
- — Robert Ashton, *This Is Heroin*, p. 208, 2002

2 the craving for food that follows the smoking of marijuana *US*

- — William D. Alsever, *Glossary for the Establishment and Other Uptight People*, p. 6, December 1970

3 high-top sports shoes, especially Converse's Chuck Taylor™ shoes *US*

- — Connie Eble (Editor), *UNC-CH Campus Slang*, p. 2, Fall 1984

chuck up *verb*

1 to yield, to abandon, to give in *UK, 1864*

From pugilism, specifically from the traditional method of conceding defeat; a shortening of 'chuck up the sponge'.

2 to vomit *AUSTRALIA*

Reported by Barry Prentice, 1984.

chuck wagon *noun*

1 a truck stop or roadside restaurant *US*

A jocular reference to the cooking wagon on cattle drives in the Old West.

- — "Slingo", *The Official CB Slang Dictionary Handbook*, p. 15, 1976

2 a brakevan (caboose) *US*

- — Ramon Adams, *The Language of the Railroader*, p. 32, 1977

chuck you, Farley!

used as an expression of derision *CANADA*

An intentional corruption of 'Fuck you, Charley!', favoured by school children.

- — Bill Casselman, *Canadian Sayings*, p. 118, 2002

chud *noun*

a disgusting person *US*

From the film *Cannabalistic Humanoid Underground Dwellers*.

- Besides being the perfect film for study, it can drive home the message that these "CHUDS" ain't nothing compared to some of the people you'll have to meet in the movie business. — John Waters, *Crackpot*, p. 131 – 132, 1986
- — Pamela Munro, *U.C.L.A. Slang*, p. 30, 1989

chuddie; chuddy *noun*

chewing gum *UK, 1984*

Used by teenagers.

chuddies *noun*

underpants *UK*

Directly from Punjabi into **HINGLISH** (Asian English); widely popularised as a catchphrase **KISS MY CHUDDIES!** coined by *Goodness Gracious Me*, a BBC comedy sketch show scripted and performed by four British Asian comedians, first heard on Radio 4 in 1996 but better known from television, since 1999; often misunderstood to mean **ARSE**.

chuff *noun*

1 the buttocks *AUSTRALIA, 1945*

- — David McGill, *David McGill's Complete Kiwi Slang Dictionary*, p. 28, 1998
- He looks a right chuff in that hat — *The Last Of The Summer Wine*, 29th April 2001
- The immaculately dressed bull-worrier was gored up the chuff, resulting in what doctors described as "horrendous internal injuries". — *FHM*, p. 152, June 2003

2 the vagina *UK*

- — *Roger's Profanisaurus*, p. 8, December 1997

3 pubic hair *US*

- — Dale Gordon, *The Dominion Sex Dictionary*, p. 43, 1967
- — *Maledicta*, p. 131, Summer/Winter 1982: 'Dyke diction: the language of lesbians'

4 a homosexual male *UK, 1961*
A sexual objectification from the sense as 'buttocks'.

▸ **the chuff**
replaces 'the hell' in phrases such as 'where the hell?'; a euphemism for 'the fuck' *UK*
From **CHUFF** (the buttocks).
- Who the chuff's gonna come Sunday afternoons? — **Nicholas Blincoe**, *Ardwick Green (Disco Biscuits)*, p. 3, 1996
- I don't see why the chuff not, Gerald. — *The Full Monty*, 1997

chuff *verb*
to fart *UK*
- Ooops! Best open a window vicar. I've just chuffed. — *Roger's Profanisaurus*, 1998

chuff all
nothing, nothing at all *UK*
- Chuff all else to do. — *The Full Monty*, 1997

chuff box *noun*
the vagina; in later use, the anus *UK, 1961*

chuff chum *noun*
a male homosexual *UK, 1961*
An elaboration of **CHUFF** (a male homosexual). Derogatory.

chuffdruff; muffdruff *noun*
dried flakes of sexual secretions (male and/or female) clinging to the female pubic hair *UK*
An ellipsis of **CHUFF** (the vagina) or **MUFF** (the vagina, etc.) and 'dandruff'. Recorded by, perhaps coined for, *Roger's Profanisaurus*, 1998, then into slightly wider currency.

chuffed *adjective*
1 pleased, delighted; flattered; very excited *UK, 1957*
Originally northern English dialect meaning 'proud', adopted by military, then wider society. The current, more generalised usage was possibly spread by jazz fans. Embellishments include 'chuffed to fuck'; 'chuffed to arseholes'; 'chuffed to buggery'; 'chuffed pink'; 'chuffed to little mint-balls'; 'bo-chuffed'; 'chuffed to little naffy breaks'; 'chuffed to naffy breaks' and 'chuffed to oil-bumps'. Often qualified by intensifiers **DEAD**, **REAL**, **WELL**, etc.
- Janet Murray says: "I'd be chuffed" (current 'Cat' word for flattered). "It's nice to think someone fancies you." — *Woman's Own*, 1959
- I was really chuffed. — **Ann Barr and Peter York**, *The Official Sloane Ranger Handbook*, p. 158, 1982
- I'm chuffed to see her[.] — **Mike Benson**, *Room full of Angels (Disco Biscuits)*, p. 27, 1996
- You would be well and truly pretty fucking chuffed, wouldn't you? — **Dave Courtney**, *Raving Lunacy*, p. 52, 2000
- Caleb's chuffed to fuck it was his men that did it. — **Jack Allen**, *When the Whistle Blows*, p. 161, 2000
- And Ian [Dury], he'd be well chuffed. — **BP Fallon**, *Brand New Boots And Panties*, 2001

2 displeased, disgruntled *UK*
Qualifiers and context may be required to distinguish usage from the previous sense as 'pleased'. Variants include 'dischuffed' and 'dead chuffed'.

chuffer *noun*
1 a person, euphemistic for 'fucker' *UK*
- NATHAN: I don't feel well. GAZ: 'Course you don't, you cheeky chuffer, you've got a hangover. — *The Full Monty*, 1997

2 a cigarette-smoker *UK*
A play on 'puffer' and **CHUFF** (the buttocks/an arse).
- The fact wolves rarely smoke and would merrily kill a chuffer long before the cancer gets him is neither here nor there. — *Loaded*, p. 32, June 2003

3 a train *UK*
From nursery use.
- We went up the escalator [and] got our seats in the chuffer. We were made up. — **Jeremy Cameron**, *Brown Bread in Wengen*, p. 89, 1999

4 the buttocks *UK*
An elaboration of **CHUFF**.
- MC5 gave rock'n'roll a major kick up the chuffer during the early 1970s[.] — *Kerrang!*, 28th August 2004

chuffing *adjective*
used as an intensifier, a euphemism for 'fucking' *UK*
- Dave, are you gonna play the prince in the chuffin' tower all day, or what? — *The Full Monty*, 1997

chuffing Nora!
used for registering surprise, anger, amazement, etc *UK*
A variation of **FLAMING NORA!**.
- — *The Full Monty*, 1997

chuff it!
a general declaration of rejection or dimissal; may also imply resignation to or acceptance of a situation *UK*
FUCK IT! euphemistically.

chuff muncher *noun*
a lesbian *UK*
From **CHUFF** (the vagina).
- — *Roger's Profanisaurus*, 1998

chuff nut *noun*
a piece of faecal matter clinging to anal hair *UK, 1961*
Elaborated on **CHUFF**.

chuff piece *noun*
the anus, the arse *UK*
An elaboration of **CHUFF**.
- I got to wash a shift every night – if I don't want to feel like an old cow's chuff-piece that is. — **Christopher Hawke**, *For Campaign Service*, 1962

chuftie *noun*
the vagina *UK, 1998*
A variation of **CHUFF** (the vagina).

chuftie plug *noun*
a tampon *UK*
- — *Roger's Profanisaurus*, 1998

chug *noun*
a long, sustained swallow of a drink *US, 1969*
- — **J.E. Lighter**, *Historical Dictionary of American Slang, Volume 1*, p. 420, 1994

chug *verb*
1 to swallow a drink in a single draught *US*
An abbreviation of **CHUGALUG**.
- — **Connie Eble (Editor)**, *UNC-CH Campus Slang*, p. 2, Fall 1989
- [T]he man chugged the rest of his vodka and tonic[.] — **Greg Williams**, *Diamond Geezers*, p. 36, 1997
- Bacon, Moon and Lee are in the bar chugging beers. — **Bernard Dempsey and Kevin McNally**, *Lock, Stock... & Two Sips*, p. 302, 2000
- DeChooch chugged three fingers and got some color back into his face. — **Janet Evanovich**, *Seven Up*, p. 277, 2001

2 in computing, to operate slowly *US*
- The disk is chugging like crazy. — **Eric S. Raymond**, *The New Hacker's Dictionary*, p. 95, 1991

chugalug; chuglug *verb*
to drink without pausing to breathe *US, 1936*
- Chug-a-lug, chug-a-lug / Make you want to holler hi-de-ho / Burns your tummy, don'tcha know / Chug-a-lug, chug-a-lug — **Roger Miller**, *Chugalug*, 1964
- Pooks, I couldn't care less how fast Schoons can chug-a-lug a beer. — **John Nichols**, *The Sterile Cuckoo*, p. 163, 1965
- They were both over six feet and could chugalug a can of beer in less than twenty seconds. — **Elmore Leonard**, *The Big Bounce*, p. 170, 1969
- [J]ust chuglug two quarts of coffee and throw on side one of the first Clash album[.] — **Lester Bangs**, *Psychotic Reactions and Carburetor Dung*, p. 301–302, 1980
- Paco fetching another bursting-full bus pan of dishes in the meantime, chugalugging his coffee, going to take a whiz[.] — **Larry Heinemann**, *Paco's Story*, p. 112, 1986
- Chugalugging half the can, he cocked a thumb and foreigner at the Roberto Duran poster and giggled[.] — **James Ellroy**, *Suicide Hill*, p. 629, 1986

chug-a-lug!
used as a drinking toast *AUSTRALIA, 1984*

chugger *noun*
a professional fundraiser who is tasked to confront passers-by in the street with a charity's need for regular income and persuade people to sign agreements to make regular donations *UK, 2002*
A blend of 'charity' and **MUGGER** (a street robber).
- What do you do when a chugger moves into view? Do you cross the road, look the other way, go into reverse or pretend to take a mobile phone call? — *The Guardian*, 9th August 2003

chugging *noun*

a method of professional fundraising by persuading passers-by in the street to sign financial agreements for regular donations *UK*

A blend of 'charity' and MUGGING (street robbery).

- Charities and fundraising companies point to the thousands of donors recruited this way, while the technique has been dubbed "charity mugging" – or "chugging" – by those who resent being stopped[.] — *The Guardian*, 27th November 2003
- Public irritation forces charities to end 'chugging'[.] — *The Observer*, 7th March 2004

chuke *noun*

a knitted cap *US, 1966*

- — Frederic G. Cassidy, *Dictionary of American Regional English*, p. 662, 1985

▷ see: CHUC

chukka chap *noun*

a man associated with the game of polo *UK*

A 'chukka' is a period of play in a polo match.

- [A] wider range of people than the "chukka chicks" and "chukka chaps" featured on the inside back cover of Polo Times[.] — *The Guardian*, 29th July 2003

chukka chick *noun*

a woman associated with the game of polo *UK*

chum *noun*

1 an associate, a regular companion or a close friend *UK, 1684*

Originally in conventional use; slipped into colloquial use in C19.

- Seventeen-year-old Tasleema is under pressure from her dad to marry a nice Bengali boy, while her Hindu chum, Lux, is hassled for hanging out with a white guy[.] — *The Guardian*, 29th March 2003

2 used (of a male) as a form of address, often patronising *UK, 1684*

- Don't give me that stuff, chum. — Mickey Spillane, *I, The Jury*, p. 17, 1947
- Are you sure you've come to the right camp, chum? — Graeme Kent, *The Queen's Corporal [Six Granada Plays]*, p. 83, 1959

chum *verb*

1 in aerial combat, to fly low over enemy territory in order to draw enemy ground fire, which is then answered by airpower flying higher and out of sight *US*

- — Gregory Clark, *Words of the Vietnam War*, p. 101, 1990

2 to vomit *US*

- — Judi Sanders, *Cal Poly Slang*, p. 2, 1990

chuma *verb*

to kiss *FIJI*

From the Hindi.

- Don't they make you sick? Look at them, chuma, chuma all the time! — Jan Tent, 1996

chum buddy *noun*

a close friend *US, 1952*

- — Harold Wentworth and Stuart Berg Flexner, *Dictionary of American Slang*, p. 105, 1960
- Don't gorget when you gather your chum-buddies for your Friends watch party that tonight's episode has been "supersized." — *Arkansas Democrat-Gazette*, 12th February 2004

chummery *noun*

in India, a bungalow (or similar) shared by friends (now, usually young and single) *INDIA, 1888*

From CHUM (a friend).

- [O]ur mess mate and chummerian in the Lodi Colony bachelors' chummery where I used to stay[.] — *The Times of India*, 4th February 2004

chummified *adjective*

drunk *US*

- — Collin Baker et al., *College Undergraduate Slang Study Conducted at Brown University*, p. 96, 1968

chummy *noun*

1 a civilian; a prisoner; a prime suspect; also used as a patronising form of address *UK, 1948*

Metropolitan Police slang; a diminutive of CHUM (a friend) that threatens intimacy.

- — Peter Laurie, *Scotland Yard*, p. 321, 1970

2 loose and broken pieces of anything *CANADA*

A closely related word with a different but perhaps related meaning is used in New England and the Canadian Maritime Provinces fishing: 'chum bait', 'chumming'.

- When the pull-cord on the chainsaw stuck, she broke, and all that chummy come out of her. — Lewis Poteet, *The South Shore Phrase Book*, p. 31, 1999

chummy *adjective*

very friendly, intimate, sociable *US, 1884*

- And, if you ask me, Trent's being awfullly chummy too. — C.D. Payne, *Youth in Revolt*, p. 390, 1993

chump *noun*

1 a fool; a naive person who is easily duped *US, 1876*

- I'd acted like a chump. — Jim Thompson, *The Killer Inside*, p. 9, 1952
- That Carlisle was a big, fatheaded chump. — Clarence Cooper Jr, *The Scene*, p. 101, 1960
- Don't be a chump. Don't bet any more money on that damn fool shot. — *The Hustler*, 1961
- — *Current Slang*, p. 15, Fall 1968
- He said, "Gonzi, Miles and Vernon were trying to use me so I burned both them chumps." — Babs Gonzales, *Movin' On Down De Line*, p. 63, 1975
- How about laying some more fast run-down on me ... like has her old man got any chump shortcomings ... craps, hard shit or what not? — Iceberg Slim (Robert Beck), *Airtight Willie and Me*, p. 24, 1979
- I said to her, "Baby, nobody makes a chump outta me." Now I'm living at the Travel-Lodge, and she's living in my house for free. — *Airheads*, 1994
- I don't want to do any coke. It's a terrible drug. It's for chumps. — Kenneth Lonergan, *This is Our Youth*, p. 47, 2000

2 the head *UK, 1859*

- People thought he'd gone off his chump. They thought he was a hopeless drunk. — *The Guardian*, 14th February 2004

▸ **off your chump**

in any degree, mad *UK, 1864*

- CLARICE: I'm getting worried – he's gone off his chump. TOM: Not he, not he — John O'Toole, *The Bush and the Tree*, p. 27, 1960
- C: Eric the Half-Bee. He had an accident. S: You're off your chump. C: Look, if you intend by that utilization of an obscure colloquiallism to imply that my sanity is not up to scratch, or indeed to deny the semi-existence of my little chum Eric the Hallittle chum Eric the Half-Bee, I shall have to ask you to listen to this! — Graham Chapman, *Monty Python's Fling Circus*, 1970

chump *verb*

1 to act foolishly *US*

- Most pimps chump off their money. They blow it on drugs, clothes, jewelry, cars and in chrome and leather cesspools. — Iceberg Slim (Robert Beck), *The Naked Soul of Iceberg Slim*, p. 68, 1971

2 to swindle someone, to cheat someone *US, 1930*

- He wouldn't be rimmed no sir, not him, because he wasn't the kind of a chump who allowed himself to be chumped by a cheap kike auctioneer. — James T. Farrell, *Willie Collins*, p. 107, 1946

chump change *noun*

a small amount of money *US*

- — *Current Slang*, p. 15, Fall 1968
- They said that Western whores were lazy and were satisfied with making "chump change." — Iceberg Slim (Robert Beck), *Pimp*, p. 285, 1969
- Why should they keep their job as a delivery boy for "chump change" when they could be making big money? — Christina and Richard Milner, *Black Players*, p. 141, 1972
- — Carl J. Banks Jr, *Banks Dictionary of the Black Ghetto Language*, 1975
- Whatever she was doing in partners with the Mafia asshole, who was not even a made man, she calls on him to do a job and treats him like a turd. Knocks him down from his regular rate and pays him off with chump change. — Robert Campbell, *Alice in La-La Land*, p. 243, 1987
- He pays you chump change. Know what a real driver gets for haulin' poison waste? — Joseph Wambaugh, *Finnegan's Week*, p. 39, 1993

chump educator *noun*

1 a trade newspaper or magazine used to educate outsiders on the industry's secrets *US*

- — Don Wilmeth, *The Language of American Popular Entertainment*, p. 53, 1981

2 in the circus or carnival, *Billboard* magazine *US*

- — Joe McKennon, *Circus Lingo*, p. 26, 1980

chump expenses *noun*

minor expenses *US*

- At least she'd make enough scratch for chump expenses. — Iceberg Slim (Robert Beck), *Pimp*, p. 252, 1969

chump heister *noun*
a carnival ferris wheel *US*
- —Joe McKennon, *Circus Lingo*, p. 26, 1980

chump job *noun*
a legal, legitimate job, especially a low-paying and menial one *US*
- Why should I work a chump job for chump change when I can make real money and be independent of the Man?—Christina and Richard Milner, *Black Players*, p. 257, 1972

chump off *verb*
to better or out-insult someone in a verbal duel *US*
- —David Claerbaut, *Black Jargon in White America*, p. 60, 1972

chump twister *noun*
a carousel *US, 1961*
- —J.E. Lighter, *Historical Dictionary of American Slang, Volume 1*, p. 421, 1994

chunck *verb*
in pinball, to hit the ball into a scoring bumper with such force that the bumper fails to respond *US*
- —Bobbye Claire Natkin and Steve Kirk, *All About Pinball*, p. 111, 1977

chunder *noun*
1 vomit *AUSTRALIA, 1953*
- When the ship righted itself the surface of the solidified chunder remained at an angle, not to be removed until we docked in Singapore.—Clive James, *Unreliable Memoirs*, p. 169, 1980
- He was disqualified under the no chunder rule.—Frank Hardy, *Hardy's People*, p. 201, 1986

2 an instance of vomiting *AUSTRALIA, 1983*
- Petrified, I hovered over him, only once or twice forgetting to dodge a projectile chunder.—Kathy Lette, *Girls' Night Out*, p. 80, 1987

3 in poker, a weak hand that wins *US*
- —John Vorhaus, *The Big Book of Poker Slang*, p. 10, 1996

chunder *verb*
1 to vomit *AUSTRALIA, 1950*
Probably rhyming slang for 'Chunder Loo' (spew); from the name of an advertising comic strip character that ran in the early C20. The widely held theory that it derives from a clipping of the phrase 'Watch under!', used by seasick passengers on liners to warn the lower decks of an impending vomit-shower, is nothing but ingenious trifling.
- She objected to pale blue satin clad girls chundering all over her tulle toilet seat covers[.]—Sue Rhodes, *Now you'll think I'm awful*, p. 142, 1967
- If you wanna throw your voice / Mate, you won't have any choice / But to chunder in the old Pacific Sea.—Barry Humphries, *The Wonderful World of Barry McKenzie*, p. 15, 1968
- Jeez, if I touch another drop of this rot gut I'll chunder for a certainty.—Barry Humphries, *The Wonderful World of Barry McKenzie*, p. 8, 1968
- [H]e felt as if he'd chunder if he lay down.—Allan Skerman, *Beyond Indigo*, p. 356, 1989
- And if I yack, chances are someone else will chunder.—*Wayne's World 2*, 1993

2 to mangle someone *AUSTRALIA*
- Out the way, bunny, you'll get chundered by the car that's bringing me Dad home.—Tim Winton, *That eye, the sky*, p. 47, 1986
- Convinced I had been chundered, the Bob Hawke Surf Team gawked at me as I paddled out the back.—Kathy Lette, *Girls' Night Out*, p. 195, 1987

3 to churn *AUSTRALIA*
- Across the passageway from the transmitting station, water chundered and soughed rebelliously through the non-return valves of the seaman's heads.—John Wynnum, *Tar Dust*, p. 9, 1962

chunderer *noun*
a person who habitually vomits, especially as a result of excessive drinking *AUSTRALIA*
- Well, I was going to tell you my latest yarn 'the fantastic farter from Finnigan's Falls' but, seeing as there are ladies present I'll settle for the 'The Champion Chunderer from Cooper's Creek'—Frank Hardy, *The Outcasts of Foolgarah*, p. 198, 1971

chundering *noun*
vomiting *AUSTRALIA*
- We had a keg in the boot and a few dozen tubes between us so there was much chundering en route—Barry Humphries, *A Nice Night's Entertainment*, p. 77, 1964

chunderish *adjective*
bilious *AUSTRALIA*
- Never drunk liquor before, really. Yer feelin chunderish? No. Well. Praps.—Tim Winton, *Cloudstreet*, p. 102, 1991

chunderous *adjective*
sickening *AUSTRALIA*
- I hope to hell I never see another society ball. At least I can congratulate myself on the fact that I haven't been near one since I gave up writing that chunderous chatter page.—Sue Rhodes, *Now you'll think I'm awful*, p. 134, 1967
- 'Well, quite apart from the metaphysical implications, it must have been a particularly chunderous undertaking.—Alexander Buzo, *Rooted*, p. 95, 1969
- The news of Sir Mark was bad enough, but the thought of that yobbo Patterson, whom I had known of old, stepping into my job, was chunderous!—Edna Everage (Barry Humphries), *My Gorgeous Life*, p. 277, 1989

chunk *noun*
a large amount *US*
- WADE: Well, seven hundred and fifty thousand dollars is a lot. JERRY: Yah, well, it's a chunk.—*Fargo*, 1996

chunk *verb*
1 to throw something *US, 1835*
- "You know how to make pigeons fly?" Sonny hesitated. "Chunk rocks at 'em?"—Chester Himes, *The Real Cool Killers*, p. 51, 1959
- "Hey, quit chunkin' them balls, you little dumb-asses," Coach Popper yelled.—Larry McMurtry, *The Last Picture Show*, p. 36, 1966
- Everybody's mother knew a little boy "got his eye put out like that," whether we were chunkin' rocks at each other or fighting with homemade bullwhips.—Ken Weaver, *Texas Crude*, p. 107, 1984

2 to vomit *US*
- —Judi Sanders, *Mashing and Munching in Ames*, p. 5, 1994

3 in American casinos, to bet a great deal, especially to do so unwisely *US*
- —Steve Kuriscak, *Casino Talk*, p. 12, 1985

4 to engage in a fist fight *US*
- —Charles Shafer, *Folk Speech in Texas Prisons*, p. 201, 1990
- —Rick Ayers (Editor), *Berkeley High Slang Dictionary*, p. 16, 2004

chunka-chunka *adjective*
used for representing a steady musical rhythm *UK*
Echoic.
- [G]uitarist [Dave] Fiuczynski moves between Hendrixian psychedelic and Stax/Volt chunka-chunka rhythm guitar riffs.—*www.jazzweekly.com*, 10th June 2003

chunk down *verb*
to eat *US*
- —Collin Baker et al., *College Undergraduate Slang Study Conducted at Brown University*, p. 96, 1968

chunker *noun*
an M79 grenade launcher *US, 1975*
Vietnam war usage.
- —*Maledicta*, p. 259, Summer/Winter 1982: 'Viet-speak'
- "Use your chunker! the team leader yelled to Bruce Judkins who nodded and brought the short, compact weapon up to fire. The chunker was actually an M-79 grenade launcher, a six-pound, single-shot break-open weapon like a fat sawed-off shotgun that could fire a 40mm high-explosive round up to four hundred yards.—Kregg P. Jorgenson, *LRRP Company Command*, p. 121, 2000

chunk of beef; chunka; chunker *noun*
a chief, a boss *AUSTRALIA, 1942*
Rhyming slang; probably no longer in use.

chunk of change
a lot of money *US*
- But believe me when I say the whole thing isn't just about a chunk of change.—Christopher Brookmyre, *The Sacred Art of Stealing*, p. 238, 2002
- —Victor H. Royer, *Casino Gamble Talk*, p. 33, 2003

chunky; chunks; chunkies *noun*
hashish *US*
From the similarity in appearance to a block of chocolate.
- —Eugene Landy, *The Underground Dictionary*, p. 50, 1971
- —Richard A. Spears, *The Slang and Jargon of Drugs and Drink*, p. 108, 1986
- —Mike Haskins, *Drugs*, p. 287, 2003

chunt *noun*
an inept, unlikeable person *US*
- —Connie Eble (Editor), *UNC-CH Campus Slang*, p. 2, April 2004

church *noun*
LSD *UK*
- —Mike Haskins, *Drugs*, p. 285, 2003

▸ **the church**
the Investigations Department of HM Customs & Excise *UK*
• I've been in touch with one of the National Crime Squad teams who have been working alongside the Church on this. —Garry Bushell, *The Face*, p. 98, 2001
• "What The Church don't know doesn't fucking hurt them," Simon said crisply. "Church? What's religion got to do with it?" I'd never heard the expression. "Cuzzies. We call them The Church. 'C and E' – close enough to Church of England." "Oh... Customs..." —Duncan MacLaughlin, *The Filth*, p. 178, 2002

church boys *noun*
▷ see: C OF E

churchie *noun*
a religious proponent of virtue *NEW ZEALAND, 1997*
• —Harry Orsman, *A Dictionary of Modern New Zealand Slang*, p. 29, 1999

church is out
1 an opportunity has passed *US*
• —*Current Slang*, p. 2, Summer 1966
2 no hope remains; there is nothing to be done *US, 1966*
• —Frederic G. Cassidy, *Dictionary of American Regional English*, p. 665, 1985

church key *noun*
a can and bottle opener *US, 1951*
With the advent of pull-ring (1962), the pop-top (1963), and the stay-on tab can (1974), the device and term all but disappeared.
• —*American Weekly*, p. 2, 14th August 1955
• She hooked the church key over the top of each bottle and with a sharp rap of her hand that made a sharp, sucking pok, opened the bottles and handed them up. —Larry Heinemann, *Close Quarters*, p. 70, 1977
• The real hoods, the serious ones who'd been up the night before fighting with churchkeys and tireirons or knocking up "cheap" girls, spent the days dozing fully clothed[.] —Eve Babitz, *Eve's Hollywood*, p. 59, 1984

Church of England *noun*
in craps, a bet that the next roll will be 1, 2, 11 or 12 *US, 1983*
A back-formation from C AND E, itself the initials of 'crap-eleven', the conventional name of the bet.
• —Thomas L. Clark, *The Dictionary of Gambling and Gaming*, p. 44, 1987

church rat *noun*
a self-serving, pious person *TRINIDAD AND TOBAGO, 1993*
• —Lise Winer, *Dictionary of the English/Creole of Trinidad & Tobago*, 2003

church tramp *noun*
a student who changes his church affiliation as necessary to attend various church social functions *US*
• —*American Speech*, p. 272, December 1963: 'American Indian student slang'

church warden *noun*
a pipe with a long stem *UK, 1863*
Originally made of clay but the name refers to the shape not the material. In 2003 this type of pipe is enjoying a small revival in fashion as a result of the films in the *Lord of the Rings* trilogy.

churn *verb*
to schedule unnecessary return visits to a doctor to increase fees *US, 1991*
• —*American Speech*, p. 254, Fall 1993: 'Among the new words'

▸ **churn butter**
to have sex *US*
Vietnam war usage; slang based on visual images.
• —Linda Reinberg, *In the Field*, p. 43, 1991

churn out *verb*
to produce a large quantity of something, especially without too much concern for the finished article's quality *UK, 1912*
• [J]ust to inform you that the author did go to Cambridge and is churning out this tripe only so she can upgrade her postcode. —*The Guardian*, 15th June 2004

churus *noun*
▷ see: CHARAS

chut *noun*
a male homosexual; homosexual practices between men *UK, 1977*
Possibly from CHUTE (the rectum), CHUTNEY (sodomy) or as a variation of CHUFF (a homosexual male).

chut *verb*
to chew chewing gum *AUSTRALIA*
• It won't chut properly. —Sidney J Baker, *The Australian Language*, p. 205, 1945

chute *noun*
1 the rectum *US, 1976*
• [S]lim blonde anal lover Chrissy Ann, who lets Cal Jammer slide up her chute. —*Adult Video News*, p. 56, February 1993
2 the coin slot on a pinball machine *US*
• —Bobbye Claire Natkin and Steve Kirk, *All About Pinball*, p. 111, 1977
3 especially in Quebec, a waterfall *CANADA*
• On Porcupine Lake a dam had been built to control the flow of water, and the chute itself was nineteen hundred and fourteen feet long. —Audrey Saunders, *Algonquin Story*, p. 44, 1947
• The river leaves Isaac Lake by a short fast chute. —*Islander*, p. 13/1, 14th November 1965
4 in sailing, a spinnaker *US*
• "Okay!" Winnie shouted. "Let's pop the chute!" —Joseph Wambaugh, *The Golden Orange*, p. 286, 1990
5 a parachute *UK, 1920*
• [A]s lucky as a man whose 'chute has failed[.] —James Hawes, *Dead Long Enough*, p. 26, 2000
6 in the usage of youthful model road racers (slot car racers), a straight portion of track *US*
• —Phantom Surfers, *The Exciting Sounds of Model Road Racing (Album cover)*, 1997

▸ **through the chute**
smuggled from Venezuela *TRINIDAD AND TOBAGO, 1987*
• —Lise Winer, *Dictionary of the English/Creole of Trinidad & Tobago*, 2003

chutes *noun*
a subway (underground) system *US*
• —Hyman E. Goldin et al., *Dictionary of American Underworld Lingo*, p. 44, 1950

chutney *noun*
sodomy *UK, 1984*
From a similarity in colour and texture between conventional 'chutney' and faecal matter.

chutney farmer; chutney ferret *noun*
a male homosexual *UK*
Derogatory. From CHUTNEY (sodomy).
• —Angela Devlin, *Prison Patter*, p. 37, 1996

chutty *noun*
chewing gum *AUSTRALIA, 1942*

chutzpah; chuzpah *noun*
gall, intestinal fortitude, extreme self-confidence *US, 1892*
One of the several most well-known Yiddish words in the US.
• Next to his adroitness in fleecing the philanthropic sheep was his chutzpah, his unmitigated impudence. —Nathan Ausubel, *A Treasury of Jewish Folklore*, p. 267, 1948
• —Collin Baker et al., *College Undergraduate Slang Study Conducted at Brown University*, p. 96, 1968
• It takes chutzpah as well as millions to win the America's Cup. —Joseph Wambaugh, *Floaters*, p. 267, 1996
• Bill Gates, the company's chairman, even had the chutzpah to say that this week's ruling was a challenge to "healthy competition in the software industry". —*The Economist*, 10th June 2000
• I'm talking about Vice President Dick Cheney. For him to be questioning Sen.John Kerry's ability and/or willingness to protect this nation takes, well, chutzpah. —*Oakland Tribune*, 2nd May 2004

CHV *noun*
Council House Vermin, i.e. people who, it appears, can only afford to live in council houses *IRELAND*
• He calls in his secretary, roysh [right], quite good-looking bird I have to say, but CHV – we're talking TOTAL Council House Vermin here – and he sends her out to the shop...' —Paul Howard, *Ross O'Carroll-Kelly*, p. 79, 2003

chyack *verb*
▷ see: CHIACK

ciacito, baby
used as a farewell *US*
A catchphrase television sign-off of Daisy Fuentes, the too-hip host on the MTV cable network in the 1990s. Repeated with referential humour.

ciao; ciaou

goodbye *UK, 1959*

From an Italian greeting and farewell, affected by English-speakers as a fashionable or ironic farewell.

- NICKY: See you. ANDREW: Ciao! NICKY: 'Bye, Trish! —Peter Nichols, *Promenade [Six Granada Plays]*, p. 49, 1959
- BARRY: See youse later, sport! TORQUIL: Ciaou! And loads of luck! —Barry Humphries, *Bazza Pulls It Off!*, 1971
- —Connie Eble (Editor), *UNC-CH Campus Slang*, p. 2, Fall 1981
- Hey, you're still my main man and I love you, bro. Ciao. —Elmore Leonard, *Be Cool*, p. 106, 1999
- CECILE: Nice meeting you. Sebastian: CIAO. —*Cruel Intentions*, 1999

'cid; cid; sid *noun*

LSD *US*

An abbreviation of **ACID**.

- —Connie Eble (Editor), *UNC-CH Campus Slang*, p. 2, October 1986
- —US Department of Justice, *Street Terms*, October 1994

-cide; -icide *suffix*

the conventional suffix, that creates the meaning 'murder' or 'murderer', when used to make a flippant or nonce-word *UK, 1866*

In June 2003 a quick search of the Internet reveals 'Bushicide', 'Saddamicide' and 'Iraqicide'.

Cider City *nickname*

Hereford, Herefordshire; Taunton, Somerset *UK*

Both are historic centres of cider-making.

- There is more than one Cider City[.] —Peter Chippindale, *The British CB Book*, p. 168, 1981

ciderhead *noun*

a cider drinker *UK*

Combines conventional 'cider' with **-HEAD** (a habitual user).

- [S]trong cider has become the cheap youth intoxicant of choice in Someset and Devon, and local police have been blaming ciderheads for public-order disturbances. —David Rowan, *A Glossary for the 90s*, p. 4, 1998

cig *noun*

a *cig*arette or *cig*ar *US, 1894*

- [T]hey heard him say to Polly, 'Have a cig?' while offering a silver cigarette-case with a flourish. —Norman Lindsay, *Halfway to Anywhere*, p. 44, 1947
- While I fired a cig he called an extension number and was connected. —Mickey Spillane, *My Gun is Quick*, p. 13, 1950
- I see her standing, with her black velvet slacks, handsapockets, thin, slouched, cig hanging from lips[.] —Jack Kerouac, *The Subterraneans*, p. 50, 1958
- We carried the tax stampless cigs down into the cellar in the nick of time. —Ed Sanders, *Tales of Beatnik Glory*, p. 29, 1975
- When we finished Susie went for the john, I went for my cigs. —Larry Heinemann, *Close Quarters*, p. 187, 1977
- So at two o'clock one morning, Whokka left two packets of cigs outside his room on the 'Welcome' mat, and to his delight, they were gone when he woke up. —Max Walker, *How To Tame Lions*, p. 109, 1988
- [P]ast an old mechanical cig machine[.] —Nicholas Blincoe, *Ardwick Green (Disco Biscuits)*, p. 4, 1996
- Guns at this side, Freddy Heflin walks slowly, steadily, down the middle of the street, towards the Four Aces. He lights a cig. —James Mangold, *Copland*, p. 147, 1997

cigar *noun*

1 a reprimand, especially at work *US*

- —Harold Wentworth and Stuart Berg Flexner, *Dictionary of American Slang*, p. 105, 1960

2 in circus and carnival usage, any compliment *US*

- —Don Wilmeth, *The Language of American Popular Entertainment*, p. 53, 1981

cigar!

correct! *US*

An extrapolation from 'Close, but no cigar'.

- —Trevor Cralle, *The Surfin'ary*, p. 21, 1991

cigarette *noun*

an untalented or personality-free roller derby skater *US*

The cigarette lagged back in the packet, hence the punning term.

- Skaters who were washed up, problem children looking for a way back in, and rookies who would probably never amount to anything were cigarettes. Virtually every team had at least one. —Keith Pollage, *Roller Derby to Rollerjam*, p. 126, 1999

cigarette holder *noun*

the shoulder *UK*

Rhyming slang.

- —Ray Puxley, *Fresh Rabbit*, 1998

cigarette paper *noun*

a packet of heroin or another drug *US, 1936*

- —Robert Ashton, *This Is Heroin*, p. 208, 2002

cigarette pimp *noun*

a pimp whose lack of professional pride leads him to solicit customers for his prostitutes *US*

- Black pimps never solicit for their women if they are "true pimps," and call a man who does a cigarette pimp, popcorn pimp, or chile pimp. —Christina and Richard Milner, *Black Players*, p. 33, 1972
- —Burgess Laughlin, *Job Opportunities in the Black Market*, p. 2, 1978

cigarette roll *noun*

a type of parachute malfunction *US, 1962*

- —Robert W. Black, *Rangers in Korea*, p. 335, 1989
- The cigarette roll was a rigging error which caused the parachute to unfold, but not fill with air, not opening to full deployment. —Gregory Clark, *Words of the Vietnam War*, p. 498, 1990
- The main parachute of an experienced jumper failed to open; it streamed upward in what was known as a cigarette roll. —Robert W. Black, *A Ranger Born*, p. 44, 2002

cigarette swag; cigarette paper swag *noun*

a small pack of possesions and necessary items carried by a tramp *AUSTRALIA, 1938*

From the size and shape of the pack.

cigarette with no name *noun*

a marijuana cigarette *US*

- —Edith A. Folb, *runnin' down some lines*, p. 232, 1980

cigger *noun*

a cigarette *AUSTRALIA, 1922*

- P'raps you're smiled at by a bearer who is muscular and big, / Fishing fags out of his pocket with a 'Have a cigger, Dig?' —Tip Kelaher, *The Digger Hat and other verses*, p. 29, 1942
- —Jim Ramsay, *Cop It Sweet!*, p. 23, 1977

ciggy; ciggie *noun*

a cigarette *US, 1915*

- The youngsters eat at Walgreen's drugstore, 44th Street and Broadway, and the drugstore, in the Astor; instead of cocktails they sip cokes and smoke ciggies. —Jack Lait and Lee Mortimer, *New York Confidential*, p. 39, 1948
- Marijuana (we hear) is now peddled in the form of phony cigars. Called "atomics." A box (less conspicious than ciggies) sells at $35[.] —*San Francisco Call-Bulletin*, p. 8G, 11th March 1953
- Won't be a sec, mummy, just popping around to the hotel for a few ciggies. —Barry Humphries, *The Wonderful World of Barry McKenzie*, p. 41, 1968
- "You got a ciggy?" The messenger gives him a cigarette and Billy puts one hand beneath his head and smokes. —Darryl Ponicsan, *The Last Detail*, p. 3, 1970
- Give me a ciggy. —Jennifer Saunders, *Absolutely Fabulous*, p. 62, 1992
- "Do you know what's in those boxes?" "First-quality ciggies. You want some?" —Janet Evanovich, *Seven Up*, p. 57, 2001
- Ophelia took the unlit ciggy that Hot Buns had been clenching in her mouth[.] —Gretel Killeen, *Hot Buns and Ophelia get shipwrecked*, p. 46, 2001

ciggyboo; ciggieboo *noun*

a cigarette *UK, 1958*

- The ciggyboos are kept in counter under the trash locked behind a wooden board. —Allen Ginsberg, *Journals*, p. 204, 5th May 1961
- —Andy Anonymous, *A Basic Guide to Campusology*, p. 6, 1966
- —Collin Baker et al., *College Undergraduate Slang Study Conducted at Brown University*, p. 96, 1968

ciggybutt *noun*

a cigarette *US*

- —Connie Eble (Editor), *UNC-CH Campus Slang*, p. 2, Fall 1998

Cilla Black; Cilla *noun*

the back *UK*

Rhyming slang, formed on the name of singer and television presenter Cilla Black (b.1943).

- A "dodgy Cilla" is a television script writer's term for a bad back. —Ray Puxley, *Cockney Rabbit*, 1992

CIL spinner *noun*

an illegal charge of dynamite to 'catch' fish in the water without using hooks or nets *CANADA, 1989*

- A stick of dynamite exploded underwater to stun fish so they will float to the surface for easy 'fishing'. Known around the [BC] Saanich Peninsula as a James Island Spinner, for the Canadian Industries Limited explosives plant once located there. —Tom Parkin, *WetCoast Words*, p. 26, 1989

cinch *noun*

1 a certainty *US, 1890*

- For me it's always a cinch. I got a much better chance than the local talent. — *It Happened One Night*, 1934

2 in horse racing, a horse that is virtually certain to win *US*

- — Robert Saunders Dowst and Jay Craig, *Playing the Races*, p. 161, 1960

cinchers *noun*

brakes *US, 1942*

- — Montie Tak, *Truck Talk*, p. 31, 1971

Cincy; Cinci *nickname*

Cincinatti, Ohio *US, 1899*

- We were in Cincy in April and had a free day on our hands because this exhibition game was called off. — Bernard Malamud, *The Natural*, p. 47, 1952
- Keep out of Cincy in the fall – mean cops. — John Clellon Holmes, *The Horn*, p. 160, 1958
- Cinci, just another forlong border-south Queen City, the Gateway to something or other — Bill Cardoso, *The Maltese Sangweech*, p. 175, 1984

cinder dick *noun*

a railway detective *US, 1925*

- And, when nosing around the freight yards, he almost got picked up by a cinder dick, he did the most direct and logical thing. — Wallace Stegner, *The Big Rock Candy Mountain*, p. 27, 1943
- — Norman Carlisle, *The Modern Wonder Book of Trains and Railroading*, p. 260, 1946
- At first, it specialized in providing police – "cinder dicks" – for half a dozen railroads. — J. Anthony Lukas, *Big Trouble*, p. 78, 1997

cinderella *noun*

the nose *UK*

Rhyming slang for 'smeller'.

- — Ray Puxley, *Cockney Rabbit*, 1992

cinderella *adjective*

1 the colour yellow; in snooker, the yellow ball *UK*

Rhyming slang.

- — Ray Puxley, *Cockney Rabbit*, 1992

2 cowardly *UK*

Rhyming slang for **YELLOW**.

- — John Ayto, *The Oxford Dictionary of Rhyming Slang*, p. 81, 2002

Cinderella liberty *noun*

a short release from military duty and from base restrictions *US, 1961*

Cinderella had to be home by midnight, as do navy and marine troops.

- Wagoner said yes, ten percent of the battalion would be allowed Cinderlla liberty (ending at midnight) in Danang. — Philip Caputo, *A Rumor of War*, p. 129, 1977
- — Gregory Clark, *Words of the Vietnam War*, p. 279, 1990
- Large signs were strategically placed along the way that stated the penalty fo being caught out in town after midnight, when curfew began for all enlisted men holding the pay grade of E-5 or below, and remained in effect until 5:00 a.m. This was commonly known as "Cinderella Liberty" — Bruce H. Norton, *Force REcon Diary*, p. 5, 1992
- "NoFuck Virginia." Recruits learn to say "NoFuck"on their first Cinderella liberty when they have to be back on base by midnight without getting "any." — Maria Flook, *My Sister Life*, p. 62, 1998

Cinderella team *noun*

a sports team that wins a tournament or championship that it had little hope of winning *US*

- — Zander Hollander and Sandy Padwe, *Basketball Lingo*, p. 21, 1971

cinders *noun*

▸ **take to the cinders**

on the railways, to quit a job *US*

- — Ramon Adams, *The Language of the Railroader*, p. 153, 1977

cinder trail *noun*

a railway track *US*

- Now, you know, all my life I've been a wanderer / up and down that old cinder trail. — Bruce Jackson, *Get Your Ass in the Water and Swim Like Me*, p. 72, 1962

cinnamon stick *noun*

a penis with faeces stains after anal sex *US*

- — *Maledicta*, p. 231, 1979: 'Kinks and queens: linguistic and cultural aspects of the terminology for gays'

cipaille *noun*

in Quebec, a deep-dish meat pie *CANADA*

- Both French and English claim origins for "cipaille." [It may be] English "sea pie" wearing French spelling–from British nautical slang. Now a Quebec Christmas dish, it is layers of meat, vegetables, herbs, bouillon, cooked in pastry. — Bill Casselman, *Canadian Food Words*, p. 149–150, 1998

ciphering *noun*

arithmetic *US, 1905*

- I liked ciphering all right, but I didn't care much for spelling and studying the Bible and memorizing psalms. — James Lincoln Collier, *My Brother Sam is Dead*, p. 66, 1974

circle *noun*

any group of people playing footbag *US*

- — Jim Crotty, *How to Talk American*, p. 122, 1997

circle *verb*

▸ **circle a game**

(of a bookmaker) to limit the amount that may be bet on a given game or race when the bookmaker suspects that the game or race is fixed *US*

- — Burgess Laughlin, *Job Opportunities in the Black Market*, p. 5, 1978

▸ **circle the drain**

1 to be near death *US*

- — *Los Angeles Times*, p. B1, 19th December 1994

2 by extension, said of a project or enterprise that is nearing collapse *US*

- — Vann Wesson, *Generation X Field Guide and Lexicon*, p. 38, 1997

Circle City *nickname*

Leeds, West Yorkshire *UK*

- You only have to try to find your way round the motorway network in Leeds to realize why it is called Circle City[.] — Peter Chippindale, *The British CB Book*, p. 169, 1981

circled *adjective*

married *US*

- — *San Francisco Examiner*, p. III-2, 22nd March 1960

circle jerk *noun*

1 group male masturbation, sometimes mutual and sometimes simply a shared solitary experience *US*

- The "circle jerk," or mass masturbation, is a common sex activity. — Harrison E. Salisbury, *The Shook-up Generation*, p. 32, 1958
- He is also a participant in the circle-jerks held with the shades pulled down in Smolka's living room after school[.] — Philip Roth, *Portnoy's Complaint*, p. 194, 1969
- "One was gobbling another's joint, and the other six were standing around fondling anything they could find." "A real circle jerk," said Ranatti. — Joseph Wambaugh, *The New Centurions*, p. 190, 1970
- If there are several persons present, and somehow it has been determined that all are "O.K.", a circle jerk will result. — John Francis Hunter, *The Gay Insider*, p. 191, 1971
- Sometimes the event [a college fraternity hazing] is a circle-jerk, with each guy fisting the cock of the guy next to him. — *Drummer*, p. 73, 1977
- In a circle jerk, the members of the company each bring themselves off by masturbation, sometimes competing for phallus size and distance of ejaculation. — Wayne Dynes, *Homolexis*, p. 105, 1985
- As a little girl, I never got to be part of a circle jerk. Girls didn't get to jerk off in circles. Little boys bonded through showing off their penises. — Susan Crain Bakos, *Sexational Secrets*, p. 69, 1996

2 any non-productive, time-wasting exercise *US, 1973*

- The grand jury is off on a giant circle jerk. They've got nothing. — Steven Paul Martini, *The Judge*, p. 42, 1995
- Reality was troubling and deeply relevant, a refreshing departure from the usual circle jerk of undergraduate publishing. — Tom Perrotta, *Joe College*, p. 36, 2000

3 a series of exit consoles on websites that link back on themselves, creating an infinite loop *US*

- — *www.adultquarter.com/blossary.html*, January 2004

circle-jerk *verb*

to participate in group male masturbation *US*

- [S]ucking, fucking, circle-jerking, all anonymously performed[.] — John Francis Hunter, *The Gay Insider*, p. 26, 1971
- [F]or some reason the idea of circle jerking with a needle-dicked lard-arse didn't appeal. — Kitty Churchill, *Thinking of England*, p. 132, 1995

Circle K *noun*

the recreational drug ketamine *US*

A punning allusion to a US national chain of convenience stores.

- The stolen drugs include pentobarbital, Valium, and ketamine – known on the streets as "Circle K." —*Press Journal (Vereo Beach, Florida)*, p. A3, 14th March 1998

circle work *noun*

the driving of a car in tight circles to form circular tracks on the ground *AUSTRALIA*

- Utes are also essential for 'circle work', a rural mating ritual at B&S balls in which farm boys wearing tuxedos do doughnuts in paddocks while girls watch on, ideally weak with lust and admiration. —*Sydney Morning Herald*, p. 8s, 29th June 1996
- —Phillip Gwynne, *Deadly Unna?*, p. 40, 1998

circs *noun*

*circ*umstances *UK, 1883*

- [F]ine by him in the circs. —John Williams, *Cardiff Dead*, p. 19, 2000
- In different circs [...] I could run rings round these lads. —Kevin Sampson, *Outlaws*, p. 216, 2001

circuit *noun*

a series of homosexual parties held each year around the US, with participants flying from city to city for the festivities *US, 1990s*

- —Kevin Dilallo, *The Unofficial Gay Manual*, p. 238, 1994
- The gay urban scene today encompasses what has come to be known as the "circuit," a series of large gay dance parties that occur throughout the year in cities around the country and around the world, attended by tens of thousands of gay men. —Michelangelo Signorile, *Life Outside*, p. xxiv, 1997

circuit girl *noun*

a travelling prostitute *US*

- Laticia says the pimps use "tudge boys," street slang for hired enforcers, not only to rough up circuit girls who get out of line, but also to patrol Colfax, looking for crack whores out of bounds. —*Denver Westword*, 2nd May 2002

circuit queen *noun*

a male homosexual who follows the circuit from party to party *US*

- —Kevin Dilallo, *The Unofficial Gay Manual*, p. 238, 1994
- Whether you're a circuit queen or a suburban dad, just coming out or stoically postgay, Drama Queen takes you kindly by the hand and leads you on an exploratoin of the unique and oft-misunderstood dynamics of our daily lives. —Patrick Price, *Drama Queen*, p. xviii, 2001

circular file *noun*

a wastebasket *US, 1947*

- Cladny is one of many who has loaded the circular file with fund-raising literature from organiations to which he has already contributed. —*Washington Post*, p. C14, 24th December 1981
- It's going right into the old circular file as soon as I make a couple routine calls to the feds. —Carl Hiaasen, *Tourist Season*, p. 21, 1986

circulation *noun*

traffic *CANADA*

- —Victor Trahan, *The City of Montreal Style Guide*, p. 119, 2001

circus *noun*

1 sexual behaviour that is public, fetishistic or both *US, 1878*

- Brenda described a "party" or "circus" at the request of a grand juror. She said there would be a group of girls and paying customers – "three or four men from the studios whose names I won't mention because they're all professionals." All would be in the nude. —*San Francisco Examiner*, p. 6, 9th August 1949
- A dozen or so convicts stripped naked and had a "circus" in one of the schoolrooms. Convicts came from all over the prison to watch. —Chester Himes, *Cast the First Stone*, p. X, 1952
- I'll do anything. I'll be your woman, or a circus girl. —Chester Himes, *A Rage in Harlem*, p. 209, 1957
- When I came in here, our deal included no circuses, no shows, no peeping. —Robert Leslie, *Confessions of a Lesbian Prostitute*, p. 66, 1965
- [W]here the skinpoppers and schmeckers (those who used the needles and those who sniffed the powder), the pushers and the weedheads gathered for sex circuses and to listen to the real cool jive. —Chester Himes, *Come Back Charleston Blue*, p. 150, 1966
- We would snort it [cocaine] through alabaster horns and then in the mirrored bedroom we made "circus" love until our nerve ends shrieked. —Iceberg Slim (Robert Beck), *Pimp*, p. 61, 1969
- A circus, Porky thought as he watched another girl cross the room and sit down on the floor between Jean's legs. —Donald Goines, *Dopefiend*, p. 12, 1971

2 a state of affairs; a noisy and confused institution, place, scene or assemblage *US, 1899*

- Oh what a circus / Oh what a show / Argentina has gone to town / Over the death of an actress called Eva Peron —Tim Rice, *Oh, What a Circus*, 1978
- The absolute pits, for everyone concerned, are the hotel circuses where a Hollywood star is flown into London for a couple of days to do 'European publicity'. —*The Observer*, 27th January 2002
- [A] media circus[.] —*The Guardian*, 12th July 2002

3 a temporary company of people (often moving from place to place), engaged in the same endeavour, e.g. lawn tennis, motor racing, etc *UK, 1958*

A specialisation of **CIRCUS** (an assemblage).

4 a group of aircraft engaged in displays of skillful flying *UK, 1916*

Military origins.

5 feigned spasms by a drug addict to convince a doctor to prescribe a narcotic *US*

- —Vincent J. Monteleone, *Criminal Slang*, p. 50, 1949
- —J.E. Schmidt, *Narcotics Lingo and Lore*, p. 30, 1959

circus bees; circus squirrels *noun*

body lice *US*

- —Don Wilmeth, *The Language of American Popular Entertainment*, p. 54, 1981

circus cowboy *noun*

a youthful, attractive homosexual male prostitute *UK*

A matching of the US **MIDNIGHT COWBOY** with London geography.

- —*Maledicta*, p. 144, Summer/Winter 1986 – 1987: 'Sexual Slang: prostitutes, pedophiles, flagellators, transvestites, and necrophiles'

circus simple *adjective*

obsessed with the circus *US, 1975*

- —Joe McKennon, *Circus Lingo*, p. 26, 1980

circus tent *noun*

an apartment or house where customers pay to view sexual exhibitions *US*

- And behind the respectable-looking facades of the apartment buildings were the plush flesh cribs and poppy pads and circus tents of Harlem. —Chester Himes, *The Real Cool Killers*, p. 61, 1959

ciss!

▷ see: **CESS!**

cissy *adjective*

effeminate *CANADA, 1915*

From 'sister'.

- Unpopular with me were the "cissy" cowboys Roy Rogers and Gene Autry.They also sang. Yuk. —Brian McDonald, *Elephant Boys*, p. 40, 2000

cits *noun*

▸ **the cits**

Minneapolis and St Paul, Minnesota *US*

- —John D. Bell et al., *Loosely Speaking*, p. 4, 1966

citizen *noun*

1 an ordinary person outside a gang or club *US*

- As Hell's Angels, we lived in our own underground world, barely part of the citizens' world and having as little to do with them as possible. —Ralph "Sonny" Barger, *Hell's Angel*, p. 109, 2000

2 a fellow member of a youth gang *US*

- —Dale Kramer and Madeline Karr, *Teen-Age Gangs*, p. 174, 1953

3 a prisoner who has earned the respect of other prisoners *US*

- —James Harris, *A Convict's Dictionary*, p. 30, 1989

City *noun*

▸ **The City**

San Francisco, California *US*

Uniformly used by northern Californians, who shun **'FRISCO**.

- [F]rom LA I ride the frieght on up to the City and en route I want to visit the Buddhist Monastery at Santa Barbara[.] —Jack Kerouac, *Letter to Malcolm Crowley*, p. 502 – 503, 19 July 1955

-city *suffix*

a good example of the precedent noun *US, 1930*

- Weep City was just around the turn, and we were traveling on the express. —Mezz Mezzrow, *Really the Blues*, p. 160, 1946
- Fat City: an extremely favorable situation —Collin Baker et al., *College Undergraduate Slang Study Conducted at Brown University*, p. 115, 1968
- "One of my prize suckers is taking a cue stick from the rack to make the trip to trim city." —Iceberg Slim (Robert Beck), *Trick Baby*, p. 183, 1969

- This has never failed. Poon City! You are there! —Terry Southern, *Now Dig This: The Unspeakable Writings of Terry Southern 1950–1995*, p. 5, 1986
- The reporters ignored him – snore city. —James Ellroy, *White Jazz*, p. 64, 1992
- It's Kickback City. — *Casino*, 1995

city block *noun*
in horse racing, a large margin of victory or a large lead *US*
- —David W. Maurer, *Argot of the Racetrack*, p. 19, 1951

city college *noun*
a jail, especially the New York City jail *UK, 1796*
- —Vincent J. Monteleone, *Criminal Slang*, p. 51, 1949
- —Jay Robert Nash, *Dictionary of Crime*, p. 67, 1992
- He was sent first to the Tombs, a jail his old gangster firends called City College. —Rich Cohen, *Tough Jews*, p. 79, 1999

city flyer *noun*
a small truck used for local deliveries *US*
- —Montie Tak, *Truck Talk*, p. 31, 1971

city Jake *noun*
a person sophisticated in urban ways *US, 1966*
- —Frederic G. Cassidy, *Dictionary of American Regional English, Volume 1*, p. 673, 1985

city kitty *noun*
a local police official *US*
- —Lanie Dills, *The Official CB Slanguage Language Dictionary*, p. 24, 1976

city light *noun*
the low-intensity setting on headlights *US, 1950*
- —Frederic G. Cassidy, *Dictionary of American Regional English, Volume 1*, p. 673, 1985

city mouse *noun*
in Antarctica, a support personnel who never leaves McMurdo Station *ANTARCTICA*
- — *Cool Antarctica*, 2003: 'Antarctic slang'

city of the newly-wed and nearly-dead *nickname*
Victoria, British Columbia *CANADA*
- —Tom Parkin, *WetCoast Words*, p. 35, 1989

city slicker *noun*
a smoothly persuasive rogue of a type stereotypically associated with city life; a sophisticated city-dweller *US, 1924*
The second sense is derogatory.
- [He] has to face down the snobbery of his city-slicker fellow students towards a country boy. — *The Guardian Weekly*, 11th June 2003

city titties *noun*
small bumps delineating lanes on motorways and roads *US*
- —Lewis Poteet, *Car & Motorcyle Slang*, p. 51, 1992

city tote *noun*
a coat *UK*
Rhyming slang, formed on the name of a bookmaking firm.
- —Ray Puxley, *Fresh Rabbit*, 1998

civilian *noun*
1 anyone who is not a member of the group with which the speaker identifies, especially a motocyle gang *US, 1946*
- Ricky finished his glass of red while they argued who was meaner, dirtier, who'd stomped more civilians, hit more cops, got brought up on more charges. —Elmore Leonard, *Glitz*, p. 240, 1985
- Generally, they held themselves to a higher standard of honesty and commitment than most civilians I knew. —Peter Coyote, *Sleeping Where I Fall*, p. 112, 1998

2 a non-regular officer *US*
- Patton recommended only seven full colonelcies – four Regulars, three "civilians." —Robert S. Allen, *Patton's Third U.S. Army*, p. 45, 1947

3 in twelve-step recovery programmes such as Alcoholics Anonymous, a person who is not involved in and does not need to be involved in a recovery programme *US*
- —Christopher Cavanaugh, *AA to Z*, p. 68, 1998

civil serpent *noun*
used as a humorous synonym for 'civil servant' *US, 1980*
- If not corrupted or manipulated by development interests, pandering politicians or civil serpents, the boards hold the promise of a planning process more sensitive to the needs and desires of the city's diverse neighborhoods. — *Los Angeles Times*, p. 2 (Part 8), 23rd November 1986

civvies *noun*
1 civilian clothes *UK, 1889*
Military usage.
- Probably an admiral in civies, spying out the next war. —Philip Wylie, *Opus 21*, p. 142, 1949
- When she saw Harry walk in wearing his pre-war civvies, his wrists and ankles sticking out like Huck Finn's, she promptly burst into laughter. —Max Shulman, *Rally Round the Flag, Boys!*, p. 24, 1957
- He slammed a plastic bag down on the counter. "These are the civies you came in with. Put 'em on." —Gerald Petievich, *One-Shot Deal*, p. 157, 1981

2 manufactured cigarettes *UK*
Prison slang, remembering the pleasures of being a **CIVVY** (a civilian) and a gentle play on **CIGGY**; **CIGGIES**.
- —Angela Devlin, *Prison Patter*, p. 37, 1996

civvy *noun*
a member of the general public, not a member of the uniformed services: military, police, prison, fire, etc *UK, 1895*
Abbreviated from 'civilian'.
- CIVVIE: the amorphous British public that is always getting lost and wanting to know the time. —Peter Laurie, *Scotland Yard*, p. 321, 1970

civvy *adjective*
civilian *UK, 1915*
Military use.
- It gives me outlets that I can't get in civvy life. We have opportunities to go places and do things we can't do in civilian life. — *The Guardian*, 31st January 2003

civvy street *noun*
civilian life; non-military life *UK, 1943*
- Stay with the army in the knowledge that the best was behind him or bale out and take his chances in civvy street? —Chris Ryan, *The Watchman*, p. 187, 2001

CJ *noun*
phencyclidine, the recreational drug known as PCP or angel dust *US*
- —US Department of Justice, *Street Terms*, October 1994

C-jam *noun*
cocaine *US*
- —Richard A. Spears, *The Slang and Jargon of Drugs and Drink*, p. 109, 1986

c-jame *noun*
cocaine *US*
- — *Current Slang*, p. 15, Fall 1968

C-joint *noun*
a place where cocaine is sold *US*
- —Nick Constable, *This is Cocaine*, p. 182, 2002

CJ's *noun*
a pair of men's close-fitting and revealing nylon swimming trunks *AUSTRALIA*
Standing for **COCK JOCKS**.
- CJ's or Cockjocks, were a pretty common term for speedos when I was growing up in WA, and still are now. — *Wordmap (www.abc.net.au/wordmap)*, 2003

CK *noun*
1 Calvin Klein™ clothing *US*
Favoured by members of the Bloods youth gang, to whom the initials also stand for 'Crip Killer'.
- —Bill Valentine, *Gangs and Their Tattoos*, p. 77, 2000

2 a mixture of cocaine and the recreational drug ketamine *US*
- Users pay from $20 to $40 per dose, or "bump," usually to be mixed with heroin or cocaine and snorted (the coke/ketamine combo is called CK or the "Calvin Kelin Special")[.] — *The Record [Bergen County, New Jersey]*, p. A1, 5th December 1995

3 cocaine *US*
- —Eugene Landy, *The Underground Dictionary*, p. 51, 1971

4 a man who feels that he has to disparage other men in front of women *US*
An abbreviation of **COCK-KNOCKER**. Recorded in Los Angeles, August 2002.

CK1 *noun*
a mixture of nine parts cocaine and one part the recreational drug ketamine *UK*
The brand name of a popular fragrance by Calvin Klein.
- Meanwhile in London, a ready-mixed wrap of powder called CK1 is doing the rounds. — *Sky Magazine*, p. 76, July 2001
- —Mike Haskins, *Drugs*, p. 293, 2003

clack *verb*
to rattle the dice when switching altered dice in or out of a game; always inadvertent and usually disastrous to the cheat *US*
- —*The Annals of the American Academy of Political and Social Sciences*, p. 123, May 1950

clacker *noun*
1 the backside; the anus *AUSTRALIA*
Probably from 'clacker' a ratcheted noise-making device, alluding to farting. Not a perversion of 'cloaca'.
- Come on then up there, off your clackers! —J.E. MacDonnell, *Don't Gimme the Ships*, p. 135, 1960
- And it still hurts to think of his size 12 boots right up my clacker. —Rex Hunt, *Tall Tales – and True*, p. 79, 1994
- —Paul Vautin, *Turn It Up!*, p. 95, 1995
- [S]he relentlessly interrogates notions of immutable identity AND takes a great big red ribbon out of her clacker. — *Sydney Scope Magazine*, p. 2, 2001

2 a young woman; a group of young women; young women in general *UK*
Military.
- [A] nice piece (or bit) of clacker. — Beale, 1984

3 a dollar *US, 1918*
- Commencing shortly after the first of the year, he'll get some 25,000 clackers per annum[.] — *San Francisco Examiner*, p. 19, 20th December 1945
- In Alameda County, where the officials have a thrifty eye toward the public clacker, the Supervisors and their lawyers have been recovering assessment losses. — *San Francisco Examiner*, p. 35, 3rd February 1966

4 a triggering device for claymore mines *US*
- —Gregory Clark, *Words of the Vietnam War*, p. 104, 1990

clackers *noun*
the teeth; false teeth *US, 1950*
- —Frederic G. Cassidy, *Dictionary of American Regional English, Volume 1*, p. 675, 1985
- [R]emembering my father's ugly pink clackers soaking in their bedside glass of water. —Leonard Garment, *Crazy Rhythm*, p. 265, 2000

clacker valve *noun*
the female genitalia *UK*
- —Chris Lewis, *The Dictionary of Playground Slang*, p. 59, 2003

clag *noun*
excreta, faeces; rubbish *UK*
- These are modern clag. We could find cheaper antique ones. —Jonathan Gash, *The Ten Word Game*, p. 31, 2003

claggy *adjective*
unpleasantly bedaubed with excreta *UK*
From **CLAG**.
- Oh Geez... I trod in dog chocolate, now my shoes are all claggy! —Chris Lewis, *The Dictionary of Playground Slang*, p. 59–60, 2003

clag nut *noun*
a small lump of excreta or toilet paper that clings to the anal hair *UK*
From **CLAG** (faeces).
- —Chris Lewis, *The Dictionary of Playground Slang*, p. 60, 2003

claim *verb*
1 to arrest someone *UK*
- —Peter Laurie, *Scotland Yard*, p. 321, 1970

2 to challenge someone to a fight *IRELAND*
- The Mulryans was doing a lot of braggin' about what they'd do to us, so we sent them word that we was claimin' them. —Murphy Tom, *A Whistle in the Dark*, p. 18, 1989

claiming *noun*
a method of casino cheating, in which a cheat claims that a slot machine malfunctioned and they received no payment or inadequate payment from a win *US*
- It is informally called claiming and can occur in a variety of situations in which the players falsely claim that the slot machine has malfunctioned. —Jim Regan, *Winning at Slot Machine*, p. 67, 1985

Claire Rayners *noun*
trainers (footwear) *UK, 1997*
Based on the name of Claire Rayner, popular agony aunt and novelist.
- —John Ayto, *The Oxford Dictionary of Slang*, p. 173, 1998

clam *noun*
1 the vagina *US, 1916*
- I was gobblin' her clam like it was the last supper. —Richard Price, *The Wanderers*, p. 37, 1974
- Further down the beach, a beautiful woman was sunning as three tourists with camcorders zoomed in our her shaved clam. —Anka Radakovich, *The Wild Girls Club*, p. 78, 1994
- I will not shake my clam in front of a tragically hip East Village audience for $35 a night when I can be doing the same in Jersey for $300 a night. —James Ridgeway, *Red Light: Inside the Sex Industry*, p. 153, 1996

2 the anus *US*
- —*Maledicta*, p. 197, 1983: 'Ritual and personal insults in stigmatized subcultures'

3 the mouth *US, 1825*
- —J.E. Lighter, *The Historical Dictionary of American Slang*, p. 426, 1994

4 a dollar *US, 1886*
- I take him for fifty clams a day. —Horace McCoy, *Kiss Tomorrow Good-bye*, p. 354, 1948
- "Connie," Mort said, "got fifteen clams on you?" —Bernard Wolfe, *The Late Risers*, p. 28, 1954
- Oh, it ain't going to cost nothing, like something like little old two million clams. —William "Lord" Buckley, *Hip Einie*, 1955
- I laugh and we move up the street to Hermes where I buy a hideous purse that looks just like a doctor's bag for five hundred clams. —Julia Phillips, *You'll Never Eat Lunch in this Town Again*, p. 148, 1991
- Thousand, yes, bones or clams or whaever you call them. — *The Big Lebowski*, 1998

5 a betting chip in a poker game *US*
- —George Percy, *The Language of Poker*, p. 21, 1988

6 in a musical performance, a missed cue or an off-key note *US, 1955*
- —Robert S. Gold, *A Jazz Lexicon*, p. 58, 1964
- —David Shenk and Steve Silberman, *Skeleton Key*, p. 39, 1994

clam; clam up *verb*
to stop talking *US, 1916*
- I haven't got enough to lean on you and make you open up, but you can believe it that I'm going to get something that'll make you give this clamming up another thought. —Robert Campbell, *The Cat's Meow*, p. 113, 1988
- Phil, I'm just scared he's gonna clam up on me with all these sheriffs all over the place. — *Natural Born Killers*, 1994

clambake *noun*
a session in which jazz musicians collectively improvise *US, 1937*
From **CLAM** (a missed note).
- —Arnold Shaw, *Lingo of Tin-Pan Alley*, p. 9, 1950
- —Robert S. Gold, *A Jazz Lexicon*, p. 58, 1964

clam dam *noun*
a condom *US, 1990s*
Combines **CLAM** (the vagina) with 'dam' (a barrier).

clam-diggers *noun*
calf-length trousers *US*
The suggestion is that the trousers are an appropriate length for digging for clams in mud flats.
- They go over any skirt and top off all the shorts, clam-diggers and slacks combinations you have for the summer. — *San Francisco Examiner*, p. 11, 15th June 1947
- Mario Villalobss watchd te bearded young vice cop, who wore a tank top and clam diggers[.] —Joseph Wambaugh, *The Delta Star*, p. 17, 1983

clam gun *noun*
a shovel or other digging implement *US, 1927*
- —Russell Tabbert, *Dictionary of Alaskan English*, p. 165, 1991
- (Canadian Forces, present) The "clam-gun" is the weapon used to hunt the wily clam. —Tom Langeste, *Words on the Wing*, p. 60, 1995
- There may be days when you beachcomb or laze around camp until the tide is nearly out, then grab your trusty clam gun and dig up a meal of luscious razor clams from the long sand beach of McIntyre Bay[.] —Neil G. Carey, *A Guide to the Queen Charlotte Islands*, p. 29, 1998

clamp *verb*
▸ **clamp it to**
to have sex *US*
- "Generally, I talk about clamping it to some old girl, becuase you start talking about sex around here and half these guys lose their minds." [Interview with Walt Grove] — *Playboy*, p. 130, May 1963

clam patch *noun*
the passenger seat on a motorcyle *US*
Biker (motorcyle) slang, coarsely referencing women as **CLAM** (the vagina).

clampers *noun*
the teeth *US, 1970*
• —Frederic G. Cassidy, *Dictionary of American Regional English, Volume 1*, p. 677, 1985

clamp it!
be quiet! *UK: SCOTLAND*
• —Michael Munro, *The Patter, Another Blast*, 1988

clamps *noun*
handcuffs *US*
• —Vincent J. Monteleone, *Criminal Slang*, p. 51, 1949

clams *noun*
money *AUSTRALIA, 1992*
• This sorry situation leads me to believe the majority of you out there...are simply closet Sick Puppy readers who really don't want it known that they actually fork out their hard-earned clams for this trash. —*Sick Puppy*, p. 2, 1998

clam-shelled *adjective*
▸ to get clam-shelled
to be engulfed by a wave while surfing *US*
• —Trevor Cralle, *The Surfin'ary*, p. 21, 1991

clam squirt *noun*
vaginal secretions *US*
• Anyways, I get this knife an' some bread and I stuck the knife up her ol' patoot, got a nice gob of clam squirt, an' I spread it on the bread. —Richard Price, *The Wanderers*, p. 37, 1974

Clan *noun*
▸ the Clan
a group of performers and friends surrounding Frank Sinatra in the 1950s and 60s *US*
Better known as the Rat Pack.
• "The Clan," as they've been dubbed by others, possess talent, charm, romance, and a devil-may care nonconformity that gives them immense popular appeal. —*Playboy*, p. 34, June 1960

clanger *noun*
1 an error, a mistake *UK, 1957*
• I thought, "Christ, I've made a dreadful clanger here." —*The Guardian*, p. 9, 14th January 2002
2 a coward *AUSTRALIA*
• —Sidney J. Baker, *Australia Speaks*, 1953
3 in poker, a drawn card that does nothing to improve your hand *US*
Also known as a 'clang'.
• —John Vorhaus, *The Big Book of Poker Slang*, p. 10, 1996

clangeroo *noun*
a memorably bad misjudgement *UK*
An intensification of **CLANGER** (an error) with the suffix **-EROO**; mainly theatrical in use.
• Not just a floater [a mistake] but a real old-fashioned clangeroo. —Terence Rattigan, *Theatrical Companion to Coward*, 1957

clangers *noun*
testicles *UK, 1961*
• You like real clangers? I'll show you a pair that gong like Big Ben! —Joseph Wambaugh, *The Secrets of Harry Bright*, p. 47, 1985

clank *noun*
an armoured tank *US, 1982*
• —J.E. Lighter, *The Historical Dictionary of American Slang*, p. 427, 1994

clank *verb*
1 to be nervous *US, 1955*
• For a fellow down to his last fuel, it's "bingo." If he "clanks," he's nervous and if he "augers in" he crashed. —*San Francisco Examiner*, p. 10 (II), 2nd June 1957
2 to reject a romantic overture or partner *US*
• —*Time Magazine*, p. 46, 24th August 1959

clank clank!
used in response to an Australian's claim of ancestry that goes back to the days of the early settlers *AUSTRALIA*
Echoic of transported prisoners' chains. Reported by Warrant Officer Ron Tyler of the Royal Australian Air Force, 1968.

clanked up *adjective*
anxious, nervous *US, 1953*
• —J.E. Lighter, *The Historical Dictionary of American Slang*, p. 427, 1994

clanks *noun*
delirium tremens *US, 1980*
• —Ralph de Sola, *Crime Dictionary*, p. 28, 1982

clap *noun*
gonorrhoea *UK, 1587*
From old French *clapoir* (a sore caused by venereal disease); the term was normal register for centuries, slipping into colloquial or slang in mid-C19.
• The girls stayed put until they ground out the thousand or got a slap from Mr. Clap. —Mezz Mezzrow, *Really the Blues*, p. 59, 1946
• [B]y the time she was fifteen she had been plain lousy with clap and syphy, and she had had gonorrheal rheumatism, and one day she had just jumped into the Jackson Park lagoon and polluted the drinking water for the gold fish. —James T. Farrell, *Saturday Night*, p. 30, 1947
• I already spent every kurd of it buying Penstrep for Ali's clap. —William Burroughs, *Naked Lunch*, p. 180, 1957
• But all the way out west, to Washington, he kept worrying about whether he was going to get a clap. —Clancy Sigal, *Going Away*, p. 135, 1961
• But how do you get the clap? By doing it, and anybody who does that dirty thing obviously deserves to get the clap. —Lenny Bruce, *How to Talk Dirty and Influence People*, p. 54, 1965
• There is an awful lot of clap loose in the U.S. – and while rubbers are a drag, the clap is something else again. —*Berkeley Barb*, p. 10, 2nd June 1967
• I tried to close down this bad news commune on 11th Street run by Spade Charlie, a real amphetamine, V.D., clap headquarters. —Abbie Hoffman, *Revolution for the Hell of It*, p. 175, 1968
• After they came back on board, come to find out that four of them had picked up the clap. —Darryl Ponicsan, *The Last Detail*, p. 15, 1970
• In the beginning, Estelle had been just another cunt by the roadside as likely to give the clap to him as the other way around. —Gurney Norman, *Divine Right's Trip (Last Whole Earth Catalog)*, p. 43, 1971
• Joy, there's no way you can get the clap unless you go to the Heart O' Texas Motel with roy Kennerdine or Billy Bob Simpson or any of those other off-brand, drop-case guys you hang around with in the afternoons. —Dan Jenkins, *Dead Solid Perfect*, p. 77, 1986

clap *verb*
to kill someone *US*
• Check reportedly screamed obscenities at the woman and threatened to "clap" her and her sister. "Clap" is street slang for murder, police said. —*Connecticut Post*, 8th April 2002

▸ clap beef
to have sex with a woman *JAMAICA, 1980*
• —Thomas H. Slone, *Rasta is Cuss*, p. 37, 2003

▸ clap eyes on
to see someone or something *UK, 1838*
• [O]ne of the most beautiful unspoiled stretches of golden sand you will ever clap eyes on —*The Guardian*, 2nd February 2003

clap checker *noun*
a member of the Medical Corps *US*
Vietnam war usage, identifying medics by the least glorious of their duties.
• —Linda Reinberg, *In the Field*, p. 44, 1991

clap clinic *noun*
a medical pratice that treats all sexually transmitted disease *US*
• —Susan Quist, *On the Way to the Clap Clinic*, 1976
• You were down the clap clinic so many times last season you were on first-name terms with all the doctors. —Colin Butts, *Is Harry on the Boat?*, 1997

clapped-out; clapped *adjective*
1 unservicable as a result of use or neglect *UK, 1946*
• [P]oor saps who are obsessively smitten by clapped-out Jaguars. —Jenny Eclair, *Camberwell Beauty*, p. 347, 2000
2 (of persons) exhausted, no longer effective *UK, 1946*
• —Hugh Tracy, *Death in Reserve*, 1976
• —Louis S. Leland, *A Personal Kiwi-Yankee Dictionary*, p. 26, 1984

clappers *noun*
the testicles *UK*
Derives from the clapper of a bell, and is almost always in the plural.
• Don't let me hear you making another report like that or I'll have your clappers for a necktie. —John Winton, *We Joined the Navy*, 1959

▸ like the clappers; like the clappers of hell; like the clappers of fuck
very fast; very hard *UK, 1948*
Possibly rhyming slang for 'clappers of a bell', 'hell'.

- DAVE: He wanted to know if you're a goer. DENISE: What did you say? DAVE: I said you go like the clappers. — Caroline Aherne and Craig Cash, *The Royle Family*, 1999
- What it all boils down to is that the Ducati 999 goes like the clappers. — *The Guardian*, 10th September 2002

clappy *adjective*

infected with a sexually transmitted infection, especially gonorrhoea *US, 1937*

- Before I'd touch your slimy thighs / which a thousand crabs has bit / I'd drink a gallon a drunkard's puke / and suck a clappy dick. — Bruce Jackson, *Get Your Ass in the Water and Swim Like Me*, p. 124, 1964

claps *noun*

gonorrhoea *US, 1965*

Largely black usage.

- "She had the claps," he said, "and those Texas claps got bigger monster bugs." — Christina and Richard Milner, *Black Players*, p. 72, 1972
- [T]hese beast ain't got NO IDEA how to help a man get rid of the claps. — A.S. Jackson, *Gentleman Pimp*, p. 62, 1973
- — John A. Holm, *Dictionary of Bahamian English*, p. 43, 1982

clap shack *noun*

a clinic or hospital ward where sexually transmitted infections are treated *US, 1952*

- The place their unfortunate owners are sent for treatment is the clap shack. — Paul Fussell, *Wartime*, p. 257, 1989

clap sticks *noun*

in the television and film industries, the clapboard used for synchronising sound and picture *US*

- — Ira Konigsberg, *The Complete Film Dictionary*, p. 52, 1987

claptrap *noun*

1 nonsense, rubbish *UK, 1915*

From the conventional sense (language designed to win applause).

- How could this jury listen to such Stella Dallas claptrap? — Edwin Torres, *After Hours*, p. 425, 1979
- This year we've heard the shortlist for the Turner prize described as "conceptual bullshit" (Kim Howells) and "rehashed claptrap" (Charles Saatchi). — *The Guardian*, 11th December 2002

2 a brothel with a high incidence of sexually transmitted infections *US*

- — *Maledicta*, p. 150, Summer/Winter 1986–1987: 'Sexual slang: prostitutes, pedophiles, flagellators, transvestites, and necrophiles'

clarabelle *noun*

tetrahydrocannabinal (THC), the psychoactive ingredient in marijuana *US*

- — Eugene Landy, *The Underground Dictionary*, p. 51, 1971

Clarence *nickname*

a cross-eyed person *UK: SCOTLAND*

From Clarence, a cross-eyed lion that out-acted the human cast in BBC television's *Daktari*, 1966–69.

- — Michael Munro, *The Patter, Another Blast*, 1988

claret *noun*

blood *UK, 1604*

Conventional claret is a fortified Bordeaux red wine; the visual connection is obvious.

- [S]creaming blue murder and holding the side of his face, and claret is pouring out from between his fingers[.] — Frank Norman, *Bang To Rights*, p. 28, 1958
- "I want blood. Blood, Arthur." He thumped on the desk to underline his words. Arthur nodded uneasily. "I like a bit of claret myself." — Anthony Masters, *Minder*, p. 19, 1984
- Teach him a thing or two. Spill some claret. — Greg Williams, *Diamond Geezers*, p. 133, 1997
- I'm sure if the Old Bill [police] had seen the claret I would have had my collar felt. — Martin King and Martin Knight, *The Naughty Nineties*, p. 41, 1999
- Claret is now trickling down the bridge of my nose. — Jimmy Stockin, *On The Cobbles*, p. 36, 2000

Clarisse *noun*

used as a term of address among male homosexuals *US*

- — *Fact*, p. 26, January-February 1965

clarity *noun*

MDMA, the recreational drug best known as ecstasy *US*

- — Bruce Eisner, *Ecstasy*, p. 1, 1989
- — *Miramonte High School Parents Club Newsletter (Orinda, California)*, p. 1, 26th November 2001
- — Mike Haskins, *Drugs*, p. 289, 2003

Clark Gable *noun*

a table *UK*

Rhyming slang, formed on the name of US film actor Clark Gable, 1901–60.

- — Ray Puxley, *Cockney Rabbit*, 1992

Clark Kent *adjective*

homosexual *UK*

Rhyming slang for **BENT**, formed from the 'secret-identity' of Superman.

- [H]e's completely Clark Kent. — Bodmin Dark, *Dirty Cockney Rhyming Slang*, 2003

clart *noun*

1 used as a term of friendly address *UK*

Most likely from UK black **BLOODCLAAT** or **PUSSYCLAAT** (a contemptible person) into wider youth usage.

- Aright, clart. What're you doing, spar? — Goldie Looking Chain, *Soap Bar*, 2004

2 excrement; also as a euphemism for all senses of 'shit' *UK*

From Scottish and dialect *clarty* (sticky with dirt; sticky; dirty). Also used in the plural.

- — Clement and La Frenais, *A Further Stir of Porridge*, 1977

clary *noun*

a clarinet *US, 1942*

- — Robert S. Gold, *A Jazz Lexicon*, p. 59, 1964

▷ **see: JULIAN CLARY**

class *noun*

elegant style or behaviour, refined taste, a state of excellence *UK, 1874*

Originally sports usage.

- You look like you got class. Yessir! With a capital K. And I'm a guy that knows class when he sees it, believe you me. — *It Happened One Night*, 1934
- I could've been a contender. I could've had class and been somebody. Real class. — Budd Schulberg, *On the Waterfront*, 1954

class *verb*

to attend a class *US*

- — Connie Eble (Editor), *UNC-CH Campus Slang*, p. 3, October 2002

class A's *noun*

1 cocaine, heroin and other drugs that are legally categorised as Class A narcotics *UK*

- I slowly slipped into a farcical but forceful world of contention, materialism... and class-As. — Wayne Anthony, *Spanish Highs*, p. 1, 1999

2 in the US Army, the dress uniform *US*

- — Carl Fleischhauer, *A Glossary of Army Slang*, p. 10, 1968

classic *adjective*

1 excellent *US*

- — John Severson, *Modern Surfing Around the World*, p. 166, 1964
- — Connie Eble (Editor), *UNC-CH Campus Slang*, p. 2, Spring 1990

2 handsome, well-dressed *US*

- — Ethan Hilderbrant, *Prison Slang*, p. 25, 1998

classic six *noun*

a common layout of an apartment in Manhattan – two bedrooms, living room, dining room, kitchen and small maid's room *US*

- — Amy Sohn, *Sex and the City*, p. 154, 2002

class up the ass *noun*

a superlative style *US*

- Man, that is true punk; that is so fucked up it's got class up the ass. — Lester Bangs, *Psychotic Reactions and Carburetor Dung*, p. 113, 1972

classy *adjective*

of superior quality; stylish *UK, 1891*

To have **CLASS**.

- [S]ilver-grey fur coat, miniskirt, leggings, boots, expensively shaggy hair – she's ... classy. That's the only word for it. She looks like a high-class Goldie Hawn. — Kevin Sampson, *Outlaws*, p. 110, 2001

classy chassis *noun*

an attractive female body *US*

- — *American Weekly*, p. 2, 14th August 1955
- — Clarence Major, *Dictionary of Afro-American Slang*, p. 37, 1970

clat *noun*
a dirty person *UK: SCOTLAND*
- To call somebody a clat means that you think he is dirty, whether physically or mentally. — Michael Munro, *The Original Patter*, p. 16, 1985

clatch *noun*
your personal belongings *ANTARCTICA, 1989*
- — Bernadette Hince, *The Antarctic Dictionary*, p. 85, 2000
- — *Cool Antarctica*, 2003: 'Antarctic slang'

clatter *verb*
to smack someone, to hit someone, to beat someone up *UK*
- I clattered him. — Patrick O'Shaughessy, *Market Traders' Slang*, 1979
- — Angela Devlin, *Prison Patter*, p. 37, 1996

clatters *noun*
a smacking *UK*
From CLATTER (to smack).
- — Patrick O'Shaughnessy, *Market Traders' Slang*, 1979

'clavaed up *adjective*
used when a bala*clava* helmet is worn *UK*
- Various guys, bandanaed and 'clavaed up, darting across the sideroad. — Diran Adebayo, *My Once Upon A Time*, p. 274, 2000

Claven *noun*
someone who purports to know everything *US*
From the Cliff Claven character on the television comedy *Cheers*.
- — Connie Eble (Editor), *UNC-CH Campus Slang*, p. 2, Fall 1991

claw *noun*
a pickpocket *US, 1914*
- — Hyman E. Goldin et al., *Dictionary of American Underworld Lingo*, p. 44, 1950
- — Don Wilmeth, *The Language of American Popular Entertainment*, p. 55, 1981

claw *verb*
to pick a glass up from its top *US*
- — Kathryn Leigh Scott, *The Bunny Years*, 1998
- You learned never to 'claw' a glass by picking it up from the top so your fingers touched the rim. You always used a napkin and handled the glass in the middle. — Kathryn Leigh Scott, *The Bunny Years*, p. 173, 1998

▸ **claw off a lee shore**
to face serious difficulties in a task or project *US*
Nautical origins.
- — Charles F. Haywood, *Yankee Dictionary*, p. 30–31, 1963

clay *noun*
1 a claymore mine *US*
- — J.E. Lighter, *The Historical Dictionary of American Slang*, p. 429, 1994

2 tetrahydrocannabinal (THC), the psychoactive ingredient in marijuana *US*
- — Eugene Landy, *The Underground Dictionary*, p. 51, 1971

3 hashish *US*
- — Jay Robert Nash, *Dictionary of Crime*, p. 68, 1992

clay eater *noun*
a poor rural dweller *US, 1841*
- "Clay-eaters" was a term often applied to far-flung denizens of the unsettled South. — Jim Goad, *The Redneck Manifesto*, p. 85, 1997

clay pigeon *noun*
a person who is easily victimised *US*
- — Helen Dahlskog (Editor), *A Dictionary of Contemporary and Colloquial Usage*, p. 13, 1972
- — Ralph de Sola, *Crime Dictionary*, p. 28, 1982

Clayton's *noun*
any substitute for a desired thing *NEW ZEALAND*
- — Sonya Plowman, *Great Kiwi Slang*, p. 47, 2002

Clayton's *adjective*
false, pretend, faux *AUSTRALIA, 1984*
From the proprietry name of a substitute alcoholic drink which was widely advertised as 'the drink you have when you're not having a drink'.
- 'Was it meant to be a Clayton's royal commission?' asked Masters. 'I'm afraid that's so,' said Woodward, 'The Government expects whitewashing.' — *Sydney Morning Herald*, p. 14, 25th June 1986

clean *verb*
1 by gambling, fraud or theft, to take all of someone's money *UK, 1812*
A variant is 'clean out'.
- When some man comes along and claims a godly need / He will clean you out right through your tweed / ("That's right, you asked for it, remember there is a big difference between kneeling down and bending over . . .") He's got twenty million dollars in his Heavenly Bank Account. — Frank Zappa, *Heavenly Bank Account*, 1981

2 to remove seeds, stems and foreign matter from marijuana leaves *US, 1967*

3 to rid yourself of altered dice, altered cards or any evidence of cheating *US*
- — *The Annals of the American Academy of Political and Social Sciences*, p. 123, May 1950

4 in mountain biking, to succeed in negotiating an obstacle or set of obstacles without accident *US*
- [A] series of five to seven small obstacles that I know I can clean without much thought. — *Mountain Bike Magazine's Complete Guide To Mountain Biking Skills*, p. 41, 1996

▸ **clean it up**
to clarify or explain something *US*
- — William K. Bentley and James M. Corbett, *Prison Slang*, p. 14, 1942

▸ **clean out the kitchen; clean up the kitchen**
to perform oral sex on a woman *US, 1941*
- — Roger Blake, *The American Dictionary of Sexual Terms*, p. 51, 1964

▸ **clean the books**
to induce a criminal to confess to a series of unsolved crimes *US*
- — Inez Cardozo-Freeman, *The Joint*, p. 488, 1984

▸ **clean the cage out**
to perform oral sex on a woman *UK*
- — Paul Baker, *Polari*, p. 169, 2002

▸ **clean the clock**
on the railways, to make an emergency stop *US*
An allusion to the air gauge that drops to zero in an emergency stop.
- — Ramon Adams, *The Language of the Railroader*, p. 33, 1977

▸ **clean the kitchen**
to lick your sex-partner's anus *UK*
- — Paul Baker, *Polari*, p. 169, 2002

▸ **clean the pipes**
to ejaculate; to masturbate *US*
- DOM: You know, clean the pipes. TED: Pipes? What are you talking about? DOM: You jerk off before all big dates, right? — *Something About Mary*, 1998

▸ **clean the table**
in pool, to shoot all of the remaining balls in one turn *US, 1989*
- — Mike Shamos, *The Illustrated Encyclopedia of Billiards*, p. 51, 1993

▸ **clean the tube**
(of a male) to masturbate *US*
Using 'tube' to mean 'the penis'.
- "The boy is masturbating" [...] Cleaning the tube[.] — Erica Orloff and JoAnn Baker, *Dirty Little Secrets*, p. 89, 2001

▸ **clean up the calendar**
(used of the police) to extract from a criminal confessions clearing up a number of crimes, regardless of his actual guilt, in exchange for lenient treatment on another crime *US*
- — Jay Robert Nash, *Dictionary of Crime*, p. 68, 1992

▸ **clean your bones**
to thrash or defeat someone soundly in a fight *US*
- — *American Speech*, p. 276, December 1963: 'American Indian student slang'

▸ **clean your clock**
1 to severely defeat someone, physically or in a competition *US, 1959*
- [S]ince Turnipseed had got his clock cleaned in his own cell it wasn't difficult to determine who deserved the credit. — Malcolm Braly, *On the Yard*, p. 202, 1967
- "We played poker," added Jeremiah-Dumpling. "Cleaned his fucking clock." — Carl Hiaasen, *Native Tongue*, p. 356, 1991

2 in trucking, to pass another vehicle, especially another truck, at high speed *US*
- — Montie Tak, *Truck Talk*, p. 32, 1971

clean *adjective*

1 drug-free *US, 1949*

- "Look, I kicked. I'm clean, I tell yah!" Fay repeated.—Alexander Trocchi, *Cain's Book*, p. 156, 1960
- I was thinkin' about askin' you to see what you can do for me. I mean, like, when I get clean.—Nathan Heard, *Howard Street*, p. 79, 1968
- And yet, while we sat and rapped, he was hooked and I was clean. —A.S. Jackson, *Gentleman Pimp*, p. 134, 1973
- "If I don't get anything else out of all this," he said, "I'm going to get clean."—Seth Morgan, *Homeboy*, p. 102, 1990
- —Angela Devlin, *Prison Patter*, p. 37, 1996
- I have to take a drug test every six months to make sure I'm clean. —*American Beauty*, 1999
- It probably took another two years to get off the gear altogether, but I've been clean since.—Robert Ashton, *This Is Heroin*, p. 78, 2002

2 unarmed *US, 1952*

- —Angela Devlin, *Prison Patter*, p. 37, 1996

3 innocent; free of suspicion; without a trace of guilt; without a criminal record *US, 1925*

- This is clean shit. No serial numbers and never been used.—*48 Hours*, 1982
- I've been picked up a couple times. Loan sharking. Racketeering. But I was never convicted. I'm clean.—*Get Shorty*, 1995

4 not subject to police surveillance *US*

- If some punk asks you if your ride is "clean," he wants to know if it was tailed or not.—Henry Hill and Byron Schreckengost, *A Good Fella's Guide to New York*, p. 13, 2003

5 (used of an illegal betting operation) unafraid of police intervention because of bribes paid to the police *US*

- —David W. Maurer, *Argot of the Racetrack*, p. 20, 1951

6 excellent, fashionable, stylish *US*

- —*San Francisco Examiner*, p. 8, 27th October 1963
- —Miss Cone, *The Slang Dictionary (Hawthorne High School)*, 1965
- It was the one who had a Thunderbird, and some clean vines.—H. Rap Brown, *Die Nigger Die!*, p. 9, 1969
- It was lowered to da ground, had twice-pipes, candy-apple red and button top. Ooo, clean!—Cheech Marin and Tommy Chong, *Santa Calus and his Old Lady*, 1971
- I damn near didn't know who he was, he was so clean.—A.S. Jackson, *Gentleman Pimp*, p. 28, 1973
- Now we were big-time pimps from the New York scene / And believe me, Jim, we were both real clean.—Dennis Wepman et al., *The Life*, p. 36, 1976

7 (used of a theatrical performance) completely sold-out *US*

- —Sherman Louis Sergel, *The Language of Show Biz*, p. 49, 1973

8 in circus and carnival usage, without value *US*

- —Don Wilmeth, *The Language of American Popular Entertainment*, p. 55, 1981

9 (of an object ball in pool) directly into the pocket without touching a cushion or another ball *US*

- —Mike Shamos, *The Illustrated Encyclopedia of Billiards*, p. 51, 1993

▸ **clean road for monkey to run**

to labour for someone else's benefit *TRINIDAD AND TOBAGO*

- —Lise Winer, *Dictionary of the English/Creole of Trinidad & Tobago*, 2003

clean *adverb*

completely *UK*

- GUNN: Alone? ALONNA: No, Jason had his back. They got away clean.—*Angel*, 1999
- The prisoner got clean away.—*BBC News*, 26th April 2002
- One of the actors just clean forgot his lines[.]—*The Guardian*, 10th March 2003

clean and ready *adjective*

prepared; dressed nicely *US*

- —Edith A. Folb, *runnin' down some lines*, p. 232, 1980

cleaner *noun*

1 in the used car business, a customer who does not have a car to trade in *US*

- It's a cleaner but he's got no D.P. so I sent him to the happy man and now I find they couldn't get together because he's got no sticks.—*San Francisco Examiner*, p. II-1, 24th February 1956

2 a hired killer *US*

- Tiny stars placed on the arm in any fashion indicate that the wearer is a hitter (also known as a "cleaner" or "torpedo").—Bill Valentine, *Gangs and Their Tattoos*, p. 36, 2000

3 in circus and carnival usage, the person who retrieves money from paid players who have been allowed to win a concession game to drum up business *US*

- —Don Wilmeth, *The Language of American Popular Entertainment*, p. 55, 1981

cleaners *noun*

▸ **take to the cleaners**

1 to thrash someone *UK*

- MR. BIG NOSE: One more time, mate; I'll take you to the fuckin' cleaners! [...] MRS. BIG NOSE: And don't pick your nose [...] MR. BIG NOSE: I wasn't going to pick my nose. I was going to thump him! —Monty Python, *Life of Brian*, 1979

2 to thoroughly swindle; to rob *US, 1907*

- —Angela Devlin, *Prison Patter*, p. 37, 1996
- "I hope he's happy with his trashy little whore because she's costing him a fortune." Peter barked a laugh. "You took him to the cleaners, huh?" ""Bet your ass," Christian said.—Judith Gould, *Time to Say Good-Bye*, p. 29, 2000

3 to forcibly strip someone *UK*

- —Angela Devlin, *Prison Patter*, p. 37, 1996

clean freak *noun*

a person who is obsessed with cleanliness *US*

- He blamed his affliction on dirt, and he was a tireless clean freak who liked the cell spotless.—Malcolm Braly, *On the Yard*, p. 7, 1967

cleaning crew *noun*

the members of a criminal enterprise who rid the crime scene of possible evidence and at times any bodies resulting from the crime *US*

- Tommy had decided not to use a contracted cleaning crew. On some hits a crew of "sanitation specialists" would follow in right behind to wash the crime scene down with detergents and vaccum the carpets, eliminating trace evidence.—Stephen Cannell, *King Con*, p. 20, 1997

cleaning kit *noun*

the equipment needed to rid a crime scene of possible evidence *US*

- "Okay," Texaco said, looking at the cleaning kit in a Gucci leather suitcase beside him."—Stephen Cannell, *King Con*, p. 20, 1997

clean out *verb*

to thrash someone *US, 1862*

- Oh yeah. I got in a bar fight in the Eighties and got cleaned out – got marked up pretty good.—*The Times Magazine*, p. 44, 23rd February 2002

clean peeler *noun*

to a surfer, a perfect wave *US*

- —Vann Wesson, *Generation X Field Guide and Lexicon*, p. 38, 1997

clean sheets *noun*

a bed or cot *US*

Vietnam war usage.

- —Linda Reinberg, *In the Field*, p. 44, 1991

cleanskin *noun*

1 a person without a criminal record *AUSTRALIA, 1943*

Originally applied to an unbranded sheep. Used during a report on a bomb explosion in Ealing, west London, *BBC Television News*, 3rd March 2001.

- Of course Thomas Moore was a cleanskin without even the slightest hint of scandal attached to his name.—Clive Galea, *Slipper*, p. 67, 1988
- Even more annoying, both of the Tudors were cleanskins, as was Sandra Halley.—Stephen Dedman, *Shadows Bite*, p. 91, 2001

2 a novice *AUSTRALIA, 1907*

From the conventional sense (an unbranded stock animal).

- The squad leader was one of the most experiencd operators in the MEU and he was the only member of the squad with any previous gaol-riot experience – the rest of us were cleanskins.—William Dodson, *The Sharp End*, p. viii, 2001

3 a person of integrity, especially in a political context *AUSTRALIA, 1942*

From the sense of 'a person without a police record'.

4 in horse racing, a jockey who has never been disqualified in a race *AUSTRALIA*

- —Ned Wallish, *The Truth Dictionary of Racing Slang*, p. 15, 1989

cleansleeve *noun*

a low-ranking military recriut *US, 1909*

- Yet only five years after graduating – "clean sleeve," with no rank chevrons – Davison had commanded a battalion in France.—Rick Atkinson, *The Long Gray Line*, p. 65, 1989

clean-the-kitchen *noun*

corned beef hash *US*

- —*American Speech*, p. 89, April 1946: 'The language of west coast culinary workers'

clean time *noun*
the amount of time that has passed since a prisoner was last in trouble *US*
• —James Harris, *A Convict's Dictionary*, p. 30, 1989

clean-up *noun*
1 a good alibi *US*
• —Charles Shafer, *Folk Speech in Texas Prisons*, p. 201, 1990
2 a wave that breaks seaward of most surfers, causing them to lose their boards and thus cleaning up the area *US*
• —John Severson, *Modern Surfing Around the World*, p. 166, 1964

clean up *verb*
to make a profit, especially a big one *US, 1831*
• —Angela Devlin, *Prison Patter*, p. 37, 1996

cleanup team *noun*
the members of a criminal enterprise who rid a crime scene of any possible evidence and at times bodies resulting from the crime *US*
• Problem was, you had to know the cleanup team was solid. —Stephen Cannell, *King Con*, p. 20, 1997

clean wheels *noun*
a motor vehicle to be used in crime that has never been previously stolen or come under prior police suspicion in any way *UK*
• —David Powis, *The Signs of Crime*, 1977

clean works *noun*
a new needle and syringe *US*
A concept and term new in the age of AIDS.
• —Peter Johnson, *Dictionary of Street Alcohol and Drug Terms*, p. 41, 1993

clear *noun*
▸ **in the clear**
with no evidence against you; therefore, innocent or apparently so *UK, 1934*

clear *verb*
to steal something *UK*
• They're standing outside a top sports store. "Go in and clear what you can," Candice orders. "What? Steal?" "No, bake a freakin' cake." —Karline Smith, *Letters to Andy Cole*, p. 141, 1998

▸ **clear the channel**
to stop talking *US*
• — *Dobie Gillis Teenage Slanguage Dictionary*, 1962

▸ **clear your tubes**
to ejaculate; to masturbate *AUSTRALIA*
• — Thommo, *The Dictionary of Australian Swearing and Sex Sayings*, p. 26, 1985

clear as mud *adjective*
anything but clear; confused *UK, 1842*
• [T]he situation is still as clear as mud. — *The Observer*, 29th September 2002

clearinghouse *noun*
an illegal lottery *US, 1951*
More commonly known as a **NUMBERS** game.
• —Thomas L. Clark, *The Dictionary of Gambling and Gaming*, p. 44, 1987

Clear Lake *noun*
methamphetamine purportedly manufactured in the Clear Lake region of northern California *US*
• —Geoffrey Froner, *Digging for Diamonds*, p. 68, 1989: 'Types of speed'.

clear light *noun*
a stage in some LSD experiences in which the user feels receptive to enlightment *US*
• —Edward R. Bloomquist, *Marijuana*, p. 336, 1971

clearly!
I agree! *US*
• —Connie Eble (Editor), *UNC-CH Campus Slang*, p. 2, November 2002

clear off *verb*
to depart *UK, 1816*
Often used as an imperative.
• Pinochet may, or may not, clear off. But [Lord] Hoffmann certainly should[.]— *The Guardian*, 19th January 1999

clearskin *noun*
used as a variation of all senses of 'cleanskin' *AUSTRALIA, 1943*

clear-skinned *adjective*
with a light complexion *BARBADOS*
• —Frank A. Collymore, *Barbadian Dialect*, p. 31, 1965

clef *verb*
to compose a tune or song *US, 1948*
• —Harold Wentworth and Stuart Berg Flexner, *Dictionary of American Slang*, p. 108, 1960

Clem *noun*
in the circus or carnival, a fight with customers *US, 1891*
• —Joe McKennon, *Circus Lingo*, p. 26, 1980

Clement Freud *noun*
a haemorrhoid *UK*
Rhyming slang, formed from the name of British writer, broadcaster and politician, Sir Clement Freud (b.1924), father of **EMMA FREUD** whose name has a synonymous purpose.
• I've got one Clement Freud so big that I thought my brain had fallen out of my Khyber [anus]. —Bodmin Dark, *Dirty Cockney Rhyming Slang*, 2003

clemo *noun*
executive clemency granted to a convicted prisoner *US*
• —Harold Wentworth and Stuart Berg Flexner, *Dictionary of American Slang*, p. 108, 1960

clennedak *noun*
in Quebec, a child's taffy cone (a sweet confection) *CANADA*
• Clennedak, a children's candy, is named after a brand name, Klondyke, and also referred to in spoken Quebecois as "kiss" of "tire." —Bill Casselman, *Canadian Food Words*, p. 151, 1998

clerk *noun*
in American casinos, an exceptionally skilled dealer *US*
• —Lee Solkey, *Dummy Up and Deal*, p. 109, 1980
• —Steve Kuriscak, *Casino Talk*, p. 12, 1985

clerks and jerks *noun*
clerical support personnel and officers *US, 1975*
Vietnam war usage. The high degree of cynicism about officers found in enlisted men was even more intense in Vietnam.
• Running a god-damned club when there's nobody on the rear except clerks and jerks. —John M. Del Vecchio, *The 13th Valley*, p. 461, 1982
• —Linda Reinberg, *In the Field*, p. 44, 1991
• [T]he second plane was filled with the clerks and jerks – the Ranger support company, whose weapons probably weren't even loaded. —Richard Marcinko, *Rogue Warrior*, p. 329, 1992

clever *adjective*
▸ **damned clever these Chinese; dead clever these Chinese; clever chaps these Chinese**
a catchphrase used as a comment upon an explanation given about some device or machine, especially if the explanation has not been understood *US*
A back-handed tribute to Chinese ingenuity.
• GRAMS: GIANT EXPLOSION, GLASS SMASHING AND OBJECTS FALLING ON FLOOR GRYTPYPE: Damned clever these Chinese! —Spike Milligan, *The Goon Show*, 18th January 1955
• Her left ear, from my point of view, was on the right, and her right ear was on the left, both the opposite way round form my own, just as the book said. Damn clever these Chinese. — *The Express*, p. 26, 22nd October 2001

clever bollocks *noun*
a clever person *UK*
• No, actually, clever bollocks[.]—Dave Courtney, *Dodgy Dave's Little Black Book*, p. 22, 2001

clever clogs *noun*
a clever person *UK, 1866*
A variation of 'clever boots'.
• Isaac Newton may have thought he was a clever clogs for coming up with his theory of gravity after that apple supposedly hit him on his 17th century head. — *The Guardian*, 29th July 2002

clever creep *noun*
a forensic chemist *UK*
Police use.
• —John Wainwright, *Dig His Grave and Let Him Lie*, 1971

clever dick *noun*

1 a clever, rather too clever, person *UK, 1887*
Derisory or sarcastic in use.
- Well, if you must know, Mr Clever Dick, it was to teach Frank and Joe a lesson. —Ray Galton and Alan Simpson, *Hancock's Half Hour*, 22nd April 1958
- A tax-man hates a clever dick – and that's what you are, Arthur. —Anthony Masters, *Minder*, p. 125, 1984
- Lewis scrambled up, his face nearly purple with embarrassment and anger. "You're the clever-dick, aren't you!" —Greg Iles, *Black Cross*, p. 174, 1995
- Or would some clever-dick theorist simply redefine the strike as an alternative form of conceptual creativity and have done with it? —*The Guardian*, 8th October 2002

2 a brick *UK*
Rhyming slang.
- —Ray Puxley, *Cockney Rabbit*, 1992

clever Dickie *noun*
a bricklayer *UK*
Rhyming slang for 'brickie', extended from CLEVER DICK (a brick).
- —Ray Puxley, *Cockney Rabbit*, 1992

clever drawers *noun*
a knowledgable person *UK*
Disparaging.
- PETE: He was always boasting about things he knew. DUD: Old clever drawers, weren't he, eh? —Peter Cook, *Not Only But Also*, 1966

cleverguts *noun*
a clever person *UK, 1959*
Childish and sarcastic.

cleverkins *noun*
a clever person *UK, 1937*

cleverly *adverb*
(used of a racehorse winning a race) easily *US*
- —Robert Saunders Dowst and Jay Craig, *Playing the Races*, p. 161, 1960

clever Mike *noun*
a bicycle *UK, 1961*
Rhyming slang for 'bike'.

clever sticks *noun*
a clever person *UK, 1946*
A variation on the theme of 'clever boots'; often used as a juvenile taunt.

clevie *noun*
the vagina *UK*
- —Paul Baker, *Polari*, p. 169, 2002

clew up *verb*
to hide, to go into hiding *UK*
Of naval origins.
- They caught up with him three weeks later in Blackpool. Clewed up in a dosshouse, he was stone broke. —Colin Evans, *The Heart of Standing*, 1962

click *noun*

1 a gang *US, 1879*
A corrupted spelling of 'clique'.
- You know there's a lot of streets where a whole 'click' is made out of punks who can't fight[.] —Piri Thomas, *Down These Mean Streets*, p. 49, 1967
- I'd been hearing about him on the street in Harlem, he was the war counselor of some click uptown on Lenox Avenue. —Edwin Torres, *Carlito's Way*, p. 20, 1975
- Just remember, if you join a prison tip or click, you'll never fit in out there again. —Seth Morgan, *Homeboy*, p. 153, 1990
- Everyone in here is associated in "clicks" or gangs. Since I am an outsider to these "clicks" I live a fearful existence. —Miles Harvey, *The Island of Lost Maps*, p. 213, 2000

2 a kilometer *US, 1962*
Also spelt 'klick' or 'klik'. Vietnam war usage.
- —Carl Fleischhauer, *A Glossary of Army Slang*, p. 30, 1968
- So the helicopter takes off and after going out maybe four clicks it crashes, and the wounded and everybody on board dies. —John Kerry, *The New Soldier*, p. 98, 1971
- A LOH fired up a sampan on the river at 131324, that's about a klick en a half downriver from that big tree that sticks up. —John M. Del Vecchio, *The 13th Valley*, p. 281, 1982
- [E]verything was transformed into Crispy Critters for half a dozen clicks in any direction you would have cared to point. —Larry Heinemann, *Paco's Story*, p. 15, 1986
- I saw some bodies about half a klick this side of Phy Cam Canal. —*Full Metal Jacket*, 1987
- "There I was, thinkin I was forty clicks outta Da Nang." —Joseph Wambaugh, *The Golden Orange*, p. 54, 1990
- I have never learned to call kilometres "clicks," and my idea of a good time is for someone else to take the wheel. —David Helwig, *Living Here*, p. 94, 2001

click *verb*

1 to have a successful encounter with a hitherto unknown member of the opposite sex *UK, 1937*
- The journalist met the keeper's wife, clicked with her, and when the World Cup began, returned to the house to see her again. —*The Observer*, 30th September 2001

2 to get along instantly and famously *UK, 1915*
- We just seemed to click, though, didn't we? —Mary Hooper, *(megan)2*, p. 163, 1999
- —Connie Eble (Editor), *UNC-CH Campus Slang*, p. 3, Fall 1999

3 to suddenly understand something; to suddenly make sense in context *UK, 1939*
- Something, you know, just clicked. —*The Guardian*, 10th July 2001

4 to perform at the right moment as needed by a friend *US*
- —Terry Williams, *The Cocaine Kids*, p. 136, 1989

5 to enjoy an amorous relationship *IRELAND*
- In less than a year he had managed to click in some hungry way with Madonna McManus[.] —John Kelly, *The Sophisticated Boom Book*, p. 39, 2003

6 of a woman, to become pregnant (or in Australia, of a cow) *UK, 1937*
- —Sidney Baker, *Australian Slang*, 1953

7 in the theatre or other forms of entertainment, to be a success *US, 1926*
- [Ray] Bolger always had the brains to know what made him click with audiences. —Michael Kantor and Laurence Maslon Broadway, *The American Musical*, p. 2, 2004

8 in horse racing, to win a race *US*
- —David W. Maurer, *Argot of the Racetrack*, p. 20, 1951

9 to be well accepted *US*
- —Arnold Shaw, *Dictionary of American Pop/Rock*, p. 78, 1982

10 to be selected or accepted for a duty or a fate; to be killed *UK, 1917*
A military colloquialism.

clicker *noun*

1 crack cocaine mixed with phencyclidine, the recreational drug known as PCP or angel dust *US*
- —US Department of Justice, *Street Terms*, October 1994
- —Mike Haskins, *Drugs*, p. 293, 2003

2 a brick *US, 1989*
- —Ellen C. Bellone (Editor), *Dictionary of Slang*, p. 7, 1989

3 in circus and carnival usage, a free pass *US*
- —Don Wilmeth, *The Language of American Popular Entertainment*, p. 55, 1981

clickers *noun*
false teeth *US, 1950*
- —Frederic G. Cassidy, *Dictionary of American Regional English, Volume 1*, p. 685, 1985

clicks *noun*
approval; applause *US*
- —Connie Eble (Editor), *UNC-CH Campus Slang*, p. 2, Fall 1997

clicks and mortar; C&M *noun*
a business that combines trading from traditonal business premises with Internet-based commerce *US*
A play on 'bricks and mortar', a traditional business.
- He struck a chord with his audience by saying companies that learn how to seamlessly blend virtual and physical assets will emerge as big winners in what he called the new "clicks and mortar" economy. —*Washington Post*, p. E1, 22nd July 1999
- The merger of AOL and Time Warner will create the first big "clicks and mortar" company. "Clicks and mortar" describes the so-far mythical union between internet growth and traditional levels of profit. —*BBC News*, 11th October 2000
- Such "clicks and mortar" retailers give customers the option to purchase or order on-line and then pick up the product at a bricks-and-mortar branch. —Harvard Business Review, *Harvard Business Review on Marketing*, p. 61, 2001

clientised *adjective*
having come to a point of view that is in sympathy with a client's or subject's outlook or situation *UK*
- —Susie Dent, *The Language Report*, p. 10, 2003

Cliffie *noun*
a student or alumna of Radcliffe College, Harvard University *US, 1961*
- Obviously the 'Cliffie who greeted me read the Crimson and knew who I was. —Erich Segal, *Love Story*, p. 25, 1970

C light *noun*
in the pornography industry, a light used to illuminate the genitals of the performers *US*
'C' is in **CUNT**.
- This is Randy's dick here. We lit it so it wouldn't look so white and unreal: a little light called the C light. —Robert Stoller and I.S. Levine, *Coming Attractions*, p. 131, 1991
- —*Adult Video News*, p. 50, October 1995
- The c-light is a light shined directly on the action (whether you want to call it crotch or cookie or cunt). It helps us see the "c" better. Makes the "c" brighter. —*The Village Voice*, 3rd April 2001

climax *noun*
1 amyl nitrite *US*
Because of the orgasm-enhancing characteristics of the drug.
- —Jay Robert Nash, *Dictionary of Crime*, p. 69, 1992

2 heroin *UK, 1998*
- —Mike Haskins, *Drugs*, p. 283, 2003

climb *noun*
1 cat burglary *UK, 1936*
- [A]ll sorts of dimwitted screwsmen have a go at the climb, as they call it, now and again[.] —Charles Raven, *Underworld Nights*, p. 142, 1956

2 a marijuana cigarette *US, 1946*
A climb is necessary if you wish to get **HIGH** (intoxicated).
- —Richard A. Spears, *The Slang and Jargon of Drugs and Drink*, p. 110, 1986
- —Mike Haskins, *Drugs*, p. 287, 2003

climb *verb*
▸ **climb the wooden hill; climb the wooden hill to Bedfordshire**
to go upstairs to bed *UK, 1984*
A combination of **WOODEN HILL** (the stairs) and **BEDFORDSHIRE** (a bed).
- I waited till 'er [the speaker's wife] had climbed the wooden hill to Bedfordshire, got on the dog [telephone] and rang the number. —Andrew Nickolds, *Back to Basics*, p. 146–147, 1994

climbing trees to get away from it
used as a catchphrase reply to the question 'getting any (sexual satisfaction)?' *AUSTRALIA, 1984*

climb into *verb*
to criticise someone, to launch a verbal attack on someone *NEW ZEALAND*
- You can go to certain suburbs where you will have people climbing into Polynesians for under-achieving and in the next breath criticizing Asians for over-achieving. —*Dominion*, p. 1, 6th July 1993

climey *noun*
a British social 'climber' in the US, especially New York *UK, 1990s*
A contraction of 'climber' and **LIMEY** (a Briton).
- —Alon Shulman, *The Style Bible*, p. 55, 1999

clinch *noun*
a prolonged or passionate embrace *US, 1901*
- That weakness is probably what prompted Angel to present Buffy with her own cross, a weakness he proves equally susceptible to when his passionate clinch with Buffy results in a cross-shaped burn on his chest. —Ngaire E. Genge, *Buffy Chronicles*, p. 8, 1998

clinch *verb*
in bird-watching circles, to identify a rare bird *UK*
- —*New Society*, 17th November 1977

cling *verb*
▸ **cling to the belt**
(used of South Vietnamese troops) to stay close to US troops *US*
- [T]he Vietnamese did all they could to keep the killing on an infantry-against-infantry basis by staying as close to the Americans as possible, a tactic they called "clinging to the belt." —Neil Sheehan, *A Bright Shining Lie*, p. 574, 1988

clinic *noun*
1 a poker game characterised by over-analysis of each hand *US*
- —George Percy, *The Language of Poker*, p. 21, 1988

2 a poker game played by doctors *US*
- —George Percy, *The Language of Poker*, p. 21, 1988

clink *noun*
a jail; a police station *UK, 1785*
Originally an infamous prison in Southwark, London, and then by the mid-C19 applied to any jail, prison or cell.
- Mom left a big hole in his life, which he filled by marrying Betty Bugbee when she got out of the clink. —Bernard Wolfe, *The Late Risers*, p. 301, 1954
- I heard that after the fracas in Harlem she landed in the clink[.] —Ross Russell, *The Sound*, p. 287, 1961
- The Office, Barlow called it. Home, John Watt called it. The Stir, Clink, Bog, Nick, depending on what your are, and where you come from. —Troy Kennedy Martin, *Z Cars*, p. 21, 1962
- [T]he western lead will be Rusty Godowsky who is aimed for stardom if he stays out of the clink[.] —Gore Vidal, *Myra Breckinridge*, p. 102, 1968
- He just laughed and said he'd probably see me in the clink before he got out. —Oscar Zeta Acosta, *The Revolt of the Cockroach People*, p. 253, 1973
- There were interviews with black neighborhood residents who said the police had to start hooking the kids up and throwing them in the clink. —Elmore Leonard, *Switch*, p. 100, 1978
- Rings was like, Wow, I never thought to find love in the clink! —Seth Morgan, *Homeboy*, p. 83, 1990
- In those days, simply being a suspicious character could land you in the clink for three days without charges being pressed, a handy method for dealing with undesirables. —Kim Rich, *Johnny's Girl*, p. 47, 1993

clinker *noun*
1 in the entertainment industry, a failure *US, 1961*
- This is, mind you, the definitive list of clinkers released in 1973. —*San Francisco Examiner and Chronicle, Sunday Scene*, p. 12, 13th January 1974

2 a small piece of faeces clinging to anal hairs *UK, 1904*
- —James McDonald, *A Dictionary of Obscenity, Taboo and Euphemism*, p. 20, 1988

3 a wrong note in a musical performance *US, 1937*
- —Kenn "Naz" Young, *Naz's Underground Dictionary*, p. 20, 1973
- —Arnold Shaw, *Dictionary of American Pop/Rock*, p. 79, 1982

4 a mistake *US, 1937*
- —Robert S. Gold, *A Jazz Lexicon*, p. 59, 1964

5 a piece of broken-up ice on the water *CANADA*

clinkeroo *noun*
a jail or prison *US*
- —Jay Robert Nash, *Dictionary of Crime*, p. 69, 1992

clinkers *noun*
1 handcuffs *US*
- —Vincent J. Monteleone, *Criminal Slang*, p. 52, 1949

2 leg irons; foot shackles *UK, 1699*
- —Hyman E. Goldin et al., *Dictionary of American Underworld Lingo*, p. 45, 1950

clip *noun*
1 a rate of speed *UK, 1867*
- The Metropolitan Police Authority are proceeding at a fair old clip to put in place the changes to their structures that will unleash and build up a series of savings during the coming financial year. —Mayor Ken Livingstone, *London Assembly*, 19th September 2001

2 an occurence or instance *US*
- Since then, I been on half a dozen scores – three, four thousand a clip – when I'm pressed to the wall. —Vincent Patrick, *The Pope of Greenwich Village*, p. 30, 1979

3 a blow *UK, 1830*
- nothing more daring than allowing them to say "bloody" without getting a clip round the ear. —*The Guardian*, 28th May 2004

4 a swindle or other act of dishonest trickery *US, 1941*
- He felt it expedient to do so each day after he had put a hard clip on some sucker who might be inclined to wake up sober and call for the bluecoats. —Robert Sylvester, *No Cover Charge*, p. 208, 1956
- [G]uys sitting around talking about the clip they'd made. —Herbert Huncke, *Guilty of Everything*, p. 43–44, 1990

5 a string of bottles containing doses of crack cocaine *US*
- She could carry two clips down in her panties, another two up top, and the Fury couldn't do anything unless they pulled her into the precinct for a strip search. —Richard Price, *Clockers*, p. 5, 1992

6 a vasectomy *US*
- —Judi Sanders, *Faced and Faded, Hanging to Hurl*, p. 40, 1993

7 in the circus or carnival, a patron *US*

- —Joe McKennon, *Circus Lingo*, p. 26, 1980

clip *verb*

1 to steal something; to swindle someone; to win something, especially through cheating *US, 1922*

- The only time the board of aldermen ever had a meeting was when enough of the waiters ganged up around the bar to talk about the laines they clipped, and the police chief was too busy mixing drinks to bust himself under the prohibition act. —Mezz Mezzrow, *Really the Blues*, p. 66, 1946
- Generally a runner made plenty for himself, taking a chance that the dough he clipped wasn't on the number that pulled in the shekels. —Spillane, *I, The Jury*, p. 46, 1947
- Of course, about price – how much was he going to clip you? —Bernard Wolfe, *The Late Risers*, p. 168, 1954
- What with the frigging cop butting in, I have to go all the way down to Seventh Street to clip a bag of coal[.] —Rocky Garciano (with Rowland Barber), *Somebody Up There Likes Me*, p. 50, 1955
- I Just clip a buck here and a buck there. It mounts up, but nobody gets hurt. —Jim Thompson, *The Grifters*, p. 72, 1963
- Immediately Skippere had a plan to clip the score[.] —John Rechy, *City of Night*, p. 113, 1963
- I clipped a dance moll for a swab, it paid a trey or a fin. —Bruce Jackson, *Get Your Ass in the Water and Swim Like Me*, p. 85, 1965
- She began to make more, especially when she learned how to clip a trick as he concentrated on his kicks, or was drunk. —Nathan Heard, *Howard Street*, p. 97, 1968
- Boy, you clipped me for ten grand and the others for at least another five. —Iceberg Slim (Robert Beck), *Airtight Willie and Me*, p. 112, 1979
- Let me tell you about clipping. It has many variations. Sometimes it ain't exactly subtle. —Jake Arnott, *He Kills Coppers*, p. 18, 2001

2 to kill someone, especially by gunshot *US, 1928*

- "You are the only one who can get close enough to her to do it," his father said. "Zotz her? Clip Irene?" —Richard Condon, *Prizzi's Honor*, p. 304, 1982
- [S]ick or no fuckin' sick, you knew people were gonna get clipped. —*Casino*, 1995
- Hey, guys like Joe Loop get clipped all the time. It's what they do, man, they get pissed off about something or bored and shoot each other; it's their fate. —Elmore Leonard, *Be Cool*, p. 284, 1999

3 to hit someone *US, 1855*

- And I haven't had to really clip a young Negro in years. —Ralph Ellison, *Invisible Man*, p. 144, 1947

▸ **clip a steamer**

to defecate *US*

- —Chris Lewis, *The Dictionary of Playground Slang*, p. 61, 2003

clip and clean *adverb*

completely *US*

- The jolt took out his front tooth clip and clean. —John Gould, *Maine Lingo*, p. 53, 1975

clip-a-nines *noun*

a 9 mm ammunition clip *US*

- I've sen fifteen-year-olds roll pipe bombs under taxis and peel a clip-a'-nines at a passing squad car. —Stephen J. Cannell, *The Tin Collectors*, p. 34, 2001

clip girl *noun*

an attractive woman employed in a clip joint to encourage customers to part with their money on the promise of (sexual) services to be delivered *UK*

- "Here's comes trouble," I joked to Dave when this clip girl sauntered over to us. —Jake Arnott, *He Kills Coppers*, p. 17, 2001

clip joint; clip dive *noun*

a bar, gambling house or other business where customers are routinely cheated *US, 1932*

- Clip Joints: To be avoided, unless you are looking for grief. —Jack Lait and Lee Mortimer, *New York Confidential*, p. 215, 1948
- Baltimore clip-dives operate more closely to the orthodox custom. —Jack Lait and Lee Mortimer, *Washington Confidential*, p. 283, 1951
- About the only real aggravation in those days, Watkins remembers, was a parking lot which separated the "legitimate" Stables from a clip joint a few yards East. —Robert Sylvester, *No Cover Charge*, p. 82, 1956
- Ralph got a job in a clip joint on West 49th Street and soon acquired a good reputation among the whores he protected from tricks complaining about being robbed. —Babs Gonzales, *I Paid My Dues*, p. 104, 1967
- There are around six clip-joints in Soho (also called hostess bars and near-beer bars) which promise both alcohol and sex and deliver neither. —Kitty Churchill, *Thinking of England*, p. 190, 1995
- The regular West End Central officers had already gone around the clubs and clip joints and given the "warning formula". —Jake Arnott, *He Kills Coppers*, p. 16, 2001

clip off *verb*

(used of ammunition) to explode because of heat from a surrounding fire *US*

- —Gregory Clark, *Words of the Vietnam War*, p. 123, 1990

clipped dick *noun*

a Jewish person *US*

Derogatory.

- —Harold Wentworth and Stuart Berg Flexner, *Dictionary of American Slang*, p. 109, 1960

clipper *noun*

1 a thief *US*

- No security staff could hope to beat this army of clippers without a lot of help. —*I was a House Detective*, p. 120, 1954
- —*Woman*, 11th December 1965

2 a person who collects film clips, usually of a single subject *US*

- —*American Speech*, p. 53, Spring 1978: 'Star trek lives: trekker slang'

3 a disposable cigarette lighter *UK*

A generic from the Clipper™ brand.

- —Angela Devlin, *Prison Patter*, p. 37, 1996

Clipper Club *noun*

the abstract brotherhood of men who have undergone a vasectomy *US*

- —Connie Eble (Editor), *UNC-CH Campus Slang*, p. 4, Fall 1995

clippie; clippy *noun*

1 a female conductor on a bus or train *UK, 1941*

From clipping tickets.

2 an employee who checks and clips tickets at railway stations *AUSTRALIA, 1953*

clipping *noun*

a robbery facilitated by posing as a prostitute and knocking out the clients with sleeping pills *UK*

- —*New Society*, 7th July 1977

clique *noun*

a youth gang *UK*

A nuance of the conventional sense.

- [Y]our Kru, or your Massive, your Thugs, or Bredrins; Dawgs, Homies, your Clique, or your Posse. —Julian Johnson, *Urban Survival*, p. 264, 2003

clique up *verb*

to form small groups *US*

- There's other characters, as soon as they walk in the wing, they'll just clique right up with a group. —Bruce Jackson, *Outside the Law*, p. 155, 1972

clit *noun*

1 the clitoris *US*

- Why, I've only to give my clit a tiny flick right now and I'd be sopping. —Terry Southern, *Candy*, p. 49, 1958
- I'll blip her clit up and I'll blip it down, and I'll blip it east and west[.] —Robert Gover, *Poorboy at the Party*, p. 82, 1966
- —Collin Baker et al., *College Undergraduate Slang Study Conducted at Brown University*, p. 97, 1968
- The good guys who think they know what "Women's Lib," as they so chummily call it, is all about – and who then proceed to degrade and destroy women by almost everything they say and do: The token "pussy power" or "clit militancy" articles. —Loren Baritz, *The American Left*, p. 501, 1971
- She told me her clit was so sensitive when I got through that she didn't think she could touch it for a week. —Roger Blake, *What you always wanted to know about porno-movies*, p. 244, 1972
- She closed her eyes and woke up with Kiki's head moving between here legs. His tongue was teasing her clit. —Robert Deane Pharr, *Giveadamn Brown*, p. 51, 1978
- And there's a Tarzan take-off where the man of the jungle cuts the yodeling and gets down to kicking the well-lubed clit of the professor's daugther[.] —*Adult Video*, p. 65, August/September 1986
- There's the clit moan (a soft, in-the-mouth sound), the vaginal moan (a deep in-the-throat sound), the combo clit-vaginal moan. —Eve Ensler, *The Vagina Monologues*, p. 110, 1998
- [T]he very tip of my tongue making dollar signs on her clit, $$$$$$$$. —J.J. Connolly, *Layer Cake*, p. 77, 2000

2 a despicable person *UK*

A figurative application, similar to **PRICK**.

- [H]ate myself – too thin too fat wimp clit mammy's boy[.] —Patrick Jones, *Unprotected Sex*, p. 225, 1999

clithopper *noun*

a promiscuous lesbian *US*

- —*Maledicta*, p. 136, Summer/Winter 1982: 'Dyke diction: the language of lesbians'

clit lit; cliterature *noun*
good quality erotica for women *US*
Formed from CLIT (the clitoris) and 'lit' (literature). 'Cliterature' is used as a chapter heading in Jaye Zimet, *Strange Sisters*, 1999.
- "Cliterature" looks at the broad expanse of women's desire, with a particular eye on those things not usually seen as erotic.—Madelena M. Christian (Editor), *Cliterature*, 2001
- So is it ghettoization to classify female artists and their art under a single label, whether jocular..."chick flicks," "clit lit"[?]—*Windy City Times*, 18th September 2002

clitoris *noun*
any popular model of car *UK*
Motor trade slang. Explained as 'every cunt has one' by a car salesman, 4th August 2004.
- Is she trying to get out of that clitoris?—The Stranglers *Peaches*, 1977

clit ring *noun*
a piece of jewellery for a clitoral piercing *US*
As body piercing became more popular through the 1990s this prosaically-named ornamentation, based on an abbreviation of 'clitoris' became a familiar possibility.
- I asked Elaine Beastie if she had any underwear on. "No, my clit ring's hanging out" she said.—Howard Stern, *Miss America*, p. 402, 1995
- I have to take my clit-ring out," she says, "it'll tear the condon."—Darren Francis, *The Sprawl [britpulp]*, p. 315, 1999

clit stick *noun*
a small vibrating sex-aid designed for clitoral stimulation *UK*
An abbreviation of 'clitoris' combined with the lipstick-sized vibrator's shape.
- Oh, it's a clit-stick!—*A - Z of Rude Health*, 11th January 2002

clit tease *noun*
a heterosexual woman who socialises with lesbians without revealing that she is heterosexual *US*
- —Amy Sohn, *Sex and the City*, p. 154, 2002

clitter *noun*
a slap with the open hand *IRELAND*
From the Irish *cliotar*.
- I gave him a clitter across the face—Liam Irwin, *North Munster Antiquarian Journal*, p. 77, 2000

clitty
the clitoris *UK, 1866*
- We got chocolate clitty onstage for ya now.—Josh Alan Friedman, *Tales of Times Square*, p. 65, 1986
- She may want you to use your best soft, sloppy tongue for caressing her clit, or if she has a tough li'l clitty, a firm tongue might be just fine.—Jamie Goddard, *Lesbian Sex Secrets for Men*, p. 142, 2000

clitty clamp *noun*
a device that is attached to a clitoris and is designed to cause discomfort or pain in the cause of sexual stimulation *UK*
- Her punishment from her master took a variety of forms "from the caning of my bottom and breasts through torturous bondage, inflatable appendages, nipple and clitty clamps, enemas and electrical stimulation."—Kitty Churchill, *Thinking of England*, p. 105, 1995

clitwobble *noun*
a woman's desire for sex *UK*
- [W]hen he has a knob throb for her and she has a clitwobble for him.—Ray Puxley, *Fresh Rabbit*, p. 79, 1998

cloak *verb*
to send an electronic message in a manner that disguises the true origin of the message *US*
- —Andy Ihnatko, *Cyberspeak*, p. 40, 1997

cloak-and-dagger *adjective*
very secret; pertaining to espionage *US, 1944*
- The capital is overrun by snoops and spies, not only using every cloak-and-dagger device for foreign transmission, but assigned and trained to catch and report inter-bureau information, rumors included.—Jack Lait and Lee Mortimer, *Washington Confidential*, p. 245, 1951

clobber *noun*
clothes, especially any outfit of good or noticeable quality *UK, 1879*
Probably Yiddish *klbr*, but 'to clobber' is 'to CLOUT' ('to hit' and may also be 'clothing').
- [A] friend in the second-hand car business who let him kip on his sofa, and lent him some clobber.—Charles Raven, *Underworld Nights*, p. 19, 1956
- We didn't have to wear our best clobber for parades and all that rubbish[.]—Johnny Speight, *It Stands to Reason*, p. 67, 1973
- [I]t's a decade since Manchester took the pop world in a surge of loose clobber, street swagger, wild drugs and great pop.—John Robb, *The Nineties*, p. 61, 1999
- [T]hey ends up getting chased through the club in their boxies [boxer shorts] with half their clobber still un the lockers.—Kevin Sampson, *Outlaws*, p. 167, 2001

clobber *verb*
1 to strike someone forcefully *US, 1944*
- For no reason they were going to clobber us.—Nat Hentoff, *Jazz Country*, p. 54, 1965
- [H]e could clobber some greedy local who got a bit cheeky up-country.—*The Times Magazine*, p. 24, 23rd February 2002

2 to criticise someone or something harshly *UK, 1956*
- Nothing else is clobbered like heavy metal[.]—*Ask*, p. 72, 8th May 1981

3 in computing, to overwrite a program *US*
- —Eric S. Raymond, *The New Hacker's Dictionary*, p. 96, 1991

4 to impose an onerous duty or unwelcome burden on someone *UK, 1984*
Usually before 'with'; for example, 'I got clobbered with finishing the weeding'.

clobbered *adjective*
drunk *US, 1951*
- You know. Drunk, stewed, clobbered, gone, liquored up, oiled, stoned, in the bag.—Max Shulman, *Guided Tour of Campus Humor*, p. 106, 1955
- —*American Speech*, p. 156, May 1959: 'Gator (University of Florida) slang'

clobbering machine *noun*
the notional machine that creates conformity *NEW ZEALAND*
- —David McGill, *David McGill's Complete Kiwi Slang Dictionary*, p. 29, 1998

clock *noun*
1 a milometer (odometer) *UK, 1967*
- —Lewis Poteet, *Car & Motorcyle Slang*, p. 53, 1972
- It had nothing on the clock but its springs were shot[.]—Peter Corris, *Make Me Rich*, p. 78, 1985
- [P]robably worth around £3,000 in immaculate condition with 60,000 miles on the clock.—*The Guardian*, 8th February 2002

2 a speedometer *UK, 1942*

3 a taxi meter *UK, 1930*
Often in the enquiry 'How much is on the clock?'.

4 an air gauge used with air brakes *US*
- —Norman Carlisle, *The Modern Wonder Book of Trains and Railroading*, p. 261, 1946

5 a watch *UK*
In conventional use from 1559, in slang use since late C19; noted by the *Oxford English Dictonary* as obsolete 'except in modern slang'.

6 the face *UK, 1918*
- —John Ayto, *The Oxford Dictonary of Slang*, p. 2, 1998

7 a punch to the face *NEW ZEALAND, 1959*
From the verb.

8 a look *UK*
From the verb.
- One stushed-up establishment had had one clock of my typically attired friend and barred the door.—Diran Abedayo, *My Once Upon A Time*, p. 267, 2000

9 a one-year prison sentence *AUSTRALIA, 1941*
- —Garry Simes, *A Dictionary of Australian Underworld Slang*, p. 47, 1993

10 a prisoner who is at the beginning of their sentence *US*
- —Frank Prewitt and Francis Schaeffer, *Vacaville Vocabulary*, 1961 – 1962

11 bravery, courage *US*
- —Hyman E. Goldin et al., *Dictionary of American Underworld Lingo*, p. 45, 1950

clock *verb*
1 to catch sight of or notice someone or something; to watch someone or something *US, 1929*
- The boys down at Chelsea nick every time they clock my boat[.]—Derek Raymond (Robin Cook), *The Crust on its Uppers*, 1962
- Big, gap-toothed smile of surprise, like we wasn't clocked before we came in the door, comes up from the pool table.—Edwin Torres, *After Hours*, p. 170, 1979
- When you walked in, Eddie, did you clock the two chinks?—Vincent Patrick, *The Pope of Greenwich Village*, p. 36, 1979

- [S]ome geezer I ain't never clocked before who keeps asking me stupid questions. —Greg Williams, *Diamond Geezers*, p. 35, 1997
- We sat back sipping our teas clocking Slip gobbing his apples. —Jeremy Cameron, *Brown Bread in Wengen*, p. 114, 1999

2 to watch someone patiently; especially to follow someone with the purpose of discovering the details of a bet *UK*
- —Frank Norman, *Bang to Rights*, 1958
- To "clock" someone is to follow someone and see what he backs. This is sometimes expressed as "Get on his daily [tail]". —*Sunday Telegraph*, 7th May 1967

3 to keep track of a slot machine in an effort to make an educated guess as to when it will pay off *US*
- There's a machine I'm clocking. Jackpot's getting up where it's getting interesting. —J. Edward Allen, *The Basics of Winning Slots*, p. 56, 1984

4 to keep track of the money involved in a game or an enterprise *US*
- —Robert C. Prus and C.R.D. Sharper, *Road Hustler*, p. 169, 1977

5 to register on the speedometer; to attain a particular speed *UK, 1984*
From **CLOCK** (a speedometer).

6 to figure something out, to evaluate something *US, 1961*
- I mean, he was already in Vegas a couple of years and he had the fuckin' place clocked. —*Casino*, 1995

7 to earn something *US*
- —Ellen C. Bellone (Editor), *Dictionary of Slang*, p. 7, 1989

8 to punch, to strike with the fist *UK, 1932*
Perhaps, originally, 'to hit in the **CLOCK**' (the face).
- Peter was so mad he clocked Perce good and hearty. —Charles Raven, *Underworld Nights*, p. 45, 1956
- "Finally the fool clocked a sergeant in the locker room at the end of a shift. Knocked him cold." —Vincent Patrick, *The Pope of Greenwich Village*, p. 112, 1979
- —Connie Eble (Editor), *UNC-CH Campus Slang*, p. 2, April 1997
- "How about the guy you clocked?" "He tried to stiff [cheat] me.["] —Janet Evanovich, *Seven Up*, p. 94, 2001
- One day I'd clock Kev. I could see it coming. —Jonathan Gash, *The Ten Word Game*, p. 187, 2003
- Butler then clocked the victor with his best punch of the night[.] —*FHM*, p. 158, June 2003

9 to sell drugs on the street *US*
- This kid Strike is now out there on the streets clocking for Rodney, like his lieutenant or something, OK? —Richard Price, *Clockers*, p. 447, 1992
- —Mark S. Fleisher, *Beggars & Thieves*, p. 287, 1995

10 to wind back the mileometer (odometer) of a vehicle to increase its sale value *US*
- —*American Speech*, p. 309–310, Winter 1980: 'More jargon of car salesmen'.
- About 90% of the used cars coming into New Zealand had done more miles than their odometers indicated. They had been 'clocked.' —*Sunday Star-Times*, p. C13, 23rd July 1995

▸ clock in
to visit your boyfriend or girlfriend only out of a sense of duty *US*
- I'd love to drink and throw stuff off the roof with you guys, but I have to clock in with the boss or she''ll cut me off. —Ben Applebaum and Derrick Pittman, *Turd Ferguson & The Sausage Party*, p. 13, 2004

▸ clock in the green room
while surfing, to take a long ride inside the hollow of a breaking wave *US*
- —Trevor Cralle, *The Surfin'ary*, p. 21, 1991

▸ clock the action
to understand what is happening and what is being said *US*
- —*Dobie Gillis Teenage Slanguage Dictionary*, 1962

clock and house *verb*
to see and remember suspects' faces, and then follow them to their home *UK*
From **CLOCK** (to see; to watch and follow).
- —David Powis, *The Signs of Crime*, 1977

clocker *noun*
1 a street drug dealer, especially of crack cocaine *US*
- Strike's clockers got jumpy if they thought they were being watched. —Richard Price, *Clockers*, p. 5, 1992

2 a watchman or guard, especially one who punches a time clock while making his rounds *US*
- —Vincent J. Monteleone, *Criminal Slang*, p. 52, 1949
- —Jay Robert Nash, *Dictionary of Crime*, p. 69, 1992

3 an onlooker *US*
- He bounced over and they giggled and kissed and performed a young lovers' routine for the benefit of the clockers and watchers in all the other cars. —Emmett Grogan, *Final Score*, p. 220, 1976

clocking *noun*
a fraudulent act of turning back a vehicle's mileometer (odometer) *UK, 1974*
From the verb **CLOCK**.

clock out *verb*
to act in a psychotic manner *US*
- —Terry Williams, *The Cocaine Kids*, p. 136, 1989

clock puncher *noun*
an employee whose working day is measured by a time-clock *US*
A worker must 'punch in' and 'punch out' at a time-clock.
- Try to become something more than just a clock puncher in a small-town shoe factory. —*I Am a Fugitive from a Chain Gang*, 1932

clock watcher *noun*
1 an employee who takes care to work only for as long and as hard as is minimally required *UK, 1911*
- I don't want a clock-watcher. If you arrive late, you don't want a frosty reception in the bar. —*The Observer*, 9th March 2003

2 a person completey lacking in generosity *US, 1956*
- —Harold Wentworth and Stuart Berg Flexner, *Dictionary of American Slang*, p. 110, 1960

clock watching *noun*
the act of working no harder, or for no longer, than is minimally required *UK, 1942*
- This survey shows many firms are worried that they are spending too much of their time form filling or clock watching rather than actually doing business. —*BBC News*, 12th September 1999

clockweights *noun*
the testicles *UK*
From the workings of a longcase clock.
- [T]he ward sister whips off his bed sheets, strips him and has a good poke round his clockweights. —*FHM*, p. 31, June 2003

clockwork along *verb*
to go smoothly *UK, 1990s*
As in 'to go like clockwork'.
- Everythin's clockworkin' along. Eddie's all set to cave in. —Nick Barlay, *Curvy Lovebox*, p. 74, 1997

clockworks *noun*
the brain *US*
- —Marcus Hanna Boulware, *Jive and Slang of Students in Negro Colleges*, 1947

clocky *noun*
sudden waving arm movements of a surfer trying to get his balance *US*
- The judges took off half a point for each of those clockies you did on take-off. —Trevor Cralle, *The Surfin'ary*, p. 21–22, 1991

clod *noun*
a stupid person *UK, 1605*
- You also need to convince yourself that there is nothing worse than stupid clods who ask pointless unnecessary questions. —Mad Magazine, *Mad About the Sixties*, p. 129, 1995

clodbuster *noun*
a farmer *US, 1950*
- You'll end up marrying a clod-buster's daughter and spend the rest of your life raising chickens. —Robert Tyre, *Saddlebag Surgeon*, p. 141, 1954

cloddy *noun*
a prison officer *UK*
- —Angela Devlin, *Prison Patter*, p. 38, 1996

clodge *noun*
the vagina *UK*
- [H]ave my hand brush against the techer's stocking-top rather than thump into her red-hot clodge. —Frank Skinner, *Frank Skinner*, p. 51, 2001

clodhopper *noun*
1 a person with big feet; big feet or big shoes *UK, 1836*
Evoking the image of a ploughman with large, coarse boots.
- [S]o the Negro's supposed to lie down and let the paddy climb upon his chest with his clodhoppers. —Piri Thomas, *Down These Mean Streets*, p. 126, 1967

- —Janey Ironside, *A Fashion Alphabet*, p. 132, 1968
- He shifts his clodhopper feet as he exhales tension relief to discover her apparently innocent.—Iceberg Slim (Robert Beck), *Doom Fox*, p. 150, 1978

2 a clumsy person *UK, 1824*
- Frol danced with every clodhopper who asked[.]—Tom Robbins, *Jitterbug Perfume*, p. 38, 1984

3 a police officer *UK*
Rhyming slang for **COPPER**; sometimes shortened to 'clod'.
- "Plod the Clod" now pounds the beat. Or, depending where you live, doesn't.—Ray Puxley, *Fresh Rabbit*, 1998

4 a copper coin, a penny *UK, 1925*
Rhyming slang for 'copper'. Sometimes shortened to 'clod'.
- —Patrick O'Shaughnessy, *Market Traders' Slang*, 1979

clog *verb*
to take a picture with a moblile phone and upload it to a website *US*
A contraction of 'camera' and 'log'.
- —Susie Dent, *The Language Report*, p. 12, 2003

clog down *adverb*
of driving, very fast or accelerating *UK, 1984*
Military; from the sense of putting your foot down on an accelerator pedal.

clogger *noun*
a footballer who has a reputation for fouling when tackling an opponent *UK, 1970*
- [Tony] Adams is the first robust English clogger to scale such heights[.]—*The Guardian*, 19th October 2002
- —Susie Dent, *The Language Report*, p. 52, 2003

cloggie *noun*
1 a clog dancer *UK*
Popularised in the late 1960s by *The Cloggies*, a cartoon strip about a clog dancing team, written and drawn by Bill Tidy.

2 a Dutch person *UK*
Derogatory. Originally military usage, from the extensive use of clogs as a symbol of Netherlands' folk-culture. Also variant 'clog head'.
- —Nigel Foster, *The Making of a Royal Marine Commando*, 1987
- Since Europe is now an open market, we need to keep up with the times. It's where these two clog heads come in.—Guy Ritchie et al., *Lock, Stock... & Four Stolen Hooves*, p. 6, 2000

cloggy *noun*
the Dutch language *UK*
From the extensive use of clogs as a symbol of the Netherlands' folk-culture.

clomp *verb*
to walk in a noisy and demonstrative fashion *UK, 1829*
- There he was clomping along in front of me on the trail[.]—Jack Kerouac, *The Dharma Bums*, p. 164, 1958

clone *noun*
1 a highly stylised, fashion-conscious homosexual male *US*
- [T]he Castro Street lot (often called clones) has a typical admixture of leather queens mostly "South of Market types".—*Maledicta*, p. 247, 1979
- First attracting attention as a definite type, it seems, in San Francisco and New York's Greenwich Village, the gay clone wears short hair and a clipped mustache, and (if possible) sports a sculpted chest with prominent pectorals.—Wayne Dynes, *Homolexis*, p. 31-32, 1985

2 a personal computer that closely duplicates the functions and operations of a leading brand *US*
- —Eric S. Raymond, *The New Hacker's Dictionary*, p. 96, 1991
- I am writing this in the tenuous privacy of my bedroom on my annoyingly obsolete AT clone.—C.D. Payne, *Youth in Revolt*, p. 3, 1993

clone *verb*
to reconfigure a stolen mobile phone so that an existing subscriber is charged for all calls *US*
- To clone a regular cellular telephone, thieves steal the over-the-air electronic signal that identifies each cellular caller for billing purposes.—*Newsday (New York)*, p. 3, 9th January 1994

clonk *verb*
to hit someone *UK, 1943*
- Alexandra envelops Sarah in a big hug, nearly clonking her on the head with one of her shopping bags.—Emma McLaughlin, *The Nanny Diaries*, p. 4, 2002

clonked; clonked out *adjective*
of a mechanical device, not working *UK*
A teenagers' variation of **CONKED**; **CONKED OUT**, used by Joanna Williamson, 1982.

clonk out *verb*
▷ **see:** CONK OUT

close *verb*
▸ **close the back door**
in bombing missions, to provide rear guard protection for the bombers *US*
- —Gregory Clark, *Words of the Vietnam War*, p. 106, 1990

▸ **close the door**
in motor racing, to pass another car and then pull sharply in front of it to minimise its chances of passing you *US*
- —John Lawlor, *How to Talk Car*, p. 33, 1965

close *adjective*
skilled *US*
- "Like he's close, man" (he is quite capable) and "touches home" (really makes sense).—*Look*, p. 49, 24th November 1959

close but no cigar; no cigar *adverb*
incorrect *US*
From carnival games giving cigars as prizes.
- I show him the picture of Helen in the summer dress. "Still no cigar," he says.—Robert Campbell, *Junkyard Dog*, p. 163, 1986
- The red-tail youngster went after the mouse, but it scurred away – close, but no cigar.—Marie Winn, *Red-Tails in Love*, p. 229, 1999

close call *noun*
a near thing, a narrow escape *US, 1881*
- Sharing the terror of a close call and then the euphoria of survival is an experience that binds for a lifetime.—*The Observer*, 25th November 2001

closed *adjective*
subject to strict law enforcement; unfriendly to criminal enterprises *US*
- Here I was with four idle whores in a closed town where I had fallen [been arrested] three times.—Iceberg Slim (Robert Beck), *Pimp*, p. 279, 1969

closed door *noun*
a surf condition where waves are breaking simultaneously all along a beach, creating no shoulder to ride *US*
- —Grant W. Kuhns, *On Surfing*, p. 115, 1963

closed for maintenance *adjective*
in the bleed period of the menstrual cycle *US*
- —*The Museum of Menstruation and Women's Health*, November 2000

closed game *noun*
a private gambling game, especially poker, usually for high stakes *US*
- —Jay Robert Nash, *Dictionary of Crime*, p. 69, 1992

close out *verb*
(of waves) to become unsuitable for surfing, either because of their size or their breaking pattern *US*
- It's closing out completely. Let's call it.—*Point Break*, 1991

closer *noun*
in a sales team, the individual responsible for the final stages of negotiations *US*
- MASTER: Told them the job was free. Then you sent in your closer with some cover story about how you had suffered a nervous breakdown, and a sale was ultimately made for $2375.00.—*Tin Men*, 1987

closet *noun*
a person who is secretly homosexual *UK*
- I'm not saying he's a closet, but well, it makes you think, dunnit? —Garry Bushell, *The Face*, p. 141, 2001

▸ **in the closet**
hidden, not avowed *US, 1967*
Almost always applied to homosexuality.
- Do you know what it means to be "in the closet?"—Mart Crowley, *The Boys in the Band*, p. 169, 1968

- While gays who are prominent in businesses or professions in Manhattan many live in the closet in the city, they tend to be most relaxed and casual and open while in residence in The Hamptons[.] —John Francis Hunter, *The Gay Insider*, p. 253, 1971
- It sure puts you guys in the closet for a while. —George V. Higgins, *The Friends of Eddie Doyle*, p. 46, 1971
- Okay. So he's in the closet. —Edwin Torres, *Q & A*, p. 111, 1977

▸ on the closet

(of a prisoner and prison officer) to be handcuffed together but separated by a long chain that is intended to reduce embarrassment when using the water *closet* UK

- You'll be on the Closet, Smith [...] It's the rules, I'm afraid. — *The Guardian*, 22nd June 2000

▸ out of the closet

avowed, open *US, 1971*

- So come on outa the closet, James[.] —Lester Bangs, *Psychotic Reactions and Carburetor Dung*, p. 115, 1973
- Yeah, well the only woman of the Indian's we ran into was shacked up with her dyke girlfriend. I guess she went with him before she came outta the closet. — *48 Hours*, 1982
- Espeically with priests coming out of the closet and saying they're queer[.] —Robert Campbell, *The Cat's Meow*, p. 51, 1988

closet *adjective*

hidden, not admitted *US, 1952*

Most often but not always, and not first, used in conjunction with homosexuality.

- —Dale Gordon, *The Dominion Sex Dictionary*, p. 45, 1967
- "Well," she said, 'a closet intellectual." —Walter Tevis, *The Color of Money*, p. 52, 1984
- He was a middle-aged closet pervert from over in the Valley. He thought we didn't know. —Robert Campbell, *Alice in La-La Land*, p. 77, 1987
- Debbie thought I was just a frustrated closet bull dyke, and hung around all night, spitefully, I felt. —Jennifer Blowdryer, *White Trash Debutante*, p. 78, 1997
- —Christopher Cavanaugh, *AA to Z*, p. 69, 1998

close-talker *noun*

a person who speaks to others without respecting the usual cultural protocols on not standing too close to someone you are talking to *US*

A term popularised on Jerry Seinfeld's television programme in an episode 'The Raincoat Party' first aired on 28th April 1994.

closet case *noun*

1 a person who is secretly homosexual *US, 1969*

- "[S]omeone from Dallas – I think he's a closet case – wrote a horrible letter, from a Christian point of view. —Dan Woog, *Jocks*, p. 211, 1998

2 someone to be ashamed of *US*

Teen slang, without any suggestion of the homosexuality later associated with the term.

- — *Look*, p. 88, 10th August 1954

3 a potential romantic interest whom you are keeping away from your friends *US*

- [F]raternity and sorority has its share of closet cases. —Max Shulman, *Guided Tour of Campus Humor*, p. 75, 1955
- — *McCall's*, April 1967

closet dyke *noun*

a lesbian who conceals her sexual orientation *US*

- —Dale Gordon, *The Dominion Sex Dictionary*, p. 45, 1967

closeted *adjective*

living with an unrevealed fact, especially homosexuality *US*

- It's not like he can't change. I was closeted once myself. —Armistead Maupin, *Maybe the Moon*, p. 220, 1992

close to the door *adjective*

about to be released from prison *US*

- —James Harris, *A Convict's Dictionary*, p. 30, 1989

close to the skin *adjective*

lacking subcutaneous fat *US*

- — *American Speech*, p. 199, Fall 1984

closet queen *noun*

a male homosexual who conceals his sexual orientation *US*

- All the fairies in her town were closet queens or pinkteas[.] —Hubert Selby Jr, *Last Exit to Brooklyn*, p. 60, 1957
- —Donald Webster Cory and John P. LeRoy, *The Homosexual and His Society*, p. 262, 1963: 'A lexicon of homosexual slang'
- They call them "closet queens." The implicationis queen. It derives from the English word for lavatory, water closet. —Antony James, *America's Homosexual Underground*, p. 66, 1965
- Closet queens are abundant too. —Angelo d'Arcangelo, *The Homosexual Handbook*, p. 161, 1968
- Have you heard the term "closet queen"? —Mart Crowley, *The Boys in the Band*, p. 169, 1968
- These are the "closet queens," the "aunties" and the furtive, secretive types. — *Screw*, p. 14, 25th April 1969
- It's rather obvious that you are, to use vulgar slang, a closet queen. —John Waters, *Pink Flamingos*, p. 49, 1992

close work *noun*

sexual activity *US*

- That boy up on the stage singing to them from his heart is clearly country, even as they are, and they find it not at all unthinkable that he might be available for some close work after the show. —Max Shulman, *Rally Round the Flag, Boys!*, p. 164, 1957

clot *noun*

a dolt *UK, 1632*

- [A]ll these thick clots could do was shuffle about and talk to each other. —Johnny Speight, *It Stands to Reason*, p. 92–93, 1973
- —Louis S. Leland, *A Personal Kiwi-Yankee Dictionary*, p. 26, 1984

cloth *noun*

▸ down to the cloth

(used of a player in a game of poker) almost out of money *US*

- —David M. Hayano, *Poker Faces*, p. 186, 1982

cloth-eared *adjective*

deaf *UK, 1965*

- [I]f he had been singing through that microphone none of those cloth-eared creeps would have known the difference anyway. —Johnny Speight, *It Stands to Reason*, p. 93–93, 1973

cloth-ears *noun*

a person with a poor sense of hearing; a person affecting deafness; a condition of convenient deafness *UK, 1912*

From the ear-flaps on certain headgear.

- If the Halle audience didn't take to his Rose of Sharon it would have stood condemned for its cloth ears. — *The Guardian*, 2000

clothes *noun*

1 in horse racing, a horse blanket *US*

- —David W. Maurer, *Argot of the Racetrack*, p. 21, 1951

2 a plainclothes police officer or division *US, 1971*

- —J.E. Lighter, *The Historical Dictionary of American Slang*, p. 438, 1994

clotheshorse *noun*

a person who pays a great deal of attention to fashions and the clothing they wear *US, 1850*

- Everybody in a Technicolor movie seems to feel obliged to wear a lurid costume in each new scene and to stand around like a clotheshorse with a lot of very green trees[.] —Sylvia Plath, *The Bell Jar*, p. 42, 1971
- "Don't see no reason to be a clotheshorse." Hawk was wearing white Puma track shoes with a black slash on them. White linen slacks, and a matching white linen vest with no shirt. —Robert Parker, *Promised Land*, p. 82, 1976

clothesline *noun*

the line used to lead a glider plane into the air *US*

- However, there was nothing he could do about it except hope that the hook trailing behind the C-47 missed the "clothesline" tow rope. —Ian Padden, *U.S. Air Commando*, p. 61, 1985

clothes-peg *noun*

1 the leg *UK, 1931*

Rhyming slang, usually in plural.

- —Ray Puxley, *Cockney Rabbit*, p. 37, 1992

2 an egg *UK, 1961*

Rhyming slang.

clothes queen *noun*

a homosexual man who is drawn to ostentatious, flamboyant clothing *US*

- —Donald Webster Cory and John P. LeRoy, *The Homosexual and His Society*, p. 263, 1963: 'A lexicon of homosexual slang'

clotted cream *noun*

a student at the Royal Agricultural College in Cirencester *UK*

A jocular representation of a thick and rich elite.

- — *Popbitch*, 28th October 2004

clotty *adjective*

slovenly, untidy *IRELAND*

- "Ten years ago garden centres in Ireland were clotty affairs but the competition has changed all that," he said[.] — *Irish Farmers Journal*, 5th February 2000

cloud *noun*

1 crack cocaine *US*

From the thick white smoke produced when smoked.

- — US Department of Justice, *Street Terms*, October 1994

2 the intoxication from smoking freebase or crack cocaine *US*

- — Terry Williams, *Crackhouse*, p. 147, 1992

cloudhopper *noun*

an air pilot, especially in the bush *CANADA*

- Remember, it is better to have a red face with a few scars of humiliation, and live to be an old pilot than to die a bold smooth-faced young cloudhopper. — W.A. Leising, *Arctic Wings*, p. 170, 1959

cloud nine *noun*

1 a condition of perfect happiness, euphoria *US, 1935*

Probably derives as a variation of **CLOUD SEVEN**; possibly from US weather forcasting terminology which divides clouds into nine types, the highest being number nine; or, less likely, a spiritual possibility: of the ten names for Buddha, the ninth is 'enlightened one'. It is probable that the US radio adventure series *Johnny Dollar*, 1949–62, popularised the term's usage.

- Depressed and down-hearted, I took to Cloud 9. / I'm doing...(fine) / Up here. (On cloud nine) / Listen one more time. / I'm doing...(fine) / Up here. (On cloud nine) — The Tempations, *Cloud Nine*, 1969
- Frank is, of course, delirious way past Cloud Nine. — Stephen King, *On Writing*, p. 245, 2000
- [Golfer, Paul] McGinley still floating on cloud nine. — *The Guardian*, 3rd October 2002

2 MDMA, the recreational drug best known as ecstasy *UK*

From the blissed-out state.

- — Mike Haskins, *Drugs*, p. 289, 2003

3 crack cocaine *US*

- — US Department of Justice, *Street Terms*, October 1994
- — Mike Haskins, *Drugs*, p. 281, 2003

cloud seven *noun*

a condition of perfect happiness, euphoria *US, 1956*

Derives, possibly, from 'seventh heaven'. Still current but **CLOUD NINE** attracts more attention.

clout *noun*

1 a heavy blow *UK*

Conventional from about 1400, hardly literary by 1770, and has since slipped into dialect and colloquial use.

- Oh, he may well lose his rag early on and give somebody – lots of people – a clout. It is a sort of pressure valve. — *The Observer*, 30th March 2003

2 power, influence, especially political *US, 1868*

- I don't like admitting my stomach has more clout than my mind[.] — Rhiannon Paine, *Too Late for the Festival*, p. 18, 1999

clout *verb*

1 to hit a person with a heavy blow of your hand *UK*

Conventional from early C14, by late C19 had slipped into dialect and colloquial use.

- She saw Martin hit Robin, and Robin clout him back. — *The Observer*, 2nd July 2000

2 to rob or steal something *UK, 1708*

- In the reformatory. They tried to clout a color TV among other things, and got busted for it. They'd been playing that caper for quite a while. — Hugh Garner, *The Intruders*, p. 83, 1976
- The Prizzis had been clouted for a gang of money! — Richard Condon, *Prizzi's Honor*, p. 59, 1982
- A black-white stick-up gang had been clouting markets and juke joints on West Adams[.] — James Ellroy, *Hollywood Nocturnes*, p. 127, 1994

3 to fail to bet a debt *AUSTRALIA*

- — Ned Wallish, *The Truth Dictionary of Racing Slang*, p. 15, 1989

4 to arrest someone *US*

- — Jay Robert Nash, *Dictionary of Crime*, p. 70, 1992

clouter *noun*

a thief who steals from parked cars *US*

- — Kenn "Naz" Young, *Naz's Dictionary of Teen Slang*, p. 23, 1993
- A recent Associated Press story described a car clouter who dressed like a hiker and used his walking stick to break windows at a trailhead in a national park, snatching $9,400 worth of valuables the day he got caught with the goods. — *Statesman Journal (Salem, Oregon)*, p. 1D, 18th July 2003

clouting *noun*

the palming of cards *AUSTRALIA*

- — Sidney J. Baker, *Australia Speaks*, 1953

clover *noun*

money *US*

- — David W. Maurer, *Argot of the Racetrack*, p. 21, 1951

clown *noun*

1 a fool, an incompetent person *US, 1898*

- Lieutenant Colonel Henry Braymore Blake. One of them regular army clowns. — *M*A*S*H*, 1970
- My voice shook, talking with this clown was doing me a lot of good. — Jim Thompson, *Savage Night*, 1985
- Least of all the pushy broad, the smart Jew, and the Harvard clown. — *A Few Good Men*, 1992

2 in carnival usage, a local police officer *US, 1929*

- — J.E. Lighter, *The Historical Dictionary of American Slang*, p. 439, 1994

3 a railway pointsman or yard brakeman *US*

- — Norman Carlisle, *The Modern Wonder Book of Trains and Railroading*, p. 261, 1946
- — Ramon Adams, *The Language of the Railroader*, p. 34, 1977

clown alley *noun*

on a circus lot, the area of tents where performers, especially clowns, dress and live *US, 1956*

- "The old-fashioned clown alley ended after the 1997 season," said Renee Storey, the circus's vice president for administration. — *New York Times*, p. G11, 12th August 1999
- In clown alley, Felix Adler was preparing for the walkaround. — Stewart O'Nan, *The Circus Fire*, p. 70, 2000

clown bookie *noun*

a bookmaker who operates in carnivals *AUSTRALIA*

- — Ned Wallish, *The Truth Dictionary of Racing Slang*, p. 16, 1989

clown wagon *noun*

a brakevan (caboose) *US, 1931*

- — Norman Carlisle, *The Modern Wonder Book of Trains and Railroading*, p. 261, 1946
- — Mike Schafer, *Caboose*, p. 24, 1997

club *noun*

1 in pool, a heavier-than-usual cue stick *US*

- — Steve Rushin, *Pool Cool*, p. 10, 1990

2 in trucking, a dilapidated trailer *US*

- — Montie Tak, *Truck Talk*, p. 32, 1971

▸ **in the club**

pregnant *UK, 1890*

A shortening of **IN THE PUDDING CLUB**.

- — Sonya Plowman, *Great Kiwi Slang*, p. 99, 2002

▸ **put in the club**

to make someone pregnant *UK, 1943*

club *verb*

to spend an evening in a nightclub or several nightclubs *US*

- The few who stayed, and the tourists, kept to the Gay White Way as they used to name it, clubbing, bar hopping or taking in a show. — Mickey Spillane, *Return of the Hood*, p. 80, 1964
- The status-conscious dress codes of '80s clubbing dissolved in all-night raves[.] — Steven Daly and Nalthaniel Wice, *alt.culture*, p. 2, 1995
- At nights we'd go clubbing and spend time in the bathroom snorting and giggling. — Cleo Odzer, *Goa Freaks*, p. 69, 1995
- The terms "clubbing" and "clubber" are used [...] in preference to night-clubbing" and "night-clubber" – terms which clubbers rarely use. — Ben Malbon, *Cool Places*, p. 282, 1998

clubber *noun*

a patron of nightclubs *US*

- Clubbers have long known that a great DJ can toy with them like a great lover. — Frank Broughton, *How to DJ Right*, p. 14, 2003

clubbers' cold *noun*

a runny nose, as a side-effect of drug use *UK*

- [I]f you are genuinely unwell you don't dare blow your nose in a club without risking attracting hordes of bimbos, people after a toot or bouncers eager to search you. — Alon Shulman, *The Style Bible*, p. 56, 1999

clubbie *noun*

a beach lifeguard *AUSTRALIA*

An abbreviation of 'life-saving *club*'.

- —Gary Fairmont R. Filosa II, *The Surfer's Almanac*, p. 183, 1977
- Like stopping Clubbies from dropping in on me and dingin' me board. —Kathy Lette, *Girls' Night Out*, p. 142, 1987
- It had been a great day at the beach. The bronzed clubbies and their girls were enjoying drinks, blackened steaks and sausages with their mates. —Clive Galea, *Slipper*, p. 91, 1988
- —Harry Orsman, *A Dictionary of Modern New Zealand Slang*, p. 30, 1999

club-crawl *verb*

to move as a group of friends from one nightclub to another *US*

- But instead of club crawling, she's been spending her nights working as a second assistant director[.]—*Vogue*, p. 86, June 1994

Club Fed *noun*

a minimum-security, well-equipped federal prison housing white-collar criminals, especially the federal prison camp in Lompoc, California *US*

A punning reference to Club Med, a group of holiday resorts.

- Big Springs has no walls and is called Club Fed by critics because of its elaborate recreational facilities and college dormitory atmosphere. —*Washington Post*, p. A1, 8th September 1985
- That was Lompoc FPC, federal prison camp, the one they used to call Club Fed. No fence, no guys with shanks or razor blades stuck in toothbursh handles. The worst that could happen to you, some guy hits you over the head with a tennis racquet. —Elmore Leonard, *Out of Sight*, p. 45, 1996
- Hopefully, you'll never experience the pleasures of a "Club Fed vacation." —Suroosh Alvi et al., *The Vice Guide*, p. 223, 2002

club-fight *verb*

to engage in youth gang warfare *US*

- I ain't club-fighting no more. I ain't sham-battling or nothing else. I'm out. —Hal Ellson, *Duke*, p. 144, 1949

club-hop *verb*

to move from one nightclub to another, especially with a group of friends *US*

- Sophomore year. I'm going down on Cynthia Slater in her dorm room after we went club-hopping. —*Chasing Amy*, 1997

clubhouse lawyer *noun*

an athlete who is quick to criticise his team's management when presented with an audience of fellow players *US, 1937*

- —Zander Hollander and Paul Zimmerman, *Football Lingo*, p. 22, 1967
- —Richard Scholl, *Running Press Glossary of Baseball Language*, p. 24, 1977
- Sheffield is not the same man who earned a reputation as a malcontent early in his career, who's known as a clubhouse lawyer who stirs up trouble among his teammates[.]—*Daily News (New York)*, p. 66, 21st December 2003

club kid *noun*

a fashionable, attractive young person paid to attend a nightclub in the hope of attracting others *US*

- The epithet "club kids" gained currency in 1988, when a New York magazine cover story featured a posse of young nightcrawlers who managed to parlay their exhibitionist antics and fondness for glitzy, flamboyant get ups into budding careers. —Steven Daly and Nalthaniel Wice, *alt.culture*, p. 42, 1995

clubland *noun*

an area of London bounded by and mainly comprising St James's Street and Pall Mall; subsequently, with the coming of nightclubs and club culture, any area where a number of clubs are to be found *UK, 1885*

club sandwich *noun*

sex involving three people at once *US*

Surviving in the shortened form of a simple 'sandwich'.

- —*Current Slang*, p. 5, Winter 1970

club widow *noun*

a woman whose husband's pursuits at a country club or other club often leave her at home alone *US, 1928*

- —Jospeh A. Weingarten, *An American Dictionary of Slang*, p. 72, 1954

clubzine *noun*

a single-interest fan magazine published by a fan club *US*

- —*American Speech*, p. 24, Spring 1982: 'The languge of science fiction fan magazines'

cluck *noun*

1 a gullible fool *US, 1906*

- Don't be a cluck! Sure, New York is the home of Tiffany and Cartier, Bonwit and Saks, Milgrim and Bergdorf-Goodman. But Gotham gals don't flop for samps, simps, or retail buyers. —Jack Lait and Lee Mortimer, *New York Confidential*, p. 126, 1948
- Some other time, baby. I got to go find that cluck. —Philip Wylie, *Opus 21*, p. 288, 1949
- I find myself eating at some greasy spoon next to a liquor store and talking to the most embittered cluck this side of the Continental Divide. —Clancy Sigal, *Going Away*, p. 134, 1961
- Don't a one of you clucks know what I'm talking about enough to give us a hand? —Ken Kesey, *One Flew Over the Cuckoo's Nest*, p. 136, 1962
- Guy that's worth, easy, forty fifty million, he cheats on a hundred-dollar round of golf and all the clucks, the guys that play with him, know it. —Elmore Leonard, *Cat Chaser*, p. 27, 1982

2 a crack cocaine user *US*

- — US Department of Justice, *Street Terms*, October 1994
- —Mark S. Fleisher, *Beggars & Thieves*, p. 288, 1995

3 counterfeit money *US*

- —Vincent J. Monteleone, *Criminal Slang*, p. 53, 1949

cluck *verb*

to withraw from any drug *UK*

Perhaps this derives from a confused attempt at the sound of a **COLD TURKEY** (the withdrawal period and its symptoms).

- I came off with spliff [marijuana], mainly because that helped with the comedowns when I was fully "clucking". —Macfarlane, Macfarlane and Robson, *The User*, p. 106, 1996
- [T]hey got four days clucking, get the sweats and no sleep and then hallucinations, problem. —Jeremy Cameron, *Brown Bread in Wengen*, p. 112–113, 1999
- Anyone who get webbed up in the brown [heroin] get seriously dropped out cos it's a known fact that they'll bubble you up when they're clucking. —J.J. Connolly, *Layer Cake*, p. 15, 2000

cluck and grunt *noun*

ham and eggs *US*

- —Helen Dahlskog (Editor), *A Dictionary of Contemporary and Colloquial Usage*, p. 13, 1972

clucker *noun*

1 in the urban drug culture, someone who brings buyers to sellers *US*

- — *Detroit News*, p. 5D, 20th September 2002

2 a fool *US*

- —Lou Shelly, *Hepcats Jive Talk Dictionary*, p. 8, 1945

3 the two halves of a scallop shell still closed after the scallop has died of natural causes *CANADA*

- Numbers of empty shells, called "cluckers" by the fishermen, are brought up in the drags among the living scallops. —*Fisheries Research Board Journal*, p. 811, 1955

cluckhead *noun*

a crack cocaine addict *US*

- —Bill Valentine, *Gang Intelligence Manual*, p. 75, 1995

cluckiness *noun*

the state of wanting to be pregnant *AUSTRALIA*

- I bought some books on the subject and proceeded to talk myself out of my unprecedented cluckiness[.]—Bettina Arndt, *The Australian Way of Sex*, p. 73, 1985
- —Ignatius Jones, *True Hip*, p. 83, 1990

clucking *adjective*

showing an addict's hunger for drugs, especially crack cocaine *UK*

- I was clucking for crack. —Angela Devlin, *Prison Patter*, p. 38, 1996
- There is nothing more devious and dangerous than a "clucking" junkie on the make. —*Inside Times*, p. 13, May-July 2003

clucky *adjective*

1 (of a hen) to be sitting on an egg or eggs *CANADA, 1988*

This term was in use in the US in the 1940s, but persists in Canadian country areas.

- When a hen is on her nest, Island women say "she's gone clucky," and the McAndrew birds are forever going clucky. —Harry Bruce, *Down Home*, p. 238, 1988

2 (of a woman) showing signs of pregnancy or of an intense desire for children *AUSTRALIA, 1941*

Extended from the conventional use referring to a broody hen. Originally and especially used of women, but now also of men.

- —Jim Ramsay, *Cop It Sweet!*, p. 23, 1977
- I've never been one of these real clucky sort of females, you know, how some girls, you know, go absolutely ga-ga over a baby.—Lyn Richards, *Having Families*, p. 112, 1985
- Win's been quite clucky of late. You haven't duffed her, have you, Brian?—David McGill, *David McGill's Complete Kiwi Slang Dictionary*, p. 29, 1998

cludgie; cludge *noun*

a (public) lavatory *UK, 1985*

Scottish dialect, now in wider use.

- [I]n a few months he could be wishing he was the one staking out rural cludgies, because at least it was a pay check.—Christopher Brookmyre, *Boiling a Frog*, p. 298, 2000
- [O]n her hands and knees in piss in the London Road cludgies[.]—Niall Griffiths, *Kelly + Victor*, p. 49, 2002

clue *noun*

▸ **have no clue; have not a clue; haven't a clue**

to be ignorant *UK, 1948*

As in the title of a BBC Radio 4 programme, *I'm Sorry, I Haven't a Clue*, on air since 1981.

- [W]hat they are and how they are done I have no clue.—*The Guardian*, 30th October 2002

clue; clue in *verb*

to inform someone, to update someone *UK, 1948*

- —*Newsweek*, p. 28, 8th October 1951
- "I'll clue you," said Grady. "There's gotta be a rumble."—Max Shulman, *Rally Round the Flag, Boys!*, p. 231, 1957
- Well's she's out of your price range, man. My brother's been out with her. He clued me in.—*American Graffiti*, 1973

clued up *adjective*

well-informed *UK, 1970*

- [L]ocking the cars up in the local Kwik-Fit overnight so that the really clued-up mechanics cannot give their man (Michael Schumacher) the edge[.]—*The Guardian*, 10th April 2003

clueless *adjective*

unaware, especially of fashion, music and other social trends *UK, 1943*

- —*USA Today*, 29th September 1983
- Would you look at that girl? She is so adorably clueless.—*Clueless*, 1995

clue up *verb*

to brief someone, to inform someone *UK, 1984*

- —Angela Devlin, *Prison Patter*, p. 38, 1996

cluey *noun*

a well-informed person *AUSTRALIA*

- —Alex Buzo, *Norm and Ahmed*, 1968

cluey *adjective*

wise; in the know *AUSTRALIA, 1967*

- He's a real cluey bloke, no rick. We were very proud of him when he graduated from Sydney Uni.—Alexander Buzo, *Norm and Ahmed*, p. 15, 1969
- —Alexander Buzo, *Rooted*, p. 78, 1969
- —Jim Ramsay, *Cop It Sweet!*, p. 23, 1977
- —Ryan Aven-Bray, *Ridgey Didge Oz Jack Lang*, p. 21, 1983

clump *noun*

1 a person whose main talent is hitting other people *UK*

- [T]hick-necked clumps[.]—Dave Courtney, *Raving Lunacy*, p. 99, 2000

2 a heavy blow with the hand *UK, 1889*

- I saw him out in a mate's club and gave him a clump there as well, for good measure.—Dave Courtney, *Raving Lunacy*, p. 100, 2000

clump *verb*

to hit someone heavily, to thump someone *UK*

- I wanted to see everyone who had clumped and been clumped for Chelsea.—Martin King and Martin Knight, *The Naughty Nineties*, p. 211, 1999

clumping *adjective*

used as an occasional variant of 'thumping' (large) *UK*

- [A] clumping great thing – I wouldn't give it house-room!—*Beale*, 1984

clumsome; clumbsome *noun*

in electric line work, a worker who is not a journeyman lineman but who claims some climbing experience *US, 1942*

From the worker's claim that while not a journeyman, he has 'climb some'.

- —A.B. Chance Co., *Lineman's Slang Dictionary*, p. 4, 1980

clumsy as a cub-bear handling his prick *adjective*

very clumsy indeed *CANADA, 1984*

clunk *noun*

1 an ill-bred or ill-mannered person; a fool *US, 1929*

- —Sidney J. Baker, *Australia Speaks*, 1953

2 a man *AUSTRALIA*

- —Ruth Park, *The Harp in the South*, 1948

▸ **the clunk**

a CF-100 Canuck jet fighter aircraft *CANADA*

The aircraft first flew in 1950, and is also known as **ALUMINIUM CROW** and **LEAD SLED**.

clunk!; ker-lunk!

used for approximating the sound of a hard object hitting another *UK, 1823*

As in Jimmy Saville's catchphrase 'Clunk clip every trip', in public information films of the 1970s, in which 'clunk' represents a car door closing and 'click' a seatbelt slotting home.

- [Madonna was] desperate to be Evita, desperate to be loved, more failed love – "she wasn't very adventurous in bed" – more albums. Clunk, clunk, clunk.—*The Guardian*, 24th November 2001

clunker *noun*

1 an old, beat-up car *US, 1942*

The original military usage in the 1940s applied to any old vehicle or machine. By the 1960s, applied almost exclusively to a car.

- The parking lot at Devil's Slide was jammed with vehicles: flowered hippie vans, city clunkers, organic pickups with shingled gypsy houses, and a dusty pack of Harley-Davidsons.—Armistead Maupin, *Tales of the City*, p. 99, 1978
- Banged up, pounded out, dented-in old clunkers with "21" or "99" or "45" painted haphazardly on their doors and tops.—*San Francisco Examiner and Chronicle*, p. 6, 1st July 1979
- He had made friends with the few attractive women who had wandered in, deciding he was more interesting than the rusting clunkers he was selling.—Stephen Cannell, *Big Con*, p. 28, 1997

2 an inferior item *US*

- [O]ne of the all-time clunkers of history[.]—Lester Bangs, *Psychotic Reactions and Carburetor Dung*, p. 14, 1971

clunkhead *noun*

a dolt *US, 1952*

- The minute I ever decided to become a clunkhead enough to take a shot, the real big boys would goose me out of business[.]—Morton Cooper, *High School Confidential*, p. 115–116, 1958
- The people in the Department of State are equally convinced that if they don't watch those clunkheads in the field who are so immersed in the problem, they will disregard policy and get everyone in trouble.—*Washington Post*, p. 5 (Book World), 13th February 1983
- There is a clique of right-wing cranks, yahoos and assorted clunkheads who make a career and a living off direct-mail propaganda in complaining about public broadcasting.—*Boston Globe*, p. 17, 20th January 1995
- Some wonder aloud why UTEP doesn't look for coaches like Don Haskins, who win and still stick around all 38 years of their career. Clunkheads, all.—*El Paso Times*, p. 1C, 26th December 2003

clunky *adjective*

awkward, clumsy, inelegant *US, 1968*

- Older people look funny when they're on the [mobile] phone, a bit clunky. You're supposed to be cool, relaxed and confident.—*The Times Magazine*, 21st June 2003

clusterfuck *noun*

1 group sex, heterosexual or homosexual *US, 1966*

- Oh, those big cluster fucks! I can't stand them. I think it's revolting, you know, more or less getting punked by anybody who happens to be standing near you, man, woman, child, or dog.—Nicholas Von Hoffman, *We Are The People Our Parents Warned Us Against*, p. 182, 1967
- You may see many of the people at your "do" only at other "cluster fucks," having nothing in common with them but a taste for orgies.—Angelo d'Arcangelo, *The Homosexual Handbook*, p. 115, 1968
- If Chris likes an occasional clusterfuck, and feels he has to do this "mascline" sex thing for himself (with the girls), remember he is doing it partly for you too.—*Screw*, p. 8, 18th August 1969
- —Bruce Rodgers, *The Queens' Vernacular*, p. 148, 1972
- —H. Max, *Gay (S)language*, p. 8, 1988
- The last scene shot was the Clusterfuck, beginning around 11 p.m. —*Cult Movies No. 17*, p. 47, 1996

2 a disorganised, chaotic situation *US, 1969*

- Now what's happenin? We gonna get this clusterfuck in the air?—John M. Del Vecchio, *The 13th Valley*, p. 137, 1982
- This fire's been the shits," he said, pushing back his hard hat. "Welcome to the first clusterfuck of the year.—Murry A. Taylor, *Jumping Fire*, p. 80, 2000

clusterscrew *noun*

chaos; momumental lack of organisation *US*

- You saw what a clusterscrew that outfit was. It only took ten gooks to fuck that Company up bad. —Charles Anderson, *The Grunts*, p. 65, 1976

clutch *noun*

1 a despised person *US, 1961*

- —Harold Wentworth and Stuart Berg Flexner, *Dictionary of American Slang*, p. 686, 1976

2 in poker, a hand that is certain to win *US*

- —Albert H. Morehead, *The Complete Guide to Winning Poker*, p. 259, 1967

clutch *verb*

▸ **clutch the gummy**

to be caught and blamed for something *US*

An elaboration of **HOLD THE BAG**.

- —Harold Wentworth and Stuart Berg Flexner, *Dictionary of American Slang*, p. 112, 1960

clutch *adjective*

1 serving as a replacement *US*

Korean war usage.

- We have been standing "clutch duty" lately, which means that we are on call as reinforcements or replacements for the front-line troops. —Martin Russ, *The Last Parallel*, 1957
- The replacement platoon, or "clutch platoon" as it is called, arrived, the morning watches were occupied, and we departed. —Martin Russ, *The Last Parallel*, p. 122, 1957

2 unkind *US*

- "I bet the witch child ran away!" he said. Cherokke began to cry. "I"ve been so clutch to her." —Francesca Lia Block, *Witch Baby*, p. 136, 1991

clutched *adjective*

scared, anxious *US, 1952*

- —J.E. Lighter, *The Historical Dictionary of American Slang*, p. 441, 1994

clutz *noun*

▹ see: **KLUTZ**

Clyde *noun*

1 a misfit; an outcast *US, 1950*

- "Clyde" – a loser, a shmendrick. Also, "a cantaloupe." — *Washington Post*, p. B1, 17th January 1985
- You hear that, Clyde? That's got to be the most spooky-ass question I've ever heard. — *Heathers*, 1988
- Just men, maybe ten guys in clothes you haven't seen in twenty years, like it's the Misfits Convention, all these fuckin' Clydes in one place. Except these Clydes are gangsters and they're all looking at us now like, what's going on? —Elmore Leonard, *Be Cool*, p. 240, 1999

2 during the Vietnam war, a Viet Cong or North Vietnamese regular *US*

- —Linda Reinberg, *In the Field*, p. 45, 1991

3 used to refer to any object the name of which you cannot remember or do not know *US*

- —Lewis Poteet, *Car & Motorcyle Slang*, p. 53, 1992

▸ **as deep and dirty as the Clyde**

used of someone who is devious, dishonest, secretive or untrustworthy *UK: SCOTLAND*

Glasgow use, formed on the River Clyde.

- —Michael Munro, *The Original Patter*, 1985

C-man *noun*

a sexually successful male student *US*

An abbreviation of 'cunt-man' or **COCKSMAN**.

- —Collin Baker et al., *College Undergraduate Slang Study Conducted at Brown University*, p. 93, 1968

c'mon

1 used to require a reasonable or common-sense response *UK*

Also used in the long form 'come on'.

- C'mon, I was raised with this music. — *Hip-Hop Connection*, p. 38, July 2002

2 used imperatively in a citizens' band radio transmission to request a reply *US*

Slovening of 'come on'.

- PIGPEN: By golly, it's clean clear to Flagtown. C'mon. RUBBER DUCK: Yeah, that's a big ten-four there, Pigpen. —C.W. McCall, *Convoy*, 1976

C-note *noun*

1 a one hundred dollar note *US, 1930*

- Van shrugged. "I expect I'm out one C-note." —Ross Russell, *The Sound*, p. 65, 1961
- You could find a dozen punks in Harlem who'd kill him for a C-note. —Chester Himes, *Cotton Comes to Harlem*, p. 15, 1965
- She seemed to wake up, staring at that C-note. —Elmore Leonard, *Glitz*, p. 30, 1985
- [P]ast the jag-off guard who gets an extra c-note a week just to watch the door[.] — *Casino*, 1995

2 a prison sentence of 100 years *US*

- —Charles Shafer, *Folk Speech in Texas Prisons*, p. 201, 1990

C-note charlie *noun*

in a casino, a gambler who insists on betting with hundred-dollar notes, not betting chips *US, 1949*

- —Thomas L. Clark, *The Dictionary of Gambling and Gaming*, p. 45, 1987

CNS-QNS

(in doctors' shorthand) unintelligent *UK*

An initialism of 'central nervous system – quantity not sufficient'; recorded in an article about medical slang in British (3 London and 1 Cambridge) hospitals.

- — *Ethics and Behaviour*, August 2003

coachman's knob *noun*

an erection of the penis caused by the vibrations whilst travelling on public transport *UK*

- —Chris Lewis, *The Dictionary of Playground Slang*, p. 61, 2003

coal *noun*

a marijuana cigarette *US*

- I like a blunt or a big fat coal/But my double-barrel bong is gettin me stoned. — Cypress Hill, *Hits from the Bong*, 1993

▸ **burn coal; deal in coal**

(of a white person) to have sex with a black person *US, 1922*

- The Harlem community accepts – though it despises – these Caucasians who cross the color line, or as it is known above 110th Street, "change their luck" or "deal in coal." —Jack Lait and Lee Mortimer, *New York Confidential*, p. 101, 1948
- Antoine, my contract says no nigers. I dont . . . burn . . . coal. —Seth Morgan, *Homeboy*, p. 155, 1990

coal and coke; coals and coke *adjective*

penniless *UK, 1937*

Rhyming slang for **BROKE**.

- —Jim Wolveridge, *He Dont Know "A" from a Bull's Foot*, 1978

coal candy *noun*

hard black licorice *US*

- —Amy and Denise McFadden, *CoalSpeak*, p. 4, 1997

coal cracker *noun*

a resident of the anthracite coal region of northeastern Pennsylvania *US*

- —Amy and Denise McFadden, *CoalSpeak*, p. 4, 1997

coalface *noun*

▸ **at the coalface**

used to signify the place where actual work is done (as opposed to management or administration) *UK*

A figurative use of the mining reality.

- Certainly none of us at the coalface [as a soldier on active duty] was ever told what the big plan was. —Andy McNab, *Immediate Action*, p. 51, 1995

coal hole *noun*

1 a coal mine, especially a closed mine *US*

- —Amy and Denise McFadden, *CoalSpeak*, p. 4, 1997

2 the anus *UK*

- Sugar paste [...] can also be used directly on your coal-hole, unlike paraffin-based waxes. — *The FHM Little Book of Bloke*, p. 9, June 2003

coalie *noun*

a wharf labourer who loads and unloads coal *AUSTRALIA, 1882*

- In any event fresh efforts would be made tomorrow morning to induce the rebellious coalies to at least accept work on interstate colliers. —John Morrison, *Stories of the Waterfront*, p. 145, 1955

coalman's sack *adjective*

very dirty *UK*

Rhyming slang for 'black'.

- —Ray Puxley, *Cockney Rabbit*, 1992

coalminer's breakfast *noun*

a shot of whisky served in a glass of beer *US*

- [A] "Coalminer's Breakfast," or "Depth Charge" (when a shot of whiskey is dropped into a glass of beer. —Roger E. Axtell, *The Do's and Taboos of Hosting International Visitors*, p. 76, 1990

coal oil *noun*
kerosene *US*
• —Joe McKennon, *Circus Lingo*, p. 26, 1980

Coaly *noun*
the devil *US, 1950*
• "Okay, the first thing I want to do is decide on a model juror." "Black," said Lucien. "Black as old Coaly's ass," said Harry Rex.—John Grisham, *A Time to Kill*, p. 329, 1989

Coast *noun*
▸ **the Coast**
1 the west coast of the US *US, 1930*
• He came from the Coast. He saw a way to get back East without arousing suspicion.—Mickey Spillane, *My Gun is Quick*, p. 150, 1950
• Sophia's husband was away on one of his trips to the coast when I told her and her sister.—Malcolm X and Alex Haley, *The Autobiography of Malcolm X*, p. 141, 1964
• You can tell they're not from the coast.—Nicholas Von Hoffman, *We Are The People Our Parents Warned Us Against*, p. 13, 1967
• We'll have to expose it over that Don Honoroff footage he sent us from the coast.—Fred Baker, *Events*, p. 32, 1970
2 the northwest coast of Tasmania *AUSTRALIA, 1987*
• —Maureen Brooks and Joan Ritchie, *Tassie Terms*, p. 32, 1995

coast *verb*
1 to idle; to relax *US*
• —Douglas Simonson, *Pidgin to da Max*, 1981
• —*San Jose Mercury News*, 11th May 1999
2 to relax and experience the effects of a drug *US*
• All I wanted to do was bang 'H' and 'coast.'—Iceberg Slim (Robert Beck), *Pimp*, p. 99, 1969
• —Eugene Landy, *The Underground Dictionary*, p. 52, 1971

coaster *noun*
someone who lives near the beach; a surfer *US*
• Like you know, this beasty coaster goes, 'You wanna bag some rays?' and like I totally go, 'Bag your face, surf punk.'—Mary Corey and Victoria Westermark, *Fer Shurr!*, 1982

Coastie; Coasty *noun*
a member of the US Coast Guard; a Coast Guard ship *US, 1970*
• And when the Strike Team Coasties have done their duty and cleaned up a mess that somebody else made, they get homage from a grateful news media[.]—Hans Halberstadt, *USCG*, p. 89, 1986
• Get the XO to set up a track to rendezvous with the Coastie.—P.T. Deutermann, *Scorpion in the Sea*, p. 122, 1992

coasting *adjective*
drug-intoxicated to a pleasant degree *US, 1936*
• —Richard A. Spears, *The Slang and Jargon of Drugs and Drink*, p. 111, 1986
• —Mike Haskins, *Drugs*, p. 291, 2003

coast-to-coast *noun*
a powerful amphetamine or other central nervous system stimulant *US*
Purportedly strong enough to keep a truck driver awake long enough to drive the 3000 miles from coast to coast.
• —*American Speech*, p. 203, Fall 1969: 'Truck driver's jargon'
• —Mike Haskins, *Drugs*, p. 279, 2003

coat *noun*
▸ **on the coat**
ostracised *AUSTRALIA, 1940*
Tugging on the lapel of the coat was used as a signal to be silent by criminals.
• —Jim Ramsay, *Cop It Sweet!*, p. 65, 1977

coat *verb*
1 to belittle someone, to defeat someone with words *UK*
From the sense 'to reprimand someone'.
• Woodsy [a comedian] spent five minutes just coating 'im [a heckler] until everyone in the place was crying with laughter.—Colin Butts, *Is Harry on the Boat?*, p. 93, 1997
2 to reprimand someone, especially of a warder reprimanding a prisoner *UK*
• —Angela Devlin, *Prison Patter*, p. 38, 1996
3 to ostracise someone *AUSTRALIA*
• —Jim McNeil, *The Chocolate Frog [and] The Old Familiar Juice*, 1973
4 in tournament pool, to obscure the view of the tournament judge when making a shot, thus jeopardising the point *US, 1972*
• —Mike Shamos, *The Illustrated Encyclopedia of Billiards*, p. 1972, 1993

coat and badge *noun*
▸ **on the coat and badge**
scrounging; on the cadge *UK, 1960*
Rhyming slang, from the verb **COAT AND BADGE** (to cadge).

coat and badge *verb*
to cadge something *UK, 1936*
Rhyming slang, formed on Doggett's Coat and Badge Race, the oldest annual sporting event in Britain, a boat race from London Bridge to Chelsea, first contested by Thames' watermen in 1715 and continuing still.
• —Ray Puxley, *Cockney Rabbit*, 1992

coathanger *noun*
1 in rugby, a straight-arm, neck-high tackle *NEW ZEALAND*
• —David McGill, *David McGill's Complete Kiwi Slang Dictionary*, p. 29, 1998
2 a horizontal branch that needs to be removed from trees destined for timber *NEW ZEALAND*
• Make sure not to leave any coathangers.—*Journal of Agriculture (NZ)*, p. 18, February/March 1988

coathanger *nickname*
the Sydney Harbour Bridge *AUSTRALIA, 1943*
• —Jim Ramsay, *Cop It Sweet!*, p. 23, 1977
• [R]esidents lined the Harbour on Saturday night with their champagne, families and picnic blankets, assuming that a great view of the old coathanger would afford simultaneously a great view of the pyrotechnics.—*Sydney Morning Herald*, p. 36, 6th October 1988

coat of varnish *noun*
a reprimand; a prison sentence *UK*
An elaboration of **COAT** (to reprimand).
• So, when Peter and Mick went up the steps [into court] at the next sessions they got a very light coat of varnish[.]—Charles Raven, *Underworld Nights*, p. 196, 1956

coat puller *noun*
someone who tips in return for a favour and in the hope of future favours *AUSTRALIA*
• —Ned Wallish, *The Truth Dictionary of Racing Slang*, p. 16, 1989

coaxer *noun*
in horse racing, a battery-powered device used illegally by a jockey to shock a horse during a race *US*
• Frank Wolverton of Santa Rosa, Cal., "a track follower," today was suspended by the Lone Oak Racing Track Board of Stewards for manufacturing electrical "coaxers" allegedly used to stimulate horses in two races.—*San Francisco News*, p. 21, 7th September 1951

cob *noun*
1 a mate, a friend *AUSTRALIA*
Shortening of **COBBER**.
• 'You watch it, cobs. You don't wanna clew up as cox'n of a pram.' 'She'll be apples.'—J.E. MacDonnell, *Don't Gimme the Ships*, p. 38, 1960
• You weren't actually married, of course. Not me, cob. She was keen enough, though.—Robin Muir, *Word for Word*, p. 254, 1960
• The cobs weren't expecting to get off here.—John Wynnum, *Tar Dust*, p. 118, 1962
• Too right I will, cob.—Lance Peters, *The Dirty Half-Mile*, p. 175, 1979
2 the penis, literally and in the figurative sense of a disagreeable man *US, 1954*
• The president, a fairly rough old cob, said just a little angrily, "Look, don't be so surprised."—Clancy Sigal, *Going Away*, p. 141, 1961
3 the testicle *UK: NORTHERN IRELAND*
• Now, no knee and nut stuff and no catching by the cobs.—Brendan Behan, *Borstal Boy*, 1958
4 prison food, originally and especially bread *UK*
From a 'cob loaf'.
• —Angela Devlin, *Prison Patter*, p. 38, 1996
5 brown skin *BARBADOS*
Collected by Richard Allsopp.

▸ **have a cob on; get a cob on**
to be annoyed, moody or angry; to become annoyed, moody or angry *UK, 1937*
First recorded as Merchant Navy slang, then Royal Navy before more general usage; possibly northern dialect in origin.
• I don't know why Dixie's got a cob on with us for.—Alan Bleasdale, *Boys From the Blackstuff*, 1982

- [N]o-one ever talked back to him or answered him back, which is obviously why he got such a cob on when I told him to fuck off. —Dave Courtney, *Stop the Ride I Want to Get Off*, p. 271, 1999
- What's the friggin matter with you? What's the cob on for? —Niall Griffiths, *Kelly + Victor*, p. 45, 2002

▸ **off the cob**
overly sentimental *US, 1935*
A play on words to achieve 'corny'.
- —Jack Lait and Lee Mortimer, *New York Confidential*, p. 236, 1948

cobalt bomb *noun*
a nuclear device to enable the use of cobalt in medicine *CANADA*
- At the Chalk River atomic pile, the cobalt had become highly charged – one cobalt bomb unit has more than half the power of all the radium units used in medical work throughout the world. —Robert Moon, *This is Saskatchewan*, p. 137, 1953

Cobar shower *noun*
1 a dust storm *AUSTRALIA, 1945*
Cobar is an inland town in New South Wales. Other locations similarly used by nature, weather and irony: Bourke, Bogan, Bedourie, Darling, Wilcannia and Wimmera.

2 a flower *AUSTRALIA, 1945*
Rhyming slang.

cobb *noun*
lung phlegm *US*
- —Chris Lewis, *The Dictionary of Playground Slang*, p. 61, 2003

cobber *noun*
a mate, friend, companion *AUSTRALIA, 1893*
Perhaps originally the agent noun of the Suffolk dialect *cob* (to take a liking to a person). The Yiddish *chaber* (comrade) seems a less likely source. Formerly extremely common but now more well known than actually used.
- In the opinion of many of the British, the great strength of the Australians in the jungle lay in their ability to adapt themselves to the most adverse circumstances, and in the strength of the "cobber" bond between individuals, especially between men of the same unit. —Rohan D. Rivett, *Behind Bamboo*, p. 240, 1946
- And for six years Jock and Jimmy have been cobbers all over Australia. —*Weekend*, p. 3, 1st June 1957
- Hey, Bazza! Is this Pom a cobber of yours? 'Cause if he's not I'll give him the bum's rush!!! —Barry Humphries, *The Wonderful World of Barry McKenzie*, p. 28, 1968
- I have become good cobbers with the whole staff from the gardener to the manager and they are a terrifically friendly bunch. —Sam Weller, *Old Bastards I Have Met*, p. 30, 1979
- When the first finished he gave the rubber to his mate and said, 'Turn it inside out and you'll be right cobber.' —Martin Cameron, *A Look at the Bright Side*, 1988
- Only last year, the Australian novelist Kate Grenville wrote in desperation that – to get noticed as an author outside her country – she virtually had to wear corks in her hat and call everybody cobber. —*The Guardian*, 6th June 2001
- Be a good mate even to blokes who are rotten to you, be a cobber even if they stab you in the back. —Kel Richards, *The Aussie Bible*, p. 32, 2003

cobber dobber *noun*
a person who informs on a friend, workmate or the like *AUSTRALIA, 1966*
As appealing as this rhyming couplet seems it never attained great popularity.
- If your Grandma's funeral once again falls on Melbourne Cup day, it's a cobber dobber who asks the boss if he's ever counted your deceased grandmothers. —Arthur Chipper, *The Aussie Swearer's Guide*, p. 33, 1972

cobber up *verb*
to become friends with someone *AUSTRALIA, 1918*
- He and our disreputable Tracker Dick had cobbered up on sight, and were an example of utter opposites. —Vic Hall, *Outback Policeman*, p. 147, 1970
- —Jim Ramsay, *Cop It Sweet!*, p. 23, 1977

cobbing *noun*
a beating *UK, 1769*
Listed as 'obsolete' and 'of nautical origin' by the *Oxford English Dictionary*, this term is still in use in the Canadian Maritime Provinces.

cobbler *noun*
a forger of official documents *US*
- —Ralph de Sola, *Crime Dictionary*, p. 29, 1982

cobblers *noun*
nonsense *UK, 1955*
From the earlier sense (testicles).
- [A]fter which homespun cobblers I shall have it away [leave] in the jam [car][.] —Derek Raymond (Robin Cook), *The Crust on its Uppers*, p. 99, 1962
- —Angela Devlin, *Prison Patter*, p. 38, 1996
- If you think what I've just told you is so much cobblers, just wait! —Duncan MacLaughlin, *The Filth*, p. 57, 2002

▸ **load of cobblers; load of old cobblers**
nonsense; lies *UK, 1968*
An elaboration, but not necessarily an intensification, of **COBBLERS** (nonsense).
- Does he like it, or does he think it's a load of cobblers? —Philip Pullman, *The Shadow in the North*, p. 97, 1988
- You're fifteen feet under, mate, and your mouth's full of shit. You're talking a load of old cobblers. What clinics? What infirmaries? —Eduardo de Filippo (translated by Peter Tinniswood), *Napoli Milionaria*, 1992

cobbler's awls; cobbler's stalls; cobblers *noun*
the testicles *UK, 1936*
Rhyming slang for **BALLS** (the testicles).
- I see Johnny as a mate. I also value my cobblers. —Garry Bushell, *The Face*, p. 181, 2001

cobblers to you!
used for expressing rejection of someone *UK, 1974*
Originally, a euphemistic application of testicles in a form in which **BALLS!** and **BOLLOCKS!** also serve. Now so inoffensive that it has been co-opted by shoe-repairers.

cobitis *noun*
a dislike of prison food *UK, 1950*
A combination of **COB** (prison food) and the suffix **-ITIS** (used to create imaginary medical conditions).
- —Angela Devlin, *Prison Patter*, p. 38, 1996

COBOL Charlie *noun*
in computing, a COBOL programmer who can use the language but does not fully understand how it works *US*
- —Karla Jennings, *The Devouring Fungus*, p. 218, 1990

coby *noun*
morphine *US*
- —Jay Robert Nash, *Dictionary of Crime*, p. 70, 1992

coca; coka *noun*
cocaine *US*
- —Richard A. Spears, *The Slang and Jargon of Drugs and Drink*, p. 111, 1986
- —Mike Haskins, *Drugs*, p. 280, 2003

cocaine-voucher *noun*
a currency note *UK*
A contemporary variation on **BEER VOUCHERS**.
- I completely forgot to go to the cocaine-voucher machine, silly of me[.] —James Hawes, *White Powder, Green Light*, p. 216, 2002

cochornis *noun*
marijuana *US, 1980*
- —Richard A. Spears, *The Slang and Jargon of Drugs and Drink*, p. 112, 1986
- —Mike Haskins, *Drugs*, p. 287, 2003

cock *noun*
1 the penis *UK, 1450*
Probably from 'cock' (a male bird).
- The success of Allen is due to the fact that no one since Henry Miller has had the guts to say cock and cunt in public. —Jack Kerouac, *Letter to Lucien Carr*, p. 563, 24th February 1956
- Jesus she was hot! I thought she'd tear the cock off me. —Henry Miller, *Tropic of Cancer*, p. 102, 1961
- What he's doing is staring at Johnny's cock[.] —John Rechy, *Numbers*, p. 41, 1967
- A hand on your cock is more moral – and more fun – than a finger on the trigger. —Richard Neville [quoting Lawrence Lipton], *Play Power*, p. 71, 1970
- —Richard Herring, *Talking Cock*, 2003

2 the vagina *US, 1867*
- The third whore said, "My old cock is bigger 'n the world." —*Get Your Ass in the Water and Swim Like Me*, p. 102, 1964
- —Roger D. Abrahams, *Deep Down in the Jungle*, p. 259, 1970
- Say, "Yes, your mama got a cock big as a whale is true / And your sister got a big cock, too!" —Roger Abrahams, *Positively Black*, p. 90, 1970
- Jerry, do you think it feels as nice to a bitch when she has her cock socked? —Christina and Richard Milner, *Black Players*, p. 218, 1972

- What I wanted was for a white whore to hit on me to spend some money with her, that way I'd have a chance to "georgia" her out of some cock. —Donald Goines, *Whoreson*, p. 203, 1972
- Cock mean pussy down here, boy. so don't you go takin' no offense, y'hear. —Emmett Grogan, *Ringolevio*, p. 159, 1972

3 used as a male-to-male term of address *UK, 1837*
Decidedly casual.

- "Is that Father Christmas?" There was a night-light burning beside the bed. ""Yes, cock – I mean Sonny," hissed Sapphire[.] —Charles Raven, *Underworld Nights*, p. 207, 1956
- 'Listen, cock,' I told him, 'this old cab's in such a state of disrepair it rattled and shook until the whistle fell off.' —Patsy Adam-Smith, *Folklore of the Australian Railwaymen*, p. 286, 1969
- —Maureen Brooks and Joan Ritchie, *Tassie Terms*, p. 33, 1995
- I am in Newcastle, but worked in Hobart for 3 years. Nearly fainted when someone first said, "G'day Cock!" —*www.abc.net.au/wordmap*, 2003

4 a man who buys more than his share of drinks in a public house or club so as to have company pleasing to him *UK*

- —David Powis, *The Signs of Crime*, 1977

5 rubbish, nonsense *UK, 1937*
From 'poppycock' (nonsense) or 'cock and bull story' (a fictitious narrative).

- —Paik Choo, *The Coxford Singlish Dictionary*, p. 31, 2002
- I don't believe there's a God who says, If you drink, do drugs and swear and rob houses you're not sitting on my cloud. It's all cock. It's all fanny. —*Q*, p. 100, May 2002

6 a man who fights without restraint *US*

- —R. Frederick West, *God's Gambler*, p. 223, 1964

▸ **get cock**
to have sex *US*

- —Bruce Jackson, *Outside the Law*, p. 57, 1972

▸ **give six inches of hot cock**
from a male perspective, to have sex *UK, 1974*
The measurement is flexible.

cock *verb*

1 to have sex *US*

- —Malachi Andrews and Paul T. Owens, *Black Language*, p. 111, 1973

2 to prepare an aircraft for take-off *US*

- When the crews were not preflighting the airplanes, "cocking" them for instant takeoff, they were flying the simulator[.] —Walter J. Boyne and Steven L. Thompson, *The Wild Blue*, p. 265, 1986

3 to trick someone; to outsmart someone *GUYANA, 1975*

- —Richard Allsopp, *Dictionary of Caribbean English Usage*, p. 159, 1996

▸ **cock a deaf 'un**
to pretend not to hear someone; or deliberately not listen to, or ignore someone *UK*
A variant, possibly a mishearing, of **COP A DEAF 'UN**.

- [W]hen the name of Signalman Speight was called over the tannoy I just cocked deaf-uns, and spent some of the most marvellous months of the war[.] —Johnny Speight, *It Stands to Reason*, p. 63, 1973

▸ **cock ten**
to sit with your legs crossed as others work *GUYANA*

- —Richard Allsopp, *Dictionary of Caribbean English Usage*, p. 159, 1996

cock!
used as an expression of displeasure *CANADA*

- Cock! I got a 4 a.m. wakeup call from Mike this morning. —Jack Chambers (Editor), *Slang Bag 93 (University of Toronto)*, p. 2, Winter 1993

cockadau *verb*
to kill someone *US, 1987*
On loan from Vietnamese.

- "Cockadau!" Harris suddenly yelled in Vietnamese. He sounded a little nuts. "Cockadau means kill," Sampson told me. —James Patterson, *Four Blind Mice*, p. 313, 2002

cock-a-doodle-don't *noun*
a condom *UK*
Contrived play on **COCK** (the penis) and the feathered variety's crow; possibly informed by **DOODLE** (the penis) and, less likely, 'doodle' (to make a fool of).

- —David Rowan, *A Glossary for the 90's*, 1998

cockaleekie *adjective*
impudent, cheeky *UK*
Rhyming slang, formed on a type of soup.

- Don't get cockaleekie or I'll smack your legs. —Ray Puxley, *Fresh Rabbit*, 1998

cockalize; kokalize *verb*
to thrash someone *US*

- I kokalized him in Scranton. —Marvin Wald and Albert Maltz, *The Naked City*, 1947

cock-almighty *noun*
the best *UK*
Obsolete euphemism of 'cock' for 'God', hence 'God almighty', with reference to more modern nuances of **COCK** (chief, man, etc.).

- "Turn down Top of the Pops?" "Sure. It's not the cock-almighty now, anyway. Anyone can get on." —Kevin Sampson, *Powder*, p. 66, 1999

cockamamie; cockamamy *adjective*
implausible, not credible *US, 1941*
Neither Yiddish nor Hebrew, but born of Jewish immigrants in the US.

- Did you ever hear such a cockamamy story? —Leo Rosten, *The Joys of Yiddish*, p. 94, 1968
- Through some cockamamie appeal you're back on the street. —Edwin Torres, *After Hours*, p. 387, 1979
- [W]hy would you approach a sarcastic, honest-to-a-fault asshole like me with such a cockamamie idea? —Howard Stern, *Miss America*, p. 71, 1995
- I couldn't for the life of me figure out where he had gotten that cokamamy idea[.] —Rita Ciresi, *Pink Slip*, p. 75, 1999

cock and bull story *noun*
a fanciful, exaggerated or outright untrue story *US, 1795*

- I debated about going back with some cock-and-bull story, anything to forestal her tipping him off to my deception. —Sue Grafton, *J is for Judgment*, p. 170, 1993
- Taylor shot me a look that asked, Are you going to back up this cock-and-bull story? I gave im a sheepish smile and nodded my head. —Douglas C. Waller, *The Commandos*, p. 184, 1994

cockapoo *noun*
a crossbreed of cocker spaniel and poodle *US*

- [C]ockapoos – or terra-poos, peke-a-poos, or labradoodles. Lots of mixes are out there, great pets one and all. But a breed? No. —Gina Spadafori and Marty Becker, *Dogs for Dummies*, p. 28, 2001

cockatoo *noun*

1 a person acting as lookout, especially for an illegal activity *AUSTRALIA, 1827*
Flocks of feeding cockatoos often have one or more birds posted up high as sentries to warn of approaching danger.

- [H]e drifted along Sussex Street and asked one of the cockatoos for a match to light his cigarette. —Vince Kelly, *The Bogeyman*, p. 9, 1956
- —Ned Wallish, *The Truth Dictionary of Racing Slang*, p. 16, 1989
- This time they had brought along two extra players to act as 'cockatoos'[.] —William Dodson, *The Sharp End*, p. 158, 2001

2 a small-scale farmer *AUSTRALIA, 1845*

- —A.B. Paterson, *Rio Grande and Other Verses*, p. 46, 1902
- The Delahuntys were not bad employers as Australian cockatoos went in the hungry thirties; but they were nearly as poor as the men they exploited. —Frank Hardy, *Legends From Benson's Valley*, p. 232, 1963
- —Bill Hornadge, *The Ugly Australian*, p. 39, 1975

cockatoo *verb*
to act as a lookout *AUSTRALIA, 1954*

cockatoo farmer *noun*
a small-scale farmer *AUSTRALIA, 1849*

- The store supplied every sheep station and cockatoo farmer within fifty or a hundred miles[.] —Harold Lewis, *Crow On A Barbed Wire Fence*, p. 30, 1973

cockatooing *noun*
the act or job of being a lookout *AUSTRALIA, 1945*

- Fatty, in a perverse sort of way, was rather grateful to Church for making the profession of cockatooing so important. —Lance Peters, *The Dirty Half-Mile*, p. 10, 1979

Cockbang *noun*
Bangkok, Thailand *US*
Offensive. A near-Spoonerism that aptly describes Bangkok's reputation and role as a sex destination during the Vietnam war.

- —Linda Reinberg, *In the Field*, p. 46, 1991

cock bite *noun*
an unpleasant person *US*
- —Eugene Landy, *The Underground Dictionary*, p. 53, 1971

cockblock *verb*
to interfere with someone's intentions to have sex *US, 1971*
- So you both jus' gonna set dere and cock block and neither one o' you gonna get nothin. —Geneva Smitherman, *Talkin that Talk*, p. 85, 1999
- I wanted to tell her how pissed I was that she had cock-blocked me, but I didn't feel like we knew each other well enough for me to have a right to be mad. —Amy Sohn, *Run Catch Kiss*, p. 82, 1999
- —Connie Eble (Editor), *UNC-CH Campus Slang*, p. 2, Spring 1999
- Every night when I try to think of someone else, Javon cockblocks me. —Carol Taylor (Editor), *Brown Sugar*, p. 26, 2001

cock book *noun*
a sexually explicit book *US*
- —Carl Fleischhauer, *A Glossary of Army Slang*, p. 10, 1968

cock cap *noun*
a condom *UK*
Combines **COCK** (the penis) with protective wear.
- —David Rowan, *A Glossary for the 90's*, 1998

cock cheese *noun*
smegma *UK, 1961*
- —Roger Blake, *The American Dictionary of Sexual Terms*, p. 38, 1964

cock chokers *noun*
a pair of men's close-fitting and revealing nylon swimming trunks *AUSTRALIA*
- —*Wordmap (www.abc.net.au/wordmap)*, 2003

cock Corpsman *noun*
a military doctor or medic who inspects male recruits for signs of sexually transmitted disease *US*
- —Roger Blake, *The American Dictionary of Sexual Terms*, p. 39, 1964
- —Dale Gordon, *The Dominion Sex Dictionary*, p. 119, 1967

cock custard *noun*
semen *UK*
- He's a jumped up squirt of cock custard. —Harry Enfield, *We Know Where You Live. Live*, 2001

cock-diesel *adjective*
muscular *US, 1988*
- Or "Stupid cock diesel" – slang for a boy who was muscular from lifting weights." —Tom Wolfe, *Hooking Up*, p. 1, 2000

cockeater *noun*
a person who enjoys performing oral sex on men *US*
- —Dale Gordon, *The Dominion Sex Dictionary*, p. 45, 1967

cocked *adjective*
drunk *US, 1737*
- —J.E. Lighter, *Historical Dictionary of American Slang, Volume 1*, p. 446, 1994

cocked hat *noun*
an informer; an untrustworthy person *UK*
Rhyming slang for **RAT**.
- —Ray Puxley, *Cockney Rabbit*, 1992

cocker *noun*
1 the penis *US*
- Those black cockers are the longest, the fattest, the hardest in the world. —John Folger, *Black on White*, p. 27, 1967

2 a man *US, 1946*
From the Yiddish *kakker*; used with a lack of kindness.
- Yeah, I know the old Cocker. Lives across the Avenue in those apartments. —George Pelecanos, *A Firing Offense*, p. 23, 1992

3 used as a male-to-male form of address *UK, 1888*
- It was good of you to help us cocker. —Arnold Wesker, *Talking About Jerusalem*, 1960

4 a cockroach *AUSTRALIA*
- —Ruth Park, *A Power of Roses*, 1953
- —Elleston Trevor, *Gale Force*, 1956

cockernee *noun*
a Cockney; a Londoner *UK*
A jocular attempt at Cockney pronunciation; a Cockney is anyone born within the sound of Bow Bells, although world-usage has moved the boundaries to include all of a vaguely defined London.
- "Parklife", a rollicking good tune with actor Phil Daniels handling the cockernee vocals[.] —John Robb, *The Nineties*, p. 130, 1999

cockers-p *noun*
a cocktail party *UK*
- —*New Society*, p. 384, 10th March 1983

cockerwitter *noun*
a person from the Woods Harbor and Shag Harbor areas of Shelburne County, Nova Scotia *CANADA*
The name is derived from Cockerwit Passage, the narrow strip of navigable water between Woods Harbour and Soloman, Vigneau, and St John Islands.
- —Robie Tufts, *Birds of Nova Scotia*, 1979

cock eye *noun*
a wink *TRINIDAD AND TOBAGO*
- —Lise Winer, *Dictionary of the English/Creole of Trinidad & Tobago*, 2003

cock-eye Bob; cock-eyed Bob; cocky Bob *noun*
a sudden squall or thunderstorm in northwest Australia *AUSTRALIA, 1894*
Occasionally shortened to 'cock-eye'.

cock-eyed *adjective*
1 squint-eyed *UK, 1821*

2 drunk *US, 1737*
First recorded by Benjamin Franklin.
- There, one night, cockeyed, he shot two inoffensive customers. —Jack Lait and Lee Mortimer, *New York Confidential*, p. 160, 1948
- Thursday night I took a bottle up to my room with me, and I got half cockeyed. —Jim Thompson, *Savage Night*, p. 124, 1953

3 absurd, ridiculous, topsy-turvy *UK, 1896*
- Film extras need three things: thick skin [...], endless patience, and cock-eyed optimism. —*Guardian Unlimited*, March 2002

cock-eyes *noun*
in craps, a three *US, 1968*
- —Thomas L. Clark, *The Dictionary of Gambling and Gaming*, p. 45, 1987

cockfest *noun*
a party with many more males than females in attendance *US*
- —Don R. McCreary (Editor), *Dawg Speak*, 2001

cock-happy *adjective*
over-confident *UK*
- We won, but remember, it might not be so easy another time, so don't get cock-happy about it. —*Spearhead in Malaya*, 1959

cock hound *noun*
a man obsessed with sex *US, 1947*
- For a minute or two, he was completely unable to think of what he could possibly say to her that would not make him sound like a cock hound[.] —Cecil Brown, *The Life & Loves of Mr. Jiveass Nigger*, p. 68, 1969
- Everyone in Hollywood knows my father as a real cockhound. Once when I came home from boarding school he had these two Puerto Rican women in his bedroom. —Gerald Petievich, *To Die in Beverly Hills*, p. 48, 1983

cockie *noun*
the penis *UK*
An elaboration of **COCK**.
- I don't mean cockies in general like, but they don't want the real thing. No way. —Niall Griffiths, *Sheepshagger*, p. 186, 2001

▷ **see: COCKY**

cockiness *noun*
a personal quality of smug over-confidence *UK, 1864*
- Strangely this wimpishness has been shot through with mega-self-confidence, verging on cockiness[.] —Frank Skinner, *Frank Skinner*, p. 27, 2001

cocking stocking *noun*
a condom *UK*
- —David Rowan, *A Glossary for the 90's*, 1998

cock it on; cock on *verb*
to exaggerate; to overcharge someone *UK*
The supplement to the 5th edition of Partridge's *Dictionary of Slang and Unconventional English* records this term as occuring since about 1910 and in virtual disuse by 1960.

cock it up *verb*

1 to make a complete mess of something *UK*

- He is a piece of slimy refuse, unable to carry out the simplest murder plot without cocking it up[.] — Peter Cook, *Entirely a Matter for You.*, 1979
- And the next minute I really cocked it up and proper mugged myself off. — Dave Courtney, *Raving Lunacy*, p. 102, 2000

2 (of a woman) to offer yourself sexually *AUSTRALIA*

- [T]hat nervous that if you cocked it up to him he'd put his hat over it and run[.] — X. Herbert, *Soldiers' Women*, 1961
- — G.A. Wilkes, *A Dictionary of Australian Colloquialisms*, 1978

cock jacket *noun*

a reputation for sexual prowess *US*

- Me, I had a cock jacket. They thought every broad that rode my bike, with the exception of my mother, got laid. — Joseph Wambaugh, *Lines and Shadows*, p. 51, 1984

cock-jockey *noun*

a man who thinks that sex is more important than anything else and that his contribution is paramount *UK*

- One thing, tho; cock-jockey forgot to ask for his change before he stamped off. — Niall Griffiths, *Kelly + Victor*, p. 292, 2002

cock jocks *noun*

a pair of men's close-fitting and revealing nylon swimming trunks *AUSTRALIA*

- I might wear cock jocks in the race to go faster than boardies. — *Wordmap (www.abc.net.au/wordmap)*, 2003

cock-knocker *noun*

a despised person *US, 1959*

- Goggles so big you can't see his motherfuckin face. Spooky old cock-knocker, ain't he? — Stephen King, *The Stand*, p. 504, 1978
- The little shit. The little brass-balled cock-knocker. Screw him. — Pat Cadigan, *Synners*, p. 281, 1991
- He started it! Fucking cock-knocker! — *Chasing Amy*, 1997

cockle and hen *noun*

ten shillings; ten pounds; in betting, odds of 10–1; in prison, a ten year sentence; in Bingo (also House and Tombola), the number ten *UK, 1960*

Rhyming slang; usually as 'cockle', which is a slovening of 'cockerel'. Other variants include 'cockle', 'cock and hen', 'cocks and 'en' and 'cockun'.

- — Peter Wright, *Cockney Dialect & Slang*, p. 109, 1981
- — John McCririck, *John McCririck's World of Betting*, p. 59, 1991
- — Angela Devlin, *Prison Patter*, p. 38, 1996
- I gives him a tenner and that. Gives him a cockle, should I say. — Kevin Sampson, *Clubland*, p. 164, 2002
- A jacks is £5; a cockun (cock & hen) £10[.] — *The Guardian*, 30th October 2002

cockleburr *noun*

any central nervous system stimulant *US*

- — Lanie Dills, *The Official CB Slanguage Language Dictionary*, p. 25, 1976

cockle to a penny *noun*

in gambling, odds of 10–1 *UK, 1984*

Rhyming slang, combining **COCKLE AND HEN** (ten) and **PENNY BUN** (one); mainly in racecourse use.

cock linnet *noun*

a minute *UK, 1909*

Rhyming slang, formed on the singing bird that is a familiar symbol of Cockney mythology.

- Won't be a cock linnet, I've just got to put my boots on. — Ray Puxley, *Cockney Rabbit*, 1992

cock, lock and rock *verb*

to prepare for and go into armed conflict *UK*

A variation of 'lock and load'.

- Let's cock, lock and rock. — Chris Ryan, *The Watchman*, p. 347, 2001

cock loft *noun*

the observation tower of a brakevan (caboose) *US*

- — Norman Carlisle, *The Modern Wonder Book of Trains and Railroading*, p. 261, 1946

cockmaster *noun*

a male proud of his sexual prowess *US*

- In a jiff I was in; but for some strange reason I couldn't come; all 19-year-old cockmasters can't come, you know this as well as I do. — Jack Kerouac, *Letter to Neal Cassady*, p. 299, 10th January 1951

cockmeat *noun*

the penis, specifically or as a generality *US*

- Hey girls, who needs some cockmeat from a real man? — Howard Stern, *Miss America*, p. 15, 1995

cock movie *noun*

a pornographic film *US*

- — *American Speech*, p. 228, October 1967: 'Some special terms used in a University of Connecticut men's dormitory'

cock off!

go away! *UK*

- Cock off back to the coffee table you charlatans. — *X-Ray*, p. 29, May 2003

cock of the walk *noun*

an important man in any given circumstance *UK, 1855*

A fighting cock allows no other into its enclosure or 'walk'.

- Englishmen wear luxuriant mustaches, trick clothes, loud vests – sometimes monocles. Just conceited little cocks of the walk. — Lee Mortimer, *Women Confidential*, p. 186, 1960
- [T]he main man,the cock of the walk, the king of this particular little hill[.] — James Hawes, *Dead Long Enough*, p. 105, 2000

cock on *verb*

▷ **see: COCK IT ON**

cockpit *noun*

1 the vagina *UK, 1891*

- — Dale Gordon, *The Dominion Sex Dictionary*, p. 45, 1967

2 the clitoris *US*

- — *Maledicta*, p. 131, Summer/Winter 1982: 'Dyke diction: the language of lesbians'

cockpit queen *noun*

a flight attendant who is more interested in the men flying the plane than doing her job with the passengers *US*

- — Rene Foss, *Around the World in a Bad Mood*, p. 34, 2002

cockrag *noun*

a loincloth *AUSTRALIA, 1964*

cock ring *noun*

a device worn on the penis to enhance sexual performance *US*

- The other man wears a cock ring – a current fad, a ring of metal, like his, or of studded leather, around the base of the cock and balls, supposedly insuring harder hard-ons, better orgasms. — John Rechy, *The Sexual Outlaw*, p. 202, 1977
- There are those items which in some way prohibit normal bodily functions [...] gags, cock-rings, harnesses, handcuffs[.] — Kitty Churchill, *Thinking of England*, p. 29, 1995

cockroach *noun*

1 a white person *TRINIDAD AND TOBAGO*

- — Lise Winer, *Dictionary of the English/Creole of Trinidad & Tobago*, 2003

2 a motor coach *UK, 1960*

Rhyming slang, noted by Julian Franklyn, 1961, as having 'been evolved since the war'.

- — Ray Puxley, *Cockney Rabbit*, 1992

3 a racing greyhound that never wins *AUSTRALIA*

- — Ned Wallish, *The Truth Dictionary of Racing Slang*, p. 16, 1989

cockroach *verb*

to steal something *US*

Hawaiian youth usage.

- Who wen cockaroach da cookies? — Douglas Simonson, *Pidgin to da Max*, 1981

cockroach bite *noun*

any lip sore *TRINIDAD AND TOBAGO, 1996*

- — Lise Winer, *Dictionary of the English/Creole of Trinidad & Tobago*, 2003

cockroach killers *noun*

pointed shoes or boots *US, 1970*

- — Peter A. Smith and Fred M. Barritt, *Bermewjan Vurds*, 1985
- "Cockroach killers" (a term you may also hear in the American Southwest) are pointy-toed shoes. — Darwin Porter, *Frommer's Bermuda 2004*, p. 225, 2003

cock robin *noun*

the penis *UK*

- I hope no-one's seriously suggesting we've more than one artist bucketing about with a knife in one hand and his cock-robin in the other. — Michael Kenyon, *The Rapist*, 1977

cock rock *noun*

aggressively macho heavy rock music performed with pelvic-thrusting posturing *US*

Combines **COCK** (the penis) and 'rock'.

- You get straight-up funk, vintage Seventies cock-rock, anarchic hard-core and enough psychedelia to make this the pot-smoking album of the year. — *Phoenix (Arizona) New Times*, p. 97, 23rd December 1992
- The typical guitar oriented thrashy pop would at times evolve into a sound described perfectly by the band as 'cock rock'. — *Beat*, p. 46, 9th July 1996
- They're going to be the ones responsible for this corporate, alternative and cock-rock fusion. — *Jabberrock*, p. 237, 1997
- [B]y 1992 grunge had totally destroyed the LA cock rock scene. — John Robb, *The Nineties*, p. 227, 1999
- Ten music-related university courses that really exist [...] 5 PHALLIC MASCULINITY IN COCK ROCK – POPULAR MUSIC, GENDER AND SEXUALITY, Leeds University — *Q*, p. 38, December 2001

cock rocker *noun*

a performer of cock rock *UK*

Mainly in the 1970s and 80s.

- [W]henever you see a picture of one of these cock rockers with long hair and leathers you piss yourself because they're all weedy-looking wankers acting hard for a camera[.] — John King, *Human Punk*, p. 75, 2000

cock rot *noun*

an unspecified sexually transmitted disease *US*

- — Gregory Clark, *Words of the Vietnam War*, p. 108, 1990

cocksman *noun*

1 a man who prides himself on his sexual prowess *US, 1896*

- The adolescent cocksman having made his conquest barely broods at home the loss of the love of the conquered lass[.] — Jack Kerouac, *The Subterraneans*, p. 18, 1958
- "I thought Aggies was all irresistible cocksmen," Duane said. — Larry McMurtry, *The Last Picture Show*, p. 137, 1966
- Lenny Bruce and John F. Kennedy had something in common. They were both great cocksmen. — Richard Neville, *Play Power*, p. 74, 1970
- You know that guy, that guy is the cocksman of Bay Ridge. — *Saturday Night Fever*, 1977
- Must've been a terrible temptation for a cocksman like Younger. — Robert Campbell, *Sweet La-La Land*, p. 234, 1990
- Allen was still so unsure of himself and here was Neal the confident cocksman if there ever was one. — Herbert Huncke, *Guilty of Everything*, p. 92, 1990

2 a male prostitute *US*

- — Clarence Major, *Dictionary of Afro-American Slang*, p. 38, 1970

cocksmith *noun*

a sexually expert man *US, 1959*

- Nevertheless, the latter scene is one of the most scorching four-ways ever comitted to film with Siffredi proving to be arguably the best living cocksmith in the business. — *Adult Video News*, p. 48, February 1993

cock-sparrow *adjective*

mad *AUSTRALIA*

Rhyming slang for **YARRA** (mad, stupid).

- — Jim McNeil, *The Chocolate Frog*, 1973

cockstand; stand *noun*

an erection *UK, 1866*

- Fighting gives ye a terrible cockstand, after. Ye want me, do ye no? — Diana Gabaldon, *Outlander*, p. 343, 1991
- — Lise Winer, *Dictionary of the English/Creole of Trinidad & Tobago*, 2003

cocksuck *noun*

an act of oral sex on a man *US, 1940*

- He'd grin grotesquely, rolling his eyes and darting his tongue in and out of his cadaverous mouth – more in an approximation, or so it seemed to me, of clit-lick than of cock-suck. — Terry Southern, *Now Dig This*, p. 33, 2001

cocksuck *verb*

to perform oral sex on a man *US*

- She cock-sucked him like crazy, and then he lost all control. — Roy Hawkins, *Bimbos by the Bay*, p. 105, 1977

cocksucker *noun*

1 used as a generalised term of abuse for a despicable person *US, 1918*

- I don't see how these cocksuckers could have done a better job trying to fuck me up as a first & second novelist if they had laid out a blueprint in an attic. — Jack Kerouac, *Letter to Neal Cassady*, p. 239–240, 3rd December 1950
- I said, what if the three months comes at a time when the writing is going well? Marty said, "Cocksucker." — Clancy Sigal, *Going Away*, p. 46, 1961
- — *The Guild Dictionary of Homosexual Terms*, p. 8, 1965
- He died on account of this silly cocksucker here. So I promised him I'd have this silly cocksucker shot after the war. — Kurt Vonnegut, *Slaughter-houseFive*, p. 141, 1969
- All the way to the station house I was called 110 cocksuckers, etc. — Babs Gonzales, *Movin' On Down De Line*, p. 55, 1975
- Every natural urge has been thwarted in one way or another, so that some cocksucker gets to make a dollar off your guilt. — Frank Zappa, *The Real Frank Zappa Book*, p. 233, 1989
- [H]e a ace number-one cocksucker, but he an honorable cock-sucker. — Joel Rose, *Kill Kill Faster Faster*, p. 75, 1997
- You cocksuckers as good as killed my little girls and I want you out of my house! — Robert Crais, *L.A. Requiem*, p. 46, 1999

2 a person who performs oral sex on a man, especially a male homosexual *UK, 1891*

The most well-known use of the term in the US is in a statement attributed to former President Richard Nixon, who upon learning of the death of FBI Director J. Edgar Hoover on 2nd May 1972, is reported to have said 'Jesus Christ! That old cocksucker!'. Nixon was reflecting the widespread belief that Hoover was homosexual.

- Besides I don't hafta take any shit off any uncircumcised cocksucker. — William Burroughs, *Naked Lunch*, p. 113, 1957
- Later, in his apartment, he said, "Why are you so nervous, aint you been with a cocksucker before?" — John Rechy, *City of Night*, p. 28, 1963
- 'Homosexual' is a kind of neutral, scientific term which might in a given context itself have a freight of significance or beauty or artistic merit. But it's less likely to than the word 'cocksucker,' which is closer to colloquial, idiomatic expression. — Lenny Bruce, *How to Talk Dirty and Influence People*, p. 117, 1965
- So I turned around with my head hung in sorrow / I was a playboy today, but I'll be a cocksucker tomorrow. — Bruce Jackson, *Get Your Ass in the Water and Swim Like Me*, p. 127, 1965
- He left these jungles in a hell of a rage / Like a young cocksucker full of his gays. — Roger Abrahams, *Positively Black*, p. 88, 1970
- Abbey proved herself to be a first-rate cock-sucker. — Roy Hawkins, *Bimbos by the Bay*, p. 23, 1977
- With an expert cocksucker, a rubber is no barrier to pleasure. — *Letters to Penthouse V*, p. 155, 1995

3 a person who performs oral sex on a woman *US, 1942*

- The man said, "I'm a cocksucker [a performer of cunnilingus]." — Roger Abrahams, *Positively Black*, p. 104, 1970

4 during the Vietnam war, a leech *US*

Especially the huge, reddish-black, slimy leeches of the Mekong Delta.

- — Linda Reinberg, *In the Field*, p. 46, 1991

▸ **third assistant cocksucker at a Mongolian clusterfuck**

a lowly assistant *US*

- — *Maledicta*, p. 18, Summer 1977: 'A word for It!'

cocksucker red *adjective*

a bright red shade of lipstick *US*

Not a brand name. Garish and conveying a low-life, whorish image.

- [S]o I said just let me handle this because my grandma is getting nothing less than Cocksucker Red when they put her in the ground... — Armistead Maupin, *Further Tales of the City*, p. 74, 1982
- — *Adult Video News*, p. 42, August 1995

cocksucker's teeth *noun*

used as the epitome of uselessness *US*

- — Robert A. Wilson, *Playboy's Book of Forbidden Words*, p. 73, 1972

cocksucking *noun*

oral sex performed on a man *UK, 1895*

- I don't know what it is, but the Trailways and the Greyhound people have done more to popularize impersonal cocksucking than Army chaplains. — Angelo d'Arcangelo, *The Homosexual Handbook*, p. 47, 1968
- Frank's dick was almost fully hard from the cock-sucking; it stuck halfway up from his naked lap. — Roy Hawkins, *Bimbos by the Bay*, p. 9, 1977
- Though I enjoyed sucking David's dick, it's true that I considered cocksucking to be strictly foreplay and not the main course. — *Letters to Penthouse V*, p. 58, 1995

cocksucking *adjective*

despicable, loathsome *US, 1902*

- But these next five years are not to be wasted "waiting" for these cocksucking bastards with their sheep's brains who will some day come bleating all over my premises. — Jack Kerouac, *Letter to Neal Cassady*, p. 173, 8th December 1948

- "Listen, you bitch," he says, still gripping the front of her dress, "you cock-sucking whore. Just fucking shut it or I'll shut it for you." —Ted Lewis, *Jack Carter's Law*, p. 71, 1974
- [A] bunch of cocksucking pharmaceutical companies want to sell their poisons. —Howard Marks, *The Howard Marks Book of Dope Stories*, p. 299, 2001

cocksy *noun*
▷ see: COXEY

cocktail *noun*

1 a marijuana cigarette, partially smoked and inserted into a regular cigarette *US*
- — *Mr.*, p. 9, April 1966: 'The hippie's lexicon'
- —Eugene Landy, *The Underground Dictionary*, p. 53, 1971
- As the cigarette began to burn his finger, Prince put the reefer out and made a cocktail out of the roach. —Donald Goines, *Black Gangster*, p. 224, 1977

2 cocaine *UK*
- —Mike Haskins, *Drugs*, p. 280, 2003

3 any mixture of drugs *CANADA*
- But sanity for Stephen had become sticking a needle in his arm every fifteen minutes, shooting up a heroin and cocaine cocktail. —Suroosh Alvi et al., *The Vice Guide*, p. 171, 2002

cocktail *verb*
to insert a partially smoked marijuana cigarette into a tobacco cigarette *US, 1960*
- The bomber in her hand was now a "roach." I cocktailed it for her. —Iceberg Slim (Robert Beck), *Pimp*, p. 182, 1969
- Marlene sighed impatiently and cocktailed the roach, waited for a light and took a deep hit before passing it on. —Odie Hawkins, *Amazing Grace*, p. 142–143, 1993
- I cocktailed the last of a roach I had now three days in my wallet, smoked it, a mellow high, boss shit from North Africa, I think the dude said. —Clarence Major, *All-Night Visitors*, p. 54, 1998

cocktailery *noun*
a cocktail lounge *US*
- —Don Wilmeth, *The Language of American Popular Entertainment*, p. 56, 1981

cocktail hour *noun*
the time when all patients in a hospital ward are given medication *US*
- — *American Speech*, p. 154, April 1946: 'GI words from the separation center and proctology ward'

cocktail party *noun*
the use of Molotov cocktails *US*
- —H. Craig Collins, *Street Gangs*, p. 222, 1979

cock tax *noun*
spousal support; alimony *AUSTRALIA*
- —Ian Fleming, *You Only Live Twice*, 1964
- —James McDonald, *A Dictionary of Obscenity, Taboo and Euphemism*, p. 26, 1988

cocktease *noun*
a cockteaser *US*
- He wanted to hit the supercilious little cocktease. —John Nichols, *The Nirvana Blues*, p. 426, 1981

cocktease *verb*
to tempt a man with the suggestion of sex *UK, 1957*
- —Angus Wilson, *A Bit off the Map*, 1957
- I knew I couldn't cocktease him any lower without walking off the lot[.] —Rita Ciresi, *Pink Slip*, p. 310, 1999

cockteaser *noun*
a sexually attractive woman who flaunts her sexuality *UK, 1891*
- Nobody likes a cockteaser. Either you put out or you dont. —Hubert Selby Jr, *Last Exit to Brooklyn*, p. 107, 1957
- The bad thing about a cockteaser like Angela is she turns her man loose on the world and lets a lot of other women in for trouble. —John Updike, *Couples*, p. 125, 1968
- I am really a professional cockteaser. —George Paul Csicsery (Editor), *The Sex Industry*, p. 137, 1973
- JOAN: My little boy is sick, and I really should be getting home. BERNIE: Cockteaser. JOAN: I beg your pardon? BERNIE: You heard me. JOAN: I have never been called that in my life. BERNIE: Well, you just lost your cherry. —David Mamet, *Sexual Perversity in Chicago*, p. 21, 1974
- So, you heavenly cock teaser, you will date me a couple times. —Iceberg Slim (Robert Beck), *Death Wish*, p. 26, 1977
- Ain't just dancing. You're a cock-teaser. — *Saturday Night Fever*, 1977
- She fitted none of the categories they commonly used when talking about girls; she wasn't a cock-teaser, a cold fish, an easy lay or a snarky bitch; she was an honorary person. —Margaret Atwood, *Dancing Girls*, p. 29, 1977
- He was still with Cindy of the blond hair and cute ass. Cockteaser was a name invented specially for Cindy. —Jackie Collins, *Chances*, p. 130, 1980

cock-up *noun*
an error, a mistake *UK, 1948*
A number of etymologies have been suggested, among them: bookkeeping amendments written at a tilt, and the 'cock' (spigot) of ale-barrels; while it is possible that the origins lurk in such innocence it is certain that modern usage is influenced by 'fuck-up', 'balls-up', etc., which presumes 'cock' is a 'penis'.
- [U]ntil this cock-up with our radio sets, you see[.] —Mike Stott, *Soldiers Talking, Cleanly*, 1978
- I haven't really seen Dixie since, since that cock-up in Middlesbrough – y'know. —Alan Bleasdale, *Boys From the Blackstuff*, 1982
- [S]ince the Carlisle cock-up story broke[.] —John McCririck, *John McCririck's World of Betting*, p. 157, 1991
- We can't be having none of this amateurism no more. I thought we'd left cock-ups behind[.] —Kevin Sampson, *Powder*, p. 226–227, 1999

▸ **couldn't organise a cock-up in a brothel**
used of an inefficient person *UK*
A later variation of **COULDN'T ORGANISE A FUCK IN A BROTHEL** with a neat pun on **COCK-UP** (an error) and **COCK** (the penis).

cock up *verb*
to make a mess of something; to make a mistake *UK*
Military in origin.
- I don't want your enthusiam for your work cocking up the whole operation. —Ted Lewis, *Jack Carter's Law [britpulp]*, p. 42, 1974

cockwood *noun*
firewood stolen from work *UK, 1984*
Coalminers' use.
- — *Pit-Talk*, 1970

cocky; cockie *noun*

1 a cockroach *AUSTRALIA, 1984*
- Proof that cockies were a more intelligent life force. So, they would inherit the earth, after all. —Kathy Lette, *Girls' Night Out*, p. 115, 1987

2 a cockatoo *AUSTRALIA, 1834*
Occasionally used loosely of other parrots. Frequently as a name for a pet cockatoo.
- 'Scratch Cocky's comb,' the bird invited, inclining the sulphur crest[.] —Dymphna Cusack, *Picnic Races*, p. 140, 1962
- When I got home I would put her in the old cage the cocky had lived in until he had died[.] —T.A.G. Hungerford, *Stories From Suburban Road*, p. 2, 1983

3 a sheep which has lost some of its wool *AUSTRALIA*
- —Sidney J. Baker, *The Drum*, 1959

4 a small-scale farmer *AUSTRALIA, 1871*
Often preceded by the crop or livestock farmed, such as **COW COCKY** and **SPUD COCKY**.
- We was helping a cocky keep the fire off his wheat and the wind turns round and our camp cops the lot. —Kylie Tennant, *The Honey Flow*, p. 15, 1956
- That's when we won the Quilpie Polo Gold Cup against all the cockies[.] —Herb Wharton, *Cattle Camp*, p. 105, 1994

5 used as a term of endearment; hence as a more general form of address *UK, 1687*
- "We dont know how long I've got," says Simon [Cadell] [...] "so we'd better get on with it, eh, cockie?" —Gyles Brandreth, *Breaking the Code*, p. 220, 1999

▸ **like cocky on the biscuit tin**
left out; on the outside looking in *AUSTRALIA*
Referring to Arnott's™ biscuits which have since at least 1910 had a logo of a parrot eating a biscuit adorning their biscuit tins.
- Like those gaily-painted customers' chairs in general stores promoting biscuits – the same biscuits, incidentally, that gave the Australian language that useful phrase "sitting round like a cocky on a biscuit tin." —Suzy Jarratt, *Permissive Australia*, p. 160, 1970
- Out here like the bloody cocky on the bloody biscuit tin. —Richard Beckett, *The Dinkum Aussie Dictionary*, p. 15, 1986

▸ **like the bottom of a cocky's cage**
(of the mouth or tongue) in a disgusting state from being hungover *AUSTRALIA*
- When Curly woke up with roadmap eyes and a mouth like the bottom of a cocky's cage, he was under the kitchen table. —Frank Hardy, *Hardy's People*, p. 128, 1986
- One is said to have 'a mouth like the bottom of a cocky's cage' when one is suffering from a terminal hangover. —Richard Beckett, *The Dinkum Aussie Dictionary*, p. 15, 1986

cocky *adjective*

over-confident; smug; arrogant *UK, 1768*

From the strutting nature of the rooster.

- They think we are cocky, flash and cowardly.— Martin King and Martin Knight, *The Naughty Nineties*, p. 151, 1999
- I began to regret having been so cocky with them.— Malcolm Pryce, *Aberystwyth Mon Amour*, p. 68, 2001

cocky Bob *noun*

▷ see: COCK-EYE BOB

cocky dickie *noun*

an over-confident individual *UK*

- He used to wear loud suits and did outrageous things to get us attention. He was a cocky dickie and Ian liked that.— Jim Drury, *Ian Dury and the Blockheads*, p. 62, 2003

cocky's crow *noun*

dawn *AUSTRALIA, 1945*

Extended from a conventional 'cock's crow', playing on **COCKY** (a small-scale farmer).

cocky's joy *noun*

1 golden syrup or treacle *AUSTRALIA, 1902*

- Honest selectors, on the other hand, were traditionally supposed to live almost entirely on nothing but bread (or damper) and treacle, known contemptuously to the bushmen as 'cocky's joy'.— Russel Ward, *The Australian Legend*, p. 199, 1960
- — Jim Ramsay, *Cop It Sweet!*, p. 24, 1977
- I remember being astounded that this girl preferred Golden Syrup to jam, but that was apparently what she was used to. We called it cocky's joy and thought it was only for poor people.— Bert West, *A Beaut Life*, p. 22, 1993

2 rum *AUSTRALIA*

- Rum is variously known as blackfellow's delight, cocky's joy and whip.— Sidney J. Baker, *The Australian Language*, p. 227, 1953

cocky's string *noun*

fencing wire, especially number eight fencing wire *NEW ZEALAND*

From **COCKY** (a small-scale farmer).

- — David McGill, *David McGill's Complete Kiwi Slang Dictionary*, p. 31, 1998

co-co *noun*

cocaine *US*

- RUCKER: My girl at Chase says Figsy was missing payments – what with the his and her co-co problems and whatnot.— *Copland*, 1997

cocoa *noun*

semen *UK, 1984*

In the phrase 'come your cocoa'.

▸ **come cocoa**

to make a complete confession of guilt *UK*

- — David Powis, *The Signs of Crime*, 1977

cocoa puff *noun*

a combination of marijuana and cocaine *UK*

- — Mike Haskins, *Drugs*, p. 293, 2003

cocoa puff *verb*

to smoke cocaine mixed with marijuana *UK, 1998*

Punning on a branded breakfast cereal.

cocobay on top of yaws *noun*

more trouble than you can handle *GUYANA*

- — Richard Allsopp, *Dictionary of Caribbean English Usage*, p. 161, 1996

cocolo *noun*

the penis *TRINIDAD AND TOBAGO*

- — Lise Winer, *Dictionary of the English/Creole of Trinidad & Tobago*, 2003

coconut *noun*

1 a Mexican-American who rejects his heritage and seeks to blend in with the white majority *US*

Like a coconut, brown on the outside but white on the inside.

- — Dagoberto Fuentes and Jose Lopez, *Barrio Language Dictionary*, p. 32, 1974
- Shot full of holes, he apparently only had one worry: that these coconut assholes might accidentally drop him over a cliff and kill him.— Joseph Wambaugh, *Lines and Shadows*, p. 138, 1984
- — Multicultural Management Program Fellows, *Dictionary of Cautionary Words and Phrases*, 1989

2 a black person who is considered to have exchanged heritage and community values for acceptance by white society *UK*

A coconut is brown on the outside, white on the inside.

- — *New Society*, p. 515, 24th September 1981
- [A]ll he got from the community, his community, was [...] a lot of abuse about being an "Uncle Tom", a "house nigga", a "coconut".— Karline Smith, *Moss Side Massive*, p. 181, 1994
- — Angela Devlin, *Prison Patter*, p. 38, 1996

3 an Australian Aboriginal who has adopted the values of white society *AUSTRALIA, 1980*

- Ambrose and the Talbots don't get on. He reckons they're coconuts.— Shane Maloney, *Nice Try*, p. 42, 1998

4 a Pacific Islander *NEW ZEALAND*

- This is the elite part of town. Islanders, Chiamen and Maoris, Coconuts, horis and chinks.— Charles Frances, *Johnny Rapana*, p. 121, 1964

5 a clod, a dolt *US*

- — Miss Cone, *The Slang Dictionary (Hawthorne High School)*, 1965

6 cocaine *US*

- — US Department of Justice, *Street Terms*, August 1994

coconuts *noun*

1 cocaine *US*

- — *American Speech*, p. 25, February 1952: 'Teen-age hophead jargon'

2 money *US*

- — Don Wilmeth, *The Language of American Popular Entertainment*, p. 58, 1981

coconut tackle *noun*

in rugby, a head-high tackle *NEW ZEALAND*

- — David McGill, *David McGill's Complete Kiwi Slang Dictionary*, p. 31, 1998

coconut telegraph *noun*

the informal way in which news travels in the Caribbean *US*

- Kirk can get in touch with me on the Coconut Telegraph and I will meet you there.— Jimmy Buffett, *Tales from Margaritaville*, p. 61, 1989

cocoon *verb*

to stay at home enjoying sedentary activities *US, 1987*

- — *American Speech*, Fall 1988

coco rocks; cocoa rocks *noun*

crack cocaine combined in its production with a chocolate-flavoured milk powder *UK*

- — Mike Haskins, *Drugs*, p. 293, 2003

Coco the Clown *noun*

cocaine *UK*

A disguise for **co-co**; formed from the professional name (sometimes 'CoCo') of Latvian-born Nicolai Polakovs, 1900–74, who, for forty years from 1930, worked for Bertram Mills' Circus and became the best-known clown in the UK; subsequently the name has become almost a generic for any clown.

- He had done it. Knocked Coco the Clown on the head.— James Hawes, *White Powder, Green Light*, p. 7, 2002

COD *noun*

the product a male prostitute sells – *c*ock *o*n *d*emand *UK*

- — *Maledicta*, p. 147, Summer/Winter 1986–1987: 'Sexual slang: prostitutes, pedophiles, flagellators, transvestites, and necrophiles'

cod *verb*

to hoax someone, to fool someone *UK, 1864*

- The Doctor would cod the lady of the flat or her maid into holding the torch for him.— Charles Raven, *Underworld Nights*, p. 53, 1956

cod *adjective*

1 mock, parodic, ersatz *UK*

Originally theatrical; usually in combination with the term that is being qualified.

- [T]he most superficial, cod-Celtic twat who ever walked the earth[.] — James Hawes, *Dead Long Enough*, p. 54, 2000

2 bad *UK*

Variants include 'codalina', 'codette' and 'codettareenaronee'.

- JULIAN: Haaaaa! What a naff lot! SANDY: It is a bit cod, isn'y it?— Barry Took and Marty Feldman, *Round The Horne*, 17th March 1968
- [T]he omi-palone [gay man] with a vogue [cigarette] on and the cod sheitel [wig].— James Gardiner, *Who's a Pretty Boy Then?*, p. 123, 1997

cod and hake; cod *noun*

the penis *UK*

Rhyming slang for **TROUSER SNAKE**.

- He's got a cod big enough to close a convent.— Bodmin Dark, *Dirty Cockney Rhyming Slang*, 2003

coddy *noun*
▷ see: LUCODDY

coddy; cody *adjective*
bad, amateurish *UK*
An elaboration of **COD**.
- What a coddy kaffall dear. Oh vada [observe] the schnozzle [nose] on it dear. —David McKenna, *Storm in a Teacup*, 1993
- —Paul Baker, *Polari*, p. 169, 2002

code brown *noun*
used as a vaguely humorous notification that a hospital patient has defecated *US*
An allusion to the colour code jargon heard in hospitals.
- —*Maledicta*, p. 31, 1988–1989: 'Medical maledicta from San Francisco'
- —Adam T. Fox, St Mary's Hospital, London, 10th October 2002

code R *noun*
rape *NEW ZEALAND*
Prison slang.
- —*NZWords*, p. 2, 2nd October 1999

coder-boder *adjective*
▷ see: COOLABOOLA

code red *noun*
in the military, punishment meted out by a group to soldiers to a non-conforming peer *US*
- Sir, a Code Red is a disciplinary engagement. —*A Few Good Men*, 1992

code two *noun*
an escape from prison *CANADA*
- —A. Schroeder, *Shaking it Rough*, 1976

codfish flats *noun*
a poor section of town *US, 1969*
- —Frederic G. Cassidy, *Dictionary of American Regional English, Volume 1*, p. 713, 1985

codger *noun*
a pleasantly eccentric old man *UK, 1756*
Often found as 'old codger'.
- My grandfather was a tough old codger, but that's one thing you can say for him, he was always a believer in giving folks a second chance. —Gurney Norman, *Divine Right's Trip (Last Whole Earth Catalog)*, p. 49, 1971
- When Bobbie questioned Fin about the age of all the fun-loving fogies, coots, geezers, codgers, duffers and biddies she'd met in the saloon, he didn't know how to tell her that the oldest fossil in the joint wasn't fifteen years his senior. —Joseph Wambaugh, *Finnegan's Week*, p. 230, 1993
- [T]here are invisible people there, old codgers with lots of coats and a cup of tea. —Jane Rogers, *Lucky*, p. 16, 1999
- [T]he self-indulgent ramblings of an old codger who would have been wiser to let someone else tell his story[.] —*The Guardian*, 12th October 2002

codi *noun*
a codeine tablet *UK*
- —Roderic Jeffries, *A Traitor's Crime*, 1968

codjocks *noun*
a pair of men's close-fitting and revealing nylon swimming trunks *AUSTRALIA*
- Are we wearing boardies or codjocks for the carnival? —*Wordmap (www.abc.net.au/wordmap)*, 2003

cod ogle *noun*
a contact lens *UK*
- —the cast of 'Aspects of Love', Prince of Wales Theatre, *Palare (Boy Dancer Talk) for Beginners*, 1989–92

codology *noun*
nonsense *IRELAND*
- Mr Henry is quoted as saying that a city of almost 1 million people cannot afford 100 gardai to monitor rush hour traffic all the year round. It is Operation Bluff and Bluster at best; Operation Codology at worst. —*Irish Times*, 4th September 1997
- I can tell you there were less than 20 spectators there so their argument that it would inconvenience their supporters is all codology. —*Irish Examiner*, 21st October 1999

cod-riah *noun*
a wig *UK*
- So I varded the cod-riahs but they were much too butch pour moi —the cast of 'Aspects of Love', Prince of Wales Theatre, *Palare (Boy Dancer Talk) for Beginners*, 1989–92

cods *noun*
1 the testicles *UK, 1632*
- He don't have cods enough to steal and all he wants to do is stand around and whip some gal, you know. —Bruce Jackson, *Outside the Law*, p. 157, 1972
- She stepped aside, reaching out and cupping his cock and cods in her lump, liver-spotted hand. —Earl Thompson, *Tattoo*, p. 195, 1974

2 courage, daring *US*
Synonymous with **BALLS**.
- He don't have cods enough to steal and all he wants to do is stand around and whip some gal, you know. —Bruce Jackson Outside the Law, p. 157, 1972

3 a mess, a state of confusion *UK*
Possibly rhyming slang for 'cod and skate', **STATE**.
- Make no mistake, the Church is in a right cods. —Andrew Nickolds, *Back to Basics*, p. 163, 1994

cod's roe *noun*
money *UK*
Rhyming slang for **DOUGH**.
- A losing punter [gambler] may often be heard to complain that he has "done his cod's". —Ray Puxley, *Fresh Rabbit*, 1998

codswallop; cods *noun*
nonsense *UK, 1963*
- That's codswallop, and dangerously cynical codswallop at that. —*The Guardian*, 5th April 2004

Cod War *noun*
1 the political friction in the early to mid-1970s between Britain and Iceland, especially between the British and Icelandic fishing fleets and fishermen, over the fishing rights off Iceland *UK*
A journalists' term that allowed the consequent pun: 'Cod peace'.
- A compensation scheme was introduced last year by the Labour government which acknowledged the problem 24 years after the cod war. —*The Guardian*, 26th October 2001

2 a female prisoner *US*
- —Vincent J. Monteleone, *Criminal Slang*, p. 53, 1949

cody *adjective*
▷ see: CODDY

coeey *noun*
a rat *UK*
English gypsy use.
- —Jimmy Stockin, *On The Cobbles*, p. 10, 2000

coey *noun*
a thing; any object *UK*
- —Patrick O'Shaughnessy, *Market Traders' Slang*, 1979

C of E; church boys *noun*
HM Customs & Excise *UK*
A play on the initial similarity to the Church of England.
- ROBBIE: There's a certain amount of, er, interest in gear of this quality from the Church boys... LEE: Church boys? ROBBIE: C of E. Lee still looks puzzled. Robbie rolls his eyes. ROBBIE (CONT'D): Anyone speak English? Customs and Excise. —Bernard Dempsey and Kevin McNally, *Lock, Stock ... & Two Hundred Smoking Kalashnikovs*, p. 107, 2000

coffee *noun*
LSD *US*
A euphemism created in Boston, alluding to the fact that LSD was often sold in Cambridge coffee houses.
- —Richard Lingeman, *Drugs from A to Z*, p. 47, 1967

coffee-and *noun*
a light meal *US, 1901*
- —Hyman E. Goldin et al., *Dictionary of American Underworld Lingo*, p. 46, 1950
- They sprawled at the counter and at the tables and ordered coffeeand. —Hubert Selby Jr, *Last Exit to Brooklyn*, p. 239, 1957
- I drank coffee in Skid Row coffee houses, South Main Street, coffee-and, seventeen cents. —Jack Kerouac, *The Dharma Bums*, p. 93, 1958

coffee-and *adjective*
small-time, insignificant *US, 1937*
- "That coffe-an' mac you got," a French girl would crack to a straight one, and then it was on – hair came out by the handful. —Mezz Mezzrow, *Really the Blues*, p. 23, 1946
- —Hyman E. Goldin et al., *Dictionary of American Underworld Lingo*, p. 46, 1950

• [C]offee-and habit: a small drug habit[.]—Richard A. Spears, *The Slang and Jargon of Drugs and Drink*, 1986

coffee-and-cakes *noun*

a small salary *US, 1925*

• —Harold Wentworth and Stuart Berg Flexner, *Dictionary of American Slang*, p. 113, 1960

coffee and tea; coffee *noun*

the sea *UK*

Rhyming slang.

• —Ray Puxley, *Cockney Rabbit*, 1992

coffee grinder *noun*

1 in oil drilling, a worn-out rig *US*

• —Jerry Robertson, *Oil Slanguage*, p. 38, 1954

2 a sexual dancer who makes grinding motions with her pelvis *US*

• —Harold Wentworth and Stuart Berg Flexner, *Dictionary of American Slang*, p. 114, 1960

coffeehouse *verb*

in poker, to try to deceive your opponents by idle speech and deliberate mannerisms *US, 1949*

• —Albert H. Morehead, *The Complete Guide to Winning Poker*, p. 259, 1967
• —Thomas L. Clark, *The Dictionary of Gambling and Gaming*, p. 46, 1987

coffeemate *noun*

any central nervous system stimulant *US*

Punning on a non-dairy coffee cream-substitute.

• —Lanie Dills, *The Official CB Slanguage Language Dictionary*, p. 25, 1976

coffee pot *noun*

a restaurant *US, 1928*

• —Montie Tak, *Truck Talk*, p. 33, 1971
• —Peter Chippindale, *The British CB Book*, p. 153, 1981

coffee shop *noun*

a café-style business open for the smoking, or other consumption, of marijuana in its various forms

Originally in Amsterdam.

• —Nick Jones, *Spliffs*, p. 250, 2003

coffee stalls *noun*

the testicles *UK*

Rhyming slang for **BALLS**; not as popular as **ORCHESTRA STALLS**.

• —Julian Franklyn, *A Dictionary of Rhyming Slang*, 1961

coffin *noun*

1 a surfing manoeuvre in which the surfer lines prone on the board, his arms crossed over his chest *AUSTRALIA*

• —*Pix*, 28th September 1963
• —John M. Kelly, *Surf and Sea*, p. 282, 1965

2 in skateboarding, a manoeuvre in which the rider lies completely horizontally on the board, feet first *US*

• You can do the tricks the surfers do / Just try a Quasimodo or The Coffin too.—Jan Berry and Dean Torrance, *Sidewalk Surfin'*, 1964
• —Albert Cassorla, *The Skateboarder's Bible*, p. 199, 1976

3 the canvas bag used to carry cricket equipment *NEW ZEALAND, 1993*

• —Harry Orsman, *A Dictionary of Modern New Zealand Slang*, p. 31, 1999

4 a case housing weapons *US*

• In the trunk of the squad car was a wooden box known as the coffin. It contained two Remington 12-gauge automatic shotguns, with ammunition[.]—Jon A. Jackson, *The Blind Pig*, p. 7, 1978

5 a safe within a safe *US*

• —Vincent J. Monteleone, *Criminal Slang*, p. 53, 1949

6 in poker, the smallest possible raise in a game with a limited number of raises permitted *US*

• —Albert H. Morehead, *The Complete Guide to Winning Poker*, p. 256, 1967

coffin box *noun*

in trucking, a sleeping compartment added onto a conventional cab *US*

• —Montie Tak, *Truck Talk*, p. 33, 1971

coffin corner *noun*

in battle, a vulnerable position *US, 1995*

• I ain't surprised. We're flying in coffin corner to start with. And we were so goddamn low by the time we jumped that the squadron had already left us behind.—Greg Iles, *Black Cross*, p. 138, 1995

coffin-dodger *noun*

an old or elderly person, especially if infirm *UK*

Recorded in an article about medical slang in British (3 London and 1 Cambridge) hospitals.

• —Chris Donald, *Roger's Profanisaurus*, 1998
• I can't wait to see him sitting there, all nervous with loads of coffin dodgers nagging him.—Colin Butts, *Is Harry Still on the Boat?*, p. 120, 2003
• —*Ethics and Behaviour*, August 2003

coffin hoist *noun*

in electric line work, any type of chain hoist *US*

• —A.B. Chance Co., *Lineman's Slang Dictionary*, p. 4, 1980

coffin lid *noun*

a child *UK*

Rhyming slang for **KID**.

• [A]ll the other cozzers [police officers] gone home to the wife and coffin lids.—J.J. Connolly, *Layer Cake*, p. 152, 2000

coffin nail *noun*

a cigarette *US, 1900*

From the link between smoking cigarettes and death. In the C19, it referred to 'a cigar'.

• —Lou Shelly, *Hepcats Jive Talk Dictionary*, p. 23, 1945
• "Say, got a fag?" asked Buddy. "Here's a coffin nail," Phil said, talking out of the side of his mouth and extending a pack to Buddy.—James T. Farrell, *Saturday Night*, p. 28, 1947
• And that's what the so-called Surgeon General has going for him – a black hat: cigarettes. Coffin nails, gaspers – a black hat if ever there was one.—Max Shulman, *Anyone Got a Match?*, p. 42, 1964
• It's why I didn't take a drink or smoke a coffin nail or lay a broad until I was nineteen.—Iceberg Slim (Robert Beck), *Doom Fox*, p. 199, 1978
• If I had just turned twenty-two, I wouldn't be suckin' on these ol' coffin nails myself, but I ain't got a thing to lose, not at my age.—Odie Hawkins, *The Busting Out of an Ordinary Man*, p. 143, 1985

coffin spike *noun*

a cigar *US*

• —Kenn "Naz" Young, *Naz's Underground Dictionary*, p. 20, 1973

coffin tank *noun*

a motorcyle petrol tank shaped like a coffin *US, 1970s*

• —Ed Radlauer, *Motorcylopedia*, p. 12, 1973
• Same with the other practical features Harley built into the FLH – the front brakes, sprung seats, 16-inch tires, electric starts, and shock absorbers, 19 and 21-inch front tires on extended forks, tiny "peanut" and coffin tanks, stepped saddles, and hardtail frames.—Greg Field, *Harley-Davidson Evolution Motorcyles*, p. 44, 2001
• Tony designed this Sporters model with extended front forks and a coffin tank which, in retrospect, was an ominous sign—Phil Kaufman, *'Parson's Folly' in Mammoth Book of Sex, Drugs and Rock 'n' Roll*, p. 198, 2001

cog *verb*

to copy from another's work *TRINIDAD AND TOBAGO*

• —Lise Winer, *Dictionary of the English/Creole of Trinidad & Tobago*, 2003

cogger *noun*

a Catholic *UK*

• —Fritz Spiegl, *Lern Yerself Scouse*, 1966

Coggy *adjective*

Catholic, especially Roman Catholic *UK*

• More Coggy than the friggin Pope, me.—Niall Griffiths, *Kelly + Victor*, p. 51, 2002

cogs *noun*

sunglasses *US*

• —Lou Shelly, *Hepcats Jive Talk Dictionary*, p. 8, 1945

cog-stripper *noun*

in trucking, a driver who has problems shifting gears *US*

• —Montie Tak, *Truck Talk*, p. 33, 1971

cohangas *noun*

the testicles, literally and figuratively as a measure of courage *US*

An intentional butchering of the Spanish *cojones*.

• —Judi Sanders, *Kickin' like Chicken with the Couch Commander*, p. 6, 1992

coin *noun*

money *UK, 1820*

• If you intend to seek coin or a career here (or just a job) do not come at all[.]—Jack Lait and Lee Mortimer, *New York Confidential*, p. 122, 1948

- "You're going to blow the coin?" he asked, incredulously. "You don't have to if you don't want to." — James Simon Kunen, *The Strawberry Statement*, p. 76, 1968
- You're only sending coin to Larry in the brig, you ain't writing a noble prize. — Darryl Ponicsan, *The Last Detail*, p. 168, 1970
- I've had you dad, I've had your uncle Elvin, an individual I think of as a model repeat offender. Smuggling, armed robbery, hitting people over the head for their coin. — Elmore Leonard, *Maximum Bob*, p. 12, 1991
- Because it's not just the money I deserve. It's not just the coin. — *Jerry Maguire*, 1996

coin *verb*

to earn an amount of money *US*

- [W]ith the chuck-luck and Indian-dice games at the cigar counter I was coining at least two C-notes a week. — Mezz Mezzrow, *Really the Blues*, p. 44, 1946

coin it; coin it in *verb*

to make money, especially easily or quickly *UK, 1984*

From the earlier 'coin money'.

- If your destination becomes the next hot place to visit, you can coin it in: one Rough Guides author has become a millionaire from his well-timed book on Thailand. — *Freelance [Newsletter of the London Freelance Branch of the NUJ]*, June 2003

coinkidink *noun*

a coincidence *US*

Multiple creative spellings are to be found.

- Is it just more of what Kendall calls "coincidence-a-dinkies?" — Beatrice Sparks (writing as 'Anonymous'), *Jay's Journal*, p. 54, 1979
- — Pamela Munro, *U.C.L.A. Slang*, p. 30, 1989
- NOT AN item but a heckuva coinkydink: Winifred Giannini, whose care bears plates reading "2 VJH 135," parked and 19th and Ocean behind a car with plates "2 VJH 124." — *San Francisco Chronicle*, p. E1, 6th March 1992
- "I wouldn't want to sleep there alone," she said. "What a coinkydink," I said in my best Three Stooges voice. "Neither does Mrs. Swanson. — Alice McDermot, *Child of My Heart*, p. 181, 2002
- What struck me as a little 'coinkydinky,' Colonel, is that three times in the space of ten days, you were witness to some sort of cover-up there. — *Real Time with Bill Maher*, 13th February 2004

coin-op *noun*

a coin-operated pool table *US*

- — Steve Rushin, *Pool Cool*, p. 10, 1990

COIO *noun*

a Canadian whose origins are in India *CANADA*

- Although hundreds of Canadians died in the [1987 Air India bombing], it was seen as only an Indian problem. "These were Canadians of Indian origins – COIOs," said Clark Blaise. — *National Post*, p. B5, 29th June 2002

cojones *noun*

the testicles; courage *US, 1932*

From Spanish.

- It had been raining like a bastard, and the baseball field was mud up to your cojones. — Truman Capote, *In Cold Blood*, p. 331, 1965
- [A]nd would be if the anthropologists had a shred of imagination or the dimmest sense of wonder, or the cojones, the bollocks to look at the big picture, to help focus and enlarge the big picture. — Tom Robbins, *Fierce Invalids Home from Hot Climtes*, p. 74, 2000

coke *noun*

1 cocaine *US, 1903*

- H and coke. You can smell it going in. — William Burroughs, *Junkie*, p. 66, 1953
- I've got some Coke. What's you think we're celebrating for? Coke and champagne, Kitty, get champagne for everyone. — Susan Hall, *Gentleman of Leisure*, p. 130, 1972
- Wow, I don't believe it. You mean to tell me you guys have never snorted coke? — *Annie Hall*, 1977
- Here were two coke fiends who came into court because their marriage didn't seem to be working and the children were getting nervous. — Hunter S. Thompson, *Songs of the Doomed*, p. 197, 1983
- Is there gonna be coke at this party, Colonel? — *Boogie Nights*, 1997

2 crack cocaine *UK*

From the previous sense.

- But the drug of choice now was crack cocaine. Coke. Rock. White. Stones. Charlie. — Lanre Fehintola, *Charlie Says...*, p. 129, 2000

coke bar; coke joint *noun*

a bar, club or pub where cocaine or crack cocaine is used openly

- — Nick Constable, *This is Cocaine*, p. 182, 2002

coke biscuit *noun*

a pill of MDMA, the recreational drug best known as ecstasy *UK*

Presumably marketed, illegally, under this name to tempt custom with a partial (in fact, non-existent) content of cocaine or, perhaps, Coca-Cola.

- — Gareth Thomas, *This Is Ecstasy*, p. 54, 2002

Coke bomb *noun*

a crude hand grenade fashioned by the Viet Cong, packed inside a drinks can *US*

- — Gregory Clark, *Words of the Vietnam War*, p. 53, 1990

cokebottle *noun*

in computing, any character that is not found on a normal computer keyboard *US*

- A program written at Stanford, for example, is likely to have a lot of "control-meta-cokebottle" commands, that is, commands that you can only type on a Stanford keyboard[.] — Guy L. Steele et al., *The Hacker's Dictionary*, p. 44, 1983

Coke bottle glasses *noun*

spectacles with very thick lenses *US, 1986*

- [S]ome skinny jerk-off with Coke-bottle glasses[.] — Carl Hiaasen, *Strip Tease*, p. 4, 1993
- Nuggy was a barber, I think a teach-yourself, do-it-yourself barber, he was 70, had Coke bottle glasses and Dad loved him. — Paul Vautin, *Turn It Up!*, p. 111, 1995
- Mind that cunt? Coke-bottle glasses? — Irvine Welsh, *The State of the Party (Disco Biscuits)*, p. 32, 1995
- A few weeks earlier, Senator Pothole [D'Amato] had been on the Imus radio show and done an over-the-top Japanese stereotype impression of Judge Ito. It was real Jerry-Lewis-bucktooth-Coke-bottle-glasses stuff[.] — Al Franken, *Rush Limbaugh is a Big Fat Idiot*, p. 189, 1996

Coke bottles *noun*

a person with poor eyesight and thick glasses *US*

- The labels were cruel: Gimp, Limpy–go-fetch, Crip, Lift-one-drag one, etc. Pint, Half-a-man, Peewee, Shorty, Lardass, Pork, Blubber, Belly, Blimp. Nuke-knob, Skinhead, Baldy. Four-eyes, Specs, Coke bottles. — *San Francisco Examiner*, p. A15, 28th July 1997

coke bugs *noun*

a cocaine-induced conviction that insects or snakes are crawling beneath the skin

- — Nick Constable, *This is Cocaine*, p. 182, 2002

coke burger

a tablet of MDMA, the recreational drug best known as ecstasy *UK*

The name leads to unrealistic hopes that the tablet may contain a trace of cocaine.

- — Gareth Thomas, *This Is Ecstasy*, p. 55, 2002

coked; coked out; coked up *adjective*

cocaine-intoxicated *US, 1924*

- I was real hungup on it two years ago, you understand – coked most of the time. — John Clellon Holmes, *Go*, p. 121, 1952
- I knew what a devil she could be when she was coked up[.] — Polly Adler, *A House is Not a Home*, p. 47, 1953
- They're coked to the gills. — Edwin Torres, *Q & A*, p. 98, 1977
- "You look just like David Bowie," Alana, who is obviously coked up out of her mind, tells Daniel. — Bret Easton Ellis, *Less Than Zero*, p. 16, 1985
- Coked-out as we were, nobody ate much, but we nibbled, and I felt safe, saved from catastrophe. — Cleo Odzer, *Goa Freaks*, p. 50, 1995
- I even know the occasional person who gets coked up when they go on stage. — Macfarlane, Macfarlane and Robson, *The User*, p. 11, 1996
- [C]oked off his box[.] — Dave Courtney, *Stop the Ride I Want to Get Off*, p. 158, 1999
- I'd rather watch the history channel than listen to some coked-up twat. — *Drugs An Adult Guide*, p. 16, December 2001

cokehead *noun*

a cocaine addict *US, 1922*

- [H]ard-core, career dope fiends, and even the cokeheads like the number runners from way back – Cisco Kid and Billy Bucks – be comin' into the clubs to get a taste of the base. — *New Jack City*, 1990
- Americans are all fucking coke heads. Even the respectable ones. — Shaun Ryder, *Shaun Ryder... in His Own Words*, 1991
- You were never an alky, you were a cokehead. — *Something About Mary*, 1998
- Ye's a pyscho-cokehead-hitman. — *Traffic*, 2000

coke house *noun*

a building or dwelling where cocaine is sold *US*

- I told two of my old roomies about the coke house, but I didn't say I worked here or nothing. — Terry Williams, *The Cocaine Kids*, p. 40, 1989

coke jumbie *noun*
a cocaine user or addict *TRINIDAD AND TOBAGO, 1989*
- —Lise Winer, *Dictionary of the English/Creole of Trinidad & Tobago*, 2003

coke out *verb*
to use cocaine to an excess *US*
- The ritual was to coke out every night, for the whole night, and not to stay too long with any particular group.—Cleo Odzer, *Goa Freaks*, p. 39, 1995

coke, smoke, and a puke *noun*
a fighter pilot's breakfast *US*
- —*United States Naval Institute Proceedings*, p. 108, October 1986

coke whore *noun*
a person who trades sex for cocaine *US*
- —Jay Robert Nash, *Dictionary of Crime*, p. 72, 1992

Cokey Stokey *nickname*
Stoke Newington in north London *UK*
A rhyme based on 'Hokey Cokey' (a dance), combining the first element of Stoke Newington and **COKE** (cocaine), from the reputation of the area as a centre for drugs and other criminal endeavours.
- My biggest fear was to be sent to Stoke Newington, popularly known by both police and criminals alike as Cokey Stokey[.]—Duncan MacLaughlin, *The Filth*, p. 145, 2002

cokie *noun*
1 a frequent user of cocaine *US, 1916*
- A competitor in the same block was Wilbur Kenny, known to the cokies merely as "Y."—Jack Lait and Lee Mortimer, *Washington Confidential*, p. 51, 1951
- The girls never bother the alkies and cokies of the street with their joke[.]—John M. Murtagh and Sara Harris, *Cast the First Stone*, p. 4, 1957

2 a junior member of a youth gang *US*
- I see one of their cokies standing in a doorway with his hands in his pockets.—Hal Ellson, *Duke*, p. 39, 1949

Cokomo Joe; Kokomo Joe; kokomo *noun*
a cocaine user *US, 1938*
- —J.E. Schmindt, *Narcotics Lingo and Lore*, p. 98, 1959
- —Mike Haskins, *Drugs*, p. 282, 2003

cola *noun*
1 cocaine *US*
Playing off the popular soft drink.
- —Jay Robert Nash, *Dictionary of Crime*, p. 72, 1992

2 a marijuana bud or buds, especially the long top bud on a marijuana plant *UK*
From Spanish *cola* (a tail).
- —Steven Wishnia, *The Cannabis Companion*, p. 151, 2004

cold *noun*
▸ **out in the cold**
stranded, neglected, imperiled *UK*
A phrase popularised by John LeCarre's *The Spy Who Came in From the Cold*.
- JULES: But what I can say is my ass is out in the cold and I'm askin' you for some sanctuary 'till our people can bring us in.—*Pulp Fiction*, 1994

▸ **too slow to catch a cold**
applied to someone or something that moves slowly, or someone whose thought processes are sluggish *UK, 1917*
- "Hurry up, Pigman!" shouted the sows. "Stir your stumps, you lazy thing!" "He's too slow to catch a cold!"—Dick King-Smith, *Pigs Might Fly*, p. 5, 1990
- The car was noisy, too slow to catch a cold and had antiquated road-holding properties.—Laurence Meredith, *Original Vw Beetle*, p. 126, 1999

cold *adjective*
1 heartless, cruel *US, 1962*
- That's pretty cold, ain't it, lady?—*Basic Instinct*, 1992
- "If you do something to offend someone, then that's cold, " said Ryan Hoskin, 17, a senior at Stuart.—*The Washington Post*, 19th March 2002

2 bad *US, 1934*
- And the bitch had cuffs on at the time, but I being the warm and he being the cold, I was able to get her to give up the source of her supplier which was all we wanted from the jump.—A.S. Jackson, *Gentleman Pimp*, p. 131, 1973

3 absolute *US*
- "They don't want their wives to know they're cold freaks," she explains. "They bring their sex hang-ups to us."—George Paul Csicsery (Editor), *The Sex Industry*, p. 9, 1973

4 not capable of being traced to an owner *US*
Back-formed from **HOT** (stolen).
- "He could feel the bump of Dan's service revolver, unwrapped and loaded now against his leg. A cold piece, its registry lost in a mountain of old records somewhere if they existed at all.—Robert Campbell, *Boneyards*, p. 276, 1992

5 innocent of charges under which someone was convicted *AUSTRALIA, 1944*
Prison usage.

6 in gambling, unlucky *US*
- Duffy ended up being the only player shooting at table three because he was so cold he had become a plague on everybody's luck.—Stephen Cannell, *Big Con*, p. 202, 1997

7 without preparation; in ignorance *US, 1896*
Generally used quasi-adverbially.

8 used as a substitute for 'cool' in any of its senses *US*
- The dress Mary's wearing today is too cold.—Joan Fontaine et al., *Dictionary of Black Slang*, 1968
- —*Columbia Missourian*, p. 8A, 19th October 1998
- —Julian Johnson, *Urban Survival*, p. 258, 2003

9 (used of a take-off from an aircraft carrier) failed, resulting in a crash *US*
- What had it been? A "cold-cat" shot, whatever that was, from a carrier. A crash at take-off, anyway, into the waters off Iwo-Jima[.]—Hank Searls, *The Big X*, p. 221, 1959

cold *adverb*
suddenly, completely *US, 1889*
- Talking about a stretch in Atlanta, where he kicked a habit cold: "Fourteen days I was beating my head against the wall."—William Burroughs, *Junkie*, p. 68, 1953
- They had me cold.—Clarence Cooper Jr, *The Farm*, p. 63, 1967

cold and hot *noun*
cocaine and heroin combined for injection *US*
Based on the initials.
- —Richard A. Spears, *The Slang and Jargon of Drugs and Drink*, p. 115, 1986

cold and hungry *noun*
in trucking, a C & H truck *US*
- —Wayne Floyd, *Jason's Authentic Dictionary of CB Slang*, p. 12, 1976

cold as a Bay Street banker's heart *adjective*
very ungenerous, or in metaphor, very cold *CANADA*
This expression is from the Canadian prairies, and refers both to its peoples' resentment of Toronto bankers (Bay is the main banking street) and to the legendary cold winters of Saskatchewan, Manitoba and Alberta.

cold as a nun's cunt *adjective*
extremely cold *AUSTRALIA, 1955*

cold as a nun's nasty *adjective*
extremely cold *AUSTRALIA*
- He might be as cold as a nun's nasty!—Barry Humphries, *Bazza Pulls It Off!*, 1971

cold biscuit *noun*
1 a female who does not respond to sexual overtures *US*
- —Helen Dahlskog (Editor), *A Dictionary of Contemporary and Colloquial Usage*, p. 14, 1972

2 a person lacking any apparent sex appeal *US*
High school usage.
- —*Washington Post*, 23rd April 1961

cold-blooded *adjective*
1 competent; admirable *US*
Also shortened to 'cold'.
- —William K. Bentley and James M. Corbett, *Prison Slang*, p. 31, 1992

2 in horse racing, said of any horse that is not a thoroughbred *US*
- —Robert Saunders Dowst and Jay Craig, *Playing the Races*, p. 161, 1960

cold blow *noun*
air conditioning *US*
- —Montie Tak, *Truck Talk*, p. 33, 1971

cold bluff *noun*
in poker, a large bet on a poor hand designed to mislead other players *US, 1980*
- —Thomas L. Clark, *The Dictionary of Gambling and Gaming*, p. 46, 1987

cold-bust *verb*
to catch someone in the act; to reveal your own guilt inadvertently *US*
- —Connie Eble (Editor), *UNC-CH Campus Slang*, p. 2, Fall 1986
- It was too late to make a run for it. We were cold busted. —L.L. Cool J, *I Make My Own Rules*, p. 56, 1997
- "I figured I was cold busted so I pulled over and was ready to give myself up," Andreas said. —Mike Seate, *Streetbike Extreme*, p. 81, 2002

cold-call *verb*
to go into a pub hoping to make a sexual contact *UK*
Adopted from sales jargon.
- —Paul Baker, *Polari*, p. 169, 2002

coldcock *verb*
to hit someone without warning, especially with a blow to the head that knocks the person to the ground *US, 1918*
- You killed her. You coldcocked her and set fire to her. —Jim Thompson, *The Nothing Man*, p. 172, 1954
- Then he cold-cocked his two principal tormentors with a short left and a short right respectively, and the ragging stopped. —Max Shulman, *Rally Round the Flag, Boys!*, p. 165, 1957
- I wish he was a wise-ass messcook who coldcocked a commander and went over the hill. —Darryl Ponicsan, *The Last Detail*, p. 148, 1970
- Jackie got up and cold cocked him with two punches and then announced, "Let 'em roll." —Babs Gonzales, *Movin' On Down De Line*, p. 47, 1975
- I screamed, "Look out Papp!" too late for him to duck Jenkins' boot kick to his jaw that cold-cocked him flat on his back with his crooked mouth leaking blood." —Iceberg Slim (Robert Beck), *Doom Fox*, p. 119, 1978
- Nino cold-cocks the woman with left hook – she's out like a light. —*New Jack City*, p. 4, 1990

cold coffee *noun*
beer *US*
- —Wayne Floyd, *Jason's Authentic Dictionary of CB Slang*, p. 12, 1976

cold comfort *noun*
in necrophile usage, sexual activity with a corpse *US*
- —*Maledicta*, p. 180, Summer/Winter 1986–1987: 'Sexual slang: prostitutes, pedophiles, flagellators, transvestites, and necrophiles'

cold crotch *noun*
the application of an ice pack on the scrotum of a man who has overdosed on heroin *US*
- —Peter Johnson, *Dictionary of Street Alcohol and Drug Terms*, p. 45, 1993

cold-cunt *verb*
(used of a woman) to treat someone with hostility *US*
- [E]ven my female helpers if detected as not sympatica have been cold-cunted and brushed off. —*Maledicta*, p. 134, Summer/Winter 1982

cold deck *noun*
1 in card games, a stacked deck of cards *US, 1857*
- —Lou Shelly, *Hepcats Jive Talk Dictionary*, p. 23, 1945
- Was back in thirty-two when times were hard/I had a sawed-off shotgun and a cold deck a cards. —Bruce Jackson, *Get Your Ass in the Water and Swim Like Me*, p. 50, 1964
- —Jim Glenn, *Programmed Poker*, p. 155, 1981

2 logs swept into a stack to be moved after drying *CANADA*
British Columbia logging usage.
- Logs which are piled together for loading immediately make up a hot deck, those left in a pile to be moved later form a cold deck. —John Gough, *The Story of British Columbia*, p. 185, 1952

cold dope *noun*
in horse racing, information based on empirical evidence *US*
- —David W. Maurer, *Argot of the Racetrack*, p. 21, 1951

cold draw *noun*
in curling, a rock curled into an open house or into the house without rubbing or knocking out another rock *CANADA*
- Another cold draw to the four-foot with the last rock by Dagg bailed out Canada. —*Calgary Herald*, p. 16/6, 20th March 1964

colder than a witch's tit *adjective*
extremely cold; extremely unfriendly *AUSTRALIA*
- The pool is as cold as a witch's tit. —Barry Humphries, *A Nice Night's Entertainment*, p. 175, 1978
- We're standing out there on the sidewalk, colder than a witch's tit[.] —George V. Higgins, *Penance for Jerry Kennedy*, 1985
- Maybe the rellies are truly freezing their cojones off back in Tulsa, but you still want to believe it's colder than a witch's tit outside. —*Metropolitan [San Francisco]*, 18th January 1999

cold feet *noun*
fear or a reluctance to proceed *US, 1896*
- TAYLOR: [...] You'd better watch your step now that he's back. O'MALLY: Are you gettin' cold feet or something? —Graeme Kent, *The Queen's Corporal [Six Granada Plays]*, p. 93–94, 1959
- Maybe he just got cold feet. —Michael Chabon, *The Amazing Adventures of Kavalier & Clay*, p. 495, 2000

cold finger work *noun*
picking the pocket of a man preoccupied with sex *US*
- The woman goes through the man's clothes while he is in no frame of mind to keep his hands on his pockets. This is subtly known in Harlem as "cold finger work." —Jack Lait and Lee Mortimer, *New York Confidential*, p. 99, 1948

cold fish *noun*
1 an unfriendly person *US, 1924*
- He's a cold fish all right. —Jack Kerouac, *Letter to Carolina Kerouac Blake*, p. 89, 14th March 1945
- But I know I have to talk to Chichi if I want any kind of emotional angle, a point of view, because Robbie's such a cold fish. He thinks he's Mr. Personality, but he's basically a very dull person. —Elmore Leonard, *Split Images*, p. 213, 1981

2 a standoffish, unwelcoming girl *CANADA*
- She wasn't a cock-teaser, a cold fish, an easy lay or a snarky bitch. —Margaret Atwood, *Dancing Girls*, p. 29, 1977

cold-footer *noun*
a cowardly soldier, or someone too cowardly to become a soldier *AUSTRALIA, 1916*
From having **COLD FEET** (fear).

cold hole *noun*
during Vietnam, an enemy tunnel that has been verified as empty *US*
- —Linda Reinberg, *In the Field*, p. 46, 1991

coldie *noun*
a cold beer *AUSTRALIA, 1953*
- —Nino Culotta (John O'Grady), *They're A Weird Mob*, p. 126, 1957
- Don't know about you, but I could go a few swift coldies! —Barry Humphries, *The Wonderful World of Barry McKenzie*, p. 41, 1968
- —Ivor Limb, *Footy's No Joke!*, p. 45, 1986
- —Kathy Lette, *Girls' Night Out*, p. 139, 1987

cold in the dong *noun*
gonorrhea *US*
- —*Maledicta*, p. 228, Summer/Winter 1981: 'Sex and the single soldier'

cold like dog nose *adjective*
very cold *TRINIDAD AND TOBAGO*
- —Lise Winer, *Dictionary of the English/Creole of Trinidad & Tobago*, 2003

cold meat party *noun*
a funeral or wake *US, 1908*
- My favourite euphemism for a funeral wake is cold meat party, partly because the attempt at euphemistic disguise (deliberately) fails. —Andrew Goatly, *Critical Reading and Writing*, p. 109, 2000

cold one *noun*
1 a cold beer *US, 1927*
- Hurry up Jack. Give us a carton and a cold one. I'm in a hurry. —Sam Weller, *Old Bastards I Have Met*, p. 22, 1979
- "You want a cold one?" The guy stared at him. "That means a beer. You want one? You like beer?" —Elmore Leonard, *Bandits*, p. 106–107, 1987

2 an empty wallet, purse or safe *US*
- —Joseph E. Ragen and Charles Finston, *Inside the World's Toughest Prison*, p. 795, 1962

cold pit *noun*
in motor racing, a member of the pit crew who works behind the wall separating the pit from the race track *US*
- —John Edwards, *Auto Dictionary*, p. 125, 1993

cold-plate *verb*
to attach a legitimate licence plate to a stolen vehicle that matches the description of the vehicle to which the licence plate belongs *US*

- The shop in Old Town might be in cahoots with Tijuana thieves who steal trucks and cold-plate them. —Joseph Wambaugh, *Finnegan's Week*, p. 132, 1993

cold potato *noun*

a waiter, especially a slow or inefficient one *UK*

Cockney and theatrical rhyming slang.

- —Julian Franklyn, *A Dictionary of Rhyming Slang*, 1960
- —Ray Puxley, *Cockney Rabbit*, 1992

cold prowl *noun*

an assumed easy house to rob *CANADA, 1976*

- "I got us a cold prowl lined up over on Dundonald Street." "Where's that?" "South a Bloor off Yonge. It's a lead pipe cinch." —Hugh Garner, *The Intruders*, p. 135, 1976

cold-read *verb*

(used of a fortune teller) to tell a fortune without background information on the customer, relying on observations and the customer's answers for the predictions *US*

A term borrowed from acting, where it means 'to read a script outloud without having studied it'.

- —Lindsay E. Smith and Bruce A. Walstad, *Sting Shif*, p. 115, 1989

cold shake *noun*

a method of preparing pills for injection by crushing and then dissolving them in cold water instead of heating with a flame *US*

- —Geoffrey Froner, *Digging for Diamonds*, p. 20, 1989

cold spot *noun*

a glass of iced tea *US*

- —*American Speech*, p. 61, February 1967: 'Soda-fountain, restaurant and tavern calls'

cold storage *noun*

1 a morgue *US*

- —Vincent J. Monteleone, *Criminal Slang*, p. 55, 1949

2 solitary confinement *US*

- —Vincent J. Monteleone, *Criminal Slang*, p. 55, 1949
- —Marlene Freedman, *Alcatraz*, 1983

Coldstream Guards; coldstreams *noun*

playing cards *UK*

Rhyming slang, formed on the name of the oldest serving regular regiment in the British Army.

- —Ray Puxley, *Cockney Rabbit*, 1992

cold tea sign *noun*

an irreverent indicator of a geriatric's death in hospital *UK*

A blackly humorous medical symptom, glossed as 'when positive, refers to the several cups of cold tea on the bedside cabinet besides a dead geriatric'.

- —Adam T. Fox, St Mary's Hospital, London, 10th October 2002

cold turkey *noun*

1 an act of withdrawing from addictive drugs suddenly; the time period of that withdrawal *US, 1925*

- If you didn't bring a trained nurse with you, you're just sneezed down, and it's piddle and cold turkey for you. —*The New American Mercury*, p. 711, 1950
- "I've tried, Tom. Honestly I have. But no-one knows what a spell of cold turkey is like – " "Cold turkey?" "Trying to kick the habit." —Douglas Rutherford, *The Creeping Flesh*, p. 83–84, 1963
- I promise you anything / Get me out of this hell / Cold turkey has got me / on the run. —John Lennon, *Cold Turkey*, 1970
- I'm clean now. On my children. Believe me! Two weeks cold turkey waiting for bail got my head together. —*Goodfellas*, 1990
- [H]e didn't realise I'd started my cold turkey already. —Lanre Fehintola, *Charlie Says...*, p. 195, 2000

2 in blackjack, a hand comprised of two face cards *US*

- —Lee Solkey, *Dummy Up and Deal*, p. 110, 1980

3 in poker, two kings dealt consecutively *US*

- —George Percy, *The Language of Poker*, p. 22, 1988

cold turkey *verb*

to withdraw from a habit or addiction suddenly and without any tapering off *US, 1949*

- Two days later, Chico told himself, "I'm going to cold turkey it. That's the hard way but the only way to bust my habit." —Hal Ellson, *The Golden Spike*, p. 47, 1952
- "You gonna cold-turkey it!" Dincher yelled on his feet. —George Mandel, *Flee the Angry Strangers*, p. 250, 1952
- I fuckin remember yew down Plas Crug with spew down-a front of yewer fuckin shirt screamin at passers-by cos ey wouldn't lend yew any fuckin money. Cold turkeyin like. —Niall Griffiths, *Sheepshagger*, p. 138, 2001

cold turkey *adjective*

(used of an attempt to break a drug addiction) sudden and complete without narcotics or medication to ease the withdrawal symptoms *US*

- Mae said she'd prefer to get the agony over with as quickly as possible so I might as well give her the Cold Turkey cure. —Polly Adler, *A House is Not a Home*, p. 155, 1953

cold turkey *adverb*

(used of an attempt to break a drug addiction) suddenly and completely without narcotics or medication to ease the withdrawal symptoms *US, 1922*

- Included as a medical record from the hospital when he had made her go cold turkey, which is dope-addict talk for an all-out cure. —Mickey Spillane, *I, The Jury*, p. 12, 1947
- You did it cold turkey, man? —Willard Motley, *Let No Man Write My Epitaph*, p. 120, 1958
- Like the worst habit I ever had was $135 a day. And I kicked that one cold-turkey 'cause I didn't know what I was in for. —James Mills, *The Panic in Needle Park*, p. 99, 1966
- Each time take less and less and bang, you've kicked, cause trying to kick it cold turkey is a bitch. —Piri Thomas, *Down These Mean Streets*, p. 204, 1967
- I kicked the habit 'cold turkey' in city jail. —Iceberg Slim (Robert Beck), *Pimp*, p. 101, 1969
- You might as well make up your mind to kick cold turkey, 'cause we ain't got nothing for you. —Donald Goines, *Dopefiend*, p. 230, 1971
- It was in the Tombs that I kicked the hardest habit that I'd ever kicked cold turkey in my life. —A.S. Jackson, *Gentleman Pimp*, p. 126, 1973
- When I came out – I had of course kicked my habit – cold turkey – while in prison – I was very careful[.] —Herbert Huncke, *The Evening Sun Turned Crimson*, p. 57, 1980
- —Angela Devlin, *Prison Patter*, p. 38, 1996

cold weather indicators *noun*

a woman's nipples *US*

- —Don R. McCreary (Editor), *Dawg Speak*, 2001

colgate *noun*

any toothpaste *TRINIDAD AND TOBAGO*

- —Lise Winer, *Dictionary of the English/Creole of Trinidad & Tobago*, 2003

coli *noun*

marijuana *US, 1978*

A shortening, perhaps, of **BROCCOLI** (marijuana) or **COLIFLOR TOSTAO** (marijuana).

- —Richard A. Spears, *The Slang and Jargon of Drugs and Drink*, p. 116, 1986
- —Mike Haskins, *Drugs*, p. 287, 2003

colifor tostao *noun*

marijuana *US, 1973*

A 'toasted cauliflour' in unconventional Spanish.

- —Richard A. Spears, *The Slang and Jargon of Drugs and Drink*, p. 116, 1986
- —Mike Haskins, *Drugs*, p. 287, 2003

colin *noun*

an erection *UK*

- —Paul Baker, *Polari*, p. 169, 2002
- —*Attitude*, p. 60, July 2003

coliseum curtains *noun*

the foreskin *UK*

- —Paul Baker, *Polari*, p. 169, 2002

collabo *noun*

an artistic collaboration *UK*

A hip-hop term.

- [E]verything from the best posse cuts and collabos to the most underrated artist[.] —Patrick Neate, *Where You're At*, p. 35, 2003

collar *noun*

1 an arrest *US, 1871*

- One of the cops, the handsomest, made the pick-up, and his confederates were supposed to crash in five minutes after he entered the room, which would give both time to disrobe, and that is enough evidence to make a collar. —Jack Lait and Lee Mortimer, *Washington Confidential*, p. 23, 1951
- In those days one big collar and you were in the Detective Bureau. —Edwin Torres, *Q & A*, p. 17, 1977

- Cocaine. Dirty cops. Hollywood. This is Crocket and Tubbs all the way. And we found it, so we want the fucking collar. — *True Romance*, 1993
- [M]ake ten collars by the witching hour and cop a microwave for a bonus. — Andrew Nickolds, *Back to Basics*, p. 46, 1994
- [C]oppers looking for a collar[.] — Irish Jack (writing of the 1960s), *History, The Sharper Word*, p. 31, 1998

2 a police officer *US*

- — Kenn "Naz" Young, *Naz's Underground Dictionary*, p. 22, 1973

3 hard, laborious work *UK*

English gypsy use; shortened from conventional 'collar-work'.

- [W]e repaid them [farmers] by doing a bit of collar and treating their land with respect in turn. — Jimmy Stockin, *On The Cobbles*, p. 49, 2000

4 an improvised seal between a dropper and needle used to inject drugs *US*

- Siphoning up the liquid again, applying the needle with its collar (a strip from the end of a dollar bill) to the neck of the dropper, twisting it on, resting the shot momentarily while he ties up[.] — Alexander Trocchi, *Cain's Book*, p. 81, 1960
- The hypodermic needle is secured to a common eyedropper by means of a narrow cardboard "collar." — Leonard Cohen, *Beautiful Losers*, p. 238–239, 1966
- — *Current Slang*, p. 15, Fall 1968

5 the steering column of a car *US*

- I don't care what kind of car it is, how fancy, how expensive, how new. You pop the collar, it's 1966 all over again. — *Gone in 60 Seconds*, 2000

▸ **finger a collar**

to make an arrest *UK*

Police slang; a variation of 'feel your collar'.

- — Martin Fido and Keith Skinner, *The Official Encyclopaedia of New Scotland Yard*, 1999

▸ **have your collar felt; have your collar touched**

to be arrested or stopped by the police *UK, 1949*

The active verb **COLLAR** (to seize, to arrest) dates from the early C17. In those and other gentler times officers of the law would, reputedly, touch their suspect on the collar or shoulder to signify capture.

- [S]tart grassing even before they've been whacked, soon as they get their collar felt[.] — Derek Raymond (Robin Cook), *The Crust on its Uppers*, p. 24, 1962
- "Mr. Regan," he said and wondered if he was about to have his collar felt. — *The Sweeney*, p. 49, 1976
- I'm sure that if the Old Bill had seen the claret [blood] I would have had my collar felt. — Martin King and Martin Knight, *The Naughty Nineties*, p. 41, 1999
- "Gene's been looking to get that felt." He grabs his collar and tugs. — J.J. Connolly, *Layer Cake*, p. 264, 2000

collar *verb*

1 to grab someone by the collar, literally or figuratively; to arrest someone *UK, 1613*

- We collared everybody on campus; we applied all possible pressures. — Max Shulman, *The Many Loves of Dobie Gillis*, p. 34, 1951
- And being a girl, I supposed they figured they'd collar me. — James Mills, *The Panic in Needle Park*, p. 101, 1966
- I'm going to collar the rats who operate this ring or else! — *The Sweeney*, p. 29, 1976
- Didn't I tell you, when I collared you, your next step was going to be the place where they're so concerned about whether you get nightmares, that they keep guards around all night? — George V. Higgins, *The Rat on Fire*, p. 178, 1981
- He didn't look like a guy who shot alligators or collared offenders. — Elmore Leonard, *Maximum Bob*, p. 94, 1991
- The geezer said if we're collared doing anything untoward in the firm's uniform, that was it – curtains. — Martin King and Martin Knight, *The Naughty Nineties*, p. 53, 1999
- I was sober when I was collared[.] — Danny King, *The Burglar Diaries*, p. 148, 2001

2 to appropriate something; to steal something *UK, 1700*

- [H]e slipped from the mess tent, collaring a bottle of rum as he went. — Chris Ryan, *The Watchman*, p. 63, 2001

3 to understand something, to grasp something *US, 1938*

- I began to collar that all the evil I ever found came from ounce-brain white men who hated Negroes and me both, while all the good things in life came to me from the race. — Mezz Mezzrow, *Really the Blues*, p. 44, 1946

4 in horse racing, to run neck-and-neck *US*

- — David W. Maurer, *Argot of the Racetrack*, p. 21, 1951

5 (from a male perspective) to have sex *AUSTRALIA*

A shortening of **HOP INTO THE HORSECOLLAR**.

- — Barry Humphries, *Bazza Pulls It Off!*, 1971

▸ **collar a hot**

to eat a meal *US*

- — Marcus Hanna Boulware, *Jive and Slang of Students in Negro Colleges*, 1947

▸ **collar the jive**

to understand what is being said *US*

- — Marcus Hanna Boulware, *Jive and Slang of Students in Negro Colleges*, 1947

collar and cuff *noun*

a homosexual male *UK, 1934*

Rhyming slang for **PUFF**.

- — Julian Franklyn, *A Dictionary of Rhyming Slang*, 1961

collars and cuffs *noun*

▸ **matching collars and cuffs; collars and cuffs that match**

applied to a person, usually a woman, whose hair is neither bleached nor dyed *US*

A jocular suggestion that the hair on the head is of the same natural shade as the pubic hair.

- — Ken Weaver, *Texas Crude*, p. 81, 1984
- "Do the collars match the cuffs?" "What?" "Do the curtains match the carpets?" "I don't understand." "Your pubic hair. Does it match the color of the hair on your head?" — Andrew Lewis Conn, *P: A Novel*, p. 16, 2003

collars-for-dollars *noun*

a situation in which an arresting officer trades the criminal's release for a share of the proceeds of the crime *US*

- You think it's some kinda buy-down? Some bullshit collars-for-dollars scheme? — Stephen J. Cannell, *The Tin Collectors*, p. 174, 2001

collats *noun*

money *UK*

Abbreviated and adapted into predominantly black usage from 'collateral' (a pledge of equal value).

- A client it seemed. Who knows, maybe one with serious collats. That would be nice. — Diran Adebayo, *My Once Upon A Time*, p. 5, 2000

collect *noun*

a win at gambling *AUSTRALIA*

- — James Holledge, *The Great Australian Gamble*, p. 22, 1966
- Collects of £10,000 were common. — James Holledge, *The Great Australian Gamble*, p. 56, 1966
- The girls took two-dollar quinellas and doubles and actually managed a collect. — Clive Galea, *Slipper*, p. 137, 1988

collect *verb*

1 to call for a person and proceed with him or her *UK, 1937*

- [T]he PR agent organising publicity for the diaries, collected her by car and they sped to the BBC in Portland Place[.] — *The Guardian*, 3rd October 2002

2 to win at gambling; to take your winnings *AUSTRALIA*

- [I]t looked as though the majority were going to collect. — Joe Andersen, *Winners Can Laugh*, p. 76, 1982
- Weight was right and Joe hurried back to the pub to collect. — Clive Galea, *Slipper*, p. 7, 1988

collect call *noun*

a citizens' band radio message for a specific named person *US*

- — Elementary Electronics, *Dictionary of CB Lingo*, p. 58, 1976

collection box *noun*

the vagina *BAHAMAS*

- — John A. Holm, *Dictionary of Bahamian English*, p. 45, 1982

college *noun*

jail *UK, 1699*

- — Lou Shelly, *Hepcats Jive Talk Dictionary*, p. 9, 1945
- — Hy Lit, *Hy Lit's Unbelievable Dictionary of Hip Words for Groovy People*, p. 9, 1968

college classique *noun*

in Quebec, a specialised, college-preparatory school *CANADA*

These Catholic schools, absorbed into the state system of junior colleges, are still known by their French name, even among anglophones.

- The colleges classiques of Lower Canada were turning out lawyers, journalists, and doctors. — A.S. Morton, *Kingdom of Canada*, p. 218, 1963
- In Quebec, 21 tertiary educational colleges, the College Classique, may now join CUS because of the change. — *Gauntlet*, p. 5/3, 11th October 1963

College Eye *noun*

a Lockheed EC-121 Warning Star aircraft *US*

Vietnam war usage.

- — Linda Reinberg, *In the Field*, p. 46, 1991

college hill *noun*
a well-off section of town *US, 1970*
- —Frederic G. Cassidy, *Dictionary of American Regional English, Volume 1*, p. 725, 1985

College Joe *noun*
a quintessential college student *US*
- In come this trick by hisseff. College Joe. —Robert Gover, *One Hundred Dollar Misunderstanding*, p. 19, 1961

college try *noun*
a sincere effort, despite the likelihood of failure *US, 1918*
Especially common as 'the old college try'.
- He thought of everything in terms of the old college try, and he had told students to attack their studies, their sports, religious waverings, sexual maladjustments, physical handicaps and a constellation of other problems with the old college try. —John Knowles, *A Separate Peace*, p. 174, 1954
- WAYNE: You can't escape like this. MICKEY: Probably not, but we're gonna give it the old college try. —*Natural Born Killers*, 1994
- You gave it the old college try. No hard feelings. —Stephen Cannell, *Big Con*, p. 44, 1997

college widow *noun*
a woman who lives in or near a college town and dates men from the college year after year *US, 1900*
- She made me think of a collge widow. Actually, she was a serious girl, in her own inscrutable way. —Mary McCarthy, *Memories of a Catholic Girlhood*, p. 174, 1957

collie *noun*
marijuana *JAMAICA*
From **KALI**.
- —Glen Brown, *Collie and Wine*, 1970
- —Jay Robert Nash, *Dictionary of Crime*, p. 73, 1992
- [A] variety of ganja, nowadays rendered as colley or colly[.] —Harry Shaphiro, *Waiting For The Man*, 1999
- Marley remains shrouded in myth, trailing smoke screens of collie weed from the ever-present cutchie — *Uncut*, p. 53, March 2001

Collie; Colly *nickname*
Colchester; hence the Military Corrective Establishment at Colchester; detention therein *UK*
Military.
- [A]nd 'fore he knew where he was, he'd landed six month's Collie. — Beale, 1974

collie dug *noun*
a man; implying that to some degree the person is a fool or a victim *UK: SCOTLAND*
Glasgow rhyming slang for **MUG**, formed from the local pronunciation of 'collie dog'.
- [A] right collie dug[.] — *The Guardian*, 29th April 2002

Collie Knox *noun*
the pox *UK*
Rhyming slang, noted by Red Daniells, 1980.

collie man *noun*
a marijuana dealer *JAMAICA*
- Quaju Peg the collie-man / Sell the best collie in sea port town — Congos, *Row Fisherman Row*, 1977
- Heart of the Congos is an unparalleled showcase of Jamaican vocal technique. Just hear Watty Burnett dropping down to bass in praise of the collie man on Fisherman. —Steve Barrow, *The Rough Guide to Reggae*, p. 129, 1999

colly *noun*
1 an erection *UK*
Derives from earlier rhyming slang, 'colleen bawn' for **HORN**; formed on the name of the heroine of *The Lily of Killarney*, an 1862 opera by Julius Benedict.
- —Julian Franklyn, *A Dictionary of Rhyming Slang*, 1960

2 cauliflower *UK, 1961*
Also variant 'cauli'.

collywobbles *noun*
an unsettled condition of the stomach *UK, 1823*
Derives from the conventional senses of 'colic' and 'wobble'.
- Have you got the collywobbles or something? You feeling a bit peaky? —Peter Cook, *Not Only But Also*, 1970
- —Louis S. Leland, *A Personal Kiwi-Yankee Dictionary*, p. 27, 1984
- The name will mean nothing but it's enough to induce serious collywobbles in the fashion world for Carine [Roitfield] is the most stingingly hip of stylists and editor of French Vogue. —*The Guardian*, 30th March 2001

Colney Hatch; colney *noun*
a match *UK*
Rhyming slang, formed on the one time lunatic asylum in north London.
- —Julian Franklyn, *A Dictionary of Rhyming Slang*, 1960
- —Ray Puxley, *Cockney Rabbit*, 1992

Colombian *noun*
extremely potent marijuana from Colombia *US, 1971*
- I think you better hit on a couple pounds of good Colombian. —Elmore Leonard, *City Primeval*, p. 107, 1980

Colombian gold *noun*
marijuana from Colombia, yellow in colour *US, 1976*
- —Ernest Abel, *A Marijuana Dictionary*, p. 26, 1982

Colombian marching powder *noun*
cocaine *UK, mid-1980s*
Less common than Bolivian or Peruvian.
- And what about the ... Colombian Marching Powder, shouted, then hissed Jan, suddely remembering we were in a cab. —James Hawes, *Dead Long Enough*, p. 72, 2000
- [P]erhaps music's most famous fan of Colombian marching powder was Elton John. — *Drugs An Adult Guide*, p. 17, December 2001

Colombian necklace *noun*
a form of execution intended to set an example in which the victim's throat is slit *US*
Probably formed after the more elaborate **COLOMBIAN NECKTIE**.

Colombian necktie *noun*
a form of execution intended to set an example in which the victim's throat is slit and the toungue pulled down through the gaping wound *US*
From a well-dressed image in which the tongue replaces a tie. A **COLOMBIAN NECKLACE** is less elaborate.
- [T]he 'Colombian necktie' in which the victim's throat is cut and his tongue is brought out through the wound. Something like that. —John E. Douglas and Mark Olshaker, *Journey into Darkness*, p. 342, 1997
- [J]ust before she kneed him in the balls and tried to give him a Colombian necktie[.] —Cherry Adair, *Kiss and Tell*, p. 59, 2000

Colombian red *noun*
marijuana from Colombia, reddish in colour *US, 1976*
- —Ernest Abel, *A Marijuana Dictionary*, p. 26, 1982

Colonel Blimp *noun*
1 a shrimp (seafood) *UK*
Rhyming slang, formed on the name of a character invented in the 1930s by cartoonist David Low and subsequently adopted as a conventional standard of bigotry and pompousness.
- —Ray Puxley, *Cockney Rabbit*, 1992

2 a very conservative, reactionary man *UK, 1934*
Often shortened to 'blimp'. From the cartoon character invented by British cartoonist David Low, 1891–1963, and brought to life by Welsh actor Roger Livesey, 1906–76, in the film *The Life and Death of Colonel Blimp*, 1943.
- I realized I was in serious danger of turning into one of the Colonel Blimp types who sat around me in considerable numbers[.] —Bill Bryson, *Notes from a Small Island*, p. 249, 1995

Colonel Gadaffi; colonel *noun*
a café *UK*
Rhyming slang, formed on the name of the Libyan leader Colonel Muammar al-Qaddafi (b.1942).
- —John Ayto, *The Oxford Dictionary of Rhyming Slang*, 2002

Colonel Klink *noun*
any high-ranking prison officer *US*
A reference to *Hogan's Heroes*, a popular television comedy of the late 1960s.
- —Gary K. Farlow, *Prison-ese*, p. 14, 2002

Colonel Prescott; colonel *noun*
a waistcoat *UK*
Rhyming slang, recorded by Julian Franklyn in 1960 but thought to date from the 1930s.

Colonel Sanders *noun*
a mature male homosexual who is especially attracted to boys or young men *US*
An allusion to the founder of the Kentucky Fried Chicken™ franchise.
- — *Maledicta*, p. 220, 1979: 'Kinks and queens: linguistic and cultural aspects of the terminology for gays'

color *noun*
1 in roller derby, any type of theatrics that would make the skater stand out to fans *US*
- — Keith Coppage, *Roller Derby to Rollerjam*, 1999

2 money *US*
- — Hyman E. Goldin et al., *Dictionary of American Underworld Lingo*, p. 47, 1950

3 in a casino, any betting token worth more than one dollar *US, 1977*
- — Thomas L. Clark, *The Dictionary of Gambling and Gaming*, p. 47, 1987

color *verb*
▸ **color it dos**
make that a double *US*
- — Anna Scotti and Paul Young, *Buzzwords: L.A. Freshspeak*, p. 57, 1997

colorado *noun*
1 cocaine
- — Mike Haskins, *Drugs*, p. 280, 2003

2 a red barbiturate capsule, especially if branded Seconal™ *US*
From Spanish *colorado* (the colour red). Often abbreviated to 'colie'.
- — Eugene Landy, *The Underground Dictionary*, p. 54, 1971
- — Richard A. Spears, *The Slang and Jargon of Drugs and Drink*, p. 117, 1986
- Got any colorados, chico? — Lois Stavsky et al., *A2Z*, p. 22, 1995

Colorado cocktail *noun*
marijuana *UK, 1998*
- — Mike Haskins, *Drugs*, p. 287, 2003

Colorado Kool Aid *noun*
Coors™ beer *US*
Brewed in Colorado, and for several decades not marketed nationally.
- "Oh, he'll drink that Colorado Kool-Aid," said Jim Tom "He don't like it any more than he likes gettin' fed and fucked before sundown." — Dan Jenkins, *Semi-Tough*, p. 24, 1972
- — Ellen C. Bellone (Editor), *Dictionary of Slang*, p. 7, 1989

colored people's time *noun*
used for denoting a lack of punctuality *US*
One of the very few instances in which the former ameliorative 'colored people' is still used in the US.
- Their lives run by a clock that keeps C.P.T., Colored People's Time, which assumes that appointments won't be kept, work promised won't be delivered, jobs found won't be gone to, since those are all part of the outside world. — Paul Jacobs, *Prelude to a Riot*, p. 12, 1967
- CPT – Colored Pepole's time (i.e., on time when they WANT to be, otherwse NOT). — *San Francisco Examiner*, p. 33, 9th May 1967
- I be trying to hook you up, mama. So cut all the hoorah, we wain't on colored people's time here. — Stephen Cannell, *Big Con*, p. 49, 1997
- "Well, now, I don' rightly know de answer to dat. Counselor Tubbs, he operates on C.P.T." Colored People's Time. — Tom Wolfe, *A Man in Full*, p. 21, 1998

colored showers *noun*
a sexual fetish involving urination on your partner *US*
- — J.R. Schwartz, *The Official Guide to the Best Cat Houses in Nevada*, p. 164, 1993

colored town *noun*
a neighbourhood with a large population of black people *US*
- Colored town. It's on fire. — Jim Thompson, *Pop. 1280*, p. 150, 1964

color for color *adverb*
in American casinos, the method of paying bets – one denomination at a time *US*
- — Lee Solkey, *Dummy Up and Deal*, p. 110, 1980

color me *verb*
used ironically in conjunction with an adjective for describing a personal condition *US, 1962*
- Color me Naive. — Erma Brombeck, *At Wit's End*, p. 121, 1967
- — Connie Eble (Editor), *UNC-CH Campus Slang*, p. 2, Spring 1980
- HEATHER CHANDLER: Grow up, Heather. Bulimia's so '86. HEATHER MCNAMARA: Color me nauseous. — *Heathers*, 1988
- What the hell. Color me stupid. — Charles W. Sasser, *Raidre*, p. 45, 2002

colors *noun*
1 insignia that indentify group membership, especially in motorcyle gangs *US*
- All that remained was the gathering of any loose money or marijuana that might be lying around, lashing the sleeping bags to the bikes and donning the infamous "colors." The all-important colors ... the uniform as it were, the crucial idenity[.] — Hunter S. Thompson, *Hell's Angels*, p. 8, 1966
- We got to play out of town twice, once in an ex-biker club in Sacramento that thrilled me by making me take off my Harley Wings because they were "colors"[.] — Jennifer Blowdryer, *White Trash Debutante*, p. 78, 1997

2 the coloured clothing worn as a signal of gang affiliation *US*
- So we pulled off our jackets and showed them our colors[.] — Terry Williams, *The Cocaine Kids*, p. 60, 1989

color-struck *adjective*
overly conscious of skin colour *US*
- I ain't got nothin' against dark-skin girls. I ain't never been color struck, and I never try to let none-a my chillun be color struck. — Claude Brown, *Manchild in the Promised Land*, p. 133, 1965
- You just color-struck, that's why you givin' your money to a white man[.] — Nathan Heard, *Howard Street*, p. 143, 1968
- Either you want a black man, or it's really true that you done got color-struck and you won't be satisfied unless you get your own white owl. — Donald Goines, *Whoreson*, p. 260, 1972

color up *verb*
in casino gambling, to trade chips of one denomination for chips of a higher denomination *US*
- — Michael Dalton, *Blackjack*, p. 39, 1991

colour *noun*
an Aboriginal Australian *AUSTRALIA*
- I brought the subject back to Australia, intending to rhapsodize about the wonderful skies and landscapes. "The colours there are so..." "You mean the Aborigines. Ugh!" interrupted Martin. — Kitty Churchill, *Thinking of England*, p. 137, 1995

colourful *adjective*
(of language) robust and lively, some may say offensive *UK*
- [A]n old soldier [...] abuses the French in the most colourful language when he hears that Bonaparte means to march on Moscow[.] — Leo Tolstoy translated by Rosemary Edmunds, *War and Peace*, p. 885, 1957
- One speaker who became renowned for his "colourful language" (as it was officially described in parliamentary records) was [Australian] Prime Minister Paul Keating. — Adrian Beard, *The Language of Politics*, p. 110, 2000
- For a Foreign Office mandarin, it was unusually colourful language [...] Edward Clay, the high commissioner [to Kenya], told his audience that ministers "could hardly expect us not to care when their gluttony causes them to vomit all over our shoes". — *The Guardian*, 16th July 2004

colour of his eyes *noun*
the size of the penis *UK*
Rhyming slang for 'size'.
- — Paul Baker, *Polari*, p. 169, 2002

Columbia clutch *noun*
an overdrive gear *US*
- He had twin pots and a Columbia clutch / An' speed that no other car could touch / An' to you folks who don't dig the jive / That's two carburetors and an overdrive. — George Wilson (performed by Bob Williams), *Hot Rod Race*, 1960

Columbian *noun*
marijuana *US, 1971*
A misspelling of **COLOMBIAN**, also seen as 'Columbian red', 'Columbian gold', etc.
- — Richard A. Spears, *The Slang and Jargon of Drugs and Drink*, p. 117, 1986
- — Mike Haskins, *Drugs*, p. 287, 2003

Columbus black *noun*
marijuana claimed to originate in Columbus, Ohio *US, 1982*
- — Richard A. Spears, *The Slang and Jargon of Drugs and Drink*, p. 117, 1986
- — Mike Haskins, *Drugs*, p. 287, 2003

Columbus Circles *noun*
dark circles beneath an actor's eyes *US*
- — Wilfred Granville, *The Theater Dictionary*, p. 14, 1952

com *noun*
a safe or vault's combination *US*
- —Vincent J. Monteleone, *Criminal Slang*, p. 55, 1949

Coma *noun*
▸ **the Coma off Point Loma**
the 1988 World's Cup, in which Team Dennis Connor sailing a catamaran enjoyed large leads over, and defeated, New Zealand *US, 1988*

combat fishing *noun*
sport fishing at a crowded fishing spot *US*
- —Mike Doogan, *How to Speak Alaskan*, p. 22, 1993

combat-happy *adjective*
deranged by the horrors of combat *US, 1962*
- And Leo's Duvall-like portrayal, though sometimes over the top, is an interesting study of a combat-happy maniac whose unstable emotional state is exacerbated when he's given virtual carte blanche to kill in the name of his country. —*Denver (Colorado) Westword*, 26th November 1998

combat jack *noun*
an act of masturbation by a combat soldier to relieve the tension or boredom of combat *US*
- After surviving their first ambush at Al Gharraf, a couple of Marines even admitted to an almost frenzied need to get off combat jacks. —*Rolling Stone*, 24th July 2003

combat professor *noun*
in Vietnam, an American military advisor *US*
Faint praise.
- —Linda Reinberg, *In the Field*, p. 47, 1991

combats *noun*
fashionable trousers with a military design
An abbreviation of 'combat trousers'.
- [G]ot to please the little twats in combats and daps[.] —James Hawes, *Dead Long Enough*, p. 44, 2000

Combat Zone *nickname*
an unsavory area in downtown Boston, dominated by sex shops, bars and drug dealers *US, 1971*
- Get-down time in the Combat Zone and Inez was waiting to draw first blood. —John Sayles, *Union Dues*, p. 180, 1977
- —Laurence Urdang, *Names and Nicknames of Places and Things*, p. 68, 1987
- The wheelchair-bound friends and the then teenaged boys ended up at a girlie show in the Combat Zone. —*Boston Herald*, p. 23, 13th January 2004

comber *noun*
a large wave that breaks on a reef or a beach *US*
- —Gary Fairmont R. Filosa II, *The Surfer's Almanac*, p. 183, 1977

combine harvester *noun*
a class 9 goods locomotive *UK*
- —Harvey Sheppard, *A Dictionary of Railway Slang*, 1970

combo *noun*
1 a combination of anything physical or abstract *US, 1921*
- —*American Speech*, p. 78–79, February 1962
- [H]e reaches over to Edward with the cup an' saucer combo an' y'can't so much as hear a rattle. —Nick Barlay, *Curvy Lovebox*, p. 72, 1997
- I just told you, she's half Asian, half American. They're all good looking. You could mate Don Rickles and Yoko Ono and they're going to have a gorgeous kid. It's a foolproof combo. —*Something About Mary*, 1998
- There's the clit moan (a soft, in-the-mouth sound), the vaginal moan (a deep in-the-throat sound), the combo clit-vaginal moan. —Eve Ensler, *The Vagina Monologues*, p. 110, 1998

2 a white man who cohabits with an Aboriginal woman *AUSTRALIA, 1896*
A term of derision. From 'combination', as they combine both black and white.
- A 'Combo' is a degenerate white and so on. The north has its own vocabulary. —Patsy Adam-Smith, *Folklore of the Australian Railwaymen*, p. 279, 1969
- —Jim Ramsay, *Cop It Sweet!*, p. 24, 1977

3 a small jazz band *US, 1924*
- —*American Speech*, p. 78–79, February 1962
- Some skinny joker with scald burns on his face was fronting a combo. —Iceberg Slim (Robert Beck), *Pimp*, p. 95, 1969

4 in pool, a combination shot, or one in which the cue ball is shot into a numbered ball that then hits the object ball *US*
- Balls shot in combination are preceded by the call of "combo," much the same as a basketball player cries "glass" to acknowledge that he intends to make his shot off the backboard. —Steve Rushin, *Pool Cool*, p. 10, 1990

5 a combination lock *UK*
- —Angela Devlin, *Prison Patter*, p. 39, 1996

combo *adverb*
▸ **go combo**
of a white man, to live with an Aboriginal woman *AUSTRALIA, 1896*
- —Sidney J. Baker, *The Drum*, 1959

combol *noun*
cocaine *UK*
- —Mike Haskins, *Drugs*, p. 280, 2003

comb-over *noun*
a male hairstyle in which a few long strands grown on one side of the head are contrived to cover a bald pate *UK*
- Bobby Charlton's infamous comb-over hairstyle has been named as "the worst hairstyle in history", according to a survey published today. —*The Guardian*, 3rd December 2002

combusse *noun*
a married man's lover *TRINIDAD AND TOBAGO*
Winer theorises that she '*comes bust* up the marriage'.
- —Lise Winer, *Dictionary of the English/Creole of Trinidad & Tobago*, 2003

come; cum *noun*
1 semen *US, 1923*
- —Donald Webster Cory and John P. LeRoy, *The Homosexual and His Society*, p. 263, 1963: 'A lexicon of homosexual slang'
- "Well, dammit, it was full of his come!" she retorted with an indignant toss of her head. —Nathan Heard, *Howard Street*, p. 20, 1968
- Help! I'm a prisoner in a cum-stained comic! —*Screw*, p. 5, 19th March 1971
- His rich rich come made the bitch's body numb / And the whore went blind in both eyes. —Dennis Wepman et al., *The Life*, p. 111, 1976
- Jim feels the other's warm cum on his stomach, and his own cock stretches[.] —John Rechy, *The Sexual Outlaw*, p. 32, 1977
- He saw the Jimi poster in my room and goes, 'That nigger looks like he's got a mouth full of cum.' —Francesca Lia Block, *Baby Be-Bop*, p. 391, 1995
- I touch her pussy now, the dry hair. My sperm dry on it. Little streaks of dry cum. —Clarence Major, *All-Night Visitors*, p. 4, 1998
- I pulls out and stands back. Two strong jets of cum, one after another, right into her face. —Kevin Sampson, *Outlaws*, p. 117–118, 2001

2 an orgasm *US, 1967*
From the verb sense (to experience an orgasm).
- [In Cairo, 1992] the price was about 50 piastres (8p) for one come whether you took a minute or hours. —Fiona Pitt-Kethley, *Red Light Districts of the World*, p. 42, 2000

▷ **see:** COME AND GO

come; cum *verb*
1 to experience an orgasm *UK, 1600*
- In a jiff I was in; but for some strange reason I couldn't come; all 19-year-old cockmasters can't come, you know this as well as I do. —Jack Kerouac, *Letter to Neal Cassady*, p. 299, 10th January 1951
- "Who's talking about 'go?" demanded Liv. "The girls want to come! Am I right, Can?" —Terry Southern, *Candy*, p. 49, 1958
- You're doing this just to give me the pleasure of coming, you're so kind. —Jack Kerouac, *The Subterraneans*, p. 47, 1958
- "You came, Boston," he remarked with the air of a satisfied instructor. —Mary McCarthy, *The Group*, p. 37, 1963
- Tom licked every inch of Johnny's body, and Johnny came in his mouth – sometimes several times a day. —John Rechy, *Numbers*, p. 32, 1967
- He was afraid she would come too soon; he was afraid he might come too soon. —Cecil Brown, *The Life & Loves of Mr. Jiveass Nigger*, p. 75, 1969
- That's some chick, coming under these kinda conditions. —*Saturday Night Fever*, 1977
- "I can come eighteen times in one day, easily," Levenson bragged to Al while visiting the Screw executive offices. —Josh Alan Friedman, *Tales of Times Square*, p. 98, 1986
- He reached under the covers and touched his groin. Maybe if he came he wouldn't need to cry. —Francesca Lia Block, *I Was a Teenage Fairy*, p. 97, 1998
- Fuck that, I didn't get to cum yet. —Kevin Smith, *Jay and Silent Bob Strike Back*, p. 94, 2001

2 to yield to bribery or persuasion *UK*
- —G.F. Newman, *Sir, You Bastard*, 1970

3 to behave in a specified way *UK, 1837*
- Don't change your mind, don't come all orchid eyes; don't change your mind, don't disguise the fear you feel[.] — Peter Hammill, *Rubicon*, 1972

▸ come a cropper
to fall heavily; to be the victim of an accident *UK*
From hunting jargon, 'a cropper' (a fall).
- [T]he law of averages says the more fights you have, the chance of you coming a cropper increases. — Dave Courtney, *Stop the Ride I Want to Get Off*, p. 225, 1999

▸ come a tumble
to detect something, to fathom something, to understand something *UK*
Rhyming slang for **RUMBLE**.
- If your boss comes a tumble he'll march you straight down the nick. — Ray Puxley, *Cockney Rabbit*, 1992

▸ come big
(of a bettor in horse racing) to bet more than usual on a race *AUSTRALIA*
- — Ned Wallish, *The Truth Dictionary of Racing Slang*, p. 16, 1989

▸ come down like trained pigs
in horse racing, to finish a race exactly as predicted *US*
- — David W. Maurer, *Argot of the Racetrack*, p. 21, 1951

▸ come from
to emanate from; to expose the philosophical basis for a statement or action *US*
Another vague term of the 1960s.
- If you can check where I'm coming from, I'm talking about the class struggle. — Bobby Seale, *A Lonely Rage*, p. 295, 1978

▸ come high or come low
no matter what *TRINIDAD AND TOBAGO*
- — Lise Winer, *Dictionary of the English/Creole of Trinidad & Tobago*, 2003

▸ come home
(of the effects of LSD) to dwindle, diminish and vanish *US*
- — Jim Crotty, *How to Talk American*, p. 87, 1997

▸ come home early
in horse racing, to establish and hold an early lead to win a race *US*
- — David W. Maurer, *Argot of the Racetrack*, p. 21, 1951

▸ come hot
in a confidence swindle, to complete the swindle which the victim immediately understands to have been a swindle *US*
- — M. Allen Henderson, *How Con Games Work*, p. 218, 1985

▸ come like salt
to be in great abundance *TRINIDAD AND TOBAGO*
- — Lise Winer, *Dictionary of the English/Creole of Trinidad & Tobago*, 2003

▸ come over all peculiar
to feel suddenly physically indisposed or emotionally upset *UK*
A later variant of **COME OVER ALL QUEER**, avoiding the ambiguous and politically incorrect **QUEER** (unwell/homosexual).
- The contribution of these two to April Fools' Day was to stage a dance routine in one of their shows during which Dec came over all peculiar and passed out on the floor. — *Evening Standard (London)*, 2nd April 2003

▸ come over all queer
to feel suddenly physically indisposed or emotionally upset *UK, 1937*
- [O]wners who come over all queer at the sight of someone in a camouflage jachet are gradually becoming the minority. — *The Scotsman*, 31st July 2004

▸ come over all unnecessary; go all unnecessary
to become sexually excited *UK, 1984*
- The Bride Stripped Bare might sound like the sort of novel to make a chap come over all unnecessary[.] — *The Times*, 2nd July 2003

▸ come sick
to experience the bleed period of the menstrual cycle *US, 1948*
- — Frederic G. Cassidy, *Dictionary of American Regional English, Volume 1*, p. 737, 1985

▸ come the acid; come the old acid; come the old acid drop
to be heavily sarcastic or especially impudent *UK, 1962*
From **ACID** (sarcasm).
- Tried to come the old acid wiv me. — Viv Stanshall, *Ginger Geezer*, 1981

▸ come the bludge on
to sponge upon someone *AUSTRALIA*
From **BLUDGE** (to cadge).
- What's the big idea, coming to bludge on us? — D'Arcy Niland, *Call Me...*, 1958

▸ come the cunt; come the old cunt
to be particularly obstreperous or unpleasant *UK*
From **CUNT** (an unpleasant or despicable person).
- "Don't come the cunt with me, mate!" uttered as a threat. — Beale, 1984

▸ come the old soldier
1 to wheedle, to impose on someone *UK, 1818*
Of military origin.
- If your builder's trying to come the old soldier and kid you up that the garage he's building is just like the swimming pool you ordered, your arquitecto's on hand to say oi, get your finger out.. — *buyaspanishhome.com*, 26th June 2003

2 to hector someone, to domineer someone by virtue of supposed greater knowledge *UK, 1984*
Deriving from the likely behaviour of the longest-serving soldier in the barracks.
- I don't want to come the old-soldier-back-from-the-wars here, but I am certain that if Tony Blair went out and smelt the burning carcasses – and the despair – he would instantly reach the same conclusion. — *The Guardian*, 20th March 2001

▸ come the raw prawn
1 to try to deceive someone or impose upon them *AUSTRALIA, 1942*
A raw prawn is hard to swallow.
- Now look here Eric don't come the raw prawn with me. — Barry Humphries, *Bazza Pulls It Off!*, 1971

2 to behave in a recalcitrant manner *UK, 1979*
Heard among Irish labourers.

▸ come the tin man
to bluff; to make yourself a nuisance *UK, 1962*

▸ come the tin soldier; come the old tin soldier
to be impertinent or obstructive *UK*
An elaboration and slight shift in sense from **COME THE OLD SOLDIER**.
- [D]on't come the old tin soldier with me! — David Powis, *The Signs of Crime*, 1977

▸ come to grief
1 to get into serious trouble; to fail *UK, 1850*
- I used to tell people in the 60s and 70s – a long, long time ago – that the Soviet Union will come to grief[.] — M. Job, *Trinidad and Tobago Parliament (Hansard)*, 15th October 1999

2 to take a tumble; to have a fall *UK, 1854*
Usually sporting. Novelist and former jockey Dick Francis, puns both senses in the book title *Come to Grief*, 1995.

▸ come your lot
to experience an orgasm *UK*
An elaboration of **COME**.
- I got the feeling that he was coming his lot in his trousers. — John Peter Jones, *Feather Pluckers*, p. 150, 1964

▸ come your mutton
(of a male) to masturbate *UK, 1961*

▸ come your turkey
(of a male), to masturbate *UK, 1961*

come across *verb*
1 (generally of a woman) to take part in sexual intercourse *AUSTRALIA*
- [B]ecause he's bought you three meat pies, and two seats at the movies, and you haven't come across, you're suddenly a waste of time. — Sue Rhodes, *Now you'll think I'm awful*, p. 98, 1967
- By cripes if she doesn't come across after the show tonight the Pope's a Jew. — Barry Humphries, *The Wonderful World of Barry McKenzie*, p. 19, 1968
- Starve the lizards! No doubt about you sheilas. I mean, one minute you're coming across, now you're not! — *The Adventures of Barry McKenzie*, 1972
- 'I have a job for you.... Will you come across?' 'Don't I always?' — *Kings Cross Venus*, p. 20, 1st November 1972

2 to have sex as the result of persuasive insistence *US, 1921*
- He had gone dancing there a week ago, picked up a dame, shot her a line, and she had come across. — James T. Farrell, *The Life Adventure*, p. 182, 1947

- "Yeah," another one agreed, "a babe would have to come across to ride in that car with me." —Irving Shulman, *The Amboy Dukes*, p. 52, 1947
- Jazz groupies in those days came across as weird but did not necessarily come across. —Larry Rivers, *What Did I Do?*, p. 50, 1992
- [I]f Mel hadn't of come across with the goods when she did[.] —Danny King, *The Burglar Diaries*, p. 29, 2001

3 to agree to become an informer *US*
- You'd better realize that if you come across, you've got to come across all the way; we don't want to hear anything from you that isn't true just because you think we'd like to hear it. —Leonard Shecter and William Phillips, *On the Pad*, p. 50, 1973

4 to give the appearance of having a specified characteristic *UK*
- [H]e always come across like he was half-bevvied [drunk]. —Kevin Sampson, *Clubland*, p. 112, 2002

come again?

please repeat or restate what you just said *US*
- —Clarence Major, *Dictionary of Afro-American Slang*, p. 39, 1970

come-along; cum-along *noun*

a wire grip used for holding wire or conductor under strain *US, 1944*
- —A.B. Chance Co., *Lineman's Slang Dictionary*, p. 5, 1980

come and go; come *noun*

snow *UK*

Rhyming slang, which extends as verb and adjective: 'coming and going' (snowing).
- —Ray Puxley, *Cockney Rabbit*, 1992

comeback *noun*

1 a return to a formerly successful status *US, 1908*
- Shane Warne, who has 366 victims, could make a come back for Victoria in a one-day match in Perth tomorrow, more than two months after breaking his spinning finger. —*The Guardian*, 1st January 2001
- Suddenly, the paper [Daily Mail] says, the kind of rhetoric and wrecking tactics once thought banished for good by Margaret Thatcher's hard-won union reforms are making a come-back. —*BBC News*, 2nd December 2002

2 a repercussion; repercussions *UK, 1894*
- [S]uffer absolutely no come-back for it whatsoever[.] —Danny King, *The Burglar Diaries*, p. 206, 2001

3 revenge *US*
- —*American Speech*, p. 306, December 1964: 'Lingua cosa nostra'

4 a return call on a citizens' band radio *US*
- —Wayne Floyd, *Jason's Authentic Dictionary of CB Slang*, p. 13, 1976

5 a boomerang *AUSTRALIA, 1878*

6 an adulterant used to dilute crack cocaine *US*

A chemical that when baked looks, smells and tastes like **CRACK**.
- Max's recipe calls for an "eighth" of cocaine (1/8 kilo, or 125 grams), 60 grams of bicarbonate of soda (ordinary baking soda) and 40 grams of "comeback," an adulterant that has allowed Max to double his profits from crack. —Terry Williams, *The Cocaine Kids*, p. 17, 1989
- And like you Gee Money I have also been doing some experimenting and discovered by cutting the caine with comeback we make more product not less. —*New Jack City*, 1990

come back *verb*

1 to reply *US, 1896*
- Even today in question period, we asked questions about change in a nice way. The government House leader came back with a smart aleck answer[.] —John Reynolds, *Parliament of Canada (Hansard)*, 1st February 2002

2 to reply to a citizens' band radio broadcast *US, 1976*
- Breaker asking for a copy you've got the Gooseman here. Come back. —Peter Chippindale, *The British CB Book*, p. 16, 1981
- From the opening whistle, he'd be as mad as a redneck truckdriver who'd heard a fag come back on his CB. —Dan Jenkins, *Life Its Ownself*, p. 18, 1984

3 to retract something, to take something back, especially to apologetically cancel a previous remark *AUSTRALIA*
- Now I've put my foot in it – skin deep. Come back all I said. —Vance Palmer, *Seedtime*, 1957

comeback kid *noun*

a thief who breaks into a hotel room where he has previously stayed, using a key he failed to return *US*
- A combeback kid was a room-rifler who operated by the simple procedure of checking in and checking right out again the next day but "forgetting" to turn in the room key when he left. —Dev Collans with Stewart Sterling, *I was a House Detective*, p. 11, 1954

come-back money *noun*

in horse racing, money from off-track betting operations that is wired to a race track just before a race *US*
- —David W. Maurer, *Argot of the Racetrack*, p. 21, 1951

come chugger *noun*

a person who performs oral sex on men *US*
- He's not a fudgepacker. Cum chugger yes, but not a fudgepacker. —*Cruel Intentions*, 1999

come clean *verb*

to tell the truth, to confess *US, 1919*
- —Angela Devlin, *Prison Patter*, p. 39, 1996

come day, go day; come day, go day, God send Sunday *adjective*

laid back, unruffled *US, 1918*
- "Come day, go day, God send Sunday" is more the motto of the free and go-easy life of the Boyds. —Edward L. Ayers, *Southern Crossing*, p. 19, 1995

comedown *noun*

1 a person, thing or event that dampens your spirits or depresses you *US*
- Well, this is really a comedown. —John Clellon Holmes, *Go*, p. 143, 1952

2 a period during which the diminishing sensations of a drug are felt *UK, 1984*
- Lacking the harsh edge and crashing "come-downs" associated with stronger stimulants like speed or coke, acid's mild stimulant effect often lingers for a while after the psychedlic effects have dissipated. —Cam Cloud, *The Little Book of Acid*, p. 16, 1999

come down *verb*

1 to experience the easing of drug intoxication *US, 1959*
- —Burton H. Wolfe, *The Hippies*, p. 203, 1968
- —Angela Devlin, *Prison Patter*, p. 39, 1996
- You're high and you need to come down. Sleep it off, Dirk. —*Boogie Nights*, 1997

2 to arrive in prison *US*
- —Bruce Jackson, *Outside the Law*, p. 56, 1972
- You take a lot of guys that when they come down the first or second time to the penitentiary, they come down with a good reputation from the streets[.] —Bruce Jackson, *Outside the Law*, p. 170, 1972

3 (of a river) to flood; to be inundated *AUSTRALIA, 1868*

Many Australian rivers are mostly dry for a large part of the year and then fill, often quite suddenly, during the wet season.
- This was the last train to get over the Finke [river] for more than a week because it came down again almost immediately. —Patsy Adam-Smith, *Folklore of the Australian Railwaymen*, p. 39, 1969

come down!

in the sport of archery, used as an imperative to instruct a pupil to refrain from completing a shot *UK*
- —*Archery Today*, p. 149, 1988

come dumpster; cum dumpster *noun*

a promiscuous female *US*
- —Connie Eble (Editor), *UNC-CH Campus Slang*, p. 1, Spring 2001

come freak; cum freak *noun*

a person who is obsessed with sex *US, 1966*
- Maybe I'm turning into a come freak. —Malcolm Braly, *On the Yard*, p. 326, 1967
- —*Current Slang*, p. 19, Fall 1968
- A pimp does not want a promiscuous woman, a "come-freak," who "lives only on the physical plane." —Christina and Richard Milner, *Black Players*, p. 89, 1972
- Body have to be stuck with a mean case of horniness to even think about it in this weather, much less do anything about it. Have to be a stone come-freak. —John Sayles, *Union Dues*, p. 180, 1977

come-fuck-me *adjective*

sexually alluring *US*

An embellished **FUCK-ME**.
- Then Paco hears Cathy and Marty-boy leave her apartment (the two of them dressed for a hot day's traveling; Cathy in one of her famous low-cut, summery "come-fuck-me" dresses). —Larry Heinemann, *Paco's Story*, p. 187, 1986
- I buy a pair of shoes like Tiffany's – come-fuck-me shoes – with heels high as candy canes. —Cathi Hanauer, *My Sister's Bones*, p. 24, 1996
- Sharlene looked so good in that skintight jumpsuit and come-fuck-me boots. —Elizabeth Atkins Bowman, *Dark Secret*, p. 63, 2000
- Does Madonna walk around the house in cone bras and come-fuck-me bustiers? —Steven Pressfield, *The War of Art*, p. 86, 2002

- [T]he woman had looked away from her sketch long enough to favor him with a come-fuck-me stare so blatant it allowed for no other interpretation. — David Cray, *Partners*, p. 148, 2004

come gum; cum gum *noun*

chewing gum with a liquid centre *US*

- — *Maledicta*, p. 284, 1984–1985: 'Food names'

come-here *noun*

a person originally from outside a community *US*

- — Frederic G. Cassidy, *Dictionary of American Regional English, Volume 1*, p. 735, 1985

come-hither look *noun*

a flirtatious and inviting glance *UK, 1961*

- [W]ith a come-hither look, the adultress lures Papa away to leave Mum and the kids to look after themselves[.] — *The Guardian*, 25th August 2002

come-in *noun*

in a circus, the hour period before the performance, during which patrons are allowed to enter the big top *US*

- — Joe McKennon, *Circus Lingo*, p. 27, 1980

come in, Berlin

used as a humorous request that someone joins a conversation *US*

Often said with a melodramatic flourish, mimicking a military communication.

- — Connie Eble (Editor), *UNC-CH Campus Slang*, April 1978

come in if you're pretty

used in response to a knock on a dressing room door *UK*

Theatrical camp; certainly in use since the mid-1980s.

come in spinner!

1 in the gambling game two-up, used as a call signalling that all bets are laid and it is time to spin the coins *AUSTRALIA, 1943*

- The boxer calls, 'Come in, Spinner,' or sometimes, 'Fair go, Spinner.' — James Holledge, *The Great Australian Gamble*, p. 100, 1966
- I'd be too scared – that once again I might be caught by the heady excitement that goes with the boxer's call, 'Come in, spinner.' — James Holledge, *The Great Australian Gamble*, p. 104, 1966
- The keeper put the remainder in his pocket and said, 'Come in, spinner.' — John O'Grady, *It's Your Shout, Mate!*, p. 25, 1972

2 begin!, commence! *AUSTRALIA*

- 'Know the words?' He began to play. 'Yes. I know the words.' 'Come in, spinner.' — Nino Culotta (John O'Grady), *They're A Weird Mob*, p. 117, 1957
- — Jim Ramsay, *Cop It Sweet!*, p. 24, 1977

come it *verb*

1 to behave impudently *UK: SCOTLAND, 1934*

- Blimey – you do come it, don't you? — Anthony Masters, *Minder*, p. 12, 1984

2 to wheedle something, to impose something *UK, 1925*

Of military origins; a variation of **COME THE OLD SOLDIER**.

come-off *noun*

an event or result *US, 1887*

- By this time, the Hotsy Totsy Club "come off," as the hoodlum expression describes such unfortunate occurrences, was making both press and police forget the irritating lack of an arrested culprit[.] — Robert Sylvester, *No Cover Charge*, p. 16, 1956

come off *verb*

1 to happen, especially to happen successfully *UK, 1864*

- — John Ayto, *The Oxford Dictionary of Slang*, p. 410, 1998
- [S]ooner or later another attack will come off successfully. — *The Guardian*, 5th September 2003

2 to orgasm *UK, 1937*

A variation of **COME**.

3 to give the appearance of whatever characteristic is specified *US*

- I know I may come off quiet, may come off shy / But I feel like talking, feel like dancing when I see this guy — Britney Spears, *I 'm a Slave 4 U*, 2003

come off it!

don't exaggerate!; don't keep trying to fool me! *UK, 1912*

Elaborated from the earlier US usage: 'come off!' and phrases like 'come off your perch!' and 'come off the 'grass!'.

- Come off it, we all love Harry Potter. — *The Observer*, 2nd July 2000

come-on *noun*

1 a challenge to fight, often unspoken *UK*

- I was never involved in serious trouble – no heavy come ons – no fights. — Jamie Mandelkau, *Buttons*, p. 82, 1971

2 an invitation, especially unspoken and especially sexual *US, 1942*

- Can't a man say a woman is attractive without it being a come-on? — *When Harry Met Sally*, 1989
- She had the talent, she had the cool expression on her face, like a good stripper who doesn't overdo it, just gives you enough of a come-on. — Elmore Leonard, *Be Cool*, p. 53, 1999

3 an inducement *UK*

- the come-ons the industry intend. — Simon Napier-Bell, *Black Vinyl White Powder*, p. 206, 2001

come on *verb*

1 to demonstrate sexual interest *US, 1959*

- Now Johnny Rio is not coming on with this queen – although he spoke to her and winked. — John Rechy, *Numbers*, p. 69, 1967
- So you're coming on to me. — *When Harry Met Sally*, 1989
- This fucking pervert just came on to Nance! — *Something About Mary*, 1998
- Some of our customers – wealthy, older men – felt free to come on to us. — Kathryn Leigh Scott, *The Bunny Years*, p. 74, 1998
- But I saw her last week and she was coming on to me all over the place. — Kenneth Lonergan, *This is Our Youth*, p. 34, 2000

2 to commence the bleed period of the mentrual cycle *UK, 1984*

Euphemistic.

- Some bird come on all of a sudden. We had to send her 'ome cos the Tampax machine in the Ladies is fucked[.] — Garry Bushell, *The Face*, p. 39, 2001

3 (of drugs) to start having an effect *US, 1946*

- I make Koolaid that makes purple Owlsey come on like piss. — *Apocalypse Now*, 1979
- She hung out with me while I was coming on when I had been dosed by what I think was something apporaching 3500 mikese[.] — Stephen Gaskin, *Amazing Dope Tales*, p. 115, 1980

4 to give the appearance of whatever characteristic is specified *UK, 1942*

Originally used in jazz circles but exampled here as a song title and lyric by melodic heavy metal band Pretty Maids.

- — Pretty Maids, *Come On Tough, Come On Nasty*, 1992

come on snake, let's rattle!

let's dance! *US*

Teen slang.

- — *San Francisco News*, p. 6, 25th March 1958

come on worm, let's wiggle

let's dance *US*

- — *This Week Magazine, New York Herald Tribune*, p. 47, 28th February 1954

come out *verb*

1 to declare your homosexuality openly or publicly *US, 1941*

- Not all homosexuals are "gay." That term is applied especially to those who are just "coming out" or acknowledging their membership in a minority group. — Helen P. Branson, *Gay Bar*, p. 9, 1957
- — Donald Webster Cory and John P. LeRoy, *The Homosexual and His Society*, p. 263, 1963: 'A lexicon of homosexual slang'
- I was 16 when I really 'came out.' — Antony James, *America's Homosexual Underground*, p. 110, 1965
- I didn't come out until I left college. — Mart Crowley, *The Boys in the Band*, p. 37, 1968
- When we first "came out" we spent many happy and exciting times in gay bars from one coast to the other. — *Screw*, p. 8, 24th November 1969
- When any male anywhere "comes out" he is faced with the problem of where to find sex partners and/or lovers. — John Francis Hunter, *The Gay Insider*, p. 5–6, 1971

2 to declare or admit to a personal fact *UK, 2000*

- I have decided it's time to come out — Prime Minister Tony Blair, *confessing to needing reading glasses at the London Press Awards*, May 2001
- Now the phrase "come out" has become a piece of post-modern irony available to all. In an exemplary usage, the general secretary of the National Secular Society recently grumbled, "It's much easier for a member of parliament to come out as gay than come out as an athelst. — *The Guardian*, p. 23, 9th May 2001

3 to leave college or high school amateur athletics and sign a contract to play professionally *US*

- — *American Speech*, Winter 1990

4 to leave the bush to return to an urban or settled area *CANADA*

- [A]fterwards, when we had 'come out" and were in Toronto[.] — E. Gillis, *North Pole Boarding House*, p. 136, 1951

▸ come out of the closet
to declare your homosexuality openly or publicly *US*
- It took me almost fifty years to come out of the closet, to stop pretending to be something I was not [...] Anyway I'm out of the closet. Here I am. — Milton Merle, *On Being Different*, p. 98, 1971

come outside!; outside!
used as a challenge to fight *UK, 1984*
A shortening of any number of variations on 'Come outside and fight!'.

comer *noun*
a promising prospect *US, 1879*
- Bana was twenty-seven and a comer. His foot was on the ladder. — Robert Campbell, *Alice in La-La Land*, p. 195, 1987

come scab *noun*
a dried-on patch of semen on skin *UK*
- [E]xhaust-soot and dried sweat, come scabs [...] all down the plug an into the Mersey[.] — Niall Griffiths, *Kelly + Victor*, p. 186, 2002

come shot; cum shot *noun*
a scene in a pornographic film or a photograph of a man ejaculating *US*
- The film [Deep Throat] features a couple of ass-fucking sequences and three come shots, two in that wonderful mouth. — *Screw*, p. 21, 19th June 1972
- Among other things, he eliminated the external cum shot, in which an ejaculating male suddenly withdraws his member from whatever female orifice it happens to be in, and has his orgasm on the outside of the woman's body, preferably spraying her in the face[.] — George Paul Csicsery (Editor), *The Sex Industry*, p. 170, 1973
- A lot of it is faked, except the come-shots. (Quoting Harry Reems). — *Adam Film Quarterly*, p. 23, December 1975
- This shot is known as the "come shot." On a porno-movie set it is also referred to as the "money shot." — Stephen Ziplow, *The Film Maker's Guide to Pornography*, p. 78, 1977
- What you see now is the "cum shot," and it has become a big item in sexflicks. You can watch his jism jettison, and this removes all doubt that there is anything simulated about this sex scene. — *Adam Film World*, p. 58, 1977
- Bask and glow and then we get another cum shot on her ass, he's got both cum shots, he's got the money shots in this whole set-up now. — Robert Stoller and I.S. Levine, *Coming Attractions*, p. 30, 1991
- After one giant come-shot Emily put her tea down and took a deep breath and puffed out her cheeks and smiled. — Nicholson Baker, *Vox*, p. 115, 1992
- "You know what a cum shot is?" Sabrina said she did not. Erin explained. "Yukky." — Carl Hiaasen, *Strip Tease*, p. 335, 1993
- This film was released in 1966. Cum shots didn't appear in wide-screen close-up in commerical cinema until five years later. — Darius James, *That's Blaxploitation!*, p. 159, 1995
- What do you want to do about the come shot? We could go to the stock footage, get a close-up. — *Boogie Nights*, 1997
- ANA: DId you specifiy that you didn't want cum shots in the face? MARIAH: Yeah, I told them I didn't want it on my face. — Ana Loria, *1 2 3 Be A Porn Star!*, p. 54, 2000

come the revolution
at some unknown point in the future everything will change for the better, used as a catchphrase response to an unanswerable complaint, or as a vague, unmeant threat of revenge *US*
- When disputes erupted, "Come the revolution!" could mean "Later for that – much later." — Todd Gitlin, *The Sixties*, p. 346, 1987
- But the lawyers have not disappeared from either side. Nor, I suspect, will they ever, even come the revolution. — *The Guardian*, 10th May 2001

come the revolution you'll be first against the wall
used in complaint against any figure of authority *UK*
- You don't admit to anything you think you'll never fall / But come the revolution you'll be first against the wall. — Saxon, *Unleash the Beast*, 1997

come-through *noun*
in a big store confidence swindle, the stage when the victim learns that he has been swindled and goes after the swindlers *US*
- Dakota has to remain behind after we run so she can tell the tale to Tommy and control the 'come-through. — Stephen Cannell, *Big Con*, p. 193, 1997

come-to-bed-eyes *noun*
male or female eyes that offer a glimpse of sexual promise, allegedly *UK*
- — Roy Harper, *Come To Bed Eyes*, 1982

come to that!
in point of fact!; since you mention it! *UK, 1923*

come undone *verb*
in a literal and figurative sense: to fall to pieces; also, to meet with difficulties or disaster *UK, 1937*
- I'm contemplating, thinkin' about thinkin' / It's overrated, just get another drink and / Watch me come undone [...] Because I'm scum, and I'm your son / I come undone / I come undone — Robbie Williams, *I Come Undone*, 2002

come unstuck *verb*
in a literal and figurative sense: to fall pieces; also, to meet with difficulties or disaster *UK, 1928*
Earlier variations are 'come unput' and **COME UNDONE**. All have the sense 'to fall apart'.
- [T]he fencing [a trade in stolen goods] came unstuck[.] — Derek Raymond (Robin Cook), *The Crust on its Uppers*, p. 42, 1962
- [T]his bet that their values would fall came unstuck as the bonds soared to their highest values for 40 years. — *The Guardian*, 14th December 2002

come-up *noun*
a robbery *US*
- In two expletive-laced calls to friends Jan. 5, two days after his arrest, Rawls admitted he knew Ramirez was planning a "come up," which is street slang for a robbery. — *The Oregonian*, p. B2, 10th November 2003

come up *verb*
1 (of drugs) to start having an effect *UK*
A variation of the earlier **COME ON**.
- [J]ust dropped a tab. Should be coming up nicely in a moment[.] — Nicholas Blincoe, *Ardwick Green (Disco Biscuits)*, p. 11, 1996
- [W]e're sort of staring at each other and coming up SO massively we had to go and sit down[.] — Ben Malbon, *Cool Places*, p. 272, 1998
- I had an E with ketamine in it. I came up in three minutes[.] — *Mixmag*, p. 89, February 2002

2 to grow up; to be raised *US*
- The reason I tell you all I do is because when I was coming up I didn't have my father around to tell me things. — *Boyz N The Hood*, 1990

3 of a racehorse (that has been bet on), to win *UK, 1937*

▸ come up trumps
to succeed; to turn out well *UK*
An image of card playing.
- If that slippery no-mark comes up trumps, I'll kiss his fat head and that's the God's honest truth. — Kevin Sampson, *Outlaws*, p. 205, 2001

come up on *verb*
to have a win on a lottery, or football pool, or the like *UK, 1984*
- Daddy screamed with joy. He told us that he had 'come up on the football pools'. — Cosette Allisopp, *Both Sides of the River*, 2002

comfort lady *noun*
a prostitute *US*
- Comfort Ladies are mostly in their thirties, short stout and ugly. — Fiona Pitt-Kethley, *Red Light Districts of the World*, p. 84, 2000

comfy *adjective*
comfortable *UK, 1829*
- His voice in the dark, breathing on her, said, "You comfy?" — Elmore Leonard, *Out of Sight*, p. 40, 1996

comfy wing *noun*
in prison, the enhanced wing for prisoners who have earned the privilege of greater comfort *UK*
From **COMFY** (comfortable).
- There's no danger of confrontation when Bob lands on the comfy wing. — Erwin James, *The Guardian*, 17th February 2000

comical *adjective*
used as a humorous synonym for 'chemical' *US*
- — Carl Fleischhauer, *A Glossary of Army Slang*, p. 10, 1968

comical Chris *noun*
an act of urination *UK*
Rhyming slang for **PISS**.
- — Red Daniells, 1980

comic book *noun*
a truck driver's daily log book *US*
A reflection of the degree of attention given to the log book by some drivers.
- — Wayne Floyd, *Jason's Authentic Dictionary of CB Slang*, p. 13, 1976

comic cuts *noun*

the guts *AUSTRALIA, 1945*

Rhyming slang.

- —Frank Hardy, *The Yarns of Billy Borker*, p. 122, 1965
- Tom kept shovelling food into his jaws and beaming, voicing often his pleased surprise concerning the disappearance of his obscure 'trouble in the comic cuts'. —Geoff Wyatt, *Saltwater Saints*, p. 34, 1969
- —Frank Hardy, *The Outcasts of Foolgarah*, p. 76, 1971
- —Jim Ramsay, *Cop It Sweet!*, p. 24, 1977
- —Ryan Aven-Bray, *Ridgey Didge Oz Jack Lang*, p. 21, 1983

comics *noun*

1 the testicles *UK*

A shortening of 'comic cuts' rhyming slang for **NUTS**.

- —Ray Puxley, *Cockney Rabbit*, p. 40, 1992

2 topographical maps *US*

Cynical Vietnam war usage.

- —Linda Reinberg, *In the Field*, p. 48, 1991

3 weekly motorcycle newspapers and magazines *UK*

- —Douglas Dunford, *Motorcycle Department, Beaulieu Motor Museum*, 1979

comic strip *noun*

a person with many tattoos *US*

- —*Los Angeles Times Magazine*, p. 7, 13th July 1997

coming down!; coming through!

used as a warning by a surfer to other surfers that he is starting a ride on a wave *US*

- —Trevor Cralle, *The Surfin'ary*, p. 23, 1991

coming out party *noun*

discharge from prison *US*

- —Marlene Freedman, *Alcatraz*, 1983

comings *noun*

semen *UK, 1961*

From **COME** (to orgasm).

comm *noun*

a commission *AUSTRALIA*

- —Ned Wallish, *The Truth Dictionary of Racing Slang*, p. 17, 1989

commando *noun*

a person with rough sexual tastes *US*

- —Roger Blake, *The American Dictionary of Sexual Terms*, p. 43, 1964

▸ **go commando**

to wear no underwear *US*

Commandos are always ready for action.

- JULIE BRADLEY: Do you approve of girls going commando? Philip OLIVER: No knickers? Definitely. —*Sky Magazine*, p. 83, July 2001
- Knowing her daughter's penchant for going commando, the first thing she did was whip off her pants for Letitia to wear while she was examined. —*Ariel*, 12th August 2003

commercial *noun*

1 a male homosexual prostitute *US*

- Commerical – One who is a male prostitute, whether brazenly or discreetly, homosexual or not. —Anon., *The Gay Girl's Guide*, p. 5, 1949
- —Guy Strait, *The Lavendar Lexicon*, 1964

2 a sex scene in a pornographic film *US*

An intentionally misleading term which makes a public discussion about the production of pornography possible without offending those nearby.

- —*Adult Video News*, p. 42, August 1995

commercial highway engineer *noun*

a truck driver *US*

A humorous glamourisation of the job.

- —Montie Tak, *Truck Talk*, p. 44, 1971

commercial traveler *noun*

a ram that escapes its paddock *NEW ZEALAND*

- Dry humour runs thick through this collection; for example commercial traveler – a ram that jumps the fence into a neighbouring paddock; to put into neutral – to castrate male lambs or calves; career girl – a ewe that refuses to mother her lamb; double-yolker – a ewe carrying twins; body-snatcher – a stock buyer. —*Dominion Post*, p. C6, 22nd November 2002

commercial traveller *noun*

a person with bags under his eyes *UK, 1961*

From a music-hall joke current in the 1930s.

commie *noun*

1 a Communist, literally or approximately *US, 1939*

- I had one, good, efficient, enjoyable way of getting rid of cancerous Commies. I killed them. —Mickey Spillane, *One Lonely Night*, p. 175, 1951
- Not all who reside in Georgetown are rich, red or queer, nor do all Washington millionaires, Commies and/or fags dwell in Georgetown. —Jack Lait and Lee Mortimer, *Washington Confidential*, p. 8, 1951
- [T]his slush [counterfeit money] is from the commies and their agent [...] This is commie shock tactics. —Derek Raymond (Robin Cook), *The Crust on its Uppers*, p. 53, 1962
- Now there are no more dirty Japs; there are dirty Commies! —Lenny Bruce, *How to Talk Dirty and Influence People*, p. 17, 1965
- They call us "scum-bags" and "fairies" and "Jew-bastards" and "commies". —Abbie Hoffman, *Revolution for the Hell of It*, p. 49, 1968
- Since that exchange, Myra Breckinridge has been thought by some to be a Commie, not the worst thing to be known as at the Academy[.] —Gore Vidal, *Myra Breckinridge*, p. 41, 1968
- Aunt Sadie, long hair is a commie plot! Long hair gets people uptight – more uptight than ideology, cause long hair is communication. —Jerry Rubin, *Do It!*, p. 93, 1970
- She's a Commie pig. —*Harold and Maude*, 1971
- All free? Free my ass. What are you, a fucking commie? —*Repo Man*, 1984
- I'm Jack Malone, and you look like a Commie. —*The Guardian*, 19th May 2001

2 a computer *UK*

- —Angela Devlin, *Prison Patter*, p. 39, 1996

commish *noun*

1 a *commiss*ion, a percentage on sales *US, 1862*

- They find some mug punter eager to make a quick commish [...] then stitch him up. —Andrew Nickolds, *Back to Basics*, p. 97, 1994

2 a *Commiss*ioner *US, 1910*

- "Commish," he pleaded, "don't get us wrong.["] —Harry J. Anslinger, *The Murderers*, p. 101, 1961

commo *noun*

1 a Communist *AUSTRALIA*

- —*The Daily Express*, 20th December 1946
- The boss plays one group against another and one teacher against another and he's got a bee in his bonnet about discipline and Commos. —Michael Peters, *Pommie Bastard*, p. 58, 1969
- She came to a bad end and joined the Commos. —Dorothy Hewett, *The Chapel Perilous*, p. 66, 1972
- You rotten, bloody, poofter, commo, mongrel bastard. —Bill Hornadge, *The Ugly Australian*, p. 113, 1973
- I'm not a Commo but my favourite hobby / Is fart-arsing around with the environment lobby. — Barry Humphries, *Les Patterson's Australia*, p. 61, 1978
- —David McGill, *David McGill's Complete Kiwi Slang Dictionary*, p. 30, 1998

2 a military radio; communications *US, 1964*

- "While we were on the attack my commo (radio) went out," said one solider to a center observer. "Then by a miracle, I got my commo back." —*Houston Chronicle*, p. 4A, 20th March 1989

3 purchases from a prison shop *US*

- —Jay Robert Nash, *Dictionary of Crime*, p. 74, 1992

commo *adjective*

Communist *UK, 1942*

- It wasn't the financiers that stopped this country from going commo: it was the courage and guts of the battler. —Patsy Adam-Smith, *Folklore of the Australian Railwaymen*, p. 188, 1969
- —Frank Hardy, *The Outcasts of Foolgarah*, p. 26, 1971

commodore *noun*

the sum of fifteen pounds (£15) *UK*

Extended from rhyming slang **LADY**; **LADY GODIVA** (a **FIVER**, £5) – via the song 'Three Times a Lady', by the Commodores, 1978.

- —Chris Roberts, *Heavy Words Lightly Thrown*, 2003

common *noun*

common sense *UK, 1936*

A familiar form in the 1950s and 60s, especially as 'a bit of common', now rare.

common *adjective*

▸ **as common as cat shit and twice as nasty**

extremely ordinary; very cheap and nasty; morally or socially beneath you *UK*

Noted by Julian Franklyn in 1968.

common dog *noun*

common sense *UK*

Military.

- —Nigel Foster, *The Making of a Royal Marine Commando*, 1987

commo wire *noun*

electrical wire used for a wide variety of tasks *US*

- Jones (Jonesy for short, James) had thirty-nine pairs of blackened, leathery, wrinkly ears strung on a bit of black commo wire and wrapped like a garland around that bit of turned-out brim of his steel hat.—Larry Heinemann, *Paco's Story*, p. 7, 1986
- —Gregory Clark, *Words of the Vietnam War*, p. 118, 1990

comms *noun*

communications

- [A] scheduled comms burst from base.—Chris Ryan, *The Watchman*, p. 25, 2001

community chest *noun*

a sexually available girl *US*

- Boys look down on a "community chest," meaning a promiscuous girl.—Joe David Brown, *Sex in the '60s*, p. 19, 1968

commute *verb*

to take DMT, a short-lasting hallucinogen *US*

- —William D. Alsever, *Glossary for the Establishment and Other Uptight People*, p. 9, December 1970

Como *noun*

a Fred Perry™ shirt, a fashion item with iconic status among skinheads *UK*

Via singer Perry Como (1912–2001).

- [T]hese older lads, skins they were, Bennies [a Ben Sherman shirt], Comos, Flemmings [brand-name], full kit, come ambling over.—Kevin Sampson, *Outlaws*, p. 245, 2001

comp *noun*

1 a *comp*etition *UK, 1929*

Also called a 'compo'.

- World Cup comp winners— *BBC Sport*, 11th April 2002

2 a *comp*limentary benefit given to valued customers *US*

- Comps, the giving away of food, rooms, drink, girls, free airplane tickets, and show entertainment, started in Vegas in the 1940s. —Mario Puzo, *Inside Las Vegas*, p. 285, 1977
- "You're gonna be a comp." "Yeah? What's that, Vincent, a comp?" "Like the champagne, a gift. You're gonna get handed out, passed around."—Elmore Leonard, *Glitz*, p. 77, 1985

3 *comp*ensation *US, 1953*

- [J]ust a little bit of comp for them in case the company decides to get iffy[.]—Kevin Sampson, *Outlaws*, p. 235, 2001

4 a *comp*ositor; a typesetter *US, 1842*

- Cliff and I outpaced the journeymen "comps"[.]—Brian McDonald, *Elephant Boys*, p. 162, 2000

comp *verb*

1 to issue something on a *comp*limentary basis *US, 1961*

- This is the end result of all the bright lights and the comped trips[.] — *Casino*, 1995
- I play long enough and hard enough to get a comped room and put food in my stomach.— *Hard Eight*, 1996

2 to accompany someone musically *US, 1949*

- —Robert S. Gold, *A Jazz Lexicon*, p. 63, 1964

compa *noun*

a very close friend *US*

Border Spanish used in English conversation by Mexican-Americans; from the more formal *compadre* (godfather to one's child).

- —Dagoberto Fuentes and Jose Lopez, *Barrio Language Dictionary*, p. 33, 1974

compadre *noun*

a close and trusted male friend *US, 1833*

From the Spanish word (the godfather of your child).

- [T]he slim blond boy continued to run like a streak toward his friends, his long lost compadres, his School pals.—James Patterson, *When the Wind Blows*, p. 340, 1998

company *noun*

sex *US*

Used as a euphemism by prostitutes soliciting customers.

- —William T. Vollman, *Whores for Gloria*, p. 139, 1991

company girl *noun*

a prostitute hired to enliven a corporate event or outing *US*

- Whores are now "call girls," "party girls" or "company girls." Instead of visiting them, they come to see you.—Lee Mortimer, *Women Confidential*, p. 140, 1960

company jewelry *noun*

a railwayman's company hat, badge and switch keys *US*

- —Norman Carlisle, *The Modern Wonder Book of Trains and Railroading*, p. 261, 1946

company patsy *noun*

the person within an organisation who is blamed for everything that goes wrong *US*

- —Sherman Louis Sergel, *The Language of Show Biz*, p. 56, 1973

complain *verb*

▸ **can't complain!; musn't complain!**

things are tolerable, nothing to *really* complain about *UK, 1847*

A catchphrase, often given as a by-rote reply without consideration of the sense.

- [She] said the things she always said: "How's tricks?" and "Can't complain" and "Bye now."—Jean Potts, *An Affair of the Heart*, 1970

comp list *noun*

a list kept at the door of a club or concert, identifying those who are to be admitted free of charge *US*

- Chili was on his way in, waiting for the doorman to find his name on the comp list, as Hy Gordon was coming out and they stopped to say hello.—Elmore Leonard, *Be Cool*, p. 51, 1999

compo *noun*

1 compensation *UK*

- [H]e's still got to have a few bob compo from somewhere[.] —J.J. Connolly, *Layer Cake*, p. 195, 2000
- Aye, alright. Compo off you if I lose me friggin licence, tho.—Niall Griffiths, *Kelly + Victor*, p. 339, 2002

2 worker's compensation *AUSTRALIA, 1941*

- — *The Daily Express*, 20th December 1946
- Now, just a minute, mate, what hope would a working man have without a bit of honest compo? As a matter of fact, my back is real crook but the doctor didn't believe me, either.—Frank Hardy, *The Yarns of Billy Borker*, p. 134, 1965
- —David McGill, *David McGill's Complete Kiwi Slang Dictionary*, p. 30, 1998

3 a composition *TRINIDAD AND TOBAGO*

- —Lise Winer, *Dictionary of the English/Creole of Trinidad & Tobago*, 2003

4 mixed mortar, plaster or the like *AUSTRALIA*

- Jesus. They've locked. The compo's set. (He tries to walk in vain). —Jack Hibberd, *A Stretch of the Imagination*, p. 6, 1971
- [T]he mixer blades stirred the powdered clay, earth and asbestos in the compo.—Graham Sheil, *War's End*, p. 65, 1981

comprehensively *adverb*

thoroughly, indisputably; in a very big and a delightfully humorous way *UK, 1979*

Sporting.

- For Everton this was a dreadful night. Comprehensively beaten by a Chelsea team they meet again in the league at Goodison Park on Saturday[.]— *The Guardian*, 5th December 2002

comprehensive physician *noun*

a proctologist, a doctor specialising in diseases of the rectum *US*

Based on any number of pale puns about 'holes' and 'whole patients'.

- — *Maledicta*, p. 57, Summer 1980: 'Not sticks and stones, but names: more medical pejoratives'

comprenday *verb*

to understand *UK*

Cod-French, from *comprendre* (to comprehend).

- Takes a while to fucking comprenday what's going on[.]—Kevin Sampson, *Outlaws*, p. 275, 2001

comprende?

do you understand? *US*

Spanish used by English speakers without regard to their fluency in Spanish, and with multiple variations reflecting their lack of fluency.

• Fuck with me, bitch, even a little bit, even a little bit, you're gonna get accidentally shot! Comprehende? — *Natural Born Killers*, 1994

comps *noun*

comprehensive college examinations *US*

• I spent most of my time boning up for my final examination, the "comps." — Clancy Sigal, *Going Away*, p. 407, 1961

compsci *noun*

a *comp*uter *sci*ence student *UK, 2002*

A shortening and compounding of the discipline, pronounced 'comp-ski'.

compty *adjective*

mentally deficient *UK*

Army, possibly of Hindustani derivation.

compute *verb*

to make sense *US, 1964*

Almost always heard in the negative – 'does not compute'. Popularised in the 1960s television situation comedy *My Living Doll*, in which the robotic character played by Julie Newmar would respond to anything that she did not understand by saying 'That does not compute'.

• Because good news does not compute for me right now. — Anna Quindlen, *One True Thing*, p. 151, 1994

• On the very next page, we find out that in the 71 days since combat operations ended in Iraq, 77 American soldiers have died. This does not compute! [Letter to Editor] — *Times Herald (Port Huron, Michigan)*, p. 9AQ, 18th July 2003

computer geek *noun*

a person whose life is centred around computers to the exclusion of all other outlets *US*

• — Eric S. Raymond, *The New Hacker's Dictionary*, p. 102, 1991

computer nerd *noun*

a student whose enthusiasm for computers has interfered with the development of a well-rounded personality *US*

• I'm not at all impressed by those movies about computer nerds in high school who triumph in some improbable way over the jocks[.] — *Wasington Post (reprinted from The Nation)*, p. C5, 22nd December 1985

compy *noun*

a competition *AUSTRALIA*

• They got kicked out of the compy for brawling. — Phillip Gwynne, *Deadly Unna?*, p. 20, 1998

compy?

do you understand? *US*

A complete corruption of the French or Spanish.

• — Marcus Hanna Boulware, *Jive and Slang of Students in Negro Colleges*, 1947

comrat *noun*

a political liberal *US*

A derogatory play on the communist use of the term 'comrade'.

• The Nat'l Laywers Guild (listed as a commy front by the Cong-probers) is trying to find some way to intervene in the proceedings against the comrats by the McCarran Act. — *San Francisco Call-Bulletin*, p. 11, 12th June 1951

comred *noun*

a political liberal *US*

A play on the term 'comrade'.

• What this cultural group did not select is an ex-Commy such as Chambers, Budenz, Bentley, Rushmore and other one-time Reds, who proved their loyalty to the U.S. by publicly named comreds. — *San Francisco Call-Bulletin*, p. 60, 3rd February 1953

comsymp *noun*

a liberal; a *com*munist *symp*athizer *US*

• Therefore, the defeat of that proposal put forward by those wild-eyed comsymps in Welfare, due to come before the board at Monday's meeting, was the big skyhook[.] — Robert Gover, *Here Goes Kitten*, p. 91, 1964

con *noun*

1 a *con*vict or ex-*con*vict *US, 1888*

• Get the helll over there and help those cons pile up them bricks[.] — Mezz Mezzrow, *Really the Blues*, p. 36, 1946

• Shortie was a con and he was more than anxious to stay away from murder. — Mickey Spillane, *My Gun is Quick*, p. 57, 1950

• Johnny Berger is a con. And like all cons he's dreaming that favorite dream of the caged – "another chance." — *San Francisco Examiner*, p. 35, 27th May 1956

• I listen to the other cons making with the patter – kidding each other about the great things they're going to do to celebrate release. — Colin Johnson, *Wild Cat Falling*, p. 4, 1965

• And whenever they see his ugly cara, they'll know that I did it, and every con in the joint will know I got a rep for pure hombre and cool himself. — Piri Thomas, *Down These Mean Streets*, p. 253, 1967

• I was astonished to see the old grizzled cons playing marbles. — Eldridge Cleaver, *Soul on Ice*, p. 43, 1968

• In the recreation room there were some fifty gas ranges that cons used to cook on. — A.S. Jackson, *Gentleman Pimp*, p. 128, 1973

• Neil, just as well this Old Bastard's honest, because if he was a "Con" you blokes would go cockeyed trying to watch him. — Sam Weller, *Old Bastards I Have Met*, p. 4, 1979

2 a criminal *con*viction *UK, 1925*

• Well, nothing recent if it was a conviction for shit-all, because a con for shit-all meant you weren't much of a villain. — Garry Bushell, *The Face*, p. 33, 2001

3 deception; an act intended to trick or deceive; a tale intended to deceive *US, 1896*

• The nature of the con, which Carey thought sounded like an urban myth, is tricky to summarise, so you will just have to buy the book. — *The Guardian*, 16th July 2002

4 a *con*vention *US*

Especially popular among fans of science fiction and comic books.

• — *American Speech*, p. 53, Spring 1978: 'Star Trek lives: trekker slang'

• I swear – the next con I attend and they ask me to be on the minority panel, if I see your name anywhere near the list, I'm passing. — *Chasing Amy*, 1997

5 in horse racing, a *con*cession wager *AUSTRALIA*

• "The con" is a form of betting that allows the backer to receive his stake back should his selection fail to win but run 2nd or 3rd. — Ned Wallish, *The Truth Dictionary of Racing Slang*, p. 17, 1989

6 a *con*ference; a *con*sultation *UK, 1961*

Lawyers' use.

• — Collin Brooks, *The Swimming Frog*, 1951

7 a lavatory attendant *UK, 1961*

con *verb*

to subject someone to a *con*fidence trick; to dupe the victim of a criminal enterprise *US, 1892*

• He started telling me how he con[n]ed all this gilt off the old dear. — Frank Norman, *Bang To Rights*, p. 108, 1958

• He's been associated with race tracks and track people and had a great deal of school difficulties. He was quite proficient in 'conning' people. — *San Francisco News*, p. 4, 5th June 1959

• But you better try and try hard. And don't try to con the parole board. — *San Francisco Chronicle*, p. 36, 16th April 1966

• She was going to con a con man. Ha! — Edwin Torres, *Carlito's Way*, p. 36, 1975

Con-Air *noun*

any aeroplane flown by the federal Bureau of Prisons to transport prisoners *US*

• — Reinhold Aman, *Hillary Clinton's Pen Pal*, p. 25, 1996

Conan Doyle; conan *noun*

a boil *UK, 1932*

Rhyming slang, formed on the name of Sir Arthur Conan Doyle, author and creator of Sherlock Holmes. As the current use is almost exclusively of the shortened form, to many the source of the rhyme, and hence the rhyme itself, has been lost.

con artist *noun*

a skilled confidence swindler *US, 1937*

• Every con artist that has ever lived had to gain the mark's confidence during the scam. — Dennis M. Marlock, *How to Become a Professional Con Artist*, p. 34, 2001

concert *noun*

a play; a show; any theatrical entertainment *UK*

• [T]onight's concert with those camp munchkins [children], all ogles and pots [teeth] and nante voce [voice]. — the cast of 'Aspects of Love', Prince of Wales Theatre, *Palare (Boy Dancer Talk) for Beginners*, 1989–92

concertina *noun*

a sheep that is hard to shear because of the wrinkles on its skin *AUSTRALIA*

• — Sidney J. Baker, *The Drum*, 1959

conch *noun*

1 a conscientious student *AUSTRALIA*

Used contemptuously.

- And she was so happy today cos we got our report cards, and on hers the teachers writ stuff like, 'Amanda is a delight to teach.' Wot a conch! — Kylie Mole (Maryanne Fahey), *My Diary*, p. 82, 1988

2 a white native of the Bahamas, especially a poor one *BAHAMAS, 1840*

- — John A. Holm, *Dictionary of Bahamian English*, p. 47, 1982

▸ **have the conch**

to be your turn to speak *UK*

From the symbolic value of a conch-shell in William Golding's *Lord of the Flies*, 1954.

conchie; conchy *noun*

a conscientious objector *UK, 1917*

- Some 30 of the conchies (half the camp population) worked hard at a campaign of studied defiance of camp officials. — *Time*, p. 21, 19th February 1945

Conchie Joe; Conchie Joe *noun*

a local white Bahamian *BAHAMAS, 1978*

Collected by Richard Allsopp.

Conchy Joe *noun*

▷ see: CONKY JOE

Con Club *noun*

any provincial headquarters of the Conservative and Unionist Association *UK*

Described in *The Sunday Times*, 20th August 1978, as 'that ambiguous abbreviation'.

con-con *noun*

the residue that remains after smoking freebase cocaine *US*

- — Terry Williams, *Crackhouse*, p. 147, 1992

concrete overcoat *noun*

a covering of a corpse with concrete to facilitate its disposal in a body of water *US, 1971*

- I see a few wrinkles in this scheme now (the words "concrete overcoat" come to mind), but I did not then. — Joan Didion, *The White Album*, p. 182, 1979

concrete overshoes *noun*

concrete poured around a person or body's feet to faciliate disposal in a body of water *US, 1976*

- We guessed that most of them were where you couldn't see them, at the bottom of Lake Michigan, wearing concrete overshoes. — Richard Peck, *A Long Way from Chicago*, p. 1, 1998

concrete wheels *noun*

a citizens' band radio transmitter situated in a building *UK*

Citizens' band radio slang.

- — Peter Chippindale, *The British CB Book*, p. 153, 1981

concuss *adjective*

suffering the symptoms of a concussion *SINGAPORE*

- — Paik Choo, *The Coxford Singlish Dictionary*, p. 32, 2002

condo *noun*

an owner-occupied flat, a *condo*minium *US, 1964*

- [B]uy apartments freehold in purpose-built blocks – condominiums, or 'condos'. — *The Observer*, 30th November 2003

condom *noun*

1 in computing, the plastic bag that protects a 3.5 inch disk *US*

- — Eric S. Raymond, *The New Hacker's Dictionary*, p. 103, 1991

2 in pool, a removable rubber sleeve for a cue stick *US*

- — Mike Shamos, *The Illustrated Encyclopedia of Billiards*, p. 56, 1993

condominiums *noun*

in bar dice games, a roll from the cup in which some dice are stacked on top of others, invalidating the roll *US*

- — Gil Jacobs, *The World's Best Dice Games*, p. 201, 1976

conducer *noun*

a railway conductor *US*

- — Norman Carlisle, *The Modern Wonder Book of Trains and Railroading*, p. 261, 1946

conductor *noun*

1 an experienced LSD user who acts as a guide for another who is experiencing the drug's effects; LSD *US, 1982*

- — Richard A. Spears, *The Slang and Jargon of Drugs and Drink*, p. 119, 1986
- — Mike Haskins, *Drugs*, p. 285, 2003

2 the second active participant in serial sex with a single passive partner *US*

From PULL A TRAIN (serial sex).

- Carolina Moon announced that she was going to take her blanket into the bushes and pull the train. "I'm first! I'm the engineer!" cried Harold Bloomguard. "I'm second! I'm conductor!" cried Spencer Van Moot. — Joseph Wambaugh, *The Choirboys*, p. 333, 1975

cone *noun*

1 a detachable conical receptacle of a pipe or bong; the contents of one of these *AUSTRALIA*

- He lit up, drew the cone and shotgunned it[.] — Harrison Biscuit, *The Search for Savage Henry*, p. 60, 1995
- Speed was matching Hoover cone for cone without any appreciable loss of motor function. — Harrison Biscuit, *The Search for Savage Henry*, p. 74, 1995

2 a cone-shaped marijuana cigarette *UK*

- He was sitting alone on a small brick wall, smoking what I recognised, before I could even smell it, as a cone of grass. — Ken Lukowiak, *Marijuana Time*, p. 1999, 2000

3 a socially inept person *US*

An abbreviation of CONEHEAD.

- — Elena Garcia, *A Beginner's Guide to Zen and the Art of Snowboarding*, p. 121, 1990

▸ **give cone**

to perform oral sex *US*

- — Mimi Pond, *The Valley Girl's Guide to Life*, p. 57, 1982

▸ **pull a cone**

to smoke the entire contents of a a detachable conical receptacle of a marijuana pipe *AUSTRALIA*

- He offered her his home-made bong. 'Pull a cone,' he said magnanimously. — Kathy Lette, *Girls' Night Out*, p. 145, 1987
- Warren had a good soul and he pulled cones like a trooper[.] — John Birmingham, *He Died With a Felafel in his Hand*, p. 33, 1994
- They were pulling cones. — Linda Jaivin, *Rock n Roll Babes from Outer Space*, p. 102, 1996

conehead *noun*

1 a habitual smoker of marijuana *AUSTRALIA*

- — Kathy Lette, *Girls' Night Out*, p. 187, 1987
- 'Bong brains' or 'Cone heads' derive their names from inhaling vast amounts of marijuana smoke. — *Sydney Morning Herald*, p. 7, 3rd January 1987

2 a socially inept person *US*

From a recurring skit on *Saturday Night Live*, first appearing in 1983; Dan Ackryod played alien Beldar Conehead and Jane Curtin his wife Prymaat.

- — Elena Garcia, *A Beginner's Guide to Zen and the Art of Snowboarding*, p. 121, 1990

3 a young person with a shaved head and radical racist views *NEW ZEALAND*

Another name for the common SKINHEAD.

- — Diana Looser, *Lexicon*, p. 46, 2001

coner *noun*

a pickpocket who distracts a targeted victim by dropping an ice-cream cone at the victim's feet *UK*

- — *Sunday Times*, 11th May 1969

Coney Island *noun*

1 any room in a police station where suspected criminals are forcefully interrogated *US*

- — Vincent J. Monteleone, *Criminal Slang*, p. 57, 1949
- — Hyman E. Goldin et al., *Dictionary of American Underworld Lingo*, p. 47, 1950

2 a lunch cart; a condiment-rich lunch served from a lunch cart *US*

- — Harold Wentworth and Stuart Berg Flexner, *Dictionary of American Slang*, p. 118, 1960

3 any travelling carnival or amusement park *TRINIDAD AND TOBAGO, 1927*

- — Lise Winer, *Dictionary of the English/Creole of Trinidad & Tobago*, 2003

Coney Island butter *noun*

mustard *US, 1947*

- — Frederic G. Cassidy, *Dictionary of American Regional English, Volume 1*, p. 749, 1985

Coney Island whitefish *noun*

a used condom *US*

The most prominent use of the term is probably in the title of the 1979 Aerosmith song 'Bone to Bone (Coney Island White Fish Boy)'.

- Abrams spotted a flaccid rubber sheath that in his youth had been called a Coney Island whitefish.—Nelson DeMille, *The Talbot Odyssey*, p. 346, 1984
- Coney Island also gave its name, probably in the 1930s, to the Coney-Island whitefish, a used condom floating in the water at the bathing beach – a common sight then and now.—Irving Lewis Allen, *The City in Slang*, p. 102, 1993
- I recall how surfers objected to sharing their waves with the schools of "Coney Island whitefish," the name we gave used condoms that drifted east, along Long Island's South Shore, from the city sewer system.—Russell Drumm, *In the Slick of the Cricket*, p. 212, 1997
- —Samuel M. Katz, *Anytime Anywhere*, p. 386, 1997
- In Brooklyn, in what many people have been taught by crack journalists to call "a more innocent time," floating condoms were often called "Coney Island whitefish."—Gilbert Sorrentino, *Little Casino*, p. 35, 2002

conference *noun*

a poker game *US*

An intentionally misleading euphemism.

- —George Percy, *The Language of Poker*, p. 24, 1988

confessional *noun*

a police interview room *UK*

- Coppers have their own pet names for interview rooms. "The Confessional", "The Sweat Box", "The Truth Chamber".—John Wainwright, *The Last Buccaneer*, 1971

confetti *noun*

1 bricks *US, 1950*

An abbreviation of **IRISH CONFETTI**.

- —Harold Wentworth and Stuart Berg Flexner, *Dictionary of American Slang*, p. 119, 1960

2 snow *UK*

Obviously, 'wet confetti' is 'sleet'.

- —Peter Chippindale, *The British CB Book*, p. 153, 1981

confidencer *verb*

an electronic device that screens out background noise from a telephone mouthpiece *US*

- —M. Allen Henderson, *How Con Games Work*, p. 219, 1985

confo *noun*

a conference *AUSTRALIA*

- —Sidney J. Baker, *The Australian Language*, 1953

confound! *verb*

curse!, especially as 'confound it!', 'confound you!', etc; used for mild oaths or imprecations *UK*

- SERGEANT: Oh, don't misunderstand me, sir. I'm willing enough to try, but you see, ah... we're not used to pulling officers out of pits. ALGERNON: Confound it, man, what are you jabbering about?—*The Highlanders*, 24th December 1966

confounded *adjective*

inopportune, unpleasant, odious, excessive *UK, 1760*

- This isn't as much of a confounded nuisance as it sounds: once registered, friends don't need permission again[.]—*Maxim Magazine*, June 2003

Confucius he say

used as an introduction to either a genuine or cynical philosophical proposition, or as a set-up to a joke that is archly stylised: its lack of the use of 'a' or 'the' approximates 'oriental' words of wisdom *UK*

An example (selected at random from a wealth of Internet sites that celebrate this comedic formula): 'Crowded elevator small different to midget'. Confucius, 551–479 BC, was a great Chinese philosopher not best remembered for his jokes and double entendres.

- Tomsett drained his glass. "... I've always been a bit dubious about this rape business." "Confucius, he say girl with skirt up, she run faster than man with trousers down, eh?" The two older [dons] smiled politely at the tired old joke[.]—Colin Dexter, *Last Bus to Woodstock*, 1975

confuddle up *adjective*

confused *BAHAMAS*

- —John A. Holm, *Dictionary of Bahamian English*, p. 48, 1982

confuffle *noun*

confusion *TRINIDAD AND TOBAGO, 1993*

- —Lise Winer, *Dictionary of the English/Creole of Trinidad & Tobago*, 2003

confusion *noun*

a street fight; a quarrel leading to a fight *JAMAICA, 1873*

Noted as of West Indian origin.

- —David Powis, *The Signs of Crime*, 1977

Cong *noun*

a Congregational chapel; a follower of the Congregational faith *UK, 1961*

The *Book of Congregational Praise* was known as 'Cong Praise'. The term faded from use after the Congregational Church merged with the Presbyterian Church of England in 1972. Members of the newly formed United Reformed Church soon became 'Urks'.

Congo *noun*

a Congregationalist *AUSTRALIA*

- —Sidney J. Baker, *Australia Speaks*, 1953

Congo brown; Congo dirt *noun*

marijuana purportedly grown in Africa *US*

- —Jay Robert Nash, *Dictionary of Crime*, p. 76, 1992

Congolese *noun*

an extremely potent variety of marijuana cultivated in the Republic of Congo *UK*

- You will wake in the morning new born, without a hangover (unless it's that deadly Congolese).—Richard Neville, *Play Power*, p. 135, 1970

congrats *noun*

congratulations *UK, 1894*

- This one's received with no fanfare or congrats.—Josh Alan Friedman, *Tales of Times Square*, p. 122, 1986

conhanger *noun*

the co-signer of a purchase contract or loan *US*

- —*American Speech*, p. 312, Autumn-Winter 1975: 'The jargon of car salesmen'

con into; con out of *verb*

to subject someone to a criminal trick; to fool a victim into giving up something of value

Derives from **CON** (confidence trick).

- I had a bunny with some geezer who was doing a lagging for conning some old dear out of a few grand.—Frank Norman, *Bang To Rights*, p. 108, 1958

conjugals *noun*

conjugal rights *UK, 1937*

- Later, the governor's ban on conjugals and smoking riles the inmates.—*OZ Episode Guide*, 2003

conk; konk *noun*

1 the head *US, 1870*

- The halo that started to shape up around my conk was so big and bright, I felt like an overgrown glow-worm.—Mezz Mezzrow, *Really the Blues*, p. 89, 1946

2 the nose; hence, a nickname for anyone blessed with a big nose *UK, 1812*

Possibly from 'conch' (a large shell) with Latin and Greek derivations.

- No thanks. I once shoved that stuff up me conk and me hankie turned brown.—Barry Humphries, *Bazza Pulls It Off!*, 1971
- [A]ll the charlie [cocaine] he'd ever shoved up his conk[.]—*Drugs An Adult Guide*, p. 17, December 2001

3 a hairstyle in which naturally curly hair is chemically straightened; hence, the hair straightening process; the chemical preparation required *US, 1942*

- Even the solid cats in their pancho conks didn't ruffle me.—Chester Himes, *If He Hollers Let Him Go*, p. 43, 1945
- Three brown-faced youngsters – all not yet twenty – whom Teese knew, lunged importantly at the glazed-glass front of the billiard hall, hair slicked and twirled in the fashionable konk[.]—Clarence Cooper Jr, *Black*, p. 189, 1963
- I couldn't get over marveling at how their hair was straight and shiny like white men's hair; Ella told me this was called a "conk."—Malcolm X and Alex Haley, *The Autobiography of Malcolm X*, p. 43, 1964
- —Janey Ironside, *A Fashion Alphabet*, p. 190, 1968
- He'd drop by the school and be vined down. He was clean, Jim. Had him a conk then and he knew he was ready.—H. Rap Brown, *Die Nigger Die!*, p. 24, 1969
- Some of them look like, you know, with the fancy hair [referring to high conks or "process," straightened and teased hair].—Christina and Richard Milner, *Black Players*, p. 114, 1972
- I went to a barber shop way up in the wilds of the South Bronx, recommended by some walking exponents of one hair-straightening process known as the "konk."—Piri Thomas, *Stories from El Barrio*, p. 50, 1978

conk *verb*

1 to straighten hair using any number of chemical processes *US, 1944*

- The face of a colored youth with slick conked hair and beardless cheeks stared up.—Chester Himes, *The Real Cool Killers*, p. 25, 1959

- Everybody understood that my head had to stay kinky a while longer, to grow long enough for Shorty to conk it for me. —Malcolm X and Alex Haley, *The Autobiography of Malcolm X*, p. 51, 1964
- He had his hair conked, but around his ears and at the nape of his neck were the hard, tight burrs he wanted so much to hide. —Nathan Heard, *Howard Street*, p. 86, 1968
- [S]ince I had my hat conked in them days, I had no 'do-rag' round my skull. —Odie Hawkins, *Ghetto Sketches*, p. 119, 1972
- Then you had a pimp name of Red Conk on account of he conked his hair red (hair was straight in them days one way or other – Dixie Peach or Sulfur 8). —Edwin Torres, *Carlito's Way*, p. 13, 1975
- Wasn't but yesterday you was conkin' yo' head with a steam iron at your ol' lady's beauty parlor. —Edwin Torres, *Q & A*, p. 18, 1977

2 to hit someone, especially on the head *UK, 1821*

- Mac would conk the ugly customers on the top and carry them outside[.] —Mezz Mezzrow, *Really the Blues*, p. 70, 1946
- Larry Fay liked to roam around his own night clubs – which were sometimes multiple – with a roll of nickels (like the cashiers have) in his hand and look for an excuse to conk somebody[.] —Robert Sylvester, *No Cover Charge*, p. 200, 1956
- "Sam," he said, "I think I'll get up and conk him." —Jack Kerouac, *On the Road*, p. 78, 1957

3 to kill someone *US, 1918*

- He was yellow. That's what caused him to get conked. —Horace McCoy, *Kiss Tomorrow Good-bye*, p. 41, 1948

conkbuster *verb*

inexpensive, potent whisky *US*

- —Marcus Hanna Boulware, *Jive and Slang of Students in Negro Colleges*, 1947

conked; conked out *adjective*

(of a machine) not working; (of a person) exhausted *UK, 1984*

- Oh yeah. I've slept plenty. I've been pretty much conked out since Bakerfield. —Emily Toll, *Murder Pans Out*, p. 11, 2003

conker *noun*

a line of traffic that builds up behind a slow driver *UK*

- [A slow, careful, trundling driver] can establish behind him what we call a "conker" of up to 50 other road users. —*Daily Telegraph*, June 1972

conk out; konk out; clonk out *verb*

to fall asleep; to pass out; to stop operating *UK, 1917*

- I don't conk out on grape! —Dan Burley, *Diggeth Thou?*, p. 34, 1959
- The Plymouth conked out on La Brea avenue, and we had to take three buses out to Boyle Heights. —Clancy Sigal, *Going Away*, p. 65, 1961
- He told me he'd stolen a car and it conked out on him. —Claude Brown, *Manchild in the Promised Land*, p. 142, 1965
- He just crawled into the back seat, said "West 45th Street," and conked out. —*Taxi Driver*, 1976
- [T]he engine is diabolical. British Leyland. Conks out, all the time. —Mike Stott, *Soldiers Talking, Cleanly*, 1978
- It was dawn and I wanted to conk out. —Edwin Torres, *After Hours*, p. 290, 1979
- At this point Iris lay back in her chair and konked out on him. He could slap her face all he wanted, throw water in it, hold her under the shower – he could see she wasn't about to come around for the rest of the night. —Elmore Leonard, *Glitz*, p. 190, 1985
- I switched myself to auto-pilot and, like a clonked-out zombie, just rode and rode. —Josie Dew, *The Sun In My Eyes*, p. 307, 2001

conky *noun*

1 a nose *UK*

Market traders' elaboration of **CONK**. Variants include 'conkey' and 'conkie'.

- —Patrick O'Shaughnessy, *Market Traders' Slang*, 1979

2 used of any person with a large nose *UK*

From **CONK** (a nose). Arthur Wellesley, Duke of Wellington (1769–1852) is perhaps the best known of people so profiled; he was known first as 'conkey', then 'old conkey'. Another variant spelling is 'konsky'.

3 the penis *BAHAMAS*

- —John A. Holm, *Dictionary of Bahamian English*, p. 48, 1982

Conky Joe; Conchy Joe *noun*

a white person, or a person with very light-coloured skin *BAHAMAS, 1942*

- —John A. Holm, *Dictionary of Bahamian English*, p. 49, 1982

con man *noun*

a confidence swindler *US, 1889*

- Cherie Blair let a notorious conman help purchase a flat in Bristol for her student son, Euan. —*The Guardian*, 2nd December 2002

con merchant *noun*

a confidence swindler *US*

- In short, since a con merchant must swindle his clients under those circumstances where clients appreciate that a confidence game could be employed, the con man must forestall the immediate impression that he might be what in fact he is. —Erving Goffman, *The Presentation of Self in Everyday Life*, p. 225, 1959

connect *noun*

a connection from which an illicit substance may be obtained; a drug dealer *US*

- The connect ain't come through the last week, and the Man's downtown. —Clarence Cooper Jr, *The Scene*, p. 23, 1960
- "If my connect gets the wire I gave his name to somebody," he said, "splittin aint going to help me none." —Charles W. Moore, *A Brick for Mister Jones*, p. 34, 1975
- He knew just the people to go to for sugar connects, where he could buy twenty thousand pounds of sugar without any static. —Donald Goines, *Black Gangster*, p. 13, 1977
- We all went back to the Village to MacDougal Street near the Fat Black Pussy Cat where we hung around until Joe made my connect for me. —Herbert Huncke, *The Evening Sun Turned Crimson*, p. 136, 1980
- The price is going up, because the connect wants thirty [$30,000] for each [kilo] package, and I got to make at least ten on each package for myself. —Terry Williams, *The Cocaine Kids*, p. 34, 1989
- Because it's my connect. I'm providing the connect. —Kenneth Lonergan, *This is Our Youth*, p. 37, 2000

connect *verb*

to make a sexual conquest *US*

- —*American Speech*, p. 19, Spring 1985: 'The language of singles bars'

connected *adjective*

associated with, if not a formal part of, organised crime *US, 1977*

- You can't print me. I'm, a connected guy. —Edwin Torres, *Q & A*, p. 157, 1977
- No, I never heard that name. He could be connected, but I can tell you he's not family. —Elmore Leonard, *Killshot*, p. 230, 1989

connection *noun*

1 a drug dealer; a drug deal *US, 1928*

- "I need a jolt," one addict might remark. "I gotta see my connection." —William J. Spillard and Pence James, *Needle in a Haystack*, p. 148, 1945
- Then my supply ran out and my connection got a ship. —John Clellon Holmes, *Go*, p. 47, 1952
- "Then you don't get my business, either," Angel said. "We got other connections." —Hal Ellson, *The Golden Spike*, p. 30, 1952
- I drank all day in a wild poolhall-bar-restaurant-saloon two-part joint, also got burned for a fin (Mexican, 5 pesos, 60 cents) by a connection. —Jack Kerouac, *Letter to Neal and Carolyn Cassady*, p. 359, 27th May 1952
- Why don't we go uptown? I know several good connections we can probably catch about now. —William Burroughs, *Junkie*, p. 29, 1953
- Couldn't you make a connection last night? —John D. McDonald, *The Neon Jungle*, p. 71, 1953
- The connection came in and motioned me to the cellar toilet[.] —Jack Kerouac, *On the Road*, p. 88, 1957
- I didn't tell Casanova anything. Nothing about you and Red, although they seem to have plenty of information at their disposal. And nothing at all about our connection. —Ross Russell, *The Sound*, p. 238, 1961
- "Knock three times, then once, then twice." "All that? He must be a connection." —Chester Himes, *Cotton Comes to Harlem*, p. 38, 1965
- As a matter of fact, he was selling horse, and he wanted to know if I wanted to sell some. He had a connection for me. —Claude Brown, *Manchild in the Promised Land*, p. 153, 1965
- I'd better go see my connection. —Piri Thomas, *Down These Mean Streets*, p. 203, 1967
- He also explained how hard it was for Eastern cats to cop and spoke of the big bread I could make if I could find a connection. —Babs Gonzales, *I Paid My Dues*, p. 26, 1967
- THE CONNECTION sniffs powder, cocks his head and smiles. —Peter Fonda, *Easy Rider*, p. 47, 1969
- I saw her today at the reception / A glass of wine in her hand / I knew she was gonna meet her connection / At her feet was a footloose man — Rolling Stones, *You Can't Always Get What You Want*, 1969
- I had to make a connection for sleeping pills. Now! —Iceberg Slim (Robert Beck), *Trick Baby*, p. 267, 1969
- Is there a connection around, man? I have to cop. I'm alright, but my old lady is getting sick. —Herbert Huncke, *The Evening Sun Turned Crimson*, p. 72, 1980

2 a sexual partner *US*

- —*American Speech*, p. 19, Spring 1985: 'The language of singles bars'

3 a friend *SOUTH AFRICA*

- Jimmy's my big connection bru. We surf together every day. —*Surfrikan Slang*, 2004

connections *noun*

in horse racing, a horse's owner, trainer and the trainer's assistants *US*

- —Robert Saunders Dowst and Jay Craig, *Playing the Races*, p. 161, 1960

connectors *noun*

in poker, several sequenced cards that might be improved to a five-card sequenced straight *US*

- —Anthony Holden, *Big Deal*, p. 299, 1990

conneroo *noun*

a confidence swindler *US, 1949*

- Glenn made Jack feel as he had around his stepfather – a master barroom conneroo who would afterwards deride those who always stood him a drink[.]—Earl Thompson, *Tattoo*, p. 227, 1974

connie *noun*

1 a tram or train conductor *AUSTRALIA, 1933*

- This passenger said to the old connie, 'Throw me off at Gladstone, will you?'—Patsy Adam-Smith, *Folklore of the Australian Railwaymen*, p. 207, 1969
- —Ramon Adams, *The Language of the Railroader*, p. 36, 1977

2 a convict *AUSTRALIA*

- —Ross Campbell, *Mummy, Who is Your Husband?*, 1964

3 the vagina *US*

A common name as a euphemism (perhaps for **CUNT**).

- There's [...]"a ghoulie," "possible," "tamale," "tottita," "Connie, a "Mimi" in Miami[.]—Eve Ensler, *The Vagina Monologues*, p. 6, 1998

4 a type of playing marble *AUSTRALIA, 1966*

A shortening of **CONNIE AGATE**.

- Years older than I, Mick dated up clay-dabs against my connies.—Clive James, *Unreliable Memoirs*, p. 19, 1980

5 especially eastern mainland, a small stone or rock, especially one for throwing *AUSTRALIA, 1978*

Possibly from an Australian Aboriginal language.

- — *Wordmap (www.abc.net.au/wordmap)*, 2003

Connie *noun*

1 a Constellation airliner *US, 1953*

An aircraft that in the 1950s and 60s linked countries and continents. In 2004, the Dutch National Aviodrome museum completed the restoration of a Lockheed L-749 Constellation. The project was titled 'Connie Comeback'.

- Nobody from L.A. wants to ride a DC-3 over mountains when he can take a Connie and make it in seven hours to Mexico City.—Raymond Chandler, *The Long Goodbye*, p. 26, 1953

2 a Royal Enfield 'Constellation' motorcycle, introduced in 1958 *UK*

- —Douglas Dunford, *Motorcycle Department, Beaulieu Motor Museum*, 1979

3 a Lincoln Continental car *US*

- They're the owners of record for about nine Lincoln Connies and at least four Cads.—George V. Higgins, *The Friends of Eddie Doyle*, p. 98, 1971

connie agate *noun*

a type of playing marble made from agate *AUSTRALIA, 1916*

Perhaps from 'cornelian', with elision of the 'r'.

- TEACHER: "Well, what's the matter now?" SMALL BOY: "Please, I've swallered Brown's conny agate, an' he wants it back."—Norman Lindsay, *Comic Art of Norman Lindsay*, p. 211, 1916
- My collection of marbles consisted mainly of priceless connie agates handed down by Grandpa.—Clive James, *Unreliable Memoirs*, p. 19, 1980

Connie's army *noun*

the flotilla of supporters of the racing yacht *Constellation* in the 1962 America Cup races *US*

An obvious allusion to 'Arnie's army'.

- "Connie's Army," the spectator fleet which stayed close to the leading Constellation, affected both boats with their wakes and the British were informed that the Coast Guard would study how to remedy the situation today.—*San Francisco News Call-Bulletin*, p. 56, 19th September 1964

conniver about *verb*

to wander aimlessly *AUSTRALIA*

- —Sidney J. Baker, *The Australian Language*, 1953

con out of *verb*

▷ see: CON INTO

conrod *noun*

a connecting rod *UK, 1931*

Used by engineers and mechanics.

cons *noun*

1 a prison sentence *UK*

- —Angela Devlin, *Prison Patter*, p. 39, 1996

2 previous convictions *UK*

Metropolitan Police slang.

- —Peter Laurie, *Scotland Yard*, p. 322, 1970

cons *verb*

in computing, to add an item to a list *US*

- —Guy L. Steele et al., *The Hacker's Dictionary*, p. 48, 1983

con safos

used as a warning not to deface the writer's grafitti *US*

- Of course at the bottom of the wall was the inenvitable "CON SAFOS," the crucial gang incantation not to be found in any Spanish dictionary[.]—Joseph Wambaugh, *The New Centurions*, p. 105, 1970

conscious *adjective*

socio-politically aware of black race issues *UK*

- Lloyd was impressed with the reasoning of this obviously conscious black woman.—Donald Gorgon, *Cop Killer*, p. 29, 1994

con's con *noun*

in prison, an ideal prisoner in the opinion of other inmates *UK*

From **CON** (a convict).

- Jack always gave the impression he was a "con' scon" – a stalwart defender of the prison culture.—Erwin James, *The Guardian*, 1st March 2001

consent job *noun*

any crime committed with the consent of the victim, who then collects on an insurance policy *US*

- —Hyman E. Goldin et al., *Dictionary of American Underworld Lingo*, p. 48, 1950

conshie *noun*

a conscientious person *AUSTRALIA*

In contrast to the sense of 'conscientious objector', which seems to have little or no purchase in Australia.

- One lousy stripe, and as soon as you tried to do the right thing you were a "military maniac" or "Army-happy" or, worst of all, a "conshie".—R. Beilby, *No Medals for Aphrodite*, 1970

consig *noun*

in an organised crime enterprise, a trusted advisor *US*

Shortened from the Italian *consigliore*.

- Now they say he's like an honorary consig, a counsellor, reactivated while Sale's doing his two years.—Elmore Leonard, *Glitz*, p. 170, 1985

constant screecher *noun*

a teacher *UK*

Rhyming slang.

- —Ray Puxley, *Cockney Rabbit*, 1992

consti *noun*

*consti*pated *UK*

Slightly embarrassed if not entirely euphemistic; recorded as a young woman's use by Joanna Williamson in 1982.

constipated *adjective*

in tiddlywinks, said of a position in which your winks are tied down and useless *US*

- — *Verbatim*, p. 525, December 1977

constipation *noun*

a railway station *UK*

Rhyming slang; punning, perhaps, on a lack of movement.

- —Ray Puxley, *Cockney Rabbit*, 1992

constitutional *noun*

a drug addict's first injection of the day *US*

- —J.E. Schmidt, *Narcotics Lingo and Lore*, p. 33, 1959

contact *noun*

1 (of any situation of any degree of criminality or legality) an acquaintance, especially in business or trade; someone you can call on for assistance or information; a connection; an agent *US, 1931*

- I trotted down to the local AA [Alcoholics Anonymous] because I had lost my contacts book.—*The Observer*, 1st December 2002

2 a reliable source for something, especially drugs *US*

- —J. L. Simmons and Barry Winograd, *It's Happening*, p. 168, 1966

3 a police informer *US*

- — *American Speech*, p. 268, December 1962: 'The language of traffic policemen'

4 a *contact* lens *US, 1961*

Usually used in the plural.

- I tried coloured contacts. Just to see what I'd look like with blue eyes. — *The Guardian*, 18th June 2004

contact high *noun*

a vicarious, sympathetic experience caused by witnessing another person's drug-induced experience *US, 1955*

- — J. L. Simmons and Barry Winograd, *It's Happening*, p. 168, 1966
- — Edward R. Bloomquist, *Marijuana*, p. 157, 1968

contact lens *noun*

LSD; LSD mixed with another drug *US, 1977*

Possibly from the small size of a dose and its ability to change your view of the world.

- — Richard A. Spears, *The Slang and Jargon of Drugs and Drink*, p. 119, 1986
- — Mike Haskins, *Drugs*, p. 285, 2003

containered *adjective*

locked in a cell *UK*

- — Angela Devlin, *Prison Patter*, p. 40, 1996

content-free *adjective*

said of a computer message that adds nothing to the substance of a discussion or to the reader's knowledge *US*

- Though this adjective is sometimes applied to flamage, it more usually connotes derision for communication styles that exalt from over substance or are centered on concerns irrelevant to the subject ostensibly at hand. — Eric S. Raymond, *The New Hacker's Dictionary*, p. 104, 1991

continental cuisine *noun*

frozen food served to firefighters in remote but not inaccessible locations *US*

- — *American Speech*, p. 205 – 209, Summer 1991: 'The language of smokejumping – again'

continental kit *noun*

in hot rodding, a spare tyre fastened on the boot (trunk) of the car *US*

- — *Good Housekeeping*, p. 143, September 1958

contour *adverb*

(used of an aircraft) at treetop level *US*

- There would be no warning beyond a minute or two if the pilots flew "contour" – that is, at treetop level – for the last few miles, which they did whenever they could. — Neil Sheehan, *A Bright Shining Lie*, p. 74, 1988

contours *noun*

the curves of a woman's body *UK, 1886*

Somewhere between poetry and pornography.

- The woman in the Balthus drawing [a 1948 sketch for Femme couchée] has the same wistful, melancholic look as characters in David's work, but her contours are softer and the effect more ethereal. — *Time Europe*, 24th June 2002

contract *noun*

1 an order to kill someone or a reward offered to anyone who kills the target *US, 1941*

- — *American Speech*, p. 306, December 1964: 'Lingua cosa nostra'
- "We'll let a contract out on him," Teddybear says. (The Haight thinks gangsters talk this way.) — Nicholas Von Hoffman, *We Are The People Our Parents Warned Us Against*, p. 45, 1967

2 a promise made by one police officer to do a favour for another *US*

- — *New York Times Magazine*, p. 87, 16th March 1958

contract rider *noun*

in horse racing, a jockey who is under contract with one stable *US*

- — Dean Alfange, *The Horse Racing Industry*, p. 212, 1976

contra-rotating death banana *noun*

a Chinook helicopter *UK*

In Royal Air Force use, 2002.

contrary *adjective*

(of someone's personality or disposition) adverse, antagonistic, perverse *UK, 1850*

The earliest example is the undated nursery rhyme 'Mary, Mary, quite contrary' which is supposed to be about Mary Stuart, 1542 – 87.

- It is unlikely that I would have phoned up for tickets if I wasn't a contrary so-and-so. — *The Guardian*, 14th February 2003

Control-Alt-Delete *noun*

▷ **see: CTRL-ALT-DELETE**

control C *verb*

to stop what it is that you are doing *US*

A borrowing from the command used on many computer operating systems to interrupt a program.

- — Eric S. Raymond, *The New Hacker's Dictionary*, p. 105, 1991

control freak *noun*

a person with an obsessive need to control people and events *US, 1977*

- You know that, Mike? You're a maniac control freak. — *The Deer Hunter*, 1978
- Oh, so that was it. Control freak. — Francesca Lia Block, *I Was a Teenage Fairy*, p. 77, 1998
- This girl, an absolute adolescent, is a control freak's nightmare, an accident waiting to happen[.] — Elizabeth Wurtzel, *Bitch*, p. 146, 1999
- And why worry about the ending anyway? Why be such a control freak? — Stephen King, *On Writing*, p. 161, 2000
- John McGraw, obsessive control freak that he was, reviewed the hotel dinner checks to see what his players were eating. — Bill James, *The New Bill James Historical Baseball Abstract*, p. 426, 2001

controller *noun*

a mid-level operative in an illegal gambling enterprise who is in charge of a number of runners *US*

- A controller might have as many as fifty runners working for him, and the controller got five percent of what he turned over to the banker. — Malcolm X and Alex Haley, *The Autobiography of Malcolm X*, p. 85, 1964
- A lot of the junkies started sticking up the numbers writers and sticking up the controllers. — Claude Brown, *Manchild in the Promised Land*, p. 191, 1965
- A banker usually has working for him several "controllers," each of whom in turn controls a number of runners. — *The Knapp Commission Report on Police Corruption*, p. 79, 1972
- Then you got to be an administrator; then you got labor problems – what controller is humpin' what runner's wife. — Edwin Torres, *Carlito's Way*, p. 30, 1975

control O *verb*

to stop talking *US*

From the character used on some computer operating systems to abort output but allow the program to keep on running. Generally means that you are not interested in hearing anythimg more from that person, at least on that topic.

- — Eric S. Raymond, *The New Hacker's Dictionary*, p. 105, 1991

Con U *nickname*

Concordia University, Montreal *CANADA, 1972*

After the formation of Concordia University out of two existing institutions, this short form expressed student dissatisfaction with procedures and policies.

conversate *verb*

to converse in a loud and lively style *US*

From the conventional 'conversation'.

- Most of the folk that lined the poorly lit alley, drinking and conversating in little groups, looked my age or thereabouts. — Diran Abedayo, *My Once Upon A Time*, p. 69, 2000

conversion job *noun*

a disfigurement caused by a violent beating *UK, 1969*

From the conventional sense.

- If you don't knuckle under, someone will do a conversion job on you. — *Beale*, 1984

convert *noun*

a newly addicted drug addict *US*

- — Vincent J. Monteleone, *Criminal Slang*, p. 57, 1949

convert *verb*

to steal something *NEW ZEALAND*

- — Louis S. Leland, *A Personal Kiwi-Yankee Dictionary*, p. 28, 1984

convict *noun*

in circus usage, a zebra *US, 1926*

An allusion to the zebra's striped coat, evocative of a prison uniform.

- — Don Wilmeth, *The Language of American Popular Entertainment*, p. 63, 1981

convincer *noun*
the stage in a confidence swindle when the victim is fully committed to the scheme *US, 1940*
- White grifters call it the convincer. When con is played for money alone, it's that point at which the sucker is hooked or convinced by actual or paper profits that he can reap a bonanza. —Iceberg Slim (Robert Beck), *Trick Baby*, p. 55, 1969

convo *noun*
a conversation *AUSTRALIA*
- You could have great convos with her. —Kathy Lette, *Girls' Night Out*, p. 62, 1987

convoy *noun*
1 a group of trucks driving as a group, in communication with each other *US*
- —Montie Tak, *Truck Talk*, p. 37, 1971
- Mercy sakes alive, looks like we got us a convoy. —C.W. McCall, *Convoy*, 1976

2 serial sex between a woman and multiple male partners *FIJI*
Recorded by Jan Tent.

con wise *adjective*
extremely sophisticated in the ways of the world based on lessons learned in prison *US, 1912*
- Why didn't he tell his jailers about this? He was an ex-con. No con-wise con squeals. — *San Francisco Examiner*, p. 4 (II), 4th August 1957
- He's con wise, told me what I already know. —Gerald Petievich, *Money Men*, p. 56, 1981

coo *noun*
the vagina *UK, 1879*
- —J.E. Lighter, *Historical Dictionary of American Slang, Volume 1*, p. 470, 1994

coo!; coo-er!
used for expressing astonishment, disbelief or wonderment *UK, 1911*

cooch *noun*
the vagina; sex with a woman *US*
- There are plenty of queer women who work as porn stars, strippers, and sex workers, but there are a lot fewer of us willing to fork over cash for cooch. — *The Village Voice*, 7th August 2001

cooch dancer *noun*
▷ see: COOTCH DANCER

coocher *noun*
a sexually suggestive dancer *US, 1927*
- [I]mmediately after each coarse coocher has given her exhibition, your waitress solicits you for her. —Jack Lait and Lee Mortimer, *Chicago Confidential*, p. 60, 1950
- Coochers is the term applied to the solo dancers. It derives from hootchee cootchee, a descriptive label traced to Little Egypt's belly dancing at the 1893 Chicago World's Fair. —William Green, *Strippers and Coochers*, p. 161, 1977

coochie *noun*
the vagina; sex with a woman; a woman as a sex object *US*
- She ain't giving up no coochie. —*A2Z*, p. 22, 1995
- So what you had your little coochie in your dad's mouth? —Eminem (Marshall Mathers), *My Fault*, 1999
- There are '80s goths and foppish glam boys and women dressed like schoolgirls and schoolgirls dressed like hookers and endless Lil' Kim coochies in blond wigs and crop-tops that bear obtuse English phrases like "Sexy Kitty" or "Culture Style" and their eyes are manga wide and their make-up is as thick and as solid as cement. —Patrick Neate, *Where You're At*, p. 50, 2003

coochie-cutters *noun*
very short shorts *US*
- —Connie Eble (Editor), *UNC-CH Campus Slang*, p. 3, October 2002

coochi snorcher *noun*
the vagina *US*
Elaboration of COOCHIE (the vagina).
- She transformed my sorry-ass coochi snorcher and raised it up into a kind of heaven. —Eve Ensler, *The Vagina Monologues*, p. 82, 1998

cooder *noun*
a hairdresser *UK*
Probably contrived from the name of US guitarist Ry Cooder (b.1947) as a play on 'riah' (hair), 'Ry' forming a pun on 'hair cut'. Used in contemporary gay society.
- — *Attitude*, p. 60, July 2003

cooee *noun*
the call 'cooee' *AUSTRALIA, 1831*
- Laughter and gay calls echoed along the bank, and a coo-ee sounded from higher up. —Dymphna Cusack, *Picnic Races*, p. 131, 1962

▸ **within cooee**
within calling distance of a 'cooee'; nearby, close *AUSTRALIA, 1836*
- Never come within cooee of the place but someone's stuck in it. —Kylie Tennant, *The Honey Flow*, p. 61, 1956
- If your team 'didn't finish within cooee' or a 'bull's roar' of the opposition then you've been soundly beaten. —Ivor Limb, *Footy's No Joke!*, p. 18, 1986
- I dashed off. He never got within cooee of me after that. —Sally Morgan, *My Place*, p. 82, 1987

cooee *verb*
to make the call 'cooee' *AUSTRALIA, 1824*
- Someone was cooee-ing, and Harmon stirred and began reversing the pose preparatory to going to ground. —Arthur Upfield, *Bony and the Mouse*, p. 83, 1959
- —Dymphna Cusack, *Picnic Races*, p. 65, 1962

cooee!
used as a call to communicate whereabouts over distance *AUSTRALIA, 1793*
A direct borrowing of the call in the extinct Australian Aboriginal language Dharug, from the Sydney region. Adopted by the early white colonists, the call is used in the bush to mean both 'where are you?' and the answer 'I am here'. The 'coo' is drawn out and followed by a sharp, rising 'ee'.
- Where is that little blighter, Rory? He could come and give this a burl. Hey...Cooee...Rory... —Nourma Handford, *Carcoola Holiday*, p. 184, 1953

cook *noun*
1 a musician who plays with great passion and energy *US, 1962*
- —Robert S. Gold, *A Jazz Lexicon*, p. 65, 1964

2 on the railways, a rear brakeman *US*
- —Ramon Adams, *The Language of the Railroader*, p. 37, 1977

3 a look, in the phrases 'give a cook', 'have a cook', 'take a cook' *UK, 1960*
Possibly rhyming slang, or may simply be an accidental rhyme formed by confusion with the Yiddish use of German *guck* (a look).

4 extreme criticism *AUSTRALIA*
- After a poor ride, a dissatisfied trainer might give his jockey or apprentice a "nice old cook". —Ned Wallish, *The Truth Dictionary of Racing Slang*, p. 17, 1989

cook *verb*
1 to melt a powdered narcotic, especially heroin, in water, prior to injecting or inhaling *US*
The drug is 'cooked up' and 'cooked down'.
- Angel watched him begin preparations again and didn't move until all six caps were in the spoon, ready to be cooked. —Hal Ellson, *The Golden Spike*, p. 7, 1952
- Cook up a fix, Busser. Cook it up, boy. —George Mandel, *Flee the Angry Strangers*, p. 281, 1952
- You cook and I'll fix the hypo[.] —John D. McDonald, *The Neon Jungle*, p. 76, 1953
- "Yes, yes, we gonna cook." Red stood over the double gas plate and fined the flame down low. —Ross Russell, *The Sound*, p. 244, 1961
- I finally got enough to get me a ten-dollar bag. I came home and cooked my stuff. —Claude Brown, *Manchild in the Promised Land*, p. 259, 1965
- Cono, man, cook this shit up. —Piri Thomas, *Down These Mean Streets*, p. 5, 1967
- With slightly trembling hands he cooked it, and shot half the bag. —Nathan Heard, *Howard Street*, p. 96, 1968
- So cook me up when you're good and ready / And you won't remember if you're Johnnie or Eddie. —Dennis Wepman et al., *The Life*, p. 171, 1976
- Hey, man, gimme something cooked! — *The Bad Lieutenant*, 1992

2 to boil dynamite to extract nitroglycerine *US*
- —Jay Robert Nash, *Dictionary of Crime*, p. 79, 1992

3 to prepare crack cocaine, heating a mixture of cocaine, lidocaine, baking soda and other chemicals to remove the hydrochloride *US*
- —Terry Williams, *Crackhouse*, p. 147, 1992

4 to excel, to excite people *US, 1942*
- You're cooking when you can play everything that jumps into your mind. —Nat Hentoff, *Jazz Country*, p. 25, 1965

- I got there at 1 P.M. and he took me down in the basement and staked me in the game. Between shows all that day, I really "cooked." — Babs Gonzales, *I Paid My Dues*, p. 28, 1967

5 to falsify accounting figures; to manipulate them *UK, 1636*
- So when Harald found out that these Communists in the management were cooking the books, he organized the actors and threw a picket line around the theatre. — Mary McCarthy, *The Group*, p. 213, 1963
- I think he's got the real books at home, and he's got this set here that's been cooked he shows to artists, the ones that think he's holding out on 'em and they want to see the books. — Elmore Leonard, *Be Cool*, p. 193, 1999

6 to make something radioactive; to become radioactive *US, 1950*

7 (used of a car radiator in hot rodding) to boil over *US*
- — Fremont Drag Strip, *Guide to Drag Racing*, 1960

8 to execute someone by electrocution *US, 1932*
- [H]e was still going to cook in the hot squat up the river. — Mickey Spillane, *Kiss Me Deadly*, p. 139, 1952
- I think most of the guys my age looked upon them as heroes when they were getting cooked at Sing Sing. — Claude Brown, *Manchild in the Promised Land*, p. 220, 1965

▸ cook on all four
to be very busily employed *CANADA, 1984*
Adopted from **COOK WITH GAS** or **COOK ON THE FRONT BURNER**.

▸ cook on the front burner
to excel; to go fast *US*
- — *American Speech*, p. 227, October 1956: 'More United States Air Force slang'

▸ cook with gas
to perform successfully, especially after a period of trying and failing; to do very well *US, 1941*
- — Lou Shelly, *Hepcals Jive Talk Dictionary*, 1945
- He goes to the jukery to watch and wait and cut a rug with a solid gate he snatches a quail with hep and class and they go to town cooking with gas! — Haenigsen *Jive's Like That*, 1947
- We are well down the road. Robbie [Coltrane] is on board, Mervyn Gill-Dougherty is now producing, we're cooking with gas and I have arranged to shadow a Scottish QC for a couple of weeks. — *Sunday Herald [Scotland]*, 30th March 2003

▸ cook your goose
1 to ruin someone; to kill someone *UK, 1851*
- In trying to get Martin Scorsese a golden egg, has Miramax cooked his goose instead? — *New York Daily News*, 17th March 2003

2 to drink to the point of being drunk *US*
- — R. Frederick West, *God's Gambler*, p. 223, 1964

cookbook *noun*
in computing, a book of code segments that can be used to enhance programs *US*
- Cookbooks, slavishly followed, can lead one into voodoo programming, but are useful for hackers trying to monkey up small programs in unknown languages. — Eric S. Raymond, *The New Hacker's Dictionary*, p. 105, 1991

cooked *adjective*
1 drunk or drug-intoxicated *US*
- — Anna Scotti and Paul Young, *Buzzwords*, p. 57, 1997

2 in trouble *US*
- I knew she would soon make her choice and I would be cooked for good and all. — Max Shulman, *I was a Teen-Age Dwarf*, p. 28, 1959

3 embalmed *US*
- — *Maledicta*, p. 180, Summer/Winter 1986–1987: 'Sexual slang: prostitutes, pedophiles, flagellators, transvestites, and necrophiles'

4 finished, exhausted *UK, 1925*
- You is fucked and you is cooked and you is over. — Joel Rose, *Kill Kill Faster Faster*, p. 119, 1997

cookem fry *verb*
to die *UK*
Rhyming slang, from an earlier naval use as 'hell'.
- — John Laffin, *Jack Tar*, 1969

cooker *noun*
1 any object used to heat heroin preparatory to injecting it *US*
- The cookers are metal caps off wine bottles with the cork lining taken out. — Willard Motley, *Let No Man Write My Epitaph*, p. 157, 1958
- A gland in his neck was making the ducts in his mouth water at the thought of drugs: cooker, matches, needle, eye-dropper, and pacifier. — Clarence Cooper Jr, *The Scene*, p. 15, 1960
- When he awakes in the morning, he reaches instantly for his "works" – eyedropper, needle ("spike," he calls it), and bottle top ("cooker"). — James Mills, *The Panic in Needle Park*, p. 14, 1966
- Joe Green, better known to his friends and acquaintances as Jo-Jo, poured the rest of the heroin out of a small piece of tin foil into the Wild Irish Rose wine bottle top that had been converted into what drug users call a cooker. — Donald Goines, *Crime Partners*, p. 7, 1978

2 a person who prepares crack cocaine *US*
- — Terry Williams, *Crackhouse*, p. 147, 1992

3 a person or thing that excels or excites *US, 1943*
- Baby, this is Bernie, Bernie is a real heavy cooker on piano. — Ross Russell, *The Sound*, p. 190, 1961
- — Stewart L. Tubbs and Sylvia Moss, *Human Communication*, p. 120, 1974

cooker *verb*
to inject a drug intravenously *UK*
- — Mike Haskins, *Drugs*, p. 290, 2003

cookie *noun*
1 a person *US, 1917*
- There's your answer. He's a smart cookie. — Horace McCoy, *Kiss Tomorrow Good-bye*, p. 207, 1948
- When that girl comes back she be one mad cookie, you bet! — Mickey Spillane, *One Lonely Night*, p. 146, 1951
- He was a sharp cookie, West, and Miller was just as sharp[.] — Evan Hunter, *The Blackboard Jungle*, p. 64, 1954
- But in the 'twenties a cookie who knew something about sex appeared in a cafe and, instead of showing herself nude, showed herself naked. — Lee Mortimer, *Women Confidential*, p. 134, 1960

2 the vagina *US*
- — Clarence Major, *Dictionary of Afro-American Slang*, p. 40, 1970
- I promise you, kiddo, if you can't get a boner, I'll let you cop a feel of my cookie. — Thomas Sanchez, *The Zoot Suit Murders*, p. 58, 1978

3 a material reward or inducement; money *US*
- Cookies are the prizes to be won in a game, and the term usually refers to money. — Christina and Richard Milner, *Black Players*, p. 48, 1972
- Now that you're on the streets, you'll need cookies in your kick [wallet], and always try to keep some there. — A.S. Jackson, *Gentleman Pimp*, p. 30, 1973

4 a sweet confection that has marijuana as a major ingredient *US*
- [I]t is an offence to possess even one seed or leaf of cannabis. This includes cookies. Don't get casual. — Brian Preston, *Pot Planet*, p. 95, 2002

5 cocaine *US*
- — Vincent J. Monteleone, *Criminal Slang*, p. 58, 1949

6 a large chunk of processed crack cocaine *US*
- Cocaine had to be turned into what we called a cookie. Then you could break it off and sell it as rocks. — *Menace II Society*, 1993

7 a cigarette *US*
- — Wayne Floyd, *Jason's Authentic Dictionary of CB Slang*, p. 13, 1976

8 a cigarette adulterated with crack cocaine *US*
- — Anna Scotti and Paul Young, *Buzzwords*, p. 131, 1997

9 a file that an Internet webpage leaves on the hard drive of a user's computer, that is retrieved whenever the user returns to that webpage *US*
- — Eric S. Raymond, *The New Hacker's Dictionary*, p. 117, 1993
- — Andy Ihnatko, *Cyberspeak*, p. 40, 1997

10 a blood clot travelling through the arteries *US*
- — Sally Williams, *"Strong" Words*, p. 137, 1994

11 in television and film making, a light screen designed to cast shadows *US*
- — Ralph S. Singleton, *Filmaker's Dictionary*, p. 91, 1990

▸ that's the way the cookie crumbles
that's how things turn out *US, 1956*
- — *Independent Record (Helena, Montana)*, 27th November 1955
- Well, you know what they say, that's the way the cookie crumbles sometimes. — Odie Hawkins, *Ghetto Sketches*, p. 179, 1972
- [I]f the conversation happens to turn to gossip about sex in the office, well, that's the way the cookie crumbles. — Michael Crichton, *Disclosure*, p. 223, 1993

cookie breath *noun*
the alcoholic fumes arising from someone who has drunk lemon extract or vanilla flavouring *CANADA*
- He gets drunk any way he can – he has cookie breath all the time. — Lewis Poteet, *The South Shore Phrase Book*, p. 33, 1999

cookie cutter *noun*

1 in circus and carnival usage, a police badge *US, 1926*

- —Don Wilmeth, *The Language of American Popular Entertainment*, p. 63, 1981

2 the cap badge worn by officers of the Canadian Cadet Instructors Cadre *CANADA*
The CIC cap badge is brass and maple leaf-shaped. As such, its irregular edges are reminiscent of the serrated edge of a kitchen biscuit cutter.

- —Tom Langeste, *Words on the Wing*, p. 66, 1995

cookie duster *noun*

a mustache *US, 1930*

- One's ten, the other's four and half, living up there with their mom and a real estate man she married name of Gary, has a little cookie-duster mustache.—Elmore Leonard, *Riding the Rap*, p. 9, 1995

cookies *noun*

the contents of a person's stomach *US, 1927*

- —J.E. Lighter, *Historical Dictionary of American Slang, Volume 1*, p. 472, 1994
- The body's response to fear is simple: fight or flight. Either lose your cookies while scampering off to safety, or hope to find an incontinence pad before being embarrassed to death[.]—Karen Moline, *No Parachutes [Tart Noir]*, p. 49, 2002

▸ **blow your cookies**

to vomit *US, 1976*

- My lunch – a tahini-and-bean-sprout pita – came back into my throat, and I practically blew my cookies all over my calendar.—Rita Ciresi, *Pink Slip*, p. 54, 1999

▸ **get your cookies**

to experience pleasure, especially in a perverted way *US, 1956*

- A fart smeller, way over in the corner, grabbed them, started sniffing, getting his cookies.—Steve Cannon, *Groove, Bang, and Jive Around*, p. 71, 1969

cookie toss *noun*

vomit *US*

- Then we filled the salad bathtub with a concotion of Martian cookie-toss that was genuinely disgusting.—Ed Sanders, *Tales of Beatnik Glory*, p. 32, 1975

cooking *adjective*

1 in shuffleboard, used for communicating the fact that a disc is in the kitchen *US*

- —Omero C. Catan, *Secrets of Shuffleboard Strategy*, p. 65, 1967

2 (used of surf conditions) excellent *US*

- —Gary Fairmont R. Filosa II, *The Surfer's Almanac*, p. 183, 1977

cooking fuel *noun*

low-octane petrol *UK*

- —Douglas Dunford, *Motorcycle Department, Beaulieu Motor Museum*, 1979

cooking lager *noun*

a lager of no more than average strength *UK*

- —Andrew Holmes, *Sleb*, p. 150, 2002

cook off *verb*

(used of ammunition) to explode because of heat from a surrounding fire *US*

- —Gregory Clark, *Words of the Vietnam War*, p. 123, 1990

cook shack *noun*

1 a truck stop or roadside restaurant *US*

- —"Slingo", *The Official CB Slang Dictionary Handbook*, p. 17, 1976

2 a brakevan (caboose) *US*

- —Ramon Adams, *The Language of the Railroader*, p. 37, 1977

cook up *verb*

1 to concoct something; to fabricate something; to falsify something *UK, 1817*
Often in the form 'cook up a story'.

- "What you got cooked up?" he asked.—Chester Gould, *Dick Tracy Meets the Night Crawler*, p. 168, 1945
- [I]f I hadn't refused to come in, this charge would never have been cooked up in the first place.—Martin Waddell, *Otley*, p. 105, 1966
- The Man be cooking up the conspiracies again, but the sentences are gonna be a motherfucker – I ain't jiving you.—Edwin Torres, *Carlito's Way*, p. 66, 1975
- Police yesterday accused Runyenjes MP Njeru Kathangu of cooking up a story about his daughter's kidnapping.—*Daily Nation [Kenya]*, 21st March 2001

2 to manufacture amphetamine *US*

- They cook up speed in those shacks, but it's almost impossible to get probable cause to bust them.—Joseph Wambaugh, *The Secrets of Harry Bright*, p. 108, 1985

3 to process cocaine hydrochoride into crack cocaine *UK*

- —Nick Constable, *This is Cocaine*, p. 182, 2002

cooky *noun*

in sabre fencing, a hit on the guard not on the target *UK*
A corruption of 'coquille' (the guard).

- —E.D. Morton, *Martini A-Z of Fencing*, 1988

cool *noun*

1 self-control, composure *US, 1953*

- An Open Letter to Tom Jones – YOU BLEW YOUR COOL, TOM JONES [Full-page advertisement]—*Record Beat*, p. 9, 12th April 1966
- Then Our Mayor hotly blew his cool and launched the now-historic raids on the North Beach nudie nooks.—*San Francisco Chronicle*, p. 29, 8th July 1966

2 a truce between street gangs *US*

- A "cool" was negotiated by street club workers. But it was an uneasy truce, often broken.—Harrison E. Salisbury, *The Shook-up Generation*, p. 38, 1958

3 a look *UK*
Back slang.

- [T]ake a cool at that.—David Powis, *The Signs of Crime*, 1977

cool *verb*

1 to calm down; to become less dangerous *US*

- Jim will last out the cops. He'll go to the hustling bar a few streets away, until the street cools.—John Rechy, *The Sexual Outlaw*, p. 48, 1977

2 to idle; to pass time doing nothing *US*

- I was coolin with Rick.—*Boyz N The Hood*, 1990

3 to kill, or at least immobilise someone *US*

- —*American Speech*, p. 268, December 1962: 'The language of traffic policemen'

4 to die *US*

- —Sally Williams, *"Strong" Words*, p. 137, 1994

▸ **cool it**

to unwind, to calm down; to slow down, to ease off; to stop whatever activity you are engaged in *US, 1953*
Often used in the imperative.

- Let's cool it—Lavada Durst, *The Jives of Dr. Hepcat*, 1953
- "Man, we'd be sitting over there in the bar," said one, "just coolin it around the pool table with a few beers[.]—Hunter S. Thompson, *Hell's Angels*, p. 40, 1966
- [T]he black friends of the white power structure issued a pamphlet with the headline COOL IT, BABY!—Eldridge Cleaver, *Soul on Ice*, p. 90, 1968
- [S]he insisted on carrying [drugs] even after I warned her to cool it while I was heavy into my dealing changes.—Robert Bingham, *Planted, Burnt, and Busted [The Howard Marks Book of Dope Stories]*, p. 339, 1970
- "Cool it. The guard's coming," I whispered.—Bobby Seale, *A Lonely Rage*, p. 263, 1978
- Meaning we'll have to cool it for a while, right?—*Sex, Lies and Videotape*, 1989

▸ **cool your brains**

to calm down *TRINIDAD AND TOBAGO, 1928*

- —Lise Winer, *Dictionary of the English/Creole of Trinidad & Tobago*, 2003

▸ **cool your heels**

to rest *UK, 1633*

- A half hour later Rocco walked into the amber glow of the old Juvie annex behind the Western District station house and found four kids cooling their heels[.]—Richard Price, *Clockers*, p. 591, 1992

▸ **cool your jets**

to calm down; to back off *US, 1973*

- I'm just going to cool my jets, no matter what!—Beatrice Sparks (writing as 'Anonymous'), *Jay's Journal*, p. 62, 1979
- WURLITZER: How 'bout Mallory? SCAGNETTI: Coolin' her jets in a holding cell.—*Natural Born Killers*, 1994

▸ **cool your liver**

to drink alcohol *BARBADOS*

- Then, later at night, the drum and kettle men would come around asking for something to cool their liver.—*Advocate*, 20th December 1998

cool *adjective*

1 fashionable, attractive, admired *US*

- —Marcus Hanna Boulware, *Jive and Slang of Students in Negro Colleges*, 1947
- He had been half-heartedly trying to explain to her what was suggested by the term "cool," as hipsters used it.—John Clellon Holmes, *Go*, p. 173, 1952

- I learned the new hipster vocabulary; "pot" for weed, "twisted" for busted, "cool," an all-purpose word indicating anything you like or any situation that is not hot with the law. —William Burroughs, *Junkie*, p. 120, 1953
- Things were "cool" and cool things "gassed" the initiates and anything that was particularly cool was "crazy." —Robert Sylvester, *No Cover Charge*, p. 287, 1956
- [N]ow it is no longer 1948 but 1953 with cool generations and I five years older, or younger[.] —Jack Kerouac, *The Subterraneans*, p. 9, 1958

2 acceptable, agreeable *US*
- BUTCH: So we're cool. MARSELLUS: Yeah man, we're cool— *Pulp Fiction*, 1994
- I guess he's pretty, huh, racially pretty cool. — *The Big Lebowski*, 1998
- My friend and I were messing about with a gun and I accidentally shot him in the face [...] But we're cool. We're still good friends. — *The Times Magazine*, p. 44, 23rd February 2002

3 (of jazz or the style of a jazz performer) relaxed, good, modern *US*
- — *Cool Blues*, 19th February 1947
- — *The Observer*, 16th September 1956

4 discreet, under control *UK, 1952*
Similar to the earlier **COOL AS A CUCUMBER**.
- Staying cool in Marrakesh would be like Alice not falling down a well. —Richard Neville, *Play Power*, p. 233, 1970

5 retaining complete personal control of the need for drugs or whilst drug-exhilarated, or so the user believes *UK*
- —John Wyatt, *Drugs*, 1973

6 not carrying illegal drugs *UK*
- — *The Observer*, 3rd December 1967

7 used for emphasising an amount of money *UK, 1728*
- Depending on the size of the casino and the day of the week, that sum can fluctuate between a half-million and a cool million dollars, sheer cash. —Edward Lin, *Big Julie of Vegas*, p. 80, 1974
- "Wot's it worth, Johnny?" "A cool fifty grand, Rag! The boss knows how to pick 'em, eh?" — *The Sweeney*, p. 54, 1976
- Ingram played by George Clooney in Ocean's 11-type conman mode, liberating a cool million from the people who have encouraged a nation to daydream of fast bucks and obscene wealth. — *The Guardian*, 22nd April 2003

▸ **cool like Gokool**
very successful *TRINIDAD AND TOBAGO, 1938*
- —Lise Winer, *Dictionary of the English/Creole of Trinidad & Tobago*, 2003

coolaboola; coder-boder *adjective*
excellent, admirable, acceptable *IRELAND*
An elaboration of **COOL** (acceptable) combining a slangy abridgement of the Irish *ruaille-buaille* (a row, noisy confusion, noise).
- "COOLABOOLA." It's not a Bornean call of the wild. Nor a fancy greeting that will get you a first class meal in a tropical rainforest. No, it just means "cool". — *Irish Times*, 24th August 1996
- Everything was 'cooler-booler' to her except me. —Ardal O'Hanlon, *The Talk of the Town*, p. 202, 1998

cool as *adjective*
extremely pleasing, very good *UK*
An intensification of **COOL**, shortened from **COOL AS FUCK**, etc.
- Did yer see Orbital? - Yeh. - Aw cool as. - Yeh. —Niall Griffiths, *Kelly + Victor*, p. 34, 2002

cool as a cucumber *adjective*
self-possessed *UK, c.1732*
- She might look as cool as a cucumber when she gives evidence[.] — *The Guardian*, 13th April 2003

cool as a fish's fart *adjective*
calm, composed *IRELAND*
- Here comes Townsend. What a player. Cool as a fish's fart. —Howard Paul, *The Joy*, p. 155, 1996

cool as fuck *adjective*
extremely pleasing, very good
An intensification of **COOL**. In 1990, the phrase 'cool as fuck' was part of the logo-styling for UK band the Inspiral Carpets.

cool bananas!
great! excellent! *AUSTRALIA, 1987*
- It is now de rigueur, we discovered in a variety of calls with people yesterday, to end the conversation with an expression such as 'cool bananas', 'rage on', 'right on man', etc. — *Courier-Mail*, p. 2, 15th February 1989

cool beans!
used as an expression of intense approval *US*
- —Connie Eble (Editor), *UNC-CH Campus Slang*, p. 2, Spring 1987
- — *Merriam-Webster's Hot Words on Campus Marketing Survey '93*, p. 3, 13th October 1993
- Okay, cool beans, a party. I'm into it. —Joel Rose, *Kill Kill Faster Faster*, p. 29, 1997
- —Vann Wesson, *Generation X Field Guide and Lexicon*, p. 40, 1997

cool breeze *noun*
used as a term of address, generally with admiration *US, 1961*
- —J.E. Lighter, *Historical Dictionary of American Slang, Volume 1*, p. 475, 1994

cool breeze *adjective*
calm, collected *US*
- Good when I'm cool breeze and bad when I'm down. —Piri Thomas, *Down These Mean Streets*, p. 48, 1967

cool breezer *noun*
a carefree, casual surfer *US*
- —Michael V. Anderson, *The Bad, Rad, Not to Forget Way Cool Beach and Surf Discriptionary*, p. 4, 1988

Cool Britannia *noun*
a marketing categorisation for fashionable British culture *UK*
Puns 'Rule Britannia'; originally coined by the Bonzo Dog Doo Dah Band: 'Cool Britannia / Britannia you are hip': 1967.
- [Britpop] had been the soundtrack to the mid nineties, the so-called "Cool Britannia". —John Robb, *The Nineties*, p. 141, 1999

cool-cool; cool-cool so *adverb*
as if normal *TRINIDAD AND TOBAGO*
- —Lise Winer, *Dictionary of the English/Creole of Trinidad & Tobago*, 2003

coolcrack *verb*
to kill someone *US*
- Give it to him, Maceo, coolcrack the motherfouler! —Ralph Ellison, *Invisible Man*, p. 488, 1947

cool dad *noun*
a well-dressed, popular male *US*
College student usage.
- — *Time Magazine*, p. 46, 24th August 1959

cool deal!
used as an expression of assent or praise *US*
- —Connie Eble (Editor), *UNC-CH Campus Slang*, p. 2, Fall 2001

cool down *verb*
to calm down *UK, 1882*
- When he cooled down, he spoke of his hostility to secondary selection in a way that completely convinced me of his sincerity. — *The Guardian*, 28th October 2002

cooler *noun*

1 a jail or prison *US, 1872*
- I was in cooler with poor Spick husbands for 30 mins. —Jack Kerouac, *Letter to Neal Cassady*, p. 326, 1 October 1951
- [H]e was swinging by his belt from the windowbars of the courthouse cooler. —Jim Thompson, *The Killer Inside*, p. 150, 1952
- You sure you want to mix it with a guy who has been in the cooler —Raymond Chandler, *The Long Goodbye*, p. 71, 1953
- "Any analysis, any time spent in any other institutions?" "Well, counting state and county coolers-" —Ken Kesey, *One Flew Over the Cuckoo's Nest*, p. 44, 1962
- I didn't know you were out of the cooler yet, Dally. —S.E. Hinton, *The Outsiders*, 1967
- Your mate can start by getting him out of the cooler pronto! —Barry Humphries, *Bazza Pulls It Off!*, 1971
- While Gigi cooled his heels in the cooler, a private detective named Whelan, a retired homicide cop, was out working on his behalf. —Leonard Shecter and William Phillips, *On the Pad*, p. 214, 1973

2 a cell used for solitary confinement; a segregation unit *US, 1899*
- —John M. Murtagh and Sara Harris, *Cast the First Stone*, p. 259, 1957
- —Angela Devlin, *Prison Patter*, p. 40, 1996

3 an infirmary *US*
Where one's social activities are 'put on ice'.
- — *Concord (New Hampshire) Monitor*, p. 17, 23rd August 1983

4 a morgue *US*
- —Sally Williams, *"Strong" Words*, p. 137, 1994

5 a silencer attached to a hand gun *US*
- —Joseph E. Ragen and Charles Finston, *Inside the World's Toughest Prison*, p. 795, 1962

6 a cigarette laced with cocaine *US*
- — US Department of Justice, *Street Terms*, October 1994

7 a stacked deck of cards used by a cheat *US, 1935*
- —Robert C. Prus and C.R.D. Sharper, *Road Hustler*, p. 169, 1977
- —Michael Dalton, *Blackjack*, p. 40, 1991

8 in horse racing, a horse that is not expected to win the race *US, 1935*
- —Dan Parker, *The ABC of Horse Racing*, p. 145, 1947

9 a lightweight cotton blanket put on a horse after a warm-up *US*
- —George Sullivan, *Harness Racing*, p. 102, 1964

cooler-bagger *noun*
a man with a paunch *SOUTH AFRICA*
Teen slang; coined in humorous reference to **SIX-PACKER** (a well-built man).
- —*Sunday Times (South Africa)*, 1st June 2003

coolgardie safe; Coolgardie *noun*
a type of storage locker for keeping foodstuffs cool *AUSTRALIA, 1924*
From the name of a Western Australian mining town.
- When we got to Jessops Wells a fettler came over with a bottle he'd kept cool – well off the boil anyway – in a coolgardie safe.—Patsy Adam-Smith, *Folklore of the Australian Railwaymen*, p. 82, 1969
- Relax, pal, while I repair to the Coolgardie and knock up a snack.—Jack Hibberd, *A Stretch of the Imagination*, p. 8, 1971
- —Jim Ramsay, *Cop It Sweet!*, p. 24, 1977

cool head main thing!
used for urging others to calm down *US*
Hawaiian youth usage.
- —Elizabeth Ball Carr, *Da Kine Talk*, p. 128, 1972
- —Douglas Simonson, *Pidgin to da Max*, 1981

cool-hunter *noun*
a person engaged in the identification of up-coming trends, especially in the media or fashion industry *UK*
Formed on **COOL** (fashionable).
- In a world built on artifice, on the cool-hunter's spin and the stylist's gloss *coolie noun*, reality is hard to come by.—*The Observer*, 13th October 2002

coolie *noun*

1 a loner; a person who refuses to join a gang *US*
- The concept of the coolie is common to all the street gangs. The coolie is a boy who does not belong to a street club.—Harrison E. Salisbury, *The Shook-up Generation*, p. 29, 1958
- Coolies is something like whores, you know. Can't stop nothing because they all alone in the world.—Sara Harris, *The Lords of Hell*, p. 128, 1967

2 a hip, street-smart person *US*
- "I hear you 104th Street coolies are supposed to have heart," I said. —Piri Thomas, *Down These Mean Streets*, p. 49, 1967

3 a cigarette to which crack cocaine has been added *US*
- —Terry Williams, *Crackhouse*, p. 147, 1992
- —Mike Haskins, *Drugs*, p. 293, 2003

Coolie *noun*

1 in South Africa, a person of Indian descent *INDIA, 1873*
Offensive, insulting.
- [S]he went into hospital to have her (Gesturing) "wardrobe" taken out. Dripping in jewellery like a bladdy coolie! Looks like a damn Christmas tree, if you ask me.—Lueen Conning, *A Coloured Place*, 1998
- He leans into Maxim as Lili plops down beside her man. "Coolie?" he asks, indicating Lili with his chin. "Guyanese?" "India," Maxim says, putting his arm around her shoulders. "She's Indian."—V.K. Mina, *Splintered Day*, p. 56, 1999

2 a Vietnamese civilian *US*
The C19 term for Chinese or other East Asians was revived by US soldiers in Vietnam.
- —Linda Reinberg, *In the Field*, p. 49, 1991

3 an Asian servant *AUSTRALIA*
- The talk turned to Coolies and how they simply had to use an electric cattle prod on some of their Asian servants to get them to do any work.—Kitty Churchill, *Thinking of England*, p. 137, 1995

4 a locomotive fireman *UK*
- —Frank McKenna, *A Glossary of Railwaymen's Talk*, 1970

coolie *adjective*
of East Indian origin *TRINIDAD AND TOBAGO, 1880*
- —Lise Winer, *Dictionary of the English/Creole of Trinidad & Tobago*, 2003

coolie colours *noun*
bright colours, especiallly in combination in dress *GRENADA*
From the association of these bright colours with Indians.

coolie-do *noun*
the vagina *US*
- —Helen Dahlskog (Editor), *A Dictionary of Contemporary and Colloquial Usage*, p. 15, 1972

coolie food *noun*
Indian food *TRINIDAD AND TOBAGO*
- —Lise Winer, *Dictionary of the English/Creole of Trinidad & Tobago*, 2003

coolie pink *noun*
a garish, bright pink *SOUTH AFRICA*
Associated with the bright colours favoured by East Indians.
- —Jean Branford, *A Dictionary of South African English*, 1978
- —Lise Winer, *Dictionary of the English/Creole of Trinidad & Tobago*, 2003

coolie tonic *noun*
any liquid poison *TRINIDAD AND TOBAGO*
In Trinidad, poison is associated with Indian suicides.
- —Lise Winer, *Dictionary of the English/Creole of Trinidad & Tobago*, 2003

cooling *adjective*
unemployed *US*
- —Babs Gonzales, *Be-Bop Dictionary and History of its Famous Stars*, p. 9, 1949

cooling glasses; coolers *noun*
sunglasses *INDIA*
- I bought a pair of cooling glasses today – the sun was so bright. —Paroo Nihalini, R.K. Tongue and Priya Hosali, *Indian and British English*, 1979

coolio *adjective*
fashionable; acceptable *US*
An elaboration of **COOL**; probably also a reference to rapper Coolio who enjoyed a huge international success in the mid-1990s.
- —Connie Eble (Editor), *UNC-CH Campus Slang*, p. 2, April 1997
- It's not supposed to be Coolio to be early all the time, but it does always seem to work out that I'm the first one there.—Kevin Sampson, *Outlaws*, p. 3, 2001

cool it back *verb*
to become calm and composed under pressure *US*
- —Inez Cardozo-Freeman, *The Joint*, p. 489, 1984

cool Muther John *noun*
a boy who is fashionable, knowledgeable and trendy *US*
- —*American Weekly*, p. 2, 14th August 1955

coolness!
used for expressing agreement or approval *US*
- —Connie Eble (Editor), *UNC-CH Campus Slang*, p. 3, Spring 1988

cool off *verb*
to calm down *UK, 1887*
- [T]he woman who says she cooled off her affair once "the excitement of being with a famous person had worn off"[.]—*The Guardian*, 15th June 2003

cool-off man *noun*
in a confidence swindling or cheating scheme, the member of the swindling group who stays with the victim calming him down after he learns that he has been swindled *US, 1977*
- —Thomas L. Clark, *The Dictionary of Gambling and Gaming*, p. 52, 1987

cool-out *noun*
in police interrogations, the practice of leaving the accused alone in the interrogation room before the interrogation begins *US*
- I know this routine, guys. I pulled a this cool-out a hundred times myself.—Stephen Cannell, *Big Con*, p. 320, 1997

cool out *verb*

1 to idle *BARBADOS*
- Look at we all working and he at home cooling out!—Frank A. Collymore, *Barbadian Dialect*, p. 35, 1965
- Most kids use [glue-sniffing] to cool out from pressure[.]—*Time Out*, 8th January 1982
- If you need to cool out, markie says you're welcome to go down to the apartment. Cool out there in comfort.—Joel Rose, *Kill Kill Faster Faster*, p. 25, 1997

2 in police interrogations, to perform a cool-out on someone *US*
- She'd been a prosecutor for five years, so she knew that there were basically two reasons why cops cool out a suspect like this. —Stephen Cannell, *Big Con*, p. 320, 1997

3 (used of a confidence swindler or a tout who has given bad tips) to calm a bettor who has lost *US*
- —David W. Maurer, *Argot of the Racetrack*, p. 22, 1951
- —Robert C. Prus and C.R.D. Sharper, *Road Hustler*, p. 169, 1977

cool points *noun*
an imaginary tally of points awarded for cool behaviour and subtracted for uncool behaviour *US*
- —Connie Eble (Editor), *UNC-CH Campus Slang*, p. 2, Spring 1989

cool the beans!
calm down!, be patient! *UK: SCOTLAND*
- —Michael Munro, *The Patter, Another Blast*, 1988

cool wash; coul wash *noun*
a pelting with stones *DOMINICA*
Probably a corruption of the French *coup de roche* (blow with a stone) to Creole *koul woche*.

cool water *noun*
strong, illegally manufactured whisky *US*
- —*Star Tribune (Minneapolis)*, p. 19F, 31st January 1999

cooly *noun*
marijuana *JAMAICA*
Perhaps a deliberate mispronunciation of **KALI**.

cool your jets!
calm down! *US*
- —Connie Eble (Editor), *UNC-CH Campus Slang*, p. 1, Fall 1982
- [E]verybody should just cool their jets. —Christopher Brookmyre, *The Sacred Art of Stealing*, p. 200, 2002

cool yule
happy Christmas
A very uncool turn of phrase, generally heavily ironic or knowingly *infra dig* for humorous effect.
- Have a Cool Yule, dude! —Kevin Sampson, *Powder*, p. 461, 1999

coon *noun*
in the UK and US, a black person; in Australia, an Aborigine; in New Zealand, a Pacific Islander; in South Africa, a black-faced minstrel *US, 1834*
Offensive.
- The cop leaned over to see me better. "A coon," he said. Then he looked at Alice again. "Both coons." —Chester Himes, *If He Hollers Let Him Go*, p. 63, 1945
- "Ring the bell before Jackson kills him a coon!" someone boomed in the sudden silence. —Ralph Ellison, *Invisible Man*, p. 22, 1947
- I'll tell that coon over there to turn it off or get his fat little ass kicked. —Ken Kesey, *One Flew Over the Cuckoo's Nest*, p. 77, 1962
- Heard these little coons are hung like horses[.] —Dick Gregory, *Nigger*, p. 10, 1964
- White people always associated watermelons with Negroes, and they sometimes called Negroes "coons" among all the other names[.] —Malcolm X and Alex Haley, *The Autobiography of Malcolm X*, p. 15, 1964
- "The coon's loaded," he muttered, craning his neck out the window to look behind us. —Terry Southern, *Now Dig This*, p. 118, November 1968
- Don't want any of that fucking coon music. —Johnny Speight, *It Stands to Reason*, p. 93, 1973
- Stand up, coon. Name and number. —*Scum*, 1979
- Come on you fuckin' coon, move that fuckin' motor! —Donald Gorgon, *Cop Killer*, p. 2, 1994
- —Harry Orsman, *A Dictionary of Modern New Zealand Slang*, p. 31, 1999
- Non-stop [...] poisonous invective against fucking queers, lezzies – I wouldn't mind fuckin' one of them though – pakkies, coons and the cuntin' Common Market. —Stuart Browne, *Dangerous Parking*, p. 44, 2000

coon *verb*
1 to steal something; someone to cheat *US*
- [S]ome of us boys would slip out down the road, or across the pastures, and go "cooning" watermelons. —Malcolm X and Alex Haley, *The Autobiography of Malcolm X*, p. 15, 1964
- —Clarence Major, *Dictionary of Afro-American Slang*, p. 40, 1970
- Monkey said, "Find a stump to fit your rump / And I'll coon you till your asshole jump." —Dennis Wepman et al., *The Life*, p. 33, 1976

2 to bet *US*
- —Marcus Hanna Boulware, *Jive and Slang of Students in Negro Colleges*, 1947
- Say, "Why don't you get you a deck of cards where I can coon you some?" —Bruce Jackson, *Get Your Ass in the Water and Swim Like Me*, p. 175, 1962

3 on the railways, to travel over the tops of goods wagons while a train is moving *US*
- —J. Herbert Lund, *Herb's Hot Box of Railraod Slang*, p. 56, 1975

coon-ass *noun*
a resident of Louisiana; a Cajun *US, 1943*
Often, not always, considered a slur.
- —Jerry Robertson, *Oil Slanguage*, p. 40, 1954
- —*American Speech*, p. 57, Spring-Summer 1975: 'Razorback slang'
- How a coon ass like me merits the time and patience of two such eminent editors is hard to figure. —James Carville, *We're Right, They're Wrong*, p. x, 1996
- He talks like a coon-ass. —James Lee Burke, *Sunset Limited*, p. 174, 1998
- When he called the name Terry Hubert, I whispered, "A-Bear, Sir, not Hubert. That's a coon-ass name, Sir!" —Franklin D. Rast, *Don's Nam*, p. 42, 1999

coon bottom *noun*
a poor part of town, especially one where poor black people live *US, 1968*
- Others suggest that these sections are not urban at all but intolerably countrified: Frogtown and Goosetown (3 responses each), Gooseville, Coontown, and Coon Bottom (1 each). —Erin McKean (Editor), *Verbatim*, p. 37, 2001

coondie *noun*
a stone or rock, especially a small stone suitable for throwing *AUSTRALIA, 1941*
Usage chiefly in Western Australia.
- I remember boondies being larger rocks (still big enough to throw) and smaller ones called coondies[.] —*Wordmap (www.abc.net.au/wordmap)*, 2003

cooney *noun*
1 a white resident of Louisiana *US*
A diminutive of **COON-ASS**.
- —*American Speech*, p. 57, Spring-Summer 1975: 'Razorback slang'

2 a woman, especially a wife *CANADA*
Northern Canadian usage. Also spelled 'kuni'.
- "It can't be," murmured the old lady, "Whatever will the kunis think of them curly locks?" —W. A. Anderson, *Angel of Hudson Bay*, p. 39, 1961

coon killer *noun*
a club *US*
- —Ralph de Sola, *Crime Dictionary*, p. 31, 1982

coon light *noun*
a light mounted on a truck tracking on the right edge of the road *US*
- —Montie Tak, *Truck Talk*, p. 37, 1971

coon's age *noun*
a long time *US, 1843*
- Hell, I haven't been in a brawl in a coon's age. —Darryl Ponicsan, *The Last Detail*, p. 77, 1970
- "If it ain't Bertha Grimmitt – you ain't been in here in a coon's age," Cleve Goins shouted. —Pat Conroy, *The Great Santini*, p. 173, 1976
- I found this old address book in a jacket I ain't worn in a coon's age. Toby what? What the fuck was her last name? —*Reservoir Dogs*, 1994
- "I have a sneaking suspicion you haven't sat in a coon's age." "However the hell long that is," said Switters. —Tom Robbins, *Fierce Invalids from Hot Climates*, p. 130, 2000

coon stopper *noun*
a powerful gun *US*
- "And this, Wiftoe," he said pointing to Condo's revolver, "is a Colt Trooper .357. The kind you stop coons with. A coon-stopper." —John Sayles, *Union Dues*, p. 313, 1977

Coon Town *noun*
a neighbourhood populated largey by black families *US*
Offensive.
- —*Maledicta*, p. 52, 1986–1987: 'A continuation of a glossary of ethnic slurs in American English'

coop *noun*
1 a house or apartment *US*
- [S]crams on ahead to grandma's coop[.] —Haenigsen, *Jive's Like That*, 1947

2 a police stationhouse *US*
- —Joseph E. Ragen and Charles Finston, *Inside the World's Toughest Prison*, p. 795, 1962

3 a place where police sleep or idle during their shift *US*
- "First, though, he went down to his little coop, a room in the basement of an apartment house where police could, while on duty, rest, sleep, play cards, use a toilet, hide from the sergeant. —Leonard Shecter and William Phillips, *On the Pad*, p. 91, 1973

4 in craps, a roll of 12 *US, 1983*
An abbreviated nickname of Gary Cooper, star of the Western film *High Noon*.
- — Thomas L. Clark, *The Dictionary of Gambling and Gaming*, p. 90, 1987

coop *verb*
to sleep or relax while on duty *US, 1962*
- When policemen sleep on duty in New York, they "coop"; when they sleep in Washington, they "huddle." — *New York Times*, 15th February 1970
- As a rookie cop, Serpico was also introduced to the fine art of "cooping," or sleeping on duty, a time-honored police practice that in other cites goes under such names as "huddling" and "going down." — Peter Maas, *Serpico*, p. 63, 1973
- A big four cops – and two of them moonlight days driving cabs, so they spend half their shift cooping. — Vincent Patrick, *The Pope of Greenwich Village*, p. 37, 1977
- He suggested I sleep, I didn't intend to do any cooping on that job, but all of a sudden I couldn't keep my eyes open. — George Chesbro, *Shadow of a Broken Man*, p. 56, 1977
- He's in there with the guy who takes your quarter, drinking. Cooping, they call it in the city, in New York. — John Sayles, *Union Dues*, p. 367, 1977

coop delight *noun*
the body of a murder victim *US*
From the Latin *corpus delicti*.
- — John R. Armore and Joseph D. Wolfe, *Dictionary of Desperation*, p. 25, 1976

cooper *verb*
to silence or humiliate someone *CANADA*
- To be coopered is to get tied up in an argument or beaten in a fight or contest and be silenced like a barrel is when it is coopered with all the staves in, the hoops on, and the head 'coopered.' — Lewis Poteet (citing a letter from Danny Bower), *The South Shore Phrase Book*, p. 33, 1999

coop-happy *adjective*
deranged from confinement *US*
- — Harold Wentworth and Stuart Berg Flexner, *Dictionary of American Slang*, p. 122, 1960

coo's arse; cow's arse *noun*
1 a cigarette end over-moistened with a smoker's saliva *UK: SCOTLAND*
- OK, ye can have a drag a ma fag but don't gie it a coo's arse. — Michael Munro, *The Patter, Another Blast*, 1988

2 by extension, a botched job *UK: SCOTLAND*
- Whoever hung this wallpaper made a coo's arse of it. — Michael Munro, *The Patter, Another Blast*, 1988

coosie *noun*
a Chinese person or other South Asian *US*
- — *American Speech*, p. 30, February 1949: 'A.V.G. lingo'

coot *noun*
1 a harmless simpleton, especially an old one; a fellow *US, 1766*
Probably from the behavioural characteristics of the bird. Current in south London according to *Johnny Vaughan Tonight*, 13th February 2002.
- I hunched behind the wheel when I began thinking of the old coot who took the easy way out. — Mickey Spillane, *One Lonely Night*, p. 144, 1951
- After Howard Blakely wandered away, the old coot sat there, scattering crumbs and listening to the pings from the shooting gallery across the way. — Bernard Wolfe, *The Late Risers*, p. 33, 1954
- No one worried about the poor coot except Chuck. — Vince Kelly, *The Bogeyman*, p. 99, 1956
- Never mind the old coot down below, love. — Arthur Upfield, *Bony and the Mouse*, p. 26, 1959
- Hey, Mum, there's a silly coot in there who thinks it's Christmas. — Bill Wannan, *Folklore of the Australian Pub*, p. 6, 1972
- He's the troublemaker,' Clurry went on. 'This fair-headed coot. — Max Fatchen, *Chase through the Night*, p. 84, 1976
- — Multicultural Management Program Fellows, *Dictionary of Cautionary Words and Phrases*, 1989
- This coot was maybe sixty; tall and stooped, with a beaklike nose dropping in a straight line from his high liverspotted pate. — Seth Morgan, *Homeboy*, p. 168, 1990
- When Bobbie questioned Fin about the age of all the fun-loving fogies, coots, geezers, codgers, duffers and biddies she'd met in the saloon, he didn't know how to tell her that the oldest fossil in the joint wasn't fifteen years his senior. — Joseph Wambaugh, *Finnegan's Week*, p. 230, 1993
- I was never the brainiest coot, either at school or in the police force. — Rex Hunt, *Tall Tales – and True*, p. 108, 1994

2 the vagina; a woman as a sex object; sex with a woman *US*
- — *American Speech*, p. 57, Spring-Summer 1975: 'Razorback slang'

coot *verb*
to have sex *BAHAMAS*
- — John A. Holm, *Dictionary of Bahamian English*, p. 50, 1982

cootch dancer; cooch dancer *noun*
a woman who performs a sexually suggestive dance *US, 1910*
A shortened form of **HOOCHY KOOCHY**.
- A good colored singer doesn't have to wrap her sex in a pacakge and peddle it to the customer like a cootch dancer in a sideshow. — Mezz Mezzrow, *Really the Blues*, p. 27, 1946
- In sentencing the Cootch-Dancer Schmidt to 15 years for manslaughter (Time, Beb. 2), the judges had chided her for "appearing nude on the deck of [Mee's] yacht like a nymph," and for "swimming naked in [Havana] Bay." — *Time*, 11th October 1948

cootchy-coo; kootchy-koo; kitchy-koo *noun*
used as a lexicalisation of talk used with babies *UK, 1984*
From Irish dialect *kitchy, kitchy, kaw*.
- The clerk gave the baby a hunched-up kootchy-koo, impervious to Rodeny's rage. — Richard Price, *Clockers*, p. 571, 1992

cooter *noun*
the vagina *US*
- — Connie Eble (Editor), *UNC-CH Campus Slang*, p. 2, Fall 1986
- And then they shoved frozen polar bear sperm pencils up their cooters. — Tony Kushne, *Angels in America*, p. 34, 1994
- There's [a...] "cooter," "labbe," "Gladys Siegelman," "VA," "wee wee[".] — Eve Ensler, *The Vagina Monologues*, p. 6, 1998
- Cunt, Pussy, Coochie, Slit, Twat, Cooter, Snatch, Hole, Beaver, Bearded clam, Crack, Mound. — Mark Burnett, *Girlstellall.Com*, p. 211, 2002

cootie catcher *noun*
a somewhat intricately folded piece of paper, manipulated by the fingers, used by children to tell fortunes or to catch imaginary cooties *US*
- To American children, the salt cellar construction is traditionally known as a 'cootie catcher'. — Eric Kenneway, *Complete Origami*, p. 154, 1987
- Folk toys can be made by children themselves, in which case they are often temporary ("cootie catchers" and paper folded into a specific form and used to tell fortunes). — Jan Harold Brunvand, *American Folklore*, p. 712, 1996
- [A] playmate's folding paper toy (we used to call them "coottie catchers") unfolded to show him the words "dream is destiny." — Roger Ebert, *Roger Ebert's Movie Yearbook*, p. 652, 2002

cooties *noun*
an imaginary disease or infestation that could be transmitted by close contact, thus creating a stigma for the person who is said to have it *US, 1971*
A children's corruption of the older sense of the term (a body louse).
- Get your cooties off me. — *American Graffiti*, 1973
- Pretend you're a missionary saving a colony of cootie victims. — *Heathers*, 1988
- More than mouthwash would be required to slay those cooties. — C.D. Payne, *Youth in Revolt*, p. 39, 1993
- You can use my straw, I don't have kooties. — *Pulp Fiction*, 1994
- The tight-lipped way Peggy eked out the words placenta previa made it sound as if Karen had contracted crabs or cooties. — Rita Ciresi, *Pink Slip*, p. 66, 1999

Coot-sac *noun*
a cove or bay without an outlet *CANADA*
From the French *cul de sac* (dead end).

coover *noun*
any article or thing *UK*
English gypsy use, from Romany *kova* (this; thing).
- — Jimmy Stockin, *On The Cobbles*, p. 10, 2000

cooze; coozie *noun*
1 the vulva; the female genitals *US, 1927*
- — *The Guild Dictionary of Homosexual Terms*, p. 9, 1965
- Maybe it's just something to hold on to ... an extension of her thing, you know, her cooze. — Terry Southern, *Blue Movie*, p. 37, 1970
- "Snatch," "hole," "kooze," "slash," "pussy" and "crack" were other terms referring variously to women's genitals, to women as individuals, or to women as a species. — *Screw*, p. 5, 3rd January 1972
- [S]ee to it that their sweet-kooze don't get hassled by any rampaging perverts[.] — Lester Bangs, *Psychotic Reactions and Carburetor Dung*, p. 152, 1975
- The cooze light. The pussy light, the cunt, the C light, a little light. — Robert Stoller and I.S. Levine, *Coming Attractions*, p. 131, 1991
- She also possesses a truly attractive cunt: cooze lips which aren't flappy, crinkly, or rundown[.] — Anthony Petkovich, *The X Factory*, p. 16, 1997

2 a woman, especially a promiscuous woman *US, 1921*
- "Who's that fine-looking coozie?" hollered another one. —Frederick Kohner, *Gidget*, p. 15, 1957
- See, in the lounge, they got these coozie that carry lights, take you to a table. —Robert Gover, *Here Goes Kitten*, p. 25, 1964
- "There's enough white stuff around." Vess grinned slyly, and as he did it occurred to me that the word "stuff" involved me more than it was comfortable to admit, since it was not oriented towards the coozies. —Phil Andros (Samuel M. Steward), *Stud*, p. 88–89, 1966
- Brad says you're being a real cooze. —*Heathers*, 1988
- Let me tell ya what 'Like a Virgin's' about. It's about some cooze who's a regular fuck machine. —*Reservoir Dogs*, 1992
- Listen, you little cooze[.] —*Gone in 60 Seconds*, 2000

cooze light *noun*

in the pornography industry, a light used to illuminate the genitals of the performers *US*
- —*Adult Video News*, p. 50, October 1995

coozie stash *noun*

contraband, especially drugs, hidden in the vagina *US*
- —Jay Robert Nash, *Dictionary of Crime*, p. 79, 1992

cop *noun*

1 a police officer *US, 1859*

False etymologies abound, with formation suggestions of 'copper badges', 'copper buttons', or an abbreviatoin of 'Constable On Patrol' at the head of the unruly pack. The verb sense 'to grab' leads to the verb sense 'to arrest' which leads to **COPPER** which was shortened to 'cop'. No buttons, no badges, no initialisms.
- J. Edgard Hoover, director of the F.B.I., recently tried to enlist the help of a television program in what seems to be a campaign on the part of certain high-ranking cops to eliminate a word from the language. The word is "cop", as a noun, in its most popular usage. —*New Yorker*, p. 51, 18th July 1959
- 'Hagger, the cop, is out on patrol[.]' —Wal Watkins, *Race the Lazy River*, p. 16, 1963
- You must be Murdock and Salazar, the crooked cops. —Carl Hiaasen, *Skin Tight*, p. 151, 1989
- The first thing he said to me, "We are police officers." I said, "You're cops to me." —Herbert Huncke, *Guilty of Everything*, p. 22, 1990
- You were doing good here. You did that nice short thing on the gay cop. —Anna Quindlen, *One True Thing*, p. 36, 1994
- Setups with regional police became routine, sparked by America's historic phobia about "niggers with guns," and in the aftermath, some thirty-eight Panthers were shot down by racist cops. —Mumia Abu-Jamal, *Live from Death Row*, p. 147, 1996
- But during the ten years I worked with the Bastone crew, I became more than just a crooked cop who turned his head for a price. —Sam Giancana, *Double Deal*, p. 11, 2003
- Then he suggested renting a drug-sniffing dog from a corrupt cop and checking out warehouses on the Brooklyn and New Jersey water-front. —Greg B. Smith, *Made Men*, p. 81, 2003

2 an arrest *UK, 1844*

Especially familiar in the phrase **IT'S A FAIR COP**.

3 a job or employment; a position *AUSTRALIA, 1915*
- It's a pretty soft cop. The money's money's good. Plenty of supper. —Alexander Buzo, *Rooted*, p. 40, 1969
- COP: Good job obtained by shrewdness or luck; Agreeable proposition. —Jim Ramsay, *Cop It Sweet!*, p. 24, 1977

4 treatment; a deal *AUSTRALIA*
- I've had a rotten cop ever since I came to this flamin' country but this beats the bloody lot! —Barry Humphries, *The Wonderful World of Barry McKenzie*, p. 24, 1968
- Be that as it may, if I come across with this flamin' autobiography of meself I'll require something in the vicinity of a fair cop money-wise. —Barry Humphries, *The Wonderful World of Barry McKenzie*, p. 56, 1968

5 in carnival usage, a small prize won at a game concession *US*
- —Joe McKennon, *Circus Lingo*, p. 27, 1980
- —Don Wilmeth, *The Language of American Popular Entertainment*, p. 64, 1981

6 winnings from gambling *US, 1930*
- Put that heavy cop in your mitt flat against your thigh furthest from the mark. —Iceberg Silm (Robert Beck), *Trick Baby*, p. 93, 1969

7 a gratuity *AUSTRALIA*
- —Ned Wallish, *The Truth Dictionary of Racing Slang*, p. 17, 1989

▸ it's a fair cop

used of a good or legal arrest; in later use, as a jocular admission of anything trivial *UK, 1891*
- The old Ken would have stood up and said 'it's a fair cop', or else that he didn't do anything. —*The Guardian*, 21st June 2002

▸ no cop; not much cop

worthless, valueless, useless *UK, 1902*
- She's not much cop as a singer[.] —*BBCi Leicester*, 17th September 2002

cop *verb*

1 to obtain, to take or to purchase something, especially drugs *US, 1867*
- Slicker Morrie made more dames and copped more cherries than any lad in the history of Louisa Nolan's dance hall. —James T. Farrell, *Saturday Night*, p. 30, 1947
- Now cop a walk, you're screwing our game. —Irving Shulman, *The Amboy Dukes*, p. 54, 1947
- He had gotten nicked too, and it gave him a good excuse to cop a day off now and then. —Mickey Spillane, *One Lonely Night*, p. 63, 1951
- "Get ready to cop," I said, and dropped the caps into his hands. —William Burroughs, *Junkie*, p. 56, 1953
- Now all the Cats are out to cop the Chicks[.] —Dan Burley, *Diggeth Thou?*, p. 5, 1959
- You're out here to pull them tricks and cop that bread, dig? —Clarence Cooper Jr, *The Scene*, p. 10, 1960
- One night "Mel Torme" didn't show up and the guys had me do a few tunes and I copped the gig. —Babs Gonzales, *I Paid My Dues*, p. 23, 1967
- [T]his is the way they have been living for months, for years, some of them, across America and back, on the bus, down to the Rat lands of Mexico and back, sailing like gypsies along the Servicenter fringes, copping urinations[.] —Tom Wolfe, *The Electric Kool-Aid Acid Test*, p. 16, 1968
- He would know where to cop "C," [cocaine], and probably gangster [marijuana] for the runt. —Iceberg Slim (Robert Beck), *Pimp*, p. 126, 1969
- I discovered where pot was easily obtained and copped steadily from then on. —Herbert Huncke, *The Evening Sun Turned Crimson*, p. 28, 1980
- I remember when there wasn't one album you had to cop; there was ten. —*Hip-Hop Connection*, p. 38, July 2002

2 to seduce someone, to have sex with someone *US, 1965*
- I played stickball, marbles, and Johnny-on-the-Pony, copped girls' drawers and blew pot. —Piri Thomas, *Down These Mean Streets*, p. 13, 1967
- Copped regular after that. Her desk, Kleinfeld's desk, broom closet, even on the washbasin. —Edwin Torres, *After Hours*, p. 220, 1979
- Billy Woods, like most of the dudes in and around the neighborhood wanted to cop Phyllisine. —Donald Goines, *The Busting Out of an Ordinary Man*, p. 19, 1985
- Ey, I think Twiggy's trying to cop with me. —Caroline Aherne and Craig Cash, *The Royle Family*, 1999

3 to come upon someone; to catch someone out *AUSTRALIA, 1933*
- Wait till me brother cops yer with our crowd – knock yer bandy. —Norman Lindsay, *Saturdee*, p. 42, 1934
- 'We'd get copped in the passage,' said Plugger. —Gavin Casey, *It's Harder for Girls*, p. 27, 1941
- When the Ord'ly Officer cops you with a fag, or off your beat, / And you'd think you'd lost the war the way he tells you off a treat —Tip Kelaher, *The Digger Hat and other verses*, p. 23, 1942
- Strength of it was old Ma Randal copped old Randal absolutely doing a bear up in that piece's bed. —Norman Lindsay, *Halfway to Anywhere*, p. 42, 1947
- —Norman Lindsay, *Halfway to Anywhere*, p. 67, 1947
- I copped him fair and square. He was lowerin' the belt of ammo over the side of the platform. —J.E. MacDonnell, *Sabotage!*, p. 102, 1964
- —John Wynnum, *Jiggin' in the Riggin'*, p. 22, 1965

4 to catch sight of someone or something; look at someone or something *AUSTRALIA, 1925*
- It was after dark when I got there, and I was staggerin' all over the road, when a police sergeant cops me. —Erle Cox, *Out of the Silence*, p. 255, 1925
- —Leonard Mann, *Flesh in Armour*, p. 112, 1932
- When we got there they both said 'G'day, Pat' and Pat slapped the ticket in front of Stevo and said 'Cop that.' —Sam Weller, *Old Bastards I Have Met*, p. 116, 1979

5 to see something; to notice something *UK*
- He'll live with any luck! Did he cop your face? —*The Sweeney*, p. 49, 1976

6 to catch someone *AUSTRALIA, 1889*
- —Norman Lindsay, *Saturdee*, p. 30, 1934
- Your old man's a pretty stinkin' good runner, would have copped me if I hadn't bunked into the furze. —Norman Lindsay, *Halfway to Anywhere*, p. 121, 1947
- 'What convictions?' Rufe grinned. Hell, he'd only been copped the once. —Wilda Moxham, *The Apprentice*, p. 112, 1969

7 to inform; to betray someone *US, 1895*
- Louis went up without copping – naming any names to have his time cut – and was respected among the population, all the homeboys up at Starke, where he met Bobby Deo. —Elmore Leonard, *Riding the Rap*, p. 55, 1995

8 to endure something *AUSTRALIA*
- We can't cop this. —Frank Hardy, *The Outcasts of Foolgarah*, p. 36, 1971
- I can't cop it in here for much longer. —Ray Denning, *Prison Diaries*, p. 140, 1979
- When Jack Denning was a young criminal the attitude was 'do the crime, cop the time.' —Donald Catchlove, *Ray Denning My Life and Time*, p. 16, 1994

9 to take or receive a bribe *UK*

- "Did he cop?" means "Did he receive a gratuity (or bribe)?" —David Powis, *The Signs of Crime*, 1977

10 to steal something *AUSTRALIA*

- He was good at pinching things, too. They pulled nails out of other people's fences, knocked off the odd fourbetwo from wood heaps and even copped a shovel. —Tim Winton, *Cloudstreet*, p. 122, 1991

11 in trainspotting, to record a train's number *UK*

- I should, at this juncture, point out that while trainspotters "cop" engine numbers planespotters "make" aircraft numbers. —Iain Aitch, *A Fête Worse Than Death*, p. 73, 2003

12 (used of a rigged carnival game) to malfunction, allowing a player to win *US*

- —Gene Sorrows, *All About Carnivals*, p. 14, 1985

▸ **cop a breeze**

to leave, especially without calling attention to yourself *US*

- —Hyman E. Goldin et al., *Dictionary of American Underworld Lingo*, p. 49, 1950

▸ **cop a deaf 'un**

to pretend not to hear; to deliberately not listen to, or ignore, someone *UK, 1920s*

- [T]he best thing to do is cop a deaf un to everything that's said to you. —Frank Norman, *Bang To Rights*, p. 93, 1958

▸ **cop a drop**

to take a bribe *UK*

Combines **COP** (to obtain) with **DROP** (a bribe).

- —Peter Laurie, *Scotland Yard*, p. 322, 1970
- —Angela Devlin, *Prison Patter*, p. 40, 1996

▸ **cop a feel**

to touch someone sexually without their consent *US, 1935*

- I knew before he started copping feels what he wanted. —Antony James, *America's Homosexual Underground*, p. 111, 1965
- DENOUNCE the poor Nigger male who cherishes his whiteness, and allows the Caucasian male's "copping-a-feel" his own black wife's ass, at a social. —Robert deCoy, *The Nigger Bible*, p. 132–133, 1967
- She was the only woman that I've ever met that I could kiss without copping a feel. Except for my mama and sisters, of course, and I'm not too sure about my sisters. —Tom Robbins, *Another Roadside Attraction*, p. 165, 1971
- Is this what they call copping a feel? —*American Graffiti*, 1973
- Remember 'copping a feel?' Boggie was the first. Said it was great. —*Diner*, 1982
- But would a company yes-man (who I suspected would never dare cop a feel unless it was written into the annual strategic plan) really risk so much to show his interest in me? —Rita Ciresi, *Pink Slip*, p. 85, 1999

▸ **cop a heel**

to leave; to run away; to escape *US*

- Kid said, "Then cop a heel and pee." She muttered an inaudible expletive as she gave him a filthy look and stomped away. —Iceberg Slim (Robert Beck), *Long White Con*, p. 20, 1977
- —M. Allen Henderson, *How Con Games Work*, p. 219, 1985
- —Angela Devlin, *Prison Patter*, p. 40, 1996

▸ **cop a joint**

to perform oral sex on a man *US, 1962*

- —Guy Strait, *The Lavendar Lexicon*, 1 June 1964
- I was staying at the Y once, and this guy kept following me in the showers, wanting to cop my joint. —John Rechy, *Numbers*, p. 65, 1967
- [S]he smiles and says, 'How about if I cop your joint instead?' —Terry Southern, *Blue Movie*, p. 149, 1970
- Somebody cops your joint, Kid Kilo would always say, it's ten bills. —John Sayles, *Union Dues*, p. 290, 1977
- I kept my hands on my private parts, broke a boy's arm tried to cop my joint and came out [of prison] a two hundred and five pound virgin. —Elmore Leonard, *Gold Coast*, p. 17, 1981

▸ **cop a load**

to take a look, especially to take a good look; to pay attention to something *UK, 1984*

- You haven't got a f**kin' clue. Cop a load of this, the real deal, the Dead f**kin' Kennedys, recorded live at their peak from the San Francisco Bay in pristine quality. —*Kerrang!*, 17th March 2001

▸ **cop a minty wrapper**

in horse racing, to receive a very small gratuity, or no gratuity at all, after winning a race *AUSTRALIA*

- —Ned Wallish, *The Truth Dictionary of Racing Slang*, p. 17, 1989

▸ **cop a mope**

to escape *US*

- —*American Speech*, p. 194, October 1951: 'A study of reformatory argot'

▸ **cop a nod**

to sleep *US*

- —Marcus Hanna Boulware, *Jive and Slang of Students in Negro Colleges*, 1947
- —Robert S. Gold, *A Jazz Lexicon*, p. 69, 1964

▸ **cop a packet**

1 to be severely wounded *UK*

Originally military.

- And he asks her where she's been / She's only thirty-five going on seventeen / She's going to cop a packet if he ever finds her / In between the sheets —Elvis Costello (Declan McManus), *...And In Every Home*, 1982

2 to become infected with a sexually transmitted disease *UK, 1984*

3 to be sentenced to preventive detention *UK*

Prison use.

- —Paul Tempest, *Lag's Lexicon*, 1950

▸ **cop a plea**

to enter a guilty plea to a criminal charge *US, late 1920s*

- Only plea I ever copped cost me three years in the slams. —Edwin Torres, *Carlito's Way*, p. 10, 1975

▸ **cop a pose**

to adopt the posture of a fashion or shop-window mannequin *UK*

- They are 13 and 15. "We change our clothes every 15 minutes," says Lily, copping a pose. —*The Times*, p. 9, 26th April 2003

▸ **cop deuces**

to assume a submissive or defensive position *US*

- —John R. Armore and Joseph D. Wolfe, *Dictionary of Desperation*, p. 25, 1976

▸ **cop it sweet**

1 to enjoy the situation *AUSTRALIA*

- She was a wild bitch but a bloody good plug. She could move all right. Not a bad cook either, that was saving wages, so he may as well cop it sweet. —Bluey *Bush Contractors*, p. 185, 1975
- Copping it sweet: Taking things easy; having a quiet and pleasant day with a case of beer and a bag of prawns. —Richard Beckett, *The Dinkum Aussie Dictionary*, p. 16, 1986

2 to receive something graciously *AUSTRALIA*

- A jockey or trainer may "cop it sweet" when receiving a penalty[.] —Ned Wallish, *The Truth Dictionary of Racing Slang*, p. 17, 1989

3 in prison, to take punishment without complaint *AUSTRALIA, 1950*

- He continued to cop it sweet and did his two years for illegal possession of a lethal weapon without a word. —Criena Rohan, *Down by the Dockside*, p. 205, 1963
- He copped it sweet and when he was released Joe was there to meet him. —Clive Galea, *Slipper*, p. 149, 1988

4 to endure unpleasantness without complaint; to resignedly put up with something bad *AUSTRALIA*

- So he copped it sweet like tha mangy dog he was. —Clive Galea, *Slipper*, p. 60, 1988
- So Davo just had to cop it sweet as they say and even though he wasn't the type to bear a grudge he was deeply hurt – no two ways about it. —Robert G. Barrett, *Davo's Little Something*, p. 6, 1992
- What would they have done in my position. Nothing. Shit themsleves and copped it sweet. —Robert G. Barrett, *Davo's Little Something*, p. 211, 1992
- —Shane Maloney, *Nice Try*, p. 291, 1998

▸ **cop on to**

catch on to something; become aware of something *AUSTRALIA*

- Sounds simple 'nuff, doesn't it? Yet you'd be surprised how few women can cop on to it. —Ray Lawler, *Summer of the Seventeenth Doll*, p. 40, 1957

▸ **cop the lot**

to receive everything *AUSTRALIA, 1911*

- We was helping a cocky keep the fire off his wheat and the wind turns round and our camp cops the lot. —Kylie Tennant, *The Honey Flow*, p. 15, 1956
- —Harvey E. Ward, *Down Under Without Blunder*, p. 37, 1967
- [T]his bloke came up and started picking a blue with Simmo. Christ! It was suicide! Well, anyway, he copped the lot from Simmo, as you can well imagine. —Alexander Buzo, *Rooted*, p. 77, 1969
- The Bitch, he decided, would surely cop the lot tomorrow. Or he would die in the attempt. —Gerald Sweeney, *The Plunge*, p. 49, 1981

▸ **cop z's**

to sleep *US, 1961*

- —Robert S. Gold, *A Jazz Lexicon*, p. 70, 1964

cop *adjective*

good, worth having, of value *UK*

- Malcolm had sed that this E [MDMA] wasunt much cop but, fuck, this initial rush is fuckin incredible. — Niall Griffiths, *Grits*, p. 33, 2000
- BEEFA: was it any cop this year? — *Ministry*, p. 7, October 2002

copacetic; copasetic *adjective*

good, excellent; safe; attractive *US, 1919*

Etymology unknown; Chinook jargon, French, Italian and Yiddish sources have been suggested.

- — Bernard Wolfe, *The Late Risers*, p. 189, 1954
- It was not copasetic / It was not right. — The Rulers, *Copasetic*, 1966
- Good bread coming in. Everything was copasetic. Too good to last. — Edwin Torres, *Carlito's Way*, p. 29, 1975
- Everything was copasetic. — Donald Gorgon, *Cop Killer*, p. 161, 1994

cop and blow *noun*

the rule of thumb governing a pimp's *modus operandi*, acquiring and losing prostitutes *US*

- He reconciled himself to the name of the game, "Cop and Blow" (win and lose) and made his way uptown[.] — Babs Gonzales, *I Paid My Dues*, p. 101, 1967
- "You know the name of the game: Cop and Blow. You lose on this end, but you gain on another." — Nathan Heard, *Howard Street*, p. 254, 1968
- I bombarded him with street logic and begged him to recognize the hard pimp law of "cop and blow": somebody has to lose when somebody wins. — Iceberg Slim (Robert Beck), *The Naked Soul of Iceberg Slim*, p. 123, 1971
- You ain't got to take that attitude, baby. After all, the game is cop and blow. — Donald Goines, *Whoreson*, p. 83, 1972
- What they consider my salary is the money I've made all year from girls who cop and blow – they just come and go. — Susan Hall, *Gentleman of Leisure*, p. 13, 1972
- Cop and blow is the name of the game. — A.S. Jackson, *Gentleman Pimp*, p. 100, 1973
- Bitch, you ain't no lame, you know the Game / They call it cop and blow. — Dennis Wepman et al., *The Life*, p. 86, 1976

cop and blow *verb*

to acquire something and then leave *US*

- But he had no hangups or any peculiarly excessive style of stealing like his two partners – his way was simply to cop and blow. — Emmett Grogan, *Ringolevio*, p. 46, 1972

cop and hold; cop and lock *verb*

(of a pimp) to acquire and retain a prostitute *US*

- My regulars – whom I've copped and locked – that's Sandy and Kitty and Linda – they each made around seventy-five thousand last year. — Susan Hall, *Gentleman of Leisure*, p. 13, 1972

cop caller *noun*

a truck with squeaky brakes or noisy recapped tyres *US, 1938*

- — Montie Tak, *Truck Talk*, p. 37, 1971

cope *verb*

to function in normal situations while under the influence of a hallucinogenic drug *US*

- — J. L. Simmons and Barry Winograd, *It's Happening*, p. 169, 1966

Copenhagen capon *noun*

a transexual *US*

Homosexual usage; an allusion to the sex-altering operation performed on Christine Jorgensen in Denmark.

Copenhagen snoose *noun*

damp, grated chewing snuff *CANADA*

- The smell of a pine-knot fire / From a stovepipe that's come loose / Mingles sweetly with the boot grease / And the Copenhagen snoose. — *B.C. Digest*, p. 8/2, 1964

cop for *verb*

to get into an intimate relationship with someone *UK*

From **cop** (to catch).

- RUDE BOY: [...] I've never been there without copping for it. SLOANE: Copping for what? RUDE BOY: Totty. Copping for totty. Skirt. — Henry Sloane, *Sloane's Inside Guide to Sex & Drugs & Rock 'n' Roll*, p. 34, 1985
- Simon Le Bon [a singer] [...] managed to cop for Yasmin Pervanneh off the hair adverts. — Kevin Sampson, *Powder*, p. 23, 1999

cop house; cop factory *noun*

a police station *US, 1928*

- I have to go to the cop house just about now. — Raymond Chandler, *Playback*, p. 152, 1958
- — Jay Robert Nash, *Dictionary of Crime*, p. 80, 1992

copilot *noun*

1 a tablet of dextroamphetamine sulphate (trade name Dexedrine™), or any other central nervous system stimulant *US, 1965*

- — Donald Louria, *Nightmare Drugs*, p. 28, 1966
- — *Daily Mirror*, 14th June 1966
- — *American Speech*, p. 203, Fall 1969: 'Truck driver's jargon'
- — Montie Tak, *Truck Talk*, p. 37, 1971
- Jackie slipped me a couple of co-pilots in English when she passed out the test papers. — Anonymous, *Go Ask Alice*, p. 94, 1971
- — Richard A. Spears, *The Slang and Jargon of Drugs and Drink*, p. 122, 1986
- — Mike Haskins, *Drugs*, p. 279, 2003

2 the co-signer of a purchase contract or loan *US*

- — *American Speech*, p. 312, Autumn-Winter 1975: 'The jargon of car salesmen'

cop it *verb*

1 to get or receive something painful, such as a beating; to receive punishment *AUSTRALIA, 1916*

- The silly twerp'll cop it hot if Hankinson gets to hear. — W.R. Bennett, *Wingman*, p. 20, 1961
- Well, old Truthful copped it from the mosquitoes, I can tell you[.] — Frank Hardy, *The Yarns of Billy Borker*, p. 29, 1965
- Boy did I cop it! Dad rekons I blunted his razor. — Kylie Mole (Maryanne Fahey), *My Diary*, p. 70, 1988
- Both these guys tried to do in Hitler and copped it in no uncertain terms as a result. — Ignatius Jones, *The 1992 True Hip Manual*, p. 196, 1992
- The standover merchants were always on the go and whenever one of the inmates got done over there was always a reason for it, a motive. No one ever copped it just for the hell of it. — William Dodson, *The Sharp End*, p. 31, 2001

2 to take or receive something *AUSTRALIA*

- Does he think there's some prize or something for every kid whose ma's copping it from a Yank sailor? — Ward McNally, *Supper at Happy Harry's*, p. 24, 1982
- [T]he way Ailie was going on she would have laid there and copped it all night. — Robert G. Barrett, *Davo's Little Something*, p. 272, 1992

3 to be killed *AUSTRALIA*

- Windy looked down at her, remembering, and he thought: maybe you're right, at that. I might cop it myself next week, next month. — J.E. MacDonnell, *Don't Gimme the Ships*, p. 43, 1960
- We all exercise the same care but if he cards fall wrong one day for some man, and if it's you, you've copped it. — Patsy Adam-Smith, *Folklore of the Australian Railwaymen*, p. 52, 1969
- Just hack you up a bit or shoot yer in the gut. Might be hours before you cop it. — Chris Baker and Andrew Day, *Lock, Stock... & A Good Slopping Out*, p. 416, 2000

4 to be hit with enemy fire *AUSTRALIA, 1932*

- A Company copped it. — Eric Lambert, *The Veterans*, p. 153, 1954

cop man *noun*

a low-level drug dealer who must pay cash to the supplier for the drugs to be sold *US*

- Many are taken on in a variety of tangential roles and work as steerers, touts, guards, runners, and "cop men" – dealers whom suppliers will only sell to on a cash basis. — Terry Williams, *The Cocaine Kids*, p. 33, 1989

cop off *verb*

1 to form a liaison with someone based on mutual sexual attraction *UK*

Ultimately from **cop** (to catch).

- And if you did happen to cop off and find somewhere to have a shag, and you'd both had an E, then you had a really blindin' bonk. — Dave Courtney, *Raving Lunacy*, p. 267, 2000

2 to fondle someone intimately; to engage in foreplay; to have sex *UK*

- He shoves The Joy of Sex at me, and I can't help looking at a few pages: endless pictures of horrible hippies copping off. — *The Guardian*, p. 9, 28th November 2001

3 to masturbate *UK*

- Well, we'd better get those tapes back cos I've got a couple of 'undred desperate perverts itching to cop off on 'em. — Chris Baker and Andrew Day, *Lock, Stock... & Spaghetti Sauce*, p. 227, 2000

4 to shirk, to skive, to play truant *UK*

- Soon [George Harrison] was copping off with a bunch of mates to smoke "Woodies" [a branded cigarette][.] — *Uncut*, p. 40, February 2002

cop on *noun*

understanding, common knowledge *IRELAND*

- You have a bit of cop on, you're a sensible man and we think you might be able to tell us what's going on. — Eamonn Sweeney, *Waiting for the Healer*, p. 193, 1997

cop on *verb*
to understand something; to start behaving reasonably *IRELAND*
Sometimes said in angry response to a person's undesirable behaviour: 'cop (yourself) on'.
- And Veronica would ask him why he couldn't get a job like Bimbo – but that wasn't the reason he wanted Bimbo to cop on to himself. —Roddy Doyle, *The Van*, 1991

cop-out *noun*
a drastic compromise of principle *US, 1956*
- I considered crossing over to the other side of the highway and trying to get back to New Haven for a bus. But that would be an incredible cop out. —James Simon Kunen, *The Strawberry Statement*, p. 81, 1968
- Kesey has sold out to keep from getting a five-year sentence or worse. Next he'll nail it down by calling all the kids to Winterland and telling them to stop taking LSD ... Freaking cop-out ... —Tom Wolfe, *The Electric Kool-Aid Acid Test*, p. 336, 1968

cop out *verb*
1 to avoid an issue by making excuses; to go back on your word *US*
- [O]ff we go, 2 girls and me and Neal, bleary, driving into woods of California for orgy, but one girl cops out[.] —Jack Kerouac, *Letter to John Clellon Holmes*, p. 339, 8th February 1952
- So I cop out, from the lot, from life, all of it, go to sleep in the bedroom[.] —Jack Kerouac, *The Subterraneans*, p. 90, 1958
- I'm not trying to cop out, but I was playing it too safe that afternoon at your house. —Nat Hentoff, *Jazz Country*, p. 32, 1965
- He stuttered and blinked trying to "cop out" because we'd surprised him. —Babs Gonzales, *I Paid My Dues*, p. 59, 1967
- Even Flo Kennedy, our chief lawyer, copped out – though some of the younger legal-beagels (women, bless'em) were ready to carry the fight to the floor of the Pageant[.] —*Screw*, p. 14, 13th October 1969
- The line between madness and masochism was already hazy; the time had come to pull back ... to retire, hunker down, back off and "cop out," as it were. —Hunter S. Thompson, *Fear and Loathing in Las Vegas*, p. 81, 1971
- All the way over here I was telling you how he would cooperate. Now, he's just copping out. —Donald Goines, *Inner City Hoodlum*, p. 60, 1975

2 to confess; to enter a guilty plea *US, 1938*
- "She's gonna cop out," Davis told him. —Clarence Cooper Jr, *The Scene*, p. 115, 1960
- I was supposed to take a jury trial, but the lawyer told me he'd get me eighteen months if I'd cop out. —Henry Williamson, *Hustler!*, p. 141, 1965
- I copped out to attempted larceny and was given one to two years in the state prison at Jackson, Michigan. —A.S. Jackson, *Gentleman Pimp*, p. 59, 1973

cop-out man *noun*
in a crooked version of the coin-tossing game two-up, the person who by arrangement takes the winnings *AUSTRALIA*
- —Sidney J. Baker, *The Australian Language*, 1953

cop out on *verb*
to inform on someone *UK*
- —Angela Devlin, *Prison Patter*, p. 40, 1996

copped-out *adjective*
conventional *UK*
From **COP OUT** (to make excuses, to cease trying).
- [Y]ou think that all these ancient tossers over twenty-five have somehow chosen their copped-out lives[.] —James Hawes, *Dead Long Enough*, p. 21, 2000

copper *noun*
1 a police officer *UK, 1846*
Derives from **COP** (to catch).
- I couldn't figure out why a copper would go poking his nose under the seat of a respectable-looking cab at six in the A.M. —Mezz Mezzrow, *Really the Blues*, p. 32, 1946
- [T]here was a chance that either the police might walk in on me or the little guy get suspicious enough of my being away so long he'd call a copper. —Mickey Spillane, *I, The Jury*, p. 58, 1947
- Now how did I know you were a copper? —Marvin Wald and Albert Maltz, *The Naked City*, 1947
- Sheik looked dazed. "Can't no copper hurt me," he muttered thickly[.] —Chester Himes, *The Real Cool Killers*, p. 92, 1959
- Well, this big fat copper looks at him dead savage[.] —John Peter Jones, *Feather Pluckers*, p. 7, 1964
- You bloody copper bastard! —D.E. Charlwood, *All the Green Year*, p. 66, 1965
- And every copper is on the take, you know, up and down the line. —Sara Harris, *The Lords of Hell*, p. 117, 1967
- —Angela Devlin, *Prison Patter*, p. 40, 1996
- So the coppers walked off[.] —Dave Courtney, *Raving Lunacy*, p. 12, 2000
- Most of the coppers I worked with at street level are ace guys[.] —Duncan MacLaughlin, *The Filth*, p. 11, 2002

2 a police informer *UK, 1937*

3 a prison informer *UK, 1961*

4 a pre-decimal penny or halfpenny coin; a post-decimal two-penny or one-penny coin; such coins mixed *UK*
Originally, about 1840, of coins actually made of copper; the term has survived bronze and further debasement.

copper *verb*
1 in craps, to bet that the shooter will lose *US*
- —*The Annals of the American Academy of Political and Social Sciences*, p. 123, May 1950

2 to inform against someone *UK, 1924*

3 to be engaged as a working police officer *UK, 1984*

copper chopper *noun*
a police helicopter *US*
- Most of it was growing outside on a porch, clearly visible to anybody at a higher elevatoin, such as, say, a snooping copper chopper. —Larry "Ratso" Sloman, *Reefer Madness*, p. 420, 1979
- That game's halftime show will include an exhibition by LAPD's Special Weapons and Tactics (SWAT) unit, as well as helicopter-borne officers flying into the stadium and rappelling from the "copper choppers" to a simulated crime scene on the Coliseum floor. —*San Francisco Chronicle*, p. D6, 24th January 1990

copper jitters *noun*
an excessive fear of contact with the police *US*
- Pushing junk is a constant strain on the nerves. Sooner or later you get the "copper jitters," and everybody looks like a cop. —William Burroughs, *Junkie*, p. 58, 1953
- —Angela Devlin, *Prison Patter*, p. 40, 1996

coppers *noun*
money *BARBADOS*
- He can buy a car; he got the coppers. —Frank A. Collymore, *Barbadian Dialect*, p. 35, 1965

Coppers in Disguise *nickname*
the Criminal Investigation Department *UK, 1984*
An jocular play on the well-known initials CID; substituting **COPPER** (a police officer) for 'criminal' and referring to the non-uniformed status of the officers as 'in disguise'.

copper's nark *noun*
a police informer *AUSTRALIA, 1945*
- Anyway, Brown Tongue decided to play his well-known role of copper's nark once too often. —Frank Hardy, *The Outcasts of Foolgarah*, p. 21, 1971
- —Angela Devlin, *Prison Patter*, p. 40, 1996

copper time *noun*
the reduction of a prison sentence for good behaviour *US*
- —William K. Bentley and James M. Corbett, *Prison Slang*, p. 25, 1992

copping neighborhood *noun*
a neighbourhood where buyers and sellers know that drugs are sold *US*
- The street corners were literally teeming with sick addicts in the copping neighborhoods. —Herbert Huncke, *Guilty of Everything*, p. 130, 1990

copping zone *noun*
an area in a city where buyers and sellers of drugs know to congregate and do business *US*
- It was a place to "cop" (buy), a "copping zone". —Terry Williams, *The Cocaine Kids*, p. 14, 1989
- —Terry Williams, *Crackhouse*, p. 147, 1992

coppist *noun*
a trainspotter, especially one positioned at a level crossing *UK*
From **COP** (to see something).
- —*Daily Mirror*, 19th September 1946

cop shop *noun*
a police station *AUSTRALIA, 1941*
- They took us downtown to the copshop and backed the wagons up against the doors. —Jamie Mandelkau, *Buttons*, p. 104–105, 1971
- —Helen Dahlskog (Editor), *A Dictionary of Contemporary and Colloquial Usage*, p. 15, 1972
- Then I dropped him off at the cop shop. They took him. —*Taxi Driver*, 1976
- —Wayne Floyd, *Jason's Authentic Dictionary of CB Slang*, p. 13, 1976
- Well, eventually the walloper decides to take Mo to the cop shop. He's going to vag him. —*Sydney City Hub*, p. 5, 4th April 1996

- Two options then coming out the cop shop.—Jeremy Cameron, *Brown Bread in Wengen*, p. 22, 1999

cop spotter *noun*

a rearview mirror *US*

- —Montie Tak, *Truck Talk*, p. 37, 1971

cop's rub *noun*

a frisking or pat-down for weapons or contraband *US*

- They ordered the white guys out of the car, put the cop's rub on 'em, then asked them to open the trailer.—A.S. Jackson, *Gentleman Pimp*, p. 8, 1973

cop's tang *noun*

a Ford Mustang modified and enhanced for police use *US*

- —Lewis Poteet, *Car & Motorcyle Slang*, p. 56, 1992

cops' tank *noun*

a jail cell reserved for policemen/criminals *US*

- O.A. Joness mumbled, hoping that he would get put in the cops' tank at the county jail[.]—Joseph Wambaugh, *The Secrets of Harry Bright*, p. 33, 1985

'copter; copter *noun*

a heli*copter* *US, 1947*

- [W]atching the pictures relayed by the 'copters sweeping back and forth[.]—Christopher Brookmyre, *Not the End of the World*, p. 244, 1998

cop that lot!

just look at them!, or that!: especially to express admiration, astonishment or derision *AUSTRALIA*

- —Nino Culotta, *Cop This Lot*, 1960

copy *noun*

a received radio-communication; a message confirming reception *US*

- Ah, breaker one-nine, this here's the Rubber Duck. You got a copy on me.—C.W. McCall, *Convoy*, 1976
- Breaker asking for a copy you've got the Gooseman here. Come back.—Peter Chippindale, *The British CB Book*, p. 16, 1981

copy *verb*

to understand what has been said *US, 1984*

Shortwave radio slang that spread well outside the world of radio.

- I want no firing, period, unless your hear shots. Copy that, Mace? —*Airheads*, 1994

copybroke *adjective*

descriptive of a computer program in which the copyright scheme has been disabled *US*

- —Eric S. Raymond, *The New Hacker's Dictionary*, p. 106, 1991

copy, copy

I am receiving

Citizens' band radio slang.

- [S]ay, "Copy, copy" and then wait.—Peter Chippindale, *The British CB Book*, p. 17, 1981

cop you later

goodbye *AUSTRALIA*

With an intentional, if somewhat feeble, pun on 'copulator' or 'copulate her'.

- —Lenie Johansen, *The Dinkum Dictionary*, 1988
- —Susan Butler, *The Macquarie Dictionary of New Words*, p. 70, 1990
- —Sonya Plowman, *Great Kiwi Slang*, p. 49, 2002

cor!

used for registering shock, surprise or sexual desire *UK, 1931*

A euphemistic rendering of 'God!'.

- Cor, the currant [sun]'s 'ot today[.]—*The Sweeney*, p. 6, 1976
- Cor, you were giving it some this morning weren't you?—Mark Steel, *Reasons to be Cheerful*, p. 176, 2001
- Cor! Look at the tits on that!—*overheard in a London pub*, May 2001

coral *noun*

a capsule of chloral hydrate *US, 1970*

- —Richard A. Spears, *The Slang and Jargon of Drugs and Drink*, p. 122, 1986
- —Mike Haskins, *Drugs*, p. 282, 2003

corals *noun*

▷ **see:** CHORALS

coral stomper *noun*

a Pacific Islander *NEW ZEALAND*

Derogatory.

- —David McGill, *David McGill's Complete Kiwi Slang Dictionary*, p. 30, 1998

cor blimey!; gorblimey!

used for registering shock or surprise *UK, 1896*

A euphemistic rendering of 'God blind me!'; abbreviates to **BLIMEY!**.

- Cor blimey, twelve o'clock. It's Monday at last.—Ray Galton and Alan Simpson, *Hancock's Half Hour*, 22nd April 1958
- Cor blimey, where's the fire?—Graeme Kent, *The Queen's Corporal [Six Granada Plays]*, p. 87, 1959

cords *noun*

corduroy trousers *US, 1926*

In the 1960s, Los Angeles radio disc jockey Dick 'Huggy Boy' Hugg called teenagers to dances at the El Monte Legion Stadium with a charged 'Guys wear ties, gals dress nice – no cords or levis please'.

- [M]any of us bought him a beer and a Polish sausage when he came in with his paint-splattered cords and brown brogans, broke as ever. —Oscar Zeta Acosta, *The Autobiography of a Brown Buffalo*, p. 47, 1972

corduroy *noun*

in surfing, a swell lined up like ribbing *US*

- —Trevor Cralle, *The Surfin'ary*, p. 24, 1991

corduroy road *noun*

a road built over a swamp or muddy land by laying logs side by side at right angles to the way *CANADA*

- Floating muskeg surrounded the lake, so we moved onto higher ground and built a corduroy road back to the lake.—*Edmonton Journal*, p. 1/1, 1st August 1961

core *adjective*

1 said of pornography that shows penetration *US*

A shortened **HARDCORE**.

- —*Adult Video News*, p. 42, August 1995

2 serious, weighty, important *US*

- —Connie Eble (Editor), *UNC-CH Campus Slang*, p. 3, Fall 1986

-core *suffix*

when in combination with a (modern) musical style, used for creating a less-compromising genre title *UK*

- [A] nu-metal band, or a hardcore band or even the wettest of emo-core bands[.]—*Kerrang!*, 27th May 2000
- Bostonian grindcore rockers Anal Cunt, for instance, who apparently took their name from a GG Allin lyric, are unlikely to appear on Saturday morning TV any time soon.—*The Guardian*, 25th February 2005

corella *noun*

a sheep with patches of wool hanging loose *AUSTRALIA*

- —Sidney J. Baker, *The Australian Language*, 1953

co-respondent shoes *noun*

black and white or brown and white shoes of a type *UK, 1934*

Deriving, apparently, from the type of people who wore them: co-respondents in divorce cases; they were originally called 'co-respondent's shoes'. Originally fashionable between the World Wars, they were worn in the 1950s by entertainers as diverse as Max Miller and Elvis Presley. They have long been fashionable with golfers and are still available to buy.

- [T]he only colour is provided by the disguises the men adopt – sharp, spivvy suits, waxed, toothbrush moustaches and co-respondent shoes – cads down to the last detail.—*The Guardian*, 30th May 2002

corey; cory; corie *noun*

the penis *UK*

English gypsy use; probably from Romany *kori* (a thorn).

- 12 red-faced young men energetically shaking the drips from their coreys—Jimmy Stockin, *On The Cobbles*, p. 81, 2000

corflu *noun*

correction fluid, especially the fluid used for correcting mimeograph stencils *US*

- —*American Speech*, p. 25, Spring 1982: 'The language of science fiction fan magazines'

Corine *noun*

cocaine *US*

- —John B. Williams, *Narcotics and Hallucinogenics*, p. 111, 1967
- —Mike Haskins, *Drugs*, p. 280, 2003

cork *noun*

a tampon *US*

- Hey Barb, you got your cork in?—*Maledicta*, p. 57, Summer/Winter 1981
- Could I steal a cork? I'm dying.—a correspondent *The Museum of Menstruation and Women's Health*, January 2001

cork *verb*

1 to have sex *US*

- — *Maledicta*, p. 250, 1983: 'A connotative analysis of synonyms for sexual intercourse'

2 to set your fishing gear to obstruct that of another fisherman *CANADA, 1989*

- — Tom Parkin, *WetCoast Words*, p. 39, 1989

▸ **cork the air**

to sniff cocaine *US*

- — Hyman E. Goldin et al., *Dictionary of American Underworld Lingo*, p. 50, 1950
- — Mike Haskins, *Drugs*, p. 291, 2003

▸ **cork the bottle**

(used of a relief pitcher in baseball) to enter a game and pitch effectively *US*

- — Zander Hollander, *Baseball Lingo*, p. 37, 1967
- [E]xhaling finally when Edgar Martinez drove in Ichiro with the cushion run and a bullpen of Nelson, Arthur Rhodes and Kazuhiro Sasaki marched in to cork the bottle[.] — *Rocky Mountain News (Denver)*, p. 2C, 16th October 2001

▸ **cork your cryhole**

to stop complaining *US*

- — Connie Eble (Editor), *UNC-CH Campus Slang*, p. 3, October 2002

corker *noun*

1 something or someone attractive, desirable or wonderful; a stunner *UK, 1882*

- I've been to Majorca, and by that's a corker[.] — Ivor Biggun, *The Charabanc Trip*, 1978

2 something that closes or settles an argument *US, 1835*

3 an inconsistent, unpredictable poker player *US*

- — George Percy, *The Language of Poker*, p. 24, 1988

cork in *verb*

to become wedged after falling into a snow crevasse *ANTARCTICA*

- — *Cool Antarctica*, 2003: 'Antarctic slang'

corking *adjective*

unusually large, fine or good *US, 1895*

- A corking over from the lad: tip-top. — *The Guardian*, 22nd August 2002

cork off *verb*

to sleep *US*

- Pa blew up the mattress and corked off for a couple of hours while I read the book[.] — Max Shulman, *I was a Teen-Age Dwarf*, p. 4, 1959

corkscrew *noun*

a black woman's hair temporarily set in neatly aligned clumps to facilitate drying *BARBADOS*

- — Richard Allsopp, *Dictionary of Caribbean English Usage*, p. 169, 1996

corkscrew *verb*

to move spirally, or cause something to move spirally *UK, 1837*

- He gasps as one of her knuckles pushes between the powdered cheeks of his arse, gently corkscrewing into him. — *The Guardian*, 23rd September 2002

cork top *noun*

a surfer *US*

- — *Paradise of the Pacific*, p. 27, October 1963

corky *noun*

a corked muscle *AUSTRALIA*

- He's copped a corky and he's sure to miss a couple. — Ivor Limb, *Footy's No Joke!*, p. 18, 1986

cor love-a-duck!

▷ see: GAWD LOVE-A-DUCK!

cor lummie!; cor lumme!; cor lummy!

used as a general-purpose expletive *UK, 1961*

A Cockney variation of 'God love me!'; almost stereotypically Cockney but later use tends towards irony.

corn *noun*

1 something that is excessively sentimental *US, 1936*

Originally applied to all music that was not jazz in the 1930s, and then eased into general usage.

- [A]nd, to top off the ridiculous and embarrassing performance, she threw on the corn. — Jim Thompson, *The Grifters*, p. 12, 1963

2 sentimental, maudlin, mawkish music *US, 1936*

- I thought George was going to knock out some of the usual corn. — Mezz Mezzrow, *Really the Blues*, p. 25, 1946

3 whisky *US*

- If "Harry Belfonte" could make it after being a restauranteur, I can sure do alright "pouring the corn." — Babs Gonzales, *I Paid My Dues*, p. 157, 1967

4 any alcoholic beverage *TRINIDAD AND TOBAGO, 1986*

- — Lise Winer, *Dictionary of the English/Creole of Trinidad & Tobago*, 2003

5 money *US, 1837*

Both corn and money are seen as staples of life.

- Clifton was bringing home corn and, in her eyes, that meant her elder son was doing well[.] — Karline Smith, *Moss Side Massive*, p. 54, 1994
- C.R.E.A.M. Cash Rules Everything Around Me. It's just an old word for money. After bread and readies, but before corn and cheddar and ducats and collats. About the same time as wonga. — Diran Adebayo, *My Once Upon A Time*, p. 59, 2000
- I was really relying on that corn. — *Dog Eat Dog*, 2000
- when the establishment Mafioso realise how much gilt, paper, cashish, wonga, wedge, corn, cutter, loot, spondos, dollar, readies, shillings, folding, dough, money is on offer — J.J. Connolly, *Layer Cake*, p. 94, 2000

6 a hard scar produced by repeated drug injections *US*

- — Eugene Landy, *The Underground Dictionary*, p. 58, 1971

corn *verb*

to make a great deal of money without apparent effort *BARBADOS*

- — Richard Allsopp, *Dictionary of Caribbean English Usage*, p. 170, 1996

Corn and Brocoli Channel *nickname*

the Canadian Broadcasting Corporation *CANADA*

A jocular formation from the network's initials.

- The CBC [is known as] the Corn and Broccoli Channel because it has nationally approved humour and wholesome programming[.] — *Toronto Globe and Mail*, p. D12, 3rd August 2002

corn and bunion *noun*

an onion *UK, 1931*

Rhyming slang; the plural is 'corns and bunions'. Also applied in idiomatic use.

- He knew his corns and bunions when it came to painting. — Ray Puxley, *Cockney Rabbit*, 1992

cornball *adjective*

clichéd; overly sentimental *US, 1948*

- I was half tempted but decided that would have been too cornball. — Clancy Sigal, *Going Away*, p. 353, 1961

cornbeef-and-biscuits politics; cornbeef-and-rum politics *noun*

the practice of seeking to capture the votes of poor people by offering them gifts of corned beef, biscuits and rum as a bribe during political campaigns *BARBADOS*

- There's no doubt that the days of corned beef and biscuit politics are over. Barbados has ushered in a new political era where pizza, snack boxes, rum, brandy and stouts are the orders of the day. — *Saturday Sun*, p. 11, 2nd November 1996

corn belt *noun*

the mid-western United States *US*

- [Z]igzagged through corn belts and cotton belts (this is not too clear, I am afraid, Clarence, but I did not keep anynotes)[.] — Vladimir Nabokov, *Lolita*, p. 154, 1955
- Setting out on a tour of the Corn Belt in a tubercular jalopy, Oscar informed the suckers that research had disclosed that they were descendants of the illegitimate Drake boy. — *San Francisco Examiner, American Weekly*, p. 17, 24th May 1959
- In addition, those photographs could earn those corn-belt clods a fortune in some photographic contest. — John Kennedy Toole, *A Confederacy of Dunces*, p. 231 – 232, 1980
- Dean could have come out of the Corn Belt with a dismal third-placing showing. But finish third and appear un-presidential in the process? — *Arizona Republic*, p. 10B, 28th January 2004

corn binder *noun*

any International Harvester™ truck *US*

- — Montie Tak, *Truck Talk*, p. 37, 1971

cornbread *noun*

a simple, rural southern black person *US, 1954*

Cornbread is a staple in the diet of poor rural southerners, black and white.

- — J.E. Lighter, *Historical Dictionary of American Slang, Volume 1*, p. 488, 1994

corn cob *noun*
in electric line work, a thimble adapter pin *US*
• —A.B. Chance Co., *Lineman's Slang Dictionary*, p. 5, 1980

corned *adjective*
drunk *UK, 1785*
• —Helen Dahlskog (Editor), *A Dictionary of Contemporary and Colloquial Usage*, p. 15, 1972

corned beef *noun*
1 in prison, a chief officer *UK*
Rhyming slang.
• —Paul Tempest, *Lag's Lexicon*, 1950
2 a thief *UK, 1984*
Rhyming slang. Also known as 'bully beef'.

corned beef; corny *adjective*
deaf *UK: SCOTLAND*
Glasgow rhyming slang, reliant on Glasgow pronunciation.
• —Michael Munro, *The Original Patter*, 1985
• Are ye corned beef? I said sit doon on yer chorus [backside] and we'll have a wee Salvador [drink]. Mine's a Mick Jagger [lager] by the way. — *The Guardian*, 29th April 2002

cornelius *noun*
marijuana *US*
• —Anna Scotti and Paul Young, *Buzzwords*, p. 131, 1997

Cornel Wilder *noun*
a hair-fashion of the 1950s, popular with youths in Sydney *AUSTRALIA*
Named after US film actor Cornel Wilde (b.1915) who actually wore his hair shorter than the fashion he inspired.
• —Sidney J. Baker, *The Australian Language*, 1953

corner *noun*
1 in horse racing, a share of the winnings *AUSTRALIA*
• One might ask another, "Did you get your corner?"—Ned Wallish, *The Truth Dictionary of Racing Slang*, p. 17, 1989
2 the block in a prison where the cells for solitary confinement are found *US*
• —Joseph E. Ragen and Charles Finston, *Inside the World's Toughest Prison*, p. 795, 1962

▸ **around the corner**
in poker, said of a sequence of cards that uses the ace as both a high and low card *US*
• —George Percy, *The Language of Poker*, p. 6, 1988

▸ **cut a corner; cut corners; cut the corners**
to perform any task in a manner that minimises time, effort or expense, but for equal profit or even greater gain, and perhaps at the cost of safe-practice or legality *UK, 1957*
From the conventional, literal sense.
• Nobody was cutting corners, nobody was trying to do it on the cheap, nobody was putting lives at risk.— *The Guardian*, 30th May 2003

▸ **in the corner**
on a fishing or lobstering boat, fully throttled *US*
• —Kendall Merriam, *The Illustrated Dictionary of Lobstering*, p. 51, 1978

corner *verb*
1 to force someone into an embarrassing or difficult position *US, 1824*
Figurative.
• Mugabe is cornered[.] As even his police force begins to abandon him, and strikes rock the country, Zimbabwe's increasingly desperate president is stepping up the level of repression.— *The Guardian*, 5th June 2003
2 to go around a corner of a racecourse; to drive a vehicle around a corner, especially at speed *UK, 1861*
• Hyundai argued that the blurred wheels were intended to indicate movement as the car cornered a bend[.]— *The Guardian*, 19th September 2001

corner boy *noun*
1 an urban youth who idles in the street *US*
• —Hermese E. Roberts, *The Third Ear*, 1971
• —John A. Holm, *Dictionary of Bahamian English*, p. 50, 1982
2 a fellow prisoner from a prisoner's neighbourhood *US*
• —Lee McNelis, *30 + And a Wake-Up*, p. 1, 1991

corner game; cornering *noun*
a confidence trick in which payment is received before the promised delivery of goods or sexual services will take place 'around the corner' – the delivery, of course, is never made *UK*
• I first met him when a rather neat little corner game I'd been playing came unstuck.—Charles Raven, *Underworld Nights*, p. 90, 1956
• —Angela Devlin, *Prison Patter*, p. 40, 1996
• If they are working the Corner Game it is, of course, very hard to track them down.—Jake Arnott, *He Kills Coppers*, p. 18, 2001

corner man *noun*
a person who is not part of the criminal underworld but whose sympathies lie with the underworld in its constant strife with law enforcement *US*
• —R. Frederick West, *God's Gambler*, p. 223, 1964

cornet player *noun*
a cocaine user *US*
• I can see you are a heavy cornet player, Roger.—Edwin Torres, *Q & A*, p. 114, 1977

corn-fed *adjective*
unsophisticated, simple, rustic *US, 1924*
• Certainly it generated televised images of a feminized home front – small Midwestern towns waving with yellow ribbons and corn-fed women trying to keep back the tears.— *Feminist Studies*, p. 72, 1994

cornfield clemency *noun*
escape from a rural prison *US*
• —Jay Robert Nash, *Dictionary of Crime*, p. 81, 1992

cornfield meet *noun*
a head-on train collision *US, 1931*
• —Norman Carlisle, *The Modern Wonder Book of Trains and Railroading*, p. 261, 1946
• To keep opposing trains from hitting each other head on (a "cornfield meet" in railroad jargon), "meets" are staged at passing-track sections.—Gerry Souter, *The American Toy Train*, p. 143, 1999

cornflake *noun*
1 a youthful, sexually inexperienced male who is the object of an older homosexual's desire *US*
• — *Maledicta*, p. 221, 1979: 'Kinks and queens: linguistic and cultural aspects of the terminology for gays'
2 the cap badge worn by Canadian Forces recruits *CANADA*
Named because of its resemblance to a cornflake in colour and shape.

cornflake *adjective*
fake *UK*
Rhyming slang.
• —Ray Puxley, *Cockney Rabbit*, 1992

corn game *noun*
in a carnival, a Bingo game *US*
• — *American Speech*, p. 308–309, December 1960: 'Carnival talk'
• —Joe McKennon, *Circus Lingo*, p. 27, 1980
• —Don Wilmeth, *The Language of American Popular Entertainment*, p. 64, 1981

cornhead *noun*
a long-haired adherent to the racist, fascist philosophy espoused by shaved-head skinheads *US*
• Today, most skinheads continue to wear close-cropped hair; however, there are long-haired skinheads, who are referred to as "cornheads."—Bill Valentine, *Gangs and Their Tattoos*, p. 59, 2000

cornhole *noun*
the anus *US, 1922*
• They may want you to show your corn hole. A lot of them are very anal.—James Ridgeway, *Red Light*, p. 153, 1996

cornhole *verb*
1 to take the active role in anal sex *US, 1938*
• —Hyman E. Goldin et al., *Dictionary of American Underworld Lingo*, p. 50, 1950
• 'Now look are you going to cooperate" – three vicious diddles – "or does the ... does the Man cornhole you???"—William Burroughs, *Naked Lunch*, p. 196, 1957
• Jus' take your pants down an' we jus' do a li'l corn-holin' with you-all.—Piri Thomas, *Down These Mean Streets*, p. 161, 1967
• Al had never 'cornholed' before.—James Harper, *Homo Laws in all 50 States*, p. 177, 1968

- Fans expressed their profound interest in dirty, unsheathed cornholing by expressing total uninterest in such safe sex features[.] —Anthony Petkovich, *The X Factory*, p. 10, 1997

2 to victimise someone; to force someone into submission *US, 1974*
A figurative use of the previous sense.
- I guess he felt safe, ninety miles away, but he was about to be cornholed by yours truly[.] —Howard Stern, *Miss America*, p. 272, 1995

corn husk *noun*
a condom, especially one manufactured for anal intercourse *UK*
Derives from **CORNHOLE** (anal sex); conventionally, 'husk' is the membranous outer covering of the maize plant.
- —David Rowan, *A Glossary for the 90's*, 1998

Cornish pasty; Cornish *adjective*
appetising; sexually alluring *UK*
Rhyming slang for 'tasty'.
- She's a bit Cornish. —Ray Puxley, *Cockney Rabbit*, 1992

corn man *noun*
a man who is emotionally and sexually inexperienced *TRINIDAD AND TOBAGO*
- —Lise Winer, *Dictionary of the English/Creole of Trinidad & Tobago*, 2003

corn mule *noun*
homemade alcohol using corn as a base *US*
- —Vincent J. Monteleone, *Criminal Slang*, p. 59, 1949

corn off the cob *noun*
mawkish, sentimental music or entertainment *AUSTRALIA, 1984*
An elaboration of **CORN**.

corn on the cob *adjective*
used as an intensifier *UK*
- One step ahead. Corn on the fuckin' cob double bluff. —Nick Barlay, *Curvy Lovebox*, p. 84, 1997

cornpone *noun*
an unsophisciated, crude rural southerner *US, 1919*
Poet Lawrence Ferlinghetti regularly referred to US President Lyndon B. Johnson as 'Colonel Cornpone' in his poems; cartoonist Al Capp created General Jubilation T. Cornpone, master of grabbing defeat from the jaws of victory.
- Consequently, I head Dan Rather, CBS's king of cornpone, begin the evening with his now infamous promise. —*Commonweal*, p. 1, 12th January 2001

cornrip *noun*
a prostitute *BARBADOS*
- —Frank A. Collymore, *Barbadian Dialect*, p. 35, 1965

corn row *noun*
hair tied in tight braids separated by rows of bare scalp *US, 1946*
- —*American Speech*, Fall-Winter 1971
- After several trips to Africa he decided to give up his "natural" and wear what the black brothers call "corn rows." —*San Francisco Chronicle*, p. 54, 5th June 1972
- —Edith A. Folb, *runnin' down some lines*, p. 233, 1980
- As we speak, they're braiding each other's hair into corn rows. —Kpjm Berendt, *Midnight in the Garden of Good and Evil*, p. 293, 1994

corn-row *verb*
to fix hair in tight braids *US*
- —*American Speech*, Fall-Winter 1971
- Sapphire knows how to corn-row hair. —Carolyn Greene, *70 Soul Secrets of Sapphire*, p. 25, 1973

corn snake *noun*
a dried corn stalk gusting across a road *US*
Biker (motorcycle) usage.

corn stalker *noun*
a marijuana cigarette rolled in the outer leaf of a corn cob and sealed with honey *US*
- —Mike Haskins, *Drugs*, p. 287, 2003

corny *adjective*
mawkish, sentimental, hackneyed *US, 1932*
- The piano player in the band was an old maid about forty-five who knew every song that had been published in the last hundred years and could play in any key you named, each one cornier than the other. —Mezz Mezzrow, *Really the Blues*, p. 60, 1946
- Christ, I'm getting corny. —Jack Neal Cassady, *Letter to Jack Kerouac*, p. 135, 5th October 1947
- They were full of corny quips and Eastern college talk[.] —Jack Kerouac, *On the Road*, p. 227, 1957
- ["]New York meant beautiful women and street-smart guys who seemed to know all the angles." Nah, no... corny, top corny... for... my taste. —*Manhattan*, 1979

▷ **see: CORNED BEEF**

corp *noun*
a corporal, generally as a term of address *UK*
Military.
- How long you been out the army, Corp? —Clive Exton, *No Fixed Abode [Six Granada Plays]*, p. 119, 1959

corpie *noun*
a police officer *SAINT KITTS AND NEVIS*
- —Richard Allsopp, *Dictionary of Caribbean English Usage*, p. 171, 1996

Corpo *nickname*
Dublin Corporation *IRELAND*
- But yesterday the EIS was published and it says the spike would look only gorgeous, and the Corpo is already stocking up on red ribbon for the official unveiling. —*The Examiner*, 15th June 2000

corporation *noun*
a prominent belly *UK, 1753*
- [E]asing his chair back from the table, he loosened his embroidered waistcoat, then slapped his ample corporation. —Jenny Chaplin, *Childhood Days in Glasgow*, 1992

corporation cocktail *noun*
an intoxicating drink made by bubbling coal gas through milk *UK*
Current in the 1970s, until wholesale conversion to natural gas.

corporation pop *noun*
tap water *UK: ENGLAND*
Formed from 'pop' (a soft drink) and the 'corporation' that supplied water to domestic consumers; used in northern England.
- I borrowed Brasso, silver polish, perfume; / yet no amount of elbow grease or corporation pop / would cut through centuries of use and blame. —Peter Robinson, *The Bargain*, 1997

corpse *noun*
1 an actor's on-stage blunder or fit of laughter *UK*
From the verb.
- And how typical of The Backstagers [an amateur dramatic society] that they should have all the theatrical slang. A "corpse" was a breakdown into laughter on stage. —Simon Brett, *An Amateur Corpse*, 1978

2 a corporal *UK*
In Royal Air Force use, 2002.

corpse *verb*
of an actor, to blunder and so confuse yourself or another actor; while acting, to fall prey to irresistible laughter *UK, 1873*
- [A] classical actor who has recently corpsed during a first-night speech[.] —*The Guardian*, 16th September 2000

corpse cop *noun*
a homicide detective *US*
- Sidney, I realize an old corpse cop like you has instincts about dead bodies. —Joseph Wambaugh, *The Secrets of Harry Bright*, p. 168, 1985

corpser *noun*
an actor who is prone to disruptive laughter *UK*
From **CORPSE** (to blunder).
- Meanwhile Jason Isaacs (Lucius Malfoy) describes him [Daniel Radcliffe] as the 'worst corpser' he's ever worked with. —*Sunday Herald [Scotland]*, 3rd November 2002

corpsing *noun*
involuntary laughter, especially among actors *UK*
From the verb.
- Actors, I think, call it corpsing. They do it all the time and most Saturday evening television is taken up with clips of them falling about[.] —Danny King, *The Bank Robber Diaries*, p. 3, 2002

corpuscle *noun*
used as a humorous synonym for 'corporal' *US*
- —Carl Fleischhauer, *A Glossary of Army Slang*, p. 11, 1968

corr *noun*

a fight *UK*

English gypsy use, from Romany *koor* (to fight).

- —Jimmy Stockin, *On The Cobbles*, p. 10, 2000

corral *noun*

a group of prostitutes working for a single pimp *US*

- —Eugene Landy, *The Underground Dictionary*, p. 58, 1971

corroboree *noun*

any gathering or party; a celebration *AUSTRALIA, 1833*

Figurative use of the original sense as 'a traditional dance ceremony held by Australian Aboriginals', from the extinct Australian Aboriginal language Dharug, spoken in the Sydney region. Now considered politically incorrect.

- But Sydney must have its corroboree,—Sutton Woodfield, *A for Artemis*, p. 116, 1960
- —Harvey E. Ward, *Down Under Without Blunder*, p. 37, 1967
- —Jim Ramsay, *Cop It Sweet!*, p. 25, 1977

corroded *adjective*

ugly *US*

- —Edith A. Folb, *runnin' down some lines*, p. 233, 1980

corset *noun*

a bullet-proof vest *US*

- —Vincent J. Monteleone, *Criminal Slang*, p. 59, 1949

corvey; corvee *noun*

in Quebec, a community work project *CANADA*

Originally the word, from French, meant 'community work repairing the road in the spring'. In French, it carries the sense of 'what a bore!' but in English, it is still used.

- About 500 volunteers collected litter or planted trees during the Corvee du Mont Royal, the annual organized cleanup of the mountain. The annual corvey has developed into an event that is part work, part spring festival, part family outing.—*Montreal Gazette*, p. A3, 6th May 2002

cory *noun*

▷ **see:** COREY

corybungus *noun*

the buttocks *UK*

Homosexual usage; perhaps from **COREY** (the penis).

- —Paul Baker, *Polari*, p. 169, 2002
- —*Attitude*, p. 60, July 2003

cos

▷ **see:** 'CAUSE

cosa *noun*

marijuana *US*

From the Spanish for 'thing', so functionally the equivalent of 'stuff', an intentionally vague inreference to the drug.

- —Jay Robert Nash, *Dictionary of Crime*, p. 81, 1992

cosh; kosh *noun*

a bludgeon, a truncheon *UK, 1869*

- Miss Hope-Baldwin was a private woman who was terrified of intrusion and kept a cabinet full of weapons, including an axe, crossbow, machete, sword stick, cosh and an air rifle and two revolvers, the court was told.—*The Guardian*, 21st January 2003

▸ **under the cosh**

at a disadvantage; under control *UK, 1958*

- —Frank Norman, *Bang to Rights*, 1958
- [H]e's got it, the loyals, and the punters, right under the cosh[.] —Derek Raymond (Robin Cook), *The Crust on its Uppers*, p. 56, 1962
- Poll result puts [Ian] Duncan Smith under the cosh as Tories slump to a four-year low, modernisers and traditionalists are united in their urge to hold leader to account .—*The Guardian*, 18th December 2002

cosh *verb*

to strike someone with a cosh *UK, 1896*

- And when you're coshed, stay coshed.—Derek Bickerton, *Payroll*, p. 9, 1959
- [O]ne of them coshed the train's engineer on the head with an axe-handle, making it a crime with violence.—Emmett Grogan, *Ringolevio*, p. 201, 1972

co-signer *noun*

a fellow prisoner who is willing to vouch for you or to defend you with action *US*

- —James Harris, *A Convict's Dictionary*, p. 30, 1989

coskel *adjective*

dressed in conflicting, clashing colours *TRINIDAD AND TOBAGO*

- —Richard Allsopp, *Dictionary of Caribbean English Usage*, p. 171, 1996

cosmic *adjective*

1 wonderful, excellent, fabulous *UK*

The teenage appetite for superlatives is **OUT OF THIS WORLD**.

- The holiday was better than lovely – it was cosmic!—Miss Nicola Hardy, 1977

2 esoteric, difficult to grasp *US*

- —Connie Eble (Editor), *UNC-CH Campus Slang*, p. 2, Fall 1980

cosmic rays *noun*

the source of an unexplained computing problem *US*

- "Hey, Eric – I just got a burst of garbage on my tube, where did that come from?" "Cosmic rays, I guess."—Eric S. Raymond, *The New Hacker's Dictionary*, p. 107, 1991

cosmos *noun*

phencyclidine, the recreational drug known as PCP or angel dust *US*

- —*Drummer*, p. 77, 1977
- —Jay Robert Nash, *Dictionary of Crime*, p. 82, 1992

cossie; cozzie *noun*

1 a theatrical costume *UK*

- JULIAN: What cossy did they say? MR HORNE: Cossy? JULIAN: Costume. Polari for costume.—Barry Took and Marty Feldman, *Round The Horne*,
- I knew I'd have to put £6 in the slot for long enough to see her breasts and £9 if the cossie was going to come all the way off.—Kitty Churchill, *Thinking of England*, p. 187, 1995
- Based on Shaw's Pygmalion, to which lyricist and composer Alan Jay Lerner and Frederick Loewe lent a romantic gloss and opportunities for lots of very nice cossies, My Fair Lady shouldn't by rights work at all.—*The Guardian*, 22nd May 2002

2 a swimming costume *AUSTRALIA, 1926*

- —Jim Ramsay, *Cop It Sweet!*, p. 25, 1977
- On hot nights before the nor'easter came you changed into your cossie and ran under the sprinkler.—Clive James, *Unreliable Memoirs*, p. 174, 1980
- Hadn't I discovered that mouldy old convict cozzie tucked away in Nana's chest of drawers?—Edna Everage (Barry Humphries), *My Gorgeous Life*, p. 6, 1989
- [T]hink of those lifeguards with their cossies up their botties!—*New York Observer*, 17th March 2003

cost *verb*

to be expensive *UK, 1933*

- That double click will cost you.—*New Scientist*, 12th June 2004

▸ **cost a bomb**

to be very, or unexpectedly, expensive *UK, 1984*

- A word to the wise – he'd be better off steering clear of the cafe; the muffins cost a bomb.—*The Guardian*, 21st November 2002

▸ **cost a packet**

to be very, or unexpectedly, expensive *UK, 1984*

- Getting from Sardinia to Sicily would cost a packet.—*The Observer*, 7th November 1993

▸ **cost an arm and a leg**

to be very, or unexpectedly, expensive *US, 1974*

- [It] costs you an arm or leg to get it back – worse if you try to climb over the barbed wire.—Andrew Nickolds, *Back to Basics*, p. 36, 1994
- [B]uses still far too infrequent, taxis which cost an arm and a leg, average road speeds down to 10mph[.]—*The Guardian*, 13th March 2003

Costa del *noun*

when combined with a place name, an area that is peopled with criminals *UK*

After **COSTA DEL CRIME**.

- Costa del Ambridge.—*The Archers*, 17th August 2003

Costa del Crime *noun*

Spain's Costa del Sol *UK*

In the late 1970s, a diplomatic breakdown between Britain and Spain (over Gibraltar) created a safe haven for British criminals. One of the effects of a major armed robbery in London in 1983 was this journalistic coinage.

- [T]he operation against the UK drugs gangs on what is sometimes known as the "costa del crime", which has netted 3 tonnes of hashish so far, was continuing yesterday.—*The Guardian*, 17th June 2003

Costa del Sludge *noun*
the Spanish Riviera *UK*
A bitter reference to pollution.
- —G. Moorhouse, 19th June 1980

Costa Geriatrica *noun*
the south coast of England; Spain's Costa Brava; any coastal area popular as a retirement destination; hence, also applied to non-coastal areas such as Henley-on-Thames *UK*
A jocular but nevertheless derisory reference to the number of old people that retire to the seaside.
- —*New Society*, 21st April 1977
- [M]akes my dosh fetching them motors back off the Costa Geriatrica.—Jeremy Cameron, *Brown Bread in Wengen*, p. 16, 1999
- "Madeira?" a friend had snorted. "Isn't it a bit costa geriatrica?" Well, yes, there are a lot of older types snoozing by the pool[.]—*The Guardian*, 13th October 2001

cosy *noun*
an act of sexual intercourse *UK*
Used by upper-class society females; from the verb sense (to snuggle).
- —Ann Barr and Peter York, *The Official Sloane Ranger Handbook*, p. 158, 1982

cot *noun*
bed *AUSTRALIA*
- Come on, Billy. The cot for you.—Eric Lambert, *The Veterans*, p. 69, 1954
- 'Because I'm good in the cot.' 'Whoever told you that is a liar.' —Paul Vautin, *Turn It Up!*, p. 126, 1995

cot case *noun*
an incapacitated person, such as a drunk or insane person *AUSTRALIA, 1932*
That is, 'a person who should be confined to a bed'.
- [S]ergeant Burke was boozing and no better than a cot case. —Leonard Mann, *Flesh in Armour*, p. 144, 1932
- If I don't get a bit of shut-eye soon I'll be a flamin' cot-case so help me!—Barry Humphries, *The Wonderful World of Barry McKenzie*, p. 51, 1968
- I'll be a flaming cot-case if I don't get an amber transfusion. —*The Adventures of Barry McKenzie*, 1972
- [I]t's all she can do to conjure up a measure of pity for a sorry self-deluded fucking cot case like me.—Harrison Biscuit, *The Search for Savage Henry*, p. 56, 1995
- —David McGill, *David McGill's Complete Kiwi Slang Dictionary*, p. 30, 1998

cotch *noun*
any improvised place to sleep *JAMAICA, 1972*
- —Richard Allsopp, *Dictionary of Caribbean English Usage*, p. 171, 1996

cotch *verb*
to vomit *SOUTH AFRICA, 1974*
Directly from Afrikaans *kots*.
- —Jean Branford, *A Dictionary of South African English*, 1978

cotched *adjective*
relaxed, especially in a post-dance or post-drug-use situation *UK*
Used by some teenagers for 'chilled out'.
- —Susie Dent, *The Language Report*, p. 76, 2003

cotics *noun*
narcotics, especially heroin *US, 1942*
- —US Department of Justice, *Street Terms*, October 1994

cottage *noun*
a public lavatory used for homosexual encounters *UK, 1932*
- In Newcastle-upon-Tyne, for instance, the public WC in Shakespeare Street is nicknamed "Anne Hathaway's Cottage."—*Maledicta*, p. 233, Winter 1980
- [T]he ome-pallone [homosexual man] outside the cottage on Victoria Station.—the cast of 'Aspects of Love', Prince of Wales Theatre, *Palare (Boy Dancer Talk) for Beginners*, 1989–92
- In British parks, the "facilities" provided tended to look like miniature country cottages, with a sloping roof and windows, and gay men started to refer to them as such.—Paul Baker, *Polari*, p. 170, 2002

cottage *verb*
to seek homosexual contact in a public urinal *UK, 1971*
After COTTAGE (a public lavatory).
- Did you see anything? Were you perhaps cottaging in the area that night[?]—Christopher Brookmyre, *Boiling a Frog*, p. 297, 2000
- I'm just back from a lovely cottaging holiday in the Lake District. —Paul Baker, *Polari*, p. 170, 2002

cottage cheese *noun*
cellulite *US*
A purely visual coining.
- —Pamela Munro, *U.C.L.A. Slang*, p. 53, 1997

cottage queen *noun*
a homosexual man who seeks sexual contact in public toilets *UK*
A combination of COTTAGE (a public lavatory) and QUEEN (a homosexual man).
- Makes a change from those cottage queen chorines[.]—the cast of 'Aspects of Love', Prince of Wales Theatre, *Palare (Boy Dancer Talk) for Beginners*, 1989–92

cottager *noun*
a homosexual man who seeks sexual contact in public toilets *UK*
After COTTAGE (a public lavatory).
- hanging around secluded highland public conveniences all night, in the hope of running into the headhunter, or at least some would-be cottager they could accuse—Christopher Brookmyre, *Boiling a Frog*, p. 296, 2000

cottaging *noun*
1 the practice of engaging in homosexual encounters in public toilets *UK, 1972*
- The vote came on a Conservative amendment saying anybody caught involving in "cottaging" should face prosecution and face jail terms of up to two years.—*BBC News*, 9th June 2003

2 the practice of going down to your 'cottage' – a second and often quite a large house – in the country for the weekend *UK, 1984*

cotton *noun*
1 cotton used for straining a dissolved narcotic (heroin, cocaine or morphine) before injection; the bits of cotton saturated with drugs can be aggregated for an injection *US, 1933*
- I was all out of junk at this point and had double-boiled my last cottons.—William Burroughs, *Junkie*, p. 37, 1953
- But when I make that big sting, I'll straighten you / If you'll save me a little on the cotton.—Dennis Wepman et al., *The Life*, p. 78, 1976
- Of course that's where Rooski would go to ground, there to run errands for the Troll and beg cottons from the other dopefiends. —Seth Morgan, *Homeboy*, p. 60, 1990

2 female pubic hair *US*
- —Roger D. Abrahams, *Deep Down in the Jungle*, p. 259, 1970

▷ **see:** COTTON WOOL

cotton ball *noun*
a burst of flak fire as perceived from the air *US*
- —Gregory Clark, *Words of the Vietnam War*, p. 125, 1990

cotton brothers *noun*
cocaine, heroin and morphine *US, 1938*
From the cotton strainer used when prepararing these drugs.
- —Robert Ashton, *This Is Heroin*, p. 208, 2002
- —Mike Haskins, *Drugs*, p. 283, 2003

cotton-chopper *noun*
used as a term of address, especially to someone with a southern accent *US*
- Terms such as Bud, cottonpicker, cottonchopper, guy, and good buddy are affectionate-type terms used among truckers. —Gwyneth A. "Dandalion" Seese, *Tijuana Bear in a Smoke 'Um Up Taxi*, p. 18, 1977

cotton fever *noun*
an intense illness sometimes suffered after injecting heroin leached from used cottons *US*
- —Geoffrey Froner, *Digging for Diamonds*, p. 22, 1989

cottonhead *noun*
a heroin addict who habitually uses cotton used by other addicts to leach out heroin for his use *US*
- —Richard Horman and Allan Fox, *Drug Awareness*, p. 465, 1970

cotton mouth *noun*
a dryness of the mouth as a result of smoking marijuana or hashish
- —Nick Jones, *Spliffs*, p. 250, 2003

cotton on to; cotton on; cotton to *verb*

to form, or have, a liking or fancy for something or someone; to understand or come to understand *AUSTRALIA, 1907*

- Me and him met at a peace officer's convention one year, and we kind of cottoned to each other right away. — Jim Thompson, *Pop. 1280*, p. 18, 1964
- But what if he cottons on to what I'm doing? — J.J. Connolly, *Layer Cake*, p. 148, 2000
- Not every Formula one star has cottoned on to the marketing power of the web. — *The Guardian*, 16th June 2001

cottonpicker *noun*

a fellow; used as a term of address, especially from trucker to trucker *US, 1919*

- — Lanie Dills, *The Official CB Slanguage Language Dictionary*, p. 26, 1976

cotton-picking *adjective*

used as a folksy intensifier *US, 1952*

- That's the sum cottinpickin total[.] — Robert Gover, *Here Goes Kitten*, p. 54, 1964

cotton shooter *noun*

a drug addict who injects residue aggregated from cotton swatches used to strain drugs *US*

- Down-and-out addicts are "cotton shooters." They collect discarded cottons, soak out the narcotic residue and come up with an anemic shot. — *San Francisco News*, p. 1, 5th December 1951

cotton slut *noun*

a person who will attend an event for the sole purpose of obtaining a tee-shirt being given to those in attendance *US*

- — Don R. McCreary (Editor), *Dawg Speak*, 2001

cottontail *noun*

an attractive woman *US, 1962*

- — J.E. Lighter, *Historical Dictionary of American Slang, Volume 1*, p. 492, 1994

cotton-top *noun*

an old person *US*

An allusion to the white hair with which some older people are blessed.

- — Connie Eble (Editor), *UNC-CH Campus Slang*, p. 3, Spring 2000

cotton wool; cotton *noun*

a casual quest for a sexual partner *UK*

Rhyming slang for **PULL**, in the phrase **ON THE PULL** (to quest or be questing for a sexual partner).

- The hunt for sexual quarry is known as going on the "cotton". — Ray Puxley, *Fresh Rabbit*, 1998

▸ **wrap in cotton-wool; keep in cotton-wool**

to cosset; to be extremely protective of someone *UK, c.1890*

- There is something that sticks in the craw about the way the FA wraps the [England football] team in cotton wool. — *The Guardian*, 28th May 2003

couch *noun*

▸ **on the couch**

1 undergoing psychotherapy *US*

- — *American Speech*, p. 145–148, May 1961: 'The spoken language of medicine; argot, slang, cant'

2 in gambling, without further funds *US*

- — John Vorhaus, *The Big Book of Poker Slang*, p. 27, 1996

couch casting *noun*

the practice of casting roles in performances based on the actor's willingess to have sex with the casting director *US*

- — Sherman Louis Sergel, *The Language of Show Biz*, p. 60, 1973

couch commander *noun*

someone watching television with a remote control *US*

- — Judi Sanders, *Don't Dog by Do, Dude!*, p. 8, 1991

couch dance *noun*

a sexual dance performed in a sex club, with the dancer grinding on the lap of a man seated on a couch *US*

- Additionally, some officers are pulling the tough duty of sitting around in topless clubs and paying for table or couch dances, waiting to be "wrongly touched." — *Seattle Times*, p. D1, 20th June 1990
- "What's a couch dance?" "You take the guy into a private room filled with couches. No door, and a bouncer standing outside, keepin' an eye on things. You dance on his lap and he gropes you for three, or four minutes." — Richard N. Cote, *The Redneck Riviera*, p. 126, 2002
- Some of the girls sashay over to chat with the generous tippers or give private "couch dances" in circular booths along back walls. — *Cincinnati Enquirer*, p. 1B, 19th May 2003

couchie *noun*

▷ see: **KOUTCHIE**

couch lock *noun*

a feeling of inertia as a result of smoking marijuana *UK*

- — Steven Wishnia, *The Cannabis Companion*, p. 151, 2004

couch potato *noun*

a person who habitually idles, watching television *US, 1976*

Possibly a pun on 'boob-tuber' (a television addict) and a 'potato' as a 'tuber'; it may also play on **VEGETABLE** (a person with an undemanding existence); the 'couch', of course, is where the potato is planted. One of the very few slang words or phrases where it is seemingly possible to trace the coining; in July 1976 a group of friends in California coined the term, which was first used in commerce in 1977 and then hit the bigtime with the *Official Couch Potato Handbook* (1983).

- — Connie Eble (Editor), *UNC-CH Campus Slang*, p. 2, Spring 1984
- I'd be ready to give odds he's a couch potato, sitting in watching television while the other kids are out batting the baseball around or playing soccer. — Robert Campbell, *The Cat's Meow*, p. 75, 1988
- — *American Speech*, Fall 1988
- For me the Couch Potato of TV Demonology looks like Dandy Nichols in the early seventies. — Stuart Jeffries, *Mrs Slocombe's Pussy*, p. xix, 2000
- Steady, gray drizzle that encourages statewide bad hair and couch potato mentality. — Janet Evanovich, *Seven Up*, p. 77, 2001

couch surfer *noun*

a person who sleeps on a friend's couch overnight *NEW ZEALAND*

- Most are aged between 16 and 20, and are making the transition from living at home to flatting. "They're the couch surfers'. — *(Wellington) Contact*, p. 1, 7th August 2003

cough *noun*

1 a confession *UK*

After **COUGH** (to confess).

- I've had a cough on less than this, before they [suspects] collect their wits. — Roger Busby, *Garvey's Code*, 1978
- Is that a cough? — a Police Constable in Bristol, UK, 25th March 2002

2 a piece of information or good evidence *UK*

Police use; from **COUGH UP** (to disclose).

3 money paid out *US*

From **COUGH UP** (to pay).

- It's a bit of an outlay given our present cash flow [...] but the profit margin more than compensates for the cough [...] injecting much needed funds into our accounts. — Bernard Dempsey and Kevin McNally, *Lock, Stock ... & Two Hundred Smoking Kalashnikovs*, p. 108–109, 2000

cough *verb*

1 to confess *US, 1899*

- They told me that the others have coughed it. That is their pigeon. — *Bournemouth Evening Echo*, 20th April 1966
- He coughed for them. What more do you want? — David Peace, *Nineteen Seventy-Four*, p. 167, 1999

2 in drag racing, to suffer complete engine failure *US*

Used as a transitive verb; 'you cough your engine'.

- — Ross Olney, *Kins of the Drag Strip*, p. 186, 1968

▸ **cough your cud**

to vomit *NEW ZEALAND*

- The poor townie turned green and as we say in the country, coughed his cud. — Bill Richards, *A Pioneer's Life*, p. 91, 1989
- — Harry Orsman, *A Dictionary of Modern New Zealand Slang*, p. 32, 1999

cough!

said humorously while pretending to grab at another man's testicles *UK, 1984*

From the practice in medical examinations of cupping the testicles and testing the healthy movement that is occasioned by a cough.

cough and a spit *noun*

1 a small part in a play or a film *UK, 1984*

- A lot of actors are very happy with 'a cough and a spit', which is a phrase I loathe. — *The Guardian*, 29th January 2003

2 a short distance *UK*

- Any AA map will tell you that March is just a 40-minute cough and a spit away from where Pod lives[.] — *The Guardian*, 10th May 2003

cough and choke *verb*
to smoke *UK*
Also used as a noun to mean 'a cigarette'.
- — Ray Puxley, *Fresh Rabbit*, 1998

cough and die *verb*
(used of a computer program) to cease operating by virtue of a design feature *US*
- The parser saw a control-A in its input where it was looking for a printable, so it coughed and died. — Eric S. Raymond, *The New Hacker's Dictionary*, p. 109, 1991

cough and drag *noun*
a cigarette *UK*
Rhyming slang for **FAG** (a cigarette), pitched somewhere between irony and black humour.
- [C]over me while I nip out for a cough and drag. — Ray Puxley, *Cockney Rabbit*, 1992

cough and sneeze *noun*
cheese *UK*
Rhyming slang, generally thought to date from late C19.
- — Julian Franklyn, *A Dictionary of Rhyming Slang*, 1961
- — Ray Puxley, *Cockney Rabbit*, 1992

cough and splutter *noun*
butter *UK, 1978*
Rhyming slang.
- — Ray Puxley, *Cockney Rabbit*, 1992

cough drop *noun*
an attractive girl *SOUTH AFRICA*
- — *Cape Argus*, 4th July 1946

cough it up – it might be a gold watch!
used as jocular encouragement to someone with a hacking cough *UK, 1978*

cough syrup *noun*
money paid to police informers *US*
- — *American Speech*, p. 155, May 1951: 'Hermann collitz and the language of the underworld'

cough up *verb*
1 to pay; to hand over something *US, 1890*
- After the usual stalling the insurers had dug in and decided they weren't going to cough up. — Greg Williams, *Diamond Geezers*, p. 46, 1997

2 to disclose something *US, 1896*

couillon *noun*
a lacrosse-like two ball game played by eastern Canadian Indian women on ice or in a clearing *CANADA*
- He even tried his hand at the women's game of couillon on the river ice. — Walter O'Meara, *The Grand Portage*, p. 195, 1951

couldn't-care-less *adjective*
indifferent, uncaring *UK, 1947*
- These discussions made Felix afraid, which expressed itself in a couldn't-care-less attitude[.] — Ajith Fernando, *Acts*, p. 580, 1998

coul wash *noun*
▷ see: COOL WASH

council gritter; council *noun*
the anus *UK*
Rhyming slang for **SHITTER**.
- Does she take it up the council? — *www.LondonSlang.com*, June 2002

council houses *noun*
trousers *UK, 1934*
Rhyming slang.

count *noun*
the ratio by which a drug is diluted *US*
- They say it's supposed to be six and one, but if the dealer is wise, he wants everybody to keep coming to him, and he wants to give them a nice count so they can fall out, he will go and cut it two and one, or three and one, and make it nice and strong. — Jeremy Larner and Ralph Tefferteller, *The Addict in the Street*, p. 38, 1964

count *verb*
in pool, to make a shot *US*
- I started in there when I was 13 and when I was 14 I got my stroke. I got my stroke and learned to count [pocket the balls]. — Ned Polsky, *Hustlers, Beats, and Others*, p. 89, 1967

▸ **count days**
in twelve-step recovery programmes such as Alcoholics Anonymous, to track your recovery from addiction *US*
- We count our days since we last incurred unsecured debt. — Christopher Cavanaugh, *AA to Z*, p. 74, 1998

▸ **count your money**
to use the toilet *US*
- — Jerry Robertson, *Oil Slanguage*, p. 41, 1954

counter *noun*
1 in poker, a player who to the annoyance of other players repeatedly counts his chips or money *US*
- — Irwin Steig, *Common Sense in Poker*, p. 183, 1963

2 a prostitute's customer *US*
- — Roger Blake, *The American Dictionary of Sexual Terms*, p. 48, 1964

3 in lobstering, a lobster that meets the legal measurement requirements *US*
- — Kendall Meriam, *The Illustrated Dictionary of Lobstering*, p. 26, 1978

counter hopper *noun*
a dedicated follower of youth fashion *UK*
- — Tom Hibbert, *Rockspeak!*, p. 44, 1983

countess *noun*
an older homosexual man *US*
- — *Maledicta*, p. 222, 1979: 'Kinks and queens: linguistic and cultural aspects of the terminology for gays'

country *noun*
▸ **in country**
during the Vietnam war, in Vietnam *US*
- How much longer do you have in country? — Ronald J. Glasser, *365 Days*, p. 177, 1971
- After a few months "in country," the advisers and experts usually came to the conclusion that the United States was not sending enough commodities for them to do their job properly. — Frances Fitzgerald, *Fire in the Lake*, p. 347, 1972

country *adjective*
unsophisticated, rural, not world-wise *US*
- You know what Otis? What. You're country. It's alright. — Otis Redding, *Tramp*, 1964
- Cuz you're so country. So Bama. I didn't know niggers like you still existed. — *Mo' Better Blues*, 1990

country bama *noun*
a naive, gullible rustic *US*
- I can't imagine no country bama muthafucka talking bout. — *Boyz N The Hood*, 1990
- But he wasn't what Tracy used to call a "country bama," either. — Felicia Mason, *Truly, Honestly*, p. 304, 2000
- Because he's a big old country 'bama, ain't got no good sense. — Sandra Jackso Opoku, *Hot Johny (and the Women Who Loved Him)*, p. 172, 2001
- In fact, I was gonna ask your country Bama ass why do you put those Jheri Curl drip-drip chemicals in your Black nappy hair? — Ayana Byrd, *Hair Story*, p. 112, 2001

country booboo *noun*
any naive, gullible person *VIRGIN ISLANDS, BRITISH*
- — Richard Allsopp, *Dictionary of Caribbean English Usage*, p. 172, 1996

country bookie *noun*
a naive rustic *TRINIDAD AND TOBAGO, 1904*
- — Lise Winer, *Dictionary of the English/Creole of Trinidad & Tobago*, 2003

country Cadillac *noun*
a pickup truck *US*
- — Wayne Floyd, *Jason's Authentic Dictionary of CB Slang*, p. 13, 1976

country club *noun*
1 a minimum security, comfortable prison generally reserved for corporate and banking criminals *US*
- Once, when jailed briefly in the early 50's, Costello was sent to a Federal country club near Flint, Michigan[.] — Lee Mortimer, *Women Confidential*, p. 34, 1960
- Chino, California's "country club" prison, yesterday had its first murder. — *San Francisco Examiner*, p. 18, 18th July 1972
- I should be going to one of those country-club joints like where they sent those Watergate assholes[.] — Elmore Leonard, *Freaky Deaky*, p. 13, 1988

2 anything that appears to be relatively comfortable and undemanding *US*
- His instructors had spoken of some precincts that were "country clubs" – in the quieter residential sections of the city[.] — Peter Maas, *Serpico*, p. 58, 1973

country cousin *noun*

1 the bleed period of the menstrual period *US, 1908*

- —Frederic G. Cassidy, *Dictionary of American Regional English, Volume 1*, p. 802, 1985

2 a dozen *UK, 1909*
Rhyming slang.

- —Ray Puxley, *Cockney Rabbit*, p. 41, 1992

country dunny *noun*

▸ all alone like a country dunny
completely alone; by yourself; friendless *AUSTRALIA*

- —Lenie Johansen, *The Dinkum Dictionary*, 1988

▸ like a country dunny
glaringly obvious; standing out *AUSTRALIA*

- You still haven't stained your webbing – you stand out on parade like a country dunny.—Eric Lambert, *The Veterans*, p. 100, 1954

country mile *noun*
a long distance or margin *US*

- —David W. Maurer, *Argot of the Racetrack*, p. 22, 1951
- I love my job, it's the best I've ever had by a country mile and turning up for work is an absolute delight.—Paul Vautin, *Turn It Up!*, p. 103, 1995

country mouse *noun*
in Antarctica, a scientist or scientist's assistant whose work takes them into the field, away from McMurdo Station *ANTARCTICA*

- — *Cool Antarctica*, 2003: 'Antarctic slang'

country send *noun*
in a big con, sending the victim away to retrieve money *US*

- In the old days once a mark was hooked on the con, the sharpers would always send him home to get more money. It was called "The Country Send."—Stephen Cannell, *Big Con*, p. 292, 1997

country store *noun*
in the Vietnam war, a military self-service supply centre *US*

- —Carl Fleischhauer, *A Glossary of Army Slang*, p. 11, 1968

country straight *noun*
in poker, a hand consisting of four sequenced cards which can be converted into a five-card sequence with the correct draw at either end of the sequence *US, 1978*

- —Thomas L. Clark, *The Dictionary of Gambling and Gaming*, p. 53, 1987

country wool *noun*
homespun wool *CANADA*

- He always wore a pair of long country-wool stockings.—Thomas Raddall, *Wings*, 1956

count store *noun*
a rigged carnival game *US*

- —Gene Sorrows, *All About Carnivals*, p. 15, 1985

count the hooks!; count the hoops!
in the Canadian military, used for demanding that a subordinate recognises the uniform and rank of the superior rebuking him or her *CANADA*

- "Count the hooks!" and "Count the hoops!" are a forceful reminder that he or she is a subordinate and should do as ordered. Hooks are the chevrons worn by NCOs, and hoops are officer's rank braid. —Tom Langeste, *Words on the Wing*, p. 67, 1995

county *noun*
any county jail, where the accused are held before trial and prisoners convicted of misdemeanors are incarcerated for short sentences *US*

- So there we were in County.—William Burroughs, *Junkie*, p. 66, 1953
- About a month ago, your 'boon coon' 'Party' caught sixty in the county.—Iceberg Slim (Robert Beck), *Pimp*, p. 79, 1969
- Teddy Laursen is in County. He's very anxious to talk to you.— *Body Heat*, 1980
- I mean like I just met you in County last night and I really haven't had time to check you out.—Gerald Petievich, *Money Men*, p. 52, 1981
- [N]ow he walked from Weehawken toward the benches, thinking about Victor, realizing that his brother was about to spend his second night in County.—Richard Price, *Clockers*, p. 383, 1992
- A week in the County wasn't s'pose to be shit, but I still didn't feel like tain' my ass up off in that muthafucka.— *Menace II Society*, 1993
- Okay gentlemen, you've both been to County before, I'm sure. Here it comes.— *Pulp Fiction*, 1994
- Judge said if we go within a hundred feet of the stores, we get thrown into County.—Kevin Smith, *Jay and Silent Bob Strike Back*, p. 14, 2001

county *adjective*
in the manner of the landed gentry; snobbish, pretentious in the manner of, or with pretentions to, the gentry *UK, 1921*

- [T]he winds of change are also blowing through the respectable county set.— *The Observer*, 27th February 2000

county blues *noun*
a blue uniform issued to prisoners in a county jail *US*

- Caine is dressed in the "County Blues;" that's the jumpsuit that they give all inmates.— *Menace II Society*, 1993

County Kilburn *nickname*
the northwest London district of Kilburn *UK*
Formed in the manner of an Irish County in recognition of the high density of Irish in Kilburn's population.

- See, in the boob [jail] ninety per cent of the cons are complete fuckin gobshites, as they say up in County Kilburn[.]—J.J. Connolly, *Layer Cake*, p. 38, 2000

county mountie *noun*

1 a member of the Ulster Defence Regiment (1970–1992) *UK*
Adopted from the US meaning (a local police officer); a reference to the six counties of Ulster.

- —Peter Chippindale, *The British CB Book*, p. 153, 1981

2 a local police officer *US, 1975*

- —Wayne Floyd, *Jason's Authentic Dictionary of CB Slang*, p. 13, 1976
- Peter, what's the name of that county mountie who's heading up the search for the gas station kid?—Dan Simmons, *Carrion Comfort*, p. 627, 1989
- It was the perfect spot for a speed trap. A County Mountie clocked the red Porsche at over one hundred miles per hour, set his blue and reds flashing, and gave chase.—Homer Hickam, *Back to the Moon*, p. 265, 1999

count your fingers!
used with heavy humour to suggest distrust of a person who is shaking, or has just shaken, someone's hand *UK*

- "I knew quite a few Taffs in those days." He winced as the handshake continued and was then mercifully terminated. "Still," said Eric with his too easy smile, "count your fingers though," he said. —Anthony Masters, *Minder*, p. 18, 1984

county shoes *noun*
inexpensive shoes issued to prisoners by a county jail *US*

- One of them is still wearing his 'county shoes'. That tells me he just could out of county jail[.]—Joseph Wambaugh, *The Blue Knight*, p. 9, 1973

county time *noun*
time served in a local county jail, as opposed to a state or federal prison *US*
Less than 'state time' or 'hard time'.

- Add county time awaiting hearings, and that hole we just left, that's more'n a decade of correctional living.—Elmore Leonard, *Out of Sight*, p. 45, 1996

coup *noun*

1 a crime *UK*

- On this coup, though, he was the lookout.—Dave Courtney, *Dodgy Dave's Little Black Book*, p. 167, 2001

2 in horse racing, a secret betting plunge in which a great deal of money is bet at favourable odds *AUSTRALIA, 1895*

- As so often happened with coups wholly or partly engineered by Mr Connolly, the betting plunge on Nightmarch was successful. —Maurice Cavanough and Meurig Davies, *Cup Day*, p. 203, 1960
- —Wilda Moxham, *The Apprentice*, p. 141, 1969
- —David Bennet, *Know Your Bets*, p. 26, 2001

Coupe *noun*
a Cadillac Coupe de Ville car *US*

- —Edith A. Folb, *runnin' down some lines*, p. 233, 1980

coupla *noun*
two *UK*
A slovening of 'couple of'.

- CORP: [...] How long you been out [of prison], Tich? TICH: Coupla weeks.—Clive Exton, *No Fixed Abode [Six Granada Plays]*, p. 121, 1959

couple *noun*
several drinks, especially beers, not necessarily two *UK, 1935*

- 'We'll have a couple at the Prince o' Wales.' When Nowra was behind us, he said we would have a couple more at Milton.—Nino Culotta (John O'Grady), *Gone Fishin'*, p. 99, 1962
- That afternoon Reg dropped me home and we popped into the 'Ulster' for a couple.—Sam Weller, *Old Bastards I Have Met*, p. 19, 1979

• Was in the back bar at the "Queen's" in Southport one day having a couple with two Demons. —Sam Weller, *Old Bastards I Have Met*, p. 18, 1979

couple of bob *noun*

1 a non-specific amount of money *UK, 1980*
Pre-1971, when decimalisation changed the face and value of sterling, a **BOB** was 'a shilling' (5p).

2 a job *UK*
Rhyming slang.
• —Ray Puxley, *Cockney Rabbit*, 1992

3 a lump of phlegm *UK*
Rhyming slang for **GOB** (to spit).
• —Ray Puxley, *Cockney Rabbit*, p. 41, 1992

coupon *noun*

1 the face *UK, 1980*
Often in the phrase 'fill in your coupon' (attack your face).
• All those smiling coupons, all gloating at me. —Ian Pattison, *Rab C. Nesbitt*, 1988
• Even with so many bodies milling about and a loudhailer obscuring his coupon, McMaster was not difficult to spot[.] —Christopher Brookmyre, *The Sacred Art of Stealing*, p. 106, 2002

2 an 'I owe you' which has not and will not be paid off *US*
• I haven't seen Big Larry in three months; I think I'm holding a coupon. —John Vorhaus, *The Big Book of Poker Slang*, p. 11, 1996

3 in trucking, a speeding ticket *US*
• —Elementary Electronics, *Dictionary of CB Lingo*, p. 60, 1976

courage *noun*
sexual potency *BAHAMAS*
• —John A. Holm, *Dictionary of Bahamian English*, p. 52, 1982

courage pill *noun*

1 a capsule of heroin *US, 1933*
• —Vincent J. Monteleone, *Criminal Slang*, p. 59, 1949
• I was discovering why heroin caps are so often called "courage pills." —Douglas Rutherford, *The Creeping Flesh*, p. 149, 1963
• —Mike Haskins, *Drugs*, p. 283, 2003

2 a central nervous system despressant *UK*
• —Mike Haskins, *Drugs*, p. 282, 2003

'course
of course *UK, 1886*
• NATHAN: I don't feel well. GAZ: 'Course you don't, you cheeky chuffer, you've got a hangover. —*The Full Monty*, 1997

course-a-grunt; course-a-pig *noun*
an error in bricklaying in which opposite ends of a new wall meet at different heights *UK*
Recorded by Jack Stearn, building instructor, 1978.

course note *noun*
paper money in denominations of $5 or greater *US*
• —Hyman E. Goldin et al., *Dictionary of American Underworld Lingo*, p. 50, 1950

court *noun*

▸ **hold court in the street**
to mete out what a police officer deems justice through physical beatings *US*
• He was busting heads and holding court in the street, then getting you dummies to take the heat for him if complaints came down. —Stephen J. Cannell, *The Tin Collectors*, p. 179, 2001

court *verb*

▸ **court Cecil**
to become addicted to morphine *US*
• —Jay Robert Nash, *Dictionary of Crime*, p. 83, 1992

court card *noun*
in a deck of playing cards, any jack, queen or king *US*
• —Irv Roddy, *Friday Night Poker*, p. 217, 1961

courtesy flush *noun*
a mid-defecation flush of the toilet as a courtesy to others in a bathroom or other prisoners in the cell *US*
• —Reinhold Aman, *Hillary Clinton's Pen Pal*, p. 33, 1996

court-in *noun*
a ceremonial beating to initiate a new member into a gang *US*
• Giggles, Shygirl and Rascal performed the initiation they call a court-in, a 13-second beating that ended with tangled hair, smudged lipstick and a bloody nose. —*Houston Chronicle*, p. 3A, 4th February 1990
• —Mark S. Fleisher, *Beggars & Thieves*, p. 288, 1995

court-out *noun*
a ceremonial beating of a person leaving a gang *US*
• If she fails to do her part as a loyal gang member – if she is not, as the girls say, down for her neighborhood – she can face a "court-out," in which there is no time limit to the beating. —*Houston Chronicle*, p. 3A, 4th February 1990

Cousin Charlie *nickname*
the Federal Communications Commission *US*
• —Radio Shack, *CBer's Handy Atlas/Dictionary*, p. 25, 1976

cousin Ella *noun*
an umbrella *UK*
Rhyming slang.
• —Ray Puxley, *Cockney Rabbit*, 1992

Cousin Jack *noun*
a Cornish man, especially a miner *AUSTRALIA, 1863*
• This appreciable number of Irish did not swamp the humour of the bulk of railwaymen, 'Cousin Jacks' (miners from Cornwall who flocked to the railways when the mines failed), the Welsh, English and Scots. —Patsy Adam-Smith, *Folklore of the Australian Railwaymen*, p. 204, 1969

cousins *noun*
curly hair on the back of the neck *BAHAMAS*
• —John A. Holm, *Dictionary of Bahamian English*, p. 52, 1982

cousin Sis *noun*
a piss (an act of urination); piss (alcohol), especially in the phrase 'going on the cousin Sis' *UK*
Rhyming slang.
• —Ray Puxley, *Fresh Rabbit*, 1998

couta *noun*
a barracouta *AUSTRALIA, 1933*

cove *noun*
a fellow, bloke *UK, 1567*
From Romany *kova* (a thing, a person).
• We're looking for a cove that leases a lot of timber country. —Kylie Tennant, *The Honey Flow*, p. 62, 1956
• —Arthur Upfield, *Bony and the Mouse*, p. 51, 1959
• —John Wynnum, *Jiggin' in the Riggin'*, p. 27, 1965
• I'm Captain Fossliner, I've been waiting for you coves all afternoon. —Ray Slattery, *Mobbs' Mob*, p. 58, 1966
• Didn't you ever meet the cove? —Jean Brooks, *The Opal Witch*, p. 122, 1967
• —Patsy Adam-Smith, *Folklore of the Australian Railwaymen*, p. 187, 1969
• Strike me! This cove's stashin' it away in bundles. —Gerald Sweeney, *The Plunge*, p. 192, 1981
• [A] cove whose boat [face] lacked only a pencil moustache for him to have the word 'Spiv' stamped in his passport[.] —Andrew Nickolds, *Back to Basics*, p. 90, 1994
• He was just such a queer cove to find in here. —John Milne, *Alive and Kicking*, p. 128, 1998

Covent Garden
pardon, especially as a shortened version of 'I beg your pardon' *UK*
Rhyming slang, replacing the original (1857) sense as 'a farthing' (a coin that was worth 1/4 of a penny); formed on the name of a fashionable area of central London when it still had a reputation as a market for fruit and vegetables.
• —Ray Puxley, *Cockney Rabbit*, 1992

cover *noun*

1 an admission fee paid to enter a bar or club *US*
A shortened 'cover charge'.
• Bellamy was so snockered he didn't even blink at the ten-dollar cover. —Carl Hiaasen, *Tourist Season*, p. 2, 1986

2 a single large-denomination note wrapped around small-denomination notes, giving the impression of a great deal of money *US*
• He loved to flash his "Kansas City roll," probably fifty one-dollar bills folded with a twenty on the inside and a one-hundred dollar bill on the outside. We always wondered what Dollarbill would do if someone ever stole his hundred-dollar "cover." —Malcolm X and Alex Haley, *The Autobiography of Malcolm X*, p. 89, 1964

3 a recording which has been popularised by someone else *US, 1970*
A shortened form of the more formal 'cover version'.

- Listen, it isn't bad enough, we have to do covers, we're doing the Spice Girls, and those chicks can't even fucking sing. —Elmore Leonard, *Be Cool*, p. 35, 1999

4 the disguise and staged personality assumed by an expert card counter playing blackjack in a casino in the hope of avoiding detection and ejection *US*

- —Michael Dalton, *Blackjack*, p. 25, 1991

cover *verb*

1 (used of a male) to have sex with a woman *TRINIDAD AND TOBAGO, 1980*

Conventionally applied to a stallion with a mare.

- —Lise Winer, *Dictionary of the English/Creole of Trinidad & Tobago*, 2003

2 (used of a favourite by sports gamblers) to win by at least the margin established as the pointspread by the bookmakers *US*

- —*Bay Sports Review*, p. 8, November 1991

covered wagon *noun*

1 an aircraft carrier, especially the USS Langley *US, 1933*

- The nickname "covered wagon" describes the way the Langley looked with its rooflike landing strip over the deck. —*Sunday Telegram (Worcester, Massachusetts)*, p. B1, 4th May 1997
- They called it a covered wagon because the flight deck was above the well deck making the ship sort of look like a covered wagon. —*Virginian-Pilot (Norfolk, Virginia)*, p. 5, 5th September 1997

2 an ugly or unpleasant woman *UK*

Rhyming slang for **DRAGON**.

- —Ray Puxley, *Cockney Rabbit*, 1992

covered with horseshoes *adjective*

extremely lucky *US*

- —George Percy, *The Language of Poker*, p. 24, 1988

cover for *verb*

1 to act as a substitute for another worker *UK, 1976*

- The firefighters' strike highlighted the relatively poor pay of many of the soldiers, sailors, and RAF personnel who were covering for people demanding significant increases and already earning more than they earned. —*The Guardian*, 30th December 2002

2 to conceal someone's crime or mistake *UK, 1968*

covers *noun*

▸ **pull the covers off**

to reveal someone's homosexuality *US*

- —*Maledicta*, p. 265, Summer/Winter 1981: 'By its slang, ye shall know it: the pessimism of prison life'

covey *noun*

a group of gullible people, likely victims for a swindle or crime *US*

- —R. Frederick West, *God's Gambler*, p. 223, 1964

cow *noun*

1 a contemptible woman *UK, 1696*

- Jimmy says, "You rotten mingy old cow." —John Peter Jones, *Feather Pluckers*, p. 18, 1964
- You stupid, sad, old cow. —Jennifer Saunders, *Absolutely Fabulous*, p. 5, 1992
- Too fuckin' late now I tells the fat cow, too fuckin' late now. —Paul Fraser and Shane Meadows, *TwentyFourSeven*, p. 9, 1997
- What a cow! I bet she's taken a sickie. —Diran Abedayo, *My Once Upon A Time*, p. 247, 2000

2 a fellow, bloke *AUSTRALIA, 1941*

- You're a lucky cow; there's no doubt about it. —Alan Marshall, *I Can Jump Puddles*, p. 243, 1955
- You're a bloody long-winded cow, Ossie. —Dymphna Cusack, *Picnic Races*, p. 105, 1962
- 'Ah, he's keeping up appearances, poor old cow,' Darky said. —Frank Hardy, *Legends From Benson's Valley*, p. 160, 1972

3 a despicable person *AUSTRALIA, 1894*

- By cripes, they let that cow Gilbert go to university and now the old man reckons he can't afford to send me. —Norman Lindsay, *The Cousin from Fiji*, p. 135, 1945
- You're a lucky cow; there's no doubt about it. —Alan Marshall, *I Can Jump Puddles*, p. 243, 1955
- Of course the stupid cow knew what to do! —W.R. Bennett, *Wingman*, p. 17, 1961
- Oh well fuck you stupid cow shit bloody prick bastard. —Gretel Killeen, *Hot Buns and Ophelia get a Bloke*, p. 53, 2000

4 a prostitute attached to a pimp *US, 1859*

- Her tricks, when she functioned as an independenet instead of a cow, had been hundred-dollar babies who came highly recommended. —John M. Murtagh and Sara Harris, *Cast the First Stone*, p. 128, 1957
- Pimps also refer to the women as "cows" and "shitkickers." —Sara Harris, *The Lords of Hell*, p. 48, 1967

5 something that causes annoyance *AUSTRALIA, 1904*

- —Arthur Chipper, *The Aussie Swearer's Guide*, p. 34, 1972
- Cow of a day, love. —Peter Corris, *Pokerface*, p. 16, 1985

6 any unpleasant situation or experience *NEW ZEALAND*

- 'This is the crookest road I've ever struck,' said Cyril. 'It's a cow all right,' said Penelope. —Ronald Hugh Morrieson, *Came a Hot Friday*, p. 110, 1964

7 a can of evaporated milk *US*

Follows 'the'.

- When the cow is called for, the standard reply is, "Send down the milk, the calf's blattin'!" —John Gould, *Maine Lingo*, p. 62, 1975

8 a transport aircraft, usually a C-123 or C-130, outfitted with pumps and large rubberised drums *US*

- —Linda Reinberg, *In the Field*, p. 53, 1991

▸ **have a cow**

to become emotionally overwrought; to lose control *US, 1966*

- —Collin Baker et al., *College Undergraduate Slang Study Conducted at Brown University*, p. 100, 1968
- —Connie Eble (Editor), *UNC-CH Campus Slang*, April 1978
- My mom had a cow. —Francesca Lia Block, *I Was a Teenage Fairy*, p. 134, 1998
- Martha Stewart would have a cow over my apartment. —Janet Evanovich, *Seven Up*, p. 99, 2001

▸ **run cow; work cow**

to work for personal gain while in the employ of another *GUYANA, 1952*

Recorded by Richard Allsopp.

Cow & Gate *adjective*

late, in the sense that the bleed period of the menstrual cycle is overdue *UK*

Rhyming slang, formed, with heavy irony, on the name of a well-known baby food manufacturer.

- —Ray Puxley, *Fresh Rabbit*, 1998

cowabunga; cuyabunga!

used as an expression of triumph *US, 1955*

Originally a signature line uttered by Chief Thunderthud on *The Howdy Doody Show* (NBC, 1947–60). Embraced by surfers, American soldiers in Vietnam, and the writers of *Teenage Mutant Ninja Turtles* and *The Simpsons*.

- —*Paradise of the Pacific*, p. 27, October 1963
- Those hopsotch poledads and pedestrains too, will bug ya / Shout "Cuyabunga!" now and skate right on through. —Jan Berry and Dean Torrance, *Sidewalk Surfin'*, 1964
- —John M. Kelly, *Surf and Sea*, p. 282, 1965
- —Hy Lit, *Hy Lit's Unbelievable Dictionary of Hip Words for Groovy People*, p. 10, 1968
- Gene Brabender sometimes walks around bellowing "cowabunga!" So I threw some trivia at him. "Bender, who first said 'cowabunga?'" —Jim Bouton, *Ball Four*, p. 314, 1970

cow and calf *noun*

1 half; thus, 50 pence (half £1) *UK, 1950*

Rhyming slang. Variants are 'cow calf' and 'cows'.

- —Angela Devlin, *Prison Patter*, p. 40, 1996

2 a laugh *UK*

Rhyming slang. Also used as a verb.

- —Ray Puxley, *Cockney Rabbit*, 1992

cow and horse; cow *noun*

sexual intercouse *UK*

Rhyming slang.

- Six months and we still haven't had any cow. —Bodmin Dark, *Dirty Cockney Rhyming Slang*, 2003

cowardy custard; cowardy, cowardy custard *noun*

a coward *UK, 1836*

Custard is **YELLOW** (the colour applied as an adjective for cowardice) and so reinforces the accusation.This taunting form of address is usually hurled or chanted by children.

- It wasn't just drunken convenience. There was a touch of the cowardy custard about it. —John Milne, *Alive and Kicking*, p. 141, 1998
- "You want money on it?" No. "Oh, come on, Cowardy, Cowardy, Custard." —*The Guardian*, 24th May 1999

cow belt *noun*

the rural areas of the Indo-Gangetic plain *INDIA*

Journalistic, from the perception that more traditional Hindu values hold sway in such communities, and, therefore, a cow is revered more there than elsewhere in modern India.

• Cow belt comedies make Sangma say "Cheese". — *The Times of India*, 22nd August 2001

cowboy *noun*

1 a reckless, impulsive, undisciplined person *US, 1926*
• A Cuban has trouble getting in and out; and besides, this is not a cowboy job. — Edwin Torres, *Carlito's Way*, p. 72, 1975
• Am I crazy? I got a business. What do I need cowboy stuff for? — Richard Condon, *Prizzi's Honor*, p. 234, 1982
• He's a good kid, but he's crazy. He's a cowboy. He's got too much to prove. — *Goodfellas*, 1990
• Who's behind this? Which cunt is backing this cowboy up? — Kevin Sampson, *Outlaws*, p. 69, 2001

2 a flash fellow; a know-all *UK*
• — Home Office, *Glossary of Terms and Slang Common in Penal Establishments*, 1978

3 a young and inexperienced, or irresponsible, driver *UK, 1984*

4 a motorist prone to breaking the rules of the road *US, 1928*
• — *New York Times Magazine*, p. 88, 16th March 1958

5 any tradesman (such as a builder, electrician, mechanic or plumber) who is unreliable, irresponsible and, perhaps, unqualified; the sort to make quick money by undercutting regular, trained craftsmen *UK, 1984*
As in the sign for Patel Brothers Builders: 'You've tried the Cowboys, now try the Indians!'.

6 a minor criminal given to violence *UK*
From such a person's tendency to 'come out shooting'.
• — G.F. Newman, *The Guvnor*, 1977

7 during the Vietnam war, an unprincipled, untrustworty, hustling Vietnamese person *US*
• — Linda Reinberg, *In the Field*, p. 53, 1991

8 a beginner *CANADA*
Mining usage.
• "Cowboy" alone has acquired a romantic connotation (except in the mines where it is a synonym for "greenhorn." — *Vancouver Press*, p. 13, August 1959

9 used as a humorous term of address *US*
• Whoa. Put a little more in there, cowboy. — *American Beauty*, 1999

10 in horse racing, any jockey with an unconventional style of riding *AUSTRALIA*
• — Ned Wallish, *The Truth Dictionary of Racing Slang*, p. 19, 1989

11 a bow-legged man *UK, 1984*
From the gait of such a horse-rider.

12 in computing, a person with an intelligence, knowledge and dedication to programming *US*
• — Eric S. Raymond, *The New Hacker's Dictionary*, p. 109, 1991

13 in a deck of playing cards, a king *US*
• — Albert H. Morehead, *The Complete Guide to Winning Poker*, p. 260, 1967

14 a perfunctory cleaning of the body with a wash cloth but not a full bath or shower *BAHAMAS*
• — John A. Holm, *Dictionary of Bahamian English*, p. 52, 1982

cowboy *verb*

1 to murder someone in a reckless manner *US, 1946*
• And the wops are gonna cowboy me on sight. Open contract. — Edwin Torres, *Q & A*, p. 180, 1977

2 to gang-rape someone *US*
• They cowboyed him in the steam room. — William Burroughs, *Naked Lunch*, p. 188, 1957

Cowboy *nickname*

Nguyen Cao Ky, Prime Minister of South Vietnam after the murder of Diem *US*
So named by President Diem. 'Cowboy' is a term the Vietnamese then reserved for only the most flamboyant of gangsters. US Secretary of Defense McNamara condemned Ky as 'the absolute bottom of the barrel'.
• — Linda Reinberg, *In the Field*, p. 53, 1991

cowboy Bible *noun*

a packet of cigarette rolling papers *US, 1970*
• — Frederic G. Cassidy, *Dictionary of American Regional English, Volume 1*, p. 809, 1985

cowboy Cadillac *noun*

any pickup truck *US*
• — Wayne Floyd, *Jason's Authentic Dictionary of CB Slang*, p. 13, 1976
• Came back to town once in a cowboy Cadillac, big old bull horns on the hood and six-shooters for door handles." — Craig Lesley, *The Sky Fisherman*, p. 78, 1995

cowboy coffee *noun*

coffee boiled in an open pot, served without milk or sugar *US, 1943*
• I taught him how to make cowboy coffee by merely throwing the grinds into the pot, and I drank plenty of it, loving the smell of it. — Anne Rice, *Servant of the Bones*, p. 15, 1996

cowboy cool *adjective*

(used of beer) room temperature *US*
• I don't have any cold beers, but you're welcome to one of these if you don't mind it being cowboy cool. — Ken Weaver, *Texas Crude*, p. 63, 1984

cowboy coupe *noun*

a pickup truck decked out with accessories *US*
• — *American Speech*, p. 268, December 1962: 'The language of traffic policemen'

cowboy hat *noun*

a disposable paper toilet seat cover *US*
• — Judi Sanders, *Kickin' like Chicken with the Couch Commander*, p. 6, 1992

cowboys *noun*

the police; police officers *UK*
• — *Observer*, 15th May 1960

Cowboys *noun*

▸ **the Cowboys**
third battalion, Royal Green Jackets *UK*
• — Andy McNab, *Immediate Action*, p. 17, 1995

cowboys and Indians *noun*

a prison sentence of 99 years *US*
• — Charles Shafer, *Folk Speech in Texas Prisons*, p. 201, 1990

cow cage *noun*

a livestock carriage on a freight train *US*
• — Norman Carlisle, *The Modern Wonder Book of Trains and Railroading*, p. 261, 1946

cow cocky *noun*

a dairy farmer *AUSTRALIA, 1902*
• She was nagging him now almost like he was just a hired cow-cocky. — Jon Cleary, *The Long Shadow*, p. 35, 1949
• — Arthur Chipper, *The Aussie Swearer's Guide*, p. 34, 1972
• — Bill Wannan, *Folklore of the Australian Pub*, p. 61, 1972
• I'll show those smart Western Districts cow-cockies a thing or two. — Roy Higgins and Tom Prior, *The Jockey Who Laughed*, p. 15, 1982

cow college *noun*

a small rural college, especially one offering degrees in agriculture *US, 1906*
• Your career would have been different – you might have been stuck in some cow college. — Wallace Stegner, *Crossing to Safety*, p. 8, 1987

cow confetti; cowyard confetti *noun*

nonsense, rubbish *AUSTRALIA, 1941*
A euphemism for **BULLSHIT**.
• I wouldn't have dared offer Fred money, but I determined I would do him a favour some time, and thanked him so heartily that I was asked not to sprinkle any cow confetti. — Kylie Tennant, *The Honey Flow*, p. 32, 1956

cow cunt *noun*

a despicable person *US*
• A retard. A cow cunt. — Joyce Carol Oates, *Foxfire*, p. 149,
• Creepy cow cunt like Krystal! — Mary Mcgary Morris, *Vanished*, p. 61, 1988

cow-cunted *adjective*

possessing a slack and distended vagina *US*
• — *Maledicta*, p. 184, Winter 1980: 'A new erotic vocabulary'
• — Michael Dalton Johnson, *Talking Trash with Redd Foxx*, p. 64, 1994

Cowdenbeath *noun*

the teeth *UK: SCOTLAND*
Glasgow rhyming slang, formed from a Scottish town (and football team).
• — Michael Munro, *The Patter, Another Blast*, 1988

cow dust time *noun*
evening *INDIA*
A direct translation from Belgali *go-dhuli*, describing the dust that hangs in the air at that time of day when the cattle are returned from the fields.
- It was getting late, and the sun was setting over the Ajoy – the time Bengalis call go dhuli bhela, or cow dust time. — *The Guardian*, 7th Febrary 2004

cowgirl *noun*
a sexual position in which the woman is on top, astride and facing her partner *US*
- — *Adult Video News*, p. 42, August 1995
- [I]n describing one of these positoins (called the "cowgirl," in which the woman is facing the man and sitting up, or the "reverse cowgirl," in which she faces away from him) a pornographic director has said: "Very unnatural position. The girls hate it.["] — Gail Dines, *Pornography*, p. 76, 1998
- These include fellatio, cunniligus, missionary-style, doggie-style, cowgirl, reverse cowgirl, double penetration, double-pussy penetration and double-anal penetration. — Carolina Vegas Starr, *Jobs Your Mother Never Wanted You to Have*, p. 77, 2002

cow grease *noun*
butter *UK*
Originally 'cow's grease', 1857.

cowing *adjective*
used to intensify *UK, 1962*
Probably military origins; a euphemism for **FUCKING**.
- ["I]s it true what they all say about black men?" "What? That we all make great lawyers, accountants, politicians?" "No, yer pillock, that you've all got cowin' bug dadgers [penises]. — Colin Butts, *Is Harry on the Boat?*, p. 19, 1997

cowing lush *adjective*
marvellous, wonderful; used as an all-purpose expression of admiration *UK: WALES*
- Cowing lush he is. — overheard in Cardiff August 2001

cow juice *noun*
milk *UK, 1796*
- 4 slices o' plain breid / a quarter pun o' gammon / hauf a pun o' butter / hauf pint o cow juice — *Chewin' the Fat*, 6th July 2003

cow-kick *verb*
(of a horse) to kick outward and upward like a cow *CANADA*
- Among them were stampeders, kickers, strikers, and the odd one that would cow-kick or bite. — E.F. Hagell, *When the Grass Was Free*, p. 59, 1954

cow lick *noun*
in publishing, inexpensive varnish used on a book cover *US*
- — Rachel S. Epstein and Nina Liebman, *Biz Speak*, p. 50, 1986

cowpat *noun*
a single dropping of cow dung *UK, 1954*
- I was greeted on my first day there by a snot-nosed 13-year-old who looked me up and down like I'd just dragged myself in off a cowpat. — Sue Rhodes, *Now you'll think I'm awful*, p. 132, 1967
- He brought back two dehydrated cow-pats. — Kerry Cue, *Crooks, Chooks and Bloody Ratbags*, p. 154, 1983
- "Please sit," she said, pointing to the wobbly mound of sticky, dark brown goo, which looked like a giant cow pat. — *The Guardian*, 14th July 2001

cowpath *noun*
a narrow back road *US*
- — Montie Tak, *Truck Talk*, p. 38, 1971

cowpat lotto *noun*
a lottery in which the winner is decided by which part of a paddock a cow first drops dung *AUSTRALIA, 1995*
- — *Macquarie Dictionary (Federation Edition)*, 2001

cow poke *noun*
a wooden device to keep a cow from going through a fence *CANADA*
The *Dictionary of American Regional English* lists this word and meaning in the US in 1968.
- A "cow poke" is a large wooden Y, usually a naturally forked branch of a tree, placed and lashed around a cow's neck to prevent the cow from getting through a fence. — Chris Thain, *Cold as a Bay Street Banker's Heart*, p. 47, 1987

cow's arse *noun*
▷ see: **COO'S ARSE**

cow's breakfast *noun*
a straw hat *CANADA*
- He returned through the streets quite oblivious of the very un-naval "cow's breakfast" [straw hat] still on his head. — *Weekend*, p. 28/3, 1st August 1959

cow's calf; cow and calf; cow's; calf *noun*
until 1971, ten shillings; thereafter, fifty pence *UK, 1941*
Rhyming slang for 'half' (of £1). Pre-decimalisation, mainly reduced to 'calf'; in later C20 'cows' predominates.

cowsh *noun*
cattle excrement; nonsense *AUSTRALIA, 1937*
An abbreviation of 'cow shit'. In 2003 it is used in its literal sense by UK cavers.

cow's lick *noun*
prison; a prison *UK, 1962*
Rhyming slang for **NICK** (a prison).
- — Ray Puxley, *Cockney Rabbit*, 1992

cowson *noun*
a contemptible man *UK, 1936*
Literally, 'the son of a cow'.
- — Chas & Dave, *Gertcha!*, 1979
- "We'll deal with that cowson later," said Tony. — Garry Bushell, *The Face*, p. 36, 2001

cowstroke *noun*
in cricket, a hefty stroke to the leg side *UK, 1978*
- — Simon Hughes, *Cricket 4*, 2001

cow-tongue *noun*
a gossip *TRINIDAD AND TOBAGO*
- — Lise Winer, *Dictionary of the English/Creole of Trinidad & Tobago*, 2003

Cow Town *nickname*
1 Forth Worth, Texas *US*
- — Lanie Dills, *The Official CB Slanguage Language Dictionary*, p. 27, 1976

2 Calgary, Alberta *CANADA*
- Southern Alberta still has many ranches, and Calgary is still a cowtown. — Donalda Dickie, *The Great Golden Plain*, p. 293, 1962
- And, like most Calgarians, they're quick to boost Cowtown as a "most progressive city." — *Calgary Herald Magazine*, p. 7/5, 5th October 1963

cow trail *verb*
to take a motorcyle cruise in the country for recreation *US*
- — Ed Radlauer, *Motorcylopedia*, p. 12, 1973

cowyard *noun*
an inexpensive brothel *US, 1964*
- The worst conditions for prostitutes were found in 6-foot by 6-foot cribs and multi-story "cowyards" off Pacific Street, which was known to sailors everywhere as Terrific Street. — *San Francisco Examiner*, p. A17, 26th December 1994

cowyard cake *noun*
a cake or bun containing a few sultanas *AUSTRALIA*
- — Sidney J. Baker, *The Australian Language*, 1953

cowyard confetti *noun*
▷ see: **COW CONFETTI**

cox box *noun*
an electronic device that includes an amplifier/microphone system as well as various measurement functions, used by a coxswain in competitive rowing *US*
- Cox box: The in-boat intercom used by the coxswain to be sure all eight rowers can hear the commands. — Sue Muller Hacking, *Boatless in Seattle*, p. 76, 1999

coxed *adjective*
(of a boat) under the control of a *cox*swain *UK*
- The women's squad and men's coxed four also reached finals[.] — *The Guardian*, 23rd August 2001

coxey; cocksy *noun*
an inexperienced swindler working on a scam by telephone who makes the initial call to potential victims *US*
- — Kathleen Odean, *High Steppers, Fallen Angels, and Lollipops*, p. 132, 1988

coxy *noun*

a *coxswain* US

- He's coxy on the Olympic crew. —Richard Farina, *Been Down So Long*, p. 39, 1966
- —Judy's Enterprises, *Coxswain Postcard*, 2001

coyote French *noun*

the mixture of Canadian French, Cree and English spoken by the older Metis CANADA

- Did you use spurs on those bronc? his father called in his excitable Coyote French. —Dan Cushman, *Stay Away, Joe*, p. 3, 1963

coyote ugly *adjective*

very ugly *US, 1985*

The conceit of the term is that a man who wakes up with a 'coyote ugly' woman sleeping on his arm will, like a coyote caught in a trap, gnaw off his arm to escape.

- In an interview, [Judge Bernard] Avellino said the victim "was the ugliest girl I have ever seen in my entire life ... in the top 10." Avellino was also quoted as calling the vicitm "coyote ugly." —*Los Angeles Times*, p. 2, 5th February 1986
- —*Philadelphia Inquirer*, p. A1, 27th January 1986
- [A] judge chastised a defendant accused in an attempted rape case for having picked an "unattractive girl" and later, in a subsequent interview, described the victim as "coyote ugly," society is again sent a clear message. —Laura A. Otten, *Women's Rights and the Law*, p. 9, 1993

coz

▷ **see: 'CAUSE**

cozmo *noun*

phencyclidine, the recreational drug known as PCP or angel dust US

- —US Department of Justice, *Street Terms*, October 1994

cozy *adjective*

dull, boring US

- —Kenn "Naz" Young, *Naz's Dictionary of Teen Slang*, p. 25, 1993

cozzer *noun*

a police officer; the police UK

A confusion of Hebrew *chazar* (pig) and **COPPER** (a police officer).

- So one of the coszers [sic] told me that I was nicked for conning the old bag[.] —Frank Norman, *Bang To Rights*, p. 113, 1958
- There were four hundred cozzers holding riot shields —Ian Dury, *Itinerant Child*, 1998

cozzie *noun*

▷ **see: COSSIE**

CP *noun*

corporal punishment *US, 1987*

- Well, most of them want the same thing; bit of abuse, bit of CP, like. —Niall Griffiths, *Kelly + Victor*, p. 229, 2002

c phone *noun*

a mobile telephone US

'C' is for 'cellular'.

- —Pamela Munro, *U.C.L.A. Slang*, p. 49, 1997

CP pill *noun*

a large, orange anti-malaria pill taken once a week US

Chloroquine-Primaquine.

- —Linda Reinberg, *In the Field*, p. 53, 1991

CPR strawberry *noun*

a prune CANADA

- During construction and depression, the railroad made prunes handy, inexpensive, could be kept in all weather, so our fathers ate more prunes than they care to remember, and to this day prunes are known throughout the West as CPR strawberries. —Chris Thain, *Cold as a Bay Street Banker's Heart*, p. 48, 1987

CPT; CP time *noun*

a notional system of time in which punctuality is not important *US, 1925*

An abbreviation of **COLORED PEOPLE'S TIME**.

- And come on time, not C.P.T. —*Letter from Langston Hughes to Carl Van Vechten*, 23rd September 1949
- Their lives run by a clock that keeps C.P.T., Colored People's Time, which assumes that appointments won't be kept, work promised won't be delivered, jobs found won't be gone to, since those are all part of the outside world. —Paul Jacobs, *Prelude to a Riot*, p. 12, 1967
- CPT – Colored Pepole's time (i.e., on time when they WANT to be, otherwse NOT). —*San Francisco Examiner*, p. 33, 9th May 1967
- —Malachi Andrews and Paul T. Owens, *Black Language*, p. 91, 1973
- In recognition of the fact that a stereotype has developed regarding C.P. Time, the first 15 minutes of any meeting shall henceforth be known as J.T. (Jive Time). —Carolyn Greene, *70 Soul Secrets of Sapphire*, 1973
- —Connie Eble (Editor), *UNC-CH Campus Slang*, Spring 1980
- Although there are cultural jokes about "CP time" (being chronically or consistently late), I was once told by a brother from Kenya that "things begin when the people gather." —Teresa L. Fry Brown, *God Don't Live Ugly*, 2000
- "We couldn't possibly expect this thing to start on time," he says, pointing to a truth that, between Harvard and CP time – "colored People's time" – should be more obvious to this crowd. —*FM*, 4th May 2000

crab *noun*

1 a contemptible person *UK, 1580*

- I had to swallow it when the little crab told me that the two and a half single stone I had nicked the previous afternoon was jargoon [fake]. —Charles Raven, *Underworld Nights*, p. 167, 1956

2 in the language of members of the Bloods youth gang, a member of the Crips youth gang US

- "We keep Crabs out of our 'hood," he said, referring to area Crip gang members. —*Los Angeles Times*, p. 6 (Metro), 8th November 1987
- —Bill Valentine, *Gang Intelligence Manual*, p. 75, 1995
- "There's crabs in the 'hood," she said, using the derogatory slang for "Crips," a rival gang. —*Omaha World-Herald*, p. 1A, 18th September 2002

3 a member of the Royal Air Force UK

- "It's OK, it's only the Crabs," said a man with a pair of high-powered binoculars. —Robert McGowan and Jeremy Hands, *Don't Cry for Me, Sergeant-Major*, p. 80, 1983
- —Nigel Foster, *The Making of a Royal Marine Commando*, 1987

4 a first-year college student US

- —Marcus Hanna Boulware, *Jive and Slang of Students in Negro Colleges*, 1947

5 the vulva BAHAMAS

Sometimes expanded to 'crabby'.

- —John A. Holm, *Dictionary of Bahamian English*, p. 52, 1982

6 in the television and film industries, a device used to support a tripod on a slippery or uneven surface UK

- —Oswald Skilbeck, *ABC of Film and TV Working Terms*, p. 28, 1960

▷ **see: HAMSTER CRAB**

crab *verb*

1 (of an aircraft) to fly close to the ground or water; to drift or manoeuvre sideways *UK, 1943*

From the sideways movement of a crab. In 1945, Robert Hinde noted of this word that an aircraft flying close to the ground will appear to fly diagonally.

2 in the language of parachuting, to direct the parachute across the wind direction US

- —Dan Poynter, *Parachuting*, p. 166, 1978: 'The language of parachuting'

3 in the television and film industries, to move the camera sideways US

- —Ira Konigsberg, *The Complete Film Dictionary*, p. 67, 1987

4 to spoil something *UK, 1812*

- Dope crabbed Phil's effect by saying that Garrity had cleaned up some jack playing the market. —James T. Farrell, *Saturday Night*, p. 32, 1947

5 in horse racing, to belittle a horse's performance UK

- —Rita Cannon, *Let's Go Racing*, p. 71, 1948

crab *adjective*

perverse; ill-humoured, perpetually mean, cross UK

A shortening of **CRABBY**.

crab air *nickname*

the Royal Air Force (RAF) UK

Military use; extends from **CRAB** (a member of the Royal Air Force).

- —Nigel Foster, *The Making of a Royal Marine Commando*, 1987

crab bait *noun*

a newly arrived prisoner US

- —John R. Armore and Joseph D. Wolfe, *Dictionary of Desperation*, p. 25, 1976

crabbie *noun*

the vagina BAHAMAS

- —Patricia Clinton-Meicholas, *More Talkin' Bahamian*, p. 35, 1995

crabby *adjective*

ill humoured, perpetually mean, cross *US, 1908*

The villain of the extremely popular 1957 *Tom Terrific* cartoon series from Terry-Toon Cartoon Studios was the aptly named Crabby Appleton, who was, we remember, 'rotten to the core'.

- It was something else bothering her, or her life in general that made her crabby. Sitting there pissed off in her black bra and panties. —Elmore Leonard, *Glitz*, p. 188, 1985
- All right, crabby arse, all right. Where's the bloody remote off the television? —Caroline Aherne and Craig Cash, *The Royle Family*, 1999

crab-fat *noun*

an airman in the Royal Air Force *UK*

In army and navy use. From the colour and consistency of a blue ointment used to treat **CRABS** (pubic lice); the blue is of a similar shade to the Royal Air Force uniform. However, this derivation may not be direct, nor strictly accurate. From the early C20, Admiralty grey paint was called 'crab-fat' and the anti-lice ointment was claimed as the inspiration for that shade. It seems equally likely, therefore, that this later use should derive from the grey paint.

crabfats *noun*

the Royal Air Force *UK, 1961*

In army and navy use; from the singular sense **CRAB-FAT** (an airman).

- —John W. Mussell, *Militarisms*, 1995

crab-foot *noun*

childlike, scratchy handwriting *BELIZE*

- —Richard Allsopp, *Dictionary of Caribbean English Usage*, p. 175, 1996

crab hole *noun*

a depression in swampy ground *NEW ZEALAND*

- Most of this area consisted of low-lying swamp and crab holes covered with flax and toe-toe. —John Deans, *Pioneers on Port Cooper Plains*, p. 114, 1964

crab in a barrel *noun*

used as a representation of the inability of people to work together *TRINIDAD AND TOBAGO*

- —Lise Winer, *Dictionary of the English/Creole of Trinidad & Tobago*, 2003

crab-mash *verb*

to do a poor job ironing clothes *BARBADOS*

- —Frank A. Collymore, *Barbadian Dialect*, p. 36, 1965

crabs *noun*

1 pubic lice *UK, 1707*

- If I'd meet a stranger on the street, I'd say: "You look itchy. What's the matter? You got the crabs?" —Ethel Waters, *His Eye is on the Sparrow*, p. 36, 1951
- The Inspector opens his fly and begins looking for crabs, applying ointment from a little clay pot. —William Burroughs, *Naked Lunch*, p. 73, 1957
- Before I'd touch your slimy thighs / which a thousand crabs has bit / I'd drink a gallon a drunkard's puke / and suck a clappy dick. —Bruce Jackson, *Get Your Ass in the Water and Swim Like Me*, p. 124, 1964
- I'll stay a week / And get the crabs / And take a bus back home. —Frank Zappa, *Who Needs The Peace Corps?*, 1968
- And I've never had VD, never had the crabs, no syphilis, clap, gonorrhea, nothing. (Quoting John C. Holmes, porn star who died of AIDS in 1988). —Kenneth Turan and Stephen E. Zito, *Sinema*, p. 120, 1974
- Ho Chi Minh is a son of a bitch / Got the blueballs, crabs, and the seven-year itch. —*Full Metal Jacket*, 1987
- The French call them papillons d'amour, i.e., the "butterflies of love." I call them crabs, the tiny parasites of crotch. —Jim Carroll, *Forced Entries*, p. 4, 1987
- Instead, I told him I had to go home because I was having a heavy flow, and besides, I was still recovering from a bad case of crabs. —Anka Radakovich, *The Wild Girls Club*, p. 47, 1994
- When we were kids in the Navy, he had such a bad case of crabs, we used to call him the Governor of Maryland. —*The Sopranos (Episode 60)*, 2004

2 in craps, a three *US, 1938*

- —Thomas L. Clark, *The Dictionary of Gambling and Gaming*, p. 53, 1987

3 by extension, in a deck of playing cards, any three *US, 1981*

- —Thomas L. Clark, *The Dictionary of Gambling and Gaming*, p. 53, 1987

crabs on the rocks *noun*

an itching of the scrotum *UK*

A play on **CRABS** (pubic lice).

crack *noun*

1 crystalline lumps of concentrated cocaine *US, 1985*

- When cocaine got too expensive for the 'hood, crack was invented. Now brothers with fourth-grade educations go down into their basements and become mad scientists. —Chris Rock, *Rock This!*, p. 68, 1997
- The simple technique used in the preparation of crack consists of heating cocaine hydrochloride in a baking soda and water solution[.] —Richard Rudgley, *The Encyclopaedia of Psychoactive Substances*, p. 69, 1998
- Hip hop 'bin around since 1970. It got exposed in 1979. So once it's exposed, this is it. Just like crack. Crack 'bin around, till Richard Pryor got burnt up, then it went: whoosh! —Alex Ogg, *The Hip Hop Years [quoting Kool Herc]*, p. 45, 1999
- I know I shouldn't have but crack, mixed with a sprinkling of heroin to take away the edginess, was just what I needed[.] —Lanre Fehintola, *Charlie Says...*, p. 1, 2000

2 entertaining conversation in good company *IRELAND, 1966*

Irish neologism *craic* (an informal entertainment) combines with earlier Eirrean use of 'the crack' (brisk talk, news); ultimately from Old English *cracian* (crack, a loud noise).

- [A] couple of pints of good beer, maybe the first in the week and the crack... the crack... we'd talk of many things... —Alan Bleasdale, *Boys From the Blackstuff*, 1982
- There's nothing comes close to the crack you have on the train down to a London match. —Kevin Sampson, *Outlaws*, p. 161, 2001

3 a witticism; a quick and funny remark *US, 1884*

- I sat there in the tree-shaded yard, listening to Axel talk and Marie make cracks[.] —Clancy Sigal, *Going Away*, p. 240, 1961

4 a witty person *US*

- —Connie Eble (Editor), *UNC-CH Campus Slang*, November 1976

5 a smart person *FIJI, 1993*

- You must be a real crack to lecture at USP. —Jan Tent, 1996

6 a top class racehorse *AUSTRALIA*

- The third horse, Postillion, ran a wonderfully good race to finish only two lengths behind the cracks[.] —Maurice Cavanough and Meurig Davies, *Cup Day*, p. 125, 1960
- From that win, and another soon after in the All-Aged Stakes, when the little mare vanquished the best weight-for-age cracks, he pocketed £50,000 in stakes and bets. —James Holledge, *The Great Australian Gamble*, p. 84, 1966
- —Jim Ramsay, *Cop It Sweet!*, p. 25, 1977

7 the vagina *UK, 1775*

The imagery from which this derives should be apparent; it remains in widespread use.

- "Snatch," "hole," "kooze, "slash," "pussy" and "crack" were other terms referring variously to women's genitals, to women as individuals, or to women as a species. —*Screw*, p. 5, 3rd January 1972

8 the cleft between the buttock muscles; loosely, the bottom; or, more narrowly, the anus *UK*

- If they decide to shine their lovelight on you [...] the journos [journalists]'ll suck the fart sediment out of your crack. —Kevin Sampson, *Powder*, p. 101, 1999

9 a passing of wind *US*

- I let farts to be sure, but hardly ever a real crack, they oozed out with a sucking noise, melted in the mighty never. —Samuel Beckett, *The Complete Short Prose (The End)*, p. 97, 1946

10 an instance; one item *US, 1937*

- He and I and Alvah drove to Oakland in Morley's car and went first to some Goodwill stores and Salvation Army stores to buy various flannel shirts (at fifty cents a crack) and undershirts. —Jack Kerouac, *The Dharma Bums*, p. 84, 1958

11 an opportunity or chance *US, 1893*

- Okay, who wants to take a crack at wiring Mr. Zimm's jaw? —*Get Shorty*, 1995

12 an attempt *US, 1836*

In phrases 'have a crack', 'take a crack', 'give a crack', etc.

- I'm not blaming anyone but it would have been nice to have a crack at the job and there should have been an open competition. —*The Guardian*, 7th December 2002

13 of dawn or day, the break, the instant it commences *US, 1887*

- Yeah, the bed in my room has a loose spring / It pokes my back till crack of day —This Euphoria, *I'd Rather Be Lost*, 1994
- [G]etting up at the crack of dawn to buy flowers at St Philips Market[.] —*BBC Radio Bristol*, 5th March 2003

14 the latest news *UK*

Anglo-Irish. Heard on a construction site in Lancashire.

- What's the latest crack? —John Davies, 1979

15 wood; firewood *UK, 1851*
English gypsy use.
- —Jimmy Stockin, *On The Cobbles*, p. 10, 2000

▸ **on crack**
out of your mind *US*
Used in situations where there is no crack cocaine involved, usually humorously in a statement such as 'What are, on crack?'.
- —Connie Eble (Editor), *UNC-CH Campus Slang*, p. 7, April 1995

crack *verb*

1 to speak *US, 1897*
- I said, "Have you cracked anything about me to him?"—Iceberg Silm (Robert Beck), *Pimp*, p. 155, 1969
- As I was about ready to end my spiel, my man Walter cracked "Go on and pimp, Stoney, to hell with what any black-ass pimping sonuvabitch gotta say!"—A.S. Jackson, *Gentleman Pimp*, p. 45, 1973
- When I crack on a female 'how you livin?' she got to respond to me in the positive, or I don't waste my time.—Terry Williams, *The Cocaine Kids*, p. 87, 1989

2 to ask for something *US, 1928*
- Oh yeah, you can cop a 'spike' [needle] at any drug store. You gotta crack for insulin with it.—Iceberg Silm (Robert Beck), *Pimp*, p. 135, 1969
- When I cracked for seconds, the hack stood there looking / I said, "Serve it raw, punk. The chair'll do the cooking."—Dennis Wepman et al., *The Life*, p. 118, 1976

3 to reveal a secret; to inform on someone *US, 1922*
- [I]t was easy going through the usual jailhouse bullshit, answering a lotta things, like who's doing what, how long Joe Blow been dealing, how'd I get cracked, who cracked me.—A.S. Jackson, *Gentleman Pimp*, p. 127, 1973

4 to tease someone; to taunt someone; to insult someone *US, 1930*
- The girls used to fight over their macs. "That coffee-an' mac you got," a French girl would crack to a straight one, and then it was on – hair came out by the handful.—Mezz Mezzrow, *Really the Blues*, p. 23, 1946
- Rodney, man, I was just crackin'.—Richard Price, *Clockers*, p. 181, 1992
- —Vann Wesson, *Generation X Field Guide and Lexicon*, p. 42, 1997
- There are many different terms for playing the dozens, including "bagging, capping, cracking, dissing, hiking, joning, ranking, ribbing, serving, signifying, slipping, sounding and snapping".—James Haskins, *The Story of Hip-Hop*, p. 54, 2000

5 to arrrest someone *US, 1952*
- Did you know that was the time I got cracked? That the Man swooped down on me?—Clarence Cooper Jr, *The Farm*, p. 46, 1967
- I had spent the two months in County Jail where I had been taken after Captain Churchill, a "House" bloodhound, backed by city police, crashed my pad and cracked me on an ancient fugitive warrant for the escape from the "House."—Iceberg Slim (Robert Beck), *The Naked Soul of Iceberg Slim*, p. 21, 1971
- How did you get cracked on that there rape beef, anyway, Green Grass?—Charles W. Moore, *A Brick for Mister Jones*, p. 103, 1975

6 to break and enter using force with the intent of committing a crime within *UK, 1725*
- I'm going out to crack safes.—Jack Kerouac, *Letter to Neal Cassady*, p. 174, 8th December 1948
- Are you game to crack another store?—Hal Ellson, *Tomboy*, p. 6, 1950
- Their method of "cracking" a home was this.—Jack Lait and Lee Mortimer, *Washington Confidential*, p. 121, 1951
- [B]ecause three blocks away, a short walk for a sick junkie, are respectable neighborhoods good for burglary and "cracking shorts" (breaking into cars).—James Mills, *The Panic in Needle Park*, p. 19, 1966
- That's what happened when I and another guy planned on cracking a joint[.]—Herbert Huncke, *Guilty of Everything*, p. 102, 1990
- They ran nightclubs, numbers rackets, and girls; they cracked safes and fenced stolen property.—Kim Rich, *Johnny's Girl*, p. 62, 1993

7 to change paper money into coin *UK, 1961*
Originally used by seamen in Liverpool; phrased in use as, for example: 'Can you crack a fiver?' 'Can you change a five pound note?'.

8 to have sex with a girl who is a virgin *FIJI, 1992*
- She too young to crack, man.—Jan Tent, 1995

9 in surfing, to catch a wave *AUSTRALIA*
- We spent two weeks in a rented cottage at Coff's Harbour, and I finally learned to crack a wave, and was very proud of myself.—Nino Cluotta (John O'Grady), *They're A Weird Mob*, 157
- So I'm in the surf cracking waves when all of a sudden a near tidal job smashed me[.]—Paul Vautin, *Turn It Up!*, 1957

10 to strike something or someone in such a way that a sharp noise is produced; to slap, to smack, etc *UK*
- Chanderpaul suffered a dual indignity when a delivery which pitched outside leg stayed down and cracked him on the inside of his knee, sending him sprawling on the pitch in agony.—*The Advertiser (South Australia)*, 12th April 2003

11 in cricket, to hit a ball hard *UK, 1882*
- Sehwag cracked the third ball of his second spell behind point for four[.]—*The Guardian*, 9th August 2002

12 to drum with expertise *TRINIDAD AND TOBAGO*
A shortening of 'crack a hand'.
- —Lise Winer, *Dictionary of the English/Creole of Trinidad & Tobago*, 2003

▸ **crack a bennie**
to break a Benzedrine™ (amphetamine sulphate) inhaler open *US*
- —William D. Alsever, *Glossary for the Establishment and Other Uptight People*, p. 7, December 1970

▸ **crack a fat**
to achieve an erection *AUSTRALIA*
- Pommy sheilas? Aw, they're apples I s'pose – but the way I feel now I don't reckon I could crack a fat!—Barry Humphries, *The Wonderful World of Barry McKenzie*, p. 52, 1968
- If you can't crack a fat or anythink, youse'll owe me double, see. —David McGill, *David McGill's Complete Kiwi Slang Dictionary*, p. 34, 1998

▸ **crack a grain**
to suffer aching testicles *TRINIDAD AND TOBAGO*
- —Lise Winer, *Dictionary of the English/Creole of Trinidad & Tobago*, 2003

▸ **crack a Judy; crack a Judy's tea-cup**
to take a woman's virginity *UK, 1937*
Formed from conventional 'crack' (to break, to open) and **JUDY** (a girl or woman).
- Baby baby baby let me pick your cherry / Go star-gazin' on yer back / To crack a Judy's teacup I'll give you a little upshot / Doncha say your mama's comin' back—Savage Garden, *Smashed 'n' Trashed*, 1995

▸ **crack a laugh**
to burst into laughter *TRINIDAD AND TOBAGO*
- —Lise Winer, *Dictionary of the English/Creole of Trinidad & Tobago*, 2003

▸ **crack a lay**
to divulge something secret *AUSTRALIA, 1941*
- Of course, I didn't crack a lay who I was.—Sam Weller, *Old Bastards I Have Met*, p. 121, 1979

▸ **crack an egg**

1 in bowls, to play with just sufficient weight to move a bowl or a jack an inch or two *SOUTH AFRICA*
- —*Partridge*, 1968

2 in curling, to touch a stone lightly with the bowled stone *CANADA*
- —*Weekend*, p. 34, 26th November 1960

▸ **crack a rat**
to fart *US*
- —Peter Furze, *Tailwinds*, p. 39, 1998

▸ **crack a short**
to break into a car *US*
- —William D. Alsever, *Glossary for the Establishment and Other Uptight People*, p. 7, 1970

▸ **crack a smile**
to smile broadly, especially of someone who is usually serious *UK, 1990*
- Designer coffins are the way to go these days. If you want your mourners to crack a smile then the Return to Sender model painted to look like a courier package may be just the ticket.—*The Guardian*, 2nd March 2000

▸ **crack the nut**
to meet an operation's daily operating expenses *US*
- —Joe McKennon, *Circus Lingo*, p. 29, 1980

▸ **crack wise**
to insult someone with a degree of sarcasm and humour *US, 1921*
Imparts a slight air of the old gangster life.
- If he was all hopped up, cracking wise, acting big buying drinks for the house, he was on his way.—Mezz Mezzrow, *Really the Blues*, p. 59, 1946
- He came up to me cracking wise all the way and we shook hands. —Clancy Sigal, *Going Away*, p. 350, 1961

- Such a wiseass. But go ahead. Crack wise. That's why you're jockeying a register in some fucking local convenience store instead of doing an honest day's work. — *Clerks*, 1994

▶ crack your cherry
to lose your innocence or virginity *US*
- He had no idea he was talking to a young man who cracked his cherry in the thievery business with forty times that at Ludwig's. — Red Rudensky, *The Gonif*, p. 76, 1970

▶ crack your face
to smile broadly, especially of a usually serious person *UK, 1966*
- That Eunice is a miserable bugger – she's never been known to crack her face. — *The Guardian*, 3rd January 2000

▶ get cracking
to start, to begin work *UK, 1937*
- In, out – let's get crackin'! — Stephen Sondheim, *West Side Story*, 1957
- Let's skiddadle [go hurriedly] down the nearest tube [London underground] and get cracking. — Barry Humphries, *Bazza Pulls It Off!*, 1971
- Get cracking, you bunch of fairies! — *The Guardian*, 25th January 2003

crack *adjective*
excellent *UK, 1793*
- I rode all the way back on The Chief, the crack train on the Santa Fe[.] — Mezz Mezzrow, *Really the Blues*, p. 137, 1946

crack about *verb*
to act vigorously and aggresively *UK*
Field Marshal Montgomery spoke of his army, after it had crossed the Rhine in 1945, as having the chance to 'crack about on the plains of North Germany'.

crackalacking; crackalackin' *verb*
happening; doing; occuring; working *US*
Also, in the greeting 'what's crackalackin?'.
- I keep it crackalackin' / I'm all about them plaques and figures / I'm a platinum nigga — Roscoe, *What I Look Like*, 2003
- What's poppin' wit'chu? What's happenin'? What's crackalackin'? You still mackin'? You still bad actin.? — Aceyalone, *Let Me Hear Sumn*, 2003

crack along; crack on *verb*
to move swiftly *UK, 1837*
From the use of a whip to encourage speed.
- With a wind gusting up to force five and six, we cracked along briskly. — *The Guardian*, 9th February 2002

crack attack *noun*
the intense craving for crack cocaine felt by an addict *US*
- — Terry Williams, *Crackhouse*, p. 148, 1992

crack baby *noun*
1 a child born with an addiction to crack cocaine *US*
- These are cocaine and crack babies. Born carrying a psychic ball and chain they didn't ask for. — *New Jack City*, 1990

2 someone who is behaving very foolishly *US*
Comparing the person to a baby born addicted to crack cocaine.
- — Connie Eble (Editor), *UNC-CH Campus Slang*, p. 2, Fall 1993

crack back *noun*
marijuana mixed with crack cocaine *UK, 1998*
- — Mike Haskins, *Drugs*, p. 287, 2003

CrackBerry *nickname*
the BlackBerry™, a wireless instant-messaging device from Waterloo, Ontario *CANADA*
- [The use of the Blackberry] is so addictive that it's also known as the CrackBerry. — *Toronto Globe and Mail*, p. A17, 21st June 2002

crack cooler *noun*
pieces of crack cocaine soaked in a wine cooler drink *US*
- — US Department of Justice, *Street Terms*, 1994

crack-crack *noun*
hands that are badly chapped *NORFOLK ISLAND*
- — Beryl Nobbs Palmer, *A Dictionary of Norfolk Words and Usages*, p. 9, 1992

crack down *verb*
1 to repress; to supress by Draconic means, especially used of campaigns against lawless persons or acts *UK, 1940*
Usually before 'on' or 'upon'.
- Israel maintains that Mr Arafat is not cracking down on militants[.] — *The Guardian*, 27th October 2001

2 in horse racing, to be determined to win a race *US*
- — Igor Kushyshyn et al., *The Gambling Times Guide to Harness Racing*, p. 114, 1994

crack down on *verb*
to seize or make off with something *AUSTRALIA, 1961*

cracked *adjective*
mentally impaired *UK, 1692*
- — John Ayto, *The Oxford Dictionary of Slang*, p. 303, 1998

cracked ice *noun*
diamonds that have been removed from their settings *US*
- — Joseph E. Ragen and Charles Finston, *Inside the World's Toughest Prison*, p. 795, 1962

cracked out *adjective*
suffering symptoms of heavy crack cocaine usage *US, 1988*
- The way it is now, Ronnie could do it, play himself, some cracked out asshole. — *Get Shorty*, 1995
- She was whispering it in his ear, scraping his neck, that hard, cracked-out voice croaking to him[.] — Kevin Sampson, *Powder*, p. 56, 1999

cracked squash *noun*
a fractured skull *US*
- — *Maledicta*, p. 117, 1984–1985: 'Milwaukee medical maledicta'

crack 'em up *noun*
a vehicular accident *US*
- — Bill Davis, *Jawjacking*, p. 32, 1977

cracker *noun*
1 a poor, uneducated, racist white from the southern US *US, 1766*
- Tommy was another cracker bastard. — Chester Himes, *If He Hollers Let Him Go*, p. 26, 1945
- Just a flunkey, a northern redneck, a Yankee cracker! — Ralph Ellison, *Invisible Man*, p. 200–201, 1947
- "I'm Ethel Waters," I told him, "and I'm standing on my grounds. And you or no other cracker sonofabitch can tell me what to do." — Ethel Waters, *His Eye is on the Sparrow*, p. 203, 1951
- Like I'd walk up to some big, fat-assed cracker policeman and hold my hands inside my sleeves and bow and ask him directions[.] — Ross Russell, *The Sound*, p. 73, 1961
- The horror is the Georgia "cracker." Depravity rigid. — Clancy Sigal, *Going Away*, p. 452, 1961
- I was working down the aisle and a big, beefy, red-faced cracker soldier got up in front of me[.] — Malcolm X and Alex Haley, *The Autobiography of Malcolm X*, p. 77, 1964
- No, the crackers down South is white people, real mean white people. — Claude Brown, *Manchild in the Promised Land*, p. 44, 1965
- Everyone was supposed to be non-violent, but when these crackers started to beat women and children there was a hell of a rumble. — Babs Gonzales, *I Paid My Dues*, p. 134–135, 1967
- I think we ought to just challenge for the heck of it every two hours or so, just to let those crackers know that we are on our toes and they'd better not try anything. — Stokely Carmichael and Charles V. Hamilton, *Black Power*, p. 110, 1967
- [A] number-one-all-Amerikian cracker[.] — Abbie Hoffman, *Woodstock Nation*, p. 41, 1969
- They went out to the highway and caught a ride with a young cracker in a '55 Ford. — Cecil Brown, *The Life & Loves of Mr. Jiveass Nigger*, p. 27, 1969
- I mean, jail up north is gotta be like summer camp compared to jail down in cracker country. — *Raging Bull*, 1980
- I was with the two producers once when they were talking about casting the role of "Slade," the decadent, wealthy cracker[.] — Terry Southern, *Now Dig This*, p. 8, 1986
- You got cracker farm-boy Luke Skywalker, Nazi poster boy – blond hair, blue eyes. — *Chasing Amy*, 1997

2 a person of Anglo-culture *CANADA*
- "What is a cracker?" "Someone like a white guy, like a cracker jack." — Alroy, *Cultural Identity and Identity Performance among Latin American Youths in Toronto*, p. 132, 2001

3 anything excellent *UK, 1914*
From CRACK (excellent). Contemporary usage is due in part to comedian Frank Carson who has 'It's a cracker!' as a catchphrase.
- We did some crackers. — Val McDermid, *Keeping on the Right Side of the Law*, p. 181, 1999
- I was at one [a party] the other year, fucking cracker it were[.] — Kevin Sampson, *Outlaws*, p. 41, 2001

4 an excellent performance in a game *AUSTRALIA*
- You will have played well when the pundits describe your performance as a 'cracker'[.] — Ivor Limb, *Footy's No Joke!*, p. 20, 1986

5 an attractive woman *UK, 1914*
- I saw a pretty girl coming along the street. "Ain't she a cracker? Look at her, she's like a film star." — Joe Morgan, *Eastenders Don't Cry*, p. 58, 1994

6 the buttocks *US*

- And the loudest cusser is generally the first one knocked on his cracker and sent to the bench for repairs. —*Fortnight*, p. 11, 31st December 1948
- Now their fear of missing something has carried them almost, but not quite, to the point of hoping that Clay wins so that the beautiful sight they want most to see – that of Clay on his cracker – might be "saved" for their eyes at some later date. —*San Francisco Examiner*, p. 61, 23rd March 1966

7 a person who breaches a computer system's security scheme *US*

Coined c. 1985 by hackers in defence against journalistic misuse of the word.

- —Eric S. Raymond, *The New Hacker's Dictionary*, p. 110, 1991

8 a criminal who specialises in breaking into safes *US*

An abbreviation of 'safe cracker'.

- —Ralph de Sola, *Crime Dictionary*, p. 33, 1982

9 a safe *CANADA, 1976*

- Maybe he [the store manager] adds it up first in his office, takes it home, stashes it in the cracker, or maybe behind the corn flakes. —Hugh Garner, *The Intruders*, p. 107, 1976

10 a pound (£1); a pound-note *AUSTRALIA, 1934*

In *A Dictionary of Australian Colloquialisms*, 1978, G. A. Wilkes argues that there is no evidence that a 'cracker' has ever been used to mean 'a pound', which is the sense that both Sidney J. Baker and the *Oxford English Dictionary* favour, but he (Wilkes) offers no alternative. Often used in phrases such as 'not have a cracker'.

11 the least amount of money *AUSTRALIA, 1934*

- Three years before he hadn't a cracker. —Eric Lambert, *The Veterans*, p. 64, 1954
- He didn't have a cracker when he lived on the Terrace. —Wilda Moxham, *The Apprentice*, p. 52, 1969

12 a firework *AUSTRALIA, 1907*

- Now and then fountains of red sparks shot up out of Lick Jimmy's backyard, where he was letting off crackers in some solitary celebration[.] —Ruth Park, *Poor Man's Orange*, p. 28, 1949

13 a phonograph record *US*

- — *Time Magazine*, p. 92, 20th January 1947

14 a brothel *AUSTRALIA, 1955*

- —G.A. Wilkes, *A Dictionary of Australian Colloquialisms*, 1978

15 a tooth *UK*

Usually in the plural.

- When I saw Davis the other day his crackers seemed to be in good shape... no sign even of tartar. —Graham Greene, *The Human Factor*, 1978

▸ **go off like a cracker**

to explode into a rage *AUSTRALIA*

- But tell him I paid $100 for someone to clean the windows and he goes off like a cracker. —Paul Vautin, *Turn It Up!*, p. 134, 1995

▸ **not worth a cracker**

entirely worthless *AUSTRALIA, 1941*

- 'He's got guts, anyway,' said Sayers. 'I didn't think he was worth a cracker.' —Gavin Casey, *It's Harder for Girls*, p. 126, 1941
- Circumstantial evidence isn't worth a cracker in court, on something like this. —Ricki Francis, *Hotel Kings X*, p. 83, 1973

cracker *adjective*

excellent *NEW ZEALAND*

- The huge Maori put the Yank down. 'By Kori,' he said with a kind smile, 'That was a cracker yarn, mate.' —John Sinclair and Margaret Trotter, *From Caithness to Southland*, p. 24, 1994

cracker!

used for expressing approval *UK*

- — Susie Dent, *The Language Report*, p. 75, 2003

cracker-ass *noun*

a thin person *US, 1966*

- —Frederic G. Cassidy, *Dictionary of American Regional English, Volume 1*, p. 826, 1985

crackerbox *noun*

1 a plain, box-like house *US, 1945*

- The people sweltering through the early dog days of late spring ... not warm enough to stay outside all the time, but too warm to stay inside the crackerbox walls[.] —Odie Hawkins, *Ghetto Sketches*, p. 9, 1972
- The house was a frame crackerbox with a pair of dormer windows sticking out of the roof and no style at all until Richard fixed up the front with imitation ledgerock, a grillwork porch and striped aluminum awnings over the proch and windows. —Elmore Leonard, *Switch*, p. 37, 1978
- Why on earth didn't I sell this run-down little cracker box and return to my hometown[?] —Armistead Maupin, *Maybe the Moon*, p. 19, 1992

2 a jail from which escape is simple; a safe which is simple to break into *US*

- —Hyman E. Goldin et al., *Dictionary of American Underworld Lingo*, p. 51, 1950

3 a brakevan (caboose) *US*

- —Ramon Adams, *The Language of the Railroader*, p. 38, 1977

4 a military truck used as an ambulance *US, 1950*

- —J.E. Lighter, *Historical Dictionary of American Slang, Volume One*, p. 504, 1994

cracker-box *adjective*

plain, simple, unsophisticated *US, 1911*

- [H]earing for month after month after month of the achievements of bums like Floyd and Karpis and Nelson and Dillinger, who were getting rich off cracker-box banks. —Horace McCoy, *Kiss Tomorrow Good-bye*, p. 7, 1948

Crackerdom *noun*

an area inhabited predominantly by racist white people *US*

- My Lady saved me form Georgia, the Georgia that I had thought of, the world that represented Crackerdom, was undermined by people from another place. —Odie Hawkins, *Scars and Memories*, p. 82–83, 1987

cracker factory *noun*

a mental hospital *US*

- You'd have me sent to a cracker factory if I told you. —Sidney Sheldon, *The Naked Face*, p. 160, 1970
- Six months in a five-star cracker factory, and that woman is home free. —Judith Kelman, *One Last Kiss*, p. 70, 1994

crackerjack *noun*

an excellent example of something *US, 1895*

- We've got a crackerjack here, Miss Chambers, who's been with us twenty years. —Mary McCarthy, *The Group*, p. 199, 1963

crackerjack *adjective*

highly skilled, excellent *US, 1899*

- Everything is shipshape, jim-dandy, and crackerjack[.] —Jim Thompson, *The Nothing Man*, p. 189, 1954
- "Yes, sir," interrupted Jefferson, "we have gone and made us a real crackerjack of a college." —Max Shulman, *Anyone Got a Match?*, p. 125, 1964
- I've been getting crackerjack reports from them, particularly in Empathy[.] —Gore Vidal, *Myra Breckinridge*, p. 48, 1968
- I know some cracker jack pool hustlers solo sharking that are starving to death. —Iceberg Slim (Robert Beck), *Mama Black Widow*, p. 158, 1969

cracker night *noun*

a night which is celebrated with fireworks *AUSTRALIA, 1951*

Currently this is used to commemorate the birthday of Queen Elizabeth II, though it was previously used to celebrate other occasions.

- Because they're getting ready for another big cracker night. —Hesba Brinsmead, *Longtime Dreaming*, p. 91, 1982

crackers *noun*

LSD *US*

From the practice, at least in Boston, of saturating animal cracker biscuits with LSD and selling it in that form.

- —John Williams, *The Drug Scene*, p. 111, 1967

crackers *adjective*

crazy, mad *UK, 1925*

- I guess he and Kurt told me all that crap just to see exactly how crackers I was! —Beatrice Sparks (writing as 'Anonymous'), *Jay's Journal*, p. 40, 1979
- [H]e murdered some poor fucker to make isself feel better. That's all yer [there] was to it. Psycho. – Crackers. – Yeh, psycho[.] —Niall Griffiths, *Sheepshagger*, p. 159, 2001
- Councillor Clyne said he agreed with Lambeth Mayor Councillor June Fewtrell's statement that the council's current housing allocation policy is "crackers". —*Streatham Guardian*, 14th March 2003

crack gallery *noun*

a building or room where crack cocaine is sold and smoked *US*

- —Terry Williams, *The Cocaine Kids*, p. 136, 1989

crack girl *noun*

a girl or woman addicted to crack cocaine *US, 1980s*

- If you catch the crack girl early on she can still look fine. Three weeks into the addiction, no one can tell the difference – except that a girl who would normally never talk to you ... will fuck you for five or ten dollars. —Chris Rock, *Rock This!*, p. 79, 1997

crack hardy *verb*

to endure something bravely; to put on a brave face *AUSTRALIA, 1904*

- Good-oh, but there's no sense cracking hardy at your age. —Dymphna Cusack, *Picnic Races*, p. 77, 1962
- —Jim Ramsay, *Cop It Sweet!*, p. 25, 1977

crackhead *noun*

1 a person addicted to crack cocaine *US*

- "I want quality young people in this organization, not crackheads, is that understood?" he said again. — *New York Times*, p. 8 (Section 11), 10th August 1986
- —Terry Williams, *Crackhouse*, p. 148, 1992
- The guy could be a crackhead. — *Sleepless in Seattle*, 1993
- Marion Barry at the Million Man March. Do you know what that means? Even in our finest hour we had a crackhead on stage. —Chris Rock, *Rock This!*, p. 187, 1997
- 60 grand on the premises. Even a third of that is enough to make some people go home and get out the sawn-off [...]. Or on 60th of it for a crackhead. —Dave Courtney, *Raving Lunacy*, p. 224, 2000

2 a crazy person *UK*

From **CRACKED** (mentally impaired).

- I'm still a crackhead... No, after a couple of kids I've changed. —*Q*, p. 98, May 2002

crack house *noun*

a building or room where crack cocaine may be bought and consumed *US*

- Meanwhile, narcotics officers of the New York City Police Department have shut down a few of the so-called crack houses, the rough equivalent of heroin-shooting galleries, where sales are made and users gather for smoking binges that can last for several days. — *New York Times*, p. A1, 29th November 1985
- You know, they turned that spot into a crack house, it's just crack and more crack. —Terry Williams, *The Cocaine Kids*, p. 70, 1989

crackie *noun*

1 a crack cocaine user *US*

- Back in 1989–1990, I spent many nights in the East Village of New York hanging out with "crackies" of all stripes around makeshift bonfires of the insanities. —Jim Crotty, *How to Talk American*, p. 90, 1997

2 in the Maritime Provinces, a small yapping dog *CANADA*

- Newfoundland figures of speech include saucy as a crackie. —L.E.F. English, *Newfoundland*, p. 39, 1959

crack-in *noun*

a burglary *US*

- —Vincent J. Monteleone, *Criminal Slang*, p. 60, 1949

cracking *adjective*

1 very fast, vigorous *UK, 1825*

Also used as an adverb.

- The book sets off at a cracking rate, with bodies piling up in the first few chapters. — *The List' reviewing 'Set in Darkness' by Ian Rankin*, 2001

2 excellent *UK, 1833*

Also used as an adverb.

- To be fair, they always do have these cracking stories. —Kevin Sampson, *Outlaws*, p. 165, 2001
- Guinness is a cracking good pint you might enjoy next time you are in the pub[.] — *The Guardian*, 9th September 2002
- [A] cracking good thriller that looks set to be the beach book of the summer[.] — *The Observer*, 4th July 2004

crack in the shack *noun*

a homosexual in a jail cell *US*

- "What's happening in there?" "We got us a crack in the shack, man. Want to get down? —Inez Cardozo-Freeman, *The Joint*, p. 490, 1984

crack it *verb*

1 to succeed in some endeavour; to attain a desire *AUSTRALIA, 1936*

- Keep on with your art, mate. You'll crack it one day, I'm sure of it. —Alexander Buzo, *Rooted*, p. 78, 1969
- The buggers are always wanting to visit. Especially around Christmas. In the hope of cracking it for a presso. —Phillip Adams, *The Unspeakable Adams*, p. 181, 1977
- He cracked it for a lift out to the Territory[.] —Sam Weller, *Old Bastards I Have Met*, p. 140, 1979
- I think he's cracked it. — *The Observer*, 14th June 2002

2 to succeed in gaining sexual intercourse; to have sex *AUSTRALIA, 1941*

- Be careful of wogs though. I won't get off with them myself. Rather not crack it than crack it with a wog. —Kevin Mackey, *The Cure*, p. 88, 1970
- —Harry Orsman, *A Dictionary of Modern New Zealand Slang*, p. 33, 1999

3 to work as a prostitute *AUSTRALIA, 1945*

- I knew he cracked it along the big stone wall of East Sydney Tech, opposite the police station. —Kathy Lette, *Girls' Night Out*, p. 79, 1987

crackle *noun*

banknotes *UK*

From the sound of new money.

- —Paul Tempest, *Lag's Lexicon*, 1950

crackling *noun*

a woman or women regarded as sexual pleasure *UK*

This probably blends the pleasures to be had from tender, juicy meat and **CRACK** (the vagina). Conventionally 'crackling' is the crisped skin of roast pork.

crack mama *noun*

a homeless woman addicted to crack cocaine *US*

- —Judi Sanders, *Da Bomb*, p. 4, 1997

crack off *verb*

(of a male) to masturbate *UK*

- I had cracked off twice that day – so it was understandable. —Richard Herring, *Talking Cock*, p. 167, 2003

crack on *verb*

1 to tell someone something; to reveal a secret *AUSTRALIA*

- Well, it appears that between us we had a sprog, but she never cracked on about it, and I didn't tumble to it. —John Wynnum, *Jiggin' in the Riggin*, p. 58, 1965
- Everywhere people asked, 'How long have you owned it?' But we never cracked on that the Jaguar wasn't ours[.] — *The Times*, 27th April 2003

2 to go ahead *UK*

A variation of the sense 'to hurry', hence 'to move forward'.

- [I]f it meant me not having to put my hand in my pocket for his fee, then fuck it, crack on. —Danny King, *The Burglar Diaries*, p. 97, 2001

3 to flirt; to try to seduce someone *US*

- —Connie Eble (Editor), *UNC-CH Campus Slang*, p. 1, Fall 1982

4 to succeed in gaining sexual favours from another *AUSTRALIA, 1955*

- How did a poonce like Bentley ever crack on to a horny bird like Sandy? —Alexander Buzo, *Rooted*, p. 96, 1969

▷ **see:** CRACK ALONG

crack out *verb*

1 to escape from prison *US*

- —Hyman E. Goldin et al., *Dictionary of American Underworld Lingo*, p. 51, 1950

2 in a swindle, to relieve the victim of his money quickly *US*

- —Robert C. Prus and C.R.D. Sharper, *Road Hustler*, p. 169, 1977

crackpot *noun*

a person who is somewhere in the continuum between odd and crazy *UK, 1883*

- When Washington was suddenly flooded with a horde of crackpots from the campuses, Communists, ballet-dancers and economic planners, there was no place for them to live. —Jack Lait and Lee Mortimer, *Washington Confidential*, p. 9, 1951
- What the hell, we were supposed to be here as observers, not as participants in any of Allen's crackpot schemes. —Terry Southern, *Now Dig This*, p. 122, November 1968
- "The Beach police think it's a crackpot," Garcia added in a noncommittal way. —Carl Hiaasen, *Tourist Season*, p. 54, 1986
- "Just remember," Rebus warned, "the person we're looking for might be a crackpot too." —Ian Rankin, *The Falls*, p. 99, 2001

crackpot *adjective*

(of ideas and schemes) crazy, fantastic, unrealistic *US, 1934*

- They're going to fund this crackpot scheme by selling Ronaldinho. — *The Guardian*, 27th February 2003

crack regiment *noun*

the Women's Royal Army Corps, and its predecessor (from 1938–46), the Auxiliary Territorial Service *UK, 1995*

A pun on **CRACK** (excellent) and **CRACK** (the vagina).

crack salesman *noun*

1 a youthful, attractive homosexual male prostitute *US*

- — *Maledicta*, p. 220, 1979: 'Kinks and queens: linguistic and cultural aspects of the terminology for gays'

2 a pimp *US*

- —Vincent J. Monteleone, *Criminal Slang*, p. 60, 1949

cracksman *noun*
a burglar; a safe-breaker *US, 1797*
Originally 'a house-breaker'. As in the title of the 1963 film starring Charlie Drake.

crack smile *noun*
a slash from ear to mouth, especially one inflicted for failure to pay for drugs *US*
- —Kenn "Naz" Young, *Naz's Dictionary of Teen Slang*, p. 26, 1993

cracksmoker *noun*
a person whose sanity is open to question, whether or not they actually smoke crack *US*
- — *Maybeck High School Yearbook (Berkeley, California)*, p. 28, 1997

crack troops *noun*
female soldiers *US, 1947*
A pun on 'crack' – here used in the vaginal sense, not the expected expert sense.
- —J.E. Lighter, *Historical Dictionary of American Slang, Volume One*, p. 506, 1994

crack-up *noun*
1 a nervous breakdown *US, 1936*
- So return with us now to Los Angeles where Brenda (Griffiths) is headed for a crack-up even before she hits her mother, the crazy psychiatrist Joanna Cassidy[.]— *New York Metro*, 4th March 2002

2 a cause for laughter *US, 1961*
- Yes sir, I was definitely the life of the party. A real crack-up. —Bill Myers, *The Incredible Worlds of Wally Mcdoogle #7*, p. 33, 1994

crack up *verb*
1 to undergo a nervous breakdown *US, 1917*
- Same thing Day after day – Tube-Work-Dinner-Work-Tube-Armchair-TV-Sleep-Work. How Much More Can You Take. One in Five Go Mad, One in Ten Cracks Up. —Richard Neville, *Play Power*, p. 253, 1970
- Lank lizards, as Weetzie would say. Maybe I am cracking up. —Francesca Lia Block, *Missing Angel Juan*, p. 293, 1993

2 to praise someone highly *US, 1829*
- So people are beginning to believe that organic food is a bit of a con, that it is not all that it is cracked up to be and they resent having to pay a premium for it. — *The Guardian*, 4th January 2002

3 to amuse someone greatly; to cause laughter *US, 1942*
- And, wow, the cricket on the car radio really cracks me up. — *The Guardian*, 4th August 2000

crack weed *noun*
marijuana laced with crack cocaine *UK*
- —Mike Haskins, *Drugs*, p. 287, 2003

crack whore *noun*
a prostitute motivated by a desire to buy crack cocaine *US, 1980s*
- A crack whore named Princess from the Forties House in South Jamaica had turned up dead in the grass near an exit ramp to Greenwich, Connecticut. — *San Francisco Chronicle*, p. 5 (Sunday Review), 19th August 1990
- See, he likes to smoke crack; she's a crackhead. There's a difference. She leaves because she's a drifting crack whore and she literally sleeps where she ends up. —Chris Rock, *Rock This!*, p. 75, 1997
- She puts me in mind of the crackwhore, my crackwhore, the crackwhore in my crackwhore story[.]—Niall Griffiths, *Kelly + Victor*, p. 67, 2002

cracoid *noun*
a crack cocaine addict *US*
- A turf challenge was slanting across the Strip, a precision patrol of cracoids swivelhipping between stalled bumpers straight for the Blue Note. —Seth Morgan, *Homeboy*, p. 17, 1990

cradle *noun*
1 your domicile, be it a room, apartment or house *CANADA*
- —Jack Chambers (Editor), *Slang Bag 93 (University of Toronto)*, p. 2, Winter 1993

2 any open-top railway goods wagon, such as a gondola *US*
- —Ramon Adams, *The Language of the Railroader*, p. 38, 1977

cradle baby *noun*
a novice citizens' band radio user *US*
Based on the initials CB.
- — *Complete CB Slang Dictionary*, 1976
- —Peter Chippindale, *The British CB Book*, p. 154, 1981

cradle rape *noun*
sex with a girl under the age of consent *US*
- What's your story, morning glory? It costs three grand to fix cradle rape. —Iceberg Slim (Robert Beck), *Trick Baby*, p. 161, 1969

cradle-rocker *noun*
in placer mining, a trough on a rocker shaken to separate gold flecks from sand and earth *CANADA*
- A cradle-rocker is a trough on a wooden or metal rocker, to wash and shake [potentially gold-bearing] muddy gravel in water. The prospector who performs such a task may also be called a cradle-rocker. —Bill Casselman, *Canadian Words*, p. 166, 1995

cradle-snatch *verb*
to have a sexual relationship with someone much younger than yourself *UK, 1938*
The image of the partner as a baby.
- The crew would think I've gone in for cradle snatching. —Frederick Kohner, *Gidget*, p. 98, 1957
- The women, he meant. Too fucking young for the most part. Even the ones where it wasn't out and out cradle-snatching[.]—John Williams, *Cardiff Dead*, p. 109, 2000

cradle-snatcher *noun*
a person who has a noticeably younger lover *US, 1907*
Also known as a 'cradle-robber'.
- [Joan Collins] has worked through all the stereotypes: happy marriage, broken marriage, fulfilled mother, sex goddess, vampire, porn pin-up, tabloid whore, cradle snatcher, stage luvvie, and always she emerges as Joan. — *The Guardian*, 24th July 2001

Craft's disease *noun*
senile dementia *AUSTRALIA*
From the spurious acronym '*c*an't *r*emember *a* *f*ucking *t*hing'.
- —James Lambert, *The Macquarie Book of Slang*, 1996

craftsman *noun*
a socially inept dolt *US*
- [T]he cha ("very cool") worlds include: "winded" for hung over; "craftsman" for a complete idiot; and "ass" for awful. — *Washington Times*, p. C3, 26th August 1992

crafty Alice *noun*
used as the epitome of a woman's wiles *UK*
A Lancashire saying noted by Laurie Atkinson, 1969.
- —Martin Shovel, *101 Ways to Sneak a Crafty Smoke*, 1997

crafty butcher *noun*
a male homosexual *UK*
Punningly derived, with Chrismas-cracker-motto corniness, because 'a crafty butcher takes his meat through the back door'.
- —Chris Lewis, *The Dictionary of Playground Slang*, p. 65, 2003

cram *verb*
to study hastily for an examination *UK, 1810*
- If you crammed last time around it was a bad thing. —Michael Moiso, *How to Pass When You Failed the Bar Exam*, p. 77, 2004

cram-book *noun*
a book used for hasty study *UK, 1883*
- A very good cram book. —a customer review of 'A+ Exam Cram', James G. Jones and Craig Landes, 1998, 6th March 1999

cram it!
used for registering an imperative rejection *US, 1957*
- "Hey, did the mirror fog up, Susan? Did you touch yourself?" "Would you just cram it?" Susan said. —Howard Stern, *Miss America*, p. 277, 1995

crammer *noun*
1 a period of intense studying for an examination *UK*

2 a teacher who prepares students for examination; a student in a period of intense study for an examination; hence, an institution where students are given such intense preparation *UK, 1813*
- I even took my A levels from my crammers on whizz [amphetamines]. —Macfarlane, Macfarlane and Robson, *The User*, p. 91, 1996

cramming *noun*
intensive study especially in preparation for an examination *UK, 1821*
- Euan and Nicky Blair receive private "cramming" tuition in history and other subjects for their A-levels. — *The Guardian*, 4th July 2002

cramp *noun*

an unpleasant person *US*

- Stupkid cramp, man! —Jess Mowry, *Way Past Cool*, p. 32, 1992

cramp *verb*

▸ **cramp your style**

to hamper or prevent you from doing, or being at, your best *US, 1917*

From sporting use.

- Maybe the overwhelmingly partisan crowd cramped his style. — *Daily Telegraph*, 30th June 2003

cramper *noun*

a small cage in which a prisoner of war is confined *US*

- The cage, with a locked drop gate facing the open end of the horseshoe of buildings, was not large enough for him to stand or fully extend himself on the ground, and Veil had to shuffle on all fours in order to turn around. It was what, in Vietnam, had been called a tiger cage, or "cramper". —George C. Chesbro, *Veil*, p. 123, 1986

cran *noun*

a hiding-place for stolen goods *UK*

- "Use the cran in Dragonsdale." A cran is a place – hole in a wall, hollow tree, a disused belltower in some church – where thieves leave stolen goods until fuss has died down. —Jonathan Gash, *The Ten Word Game*, p. 47, 2003

crane *noun*

1 in skateboarding, a manoeuver in which the rider crouches on one foot, extending the other leg outwards *US*

- —Laura Torbet, *The Complete Book of Skateboarding*, p. 105, 1976

2 a superior with a great deal of influence *US*

New York police slang.

- The Extremely Unofficial and Completely Off-the-Record NYPD/ESU Truck-Two Glossary —Samuel M. Katz, *Anytime Anywhere*, p. 387, 1997

crank *noun*

1 methamphetamine hydrochloride in powdered form; any amphetamine; methcathinone *US*

On 15th September 1966, jazz critic Ralph J. Gleason wrote to slang lexicographer Peter Tamony, reporting that on 6th September he had heard the word 'crank' used by a 'young Negro pusher' in San Francisco's Fillmore district. On 9th October 1967, Gleason wrote Tamony a second note, clarifying that 'crank' was the same as 'meth', not 'heroin'. Peter Tamony heard the term again on 12th April 1968, in a speech at a meeting of the California Folklore Society in Berkeley.

- —William D. Alsever, *Glossary for the Establishment and Other Uptight People*, p. 7, December 1970
- I ain't trading no uptown crank for no downtown trash. — *Drugstore Cowboy*, 1988
- Are you saying you never made crystal meth, crank, methamphetamine, what ever you want to call it, with these chemicals? —Eleusis *Lightning on the Sun [The Howard Marks Book of Dope Stories]*, p. 322, 2001
- —Mike Haskins, *Drugs*, p. 279, 2003

2 a mentally unstable person; an unreliable, unpredictable person; a person who is obsessed by a single topic or hobby *US, 1833*

- Since you seem to be unwilling to accept the note as the work of some crank who has observed Mr. Bigelow's movements and who profited by an unfortunate but by no means extraordinary coincidence. —Jim Thompson, *Savage Night*, p. 135, 1953

3 a prison guard who takes pleasure in making life difficult for prisoners *US*

- — *Maledicta*, p. 264, Summer/Winter 1981: 'By its slang, ye shall know it: the pessimism of prison life'

4 a prison bully *US*

- The next thing anyone knows is this crank is screaming blue murder and holding the side of his face —Frank Norman, *Bang To Rights*, p. 28, 1958

5 a crankshaft *US*

Hot rodder usage.

- — *Hot Rod Magazine*, p. 13, November 1948

6 the penis *US, 1968*

- Right soon after that, his crank was hard. It rose up like it wanted to have a look around. —Tom Abrams, *A Piece of Luck*, p. 47, 1994
- So, to save time, he simply pulls out his crank and pisses into his now-empty Diet Coke cup. —Rick Reilly, *Who's Your Caddy?*, p. 51, 2003

7 an act of masturbation *AUSTRALIA*

- — Thommo, *The Dictionary of Australian Swearing and Sex Sayings*, p. 29, 1985

crank *verb*

1 to use amphetamines or methamphetamine, central nervous system stimulants *US*

- —William D. Alsever, *Glossary for the Establishment and Other Uptight People*, p. 7, December 1970

2 to inject a drug *UK*

Also known as 'crank up'.

- —Home Office, *Glossary of Terms and Slang Common in Penal Establishments*, 1978
- —Mike Haskins, *Drugs*, p. 290, 2003

3 to turn up the volume of music to very loud *US*

- Hey! Turn your radios up! Crank it up so's we can hear it! — *Airheads*, 1994
- I had the tunes cranked, I had nine grand sitting in front of me. — *Empire Records*, 1995
- I've got it modified with the TK 421, which is a bass unit that basically kicks in another two, maybe three quads when you really crank. — *Boogie Nights*, 1997

4 to excel *US*

- UNREAL, it's cranking out there. —Michael V. Anderson, *The Bad, Rad, Not to Forget Way Cool Beach and Surf Discriptionary*, p. 5, 1988

5 in computing, to perform well *US*

- This box cranks (or, cranks at) about 5 megaflops, with a burst mode of twice that on vectorized operations. —Eric S. Raymond, *The New Hacker's Dictionary*, p. 110, 1991

6 in a card game, to deal the cards *US*

- —George Percy, *The Language of Poker*, p. 25, 1988

▸ **crank tail**

to physically assault someone *TRINIDAD AND TOBAGO, 1971*

- —Lise Winer, *Dictionary of the English/Creole of Trinidad & Tobago*, 2003

crank *adjective*

insane *FIJI*

- When you drink too much grog and get dope all the itme, then you go crank. —Jan Tent, 1995

crank bug *noun*

an insect that is seen by someone under the influence of methamphetamine but not by others *US*

- —Walter L. Way, *The Drug Scene*, p. 107, 1977

crankcase *verb*

the head *US*

- You're not responsible to desk sergeants any more, sweets, can't you get that through your crankcase? —Clarence Cooper Jr, *The Scene*, p. 50, 1960

crank commando *noun*

an amphetamine or methamphetamine addict *UK*

- —William D. Alsever, *Glossary for the Establishment and Other Uptight People*, p. 30, December 1970

cranked; cranked out; cranked up *adjective*

1 stimulated by methamphetamine or amphetamines *US*

- "There's another worrier," said my attorney. "He's probably all cranked up on speed." —Hunter S. Thompson, *Fear and Loathing in Las Vegas*, p. 14, 1971
- They're all crazy cranked-out animals! —Joseph Wambaugh, *The Secrets of Harry Bright*, p. 243, 1985
- "Go on home, man," the ox said to him. "Take my pickup. I gotta git cranked." —Joseph Wambaugh, *Finnegan's Week*, p. 202, 1992
- Akerlund rounds up a troupe of Hollywood B-listers – Mena Suvari, Brittany Murphy, Jasosn Schwartzman, and Patrick Fugit – for an hour and a half of cranked-out obnoxiousness. — *Boston Globe*, p. D8, 28th March 2003

2 excited; intensified *US, 1957*

Mechanical imagery.

- Only a fool would try to explain why four thousand Japanese ran at top speed past the U.S.S. Arizona, sunken memorial in the middle of Pearl Harbor, along with another four or five thousand certified American liberals cranked upon beer and spaghetti[.] —Hunter S. Thompson, *Songs of the Doomed*, p. 189, 1980

cranker *noun*

a bowler who in delivering the ball lifts it high over his head in the backswing *US*

- —Dawson Taylor, *How to Talk Bowling*, p. 32–33, 1987

cranking; cranking up *noun*

the act of injecting a drug *UK*

- [H]e's got cranking down to a fine art[.] —Lanre Fehintola, *Charlie Says...*, p. 97, 2000

cranking *adjective*
amusing; pleasing; exciting; good *US*
- — Mary Corey and Victoria Westermark, *Fer Shurr! How to be a Valley Girl*, 1982
- [T]hat's crankin', man – fuckin' majeek [magic]! — Stuart Browne, *Dangerous Parking*, p. 40, 2000

crank off *verb*
to consume something *US*
- I'm busy crankin' off an eight-ball, dude. — Stephen J. Cannell, *The Tin Collectors*, p. 116, 2001

crank out *verb*
to create something, to make something
The implication is of mechanical manufacture, but that is not necessarily the intention.
- I laid down some "dummy vocals" [for the song Guilty Conscience] while [Dr] Dre learned his parts and we cranked it out[.] — Eminem (Marshall Mathers), *Angry Blonde*, p. 53, 2001

crank time *noun*
the time set or needed to start up a helicopter *US*
- — Linda Reinberg, *In the Field*, p. 53, 1991

cranny *noun*
1 the vagina *UK*
An adoption, probably in C19, of the conventional sense; it remains in circulation mainly as an occasional variation of a pornographer's theme; the male-inspired 'cranny-hunter', however, is no longer evident.
2 a toilet *US, 1968*
- — Frederic G. Cassidy, *Dictionary of American Regional English, Volume 1*, p. 832, 1985

crap *noun*
1 nonsense *UK, 1898*
- And I think that stuff about women wanting it just as bad is crap. — *Sex, Lies and Videotape*, 1989

2 excrement *UK, 1846*
- It's still quite a shocking moment though, when you see Divine eat the dog crap[.] — *The Guardian*, 17th November 1998

3 an act of defecation *US, 1926*
- [H]ow, in the crowded, ever-moving convoys, they dealt with menstruation or simply going for a crap[.] — *The Guardian*, 6th July 2002

4 marijuana *US*
- — Francis J. Rigney and L. Douglas Smith, *The Real Bohemia*, p. xiii, 1961

5 weak or highly diluted heroin *US, 1942*
- — Richard Lingeman, *Drugs from A to Z*, p. 51, 1969
- — Robert Ashton, *This Is Heroin*, p. 208, 2002

▸ **take a crap**
to defecate *US*
- I took a crap in a 1000-year old Indian stone crapper in the outdoors. — Jack Kerouac, *Letter to Allen Ginsberg*, p. 350, 10th May 1952

crap *verb*
to defecate *UK, 1673*
- Didn't seem possible that the git who owned this motor could have been crapping all that long. — John Peter Jones, *Feather Pluckers*, p. 39, 1964

crap *adjective*
inferior, shoddy, valueless, unpleasant, disliked for whatever reason *US, 1916*
From the earlier sense (excrement).
- I fell into a crap sleep beneath the bright office lights. — David Peace, *Nineteen Seventy-Four*, p. 101, 1999
- He hated me because he wanted a proper mum, one who wasn't crap at it. — Mary Hooper, *(megan)2*, p. 148, 1999

crap antenna *noun*
the ability to detect when someone is speaking nonsense *AUSTRALIA*
- I was an apprentice fanny farter, with an okay vocabulary and had a very finely-tuned crap antenna. — Kathy Lette, *Girls' Night Out*, p. 64, 1987

crap around *verb*
to idle; to pass time doing nothing; to waste time *US, 1935*
- Tell him I'm not going to crap around bargaining. — James Clavell, *King Rat*, p. 221, 1962

crap artist *noun*
a convincing liar *US, 1934*
- Oh, hell, I hate them, those crap artists. — Saul Bellow, *Humboldt's Gift*, p. 142, 1975
- Wassamatter, all the big girls found out you're a crap artist? — Jackie Collins, *CHances*, p. 577, 1980

crap-ass *noun*
a despicable person *US, 1975*
- [E]ven though architects are always trying to take credit for it – crap-asses. — Todd McEwen, *Who Sleeps with Katz?*, p. 40, 2003

crap-ass *adjective*
shoddy, inferior *US*
- I'm a dull, boring hack writing copy for crap-ass products and sucking up to a bunch of corporate dildos. — Linda Watanabe McFerrin, *Hand of Buddha*, p. 51, 2000

crapaud-foot writing; crapaud hand *noun*
illegible penmanship *TRINIDAD AND TOBAGO*
- — Lise Winer, *Dictionary of the English/Creole of Trinidad & Tobago*, 2003

crapaud-going-to-wedding *noun*
childlike, scratchy handwriting *GRENADA*
- — Richard Allsopp, *Dictionary of Caribbean English Usage*, p. 175, 1996

crap course *noun*
an easy college course *US, 1956*
- But you were having an affair with your college professor. That jerk that teaches that incredible crap course "Contemporary Crisis in Western Man"! — *Annie Hall*, 1977

crape-hanger *noun*
a doomsayer *US*
- The crapehangers love to bury me. They think I'm making more money than I should. — *Time*, p. 54, 27th June 1949
- The crape hangers were out in full force. — Vincent Curcio, *Chrysler*, p. 269, 2000

crap hat *noun*
in a paratroop regiment, a non-jumper *UK*
From the different colour of the uniform beret (a non-jumper is not allowed to wear the red 'cherry berry' beret).
- Without a doubt, the major at Sutton Coldfield was my very first breathing example of what we paras called a "crap-hat Rupert [officer] wanker". — Ken Lukowiak, *Marijuana Time*, p. 12–13, 2000

crap heap *noun*
a dilapidated vehicle *AUSTRALIA*
- It's a moral they'll flog you some biffed-up grunter, some souped-up amateur crap heap with a dudded date[.] — Barry Humphries, *A Nice Night's Entertainment*, p. 147, 1974

craphole *noun*
a bad place, a disgusting place *US, 1939*
- Listen, the only reason I came back to this craphole was to find out who did it. — Mike Hodges, *Get Carter*, p. 49, 1971
- Ah walked out of Francois' craphole[.] — Ben Elton, *High Society*, p. 148, 2002

craphouse *noun*
1 a toilet *US, 1934*
- I'm got the ol' experience, I'm smart as a craphouse rat. — Nelson Algren, *Never Come Morning*, p. 10, 1963

2 a dirty, unpleasant place *US, 1934*
- You don't need to snake their dirty whores in some enlisted man's off-limits craphouse, then cover your ass with that Jesus talk of yours. — David Poyer, *The Med*, p. 54, 1988

crapness *noun*
a lack of style or worth *UK*
- I'm going to Dublin to have a laugh at its crapness and hence my own crapness for going there. — James Hawes, *Dead Long Enough*, p. 73, 2000

crap off *verb*
to annoy someone *AUSTRALIA*
- Crapped off with one-night stands, shat off with shallowness, quiet camp guy, twenty-five, would like to meet couple under thirty willing to dally discreetly during daytime. — *Alvin Purple*, p. 96, 1974

crapola *noun*
used as an embellished 'crap' in any and all of its senses *UK*
- "The Prime Minister expressed his hope that the Greek and Turkish Governments would reconsider the British proposals in the light of..." "Crapola," Mellors said. — Derek Bickerton, *Payroll*, p. 77, 1959
- Let us cope with the preliminary part of that farrago of crapola by citing the handiest record of the net assessment of the Shah's reign[.] — *San Francisco Examiner*, p. 34, 10th December 1979
- And you got to know that statue will be some dipped-in-shit, John Wayne crapola[.] — Larry Heinemann, *Paco's Story*, p. 157, 1986
- Tell me you've finished your crapola Foreign Legion movie. — Gerald Petievich, *Shakedown*, p. 133, 1988

crap out *verb*

1 to be completely exhausted; to go to sleep *US*

- — *American Speech*, p. 227, October 1956: 'More United States Air Force slang'
- Four in the morning / crapped out, yawning — Paul Simon, *Still Crazy After all these Years*, 1976

2 to die *US, 1929*

- Suppose I crap out? — Mickey Spillane, *Me, Hood!*, p. 14, 1963

3 to come to an end of a horizontal passage while caving or pot-holing *UK*

The horizontal equivalent of the conventional mining-term 'bottom out'.

- — David Morrison of Wessex Cave Club, 29th February 2004

crapper *noun*

1 a toilet *US, 1927*

- "Him, we wouldn't let a guy like him even touch the crapper," said Willie. — James T. Farrell, *Willie Collins*, p. 115, 1946
- "Ain't you supposed to be in the crapper?" he asked. — Horace McCoy, *Kiss Tomorrow Good-bye*, p. 9, 1948
- I took a crap in a 1000-year old Indian stone crapper in the outdoors. — Jack Kerouac, *Letter to Allen Ginsberg*, p. 350, 10th May 1952
- Gus said to Paco, "Let's go to the crapper." — Willard Motely, *Let No Man Write My Epitaph*, p. 304, 1958
- I try and try, ma'am, but I'm afraid I'll never make my mark as head man of the crappers. — Ken Kesey, *One Flew Over the Cuckoo's Nest*, p. 151, 1962
- Inside the crapper, I ripped a wad of paper from it's holder. — Iceberg Slim (Robert Beck), *Pimp*, p. 81, 1969
- Franny, on the other hand, is very impressed and ends the story valiantly trying to cool herself out by lipping the little prayer as she sits on the crapper in the girl's john. — *The Last Supplement to the Whole Earth Catalog*, p. 26, 1971
- Ernesto Cabal, alias Little Ernie, alias No-Way Jose, was sitting disconsolately on the crapper when the trusy opened the cell for Brian Keyes. — Carl Hiaasen, *Tourist Season*, p. 13, 1986
- Give her half of one, Bob, that'll keep her in the crapper all afternoon. — *Drugstore Cowboy*, 1988
- [T]he worst place to be, outside of being caught on the crapper[.] — Dave Courtney, *Stop the Ride I Want to Get Off*, p. 252, 1999

2 the anus, the rectum; the buttocks *UK, 1998*

- "Oi want you to blow some charlie [cocaine] op moi [up my] crapper, Tom." West Country accent, an' all[.] — Ben Elton, *High Society*, p. 215, 2002

▸ **in the crapper**

in horse racing, a finish in fourth place or worse *US*

- — Tom Ainslie, *Ainslie's Complete Guide to Thoroughbred Racing*, p. 333, 1976

crapper dick *noun*

a police officer who patrols public toilets in search of illegal homosexual activity *US*

- — Hyman E. Goldin et al., *Dictionary of American Underworld Lingo*, p. 52, 1950
- — Angela Devlin, *Prison Patter*, p. 40, 1996

crappereena *noun*

a toilet *UK*

- — Patrick O'Shaughnessy, *Market Traders' Slang*, 1979

crappers *noun*

▸ **in crappers ditch**

in severe trouble *NEW ZEALAND*

A strikingly unpleasant image akin to **UP SHIT CREEK**.

- — David McGill, *David McGill's Complete Kiwi Slang Dictionary*, p. 34, 1998

crappers *adjective*

very drunk *UK*

- — Nigel Foster, *The Making of a Royal Marine Commando*, 1987

crappo *noun*

a resident of Jersey (in the Channel Islands) according to those on Guernsey *UK*

- The locals call themselves Jersey beans. Residents of Guernsey call residents of Jersey crappos. — John Lahr, *Dame Edna Everage and the Rise of Western Civilisation*, p. 198, 1991

crappy *adjective*

1 of poor quality *US, 1942*

From **CRAP** (excrement), synonymous with **SHITTY**.

- He'd clip out cartoons and weather reports and crappy poems and health columns. — Jim Thompson, *The Killer Inside*, p. 96, 1952
- I'm a crappy little agency with crappy little clients nobody else will touch[.] — Max Shulman, *Anyone Got a Match?*, p. 24, 1964
- [W]e were having a fairly high-level meeting, about some crappy exercise or other[.] — Mike Stott, *Soldiers Talking, Cleanly*, 1978
- It's a crappy old banger. — Chris Ryan, *Stand By, Stand By*, p. 82, 1996
- I have my cats. Me and my two cats in a crappy place. — *Hard Eight*, 1996
- Yeah, but the animation's all crappy – it probably can't sustain itself over ninety minutes. — *South Park*, 1999

2 befouled with excrement *UK, 1846*

- I'll give you a beltin' when I've changed this crappy nappy! — Barry Humphries, *Bazza Pulls It Off!*, p. [18], 1971

craps *noun*

dice, especially used in craps *US*

- And I'd take some loaded craps down there, some bones, and I would beat the paddy boys out of all their money. — Claude Brown, *Manchild in the Promised Land*, p. 151, 1965

craps!

used for expressing disgust *TRINIDAD AND TOBAGO*

- — Lise Winer, *Dictionary of the English/Creole of Trinidad & Tobago*, 2003

crapshoot *noun*

an unpredictable, risky situation *US, 1971*

- All oil field exploration is a crap shoot at best, with only one in ten or fifteen fields panning out. — Stephen Cannell, *Big Con*, p. 137, 1997

craptitude *noun*

a state of existence comprising generally negative qualities such as poor taste and feebleness *UK*

A variation of **CRAPNESS** that seems to carry a suggestion of decrepitude.

- The ultimate cunting Irish experience awaits you in all its crapitude. — James Hawes, *Dead Long Enough*, p. 100, 2000

crap up *verb*

1 to fill something with clutter *US, 1946*

- It was still all crapped up. Boxes of car parts were stacked all the way to the ceiling. Tires were rolled over in the corners. Oil cans and carburetors and anything else that didn't have a box were all crammed together on a bunch of shelves. — Sam Giancana, *Double Deal*, p. 65, 2003

2 to spoil something; to ruin something *US, 1953*

- I'm sick and tired of Him and His whole choir of Guardian Angels – all they do is crap up my life! — Laura Esquivel, *The Law of Love*, p. 134, 1996

3 to address someone with a complete lack of sincerity *US*

- "[Y]ou don't have to give me any crap." "Well, for Christ's sake, who's crapping you up?" — Hal Ellson, *Tomboy*, p. 121, 1950

crash *verb*

1 to enter a party or social event without an invitation *US, 1921*

- The newcomers intended to crash, as everyone in the room knew. — Hal Ellson, *The Golden Spike*, p. 69, 1952
- On this particular night, the Wolf "crashed" a rather high-class party. — Max Shulman, *Guided Tour of Campus Humor*, p. 70, 1955
- Needless to say, nobody with an ounce of good manners or a thimbleful of concern for the feelings of others ever crashes a party. — Dick Clark, *To Goof or Not to Goof*, p. 130, 1963
- Frank crashed the party? — Terry Southern, *Now Dig This*, p. 220, 1978

2 to enter a place with force with the intention of commiting a crime *US, 1924*

- — Mickey Spillane, *My Gun is Quick*, p. >, 1950
- I told her somebody had crashed the place before I got there and liked to knock it apart. — Mickey Spillane, *My Gun is Quick*, p. 24, 1950
- We had a pretty good bunch of O'Sullivans, a torch man, a mechanic, a jigger and a hard-shell biscuit who'd been with a gopher mob. We crashed with a get-in betty. — *The New American Mercury*, p. 709, 1950
- It wasn't really fear even though he had never crashed a joint before. — Donald Goines, *Dopefiend*, p. 162, 1971

3 to stay somewhere temporarily; to sleep somewhere *US, 1945*

- As we walked up the steps a neighbor said "Here come two more kids looking for a place to crash." — James Simon Kunen, *The Strawberry Statement*, p. 96, 1968
- Well, she lets me crash at her place. — *Airheads*, 1994
- Then I realized that I owned my own apartment and had an American Express card while he was still crashing on his friend's couch and thrilled to have a new library card. — Anka Radakovich, *The Wild Girls Club*, p. 158, 1994
- I was just planning to crash on the floor for a few days till I figure out what I'm doing. — Kenneth Lonergan, *This is Our Youth*, p. 54, 2000

4 to go to sleep *UK, 1943*

- With that I think I'm ready to crash. — Darryl Ponicsan, *The Last Detail*, p. 100, 1970
- Then I returned to my room at Lennon's, showered, changed into pyjamas, ordered an early dinner, ate it, and crashed. — John O'Grady, *It's Your Shout, Mate!*, p. 76, 1972

5 to return to normal perceptions after a drug intoxication; to experience an associated feeling of post-intoxication depression or dismay *US, 1967*

- WYATT: Wow! I think I'm gonna crash. BILLY: Ah, man. I think you have crashed, man. —Peter Fonda, *Easy Rider*, p. 71, 1969
- 'I'm crashing, man,' Manny says. He lies on the floor. —John Rechy, *The Fourth Angel*, p. 114, 1972
- —Nick Constable, *This is Cocaine*, p. 182, 2002

6 (used of a computer program) to fail completely without warning *US*

- —Guy L. Steele et al., *The Hacker's Dictionary*, p. 49, 1983

7 (used of a police case) to fail or be dropped *UK*

- —Angela Devlin, *Prison Patter*, p. 41, 1996

8 to hit something, to strike something *US*

- —Terry Williams, *The Cocaine Kids*, p. 136, 1989

9 to escape from jail or prison *US*

- —Red Rudensky, *The Gonif*, p. a, 1970

10 in circus and carnival usage, to change money *US*

- —Don Wilmeth, *The Language of American Popular Entertainment*, p. 66, 1981

11 to pass something; to give something out *UK: ENGLAND*
Teen slang, recorded in Leicestershire.

- Crash the sugar, yoof [youth]. —D. and R. McPheely, 1977

12 to intubate a hospital patient quickly and urgently *US*

- —Sally Williams, *"Strong" Words*, p. 137, 1994

13 to perform a high-priority job as soon as possible *US*

- — Department of the Army, *Staff Officer's Guidebook*, p. 58, 1986

▸ **crash the ash**
to offer someone a cigarette *UK, 1984*
Probably since the 1950s; recorded as current by BBC Radio Leicester, May 2003.

crash and burn *verb*

1 to fail *US*

- And anyway, roysh [right], the goys were all stood behind him, giving it 'Crash and burn, crash and burn,' and this friend of my, roysh, he was just there, 'Oh my God, I SO love a challenge.' —Paul Howard, *Ross O'Carroll-Kelly*, p. 9, 2003

2 in computing, to fail in a dramatic and spectacular fashion *US*

- —Eric S. Raymond, *The New Hacker's Dictionary*, p. 110, 1991

crash box *noun*
in cars, a manual transmission not equipped with synchromesh, requiring forceful gear shifts *US*

- —John Lawlor, *How to Talk Car*, p. 35, 1965

crash car *noun*
an old, inexpensive car used in the distribution of illegal alcohol *US*

- —David W. Maurer, *Kentucky Moonshine*, p. 115, 1974

crash cart *noun*
a mobile cart used to carry equipment *US, 1982*
Originally hospital use, since expanded.

- Next to me was the "crash cart" they had used for Marcus. Rubber tourniquets hung like streamers from the black handles of the cart. —James Patterson, *Kiss the Girls*, p. 29, 1995
- Usually, the crew chief sits on top of a big box, called a crash cart, which is filled with equipment used for quick repairs[.] —Mark Martin, *NASCAR for dummies*, p. 152, 2000

crash-course *noun*
a short, intensive course on a particular subject *UK, 1973*

- Welcome to the world of the crash course. To employers, the idea of sending out employees to learn the basics in a week [...] is irresistible. — *The Guardian*, 14th October 2002

crasher *noun*

1 a person temporarily sleeping in someone else's house or apartment *US*

- Crasher could only cop about six hours sleep, however, because John and Paul had to wake everybody up by 10 A.M. in order to sweep and to get the breads in the ovens in time to open for the noon-hour soup rush. —Ed Sanders, *Tales of Beatnik Glory*, p. 30, 1975

2 a very tedious or tiresome person or thing *UK*
A variation of CRASHING BORE.

- —Noel Coward, *Pomp and Circumstance*, 1960

3 a powerful, hard-breaking wave *US*

- —John Severson, *Modern Surfing Around the World*, p. 165, 1964

crash hat *noun*
a safety helmet *US*

- Brainbucket, skid lid, melon gear, crash hat. It doesn't matter what you call it, just as long as you have one – a helmet for hitting the slopes, trails, skating rinks and half-pipes. —*Times Union (Albany, New York)*, p. D1, 23rd December 2003

crash helmet *noun*
a condom *UK*
Figurative use of motorcyclists' safety wear: in both uses worn in case of accident. Possibly also a punning reference to 'helmet' (the head of the penis).

- —David Rowan, *A Glossary for the 90's*, 1998

crash hot *adjective*
excellent *AUSTRALIA*

- You blokes did a crash-hot job tonight, feller. —W.R. Bennett, *Target Turin*, p. 66, 1962
- Gary's a good bloke and his Mum cooks a crash hot rissole. —Alexander Buzo, *Rooted*, p. 86, 1969
- Unless I can borrow the loan of a really crash-hot hygiene publication to peruse I reckon I've done me lot for tonight. —Barry Humphries, *Bazza Pulls It Off!*, 1971
- —Sonya Plowman, *Great Kiwi Slang*, p. 51, 2002

crash hot!
used for expressing enthusiastic approval *NEW ZEALAND*

- —David McGill, *David McGill's Complete Kiwi Slang Dictionary*, p. 34, 1998

crashing bore *noun*
a very tedious or tiresome person or thing *UK, 1934*

- What a crashing bore it [cleaning] is. — *The Guardian*, 2nd December 2002

crash-out *noun*
an escape from prison or jail *US, 1940*

- He was the last guy I would have picked as a partner in a crash-out; he was very young, this would be his first break, and Christ alone knew how his reflexes would work if something went wrong. —Horace McCoy, *Kiss Tomorrow Good-bye*, p. 7, 1948

crash out *verb*
to escape from prison *US*

- He's on the lam from a pen back east, crashed out with twenty years to serve of a thirty-year bank-robber rap. —Jim Thompson, *A Swell-Looking Babe*, p. 77, 1954

crash pad *noun*

1 a room, apartment or house where people stay for the night or temporarily, with or without knowing the owner, with or without formal invitation *US, 1967*

- In one week, four Digger-sponsored crash pads were busted by the cops. —Abbie Hoffman, *Revolution for the Hell of It*, p. 54, 1968
- [R]ent or work deals with the urban gov't to take over spaces that have been abandoned for use as carpentry shops, garages, theaters, etc., rent whole houses, but don't let them turn into crash pads. —*The Digger Papers*, p. 15, August 1968
- Landis was taken into custody at his home at 243 Bradford street, which police said was being used as a "crash pad" for assorted homeless hippies. — *San Francisco Chronicle*, p. 3, 19th June 1968
- The White House will become a crash pad for anybody without a place to stay in Washington. —Jerry Rubin, *Do It!*, p. 256, 1970
- As you read this, hundreds of world travellers are huddled together in crash pads, town squares, or on the backs of buses[.] —Richard Neville, *Play Power*, p. 212, 1970
- Forty Berkeley police who made simultaneous raids at 6 a.m. on 220 suspected "crash pads" suspected of harboring scores of runaway juveniles found only four youngsters and five adults. — *San Francisco Examiner*, p. 7, 31st July 1970
- But for eighteen-year-old Linda, the Village was a different scene: crash pads and acid trips, freaking out and psychedelic art, witches and warlocks. —J. Anthony Lukas, *Don't Shoot – We Are Your Children*, p. 169, 1971

2 a pit of soft dirt or sand used for low-level stunt falls *US*

- —John Cann, *The Stunt Guid*, p. 57,

-crat; -ocrat *suffix*
when linked with a subject, used to designate a person that may be dominant, or aspiring to dominance, or pretending superiority within that subject-area *UK, 1937*
A sarcastic or humorous application of the conventional sense found in such words as 'aristocrat', 'democrat', 'plutocrat', etc. The root in most conventional senses ends with an 'o'; in colloquial or journalistic usage the 'o' is generally incorporated.

- [A] fellow mediacrat who writes for a Jewish newspaper in the US[.] —*Jerusalem Post*, 3rd February 1999

crate *noun*

1 an old and dilapidated car *US, 1927*

- The stink they raised was so funky that the manager at the bus terminal tried to shift the whole party to a dirty creaky old crate.[.]freight car, —Mezz Mezzrow, *Really the Blues*, p. 234, 1946
- An instant later he saw Taylor suddenly bomb the Pontiac forward. Collucci said, "Kick the piss out of this crate!" —Iceberg Silm (Robert Beck), *Death Wish*, p. 238, 1977

2 a railway boxcar *US*

- —Ramon Adams, *The Language of the Railroader*, p. 38, 1977

crate of sand *noun*

a truck hauling sugar *US*

- —Montie Tak, *Truck Talk*, p. 39, 1971

crater *noun*

1 a deep sore caused by repeated injections *US*

- I had cultivatd a crater and always shot through the same hole. It sure looked awful, though. —Piri Thomas, *Down These Mean Streets*, p. 202, 1967
- —Edward R. Bloomquist, *Marijuana*, p. 337, 1971

2 a facial blemish *US*

- —Collin Baker et al., *College Undergraduate Slang Study Conducted at Brown University*, p. 101, 1968

crates *noun*

the female breasts *NEW ZEALAND*

- —Louis S. Leland, *A Personal Kiwi-Yankee Dictionary*, p. 29, 1984

c-rat grenade *noun*

a crude hand grenade fashioned by the Viet Cong using a US combat rations can as the grenade shell *US*

- —Gregory Clark, *Words of the Vietnam War*, p. 79, 1990

c-rats *noun*

US Army combat rations *US, 1965*

Vietnam war coinage, used since.

- It brought the usual water, C-rats and mail. —Charles Anderson, *The Grunts*, p. 106, 1976
- Negative, m' man, fuck a bunch a C rats. I mean meat. —Larry Heinemann, *Close Quarters*, p. 142, 1977
- —Keith Nolan, *Battle for Hue*, p. 191, 1983
- —Linda Reinberg, *In the Field*, p. 53, 1991
- The bombs thudded, the ground trembled, Taylor cranked the volume higher. "Rock 'n' roll is C-Rats for the soul," he said, using the military slang for field rations. —*Boston Globe*, p. 1, 27th January 1991

craven *adjective*

gluttonous, greedy *GRENADA*

- —Richard Allsopp, *Dictionary of Caribbean English Usage*, p. 175, 1996

cravenous *adjective*

gluttonous, greedy *VIRGIN ISLANDS, BRITISH*

- —Richard Allsopp, *Dictionary of Caribbean English Usage*, p. 175, 1996

cravetious *adjective*

greedy *TRINIDAD AND TOBAGO, 1956*

- —Lise Winer, *Dictionary of the English/Creole of Trinidad & Tobago*, 2003

cravicious *adjective*

gluttonous, greedy *BARBADOS*

- —Richard Allsopp, *Dictionary of Caribbean English Usage*, p. 176, 1996

crawfish *verb*

to evade someone or something *US, 1842*

In nature, the only defence available to the crawfish is to bury itself in mud or silt, moving backwards.

- "Aw shut up," Green said impatiently. "You're crawfishing and you know it." —Raymond Chandler, *The Long Goodbye*, p. 33, 1953

crawl *noun*

1 in television and film making, titles that roll from the bottom of the screen to the top *US*

- —Ralph S. Singleton, *Filmaker's Dictionary*, p. 39, 1990

2 in pool, backspin applied to the cue ball *US, 1954*

- —Mike Shamos, *The Illustrated Encyclopedia of Billiards*, p. 63, 1993

crawl *verb*

1 to behave sycophantically *AUSTRALIA, 1880*

- He fears no one, crawls to no one, bludges on no one, and acknowledges no master. —Nino Culotta (John O'Grady), *They're A Weird Mob*, p. 204, 1957
- So what makes you think I'll crawl to you? —*Janie Stagestruck*, p. 113, 1972
- Well, yes, she (and we) certainly crawled to Ron [US President Ronald Reagan] very humiliatingly indeed. —*The Guardian*, 20th April 2001

2 to search somewhere *US*

- But the dresser had been pulled out, and the three scrapbooks stacked across it had been replaced unevenly, one upside down. The pad had been crawled. —James Ellroy, *Suicide Hill*, p. 740, 1986

crawler *noun*

1 a sycophant *AUSTRALIA, 1827*

- 'Yeah. I'm on the side of the law.' 'A crawler,' Porter said disgustedly[.] —Jon Cleary, *The Long Shadow*, p. 79, 1949
- Otherwise you could be called a 'crawler', or a 'brown nose', and these are not good things to be called. —John O'Grady, *Aussie Etiket*, p. 19, 1971

2 a despicable or contemptible person; a low person *AUSTRALIA, 1917*

- This was soft stuff; married men's stuff! Admit this sort of thing and any sort of crawler could pass himself off as a man! —Frank Dalby Davison, *The Wells of Beersheba*, p. 90, 1965

crawling *adjective*

verminous *UK, 1961*

Shortened from 'crawling with lice'.

crawling horror *noun*

in computing, obsolete hardware or software *US*

- —Eric S. Raymond, *The New Hacker's Dictionary*, p. 110, 1991

crawl with *verb*

to be alive, or filled with, people of a specified type *UK, 1925*

- [T]his Italian region [Tuscany] is crawling with tourists in summer. —*The Independent*, 31st August 2002
- A lot of stories break there [the BBC News website], and at the moment it's crawling with journalists. —*The Guardian*, 25th March 2002

cray *noun*

1 a one-hundred dollar note *NEW ZEALAND*

From the note's red colour, shared with the crayfish.

- —David McGill, *David McGill's Complete Kiwi Slang Dictionary*, p. 31, 1998

2 a crayfish *AUSTRALIA, 1909*

- Tasmanians attempt to solve it by decreasing the population of scallops and crays. —Douglas Baglin and John O'Grady, *Ladies and Gentlemen*, p. 21, 1966

crayon *noun*

a programmer who works on a supercomputer designed by Cray Research *US*

- —Eric S. Raymond, *The New Hacker's Dictionary*, p. 111, 1991

craythur *noun*

strong alcohol, usually whiskey *IRELAND*

The spelling reflects the Hiberno-English pronunciation of 'creature'.

- A scrumptious meal was served to all, plus a drop of the Craythur and a free raffle for numerous prizes was held. —*Laois Nationalist*, 15th October 2002

crazies *noun*

phencyclidine, the recreational drug known as PCP or angel dust *US*

- —Peter Johnson, *Dictionary of Street Alcohol and Drug Terms*, p. 50, 1993

crazy *noun*

a person who engages in erratic or unpredictable behaviour *US, 1867*

- Such groups have become known as "crazies." —*San Francisco Examiner and Chronicle*, p. 1, 23rd February 1969
- In one room crazies planned to rent planes and fly over the Rose Bowl dropping antiwar leaflets on the crowd. —Jerry Rubin, *Do It!*, p. 38, 1970
- The "crazies" might still be winning headlines, but largely they had lost the campuses. They had taken to playing revolution mostly with themselves. —William Tulio Divale, *I Lived Inside the Campus Revolution*, p. 195, 1970
- And the "crazies" are beginning to get to me too. I wonder if we really are going to have a full scale revolution in this country. —Anonymous, *Go Ask Alice*, p. 78, 1971
- In a town full of bedrock crazies, nobody even notices an acid freak. —Hunter S. Thompson, *Fear and Loathing in Las Vegas*, p. 24, 1971
- This town has always had its share of craizies. —*Slacker*, 1992

crazy *adjective*

1 excellent, exciting, superlative *US, 1948*

- It's "crazy," it's the "world's best." —*San Francisco Call-Bulletin*, 31st October 1947

- Look at all those poor innocent souls who go to sleep and get up early for work while we're still having a crazy time. —Hal Ellson, *The Golden Spike*, p. 113, 1952
- "Crazy," said her mother, returning to her household chores. —Steve Allen, *Bop Fables*, p. 4, 1955
- Isn't this the craziest! — *Rebel Without a Cause*, 1955
- Things were "cool" and cool things "gassed" the initiates and anything that was particularly cool was "crazy." —Robert Sylvester, *No Cover Charge*, p. 287, 1956
- [H]e blew his now-settled-down-into-regulated-design "crazy" notes[.] —Jack Kerouac, *The Subterraneans*, p. 13, 1958
- — *The Daily Colonist (Victoria)*, 16th April 1959
- Andy used first. "Crazy." —Clarence Cooper Jr, *The Scene*, p. 17, 1960
- —J. L. Simmons and Barry Winograd, *It's Happening*, p. 169, 1966
- At other times, it is wonderfully descriptive, such as when dealers talk about making "crazy dollars" with which to buy a "baby Benz," a Mercedes 190. — *Washington Post*, p. 9, 12th September 1989
- —Connie Eble (Editor), *UNC-CH Campus Slang*, p. 2, Fall 1996

2 enthusiastic *for, about* or *to do* something *UK, 1779*

- Great hamburgers and french fries. You're just not crazy about the decor, with those golden arches. —Kenneth C. Davis, *Don't Know Much About Geography*, p. 61, 1992
- Everyone is going crazy about Wap phones – but nobody really knows how they will change the world. — *The Guardian*, 13th April 2000
- —James Villas, *Crazy For Casseroles*, 2003

3 (used of a particular card in poker and other card games) capable of being played as a card of any value *US*
The same as the more common 'wild'.

- —Albert H. Morehead, *The Complete Guide to Winning Poker*, p. 260, 1967

4 many *US*

- Everybody thinks they can make crazy dollars, but they confused. —Terry Williams, *The Cocaine Kids*, p. 86, 1989

crazy *adverb*

▸ **like crazy**
of behaviour, to the utmost *US, 1924*

- We will be studying this thing like crazy for the next year. — *BBC News*, 16th November 1999

crazy alley *noun*
the area in a prison in which mentally ill patients are confined *US*

- —William K. Bentley and James M. Corbett, *Prison Slang*, p. 3, 1992

crazy as a bedbug *adjective*
extremely eccentric, mad *US, 1918*

- Every character in this movie, with the possible exception of the fresh-cheeked local lass Betty of Cardiff (Tara Fitzgerald) is crazy as a bedbug, and none of them know it[.] — *Chicago Sun-Times*, 12th May 1995

crazy-ass *adjective*
very crazy *US*

- They're like that crazy mother in the first Dirty Harry movie. 'Member that crazy-ass mother? — *Natural Born Killers*, 1994

crazy doctor *noun*
a psychiatrist or other psychotherapist *US*

- —Leo Rosten, *The Joy of Yinglish*, p. 119, 1989

crazy Eddy *noun*
high quality phencyclidine, the recreational drug known as PCP or angel dust *US*

- —Peter Johnson, *Dictionary of Street Alcohol and Drug Terms*, p. 50, 1993

crazy eight; crazy 8 *noun*
a discharge from the US Army for mental unfitness *US*
From US Army Regulation 600–208.

- —Carl Fleischhauer, *A Glossary of Army Slang*, p. 12, 1968

crazy freak *noun*
a pretty girl *US*

- — *American Speech*, p. 302, December 1955: 'Wayne University slang'

crazy house *noun*
a mental hospital *US, 1887*

- I just hope no one sees me down in those bottoms talking to a monkey. Why, they would put me in the crazy house sure as shootin'. —Wilson Rawls, *Summer of the Monkeys*, p. 120, 1976

Crazy Joey *nickname*
Joey Gallo, reputed member of the Gambino crime family in New York, shot to death at Umberto's Clam House in 1972 *US*

- It was before Apalachin and before Crazy Joey decided to take on a boss and start a war. — *Goodfellas*, 1990

crazy large *adjective*
doing very well *US*

- —Kenn "Naz" Young, *Naz's Dictionary of Teen Slang*, p. 26, 1993

crazy like a fox; crazy as a fox *adjective*
eccentric; cunning *US, 1935*

- He was crazy as a fox but there was nothing you could do about it, not even when he insisted on going out screwing in spats and a straw hat. —Charles Raven, *Underworld Nights*, p. 31, 1956

crazy oats *noun*
wild rice *CANADA*

- The French settlers came closer to the truth when they called it "crazy oats" since it is a close relative to the oat family. — *Saskatchewan News*, p. 4/1, November 1963

crazyweed *noun*
marijuana *UK, 1998*

- —Mike Haskins, *Drugs*, p. 287, 2003

creaker *noun*
an old person *US, 1958*

- This family is full of creakers. We creak along to about the age of 96. —Flannery O'Connor, *Letter to Richard Stern*, p. 574, 14th April 1964

cream *noun*

1 a bribe *US*

- —Bill Reilly, *Big Al's Official Guide to Chicagoese*, p. 23, 1982

2 a variety of hashish from the Parvatti Valley in Northern India *UK*

- —Nick Jones, *Spliffs*, p. 83, 2003

CREAM; cream *noun*
money *US*

- —Wu-Tang Clan, *C.R.E.A.M. (Cash Rules Everything Around Me)*, 1994
- "This "cream" that they keep chanting about getting," he pointed to Sinbad and co., "what do they mean?" "C.R.E.A.M. Cash Rules Everything Around Me. It's just an old word for money." —Diran Adebayo, *My Once Upon A Time*, p. 59, 2000
- —Connie Eble (Editor), *UNC-CH Campus Slang*, p. 3, October 2002

cream *verb*

1 to ejaculate; to secrete vaginal lubricants during sexual arousal *US, 1915*

- Sometimes, though, I'd go home afterwards, after having had a hard-on for four hours of making out on the floor and in the bleachers, but without creaming, and it really gave you a sore dick. — *The Berkeley Tribe*, p. 13, 5th-12th September 1969
- Rich whores cream, poor whores dream. —Dennis Wepman et al., *The Life*, p. 149, 1976
- Blowjob to orgasm? They call it "full French" here. Usually runs five dollars more than half-and-half. Cream in her mouth? —Gerald Paine, *A Bachelor's Guide to the Brothels of Nevada*, p. 15, 1978
- Leslie gives the gorgeous geisha a raunchy workout, which ends with him creaming all over her grateful face, after which he goes to work on Mai's still-smouldering snatch[.] — *Adult Video*, p. 23, August/September 1986
- Geezers like him have been creamin' over it[.] —Nick Barlay, *Curvy Lovebox*, p. 56, 1997
- [P]orn directors demanding bigger tits and porn stars creaming themselves to hot sweaty house music[.] — *Mixmag*, p. 4, April 2003

2 by extension, to gush with excitement *US*

- It is only "history" that today critics cream all over Moby Dick, the dear perceptive things. —Jack Kerouac, *Letter to Neal Cassady*, p. 173, 8th December 1948
- Wouldn't he cream his jeans if he saw me and knew what I was there for! —Mickey Spillane, *My Gun is Quick*, p. 153, 1950
- Movement, it creams me to be talking to you. —Bernard Wolfe, *The Late Risers*, p. 228, 1954
- Inneresting, inneresting, you cream over that word. Inneresting. — *Saturday Night Fever*, 1977
- [T]he idea of no more school nearly made him cream in his jeans. —James Ellroy, *Blood on the Moon*, p. 19, 1984
- The PD's office would cream over something like this. —Carl Hiaasen, *Tourist Season*, p. 21, 1986
- I mean, you'll just cream your jeans when you see it. — *Drugstore Cowboy*, 1988

3 to defeat someone convincingly *US, 1940*

- [H]e had benched his regulars and sent in his scrubs, and as a result, the Rockets had been creamed the next three times in a row. —Max Shulman, *Rally Round the Flag, Boys!*, p. 224, 1957
- I'm doing almost seventy, not bad for two up. Then Jim Lush creams past me on a big new lilac Vespa S.S. —Ian Hebditch, *Weekend, The Sharper Word*, p. 135, 1969
- We creamed them 7-0. —Erich Segal, *Love Story*, p. 11, 1970

- We're gonna get creamed. —*A Few Good Men*, 1992
- "Bruno left it on the bus after Friday's game," sniffed Fuzzy indignantly. "I guess he was bummed we got creamed again." —C.D. Payne, *Youth in Revolt*, p. 198, 1993
- I took on three gypsies, creamed the lot of them and was back home by eight o'clock that night. —Lenny McLean, *The Guv'nor*, p. 95, 1998

4 to kill someone *US, 1940*

- [W]hen she had the chance to get Evello creamed before that congressional committee she put in her bid[.] —Mickey Spillane, *Kiss Me Deadly*, p. 143, 1952

5 to hit someone or something *US, 1942*

- When Ali creamed him in the eighth, Foreman pirouetted, spiraled downward using the whole ring for his fall[.] —Bill Cardoso, *The Maltese Sangweech*, p. 304, 1984
- You can't strap into your seat belt, without almost getting creamed by a bus. —*Gone in 60 Seconds*, 2000

6 to rob someone *UK*

- I said to Andrew, "Andy, do you reckon you can cream that place?" He said, "No problem, just keep a look out for me." —Lenny McLean, *The Guv'nor*, p. 22, 1998

▸ cream the rag
to boast in an offensive manner *US*
The mastubatory image is powerful.

- —*American Speech*, p. 233, Autumn-Winter 1971: 'Checkschmuck! The slang of the chess player'

▸ cream your jeans
while dressed, to respond to a sexual stimulus by secreting fluids *US, 1942*

- I reckon the first bastards who cop an eyeful of this lot will either cream their jeans or come across swiftly with the folding stuff. —Barry Humphries, *Bazza Pulls It Off!*, 1971
- By the end they were squirming and squealing and carrying on like they were creaming in their jeans. —Guy Owen, *The Flim-Flam Man and the Apprentice Grifter*, p. 226, 1972

▸ get creamed
to be knocked from your surfboard and pounded into the ocean, ocean bottom or pilings of a pier *US*

- —Dennis Aaberg and John Milius, *Big Wednesday*, p. 208, 1978

cream bun *noun*
a Protestant *UK: SCOTLAND*
Glasgow rhyming slang for **HUN**.

- —Michael Munro, *The Complete Patter*, 1996

cream cookie *noun*
a bookmaker; a betting shop *UK: SCOTLAND*
Glasgow rhyming slang for **BOOKIE**.

- —Michael Munro, *The Patter, Another Blast*, 1988

cream cracker *noun*
an unsavoury lower-class person *IRELAND*
Rhyming slang for **KNACKER**; also abbreviated to 'creamers'.

- Then the bird, roysh [right], you'd have to feel sorry for her, she puts on the life jacket and all the cream crackers down the back are giving it, 'Very sexy on ye.' —Paul Howard, *Ross O'Carroll-Kelly*, p. 92, 2003

cream crackered *adjective*
tired out, exhausted *UK, 1992*
Rhyming slang for **KNACKERED** (exhausted); a conventional 'cream cracker' is a savoury biscuit.

- He was cream crackered after fucking last night and all he wanted was to watch some telly[.] —Greg Williams, *Diamond Geezers*, p. 109, 1997
- We already did it up and down and side to side and follow the leader and round the houses. I was cream crackered. —Jeremy Cameron, *Brown Bread in Wengen*, p. 62, 1999

creamed *adjective*
soiled by vaginal secretions as a result of sexual arousal *UK*

- [W]e exchanged numbers like French kisses, at 2 a.m. / my creamed knickers rode the night bus home —Bernadine Evaristo, *Lara*, 1997

creamer *noun*

1 an employee who steals from the till *UK*

- —Angela Devlin, *Prison Patter*, p. 41, 1996

2 someone who is over-excited or scared; by implication, someone who is not in control of his emotions or his affairs *AUSTRALIA*

- —Alex Buzo, 1973

3 in the car sales business, an excellent car *US*

- —*Cars*, p. 40, December 1953

creamie *noun*

1 a sexually attractive young woman *UK*

- [P]ick up a creamie an' where can I take her for a bit of recreation? —Alan Bleasdale, *Boys From the Blackstuff*, 1982

2 an outstanding student selected after advanced flying training to become a flying instructor *UK*
Also variant 'creamy'.

- —Colin Strong and Duff Hart-Davis, *Fighter Pilot*, 1981

creamies *noun*
the viscuous discharge of a sexually transmitted infection *US*

- —*Kiss*, 1969

cream off *verb*
to orgasm *UK*
Based on **CREAM** (to ejaculate).

- JAMIE: Yer not lookin' for that kind of movie then? DEEP THROAT: I could cream off quicker to "Aerobics Oz Style". —Chris Baker and Andrew Day, *Lock, Stock... & Spaghetti Sauce*, p. 250, 2000

creampie *noun*
semen seeping from a vagina, anus or mouth *US*
A fetish that oozed from US Internet pornography in the early 2000s; the semen is as often as not an artificially concoted look-alike.

- Creampie vids mean to correct this by showing sex as it actually happens, plus bodily fluids getting licked off the floor. —*Village Voice*, p. 179, 23rd April 2002
- Howard Schiffer is not the first parent to be alarmed that his teenager was learning about sex from either sniggering peers or a deeply confused culture that veers between sexual repression and Internet "creampie" raunch. —*Salon.com*, 12th May 2004

cream puff *noun*

1 a huff *UK*
Glasgow rhyming slang.

- Aw, don't take the cream puff. —Michael Munro, *The Original Patter*, 1985

2 an effeminate male *US*

- —Lou Shelly, *Hepcats Jive Talk Dictionary*, p. 9, 1945

3 an easy target, easy prey *US, 1915*

- Blue had been right about Frascati. He was a real cream puff. He didn't give us an anxious moment all during the play. —Iceberg Slim (Robert Beck), *Trick Baby*, p. 299, 1969

4 in the used car business, a well-preserved car *US, 1949*

- If you're in the market for a real good used car, ask your Chrysler dealer to show you through his cream puff row. —*Of Anchors, Bezels, Pots and Scorchers*, September 1959
- —John Edwards, *Auto Dictionary*, p. 37, 1993

creamy *noun*
a person of mixed European and Australian Aboriginal heritage *AUSTRALIA, 1912*

- Poor old Billy Button, railway ganger at the Caroline, married to a yeller piece, father of a mob o' creamies, got a bit of a stock-run, tryin' to win a race for twenty years – and now he's done it! —Xavier Herbert, *Poor Fellow My Country*, p. 88, 1975

creamy *adjective*

1 quarter-caste Australian Aboriginal *AUSTRALIA, 1912*

- The only stock he has is creamy children. —Xavier Herbert, *Poor Fellow My Country*, p. 43, 1975

2 sexually attractive *US, 1947*
Influenced by 'creamy' (delightful), this use is from **CREAM** (to secrete fluids when sexually aroused).

- [Y]ou meet some creamy bird, say she's twenty-six or whatever, right? —James Hawes, *Dead Long Enough*, p. 265, 2000

3 pleasing, excellent *UK, 1889*
Teen slang.

- —*American Weekly*, p. 2, 14th August 1955
- He drove a creamy Corvette with red leather upholstery – on those rocket jobs that does three hundred miles an hour. —Frederick Kohner, *Gidget*, p. 47, 1957

crease *noun*
in sports betting, a distortion created when strong fan support for one team or contestant creates an imbalance in the odds which can be exploited by a clever bettor *US*

- —Avery Cardoza, *The Basics of Sports Betting*, p. 43, 1991

crease; crease up *verb*

to laugh immoderately, to collapse with laughter; to cause such a condition *UK, 1984*

An image of being bent double with laughter.

- [T]he first fight was played out and they again creased with laughter. — *Guardian Unlimited*, 1st February 2001
- [H]is younger brother would make cutting jokes – things which Ian interpreted as genuinely rude – and have everyone creased up with laughter. — *The Observer*, 20th May 2001

cred *noun*

credibility *UK*

- [G]unpoint abduction didn't have enough cred to be anything more than an implausible but as-yet-uneliminated possibility. — Christopher Brookmyre, *Not the End of the World*, p. 192, 1998
- When the Hollister incident cut deep into their cred, they labeled rowdy, outlaw motorcylists the "one-percenters." — Ralph "Sonny" Barger, *Hell's Angel*, p. 41, 2000

cred *adjective*

acceptable to your peers; hence, fashionable *UK*

Abbreviated from **STREET-CRED** (the quality of being understood by urban youth), in turn shortened from 'street-credible'.

- The Prodigy [...] seem to have been dumbed down, put on a critical backburner, lost their cred edge. — John Robb, *The Nineties*, p. 213, 1999
- In the glam era, Bolan was "cred" only to start with while Bowie was never anything else. — Simon Napier-Bell, *Black Vinyl White Powder*, p. 277, 2001

credentials *noun*

the genitals *US, 1968*

- — J.E. Lighter, *Historical Dictionary of American Slang, Volume One*, p. 518, 1994

credit *noun*

1 an achievement or accomplishment *US*

From the acknowledgement of service rendered in the entertainment industry.

- He asked me if I ever done armed robbery before. I read him my credits. — *Reservoir Dogs*, 1992

2 a reduction of a jail sentence due to good behaviour *US*

- — Vincent J. Monteleone, *Criminal Slang*, p. 61, 1949

credit card *noun*

1 a boyfriend *UK*

- — Peter Chippindale, *The British CB Book*, p. 154, 1981

2 a favour owed *US*

- If he wants to screw Amad he'll call in some credit cards at Vacaville. — Vincent Patrick, *Family Business*, p. 244, 1985

creek *noun*

▸ down the creek

in oil drilling, wasted or lost *US*

- He let his grease go down the creek and got run-off (fired). — Jerry Robertson, *Oil Slanguage*, p. 47, 1954

▸ up the creek

in trouble *US, 1918*

Variant phrases include 'up the creek without a paddle' and 'up the creek with a paddle in a barbed-wire canoe'.

- The local bogies [police] made inquiries and he was up the creek. — Charles Raven, *Underworld Nights*, p. 31, 1956
- If not you're up the creek without a paddle, and no mistake. — Troy Kennedy Martin, *Z Cars*, p. 135, 1962

creep *noun*

1 an objectionable or unpleasant person; a dull or insignificant person *US, 1926*

- Then some nits comes in and stands near me; some middle-aged creeps with toffee-nosed accents[.] — John Peter Jones, *Feather Pluckers*, p. 102, 1964
- What's this! Women's magazines. You poor creep! — Geoff Brown, *I Want What I Want*, p. 75, 1966
- I got this here album by this bunch of Limey creeps called Jethro Tull[.] — Lester Bangs, *Psychotic Reactions and Carburetor Dung*, p. 133, 1973
- My name's Dawn, you creep[.] — Jay Saporita, *Pourin' It All Out*, p. 86, 1980
- I'm a creep / I'm a weirdo[.] — Radiohead, *Creep*, 1993
- He was a wart in creep's clothing. — Jonathan Gash, *The Ten Word Game*, p. 190, 2003

2 a prisoner who is neither respected nor liked *US*

- Very often, a 'creep' to escape general harassment will pay tribute to one particular 'gee' and will be taken under his protection. — *American Speech*, p. 194, October 1951: 'A study of reformatory argot'

3 a thief who operates in hotels, entering unlocked rooms as the guests sleep *UK, 1877*

- Often creeps would check into the hotel, in order to have a plausible explanation if challenged by a corridor patrol. — Dev Collans with Stewart Sterling, *I was a House Detective*, p. 32, 1954
- Some Creeps wear thick woollen socks over their shoes. — Charles Raven, *Underworld Nights*, p. 11, 1956

4 a drug addict who relies on the kindness of other addicts for small amounts of drugs *US*

- — Eugene Landy, *The Underground Dictionary*, p. 60, 1971

5 a furtive arrival or departure *US*

- The Chicagoans, including some of the Austin High Gang, were pulling a creep in a dozen different directions. — Mezz Mezzrow, *Really the Blues*, p. 129, 1946

▸ on the creep

used of a thief who is working *UK*

- — Angela Devlin, *Prison Patter*, p. 82, 1996

creep *verb*

1 to work as a sneak-thief *US, 1928*

- Sapphire Harris, the King of Creeps, had crept a gaff on a tip-off passed on to him by Larry[.] — Charles Raven, *Underworld Nights*, p. 191, 1956

2 to ambush someone with the intent of seriously injuring or killing them *US*

Prison usage.

- — Paul Glover, *Words from the House of the Dead*, 1974

3 to attempt to have a secret sexual relationship with someone's boyfriend or girlfriend *US*

- — Don R. McCreary (Editor), *Dawg Speak*, 2001

4 to be sexually unfaithful *US*

- — David Claerbaut, *Black Jargon in White America*, p. 61, 1972

5 to dance *UK, 1984*

A late 1950s usage, not necessarily in reference to 'the Creep', a short-lived 1950s dance sensation.

6 to escape *US*

- Still even those who managed to creep were reapprehended with stifling regularity. — Malcolm Braly, *On the Yard*, p. 205, 1967

creep!

go away! *UK*

- — *News Chronicle*, 22nd May 1958

creep-and-cuss *adjective*

(used of car traffic) extremely congested *US*

- It was creep-and-cuss traffic for two hours, beginning at 11:30 a.m. On Bayshore Freeway, autos were bumper-to-bumper from Candlestick south to San Bruno, about eight miles. — *San Francisco Examiner*, p. 1, 17th August 1964

creeped out *adjective*

worried, disturbed *US*

Extends from **THE CREEPS** (a feeling of dread).

- It was midafternoon, and I was more than a little creeped out[.] — Janet Evanovich, *Seven Up*, p. 15, 2001

creeper *noun*

1 a burglar *US, 1906*

- Bill had been a creeper at one time, who had made his living by breaking into homes and apartments. — Nathan Heard, *Howard Street*, p. 36, 1968
- He was a daytime hotel creeper and hitting maybe four to six hotel rooms in the best downtown hotels every time he went to work. — Joseph Wambaugh, *The Blue Knight*, p. 20, 1973
- — Angela Devlin, *Prison Patter*, p. 41, 1996

2 a prostitute or prostitute's accomplice who steals from the clothes of the prostitute's customer *UK*

- "And what about the two creepers -?" "Not my friends[.]" — Anthony Masters, *Minder*, p. 167, 1984

3 a marijuana cigarette *US*

- — Jim Emerson-Cobb, *Scratching the Dragon*, April 1997

4 in trucking, a very low gear *US, 1937*

- — Mary Elting, *Trucks at Work*, 1946
- — *American Speech*, p. 42, February 1963: 'Trucker's language in Rhode Island'

5 in car repair, a platform on casters that allows a mechanic to lie on their back and roll under a car to work on it *US*

- — Lewis Poteet, *Car & Motorcyle Slang*, p. 57, 1992

creeperbud; creeper *noun*

a subtly potent variety of marijuana *US, 1981*

Because it 'creeps up on you'.

- —Richard A. Spears, *The Slang and Jargon of Drugs and Drink*, p. 128, 1986
- —Mike Haskins, *Drugs*, p. 287, 2003

creepers *noun*

soft-soled, quiet shoes favoured by burglars *US*

- —Vincent J. Monteleone, *Criminal Slang*, p. 61, 1949
- —Joseph E. Ragen and Charles Finston, *Inside the World's Toughest Prison*, p. 796, 1962
- —Inez Cardozo-Freeman, *The Joint*, p. 491, 1984

creepers!

used for expressing surprise *US, 1944*

An abbreviated version of **JEEPERS, CREEPERS!**.

- Creepers! If any of my buddies in the lower income group could see me here, I wonder what they'd say. [Freckles and his Friends comic strip]—*San Francisco News*, p. 29, 17th October 1946

creep game *noun*

a scheme in which a prostitute and her confederate rob the prostitute's customer *US, late 1960s*

- Lying in bed, he explained to her the new hap-nings and also started to teach her in the art of using knock-out drops plus, "The Creep game" where one girl does the physical work while another would rob the victims pockets.—Babs Gonzales, *I Paid My Dues*, p. 97, 1967

creep house *noun*

a brothel where customers are routinely robbed *US, 1913*

- Warnings of immorality were probably less effective than warnings that some brothels were creep houses or panel houses wherein visitors were robbed of money and gold watches.—Irving Lewis Allen, *The City in Slang*, p. 180, 1993

creepie-peepie *noun*

a small, hand-held television camera *US, 1952*

An unsuccessful attempt to recreate the popularity of **WALKIE-TALKIE**.

- —*American Speech*, October 1953

creeping crud *noun*

any skin rash suffered in tropical and jungle environments *US*

- "Jungle rot," "New Guinea crud" or "the creeping crud" are U.S. servicemen's names for any & every kind of tropical skin disease. —*Time*, p. 76, 13th August 1946

creeping Jesus *noun*

a hypocritically pious, sneak and coward *UK, 1818*

- I am a cranky frustrated mature spinster employed as a kind of ... creepin Jesus sprat-catcher[.]—Alan Bleasdale, *Boys From the Blackstuff*, 1982

creeping Jesus!

used as an expression of surprise, frustration, anger, etc *AUSTRALIA, 1961*

- Creeping Jesus, I thought. That screws the press credentials.—Hunter S. Thompson, *Fear and Loathing in Las Vegas*, p. 269, 1971
- I had cancer of the yoni! Creeping Jesus, I thought, how embarrassing.—Annie Lamott, *Hard Laughter*, p. 153, 1980

creeping mocus *noun*

a non-existent disease *US*

- —*American Speech*, p. 304, December 1947: 'Imaginary diseases in army and navy parlance'

creep joint *noun*

a brothel where customers' clothes are searched and robbed *US, 1921*

- Took my public-school training in three jails and a plenty of poolrooms, went to college in a gang of tea-pads, earned my Ph.D. in more creep joint and speakeasies and dancehalls than the law allows.—Mezz Mezzrow, *Really the Blues*, p. 3, 1946
- What kinda creep joint you run here?—William Burroughs, *Naked Lunch*, p. 200, 1957
- [W]e went through plush lavender and redwood catacombs to the inner sanctum of a florid-faced wheeler dealer in a four-hundred dollar suit who was oozing distractive charm like a pickpocket whore in a creep joint.—Iceberg Slim (Robert Beck), *The Naked Soul of Iceberg Slim*, p. 142, 1971

creepo *noun*

a contemptible person *US, 1960*

- Remember that I did for love of you, you creepo; this gives me rights.—Salman Rushdie, *The Satanic Verses*, p. 343, 1988

creep out *verb*

to create a very uncomfortable feeling in someone *US, 1983*

- Actually, Dad, that room creeps me out.—Francince Pascal, *Tearing Me Apart (Sweet Valley High Senior Year No. 36)*, p. 87, 2001

creep pad *noun*

a creep joint *US*

- I swear I'm no sky-pilot, but a creep pad turns into a confession booth as soon as I squat in it.—Mezz Mezzrow, *Really the Blues*, p. 88, 1946

creeps *noun*

▸ **the creeps**

a sensation of dread *UK, 1849*

- What was waiting for us up ahead, if we'd got a preview, would have given us the creeps.—Mezz Mezzrow, *Really the Blues*, p. 139, 1946
- That Johnny – he gave me the creeps.—Derek Bickerton, *Payroll*, p. 27, 1959
- She gave me the creeps, though. I don't know why.—*Basic Instinct*, 1992
- Cocky men like that gave me the creeps – yet sometimes they had their uses.—Rita Cirtesi, *Pink Slip*, p. 2, 1999
- Ian McLagan of the Small Faces remembers being with [Andrew Oldham...] when he punched a journalist. "It gave me the creeps, and I realised then that maybe he wasn't just the fun-loving, pot-smoking head he pretended to be."—Simon Napier-Bell, *Black Vinyl White Powder*, p. 61, 2001

creeps!

used as an all-purpose, non-profane expression of surprise *US*

- Creeps! What the heck is that? [Tiffany Jones comic strip]—*San Francisco Chronicle*, p. 24, 24th May 1971

creepster *noun*

a revolting person *US*

An embellished **CREEP**.

- Look at this crazy girl following some stranger into his diner trying to save her boyfriend who isn't even her boyfriend anymore because of some weird creepster dream.—Francesca Lia Block, *Missing Angel Juan*, p. 349, 1993

creepy *adjective*

annoying; producing anxiety or nervousness in others *US, 1919*

- Do you have any control over how creepy you allow yourself to get? —*As Good As It Gets*, 1997

creepy-crawly *noun*

an insect; a spider *UK, 1960*

- [T]urning over rocks and then going all squeamish when lots of little creepy-crawlies all scurry away[.]—*The Guardian*, 6th June 2003

creepy-peepy *noun*

1 battlefield radar *US*

Vietnam war usage.

- —*Time*, p. 32, 10th December 1965
- —Carl Fleischhauer, *A Glossary of Army Slang*, p. 12, 1968

2 a television mini-camera *US*

- —Rachel S. Epstein and Nina Liebman, *Biz Speak*, p. 52, 1986

crem *noun*

a *crem*atorium *UK*

Cremation has been legal in the UK since 1884; it is a matter of conjecture how soon this familiar shortening took a hold.

- —John Betjeman, *A Wembley Lad' and 'The Crem*, 1971

Creme de Menthe French *noun*

oral sex performed with a mouth full of creme de menthe alcohol *US*

- —J.R. Schwartz, *The Official Guide to the Best Cat Houses in Nevada*, p. 164, 1993

cremmie; cremmy *noun*

a *crem*atorium *AUSTRALIA*

An elaboration of **CREM**.

- —Barry Humphries, *A Nice Night's Entertainment*, 1982
- The relatives are wantin hauf [half]-price at the cremmy.—Michael Munro, *The Patter, Another Blast*, 1988

crepes *noun*

trainers (sneakers) *JAMAICA*

- —Richard Allsopp, *Dictionary of Caribbean English Usage*, p. 178, 1996

crepesoles *noun*

trainers (sneakers) *GUYANA*

- —Richard Allsopp, *Dictionary of Caribbean English Usage*, p. 178, 1996

crest *verb*

to smile *US*

From the branded toothpaste.

- —Vann Wesson, *Generation X Field Guide and Lexicon*, p. 42, 1997

cretin *noun*

an incompetent and despicable person *US*

- — *Coevolution Quarterly*, p. 29, Spring 1981: 'Computer slang'
- — Eric S. Raymond, *The New Hacker's Dictionary*, p. 112, 1991

cretinous *adjective*

in computing, incompotent, dysfunctional *US*

- — *Coevolution Quarterly*, p. 29, Spring 1981: 'Computer slang'
- — Eric S. Raymond, *The New Hacker's Dictionary*, p. 112, 1991

crevice *noun*

the vagina *UK, 1937*

Widespread in pornographic literature.

crew *noun*

1 a criminal gang *US, 1946*

- Most of my crew got washed on the way. — Edwin Torres, *Carlito's Way*, p. 6, 1975
- Even after expenses on the machines and kicking money back to his crew boss, he's got to wind up with a thousand a week. — Vincent Patrick, *The Pope of Greenwich Village*, p. 11, 1979
- After any kind of a drug haul, everyone in the crew indulged to the utmost. — *Drugstore Cowboy*, 1988
- His troubles with these two were to prove typical of the problems he encountered when he first tried to establish a crew. — Terry Williams, *The Cocaine Kids*, p. 14, 1989
- To become a member of a crew, you've got to be one hundred percent Italian so that they can trace all your relatives back to the old country. — *Goodfellas*, 1990
- They could have a lovers' quarrel, give the dope to a new boyfriend not in the crew, sell it themselves, smoke it themselves. — Richard Price, *Clockers*, p. 5, 1992
- Bout the Crew gonna smoke us? — Jess Mowry, *Way Past Cool*, p. 21, 1992
- I wasted most of it with your brother and his crew. — *Gone in 60 Seconds*, 2000

2 a tightly-knit group of close friends *US*

- [T]hose guys made me a member of the crew. — Frederick Kohner, *Gidget*, p. 37, 1957
- — *San Francisco Sunday Examiner & Chronicle*, p. 20, 2nd September 1984
- — Ellen C. Bellone (Editor), *Dictionary of Slang*, p. 8, 1989
- So, anyway, the whole crew is going to this party in the Valley. — *Clueless*, 1995
- The crew won't be visiting school today. — Karline Smith, *Letters to Andy Cole*, p. 139, 1998

3 a group of graffiti artists who work together *US*

- — Jim Crotty, *How to Talk American*, p. 141, 1997

crew chief *noun*

the leader of a unit of a criminal gang *US*

- It was exactly the one Andre had given to him, complete with hug, when Strike's mother had gone to Andre four years ago, after some long-gone local crew chief had taken Strike out for his haircut. — Richard Price, *Clockers*, p. 281, 1992

crew dog *noun*

a crew chief in the US Air Force *US*

- — *Seattle Times*, p. A9, 12th April 1998

crew hog *noun*

a miscellaneous member of a film crew *US*

- The typical porn crew – camera operators, assistant directors, box-cover photographers, and other 'crew hogs' – does not have as good a time as you might think. — Ana Loria, *1 2 3 Be A Porn Star!*, p. 30, 2000

crew pie *noun*

a pizza made by a pizza parlour's employees *US*

- — *Maledicta*, p. 10, 1996: 'Domino's pizza jargon'

crew runner *noun*

the leader of a criminal gang *US*

- Kip's become quite the litte crew runner since you left. — *Gone in 60 Seconds*, 2000

crew up *verb*

to form a group to commit a crime *US*

- If we put out the word that we're crewing up for a one-time-only job, what do you think that'll yield. — *Gone in 60 Seconds*, 2000

cri!

used as an expression or shock, surprise, etc *UK, 1984*

A shortening of **CRIKEY!**.

crib *noun*

1 a person's dwelling; an apartment or house *US, 1809*

- He had chicks sleeping with cats in nice cribs downtown. — Claude Brown, *Manchild in the Promised Land*, p. 109, 1965
- Nat wasn't making but twenty dollars ($20) a night but he told me when I got out I could shack up at his crib for a few weeks while getting my strength back. — Babs Gonzales, *I Paid My Dues*, p. 25, 1967
- But I'll tell you what, you meet me over to my crib in about an hour. — Donald Goines, *El Dorado Red*, p. 78, 1974
- So you hang 'round your crib a lot, waiting for something to happen. — Edwin Torres, *San Francisco*, p. 52, 1975
- Next time you bogart your way into a nigger's crib, an' get all in his face, make sure you do it on white boy day. — *True Romance*, 1993
- This is all right. Two minutes from your crib, ten minutes from your work. — *Jackie Brown*, 1997
- You bring a woman back to your crib for some lovemaking, the song you put on depends on the woman, the type of lovemaking you intend to do, right? — *Gone in 60 Seconds*, 2000

2 a room or shack where a prostitute plies her trade *US, 1846*

- All of nigger Chicago is lousy with police stations, gambling joints, and whore cribs. — Iceberg Slim (Robert Beck), *Mama Black Widow*, p. 74, 1969

3 a house or shop chosen for a robbery *CANADA, 1976*

- What we gotta do is wait till we got a crib set up, clout a good car for the getaway, then change to the truck a few blocks from the job. — Hugh Garner, *The Intruders*, p. 106, 1976

4 in trucking, the sleeping compartment behind the driver *US*

- — "Slingo", *The Official CB Slang Dictionary Handbook*, p. 18, 1976

5 a holiday cottage *NEW ZEALAND*

Reported by Margaret Moore in 1980.

6 a prison cell *US*

- — Charles Shafer, *Folk Speech in Texas Prisons*, p. 202, 1990

7 a gambling establishment *UK, 1823*

- — *The Annals of the American Academy of Political and Social Sciences*, p. 123, May 1950

8 a brakevan (caboose) *US*

- — Ramon Adams, *The Language of the Railroader*, p. 39, 1977

9 a safe *US*

- — Joseph E. Ragen and Charles Finston, *Inside the World's Toughest Prison*, p. 796, 1962

10 a receptacle for carrying a meal to work *AUSTRALIA, 1941*

- As most Australians know the enduring popularity of the dog on the tucker box at Gundagai, a famous sculpture notwithstanding, is not because the dog faithfully sat guarding the tucker box, but because it shat on its master's 'crib'. — Nancy Keesing, *Lily on the Dustbin*, p. 49, 1982

11 a meal taken during the major break at work *AUSTRALIA, 1890*

- Joe Allingham was telling me about one day they were out mustering and the black lad had forgotten his crib. — Sam Weller, *Old Bastards I Have Met*, p. 40, 1979

12 any form of written aid to cheating in examinations *UK, 1900*

The original (1841) meaning was specifically 'a literal translation illicitly used by students'; the current vaguer sense gained purchase during C20.

13 *crib*bage (a card game) *UK, 1885*

14 crack cocaine *UK, 1998*

- — Mike Haskins, *Drugs*, p. 281, 2003

crib *verb*

1 to reside somewhere *US*

- I coasted the 'Hog' into the curb outside the hotel where Kim, my newest, prettiest girl, was cribbing. — Iceberg Slim (Robert Beck), *Pimp*, p. 272, 1969
- All the chorus chicks from the Lido was cribbing there (20) so I knew I was gonna have a ball. — Babs Gonzales, *Movin' On Down De Line*, p. 15, 1975

2 to cheat in an examination *UK, 1891*

- Cribbing on examinations is apparently a world-wide practice. — Max Shulman, *Guided Tour of Campus Humor*, p. 3, 1955

3 to plagiarise something; to copy something *UK, 1941*

- It's an easy act for a dcotor to crib. — Philip Wylie, *Opus 21*, p. 159, 1949
- But Recess [a children's TV catroon] is the runt of the genre: malnourished and over-eager; cribbing from its neighbours as it struggles to make the grade. — *The Guardian*, 27th July 2001

cribbage peg *noun*

the leg *UK, 1923*

Rhyming slang.

cribber *noun*

a horse that chews the wood of its stall *US*

- — Dan Parker, *The ABC of Horse Racing*, p. 145, 1947

crib course *noun*
a basic, easy course of study *US, 1970*
• Crib course in wireless basics. —Clint Smith, *Wireless Telecommuincations FAQs*, p. Back Cover, 2001

crib girl *noun*
a woman working in a supply shack or supply room *US*
• I turned to the crib girl and said, "Let me have S-14." —Chester Himes, *If He Hollers Let Him Go*, p. 17, 1945

cribhouse *noun*
a brothel *US, 1916*
• He wasn't anything, for he got cut by a coke-frisky piano player in a cribhouse where he had gone to take out a little in trade on his protection account. —Robert Penn Warren, *All the King's Men*, p. 13, 1946

cribman *noun*
a professional safecracker *US*
• —John R. Armore and Joseph D. Wolfe, *Dictionary of Desperation*, 1976
• He's in the big house for all day and night, a new fish jammed into a drum with a cribman, who acts like a gazoonie. —*San Francisco Examiner*, p. 26, 17th August 1976

crib sheet *noun*
a piece of paper with information used for studying or cheating in a examination or test *US, 1960*
• Finally, do not carry notes or crib sheets on your person – this can only reuslt in the gravest of problems. —O. Ray, *Auditin*, p. 33, 2003

crib time *noun*
a meal time during work hours *AUSTRALIA, 1890*
• I was fencing near a per-way gang and I joined them to share their billy at crib time[.] —Patsy Adam-Smith, *Folklore of the Australian Railwaymen*, p. 154, 1969

cricket *adjective*
fair, following customs and rules *UK, 1900*
• Why don't we just get hold of them and – It's not cricket maybe but —Herman Wouk, *The Caine Mutiny*, p. 85, 1951

cricket score odds *noun*
in horse racing, odds of 100–1 or higher *AUSTRALIA*
• —Ned Wallish, *The Truth Dictionary of Racing Slang*, p. 19, 1989

cricket team *noun*
a very sparse moustache *AUSTRALIA*
There are eleven men – or hairs – on each side. Noted by Barry Prentice, 1984.

cricks; crix *noun*
theatre critics *US*
• —Wilfred Granville, *The Theater Dictionary*, p. 47, 1952

crigs *noun*
the testicles *UK: NORTHERN IRELAND*
From the Irish *creig* (rock) or *cnag* (knob).
• He was so big I could nearly run in between his legs. Before I kicked the crigs off him that is. —Patrick McCabe, *The Butcher Boy*, p. 65, 1992

crikey!
used as an expression of surprise, frustration, etc *UK, 1838*
A euphemism for **CHRIST!**.
• Crikey, I remember a billy [goat] we met in Aden. —Dymphna Cusack, *Picnic Races*, p. 102, 1962
• Crikey, it was only a dollar last time I was here. —Bill Wannan, *Folklore of the Australian Pub*, p. 4, 1972
• "Hush-hush all the way, Mr . Regan," Kelly said. "Crikey, nobody knows who did the blag" —*The Sweeney*, p. 50, 1976
• —Ivor Limb, *Footy's No Joke!*, p. 20, 1986

crikey Moses!
used for registering surprise or anguish *UK*
• Ooooh. It stings. Oh crikey Moses. Now look what I've done. —Elizabeth George, *Missing Joseph*, p. 182, 1993
• "Gay?" said Virginia, smiling with tremendous satisfaction. "Crikey Moses." I took her reverting to the Bunty lexicon of swearing to mean she was much moved. —Mavis Cheek, *The Sex Life of My Aunt*, p. 254, 2002

crill *noun*
a marijuana cigarette laced with cocaine *UK*
A lazy pronounciation of **CRIPPLE**.

crill *adjective*
inferior *US*
• —Kenn "Naz" Young, *Naz's Dictionary of Teen Slang*, p. 27, 1993

crills *noun*
crack cocaine *US*
• —Maria Hinojas, *Crews*, p. 167, 1995

crillz *noun*
an abode *US*
• —Connie Eble (Editor), *UNC-CH Campus Slang*, p. 3, April 1997

crim *noun*
a *crim*inal *US, 1909*
• [Y]ou get sick of hearing the same old stories – crims have a rich but repetitive fantasy life. —Kevin Mackey, *The Cure*, p. 100, 1970
• —Louis S. Leland, *A Personal Kiwi-Yankee Dictionary*, p. 30, 1984
• Women think I'm a rough old crim. —Shaun Ryder, *Shaun Ryder... in His Own Words*, 1996
• Spain is populated entirely by leather-skinned crims and dodgy pool-boys armed with shotguns. —*FHM*, p. 25, June 2003

crim *adjective*
involved in crime; criminal *AUSTRALIA*
• You promised not to see any of your old crim mates. —Kathy Lette, *Girls' Night Out*, p. 180, 1987

Crimble *noun*
▷ see: **CHRIMBO**

crime *noun*
someone who doesn't pay debts *AUSTRALIA*
From the addage 'crime doesn't pay'.
• —Ned Wallish, *The Truth Dictionary of Racing Slang*, p. 19, 1989

crime *verb*
in the military, to discipline someone *AUSTRALIA, 1932*
• He hasn't even threatened to crime anyone yet. —Eric Lambert, *The Veterans*, p. 100, 1954

Crime Dog *nickname*
Fred McGriff (b.1943), a first baseman (1986–2001) with a large impact on the defence of the team he was playing for *US*
An allusion to the comic strip character McGruff, a crime-fighting dog.

crimey *noun*
a criminal *US, 1969*
• "My crimey here thinks the way to go is more drugs," he says[.] —Terry Williams, *The Cocaine Kids*, p. 86, 1989

crimp *noun*
1 an obstacle or impediment *US, 1896*
• I can understand that must have been a bitch of a crimp. —Iceberg Slim (Robert Beck), *Airtight Willie and Me*, p. 59, 1979

2 a discreet bend or crease in a playing card that assists a cheat or a conjuror to prosper
• The crimp can be put anywhere on the card, but the corners or long sides are generally used. —*Card Trick Central*, 2003

crimp *verb*
to intrude; to impede something *US*
• That hump of a husband of hers was crimpin' on my time. —Edwin Torres, *After Hours*, p. 218, 1979

crimp cut *noun*
in a card game, a cheating move in which the cheater cuts the deck of cards to an intended spot *US*
• —Peter O. Steiner, *Thursday Night Poker*, p. 409, 1996

crimper *noun*
1 a hairdresser *UK*
• —Janey Ironside, *A Fashion Alphabet*, p. 190, 1968
• —Paul Baker, *Polari*, p. 170, 2002

2 in gambling, a person who crimps cards so as to be able to identify them in future hands *US*
• Besides dice tats and 7UPS, there were volumes for nail nickers and crimpers (card markers), hand muckers and mit men (card switchers), as well as card counters and shiner players. —Stephen Cannell, *Big Con*, p. 143, 1992

crimps *noun*
tight curls of hair *BAHAMAS*
• —John A. Holm, *Dictionary of Bahamian English*, p. 54, 1982

crimson butterfly *noun*
the penis *UK*
• —Richard Herring, *Talking Cock*, p. 30, 2003

crimson rambler *noun*
a bedbug *US, 1906*
• —Vincent J. Monteleone, *Criminal Slang*, p. 61, 1949

crimson tide; crimson wave *noun*
the bleed period of the menstrual cycle *US*
• — *The Museum of Menstruation and Women's Health*, January 2001

cringe *noun*
methamphetamine *US*
Probably from **CRANK**, but the image of cringing is powerful when discussing a methamphetamine user.
• Teener means one sixteenth of an ounce. One eighth is called a eightball. You ever do cringe? That's what we call meth, cringe. —Joseph Wambaugh, *Finnegan's Week*, p. 40, 1993

cringe!; oh cringe!
used as an expression of abject embarrassment, apology or regret; also, in sympathy with another's embarrassment *UK, 1984*
A vocalisation of a probable physical reaction to such embarrassment.

crink *noun*
1 a sharp, searing pain *US, 1970*
• [T]hat was the direction in which she turned in order to ease a crink in her neck. —Roger Zelazny, *Bring Me the Head of Prince Charming*, p. 187, 1991
2 methamphetamine sulphate in powdered form *US*
• —Walter L. Way, *The Drug Scene*, 1977

crinkle *noun*
paper money *UK, 1954*
• [T]he penman, who never drops [passes forged cheques] himself, has to send a minder, known as a topper, to keep an eye on the dropper, make sure he doesn't pocket the crinkle[.] —Charles Raven, *Underworld Nights*, p. 81, 1956

crinkle-top *noun*
a black person with natural or afro hair *US*
• —Edith A. Folb, *runnin' down some lines*, p. 233, 1980

crip *noun*
1 an easy course in school or college *US, 1923*
• — *Time Magazine*, p. 46, 24th August 1959
• —Andy Anonymous, *A Basic Guide to Campusology*, p. 7, 1966
2 a *cripple* *US, 1893*
• In the middle of the second month we attended a wedding of an old whore and a crip on the abandoned stage of a Main Street theater closed for repairs. —Clancy Sigal, *Going Away*, p. 238, 1961
• The stump [of a rat's foot] was ragged like a trap had hacked off the foot, or perhaps the old crip had chewed it off in a valorous escape from the trap. —Iceberg Slim (Robert Beck), *Mama Black Widow*, p. 71, 1969
• —Multicultural Management Program Fellows, *Dictionary of Cautionary Words and Phrases*, 1989
• How'd dem crips get the jack inside? —Seth Morgan, *Homeboy*, p. 331, 1990

cripes!
used as a euphemistic exclamation in place of 'christ!' *AUSTRALIA, 1903*
• Cripes, how I wanted her to open up. —Mickey Spillane, *One Lonely Night*, p. 59, 1951
• [H]it cripes knows many sex-starved Brit sheilahs[.] —Barry Humphries, *Bazz Pulls It Off!*, 1971
• 'I hope nothing has happened to your mate.' 'Cripes no,' said Clancy. —Bill Wannan, *Folklore of the Australian Pub*, p. 57, 1972
• Oh, cripes. Do you have change for a dollar? All I have is these stupid Nepalese coins. — *Something About Mary*, 1998

crippen!
used for registering surprise or annoyance *UK, 1984*
Using the name of notorious murderer Dr H. H. Crippen, 1860–1910; ultimately a variation of **CHRIST!**.

crippie *noun*
high quality marijuana *US*
• The top grade marijuana, known in street slang as "crippie," sold for about $5,000 a pound. — *Sun Sentinel (Fort Lauderdale, Florida)*, p. 1B, 4th June 2002

cripple *noun*
1 a marijuana cigarette *US*
Evolves from **CRUTCH** (a device to support the butt).
• — *American Speech*, p. 87, May 1955: 'Narcotic argot along the Mexican border'
• —Richard A. Spears, *The Slang and Jargon of Drugs and Drink*, p. 128, 1986
• —Mike Haskins, *Drugs*, p. 287, 2003
2 a knee-boarder; a surfer who rides kneeling rather than standing *US*
Derogatory, spoken with disdain by experienced surfers.
• — Surf Punks, *Oh No! Not Them Again!*, 1988
3 in pool, a shot that cannot be missed or a game that cannot be lost *US, 1964*
• —Steve Rushin, *Pool Cool*, p. 11, 1990
• —Mike Shamos, *The Illustrated Encyclopedia of Billiards*, p. 63, 1993
4 a disabled railway carriage *US*
• —Norman Carlisle, *The Modern Wonder Book of Trains and Railroading*, p. 261, 1946

cripple-cock *noun*
1 cider *UK: ENGLAND*
Dorset slang, subsequently adopted as a brand name. Possibly playing on **BREWER'S DROOP** (an inability to acheive an erect penis symptomatic of drunkenness).
• —J.B. Smith, *Somerset & Dorset Notes & Queries*, 1979
2 used as a general pejorative *UK*
A slur on virility.
• —Sean McConville, *The State of the Language*, 1980

crippleware *noun*
computer software that operates up to a point but then is disabled until payment for a full working version is made *US*
• —Eric S. Raymond, *The New Hacker's Dictionary*, p. 112, 1991

crip up *verb*
(of an able-bodied actor) to play the rôle of a disabled character *UK*
From **CRIP** (a cripple).
• — *Should We Be Laughing?*, 17th February 2004

cris *noun*
amphetamines *US, 1971*
A misspelling and/or a play on **CRYSTAL** (methamphetamine), or an abbreviation of Spanish *cristal*.

Crisco Frisco *nickname*
San Francisco, California *US*
An allusion to the vegetable shortening often used as a sexual lubricant and San Francisco's reputation as a city with a large homosexual population.
• — *Maledicta*, p. 226, 1979: 'Kinks and queens: linguistic and cultural aspects of the terminology for gays'

crisp *noun*
1 crack cocaine mixed with marijuana *US*
• —Lois Stavsky et al., *A2Z*, p. 24, 1995
2 any alcohol *US*
• —Don R. McCreary (Editor), *Dawg Speak*, 2001

crisp *adjective*
1 excellent, perfect, appealing *US*
• —Lois Stavsky et al., *A2Z*, p. 24, 1995
2 said of a table in pool where there is no need to adjust a shot to compensate for the table surface *US*
• —Mike Shamos, *The Illustrated Encyclopedia of Billiards*, p. 63, 1993

crisper *noun*
a commissioned act of arson *UK*
• Gerbil who does crispers – translated, means he burns houses of drugs dealers and the like – for Glasgow and Liverpool folk, for a small fee. —Jonathan Gash, *The Ten Word Game*, p. 164, 2003

crispie *noun*
a currency note; hence the plural is also generalised as money *UK*
Extended from 'crisp', the quality of new notes.
• [They buy] each other a drink and pay for it with greenies, crispies, lottery tickets, drinking vouchers. —Ann Barr and Peter York, *The Official Sloane Ranger Handbook*, p. 117, 1982

crispo *adjective*
mentally deficient due to drug abuse *US*
• —Kenn "Naz" Young, *Naz's Dictionary of Teen Slang*, p. 27, 1993

crisp packet *noun*
a prison bed *UK*
• —Angela Devlin, *Prison Patter*, p. 41, 1996

crispy *noun*
a badly burnt person or corpse *US, 1981*
An abbreviation of **CRISPY CRITTER**.
• —J.E. Lighter, *Historical Dictionary of American Slang, Volume One*, p. 523, 1994

crispy *adjective*
1 good, stylish, fashionable, pleasing *US*
• You're crispy, you're the shit, you really are, Joey. You're the man. —Joel Rose, *Kill Kill Faster Faster*, p. 141, 1997
• Even a Fubu sweat suit; I like it to be fresh, crispy, brand-new, looking right. —*Style*, p. 96, July 2001
2 slightly diminished in mental facilities due to prolonged alcohol and/or drug use *US*
• —Connie Eble (Editor), *UNC-CH Campus Slang*, p. 2, March 1979

crispy critter *noun*
1 a burnt corpse, especially one burnt by napalm *US, 1967*
The term was borrowed from the branded name of a sugar-frosted oat cereal cut out in animal shapes, popular in the US in the 1960s.
• —*Current Slang*, p. 15, Summer 1970
• [E]verything was transformed into Crispy Critters for half a dozen clicks in any direction you would have cared to point; everything smelling of ash and marrow and spontaneous combustion[.] —Larry Heinemann, *Paco's Story*, p. 15, 1986
• While the white-hot cloud drained out, dissipating in the slight afternoon breeze, a squad found two crispy critters inside. —Charles W. Sasser and Craig Roberts, *One Shot One Kill*, p. 198, 1990
• —Linda Reinberg, *In the Field*, p. 54, 1991
• It's a two-story dump on North Bond Street and, of course, there are no witnesses – just a bunch of burned furniture and one crispy critter in the middle room. —David Simon, *Homicide*, p. 447, 1991
2 a badly burnt hospital patient *US*
• —*Maledicta*, p. 35, 1988–1989: 'More Milawukee medical maledicta'
3 a burnt pizza *US*
• —*Maledicta*, p. 10, 1996: 'Domino's pizza jargon'

criss; kris *adjective*
stylish, attractive, fashionable; used of the new or desirable *JAMAICA*
Adapted from an abbreviation of 'crisp' (fresh). UK black usage.
• —L. Emilie Adams, *Understanding Jamaican Patois*, p. 53, 1991
• [S]omeone said that the party was going to have "two criss gal fe every man"[.] —Karline Smith, *Moss Side Massive*, 1994
• [There] was usually an assortment of some criss-looking vehicles parked outside. —Donald Gorgon, *Cop Killer*, 1994
• —Chester Francis-Jackson, *The Official Dancehall Dictionary*, p. 12, 1995
• I had a cris' pair ah Versace jeans dat got bun [burnt] up. —Courttia Newland, *Society Within*, p. 11, 1999
• "[Y]ou tink she the one?" "Mmm. I feel so." "She kris, no question. Young still –" "That's it !" I interrupted. "Exactly. A new bird. Not tired, or damaged, Y' unnerstan'?" —Diran Abedayo, *My Once Upon a Time*, 2000
• —Peter L. Patrick, *Some Recent Jamaican Creole Words*, 2003

crissake; crisake; krissake
used for expressing frustration or annoyance
• Oh, for crissake woman stop your bloody nattering. Stop your damn mouth. —John Peter Jones, *Feather Pluckers*, p. 18, 1964
• Well spruce up with this Wettex anyway for krissake me jolly old tar. —Barry Humphries, *Bazza Pulls It Off!*, 1971
• [I]t slept two of us, for crisake. —Johnny Speight, *It Stands to Reason*, p. 20, 1973

criss-cross *noun*
an amphetamine tablet, especially Benzadrine™ (amphetamine sulphate) *US*
From the cross scoring on the tablet; possibly a play on **CRIS**, a central nervous system stimulant (amphetamine).
• —US Department of Justice, *Street Terms*, August 1993
• —Mike Haskins, *Drugs*, p. 279, 2003

criss-cross *verb*
to simultaneously ingest lines of heroin and cocaine by nasal inhalation
• —Robert Ashton, *This Is Heroin*, p. 208, 2002
• —Mike Haskins, *Drugs*, p. 274, 2003

cristal *noun*
MDMA, the recreational drug best known as ecstasy *UK*
• —Mike Haskins, *Drugs*, p. 289, 2003

cristina; cris; crist; christina *noun*
methamphetamine *US, 1971*
A personification of **CRYSTAL** (powdered methamphetamine).
• —Walter L. Way, *The Drug Scene*, 1977
• And amidst all this Crist' poppin' and wristwatches / I just sit back and just watch[.] —Eminem (Marshall Mathers), *Marshall Mathers*, 2000
• —Mike Haskins, *Drugs*, p. 279, 2003

crit *noun*
1 a critic *UK, 1743*
• The release of Radiohead's Hail to the Thief is finally upon us, meaning that pop crits can assume their most chin-stroking stance and pontificate at length. —*The Guardian*, 10th June 2003
2 a criticism; a critique *UK, 1908*
3 a state of critical mass; critical size *US, 1957*
A colloquialism from nuclear physics.

crit-hit *noun*
a critical success *UK*
A combination of **CRIT** (a critic) and 'hit' (a success).
• "My Little Eye" is a ruthless horror movie whose innovative extra features only make it more troubling. A low-budget crit-hit, it follows five twenty something contestants in a 'reality TV' webcast. —Nev Pierce, *BBCi*, 11th April 2003

critical *adjective*
1 dangerously ill or injured *UK*
• A Middleton man has appeared before Rochdale magistrates accused of attempting to kill his partner, who is critical in hospital after white spirits ignited on her. —*Middleton Guardian (Manchester)*, 18th July 2003
2 impressive, amazing *US*
• —Connie Eble (Editor), *UNC-CH Campus Slang*, p. 3, November 1990
• —Vann Wesson, *Generation X Field Guide and Lexicon*, p. 42, 1997
3 (used of a wave) very steep, threatening to break at any moment *US*
• —Grant W. Kuhns, *On Surfing*, p. 115, 1963

criticism/self-criticism *noun*
a structured group discussion in which members of the group analyse and comment on their own behaviour and that of other members of the group *US*
Popular in leftist groups in the US in the late 1960s and early 70s.
• Hanisch understood the process of consciousness-raising, gleaned from Chinese cadre criticism/self-criticism and speaking bitterness sessions as "a political action," not a therapeutic one. —Paula Rabinowitz, *Black & White & Noir*, p. 206, 2002
• And a lot more interesting than "It Ain't Me Babe" which is bogged down by the criticism/self-criticism mania common in the early 70's. —Aaron Cometbus, *Despite Everything*, p. 312, 2002

critter *noun*
a creature, especially a horse or a cow; a person (usually disparaging) *US, 1815*
• So, slimy critter that he is, we're right back where we started from. —Lester Bangs, *Psychotic Reactions and Carburetor Dung*, p. 194, 1976

crivens!
used for registering shock, horror or astonishment *UK*
Probably a compound of 'Christ!' and 'heavens!'.
• The Purple played on Radio One! Crivens. —Kevin Sampson, *Powder*, p. 106, 1999
• A fairly inoffensive question you would have thought, but crivens! —*Ministry*, p. 7, October 2002

crix *noun*
▷ see: **CRICKS**

cro *noun*
a prostitute *AUSTRALIA*
A variation of **CROW**.
• —Kylie Tennant, *The Joyful Condemned*, 1953

croack *noun*
a mixture of crack and an amphetamine *US*
• —Peter Johnson, *Dictionary of Street Alcohol and Drug Terms*, p. 51, 1993

croagies *noun*
the testicles *US*
• She didn't do anything like that, try to kick me in the croagies or anything. —George V. Higgins, *Penance for Jerry Kennedy*, p. 191, 1985

croak *noun*

a combination of crack cocaine and methamphetamine *UK, 1998*

A variation of **CRACK** with fatal forebodings: **CROAK** (to die).

• —Mike Haskins, *Drugs*, p. 293, 2003

croak *verb*

1 to die *UK, 1812*

From the death-rattle.

• Old Mr. Keller croaked, but he was almost eighty yeas old, he shoulda croaked[.]—Darryl Ponicsan, *The Last Detail*, p. 59, 1970
• You mean all them under them sheets croaked it?—Barry Humphries, *Bazza Pulls It Off!*, 1971
• It would be a great sensation to croak out on a bike ... I'd like a fucking smash, got to be a good one, or I don't want to go.—Paul E Willis, *Profane Culture*, p. 58, 1978
• Wasn't Jimmy about your age when he croaked?—Anthony Masters, *Minder*, p. 164, 1984
• [A] couple of years later he went and croaked it, coke-induced heart attack.—Jenny Eclair, *Camberwell Beauty*, p. 96, 2000

2 to kill someone *UK, 1823*

• Let her go ahead and croak him.—Chester Himes, *The Real Cool Killers*, p. 45, 1959
• I recall pointing to the loaded double-barreleled shotgun on my wall and replying, with a smile, that I would croak at least two of them before they go away.—Hunter S. Thompson, *Hell's Angels*, p. 143, 1966
• "Party" tried his fists and muscle until the pimp game croaked him. —Iceberg Slim (Robert Beck), *Pimp*, p. 41, 1969
• When I heard they croaked Charlie I freak out, almost went back to shootin scag.—Charles W. Moore, *A Brick for Mister Jones*, p. 105, 1975

3 to inform on someone, to betray someone *US*

• —R. Frederick West, *God's Gambler*, p. 223, 1964

4 in pool, to miscue *CANADA, 1988*

• —Mike Shamos, *The Illustrated Encyclopedia of Billiards*, p. 63, 1993

croaker *noun*

1 a doctor, especially a company doctor *UK, 1879*

Sometimes abbreviated to 'croak'.

• We'll knock off this croaker.—William J. Spillard and Pence James, *Needle in a Haystack*, p. 18, 1945
• He was just having a stomach attack from overeating and constipation, and the most he needed was some bicarbonate of soda and a physic, not a croaker.—Mezz Mezzrow, *Really the Blues*, p. 95, 1946
• —Norman Carlisle, *The Modern Wonder Book of Trains and Railroading*, p. 261, 1946
• The old croaker on 102nd finally lost his mind altogether and no drugstore would fill his scripts[.]—William Burroughs, *Junkie*, p. 25–26, 1953
• From this croaker up on 76th Street. He used to write for me, you know, scripts, prescriptions. I turned a trick with him.—James Mills, *The Panic in Needle Park*, p. 91, 1966
• He told me he knew of a couple of people who were keeping up habits making croakers.—Herbert Huncke, *The Evening Sun Turned Crimson*, 1980
• TERRY SOUTHERN: Bill, these are the pharmaceutical samples, sent by the drug companies [...] to Doc Tom Adams, the writing croak. —Victor Bockris, *With William Burroughs [The Howard Marks Book of Dope Stories]*, p. 31, 1997

2 a doctor who provides narcotics for an addict *US*

A specialisation of the previous sense.

• —Home Office, *Glossary of Terms and Slang Common in Penal Establishments*, 1978

3 a habitual complainer *AUSTRALIA, 1882*

In C19 US use, but now obsolete there.

• —Gilbert H. Lawson, *A Dictionary of Australian Words and Terms*, 1924
• It was only the croakers made a fuss.—Wilda Moxham, *The Apprentice*, p. 142, 1969
• The croakers did a right about turn after the Caulfield Stakes.—Wilda Moxham, *The Apprentice*, p. 178, 1969

4 a dying person, or one who has just died *UK, 1873*

From **CROAK** (to die).

croc *noun*

a crocodile *AUSTRALIA, 1884*

• Crocs are meaner, more aggressive. Gators get fat and lazy.—Carl Hiaasen, *Tourist Season*, p. 115, 1986

crock *noun*

1 an unpleasant or worthless person, object or experience; a waste of time *US, 1944*

Contemptuously abbreviated from the familiar **CROCK OF SHIT**.

• Your ideas are a crock, I added to myself.—Jack Kerouac, *The Dharma Bums*, p. 72, 1958
• We may all know that Sensira are a crock, yeah? But the fact at the moment is that the country likes them.—Kevin Sampson, *Powder*, p. 126, 1999

2 an old and worn-out person or thing *UK, 1889*

• It's the old crocks' house you want to put him up at.—Troy Kennedy Martin, *Z Cars*, p. 82, 1962

3 a person with medical problems which are the result of abusive living *US*

• —*Maledicta*, p. 68, Summer/Winter 1978: 'Common patient-directed pejoratives used by medical personnel'

4 a computer program that normally functions but fails if modified at all *US*

• —Guy L. Steele et al., *The Hacker's Dictionary*, p. 50, 1983

5 nonsense *US*

An abbreviation of **CROCK OF SHIT**.

• "Now what kind of crock are you giving us?" No crock. It's every word gospel.—Ken Kesey, *One Flew Over the Cuckoo's Nest*, p. 297, 1962

crock *adjective*

broken; no good *AUSTRALIA*

• He spends an hour rummaging for fresh crock clocks and two hours on repair work.—*Weekend*, p. 7, 1st June 1957

C rock *noun*

crack cocaine *UK*

c (cocaine) plus **ROCK** (crack cocaine).

crock cut *noun*

a haircut which gives the appearance of having been achieved by placing a bowl over the subject's head *US, 1947*

• —Frederic G. Cassidy, *Dictionary of American Regional English, Volume One*, p. 855, 1985

crocked *adjective*

1 wrong, awry *UK*

• [R]etain all the best lawyers and barristers just in case it all goes crocked and avoid any kinda attention.—J.J. Connolly, *Layer Cake*, p. 31, 2000

2 drunk *US, 1917*

• In the first place, they were both slightly crocked.—J.D. Salinger, *Catcher in the Rye*, p. 86, 1951
• I had traveling money and got crocked in the bar downstairs.—Jack Kerouac, *On the Road*, p. 76–77, 1957
• He was pretty well crocked, which made me apprehensive. If Dally was drunk and in a dangerous mood..."—S.E. Hinton, *The Outsiders*, p. 54, 1967
• —Collin Baker et al., *College Undergraduate Slang Study Conducted at Brown University*, p. 102, 1968
• The rollers [police] finally got crocked. The whores took them around the Chinese screen into bedrooms.—Iceberg Slim (Robert Beck), *Pimp*, p. 214, 1969
• Both of them were half-crocked, drunken leers on their faces. —Herbert Huncke, *The Evening Sun Turned Crimson*, p. 119, 1980
• "[P]iss artists" are "boozy", "fluffy", "well-gone", "legless", "crocked"[.]—Peter Ackroyd, *London The Biography*, p. 359, 2000

crock of shit *noun*

1 an unpleasant or worthless person, object or experience; a waste of time *US, 1951*

A conventional 'crock' (a pot) of **SHIT** (excreta).

• Now, stop stallin', man, or else admit all this professional stuff you're talkin' about is a crock of shit.—*48 Hours*, 1982
• [T]ell 'em that the cruise is a crock of shit an' not worth getting up for.—Colin Butts, *Is Harry on the Boat?*, p. 130, 1997
• I've seen the end of the Ecstasy rainbow and it's not a pot of gold, but a crock of shit.—Wayne Anthony, *Spanish Highs*, p. 187, 1999

2 nonsense, lies *US, 1945*

• They said God took her away. That's a crock of shit. God don't do evil things like that[.]—Rita Mae Brown, *Rubyfruit Jungle*, p. 27, 1973
• Now, stop stallin', man, or else admit all this professional stuff you're talking about is a crock of shit.—*48 Hours*, 1982

crocky *noun*

a crocodile *AUSTRALIA, 1943*

Mostly juvenile.

crocodile *noun*

1 a long line of school children walking two abreast *UK, 1870*

• Parents, teachers, girls: on this speech day I welcome back our old pupil, Sally Banner who was once one of your number, who walked in the school crocodile to the school chapel[.]—Dorothy Hewett, *The Chapel Perilous*, p. 9, 1972

2 a smile *UK*

Rhyming slang.

• Come on, give us a crocodile.—Ray Puxley, *Cockney Rabbit*, 1992

3 a horse *AUSTRALIA, 1897*
Possibly a jocular elaboration of **CROCK** (a worthless or worn-out thing, hence a broken-down horse).

crocus *noun*

1 a doctor *UK, 1785*
Originally 'croakus'.
- —Paul Baker, *Polari*, p. 170, 2002

2 a fair-weather trader who appears for a while when winter is over *UK*
- —Patrick O'Shaughnessy, *Market Traders' Slang*, 1979

Croker *nickname*
Croke Park, the official head quarters of the Gaelic Athletic Association (GAA) *IRELAND*
- Sure, the new Croker's an absolute gobsmacker, a monolith to rival the Nou Camps and Rose Bowls of this world and, for those fortunate enough to secure a corporate sponsored seat, the pre-match spread is lavish. It is but a single venue, however, and the GAA is a national organisation. — *Irish Times*, 15th April 2000

Cromwell *noun*
a Vauxhall Cavalier car *UK*
Citizens' band radio slang; Cromwell and the Cavaliers were on opposing sides in the English Civil War.
- —Peter Chippindale, *The British CB Book*, p. 161, 1981

cronky *adjective*

1 fraudulent, dishonest *AUSTRALIA*
From 'cronk' (corrupt).
- I only came down here yesterday, you cronky tart – I haven't even had the chance to unbutton the mutton!!! —Barry Humphries, *Bazza Pulls It Offl*, 1971

2 applied generally as a disdainful descriptor *UK*
Reported among Leicestershire schoolchildren by Miss Rebecca Walton, 1983.

3 inferior; 'wonky' *UK, 1961*

crook *adjective*

1 dishonest; illegal; (of an item) illegally gained, stolen, illicit *AUSTRALIA, 1898*
- Nothin' crook about it, boy; just good business. —Frank Hardy, *Power Without Glory*, p. 453, 1950
- Snow here says the Steward's that crook you could bring Bernborough here and call him 'Jakerloo' and no one would be any the wiser. —Dymphna Cusack, *Picnic Races*, p. 155, 1962
- That reminds me, did I ever tell you about the crookest raffle ever run in Australia? —Frank Hardy, *The Yarns of Billy Borker*, p. 17, 1965

2 (of a racehorse) not being run to win; (of a jockey) not riding to win *AUSTRALIA, 1895*
- 'Jack knew the horse and was of the opinion that Sam would win easily. 'That's what everyone seemes to think, but I'm crook, owners instructions,' replied Sam. —Joe Andersen, *Winners Can Laugh*, 1982
- There were 10 horses in the race and Sam had been elected as the one to carry their combined investments. The other nine were crook. —Joe Andersen, *Winners Can Laugh*, p. 114, 1982

3 bad; no good *AUSTRALIA, 1900*
- Things looked crook enough then alright. —Robert S. Close, *Love Me Sailor*, p. 206, 1945
- I've got a crook headache, so I dodged it. —Eric Lambert, *The Veterans*, p. 10, 1954
- That's pretty tough work, isn't it? Crook hours, I mean. —John Wynnum, *Jiggin' in the Riggin'*, p. 45, 1965
- Well take it easy goin' down. Bloody fog's still crook. —John O'Grady, *It's Your Shout, Mate!*, p. 76, 1972

4 ill; unwell; injured *AUSTRALIA, 1908*
- Jesus, you look crook!...What's the matter Paddy? —Robert S. Close, *Love Me Sailor*, p. 104, 1945
- I was over in this dump last year, but I had to shoot through back to Aussie unexpectedly when me auntie took crook. —Barry Humphries, *The Wonderful World of Barry McKenzie*, p. 38, 1968
- I felt like falling to weeping but had a crook back. —Barry Dickins, *What the Dickins*, p. 19, 1985
- You know how you feel when you're crook in the guts? —Kathy Lette, *Girls' Night Out*, p. 53, 1987

▸ **go crook**
to express anger verbally *AUSTRALIA, 1910*
- No use going crook at the Yanks. —Eric Lambert, *The Veterans*, p. 159, 1954
- —Nino Culotta (John O'Grady), *They're A Weird Mob*, p. 136, 1957
- No use going crook about it. —Dymphna Cusack, *Picnic Races*, p. 21, 1962
- —Harvey E. Ward, *Down Under Without Blunder*, p. 37, 1967
- He went crook. He said, 'You can eat them bastards out in the bush, but not in my bloody camp!' —Herb Wharton, *Cattle Camp*, p. 97, 1994

crook *adverb*
badly *AUSTRALIA*
- He was in my hair, but not that crook that I'd bump him. —Arthur Upfield, *Bony and the Mouse*, p. 48, 1959

crook as a dog *adjective*
very unwell *AUSTRALIA*
- I'm crook as a mangy dog this morning. —Alan Marshall, *I Can Jump Puddles*, p. 186, 1955
- The diarrhoea I got occasionally became a full-time thing with me, and I felt as crook as a dog. —William Dick, *A Bunch of Ratbags*, p. 288, 1965
- In fact, there are bad days when they must positively be crook as dogs, which is exactly what a God would feel like in reverse. —Geoff Wyatt, *Saltwater Saints*, p. 79, 1969

crook as Rookwood *adjective*
(especially in Sydney) very unwell *AUSTRALIA*
Rhyming phrase referring to Rookwood Cemetery, the main cemetery serving Sydney for many years.
- In point of established fact sport, I'm as crook as Rookwood!! I reckon I might have to cry Ruth [vomit] pretty soonish!!! —Barry Humphries, *Bazza Pulls It Offl*, 1971
- In other words it makes you feel 'as crook as Rookwood'. —Nancy Keesing, *Lily on the Dustbin*, p. 124, 1982

crook book *noun*
a piece of crime fiction *UK*
- Now, what's the idea of meeting in a place like this? You get it out of some crook book or something? —Derek Bickerton, *Payroll*, p. 6, 1959

crooked *adjective*

1 dishonest; of dishonest manufacture *UK, 1864*
- The Tories are either innumerate or crooked, and certainly doomed. — *The Guardian*, 15th November 2004

2 annoyed *AUSTRALIA, 1942*
- 'Are you not ashamed of yourself?' 'Yeah, I'm real crooked on me.' —Nino Culotta (John O'Grady), *They're A Weird Mob*, p. 86, 1957

crooked *adverb*
illicitly, in a criminal manner, furtively *UK, 1936*
- 'When you live crooked', Batman Güemes repeated, 'you've got no choice but to work straight'. —Arturo Perez-Reverte (translated by Andrew Hurley), *The Queen of the South*, p. 40, 2002

crooked as a dog's hind leg
extremely crooked *AUSTRALIA*
Both literally and figuratively 'crooked'.
- I commented once on the straightness of a furrow he had just turned in starting the winter ploughing-out in the four-year-old orchard. "Straight!" said he. "Oh, no, boy! That's as crooked as a dog's hind-leg!" —Frank Dalby Davison, *The Wells of Beersheba*, p. 293, 1965
- Crooked. Bent, dishonest. He was as crooked as a dog's hind leg. —*The Dinkum Dictionary Of Australian English*, p. 20, 1990

crookie *noun*
a wrong or weak person or thing *NEW ZEALAND*
- These West Coast publicans are usually a pretty good team but there's a crookie in every bunch of blokes. —Barry Crump, *One of Us*, p. 104, 1962

crook on *adjective*
annoyed with *AUSTRALIA*
- You're crook on me because I stayed up there with Dowdie and didn't walk out with you. —Ray Lawler, *Summer of the Seventeenth Doll*, p. 36, 1957
- So the only thing I'm crook on is they didn't let me in on the attack. —Frank Hardy, *The Outcasts of Foolgarah*, p. 214, 1971

croop *noun*
a croupier *UK*
- The croupier, provided by the club, took something out of the pot from every winning run, or winners would "see the croop" by tossing him a portion of their winnings. —Brian McDonald, *Elephant Boys*, p. 17–18, 2000

croot *noun*
▷ **see: CRUIT**

crop *noun*

1 a fifth of a gallon of wine *US*
- —*American Speech*, p. 57, Spring-Summer 1975: 'Razorback slang'

2 inferior quality heroin
A variation of **CRAP**.
- —Robert Ashton, *This Is Heroin*, p. 208, 2002

crop dusting *noun*
farting while walking down the aisle of an airliner *US*
- —Rene Foss, *Around the World in a Bad Mood*, p. 35, 2002

crop-head *noun*
a male with closely cut hair *UK*
- —Tom Hibbert, *Rockspeak!*, p. 45, 1983

cropper *noun*
1 a man who seeks to have sex with a transexual *UK*
Named after *Coronation Street* character Roy Cropper whose 1999 soap opera story-line had him involved with a transexual.
- —*Attitude*, p. 60, July 2003

2 a fail; a setback *AUSTRALIA, 1921*
- Second cropper happened soon after the first – you should have seen me – mud from head to feet[.],—Patsy Adam-Smith, *The ANZACS*, 1978

▸ **come a cropper**
to take a heavy fall; to go wrong *UK, 1874*
This is the most familiar phrase based-on 'cropper' (a fall, 1858); others are 'get a cropper' and 'fall a cropper'.
- Bloke's got to help a girl where it's rough case she slips and comes a cropper in the dark.—Norman Lindsay, *Halfway to Anywhere*, 1947
- [T]errific crash as Tony comes a cropper.—Ray Galton and Alan Simpson, *Hancock's Half Hour*, 28th June 1959
- He's making a big name for himself, alright.' 'One of these days I'm afraid he's going to come a cropper.—Murray Bail, *Holden's Performance*, p. 117, 1988
- I was just a normal schoolboy with normal schoolboy habits and a propensity for mishap, as evidenced by the day I came a cropper in tar at Mentone.—Rex Hunt, *Tall Tales – and True*, 1994
- But like the best-laid plans, the best-planned lays can come a cropper.—Duncan MacLaughlin, *The Filth*, p. 50, 2002

croppie *noun*
a crop circle researcher *UK*
- The various groups of croppies spend most of the summer photographing crop circles from the air[.]—Iain Aitch, *A Fête Worse Than Death*, p. 219, 2003

crop-topped *adjective*
with short hair, cropped on top
- [A] six-foot-four triangular-torsoed, crop-topped GI [...] told me the forecast was for a fine weekend.—Josie Dew, *The Sun In My Eyes*, p. 294, 2001

cross *noun*
an act of betrayal, a double*cross* *UK*
- They're double into this because it's a cross. It's the old guard getting fucked up the arse and I know they're going to be bang into that. —Kevin Sampson, *Outlaws*, p. 253, 2001

▸ **in a cross**
in trouble *US*
- I go for you, Sam, I think you're boss / but don't think you can ever put me in a cross.—Dennis Wepman et al., *The Life*, p. 40, 1976

▸ **on the cross**
dishonestly *UK, 1819*

Cross *noun*
▸ **the Cross**
the King's *Cross* district of Sydney *AUSTRALIA, 1946*
- The Cross is a heterosexual playground. It is well policed and there's rarely more trouble than a few drunks having a fight.—*sydney.visitors-bureau.com*, July 2003

cross *verb*
1 to betray someone *UK, 1821*
- Seven years later she would tally up and happily cross me into prison.—Iceberg Slim (Robert Beck), *Pimp*, p. 110, 1969

2 to cheat a cheat *US, 1950*
- —Thomas L. Clark, *The Dictionary of Gambling and Gaming*, p. 55, 1987

cross bar hotel *noun*
a jail or prison *US, 1865*
- —*Swinging Syllables*, 1959
- the poor jerk from Camden you take up the river to the Crossbars Hotel.—Darryl Ponicsan, *The Last Detail*, p. 181, 1970
- So Butch said he could keep me out of the Crossbar Hotel for a while if I would send him another hundred[.]—Joe Bob Briggs, *Joe Bob Goes to the Drive-In*, p. 32, 1987
- "If they ignore [the laws] they're going to end up staying in the Virginia Beach crosssbar hotel," says Virginia Beach police Officer Lou Thruston.—*Washington Times*, 24th May 1996

cross-comical *adjective*
foolish *BARBADOS*
- —Frank A. Collymore, *Barbadian Dialect*, p. 36, 1965

crosscut *noun*
a Chinese woman; a Jewish woman *UK*
A Liverpudlian term, derived from the notion that Asian women's genitals have a different orientation to those of Western women; hence, its yet more ill-informed application to Jewish women.
- —Fritz Spiegl, *Lern Yerself Scouse*, 1966

crossed wires *noun*
a misunderstanding *UK, 1932*
From the hazards of telephony.
- A Man Booker spokeswoman said the posting must have been an error caused by crossed wires between the prize's development website and the actual site.—*The Guardian*, 17th October 2002

cross-eye; cross-eyes *noun*
a person with a squint *UK, 1937*
From the conventional sense describing the condition.

cross-eyed *adjective*
annoyed, angry *UK*
- He went a bit cross-eyed until he saw me laughing.—Lenny McLean, *The Guv'nor*, p. 191, 1998

crossfire *noun*
in confidence games, conversation between confederates in the swindle that draws the victim into the swindle *US, 1940*
Originally used to describe the quick banter of vaudeville, then adapted to criminal purposes.
- Now, when Blue came back he'd need me to set up the crossfire to make it logical to Dot that the flue and the mail-away were necessary and fair arrangements for us all.—Iceberg Slim (Robert Beck), *Trick Baby*, p. 27, 1969

crossfire *verb*
(used of a racehorse) to clip the rear hooves together while running *US*
- —David W. Maurer, *Argot of the Racetrack*, p. 22, 1951

crosshairs *noun*
▸ **put in the crosshairs**
to target something *US*
From military sniper/target competition shooting.
- This wasn't the first time opponents had put rap in their crosshairs. —*The Source*, p. 74, March 2002

crosshaul *noun*
a notional tool that a novice logger is often sent to fetch *US, 1913*
- —Frederic G. Cassidy, *Dictionary of American Regional English, Volume One*, p. 860, 1985

crosslift *noun*
in poker, a cheating technique in which two confederates on either side of the victim continue raising the bet until the victim withdraws from the hand *US, 1968*
- —Thomas L. Clark, *The Dictionary of Gambling and Gaming*, p. 55, 1987

cross my heart and hope to die
used as an oath, often with humour *US, 1926*
- No jive, cross my heart and hope to die, Darling.—Iceberg Slim (Robert Beck), *Airtight Willie and Me*, p. 75, 1979

cross my heart and hope to spit
used as an oath and pledge *US*
Popularised by Theodore 'Beaver' Cleaver on the US television comedy *Leave it to Beaver* (CBS and ABC, 1957–63), in place of the more common 'cross my heart and hope to die'. Used with referential humour by those who had watched the show as children.

Crossmyloof *noun*
a male homosexual *UK: SCOTLAND*
Glasgow rhyming slang for **POOF**, formed from an area of the south side of Glasgow.
- —Michael Munro, *The Patter, Another Blast*, 1988

cross of the north *noun*
a stance assumed by a canoer on a portage when meeting someone on a trail *CANADA*
- When you are on a portage with a pack on your back and you meet a fellow and stop to speak, you just naturally lean forward on your paddles to ease the load of your pack, and so the blade cross between

you making what we call "the cross of the north." —John Rowlands, *Cache Lake Country*, p. 165, 1947

crossover *verb*
to leave one youth gang and join a rival gang *US*
- —Bill Valentine, *Gang Intelligence Manual*, p. 75, 1995

cross-patch *noun*
a peevish, ill-tempered person *UK, 1700*
A combination of 'cross' (angry, peevish) and obsolete 'patch' (a fool). Originally applied to a girl or a woman; the general sense is first recorded in 1818.

crossroad *noun*
an amphetamine tablet identified by its cross-scoring *US*
Less commonly heard than **CROSS TOP**.
- —National Institute on Drug Abuse, *What do they call it again*, 1980
- —Mike Haskins, *Drugs*, p. 279, 2003

crossroader *noun*
an itinerant card cheat *US, 1889*
- —John Scarne, *Scarne on Dice*, p. 463, 1974
- [I]n a court of law, if a blackjack Dealer gets terribly unlucky and his table keeps losing fifteen nights in a row, there is no legal proof that he is cheating for the benefit of an "outside" man or "crossroader," that he is "dumping out." —Mario Puzo, *Inside Las Vegas*, p. 180, 1977

cross-talk *noun*
in a radio or television broadcast, speaking simultaneously and thus possibly obscuring what is said *US*
- I don't have the same negative feelings about cross-talk that some of my predecessors did. Cross-talk often adds to the excitement of a telecast. —Dan Jenkins, *Life Its Ownself*, p. 222, 1984

cross-thread *adjective*
contrary *TRINIDAD AND TOBAGO, 1960*
- —Lise Winer, *Dictionary of the English/Creole of Trinidad & Tobago*, 2003

cross top *noun*
a tablet of Benzedrine™ (amphetamine sulphate), a central nervous system stimulant *US, 1971*
From the appearance: white tablets with a cross cut into the surface.
- —Walter L. Way, *The Drug Scene*, 1977
- Actually, the cross tops from the early '70s were sometimes decent-grade methamphetamines, not the early '80s-style caffeine crap. —Don Bolles, *Retrohell*, p. 50, 1997
- —Mike Haskins, *Drugs*, p. 279, 2003

crossword spanner *noun*
a pencil *UK*
Recorded by Wilfred Granville, 1962, as a term used by Royal Navy engineers.

crot *noun*
excrement, especially as 'soft crot', a loose stool *UK*
A schoolboys' term recorded by Peter Jones, 1957.

crotch *noun*
a woman *US*
- I come in here, I open the door, and there's this crotch at the desk there. —George V. Higgins, *The Digger's Game*, p. 180, 1973

Crotch *nickname*
the US Marines Corps *US, 1953*
- I been busted so many times I couldn't make lance corporal if I stayed in the Crotch for thirty years. —Philip Caputo, *A Rumor of War*, p. 133, 1977
- Anyway, I go, 'Were you in the Crotch?' He says, 'The Crotch?' I say, 'Yeah, the Marine Corps. Where yo around Da Nang?' —James Lee Burke, *Sunset Limited*, p. 134, 1998
- —Charles D. Melson, *US Marine in Vietnam: 1965–1974*, p. 58, 1998

crotch ball *noun*
in handball, a ball that strikes the intersection of two playing surfaces *US*
- —Paul Haber, *Inside Handball*, p. 65, 1970

crotch crickets *noun*
pubic lice *US, 1971*
- Oh shit, I've never had saber-toothed crotch crickets before. —Beatrice Sparks (writing as "Anonymous"), *Jay's Journal*, p. 130, 1979
- On top of being skinny, our crotch crickets were very prevalent, and the bedbugs were everywhere. —Donald Knox, *Death March*, p. 401, 1981
- —Michael Dalton Johnson, *Talking Trash with Redd Foxx*, p. 51, 1994

crotchety *adjective*
ill-tempered, cross *UK, 1825*
- Option One, knock on crotchety-matron-across-the-way's door. —Emma McLaughlin, *The Nanny Diaries*, p. 4, 2002

crotch light *noun*
in the pornography industry, a light used to illuminate the genitals of the performers *US*
- They said, "What am I doing here" and see all these strange faces and people holding crotch lights. —Stephen Ziplow, *The Film Maker's Guide to Pornography*, p. 14, 1977

crotch magazine *noun*
a pornographic magazine *US*
- "My name's Whistler," he said when the attendant looked up from his crotch magazine, open to the centerfold in which a girl of stunning beauty opened her legs for anyone who cared to ogle her. —Robert Campbell, *In La-La Land We Trust*, p. 95, 1986

crotch rocket *noun*
a motorcyle, usually a fast racing motorcyle *US, 1974*
- —Lewis Poteet, *Car & Motorcyle Slang*, p. 58, 1992
- —Connie Eble (Editor), *UNC-CH Campus Slang*, p. 2, Fall 1995
- Yeah. You're going to need more than that crotch rocket. —*The Fast and The Furious*, 2001

crotch rot *noun*
any fungal infection in the crotch *US, 1967*
- Sometimes your chops for action and your terror would reach a different balance and you'd go looking for it everywhere, and nothing would happen, except a fire ant would fly up your nose or you'd grow a crotch rot[.] —Michael Herr, *Dispatches*, p. 1962, 1977
- —Sally Williams, *"Strong" Words*, p. 137, 1994
- Aside from some improvement in my jungle sores, crotch rot, and immersion foot, I rejoined my unit in much worse shape than when I'd left. —Nelson DeMille, *Up Country*, p. 280–281, 2002

crotch row *noun*
in a striptease performance, seats very near the performers *US*
- —Sherman Louis Sergel, *The Language of Show Biz*, p. 63, 1973
- —Don Wilmeth, *The Language of American Popular Entertainment*, 1981

crotch shot *noun*
a photograph focused on a person's genitals *US*
- Customer always want smiling crotch shots. —George Paul Csicsery (Editor), *The Sex Industry*, p. 163, 1973
- The explicitness of the crotch shots was made for pigs like you who need the anatomy lesson. —*The Village Voice*, 25th July 2000

crotch strap *noun*
in motor racing, a safety device that attaches to the buckle of the lap belt and is attached to the chassis under the seat *US*
- —Don Alexander, *The Racer's Dictionary*, p. 19, 1963

crotch walker *noun*
a shoplifter who conceals booty between the thighs *UK*
- —Angela Devlin, *Prison Patter*, p. 41, 1996

crovey!
used for expressing approval *UK*
- — Susie Dent, *The Language Report*, p. 75, 2003

crow *noun*

1 a black person *US, 1823*
Offensive.
- It was a dangerous practice to call a Negro anything that could be loosely construed as insulting because of the centuries of their having been called niggers, jigs, dinges, blackbirds, crows, boots and spooks. —Maya Angelou, *I Know Why the Caged Bird sings*, p. 106, 1969

2 a female prostitute *AUSTRALIA, 1944*
Occasionally also spelt 'cro'. Perhaps influenced by **CHROMO**.
- Marry you, an amateur moll like you? Marry a crow who deserted her husband and kid! —Dorothy Hewett, *The Chapel Perilous*, p. 75, 1972
- —Jim Ramsay, *Cop It Sweet!*, p. 26, 1977

3 a mawkish, old-fashioned person *US*
- A corny peson is a "cornball" or a "crow." — *Women's Digest*, p. 40, September 1945

4 a drinking friend *BERMUDA*
- —Peter A. Smith and Fred M. Barritt, *Bermewjan Vurds*, 1985

5 an undertaker; an undertaker's employee *UK*
From their black clothing.
- —Margery Allingham, *More Work for the Undertaker*, 1947

6 used as an abusive term of address *UK*
- Don't get fucking gobbie with me, you crow, or I'll fucking drop you. —Ken Lukowiak, *A Soldier's Song*, p. 78, 1993

7 cocaine *UK*
- —Mike Haskins, *Drugs*, p. 280, 2003

8 an electronic warfare specialist *US*
Vietnam war usage.
- He knew the "crows" in the back of the plane – four electronic warfare officers – were doing the same. —William C. Anderson, *Bat 21*, p. 3, 1980

9 an eagle insignia in the US Navy *US, 1905*
- She hadn't felt so powerful since those days when she'd first earned the "crow" of a petty officer, taking on the responsibility of command over subordinates. —Joseph Wambaugh, *Finnegan's Week*, p. 29, 1993

▸ **as the crow flies**
directly; in a straight line *AUSTRALIA, 1902*
- The way the crow flies, it's about six miles to Omana. —Wal Watkins, *Race the Lazy River*, p. 105, 1963
- As the crow flies that trip would be about 600 kilometres, but it was much further the way they travelled[.] —Herb Wharton, *Cattle Camp*, p. 135, 1994

Crow *nickname*
the Crow's Nest Pass railway freight rates *CANADA*
- In western Canada, any reference to the Crow has nothing to do with birds; it refers to the controversial, much altered Crow's Nest Pass freight rates. —Chris Thain, *Cold as a Bay Street Banker's Heart*, p. 49, 1987

crowbait *noun*
a horse, especially an older horse *US, 1851*
- —*American Speech*, p. 270, December 1958: 'Ranching terms from eastern Washington'

crowbar palace *noun*
a jail *US, 1941*
- Three months in Fort Smith's crowbar palace may have a most salutary effect on the young man concerned. —*News of the North*, p. 2/1, 29th August 1963

crowd *noun*
1 a company of people defined by a common-denominator, a set *US, 1840*
- I'm in with the "In" crowd / I go where the "In" crowd goes / I'm in with the "In" crowd / And I know what the "In" crowd knows[.] —Dobie Gray, *The 'In' Cowd*, 1964

2 a fat person *US*
- —William D. Alsever, *Glossary for the Establishment and Other Uptight People*, p. 8, 1970

crowd *verb*
1 to put pressure on someone, to coerce someone *US, 1828*
- "I can tell just by you saying that that you like the guy." "Sure, I like him. But don't crowd me into making any other declarations. I'm not ready for them yet." —Sara Paretsky, *Guardian Angel*, p. 401, 1992

2 to verge on a specified age *US, 1943*
- I got my first guitar when I was fourteen / Now I'm crowding thirty and still wearing jeans. —Bob McDill, *Amanda*, 1973

crowded cabin *noun*
in poker, a hand consisting of three cards of one rank and a pair *US*
Conventionally known as a 'full house'.
- —George Percy, *The Language of Poker*, p. 25, 1988

crowded space *noun*
a suitcase *UK*
Rhyming slang; especially, by thieves stealing luggage in crowded spaces.
- —Julian Franklyn, *A Dictionary of Rhyming Slang*, 1961

crowd engineer *noun*
a police dog *US*
- —Jay Robert Nash, *Dictionary of Crime*, p. 90, 1992

crowd-surf *verb*
to pass over the heads of a crowd, propelled and supported by the hands of that crowd *US*
- With the club's tables and chairs tucked away, the flannel-clad crowd had plenty of room to dance and crowd-surf, which the band encouraged. —*Buffalo (New York) News*, p. 5, 25th October 1993
- Suddenly there was a thunderous roar from the crowd. "Oh, shit. He's gone crowd-surfing." —Ben Elton, *High Society*, p. 172, 2002
- They had a bunch of people, and they would make guys crowd surf. —Suroosh Alvi et al., *The Vice Guide*, p. 313, 2002
- Instead he [Grant Nicholas, Feeder] is positively cheery between songs – quipping to fans "getting crushed at the front" and expressing bemusement when some crowd-surf "to a song with strings"[.] —*The Guardian*, 21st February 2003

crow-eater *noun*
a person from the state of South Australia *AUSTRALIA, 1881*
- I learnt later – in Sydney – that West Australians are called 'sandgropers', and South Australians are 'crow-eaters'. —John O'Grady, *It's Your Shout, Mate!*, p. 28, 1972
- —Jim Ramsay, *Cop It Sweet!*, p. 26, 1977

crow foot *noun*
1 in car repair, an open-ended wrench with an extension *US*
- —John Edwards, *Auto Dictionary*, p. 37, 1993

2 in the television and film industries, a device used to support the legs of a tripod on a slippery or uneven surface *UK*
- —Oswald Skilbeck, *ABC of Film and TV Working Terms*, p. 35, 1960

crowhop *noun*
in western Canadian rodeos, a mild bucking *CANADA*
The Historical Dictionary of American Slang lists this term with a similar meaning in use in the US.
- The term is heard on the rodeo circuit where a horse or bull that is doing a pathetic job of bucking is referred to as doing a crowhop. —Chris Thain, *Cold as a Bay Street Banker's Heart*, p. 49, 1987

crowie *noun*
an old woman *UK*
From a resemblance to the crow in colour (of plumage/clothing) and tone of voice.
- —Patrick O'Shaughnessy, *Market Traders' Slang*, 1979

Crow Jim *noun*
anti-white racial discrimination by black people *US, 1956*
A reversal of the common term **JIM CROW** for anti-black discrimination.
- Even in their chosen field of "traditional" jazz the authors are unreliable due to the constant intrusion of a form of racial bias known in the trade as "Crow-Jim." —*San Francisco Examiner*, p. 3 (II), 7th January 1957
- It is the perfect Crow Jim production of all time. —Peter Tamony, *Letter to Ralph J. Gleason*, 3rd November 1959
- —Robert S. Gold, *A Jazz Lexicon*, p. 72, 1964
- Archie Shepp had not yet passed form Fire Music into increasingly virulent Crow-Jim nihilism. —Lester Bangs, *Psychotic Reactions and Carburetor Dung*, p. 41, 1987

crown *noun*
1 a type of MDMA, the recreational drug best known as ecstasy *UK*
From the imprint on the pink pill.
- —Angela Devlin, *Prison Patter*, p. 41, 1996
- Oh, these Crowns beat Mizzis any time! —James Hawes, *Dead Long Enough*, p. 154, 2000

2 a hat *US*
- A candy-striped tie hung down to his fly / And he sported a gold-dust crown. —Dennis Wepman et al., *The Life*, p. 54, 1976
- —Bill Valentine, *Gang Intelligence Manual*, p. 110, 1995

3 a condom *UK*
- —David Rowan, *A Glossary for the 90's*, 1998

Crown *noun*
a Crown Prosecutor *CANADA*
- "We are going to do more screws," Boucher said before being warned the guards were under heavy protection. "It doesn't matter. We will do pigs, judges and Crowns." —*Montreal Gazette*, p. A3, 30th April 2002

crown *verb*
1 to hit someone on the head *UK, 1746*

2 to couple a brakevan (caboose) to a freight train *US*
- —Norman Carlisle, *The Modern Wonder Book of Trains and Railroading*, p. 261, 1946

crown and anchor *noun*
a despicable person *UK*
Rhyming slang for **WANKER**, formed on the name of a dice game.
- —Ray Puxley, *Cockney Rabbit*, 1992

crown crap *noun*
heroin *US, 1975*
- —Richard A. Spears, *The Slang and Jargon of Drugs and Drink*, p. 130, 1986
- —Robert Ashton, *This Is Heroin*, p. 205, 2002
- —Mike Haskins, *Drugs*, p. 283, 2003

crownie *noun*
a tram or bus inspector *AUSTRALIA*
After the emblem of that rank.
- —Sidney J. Baker, *Australia Speaks*, 1953

crown jewels *noun*
1 the male genitals, especially the testicles *AUSTRALIA, 1970*
- There's probably a hairline fracture there or some cartilage damage. How are the crown jewels?—Robert G. Barrett, *Davo's Little Something*, p. 107, 1992
- This was tragic, Minnie Mouse was a bloke. I quickly raced the kids away to protect them from this heartbreaking tragedy and left Minnie laying there clutching her crown jewels.'—Paul Vautin, *Turn It Up!*, p. 40, 1995
- When the river ambulance turned up they wheeled him away still wearing his loose silk suit, a bag of limbs dead to the world and with his crown jewels hanging out.—Mark Paytress, *Siouxsie and the Banshees*, p. 138, 2003
- [A] drunk fan ran into the ring with his trousers by his ankles, joyfully parading his crown jewels.—*Sunday Times (South Africa)*, 6th April 2003

2 tools *UK*
Rhyming slang, perhaps taking its inspiration from the value a tradesman places on his tools.
- —Ray Puxley, *Cockney Rabbit*, 1992

3 jewels, usually ostentatious if not tacky, worn by a drag queen *US*
The royalty punning thanks to 'queen'.
- —*Fact*, p. 26, January-February 1965

Crown Vic *noun*
a Ford Crown Victoria car *US*
- They were in Darryl's Crown Vic in the second row of cars facing the Ralphs sign, the big oval up there, the eye-catcher of the shopping center on Fairfax at Santa Monica.—Elmore Leonard, *Be Cool*, p. 178, 1999
- Crown Vics were senior staff vehicles[.]—Stephen J. Cannell, *The Tin Collectors*, p. 142, 2001

crows *noun*
▸ **where the crows fly backwards**
an arid, desolate region *AUSTRALIA, 1932*
- [T]hat's where the heat buckles the rails like a dog's hind leg, the line gets lost in the sand and the crows fly backwards to keep the dust out of their eyes.—Patsy Adam-Smith, *Folklore of the Australian Railwaymen*, p. 26, 1969
- Woop Woop: Where the crows fly backwards or 'the arse end of nowhere'.—Richard Beckett, *The Dinkum Aussie Dictionary*, p. 57, 1988

crow's feet *noun*
1 wrinkles at the corner of the eyes *UK, 1374*
- I told you, he's got that outdoor good-guy look. even has crow's-feet when he squints.—Elmore Leonard, *Riding the Rap*, p. 103, 1995

2 MDMA, the recreational drug best known as ecstasy *UK*
Specifically used of any tablet of MDMA stamped with an image similar to the single print of a bird's track.
- —Harry Shapiro, *Recreational Drugs*, p. 212, 2004

crow's foot *noun*
in electric line work, a device formally known as an Epoxirod tri-unit *US*
- —A.B. Chance Co., *Lineman's Slang Dictionary*, p. 5, 1980

crow's nest *noun*
1 the uppermost balcony in a cinema *US, 1970*
A pun on the nautical term, acknowledging that the upper balconies were reserved for black people (**CROW**s).
- —J.E. Lighter, *Historical Dictionary of American Slang, Volume One*, p. 529, 1994

2 the observation tower of a brakevan (caboose) *US, 1940*
- —Norman Carlisle, *The Modern Wonder Book of Trains and Railroading*, p. 261, 1946

crow storm *noun*
a flocking up of noisy crows as cold weather approaches in the antumn *CANADA*
- "You've got to have a few crow storms before you can have a snow storm." – from Quebec's Eastern Townships. By local legend, the crows are being punished for failing to report to Noah in the Ark that the flood was receding.—Lewis Poteet, *Talking Country*, p. 34, 1992

CRS disease *noun*
a sudden loss of memory *US*
The person in question 'can't remember shit'.
- —Anna Scotti and Paul Young, *Buzzwords*, p. 58, 1997

crucial *adjective*
very good *BERMUDA*
Recorded in Bermudan and American youth culture.
- —Peter Smith and Fred M. Barritt, *Bermewjan Vurds*, 1985
- —Connie Eble (Editor), *UNC-CH Campus Slang*, p. 2, Fall 1987
- —Rick Ayers (Editor), *Slang Dictionary*, p. 7, 2001

crud *noun*
1 a contemptible person *US, 1930*
Originally Scottish dialect for 'excrement'.
- The crud pulled out his money to try to bribe me. [Steve Canyon comic strip]—*San Francisco Examiner*, p. 14, 24th March 1947
- No bums like these cruds.—Hubert Selby Jr, *Last Exit to Brooklyn*, p. 123, 1957
- The furious District Attorney of Fort Lauderdale, Fla., who describes his town's Easter vacation visitors as "College cruds," put it too mildly.—*Los Angeles Herald-Examiner*, p. B3, 5th April 1967
- Little crud,' says Galvin. 'He'll pump that up into a load of bullshit. Page six of the scandal sheet, just past the bikinis and the big tits. —Barry Oakley, *A Salute to the Great McCarthy*, p. 79, 1970
- Do as you're telt [told]. Wee crud!—Ian Pattison, *Rab C. Nesbitt*, 1988

2 rubbish, filth, shit *US, 1943*
Originally Scottish dialect *crud* (curdled matter); the first appearance, noted by J.E. Lighter, is 1508 in the UK, but not truly in currency in this sense until the 1940s.
- [T]he oil and crud getting washed into the canal.—*The Times Magazine*, p. 24, 23rd February 2002

3 dried or sticky semen *US*
- —Dale Gordon, *The Dominion Sex Dictionary*, p. 52, 1967

4 any sexually transmitted infection *US, 1951*
- —Dale Gordon, *The Dominion Sex Dictionary*, p. 52, 1967

5 a common cold or the flu *ANTARCTICA*
- —*Cool Antarctica*, 2003: 'Antarctic slang'

6 a notional disease, covering many ailments, real and imaginary *US, 1932*
- —*American Speech*, p. 304, December 1947: 'Imaginary diseases in army and navy parlance'

7 snow that does not produce good snowboarding *US*
- —Elena Garcia, *A Beginner's Guide to Zen and the Art of Snowboarding*, p. 121, 1990

crudded up *adjective*
infected with a sexually transmitted disease *US*
- It's not possible that she's all crudded up?—*Chasing Amy*, 1997

cruddy *adjective*
1 useless, worthless, unpleasant, disgusting *US, 1947*
Created from **CRUD** (filth).
- Oh, my aching, breaking, cruddy, bloody back!—Max Shulman, *Rally Round the Flag, Boys!*, p. 20, 1957
- Is this the Mothers of Invention recording under a different name in a last ditch attempt to get their cruddy music on the radio?—Frank Zappa, *Cruising With Ruben & The Jets*, 1968
- Hey! That cruddy Reppo runt's still at our joint!—Geoff Wyatt, *Saltwater Saints*, p. 63, 1969

2 encrusted with dirt or filth *US, 1949*
- This is where you're heading. A cruddy lung, smoking through a hole in your throat. Do you really want that?—*Clerks*, 1994
- Can I sit on the chair? I don't want to get all cruddy.—*Airheads*, 1994

crudie *noun*
an unsophisticated rustic *US*
- —Mary Swift, *Campus Slang (University of Texas)*, 1968

crud up *verb*
to foul something; to spoil something *US, 1963*
- There never was much around Houston or Dallas to crud up, but the limestone hills and fast rivers of Central Texas – that's a shame. —Molly Ivins, *Molly Ivins Can't Say That, Can She?*, p. 26, 1991

crudzine *noun*
a poorly written and/or poorly produced fan magazine *US, 1976*
- —*American Speech*, p. 53, Spring 1978: 'Star trek lives: trekker slang
- —*American Speech*, p. 25, Spring 1982: 'The language of science fiction fan magazines'

cruel *verb*

to spoil something, especially to spoil a person's chances *AUSTRALIA, 1899*

Also spelt 'crool' in an effort to represent an uneducated pronunciation.

- But I kept quiet, I didn't want to crool meself. —Alexander Buzo, *Norm and Ahmed*, p. 8, 1969
- If you get too hungry, you'll cruel the deal. —Arthur Chipper, *The Aussie Swearer's Guide*, p. 38, 1972
- —Jim Ramsay, *Cop It Sweet!*, p. 26, 1977
- [A]ttacks by Palestinian militants have before cruelled the Israeli Labour Party's political hopes against Likud[.] —*ABC Local Radio (Australia)*, 6th January 2003

▸ cruel the pitch

to spoil your chances; to ruin an opportunity *AUSTRALIA, 1915*

- His old man nearly burst a blood vessel and Roddy reckons he's cruelled his pitch for that 1960 Goddess. —Barry Humphries, *A Nice Night's Entertainment*, p. 42, 1960
- Blimey, it's cruelled my pitch properly. —John Wynnum, *Tar Dust*, p. 19, 1962
- [T]he Bre-X fiasco (the salted gold discovery in Indonesia) had, at a single blow, cruelled the pitch for junior explorers several years earlier[.] — *The Australian*, 17th October 2002

cruel *adjective*

very *US*

- —Frederic G. Cassidy, *Dictionary of American Regional English, Volume One*, p. 868, 1985

cruel; cruelly *adverb*

severely; extremely hard *UK*

In conventional use until later C19.

cruet *noun*

the head *AUSTRALIA, 1941*

- As I was saying, they had these holes cut into the tabletop and they used to get the monkey and jam his skull up under it, so the top of his cruitt [*sic*] used to be before the eater —Geoff Wyatt, *Saltwater Saints*, p. 74, 1969
- His cruet's as good as yours and mine. —D'Arcy Niland, *Dead Men Running*, p. 77, 1969

▸ do your cruet

to lose your temper *AUSTRALIA, 1976*

cruft *noun*

any unpleasant, unidentified substance *US*

- —Guy L. Steele et al., *The Hacker's Dictionary*, p. 50, 1983

crufty *adjective*

in computing, poorly designed or poorly built *US*

- —Guy Steele, *Coevolution Quarterly*, p. 29, Spring 1981: 'Computer slang'
- —Eric S. Raymond, *The New Hacker's Dictionary*, p. 114, 1991

cruise *noun*

a male homosexual who picks up multiple short-term sexual partners *US*

- That cruise we rob bed looked like a bum but he went for four C's on the shake. —Hyman E. Goldin et al., *Dictionary of American Underworld Lingo*, p. 53, 1950

cruise *verb*

1 to search for a casual sex-partner, usually homosexual; to pursue a person as a casual sex-partner, especially by eye contact *US, 1925*

- —Donald Webster Cory and John P. LeRoy, *The Homosexual and His Society*, p. 263, 1963: 'A lexicon of homosexual slang'
- [T]wo anxious fairies cruise me. —John Rechy, *City of Night*, p. 194, 1963
- — Florida Legislative Investigation Committee (Johns Committee), *Homosexuality and Citizenship in Florida*, 1964: 'Glossary of homosexual terms and deviate acts'
- A man who spends long evenings in a "gay bar" hoping to "cruise" what he knows is going to be a one-night stand cannot fulfill his office functions the next morning. —Antony James, *America's Homosexual Underground*, p. 59, 1965
- She is aggressive in all of her homosexuality, from making the first overture to a girl while "cruising" to her actions in bed. —Ruth Allison, *Lesbianism*, p. 20, 1967
- Another homosexual trait noted by Bergler and others is chronic dissatisfactoin, a constant tendency to prowl or "cruise" in search of new partners. —Joe David Brown, *Sex in the '60*, p. 69, 1968
- I don't get it – you cruise Atlantic City or something? —Mart Crowley, *The Boys in the Band*, p. 121, 1968
- At first it simply didn't occur to me that this number was cruising me. —John Francis Hunter, *The Gay Insider*, p. 35, 1971
- [T]he third episode begins with Donovan, quite naked, wandering around his house, "cruising" a black telephone lineman. —Kenneth Turan and Stephen E. Zito, *Sinema*, p. 191, 1974
- An attractive man begins to cruise him. —John Rechy, *The Sexual Outlaw*, p. 74, 1977
- What are you doing, cruising him? —*As Good As It Gets*, 1997

2 to join others in driving slowly down chosen downtown streets, usually on a weekend night, seeing others and being seen *US, 1957*

- The Fearless Four, as we called ourselves, went cruising Tenth Street in Modesto, circling Burgi's Drive Inn or dragging the Okies along the canal banks with the trunk loaded with Goebel beer every night for three years. —Oscar Zeta Acosta, *The Autobiography of a Brown Buffalo*, p. 107, 1972
- —John Edwards, *Auto Dictionary*, p. 38, 1993

3 to drive *US*

With a suggestion of carefree elan.

- "Whaddya say, hey?" he said to Comfort. "Let's do some cruisin'." —Max Shulman, *Rally Round the Flag, Boys!*, p. 58, 1957
- Wait, wait, I gotta cruise by this afternoon and run a little business if you know what I'm talking about. — *Dazed and Confused*, 1993

4 to take someone, to lead someone *US*

- Rue Auberg; fly little chick gets stranglehold on my lapel, tries to cruise me up to her apartment[.] —Mezz Mezzrow, *Really the Blues*, p. 197, 1946

▸ cruisin' for a bruisin'

headed for trouble, especially a physical beating *US, 1947*

- — *Newsweek*, p. 28, 8th October 1951
- — *Dobie Gillis Teenage Slanguage Dictionary*, 1962
- Your dad is really cruising for a bruising, Carlotta. —C.D. Payne, *Youth in Revolt*, p. 376, 1993

cruise and kill *verb*

(of light scout teams during the Vietnam war) to go around looking for solders to kill *US*

- —Linda Reinberg, *In the Field*, p. 54, 1991

cruise joint *noun*

a bar or other establishment where people gather in search of sexual partners *US*

- "We'd hit the cruise joints aorund Chicago looking for a well-heeled out of town faggot in the city for kicks," explained Gene. —Johnny Shearer, *The Male Hustler*, p. 36, 1966

cruisemobile *noun*

any desireable car *US, 1978*

- —Lillian Glass with Richard Liebmann-Smith, *How to Deprogram Your Valley Girl*, p. 27, 1982
- The hot exhausts of Chevy Biscaynes, Pontiac Catalinas, Mercury Montereys, and the rest of the road's superwide, electraglide, V8 cruisemobiles muddy the atmosphere[.] —William Clark, *Temples of Sound*, p. 193, 2003

cruiser *noun*

1 a person who habitually searches regular haunts for casual sex-partners, usually homosexual *UK*

- —Angela Devlin, *Prison Patter*, p. 41, 1996

2 a prostitute *US, 1868*

- —Ruth Todasco et al., *The Intelligent Woman's Guide to Dirty Words*, p. 3, 1973

3 a surfer who approaches surfing with a casualness that borders on laziness *US*

- —Michael V. Anderson, *The Bad, Rad, Not to Forget Way Cool Beach and Surf Discriptionary*, p. 5, 1988

cruising *noun*

the recreational activity of searching for a casual sex-partner, usually homosexual *UK, 1927*

- There was quite a bit of forthright cruising (that's the gay word for giving a guy "the eye") going on[.] — *Screw*, 24th November 1969
- Cruising, he had long ago decided, was a lot like hitchhiking. It was best to dress like the people you wanted to pick you up. —Armistead Maupin, *Tales of the city*, 1978
- Jane came back to her little terraced house in Cardiff at 10 p.m., having left Dickie and his friends to their cruising before it got too obvious that they were itching to leave her and go out into the locker rooms of the night. —James Hawes, *White Powder, Green Light*, 2002

cruisy *adjective*

1 relaxing, enjoyable *NEW ZEALAND*

- If you want a cruisy, clear day, smoke some really good, locally grown dak. — *Dominion*, p. 13, 29th June 1998

2 characterised by a high degree of activity by homosexual men looking for sexual partners *US, 1949*

Also spelt 'cruisey'.

- Third Avenue is also cruisy in the later afternoon.—John Francis Hunter, *The Gay Insider*, p. 120, 1971
- A place where one can expect to find many persons on the make is termed cruisy.—Wayne Dynes, *Homolexis*, p. 39, 1985
- You can go out and make good friends without it being a cruisey scenario.—*Attitude*, p. 34, October 2003

cruit; croot *noun*
a new military recruit *US, 1897*
- —Carl Fleischhauer, *A Glossary of Army Slang*, p. 12, 1968

cruller *noun*
the head *US, 1942*
- Toady to the turban, drooop, or snipe a Stayman off your son's cruller with a bow and arrow at a hundred paces," says Mr. Big.— Haenigsen, *Jive's Like That*, 1947

crumb *noun*
1 a despicable person *US, 1919*
- "One move outa you or your other crumbs and I'll have this in your guts," Crazy rasped.—Irving Shulman, *The Amboy Dukes*, p. 213, 1947
- I think I remember Larry sayin' – "Mayor Lindsay is a crumbe!" —Eugene Boe, *The Wit & Wisdom of Archie Bunker*, p. 102, 1971

2 a body louse *US, 1863*
- —Joseph E. Ragen and Charles Finston, *Inside the World's Toughest Prison*, p. 796, 1962
- —Joe McKennon, *Circus Lingo*, p. 29, 1980
- A crumb was a body louse, so crummy as an adjective has also come to mean undesirable.—Tom Parkin, *WetCoast Words*, p. 42, 1989

3 a small piece of crack cocaine *US*
- — US Department of Justice, *Street Terms*, october 1994

▸put on the crumb act
to impose something on another person *AUSTRALIA*
- —Sidney J. Baker, *The Drum*, 1959

crumb box *noun*
1 in circus and carnival usage, a small suitcase or box containing personal belongings *US*
- —Don Wilmeth, *The Language of American Popular Entertainment*, p. 67, 1981

2 a brakevan (caboose) *US, 1945*
- —Ramon Adams, *The Language of the Railroader*, p. 40, 1977

crumb bum *noun*
1 a lowly, inept person *US, 1934*
- All the guys have gone into the army; only the crumb-bums are left. —Hal Ellison, *Summer Street*, p. 15, 1953

2 a gambler who places very small and very conservative bets *US*
- — *The Annals of the American Academy of Political and Social Sciences*, p. 123, May 1950

crumb castle *noun*
in circus and carnival usage, a dining tent *US*
- —Don Wilmeth, *The Language of American Popular Entertainment*, p. 67, 1981

crumb-catcher *noun*
a young child *US, 1962*
- I said, "Well, I can dig it, buddy, 'cause I'm hooked up myself. I got a dough-roll [wife] and two crumb-catchers [children], you know." —Bruce Jackson, *In the Life*, p. 152, 1972
- What about this little crumb-catcher you got in the oven here?—Edwin Torres, *After Hours*, p. 378, 1979

crumb crunchers *noun*
the teeth *US*
- —Lou Shelly, *Hepcats Jive Talk Dictionary*, p. 23, 1945

crumb-crusher; crumb-cruncher *noun*
a child, especially a very young one *US, 1959*
- —Robert George Reisner, *The Jazz Titans*, p. 153, 1960
- —Frank Prewitt and Francis Schaeffer, *Vacaville Vocabulary*, 1961–1962
- I hadn't heard about a "crumb crusher."—Iceberg Slim (Robert Beck), *Pimp*, p. 114, 1969
- The little bitch – outta the clear blue – told me one night that she was going to have a crumb crusher!—A.S. Jackson, *Gentleman Pimp*, p. 45, 1973
- She ain't into nothin', with two crumbcrushers and no ambition. —Donald Goines, *The Busting Out of an Ordinary Man*, p. 21, 1985

crumb-hunting *noun*
housework *CANADA*
Teen slang, reported by a Toronto newspaper in 1946, and reported as 'obsolescent or obsolete' by Douglas Leechman, 1959. From military use in the early 1940s of 'crumb hunt' as meaning 'a kitchen inspection'.

crumble *noun*
in hospital, an elderly patient *UK*
Medical slang.
- —Adam T. Fox, St Mary's Hospital, London, 10th October 2002

crumbly; crumblie *noun*
an older person, certainly one who is over 50 years old *UK*
An upper-class society image of crumbling with decay.
- —Ann Barr and Peter York, *The Official Sloane Ranger Handbook*, p. 158, 1982
- [W]hat most of the crumblies really seem to want is a free TV licence.—Gyles Brandreth, *Breaking the Code*, 1999

crumbo *noun*
▸el crumbo
a socially inept person *US*
Pseudo Spanish.
- —*American Speech*, p. 155, May 1959: 'Gator (University of Florida) slang'

crumbs *noun*
a small amount of money *US*
An offshoot of **BREAD**.
- —Clarence Major, *Dictionary of Afro-American Slang*, p. 42, 1970
- —Kenn "Naz" Young, *Naz's Underground Dictionary*, p. 23, 1973

crumbs!
used as a mild exclamation *UK, 1922*
A euphemism for **CHRIST!**.
- What's Cliff Richard's favourite biscuit? Oh my goodness. I would say [playing for time] ... oh crumbs... I like chocolate-chip cookies, that kind of thing[.]— *The Guardian*, 19th December 2003

crumb-snatcher *noun*
a child; a baby *US, 1958*
- —Robert George Reisner, *The Jazz Titans*, p. 153, 1960
- —Frank Prewitt and Francis Schaeffer, *Vacaville Vocabulary*, 1961–1962

crummy *noun*
1 a brakevan (caboose) *US, 1916*
- —Norman Carlisle, *The Modern Wonder Book of Trains and Railroading*, p. 261, 1946
- "He" the Conductor who made me ride outside the crummy.—Jack Kerouac, *Letter to John Clellon Holmes*, p. 407, 19th February 1953
- He stayed in New York three days and hastily made preparations to get back on the train with his railroad pass and again recross the continent, five days and five nights industry coaches and hard-bench crummies[.]—Jack Kerouac, *On the Road*, p. 308, 1957

2 a truck, a boxcar or an old brakevan (caboose), converted to passenger carrying by adding wooden benches *CANADA*
- Loggers ride in cold and heat in old trucks or rail cars called crummies, which are "crummy."— *Vancouver Sun*, p. 5/2, 30th May 1964
- The word [crummy] developed from a car on logging railways used for the same purpose.—Tom Parkin, *WetCoast Words*, p. 42, 1989

crummy *adjective*
1 inferior *US, 1915*
- "Of all the lousy, crummy, garish, flamboyant, undisciplined, stupid, corny writing," continued Mr. Oliver, "that I have ever had the misfortune to read, this is absolutely the – Will you stop blubbering?"—Max Shulman, *The Many Loves of Dobie Gillies*, p. 149–150, 1951
- When it came to a choice of being nice and dead or crummy and alive, the guy would work overtime at being a heel.—Jim Thompson, *Savage Night*, p. 40, 1953
- Before the crummy day's over, every crummy soul in this crummy school's gonna know who Tony Baker is.—Morton Cooper, *High School Confidential*, p. 12, 1958
- Once at Ames with Minnesota Fats and then again at Arthur's in that cheap, crummy poolroom.— *The Hustler*, 1961
- Maybe he wasn't just a crummy car burglar trying to get by.—Carl Hiaasen, *Tourist Season*, p. 36, 1986

2 lice-infested *UK, 1859*
- —Joe McKennon, *Circus Lingo*, p. 29, 1980

crump *verb*
1 to die *US, 1958*
- —Sally Williams, *"Strong" Words*, p. 137, 1994

2 (used of a hospital patient) to become suddenly sicker, especially without hope of recovering *US, 1980*
- — *Maledicta*, p. 31, 1988–1989: 'Medical maledicta from San Francisco'

crumpet *noun*
1 sexually desirable women considered collectively; hence, desirable men *UK, 1936*
Originally of women only; men weren't so categorised until the 1980s.

- Christ, it's rife up the country, mate. Crumpet for the taking. —Alexander Buzo, *Rooted*, p. 90, 1969
- I gave up on her and went in search of love, affection and a bit of crumpet elsewhere. —Paul Vautin, *Turn It Up!*, p. 83, 1995
- I thought you were the thinking girl's crumpet, Jake. I'm a bit disappointed in you. —Linda Jaivin, *Rock n Roll Babes from Outer Space*, p. 243, 1996
- [T]his party should be stacked out with crumpet. —John King, *Human Punk*, p. 120, 2000
- It wasn't difficult going along with the comments about "crumpet", the jokes about queers and pansies. —Jake Arnott, *He Kills Coppers*, p. 62, 2001
- [T]he bright and attractive host Joan Bakewell (dubbed by the contemporary media "the thinking man's crumpet")[.] —Mick Farren, *Give the Anarchist a Cigarette*, p. 99, 2001

2 the head *UK, 1891*

- Cripes, it's enough to send a bloke off his crumpet[.] —Norman Lindsay, *Halfway to Anywhere*, p. 101, 1947

▸ a bit of crumpet
sexual intercourse *NEW ZEALAND*

- —Louis S. Leland, *A Personal Kiwi-Yankee Dictionary*, p. 15, 1984

▸ bow the crumpet
to plead guilty *AUSTRALIA*
Formed on **CRUMPET** (the head); from bending the head in unspoken affirmative.

- — *The (Sydney) Bulletin*, 26th April 1975

▸ not worth a crumpet
worthless *AUSTRALIA, 1944*

- A bomb is what his stable needs. None of his string is worth a crumpet. —Wilda Moxham, *The Apprentice*, p. 79, 1969

crumpet man *noun*
a womaniser *UK*

- —David Powis, *The Signs of Crime*, 1977

crump out *verb*
to succumb to exhaustion; to die *US, 1953*

- Just the implication that, if she keeps her equipment in regular use, she'll be all set for sex until she crumps out altogether. —Susan Rako, *The Hormone of Desire*, p. 33, 1996

crunch *noun*

1 a most severe test of strength, courage, nerve, skill, etc *UK, 1939*

- A kid points out that we've come to the big crunch. If you don't go to the dean you're suspended and you have the draft and prison. —James Simon Kunen, *The Strawberry Statement*, p. 62, 1968
- "Crunch" is a word currently favored by the keener journalists. It means the showdown, the moment of truth. —Gore Vidal, *Myra Breckinridge*, p. 202, 1968
- CHARLIE [Michael Caine]: Right, here's the crunch: do you all know how to get there? —Troy kennedy Martin, *The Italian Job [uncut script]*, 1969

2 a number sign (#) on a computer keyboard *US*

- —Eric S. Raymond, *The New Hacker's Dictionary*, p. 39, 1991

3 a hospital patient with multiple fractures *US*

- — *Maledicta*, p. 32, 1988–1989: 'Medical maledicta from San Francisco'

4 an Afrikaner *SOUTH AFRICA, 1970*
Also 'crunchie'. Derogatory and offensive.

▸ do your crunch
to become enraged *UK*
Army use.

- You shoulda seen 'im when 'e found it – done 'is crunch, 'e did. —1984

crunch *verb*
to analyse something, especially a large amount of data *US*

- —Guy L. Steele, *Coevolution Quarterly*, p. 29, 1981: 'Computer slang'
- —Guy L. Steele et al., *The Hacker's Dictionary*, p. 51, 1983
- We did it by crunching data. — *Point Break*, 1991

crunch and munch *noun*
crack cocaine *US*
From the drug's arguable resemblance to breakfast cereal or a snack food.

- —Peter Johnson, *Dictionary of Street Alcohol and Drug Terms*, p. 51, 1993

crunch cap *noun*
a fatigue hat, made of cotton canvas with a brim around, that kept the sun and rain off the heads of American soldiers in Vietnam *US*
It could be folded or 'crunched up' easily.

- —Linda Reinberg, *In the Field*, p. 54, 1991

crunch case *noun*
a hospital patient with a severe head injury *US*

- —Sally Williams, *"Strong" Words*, p. 137, 1994

cruncher *noun*

1 a dent in a surfboard that can be repaired without a resin filler *US*

- —George Colendich, *The Ding Repair Scriptures*, p. 88, 1986

2 a foot *US*

- Gee, you feel it way down to your crunchers. —Mezz Mezzrow, *Really the Blues*, p. 100, 1946

crunch hat *noun*
in motor racing, a safety helmet *US*

- —John Edwards, *Auto Dictionary*, p. 38, 1993

crunch time *noun*
the critical moment *AUSTRALIA*

- Confounding the whole stunning situation, is that SA has not won a national title for 34 years! Surely it's crunch time[.] — *News*, p. 59, 1st March 1990
- —Shane Maloney, *Nice Try*, p. 6, 1998
- —William Dodson, *The Sharp End*, p. 65, 2001

crunchy *noun*

1 the pavement or sidewalk *US*

- —Lou Shelly, *Hepcats Jive Talk Dictionary*, p. 9, 1945

2 a foot soldier, or member of the infantry *US, 1951*
Korean and then Vietnam war usage.

- Armed helicopters were especially reassuring to the "crunchies," the ground infantrymen who depended on them to deliver accurate supporting fire. —Shelby L. Stanton, *The Rise and Fall of an American Army*, p. 86, 1985
- —Linda Reinberg, *In the Field*, p. 54, 1991

crunchy *adjective*
embodying the values or at least the trappings of the 1960s counterculture; a person who embodies these values *US*
An adjective often associated with **GRANOLA**, used to describe the throwback person.

- —Connie Eble (Editor), *UNC-CH Campus Slang*, p. 2, Spring 1990
- "A crunchy is a '90s hippie," says Scott Blasik, a young poet from Durham, New Hampshire. "A hiking-boot-wearing, granola-eating, Grateful Dead/Blues Traveler-listening type of person." —David Shenk and Steve Silberman, *Skeleton Key*, p. 48, 1994
- —Andy Ihnatko, *Cyberspeak*, p. 48, 1997
- True, they [the Indigo Girls] are crunchy lesbian-coffeehouse-alterna-rock, and I know you hide the CD when people come over, but it's time we make these girls cool again. —Suroosh Alvi et al., *The Vice Guide*, p. 17, 2002

crunk *noun*
an excited state *US*

- Iconz take a geeky, white American family clubbing and they all get their crunk on. — *Mixmag*, p. 38, December 2001

crunk *adjective*
excellent; intense *US, 1995*
Rap coinage; a variation of **CRANKED** (intensified).

- I go out to clubs. I love to dance and get "crunk." —Alison Pollet, *MTV's Real World Chicago*, p. 104,
- Take him out and take his money / Then I spit on the punk / Now I'm crunk[.] — Three 6 Mafia, *Tear Da Club Up*, 1996
- But around here we get it crunk when ya / Bounce with me —Lil Bow Wow, *Bounce With Me*, 2000

crunked *adjective*

1 excited *US*
Rap usage; a variation of **CRUNK** (excellent).

- Best bit: When overcrunked dad grabs a podium dancer and gets a smack. — *Mixmag*, p. 38, December 2001
- —Connie Eble (Editor), *UNC-CH Campus Slang*, p. 3, October 2002

2 very drunk *US*

- —Connie Eble (Editor), *UNC-CH Campus Slang*, p. 3, Spring 2003

Crusaders *nickname*
the 523rd Fighter Squadron, which served in Korea and briefly in Vietnam *US*

- —Linda Reinberg, *In the Field*, p. 54, 1991

crush *noun*

1 a romanticised affection for someone; an infatuation *US, 1884*
- RUTH: Do you remember your first crush?. LIANNA: My first crush... I used to go to camp up north in the summer. There was this one counselor, she was fifteen maybe sixteen [...] I had sort of a crush on her. —John Sayles, *Lianna*, 1983
- I've a bit of a crush on you mysel. —Ian Pattison, *Rab C. Nesbitt*, 1988

2 the object of an infatuation *AUSTRALIA*
In C19 US use, but now obsolete there.
- You're delirious that your crush has finally noticed you, then you realise that he's just using you to make a move on your bud. — *Dolly*, p. 54, 1996
- He was a huge crush of mine in highschool, and it ended up being very awkward. — *Passing Show*, p. 16, 2002

3 the vagina *US*
- — *Maledicta*, p. 131, Summer/Winter 1982: 'Dyke diction: the language of lesbians'

4 a hat *US, 1916*
- —Marcus Hanna Boulware, *Jive and Slang of Students in Negro Colleges*, 1947

5 in pool, the opening or break shot *US*
- —Mike Shamos, *The Illustrated Encyclopedia of Billiards*, p. 66, 1993

crush *verb*

to do very well *US*
- —Connie Eble, *UNC-CH Campus Slang*, March 1986

crushed *adjective*

ugly *US*
- — *People Magazine*, p. 73, 19th July 1993

crusher *noun*

1 in horse racing, a person who works the odds as they shorten *AUSTRALIA*
- A crusher's a bloke who backs a horse at, say, five to one; then lays it in a bookmaker's bag, at say three to one. Has two points going to nothing. —Frank Hardy, *The Yarns of Billy Borker*, p. 59, 1965
- He could smell trouble before a bet was laid in the shape of a big plunge or a favourite about to blow out the backdoor. He avoided the big punting credit clients and taking bet-back bets from other bookies. The crushers knew better than to try to get on with Duvi. —Clive Galea, *Slipper!*, p. 26, 1988

2 a powerful, hard-breaking wave *US*
- —John Severson, *Modern Surfing Around the World*, p. 165, 1964

3 something overpowering or overwhelming *UK, 1840*

4 a police officer *UK, 1835*
Now rare.

crushers *noun*

fashionable, stylish sunglasses *US*
Biker (motorcyle) usage.

crushman *noun*

a good-looking boy *US*
- —Connie Eble (Editor), *UNC-CH Campus Slang*, p. 3, Spring 1982

crust *noun*

1 a livelihood *AUSTRALIA, 1888*
- 'What's he do for a crust?' 'He's got a small factory.' —Eric Lambert, *The Veterans*, p. 67, 1954
- "And what do you do for a crust?" I gaily asked. —Sue Rhodes, *Now you'll think I'm awful*, p. 84, 1967
- What do youse do for a crust? —Barry Humphries, *Bazza Pulls It Off!*, 1971
- —David McGill, *David McGill's Complete Kiwi Slang Dictionary*, p. 35, 1998
- Mr and Mrs Beckham will always be able to earn a crust – at least, as long as they can keep middle age at bay[.] — *The Guardian*, 25th June 2002

2 in the UK, members of an alternative culture underclass *UK*
Back-formation from **CRUSTY** (a member of an alternative culture underclass).
- There's a lot of crust here [Glastonbury], a lot of French-style armpits. — *The Guardian*, p. 2, 28th June 2004

3 nerve, courage, gall *US, 1900*
- You got a crust asking Allbright to use ammuintion on that slob. —Raymond Chandler, *The Long Goodbye*, p. 75, 1953

crust *verb*

to insult someone *US*
- —Lou Shelly, *Hepcats Jive Talk Dictionary*, p. 9, 1945

crustie *noun*

an old person *NEW ZEALAND, 1997*
- —Harry Orsman, *A Dictionary of Modern New Zealand Slang*, p. 34, 1999

crust of bread; crust *noun*

the head, epecially as a source of intelligence *UK*
Rhyming slang.

crusty *noun*

a young person who many years later embraces the counter-culture values of the late 1960s *UK, 1990*
- Next in the queue was a clump of crusties. They were standing so close to each other that it looked as though their dreads had all velcroed together. —Linda Jaivin, *Rock n Roll Babes from Outer Space*, p. 166, 1996
- It's wet but the festival is up and running and the counter culture is at play: crusties, rastas, schoolies, hippies, freaks, straights, dopers, acid-heads, nightclubbers and parents and kids are all in for the long haul together. — *Sun-Herald*, p. 121, 7th January 1996
- —Vann Wesson, *Generation X Field Guide and Lexicon*, p. 42, 1997
- Crusties are notorious for not believing in baths and synthetic inventions such as deodorant and shampoo – hence their name. Instead they prefer growing dreadlocks and tying dogs on pieces of string. —Ben Osborne, *The A-Z of Club Culture*, p. 61, 1999
- [He] had turned Crusty and gone to live in an old gypsy caravan by the side of the road in the middle of nowhere. —Pete McCarthy, *McCarthy's Bar*, p. 19, 2000
- '[A] good-looking posh young trustafarian juggling crustyboy she'd met at some Arts Festival[.] —James Hawes, *Dead Long Enough*, p. 34, 2000
- Roy had his flat turned over last week like an I'm fuckin sure it was one-a those crusties, fuckin sure of it, mun. —Niall Griffiths, *Sheepshagger*, p. 162, 2001

crusty *adjective*

1 dirty, shabby *US*
- —Helen Dahlskog (Editor), *A Dictionary of Contemporary and Colloquial Usage*, p. 16, 1972
- A crustie boy examined his bourbon-and-scotch soaked trousers and scratched his head, raising a small cloud of dust —Linda Jaivin, *Rock n Roll Babes from Outer Space*, p. 138, 1996
- "I couldn't stand sitting next to that crusty man in the theater." —Rick Ayers (Editor), *Berkeley High Slang Dictionary*, p. 17, 2004

2 crude, vulgar *US*
- —J. R. Friss, *A Dictionary of Teenage Slang (Mt. Diablo High)*, 1964
- — *Current Slang*, p. 2, Fall 1966

crusty treats *noun*

cocaine *UK*
- —Mike Haskins, *Drugs*, p. 280, 2003

crut *noun*

1 filth, nastiness, dirt *US, 1940*
- —J.E. Lighter, *Historical Dictionary of American Slang, Volume One*, p. 535, 1994

2 a disease *US*
- Benny clutched his stomach and rolled his eyes. "Me too. I got the crut." —Irving Shulman, *The Amboy Dukes*, p. 73, 1947

crutch *noun*

1 an improvised holder for the short butt of a marijuana cigarette *US, 1938*
The term of choice before **ROACH CLIP** came on the scene.
- She doubled the empty match cover over backward and put the butt of the cigarette up in the fold to make a crutch, and she brought the cardboard up to her lips and took three deep final drags off the short roach. —Thurston Scott, *Cure it with Honey*, p. 69, 1951

2 in pool, a device used to support the cue stick for a hard-to-reach shot *US*
As the terminology suggests, the device is scorned by skilled players.
- —Steve Rushin, *Pool Cool*, p. 11, 1990

3 in skating, an experienced skater supporting a novice *UK, 1961*

crutch *verb*

to conceal goods (stolen property or contraband) in the vagina – usually contained in a condom and often further protected from discovery by the insertion of a tampon *UK*
- —Angela Devlin, *Prison Patter*, p. 41, 1996

crutcher *noun*

a female thief or smuggler who hides goods in her crutch
From **CRUTCH**. Recorded by a Jamican inmate of a UK prison, August 2002.

Crutches *nickname*

Las Cruces, New Mexico *US*
- — *Current Slang*, p. 16, Spring 1970

cry *noun*

▸ **the cry**

the best *US*

- Q: Charlie, how would you describe the house parties? A: It's the cry! The latest! —Max Shulman, *Guided Tour of Campus Humor*, p. 106, 1955

cry *verb*

▸ **cry all the way to the bank**

used ironically by, or of, someone whose artistic work is a commercial success yet attracts adverse criticism *US*

Credited to musician and entertainer (Wladziu Valentino) Liberace who, from the mid-1950s, enjoyed great popular success and, in the face of critical disdain, quipped and then included the following quotation in his stage act: 'When the reviews are bad I tell my staff that they can join me as I cry all the way to the bank'. The phrase survives but has also become the more straightforward 'laugh all the way to the bank'.

▸ **cry a river**

to regret something deeply *US*

- And I want you to know, we'll all cry a river when you're gone. —*Natural Born Killers*, 1994

▸ **cry Bert**

to vomit *AUSTRALIA*

- [T]he wretch who "cries Bert" after a hastily ingurgitated lunch of curried prawns and creme de menthe. —Barry Humphries, *Bazza Pulls It Off!*, 1971

▸ **cry blue ruin**

to proclaim a family financial disaster *CANADA*

The Historical Dictionary of American Slang records this term in use in the US, but with the meaning 'a cheap, powerful liquor' only.

- Now you'll have to wait till next year to cry blue ruin. —Morley Callaghan, *Stories*, p. 146, 1959

▸ **cry Ruth**

to vomit *AUSTRALIA*

Self-descriptive of its echoic origins.

- [Lew:] "Cry Ruth"?? I don't get your meaning skipper! [Barry:] You know cry Ruth! Chuck! Make love to the lav!!! [Lew:] My God man quick the window!! [Barry:] RUTH RUTH ROOOOOTH!!! —Barry Humphries, *Bazza Pulls It Off!*, 1971

▸ **cry your eyes out; cry your heart out**

to weep long and bitterly *UK, 1704*

- Don't cry your heart out / Don't tell your preacher[.] —Alice Cooper, *Not That Kind of Love*, 1987
- Alistair, who you might think would eat your liver, unable to forget his mum crying her eyes out in the court. —*The Guardian*, 22nd January 2002

cry baby *noun*

a child swindler who appeals for money from strangers with pitiful tales of woe, accompanied if need be by tears *US*

- —Bill Reilly, *Big Al's Official Guide to Chicagoese*, p. 23, 1982

cry baby grenade *noun*

a hand grenade loaded with tear gas for use in riots and to clear bunkers and tunnels *US*

- —Gregory Clark, *Words of the Vietnam War*, p. 207, 1990

cry down *verb*

to disparage someone or something *TRINIDAD AND TOBAGO, 1988*

- —Lise Winer, *Dictionary of the English/Creole of Trinidad & Tobago*, 2003

crying *adjective*

used as a negative intensifier *US, 1942*

- Yet no one came up with a crying dime. —Nelson Algren, *The Man With the Golden Arm*, p. 136, 1949

crying towel *noun*

a notional linen given to someone who is a chronic complainer *US, 1928*

- Give Challee a crying towel, with the compliments of the *Caine!* —Herman Wouk, *The Caine Mutiny*, p. 479, 1951
- —Zander Hollander and Paul Zimmerman, *Football Lingo*, p. 28, 1967

crying weed *noun*

marijuana *US, 1953*

The WEED that invites emotional involvement.

- —Richard A. Spears, *The Slang and Jargon of Drugs and Drink*, p. 130, 1986
- —Mike Haskins, *Drugs*, p. 287, 2003

cry me a river!

used for expressing a lack of sympathy in the face of an implicit solicitation of same *US*

- —Connie Eble (Editor), *UNC-CH Campus Slang*, p. 3, April 1995
- Huh, cry me a river. Three kings. —David Chase, *Sopranos*, 25th August 1997

cryppie; crippie *noun*

in computing, a cryptographer *US*

- —Eric S. Raymond, *The New Hacker's Dictionary*, p. 115, 1991

crypto *noun*

a person who is a secret-sympathiser or -adherent of a political group, especially of a communist *UK*

Adapted from the conventional prefix *crypto-* (concealed, hidden, secret) in such uses as 'crypto-facist'; ultimately from Greek *kruptos* (hidden).

- Labour MPs of various shades of opinion – not by any means only the Communist 'fellow-travellers' or so-called 'crypto's'. —Tom Driberg, *Reynolds News*, 10th March 1946

cryptonie; cryppie *noun*

marijuana *UK*

- —Mike Haskins, *Drugs*, p. 287, 2003

crystal *noun*

1 a powdered narcotic, especially methamphetamine *US*

- She believes crystals are a form of Methedrine and that "they're called chicken feed because they're actually given to chickens." —*San Francisco News Call Bulletin*, p. 3, 17th February 1964
- "You can get awful damn high shooting crystal, and smack can be used to bring you down —Joan Didion, *Slouching Toward Bethlehem*, p. 115, 1967
- But the three staples of the market are methamphetamine (usually called crystal, speed, or by the trade name Methedrine), marijuana (pot), and acid, as LSD is always referred to. —Nicholas Von Hoffman, *We Are The People Our Parents Warned Us Against*, p. 31, 1967
- Sure, I appreciated the crystal blow and his plans to celebrate my birthday. —Iceberg Slim (Robert Beck), *Airtight Willie and Me*, p. 21, 1979
- He could "requisition" oz. bottles of "fluffy flake Merc crystal" for about twelve dollars each. —Terry Southern, *Now Dig This*, p. 11, 1986
- —Geoffrey Froner, *Digging for Diamonds*, p. 68, 1989
- The tweaker said, "Dude, you shouldn't be doin that crystal so early in the morning." —Joseph Wambaugh, *Finnegan's Week*, p. 310, 1993
- ROLLERGIRL: This stuff burns. DINK: It's crystal. —*Boogie Nights*, 1997

2 phencyclidine *US*

Recorded as a current PCP alias.

- —*Drummer*, p. 77, 1977

3 a type of marijuana

- Crystal may well be so named because of the clarity of the high it delivers. —*Spliffs*, p. 67, 2003

crystal *adjective*

perfectly understandable *UK*

A reduction of 'crystal-clear'.

- [I]t became crystal that the National Lottery was a closed book[.] —Andrew Nickolds, *Back to Basics*, p. 27, 1994

crystal chin *noun*

a fighter who is easily injured with blows to the chin *US*

- Redbeard Mahoneey in his time had been a merchant seaman, a renowned arm wrestler, and a pretty good professional boxer, except for his crystal chin. —Joseph Wambaugh, *The Glitter Dome*, p. 83, 1981

crystal cylinder *noun*

the hollow of a breaking wave *AUSTRALIA*

- Here I am in search of the pure source beyond the land of the crystal cylinder[.] —*Tracks*, p. 31, October 1992

crystal meth; crystal meths *noun*

powdered methamphetamine *US*

- Every fucking fucker in the fucking band [Oasis] and crew had been up two days straight solid doing coke and crystal meths, right up to showtime. —Simon Napier-Bell, *Black Vinyl White Powder*, p. 318, 2001
- Now all I see is a bunch of little kids tweaking on crystal meth, ring their ass off so hard they can't dance. —Tara McCall, *This is Not a Rave*, p. 7, 2001
- Don't expect to sleep. The pill (Yabba) is like super-strong base speed and can last up to 24 hours. If smoked (crystal meth), users can be awake for days. —*Mixmag*, p. 38, December 2001

crystal palace *noun*

an apartment or house occupied by amphetamine and/or methamphetamine abusers *US*

- —Walter L. Way, *The Drug Scene*, p. 107, 1997

crystal pop *noun*

a combination of cocaine and phencyclidine, the recreational drug known as PCP or angel dust *UK*

Possibly playing on 'Krystal' champagne.

- —Mike Haskins, *Drugs*, p. 293, 2003

crystal ship *noun*

a syringe filled with a melted powdered drug *US*

- —Jay Robert Nash, *Dictionary of Crime*, p. 91, 1992

crystal tea *noun*

LSD *UK, 1998*

From the appearance of the drug in crystalline form.

- —Mike Haskins, *Drugs*, p. 285, 2003

crywater *noun*

tears *ANTIGUA AND BARBUDA*

Collected by Richard Allsopp.

c's *noun*

1 combat rations, the standard meals eaten by US troops in the field, consisting of an individual ration of packaged pre-cooked foods which can be eaten hot or cold *US*

- Have your people shaved by noon tomorrow and tell them to eat up all their Cs – we gotta pallet coming in the morning.—Charles Anderson, *The Grunts*, p. 90, 1976
- "You hungry any?" "Inna sorta gen'ral way, yeah. You mean C's?" —Larry Heinemann, *Close Quarters*, p. 142, 1977
- —Linda Reinberg, *In the Field*, p. 32, 1991

2 food *US*

An abbreviation of 'calories'; 'to get your c's' is 'to eat'.

- —Collin Baker et al., *College Undergraduate Slang Study Conducted at Brown University*, p. 93, 1968

CS *noun*

1 used as a euphemism for 'chickenshit' *US, 1944*

Far less common than **BS** (**BULLSHIT**).

- —J.E. Lighter, *Historical Dictionary of American Slang, Volume One*, p. 536, 1994

2 marijuana *UK*

- —Mike Haskins, *Drugs*, p. 287, 2003

C sponge *noun*

a contraceptive sponge *US*

- They'd blame it on the fact that I was wearing a c-sponge, saying it would make them numb.—Anthony Petkovich, *The X Factory*, p. 99, 1997

CT *noun*

a woman who signals an interest in sex with another woman but does not have sex with her *US, 1923*

An abbreviation for **CUNT TEASE**.

- —Eugene Landy, *The Underground Dictionary*, p. 61, 1971

CTD

(in doctors' shorthand) expected to die soon *UK*

An initialism for '*c*ircling *t*he *d*rain'.

- —*Ethics and Behaviour*, August 2003

CTN

used as shorthand in Internet discussion groups and text message to mean '*c*an't *t*alk *n*ow' *US*

- —Gabrielle Mander, *WAN2TLK? ltl bk of txt msgs*, p. 44, 2002

Ctrl-Alt-Delete; Control-Alt-Delete *noun*

a notional device or technique which causes something to be reconsidered or restarted *US, 1995*

From the combination of character-keys used as a 'short-cut' to restart a computer; the former is written, the latter spoken.

- Wouldn't it be nice if whenever we messed up our life, we could simply press Ctrl-Alt-Delete and start all over again?—*The Indianapolis Star*, 8th September 2003
- [I]t's a tribute to the cultural penetration of Ctrl-Alt-Delete that the term is so often used in non-computing contexts[.]—*Word Spy*, 12th February 2004

Cuban pumps *noun*

in homosexual usage, heavy work boots *US*

- —*Maledicta*, p. 53, 1986–1987: 'A continuation of a glossary of ethnic slurs in american english'

cubbitch *adjective*

greedy *TRINIDAD AND TOBAGO, 1960*

- —Lise Winer, *Dictionary of the English/Creole of Trinidad & Tobago*, 2003

cubby *noun*

a room, apartment or house *US*

- —Jack Lait and Lee Mortimer, *New York Confidential*, p. 235, 1948: 'A glossary of Harlemisms'

cube *noun*

1 a complete conformist *US*

An intensification of **SQUARE** (a conventional person).

- Youngsters of both sexes used to call a person who wasn't hip a "square," but now the phrase is "cube" (that's a square in 3-D). —*American Weekly*, p. 2, 14th August 1955
- Man, what a cube. This I gotta dig.—William Bast, *The Myth Makers [Six Granada Plays]*, p. 176, 1958
- "A cube is a new fangled square, isn't it?" she teased.—Morton Cooper, *High School Confidential*, p. 138, 1958
- —*San Francisco News*, p. 6, 25th March 1958

2 LSD *US*

From the fact that LSD was often administered in sugar cubes.

- —Donald Louria, *Nightmare Drugs*, p. 45, 1966

3 a tablet of marijuana, approximately one gram in weight *US, 1984*

From the shape.

- —Richard A. Spears, *The Slang and Jargon of Drugs and Drink*, p. 130, 1986
- —Mike Haskins, *Drugs*, p. 287, 2003

4 a tablet of morphine *US*

- —Hyman E. Goldin et al., *Dictionary of American Underworld Lingo*, p. 54, 1950
- —Angela Devlin, *Prison Patter*, p. 41, 1996

5 a cubic inch *US*

- When someone says his engine has 440 cubes, he means that his engine has a cylinder capacity of 440 cubic inches.—Ed Radlauer, *Drag Racing Pix Dix*, p. 15, 1970
- The GS versions were powered by the 350-cube power plant, now rated at 260 horses.—William G. Holder, *American Muscle Cars*, p. 10, 1992

6 a work space in an open-area office *UK, 1936*

An abbreviation of 'cubicle'.

- I've got the manuals in my cube.—Eric S. Raymond, *The New Hacker's Dictionary*, p. 115, 1991

cubeb *noun*

a herbal cigarette, pungent and spicy, made from the cubeb berry *US*

- "Granny will smell it if you smoke in here," Sissie said. "She thinks they're cubebs."—Chester Himes, *The Real Cool Killers*, p. 93, 1959

cube head *noun*

a regular LSD user *US, 1966*

- —Eugene Landy, *The Underground Dictionary*, p. 61, 1971

cubes *noun*

1 the testicles *US*

- —Collin Baker et al., *College Undergraduate Slang Study Conducted at Brown University*, p. 103, 1968

2 dice *US, 1918*

- He lit a cigarette, exhaled, and said with hazel eyes ashine, "Say, Speedy, how's your cube game?'—Iceberg Slim (Robert Beck), *Long White Con*, p. 168, 1977

3 morphine *US*

- —Edith A. Folb, *runnin' down some lines*, p. 233, 1980

4 crack cocaine *UK*

- —Mike Haskins, *Drugs*, p. 281, 2003

cubicle *noun*

a Mini Metro car *UK*

- —Peter Chippindale, *The British CB Book*, p. 161, 1981

cub reporter *noun*

a young, naive and untrained reporter *US, 1908*

The term is a popular culture allusion to the Superman legend. When Clark Kent went to work at the *Daily Star*, Jimmy Olsen was an office boy with aspirations to be a great reporter. With help from Superman, Olsen, who was forever tagged with the label 'cub reporter', became a member of the reporting staff. From the much earlier (1845) sense of a 'cub' as an 'apprentice'.

- For two weeks out of every year, students were required to go to work as cub reporters on the downtown Minneapolis newspapers, where they covered real news stories and helped to put out a real metropolitan daily.—Max Shulman, *The Many Loves of Dobies Gillis*, p. 142, 1951

- Leon Daniel, a fine and dedicated newsman, gave me my start by hiring me as a cub reporter for UPI in London. —Thomas L. Friedman, *From Beirut to Jerusalem*, p. 573, 1995

cuck *verb*
to defecate *CANADA*
- "Cuck" is number two. 'Maman, I gotta cuck.' —David Mazerolle, *LAvant tu take off, please close the lights*, p. n.p., 1993

cuck *adjective*
very bad, awful *IRELAND*
- That's bad now, Paul. It's a gammy chant. It's cuck melodeon, Mam. —Eamonn Sweeney, *Waiting for the Healer*, p. 50, 1997

cuckle bucks *noun*
curly or kinky hair that has not been chemically straightened *US*
- —Malachi Andrews and Paul T. Owens, *Black Language*, p. 88, 1973

cuckoo *noun*
a fool; a crazy person *UK, 1889*
- Listen, I got another one of those phone calls this morning. Some cuckoo, he'll get picked up and thrown in jail. —Elmore Leonard, *Maximum Bob*, p. 245, 1991

cuckoo *adjective*
crazy, mad, distraught *US, 1906*
- You can't leave the kids with that girl. She's cuckoo!" "Now, Harry-" "Don't give me the 'Now Harry' bit. I tell you this girl is a certifable maniac!" —Max Shulman, *Rally Round the Flag, Boys!*, p. 82, 1957
- Look, honey, if that man is cuckoo for kids, that's his problem, not yours. —Armistead Maupin, *Further Tales of the City*, p. 223, 1982
- —Angela Devlin, *Prison Patter*, p. 41, 1996
- It's only fair to tell you / I'm absolutely cuckoo —Stephin Merritt, *Absolutely Cuckoo*, 1999
- He's boo-koo koo-koo. — *Gone in 60 Seconds*, 2000

cuckoo farm *noun*
a mental hospital *UK*
A variation of **FUNNY FARM**.
- The zealots who saw truth as indivisible ended up in [...] the cuckoo farm. —D. Kavanagh, *Duffy*, 1980

cuckoo house *noun*
a mental hospital *US, 1930*
- —J.E. Lighter, *Historical Dictionary of American Slang, Volume One*, p. 537, 1994

cuckoo's nest *noun*
1 the vagina *UK, 1840*
Survives in folk songs of the US and UK.
- But I like a girl with the bubbies on her breast / And a road that's easy traveled to her cuckoo's nest. — Traditional, *The Cuckoo's Nest*

2 a mental hospital *US, 1962*
- Her antics gave our neurology section a heady "cuckoo's nest" atmosphere. —Jean-Dominique Bauby, *The Diving Bell and the Butterfly*, p. 96, 1997

cucumber *noun*
1 a number, usually a telephone number *UK*
Rhyming slang.
- Give me your cucumber and I'll ring you back. —Ray Puxley, *Cockney Rabbit*, 1992

2 in gambling, an ignorant victim of a cheat *US*
A play on 'green', the colour of the cucumber and a slang term for 'inexperienced'. Often shortened to 'cuke'.
- —Frank Garcia, *Marked Cards and Loaded Dice*, p. 261, 1962

cucumbers *noun*
▸ **the cucumbers**
in prison, Rule 43, which allows a prisoner to be kept apart from the main prison community for 'safety of self or others' *UK*
Rhyming slang.
- Take the cucumbers, take the cucumbers. —ex-Cabinet Minister Jonathan Aitken recalling his arrival in prison in 1999, *Have I Got News for You*, 28th November 2003

cuda *noun*
1 a barracuda *US, 1949*
- "Wait, don't cast yet, those are just cudas," he cautioned as he threw more live aits oer the rising cloud of snook. — *Inshore Salt Water Fishing*, p. 45, 2001

2 a Plymouth Baracuda car *US*
- —John Lawlor, *How to Talk Car*, p. 35, 1965
- — Elementary Electronics, *Dictionary of CB Lingo*, p. 58, 1976

cuddle and kiss *noun*
1 an act of urination *UK*
Rhyming slang for **PISS**. Sometimes shortened to 'cuddie'.
- Watch my beer I'm going for a cuddle. —Ray Puxley, *Cockney Rabbit*, 1992

2 a girl; a girlfriend *UK, 1938*
Rhyming slang for 'miss'; formed in a time when a cuddle and kiss were the only realistic objectives for a young man with love on his mind.
- —Julian Franklyn, *A Dictionary of Rhyming Slang*, p. 54, 1960

3 piss, in the phrase 'take the piss' (to make a fool of) *UK*
Rhyming slang.
- —Ray Puxley, *Cockney Rabbit*, 1992

cuddle bunny *noun*
an attractive girl *US*
- Hey, Cuddle-bunny, come on over. I'm tired of being a chair-warmer for this drip-bait. [Freckles and his Friends comic strip] —*San Francisco Examiner*, p. 15, 9th February 1946

cuddled and kissed; cuddled *adjective*
drunk *UK*
Rhyming slang for **PISSED**.
- —Ray Puxley, *Fresh Rabbit*, 1998

cuddle puddle *noun*
a group of people laying together, especially after taking the type of recreational drugs that enhance feelings of togetherness; a communal jacuzzi *UK*
- —Susie Dent, *The Language Report*, p. 12, 2003

cuddle seat *noun*
in a cinema, a double seat provided for a couple's convenience *AUSTRALIA*
Probably adopted from the brand name Cuddleseat™ (a baby carrier) introduced in 1947.

cuddy *noun*
a horse *AUSTRALIA, 1897*
From British dialect *cuddy* (a donkey).
- Two owners with a maiden horse each were discussing the problem of making a profit out of their cuddies. —Frank Hardy and Athol George Mulley, *The Needy and the Greedy*, p. 89, 1975

cudja?
could you? *UK*
Apparently coined by television production company Brighter Pictures but rapidly gained wider use.

cuds *noun*
the countryside *UK*
- We used to go out on patrol in the cuds with welly boots on because of the mud. —Andy McNab, *Immediate Action*, p. 23, 1995

cue *noun*
1 barbecued meat *US*
- Probably, Earl got to have him some 'que on Memorial Day. —Odie Hawkins, *Black Chicago*, p. 149, 1992

2 barbecue *US, 1908*
- The term barbecue (a.k.a. Bar-B-Q, BBQ, 'cue, or, to the real aficionados, simply Q) is often used synonymously with grilling. —Omaha Steaks, *Omaha Steaks*, 2001

3 a tip or gratuity *US*
- —Roger D. Abrahams, *Deep Down in the Jungle*, p. 259, 1970

▸ **put your cue in the rack**
to die; to retire *AUSTRALIA*
- —Ned Wallish, *The Truth Dictionary of Racing Slang*, p. 20, 1989

cueball *noun*
1 a bald person *US, 1941*
- —Don R. McCreary (Editor), *Dawg Speak*, 2001

2 a crew-cut haircut *US*
- — *American Speech*, p. 303, December 1955: 'Wayne University slang'

3 one-eighth of an ounce of cocaine *US*
- —Kenn "Naz" Young, *Naz's Dictionary of Teen Slang*, p. 27, 1993

cue biter *noun*
an actor who proceeds with his lines without letting the audience react appropriately to the cue line *US*
- —Sherman Louis Sergel, *The Language of Show Biz*, p. 63, 1973

cue-bow *noun*

a charge of 'conduct unbecoming an officer' filed against a police officer *US*

- The charge was conduct unbecoming an officer, or CUBO, called "cue-bow" by the policemen. —Joseph Wambaugh, *The Choirboys*, p. 20, 1975

cues *noun*

headphones worn by musicians overdubbing a tape *US, 1979*

- —Arnold Shaw, *Dictionary of American Pop/Rock*, p. 100, 1982

cuff *noun*

▸ off the cuff

unrehearsed, improvised *US, 1938*

From the discreet *aide-memoire* some performers or speakers jot on their cuffs.

- [C]onsidering his personal record for acting off the cuff. — *The Sweeney*, p. 51, 1976

▸ on the cuff

1 on credit *US, 1927*

- [A]rrangers worked for us on the cuff[.] —Mezz Mezzrow, *Really the Blues*, p. 288, 1946
- —Arnold Shaw, *Lingo of Tin-Pan Alley*, p. 10, 1950
- A shrewdie can live here forever on the cuff. —Jack Lait and Lee Mortimer, *Washington Confidential*, p. 277, 1951
- Look, boys, I'm a little short. You don't mind putting this one on the cuff, do you? You know I'm good for it. —William Burroughs, *Junkie*, p. 76, 1953
- He's got the capital, he can let you ride on the cuff a little while. —John Sayles, *Union Dues*, p. 244, 1977
- You owe me folding, plus the juice. When you are on the cuff you speak to me. You hide, you only make it worse. —Greg Williams, *Diamond Geezers*, p. 10, 1997

2 admitted to a theatre without paying for a ticket *US*

- —Sherman Louis Sergel, *The Language of Show Biz*, p. 64, 1973

cuff *verb*

1 to handcuff someone *UK, 1851*

- I just got cuffed again/ Now I'm going to dizz knee land. — Dada, *Dizz Knee Land*, 1992
- —Angela Devlin, *Prison Patter*, p. 42, 1996
- You are under arrest! Cuff 'em! — *South Park*, 1999
- There's a pair of handcuffs in my pocket, take them out and cuff her wrists. —Stewart Home, *Sex Kick [britpulp]*, p. 259, 1999

2 to shine something, to polish something *US*

- While the cat was cuffing my boots, my brother came in. —A.S. Jackson, *Gentleman Pimp*, p. 27, 1973

3 to drink to excess *TRINIDAD AND TOBAGO, 1956*

- —Lise Winer, *Dictionary of the English/Creole of Trinidad & Tobago*, 2003

4 to admit someone to an entertainment without charge *US*

- But the two assigned to keep the visitors happy had worked the bright-light belt, so they knew where they could cuff a few small night clubs. —Jack Lait and Lee Mortimer, *Washington Confidential*, p. 223, 1951
- —Don Wilmeth, *The Language of American Popular Entertainment*, p. 67, 1981

5 in an illegal betting operation, to accept bets at odds and in a proportion guaranteed to produce a loss for the book-maker *US*

- —David W. Maurer, *Argot of the Racetrack*, p. 23, 1951

cuff down; cuff up *verb*

to assault someone; to beat someone *TRINIDAD AND TOBAGO, 1966*

- —Lise Winer, *Dictionary of the English/Creole of Trinidad & Tobago*, 2003

cuff link faggot; cuff link queen *noun*

a wealthy, ostentatious homosexual male *US*

- In this rarified area, johns are not johns but cuff link faggots or queens, an expression derived from their tendency to wear extravagant looking jewelry. They are also called "finger bowl faggots." —Antony James, *America's Homosexual Underground*, p. 29, 1965

cuff links *noun*

handcuffs *US*

- —Ralph de Sola, *Crime Dictionary*, p. 37, 1982

cuffs *noun*

handcuffs *UK, 1861*

Originally used of C17 iron fetters, now used as a shortening of 'handcuffs'.

- "Got any 'cuffs, Rog?" asked one. "Used mine on some paki kid down the road." —Greg Williams, *Diamond Geezers*, p. 207, 1997

cuke *noun*

a cucumber *US, 1903*

A domestic colloquialism.

- I got tomatoes, cukes, and a jar of mayonnaise. She wanted bacon, but all the bacon was gone. —Stephen King, *Skeleton Crew*, p. 52, 1985

CUL

used in computer message shorthand to mean 'see you later' *US*

- —Eric S. Raymond, *The New Hacker's Dictionary*, p. 342, 1991

culchie *noun*

a person from rural Ireland *IRELAND, 1958*

A derogatory term coined during the 1940s at University College Galway for students of agriculture; probably from Irish *Coillte Mach* (County Mayo), regarded (wrongly) as a remote place. Other possible etymologies: *coillte* (woods) and *cúl and tí* (a rear entrance to an important house, used by social inferiors).

- He said he was a culchie little chancer who plamased his way to the top. —Joseph O'Connor, *Red Roses and Petrol*, p. 6, 1995
- You really do think we're all a bunch of eejit [idiot] culchies, don't you? —James Hawes, *Dead Long Enough*, p. 262, 2000

cull *noun*

1 a prisoner re-assigned to an undemanding job after failing at a more challenging one *US*

- —Charles Shafer, *Folk Speech in Texas Prisons*, p. 202, 1990

2 in horse racing, a horse that is cast off by a stable because it has failed to perform well *US*

- —Dan Parker, *The ABC of Horse Racing*, p. 145, 1947

▸ on the cull list

unmarried *US, 1933*

- —Frederic G. Cassidy, *Dictionary of American Regional English, Volume One*, p. 877, 1985

cully; cull; cul *noun*

a man, a fellow, a companion *UK, 1661*

- Get into these, cul, somebody's got to come into the ring tonight. —Butch Reynolds, *Broken Hearted Clown*, p. 16, 1953
- —Paul Baker, *Polari*, p. 171, 2002

cultural jammer; jammer *noun*

a cultural activist who creatively subverts advertising material *US*

- These artists are "cultural jammers," exposing the ways in which corporate and political interests use the media as a tool of behavior modification. — *New York Times*, p. 1 (Section 2), 23rd December 1990
- [T]o paint jammers as "vigilante censors" in the media[.] —Naomi Klein, *No Logo*, p. 288, 2001

culture fruit *noun*

watermelon *US*

- Black people did not want to reject the fruit because of the white man's mechanism of perpetuating racisim in relation to it, so we made it a positive thing by calling it CULTURE FRUIT cause it was too good to let go. —Malachi Andrews and Paul T. Owens, *Black Language*, p. 96, 1973

culture jam; jam *noun*

a message subverted by anticorporate activists *US*

- My favourite truth-in-advertising campaign is a simple jam on Exxon that appeared after the 1989 Valdez spill: "Shit Happens. New Exxon," two towering billboards announced[.] —Naomi Klein, *No Logo*, p. 282, 2001
- [J]ams that change Absolut Vodka to "Absolut Hangover" or Ultra Kool cigarette to "Utter fool"[.] —Naomi Klein, *No Logo*, 2001

culture jamming; jamming *noun*

the act of inverting and subverting advertising matter by anticorporate activists *US*

Derives from the conventional sense of 'jam' (to disrupt a signal).

- Next Friday: Craig Baldwin's latest experimental documentary, "Sonic Outlaws," which deals with copyright infringement and "culture jamming." — *Seattle Times*, p. H17, 7th July 1995
- Culture jamming baldly rejects the idea that marketing – because it buys its way into our public spaces – must be passively accepted as a one-way information flow. —Naomi Klein, *No Logo*, p. 281, 2001

culture vulture *noun*

an enthusiast for intellectual and artistic culture and cultural events *US, 1947*

- Go neon in Tokyo, be a culture vulture in Kyoto, explore nature at Daisetsuzan National Park. — *Guardian Unlimited*, July 2003

cultus *adjective*

worthless, bad, useless, insignificant *US, 1851*

From the Chinook trading jargon.

- "Bad medicine," "chaffy," "snide," "jim-crow," "and "pizen" are applied to anything worthless on the Eastern slope of the Rockies while "cultus," a Chinook Indian word – is most frequently employed with like significance upon the BC side. — *Alberta Historical Review*, p. 14/2, 1962

cultus coulee *noun*

a stroll or ride for pleasure *CANADA*

- These Indians always seemed to be travelling "cultus coulee," which means moving about with no set destination, and stopping wherever there was good hunting or fishing. — R. D. Symons, *Many Trails*, p. 75, 1963

cultus potlatch *noun*

a present for which nothing is expected in return, especially one of little value *CANADA*

- At Christmas-time Chief Gregior would come and receive tobacco as a cultus potlatch. — *BC Historical Quarterly*, p. 200, July 1940

cum *noun*

amyl nitrite *US*

A drug associated with sex.

- — Jay Robert Nash, *Dictionary of Crime*, p. 91, 1992

▷ **see:** COME *and variants*

cumbucket *noun*

a despised person *US*

- "Scumbags?" "Naw." "Cumbuckets?" "Too long." — Joseph Wambaugh, *The Choir Boys*, p. 33, 1975
- She heard him call me disgusting names, like the time we were sitting in the kitchen and he yelled to me from the living room, "Hey, cumbucket, get out here with a beer." — Robert Davidson, *Fighting Back*, p. 167, 2000

cum catcher *noun*

a condom *UK*

Uses COME; CUM (semen) to describe a condom's purpose.

- — David Rowan, *A Glossary for the 90's*, 1998

cum drum *noun*

a condom; especially a condom with a bulbous extension to collect semen *US*

Phonetically similar to 'condom'.

- — *Maledicta*, p. 150, Summer/Winter 1986–1987: 'Sexual slang: prostitutes, pedophiles, flagellators, transvestites, and necrophiles'

cummy face *noun*

in a pornographic film or photograph, a close-up shot of a man's face as he ejaculates *US*

- — *Adult Video News*, p. 42, August 1995

cum shaw *noun*

anything procurred through other than legitimate channels *UK, 1925*

From the Chinese for a 'present' or 'bonus', originally applied to a payment made by ships entering the port of Canton.

- Belmonte was the Vance's acknowledged "cum shaw" expert, the man (there is one on every ship) who does the semilegal horse trading for items the ship wants and cannot obtain through regular supply channels. — Neil Sheehan, *The Arnheiter Affair*, p. 61, 1971

cung *noun*

marijuana *US*

- — Bill Valentine, *Gang Intelligence Manual*, p. 130, 1995

cunkerer *noun*

a blundering, poorly trained technician *GUYANA*

From 'cunk', imitative of the metallic sound of a clumsily handled tool.

cunning as a Maori dog *adjective*

very cunning; sly *NEW ZEALAND, 1947*

In *A Dictionary of Modern New Zealand Slang*, 1999, Harry Orsman notes that *'Maori dog* is now usually replaced by less objectionable epithets like *shithouse rat'*.

cunning as an outhouse rat *adjective*

very cunning indeed *NEW ZEALAND*

- Fulton is described as being as cunning as the proverbial outhouse rat. — *Sunday Star-Times*, p. A5, 7th July 1996

cunning as a shithouse rat *adjective*

extremely crafty *NEW ZEALAND, 1917*

- I dunno how the bastard beat us. He must be cunning as a — rat. — Jon Cleary, *The Long Shadow*, p. 131, 1949
- Mrs. Hansen called Lola a dirty little half-bred, over-sexed slut, no better than the bloody blacks and cunning as a shit-house rat. — Criena Rohan, *The Delinquents*, p. 32, 1962
- — Clive Galea, *Slipper*, p. 51, 1988
- [T]his rolled-gold, 24-carat nong [Saddam Hussein] who, cunning as a shithouse rat, has tried to con the world while acting like a low mongrel towards his own citizens — *The Daily Telegraph*, 14th February 2003

cunning kick *noun*

a place for secreting money *AUSTRALIA*

- It was Jack's 'cunnin' kick' for what he could divert on its way to the till. — Sam Weller, *Old Bastards I Have Met*, p. 114, 1979

cunny *noun*

the vagina *UK, 1615*

A play on CUNT (the vagina) and 'con(e)y' (a rabbit).

- I kept touching her breasts and her cunny (that's what she calls it) and at last I got on her between her legs and she guided my prick into her cunt[.] — Frank Harris, *My Life and Loves (Grove Press Reader)*, p. 168, 1963
- Some "cherries" completely close the cunny hole and have to be opened by surgery. — *Screw*, p. 9, 29th December 1969
- LESSEE YA LAP THAT CUNNY UP[.] — Lester Bangs, *Psychotic Reactions and Carburetor Dung*, p. 364, 1981
- I must have been wearing loose-fitting shorts because, as I was waiting to see my friend, her puppy came to me and licked me several times on my little cunny. — Nancy Friday, *Women on Top*, p. 221, 1991
- Does he ever get down there and tongue my cunny? No sir, no how, no way. — *Letters to Penthouse XV*, p. 303, 2002

cunny fingers; cunny thumbs *noun*

an awkward, clumsy person *US, 1892*

A term originally applied to a weak shooter.

- Oh, give it here, cunny-thumbs. I know my way 'round a cork. — Dewey Lambdin, *King's Captain*, p. 345, 2000

cunt *noun*

1 the vagina *UK, 1230*

The most carefully avoided, heavily tabooed word in the English language.

- I bet her cunt is juicy & ripe, hunh? — Neal Cassady, *The First Third*, p. 197, 1950
- O Tania, where now is that warm cunt of yours, those fat, heavy garters, those soft, bulging thighs? — Henry Miller, *Tropic of Cander*, p. 5, 1961
- One way to a girl's mind is through her cunt. — Richard Neville, *Play Power*, p. 92, 1970
- The Phoenix Art Gallery in Berkeley is a perfect example of how men find excuses to portray women as cunts. — *The Berkeley Tribe*, p. 5, 26th June-3rd July 1970
- You know: well-scrubbed, blonde bangs, china blue eyes, apple cheeks, little cunt that smells like a gouda cheese. — Tom Robbins, *Another Roadside Attraction*, p. 78, 1971
- Many women today do freely use words like "fuck," "cunt," "prick" in bed and on the street. — *Screw*, p. 7, 1st July 1972
- Every time I see your dick I see her cunt in my bed. — Marianne Faithfull, *Why'd Ya Do It*, 1979
- The Melody girls orchestrate their stripteases over five-song cassette sound tracks; the generous ones reach cunt by the fourth number, while the ones who fancy themselves jazz ballerinas wait till the fifth. — Josh Alan Friedman, *Tales of Times Square*, p. 9, 1986
- ROBIN: Well, you know I'm not going to say it. JANE: Oh, come on! C-U-N-T. Come on, please? ROBIN: I don't think so. — *Boys on the Side*, 1995
- She talked to me for a half-hour more about the word "cunt" and when she was finished, I was a convert. I wrote this for her. — Eve Ensler, *The Vagina Monologues*, p. 84, 1998

2 a woman, especially as an object of sexual desire *UK, 1674*

- After that, Mexico, and this time a cunt will live with me. — Jack Kerouac, *Letter to Neal Cassady*, p. 400, April 1953
- And those rotten bitches. Two cent cunt. — Hubert Selby Jr, *Last Exit to Brooklyn*, p. 55, 1957
- Somewhere in the middle of Missouri, for the first time, this sailor, who never called a woman a woman if he could call her a cunt, and a Negro a nigger (I'd advertised for him in the New York Times), finally boiled over. — Clancy Sigal, *Going Away*, p. 175, 1961
- Next to Miss Destinee's pad theres this real swell cunt an she walks aroun all day in her brassiere – standing by the window[.] — John Rechy, *City of Night*, p. 105, 1963
- Jesus, I don't know anyone who has stuff to waste on high-school cunt. — Malcolm Braly, *On the Yard*, p. 28, 1967
- Ha, you bet your sweet ass they could be improved! Get some halfway decent cunt in there for openers! — Terry Southern, *Blue Movie*, p. 25, 1970
- In the beginning, Estelle had been just another cunt by the roadside as likely to give the clap to him as the other way around. — Gurney Norman, *Divine Right's Trip (Last Whole Earth Catalog)*, p. 43, 1971

- And all because of a stupid blond cunt in a cold water flat who knew how to assuage his sex problems[.] —Mickey Spillane, *Last Cop Out*, p. 7, 1972
- "Some cunt phoned for you." "Any cunt could do that." —Brian Preston, *Pot Planet*, p. 88, 2002

3 sex with a woman *UK, 1670*

- [A]t the same time depriving him of cunt and subjecting him to homosex stimulation[.] —William Burroughs, *Naked Lunch*, p. 27, 1957
- They would run down a story to them about selling them some cunt from some of the finest bithces they ever saw. —Claude Brown, *Manchild in the Promised Land*, p. 160, 1965
- All the cats laughed at me all the way to Frisco, "Ole Babs spent Fifty Dollars and still didn't get no cunt, so that makes Babs a trick." —Babs Gonzales, *Movin' On Down De Line*, p. 22, 1975

4 a despicable person, female or male *UK, 1860*
When used as a reductive term of abuse, 'cunt' is usually more offensive than the male equivalents.

- He's just a great big lazy cunt. —Sumner Locke Elliott, *Rusty Bugles*, p. 28, 1948
- I was hi & she was nice to me instead of being antagonistic as per most cunts, & she looks fine, what tits & slim body. —*The First Third*, p. 197, 5th November 1950
- She said, "Please don't tell me my son is dead." / I said, "If you don't believe it, cunt, look at the hole in his head." —Bruce Jackson, *Get Your Ass in the Water and Swim Like Me*, p. 50, 1964
- I glance at his Mercedes-Benz – capitalist swine, barbiturate pushing pig, member of the suburban nouveau riche, cunt. —Kevin Mackey, *The Cure*, p. 40, 1970
- Do you know what that cunt said? —Eve Babitz, *Eve's Hollywood*, p. 117, 1974
- "Listen, cunt," I tell him, "what's in this envelope is all you get for your favours." —Ted Lewis, *Jack Carter's Law*, p. 7, 1974
- DEREK: I said "you cunt". I said "you fucking cunt." I said "who are you fucking calling cunt, cunt?" CLIVE: Yeah? What did he say, cunt? DEREK: He said "you fucking cunt." —Peter Cook and Dudley Moore, *Derek & Clive (Live)*, 1976
- This is no fucking good to me, you cunts treating me like an animal. —Ray Denning, *Prison Diaries*, p. 31, 1978
- You titless cunt! —Robert English, *Toxic Kisses*, p. 5, 1979
- Her new husband makes potato chips. And she's a cunt. —Armistead Maupin, *Babycakes*, p. 206, 1984
- What's a man got to do? Go 'n talk to some cunt in Parliament? —Peter Corris, *Make Me Rich*, p. 105, 1985
- You talk like a pissed-off dishwasher: "Fuck those cunts and their fucking tips." —*Reservoir Dogs*, 1988
- Both bookies then slept, content that those smart arse dago cunts would get their comeuppance come Slipper time. —Clive Galea, *Slipper*, p. 209, 1988
- 'Last time I vote for those bastards,' exclaimed one distraught resident. 'Cunts promised us no aircraft noise if they got into office.' —Linda Jaivin, *Rock n Roll Babes from Outer Space*, p. 289, 1996
- [I]t's always nice to get a result over those [wheel] clamping cunts, ain't it? —Dave Courtney, *Raving Lunacy*, p. 88, 2001
- I tabulated the votes and you're all a pack of cunts! I didn't get one measly vote in that category. —*Inpress Magazine*, p. 58, 4th April 2002
- "You fucking Communist cunt, get out of here," he [Richard Mellon Scaife' said to Karen Rothmyer of the Columbia Journalism Review. —Al Franken, *Lies*, p. 132, 2003
- You're a terrific person. You're my favorite person. But every once in a while, you can be a real cunt. —*Kill Bill*, 2003

5 among homosexuals, a boy or young man as a sexual object *US*

6 among homosexuals, the buttocks, anus and rectum *US*

- Move your cunt – Mama wants to sit down. —Bruce Rodgers, *The Queens' Vernacular*, p. 57, 1972

7 among homosexuals, the mouth *US*

- Close your filthy cunt; I don't want to hear any more about it. —Bruce Rodgers, *The Queens' Vernacular*, p. 57, 1972

8 a person you admire or pretend to grudgingly admire; a form of address between friends *UK*
Mainly jocular usage.

- So he'd whizzed up (laced with amphetamines) all the sandwiches, bless him. Cunt. —Dave Courtney, *Raving Lunacy*, p. 139, 2001

9 an idiot, a fool *UK, 1922*

- If you want to get on, become a stupid cunt, the Establishment will love you. London's full of them. —Robin Page, *Down Among the Dossers*, p. 115, 1973
- [T]hey ask for my name, and like a cunt I give it to them without thinking[.] —James Hawes, *Dead Long Enough*, p. 219, 2000
- Stony-faced she is. Only cracks up once she's made a cunt out of you. —Kevin Sampson, *Clubland*, p. 47, 2002

10 to a drug addict, a vein used for injecting a drug, especially the vein found on the inside of the elbow *US*

- [I]t looks like a small purple cyst . . . into which she drives the needle each time she fixes. "That's your cunt, Jody," I said once[.] —Alexander Trocchi, *Cain's Book*, p. 31, 1960
- —Stewart L. Tubbs and Sylvia Moss, *Human Communication*, p. 119, 1974

11 an unfortunate or difficult situation; an unpleasant task; a problem *UK, 1931*
A logical extension of earlier, still current senses (an irritating person or object).

- What a cunt, though, if the geezer got so stoned one night that he tried to take out the wrong eye? —Dave Courtney, *Raving Lunacy*, p. 4, 2001

cunt and a half *noun*
an extremely unpleasant person *UK, 1984*
This intensification of **CUNT** (an unpleasant person) was originally used exclusively of males.

cunt book *noun*
a pornographic book, especially one with photographs or illustrations *US*

- Goldstein showed that it wasn't just perverts that bought cunt books. —*Screw*, p. 2, 4th July 1969
- You sanitize everything? Take out the rubbers and cunt books? —David Poyer, *The Passage*, p. 192, 1995

cunt breath *noun*
a despicable person *US*

- And leave those cocksucking, cunt-breath, pusnuts, shit-for-brains, pencil-pushing Pentagon assholes to me. —Richard Marcinko, *Rogue Warior I*, p. 266, 1992
- Little five-foot-six-inch Roten stands up and says, "He said suck my shorts, cunt breath!" —Daniel E. Kelly, *U.S. Navy Seawolves*, p. 31, 2002

cunt cap *noun*
a narrow green garrison cap worn by enlisted men *UK, 1923*
Probably of World War 1 vintage. Beale noted, in 1984, that the Chinese Army refer to the same article as a 'cow's-cunt-cap'. Soldiers learn the term in the first few days of training. They now learn not to use the term in the presence of women.

- —*Argosy*, p. 81, July 1966
- —Carl Fleischhauer, *A Glossary of Army Slang*, p. 13, 1968
- Shaerbach's kid brother in his uniform, his cunt cap pushed back on his shaved, Neanderthal skull[.] —Gilbert Sorrentino, *Steelwork*, p. 59, 1970
- A white soldier, his shirttail out behind, his cunt cap crosswise on his dome, staggered along happily[.] —Earl Thompson, *Tattoo*, p. 121, 1974
- Since at least as long ago as 1940, the soldier's name for the Army's garrison cap has been cunt cap. —*Maledicta*, p. 222, Winter 1980
- —Linda Reinberg, *In the Field*, p. 55, 1991

cunt collar *noun*
a desire for sex *US*

- But then they got so bad that even cats with long cunt collars would get tired of screwing these cold junkie bitches. —Claude Brown, *Manchild in the Promised Land*, p. 193, 1965
- He had a cunt collar around his neck bigger than this galaxy[.] —Steve Cannon, *Groove, Bang, and Jive Around*, p. 29, 1969
- Spoon's cunt collar was tight / which was understandably right / after serving three years and day. —Lightnin' Rod, *Hustlers Convention*, p. 16, 1973
- She began to wonder what made this dude uptight ... have what Ranger called a 'cunt collar.' —Robert Deane Pharr, *Giveadamn Brown*, p. 60, 1978

cunt eater *noun*
any person who performs oral sex on a woman *US*

- I want so much to really get down there and examine her cunt. But I am ashamed to do it. I might be called a "Cunt Eater," for even getting that close. —Clarence Major, *All-Night Visitors*, p. 20, 1998

cunted *adjective*
drunk *UK*

- —Pete Brown, *Man Walks into a Pub*, 2003

cunt-eyed *adjective*
squinting *UK, 1916*

- Bawl, little baby. Bawl, you fucking cunt-eyed baby. —Pat Conroy, *The Lords of Discipline*, p. 106, 1980

cunt face *noun*
a despicable person *US, 1948*

- [G]enerations of academy maintenance men had sanded away the more flragrant obscenities, although an occasional "dork-brain" or "cunt-face" was freshly etched in the wooden slats[.] —John Irivng, *A Prayer for Owen Meany*, p. 111, 1989
- And I want it all, whether it's from an ugly Indian-curry-quaffing cunt-face – the Bureau butt-wiping baloney-beaters – or Michael Ei. —Robert Eringer, *Lo Mein*, p. 157, 2000

cunt-faced *adjective*
despicable *US*

- We can't let these cunt-faced white-assed motherfuckers get away with this shit no longer. —James Baldwin, *If Beale Street Could Talk*, p. 159, 1974

- He said she was a heartless lying evil cunt-faced bitch just like her goddamn fucking mother was.—Buddy Giovinazzo, *Life is Hot in Cracktown*, p. 6, 1993
- She kept her eyes off the mess he was making of her crime scene, reading the words on the wall, cocksucker, disgusting cunt faced pig.—Michele Jaffe, *Bad Girl*, p. 295, 2003

cunt fart *noun*
a despicable person *US*
- This is your wake-up call, you cunt fart.—Bruce Wagner, *I'm Losing You*, p. 151, 1996

cuntfuck *noun*
an extremely unpleasant individual *UK*
Both **CUNT** and **FUCK** are synonymous here, each serving to intensify the other.
- The thing that still pisses me off to this day is that cuntfuck said we engineered the battle with his bunch of wankers.—*Q*, p. 100, May 2002

cunt hair *noun*
a very small distance *US*
- Ill be home just a cunt-hair less than every two days and for twelve hours and at a stretch[.]—Jack Kerouac, *On the Road*, p. 134, 1957
- —Carl Fleischhauer, *A Glossary of Army Slang*, p. 13, 1968
- Well, we the side of the angels in the censorship fight, won one recently by the margin of a cunt's hair[.]—*Screw*, p. 12, 8th March 1970
- [A] quick, but competent one arm chin with both hands, satisfactory enough with the right hand and a cunt hair short with the smaller left.—Neal Cassady, *The First Third*, p. 165, 1971
- You yank the ring and pull the pin all but half a cunt hair. See?—Larry Heinemann, *Close Quarters*, p. 45, 1977

cunt hair grass *noun*
an oatgrass or spike rush *US, 1945*
- —Frederic G. Cassidy, *Dictionary of American Regional English, Volume One*, p. 880, 1985

cunt hat *noun*
a felt hat *UK, 1923*
Probably from the shape of the crease in the crown.

cunthead *noun*
a despised fool *US, 1971*
- Wilson was looking for some diversion, and he clearly didn't like Kent's looks. "Shove off, cunt-head," he snapped.—John Irving, *The Water-Method Man*, p. 239, 1972

cunt-holes!
used for registering frustration, annoyance or anger *UK*
- [F]ucky dingnuts and bastardy cunt-holes[.]—Jenny Eclair, *Camberwell Beauty*, p. 208, 2000

cunt hook *noun*
the hand *US*
Usually in the plural.
- —Michael Dalton Johnson, *Talking Trash with Redd Foxx*, p. 114, 1994

cunt-hooks *noun*
1 a gesture that is used to insult or otherwise cause offense, in which the forefinger and middle-finger are extended to form a V-shape, the palm turned in towards the gesturer *UK, 1984*
An alternative name for a **V-SIGN**.
2 an unpleasant person *UK*
- I was sober when I was collared and so cunt-hooks should judge me on the events of the night.—Danny King, *The Burglar Diaries*, p. 148, 2001

cunt hound *noun*
a man obsessed with the seduction of women *US, 1960*
- It was shocking, but I knew Joe was 1 helluva cunthound, or so he said[.]—Clarence Cooper Jr, *The Farm*, p. 187, 1967
- —*Maledicta*, p. 10, Summer 1977: 'A word for it!'
- Ralston is a notorious well-endowed cunthound and he's had years to work on you.—James Ellroy, *Brown's Requiem*, p. 175, 1981

cuntie *noun*
a contemptible person *UK: NORTHERN IRELAND*
A patronising elaboration of **CUNT**.
- There's not a lot we don't know about ye, cuntie, ye can thank yer Regimental magazine for that[.]—Chris Ryan, *The Watchman*, p. 10, 2001

cuntiness *noun*
unpleasant or stupid characteristics of a person *UK*
- [F]all into line with the rest of the world with regards to Norris and cuntiness.—Danny King, *The Burglar Diaries*, p. 34, 2001
- I have no doubt that beating brought me back from the brink of lifelong cuntiness.—Frank Skinner, *Frank Skinner*, p. 239, 2001

cunting *adjective*
used as an intensifier, generally denoting disapproval *UK*
- pakkies, coons and the cuntin' Common Market—Stuart Browne, *Dangerous Parking*, p. 44, 2000
- The ultimate cunting Irish experience awaits you[.]—James Hawes, *Dead Long Enough*, p. 100, 2000
- [F]ucking stuck yer in some cunting prison[.]—Patrick Jones, *Everything Must Go*, p. 146, 2000
- [F]uck knows how many cunting times.—Ken Lukowiak, *Marijuana Time*, p. 22, 2000
- We'll give him the old oil and have him typing letters and licking envelopes before you can say Arrogant Cunting Upper Fucking Class Arseholes.—Stephen Fry, *Revenge*, p. 48, 2000
- Fuckin Jesus Christin twattin cuntin fuckin hell!—Niall Griffiths, *Grits*, p. 42, 2000
- lug boxes around a cuntin warehouse—Niall Griffiths, *Kelly + Victor*, p. 140, 2002
- The barrage of profanity [in "Jerry Springer – the Opera"] has its peaks of hilarity, not least when Satan is described as a "cunting cunting cunting cunt".—*The Guardian*, 11th November 2003

-cunting- *infix*
used as an intensifier, generally negative *UK*
- Afan Taff road Blackwood South bastard Wales UcuntingK the fucking world[.]—Patrick Jones, *Everything Must Go*, p. 162, 2000

cuntish *adjective*
1 unpleasant; stupid *UK*
- [I]f you're only going to ask cuntish quesitons we're leaving the room.—Alan Woods, *The Map Is Not the Territory*, p. 180, 2000
- All the same, it's a cuntish way to end up.—J.J. Connolly, *Layer Cake*, p. 180, 2000
- I never touch wedding rings. It's too cuntish.—Danny King, *The Burglar Diaries*, p. 188, 2001
- — Fleapit, *Cuntish Behaviour*, 2001

2 weak, cowardly *US*
- "Don't go cuntish on me!" Roscoe snarled when he drove away from the station.—Joseph Wambaugh, *The Choir Boys*, p. 53, 1975
- Danny stood up, feeling warm and loose, wondering if he should muscle Lembeck for going cuntish on him.—James Ellroy, *The Big Nowhere*, p. 83, 1988

cunt juice *noun*
vaginal secretions *US*
- Cunt juice is a perfume.—Kathy Acker, *In Memorian to Identity*, p. 128, 1990
- My cock slides in almost too easily – her cunt is too wet, drenched with her own cunt juice and Christie's saliva, and there's no friction.—Brett Easton Ellis, *American Psycho*, p. 175, 1991
- I eased myself into her ass, very slowly, greasing myself well with her cunt juice.—Pedro Juan Gutierrez, *Dirty Havana Trilogy*, p. 5, 1998
- I could see steam rising up from the tank barrel where her warm cunt juices had bathed it.—*Letters to Penthouse XV*, p. 147, 2002

cunt-lapper *noun*
a person who performs oral sex on a woman *US, 1916*
- "Wait a minute," he yelled, "don't you cunt-lappers know that's Agnes, she's got the biggest dose in Hartford, everybody knows that."—Jack Kerouac, *Letter to Neal Cassady*, p. 298, 10th January 1951
- —Helen Dahlskog (Editor), *A Dictionary of Contemporary and Colloquial Usage*, p. 17, 1972
- Well, cock-suckers and reluctant cunt-lappers, the revolution is here!—*Screw*, p. 5, 12th June 1972

cunt-lapping *noun*
oral sex on a woman *US*
- Is Cunt-Lapping Better Than the Pill? (Headline)—*Screw*, p. 13, 22nd March 1970

cunt-lapping *adjective*
depised *US, 1923*
- The public-relations value of appearing to send all the pot-smoking, cunt-lapping, ad-men for the revolution to Brixton, or even Parkhurst, is enormous.—Germaine Greer, *The Madwoman's Underclothes*, p. 45, 1986
- I know you and Boyd wanted that cunt-lapping faggot to win.—James Ellroy, *American Tabloid*, p. 1, 2001

cunt-licking *noun*
oral sex on a woman *US*
- It took a good ten minutes of wrestling and another five were given over to cunt-licking before Samson got to sink his sausage in Walker's tunnel of love.—Stewart Home, *Slow Death*, p. 107, 1996
- Elsewhere there's all the stuffed cunts, finger jobs, and cunt-licking you can handle – and then some.—*The Penthouse Erotic Video Guide*, p. 196, 2003

cunt-licking *adjective*
despised *US, 1985*
• "I'm not gonna be any cunt-licking nurse," Natalie snapped. —Augusten Burroughs, *Running with Scissors*, p. 44, 2002

cunt light *noun*
in the pornography industry, a light used to illuminate the genitals of the performers *US*
• —*Adult Video News*, p. 50, October 1995

cunt like a Grimsby welly *noun*
an unusually large and pungent vagina *UK*
Grimsby is a fishing port on the northeast coast of England; the comparison to a 'welly' (Wellington boot) is obvious.
• Fackin' slag. Cunt like a Grimsby welly, arse like a wizard's sleeve. —Andrew Holmes, *Sleb*, p. 151, 2002

cunt man *noun*
a heterosexual man; a womaniser *UK*
Uses **CUNT** in the generalised sense as 'women'.
• I hear you're a bit of a cunt man, Mr Dunford. So I apologise for the vile content of these snaps. —David Peace, *Nineteen Seventy-Four*, p. 184, 1999

cunt off *verb*
to make someone angry; to annoy someone *UK*
• I fucking hate all that, Carole ... I fucking hate it ... it cunts me right off[.] —John King, *White Trash*, p. 116, 2001

cunt pie *noun*
the vagina, especially as an object of oral sex *US*
• There, in public, making herself hotter and hotter, finger in cunt pie going round and round, as finger slips black panties lower, she breathes harder and harder. —Kathy Acker, *Portrait of an Eye*, p. 147, 1980

cunt prick *noun*
a despicable person *UK*
A compound of two terms of abuse that may need strengthening after overuse.
• Ya cuntprick, one's sayin' with harsh breath, ya sang to the fuckin' rozzers. —Nick Barlay, *Curvy Lovebox*, p. 19, 1997

cunt racket *noun*
prostitution *US*
• Must be some hod times in the cunt racket. —John Sayles, *Union Dues*, p. 152, 1977

cunt rag *noun*
1 a sanitary towel *US*
• A bitch was nothing but a bitch no matter who she was; they spread their legs the same wore cunt-rags the same when they had their periods, and sat on the toilet to do the same things[.] —Nathan Heard, *Howard Street*, p. 177, 1968
• You'd have to go to the bottom of the Hudson River and bring me back Lena Horn's cunt rag. —Dennis Wepman et al., *The Life*, p. 151, 1976
• She's putting that cunt rag back in. —James Ellroy, *My Dark Places*, p. 350, 1996
• And I saw Anna's dead blood cunt rag last week. —John Alfred Williams, *Clifford's Blues*, p. 154, 1999

2 a despicable person or thing *US*
• You ever seen a nun call a small child a "fucking cunt rag?" Wasn't pretty. —*Chasing Amy*, 1971

cunt's act *noun*
a major deception *AUSTRALIA*
• —Thommo, *The Dictionary of Australian Swearing and Sex Sayings*, p. 31, 1985

cunt screen *noun*
a strip of canvas stretched between the open rungs of the accommodation ladder up which lady guests would ascend above the heads of the boat's crew *UK*
Similar in purpose and effect to a **VIRGINITY CURTAIN**.

cunt-simple *adjective*
obsessed with sex; easily distracted by women *US*
• With her mind, and with her body, she had to organize Louis Palo, that cunt-simple schmuck, and her own husband, to steal the money then to take the fall for her. —Richard Condon, *Prizzi's Honor*, p. 70, 1982

cunt sniff *noun*
a contemptible or loathesome individual *UK*
As usage of **CUNT** (a contemptible person) becomes evermore mainstream, elaborations are necessary to maintain the derogatory effect. 'Cunt sniff' contrives **CUNT** (vagina) and conventional 'sniff' (to inhale, to smell) to suggest something of no more worth than the odour of a woman's genitals.
• It Took Us Ages to Film This, so the Least You Ungrateful Little Cuntsniffs Could Do is to Pay Some Fucking Attention for Once[.] —*Esquire*, p. 40, November 2001

cunt splice *noun*
any improvised splice *US, 1956*
• —Peter Kemp, *The Oxford Companion to Ships and the Sea*, p. 218, 1976

cunt starver *noun*
a prisoner serving time for not making maintenance payments *AUSTRALIA, 1950*
• —Gary Simes, *A Dictionary of Australian Underworld Slang*, 1993

cunt stretcher *noun*
the penis *US*
• What price now, 'cunt plugger', 'cunt prober', 'cut prodder', 'cunt rammer', 'cunt stopper', 'cunt stretcher', 'cunt whacker'? —Ian Gibson, *The Erotomaniac*, p. 184, 2001

cunt-struck *adjective*
obsessed with sex with a woman or women *UK, 1866*
• I do not agree, for instance, that he is a philosopher, or a thinker. He is cunt-struck, that's all. —Henry Miller, *Tropic of Cander*, p. 4, 1961
• —John D. Bell et al., *Loosely Speaking*, p. 6, 1966
• —Michael Dalton Johnson, *Talking Trash with Redd Foxx*, p. 62, 1994

cunt-sucker *noun*
1 a person who performs oral sex on women *UK, 1868*
• He can become a world-class cunt sucker who will have women standing in line waiting to be next. —Betty Dodson, *Orgasms for Two*, p. 172, 2002

2 a despised person *US, 1964*
• Meal mouthed cunt suckers flow through you. —William S. Burroughs, *The Soft Machine*, p. 47, 1966
• You ain't been here twety minutes you finished already, you cheap quickie cuntsucker ... in and out .. that's what she likes, the cold bitch. —Grace Paley, *Enormous Changes at the Last Minute*, p. 112, 1974

cunt-sucking *noun*
oral sex on a woman *US*
• I sat right down on Joe's mouth and he gave me the most comprehensive cunt-sucking that I've ever had in my life. —Graham, Masterson, *Secrets of the Sexually Irresistible Woman*, p. 244, 1998

cunt-sucking *adjective*
despised *US*
• And you just let me tell you how much all the kids in the office and the laboratory hate you thinking heavy metal assed cunt sucking board bastards. —William S. Burroughs, *Nova Express*, p. 48, 1964
• I didn't foresee that my editors at Columbia University Press would be called "cunt-sucking maggots to let this one slighter through." —Elaine Showalter, *Hystories*, p. x, 1997

cunt tease *noun*
a woman who signals an interest in sex with another woman but does not have sex with her *US*
• —Eugene Landy, *The Underground Dictionary*, p. 61, 1971

cunt-tickler *noun*
a mustache *US*
• I was you was an Italianate Jew, all earthy and Levantine and suave and had a cunt-tickler of a mustache[.] —Norman Mailer, *Why Are We in Vietnam?*, p. 15, 1967

Cunt Town *nickname*
Norfolk, Virginia *US*
A major naval base, and hence a hotbed of prostitution.
• —Ralph de Sola, *Crime Dictionary*, p. 198, 1982

cunt wagon *noun*
a car perceived to attract women *US*
• "A real cunt wagon," the salesman had whispered confidentially in his ear. —Earl Thompson, *Tattoo*, p. 435, 1974

cunty *adjective*
unpleasant *US*
• [S]he was also smart, tough, feisty and knew her way around without being foul-mouthed and cunty. —Emmett Grogan, *Ringolevio*, p. 198, 1972
• [A] couple of big cunty brothers in jumpers[.] —Ben Elton, *High Society*, p. 23, 2002

cup *noun*

1 the vagina *US*

- Satin was a bitch that had one of those real rarel fuzzy cups, the kind a man runs into once in a lifetime. —A.S. Jackson, *Gentleman Pimp*, p. 108, 1973

2 a cup of tea *UK*

Both figurative and practical.

- Anyway, none of it would be your cup, darling. —Angus Wilson, *Hemlock and After*, 1952

Cup *noun*

▸ **the Cup**

the annual Melbourne Cup horse race *AUSTRALIA, 1864*

The most prestigious Australian horse racing event.

- I don't know anything about the Cup, mate. —James Holledge, *The Great Australian Gamble*, p. 118, 1966
- The trainer took him to the saddling paddock about a half an hour before the Cup, which was run at two-forty in the afternoon. —Wilda Moxham, *The Apprentice*, p. 2, 1969
- Son I'm taking the train down for the Cup. —Clive Galea, *Slipper*, p. 5, 1988

cup and saucer *noun*

the fifth wheel on a tractor trailer *US*

- —*American Speech*, p. 273, December 1961: 'Northwest truck drivers' language'

cupcake *noun*

1 a cute girl *US, 1939*

- It's Art Linkletter, assisted by a cupcake named Jean Lewis, setting up one of his harebrained stunts for "People Are Funny." [Caption] —*San Francisco News*, p. 4T, 25th September 1954
- Not so long ago the Korbel vineyards got hoooked up with a conventoin in town and some bright young man conceived the idea of having an unclothed cupcake take a bath in champagne. —*San Francisco Call-Bulletin*, p. 13, 21st August 1957
- He gets a look at the cupcakes and he's staggering all over the place, and he grabs her right by the left tit and gives her a nice little milkshake, on the house. —George V. Higgins, *The Rat on Fire*, p. 126, 1981
- Give me that cupcake shot first. —Robert Stoller and I.S. Levine, *Coming Attractions*, p. 195, 1991
- "Hi Nick," said Jerry, toweling his hair. "You get a piece off your cupcake yet?" —C.D. Payne, *Youth in Revolt*, p. 48, 1993
- He unsnapped my jeans, hooked a finger into the waistband, and pulled me to him. "About that proposal, cupcake..." he said. —Janet Evanovich, *Seven Up*, p. 2, 2001

2 a male homosexual, especially if young *US*

- —Angela Devlin, *Prison Patter*, p. 42, 1996

3 a haircut shaped like a box *US*

- —Ellen C. Bellone (Editor), *Dictionary of Slang*, p. 8, 1989

cupcakes *noun*

1 the female breasts *UK*

Possibly informed, if not inspired, by a brassiere's 'cups'.

- I'm banging away, looking at those tight little cup cakes jiggling about[.] —Ben Elton, *High Society*, p. 20, 2002

2 well-defined, well-rounded buttocks *US, 1972*

- —H. Max, *Gay (S)language*, p. 9, 1988

3 LSD *UK*

- —Mike Haskins, *Drugs*, p. 285, 2003

Cup Day *noun*

the day on which the Melbourne Cup horse race is run *AUSTRALIA, 1876*

- On our first Cup day at Monomeith the goods train pulled in just before 3 p.m. —Patsy Adam-Smith, *Folklore of the Australian Railwaymen*, p. 189, 1969

cupful of cold sick *noun*

the eptiome of worthlessness *NEW ZEALAND*

- —David McGill, *David McGill's Complete Kiwi Slang Dictionary*, p. 36, 1998

cupid's itch *noun*

any sexually transmitted infection *US, 1930*

- —Joseph E. Ragen and Charles Finston, *Inside the World's Toughest Prison*, p. 796, 1962
- "So your client goes in on Monday complaining that he is," she reads from a page, "as he describes it, 'pissing battery acid,' and wondering if he has to tell his wife about a little bout of Cupid's itch." —Richard Dooling, *Brain Storm*, p. 261, 1998
- [T]he gals all had Cupid's Itch and the whiskey was two dollars a glass. —Jake Logan, *Hot on the Trail*, p. 101, 2002

cupid's measles *noun*

syphilis; any sexually transmitted infection *US*

- You say only three people know that this Prince has Cupid's measles? —George MacDonald Fraser, *Royal Flash*, p. 98, 1970

cupla focal

a paltry knowledge of Irish, literally a few words, enough for a display of national pride but not nearly enough for a conversation *IRELAND*

- Maybe it's all down to TnaG but suddenly everyone seems dead keen to trot out the cupla focal. —*Irish Times*, 16th November 1996
- What could be closer to perfect manhood, than to go tearing out onto a playing pitch armed with ash and steeled for battle, to knock skin and hair out of the enemy until, ascending dizzy heights, you end up clutching a cup to the clouds victorious and bellowing the koopla focal in God's face? —*Clare Champion*, 2nd March 2001

cup of chino; cup of cheeno *noun*

a cappuccino *AUSTRALIA*

- While the gingerbread browned, Bill loffered us 'lemictons' and Tony made 'cups of chino'. —Kathy Lette, *Girls' Night Out*, p. 111, 1987
- —James Lambert, *The Macquarie Book of Slang*, 1996

cup of tea *noun*

1 something that is to your taste *UK, 1932*

Variants are 'cup of char' and 'cuppa'.

- That's about your mark, I should think. That's about your cup of tea. Isn't it? —Clive Exton, *No Fixed Abode [Six Granada Plays]*, p. 122, 1959
- I'm surprised. I wouldn't have thought it would be, like, your cup of tea. —Melanie McGrath, *Hard, Soft & Wet*, p. 106, 1998
- "Well," I had to acknowledge, "not my own cuppa." —Claire Mansfield and John Mendelssohn, *Dominatrix*, p. 16, 2002
- He's not really my cup of char musically, but the small crowd keep dancing, and the beats are big. —Donna Legge, *BBCi*, 27th May 2003

2 an act of urination *UK*

Rhyming slang for **PEE** or **WEE**.

- If you hear someody in the pub announce that he is going for a 'cup of tea' he isn't. —Ray Puxley, *Cockney Rabbit*, p. 43, 1992

cup of tea *verb*

to see *UK*

Rhyming slang.

- —Ray Puxley, *Cockney Rabbit*, p. 43, 1992

cuppa; cupper *noun*

a cup of tea or coffee *UK, 1934*

- Gawd, I could do a cuppa. —Ruth Park, *Poor Man's Orange*, p. 80, 1949
- [I] had visions of cuppers and snout [cigarettes]. —Charles Raven, *Underworld Nights*, p. 201, 1956
- Take five. Have a cuppa. —Nick Barlay, *Curvy Lovebox*, p. 33, 1997
- Oh good, Number Two, I do enjoy a good cuppa joe. —*Austin Powers*, 1999
- [H]e popped into Burtonwood for a fucking cuppa. —Kevin Sampson, *Outlaws*, p. 15, 2001

cuppie *noun*

a female hanger-on at a World Cup sailing competition *US*

- The cuppies, many of whom were dressed in upscale sailing togs, outnumbered sailors and sailing wannabes by a wide margin. —Joseph Wambaugh, *Floaters*, p. 55, 1996

cups *noun*

sleep *US*

- —Jack Lait and Lee Mortimer, *New York Confidential*, p. 235, 1948: 'A glossary of Harlemisms'

▸ **in your cups**

drinking; drunk *UK, 1406*

- Well, Collie, is this part of your college training? Not to take advantage of a lady in her cups? —Jim Thompson, *After Dark, My Sweet*, p. 35, 1955
- In his cups, of course. Meant no harm. —Max Shulman, *Anyone Got a Match?*, p. 68, 1964

Cup week *noun*

the week during which the Melbourne Cup horse race is run *AUSTRALIA, 1882*

- I once had high hopes for a suitor – a wealthy and well travelled grazier – until he arrived in Melbourne (where I lived at the time) to attend the festivities which accompany Cup week. —Sue Rhodes, *Now you'll think I'm awful*, p. 9, 1967

cura *noun*

heroin; specifically an injection of heroin at a moment of great need *US, 1969*

From Spanish for 'cure'.

- —Richard A. Spears, *The Slang and Jargon of Drugs and Drink*, p. 132, 1986
- —Mike Haskins, *Drugs*, p. 283, 2003

curate's egg *noun*
something that is good in parts *UK, 1961*
From the phrase 'good in parts – like a curate's egg'.
- Perhaps supermarket wine departments should create a special section marked Curate's Eggs – the honesty of this, allied to the fact that many drinkers simply do not care that a wine is deficient in one area though excellent in another (a weedy aroma, say, but substantial body) would have great appeal. — *The Guardian*, 7th June 2003

curb *noun*
▸ **against the curb**
without money *US*
- — Bill Valentine, *Gang Intelligence Manual*, p. 74, 1995

▸ **to the curb**
1 destitute; suffering from hard times *US*
- — James Harris, *A Convict's Dictionary*, p. 40, 1989

2 rejected in romance *US*
- — *Washington Post*, 14th October 1993

3 vomiting *US*
- — Pamela Munro, *U.C.L.A. Slang*, p. 19, 1989

curb *verb*
to stop or slow down *US*
- — Lavada Durst, *The Jives of Dr. Hepcat*, p. 12, 1953

curb hop *noun*
a person who takes orders and serves food to customers seated in their cars *US, 1937*
- I decided to leave that job after a slightly retraded curb hop choked me into unconscoiusness[.] — Walter Cronkite, *A Reporter's Life*, p. 16, 1996

curb serve *verb*
to sell crack cocaine on a street corner *US*
- — Bill Valentine, *Gang Intelligence Manual*, p. 75, 1995

curbstoner *noun*
in the used car business, a dealer who operates with low overheads and a small inventory *US*
- — *Esquire*, p. 118, March 1968

cure *noun*
1 treatment for drug addiction *US*
Generally after 'the'.
- In fact, the owner's son was a user – at this time in a sanitarium taking the cure. — William Burroughs, *Junkie*, p. 52, 1953

2 suicide *US*
- — Vincent J. Monteleone, *Criminal Slang*, p. 63, 1949

cured *adjective*
▸ **get cured**
to get rich *US*
- Salvador, known as Sally to his friends – he always keeps a few "friends" around and pays them by the hour – got cured in the slunk business in World War 2. — William Burroughs, *Naked Lunch*, p. 156, 1957

Curehead *noun*
someone who dresses in black similar to members of the band the Cure or other goth-rock bands, wears makeup and has the specific hairstyle of the lead singer *IRELAND*
- She was a bit of a Curehead but not that bad: she had a mind of her own. It was just the look, the image she followed, the hair and the Docs. She was into the Cure as well but not only the Cure. — Roddy Doyle, *The Van*, p. 25, 1991

curer *noun*
an alcoholic drink taken to alleviate the symptoms of a hangover *UK: SCOTLAND*
- C'mon for a wee curer and ye'll be bran new. — Michael Munro, *The Complete Patter*, 1996

cure-the-plague *noun*
the bleed period of the menstrual cycle *US*
From the C14 belief that drinking menstrual blood was a remedy for bubonic plague.
- — *The Museum of Menstruation and Women's Health*, November 2000

curfuffle; gefuffle; kerfuffle *noun*
a disturbance or disorder of any kind *UK: SCOTLAND, 1813*
- [I]f Mr Blair's Commons statement on the reshuffle kerfuffle goes badly later today[.] — *The Guardian*, 18th June 2003

curl *noun*
the concave face of a wave as it breaks *US*
- — Grant W. Kuhns, *On Surfing*, p. 115, 1963

Curl *noun*
used of a bald man, or one with *curly* hair, as a form of address *AUSTRALIA, 1984*
A barely abbreviated form of **CURLY**.

curlies *noun*
pubic hair *US*
Used both literally and figuratively to suggest complete control over someone.
- You're in no position to make deals. We got you by the curlies. — Joseph Wambaugh, *The Blue Knight*, p. 146, 1973

curl the mo; curl a mo *adjective*
great; terrific; excellent *AUSTRALIA, 1941*
- The Blue Orchids are curl the Mo. — Sumner Locke Elliott, *Rusty Bugles*, p. 10, 1948

curl the mo!; curl a mo!
terrific! *AUSTRALIA*
- And the S.P. [bookmaker] had paid the full starting price – fifty to one! Curl a mo! — Eric Lambert, *The Veterans*, p. 27, 1954
- — Jim Ramsay, *Cop It Sweet!*, p. 26, 1977

curly *noun*
a challenging situation *NEW ZEALAND*
McGill suggests that the term is 'derived possibly from googly ball in cricket'.
- — David McGill, *David McGill's Complete Kiwi Slang Dictionary*, p. 33, 1998

Curly *noun*
used of a bald-headed man *UK, 1961*
Ironic or, perhaps, the man so-dubbed began with curly hair and, like the word itself, evolved into this sense.

curly *adjective*
1 (mainly of decisions, questions, etc) difficult *AUSTRALIA, 1963*
- [A] curly one for Beckham and fans[.] — *The Australian*, 12th June 2003

2 excellent, attractive *UK, 1981*
Possibly a shortened variation of **CURL THE MO**.

▸ **to give someone the curly lip**
to say something displeasing *US*
- Most people call me Jimmy. One or two call me Jimbo when they want to give me the curly lip. — Robert Campbell, *Nibbled to Death by Ducks*, p. 2, 1989

curly do *noun*
a curly hair style popular with black men and women in the mid-1970s *US*
- It's goodbye Afro, hello curls for scads of local hip black men who are part of the international, unisex trend to curly hair. They call the style "a Superfly," "a Lord Jesus" or just "a Curly Do" and they're spending lots of time and money to get the look. — *San Francisco Examiner*, p. 34, 13th April 1975

curly wolf *noun*
an aggressive, belligerent man *US, 1910*
A term from the American west.
- I think I'll pick a flower and maybe call on the old curly wolf himself. — Kerry Newcomb, *Texas Anthem*, p. 121, 1986

curp *noun*
the penis *UK, 1981*
Back slang, 'kcirp' for **PRICK** (the penis). Only ever in limited use, by 2003 completely redundant.

currant bread *adjective*
dead *UK*
Rhyming slang.
- — Ray Puxley, *Cockney Rabbit*, 1992

currant bun *noun*
1 a nun *UK*
Glasgow rhyming slang.
- — Michael Munro, *The Complete Patter*, 1996

2 the sun *UK, 1938*
Rhyming slang. Sometimes shortened to 'currant'.
- Cor, the currant [sun]'s 'ot today[.] — *The Sweeney*, p. 6, 1976

- [T]he Empire, on which the currant bun never sets[.] —Ronnie Barker, *Fletcher's Book of Rhyming Slang*, p. 39, 1979

▸ **on the currant bun**
on the run *UK*
Rhyming slang, in underworld and police use.
- —John Gosling, *The Ghost Squad*, 1959

Currant Bun *nickname*
The Sun, a daily newspaper *UK*
Rhyming slang, acquired from the solar original.
- I had to go further down the road to get me currant bun, / Hello – Isn't that George on page one? —Madness *In the Middle of the Night*, 1979
- —*The Times*, 10th June 1982
- [S]uch masterpieces of the scribe's art as Magna Carta, Hansard and the Currant Bun[.] —Andrew Nickolds, *Back to Basics*, p. 32, 1994
- Patient confidentiality, remember. Just her. No nurses or theatre orderlies ready to spill their guts for a backhander from the Currant Bun. —Christopher Brookmyre, *Boiling a Frog*, p. 86, 2000
- That lot in the Currant Bun? —Garry Bushell, *The Face*, p. 153, 2001

currant cake *adjective*
awake *NEW ZEALAND*
Prison rhyming slang.
- —Harry Orsman, *A Dictionary of Modern New Zealand Slang*, p. 35, 1999

currant-cakes *noun*
delirium tremens *UK*
Rhyming slang for **SHAKES**; a back-formation from **CURRANT-CAKEY** (shakey).
- —Ray Puxley, *Cockney Rabbit*, 1992

currant-cakey; currant-cakie *adjective*
shakey *UK, 1932*
Rhyming slang.

currants and plums *noun*
the gums *UK*
Rhyming slang.
- —Ray Puxley, *Cockney Rabbit*, 1992

curry *noun*
verbal support on the emphatic end of the scale *NEW ZEALAND*
- —David McGill, *David McGill's Complete Kiwi Slang Dictionary*, p. 36, 1998

▸ **give someone currry**
1 to attack someone *AUSTRALIA, 1936*
That is, make it 'hot' for them.
- He give 'em some curry. He didn't have to lay down like a sheila to them, he told 'em[.] —D'Arcy Niland, *The Shiralee*, p. 44, 1955
- —Arthur Chipper, *The Aussie Swearer's Guide*, p. 48, 1972
- If someone give you curry, be nice to them. —Kel Richards, *The Aussie Bible*, p. 32, 2003

2 to make someone's life difficult, to reprove someone *AUSTRALIA, 1936*
Possibly from the hot nature of curry.
- Yeah. He really gave him curry at the end [...] of his summing up. —Robert Hughes, *PM*, 10th May 2000

Curry *noun*
▸ **the Curry**
Cloncurry, generally called 'The Curry', is the western Queensland base of the Flying Doctor Service *UK*
- —Jock Marshall and Russell Drysdale, *Journey Among Men*, p. 21, 1962

curry city *nickname*
Bradford, West Yorkshire *UK*
Citizens' band radio slang, reflecting the large immigrant population.
- [I]t will take more than the Commission for Racial Equality to change Bradford's name from Curry City. —Peter Chippindale, *The British CB Book*, p. 169, 1981

curry-mouth *adjective*
fond of Indian food *TRINIDAD AND TOBAGO, 1987*
- —Lise Winer, *Dictionary of the English/Creole of Trinidad & Tobago*, 2003

curry muncher *noun*
a person from the Indian subcontinent *NEW ZEALAND*
Derogatory.
- One Fiji Indian representative at the meeting said Indian children were generally referred to as curry-munchers and niggers. —*(Wellington) Dominion*, p. 9, 6th May 1991
- Chinny chin chins on my left has got hers in her right hand at about the same level as the curry muncher. —Paul Vautin, *Turn It Up!*, p. 208, 1995

curse *noun*
1 the bleed period of the menstrual cycle *US, 1930*
Used with 'the'.
- I've got the curse. But call me again. —James T. Farrell, *Rendezvous*, p. 139, 1955
- —Collin Baker et al., *College Undergraduate Slang Study Conducted at Brown University*, p. 102, 1968
- And was surprised when she told him she was going to call in and say she was in bed with the curse. —Elmore Leonard, *Swag*, p. 115–116, 1976
- I was praying all these past four days I wouldn't get the curse. I'm overdue. —Elmore Leonard, *Switch*, p. 158, 1978
- —*The Museum of Menstruation and Women's Health*, April 2002

2 a swagman's bundle of personal effects, a swag *AUSTRALIA, 1921*
Variants are 'curse of Cain' and 'curse of God'.

▸ **carry the curse; hump the curse**
to go on the tramp *AUSTRALIA*
After **CURSE** (a swag).
- —Sidney J. Baker, *The Drum*, 1959

curse *verb*
▸ **curse stink; cuss stink**
to use a great deal of profanity *TRINIDAD AND TOBAGO, 1960*
- —Lise Winer, *Dictionary of the English/Creole of Trinidad & Tobago*, 2003

curse of Eve *noun*
the bleed period of the menstrual cycle *UK, 1929*
Adopted from poetic and literary use.
- We may not be able to lift the curse of Eve completely. But we think we can help you keep your sense of humour during what amounts to a quarter of your adult life. —advertisment for 'Dr White's' tampons, *Company*, June 1987

curse of Mexico *noun*
in a deck of playing cards, the two of spades *US, 1949*
- —Thomas L. Clark, *The Dictionary of Gambling and Gaming*, p. 57, 1987
- —George Percy, *The Language of Poker*, p. 25, 1988

curse of Scotland *noun*
in a deck of playing cards, the nine of diamonds *UK, 1715*
- —Albert H. Morehead, *The Complete Guide to Winning Poker*, p. 260, 1967

curse rag *noun*
a sanitary towel *UK, 1961*
Formed on **CURSE** (the bleed period of the menstrual cycle).

curtain *noun*
used in conjunction with a precedent noun, indicating isolation, hostility, aggression and/or danger *US*
- —*American Speech*, p. 186–189, October 1955: 'A new look at the Iron Curtain'

curtain-climber *noun*
a small child *US*
- —Kenn "Naz" Young, *Naz's Underground Dictionary*, p. 23, 1973
- —Peter Chippindale, *The British CB Book*, p. 154, 1981

curtain-raiser *noun*
the first game of a season *US*
- —Parke Cummings, *Dictionary of Baseball*, p. 15, 1950
- I spent last Saturday night TV surfing, going from "The Godfather" on ABC, the Corleones vs. those other families, to the XFL curtain-raiser on NVC[.] —*Times-Picayune (New Orleans)*, p. 1 (Sports), 9th February 2001

curtains *noun*
1 the end, implying death or dismissal *US, 1901*
Theatrical origin (the final curtain of a play).
- If I fire this rod it's curtains for you – It's a curtain rod! —*old joke*,
- Now, when we get out there, you do what we say or its curtains. —*Natural Born Killers*, 1994
- [I]f we're collared doing anything untoward in the firm's uniform, that was it – curtains. —Marting King and Martin Knight, *The Naughty Nineties*, p. 53, 1999

2 the *labia majora* *US*
- —*Maledicta*, p. 132, Summer/Winter 1982: 'Dyke diction: the language of lesbians'

▸ **curtains and carpet that match; matching curtains and carpet**
said when a person's hair colour matches the colour of their pubic hair *US*
- "Do the curtains match the carpets?" "I don't understand." "Your pubic hair? Does it mach the color of the hair on your head?" —Andrew Lewis Conn, *P: A Novel*, p. 16, 2003

curtain-twitcher *noun*

a person who spies on the comings and goings of the world from behind a curtained window *UK*

- More than once I had to hop back quickly to avoid being spotted. I began to feel like a curtain-twitcher. — *The Guardian*, 7th February 2002

curve *noun*

▸ **ahead of the curve**

anticipating events or trends; on the cutting edge *US, 1980*

- — *American Speech*, Fall 1990

▸ **behind the curve**

lagging behind trends or developments *US, 1989*

- — *American Speech*, Fall 1990

curve-breaker *noun*

a diligent, smart student *US*

A student whose performance upsets the grading curve.

- A. I've had two guts all lined up, but they backfired. Q. Why? A. Too many curve breakers. — Max Shulman, *Guided Tour of Campus Humor*, p. 105, 1955

curved *adjective*

corrupt, crooked, criminal *UK*

A variation of **BENT**.

- Always the straight goer George, never liked a curved copper. — Jeremy Cameron, *Brown Bread in Wengen*, p. 149, 1999

curve-killer *noun*

a student who excels *US*

A reference to the grading curve.

- — *Time Magazine*, p. 46, 24th August 1959
- — Helen Dahlskog (Editor), *A Dictionary of Contemporary and Colloquial Usage*, p. 17, 1972

curvy crawler *noun*

a prostitute, a streetwalker *UK*

A play on **KERB CRAWLING** (soliciting prostitutes from a vehicle).

- — Peter Chippindale, *The British CB Book*, p. 154, 1981

cush *noun*

1 the vagina; sex; a woman as a sexual object *US, 1960*

- No, it was a walking, living round balloon with a fat "poke" [wallet] and a flaming itch for black "Cush." — Iceberg Slim (Robert Beck), *Pimp*, p. 40, 1969

2 loose tobacco *US, 1950*

- — Frederic G. Cassidy, *Dictionary of American Regional English, Volume One*, p. 889, 1985

3 money *US, 1900*

- — Inez Cardozo-Freeman, *The Joint*, p. 492, 1984

cush *adjective*

comfortable, unstrained *US, 1931*

A shortened form of **CUSHY**.

- I called Homeboy at Folsom, got through 'cause he got this cush orderly job. — James Ellroy, *Suicide Hill*, p. 796, 1986

cushion *noun*

a passenger railway carriage *US, 1913*

- — Norman Carlisle, *The Modern Wonder Book of Trains and Railroading*, p. 261, 1946

cushty *adjective*

excellent, great *UK*

A roughly contemporaneous variation of **CUSHY** (easy, comfortable); attributed to market traders since the late 1910s; much more widespread since 1981 through usage in BBC television comedy series *Only Fools and Horses*.

- DEL: Nice thick frost is there? ALBERT: Bit slippery underfoot, yeah! DEL: Oh cushty! — John Sullivan, *Only Fools and Horses*, p. 219, 1985
- Wally got a cushty Chopper bike one year. — Jimmy Stockin, *On The Cobbles*, p. 50, 2000
- Cushty. You crack it [a bottle of wine] open, I'll make the sarnies. — Danny King, *The Burglar Diaries*, p. 92, 2001

cushy *adjective*

easy, comfortable, unstrained *UK, 1915*

From Hindu *khush* (pleasant) or Romany *kushto* (good).

- There was a cushy career spot in State arranged by his father Sam'l and waiting for him when he got his very own Ph.D. — Bernard Wolfe, *The Magic of Their Singing*, p. 8, 1961
- I've got a cushy job. — Ann Barr and Peter York, *The Official Sloane Ranger Handbook*, p. 158, 1982

cuspy *adjective*

(used of a computer program) well-designed, highly functional *US*

- — Guy L. Steele, *Coevolution Quarterly*, p. 29, Spring 1981: 'Computer Slang'
- — Guy L. Steele et al., *The Hacker's Dictionary*, p. 52, 1983

cuss *noun*

1 a person; a creature *US, 1775*

Usually, slightly contemptuous, reproachful or humorous; probably derived as a shortening of **CUSTOMER**, pehaps influenced in later usage by **CUSS** (a curse).

- "You're not a bad cuss really, are you?" I said pleasantly[.] — Petra Christian, *The Sexploiters*, p. 48, 1973
- Jim Watson is, if nothing else, an awkward cuss, albeit a talented one. — *The Observer*, 14th October 2001

2 a curse *US, 1848*

A dated euphemism that survives in the term **TINKER'S CUSS** (a thing of little value).

cussbud *noun*

a person who uses a great deal of profanity *TRINIDAD AND TOBAGO, 1977*

- — Lise Winer, *Dictionary of the English/Creole of Trinidad & Tobago*, 2003

cuss-cuss *noun*

insults, profanity *BAHAMAS*

- — John A. Holm, *Dictionary of Bahamian English*, p. 56, 1982

cussedness *noun*

cantankerousness, contrariness *US, 1866*

- [H]is team were too soft-hearted in the spells when they dominated. Nor did they quite have the cussedness to see out stoppage time. — *The Guardian*, 20th January 2003

cuss fight *noun*

a loud, angry argument *US, 1923*

- He rushed to the White House and they had a huge cuss fight[.] — John Grisham, *The Pelican Brief*, p. 100, 1992

cussie *noun*

an HM Customs & Excise official *UK*

- a special filter system attached to the loo so that the poor Cussie who draws the short straw can fish around — Duncan MacLaughlin, *The Filth*, p. 189, 2002

cuss out *verb*

to reprimand someone with a heavy reliance on profanity *US, 1863*

- She hates to drive anywhere with me because I am inclined to cuss out drivers who don't please me. — Wallace Earle Stegner, *The Spectator Bird*, p. 10, 1976

cuss word *noun*

a profanity *US, 1872*

After **cuss** (a curse).

- If I was a fat bitches thong I'd be like "Hell naw!' / If I was a hotties thong I'd be like "Awwww..." / If I was a cuss word I'd just be like "fuck" — Insane Clown, Posse *If*, 2000

custard and jelly; custard *noun*

television; a television *UK, 1974*

Rhyming slang for **TELLY**.

- [T]here's nothing on the custard. — Ray Puxley, *Cockney Rabbit*, 1992
- It might even persuade "saucepan lids" (kids) to spend more time reading and less time in front of the "custard and jelly" (telly). — *BBC News*, 26th February 2001

custard cream; custard *verb*

to dream *UK*

Rhyming slang, formed on a biscuit.

- — Ray Puxley, *Cockney Rabbit*, 1992

custards *noun*

acne, pimples, spots *AUSTRALIA, 1942*

From the colour of the swelling or the pus.

- — *BBCi Body Files*, July 2003

custard tart *noun*

a traffic warden *UK*

- — Peter Chippindale, *The British CB Book*, p. 154, 1981

custer *noun*

a person who poses as a member of a youth gang but is not accepted as a gang member *US*

- —Bill Valentine, *Gang Intelligence Manual*, p. 75, 1995

custie *noun*

a buyer of illegal drugs *US*

Simply put, an abbreivation of 'customer'.

- —Jim Crotty, *How to Talk American*, p. 352, 1997

customer *noun*

1 a person, or any creature, generally qualified as a type *UK, 1589*

- Should you so wish, you can typecast the most awkward customer to your whim.—*The Guardian*, 3rd August 2002

2 any person who is subject to a social worker's professional or charitable attention *UK*

A patronising categorisation, now replaced with the equally dishonest 'client'.

- Do-gooders who visit patients in hospitals, or elderly people in their homes, sometimes call them "customers".—Albert E. Petch, 1966

3 a motorist being stopped by a police officer for a traffic violation *US*

- —*American Speech*, p. 268, December 1962: 'The language of traffic policemen'

4 a potential shop-lifter *UK*

In UK Disney Stores in the mid-1990s staff were instructed to refer to customers as 'guests' – anyone referred to as a 'customer' was instantly the subject of an unwelcome attention.

5 a prisoner *US*

- —Vincent J. Monteleone, *Criminal Slang*, p. 63, 1949

cut *noun*

1 an adulterant used to dilute a drug; a dilution of a drug *US*

- Now today, if you buy your piece, you'd be very lucky if you could get a three-to-one cut[.]—James Mills, *The Panic in Needle Park*, p. 44, 1966
- New York Pure, no more than a one cut, if that.—Vernon E. Smith, *The Jones Men*, p. 88, 1974
- Bout sixty-five hunnerd for half a pound a meth plus half a pound a cut.—Joseph Wambaugh, *The Secrets of Harry Bright*, p. 191, 1985
- Probably all the lactose in the cut: you were shooting ten times more sugar than junk.—Seth Morgan, *Homeboy*, p. 139, 1990
- Buy four, bleed in a ounce of cut, make it five.—Richard Price, *Clockers*, p. 185, 1992
- Because we extract a quarter ounce for ourselves, throw back in a quarter ounce of cut, sell it for like a hundred twenty-five a gram, clear around thirty-six hundred bucks.—Kenneth Lonergan, *This is Our Youth*, p. 35, 2000

2 a share, usually of profits, often of ill-gotten gains *AUSTRALIA, 1911*

- You'll never see the bill of lading until my cut is deposited in escrow!—William Burroughs, *Naked Lunch*, p. 180, 1957
- They sent me to offer you a cut. We could use a fifth man – a driver.—*The Usual Suspects*, 1995
- None of [Ray Davies' managers and publishers] sued for libel, instead they just took their cut on this song, just as they had on all the others.—Simon Napier-Bell, *Black Vinyl White Powder*, p. 272, 2001

3 a reduction of a prison sentence *US*

- Gary went back to court to try to get a time cut.—Gary K. Farlow, *Prison-ese*, p. 15, 2002

4 any district where goods are bought and sold with a minimum of questions asked *UK*

- —Paul Tempest, *Lag's Lexicon*, 1950

5 any place where young people congregate to socialise *US*

- —Lavada Durst, *The Jives of Dr. Hepcat*, p. 12, 1953

6 someone's appearance *IRELAND*

Usually derogatory.

- He would have been an impressive sort of a cut of a skin if it hadn't been for the sickly yellow-white belly peeping from underneath the T-shirt—Eamonn Sweeney, *Waiting for the Healer*, p. 136, 1997
- You can tell, just by the cut of him that he's done great deeds in his too brief lifetime. Skulls have cracked and foes been scattered—*Clare Champion*, 2nd March 2001

7 a stage or a degree *UK, 1818*

- Rod [Stewart]'s a cut above Geri [Halliwell] as Labour's new mood music—*The Guardian*, 22nd May 2001
- I think Taggart, in writing, filming and performance, is a cut above most other cop shows.—Rob Gowland, *The Guardian*, 19th June 2002

8 of music, a recording or a special part of one *US*

From the verb sense.

- —Roy Carr and Tony Tyler, *The Beatles*, 1975

9 in hip-hop music, a sample or part of a tune that is played repeatedly *US*

- —James Haskins, *The Story of Hip-Hop*, p. 137, 2000

10 the vagina *US*

- —Dale Gordon, *The Dominion Sex Dictionary*, p. 54, 1967

11 a press cutting *UK*

- They were helping me to sort out my press cuttings (or "cuts" as we journalistas call them) from the last season of fashion shows.—*The Times*, p. 9, 26th April 2003

12 a hitting of the open hand with a cane for corporal punishment *AUSTRALIA, 1915*

Formally common in the Australian school system, now the practice is obsolete. The term is commonly found in the plural as the punishment was generally so given.

- It was a long walk to school and quite often we were late. This meant that we were punished with the cuts.—*People Magazine*, p. 52, 26th August 1981

cut *verb*

1 in the drug trade, to dilute drugs *US, 1937*

- Ray just sat there and watched while Chico went to work cutting the horse with milk sugar.—Hal Ellson, *The Golden Spike*, p. 166, 1952
- We bought the stuff for ninety dollars per quarter-ounce, cut it one-third with milk sugar and put it in one-grain caps.—William Burroughs, *Junkie*, p. 50, 1953
- They cut it, cap it, and retail it at about a hundred per cent profit.—John D. McDonald, *The Neon Jungle*, p. 61, 1953
- When you break it down, it comes out to something like eight ounces after cutting it[.]—Clarence Cooper Jr, *The Scene*, p. 27, 1960
- He bought heroin in "pieces" (ounces), cut it, bagged it, and handed it over on consignment to a handful of pushers.—James Mills, *The Panic in Needle Park*, p. 19, 1966
- I invest half a grand in cocaine and H. It's good enough so I can cut it twice with milk, sugar, and still have the best stuff on Thirty-fifth Street.—Iceberg Slim (Robert Beck), *Trick Baby*, p. 184, 1969
- I ain't never tried to step on this much heh-rawn in my life. We got a few bags cut but the suitcase is still full.—Vernon E. Smith, *The Jones Men*, p. 48, 1974
- If it wasn't for the efforts of the two ladies (sic) of the house, Palo would cut the dope to shreds.—Jim Carroll, *Forced Entries*, p. 11, 1987
- She got her start in the business by learning to cut the pure stuff that these guys used to get[.]—Herbert Huncke, *Guilty of Everything*, p. 4, 1990
- It's good shit. From when they busted those Columbians uptown. You can cut it in half.—*The Bad Lieutenant*, 1992
- [I]t was proably the dope I'd brought in msyelf – cut three times.—Cleo Odzer, *Goa Freaks*, p. 201, 1995

2 to dilute anything by the addition of a secondary ingredient *US*

Extended from the previous sense (to dilute drugs).

- They're cutting the butter with Vaseline.—William Burroughs, *Queer*, p. 36, 1985

3 (of a drug) to take effect *UK*

- By the time the E really started cutting I was well into the dancing thing.—Ben Malbon, *Cool Places*, p. 278, 1998

4 to fart *US, 1967*

- [S]ome American speakers use "cut" as a variant of "lay" or "let" and refer to "cutting" or "cutting a fart".—Peter Furze, *Tailwinds*, p. 55, 1998

5 to engage in an informal musical competition in which musicians attempt to better each other in extended jazz solos *US, 1937*

- When one jazz musician cuts another, he merely outplays him, does it better, shows him how, establishes who's boss of the instrument.—Robert Sylvester, *No Cover Charge*, p. 48, 1956
- "But I can still cut all these cats two choruses to one," he spat out[.]—John Clellon Holmes, *The Horn*, p. 51, 1958

6 to record a song *US, 1937*

- —Arnold Shaw, *Lingo of Tin-Pan Alley*, p. 10, 1950
- He finally came half an hour late, borne up (as it were) by ajostling, haggard bunch of hangers-on, among whom was the white boy for whose phantom company the records were to be cut.—John Clellon Holmes, *The Horn*, p. 67, 1958
- They can cut discs which are played on our Muzak-type system.—Gore Vidal, *Myra Breckinridge*, p. 52, 1968
- When you get my backups straight, then we'll talk about cutting this tune here.—*Nashville*, 1992

7 to skip something, to fail to attend something *UK, 1794*

- You're not going to cut again. Get up.—Irving Shulman, *The Amboy Dukes*, p. 19, 1947

- He cuts a lot of classes. He got thrown out of schools.—John D. McDonald, *The Neon Jungle*, p. 94, 1953
- The fact that you're cutting gym so you can T.A. Sophomore English just to hear his name, is a little without in itself if you ask me.—*Ten Things I Hate About You*, 1999

8 to leave quickly *UK, 1790*

- "Let's cut," I said. We started down the platform.—William Burroughs, *Junkie*, p. 48, 1953
- [S]uddenly he gets up and says to Miss Van Allen, 'I got to cut. This isn't my scene.'—Gore Vidal, *Myra Breckinridge*, p. 207, 1968

9 to ignore a person, either as a single act or as continuing behaviour *UK, 1634*

- When King stood at the press conference and launched his own verbal assault on Maloney, Lewis cut him dead.—*The Daily Telegraph*, 8th November 2001

10 to tease or disparage someone *US*

- —*American Speech*, p. 57, Spring-Summer 1975: 'Razorback slang'

11 to divide or share out legal profits or criminal gains *UK, 1928*

12 to perform surgery *US*

- You just sit up front and sign the mail, and leave the cutting to us. —*M*A*S*H*, 1970

▸ be cut out for

to have the appropriate qualities for something *UK, 1645*

- Modern Germany, however, is not cut out for Thatcherism (nor was the UK really)[.]—*The Guardian*, 17th March 2003

▸ cut a chogie

to leave quickly *US*

Korea and Vietnam war usage.

- It was time for us to "cut-a-chogie," to haul our asses out of the area.—C.S. Crawford, *The Four Deuces*, p. 251, 1989
- —Linda Reinberg, *In the Field*, p. 55, 1991
- Our pay was burning a hole in our fatigue pockets, so we "cut a chogie" down to the Dragon's Lair and exchanged a good share of it for cold cans of beer.—Robert Peterson, *Rites of Passage*, p. 473, 1997

▸ cut a fat one

in drag racing and hot rodding, to drive at top speed *US*

- —Lyle K. Engel, *The Complete Book of Fuel and Gas Dragster*, p. 150, 1968

▸ cut a hus

to do someone a favour *US*

Marine slang in Vietnam.

- —Linda Reinberg, *In the Field*, p. 55, 1991

▸ cut a melon

to fart *UK*

- —Peter Furze, *Tailwinds*, p. 55, 1998

▸ cut a rat

to fart *US*

- I tried to cut a rat the whole show but I didn't have any gas.—Howard Stern, *Miss America*, p. 219, 1995

▸ cut a rug

to dance expertly *US, 1942*

- We gave the customers a ham-and-cheese sandwich and a bottle of pop for a dollar, and they had the right to hang around all night to cut some rug or dig the band.—Mezz Mezzrow, *Really the Blues*, p. 86–87, 1946
- He goes to the jukery to watch and wait and cut a rug with a solid gate: he snatches a quail with hep and class and they go to town cooking with gas!—Haenigsen, *Jive's Like That*, 1947
- "I'm ... ah, curious to know if you can still cut a bad rug."—Iceberg Slim (Robert Beck), *Doom Fox*, p. 253, 1978
- Come on. Let's cut a rug.—*Empire Records*, 1995
- [A] few of the more daring couples – from the looks of it mostly older folks who wanted to show they still knew how to cut the rug – were swaying to Perry Como.—Rita Ciresi, *Pink Slip*, p. 323, 1999

▸ cut a rusty

to show off *US, 1838*

- "You're still spunky," the voice responded. "Ain't no one able to cut a rusty like you."—Gwyn Hyman Rubio, *Icy Sparks*, p. 204, 1998

▸ cut ass; cut arse

1 to leave, especially in a hurry *US*

- —Helen Dahlskog (Editor), *A Dictionary of Contemporary and Colloquial Usage*, p. 5, 1972

2 to assault someone *TRINIDAD AND TOBAGO, 1980*

- —Lise Winer, *Dictionary of the English/Creole of Trinidad & Tobago*, 2003

▸ cut brush

to drive off the road into brush *US*

- —*American Speech*, p. 268, December 1962: 'The language of traffic policemen'

▸ cut cake; cut the strawberry cake

to short-change someone *US*

- —Vincent J. Monteleone, *Criminal Slang*, p. 64, 1949
- —Don Wilmeth, *The Language of American Popular Entertainment*, p. 69, 1981

▸ cut card straight

to deal in a direct and honest manner *TRINIDAD AND TOBAGO*

- —Lise Winer, *Dictionary of the English/Creole of Trinidad & Tobago*, 2003

▸ cut down to size

to reduce someone to a true understanding of his or her status or worth *US, 1927*

- Young guns swiftly cut down to size.—*The Observer*, 20th July 2003

▸ cut it

to perform satisfactorily and so meet a requirement *US*

From **CUT THE MUSTARD**.

- Poetry readings just don't cut it for me the way they used to.—Jim Carroll, *Forced Entries*, p. 58, 1987
- If they couldn't or wouldn't be arsed to cut it, they were out—Wayne Anthony, *Spanish Highs*, p. 54, 1999

▸ cut loose

1 to leave someone alone *US*

- —Stewart L. Tubbs and Sylvia Moss, *Human Communication*, p. 120, 1974

2 to enjoy yourself unrestrained by any sense of moderation *US, 1808*

- After that, maybe I'd cut loose a little bit.—Mickey Spillane, *My Gun is Quick*, p. 6, 1950
- I guess I cut pretty loose in my day too.—*Rebel Without a Cause*, 1955

▸ cut no ice

to make no difference *US, 1896*

- A curt rejection from Whitehall mandarins cuts no ice with the confirmed Eurosceptic Iain Duncan Smith[.]—*The Guardian*, 22nd August 2001

▸ cut one off

in the police, to salute a superior officer *UK*

Usually in the form 'cut *someone* one off'.

- —*Free-Lance Writer*, April 1948

▸ cut out to be a gentleman

circumcised *UK, 1961*

- —Roger Blake, *The American Dictionary of Sexual Terms*, p. 53, 1964

▸ cut skin; cut tail

to physically assault someone; to beat someone *TRINIDAD AND TOBAGO, 1959*

- —Lise Winer, *Dictionary of the English/Creole of Trinidad & Tobago*, 2003

▸ cut someone's lunch

to cuckold; to steal someone's partner; to move in on another's potential pick-up *AUSTRALIA, 1996*

- I often heard of someone 'cutting someone's lunch' which usually meant that a man's best mate was sleeping with his wife.—*Wordmap (www.abc.net.au/wordmap)*, 2003

▸ cut some slack

to relax the pressure *US*

- I was trying to cut Eddie DeChooch some slack because he was old and depressed[.]—Janet Evanovich, *Seven Up*, p. 31, 2001

▸ cut ten

to sit with your legs crossed as others work *JAMAICA, 1977*

Collected by Richard Allsopp.

▸ cut the cheese

to fart *US, 1959*

- —*Esquire*, p. 180, June 1983
- [A] a co-worker/subordinate who had gone to prep school at Millbrook used to reveal his social superiority by saying "Who cut the brie?" —Peter Furze, *Tailwinds*, p. 54, 1998

▸ cut the coax

to turn off a citizens' band radio *US*

- —Wayne Floyd, *Jason's Authentic Dictionary of CB Slang*, p. 13, 1976

▸ cut the gas

to stop talking *US*

Teen slang.

- —*Newsweek*, p. 28, 8th October 1951

▸ cut the mustard

1 to perform satisfactorily and so meet a requirement *US, 1902*

2 to fart with especially noxious effect *UK*

- "Cut the mustard" refers instead [of cut the cheese] to breaking wind in an especially smelly way. — Peter Furze, *Tailwinds*, p. 54, 1998

3 to have sex *UK*

- A lady from New Zealand expressed dismay at the sight of a pair [of lovers] energetically cutting the mustard in broad daylight. — *Sunday Telegraph*, 9th October 1977

▸ **cut throat**
to have sex with a female virgin *TRINIDAD AND TOBAGO*

- — Lise Winer, *Dictionary of the English/Creole of Trinidad & Tobago*, 2003

▸ **cut to the chase**
to get on with it *US, 1983*
Cinematic imagery; 'to jump to the next exciting sequence'.

- "Cut to the chase," he muttered irritably. "What the hell is it you want us to do?" — Carl Hiaasen, *Native Tongue*, p. 83, 1991
- ["]We can come to an arrangement." "Cut to the fuckin' car-chase. What do you want?" "Fifty grand." — Christopher Brookmyre, *Boiling a Frog*, p. 255, 2000

▸ **cut up jackies**
in the circus or carnival, to tell stories about the past *US*

- — Joe McKennon, *Circus Lingo*, p. 29, 1980

▸ **cut up jackpots**
(used of carnival workers) to engage in carnival insider conversation *US*

- — Gene Sorrows, *All About Carnivals*, p. 19, 1985

▸ **cut up pipes**
in circus and carnival usage, to gossip, brag or disparage someone *US*

- — Don Wilmeth, *The Language of American Popular Entertainment*, p. 69, 1981

▸ **cut your eyes**
to look at someone or something with disdain *BARBADOS*

- — Frank A. Collymore, *Barbadian Dialect*, p. 37, 1965

▸ **cut your own hair**
to be extremely frugal *AUSTRALIA*

- — Ned Wallish, *The Truth Dictionary of Racing Slang*, p. 20, 1989

▸ **cut your water off**
in shuffleboard, to hold an oponent to a scoreless half round *US*

- — Omero C. Catan, *Secrets of Shuffleboard Strategy*, p. 65, 1967

▸ **cut Z's**
to sleep *US*

- — Linda Reinberg, *In the Field*, p. 55, 1991

cut *adjective*

1 circumcised *US*

- — H. Max, *Gay (S)language*, p. 10, 1988
- I've got six-pack abs. I'm eight inches cut. — *The Village Voice*, 4th April 2000

2 physically fit, conditioned, well-toned *US*

- — Connie Eble (Editor), *UNC-CH Campus Slang*, p. 2, Fall 1998

cut!; cut it!; cut it out!
stop!, cease! *UK, 1859*

- Cut it out please, and get on. — Spike Milligan, *The Goons*, 22nd December 1958
- Claimin' you's a hustlin' type of nigga, cut it out / You's an average type of cat / No money, no clout[.] — Eve *Ain't Got No Dough*, 1999

cut along *verb*
to depart *UK, 1902*
Often as an imperative.

- Better cut along to this fitting, then, so that you can give me the low down on Saturday. — Liz Fielding, *The Best Man and the Bridedmaid*, 2000

cut and carried *adjective*
married *UK*
Rhyming slang.

- — Julian Franklyn, *A Dictionary of Rhyming Slang*, 1960

cut and paste *noun*
cosmetic surgery *US*

- — Anna Scotti and Paul Young, *Buzzwords*, p. 108, 1997

cut and paste *verb*
to open a patient's body in surgery only to discover an inoperable condition, and then to close the patient back up *US*

- — Sally Williams, *"Strong" Words*, p. 137, 1994

cut and run *verb*
to depart promptly; to decamp hurriedly *UK, 1826*
Of nautical origin.

- Lizzi fears she in now in a worse position than if she had cut and run. — *The Observer*, 22nd July 2001

cut and scratch *noun*
a match, safety or non-safety *UK*
Rhyming slang.

- — Julian Franklyn, *A Dictionary of Rhyming Slang*, 1960

cut and shut *adjective*
used to describe a secondhand car that has been illegally contrived from the best parts of two damaged cars *UK*
Often hyphenated as a noun.

- — *Woman's Own*, 28th February 1968

cut and tuck *noun*
a male transexual who has had his penis removed and an artificial vagina surgically constructed *AUSTRALIA*

- — Thommo, *The Dictionary of Australian Swearing and Sex Sayings*, p. 31, 1985

cut-ass *noun*
a beating *TRINIDAD AND TOBAGO, 1959*

- — Lise Winer, *Dictionary of the English/Creole of Trinidad & Tobago*, 2003

cutback *noun*
in surfing, a turn back into the wave *US*

- I've admired your nose-riding for years. I like your cutback too. — *Apocalypse Now*, 1979

cut buddy *noun*
a close friend *US, 1954*

- — Robert George Reisner, *The Jazz Titans*, p. 153, 1960
- We greeted each other like we were ol' cut-buddies, but after all the greeting and slapping hands, we found it hard to talk to each other. — H. Rap Brown, *Die Nigger Diel*, p. 24, 1969
- Most Black males have at least one close male friend – often called "Cuz," "Running Buddy," "Ace Boon Coon," "Cut Buddy," Road Dog," Homeboy," or "Main Man". — Joseph L. White, *Black Man Emerging*, p. 134, 1999

cutchie *noun*
▷ see: KOUTCHIE

cut dead *verb*
to ignore someone completely *UK, 1826*
An emphasised use of **CUT** (to ignore).

- "I seen the dweeb around," Baborak replied, cutting me dead and walking away. — C.D. Payne, *Youth in Revolt*, p. 243, 1993

cut-down *noun*
a half bottle of rum *BARBADOS*

- — Frank A. Collymore, *Barbadian Dialect*, p. 37, 1965

cute *adjective*
a*cute*, sharp-witted, clever, shrewd *UK, 1731*

- You sure you wanna get cute with me? — Tommy Lee Jones, *U.S. Marshals*, 1998

cute hoor *noun*
any person, female or male, who is corrupt *IRELAND*
May be used affectionately as well as pejoratively. The present Hiberno-English pronunciation was common in England in C16 and C17, and lasted in common use into C19.

- In this country of the cute hoor, misleading the Dáil or Seanad is considered little more than a minor stroke. — *Irish Times*, 27th January 2001
- However, my dislike of Lucan does not stem entirely from cute hoor developers flogging unimaginatively designed houses. — Donal Ruane, *Tales in a rear view mirror*, p. 57, 2003

cutemup *noun*
a prison doctor *US*

- — Frank Prewitt and Francis Schaeffer, *Vacaville Vocabulary*, 1961 – 1962

cuter *verb*
a twenty-five cent piece *US, 1927*
A corruption of 'quarter'.

- — Lou Shelly, *Hepcats Jive Talk Dictionary*, p. 9, 1945

cuteration *noun*
the zenith of cuteness *US*

- — *American Speech*, p. 275, December 1963: 'American Indian student slang'

cutesy *adjective*
cloying, annoyingly cute *US, 1914*
- Don't take all that cutesy-kitschy fuckin' retro-Sixties bullshit out in my apartment. —Kenneth Lonergan, *This is Our Youth*, p. 32, 2000

cut-eye *noun*
a disapproving look *TRINIDAD AND TOBAGO, 1960*
- —Lise Winer, *Dictionary of the English/Creole of Trinidad & Tobago*, 2003

cut fine; cut it fine *verb*
to narrow something down to a minimum *UK, 1891*
- Andrew Hay, 36, a van driver from Gosport, thought he was cutting it fine when he arrived on Thursday night. —*The Guardian*, 6th April 2002

cut from timber to bramble *adjective*
(used of a man) sexually active and indiscriminate *TRINIDAD AND TOBAGO, 1987*
- —Lise Winer, *Dictionary of the English/Creole of Trinidad & Tobago*, 2003

cut-glass sledgehammer *noun*
a notional tool that a young, inexperienced novice is sent to fetch *US, 1960*
- —Frederic G. Cassidy, *Dictionary of American Regional English, Volume One*, p. 895, 1985

cut-hip *noun*
a physical beating; a thrashing *BAHAMAS*
Recorded by Richard Allsopp.

cutie *noun*
an attractive or clever young woman *US, 1911*
Originally (UK, C18) a 'clever but shallow person'; this sense is an early example of a US term moved into wider usage by Hollywood films.
- "The Snake Pit" is that – the mad gathering place at cocktail time for the local celebs – the Senators, lobbyists, army brass and blondest cuties. —Jack Lait and Lee Mortimer, *Washington Confidential*, p. 132, 1951
- I started getting it on with some little cutie with a D cup[.] —Howard Stern, *Miss America*, p. 49, 1995
- "Hello, cutie," Mr Morganstern said. —Janet Evanovich, *Seven Up*, p. 156, 2001

cutie-pie *noun*
an attractive woman *US*
- Les Harrison attempted to intercept her and introduce her to the cutie-pie starlet. —Terry Southern, *Blue Movie*, p. 17, 1970
- And there were leggy cutie-pie vultures and cold-blooded toothy hustlers staked out in the plush murk to ambush celebrity bank-rools. —Iceberg Slim (Robert Beck), *The Naked Soul of Iceberg Slim*, p. 80, 1971
- I only like cutie pies massaging me. When you're massaged, you like to open up your eyes and see a cutie pie there. —Susan Hall, *Gentleman of Leisure*, p. 93, 1972
- The girl was getting under my skin – and a veritable cutie-pie she was too. —Terry Southern, *Now Dig This*, p. 131, 2001

cut-in *noun*
the initial contact with the intended victim in a confidence swindle *US*
- Folks left the office and went to the elevator athrob with satisfaction that the Bates cut-in had come off so sweetly. —Iceberg Slim (Robert Beck), *Long White Con*, p. 94, 1977

cut in *verb*
1 to attempt a romantic relationship with someone already romantically involved *US*
- That makes her his chick. You've both been playing around when you're not supposed to. Happy don't fancy that crap and neither do we 'cause there's not supposed to be any cutting in. —Hal Ellson, *Tomboy*, p. 76, 1950

2 to seize a share of a business or enterprise *US, 1980*
- I wanted to be in the swim so I cut in on a chick. She was not much to look at, but she made good money[.] —Louis Armstrong, *Satchmo*, p. 86, 1954

cut into *verb*
to approach someone and draw them into a swindle; to introduce someone to something *US, 1940*
- He doesn't know a diamond from a seashell. I've already cut into him and told him the tale. —Iceberg Slim (Robert Beck), *Trick Baby*, p. 298, 1969
- Prince cut me into a choice little crib for fifteen cents a week. —Babs Gonzales, *Movin' On Down De Line*, p. 15, 1975

cut it!; cut it out!
▷ **see:** CUT!

cutlass carpenter *noun*
an unskilled carpenter *TRINIDAD AND TOBAGO*
- —Lise Winer, *Dictionary of the English/Creole of Trinidad & Tobago*, 2003

cut lunch *noun*
a circumcised penis as an object of oral sex *AUSTRALIA*
- —Thommo, *The Dictionary of Australian Swearing and Sex Sayings*, p. 31, 1985

cut-lunch commando *noun*
a soldier who does not see active service, especially a reservist *AUSTRALIA, 1952*
A contemptuous term implying that they get a prepared lunch rather than real army rations.
- —Ryan Aven-Bray, *Ridgey Didge Oz Jack Lang*, p. 22, 1983

cut man *noun*
the member of a boxer's entourage responsible for treating cuts between rounds *US*
- Of course he had a great cut man, Whitey Bimstein, and Charley Goldman, a great trainer, taught him to shorten up his shots and develop a left hook. —Edwin Torres, *Carlito's Way*, p. 135, 1975
- The cutman should have told him not to clear his nose after taking the shot in the eye from Palomino. —Elmore Leonard, *Out of Sight*, p. 113, 1996

cut off *verb*
to lay someone off due to lack of work *US*
- —Linda Niemann, *Boomer*, p. 248, 1990

cut off the joint *noun*
from the male perspective, an act of sexual intercouse *UK, 1961*

cut of your jib *noun*
your general appearance, hence, nature, character and temperament *UK, 1825*
- I like the cut of his jib. —*The Guardian*, 19th June 2001

cutor *noun*
a prosecuting attorney *US*
- —Joseph E. Ragen and Charles Finston, *Inside the World's Toughest Prison*, p. 796, 1962

cut out *verb*
1 to leave *US, 1827*
- Five of us piled into a cab and cut out for the colored district on the South Side. —Milton Mezzrow, *Really the Blues*, p. 25, 1946
- —Marcus Hanna Boulware, *Jive and Slang of Students in Negro Colleges*, 1947
- Now, look, man, we ought to be cutting out. —John Clellon Holmes, *Go*, p. 98, 1952
- "This joint must have just been raided," she said. "Looks like everybody cut out." —Steve Allen, *Bop Fables*, p. 6, 1955
- With her pretty nose in the air she cut out of there[.] —Jack Kerouac, *On the Road*, p. 89, 1957
- Then E.J. and I had cut out, bumming around and fruit-picking[.] —Clancy Sigal, *Going Away*, p. 84, 1961
- —J. L. Simmons and Barry Winograd, *It's Happening*, p. 169, 1966
- Looks like you decided to cut out early. —*Empire Records*, 1995
- I'd never seen so many glittering angora sweaters, gold-lame tops, jingle-bell necklaces, and Jolly Old Saint Nicholas earrings gathered under one roof in my life. —Rita Ciresi, *Pink Slip*, p. 321, 1999

2 to die *US*
- The bad jazz that a cat blows wails long after they've cut out. —William "Lord" Buckley, *Marc Anthony's Funeral Oration*, 1955

3 to take goods in payment instead of money *AUSTRALIA*
- After the refund we had a fiver left over so, with Alan's permission, we proceeded to cut it out over the bar. —Joe Brown, *Just for the Record*, p. 54, 1984

4 to pay for something by having sexual intercourse rather than using money *AUSTRALIA*
- Beyond the moat, a group of taxi drivers (telling each other lies about long jobs they'd got, and women who cut out the fare in the back seat)[.] —Frank Hardy, *The Outcasts of Foolgarah*, p. 49, 1971
- So she suggested that the old fulla might like to come in an cut it out. —Sam Weller, *Old Bastards I Have Met*, p. 63, 1979

5 (of a power-source controlled by automatic technology) to switch off; to break (electrical) contact *UK, 1984*

6 to serve time in prison rather than paying a fine *AUSTRALIA, 1939*
- Take the parking fines you're always on about: some people pay them, some cut them out in jail[.] —Frank Hardy, *Hardy's People*, p. 183, 1986
- —Harry Orsman, *A Dictionary of Modern New Zealand Slang*, p. 35, 1999

cuts *noun*

1 the definition of body muscle from spaces between the muscle that have no fat *US*

- — *American Speech*, p. 199, Fall 1984: 'The language of bodybuilding'

2 any remote location *US*

- We had to drive to the cuts to pickup my friend. — Peter Smith and Fred M. Barritt, *Bermewjan Vurds*, p. 17, 1985
- — Rick Ayers (Editor), *Berkeley High Slang Dictionary*, p. 17, 2004

3 permission from a friend to step into a queue at their place *US*

- — Pamela Munro, *U.C.L.A. Slang*, p. 43, 1989

4 clothing *US*

- Whooh! This preacher got some cuts, I thought, admiring the sharp clothes he was wearing. — Bobby Seale, *A Lonely Rage*, p. 133, 1978

cutter *noun*

1 a surgeon *US*

- Y'all were short a couple cutters and we're what the Army sent. — *M*A*S*H*, 1970

2 an illegal abortionist *FIJI, 1994*

Recorded by Jan Tent.

3 a person who is proficient with the use of a knife or of a weapon *US*

- Crazy's reputation as a cutter and potential killer was well known in Brownsville. — Irving Shulman, *The Amboy Dukes*, p. 214, 1947

4 a pistol *US, 1908*

- — *American Speech*, p. 193, October 1957: 'Some colloquialisms of the handgunner'

5 a musician who betters another in a competition of solos *US*

- Mexico's "cutters" must have played variations on it for three straight, solid hours. — Robert Sylvester, *No Cover Charge*, p. 49, 1956

6 any substance used to dilute a drug, thereby expanding volume while reducing potency *US*

- — Mark S. Fleisher, *Beggars & Thieves*, p. 288, 1995

7 in American casinos, twenty-five cents *US*

Playing on the sound of 'quarter'.

- — Steve Kuriscak, *Casino Talk*, p. 17, 1985

8 money *UK*

- [W]hen the establishment Mafioso realise how much gilt, paper, cashish, wonga, wedge, corn, cutter, loot, spondos, dollar, readies, shillings, folding, dough, money is on offer[.] — J.J. Connolly, *Layer Cake*, p. 94, 2000

cut the cackle!

stop talking! *UK, 1889*

From **CACKLE** (to chatter inconsequentially). When extended to: 'cut the cackle and come to the 'osses [Horses]', the meaning is 'stop the preliminaries and get down to business'.

- It is time, as James Agate used to say, to cut the cackle and come to the 'osses: to discuss, in other words, the productions rather than the policy of the RSC. — *The Guardian*, 15th April 2002

cut the crap!

stop talking nonsense! *US, 1956*

- Dat blood yu shed is mine / Yu paper I won't sign, / Cut de crap and set I free — Benjamin Zephaniah, *Cut de crap*, p. 46, 1992

cutting *noun*

the preparation of cocaine for inhalation by chopping lines of powder with a razor blade or credit card

- — Nick Constable, *This is Cocaine*, p. 182, 2002

cutting *adjective*

good, excellent *UK*

- — Julian Johnson, *Urban Survival*, p. 258, 2003

cutting gear *noun*

oxyacetylene apparatus used to break into safes *UK*

- — David Powis, *The Signs of Crime*, 1977

cutting house *noun*

a place where drugs are diluted for resale *US*

- Well, that was Willis McDaniel's main cuttin' house they hit. — Vernon E. Smith, *The Jones Men*, p. 54, 1974

cutting man *noun*

a best friend *US*

- — Roger D. Abrahams, *Deep Down in the Jungle*, p. 259, 1970

cutting plant *noun*

a shop where stolen cars are dismantled or altered *US*

- But wait – and both of them had been in there for grand theft auto, supplying new Sevilles and Continentals to body shops and cutting plants down near Columbus. — Elmore Leonard, *Switch*, p. 16, 1978

cuttings merchant *noun*

in prison, a prisoner who wields power by collecting newspaper cuttings of reported crimes *UK*

- — *The Guardian*, 2nd March 2000

cutty *noun*

1 a cousin *US*

- On the west side, Mexicans and blacks started calling him "Cutty," street slang for cousin. — *Los Angeles Times*, p. 1, 26th August 2002

2 a playful girl *IRELAND*

- She's a fine cutty that one – there's plenty of go in her. — Terence Dolan, *A Dictionary of Hiberno-English*, p. 85, 1999

cut-up *noun*

a dishonestly fixed outcome of any event, e.g. a competition, an election, a lottery, a job application, etc *UK, 1985*

- You'd hee-haw [none, nothing at all, no] chance of gettin the job; it was a cut-up from the start. — Michael Munro, *The Complete Patter*, 1996

cut up *verb*

1 to behave without restraint *US, 1846*

- The lowlier links lam the 36 miles to Baltimore to cut up. — Jack Lait and Lee Mortimer, *Washington Confidential*, 1951

2 (when driving) to overtake in such a manner that other vehicles are adversely affected *UK*

- I cuts up quite a few old toffee noses on me way down to the nob end of the town. — John Peter Jones, *Feather Pluckers*, p. 38, 1964

cut-up *adjective*

upset, emotionally distressed *UK, 1844*

- Olivia [...] was really cut up about being rejected by a state comprehensive on the grounds that she lived too far away. — *The Guardian*, 18th March 2003

cut up rough *verb*

1 to be, or become, quarrelsome or difficult *UK, 1837*

- So when the Pope cuts up rough about the divorce [...] Henry decides to go it alone and open his own church. — Andrew Nickolds, *Back to Basics*, p. 165, 1994
- [S]ome party officials fear that Mr Livingstone would cut up rough if the shortlist was "fixed." — *The Guardian*, 1st October 1999

2 to resist or show resentment with violence *AUSTRALIA, 1944*

- — Gary Simes, *A Dictionary of Australian Underworld Slang*, 1993

cut war *noun*

in lobstering, a rivalry that has escalated to the point where lobstermen are cutting each other's buoys *US*

- — Kendall Merriam, *The Illustrated Dictionary of Lobstering*, p. 29, 1978

cuyabunga!

▷ see: COWABUNGA!

cuz *noun*

a friend *US, 1979*

- — *The Bell (Paducah Tilghman High School)*, p. 8–9, 17th December 1993

cuz

▷ see: 'CAUSE

cuzz *noun*

a term of address used by one member of the Crips youth gang to another *US*

- RICK ROC catches the ball and throws Ricky a gang sign. RIC ROCK: Thanks cuzz. — *Boyz N The Hood*, 1990
- — Ethan Hilderbrant, *Prison Slang*, p. 169, 1998
- One of the Crips named Cunningham had been tagged with the moniker "Young Cousin." This was subsequently shortened to "Young Cuzz," and then to, "Cuzz." Many of the other Crips started calling each other Cuzz[.] — Bill Valentine, *Gangs and Their Tattoos*, p. 75, 2000

cuzzies *noun*

HM Customs & Excise *UK*

- "Cuzzies. We call them The Church. 'C and E' – close enough to Church of England." "Oh... Customs..." — Duncan MacLaughlin, *The Filth*, p. 178, 2002

cuzzy-bro *noun*

a close and loyal friend *NEW ZEALAND*

- I want to give these chaps responsibility – they're the 'cuzzy-bros' from in these gangs. — *(Wellington) Dominion*, p. 1, 14th August 1991

cwazy *adjective*

used as a jocular substitute for 'crazy' *US*

- After all these years, the hamburgers at Vanessi's – when Mario makes 'em – are still the endest, the gonest, the cwaziest. — *San Francisco*, p. 29, 23rd March 1952
- Monkey Flees Its Cage and Cwazy People [Headline]— *San Francisco Examiner*, p. 5, 15th March 1956

c-word *noun*

the word cunt *UK*

Usually after 'the'.

- The questionnaire was given to boarders at St. Joseph's Convent, Lochinvar, and listed "f" and "c"words as well as the words "bitch" and "bastard." — *The Advertiser*, 11th July 1986
- Chapman argued, on MacKenze's behalf, that the Independent had used language which was 'foul and offensive' and that the C-word had never been used before in a national newspaper. — *The Times*, 6th March 1988
- Dr Hoffman reportedly broke down after an editor grilled her about her use of the c-word while she was giving testimony in a court case. — *The Guardian*, 30th June 2004

CYA *verb*

to protect yourself from future criticism for actions being taken now *US, 1959*

An abbreviation of 'cover your ass'.

- In World War II, the Army coined its special code word – SNAFU, or politely translated, Situation Normal All Fouled Up. Today's Army has its code word too – CYA, or Cover Your Ass. — *New York Times*, p. SM10, 5th September 1971
- "I can't cover for you there, even if I wanted to," he said, laying out the usual C.Y.A. office ground rules. That's the way it was in the District Attorney's office. You had to "Cover Your Ass," because Gil always covered his. — Stephen Cannell, *King Con*, p. 46, 1997
- Pumping up a coalition that existed mostly in name, putitng out CYA statements, refusing to concede a war plan had obvious problems, hyping one of the more dramatic (and cinematic) moments of the war – none of this was surprising behavior for the Pentagon[.] — David Corn, *The Lies of George W. Bush*, p. 267, 2003

c-ya

used in computer messages as shorthand to mean 'see you' *US*

- — Christian Crumlish, *The Internet Dictionary*, p. 44, 1995

cyber *adjective*

denoting an on-line, Internet or digital state or existence *US, 1966*

A back-formation from 'cybernetics' (scientific and mechanical systems of control and communication), coined in 1948 by Norbert Wiener (1894–1964) from the Greek *kybernan* (to steer, to govern). Mainly used in unhyphenated combinations as a prefix, but can stand alone.

- The Los Angeles Times and San Francisco Chronicle are stuffed with features on cyberlove, cybersex, cyberfashion, cyberfun, cyberscare, cyberwork, cyberplay, cyberscene... Nancy comes to the conclusion that the Information Age is nothing more than a media invention. — Melanie McGrath, *Hard, Soft & Wet*, p. 135, 1998

cyberspace *noun*

the notional locus where on-line communication takes place and from where a digital existence is supposed *US, 1984*

Coined by science fiction author William Gibson (b.1948) to describe 'the hallucinatory world existing between computers' in *Neuromancer*, 1984.

cycle *noun*

anabolic steroids *US*

Steroids are taken for a fixed time period – a 'cycle' – and then not taken for the same time period. Professional wrestling usage.

▸ **having your cycle**

experiencing the bleed period of the menstrual cycle *US*

- — *The Museum of Menstruation and Women's Health*, April 2001

cycle-lifter *noun*

a bicycle thief *INDIA*

- Cycle-lifters have a field day in the twin cities. — Paroo Nihalini, R.K. Tongue and Priya Hosali, *Indian and British English*, 1979
- Cycle-lifter arrested. — *Indian Express*, 3rd September 1999

cyclo *noun*

a rickshaw pulled by a bicycle *US*

- [F]rom the poor cyclo drivers of Hue to the most sophisticated intellectuals[.] — Frances Fitzgerald, *Fire in the Lake*, p. 244, 1972
- He drove out of the old French cavalry camp and then maneuvered in his impatient way through Saigon's vehicular extravangza of trucks and gaudily painted buses coming and going from the countryside, Vespa scooters and Lambretta motorbikes, cyclos[.] — Neil Sheehan, *A Bright Shining Lie*, p. 41, 1988

cyclone *noun*

phencyclidine, the recreational drug known as PCP or angel dust *US*

- — US Department of Justice, *Street Terms*, October 1994

Cyclops sausage dog *noun*

the penis *UK*

Probably jocular imagery of a mythical one-eyed giant crossed with a dachshund.

- So who's in control, the man or his Cyclops sausage dog? — Richard Herring, *Talking Cock*, p. 250, 2003

cylinder *noun*

the vagina *AUSTRALIA, 1984*

A mechanics' simile.

Cyp *noun*

a *Cypriot* *UK, 1984*

Pronounced 'sip'.

Cyril Lord *adjective*

bald *UK*

Rhyming slang; an imperfect rhyme formed on the name of a British carpet manufacturer (now Carpets International) probably best remembered for an incredibly annoying advertising jingle that haunted the 1960s and 70s. Ray Puxley notes that Cyril Lord made rugs and, appropriately, a **RUG** is 'a hair piece'.

- — Ray Puxley, *Cockney Rabbit*, 1992

Cyril Sneer; cyril *noun*

a male homosexual *UK*

Rhyming slang for **QUEER** formed from a character in the Canadian cartoon series *The Raccoons* from the 1980s.

- You look like a Cyril in that pink shirt. — Bodmin Dark, *Dirty Cockney Rhyming Slang*, 2003

cyring call *noun*

in poker, a bet equal to the last bet made in a hesitating fashion *US*

- — David M. Hayano, *Poker Faces*, p. 186, 1982

Dd

D *noun*

1 LSD *US, 1971*

- —Richard A. Spears, *The Slang and Jargon of Drugs and Drink*, p. 134, 1986
- —Mike Haskins, *Drugs*, p. 285, 2003

2 Dilaudid™, a synthetic opiate *US, 1954*

- All right, we was just gonna shoot this little bitty bottle of D.—Bruce Jackson, *In the Life*, p. 220, 1972
- —William K. Bentley and James M. Corbett, *Prison Slang*, p. 65, 1992

3 narcotics *US*

- —John R. Armore and Joseph D. Wolfe, *Dictionary of Desperation*, p. 26, 1976

4 used as a term of address, young man to young man *US*

An abbreviation of DUDE.

- Look out, dude, no reason to be rude, dude, I'm just asking, d. When you get out and about?—Joel Rose, *Kill Kill Faster Faster*, p. 59, 1997

5 a police detective *AUSTRALIA, 1882*

- The waterfront D's were always searching his gladstone bag, but they never caught him.—Frank Hardy, *The Yarns of Billy Borker*, p. 130, 1965

6 a (pre-decimalisation, 1971) penny *UK, 1387*

From Latin *denarius*, a rough equivalent of an old penny, used in the standard abbreviation for pre-decimal Sterling: £1sd.

7 in poker, the fourth player to the left of the dealer *US*

- —George Percy, *The Language of Poker*, p. 26, 1988

8 a demilitarised zone *US*

A shortening of DMZ, the official abbreviation.

- —Linda Reinberg, *In the Field*, p. 56, 1991

D-5 *noun*

a Sony TCD-5M analogue recording tape deck *US*

Favoured by tapers of Grateful Dead concerts until the advent of digital audio tape in the early 1990s.

- —David Shenk and Steve Silberman, *Skeleton Key*, p. 49, 1994

da *noun*

father, a father *UK, 1851*

An abbreviation of affectionate, informal or childish 'dad' or 'dada', especially in Scotland.

- My Da had some strange ideas [...] My Da thought of boxing as folk art.—Anthony Masters, *Minder*, p. 18, 1984
- Thanks very much, da.—Ian Pattison, *Rab C. Nesbitt*, 1988
- He's had a call from the hozzy [hospital]. His da's had a stroke.—Kevin Sampson, *Outlaws*, p. 144, 2001

DA *noun*

1 a hair-style popular in the early 1950s; the hair was tapered and curled on the nape of the neck like the feathers of a duck's tail *US, 1951*

Abbreviated from DUCK'S ARSE/ASS.

- The D.A. haircut reqiures nothing more than finding a barber who is not a sqaure (i.e. one who would think it was named for the district attorney).—*Life*, p. 137, 25th January 1954
- [S]moothing their hair lightly with the palms of their hands, pushing their DA's gently and patting them in place.—Hubert Selby Jr, *Last Exit to Brooklyn*, p. 28, 1957
- I noticed they were dressed in peg pants with pistol pockets, wearing DA's, like everybody except me.—Bobby Seale, *A Lonely Rage*, p. 86, 1978
- Her hair was done in a salt-and-pepper DA.—Armistead Maupin, *Tales of the City*, p. 25, 1978

2 a *d*rug *a*ddict *US*

- I sure didn't want to be classed as a junkie, no matter how many "D.A.'s" they stamped on my card.—Mezz Mezzrow, *Really the Blues*, p. 311, 1946

3 a *d*umb *a*ss *US*

da

1 the *US*

Fashionable respelling of phonetic slovening; an essential element in Hawaiian youth usage.

- —Douglas Simonson, *Pidgin to da Max*, 1981
- [P]lay some real joints from da street.—*Hip-Hop Connection*, p. 9, July 2002

2 so; very *US*

Hawaiian youth usage.

- Oh, da hot!—Douglas Simonson, *Pidgin to da Max*, 1981

dab *noun*

1 a fingerprint *UK, 1926*

Police jargon, in everyday use, usually in the plural.

- Hope he doesn't lamp [see] my dabs in the dust on the bottle.—Derek Raymond (Robin Cook), *The Crust on its Uppers*, p. 119, 1962
- [T]he maniac that had done for him left nothing but his dabs all over the cashier's box[.]—Troy Kennedy Martin, *Z Cars*, 1962
- The handwriting on the application form was clearer evidence of his presence than any finger dabs.—Emmett Grogan, *Ringolevio*, p. 108, 1972
- —Angela Devlin, *Prison Patter*, p. 43, 1996
- [W]e wanted to get away before he takes our dabs and rats [informs] to the soshe [Social Security, a UK government agency].—Kevin Sampson, *Powder*, p. 28, 1999

2 a moistened finger-tip covered in powdered amphetamine *UK*

Possibly, and then only partly inspired, as a nostalgic reference to a children's sweet, the Sherbert Dib Dab™, a lolly dipped into a powdered sugar confection.

- It ain't no secret that I indulge in the odd dab myself.—Dave Courtney, *Raving Lunacy*, p. 5, 2000

3 in rugby, a short, darting run with the ball *NEW ZEALAND*

- An audacious dab by Mill surprised Southland and Stringfellow cut past to score halfway out.—Gordon Slatter, *On the Ball*, p. 110, 1970

4 in cricket, a batsman's stroke that deflects the ball gently behind the wicket *UK, 1969*

- —Michael Rundell, *The Dictionary of Cricket*, p. 59, 1985
- —Keith Foley, *A Dictionary of Cricketing Terminology*, p. 95, 1998

5 a criminal charge; a prison disciplinary charge *UK*

- —Angela Devlin, *Prison Patter*, p. 82, 1996

dab *verb*

1 to ingest a powdered drug by sucking or licking the powder collected on a moistened finger *UK*

- [Y]ew've necked two Es and dabbed a gramme-a whizz an smoked endless spliffs and necked a bottle of vodka[.]—Niall Griffiths, *Sheepshagger*, p. 76, 2001

2 in mountain biking, to touch the ground unintentionally with any part of the body *US*

- —William Nealy, *Mountain Bike!*, p. 160, 1992: 'Bikespeak'

3 of a batsman in cricket, to play a tentative stroke that gently deflects the ball behind the wicket *UK*

- —Michael Rundell, *The Dictionary of Cricket*, p. 59, 1985
- —Keith Foley, *A Dictionary of Cricketing Terminology*, p. 95, 1998
- Gayle is doing as he pleases now, pulling Flintoff for two, then dabbing him past point for a single.—*The Guardian*, 10th April 2004

dabble *noun*

stolen property *UK*

- —R. Samuel (Editor), *East End Underworld*, 1981

dabble *verb*

1 to use addictive drugs without succumbing to the addiction *US*

- —Vincent J. Monteleone, *Criminal Slang*, p. 64, 1949
- How long have you been dabblin' in stuff?—Claude Brown, *Manchild in the Promised Land*, p. 322, 1965
- —Eugene Landy, *The Underground Dictionary*, p. 64, 1971

2 to experiment with homsexuality *UK*

- —Angela Devlin, *Prison Patter*, p. 43, 1996
- Also, I've dabbled. I mean, perform fellatio once and you're a poet, twice and you're a homosexual.—*Austin Powers*, 1999

3 to operate an (occasional) trade in stolen or illegal goods, especially antiques or drugs *UK*

- —Angela Devlin, *Prison Patter*, p. 43, 1996

dab-dab *noun*
to participate in homosexual sex *US*
Prison usage.
- —Charles Shafer, *Folk Speech in Texas Prisons*, p. 202, 1990

dacha; daiture; deger *adjective*
ten *UK*
From Italian *dieci*, via lingua franca into polari.
- [Y]ou might like to count to ten in Polari: una, duey, trey, quater, chicker, sey, setter, otto, nobber, dacha.—Michael Quinion, *World Wide Words*, 1996
- —Paul Baker, *Polari*, p. 171, 2002

Dachau *noun*
any military stockade *US*
Vietnam war usage.
- —Carl Fleischhauer, *A Glossary of Army Slang*, p. 13, 1968

dachs *noun*
a *dachs*hund *UK, 1886*
- There's no need for a coat when your dachs goes for walks with you. —*The Times*, 1st October 2002

dachsie; dachsy *noun*
a *dachs*hund *UK, 1961*
An affectionate elaboration of **DACHS**.

dack *verb*
▷ **see:** **DAK**

dack up *verb*
to light or smoke (a marijuana cigarette) *NEW ZEALAND*
- You all moved up the street and drank more piss, went outside to dack up with a few of the boys, back inside for more laughs.—Alan Duff, *One Night Out Stealing*, p. 102, 1991

dad *noun*
1 used as a term of address for a man *US, 1928*
- —Robert S. Gold, *A Jazz Lexicon*, p. 76, 1964

2 a homosexual prisoner's 'owner' (protector and lover) *US*
- —William K. Bentley and James M. Corbett, *Prison Slang*, p. 59, 1992

Dad *noun*
used as a patronising form of address to an older man *US, 1847*
- The young man pointed down down a flight of rickety stairs that were covered in debris. "That's not safe," said Arthur. "Neither am I, Dad. Now move it."—Anthony Masters, *Minder*, p. 169, 1984

▸ **be like Dad**
to keep quiet; to say nothing *UK*
From the World War 2 slogan 'be like Dad: keep Mum', playing on **MUM** (quiet).
- —Angela Devlin, *Prison Patter*, p. 26, 1996

-dad *suffix*
used as a nonce suffix attached to a friend's name *US*
- [A]dded to a bro's name, for example, Sean-dad, Jaime-dad, Betty-dad.—Jim Humes and Sean Wagstaff, *Boarderlands*, p. 221, 1995

da-dah!
used as a mock fanfare *UK*
- Then suddenly – da-dah! – one of the young German ladies breaks off from her moment of passion to take a ready-made "reefer" from her purse.—Ken Lukowiak, *Marijuana Time*, p. 4, 2000

Dad and Dave *noun*
1 a shave *AUSTRALIA, 1944*
Rhyming slang, after the characters Dad and Dave, the subject of well-known and well-loved humorous sketches concerning pioneering life by 'Steele Rudd' (Arthur Hoey Davis, 1868–1935).

2 a grave *AUSTRALIA*
Rhyming slang.
- [O]ld man McKakie was rotating faster in the old Dan and Dave as news came through of the activities of young Albert.—Frank Hardy, *The Outcasts of Foolgarah*, p. 152, 1971

dad-blamed *adjective*
used as a euphemism for 'damned' *US, 1844*
'Dad' is a euphemism for God.
- "What you always writing in that dad-blamed book for?" she asked with a sour little face.—Louise Fitzhugh, *Harriet the Spy*, p. 36, 1964
- When they're located, the whole dad-blamed family is going to be whisked off to a mansion in Beverly Hills[.]—*Portland Mercury*, 18th September 2002

dad-blasted *adjective*
damned, confounded *US, 1840*
In which 'dad' is a euphemism for God.
- [A]n integral part of newspaper paste-up until these dad-blasted computers took over the world—*The Morning News (North West Arkansas)*, 6th July 2003

daddy *noun*
1 the very best *US, 1865*
- —Connie Eble (Editor), *UNC-CH Campus Slang*, p. 2, Fall 1991
- I've seen a bird which has finally killed its opponent [in a cock fight...] start crowing like it's shouting, "I'm the daddy, I'm the daddy." —Jimmy Stockin, *On The Cobbles*, p. 107, 2000
- It's The Daddy—*Holsten Pils television advertising.*, 2001
- Harley claims the V-Rod is the most radical motorcycle in the company's 100-year history, as well as being its most powerful production bike ever. They're not wrong. This bike is the daddy of them all.—*The Guardian*, 25th May 2003

2 the most powerful inmate in a borstal (a juvenile offenders penal institution); in prison, the most powerful or very strong inmate, or the prisoner who runs a racket *UK, 1978*
- You're nothing. I'm the daddy here.—*Scum*, 1979
- —Angela Devlin, *Prison Patter*, p. 43, 1996
- "Lenny," he said, "the Daddy is telling everybody that you're a cockney poof."—Lenny McLean, *The Guv'nor*, p. 30, 1998

3 a leader *UK*
Originally prison slang, especially of a forceful personality among borstal inmates; now in wider use.
- I'm looking round for the Number One, the daddy.—Kevin Sampson, *Outlaws*, p. 177, 2001

4 the dominant partner in a male homosexual relationship *US, 1932*
- They are usually long-terms and are familiarly known to inmates by such local cognomens as "wolves," "top men," "jockers" or "daddies."—*Ebony*, p. 82, July 1951
- [T]he queens will go on looking for their own legendary permanent "Daddies" among the older men who dig the queens' special brand of gone sexplay[.]—John Rechy, *City of Night*, p. 108, 1963
- But the homosexual daddies would pretend to have more money than they really had.—Geoff Brown, *I Want What I Want*, p. 47, 1966
- It must have been your night to play daddy.—Malcolm Braly, *On the Yard*, p. 333, 1967
- Well, they're more hard-working, because to them it's just a front and they got to prove that they are daddy.—Bruce Jackson, *In the Life*, p. 119, 1972
- He truly was my bitch, and I was his daddy.—Howard Stern, *Miss America*, p. 307, 1995

5 an aggressive, predatory male homosexual *US*
- Inmates subject to rape ("punks") face threats and violence perpetrated by stronger inmates ("daddies," "jockers," or "booty bandits") who initiate unwanted sexual acts.—*Corrections Today*, p. 100, December 1996

6 the woman who plays the active, masculine role in a lesbian relationship *US, 1940s*

7 in the US Army, your supervising officer *US*
- —Carl Fleischhauer, *A Glossary of Army Slang*, p. 13, 1968

8 used as a term of address to a man *UK, 1681*
- She say, 'No, Daddy, my money ain't short.—Christina and Richard Milner, *Black Players*, p. 87, 1972

9 a marijuana cigarette *UK*
- —Mike Haskins, *Drugs*, p. 287, 2003

daddy-come-to-church *noun*
an unusual event *US*
- All that hard work and deep breathing had put breasts on her like daddy-come-to-church.—Jim Thompson, *Savage Night*, p. 22, 1953

daddy mac *noun*
an attractive young man *US*
- —Vann Wesson, *Generation X Field Guide and Lexicon*, p. 48, 1997

daddy-o *noun*
1 a term of address for a man *US*
Also variant 'daddio'.
- Wait a minute, daddy-o, I'm going your way!—Ralph Ellison, *Invisible Man*, p. 173, 1947
- Coined during the Beat era, used there without irony for a brief period and then used with mocking irony since.—Arnold Shaw, *Lingo of Tin-Pan Alley*, p. 10, 1950

- You just burned down the town last Wednesday, daddy-o. — William 'Lord' Buckley, *Nero*, 1951
- You know who I want to marry, Daddio, you know. — George Mandel, *Flee the Angry Strangers*, p. 358, 1952
- "Sorry, Daddy-o," said Red. "Some other time." — Steve Allen, *Bop Fables*, p. 38, 1955
- RIFF: Spread the word, Diesel. DIESEL: Right, daddy-0. — Stephen Sondheim, *West Side Story*, 1957
- Evan Hunter, author of MGM's movie "Blackboard Jungle," was sued for using the expression "daddy-o" in the script. A Midwest disc jockey claimed he coined the term. — *San Francisco Chronicle, This Week*, p. 10 (II), 26th August 1962
- Daddy-o, I'm going to make like I didn't dig what you just put down. — Piri Thomas, *Down These Mean Streets*, p. 110, 1967
- You can get a steak here. Hey daddy-o, dont be a [Mia makes the international symbol for square, made popular by Pebbles Flintstone.] — *Pulp Fiction*, 1994
- Pop [music] is now old. It's no longer the noo scene daddio. — John Robb, *The Nineties*, p. 115, 1999

2 the US Federal Communications Commission *US*

- — Bill Davis, *Jawjacking*, p. 33, 1977

daddypoo *noun*

used as an embellishment of 'daddy', usually from a woman to a man *US*

- All the other girls are ahead of me this month, daddypoo! [Steve Roper comic strip] — *San Francisco Chronicle*, p. 54, 1st March 1966

daddy's yacht *noun*

used rhetorically as a representation of the privileges of civilian life *UK*

Military sarcasm, in several variations, most commonly 'Where do you think you are? On your daddy's yacht'; directed mainly at National Service recruits (1945–62).

- — Colin Evans, *The Hearts of Standing*, 1962

daddy tank *noun*

a jail cell reserved for lesbian prisoners *US*

- — Eugene Landy, *The Underground Dictionary*, p. 64, 1971
- — Ralph de Sola, *Crime Dictionary*, p. 37, 1982
- — William K. Bentley and James M. Corbett, *Prison Slang*, p. 10, 1992

dadger *noun*

the penis *UK*

Variation of TADGER (the penis).

- ["I]s it true what they all say about black men?" "What? That we all make great lawyers, accountants, politicians?" "No, yer pillock, that you've all got cowin' big dadgers." — Colin Butts, *Is Harry on the Boat?*, p. 19, 1997

dadrock *noun*

1990s rock music that sounds like music from a generation earlier, e.g. Oasis play dadrock that bears obvious similarities to the Beatles *UK*

- The fashion that goes with the music – including haircuts, clothes and the predictable rock star antics – has created dadrock and has made criticism difficult for those who remember it (and thought it was fab) first time around. — Alon Shulman, *The Style Bible*, p. 70, 1999
- Cheered on the dadrock supergroup of Liam [Gallagher], Noel [Gallagher], Paul Weller and the Stereophonic's Kelly Jones[.] — *FHM*, p. 16, June 2003

dads *noun*

a father, or in general address, a man *UK, 1984*

A variation of 'dad'.

dad's army *adjective*

barmy, foolish *UK*

Rhyming slang, after the 1970s television comedy of the UK's World War 2 Home Guard.

- I don't trust him, he looks a bit dad's army to me. — Ray Puxley, *Cockney Rabbit*, p. 45, 1992

Dad's Army *nickname*

the Home Guard (1940–45); hence, any grouping of older men with a united purpose *UK*

Gently derogatory. The term survives essentially as a piece of familiar nostalgia mainly because of the popularity of BBC television comedy series *Dad's Army* (1968–77, and which is still being repeated in 2003). The modern sense is therefore informed by the nature of the characters in the programme; variously bumptious and bumbling, etc.

- [On the QE2] a Dad's Army of doddery doctors, senescent solicitors, geriatric taxi drivers and antiquated accountants. — *The Guardian*, 14th October 2001

daff *noun*

excrement *IRELAND*

- Go on, Des, tell him he's the colour of his own daff. — Tom Murphy, *A Whistle in the Dark*, p. 17, 1989

daffies *noun*

strong alcohol *UK*

- — Patrick O'Shaughnessy, *Market Traders' Slang*, 1979

daffodil *noun*

a homosexual man *US, 1935*

- — Fred Bason, *Second Diary*, 1952
- — *Maledicta*, p. 227, 1979: 'Kinks and queens: linguistic and cultural aspects of the terminology for gays'

daffy *noun*

a skiing stunt in which one ski is swung up in front of the skier while the other is brought up behind and parallel to the first, the whole being a form of mid-air splits *UK, 1984*

'Daffy' is listed under the heading Freestyle skiing in the official lexicon for the 2002 Winter Olympic Games.

daffy *adjective*

odd, eccentric, silly *UK, 1884*

The original meaning of 'slightly mad' has softened over the years.

- [T]he whole thing was making a young girl who wasn't too bright to begin with into some kind of a daffy basket case. — George V. Higgins, *The Rat on Fire*, p. 149, 1981
- Before Lynn could get into his Rambler, Nelson showed him that daffy grin and said, "If we get him, I hope you'll put in a good word for me with your ex-captain." — Joseph Wambaugh, *Fugitive Nights*, p. 103, 1992
- Tuesday, 20 April [1993] [Lord James Douglas-Hamilton] can't be as bumbly and daffy as he pretends to be. — Gyles Brandreth, *Breaking the Code*, p. 172, 1999
- [Jane Birkin] somehow combines the auras of an implausibly sophisticated and svelte grande dame and a daffy language teacher doing a turn at the end-of-term concert. — *The Guardian*, 4th March 2003

daffydowndilly; daffadowndilly *adjective*

silly *UK*

Rhyming slang, formed on an informal name for the 'daffodil', or perhaps it is simply an elaboration of DAFFY (silly, daft).

- Current in the theatrical world[.] — Julian Franklyn, *A Dictionary of Rhyming Slang*, 1960

daffy-headed *adjective*

feather-brained, daft *UK*

- The daffy-headed dimmo who worries about glove compartments doesn't exist. — *Sunday Express*, 25th October 1981

daft *nickname*

Nova Scotia's Department of Fisheries and Oceans *CANADA*

- The bills were presented to me at my retirement party, by the Minister of the Department of Fishy Things, officially shortened to DOFT but referred to by my department staff as DAFT). — Vincent Russell, *Over the Grey in Jilted Angels*, p. 63, 2002

daft and barmy *noun*

an army *UK*

Rhyming slang. Note also the reversed rhyme: DAD'S ARMY for 'barmy'.

- [I]n the daft and barmy maintaining law and order[.] — Ronnie Barker, *Fletcher's Book of Rhyming Slang*, p. 39, 1979

daft as a brush; mad as a brush *adjective*

crazy; stupid *UK, 1945*

- [H]er with one son in jail and the other one daft as a brush. — Livi Michael, *Robinson Street*, p. 28, 1999

daft Doris *noun*

a foolish woman *UK*

- Well thanks very fucking much for that, you daft Doris. — Ken Lukowiak, *Marijuana Time*, p. 177, 2000

daftie *noun*

a daft person *UK, 1872*

- Geordie, who is regarded in the Newcastle of the 1960s as the local "daftie" but is in fact an autistic savant. — *The Guardian*, 14th December 2002

dag *noun*

1 a matted lock of wool and excrement on a sheep's behind *AUSTRALIA, 1891*

From British dialect.

- Get a load of me, will you? Dags on every inch of me hide; drinking me own sweat; swallowing dirt with every breath I breathe; shearing sheeps that should have been dog's meat years ago[.] —Frank Hardy, *The Yarns of Billy Borker*, p. 147, 1965
- [H]e's a dag. —Sumner Locke Elliott, *Rusty Bugles*, p. 52, 1968
- He was a bit of a dag. —Douglas Lockwood, *My Old Mates*, p. 118, 1979

2 a person who is eccentric and humorous; a real character; a wag *AUSTRALIA, 1875*

Formerly common, now obsolete (but see gloss at sense 3). Some have suggested that the origin of this term lies in the British dialect term 'a feat set as a dare', but the examples given in the *English Dialect Dictionary* make these feats more skilful than amusing or eccentric.

- Let's shoot through [go] before this dag yells for the blues [police]. —Barry Humphries, *Bazza Pulls It Off!*, 1971
- —Jim Ramsay, *Cop It Sweet!*, p. 27, 1977
- — *The Traveller's Tool*, p. 138, 1985
- But some dag said that the plastic Prime Minister once had 73 per cent support[.] —Frank Hardy, *Hardy's People*, p. 119, 1986
- —David McGill, *A Dictionary of Kiwi Slang*, p. 34, 1988

3 a person who is dull and conservative; a person who has no sense of fashion; an uncool or unhip person *AUSTRALIA, 1966*

Now the commonest meaning. It is widely believed that it derives from sense 1, but this is not the case. Probably partially from sense 2 and partially a backformation from **DAGGY** sense 2. Formerly and still to some extent quite an insult, equivalent to **GEEK** and **NERD**, but recently also used in an affectionate manner, and jocularly 'reclaimed' as a term of approval. This reclamation has led to a semantic shift where the meaning can be 'uncool in an amusing or eccentric way', and thus this sense now overlaps with that of sense 2.

- Hang on a sec you silly dag while I square off this four-by-two. — *The Adventures of Barry McKenzie*, 1972
- Don't be a dag. Control the impulse to call. —Kathy Lette, *Girls' Night Out*, p. 15, 1987
- Next night I went to the local dive for deviants. It was downstairs with dags for two bucks. And upstairs with phonies, for four. —Kathy Lette, *Girls' Night Out*, p. 87, 1987
- Why don't you dump him Mouche? He's a total dag. —Kathy Lette, *Girls' Night Out*, p. 96, 1987
- Promise him that your Dag Days are over. No longer will you wear blue with black or sprout maverick patches of armpit hair. —Kathy Lette, *Girls' Night Out*, p. 208, 1987
- The Dag's clothes on the other hand look like they were made in Sorrow rather than in Anger, and simply serve to cover his body – a pale, flabby embarrassment that should be kept covered at all costs. —Ignatius Jones, *True Hip*, p. 32, 1990
- Like, right, you think I'm a dag, don't you? —Christos Tsiolkas, *Loaded*, p. 39, 1995

4 a daring act *NEW ZEALAND*

Originally and literally 'a clump of faecal matter stuck on a sheep's tail'.

- —Louis S. Leland, *A Personal Kiwi-Yankee Dictionary*, p. 31, 1984

dag *verb*

1 to engage in anal sex *US*

- — *The Correctional Officer's Guide to Prison Slang*, 2001

2 to participate in serial, reciprocal, homosexual oral sex *US*

- —Charles Shafer, *Folk Speech in Texas Prisons*, p. 202, 1990

dag!

used for expressing surprise *US*

- "I made four goals in the game yesterday." "Dag! You were hot!" —Connie Eble (Editor), *UNC-CH Campus Slang*, p. 3, Spring 1987
- "Oh hell, I might as well try 'em [psychoactive mushrooms], this party is so drab." "Oh dag!" "What?" "I ain't mean for you to eat the whole bag!" —Eminem (Marshall Mathers), *My Fault*, 1999

dagdom *noun*

the notional realm of dags *AUSTRALIA*

- While the symbol of Hip Dressing is the Well-Cut Suit, a sure sign of Dagdom is the wearing of *Slacks*. —Ignatius Jones, *True Hip*, p. 32, 1990

dage *noun*

a foreigner, an immigrant *AUSTRALIA*

From **DAGO** (a foreigner, an immigrant, etc.).

- —Vince Kelly, *The Shadow*, 1955

Dagenham dustbin *noun*

a Ford car *UK*

Citizens' band radio slang. Dagenham in Essex is best-known as the major manufacturing base for Ford cars.

- —Peter Chippindale, *The British CB Book*, p. 161, 1981

dagga *noun*

1 marijuana *SOUTH AFRICA, 1955*

Dagga is the common name in South Africa for a relatively non-toxic herb (genus: *Leonotis*, varieties: *Cape*, *red* and *wilde*) which is smoked like tobacco; however, for a slang user one herb predominates.

- — *Current Slang*, p. 4, Spring 1968
- In South Africa they call it dagga and it is laughing grass. It is very green and the best stuff comes from Durban. —Richard Neville, *Play Power*, p. 223, 1970
- Although smoking dagga is illegal, it is readily available. — *San Francisco Chronicle*, p. 36, 21st September 1971
- I was standing against the wall in the toilets smoking dagga. — *Sunday Times (South Africa)*, 28th February 1999
- —Mike Haskins, *Drugs*, p. 287, 2003

2 a marijuana cigarette *US*

- — *American Speech*, p. 87, May 1955

dagga rooker *noun*

a marijuana smoker *SOUTH AFRICA*

Combines **DAGGA** with Africaans *rooker* (a smoker). In respectable circles a 'dagga rooker' is recorded as 'a scoundrel; a wastrel'.

dagger *noun*

a lesbian *US*

An abbreviation of the full **BULLDAGGER**.

- —Edith A. Folb, *runnin' down some lines*, p. 234, 1980

dagger of desire *noun*

the erect penis *UK*

Jocular.

- I realised that I could only do the dagger of desire justice by writing a book —Richard Herring, *Talking Cock*, p. 17, 2003

daggers *noun*

▸ throw daggers; give the daggers

to look angrily at someone *UK*

Variations of the conventional form 'look daggers'.

- She kisses Lobelia and throws Judy daggers and then she disappears in a whisper of heavy satin. —Lisa Jewell, *Labia Lobelia [Tart Noir]*, p. 241, 2002
- Gavin shouted at me and gave me the daggers. —Danny King, *The Bank Robber Diaries*, p. 2, 2002

daggily *adverb*

in a daggy manner *AUSTRALIA*

- —Arthur Chipper, *The Aussie Swearer's Guide*, p. 86, 1972

dagginess *noun*

the state of being daggy *AUSTRALIA*

- The problem here is that a kind of Pervasive Dagginess is thought to be essential for advancement in this kind of profession [banking]. —Ignatius Jones, *True Hip*, p. 11, 1990

daggy *adjective*

1 unfashionable; uncool *AUSTRALIA, 1981*

- We have the same daggy sense of humour. He's great. It's hard to tell whose is daggier, but we laugh at each other's jokes, if nobody else does. — *Weekend Australian*, p. 10, 29th December 1984
- Come on, Deb, she couldn't be interested in Paul – that daggy coat, and looking like he hasn't eaten since he was twelve. —Jenny Pausacker, *What are ya?*, p. 41, 1987
- Charley and Bruce helped me renovate my wardrobe. Out with the daggy. In with what I think we can call 'restrained fashionable'. —Terry Lane, *Hectic*, p. 98, 1993
- There was a puzzled look on his face, a look that said he was almost worried. He looked quite odd without his usual daggy grin. You got used to the mad, cheerful look on the Sarge's face; it was a surprise to see it gone. —Tim Winton, *Lockie Leonard*, p. 14, 1997
- And even though the motorbike is really old-fashioned looking and the leather jacket is pretty daggy, there's something about him. —Phillip Gwynne, *Deadly Unna?*, p. 82, 1998
- And anyhow Paula wasn't going to look like Mary from the dairy by admitting she didn't know what was going on in this sophisticated ambience of fashionably daggy movie people. —Peter Robb, *Pig's Blood and other fluids*, p. 61, 1999
- Knitting is not daggy any more. — *Who*, p. 69, 27th July 2003

2 (of clothes, personal appearance, etc) dirty, filthy *AUSTRALIA, 1967*

- She's married to a daggy artist in daggy jeans in a daggy Paddo flat with fifteen daggy dogs.—Arthur Chipper, *The Aussie Swearer's Guide*, p. 37, 1972
- 'A month ago I see him in a pub in Tamworth, all daggy. Gone to pieces.'—David Ireland, *The Glass Canoe*, p. 148, 1976
- Would I make love to an Aboriginal woman? No, it has never occurred to me. No. They're too daggy.—Sandra Jobson, *Blokes*, p. 166, 1984
- Her shoes were scuffed and daggy and she had no stockings to wear[.]—Tim Winton, *Cloudstreet*, p. 180, 1991

3 cheap or trashy looking in a sexually promiscuous way *US*

- —Anna Scotti and Paul Young, *Buzzwords*, p. 90, 1997

4 (of sheep) having dags; (of wool) soiled with excrement *AUSTRALIA, 1895*

- Not like the western slopes where the bosses are out on the run from sun-up ter sun-down musterin' and inoculatin' and takin' out and musterin' and crutchin' and pickin' daggy wool and takin' out again.—Dymphna Cusack, *Picnic Races*, p. 192, 1962
- Curly got two for one for daggy and maggoty sheep at the Shepparton Abbatoirs in 1936.—Frank Hardy, *Hardy's People*, p. 150, 1986

dago *noun*

1 an Italian or Italian-American; Italian *US, 1857*

A slur, originally applied to Spaniards, then to Spaniards, Portuguese and Italians, and now only to Italians.

- "He called me a dago son of a b——," explained Sinatra as he told how he had clouted Mortimer at the entrance of Ciro's.—*Fortnight*, p. 20, 21st April 1947
- You know that Bleecker Street is evil with all them wild Dago kids after dark.—George Mandel, *Flee the Angry Strangers*, p. 20, 1952
- Who gets the jobs over there in the NMU Hall? American white men like you and me? No. Dagos and Spiks and Niggers.—William Burroughs, *Junkie*, p. 72, 1953
- He used to arrive about six in the evening, loaded with chickens from the rotisserie and bottles of Dago red.—Polly Adler, *A House is Not a Home*, p. 42, 1953
- They were sitting around drinking dago red and Lovis asked where his folks came from.—Bernard Wolfe, *The Late Risers*, p. 183, 1954
- I had so much of that hot greaser dago cock that I stopped menstruating and started minstroning!—Terry Southern, *Candy*, p. 211–212, 1958
- The Old Digger looked up from his rifle cleaning to observe, 'nothing personal, mate, when I spoke before about dagos not liking cold steel.'—Frank Hardy, *The Outcasts of Foolgarah*, p. 187, 1971
- You a dago or an Abo?—Shane Maloney, *Nice Try*, p. 98, 1988
- In '77 he smoked a bag of dust he bought from a dago.—*New Jack City*, 1990
- I mean, around here a cultured person is one that don't drink dago red from a jar.—Joseph Wambaugh, *Finnegan's Week*, p. 9, 1993
- I like the word wog, can't stand dago, ethnic or Greek-Australian. —Christos Tsiolkas, *Loaded*, p. 115, 1995
- Now, if I can attract the fat dago's attention, I'll get us all a drink[.] —Colin Butts, *Is Harry on the Boat?*, p. 17, 1997

2 any foreigner *UK*

Liverpool use.

- United nations it were round the Southern Neighbourhoods [...] – mainly Filipino families when we was growing up. Sometimes they'd get called dagos and that. Nothing was meant by it.—Kevin Sampson, *Outlaws*, p. 7, 2001

3 in hot rodding, a dropped front axle, especially on older Fords *US*

- The "dago" part of the term is California slang for the city of San Diego, where this type of axle was originated.—John Lawlor, *How to Talk Car*, p. 37, 1965
- I took apart the cars I saw and put them back together in more interesting ways, lowered, louvered, dagoed, chopped-and-channeled.—Tobias Wolff, *This Boy's Life*, p. 122, 1989

dago *adjective*

foreign *AUSTRALIA, 1900*

Dago *nickname*

San Diego, California *US, 1931*

- We don't do it in Dago.—Raymond Chandler, *Playback*, p. 13, 1958
- I made a connection with some Mexican pushers in 'Dago, and they kept me supplied.—John O'Day, *Confessions of a Male Prostitute*, p. 105, 1964
- I caught the six o'clock bus to Dago and walked across the border. —James Ellroy, *Brown's Requiem*, p. 128–129, 1981

▸ **the Dago**

Frank Sinatra, American singer (1915–1998) *US*

- The latest casino owner in Las Vegas to embark on the hearts-and-flowers route is Francis Albert Sinatra, better known as The Leader, The General, The Dago, The Pope, and Frankie Boy.—Ed Reid and Ovid Demaris, *The Green Felt Jungle*, p. 74, 1963

dago bomb *noun*

a type of firework *US, 1960*

- Now loo, when the Dago bomb goes off I want all of you to be ready.—Jean Shepherd, *The Ferrari in the Bedroom*, p. 187, 1972

dago red *noun*

inexpensive, inferior red wine *US, 1906*

- —Vincent J. Monteleone, *Criminal Slang*, p. 65, 1949
- "You're real smooth and sophisticated," Buster said to his partner. "Like dago red in a fruit jar."—Joseph Wambaugh, *The Golden Orange*, p. 176, 1990

dagotown *noun*

a neighbourhood dominated by Italian-Americans *US*

- Even the dago-town pusher was wary of him now, just because of Sonny.—Clarence Cooper Jr, *The Scene*, p. 12, 1960

Dagwood *noun*

a large and elaborate sandwich *US, 1948*

Named after the sandwiches made by the Dagwood Bumstead character in the *Blondie* comic strip.

- Sol had a saltine Dagwood going: peanut butter, lox spread, sardines.—James Ellroy, *Hollywood Nocturnes*, p. 96, 1994

Dagwood dog *noun*

a deep-fried battered frankfurter on a stick *AUSTRALIA*

- Makin', Bakin', Cookin' all the while, the hot 'n tasty Dagwood dog on a stick. Every year at the local Ag show when I was a kid for as long as I can remember.—*Wordmap (www.abc.net.au/wordmap)*, 2003

daikon legs *noun*

short, pale and fat legs *US*

Hawaiian youth usage. The 'daikon' is also known as an Asian, Oriental or Chinese radish; it is stubby and white.

- —Douglas Simonson, *Pidgin to da Max*, 1981

dailies *noun*

film scenes filmed one day, rush processed and delivered for viewing by the director and others the same or next day *US, 1970s→*

- The boot. T and A. Gaffer. Another one he used, "dailies," referring to the videotapes. The guy loved to use words nobody knew what they meant.—Elmore Leonard, *Split Images*, p. 214, 1981

daily *noun*

a regular (daily) bet with a bookmaker *UK, 1984*

daily-daily *noun*

during the Vietnam war, anti-malaria pills taken daily, in addition to a second medication taken once a week *US*

- Doc McCarthy came by with the daily-daily (anti-malaria) pills.—John M. Del Vecchio, *The 13th Valley*, p. 243, 1982

daily double *noun*

in poker, two consecutive winning hands *US*

A borrowing from horse racing.

- —John Vorhaus, *The Big Book of Poker Slang*, p. 12, 1996

daily dozen *noun*

physical exercises, performed on rising; hence, a limited group (or the measure thereof) of anything (voluntarily) experienced on a daily basis *UK, 1919*

It is unlikely that the 'dozen' was ever a precise sum.

- Using twelve basic poses ("The Daily Dozen") along with "Myth Busters," "Jargon Alerts," and "Tips"[.]—*Barnes & Noble review of the video 'Basic Yoga Workout for Dummies'*, 2001
- [T]he place where Hemingway drank his daily dozen mojitos (rum with sugar, limejuice and mint) [.]—*The Guardian*, 10th February 2001

Daily Express *noun*

a dress *UK*

Rhyming slang, formed on the title of a leading national newspaper.

- —Ray Puxley, *Cockney Rabbit*, 1992

Daily Express *verb*

to dress *UK*

Rhyming slang, formed on the title of a leading national newspaper.

- —Ray Puxley, *Cockney Rabbit*, 1992

Daily Getsmuchworse *nickname*

the *Daily Express* *UK*

Coined in the 1970s by satirical magazine *Private Eye*.

Daily Liar *nickname*

the *Daily Mail* *UK, 1984*

Jocular.

Daily Mail; daily *noun*

1 a tail; hence, rectum, arse *UK*

Rhyming slang, based on the title of a major newspaper.

- But this time Nat and I were right on his daily[.] —Charles Raven, *Underworld Nights*, p. 127, 1956
- He found another car up his daily. —G.F. Newman, *The Guvnor*, 1977
- He fell on his Daily Mail. —David Powis, *The Signs of Crime*, 1977

2 a tale, especially 'glib patter' or the story told by an informer; a confidence-trickster's patter *UK, 1960*

Rhyming slang, formed on the title of a leading national newspaper.

- He spun me a Dail (Mail) I just couldn't believe. —David Powis, *The Signs of Crime*, 1977

3 a prostitute; a sexually available woman *UK*

Rhyming slang for TAIL (a woman objectified sexually) or BRASS NAIL (a prostitute), formed on the title of a leading national newspaper.

- She's Daily Mail all right, (she's accommodating in the sexual sense. —David Powis, *The Signs of Crime*, 1977

4 bail *UK*

Rhyming slang, formed on the title of a leading national newspaper.

- Guvnor, what's the chances of the old Daily Mail? —David Powis, *The Signs of Crime*, 1977

5 a nail *UK*

Rhyming slang, formed on the title of a leading national newspaper; used by carpenters.

- —Julian Franklyn, *A Dictionary of Rhyming Slang*, 1961

6 ale *UK*

Rhyming slang.

- —Julian Franklyn, *A Dictionary of Rhyming Slang*, p. 55, 1960

Daily-Tell-the-Tale *nickname*

the *Daily Mail* *UK*

- —Julian Franklyn, *A Dictionary of Rhyming Slang*, 1960

Daily Torygraph *nickname*

the *Daily Telegraph* *UK*

From the paper's political bias.

- But editors, Brother Boris at the Spectator and Comrade Charles on the *Daily Torygraph*, will soon be talking collective agreements after – whisper it – even their columnists voted in a secret ballot to be represented by the National Union of Journalists. —*The Guardian*, 16th May 2003

dainties *noun*

underwear, especially women's underwear worn by transvestites *US*

- —Bruce Rodgers, *The Queens' Vernacular*, p. 59, 1972

dairy; dairies *noun*

the female breast(s) *UK*

Elaborated as 'dairy arrangements' in 1923; most later use tends towards 'dairy' for 'a breast', with 'dairies' as a natural plural; however, 'dairy' is originally recorded as both singluar and plural (in the context of a single female) by Francis Grose in 1788; it is current in the plural sense in Scamto (urban youth slang in South African townships) in 2005.

- —*The Times*, 12th February 2005

▸ **the dairy**

the best *UK*

A play on conventional 'cream'.

- Ian [Dury] was an editor's dream come true, so he was bound to get the dairy. —Will Birch, *No Sleep Till Canvey Island*, p. 268, 2003
- I realise we're successful now and I'm getting all the dairy because it's my record deal[.] —ascribed to Ian Dury, 1978 Jim Drury, *Ian Dury and the Blockheads*, p. 128, 2003

dairy box *noun*

a sexually transmitted infection *UK*

Rhyming slang, formed on a branded chocolate assortment manufactured by Nestlé.

- —Ray Puxley, *Cockney Rabbit*, 1992

daisy *noun*

1 an excellent thing or person *US, 1757*

- Behind all this lackadaisical exterior, he [Peter Falk]'s a daisy. In our judgment, he can act with anyone on the stage or screen today[.] —Cleveland Amory, *quoted in 'TV Guide Online' 2003*, 1972

2 an attractive young woman *US, 1876*

- Who was she? Just some blonde daisy, getting into the Jag. —John Milne, *Alive and Kicking*, p. 33, 1998

3 a male homosexual *US, 1944*

Often used in Peter O'Donnell's *Modesty Blaise* stories, 1962–2001.

daisy bell!

hell! *UK*

Rhyming slang, formed on the name of a music hall song ('Daisy Bell' also known as 'A Bicycle Made for Two', by Harry Dacre, 1892).

- Expressions of anger, disappointment or frustration are "blooming", "bloody", or "fucking daisy"[.] —Ray Puxley, *Cockney Rabbit*, 1992

daisy chain *noun*

1 a group of people, arranged roughly in a circle, in which each person is both actively and passively engaged in oral, anal or vaginal sex with the person in front of and behind them in the circle *US, 1927*

A term that is much more common than the practice.

- Past the Horseshoe Club, with its modified burlesque, and where for five bucks extra you can watch three naked women form a daisy chain on the floor of a basement room anytime after one a.m. —*Rogue for Men*, p. 46, June 1956
- [T]hey left and came back with cans of beer which were passed around the daisychain[.] —Hubert Selby Jr, *Last Exit to Brooklyn*, p. 126, 1957
- Robert Christie, mass strangler of women – sounds like a daisy chain – hanged in 1953. —William Burroughs, *Naked Lunch*, p. 225, 1957
- —Donald Webster Cory and John P. LeRoy, *The Homosexual and His Society*, p. 263, 1963: 'A lexicon of homosexual slang'
- We had sort of a daisy chain, with Ned in the middle. Ned's boyfriend performed fellation on him while Ned used his hand on me and I masturbated his friend. —Ruth Allison, *Lesbianism*, p. 117, 1967
- The orgy scene is to involve, primarily, three different sexual activities in the following chronological order: oral sex in a "daisy-chain" configuration with all five performers involved. —Vincent Barth, *Porno Films and the People Who Make Them*, p. 121, 1973
- His appearance signals a nine-person orgy that features a delicious daisy-chain of joined cocks and cunts and mouths. —*Adult Video*, p. 29, August/September 1986

2 an abstract grouping of people who have had sex with the same person at different times *US*

- —Connie Eble (Editor), *UNC-CH Campus Slang*, p. 3, Spring 1990

3 figuratively and by extension, a series of events that return to the beginning *US*

- Randolph is suing. Stanley is suing Stuyvessant North. It's a daisy chain. —*San Francisco Call-Bulletin*, p. 15, 6th May 1954
- But the cool nurse who's no longer cool goes immediately to the feds, who've been talking to her anyway, and now the fucking daisy chain comes around again." —Elmore Leonard, *Bandits*, p. 140, 1987

4 in computing, a network architecture in which a single cable connects all nodes *US*

- —Christian Crumlish, *The Internet Dictionary*, p. 47, 1995

5 a confidence swindle where funds from successive victims are used to keep the swindle alive with the earlier victims *US, 1985*

- He has a girlfriend named Monica Brown, a con artist who's working a gold-mine scam, a daisy chain. —Gerald Petievich, *Shakedown*, p. 154, 1988

6 a series of (Claymore) mines attached to each other and rigged for sequential detonation *UK*

From the general appearance.

- We used a device christened the "daisy chain", made from gun-cotton primers threaded on a five-foot chain of prima cord [...] Five primers went to each daisy chain spaced out and held by knots in the cord. —Vladimir Peniakoff, *(writing of the North Afrian campaign, 1942–3), Private Army*, 1950
- —Linda Reinberg, *In the Field*, p. 56, 1991

daisy cutter *noun*

1 a 10,000 to 15,000 pound bomb used to clear jungle and create an instant landing zone in Vietnam *US, 1967*

- —Gregory Clark, *Words of the Vietnam War*, p. 133, 1990
- A "Daisy Cutter" is a huge bomb that can cause massive destruction [...] The type depicted in the leaflets, and also used in Afghanistan, is

the BLU-82B Commando Vault or Big Blue 82, also known as the Daisy Cutter. — *BBC News*, 6th November 2001

2 in cricket, a fast ball, bowled conventionally or thrown underarm, that barely clears the surface of the pitch *UK, 1863*

- — Michael Rundell, *The Dictionary of Cricket*, p. 59, 1985
- — Keith Foley, *A Dictionary of Cricketing Terminology*, p. 95, 1998
- One delivery from Kirtley is an old-fashioned daisy cutter. — *The Guardian*, 15th August 2003

Daisy Dormer *adjective*

warmer, especially of the weather *UK*

Rhyming slang, formed on the name of a music hall entertainer; originally used as a noun in the sense as a 'bed-warmer'.

- — Julian Franklyn, *A Dictionary of Rhyming Slang*, 1960
- — Ray Puxley, *Cockney Rabbit*, 1992

Daisy Dukes *noun*

very short and very tight shorts *US*

Named after a character on the unforgettable US television programme *Dukes of Hazard*.

- — Connie Eble (Editor), *UNC-CH Campus Slang*, p. 2, Spring 1993
- Daisy Dukes gets props / Hair and nails fresh from the shop. — The Dove Shack, *Summertime in the LBC*, 1995

daisy roots; daisies; daisys *noun*

boots *UK, 1859*

Rhyming slang, always in the plural.

- He looks a proper nana / In his great big hobnail boots / He's got such a job to pull them on / That he calls them daisy roots. — Lonnie Donegan, *My Old Man's a Dustman*, 1960
- It's me new daisy roots, they're killing me plates [feet]. — *The Sweeney*, p. 6, 1976
- Spruced up in me piccolo [suit], me titfer [hat] and me daisys. — Viv Stanshall, *Ginger Geezer*, 1981

daiture *adjective*

▷ see: DACHA

dak *noun*

1 marijuana *NEW ZEALAND*

- If you want a cruisy, clear day, smoke some really good, locally grown dak. — *Dominion*, p. 13, 29th June 1998

2 a C-47A Skytrain plane, also known as a DC-3, most commonly used to transport people and cargo, but also used as a bomber and fighter *US*

- She was known affectionately as the "Gooney Bird," "Dak," and "Dizzy Three" to the men who flew her during World War II. — *San Francisco Chronicle*, p. 60, 18th January 1975

dak; dack *verb*

to pull another's trousers down as a prank *AUSTRALIA*

- Someone dacked Daniel yesterday and he had blue undies on. — June Factor, *Kidspeak*, p. 52, 2000

dakhi *noun*

a black person *SOUTH AFRICA*

Scamto youth street slang (South African townships).

- — *The Times*, 12th February 2005

da kine

used at any time to mean anything *US, 1951*

Hawaiian youth usage. Elizabeth Ball Carr describes the term in *Da Kine Talk* (1972) as 'a shibboleth – a phrase distinctive of Hawaii's local talk'. She cites usages as a noun, pronoun, adjective and suffix.

- — Douglas Simonson, *Pidgin to da Max*, 1981
- — Mitch McKissick, *Surf Lingo*, 1987

daks; dacks *noun*

shorts or trousers *AUSTRALIA*

From a proprietary name.

- I sit there, daks down, staring at the shiny side of his shoes, just visible under the gap in the partition. — Barry Oakley, *A Salute to the Great McCarthy*, p. 105, 1970
- I've got a bundle of lettuce [money] and a clean pair of thunder-bags under me daks [trousers]. — Barry Humphries, *Bazza Pulls It Off!*, 1971
- It is well known even by English children that all Aussies are called Bruce and that, if male, they are large, sweaty and drunken, and given to dropping their daks without provocation especially at Munich beer festivals. — *Sydney Morning Herald*, p. 8, 4th May 1984
- Drop your dacks and give 'em to Abdul. — Roy Slaven (John Doyle), *Five South Coast Seasons*, p. 91, 1992
- — David McGill, *David McGill's Complete Kiwi Slang Dictionary*, p. 37, 1998

dallacking *verb*

play acting, fooling *IRELAND*

- Stop that dallacking. — *North Munster Antiquarian Journal*, p. 84, 2000

Dallie; Dally *noun*

a Dalmatian, especially an immigrant to New Zealand from that area or the Balkans in general *NEW ZEALAND, 1940*

- — Miss Margaret Rowland, 1978

Dally *noun*

a New Zealander whose heritage is Croatian (Dalmatian) *NEW ZEALAND, 1950*

- — Harry Orsman and Des Hurley, *The Beaut Little Book of New Zealand Slang*, 1994
- Her [Dr Nina Nola's] talk entitled "The Making of a [Dalmatian] New Zealander" will look at the literary identity of "Dally Kiwis" and how it was forged by writers such as Amelia Batistich from the 1940s onwards. — *Massey News, Massey University*, 7th August 2002

dally *verb*

in western Canadian rodeos, to loop the lariat around the saddle horn *CANADA*

- When watching the steer-roping at the rodeo you will see the cowboy, after roping the steer, dally his lariat so that the horse may hold the rope taut while he dismounts. — Chris Thain, *Cold as a Bay Street Banker's Heart*, p. 51, 1987

dally *adjective*

good, kind, nice, sweet *UK*

Possibly a variation of DOLLY (attractive).

- — Paul Baker, *Polari*, p. 171, 2002
- — *Attitude*, p. 60, July 2003: 'Old palare lexicon'

dam *noun*

a menstrual cup (a device worn internally, used instead of tampons) *US*

- The first day, our "floodgates open up." And, my friends and I are all converts to the Keeper menstrual cup, so it's our "dam." — a contributor *The Museum of Menstruation and Women's Health*, May 2001

Dam *noun*

▸ **the Dam**

Amsterdam *UK*

- I had me first E in the Dam. — Shaun Ryder, *Shaun Ryder... in His Own Words*, 1996
- The ganja [marijuana] is awesome, a hybrid of that skink weed just come over from the 'Dam, and I'm so totally stoned. — Lanre Fehintola, *Charlie Says...*, p. 114, 2000
- Johnny had got the internet bug after he started ordering his CDs from Amazon, and his puff [marijuana] from the Dam. — Garry Bushell, *The Face*, p. 24–25, 2001
- Just come in from the Dam, best fucking quality. — Tony Wilson, *24 Hour Party People*, p. 178, 2002

dama blanca *noun*

cocaine *US, 1976*

Spanish for 'white lady'.

- — R.C. Garrett, *The Coke Book*, p. 200, 1984
- — US Department of Justice, *Street Terms*, August 1994
- — Mike Haskins, *Drugs*, p. 280, 2003

damage *noun*

1 expense; cost *UK, 1755*

Probably from damages awarded at law. Especially familiar in the (jocular) phrase, 'what's the damage?' (how much?).

- I handed over the damage to a City Circle Promotions lady[.] — Diran Abedayo, *My Once Upon A Time*, p. 138, 2000
- What's the damage? A double room will set you back £205. — *The Observer*, 20th January 2002

2 a problem *US*

- What's your damage, Heather? — *Heathers*, 1988

▸ **do damage**

to cost a lot *US*

- — Anna Scotti and Paul Young, *Buzzwords*, p. 90, 1997

damaged goods *noun*

1 an ex-virgin *US, 1916*

- — Vincent J. Monteleone, *Criminal Slang*, p. 65, 1949

2 a person who is mentally unstable *UK*

- Fuckin psychopath, that knobhead. Damaged bleedin goods, like. — Niall Griffiths, *Kelly + Victor*, p. 44, 2002

dame *noun*

1 a woman *UK, 1720*

While the term originally reflected on the woman involved (an implication of common status), it now reflects more on the speaker, suggesting a tough or old-fashioned viewpoint.

- Prosperous now, he drifted into Broadway life – and immediately tangled with a new breed of dames. — Bernard Wolfe, *The Late Risers*, p. 48, 1954

2 in a deck of playing cards, a queen *US*

- — Peter O. Steiner, *Thursday Night Poker*, p. 409, 1996

Dame Judi Dench; Dame Judi; Judi Dench; Judi *noun*

a stench *UK, 1998*

Rhyming slang, formed from the name of celebrated actress Dame Judi Dench (b.1934).

- — *Antiquarian Book Review*, p. 18, June 2002
- A rat died under the floorboards and the Judi is awful. — Bodmin Dark, *Dirty Cockney Rhyming Slang*, 2003

damfino

used as a jocular abbreviation of 'damned if I know' *US, 1882*

- "Then why are we doing this?" "Damfino." — Jerry Pournelle and Jerry Pournelle, *Football*, p. 514, 1985

dammit *noun*

used, for the purposes of comparison, as the representation of something insignificant *UK, 1908*

Adapted from 'damn-it'. In 'soon as dammit' (exceedingly quick, or almost immediate); 'near as dammit' (very close indeed); etc.

- [W]ith a bit of extra money to reflect the changing nature of the job, [firefighters] would be as near as dammit on the 30,000 a year they are calling for. — *The Guardian*, 15th November 2002
- [K]issing babies and praising troops, this was as near as dammit a prime ministerial triumph. — *The Guardian*, 30th May 2003

damn *noun*

something of little or no worth *UK, 1760*

Usually in phrases like 'not worth a damn', 'not care a damn' and 'not give a damn'. 'Who gives a damn about that?' (R.F. Delderfield, *Give Us This Day*, p. 57, 1973). There is a stongly fought historical argument (*Hobson-Jobson*, 1903, and Partridge's 1931 annotated reprint of Francis Grose's *Dictionary of the Vulgar Tongue*) that this derives from 'dam' (an Indian coin of little value); the *Oxford English Dictionary* prefers 'damn' (a 'profane utterance') as the object of this etymology.

- Life's not worth a damn / Till you can say / I am what I am. — Jerry Herman, *I Am What I Am*, 1983
- I was bare arsed and fancy free in front of everyone. But I didn't care a damn. — Bryce Courtenay, *The Power of One*, p. 254, 1989
- David O. Selznick was fined $5,000 for allowing Clark Gable to say "Frankly, my dear, I don't give a damn" in Gone With The Wind (1939). — Aubrey Dillon-Malone, *I Was A Fugitive From A Hollywood Trivia Factory*, p. 99, 1999
- I mean it. I don't give a damn who you are. — James N. Frey, *How to Write a Damn Good Mystery*, p. 46, 2004

damn'; damn *adjective*

damned; used for implying anything from distaste to hate for whoever or whatever is so described *UK, 1775*

A shortening of **DAMNED**.

- Damn Yanks. They asked for it. Serve 'em right. All Bush's fault. — *The Guardian*, 30th October 2002

-damn- *infix*

used as an intensifier *US, 1867*

- "And I'll guaran-damn-tee you they won't be back," and he put his hat on and left. — Fannie Flagg, *Fried Green Tomatoes at the Whistlestop Cafe*, p. 206, 1987

damn!; damn it!

used for registering annoyance or irritation *UK, 1589*

- [Y]ou're just busy, damn it. — *The Guardian*, 9th December 2000

damn all *noun*

nothing *UK, 1922*

- [T]he LA Dodgers, are owned by a Mr Murdoch and have done damn all since his takeover. — *The Guardian*, 10th October 2002

damn and bastardry!

used as a mild oath *UK*

Modelled on conventional 'damn and blast'.

- Damn and bastardry, I still remember that stuff after all[.] — James Hawes, *Dead Long Enough*, p. 276, 2000

damn and blast *noun*

the last position in a race *UK*

Rhyming slang.

- Damn and blast, my horse came in damn and blast. — Ray Puxley, *Cockney Rabbit*, 1992

damn and blast *verb*

to curse, to condemn *UK*

- But last week, Pan Trinbago came forward to damn and blast the Maha Sabha for having criticised an NLCB handouts policy[.] — *Trinidad Guardian*, 22nd June 2003

damn and blast!

used for expressing anger or frustration *UK, 1943*

A common coupling of **DAMN!** and **BLAST!**.

- [T]he Irish XV dragged the Australians down to their level of thud and blunder, hit and hope, damn and blast it[.] — *The Guardian*, 11th October 1999

damnation alley *noun*

in roulette, the twelve-number column on the left of the layout *US, 1979*

So named because a dealer may not see a cheat place a late bet in the column, which is sometimes out of the dealer's line of sight.

- — Thomas L. Clark, *The Dictionary of Gambling and Gaming*, p. 58, 1987

damned *adjective*

used as an all-purpose intensifier, generally to negative effect *UK, 1596*

- Not a damned thing has changed in more than 120 years. — *The Guardian*, 30th March 2002

▸ as be damned

very, extremely *IRELAND, 1939*

- Most of us freely admit they are cheesy as be damned. — *Michigan Daily*, 10th April 2003

damned tooting

used for expressing emphatic agreement *US*

Folksy.

- Simms said he was damned tootin' he was right. — Jim Thompson, *The Grifters*, p. 17, 1963
- You're damned tootin' ol LB ain't gonna take no money from the members of the Bar. — Oscar Zeta Acosta, *The Autobiography of a Brown Buffalo*, p. 21, 1972

damn-fool; damfool *adjective*

foolish, silly *UK*

From 'damned fool' (an absolute fool).

- That was a damn-fool thing to say. — Graeme Kent, *The Queen's Corporal [Six Granada Plays]*, p. 92, 1959

damn skippy

absolutely! without a doubt! *US*

An intensive affirmative.

- We got them on our side and damn skippy we'll use them. — William Upski Winsatt, *Bomb the Suburbs*, p. 51, 1994
- "I'm telling you, you can't trust nobody anymore." "He snookered us." "Damn skippy." — Janet Evanovich, *Seven Up*, p. 12, 2001
- You say to people, "What? You don't know that?" And they're, like, "Damn skippy I don't know that! Come to think of it, I don't know shit!" Real proud. — Patrick Neate, *Where You're At*, p. 41, 2003

damn well *adverb*

certainly, assuredly, very much *UK, 1934*

- Mr Blair replied with increasing testiness that the normal proprieties would be observed, which we all took to mean that he would do what he damn well pleased, or at least what damn well pleased George Bush. — *The Guardian*, 25th July 2002

Damon Hill; damon *noun*

a pill, especially an amphetamine *UK*

Rhyming slang, formed on the name of the UK's Formula 1 World Champion (1996) racing driver Damon Hill (b.1960); a discreetly playful reference to **SPEED** (an amphetamine).

- — Ray Puxley, *Fresh Rabbit*, 1998

damp *adjective*

allowing the importation of alcohol for personal consumption but not for public sale *US*

A play on the extremes of 'wet' and 'dry'.

- — Russell Tabbert, *Dictionary of Alaskan English*, p. 89, 1991

damp blanket *noun*

in the theatre, a bad review *US*

- — Don Wilmeth, *The Language of American Popular Entertainment*, p. 70, 1981

damper *noun*

1 a solitary confinement cell; a cell *US*

- —William K. Bentley and James M. Corbett, *Prison Slang*, p. 10, 1992
- —Angela Devlin, *Prison Patter*, p. 43, 1996

2 a safe deposit box in a bank *US, 1872*

- —Clarence Major, *Dictionary of Afro-American Slang*, p. 44, 1970

3 a bank *US, 1932*

- He was a pretty good fake in his day, but he couldn't show his mug around any of the dampers in the Apple.—A.S. Jackson, *Gentleman Pimp*, p. 134, 1973

4 a simple, unleavened, savoury bread traditionally cooked in the ashes of a campfire *AUSTRALIA, 1825*

So named because it 'dampens' the appetite. Now also applied to a similar style of bread available at bakershops.

- —Harvey E. Ward, *Down Under Without Blunder*, p. 37, 1967
- —Arthur Chipper, *The Aussie Swearer's Guide*, p. 40, 1972
- At dawn he boiled a billy, made same damper for breakfast and then deliberately made noises to wake up Morgan.—Bob Ellis and Anne Brooksbank, *Mad Dog Morgan*, p. 120, 1976
- —Jim Ramsay, *Cop It Sweet!*, p. 27, 1977
- If you're God's Son, use your powers to turn this lump of rock into a nice piece of fresh damper.—Kel Richards, *The Aussie Bible*, p. 22, 2003

damper *verb*

to mute, to quiet *US*

- Pallies, damper the rapping!—Iceberg Slim (Robert Beck), *Airtight Willie and Me*, p. 29, 1979

damps *noun*

central nervous system depressants *US*

A playful allusion to 'amps' as 'amphetamines'.

- —Jay Robert Nash, *Dictionary of Crime*, p. 94, 1992

damp squib *noun*

a failure; a dud; a fizzler *AUSTRALIA*

A 'damp squib' is, literally, a 'wet firework'.

- It was all a damp squib Lucinda said to Marian when they had gone. —Martin Boyd, *Lucinda Brayford*, p. 437, 1946

Dan *noun*

1 a man in charge of a male public convenience *UK*

From the children's rhyme, 'Dan, Dan, dirty old man, / Washed his face in the lavatory pan'.

- —Neil Bell, *Many Waters*, 1954

2 a Roman Catholic *UK: SCOTLAND*

Glasgow slang.

- Are you a Billy [Protestant] or a Dan?—Michael Munro, *The Patter, Another Blast*, p. 19, 1988

dance *noun*

a fight *CANADA*

Ice hockey usage.

- Once in a while we have a dance, even with a black eye.—Bobby Orr, *Orr on Ice*, p. 150, 1970

▸ **what's the dance?**

what's going on?; what's going to happen? *UK, 2002*

Collected in April 2002 in private correspondance with an inmate of one of Her Majesty's prisons.

dance *verb*

1 of a batsman in a game of cricket, to swiftly advance beyond the crease to meet the pitch of a ball *UK, 1995*

- —Keith Foley, *A Dictionary of Cricketing Terminology*, p. 96, 1998

2 (used of a wink in tiddlywinks) to wobble around *US*

- —*Verbatim*, December 1977

3 to cause a car to bounce up and down by use of hydraulic lifts *US*

- —Edith A. Folb, *runnin' down some lines*, p. 234, 1980

▸ **dance ass**

to ignore the needs of others *TRINIDAD AND TOBAGO*

- —Lise Winer, *Dictionary of the English/Creole of Trinidad & Tobago*, 2003

▸ **dance in the rain room**

to take a shower in prison *US*

- —James Harris, *A Convict's Dictionary*, p. 30, 1989

▸ **dance on the carpet**

to be called into a superior's office for questioning about possible misconduct or poor work performance *US*

- —Norman Carlisle, *The Modern Wonder Book of Trains and Railroading*, p. 261, 1946

dance fever *noun*

Fentany™, a synthetic narcotic analgesic that is used as a recreational drug *UK*

- —Harry Shapiro, *Recreational Drugs*, p. 154, 2004

dancehall *noun*

1 in a prison in which death sentences are executed, the execution chamber *US, 1928*

- —Troy Harris, *A Booklet of Criminal Argot, Cant and Jargon*, p. 8, 1976

2 in oil drilling, a large flat-bed truck *US*

- —Jerry Robertson, *Oil Slanguage*, p. 44, 1954

dance of death *noun*

a relationship or marriage between two addicts *US*

Used in twelve-step recovery programmes such as Alcoholics Anonymous.

- —Christopher Cavanaugh, *AA to Z*, p. 75, 1998

dancer *noun*

1 a boxer who evades his opponent rather than engaging him *US, 1949*

- —Harold Wentworth and Stuart Berg Flexner, *Dictionary of American Slang*, p. 139, 1960

2 a cat burglar; a sneak thief *UK, since C19*

- —Angela Devlin, *Prison Patter*, p. 43, 1996

dancers *noun*

▸ **have it on your dancers**

to run away *UK*

A variation of (have it) **ON YOUR TOES**.

- He had it on his dancers.—David Powis, *The Signs of Crime*, 1977

dancing *noun*

in railway slang, the condition of locomotive wheels slipping on the rail *UK*

- —Frank McKenna, *A Glossary of Railwaymen's Talk*, 1970

dancing academy *noun*

used as a euphemism and legal dodge for an after-hours homosexual club *US*

- Although it appears an unlikely hour for serious study, private dancing academies offering instruction between 2 a.m. and 6 a.m. have opened in San Francisco, the police reported to the Board of Supervisors yesterday.—*San Francisco Chronicle*, p. 4, 12th April 1974

dancing girls *noun*

in dominoes, the seven tiles with a five *US*

- —Dominic Armanino, *Dominoes*, p. 16, 1959

Dan Dares *noun*

flared trousers *UK*

Rhyming slang for 'flares', formed on Dan Dare, the comic strip 'pilot of the future', first seen in *The Eagle* in 1950.

- —Michael Munro, *The Complete Patter*, 1996
- —Ray Puxley, *Fresh Rabbit*, 1998

D&D *noun*

*d*ungeons and *d*ragons (a genre of fantasy roleplay games) *UK*

- "It's D & D but they might be able to help." "D & D?" "Sword and sorcery, dungeons and dragons."—Ian Rankin, *The Falls*, p. 109, 2001

D and D *verb*

1 to leave a restaurant without paying your bill *US*

An abbreviation of **DINE AND DASH**.

- —Anna Scotti and Paul Young, *Buzzwords*, p. 60, 1997

2 to fail to lead; to escape responsibility *CANADA*

Said to stand for (to) 'delegate and disappear'.

- (Canadian Forces, current) D and D is an irreverent play on the initials DND, Department of National Defence.—Tom Langeste, *Words on the Wing*, p. 73, 1995

D and D *adjective*

1 *d*runk and *d*isorderly *UK, 1899*

Abbreviated from an official cause of arrest.

- In comes a bright bogey [policeman] who knows who she is and nicks her on the spot for being d and d, which she is by this time[.]—Charles Raven, *Underworld Nights*, p. 22, 1956
- Chances were, an old drunk told him, they'd give him two days on the D and D and credit for time served.—Robert Campbell, *In La-La Land We Trust*, p. 112, 1986

2 *d*eaf and *d*umb *US, 1937*
Usage is both literal (applied to beggars) and figurative (applied to someone who knows nothing and will say nothing).
- —Harold Wentworth and Stuart Berg Flexner, *Dictionary of American Slang*, p. 139, 1960

dander *noun*
1 anger *UK, 1831*
Possible etymologies: 'dander' (dandruff), 'dunder' (ferment) or Romany *dander* (to bite), *dando* (bitten).

2 a leisurely stroll *IRELAND*
Also used as a verb. In the north of Ireland it is pronounced 'donder'.
- Fancying a dander during the Easter holidays, I opted for a leisurely stroll around the Forest Park.— *Down Democrat*, 16th April 2002

▸ get your dander up
to become annoyed or angry *US, 1831*
- [H]e scoffs so much he gets the gypsy's dander up, an action he'll regret.—Lester Bangs, *Psychotic Reactions and Carburetor Dung*, p. 124, 1973

Dandies *noun*
▸ the Dandies
the Dandenong Ranges outside Melbourne *AUSTRALIA*
- —Barry Humphries, *A Nice Night's Entertainment*, 1981

D and M *noun*
a serious conversation, generally relating to personal relationships *AUSTRALIA*
Standing for **DEEP AND MEANINGFUL**.
- —James Lambert, *The Macquarie Book of Slang*, 1996

dandruff *noun*
1 snow *US*
- — *Complete CB Slang Dictionary*, 1976
- —Peter Chippindale, *The British CB Book*, p. 154, 1981

2 cocaine *UK*
- —Dave Courtney, *Dodgy Dave's Little Black Book*, p. 8, 2001

dandy *noun*
1 anything first-rate or execellent *UK, 1784*
- [I]t's a dandy of a place you'd be a fool to leave.— *The Guardian*, 31st January 2001

2 a grade of 'D' *US*
- — *Time*, p. 57, 1st January 1965: 'Students: the slang bag'

3 in South Australia, a small container for ice-cream *AUSTRALIA, 1954*
Origin unknown. Perhaps originally a brand name.
- As far as I know, the word "Dandy" is used, because that was the original brand.— *Wordmap (www.abc.net.au/wordmap)*, 2003

D and Z *noun*
a demilitarised zone *US*
- —Linda Reinberg, *In the Field*, p. 56, 1991

dang
used as a mild oath or intensifier *US, 1821*
A euphemised 'damn'.
- Dang me, dang me / They oughta take a rope and hang me.—Roger Miller, *Dang Me*, 1964
- It's those dang judgment calls!—Dan Jenkins, *Life Its Ownself*, p. 193, 1984
- LUCY: Get me a beer. VELMA: Hey, we quit drinking. LUCY: Dang, that's right, enit? I forgot.— *Smoke Signals*, 1998

dange *adjective*
extremely good *CANADA*
Rhymes with 'strange', short for 'dangerous'.

danged *adjective*
used as a euphemism for 'damned' *US*
- When did they sneak that danged glass in there?—Ken Kesey, *One Flew Over the Cuckoo's Nest*, p. 195, 1962
- Because the danged place was being painted, and the painters had left their ladders and cans scattered all over everywhere.—Jim Thompson, *Pop. 1280*, p. 10, 1964

danger *noun*
an aggresive flirt *FIJI*
Recorded by Jan Tent in 1993.

danger is my business
used as a humorous response to a suggestion that a proposed activity is dangerous *US*
The motto of cartoon secret agent *Cool McCool* (NBC, 1966–69), used with referential humour.

danger wank *noun*
an act of masturbation with the threat of being discovered as an added stimulus *UK*
- [T]hrill-seeking masturbation, while your mum is walking upstairs to your bedroom after you have called her. The object of the game is to come before she opens the door and catches you.—Chris Lewis, *The Dictionary of Playground Slang*, p. 69, 2003

dangle *noun*
the penis *US, 1936*
- On the wall was a nude drawing of Dean, enormous dangle and all, done by Camille.—Jack Kerouac, *On the Road*, p. 44, 1957
- —Collin Baker et al., *College Undergraduate Slang Study Conducted at Brown University*, p. 103, 1968
- She must have featured the angle of his dangle.—J.F. Freedman, *Against the Wind*, p. 88, 1991

dangle *verb*
▸ dangle the cat
to drive a Caterpillar truck *US*
- —Montie Tak, *Truck Talk*, p. 40, 1971

dangleberries *noun*
pieces of dried faecal matter clinging to the hairs surrounding the anus *UK, 1984*
- Why do speakers in post-industrial Britain and Australia still need a dozen or more words to denote the flakes of dung that hang from the rear of sheep and other mammals, words like dags, dangleberries, dingleberries, jub-nuts, winnets and wittens?.—Tony Thorne, *Slang and the Dictionary*, 2002

dangle from *verb*
from a male perspective, to have sex *UK, 1961*
Heard in the 1970s: 'Cor! I could dangle from *that*!'.

dangler *noun*
1 the penis *US*
- At which point he unzipped his fly and yanked out his dangler and waved it at me.—John Francis Hunter, *The Gay Insider*, p. 204, 1971

2 a person who has died by hanging *US*
- — *Maledicta*, Summer/Winter 1986–1987

3 a lorry's trailer *UK*
- — *British Road Services Magazine*, December 1951

4 a freight train *US*
- —Ramon Adams, *The Language of the Railroader*, p. 42, 1977

dangling bits *noun*
the external male genitals *AUSTRALIA*
Variant of **DANGLY BITS**.
- Then [the dog] spotted the dangling bits and jumped up and grabbed a real good mouthful.—Sam Weller, *Old Bastards I Have Met*, p. 18, 1979

dangly bits *noun*
the external male genitals *AUSTRALIA, 2000*
- — *A - Z of Rude Health*, 11th September 2002
- Warning: zippers can be a health hazard – especially for those with dangly bits.— *AAP News Service*, 6th September 2002

daniel *noun*
the buttocks *US*
- Man, we oughta git up off our daniels and dig what's goin' on.—Mezz Mezzrow, *Really the Blues*, p. 250, 1946

Daniel Boone squad; Daniel Boone team *noun*
US soldiers who engaged in cross-border reconnaissance in Cambodia during the Vietnam war *US*
- —Linda Reinberg, *In the Field*, p. 57, 1991

Daniels *noun*
the buttocks *US*
- —Kenn "Naz" Young, *Naz's Underground Dictionary*, p. 24, 1973

Danish pastry *noun*
a transexual *US*
An allusion to Denmark's standing as an early pioneer in sex-change operations.
- —Jim Crotty, *How to Talk American*, p. 138, 1997

dank *noun*

a very potent marijuana *US, 1998*

In conventional English, 'dank' conjures the 'stinky' **STINKWEED** (marijuana) smell of **WEED** (marijuana) growing in a damp place; or possibly from the slang adjective 'dank' (excellent). Recorded with the use of 'the'.

- —Mike Haskins, *Drugs*, p. 287, 2003

dank *adjective*

1 inferior; inefficient; bad; unpleasant *UK*

Originally recorded as a military term, the semi-conventional usage arrived on a US campus 40 years later providing the spur for the sense that follows.

2 excellent; brilliant *US*

BAD is 'good', **WICKED** is 'excellent'.

- —Pamela Munro, *U.C.L.A. Slang*, p. 33, 1989
- —Connie Eble (Editor), *UNC-CH Campus Slang*, p. 2, Fall 1996

Dan Leno *noun*

a festive event, a jollification, especially a coach trip to the seaside *UK*

Rhyming slang for 'a beano' (a jollification); formed on the professional name of Victorian comedian Dan Leno (George Galvin), 1860–1904.

- —Ray Puxley, *Cockney Rabbit*, 1992

Danny La Rue; Danny *noun*

a clue *UK*

Rhyming slang, based on popular 'comic in a frock' Danny La Rue (b.1926).

- I haven't a Danny mate! — *www.LondonSlang.com*, June 2002

Danny La Rue *adjective*

blue, applied to any shade whether actual or figurative *UK*

Rhyming slang, formed on the name of popular 'comic in a frock' Danny La Rue (b.1926).

- —Ray Puxley, *Cockney Rabbit*, 1992

Danny Marr *noun*

a car *UK*

Rhyming slang, based on an unrecognised source.

- —Angela Devlin, *Prison Patter*, p. 43, 1996

Dan O'Leary *noun*

a tour of police duty in which the police officer works every possible minute *US*

- — *New York Times Magazine*, p. 88, 16th March 1958

dan up *verb*

to spruce up *TRINIDAD AND TOBAGO*

- —Lise Winer, *Dictionary of the English/Creole of Trinidad & Tobago*, 2003

dap *noun*

a handshake hooking thumbs, used by black US soldiers in Vietnam *US, 1972*

- [R]ace consciousness took the form of sybmolic cultural behavior, for example, involved handshakes or the "dap." —Charles R. Figley, *Strangers at Home*, p. 79, 1980
- This was a dap, among "in-country" vets a sign that they had been in Vietnam. —Wukkuan Diehl, *Thai Horse*, p. 249, 1987
- —Linda Reinberg, *In the Field*, p. 57, 1991

dap *verb*

to greet another with a ritualistic handshake; to show respect in greeting *US, 1973*

- Even if you just hate my fuckin guts go 'head and dap me / Cause I'm gon' dap you anyway and then go home and pray for yo' ass later. — Outkast, *Wailin'*, 1996

dap *adjective*

well-dressed, fashionable *US, 1956*

A shortened 'dapper'.

- —Robert George Reisner, *The Jazz Titans*, p. 153, 1960
- — *Current Slang*, p. 19, Fall 1968
- —Hermese E. Roberts, *The Third Ear*, 1971

DAP *adjective*

*d*ead-*a*ss *p*erfect *US*

Golf usage.

- —Hubert Pedroli and Mary Tiegreen, *Let the Big Dog Eat!*, p. 29, 2000

dap down *verb*

to dress nicely *US*

- —Edith A. Folb, *runnin' down some lines*, p. 234, 1980

dapper *noun*

a person dressed in style *US*

- When she hesitated and put her hands on her hips, two young dappers yelled from the middle of the bar. —Donald Goines, *Never Die Alone*, p. 46, 1974

dapper *adjective*

perfect, excellent, admirable *UK*

Possibly punning on the conventional sense of 'dapper' (neat and tidy) and **TIDY** (good, correct). Black usage.

- Yeah? Dapper, C-C. You just dapper for that. Thank you! —Diran Abedayo, *My Once Upon A Time*, p. 210, 2000

dapper Dan *noun*

any well-dressed man *US*

- I asked famed fashion designer Bill Blass the difference between a slob and a Dapper Dan last night at an I. Magnin party. — *San Francisco Examiner*, p. 37, 21st October 1970

daps *noun*

1 gym shoes, plimsoles, tennis shoes, trainers *UK*

Originally 'slippers', certainly in this general sense since the 1950s, adapting to succeeding fashions.

- [G]ot to please the little twats in combats and daps[...] – Daps? I asked, as Harry sat down with us. – Trainers to you, you Saxon gobshite[.] —James Hawes, *Dead Long Enough*, p. 44, 2000

2 proper respect *US*

- —Pamela Munro, *U.C.L.A. Slang*, p. 56, 1997

Dapto dog *noun*

an person of Mediterranean or Middle Eastern background *AUSTRALIA, 1983*

Rhyming slang for **WOG**. Named after the Dapto Dogs, a greyhound racing track at Dapto, south of Sydney.

- —Ryan Aven-Bray, *Ridgey Didge Oz Jack Lang*, p. 24, 1983
- —Kathy Lette, *Girls' Night Out*, p. 222, 1987
- The badly-maligned 'Wogs' (Dapto dogs/Chocolate frogs) are finally wreaking revenge on Anglo-Saxon kids. 'Aussies' are 'Skips' or 'Joeys'. — *Sydney Morning Herald*, p. 7, 3rd January 1987

DAR *noun*

a hard-working student; a *d*amned *a*verage *r*aiser *US*

- — *American Speech*, p. 303, December 1955

darb *adjective*

in circus usage, excellent *US*

- —Don Wilmeth, *The Language of American Popular Entertainment*, p. 70, 1981

darbies *noun*

1 a set of handcuffs or fetters; shackles *UK, 1665*

Derives from a C17 moneylender's bond called Father Darby's or Derby's bands.

- Until this sweed [swede] next to me moved his hand, and by doing so moved mine as we were joined together like siames[e] twins by the darbies. —Frank Norman, *Bang To Rights*, p. 39, 1958

2 fingerprints *UK*

- —Paul Tempest, *Lag's Lexicon*, 1950

Darby *noun*

▸ **on your Darby**

alone, on your own *UK, 1942*

Rhyming slang, formed on **DARBY AND JOAN** (the conventional archetype of an elderly married couple or inseparable companions).

Darby and Joan *noun*

1 an inseparable couple, with connotations of possible homosexuality *UK*

Extending the conventional sense of 'an archetypal elderly married couple'.

- —Charles Allen, *Plain Tales from the Raj*, 26th October 1975

2 a telephone *UK*

Rhyming slang, formed on the conventional archetype of an elderly married couple or inseparable companions. First noted by Julian Franklyn, *A Dictionary of Rhyming Slang*, 1961, but thought to date from the end of C19.

3 a loan *AUSTRALIA*
Rhyming slang.
- —John Ayto, *The Oxford Dictionary of Rhyming Slang*, 2002

Darby and Joan *verb*
to moan *UK*
Rhyming slang, formed (perhaps ironically) on the conventional archetype of an elderly married or inseperable couple.
- —Ray Puxley, *Cockney Rabbit*, 1992

Darby bands *noun*
the hands *UK*
Rhyming slang, from the old (possibly C16) expression 'Father Darby's bands' (a binding agreement between a money lender and a borrower).
- —Ray Puxley, *Cockney Rabbit*, 1992

darby kelly; darby *noun*
▷ **see:** DERBY KELLY

dare *noun*
a challenge, an act of defiance *UK*
In conventional use from late C16 to late C19, usage thereafter is colloquial.
- Once, for a dare, / He filled his heart-shaped swimming pool / With bank notes.— *The Guardian*, 19th January 2002

darg *noun*
a certain fixed amount of work for a given time period *AUSTRALIA, 1927*
- Miners at the State Coal Mine today suspended for two weeks a miner who allegedly exceeded a darg – an output limit imposed by the union.— *Daily Telegraph*, p. 9, 8th February 1950

dark *noun*
▸ **in the dark**
(used of a bet in poker) made without having seen your cards *US*
- —Anthony Holden, *Big Deal*, p. 302, 1990

dark *verb*
to spoil, especially by behaving aggressively *UK, 1990s→*
- Those fools were looking to dark someone's evening and they just decided to come our way.—Diran Adebayo, *My Once Upon A Time*, p. 76, 2000

dark *adjective*
1 bad, inferior, unpleasant, nasty; used as an all-purpose negative *UK*
- Have you spat on the sausages as well? Benny nods again. That's dark, that is.—Paul Fraser and Shane Meadows, *TwentyFourSeven*, p. 7–8, 1997

2 unreachable by telephone *US*
A condition usually resulting from a failure to pay your bill.
- —Ben Applebaum and Derrick Pittman, *Turd Ferguson & The Sausage Party*, p. 24, 2004

3 good *UK*
On the **BAD** (good) model, the reverse of sense 1.
- She's bubbly, her clothes always the latest fashion. Well dark. She's got money[.]—Karline Smith, *Letters to Andy Cole*, p. 139, 1998
- —Julian Johnson, *Urban Survival*, p. 258, 2003

4 evil
- [T]o invite your tightest to your cousin's wedding and introduce him to the man you're sending to end him – that's dark.—Diran Adebayo, *My Once Upon A Time*, p. 109, 2000

5 secret *AUSTRALIA, 1877*
- —Norman Lindsay, *Halfway to Anywhere*, p. 119, 1947
- 'Well, listen, Ted,' came Tully voice, 'keep it dark, will you?'—Eric Lambert, *The Veterans*, p. 204, 1954
- 'He's an Itie.' 'I'll keep ut dark,' said Bill.—Nino Culotta (John O'Grady), *They're A Weird Mob*, p. 91, 1957
- —James Holledge, *The Great Australian Gamble*, 1966

6 untelevised *US*
- Dark matches serve numerous purposes. Wrestlers who've shined on the independent circuit – cards staged by small promoters in high school gyms, Grange halls and fraternal lodges – are invited to World Wrestling Federation TV tapings to audition for Federation officials. — *Raw Magazine*, p. 48, September 2000
- Just as non televised under-card bouts are called "dark matches," non televised arena events are called "dark shows.!" Yeah, sure, the results show up in the rankings, but not on the boob tube.— *Rampage Magazine*, p. 18, September 2000

dark and dirty *noun*
rum and coke (Coca-Cola™ or similar) *UK*
The drink is made, and the term is formed, of *dark* rum and a fizzy accompaniment the colour (some may think) of dirty water. Royal Marines coinage.
- —Christopher Hawke, *For Campaign Service*, 1979

dark as an abo's arsehole *adjective*
extremely dark *AUSTRALIA*
- Funny, door's still open but the shop's as dark as an abo [aborigine]'s arsehole – and what's that noise?—Barry Humphries, *Bazza Pulls It Off!*, 1971

dark brown *adjective*
of a voice, low, well-modulated and sexually attractive *UK*
Originally of a female voice, then more general.
- [She] spoke seldom, but when she did it was in a voice like dark brown velvet and no one interrupted her.—Josephine Tey, *Miss Pym Disposes*, 1946
- Andrew Sachs's dark-brown voice reading Silas Marner[.]— *The Guardian*, 18th March 2000

dark cheaters *noun*
sunglasses *US*
- Don't think for a minute those dark cheaters fool little Flackie. —Raymond Chandler, *The Little Sister*, p. 65, 1949

dark days *noun*
a type of bet in an illegal numbers game lottery *US*
- Then to be on the safe side he also played jail house, death row, lady come back, two-timing woman, pile of rocks, dark days and trouble.—Chester Himes, *A Rage in Harlem*, p. 23, 1957

darkers *noun*
sunglasses *TRINIDAD AND TOBAGO, 1987*
- —Lise Winer, *Dictionary of the English/Creole of Trinidad & Tobago*, 2003

dark eyes *noun*
dizziness *BARBADOS*
- —Frank A. Collymore, *Barbadian Dialect*, p. 38, 1965

Dark Gable *noun*
a handsome black man *US*
Punning on the name Clark Gable. The nickname has been taken by more than one, but perhaps nobody more prominent than Mohammed Ali who briefly called himself Dark Gable in 1981.
- You make like a Dark Gable but you can't dig my fable.—Dan Burley, *Diggeth Thou?*, p. 45, 1959

dark-green *adjective*
1 excellent *US*
- "Dark Green," he explained, "is what the hipsters are saying now instead of "real crazy."— *San Francisco Examiner*, p. 31, 7th May 1954

2 black *US*
Marine humour in Vietnam – a black marine was said to be 'dark-green'.
- —Linda Reinberg, *In the Field*, p. 57, 1991

dark horse *noun*
1 in horse racing, a horse that is deemed a poor performer but one that might surprise all and win *US*
- —David W. Maurer, *Argot of the Racetrack*, p. 23, 1951

2 a racehorse that has been trained in secret *AUSTRALIA, 1877*
- He was on the favourite in a Novice at Wyong, where he met up with a dark horse that had been kept under wraps.—Wilda Moxham, *The Apprentice*, p. 97, 1969

3 a person who keeps things about themselves secret *AUSTRALIA, 1917*
- —Nino Culotta (John O'Grady), *They're A Weird Mob*, p. 159, 1957
- I believe the silly old bugger really missed me while I was away, she thought, in surprise. What a dark horse he is!—Jean Brooks, *The Opal Witch*, p. 103, 1967

4 a candidate or competitor of whom little is known *UK, 1865*
A figurative use of racing slang.
- Helen has been A BIT depressed since she split up with Guy, but is a bit of a dark horse. Graham and Helen ALMOST get off with one another.— *The Guardian*, 25th February 2000

darkie *noun*
1 used as a flattering and affectionate term of address for an attractive, dark-skinned woman *TRINIDAD AND TOBAGO, 1990*
- —Lise Winer, *Dictionary of the English/Creole of Trinidad & Tobago*, 2003

2 a piece of excrement *AUSTRALIA*
- 'A giant's been here.' 'What evidence have you?' we asked. 'In the lav,' he said. We went to look. Lying indolently on its side was a twelve inch darky about this big and this round and sliced off at both ends like a loaf of bread. —David Ireland, *The Flesheaters*, p. 126, 1972

dark meat *noun*

a black person as a sexual object *US, 1888*
- All white men hanker after dark meat. The reader has the preacher's word for that. —*Pacific Spectator*, p. 108, Winter 1947
- I tell them dark meat's all the same as white in the dark, but I think they can't believe it. —John M. Murtagh and Sara Harris, *Cast the First Stone*, p. 11, 1957
- He remembered all the nasty sayings of his friends: Dark meat. —Willard Motely, *Let No Man Write My Epitaph*, p. 327, 1958
- You got eyes for dark meat? You want to rub some kink hair for luck? —Bernard Wolfe, *The Magic of Their Singing*, p. 103, 1961
- Vess's remarks really started me to wondering, however, why I really did like dark meat so much. —Phil Andros (Samuel M. Steward), *Stud*, p. 89, 1966
- "You havin' fun with that dark meat, Tony? She don't move me at all," he said in a matter-of-fact voice. —Donald Goines, *Black Gangster*, p. 166, 1977
- This torrid tribute to the joys of dark meat features a chorus line of ebony beauties bouncing and boffing through a series of raunchy, relentlessly racist, and often unbearably funny skits that mine just about every sick cliche[.] —*Adult Video*, p. 16, August/September 1986
- [S]he had her share of sex appeal – she liked dark meat anyway. —Duncan MacLaughlin, *The Filth*, p. 173, 2002

dark money; dark time *noun*

extra wages paid for night work *UK*
- —Frank McKenna, *A Glossary of Railwaymen's Talk*, 1970

dark o'clock *noun*

night *UK*
- We practised from seven-thirty each morning until dark o'clock. —Andy McNab, *Immediate Action*, p. 129, 1995

darks *noun*

dark glasses *BERMUDA*
- —Peter A. Smith and Fred M. Barritt, *Bermewjan Vurds*, 1985

dark shadow *noun*

a tightly-cropped hair cut that stops short of absolute baldness *UK*
- Some skins [skinheads] wore a so-called "dark shadow", where the razor was used with no guard. Baldness was not popular. —Martin Roach, *Dr. Marten's Air Wair*, 1999

darkside *noun*

a category of rave music *UK*
- —Gareth Thomas, *This Is Ecstasy*, p. 43, 2002

dark thirty *noun*

late at night *US*
- To work from dawn till dark thirty. —Ken Weaver, *Texas Crude*, p. 91, 1984

dark time *noun*

night *US*
- — Elementary Electronics, *Dictionary of CB Lingo*, p. 60, 1976

darktown *noun*

a neighbourhood populated largely by black people *US, 1916*
- The black ghettos of the "Darktown" slums in every Southern city were the consequence mainly of the Negro's economic status, his relegation to the lowest rung of the ladder. —C. Vann Woodward, *The Strange Career of Jim Crow*, 1974
- "It might be a window peeper who's been working Darktown lately." —James Ellroy, *White Jazz*, p. 54, 1992
- Lorenzo had guessed as much, Gannon being the mostly white blue-collar town bordering the so-called Darktown section of Dempsy. —Richard Price, *Freedomland*, p. 37, 1998

dark 'un *noun*

of dock-workers, a 24-hour shift *AUSTRALIA, 1957*
- —G.A. Wilkes, *A Dictionary of Australian Colloquialisms*, 1978

dark-white paint *noun*

used as the object of a prank errand for a novice painter *US, 1966*
- —Frederic G. Cassidy, *Dictionary of American Regional English, Vol. II*, p. 14, 1991

darky; darkie *noun*

1 a black person *US, 1775*

Originally used in a paternalistic, condescending manner, but now mainly to disparage.
- The darky maid was at the door to greet me, but this time she had on her hat and coat. —Mickey Spillane, *I, The Jury*, p. 49, 1947
- In fact, there's a saying in Georgetown now that you're not "smart" unless darkies live next door to you. —Jack Lait and Lee Mortimer, *Washington Confidential*, p. 10, 1951
- She's that nun who stools for them two darky dicks, ain't she? —Chester Himes, *A Rage in Harlem*, p. 150, 1957
- My Dad has taught me that in England some foolish man may call me sambo, darkie, boot or munt or nigger, even. —Colin McInnes, *City of Spades*, 1957
- Darkies are always singing. You people know that. —James Baldwin, *Blues for Mister Charlie*, p. 73, 1964
- "All us darkies don't have that thing, do we?" Tim said. —Nat Hentoff, *Jazz Country*, p. 22, 1965
- Well, what the hell is your problem that you and that other darky would come here to my house with the city lousy with government agents? —Iceberg Slim (Robert Beck), *Long White Con*, p. 148, 1977
- I mean in the East End it's, like, there is a lot of darkies because it is a working class area I s'pose —*Ask*, p. 74, 8th May 1981
- You would be totally shafted if you shot some old darkie and there was no evidence[.] —Donald Gorgon, *Cop Killer*, p. 8, 1994
- I don't do that darky street shit. —Elmore Leonard, *Be Cool*, 1999
- But who was using em? Chinese immigrants. Slave labor. And the darkies up in the inner cities[.] —*Traffic*, 2000
- [T]he wee darkie lassie with the funny name[.] —Christopher Brookmyre, *The Sacred Art of Stealing*, p. 53, 2002

2 an Australian Aboriginal *AUSTRALIA, 1845*
- Lord, you're a goon. You look like a darkie going to a corroboree. —Ruth Park, *Harp In The South*, p. 211, 1948
- I saw these abo fellas all getting onto the other darkie, not Billy. —Petru Popescu, *The Last Wave*, p. 179, 1977
- —Shane Maloney, *Nice Try*, p. 133, 1998

3 a Polynesian person *NEW ZEALAND, 1863*
- —Harry Orsman, *A Dictionary of Modern New Zealand Slang*, p. 37, 1999

Darky Cox *noun*

a *box* in a theatre auditorium *UK*

Rhyming slang, of unknown derivation.
- —Julian Franklyn, *A Dictionary of Rhyming Slang*, 1961
- —Ray Puxley, *Fresh Rabbit*, 1998

darkytown *noun*

a neighbourhood with a large population of black people *US*
- Roy felt it when he ventured out of darky town onto the broad reaches of Court Square the center of white power and prestige in Holly Springs, —J. Anthony Lukas, *Don't Shoot – We Are Your Children*, p. 79, 1971

darl; darls *noun*

used as an address or endearment, darling *UK, 1930*
- —Jon Cleary, *The Sundowners*, 1952
- You jus' got yourself a job, darl. —Jean Brooks, *The Opal Witch*, p. 192, 1967
- Good on ya, darl,' yelled seven million Australian women parked around TV sets in their living rooms. —Gretel Killeen, *Hot Buns and Ophelia get shipwrecked*, p. 92, 2001

darling *noun*

1 used both as a general and a theatrically arch form of address *UK, 1933*

In 1979, Beale noted: '[I]t is used in address as indiscriminately as the Londoner's "Love" or Durham "Flower"'.
- When did we start calling people "darling"? I can remember finding it impossible. It was a word your parents used for each other. I could say "man" and "babe", but not "darling". And now I can't stop saying it. Darling, darling, darling, darling[.] —Jennifer Saunders, *Absolutely Fabulous*, p. 128, 1992
- Everything all right, darlings? —Kevin Sampson, *Powder*, p. 21, 1999

2 used as a term of address between male homosexuals *US*
- Darling – Meaningless vocative loosely used in "bitchy" conversation. — Anon., *The Gay Girl's Guide*, p. 6, 1949

darling *adjective*

charming, sweet *UK, 1805*

An affectedly feminine or effeminate usage.
- "I can't believe how darling this stuff is," said one woman who was loading up a box of ornaments to give away. — *Santa Paula Times*, 29th November 2002

Darling Buds of May; Darling Buds *adjective*

homosexual *UK*

Rhyming slang for **GAY** formed on the title of a 1958 novel by H.E. Bates and, especially, from a 1991 BBC television adaptation.
- [T]his TV series ["The Darling Buds of May"] was on in spring of '91 and by summer a gay barman was nicknamed "Darling Buds'. —Ray Puxley, *Cockney Rabbit*, 1992

darling daughter *noun*
water *UK*
Rhyming slang. One of several terms that have 'daughter' as the common (dispensible) element.
- —Ray Puxley, *Cockney Rabbit*, 1992

darlings *noun*
the prostitutes of Darlinghurst and King's Cross, Sydney *AUSTRALIA, 1984*
- Darlo darlings ... Rebecca waits for a client on one of the residential back streets of Darlinghurst. [...] Who owns the streets of Darlinghurst – the prostitutes who have always worked there or the residents who say the law must be upheld? —*Sydney Morning Herald*, 18th July 2001

Darling shower *noun*
a dust storm *AUSTRALIA, 1945*
Ironic; probably from areas of the outback by the western reaches of the Darling River.

Darlo *nickname*
1 Darlington, County Durham *UK, 1984*
- [C]overing all aspects of Darlo history. —*www.darlingtontown.co.uk*, August 2003

2 Darlinghurst, Sydney *AUSTRALIA, 1937*
- Darlo darlings ... Rebecca waits for a client on one of the residential back streets of Darlinghurst. —*Sydney Morning Herald*, 18th July 2001

darls *noun*
darling *AUSTRALIA*
- 'I know, darls,' he screeched. —Sue Rhodes, *Now you'll think I'm awful*, p. 110, 1967
- —Alexander Buzo, *The Roy Murphy Show*, p. 103, 1970
- Sorry, darls. I told you yesterday, I'm regular as clockwork since I went on the pill. —Frank Hardy, *The Outcasts of Foolgarah*, p. 17, 1971
- —Lance Peters, *The Dirty Half-Mile*, p. 35, 1979

darn!; darn it!
used for registering annoyance, frustration, etc *US, 1781*
A euphemistic variation of **DAMN!**.
- My friend hit her fist into the palm of her other hand and exclaimed: "Darn! I saw that ad but thought it was a typo!" —Dolf de Roos, *Real Estate Riches*, p. 78, 2001

darnation *noun*
damnation *US, 1798*
Euphemistic; despite the weakening of 'damnation', there is still evidence of use.

darned *adjective*
used as an intensifier *US, 1807*
Euphemistic for **DAMNED**.
- Each week at the conclusion of Scooby Doo, the evil, ugly, old guy [...] will blame those "darned kids" for trapping him. —Stuart Jeffries, *Mrs Slocombe's Pussy*, p. 216, 2000

darned tooting!
used as a mock oath affirming that which has just been said *US*
Usually used in a self-mocking way, conjuring the image of an older, confused, country bumpkin.
- Simms said he was damned tootin' he was right. —Jim Thompson, *The Grifters*, p. 17, 1963
- You're darned tootin'! —*Fargo*, 1996

darn straight!
you are right! *US*
Used with irony, playing with the use of the heavily euphemised 'darn'.
- —Connie Eble (Editor), *UNC-CH Campus Slang*, p. 3, Spring 1994

Darren Gough *noun*
a cough *UK*
Rhyming slang, formed on the name of Yorkshire and England cricketer (b.1970).
- —Ray Puxley, *Fresh Rabbit*, 1998

dartboard *noun*
▸ **had more pricks than a second-hand dartboard**
used of a sexually promiscuous woman *UK*
According to Ted Walker, writing of the 1940s in *High Path*, 1982, such a woman may be described as 'a second-hand dartboard'. As the punch-line of a joke from the early 1980s 'second-hand' is dispensible. Currently popular in Australia.
- —Ted Walker, *High Path*, 1982

daru *noun*
rum *BARBADOS*
From Hindi.
- —Frank A. Collymore, *Barbadian Dialect*, p. 38, 1965

Darwin rig *noun*
an adaptation of the typical business suit worn by men in far northern Australia *AUSTRALIA, 1964*
Generally a short-sleeved shirt, and often short trousers. A tie is normally included, but a jacket is definitely not. Named after Darwin, a major city in the tropical north.
- The same as for 'Territory rig', but it was always 'Darwin rig' in Darwin from the 1950s to the mid-70s. —*Wordmap (www.abc.net.au/wordmap)*, 2003

Darwin stubbie; Darwin stubby *noun*
a 2.25 litre bottle of beer *AUSTRALIA*
An ironic term: a **STUBBIE** is one of the smallest bottle sizes. The city of Darwin is located in the tropical north and is well known for prodigious beer-drinking.
- They're not the same as our stubbies. A Darwin stubby holds forty ounces. —John O'Grady, *It's Your Shout, Mate!*, p. 87, 1972
- [H]e moved onto a story about a Brahman bull in the Northern Territory that could drink a Darwin stubbie in fifteen seconds. —Robert G. Barrett, *Davo's Little Something*, p. 93, 1992

dash *noun*
1 a dashboard *UK, 1902*
- [T]he clock on the Mercedes's dash caught his eye. —Francine Pascal, *Control Freak*, p. 23, 2001

2 an escape from custody *US*
- —*American Speech*, p. 25, February 1952: 'Teen-age hophead jargon'

▸ **have a dash at**
to make an attempt, to try *AUSTRALIA, 1923*
The surviving form of 'do your dash'.
- I think I'll go and try out something new, you know, just to see how it feels / I think I'll have a dash at some jellied eels. —Rolf Harris, *Someone's Pinched Me Winkles*, 1962

dash *verb*
to depart in a hurry *UK, 1932*
- Well, that concludes our meeting. If you would excuse me, I must dash, the last bus leaves in five minutes. —*The Times*, 5th May 2004

dash!; dash it!; dash it all!
used as a general purpose expletive *UK, 1800*
Euphemistic only when deliberately replacing **DAMN!** but note that **SHIT** is disguised in the extended variations.

dashed *adjective*
damned *UK, 1881*
Euphemistic; dated.

dash on to *verb*
to chastise *UK*
- —Patrick O'Shaughnessy, *Market Traders' Slang*, 1979

dash-pot *noun*
a device that can be installed in a car engine to prevent the car from stalling when the driver suddenly lifts their foot off the accelerator *US*
- —Tom MacPherson, *Dragging and Driving*, p. 137, 1960

dash up the channel *noun*
from the male perspective, sexual intercourse *UK*
A work-related coinage used by (southern) England coastal fisherman.

dat *noun*
pork *JAMAICA*
- —Velma Pollard, *Dread Talk*, p. 42, 2000

date *noun*
1 a person with whom an appointment or romantic engagement is made *US, 1925*
From the conventional sense that defines the appointment.
- How does my date tackle that gap? Does he kiss me? Does he envelop me in his arms? —*The Guardian*, 19th July 2003

2 a prostitute's customer *US*

- This John is a real honest-to-goodness hundred-dollar date, the way it used to be during the war. —Ross Russell, *The Sound*, p. 181, 1961
- I understand that a lot of girls get customers or Johns or dates or whatever you want to call them who are perverted in one way or the other. —John Warren Wells, *Tricks of the Trade*, p. 38, 1970
- I put her to work on the same edge on Hastings Street and fixed it where she could take her dates to a pal's pad to turn em. —A.S. Jackson, *Gentleman Pimp*, p. 88, 1973
- Since each girl usually had between five and twenty dates a day, the average would be about twelve. —Jan Hutson, *The Chicken Ranch*, p. 83, 1980
- They told him that he was her first date of the night, but her cunt seemed to be full of something viscous like come or corn syrup. —William T. Vollman, *Whores for Gloria*, p. 15, 1991

3 a sexual liaison between a prostitute and a customer *US, 1957*
An ironic euphemism.

- The men involved on these "dates" were always Chinese. —Harry J. Anslinger, *The Murderers*, p. 38, 1961
- She was hooking when I met her. So I didn't go for that at all. 'Cause I never made it with a hooker before. So one night she had a date, so she told me to come back late, in an hour or something like that. —James Mills, *The Panic in Needle Park*, p. 56, 1966
- The polite form is to have a date, to turn a date, or dating. —Christina and Richard Milner, *Black Players*, p. 38, 1972
- But there were no $5 dates in my house. —Bruce Jackson, *In the Life*, p. 78, 1972
- You want a date, honey? —Vernon E. Smith, *The Jones Men*, p. 111, 1974
- Since each girl usually had between five and twenty dates a day, the average would be about twelve. —Jan Hutson, *The Chicken Ranch*, p. 83, 1980
- She said doll you want a date? —William T. Vollman, *Whores for Gloria*, p. 12, 1991
- Oliver had assured her that she was his top bitch but demanded to know why she couldn't catch as many dates as Alice, his bottom bitch. —Joseph Wambaugh, *Floaters*, p. 67, 1996

4 a prisoner's expected date of release from prison *US*

- —James Harris, *A Convict's Dictionary*, p. 30, 1989

5 a foolish or silly person *UK, 1914*
Especially in the phrase 'soppy date'; later use is generally affectionate.

6 the anus; the buttocks *AUSTRALIA, 1961*
First recorded in Australia in 1919 as 'a word signifying contempt'. Harry Orsman, *A Dictionary of Modern New Zealand Slang*, 1999, makes an unsubstantiated claim on coinage around 1940. However, a case for a piece of rhyming slang always reduced to its first element, **DATE AND PLUM**, **BUM**, is made by Ray Puxley, *Fresh Rabbit*, 1998, with the following illustration: 'WIFE: The dog's been full of mischief today. HUSBAND: Yeah? Well, his date'll be full of my boot if he keeps on'.

- [D]ue to its resmblance in appearance to a date fruit. —Thommo, *The Dictionary of Australian Swearing and Sex Sayings*, 1985
- [I]t's a dead-set short cut to a fat ear, a thick lip and a full load of number 12s up the date. —Roy Slaven (John Doyle), *Five South Coast Seasons*, p. 27, 1992

date *verb*

1 (used of a prostitute) to have sex with a customer for pay *US*

- A white prostitute tried to date us at the Mai Fong restaurant, in Chinatown[.] —Jack Lait and Lee Mortimer, *Washington Confidential*, p. 26, 1951
- His name is Milt. I've dated him before, he only gets to the Apple once or twice a year. —Ross Russell, *The Sound*, p. 182, 1961
- The polite form is to have a date, to turn a date, or dating. —Chrfistina and Richard Milner, *Black Players*, p. 38, 1972

2 to be or become old-fashioned *UK, 1896*
From the conventional sense (to fix definitely in a period).

- It is also feared that when the buildings become dated in a few years' time the government will still be paying for them. — *The Guardian*, 1st October 2002

3 to caress the buttocks *AUSTRALIA, 1984*
From **DATE** (the buttocks).

4 to poke in the anus; to goose *AUSTRALIA*

- He went past them to get a can of beer and the Glass Canoe dated him savagely, making him jump. —David Ireland, *Unknown Industrial Prisoner*, p. 163, 1972

date and plum; date *noun*
the buttocks, the backside, the anus *UK*
Rhyming slang for **BUM**.

- Well, his date will be full of my boot if he keeps on. —Ray Puxley, *Fresh Rabbit*, 1998

date bait *noun*

1 an attractive person of either sex who is sought-after as a date *US, 1944*

- She was not somebody who was considered date bait, because of her weight and her presentation. —David Brock, *The Seduction of Hilary Rodham*, p. 40, 1996

2 anything that might serve as an incentive for a date *US, 1986*

- What a fun, sweet, terrific movie. Great date bait. —Roger Ebert, *Questions for the Movie Answer Man*, p. 163, 1997

date driller *noun*
the active participant in anal sex *NEW ZEALAND*

- —David McGill, *David McGill's Complete Kiwi Slang Dictionary*, p. 38, 1998

date-packer *noun*
a male homosexual *AUSTRALIA*

- [I]v'e got it on reliable authority that most of our museum directors are demon date-packers. — *The Traveller's Tool*, p. 19, 1985

date roll *noun*
toilet paper *AUSTRALIA*

- [My uncle] came home from the shops and said he'd bought, amongst other things, some date roll. Being unfamiliar with the term I imagined it to be some type of bun or cake with dates. Later on in the arvo my aunt asked me what I was hunting for in the kitchen – when I told her "date roll" she killed herself laughing. — *Wordmap (www.abc.net.au/wordmap)*, 2003

date with DiPalma *verb*
(of a male) an act of masturbation *US*
DiPalma alias 'the hand'.

- Another way to say "the boy is masturbating" [...] a date with DiPalma[.] —Erica Orloff and JoAnn Baker, *Dirty Little Secrets*, p. 65, 2001

daughter *noun*

1 a form of address between homosexual men *UK*
This **CAMP** adoption of the feminine form is also reflected in the cross-gender assignment of pronouns.

- She has a permanent vogue [cigarette] in her screech [mouth] and her droje is mega ribena on toast [awful], daughter. —the cast of 'Aspects of Love', Prince of Wales Theatre, *Palare (Boy Dancer Talk) for Beginners*, 1989–92

2 a male homosexual in relation to the man who has introduced him to homosexuality *US*

- — Anon., *The Gay Girl's Guide*, p. 6, 1949
- — *American Speech*, p. 56, Spring-Summer 1970: 'Homosexual slang'

dauncey *adjective*
pregnant *US*
The 'Lucy is Enceinte' episode of the television comedy *I Love Lucy* (CBS, 1950–57), which aired on 8th December 1952, was the first US television treatment of pregnancy. Lucy avoided the word 'pregnant', instead saying that she was 'feeling real dauncey', explaining that it was a word that her grandmother 'made up for when you're not really sick but you just feel lousy'. The word enjoyed brief popular usage.

Dave Clark *adjective*
dark *UK*
Rhyming slang, formed from the name of UK drummer, leader of the Dave Clark Five (b.1942).

- [H]aving no Mott the Hooples [scruples] he goes out when it's a bit Dave Clark[.] —Mervyn Stutter, *Getting Nowhere Fast*, 21st May 2004

Dave Dee, Dozy, Beaky, Mick and Tich *adjective*
rich *UK*
Rhyming slang, jocularly contrived from a 1960s UK pop group.

- [A]ll because some little git to get Dave Dee, Dozy, Beaky, Mick and Tich [...] quick. —Mervyn Stutter, *Getting Nowhere Fast*, 21st May 2004

David Bowie *adjective*
windy *UK*
Rhyming slang for 'blowy', formed on the name of singer and musician David Bowie (David Robert Jones, b.1947).

- —Ray Puxley, *Cockney Rabbit*, 1992

David Gower; David *noun*
a shower *UK, 2002*
Rhyming slang, based on the name of cricketer and television personality David Gower (b.1957).

- I've gotta go for a David. — *www.LondonSlang.com*, June 2002

- Typical! No rain for weeks and then a David Gower just when I want to mow the lawn. —Bodmin Dark, *Dirty Cockney Rhyming Slang*, 2003

Davina McCalls *noun*
nonsense *UK*
Rhyming slang for **BALLS**, formed from the name of UK television presenter Davina McCall (b.1967).
- [I]t sounds like a right load of Davina McCalls to me. —Mervyn Stutter, *Getting Nowhere Fast*, 21st May 2004

davvy *noun*
a sofa or couch *US*
A corruption of 'Davenport'.
- —Amy and Denise McFadden, *CoalSpeak*, p. 5, 1997

Davy Crockett *noun*
a pocket *UK*
Rhyming slang, formed on the name of an American folk-hero who lived from 1786–1836; he was not an inspiration for slang until the actor Fess Parker brought him to life in 1954 and a succession of Disney-made television adventures.
- —Julian Franklyn, *A Dictionary of Rhyming Slang*, 1961

Davy Jones's locker; Davy Jones's; Davy's locker *noun*
1 the last resting place of those lost at sea; the sea *UK*
Davy Jones has been used as a personification for the 'spirit of the sea' since 1751, his locker is mentioned in *The Journal of Richard Cresswell, 1774–7*; the etymology, however, is another mystery of the deep. Jones may arise from Jonah (and his biblical history of the sea), Davy may have been added by Welsh sailors in honour of St David.

2 a door knocker *UK*
Rhyming slang.
- Many a rent man, tally man or anyone who comes to the house requiring payment has had to "take it out of Davy Jones's till payday'. —Ray Puxley, *Cockney Rabbit*, 1992

Davy Large *noun*
a barge *UK*
Rhyming slang, formed on the name of a docker who later became a trades union official.
- —Julian Franklyn, *A Dictionary of Rhyming Slang*, 1961

daw *noun*
a silly, empty person; an obdurate, unreasoning person *IRELAND*
- I know the Kellys is [sic] no daws. I want you to help me on this. The rest of our crowd wouldn't do it right. —Eamonn Sweeney, *Waiting for the Healer*, p. 122, 1997

dawamesk *noun*
marijuana *UK*
- —Mike Haskins, *Drugs*, p. 287, 2003

daw-daw; daw-yaw *adjective*
slow-witted *UK*
This seems to derive from a yokelish **DOH!**. Certainly the metropolitan notion of countrysiders at the time this slipped into usage was through BBC radio's 'everyday story of country folk', *The Archers*, first broadcast nationally in 1951; actor Robert Mawdesley certainly introduced such a meaningless syllable into his portrayal of Walter Gabriel, an irascible rogue who gave the appearance of being more slow-witted than he actually was.

dawg *noun*
1 a dog *US*
A rural, southern 'dog'.
- Kleinfeld put his hand out and Carlito slapped it. "You dawg," Brigante said. —Edwin Torres, *After Hours*, p. 208, 1979

2 a fellow youth gang member *US*
- [Y]our Kru, or your Massive, your Thugs, or Bredrins; Dawgs, Homies, your Clique, or your Posse. —Julian Johnson, *Urban Survival*, p. 264, 2003

dawner *noun*
an engagement between a prostitute and customer that lasts all night, until dawn *US*
- Rialto was supposed to be waitin' on Felita to say was it going to be a quick trick or a dawner. But Rialto wasn't there. —Robert Campbell, *Alice in La-La Land*, p. 328, 1987

dawn patrol *noun*
any activity that requires staying up all night or getting up very early *US, 1945*
Originally a military term, later applied figuratively.
- —Lou Shelly, *Hepcats Jive Talk Dictionary*, p. 44, 1945
- "I suffered through those dawn patrol meetings myself," says Masters. —*San Francisco News*, p. 23, 19th September 1951
- —Dawson Taylor, *How to Talk Golf*, p. 27, 1985
- —Mitch McKissick, *Surf Lingo*, 1987
- Dawn patrol – major dawn patrol. My son had a full blown attack. —*As Good As It Gets*, 1997

day *noun*
▸ **not your day; it's not your day; it just isn't your day**
used for expressing a rueful, philosophical acceptance of a day when everything seems to go wrong *UK, 1984*
- His deft touch sets up Keane for United's clearest chance of the game. Keane leans back and fires over [the goal]. It is not his day. — *The Guardian*, 19th April 2000

day!
good day!, hello! *UK, 1907*
An shortening of **G'DAY**.
- "Gooday," Joe said. "Day". —Nino Culotta (John O'Grady), *They're A Weird Mob*, p. 146, 1957
- "Day, Nat," he greeted Bony[.] —Arthur Upfield, *Bony and the Mouse*, p. 45, 1959

day and night *noun*
1 a *light* ale *UK*
Rhyming slang, first recorded by Julian Franklyn, *A Dictionary of Rhyming Slang*, 1960, with the remark: 'This seems to be a post-second war formation, and has a restricted currency. It will be interesting to observe "whether it flame or fade" in the next decade'. If not flaming it has continued to glow, according to Ray Puxley, *Cockney Rabbit*, 1992, with the definition: 'Another term for bottled sunshine.'

2 light (illumination) *UK*
Rhyming slang.
- —Ray Puxley, *Cockney Rabbit*, 1992

day-and-night merchant *noun*
a lorry driver who breaks the law by driving more than 11 hours in 24 to undercut other drivers *UK*
Peter Sanders, *Daily Telegraph*, 26th January 1964, since which date more stringent rules have been implemented.

day-for-day *adverb*
serving a prison sentence without any reduction in the sentence for good behaviour *US*
- —Charles Shafer, *Folk Speech in Texas Prisons*, p. 202, 1990

dayglo; day-glo *adjective*
used of dazzlingly vivid, rebelliously bright, flourescent colours *UK*
Day-Glo™ paints were introduced in 1951, the name was soon applied to the wider world of tastelessness.
- [O]ff to the Ritz in our dayglo school ties[.] —Derek Raymond (Robin Cook), *The Crust on its Uppers*, p. 30, 1962
- [S]himmering flower children, splashed with Day-Glo, spotted with marcasite[.] —Richard Neville, *Play Power*, p. 30, 1970
- [T]he weather bloke in the day-glo sports jacket told us "There won't be a hurricane"[.] —Andrew Nickolds, *Back to Basics*, p. 33, 1994

day job *noun*
a conventional job, usually used to finance a person's true interest or passion *US*
- HONEY BUNNY: Well, what else is there, day jobs? PUMPKIN: Not this life. — *Pulp Fiction*, 1994

daylight *noun*
in horse racing, the non-existent second-place finisher in a race won by a large margin *AUSTRALIA*
Used with humour.
- —Ned Wallish, *The Truth Dictionary of Racing Slang*, p. 21, 1989

▸ **he (she) wouldn't give you daylight in a dark corner**
said of a person with a reputation for meanness *UK*
Glasgow use.
- —Michael Munro, *The Patter, Another Blast*, 1988

daylight in the swamp!

used for rousing people from bed *US, 1936*

A logger term.

- My father woke us early, hours before it's light out, pounding on our doors, bellowing "Reveille, reveille, it's daylight in the swamp!" —Susan Fox Rogers, *Solo*, p. 17, 1996

daylight robbery *noun*

an exorbitant price *UK, 1949*

- 'Three-ten a week, take it or leave it, there's plenty waiting.' 'That's daylight robbery!'—Eric Lambert, *The Veterans*, p. 60, 1954
- —Frank Hardy, *The Outcasts of Foolgarah*, p. 137, 1971
- —Shane Maloney, *Nice Try*, p. 152, 1998

daylights *noun*

▷ **see: LIVING DAYLIGHTS**

day number *noun*

in an illegal number gambling lottery, a wager on a number for a single day's drawing *US*

- —*American Speech*, p. 191, October 1949

day player *noun*

an actor who is called for a single day's work on a television programme or film set *US*

- I mean was it a pretty big part or were you just – were you a day player?—Robert Campbell, *Juice*, p. 28, 1988

days *noun*

▸ **good old days**

the past, remembered fondly and better than it ever was *UK*

Evolved from the early C19 'good old times'.

- "It used to be you could shoot yourself in the leg and get in People and on Face the Nation." "Them was the good old days."—Robert Campbell, *Junkyard Dog*, p. 42, 1986

day's dawning; days a dawning *noun*

morning *UK*

Rhyming slang.

- —Julian Franklyn, *A Dictionary of Rhyming Slang*, 1960

days of rage *noun*

a series of violent confrontations between radical members of the Students for Democratic Society and the police in downtown Chicago in the autumn of 1969 *US*

- —J. Anthony Lukas, *The Barnyard Epithet and Other Obscenities*, p. 10, 1970

day to day *adjective*

unencumbered by thoughts of the long term, living one day at a time *US*

- "Let me explain something so you understand," Stick said. "See, I did seven years straight up day to day in a room six and half feet wide by ten feet deep."—Elmore Leonard, *Stick*, p. 84, 1983

dazzle dust *noun*

face powder *CANADA*

Teen slang, reported by a Toronto newspaper in 1946, and reported as 'obsolescent or obsolete' by Douglas Leechman, 1959.

DB *noun*

1 a *d*ead *b*ody *US*

- "I think a guy might be dead upstairs." "What the hell made you think so?" I said sarcastically, as we started up the stairs and I smelled the d.b. from here.—Joseph Wambaugh, *The Blue Knight*, p. 131, 1973

2 a socially inept person *US*

An abbreviation of **DOUCHE BAG**.

- —Connie Eble (Editor), *UNC-CH Campus Slang*, p. 3, November 2003

DBI

a doctors' (unofficial) code for classifiying a despicable, offensive or unhygeinic person, in a measure indicated by a suffixed numeral *UK*

An initialism for '*d*irt *b*ag *i*ndex'.

- DBI refers to "Dirt Bag Index", and multiplies the number of tattoos with the number of missing teeth to give an estimate of the number of days since the patient last bathed.—*Ethics and Behaviour*, August 2003

DC *noun*

a hamburger with every possible trimming and condiment *US*

- —*American Speech*, p. 280, December 1966: 'More carnie talk from the west coast'

DD *noun*

a person who is *d*eaf and *d*umb *US, 1926*

- —Vincent J. Monteleone, *Criminal Slang*, p. 68, 1949

DD *adjective*

by extension, said of a criminal who gives up no information at all if arrested *US*

- —Hyman E. Goldin et al., *Dictionary of American Underworld Lingo*, p. 56, 1950

D day *noun*

used as a designation for the start of an action *US*

Originally applied to military actions, then expanded to general use. For example, in a US veteran's hospital, it is the routine day that Ducolax™ suppositories are given to bed-bound patients.

- —*American Speech*, December 1944
- —*Maledicta*, p. 55, Summer 1980: 'Not sticks and stones, but names: more medical pejoratives'

DDD *noun*

▷ **see: DERRY-DOWN-DERRY**

d-dog *noun*

a dog trained to detect hidden drugs *US*

- —Jay Robert Nash, *Dictionary of Crime*, p. 95, 1992

DDT!

used for disparaging, urging the listener to *d*rop *d*ead *t*wice *US*

Youth usage; punning on the insecticide now banned but used with great effectiveness to kill mosquitos in the years after World War 2. Recorded in *Time*, 3rd October 1949.

- Last year's "drop dead" is now "D.D.T." (drop dead twice) or, more formally, "Please do me the personal favor of dropping dead."—*Life*, p. 119, 17th November 1947
- But when Batsy feels like snoozing nice ... "DDT," you all ... "Drop Dead Twice." [They'll Do It Every Time comic strip]—*San Francisco Call-Bulletin*, 10th November 1950
- —*American Weekly*, p. 2, 14th August 1955
- He remembers Winchell's famous handwritten notes on top of wrongo items returned to the sender: "DDT" wihch meant "Drop Dead Twice."—*Daily Variety*, p. 2, 19th November 1998

deacon *noun*

a prison warden *US*

- —Vincent J. Monteleone, *Criminal Slang*, p. 66, 1949

deacon *verb*

to present a job or product in the best possible light, placing more importance on the first impression than on the actual quality *US, 1855*

- He deaconed his barn by painting the side toward the ro'd.—John Gould, *Maine Lingo*, p. 70, 1975

deacon seat *noun*

1 the seats nearest a fire *US*

- Because the deacons usually sat down front in church, the deacon-seat became the bench nearest the fire in a lumber camp.—John Gould, *Maine Lingo*, p. 70, 1975

2 in a lumber camp, the long bench in the bunkhouse *US, 1851*

- Along three sides of the single room ran double tiers of bunks, below which stood the benches or "deacon seats" on which the men sharpened their tools, mended their harness, ate their meals, and took their ease.—G.R. Stevens, *The Incompleat Canadian*, p. 36, 1965
- In front of each row of bunks were long benches made from split logs, called deacon seats.—A.S. Gintzler, *Rough and Ready Loggers*, p. 20, 1994

deacon's nose *noun*

the flat lobe at the nether end of a chicken which is like a mammal's tail, base for the tail-feathers *CANADA*

This part of the chicken or turkey is also known in the US as 'the pope's nose'.

- —Walter Avis, *Dictionary of Canadianisms*, p. 197, 1967

dead *noun*

1 a corpse *BARBADOS, 1971*

- —Richard Allsopp, *Dictionary of Caribbean English Usage*, p. 189, 1996

2 in any card game, cards that have been discarded *US*

- I buried their dead / then did what they said / dealing each man their hand.—Lightnin' Rod, *Hustlers Convention*, p. 90, 1973

dead *adjective*

1 absolute *UK, 1894*

- What a dead coot!—Eric Lambert, *The Veterans*, p. 102, 1954
- After the Damoclean sword there is relief in dead certainty.—*The Guardian*, 18th March 2002

2 used for expressing a very high degree of trouble *UK*
- Oh no! I'm dead. — *Coronation Street*, 18th February 2002

3 (of a place) dull, boring; without interest *AUSTRALIA*
- I don't know what fun you expect knocking round this dead hole. — Norman Lindsay, *The Cousin from Fiji*, p. 135, 1945

4 in a bar, used for describing any drink that has been abandoned *UK*
- Is this pint dead? — Michael Munro, *The Original Patter*, 1985

5 (of a racehorse) not run on its merits; ridden to lose deliberately *AUSTRALIA*
- Ut wasn't pulled. Ut was dead. — Nino Culotta (John O'Grady), *They're A Weird Mob*, p. 73, 1957
- Punters will put up with anything – except dead favourites. — Frank Hardy, *The Yarns of Billy Borker*, p. 48, 1965
- If it drifts in the market, I won't back it, it'll be dead. — Frank Hardy, *The Yarns of Billy Borker*, p. 107, 1965
- At one stage of my career, some punters booed nearly every time I lost a race. They seemed to think that if I got beaten, I had to be dead. — Frank Hardy and Athol George Mulley, *The Needy and the Greedy*, p. 18, 1975
- 'Think you're smart, don't you?' he snarled. 'But you're a mug. You didn't know I owned that horse and it was dead.' — Frank Hardy and Athol George Mulley, *The Needy and the Greedy*, p. 61, 1975
- One morning, Pat rushed in and said 'Did you know the Pope's dead?' Mick replied, 'I'll bet that bastard Mulley is riding him!' — Roy Higgins and Tom Prior, *The Jockey Who Laughed*, p. 59, 1982
- He's dead alright. He's just blown from sixes to thirty-threes. — Joe Andersen, *Winners Can Laugh*, p. 198, 1982

6 (used of dice) weighted to have one face land up more often than the law of averages would predict *US*
- — Frank Scoblete, *Guerrilla Gambling*, p. 304, 1993

7 in bar dice games, no longer wild *US*
If a game is played with 'aces wild' (assuming the point value of any other die), a call of 'aces dead' after the first call of a hand nullifies the 'wild' status.
- — Gil Jacobs, *The World's Best Dice Games*, p. 191, 1976

8 in pinball, said of a bumper that scores when hit but does not propel the ball back into play *US*
- — Bobbye Claire Natkin and Steve Kirk, *All About Pinball*, p. 111, 1977

9 in pool, said of a shot made such that the cue ball stops completely after striking the object ball *US*
- — Steve Rushin, *Pool Cool*, p. 11, 1990

▸ **not be found dead with; not be seen dead with**
used to deny the possibility that you will have anything whatsoever to do with someone or something *UK, 1915*
- Nick Hornby's Fever Pitch remains the best Christmas bet – even if dyed-in-the-wool denizens of White Hart Lane wouldn't be seen dead with it these days. — *The Guardian*, 30th November 2001
- I was going to say I wouldn't be found dead in Nottingham, but on reflection, the opposite is more likely! — Cavan Duval, *BBCi*, 29th July 2002

▸ **not be seen dead in; not be found dead in**
used in expressions of dislike and dismissal for items of clothing; may also, with slight variation, be applied to a place *UK, 1961*
- The dress at hunt balls is white tie, which means tails for the men and long dresses for the women. Not the kind of gear Gordon Brown would be seen dead in, but then he can afford to be blase about grand events. — *The Guardian*, 7th December 1999
- There are two categories of Sydney pub – one people die to be seen in and the other they wouldn't be seen dead in. — *The Guardian*, 30th October 1999

dead *adverb*
very, absolutely, extremely, completely *UK, 1589*
A general intensifier.
- She's dead off bloke who do a bear-up with girls. — Norman Lindsay, *Halfway to Anywhere*, p. 100, 1947
- I was dead charlie (=scared) — Frank Norman, *Bang To Rights*, p. 49, 1958
- It was dead easy. — Ward McNally, *Supper at Happy Harry's*, p. 41, 1982
- I saw this kid with a dead little body and a dead massive head. — Shaun Ryder, *Shaun Ryder... in His Own Words*, 1993
- [H]e was dead loud. — Kevin Sampson, *Outlaws*, p. 7, 2001

dead air *noun*
silence *US*
Telecommunications usage.
- I tell the bitch at the desk to buzz in on the creep and tell him Bangs wants to talk to him. I get dead air. — Lester Bangs, *Psychotic Reactions and Carburetor Dung*, p. 186, 1976

dead-alive *adverb*
extremely slowly *TRINIDAD AND TOBAGO, 1971*
- — Lise Winer, *Dictionary of the English/Creole of Trinidad & Tobago*, 2003

dead as disco *adjective*
completely dead *US*
From the meteoric rise and fall of the disco fad in the 1970s.
- By Friday, man, or you're fuckin' dead as disco. — *Get Shorty*, 1995

dead ass *noun*
the buttocks in seated repose *US, 1950*
- Look, we have this date scheduled. I can't perform unless you get off your dead ass. — Rosabeth Moss Kanter, *Change Masters*, p. 81, 1983

dead-ass *adjective*
lacking energy *US, 1958*
- I gave a dead-ass performance. — Andrea Siegel, *Women in Aikido*, p. 80, 1993

dead-ass *adverb*
absolutely *US, 1971*
- "We've got three infantry brigades," he said. "Yours is dead-ass last." — Joseph Persico, *My American Journey*, p. 204, 1995

dead babies *noun*
semen *US*
- — Ethan Hilderbrant, *Prison Slang*, p. 36, 1998

dead-bang *adjective*
beyond debate *US, 1934*
- We were both hungry for jurywork, and therefore we agreed to try a dead-bang loser of a rape case on reassignment from somebody smarter. — Scott Turow, *Presumed Innocent*, p. 174, 1987

dead-bang *adverb*
absolutely *US, 1919*
- I don't need to turn you, Vicky. I got you dead bang. — Stephen Cannell, *Big Con*, p. 323, 1997

deadbeat *noun*
1 a person who won't pay his debts, especially one who does not pay child support after divorce *US, 1871*
In modern use, often construed with 'dad' or 'parent'.
- So you want a financial, is he a deadbeat? — *Sleepless in Seattle*, 1967
- You sonofabitch fuck. Are you calling me a deadbeat? The money I spent here? — *Goodfellas*, 1990
- I said Dad was in arrears on his child-support payments, was not seriously looking for worik, and had turned down the offer of a very good job. ... "And don't worry. We'll light a fire under that deadbeat." — C.D. Payne, *Youth in Revolt*, p. 107, 1993
- There's a lot more money in getting deadbeats to pay up, isn't there? — Elmore Leonard, *Riding the Rap*, p. 158, 1995

2 a destitute person; a bum or derelict *AUSTRALIA, 1892*
- You weren't so keen on him last election when he reckoned a Liberal Party feller would do some more good for Gubba than that Country Party dead-beat we've been carrying for years. — Dymphna Cusack, *Picnic Races*, p. 22, 1962
- Investigate two-up with an open mind and you will find evidence of suicides, the loss of businesses, the degradation of professional men into dead-beats and 'no-hopers'. — James Holledge, *The Great Australian Gamble*, p. 103, 1966
- An old white deadbeat was waving from his chair by the wall. — Petru Popescu, *The Last Wave*, p. 33, 1977
- Fucking deadbeat that I am, plonkie fucking half a playboy that I've become[.] — Kevin Sampson, *Outlaws*, p. 190, 2001

dead beat *adjective*
exhausted *UK, 1821*
- A man who says he is "dead beat" at the end of a recording session must have given his all. — *CD liner notes of Prince Buster's 'The Prophet'*, 1994

dead bird *noun*
in horse racing, a certainty *AUSTRALIA, 1889*

Dead board *noun*
an Internet bulletin board system designed by, and for, fans of the Grateful Dead *US*
- — David Shenk and Steve Silberman, *Skeleton Key*, p. 53, 1994

dead cat *noun*
in circus usage, a lion, tiger or leopard that is on display but does not perform *US*
- — Don Wilmeth, *The Language of American Popular Entertainment*, p. 71, 1981

dead cat on the line *noun*

used as a representation of something that is wrong or immoral *US, 1970*

- There's a dead cat on the line, Eleanor. And you'd better wake up and smell it.—Candy Dawson Boyd, *Charlie Pippin*, p. 32, 1987
- If one comes in there like a scalded dog, the others in that hole know there's a dead cat on the line somewhere.—Foxfire Fund, *Foxfire 11*, p. 266, 1999

dead centre *noun*

a cemetery *UK, 1961*

Jocular.

- Where's the dead centre of Dublin?...Well the dead centre of Dublin is Glasnevin Cemetery.—?monn MacThom?, *Gur Cake and Coal Blocks', O'Brien*, p. 27, 1976

dead cert *noun*

a *cert*ainty *UK, 1889*

Originally sporting and gambling usage.

- He's a dead cert for fourteen [years] PD (=penal detention) when he's old enough.—Frank Norman, *Bang To Rights*, p. 158, 1958
- —Barry Humphries, *The Traveller's Tool*, 1985
- And if this year's show is anything to go by, that'll be a dead farkin' cert.—*Picture*, p. 14, 7th December 1994
- LEE: ...3.30 tomorrow, Fontwell [...] FIREBUG: Dead cert? LEE: Oh yeah.—Guy Ritchie et al., *Lock, Stock... & Four Stolen Hooves*, p. 25, 2000

dead-cert *adjective*

certain *AUSTRALIA*

- Mind you, there have been a lot of tears and muttered curses as well – from mug punters who put their beer money on the 'red-hot, dead-cert, sure-fire' tips these boys purport to have the mail on every week.—*TV Week*, p. 24, 13th February 1993

dead cinch *noun*

a certainty *UK, 1927*

An intensification of **CINCH** (a certainty).

- There are even people today who are saying it [the Dow Jones Industrial Average] 's a dead cinch to pass 10,000 this year.—*San Angelo Standard-Times (West Texas)*, 17th January 1999

dead-cinch *adjective*

certain *UK*

From the noun sense.

- The Republicans have a dead-cinch lock on power in Lansing. —*Times Herald (Port Huron)*, 14th January 2001

dead drop *noun*

in espionage or a sophisticated criminal venture, a location where a message can be left by one party and retrieved by another *US*

- —Henry Becket, *The Dictionary of Espionage*, p. 52–53, 1986
- That bank could be the dead-drop.—Stephen Cannell, *King Con*, p. 119, 1997

dead duck *noun*

an absolute failure, a person or thing with no possibility of success *US, 1829*

- Senator Hugh Burns (F. Fresno) said his bill to make the present closing hours permanent apparently is a "dead duck."—*San Francisco News*, p. 1, 10th June 1947

dead end *noun*

in bowls, an end (a stage of play) that has to be replayed when the jack is driven out of bounds *UK*

- —David Bryant, *The Game of Bowls*, p. 38, 1990

deaders *noun*

meat *JAMAICA*

- —Velma Pollard, *Dread Talk*, p. 49, 2000

dead eye dick *noun*

a person who is an excellent shot *AUSTRALIA*

- 'He's a dead eye dick' – a footballer with exceptional goal kicking accuracy.—Ivor Limb, *Footy's No Joke!*, p. 21, 1986

deadfall *noun*

a dishonest, disreputable, vice-ridden drinking establishment *US, 1837*

- They worked the come-on joints and dead-falls on West Fifty-second Street, between Sixth and Seventh Avenues[.]—Lee Mortimer, *Women Confidential*, p. 138, 1960

dead finish *noun*

the end *AUSTRALIA, 1881*

- That's your dead finish here, Rita dear.—Norman Lindsay, *Dust or Polish?*, p. 38, 1950

dead fish *noun*

a gambler who places small bets to prolong the inevitable *US, 1963*

- —Thomas L. Clark, *The Dictionary of Gambling and Gaming*, p. 58, 1987

deadfoot *noun*

a slow vehicle *US*

- —*Complete CB Slang Dictionary*, 1976
- —Peter Chippindale, *The British CB Book*, p. 154, 1981

dead from the neck up *adjective*

brainless, stupid, insensitive *UK, 1930*

- You gotta drag yourself to work / Drug yourself to sleep / You're dead from the neck up / By the middle of the week—The Clash *All the Young Punks (New Boots and Contracts)*, 1978

dead gaff *noun*

a premises with no-one in *UK*

- You pick a dead gaff – a house you know or think is empty – sound the drum by knocking at the front door to make sure[.]—Charles Raven, *Underworld Nights*, p. 32, 1956

dead give-away *noun*

a notable indication, or betrayal, of guilt, or defect *US, 1882*

- The vivid orange mark on the back of her head is a dead give-away of her supposedly barren status, but the lamb is well and a bonus.—*The Guardian*, 9th May 2001

dead hand *noun*

in poker, any hand held by a player who has bet all of his chips or money on the hand *US*

- —Oswald Jacoby, *Oswald Jacoby on Poker*, p. 141, 1947

deadhead *noun*

1 a person who rides free on a railway, bus or aeroplane, usually because of their employment with the carrier *US, 1841*

- —Norman Carlisle, *The Modern Wonder Book of Trains and Railroading*, p. 261, 1946
- The only other people on the plane were a half dozen or so off-duty pilots: "deadheads" as they say in the business.—Hunter S. Thompson, *Generation of Swine*, p. 137, 7th July 1986

2 a boring person *US, 1907*

- —*Newsweek*, p. 28, 8th October 1951
- —Helen Dahlskog (Editor), *A Dictionary of Contemporary and Colloquial Usage*, p. 18, 1972

3 a non-playing observer of gambling *US*

- —John Scarne, *Scarne on Dice*, p. 465, 1974

4 a person given a ticket or tickets for having performed minor services in a theatrical production *US*

- —Sherman Louis Sergel, *The Language of Show Biz*, p. 69, 1973

Deadhead *noun*

a follower of Grateful Dead, a band strongly associated with psychedelic drugs, seen by many to epitomise the hippie ideal *US, 1972*

Grateful Dead's choice of name was the result of browsing a dictionary; usually abbreviated to 'The Dead'; their 30 year career as a live band came to an end in 1995 with the death of guitarist Jerry Garcia.

- —Connie Eble (Editor), *UNC-CH Campus Slang*, p. 2, Fall 1982
- Someone who loves – and draws meaning from – the music of the Grateful Dead and the experience of Dead shows, and builds community with others who feel the same way.—David Shenk and Steve Silberman, *Skeleton Key*, p. 60, 1994
- [J]ust hanging out, doing drugs with their dead-head clothes on[.] —Tim Lucas, *Cool Places*, p. 154, 1998
- Ten music-related university courses that really exist [...] 2 DEAD-HEAD 101, University of North Carolina, Greensboro—*Q*, p. 38, December 2001
- A dear junkie friend from Cambridge [UK], Dead-head and antiquarian bookseller[.]—Tony Wilson, *24 Hour Party People*, p. 22, 2002

deadhead *verb*

1 to discourage *UK*

A gardening image of deadheading roses to discourage growth.

- I try to deadhead his questions.—Kevin Sampson, *Outlaws*, p. 240, 2001

2 to ignore *UK*

- Usually I wave away or dead-head prozzies on the make, like[.]—Niall Griffiths, *Kelly + Victor*, p. 67, 2002

3 to coast in a car with a depleted petrol supply *US*

- "Lady," the Hulk said, "you mean you were deadheading when you rolled up here?" "If that means running empty," Joanie said, "yeah." —Emmett Grogan, *Final Score*, p. 82, 1976

4 (used of an airline or railway employee) to ride as a passenger in available seating *US, 1854*

- Deadheaded up there like a bat out of fuckin' hell.—George V. Higgins, *The Rat on Fire*, p. 105, 1981

deadhead *adverb*

without cargo *US*

- They'll take any cargo you got rather than go dead-head.—Elmore Leonard, *Bandits*, p. 270, 1987

dead heart *noun*

the arid inland regions of Australia *AUSTRALIA, 1906*

- The sands of the "dead heart" swept over them, even silting over the graves.—George Farwell, *Land of Mirage*, p. 157, 1950
- —Jim Ramsay, *Cop It Sweet!*, p. 27, 1977

dead horse *noun*

tomato sauce *AUSTRALIA, 1966*

Rhyming slang.

- It will be no surprise if he finishes up in Sir Reggie's personal office asking for his Four-and-Twenty pie with dead horse.—Max Harris, *The Angry Eye*, p. 116, 1973
- —Jim Ramsay, *Cop It Sweet!*, p. 27, 1977
- And if nothing else, it [Harry's Cafe de Wheels, Cowper Wharf Road, Woolloomooloo]'s a great place to learn local lingo such as "pass the dead horse tomato sauce mate". Indeed.— *The Guardian*, 24th July 2003

dead house *noun*

a funeral parlour *BARBADOS*

- —Frank A. Collymore, *Barbadian Dialect*, p. 38, 1965

dead-leg *noun*

1 a useless person *UK*

- He's our village policeman, a real dead-leg. He couldn't catch a cold.—Jonathan Gash, *The Ten Word Game*, p. 194, 2003

2 a corking of the thigh *AUSTRALIA*

- —James Lambert, *The Macquarie Book of Slang*, 1996

dead letter perfect *adjective*

of an actor, absolutely certain of your lines *UK*

- —William Granville, *A Dictionary of Theatrical Terms*, p. 58, 1952

dead lice *noun*

▸**dead lice are falling off; dead lice are dropping off**

used for describing someone who is very slow-moving or lazy *US, 1960*

- Look at those good-for-nothing loafers, so lazy that dead lice wouldn't drop off them.—Robert Ruark, *The Old Man and the Boy*, p. 119, 1957

dead line *noun*

in prison, a line the crossing of which will bring gun fire from guards *US*

- —Frank Prewitt and Francis Schaeffer, *Vacaville Vocabulary*, 1961–1962

deadline *verb*

to remove from action for repairs *US*

Vietnam war usage.

- —Linda Reinberg, *In the Field*, p. 58, 1991

dead loss *noun*

1 a person or thing that is utterly inefficient, or a complete failure or an absolute waste of time or money *UK, 1927*

- [Geena] Davis's husband is a boor, [Susan] Sarandon's boyfriend a dead loss[.]— *The Guardian*, 11th July 1991

2 a boss *UK*

Rhyming slang, adopting the non-rhyming sense: 'a person that is utterly inefficient or an absolute waste of money'.

- —Ray Puxley, *Cockney Rabbit*, 1992

deadly *adjective*

1 excellent *US*

Especially common in Australian Aboriginal English.

- —Clarence Major, *Dictionary of Afro-American Slang*, p. 45, 1970
- Right now I'm enjoying a Jolt cola with a dash of Henson's Orange soda. It's deadly.— *Wayne's World 2*, 1993
- She really knew how to smoke, all right. Probably blow smoke rings and all. 'Deadly,' she said, and passed me the durrie.—Phillip Gwynne, *Deadly Unna?*, p. 123, 1998
- Used when I was growing up in Darwin, still used by my friends when I go back there. Commonly used to describe things which are pretty cool, like a deadly car , bike or clothes, also used as a general exclamation like 'that's deadly' or 'too deadly for you'.— *Wordmap (www.abc.net.au/wordmap)*, 2003

2 very boring *US*

- — *American Speech*, p. 303, December 1955: 'Wayne university slang'

deadly *adverb*

excessively, extremely, very *UK, 1688*

- It was deadly quiet on account of the heavy fire doors every ten feet or so.—J.J. Connolly, *Know Your Enemy [britpulp]*, p. 155, 1999

deadly embrace *noun*

in computing, the condition resulting when two processes cannot proceed because each is waiting for another to do something *US*

- — *'Computer slang'*, p. 29, Spring 1981

deadly treadly *noun*

a bicycle *AUSTRALIA*

Rhyming elaboration of **TREADLY**, with the suggestion that it is risky to ride.

- I raced my friend around the park on my deadly treadly.— *Wordmap (www.abc.net.au/wordmap)*, 2003

dead man *noun*

an earth anchor for a wire or cable *UK, 1840*

- —A.B. Chance Co., *Lineman's Slang Dictionary*, p. 5, 1980

dead man's arm *noun*

a steamed roll pudding *NEW ZEALAND, 1985*

- —Harry Orsman, *A Dictionary of Modern New Zealand Slang*, 1999

dead man's ears *noun*

stewed dried apricots *NEW ZEALAND, 1992*

- —Harry Orsman, *A Dictionary of Modern New Zealand Slang*, 1999

dead man's hand *noun*

in poker, a hand with a pair of aces and a pair of eights *US, 1888*

Although it is the modern belief that this was the hand held by Wild Bill Hickcok when shot to death in 1876 in Deadwood, Dakota Territory, early uses of the term (which also sometimes referred to three jacks with two red sevens) make no mention of Hickok. In 1942, Damon Runyon wrote that the hand with jacks was sometimes called the 'Montana dead man's hand'.

- —John Scarne, *Scarne's Guide to Modern Poker*, p. 277, 1979

dead man's head *noun*

a spherical plum pudding *NEW ZEALAND, 1994*

- —Harry Orsman, *A Dictionary of Modern New Zealand Slang*, 1999

dead man's pull-ups *noun*

an exercise in which a person hangs with their arms extended from a bar, lifts their chin over the bar and then lowers themself to the full arm-extended position *US*

- Her hands had looked like chopped sirloin from all the training, until at last she could pump out twenty. All the way down. All the way up. Dead man's pull-ups.—Joseph Wambaugh, *Floaters*, p. 140, 1996

dead man's rounds *noun*

ammunition held pointed toward the bearer *US*

- —Linda Reinberg, *In the Field*, p. 58, 1991

dead man's zone; dead Marine zone *noun*

a demilitarised zone *US*

Back-formation from the initials DMZ.

- —Linda Reinberg, *In the Field*, p. 58, 1991

dead marine *noun*

an empty bottle *AUSTRALIA, 1854*

- So they drank, and the dead marines mounted up in the corner, where Roie's clothes had once hung.—Ruth Park, *Poor Man's Orange*, p. 152, 1949
- —Jim Ramsay, *Cop It Sweet!*, p. 28, 1977

dead meat *noun*

1 used for expressing a very high degree of trouble *US, 1974*

Originally applied only in situations where death was certain, but then softened to include lesser consequences.

- 'You're dead meat,' I said.—Armistead Maupin, *Maybe the Moon*, p. 179, 1992
- It's a good thing you had that plane ticket to get out of the country. You'd be dead meat for sure here.—C.D. Payne, *Youth in Revolt*, p. 347, 1993
- "He's fuckin' dead meat!" [...] They are using the domestic implements to beat a third prisoner, who cowers in a cell doorway. "He's fuckin' dead meat!" "Nonce [a sex-offender]! He's fuckin' dead meat!"— *The Guardian*, 29th January 2001: 'A life inside'

2 a prostitute *UK, 1961*

An allusion to the flesh that is sold in a butcher's shop, as opposed to that which is freshly given.

dead money *noun*

1 obviously counterfeit paper money *US*

• —*American Speech*, p. 100, May 1956: 'Smugglers' argot in the southwest'

2 in poker, money bet by a player who has withdrawn from a hand *US*

• —Edwin Silberstang, *Winning Poker for the Serious Player*, p. 218, 1992

deadner *noun*

a blow, a thump *IRELAND*

• The other punch was known as the deadner. You formed a fist, the middle knuckle slightly raised, and you punched your victim high up on the outside of the arm, aiming for a nerve. —Bernard Share, *Slanguage*, p. 81, 2003

dead-nuts *adverb*

completely *US, 1887*

• I catch you dead nuts in the middle of the act, you don't even act nervous or anything. —Elmore Leonard, *Swag*, p. 9, 1976
• Ordinarily Marine Corps noncoms were dead-nuts certain about everything. Even when they were wrong. —Stephen Coonts, *Victory*, p. 436, 2003

deado *noun*

a corpse *US, 1919*

• —David Craig, *Faith, Hope and Death*, 1976

deado; dead-oh *adjective*

deep asleep; unconscious *UK*

Possibly from the earlier sense (very drunk), however **DEAD** in 'dead drunk' serves as an intensifier, whereas the sense here may be a literal allusion.

dead-on *adjective*

accurate *UK, 1889*

Used by Brendan Behan, *Borstal Boy*, 1958.

• I'll do a dead-on Kingfish voice as O.J. [Simpson][.] —Howard Stern, *Miss America*, p. 138, 1995

dead on arrival *noun*

1 heroin *UK, 1998*

From official jargon for those who are delivered to hospital too late.

• [S]lang [names for heroin] draws on words associated with death ("heaven dust", "dead on arrival", " hell dust")[.] —Robert Ashton, *This Is Heroin*, p. 55, 2002
• —Mike Haskins, *Drugs*, p. 283, 2003

2 phencyclidine, the recreational drug known as PCP or angel dust *US*

In honour of the drug's fatal overdose potential.

• —Peter Johnson, *Dictionary of Street Alcohol and Drug Terms*, p. s, 1993

dead pan *noun*

a complete lack of facial emotion *US, 1927*

• The more effective technique is dead pan. —Madeleine L'Engle, *Walking on Water*, p. 184, 1980

deadpan *adjective*

without expression; displaying no emotion *US, 1928*

• With his sunken cheeks, deadpan kisser and wig that looked like a Fuller brush, he used to give us hysterics up on the bandstand[.] —Mezz Mezzrow, *Really the Blues*, p. 85, 1946

dead pigeon *noun*

1 in a criminal enterprise, a double-crosser *US*

• —R. Frederick West, *God's Gambler*, p. 225, 1964: 'Appendix A'

2 a person who is destined to lose *US, 1919*

• Well, sir, Mary is a dead pigeon, the way I see it, and Barney goes for that kind of case. —Herman Wouk, *The Caine Mutiny*, p. 377, 1951

dead pony gaff *noun*

of circus and fairgrounds, a bad site *UK, 1961*

Used by travelling showmen.

dead presidents *noun*

US currency notes of any dollar denomination; hence, generically, US money *US, 1944*

From the portraits of Washington, Lincoln, Hamilton etc., printed on the different value notes.

• —Lou Shelly, *Hepcats Jive Talk Dictionary*, p. 23, 1945
• Say, if you overhear some conversation about "a lot of dead Presidents," don't phone J. Edgar. It's accepted American slang for money – especially bills. Broadway's Gentleman Georgie Solotaire coined it. It's catching on all over. —*San Francisco Examiner*, p. 24, 17th December 1952
• Then after everything is nice and groovy we just sit down and knock out a couple of those good old goone ones and pry Jimmy Vann loose from some of them dead presidents. —Ross Russell, *The Sound*, p. 191, 1961
• I say, 'Bitch, what about those dead Presidents?' —Christina and Richard Milner, *Black Players*, p. 87, 1972
• "If I see you again," Slick had told her, "it better be behind a pile of dead Presidents. Take a load of Jacksons and Grants get you off my shit list, girl." —John Sayles, *Union Dues*, p. 181, 1977
• [L]eave my residence / Thinkin how could I get some dead presidents / I need money, I used to be a stick-up kid[.] —Eric B. and Rakim, *Paid in Full*, 1987
• Maurice, the Blue Note's manager, no matter how often or eloquently he promised a bonus percentage of gross receipts over a certain figure, always kicked the same lousy fifty dead presidents across the bar at closing. —Seth Morgan, *Homeboy*, p. 13, 1990
• Infotech is worth too many dead presidents for the backlash to bite. —Melanie McGrath, *Hard, Soft & Wet*, p. 129, 1998

dead rabbit *noun*

the penis in a flaccid state *US*

• —Roger Blake, *The American Dictionary of Sexual Terms*, p. 54, 1964

dead ring *noun*

an exact likeness *AUSTRALIA, 1915*

• —Dymphna Cusack, *Picnic Races*, p. 201, 1962
• God knows you're the dead ring of her in everything[.] —Wilda Moxham, *The Apprentice*, p. 52, 1969

dead ringer *noun*

an exact likeness *US, 1891*

• He had black hair, combed up in a pompadour; an oily, showbiz smile plastered across a jowly face and was a dead ringer for Tommy Lee Jones. —Robert G. Barrett, *The Wind and the Monkey*, p. 150, 1999
• The vicar's little daughter is a dead ringer for Drew Barrymore from E.T. —*The Observer*, 15th September 2002

dead road *noun*

MDMA, the recreational drug best known as ecstasy *UK*

• —Mike Haskins, *Drugs*, p. 289, 2003

dead set; dead-set; deadset *adjective*

complete, utter *AUSTRALIA*

• I'm a real crusader against stomach acid, got a dead-set cure for it: Quick-Eze. —Frank Hardy, *The Yarns of Billy Borker*, p. 119, 1965
• —Barry Humphries, *A Nice Night's Entertainment*, p. 147, 1974
• "Up your arse," says Rogers. "See I told you, a dead set queen." —William Nagel, *The Odd Angry Shot*, p. 12, 1975
• It was a deadset nightmare. —Paul Vautin, *Turn It Up!*, p. 50, 1995
• Now there was an old codger in Jerusalem named Simeon who was a dead-set good bloke. —Kel Richards, *The Aussie Bible*, p. 15, 2003

dead set; dead-set; deadset *adverb*

1 completely, utterly *AUSTRALIA*

From the common collocation of 'dead completely' and 'set against/for/on' (determined (not) to do or have happen). The Lindsay quotation can be read either as a collocation or an adverb and perhaps represents the period of grammatical and semantic transition.

• My mother's dead set against girls going walks with boys at night. —Norman Lindsay, *Halfway to Anywhere*, p. 110, 1947
• I don't believe this. I dead set, fair dinkum, don't bloody well believe it. —Robert G. Barrett, *Davo's Little Something*, p. 205, 1992

2 really; honestly *AUSTRALIA*

• We 're going to make a killing. Just for the extra time it takes to get there. We've got enough fuel. Dead set. —Rodney Hall, *Kisses of the Enemy*, p. 10, 1987
• Youse two should sing topless. Then you'd make some moolah. I would. Deadset. —Kathy Lette, *Girls' Night Out*, p. 76, 1987
• He raised an open palm, swearing an oath. "This isn't down to us, dead set." —Shane Maloney, *Nice Try*, p. 178, 1988
• Dead-set, the whole thing looked off to me. —Roy Slaven (John Doyle), *Five South Coast Seasons*, p. 129, 1992
• Red hair all over the place, I deadset thought it was Ronald McDonald who walked into the bank to share my teller's box back in 1979. —Paul Vautin, *Turn It Up*, p. 131, 1995

deadshit *noun*

a despicable person *AUSTRALIA*

• And you can tell him if he don't come up with some cash, I'll trace the deadshit through the Red Cross and leave a little bundle of joy on his doorstep, quickfuckinsmart. —Geoff Mill, *Nobody Dies But Me*, p. 122, 1961
• As a young journalist I'd been told many stories of Horne the deadshit and Horne the right-wing polemicist. —Frank Moorhouse, *Days of Wine and Rage*, p. 109, 1976

- As I slammed the drawers of the filing cabinet, I told Aussie where I kept him filed – under D for deadshit. —Kathy Lette, *Girls' Night Out*, p. 106, 1986

dead skin *noun*
the white inner peel of an orange *BAHAMAS*
- —John A. Holm, *Dictionary of Bahamian English*, p. 59, 1982

dead sled *noun*
in the used car business, a car in extremely poor condition *US*
- For the last two weeks, Beano had been selling dead-sleds and junkers to unsuspecting blue hairs at Bob's Auto Ranch. —Stephen Cannell, *Big Con*, p. 28, 1997

dead soldier *noun*
an empty alcohol bottle or beer can *US, 1899*
- First toast: "May the war be over before this bottle becomes a dead soldier." —*San Francisco Chronicle*, p. 24, 29th June 1966
- My foot struck a bottle. I looked down. It was the dead gin soldier. —Iceberg Slim (Robert Beck), p. 128, 1969
- Dead soldiers of all cheap and barely legal brands were kicked into the corners[.] —Earl Thompson, *Tattoo*, p. 23, 1974
- The last can was crushed and wedged between the ceiling and the aluminum pyramid below to give the shaky structure support. Bull's Eye called it dead soldier's wall. —Jack W. Thomas, *Heavy Number*, p. 23, 1976
- Nother dead soldier and the brandy's near touching bottom. —Elmore Leonard, *Cat Chaser*, p. 13, 1982

dead spit *noun*
an exact likeness of *UK, 1901*
- She was a lovely girl. Dead spit of Beryl, she was. —Alexander Buzo, *Norm and Ahmed*, p. 23, 1969
- A parcel of Italians, the dead spit of their Mario, talked and laughed[.] —Wilda Moxham, *The Apprentice*, p. 85, 1969
- —Jim Ramsay, *Cop It Sweet!*, p. 28, 1977
- [George] Clooney, playing an escaped southern convict is a dead spit for Errol Flynn. —*The Guardian*, 15th May 2000

dead-stick *verb*
to land an aircraft without engine function *US, 1962*
- My only alternative was to dead-stick the plane into the chilly waters. —Bob Hoove, *Forever Flying*, p. 29, 1996

dead-stick *adjective*
(used of landing an aircraft) without engine function *US*
- The dead-stick ditching of a plane into the ocean wasn't something you could practice; you had to get it right the first time. —Elgen M. Long, *Amelia Earhart*, p. 30, 1999

Dead threads *noun*
in the language surrounding the Grateful Dead, the layers of clothes worn by a concert-goer *US*
- —David Shenk and Steve Silberman, *Skeleton Key*, p. 59, 1994

dead time *noun*
time served in jail which does not count towards fulfilment of the prisoner's sentence *US*
- It ain't dead time no more like it used to be. Now they give a man all the time he spends in the county jail. —Donald Goines, *White Man's Justice, Black Man's Grief*, p. 32, 1973

dead to rights
denoting an absolute certainty that fully justifies arrest on a criminal charge, as when caught red-handed *UK, 1859*
DEAD intensifies 'to rights' (fairly, legally).
- We got you dead to rights! —*The Sweeney*, p. 43, 1976

dead to the world *adjective*
unconscious, deeply and soundly asleep; unaware of any outside stimulus *UK, 1899*
Earlier use may also have connoted 'drunk'.
- Zen was dead to the world. Under the next umbrella, Massimo Rutelli was just dead. —Michael Dibdin, *And The You Die*, 2002

dead tree format
printed on paper *UK, mid-1990s →*
- We're putting out this newsletter about freedom. It's only in dead tree format presently, but Greg wants it up on the Net too. —Melanie McGrath, *Hard, Soft & Wet*, p. 119, 1998

dead trouble *noun*
an extremely difficult situation, deep trouble *UK, 1971*
- [I]n a few years' time, if someone like Mrs Young were going to a university that would be charging the £1,900 top-up fees, "she would be in dead trouble". —*BBC News Online*, 4th July 2003

dead 'un *noun*
1 unoccupied premises *UK*
Criminal use.
- [A]n ex-member of the Surrey constabulary who had been nicked for screwing dead-uns on his beat. —Charles Raven, *Underworld Nights*, p. 186, 1956

2 a racehorse deliberately ridden to lose *AUSTRALIA, 1877*
- More rumours of rigged races, bought jockeys, "dead 'uns" and the like circulated. —James Holledge, *The Great Australian Gamble*, p. 33, 1966
- 'You dirty little mug,' the undertaker said, 'you pulled that horse up on me.' The jockey replied: 'What are you going crook about? You have been getting money out of dead'uns all your life.' —Frank Hardy and Athol George Mulley, *The Needy and the Greedy*, p. 75, 1975

deadwood *noun*
1 an incompetent or otherwise useless person *US, 1887*
- He'd have a lot of deadwood to clear out, or put some sap back into 'em. —Jim Thompson, *The Grifters*, p. 122, 1963
- Luke Zigman was surprised to see the old deadwood player being rolled by into the casino by his nephew at three in the morning. —Stephen Cannell, *Big Con*, p. 224, 1997

2 a flaccid penis *US*
Extended from WOOD (the erect penis).
- —*Adult Video News*, p. 51, October 1995

3 unsold tickets for a performance *US, 1934*
- —Wilfred Granville, *The Theater Dictionary*, p. 54, 1952
- —Joe McKennon, *Circus Lingo*, p. 30, 1980

4 non-playing observers of gambling *US*
- —John Scarne, *Scarne on Dice*, p. 482, 1974

5 a person caught outright commiting a crime *US*
- —William K. Bentley and James M. Corbett, *Prison Slang*, p. 92, 1992

dead yard *noun*
a ceremony after burial in the deceased's yard *JAMAICA*
- —Peter L. Patrick, *Some Recent Jamaican Creole Words*, 2003

deaf and dumb *noun*
the buttocks, the backside, the anus *UK*
Rhyming slang for BUM.
- [S]omeone offering anything that is unwanted may be told to "Shove it up your deaf and dumb". Or it may be used in glowing terms of reference, e.g., "She's got a lovely little deaf and dumb." —Ray Puxley, *Cockney Rabbit*, 1992

deafie *noun*
a deaf person *TRINIDAD AND TOBAGO, 1972*
Prominently applied to Dr Eric Williams, Prime Minister of Trinidad from 1956 until 1981.
- —Lise Winer, *Dictionary of the English/Creole of Trinidad & Tobago*, 2003

deal *noun*
1 a business transaction, a trade or a bargain *US, 1838*
- Around 10% comes from licensing and merchandising deals – such as Lego's Willams cars and Puma's Jordan-branded products. —*The Guardian*, 22nd February 2002

2 an underhand or secret transaction; a trade of questionable legality; a mutually beneficial commercial or political arrangement *US, 1881*
A nuance of the broader sense (a trade, a bargain).
- It would have to be at the end a deal, which guarantees some independence for a large chunk of the ethnic Albanian population. —*The Guardian*, 18th April 1999

3 a small amount of marijuana or hashish *UK*
- —Home Office, *Glossary of Terms and Slang Common in Penal Establishments*, 1978

▸ **bad deal; raw deal; rough deal**
ill-treatment, exploitative or unfair usage; a swindle *US, 1912*
- You got yourself a load of trouble now / You got yourself a bad deal / You say I've got a bad attitude / How d'you think I feel? —Deep Purple, *Bad Attitude*, 1987
- But I think the working classes get a rough deal whoever gets in [elected]: we tend to get overlooked. —*The Observer*, 13th May 2001
- MNCs' raw deal to shareholders. —*The Times of India*, 9th June 2003

▸ **fair deal; square deal**
an honest and equitable usage *US, 1876*
The *locus classicus* of 'square deal' is in a speech delivered by US President Theodore Roosevelt in 1903: 'We must treat each man on his worth and merits as a man. We must see that each is given

a square deal, because he is entitled to no more and should receive no less'.
- It's a fair deal. Students benefit from their education – why shouldn't they give something back after they graduate? — *The Observer*, 26th January 2003
- Overtime rules not a square deal. — *Middletown Journal (Ohio)*, 16th July 2003

▸ **new deal**
a new arrangement *US, 1834*
- New deal for jobless gets cash to carry on . — *The Guardian*, 18th July 2000

▸ **the deal; the real deal**
the very best *US*
- — Connie Eble (Editor), *UNC-CH Campus Slang*, p. 3, Fall 1986

deal *verb*
1 to sell drugs *US, 1958*
- Frankie has been dealing for six years without a bust. — Abbie Hoffman, *Woodstock Nation*, p. 66, 1969
- We are all outlaws in the eyes of America / In order to survive we steal cheat lie forge fuck hide and deal — Jefferson Airplane, *We Can Be Together*, 1970
- Seems like dealing is all I'm good at, so be it. — Edwin Torres, *Carlito's Way*, p. 66, 1975
- The fuzz dug everybody dealing. — Babs Gonzales, *Movin' On Down De Line*, p. 81, 1975
- DANTE: How many times I gotta tell you not to deal outside the store. JAY: I'm not dealing. KID: You got anything, man? JAY: Yeah, what do you want? — *Clerks*, 1994

2 to supervise the blackjack game in a casino *US*
- How many games do you deal? — Lee Solkey, *Dummy Up and Deal*, p. 111, 1980

▸ **deal off the top**
to treat fairly *US*
From the gambling scheme of cheating by dealing off the bottom of a deck.
- After I had been in town six months, fate dealt me one off the top for a change. — Iceberg Slim (Robert Beck), *Pimp*, p. 288, 1969

deal *adverb*
much *UK, 1756*
After the noun sense (a considerable amount).
- [I]if there was, results would be a deal better. — *The Guardian*, 18th June 2003

dealer's band *noun*
an elastic band used by a drug dealer to secure or to facilitate the jetisoning of drugs for sale *US*
- Many addicts – especially pushers – wear a rubber band on their wrists (a dealer's band, some call it) which, if hooked properly around a deck of heroin, will send it flying if an approaching detective is spotted. — James Mills, *The Panic in Needle Park*, p. 15, 1966

dealy *noun*
a thing the correct name of which escapes or is not important to the speaker *US*
- — Pamela Munro, *U.C.L.A. Slang*, p. 59, 2001

dean *noun*
1 a shark *AUSTRALIA*
- — Gary Fairmont R. Filosa II, *The Surfer's Almanac*, p. 184, 1977

2 a skilled and experienced poker player *US*
- — John Scarne, *Scarne's Guide to Modern Poker*, p. 277, 1979

deaner; deener; dener; diener *noun*
a shilling *UK, 1857*
Until decimalisation in 1971; probably from *denier* (a French coin, the twelth part of a sou). After the introduction of decimal currency in Australia in 1966, it came to mean a ten cent piece, or its value, a similar coin with about the same comparative value; dying out from the 1980s, now seldom heard.
- An' while yez are fillin' up, Bill's goin' round collectin' subs. Ten deaners a head. — Nino Culotta (John O'Grady), *They're A Weird Mob*, p. 118, 1957
- 'I'll bet a deener you wouldn't go pickin' on young Temple the way y'hammer jokers like me,' he said darkly. — W.R Bennett, *Wingman*, p. 98, 1961
- An' that redhead up there gives me three bob. Three lousy little deaners sittin' there in me hand. — Nino Culotta (John O'Grady), *Gone Fishin*, p. 124, 1962
- Whatever the complaint is, you can lay an even deener Sloppy has had it. — John Wynnum, *Tar Dust*, p. 118, 1962
- He [Prime Minister Keating] said his income tax cuts were designed to put some extra deeners in the pocket of the bloke who was willing to get off his backside and earn a few extra bucks. — *Sun-Herald*, p. 15, 16th June 1985
- — Paul Baker, *Polari*, p. 171, 2002

dean of men *noun*
a prison warden *US*
- — Vincent J. Monteleone, *Criminal Slang*, p. 66, 1949

dear!; oh dear!; dear oh dear!
used as a mild register of anxiety, irritation, regret, etc *UK, 1694*
Probably 'dear God!' or 'dear Lord!'.
- Cor dear oh dear. Not in my ear, please. You frightened the life out of me. — Ray Galton and Alan Simpson, *Hancock's Half Hour*, 22nd April 1958
- Oh drat is the coffee delayed? Oh dear. Oh yeh. — Mike Stott, *Soldiers Talking, Cleanly*, 1978
- Oh dear, what a time to pick a war with Murdoch. — *The Observer*, 4th November 2001

dear dear!
used as a mild exclamation or oath; often used to add a mild or ironic emphasis to what is being said *UK, 1849*
By reduplication of **DEAR!**.
- [T]here she is, slagging him off left right and centre ... dear dear dear, what is this country coming to when a defenceless disabled person is attacked in this way? Oh deary deary dear. — Damon Rose, *Ouch!*, 7th March 2003

dear dyin' Moses!
used as an elaborate, original curse in coastal Nova Scotia *CANADA*
- — Lewis Poteet, *The South Shore Phrase Book*, p. 37, 1999

dearg *noun*
a stab or a shot, a sharp punch *IRELAND*
- He gave him the dearg — *North Munster Antiquarian Journal*, 2000

dear heart *noun*
used as a term of address *UK*
Often conveys sarcasm, or may be affectedly theatrical.
- "Dear heart," I said [...] "how nice of you to call." — Martin Waddell, *Otley*, p. 135, 1966
- Yep, she walked in about the time he mounted one of his lady patients, and asked him, "What's this, dear heart, your famous meat injection?" — Ken Weaver, *Texas Crude*, p. 108, 1984

dearie *noun*
1 used by women as a form of address *UK, 1681*
A less intimate variation of conventional 'dear' (a loved one).
- I hope you're enjoying your fags, I said. I'm enjoying them a treat, dearie. That's what old Beth says. — Geoffrey Fletcher, *Down Among the Meths Men*, p. 35, 1966

2 used as an affected form of address among male homosexuals *UK*
Camp adoption of the previous sense.
- Don't ask me what it was, dearie; it certainly wasn't art. — Derek Raymond (Robin Cook), *The Crust on its Uppers*, p. 31, 1962
- Lee touched his sweater. "Sweet stuff, dearie," he said. — William Burroughs, *Queer*, p. 53, 1985

dearie me!; deary me!
used for registering regret *UK, 1785*
An elaboration of **DEAR ME!** that is more sorrowful in tone.
- Another import we want to rebuff, dearie me yes, is European culture. — Andrew Nickolds, *Back to Basics*, p. 83, 1994
- Did I really say that? Dearie me, what a toss. — James Hawes, *Dead Long Enough*, p. 300, 2000

Dear Jane *noun*
a letter to a girlfriend or wife breaking off the relationship *US*
- Oh, you mean the "Dear Jane" routine? — Clarence Cooper Jr, *Black*, p. 64, 1963

Dear John; Dear John letter; Johnny letter *noun*
a letter from a woman to her husband or boyfriend ending their relationship *US, 1945*
- She left me about a year ago. I got a Dear John. — Norman Mailer, *Naked and Dead*, p. 316, 1948
- — *American Speech*, p. 303, December 1955: 'Wayne university slang'
- 389 pieces of mail (which included one birth announcement and three Dear Johns) received. — Charles Anderson, *The Grunts*, p. 121, 1976
- She wrote him a Dear John last month. — Gerald Petievich, *Money Men*, p. 39, 1981
- Hey, Crutcher, I hear you got a Dear John from your gal. — *Platoon*, 1986
- They all tensed up. They knew the sound well. Someone receiving a Dear John letter[.] — Odie Hawkins, *Great Lawd Buddha*, p. 44, 1990
- Aboard the nuclear-powered carrier USS Theodore Roosevelt, with a crew of 5,000, the chaplains spent hours last Sunday night counseling men who'd received one version or another of the dreaded "Dear John" lettter. — *Washington Times*, 1st February 1991

- —Angela Devlin, *Prison Patter*, p. 66, 1996
- In Baghdad, the worst of the fighting over and the soldiers bunking in a former train station, the mail watch began again. A letter arrived for Tielbar and he recognized it wasn't what he'd hoped. It was a "Dear John" letter. She couldn't wait any longer. —*Hartford (Connecticut) Courant*, p. 6, 9th November 2003

dear me!
used as a mild exclamation or oath; often used to add a mild or ironic emphasis *UK, 1773*
- John McEnroe, who had to work himself into a raging fury just to compare an umpire to an armpit. Dear me, if he'd ever called somebody poo-poo pants he'd have likely exploded. —*The Guardian*, 28th June 2003

dear old thing *noun*
▷ see: OLD THING

death *noun*
1 paramethoxyamphetamine or 4-methoxyamphetamine (PMA), a synthetic hallucinogen *AUSTRALIA*
- Known on the streets as "Death", PMA looks like Ecstasy and has similar effects, but it is a chemical killing machine. —*Glasgow Herald (Australia)*, 23rd August 1997
- I know Es are lethal and kill people, but not like this drug does. It's nicknamed "Death", for God's sake. —Wayne Anthony, *Spanish Highs*, p. 78, 1999

2 someone or something that is exquisitely perfect *US, 1965*
- David Frazer said she was death. —*Diner*, 1982
- — Levi Straus & Company, *Campus Slang*, p. 2, January 1986
- —Trevor Cralle, *The Surfin'ary*, p. 28, 1991

3 a difficult situation, such as an exam, a hangover, etc *US*
- —Connie Eble (Editor), *UNC-CH Campus Slang*, p. 3, Fall 1987

4 in harness racing, the position just behind and outside the leader *US*
Because the horse in that position has to travel farther than horses on the inside and does not have the benefit of a lead horse breaking the wind resistance.

▸ **at the death**
in the finish *UK*
Figurative sense of a conventional 'end'.
- I persuade him at the death[.] —Derek Raymond (Robin Cook), *The Crust on its Uppers*, p. 55, 1962

▸ **like death; like death warmed up**
feeling or appearing extremely unwell *UK, 1939*
- —John Wynnum, *Tar Dust*, p. 105, 1962
- Won't be a move outta 'im fer today anyhow. Right now he looks like death warmed up. —John Wynnum, *Tar Dust*, p. 105, 1962
- —John O'Grady, *It's Your Shout, Mate!*, p. 53, 1972
- [L]eaving some of the Leicester players "looking like death warmed up with the shock". —William Fotheringham, *The Guardian*, 7th April 2003
- I'm coming off the tablets and I'm going to feel like death, so don't ask me to do anything. —Michele Kirsch, *The Observer*, 3rd February 2003

▸ **to death**
1 to the extreme; superlative *UK*
- At home, Mum had my little sister Sherry and I loved her to death. —Lenny McLean, *The Guv'nor*, p. 19, 1998
- —Gary K. Farlow, *Prison-ese*, p. 74, 2002

2 frequently and *ad nauseum* *UK, 1937*
- [W]hen you're a writer you've got to look hard for new experiences. Coke and smackalogues have been done to death. —*The Guardian*, 23rd February 2002

death adder; death adder man *noun*
an unwelcoming man who lives a solitary life in the Australian outback *AUSTRALIA, 1951*
From the name given to several species of venomous snake found in Australia. Historically 'an outback gossip' was also known as a 'death adder'.
- These solitary men are usually known as hatters. Some of them go under the name of death adder men, for it is reckoned they will bite your head off if spoken to before noon. —Jock Marshall and Russell Drysdale, *Journey Among Men*, p. 56, 1962

death adders *noun*
▸ **have death adders in your pockets**
to be stingy *AUSTRALIA*
- Why doancher buy a drink? Get them death adders outa ya pockets. —Lawson Glassop, *We Were The Rats*, p. 118, 1944

death ball *noun*
in cricket, any bowled-delivery that takes a wicket *UK, 1996*
- —Keith Foley, *A Dictionary of Cricketing Terminology*, p. 98, 1998

death benefit *noun*
in poker, money given to a player to complete a bet *US*
- —John Vorhaus, *The Big Book of Poker Slang*, p. 12, 1996

death box; fun box *noun*
in snowboarding and skateboarding, an improvised hollow platform such as a wooden or plasic box or barrel, from which to bounce the board *US*
- —Jim Humes and Sean Wagstaff, *Boarderlands*, p. 222, 1995
- A teenager has just leapt onto my box with his skateboard and he's giving me dirty looks. "I think you might be sitting on a death box," said the American dad. "It's part of the equipment." —*The Times*, p. 16, 26th April 2003

death cookie *noun*
in snowboarding, a rock hidden in snow *US*
- —Jim Humes and Sean Wagstaff, *Boarderlands*, p. 221, 1995

death drinker *noun*
a vagrant alcoholic *UK*
- Today's vagrant drinkers of Spitalfields, Stepney, Camden, Waterloo and parts of Islington, are known as the "death drinkers". —Peter Ackroyd, *London The Biography*, p. 359, 2000

death drop *noun*
butyl chloride when taken recreationally *UK, 1984*

death metal; deathcore *noun*
a category of heavy metal music that draws on violent, blasphemous and mysogynistic imagery *UK, 1992*
- Slayer and others in the industry have developed sophisticated strategies to sell death metal music to adolescent boys. —*The Guardian*, 24th January 2001

death mitten *noun*
bags slipped over the hands of murder victims to preserve evidence *US*
- Death mittens, in case something's under the nails. You know, like hair, skin, from a struggle. —Richard Price, *Clockers*, p. 137, 1992

death on call *noun*
Battery C, 4th Battalion, 77th Infantry of the US Army *US*
A gunship unit with the boast of 'kill by profession'.
- —Gregory Clark, *Words of the Vietnam War*, p. 136–137, 1990

death on truckers *noun*
the US Department of Transportation *US*
From the agency's initials: DOT.
- —Montie Tak, *Truck Talk*, p. 41, 1971

death pen *noun*
a designated pen with black indelible ink used in hospitals for filling out death certificates *US*
- —Sally Williams, *"Strong" Words*, p. 138, 1994

death rattle *noun*
in cricket, the noise made when a batsman's wicket is hit by the ball *UK, 1958*
- —Keith Foley, *A Dictionary of Cricketing Terminology*, p. 98, 1998

death rim *noun*
any expensive car wheel rim *US, 1995*
The rim is an invitation to crime and violence, hence the name.
- —*American Speech*, p. 303, Fall 1996: 'Among the new words'

death row *noun*
a type of bet in an illegal numbers game lottery *US*
- Then to be on the safe side he also played jail house, death row, lady come back, two-timing woman, pile of rocks, dark days and trouble. —Chester Himes, *A Rage in Harlem*, p. 23, 1957

death seat *noun*
1 the front passenger seat of a car or truck *US*
From the probability, actual or notional, that the passenger is the least likely to survive an accident.
- [Y]es, he was sitting in the death seat I think you call it in the insur, the phrase they used in the paper that is to say beside the driver. —William Gaddis, *JR*, p. 239, 1975
- I could tell Franny had taken the wheel when the car began to careen between the trees, great slithers of the spring mud flying – and the wild, half-seen gestures of Frank's arms waving in what is popularly called the death seat. —John Irving, *The Hotel New Hampshire*, p. 199, 1981

2 in a trotting race, the position on the outside of the leader *AUSTRALIA, 1982*
Derives from the difficulty of overtaking from such a position.

death spiral *noun*
a downward spiral of an aeroplane from which recovery is nearly impossible and as a result of which impact with the ground is inevitable *US*
- The two, in the course of the fight, found themselves in what some call "the death spiral." —Robert K. Wilcox, *Scream of Eagles*, p. 157, 1990

death tourist *noun*
a person who travels to a country where euthanasia is legal for the purpose of achieving a medically assisted suicide *US*
- Assisted suicides are legal in Switzerland but not in the UK, making the country a draw for "death tourists." — *CNN*, 20th January 2003

death trip *noun*
1 LSD enhanced with botanical drugs from plants such as Deadly Nightshade or Jimsonweed *US*
- —William D. Alsever, *Glossary for the Establishment and Other Uptight People*, p. 3, December 1970

2 heroin *UK*
- Ecstasy is "disco biscuits" and "happiness", heroin is "death trip". —Robert Ashton, *This Is Heroin*, p. 55, 2002

3 a fascination with death *US, 1969*
- The herding tribes gradually overran the feminist states, replacing the Great Mother with God the Father, substituting the Christian death trip for the pagan glorification of life. —Tom Robbins, *Even Cowgirls Get the Blues*, p. 331, 1976

death watch *noun*
attendance upon a man condemned to death *UK*
Hanging was institutionalised in C5 Britain; the death penalty was abolished in the UK in November 1965 – except for the crimes of treason, piracy with violence and arson in Royal Dockyards.
- —Paul Tempest, *Lag's Lexicon*, 1950

death wish *noun*
phencyclidine, the recreational drug known as PCP or angel dust *US*
- —Richard A. Spears, *The Slang and Jargon of Drugs and Drink*, p. 138, 1986

deathy *noun*
a death adder *AUSTRALIA*
- —Sidney H. Courtier, *The Glass Spear*, 1951

deazingus *noun*
a dingus, or eye dropper, used in drug injecting *US*
- Deazingus taken from a carnival grifter's usage and an example of cezarney, an argot based on phonetic distortion. —David Maurer and Victor Vogel, *Narcotics and Narcotic Addiction*, p. 402, 1973

deb *noun*
1 a *deb*utante *US, 1920*
- [A]ll the debs and dowagers let their hair down and danced[.] —Charles Raven, *Underworld Nights*, p. 102, 1956
- You'll meet her. She's one of the debs I invited over. —Dan Jenkins, *Life Its Ownself*, p. 127, 1984

2 a girl associated with a youth gang, either directly as a member or through a boyfriend *US, 1946*
A lovely if ironic borrowing from 'debutante'.
- The Debs and Sub-Debs are usually from 50 to 500 feet behind the warriors. —Jack Lait and Lee Mortimer, *New York Confidential*, p. 106, 1948
- —Vincent J. Monteleone, *Criminal Slang*, p. 67, 1949
- Why isn't she like the rest of the debs in the gang, or any other girl? —Hal Ellson, *Tomboy*, p. 2, 1950
- Each gang has its following of girls. In some cases, they are organized into ladies' auxiliaries – usually called "debs." Sometimes, the debs constitute a fighting gang which engages in combat with other girl gangs. —Harrison E. Salisbury, *The Shook-up Generation*, p. 31, 1958
- She's the head guy's deb. You stick your nose in there any more, the Mau Maus'll slice it off. — *Man's Magazine*, p. 12, February 1960
- Our debs sat on the stoops watching for the fuzz or for any wrong shit from the Jolly Rogers. —Piri Thomas, *Down These Mean Streets*, p. 52, 1967
- I want you to take over absolute control of all the debs until Ruby is released. Your main job will be to see that most of the girls lead at least two tricks a night someplace where the boys can roll them without too much trouble. —Donald Goines, *Black Gangster*, p. 35–36, 1977

3 a depressant, sedative or tranquillizer tablet *US, 1975*
From a slovenly pronunciation of 'deps' (depressants); also recorded in the plural.
- —Richard A. Spears, *The Slang and Jargon of Drugs and Drink*, p. 138, 1986

4 a tablet or capsule of amphetamine *UK*
A reversal of the chemical effect in the earlier usage; also noted as a plural.
- —Mike Haskins, *Drugs*, p. 279, 2003

5 a tablet of MDMA, the recreational drug best known as ecstasy *UK*
- —Mike Haskins, *Drugs*, p. 289, 2003

debag *verb*
to remove someone's trousers, often with humorous intention, always with some degree of force *UK, 1914*
From **BAGS** (trousers).
- After being caught, debagged, and ducked in a fountain, he gave up[.] —Charles Raven, *Underworld Nights*, p. 15, 1956

deball *verb*
to castrate *US, 1961*
- I'll gut and deball the old bastard if he's touched you. —Keri Hulme, *The Bone People*, p. 137, 1983
- We're a rock & roll group; or at least, we used to be until you came round and tried to deball us. —Larry Kirwan, *Liverpool Fantasy*, p. xiv, 203

debaucherama *noun*
an orgy *UK*
Combines conventional 'debauch' with a variation of the suffix '-orama' (indicates largeness).
- Makes sense they'd put a tail on me at a debaucherama like that, I suppose, and unfortunately I didn't disappoint. —Christopher Brookmyre, *Boiling a Frog*, p. 184, 2000

Debbie Chon *noun*
an overweight soldier *US*
From the Korean; Korean war usage.
- —Frank Hailey, *Soldier Talk*, p. 17, 1982

debone *verb*
to bend a playing card so that it can be identified later in another player's hand *US, 1968*
- —Thomas L. Clark, *The Dictionary of Gambling and Gaming*, p. 60, 1987

debriefing *noun*
an after-flight hotel party attended by a flight crew and flight attendants *US*
- —Rene Foss, *Around the World in a Bad Mood*, p. 35, 2002

debris *noun*
marijauna seeds and stems remaining after cleaning *US*
- —Eugene Landy, *The Underground Dictionary*, p. 64, 1971

debthead *noun*
a prisoner who is continually in debt and, therefore, untrustworthy *UK*
A combination of conventional 'debt' with **-HEAD** (a person considered as a single attribute).
- —Angela Devlin, *Prison Patter*, p. 43, 1996

debtor's colic *noun*
any feigned illness whereby a man can get into hospital, or remain sick in his cell, in order to avoid meeting his creditors *UK*
- Every prison has its bad payers and when these report sick the word goes round that "so-and-so" has debtor's colic. —Paul Tempest, *Lag's Lexicon*, 1950

debts *noun*
in prison, a placing (of an inmate) on report *UK*
- I got my debts for calling that kanga [a warder] a bastard! —Angela Devlin, *Prison Patter*, p. 43, 1996

debug *verb*
1 to clear an area of listening devices *US, 1964*
- "We were first on the scene and concluded that Rove had hired a company to debug his office and the same company had planted the bug[.]" —Lou Dubose, *Boy Genius*, p. 34, 2003

2 to rectify faults of electrical, mechanical or operational nature; to remove faulty programming from a computer *UK, 1945*
- He still has to get the circuit pack, get parts (a nontrivial task), and debug it. —Robert Pease, *Troubleshooting Analog Circuits*, p. 171, 1991

debut *verb*
1 to subject a boy to his first homosexual experience *UK*
- — Anon., *King Smut's Wet Dreams Interpreted*, 1978
- — *Maledicta*, p. 155, Summer/Winter 1986–1987: 'Sexual slang: prostitutes, pedophiles, flagellators, transvestites, and necrophiles'

2 to acknowledge your homosexuality *US*

- —Roger Blake, *The American Dictionary of Sexual Terms*, p. 55, 1964

decadence; deccadence *noun*

MDMA, the recreational drug best known as ecstasy *UK, 1998*

- —Mike Haskins, *Drugs*, p. 289, 2003

decaf *noun*

decaffeinated coffee *US, 1956*

- GUY WITH NECK-SUPPORT: I'll have a decaf coffee. TRUDI: I'll have a decaf espresso. MOVIE CRITIC: I'll have a double decaf cappuccino. POLICEMAN: Give me decaffeinated coffee ice cream. HARRIS K. TELEMACHER: I'll have a half double decaffeinated half-caf, with a twist of lemon.—Steve Martin, *LA Story*, 1991
- I relaxed in the Salvador Allende Community Photography Project Coffee Bar with a cup of decaff and looked at my prints.—John Milne, *Alive and Kicking*, p. 90, 1998
- Bugger it! I hate decaff.—Stuart Browne, *Dangerous Parking*, p. 321, 2000

decaf *adjective*

decaffeinated *US, 1981*

- She stopped all her caffeine sodas and only had one decaf soda a week.—Juliana van Olphen-Fehr, *Diary of a Midwife*, p. 150, 1998

decapitation *noun*

the assassination of a head of state *US*

Media-friendly military jargon.

- American officials described the overnight precision bomb attack as a "decapitation exercise". Such a mission is designed to kill the leadership of a hostile regime, or, as the US officials describe it, to "cut the head off the snake"[.]—*The Guardian*, p. 3, 21st March 2003

decapitation strike *noun*

a military attack intended to kill (or render impotent) an enemy's leader *US*

- —Susie Dent, *The Language Report*, p. 10, 2003

decayed *adjective*

drunk *US*

- —*Current Slang*, p. 2, Fall 1966
- —Helen Dahlskog (Editor), *A Dictionary of Contemporary and Colloquial Usage*, p. 18, 1972

dece *adjective*

exceptionally good, 'wonderful' *UK*

A shortening of '*dec*ent', pronounced 'deece'; noted by Mrs C. Raab, 1977.

decent *adjective*

1 sufficiently dressed for standards of propriety, especially in the phrase 'are you decent?' *UK, 1949*

A specialised sense of 'decent', probably of theatrical origins.

- A sharp knock sounded on the bathroom door, followed by a cheerful "Are you decent?" and just barely preceded by Donovan's entrance into the room.—Kay Hooper, *Kissed by Magic (in Enchanted)*, p. 55, 1983
- Kyle enters Lucy's suite, calling out, "Are you decent?" Discovering she has left for the airport, he muses, "I guess she was."—Roger Ebert, *writing of the film 'Written on the Wind', on the Chicago Sun-Times website*, August 2003

2 good, pleasing, excellent *US*

- —*Detroit Free Press*, 4th November 1979
- —Connie Eble (Editor), *UNC-CH Campus Slang*, p. 3, November 1990
- —Lee McNelis, *30 + And a Wake-Up*, p. 7, 1991

decider *noun*

of a sporting contest, the deciding factor: the final heat, the final set; the winning stroke, the winning run, the winning play *UK, 1883*

From racing, when a 'decider' is a heat run after a dead-heat. Generally used with 'the'.

- Now for the decider. BBC Sport's Alastair Hignell says it is all to play for in the third Test in Sydney.—*BBC Sport*, 9th July 2001

decimated *adjective*

drunk *UK*

- —*e-cyclopaedia*, 20th March 2002

decision *noun*

▸ **take a decision**

in Quebec, to make a decision *CANADA*

This usage is part of the widespread use of Frenglish in Montreal.

- He took the decision himself.—*Montreal Gazette*, p. A1, 27th July 2002

decision *verb*

to win a boxing match by a decision of the judges as opposed to with a knock-out *US*

- One of the boys from the old neighborhood was parkin' the cars on 60th Street (used to be a good pug, had decisioned Bethea in the Garden).—Edwin Torres, *After Hours*, p. 329, 1979

deck *noun*

1 a packet of a powdered drug *US, 1916*

- The stuff is usually paid for in advance, with the peddlers hoping they come through with enough decks to make money on it.—Mickey Spillane, *I, The Jury*, p. 23, 1947
- Now you can pull up in your car in front of a newsdealer there, at any hour, day or night, and place a bet on a horse, buy a deck of junk or get a girl[.]—Jack Lait and Lee Mortimer, *Washington Confidential*, p. 20, 1951
- Once he was too feeble to leave the house and sent me out for a deck of junk.—Ethel Water, *His Eye is on the Sparrow*, p. 148, 1952
- "He promised to let me have some stuff." "What sort of stuff? Reefers?" "No. A deck of H."—Douglas Rutherford, *The Creeping Flesh*, p. 102, 1963
- Many addicts – especially pushers – wear a rubber band on their wrists (a dealer's band, some call it) which, if hooked properly around a deck of heroin, will send it flying if an approaching detective is spotted.—James Mills, *The Panic in Needle Park*, p. 15, 1966
- When we saw him choking, we knew he'd been eating the decks he had on him, so before he could digest them we got enough out of him to convict him of possession anyway.—Chester Himes, *Come Back Charleston Blue*, p. 28, 1966
- Walbert was steady nickel-and-dime decks and street pimpin'.—Edwin Torres, *After Hours*, p. 210, 1979
- Phil Vittimizzare was eating a Danish while he played the pinball machine and two dealers were counting out decks of heroin at a table in the back.—Richard Condon, *Prizzi's Honor*, p. 34, 1982
- She would give me piddling amounts of H. They used to sell it in decks in those days. Instead of glassine bags they'd fold a piece of paper into a little package.—Herbert Huncke, *Guilty of Everything*, p. 31, 1990
- You show me one fucking junkie out there who don't know how you catch the Virus [HIV], I'll buy you a whole deck of heroin, how's that?—Richard Price, *Clockers*, p. 238, 1992
- The man, identified as Reynaldo Colon, 33, of Ridgewood, Queens, approached the detective with a folding Leatherman, a metal-colored multipurpose tool, and said, "Give me the decks," using street slang to refer to the small glassine packages of heroin.—*New York Times*, p. B3, 21st October 2000

2 a packet of cigarettes *US, 1923*

- I sat there until a quarter to nine trying to smoke my way through a deck of Luckies.—Mickey Spillane, *One Lonely Night*, p. 103, 1951
- —*Newsweek*, p. 98, 8th October 1951

3 a phonograph turntable *US*

A critical component of a **DJ** in the modern sense of the term.

- —Judi Sanders, *Da Bomb*, p. 5, 1997

4 the ground *UK, 1836*

- [S]ome mug was laying stark out [spark out] on the deck, with a load of claret pouring out of his mouth.—Frank Norman, *Bang To Rights*, p. 26, 1958

5 in cricket, the pitch *UK, 1995*

- —Keith Foley, *A Dictionary of Cricketing Terminology*, p. 98, 1998

6 a pack of playing cards *UK*

In conventional use from late C16 until about 1720, then dialect and colloquial. In the early part of C20, usage was confined, more or less, to the underworld; from the end of World War 2 it was in common use in the UK and Australia and, by the 1970s, in general and widespread informal use. 'Deck of cards' was a UK number one hit for Max Bygraves in 1973.

- Those of the boys who had a prayer book took them out, but this one boy had only a deck of cards, and so he spread them out.—Tex Ritter, *Deck of Cards*, 1948

deck *verb*

to knock to the ground *US, 1945*

- Irrigated his face with the shot of J and B I'd just poured him. Then I tried to deck the sucker.—*48 Hours*, 1982
- [I]f people weren't performing they'd get decked.—Andy McNab, *Immediate Action*, p. 48, 1995
- Doesn't say a word, walks up and decks the guy and throws him out on the street.—Elmore Leonard, *Be Cool*, p. 183, 1999
- AUNT GERALDINE, a woman in her forties with straw-blonde hair and tattoos up both arms decks the Senior Attendant with one punch.—Guy Ritchie, *Lock, Stock... & Four Stolen Hooves*, p. 38, 2000

deck ape *noun*

an enlisted sailor in the US Navy *US, 1944*

- Deck apes worked in whites, not dungarees.—Earl THompson, *Tattoo*, p. 309, 1974

- Shelby said, "Look at all them lazy deck apes, smokin n' jokin'. Can't tell me anbody works in the navy. I shoulda been a swab." —Joseph Wambaugh, *Finnegan's Week*, p. 39, 1993

decked *adjective*

1 unconscious from abuse of alcohol or drugs *US, 1961*

- —J.E. Lighter, *Historical Dictionary of American Slang, Vol. I*, p. 574, 1994

2 dressed stylishly *US*

- —David Claerbaut, *Black Jargon in White America*, p. 62, 1972

decker *noun*

a look *AUSTRALIA*

- 'Nice office you've got here, Jimmy,' he says taking a decker round the room. —Dal Stivens, *Jimmy Brockett*, p. 65, 1951

deckie *noun*

a deck-hand *UK, 1913*

Nautical.

deck monkey *noun*

a deckhand *US, 1941*

- [T]wo other "deck monkeys" besides himself, who would grind the winches and provide ballast. —Mark L. Friedman, *Everyday Crisis Management*, p. 101, 2002

decknician *noun*

a disc jockey who is admired for skilful manipulation and mixing of music on turntables *UK*

- —Susie Dent, *The Language Report*, p. 44, 2003

decko; dekko *noun*

a look *UK, 1894*

Originally military; from Hindu *dekho* (look) or Romany *dic* (to look).

- She took one dekko at it, knew by instinct it was good[.] —Charles Raven, *Underworld Nights*, p. 23, 1956
- Now let's 'ave a dekko at yer 'at. —Nino Culotta (John O'Grady), *They're A Weird Mob*, p. 140, 1957
- Tim Cadey's coming out this morning to take a dekko at the filly. —Dymphna Cusack, *Picnic Races*, p. 52, 1962
- [O]nly bastards with really twisted minds would want to take a dekko at my nut-chokers [men's pants]!!! —Barry Humphries, *Bazza Pulls It Off!*, 1971
- Do you want to know what I thought when I got a dekko at that photo of youse? —*The Adventures of Barry McKenzie*, 1972
- He used a little wooden icy-pop stick to lift each penis up while he had a good dekko at the underside of the shaft and glans. —Bettina Arndt, *The Australian Way of Sex*, p. 8, 1985
- [H]ave a dekko at some prefab with a plywood extension. —Andrew Nickolds, *Back to Basics*, p. 126, 1994
- [H]ave a decko at Iron Gob's mates[.] —John King, *Human Punk*, p. 25, 2000
- I takes a little decko at him. —Kevin Sampson, *Outlaws*, p. 194, 2001

deck off *verb*

to dress up *TRINIDAD AND TOBAGO, 1973*

- —Lise Winer, *Dictionary of the English/Creole of Trinidad & Tobago*, 2003

decks *noun*

trousers *UK*

- —Tom Hibbert, *Rockspeak!*, p. 47, 1983

deck up *verb*

to package a powdered drug for sale *US*

- We could deck up two-three hundred in an evening's time. It all depends on how much you got and how fast you deck up. —Jeremy Larner and Ralph Tefferteller, *The Addict in the Street*, p. 207, 1964
- —Eugene Landy, *The Underground Dictionary*, p. 64, 1971

declare *verb*

▸ **declare a gang**

(used of warring youth gangs) to agree to discuss a truce *US*

- —Dale Kramer and Madeline Karr, *Teen-Age Gangs*, p. 174, 1953

declare out *verb*

(of the Canadian Armed Forces) to opt out of service, to resign a commission *CANADA*

- Those who come in from university enter on permanent commissions, but may declare out if they wish after four years. —*Toronto Globe and Mail*, p. 8/6, 10th July 1959

decomp room *noun*

the room in a morgue housing decomposed bodies *US*

- There were bunches of bodies in the "decomp" room, decomposed bodies, lying putrid under ceiling fans[.] —Joseph Wambaugh, *The Delta Star*, p. 42, 1983
- She gagged as she passed the decomp room, where decomposing bodies lay under plastic sheets, waiting for autopsies. —Stephen Cannell, *King Con*, p. 62, 1992

decorate *verb*

to pay for something at a restaurant or bar *US, 1908*

Most commonly in the phrase 'decorate the mahagony' for buying drinks at a bar.

- Decorating the booths in the ice-cream parlor. —Dick Clark, *To Goof or Not to Goof*, p. 103, 1963

decorated with red roses *adjective*

in the bleed period of the menstrual cycle *US*

Remembered as World War 2 usage.

- —Karen Houppert, *The Curse*, 1999

decoy *noun*

an undercover police officer whose appearance leads criminals to assume the officer is a promising victim *US*

- We go in teams in a hot street-crime area, inner city. Dress like you live around there. One guy's the decoy, the target. —Elmore Leonard, *Split Images*, p. 23, 1981

dedo *noun*

an informant *US*

From the Spanish for 'finger', used by English speakers in the American southwest.

- —Bill Valentine, *Gang Intelligence Manual*, p. 41, 1995: 'Hispanic gang terminology'

dedud *verb*

to clear unexploded artillery shells from a practice range *US*

- —Carl Fleischhauer, *A Glossary of Army Slang*, p. 14, 1968

dee *noun*

1 a capsule of Dilaudid™, a pharmaceutical narcotic *US*

- —Richard A. Spears, *The Slang and Jargon of Drugs and Drink*, p. 138, 1986

2 a police detective *AUSTRALIA, 1882*

Variant spelling of **D**.

- So th' dees hassled youse a bit, did they? —Ward McNally, *Supper at Happy Harry's*, p. 68, 1982

deeda *noun*

LSD *US*

John Williams reported this term from Harlem, which was not a hotbed of LSD activity.

- —John Williams, *The Drug Scene*, p. 111, 1967

dee dee *noun*

the vagina *US*

- There's [a...] "toadie," "dee dee," "nishi," "dignity," "monkey box[".] —Eve Ensler, *The Vagina Monologues*, p. 6, 1998

deedee *noun*

a drug (or dope) dealer *UK*

A pronounced initialism.

- Deedees're always paranoid about everythin'. —Nick Barlay, *Curvy Lovebox*, p. 28, 1997

dee-dee *verb*

▷ **see: DIDI**

deefa *noun*

a dog *NEW ZEALAND*

Playing on 'd for dog'.

- —David McGill, *David McGill's Complete Kiwi Slang Dictionary*, p. 38, 1998

deefer, deejay *nouns*

▷ **see: D FOR DUNCE, DJ**

deek *verb*

to decoy an opposing player into making a wrong move *CANADA, 1942*

- —Zander Hollander, *Baseball Lingo*, p. 41, 1967
- I was watching a game the other day when Larry Walker deeked a baserunner and it saved a run. —*Denver Post*, p. C-20, 25th July 1999
- He deeked the goalie. —*sjm/canusdic.html*, p. 1, 10th November 2001
- Gale skated around him, stood in front of Ayers, deeked him, then slid the puck in the goal after Ayers committed. —*Buffalo (New York) News*, p. C1, 26th October 2003

deelish *adjective*

▷ **see: DELISH**

deemer *noun*

a ten-cent piece *US, 1926*

From the colloquial 'dime'.

- "If I stepped out on that street and played chump Santa Claus to my last deemer, that would be Blue's happiness, not yours." — Iceberg Slim (Robert Beck), *Trick Baby*, p. 12, 1969

deener *noun*
▷ see: DEANER

deep *adjective*
1 filled with the specified number of referential objects *US*
For example, 'four deep' would mean 'four people in a car'.
- — Malachi Andrews and Paul T. Owens, *Black Language*, p. 86, 1973

2 serious, intense *US*
- Damn, Furious is deep, he used to be a preacher or something? — *Boyz N The Hood*, 1990

3 (used of language) standard *BAHAMAS*
- — John A. Holm, *Dictionary of Bahamian English*, p. 60, 1982

4 habitual *UK*
This seems to be used in the black community only.
- Come to my yard and none of your deep lateness. — Diran Abedayo, *My Once Upon A Time*, p. 20, 2000

deep!
used for expressing approval *UK*
- — Susie Dent, *The Language Report*, p. 75, 2003

deep and meaningful *adjective*
a serious conversation, generally about emotions and relationships *AUSTRALIA*
- — Kylie Mole (Maryanne Fahey), *My Diary*, p. 66, 1988
- Feel like the whole human race is on your case and in your face just when you're not in the mood for hard and heavy deep and meaningfuls? — *Echo Newspaper (www.echo.net.au)*, 6th May 2003

deep-dick *verb*
(from the male point of view) to have sex *US*
- Can I at least tell people that all you needed was some serious deep-dicking? — *Chasing Amy*, 1997

deep end *noun*
▸ **go off the deep end; go in off the deep end**
to become excited, angry, emotional, passionate, maddened *UK, 1921*
A figurative application of the deep end of a swimmng pool.
- Syd [Barrett] went off the deep end through too much LSD, or because he was simply too fragile for the pressures of pop fame. — *The Guardian*, 27th October 2002

deep freeze *noun*
solitary confinement *US*
- And in a couple of hours from now he wouldn't have a job, even if the cops didn't grab him and toss him into the deep freeze. — Raymond Chandler, *Playback*, p. 72, 1958
- — Inez Cardozo-Freeman, *The Joint*, p. 492, 1984

deep house *noun*
a sub-category of house music but with a mellower feel, often featuring profound, rolling bass lines and samples from jazz records *UK*
- — *The Sunday Times Magazine*, p. 49, 1st June 2003: 'The parents' guide to the music maze'

deep kimchi *noun*
serious trouble *US*
Based on the unflattering comparison of the Korean pickled delicacy with excrement.
- — *Seattle Times*, p. A9, 12th April 1998: 'Grunts, squids not grunting from the same dictionary'

deep magic *noun*
in computing, an understanding of a technique in a program or system not known by the average programmer *US*
- Compiler optimization technqiues and many apsects of OS design used to be deep magic; many techniques in cryptography, signal processing, graphics, and AI still are. — Eric S. Raymond, *The New Hacker's Dictionary*, p. 122, 1991

Deep North; deep north *noun*
the far northern parts of the eastern state of Queensland *AUSTRALIA, 1972*
Modelled on US 'deep south', with identical connotations.
- We southerners call Queensland the Deep North. — Kathy Lette, *Girls' Night Out*, p. 171, 1987
- Ah, the eighties, you just had to love them. I tell you, they were some wild fucking times. Especially in the deep north. — Harrison Biscuit, *The Search for Savage Henry*, p. 6, 1995

deep-pocket *adjective*
(used of a defendant in civil litigation) wealthy, possessing considerable financial reserves *US, 1976*
- If the latter is ever spotted, do not attempt to feed ordinary lawyer bait: i.e., greenbacks, cocaine, hookers, deep-pocket defendants, adolescent boys. — Joseph Wambaugh, *Fugitive Nights*, p. 93, 1992

deep-sea diver *noun*
a fiver (£5) *UK*
Rhyming slang. Used in an advertisement for Olympus Cameras Centre in *Amateur Photographer*, 6th December 1980.

deep sea fishing *noun*
exploratory surgery *US*
- — Sally Williams, *"Strong" Words*, p. 138, 1994

deep serious *adjective*
extremely critical, as bad as it gets *US*
Vietnam war coinage and usage.
- Armed helicopters were especially reassuring to the "crunchies," the ground infantrymen who depended on them to deliver accurate supporting fire whether conducting raids or in "deep serious" trouble trying to disengage. — Shely L. Stanton, *The Rise and Fall of an American Army*, p. 86, 1985
- — Linda Reinberg, *In the Field*, p. 59, 1991

deep shaft *noun*
strong, illegally manufactured whisky *US*
- It is called corn liquor, white lightning, sugar whisky, skully cracker, popskull, bush whiskey, stump, stumphole, 'splo, ruckus juice, radiator whiskey, rotgut, sugarhead, block and tackle, wildcat, panther's breath, tiger's sweat, Sweet spirits of cats a-fighting, alley bourbon, city gin, cool water, happy Sally, deep shaft, jump steady, old horsey, stingo, blueye John, red eye, pine top, buckeye bark whiskey and see seven stars. — *Star Tribune (Minneapolis)*, p. 19F, 31st January 1999

deep six *verb*
to discard; to reject *US, 1952*
- We pulled over to the side of the road, and like a couple of Mafiosi getting rid of the guy who betrayed the family honor, we deep-sixed him into the ditch. — Rita Ciresi, *Pink Slip*, p. 32, 1999

deep throat *noun*
oral sex performed on a man in which the person doing the performing takes the penis completely into their mouth and throat *US*
A term from the so-named 1972 classic pornography film.
- She was beaten on an almost daily basis, humiliated, threatened, including with guns, kept captive and sleep-deprived, and forced to do sex acts ranging from "deep throat" oral sex to intercourse and sodomy. — Andrea Dworkin, *Mercy*, p. 344, 1991
- — *Adult Video News*, p. 48, August 1995
- On Saturday night a game of deep throat was being played. The Marines had drawn a line on the rhino's dildo and chanted, "Beat the line, beat the line," as a woman would simulate performing oral sex. — Gregory L. Vistica, *Fall from Glory*, p. 328, 1997
- Once you've mastered the basic techniques of fellatio and cunnilingus, you might want to experiment with '69', deep throat and other oral tricks for adventurous lovers! — Siobhan Kelly, *The Wild Guide to Sex and Loving*, p. 64, 2002

deep throat *verb*
to take a man's penis completely into the mouth and throat *US*
- [S]tudents expecting to see "Kermit's Wild West Adventure" were instead exposed to a mattress-level montage of Latin porn star Pina Kolada deepthroating a semi-pro soccer team. — Carl Hiaasen, *Native Tongue*, p. 47, 1991
- I know he is ready to shoot his thick creamy come down my throat, as I deep-throat him. — Nancy Friday, *Women on Top*, p. 81, 1991
- You may have to deep-throat using a "69" position in order for his and your angles to match up. — Craig Nelson, *Finding True Love in a Man-Eat-Man World*, p. 82, 1996
- So if you're giving him head, you've got to deep throat it so you can touch that part. — Anthony Petkovich, *The X Factory*, p. 86, 1997

deep-water Baptist *noun*
a member of a Baptist sect that practises full-immersion baptism *US, 1949*

• I came to, under a steaming pile of trash / In the narrow alley-way / Behind that old Deep Water Baptist mission. —Paul Muldoon, *Immram*, p. 98, 1977

deez-nuts

me *US*

The reference to 'these nuts' is an intimate, if crude, reference to yourself.

• I'm not going to let anyone mess with deez-nuts. —Peter Smith and Fred M. Barritt, *Bermewjan Vurds*, p. 18, 1985

• —Rick Ayers (Editor), *Berkeley High Slang Dictionary*, p. 18, 2004

def *adjective*

excellent, superlative *US, 1979*

• —Connie Eble (Editor), *UNC-CH Campus Slang*, p. 2, Fall 1987

• —Ellen C. Bellone (Editor), *Dictionary of Slang*, p. 9, 1989

• —Terry Williams, *The Cocaine Kids*, p. 136, 1989

• [E]ven "stoopid fresh," which could also be "def" when it wasn't "dope." —Nelson George, *Hip Hop America*, p. 209, 1998

• —James Haskins, *The Story of Hip-Hop*, p. 137, 2000

def *adverb*

definitely *US, 1942*

• [Jim] Morrison, def, does not get a pie in the face! He 'fessed up! —Lester Bangs, *Psychotic Reactions and Carburetor Dung*, p. 36, 1970

• —Connie Eble (Editor), *UNC-CH Campus Slang*, p. 2, Fall 1996

• We'll talk yeah? - Yeh yeh def... - We'll talk... - Yeh... I said. —Nick Barlay, *Curvy Lovebox*, p. 178, 1997

• "I feel certain that you and I share the same agenda on drugs, Tommy." "Yeah, def', big time." —Ben Elton, *High Society*, p. 69, 2002

de facto *noun*

a partner in a de facto relationship *AUSTRALIA, 1952*

• —Frank Hardy, *The Outcasts of Foolgarah*, p. 51, 1971

• You're a de facto, living in a pokey bed-sit in the suburbs. —Dorothy Hewett, *The Chapel Perilous*, p. 75, 1972

• —Kathy Lette, *Girls' Night Out*, p. 223, 1987

defect *noun*

a school prefect *UK, 1961*

A pun to delight the childish.

deffo; defo *adverb*

definitely *UK*

• Make sure Didi and Sander and Tinhead are deffo coming[.] —Kevin Sampson, *Outlaws*, p. 29, 2001

• Unmistakable, a come-here-and-talk-to-me grin, that was. Deffo. And fuck it, I friggin well will. —Niall Griffiths, *Kelly + Victor*, p. 7, 2002

• No, I am, defo. —Niall Griffiths, *Kelly + Victor*, p. 213, 2002

• Five years down the line maybe, but deffo not at the moment. —*Q*, p. 100, May 2002

defiled *adjective*

drunk *US*

• —Connie Eble (Editor), *UNC-CH Campus Slang*, p. 3, April 1997

definite *adjective*

used as a meaningless embellishment *US*

• "Definite" - all-purpose Rat Pack prefix, as in "I'll hail a definite cab." —*Washington Post*, p. B1, 17th January 1985

deft and dumb *adjective*

a catchphrase that defines desirable qualities in a wife or mistress *US, 1961*

First recorded as the title of a 1937 detective story by Octavus Roy Cohen.

deger *adjective*

▷ see: DACHA

degomble *verb*

to remove snow stuck to your clothes and equipment before going indoors *ANTARCTICA, 1989*

• —Bernadette Hince, *The Antarctic Dictionary*, p. 98, 2000

• —*Cool Antarctica*, 2003: 'Antarctic slang'

dehorn *noun*

1 denatured alcohol (ethyl alcohol to which a poisonous substance has been added to make it unfit for consumption) *US, 1926*

• [H]e lived on dehorn alcohol, mullligan, dayolds, misery[.] —John Clellon Holmes, *The Horn*, p. 159, 1958

2 a person who is addicted to denatured alcohol (ethyl alcohol to which a poisonous substance has been added to make it unfit for consumption) *US, 1926*

• The Jolity Theater is a crummy burlesque house on Minneapolis's skid row. It is patronized largely by vagrants, winos, dehorns, grifters, and other such unsanitary persons. —Max Shulman, *The Many Loves of Dobie Gillis*, p. 203, 1951

dehorn *verb*

1 to have sex after a long period of celibacy *US*

• —Helen Dahlskog (Editor), *A Dictionary of Contemporary and Colloquial Usage*, p. 18, 1972

2 to demote or discharge from employment *US*

• —Norman Carlisle, *The Modern Wonder Book of Trains and Railroading*, p. 261, 1946

3 to cut someone's hair *US*

• —Helen Dahlskog (Editor), *A Dictionary of Contemporary and Colloquial Usage*, p. 18, 1972

dehose *verb*

to return a computer that is suspended in an operation to functioning *US*

• —Eric S. Raymond, *The New Hacker's Dictionary*, p. 122, 1991

dehydrate *verb*

to become thirsty, especially for alcohol *UK*

Coined at around the same time as dehydrated foods became fairly common.

• Let's have a drink, all this talking dries me - dehydrates me, to use the modern slang. —Manning Coles, *The Fifth Man*, 1946

dehydrated water *noun*

the object of a prank errand for a new or inexperienced worker *US, 1970*

• —Frederic G. Cassidy, *Dictionary of American Regional English, Vol. II*, p. 36, 1991

deja dit *noun*

a sensation of having said something before; the consequent boredom *UK, 1994*

Adopted directly from French (already said), following 'deja vu'.

• —*The Word Spy*, 12th September 2003

deja fuck *noun*

the unsettling sensation that the person with whom you are now having sex is a former sexual partner *US*

• —Amy Sohn, *Sex and the City*, p. 154, 2002

deja vu all over again *noun*

the same thing, once again, repeated *US*

An assault on the language attributed to baseball great Yogi Berra.

• "It's deja vu all over again," as Yogi Berra probably didn't say. We are out to get a new baseball stadium, according to the gazettes. —*The Seattle Times*, p. B1, 30th May 1995

• When his teammates Mickey Mantle and Roger Maris slugged back-to-back home runs for what he described as "the umpteenth time," he [Berra] grunted, "It's deja vu all over again." —*New York Times*, p. 4, 8th August 1999

• Bush Plan: Deja Vu All Over Again —*Washington Post*, 17th May 2001

deke *noun*

a decoy *US*

• We found an unoccupied blind, put out our "dekes" and sat down to await developments. —*San Francisco News*, p. 12, 16th December 1950

dekko *noun*

▷ see: DECKO

delay *verb*

in Quebec, a time limit, an extension *CANADA*

• —Victor Trahan, *The City of Montreal Style Guide*, 2002

delayer *noun*

a railway dispatcher *US*

• —Norman Carlisle, *The Modern Wonder Book of Trains and Railroading*, p. 261, 1946

delec *adjective*

attractive *NEW ZEALAND*

An abbreviation of 'delectable'.

• —David McGill, *David McGill's Complete Kiwi Slang Dictionary*, p. 35, 1998

delete *verb*

to leave *US*

• —Kenn "Naz" Young, *Naz's Dictionary of Teen Slang*, p. 30, 1993

Delhi belly *noun*
diarrhoea suffered by tourists *US, 1944*
- Anyone suffering from art-gallery gout, Delhi belly, jaded eyeballs or other ills of the traveler on the high road, is hereby advised to relax while suffering. — *Washington Post, Times Herald*, p. F17, 24th July 1955
- When it comes to where you can get Delhi Belly, Tut's Trot, or Montezuma''s revenge, there are no surprises here. — Robert Young Pelton, *The world's Most Dangerous Places*, p. 15, 2003

deli *noun*
a *deli*catessen *US, 1954*
- You'll have to run down to the deli for biscuits. We're right out. — *Janie Stagestruck*, p. 17, 1972
- I went out to the street, and then only to buy a can of food for the starving cat. I wandered up to the corner deli. — *The Observer*, 23rd September 2001

Delia *noun*
a recipe *UK*
From Delia Smith (b.1941), arguably the UK's most celebrated cookery writer and broadcaster.
- "I only took the recipes." "You nicked the Delias? You could go to prison for that[.]" — Mervyn Stutter, *Getting Nowhere Fast*, 21st May 2004

delicacies *noun*
the testicles *UK*
- — *A–Z of Rude Health*, 11th January 2002

delicate *adjective*
▸ **in a delicate state of health; in a delicate condition**
pregnant *UK, 1850*
Now rare, but still understood.
- In 1835, when Marie Taglioni found herself pregnant [...], the ballerina superstar was obliged to fake a knee injury to explain her disappearance from the stage. For years afterwards, un mal au genou was the euphemism used by dancers in the same delicate condition. — Judith Mackrell, *The Guardian*, 12th December 2001

delicatessen book *noun*
a betting operation where the odds are constantly cut *US*
- — Dan Parker, *The ABC of Horse Racing*, p. 145, 1947

delish; deelish *adjective*
delicious *UK, 1920*
- I took her first to dinner. "Gee, that was a delish dinner," she said as we left the restaurant. — Max Shulman, *The Many Loves of Dobie Gillis*, p. 43, 1951
- "No, tell me how you like it with my hair over one eye!" "De-lish!" she exclaimed. — Eve Babitz, *L.A. Woman*, p. 119, 1982
- — Judi Sanders, *Da Bomb*, p. 5, 1997
- Thuh lasagne's done a treat, thuh top all bubbly brown an crispy, smells fuckin deelish, thuh garlic bread as well[.] — Niall Griffiths, *Grits*, p. 14, 2000

delivery boy *noun*
in poker, any young, inexperienced, unskilled player *US*
- — John Vorhaus, *The Big Book of Poker Slang*, p. 13, 1996

delivery order *noun*
a request that a certain type of car be stolen and sold to the requesting party *US*
- [A] brand-new Corvette he could get five grand for easy, even without a delivery order. — Elmore Leonard, *Stick*, p. 67, 1983

dell *verb*
to hit *UK*
English gypsy use.
- [He] had no idea why the mush would want to dell him and then jell [run off]. — Jimmy Stockin, *On The Cobbles*, p. 144, 2000

delo *noun*
a delegate *AUSTRALIA, 1961*
- This could take the form of a regular monthly or quarterly meeting open to all union delos in the MP's electorate, &/or other meetings with delos that are specific to a particular union or sector or geographic part of the electorate — *Workers Online (workers.labor.net.au)*, 12th April 2002

delosis *noun*
a pretty girl *US*
- — Lavada Durst, *The Jives of Dr. Hepcat*, p. 12, 1953

delouse *verb*
to clear an area of listening devices *UK, 1969*
A pun on synonymous **DEBUG**.

delph *noun*
the teeth *UK*
Possibly from a play on Delft china.
- — Paul Baker, *Polari*, p. 171, 2002

Delta delta *noun*
a female Red Cross volunteer in Vietnam *US*
- — Gregory Clark, *Words of the Vietnam War*, p. 151, 1990

Delta dust *noun*
marijuana grown in Vietnam *US*
A subtle pun on the several scientific names for marijuana and its psychoactive component that include 'Delta 1' or 'Delta 9'.
- — Linda Reinberg, *In the Field*, p. 60, 1991

delta sierra *noun*
a stupid person *US, 1987*
Using the phonetic alphabet for DS – 'dumb shit' or 'dog shit'.
- — J.E. Lighter, *Historical Dictionary of American Slang, Vol. I*, p. 576, 1994

Delta sox *noun*
nylon socks that replaced wool socks for US Army troops in Vietnam in 1970 *US*
The army concluded that nylon socks were more suited for tropical wear, especially in areas such as the Mekong Delta, than were wool socks.
- — Gregory Clark, *Words of the Vietnam War*, p. 139, 1990

delts *noun*
the deltoid muscles *US, 1981*
- — *American Speech*, p. 199, Fall 1984: 'The language of bodybuilding'

delurk *verb*
to post a message on an Internet discussion group after previously observing without posting *US*
- — Christian Crumlish, *The Internet Dictionary*, p. 51, 1995

deluxe *noun*
in circus usage, a box seat *US*
- — Don Wilmeth, *The Language of American Popular Entertainment*, p. 72, 1981

dem *noun*
1 a *dem*onstration; also, as a verb, to *dem*onstrate, especially how an article works *UK*
- — Michael Butterworth, *Walk Softly in Fear*, 1968

2 a capsule of merperidine (trade name Demerol™), a synthetic opiate *US*
- — Jay Robert Nash, *Dictionary of Crime*, p. 98, 1992

Dem *noun*
a *Dem*ocrat *US, 1875*
- When the Dems found out he knew Republicans, and vice versa, they began to use him as a channel to square things they didn't want to talk about directly to each other[.] — Jack Lait and Lee Mortimer, *Washington Confidential*, p. 161, 1951

dem *adjective*
their *UK*
West Indian and black English rendering of 'them' used ungrammatically or shortened from 'belonging to them'.
- [S]hould baby fathers take more responsibility for dem pickney? — Donald Gorgon, *Cop Killer*, p. 89, 1994

dem
them *JAMAICA, 1868*
West Indian and black English phonetic variation.

demented *adjective*
in computing, not functional and not useful *US*
In computing, the condition resulting when two processes cannot proceed because each is waiting for another to do something.
- — Guy L. Steele et al., *The Hacker's Dictionary*, p. 55, 1983

demento *noun*
a deranged person *US, 1977*
- "I don't have a clue about you, old sport," he says. "You're just another New York demento, as far as I can tell." — Pete Hamill, *Forever*, p. 573, 2003

demi-god *noun*
1 a good-looking boy *US*
- — Connie Eble (Editor), *UNC-CH Campus Slang*, p. 2, November 1983

2 a person recognised by the computing community as a major genius *US*

- To qualify as a genuine demigod, the person must recognizably identify with the hacker community and have helped shape it. — Eric S. Raymond, *The New Hacker's Dictionary*, p. 123, 1991

demmy *noun*

a capsule of Demerol^{TM} (merperidine), a powerful and habit-forming painkiller *US, 1956*

- — Richard A. Spears, *The Slang and Jargon of Drugs and Drink*, p. 139, 1986

demo *noun*

1 a *demon*stration model or recording *US, 1963*

- I don't have to sell this ripper nineteen-sixty-eight John Olsen neither, because it's my own demo[.] — Barry Humphries, *A Nice Night's Entertainment*, p. 146, 1974
- You don't happen to have a tape or a demo that we might listen to? — *King of Comedy*, 1976
- "Mebbe you should let me decide that -" "What?" "Whether she's very good. Got a demo?" "Eh?" "Cassette." — Anthony Masters, *Minder*, p. 70, 1984
- I wanted the money to make a demo [demonstration record] and go into the record business. — Terry Williams, *The Cocaine Kids*, p. 89, 1989
- You guys are an unsigned band, and you broke into the radio station to get your demo tape played on the air? — *Airheads*, 1994
- Bobby Beck, the owner, used to let me come in and play drums on the demo kit. — *Empire Records*, 1995
- They can listen to a demo and tell right away if they can break it. — Elmore Leonard, *Be Cool*, p. 69, 1999

2 an act of having sex in front of observers *AUSTRALIA*

Apparently this had a vogue amongst yobbo blokes during the 70s.

- 'What about a demo from Disneyland?' called the Humdinger. 'Yeah!' chorused several urgers. 'Come on, Disneyland. Pull 'em down and let's see you give the girls a bang. Hey, Sandpiper!' But his plans foundered. Disneyland wouldn't take them off. — David Ireland, *The Unknown Industrial Prisoner*, p. 303, 1971
- [D]emo: demonstration, usually referring to sex. — Jim Ramsay, *Cop It Sweet!*, p. 28, 1977

3 a political *demon*stration *AUSTRALIA, 1904*

- I've just heard on 2GF that nine people from the PAG have been arrested as a result of a peaceful demo over my bashing. — Ray Denning, *Prison Diaries*, p. 62, 1978
- Would anything get them going again. Put a bit of spark in the demo? — Harrison Biscuit, *The Search for Savage Henry*, p. 68, 1995
- — Shane Maloney, *Nice Try*, p. 150, 1998
- Fair trade demo attracts record numbers. — *The Guardian*, 20th June 2002

4 a *demon*stration of how something works or how an action or activity ought to be done *UK, 1961*

- I've gotta give a demo of the drool-proof interface; how does it work again? — Eric S. Raymond, *The Hacker's Dictionary*, p. 139, 1993

5 *demo*lition *US, 1943*

- [B]ig baskets like you see demo boys filling up with stuff when they're knocking a dump down. — Alfred Draper, *Swansong for a Rare Bird*, 1970

6 a laboratory pipette used to smoke crack cocaine *US*

- — Terry Williams, *Crackhouse*, p. 152, 1992

demob *noun*

a release from conscription or other contract of military service *UK, 1945*

An abbreviation of officialese 'demobilisation'; hence 'demob suit' (clothes issued on return to civilian life), etc.

- Roll on death, demob's too far away. — Graeme Kent, *The Queen's Corporal [Six Granada Plays]*, p. 85, 1959
- After demob he got a job driving a van in North London. It bored him shitless. — Jake Arnott, *He Kills Coppers*, p. 38, 2001

demob *verb*

to demobilise *UK, 1918*

- This outbreak of mass fecklessness was blamed on immigrants and soldiers demobbed from the civil war. — *The Guardian*, 28th February 2004

demoiselle *noun*

an odd-shaped pillar of clay or cemented gravel, caused by erosion *CANADA*

The word comes from the French, meaning 'young woman', and is likely to be suggested by the shape, or the shape as it appears to a plains rider who hasn't seen a woman for a long time.

- In places along Medicine Lake highway the thick deposits of glacial drift or boulder clay have been cut into high, fantastic earth pillars called "hoodoos" or "demoiselles." — *Canadian Geographical Journal*, p. 161/2, April 1952

demolish *noun*

crack cocaine *UK, 1998*

- — Mike Haskins, *Drugs*, p. 281, 2003

demolition party *noun*

a party held on the last night of a lease for the purpose of destroying furniture, fixtures, etc *NEW ZEALAND, 1987*

- — Harry Orsman, *A Dictionary of Modern New Zealand Slang*, p. 37, 1999

demon *noun*

a police detective, or, loosely, a police officer *AUSTRALIA, 1898*

Originally criminal slang. The suggestion in the *Oxford English Dictionary Supplement* (1972) that it is somehow extracted from Van *Diemen*'s Land, a former name of the penal colony of Tasmania, seems tenuous at best.

- Rufe had been depending on him for a handout to take him north maybe, or to the sugar canefields; west even, to the pearling grounds. Heck, anywhere out of reach of the demons. — Wilda Moxham, *The Apprentice*, p. 8, 1969
- Was in the back bar at the "Queen's" in Southport one day having a couple with two Demons. — Sam Weller, *Old Bastards I Have Met*, p. 18, 1979

demon *adjective*

1 applied to someone, especially in cricket and other sports, who seems superhuman in action *UK, 1883*

Originally used of Australian cricketer Fred Spofforth, 1853–1926.

- I've got a personal theory that one reason he [Merv Hughes] was such a demon bowler was that luckless batsman were unsighted by the facial foliage. — *The Guardian*, 27th February 2003

2 excellent *US*

- — Tom Hibbert, *Rockspeak!*, p. 47, 1983
- — Connie Eble (Editor), *UNC-CH Campus Slang*, p. 4, Spring 1988

demon tweak *noun*

1 a motocycle enthusiast who does his own tuning at home *UK*

- — Douglas Dunford, *Motorcycle Department, Beauliey Motor Museum*, 1979

2 in motor racing, a highly clever modification which may or may not improve the car's performance *US*

- — Don Alexander, *The Racer's Dictionary*, p. 19, 1980

demoto *noun*

a person lacking motivation; a self-non-starter *US*

- — *Washington Post*, 14th October 1993

dems *noun*

demolitions *UK*

Military.

- Joe, the dems instructor, was coming to the end of his two years in the job. — Andy McNab (writing of the late 1970s/early 80s), *Immediate Action*, p. 183, 1995

denari; denarli; dinarlee; dinali; denali *noun*

money *UK, 1914*

Polari.

- [T]he mush said he would not go until he got the denali that was coming to him. — Butch Reynolds, *Broken Hearted Clown*, p. 28, 1953
- [I]t was heavy "graft" (work) and very little "denari" (money – "wonger" and "denali" are also used for this). — Butch Reynolds, *Broken Hearted Clown*, p. 30, 1953

dener *noun*

▷ **see:** DEANER

Denis Law *noun*

a carpenter's saw *UK*

Rhyming slang, formed on the name of Scottish footballer (b.1940).

- — Ray Puxley, *Cockney Rabbit*, 1992

Denmark *noun*

▸ **go to Denmark**

to undergo a sex change operation *US*

Homosexual usage; an allusion to the sex-altering operation performed on Christine Jorgensen in Denmark.

- I'll makeya a real woman without goin to Denmark. — Hubert Selby Jr, *Last Exit to Brooklyn*, p. 46, 1957
- — *The Guild Dictionary of Homosexual Terms*, p. 19, 1965
- — *Maledicta*, p. 53, 1986–1987: 'A continuation of a glossary of ethnic slurs in American English'

den mother *noun*
an older, unofficial leader of a group of homosexual men *US*
• —Jim Crotty, *How to Talk American*, p. 138, 1997

Dennis the Menace *noun*
a variety of MDMA, the recreational drug best known as ecstasy *UK*
From the similarity between the red and black stripes on the comic book character's jumper and those on the tablet.
• —Angela Devlin, *Prison Patter*, p. 43, 1996
• —Macfarlane, Macfarlane and Robson, *The User*, p. 74, 1996
• Street names [...] California sunrise (also sometimes LSD), Dennis the Menace, disco biscuits[.]—James Kay and Julian Cohen, *The Parents' Complete Guide to Young People and Drugs*, p. 136, 1998
• Doves would make your head light and warm your emotions; Dennis the Menaces would make your legs heavy and blank your brain.—Dave Haslam, *Adventures of the Wheels of Steel*, p. xxv, 2001
• —Gareth Thomas, *This is Ecstasy*, p. 55, 2002

Dennistoun Palais *noun*
aluminium *UK: SCOTLAND*
Glasgow rhyming slang, on 'ally', formed from a venue in the Dennistown area of the city; used by local scrap-dealers.
• —Michael Munro, *The Patter, Another Blast*, 1988

dental floss *noun*
LSD *UK*
• —Mike Haskins, *Drugs*, p. 285, 2003

dental flosser *noun*
someone who is considered to be worthless or despicable *UK*
Rhyming slang for **TOSSER**.
• —Bodmin Dark, *Dirty Cockney Rhyming Slang*, 2003

dent for an E-flat bugle *noun*
an imaginary item for which a novice musician may be sent *UK*
Military in origin, but remembered as a fool's errand enjoyed in the Boy's Brigade during the early 1960s.

dentist *noun*
in oil drilling, a cement worker *US*
• —Jerry Robertson, *Oil Slanguage*, p. 44, 1954

dentist's friend *noun*
in circus and carnival usage, any sweet *US*
• —Don Wilmeth, *The Language of American Popular Entertainment*, p. 72, 1981

Denver mud *noun*
a patent medicine applied as a poultice *US, 1970*
• Strange things surfaced, like the taste of the Denver mud Mama applied to my chest when I had a cold. She heated the mud in the lid on the burner, then spread it on my chest.—Kay Allenbaugh, *Chocolate for a Woman's Soul*, p. 215, 1997

dep *noun*
1 a *dep*osition (a copy of a transcript of evidence) *UK*
Usually in the plural.
• —Angela Devlin, *Prison Patter*, p. 43, 1996
• Feckles had had his locker broken into. "Deps" (court depositions) in which it was stated that he had been an official police informant up until 1998 had been stolen and circulated.—Erwin James, *The Guardian*, 15th March 2001: 'A life inside'

2 a *dep*uty *UK, 1851*
• —Hyman E. Goldin et al., *Dictionary of American Underworld Lingo*, p. 57, 1950

3 a *dep*uty prison governor *UK, 1950*
• —Angela Devlin, *Prison Patter*, p. 43, 1996

4 in the theatre, a company representative of Equity (the actors' union) *UK*
• If you are currently a dep, recently been a dep or would like to be a dep give us a call.—*Equity Journal*, p. 8, June 2001

5 in Quebec, a corner store *CANADA*
A short form of the French word *depanneur*, which is also used by anglophones and allophones as well as Quebec French speakers, and is often used to describe what in Ontario is known as a 'confectionery', and in south and central Texas as an 'icehouse'.
• "Deps," as they have been known to generations of local students, differentiate themselves from their counterparts in other Canadian urban centres through the sale of beer and infamously low-quality wine.—*The McGill Daily*, 5th November 2001

depart *verb*
in the language of fighter pilots, to accelerate through the plane's limits *US*
• If that failed, McKeown would dleiberately "depart' the plane (take it outside its flight envelope) as a last resort maneuver.—Robert K. Wilcox, *Scream of Eagles*, p. 140, 1990

department of fishy things *nickname*
Nova Scotia's Department of Fisheries and Oceans *CANADA*
• The bills were presented to me at my retirement party, by the Minister of the Department of Fishy Things, officially shortened to DOFT but referred to my department staff as DAFT).—Vincent Russell, *Over the Grey in Jilted Angels*, p. 63, 2002

Department of Holidays *nickname*
the British Columbia Ministry of Transportation and Highways *CANADA, 1989*
• Before the Ministry of Transportation and Highways was 'privatized', the advanced inaction of many government employees on the roadside gave rise to this colloquial phrase. In a state of nervousness, I once [used it] in court, to laughter.—Tom Parkin, *WetCoast Words*, p. 45, 1989

department of the obvious *noun*
a mythical agency that employs people to state the obvious *US*
• —Connie Eble (Editor), *UNC-CH Campus Slang*, p. 2, Fall 1991

departure lounge *noun*
in hospital, a geriatric ward *UK*
Medical slang, using humour to cope with imminent death.
• —Adam T. Fox, St Mary's Hospital, London, 10th October 2002

depeditate *verb*
in computing, to place text in a fashion that cuts off the feet of the letters *US*
• —Eric S. Raymond, *The New Hacker's Dictionary*, p. 124, 1991

depending on what school you went to
a catchphrase used when two distinct pronunciations of a word are offered *AUSTRALIA, 1977*

depend on it!; depend upon it!
be certain; used as an assurance that a statement is, or will be, true *UK, 1738*
• Barç lose to Real at the Camp Nou and other results do not go the club's way, he [Van Gaal] will be out – depend upon it – by Christmas.—*The Observer*, 17th November 2002

depth bomb *noun*
an amphetamine tablet *UK*
• [F]or five shillings you can buy enough pills – "purple hearts," "depth bombs" and other lovelies of the pharmacological arts.—Tom Wolfe, *The Noonday Underground*, p. 66, 1968

depth charge *noun*
1 a shot of whisky served in a glass of beer *US, 1956*
• [A] "Coalminer's Breakfast," or "Depth Charge" (when a shot of whiskey is dropped into a glass of beer.—Roger E. Axtell, *The Do's and Taboos of Hosting International Vistitors*, p. 76, 1990

2 a fig or a prune *UK, 1943*
Of Royal Navy and Royal Air Force origins; comparing an explosion in the deep, which is in the power of such military hardware, to the laxative effect of the fruits.

3 any food that is heavy or stodgy *UK*
From the effects on your lower depths; recorded in prison use by Paul Tempest, *Lag's Lexicon*, 1950, who offers 'dumplings' as an example. Soon in wider use.

depth charging *noun*
a system of playing blackjack based not on a count of the value of cards played but on the depth of the deck dealt *US*
• —Michael Dalton, *Blackjack*, p. 42, 1991

deputy *noun*
a married person's lover *TRINIDAD AND TOBAGO, 1975*
• —Lise Winer, *Dictionary of the English/Creole of Trinidad & Tobago*, 2003

deputy do-right *noun*
a police officer *US*
• —Edith A. Folb, *runnin' down some lines*, p. 234, 1980

der!

you idiot! *AUSTRALIA*

In origin representing a stalling articulation such as 'um' or 'er', implying that you need to spend time thinking about something that is obvious. Always said with a sarcastic tone.

- 'Oh der,' moaned Boardie sarcastically.—Kathy Lette and Gabrielle Carey, *Puberty Blues*, p. 46, 1979
- Like they go to me, 'Kylie, we know you have been kissing boys,' and I go, 'Er der, I wood hardly be kissing fence posts.'—Kylie Mole (Maryanne Fahey), *My Diary*, p. 52, 1988
- Yes I did forget! Der!—*Macquarie Dictionary Ozcorp*, 1991

derange *verb*

to bother, to trouble *CANADA*

From the French *deranger*.

- —Victor Trahan, *The City of Montreal Style Guide*, p. 119, 2001

derby *noun*

1 oral sex *US, 1969*

- —Kenn "Naz" Young, *Naz's Underground Dictionary*, p. 24, 1973

2 any sporting contest between traditional rivals *UK*

- He was always telling us that the United/City derby was the ultimate row[.]—Martin King and Martin Knight, *The Naughty Nineties*, p. 62, 1999

derby kelly; darby kelly; derby kel; derby kell; derby; darby *noun*

the stomach, the abdomen, the belly *UK, 1906*

Rhyming slang for 'belly'.

- Boiled beef and carrots / Boiled beef and carrots / That's the stuff for your "Darby Kel" / It makes you fat and keeps you well[.]—Harry Champion, *Boiled Beef and Carrots*,
- [S]haring a pint of pig's ear [beer], or filling our Darbies [stomachs] round your Cain and Abel [table].—Ronnie Barker, *Fletcher's Book of Rhyming Slang*, p. 39, 1979
- I swung one into his derby and he woofed like a dog. I followed it with a really low one, right in the assets.—Lenny McLean, *The Guv'nor*, p. 82, 1998

derel *noun*

a person lacking in basic intelligence *US*

An abbreviation of the conventional 'derelict'.

- —Trevor Cralle, *The Surfin'ary*, p. 29, 1991

derelict *noun*

a socially inept, slightly dim person *US*

- —Connie Eble (Editor), *UNC-CH Campus Slang*, p. 2, March 1979

derm; derem *noun*

an intestine; usually in plural, guts *SOUTH AFRICA, 1970*

The phrases 'my derms are clapping together' and 'my derms are flapping together' are glossed as a 'vulgarism for "hungry"' by Jean Branford, *A Dictionary of South African English*, 1978.

dermo *noun*

dermatitis *AUSTRALIA, 1948*

- You oughta be grateful you got the dermo and was sent home. It's likely you'd've got killed with the others when the Japs bombed. —Graham Sheil, *War's End*, p. 9, 1981

dero *noun*

a derelict *AUSTRALIA, 1971*

- —G.A. Wilkes, *A Dictionary of Australian Colloquialisms*, 1978
- —Harry Orsman, *A Dictionary of Modern New Zealand Slang*, p. 38, 1999

DEROS; deros *verb*

to return to the US from combat duty in Vietnam *US, 1968*

From the abbreviation for the '*d*ate of *e*stimated *r*eturn from *o*verseas'.

- The reduction hadn't worked, but he would DEROS Vietnam and ETS the army at the same time.—Ches Schneider, *From Classrooms to Claymores*, p. 149, 1999

derrick apple; derrick fruit *noun*

in oil drilling, a nut, bolt or piece of dried mud that falls off a derrick *US*

- —Jerry Robertson, *Oil Slanguage*, p. 45, 1954

derrière *noun*

the vagina *US*

From French *derrière* (behind), a familiar euphemism for 'the buttocks', 'the behind', adopted here for a new location.

- There's "powderbox," "derriere," a "poochi," a "poopi," a "peepe[".] —Eve Ensler, *The Vagina Monologues*, p. 6, 1998

derro *noun*

a derelict *AUSTRALIA, 1972*

- Old Joe was the local reprobate and fast becoming a derro when the Salvos took him under their wing.—Sam Weller, *Old Bastards I Have Met*, p. 137, 1979
- —David McGill, *David McGill's Complete Kiwi Slang Dictionary*, p. 38, 1998

derry *noun*

a derelict house *UK*

- —Home Office, *Glossary of Terms and Slang Common in Penal Establishments*, 1978

Derry & Toms *noun*

bombs *UK*

Rhyming slang, formed during World War 2 on the name of a London department store. Ray Puxley, *Cockney Rabbit*, 1992, ponders the irony of a continuing need for the term in relation to much-bombed Derry. Derry & Toms closed in 1973.

- —Julian Franklyn, *A Dictionary of Rhyming Slang*, 1960

Derry-Down-Derry; DDD; three Ds *noun*

sherry *UK*

Theatrical rhyming slang.

- —Julian Franklyn, *A Dictionary of Rhyming Slang*, 1960

'ders *noun*

oral sex *US*

An abbreviation of 'headers', itself an embellishment of **HEAD**.

- It was a way cranking party, but I was sooo embarrassed, like I walk into the bedroom and Tricia's totally giving Sean ders!—Mary Corey and Victoria Westermark, *Fer Shurr! How to be a Valley Girl*, 1982

desert cherry *noun*

a soldier newly arrived in Kuwait or Saudi Arabia during the first Gulf war *US*

- "Desert cherries" in "Kevlars" fly the "Sand Box Express" to the "beach" and soon are complaining about "Meals Rejected by Ethiopians" if they can't find a "roach coach" run by "Bedouin Bob."—*Houston Chronicle*, p. 15, 24th January 1991

desert lamb *noun*

kid goat's meat *AUSTRALIA*

- The milk was good and we used the kids for meat. 'Desert lamb and green peas' was a choice dish[.]—Patsy Adam-Smith, *Folklore of the Australian Railwaymen*, p. 144, 1969

desert rat *noun*

any longtime resident of any desert area, especially, in modern usage, Las Vegas, Nevada *US, 1907*

- These confirmed desert dwellers are called '"desert rats" and they wouldn't give up their carefree life in the sun for anything.—*San Francisco Examiner*, p. 1, 22nd March 1964
- In the early days of Vegas an old desert rat collapsed outside a small-town casino.—Mario Puzo, *Inside Las Vegas*, p. 327, 1977
- —*Maledicta*, p. 156, Summer/Winter 1978: 'How to hate thy neighbor: a guide to racist maledicta'
- —John Vorhaus, *The Big Book of Poker Slang*, p. 13, 1996

desert rose *noun*

a military urinal used in the desert *UK*

- For the chaps, there were little "desert roses" – funnels on stalks – placed at intervals about the camp[.]—Kate Adie (writing of the Gulf war), *The Kindness of Strangers*, p. 335, 2002

deserve *verb*

▸ **deserve a medal**

said of a hard worker: to deserve some kind of reward for effort; also said in regard of an achievment, especially of some act, however trivial, that you would not like to have done (in either use, it is implicit that no reward or official acknowledgement of the act is likely) *UK, 1961*

- Anyone who has gone through this appalling winter getting up for work to face grey, cold, rain-sodden skies morning after morning deserves a medal.—*Epping Forest Guardian*, 18th May 2001

desi *noun*

someone from India *US*

- —Connie Eble (Editor), *UNC-CH Campus Slang*, p. 2, March 1996

designer *adjective*

(used of pornography) relatively high-brow, designed for couples and first-time viewers *US*

- —Ana Loria, *1 2 3 Be A Porn Star!*, p. 165, 2000: 'Glossary of adult sex industry terms'

designer drug *noun*

a recreational drug synthesized to mimic the effects of another more expensive or unlawful drug *US*

- —Angela Devlin, *Prison Patter*, p. 43, 1996
- Designer drugs are drugs made underground, often in home based labs. The chemists making these drugs modify the molecular structure of certain types of illegal drugs to produce analogs. These analogs are what are termed 'designer drugs'.—Gary L. Somdahl, *Drugs and Kids*, p. 94, 1996

desk commando *noun*

a military support worker who does not face combat *UK, 1958*

- —J.E. Lighter, *Historical Dictionary of American Slang, Vol. I*, p. 578, 1994

desk cowboy *noun*

a military or police support worker who does not face combat or street duty *US, 1942*

- If you were an experienced investigator who'd handled a few of these before, that would be one thing. But you're a desk cowboy, okay?—Boston Teran, *God Is a Bullet*, p. 47, 1999

deskfast *noun*

breakfast taken at your desk *US, 1996*

- We eat in the car (the dashboard break), in the office (the deskfast), in front of the TV.—*The Observer*, 5th January 2003

desk jockey *noun*

an office worker *US, 1953*

- —*American Speech*, p. 228, October 1956: 'More United States Air Force slang'
- As a congressional candidate in the late 1970s, he had emphasized his desk jockey job at the Pentagon as a whiz-kid planner in the nation's conversion to a peacetime economy.—Chris Matthews, *Hardball*, p. 126, 1988

desk piano *noun*

a typewriter *US*

- —Lou Shelly, *Hepcats Jive Talk Dictionary*, p. 23, 1945
- —Clarence Major, *Dictionary of Afro-American Slang*, p. 45, 1970

desk pilot *noun*

a military or police support worker who does not face combat or street duty *US, 1955*

- A pair of polyester desk pilots who smelled like hair oil and made grade by jamming up other cops.—James Lee Burke, *Purple Cane Road*, p. 354, 2000

desk rage *noun*

an outburst of enraged hostility within an office environment *US*

- Long hours and the growing pressures of the workplace are leading to increasing outbreaks of office strife or "desk rage."—John Middleton, *Writing the New Economy*, p. 230, 2000
- —Susie Dent, *The Language Report*, p. 17, 2003

desk rider *noun*

a military support worker who does not face combat; an officious bureaucrat *US, 1966*

- He'd had enough of this fat, strutting little desk rider! What did he know about the job?—Barbara Nadel, *Belshazzar's Daughter*, p. 106, 1999

desmadre *noun*

a disaster *US*

Border Spanish used in English conversation by Mexican-Americans.

- —Dagoberto Fuentes and Jose Lopez, *Barrio Language Dictionary*, p. 54, 1974

Desmond *noun*

a lower second-class degree, a 2:2 *UK*

A clever pun which may be considered rhyming slang, based on Archbishop Desmond Tutu (b.1930). Used by actor Sam West to describe his qualifications from Oxford University, *Midweek*, BBC Radio 4, 5th December 2001.

- —David Rowan, *A Glossary for the 90s*, 1998
- [H]e got a Desmond.—*Antiquarian Book Review*, p. 18, June 2002

▸ **do a Desmond**

to undress, completely or largely, especially at a rock concert *US*

From Desmond Morris, author of *The Naked Ape*.

- —Tom Hibbert, *Rockspeak!*, p. 50, 1983

desperado *noun*

1 a person who is down and out; an unemployed person scrounging a living from day to day *AUSTRALIA*

- We talked about desperadoes. 'I am fatally attracted to them,' I said.—Helen Garner, *Monkey Grip*, p. 107, 1977
- My uncle Robbie, a former hippy, turns up with a parental relief parcel one day and tells me he lived in the exact same house twenty years ago as a professional desperado in the early 1970s.—John Birmingham, *He Died With a Felafel in his Hand*, p. 69, 1994

2 a person who exhibits desperation in seeking sexual partners *AUSTRALIA*

- To get by, she made and sold elaborate western shirts and danced with desperados in a lonely guys' club 'for eight cents a minute'.—*People*, p. 21, 21st December 1987
- Anyway Laura had a real date one night. Some desperado from the office.—John Birmingham, *He Died With a Felafel in his Hand*, p. 148, 1994

3 a desperate gambler *US, 1961*

- —Ned Wallish, *The Truth Dictionary of Racing Slang*, p. 22, 1989

desperado *adjective*

desperate *UK*

A borrowed word used as an elaboration.

- I wouldn't say I'm desperado and that, but I wouldn't mind joining that Royal Liverpool [golf club].—Kevin Sampson, *Outlaws*, p. 74, 2001

desperate *noun*

1 a gambling addict *AUSTRALIA*

- The late Stan was driving his car out of the carpark at Rosehill races when a 'desperate' hailed him for a lift.—Frank Hardy and Athol George Mulley, *The Needy and the Greedy*, p. 58, 1975
- Grumpy, as they say in the racing game, was a desperate.—Roy Higgins and Tom Prior, *The Jockey Who Laughed*, p. 74, 1982
- Snowy and the other vice squad boys knew that shonky clubs would appear all over the place to cater for those desperates who must have a bet.—Clive Galea, *Slipper*, p. 101, 1988

2 a person who exhibits desperation in seeking sexual partners *AUSTRALIA*

- Most of the desperates were now turning to the massage parlours for a blow job, and sometimes you even got a massage thrown in.—Robert English, *Toxic Kisses*, p. 19, 1979
- Known globally as The Desperates, they'd driven their convertibles from all four corners of the globe in the hope of picking up one of Hot Bun's rejects.—Gretel Killeen, *Hot Buns and Ophelia get a Bloke*, p. 79, 2000

desperate *adjective*

very good *US*

Largely dependent on a melodramatic delivery to impart the slang sense.

- Oh what a desparately wonderful affair it's going to be – Harry James and a grand march and everybody goes formal. Isn't that desperate?—Max Shulman, *The Many Loves of Dobie Gillis*, p. 55, 1951

desperate *adverb*

very *CANADA*

- Other intensifiers were "desperate", as in "It's desperate cold out" and "I'm desperate glad to see you."—Harry Bruce, *Down Home*, p. 107, 1988

Desperate Dan *noun*

a tan *UK*

Rhyming slang, formed on the name of a comic strip hero who has appeared in the *Beano* since 1938.

- —Ray Puxley, *Cockney Rabbit*, 1992

desperate money *noun*

in horse racing, money bet by someone who is in a long losing streak and is very anxious to win *AUSTRALIA*

- —Ned Wallish, *The Truth Dictionary of Racing Slang*, p. 22, 1989

despizable *adjective*

worse than despicable *US*

- —John Gould, *Maine Lingo*, p. 72, 1975

des res

a *des*irable *res*idence *UK, 1986*

A cliché of estate agent jargon.

- Whether it was a des-res made out of turf, bijou caves (suit first-time hermit) or the Gorbals[.]—Andrew Nickolds, *Back to Basics*, p. 125, 1994
- It's October 1993 and I'm in the garden of our des-res, PC, five-bedroomed, original-fireplaced, dado-railed, stripped-pine, moulded-corniced, claw-foot-bathtubbed [...] house.—Stuart Browne, *Dangerous Parking*, p. 318–319, 2000

dessert crack *noun*

nitrous oxide *US*

Small containers of nitrous oxide used in canned dessert topping are a prime source of the gas for young users.

• Whippits: Otherwise known as "hippie crack" or "dessert crack." Either way, it's the best high a thirteen-year-old can get.—Suroosh Alvi et al., *The Vice Guide*, p. 20, 2002

dessie *noun*

a desert boot *UK*

• [T]hey were wearing duvet jackets, jeans and dessies.—Andy McNab, *Immediate Action*, p. 33, 1995

destat *verb*

to get rid of a property's statutory tenants *UK*

• Put in the schwarzes and de-stat it.—*Sunday Times*, 7th June 1963

destructo *noun*

in surfing, a large and powerful wave *US*

• —Dennis Aaberg and John Milius, *Big Wednesday*, p. 209, 1978

det *noun*

a *det*onator

• [A] pound of jelly [gelignite], dets, or a dodgy twirl[.]—Derek Raymond (Robin Cook), *The Crust on its Uppers*, p. 57, 1962

detainer *noun*

a railway dispatcher *US*

• —Norman Carlisle, *The Modern Wonder Book of Trains and Railroading*, p. 261, 1946

detectorist; metal detectorist *noun*

a person who, for recreation, operates a metal detector *UK*

• They were discovered by a metal detectorist who has found a little Roman figure of a god[.]—*The Guardian*, 22nd April 2002

dethrone *verb*

to order someone to leave a public toilet to prevent homosexual activity *US, 1941*

A royal image from the use of **QUEEN** (homosexual).

detox *noun*

a facility where an alcoholic or drug addict can begin treatment with the detoxification process *US, 1973*

• They're not patients till they're admitted somewhere for treatment, or we sent them to detox.—Elmore Leonard, *Maximum Bob*, p. 20, 1991

detox *verb*

to undergo, or subject to, a process of detoxification *US, 1972*

• The first sentence was nine months and I detoxed, which felt good[.]—*The Guardian*, p. 7, 26th February 2002

Detroit diesel *noun*

any General Motors engine *US*

• —Montie Tak, *Truck Talk*, p. 43, 1971

Detroit iron *noun*

a large, American car *US, 1950*

• —Edd Byrnes, *Way Out with Kookie*, 1959
• —Chrysler Corporation, *Of Anchors, Bezels, Pots and Scorchers*, September 1959
• It's underpowered. Two seats. Detroit iron. Nice, but compare it with a Jaguar XJS, which is quieter, smoother, handles better, is faster, and costs twenty thousand dollars less.—John McPhee, *Irons in the Fire*, p. 182, 1997

Detroit vibrator *noun*

a Chevrolet big-rig truck *US*

• —Montie Tak, *Truck Talk*, p. 43, 1971

deuce *noun*

1 two of anything, such as two marijuana cigarettes, two women, etc *US, 1943*

• I drove straight home to stash my frame between a deuce of lily-whites.—Mezz Mezzrow, *Really the Blues*, p. 101, 1946
• It hopped off with a deuce of studs jiving some buds about how strong they were—Dan Burley, *Diggeth Thou?*, p. 15, 1959
• [S]o out we go, motion to a deuce (a pair of girls) and we're off.—Ian Hebditch, *Weekend*, *The Sharper Word*, p. 134, 1969

2 a two-year prison sentence *US, 1925*

• Well, the faggot draws a deuce; and in the box he meets this cat who is some species of cheap hustler.—William Burroughs, *Naked Lunch*, p. 129, 1957
• He had served a bullet 'n a deuce.—Lightnin' Rod, *Hustlers Convention*, p. 10, 1973
• My man Colorado was doing a deuce, and he had a little click waiting for me when I got up there.—Edwin Torres, *Carlito's Way*, p. 46, 1975
• He pleaded guilty anyway, expecting a deuce maximum, back on the street in eighteen months tops.—James Ellroy, *Suicide Hill*, p. 579, 1986

3 two pounds or two dollars *US, 1900*

• Zaida dug in her bag. "Here's a decue for the cab."—Ross Russell, *The Sound*, p. 240, 1961
• Youll learn; sometimes youll stand around all day and wait for a 15-buck score, a 10-buck score, even a deuce – all day[.]—John Rechy, *City of Night*, p. 43, 1963
• The turnstile attendant thinks it might help me if I went for a little walk (the cops watch him while other cops watch the cops) and then returned to him with a deuce in my hand.—James Simon Kunen, *The Strawberry Statement*, p. 91–92, 1968

4 in the restaurant business, a table for two *US, 1935*

• I called the best hotel in town when I got home and made reservations for a deuce at nine o'clock.—Chester Himes, *If He Hollers Let Him Go*, p. 46, 1945
• "Let's grab that deuce," Lynn said, pointing to the table.—Joseph Wambaugh, *Fugitive Nights*, p. 141, 1992

5 an act of defecation *US*

From children's toilet vocabulary: **NUMBER TWO** (defecation).

• "I think she's in the back dropping a deuce."—*Howard Stern Radio Show*, 24 January 2003

6 in dice games, the point two *US*

• —*The Annals of the American Academy of Political and Social Sciences*, p. 123, May 1950

7 in pool, the two-ball *US, 1878*

• —Mike Shamos, *The Illustrated Encyclopedia of Billiards*, p. 76, 1993

8 in card games, a two of any suit *UK, 1680*

• In deuces wild, bear in mind that the four deuces roaming the pack make a total of eight aces!—George Coffin, *The Poker Game Complete*, p. 105, 1961

9 two dollars' worth of drugs *US*

Originally a $2 package of heroin; with inflation other drugs became more likely to fit the bill.

• —Robert Nash, *Dictionary of Crime*, p. 101, 1992

10 heroin *UK*

From **DEUCE BAG; DEUCE** (a two-dollar bag of heroin).

• —Richard A. Spears, *The Slang and Jargon of Drugs and Drink*, p. 140, 1986
• —Robert Ashton, *This Is Heroin*, p. 205, 2002
• —Mike Haskins, *Drugs*, p. 283, 2003

11 two hundred *US*

• TED: Mary's a little chubby, huh? HEALY: I'd say about a deuce, deuce and half. Not bad.—*Something About Mary*, 1998

12 two hundred dollars *US*

• This thing's worth about a deuce.—Charles Whited, *Chiodo*, p. 48, 1973

13 twenty dollars *US*

• I stood repeating, "Tis some strange midnight stud that's sounding a money beat on my pad's door. A deuce the morrow."—William "Lord" Buckley, *The Raven*, 1960

14 in television and film making, a 2000 watt spotlight *US*

• —Ralph S. Singleton, *Filmaker's Dictionary*, p. 46, 1990

15 an arrest or conviction for driving under the influence of alcohol *US, 1971*

California Penal Code Section 502 prohibits driving under the influence of alcohol, hence the 'two' reference.

• I don't wanna book a deuce right now. I wanna go get a hot pastrami.—Joseph Wambaugh, *The Secrets of Harry Bright*, p. 56, 1985
• —Judi Sanders, *Don't Dog by Do, Dude!*, p. 10, 1991

16 a 1932 Ford *US*

A favourite of car enthusiasts, immortalised by the Beach Boys in their 1963 song 'Little Deuce Coupe'.

• —*American Speech*, p. 95, May 1954: 'Hot rod terms in the pasadena area'
• —*Good Housekeeping*, p. 143, September 1958: 'Hot-rod terms for teen-age girls'

17 a Chevrolet II car made between 1962 and 1967 *US*

• —John Edwards, *Auto Dictionary*, p. 42, 1993

18 a small-time criminal *US*

• —Jay Robert Nash, *Dictionary of Crime*, p. 101, 1992

19 used as a substitute for 'the devil' or 'hell' *UK, 1694*

• I had the deuce of a time trying to find you.—Horace McCoy, *Kiss Tomorrow Good-bye*, p. 324, 1948
• I walked on down the street and turned into the subway kiosk wondering what the deuce had happened to Washington.—Mickey Spillane, *Kiss Me Deadly*, p. 45, 1952

20 the Delta Dagger fighter aircraft *US, 1970*

• The first USAF aircraft armed only with guided missiles and unguided rockets – the Convair YF-102 Delta Dagger, always called "the Deuce" – made its first flight on 24 October 1953.—James P. McCarthy, *The Air Force*, p. 81, 2002

▸ **deuce of benders**

the knees *US*

• —Marcus Hanna Boulware, *Jive and Slang of Students in Negro Colleges*, 1947

deuce *verb*

1 to shear 200 sheep in a day *AUSTRALIA, 1950*
Recorded by Hence, 'deucer' (someone capable of this feat).
- —G.A. Wilkes, *A Dictionary of Australian Colloquialisms*, 1978

2 to back down from a confrontation *US*
- You deuced. Admit it. You deuced.—Hal Ellson, *Tomboy*, p. 3, 1950

3 to supply someone with marijuana *US*
- —Robert Nash, *Dictionary of Crime*, p. 101, 1992

deuce and ace; deuce *noun*

a face *UK, 1925*
Rhyming slang, dated and rare.

deuce-and-a-half *noun*

a two-and-a-half ton cargo truck *US, 1944*
Military usage since World War 2.
- The gas truck, a deuce-and-a-half with two fuel tanks on the back, marked "Mo-gas," had begun moving up the line, refueling.—Larry Heinemann, *Close Quarters*, p. 17, 1977
- One fine day this full-bird colonel pulled up in a deuce-and-a-half and volunteered a bunch of us, so we pile in his truck, and off we go south[.]—Larry Heinemann, *Paco's Story*, p. 130, 1986
- No, we ain't seen nothin' all night 'cept some jeeps and a deuce 'n a half going up to the cavalary.—Harold Coyle, *Team Yankee*, p. 12, 1987

deuce-and-a-quarter *noun*

a Buick Electra 225 *US, 1968*
- —*Current Slang*, p. 6, Fall 1970
- In my deuce and a quarter feelin' funky funky fine...—N.P.G., *Deuce & A Quarter*, 1993
- By the time we'd graduated, he'd bought a real good toot and paid cash for a deuce-and-a-quarter, a Buick Electra 225.—Nathan McCall, *Makes Me Wanna Holler*, p. 124, 1994
- Shit, Russell, you be lucky to get you a Buick, maybe. 'Cause you know you ain't nothin' but a deuce-and-a-quarter-ridin' motherfucker. —George P. Zuckerman, *King Suckerman*, p. 71, 1997

deuce bag; deuce *noun*

a two-dollar bag of heroin *US, 1971*
- —Richard A. Soears, *The Slang of Drugs and Drink*, 1986

deuceburger *noun*

a prison sentence of two years *US*
- —Charles Shafer, *Folk Speech in Texas Prisons*, p. 202, 1990

deuced *adjective*

damned; confounded *UK, 1782*
Dated, but occasionally used with heavy irony.
- I'll be deuced if I'll forswear swearing.—*The Observer*, 29th June 2003

deuce-deal *verb*

to deal the second card in a deck *US, 1965*
- —Thomas L. Clark, *The Dictionary of Gambling and Gaming*, p. 61, 1987

deuce-deuce *noun*

a .22 calibre weapon *US*
- I got a Deuce Deuce. My brother gave it to me before he went inna county jail.—*Boyz N The Hood*, 1990
- He say how dem guinea gray cats go got him a deuce-deuce t'carry. —Stephen Cannell, *King Con*, p. 50, 1997
- Bolden broke into the Pony Express Sports Shop in North Hills and took about 25 guns – "nines," "deuce-deuces," and "deuce-fives," Dixon, also of North Hills testified[.]—*Daily News of Los Angeles*, p. N1, 27th April 2003

deuce-deuce-five *noun*

a Buick Electra 225 *US*
- Rollin' in my deuce deuce 5 / Convertible top down so I can see the honeys passin' me by[.]—N.P.G., *Deuce & A Quarter*, 1993

deuce-five *noun*

a .25 calibre gun *US*
- Bolden broke into the Pony Express Sports Shop in North Hills and took about 25 guns – "nines," "deuce-deuces," and "deuce-fives," Dixon, also of North Hills testified[.]—*Daily News of Los Angeles*, p. N1, 27th April 2003

deuce gear *noun*

a soldier's rucksack and other items carried in the field *US*
- —*Linda Reinberg, In the Field*, p. 61, 1991

deuce out *verb*

to withdraw from a situation out of fear *US*
- Hell, I felt like I was getting to be chicken. Deucing out.—Hal Ellson, *Duke*, p. 17, 1949

deuce-point *noun*

in a field patrol, the second soldier in line *US*
- —Linda Reinberg, *In the Field*, p. 61, 1991

deuces *noun*

1 dice that have been altered to have two twos, the second two being where one would expect to find a five *US*
Used in combination with **FIVES**, likely to produce a seven, an important number in craps.
- —John Scarne, *Scarne on Dice*, p. 466, 1974

2 a double line *US*
- —Charles Shafer, *Folk Speech in Texas Prisons*, p. 205, 1990

▸ **deuces are in**

in firefighter usage, pay cheques are prepared and ready to be distributed *US*
From a gong signal of 2-2-2.
- — *American Speech*, p. 275, December 1954: 'Fire terms: additional words and definitions'

deuce up *verb*

to line up in pairs *US*
- —Charles Shafer, *Folk Speech in Texas Prisons*, p. 202, 1990

deuceway *noun*

an amount of marijuana costing two dollars *US*
- Yeah, they got stoned on giggle-weed, zonked on grifa, zapped on yerba, bombed on boo, they were blitzed with snop, warped on twist, gay on hay, free on V- deuceways, nicels, dimes, lids, pounds and kilos of it.—*Hi Life*, p. 14, 1979

devil *noun*

1 a barbiturate or other central nervous system depressant, especially Seconal™ *US*
A truncated form of **RED DEVIL**.
- I said, "If your sick father can part with at least two dozen devils, I'll part with half a C-note."—Iceberg Slim (Robert Beck), *Trick Baby*, p. 268, 1969

2 the hallucinogen STP *US*
- —Eugene Landy, *The Underground Dictionary*, p. 65, 1971

3 a printer's apprentice or errand boy *UK, 1683*
- I was a printer's devil when I was ten, and I stayed till I couldn't work no more.—Lilian Jackson Braun, *The Cat Who Knew Shakespeare*, p. 99, 1988

4 a white person *US*
- —Edith A. Folb, *runnin' down some lines*, p. 234, 1980

5 in craps, a seven *US*
- —Frank Scoblete, *Guerrilla Gamblin*, p. 305, 1993

▸ **devil of a**

an extreme (originally diabolical) example of something *UK, 1767*
May be used with 'a' or 'the'.
- Hilary Mantel survived the devil of a girlhood and had to wrestle with serious illness.—*The Independent*, 10th May 2003
- We all know, when the gremlins get in there and affect your confidence, it's a devil of a job to get them out.—*The Guardian*, 12th May 2003

▸ **devil take him!; devil take you!; devil take me!; devil take it!**

used for expressing anger, impatience, frustration *UK, 1548*
Often used with 'the'.

▸ **go to the devil**

to fall into ruin *UK*
From about 1460, although it is recorded in Latin more than a hundred years earlier.
- Of course, all the scientific projects have gone to the devil and now I'm an avid reader only of Charlie and Freddie [Marx and Engels]. —Ernesto Che Guevara, *Back On The Road (translated by Patrick Camiller)*, 1956

▸ **go to the devil!**

used as an angry expression of dismissal *UK, 1859*
If not an exclamation, certainly imperative.
- Mr Möllemann was publicly none too pleased with the compliment. Mr Haider, he said, can "go to the devil".—*The Guardian*, 31st May 2002

▸ **how the devil!; what the devil!; when the devil!; where the devil!; who the devil!; why the devil!**

used as an impatient intensification of how, what, when, where, who, why *UK, 1489*

In early uses 'the Devil' was capitalised. 'What the devil' since about 1385. 'When the devil' since 1562. 'Where the devil', 1687. 'Who the devil', 1568. 'Why the devil', 1819.

- Now how the devil did you know about Ballygowan? — Agatha Christie, *At Bertram's Hotel*, 1965
- [W]hy the devil should there not be a debate across the country also? — Mr Straw, *UK Parliament Hansard*, 2nd June 1998
- "He looked right down his nose at me," Smith remembered, "like he was saying, 'Who the devil are you?'" — *The Observer*, 25th August 2001
- When the devil will you start applying the laws of Pakistan to all its citizens, without favour to some? — *The News International (Pakistan)*, 24th November 2001
- What the devil can you mean by that? — *The Guardian*, 25th June 2003
- The head honcho of a media group collared me at a function last week, playfully clipped me on the ear and tetchily asked where the devil I'd been for the past six months. — *Sunday Times (South Africa)*, 23rd March 2003

▸ **little devil; young devil**

used as a form of address *UK, 1931*

Often in tones of exasperation to, for instance, a wilful child; conspiratorial or playful to a (mischievous) adult.

- You really had me going for a while, you little devil. — *www.cannabis-news.com*, 21st February 2001

▸ **the devil made me do it!**

used as a humorous excuse for misconduct *US*

A catchphrase made wildly popular by comedian Flip Wilson on *The Flip Wilson Show* (NBC, 1970–74). Repeated with referential humour.

▸ **the devil to pay; the devil and all to pay; the very devil to pay**

very unpleasant consequences to face up to *UK, 1733*

An echo of Faust.

- There'll be the Devil to Pay: The Future of America's Recovered Memory Movement is at Stake in a $35M Lawsuit — *The Independent*, 17th October 1994

Devil *noun*

▸ **The Devil is rolling his oats**

it is thundering *CANADA*

- — T. K. Pratt, *oral informant in Prince Edward Island Sayings*, p. 104, 1998

devil and demon; devil *noun*

semen *UK*

Rhyming slang.

- She's had more of the devil inside her than the whole of the Spanish Armada. — Bodmin Dark, *Dirty Cockney Rhyming Slang*, 2003

devil bridle *noun*

spittle dried around the mouth *TRINIDAD AND TOBAGO, 1951*

- — Lise Winer, *Dictionary of the English/Creole of Trinidad & Tobago*, 2003

devil dancing hour *noun*

very late at night *TRINIDAD AND TOBAGO, 1971*

- — Lise Winer, *Dictionary of the English/Creole of Trinidad & Tobago*, 2003

devil devil *adjective*

(used of rough country) country broken up into holes and hillocks *AUSTRALIA, 1844*

From Aboriginal pidgin for an 'evil spirit'.

devil-dog *noun*

a member of the US Marine Corps *US, 1918*

- He spotted the joker which would have wiped out the Marine Corps in the administration Defense reorganization measure and tied the bill up until the Devil Dogs were assured of being more than a mere "police force." — Jack Lait and Lee Mortimer, *Washington Confidential*, p. 162, 1951
- "Nothing," crowed The New York Times, "could stop our gallant Devil Dogs." That was not entirely true. — William Manchester, *Goodbye, Darkness*, p. 25, 1979

devil drug *noun*

crack cocaine *UK*

- — Mike Haskins, *Drugs*, p. 281, 2003

devilfish *noun*

in poker, a skilled player who plays poorly to mask his skill early in a game *US*

- — John Vorhaus, *The Big Book of Poker Slang*, p. 13, 1996

devil me arse!

used as an expletive *UK, 1984*

Of Anglo-Irish origins.

Devil's Asshole *nickname*

an area in the Mekong Delta south of Sa Dec with a strong Viet Cong presence *US*

- — Gregory Clark, *Words of the Vietnam War*, p. 142, 1990

devil's bedpost *noun*

in a deck of playing cards, the four of clubs *UK, 1837*

- — Albert H. Morehead, *The Complete Guide to Winning Poker*, p. 261, 1967

devil's dancing rock *noun*

a large, smooth, flat stone found in a pasture or meadow *US*

- — Charles F. Haywood, *Yankee Dictionary*, p. 44, 1963

devil's dandruff *noun*

cocaine; crack cocaine *US*

A simile for an 'evil white powder'.

- Beware the devil's dandruff, he'd heard an actress warn. — Joseph Wambaugh, *The Glitter Dome*, p. 249, 1981
- — Mike Haskins, *Drugs*, p. 280, 2003
- [H]e "made love all night" after being introduced to the Devil's dandruff by a lap dancer. — *Q*, p. 32, October 2004

devil's dick *noun*

a crack cocaine pipe *US*

- — Terry Williams, *Crackhouse*, p. 148, 1992

devil's dust *noun*

1 crack cocaine *US*

- — US Department of Justice, *Street Terms*, October 1994

2 phencyclidine, the recreational drug known as PCP or angel dust *US*

- — Jay Robert Nash, *Dictionary of Crime*, p. 101, 1992

devil's half acre *noun*

a neighbourhood catering to vice *US, 1959*

- In a riverside neighborhood called the Devil's Half Acre, dozens of bars, bordellos, and gambling dens competed to empty the men's pockets. — Jamie Jensen, *Road Trip USA: New England*, p. 115, 2001

devil's herb *noun*

hashish (cannabis resin or pollen) *UK*

- I stopped smoking the devil's herb when I was oh... fourteen or fifteen. — Donald Gorgon, *Cop Killer*, p. 66, 1994

devil's luck; devil's own luck *noun*

unusually good luck; occasionally, bad luck *UK, 1891*

- "If ever a man had the devil's own luck," said Dr Quimper. — Agatha Christie, *4.50 From Paddington*, 1957

devil snatcher *noun*

larva of the dragon fly *CANADA*

- It was she who informed us that there would be many fish at the north end of the lake feeding on devil snatchers, which I guess you'll know, are the larvae of the dragon fly. The few elsewhere would take nothing but devil snatchers. — John Gowland, *Smoke over Sikanaska*, p. 167, 1955

devil's own *adjective*

devilish; troublesome, difficult *UK, 1729*

- [A]fter the result of the ballot was announced, we had the devil's own job to get the United States involved in the multinational force. — *The National Interest*, 17th October 1999

devil's smoke *noun*

crack cocaine *US*

- — US Department of Justice, *Street Terms*, October 1994
- — Mike Haskins, *Drugs*, p. 281, 2003

devil's tar *noun*

oil *US, 1949*

- — Frederic G. Cassidy, *Dictionary of American Regional English, Vol. II*, p. 56, 1991

devil weed *noun*

1 *Datura stramonium*, a narcotic herb *US*

A plant that can be eaten or smoked for drug intoxication and hallucinogenic effect, and is sometimes mistaken for marijuana. It is variously known as known as 'jimson weed' (corrupted from Jamestown weed), 'yerba dal diablo' (devil's herb), 'devil's apple' and 'thorn apple' (from the appearance of the fruit), 'angel's trumpet' and 'Gabriel's trumpet' (the flower). Native to south-western US, Mexico, Central America, India and Asia; an occasional weed in Britain.

- — *www.thenewforestweb.co.uk*, March 2001

2 marijuana *US, 1985*
Ironic, mocking those who condemn marijuana.

devo *noun*
a deviant *AUSTRALIA*
- For example, his dorky character "Stevo the Devo" sprang from a former life as a public servant – in the Deceased Estates Office. — *Herald*, p. 4, 7th May 1990

dew *noun*
1 marijuana; hashish *US, 1971*
- — Richard A. Spears, *The Slang and Jargon of Drugs and Drink*, p. 141, 1986
- — Mike Haskins, *Drugs*, p. 287, 2003

2 rum that has been manufactured illegally *TRINIDAD AND TOBAGO*
- — Lise Winer, *Dictionary of the English/Creole of Trinidad & Tobago*, 2003

▸ **knock the dew off the lily; shake the dew off the lily**
(of a male) to urinate *US*
- Think I'll shake a little dew off the lily then." He turned toward the door beyond the dance floor marked HIS. — Earl Thompson, *Tattoo*, p. 75, 1974
- — Pamela Munro, *U.C.L.A. Slang*, p. 54, 1989
- "While you're doing that," Elvin said, "I'm gonna go shake the dew off my lily." He got up and walked to the men's room, all the way in back. — Elmore Leonard, *Maximum Bob*, p. 201, 1991

dewbaby *noun*
a dark-skinned black male *US*
- — David Claerbaut, *Black Jargon in White America*, p. 62, 1972

dew drop *noun*
a drop of clear nasal fluid or mucus that hangs from the tip of the nose *UK, 1984*
- She stopped mixing the dough and her dew drop fell — *The Guardian*, 3rd April 1972

Dewey *noun*
a socially inept social outcast *US*
- — Michael V. Anderson, *The Bad, Rad, Not to Forget Way Cool Beach and Surf Discriptionary*, p. 5, 1988

dewey; dooe; dooey; duey *noun*
two *UK, 1937*
From Italian *due* via parleyaree into polari.
- [Y]ou might like to count to ten in Polari: una, duey, trey quater, chicker, sey, setter, otto, nobber, dacha. — Michael Quinion, *World Wide Words*, 1996
- — Paul Baker, *Polari*, p. 171, 2002

DEWLINE *noun*
the network of radar stations and airstrips for interceptor aircraft across Canada's North *CANADA*
An abbreviation of '*D*istant *E*arly *W*arning *Line*'.
- Some thought the just-finished Dewline and nearly all the rest of our defense apparatus had become obsolete. — *Maclean's*, p. 4/1, 28th September 1957

dex *noun*
1 Dexedrine™, a central nervous system stimulant *US, 1961*
- In my case, I was just on dex, and occasionally on Benzedrine. — John Warren Wells, *Tricks of the Trade*, p. 16, 1970
- He said there would be two or three doctors on hand with B1 shots and Dex and penicillin to handle various things like hang-overs, fatigue and the clap. — Dan Jenkins, *Semi-Tough*, p. 125, 1972
- I had a couple of tall-ones, a change of clothes, doubled-Dexed it, and hit the street. — Terry Southern, *Now Dig This*, p. 131, 2001

2 dextromethorphan (DXM), an active ingredient in non-prescription cold and cough medication, often abused for non-medicinal purposes *US*
- Youths' nicknames for DXM: Robo, Skittles, Triple C's, Rojo, Dex, Tussin, Vitamin D. DXM abuse is called "Robotripping" or "Tussing." Users might be called "syrup heads" or "robotards." — *USA Today*, p. 1A, 29th December 2003

3 MDMA, the recreational drug best known as ecstasy *UK*
From **DECADENCE** (MDMA).
- — Mike Haskins, *Drugs*, p. 289, 2003

dexedrine *noun*
MDMA, the recreational drug best known as ecstasy *UK*
An elaboration of **DEX** (MDMA) based on Dexedrine™, a branded amphetamine.
- — Mike Haskins, *Drugs*, p. 289, 2003

dexie; dexi; dexo *noun*
Dexedrine™, a central nervous system stimulant *US, 1951*
- Two or three people can get high on one joint (marijuana cigarette). Of course, you can take bennies (Benzedrine) or dexies (Dexedrine), but they make me nervous. I'm a hog. I don't just take one. I take three or four. You can get hooked on them. — *Time*, p. 19, 7th July 1952
- "I feel miserable today. I'm really dragging." SECOND WOMAN: "Here, take one of these Dexies." — Lenny Bruce, *How to Talk Dirty and Influence People*, p. 46, 1965
- After tomorrow, not a drop of horse, dexies, or reefer will be sold in this town without us getting some part of the money. — Donald Goines, *Black Gangster*, p. 34, 1977
- Meditation, shit! Cocaine or maybe a dexi was more like it. — Odie Hawkins, *The Busting Out of an Ordinary Man*, p. 156, 1985
- He remembered a thousand Soledad bull sessions about dope and dry-swallowed two perks and three dexies. — James Ellroy, *Suicide Hill*, p. 749, 1986
- — Angela Devlin, *Prison Patter*, p. 21, 1996

dexter *noun*
a diligent, socially inept student *US*
- The strongest competition to squid and grimbo as succesor term of nerd is dexter, a shortening of poindexter, probably based on a cartoon character. — *New York Times Magazine*, 22nd September 1985

DFFL
*d*ope *f*orever, *f*orever *l*oaded – a slogan of the Hell's Angels motorcyle gang that enjoyed somewhat wider popularity *US*
- Others, like the patch saying "DFFL" (Dope Forever, Forever Loaded) and the Playboy Rabbit (mocking birth control) were exposed by True magazine. — Hunter S. Thompson, *Hell's Angels*, p. 117, 1966
- — Paladin Press, *Inside Look at Outlaw Motorcyle Gangs*, p. 35, 1992

D for dunce; deefer *noun*
money, profits, extras, undeclared income *UK*
Rhyming slang for **BUNCE**.
- — Ray Puxley, *Cockney Rabbit*, 1992

DFP *noun*
in pornography, a scene in a film or a photograph showing two men ejaculating on a woman's face; a *d*ouble *f*acial *p*op *US*
- — *Adult Video News*, p. 44, August 1995

DFs *noun*
DF118s, painkillers manufactured from synthetic opium, used recreationally *UK*
- — Angela Devlin, *Prison Patter*, p. 43, 1996
- As well as smack, coke and spliff, we were starting to take lots of different pills, Valium, Rohypnol, Temazepan, DFs and Tempgesics – all downers of one kind or another. — Simon Napier-Bell, *Black Vinyl White Powder*, p. 283, 2001

DH
used as an exhortation while drinking *NEW ZEALAND*
An abbreviation of '*d*own the *h*atch!'.
- — David McGill, *David McGill's Complete Kiwi Slang Dictionary*, p. 39, 1998

dhobi; dhobie; dohbie *noun*
1 a native Indian washerman *INDIA, 1816*
From Hindi *dhobi* or *dhoby* (a member of the 'Scheduled Castes' born to wash and press clothes).
- — Nigel Hankin, *Hanklyn Janklyn*, 2003

2 laundry, washing *UK*
From the verb sense; originally a military usage.
- — Paul Baker, *Polari*, p. 171, 2002

dhobi; dhobie; dohbie *verb*
to wash (your clothes) *UK, 1929*
From Hindustani *dhob* (washing); originally a nautical usage, then general in all military services.
- — Paul Baker, *Polari*, p. 171, 2002

dhobi dust *noun*
any washing powder *UK, 1984*
Military; extended from **DHOBI** (laundry).

dhobi mark *noun*
a small laundry mark *INDIA*
Anglo-Indian.
- — Nigel Hankin, *Hanklyn Janklyn*, 2003

dhobi's itch *noun*

a ring-worm infection of the armpit and groin in areas of high humidity or temperature *UK, 1890*

This 'itch' appears to derive not from **DHOBI** (the washerman) but from **DHOBI** (the laundry) as the condition was thought to spread via underwear which had been washed together.

- This is one cause of tinea cruris ('dhobi itch') and 'jungle rot'. —C.H. Collins, *Collins and Lyne's Microbiological Methods*, p. 467, 1995

dhobi wallah *noun*

a native washerman serving the military *INDIA, 1937*

Of Anglo-Indian military origin. An extension of **DHOBI** (a washerman), possibly a combination of **DHOBI** (laundry) and 'wallah' (a man – in relation to his occupation).

diablo *noun*

LSD *UK*

The Spanish for 'devil'.

- —Mike Haskins, *Drugs*, p. 285, 2003

diabolical *adjective*

disgraceful *UK, 1958*

'Possessed by the devil' in a weakened sense.

- "Diabolical liberty," Monty muttered to himself, still clinging to the bar. —Derek Bickerton, *Payroll*, p. 121, 1959
- [T]he engine is diabolical. British Leyland. Conks out, all the time. —Mike Stott, *Soldiers Talking, Cleanly*, 1978

dial *noun*

the face *US, 1842*

- I gave the rest of the watch the once over, but there were no signs of scrapping on any other dial[.] —Robert S. Close, *Love Me Sailor*, p. 108, 1945
- [His] days as the shining light of the Ghost Squad were now over, his dial having become as familiar to the entire underworld of London as Big Ben's. —Charles Raven, *Underworld Nights*, p. 99, 1956

dial *verb*

1 in a prayer group, to pray first *US*

Not much language used by the religious qualifies as slang, but this certainly does.

- —Connie Eble (Editor), *UNC-CH Campus Slang*, p. 3, November 1990

2 in foot-propelled scootering, to get a trick right *UK*

- —Ben Sharpe, *Scooter Crazy*, p. 40, 2000

▸ **dial a traf**

to fart *US*

When the spelling of each word is reversed the sense is revealed: 'laid a fart'.

- Someone's dialled a traf. —Peter Furze, *Tailwinds*, p. 56, 1998

DIAL *adjective*

*d*umb *i*n *a*ny *l*anguage *US*

Said of truly incommunicative hospital patients.

- —Sally Williams, *"Strong" Words*, p. 139, 1994

dial-a-winner *noun*

a Dodge push-button automatic transmission *US*

- —Lyle K. Engel, *The Complete Book of Fuel and Gas Dragsters*, p. 150, 1968

dialed in *adjective*

1 in a state of concentration that excludes any and all distractions *US*

Punning on 'connected'. May be reduced to its first element.

- —Jim Humes and Sean Wagstaff, *Boarderlands/title>221*, 1995

2 belonging to the inner circle *US*

- —Jim Crotty, *How to Talk American*, p. 162, 1997

dialer *noun*

a telephone that when called automatically calls another telphone number *US*

- The line was used as an inexpensive alarm system, known as a "dialer." —Emmett Grogan, *Final Score*, p. 86, 1976

dial in on *verb*

to understand what motivates someone else; to grasp their personality *US*

- —Vann Wesson, *Generation X Field Guide and Lexicon*, p. 52, 1997

dial out *verb*

to ignore *US*

- Then I dialed him out because he seemed to advocate everything that had been said by his cohorts, and I could look in his face and tell he was afraid. —Clarence Cooper Jr, *The Farm*, p. 166, 1967

dialtone *noun*

a personality-free person *US*

- She knew Sunny Deelight, a real dialtone. —Seth Morgan, *Homeboy*, p. 296, 1990

diamaid *noun*

in a deck of playing cards, a diamond *TRINIDAD AND TOBAGO*

- —Lise Winer, *Dictionary of the English/Creole of Trinidad & Tobago*, 2003

diambista *noun*

marijuana *US, 1954*

- —Richard A. Spears, *The Slang and Jargon of Drugs and Drink*, p. 141, 1986
- —Mike Haskins, *Drugs*, p. 287, 2003

diamond *noun*

1 anything that is considered as the best, especially as an assessment of personal qualities *UK, 1990*

- We're diamond geezers, Russ. Diamonds —Greg Williams, *Diamond Geezers*, p. 45, 1997
- She doesn't understand football but she's a diamond, that girl. — Martin King and Martin Knight, *The Naughty Nineties*, p. 141, 1999
- I'm gonna be making a movie with this diamond geezer over the next couple of months[.] —Stewart Home, *Sex Kick*, p. 259, 1999
- He's a dad, a diamond, a man who likes a drink and a bite to eat. —John King, *Human Punk*, p. 234, 2000
- James is evidently an old-code man, with a sharp eye for separating the diamonds (good guys) from the plastics (flaky ones)[.] —*The Guardian*, p. 4, 13th May 2003

2 an amphetamine tablet scored with a diamond-shape *UK*

- —Mike Haskins, *Drugs*, p. 279, 2003

3 a tablet of MDMA, the recreational drug best known as ecstasy *UK*

- —Mike Haskins, *Drugs*, p. 289, 2003

4 a custom diamond-shaped car window *US*

- —Edith A. Folb, *runnin' down some lines*, p. 234, 1980
- Diamonds in the back, sunroof top / diggin the scene with the gangster lean. — Massive Attack, *Be Thankful for What You've Got*, 1991

Diamond *noun*

the central square of an Irish town *IRELAND*

- The fountain wasn't frozen it was spraying away goodo on the Diamond so I sat down beside it for a while. —Patrick McCabe, *The Butcher Boy*, p. 103, 1992

diamond *adjective*

excellent *UK, 1990*

- "Ah you have arrived. I hope everything is satisfactory." "Diamond so fat lady. Diamond." —Jeremy Cameron, *Brown Bread in Wengen*, p. 159, 1999

diamond cutter *noun*

the erect penis *US*

A later variation on the penis as a type of tool.

- During his one month convalescence Rosco was unable to raise what Harold Bloomguard called a "diamond cutter" or even a "blue veiner" due to the shooting pains in his groin. —Joseph Wambaugh, *The Choirboys*, p. 45, 1975
- Chubs found himself wielding something less than a world-class, diamond-cutter erection. —Carl Hiaasen, *Lucky You*, p. 366, 1997
- Then she slowly twists 360 degrees, all the while impaled on your diamond-cutter. — *The FHM Little Book of Bloke*, p. 25, June 2003

diamond dust *noun*

crystallized ice in the air *ANTARCTICA, 1958*

- —Bernadette Hince, *The Antarctic Dictionary*, p. 98, 2000

diamonds *noun*

1 a type of bet in an illegal numbers game lottery *US*

- He played the money row, lucky lady, happy days, true love, sun gonna shine, gold, silver, diamonds, dollars and whiskey. —Chester Himes, *A Rage in Harlem*, p. 23, 1957

2 the testicles *US*

An evolution from the common **FAMILY JEWELS**.

- —Roger Blake, *The American Dictionary of Sexual Terms*, p. 57, 1964

diamond season *noun*

warm weather *US*

- —Carsten Stroud, *Close Pursuit*, p. 271, 1987

Diamond Street *nickname*

47th Street just west of Fifth Avenue, New York *US*

Home to many diamond merchants.

- —Ralph de Sola, *Crime Dictionary*, p. 198, 1982

diamond white *noun*

a white Cadillac *US*

- —Ethan Hilderbrant, *Prison Slang*, p. 36, 1998

Diana Dors *noun*

knickers, drawers *UK*

Rhyming slang, formed on the professional name of 'Blonde Bombshell' actress Diana Fluck, 1931–84. A humorous reference to women's underwear, perhaps by contrast with the enhanced and marketed sexuality that was Diana Dors.

- —Ray Puxley, *Cockney Rabbit*, 1992

diaper *noun*

1 a sanitary towel *US*

- —Edith A. Folb, *runnin' down some lines*, p. 234, 1980

2 any winter covering on the front of a truck *US*

- —Montie Tak, *Truck Talk*, p. 43, 1971

3 a rubber insulating blanket used in overhead electric line work *US*

- —A.B. Chance Co., *Lineman's Slang Dictionary*, p. 5, 1980

diaper dandy *noun*

an athlete in his first year of college *US*

Coined or popularised by sports announcer Dick Vitale.

- —Connie Eble (Editor), *UNC-CH Campus Slang*, p. 2, Spring 1993

diapers *noun*

a flotation coat with between-the-legs button flaps issued by the National Science Foundation in Antarctica *ANTARCTICA, 1991*

- —Carnegie Mellon Astrophysics Peterson Group, *Antarctic Vocabulary*, 19th September 1997

diazzy *noun*

a diazepam tablet *UK*

- [N]o fucker ever died from a diazzy overdose mun. Methadone aye, but not diazepam. Mickey Mouse downer, diazepam.—Niall Griffiths, *Sheepshagger*, p. 108, 2001
- She swallows hers as well. Diazzies? What the fuck's she on diazzies for?—Niall Griffiths, *Kelly + Victor*, p. 23, 2002

dibbi dibbi *adjective*

stupid; worthless; insignificant *UK*

- Most of them cyann [cannot] deal with a strong woman like me. They just want some dibbi dibbi meek gal.—Donald Gorgon, *Cop Killer*, p. 57, 1994

dibble *noun*

an encounter with the police; the police; a police officer *UK*

Appeared in this sense during the 1990s; after Officer Dibble, the police character in cult television cartoon series *Top Cat*, Hanna Barbera, 1961.

- A cry went up into the dawn sky. "Beast! Dibbles! Beast! Beast-bwai!"—Karline Smith, *Modd Side Massive*, p. 102, 1994
- —Angela Devlin, *Prison Patter*, p. 43, 1996
- You'd think Johnny would have had the sense not to tell the Dibble who put him in hospital[.]—Val McDermid, *Keeping on the Right Side of the Law*, p. 179–180, 1999
- The squaddie Dibble resentfully handed me the money[.]—Wayne Anthony, *Spanish Highs*, p. 6, 1999

dibbler *noun*

the penis *US*

- The attraction of my hand, my fingers at her clitoris, only distracts from her skill on my dibbler.—Clarence Major, *All-Night Visitors*, p. 6, 1998

dibbly-dobbler *noun*

an accurate, medium-pace cricket bowler; such a cricketer's delivery *UK, 1997*

- —Keith Foley, *A Dictionary of Cricketing Terminology*, p. 105, 1998
- There was a need now to concentrate more on faster bowlers than the 'dibbly-dobbly' medium-pacers that have been such a part of the Black Caps' approach. 'Perhaps the days of the dibbly-dobbler are gone.'—*Dominion*, p. 60, 31st January 2001

dib-dabs *noun*

a condition of anxiety, uneasiness, nervousness *UK*

A variation of 'abdabs' reported by Commander C. Parsons, 1984.

dibs *noun*

1 first right to, first claim on *US, 1932*

Among the earliest slang a child in the US learns; derives from 'dib' (a portion or a share) which was first recorded in the UK by Barrere and Leland in 1889.

- —Helen Dahlskog (Editor), *A Dictionary of Contemporary and Colloquial Usage*, p. 18, 1972
- The black market, meaning the dope fiends who slept in our kitchen in the winter, offered us dibs on what they stole.—Odie Hawkins, *Scars and Memories*, p. 147, 1987
- But now, you understand, Homicide will have a priority, first dibs.—Elmore Leonard, *Freaky Deaky*, p. 175, 1988
- "Vijay has his dibs in on them." "But, Frank, that's not fair!" I complained. "I know, Nick. But those are the rules. Dibs is dibs. You know that."—C.D. Payne, *Youth in Revolt*, p. 284, 1993
- RANDAL: That's the movie I came for. V.A. CUSTOMER: I have first dibs. RANDAL: Says who? V.A. CUSTOMER: Says me. I've been here for half an hour. I'd call that first dibs.—*Clerks*, p. 35, 1994
- "Dibs on that bitch," I avow. "Good luck," Dylan says.—Marty Beckerman, *Death to All Cheerleaders*, p. 13, 2000

2 money *UK, 1807*

- "How you gonna raise the dibs?" "Multi-national companies. Conservation groups."—Anthony Masters, *Minder*, p. 176, 1984
- [T]he dibs being already earmarked for so-called artists who seem two Burnt Umbers short of a palate[.]—Andrew Nickolds, *Back to Basics*, p. 27, 1994

3 a living *US*

- What do you shake them for? How do you make your dibs?—Raymond Chandler, *The Little Sister*, p. 28, 1949

4 a room, apartment or house *US*

- —Kenn "Naz" Young, *Naz's Dictionary of Teen Slang*, p. 30, 1993

dibs and dabs *noun*

1 small amounts *US, 1960*

- Mom's Magic Seasoning: Mix and add all "dibs and dabs" from your almost empty spice bottles together.—Wendy Louise, *The Complete Crockpot Cookbook*, p. 131, 2003

2 pubic lice *UK*

Rhyming slang for **CRABS**.

- —Julian Franklyn, *A Dictionary of Rhyming Slang*, 1961

dic; dick *noun*

a *dic*tionary *US, 1831*

Recorded as 'The Dic and the Little Dics' by Miss K.M. Elizabeth Murray, *Caught in the Web of Words*, 1977, with the implication that this term was coined by, or within the family of, Scottish philologist and first lexicographer of the *Oxford English Dictionary*, Sir James Murray, 1837–1915; it would be nice if it were true. 'Dick', in the sense that someone who uses fine words is said to have 'swallowed the dick', is recorded in 1873.

dice *noun*

1 in motor racing, a duel between two cars within the field of competitors *US, 1962*

- A dice might be described as a race within a race as, for example, when two cars are battling closely for a specific position.—John Lawlor, *How to Talk Car*, p. 38, 1965

2 crack cocaine *UK*

- —Mike Haskins, *Drugs*, p. 281, 2003

3 Desoxyn™, a branded methamphetamine hydrochloride *US*

- —Walter L. Way, *The Drug Scene*, p. 108, 1977

▸ **dice on the floor, seven at the door**

used in casino gambling to express the superstitious gambler's belief that if the dice leave the table and land on the floor during a game of craps, the next roll will be a seven *US*

- "Dice on the floor, seven at the door." And they'll always remember when it comes back a seven.—Edward Lin, *Big Julie of Vegas*, p. 245, 1974

dice *verb*

1 to disparage or insult effectively *US*

- —Judi Sanders, *Faced and Faded, Hanging to Hurl*, p. 11, 1993

2 to reject, to throw away *AUSTRALIA, 1944*

The probable derivation is from conventional 'dice' (to lose or throw away).

3 to throw away; reject; discard *AUSTRALIA, 1943*

- Talking of cars, things must be rough for the used car boys. They've diced the pitch about the old lady who drove it to church every Sunday, are now claiming the one owner job belonged to a nympho who only used the back seat!—*Ribald*, p. 7, 1975
- —Jim Ramsay, *Cop It Sweet!*, p. 28, 1977

dice bite *noun*

a wound on the hand of a gambler in casino craps when struck by tossed dice *US, 1983*

- The stickman shouts, "there's no cure for dice bite," as a signal for the players to keep their hands up when the dice are coming out. —Thomas L. Clark, *The Dictionary of Gambling and Gaming*, p. 62, 1987

dice mob *noun*

a group of two or more cheats in a dice game *US, 1961*

- —Thomas L. Clark, *The Dictionary of Gambling and Gaming*, p. 63, 1987

dicer *noun*

1 a hat *US, 1887*

- —Lou Shelly, *Hepcats Jive Dictionary*, p. 9, 1945
- —Joseph E. Ragen and Charles Finston, *Inside the World's Toughest Prison*, p. 796, 1962: 'Penitentiary and underworld glossary'

2 a fast freight train *US, 1927*

- —Ramon Adams, *The Language of the Railroader*, p. 44, 1977

3 a 'duel' between two drivers *UK, 1984*

Car racing drivers' and commentators' use.

dice with death *verb*

to risk actual death or figurative demise *UK, 1941*

- Horace Silver has spent most of his life dicing with death.— *The Observer*, 22nd February 2004

dicey; dicy *adjective*

risky, uncertain *UK, 1944*

- [I]t's all a trifle dicey.—Colin MacInnes, *Absolute Beginners*, 1959
- The wording would be dicey, considering the publicity[.]—Carl Hiaasen, *Tourist Season*, p. 143, 1986
- [I]t was a bit dicy to rely on lots of nuclear power stations[.]—Josie Dew, *The Sun In My Eyes*, p. 294, 2001

dicey on the ubble *adjective*

balding *UK*

Used by Teddy Boys.

- — *News Chronicle*, 22nd May 1958

dick *noun*

1 the penis *US, 1888*

- Sometimes, though, I'd go home afterwards, after having had a hard-on for four hours of making out on the floor and in the bleachers, but without creaming, and it really gave you a sore dick.— *The Berkeley Tribe*, p. 13, 5th-12th September 1969
- [T]he thick cunt who stands at the door pretending to be a security guard, biceps for brains and a dick the size of my clit[.]—Stella Duffy, *Jail Bait [britpulp]*, p. 115, 1999
- People say that guns are just dicks but if my dick was this heavy I'd work with a limp.—J.J. Connolly, *Layer Cake*, p. 199, 2000
- He shook his dick and walked out.—Malcolm Pryce, *Aberystwyth Mon Amour*, p. 24, 2001

2 the clitoris *US*

- She had a dick so long she had to be circumcized.—Bruce Jackson, *Get Your Ass in the Water and Swim Like Me*, p. 148, 1964

3 a man *US, 1914*

- Hunter would remind Maureen she was a girl. Or Hunter would tell her she was just one of the dicks.—Elmore Leonard, *City Primeval*, p. 33, 1980

4 sex with a man *US, 1956*

- I bet she hasn't had any dick in years and years. Judging from the type of woman she was and her age. Old women don't get a lot of dick. —Elmore Leonard, *Glitz*, p. 320, 1983
- Women are tricky. You ask a woman how many men she's fucked, and she'll tell you how many boy friends she's had instead. A woman doesn't count all the miscellaneous dick.—Chris Rock, *Rock This!*, p. 130, 1997

5 a police officer, especially a detective; a private detective *US, 1886*

- Next morning, when the house dick began to gun us, we went into a huddle about our change.—Mezz Mezzrow, *Really the Blues*, p. 131, 1946
- I got snaky last night on Waley's bum gin, and some big foulball of a dick came along.—James T. Farrell, *Saturday Night*, p. 28, 1947
- "I know you don't believe that"- he laughed shortly – "and I guess you don't like dicks. But we aren't bad guys."—Irving Shulman, *The Amboy Dukes*, p. 105, 1947
- The dicks gave her the bum's rush too.—Jack Lait and Lee Mortimer, *New York Confidential*, p. 163, 1948
- In another hour every dick on the force'll be swarming in here. —Horace McCoy, *Kiss Tomorrow Good-bye*, p. 56, 1948
- I was cooking up some stuff, bending over and this dick kicked me dead up the can.—Hal Ellson, *The Golden Spike*, p. 152, 1952
- We were locked in a cell. A fat dick who seemed to know Pat came and stood at the door.—William Burroughs, *Junkie*, p. 85, 1953
- No doubt the dicks reckoned she was involved in it, since she was known to have been living with Jack when they picked him up. —Robert S. Close, *With Hooves of Brass*, p. 26, 1961
- They'll earn us trouble with the racecourse dicks.—Wilda Moxham, *The Apprentice*, p. 18, 1969
- The thought that hit my mind was that this guy was trying to get him some bread other than his dick's pay[.]—A.S. Jackson, *Gentleman Pimp*, p. 103, 1973
- I didn't know he was working as a store dick.—Nicholas Blincoe, *The Beautiful Beaten-up Irish Boy of the Arndale Centre*, p. 7, 1998

6 a despicable person *US, 1966*

Losing its taboo in the US, but still chancy.

- VERONICA: Don't be a dick. That stuff'll kill her.— *Heathers*, 1988
- CLARENCE: Now, they got him dressed like a dick. He's wearing these stupid-lookin' pants, this horrible sweater.— *True Romance*, 1993
- 'I guess that could be explained by the fact that he was kind of uptight, a bit of a dick, and the babes would run a mile the first time he opened his mouth.—John Birmingham, *He Died With a Felafel in his Hand*, p. 194, 1994
- Mikey, do us a favour and take your dick of a mate out of this bar before I break this bottle over 'is thick 'ead.—Colin Butts, *Is Harry on the Boat?*, p. 25, 1997
- Prancing about to infantile music in a room full of mirrors, making a complete dick of himself.—Shane Maloney, *Nice Try*, p. 12, 1998

7 a fool *UK, 1553*

- I think you're a dick but seeing you know Conrad I'll give it some thought.—Nicholas Blincoe, *Ardwick Green (Disco Biscuits)*, p. 5, 1996
- Made a real dick of himself.—Tony Wilson, *24 Hour Party People*, p. 10, 2002

8 nothing, zero *UK, 1925*

- He steals from you, you don't do dick.— *Empire Records*, 1995
- Electronic didn't "shift units" as they say. New Order hadn't done dick.—Shaun Ryder, *Shaun Ryder... in His Own Words*, 1996
- K: I need to tell you something about all your skills – as of right now they mean precisely dick.—Ed Solomon, *Men In Black*, 1997
- British readers know dick about her, pardon the phrase.—Christopher Brookmyre, *Not the End of the World*, p. 146, 1998

9 a look, a glance *UK*

A variation of DECKO; DEKKO.

- —Patrick O'Shaughnessy, *Market Traders' Slang*, 1979

10 during the Vietnam war, the enemy *US*

From the Vietnamese *dich* (enemy).

- —Linda Reinberg, *In the Field:*, p. 63, 1991

▷ see: DIC

▸ get your dick tender

to have an emotional need to be with a woman at all times *US*

- I knew that as soon as she became conscious of the fact that I had weakened in that respect, as soon as I had what they call "got my dick tender" – that means you've got to be with a woman all the time – they figure they're out working and you're out chipping some-place.—Bruce Jackson, *In the Life*, p. 179, 1972

▸ have had the dick

to be ruined *AUSTRALIA*

- This strike's just about had the dick.—Frank Hardy, *The Outcasts of Foolgarah*, p. 89, 1971

▸ have your dick sucked

to be fawned upon; to be flattered *UK*

- I don't need my dick sucked by the media or anybody else.—Shaun Ryder, *Shaun Ryder... in His Own Words*, 1993

▸ it's just a dick thing

used as a humorous excuse for typical male behaviour *US*

A catchphrase from the film *Mo' Better Blues*.

- —Connie Eble (Editor), *UNC-CH Campus Slang*, p. 2, Fall 1991

▸ put dick

(from the male point of view) to have sex *US*

- Damn but you know how to put dick to a bitch.—A.S. Jackson, *Gentleman Pimp*, p. 72, 1973

dick *verb*

1 to exploit; to take advantage of; to harm *US, 1964*

In the 1968 US presidential election, the bumper sticker 'Dick Nixon Before Nixon Dicks You' raised eyebrows.

- You've been dicking me around since we started on this turd-hunt. — *48 Hours*, 1982
- I got them on one side, I got La Cos Nostra on the other, I got more people trying to dick me than if I turned tricks for a living.—Elmore Leonard, *Glitz*, p. 289, 1985

- Time to play let's dick the old guys, huh, Harp? — *Point Break*, 1991
- The club owner is trying to dick me out of some money. — *Wayne's World*, 1992
- I know not to dick with him when it comes to matters PC. — Armistead Maupin, *Maybe the Moon*, p. 163, 1992
- DON'T DICK WITH YOUR DICK! — Richard Herring, *Talking Cock*, p. 236, 2003
- You know I haven't seen a dime off that shit. I've been dicked! — *FHM*, p. 222, June 2003

2 (from the male point of view) to have sex with *US, 1942*
- He said, "Did I ask him, you want to know, if he's dicking her? No, I didn't." — Elmore Leonard, *Split Images*, p. 16, 1981
- Shark, a newcomer to dicking onstage, comes from Cuba, perhaps a gift from Castro's boat-people exchange. — Josh Alan Friedman, *Tales of Times Square*, p. 189, 1986

3 to look *UK*
A variation of **DECKO**; **DEKKO**.
- Dick at the gorger's conkie. — Patrick O'Shaughnessy, *Market Traders' Slang*, 1979

Dick & 'Arry *noun*
a dictionary *UK*
- — Ray Puxley, *Cockney Rabbit – A Dick'n'Arry of Rhyming Slang*, 1992

dick around *verb*
1 to behave in a sexually promiscuous fashion *US, 1969*
- Wives were fools who let their husbands dick around. — Danya Rubbenberg, *Yentl's Revenge*, p. 3, 2001

2 to make a mess of; to inconvenience *US*
- Patience, for instance, wasn't a sign that you were tolerant of being dicked around[.] — Christopher Brookmyre, *The Sacred Art of Stealing*, p. 186, 2002

3 to pass time idly *US, 1947*
- — Connie Eble (Editor), *UNC-CH Campus Slang*, p. 2, Fall 1993

dickbrain *noun*
a fool *US, 1971*
- I had to ask myself: "How did I get here?" By behaving like a fucking dickbrain, mate, that's how. — Ken Lukowiak, *Marijuana Time*, p. 278, 2000
- Good place, dickbrain. Who would ever think to look there? — Stephen J. Cannell, *The Tin Collectors*, p. 6, 2001
- They're going for different ones [answers]. "Duh! That's a red herring, dick-brain!" — Kevin Sampson, *Clubland*, p. 112, 2002

dick-breath *noun*
used as a term of abuse *US, 1972*
- "Make her bark, dick-breath." "Who are you calling dick-breath?" "You, you dog-stealing fuck." — Daniel Lyons, *Dog Days*, p. 177, 1998

dick cheese *noun*
smegma *CANADA*
- Is dick cheese a major problem with uncircumcised gay slobs? — Suroosh Alvi et al., *The Vice Guide*, p. 272, 2002

dick daks *noun*
a pair of men's close-fitting and revealing nylon swimming trunks *AUSTRALIA*
From **DICK** (the penis) and **DAKS** (shorts).
- — *Wordmap (www.abc.net.au/wordmap)*, 2003

dick-dip *noun*
sex *US*
- — Dale Gordon, *The Dominion Sex Dictionary*, p. 57, 1967

dick doc *noun*
1 a urologist *US*
- — Sally Williams, *"Strong" Words*, p. 161, 1994

2 a military doctor or medic who inspects male recruits for signs of sexually transmitted disease *US*
- — Roger Blake, *The American Dictionary of Sexual Terms*, p. 58, 1964
- — Dale Gordon, *The Dominion Sex Dictionary*, p. 119, 1967

Dick Emery *noun*
memory *UK*
Rhyming slang, formed on the name of a British comedian and comedy actor, 1917–83.
- A man with a bad 'dick' needn't have a social problem. — Ray Puxley, *Cockney Rabbit*, 1992

dicken!; dickin!; dickon!
used to express disgust or disbelief *AUSTRALIA, 1894*
Perhaps from **DICKENS!**.

dickens!
used as an interjectional expletive to express surprise, impatience, etc, generally combined with how, what, where, etc *UK, 1598*
Euphemistic for 'the devil'.
- I don't know how the dickens he managed to do it. He was a fellow of infinite resource. — Sir William Dargie, *The Quiet Man*, 1st April 2002
- What the Dickens is going to happen, readers? And more to the point, who cares? — *The Guardian*, 1st August 2003

dicker *noun*
1 a look-out, a scout *UK: NORTHERN IRELAND*
- We wanted to use the ground as much as possible to keep us away from the eyes of "dickers". — Andy McNab, *Immediate Action*, p. 38, 1995
- The job of dickers was a vital one to the PIRA [Provisional Irish Republican Army] and many operations were cancelled because of a dicker's insincts[.] — Chris Ryan, *The Watchman*, p. 133, 2001

2 a *dic*tionary *UK, 1937*
By application of the Oxford **-ER**.

dickeroo *noun*
a police officer *US*
- — Lou Shelly, *Hepcats Jive Dictionary*, p. 9, 1945

dickey *noun*
(of clothing, in the Canadian north) a top covering *CANADA*
The word comes from Eskimo *attike* (a covering).
- Sealskin boots replaced rubber ones, summer clothing was packed away and heavy woolen socks, water-proof dickies and mittens replaced it. — B.J. Banfill, *Labrador Nurse*, p. 71, 1952

dickey *adjective*
1 of plans or things, tricky, risky, 'dicey' *UK, 1984*
Also spelt 'dischy'.

2 foolish *NEW ZEALAND*
- — David McGill, *David McGill's Complete Kiwi Slang Dictionary*, p. 36, 1998

▷ **see: UNCLE DICK**

dickey-bird *noun*
1 in oil drilling, a loud squeak caused by poorly lubricated equipment *US*
- — Jerry Robertson, *Oil Slanguage*, p. 45, 1954

2 the penis *CANADA*
An elaboration of **DICKY** credited to schoolboy use and noted by D.J. Barr, 1968.

dickey-dido *noun*
the external female genital parts *UK*
Originally recorded (1887) as a word for 'a fool'; this sense survives in the bawdy song 'The Mayor of Bayswater' (to the tune of 'The Ash Grove'): 'One black one, one white one / And one with a lump of shite on, / The hairs on her dickey-dido hang down to her knees'.

dick-eye *noun*
used as an offensive term of address between males *UK*
- — Chris Lewis, *The Dictionary of Playground Slang*, p. 70, 2003

dickface *noun*
a contemptible fool *US, 1975*
- "Why'd you kill Patrick?" "Why not. He's a dickface." — Sue Grafton, *G is for Gumshoe*, p. 251, 1990
- I know you've been listening to some scumhead, some bald dickface up there. — Howard Stern, *Miss America*, p. 276, 1995
- Chub said, "Then where's our ticket, dickface?" — Carl Hiaasen, *Lucky You*, p. 39, 1997

dick-fingered *adjective*
clumsy *US*
- He's so dick-fingered he can't pick his nose without puttin' his eye out. — Ken Weaver, *Texas Crude*, p. 108, 1984
- — Michael Dalton Johnson, *Talking Trash with Redd Foxx*, p. 130, 1994

dick flick *noun*
an action-oriented film that appeals to a male audience *US*
An opposite and equal reaction to **CHICK FLICK**.
- — Don R. McCreary (Editor), *Dawg Speak*, 2001

dickhead *noun*

an inept, unlikeable person; an idiot *US, 1964*

A satisfying embellishment of **DICK** (the penis). As a term of abuse this is often accompanied by, or even replaced with, a mime of the masturbation of a flaccid penis, gesturally sited in the centre of the forehead.

- Because you're such a God Damn Dickhead about the way you think life oughta be. —Clarence Cooper Jr, *The Farm*, p. 161, 1967
- — *Current Slang*, p. 7, Fall 1970
- They'll stitch you up, stick it up you and take you for a dead-set dickhead. — Barry Humphries, *A Nice Night's Entertainment*, 1974
- Don't stand there you mob of dick-heads. Come here near the heater. — Sam Weller, *Old Bastards I Have Met*, 1979
- I deserved to lose it, I was a dick-head – but haven't we all been at one time or another[?] —Alan Bleasdale, *Boys From the Blackstuff:*, 1982
- Come on dickhead! — *Repo Man*, 1984
- If it wasn't for dickheads like you, there wouldn't be any thievery in this world, would there? — *Full Metal Jacket*, 1987
- Never give a cop your name, dickhead. — Kathy Lette, *Girls' Night Out*, 1987
- [A]ll I could see was the dickhead photographer handing her some polyster yarn[.] —Nicholson Baker, *Vox*, p. 33, 1992
- Now we know something's rotten in Denmark, 'cause this dickhead had a big bag, and it's uncut too, so we're sweatin' him, tryin' to find out where he got it. — *True Romance*, 1993
- Why're you listening to a white rock station, dick-head? —*Airheads*, 1994
- Joe gets up from the table. Ari, he says, you're a dickhead. I take another swallow of whisky. His words hurt me, there is a stab right down in my gut. — *Christos Tsiolkas, Loaded*, 1995
- You're embarrassed, aren't you? You think your own dad's a dick-head. — *The Full Monty*, 1997
- What a prize dickhead I was. I'd come all that way, and I was going to miss the funeral. — *Phillip Gwynne, Deadly Unna?*, 1998
- He left! I sprung the dickhead and he cruised on me. — *Ten Things I Have About You*, 1999
- Very funny, dickhead. — *South Park*, 1999
- Not that we thought he was a dickhead or anything like that[.] — Dave Courtney, *Raving Lunacy*, p. 34, 2000

dickheaded *adjective*

foolish *AUSTRALIA, 1981*

- It's miles, Dad. Don't be daft. She's looking at him like he's the most dickheaded human she's ever encountered[.] —Tim Winton, *Cloudstreet*, p. 110, 1991

dickie *noun*

the penis *US*

Children's vocabulary.

- On the other hand, some corresponding euphemistic expressions (e.g., dickie, peepee, weewee, number one, number two, to move the bowels, to pass water, to make love, and so on), obviously evasive in their very structure, do have considerable usage. —*Eros*, p. 69, Autum 1962

dickie wacker *noun*

a disrespectful teenage boy who shows off *AUSTRALIA*

- — Thommo, *The Dictionary of Australian Swearing and Sex Sayings*, p. 34, 1985

dickjoke *noun*

any coarse joke *US*

- —*American Speech*, p. 167, Summer 1991: 'A brief annotated glossary of standup comedy jargon'

dickless *noun*

a female police officer or detective *US*

A shortened form of **DICKLESS TRACY** that plays on two meanings of dick – 'penis' and 'detective'.

- "You think I'd be a good Robbery/Homicide dick?" Lloyd laughed. "No, but you'd be a great Robbery/Homicide dickless." —James Ellroy, *Blood on the Moon*, p. 100, 1984

dickless *adjective*

used of men to intensify general abuse *US, 1984*

Literally: 'without a **DICK**' (a penis).

- I'm fifty. That's not old, dickless. — *Lethal Weapon*, 1987
- "Listen, you dickless sack of shit," I said[.] —Janet Evanovich, *Seven Up*, p. 118, 2001

dickless Tracy *noun*

a female police officer *US, 1963*

A neat pun on **DICK** (the penis) and the popular comic book hero-detective Dick Tracy created by Chester Gould in 1931; a contemptuous suggestion that a female cannot be as effective as a male.

- No-Balls Hadley, who was sometimes called Dickless Tracy, was also right when she declared fearlessly at a policewomen's meeting attended by chauvinist spies for Commander Moss that he, as well as most high ranking officers of the department, had little or no street experience[.] —Joseph Wambaugh, *The Choirboys*, p. 78–79, 1975
- —Jim Ramsay, *Cop It Sweet!*, p. 28, 1977
- They call us Dickless Tracys[.] —Joan Didion, *The White Album*, p. 21, 1979
- "I expect you to make sure she doesn't fall flat on her ass," he said, glancing pointedly at Bailey. "I don't need any Dickless Tracy problems." —Gerald Petievich, *To Die in Beverly Hills*, p. 11, 1983
- —Angela Devlin, *Prison Patter*, p. 43, 1996

dickless wonder *noun*

a person of either sex who lacks courage or conviction *US*

- —Anna Scotti and Paul Young, *Buzzwords:*, p. 17, 1997
- He dreamed he was back in boot camp, trying to do push-ups while a brawny black sergeant stood over him, calling him a faggot, a pussy, a dickless wonder. —Carl Hiaasen, *Lucky You*, p. 170, 1997

dick-lick *noun*

used as a term of abuse *US*

- Or do you get off on pigs rubbin their shoes on your ugly dick-lick face, you lowlife beefcake faggot! —John Patrick Shanley, *Danny and the Deep Blue Sea*, p. 24, 1984
- What are you smiling at, you dick-lick? —Don Ericson, *Charlie Rangers*, p. 3, 1989

dicklicker *noun*

1 a cocksucker in all its senses *US*

- Ahm sho 'nuff glad they got that dicklicker, man! —Nathan Heard, *Howard Street*, p. 236, 1968
- DCT made me what I am, in a way. Fucking dicklicker. —Ethan Coen, *Gates of Eden*, p. 104, 1998
- "Dicklickers!" she calls her two dads. —Naomi Odenkirk, *Mr. Show:*, p. 135, 2002

2 a greyhound racing enthusiast *AUSTRALIA*

Used by horse racing enthusiasts.

- —Ned Wallish, *The Truth Dictionary of Racing Slang*, p. 22, 1989

dicklicking *adjective*

despicable *US, 1978*

- He'd driven straight to the plant to get away from that dick-licking deputy[.] —Joseph Flynn, *Digger*, p. 266, 1997
- Dick-lickig bastards! How could they steal our mules? —Thomas Harlan, *The Dark Lord*, p. 299, 2002

dick mittens *noun*

hands that were not washed after urination *US*

- — Jim Goad, *Jim Goad's Glossary of Northwestern Prison Slang*, December 2001

dicknose *noun*

used as a term of abuse *US, 1974*

- At least Lou is upfront about it, which makes him more human than the rest of those MOR dicknoses. —Lester Bangs, *Psychotic Recations and Carburetor Drugs*, p. 196, 1076

dick off *verb*

to waste time, to idle, to shun work *US*

- Goldstein, you've done nothing but have ideas about who we could do something better. But when it comes down to a little goddam work, you're always dicking off. —Norman Mailer, *The Naked and the Dead*, p. 138, 1947

dickon!

▷ see: DICKEN!

dickory dock *noun*

1 the penis *UK*

Rhyming slang for **COCK** (the penis), not an elaboration of **DICK**.

- —Julian Franklyn, *A Dictionary of Rhyming Slang*, 2nd 1961

2 a clock *UK, 1961*

Rhyming slang, based on the nursery rhyme 'Hickory dickory dock / A mouse ran up the clock'.

dick partition *noun*

a condom *UK*

Combines **DICK** (the penis) with a barrier.

- —David Rowan, *A Glossary for the 90's*, 1998

dick pointers *noun*

a pair of men's close-fitting and revealing nylon swimming trunks *AUSTRALIA*

- — *Wordmap (www.abc.net.au/wordmap)*, 2003

dick pokers *noun*

a pair of men's close-fitting and revealing nylon swimming trunks *AUSTRALIA*

- — *Wordmap (www.abc.net.au/wordmap)*, 2003

dickrash *noun*
an annoying or despicable person; a jerk *AUSTRALIA*
• —James Lambert, *The Macquarie Book of Slang*, 1996

dicks *noun*
▸ **cut dicks; talk dicks**
to speak clearly and with an affected English accent *BRITISH VIRGIN ISLANDS, 1973*

Dick's hatband *noun*
used in comparisons, especially as the epitome of tightness *UK, 1781*
• [I]t locked up the kids tighter than Dick's hatband.—Tom Clancy, *Shadow Warriors*, p. 481, 2002

Dick Shot Off *noun*
the *D*istinguished *S*ervice *O*rder, (a medal for bravery) *UK, 1937*
Punning on **DICK** (the penis).

dick-skinner *noun*
the hand *US, 1971*
• You ain't going to have no skin on those dick-skinners. Remember them hands is your best girl. Rosie Palms.—Daniel Buckman, *The Names of Rivers*, p. 58, 2003

dick-smacker *noun*
a prison guard *US*
Not kind.
• Hey, you stupid dick-smacker, get down here and open this door. —Inez Cardozo-Freeman, *The Joint*, 1984

dicksmith *noun*
a US Navy hospital corpsman *US, 1974*
• I never thought them nice, clean 'Dicksmiths' knew that kind of language.—Edward Raymer, *Descent into Darkness*, p. 84, 1996

Dick Smith *noun*
a drug user or addict who does not socialise with other users *US, 1876*
• —*American Speech*, p. 87, May 1955: 'Narcotic argot along the mexican border'

dicksplash *noun*
an awkward or inept person, a fool *UK*
• —Chris Lewis, *The Dictionary of Playground Slang*, p. 71, 2003

dick-stepper *noun*
a clumsy oaf *US, 1983*
• I just don't want any dick-steppers. Don't send anyone you wouldn't want to break in on your team.—Larry Chambers, *Recondo*, p. 228, 1992

dick stickers *noun*
a pair of men's close-fitting and revealing nylon swimming trunks *AUSTRALIA, 1996*
• At school in Ballina, far north coast of NSW, we also called speedos "dick stickers".—*Wordmap (www.abc.net.au/wordmap)*, 2003

dick-string *noun*
a male's ability to achieve an erection *US, 1965*
• Ah hopes yuh busted his dick string.—Piri Thomas, *Down These Mean Streets*, p. 157, 1967

dick sucker *noun*
a homosexual male *US*
• Maybe they have a problem with each other, because, you know, they look like a couple of dick suckers.—Pete Dexter, *The Paperboy*, p. 179, 1995

dicksucking *noun*
oral sex performed on man *US*
• Her beautiful face was puckered with the size of his dick, as he plunged forward and back to give him a wild dick-sucking.—Roy Hawkins, *Bimbos by the Bay*, p. 53, 1977

dick-sucking *adjective*
despicable *US, 1972*
• [T]he Causey I know is the C.O. of the most limp-wristed, lily-livered, dick-sucking squadron in the history of flight.—Pat Conroy, *The Great Santini*, p. 326, 1976

dicktease *noun*
a woman who creates the impression of being more sexually available than she is *US*
A variant of the more common **PRICK-TEASER**.
• —Pamela Munro, *U.C.L.A. Slang*, p. 33, 1989

dick teaser *noun*
a girl who suggests that she will engage in sex but will not *US, 1962*
• —*American Speech*, p. 273, December 1963: 'American Indian Student Slang'
• I wanted to, but my muscles had atrophied. I didn't want him to think of me as a dick teaser.—Maya Angelou, *Gather Together in My Name*, p. 22, 1974
• You know Saphronia, decent women aren't dick-teasers.—Michele Andrea Bowen, *Church Folk*, p. 82, 2001

Dick the Shit *nickname*
Shakespeare's *Richard III* *UK*
A play on 'Richard the turd' in theatrical slang.
• I hear you might do Dick the Shit. Be a very brave move.—Anthony Sher quoting Pete Postlethwaite, *Year of the King*, 1985

dick togs *noun*
a pair of men's close-fitting and revealing nylon swimming trunks *AUSTRALIA*
From **DICK** (the penis) and **TOGS** (a swimming costume).
• I've only ever known these as "dick togs" or simply DT's, which seems to be a fairly universal name in Queensland.—*Wordmap (www.abc. net. au/wordmap)*, 2003

Dick Turpin *noun*
thirteen *UK, 1937*
Rhyming slang, used by dart players; formed on the name of the infamous highwayman, born in 1706, hanged in 1739.

dickwad *noun*
an unlikeable or despicable person *US, 1989*
• I get dickwad in there wantin' to play wheel of fortune so I can find out their supplier!—*Break Point*, 1991
• [A] TV personality, a fucking dickwad who could screw any hot stripper he wants[.]—Howard Stern, *Miss America*, p. 11, 1995
• Who's gonna stop me, dickwad?—Stephen J. Cannell, *The Tin Collectors*, p. 8, 2001

dick-waver; dicky-waver *noun*
a male exhibitionist *US*
• Indeed, at times the station house was so peaceful that the arrest of a "dicky waver," a man who exposed himself, was the major law-enforcement event of the day.—Peter Maas, *Serpico*, p. 107, 1973

dickweed *noun*
a despicable, dim-witted person *US, 1980*
• Not even in your dreams, Dickweed.—Sandra Bernard, *Confessions of a Pretty Lady*, p. 108, 1977
• What did you say dickweed?—*Heathers*, 1988
• You killed Ted, you Medieval dick-weed!—*Bill and Ted's Excellent Adventure*, 1989
• —Connie Eble (Editor), *UNC-CH Campus Slang*, p. 2, Fall 1993
• "What it, dickweed," Wendell squawks.—Stephen King, *Blakc House*, p. 327, 2001

dickwhacker *noun*
a fool *NEW ZEALAND*
• —Sonya Plowman, *Great Kiwi Slang*, p. 57, 2002

dick-whipped; dick-whupped *adjective*
dominated by a man *US, 1998*
Formed as an antonym for **PUSSY-WHIPPED** (dominated by a woman).
• [I]f a woman I'd previously considered strong and accomplished was being remade as a mindless booby by her male partner I'd think she was dick-whipped.—*The Guardian*, p. 3, 12th June 2003

dickwipe *noun*
a despicable person *US*
• I would have to say a dickwipe says what.—*Wayne's World*, 1992

dickwit *noun*
an idiot, a contemptible fool *UK*
• A guy called Dick Wit had an entire life raft to himself and was begging Hot Buns to join him.—Gretel Killeen, *Hot Buns and Ophelia Get Shipwrecked*, 2001
• That's why they call them the Projects; it's some dickwit's pet project.—Tony Wilson, *24 Hour Party People*, p. 54, 2002
• Freud was wrong: women do not have penis envy...not until we find out how much money Simon Morley and his friends have made from being dickwits.—*Daily Telegraph*, 30th July 2003

dicky *noun*
1 the penis *UK, 1891*
An extension of **DICK**.

- Your pa sticks his dicky boy in your ma, see, and shoots this stuff into the hole that your mother pees from. —Herman Wouk, *Inside, Outside*, p. 69, 1985
- "Pull his dicky and get milk," Jadie replied. "You don't get milk out of a cow's pisser." —Torey Hayden, *Ghost Girl*, p. 135, 1991

2 a windscreen on a motorcycle *UK*

- —Douglas Dunford, *Motorcycle Department, Beaulieu Motor Museum*, 1979

dicky *adjective*

1 inferior; in poor condition or health; insecure; having an odd quality *UK*

- "You know I got a dicky heart." "Dicky nut [head] is more like it," Mellors said. —Derek Bickerton, *Payroll*, p. 14, 1959
- [C]lubs in railway arches with very dicky toilets[.] —Dave Courtney, *Raving Lunacy*, p. 92, 2000

2 idiotic or annoying; appearing silly *NEW ZEALAND, 1982*

That is, of, or befitting, a **DICK(HEAD)**.

- —Harry Orsman, *A Dictionary of Modern New Zealand Slang*, p. 38, 1999
- Those in advertising wore their dicky bow ties and the used-car salesmen had shined their white shoes. —Gretel Killeen, *Hot Buns and Ophelia Get a Bloke*, p. 78, 2000

dickybird *noun*

1 a little bird *UK, 1781*

Childish. As in the tradional nursery rhyme, 'Two little dicky-birds sitting a wall, / One named Peter, one named Paul'.

2 a word; hence, a thing of little value, the smallest thing *UK, 1932*

Rhyming slang, most often given in full and usually in the negative context, 'not say a word', hence the second part of this sense. In the theatre, 'dickies' are an actor's script, 'the words'.

- BILL: Don't exagggerate. I wasn't bone idle last year, I must have done some work somewhere, even if it was just helping around the house. TONY: You did not. Nothing. Not a dickey bird. —Ray Galton and Alan Simpson, *Hancock's Half Hour*, 30th December 1956
- "I asked everyone that can be asked," Cross says, "and nobody knows a dicky bird." —Ted Lewis, *Jack Carter's Law*, p. 6, 1974
- [N]o-one's said a dickybird. — Martin King and Martin Knight, *The Naughty Nineties*, p. 124, 1999
- Alfonso doesn't say a dicky bird, just goes over and nuts Wells betwen the eyes. —John King, *Human Punk*, p. 6, 2000
- [O]ne of our number asked the inevitable question surrounding any actor of particularly mature years. "But can he still do the dickies, darling?" — *The Guardian*, 5th September 2001

▸ not a dickybird

nothing *UK*

- "What's going on in there? Can you see anything?" – "Not a dicky bird!" — Beale, 1975
- The Roux brothers have been honoured in France, the country of their birth, but in the country which has benefited immeasurably from their energy, enterprise and excellence, not a dicky bird. — *The Guardian*, 20th April 2002

dicky diddle; diddle *noun*

urination *UK*

Rhyming slang for **PIDDLE**; used by juveniles, perhaps playing on **DICKY** (the penis).

- —Julian Franklyn, *A Dictionary of Rhyming Slang*, 1961

dicky dirt; dicky *noun*

a shirt *AUSTRALIA, 1905*

Rhyming slang; also note conventional 'dicky' (a detachable shirt front, since 1811), in turn influenced by obsolete slang 'dicky' (a dirty shirt, 1781).

- Can't wear a whistle like this without the proper shoes, dicky [shirt] or Peckham [tie], can yer now? — *The Sweeney*, p. 6, 1976
- Her bristols [breasts] pointed at me / Through a dicky crisp and white[.] —Ronnie Barker, *Fletcher's Book of Rhyming Slang*, p. 21, 1979
- —Ryan Aven-Bray, *Ridgey Didge Oz Jack Lang*, p. 24, 1983

dicky-dunking *noun*

sex from the male perspective *US*

- When the frost is on the pumpkin, it's time for dicky dunkin. —Michael Dalton Johnson, *Talking Trash with Redd Foxx*, p. 39, 1994

dicky-waver *noun*

▷ **see: DICK-WAVER**

dicty *noun*

a snob *US, 1928*

- —J.E. Lighter, *Historical Dictionary of American Slang, Vol. 1*, p. 586, 1994

dicty *adjective*

1 excellent *US*

- 'Dicty dictionary' — *Time Magazine*, p. 92, 20th January 1947

2 arrogant, haughty *US, 1923*

Also spelt 'dichty'.

- —Lou Shelly, *Hepcats Jive Dictionary*, p. 9, 1945
- She was in a very proper and dicty mood, so she kept "correcting" Bessie's grammar, straightening out her words and putting them in "good " English until they sounded like some stuck-up jive from McGuffy's Reader instead of the real down-to-earth language of the blues. —Mezz Mezzrow, *Really the Blues*, p. 54, 1946
- He was seventeen and dicty-looking with his good hair and light compelxion[.] —John M. Murtagh and Sara Harris, *Cast the First Stone*, p. 85, 1957
- You gonna be one dicty nigger, now ain't you? —John Clellon Holmes, *The Horn*, p. 180, 1958
- I don't want no dichty gray that thinks music is a lot of hen tracks put down on a piece of paper. —Ross Russell, *The Sound*, p. 217, 1961

dicy *adjective*

▷ **see: DICEY**

did *noun*

a capsule of Dilaudid™, a pharmaceutical narcotic *US*

- —Richard A. Spears, *The Slang and Jargon of Drugs and Drink*, 1986

di-da, di-da, di-da

used to extend an explanation or complaint, especially when reporting an instance thereof *UK, 1940*

Usually mocking; but also as an alternative to **BLAH BLAH**. When used by lyricists of pop songs it tends to have no meaning whatsoever.

diddicoi *noun*

▷ **see: DIDICOI**

diddish *adjective*

used to describe anything associated with traditional travellers, especially with regard to degrading or denigratory treatment *UK*

Used by late 1980s–early 90s counterculture travellers.

- —Martin Roach, *Dr. Marten's Air Wair*, 1999: 'Glossary of travellers' terms'

diddle *noun*

1 an act of masturbation *US*

From conventional 'diddle' (to jerk from side to side).

- "You can keep the twenty [dollars]." "Do you want a diddle for it?" "No!" —Janet Evanovich, *Seven Up*, p. 94, 2001

2 a swindle, a deception *UK, 1803*

- The Bath affair was the first 'dial a diddle' fraud investigators had cracked. — *Youth International Party Line*, p. 4, December 1972

3 gin *UK*

- — *Attitude*, p. 60, July 2003: 'Old palare lexicon'

▸ on the diddle

engaged in swindling *UK*

From **DIDDLE** (a deception), on the model of **ON THE FIDDLE** (engaged in a swindle).

- [I]t would have been the sack if he had hard proof that we'd been on the diddle. —Danny King, *The Burglar Diaries*, p. 108, 2001

diddle *verb*

1 (from the male perspective) to have sex *US, 1870*

- You want to conk me out and diddle with me while I'm helpless. —George Mandel, *Flee the Angry Strangers*, p. 269, 1952
- Diddle, diddle, diddle yourself. I'm no whore. —James T. Farrell, *Ruth and Bertram*, p. 90, 1955
- Efn' Ah finds me some white mother-raper up here on my side of town trying to diddle my little gals Ah'm gonna cut his throat. —Chester Himes, *The Real Cool Killers*, p. 6, 1959
- The height of my folly / Was diddling a collie / But I got a nice price for the pups. — *Eros*, p. 62, Winter 1962
- How about you and Boo? Did you or did you not diddle her during the war? Are you or are you not still diddling her? —Max Shulman, *Anyone Got a Match?*, p. 253, 1964
- That's why she keeps you around for, to diddle her fiddle. —Jim Thompson, *Pop. 1280*, p. 191, 1964
- I used to could diddle all night long / but since I got the age I am / it takes me all night to diddle. —Bruce Jackson, *Get Your Ass in the Water and Swim Like Me*, p. 228, 1964
- I mean, he's got a wonderful wife and he prefers to, diddle this little yo-yo that – that, you know. — *Manhattan*, 1979
- Any movie that starts off with a woman being diddled by a giant katydid can't be all bad. —Joe Bob Briggs, *Joe Bob Goes to the Drive-In*, p. 19, 1987

2 to masturbate *US, 1934*

- [I]f I was you I would just go right back out that door and let her diddle herself in the powder room. —George V. Higgins, *The Rat on Fire*, p. 78, 1981
- She played with herself in chapel, at Holy Communion; she diddled in the confessional even as she was asking forgiveness for diddling. —Tom Robbins, *Fierce Invalids Home From Hot Climates*, p. 261, 2000
- Let's say you are diligently diddling her clit with a well-lubed fingertip[.] —Jamie Goddard, *Lesbian Sex Secrets for Men*, p. 61, 2000

3 to swindle *UK, 1806*

- —Louis S. Leland, *A Personal Kiwi-Yankee Dictionary*, p. 32, 1984
- So you were diddled. It's happened to us all once in a while. —Jennifer Saunders, *Absolutely Fabulous*, p. 80, 1992

4 to cheat *US*

- "Of course, once he spied those cut glass diamonds, he'd take in how we'd diddle him goodfashion. —Guy Owen, *The Flim-Flam Man and the Apprentice Grifter*, p. 163, 1972

5 in computing, to make a minor change *US*

- Let's diddle this piece of code and see if the problem goes away. —Guy L. Steele et al., *The Hacker's Dictionary*, p. 56, 1983

6 in computing, to work half-heartedly *US*

- I diddled a copy of ADVENT so it didn't double-space all the time. —Eric S. Raymond, *The New Hacker's Dictionary*, p. 125, 1991

▸ **diddled by the dirty digit of destiny**
adversely affected by fate *US*

- —*Maledicta*, p. 15, Summer 1977: 'A word for it!'

diddler *noun*

1 the penis *US*

- If I see a queer, I wave my diddler at him and show him how big it is. —*Screw*, p. 11, 4th July 1969

2 a child molestor *US*

- —John R. Armore and Joseph D. Wolfe, *Dictionary of Desperation*, p. p.27, 1976
- "Little girl diddler," he says. —Guy Vanderhaeghe, *The Last Crossing*, p. 96, 2002
- You diddler! Rat! Child molester! —Edward Mackenzie, *Street Soldier*, p. 287, 2003

diddling *noun*

petty cheating, sharp practice, trivial swindling, chronic borrowing *UK, 1849*

diddling Miss Daisy *noun*

an act of female masturbation *UK*
After the 1989 film *Driving Miss Daisy*.

- —Michelle Baker and Steven Tropiano, *Queer Facts*, p. 46, 2004

diddly *noun*

anything at all *US*
An abbreviation of DIDDLY-SHIT.

- —*American Speech*, p. 117, May 1964: 'Problems in the study of campus slang'
- Since Manny Lopez admitted he didn't know diddly about guns and ammo, Ernie Salgado volunteered to help with the weapons training. —Joseph Wambaugh, *Lines and Shadows*, p. 32, 1984

diddlybopper; diddybopper; dittybopper; diddley bop; diddy bop *noun*

a street thug *US*

- The Cobras dress like "real diddley bops" – first-class street fighters. —Harrison E. Salisbury, *The Shook-up Generation*, p. 27, 1958
- —Anthony Romeo, *The Language of Gangs*, p. 17, 4th December 1962
- Just because of that diddleybop walk, there were always fights, too. —Jeremy Larner and Ralph Tefferteller, *The Addict in the Street*, p. 143, 1964
- —*Current Slang*, p. 2, Winter 1966
- Now the lion jumped up full of rage / Like a ditty bopper ready to rampage. —Dennis Wepman et al., *The Life*, p. 23, 1976
- [I]dentifying in less time than it took to name the hookers, hustlers, thieves and thugs; pennyweight ponces and flyweight flimflammers; diddyboppers, deadbeats and dopefiends. —Seth Morgan, *Homeboy*, p. 13, 1990

diddly-dick *noun*

nothing at all *US, 1972*

- Balfry already told the fucker that the hooker's identification wasn't worth diddly-dick. —Robert Campbell, *Sweet La-La Land*, p. 252, 1990

diddly-dum *adjective*

fine, good *UK*

- A term of approval ["It's all diddly-dum"] among drop-outs at a "free" pop-festival on Exmoor. —*The Observer*, 13th June 1976

diddly-shit *noun*

anything at all *US, 1963*

- —*American Speech*, p. 117, May 1964: 'Problems in the study of campus slang'
- See, what Ed says, like half the time don't mean diddly-shit. —Elmore Leonard, *Gold Coast*, p. 95, 1980
- Without it they can't do diddly shit. —Gerald Petievich, *Money Men*, p. 92, 1981
- I never let him get away with diddly-shit and that's why we had our moments. —*Mojo*, p. 48, September 2003

diddums *noun*

1 used by adults for soothing and consoling babies and very young children; hence, a childish endearment *UK, 1893*

- Aw diddums ... big boys shouldn't cry. Only little girls cry. —Niall Griffiths, *Sheepshagger*, p. 231, 2001

2 used for offering heavily sarcastic mock-sympathy to an adult or older child and deride childish behaviour or for suggesting that such behaviour or attitude is childish *UK*
Adapted from the nonsense endearment used to soothe very young children. This nonsense is expandable: 'diddums doodums dumpling den'.

- Aw. bless. Poor diddums had suffered a spoiled Saturday night[.] —Christopher Brookmyre, *Boiling a Frog*, p. 375, 2000

diddy *noun*

1 a toilet *AUSTRALIA, 1958*
Perhaps originally a fanciful term used when speaking with small children. Also variant 'didee'.

- 'Well', his missus tells him, 'having the didee in the backyard isn't very convenient,' the wife says. —Frank Hardy, *The Yarns of Billy Borker*, p. 56, 1965
- Burglar Bill entered the first diddy, put down the empty can and tugged at the full one. —Frank Hardy, *The Outcasts of Foolgarah*, p. 150, 1971
- —Arthur Chipper, *The Aussie Swearer's Guide*, p. 33, 1972

2 the female breast or nipple *UK*
Recorded in Glasgow use by Michael Munro, *The Original Patter*, 1985, and in Australia by James McDonald, *A Dictionary of Obscenity, Taboo and Euphemism*, 1988.

- If Sophia Loren came up to yeh an' stuck her diddies in your face would you say tha' she was nice enough? —Roddy Doyle, *The Van*, p. 255, 1991

3 a fool; used as a mild insult *UK*
Glasgow slang, from the previous sense, and therefore a TIT.

- —Michael Munro, *The Original Patter*, 1985

4 a gypsy *UK*
A familiar diminutive of DIDICOI in all its variant spellings. Can be further reduced to 'did'.

- To make things worse, he said, one "diddy" was a "tealeaf" [thief][.] —Butch Reynolds, *Broken Hearted Clown*, p. 30, 1953

diddy *adjective*

small *UK*
Usage popularised by Liverpool comedian Ken Dodd (b.1927).

- We are the Diddy Men —Ken Dodd, *Song of the Diddy Men*, 1965
- All these other places are just diddy little villages. Hamlets, like. —Niall Griffiths, *Kelly + Victor*, p. 47, 2002

diddy around; diddy about *verb*

to fool around *UK: SCOTLAND, 1985*
From DIDDY (a fool).

- Chuck [stop] diddyin about wi they speakers. —Michael Munro, *The Complete Patter*, 1996

diddy bag; ditty bag *noun*

a small bag issued to soldiers for carrying their personal effects *US*

- —*American Speech*, p. 54, February 1947: 'Pacific War language'
- Next he removed the balloon from the hobby box and placed it in a ditty bag he had sewn from denim, the same type of bag, though half again as large, as the boxers and wrestlers and other athletes used to carry their personal gear to and from the gym. —Malcolm Braly, *On the Yard*, p. 303, 1967
- Fucking-ay-John Ditty-Bag well-told I don't. —Darryl Ponicsan, *The Last Detail*, p. 171, 1970
- "What the hell you got in there?" Emilio asked nodding toward the ditty bags. —Richard Price, *The Wanderers*, p. 219, 1974
- Stepik said he found a bulldog hash pipe in his ditty bag. —Larry Heinemann, *Close Quarters*, p. 102, 1977
- —Frank Hailey, *Soldier Talk*, p. 18, 1982

diddybop *verb*

to take part in gang fights *US, 1955*

- He was going to do that life term in the penitentiary at Dannemora and Kenny made a mental note to write him a short letter and mail him some money. "The diddy-boppin' fool!" he though[.] —Emmett Grogan, *Ringolevio*, p. 104, 1972

diddybopper *noun*
a racially ambitious black person who rejects black culture and embraces the dominant white culture *US*
• —Edith A. Folb, *runnin' down some lines*, p. 234, 1980

▷ **see: DIDDLYBOPPER**

diddy-dum slinger *noun*
a radar operator *US*
• —*American Speech*, p. 153, April 1947: 'Radar slang terms'

Diddys *noun*
in the entertainment industry, *per diems US*
A back formation, from *per diem* to the initials PD to the initials of rap singer P Diddy.
• "[W]hat did you spend your Diddys" on? Or "the Diddys in this job are stingy". —*Popbitch*, 16th September 2004

didee *noun*
a water-closet *AUSTRALIA*
Generally used with 'the'.
• —Frank Hardy, *Billy Borker Yarns Again*, 1967

didge *noun*
price or cost *US*
A corruption of 'digits'.
• —Jonathan Roberts, *How to California*, p. 166, 1984

didgy *noun*
a dustbin *UK: SCOTLAND*
Glasgow slang.
• —Michael Munro, *The Original Patter*, p. 20, 1985

didgy *adjective*
1 nervous, unsettled *UK*
Possibly from **EDGY** (nerves on edge).
• I was starting to feel didgy about all this talk. "Let's get done with this," I was thinking, "Send me to court for murder and be done!" —Victor Headley, *The Man Who Took Down The Great Pitpat [britpulp]*, p. 74, 1999
• Time to kill. Getting didgy now. —J.J. Connolly, *Layer Cake*, p. 245, 2000

2 digital *UK: SCOTLAND*
• Err's yer didgy watches, three fur a pound. —Michael Munro, *The Original Patter*, p. 20, 1985

didi; dee-dee *verb*
to leave *US, 1964*
From the Vietnamese word *di* (goodbye) adapted by US soldiers during the war and made into a verb.
• Man, the dinks have dee-deed. They've split, Man. You ain't got nothin to worry about. —John M. Del Vecchio, *The 13th Valley*, p. 74, 1982
• —Linda Reinberg, *In the Field*, p. 59, 1991

didicoi; diddicoi *noun*
gypsy; Romany; half-breed gypsy *UK, 1853*
• [S]ome jobsworth will accuse you of being a camped-out diddicoi and serve you with a ten quid overnight parking bill. —John Milne, *Alive and Kicking*, p. 23, 1998
• Gypsies, pikeys, travellers or didicois, call them what you will[.] —Jimmy Stockin, *On The Cobbles*, p. 13, 2000

didj; didg *noun*
a didjeridoo (an Australian Aboriginal instrument) *AUSTRALIA, 1919*
• Bring a didg or a drum before 11 for free entry. Nice. —*Mixmag*, p. 135, December 2001
• This page primarily provides links to valued sites that didj initiates maybe unaware of, and links to my own pages concentrating upon traditional music and didjeridu in the Top End of the Northern Territory. —*sites.uws.edu.au/vip/listerp/yidaki.htm*, 2003

didn't oughter *noun*
a daughter *UK*
Rhyming slang.
• —David Powis, *The Signs of Crime*, 1977

dido *noun*
1 mischief, a prank *US, 1807*
• Our youngest uncle, Billy, was not old enough to join in their didoes. —Maya Angelou, *I Know Why the Caged Bird Sins*, p. 66, 1969

2 a petty complaint filed against a police officer by a superior *US*
• —*New York Times Magazine*, p. 88, 16th March 1958

did you ever?; did you ever!
would you believe it! *UK, 1817*
• —Cole Porter, *Well Did You Evah?*, 1956

die; dye *noun*
a diazepam (trade name Valium™) tablet, used as an antianxiety agent *US*
• —Richard A. Spears, *The Slang and Jargon of Drugs and Drink*, p. p.142, 1986

die *verb*
1 to want something very much *UK, 1709*
• He's dying to meet you ... you met him once before with me at Helena's[.] —Julia Phillips, *You'll Never Eat Lunch in This Town Again*, p. 5, 1991

2 in roller derby, to fall after an extended and dramatic fight *US*
• —Keith Coppage, *Roller Derby to Rollerjam*, 1999

▸ **die for a tie**
used as a humorous sobriquet for General MacArthur's prediction that the war in Korea would end in a stalemate unless he were given approval to attack China *US*
• Eighth Army troops called thiis "die for a tie" speech, and in the words of Colonel Voorhees, "its effect on their attitude toward the future was not inspirational." —Joseph C. Goulden, *Korea: The Untold Story of the War*, p. 453, 1982
• The phrase "Why die for a tie?" was frequently used by opponents of limited war. —Carter Malkasian, *The Korean War 1950–1953*, p. 71, 2001

▸ **die in the arse; die in the bum**
to fail completely *AUSTRALIA*
• Sammy looks at Danny. He's shaking. He's died in the arse, Sammy tells himself, and moves off. —David Ireland, *The Glass Canoe*, p. 58, 1976

▸ **die on the law**
on the railways, to work the maximum allowed by the Hours of Service Act *US*
• —Linda Niemann, *Boomer*, p. 248, 1990

▸ **die on your arse**
of a comedian, to fail to entertain *UK*
• Les Dawson went down well; Lenny Bennett died on his arse. —*The Guardian*, 20th July 2004

▸ **die the death**
of an entertainer, especially a comedian, to meet with a complete lack of response from an audience *UK, 1984*
• The Comedy Store welcomed untested and daring acts, most of whom died the death[.] —*Sight and Sound*, November 2000

▸ **die with your boots on**
to die while in action *US*
• You have to say that cowboy died with his boots on[.] —Joseph Wambaugh, *The Glitter Dome*, p. 165, 1981

▸ **to die for**
spectacular, wonderful *US, 1983*
• The suspense is killing me. This is to die for. —*Empire Records*, 1995

die before me!
used for acknowledging that someone has said exactly what you said at the same time *TRINIDAD AND TOBAGO, 1987*
• —Lise Winer, *Dictionary of the English/Creole of Trinidad & Tobago*, 2003

Diefenbaker meat *noun*
canned meat distributed to the poor during the years John Diefenbaker was prime minister (late 1950s – mid-60s) *CANADA*
• Mystery meat – Spork or Spam – was distributed to institutions and needy families. There are people who still refer to canned meat as Diefenbaker meat or Diefenbaker steak. —Chris Thain, *Cold as a Bay Street Banker's Heart*, p. 52, 1987

Diefenbunker *noun*
the secure fallout shelter for high Canadian government officials to use in case of national disaster *CANADA*
• (CF, since 1950s): The Diefenbunker command and control underground complex was built at Carp, Ontario, to house essential federal facilities in the event of a nuclear attack. The word is a play on the name of the Prime Minister, John Diefenbaker. —Tom Langeste, *Words on the Wing*, p. 79–80, 1995
• Although operationally obsolete for decades, four years ago it was reopened as a novelty tourist attraction. —Jim Holt, *Montreal Gazette*, p. F4, 28th May 2002

diener *noun*
▷ **see: DEANER**

die on the floor, seven at the door; on the floor, hit the door

in casino craps, used as a prediction that the next roll after a dice has bounced onto the floor will be a seven *US, 1983*

• —Thomas L. Clark, *The Dictionary of Gambling and Gaming*, p. 64, 1987

dies *noun*

tablets of diazepam, an anti-anxiety agent with central nervous system depressant properties *US*

• — *Providence (Rhode Island) Journal-Bulletin*, p. 6B, 4th August 1997: 'Doctors must know the narcolexicon'

diesel *noun*

1 an aggressive, 'manly' lesbian *US, 1959*

An abbreviation of DIESEL DYKE.

• It means that if we get busted the nice, bright-eyed prosecutors are going to describe prison to you, tell you about the two-hundred-pound diesel with a smelly snatch who's going to share your cell and how you'll have to go down on half the guards[.] —Vincent Patrick, *Family Business*, p. 69, 1985

2 a man with a great physique *US*

• — *Washington Post*, 14th October 1993

3 prison tea *UK*

Probably suggestive of the taste or appearance.

• —Angela Devlin, *Prison Patter*, p. 44, 1996

4 heroin *UK*

• —Robert Ashton, *This Is Heroin*, p. 205, 2002

• —Mike Haskins, *Drugs*, p. 283, 2003

diesel *adjective*

projecting an aggressive and tough image *US*

Originally applied to a lesbian type, the DIESEL DYKE, then to a broader field.

• I'm gonna get mad diesel. — *Kids*, 1995

• —Connie Eble (Editor), *UNC-CH Campus Slang*, p. 2, Fall 1996

diesel digits *noun*

channel 19 on a citizens' band radio, favoured by truckers *US*

• — Elementary Electronics, *Dictionary of CB Lingo*, p. 61, 1976

diesel dork *noun*

a large penis *US*

• —Michael Dalton Johnson, *Talking Trash with Redd Foxx*, p. 77, 1994

diesel dyke; diesel dike *noun*

a strong, forceful, aggressive lesbian *US, 1959*

• Well, honey, that butch numbuh turns out to be a les-bay-an – the butchest dam diesel dike y'evuh laid yuh gay eyes on! —John Rechy, *City of Night*, p. 354, 1963

• And this one coming in – watch out for her – she's a diesel dike. —Donald Webster Cory, *The Lesbian in America*, p. 201, 1964

• Two cases in point are Maria and Dickie, the former a fem, the later a stompin' diesel dyke. —Ruth Allison, *Lesbianism*, p. 73, 1967

• On the other hand, I once overheard a man fighting with a disel-dyke over a girl they both wanted[.] — *Maledicta*, p. 11, Summer 1977

• This blunt word [dyke] is the most common vernacular term in America for "lesbian," especially one regarded as mannish – note the intensives bull-dyke (or bull-dagger) and diesel dyke. —Wayne Dynes, *Homolexis*, p. 44, 1985

• The perfect homo companion for a junkie diesel dyke who relaxed listening to CD's of the Ontario 500 while selfirrigating with homemade herbal colonics. —Seth Morgan, *Homeboy*, p. 16, 1990

• Have you ever gotten a lipstick smeared Christmas card from a two hundred pound diesel dyke? —James Ellroy, *Hollywood Nocturnes*, p. 25, 1994

diesel fitter; diesel *noun*

bitter (beer) *UK*

Rhyming slang.

• —Ray Puxley, *Cockney Rabbit*, 1992

diesel therapy *noun*

the repeated transfer of a troublesome prisoner from prison to prison *US*

• —Reinhold Aman, *Hillary Clinton's Pen Pal*, p. 33, 1996

dieso *noun*

a diesel mechanic *ANTARCTICA, 1967*

An Australian addition to the slang of the South Pole.

• —Bernadette Hince, *The Antarctic Dictionary*, p. 99, 2000

diet pill *noun*

an amphetamine tablet *US, 1972*

From the drug's association with weight-loss.

• —Richard A. Spears, *The Slang and Jargon of Drugs and Drink*, p. 142, 1986

• —Mike Haskins, *Drugs*, p. 279, 2003

diff *noun*

1 difference *US, 1896*

• "What's the dif?" Tomboy said. "I don't care." —Hal Ellson, *Tomboy*, p. 63, 1950

• What's the diff? You wanna get on? —George Mandel, *Flee the Angry Strangers*, p. 26, 1952

• But I got a fair idea what they'll do if they catch me without 'em, even, so what's the diff? —T.A.G. Hungerford, *The Ridge and the River*, p. 60, 1952

• The clerk glanced at Folks and muttered, "What the diff?" —Iceberg Slim (Robert Beck), *Long White Con*, p. 65, 1977

• Maybe when you hit maturity you'll understand the diff between a Remington University man like David and a Westerburg boy like Ram[.] — *Heathers*, 1988

• I don't root, I fuck, I tell him. – What's the diff? —Christos Tsiolkas, *Loaded*, p. 9, 1995

• Borstal boy, not schoolboy. – What's a fuckin diff? Young lad either way. —Niall Griffiths, *Sheepshagger*, p. 12, 2001

2 a differential in a motor vehicle *AUSTRALIA, 1941*

• If we tried to cross it we'd go down to the diff. —Wal Watkins, *Race the Lazy River*, p. 62, 1963

• —Harvey E. Ward, *Down Under Without Blunder*, p. 29, 1967

• —Shane Maloney, *Nice Try*, p. 68, 1998

diffabitterance *noun*

used as a humorous replacement for 'bit of difference' *US, 1921*

• —Frederic G. Cassidy, *Dictionary of American Regional English, Volume II*, p. 66, 1991

difference *noun*

1 notice *UK*

Jocular; usually phrased as follows.

• I'd bash away in my back room and no-one took a blind bit of difference. —Chris Ryan, *The Watchman*, p. 362, 2001

2 any weapon used in a fight or crime *US*

• —Hyman E. Goldin et al., *Dictionary of American Underworld Lingo*, p. 58, 1950

different *adjective*

out of the ordinary, special, unusual, recherché *UK, 1912*

• [I]n the 60s and 70s used as a polite escape formula, similar to interesting, by those called upon to admire something which, in all sincerity, they cannot: "Well, it's – er – different!" —Beale, 1984

▸ **different strokes for different folks**

different things please different people *US*

Singer Syleena 'Syl' Johnson released the song 'Different Strokes' (J. Cameron and J. Zachary) with this line in it in 1967; Sly and the Family Stone's 1968 mega-hit 'Everyday People' put the phrase on the map.

• "I got different strokes for different folks." [Quoting Cassius Clay] — *Great Bend (Kansas) Daily Tribune*, p. 6, 11th November 1966

• There are a hundred times as many people addicted to alcohol, anti-depressants and nicotine as there are to heroin or Charlie [cocaine]. Different strokes for different folks, right? —Wayne Anthony, *Spanish Highs*, p. 65, 1999

differs *noun*

difference *UK*

Anglo-Irish.

• "I don't suppose it'll make any differs, but," he said. —Desmond O'Neill, *Life Has No Price*, 1959

diffy *noun*

a car or truck's differential *NEW ZEALAND*

• In affectionate terms we discussed the innards of their 'carbies' and their 'diffies' and their 'con-rods.' —Temple Sutherland, *Green Kiwi*, p. 199, 1956

dig *noun*

1 a punch, a blow *UK*

Extends the conventional sense of 'poke'.

• [W]e have to give the lad a few digs to make it look thingy, justy mark him up a bit and that[.] —Kevin Sampson, *Outlaws*, p. 16, 2001

2 a jibe, an insult, a taunt *UK, 1849*

• Peanut went dark but was afraid to start trading digs with Strike. —Richard Price, *Clockers*, p. 203, 1992

3 an Australian or New Zealand soldier of either world war *AUSTRALIA, 1916*

An abbreviation of DIGGER. Commonly used as form of address to such a soldier. Later also a friendly form of address to any man,

and now generally only used to men of an age to have fought in a world war.
- How would you be, Dig? —Frank Hardy, *The Yarns of Billy Borker*, p. 147, 1965
- —George Blaikie, *Remember Smith's Weekly?*, p. 147, 1966
- —Jim Ramsay, *Cop It Sweet!*, p. 28, 1977

4 a form of male address *AUSTRALIA, 1916*
A shortening of **DIGGER**.

5 an archaeological excavation, an archaeological expedition *UK, 1896*
- 'An American women archeologist's story of life on a 'dig' in the Kurdish hills of Iraq. —Linda S. Braidwood, *Digging Beyond the Tigris*, 1953

6 in cricket, an innings *AUSTRALIA*
- This simple recitation of Australian injuries up to, and not including, Australia's second dig in the Third Test had a profound effect in Australia[.] —George Blaikie, *Remember Smith's Weekly?*, p. 236, 1966

7 an injection of a drug *UK*
- I sorted myself out with a dig then washed out my works[.] —Lanre Fehintola, *Charlie Says...*, p. 18, 2000

8 in volleyball, contact with the ball below the waist *US*
- Primarily, the dig is used to recover a hard-driven spike or other offensive shot. Other uses of the dig are in net recovery situations. —Bonnie Robison, *Sports Illustrated Volleyball*, p. 94, 1972

9 a fisherman's stretch or 'area' of water *AUSTRALIA*
- —Nino Culotta, *Gone Fishin'*, 1963

10 a drag racing event *US*
- —John Edwards, *Auto Dictionary*, p. 44, 1993

▷ **see:** DIG IN THE GRAVE

dig *verb*

1 to like, to appreciate *US, 1950*
- [I]n five seconds a billiard tournament was going full blast, with spectators lined up around the table digging all the fine points of each player. —Mezz Mezzrow, *Really the Blues*, p. 20, 1946
- [T]hey seemed unaware of anything outside the realities of deals, a pad to to stay in, "digging the frantic jazz," and keeping everything going. —John Clellon Holmes, *Go*, p. 38, 1952
- They rushed down the street together, digging everything in the early way they had[.[—Jack Kerouac, *On the Road*, p. 8, 1957
- 'Boy, is that sophistry!' said the young man. 'Dig that sophistry!' —Terry Southern, *Flash and Filigree*, p. 87, 1958
- The East Coast girls are hip / I really dig those styles they wear. —The Beach Boys, *California Girls*, 1965
- That's all he said, and that's why I dig my father. —Nat Hentoff, *Jazz Country*, p. 12, 1965
- In point of fact he is funny and very glib, and I dig rapping (talking) with him. —Eldridge Cleaver, *Soul on Ice*, p. 46, 1968
- I dig department stores, huge supermarkets and airports. —Jerry Rubin, *Do It!*, p. 12, 1970
- I'm going to see the folks I dig / I'll even kiss a Sunset pig / California, I'm coming home. —Joni Mitchell, *California*, 1971
- [T]he Count Five album, the one I'd dug so cool before[.] —Lester Bangs, *Psychotic Reactions and Carburetor Dung*, p. 14, 1971
- [A] one-hundred-percent Bedouin with a pedigree goes straight back to the Prophet. Dig his bearing. Such pride! —William Burroughs, *Queer*, p. 71, 1985
- You'll dig it [Amsterdam] the most. —*Pulp Fiction*, 1994
- He's had enough. He no longer digs her. —*The Big Lebowski*, 1998

2 to understand *US, 1934*
- —Lou Shelly, *Hepcats Jive Dictionary*, p. 9, 1945
- I tried to write them down because I figured the only way to dig Bessie's unique phrasing was to get the words down exactly as she sang them. —Mezz Mezzrow, *Really the Blues*, p. 53, 1946
- [T]hat will be a different kind of thing, of course. You dig? —Jack Kerouac, *Letter to Neal Cassady*, p. 155, 27th June 1948
- He's really diggin' this scene, man. —William "Lord" Buckley, *Nero*, 1951
- Now you all better dig this and dig it the most. —Stephen Sondheim, *West Side Story*, 1957
- But you don't need to have nothing except rubbers – until you can dig who's a cop. —Malcolm X and Alex Haley, *The Autobiography of Malcolm X*, p. 48, 1964
- I'd rather hear you as your old sour self, Sam, than listen to how fast you can play that horn. All of you dig what I mean? —Nat Hentoff, *Jazz Country*, p. 68, 1965
- Why don't you all f-f-fade away / Don't try and dig what we all say. —Pete Townsend (performed by The Who), *My Generation*, 1965
- We didn't dig why we needed to work towards owning bigger houses? bigger cars? bigger manicured lawns? —Jerry Rubin, *Do It!*, p. 18, 1970
- That's cool because for five months I ate and slept for no money at all, dig? —Babs Gonzales, *Movin' On Down De Line*, p. 79, 1975
- They leaned in close to dig the words. —Francesca Lia Block, *Baby Be-Bop*, p. 452, 1995

3 to bother, to concern *AUSTRALIA, 1958*
- The man was taken aback. "What's digging you?" he blustered. —D'Arcy Niland, *Call the...*, 1958
- —Lise Winer, *Dictionary of the English/Creole of Trinidad & Tobago*, 2003

4 to inject a drug intravenously, especially heroin *UK*
- —Angela Devlin, *Prison Patter*, p. 44, 1996
- [T]hey have caught me a couple of times before actually digging [injecting] gear [heroin]. —Lanre Fehintola, *Charlie Says...*, p. 20, 2000
- —Mike Haskins, *Drugs*, p. 290, 2003

5 in handball, to hit a low ball before it strikes the floor *US*
- —Paul Haber, *Inside Handball*, p. 65, 1970: 'Glossary'

6 in surfing, to paddle energetically *US*
- —Grant W. Kuhns, *On Surfing*, p. 115, 1963

▸ **dig a drape**

to buy a new dress *CANADA*
Teen slang, reported by a Toronto newspaper in 1946, and reported as 'obsolescent or obsolete' by Douglas Leechman, 1959.

▸ **dig for gold**

to pick your nose *US*
- —Connie Eble (Editor), *UNC-CH Campus Slang*, p. 3, November 2003

▸ **dig horrors**

to be suffering; to live with trouble *GRENADA, 1975*
- —Richard Allsopp, *Dictionary of Caribbean English Usage*, p. 192, 1996

▸ **dig out your eye**

to swindle; to cheat *TRINIDAD AND TOBAGO, 1935*
- —Lise Winer, *Dictionary of the English/Creole of Trinidad & Tobago*, 2003

▸ **dig the man a neat ditch**

in oil drilling, to perform any job well *US*
- —Jerry Robertson, *Oil Slanguage*, p. 46, 1954

▸ **dig with the right foot**

to be of the same religious persuasion, in Northern Ireland a Protestant *UK: NORTHERN IRELAND*
- [I]n Ireland the majority of diggers used the right foot...In Eastern Ireland, on the other hand, and particularly in Protestant districts of the north-east, the left foot is usually the digging foot. —Bernard Share, *Slanguage*, p. 85, 1997

▸ **dig with the wrong foot**

to be a Catholic *CANADA*
- I think of what my grand mother and my Aunt Tena, over in Dungannon, used to always say to indicate that somebody was a Catholic. "So-and-so digs with the wrong foot," they would say. "She digs with the wrong foot." —Alice Munro, *in The Story and Its Writer*, p. 996, 1968

dig-away *noun*

a festering sore *TRINIDAD AND TOBAGO, 1989*
- —Lise Winer, *Dictionary of the English/Creole of Trinidad & Tobago*, 2003

Digby chicken *noun*

a smoked, salted small herring *CANADA*
Digby is a fishing port on the west (Fundy) shore of Nova Scotia.
- Digby chicken is a tiny herring that is smoked and salted. Maritimers call fillets of the little fish Digby chips. —Bill Casselman, *Canadian Words*, p. 71, 1995
- Like the Frenchman says, the herring, before they take the heads off and the guts out. —Lewis Poteet, *The South Shore Phrase Book*, p. 37, 1999

dig down *verb*

to demolish *BARBADOS*
- —Frank A. Collymore, *Barbadian Dialect*, p. 38, 1965

digger *noun*

1 a goldminer *AUSTRALIA, 1849*
- Other diggers stood around and laughed in envy at the fierce enjoyment of a man temporarily rich. For the digger had just struck gold. —Bob Ellis and Anne Brooksbank, *Mad Dog Morgan*, p. 3, 1976

2 an Australian or New Zealand soldier of either world war *AUSTRALIA, 1916*
Also extended to soldiers fighting in other military conflicts such as the Korean and Vietnam wars. Originally applied only to infantry soldiers of World War 1 who spent much time digging and maintaining trenches. A term of high approbation.
- The cops don't go around pinching us Diggers. We've only got the military Jacks to worry about. —Vince Kelly, *The Bogeyman*, p. 109, 1956
- Quite all right office. An old digger myself. I understand. —Barry Oakley, *A Salute to the Great McCarthy*, p. 97, 1970

- This short story illustrates the immense courage and resolution of the Aussie digger to pursue the task at hand. —Martin Cameron, *A Look at the Bright Side*, 1988
- 'But he kept soldiering on.' 'Ahh he's a digger alright. Got a heart like a lion that boy.' —Robert G. Barrett, *Davo's Little Something*, p. 36, 1992
- Eight of their fellow Diggers who lay wounded on the Kokoda Trail were massacred by a Japanese collaborator. —*Aussie Post*, p. 4, 29th August 1998

3 by extension, a term of male address *AUSTRALIA, 1920*

4 an undertaker *US*

- —Lou Shelly, *Hepcats Jive Dictionary*, p. 9, 1945

5 a person who buys a large number of tickets to a popular entertainment and resells the tickets to a broker *US, 1927*

- —Sherman Louis Sergel, *The Language of Show Biz*, p. 71, 1973
- —Don Wilmeth, *The Language of American Popular Entertainment*, p. 73, 1981

6 a member of the Digger hippie counterculture support-network *US*

Named for a mid-C17 English sect that practised agrarian communism.

- They are THE DIGGERS. And everyday at four o'clock they provide anybody with anything to eat. —*Berkeley Barb*, p. 3, 21 October 1966
- The Diggers are hip to poetry. Everything is free, do your own thing. —*Trip Without a Ticket*, Winter 1966–67
- —Joe David Brown (Editor), *The Hippies*, p. 217, 1967: 'Glossary of hippie terms'
- The largess is open to all – the digger motto is, "Free but please do not steal." —Sidney Bernard, *This Way to the Apocalypse*, p. 59, 1968
- Why did the hippie take a job in the cemetery? He was a Digger! —Paul Laikin, *101 Hippie Jokes*, 1968
- Hapt is a free roneoed digger paper published in Colchester, linked with diggers in Europe. —Richard Neville, *Play Power*, p. 176, 1970

7 a pickpocket, especially a clumsy one *US, 1931*

- —Vincent J. Monteleone, *Criminal Slang*, p. 68, 1949
- —*The New American Mercury*, p. 707, 1950

8 a face-first fall *US*

- —Judi Sanders, *Faced and Faded, Hanging to Hurl*, p. 11, 1993

9 a solitary confinement cell *US*

- —William K. Bentley and James M. Corbett, *Prison Slang*, 1992

10 a drag racing car *US*

- The term originated to describe drag cars because they seem to "dig" themselves out of the hole as they accelerate from the starting line. —John Edwards, *Auto Dictionary*, p. 44, 1993

11 the grade 'D' *US*

- —Collin Baker et al., *College Undergraduate Slang Study Conducted at Brown University*, p. 104, 1968

diggety

used in various combinations for expressing surprise or pleasure *US, 1928*

- John claps his hands together. "Hot diggedy dog! I'll be a god-damned monkey's psychotherapist!" —Linda Keen, *Across the Universe with John Lennon*, p. 117, 1999

diggidy *noun*

marijuana *UK*

- — *www.addictions.org*, 2001

digging for worms *noun*

varicose vein surgery *UK*

Medical slang, obvious imagery.

- —Adam T. Fox, St Mary's Hospital, London, 10th October 2002

diggings *noun*

lodgings *US, 1837*

- Opal and Sesame Mae live together in nice diggings in West Harlem. —Sara Harris, *The Lords of Hell*, p. 48, 1967

diggity *noun*

heroin *UK*

- —Mike Haskins, *Drugs*, p. 283, 2003

diggys *noun*

digital scales *UK*

- Yuh still got dem diggys? What, c'n I borrow dem? —Courttia Newland, *Society Within*, p. 27, 1999

dig in *verb*

1 to eat heartily *UK, 1912*

- [D]ig in, fill your boots —William Granville, *Sea Slang of the Twentieth Century*, 1959

2 from a standstill, to accelerate a car suddenly, making the tyres squeal on the road *US*

- —*Newsweek*, p. 28, 8th October 1951

dig in the grave; dig *noun*

a shave *AUSTRALIA, 1931*

Rhyming slang.

digit *noun*

a number chosen as a bet in an illegal policy bank lottery *US*

- I stopped my man that I did my dope juggling with, and who also had the number bag going for him, and placed my diggets for that day. —A.S. Jackson, *Gentleman Pimp*, p. 154, 1973

digital manipulation *noun*

(of a female) masturbation *US*

A simple pun using computer technology.

- —Erica Orloff and JoAnn Baker, *Dirty Little Secrets*, p. 67, 2001

digithead *noun*

a person whose enthusiasm for mathematics or computers is never hidden *US*

- Megabyte me, Digithead! —Jim Davis, *Garfield's Insults, Put-Downs, and Slams*, p. 59, 1994

digits *noun*

a telephone number *US*

- Oh, Cher, he's getting her digits. —*Clueless*, 1995
- —*San Jose Mercury News*, 11th May 1999

digits dealer *noun*

an operator of an illegal numbers policy lottery *US*

- —Ralph de Sola, *Crime Dictionary*, p. 41, 1982

dignity *noun*

the vagina *US*

A political coinage.

- There's [a...] "toadie," "dee dee," "nishi," "dignity," "monkey box[".] —Eve Ensler, *The Vagina Monologues*, p. 6, 1998

dig out *noun*

help getting out of a difficult situation *IRELAND*

- Daddy was helping her out with her studies. She was falling behind, and he was giving her a dig out. With advice, you know. —Joseph O'Connor, *Red Roses and Petrol*, p. 79, 1995

dig out *verb*

1 to work cheerfully and with a will; to make a real effort *UK*

Military usage.

- —Nigel Foster, *The Making of a Royal Marine Commando*, 1987

2 to taunt, to insult *UK*

- I was so nervous of Jim Irwin digging me out in front of them that I stood behind the settee like a big dummy. —Lenny McLean, *The Guv'nor*, p. 19, 1998

3 in trucking, to start fast *US*

- —Montie Tak, *Truck Talk*, p. 44, 1971

digs *noun*

1 lodgings, be it a room, apartment, or house *UK, 1893*

An abbreviation of the earlier (1830s) 'diggings'. In the UK theatrical 'digs' have a long and colourful history with most venues still providing a 'digs-list' for touring players.

- This is an important courtesy, and one that you will appreciate, too, if you can establish it as Standard Operating Procedure around your digs. —Dick Clark, *To Goof or Not to Goof*, p. 69, 1963
- He smoked too many cigs / Lived in one room in Victoria / He was tidy in his digs[.] —Ian Dury, *My Old Man*, 1977
- "Having this messengered to your digs after numerous calls to reputed place of employ." —Jay McInerney, *Bright Lights, Big City*, p. 89, 1984
- The other tenants included a children's photographer, a C.P.A., an optometrist and an office for the landlord, who used the digs as a place to clip coupons and get away from his wife[.] —Joseph Wambaugh, *Fugitive Nights*, p. 44, 1992
- I am staying with a nice family in their digs across the river in the Deccan Gymkhana district. —C.D. Payne, *Youth in Revolt*, p. 404, 1993
- I'm stopping in digs in different towns and seeing the backstage of all these different theatres. —Ben Elton, *High Society*, p. 214, 2002

2 a job *US*

- —Kenn "Naz" Young, *Naz's Underground Dictionary*, p. 24, 1973

dig up; dig out *verb*

to research and discover, or find and obtain *UK, 1611*

- I had put such things as parties behind me, but I remembered Mavis McKinnon's crowd and wondered, as I always did, where she dug them up—Kylie Tennant, *The Honey Flow*, 1956
- Hello gorgeous! Where did Bazza dig you up? eh?—Barry Humphries, *The Wonderful World of Barry McKenzie*, 1968
- Oracle, the world's second largest software company, has admitted that it hired private detectives to dig up scandalous information on Microsoft, its biggest and most bitter rival.—*The Guardian*, 29th June 2000
- [E]ven in today's low interest, low inflation climate it is worth digging out the higher interest accounts[.]—*The Guardian*, 15th February 2003

dig you later

used as a farewell *US*

- —Marcus Hanna Boulware, *Jive and Slang of Students in Negro Colleges*, 1947

dik *adjective*

1 stupid *SOUTH AFRICA*

Derived from its literal Afrikaans sense as 'thick'

- —Jean Branford, *A Dictionary of South African English*, 1978

2 tired of something or someone *SOUTH AFRICA, 1986*

Often in the expression 'to be dik of'.

- —Penny Silva, *A Dictionary of South African English*, p. 185, 1996

3 heavy, beefy, big, fat, powerfully built *SOUTH AFRICA, 1970*

From Afrikaans.

- —Penny Silva, *A Dictionary of South African English*, p. 185, 1996

dikbek *noun*

a sulky or surly person *SOUTH AFRICA, 1970*

From Afrikaans for 'thick beak'.

- —Jean Branford, *A Dictionary of South African English*, 1978

dike *noun*

stolen brass or copper sold as scrap *US*

- —Joe McKennon, *Circus Lingo*, p. 30, 1980

▷ see: DYKE

dike *verb*

in computing, to remove or disable something *US*

Derived from the sense of 'dikes' as 'diagonal cutters used in electrical work'.

- A standard slogan is "When in doubt, dike it out". (The implication is that it is usually more effective to attack software problems by reducing complexity than by increasing it.)—Eric S. Raymond, *The New Hacker's Dictionary*, p. 126, 1991

dilberry *noun*

a fool *NEW ZEALAND*

- Any man who thinks and reads beyond the immediate requirements of getting a good job is a fool – 'wet', 'gormless', dilberry' etc. —*Landfall*, p. 221, 1952

Dilbert *noun*

1 in poker, a player with a strong grasp of the mathematics and probabilities associated with the game but a poor set of playing skills *US*

- —John Vorhaus, *The Big Book of Poker Slang*, p. 13, 1996

2 a blunder *US, 1944*

- —J.E. Lighter, *The Historical Dictionary of American Slang, Vol. I*, p. 592, 1994

dilbert *verb*

to disabuse an employee of work-place optimism *US, 1996*

From the experiences of Dilbert the eponymous anti-hero of the *Dilbert* comic strip.

- — Susie Dent, *The Language Report*, p. 49, 2003

dildo *noun*

a despicable, offensive or dim-witted person *US, 1960*

- —Collin Baker et al., *College Undergraduate Slang Study Conducted at Brown University*, p. 105, 1968
- —Helen Dahlskog (Editor), *A Dictionary of Contemporary and Colloquial Usage*, p. 18, 1972
- I take back cars from dildos who don't pay their bills.—*Repo Man*, 1984
- See, I don't think I need to sit here with you fuckin' dildos anymore! —*The Breakfast Club*, 1985
- Then these four dildos come in got a serious attitude problem towards us.—Jeremy Cameron, *Brown Bread in Wengen*, p. 56, 1999

DILF *noun*

a sexually attractive father *US*

A gender variation of **MILF** (a sexually appealing mother); an acronym of '*d*ad *I*'d *l*ike to *f*uck'.

- —Chris Lewis, *The Dictionary of Playground Slang*, p. 148, 2003

dill *noun*

1 a fool *AUSTRALIA, 1941*

Backformation from **DILLY** (foolish).

- 'You know why, you big dill.'—Eric Lambert, *The Veterans*, p. 91, 1954
- Anyway, stupid old Leo said as we were leaving the workshop "Last one home's a bit of an idiot", and being a bit of a dill I took the bait. —Roy Slaven (John Doyle), *Five South Coast Seasons*, p. 78, 1992
- But when he heard that Herod's son Archelaus had seized power in Judea he knew that only a dill would go there.—Kel Richards, *The Aussie Bible*, p. 18, 2003

2 the penis *AUSTRALIA*

- —James McDonald, *A Dictionary of Obscenity, Taboo and Euphemism*, p. 39, 1988

dillberries *noun*

excreta that cling to anal or pubic hair *UK*

The original spelling, as recorded by Francis Grose in 1811, is 'dilberries'.

dill-brain *noun*

a simpleton *AUSTRALIA*

- 'So you see, Mary,' Ron continued, 'if a cat can have feelings, so can a dill-brain like Tim, and more feelings, because Tim's not all that bad.'—Colleen McCullough, *Tim*, 1975
- The minute they get the Government on the ropes, the dill-brains start slogging themselves on the chops instead.—*(Aukland) Sunday News*, p. 37, 19th July 1987

dill-brained *adjective*

foolish *AUSTRALIA*

- He's their butt, their whipping boy, and the poor little coot's too dill-brained to realize it!—Colleen McCullough, *Tim*, p. 30, 1975

dill-dock *noun*

a dildo *US*

- Dill-dock – Artificial penis strapped on by active Lesbian partner. —Anon., *The Gay Girl's Guide*, p. 7, 1949

dillhole *noun*

an easily disliked person *US*

- —Judi Sanders, *Da Bomb*, p. 5, 1997

dilligaf

do I look like I give a fuck? US

Collected from a police recruit met at White Swan, Brecon, in 2001.

- Yeah, so it was FUBAR. I just started at the director like DILLIGAF and fired him. I mean, BFD, right?—Jennifer Duncan, *Sanctuary & Other Stories*, p. 176, 1999

dill piece *noun*

the penis *US*

- —Rick Ayers (Editor), *Slang Dictionary*, p. 8, 2001

dillpot; dillypot; dill *noun*

a fool *AUSTRALIA, 1941*

Rhyming slang for **TWOT**, possibly from **DILLY** (silly).

- Don't be such a dill, Barry[.]—Barry Humphries, *Bazz Pulls It Off!*, 1971

dilly *noun*

1 an excellent or remarkable thing or person *US, 1908*

Usually used in a sarcastic sense.

- Five minutes later another car drove up and a pair of dillies climbed out.—Mickey Spillane, *I, The Jury*, p. 70, 1947
- Judge Hitz, the humorist of the local bench, got off a dilly when he discovered the plaintiff in a matrimonial action was still living with her husband, the whole divorce proceedings being a sham to swindle creditors.—Jack Lait and Lee Mortimer, *Washington Confidential*, p. 233–234, 1951
- Every time I was up for a new cellmate they spin the bottle and give me a real dilly.—Rocky Garciano (with Rowland Barber), *Somebody Up There Likes Me*, p. 116, 1955
- You're the most impossible man i ever met. And I've met some dillies.—Raymond Chandler, *Playback*, p. 150, 1958
- Both were of the gooey sentimental type, dripping with sickly sweetness, but the latter was a real dilly.—Jim Thompson, *The Grifters*, p. 32, 1963
- —Helen Dahlskog (Editor), *A Dictionary of Contemporary and Colloquial Usage*, p. 18, 1972

2 a capsule of Dilaudid™, a synthetic morphine used by heroin addicts trying to break their habit *US, 1971*

- —Geoffrey Froner, *Digging for Diamonds*, p. 26, 1989

dilly *adjective*

silly, foolish *AUSTRALIA, 1905*

The *English Dialect Dictionary* records 'dilly' meaning 'queer' from Somersetshire. Possibly from **DILLPOT** (a fool) or, more likely as the first recording of 'dilly' predates 'dillpot' by 35 years, simple rhyming slang.

- You're bats. You've gone dilly on the idea[.]—Norman Lindsay, *Halfway to Anywhere*, 1947

Dilly *nickname*

Piccadilly, an area of central London *UK, 1936*

The area around Piccadilly Circus was a popular location for street-walkers and polari-speaking male prostitutes.

- Competition, as I have said, is strong along the Dilly.—Anonymous *Streetwalker*, p. 22, 1959
- —Paul Baker, *Polari*, p. 171, 2002

dilly bag *noun*

a bag, generally small, for carrying odds and ends *AUSTRALIA, 1906*

From *dilly* a traditional Australian Aboriginal woven bag, from the Australian Aboriginal language Yagara.

- —Harvey E. Ward, *Down Under Without Blunder*, p. 38, 1967
- He'd been brooding as he checked the contents of his dilly bag. —Wilda Moxham, *The Apprentice*, p. 61, 1969
- —Jim Ramsay, *Cop It Sweet!*, p. 29, 1977

dilly-bags *adjective*

much, plenty, many *AUSTRALIA*

An elaboration of **BAGS**.

- —Sidney J. Baker, *Australia Speaks*, 1953

dilly boy *noun*

a young male prostitute *UK*

The **DILLY** (Piccadilly Circus) is (perhaps was) renowned as a centre for male prostitution.

- — *Maledicta*, p. 220, 1979: 'Kinks and queens: linguistic and cultural aspects of the terminology for gays'
- —Paul Baker, *Polari*, p. 171, 2002

dilly-dally *verb*

to dawdle; hence to waste time *UK, 1741*

A reduplication of conventional 'dally' (to loiter).

- Kenny sensed something, so he dilly-dallied on the other side of the street[.]—Emmett Grogan, *Ringolevio*, p. 6, 1972
- it was a big thing: don't dilly-dally, make a decision.—Andy McNab, *Immediate Action*, p. 86, 1995
- Nobody should dilly-dally over this, watching the situation to see how the group develop. You have to jump on them now.—Kevin Sampson, *Powder*, p. 145, 1999
- [P]eople were not impressed with my dilly-dallying.—Lanre Fehintola, *Charlie Says...*, p. 100, 2000

dillzy *noun*

the penis *US*

A variation on 'dilly' (penis).

- She on the dillzy, I take advantage—Dr Dre, *Housewife*, 1999

dim *noun*

the night; twilight *US, 1944*

- —Lou Shelly, *Hepcats Jive Dictionary*, p. 9, 1945
- — *Time Magazine*, p. 92, 20th January 1947: 'Dicty dictionary'
- 'Twas the dim before Nicktide and all through the pad / You could dig them cats waiting and praying like mad[.]—Dan Burley, *Diggeth Thou?*, p. 42, 1959

dim *adjective*

unintelligent *UK, 1924*

An antonym for the intellectually bright.

- George Bush? He's nice but dim, says crown prince.— *The Guardian*, 15th May 2002

dimba *noun*

marijuana from west Africa *UK, 1998*

A variation of **DJAMBA**.

- —Mike Haskins, *Drugs*, p. 287, 2003

dimbo *noun*

▷ **see:** **DIMMO**

dime *noun*

1 ten dollars *US*

- A dime is ten dollars.—Willard Motley, *Let No Man Write My Epitaph*, p. 148, 1958
- Couldn't you borrow a dime from Moira, Joe?—Alexander Trocchi, *Cain's Book*, p. 35, 1960
- Here! Take this one! Gimme a dime!—Odie Hawkins, *Ghetto Sketches*, p. 59, 1972
- Gimme thirty-five of it, put fifteen in your stocking for mad money, and put the dime in your purse. Let it be that way all the time. A dime is the most you carry in your purse.—A.S. Jackson, *Gentleman Pimp*, p. 168, 1973

2 one hundred dollars *US*

- Two hundred bucks, two small, two dimes, two C-notes, all blown away.—Robert Campbell, *Juice*, p. 9, 1988
- Twenty dimes on Columbia.— *Casino*, 1995

3 one thousand dollars *US, 1974*

- You owe almost eight dimes. you never shoulda got in so deep, but you did.—Joseph Wambaugh, *The Black Marble*, p. 39, 1978
- —Michael Knapp, *Bay Sports Review*, p. 8, November 1991
- Twenty dimes on Columbia.— *Casino*, 1995

4 ten years; a ten-year prison sentence *US*

- [B]oth doing 10 years for SALE – but Tam's dime was new and Joe's was old, and he only had a year left.—Clarence Cooper Jr, *The Farm*, p. 25, 1967
- The repeater said, "The son-of-a-bitch is stir crazy. His voice-box screwed up on him a 'dime' ago."—Iceberg Slim (Robert Beck), *Pimp*, p. 51, 1969
- —Clarence Major, *Dictionary of Afro-American Slang*, p. 46, 1970
- He had to do a dime (ten years) for the Government.—A.S. Jackson, *Gentleman Pimp*, p. 88, 1973
- —Paul Glover, *Words from the House of the Dead*, 1974
- Guy did a dime – in the labor camps, froze his ass.—Edwin Torres, *After Hours*, p. 173, 1979
- Stupid fools, Lloyd thought, risking half a dime minimum for a thousand dollars top.—James Ellroy, *Blood on the Moon*, p. 74, 1984

5 a pretty girl *US*

A product of a one-to-ten scale for rating beauty, with ten being the best; thus an updated way of saying 'a ten'.

- —Connie Eble (Editor), *UNC-CH Campus Slang*, p. 4, October 2002

▸ **on a dime**

precisely, suddenly *US*

- The order was, you see anybody run, give them a warning, and if they don't stop on a dime, shoot.—Elmore Leonard, *Out of Sight*, p. 109, 1996

dime *verb*

to betray, to inform on *US, 1970*

- Cut the crap. I know you dimed me out on this. I know you went right to Sennett when I said I'd had a thing with a judge.—Scott Turow, *Personal Injuries*, p. 199, 1999

dime-a-dip dinner *noun*

a fundraising meal *US, 1967*

- He'd met Oribelle, en route, at a dime-a-dip dinner at a Baptist church in Fayetteville, Arkansas.—Sue Grafton, *F is for Fugitive*, p. 53, 1989

dime a dozen *adjective*

used of anything in very plentiful supply *US, 1930*

- And, of course, ATM machines are now a dime a dozen.—Marcus Buckingham and Curt Coffman, *First, Break All the Rules*, p. 129, 1999

dime bag; dime *noun*

a packet of drugs sold for ten dollars *US, 1970*

- The apartment is shadowy, sparsely furnished ... a portable record player, two beat-up sofas, a couple of sprung loose easy chairs, a small coffee table, holding on its top a dime bag[.]—Odie Hawkins, *Ghetto Sketches*, p. 115, 1972
- [Y]ou're gonna spend an entire summer going blind on paperwork because a Signalman Second Class bought and smoked a dime bag of oregano.— *A Few Good Men*, 1992
- But we should run by the park and get a dime.— *Kids*, 1995

dime-dropper *noun*

a police informant *US, 1966*

- —Weasel Murphy, *Professional Gambler's Handbook*, p. 123, 1997

dimelow; dinelow; dinelo *noun*

a fool, an idiot *UK, 1900*

- I won't back down from no man, but I ain't no dimelow.—Jimmy Stockin, *On The Cobbles*, p. 31, 2000

dime-nickel *noun*

a 105mm wheeled cannon capable of shooting shells at a high angle *US*

- —Linda Reinberg, *In the Field*, p. 62, 1991

dime note *noun*

a ten-dollar note *US, 1938*

- —Lou Shelly, *Hepcats Jive Talk Dictionary*, p. 23, 1945

dime paper *noun*

ten dollars worth of a powdered drug, especially heroin *US*

- Sell me and Clearhead a dime paper and we can geeze in one of the pads in the abandoned buliding down the block. —Emmett Grogan, *Ringolevio*, p. 43, 1972

dime special; dime *noun*

crack cocaine *US, 1998*

- —Mike Haskins, *Drugs*, p. 281, 2003

dime-stacking *noun*

a system of keeping track of drinks not rung up on a bar's cash register, enabling the bartender to calculate the amount that can be safely embezzled at the end of the shift *US*

- Both were working furiously to serve customers, as well as the waitresses at the serve bar, and neither was making any funny moves such as dime-stacking, one for every drink they didn't ring up on the register. —Joseph Wambaugh, *Fugitive Nights*, p. 116, 1992

dime store *noun*

1 a store selling a variety of small items *US, 1938*

- The looting of a train, the robbery of a dime store, those were the kind of things that Spence and Baker always seemed to find themselves hooked up with. —Donald Goines, *Inner City Hoodlum*, p. 23, 1975

2 a small casino or gambling establishment with low-stakes games *US, 1953*

- —Thomas L. Clark, *The Dictionary of Gambling and Gaming*, p. 64, 1987

dime's worth *noun*

the (variable) amount of heroin that is sufficient to cause death *UK*

- —Robert Ashton, *This Is Heroin*, p. 208, 2002

dimmo; dimbo *noun*

a stupid person *CANADA*

- Move it, you dumbheads, you dimmos, you jerks. —*The Guardian*, 4th September 1977
- The daffy-headed dimmo who worries about glove compartments doesn't exist. —*Sunday Express*, 25th October 1981
- PRs were a pretty dozy bunch on the whole – either clapped-out old hacks who were too sozzled even for Fleet Street, or dimbo girlfriends who thought they liked meeting creative people. —*The Observer*, 27th January 2002

Dimmo; Dimo *noun*

a Greek *UK, 1961*

From the pronunciation of '*Demo*', short for *Demosthenes*, a very common given-name among Greeks.

dimp *noun*

a cigarette-end *UK, 1940*

Originally military, then vagrants.

- —*Social Work Today*, 22nd January 1980

dimple *noun*

a dent on a car's body *US*

- —Jim Crotty, *How to Talk American*, p. 36, 1997

dimps *noun*

a small amount of money, tobacco or other prison currency *UK*

- —Angela Devlin, *Prison Patter*, p. 45, 1996

dimwit *noun*

a slow-witted fool *US, 1921*

Extends from **DIM** (not very bright).

- [H]e despised every second of his working life, surrounded as he was by dimwits, dealing with morons and hearing about their stupid prejudices[.] —John King, *White Trash*, p. 307, 2001

dimwitted *adjective*

stupid, slow *US, 1940*

The quality of a **DIMWIT**.

- Rowan Atkinson merges his moronic Mr Bean and his supercilious Blackadder as the eponymous dimwitted agent for MI7. —*The Observer*, 13th April 2003

Dinah *noun*

dynamite or nitroglycerin *US*

- —Vincent J. Monteleone, *Criminal Slang*, p. 68, 1949

dinarly; dinarla; dinaly; dinah; dinarlee *noun*

money *UK, 1851*

Ultimately from Latin *dinarii* into Italian or Spanish, via lingua franca to parleyaree; or, pehaps Larin *dinarius*, into Persian and wider Arabic *dinar* (various coins), via gypsy; thence general Cockney usage and adoption as part of the polari vocabulary.

- —Paul Baker, *Polari*, p. 171, 2002

din-din *noun*

dinner; a meal *UK, 1905*

Children's vocabulary; coy.

- If you get captured with one you'll get a few days no din-din. —Frank Norman, *Bang to Rights*, p. 93, 1958
- Really interesting din-din. —Odie Hawkins, *Scars and Memories*, p. 47, 1987
- I'm thinking, why don't you and I go out and have some din-din this evening. —Elmore Leonard, *Maximum Bob*, p. 245, 1991

din-dins *noun*

a meal *UK, 1920*

A variation of **DIN-DIN**.

- Puking and peeing seem to have displaced din-dins and dancing as desirable social activities in British comedy. —*Sunday Times (South Africa)*, 10th October 1999
- Danny's got better things to worry about than where you two eat your din-dins. —J.J. Connolly, *Layer Cake*, p. 195, 2000

dine *noun*

dynamite *US*

- —Jay Robert Nash, *Dictionary of Crime*, p. 103, 1992

dine *verb*

▸ **dine at the Y; eat at the Y**

to perform oral sex on a woman *US*

The Y is an effective pictogram for the groin of a woman.

- BARRY: Well, I dunno about you Suke – but I feel like dining at the Y. SUKE: Well darls [darling] if you wanted to yodel up the valley youse had your chance[.] —Barry Humphries, *Bazza Pulls It Off!*, 1971
- [W]hat's known in some circles as dining at the Y. Her Y. —*The Times Magazine*, p. 43, 16th February 2002

dine and dash *verb*

to leave a restaurant without paying your bill *US*

- —Anna Scotti and Paul Young, *Buzzwords*, p. 59, 1997

dine in *verb*

in prison, to eat in your cell rather than communally *UK*

Hence the derivatives 'diner-in' and 'dining in'.

- —Paul Tempest, *Lag's Lexicon*, 1950

dinelow; dinelo *noun*

▷ see: **DIMELOW**

ding *noun*

1 the penis *US*

- I say to you, Legion of Decency – you with your dings scrubbed with holy water and Rokeach soap – you're dirty. —Lenny Bruce, *How to Talk Dirty and Influence People*, p. 71, 1965
- "Ooops," Jimmy says, "I caught it in my ding." —Linda Perlstein, *Not Much Just Chilin'*, p. 65, 2003

2 the buttocks *AUSTRALIA*

A shortening of **DINGER**.

- Been sittin' on our dings the last alf hour waitin' for yer. —Nino Culotta (John O'Grady), *They're A Weird Mob*, p. 106, 1957

3 a party, especiallly a wild party *AUSTRALIA, 1956*

A shortening of **WINGDING**.

- —J.E. MacDonnell, *Don't Gimme the Ships*, p. 111, 1960
- I'm taking myself along to the Ding at the D.C.'s residence. —John Wynnum, *Tar Dust*, p. 51, 1962
- —John Wynnum, *Jiggin' in the Riggin'*, p. 76, 1965
- —George Blaikie, *Remember Smith's Weekly?*, p. 98, 1966
- —Frank Hardy, *The Outcasts of Foolgarah*, p. 181, 1971
- —G.A. Wilkes, *A Dictionary of Australian Colloquialisms*, 1978

4 marijuana *US, 1954*

- —Richard A. Spears, *The Slang and Jargon of Drugs and Drink*, p. 143, 1986
- —Mike Haskins, *Drugs*, p. 287, 2003

5 a dent, scratch, scrape or rip *US, 1945*

- —Grant W. Kuhns, *On Surfing*, p. 115, 1963
- —John Lawlor, *How to Talk Car*, p. 38, 1965
- They checked their boards for dings and stood over us as we waxed them. —Kathy Lette and Gabriel Carey, *Puberty Blues*, p. 32, 1979

6 the expenses incurred in operating a carnival concession *US*
- These are legitimate DINGS, but more and more, the poor concessionaire finds himself with paying, paying paying. — Gene Sorrows, *All About Carnivals*, p. 15, 1985

7 a mentally unstable person *US, 1929*
A shortened form of **DINGBAT**.
- You mean, dings drew these? — Thurston Scott, *Cure it with Honey*, p. 56, 1951
- "What Centennial's saying," Leo said, 'is these dings start shooting up the place, they ain't gonna pay the claim." — Emmett Grogan, *Final Score*, p. 244, 1976
- — Inez Cardozo-Freeman, *The Joint*, p. 493, 1984
- And any ding who smeared shit on his cell walls got five whacks in the ass with the lead-filled "ding-donger" Meyers carried. — James Ellroy, *Suicide Hill*, p. 585, 1986

8 a quasi-coercive request for money *US*
- — Bill Reilly, *Big Al's Official Guide to Chicagoese*, p. 24, 1982

Ding *noun*
an Italian; a Greek *AUSTRALIA, 1940*
- 'The Dings have surrendered,' Kevin O'Hara shouted. — Randolph Stow, *The Merry-Go-Round in the Sea*, p. 83, 1965
- — Jim Ramsay, *Cop It Sweet!*, p. 29, 1977

ding *verb*
1 to physically beat another person *UK, 1688*
This meaning is attributed by the *Oxford English Dictionary* to dialectal use in East Anglia.
- After he caught Robie flirting with his girl, he gave him a bad dinging. — Lewis Poteet, *The South Shore Phrase Book*, p. 37, 1999

2 to dent, scratch, scrape or rip *US, 1968*
- "He's got a dinged front left fender," Raymond said. — Elmore Leonard, *City Primeval*, p. 64, 1980
- You dinged my board, kook! — *Point Break*, 1991
- Before you know it, the phrase 'it's only money' is just a memory, and the only time you get to experience 'excess' is when you've dinged the Pajero. — *Sydney Morning Herald*, 15th March 2003

3 in circus and carnival usage, to borrow *US*
- — Don Wilmeth, *The Language of American Popular Entertainment*, p. 74, 1981

4 to reject *US*
- Headline: Malvina Dings Co-Op Hoot — *The Berkeley Barb*, p. 1, 24th September 1965
- — Connie Eble (Editor), *UNC-CH Campus Slang*, p. 3, April 1995

5 to wound *US*
- — Carl Fleischhauer, *A Glossary of Army Slang*, p. 15, 1968

6 to kill *US*
Vietnam war usage.
- — Linda Reinberg, *In the Field*, p. 62, 1991

7 to name for a duty or responsibility *UK*
Military.
- I've been dinged for mess committee. — Beale, 1984

dingage *noun*
damage to a surfboard or a surf-related injury *US*
- — Trevor Cralle, *The Surfin'ary*, p. 30, 1991

ding-a-ling *noun*
1 the penis *US*
A pet-name; 'dangle' (penis, also conventionally 'to hang down'), compounds with the nursery word 'ding-dong' (the ringing of a bell), to give an image of testicles as bells and penis as a dangling bell-rope. Originally black usage, the success of Chuck Berry's 1972 recording of a twenty-year-old song made this term widely accessible.
- I want you to play with my ding-a-ling — Dave Bartholomew, *My Ding-a-ling*, 1952
- I want you to play with my ding-a-ling — Chuck Berry, *My Ding-a-ling*, 1972
- I think with my ding-a-ling — Ice Cube, NWA, *I Aint Tha 1*, 1988
- She may be your wife but I stick my dingaling in her every night so that make her mine. — *Boyz N The Hood*, 1990
- Swingin' and swingin' my ding-a-ling in — Ultramagnetic MCs *Porno Star*, 1992

2 a fool *US, 1935*
- You may think I'm a ding-a-ling, but I had fun. — Mickey Spillane, *Last Cop Out*, p. 64, 1972
- [T]his burglar was doing ding-a-ling stuff on some of the jobs, cutting up clothing, usually women's or kids'[.] — Joseph Wambaugh, *The Blue Knight*, p. 21, 1973
- Katie, I wouldn't play a ding-a-ling like Stilwell without it. — Iceberg Slim (Robert Beck), *Long White Con*, p. 33, 1977

ding-a-ling *adjective*
foolish, crazy *US*
- What I can't understand is why professional baseball players are highly praised as bench jockeys, but professional football players are considered ding-a-ling for doing the same thing. — *San Francisco Chronicle*, p. 1H, 19th April 1959

dingbat *noun*
1 an odd, foolish or eccentric person *US, 1879*
- What they should do with that whole bunch of dingbats up there is toss a couple of grenades in the dorm. — Ken Kesey, *One Flew Over the Cuckoo's Nest*, p. 116, 1962
- You're dead, you dingbat. — Dymphna Cusack, *Picnic Races*, p. 206, 1962
- — Collin Baker et al., *College Undergraduate Slang Study Conducted at Brown University*, p. 105, 1968
- A dingbat across the aisle and Kitty Wells on the headphones. — Hunter S. Thompson, *Songs of the Doomed*, p. 127, 18th/19th February 1969
- Oh, don't be a dingbat. — Eugene Boe (Compiler), *The Wit & Wisdom of Archie Bunker*, p. 22, 1971
- "Dingbat, what you doing at my door with your shotgun?" Joe says as he seizes the lapels of Baptiste's robe[.] — Iceberg Slim (Robert Beck), *Doom Fox*, p. 169, 1978
- Objectionable term that describes women as intellectually inferior. — Multicultural Management Program Fellows, *Dictionary of Cautionary Words and Phrases*, 1989
- So you wanna be a Rock'n'Roll Star? You fool. So does every other talentless dingbat on the block. — Ignatius Jones, *True Hip*, p. 14, 1990
- The hosts (and the viewers) all think you are a couple of dingbats even though you are sooo rich, which most of them aren't, and semi-attractive, which most of them aren't, and have designer clothes, which most of them don't. — *Arkansas Democrat-Gazette*, p. 47, 7th December 2003

2 used as a (euphemistic) replacement for any noun the user cannot or will not name *US, 1923*
Perhaps this sense is the inspiration for the selection of symbols that comprise the Dingbats typeface.

3 a daredevil motorcyclist *UK*
- — Douglas Dunford, *Motorcycle Department, Beaulieu Motor Muesum*, 1979

▸ go like a dingbat
go fast *UK, 1967*
- Going like a dingbat. Looks like he's really made up his mind this time! — W.R. Bennett, *Night Intruder*, p. 34, 1962

▸ mad as a dingbat
extremely mad; very angry *AUSTRALIA, 1942*
A reference to *delirium tremens*.

dingbats *noun*
delirium tremens *NEW ZEALAND, 1911*
- How are you treating him for the ding-bats? — Arthur Upfield, *Bony and the Mouse*, p. 38, 1959

dingbats *adjective*
1 by extension, crazy, mad, delusional *AUSTRALIA, 1925*

2 stupid, foolish *AUSTRALIA, 1950*
- — Jim Ramsay, *Cop It Sweet!*, p. 29, 1977

ding-ding *noun*
a crazy person *US*
- Red, about all you have to fear is getting castrated by the ding-ding's knife. — Red Rudensky, *The Gonif*, p. 15, 1970

dingdong *noun*
1 the penis *US, 1944*
- He kept sitting around and trying to figure out what all this excitement was about over his erect ding-dong. — Johnny Shearer, *The Male Hustler*, p. 27, 1966
- [T]he man had used his handkerchief to wipe up the "funny white juice that came out of his dingdong"[.] — James Harper, *Homo Laws in all 50 States*, p. 41 – 42, 1968
- I quoted in repetitious sing-song the overheard limerick "King Kong plays pin pong with his ding dong." — Neal Cassady, *The First Third*, p. 67, 1971
- Gino had a slight, twenty three year old paunch, nappy hair curling fiercely on his black ass and a small ding dong. — Odie Hawkins, *Black Casanova*, p. 42, 1984
- I notice the eyes of some cats here, openly and secretly spying, measuring the length and width of the next guy's dingdong! — Clarence Major, *All-Night Visitors*, p. 31, 1998
- Truth is, I think naked men are kind of strange-looking, what with their doodles [testicles] and ding-dong hanging loose like they do. — Janet Evanovich, *Seven Up*, p. 134, 2001

2 a sing-song *UK, 1960*
Rhyming slang for 'a song'.
- [H]aving a bit of a ding-dong round the old Joanna [piano]. — Ronnie Barker, *Fletcher's Book of Rhyming Slang*, p. 39, 1979

3 a gas-powered railway coach used on a branch line *US, 1945*
- —Norman Carlisle, *The Modern Wonder Book of Trains and Railroading*, p. 261, 1946

4 a heated quarrel *UK, 1922*
- [W]e have ding-dongs and arguments about feminism.—Sally Cline, *Couples*, p. 143, 1998
- [I] had a massive bleedin' ding-dong row anyway!—Wayne Anthony, *Spanish Highs*, p. 105, 1999

5 a party *UK, 1936*
Extended from the sense as 'a sing-song'.
- We have quite a ding-dong going on here some weeks. The table wine flows like water.—Ray Galton and Alan Simpson, *Hancock's Half Hour*, 22nd April 1958

ding-dong *verb*
to telephone *US*
- I got up early that morning and ding-donged Carri, and this time I caught her home.—A.S. Jackson, *Gentleman Pimp*, p. 135, 1973

ding-dong *adjective*
1 of top quality; great; terrific *AUSTRALIA*
- His orders to the young warrior guards were that should a woman stray from her party the guard was to rap her on the head with his nulla hard enough to give her a ding-dong headache[.]—Ion L. Idriess, *The Red Chief*, 1953
- Always had him up for a ding-dong yarn when he blew in here. —Dymphna Cusack, *Picnic Races*, p. 218, 1962

2 (of a fight, competition, etc) hard fought *AUSTRALIA, 1924*
- This allowed Bill to go berserk with fury and tear into Herbert for a ding-dong punching match in the passage[.]—Norman Lindsay, *Halfway to Anywhere*, p. 169, 1947
- —Norman Lindsay, *Halfway to Anywhere*, p. 64, 1947
- It was a ding-dong struggle to the post, both horses giving of their best.—Joe Brown, *Just for the Record*, p. 116, 1984
- It was a ding-dong battle.—Ivor Limb, *Footy's No Joke!*, p. 22, 1986

ding-dong bell; ding-dong *noun*
hell *UK*
Rhyming slang, used originally by World War 2 Royal Air Force.
- What the ding dong dell does he think he's playing at?—Julian Franklyn, *A Dictionary of Rhyming Slang*, 2nd 1961
- Fucking ding dong.—Ray Puxley, *Cockney Rabbit*, 1992

dinge *noun*
1 a black person *US, 1848*
Derogatory, from conventional 'dingy' (dark).
- That old dinge nut!—John Clellon Holmes, *The Horn*, p. 210, 1958
- [A] punch-up at the jellied eel stall with these dinges saying we were square[.]—Derek Raymond (Robin Cook), *The Crust on its Uppers*, p. 36, 1962
- I think that you are the most beautiful colored girl ... black ... I mean dinger that I've ever seen.—Steve Cannon, *Groove, Bang, and Jive Around*, p. 129, 1969
- The dinge. The colored kid. He goofin off on you?—John Sayles, *Union Dues*, p. 56, 1977
- "Mr. Collucci, you know I'd be happy to do the job on this dinge," Phil said seriously.'—Iceberg Slim (Robert Beck), *Death Wish*, 1977
- If there wasn't a reward for shooting the little dinge he ought to get a medal, something.—Elmore Leonard, *City Primeval*, 1980
- Oh, look – it's just like a big dinge nut.—Herbert Huncke, *The Evening Sun Turned Crimson*, p. 101, 1980
- —Paul Baker, *Polari*, p. 171, 2002

2 a member of any dark-skinned race *UK*
Adopted from the US meaning 'a black person'. Note, also, that during World War 2 Royal Air Force bombing crews used 'the dinge' for 'the blackout'.

dinged *adjective*
concussed, in a confused mental state *UK*
Pronounced with a hard 'g'. From the conventional (if archaic) use (to hit).
- —*The Lancet*, 25th April 1970

dinged up *adjective*
battered *AUSTRALIA*
- They get a dinged-up old board that's going mouldy out the back and strip it.—Kathy Lette and Gabriel Carey, *Puberty Blues*, p. 33, 1979

dinge queen *noun*
a white homosexual man who finds black men attractive; a black homosexual man *US*
- —Florida Legislative Investigation Committee (Johns Committee), *Homosexuality and Citizenship in Florida*, 1964: 'Glossary of homosexual terms and deviate acts'
- A white man homosexually inerested in a Negro is known in homosexual parlance as a 'dinge queen.'—James Harper, *Homo Laws in all 50 States*, p. 147, 1968
- —*American Speech*, p. 56, Spring-Summer 1970: 'Homosexual slang'
- —*Maledicta*, p. 236, 1979: 'Kinks and queens: linguistic and cultural aspects of the terminology for gays'

dinger *noun*
1 the backside or anus *AUSTRALIA, 1943*
- In your great dinger, you rotten crawling chocko.—Sumner Locke Elliott, *Rusty Bugles*, p. 80, 1948
- Don't forget that he'll get more than a gentle tap up the dinger if something really goes wrong.—A.M. Harris, *The Tall Man*, 1958

2 an extraordinary thing or person *US, 1809*
An abbreviation of **HUMDINGER**.
- —David McGill, *David McGill's Complete Kiwi Slang Dictionary*, p. 39, 1998

3 a railway yardmaster *US, 1929*
- —Norman Carlisle, *The Modern Wonder Book of Trains and Railroading*, p. 262, 1946

4 a sniper *US, 1972*
- "The dinger would fire a round, then disappear," Moran said.—Elmore Leonard, *Cat Chaser*, p. 24, 1982
- —Linda Reinberg, *In the Field*, p. 62, 1991

5 a burglar alarm, especially an intentionally visible one *US, 1931*
- —Vincent J. Monteleone, *Criminal Slang*, p. 69, 1949

dinghy *noun*
1 a motorcycle sidecar *UK*
- —Douglas Dunford, *Motorcycle Department, Beaulieu Motor Muesum*, 1979

2 the penis *BAHAMAS*
- —John A. Holm, *Dictionary of Bahamian English*, p. 61, 1982

dingle *adjective*
(of weather) good *ANTARCTICA, 1989*
- —Bernadette Hince, *The Antarctic Dictionary*, p. 100, 2000
- —*Cool Antarctica*, 2003: 'Antarctic slang'

dingleberries *noun*
1 the female breasts *UK*
- Daddy says tits. Daddy says knockers and jugs and bazooms and dingleberries and jujubes. And then he laughs and goes "wuff! wuff!".—*Journal of British Photography*, 9th May 1980

2 the splattered molten particles near a weld *US*
- —Robert Kirk Mueller, *Buzzwords*, p. 67, 1974

dingleberry *noun*
1 a glob of dried faeces accumulated on anal hairs *US, 1938*
Although this sense is not the earliest recorded sense of the word, it is probably the original sense.
- —Bruce Rodgers, *The Queens' Vernacular*, p. 99, 1972
- At Ralph's side was his enormous, dingle-berry-decorated and constantly farting shaggy dog named Rimpoche.—John Nichols, *The Nirvana Blues*, p. 36, 1981
- —*Maledicta*, p. 151, Summer/Winter 1986–1987: 'Sexual slang: prostitutes, pedophiles, flagellators, transvestites, and necrophiles'
- What if you have extra stuff hanging around like dingleberries? —Howard Stern, *Miss America*, p. 114, 1995
- Some of your cruds are going to wipe just half-assed, so I do not want to see any – and I mean any – dingleberries in your skivvies.—Zell Miller, *Corps Values*, p. 14, 1996

2 a despicable person *US, 1924*
- —Collin Baker et al., *College Undergraduate Slang Study Conducted at Brown University*, p. 105, 1968
- You fucking little dingleberry. That's what you're like, you fucking ball of shit!—John Waters, *Pink Flamingos*, p. 19, 1972
- —Connie Eble (Editor), *UNC-CH Campus Slang*, March 1973
- But Surtees' move-out drills always started with some dingleberry housecat from the Orderly Room standing in the tent doorway and blowing his brains out on a silver MP whistle.—Larry Heinemann, *Close Quarters*, p. 150, 1977
- —Connie Eble (Editor), *UNC-CH Campus Slang*, p. 2, Spring 1993
- He said he'd snap us up if the lawyers weren't such dingle-berries. —*Airheads*, 1994

3 a military decoration *US, 1953*
- You kicked some ass out there today, boy! I'll see you get a dingleberry [personal decoration] for it!—Michael Hodgins, *Reluctant Warrior*, p. 184, 1996

dingleberry hone *noun*
in car mechanics, a hone (a tool used to enlarge and smooth the inside of a hole) that uses a silicon carbide ball attached to spring-like wires that flex *US*
- —John Edwards, *Auto Dictionary*, p. 44, 1993

dinglebody *noun*
a foolish, simple person *US*
- But then they danced down the streets like dinglebodies, and I shambled after[.]—Jack Kerouac, *On the Road*, p. 8, 1957

dingle-dangle *noun*

the penis *UK, 1937*

- —A.D. Peterkin, *The Bald-Headed Hermit and The Artichoke*, p. 103, 1999

dinglefuzzy *noun*

used in place of a person's name which has been forgotten *US*

- —John Gould, *Maine Lingo*, p. 73, 1975

ding list *noun*

a notional list of boys whom the keeper of the list does not like *US*

- —Carol Ann Preusse, *Jargon Used by University of Texas Co-Eds*, 1963

dingnuts!

used for registering annoyance or frustration as a euphemism for 'bollocks!' *UK*

An elaboration of **NUTS!**.

- Fucky dingnuts and bastardy cunt-holes.—Jenny Eclair, *Camberwell Beauty*, p. 208, 2000

dingo *noun*

1 a cowardly, treacherous or despicable person *AUSTRALIA, 1869*

From 'dingo' the Australian native dog, to which the attributes of cowardice and treachery have long been incorrectly applied by white people.

- You're a bit of a dingo yourself, aren't you?—Wal Watkins, *Race the Lazy River*, p. 34, 1963
- On the other side of the road the police dogs barked and the two-legged dingos howled at the sight of Australia's folk hero confronting them.—Frank Hardy, *The Outcasts of Foolgarah*, p. 231, 1971
- —Jim Ramsay, *Cop It Sweet!*, p. 29, 1977

2 an Australian *NEW ZEALAND*

- —Sonya Plowman, *Great Kiwi Slang*, p. 58, 2002

▶ **turn dingo on**

to betray someone *AUSTRALIA, 1945*

- Didn't everybody know Chuck was a heel, that he would use his cunning to take a mean advantage of people until he was in their confidence and trusted by them absolutely, then would turn dingo on them and betray them without a qualm?—Vince Kelly, *The Bogeyman*, p. 5, 1956

dingo *verb*

1 to behave in a treacherous or cowardly manner *AUSTRALIA, 1935*

- Joh is dingoed out already. He has withdrawn his Canberra push because he would rather be a medium-sized cane toad in a little State Billabong than a tadpole in the Canberra Pond.—Bill Hayden, *Johspeak*, p. 72, 1988

2 to cancel, especially to cancel a date or romantic assignation *UK*

Teen slang.

- — Susie Dent, *The Language Report*, p. 76, 2003

dingo's breakfast *noun*

an act of urination and a good look round; no breakfast at all *AUSTRALIA, 1965*

- I like to wake slowly, over a cup of coffee and the sports page, not scramble around in the dawn chill for socks and shoes, then hike off for a "dingo's breakfast" – a pee and a good look around.—Tony Horwitz, *One for the Road*, p. 94, 1987
- —Richard Beckett, *The Dinkum Aussie Dictionary*, p. 19, 1988
- The menu on the wall inside is the product of a local wit – particularly the Dingo's Breakfast (A piss and a look around – no charge!). —*Lonely Planet Northern Territory*, p. 193, 2003

ding string *noun*

a cord attached to a surfer and his surfboard *US*

The cord has the effect of reducing damage to the board after the surfer falls off.

- —Trevor Cralle, *The Surfin'ary*, p. 30, 1991

ding team *noun*

a scout and sniper working together *US*

- —Linda Reinberg, *In the Field*, p. 62, 1991

dingus *noun*

1 the penis *US, 1888*

- Gets to him pretty quick too, cause nex thing I know he's got his dingus out.—Robert Gover, *Here Goes Kitten*, p. 79, 1964
- He just stood there, his "dingus" flopping from his open fly.—Iceberg Slim (Robert Beck), *Pimp*, p. 56, 1969
- Half-and-half still costs you more than straight, so if you need the girl's mouth on your dingus to get you up it will set you back a total of thirty dollars[.]—Gerald Paine, *A Bachelor's Guide to the Brothels of Nevada*, p. 26, 1978
- I got a real ugly dingus.—Joseph Wambaugh, *The Secrets of Harry Bright*, p. 186, 1985
- What do you got there? A bigger dingus than God gave you?—*The Sopranos (Episode 63)*, 2004

2 an artificial penis *US*

- She greases the dingus, shoves the boy's legs over his head and works it up his ass with a series of corkscrew movements of her fluid hips. —William Burroughs, *Naked Lunch*, p. 92, 1957

3 used for identifying a thing, the correct name of which escapes the speaker or is not important in context; a gadget, a contraption *US, 1876*

- I filled the lower half of the dingus and set it on the flame.—Raymond Chandler, *The Long Goodbye*, p. 22, 1953
- —Helen Dahlskog (Editor), *A Dictionary of Contemporary and Colloquial Usage*, p. 18, 1972

4 a eye dropper used in makeshift drug-injection equipment *US*

- —David Maurer and Victor Vogel, *Narcotics and Narcotic Addiction*, p. 402, 1973

ding ward *noun*

a hospital ward for the mentally infirm *US*

- Why don't those unknown suspects have a little more imagination next time and come up with a surefire scheme to get Woofer in the ding ward at the Veterans' Hospital[?]—Joseph Wambaugh, *The Glitter Dome*, p. 77, 1981

dingy *noun*

a police van *US, 1970*

- —Claudio R. Salvucci, *The Philadelphia Dialect Dictionary*, p. 37, 1996

dingy *adjective*

eccentric, odd *US, 1907*

- Hey, do you think it's dingy, what I did to the girl?—Thurston Scott, *Cure it with Honey*, p. 162, 1951
- —Judi Sanders, *Kickin' like Chicken with the Couch Commander*, p. 7, 1992

dink *noun*

1 a person from South Asia; especially, in later use, a Vietnamese person *AUSTRALIA, 1938*

Recorded in 1938 as Australian slang for 'a Chinese person'; in 1961, Julian Franklyn recorded it as Australian rhyming slang, formed on **CHINK** (a Chinese person). It was adopted by the US military in Vietnam in 1967.

- "Hey," he said, lowering his weapon. "The dink's got cokes."—Ronald J. Glasser, *365 Days*, p. 80, 1971
- Another time we were running convoy and the road was crowded with dink kids, begging C rations just like always.—Larry Heienamann, *Close Quarters*, p. 98–99, 1977
- — *Maledicta*, p. 124, Summer 1980: 'Racial and ethnic slurs: regional awareness and variations'
- Bozwell was with a dink the night Violet met him and they talked a few words of gook.—Joseph Wambaugh, *The Glitter Dome*, p. 157, 1981
- What have we got to hold the blackness back, to keep our hides whole from the panji traps, to keep our heads whole from the urge to waste, to blow away in one conclusive burst all gooks, slants, slope-heads, dinks, and other such?—Bruce Dawe, *Sometimes Gladness*, p. 214, 1981
- Gooks could be both. Slants and slopes were civilians. Dinks could be both.—Nelson DeMille, *Word of Honor*, p. 414, 1985
- Police up your extra ammo and frags, don't leave nothing for the dinks.—*Platoon*, 1986

2 a partner in a relationship that can be defined as '*d*ouble (or *d*ual) *i*ncome, *n*o *k*ids', that is a couple with two jobs and no children; or as an adjective applied to the couple *US, 1987*

An acronym.

- —*American Speech*, Summer 1989

3 a clueless, unaware person *US, 1962*

- —Collin Baker et al., *College Undergraduate Slang Study Conducted at Brown University*, p. 105, 1968
- —*Current Slang*, p. 10, Spring 1971
- Safeway, dink. As in the supermarket.—Armistead Maupin, *Tales of the City*, p. 14, 1978
- It's an anonymous call, you dink.—Elmore Leonard, *Cat Chaser*, p. 233, 1982

4 the penis *US, 1888*

- —Collin Baker et al., *College Undergraduate Slang Study Conducted at Brown University*, p. 105, 1968
- —H. Max, *Gay (S)language*, p. 12, 1988
- Lube the shit out of her ass and your dink, and place your dink's face right at the anus.—Suroosh Alvi et al., *The Vice Guide*, p. 40, 2002

5 in volleyball, a tap of the ball after a faked hitting of the ball downward with great force *US*

- —Bonnie Robison, *Sports Illustrated Volleyball*, p. 94, 1972

6 a lift on a bicycle or, formerly, a horse *AUSTRALIA, 1934*

- Out on the road, as I began running towards the short cut, I heard Squid yell, 'I'll give y' a dink.'—D.E. Charlwood, *All the Green Year*, p. 46, 1965
- —Jim Ramsay, *Cop It Sweet!*, p. 29, 1977

dink *verb*

to give someone a lift on a bicycle or, formerly, a horse *AUSTRALIA, 1932*

British dialect had *dink* (to dangle a baby) and this may be the origin, but it is hardly conclusive.

- Dad, who said I was dinking Lynette Leahy down the street?—Kerry Cue, *Crooks, Chooks and Bloody Ratbags*, p. 185, 1983
- Well, she dinked me, cos I didn't have a bike anymore cos it isn't trendy.—Kylie Mole (Maryanne Fahey), *My Diary*, p. 34, 1988

dink *adjective*

genuine; true; honest *AUSTRALIA*

An abbreviation of **DINKUM**.

- They said he was a traitor. I've got to get down to Melbourne to see if he's dink. I said I hope he's legal mate.—Christopher Lee, *Bush Week*, p. 82, 1980

dink around *verb*

to idle or waste time *US*

- Bo said he'd like to meet the kid again when the kid learned some tennis and knew how to play instead of dinking around.—Elmore Leonard, *Switch*, p. 53, 1978

dinki-di; dinky-die *adjective*

genuine *AUSTRALIA, 1918*

An intensified variation of **DINKUM**, often associated with nationalistic values.

- I reckon they'd be smart to import a few dinki-di Australian French teachers.—Barry Humphries, *Bazza Pulls It Off!*, 1971

dinkie; dinky *noun*

a partner in a relationship that can be defined as '*d*ouble (or *d*ual) *i*ncome, *n*o *k*ids (*y*et)', that is a couple with two jobs and no children; or as an adjective applied to the couple *US, 1986*

dinkie dow *noun*

marijuana *US, 1968*

Originally used in the Vietnam war to mean 'off the wall' (crazy) – which was ascribed to marijuana, locally grown or imported by the soldiers. The US servicemen went home in 1975 and took the word with them.

- [D]inky dau (also spelt dinky dow) from the Vietnamese *dien cau dau* meaning to be literally off the wall or crazy, bad, or no good[.]—Linda Reinberg, *In The Field*, 1991
- —Mike Haskins, *Drugs*, p. 287, 2003

dinkied up *adjective*

smartened up, made lively *UK*

- [Northamptonshire] has few places dinkied up for the coach trade. —*Illustrated London News*, February 1981

dink pack *noun*

a six-pack of beer *CANADA*

The word 'dink' is so close to 'dinky' that it seems to refer to the six-pack as less than a 'real' box of beer: a twelve or a two-four.

- —David Mazerolle, *Avant tu take off, please close the lights*, p. n.p., 1993

dink tank *noun*

a condom *UK*

Combines **DINK** (the penis) with an appropriate container.

- —David Rowan, *A Glossary for the 90s*, 1998

dinkum *adjective*

1 serious *AUSTRALIA*

- 'I reckon there's going to be a dinkum blue here before this here Centen-ary's finished.—Dymphna Cusack, *Picnic Races*, 1962
- I'll have to end this strike to get a chance to have a real dinkum bit of sex.—Frank Hardy, *The Outcasts of Foolgarah*, 1971
- Hey, Sammy, this bastard's getting dinkum!—Sam Weller, *Old Bastards I Have Met*, 1979
- Billy said he'd wait to see if it was a 'dinkum' war, but I said I wanted nothing to do with it.—Ward McNally, *Supper at Happy Harry's*, 1982

2 real, genuine *AUSTRALIA, 1905*

Originally meaning 'work', or 'an allotted amount of work', 'dinkum' comes from the Lincolnshire and Derbyshire dialects of Britain. The phrase **FAIR DINKUM** was recorded from north Lincolnshire in 1881 and first recorded in Australia in 1890. The conjecture that it is from Cantonese *dim kum* (real gold), said to have been introduced by Chinese miners during the gold rush (1860s), cannot be true since it fails to explain how a Chinese mining term could have made its way to the British midlands.

- He took it to the station master who after a careful examination advised him not to ring the super until further enquiries were made as he doubted whether it was dinkum.—Patsy Adam-Smith, *Folklore of the Australian Railwaymen*,
- 'There's a kind of a scare on.' 'Dinkum one?'—Michael Peters, *Pommie Bastard*, p. 101, 1969
- I reckon that's more important than winnin' sometimes – bein' a dinkum trier.—Ward McNally, *Supper at Happy Harry's*, p. 35, 1982
- Many people think Mel Gibson is Australian, because of his dinkum accent.—*The Guardian*, 10th July 2000

3 honest; upstanding *AUSTRALIA*

- Dinkum bloke, old Joe, even if he had a bit of a kink.—Dymphna Cusack, *Picnic Races*, p. 204, 1962
- Billy said he'd wait to see if it was a 'dinkum' war, but I said I wanted nothing to do with it.—Ward McNally, *Supper at Happy Harry's*, p. 142, 1982

dinkum *adverb*

really; truly; honestly *AUSTRALIA, 1915*

- Dinkum Ziff – you won't know yerself without it!—Robert S. Close, *With Hooves of Brass*, p. 114, 1961
- E's Jack Holt's cousin. Dinkum 'e is!—Ward McNally, *Supper at Happy Harry's*, p. 22, 1982
- You're smart. Dinkum y'are. I reckon y'really smart.—Ward McNally, *Supper at Happy Harry's*, p. 25, 1982

dinkum Aussie

a person who embodies all those things seen as characteristically Australian *AUSTRALIA, 1920*

- I'll stick to me mates, like a dinkum Aussie[.]—Frank Hardy, *The Outcasts of Foolgarah*, p. 23, 1971

dinkum oil *noun*

reliable information *AUSTRALIA, 1915*

- When I got to know the dinkum oil about the New Zealand prison service, I had to admit there was a hell of a lot to be said for Irishness and Oldtimeism.—Ian Hamilton, *Till Human Voices Wake Us*, p. 50, 1954
- 'This is the dinkum oil,' Carter persisted. 'Dinkum oil, my bum!' growled Dinger.—John Wynnum, *Jiggin' in the Riggin'*, p. 19, 1965

dinky *noun*

1 an expensive car *UK, 1980*

Wealthy humour, based on Dinky Toys.

- —Ann Barr and Peter York, *The Official Sloane Ranger Handbook*, p. 158, 1982

2 an old, dilapidated car *TRINIDAD AND TOBAGO, 1986*

From the older, more common meaning (a kite).

- —Lise Winer, *Dictionary of the English/Creole of Trinidad & Tobago*, 2003

3 an electric tram with controls at each end *US, 1923*

- For Winnipeg's "dinkies," no turn-around or loop was required at the end of the line. The driver just changed the overhead electrical contact to the other end, and moved to the driver's seat there.—Chris Thain, *Cold as a Bay Street Banker's Heart*, p. 53, 1987

4 a small railway engine used for yard switching *US, 1905*

- —Norman Carlisle, *The Modern Wonder Book of Trains and Railroading*, p. 262, 1946
- —Ramon Adams, *The Language of the Railroader*, p. 45, 1977

dinky *adjective*

1 small, unassuming *US, 1895*

- I gave her the bag, mumbling awkwardly about "Merry Early Christmas," then played some dinky tune while she dug into the bag and pulled out the first one.—John Nichols, *The Sterile Cuckoo*, p. 90, 1965
- The whore was in a dinky little North Main hotel.—Larry McMurtry, *The Last Picture Show*, p. 55, 1966
- "Here you are standing in deep shit and you're worried about a little dinky melon crop."—Elmore Leonard, *Mr. Majestyk*, p. 86, 1974
- They entered the dinky apartment single file. Prince glanced around at the cheap furniture.—Donald Goines, *Black Gangster*, p. 32, 1977
- The judge that convicted Sonny and the doc is the same one gave me ten years straight up, minimum, and gave you five on that dinky violating probation charge.—Elmore Leonard, *Maximum Bob*, p. 53, 1991
- She was telling me about how she hitchhiked from some dinky little town in Illinois[.]—Clarence Major, *All-Night Visitors*, p. 3, 1998

2 neat, spruce, dainty *UK, 1788*

- [Dylan] Evans's dinky, pink-jacketed survey shows that reason can be impotent without the passions.—*The Guardian*, 10th February 2001

3 of music, pleasant, easy-listening *UK*

- "Time for a little music," the first black publican says. "Reggae?" I ask innocently. He glares. "No," he says, calming himself. "Something really dinky." The music of Bert Kaempfert oozes from the speakers.—*Illustrated London News*, June 1976

4 wildly enthusiastic, crazy *US*

- Last week the 49ers won a (one) game and the two sports fans went dinky. — *San Francisco Examiner and Chronicle, Sunday Punch*, p. 8, 2nd November 1969

5 fair; honest *AUSTRALIA*

dinky dau *adjective*

crazy *US*

From the Vietnamese for 'off the wall'. Vietnam war usage.

- Yeah, put it on my bill! Monsieur Dinky Dau from Bung Tau! — Tony Zidek, *Choi Oi: The LIghter Side of Vietnam*, p. 24, 1965
- — Carl Fleischhauer, *A Glossary of Army Slang*, p. 15, 1968
- — James Webb, *Fields of Fire*, p. 412, 1978
- At various times in the play, a character named Dinky Dau pointed an M-16 straight at Michael's head. — Peter Straub, *Koko*, p. 227, 1988

dinky-di; dinky-die; dinki-di *adjective*

real; genuine; true; honest *AUSTRALIA*

- No. I'm a dinky-di Aussie. — Alan Seymour, *The One Day of the Year*, p. 40, 1962
- Remember, your dinki-di Aussie swearer doesn't just let it rip. He lets it roll. — Arthur Chipper, *The Aussie Swearer's Guide*, 1972
- No dinky-die Aussie boy would dream of marrying a Greek girl, of course. — Xavier Herbert, *Poor Fellow My Country*, p. 172, 1975
- Twenty years out here is a long time. Dinky-di Aussie, eh? — J.E. MacDonnell, *Big Bill the Bastard*, p. 21, 1976
- They love to tell you they're battler and dinki-di, true-blue working class Aussies, but I'm not sure whether they exist any more. — Sandra Jobson, *Blokes*, 1984
- And the Bush Tucker stop is the place to head for dinky-di Aussie breakfasts, pavlovas and lammingtons. — *Sydney Morning Herald*, p. 35, 4th February 1984
- I'd like to invite you to the most dinky-di, ridgy didge, fair dinkum, no worries mate tournament that you could imagine. — *Australian Ultimate*, p. 7, 2003

dinky dows *noun*

marijuana *US*

Vietnam war usage.

- — Jay Robert Nash, *Dictionary of Crime*, p. 103, 1992

dinky inky *noun*

in television and film making, a low watt spotlight *US*

- — Ralph S. Singleton, *Filmaker's Dictionary*, p. 47, 1990

dinners *noun*

the female breasts *US*

- A schoolmarm in southwest Missouri has truly enormous breasts, and is known as "Big Dinners" by almost everybody in town. — Vance Randolph, *Down in the Holler*, p. 120, 1953

dinny *noun*

the vagina *BAHAMAS*

- — John A. Holm, *Dictionary of Bahamian English*, p. 61, 1982

dinnyhayser *noun*

an excellent thing or person *NEW ZEALAND*

From boxer Dinny Hayes.

- — David McGill, *David McGill's Complete Kiwi Slang Dictionary*, p. 37, 1998

dinnyhayzer *noun*

a heavy punch; a knockout blow *AUSTRALIA, 1907*

Sidney J. Baker in *The Australian Language* (1945) says that it 'commemorates the pugilist Dinny Hayes'.

dinosaur *noun*

1 any person who is old or considered to be out of date, or both *US, 1970*

- I mean the mob is falling apart. These guys like Chick, my uncle, they're dinosaurs. — Edwin Torres, *Carlito's Way*, p. 105, 1975
- Though their popularity had peaked a long time ago, they still toured on the "dinosaur' circuit, playing their vintage hits for diehard fans like me. — Jimmy Buffett, *Tales from Margaritaville*, p. 171, 1989
- They remind us half of our Gerrard - daft old dinosaurs. — Kevin Sampson, *Outlaws*, p. 216, 2001

2 an older heroin user *US*

- — Robert Ashton, *This Is Heroin*, p. 208, 2002
- — *Detroit News*, p. 5D, 20th September 2002

3 any computer that requires raised flooring and a dedicated power source *US*

- — Eric S. Raymond, *The New Hacker's Dictionary*, p. 126, 1991

dinosaur juice *noun*

petrol, gasoline *US*

- — *Complete CB Slang Dictionary*, 1976
- — Peter Chippindale, *The British CB Book*, p. 154, 1981

dinosaurs *noun*

a type of LSD *UK*

- — Mike Haskins, *Drugs*, p. 285, 2003

dip *noun*

1 a pickpocket *US, 1859*

- Allie had visited Houston and Galveston, convincing a coterie of dips that the fix was in in Forth Worth[.] — Jim Thompson, *Bad Boy*, p. 353, 1953
- Thus a pickpocket squad cop never molests a recognized dip at the Garden. The dip is merely there for entertainment and relaxation. — Robert Sylvester, *No Cover Charge*, p. 286, 1956
- I once knew a very clever little dip, a Welsh girl, who was in a class by herself as a pickpocket until she developed arthritis[.] — Charles Raven, *Underworld Nights*, p. 20, 1956
- — Joseph E. Ragen and Charles Finston, *Inside the World's Toughest Prison*, p. 796, 1962: 'Penitentiary and underworld glossary'
- They ran tarot scams and were excellent dips. — Stephen Cannell, *King Con*, p. 55, 1997
- Pure fucking manna, it were. Dips, snatches, cameras, purses, the odd Barbour jacket[.] — Kevin Sampson, *Outlaws*, p. 7, 2001

2 a short swim *UK, 1843*

- I stopped for a quick dip in the sea and got a costly reminder that the ocean isn't my friend. — *The Guardian*, 25th January 2002

3 a foolish person *US, 1932*

- — Miss Cone, *The Slang Dictionary (Hawthorne High School)*, 1965
- I sat there pulling my pud like a total dip and told her to take her whatchamacallit and go home[.] — Lawrence Block, *No Score [The Affairs of Chip Harrison Omnibus]*, p. 150, 1970
- You little dip! Did you come all the way back here to fix me breakfast? — Armistead Maupin, *Tales of the City*, p. 199, 1978

4 diphtheria; a patient suffering from diphtheria and, therefore, classified by disease *UK, 1961*

Medical.

5 crack cocaine *US*

- — US Department of Justice, *Street Terms*, October 1994

6 a member of the *Dip*lomatic Service *UK*

- — John le Carré, *A Small Town in Germany*, 1968

7 a cigarette that has been dipped in embalming fluid *UK*

- — Mike Haskins, *Drugs*, p. 293, 2003

8 from a male perspective, a swift act of sexual intercourse *UK*

- — Jonathan Thomas, *English as She is Fraught*, 1976

9 an injection of a narcotic *US*

- — J.E. Schmidt, *Narcotics Lingo and Lore*, p. 39, 1959

10 a pinch of chewing tobacco; the chewing tobacco itself *US*

- — Pamela Munro, *U.C.L.A. Slang*, p. 57, 1997

11 a light *UK*

Hence 'dips! ' (lights out!).

- — *The Felstedian*, December 1947

▸ on the dip

engaged in pickpocketing *US*

- — Vincent J. Monteleone, *Criminal Slang*, p. 166, 1949

dip *verb*

1 to pick pockets *UK, 1857*

- He watched the other woman's purse and wondered idly if he could dip on her before she noticed him. — Donald Goines, *Dopefiend*, p. 65, 1971
- I guess he thought he found a live one and tried to dip on me. — A.S. Jackson, *Gentleman Pimp*, p. 134, 1973

2 to display an inappropriate interest in another prisoner's business *US*

- — John R. Armore and Joseph D. Wolfe, *Dictionary of Desperation*, 1976

3 to eavesdrop *US*

- I was dippin' on my brother when he was talking to his girlfriend. — *The Washington Post*, 24th May 1987

4 to fail in the commission of a crime, especially theft or robbery *AUSTRALIA*

- — *The (Sydney) Bulletin*, 26th April 1975

5 to hurry *US*

- — Vann Wesson, *Generation X Field Guide and Lexicon*, p. 52, 1997

6 to swerve through traffic on a bicycle *BERMUDA*

- — Peter A. Smith and Fred M. Barritt, *Bermewjan Vurds*, 1985

7 to use chewing tobacco *US*

- — Don R. McCreary (Editor), *Dawg Speak*, 2001

8 to leave *US*

- — *Washington Post*, 14th October 1993

▸ **dip south**

to search your pockets for money *NEW ZEALAND*

- — Sonya Plowman, *Great Kiwi Slang*, p. 59, 2002

▸ **dip your left eye in hot cocky shit**

get stuffed! *AUSTRALIA*

- Go and dip your left eye in hot cocky cack. — *The Adventures of Barry McKenzie*, 1972

▸ **dip your lid**

to raise one's hat as a polite gesture *AUSTRALIA, 1915*

Although no longer in common use since the wearing of hats went out of fashion after World War 2, it is still used in allusion to *The Sentimental Bloke* by C.J. Dennis.

- — Jim Ramsay, *Cop It Sweet!*, p. 29, 1977
- [Heading] Most lovers of Australia's great outdoors dip their lids to Hat Head's special charms — *Aussie Post*, p. 26, 29th August 1998

▸ **dip your wick**

to have sex *UK, 1958*

- — Joseph E. Ragen and Charles Finston, *Inside the World's Toughest Prison*, p. 796, 1962: 'Penitentiary and underworld glossary'
- — Collin Baker et al., *College Undergraduate Slang Study Conducted at Brown University*, p. 105, 1968
- Plenty of other fellers seem to dip their wicks. — Barry Humphries, *Bazza Pulls It Off!*, 1971
- — Anon., *King Smut's Wet Dreams Interpreted*, 1978
- You're gonna find out if you mastrebate (sic) instead of dippin' your wick, you'll conserve energy. — Dan Jenkins, *Life Its Ownself*, p. 111, 1984
- He tries it on this one and that one, dipping his wick along the way, and finally finds the perfect fit[.] — *Adult Video*, p. xx, August/September 1986
- So I take it the reason for all this secrecy and urgency is we're protecting some big-shot who's dipped his wick where he shouldn't, now he wants us to pull his nuts out of the fire, is that it?? — *The Bill*, 25th April 2000

dip-dunk *noun*

an unpleasant person, especially one who is not in the know *US*

- SEAL Team Six trained harder than any unit had ever trained before, waiting for the opportunity to show the skeptical bureaucrat-sailors and dip-dunk bean-counters prevalent in Washington that it was possible for the U.S. Navy to fight back effectively against terrorists. — Richard Marcinko with John Weisman, *Rogue Warrior*, p. 5, 1992

diphead *noun*

a social outcast *US, 1975*

- All because his dizzy diphead of a sister couldn't behave herself. — Katherine Sutcliffe, *Darkling I Listen*, p. 278, 2001

diplomacy *noun*

deception *TRINIDAD AND TOBAGO, 1938*

- — Lise Winer, *Dictionary of the English/Creole of Trinidad & Tobago*, 2003

diply *noun*

a socially inept outcast *US*

- — *Time*, p. 56, 1st January 1965: 'Students: the slang bag'

dip out *verb*

1 to come off worse; to miss out on an opportunity; to fail *UK*

- — Nigel Foster, *The Making of a Royal Marine Commando*, 1987

2 to back out of *AUSTRALIA, 1952*

- — John Wynnum, *Tar Dust*, p. 32, 1962
- Dip out now, and you'll wait three weeks. — John Wynnum, *Jiggin' in the Riggin'*, p. 23, 1965
- — Jim Ramsay, *Cop It Sweet!*, p. 29, 1977

3 (used of a member of crack cocaine-selling crew) to remove small acounts of crack from the vials for sale, for later personal use *US*

- — US Department of Justice, *Street Terms*, October 1994

4 on a bird-watching trip, to fail to see the object of the quest *UK*

- [W]e nearly dipped out when two water authority men walked past in the open and sent the birds up. — *New Society*, 17th November 1977

dipper *noun*

a pickpocket *UK, 1889*

- — Vincent J. Monteleone, *Criminal Slang*, p. 69, 1949
- Another less flamboyant group of habitués are those who make money through wit, skill, and guile: boosters (professional shoplifters), dippers (pickpockets) and con artists. — Terry Williams, *The Cocaine Kids*, p. 102, 1989

dipping *noun*

the act of picking pockets *UK, 1882*

- — David Powis, *The Signs of Crime*, p. 181, 1977

dippy *adjective*

foolish, unstable, silly *US, 1899*

- — Joseph E. Ragen and Charles Finston, *Inside the World's Toughest Prison*, p. 796, 1962: 'Penitentiary and underworld glossary'
- Is it my fault the dippy network wants to spend a billion dollars to get a pilot they can fondle? — Dan Jenkins, *Life Its Ownself*, p. 71, 1984
- — Right Said Fred, *Deeply Dippy*, 1992
- I was always too dippy, too bubbly, never seirous. — Marilyn Suriani Futterman, *Dancing Naked in the Material World*, p. 104, 1992
- Then some dippy blouse [woman] in a Volvo gets up my nose[.] — Nick Barlay, *Curvy Lovebox*, p. 53, 1997

dippy dog *noun*

a deep-fried battered frankfurter on a stick *AUSTRALIA*

- I would like a battered sav (dippy dog) with my fish and chips. — *Wordmap (www.abc.net.au/wordmap)*, 2003

dipshit *noun*

a person of no consequence and no intelligence *US, 1962*

- — Collin Baker et al., *College Undergraduate Slang Study Conducted at Brown University*, p. 105, 1968
- [M]y eyes drilling the dipshit victim who stood there getting ready to ask more dumb questions. — Joseph Wambaugh, *The Blue Knight*, p. 205, 1973
- I do mind, dipshit. — Carl Hiaasen, *Tourist Season*, p. 124, 1986
- "This better be fucking important, dipshit!" the cop growled. — C.D. Payne, *Youth in Revolt*, p. 301, 1993
- The dipshit who's never been out of Miami. — *Get Shorty*, 1995
- [Y]ou're going to leave them alone in a jail cell with one inept guard? They'll escape, dipshit. — *Austin Powers*, 1999

dipshit *adjective*

offensive, inconsequential, lacking in intelligence *US, 1968*

- Turns out, not only am I ugly, but I have a dipshit personality. I suck. — Howard Stern, *Miss America*, p. 18, 1995

dip shop *noun*

in the used car business, a small finance company with very high interest rates that will offer loans to customers who might not otherwise qualify for financing *US*

- — Peter Mann, *How to Buy a Used Car Without Getting Gypped*, p. 190, 1975
- — *American Speech*, p. 309–310, Winter 1980: 'More jargon of car salesmen'

dipso *noun*

a person who suffers from an uncontrollable urge to drink *UK, 1880*

An abbreviated '*dipso*maniac'.

- Consider this – my father canned me and my brother and my Mom for a twenty five year old dipso with fake tits. — *Ferris Buehler's Day Off*, 1986

dipso *adjective*

drunk *UK*

- — Pete Brown, *Man Walks into a Pub*, 2003

dip squad *noun*

a police unit that targets pickpockets *UK*

Formed on **DIP** (a pickpocket).

- — *New Society*, 7th July 1977
- — Angela Devlin, *Prison Patter*, p. 45, 1996

dipstick *noun*

1 the penis *US, 1973*

- I wouldn't mind checking her oil with my dipstick. — Craig Lesley, *Winterkill*, p. 51, 1984
- Hey, Hemple, you wanna unlimber my member? Put a little lipstick on my dipstick? — James Hall, *Bones of Corl*, p. 235, 1991
- — James Lambert, *The Macquarie Book of Slang*, 1996
- A guy like that gets more sweetie-pie than the whole football team put together, more lipstick on his dipstick than- — Michael Hornburg, *Downers Grove*, p. 148, 1999
- Fellatio: blowing, deep throating, frenching, getting a facial, giving head, giving lip service, hoovering, putting lipstick on one's dipstick[.] — Ruth K. Westheimer, *Sex for Dummies*, p. 166, 2001

2 an inept fool, an idiot *US, 1963*

A euphemistic **DIPSHIT**; possibly punning on the synonymous sense of **PRICK**. In the UK, usage was popularised by BBC television situation comedy *Only Fools and Horses*, first broadcast in 1981. In 1992, Ray Puxley included the term in *Cockney Rabbit*, his 'Dick'n'Arry' of rhyming slang.

- — *Current Slang*, p. 4, Spring 1968

- —Helen Dahlskog (Editor), *A Dictionary of Contemporary and Colloquial Usage*, p. 18, 1972
- Sergeant Anson Trobridge, the platoon dipstick, also called Four-Eyes and Highpockets[.] —Larry Heinemann, *Close Quarters*, p. 125, 1977
- And the geeks and freaks and sideshow drifters of this world hear the dipstick yokels soaking up a shill like that[.] —Larry Heinemann, *Paco's Story*, p. 4, 1986
- [T]he dipstick freaking out in my ear kind of upped the tension. —Lanre Fehintola, *Charlie Says...*, p. 166, 2000

dipstick *verb*

to test the abstract qualities of someone or something *UK*

From the device used to measure the depth of oil in a car's engine; thus a play on 'take the measure of'.

- — Susie Dent, *The Language Report*, p. 41, 2003

dipsticks *noun*

a pair of men's close-fitting and revealing nylon swimming trunks *AUSTRALIA*

- When I stayed with my cousins in Kenthurst and we went to the local pool, everyone wore shorts instead and called speedo costumes 'dipsticks' for obvious reasons. — *Wordmap (www.abc.net.au/wordmap)*, 2003

dipsy *noun*

a gambling cheat *US*

- — *The Annals of the American Academy of Political and Social Sciences*, p. 124, May 1950

dipsy-doodle *noun*

1 a zig-zag motion *US*

From baseball jargon.

- "It would take a rather wild turn of events to keep it off the East Coast. ... It would have to do some kind of dipsy doodle," says hurricane center forecaster Jack Beven. — *USA Today*, 20th September 1989

2 a long, end-around-end skid *US*

- — *American Speech*, p. 268, December 1962: 'The language of traffic policemen'

dipwad *noun*

an inept outcast *US, 1976*

- He don't believe no cop would give a fuck about a dipwad like me. —LaVyrle Spencer, *Famliy Blessings*, p. 100, 1993

dire *adjective*

objectionable, unpleasant *UK, 1836*

A trivialisation of the conventional sense.

- The speeches were dire and there was much comment about dresses. — *The Observer*, 1st April 2001

direct action *noun*

a political act, especially a violent one, that may lead to arrest *US*

- There we sat in a corner of Central Park going through all the changes that you go through before direct action. —Abbie Hoffman, *Revolution for the Hell of It*, p. 24, 1968

dirge *noun*

a Dodge truck *US*

- —Montie Tak, *Truck Talk*, p. 44, 1971

dirk *noun*

1 a knife or improvised cutting weapon *US*

- Funny how ghees that ain't afraid of a roscoe chill when they see a dirk. —Hyman E. Goldin et al., *Dictionary of American Underworld Lingo*, p. 59, 1950

2 a socially unacceptable person *US*

- — *American Speech*, p. 118, May 1964: 'Problems in the study of campus slang'

dirt *noun*

1 a man or group of men who will prey upon homosexuals *US, 1927*

- Dirt – Properly, a highly specialized type of criminally psychopathic youth, self-appointed nemesis of any and all homosexuals, usually not homosexual himself (but this varies greatly since some kind of sexual abnormality or inferiority is almost always at the root of it), who guilefully leads on a homosexual interested in him until in a position to do him dirt, rolling and/or beating him up (rarely fatally), alone or with others, before or after being "blown". —Anon, *The Gay Girl's Guide*, 1949
- — Florida Legislative Investigation Committee (Johns Committee), *Homosexuality and Citizenship in Florida*, 1964: 'Glossary of homosexual terms and deviate acts'
- —Guy Strait, *The Lavendar Lexicon*, 1964

2 gossip, criticism, rumour *US, 1844*

- Being a psychologist has a certain appeal. You get paid extravagently well to sit around and listen to the most intimate dirt. —C.D. Payne, *Youth in Revolt*, p. 426, 1993
- Lord Ashcroft's lawyers opened their case in the high court to force the government to release "a file of dirt" held on the controversial businessman. — *The Guardian*, 5th June 2003

3 heroin *US*

Slightly less judgmental than 'shit'.

- —David Maurer and Victor Vogel, *Narcotics and Narcotic Addiction*, p. 402, 1973
- —Robert Ashton, *This Is Heroin*, p. 205, 2002

4 marijuana *US*

- Where can you get any dirt in this town? —Lois Stavsky et al., *A2Z*, p. 28, 1995

5 a tobacco cigarette *US*

- —Eugene Landy, *The Underground Dictionary*, p. 67, 1971

6 a trump card, epecially when played unexpectedly ('He's put a bit of dirt on it') *UK, 1945*

▷ see: DIRTY LEPER

▸ **down in the dirt**

(used of flying) close to the ground *US*

- High-flying fighter jocks aren't terribly comfortable down in the dirt, but another bunch of tactical pilots, the close-air support specialists, are in their element. —George Hall, *Top Gun*, p. 71, 1987

▸ **have the dirt on**

to know some scandal about someone or something; to have the news about someone or something *UK, 1984*

- He is considering legal action to fight the allegations and is putting pressure on those he is said to have the dirt on to use their influence to protect him. — *Sunday Times (South Africa)*, 27th December 1988

▸ **in the dirt**

in trouble *UK*

Euphemistic for IN THE SHIT.

- I'll be back in court double quick. Then I'd really be in the dirt. —John Peter Jones, *Feather Pluckers*, p. 70, 1964

dirt *adverb*

very *UK, 1821*

- —AC/DC *Dirty Deeds Done Dirt Cheap*, 1976
- The police are thick. They are dirt thick. We all know that[.] —Shaun Ryder, *Shaun Ryder... in His Own Words*, 1990
- Who makes the dirt-cheap clothes that fill Wal-Mart's shelves? — *The Observer*, 20th June 1999
- Sainsbury's has positioned itself on a broader base of quality and good service rather than dirt-cheap prices. — *BBCi*, 2nd June 2003

dirtbag *noun*

1 a despicable or offensive person *US, 1941*

- Rachel's a dirtbag. Who else? — *Ferris Buehler's Day Off*, 1986
- "Tell me about Ernesto Cabal." "Dirtbag burglar." —Carl Hiaasen, *Tourist Season*, p. 20, 1986
- I'm some kinda dirtbag. —Howard Stern, *Miss America*, p. 456, 1995

2 a prisoner with poor personal hygeine *US*

- — James Harris, *A Convict's Dictionary*, 1989

dirtball *noun*

a dirty, despicable person *US, 1974*

- Tell them to compare to every known in the county. Anybody. Any dirtball who's ever been printed. —Scott Turow, *Presumed Innocent*, p. 26, 1987
- This look like an act of international terrorism? Or does it look like some dirtball in a junker went nuts? —Carl Hiaasen, *Skin Tight*, p. 121, 1989

dirt bike *noun*

a motorcyle designed for off-road use *US, 1970s?*

- Maya was a tree-cuddler and animals rights vigilante, whose secondary mission in life was to liquidate all gun-toting rednecks who rode dirt bikes in "her peaceful desert" around Borrego Springs[.] —Joseph Wambaugh, *Finnegan's Week*, p. 65, 1993

dirtbird *noun*

a contemptible individual *IRELAND*

From the skua and its habit of forcing other birds to regurgitate their stomach contents.

- She said he called her a "whore", "prostitute" and "dirt bird" and told her children she was all of these — *Irish Times*, 12th December 1996
- Tell ye something but, he was a fookin dort burd [dirt bird], dat fella. —Paul Howard, *Ross O'Carroll-Kelly*, p. 103, 2003

dirtbox *noun*

1 the anus; the rectum *UK, 1984*

- "What we're on about, Mario lad, is 'ow many points you score if you gerrit up the dirt box." " What, you mean shoving it up their arse?" exclaimed Mario. —Colin Butts, *Is Harry on the Boat?*, p. 21, 1997

- [T]rying to fuck little boys up the dirt box. —John King, *Human Punk*, p. 82, 2000
- How embarrassing for those poor girls, having your private parts about half an inch away from your dirtbox. Planning! I mean, who thought of that? It isn't even hygienic. — *Sunday Times (South Africa)*, 13th April 2003
- Is this love at first sight? / I'll let you know when I've seen her dirt-box. — Susan Nickson, *Two Pints of Lager and a Packet of Crisps*, BBC 3, 12th April 2004

2 the vagina *AUSTRALIA*

- —James McDonald, *A Dictionary of Obscenity, Taboo and Euphemism*, p. 16, 1988
- Abjection was invoked in various ways: through reference to dirtiness (e.g., front bum, dirt box), uncooked (bloody?) meat (e.g., meat seat, chopped liver), vaginal secretions of all types (e.g., slushing fuck pit, the snail trail), smell (e.g. smelly hole, stench trench), and wounds (e.g., gash, gaping axe wound). — *Journal of Sex Research*, 2001

dirtbud *noun*

a despicable person *US*

- Hey, dirtbud, who you going to the prom with? — *Something About Mary*, 1998

dirt chute *noun*

the rectum *US*

- Proctor thought helplessly of how he could have been a big, clean career aviator instead of staring up some wise guy's dirt chute. —Thomas McGuane, *The Bushwacked Piano*, p. 198, 1971
- — *Maledicta*, p. 197, 1983: 'Ritual and personal insults in stigmatized subcultures'
- It would have been so sweet to know she'd felt that last big bang, and to feel her guts spasm as I greased her dirt chute! —Brian Lumley, *Necroscope: Invaders*, p. 431 – 432, 1999

dirt-dobber *noun*

a farmer; an unsophisticated rustic *US, 1947*

- I replied that as far as I knew, we came from a line of scrawny old dirt-dobbers, Scotch-Irish with more than one or two Indians thrown in. —Susan Wittig Albert, *Writing from Life*, p. 93, 1996

dirt farm *noun*

the mythical source of gossip *US*

- —Edith A. Folb, *runnin' down some lines*, p. 234, 1980

dirt grass *noun*

marijuana of inferior quality *US, 1971*

- —Richard A. Spears, *The Slang and Jargon of Drugs and Drink*, p. 144, 1986
- — *www.addictions.org*, 2001

dirties *noun*

work clothing *US*

- —Jerry Robertson, *Oil Slanguage*, p. 46, 1954

dirt nap *noun*

death *US, 1981*

- Despite yourself, you glance through the folder, a compendium of bad news with references to the big sleep, the deep six, the dirt nap. — *New York Times*, p. 32, 18th January 1987
- "I'm bringing some pain, baby," Tyson said. "If he [opponent Orlin Norris] makes even one mistake, he'll be taking a dirt nap." — *Las Vegas Sun*, 22nd October 1990
- "Then the firin pin hit a empty spot an you end up with jack." "Or a dirt nap," growled Gordon. —Jess Mowry, *Way Past Cool*, p. 7, 1992
- Foremost on their "to do" list, I imagine, is finding a way to delay for as long as possible their date with the state-sponsored dirt nap. — *News and Observer (Raleigh, NC)*, p. B1, 18th May 1998
- The Mike Tyson sideshow ("Step right up and take a dirt nap") hit Las Vegas this week[.] — *Toronto Star*, 18th September 1999
- Now he was struck by another gruesome possibility; maybe, instead of a dirty nap, he was about to go swimming with a forty-pound anchor. —Stephen J. Cannell, *The Tin Collectors*, p. 244, 2001

dirt road *noun*

the anus and rectum *US, 1922*

- —Vincent J. Monteleone, *Criminal Slang*, p. 69, 1949
- —Dale Gordon, *The Dominion Sex Dictionary*, p. 111, 1967
- "No dirt roads for me," he said with a smile." —Gerald Petievich, *To Die in Beverly Hills*, p. 93, 1983
- "That nigga just tore me a new asshole," said Rosalyn clutching her own butt cheeks. "Girl, you let him go down the dirt road?" "Oooh." She covered her mouth. "Shut up. My ass is killing me." —Antoine Thomas, *Flower's Bed*, p. 70, 2003

dirt surfer *noun*

a member of the counterculture who has abandoned any pretence of personal hygeine or grooming *US*

- —David Shenk and Steve Silberman, *Skeleton Key*, p. 70, 1994

Dirt Town *nickname*

McMurdo Station, Antarctica *ANTARCTICA*

- — *Cool Antarctica*, 2003: 'Antarctic slang'

dirt-tracker *noun*

a member of a touring sports team who is not selected for the major events *NEW ZEALAND*

- He stood by me all the way and when he came back from the meeting he ordered the dirt-trackers [the others were all playing the next day] all to be rounded up. — *Evening Post*, p. 12, 19th July 2001

dirt weed *noun*

low quality marijuana *US*

- —Vann Wesson, *Generation X Field Guide and Lexicon*, p. 54, 1997

dirty *noun*

▸ **do the dirty**

to have sex *US, 1968*

- — *Current Slang*, p. 16, Spring 1970
- He could understand that Twelvetree's daughter had walked in on her old man doing the dirty with the make-believe schoolgirl hooker but what was the half-naked whore doing with the daughter's boyfriend, scrambling into her skirt with her tits hanging out? —Robert Campbell, *Alice in La-La Land*, p. 289, 1987

▷ **see:** DIRTY DICK

dirty *verb*

▸ **to dirty your Christmas card**

in horse racing, to fail dramatically and suffer a great loss of reputation *AUSTRALIA*

- —Ned Wallish, *The Truth Dictionary of Racing Slang*, p. 14, 1989

dirty *adjective*

1 guilty *US, 1927*

- He said, "I try to keep an open mind. Everyone's dirty till they prove they aren't." —Elmore Leonard, *Maximum Bob*, p. 95, 1991

2 in possession of drugs or other contraband *US, 1927*

- But there was the chance that he was dirty too. —A.S. Jackson, *Gentleman Pimp*, p. 181, 1973

3 in urine testing, containing drug metabolites *US*

- One more dirty test, Miss Batista, and you're off the methadone program. —Seth Morgan, *Homeboy*, p. 187, 1990
- He had a dirty urine twice in a row so I violated him. —Elmore Leonard, *Maximum Bob*, p. 164, 1991

4 infected with a sexually transmitted infection *US*

- Dirty means diseased – a diseased girl. — *Oprah Winfrey Show*, 2nd October 2003

5 angry, upset, annoyed *AUSTRALIA, 1972*

- Two officials of a Central District Football Association team were dirty on Saturday when police pulled over their vehicle and defected it, forcing them to walk kilometres to their game. — *NT News*, p. 7, 1st May 1990

6 in betting on horse racing, said of a day of races that has produced wins for gamblers and losses for bookmakers *AUSTRALIA*

- —Ned Wallish, *The Truth Dictionary of Racing Slang*, p. 22, 1989

7 descriptive of electricity with unstable voltage that causes problems with computers *US*

- —Eric S. Raymond, *The New Hacker's Dictionary*, p. 127, 1991

8 of an aircraft, with undercarriage down and flaps suitably aligned in order to fly as slow as possible *UK*

Heard by Beale at a Leicester air show, August 1979.

dirty *adverb*

very, extremely; a general intensifier, especially of adjectives of size *UK, 1894*

- I tell yer, this dirty big copper musta been about seven feet tall[.] —John Wynnum, *Tar Dust*, p. 34, 1962
- Don't come back here, you dirty little no-good damn layabout. —John Peter Jones, *Feather Pluckers*, p. 18, 1964
- —Jim Ramsay, *Cop it Sweet!*, 1977
- [Christopher] Mayhew wrote a memo sacking him [Guy Burgess] after a few months for being "dirty drunk and idle." —David Leigh, 27th January 1978
- Imagine that! A dirty big Arab, living for a whole year on one grain of rice. It's incredible. —Peter Cook, *More Intersting Facts*, 1979
- —David McGill, *David McGill's Complete Kiwi Slang Dictionary*, p. 39, 1998
- [I]t was not getting down the slipway that caused problems for the Titanic, but a dirty great iceberg in the middle of the North Atlantic. —Larry Elliott, *The Guardian Weekly*, 17th January 1999

dirty air *noun*
in motor racing, air turbulence on the race track *US*
• —Don Alexander, *The Racer's Dictionary*, p. 20, 1980

dirty anal *noun*
a scene in a pornographic film or a photograph depicting anal sex where traces of faeces are visible on that which is being inserted anally *US*
• —*Adult Video News*, p. 44, August 1995

dirty and rude *adjective*
nude *UK*
Rhyming slang.
• —Ray Puxley, *Cockney Rabbit*, 1992

dirty arm *noun*
a drug addict's arm showing the scars and infections resulting from intravenous drug use *US*
• —Jay Robert Nash, *Dictionary of Crime*, p. 104, 1992

dirty barrel *noun*
the genitals of a person infected with a sexually transmitted disease *US*
• —Dale Gordon, *The Dominion Sex Dictionary*, p. 58, 1967

dirty basing *noun*
crack cocaine *UK, 1998*
The drug is cheaper and less pure than **FREEBASE** cocaine.
• —Mike Haskins, *Drugs*, 281 2003

dirty beast *noun*
a priest *UK*
Glasgow rhyming slang.
• —Michael Munro, *The Patter, Another Blast*, 1988

dirty bird *noun*
Old Crow™ whisky *US*
• —Clarence Major, *Dictionary of Afro-American Slang*, p. 46, 1970

dirty boogie *noun*
a sexually suggestive dance *US*
• You just didn't do the Dirty Boogie to Theresa Brewer, no sir, and not at the Totem Pole in Newton, Mass., no man, definitely not.—Abbie Hoffman, *Woodstock Nation*, p. 25, 1969
• And if anyone tried to give the Bop some joie de vivre it was immediately intercepted and was secretly known as the "dirty boogie."—Eve Babitz, *Eve's Hollywood*, p. 44, 1984

dirty case *noun*
in hospital usage, an operation in which the surgeons discover an infection *US*
• — *Maledicta*, p. 56, Summer 1980: 'Not sticks and stones, but names: more medical pejoratives'

dirty-dance *verb*
to dance in an explicitly and intentionally sexual manner *US*
• Breaking from our gabfest, we dirty-danced to Tom Jones songs. —Anka Radakovich, *The Wild Girls Club*, 1994

dirty daughter *noun*
water *UK*
Rhyming slang. One of several terms that have 'daughter' as the common (dispensible) element.
• —Julian Franklyn, *A Dictionary of Rhyming Slang*, 1961

Dirty Den *noun*
a pen *UK*
Rhyming slang, formed on the popular nickname of a character in BBC television's *EastEnders*; the villainous Dennis Watts, who appeared in the first episode, broadcast 19th February 1985, was nicknamed by the tabloid press.
• —Ray Puxley, *Cockney Rabbit*, 1992

dirty Dick; the dirty *noun*
a police station, a prison *UK*
Rhyming slang for **NICK**.
• —Ray Puxley, *Cockney Rabbit*, 1992

Dirty Dicks *noun*
a ward for sexually transmitted diseases in a military or other service hospital *CANADA, 1984*
A pun on **DICK** (the penis).

dirty-dirty *nickname*
the southern United States *US*
• I love how they [OutKast] represent the dirty-dirty with more juice than Zeus[.] (Letter to the editor).— *Village Voice*, p. 82, 2nd March 1999
• Over the last decade hip-hop has inevitably branched out into its many "coastal" facets, including the dirty-dirty (South).— *University Wire*, 15th September 2004

dirty dish *noun*
fish *AUSTRALIA*
Rhyming slang.
• —John Ayto, *The Oxford Dictionary of Rhyming Slang*, 2002

dirty dishes *noun*
evidence planted by police or investigators to incriminate someone *US*
• —Ralph de Sola, *Crime Dictionary*, p. 41, 1982
• —Jay Robert Nash, *Dictionary of Crime*, p. 104, 1992
• —Angela Devlin, *Prison Patter*, p. 45, 1996

dirty dog *noun*
a despicable or untrustworthy person; a lecher *UK, 1928*
• That is why most editions of Erskine May, the parliamentary rule book, contain a long list of unparliamentary phrases. They include murderer, swine, liar (of course), stool pigeon, guttersnipe, cad, Pecksniffian cant and – you've guessed it – dirty dog.— *The Guardian*, 5th October 2001

dirty dog *nickname*
the Greyhound Bus Lines *US*
• —Jim Crotty, *How to Talk American*, p. 383, 1997

dirty dupe *noun*
in television and film making, a crude, black and white, working print *US*
• —Ralph S. Singleton, *Filmaker's Dictionary*, p. 48, 1990

dirty end of the stick *noun*
an unfair position to be in, or inequitable treatment *UK, 1924*
• He got handed the dirty end of a dirty stick but he handled it. You've got to respect that.—F. Paul Wilson, *All The Rage*, p. 326, 2001

dirty girl *noun*
an operating theatre nurse who is not deemed sterile and who is available for tasks that do not require disinfecting *US*
• — *Maledicta*, p. 56, Summer 1980: 'Not sticks and stones, but names: more medical pejoratives'

Dirty Half Mile *nickname*
a section of the Sydney inner-city suburb of Kings Cross noted for prositution and vice *AUSTRALIA, 1934*
• The traffic policeman on duty held up even trams for him, and he was friend and counsellor to all the prostitutes of the Dirty Half Mile. —R. Eakin, *Aunts up the Cross*, p. 64, 1965
• [Detectives] took bribes to protect drug dealers, strip-club operators and standover thugs along Darlinghurst Road's 'dirty half mile' of sleaze and sex.— *Sydney Morning Herald*, 5th November 2002

dirty laundry *noun*
embarrassing information *US, 1982*
• What expectations do people learn form talk shows like those starring Jerry Springer or Jenny Jones, where people air their dirty laundry? —Keith E. Whitfield, *Fighting for Your African American Marriage*, p. 146, 2001

dirty leg *noun*
a woman with loose sexual mores; a common prostitute *US*
• —Andy Anonymous, *A Basic Guide to Campusology*, p. 7, 1966
• A dirty leg is the $5 or $10 trick.—Bruce Jackson, *In the Life*, p. 181, 1972
• —Charles Shafer, *Folk Speech in Texas Prisons*, p. 202, 1990

dirty leper; dirt *noun*
pepper *UK*
Rhyming slang, probably suggested or informed by the appearance of ground black pepper.
• —Ray Puxley, *Cockney Rabbit*, 1992

dirty look *noun*
a look of contempt or strong dislike *UK, 1961*
• The ref gives him a ticking off and Cool gives him a dirty look.— *The Guardian*, 22nd October 2002

dirty mac; dirty mackintosh *noun*

used as a generic description for any man who habitually resorts to sex-shops, strip-clubs and the purchase of 'top-shelf' publications *UK*

- The dirty mackintosh brigade pass him by without a glance. — Eric Idle, *He's the Star of the Sexy Movies*, 1975
- That little newsagent round the corner's got so many bum and tit mags on display you feel like one of the dirty mac outfit just going in for an evening newspaper. — *Journal of British Photography*, 4th January 1980

dirty Mac brigade *noun*

a notional collection of sex-oriented older men *UK*

- If the Dirty Mac brigade had been disappointed by the distinctly unsteamy output of Channel 4, Central, Yorkshire, and now Thames, in the wee small hours, what has been on offer? — *The Guardian*, 8th June 1987
- A float will probalby tie in with its next acquisition, likelier to be a mainstream media asset than sometihng for the dirty mac brigade again. — *The Times*, p. 50, 20th March 2004

dirty mack *verb*

to speak insults and slander *US*

- Talkin' that shit behind my back, dirty mackin' / Tellin' your boys that I'm on crack. — Eminem (Marshall Mathers), *Just Don't Give a Fuck*, 1999

dirty money *noun*

1 money that is the proceeds of crime, especially money that can be traced *UK*

Dirty Money (Un Flic) is a crime drama in which a policeman targets a drug-smuggling operation, directed by Jean-Pierre Melville, 1972.

- [H]ow many arrests have been made, how much "dirty money" has been "cleansed". — *The Guardian*, 28th June 2003

2 extra pay for very dirty work *UK, 1897*

An employment issue.

dirty movie *noun*

a sexual or pornographic film *US*

- As little as two years ago dirty movies, at least the kind that ran city-wide, were pitiful things indeed. — *Adam Film Quarterly*, p. 74, February 1969

dirty old man *noun*

1 a lecher; especially a middle-aged or older man with sexual appetites considered more appropriate in someone younger *UK, 1932*

Given impetus in the UK in the late 1960s – early 70s by television comedy series *Steptoe and Son*.

- O'MALLY: Did you ever see such pins [legs], did you, did you honestly? TAYLOR: You're a dirty old man you are, Paddy. — Graeme Kent, *The Queen's Corporal [Six Granada Plays]*, p. 87, 1959
- All you have to do, as every Dirty Old Man knows, is offer them a bar of candy[.] — G. Legman, *The Fake Revolt*, p. 10, 1967
- I was amazed that Pete believed somehow that he fell outside the DOM category. — Kitty Churchill, *Thinking of England*, p. 198, 1995

2 any homosexual man older than the homosexual male speaker *US*

- — Guy Strait, *The Lavendar Lexicon*, 1 June 1964

dirty on *adjective*

angry with *AUSTRALIA, 1965*

- The screws are real dirty on it, because this is what they've been trying to stop for years. — Ray Denning, *Prison Diaries*, p. 66, 1978
- As a supporter you can be 'dirty on the umpire' but it doesn't mean you're going to punch the umpire...well not always. — Ivor Limb, *Footy's No Joke!*, p. 22, 1986
- — Clive Galea, *Slipper*, p. 126, 1988
- — Robert G. Barrett, *Davo's Little Something*, p. 217, 1992

dirty pool *noun*

unfair tactics *US, 1940*

From the game of pool.

- — A Schroeder, *Shaking it Rough*, 1976

dirty Sanchez *noun*

an act of daubing your sex-partner's upper lip with a 'moustache' of his or her faeces *US*

This appears to have been contrived with an intention to provoke shock rather than actually as a practice, although, no doubt, some have or will experiment. The use of a Mexican name merely suggests the shape of a drooping moustache. Glossed, with perhaps too much information, as: 'To stick one's finger up a lady's *back bottom* during *doggy style sex*. Then one draws a moustache on her top lip, apparently' in *Roger's Profanisaurus*, 2003. Dirty Sanchez, a hardcore punk band from Seattle, released their first CD in 1999.

- — Chris Lewis, *The Dictionary of Playground Slang*, p. 73, 2003

dirty side *nickname*

the eastern coast of the US *US*

- — Book Craft Guild *Official CB Lingo*, p. 25, 1976

dirty smoke *noun*

marijuana *UK*

- Why the delay? "It's probably too much of that dirty smoke at night[."] — *Hip-Hop Connection*, p. 34, July 2002

dirty stack *noun*

in a casino, a stack of betting tokens of different denominations *US, 1983*

- — Thomas L. Clark, *The Dictionary of Gambling and Gaming*, p. 64, 1987

dirty stop-out *noun*

a person who spends more time than expected away from home in pursuit of pleasure *UK*

A jocular cliché when the stress on 'dirty' is admiring; may have an admonishing tone if used by parents, or if 'stop-out' is alone or combined with a harsher adjective.

- If you didn't want to go home, you'd see most people there at these clubs. All the other dirty stop-outs. — Dave Courtney, *Raving Lunacy*, p. 93, 2000

dirty thing *noun*

a person who behaves amorously, or flirts saucily or unsubtly, especially with heavy innuendo *UK, 1961*

Originally used by adolescent girls or amorous boys.

- "Could you really have sex?" Brian asked, referring to her constant requests that Paul spends a night in the den with her." Without a doubt. Let's have it!" Helen giggled mischievously. Brian laughed. "You dirty thing!" he said, before bursting into song[.] — *a fansite transcription of Big Brother Series 2*, 2001

dirty thirty *noun*

1 in the Vietnam war, a US soldier who had killed 30 enemy soldiers *US*

- Everyone talked about the Dirty Thirty. Every soldier worth his salt bragged he was getting closer and closer: "Killed another Charlie last night while Lurpin' thru sector seven. That brings my count to over two dozen. Only a matter of time before I'm a Dirty Thirty myself. — Jack Hawkins, *Chopper One #2: Tunnel Warriors*, p. 27, 1991

2 the US Air Force pilots who served as co-pilots with Vietnamese Airforce crews in 1963 and 1964 *US*

- — Gregory Clark, *Words of the Vietnam War*, p. 145, 1990

dirty tricks *noun*

secret tactics that are generally considered to be unfair *US, 1963*

- "Malice, Mormonism, McCarthy-Nixon dirty tricks are written all over it by extreme rightist elements in the Republican Party," Ritter wrote. — Norman Mailer, *The Executioner's Song*, p. 864, 1979
- Reverend Pat Robertson said, "Lee Atwater has used every dirty trick known to mankind." — Larry Beinhart, *American Hero*, p. 3, 1993
- A Bush family insider since 1973, when he [Karl Rove] was chairman of the College Republicans National Committee (and taught party youth"dirty tricks" according to the Washington Post), Rove worked for the elder Bush[.] — J.H. Hatfield, *Fortunate Son*, p. 264, 2001
- Instead of a dirty-tricks squad composed of over-the-hill intelligence agents, it featured a concerted effort by top Reagan officials to circumvent congressional control in order to funnel aid to rightwing Nicaraguan terrorists. — Daniel Lazare, *The Velvet Coup*, p. 86–87, 2001

dirty tyke *noun*

a bike *UK*

Rhyming slang.

- — Ray Puxley, *Cockney Rabbit*, 1992

dirty up *verb*

1 to render an entertainment (radio, television, film, book, play, etc) more sexually titillating *UK, 1974*

- [Joan Jett] dirtied up the Gary Glitter anthem, Do You Wanna Touch Me, adding appropriate expletives and dissing the Glittered one's fall from grace. — *Carbon County News Online (Montana)*, 24th July 2003

2 to modify a recording to make it sound more 'authentic' or 'raw' *US*

- — Tom Hibbert, *Rockspeak!*, p. 47, 1983

dirty water *noun*

▸ **get the dirty water(s) off your chest**

(of a male) to ejaculate, either with a partner or as a sole practitioner *UK, 1961*

- [W]hile the other bastards are busy getting the dirty waters off their chests a bloke like me runs the risk of goin' blind jerkin' the gerkin!!! —Barry Humphries, *Bazza Pulls It Off!*, 1971

dirty weekend *noun*

a romantic or sexually adventurous weekend (away from home) spent with your lover; or with your partner or spouse but without your children *UK, 1963*

- Ah yes, the dirty weekend – or in this case, the dirty night. —*The Observer*, 9th February 2003

dirty work *noun*

in a strip or sex show, movements made to expose the vagina *US*

- If strippers choose a face that is shy, it is because they want their "floor work" (crouching or lying on the floor and simulating intercourse) and "dirty work" ("flashing" and spreading their legs) to remind the audience of demure girls. —Marilyn Salutin, *The Sexual Scene*, p. 173, June 1971

dirty work at the crossroads *noun*

illegal activity, especially if concealed *US, 1938*

- It sounds to me as if there's going to be dirty work at the crossroads. —Rex Stout, *Some Buried Caesar*, p. 41, 1967

DIS *noun*

*d*eath while *i*n the *s*addle, or engaged in sexual intercourse *US*

- Coroners have been known to label it "D.I.S.," death in the saddle. —*Maledicta*, p. 58, 1979

dis; diss *verb*

1 to insult in a competitive, quasi-friendly spirit, especially in a competitive rap battle *US*

- There are many different terms for playing the dozens, including "bagging, capping, cracking, dissing, hiking, joning, ranking, ribbing, serving, signifying, slipping, sounding and snapping". —James Haskins, *The Story of Hip-Hop*, p. 54, 2000
- The guy from Scotland was virtually unknown, so I decided not to diss him, because I knew that would be a diss in itself! —J. Hoggarth (quoting Prime Cuts), *How To Be a DJ*, p. 101, 2002

2 to show disrespect, to disparage *US, 1982*

- —*The Washington Post*, 15th March 1987
- —*Atlantic Monthly*, p. 110, June 1988
- —Connie Eble (Editor), *UNC-CH Campus Slang*, p. 2, Fall 1990
- You know, I'll tell you what the whole shouting match came down to. Dis. It was all about dis. The kid disrespected me by raising up in my face. I dissed him by throwing him up against the fence[.] —Richard Price, *Clockers*, p. 368–369, 1992
- Italian people came over here. They got dissed. They said, "Yo man, fuck you! Little Italy. All right? We got our own thing." You ever heard of Little Africa? Didn't think so. —Chris Rock, *Rock This!*, p. 13, 1997

3 to release (from prison) *US*

An abbreviation of '*dis*charge'.

- —Charles Shafer, *Folk Speech in Texas Prisons*, p. 202, 1990

disappear *verb*

to kill someone and dispose of the corpse in a manner that assures it will never be discovered *US*

As a transitive verb, a favourite term – and practice – of right wing death squads and organised criminal enterprises.

- —*American Speech*, p. 306, December 1964: 'Lingua cosa nostra'
- Our two Nicaraguan doctors were disappeared one right after the other. —Elmore Leonard, *Bandits*, p. 38, 1987

dischuffed *adjective*

displeased, offended; insulted *UK*

Military usage.

- —Nigel Foster, *The Making of a Royal Marine Commando*, 1987

disco *noun*

1 an event where a DJ plays recorded music for dancing *UK*

The ubiquitous post-wedding-breakfast or after-dinner entertainment; probably derives from the mobile discoteques which proliferated in the 1970s to take advantage of the then-fashionable disco scene.

2 a venue for dancing to recorded music *US, 1964*

Abbreviated from '*disco*tèque'.

- —LAX *Dancin at the Disco*, 1979
- Last New Year I went out with him and a group of his mates to celebrate in a disco[.] —Macfarlane, Macfarlane and Robson, *The User*, p. 13, 1996

3 by extension, a genre of dance music *US, 1964*

- —Rimshots *Super Disco*, 1976
- —Trampps *Disco Inferno*, 1978
- —PIL *Death Disco*, 1979
- I fucking hate disco. Just can't help it. —John King, *Human Punk*, p. 295, 2000

disco *adjective*

1 out of date, out of fashion, out-moded *US*

- —Judi Sanders, *Faced and Faded, Hanging to Hurl*, p. 12, 1993

2 acceptable, good *US*

From the film *Pulp Fiction*.

- —Connie Eble (Editor), *UNC-CH Campus Slang*, p. 3, April 1995

disco biscuit *noun*

1 a tablet of MDMA, the recreational drug best known as ecstasy *UK*

A heavily ironic identity for a fashionable drug; 'disco' as a nightclub for an earlier generation that didn't have **ECSTASY** and hence, is considered extremely unfashionable, plus 'biscuit' in the conventional sense of 'a basic supply (ship's biscuit) which can sustain life'. In short 'MDMA brings life to clubs'.

- —Angela Devlin, *Prison Patter*, p. 45, 1996
- CALL IT... Adam, brownies, burgers, disco biscuits, doves, eckies, tulips, X[.] JUST DON'T CALL IT... MDMA – too scientific —*Drugs An Adult Guide*, p. 34, December 2001

2 the recreational drug methaqualone, best known as Quaaludes™, a tablet of methaqualone *US*

From the popularity of the drug in the 1970s disco scene.

- —Peter Johnson, *Dictionary of Street Alcohol and Drug Terms*, p. 59, 1993
- Most of the local trade in these babies was controlled by speed-freak bikers, and these were dismissively known as Disco Biscuits. —Editors of Ben is Dead, *Retrohell*, p. 169, 1997
- —Mike Haskins, *Drugs*, p. 282, 2003

disco brick *noun*

a kilogram of cocaine *UK*

- And a bag of disco bricks —Lupine Howl, *Vaporizer*, 2001

disco burger *noun*

a tablet of MDMA, the recreational drug best known as ecstasy *UK*

- —Angela Devlin, *Prison Patter*, p. 45, 1996
- Disco Burgers – Like most tablets, shaped like a hamburger – but coloured brown to add to the Big Mac look. —Gareth Thomas, *This Is Ecstasy*, p. 55, 2002

disco dancer *noun*

1 an opportunist *UK*

Glasgow rhyming slang for **CHANCER**.

- He's a bit ae a disco dancer that pal a yours. —Michael Munro, *The Patter, Another Blast*, 1988

2 cancer *AUSTRALIA*

Rhyming slang.

- —Ryan Aven-Bray, *Ridgey Didge Oz Jack Lang*, p. 25, 1983

disco dose *noun*

a mild dose of LSD *US*

- While the typical late-'60s tripper probably took about 250 mg of "acid," the average strength of the hits sold in recent years, known to old-timers as "disco doses," is less than half that. —Steven Daly and Nalthaniel Wice, *alt.culture*, p. 138, 1995

disco dust *noun*

cocaine *UK*

- [T]op DJs on the decks and lots of disco dust in carefully situated little stashes. —Wayne Anthony, *Spanish Highs*, p. 106, 1999

disco gun *noun*

a Walther PPK pistol *UK*

- [T]he Walther PPK, known as the "disco-gun" because it was nice and small, and therefore easy to conceal [...] I could slip the disco gun into my belt. —Andy McNab (writing of the late 1970s/early 80s), *Immediate Action*, p. 159, 1995

disco move *noun*

any manoeuvre executed by a novice surfer *US*

- —Trevor Cralle, *The Surfin'ary*, p. 30, 1991

discon *noun*

the criminal charge of 'disorderly conduct' *US, 1963*

- All defendants were charged with discone, disorderly conduct. —Ed Sanders, *Tales of Beatnik Glory*, p. 217, 1975

- [I]f Ray Garvey presses those pricks like he's supposed to I'll wind up with a dis-con conviction. — Vincent Patrick, *Family Business*, p. 53, 1985

disco queen *noun*

a male homosexual who frequents discos *US*

The title of a 1978 song by Paul Jabara glorifying the energy of the song's hero.

- — *Maledicta*, p. 235, 1979: 'Kinks and queens: linguistic and cultural aspects of the terminology for gays'

disgustitude *noun*

the state of being disgusted *US*

- — Karla Jennings, *The Devouring Fungus*, p. 219, 1990

dish *noun*

1 an attractive female *UK, 1909*

- I couldn't forget the way she looked through me the last time we met. What a dish. — Mickey Spillane, *I, The Jury*, p. 49, 1947
- Then they wondered when they were going to have the cash to promote a trim dish like the piece hanging onto Buggsy Stein's arm. — Irving Shulman, *The Amboy Dukes*, p. 3, 1947
- Nina Lund, niece of ex-Senator White, of Maine, was one of Washington's loveliest and most popular dishes. — Jack Lait and Lee Mortimer, *Washington Confidential*, p. 147, 1951
- Did you catch that photo on Page 1 yesterday of Liberace and his "current flame," a dish named Jan Valerie? — *San Francisco News*, p. 14, 14th January 1955
- I dreamed I was a real dish in my Maidenform bra. [Headline of advertisement]. — *Life*, p. 48, 16th May 1960
- Myra Breckinridge is a dish, and never forget it, you motherfuckers, as the children say nowadays. — Gore Vidal, *Myra Breckinridge*, p. 3, 1968
- — Collin Baker et al., *College Undergraduate Slang Study Conducted at Brown University*, p. 106, 1968
- DUKE: Just one for a start. HAWKEYE: The blonde dish. — *M*A*S*H*, 1970

2 the buttocks, the anus *UK*

Polari.

- JULIAN: I can't work in here. All the dishes are dirty. SANDY: Speak for yourself, ducky. — Barry Took and Marty Feldman, *Round The Horne*, 4th April 1965
- DISH = bum, bottom, etc — the cast of 'Aspects of Love', Prince of Wales Theatre, *Palare (Boy Dancer Talk) for Beginners*, 1989–92
- [T]o show off her rather bona dish[.] — James Gardiner, *Who's a Pretty Boy Then?*, p. 123, 1997
- — Paul Baker, *Polari*, p. 171, 2002

3 gossip, especially when disparaging, salacious or scandalous *US, 1976*

From the verb sense.

- This guy was awfully nice, but his dish seemed suspect. — Armistead Maupin, *Babycakes*, p. 20, 1984
- [T]abloids are known to pay cash for good "dish". — Erica Orloff and JoAnn Baker, *Dirty Little Secrets*, p. 115, 2001

4 on Prince Edward Island, an undefined amount of alcohol *CANADA*

- I think this deserves a cilibration. Would you like a dish? Whin I say "dish" I mane something stronger than tay. — Elmer Harris, *Johnny Belinda*, p. 15, 1956

▸ **put on the dish**

to apply lubricant to the anus in preparation for anal sex *UK*

- — Paul Baker, *Polari*, p. 186, 2002

dish *verb*

to gossip, to disparage *US, 1941*

Originally 'dish the dirt' or 'dish out the dirt'.

- — Donald Webster Cory and John P. LeRoy, *The Homosexual and His Society*, p. 263, 1963: 'A lexicon of homosexual slang'
- "Are you trying to dish me, Mary?" she says angrily. — John Rechy, *City of Night*, p. 53, 1963
- I could have dished her an earful, believe you me. — Antony James, *America's Homosexual Underground*, p. 133, 1965
- — Collin Baker et al., *College Undergraduate Slang Study Conducted at Brown University*, p. 106, 1968
- O.K., if you don't want to dish, we won't dish. — Armistead Maupin, *Tales of the City*, p. 143, 1978
- When I mentioned Denise, she dished, "She used to work for a matchmaker named Helena who was indicted for fraud." — Anka Radakovich, *The Wild Girls Club*, p. 55–56, 1994
- [T]he lads would not come dropping by my cublicle to dish. — Rhiannon Paine, *Too late for the Festival*, p. 129, 1999

▸ **dish it out**

when fighting or arguing, to attack with punishing force *US, 1930*

- [George W.] Bush, not one to flinch from dishing it out himself, has come under savage attack from [Garry] Trudeau[.] — *The Guardian*, 27th May 2004

▸ **dish soup**

to sell cocaine *US*

- — Mark S. Fleisher, *Beggars & Thieves*, p. 289, 1995: 'Glossary'

▸ **dish the dirt; dish it**

to gossip indiscreetly or with slanderous intent *US, 1926*

- Cocktail time hang-outs for models are the bars of the St. Clair and the Croydon, and the Cloverbar, where they dish the dirt. — Jack Lait and Lee Mortimer, *Chicago Confidential*, p. 113, 1950
- They drank more bouillon, popped more bennie and dished the dirt. — Hubert Selby Jr, *Last Exit to Brooklyn*, p. 59, 1957
- DENISE [VAN OUTEN]: So can you dish the dirt on the others? VICTORIA [ADAMS]: Dish the dirt on the others. Well, fashion-wise, the only thing that I can dish the dirt is Geri wears really silly shoes[.] — *Big Breakfast*, 14th March 1998
- — Paul Baker, *Polari*, p. 172, 2002

DI shack *noun*

the quarters where drill instructors live and the on-duty instructor works *US*

- — Linda Reinberg, *In the Field: The Language of the Vietnam War*, p. 62, 1991

dis-head; diss-head *noun*

a person who will not conform and show respect *US*

Combines **DIS** (to show disrespect) with **-HEAD** (an enthusiast).

- And all the other kids said, "Eminem's a diss-head / He'll never last[.] — Eminem (Marshall Mathers), *As the World Turns*, 2000

dishlicker *noun*

a dog, especially a racing greyhound *AUSTRALIA, 1983*

- Inside, it's just like a bonsai Randwick and yes, you can bet on the greyhounds (affectionately known as dishlickers) if you're game. — *Sydney Morning Herald*, 26th February 1988
- We snapped that up and sat back in the committee room waiting for our dishlicker to win so we could collect. — Doug Walters, *Two For The Road*, p. 98, 1992

dishonorable discharge *noun*

ejaculation achieved through masturbation *US*

- — Roger Blake, *The American Dictionary of Sexual Terms*, p. 60, 1964
- — Dale Gordon, *The Dominion Sex Dictionary*, p. 59, 1967
- When I was in the army, a sergeant caught me in the shower in the process of giving my dick a dishonorable discharge. I looked him straight in the eye and told him it was my dick and I could wash it as fast as I wanted to. — Ken Weaver, *Texas Crude*, p. 83, 1984

dish out *verb*

1 to distribute *UK, 1931*

Originally military and therefore used of food or medals.

- [Charles] Clarke ought to hold his nose and dish out the cash. — *The Guardian*, 28th May 2003

2 to dispense (abuse) *US, 1908*

- I began to feel plenty sore, doing a twenty-month stretch (that's the bit the parole board finally dished out to me). — Mezz Mezzrow, *Really the Blues*, p. 318, 1946

▸ **dish out the gravy; dish out the porridge**

of a judge, to deliver a severe sentence of imprisonment *UK, 1950*

- Cor, he ain' arf dishin' aht the porridge. — Paul Tempest, *Lag's Lexicon*, p. 97, 1950
- — Angela Devlin, *Prison Patter*, p. 46, 1996

dish queen *noun*

a male homosexual who takes special pleasure in gossip *US*

- — *American Speech*, p. 56, Spring-Summer 1970: 'Homosexual slang'

dishrag *noun*

a person or thing of no importance *US, 1906*

- — Frederic G. Cassidy, *Dictionary of American Regional English, Volume II*, p. 85, 1991

dish rags *noun*

in poker, poor cards *US*

- — John Vorhaus, *The Big Book of Poker Slang*, p. 14, 1996

dishwasher *noun*

a railway worker who cleans engines in a roundhouse *US*

- — Norman Carlisle, *The Modern Wonder Book of Trains and Railroading*, p. 262, 1946

dishwater *noun*

poor quality beer *AUSTRALIA*

- 'We want you to try the local drop now that you're here.' 'I've heard it's dishwater.' — *The Adventures of Barry McKenzie*, 1972

dishwater diarrhea *noun*
a notional disease that plagues those reluctant to wash their dishes *US, 1969*
- —Frederic G. Cassidy, *Dictionary of American Regional English, Volume II*, p. 86, 1991

dishy *adjective*
sexually attractive *UK, 1961*
From **DISH** (an attractive person).
- —Julian Rathbone, *Hand Out*, 1968
- My fevered daughter was whipped to a ward where she spent two days learning Italian from a dishy doctor.— *The Guardian*, 20th October 2001

disinfo *noun*
*disinfo*rmation *UK*
- A disinfo tool doesn't always survive.—Adam Hall, *The Kobra Manifesto*, 1976

disk drive *noun*
the vagina *UK*
- Women's genitalia were represented as (potential) containers (e.g., bucket, box, hair goblet), places to put things in (e.g., furry letterbox, disk drive, socket, slot), containers for semen (e.g., gism pot, spunk bin, honey pot), and containers for the penis/sex (e.g., willy warmer, wank shaft, shagbox).—*Journal of Sex Research*, p. 146, 2001

dismant *noun*
a bit of previously-used electrical or mechanical equipment *SOUTH AFRICA*
From '*dismant*le'.
- —Angus Hall, *On the Run*, 1974

dismo *noun*
a fanatic surfing enthusiast who never actually surfs *US*
- —Vann Wesson, *Generation X Field Guide and Lexicon*, p. 54, 1997

Disneyland *noun*
a prison with relaxed rules that ease the difficulty of serving a sentence *US*
- —William K. Bentley and James M. Corbett, *Prison Slang*, p. 3, 1992

Disneyland *nickname*
1 the Pentagon; military headquarters in Vietnam *US, 1963*
A critical assessment of reality and fantasy in the military leadership.
- —Linda Reinberg, *In the Field*, p. 63, 1991

2 the brothel district near An Khe, Vietnam, near the 1st Cavalry Division base *US*
- — *Time*, p. 29, 6th May 1966
- —Carl Fleischhauer, *A Glossary of Army Slang*, p. 15, 1968

Disneyland-on-the-Rideau *nickname*
National Defence Headquarters, on the Rideau Canal in Ottawa *CANADA*
- The term alludes to the fact that at NDHQ, just as at Disneyland, things happen which are mysterious and inexplicable and which cause amazement and wonder to all.—Tom Langeste, *Words on the Wing*, p. 81, 1995

disobey *verb*
▸ **disobey the pope**
1 to masturbate *UK*
While this may be another ecumenical variation of **BASH THE BISHOP** (to masturbate), it is certainly a literal reaction to the Catholic view of onanism. It is also theoretically possible to 'please the pope'.

2 to have sex *US*
Here the use of frowned-upon contraception seems to be implied.
- Another way to say "intercourse" [...] Disobeying the pope[.]—Erica Orloff and JoAnn Baker, *Dirty Little Secrets*, p. 63, 2001

dispatchers *noun*
in a dice game cheating scheme, improperly marked dice *UK, 1811*
- —John S. Salak, *Dictionary of Gambling*, p. 77, 1963

dispersal *noun*
in prison, the system of managing Category A prisoners by sending them to one of six high-security prisons rather than concentrating them all in one maximum-security facility *UK*
- Toby made a big deal of acknowledging the other prisoners as he showed his "old friend from dispersal" [...] the ropes.—Erwin James, *The Guardian*, 26th October 2000: 'A life inside'

diss *verb*
▷ see: **DIS**

distress *verb*
to impregnate outside marriage *TRINIDAD AND TOBAGO*
- —Lise Winer, *Dictionary of the English/Creole of Trinidad & Tobago*, 2003

dis war *noun*
an exchange of quasi-friendly insults as part of a rap battle; a war of words *US*
Extended from **DIS** (to show disrespect).
- He's been trying to stay deep and avoid the dis wars.—Lois Stavsky et al., *A2Z*, p. 28, 1995

dit *noun*
a tale, a yarn *AUSTRALIA, 1942*
Origin unknown.
- He looked forward to a snort up on the hill and the opportunity it offered to swop 'dits' with his offsider in the cruiser.—John Wynnum, *Tar Dust*, p. 48, 1962
- These memories are not "dits" in the strict sense – being factual and sometimes technical and not outrageously embellished fiction. —J.E. MacDonnell, *Dit Spinner*, 1967

ditch *noun*
1 the sea; the ocean; the Atlantic Ocean; the English Channel *UK, 1841*
Generally used with 'the'.
- I wish she would fall over the side or the whole bloody crew would drop into the ditch and leave only her and me aboard.—Robert S. Close, *Love Me Sailor*, p. 64, 1945

2 the antecubial vein inside the bend of the elbow, often used for injecting drugs *US*
- — *Current Slang*, p. 20, Fall 1968
- —Stewart L. Tubbs and Sylvia Moss, *Human Communication*, p. 119, 1974
- —Richard A. Spears, *The Slang and Jargon of Drugs and Drink*, p. 145, 1986

3 the Tasman Sea *NEW ZEALAND*
- —Sonya Plowman, *Great Kiwi Slang*, p. 60, 2002

4 inferior marijuana, especially from Mexico *UK, 1998*
From **DITCHWEED**.
- —Mike Haskins, *Drugs*, p. 287, 2003

ditch *verb*
1 to reject, discard, abandon; to elude *US, 1899*
- You ought to ditch the Dukes while you can.—Irving Shulman, *The Amboy Dukes*, p. 62, 1947
- We are free to go, but have to be very sneaky and ditch Bruce somewhere inside the Pentagon maze so he won't find the Acapulco Gold in the car.—Abbie Hoffman, *Revolution for the Hell of It*, p. 44, 1968
- Honey, ditching class to go shopping doesn't make you a defective. — *The Breakfast Club*, 1985
- I myself have ditched and gotten so bored I did homework. Figure that shit out.— *Ferris Buehler's Day Off*, 1986
- That's wonderful! Did she ditch him for another guy?—C.D. Payne, *Youth in Revolt*, p. 250, 1993
- You think this is too mean, ditching him this way?—*200 Cigarettes*, 1999
- Lord Archer 'ditched lover to win promotion.—Paul Kelso, *The Guardian*, 20th June 2001

2 to release (from prison) *US*
An abbreviation and corruption of 'discharge'.
- —Charles Shafer, *Folk Speech in Texas Prisons*, p. 202, 1990

3 in an emergency, to bring an aircraft down in the sea *UK, 1941*
- [T]he Sea plane which ditched in the water between Hythe Pier and Weston Shore in the Solent.— *Maritime and Coastguard Agency [Press release]*, 27th July 1998

ditchweed *noun*
marijuana of inferior quality that grows wild in roadside ditches, especially in Mexico *US, 1982*
- —Richard A. Spears, *The Slang and Jargon of Drugs and Drink*, p. 145, 1986
- —Mike Haskins, *Drugs*, p. 287, 2003

ditso *noun*
an absent-minded, somewhat dim person *US, 1976*
- Meantime, Zahna noticed, the ditso had left her bag, her books, and that bizarre cross on her blanket.—Kelly Lange, *The Reporter*, p. 246, 2002

ditso *adjective*
absent-minded, somewhat dim *US*
- Eddie really looked like the typical dumb blond of that era and he behaved off-camnera exactly the way he did on-camera, really goofy and ditso.—Patty Duke, *Call Me Anna*, p. 118, 1987

- Gold chain wearin' fried chicken and biscuit eatin' monkey, ape, baboon, fast runnin', high jumpin', spear chuckin' basketball dunkin' ditso spade, take you fuckin' pizza and go back to Africa. — *Do the Right Thing*, 1989

dit-spinner *noun*

a person adept at telling stories, anecdotes or the like *AUSTRALIA*

- — J.E. MacDonnell, *Dit Spinner*, 1967

ditto

I agree; the same goes for me *US*

- — Connie Eble (Editor), *UNC-CH Campus Slang*, p. 2, Fall 1981

ditto-head *noun*

a fan of radio entertainer Rush Limbaugh *US*

Limbaugh conditioned his callers to begin conversations on the radio with a simple 'Dittos from [hometown]' instead of gushing admiration for him.

- "Ditto-heads" fall for Rush Limbaugh's specious arguments that pointy-headed, inntellectual, godless, femi-Nazi, secular humanist, evolutionist, sexually permissive, environmentalist wackos are out to capture the world by stultifying the minds of our youth and destroying raditional family value. — *St. Petersburg Times*, p. 2, 8th January 1992
- One problem, we were told, is that some people in Washington are afraid of Mr. Limbaugh because he caters to conservatives and so-called "ditto heads," who agree with anything he says. — *Washington Times*, p. A6, 11th September 1992
- — Connie Eble (Editor), *UNC-CH Campus Slang*, p. 2, Fall 1996

ditty bag, dittybopper *nouns*

▷ see: DIDDY BAG, DIDDLYBOPPER

dity *adjective*

upset, nervous *US, 1978*

- For a minute I wonder is he going to get ditsy about us living together without benefit of wedlock. — Robert Campbell, *Junkyard Dog*, p. 61–62, 1986

ditz *noun*

an absent-minded, empty-headed person *US, 1982*

- — Multicultural Management Program Fellows, *Dictionary of Cautionary Words and Phrases*, 1989
- At the risk of sounding like some New Age ditz, the shriek of Hendrix's guitar was truly a cry of love. — Mick Farren, *Give the Anarchist a Cigarette*, p. 98, 2001

ditzy; ditsy *adjective*

(usually of a woman) scatterbrained, silly *US, 1973*

- This one was set up by Lorrie, her ditzy pal from The Fabric Barn, who knew a guy who had a friend who'd been 'out of circulation for a while' (whatever that means – prison if you ask me) and wanted his ashes hauled in the worst kind of way. — Armistead Maupin, *Maybe the Moon*, p. 222, 1992
- I had to pretend to be all vague and ditzy and lied too much[.] — Jenny Eclair, *Camberwell Beauty*, p. 149, 2000

div *noun*

a fool; a disagreeable individual *UK*

Abbreviated from DIVVY (a fool).

- "[T]he dreaded Roger" is a bit of a creep (or sometimes, these days, a "wally" or a "div"). — *New Society*, 10th March 1983
- — Angela Devlin, *Prison Patter*, p. 46, 1996
- [U]ptight, straight-arsed divs like you. — Dave Courtney, *Raving Lunacy*, p. 33, 2000
- What the fuck is this? What are you saying, you div? — *The Guardian*, p. 12, 26th February 2002

dive *noun*

1 a disreputable establishment *US, 1867*

- I've played the music in a lot of places these last thirty years, from Al Capone's roadhouses to swing joints along 52nd Street in New York, Paris nightclubs, Harvard University, dicty Washington embassies and Park Avenue salons, not to mention all the barrelhouse dives. — Mezz Mezzrow, *Really the Blues*, p. 4, 1946
- After Chicago we thought nothing could make us blink. But some of the dives on 8th Street made it. — Jack Lait and Lee Mortimer, *Washington Confidential*, p. 33, 1951
- There is a similar story about a sidestreet dive which clipped a sucker for several thousand dollars and turned him out on the street. — Robert Sylvester, *No Cover Charge*, p. 219, 1956
- Now you not going back on the road no more, and you ain't playing no more two bit sleazy dives. — *The Blues Brothers*, 1980
- My father was a Mexican magician. He never graduated from the border dives. — Seth Morgan, *Homeboy*, p. 119, 1990
- Do you call having pizza in the same dive pizzeria every night 'eating out'? — *Mallrats*, 1995
- Yeah. This place is a dive, anyway. — *200 Cigarettes*, 1999

2 an intentional loss in a sporting event *US, 1916*

- Q. You think anybody is crazy who takes a dive? A. Yah. Sure. — Rocky Garciano (with Rowland Barber), *Somebody Up There Likes Me*, p. 305, 1955
- What the fuck they want? I took the dive. — *Raging Bull*, 1980

▸ **take a dive**

to deliberately lose a boxing match or other sporting contest *US, 1942*

- Why cause contention over a tennis game? So, burying her own competitive spirit, she took a dive, surrendering the game. — Nora Roberts, *Dance upon the Air*, p. 269, 2001

dive *verb*

to lose a contest or competition intentionally, especially in boxing *US, 1921*

From the image of a boxer diving towards the mat, feigning a knock-out blow.

- Folks said, "It's interesting about his secret control of a stable of fighters. I'd guess a hog like that would set-up to bet the ones that dived." — Iceberg Slim (Robert Beck), *Long White Con*, p. 170, 1977

▸ **dive for pearls**

to work washing dishes in a restaurant *US, 1951*

- I begged for it, drawled for it, dove pearls in mission kitchens all last winter for it. — John Clellon Holmes, *The Horn*, p. 166, 1958

dive-bomb *verb*

to jump into water in a tucked position in order to make a large splash *AUSTRALIA*

- At Ramsgate Baths, weekend after weekend, year after year, I would show off with the clown diving troupe, dive-bomb near the edge of the pool to drench the girls, do mildly difficult acrobatic tricks, smoke, and comb my hair. — Clive James, *Unreliable Memoirs*, p. 98, 1980

divebombing *noun*

an act of picking up dog ends from the pavement *UK*

Vagrants' use.

- — *Social Work Today*, 22nd January 1980

divel a bissel!

used by Nova Scotians of German descent as a mild oath *CANADA*

- "Divel a bissel" is a form of "teufel ein bischen," the German for "the devil a little bit." It is mild Lunenburg profanity. — Lewis Poteet, *The South Shore Phrase Book*, p. 38, 1999

diver *noun*

1 a pickpocket *UK, 1611*

- — Vincent J. Monteleone, *Criminal Slang*, p. 6970, 1949
- — Angela Devlin, *Prison Patter*, p. 46, 1996

2 a hang glider *US*

- — Erik Fair, *California Thrill Sports*, p. 328, 1992

Diver *nickname*

Charles Jaco, CNN reporter in Saudi Arabia during the US war against Iraq in 1991 *US*

Because of Jaco's athletic dives off camera when a missile attack alert was announced.

- — *Army*, p. 48, November 1991

divhead *noun*

a fool; a disagreeable individual *UK*

Elaboration of DIV.

- [W]e 'ad a group of squaddies over. They were real div'eads an' they'd been giving us a few problems. — Colin Butts, *Is Harry on the Boat?*, p. 93, 1997

dividends *noun*

money *US*

- — Judi Sanders, *Da Bomb!*, p. 9, 1997

divider *noun*

a marijuana cigarette that is shared among several smokers *UK*

- — *www.addictions.org*, 2001

divine *adjective*

pleasant, 'nice' *UK, 1928*

A trivial use of the conventional sense.

divine blows *noun*

energetic sex *TRINIDAD AND TOBAGO*

- — Lise Winer, *Dictionary of the English/Creole of Trinidad & Tobago*, 2003

Divine Brown *noun*

▸ **go Divine Brown; go Divine**

to perform oral sex *UK*

Rhyming slang for **GO DOWN (ON)**; aptly formed on the professional name of a Los Angeles prostitute who enjoyed some minor celebrity when, in 1995, she was apprehended performing just such a service for film actor Hugh Grant (b.1960).

- —Ray Puxley, *Fresh Rabbit*, 1998

Divine Miss M *nickname*

Bette Middler, American singer born in 1945 *US*

- —Arnold Shaw, *Dictionary of American Pop/Rock*, p. 107, 1982

diving board *noun*

in electric line work, a work platform board *US*

- —A.B. Chance Co., *Lineman's Slang Dictionary*, p. 6, 1980

diving gear *noun*

a condom *US*

- —Judi Sanders, *Cal Poly Slang*, p. 3, 1990

diving suit *noun*

a condom *AUSTRALIA, 1984*

divoon *adjective*

lovely, delightful *US, 1944*

A humorous elaboration of 'divine'.

- Stooky! It's divoon!—S.J. Perlman, *Fly by Noon*, p. 540, 1958
- Ezzie Fenwick, who knew beauty when he saw beauty, had tears in his eyes. "Divoon," he said.—Dominick Dunne, *People Like Us*, p. 331, 1988

divorce *noun*

in the usage of organised pickpocket gangs, the loss of a crew member to jail *US*

- —Vincent J. Monteleone, *Criminal Slang*, p. 70, 1949

divot *noun*

a toupee *UK, 1934*

Borrowed from golf's 'sliced piece of turf'.

- —Wilfred Granville, *The Theater Dictionary*, p. 58, 1952

divvie *noun*

a person with instinctive knowledge *UK*

Probably from 'diviner'.

- Divvie? Maybe it's from the old word "diviner", as in water, but who knows? It's slang for anybody who can guess right about a thing without actually knowing. Some people have it for gems or paintings ... a precious knack that goes separate from any learning. I'm an antiques divvie.—Jonathan Gash, *Gold from Gemini*, 1978

divvies *noun*

1 used for claiming a share of something that is being divided *US*

- Ah get divvies though.—John Clellon Holmes, *The Horn*, p. 111, 1958

2 divination *UK*

- —Margery Allingham, *More Work for the Undertaker*, 1947

divvo *noun*

a fool *UK*

A variation of **DIVVY**.

- Shut up, will you, Divvo. What the fuck do you know about welding, anyroad?—*The Full Monty*, 1997

divvy *noun*

1 a share or portion; a *divi*dend *US, 1872*

- "I'm from the Prudential," I say. "I've brought your divvy."—Ted Lewis, *Jack Carter's Law*, p. 65, 1974
- Well, well, well, Whistler thought, not a bad night's divvy for the cops.—Robert Campbell, *In La-La Land We Trust*, p. 141, 1986

2 a fool *UK, 1989*

- —Angela Devlin, *Prison Patter*, p. 46, 1996
- You look a right divvy, Darcy. He's lost it, Lads.—Paul Fraser and Shane Meadows, *TwentyFourSeven*, p. 13, 1997

divvy *adjective*

daft, foolish, idiotic *UK*

From **DIVVY** (a fool).

- —Patrick O'Shaughessy, *Market Traders' Slang*, 1979
- He said I looked like the first man on the moon, taking these massive, divvy steps about the place.—Dave Courtney, *Raving Lunacy*, p. 11, 2000

divvy up *verb*

to divide into shares *US, 1876*

A phonetic abbreviation of 'divide'.

- TILLEY: OK, we'll divvy it up . . . four ways!—*Tin Men*, 1987
- The first few hours after Henry's death were spent in tying up loose ends: opponents were squared and spoils divvied-up.—David Starkey, *Elizabeth*, p. 59, 2000

divvy van; divi-van *noun*

a police van *AUSTRALIA, 1982*

From '*div*isional van'.

- The sergeant had the inmate packed in a special divi-van and carted off to the Royal Melbourne Mental Home before he could finish a decade of the rosary.—Kerry Cue, *Crooks, Chooks and Bloody Ratbags*, p. 85, 1983
- [They collided] with all the force of a runaway divvy van.—Shane Maloney, *Nice Try*, p. 295, 1998

dixie *noun*

1 (especially in Victoria and Tasmania) a small cardboard ice-cream container *AUSTRALIA, 1941*

- —Jim Ramsay, *Cop It Sweet!*, p. 29, 1977
- I set a new Bay 13 record in eating 18 dixies between the lunch and tea sessions.—Rex Hunt, *Tall Tales – and True*, p. 66, 1994

2 unnecesssary body action *BARBADOS*

Recorded by Richard Allsopp in 1980.

Dixie *nickname*

the southeastern United States *US, 1859*

- Seniority rules in the Congress, which permit one-party Southern Senators and Representatives to control more than their share of committees, acount for continuance of its Dixie slant.—Jack Lait and Lee Mortimer, *Washington Confidential*, p. 6, 1951

Dixie cup *noun*

1 the traditional navy white hat , symbol of the American sailor since the C19 *US, 1973*

- —Gregory Clark, *Words of the Vietnam War*, p. 147, 1990
- When freshmen, or "plebes" at the U.S. Naval Academy in Annapolis, Maryland, finish their summer basic training, they trade in their "dixie cups" (sailor hats) for "covers" (officer hats)[.]—Jan Harold Brunvard, *American Folklore*, p. 484, 1996
- All three wore white navy "Dixie cup" hats, while one also sported a piratical black eye patch and a foul-looking stogie cigar.—James H. Cobb, *Sea Fighter*, p. 178, 2000

2 a woman who speaks with a southern accent *US*

- —Bill Davis, *Jawjacking*, p. 34, 1977

3 a female Red Cross worker in Vietnam *US*

- —Gregory Clark, *Words of the Vietnam War*, p. 147, 1990

4 a person who is considered to be utterly dispensable, who is used and then discarded *US*

- "'Cause he's a Dixie cup." Tommy grinned and refused further comment. Texaco didn't know what the hell that meant[.]—Stephen Cannell, *King Con*, p. 18, 1997

dixie lid *noun*

a child, a kid *UK*

Rhyming slang.

- —Ray Puxley, *Fresh Rabbit*, 1998

Dixie Trail *noun*

anal sex facilitated by Dixie Peach hair dressing as a lubricant *US*

- And the few times subseqeunt to my chirstening when circumstances brought me in contact with someone via the "Dixie Trail," I relived the keenest pleasures.—Angelo d'Arcangelo, *The Homosexual Handbook*, p. 99, 1968

DIY *adjective*

do-it-yourself, especially of household maintenance or repair *UK, 1955*

A colloquial abbreviation.

- The DIY guide to the future.—*The Guardian*, 16th October 2002

DIYer *noun*

a *do-it-yourself-er*, a person who tends to do his own household repairs and maintenance *UK, 1984*

- [Y]ou pretend to be a lady DIYer in distress and ask the appetising gent of your choice for his advice on, say, rewiring the bathroom[.] —*The Guardian*, 7th August 2000

Diz *nickname*

Dizzy Gillespie (1917–1993), a jazz trumpeter instrumental in the creation of bebop *US*

- Ah, yes, the Bird – and ole Diz – then here's Mis Sarah herself. — Ross Russell, *The Sound*, p. 24, 1961
- In that atmosphere, with the spiraled hints of Bird, Prez, Diz or Miles cuttin' up on somebody's box, we'd have orgies. — Odie Hawkins, *Black Casanova*, p. 163, 1984
- All the great black musicians – Bird, Diz, Thelonius, Bud Powell, Miles, Kenny Clarke, etc., etc. were first appreciated there. — Terry Southern, *Now Dig This*, p. 4, 1986

dizz *noun*

1 an odd, absent-minded person *US, 1963*

- — J.E. Lighter, *Historical Dictionary of American Slang, Volume I*, p. 610, 1994

2 marijuana *UK*

- — Mike Haskins, *Drugs*, p. 287, 2003

dizz *verb*

sleep; to sleep *UK*

A Royal Navy variation of **zizz**, perhaps in combination with 'doze'.

- — D. Bolster, *Roll on My Twelve*, 1945

dizzy *adjective*

scatterbrained *US, 1878*

- — Paul Baker, *Polari*, p. 172, 2002

dizzy limit *noun*

the utmost *AUSTRALIA, 1916*

- Oh, Christ, Tim, you're the dizzy limit! — Colleen McCullough, *Tim*, p. 17, 1975
- — Jim Ramsay, *Cop It Sweet!*, p. 29, 1977

dizzy three *noun*

a C-47A Skytrain plane, also known as a DC-3, most commonly used to transport people and cargo, but also used as a bomber and fighter *US*

- She was known affectionately as the "Gooney Bird," "Dak," and "Dizzy Three" to the men who flew her during World War II. — *San Francisco Chronicle*, p. 60, 18th January 1975

dj; deejay *noun*

a *d*isc *j*ockey *US, 1950*

- Hang the DJ, Hang the DJ, Hang the DJ[.] — The Smiths *Panic*, 1986
- In Jamaica, the DJ isn't the guy who spins the records (that's the selector), it's the bloke who chats over the music. As misnomers go, it's a good one, though, since DJ is short for disc jockey, and the whole art of reggae deejaying is vocally riding the riddim [rhythm]. — *Uncut*, p. 108, May 2001

DJ *noun*

1 men's formal evening wear, a *d*inner *j*acket *UK, 1967*

2 an agent of the Federal Bureau of Investigation *US, 1935*

An allusion to the *D*epartment of *J*ustice, home to the FBI. May be spelt out as 'deejay'.

- — Jay Robert Nash, *Dictionary of Crime*, p. 98, 1992

dj; deejay *verb*

to work as a disc jockey *US, 1985*

- [T]he various hip hop expressions (graffiti, breaking, Djing, rapping)[.] — Nelson George, *Hip Hop America*, p. 18, 1992

djamba *noun*

marijuana *US, 1938*

A West African word, now in wider usage.

- [T]o prohibit the export of the resin obtained from Indian hemp and the ordinary preparations of which the resin forms the base (such as hashish, esrar, chiras, djamba) to countries which have prohibited their use. — *Second Opium Conference 1924–5, The League of Nations Advisory Commitee on Traffic in Opium and Dangerous Drugs*,
- — Richard A. Spears, *The Slang and Jargon of Drugs and Drink*, p. 146, 1986
- — Mike Haskins, *Drugs*, p. 287, 2003

DKDC

I *d*on't *k*now, I *d*on't *c*are *US*

Combining a lack of intelligence with apathy.

- — Judi Sanders, *Da Bomb!*, p. 9, 1997

DL *noun*

▸ **on the DL**

down low, discreetly *US*

- — Connie Eble (Editor), *UNC-CH Campus Slang*, p. 3, March 1996
- On the DL, I know where the mojo is. — Gary K. Farlow, *Prison-ese: A Survivor's Guide to Speaking Prison Slang*, p. 17, 2002

DM's *noun*

Dr Martens™ heavy-duty boots *UK*

An abbreviation of the brand name. The boots were designed for industrial use and subsequently adopted as fashionwear, initially by skinheads and bootboys, then as a general fashion item for either sex.

- [T]he safety pin or DM's were used to establish an alternative mode to the dominant forms for teenage girls. — Shane J. Blackman, *Cool Places*, p. 207, 1998
- DM's remind me of the Undertones in 1979 – good year, good boots, good drugs. — Martin Roach (quoting Alan McGee), *Dr. Marten's Air Wair*, 1999
- I'm showing off a new pair of DMs today [...] Soon as I got these Martens home I went out back and rubbed them up with a brick[.] — John King, *Human Punk*, p. 5–6, 2000
- The most sought-after article of clothing, though, was the steelies, 12- to 14-hole, calf-high, steel-toed Doc Marten boots also called DMs or Docs[.] — Bill Valentine, *Gangs and Their Tattoos*, p. 58, 2000

DMT *noun*

dimethyltryptamine, a hallucinogenic drug *US*

- To a client whom he feels is sound enough to handle it, he also will sell LSD, mescaline, STP, DMT or pysilocybin. — Tom Robbins, *Another Roadside Attraction*, p. 57–58, 1971
- Acid is like being sucked up a tube, but DMT is like being shot out of a cannon. — Hunter S. Thompson, *Songs of the Doomed*, p. 113, 1990

DMZ *noun*

any place between two opposing factions or social forces, controlled by neither yet ceded by neither *US*

Originally a military term – 'demilitarised zone' – for an area dividing North and South Korea.

- TRAVIS: He wanted to go to the DMZ. BETSY: The DMZ? TRAVIS: South Bronx. The worst. — *Taxi Driver*, 1976
- The back room vibrated with rock music blasting from an enormous set of speakers attached to a stereo system Miguel had stolen, piece by piece, from shops down in the Nineteenth Precinct just below Ninety-sixth Street, the "DMZ" of the East Side. — Thomas Larry Adcock, *Precinct 19*, p. 71, 1984
- The Camelot was on the DMZ between the Heights and the last vestiges of old-time German-Irish Dempsy, and cops were always welcome. — Richard Price, *Clockers*, p. 99, 1992

DNF

in motorcyle racing, *d*id *n*ot *f*inish a race *US, 1970s*

- — Ed Radlauer, *Motorcylopedia*, p. 16, 1973

do *noun*

1 a party or social function *UK, 1824*

- Nothin' worse than the day after a do, an' no grog left. — Nino Culotta (John O'Grady), *They're A Weird Mob*, p. 111, 1957
- Reports or not, he'd have to get along to this 'do'. — John Wynnum, *Tar Dust*, p. 48, 1962
- All the senior officers from up and down the coast are here, for tonight's big do. — Ray Slattery, *Mobbs Mob*, p. 88, 1966
- Yoko Ono is throwing a little do in her suite at the Clift. — Armistead Maupin, *Babycakes*, p. 221, 1984
- A valet-parking girl, in a white shirt with a black bow tie and black trousers, took his car, sayhing, "You won't need a ticket, sir." Which meant that the do wouldn't be as big as some he'd had to attend lately. — Joseph Wambaugh, *Floaters*, p. 87, 1996
- She even gets calls Christmas Day, but can't work then as she's putting on her annual orphans' do. — *Lesbians on the Loose*, p. 34, 1997
- Every year Joe and Mary went up to Jerusalem for a big do called Passover Day. — Kel Richards, *The Aussie Bible*, p. 19, 2003

2 an action, deed, performance or event *UK*

- CLARICE: It's a poor do if you can't do what you like with your own property. — John O'Toole, *The Bush and the Tree [Six Granada Plays]*, p. 41, 1960

3 a person considered in terms of their sexual performance or willingness *AUSTRALIA, 1950*

- I thought everyone knew Nessie's an easy do. — Ward McNally, *Supper at Happy Harry's*, p. 34, 1982

4 a dose of drugs *US*

- Damn, I'm getting boogy. I hope you saved me a do, Snake, 'cause I'm sure gettin' sick. — Donald Goines, *Dopefiend*, p. 216, 1971
- Foxy left the spike sticking in the girl's arm and started to prepare his own Do. — Vernon E. Smith, *The Jones Men*, p. 20, 1974

5 in craps, a bet on the shooter *US*

- At the dice table, the professor would bet either on or against the shooter – otherwise known as do or don't, right or wrong – at $1,000 a shot on what may or may not have been a system. — Edward Lin, *Big Julie of Vegas*, p. 47, 1974

6 a hairdo *US, 1966*

- "I'm out there this morning," Darryl said, "talking to Tiffany, girl with the indian 'do." — Elmore Leonard, *Be Cool*, p. 182, 1999

DO *noun*

in hot rodding, *d*ual *o*verhead camshafts *US*

- — *Hot Rod Magazine*, p. 13, November 1948: 'Racing jargon'

do *verb*

1 to kill *UK, 1790*

- Kenny walked all over that racketland looking for a gun he could buy to shoot the elbows and kneecaps off of the berk who paid to have Matt done. — Emmett Grogan, *Ringolevio*, p. 203, 1972
- You fucking chancer. You fucking poxy chancer. You nearly fucking done the lot of us, didn't you? — Ted Lewis, *Jack Carter's Law*, p. 182, 1974
- If I knew anyone that took them [drugs], I'd fucking do 'em. — Paul E. Willis, *Profane Culture*, p. 14, 1978
- Let's go all the way, let's go for it! Let's do the whole fucking village. — *Platoon*, 1986
- That was something he picked up at the movies, that blowing away. Armand tried to think how his brothers used to say it. They would say they were going to do a guy. — Elmore Leonard, *Killshot*, p. 74, 1989
- You never say nuthin bot doin one! You... you never even say nuthin bout hittin one! — Jess Mowry, *Way Past Cool*, p. 36, 1992

2 to charge with, or prosecute for, or convict of a crime *UK, 1784*

- — Paul Tempest, *Lag's Lexicon*, 1950
- "Done for drunk", Done for speed". — Peter Laurie, *Scotland Yard*, p. 322, 1970
- The DPP considered prosecuting the Duke of Edinburgh after a traffic accident in the mid-1960s, and other royals have been done for speeding. — *New Society*, 22nd July 1982
- He was done for speeding in a built-up area. — Beale, 1984

3 to use up your money, especially to squander *AUSTRALIA, 1889*

- You'll finish up doing your dough that way. — John Wynnum, *Tar Dust*, p. 20, 1962
- I mean it's nothing for him to go to the races, do a bundle, and come home laughing and joking like nothing's happened. — Paul Vautin, *Turn It Up!*, p. 134, 1995
- [T]hey will fight tooth and nail to prevent any compensation being paid to those who do their money in that circumstance[.] — Kelvin Thomson, *Hansard (Commonwealth of Australia)*, 12th March 1998

4 to assault, to beat up *UK, 1796*

- — Angela Devlin, *Prison Patter*, p. 46, 1996

5 to injure (a part of the body) *AUSTRALIA*

- I'm sorry, mate, but I'll have to go off. I've done it completely. — Richie Benaud, *Spin me a Spinner*, p. 120, 1963
- Chances are you'll do your back, rip your boardies or fall flat off. — *Tracks*, p. 126, October 1992
- — Phillip Gwynne, *Deadly Unna?*, p. 64, 1998

6 to rob *UK, 1774*

- How many banks was it you've done in your life, about fifty? — Elmore Leonard, *Bandits*, p. 97, 1987
- "We're not doing a house," says Becca. "There's a lot of rich bastards there though," says Kelly. — Cath Staincliffe, *Trainers*, p. 59, 1999

7 to swindle, to deceive, to trick *UK, 1641*

8 to have sex with *UK, 1650*

- I tried some sex banter with him but Axel was looking fierce. "I'd like to do some of them," he whispered, "I'd like to do some of them." — Clancy Sigal, *Going Away*, p. 258, 1961
- And men take her to loveless beds when they have nothing else and no one better to do. — Sue Rhodes, *And when she was bad she was popular*, p. 104, 1968
- DALLAS: I'll pay ya twenty if you go back there and do mah husband. BUTT-HEAD: Uh, you want us to do a guy? Huh huh. No way. BEAVIS: Umm, I don't know Butt-head. That is a lot of money. Maybe if we close our eyes and pretend he's a chick. — Mike Judge and Joe Stillman, *Beavis and Butt-Head Do America*, p. 29, 1997
- "I don't do divorced men." Karen gave me a tense smile and lowered her voice to a confidential whisper. "You know, Lisa, I probably shouldn't say this, but the word do sometimes has sexual connotations." — Rita Ciresi, *Pink Slip*, p. 29, 1999
- Gwenno might even go to bed with you. Let yew fuckin do her, like. — Niall Griffiths, *Sheepshagger*, p. 142, 2001

9 to perform oral sex upon someone *US*

- — Donald Webster Cory and John P. LeRoy, *The Homosexual and His Society*, p. 263, 1963: 'A lexicon of homosexual slang'

10 to consume, especially an alcoholic drink *UK, 1857*

- Could you do a cold stubbie? — Sam Weller, *Old Bastards I Have Met*, p. 22, 1979

11 to use drugs *US, 1967*

- Within three days, a homeless kid who finds himself or herself in Kings Cross [Sydney] will be sexually assaulted; within a week the kid will be doing drugs, and by 21 the kid will be dead. — *The Catholic Weekly*, 23rd February 2003

12 when combined with a name (of a very recognisable person or group) that is used as a generic noun, to behave in the manner of that person or group of people *UK, 1934*

- So you won't be doing a Madonna on us? — *Details Magazine*, July 1992
- I worry that the PM [Tony Blair] spends too much time listening to his beloved entrepreneurial friends advising him to 'do a Thatcher' at this stage of his government. — *The Observer*, 24th March 2002

13 to visit as a tourist or pleasure-seeker *UK, 1858*

- Our number 20 did Paris better than a tourist bus. — *The Guardian*, 27th November 1999

14 to suffice, to answer its purpose *US, 1846*

- It will do for now. — *The Guardian*, 13th September 2000

▸ do cards

to steal or forge credit cards *UK*

- — Angela Devlin, *Prison Patter*, p. 46, 1996

▸ do it

1 to have sex *IRELAND, 1923*

- Why, oh, Christ, why had he ever done it with that bitch? — James T. Farrell, *Tournament Star*, p. 68, 1946
- But how do you get the clap? By doing it, and anybody who does that dirty thing obviously deserves to get the clap. — Lenny Bruce, *How to Talk Dirty and Influence People*, p. 54, 1965
- [D]oing it everyway we could think of any-old place we happened to be, in fact, we did it in so many places that Denver was covered with our pecker-tracks. — Neal Cassady, *The First Third*, p. 153, 1971
- Louisianans do it Bayoutifully — *Maledicta*, p. 174–179, Winter 1980
- I couldn't have been a day older than six when Loretta and I started doin' it. — Odie Hawkins, *Black Casanova*, p. 9, 1984
- Well, actually, my one girlfriend who had kids, Alice, and she would compalin about how she and Gary never did it any more. — *When Harry Met Sally*, 1989
- Then you get to do it with a condom. — *Sleepless in Seattle*, 1993

2 to defecate; to urinate *UK, 1922*

Euphemistic.

- When one of us had to urinate, he just did it in his pants, knowing that the following day the heat from the sun would dry them out. — Henry Steele Commager *The Story of World War II*, p. 109, 1945

▸ do like a dinner

to overcome completely in a fight or competition; to vanquish *AUSTRALIA, 1847*

Punning on the phrase 'dinner's done' (dinner is ready).

- [I]t was election day and Labor was going to get done like a dinner[.] — Helen Garner, *Monkey Grip*, p. 184, 1977

▸ do the dirty on

to trick or otherwise treat unfairly *UK, 1914*

- Do not even have a mini thingio about doing the dirty on that cunt. — Kevin Sampson, *Clubland*, p. 167, 2002

▸ do the do

to have sex *US*

- — Kenn "Naz" Young, *Naz's Dictionary of Teen Slang*, p. 33, 1993

▸ do the Harold Holt; do the Harold

to decamp *AUSTRALIA*

From rhyming slang for 'bolt'. Harold Holt (1908–67) was an Australian prime minister whose office was cut short when he went ocean swimming one afternoon and presumably drowned – his body was never recovered.

- Then we could do the Harold Holt – 'Bolt' he decoded for me – up to Joh country. — Kathy Lette, *Girls' Night Out*, p. 169, 1987

▸ do the thing

to have sex *US*

- — *Current Slang*, p. 5, Summer 1968

▸ do your bit

to do your share and so contribute to the greater good, especially in times of trial or conflict *UK, 1902*

- You could argue that I did my bit and others didn't. — *The Guardian*, 1st February 2003

▸ do your do

to prepare your hairdo *US*

- — *Adult Video News*, p. 44, August 1995

▸ do yourself in

to commit suicide *UK*

A personalised variation of **DO IN** (to kill).

- He'd probably, quite seriously, do himself in. There'd be nothing else to live for. — Kevin Sampson, *Powder*, p. 33, 1999

▸ you'll do me/us

you are entirely suitable for a task; we are more than happy to be supporting you *AUSTRALIA, 1952*

Used as a cry of encouragement and support.

- Rock it in, Harry! You'll do us. —John Morrison, *Stories of the Waterfront*, p. 138, 1955
- He'll do me, old Nesbitt. —J.E. MacDonnell, *Don't Gimme the Ships*, p. 21, 1960
- You'll do me for a mate in a brawl, Ivor. —Wal Watkins, *Andamooka*, p. 167, 1971
- "Good on yer padre." "You're OK, mate." "You'll do us, padre." —William Nagel, *The Odd Angry Shot*, p. 50, 1975

DOA *noun*

1 a more than usually dangerous variety of heroin *UK, 1998*

From the acronym DOA (dead on arrival); **DEAD ON ARRIVAL** (heroin).

- —Robert Ashton, *This Is Heroin*, p. 205, 2002
- —Mike Haskins, *Drugs*, p. 283, 2003

2 phencyclidine, the recreational drug known as PCP or angel dust *US*

The abbreviation is for **DEAD ON ARRIVAL** – the results of a PCP overdose.

- —Peter Johnson, *Dictionary of Street Alcohol and Drug Terms*, p. 60, 1993

doable *adjective*

sexually attractive enough as to warrant the speaker's gift of having sex *US*

- —Pamela Munro, *U.C.L.A. Slang*, p. 58, 1997
- —Don R. McCreary (Editor), *Dawg Speak*, 2001

do as you like *noun*

a bicycle *UK, 1960*

Rhyming slang for 'bike'.

- Hey, that's a new do as you like! Where are you going? —*The Sweeney*, p. 9, 1976

doat *noun*

someone or something fit to be doted on *IRELAND*

- —Honor Tracey, *Year of Grace*, 1975

dob *noun*

a small lump or dollop, usually applied to butter, jam, cream, etc *UK, 1984*

Originally dialect.

DOB *noun*

a lesbian *US*

An abbreviation of '*d*aughters *o*f *B*ilitis'.

- —*Maledicta*, p. 138, Summer/Winter 1982: 'Dyke diction: the language of lesbians'

dob *verb*

to inform on someone *AUSTRALIA, 1955*

- The one moral code passed on to each generation of Australians since the convict days, is never to dob. —Kathy Lette, *Girls' Night Out*, p. 98, 1987
- —Kylie Mole (Maryanne Fahey), *My Diary*, p. 93, 1988
- Are you gunna dob on me, Beryl? —Tim Winton, *Cloudstreet*, p. 259, 1991
- —Harry Orsman, *A Dictionary of Modern New Zealand Slang*, p. 40, 1999

dobber *noun*

1 a despicable person *UK*

- And it keeps him away – it keeps the big dobber out of our hair. —Kevin Sampson, *Clubland*, p. 41, 2002
- We aren't at all impressed you dobber. —*X-Ray*, p. 29, May 2003

2 an informer; a telltale *AUSTRALIA, 1955*

- Jees, you dob me...and it's the last bit o' dobbin' you'll ever do. My mob don't take dobbers easy. —Xavier Herbert, *Poor Fellow My Country*, p. 954, 1975
- He was a champion dobber. And of course he always got belted up after school. —Phillip Gwynne, *Deadly Unna?*, p. 128, 1998

3 a fool, an idiot *UK: SCOTLAND*

Glasgow slang.

- Ah telt ye Ah wantit decaf, ya dobber! —Michael Munro, *The Complete Patter*, p. 43, 1996

4 the penis *US, 1974*

Also 'dob'.

- Lad had a big mad hairy dobber on him. —Kevin Sampson, *Outlaws*, p. 12, 2001
- Pullin yer little dobber ten times a day. —Niall Griffiths, *Kelly + Victor*, p. 336, 2002

dobber-in *noun*

an informer; a telltale *AUSTRALIA, 1958*

- The Sergeant kept up with local events through all manner of dobbers-in. —Kerry Cue, *Crooks, Chooks and Bloody Ratbags*, p. 178, 1983

dobbing-in *noun*

informing *AUSTRALIA*

- Years later, during his dobbing-in frenzy, Ray told police that Collins' prisoner rehabilitation business, Breakout Printing, was manufacturing passports for crims on the run. —Donald Catchlove, *Ray Denning My Life and Time*, p. 12, 1994

do bears shit in the woods?

yes; a nonsense retort used as an affirmative answer to a silly question, often sarcastic *US*

Often mixed with the synonymous 'Is the Pope Catholic?' to achieve **DOES THE POPE SHIT IN WOODS?**.

- "Is it gonna be hot?" the kid said. "Does a bear shit in the woods?" Dillon said. —George V. Higgins, *The Friends of Eddie Doyle*, p. 210, 1971

dobie *noun*

a Doberman Pinscher dog *US, 1981*

- To cut the tension, he said: "Ten bucks it's a Dobie." "No way," said Danny Pogue. "I say Rotweiller." —Carl Hiaasen, *Native Tongue*, p. 170, 1991
- I was at a bachelor party for Zane where they had these two Doberman Pinschers. The Dobies were on these stairs watching everything. —Anthony Petkovich, *The X Factory*, p. 83, 1997

dob in *verb*

1 to inform against someone; to tell on someone *AUSTRALIA, 1954*

- I don't expect you to dob your shipmate in. —J.E. MacDonnell, *Don't Gimme the Ships*, p. 122, 1960
- It was Liz Short who dobbed us both in. —*Alvin Purple*, p. 99, 1974
- I break rank from C company 3 RAR and run like buggery up the hill, wondering all the way whether some mongrel had dobbed me in for going AWOL the week before to visit the Barossa Valley. —Martin Cameron, *A Look at the Bright Side*, 1988
- But they never dobbed him in. —Richard Francis, *The Rialto*, p. 87, 1999
- I'll have to dob him in to the Fathers. —Pete McCarthy, *McCarthy's Bar*, p. 318, 2000

2 to contribute funds *AUSTRALIA, 1956*

- Wharfies will always dob in for a strike fund. —Frank Hardy, *The Outcasts of Foolgarah*, p. 48, 1971

do-boy *noun*

a male who does whatever his girlfriend tells him to do *US*

- —Don R. McCreary (Editor), *Dawg Speak*, 2001

doc *noun*

1 a *doc*tor *US, 1840*

- All medicine, docs cheap, very modern. —Jack Kerouac, *Letter to Carolyn Cassady*, p. 363, 3rd June 1952
- [H]e went to see the prison doc. —Joel Rose, *Kill Kill Faster Faster*, p. 158, 1997

2 a *doc*ument *US, 1868*

Originally a military use, especially in the plural, for 'official documents of identity or record'.

3 in computing, *doc*umentation *US*

- —Eric S. Raymond, *The New Hacker's Dictionary*, p. 129, 1991

docco *noun*

a documentary *UK*

- [A]ll talking about this club they'd been to or that docco they were making. —John Williams, *Cardiff Dead*, p. 148, 2000

doc in the box *noun*

a walk-in medical clinic *US*

- —Sally Williams, *"Strong" Words*, p. 139, 1994

dock *noun*

▸ in dock

1 of a motor vehicle, being serviced or repaired *UK, 1984*

- If your car is essential to you, check that your policy undertakes to keep you on the road when your car is in dock. —*Daily Telegraph*, 21st February 2001

2 in hospital, or otherwise unable to carry on as usual due to injury or medical treatment *UK, 1785*

- "He's been in dock," Mr. Stroll whispered on, as if through frightful draughts of cigarette smoke. "Laid up. Spinal." —John Le Carré, *Tinker, Tailor, Soldier, Spy*, 1974

dock asthma *noun*

in a trial, the shocked gasps given by the accused as accusations are made or proved *UK, 1977*

The gasps are ironically considered as symptoms of a notional disease.

- —Angela Devlin, *Prison Patter*, p. 46, 1996

docker *noun*

a partially smoked cigarette that has been thrown away or extinguished for use later *UK*

- Just give me a fag. I hev to pick up dockers, no tobacco.—Geoffrey Fletcher, *Down Among the Meths Men*, p. 54, 1966
- —Jeff Nuttall, *King Twist*, 1979

docker's ABC *noun*

*a*le, *b*accy (tobacco), *c*unt *UK, 1984*

A worker's shopping-list in the spirit of 'wine, women and song', especially well used in Liverpool.

docker's hankie *noun*

the act of clearing the nostrils by blowing the contents onto the ground *UK*

- The rude peasant cheerfully discharging his snot on the ground, first through one nostril and then through the other (sometimes called a "docker's hankie").—Michael Thompson, *Rubbish Theory*, 1979

dockie *noun*

a dockside worker *AUSTRALIA, 1935*

- But scores of workers – including dockies, wharfies and chippies – regard the Pacific Hotel in Stephen St as a second home.—*Glebe and Western Weekly*, p. 2, 8th November 1989

dock monkey *noun*

a worker who loads and unloads trucks *US, 1939*

- —Montie Tak, *Truck Talk*, p. 45, 1971

dock walloper *noun*

1 a worker who loads and unloads trucks *US*

- —Montie Tak, *Truck Talk*, p. 45, 1971

2 a thief who steals cargo before it has been unloaded or passed through customs *US*

- —Rachel S. Epstein and Nina Liebman, *Biz Speak*, p. 65, 1986

doco *noun*

a documentary *AUSTRALIA*

- Since I arrived in England, in the wake of a guilty furore over the BBC's doco Cathy Come Home, the number of homeless families has doubled[.]—Richard Neville writing in 'Oz', 1972, *Out Of My Mind*, 1996

Docs *noun*

Dr Martens™ footwear *US*

- —Judi Sanders, *Faced and Faded, Hanging to Hurl*, p. 12, 1993
- —Steven Daly and Nalthaniel Wice, *alt.culture*, p. 65, 1995
- [N]o way were my eight hole Docs coming off[.]—Shaun Ryder, *Shaun Ryder... in His Own Words*, 1996
- If ever there were status symbols in the punk community, Docs rated up there with mohawks, safety pins, and black leather and flight jackets.— Editors of Ben is Dead, *Retrohell*, p. 60, 1997
- Fuck! I wish I'd worn my Docs!—Dave Courtney, *Stop the Ride I Want to Get Off*, p. 227, 1999
- The most sought-after article of clothing, though, was the steelies, 12- to 14-hole, calf-high, steel-toed Doc Marten boots also called DMs or Docs[.]—Bill Valentine, *Gangs and Their Tattoos*, p. 58, 2000

doctor *noun*

1 (used of children) the exploration of each other's genitals *US*

- We played doctor in the woods.—Leonard Cohen, *Beautiful Losers*, p. 23, 1966
- One day, the other female member and I were asked to play "Doctor" by the club's other members.—*Screw*, p. 7, 15th December 1969
- During all those school years we children had been playing "doctor" by sticking popsicles in our underpants.—Jefferson Poland and Valerie Alison, *The Records of the San Francisco Sexual Freedom League*, p. 111, 1971
- We didn't play "house" or "Doctor" or any of that. We had sexual intercourse—Odie Hawkins, *Scars and Memories*, p. 136, 1987

2 a male with a large penis *US*

Homosexual usage.

- —Roger Blake, *The American Dictionary of Sexual Terms*, p. 60, 1964
- —Dale Gordon, *The Dominion Sex Dictionary*, p. 59, 1967

3 an expert *US*

- —Connie Eble (Editor), *UNC-CH Campus Slang*, p. 3, Spring 1990

4 a bookmaker who declines to take a bet, telling the bettor he will 'get better' *AUSTRALIA*

- —Ned Wallish, *The Truth Dictionary of Racing Slang*, p. 23, 1989

5 a person who sells illegally manufactured alcohol *US, 1960*

- —Frederic G. Cassidy, *Dictionary of American Regional English, Volume II*, p. 99, 1991

6 MDMA, the recreational drug best known as ecstasy *UK, 1998*

Possibly punning on the degrees MD and MA.

- —Mike Haskins, *Drugs*, p. 289, 2003

7 (especially in Western Australia) a refreshing wind coming after a period of stifling weather *AUSTRALIA, 1870*

Preceded by a placename to form proper nouns for commonly occurring winds of this type, such as the Albany Doctor, Esperance Doctor, Fremantle Doctor, etc.

- We used to hear it coming through the bush at Norseman and say, "Here comes the Esperance Doctor".—*Wordmap (www.abc.net.au/wordmap)*, 2003

▸go for the doctor

to race a horse at top speed *AUSTRALIA*

- Don't make a forward move until the half mile, then take it steady, go for the doctor after the turn into the striaght.—Wilda Moxham, *The Apprentice*, p. 166, 1969
- There was only one thing to do – go for the doctor and make Knox chase him.—Joe Andersen, *Winners Can Laugh*, p. 153, 1982

doctor *verb*

1 to falsify, to adulterate, to tamper *UK, 1774*

- You doctored the log books!—*A Few Good Men*, 1992

2 in cricket, to illegally tamper with the condition of the ball to the bowler's advantage *UK, 1996*

- —Keith Foley, *A Dictionary of Cricketing Terminology*, p. 108, 1998

doctor and nurse; doctor *noun*

a purse *UK*

Rhyming slang.

- A mugger will snatch a "doctor" and leg it.—Ray Puxley, *Fresh Rabbit*, 1998

Doctor Blue; Dr Blue *noun*

used in hospitals as a code announcement that a patient is in cardiac arrest *US*

- —*American Speech*, p. 203, Fall-Winter 1973: 'The language of nursing'

Doctor Cotton; Dr Cotton *adjective*

rotten *UK, 1932*

Rhyming slang.

- —Julian Franklyn, *A Dictionary of Rhyming Slang*, 1960

Doctor Crippen; Dr Crippen *noun*

dripping (melted fat used like butter) *UK*

Rhyming slang, formed on the name of the celebrated murderer Dr Hawley Harvey (1862–1910).

- —Julian Franklyn, *A Dictionary of Rhyming Slang*, 1961

Doctor Dre; Dr Dre *adjective*

homosexual *UK*

Rhyming slang for **GAY**, formed from the stage name of hip-hop performer and producer Andre Young (b.1965).

- —Bodmin Dark, *Dirty Cockney Rhyming Slang*, 2003

Doctor Feelgood; Dr Feelgood *noun*

1 any doctor who specialises in energy-giving injections *US, 1973*

- Dr. Feelgood is, actually, a generic term. There are four of them in New York City, all frequented by the social elite, show business folk, and artists with money.—Jim Carroll, *Forced Entries*, p. 75, 1987
- A roadie enters the room, telling Pink it's showtime, but getting no response he calls the doctor, who administers a shot to keep the star "going for the show." 'Doctor Feelgoods', as they were known, where common on huge tours where hundreds of thousands were at stake at every gig.—Cliff Jones, *Another Brick in the Wall*, p. 132, 1996

2 heroin *UK*

- —Robert Ashton, *This Is Heroin*, p. 205, 2002
- —Mike Haskins, *Drugs*, p. 283, 2003

Doctor Jekyll and Mister Hyde; Dr Jekyll and Mr Hyde *noun*

the recreational drug methaqualone, best known as Quaaludes™ *US*

- By 1972 it was one of the most popular drugs of abuse in the United States and was known as love drug, heroin for lovers, Dr. Jekyll and Mr. Hyde, sopors, sopes, ludes, mandrakes and quacks.—Marilyn Carroll and Gary Gallo, *Methaqualone*, p. 18, 1985

Doctor K; Dr K *nickname*

Dwight Gooden (b.1964), a right-handed pitcher (1984–2000) with an immortal early career and an acceptable mid-career *US*

In the shorthand of baseball scorekeeping, a 'K' is a 'strikeout', and 'Doc' Gooden had many.

Doctor Legg; Dr Legg *noun*
an egg *UK*
Rhyming slang, formed on the name of a minor character in the BBC television soap opera *EastEnders*.
• —Ray Puxley, *Fresh Rabbit*, 1998

Doctor Livingstone, I presume
a catchphrase greeting used for any fortuitous or unexpected meeting *UK, 1891*
Adopted from Henry Morton Stanley's greeting, in 1871, to African explorer David Livingstone.

Doctor Pepper; Dr Pepper *noun*
one of the several surface-to-air missile patterns used by the North Vietnamese against American aircraft during the Vietnam war *US*
Missile approaches from the ten o'clock, two o'clock and four o'clock positions; 'ten-two-and-four' was a Dr Pepper slogan.
• —Gregory Clark, *Words of the Vietnam War*, p. 152, 1990

doctor shopping *noun*
the practice of visiting mutliple physicians to obtain multiple prescriptions for otherwise illegal drugs *US*
A common practice of drug addicts and suppliers of drug addicts. A Palm Beach, Florida, affidavit and application for a search warrant dated 25th November 2003, stated: 'Mr Limbaugh's actions violate the letter, and spirit of section 893.13(7)(a)8, commonly known as "Doctor Shopping"'.

Doctor Thomas; Dr Thomas *noun*
a black person who rejects black culture and takes on the culture of the dominant white society *US*
An elaboration of the common **UNCLE TOM**, coined long before Clarence Thomas became the prototype of the concept.
• —Edith A. Folb, *runnin' down some lines*, p. 235, 1980

Doctor White; Dr White *noun*
1 a drug addiction *US*
• —J.E. Schmidt, *Narcotics Lingo and Lore*, p. 45, 1959
• —Jay Robert Nash, *Dictionary of Crime*, p. 106, 1992

2 cocaine *US*
• —Richard A. Spears, *The Slang and Jargon of Drugs and Drink*, p. 146, 1986

Doctor Who; Dr Who *noun*
a prison warder *UK*
Rhyming slang for **SCREW** (a prison warder), based on a time-travelling television hero first seen in 1963.
• —Angela Devlin, *Prison Patter*, p. 48, 1996

docu *noun*
a *docu*mentary film or television programme *UK*
As a prefix, such as in 'docudrama' (a documentary drama), 'docu' has been conventional since 1961.
• Mondo Mod, docu about a really shit band[.]—*Mixmag*, p. 63, June 2003

docy *noun*
the female breast *BAHAMAS*
• —John A. Holm, *Dictionary of Bahamian English*, p. 62, 1982

Doc Yak *noun*
a doctor whose reputation is less than sterling *US*
From a syndicated comic strip that last appeared in 1935.
• I did come up to Your Honour's courtroom five weeks ago, but then Old Doc Yak – what is his name? The man from Washington – Oh, Dr. McNarry.—Meyer Levin, *Compulsion*, p. 378, 1956

do-dad *noun*
in American football, a blocking strategy in which offensive players cross over and block each other's defensive opposite *US*
• —Kyle Rote, *The Language of Pro Football*, p. 112, 1966

dodad *noun*
▷ see: **DOODAD**

doddle *noun*
an objective acheived with ease; in sport, an easy win or a simple victory *UK, 1937*
Probably from 'dawdle' or 'toddle', implying a 'walk-over', which is consistent with its earliest use in racing circles, but possibly from Scottish 'doddle', a lump of homemade toffee (hence something desirable and easily acquired). It is recorded with the meaning 'money very easily obtained' in Scotland in 1934.
• [O]nly too easy in fact it was a doddle[.]—Frank Norman, *Bang To Rights*, p. 111, 1958
• It's an open nick [prison]. Be a doddle.—Anthony Masters, *Minder*, p. 5, 1984
• I remember thinking that it would be a doddle – being a mum, I mean.—Mary Hooper, *(megan)2*, p. 80, 1999
• Bloody hell – you posh birds are a doddle to sucker.—Colin Butts, *Is Harry Still on the Boat?*, p. 31, 2003

doddle *verb*
to achieve; to win something very easily *UK*
• I think she [a filly] started at even money but anyway she doddled it. —John Winton, *Never Go to Sea*, 1963

dodge *noun*
a scam, a swindle *UK, 1638*
• Why, once in Cuba he even cleaned out Babe Ruth with the fixed-race dodge.—Guy Owen, *The Flim-Flam Man and the Apprentice Grifter*, p. 17, 1972
• You're up to all the dodges, son. I trust you.—Anthony Masters, *Minder*, p. 125, 1984
• "As a matter of fact, I have a friend who needs an operation." "Watch yourself," Torino advised. "I myself have been taken by the old 'I need an operation' dodge."—Robert Campbell, *Alice in La-La Land*, p. 88, 1987

▸ **on the dodge**
in hiding from the police *US*
• Leo had been living on the dodge for over three years with wanted sheets out in a dozen states, his photograh decorating every post office wall in America.—Emmett Grogan, *Final Score*, p. 22, 1976

Dodge *noun*
▸ **get out of Dodge; get the hell out of Dodge**
to leave, usually with some haste *US, 1965*
A loose allusion to the Wild West as epitomised by Dodge City, Kansas, and the seriousness of an order by the authorities to leave town.
• Coming off the target Jack made a gut decision. "Head straight for home plate, Thunder; let's get the hell out of Dodge."—Richard Herman, *The Warbirds*, p. 295, 1989
• The pilot had some problem, so he aimed it over the sea, trimmed up the controls to keep it that way till it ran out of fuel and splashed in, and then got the hell out of Dodge.—Dennis Marvicsin and Jerold Greenfield, *Maverick*, p. 92, 1990
• That gives us forty minutes to get the fuck outta Dodge, which, if you do what I say when I say it, should be plenty.—*Pulp Fiction*, 1994

dodge *verb*
▸ **dodge the column**
to shirk, to avoid your duty, work or responsibility *UK, 1919*
Originally military.
• Why do we shrink from leaving the system the way it is and improving the High Court/sheriff court structure and instead dodge the column altogether?—Lord Macauley of Bragar, *Lords Hansard*, 6th March 1997
• Young [Russian] men dodge the column partly because service is no longer seen as a patriotic duty[.]—*Daily Telegraph*, 9th September 2000

Dodge City *nickname*
an enemy-controlled area south of Da Nang, the scene of heavy fighting in November 1968; anywhere in Vietnam with a strong Viet Cong presence *US, 1969*
• —Linda Reinberg, *In the Field*, p. 64, 1991
• I got a letter from him and he said he was going on an operation into "Dodge City," which is close to An Hoa."—Joseph T. Ward, *Dear Mom*, p. 92, 1991

dodger *noun*
1 a small advertising leaflet *US, 1879*
• I'll please my bloody self whether I read the dodger or attend the rally.—Sam Weller, *Old Bastards I Have Met*, p. 110, 1979
• —Joe McKennon, *Circus Lingo*, p. 30, 1980

2 a shunting truck *UK*
• —Harvey Sheppard, *Dictionary of Railway Slang*, 1970

3 bread *AUSTRALIA, 1897*
• Smack us in the eye with another hunk o' dodger, matey.—Nino Culotta (John O'Grady), *They're A Weird Mob*, p. 51, 1957
• —Jim Ramsay, *Cop It Sweet!*, p. 30, 1977

dodger *adjective*
excellent, fine *AUSTRALIA, 1941*
• When we got through the valley mouth everything was dodger.—Dal Stivens, *The Gambling Ghost*, 1953

dodgy *noun*

an informer *UK*

From the adjectival sense as 'unreliable', perhaps shortened from 'dodgy geezer' or similar.

- —Angela Devlin, *Prison Patter*, p. 46, 1996

dodgy *adjective*

1 of doubtful character or legality; dubious *UK*

Popularised in the 1960s by the comedian Norman Vaughan as a catchphrase, with an accompanying thumbs-down gesture. The thumbs-up opposite was 'swingin!'.

- He didn't want to have to explain why he had spent so much squad money on a didgy operation.—Lance Peters, *The Dirty Half-Mile*, p. 188, 1979
- Playing it's a little dodgy for me because I don't really enjoy the environment.—*Juice*, p. 61, 1996
- I don't have a bad bone in my body. I was dodgy, but not mean or violent or anything like that.—*Sydney Morning Herald*, 15th March 2003

2 risky *UK, 1898*

- It would have been too dodgy swagging gear into Bella's drum at 3 a.m.—Charles Raven, *Underworld Nights*, p. 22, 1956

3 stolen *UK, 1861*

- [S]et him to work screwing [burgling] – send him out with a pound of jelly [gelignite], dets [detonators], or a dodgy twirl [key].—Derek Raymond (Robin Cook), *The Crust on its Uppers*, p. 57, 1962

dodo *noun*

1 a fool *US, 1898*

- Thad is acting like a complete dodo. For a man his age his daddyhood antics border on the absurd.—Sandra Brown, *Adam's Fall*, p. 31, 1988

2 an aviation cadet who has not completed basic training *US, 1933*

- In normal times a cadet who had completed primary training became an upperclassmen and was encouraged to haze the young "dodos."—Charles A. Martin, *The Last Great Ace*, p. 116, 1998

do down *verb*

to get the better of someone, financially or otherwise; to harm someone's reputation by spreading gossip or rumour *UK, 1937*

doe *noun*

a woman *UK, 1909*

- I have met a few bent does who specialised in some definite graft [criminal endeavour], but not many.—Charles Raven, *Underworld Nights*, p. 20, 1956

doer *noun*

1 an energetic person who gets on with the job; a person who tackles problems or setbacks with good humour *AUSTRALIA, 1902*

- —Wilda Moxham, *The Apprentice*, p. 177, 1969
- —Jim Ramsay, *Cop It Sweet!*, p. 30, 1977
- Then I'll be holding up my end. Proving to myself, at least, that I'm a doer as well as my older relatives.—Ward McNally, *Supper at Happy Harry's*, p. 88, 1982

2 the person responsible for a specific crime, especially a murder *US*

- Yeah, well, he says he can serve up one of the do-ers on the Henderson job.—Richard Price, *Clockers*, p. 40, 1992

3 in horse racing, a horse as a performer – either good or poor *UK*

- —Rita Cannon, *Let's Go Racing*, p. 71, 1948

doer and gone; doer 'n' gone *adjective*

very far away *SOUTH AFRICA, 1972*

From Afrikaans for 'far away'; a synonym for **HELL AND GONE**.

does Rose Kennedy have a black dress?

yes; a sarcastic nonsense retort used as an affirmative answer to a silly question *AUSTRALIA*

- —*Maledicta*, p. 93, 1986–1987: 'Australian maledicta'

does she?

used as a euphemism for 'does she (or, is she likely to) have sex?' *UK*

Likely to have been used, on and off, since the 1920s, but not recorded until 1969.

does the Pope shit in the woods?

yes; a nonsense retort used as an affirmative answer to a silly question, often sarcastic *UK*

The result of combining synonymous **DO BEARS SHIT IN THE WOODS?** and 'Is the Pope Catholic?'.

- "So you won't be wanting a fry-up then?" asked Sonia, mock-examining her nails. "Does the Pope shit in the woods?"—Greg Williams, *Diamond Geezers*, p. 134, 1997
- "Nother drink?" he said to the Colonel, picking up the pint glasses they'd both emptied quick time. "Pope shit in the woods," said the Colonel and Mazz laughed and walked over to the bar.—John Williams, *Cardiff Dead*, p. 106, 2000
- But did they give up? Does the Pope shit in the woods?—Tony Wilson, *24 Hour Party People*, p. 207, 2002

dof *adjective*

stupid, idiotic, muddled *SOUTH AFRICA, 1979*

- —Penny Silva, *A Dictionary of South African English*, p. 180, 1996

doffie *noun*

a stupid, idiotic or muddled person *SOUTH AFRICA, 1991*

- —Penny Silva, *A Dictionary of South African English*, p. 180, 1996

do-flicky *noun*

any small tool the name of which escapes the speaker *BARBADOS*

- —Frank A. Collymore, *Barbadian Dialect*, p. 40, 1965

do for *verb*

to beat severely, to kill *UK, 1740*

- —Angela Devlin, *Prison Patter*, p. 46, 1996

dog *noun*

1 an unattractive woman or man *US, 1937*

Originally by men of women which, in the UK, has remained the predominant sense.

- And Suzie better not be a dog.—Barry Humphries, *A Nice Night's Entertainment*, p. 171, 1978
- What's the difference between a dog and a fox? About six beers.—*Maledicta*, p. 291, 1988–1989
- Rex, if you are going to play up on Lynne, you could do better than that. She's a dog.—Rex Hunt, *Tall Tales – and True*, p. 9, 1994
- [T]he woman on the door of the clip-joint was the same "old dog" (as the Licensing Officer had poetically described her)[.]—Kitty Churchill, *Thinking of England*, p. 191, 1995
- [T]hey did use to bring home some right old dogs and slappers.—Dave Courtney, *Stop the Ride I Want to Get Off*, p. 237, 1999
- She might be a slag and a dog, but anybody that thinks they can fuck with my family is going to find out different.—Val McDermid, *Keeping on the Right Side of the Law*, p. 179, 1999
- Give us the fucking beasts, la, give us the dogs any fucking time.—Kevin Sampson, *Clubland*, p. 85, 2002

2 a sexually transmitted infection *US*

- —Joseph E. Ragen and Charles Finston, *Inside the World's Toughest Prison*, p. 797, 1962: 'Penitentiary and underworld glossary'
- —*Maledicta*, p. 228, Summer/Winter 1981: 'Sex and the single soldier'

3 a informer to the police or, in prison, to the prison authorities *AUSTRALIA, 1848*

- [T]he worst thing you can call a prisoner is a dog.—Ray Denning, *Prison Diaries*, p. 31, 1978
- Old Bob spat at him. 'Only dogs work wif screws.'—Bob Jewson, *Stir*, p. 31, 1980
- 'Some arsehole dog gave us up to the pigs,' he growled.—Kathy Lette, *Girls' Night Out*, p. 99, 1987
- It wasn't easy to do, I didn't want them to think I was weak or a dog but I had to get away and I did.—Clive Galea, *Slipper*, p. 155, 1988

4 a prison warder *AUSTRALIA, 1919*

- Break off, he yells, and when they disappear from view one of the yard's innumerable heros calls: Fucking dog.—Kevin Mackey, *The Cure*, p. 100, 1970
- 'I want t' keep as far away from that dog as I can.' 'Aw, he's changed, mate.' 'Screws never change,' snarled China.—Bob Jewson, *Stir*, p. 30, 1980
- —William Dodson, *The Sharp End*, p. 11, 2001

5 a traitor *AUSTRALIA, 1896*

- Man was a dog at the end of the day, no two ways about it. Lad was a fucking dog.—Kevin Sampson, *Clubland*, p. 5, 2002

6 used as a general form of friendly address (without any negative connotations) *US, 1995*

A rare positive use of 'dog', synonymous with 'man', possibly influenced by rap artist Snoop Doggy Dogg (Calvin Broadus, b.1972). Also spelt 'dogg' and 'dawg'.

- —Linda Meyer, *Teenspeak!*, p. 28, 1994
- —Connie Eble (Editor), *UNC-CH Campus Slang*, p. 3, April 1995
- The rap page biz [publishing] is murder, dog.—*The Source*, p. 36, March 2002

7 a freshman, or first-year college student *US*

- —Marcus Hanna Boulware, *Jive and Slang of Students in Negro Colleges*, 1947

8 the grade 'D' *US, 1964*

- —Collin Baker et al., *College Undergraduate Slang Study Conducted at Brown University*, p. 106, 1968

9 a cigarette-end *UK*

A shortened **DOG END**.

- —M. Harrison, *Spring in Tartarus*, 1935

10 a marijuana cigarette *US*

- —Jim Emerson-Cobb, *Scratching the Dragon*, April 1997
- —Pamela Munro, *U.C.L.A. Slang*, p. 61, 2001

11 in sports betting, the underdog *US, 1975*

- —*Bay Sports Review*, p. 8, November 1991

12 in poker, a worthless hand *US*

- —George Percy, *The Language of Poker*, p. 29, 1988

13 in horse racing, a racehorse with little value *US, 1840*

- —David W. Maurer, *Argot of the Racetrack*, p. 24, 1951
- But, anyway, a real dog had come in at a hundred-and-forty for two. —Jim Thompson, *The Grifters*, p. 63, 1963

14 in pool, a difficult shot *US*

- —Mike Shamos, *The Illustrated Encyclopedia of Billiards*, p. 79, 1993

15 in horse racing, a sawhorse used to keep horses away from the rail during a workout on a muddy track *US*

- —Dean Alfange, *The Horse Racing Industry*, p. 212, 1976

16 in poker, the fourth player to the left of the dealer *US*

- —George Percy, *The Language of Poker*, p. 26, 1988

17 a sausage; a hot dog *UK, 1845*

Derives from the belief that dog meat was used as a sausage filler; this led to a hot sausage in a roll being called a 'hot dog'. In a fine example of circular etymology 'hot dog' now abbreviates to 'dog', and 'dog' is once again a sausage; most consumers are no longer concerned about dog meat.

- Richard Branson or Sir Alan Hansen carving up the money markets over a dog roll and a cuppa[.]—Andrew Nickolds, *Back to Basics*, p. 74, 1994
- [They] bounced over a speed-bump and turned erratically into Abbey Road. "Bugger." Mo's dog had gone all over the place.—Michael Moorcock, *The Spencer Inheritance [britpulp]*, p. 3, 1998

18 the foot *US*

- —Joseph E. Ragen and Charles Finston, *Inside the World's Toughest Prison*, p. 796, 1962: 'Penitentiary and underworld glossary'

19 a piece of paper money *TRINIDAD AND TOBAGO, 1986*

- —Lise Winer, *Dictionary of the English/Creole of Trinidad & Tobago*, 2003

20 an F86-DC aircraft *US*

- —*American Speech*, p. 228, October 1956: 'More United States Air Force slang'

21 a failure of a song or film *US, 1929*

- —Arnold Shaw, *Lingo of Tin-Pan Alley*, p. 10, 1950
- The movie is a dog, but Larry likes it becaue Natalie Wood is in it and he says during the intermiossion that Carlotte looks a lot like Natalie Wood.—Darryl Ponicsan, *The Last Detail*, p. 104, 1970

▸ **dog tied up**

an unpaid debt *AUSTRALIA, 1905*

- Shot himself, poor bloody chap. In financial strife. Got too big and went bust. Left a lot of dog's tied up I shouldn't wonder.—Wilda Moxham, *The Apprentice*, p. 137, 1969

▸ **it's a dog's life**

used of a meagre existence *UK, 1969*

A catchphrase, generally used by someone enduring such a life.

▸ **it shouldn't happen to a dog**

a catchphrase used to complain about the manner in which a human has been treated *US*

Of Yiddish origin, according to Leo Rosten, *Encounter*, September 1968.

▸ **like a dog watching television**

in the position of doing something you do not understand *US*

- —Susie Dent, *The Language Report*, p. 83, 2003

▸ **on the dog**

on credit *US*

- Some bookies let reliable customers put it on the dog ... have credit.—Burgess Laughlin, *Job Opportunities in the Black Market*, p. 10–2, 1978

▸ **put on the dog**

to assume a superior, upper-class attitude *US, 1865*

- But it's really funny to watch these Californians trying to put on the dog.—Jack Kerouac, *Letter to Caroline Kerouac Blake*, p. 131, 25th September 1947
- She's always putting on the dog – saying bahth and cahn't and dahnce and like that.—Max Shulman, *I was a Teen-Age Dwarf*, p. 60, 1959

▸ **run like a dog**

to run or perform slowly *AUSTRALIA*

- In layperson's terms, this means if you don't have a Pentium *now*, then that funky program that comes out *tomorrow* will run like a dog on your 486, if at all.—*Beat*, p. 47, 3rd August 1996

▸ **the dog dead**

there is nothing more to say on the subject *BARBADOS*

- —Frank A. Collymore, *Barbadian Dialect*, p. 40, 1965

▸ **the dog has caught the car**

a person (or group of people) who has achieved a goal and is now at a loss for what to do next *US*

- It will be very difficult for Central Command to calibrate its war plan to everything taking place in the country now. The dog has caught the car.—Retired Major General Don Shepperd, *CNN*, 11th April 2003

▸ **turn dog**

to become a police informer *AUSTRALIA, 1863*

- —William Dodson, *The Sharp End*, p. xv, 2001
- There was never a problem, though, because there was always a constant stream of give-ups ready to roll over and turn dog in return for personal gain.—William Dodson, *The Sharp End*, p. 82, 2001

Dog *noun*

the Greyhound bus line *US, 1974*

A fixture in American travel until a crippling strike in the 1990s; variants include 'Grey Dog' and 'ol' Grey Dog'.

- —Gwyneth A. "Dandalion" Seese, *Tijuana Bear in a Smoke 'Um Up Taix*, p. 14, 1977
- Well, the wife left me again. Took the ol' Grey Dog to Falfurrias last night ... thank God.—Ken Weaver, *Texas Crude*, p. 110, 1984
- —Bill Casselman, *Canadian Sayings*, p. 134, 2002

dog *verb*

1 to avoid work; to work slowly *US*

- I hoped they would understand that I wasn't going what they called it – "over the hill" – because I was yellow or wanted to dog a fight. —Rocky Garciano (with Rowland Barber), *Somebody Up There Likes Me*, p. 188, 1955
- "He's not dogging it," Carbone said. "He's got a temperature and he's got a fever and he's got the trots."—George V. Higgins, *The Rat on Fire*, p. 90, 1981

2 to studiously ignore *US*

- —*Washington Post Magazine*, p. 17, 12th April 1987: 'Say wha?'

3 to abuse or harass *US*

- —William K. Bentley and James M. Corbett, *Prison Slang*, p. 92, 1992

4 in motor racing, to follow another car very closely, hoping to distract or weaken the resolve of the driver ahead *US*

- —John Lawlor, *How to Talk Car*, p. 38, 1965

5 of a male, to have sex with a partner who is kneeling on all-fours and entered from behind *UK, 1937*

- —A.D. Peterkin, *The Bald-Headed Hermit and The Artichoke*, p. 35, 1999

6 to perform sexually for money *US*

- —Terry Williams, *The Cocaine Kids*, p. 136, 1989

7 to betray *AUSTRALIA, 1896*

8 in pool, to miss a shot that should be made *US*

- The other man won it, broke the balls wide and ran half the solids before dogging a thin cut into the corner.—Walter Tevis, *The Color of Money*, p. 114, 1984
- —Steve Rushin, *Pool Cool*, p. 11, 1990

9 to play truant *UK: SCOTLAND*

Extended from a variation of 'dodge'. With variant 'dog it'.

- —Michael Munro, *The Original Patter*, p. 21, 1985

10 to hunt dingoes *AUSTRALIA, 1910*

Variant 'to wild dog'.

▹ see: **DOG IT**

dog *adjective*

standing for prison authority, generally seen as officious and corrupt by prisoners *AUSTRALIA*

- The truth hurts these screw dog bastards.—Ray Denning, *Prison Diaries*, p. 65, 1978

• I know from experience that the dog Ombudsman is a screw in disguise, and the only reason I write to him now is to make my complaints official. —Ray Denning, *Prison Diaries*, p. 121, 1979
• I think they're up to their old tricks of screws holding prisoners whilst the dog nurse gives the needle to knock the prisoner out for about 12 hours. —Ray Denning, *Prison Diaries*, p. 140, 1979
• 'Do you know why fuckin' dog screws hang around in threes?' —Kathy Lette, *Girls' Night Out*, p. 163, 1987

dogan *noun*
an Irish Roman Catholic *CANADA*
• He was a drunken Orangeman at peace with his "dogan friends." —*Kingston Whig-Standard*, p. 13/8, 1st May 1965

dog and bone; dog *noun*
a telephone *UK, 1961*
Rhyming slang.
• I'd just come out the battle [pub] / And was looking for a dog. —Ronnie Barker, *Fletcher's Book of Rhyming Slang*, p. 21, 1979
• —Ryan Aven-Bray, *Ridgey Didge Oz Jack Lang*, p. 24, 1983
• [H]aving a deep pan Hawaiian with extra cheese on the doorstep just as the dog is lifted. —Andrew Nickolds, *Back to Basics*, p. 16, 1994
• What do you fucking think? Now get on the fucking dog. —Greg Williams, *Diamond Geezers*, p. 61, 1997
• Might still be there now only the dog and bone rang. Saved the fucking day. —Jeremy Cameron, *Brown Bread in Wengen*, p. 159, 1999
• Okay, tomorrow lunch-time sounds great!" the Mexican barked into the dog[.] —Stewart Home, *Sex Kick*, p. britpup217, 1999
• And the bollocks you'd 'ear people saying on the dog, y'know[.] —Garry Bushell, *The Face*, p. 15–16, 2001

dog and boned; doggo *adjective*
drug-intoxicated *UK*
Rhyming slang for **STONED**.
• —Ray Puxley, *Fresh Rabbit*, 1998

dog and cat *noun*
a mat *UK*
Rhyming slang.
• —Ray Puxley, *Cockney Rabbit*, 1992

dog and duck *noun*
a fight *UK*
Rhyming slang for **RUCK** (a fight). Recorded, with the opinion that it was 'formed on the name of a pub where fisti-knuckles was prevalent', by Ray Puxley, *Cockney Rabbit*, 1992.

dog and pony show *noun*
an elaborate presentation *US, 1957*
• Speaking of which, I have a dog-and-pony show for Fartface Siegel this morning. —Armistead Maupin, *Tales of the City*, p. 106, 1978
• —Department of the Army, *Staff Officer's Guidebook*, p. 58, 1986
• [He] meant the lunch to be a serious discussion, not one of those "dog and pony shows," as they were called in service parlance, which Vann put on with Cao for guided tours through My Tho. —Neil Sheehan, *A Bright Shining Lie*, p. 117, 1988

dog and pup; dog *noun*
a cup (a drinking vessel or a trophy) *UK*
Rhyming slang.
• —Ray Puxley, *Cockney Rabbit*, 1992

dog-ass *noun*
a despised person *US, 1959*
• In a strangely kind tone of voice he said: "Okay, dog ass, come get some food." —John Howard Griffin, *Black Like Me*, p. 32, 1962

dog-ass *adjective*
1 shoddy, inferior *US, 1953*
• Say, now boys, I got something to tell you, just to get it off my mind / Now your dogass pimps ought to get off the line. —Bruce Jackson, *Get Your Ass in the Water and Swim Like Me*, p. 134, 1964
• That was a dog-ass amateur job. —George V. Higgins, *The Rat on Fire*, p. 22, 1981

2 despicable *US, 1953*
• NOW WHAT DO YOU HAVE TO SAY, YOU DOG-ASS SON OF A BITCH? —David McCumber, *Playing Off the Rail*, p. 87, 1996
• I knew that despite all of Trent's good qualities, he was still a dog ass niga, like all the other men I knew. —Brenda L. Thomas, *Threesome*, p. 94, 2002

dog bait *noun*
during a mass prison escape, a prisoner left by others to attract the attention of the tracking dogs *US*
• Everybody in escaping down here, they're looking for what we call dog bait. Unless you're with a guy personally, you're going to try to feed them to the dogs so you can get away. —Bruce Jackson, *In the Life*, p. 317, 1972

dogball *noun*
in a deck of playing cards, an eight *US*
• —John Vorhaus, *The Big Book of Poker Slang*, p. 16, 1996

dog-behind *verb*
to beg for a favour *TRINIDAD AND TOBAGO*
• —Lise Winer, *Dictionary of the English/Creole of Trinidad & Tobago*, 2003

dogbone *noun*
1 the weapon panel in the cockpit of an F-4 Phantom aircraft *US, 1984*
• —Linda Reinberg, *In the Field*, p. 64, 1991

2 in electric line work, an EHV yoke plate *US*
• —A.B. Chance Co., *Lineman's Slang Dictionary*, p. 6, 1980

dogbox *noun*
1 a type of small and basic compartment in a railway carriage *AUSTRALIA, 1905*
• Lucinda knew that Paul would rather travel in the dog-box than with Lord Fitzauncell[.] —Martin Boyd, *Lucinda Brayford*, p. 458, 1946
• —Jim Ramsay, *Cop It Sweet!*, p. 30, 1977

2 a truck's gear box *US*
• —Montie Tak, *Truck Talk*, p. 45, 1971

▸ **in the dogbox**
in trouble, especially with one person *NEW ZEALAND*
• Rather funny you being in the cactus at home – I'm in the dog box with my wife too. —*(Wellington) Evening Post*, p. 12, 9th March 1953

dog breath *noun*
1 a contemptible person; used as a term of abuse *US*
• Hey, dog breath, what sort of salary will I be on? —Geoff Tibbals, *The Mammoth Book of Humor*, p. 64, 2000
• See you in hell dog breath. —Danny King, *The Bank Robber Diaries*, p. 126, 2002
• The dog-breaths drugged me at the hospital. —Gayle Lynds, *The Coil*, p. 176, 2004

2 bad-smelling breath *US, 1944*
• I had horrible dog's breath and was constantly on edge. —Suzanne Somers, *Suzanne Somer's Eat Great, Lose Weight*, p. Front Matter, 1996

3 cigarette smoke *US*
• —John Vorhaus, *The Big Book of Poker Slang*, p. 14, 1996

dog catcher *noun*
any fast truck *US*
The suggestion is that the truck is fast enough to pass a Greyhound bus.
• —Montie Tak, *Truck Talk*, p. 46, 1971

dog clutch *noun*
an involuntary locking of the vaginal muscles, imprisoning the penis (*penis captivus*) *US*
Common in dogs, not so common in humans, but common enough for a term to describe it.
• —Dale Gordon, *The Dominion Sex Dictionary*, p. 121, 1967

dog cock *noun*
chub sausage *NEW ZEALAND*
• —David McGill, *David McGill's Complete Kiwi Slang Dictionary*, p. 41, 1998

dog collar *noun*
1 a white clerical collar *UK, 1861*
• —Gregory Clark, *Words of the Vietnam War*, p. 148, 1990

2 a choker necklace *UK, 1903*

dog-dance *verb*
to give the impresson that you are following someone very closely *BARBADOS*
• —Frank A. Collymore, *Barbadian Dialect*, p. 40, 1965

dog-dancing *noun*
useless or exaggerated activity *CANADA*
• [S]uch as a dog indulges in, capering with glee at the return of his master. —Douglas Leechman, 1967

dog days *noun*
a woman's menstrual period *US, 1960*
• —Helen Dahlskog (Editor), *A Dictionary of Contemporary and Colloquial Usage*, p. 19, 1972

dog do *noun*
dog faeces *US*
• Brad had somehow stuff the right toe with dog-do. —Beatrice Sparks (writing as 'Anonymous'), *Jay's Journal*, p. 72, 1979

dog doody *noun*

dog excrement *US*

Variation on **DOGGY DO**; euphemistic.

- And because Bob frequently takes in large quantities of roughage such as furniture, shoes, and houseplants, Bob frequently expels mountains of dog doody.—Janet Evanovich, *Seven Up*, p. 32, 2001

dog driver *noun*

a police officer *UK*

Insulting or contemptuous.

- —David Powis, *The Signs of Crime*, 1977

dog-eater *noun*

a member of the Sioux Indian tribe *US*

- — *American Speech*, p. 271, December 1963: 'American Indian student slang'

dog eat your shame!

used for expressing complete disgust *TRINIDAD AND TOBAGO, 1958*

- —Lise Winer, *Dictionary of the English/Creole of Trinidad & Tobago*, 2003

dog end *noun*

1 a contemptible person *UK*

- Where was the man [...] when the dog-end who snotted on my coat was about?—Andrew Holmes, *Sleb*, p. 100, 2002

2 a cigarette-end *UK, 1935*

A corruption of 'docked end' (a partially smoked cigarette that is pinched off – 'docked' – and saved for later use) and still found as 'dock end'.

- [H]e began to roll one from some dogends which he had found on the floor of the bus.—Frank Norman, *Bang To Rights*, p. 39, 1958
- [T]he dog-ends in the ashtray, they're all good and firm, right.—Joe Morgan, *Eastenders Don't Cry*, p. 54, 1994
- He sucked down on the last millimetre of nicotine and stubbed the dock end, flicking it high[.]—Kevin Sampson, *Powder*, p. 399, 1999

dog-ender *noun*

a prisoner who rolls new cigarettes from the unsmoked remains of others *UK*

- —Angela Devlin, *Prison Patter*, p. 46, 1996

dog-eye *noun*

▸ **keep dog-eye**

to keep a look-out *UK*

From the verb **DOG-EYE** (to scrutinise).

- When I meet this bird, just hang around and keep dog-eye for me. —Garry Bushell, *The Face*, p. 205, 2001

dog-eye *verb*

to scrutinise carefully *US, 1912*

- —Joseph E. Ragen and Charles Finston, *Inside the World's Toughest Prison*, p. 797, 1962: 'Penitentiary and underworld glossary'
- Here I am in these stripes – I stuck out like a sore thumb. He had been dog-eyeing me over, but he didn't know me.—Bruce Jackson, *In the Life*, p. 320, 1972

dogface *noun*

1 an ugly person; used as a general term of abuse *US, 1849*

- "Where you headed, Dogface?" "A face like yours could stop time." —Barbara Robinette Moss, *Change Me into Zeus's Daughter*, p. 211, 2000

2 a low ranking soldier *US, 1930*

- Having served in Korea as a dogface grunt, he knew a lifer when he saw one.—Joseph Wambaugh, *Finnegan's Week*, p. 27, 1993

dog-faced *adjective*

despicable *US, 1962*

- The dog-fcaed security men had tracked him somehow.—F. Paul Wilson, *All the Rage*, p. 197, 2000

dog fashion; doggie fashion *adverb*

sexual intercourse from behind, vaginal or anal, heterosexual or homosexual *UK, 1900*

- I'd always drop it down and fuck her dog fashion.—A.S. Jackson, *Gentleman Pimp*, p. 110, 1973
- One time I was with Jim and we were balling doggie fashion and his roommate came home and got turned on watching us ball.— *Adam Film Quarterly*, p. 68, October 1973
- I had terrible thoughts of being caught, doggie fashion.—Odie Hawkins, *Black Casanova*, p. 37, 1984
- "I got a three-hundred-and-fifty-pounder likes to lay on top of me as it is. Can you picture that?" "How do you do it?" "Like the bow-wows, doggie fashion. Man, it's a full-time job."—Elmore Leonard, *Pronto*, p. 336, 1993

dog finger *noun*

the index finger *US, 1926*

- And it wasn't just any finger either – it was the pointer finger, the one next to the thumb, and we called it "the dog finger" – the finger you used to curse somebody.—Cornelia Walker Bailey, *God, Dr. Buzzard,and the Bolito Man*, p. 170, 2000

dog food *noun*

1 Italian sausage *US*

- — *Maledicta*, p. 11, 1996: 'Domino's pizza jargon'

2 heroin *US*

- —Jay Robert Nash, *Dictionary of Crime*, p. 106, 1992
- —Mark S. Fleisher, *Beggars & Thieves*, p. 289, 1995: 'Glossary'
- —Robert Ashton, *This Is Heroin*, p. 205, 2002
- —Mike Haskins, *Drugs*, p. 283, 2003

dogfuck *noun*

a despicable person *US*

- You either hand it over, or I'll have my people sign their names in your flesh. And believe me, dogfuck, they got long names.—James W. Hall, *Hard Aground*, p. 56, 1993

dogfuck *verb*

to have sex from the rear, homosexual or heterosexual, vaginal or anal *US*

- —Edith A. Folb, *runnin' down some lines*, p. 235, 1980

dogger *noun*

1 a person who engages in *al fresco* sexual activities such as exhibitionism or voyeurism; especially of sexual activities (with multiple partners) in parked vehicles, generally in the countryside *UK*

When police approached 'doggers' (before they were so-named), the usual excuse offered was 'walking the dog'.

- — *Farming Today*, 26th July 2003

2 a truant *UK: SCOTLAND*

From **DOG** (to play truant).

- —Michael Munro, *The Original Patter*, p. 21, 1985

3 a hunter of dingoes *AUSTRALIA, 1890*

- One of the roaming doggers, Anderson, has since been speared.—Ion L. Idriess, *Over the Range*, p. 316, 1947
- —Patsy Adam-Smith, *Folklore of the Australian Railwaymen*, p. 280, 1969
- After that I went bush with my oldest daughter, Pat, and worked around Quilpie for a while, and ended up as a dogger on Mt Margaret Station.—Herb Wharton, *Cattle Camp*, p. 104, 1994

doggers *noun*

multi-coloured swimming trunks *AUSTRALIA, 1963*

- —John M. Kelly, *Surf and Sea*, p. 283, 1965

Doggett's *noun*

▸ **on the Doggett's**

on the scrounge, cadging *UK, 1960*

Derives from **COAT AND BADGE** (to cadge) which has, in the past, been used as 'Doggett's coat and badge'. Doggett's Coat and Badge Race, founded by Thomas Doggett, an Irish actor, in 1715, is the oldest annual sporting event in Britain, a boat race from London Bridge to Chelsea contested by Thames' watermen. The race and the slang are both very much alive.

doggie *noun*

1 an infantry soldier *US, 1937*

A shortened **DOGFACE**.

- It hits the doggies to see a man staring glassily at the shambles of the home he spent his life building.—Bill Mauldin, *Up Front*, p. 69, 1945
- "Let's go back and have a beer and I'll tell you how you can get liquor out of the doggies up at Hue," he says with a grin.—Charles Coe, *Young Man in Vietnam*, p. 25, 1968
- [E]ven a battery of the U.S. Army, "those good old worthelss fucking doggies."—Charles Anderson, *The Grunts*, p. 132, 1976
- —Linda Reinberg, *In the Field*, p. 64, 1991

2 an enlisted man in the US Army *US, 1945*

- Once in a while a doggie or seaman came in for a hamburger and played the jukebox.—Hubert Selby Jr, *Last Exit to Brooklyn*, p. 27, 1957
- Some doggies – both draftees and enlisted men – frequently jumped the fence and went AWOL, wondering why on earth they ever joined up in the first place.—Ralph "Sonny" Barger, *Hell's Angel*, p. 22, 2000

3 a greyhound racing enthusiast *AUSTRALIA*

- —Ned Wallish, *The Truth Dictionary of Racing Slang*, p. 23, 1989

doggie cop *noun*
a police officer working with a trained dog *US*
• You wanna give up being a doggie cop, you can jist transfer over here to Ramparts. —Joseph Wambaugh, *The Delta Star*, p. 181, 1983

doggie fashion *adverb*
▷ see: DOG FASHION

doggie pack *noun*
a US Army combat field pack *US*
Used derisively by US Marines during the conflict in Vietnam.
• —*Maledicta*, p. 253, Summer/Winter 1982: 'Viet-speak'

doggie pouch *noun*
a small ammunition pouch used by the infantry *US*
• When my clip expended I started reaching in my little doggie pouch thing for more ammo. —John Kerry, *The New Soldier*, p. 68, 1971

doggie straps *noun*
rucksack straps *US*
Vietnam war usage.
• —Linda Reinberg, *In the Field*, p. 64, 1991

dogging *noun*
1 *al fresco* sexual activities such as exhibitionism or voyeurism; especially of sexual activities (with multiple partners) in parked vehicles, generally in the countryside *UK, 1998*
Originally used of the act of spying on people having sex in parked vehicles.
• Another curious habit for the looker/lookee set is called dogging. No, it doesn't mean letting your dog watch your sexual activities. —Erica Orloff and JoAnn Baker, *Dirty Little Secrets*, p. 101, 2001
• There are more and more 'dogging' websites with detailed descriptions of hundreds of renowned sites. —*Farming Today*, 26th July 2003
• Dogging is a broad term used to cover all the sexual outdoor activities that go on. This can be anything from putting on a show from your car, to a gangbang on a picnic table. —*The Guardian*, 18th September 2003
• Honk your horn if you're dogging tonight. —U Rockers, *Dogging – Parking Sex Edit*, 2004
2 the hunting of dingoes *AUSTRALIA*
• I was out dogging and poisoned a dingo. —Ion L. Idriess, *Over the Range*, p. 260, 1947

doggins *noun*
in the illegal production of alcohol, liquor sweated out of used barrel staves *US*
• —David W. Maurer, *Kentucky Moonshine*, p. 115, 1974

doggo *noun*
a sled dog handler *ANTARCTICA, 1995*
• —Bernadette Hince, *The Antarctic Dictionary*, p. 101, 2000

doggo *adjective*
1 lying prone, playing dead *UK, 1893*
• I must play by the rules, but I'll lie doggo and pretend I am hypnotized. —John Fowles, *The Magus*, p. 242, 1965
2 of a car's interior, of poor quality *UK*
• —*The Sunday Times*, 9th August 1981
▷ see: DOG AND BONED

doggone *adjective*
used as a mild, folksy euphemism for 'damn' *UK, 1826*
Multiple variants. Usually used with a conscious folksy effect in mind.
• Don't you talk to me that way! You owe every doggone cent of it and you know it, and by golly you're going to pay it. —Jim Thompson, *The Grifters*, p. 90, 1963
• I didn't have a doggone dime[.] —C.W. McCall, *Convoy*, 1976
• There really ain't too daggoned much difference between the Democrats 'n the Republicans. —Donald Goines, *The Busting Out of an Ordinary Man*, p. 57, 1985

doggy *noun*
1 the penis *BAHAMAS*
• —John A. Holm, *Dictionary of Bahamian English*, p. 63, 1982
2 a railways' platelayer *UK*
• —Harvey Sheppard, *Dictionary of Railway Slang*, 1970

doggy bag; doggie bag *noun*
1 a bag in which uneaten food from a restaurant is packed and taken home *US*
• They paid $3.50 each, left with enough uneaten steak in a "doggie bag" to feed themselves, not the dog, all next day. —*Life*, p. 47, 6th April 1947
• "Who gets the doggie bag?" The girl from the News waited. "Just put it there," Raymond said. "She doesn't take it, I will." —Elmore Leonard, *City Primeval*, p. 23, 1980
• You don't need to be Alan Greenspan to know that one of the nation's leading economic indicators – doggie-bag requests at upscale restaurants – suggests that we're headed for recessionary times. —*San Francisco Chronicle*, p. 1, 25th August 2001
• Eating cakes out of "doggie bags" —*The Times*, p. 3, 17th March 2001
2 a condom *UK*
• —David Rowan, *A Glossary for the 90s*, 1998

doggy do *noun*
dog excrement *AUSTRALIA*
• —Paul Vautin, *Turn It Up!*, p. 80, 1995
• You're a regular ice queen who treats guys as coldly as a lump of doggy do. —*Dolly*, p. 65, 1996
• —Glyn Parry, *Mosh*, p. 49, 1996

doggy style *noun*
▷ see: DOG-STYLE

doghole; doghole mine *noun*
a small mine employing less than 15 miners *US, 1943*
• The so-called dogholes are most numerous in Kerntucky, but there are many in Virginia and West Virginia. —Paul W. Thrush, *A Dictionary of Mining, Mineral and Related Terms*, p. 337, 1968
• "Now those were bad members, Clete, they gone out and joined up with these dogholes we been trying to close down." —John Sayles, *Union Dues*, p. 19, 1977

doghouse *noun*
1 in trucking, the engine covering in the driving compartment *US*
• —Montie Tak, *Truck Talk*, p. 46, 1971
2 a brakevan (caboose), or the observation tower of a brakevan *US, 1897*
• —Norman Carlisle, *The Modern Wonder Book of Trains and Railroading*, p. 262, 1946
3 the front fender, bonnet and grille of a car *US, 1934*
• —John Edwards, *Auto Dictionary*, p. 45, 1993
4 a small tool shed *US, 1918*
• —Jerry Robertson, *Oil Slanguage*, p. 46, 1954

▸ **in the doghouse**
ostracised; in disfavour *US, 1926*
Alluding to an outside kennel. Commonly used of a man being ostracised by his wife for some misdemeanor.
• My wife watches T.D.T. every night and if she sees this, I'll be in the "dog-house" for a month. —Sam Weller, *Old Bastards I Have Met*, p. 123, 1979
• —Barry Humphries, *The Traveller's Tool*, p. 35, 1985
• Former Sunderland striker Danny Dichio, still on the transfer list and in the dog house[.] —*The Guardian*, 22nd December 2002

doghouse cut *noun*
a manner of cutting a deck of cards in which a section of cards is moved from the centre of the deck to the top, leaving the bottom cards undisturbed *US*
• —Albert H. Morehead, *The Complete Guide to Winning Poker*, p. 261, 1967

dogie *noun*
heroin *US, 1969*
• —Richard A. Spears, *The Slang and Jargon of Drugs and Drink*, p. 147, 1986
• —Robert Ashton, *This Is Heroin*, p. 205, 2002
• —Mike Haskins, *Drugs*, p. 283, 2003

dog in the manger *noun*
a person who selfishly refuses to give up something that he does not want *UK, 1573*
• What you are is a dog in the manger, Kerrigan. You don't want to marry me yourself, but you just can't stand to let another man do the honest thing. —Joan Johnston, *Sweetwater Seduction*, p. 277, 1991

dog it; dog *verb*
1 to refuse to pay a lost bet or a debt *US*
• —*The Annals of the American Academy of Political and Social Sciences*, p. 124, May 1950
2 to back down from a confrontation or situation for lack of courage *US*
• —H. Craig Collins, *Street Gangs*, p. 222, 1979

dog juice *noun*
inexpensive alcohol, especially wine *US*
• —Edith A. Folb, *runnin' down some lines*, p. 235, 1980

dog leg *noun*
in oil drilling, a radical change in direction of drilling *US*
• —Jerry Robertson, *Oil Slanguage*, p. 47, 1954

dogleg *verb*
to make an angled detour, to take an angled route *UK, 1984*
Originally, perhaps, used in aviation.
- A trip to beat any tourist bus – though we did suspect we might have been doglegged. — *The Observer*, 11th August 2002

dog license *noun*
a Certificate of Exemption to allow an Aboriginal to buy a drink in a hotel *AUSTRALIA*
This term derives from the Blackfellows Act, also known as the Dog Act.
- — Sidney J. Baker, *The Drum*, 1959

dog meat *noun*
1 a person who is certain of defeat or death *US, 1977*
- If one of those gates accidentally popped open, I'd have been dog meat[.] — John C. Burnham, *A Soldier's Best Friend*, p. 97, 2000

2 an inept, worthless person *US, 1908*
- An eight-year-old makes me look like dog meat. — Elizabeth Spurr, *Surfer Dog*, p. 71, 2002

dog mouth *noun*
bad breath experienced upon waking up *US*
Hawaiian youth usage.
- — Douglas Simonson, *Pidgin to da Max Hana Hou*, 1982

do-gooder *noun*
a well-intentioned person who believes in and supports charity *US, 1927*
The term suggests both a naivite and a slightly cloying sense of self-righteousness.
- He doesn't appeal to the modern worker. They smell the do-gooder in him. — Mary McCarthy, *The Group*, p. 138, 1963
- The polio boxes are the old man's old lady's personal do-gooder project. — Darryl Ponicsan, *The Last Detail*, p. 17, 1970
- But I had to visit with a number of social workers and do-gooders[.] — Herbert Huncke, *Guilty of Everything*, p. 198, 1990
- Candy Pringle and some other do-gooder seniors from my high school just dropped by with a frozen turkey and a big bag of canned goods. — C.D. Payne, *Youth in Revolt*, p. 319, 1993

dog out *verb*
1 to keep a look out *UK*
- Higgs left Wayman dogging out at the corner. — Maurice Procter, *His Weight in Gold*, 1966

2 to criticise harshly *US, 1986*
- LEFT HAND: You dog her out because she's White. — *Mo' Better Blues*, 1990
- — *Army*, p. 48, November 1991
- — *American Speech*, p. 388, Winter 1991: 'Among the new words'

Dogpatch *nickname*
a neighbourhood of bars and shops near the Da Nang US Air Base during the Vietnam war *US*
Dogpatch was the stereotypical Appalachian town in Al Capp's *Li'il Abner* comic strip, which was very popular in the US during the Vietnam war.
- — Linda Reinberg, *In the Field*, p. 64, 1991
- Late in 1966, Steve was in a place just below Hill 327 near Da Nang that the GIs called Dogpatch, a sprawl of native huts, some made of C-ration boxes and Coke cans stamped flat and nailed together. — Peter Collier, *Destructive Generation*, p. 126, 1996
- Them girls are the cleanest in Dogpatch. Use protection and don't leave alone. — John J. Culbertson, *A Sniper in the Arizona 2nd Battalion*, p. 145, 1999

dog pile *noun*
the pile of skiers or snowboarders produced when one falls while dismounting from a lift *US*
- — Elena Garcia, *A Beginner's Guide to Zen and the Art of Snowboarding*, p. 121, 1990: 'Glossary'

dogpile *verb*
1 to jump onto someone or onto a group of people *US, 1945*
- [H]e swivled in his chair, dropped his arms and got ready to let his son dogpile him. — James Ellroy, *The Big Nowhere*, p. 110, 1988

2 to post many critical comments in response to a posting on an Internet discussion group *US*
- — Christian Crumlish, *The Internet Dictionary*, p. 54, 1995

dog-piss *adjective*
inferior, shabby *US*
- It was a scruffy dog-piss postcard off the postcard rack of broken dreams. — Tom Robbins, *Another Roadside Attraction*, p. 75, 1971

dog puncher *noun*
a driver of sled dogs *CANADA*
- Arthur Treadwell, a young dog-puncher, arrived from Dawson with a load of mail. — Pierre Berton, *The Golden Trail*, p. 37, 1964

dog race *noun*
in horse racing, a race featuring cheap racehorses *US*
- — David W. Maurer, *Argot of the Racetrack*, p. 24, 1951

dog-rob *verb*
to acquire through scrounging or pilfering *US, 1919*
- I give you Arch – that's Livingston – and Papa and anybody you can dog-rob outa some other department. — William Diehl, *Starky's Machine*, p. 92, 1978

dog-robber *noun*
1 an officer's assistant *US, 1863*
- I thought it might be stretching a point to bring the wife of the Secretary's chief horse holder, dog robber, and gofer, but Weinberger insisted. — Colin L. Powell, *My American Journey*, p. 278, 1995
- "You know he's no longer a dog-robber?" "No, I didn't." "Well' he's not. He was good at it, but he hated it." — W.E.B. Griffin, *Special Ops*, p. 94, 2001

2 a person assigned the most menial of tasks, especially the acquisition of difficult-to-acquire goods and services *US*
- Each marine hut or tent had its dog robber. Okinawans only a few months from Japanese occupation could work up a spit shine as if they had been born to it. — Earl Thompson, *Tattoo*, p. 293, 1974
- So Americans went to war with a will. They went as riflemen and machine-gunners, as cooks and dog-robbers, they went as motor-pool sergeants and as heavy equipment specialists who could reopoen a bombed harbor for the Allied invasion. — *Press Enterprise (Riverside, California)*, p. A12, 11th November 1999

3 in the film and television industries, a person whose job it is to find difficult-to-find goods for props *US*
- He is neither the biggest nor the best in his business, he tells you. There are dozens of other dog-robbers in town. Many have specialties. He's partial to military garb and gear. — *Los Angeles Times*, p. 1 (Part 6), 18th February 2002

4 during the Vietnam war, someone assigned to the rear area as seen by someone in combat *US*
- — Linda Reinberg, *In the Field*, p. 64, 1991

dog-rough *adjective*
disorderly; prone to rowdiness; unsophisticated *UK*
- Once upon a time, in a dog-rough gay pub nestling against some railway arches in south London[.] — *The Guardian*, p. 15, 14th May 2002

dogs *noun*
1 the feet; shoes *US, 1914*
- Preston had his bad dogs propped on a chair when I got back. I stumbled over his make-shift sandals beside the sofa. — Iceberg Slim (Robert Beck), *Pimp*, p. 98, 1969
- — Ellen C. Bellone (Editor), *Dictionary of Slang*, p. 9, 1989
- — Connie Eble (Editor), *UNC-CH Campus Slang*, p. 2, Fall 1997

2 in circus and carnival usage, the legs *US*
- — Don Wilmeth, *The Language of American Popular Entertainment*, p. 75, 1981

3 a safe's tumblers *US*
- — Vincent J. Monteleone, *Criminal Slang*, p. 71, 1949

▸ **go to the dogs**
to be slowly ruined *UK, 1619*
- Country going to the dogs[.] — *The Observer*, 12th November 2000

▸ **the dogs**
greyhound racing *UK, 1927*
- I have also been to the dogs. Watching six skinny greyhounds chase a bit of old rag is surprisingly good entertainment[.] — *The Guardian*, 12th July 2003

dog's abuse *noun*
very harsh abuse (that you would only give to a dog) *IRELAND*
- Sheffield Wednesday fans were giving him dog's abuse when his temper got the better of him. — *Cork Examiner*, 15th December 1998

dog's age *noun*
a very long time *US, 1836*
- Haven't seen you in a dog's age. Where you been? — William Burroughs, *Queer*, p. 76, 1985

dog's bait *noun*
a huge amount *US, 1933*
- — Frederic G. Cassidy, *Dictionary of American Regional English, Volume II*, p. 118, 1991

dog's ballocks *noun*
in typography, a colon dash (:-) *UK, 1961*

dog's balls *noun*
no money at all *FIJI*
Recorded by Jan Tent in 1993.

▸ **stick/stand out like dog's balls**
to be obvious *AUSTRALIA*
- [H]e said again, 'Cam's eyes sticking out like the proverbial...' I don't quite know why – he can be robust in language himself – but Maurice held back from 'dog's balls'. — Murray Farquhar, *Nine Words from the Grave*, p. 104, 1986
- Without it the operators stand out like dog's balls and run the risk of being shot. — William Dodson, *The Sharp End*, p. 253, 2001

dogsbody *noun*
a worker who is given the tedious menial tasks to perform, a drudge *UK, 1922*
Originally military or naval.
- DIXIE: Beggars can't be choosers. KEVIN: Can lad and dogsbody. DIXIE: I know it's not what y'want. — Alan Bleasdale, *Boys From the Blackstuff*, 1982

dog's bollock *noun*
an article of little or no value *UK*
- I don't give a dog's bollock about that. — Greg Williams, *Diamond Geezers*, p. 40, 1997

dog's bollocks; dog's ballocks; the bollocks *noun*
anything considered to be the finest, the most excellent, the best *UK, 1989*
Derived from the phrase 'It sticks out like a dog's ballocks' said of something that the speaker considers obvious, hence the sense of 'someone or something that sticks out from the rest'. Often abbreviated in speech to 'the dog's'.
- [I]n the early 70's Clive James was the dog's bollocks in erudite folk/rock circles[.] — *New Musical Express*, p. 17, 16th February 1991
- [A] black Lexus: "ABS, dual air bags, the dog's"[.] — Greg Williams, *Diamond Geezers*, p. 170, 1997
- The Dogs' Bollocks — *Melody Maker*, 23rd May 1998
- [A]ll these cunts think they're the bollocks when it comes to anything that might be a bit naughty[.] — John King, *Human Punk*, p. 307, 2000
- Ian Dury was the dog's bollocks and 'New Boots And Panties' was the cat's pyjama. — BP Fallon, *Brand New Boots And Panties*, 2001

dog's breakfast *noun*
an unmitigated mess *AUSTRALIA, 1934*
- — Louis S. Leland, *A Personal Kiwi-Yankee Dictionary*, p. 33, 1984

dog's cock; dog's prick *noun*
in typography, an exclamation mark (!) *UK, 1961*
- [K]nown in the newspaper world as a screamer, a gasper, a startler or (sorry) a dog's cock. — Lynne Truss, *Eats, Shoots and Leaves*, p. 136, 2003

dog's dick *noun*
a mess, a disgusting mess *UK*
A variation of **DOG'S DINNER** (a mess).
- Of course, you'll probably make a right dog's dick of it[.] — *FHM*, p. 44, June 2003

dog's dinner *noun*
1 used as a comparison for someone who is smartly dressed, stylishly or formally attired *UK, 1936*
Variants of the comparison include 'dolled up like a dog's dinner'; 'done up like a dog's dinner'; 'dressed up like a dogs dinner'; and 'got up like a dog's dinner'.
2 a mess, a disgusting mess *UK*
- Your garms [clothes] are wacked. You're a dog's dinner. — Nick Barlay, *Curvy Lovebox*, p. 60, 1997

dog's disease *noun*
influenza or gastro-enteritis or malaria or a hangover, etc *AUSTRALIA, 1890*
- Dog's disease to some people means 'flu, to others gastro-enteritis. — Nancy Keesing, *Lily on the Dustbin*, p. 77, 1982

dog's eye *noun*
a meat pie *AUSTRALIA*
Rhyming slang.
- — Lenie Johansen, *The Dinkum Dictionary*, 1988
- — *Sydney Morning Herald*, p. 1, 2002

dog shift *noun*
a work shift in the middle of the night *US, 1977*
- That means if you're the newest member on the force, you can expect to spend your first few years working the 'dog shift' (midnight to eight). — Larry F. Jetmore, *Police Officer Examination Preparation Guide*, p. 28, 1994

dogshit *noun*
1 anything or anyone considered to be worthless or disgusting *US, 1968*
- You dirty little faggot! Call the manager! I'm tired of listening to this dogshit! — Hunter S. Thompson, *Fear and Loathing in Las Vegas*, p. 107, 1971
- [E]verything that came from [San Francisco] was really important Art, and anything from anyplace else (especially L.A.) was dogshit. — Frank Zappa, *The Real Frank Zappa Book*, p. 68, 1989
- You look like dogshit. — *Basic Instinct*, 1992

2 Italian sausage *US*
- — *Maledicta*, p. 11, 1996: 'Domino's pizza jargon'

3 the epitome of feeling wretched or ill *UK*
- I was sitting in the Milgarth office of Detective Chief Superintendent George Oldham, feeling like dogshit. — David Peace, *Nineteen Seventy-Four*, p. 23, 1999

dogshit *adjective*
worthless or disgusting *US, 1967*
- [P]eople in positions of power in the media who know fuck all about anything and who should keep their dog-shit opinions to their stupid selves. — Frank Skinner, *Frank Skinner*, p. 151, 2001

dog show *noun*
in the military, an inspection of the feet *US*
- — Vincent J. Monteleone, *Criminal Slang*, p. 71, 1949

dog's lipstick *noun*
the uncircumcised penis when erect *UK*
From an image of the head of the penis extending beyond the protection of the foreskin in a manner reminiscent of a lipstick protruding beyond its decorative protective casing; the reference to a dog is open to interpretation.
- — Graham Norton, *V Graham Norton*, 20th May 2003

dog's lunch *noun*
a physically repulsive person *US*
- — Florida Legislative Investigation Committee (Johns Committee), *Homosexuality and Citizenship in Florida*, 1964: 'Glossary of homosexual terms and deviate acts'

dog soldier *noun*
a common soldier *US, 1950*
- [T]he department was top-heavy with managers while the ranks below were so thin that the dog soldiers on the street rarely had the time or inclination to step out of their protective machines, their cars, to meet the people they served. — Michael Connelly, *The Concrete Blond*, p. 209, 1994

dog squad *noun*
undercover police *AUSTRALIA, 1967*
- He is a member of the police "dog squad" – a form of animal life lower even than a process server. — Suzy Jarratt, *Permissive Australia*, p. 127, 1970
- — Jim Ramsay, *Cop It Sweet!*, p. 30, 1977
- — Ryan Aven-Bray, *Ridgey Didge Oz Jack Lang*, p. 25, 1983

dogster *noun*
a member of the Mongrel Mob, a prison gang *NEW ZEALAND*
Collected during an extensive survey of New Zealand prison slang, 1996–2000.

dog's tooth *noun*
truth *UK*
Rhyming slang.
- I swear that's on the dog's tooth. — Ray Puxley, *Cockney Rabbit*, 1992

dog-style; doggy style *noun*
a sexual position in which the woman or passive male kneels and the man enters her from behind *US*
- They crawl down aisle / While screwing dog-style. — *Eros*, p. 64, Winter 162
- Greek lads white as marble fuck dog style on the portico of a great golden temple. — William Burroughs, *Naked Lunch*, p. 117, 1957

dog's vomit *noun*
disgusting food *AUSTRALIA*
- — Sidney J. Baker, *The Australian Language*, p. 74, 1966

dogtag *noun*

1 an identity disc *US, 1918*

- When Billy Pilgrim's name was inscribed in the ledger of the prison camp, he was given a number, too, and an irontag in which that number was stamped. — Kurt Vonnegut, *Slaughterhouse Five*, p. 91, 1969

2 a prescription for a narcotic, possibly legal or possibly forged or illegally obtained *US*

- — J.E. Schmidt, *Narcotics Lingo and Lore*, p. 40, 1959
- — Angela Devlin, *Prison Patter*, p. 46, 1996

dog-tucker *noun*

a person or animal that consistently fails and is deemed worthless *NEW ZEALAND*

From an earlier, literal sense of the word as 'a sheep to be slaughtered for dog meat'.

- — Harry Orsman, *A Dictionary of Modern New Zealand Slang*, p. 41, 1999

dog turd *noun*

a cigar *US, 1969*

- When it came around to the man sitting on Annie's right – a heavy-set man with a red face, smoking a cigar that one of the other men had called a dog turd – the man added ten more ships. — Gary Paulsen, *The Car*, p. 144, 1994

dog wagon *noun*

1 a bus or van used to transport prisoners from jail to prison *US*

- Somebody screaming his head off in that empty dog wagon two blocks south. — Mickey Spillane, *Kiss Me Deadly*, p. 138, 1952
- — Frank Prewitt and Francis Schaeffer, *Vacaville Vocabulary*, 1961–1962

2 a lunch counter; a diner *US, 1900*

dog-wank *adjective*

worthless *UK*

- Just put the final touches to his dog-wank waffle when the phone rings in his office. — Jack Allen, *When the Whistle Blows*, p. 200, 2000

dogwash *noun*

a task that is not particularly important but is pursued in favour of a more demanding, more important task *US*

- — Eric S. Raymond, *The New Hacker's Dictionary*, p. 129, 1991

dog watch *noun*

a work or guard shift in the middle of the night *US, 1901*

- The girls we knew were all on the dogwatch, from four to twelve in the morning. — Mezz Mezzrow, *Really the Blues*, p. 22, 1946
- I was a kid dogwatch (after the last edition and before the first, next day) assistant city editor of the Chicago American. — *San Francisco Call-Bulletin*, p. 11, 19th August 1949
- — *American Speech*, p. 274, December 1954: 'Fire terms: additional words and definitions'
- A member of our battery, standing the dog watch, saw him supsended under the stern of the neighboring vessel. — Martin Russ, *The Last Parallel*, p. 28, 1957

dog water *noun*

colourless seminal fluid *US*

- Knowing that scum was white, most of the guys said that Horse was right and that it was just dog water. I said that dog water was most than he ever made. — Claude Brown, *Manchild in the Promised Land*, p. 80–81, 1965
- Slowly the initial pain subsided, ever so slowly, then it started slowly feeling good as the dog watered in her nest. — Steve Cannon, *Groove, Bang, and Jive Around*, p. 38, 1969
- "No dry spasms, piss or clear drops of 'dog water,'" according to the glib rule sheet[.] — Josh Alan Friedman, *Tales of Times Square*, p. 103, 1986

dog with two dicks; dog with two choppers; dog with two cocks; dog with two tails

used as a simile for being delighted or very pleased *UK*

Generally in phrases: '... as a dog with...' or 'like a dog with...'. 'A dog with two choppers' is first recorded by Alexander Baron, *There's No Home*, 1950; 'a dog with two tails' is noted by the *Oxford English Dictionary* in 1953.

- "That's one small step for man, one gient leap for mankind. I'm on the moon and I'm happy as a dog with two dicks, me." (Neil Armstrong, July 1969) — Chris Donald, *Roger's Profanisaurus*, 2002

doh!

used for registering frustration when things fail to turn out as planned, or at the realisation that you have said something foolish *UK, 1945*

Popularly associated with, and a catchphrase of, Homer Simpson in the television cartoon *The Simpsons* (since 1987).

- — *Beat*, p. 80, 1996
- Hang on a tic, he thought. This is tipping the weirdometer. Of course. Doh! It was the acid. — Linda Jaivin, *Rock n Roll Babes from Outer Space*, p. 22, 1996

dohbie *noun*

▷ see: **DHOBI**

doight!

used for expressing distress *US*

A wildly popular catchphrase verbalisation from *The Simpsons* television cartoon.

- — Connie Eble (Editor), *UNC-CH Campus Slang*, p. 3, Spring 1994

doily *noun*

a toupee *US*

- — Wilfred Granville, *The Theater Dictionary*, p. 205, 1952

do in *verb*

1 to kill *UK, 1905*

- Before you do me in, Mr. McManus, you will let me finish my business with Ms. Finneran first, won' you? — *The Usual Suspects*, 1995
- Mikey got shot up in the same thingio as what done Rico in. — Kevin Sampson, *Clubland*, p. 2, 2002

2 to injure *UK, 1905*

- Pierce [Brosnan] did his knee in, so by the time we actually got to the scene there'd been six months of training. — *BBCi*, 20th November 2002

3 to exhaust *UK, 1917*

Thus **DONE IN** (exhausted).

4 to defeat, to beat *AUSTRALIA, 1916*

doing a party *noun*

a tactic employed when performing a three-card-trick: a confederate of the card sharp pretends to be winning so as to encourage the unsuspecting to stake heavily *UK*

- — David Powis, *The Signs of Crime*, 1977

doings *noun*

1 used as a collective noun for unspecified necessities *UK, 1919*

Generally as 'the doings'.

2 excrement *UK, 1967*

- There's a lump of bird's doings on the windowsill. — Beale, 1984

doink *noun*

a socially inept, out-of-touch person *US*

- — Collin Baker et al., *College Undergraduate Slang Study Conducted at Brown University*, p. 106, 1968

do it!

used as an exhortation to experience life rather than analyse it *US*

- [A]s he holds the flag staunchly in his hands and marches up the aisle and then down the aisle, signifying – what? Ne'mind! But exactly! Don't explain it. Do it! — Tom Wolfe, *The Electric Kool-Aid Acid Test*, p. 167, 1968

do-it fluid *noun*

alcoholic drink *US*

Based on the observed effect of alcohol on sexual inhibition.

- — Edith A. Folb, *runnin' down some lines*, p. 235, 1980

do it now!

a catchphrase in jocular or semi-irrelevant use *AUSTRALIA*

Originally a business slogan; first recorded in this use in 1927 but dating from no later than 1910, and still common in 1965.

do it the hard way!

used in derision to an awkward worker who is struggling with a task *CANADA, 1961*

Often preceded by 'that's right!' and occasionally completed with 'standing up in a hammock'.

do-it-yourself *noun*

masturbation *UK*

- — Nicholas Monsarrat, *The Nylon Pirates*, 1960

do-it-yourself kit *noun*

a steam locomotive or locomotives *UK*

As an ironic contrast to diesel technology. Frank McKenna, author of *The Railway Workers*, credits coinage to Mr Bill Handy, a train driver.

- — Harvey Sheppard, *Dictionary of Railway Slang*, 1970

dojah *noun*

marijuana *US*

- —Rick Ayers (Editor), *Berkeley High Slang Dictionary*, p. 16, 2004

dole *noun*

▸ on the dole

in receipt of unemployment benefits *UK, 1925*

- On the dole you literally run out of money.—Mark Steel, *Reasons to be Cheerful*, p. 83, 2001

▸ the dole

unemployment benefit; the local offices from which unemployment benefit is managed *UK, 1919*

- From the perspective of the dole, everyone's a rich bastard.—Mark Steel, *Reasons to be Cheerful*, p. 84, 2001

dole bludger *noun*

a person habitually living off social security payments *AUSTRALIA, 1976*

A term of high opprobrium, often applied contemptuously to any recipient of the dole with the implication that employment could be found by anyone if they so desired.

- They talk about dole bludgers who don't want to work[.]—Frank Hardy, *Hardy's People*, p. 146, 1986
- —Kathy Lette, *Girls' Night Out*, p. 65, 1987
- —Christos Tsiolkas, *Loaded*, p. 52, 1995

dole-on-sea *noun*

a seaside resort with few visitors and high unemployment *UK*

Formed on **THE DOLE** (unemployment benefit).

- [B]y the time I left [Margate] in 1987 there were empty stretches of sand and the town had become a run down dole-on-sea.—Iain Aitch, *A Fete Worse Than Death*, p. viii, 2003

doley *noun*

a person in receipt of unemployment benefit *AUSTRALIA, 1953*

- There were four of us living in St Kilda. A student, a chef, a doley and Leo, whose parents owned restaurants.—John Birmingham, *He Died With a Felafel in his Hand*, p. 108, 1994
- Across the nation grouplets of doleys slotted into the daily ritual of sitting around each other's house with a pot of tea and homegrown grass.—Mark Steel, *Reasons to be Cheerful*, p. 83, 2001

doll *noun*

1 a young woman *US, 1840*

- If somebody else's dish (and we mean dish, not doll), looks particularly attractive, don't sample it unless you're asked to.—Jack Lait and Lee Mortimer, *New York Confidential*, p. 223, 1948
- Tappy then sent a couple of exquisite dolls to the drunk's table, everybody had drinks, and Tappy presented a $50 tab.—Robert Sylvester, *No Cover Charge*, p. 213–214, 1956
- All the wise guys 'n dolls was jammed in – place was hysteria.—Edwin Torres, *Carlito's Way*, p. 23, 1975
- Yi should see some of the hounds he's had by the way, doll.—Ian Pattison, *Rab C. Nesbitt*, 1988

2 a very attractive person of any sex that you find attractive *US*

- —Donald Webster Cory and John P. LeRoy, *The Homosexual and His Society*, p. 263, 1963: 'A lexicon of homosexual slang'
- I bet you're even more of a doll without your kit on.—Kevin Sampson, *Outlaws*, p. 130, 2001

3 used as a term of address *US*

- —Anon., *The Gay Girl's Guide*, p. 8, 1949
- Monty turned and saw a fat dyed blonde with bad teeth and too much rouge. "Wotcher, Doll," he said guardedly.—Derek Bickerton, *Payroll*, p. 119, 1959
- There y'are, dolls, no offence.—Ian Pattison, *Rab C. Nesbitt*, 1988

4 a barbiturate capsule; an amphetamine capsule or tablet *US, 1966*

Coined by Jacqueline Susann, author of *Valley of the Dolls*.

- —Richard Lingeman, *Drugs from A to Z*, p. 65, 1969
- —Edward R. Bloomquist, *Marijuana*, p. 338, 1971
- —Mike Haskins, *Drugs*, p. 279, 2003

5 a tablet of MDMA, the recreational drug best known as ecstasy *UK*

- —Mike Haskins, *Drugs*, p. 289, 2003

dollar *noun*

1 five shillings *UK, 1848*

Dating from those happy days when the rate of exchange was US$4 to £1.

- Ginger felt in his pockets. "I've got sis and six." "I've got a dollar," said Barney.—John Burke and Stuart Douglass, *The Boys*, p. 88, 1962

2 a variety of MDMA, the recreational drug best known as ecstasy *UK*

- —Angela Devlin, *Prison Patter*, p. 46, 1996

3 money *UK*

- [W]hen the establishment Mafioso realise how much gilt, paper, cashish, wonga, wedge, corn, cutter, loot, spondos, dollar, readies, shillings, folding, dough, money is on offer[.]—J.J. Connolly, *Layer Cake*, p. 94, 2000
- No, it don't work like that. No, you got to give me the dollar.—Goldie Coloured Chain, *21 Ounces*, 2004

dollar *nickname*

Route 100 in eastern Pennsylvania *US*

- —Gwyneth A. "Dandalion" Seese, *Tijuana Bear in a Smoke 'Um Up Taxi*, p. 15, 1977

dollar ride *noun*

an orientation flight on a military aircraft *US, 1975*

- The next day, they'd get their dollar ride, an orientation flight around the area.—Walter Boyne and Steven Thompson, *The Wild Blue*, p. 69, 1986
- Boyd first went on what was called the "dollar ride," an orientation flight over northeastern Mississippi, where he would be flying for the next several months.—Robert Coram, *Boyd*, p. 40, 2002

dollars *noun*

a type of bet in an illegal numbers game lottery *US*

- He played the money row, lucky lady, happy days, true love, sun gonna shine, gold, silver, diamonds, dollars and whiskey.—Chester Himes, *A Rage in Harlem*, p. 23, 1957

dollars to doughnut

very high odds, indicating a high degree of certainty *US*

- Why, I'll bet you a dollar to a doughnut my dog'll point five birds to your dog's one.—Ken Weaver, *Texas Crude*, p. 110, 1984
- I'm laying dollars to doughnuts we can pass the proposal in the '47 Special.—James Ellroy, *The Black Dahlia*, p. 20, 1987
- "Dollars to doughnuts he's at his social club," Vinnie said.—Janet Evanovich, *Seven Up*, p. 14, 2001

dollop *noun*

a lump; hence, in a figurative sense, a clumsy individual; a formless mess – 'a dollop of custard' *UK, 1812*

From an earlier sense (a tuft of grass).

- Here, a dollop of brown sauce, there, the dried mucus of a Marks and Spencer fish in white-wine sauce[.]—Jenny Eclair, *Camberwell Beauty*, p. 208, 2000

dollop; dollop out *verb*

to share out a formless mess *UK*

From the noun sense.

- [A] constant line of men walked by them [serving hatches] for us to dollop the day's menu on to their metal trays.—Ken Lukowiak, *Marijuana Time*, p. 262, 2000

doll's eyes *noun*

eyes rolling upward, suggesting neurological depression *US*

- —*Maledicta*, p. 32, 1988–1989: 'Medical maledicta from San Francisco'

doll shop *noun*

a brothel *US*

- After all, Ah Toy once worked at one of Johnny Formosa's doll shops.—Seth Morgan, *Homeboy*, p. 127, 1990

doll's house *noun*

a prison *UK*

Most likely inspired by the toy and not the Ibsen play.

- —Angela Devlin, *Prison Patter*, p. 46, 1996

doll up *verb*

to dress up, to refine *US, 1906*

- Getting themselves all dolled up and then setting out to start a row[.]—John Burke and Stuart Douglass, *The Boys*, p. 45, 1962
- I got myself all dolled up and went down – big night at the Copa.—Edwin Torers, *Carlito's Way*, p. 26, 1975
- The head of CBS Sports called from the Bel Air Hotel to say he was on the Coast for a few days to "doll up an affiliate."—Dan Jenkins, *Life Its Ownself*, p. 159, 1984

dolly *noun*

1 the vagina *UK*

In the C19, a 'dolly' was a 'penis', possibly from a 'child's dolly' (a toy a girl might play with); equally, it could derive from 'washing dolly' (a device plunged in and out of wet laundry). The etymology here is likely to be the former: 'Can I play with your dolly?'.

- —*Sky Magazine*, July 2001

2 an attractive young woman *UK, 1906*
Very much a word of its time.
- — *Newsweek*, p. 28, 8th October 1951
- In what seems like not more than two minutes, four or five dollies are on the premises. — Robert Sylvester, *No Cover Charge*, p. 266, 1956
- [A] Britain where [...] women were pneumatic dollies or sex-starved harridans[.] — Stuart Jeffries, *Mrs Slocombe's Pussy*, p. 101, 2000

3 a homosexual who lives in the suburbs *UK*
- — *Attitude*, p. 60, July 2003: 'New palare lexicon'

4 a lesbian prisoner's lover *NEW ZEALAND*
- — Harry Orsman, *A Dictionary of Modern New Zealand Slang*, p. 41, 1999

5 a very feminine fashion style of the 1960s *UK*
- — Janey Ironside, *A Fashion Alphabet*, p. 14, 1968

6 a capsule of Dolophine™, known generically as methadone *US, 1954*
- Maybe they're putting some synthetic shit in it... Dollies or something. — William Burroughs, *Naked Lunch*, p. 214, 1957
- "Even without dollies," Tom Tear said, "I could kick it in three days." — Alexander Trocchi, *Cain's Book*, p. 31, 1960
- I was clean for seven days, and after that I was on my own – without the dollies. — Jeremy Larner and Ralph Tefferteller, *The Addict in the Street*, p. 69, 1964
- I had a doctor – right up here on 14th Street – he was giving out dollies and goofballs to everyone; in fact, he got arrested. — Ralph Tefferteller, *The Addict in the Street*, p. 69, 1964
- — Sidney Cohen, *The Drug Dilemma*, p. 128, 1969
- I had one little bitty piece of dolly [Dolophine] in my aspirin box. — Bruce Jackson, *In the Life*, p. 84, 1972

7 in cricket, a simple catch *UK, 1904*
Possibly of Anglo-Indian origin. Reduced from 'dolly catch'.
- Drop a dolly. — Steve James, captain of, *Glamorgan County Cricket Club*, 18th June 2003

dolly *verb*
to interrogate *AUSTRALIA*
- — *The (Sydney) Bulletin*, 26th April 1975

dolly *adjective*
attractive, pretty; nice *UK, 1964*
Polari.
- Sitting, sipping a tiny drinkette, vadaing [watching] the great butch omis [men] and dolly little palones [women] trolling by[.] — Barry Took and Marty Feldman, *Round The Horne*, 30th April 1967
- B: You don't fancy him do you? A: Well, I'm not sure. Bona brandy [good bottom] on it. Dolly drag [clothes] too. — Emma Hindley, *Storm in a Teacup*, 1993
- — *Attitude*, p. 60, July 2003: 'Old palare lexicon'

dolly bag *noun*
the cloth bag carried by female prisoners *UK*
- — Angela Devlin, *Prison Patter*, p. 46, 1996

dolly bird *noun*
an attractive young woman *UK, 1964*
- The dolly-bird as the London female is affecitonately dubbed. — *San Francisco Chronicle*, p. 20, 24th August 1966
- While they're doing this, you drop back to give them room to drop back so they can see, and a long-hair with a dolly bird in his pocket burns into the space. — John O'Grady, *Aussie Etiket*, p. 56, 1971
- My friend Joe Barrowclough was in the bar, with a dolly bird at his one elbow and a pint of bitter at the other. — Doug Lang, *Freaks*, p. 116, 1973
- But at school there were all these little dolly birds in their school uniforms, the dresses as short as they would go so that you would glimpse their panties every time they made a move. — *Alvin Purple*, p. 15, 1974
- Loads of dolly-birds in there. — Caroline Aherne and Craig Cash, *The Royle Family*, 1999

dolly boy *noun*
a youthful, attractive homosexual male prostitute *UK*
An evolution from DILLY BOY.
- — *Maledicta*, p. 220, 1979: 'Kinks and queens: linguistic and cultural aspects of the terminology for gays'

Dolly Cotton *adjective*
rotten *UK, 1931*
Rhyming slang.

dolly dimple; dolly *adjective*
simple *UK*
Glasgow rhyming slang. Current in English prisons February 2002.
- Ye'll need tae excuse her... she's a wee bit dolly. — Michael Munro, *The Patter, Another Blast*, 1988

dolly flapper *noun*
a railway pointsman *US*
- — Norman Carlisle, *The Modern Wonder Book of Trains and Railroading*, p. 262, 1946

dolly mixtures *noun*
the cinema, the movies *UK*
Rhyming slang for 'the pictures'.
- — Ray Puxley, *Cockney Rabbit*, 1992

dolly-over-teakettles *adverb*
head-over-heels *US, 1982*
- — Frederic G. Cassidy, *Dictionary of American Regional English, Volume II*, p. 126, 1991

Dolly Parton *noun*
in craps, a roll of two ones *US, 1983*
Dolly Parton is a talented and popular American country singer and songwriter with big hair and big breasts; the single dots on the two dice suggested to someone her breasts.
- — Thomas L. Clark, *The Dictionary of Gambling and Gaming*, p. 65, 1987

dolly sweetness *noun*
a pretty girl *US*
- — Marcus Hanna Boulware, *Jive and Slang of Students in Negro Colleges*, 1947

dolo *noun*
methadone *US*
A shortened form of Dolophine™, a protected trade name for methadone.
- — Richard A. Spears, *The Slang and Jargon of Drugs and Drink*, p. 148, 1986

do lo *adverb*
secret *US*
An abbreviation of DOWNLOW.
- — Connie Eble (Editor), *UNC-CH Campus Slang*, p. 2, Spring 1999

dolphin *noun*

1 a variety of MDMA, the recreational drug best known as ecstasy *UK*
- — Angela Devlin, *Prison Patter*, p. 46, 1996

2 a flaccid penis *US*
- — *Adult Video News*, p. 51, October 1995

▸ **wax the dolphin**
of a male, to masturbate *US*
- Most guys come in here, they wax the dolphin. That's it – it's over. — *The Guru*, 2002

dolphin ball *noun*
in pinball, a ball that stays in play for a relatively long period without scoring many points *US*
- — Bobbye Claire Natkin and Steve Kirk, *All About Pinball*, p. 112, 1977

dom; domme *noun*

1 a dominatrix *US*
- [T]he most in-demand dom in the north-west. — Niall Griffiths, *Kelly + Victor*, p. 228, 2002

2 the dominant performer in a pornographic sex scene *US*
- — Ana Loria, *1 2 3 Be A Porn Star!*, p. 164, 2000: 'Glossary of adult sex industry terms'

3 a sexual dominant in sadomasochistic sexual relationships *US*
- — Thomas Murray and Thomas Murrell, *The Language of Sadomasochism*, p. 61, 1989

4 a person's room, apartment or house *US*
A shortened variant of the more common DOMMY.
- The Beatnik knocked his stroll right then, went straight down to his dom[.] — Dan Burley, *Diggeth Thou?*, p. 34, 1959

DOM *noun*
an older homosexual who is attracted to younger men and boys; a *d*irty *o*ld *m*an *US, 1966*
- — *Maledicta*, p. 221, 1979: 'Kinks and queens: linguistic and cultural aspects of the terminology for gays'

dom *adjective*

1 sexually *dom*inant *US, 1989*
- We ticked off everything – Bi, Sub, Dom, Leather, Rubber, PVC, Bondage, Water Sports[.] — Kitty Churchill, *Thinking of England*, p. 100, 1995

2 stupid, dumb *SOUTH AFRICA, 1942*
An Afrikaans word in the South African English colloquial vocabulary.
- — Jean Branford, *A Dictionary of South African English*, 1978

do me a favour; do me *noun*
a neighbour *UK*
Rhyming slang. Like many next door neighbours the rhyme is not quite perfect.
- For many the ideal "do me" is one who is not there when he's not wanted. —Ray Puxley, *Fresh Rabbit*, 1998

do me a favour!
used for expressing disbelief and refutation of a point or suggestion just raised *UK*
- Ten thousand bloody sightseers! Do me a favour, it wasn't bank holiday. —Arnold Wesker, *Chicken Soup with Barley*, 1958

dome doily *noun*
a hat *US*
- One day this top-kick hangs his dome doily on a pole in the market place and says everybody will bow to the bonnet. —Haenigsen, *Jive's Like That*, 1947

do me good *noun*
a *Wood*bine cigarette *UK, 1960*
Rhyming slang that evolved during World War 1, and survived in mid-C20 as an expression of defiance when cigarettes were scientifically linked with cancer.

domes *noun*
LSD *US*
- As we came walking along, on White Lightning and Purple Haze double domes, Owssley's first purple double domes, somebody walked up and said, "You guys have such pretty smiles.' —Stephen Gaskin, *Amazing Dope Tales*, p. 81, 1980
- —US Department of Justice, *Street Terms*, October 1994
- —Mike Haskins, *Drugs*, p. 285, 2003

dome slug *noun*
in Antarctica, a support personnel assigned to the geodesic dome at the top of the American Scott-Amundsen base *ANTARCTICA*
- —*Cool Antarctica*, 2003: 'Antarctic slang'

domie *noun*
dory-mate (short form) *CANADA*
- Your domie is a person in close relation to you, when you both work on a fishing boat and he is the other half of your pair, the other man in the dory doing hand- or long-line fishing. —Lewis Poteet, *The South Shore Phrase Book*, p. 38, 1999

Dominican Dandy *nickname*
Juan Marichal (b.1937), a high-kicking, overpowering pitcher (1960–75) *US*
From the Dominican Republic, and 'a fastidious dresser'.

domino *noun*
1 a black and white capsule containing a mixture of central nervous system stimulants and depressants *US*
- —Eugene Landy, *The Underground Dictionary*, p. 69, 1971
- —Jay Robert Nash, *Dictionary of Crime*, p. 107, 1992

2 a 12.5 mg tablet of Durophet™, an amphetamine *US, 1971*
- —Carl Chambers and Richard Heckman, *Employee Drug Abuse*, p. 204, 1972

domino *verb*
to stop or finish *US*
- —Lavada Durst, *The Jives of Dr. Hepcat*, p. 12, 1953

domkop *noun*
a fool *SOUTH AFRICA, 1910*
From Afrikaans *dom* (stupid) and *kop* (head).
- Domkop! Don't you even know your left from your right? —Bryce Courtenay, *Power of One*, p. 38, 1989

domme *noun*
▷ see: **DOM**

dommo *noun*
one who performs well *US*
Applied to skateboarding, surfing and snowboarding.
- —Vann Wesson, *Generation X Field Guide and Lexicon*, p. 56, 1997

dommo *verb*
to perform well; to dominate *US*
- —*Surfing*, p. 43, 14th March 1990

dommy; dommie *noun*
a home *US, 1943*
From '*domi*cile'.
- Harry Shapiro was crazy about musicians so we headed straight for his dommy. —Mezz Mezzrow, *Really the Blues*, p. 50, 1946
- Tis the gonest little dommy that a chick like you could pick. —Dan Burley, *Diggeth Thou?*, p. 33, 1959
- One more fine dommie that narco built. —Robert Deane Pharr, *Giveadamn Brown*, p. 123, 1978

Dom P *noun*
*Dom P*erignon champagne *UK*
- But there was nowt goin' down anywhere except cocaine, pills and vintage Dom P. —Ben Elton, *High Society*, p. 119, 2002

doms *noun*
*dom*inoes *UK*
- —*Loughborough Echo*, 4th June 1982: 'King of the doms'

don; don man *noun*
a respected leader *UK*
Ultimately from Spanish *Don* (an honorific), via gangster use. West Indian, hence UK black.
- One of the dons that cropped up in my sword-and-sorcery films was old Richard Lionheart. —Diran Abedayo, *My Once Upon A Time*, p. 151, 2000

don *verb*
▸ **don the beard**
to perform oral sex on a woman *AUSTRALIA*
- —Barry Humphries, *Bazza Pulls It Off!*, 1971

dona; donah; donna; doner *noun*
a woman, especially a girlfriend *UK, 1859*
Polari, from Spanish *doña* or Portuguese *dona* (a woman).
- She was hard to please, rather a "nark" as he put it, and easily "needled" (annoyed), but a "clever dona" (good girl) and a "grafter" (worker). —Butch Reynolds, *Broken Hearted Clown*, p. 29, 1953
- —Paul Baker, *Polari*, p. 171, 2002

dona juana *noun*
marijuana *US*
A Spanish 'Lady Jane'.
- —Richard A. Spears, *The Slang and Jargon of Drugs and Drink*, p. 148, 1986
- —Mike Haskins, *Drugs*, p. 287, 2003

dona juanita *noun*
marijuana *US, 1938*
A Spanish 'Lady Jane'.
- —Richard A. Spears, *The Slang and Jargon of Drugs and Drink*, p. 148, 1986
- —Mike Haskins, *Drugs*, p. 287, 2003

Donald Duck; donald *noun*
1 an act of sexual intercourse *AUSTRALIA*
Rhyming slang for **FUCK**.
- Donald Duck – Sexual intercourse. —Ryan Aven-Bray, *Ridgey Didge Oz Jack Lang*, p. 24, 1983
- Donald Duck: a fuck. —John Meredith, *Learn to talk Old Jack Lang*, p. 23, 1984

2 by extension, a 'fuck' in all other senses *UK*
Rhyming slang, from the Disney cartoon character.
- I don't give a Donald Duck what you think. —Ray Puxley, *Cockney Rabbit*, p. 52, 1992

3 luck *UK*
Rhyming slang, from the Disney cartoon character.
- [A] girl, very much down on her Donald Duck[.] —Ronnie Barker, *Fletcher's Book of Rhyming Slang*, p. 39, 1979
- [H]ow's your Donald Duck? —Ray Puxley, *Cockney Rabbit*, p. 52, 1992

Donald Duck *verb*
to have sexual intercourse *AUSTRALIA*
Rhyming slang for **FUCK**.
- Donald Duck – Sexual intercourse. —Ryan Aven-Bray, *Ridgey Didge Oz Jack Lang*, p. 24, 1983
- We washed down the meal with Germaine Greers and Donald Ducked on the Rory O'Moore. —Kathy Lette, *Girls Night Out*, p. 170, 1987

Donald Ducked *adjective*
exhausted *UK*
Rhyming slang for **FUCKED**.
- I'll be Donald Ducked if I'm gonny yodel for any bint. —Ian Pattison, *Rab C. Nesbitt*, 1988

Donald Duck Navy *noun*

the anti-submarine fleet of the US Navy *US, 1947*

- Most of the men and officers, Reservists and regulars, on PCs served with pride in what they called the "Donald Duck Navy." —Wm. J. Veigle, *PC Patrol Craft of World War II*, p. 79, 1998

Donald Duck suit *noun*

the blue uniform of sailors in the US Navy *US, 1972*

- He picked the Navy "because of the uniform." HIs friend had told him: "If you want to get into the Donald Duck suit, go down and sign up." —Robert S. La Forte, *Remembering Pearl Harbor*, p. 288, 1991

Donald Peers; donalds *noun*

the ears *UK*

Rhyming slang, formed on popular singer and recording artist Donald Peers, 1909–73.

- With young Justin committing GBH of the Donalds? —Anthony Masters, *Minder*, p. 23, 1984

Donald Trump *noun*

an act of defecation *UK, 2002*

Rhyming slang for **DUMP**; based on celebrated US businessman Donald Trump (b.1946), possibly an extravagant play on New York landmark Trump Tower.

- I'm just nipping out for a Donald. — *www.LondonSlang.com*, June 2002
- —Bodmin Dark, *Dirty Cockney Rhyming Slang*, 2003

donar *noun*

a steady girlfriend *US*

- —Kenn "Naz" Young, *Naz's Dictionary of Teen Slang*, p. 32, 1993

don dada *noun*

a very important person *JAMAICA*

Noted as Rasta patois for '**TOP DOG**, highest of all dons' by Paul Sullivan, *Sullivan's Music Trivia*, 2003.

donder; donner *noun*

used as an abusive term of address or reference, a bastard *SOUTH AFRICA, 1969*

From Afrikaans *donder* (a scoundrel).

- —Jean Branford, *A Dictionary of South African English*, 1978

done and dusted

1 completely finished *UK*

- [W]hen that's done and dusted, he's been picked by industry bigwigs[.] — *The Times Magazine*, p. 10, 2nd March 2002

2 beaten up *UK*

- —Paul Tempest, *Lag's Lexicon*, 1950

done deal *noun*

an agreement that has been reached *US*

Folksy, a hint of the South.

- The late-night Saturday anonymous caller said it was a "done deal." The reporter winced, having been through "done deals" before. — *Arkansas Democrat-Gazette*, 22nd January 1990
- The proposed extended-stay Saybride Suites hotel and B. Smith restaurant on the 1.24-acre site between the Waterside festival marketplace and the Spirit of Norfolk berth are called "a done deal." — *The Virginian-Pilot*, p. B8, 26th April 2001

done-done *adjective*

over-cooked *BAHAMAS*

- —John A. Holm, *Dictionary of Bahamian English*, p. 63, 1982

done in *adjective*

tired out, exhausted *UK*

- Paula and Dawn from work done in by the end of the night[.] —John King, *White Trash*, p. 88, 2001

doner *noun*

▷ see: DONA

done thing *noun*

whatever is considered to be the correct etiquette *UK, 1961*

Always with 'the'.

done up *adjective*

dressed up *UK, C20*

- My little Dolly looked a real treat. All done up with a big wide skirt and high heels. —John Peter Jones, *Feather Pluckers*, p. 19, 1964

dong *noun*

1 the penis *US, 1900*

- I'll bend his mangy dong in half and stomp on it[.] —David Markson, *The Ballad of Dingus Magree*, p. 19, 1965
- Ginger's hands quickly pulled open his trousers and she moaned as his long dong popped out rigid as a hammer. —James Harper, *Homo Laws in all 50 States*, p. 117–118, 1968
- Nevertheless, I was wholly incapable of keeping my paws from my dong once it started the climb up my belly. —Philip Roth, *Portnoy's Complaint*, p. 18, 1969
- Hugh was stroking her back and feeling hanky-panky, winking through the cartoon picture at the audience and pulling on his dong. —Steve Cannon, *Groove, Bang, and Jive Around*, p. 142, 1969
- A squeeze on the dong under the bar? —Darryl Ponicsan, *The Last Detail*, p. 72, 1970
- Wait, the mother whipped out his dong and now he's waving it flappingly, AT ME. —Paul Glover, *Words from the House of the Dead*, 1974
- There I am with my dong in my hand when a guy come up and asks if I need any help. — *Taxi Driver*, 1976
- I've got pains in my arms and my dong is growing shorter[.] —Ivor Biggun, *The Winker's Song (Misprint)*, 1978
- A quality girl likes a long word almost as much as she likes a long dong. —Sacha Baron-Cohen, *Da Gospel According to Ali G*, 2001

2 a thing of no worth *UK*

- I couldn't give a dong about anyone else. —Shaun Ryder, *Shaun Ryder... in His Own Words*, 1991

dong *verb*

to punch or hit *AUSTRALIA, 1916*

- 'You keep out of it, mister, or Socker'll dong you, too' warned Annie. —Vince Kelly, *The Bogeyman*, p. 43, 1956
- Would you dong a bloody copper if you caught the cunt alone? —S. Hogbotel and S. ffuckes, *Snatches and Lays*, p. 82, 1962

donga *noun*

1 (especially in South Australia) natural bush wilderness *AUSTRALIA*

- He stared at the darkening sky, listened to the mournful howl of a dingo across the wastes of the donga, cursing himself for his stupidity. —Jean Brooks, *The Opal Witch*, p. 25, 1967
- The whole battalion camped out in the donga. —Clive James, *Unreliable Memoirs*, p. 153, 1980

2 a temporary dwelling *AUSTRALIA, 1900*

- The air inside the closed donga was hot and stale. —James McQueen, *Uphill Runner*, p. 128, 1984

3 a watercourse *AUSTRALIA, 1902*

- —Dymphna Cusack, *Picnic Races*, p. 120, 1962
- On a flat and treeless piece of plain was a bare circle of reddish clay, shaped to form the shallowest of depressions and known as a donga. —Ray Ericksen, *West of Centre*, p. 87, 1972

4 a sleeping area *ANTARCTICA*

An Australian contribution to the language of the South Pole.

- — *Cool Antarctica*, 2003: 'Antarctic slang'

dongce *noun*

the penis *UK*

- Nonsense slang referred to vague, inoffensive terms that had little or no meanings in standard English: terms like biff, foo-foo, minky and winkie in FGTs [female genital terms], and chod, dongce, spondoolies, and winks in MGTs [male genital terms]. — *Journal of Sex Research*, p. 146, 2001

donger *noun*

the penis *AUSTRALIA, 1971*

- —Barry Humphries, *Bazza Pulls It Off!*, 1971
- [T]wo or three heavily tattooed oiks with enormous dongers, you know[.] —Mike Stott, *Soldiers Talking, Cleanly*, 1978
- Then he'd stick his donger through the hole. —Sam Weller, *Old Bastards I Have Met*, p. 18, 1979
- [A]ll they do is line up a salesman with a donger like a baby's arm who isn't fussy where he puts it. —Barry Humphries, *The Traveller's Tool*, p. 19, 1985
- —David McGill, *David McGill's Complete Kiwi Slang Dictionary*, p. 38, 1998
- Old Bill [the police] could turn round and tell us when they felt like getting their dongers out. —Jeremy Cameron, *Brown Bread in Wengen*, p. 76, 1999
- [T]he only semblance of purpose they get is waving their dongers, hither-thither. —Gretel Killeen, *Hot Buns and Ophelia get shipwrecked*, p. 45, 2001

dongle *noun*

1 a security scheme for a commerical microcomputer progam *US*

- —Eric S. Raymond, *The New Hacker's Dictionary*, p. 129, 1991

2 in computing, an Ethernet or LocalTalk connector *US*

- —Andy Ihnatko, *Cyberspeak*, p. 58, 1997

3 an electronic key that hangs on a cord around the neck *UK, 2001*

In use in the Bristol offices of the BBC during 2001.

don jem *noun*

marijuana *UK, 1998*

- —Mike Haskins, *Drugs*, p. 287, 2003

donk *noun*

1 a *donkey* *US, 1868*

- But you ought to have seen me when I was breaking in the donks and the nigs to the plough!—Ion L. Idriess, *Over the Range*, p. 242, 1947
- —Bill Hornadge, *The Ugly Australian*, p. 119, 1969

2 a racehorse *NEW ZEALAND, 1952*

An abbreviation of 'donkey'.

- —Harry Orsman, *A Dictionary of Modern New Zealand Slang*, p. 41, 1999

3 large, protruding buttocks *US*

A term often associated with celebrity Jennifer Lopez.

- —Connie Eble (Editor), *UNC-CH Campus Slang*, p. 3, November 2003

4 an engine *US, 1942*

- That damned starboard donk!—W.R. Bennett, *Wingman*, p. 16, 1961
- —W.R. Bennett, *Target Turin*, p. 32, 1962
- —W.R. Bennett, *Night Intruder*, p. 56, 1962
- I'm not weird or anything, I just put the flagpole up when I feel the vibration of a donk.—Roy Slaven (John Doyle), *Five South Coast Seasons*, p. 125, 1992

donkey *noun*

1 a black person *US, 1857*

- Tell me, Dadier, what do you think of kikes and mockies and micks and donkeys and frogs and niggers, Dadier.—Evan Hunter, *The Blackboard Jungle*, p. 209, 1954

2 a manual labourer *US, 1932*

- —Norman Carlisle, *The Modern Wonder Book of Trains and Railroading*, p. 262, 1946

3 a fool *UK, 1840*

- Some bastards take me for a donkey and that's for sure!—Barry Humphries, *Bazza Pulls It Off!*, 1971

4 (especially in South Australia) a lift on a bicycle *AUSTRALIA, 1981*

- As a child living in Adelaide we always used the word 'donkey' if we wanted a ride on the back of someones bike. It was always, "can I have a donkey?"—*Wordmap (www.abc.net.au/wordmap)*, 2003

5 a resident of Guernsey (in the Channel Islands) according to those on Jersey *UK*

- Residents of Jersey call residents of Guernsey donkeys. There is a strong rivalry between the two islands.—John Lahr, *Dame Edna Everage and the Rise of Western Civilisation*, p. 198, 1991

▸ **pull your donkey**

(used of a male) to masturbate *US*

- They'd be pulling their donkeys all night, beating their meat, whispering back and forth.—Robert Campbell, *Sweet La-La Land*, p. 136, 1990

donkey *verb*

(especially in South Australia) to give someone a lift on a bicycle *AUSTRALIA, 1981*

- Hop on the bike with me and I will donkey you home.—*Wordmap (www.abc.net.au/wordmap)*, 2003

donkey days *noun*

a very long time *BAHAMAS*

- —John A. Holm, *Dictionary of Bahamian English*, p. 63, 1982

donkey deep *adjective*

enthusiastically engaged *NEW ZEALAND*

- —David McGill, *David McGill's Complete Kiwi Slang Dictionary*, p. 41, 1998

donkey dick *noun*

1 a man with a large penis; a large penis *US*

- —*Maledicta*, p. 189, Winter 1980: 'A new erotic vocabulary'
- Mickey's got a big donkey dick.—*Natural Born Killers*, 1994
- Little fuckin' fag! Donkey dick!—*Boogie Nights*, 1997
- De Carlo was soon dubbed, by the girls, Donkey Dick Dan due to abundance in down-scope.—Ed Sanders, *The Family*, p. 108, 2002

2 sausage; unidentified pressed meat *US*

- —Carl Fleischhauer, *A Glossary of Army Slang*, p. 26, 1968

3 the flexible spout attached to the opening of a container *US*

- —Gregory Clark, *Words of the Vietnam War*, p. 150, 1990
- We would manhandle it up onto the tank, and we would put a donkey-dick (a flexible, screw-in spout) into the bung of the drum, open it up, and refuel the thing right there.—Oscar E. Gilbert, *Marine Tank Battles in the Pacific*, p. 247, 2001

4 a large electrical cable connector *US*

- —Gregory Clark, *Words of the Vietnam War*, p. 150–151, 1990

5 a prolonged, insatiable erection due to extended heroin use *US*

- —Jim Crotty, *How to Talk American*, p. 94, 1997

donkey doctor *noun*

a mechanic who works on donkey engines *US, 2003*

- It was operated by a donkeydoctor and a fireman.—Sedro-Wolley Historical Society, *Sedro-Woolley*, p. 56, 2003

donkey jammer *noun*

the operator of a donkey (auxiliary) engine *CANADA*

- I'm a donkey-jammer from hell and back, / With a Humboldt yarder a "Cracker Jack."—Robert Swanson, *Rhymes of a Haywire Hooker*, p. 41, 1953

donkey-lick *verb*

to defeat convincingly *AUSTRALIA, 1890*

- In the end, he donkey-licked his rivals[.]—*Herald*, p. 20, 1st May 1988
- —Ned Wallish, *The Truth Dictionary of Racing Slang*, p. 23, 1989

donkey punch *noun*

during homosexual anal intercourse, a sharp blow given by the active partner to the passive partner's kidneys *UK*

The sudden pain from the blow causes a clenching of the buttocks and tightening of the rectal passage, thereby enhancing the pleasure of the penetrating participant.

- Brace yourself for the "Donkey Punch"[.]—*Popbitch*, 6th April 2005

donkey-puncher *noun*

the operator of a donkey engine *US, 1920*

- There was a guy came out of the logging camp – I think he was a donkey puncher, 'cause he was making good money.—Wayde Compton, *Bluesprint*, p. 107, 2001

donkey's ages *noun*

a very long time *UK*

A variation of **DONKEY'S YEARS**.

donkey shins

thank you *US*

Intentionally butchered German.

- —Connie Eble (Editor), *UNC-CH Campus Slang*, p. 3, Spring 1990

donkey sight *noun*

an imprecise but easily manoeuvred manual sight on a tank's main gun *US*

- —Gregory Clark, *Words of the Vietnam War*, p. 150, 1990

donkey style *adjective*

(used of sex) anal *US*

- —Connie Eble (Editor), *UNC-CH Campus Slang*, p. 2, November 2002

donkey's years; donkeys' years; donkeys *noun*

a very long time *UK, 1916*

A pun on the length and sound of a 'donkey's ears'.

- Dibbs even brought his pet parrot Percy in, he's had it for donkeys' and it meant the world to him[.]—Roy Slaven (John Doyle), *Five South Coast Seasons*, p. 14, 1992
- The two of them had known each other for donkey's years, even when Mick was a civvy[.]—Andy McNab (writing of the late 1970s/early 80s), *Immediate Action*, p. 161, 1995
- We even gave him a few old books that have been knocking around donkeys, not of donkeys you understand but shit that's been on the premises too fuckin long and ain't movin.—J.J. Connolly, *Layer Cake*, p. 27, 2000
- [M]y old man and his generation who had to go round "courting" for donkey's years before getting a sniff.—Danny King, *The Burglar Diaries*, p. 29, 2001

donkey vote *noun*

a vote made by simply filling out a ballot paper in the order the candidates are listed in *AUSTRALIA*

- The system of compulsory voting at elections, with fines for non-attendance, makes the 'donkey vote' the vote of those who just vote down the list from top to bottom – a factor in political planning. —Donald Horne, *The Lucky Country*, p. 13, 1964
- —Jim Ramsay, *Cop It Sweet!*, p. 31, 1977

donkey work *noun*

difficult, menial labour *UK, 1920*

- What did God make cunts for, if not to save women from donkey-work?—Michel Faber, *The Crimson Petal and the White*, p. 13, 2002

donko *noun*
a lunchroom or tea room at a workplace *NEW ZEALAND*
• Hastening up the stairs to the 'donko' to wrap the sacking known as 'sneakers' around his boots. — Ronald Hugh Morrieson, *Pallet on the Floor*, p. 53, 1976
• In the woolstores, smoko was held in the donko, where we'd adjourn after working like billyo. — *Listener*, p. 13, 14th April 1984

donks *noun*
a very long time *UK*
An abbreviation of **DONKEY'S YEARS**, but it is worth noting the similarity to synonymous **YONKS**.
• Ah mean wi wir mates donks ago biy wi drifted apart, ken? — Irvine Welsh, *The State of the Party (Disco Biscuits)*, p. 46, 1995

don man, donna, donner *nouns*
▷ see: **DON, DONA, DONDER**

donner; donder *verb*
to thrash, to beat up *SOUTH AFRICA, 1916*
• We don't have the wooden flaps anymore – I think they were invented to try to stop black bartenders from getting donnered. — *Sunday Times (South Africa)*, 3rd February 2002

donnie; donny *noun*
a fracas *NEW ZEALAND*
An abbreviation of **DONNYBROOK**.
• 'There was a donny down at the Foresters tonight' he said. 'Couple of them was belting him with a bottle'. — Noel Hillard, *Maori Girl*, p. 257, 1960

donniker *noun*
1 a toilet *US, 1937*
• — Joe McKennon, *Circus Lingo*, p. 31, 1980
• — Gene Sorrows, *All About Carnivals*, p. 15, 1985: 'Terminology'
• "And look, there are een donnickers for the patrons." He pointed to two privy-sized boxes off to one side[.] — Gary Jennings, *The Center Ring*, p. 99, 1987
2 the penis *US, 1951*
• Otherwise he would have to have a terrifically long donniker to have her fall in love with him overnight. — Todd McCarthy, *Howard Hawks*, p. 159, 1997
3 a railway brakeman on a freight train *US, 1932*
• — Norman Carlisle, *The Modern Wonder Book of Trains and Railroading*, p. 262, 1946

donniker location *noun*
a poor location on a carnival midway *US*
• — Gene Sorrows, *All About Carnivals*, p. 15, 1985: 'Terminology'

Donniker Sam *noun*
a man who begs for money in a public toilet *US*
• — Don Wilmeth, *The Language of American Popular Entertainment*, p. 76, 1981

donny *noun*
a fight *AUSTRALIA*
• — Wilda Moxham, *The Apprentice*, p. 63, 1969
• 'You've been in a donny!' Wally said, wild instead of sorry at what had happened to his face[.] — Wilda Moxham, *The Apprentice*, p. 169, 1969

donnybrook *noun*
a riot, a tumult *UK, 1852*
• And on one such occasion we got involved in a donnybrook. I can't say how it started, and I doubt that any of the other particpants could. — Jim Thompson, *Bad Boy*, p. 386, 1953

Don Revie *noun*
an alcoholic drink, especially beer *UK*
Rhyming slang for **BEVVY** (an alcoholic drink, especially beer), formed from the name of football manager Don Revie, 1927–89, and probably coined during his tenure in charge of the England team (1974–78).
• — Ray Puxley, *Fresh Rabbit*, 1998

don't *noun*
in craps, a bet against the shooter *US*
• — *The Annals of the American Academy of Political and Social Sciences*, p. 124, May 1950
• At the dice table, the professor would bet either on or against the shooter – otherwise known as do or don't, right or wrong – at $1,000 a shot on what may or may not have been a system. — Edward Lin, *Big Julie of Vegas*, p. 47, 1974

don't ask, don't tell
used as a humorous, if jaded, reminder that some things are best left unknown *US, 1993*
An addage coined to describe the official approach to homosexuals in the US military under the Clinton administration; a soldier would not be asked about his or her sexual preference, but would be expected not to reveal their homosexuality.
• — Steven Daly and Nalthaniel Wice, *alt.culture*, p. 64, 1995

don't be rude *noun*
food *UK*
Rhyming slang.
• — Ray Puxley, *Cockney Rabbit*, 1992

don't call us, we'll call you
used as a catchphrase that is generally understood to be a polite, or not-so-polite, rejection of an application for employment *US, 1968*
Adopted from the world of entertainment where it is traditionally supposed to signal the end of an unsuccessful audition.
• Guards frequently complain that they are never consulted by the administrators. As one guard commented, "their attitude is don't call us, we'll call you." — Robert Melvin Carter and Daniel Glaser, *Correctional Institutions*, p. 211, 1977

don't-care-damn *adjective*
entirely indifferent *GRENADA, 1976*
• — Richard Allsopp, *Dictionary of Caribbean English Usage*, p. 199, 1996

don't-care-ish *adjective*
apathetic, indifferent *US, 1927*
• Well, Eleanora just went out and done what she felt like doing 'cause she was just don't care-ish. — Donald Clarke, *Billie Holiday*, p. 27, 2000

don't come the raw prawn
do not attempt to dupe me *AUSTRALIA*
Military slang from World War 2. The literal meaning of this phrase has not been satisfactorily explained. 'Prawn' has been used in Australia since C19 to mean 'fool', so a 'raw prawn' could mean a 'naive fool', and if 'come' is to be understood as 'to act the part of', the phrase would imply trying to dupe someone by feigned ignorance. Some have defined 'raw prawn' as 'something far-fetched, difficult to swallow'. If this is so, then 'come' would mean 'perpetrate', which is also possible. Simes (*A Dictionary of Australian Underworld Slang*, 1993) conjectures a link with 'prawn' meaning 'penis', but it is hard to see how this could be so.
• MAC: I heard the Crab say the Colonel said there was only eight goin' a week and that Andy and me was one of the first eight. OT: Don't come the raw prawn. What does the Crab know, and anyhow you don't think he'd tell you, do you? — Sumner Locke Elliott, *Rusty Bugles*, p. 27, 1948
• You know what I mean. Eh? Don't come the raw prawn with me! — J.E. MacDonnell, *Don't Gimme the Ships*, p. 59, 1960
• Don't come the raw prawn! I only gave her a bit of a smack on the chops, we didn't get around to the fair dinkum article! — Barry Humphries, *The Wonderful World of Barry McKenzie*, p. 12, 1968
• Don't come the raw prawn with me either or I'll drop ya you pommy drongo. — *The Adventures of Barry McKenzie*, 1972
• COME THE RAW PRAWN: Act nastily or demur from an original agreement. — Jim Ramsay, *Cop It Sweet!*, p. 24, 1977
• Come on, Dimitri, don't come the raw prawn love! Four quid's the price. I already knocked off a quid, cause I liked the look of yer. — Lance Peters, *The Dirty Half-Mile*, p. 155, 1979

don't come the uncooked crustacean
do not attempt to dupe me *AUSTRALIA*
Rare variant of **DON'T COME THE RAW PRAWN**.
• Don't come the uncooked crustacean with him, Kev – I hear tell if the pom waiters ever get cheesed with a customer they take his drink round the back and have a dip around!! — Barry Humphries, *Bazza Pulls It Off!*, p. [1], 1971
• Don't come the uncooked crustacean with me, Baz! Did you get the dirty water off your chest? I hear some of them hostesses are pretty keen[.] — *The Adventures of Barry McKenzie*, 1972

don't do anything I wouldn't; don't do anything I wouldn't do
used jocularly, as good advice, often as parting advice, and often in a sexual context *UK, 1984*
Occasionally the sentiment is changed to 'don't do anyone I wouldn't do'.
• I'll see you in a couple of weeks. In the meantime, don't do anything I wouldn't do. — *The Guardian*, 7th July 2001

don't do that, then
in computing, used as a stock response to a complaint that a certain action causes a problem *US*

- "When I type control-S, the whole system comes to a halt for thirty seconds." "Don't do that, then!" — Eric S. Raymond, *The New Hacker's Dictionary*, p. 129, 1991

don't give me that!

I don't believe you! *UK, 1984*

- Don't give me that! Because you were seen! — The Wedding Present, *Everyone Thinks he Looks Daft*, 1987

don't go there!; don't even go there!

used for expressing a lack of interest in pursuing a topic *US*

- — Connie Eble (Editor), *UNC-CH Campus Slang*, p. 2, Spring 1993
- Harry held his palms up in a don't-go-there gesture[.] — Christopher Brookmyre, *The Sacred Art of Stealing*, p. 191, 2002

don't hold your breath!

don't expect anything to happen – anything that is expected is unlikely to happen for a long time, if at all *US*

- "That air conditioning! You suppose they'll ever get around to us?" "Don't hold your breath," said Rodriguez. — Ann Blaisdell, *Practice to Deceive*, 1971

don't let today be the day!

used as an all-purpose, very serious threat *US*

- Gary went back to court to try to get a time cut. — Gary K. Farlow, *Prison-ese*, p. 18, 2002

don't mean nothin'

used as an all-purpose reaction to any bad news among American soldiers in Vietnam *US*

- — Gregory Clark, *Words of the Vietnam War*, p. 149, 1990

don't sleep!

don't kid yourself! *US*

- — Connie Eble (Editor), *UNC-CH Campus Slang*, p. 4, October 2002

don't spend it all at once!

used as a jocular injunction given when handing over a very small sum of money *UK, 1977*

- Not only do you receive the gold medal for overall achievement, as the strongest link you get to keep your final balance of £416.25. Don't spend it all at once. — *The Guardian*, 15th May 2002

don't-talk-about

not to mention *TRINIDAD AND TOBAGO*

- — Lise Winer, *Dictionary of the English/Creole of Trinidad & Tobago*, 2003

don't tense!

relax! *US*

- — *Newsweek*, p. 28, 8th October 1951
- — *American Speech*, p. 303, December 1955: 'Wayne University slang'

don't work too hard!

used as a jocular admonition by, for instance, a worker going on holiday to workmates left behind *UK, 1984*

donut dolly, donut six *nouns*

▷ see: **DOUGHNUT DOLLY, DOUGHNUT SIX**

doo *noun*

a ski*doo*, used for transport over ice and snow *ANTARCTICA*

- — *Cool Antarctica*, 2003: 'Antarctic slang'

doob; doub *noun*

an amphetamine pill or other central nervous system stimulant *UK*

- "Got any doubs (pills)?" "Too true." "Spare?" — Ian Hebditch, *Weekend, The Sharper Word*, p. 133, 1969
- Both groups took the same drug – basically "speed", alternatively known as "purple hearts", "blues", "doobs" or uppers." — Peter Burton, *Parallel Lives*, 1985

doobage *noun*

marijuana *US*

- So, Ahab, can I have my doobage. — *The Breakfast Club*, 1985
- — Connie Eble (Editor), *UNC-CH Campus Slang*, p. 4, Spring 1988
- — Ellen C. Bellone (Editor), *Dictionary of Slang*, p. 10, 1989

doober *noun*

a marijuana cigarette *US*

- "At least we can fire up a doober," he said by way of consolation, producing a fat joint from behind his ear[.] — Tom Perrotta, *Joe College*, p. 173, 2000
- But he was no head. Just a doober now and then to take the edge off. — B.A. Brittngham, *Journeys*, p. 244, 2002

doobie; dooby; doob; dube *noun*

1 a marijuana cigarette *US, 1967*

The earliest identification is as 'Negro slang for a marijuana roach'. A belief persists that the term was spawned from the 1950s American children's television show, *Romper Room*, in which children were urged to be 'good do-be's'. Alternative spelling with a 'u' for 'dubee' and 'dubbe'.

- I smoke a doobie at lunch, come back, put these babies [earphones] on and go with the flow. — Armistead Maupin, *Further Tales of the City*, p. 151, 1982
- He's got a doob in his pocket. — Judi Sanders, *Cal Poly Slang*, p. 3, 1990
- Hey man, Pickford's got a dube we're about to burn. — *Dazed and Confused*, 1993
- I think of Huggers and Deadheads as almost the same – they're not all, but you see everybody smoking doobs and getting dosed on acid. — Elmore Leonard, *Riding the Rap*, p. 285, 1995
- It is one thing to spark up a dubie and get laced at parties, but it is quite another to be fried all day. — *Clueless*, 1995
- Afterward, we both wiped off, smoked a cigarette (me) and a doobie (him), and he drove me home. — Mikki Halpin, *Retrohell*, p. 239, 1997
- [G]ently jibing stories about [...] his tendency to throw up after a couple of tokes on a doob. — Kevin Sampson, *Powder*, p. 109, 1999
- That makes Vancouver my pick as the best city in the world to smoke a doob and go for a walk. — Brian Preston, *Pot Planet*, p. 4, 2002

2 a pill *UK*

- — Paul Baker, *Polari*, p. 173, 2002

doobie-head *noun*

a smoker of marijuana in cigarette-fashion

- Dutch immigrants cultivate most of this, (an absolute must for the discerning doobie-head) — Mike Rock, *This Book*, 1999

doobious *adjective*

under the influence of marijuana *US*

A play with the conventional 'dubious' and **DOOBIE** (a marijuana cigarette).

- — Connie Eble (Editor), *UNC-CH Campus Slang*, p. 2, October 1986

doobry *noun*

used as a replacement for any noun that the user cannot or does not wish to specify *UK, 1990*

Noted as 'reportedly current since the 1950s by John Ayto, *The Oxford Dictionary of Slang*, 1998.

dooby *noun*

marijuana *UK*

- No more dooby for me today. — Ken Lukowiak, *Marijuana Time*, p. 112, 2000

dooce *verb*

to be dismissed from employment for the contents of a 'blog' (an on-line diary), website or other shared journal *US*

Named for *www.dooce.com;* established in 2001 by Los Angeles website designer Heather Armstrong, who is credited with coining the word, and who, in 2002, was fired from her job for publishing stories about her workmates on her website.

- After someone sent an unsigned, untraceable e-mail message about Ms. Armstrong's blog to her company's board in 2002, she was promptly dismissed, and 'Dooced' entered Urbandictionary.com as a term for "Losing your job for something you wrote in your online blog, Web site, etc." — *New York Times*, 30th January 2005

doocing *noun*

dismissal from employment for the contents of a 'blog' (an on-line diary), website or other shared journal *US*

From the verb sense.

- With dozens of blogs springing up in Britain every day, many work related, doocing is a risk for online diarists. — *The Times*, 15th January 2005

doodackie *noun*

an object the name of which escapes or is not important to the speaker *NEW ZEALAND*

- — Harry Orsman, *A Dictionary of Modern New Zealand Slang*, p. 42, 1999

doodackied up *adjective*

dressed up *NEW ZEALAND*

- Matron must have seen John waiting here, all doodacked up. — Hazel Walsh, *Fourth Point of Star*, p. 12, 1947

doodad; dodad *noun*

a trivial or useless object *US, 1877*

- Sam finally, as always falling over drunk, but not really, drunk-desiring, over a little lowtable covered a foot high with ashtrays piled

three inches high and drinks and doodads[.] —Jack Kerouac, *The Subterraneans*, p. 55, 1958
- I was sitting on a concrete do-dad in front of the depot restaurant during a supper break in Friarsburg, Oklahoma. —John Nichols, *The Sterile Cuckoo*, p. 7, 1965
- Chicks love to see you wearing doo-dads like that. —Darryl Ponicsan, *The Last Detail*, p. 103, 1970
- —Helen Dahlskog (Editor), *A Dictionary of Contemporary and Colloquial Usage*, p. 19, 1972
- Got all the computer electronic dodads[.] —Lester Bangs, *Psychotic Reactions and Carburetor Dung*, p. 339, 1981

doodads *noun*

the bleed period of the menstrual cycle *AUSTRALIA*
- We're on our doo-dads. —a correspondent *The Museum of Menstruation and Women's Health*, April 2001

doodah *noun*

1 used as a replacement for any noun that the user cannot or does not wish to specify *UK*
Employed to comic effect by the Bonzo Dog Doo Dah Band, formed in 1965. The 'doodah' was dropped as success beckoned.

2 the vagina *US*
- He brushed a fingertip along the back of my neck, and heat rushed through my stomach clear to my doodah. "Jesus," I said. —Janet Evanovich, *Seven Up*, p. 67, 2001

3 semen *UK*
- "[T]hey say the old doo-dah's meant to be good for it [sunburn]." "The what?" "Harry Monk." "What's that?" "Spunk." —Colin Butts, *Is Harry Still on the Boat?*, p. 255–256, 2003

doodally; doodle-ally *adjective*

▷ **see:** DOOLALLY

dooder *noun*

the female breast *BAHAMAS*
- —John A. Holm, *Dictionary of Bahamian English*, p. 64, 1982

doodle *noun*

the penis *US*
Children's vocabulary.
- — *Maledicta*, p. 190, Winter 1980: 'A new erotic vocabulary'
- Uric acid, they say is my trouble, and I don't mind telling you this, / I've to whistle 'The Last Rose of Summer', to coax the old doodle to piss. —Martin Cameron, *A Look at the Bright Side*, 1988

doodle *verb*

1 to have sex *US*
- Well, Mr. Anker, you know yourself all a Jew wants to do is doodle a Christian girl. —William Burroughs, *Naked Lunch*, p. 177, 1957

2 to play music in a whimsical, relaxed manner *US, 1955*
- —Robert S. Gold, *A Jazz Lexicon*, p. 85, 1964

doodle-a-squat *noun*

in circus and carnival usage, money *US*
- —Don Wilmeth, *The Language of American Popular Entertainment*, p. 76, 1981

doodlebug *noun*

1 in oil drilling, any mechanical or electrical device claimed as a tool to find oil *US, 1924*
- —Jerry Robertson, *Oil Slanguage*, p. 47, 1954

2 any small vehicle, such as a small tractor that pulls dollies in a warehouse *US, 1935*
- —Montie Tak, *Truck Talk*, p. 47, 1971

doodlebugger *noun*

in oil drilling, a person who claims divine powers in locating oil *US, 1936*
- [O]ilmen turned for help to "doodlebuggers" – soothsayers who claimed to be able to detect oil under foot using a forked stick. —Vijay V. Vaitheeswaran, *Power to the People*, p. 270, 2003

doodle-em-buck *noun*

▷ **see:** TOODLEMBUCK

doodle-gaze *verb*

to stare at a woman in a lingering, lustful fashion *US*
- —Charles Shafer, *Folk Speech in Texas Prisons*, p. 202, 1990

doodles *noun*

the testicles *US*
Combines the genital sense of **DOODLE** (the penis) with the vague sense (a small nameless article).
- Truth is, I think naked men are kind of strange-looking, what with their doodles and ding-dong hanging loose like they do. —Janet Evanovich, *Seven Up*, p. 134, 2001

doodly *noun*

anything at all *US, 1939*
- "Because the amount doesn't mean doodly," said the heavyset aide with the puffed face. —Robert Ludlum, *The Scorpio Illusion*, p. 27, 1993

doodly-squat *noun*

1 nothing at all *US, 1934*
- She'll stay with me and the kids 'cause he ain't gonna be worth doodly squat to her after I catch 'em. —Iceberg Slim (Robert Beck), *Doom Fox*, p. 182, 1978
- She-it, she swim better than you do, Carlito. You can't do doodley-squat. —Edwin Torres, *After Hours*, p. 379, 1979

2 low grade marijuana *US*
- Also known as doodley-squat, salt and pepper, and "amle twigs," this female-impersonator a/d/a Headache Mary is sometimes advertised as "good commercial"[.] —*Hi Life*, p. 15, 1979

doo-doo *noun*

1 excrement, literal or figurative *US, 1948*
Also as 'do-do'. A child's euphemism; by reduplication of 'do' or 'doo' (excrement).
- I came up thrashing and spitting out a mouthful of that damn duck-doodoo water[.] —Robert Edmond Alter, *Carny Kill*, p. 130, 1966
- I'm fed up with stumblin' 'round in my own doo doo every time I flush the toilet! —Odie Hawkins, *Ghetto Sketches*, p. 196, 1972
- Make sure you land on a spot where there's no dog doo-doo. — *San Francisco Chronicle*, p. 25, 22nd February 1977
- After lying in front of a freight train you can lie in bed in your underwear while two cops are visiting, asking about a certain black Buick – and while a mean-looking Walther P .38 automatic is hidden nearby at that very moment – and not worry about making doo-doo in the bed. —Elmore Leonard, *City Primeval*, p. 53, 1980
- Midget, you're doing a doo-doo job. You're fucking up. It's shit. Ca-ca. — *Mo' Better Blues*, 1990
- I think the man ah chat a whole of do-do. —Donald Gorgon, *Cop Killer*, p. 144, 1994

2 trouble *US, 1989*
- The Republicans have put up a man whose most memorable contribution to political rhetoric is "deep doo-doo." —Molly Ivins, *Molly Ivins Can't Say That, Can She?*, p. 187, 1991
- Sometimes that gut's right on and sometimes it gets me into deep do-doo, if you know what I mean. —Mel Levine, *The Myth of Laziness*, p. 79, 2003
- He'd be okay. I was the one who was in deep doodoo. —Joseph Finder, *Paranoia*, p. 387, 2004

doody; dooty *noun*

excrement *US, 1969*
Childish.
- —John A. Holm, *Dictionary of Bahamian English*, p. 64, 1982
- On any given day I'll start with a few finely crafted doody jokes. —Howard Stern, *Miss America*, p. 137, 1995

dooe; dooey *noun*

▷ **see:** DEWEY

doof *noun*

1 dance music *AUSTRALIA*
- Anyone who knows that joyously anarchic, energising trance-ey sound which reverberates periodically throughout inner city warehouses and brickpits, and at various rural haunts, can attest to doof's rhythmic and spiritual dimensions[.] — *Sydney Morning Herald (Spectrum)*, p. 7s, 4th April 1998
- Scope sunnily affirms that Gras province populated by rhinestones, daquiri fuelled parody and too-convivial doof. — *Sydney Scope Magazine*, p. 2, 2001

2 a dance music afficionado *AUSTRALIA*
- Doofs are another term for dance-club ravers, goths dress like members of the Addams Family[.] — *Sydney Morning Herald*, p. 17, 21st June 1998

3 a party open to the public, often announced and cited clanedestinely, featuring drugs, music and sensory overload *AUSTRALIA*
- A doof is Australian for rave, as in "You know: doof, doof, doof doof doof-doof-doofdoofdoofdoof…" —Brian Preston, *Pot Planet*, p. 99, 2002

4 a slow-witted person, a fool *US, 1971*
Originally a Scottish dialect word.
- "How'd you get an ID so fast?" "Doofs who found her? She had her driver's license in her shorts." —Robert Crais, *L.A. Requiem*, p. 42, 1999

doof *verb*
to hit someone *UK: SCOTLAND*
- He never says a word, jist reached ower and doofed the wee ratbag wan. —Michael Munro, *The Patter, Another Blast*, p. 19, 1988

do of *verb*
▸ **be doing of**
to be doing something *UK, 1853*
Often in a question, such as 'What are you doing of?'.

doofah; doofer *noun*
a thing, a gadget, an unnamed article *UK, 1945*
Probably from the sense that such an article will '*do for* now'.

doofball *noun*
an inept social outcast *US, 1977*
- She looks up at the gangly doofball, spreading her arms to let him see the whole of her clingy dress, her bare legs and feet. —Brian Hall, *The Saskiad*, p. 280, 1997

doofer *noun*
a dance music afficionado *AUSTRALIA*
- Many doofers' passions are directed as much at social and environmental transformation as at the pursuit of funky clothing[.] —*Sydney Morning Herald (Spectrum)*, p. 7s, 4th April 1998

doofing *noun*
dance music *AUSTRALIA*
- There's not much doofin' in *Shelter Me* but there are guitar[s], rich melodies, wonderful high notes and flashes of inspiration. —*Sydney Morning Herald*, p. Metro 7, 5th June 1997

doofus; dufus *noun*
1 a dolt, a fool *US, 1955*
- [S]miling a greatbig, stupid doffus grin comparable to the crease in her crackers. —Clarence Cooper Jr, *The Farm*, p. 26, 1967
- —*Current Slang*, p. 3, Spring 1967
- —*Current Slang*, p. 4, Winter 1971
- Whatcha do'en dufus. —Paul Glover, *Words from the House of the Dead*, 1974
- Despite howls of laughter, [David] Bowie made the yet more dismal Tin Machine II. Doofus. —*FHM*, p. 223, June 2003

2 in caving and pot-holing, an inept caver *US*
A specialist variation.
- —David Morrison of Wessex Cave Club, 29th February 2004

doogie; doojie *noun*
▹ see: DUJI

doohickey *noun*
an object the exact name of which escapes the speaker *US, 1914*
- For no reason a pencil rolled off the desk and broke its point on the glass doohickey under one of the desk legs. —Raymond Chandler, *The Little Sister*, p. 42, 1949
- Well, it's a helluva lot better than sending away for one of those plastic doohickies. —Armistead Maupin, *Tales of the City*, p. 141, 1978

doojigger *noun*
an object the name of which escapes the speaker *US, 1927*
- This chapter defines a few common things associated with your computer. It describes them by using a variety of terms, including geegaw, doojigger, and madoodle. —Dan Gookin, *DOS for Dummies*, p. 73, 1999

dook *noun*
1 in the gambling game two-up, a throw of heads three times in a row *AUSTRALIA*
- The boxer takes a percentage (generally from two shillings to four shillings in the pound) out of the centre each time the spinner has 'dooked them' or 'done a dook', which means he has tossed three straight heads. —James Holledge, *The Great Australian Gamble*, p. 102, 1966

2 a hand *AUSTRALIA, 1924*
- I looked around, stuck out my dook and said 'G'day Keith'. —Sam Weller, *Old Bastards I Have Met*, p. 13, 1979

3 a fist *AUSTRALIA*
- —Jim Ramsay, *Cop It Sweet!*, p. 31, 1977

4 (especially in Western Australia) a playing marble *AUSTRALIA*
Has the short vowel of 'book' and may be spelt 'doog'.
- 'I haven't got any dooks,' Rob said. Dooks were hard to come by, with the war on, and the big kids had pretty well cornered the supply. —Randolph Stow, *The Merry-Go-Round in the Sea*, p. 81, 1965
- D'ya want a game of doogs, Johnny? —*Wordmap (www.abc.net.au/wordmap)*, 2003

dook *verb*
1 to pass or hand over something secretly *AUSTRALIA, 1915*
- What I mean is I can dook you a caser if it's any good to you —D'Arcy Niland, *The Shiralee*, p. 138, 1955

2 to pay a bribe or gratuity *AUSTRALIA, 1945*
- 'You stop at the pub in town and ask where the best farms are', he said. 'You don't ask the manager. You ask the barman, and you dook him.' —T.A.G. Hungerford, *Stories From Suburban Road*, p. 152, 1983

▸ **dook them**
in the gambling game two-up, to throw heads three times in a row *AUSTRALIA*
- The boxer takes a percentage (generally from two shillings to four shillings in the pound) out of the centre each time the spinner has 'dooked them' or 'done a dook', which means he has tossed three straight heads. —James Holledge, *The Great Australian Gamble*, p. 102, 1966
- I'm not dooking some country publican now. —Clive Galea, *Slipper*, p. 198, 1988

dooker *noun*
a member of a criminal enterprise whose job is to distract the authorities by creating a diversion *US*
- —*American Speech*, p. 98, May 1956: 'Smugglers' argot in the Southwest'

dookie; dookey; dooky; dukey *noun*
1 excrement *US, 1969*
Children's vocabulary.
- My fighter's got nothing on his mind but punching the dooky outta the other dude. —Iceberg Slim (Robert Beck), *Death Wish*, p. 94, 1977
- Sandra, I got the squirty dukes. —Sandra Bernhard, *Confessions of a Pretty Lady*, p. 123, 1988
- Shiiit, a dukey brown Iroc? —*Menace II Society*, 1993
- —Pamela Munro, *U.C.L.A. Slang*, p. 59, 1997

2 a paymaster *US*
Carnival usage, without variant spellings.
- —*American Speech*, p. 308–309, December 1960: 'Carnival talk'

Dookie *nickname*
a student, alumni or supporter of Duke University *US*
- —Connie Eble (Editor), *UNC-CH Campus Slang*, p. 3, Spring 1990

doolacky *noun*
a thing; a thingumabob *AUSTRALIA, 1950*
- Every time I get a chance to balance on one of these amplifiers he screams 'Stand-To' and throws the entire doolacky into a flap. —John Wynnum, *Tar Dust*, p. 11, 1962

doolally; doolali; doolally tap; doodle-ally; doodally; tapped *adjective*
1 mad *UK, 1925*
From the obsolete noun 'doolally tap' (a form of madness). Deolali (a military sanitorium in Bombay) corrupted and abbreviated as 'doo-lally' plus Hundustani *tap* (fever).
- TIM: Darcy you're tapped, mate. DARCY: If anyone around here is tapped then it's you lot [...] People may think I'm a bit dolally but they know I'm harmless. —Paul Fraser and Shane Meadows, *TwentyFourSeven*, p. 23, 1997
- She's gone doolally. —Diran Abedayo, *My Once Upon A Time*, p. 96, 2000
- Ianto wrecked a house in a morning. When he went doofuckinlally. —Niall Griffiths, *Sheepshagger*, p. 55, 2001
- From 1997, public finances went doolally. The main result was graft —*The Economist*, 21st February 2002

2 extremely drunk *UK, 1943*
Extends from the previous sense.

3 in a state of sensory confusion *UK*
A compound of all senses: 'mad', 'drunk' and 'broken'.
- [H]is ma will never be my ma. Fucking doolally she is now, anyway. —Kevin Sampson, *Outlaws*, p. 33, 2001
- Ben, 24, says: "Flamers make your head go a bit doolally – it feels like it won't fit through doors!" —*Sky Magazine*, p. 89, May 2001

doolander *noun*
a powerful blow *UK: SCOTLAND*
- He gave him a doolander on the nut. —Michael Munro, *The Patter*, p. 21, 1985

dooley *noun*
1 a privvy; an outdoor toilet *US, 1968*
- —Frederic G. Cassidy, *Dictionary of American Regional English, Volume II*, p. 137, 1991

2 heroin *US*
- —US Department of Justice, *Street Terms*, October 1994
- —Robert Ashton, *This Is Heroin*, p. 205, 2002

doolie *noun*
a fool *UK: SCOTLAND, 1985*
• Never mind stauin [standing] there lik a bunch a doolies. — Michael Munro, *The Complete Patter*, p. 44, 1996

doolin *noun*
a Roman Catholic *NEW ZEALAND*
From Mickey Doolin, the quintessential Irishman.
• And in peace the civilians must have something to hate too. The Dutchies or the Pommies or the Doolins or somebody. — Gordon Slatter, *A Gun in my Hand*, p. 60, 1959

doo-mommie
go fuck your mother *US*
A phonetic approximation of the Vietnamese *du ma* (fuck your mother).
• — Linda Reinberg, *In the Field*, p. 66, 1991

DOOM pussy mission *noun*
a night bombing run flown by US bombers over North Vietnam *US*
The DOOM came from the the Da Nang Officer's Open Mess, the 'pussy' refered to the relative lack of danger in a night mission.
• — Linda Reinberg, *In the Field*, p. 66, 1991

doom tube *noun*
the hollow of a wave that does not offer a surfer the ability to leave the hollow *US*
• — Trevor Cralle, *The Surfin'ary*, p. 30, 1991

doomy *adjective*
very depressed and discouraged; dismal *UK*
• — Johnny Byrne and Jenny Fabian, *Groupie*, 1968

do one *verb*
go away, run away *UK, 2000*
• — Susie Dent, *The Language Report*, p. 77, 2003

door *noun*
1 a supplier of drugs *CANADA*
• "He was what we call a 'door.' He was the guy who could make things happen. He had contacts at all the borders, the ports, the airports and airplane companies. He was recruited by organized crime. — *Pointe Claire Chronicle*, p. A8, 17th July 2002

2 a capsule of Doriden™, a trade name for glutethimide, a sedative *US*
• — Jay Robert Nash, *Dictionary of Crime*, p. 107, 1992

▸ **from the door**
from the outset *US*
• But it was the fuzz's action from the door. They wanted me gone. — Malcolm Braly, *On the Yard*, p. 27, 1967

doorbell *noun*
the nipple of a woman's breast *US*
• "She's peeved in this one," said Glenda, leaning closer, and it was pressed against my cheek, and finally one tender doorbell went right into my ear. — Joseph Wambaugh, *The Blue Knight*, p. 24, 1973

doorcard *noun*
in seven-card stud poker, a player's first face-up card *UK*
• — Dave Scharf, *Winning at Poker*, p. 234, 2003

door-hugger *noun*
a girl who sits as far away from her date when he is driving as possible *US*
• — Andy Anonymous, *A Basic Guide to Campusology*, p. 8, 1966
• — *American Speech*, p. 59, Spring-Summer 1975: 'Razorback slang'

door jockey *noun*
a doorman *US*
• He then went back into the club, grandly exited with his escort, condescendingly told the doorman to summon a taxicab, nodded an aristocratic goodnight to the door jockey – and grandly tipped the doorman[.] — Robert Sylvester, *No Cover Charge*, p. 234–235, 1956

doorknob *noun*
1 a socially inept person *US*
• The words they are constantly coining to describe other teens – geek, nerd, doorknob, shithead, and so on – are generally intended to be derogatory. — Marcel Danesi, *Cool*, p. 43, 1994

2 a shilling *UK*
Pre-decimal rhyming slang for **BOB** (a shilling).
• — Julian Franklyn, *A Dictionary of Rhyming Slang*, 1961
• — Ray Puxley, *Fresh Rabbit*, 1998

doormat *noun*
1 a person who is easily manipulated by others *UK, 1883*
• On the other hand, we must not be so mild mannered that we become doormats and whipping posts for tohse who will take advantage of us if we give them a chance. — Joyce Meyer, *Me and My Big Mouth*, p. 191, 1997

2 a toupee *US*
• — Wilfred Granville, *The Theater Dictionary*, p. 205, 1952

3 in surfing, a bodyboarder, that is a surfer who lies down on the surfboard *SOUTH AFRICA*
Derogatory.

door pops *noun*
dice that have been altered so that they will score a 7 or 11 more frequently than normal *US*
• — *The Annals of the American Academy of Political and Social Sciences*, p. 124, May 1950

door-pusher *noun*
a girl who stays as close as possible to the passenger door while riding in a car on a date *US*
• — *Time Magazine*, p. 46, 24th August 1959

doorshaker *noun*
a night watchman *US, 1942*
• I know it's him because a the noises the doorshaker said he made. — Joseph Wambaugh, *The Choirboys*, p. 149, 1975

doorstep *noun*
▸ **not on your own doorstep**
a piece of folk-philosophy (often as an injunction): do not get sexually involved with anyone close to home, or at work *UK*
• "Extras" in general are a cardinal sin, but definately [sic] not on your own doorstep. — *www.rooferscoffeeshop.com (a forum for roofers)*, 15th July 2003

doorstep *verb*
of a journalist, to wait near a subject's door in order to obtain an interview, a photograph, etc *UK*
• Jane Drabble and I decided to doorstep him. — *The Listener*, 19th February 1981

doorstep sandwich *noun*
a sandwich that uses two very thick slices of bread *IRELAND*
• Now I thanked heaven for the rain, for without clothes to wear, he could not follow me to the Englishwomen's chalet, ply them with a fake broth-of-a-boy accent as thick as a doorstep of soda bread[.] — Hugh Leonard, *Out After Dark*, p. 99, 1989
• Pat, the confirmed bachelor is an expert on the doorstep sandwich: it consists of thick slices of bread with the contents of the fridge sandwiched between them. This is no careless construction, but one born of a long tradition. — *Irish Times*, 6th April 1999

doorstop *noun*
in computing, broken or obsolete equipment *US*
• — Eric S. Raymond, *The New Hacker's Dictionary*, p. 30, 1991

door whore *noun*
1 someone employed to welcome clubbers to a club but who actually enforces a strict exclusion policy based on the club's style requirements *UK*
• — Alon Shulman, *The Style Bible*, p. 82, 1999
• Then glam pouted and strutted its way passed the door whores. — Ben Osborne, *The A-Z of Club Culture*, p. 111, 1999

2 a restaurant hostess *US*
• — *Maledicta*, p. 47, 1995: 'Door whore and other New Mexico restaurant slang'

doos *noun*
a despicable person *SOUTH AFRICA*
• I'm going to bliksem [hit] that doos! — *Surfrikan Slang*, 2004

doosey *noun*
heroin *UK*
• — Mike Haskins, *Drugs*, p. 283, 2003

doosh *noun*
the face *UK: SCOTLAND*
Glasgow slang.
• Ah wannered [punched] um right in the doosh. — Michael Munro, *The Patter, Another Blast*, p. 19, 1988

dooty *noun*
▷ see: **DOODY**

do out of *verb*

to swindle someone out of something *UK, 1825*

- [L]ocal wine producers claim the movie star and multimillionaire wine buff [Gerard Depardieu] has done them out of a vineyard that should rightfully be theirs[.]— *The Guardian*, 5th February 2003

doover *noun*

1 a thing; a thingumabob *AUSTRALIA, 1940*

Originally in World War 2 services slang. Suggested origins include (1) a variant on **DOOFAH**, (2) from Yiddish, a variant of Hebrew *davar* (a thing), and (3) extracted from **HORSES DOOVERS**. The first two are much more likely than the last.

- —Dymphna Cusack, *Picnic Races*, p. 126, 1962
- —Arthur Chipper, *The Aussie Swearer's Guide*, p. 56, 1972
- —Jim Ramsay, *Cop It Sweet!*, p. 31, 1977
- —Sam Weller, *Old Bastards I Have Met*, p. 8, 1979

2 the penis *AUSTRALIA*

From the sense as an 'unnamed thing'.

- They always say a bloke's doover never looks up to much when you're lookin' down on it from above!—Barry Humphries, *Bazza Pulls It Off!*, 1971

do over *verb*

1 to beat someone up *UK, 1866*

- We've talked to Feeney and he says it was an abo who did him over. —Wal Watkins, *Andamooka*, p. 179, 1971
- —Jim Ramsay, *Cop It Sweet!*, p. 31, 1977
- Sometimes a prisoner was approached by a third party and asked to do someone over in the gaol[.]—William Dodson, *The Sharp End*, p. 25, 2001

2 to swindle or take advantage of *AUSTRALIA*

- In some cases (e.g.'s: Public Transport multiple hire taxis found in general newspapers etc.) the Public is aware that it is being done over – but, of course it doesn't do anything about it.— *Figure and Vigour*, p. 6, 1952
- We won't be done over like our poor old mums.—Kathy Lette, *Girls' Night Out*, p. 156, 1987

3 to frisk, to search through someone's clothing or property *UK, 1984*

- That night they stake out the warehouse and sure enough the van arrives and Rossitano and the 2 Murphy boys get out to do the place over.— *The Whistle Blower, Blue Heelers*, 1998

4 to have sex with someone *AUSTRALIA*

- Strike me...a man couldn't do her over, much...not much.—Sumner Locke Elliott, *Rusty Bugles*, p. 29, 1948
- Here he was, a one-time sailor boy who burned to do her over, but knew he would never get the chance, no matter what.—Robert S. Close, *With Hooves of Brass*, p. 76, 1961

dooverlackie; doovilackie *noun*

a thing; a thingumabob *AUSTRALIA*

- I mean, take contraception. Mou uses one of them cervical cap, doovilackies, right. God!—Kathy Lette, *Girls' Night Out*, p. 86, 1987
- One Friday arvo as we left school he told me he was working on a secret invention – but he needed some special dooverlackie to make it go.—Hugh Lunn, *Fred & Olive's Blessed Lino*, p. 53, 1993

doowally *noun*

an idiot, a person with a less than first-class grip on reality *UK: SCOTLAND*

Glasgow slang, perhaps related to **DOOLALLY** (mad).

- There's me staunin [standing] oot in the rain lik a doowally an the door's open aw the time.—Michael Munro, *The Patter, Another Blast*, p. 19, 1988

doo-wop *noun*

a musical style popular in the 1950s, featuring nonsense syllables sung in close harmony *US, 1969*

- We stood on the corners rappin' and signifyin' ("you know what, man, yo' momma is so ugy she can't even catch a cold") 'n do'wappin' (Wop doo-dooo/doo doo doo doo wop doo ddoo).—Odie Hawkins, *Men Friends*, p. 9, 1989

doozer *noun*

1 anything that is large or outstanding *CANADA*

- —J Dowell, *Pook-Off Bear*, 1975

2 an exceptional example or specimen *US, 1930*

- Players are what's important. Personalities. You must know some doozers roundabouts?—Ken Kesey, *Sailor Song*, p. 116, 1992

doozy *adjective*

an extraordinary example of something *US, 1916*

- Listen, there's a publicity angle rigged to Contino's particpation that I can't reveal the details of, but believe me, it's a doozie.—James Ellroy, *Hollywood Nocturnes*, p. 103, 1994

dop *noun*

1 the head *SOUTH AFRICA*

From Afrikaans *dop* (an empty vessel).

- —Jean Branford, *A Dictionary of South African English*, 1978

2 any brandy *SOUTH AFRICA, 1896*

From Afrikaans *doppe* (husks of grapes).

- —Penny Silva, *A Dictionary of South African English*, p. 194, 1996

3 a short drink of any spirits, a tot; the act of drinking *SOUTH AFRICA*

Variant 'doppie'.

- —Penny Silva, *A Dictionary of South African English*, p. 195, 1996

dop *verb*

to drink (alcohol) *SOUTH AFRICA, 1977*

From Afrikaans *dop* (a drink).

- You can say it's a funny kind of graft – driving around and dopping all day, occasionally clicking the shutter.— *Sunday Times (South Africa)*, 22nd June 2003

dope *noun*

1 a drug, drugs, especially if illegal *US, 1900*

- [A] great dope man, anything in the form of kicks he would want at any time and very intense[.]—Jack Kerouac, *The Subterraneans*, p. 4, 1958
- [Janis Joplin] said to a reporter not long before she died: "I wanted to smoke dope, take dope, lick dope, suck dope and fuck dope." But her mental frailty could not match her physical appetites.—Harry Shapiro, *Waiting For The Man*, 1999

2 marijuana *SOUTH AFRICA, 1946*

- They refer to it as "weed" or "dope," shunning such hipster terminology as "grass" and "pot."—Hunter S. Thompson, *Hell's Angels*, p. 215, 1966
- We had already smoked a lot of dope[.]—Doug Lang, *Freaks*, p. 8, 1973
- You guys want something to drink, or a pill, or some coke, or some dope.— *Boogie Nights*, 1997
- If LSD was the icing on the counter-cultural cake, marijuana was its basic ingredient ... For those whose folk music was heavily politicized, smoking dope became integral to the protest movement—Harry Shapiro, *Waiting For The Man*, 1999
- [Kentucky] is also the home of the "Furry Freak Brothers", whose famous motto is "Dope will get you through times of no money better than money will get you through times of no dope."—Mike Rock, *This Book*, 1999
- Yeah, then some dope to take the edge off of a long day.— *Traffic*, 2000

3 heroin *US, 1891*

- You ever hear of dope? Snow? Junk? Big H? Horse?—John D. McDonald, *The Neon Jungle*, p. 61, 1953
- The dope thing hadn't evolved into what it is now, with all the police activity. [Jazz musician Art Pepper remembering the 1950s]—Harry Shapiro, *Waiting For The Man*, 1999
- —Robert Ashton, *This Is Heroin*, p. 205, 2002

4 information, especially confidential information *US, 1902*

- For Christ's sake, Garrity, spill the dope.—James T. Farrell, *Saturday Night*, p. 21, 1947
- Sometime look up my history. Any paper will supply the dope. —Mickey Spillane, *Kiss Me Deadly*, p. 82, 1952
- Plus Fuel Facts: Inside Dope on Feeding Vitamins to your Engine — *Hot Rod Comics*, June 1952
- Had The Man given me the straight dope?—Jim Thompson, *Savage Night*, p. 62, 1953

5 a stupid fool *UK, 1851*

- I can see the big dope now. Sat outside holding his dick [patiently], first there as usual.—Kevin Sampson, *Outlaws*, p. 4, 2001

6 money *SOUTH AFRICA*

Teen slang.

- — *Sunday Times (South Africa)*, 1st June 2003

7 in oil drilling, a lubricant *US*

- —Jerry Robertson, *Oil Slanguage*, p. 47, 1954

dope *verb*

1 to use recreational drugs *US, 1889*

- As usual the party was a whirl of boozing and doping.—Jamie Mandelkau, *Buttons*, p. 73, 1971
- Doping and drinking, wisecracking and insulting[.]—Greil Marcus, *Psychotic Reactions and Carburetor Dung*, 1986

2 in the used car business, to hide a car's mechanical flaws *US*

- — *Esquire*, p. 118, March 1968

dope *adjective*

1 stylish, excellent, best *US, 1981*

A word that defines and sneers at society's failures; this common hip-hop usage, credited to rap-pioneer Chief Rocker Busy Bee, rejects the negative and promotes the positive in the 'bad-as-good' way.

- —Connie Eble (Editor), *UNC-CH Campus Slang*, p. 3, Spring 1991
- Yo Mel, kick that dope shit, homeboy. Let me see you get busy.—Chief Rocker Busy Bee, *fresh fly flavor*, 1992
- Hey, you know what would be so dope? If we got some really delicious take-out.—*Clueless*, 1995
- [E]ven "stoopid fresh," which could also be "def" when it wasn't "dope."—Nelson George, *Hip Hop America*, p. 209, 1998
- Look, we want to do this, but we don't want the whole song, we just want the dope part. That one part that the DJ plays over and over again.—Bootee (Edward Fletcher), *The hip hop years*, 1999
- I put together a group of the dopest heads from the Bronx that were making it happen—Fab Five Freddy (Fred Braithwaite), *The hip hop years*, 1999
- —Julian Johnson, *Urban Survival*, p. 258, 2003
- The guitar riff sampled from Guns N' Roses' "Sweet Child O' Mine". Dope shit.—*Muzik*, p. 24, February 2003

2 dull *SOUTH AFRICA*
Teen slang.

- —*Sunday Times (South Africa)*, 1st June 2003

dope!
used for expressing approval *UK*

- —Susie Dent, *The Language Report*, p. 75, 2003

dope cake *noun*
a baked confection which has marijuana or hashish as a major ingredient *UK*

- [H]im looking like he should be selling dope cakes at Glastonbury. —Andrew Holmes, *Sleb*, p. 89, 2002

dope corner *noun*
a street corner where drugs are usually sold *US*

- Strike preferred talking on the phone, mouth to ear – one thing about dope corners, nobody ever vandalized the phones.—Richard Price, *Clockers*, p. 6, 1992

dope daddy *noun*
a drug dealer *US, 1936*

- —*American Speech*, p. 87, May 1955: 'Narcotic argot along the Mexican border'

dopefied *adjective*
amazing *US*

- —Connie Eble (Editor), *UNC-CH Campus Slang*, p. 3, Spring 2000

dope fiend *noun*
a drug addict *US, 1895*

- I hate it when they started using 'addict' and put 'fiend' aside. A funky chump who is into serious drugs is a fuckin' Dope Fiend. Fiend, as in Fiend!—Odie Hawkins, *Midnight*, p. 147, 1995

dopehead *noun*
a regular drug user *US, 1903*

- I don't be fucking no dopeheads. I might let them suck my dick but I don't be fucking 'em. Shit, they got Aids and shit.—*Boyz N The Hood*, 1990

dope house *noun*
a house or building where drugs are bought and used *US, 1968*

- Police say the shootings appear to be another one of the city's rising dope house robberies.—Vernon E. Smith, *The Jones Men*, p. 37, 1974

dope kit *noun*
the equipment needed to prepare and inject drugs *US*

- —Kenn "Naz" Young, *Naz's Underground Dictionary*, p. 25, 1973

dopeman *noun*
a drug dealer *US*

- The dopeman they had stuck up would be getting various wires from fifty different informers, and it wouldn't take long for him to find out who was spending large sums of money.—Donald Goines, *Daddy Cool*, p. 127, 1974
- See, you you shoot the dope man, you letting his henchmen know you come in there for sho nuff business.—Vernon E. Smith, *The Jones Men*, p. 9, 1974

dope off *verb*
to fail to pay attention; to fall asleep *US, 1918*

- But I can't do anything about some silly ape who dopes off on the Betelgeuse.—Herman Wouk, *Caine Mutiny*, p. 145, 1951

dope on a rope *noun*
in the language of hang gliding, a paraglider pilot *US*

- —Erik Fair, *California Thrill Sports*, p. 336, 1992

dope out *verb*
1 to become, or spend time, intoxicated on recreational drugs *US*

- [G]o back the next day and dope out with the gang, grass, speed, reds, Romilar, who cares[.]—Lester Bangs, *Psychotic Reactions and Carburetor Dung*, p. 33, 1970

2 to discover, to ascertain, to comprehend; to work out *US, 1906*

- "Try and dope out their style of play and signals and let him have the jump," Cal told Schultz before they lined up for the next jump.—James T. Farrell, *Tournament Star*, p. 71, 1946
- I tried to dope it out, a screwy thing like that.—Jim Thompson, *Savage Night*, p. 70, 1953

dope pull *noun*
an addict's need for drugs *US*

- You got the dope pull, boyo?—Joel Rose, *Kill Kill Faster Faster*, p. 185, 1997

doper *noun*
a drug user *US, 1922*

- All the animals come out at night. Whores, skunk pussies, buggers, queens, fairies, dopers, junkies, sick, venal.—*Taxi Driver*, 1976
- And hey, good work rousting those dopers!—Carl Hiaasen, *Tourist Season*, p. 151, 1986
- Uttering "like" before any other noun may have given the dopers time to think[.]—Sean Hutchinson, *Crying Out Loud*, p. 177, 1988
- [T]he Mamas and the Papas were at once hip and hugely successful, autonomous and studio-honed – a bunch of dopers who sold records to America's suburban squares.—Barney Hoskyns, *Waiting For The Man*, p. 96, 1996
- Looking at the size of his smile, he just knew old Jack Nicholson was a doper.—Nicholas Blincoe, *Ardwick Green (Disco Biscuits)*, p. 12, 1996
- He acts like he's this big international arms dealer, when, come on, the only people he ever sold to were dopers.—*Jackie Brown*, 1997

dope rope *noun*
a cord attached to a surfer and his surfboard *US*

- —Trevor Cralle, *The Surfin'ary*, p. 30, 1991

dope sheet *noun*
1 a leaflet or pamphlet offering 'inside' tips on horse betting *US, 1900*

- —Helen Dahlskog (Editor), *A Dictionary of Contemporary and Colloquial Usage*, p. 19, 1972

2 in the television and film industries, a running report on shooting kept by an assistant director *UK*

- —Oswald Skilbeck, *ABC of Film and TV Working Terms*, p. 42, 1960
- —Ralph S. Singleton, *Filmaker's Dictionary*, p. 50, 1990

dope slope *noun*
a beginner's ski slope *US*

- —*American Speech*, p. 205, October 1963: 'The language of skiers'

dope smoke *verb*
to smoke marijuana *US, 1980*

- —Richard A. Spears, *The Slang and Jargon of Drugs and Drink*, p. 159, 1986
- —Mike Haskins, *Drugs*, p. 290, 2003

dopester *noun*
a person who analyses the past performance of racehorses and athletic teams in order to predict future performance *US, 1907*

- That is, these excellent dopesters can, presumably, assess the "real probability (as opposed to the subjective, pari-mutuel probability) that horse H will finish first[.]—Richard A. Epstein, *The Theory of Gambling and Statistical Logic*, p. 291, 1977

dope stick *noun*
a cigarette *US, 1904*

- Have you been puffing on one of those San Francisco dope sticks? —Tom Robbins, *Half Asleep in Frog Pajamas*, p. 121, 1994
- The legislative activity suggests that public attitudes were hardening, as does the proliferation of denigrating slang for cigarettes: coffin nails, dope sticks, devil's toothpicks, Satan sticks, coffin pills, joy pills, little white devils, and so forth[.]—Cassandra Tate, *Cigarette Wars*, p. 13, 1999

dope up *verb*
to use drugs *US, 1942*

- Interestingly, doping up for me has always been with older people[.]—Macfarlane, Macfarlane and Robson, *The User*, p. 2, 1996

dopey; dopie *noun*
a drug user or addict *US, 1929*

- The one thing about the Row was that it was filled with okies, weary old Wobblies, drunkies and dopies far gone, whores on their last legs – they never judged you.—Clancy Sigal, *Going Away*, p. 238, 1961

• [T]hey, none of them, giveashit for me, but they are weak dopies[.] —Clarence Cooper Jr, *The Farm*, p. 19, 1967

dopey *adjective*

1 dull-witted, foolish *US, 1903*

• Tommy's chattering away, about some dopey thing he's doing at school, with coloured paper making dopey pictures. —John Peter Jones, *Feather Pluckers*, p. 11, 1964
• You will get yourself involved in these dopey jobs. —Anthony Masters, *Minder*, p. 58, 1984

2 sleepy, lethargic, dull; half-asleep under the influence of drink, medicinal or recreational drugs *US, 1896*

• [H]e's a bit dopey. Just had an injection as well. —John King, *White Trash*, p. 153, 2001

dopium *noun*

opium; heroin *US, 1942*

• —Richard A. Spears, *The Slang and Jargon of Drugs and Drink*, p. 159, 1986
• —Mike Haskins, *Drugs*, p. 283, 2003

dor; door; dorie *noun*

a capsule of glutethimide (trade name Doriden™), a hypnotic sedative and central nervous system depressant *US*

• —Richard A. Spears, *The Slang and Jargon of Drugs and Drink*, p. 159, 1986

doradilla *noun*

marijuana *US, 1973*

The Spanish zoological name for a 'wagtail'.

• —Richard A. Spears, *The Slang and Jargon of Drugs and Drink*, p. 159, 1986
• —Mike Haskins, *Drugs*, p. 287, 2003

do-rag *noun*

a scarf worn on the head after a hair treatment process *US*

• —*Current Slang*, p. 7, Fall 1970
• [S]ince I had my hat conked in them days, I had my 'do rag 'round my skull. —Odie Hawkins, *Ghetto Sketches*, p. 119, 1972
• Nobody wears do-rags no more, you dumb nigger! —Joseph Wambaugh, *The Glitter Dome*, p. 60, 1981
• The guy in the do-rag. —Elmore Leonard, *Out of Sight*, p. 209, 1996

dorcas *noun*

used affectionately as a term of endearment *UK*

The Dorcas Society is a charitable society founded in the early C19, taking its name and biblical inspiration from the charitable nature of Dorcas recorded in Acts ix, 36. The original slang use, now obsolete, was as 'a seamstress who worked for charity'; that spirit is invested in this polari usage as 'one who cares'.

• —Paul Baker, *Polari*, p. 172, 2002

dordy!

used for registering surprise *UK*

English gypsy use, from Romany *dawdi*.

• —Jimmy Stockin, *On The Cobbles*, p. 10, 2000

do-re-mi; dough-rey-me *noun*

money *US, 1926*

Extends from **DOUGH** (money), punning on 'do-re-mi/doh-ray-mi' in the 'tonic sol-fa' system of music. Most strongly associated with Woody Guthrie's 1937 '(If You Ain't Got the) Do Re Mi'.

• —Vincent J. Monteleone, *Criminal Slang*, p. 73, 1949
• Jews know what to do with that old do-re-mi. —Red Rudensky, *The Gonif*, p. 107, 1970
• Joan's got lots of dough-rey-mi and bad QVC jewelry. —Howard Stern, *Miss America*, p. 146, 1995

dorf *noun*

a social outcast *US*

• —*McCall's*, April 1967

Dorian love *noun*

homosexual love and/or sex *US*

From Oscar Wilde's portrait.

• —*Maledicta*, p. 145, Summer/Winter 1986–1987: 'Sexual slang: prostitutes, pedophiles, flagellators, transvestites, and necrophiles'

do-right *noun*

a favour *US*

• —Connie Eble (Editor), *UNC-CH Campus Slang*, p. 3, March 1986

do-right *adjective*

righteous, diligent *US, 1936*

• If I want a do-right woman / Then I've got to be a do-right man. —B.B. King, *Lay Another Log on the Fire*, 1989

do-right boy *noun*

a police officer *US, 1970*

• —Frederic G. Cassidy, *Dictionary of American Regional English, Volume II*, p. 143, 1991

do-righter *noun*

a person who does not use drugs *US*

• —William D. Alsever, *Glossary for the Establishment and Other Uptight People*, p. 23, December 1970

Doris *noun*

1 a woman *UK*

From the slightly old-fashioned female name.

• She was one of those Dorises you didn't fancy at first[.] —Garry Bushell, *The Face*, p. 52, 2001

2 a police van *BARBADOS*

• —Frank A. Collymore, *Barbadian Dialect*, p. 41, 1965

Doris Day *noun*

1 homosexuality *UK*

Rhyming slang for **GAY**, formed from the name of American singer and actress Doris Day (b.1924), perhaps as a knowingly ironic reference to Rock Hudson, a famously closeted homosexual, with whom she co-starred on several occasions.

• —Ray Puxley, *Cockney Rabbit*, 1992
• —Susie Dent, *The Language Report*, p. 98, 2003

2 a way *UK*

Rhyming slang, which reduces to 'doris'.

• To be "on your Doris" signifies your imminent departure. —Ray Puxley, *Cockney Rabbit*, 1992

dork *noun*

1 the penis *US, 1961*

• And Roscue Rules sitting there pulling on his dork wasn't doing anything to settle his queasiness. —Joseph Wambaugh, *The Choirboys*, p. 55, 1975
• Neal wore a short kimono with his dork showing underneath it – just the tip. —William Plummer, *Holy Goof*, p. 76, 1981
• By the time I had left school, I had heard most of the euphemisms. There was dork, eric, muscle, prong, pencil (for having lead in), sausage and tonk. —Bettina Arndt, *The Australian Way of Sex*, p. 10, 1985
• He sort of matter-of-factly removed his dork, pressed the length of it against her, and jizzed on her ass[.] —Josh Alan Friedman, *Tales of Times Square*, p. 107, 1986
• [Of a phallic musical instrument] Look at this high-tech dork I'm wearing! —Frank Zappa, *The Real Frank Zappa Book*, p. 165, 1989
• I'm this innocent Jewish kid, never seen shit, and she reaches down and pulls out his dork. I mean, it's the size of a small sailboat. —Robert Stoller and I.S. Levine, *Coming Attractions*, p. 182, 1991

2 a socially inept, unfashionable, harmless person *US*

• —J. R. Friss, *A Dictionary of Teenage Slang (Mt. Diablo High)*, 1964
• —Collin Baker et al., *College Undergraduate Slang Study Conducted at Brown University*, p. 107, 1968
• I ain't nobody, dork. —*American Graffiti*, 1973
• CLAIRE: So, academic clubs aren't the same as other kinds of clubs. BENDER: Oh, but to dorks like him, they are. —*The Breakfast Club*, 1985
• We have just spent eight years being governed by dorks who acted like building a wall around Texas to ward off Sandinistas marching up through Mexico could be a super-bitchen strategic idea. —Frank Zappa, *The Real Frank Zappa Book*, p. 321, 1989
• Well, you figured wrong, dork! —*Point Break*, 1991
• A patrol car stops this dork for speeding, they walk up to the window and the guy's covered in coke. —*True Romance*, 1993
• He dresses like a dork and eats corndogs and he isn't always politically correct and he probably farts, too. —*Something About Mary*, 1998
• "Nah, we ain't company dorks," Howard snapped[.] —Stewart Home, *Sex Kick*, p. britpupl 228, 1999
• I have a boyfriend, you dork. —Marty Beckerman, *Death to All Cheerleaders*, 2000

dork *verb*

to act in a socially inept fashion *US*

• —Elena Garcia, *A Beginner's Guide to Zen and the Art of Snowboarding*, p. 121, 1990: 'Glossary'

dorkbrain *noun*

an inept outcast *US, 1974*

• [S]he was not in the habit of discussing her private affairs with dorkbrains. —James Morrison, *Broken Fever*, p. 88, 2001
• —Sonya Plowman, *Great Kiwi Slang*, p. 62, 2002

dorkbreath *noun*

used as a term of abuse *US, 1974*

• What I said, dorkbreath, is, 'Are you just good at fucking?' —R.M. Ryan, *The Golden Rules*, p. 126, 1999

dorkus *noun*

a fool *US, 1979*

An embellished **DORK**.

- You wouldn't believe the dorkus she was with when I met her.—*Body Heat,* 1980

dorky *adjective*

odd; out of step with the rest; without social skills *US, 1970*

From **DORK**.

- A dorky kid with Dumbo ears and a bad habit of mangling the petunias with his Schwinn.—Armistead Maupin, *Babycakes*, p. 87, 1984
- But I was kind of dorky in high school.—Anthony Petkovich, *The X Factory*, 1997
- In high school Dougie was the kid who wore the dorky button-down shirt when all the other kids wore T-shirts.—Janet Evanovich, *Seven Up*, p. 25, 2001
- I get awkward and dorky, and they start to think I'm a bit odd.—Frank Skinner, *Frank Skinner*, p. 186, 2001

dorm *noun*

a *dorm*itory *UK, 1900*

- I ran the whole vice-racket in the dorm, / And now there's nothing that I do not know.—James Laver, *The St. Trinian's Story*, p. 58, 1959
- [W]e can sit around in dorms and crashpads and even parents' houses[.]—Lester Bangs, *Psychotic Reactions and Carburetor Dung*, p. 75, 1971

dormie *noun*

a student living in a dormitory; a person with whom you share a dormitory room *US, 1966*

- Your visiting ex-dormie is going to have different needs than, say, your estranged billionaire father.—Paul Gilovich, *The Stranger Guide to Seattle*, p. 243, 2001

dorm rat *noun*

a person living in a dormitory *US, 1963*

- Just a dorm rat making grades, that's all.—Stephen King, *Night Shift*, p. 249, 1978

dorm rot *noun*

a bruise on the skin caused by a partner's mouth during foreplay; a suction kiss *US*

- —*Current Slang*, p. 6, Winter 1970

do-room *noun*

a room where drugs are used, especially injected *US*

- Man I swear, tryin' to keep this damn Do-room clean is a bitch.—Vernon E. Smith, *The Jones Men*, p. 15, 1974

Dorothy *noun*

a tyre *UK*

Rhyming slang, formed from the name of Welsh torch-singer Dorothy Squires, 1915–98, always used in a reduced form.

- [A] flat Dorothy or a set of Dorothys.—Ray Puxley, *Cockney Rabbit*, 1992

Dorothy Dixer *noun*

a pre-arranged question put to a minister in Parliament for which he or she has a prepared answer *AUSTRALIA, 1963*

Named after Dorothy Dix, a popular US question-and-answer columnist.

- —Jim Ramsay, *Cop It Sweet!*, p. 31, 1977

dory plug *nickname*

a member of the Royal Canadian Navy *CANADA*

- "Dory plug" was an unkind nickname. "Aw, jeez, Bill, you don't really wanna become a Dory Plug, do you?"—Tom Langeste, *Words on the Wing*, p. 85, 1995

dose *noun*

1 a case of a sexually transmitted infection *US, 1914*

- God might punish him with an automobile accident, death, a dose.—James T. Farrell, *Saturday Night*, p. 26, 1947
- "Wait a minute," he yelled, " don't you cunt-lappers know that's Agnes, she's got the biggest dose in Hartford, everybody knows that."—Jack Kerouac, *Letter to Neal Cassady*, p. 298, 10th January 1951
- And I couldn't get that, of course, until I got over the dose.—Jim Thompson, *The Kill-Off*, p. 81, 1957
- I think she's got a dose.—Willard Motley, *Let No Man Write My Epitaph*, p. 178, 1958
- Hope you don't pick up a dose or put her up the duff or anything like that.—Alexander Buzo, *Rooted*, p. 92, 1969
- I reckon I've copped a dose!!!—Barry Humphries, *Bazza Pulls It Off!*, 1971
- Ten years ago, one of her girls...one of Annie's...gave me a...dose.—Lance Peters, *The Dirty Half-Mile*, p. 298, 1979
- I partied with one girl, one and took home a dose.—Elmore Leonard, *Cat Chaser*, p. 25, 1982
- The last letter I get from her was a denial that she had given me a dose, and a ground swelling indication that she was doing the outline for a gothic novel.—Odie Hawkins, *Black Casanova*, p. 92, 1984
- Ah, Greg, you short-arsed little twat. How's the dose? Cleared up yet?—Colin Butts, *Is Harry on the Boat?*, p. 92, 1997

2 a curse, a spell *BAHAMAS*

- —John A. Holm, *Dictionary of Bahamian English*, p. 64, 1982

3 an amount or quantity of something *UK, 1607*

- Italians may make 'small doses' of torture legal[.]—*The Independent*, 23rd April 2004

4 a four-month prison sentence *UK*

In earlier use (1860) as 'three months' hard labour'.

- —Angela Devlin, *Prison Patter*, p. 46, 1996

5 a single experience with LSD *US*

- I've never had a bad one and I've taken at least two hundred doses.—Nicholas Von Hoffman, *We Are The People Our Parents Warned Us Against*, p. 95, 1967

6 a dolt *US*

- —*Current Slang*, p. 6, Summer 1969

▸ like a dose of salts

very quickly, and effectively *UK, 1837*

From the laxative properties of Epsom salts; especially as 'go through something like a dose of salts'.

- If there are signs of foetal distress, a doctor will opt for intervention like a dose of salts.—*The Observer*, 12th August 2001

dose *verb*

1 to introduce a drug, espsecially LSD, into a host substance; to give a drug to someone without their knowledge *US*

- [A]nd dosed the punch with a mixture of Yage, Hashish and Yohimbine during a Fourth of July reception at the U.S. Embassy[.]—William Burroughs, *Naked Lunch*, p. 146, 1957
- His eerily profound pictures of rocks and flowers and trees convey a concentration so intense that my first time through the book I remember feeling nauseous when I found myself tripping on the pictures to such a degree that I thought I had been dosed.—*The Last Supplement to the Whole Earth Catalog*, p. 2, March 1971
- She hung out with me while I was coming on when I had been dosed by what I think was something apporaching 3500 mikese[.]—Stephen Gaskin, *Amazing Dope Tales*, p. 115, 1980

2 to share drugs *US*

- —Anna Scotti and Paul Young, *Buzzwords*, p. 132, 1997

3 to ingest; to take a dose of *US*

- D.R. didn't learn until later that Estelle had dosed herself heavily on downers[.]—Gurney Norman, *Divine Right's Trip (Last Whole Earth Catalog)*, p. 97, 1971

4 to infect another with a sexually transmitted disease *US, 1918*

- I'm dosed, baby. Clap, if you dig. Look, one hand.—Richard Farina, *Been Down So Long*, p. 239, 1966

dosed up *adjective*

infected with a sexually transmitted disease *US*

- —*Kiss*, 1969: 'Groupie glossary'

dose of the shits *noun*

1 a case of diarrhoea *AUSTRALIA*

- [H]e was driving them at a pretty fast clip along the road when he got a bad dose of the 'what names'.—Sam Weller, *Old Bastards I Have Met*, p. 85, 1979
- Come off it, mate. All I've got is a dose of the shits. Lousy Indian food.—Blanche d'Alpuget, *Turtle Beach*, p. 66, 1981

2 a bad mood *AUSTRALIA*

- Steve might have a dose of the shits today. Listen, Davis old man, I think you should cool it.—Ricki Francis, *Hotel Kings X*, p. 78, 1973
- Sorry Tony that I barked at you – I just had a real bad dose of the shits.—Clive Galea, *Slipper*, p. 105, 1988

doses *noun*

LSD *CANADA*

- —Suroosh Alvi et al., *The Vice Guide*, p. 102, 2002

dose up *verb*

to pass a sexually transmitted infection to someone else *US*

- —Hyman E. Goldin et al., *Dictionary of American Underworld Lingo*, p. 60, 1950

dosey-doe *verb*

to dance, literally or figuratively *US*

From a basic call in American square dancing.

- Christopher gave me a big daddy-o wink behind the client's back and doz-doed out.—Clancy Sigal, *Going Away*, p. 28, 1961

dosh *noun*

money *US, 1854*

Possibly a combination of 'dollars' and 'cash'; there are also suggestions that the etymology leads to **DOSS** (temporary accommodation), hence, it has been claimed, the money required 'to doss'; and Scottish dialect *doss* (tobacco pouch, a purse containing something of value) – note, too, that tobacco is related to money via **QUID**. US 'dosh' didn't survive but in mid-C20 UK and Australia the word was resurrected, or coincidentally recoined.

- —Tom Hibbert, *Rockspeak!*, p. 53, 1983
- —Angela Devlin, *Prison Patter*, p. 47, 1996
- Don't be a twat, we haven't got enough dosh.—Stewart Home, *Sex Kick [britpulp]*, p. 216, 1999
- I need the dosh.—Danny King, *The Burglar Diaries*, p. 190, 2001

dosh *verb*

to give *UK*

- Herve doshed her his bleeding business card[.]—Jeremy Cameron, *Brown Bread in Wengen*, p. 90, 1999

doss *noun*

1 sleep *US, 1894*

- —Jack Lait and Lee Mortimer, *New York Confidential*, p. 235, 1948: 'A glossary of Harlemisms'
- I said, "Sugar, let's cop some 'doss.'"—Iceberg Slim (Robert Beck), *Pimp*, p. 116, 1969
- After I had the fix of boy it caused me to wantta get my nuts outta pawn and since I knew Chuck was beat for doss, I told him I was gonna lay and free my nuts from the pressure they were under.—A.S. Jackson, *Gentleman Pimp*, p. 71, 1973

2 a waste of time *UK*

- I'm not going to become anything, I ain't going to be able to do anything [paid work] so why bother, it [school] was a big doss. —S. Bowlby, S. Lloyd Evans and R. Mohammad, *Cool PLaces*, p. 238, 1998

3 an easy thing to do *UK*

- Fucking doss on the telly putting your skis on. Not so easy in real life.—Jeremy Cameron, *Brown Bread in Wengen*, p. 186, 1999

4 an attractive female *US*

- —*Current Slang*, p. 21, Fall 1968

5 a brakevan (caboose) *US*

- —Ramon Adams, *The Language of the Railroader*, p. 47, 1977

doss *verb*

to sleep in temporary accommodation, usually on an improvised bed – floor, sofa, etc *UK, 1744*

Sometimes embellished to 'doss down'.

- [T]here's a two on two off in the hall and those that are off doss down upstairs in Jimmy's room.—Ted Lewis, *Jack Carter's Law*, p. 203, 1974
- So, it's dossing under the arches next, is it?—Anthony Masters, *Minder*, p. 8, 1984
- I wasn't exactly sleeping rough, more just dossing down on the floors and settees of my mates.—Dave Courtney, *Stop the Ride I Want to Get Off*, p. 47, 1999

doss about; doss *verb*

to waste time *UK, 1935*

- We never usually go out anyway during the week, just doss around. —*New Society*, 13th September 1979
- Josie says to tell you that she knew she wasn't getting any [exams] because she just dossed about, and she doesn't care.—Mary Hooper, *(megan)2*, p. 66, 1999
- Smiles was dossing for ages after we left school.—John King, *Human Punk*, p. 146, 2000

dossbag *noun*

1 a sleeping bag *UK*

Gulf war usage.

- —*American Speech*, p. 388, Winter 1991: 'Among the new words'

2 a lazy or idle person *UK*

- —Chris Lewis, *The Dictionary of Playground Slang*, p. 77, 2003

dosser *noun*

a homeless person, a vagrant *UK, 1866*

Originally, 'one who frequented a **DOSS HOUSE**', now applied equally to one who sleeps rough.

- The dossers, as they liked to be called, further responded by putting on a special performance of "outcast life", and every so often one would shout: "What are we?", and the rest would reply: "DOSSERS".—Robin Page, *Down Among the Dossers*, p. 12, 1973
- —Angela Devlin, *Prison Patter*, p. 47, 1996
- There were men who looked and sounded like what are generally called dossers.—*The Times Magazine*, p. 49, 24th October 2002

doss house *noun*

a very cheap lodging-house; a shelter for the homeless *UK, 1889*

- These old fools. What they done with their lives? End your days in a lousy doss house.—Clive Exton, *No Fixed Abode [Six Granada Plays]*, p. 119, 1959

dossier *noun*

in Quebec, a project *CANADA*

This word is an example of Frenglish, as are a number of the words in the citation.

- Translator's pet dossier is to rid city of Frenglish [Headline]. Six years ago, Victor Trahan was seized of a dossier to ameliorate the English used by his employer, the city of Montreal.—*Montreal Gazette*, p. A1, 27th July 2002

doss joint *noun*

an establishment providing cheap, basic sleeping quarters *AUSTRALIA*

- Of course all the news got round amongst the railwaymen and the loco superintendent somehow found Pete in a Launceston doss joint.—Patsy Adam-Smith, *Folklore of the Australian Railwaymen*, p. 188, 1969

dossy *adjective*

daft *UK*

- Don't know what she ever saw in that dossy bastard.—Brendan Behan, *Borstal Boy*, 1958

dot *noun*

1 LSD; a dose of LSD *US*

- Look, I've got blue dots I'm selling for $1.75—Nicholas Von Hoffman, *We Are The People Our Parents Warned Us Against*, p. 43, 1967
- — US Department of Justice, *Street Terms*, October 1994
- Street names [...] blotter, cheer, dots, drop[.]—James Kay and Julian Cohen, *The Parents' Complete Guide to Young People and Drugs*, p. 141, 1998
- Very tiny, often brightly-colored pills called "microdots" or "dots" still appear with some regularity in the underground acid market.—Cam Cloud, *The Little Book of Acid*, p. 38, 1999

2 the anus *US*

- —Roger Blake, *The American Dictionary of Sexual Terms*, p. 62, 1964
- So, keeping a firm grip on the reins, he scrambled over the back of the seat, dropped his tweeds and cocked his dot over the tail-board.—Sam Weller, *Old Bastards I Have Met*, p. 85, 1979

3 the clitoris *US*

- —Roger Blake, *The American Dictionary of Sexual Terms*, p. 62, 1964

4 the bleed period of the menstrual cycle *US*

Remembered as late 1970s usage.

- — *The Museum of Menstruation and Women's Health*, 2000

5 in hot rodding, a tailight *US*

- — *Good Housekeeping*, p. 143, September 1958: 'Hot-rod terms for teen-age girls'
- —Tom MacPherson, *Dragging and Driving*, p. 136, 1960

▸ **off your dot**

out of your senses *UK, 1926*

- —C. I. Macafee, *A Concise Ulster Dictionary*, p. 57, 1996

▸ **on the dot**

exactly punctual *UK, 1909*

- [T]he rent's overdue. But I want it tonight, and on the dot every week in future.—Anonymous *Streetwalker*, p. 58, 1959
- Unwilling to break their backs for bosses, they won't be bought and want to clock off on the dot at five to take care of matters at home. — *The Guardian*, 14th July 2003

Dot *nickname*

Dorchester, Massachusetts *US*

- —Jim Crotty, *How to Talk American*, p. 35, 1997

dot *verb*

1 to drop a small amount of LSD on a piece of paper *US*

- —William D. Alsever, *Glossary for the Establishment and Other Uptight People*, p. 9, December 1970

2 to have anal intercourse *UK*

From **DOT** (the anus).

- [T]o "dot" someone is to perform anal intercourse on them (because the anus resembles a full stop)[.]—*www.LondonSlang.com*, June 2002

3 to hit someone, to strike *UK, 1895*

- He was picking on this chap – so I dotted him one[.] —*www.wiganworld.co.uk (newspaper report October 1957)*, 2005

dot-and-dash *noun*

1 money *UK*

Rhyming slang for 'cash'.

- [S]he's none too well fixed for the dot-and-dash[.]—Derek Raymond (Robin Cook), *The Crust on its Uppers*, p. 80, 1962

2 a moustache *UK*
Rhyming slang, for, in all probability, **TASH** (a moustache) and based on the morse code for 'A'.
- —Ray Puxley, *Cockney Rabbit*, 1992

dot-bomb *noun*
a failed dot-com business *US, 2001*
- —Susie Dent, *The Language Report*, p. 47, 2003

dot con artist *noun*
a criminal who operates an Internet-based fraud *US, 1999*
A play on the Internet business domain and generic 'dot com'.
- A dot-con artist who tried to capitalize on Google fever cut his last big deal yesterday, pleading guilty to wire fraud charges in Brooklyn Federal Court.—*New York Daily News*, 18th May 2004

Dot Cotton *adjective*
rotten *UK*
Rhyming slang, formed from a character played by actress June Brown in BBC television's *EastEnders*.
- —Bodmin Dark, *Dirty Cockney Rhyming Slang*, 2003

Dot Cottoned *adjective*
drunk *UK*
Possibly (imperfect) rhyming slang, 'Dot Cotton' for 'pissed rotten', from the character Dot Cotton, played by actress June Brown, in BBC television's *EastEnders* – the character is known for tipsiness.
- —*e-cyclopaedia*, 20th March 2002

dot, dot, dot
used to imply what happened next, and then, etc *UK*
A verbalisation of the written narrative device ... that is often used in romantic fiction to draw a veil over moments of intimacy.
- Belle was back on track, until she or the corporal got fed up and they parted and life's rich pageant, dot, dot, dot.—Jonathan Gash, *The Ten Word Game*, p. 160, 2003

do tell!
used for expressing doubt *US, 1891*
Ironic, sarcastic or mock-incredulous.

dot head *noun*
an Indian or Pakistani *US*
Offensive. From the caste mark which Hindu women wear on their foreheads.
- —Bill Reilly, *Big Al's Official Guide to Chicagoese*, p. 24, 1982
- Somebody oughta crack his dot-head with a baseball bat.—Eric Bogosian, *Suburbia*, p. 10, 1995
- South Asians' unique attributes are warped for use as racist artillery: attire (we are towel heads and wear loin cloths and sheets); costume (we are dot-heads).—Paula S. Rothenberg, *Race, Class and Gender in the United States*, p. 113, 1998

dot man *noun*
a Department of Transportation functionary who inspects trucks at motorway stops *US*
Based on the agency's initials: DOT.
- —Lanie Dills, *The Official CB Slanguage Language Dictionary*, p. 28, 1976

dot on the card *adjective*
definitely, no doubt *UK*
- He is definitely, one hundred per cent, dot on the card, no fuckin' question old fuckin' bill [police][.]—J.J. Connolly, *Know Your Enemy [britpulp]*, p. 155, 1999

dots *noun*
sheet music *US, 1927*
From the look of written music.
- [Y]ou can switch repertoire at a moment's notice, which you can't if you're tied to "dots" – music – and the backing.—*New Society*, 14th October 1982

dotty *adjective*
eccentric, senile *UK, 1885*
- —Lou Shelly, *Hepcats Jive Dictionary*, p. 9, 1945
- You would have thought I'd left them that morning, the way their minds kept running down that same old alley. You can't teach a dotty cat new tricks.—Mezz Mezzrow, *Really the Blues*, p. 88, 1946
- St. John of the Cross was not as dotty as certain Anglicans would have had you believe.—Joan Didion, *The White Album*, p. 119, 1971

doub *noun*
▷ **see: DOOB**

double *noun*
1 a street *UK, 1937*
- —David Powis, *The Signs of Crime*, 1977
- Only all-seeing God, some might say, could highlight the sidetracks and U-turns, the back-doubles and sudden veerings-off.—*The Observer*, 1st November 1998

2 a pimp with more than one prostitute working for him *US*
- —*Maledicta*, p. 148, Summer/Winter 1986–1987: 'Sexual slang: prostitutes, pedophiles, flagellators, transvestites, and necrophiles'

3 in gambling, a bet on two different events in which the total return on the first selection is automatically staked on the second *UK*
- —David Bennet, *Know Your Bets*, p. 30, 2001

4 a twenty-dollar note *US*
An abbreviation of **DOUBLE SAWBUCK**.
- —*American Speech*, p. 280, December 1966: 'More carnie talk from the West Coast'
- —Joe McKennon, *Circus Lingo*, p. 31, 1980

5 a lift on a bicycle or, formerly, a horse *AUSTRALIA, 1947*
- Growing up on the North Shore of Sydney in the 1960's and 70's the common term for carrying a second person on a pushbike was to 'give them a double'.—*Wordmap (www.abc.net.au/wordmap)*, 2003

▸ **on the double**
swiftly *UK, 1865*
From military use for 'marching at twice the regular speed'.
- Trouble on the double[.] William Gray and his wife planned their first family holiday with military precision. But with 10-month-old twins in tow, it was always going to be a challenge[.]—*Daily Telegraph*, 23rd April 2002

double *verb*
to give someone a lift on a bicycle or, formerly, a horse *AUSTRALIA, 1950*
- Will you double me to school on your bike?—*Wordmap (www.abc.net.au/wordmap)*, 2003

▸ **double in brass**
to perform two or more tasks at once *US*
A term from the theatre, where an actor might play a brass instrument in the orchestra while not on stage acting.
- —Charles F. Haywood, *Yankee Dictionary*, p. 48, 1963

double *adverb*
very much *UK*
Often used as an intensifier.
- Where I had be[e]n for the first four months was no good, bu the CT [Corrective Training] wing was double no good.—Frank Norman, *Bang To Rights*, p. 28, 1958
- [W]e are all double [Tom] Waits fans—Shaun Ryder, *Shaun Ryder... in His Own Words*, 1992
- [T]his is fuckin' double suspect, Roy. The cozzers [police] are gonna start wondering what we're hiding.—J.J. Connolly, *Know Your Enemy [britpulp]*, p. 148, 1999

double 8 *noun*
in the television and film industries, 16mm film *UK*
- —Oswald Skilbeck, *ABC of Film and TV Working Terms*, p. 43, 1960

double 88s
▷ **see: DOUBLE EIGHTY-EIGHTS**

double ace *noun*
in dominoes, the 1–1 piece *US*
- —Dominic Armanino, *Dominoes*, p. 17, 1959

double adaptor *noun*
1 a male who both gives and receives anal sex *AUSTRALIA*
- Some of the guys inside are double adaptors, but most become Hocks.—Kathy Lette, *Girls' Night Out*, p. 174, 1987

2 a bisexual *SOUTH AFRICA*
Scamto youth street slang (South African townships).
- —*The Times*, 12th February 2005

double-aught buck *noun*
double-O (.32 calibre) buckshot used in police shotguns *US*
- —Ralph de Sola, *Crime Dictionary*, p. 43, 1982

double bag *verb*
to use two condoms at once *US*
- —Geoffrey Froner, *Digging for Diamonds*, p. 27, 1989

double-bagger *noun*
an ugly woman *US, 1982*
- What's a double-bagger? A woman so ugly that before you'll screw her you put a bag over her head, and one over yours – just in case hers falls off. — Blanche Knott, *Blanche Knott's Book of Truly Tasteless Anatomy Jokes, Vol. 2*, p. 107, 1991

double bank *noun*
to ride as a second person on a horse, or later, a bicycle *AUSTRALIA, 1876*
- I'll double bank with you back to the homestead. — Wendy Lowenstein and Morag Loh, *The Immigrants*, p. 26, 1977

double bank *verb*
to double the number of animals pulling a load *AUSTRALIA, 1867*
- At one stretch on this 110-mile trek we had to double-bank the team to get through and at times I saw the lead camel actually crawling over the top of the sand hills. — Patsy Adam-Smith, *Folklore of the Australian Railwaymen*, p. 173, 1969

double-barreled *adjective*
extreme *US, 1867*
- I probably might just fit in one of those double-barreled accelerated courses in elementary German they've rigged up. — Sylvia Plath, *The Bell Jar*, p. 34, 1971

double-bass *noun*
a sexual position in which a man, having entered a woman from behind, simultaneously applies manual stimulation to her nipples and clitoris *AUSTRALIA, 2002*
- The position is similar to that used when playing a double bass instrument, but the sound produced is slightly different. — Chris Lewis, *The Dictionary of Playground Slang*, p. 77, 2003

double belly buster *noun*
in poker, a hand that requires two cards to make a five-card sequence *US, 1978*
- — Thomas L. Clark, *The Dictionary of Gambling and Gaming*, p. 66, 1987

double-blue *noun*
a pill containing both amphetamine and barbitutrate *UK*
- — Home Office, *Glossary of Terms and Slang Common in Penal Establishments*, 1978

double bubble *noun*
1 an amount that is twice as much, especially money *UK*
A rhyming play on 'double'.
- Bought up a load of council flats from his mum's friends in Wandsworth under the Thatcher thing, let the tenants stay there rent free and then flogged them off for double bubble when they started dying off. — Martin King and Martin Knight, *The Naughty Nineties*, p. 137, 1999
- A nice bit of double bubble [double wages for working overtime] for the Bill [police] herding potheads around[.] — Brian Preston, *Pot Planet*, p. 121, 2002

2 a water pipe with two channels, used for smoking marijuana *US*
- — Connie Eble (Editor), *UNC-CH Campus Slang*, p. 4, Spring 1998

3 cocaine in a smokable form *US*
Marketed as being twice as potent when inhaled.
- — Peter Johnson, *Dictionary of Street Alcohol and Drug Terms*, p. 63, 1993
- — Nick Constable, *This is Cocaine*, p. 181, 2002

4 in prison, interest demanded on an advance of drugs, tobacco or any other form of prison currency *UK*
With variant 'double back'.
- — Angela Devlin, *Prison Patter*, p. 47, 1996

5 a very attractive girl *US*
Teen slang.
- — *Newsweek*, p. 28, 8th October 1951

double buffalo *noun*
fifty-five miles an hour *US*
The US five-cent piece features an engraved buffalo.
- — Elementary Electronics, *Dictionary of CB Lingo*, p. 62, 1976

double carpet *noun*
1 in betting, odds of 33–1 *UK, 1967*
Dubious accounting 'doubles' the odds from a **CARPET** (3–1).
- "'Double Carpet" and all that! — John McCririck, *John McCririck's World of Betting*, p. Jacket, 1991

2 in prison, a sentence of six months *UK*
Literally, 'twice a **CARPET**' (three months).
- — Angela Devlin, *Prison Patter*, p. 47, 1996

double century *noun*
1 in cricket, a batsman's score of 200 runs or more in one innings *UK*
The earlier sense of 'two separate 100s in a single match' has been supplanted.
- — Michael Rundell, *The Dictionary of Cricket*, p. 67–68, 1985

2 in motor racing, 200 miles per hour *US*
- — John Lawlor, *How to Talk Car*, p. 38, 1965

double cheese *noun*
in pool, the situation when either player can win with one shot *US*
- — Mike Shamos, *The Illustrated Encyclopedia of Billiards*, p. 80, 1993

double cherry drop *noun*
a variety of MDMA, the recreational drug best known as ecstasy *UK*
- — Angela Devlin, *Prison Patter*, p. 47, 1996

double-choked *adjective*
extremely disappointed or disgruntled, utterly disgusted *UK*
- The bogies knew he had had it away but just couldn't pin the job on him. Which meant he was laughing and they were double-choked. — L.J Cunliffe, *Having it Away*, 1965

double click your mouse; double click *verb*
of a female, to masturbate *AUSTRALIA*
An allusion to manipulation of the clitoris.
- — Chris Lewis, *The Dictionary of Playground Slang*, p. 77, 2003

double-clutch *verb*
1 to partake of more than your share of a marijuana cigarette being passed around a group *US*
- — Edith A. Folb, *runnin' down some lines*, p. 235, 1980

2 to move quickly; to do anything quickly *US*
- — Hy Lit, *Hy Lit's Unbelievable Dictionary of Hip Words for Groovy People*, p. 12, 1968

3 to grab someone in the crotch and the buttocks *BAHAMAS*
- — John A. Holm, *Dictionary of Bahamian English*, p. 64, 1982

double-clutcher *noun*
used as a humorous euphemism for 'motherfucker' *US, 1967*
- Doubt if you remember this crazy ol' double-clutcher. — Jim Dodge, *Stone Junction*, p. 9, 1990

double-clutching *adjective*
used as a jocular euphemism for 'motherfucking' *US, 1964*
- Guys referred to the aide as a double-dealing, double-clutching, clipboard-carrying apple polisher. — Dennis Smith, *Firefighters*, p. 123–124, 1988

double-column *verb*
to pass another vehicle and stay in the passing lane *US*
- His driver swung over and to the left to "double-column it," in army parlance. — Joseph C. Goulden, *Korea*, p. 424, 1982

double cross *noun*
a double-scored tablet of amphetamine or other central nervous system stimulant *US*
- — Edward R. Bloomquist, *Marijuana*, p. 338, 1971

double-cunted *adjective*
possessing a slack and distended vagina *US*
- — *Maledicta*, p. 184, Winter 1980: 'A new erotic vocabulary'

double damn defo *adverb*
very definitely, certainly *UK*
An intensification of **DEFFO; DEFO**.
- — Chris Lewis, *The Dictionary of Playground Slang*, p. 70, 2003

double dare; double dog dare *verb*
to challenge someone to do something *US*
- I double-dig dares ye to show yore haughty face from behint th' barn. [Barney Google and Snuffy Smith comic strip] — 23rd September 1945
- And I double dare anyone to say a word against any of te adopted ones to any of the natural born members of this family. — *San Francisco Chronicle*, 23rd December 1969

double deuce *noun*
a .22 calibre gun *US*
- — Ann Lawson, *Kids & Gangs*, p. 56, 1994: 'Common African-American gang slang/phrases'

double-diamond lane *noun*
the right or slow lane on a motorway *US*
Named for the logo of the McLean Truck Line, believed to have the slowest trucks in the industry.
- — "Slingo", *The Official CB Slang Dictionary Handbook*, p. 40, 1976

double dibs!
used as a strong assertion of a claim of rights to something *US*
- Double dibs! I saw him first! [Freckels and His Friends comic strip] — *San Francisco News*, 3rd November 1947

double-digit fidget *noun*
the anxiety felt by US troops in Vietnam with less than 100 days left before leaving Vietnam *US*
- — Linda Reinberg, *In the Field*, p. 66, 1991

double-digit midget *noun*
a soldier with less than 100 days left in their tour of duty *US, 1969*
- Specialist Four Francis Anthony Cortez was a shorttimer, a double-digit midget, which mean that the six-one, 175-pound infantryman had less than a hundred days left to go on ihs tour of duty in country. — Kregg P.J. Jorgenson, *MIA Rescue*, p. 78, 1995

double dime *noun*
twenty *US*
- He's been the brass nuts here for a double dime, and guess how the bastard lost his 'rapper?' — Iceberg Slim (Robert Beck), *Pimp*, p. 51, 1969

double dime note *noun*
a twenty-dollar note *US*
- It cost mother a double dime-note only this morning. — Ross Russell, *The Sound*, p. 45, 1961

double dink *verb*
to give someone a lift on a bicycle or, formerly, a horse *AUSTRALIA, 1941*
- Kelly came down from Black Mountain every Sunday after that, and we went double dinking on his white mare[.] — Eve Langley, *The Pea-Pickers*, p. 26, 1958
- No need then to envy other kids who owned horses and double dinked to school. — *People Magazine*, p. 52, 26th August 1981

double-dip *verb*
1 to date both sexes *US*
- — Amy Sohn, *Sex and the City*, p. 155, 2002

2 to dip a piece of food into a shared sauce or relish after taking a bite *US*
- — Judi Sanders, *Faced and Faded, Hanging to Hurl*, p. 13, 1993

double dipper *noun*
a bisexual *US*
- — Anna Scotti and Paul Young, *Buzzwords*, p. 18, 1997

double-dipping *noun*
payment by two different sources for the same work or reason *US*
Slang from the ice-cream parlour, where the 'double dip' cone had two scoops of ice-cream.
- Of course Ida's Otter Creek neighbors disapproved of her extravagance and thought it tacky that she boasted of her double-dipping from Social Security. — Carl Hiaasen, *Tourist Season*, p. 109, 1986

double dome; green double dome; green single dome *noun*
LSD *US*
- — US Department of Justice, *Street Terms*, October 1994
- — Mike Haskins, *Drugs*, p. 285, 2003

doubledome *noun*
an intellectual *US, 1943*
- When those doubledomes go nuts – they still keep talking in their double-dome lingo. — Philip Wylie, *Opus 21*, p. 341, 1949
- Double-domes claim there is less juvenile delinquency in the suburbs than in the cities. — Lee Mortimer, *Women Confidential*, p. 70, 1960

double-door *verb*
in pool, to beat someone quickly *US*
The image is that the defeated player has no sooner walked in the front door than he is walking out the back door.
- — Steve Rushin, *Pool Cool*, p. 11, 1990

double dooring *noun*
an act of criminal fraud perpetrated on a hotel, in which the fraudster arrives in the manner of a legitimate customer but departs by the back door leaving the account unpaid *UK*
- — Angela Devlin, *Prison Patter*, p. 47, 1996

double duke *verb*
to arrange a deck of cards so that two players will be dealt good hands *US*
- — Robert C. Prus and C.R.D. Sharper, *Road Hustler*, p. 169, 1977: 'Glossary of terms'

double Dutch; Dutch *noun*
unintelligible speech *UK, 1876*
Double Dutch is also a secret language in which words are disguised from understanding.
- Although a lot of this was Dutch to me at the time, my friend knew how to "tell the fanny" (tell the tale)[.] — Butch Reynolds, *Broken Hearted Clown*, p. 31, 1953
- If it's all Greek or double Dutch, Bazza's the man. — *The Guardian*, 16th August 2004

double eighty-eights; double 88s
best wishes; warm wishes *US*
- — *Complete CB Slang Dictionary*, 1976
- — Peter Chippindale, *The British CB Book*, p. 154, 1981

double fever *noun*
fifty-five miles an hour *US*
From **FEVER** (five).
- — Radio Shack, *CBer's Handy Atlas/Dictionary*, p. 20, 1976

double fin *noun*
ten dollars or ten years *US*
- — Vincent J. Monteleone, *Criminal Slang*, p. 73, 1949

double-fisted *adjective*
large, imposing *US, 1853*
- The double-fisted burger was indeed thick and juicy. — Sandra Brown, *Charade*, p. 125, 1994

double fives *noun*
a hand slap of both hands used for a greeting or for expressing appreciation of that which has just been said *US*
- "But we needs the milk," Precious finished off the sentence and gave Elijah double fives. — Odie Hawkins, *Chicago Hustle*, p. 150, 1977

double-gaited *adjective*
bisexual *US, 1927*
- Rumors that Welles was double-gaited, especially when liquored up as he often was, thrived[.] — *Confidential*, p. 14, May 1956
- A certain man, who was admittedly double-gaited (bi-sexual), used to call me for his entire family. — John O'Day, *Confessions of a Male Prostitute*, p. 112, 1964
- — Guy Strait, *The Lavendar Lexicon*, 1964
- Double gaited? No. [...], I never did meet any cat who was double gaited. — Lenny Bruce, *The Essential Lenny Bruce*, p. 164, 1967
- "Robbie Daniels doesn't strike me as being double-gaited or having any abnormal ideas what his dick is for," the detective said. — Elmore Leonard, *Split Images*, p. 15, 1981
- Women who go with double-gaited Romeos invariably wind up with more pain than pleasure. — *San Francisco Examiner*, p. E9, 18th December 1981
- Think I'm getting double-gaited? — George V. Higgins, *Penance for Jerry Kennedy*, p. 147, 1985
- [I]t was already an open secret in theatrical circles that Coward was gay; and after Edna Ferber described the Lunts as "double-gaited," theater historians took the Ferber report for granted. — *Los Angeles Times*, p. 11 (Part R), 21st December 2001

double harness *noun*
marriage *AUSTRALIA, 1885*
- Don't tell me Edna's gone into double harness at long last? — John Wynnum, *Jiggin' in the Riggin'*, p. 37, 1965

double-hatted *adjective*
serving in two positions simultaneously *US*
- I remember we were double-hatted, because we were working very hard to put crews through the tactics phase of the RAG and still trying to build [thje Fighter Weapons School] syllabus. — Robert K. Wilcox, *Scream of Eagles*, p. 164, 1990

double-header; doubleheader *noun*
1 an event where two acts share the headline *UK*
- Adema and Soil: old and nu collide on genre mashing double-header[.] — *Kerrang!*, p. 40, 20th April 2002

2 an activity engaged in twice in a row on the same day, especially sex *US*

- Elijah smiled and thought to himself ... doubleheaders can wear you out. Oh well ... my dick'll rot away one day, may as well use it as much as I can now. —Odie Hawkins, *Chicago Hustle*, p. 34, 1977
- Which meant that she wasn't interested in the hundred-dollar bag of bonees who Juicy Lucy said was coming back at eight o'clock for a doubleheader. —Joseph Wambaugh, *The Glitter Dome*, p. 208, 1981

double infinity *noun*

in poker, a pair of eights *US*

Turned on its side, a figure eight is an infinity symbol.

- —John Vorhaus, *The Big Book of Poker Slang*, p. 14, 1996

double-jointed *adjective*

exceptional *US*

- "Changed my birth certificate and they accepted me." "That's double-jointed! Too much!" —Earl Thompson, *Tattoo*, p. 108, 1974

double L *noun*

a telephone *US*

An extrapolation from 'landline'.

- — *Complete CB Slang Dictionary*, p. 5, 1976

double loaded *adjective*

carrying a large amount, especially of stolen property *UK*

- The local law arrived just as Peter and Len were leaving, double loaded. —Charles Raven, *Underworld Nights*, p. 148, 1956

double net *noun*

in betting, odds of 20–1 *UK*

Literally, 'twice a **NET**' (10–1).

- —John McCririck, *John McCririck's World of Betting*, p. 59, 1991

double nickel *noun*

1 fifty-five; five-fifty *US*

- Five fifty? It's only double nickels. FIve fifty? —Ivan Doig, *Ride With Me, Mariah Montana*, p. 259, 1990
- What golfer and future PGA Tour winner once went microscopic with a double nickel, shooting an unheard-of 55 in the 1962 Premier Invitational in Longview, Texas? —Mike Towle, *The Ultimate Golf Trivia Book*, p. 52, 1999
- I want to electyrify the crowd like Michael Jordan droppin' a double nickel on the New York Knicks. —Todd Boyd, *Young Black Rich and Famous*, p. xii, 2003

2 a ten-year prison sentence *US*

- You on parole for check writing now. That liquor will get you a double nickel. —James Lee Burke, *Sunset Limited*, p. 45, 1998

3 fifty-five miles an hour, the speed limit imposed throughout the US by the federal government in 1974 *US, 1976*

- Way it was, I got on the double-nickel with the load. —George V. Higgins, *The Rat on Fire*, p. 106, 1981
- —Laurence Urdang, *Names and Nicknames of Places and Things*, p. 81, 1987

double nickels *noun*

in craps, a roll of ten made with a pair of fives *US*

- —Chris Fagans and David Guzman, *A Guide to Craps Lingo*, p. 33, 1999

double nuts *noun*

double zero *US, 1981*

- Originator of the Commander Air Group's "00" (or "double nuts" as the marking is often irreverently referred to by junior officers), recently-promoted Cdr "Jimmy" Flatley, Jr. is seen climbing down from his personal F6F-3[.] —Barrett Tillman, *Hellcat Aces of World War 2*, p. 7, 1996

double-o *noun*

a close examination *US, 1913*

- I gave him the double-o after i lamped the engraved card he handed me. —Mezz Mezzrow, *Really the Blues*, p. 261, 1946

Double-O *nickname*

rock musician Ozzy Osbourne (b.1948) *UK*

- Get your ears sonically syringed as System Of A Down, Slayer, Cradle of Filth and Tool follow The Double-O into full metal battle. —*Q*, p. 156, May 2002

double O's *noun*

Kool cigarettes *US*

- — *Maledicta*, p. 266–267, Summer/Winter 1981: 'By its slang, ye shall know it: the pessimism of prison life'

double packer *noun*

a member of the Hell's Angels who is prone to take a girlfriend with him on excursions *US*

- When I found such perennial double packers as Sonny, Terry, Tiny, Tommy and Zorro without their women, I realized the outlaws were expecting real trouble. —Hunter S. Thompson, *Hell's Angels*, p. 119, 1966

double rock *noun*

crack cocaine diluted with procaine *UK, 1998*

- —Mike Haskins, *Drugs*, p. 293, 2003

double rough *noun*

a prison sentence of 50 years *US*

- —Charles Shafer, *Folk Speech in Texas Prisons*, p. 203, 1990

double rush *verb*

to deliver in an expedited fashion *US*

Bicycle messenger slang, used as the title for a short-lived television comedy (CBS, 1995).

double saw *noun*

a twenty-year jail sentence *US*

- —John R. Armore and Joseph D. Wolfe, *Dictionary of Desperation*, p. 27, 1976

double sawbuck; double saw *noun*

a twenty-dollar note *US, 1931*

- —Lou Shelly, *Hepcats Jive Talk Dictionary*, p. 24, 1945
- I had a check for a double sawbuck coming from a booking office in Chi[.] —Mezz Mezzrow, *Really the Blues*, p. 131, 1946
- I got five double sawbucks out of my wallet and dropped them in front of him. —Raymond Chandler, *The Long Goodbye*, p. 11, 1953
- Money loves me and can't stay away from me. You see that fine 'silk' broad, I got a 'double saw' to lay her. —Iceberg Slim (Robert Beck), *Pimp*, p. 36, 1969
- On the other hand, for a double-saw, I'll tell you where you get your job done if that's your bag. —*Screw*, p. 7, 7th March 1969
- A double-sawbuck is a night out for my wife and me, or new shoes for the kids, or a hundred other things we need that twenty dollars can buy. —Dennis Smith, *Report from Engine Company 82*, p. 224, 1972
- Pimples had a meet with a fag who – so he said – was good for a double sawbuck[.] —Herbert Huncke, *The Evening Sun Turned Crimson*, p. 50–51, 1980
- Touched the barman for a double saw. —James Ellroy, *Hollywood Nocturnes*, p. 151, 1994

double sawski *noun*

a twenty-dollar note *US*

- He's into us for a double sawski. —William Burroughs, *Junkie*, p. 63, 1953

double stacked *noun*

paramethoxyamphetamine, PMA *UK*

A drug that is difficult to distinguish from MDMA (**ECSTASY**).

- Substantial quantities of the drug, known on the street as 'Double Stacked', were seized by police in the Birmingham area a few weeks before Christmas. — *The Guardian*, 14th January 2001
- They are white and 7mm diameter and 5 or 6mm thick. The Americans refer to these unusually thick tablets as "Double Stacked". — *London Toxicology Group*, February 2002

double stacks *noun*

MDMA, the recreational drug best known as ecstasy *US*

- The drug Ecstasy was called fishies or double stacks, according to the affidavit. — *Orlando Sentinel*, p. B2, 17th August 2002

double stack white Mitsubishi *noun*

an extra thick tablet of *paramethoxyamphetamine*, PMA, etched with the Japanese car manufacturer's logo, easily confused with MDMA *US*

- [H]e [Garrett Harth] reportedly offered the striking blond, brown-eyed girl [Sara Aeschlimann] a potent brand of ecstasy known as "double stack white Mitsubishi". —Ted Oehmke, *The Poisoning of Suburbia*, 6th July 2000

double-stakes-about *noun*

in gambling, a type of conditional bet *UK*

- Like single-stakes-about [see single-stakes-about], but with twice the stake on the other selection [...] If a customer requires double-stakes, this must be so stated by writing D-S-A. —David Bennet, *Know Your Bets*, p. 26, 2001

double taps *noun*

in betting, odds of 15–8 *UK*

From the **TICK-TACK** signal for the odds.

- —John McCririck, *John McCririck's World of Betting*, p. 59, 1991

double time *adverb*

very much, greatly, absolutely *UK*

Variation of **BIG TIME** (entirely) with **DOUBLE** as the intensifier.

- Blue, you fucked up double time, man. —Karline Smith, *Moss Side Massive*, p. 198, 1994

double ton *noun*

1 in cricket, a batsman's score of 200 runs or more in one innings *UK*

- —Keith Foley, *A Dictionary of Cricketing Terminology*, p. 111, 1998

2 in motor racing, 200 miles per hour *US*

- —John Edwards, *Auto Dictionary*, p. 26, 1993

double tre *noun*

six *US*

- —Ethan Hilderbrant, *Prison Slang*, p. 40, 1998

double trouble *noun*

1 a capsule of sodium amobarbital and sodium secobarbital (trade name Tuinal^{TM}), a combination of central nervous system depressants *US*

- —John B. Williams, *Narcotics and Hallucinogenics*, p. 111, 1967
- —Eugene Landy, *The Underground Dictionary*, p. 70, 1971
- —Mike Haskins, *Drugs*, p. 282, 2003

2 any combination of drugs *US*

- —Gilda and Melvin Berger, *Drug Abuse A-Z*, p. 59, 1990

3 a member of Alcoholics Anonymous who is seeking treatment for a second psychological disorder *US*

Those who succeed are known as 'double winners'.

- —Gilda and Melvin Berger, *Drug Abuse A-Z*, p. 59, 1990

double ups *noun*

vials of crack cocaine *US*

- Several minutes later, a man walked upto them and asked, "Do you have any double-ups" – street slang for crack cocaine.—*Plain Dealer (Cleveland, Ohio)*, p. C16, 25th December 1992

Double Willie *noun*

a stagehand who is paid at the doubletime rate for working through meal and rest breaks *US*

- —Sherman Louis Sergel, *The Language of Show Biz*, p. 73, 1973
- —Don Wilmeth, *The Language of American Popular Entertainment*, p. 78, 1981

double yoke *noun*

crack cocaine *UK, 1998*

Perhaps this is a reference to the 'yoke' of addiction, punning on the contents of an egg.

- —Mike Haskins, *Drugs*, p. 281, 2003

double-yolker *noun*

1 a fool *NEW ZEALAND*

Prison usage.

- —Harry Orsman, *A Dictionary of Modern New Zealand Slang*, p. 43, 1999

2 a ewe carrying twins *NEW ZEALAND*

- Dry humour runs thick through this collection; for example commercial traveler – a ram that jumps the fence into a neighbouring paddock; to put into neutral – to castrate male lambs or calves; career girl – a ewe that refuses to mother her lamb; double-yolker – a ewe carrying twins; body-snatcher – a stock buyer. —*Dominion Post*, p. C6, 22nd November 2002

double zero; zero zero; zero-zero *noun*

a high grade variety of hashish from Morocco; generally, marijuana *UK*

- —Angela Devlin, *Prison Patter*, p. 125, 1996
- Street names [...] wacky backy, weed, zero zero (or double zero) and many other names.—James Kay and Julian Cohen, *The Parents' Complete Guide to Young People and Drugs*, p. 133, 1998
- Zero-zero is the stuff of legend. Only the very finest pollen is used in preparing it and true zero-zero will contain only the barest minimum of leaf material to bind the hashish.—Nick Jones, *Spliffs*, p. 90, 2003

double zero rocky *noun*

cannabis resin *UK*

- Let's start with a look at one of these soaps on our tour. For this we need to go to Morocco to find some Double Zero (00) Rocky, so called because that is the gauge size of the screen used to sift it.—Mike Rock, *This Book*, 1999

doubting Thomas *noun*

a perpetually sceptical person *UK, 1877*

- Doubting Thomases who, whatever you show them, say, 'Let's see what you got in the back room.'—Max Shulman, *The Zebra Derby*, p. 146, 1946

douche *noun*

a shower *US*

Vietnam war military usage.

- —Linda Reinberg, *In the Field*, p. 66, 1991

douche *verb*

1 to take an enema before or after anal sex *US*

- —Bruce Rodgers, *The Queens' Vernacular*, p. 66–67, 1972

2 to reject someone's application for membership in a fraternity, sorority or club *US*

- —Collin Baker et al., *College Undergraduate Slang Study Conducted at Brown University*, p. 107, 1968

douche bag *noun*

1 a despicable person; a socially inept person *US, 1945*

- —*American Speech*, p. 238, October 1946: 'World War II slang of maladjustment'
- —Hyman E. Goldin et al., *Dictionary of American Underworld Lingo*, p. 61, 1950
- That douchebag? You should be able to do betteran that.—Hubert Selby Jr, *Last Exit to Brooklyn*, p. 119, 1957
- —*Current Slang*, p. 2, Winter 1966
- He's a real douchebag.—Richard Price, *The Wanderers*, p. 65, 1974
- [S]itting around some goddamn hotel lobby like a soggy douchebag parasite waiting for some lousy high-and-mighty rock 'n' roll band[.]—Lester Bangs, *Psychotic Reactions and Carburetor Dung*, p. 231, 1977
- Come on you douche bags.—*Repo Man*, 1984
- CLARENCE: How the fuck did you get hooked up with a douche-bag like this in the first place.—*True Romance*, 1993
- I want to see their faces when the state says "they are the worst scum-sucking, degenerate, douche bag, filthy, I don't know what's ever shit (BLEEP) out.—*Natural Born Killers*, 1994
- The great Holy Ghost was a total, one hundred percent douchebag! —Howard Stern, *Miss America*, p. 18, 1995
- I now plan to devote all my energies to destorying the douche bag. —*Cruel Intentions*, 1999
- In my opinion, all of these department guys are douche bags. Tell me who you like. I hate the whole bunch.—Stephen J. Cannell, *The Tin Collectors*, p. 88, 2001
- Hi, my name is JT, I'm an alcoholic and an addict. I'm also a TV writer, which by default makes me a douchebag.—*The Sopranos (Episode 59)*, 2004

2 a promiscuous woman prisoner *US*

- —William K. Bentley and James M. Corbett, *Prison Slang*, p. 59, 1992

3 in trucking, the windscreen wash container *US*

- —Montie Tak, *Truck Talk*, p. 50, 1971

4 a shower kit *US*

Vietnam war military usage.

- —Linda Reinberg, *In the Field*, p. 66, 1991

douched *adjective*

exhausted *US*

- —Collin Baker et al., *College Undergraduate Slang Study Conducted at Brown University*, p. 108, 1968

douche job *noun*

a wash or steam cleaning of a truck *US*

- —Montie Tak, *Truck Talk*, p. 73, 1971

douche kit *noun*

a shaving kit *US*

- Billy rinses out his razor and drops it into his douche kit.—Darryl Ponicsan, *The Last Detail*, p. 130, 1970

douche out *verb*

as a prank, to flood the floor of a room by pouring buckets of water under the crack of the door *US*

- —*American Speech*, p. 228, October 1967: 'Some special terms used in a University of Connecticut men's dormitory'

doucher *noun*

an annoying, unlikeable person *US*

- —Connie Eble (Editor), *UNC-CH Campus Slang*, p. 2, April 2004

doudou *noun*

used as a term of endearment *UK, 1998*

From French Creole, ultimately from French *doux* (sweet).

- —Susie Dent, *The Language Report*, p. 129, 2003

dough *noun*

1 money *US, 1851*

- With the dough I made for the Conn Music Company and bought an alto sax for cash.—Mezz Mezzrow, *Really the Blues*, p. 54, 1946
- Coz all the good times is over/And the squares don't have no dough.—Jimmy Witherspoon, *Skid Row Blues*, 1947
- Live off the fatta the land with dough their father left them.—Mickey Spillane, *vI, The Jury*, p. 12, 1947
- "Well, if I'd had the dough to play on Red Pepper this afternoon, I'd be swimming in good nature," Dopey said. "Me too. I was flat."—James T. Farrell, *Saturday Night*, p. 28, 1947
- "You sonofabitch!" he yelled. "Give me my dough!"—William Burroughs, *Junkie*, p. 47, 1953

- It's my experience that once a mug's been taken by the corner game [a con trick] he's kissed his dough goodbye. —Charles Raven, *Underworld Nights*, p. 91, 1956
- They maybe we can import some talent to make the hit. But we'd need some dough. —Chester Himes, *The Real Cool Killers*, p. 54, 1959
- Then he only became the line, until him and The Man couldn't get together about dough. —Clarence Cooper Jr, *The Scene*, p. 185, 1960
- Too bad in a way cause most of us used to rip off the Lion Supermarket there when we had to eat and had no dough. —Abbie Hoffman, *Woodstock Nation*, p. 21, 1969
- When you figure it up, we don't have to lay out for half of it before we got more dough back than we can use. —Richard Farina, *Long Time Coming and a Long Time Gone*, p. 211, 1969
- I just spent 60 days in the jailhouse / For the crime of having no dough. —The Band, *The Shape I'm In*, 1970
- Young man, there's a place you can go/I said, young man, when you're short on your dough. —Village People, *Y.M.C.A.*, 1978
- The guy has his wife cash the check and he takes off for Las Vegas with the dough. —*Get Shorty*, 1995

2 an American infantryman *US*
Korean war usage; shortened from the earlier **DOUGHBOY**.
- —*The Baltimore Sun*, 24th June 1951

doughball *noun*
a fool *UK: SCOTLAND*
Glasgow slang.
- Haw, doughball! That's the wrang queue ye're in. —Michael Munro, *The Patter, Another Blast*, p. 20, 1988

doughboy *noun*
1 a soldier in the infantry *US, 1847*
Many inventive, but unproved, explanations for the term's coining can be found.
- The wounded veteran of Vietnam gazed upon the World War I poster of the doughboy with the rifle. —Steve Thayer, *Silent Snow*, p. 81, 1999

2 a catering employee on a televison or film set *US*
- —Anna Scotti and Paul Young, *Buzzwords*, p. 4, 1997

dough dolly *noun*
on Prince Edward Island, a slice of bread cut off for breakfast after rising overnight *CANADA*
- "A "dough dolly" is bread that was rising from the night before, sliced off and fried. It rises in the pan." —T.K. Pratt, *oral citation from Dictionary of Prince Edward Island English*, p. 47, 1988

doughfoot *noun*
an infantry soldier *US, 1943*
World War 2's answer to the **DOUGHBOY** of World War 1.
- These – and lots of ammo – were the real essentials in a doughfoot's kit, a fact that was one of those things you just had to learn. —David H. Hackworth, *About Face*, p. 79, 1989

dough-gods *noun*
dumplings on top of a stew *CANADA*
- —Chris Thain, *Cold as a Bay Street Banker's Heart*, p. 57, 1987

dough-head *noun*
a fool *US, 1838*
From the thick consistency of conventional 'dough'.

doughnut *noun*
1 a tightly driven full circle, typically executed by young drivers who leave tyre marks from the sharp turns and acceleration *US*
- Spin a doughnut – Make a tight turn. — Fremont Drag Strip, *Guide to Drag Racing*, 1960
- He could spin donuts on that hog with is feet on the pegs. —Hunter S. Thompson, *Hell's Angels*, p. 64, 1967
- —*Current Slang*, p. 4, Winter 1971
- —John Edwards, *Auto Dictionary*, p. 46, 1993
- We fishtailed when we hit gravel, and we turned doughnuts when we hit wet spots. —James Ellroy, *Hollywood Nocturnes*, p. 185, 1994
- Utes are also essential for 'circle work', a rural mating ritual at B&S balls in which farm boys wearing tuxedos do doughnuts in paddocks while girls watch on, ideally weak with lust and admiration. —*Sydney Morning Herald*, p. 8s, 29th June 1996
- "Apparently there was some back and forth between (drivers) in two cars. They were driving in circles, doing doughnuts," Pursell said. —*San Francisco Chronicle*, p. 17, 24 December 2000

2 a tyre; in motor racing, a fat, treadless tyre *US, 1922*
- —John Lawlor, *How to Talk Car*, p. 38, 1965

3 a traffic roundabout *UK*
- —Peter Chippindale, *The British CB Book*, p. 154, 1981

4 an undersized, often illegal, steering wheel *US*
- —Edith A. Folb, *runnin' down some lines*, p. 235, 1980

5 any material produced to be played on the radio which leaves a silent space in the middle for information provided by the announcer *US*
- —Walter Hurst and Donn Delson, *Delson's Dictionary of Radio & Record Industry Terms*, p. 38, 1980

6 the anus *AUSTRALIA*
- [N]obody's ever tried to slip their pollywaffle [penis] up my dough-nut. —Barry Humphries, *The Traveller's Tool*, p. 19, 1985

7 the inside of a round, hollow wave *US*
- —Michael V. Anderson, *The Bad, Rad, Not to Forget Way Cool Beach and Surf Discriptionary*, p. 5, 1988

8 a fool, a crazy person *UK*
Probably abbreviated from **DOUGHNUT HEAD**; possibly newly coined, combining conventional 'dough' to suggest a thick consistency and **NUT** (the head); or, possibly, an elaboration of 'nut' (a crazy person). Also spelt 'donut'.
- Some right doughnuts come up with potentially great ideas only to fuck them up[.] —Danny King, *The Burglar Diaries*, p. 34, 2001
- That Sandy isn't cool – she's a donut and a Jockey Slut. —Colin Butts, *Is Harry Still on the Boat?*, p. 363, 2003

doughnut *verb*
1 to cluster around a speaker, voicing support *UK*
When television cameras were introduced in the House of Commons in 1989, their focus was exclusively on the speaker. To give the impression of support of, or even interest in, what was being said, other MPs would cluster around – 'doughnut' – the speaker, muttering words of support.
- —Nicholas Jones, *Hackers, Hotting and Hooray Henrys*, p. 23, 1992

2 to win a game without your opponent scoring *US*
- —Dick Squires, *The Other Racquet Sports*, p. 220, 1971: 'Glossary'

doughnut bumper *noun*
1 a lesbian *US*
- —Jim Crotty, *How to Talk American*, p. 139, 1997

2 an aggressive, dominant lesbian *US*
- —William K. Bentley and James M. Corbett, *Prison Slang*, p. 59, 1992

doughnut dolly; donut dolly *noun*
a female Red Cross volunteer in Vietnam *US*
Vietnam war usage. From the practice of Red Cross volunteers serving doughnuts and coffee to the troops.
- —Carl Fleischhauer, *A Glossary of Army Slang*, p. 16, 1968
- You know, one of the thingss I remember about Vietnam, besides all the war stories, are the "Doughnut Dollies" [USO girls]. They'd come out to the field to play Bingo or something. —John Kerry, *The New Soldier*, p. 78, 1971
- We don't have no officer's club out here. Ain't no band. No donut dollies to fuck. —John M. Del Vecchio, *The 13th Valley*, p. 218, 1982
- Gary peered out at the women and announced, "Doughnut Dollies," but stayed inside. —Robert Mason, *Chickenhawk*, p. 414, 1983
- I had to carry a doughnut dolly (Red Cross Worker) from Camp Eagle to Firebase Bastogne, where she would spend the day entertaining troops[.] —Tom Marshall, *Price of Exit*, p. 251, 1998

doughnut head *noun*
used as a term of abuse suggesting an empty head *US, 1977*
- My brain hears her talking and goes, Do it, doughnut head. —W.R. Philbrick, *Max the Mighty*, p. 37, 1998

doughnut six; donut six *noun*
the leader of a group of female Red Cross workers in Vietnam *US*
'Six' was radio code for a unit's commander.
- —Gregory Clark, *Words of the Vietnam War*, p. 151, 1990

dough-pop *verb*
to hit hard *US*
- "Put in there that I'll probably catch two or three balls behind Dreamer Tatum and at least once I'll dough-pop him on his black ass," he said. —Dan Jenkins, *Semi-Tough*, p. 17, 1972

dough-rey-me *noun*
▷ **see: DO-RE-ME**

dough-roll *noun*

a wife *US*

- I said, "Well, I can dig it, buddy, 'cause I'm hooked up myself. I got a dough-roll [wife] and two crumb-catchers [children], you know." — Bruce Jackson, *In the Life*, p. 152, 1972

dough-roller *noun*

1 a baker *US, 1920*

- — *American Speech*, p. 271, December 1963: 'American Indian student slang'

2 a wife or female lover *US, 1929*

- "My little dough roller be gone," sings Robert Johnson. — Donald G. Dutton, *The Batterer*, p. 139, 1995

Douglas Hurd; douglas *noun*

1 a third-class university degree *UK, 2000*

This rhyming slang, based on Britain's former Foreign and Commonwealth Secretary, succeeded a **THORA**.

- He spent three years in the pub. It's no wonder he got a Douglas. — Bodmin Dark, *Dirty Cockney Rhyming Slang*, 2003

2 a turd *UK*

Rhyming slang, formed from the name of the English Conservative politician (he was Foreign Secretary 1989–95) and novelist, Lord Douglas Hurd (b.1930).

- When a person goes to perform what for a man is a sit down job on the lavatory they have gone to "dump a Douglas". — Ray Puxley, *Cockney Rabbit*, 1992

dougla tonic *noun*

any liquid poison *TRINIDAD AND TOBAGO*

In Trinidad, suicide by Indians is associated with poison.

- — Lise Winer, *Dictionary of the English/Creole of Trinidad & Tobago*, 2003

Douk *noun*

a Doukhobor, a member of a Russian fringe religious sect with settlements in Western Canada *CANADA*

The Doukhobors were known for taking off all their clothes when brought to court.

- "It's a joke all over the rest of Canada, isn't it?" he said. "Fun and games. Cops and Douks. Douks and cops." — *Maclean's*, p. 50–51, 10th March 1962

do up *verb*

1 to inject an illegal drug *US, 1952*

- They did up two each, then went down to the stoop. — Hal Ellson, *The Golden Spike*, p. 57, 1952
- If Porky don't act funny and stop us from taking our stuff out, we can go over there and do up. — Donald Goines, *Dopefiend*, p. 47u, 1971
- But every time you start to come down it's so terrible that you do up again. — J. Anthony Lukas, *Don't Shoot – We Are Your Children*, p. 256, 1971

2 to apply a tourniquet before injecting a drug intravenously *US*

- — William D. Alsever, *Glossary for the Establishment and Other Uptight People*, p. 19, December 1970

3 to beat up *UK*

A variation of **DO**.

- You lay another finger on me mate and I do you up right. — Clive Exton, *No Fixed Abode [Six Granada Plays]*, p. 127, 1959
- — Angela Devlin, *Prison Patter*, p. 46, 1996

douse *verb*

▸ **douse the glim**

to turn off the lights *US*

- — Lou Shelly, *Hepcats Jive Talk Dictionary*, p. 24, 1945

dove *noun*

1 a five-dollar note *US*

- He owes me a dove. — Gary K. Farlow, *Prison-ese: A Survivor's Guide to Speaking Prison Slang*, p. 19, 2002

2 a tablet of MDMA, the recreational drug best known as ecstasy, identified by an embossed dove-based motif *UK*

Variously known, often depending on their appearance, as 'love dove', 'double dove' or 'white dove'.

- Doves are great. It's better than making love. — *Evening Standard (London)*, p. 19, 14th January 1992
- An E – pink, with a bird stamped on it, so a Dove, I suppose – one blotter and a little grass. — Melanie McGrath, *Hard, Soft & Wet*, p. 89, 1998
- Street names [...] shamrocks, whites, X, XTC and many others. — James Kay and Julian Cohen, *The Parents' Complete Guide to Young People and Drugs*, p. 136, 1998
- "Here y'are..." It was a little plastic packet, with a couple of white pills inside. "... in case you get bored, later. Original formula Doves. Eighty mgs of MDMA," he added proudly, and made off into the crowd. — Kevin Sampson, *Powder*, p. 239, 1999
- Doves would make your head light and warm your emotions; Dennis the Menaces would make your legs heavy and blank your brain. — Dave Haslam, *Adventures of the Wheels of Steel*, p. xxv, 2001
- [C]omes in several varieties to reflect the bird's comportment, including "both wings up", "both wings down", "one wing up and one one wing down", "double doves (which are embossed both sides)[.] — Gareth Thomas, *This Is Ecstasy*, p. 57, 2002
- — Mike Haskins, *Drugs*, p. 290, 2003

Dover boat *noun*

a coat *UK*

Rhyming slang.

- — Ray Puxley, *Fresh Rabbit*, 1998

Dover harbour *noun*

a barber *UK*

Rhyming slang.

- — Ray Puxley, *Cockney Rabbit*, 1992

doves *noun*

crack cocaine *US*

- — Kenn "Naz" Young, *Naz's Dictionary of Teen Slang*, p. 33, 1993

dowager *noun*

an elderly, usually affluent, homosexual man *US, 1941*

- — Bruce Rodgers, *The Queens' Vernacular*, p. 67, 1972

do what?

what are you saying? *UK*

- If the law had anything on me, I would've been pulled in, so I thought they were trying it on. I flared up a bit. "Do what, you c**nts?" — Lenny McLean, *The Guv'nor*, p. 78, 1998

down *noun*

1 any barbiturate or central nervous system depressant *US*

- [T]he kids take a lot of downs and dig down bands[.] — Lester Bangs, *Psychotic Reactions and Carburetor Dung*, p. 69, 1971
- Once my head is together I'll kick the speed and stabilize myself with tranks and downs[.] — Lawrence Block, *Chip Harrison Scores Again*, p. 191, 1971
- — Donald Wesson and David Smith, *Barbiturates*, p. 122, 1977
- "Ups" all day and "downs" at night. — Beatrice Sparks (writing as 'Anonymous'), *Jay's Journal*, p. 26, 1979
- DOWNS: (PERCODANS, SECONAL, TUINAL, VALIUM, DALMANE): A step away from Quaaludes (read not as powerful), downs are readily available[.] — Jay Saporita, *Pourin' It All Out*, p. 63, 1980
- I'd make that trip in from the cabin at least every two or three weeks for a fresh supply of inhalers. Sometimes I'd pick up a few downs to go along with it. — Herbert Huncke, *Guilty of Everything*, p. 88, 1990
- But what usually happened was that I'd be speeding like mad when the downs finally took effect. — Cleo Odzer, *Goa Freaks*, p. 148, 1995

2 a dislike or antipathy *AUSTRALIA, 1835*

- Some people I know think I have a down on Liverpool — Tony Wilson, *24 Hour Party People*, p. 5, 2002

▸ **have a down on**

to hold something or someone in low esteem *AUSTRALIA, 1828*

- There must be some reason why he has a down on rural people and communities[.] — Mr. Hayes, *The House of Commons Standing Committee E [Hansard]*, 20th March 2004

down *verb*

1 to finish a drink *UK, 1922*

- "I cannot see what difference another bar will make," said stockbroker Nick Hair, downing his pint outside Ozzie's. — *The Guardian*, 24th May 2003

2 to sell stolen goods *US*

- Ten minutes later he walked up to me and said, "Babs, baby, I know I downed your vines, so here's the tickets." — Babs Gonzales, *I Paid My Dues*, p. 52, 1967
- Sooner or later they have to try downing it and I want that ice hotter than a meteor, harder to move than the Rock of Gibralter. — Seth Morgan, *Homeboy*, p. 99, 1990

down *adjective*

1 excellent; loyal; fashionable *US, 1946*

- Even when the block belongs to your own people, you are still an outsider who has to prove himself a down stud with heart. — Piri Thomas, *Down These Mean Streets*, p. 47, 1967
- He explained that I didn't know him but a friend of both of ours had told him I was "down people" and to turn me on when I arrived. — Babs Gonzales, *I Paid My Dues*, p. 84, 1967
- This is the life for Kitty. She's a down ho. — Susan Hall, *Gentleman of Leisure*, p. 153, 1972
- The tigers would go to the Cabo and the BC, the down P.R.'s would go to the Palladium. — Edwin Torres, *Carlito's Way*, p. 24, 1975
- My shirts were from Brooks'; my socks cost a pound / I wore solid gold cufflinks – I knew I was down. — Dennis Wepman et al., *The Life*, p. 36, 1976

- — *Maledicta*, p. 268, Summer/Winter 1981: 'By its slang, ye shall know it: the pessimism of prison life'
- Jake the Fake held up his glass for a toast. "Here's to Taco and Slick, two of the downes' sistahs that ever did it, two of the hippes' ladies that it has ever been my purpose to meet and greet..!" — Donald Goines, *The Busting Out of an Ordinary Man*, p. 74, 1985

2 willing, prepared, eager *US, 1944*
- "Are you still down for it?" "I'm down for it." — Hal Ellson, *The Golden Spike*, p. 15, 1952
- He didn't want to make any money, or he didn't know how. He just wasn't down enough. — Claude Brown, *Manchild in the Promised Land*, p. 159, 1965
- He's a hype but he is very down with the current scene. — Eldridge Cleaver, *Soul on Ice (letter dated 19th September, 1965)*, p. 46, 1968
- Myself, I'm down for the action anytime, and I don't want to hear this ol' bullshit about the little kids in the schoolyard. — Edwin Torres, *Carlito's Way*, p. 71, 1975
- [N]ow that I wanna flap some skins Brandi ain't down for it even if I wear a jim hat. — *Boyz N The Hood*, 1990
- "Fight the Power", right, dude? We're down. — *Airheads*, 1994
- You down with the boost? — *Kids*, 1995

3 aware of the current social fashions and opinions; being or feeling a part of a general or specific social scene *US, 1944*
A narrowing of the earlier UK C18 sense (wide-awake, suspicious, aware); modern use is mainly black or trendy.
- You ain't down if you ain't heard of Method Man. — *A2Z*, p. 30, 1995
- You are a down girl. — *Clueless*, 1995
- A lady who considered herself down but who found herself frequently exasperated by the imperfections of those less together than her. — Diran Abedayo, *My Once Upon A Time*, p. 93, 2000

4 (of surf conditions) flat *US*
- — Gary Fairmont R. Filosa II, *The Surfer's Almanac*, p. 184, 1977

5 depressed *UK, 1610*
- [H]e – like everyone else at Westminster – saw it as a demotion and he was reported by friends to be 'down' for weeks afterwards. — *The Guardian*, 9th November 1998

6 in custody; imprisoned *US, 1927*
- The first time I was down I come down with assault with attempt to murder. — Bruce Jackson, *In the Life*, p. 61, 1972
- Buck, we have here Carl Edward Colbert, escapee from the West Tennessee Reception Center, down for armed robbery and assault with a deadly weapon, a pitchfork. — Elmore Leonard, *Riding the Rap*, p. 136, 1995
- — Don R. McCreary (Editor), *Dawg Speak*, 2001

down *adverb*

1 down to or down at *AUSTRALIA, 1911*
- 'Took his life, dear,' she announced, now piteously for her situation, 'on a tree down the yard.' — Patrick White, *The Tree of Man*, p. 279, 1955
- Yeah, he told Bruce down the pub that he just wouldn't look at another chick. — Kathy Lette and Gabrielle Carey, *Puberty Blues*, p. 36, 1979
- One afternoon when Ernie and I were down the Chinamen's cutting grass for our cow[.] — T.A.G. Hungerford, *Stories From Suburban Road*, p. 140, 1983

2 to hospital *BARBADOS*
- — Frank A. Collymore, *Barbadian Dialect*, p. 41, 1965

▸ **get down**
to inject (a drug) into a vein *US, 1969*
- — Ralph de Sola, *Crime Dictionary*, p. 57, 1982
- — Richard A. Spears, *The Slang and Jargon of Drugs and Drink*, p. 217, 1986
- — Mike Haskins, *Drugs*, p. 290, 2003

downalong *adjective*
in Barbados, of or pertaining to the other British West Indies islands *BARBADOS*
- But listen to she and she downalong talk. — Frank A. Collymore, *Barbadian Dialect*, p. 41, 1965

down and dirty *adjective*

1 highly competitive, no holds barred *US, 1988*
- — *American Speech*, Fall 1990

2 descriptive of the final card in a game of seven-card stud poker *US*
It is dealt face-down and it greatly affects the chances of a hand winning.
- — George Percy, *The Language of Poker*, p. 30, 1988

down and out *adjective*
homeless; without money *US, 1901*
- [W]henever time you is down and out – busted – haven't got any bread – you call yourself an Israelite[.] — Desmond Dekker, 1969

down beat *noun*

▸ **on the down beat**
declining in popularity *US*
- — Marcus Hanna Boulware, *Jive and Slang of Students in Negro Colleges*, 1947

downblouse *noun*
a type of voyeurism devoted specifically to seeing a woman's breasts looking down her blouse *US, 1994*
- "Upskirt" and "downblouse" tapes often end up on the Internet, where anyone over 18 can legally view and buy them. — *Charleston (West Virginia) Daily Mail*, p. 4C, 10th August 1998
- The Internet is littered with hundreds of Web sites dedicated to voyeuristsic "upskirts" and "downblouses" in which cameras are aimed in those locales to capture revealing images of unsuspecting women in public. — *Chicago Daily Herald*, p. 11, 13th April 2002

downer *noun*

1 a circumstance that depresses; a depressing experience *US*
From DOWN (depressed).
- Liquor's a downer! A bad trip! It'll kill you[.] — Nicholas Von Hoffman, *We Are The People Our Parents Warned Us Against*, p. 191, 1967
- They put me in gaol. Everything was a downer. — Richard Neville [quoting Otis Cook], *Play Power*, p. 245, 1970
- Everyone is a junglist now, and if you go and take an E on jungle stuff, you're going to have a downer, know what I mean? — Macfarlane, Macfarlane and Robson, *The User*, p. 3, 1996
- This job and that, it's a bit like one of them. Bit of a downer. — Kevin Sampson, *Outlaws*, p. 19, 2001

2 a barbiturate or other central nervous system depressant *US, 1965*
- — Joe David Brown (Editor), *The Hippies*, p. 217, 1967: 'Glossary of hippie terms'
- [E]verybody was saying, 'Smoke some grass or take downers'. — Nicholas Von Hoffman, *We Are The People Our Parents Warned Us Against*, p. 223, 1967
- Well, let's talk him down, give him a place to hide, get him some sugar, some milk, some food, plenty of liquids, get him some downers. — Leonard Wolfe (Editor), *Voices from the Love Generation*, p. 134, 1968
- — Edward R. Bloomquist, *Marijuana*, p. 158, 1968
- And I can't recommend downers because I've had too many friends go down and out. — *The Last Supplement to the Whole Earth Catalog*, p. 83, March 1971
- I mean is it an upper or a downer? — Oscar Zeta Acosta, *The Revolt of the Cockroach People*, p. 192, 1973
- Prisoners used to be allowed a couple of shots of whiskey in the old days prior to their execution; now they offered downers and an all-American cigarette and coffee. — Ed Sanders, *Tales of Beatnik Glory*, p. 47, 1975
- 'I don't need no more uppers," Joanie said, "but downers I could use." — Emmett Grogan, *Final Score*, p. 81, 1976

3 an animal being led to slaughter that is too sick or crippled to walk into the slaughterhouse *US*
This sense of the word began to enjoy great popularity in the US in late 2003 with the publicity surrounding Mad Cow Disease in US cattle.
- In her early thirties, she is a cocktail waitress in Minneapolis whose off-hour zeal is for ministering to stockyard animals that are too sick or crippled to walk. They are called "downers." — *Washington Post*, p. F2, 14th April 1991

▸ **have a downer on**
to hold something or someone in low esteem *AUSTRALIA, 1915*
- [T]he big [bookmaking] firms have a downer on small jumps courses staging races that, in their view, take too long[.] — *The Times*, 10th September 2003

down for mine *adjective*
willing to stand up for your group *US*
- — James Harris, *A Convict's Dictionary*, p. 31, 1989

down hill *adjective*
during the second half of a prison sentence *US*
- — Hyman E. Goldin et al., *Dictionary of American Underworld Lingo*, p. 47, 1950

down home *noun*

1 jail, especially the Manhattan Detention Pens *US*
- — Ralph de Sola, *Crime Dictionary*, p. 43, 1982

2 the US federal penitentiary in Atlanta, Georgia *US*
- — Jay Robert Nash, *Dictionary of Crime*, p. 109, 1992

3 a relatively specific place in the Maritime Provinces *CANADA, 1988*
- The term has many meanings. If a Maritimer says "Down Home" while sitting in a Toronto tavern, he could be talking about all the Maritimes, or Prince Edward Island, or a valley, cove, county, village, or the house where he grew up. — Harry Bruce, *Down Home*, p. 283–284, 1988

down home *adjective*
exemplifying the essence of black culture *US*
• —Arnold Shaw, *Dictionary of American Pop/Rock*, p. 111, 1982

downhomer *noun*
a person who identifies closely with his maritime roots *CANADA, 1988*
• Down-homer, in its gently derogatory sense, is also [like "down home"] relative. "The first time I heard the term down-homer," my father said, "it was used by Bill Fraser, a brakeman from Antigonish, to describe a freight-handler from Mulgrave 45 m. away"[.]—Harry Bruce, *Down Home*, p. 284, 1988

downie *noun*
a central nervous system depresssant *US, 1966*
• [T]he beautiful thing about downies is that there's no come down [...] you just go to sleep.—Ruth Bronsteen, *The Hippies' Handbook*, 1967
• —Eugene Landy, *The Underground Dictionary*, p. 70, 1971

Downing Street *noun*
in various games, the number ten *UK, 1943*
From *10* Downing Street, the official address of the British Prime Minister.
• —Ivan Bracklin and William Fitzgerald, *All About Darts*, p. 99, 1975
• —Peter Wright, *Cockney Dialect & Slang*, p. 109, 1981

download *verb*
to defecate *US*
Application of computer terminology to the toilet bowl.
• —Pamela Munro, *U.C.L.A. Slang*, p. 63, 2001

downlow *adjective*
secret *UK, 1990s*
Black usage.
• Cosmic approached me as I was distributing the bubbly and kissed me powerfully. "What a downlow sweetheart you are!"—Diran Abedayo, *My Once Upon A Time*, p. 201, 2000

down on *adjective*
opposed to; holding a low opinion of something *US, 1848*
• Judaism seems less down on sex than Christianity is.—Fiona Pitt-Kethley, *Red Light Districts of the World*, p. 59, 2000

down on your Mamas and Papas *adjective*
in dire financial straits *UK*
Rhyming slang for **DOWN ON YOUR UPPER**; formed on a 1960s US pop-group.
• Not bad for a man down on his Mamas and Papas.—Mervyn Stutter, *Getting Nowhere Fast*, 21st May 2004

down on your uppers *adjective*
in dire financial straits *US*
When the upper of a shoe is worn down, a person might as well be walking barefoot.
• —Charles F. Haywood, *Yankee Dictionary*, p. 49, 1963

downpressor *noun*
an oppressor *JAMAICA, 1982*
Noted as Rasta patois by Paul Sullivan, *Sullivan's Music Trivia*, p. 35, 2003.
• —Peter Tosh, *Downpresser Man*, 1976
• —Thomas H. Slone, *Rasta is Cuss*, p. 40, 2003

down south *noun*
1 below the waist; the genitals *US*
• —*Maledicta*, p. 147, Summer/Winter 1982: 'Dyke diction: the language of lesbians'
2 Antarctica *ANTARCTICA, 1913*
• —Bernadette Hince, *The Antarctic Dictionary*, p. 105, 2000
3 the US federal penitentiary in Atlanta, Georgia *US*
• —Jay Robert Nash, *Dictionary of Crime*, p. 109, 1992

▸ **it's raining down south**
experiencing the bleed period of the menstruation cycle *US*
• —Karen Houppert, *The Curse*, 1999

▸ **it's snowing down south**
your slip is showing *US*
• —*American Weekly*, p. 2, 14th August 1955

downstairs *noun*
the genital area, especially of a female *UK*
• 3) Nipples: coarse, bulbous, lacerated 4) Downstairs: bushy, trimmed, bald—Kevin Sampson, *Clubland*, p. 70, 2002

down the banks *noun*
a reprimand; a piece of your mind *IRELAND, 1968*
• I'm there [...] giving this poor cunt of a night porter down the banks.—Kevin Sampson, *Outlaws*, p. 185, 2001

down the block *adjective*
in prison, in the punishment cells *UK*
• —Home Office, *Glossary of Terms and Slang Common in Penal Establishments*, 1978

down the drain; down the drains *noun*
the brain; brains *UK*
Rhyming slang.
• —Ray Puxley, *Fresh Rabbit*, 1998

down the drain *adjective*
lost, wasted, failed *UK, 1930*
• Barton Fink, for instance, went straight down the drain and so did Billy Wilder's Fedora.—*The Guardian*, 25th June 1992

down the food chain *adjective*
to be less important in the hierarchy of a business or social organisation, further down the chain of command *UK*
An allusion to the natural organisation of species, each being the food source for the next one up the biological chain.
• [A]ll the good people down the food chain need to chop the stuff [cocaine] to keep their profits up[.]—J.J. Connolly, *Know Your Enemy [britpulp]*, p. 143, 1999

down the gurgler *adjective*
hopelessly lost *AUSTRALIA*
• I reckon there's seven grand down the gurgler and that's just to date.—*Truckin' Life*, p. 21, 12th September 1982

down the hatch!
used as a drinking toast, as a descriptive precursor to taking a drink and as an encouragement to take medicine *US, 1931*
• "Down the hatch!" The words come to us as we sit here looking at the picture of Mieuli.—*San Francisco Examiner*, 2nd June 1967

down the mine *adjective*
said of the nose of a surfboard that has knifed below the ocean surface *AUSTRALIA*
• —John Severson, *Modern Surfing Around the World*, p. 166, 1964

down the pan *adjective*
lost, wasted, failed *UK, 1961*
A variation of **DOWN THE DRAIN**.
• They can see money going down the pan and want to do something to protect it.—*The Guardian*, 7th October 2002

down there *noun*
the genitals *US*
A precious if unmistakable euphemism.
• JANE: Okay. So what do you call it? ROBIN: Down there.—*Boys on the Side*, 1995
• I come from the "down there" generation. That is, those were the words [...] that the women in my family used to refer to all female genitalia, internal or external.—Gloria Steinem, *The Vagina Monologues*, 1998
• You got an old lady to talk about her down-there. You feel better now?—Eve Ensler, *The Vagina Monologues*, p. 30, 1998

down the road *adjective*
in prison *UK*
• I'll be up in court and down the road. Because of you.—Alan Bleasdale, *Boys From the Blackstuff*, 1982

down the steps *adverb*
used to denote a sentence to imprisonment *UK*
• Fanlight went down the steps with three Christmas puddings to eat[.]—Charles Raven, *Underworld Nights*, p. 23, 1956

down time *noun*
in prison, free time *UK*
Adopted from industry, where the term means that machines aren't working, hence free time for workers.
• —Angela Devlin, *Prison Patter*, p. 47, 1996

down to *adjective*
responsible for *UK*
• X is down to Y—Peter Laurie, *Scotland Yard*, p. 322, 1970

down to
because of; attributable to *UK*
• Alright I bet you a jacks that I nick you down to larking within one moon from now.—Frank Norman, *Bang To Rights*, p. 123, 1958

down to the ground *adverb*
thoroughly, extremely well *UK, 1867*
- Under the jacket, my whole shape realigned / In ways that suited me down to the ground. — *Ten Glosses (The Guardian)*, 23rd March 2001

down to the rivets *adjective*
(used of brake pads or a clutch) extremely worn *US*
- — Lewis Poteet, *Car & Motorcyle Slang*, p. 72, 1992

downtown *noun*
1 heroin *US, 1983*
- First I'll put your Uptown on the spoon, then to make it more exciting I'm gonna add some Downtown. They call this thing a speedball, honey, but then you must know that. — *The Bad Lieutenant*, 1992

2 in pool, the foot end of the table *US*
- — Mike Shamos, *The Illustrated Encyclopedia of Billiards*, p. 82, 1993

3 during the Vietnam war, the airspace above Hanoi, North Vietnam *US, 1967*
- — *Current Slang*, p. 15, Summer 1970
- "Don't forget," Cole said, "we're going right downtown. It won't be any piece of cake." — Stephen Coonts, *Flight of the Intruder*, p. 277, 1986

downtowner *noun*
a member of the US embassy staff in Vientiane, Laos *US*
Used with more than a trace of derision by US troops in the field.
- — Linda Reinberg, *In the Field*, p. 67, 1991

down trip *noun*
any unpleasant, uninspiring experience *US*
- — Joe David Brown (Editor), *The Hippies*, p. 218, 1967: 'Glossary of hippie terms'

down trou *noun*
the voluntary lowering of your trousers *NEW ZEALAND*
- An activity sanctioned by tradition and alcohol, its practitioners are usually in their late teens or early twenties and in a bar largely patronized by their peers. — Louis S. Leland, *A Personal Kiwi-Yankee Dictionary*, p. 34, 1984

Down Under; down under *noun*
Australia *AUSTRALIA, 1915*
- — Josef Holman, *As I See Them*, p. 29, 1954
- [L]et's face it, a lot of you find it bloody convenient to come from Down Under. — Barry Humphries, *A Nice Night's Entertainment*, p. 73, 1962

Down Under; down under *adverb*
in Australia *AUSTRALIA, 1886*
- Push up bras, falsies or wads of cotton wool or Kleenex serve to give the impression that the cult of the bosom thrives down under. — Sue Rhodes, *Now you'll think I'm awful*, p. 26, 1967
- The majority of restuarants Down Under are run by ethnic minorities. — Barry Humphries, *The Traveller's Tool*, p. 80, 1985

downy *noun*
a bed *US, 1843*
A reference to the 'down' found in bedding.
- They're always coming around to our pad raving about how sensational you are in the downy. — Bernard Wolfe, *The Late Risers*, p. 131, 1954

dowry *noun*
a great deal, a lot *UK, 1859*
Probably from the value of a traditional bride's dowry.
- — Paul Baker, *Polari*, p. 172, 2002

doxy; doxie *noun*
a woman; a girlfriend *UK, 1530*
Originally, in C16, 'a beggar's trull' (the unmarried mistress of a beggar). Beginning in C19 it took on a softer and broader sense.
- It seemed he had bungled his way through a bouqeut of doxies, male and female, without anything to show for his efforts[.] — Angelo d'Arcangelo, *The Homosexual Handbook*, p. 23, 1968
- An old church doxie cracked I was cursed for killing Mama. — Iceberg Slim (Robert Beck), *Airtight Willie and Me*, p. 91, 1979
- She was an amateur doxy thinking about turning pro. — Robert Campbell, *In La-La Land We Trust*, p. 1, 1986
- Robbie, a drug dealer who works the local clubs, batters his pill-popping doxy. — *The Guardian*, 12th April 2003

Doyle Brunson *noun*
in hold 'em poker, a ten and a two as the first two cards dealt to a player *US, 1982*
Poker player Doyle 'Texas Dolly' Brunson won the World Series of Poker two years in a row with this hand.
- — Thomas L. Clark, *The Dictionary of Gambling and Gaming*, p. 67, 1987

D'Oyly Carte; d'oyly *noun*
1 a fart *UK*
Rhyming slang, formed from the name of the opera company, founded in 1875, that specialises in presenting the works of Gilbert and Sullivan. One of various backstage names for the opera company is 'The Oily Fart'.
- Generally dropped as a "D'Oyly". — Ray Puxley, *Cockney Rabbit*, 1992

2 the heart *UK*
Rhyming slang.
- "I've got a bit of wind around de oily cart." A loud artistic burp may follow. — Ray Puxley, *Cockney Rabbit*, 1992

do you kiss your mother with that mouth?
used as a rejoinder to profanity *US*
- Do you kiss your mother with that mouth? I'm gettin' out of here. — *Wayne's World*, 1992

do you know something?
used as a gentle if meaningless introduction to what might otherwise come over as unlikely, unkind or abrupt *UK, 1974*
As an example: 'Do you know something? I rather like you.'
- — Brian Foster, *The Changing English Language*, 1968

do you like the taste of hospital food?
used a jocular threat of violence *UK*
- Pick a window because now you're leaving / Do you like hospital food – You will / Can your mother sew – Have her stitch' this. — Flotsam & Jetsam, *Pick A Window*, 1995

do you want some?
used as a challenging invitation to violent conflict *UK*
- Come on then, son, do you want some? — Malcolm Pryce, *Aberystwyth Mon Amour*, p. 233, 2001
- All right then you slag, do you want some? — Mark Steel, *Reasons to be Cheerful*, p. 43, 2001

dozens *noun*
a game of ritualistic insult *US, 1915*
- "I don't play no dozens, boy," Smitty growled. "You young punks don't know how far to go with a man." — Chester Himes, *If He Hollers Let Him Go*, p. 102, 1945
- Lots of other games sprang up for the same reason: snagging, rhyming, the dirty dozens, cutting contests. — Mezz Mezzrow, *Really the Blues*, p. 230, 1946
- Playing the Dozens — *American Speech*, p. 148–149, May 1950
- "Watch out, man, I don't play the dozens," the second one said. — Chester Himes, *Cotton Comes to Harlem*, p. 63, 1965
- He would play the dozens, have rock fights, and curse us out. — Claude Brown, *Manchild in the Promised Land*, p. 84, 1965
- This was the "dozens," a game of insults. The dozens is a dangerous game even among friends[.] — Piri Thomas, *Down These Mean Streets*, p. 121, 1967
- You talking about my dead mother? I don't play the dozens, kid. — Nathan Heard, *Howard Street*, p. 71, 1968
- Hordes of children – throwing peanut shells, popcorn, dead spiders and roaches at the glass cage – followed the procession down the streets, eating cotton candy and playing the dozens about Max and the Governor. — Steve Cannon, *Groove, Bang, and Jive Around*, p. 187, 1969
- In the clean dozens some of the insults are directed at the other's mother, but most are directly personal. — Roger Abrahams, *Positively Black*, p. 40, 1970
- I hear through an open window the profane chanting of teenagers playing a merry game of ghetto dozens (dozens – the denigration of another's parents or ancestors) that explodes in a montage of pain, bright as flame, that shocks my brain. — Iceberg Slim (Robert Beck), *The Naked Soul of Iceberg Slim*, p. 19, 1971
- Two cats would meet on the street and start playin' the dozens; one guy would say, "Ashes to ashes, dust to dust, your mother has a pussy like a Greyhound bus." — Edwin Torres, *Carlito's Way*, p. 10, 1975
- [G]oing head-to-head with someone using snaps [taunts, insults] – playing the dozens – is a battle for respect. — James Haskins, *The Story of Hip-Hop*, p. 54, 2000

dozer *noun*
1 marijuana *UK*
- — Mike Haskins, *Drugs*, p. 287, 2003

2 a bulldozer *US, 1942*
- Dozers, scrapers, and dump trucks too / Scooploaders, graders, and ten tons, new. — Sandee Shaffer Johnson, *Cadences*, p. 120, 1986

dozey *adjective*
slow; stupid *AUSTRALIA*
- Those dozey bastards down at Oz House wouldn't know if a tram was up 'em till the bell rang. — *The Adventures of Barry McKenzie*, 1972

- About fifteen minutes later (it seemed and eternity) a dozey digger drives out of the plantation in a gunship and takes me to 5 RAR HQ. — Martin Cameron, *A Look at the Bright Side*, 1988

dozo *noun*

a dolt *NEW ZEALAND*

- — David McGill, *David McGill's Complete Kiwi Slang Dictionary*, p. 39, 1998

dozy *adjective*

stupid; lazy *UK*

Military coinage.

- [H]e started shouting and trying to fight, the dozy bastard! — Dave Courtney, *Stop the Ride I Want to Get Off*, p. 183, 1999

DP *noun*

1 *d*ouble *p*enetration *US*

In the pornography industry, this usually refers to a woman who is being penetrated simultaneously in the vagina and anally; viewers of American pornography have been obsessed with this type of double penetration since the 1990s. Technically, it refers to two objects or body parts inserted into the same rectum or vagina simultaneously.

- "While we're on the subject, what do you think of DP's?" "They're too hard to shoot. There's no real spontaneity in them. You know, DP actually means a double penetration in one hole – not just the pussy and the ass." — Anthony Petkovich, *The X Factory*, p. 123, 1997
- When they do sign, they specify what they will and will not do – oral, anal, girl-girl, group sex, D.P.s, gay, bi, that sort of thing. — Ana Loria, *1 2 3 Be A Porn Star!*, p. 61, 2000
- So the unattractive girls end up being he real workhorses. They're the ones who are doing all the anals and DPs. — John Bowe, *Gig*, p. 447, 2001

2 a *d*isplaced *p*erson *UK, 1945*

- Wound up carryin a load of D.P.'s out, had the misery in their eyes could break the devil's heart. — George Mandel, *Flee the Angry Strangers*, p. 63, 1952

3 Dr. Pepper™ soda *US*

A drink favoured, and hence a term heard, mostly in the southern US.

- — Andy Anonymous, *A Basic Guide to Campusology*, p. 7, 1966
- — Charles Shafer, *Folk Speech in Texas Prisons*, p. 203, 1990

DPP *noun*

a vagina simultaneously penetrated by two penises *US*

An abbreviation of '*d*ouble *p*ussy *p*enetration'.

- — Ana Loria, *1 2 3 Be A Porn Star!*, p. 164, 2000: 'Glossary of adult sex industry terms'

D.P.Q. *noun*

a *d*umb *p*assenger *q*uestion *CANADA, 1989*

- Crews of BC Ferries are asked their share [of D.P.Q.s]: among the classics are "How high above sea level are we?" "Do you catch your own seafood?" and "When do we see the whales?" — Tom Parkin, *WetCoast Words*, p. 50, 1989

DPs *noun*

a pair of men's close-fitting and revealing nylon swimming trunks *AUSTRALIA*

An initialism of **DICK POINTERS** or **DICK POKERS**.

- I remember during my teens a friend's mother referring to DPs. When I asked what they were, my friend explained that his mother was too polite to say "dick pokers." — *Wordmap (www.abc.net.au/wordmap)*, 2003

Dr *and variants*

▷ **see: DOCTOR**

drab *noun*

a pretty girl, especially one who is new in town *US*

- — Marcus Hanna Boulware, *Jive and Slang of Students in Negro Colleges*, 1947

drack *noun*

an unattractive woman *AUSTRALIA, 1960*

- — Jim Ramsay, *Cop It Sweet!*, p. 31, 1977

drack *adjective*

1 dreary; dull; awful; unpleasant *AUSTRALIA, 1944*

Ted Hartley, an amateur lexicographer, was the first to record this word in 1944, and says that it is a 'recent word derived from Dracula'. Years later he collected this quotation 'I am not a raving beauty – but I'm not exactly Dracula either', which lends some support to his initial contention. Others have suggested it is an alteration of **DRECK**, but there is little evidence of this word being known in Australia prior to 1944.

- Her parties are always drac. — Tilly Devine, *Remember Smith's Weekly?*, p. 219, 1950
- But if the tests are bad enough there is nothing so drack as a suburban cricket game or country minor league. — Sue Rhodes, *Now you'll think I'm awful*, p. 92, 1967
- A drack sort often has a mind of her own, refuses to be segregated at parties, and complains bitterly when asked to polish a car, scrape a boat, or watch footie in the rain. — Arthur Chipper, *The Aussie Swearer's Guide*, p. 38, 1972

2 (of a woman) unattractive *AUSTRALIA, 1949*

- 'She's a drack line', i.e. an uncomely woman. — Thirty-Five *The Argot*, 1950

dracs *noun*

the canine teeth *UK*

*Drac*ula, according to Hollywood at least, has overlarge pointed canines for puncturing the skin of his victims.

- Our Ratter's nickname is down to his fangs. They slope back slightly and the thingy, his dracs and that, are pointed as fuck. — Kevin Sampson, *Outlaws*, p. 12, 2001

draft beast *noun*

a student who studies hard in preparation for exams *TRINIDAD AND TOBAGO*

- — Lise Winer, *Dictionary of the English/Creole of Trinidad & Tobago*, 2003

drafty *noun*

draft beer *US*

- — *Current Slang*, p. 7, Summer 1969

drag *noun*

1 anything or anyone boring or tedious *US, 1863*

- That was a solid drag[.] — Mezz Mezzrow, *Really the Blues*, p. 132, 1946
- He wants two bucks a stick! What a drag! — John Clellon Holmes, *Go*, p. 101, 1952
- If you get to be known as a "drag" or a "bring down," you can't do business with them. — William Burroughs, *Junkie*, p. 31, 1953
- It's a funny thing how life can be such a drag one minute and a solid sender the next. — Louis Armstrong, *Satchmo*, p. 126, 1954
- "That's a solid drag, poppa," Movement said. — Bernard Wolfe, *The Late Risers*, p. 150, 1954
- "Honey, your grandma is feeling the least." "What a drag!" said Red. — Steve Allen, *Bop Fables*, p. 36, 1955
- Harlem is a drag, man, strictly a drag. — Robert Sylvester, *No Cover Charge*, p. 68, 1956
- Drag, they will tell you, is what everything is. Possession are a drag. Society is a drag. Mass government is a drag. God is a drag. Madison Avenue and General Motors are drags. — Jim Schock, *Life is a Lousy Drag*, 1958
- Well, Pops, life from then on was strictl;y a drag[.] — Dan Burley, *Diggeth Thou?*, p. 24, 1959
- Such a drag, man. They keep changing postmen and sometimes they'll just toss it on the floor. — Ross Russell, *The Sound*, p. 106, 1961
- SIMON: She's a trend setter. It's her profession! GEORGE: She's a drag. A well-known drag. We turn the sound down on her and say rude things. — *A Hard Day's Night*, 1964
- But as soon as I got up that morning, I could tell that Dad was going to be a real drag. — Claude Brown, *Manchild in the Promised Land*, p. 95, 1965
- Kind of a drag, when your baby don't love you / Kind of a drag, when you know she's been untrue. — The Buckinghams, *Kind of a Drag*, 1967
- What a drag it is getting old... — The Rolling Stones, *Mother's Little Helper*, 1967
- Plastic people! / Oh, baby, know / You're such a drag. — Frank Zappa, *Plastic People*, 1967
- Everyday he had to drive uptown to a bar to cop, and it became a daily drag. — Babs Gonzales, *I Paid My Dues*, p. 106, 1967
- Getting up early is an incredible drag, or at least I should think it would be. — James Simon Kunen, *The Strawberry Statement*, p. 69, 1968
- Jimmy was uncommunicative and even called the woman a "drag" – at which, misunderstanding, she lost her temper – but everything was a drag these days. — Nathan Heard, *Howard Street*, p. 59, 1968
- Except that the heroes were sculpted from water and sand, nobody really read the quarterlies, and the cocktail parties were a full drag. — Richard Farina, *Long Time Coming and a Long Time Gone*, p. 37, 1969
- I can't wait until I can drive next year. I walk every day. It's such a drag. — *Fast Times at Ridgemont High*, 1982
- There's like this whole big monster deal, it's endless and it's a total drag. — *The Breakfast Club*, 1985
- PIP: So you answer the phones and all? SUZZI: Yeah, for like six hours a day. PIP: What a drag, huh? — *Airheads*, 1994
- Mab would have been a drag at the club, complaining about the smoke or the possibility of being squashed by a steel-toed boot. — Francesca Lia Block, *I Was a Teenage Fairy*, p. 89, 1998

2 a conventional, narrow-minded person *US*

- — Marcus Hanna Boulware, *Jive and Slang of Students in Negro Colleges*, 1947

3 an unattractive girl *US*

- A: But that's better than being stuck. Q: Stuck? A: With a pig, a drag,a beast. — Max Shulman, *Guided Tour of Campus Humor*, p. 106, 1955

4 a transvestite *UK*

- I tell the drag barman to give me a vodka and tonic[.] —Ted Lewis, *Jack Carter's Law*, p. 23, 1974
- He knew all the drags in the township[.] —Bart Luirink (translated by Loes Nas), *Moffies*, p. 118, 2000

5 female clothing worn by men; male clothing worn by women *UK, 1870*

A term born in the theatre, but the non-theatrical sense has long dominated. He or she who wears 'drag' may or may not be a homosexual.

- It is a law violation for entertainers to appear in "drag" (clothes of the opposite sex. —Jack Lait and Lee Mortimer, *New York Confidential*, p. 68, 1948
- [H]e remembered that when Guy got bounced from the studio – for sneaking into the costume department and borrowing fancy ladies' dresses to wear at private drag parties – the kid went back to New York. —Bernard Wolfe, *The Late Risers*, p. 202, 1954
- [R]ipping and tearing Georgette's drag clothes, her lovely dresses and silks, stamping on her shoes. —Hubert Selby Jr, *Last Exit to Brooklyn*, p. 56, 1957
- "I may tell you in strictest confidence that some of these girls ..." with gambler fingers he shifts the photos in Three Card Monte Passese – are really boys. In uh drag I believe is the word???" —William Burroughs, *Naked Lunch*, p. 194–195, 1957
- [F]emale impersonation was called "drag," and "drag clubs" sprung up all over the nation, from New York to San Francisco. —Antony James, *America's Homosexual Underground*, p. 83, 1965
- [T]he rest of 'em looked like sissies in drag. —A.S. Jackson, *Gentleman Pimp*, p. 100, 1973
- I think if everyone were honest, they'd confess that the lady looks exactly like a man in drag. —*Austin Powers*, 1997

6 any kind of clothing *UK*

- Take first the Misery Kid and his trad. drag. —Colin MacInnes, *Absolute Beginners*, 1959
- Oh, couldn't be doing with all that naph drag, ducky. —Barry Took and Marty Feldman, *Round The Horne*, 10th April 1966
- —the cast of 'Aspects of Love', Prince of Wales Theatre, *Palare (Boy Dancer Talk) for Beginners*, 1989–92
- — Morrissey, *Bona Drag*, 1990

7 clout, influence *US, 1896*

- The money came in so fast and his drag was so good that he felt immune[.] —Jack Lait and Lee Mortimer, *New York Confidential*, p. 185, 1948
- I have plenty of drag around this town. —Jim Thompson, *Bad Boy*, p. 370, 1953
- Having drag in Vietnam was very important for specialized units that required special supplies or support. —Gregory Clark, *Words of the Vietnam War*, p. 154, 1990

8 a street or road, especially a major urban street *UK, 1851*

- Man, I could see myself in a sharp uniform, strutting down the main drag blowing my sax while the chicks lined up along the curb giving me the eye all the way. —Milton Mezzrow, *Really the Blues*, p. 19, 1946
- The houses thinned out and there were fewer roads intersecting the main drag. —Mickey Spillane, *One Lonely Night*, p. 126, 1951
- —Jack Lait and Lee Mortimer, *Washington Confidential*, p. >, 1951
- Washington's Main Drag is F St. if you could call it such. —Jack Lait and Lee Mortimer, *Washington Confidential*, p. 12, 1951
- [A] nosy sheriff who though I was pretty young to be hitchhiking accosted me on the main drag. —Jack Kerouac, *On the Road*, p. 230–231, 1957
- Linda would see him in a pickup truck on the "drag" Saturday nights, bumper to bumper from Wendy's down to Anthony's, where kids from both schools would hang out in the shopping center parking lot. —Elmore Leonard, *Be Cool*, p. 79, 1999

9 a car *UK, 1935*

From earlier senses as 'a coach', 'a cart', 'a wagon' and 'a van'. English Gypsy use.

- He could do things with a drag in traffic that would make a racing motorist's hair stand on end. —Charles Raven, *Underworld Nights*, p. 15, 1956
- — *San Francisco News*, p. 6, 25th March 1958
- Brum [Birmingham] was swarming with coppers who might already have the number and description of the drag. —Derek Bickerton, *Payroll*, p. 83, 1959
- —Jimmy Stockin, *On The Cobbles*, p. 10, 2000

10 a freight train, especially a slow one *US, 1925*

- —Norman Carlisle, *The Modern Wonder Book of Trains and Railroading*, p. 262, 1946
- [R]ather than await a drag, we stepped undeterred to the highway where instant luck befell us – a man on his way to Cheyenne picked us up before we'd walked a hundred yards. —Neal Cassady, *The First Third*, p. 88, 1971
- —Linda Niemann, *Boomer*, p. 249, 1990

11 an inhalation (of a cigarette, pipe or cigar) *US, 1904*

- Another minute now, just time for another quick drag on my muta[.] —Mezz Mezzrow, *Really the Blues*, p. 167, 1946
- [W]ith the smoking of two drags of te I felt constrained to open an extra button down and so show my tanned, hairy chest[.] —Jack Kerouac, *The Subterraneans*, p. 8, 1958
- Give me a drag. —*The Hustler*, 1961
- Then he settled comfortably in the chair and took a deep drag on the cigarette without watching Franchot leave the apartment. —Nathan Heard, *Howard Street*, p. 175, 1968
- They all take a drag on their reefers / And say prayers to St. Konky Mohair. —Dennis Wepman et al., *The Life*, p. 107, 1976
- Carlucci lights his cigarette and half of it disappears on the first drag. —Robert Campbell, *The Cat's Meow*, p. 50, 1988

12 a marijuana cigarette *UK*

- —Home Office, *Glossary of Terms and Slang Common in Penal Establishments*, 1978

13 the soldier at the very rear of a group of soldiers on patrol *US*

From the older term 'drag rider' (1888) for the cowhand riding at the rear of a herd.

- —Linda Reinberg, *In the Field*, p. 67, 1991

14 a sentence of three months' imprisonment *AUSTRALIA, 1877*

- — *(Sydney) Bulletin*, 26th April 1975

15 a confidence game in which a wallet is dropped as bait for the victim *US*

- — *New York Times Magazine*, p. 88, 16th March 1958

▸ **the drag**

a several-block area near Independence Square, Port of Spain, Trinidad *TRINIDAD AND TOBAGO, 1984*

- —Lise Winer, *Dictionary of the English/Creole of Trinidad & Tobago*, 2003

drag *verb*

1 to bore or annoy *US, 1944*

- I was real hung up on it two years ago, you understand – coked most of the time – but it drags me now. —John Clellon Holmes, *Go*, p. 121, 1952
- It drags me to get hit on like that. —Iceberg Slim (Robert Beck), *Pimp*, p. 126, 1969
- Of course I was never more drug in my life, but you know how it goes. —A.S. Jackson, *Gentleman Pimp*, p. 100, 1973

2 to wear clothing of the opposite sex *US*

- Dragging is just about the hardest thing to do. —*Screw*, p. 9, 15th March 1970

3 to compete in a drag race, a quarter-mile race from a standing start *US, 1950*

4 in poker, to take (chips) from the pot as change for a bet *US*

- —Albert H. Morehead, *The Complete Guide to Winning Poker*, p. 261, 1967

5 in poker, to take the house percentage out of a pot *US*

- —George Percy, *The Language of Poker*, p. 30, 1988

6 to rob vehicles *UK*

- —Peter Laurie, *Scotland Yard*, p. 322, 1970

7 to lead on, to entice *US*

- — *Maledicta*, p. 266, Summer/Winter 1981

▸ **drag the chain**

to be slow to perform some task; to lag behind *AUSTRALIA, 1912*

Metaphorically referring to Australia's convict era when prisoners were chained together, but originally in use amongst shearers and only recorded long after chain gangs were a thing of the past.

- For those of you who haven't already hit the silk, chaps, stop dragging the chain[.] —W.R. Bennett, *Night Intruder*, p. 49, 1962
- —Jim Ramsay, *Cop It Sweet!*, p. 32, 1977
- —David McGill, *David McGill's Complete Kiwi Slang Dictionary*, p. 43, 1998

▸ **drag your anchor**

to lose control of yourself and drift towards trouble *US*

Clearly understood nautical origins.

- —Charles F. Haywood, *Yankee Dictionary*, p. 49–50, 1963

drag-ass *adjective*

tired, lazy *US, 1952*

- The prospect of turning into a bureaucratic, dip-dunk, whining, drag-ass paper pusher did not excite me in the least. —Richard Marcinko, *Rogue Warrior*, p. 172, 1992
- "They were near disinegration at that point, and the drag-ass depression hung over them like a bad smell," recalls Rapeman's Steve Albini. —Michael Azerrad, *Our Band Could Be Your Life*, p. 370, 2001

drag back *verb*

to re-imprison a convict released on licence *UK*

- —Angela Devlin, *Prison Patter*, p. 47, 1996

drag ball *noun*

a dance dominated by men dressed as women *US*

- It might simply be that Harry would like to dress up as a woman and go to a drag ball, or parade down Broadway[.] — Hubert Selby Jr, *Last Exit to Brooklyn*, p. 215, 1957
- — Donald Webster Cory and John P. LeRoy, *The Homosexual and His Society*, p. 263, 1963: 'A lexicon of homosexual slang'
- It was certain to be a "drag ball" (where a goodly number of fellows are dressed as southern belles) and like many male homosexuals we had always found such affairs tedious and boring. — *Screw*, p. 14, 21st March 1969

drage; droge; droje; draje *noun*

any kind of clothing *UK*

Affected variations of **DRAG**.

- She has a permanent vogue [cigarette] in her screech [mouth] and her droje is mega ribena on toast [awful], daughter. — the cast of 'Aspects of Love', Prince of Wales Theatre, *Palare (Boy Dancer Talk) for Beginners*, 1989–92
- — Paul Baker, *Polari*, p. 173, 2002

dragged *adjective*

annoyed, depressed *US, 1952*

- Seemed real dragged. Gave me the pitch about the movies and the record date and all. — Ross Russell, *The Sound*, p. 100, 1961
- I felt so dragged, I missed a couple rehearsals of our band. — Nat Hentoff, *Jazz Country*, p. 20–21, 1965

dragger *noun*

a thief who steals vehicles or their contents *UK*

- Nowadays we call a bloke who drives off with an unattended car a "dragger", but if you met Harry prowling round a parking square he would say: "I'm at the jump-up." — Charles Raven, *Underworld Nights*, p. 46, 1956

draggin' wagon *noun*

1 a tow truck, especially a military tow truck *US, 1945*

Also known as a 'dragon wagon'.

- [T]he Logistical Vehicle System, nicknamed the "Dragon Waggon," a cab-unit with a variety of trailers that can carry more than 12 tons of cargo over rough terrain. — Allan R. Millett, *Semper Fidelis*, p. 620, 1980
- A few of the Dragon Wagons, tractor trailer trucks that hauled armored vheicles, carried twisted and burned-out 10th Cavalry tracks. — David G. Fitz-Enz, *Why a Solider?*, p. 318, 2000

2 in drag racing, a fast car *US*

- — Lyle K. Engel, *The Complete Book of Fuel and Gas Dragsters*, p. 150, 1968

draggy *adjective*

boring, tedious *US, 1868*

- Right draggy the whole thing was. — Dick Francis, *Forfeit*, 1968

drag it!

let's hurry up! *US*

Teen slang.

- — *Newsweek*, p. 28, 8th October 1951

drag king *noun*

a woman who impersonates a man, especially one who performs in a male persona *US*

- It takes a while before it becomes clear, when he takes off his suit, that this dildo-packing drag-king is a lesbian. — Paul Burston, *A Queer Romance*, p. 66, 1995
- Her club was the thiriving New York drag king scene, and made it possible for this new art form to grow and showcase itself to the world. — *The Village Voice*, 5th October 1999
- I found all these great stores in Beverly Hills and became a drag king. Then I bought a Cadillac. — Simon Doonan, *Wacky Chicks*, p. 91, 2003

drag mag *noun*

a magazine targeted at transvestites *US*

- — Bruce Rodgers, *The Queens' Vernacular*, p. 68, 1972

dragon *noun*

1 the penis *UK, 1891*

Originally in the phrase 'water the dragon' (of a man, to urinate).

2 heroin *US, 1961*

- — Angela Devlin, *Prison Patter*, p. 47, 1996
- — Robert Ashton, *This Is Heroin*, p. 205, 2002

3 an ugly or unpleasant woman *UK, 1992*

A variation of the conventional sense of 'an aggressive woman', often as 'old dragon'.

dragon drawers *noun*

brightly coloured men's underpants *TRINIDAD AND TOBAGO, 1987*

- — Lise Winer, *Dictionary of the English/Creole of Trinidad & Tobago*, 2003

dragonfly *noun*

an A-37 aircraft, used in the Vietnam war largely as a close air-support fighter for ground forces *US*

- — Ian Padden, *U.S. Air Commando*, p. 103, 1985

dragon lady *noun*

1 an aggressive, ruthless, ambitious woman *US, 1952*

Her traits make a man a leader; from a comic strip character who along with being ruthless etc. is from the Far East.

- She [Madame Ngo Dinh Nhu of Viet Nam] may be a Dragon Lady – but she's OUR Dragon Lady! — *San Francisco News Call-Bulletin*, p. 6, 12th October 1963
- A stereotypical and highly objectionable characterization of Asian women depicting them as scheming and treacherous. — Multicultural Management Program Fellows, *Dictionary of Cautionary Words and Phrases*, 1989

2 an armored cavalry assault vehicle *US*

- — Linda Reinberg, *In the Field*, p. 67, 1991

Dragon Lady *nickname*

Madame Ngo Dinh Nhu, sister-in-law of South Vietnamese President Diem *US*

Madame Nhu, married to Diem's brother, established herself as Vietnam's unofficial First Lady. She supported the abolition of divorce, birth control and abortion, and closed a number of nightclubs.

- — Linda Reinberg, *In the Field*, p. 67, 1991

the dragon on Saint George *noun*

▷ see: **RIDING SAINT GEORGE**

dragon rock *noun*

a mixture of crack cocaine and heroin *UK*

A combination of **DRAGON** (heroin) and **ROCK** (crack).

- — Robert Ashton, *This Is Heroin*, p. 208, 2002

dragon ship *noun*

any of several US helicopter gunships equipped with gatling guns during the Vietnam war *US, 1967*

- — Linda Reinberg, *In the Field*, p. 67, 1991
- Troops discovered that the "dragon ships" were especially effective in breaking up enemy night attacks. — Roger E. Bilstein, *Flightin America*, p. 252, 2001

Dragon's Jaw *nickname*

the Thanh Hoa railway and road bridge, spanning the Song Ma River three miles north of Thanh Hoa, the capital of Annam Province, North Vietnam *US*

- [T]he strike force contained fourteen planes that were headed for the Thanh Hoa Railroad Bridge, later nicknamed "The Dragon's Jaw," because of its near invincibility. — Robert K. Wilcox, *Scream of Eagles*, p. 16, 1990

drag queen *noun*

a man, usually but not always homosexual, who frequently or invariably wears women's clothing *US, 1941*

From **DRAG** (women's clothes when worn by men) and **QUEEN** (an effeminate homosexual man). The social conditions that prevailed when this term was coined allowed for less obvious and glamorous cross-dressing.

- But that is no reason for even our social scientists to remain merely tourists and write, for example, as if beats typically were devoted to "conspicuous consumption of the self" – an absurdity comparable to suggesting that most homosexuals are drag queens. — *Dissent*, p. 341, Summer 1961
- Who is to say which is more pathetic – the outlandish "drag queen" who affects thick make-up, women's skirts and high heels, or the "closet queen" who, in a much more shocking fashion, flaunts his perversion. — Antony James, *America's Homosexual Underground*, p. 67, 1965
- It was not that we were uptight about drag queens, but just that we saw no reason to associate ourselves with that tiny fringe of the gay world who dig powder puffs. — *Screw*, 21st March 1969
- At Highland and Hollywood, the queens, awesome defiant Amazons, are assuming their stations. — John Rechy, *The Sexual Outlaw*, p. 39, 1977
- Her lips are some unlikely shade of copper or violet, courtesy of her local MAC drag queen makeup consultant. — Francesca Lia Block, *I Was a Teenage Fairy*, p. 121, 1998
- Drag queens coming out of the ladies' bogs[.] — Dave Courtney, *Raving Lunacy*, p. 99, 2000

drags *noun*

drag races, a series of quarter-mile events where the cars start at rest and achieve extremely high speeds *US*

- I take her to the drags, man, and everyone flips / For her big blue eyes and her candy apple lips. — The Beach Boys, *Car Crazy Cutie*, 1963

drag show *noun*
a performance by men dressed as women *US*
- —J.D. Mercer, *They Walk in Shadow*, p. 564, 1959: 'Slang vocabulary'
- — *Maledicta*, p. 219, 1979: 'Kinks and queens: linguistic and cultural aspects of the terminology for gays.'

drag squad *noun*
the unit providing rear-guard security behind a larger body of soldiers *US*
- —Linda Reinberg, *In the Field*, p. 67, 1991

dragstser *noun*
a person who regularly asks for a puff on others' cigarettes *US*
- — *American Speech*, p. 276, December 1963: 'American indian student slang'

dragula *noun*
a tranvestite who only appears at night *UK*
A compounding of **DRAG** (female clothing worn by men) and Dracula (a legendary creature of the night).
- — *Attitude*, p. 60, July 2003: 'New palare lexicon'

drag up *verb*
1 to dress in women's clothes *UK*
- —Paul Baker, *Polari*, p. 173, 2002

2 to quit a job *US, 1930*
- —Jerry Robertson, *Oil Slanguage*, p. 103, 1954

drag weed *noun*
marijuana *US, 1949*
- —Richard A. Spears, *The Slang and Jargon of Drugs and Drink*, p. 163, 1986
- —Mike Haskins, *Drugs*, p. 287, 2003

Drain *noun*
▸ **the Drain**
the Waterloo and City underground railway *UK*
- —Harvey Sheppard, *Dictionary of Railway Slang*, 1970

drain *verb*
(used of a ball in pinball) to leave play at the bottom of the playing field *US*
- —Bobbye Claire Natkin and Steve Kirk, *All About Pinball*, p. 112, 1977

▸ **drain the dragon**
(used of a male) to urinate *AUSTRALIA*
- [T]he bloke's drained the dragon a few times and had a couple of hurls [periods of vomiting][.] —Barry Humphries, *Bazza Pulls It Off!*, 1971

▸ **drain the main vein**
(used of a male) to urinate *US*
- —Pamela Munro, *U.C.L.A. Slang*, p. 36, 1989

▸ **drain the radiator**
to urinate *US*
- —Bill Davis, *Jawjacking*, p. 36, 1977

▸ **drain the train**
(used of a male) to have sex *US*
- The bartender spoke slowly, as if to an idiot child. "You know, push the push? Slake the snake? Drain the train? Siphon the python?" —James Ellroy, *Because the Night*, p. 415, 1984

▸ **drain the vein**
to urinate *US*
- —Collin Baker et al., *College Undergraduate Slang Study Conducted at Brown University*, p. 218, 1968

▸ **drain the weasel**
(used of a male) to urinate *US*
- I gotta drain da weasel. Wanna see me write my name? — *Boyz N The Hood*, 1990

▸ **drain your crankcase**
(used of a male) to urinate *CANADA*
- —Bill Casselman, *Canadian Sayings*, p. 43, 2002

draino!
used by a golfer to celebrate a long putt falling into the hole *US*
- —Randy Voorhees, *The Little Book of Golf Slang*, p. 25, 1997

drain pipe *noun*
in poker, a conservative player who slowly but surely accumulates winnings, draining money from other players *US*
- —John Vorhaus, *The Big Book of Poker Slang*, p. 15, 1996

draje *noun*
▷ see: **DRAGE**

drama mama *noun*
an elaborately effeminate male *SINGAPORE*
- —Paik Choo, *The Coxford Singlish Dictionary*, p. 34, 2002

drama queen *noun*
someone who creates an unnecessary or excessive fuss *UK, 1990*
Originally gay usage.
- I think I'll admit to sex with a Person Unknown in Macedonia. – Macedonia? roared Jan. – God, Harry, you old drama queen. —James Hawes, *Dead Long Enough*, p. 47, 2000
- [Camille] Barbone punched her fist into a wall in frustration. Madonna walked out muttering, "What a drama queen." — *Q*, p. 102, December 2001

drammer damner *noun*
a harsh theatre critic *US*
- —Wilfred Granville, *The Theater Dictionary*, p. 52, 1952

drape *noun*
1 clothing; a man's suit *US, 1938*
- When we stripped naked and lined up for our numbers and prison clothes, my morale hit zero and kept sinking. Jack, the drapes they handed me a jungle bum wouldn't wear on workdays. —Mezz Mezzrow, *Really the Blues*, p. 33, 1946
- Them holler drapes Vann wears out in front of his band is just too much, man. —Ross Russell, *The Sound*, p. 109, 1961
- —Home Office, *Glossary of Terms and Slang Common in Penal Establishments*, 1978

2 the sag of a suit favoured by zoot suiters and their fellow travellers *US*
- What is this suit you make over and over, with the padded shoulders and the extreme drape and the pegged trousers? —Bernard Wolfe, *The Late Risers*, p. 217, 1954
- Then there was Prez, a husky, handsome blond like a freckled boxer, meticulously wrapped inside his sharkskin plaid suit with the long drape and the collar falling back[.] —Jack Kerouac, *On the Road*, p. 239, 1957

drape *verb*
to dress, to attire *US, 1942*
- Safari shirt and pants, tan colored, I'm pressed, but not like them vines Cye Martin used to drape on me. —Edwin Torres, *After Hours*, p. 272, 1979

▸ **drape the shape**
to get dressed *US*
- — *Dobie Gillis Teenage Slanguage Dictionary*, 1962

drape *adjective*
said of a stylised, baggy men's suit favoured by zoot suiters *US*
- With my paper route, my gambling in school and my other hustles, I was able to acquire a radio and two new drape suits. —Babs Gonzales, *I Paid My Dues*, p. 10, 1967

draped *adjective*
adorned with a lot of gold jewellery *US*
- —Bill Valentine, *Gang Intelligence Manual*, p. 76, 1995: 'Black street gang terminology'

drapes *noun*
bell-bottom trousers *US*
- Any kid with drapes and a duck's ass haircut on the street got his lumps right away. —Gilbert Sorrentino, *Steelwork*, p. 63, 1970
- —Douglas Simonson, *Pidgin to da Max Hana Hou*, 1982

drape shape *noun*
a baggy, loose-fitting style of clothing popular in the 1940s *US*
- During the early postwar years, the so-called "drape shape" or loose, hanging, balloon type of suit was promoted for better or for worse. — *San Francisco News*, p. 12, 11th August 1955

drat!
used as a mild expletive *UK, 1815*
From 'God rot!'.
- Oh, drat is the coffee delayed? Oh dear. —Mike Stott, *Soldiers Talking, Cleanly*, 1978

dratted *adjective*
damned *UK, 1845*
- Beveridge was a tea lady for 10 years in the officers' mess of the Ministry of Defence until she was made redundant (those dratted machines again). — *The Guardian*, 6th November 2003

draw *noun*

1 a winning bet with a bookmaker *UK*

- Finally, everyone had a draw on the favourite in the fourth race[.] —Jimmy Stockin, *On The Cobbles*, p. 196, 2000

2 marijuana; a marijuana cigarette *UK*

- [W]hen I was selling draw and things.—Shaun Ryder, *Shaun Ryder... in His Own Words*, 1987
- And this goes out to those that smoke out the bong / And all my bitches in the place who roll they own draws—Busta Rhymes, *Get High Tonight*, 1997
- Buy a bit of draw and get pissed up down the boozer Saturdays. —Jeremy Cameron, *Brown Bread in Wengen*, p. 15, 1999
- The bush was in fine, grainy pieces, courtesy of his coffee grinder; somehow the draw seemed to last longer this way.—Diran Abedayo, *My Once Upon A Time*, p. 20, 2000
- So smoke another draw / It won't matter no more—The Streets, *Stay Positive*, 2002
- Saturday afternoons are spent "all rowdy and pissed" on alcopops, "draw" is scored in petty drug deals, arguments erupt in car parks over nothing.—*The Guardian*, p. 12, 26th February 2002
- Oi blud, wanna buy a draw?—*The Guardian*, p. 9, 27th February 2002

3 a cigarette *AUSTRALIA, 1955*

- —Robert Nash, *Dictionary of Crime*, p. 110, 1992

4 in pool, backspin applied to the cue ball *US, 1866*

- —Mike Shamos, *The Illustrated Encyclopedia of Billiards*, p. 83, 1993

draw *verb*

while injecting a drug, to pull blood into the syringe to verify that the needle has hit a blood vein *US*

- —Eugene Landy, *The Underground Dictionary*, p. 70, 1971

▸**draw dead**

in poker, to draw cards into a hand that cannot win *US*

- —Anthony Holden, *Big Deal*, p. 300, 1990

▸**draw the crabs**

1 to attract the enemy's attention; to draw fire *AUSTRALIA, 1918*

- "Don't disturb those bastards," he said, indicating a flock of grotesque hornbills that crawled, feeding and quarrelling, in the high branches. "They'll damned soon draw the crabs, if anything will!"—T.A.G. Hungerford, *The Ridge and the River*, p. 91, 1952

2 to attract unwanted attention *AUSTRALIA*

- Anyway he said if he was seen out here meeting Jimmy it might draw the crabs.—Clive Galea, *Slipper*, p. 193, 1988

▸**draw the crow**

to get the worst job or the worst share of something *AUSTRALIA, 1942*

- [Punning on proper names] This is fair dinkum no 'Larkin' for its 'Smee' who wrote it for a 'Sprat' but I drew the 'Crowe' as usual. Like most railwaymen we puff and blow because its been a life of hard lines.—Patsy Adam-Smith, *Folklore of the Australian Railwaymen*, p. 211, 1969

▸**draw water**

(of the sun) to exhibit long vertical lines in the sky *CANADA, 1942*
Said in Nova Scotia to be a sign of approaching rain, it occurs also in New England, where it is said to be a sign of clear weather.

- When the sun is out and visible streaks in the sky point toward it, the sun's a-drawin' water.—Lewis Poteet, *The South Shore Phrase Book*, p. 39, 1999

draw drapes *noun*

the foreskin of an uncircumcised penis *US*

- —*Maledicta*, p. 218, 1979: 'Kinks and queens: linguistic and cultural aspects of the terminology for Gays'

drawers *noun*

sex *US*

- She didn't know why, but even after all this she was still gonna give him the drawers.—Steve Cannon, *Groove, Bang, and Jive Around*, p. 30, 1969

drawing room *noun*

a brakevan (caboose) *US*

- —Ramon Adams, *The Language of the Railroader*, p. 48, 1977

drawings *noun*

1 information; gossip; news *US*

- Sometimes I visit the shack to shoot the bull and get the latest drawings (news).—Eldridge Cleaver, *Soul on Ice*, p. 44, 1968

2 plans for a course of action *US*

- It was Joe Sing's turn to nod. "What are your drawings?"—Seth Morgan, *Homeboy*, p. 70, 1990

drawn down on *verb*

to draw out and point guns at *US*

- They, when they draw down on him and tell him to get the fuck out of the way, he just stands there sellin' wolf tickets like a goddamn fool or something.—Vernon E. Smith, *The Jones Men*, p. 202, 1974
- Cat on a family dispute almost draws down on Francis when he tried to lay the iron on his wrists after the dude had went upside Momma's head.—Joseph Wambaugh, *The Choirboys*, p. 314, 1975

draw up *verb*

to inject a drug intravenously *UK, 1998*
Derives from the initial act of drawing up blood into the syringe to mix with the narcotic before re-injection.

- —Mike Haskins, *Drugs*, p. 290, 2003

dread *noun*

1 a Rastafarian *JAMAICA*
From the distinctive dreadlocks hairstyle worn by Rastasfarians.

- I'm getting out, dread, I'm sorry.—Diran Adebayo, *My Once Upon A Time*, p. 26, 2000
- This dread Col she'd known forever[.]—John Williams, *Cardiff Dead*, p. 3, 2000
- —Lise Winer, *Dictionary of the English/Creole of Trinidad & Tobago*, 2003

2 a black person *UK*
From the previous sense; prison usage.

- —Angela Devlin, *Prison Patter*, p. 47, 1996

dread *adjective*

1 difficult, hard, impossible; used to ascribe negative qualities to any situation *UK*
West Indian and UK black.

- You know how dread it is to find a decent job out there.—Karline Smith, *Moss Side Massive*, p. 38, 1994

2 frightening *UK*

- It's dread, in the Old Bailey.—Angela Devlin, *Prison Patter*, p. 47, 1996
- —Lise Winer, *Dictionary of the English/Creole of Trinidad & Tobago*, 2003

dreaded *adjective*

1 of hair, in dreadlocks *UK*

- [H]is hair is neatly dreaded and he walks with the rolling ease of the B-Boy swagger.—Patrick Neate, *Where You're At*, p. 5, 2003

2 fashionable, popular, in style *US*

- —*Columbia Missourian*, p. 1A, 19th October 1998

dreaded lurgi; the lurgi; lerg *noun*

any malaise or minor ailment *UK*
The 'dreaded' variation is a direct quotation from *The Goon Show*, which was originally broadcast on BBC radio in 1951. So much in the world of the Goons was 'dreaded'. The 'lurgi' found a currency among school children where it was further applied to notional illnesses and any vaguely unpleasant or unclean disease that another could be accused of carrying.

- Joe will be lurching around, spreading the dreaded lurgi everywhere.—Keri Hulme, *The Bone People*, p. 238, 1983
- When you have the lurgi (some vague unidentifiable illness, usually one that's going around), then you 'feel butcher's'.—*Lonely Planet Australian Phrasebook*, p. 23, 1998
- So when I returned to school, I had deadmum disease, the screech-bump lerg, and touching me might mean catching it[.]—Andrew Holmes, *Sleb*, p. 36, 2002

dreadfully *adverb*

exceedingly *UK, 1697*
Often used to imply or intensify a pejorative sense.

- Dreadfully sorry / Dreadfully sorry[.]—The Who, *5:15*, 1973
- But since the breakfast in Paris, those radical rive gauche pavement heaters have become dreadfully common patio heaters and you can't move in B&Q without falling over one.—*The Observer*, 29th June 2003

dreadlocks *noun*

the long, bundled strands of hair worn by Rastafarians *JAMAICA, 1960*

- —Dick Hebdige, *Subculture*, 1979
- What do you think when you see someone with dreadlocks? Be honest.—*The Guardian*, 23rd August 2003

dreads *noun*

dreadlocks, a Rastafarian hairstyle in which the hair is not combed or brushed, forming matted clumps or 'locks' *US, 1977*

- —Pamela Munro, *U.C.L.A. Slang*, p. 63, 2001

dream *noun*

1 an appealing, attractive member of whatever sex attracts you *US, 1895*

- She took to me readily because she had heard of my accomplishments, and she thought I was a dream. —Phyllis and Eberhard Kronhausen, *Sex Histories of American College Men*, p. 72, 1960

2 opium *US, 1929*

- Tell me, Wst, do you know what a dream session is? —Evan Hunter, *The Blackboard Jungle*, p. 159, 1954

3 cocaine *UK, 1998*

- —Nick Constable, *This is Cocaine*, p. 181, 2002

dreamboat *noun*

1 a sexually attractive person *US, 1944*

- How was I to know wide girls like them would turn me into a ruddy dreamboat, all three of them? —Charles Raven, *Underworld Nights*, p. 119, 1956
- Ed Lakey at twenty-eight looked just like the dreamboat he had been when he went to Hollywood High[.] —Eve Babitz, *L.A. Woman*, p. 98, 1982
- When our eyes finally met through our viewfinders, I saw my video-dating dreamboat. —Anka Radakovich, *The Wild Girls Club*, p. 95, 1994

2 a well-maintained, large luxury car *US, 1945*

- Naw suh, he had a dream boat, a big green Caddy Couple de Ville. —Chester Himes, *The Real Cool Killers*, p. 100, 1959

dream book *noun*

a book that purports to interpret dreams, suggesting numbers to be played in an illegal lottery based on symbols in the dreams *US*

- Rev. Jones went back into the room for his dream book[.] —Clarence Cooper Jr, *Black*, p. 179, 1963
- What number does Madame Zora's dream book five for fish? —Louise Meriwether, *Daddy Was a Number Runner*, p. 13, 1970
- You selling plenty barbecue now, or did one of those dream bookss finally come through? —Vernon E. Smith, *The Jones Men*, p. 90, 1974
- Yet in the Pennsylvania steel town where Spencer Van Moot was born, every living soul had played numbers and consulted dream books for winners[.] —Joseph Wambaugh, *The Choirboys*, p. 64, 1975

dream cube *noun*

a sugar cube impregnated with LSD *UK*

- —Tom Hibbert, *Rockspeak!*, p. 53, 1983

dream dust *noun*

any powdered drug *US, 1957*

- And I keep getting off the subject of the rumor I picked up today from a traveling merchant into smuggling mostly ... Red Devil and Dream Dust. —William S. Burroughs, *The Place of Dead Roads*, p. 267, 1983

dreamer *noun*

1 a motorist who thinks that he can outrun a police car *US*

Police humour.

- —*American Speech*, p. 268, December 1962

2 morphine or a morphine addict *US*

- —Jay Robert Nash, *Dictionary of Crime*, p. 110, 1992

3 a blanket *US*

- —Kenn "Naz" Young, *Naz's Underground Dictionary*, p. 26, 1973

dreamers *noun*

sheets for a bed *US*

- —Lou Shelly, *Hepcats Jive Dictionary*, p. 9, 1945

dream gum *noun*

opium; heroin *US, 1934*

- —Richard A. Spears, *The Slang and Jargon of Drugs and Drink*, p. 164, 1986
- —Mike Haskins, *Drugs*, p. 283, 2003

dreamland *noun*

sleep or an unconscious state *US, 1908*

- And let's not forget stamina. I don't want him drifting off to dreamland when I've only just begun. —John Tomkiw, *Total Sex*, p. 15, 1999

dream number *noun*

in an illegal number gambling lottery, a bet based on the bettor's dream, either directly or as interpreted by a dream book *US*

- —*American Speech*, p. 191, October 1949

dreams *noun*

heroin *UK*

From earlier, obsolete sense as 'opium'. Recorded in current use.

- —Mike Haskins, *Drugs*, p. 283, 2003

dream sheet *noun*

a list created by a soldier of the places where he would like to be shipped *US, 1971*

Rarely realised.

- Owen had already filled out his Officer Assignment Preference Statement – his DREAM SHEET, he called it. —John Irving, *A Prayer for Owen Meany*, p. 416, 1989
- —Linda Reinberg, *In the Field*, p. 67, 1991

dream stuff *noun*

marijuana *US*

- "You ever smoke dream stuff?" "Charge?" "Yeah." —Hal Ellson, *Duke*, p. 34, 1949

dream team *noun*

any group made up from the best in the field *US, 1942*

- —*American Speech*, p. 182, Summer 1993: 'Among the new words'

dream ticket *noun*

an 'ideal' pairing, especially of politicians for the purposes of election *US*

Originally applied to Richard Nixon and Nelson Rockerfeller as running mates for the 1960 US Presidential election. Adopted in the UK during the 1980s, reflecting a new, more American style of political presentation.

- "New Realism", which was the view that trade unions could no longer combat employers or the government. And "dream ticket", the Labour Party choice of Neil Kinnock as its new leader and Roy Hattersley his deputy. —Mark Steel, *Reasons to be Cheerful*, p. 138, 2001

dream tobacco *noun*

marijuana *UK*

- [A] pale and bleary-eyed Dave Edmunds swigs the dregs of a bottle of whisky and takes a long slow hit of dream tobacco. —Will Birch, *No Sleep Till Canvey Island*, p. 274, 2003

dreamy *adjective*

very attractive, beautiful, desirable *US, 1941*

- Paul A. Wagner, 33-year-old former newsreel cameraman and salesman, has made things hum at Rollins College since taking over as prexy. And the coeds think he's dreamy. —*Colliers*, p. 21, 13th January 1951

dreck *noun*

1 excrement; worthless trash *IRELAND, 1922*

From the Yiddish, from the German for 'dung'.

- I'm the only one who gives her a whole can of tuna for lunch, and I'm not talking dreck, either. I'm talking Chicken of the Sea, Alex. —Philip Roth, *Portnoy's Complaint*, p. 12, 1969
- "It's not worth a penny." "Arthur-" "It's drek, Harry. All drek!" —Anthony Masters, *Minder*, p. 14, 1984
- They were the transmitters of trivia, broadcasters of banality, and disseminators of drek. —Will Self, *The Sweet Smell of Psychosis*, p. 10, 1996
- Most of it he could cheerfully dump – the packaged, niche-marketed, antiseptic dreck which constituted so much of his popmart world. —Kevin Sampson, *Powder*, p. 30, 1999

2 heroin *UK*

- —Robert Ashton, *This Is Heroin*, p. 205, 2002
- —Mike Haskins, *Drugs*, p. 283, 2003

drecky *adjective*

rubbishy, trashy, shitty *UK*

From **DRECK** (excrement, trash).

- I can only conclude that she penned her sniggering memoirs in order to give her drecky movies [...] an extra touch of notoriety. —*New Society*, 20th December 1979

dreece *noun*

three units of anything *US*

- —Hyman E. Goldin et al., *Dictionary of American Underworld Lingo*, p. 62, 1950

drenched *adjective*

drunk *US, 1926*

- —Pete Brown, *Man Walks into a Pub*, 2003

drepsley soup *noun*

(among Canadian Mennonites) a broth soup with dumplings *CANADA*

- "Drepsley" contains in its initial root a variant of the Germanic "Tropf," "drop." It might be called "drop-trick" soup: into boiling stock, a runny batter is poured through a sieve; it is boiled for four minutes and served at once – no soggy dreps! —Bill Casselman, *Canadian Food Words*, p. 180, 1998

dress down *verb*
to dress up *US*
Often intensified with 'for a motherfucker'.
• Big man be dressing down for a motherfucker tonight cause he's got two new hoes to sport around. — Inez Cardozo-Freeman, *The Joint*, p. 491, 1984

dressed *adjective*
armed *US*
• Ted didn't see the pistol that I had but I'm sure he felt I was dressed. — A.S. Jackson, *Gentleman Pimp*, p. 80, 1973

dressed up like a preacher *adjective*
overdressed, flashily dressed *US, 197*
• — Frederic G. Cassidy, *Dictionary of American Regional English, Volume II*, p. 190, 1991

dresser *noun*
a car or motorcyle with every possible accessory *US*
• — Lewis Poteet, *Car & Motorcyle Slang*, p. 72–73, 1992
• — Paladin Press, *Inside Look at Outlaw Motorcyle Gangs*, p. 35, 1992

dress for sale *noun*
a prostitute *US*
• — Lanie Dills, *The Official CB Slanguage Language Dictionary*, p. 29, 1976

dress in *verb*
to exchange the clothes worn upon arrival for prison-issued clothes *US*
• — Troy Harris, *A Booklet of Criminal Argot, Cant and Jargon*, p. 8, 1976

dressing room lawyer *noun*
an actor who is quick to recognise and address wrongs by theatre management *UK*
• — Wilfred Granville, *The Theater Dictionary*, p. 62, 1952

dress out *verb*
to exchange prison clothing for street clothes upon release from prison *US*
• — Troy Harris, *A Booklet of Criminal Argot, Cant and Jargon*, p. 8, 1976

dress-tail *noun*
a woman as a sexual object *TRINIDAD AND TOBAGO*
• — Lise Winer, *Dictionary of the English/Creole of Trinidad & Tobago*, 2003

dress-up *noun*
an unconvincing drag queen (a man dressed as a woman) *UK*
• — Paul Baker, *Polari*, p. 173, 2002

dressy casual *adjective*
of style or fashion, informal yet smart and/or expensive *US*
• The WinGS opening session is 7 p.m. Friday, and the final session ends at 4 p.m. Sunday. Dress is dressy casual. — *Worldwide News*, April 1999

drib *noun*
an unskilled poker player *US*
• — Albert H. Morehead, *The Complete Guide to Winning Poker*, p. 262, 1967

dribble *noun*
small, weak waves *US*
• — Trevor Cralle, *The Surfin'ary*, p. 31, 1991

dribble *verb*
1 to cause a car to bounce up and down by use of hydraulic lifts *US*
To 'dribble' a basketball is to bounce it, hence the transference here.
• — Edith A. Folb, *runnin' down some lines*, p. 235, 1980
2 to meander, to walk *US*
• — Robert George Reisner, *The Jazz Titans*, p. 154, 1960

dribs and drabs *noun*
pubic lice *UK*
Rhyming slang for **CRABS**.
• Said to anyone scratching themselves in the pubic area for whatever reason, "What's the matter, got the dribs and drabs?" — Ray Puxley, *Cockney Rabbit*, 1992

drift *verb*
to leave *US, 1853*
• "OKay for us to drift now, Chief?" — Evan Hunter, *The Blackboard Jungle*, p. 48, 1954

drill *verb*
1 to have sex from a male perspective *UK*
From the imagery of a long hard tool opening a hole.
• [L]ittle grains of sand ain't really knob friendly, know what I mean? So drilling away on the beach at night don't do your piping the world of good. — Dave Courtney, *Raving Lunacy*, p. 158, 2000
• When one well goes dry, we'll use another hole. — Dorothy Ellis, *Drill, Daddy, Drill*, LATE 1940S
2 to inject (a drug) *US*
• — William D. Alsever, *Glossary for the Establishment and Other Uptight People*, p. 19, December 1970
3 to shoot (with a bullet); to kill by shooting *UK, 1720*
• [I]t's just bad tactics to go and get yourself drilled. — Derek Raymond (Robin Cook), *The Crust on its Uppers*, p. 95, 1962
• Drill the fucker. I got my attorney's .357 Magnum out of the trunk and spun the cylinder. — Hunter S. Thompson, *Fear and Loathing in Las Vegas*, p. 99, 1971
4 to interrogate *US*
• They drilled us all night. Somebody was pissed about that truck getting knocked off and the cops had nothing. — *The Usual Suspects*, 1995
5 to kick, throw or bowl a ball, directly and forcefully; to score a goal with a forceful kick *AUSTRALIA*
• I was ready to bound onto the oval, grab the ball, stream down the field brushing off tackles like they were bushflies and drill the first goal of the game. — Phillip Gwynne, *Deadly Unna?*, p. 103, 1998
6 in pool, to make a shot in an emphatic and convincing manner *US*
• — Mike Shamos, *The Illustrated Encyclopedia of Billiards*, p. 83, 1993
7 to walk, to move *US*
• — Lavada Durst, *The Jives of Dr. Hepcat*, p. 12, 1953

▸ **drill for vegemite**
to have anal sex *AUSTRALIA*
From Vegemite™, a popular type of black and salty spread made from yeast extract.
• But don't run away with the idea that every Australian you meet likes drilling for vegemite. — Barry Humphries, *The Traveller's Tool*, p. 20, 1985
• Or they get a bum chum and go drilling for Vegemite. — Kathy Lette, *Girls' Night Out*, p. 174, 1987

drill down *verb*
to examine or investigate something in depth; to narrow the focus of an investigation and its results *UK*
A figurative sense of the conventional use.
• This map information can then be "drilled down" to just a few streets and transferred to a mobile. — *The Guardian*, 19th July 2001
• As someone else said you always expect driver, cleaner or shop assistant but I for one got a surprise when I drilled down through the system and found a whole category dedicated to IT related work. — *Jobseekers Advice. com*, 25th April 2003

driller *noun*
a poker player who bets very aggressisvely *US*
• — George Percy, *The Language of Poker*, p. 31, 1988

drink *noun*
1 a bribe *UK, 1977*
• Euphemism for blackmail payment or money bribe. "There's a drink in it for you" may mean there will be such payments; "Does he drink?" may mean "Is he willing to be bribed?" — David Powis, *The Signs of Crime*, 1977
• A "big drink" can be £20,000 or more; a "soppy drink" between £20 and £50 — *The Observer*, 15th August 1982
• — Angela Devlin, *Prison Patter*, p. 47, 1996
• The [the police] put it to him that for a little "drink", as they called it – or "backhander" as anyone else would call it – they'd see to it that the club didn't get in any trouble. — Dave Courtney, *Raving Lunacy*, p. 30, 2000
2 a profit *UK*
• "Bit steep. Sharpen your pencil [reduce the price] a little?" "Nah. Can't be done. You can see the quality. I'm barely getting a drink out of it meself. — Colin Butts, *Is Harry on the Boat?*, p. 287, 1997
3 a large body of water, especially an ocean *US, 1832*
• The guys I wanted to play with and listen to were all on the other side of the drink. — Mezz Mezzrow, *Really the Blues*, p. 198, 1946
• A clout in the chops is what they deserved after dropping their Austin-Healey in the drink last night[.] — Max Shulman, *Anyone Got a Match?*, p. 54, 1964
• [B]eing ditched in the drink by everything from dinghies to trans-Atlantic yachts. — *The Guardian*, 7th June 2003

▸ **in the drink**

in pool, said of a cue ball that falls into a pocket *US*

- —Steve Rushin, *Pool Cool*, p. 16, 1990

drink *verb*

▸ **drink eight cents**

to drink to excess *TRINIDAD AND TOBAGO*

- —Lise Winer, *Dictionary of the English/Creole of Trinidad & Tobago*, 2003

▸ **drink from the furry cup**

to perform oral sex on a woman *UK*

Probably coined by comedian Sacha Baron-Cohen (b.1970); his influence on late C20 UK slang is profound.

- DRINKIN FROM THE FURRY CUP WHILE AT THE EARLY STAGES OF A RELASHUNSHIP U IZ PROBABLY UP FOR EATING FROM DE BUSHY PLATE.—Sacha Baron-Cohen, *Da Gospel According to Ali G*, 2001

▸ **drink porridge**

to serve a prison sentence *UK*

A figurative use of 'drink' combined with **PORRIDGE** (imprisonment).

- But every time Club come to see him he was away, drinking porridge.—Diran Adebayo, *My Once Upon A Time*, p. 73, 2000

▸ **drink the Kool-Aid**

to be persuaded, to follow blindly *US, 1987*

From the 'Jonestown massacre', 1978, a mass murder and suicide administered through the agency of cyanide in branded soft drink Kool-Aid™.

- — Susie Dent, *The Language Report*, p. 83, 2003

▸ **drink with the flies**

to drink alone when at a public hotel or bar *AUSTRALIA, 1911*

- 'Here,' he said gently, 'don't let that joker drink with the flies.' Lasher, who was nearest to the man with the sling, turned, saw him and said: 'Come 'n have one with us, sport.'—Eric Lambert, *The Veterans*, p. 15, 1954
- —Harvey E. Ward, *Down Under Without Blunder*, p. 38, 1967
- —Jim Ramsay, *Cop It Sweet!*, p. 32, 1977

▸ **you would drink it through a shitey cloot**

applied to anyone who appears to be so thirsty, or desperate, that no obstacle will hinder the taking of a drink *UK: SCOTLAND*

Glasgow slang formed on 'shitey' (faeces-covered) and Scottish dialect *cloot* (a hoof) or, more likely, *clout* (a rag).

- —Michael Munro, *The Complete Patter*, 1996

drinkee *noun*

any alcoholic drink *US*

A jocular mock pidgin.

- "Fresheners," Nancy said. "Tighteners and fresheners. Sometimes drinkees or martin-eyes."—Elmore Leonard, *The Big Bounce*, p. 88, 1969

drinker *noun*

a public house; an after-hours drinking club (generally unlicensed) *UK*

- What is an ugly cunt like you doing in my trough? [...] – I asked what's an ugly cunt like you doing in my drinker?—Mark Powell, *Snap*, p. 39, 2001

drinkerama *noun*

a party organised around the consumption of alcohol *US*

- —Collin Baker et al., *College Undergraduate Slang Study Conducted at Brown University*, p. 109, 1968

drinker's hour *noun*

3am *US*

- Several were waking each night at the drinker's hour with night sweats and irregular heartbeats.—Joseph Wambaugh, *Lines and Shadows*, p. 305–306, 1984
- He looked at his watch. Three A.M. The Drinker's Hour. All the grief and agony of mankind happened at three A.M., after booze made the blood sugar drop.—Joseph Wambaugh, *Fugitive Nights*, p. 234, 1992

drinking voucher; green drinking voucher *noun*

a currency note, especially a £1 note *UK*

Jocular.

- [They buy] each other a drink and pay for it with greenies, crispies, lottery tickets, drinking vouchers.—Ann Barr and Peter York, *The Official Sloane Ranger Handbook*, p. 117, 1982
- The owner counted out nine quid in the old "green drinking voucher" folding money.—Stuart Maconie, *Cider with Roadies*, p. 125, 2003

drinky; drinkies *noun*

a drinking session, a drinks party *UK, 1983*

From the nursery usage.

- Let's have a little drinky to yer success. -Yeh, Vicky says. -A nice little drinkipoos.—Niall Griffiths, *Kelly + Victor*, p. 315, 2002

drinkypoo; drinki-poo *noun*

any alcoholic drink *US, 1983*

Baby talk, thought to give alcohol an innocent demeanour.

- It's time for you to have another drinky poo!—Joseph Wambaugh, *The Secrets of Harry Bright*, p. 224, 1985
- Let's have a little drinky to yer success. -Yeh, Vicky says. -A nice little drinkipoos. Forty-eight-fuckin-hour drinkipoos.—Niall Griffiths, *Kelly + Victor*, p. 315, 2002

drip *noun*

a person lacking in social skills, fashion sense or both; a simpleton, a fool *US, 1932*

- —Lou Shelly, *Hepcats Jive Dictionary*, p. 9, 1945
- In Detroit, someone who once would be called a drip or a square is now, regrettably, a nerd, or in a less severe case, a scurve.—*Newsweek*, 8th October 1951
- In the ring the joey [clown] was a "drip" (useless chap) from the "gaffs" (fairgrounds).—Butch Reynolds, *Broken Hearted Clown*, p. 31, 1953
- Ginnie openly considered Selena the biggest drip at Miss Basehoar's[.]—J.D. Salinger, *Nine Stories*, p. 39, 1953
- She had called him a drip, a creep, and a primate and had said that the best thing he could do for her was to join the French Foreign Legion.—Max Shulman, *Rally Round the Flag, Boys!*, p. 202, 1957
- —Collin Baker et al., *College Undergraduate Slang Study Conducted at Brown University*, p. 109, 1968
- George W. Bush is,. as one friend called him, a "drip" who couldn't get a date?—*Nerve*, p. 15, October-November 2000

▸ **the drip**

the payment of money owed in instalment payments *AUSTRALIA*

- —Ned Wallish, *The Truth Dictionary of Racing Slang*, p. 24, 1989

drip *verb*

to complain *UK*

- —Nigel Foster, *The Making of a Royal Marine Commando*, 1987

drip and suck *verb*

to intubate a hospital patient with intravenous and nasogastric tubes *US*

- —Sally Williams, *"Strong" Words*, p. 140, 1994

drip drop *noun*

the bleed period of the menstrual cycle *US*

- — *The Museum of Menstruation and Women's Health*, June 2000

drip dry; drip *verb*

to cry *UK*

Rhyming slang.

- Come on stop "dripping" and tell me what's wrong.—Ray Puxley, *Cockney Rabbit*, 1992

dripper *noun*

1 an old prostitute *UK*

Glossed as 'no longer controller of her emissions' by G.F. Newman, *Sir, You Bastard*, 1970.

2 an eye dropper, used in an improvised method of drug injection *US*

- — *San Francisco Call-Bulletin*, p. 6, 17th August 1953
- —Ralph de Sola, *Crime Dictionary*, p. 43, 1982

dripping *adjective*

cowardly, ineffectual *UK*

An upper-class exaggeration of **WET** (ineffectual) from conventional 'dripping wet' (soaked).

- —Ann Barr and Peter York, *The Official Sloane Ranger Handbook*, p. 158, 1982

dripping toast *noun*

a host *UK*

Rhyming slang.

- Whereby a publican becomes mine "dripping".—Ray Puxley, *Fresh Rabbit*, 1998

drippy *adjective*

mawkish, overly sentimental, insipid *US, 1947*

- [H]e was pretty as a picture in a drippy sort of way and wrote these far out pieces about the movies that I could never through[.]—Gore Vidal, *Myra Breckinridge*, p. 23, 1968

drippy dick *noun*

an unspecified sexually transmitted disease *US*

- —Gregory Clark, *Words of the Vietnam War*, p. 108, 1990

drippy faucet *noun*
the penis of a man with a sexually transmitted infection that produces a puss discharge *US*
- Do you know he has a drippy faucet?—Joseph Wambaugh, *The Glitter Dome*, p. 6, 1981

dripsy *noun*
gonorrhea *US*
- —*Maledicta*, p. 228, Summer/Winter 1981: 'Sex and the single soldier'

drive *verb*
1 to walk *US*
- —*American Speech*, p. 228, October 1956: 'More United States Air Force slang'

2 to lift weights *US*
- On November 5, 1980, while driving (lifting weights) on the lower yard, several of the Aryans spotted a white inmate who was carrying a snitch jacket[.]—Bill Valentine, *Gangs and Their Tattoos*, p. 13, 2000

3 to borrow (a radio) *US*
From **CAR** (a radio).
- —Gary K. Farlow, *Prison-ese*, p. 20, 2002

▸**drive a desk**
to do office-work; to operate a sound-desk *UK*
Usually with a derogatory or a disappointed tone. After **FLY A DESK**.
- [DJ Chris] Moyles was in pokey studios learning to drive a desk.—*The Guardian*, 18th February 1999
- The example to which I referred is a higher risk industry than driving a desk in an airconditioned office.—Hon, W.R. Baxter, Parliament of Victoria (Australia), *Hansard*, 22nd November 2000

▸**drive the bus**
to vomit *US*
- —Pamela Munro, *U.C.L.A. Slang*, p. 63, 2001

▸**drive the porcelain bus**
to kneel down and vomit into a toilet bowl *UK*
The image of the bowl's rim being held like a steering wheel.
- —Chris Donald, *Roger's Profanisaurus*, 1998

▸**drive them home**
to snore *UK*
From C18 'drive pigs to market', and its later variant 'drive the pigs home'.
- Driving them home he was, officer.—Terry Victor, *The Prince Albert Memorial Herb Garden Murder Mystery*, 1997

▸**drive wooden stake**
to irrevocably and permanently end (a project, a business, an idea) *US*
- —Robert Kirk Mueller, *Buzzwords*, p. 165, 1974

drive-by *noun*
1 a drive-by shooting, where shots are fired from a moving car *US*
- Goddamn if that dint look like the selfsame ole van what done a drive-by on us a couple days ago.—Jess Mowry, *Way Past Cool*, p. 13, 1992
- The drive-by is not a new concept, you know. The cowboys had ride-bys. They'd ride-by and shoot up a whole town.—Chris Rock, *Rock This!*, p. 77, 1997

2 a silent, smelly fart *US*
- —Jim Goad, *Jim Goad's Glossary of Northwestern Prison Slang*, December 2001

drive-by *verb*
to shoot someone, or into a crowd, from a moving car *US*
- Yo, Gordon, tell the teacher you got em all dirty gettin drive-byed.—Jess Mowry, *Way Past Cool*, p. 7, 1992

drive call *noun*
in a telephone swindle, a high-pressure, follow-up call to the victim *US*
- —M. Allen Henderson, *How Con Games Work*, p. 219, 1985: 'Glossary'

drive dark *verb*
to drive without headlights at night *US*
- —Lewis Poteet, *Car & Motorcyle Slang*, p. 73, 1992

driver *noun*
1 an amphetamine or other central nervous system stimulant *US*
- —Gilda and Melvin Berger, *Drug Abuse A-Z*, p. 59, 1990

2 a tablet of MDMA, the recreational drug best known as ecstasy *UK*
- —Mike Haskins, *Drugs*, p. 289, 2003

3 a pilot *UK, 1942*
- If this were true, the aircraft driver could count himself among the dinosaurs not too many years hence.—Tom Wolfe, *The Right Stuff*, p. 149, 1976

4 in poker, a player whose aggressive betting is dominating the game *US*
- —Peter O. Steiner, *Thursday Night Poker*, p. 409, 1996

5 the leader of a prison clique *US*
Back formation from **CAR** (a clique).
- —James Harris, *A Convict's Dictionary*, p. 31, 1989

drive-time *noun*
the hours of the morning and afternoon weekday commute, prime time on radio *US*
- This not only meant he'd had to appear on drive-time radio shows and early-morning TV shows around the country, he'd been obligated to fuck Silvia Mercer again, and then Rosemary Compton.—Dan Jenkins, *Life Its Ownself*, p. 40, 1982
- The record starts to get spins and he calls again. 'I appreciate it, bro, but could you move it into drive time?'—Elmore Leonard, *Be Cool*, p. 253, 1999

drive-up *noun*
a fresh arrival at prison *US*
- —Charles Shafer, *Folk Speech in Texas Prisons*, p. 203, 1990

driveway *noun*
a scenic road, often in a city, landscaped and planted *CANADA*
- What Ottawa needs most sorely is not more trees, parks and driveways as handouts from the taxpayers of Canada, but certain civilizing amenities which its inhabitants, officials, and businessmen can supply.—*Saturday Night*, p. 7/1, 27th September 1958

drizzles *noun*
diarrhoea *US, 1943*
- And the prisosner looks like a water bed, all shuddery and quivering, as he lies on the floor bloated by about five gallons of T.J.'s H2), guaranteed to give him the drizzles.—Joseph Wambaugh, *Lines and Shadows*, p. 128, 1984

drizzling shits *noun*
dysentery *US*
- I hope that son of a bitch dies of the drizzling shits.—*Maledicta*, p. 171, Winter 1980

dro *noun*
marijuana grown hydroponically *US*
- Sean Paul borrowed American slang for the opening line. "Just gimme the light and pass the'dro," he chants, borrowing the hip-hop term for hydroponic marijuana.—*Washington Post*, p. G01, 24th November 2002

droge; droje *noun*
▷ **see: DRAGE**

drogle *noun*
a dress *UK*
Gay slang.
- —Paul Baker, *Polari*, p. 173, 2002

droid *noun*
a low-level employee who is blindly loyal to his employer *US, 1980*
- Typical droid positions include supermarket checkout assistant and bank clerk; the syndrome is also endemic in low-leel government employees.—Eric S. Raymond, *The New Hacker's Dictionary*, p. 134, 1991

drome *noun*
in circus and carnival usage, a motordrome *US*
- —Don Wilmeth, *The Language of American Popular Entertainment*, p. 80, 1981

drone *noun*
1 a sluggard, a tedious person *UK, 1529*
- Someday, Bloodworth hoped, one of these drones would call with a hot tip, maybe even a ticket to the front page.—Carl Hiaasen, *Tourist Season*, p. 232, 1986

2 in hospital usage, a medical student *US*
- —Sally Williams, *"Strong" Words*, p. 140, 1994

drone cage *noun*
a private railway carriage *US*
- —Norman Carlisle, *The Modern Wonder Book of Trains and Railroading*, p. 262, 1946

droned *adjective*
simultaneously intoxicated on alcohol and marijuana *US*
A blend of 'drunk' and 'stoned'.
• —Pamela Munro, *U.C.L.A. Slang*, p. 60, 1997

droner *noun*
a boring, spiritless person; an objectionable person *US, 1943*
• Okay, Malcolm, Bernie, whoever else manages all those like snorners and droners all over the place[.]—Lester Bangs, *Psychotic Reactions and Carburetor Dung*, p. 242, 1977

drongo *noun*
1 a fool; a hopeless individual *AUSTRALIA, 1941*
Originally Royal Australian Air Force slang for 'a recruit'. Said in an early RAAF source to be named after the '(spangled) drongo' (a large clumsy flying bird), but drongos are not particularly large (smaller than a pigeon), and while they are somewhat aerobatic and erractic flyers they are certainly not clumsy. Otherwise it has been suggested (Sidney J. Baker, *The Australian Language*, 1945) that it is an allusion to a racehorse named Drongo which gained notoriety for never winning a race and was used as a character in satirical political cartoons in the *Melbourne Herald* in the 1920s, which may be true despite the gap of 20 years.
• Now don't call me a galah, yer stupid drongo!—Robert S. Close, *With Hooves of Brass*, p. 91, 1961
• I'll make soldiers out of you drongoes if it takes years off my life!—Ray Slattery, *Mobbs' Mob*, p. 20, 1966
• Don't come the raw prawn with me either or I'll drop ya you pommy drongo.—*The Adventures of Barry McKenzie*, 1972
• Blind Frieda could see you are a pie-eating drongo and a blithering suds-artist.—Ignatius Jones, *The 1992 True Hip Manual*, p. 158, 1992
• [They] were enjoying the sort of bacchanalian freakout usually the preserve of mushied-up [high] drongos invading Stonehenge for the Solstice.—Kevin Sampson, *Powder*, p. 27, 1999

2 a new recruit to the Royal Australian Air Force *AUSTRALIA, 1941*
Probably after Drongo, a Melbourne racehorse in the mid-1920s who, it is claimed, having failed to win a single race, was retired; hence 'a slow and clumsy individual'. An alternative etymology from the Australian Army journal, *Salt*, 1941, cited in *A Dictionary of Australian Colloquialisms*, G.A. Wilkes, 1978, offers a large and clumsy flying bird found in Australia's Cape York Peninsula as the source; in fact, the 'drongo' is a small, averagely graceful bird, but is surely the creature after which the horse was named.

drongo *adjective*
foolish *AUSTRALIA, 1945*
• 'The old story of supply and demand, I suppose.' Storm's tone became bitter. 'That, and the fact that I was drongo enough to top the course in nav. when I went through initial training school.' —W.R. Bennett, *Target Turin*, p. 104, 1962

dronk *adjective*
drunk *SOUTH AFRICA, 1983*
From Afrikaans.
• Bru, I'm going to get dronk, dronk, dronk. I already told Saras. I told he that I'm going to come home in a state.—*Sunday Times (South Africa)*, 16th December 2001

dronkie *noun*
a drunkard *SOUTH AFRICA, 1969*
From Afrikaans *dronk* (drunk).
• —Jean Branford, *A Dictionary of South African English*, 1978

droob *noun*
a hopeless individual *AUSTRALIA, 1933*
A connection with US 'droop' (an obnoxious person) is highly suspect as there is nothing to suggest that this uncommon Americanism was ever known in Australia.
• How can anyone compare a good girl like Tilly with a mob of droobs and flat-feet?—George Blaikie, *Remember Smith's Weekly?*, p. 218, 1950
• You'd have to be a bit of a droob, wouldn't you?—Barry Humphries, *The Traveller's Tool*, p. 98, 1985

droog *noun*
1 a ruffian; a henchman *AUSTRALIA, 1967*
Derives from the sense as 'a friend' in the novel and play *A Clockwork Orange* by Anthony Burgess (1917–93) and the subsequent film by Stanley Kubrick (1928–99); combined to some degree with **DRONE** (a tedious person).
• It wasn't clear whether the droog was rubbing his hands with glee or because he was suffering with pins and needles[.]—Stewart Home, *Sex Kick [britpulp]*, p. 225, 1999

2 a good friend *US*
Adopted from Russian *drug* (a friend) by Anthony Burgess (1917–93) for the novel *A Clockwork Orange*, 1962.
• This sarcasm, if I might call it such, does not become you, O my Brothers. As I am your droog and leader I'm entitled to know what goes on eh?—Stanley Kubrick, *A Clockwork Orange*, 1971

droogs *noun*
drugs *UK*
An affected mispronunciation.
• Just because it's only Nantwich or whatever, doesn't mean the kids don't want droogs. In actual fact, it means they double want droogs.—Kevin Sampson, *Outlaws*, p. 53, 2001

drool *noun*
nonsense; drivel *US, 1900*
Punning on conventional 'drivel' and 'dribble'.
• [F]or God's sake don't listen to that drool how the stuff [drugs] eat you up ... that kind of jive is for squares.—Harry J. Anslinger (US Commissioner of Narcotics), *The Murderers*, p. 174, 1961

drooling the drool of regret into the pillow of remorse
used as a humorous comment on a person who has not performed up to their expectation *US*
Coined and popularised by ESPN's Keith Olberman.
• —Keith Olberman and Dan Patrick, *The Big Show*, p. 13, 1997

droolin' with schoolin' *adjective*
said of an overly diligent student *US, 1944*
Teen slang, reported by a Toronto newspaper in 1946, and reported as 'obsolescent or obsolete' by Douglas Leechman, 1959.

drool value *noun*
sexual attractiveness *AUSTRALIA*
• It was actually a pretty fab flick and Devon has unmeasurable drool value! Where can I write to this mega-babe?—*Dolly*, p. 8, 1996

droop *noun*
a socially inept person *US, 1932*
• He's a 6-F droop, but has extra ration points.—Haenigsen, *Jive's Like That*, 1947

droop-snoot *nickname*
the supersonic airliner Concorde *UK, 1984*
After the fact that the plane's nose could be lowered. Borrowed from an earlier (1945) description of any aircraft with a downward-pointing nose.
• But the pointed nose was designed to droop, so it can be lowered at slower speeds. For take-off and landing, the "droop snoot" is put right down so that pilots have a clear view ahead.—Neal Morris, *Mega Book of Aircraft*, p. 20, 2002

droopy *adjective*
dispirited, dejected, sulky *US*
• I was not really quite prepared for her fits of disorganized boredom, intense and vehement griping, her sprawling, droopy, dopey-eyed style.—Vladimir Nabokov, *Lolita*, p. 148, 1955

droopy-drawers *noun*
1 a person, especially a child, with trousers that are too large on a comic scale *US, 1931*
• He was wearing an old black felt hat and overalls which hung down his can as though he were little Droopy-Drawers smiling up from the play pen.—Robert Penn Warren, *All the King's Men*, p. 64, 1946

2 a slovenly or incompetent person *UK, 1939*
Jocular.

drooth; drouth *noun*
a great thirst; a thirsty person; a drunk *UK: SCOTLAND, 1911*
From a dialect variation of 'drought'.
• All this shouting dousnie half give yi a drouth... (smacks his lips.)—Ian Pattison, *Rab C. Nesbitt*, 1988

drop *noun*
1 in espionage or a criminal enterprise, a place where goods, documents or money is left to be picked up later by a confederate *US, 1922*
• Sometimes the stuff is brought in direct, while at other times a 'drop' is made at an outlying area.—Clarence Cooper Jr, *The Scene*, p. 27, 1960
• There's the neighborhood cop at the numbers drop / Shaking down the run.—Dennis Wepman et al., *The Life*, p. 162, 1976

- It was a drop. It was a pass. It was a payoff to Ray Sharkey here. this City Hall Pimp you got yourself here is a shrewd sonofabitch. He wouldn't take the payoff where somebody could see. He took the payoff where everybody could see. —Robert Campbell, *Boneyards*, p. 192, 1992

2 a place where stolen goods or other criminal material may be temporarily stored *US, 1922*

- I laid these things on him for letting me use his pad as a drop. —A.S. Jackson, *Gentleman Pimp*, p. 24, 1973
- The owner was a horse lover and gambler, and used the store as a bookie drop. —James Ellroy, *Blood on the Moon*, p. 54, 1984

3 a bribe *UK, 1931*

- He knows me so I reckon he's after a drop so I put it to him and he only fucking 'as me for that too, doesn't he? —Ted Lewis, *Jack Carter's Law*, p. 125, 1974

4 in horse racing, a cash-handling error that favours the racetrack *US*

- —Bob and Barbara Freeman, *Wanta Bet?*, p. 289, 1982

5 the place where players who are invited to an illegal dice game are told where the game will be held *US*

- —*American Speech*, p. 306, December 1964: 'Lingua Cosa Nostra'

6 the ingestion of a drug *US*

- "Poor Chessman" – he muttered, still slight zonked from a late night mesc drop[.] —Ed Sanders, *Tales of Beatnik Glory*, p. 41, 1975

7 LSD *UK*

From the verb sense (to consume drugs), especially as 'drop acid'.

- Street names [...] cheer, dots, drop, flash[.] —James Kay and Julian Cohen, *The Parents' Complete Guide to Young People and Drugs*, p. 141, 1998

8 an attractive woman *AUSTRALIA*

Mimicking the language of wine connoisseurs.

- Dennis and Pat knew a couple of 'fabulous drops' that they were going 'ter take ter the pictures'. —Nino Culotta (John O'Grady), *They're A Weird Mob*, p. 46, 1957
- Second, Frosty Snow ain't told nobody but me what luscious drops they is. —J.E. MacDonnell, *Don't Gimme the Ships*, p. 137, 1960
- Wow, he croaked, that's what I really call a taut drop! He could still just faintly savour the intoxicating perfume. —John Wynnum, *Jiggin' in the Riggin'*, p. 31, 1965

9 the act of execution by hanging *UK*

Derives from: 'The new drop; a contrivance for executing felons at Newgate, by means of a platform, which drops from under them' (Francis Grose, *Dictionary of the Vulgar Tongue*, 1796). The condemned prisoner would then 'drop' to the end of a rope. Also recorded as 'the last drop'.

- There was a chap in the death cell waiting to get topped, and it comes to the morning where he is going to get the drop. —Frank Norman, *Bang To Rights*, p. 31, 1958

10 an orphan *US*

- —Clarence Major, *Dictionary of Afro-American Slang*, p. 48, 1970

11 in a casino, the amount of money taken in from betting customers *US, 1935*

- He must know that Frank Sinatra will raise the "drop" of the casino more than any other entertainer. —Mario Puzo, *Inside Las Vegas*, p. 175, 1977
- As soon as he took over, he doubled the fuckin' drop. —*Casino*, 1995

▸ get the drop on; have the drop on

to get, or have, an advantage over someone *US, 1867*

Originally, and still, 'to be quicker drawing a gun than your opponent'.

- Wasps pinch one, creeping imperceptibly slowly in a line to get the drop on the attacking side. —*The Daily Telegraph*, 23rd May 2004

drop *verb*

1 to swallow, to ingest (a drug) *US*

A favourite word of the LSD culture, but popular for other drugs of abuse before and since; if used without a direct object, almost certainly referring to LSD.

- To take orally is to "drop it." —Francis J. Rigney and L. Douglas Smith, *The Real Bohemia*, p. xx, 1961
- Everybody dropped his acid in the kitchen and for the first half hour they sat around listening to music. —Richard Alpert and Sidney Cohen, *LSD*, p. 100, 1966
- When I drop (swallow) LSD, I'm looking for an experience[.] —Roger Gordon, *Hollywood's Sexual Underground*, p. 59, 1966
- "The way they put it is that they "drop whites" to get out of bed in the morning, or whenever they get up to go to work, and "drop reds" to go to sleep," Sweeney reported at the conference. —*San Francisco Chronicle*, p. 5, 11th October 1966
- After that night, I told John I would come back and drop [acid]. —Nicholas Von Hoffman, *We Are The People Our Parents Warned Us Against*, p. 60, 1967
- Being too young to drink, he smoked pot, dropped acid, and at last sniffed heroin[.] —Raymond Mungo, *Famous Long Ago*, p. 30, 1970
- [I]t had been fourteen hours since he'd dropped the acid, and of course he was exhausted. —Gurney Norman, *Divine Right's Trip (Last Whole Earth Catalog)*, p. 103, 1971
- And we ain't dropping 'til I say so. —*Saturday Night Fever*, 1977
- Many of the Angels had obviously been dropping "belligerence," their pet name for sodium seconal (reds). —Peter Coyote, *Sleeping Where I Fall*, p. 98, 1998
- [T]he next lot decided to just find beaches, drop pills and party. —James Hawes, *Dead Long Enough*, p. 92, 2000

2 to kill, especially by shooting *UK, 1726*

In various uses and combinations 'drop' means 'to die' or 'to finish'. This variant is pro-active.

- "Fuck it!" I gasped. "Why didn't we just drop the bastards?" —Chris Ryan, *Stand By, Stand By*, p. 105, 1996
- You're his wife, and you're walking around with the shitwrap who dropped him. —Stephen J. Cannell, *The Tin Collectors*, p. 75, 2001

3 to bribe *UK*

- [A]t this stage they may try to drop you. If they do, quietly refuse[.] —Charles Raven, *Underworld Nights*, p. 92–93, 1956
- "He tried to drop the mingra [a policeman]", "I dropped him a flim [a £5 note]" —Patrick O'Shaughnessy, *Market Traders' Slang*, 1979

4 to release a music recording *UK, 1991*

- Eminem's Dr Dre-produced The Marshall Mathers LP drops in 2000 and goes platinum in one week[.] —*The Source*, p. 128, March 2002
- The LP should drop on Skint in September. —*Muzik*, p. 14, February 2003

5 to lose (especially money) *UK, 1676*

An example of C19 flash slang that has survived.

- Frank had dropped $3,200 at craps, not even shooting, betting against the shooter. —Elmore Leonard, *Switch*, p. 111, 1978

6 to cash a forged cheque *UK*

- [T]he penman, who never drops himself, has to send a minder, known as a topper, to keep an eye on the dropper[.] —Charles Raven, *Underworld Nights*, p. 81, 1956

7 to give money *UK*

- Jimmy hates your fucking guts, Charlie. He's the reason Jean doesn't drop you as much as she used to. —Ted Lewis, *Jack Carter's Law*, p. 52, 1974

8 to break off a romantic relationship with someone *AUSTRALIA*

- Drops Narrabee flat, he does, and she goes off the rails[.] —Dymphna Cusack, *Picnic Races*, p. 145, 1962
- She is doing it [petting] for him, merely for him, not for herself and it would be unladylike to appear to enjoy it. Indeed he would probably feel forced to drop her immediately if she showed any sign of enjoyment. —Sue Rhodes, *Now you'll think I'm awful*, p. 21, 1967
- —Kathy Lette, *Girls' Night Out*, p. 188, 1987
- —Kylie Mole (Maryanne Fahey), *My Diary*, p. 51, 1988
- —John Birmingham, *He Died With a Felafel in his Hand*, p. 26, 1994
- She dropped me the next day. —Paul Vautin, *Turn It Up!*, p. 81, 1995

9 to perform oral sex on a woman *US*

- I stopped dropping. It got to be too frustrating. —*Chasing Amy*, 1997

10 to fart *AUSTRALIA*

- Jeez! That packet shit my wife feeds me...drop one fart and you're hungry again. —Kathy Lette, *Girls' Night Out*, p. 140, 1987

11 to knock down with a punch *AUSTRALIA*

- She smiled. 'I'm no beauty!' 'I'll drop the first man who says so!' —Eric Lambert, *The Veterans*, p. 80, 1954
- 'I've 'ad you,' he said. 'I'm gunna drop yer.' —Nino Culotta (John O'Grady), *They're A Weird Mob*, p. 154, 1957
- 'Drop it, Jackson, or I'll drop you!' called a masked warder from the tower. —Bob Jewson, *Stir*, p. 152, 1980

12 in pool, to hit (a ball) into a pocket *US*

- —Mike Shamos, *The Illustrated Encyclopedia of Billiards*, p. 83, 1993

13 to cause a car to suddenly drop almost to the ground by use of hydraulic lifts *US*

- —Edith A. Folb, *runnin' down some lines*, p. 236, 1980

14 to include a tune in a sequence of recorded dance music *UK*

- Oakie dropped K-Klass' "Rhythm Is A Mystery". —*Mixmag*, p. 33, February 2002

▸ drop a banger

to blunder; to make a mistake, especially one of some consequence *UK, 1961*

From **BANGERS** (the testicles); a variation of **DROP A BOLLOCK**.

▸ drop a bollock; drop a ballock

to make a mistake, especially one of some consequence *UK, 1942*

Derives from **DROP A BRICK** (to make a mistake) combined with **BOLLOCKS** (the testicles).

- ROB: You dropped a bollock ain't you? ANTHONY: Yeah, I dropped a bollock... Yes... alright... I don't mind, I – ROB: You dropped one massive bollock. ANTHONY: Yes, I dropped a big fucking massive hairy bollock. — *24 Hour Party People*, 2001

▸ drop a bomb; drop one

1 to fart *UK*

- — Peter Furze, *Tailwinds*, p. 59, 1998

2 to defecate *US*

- — Don R. McCreary (Editor), *Dawg Speak*, 2001

▸ drop a brick

to make a *faux pas* *UK, 1923*

▸ drop a bundle

to give birth *NEW ZEALAND, 1948*

- [T]he poor old shielah [woman]'s just dropped another bundle!! — Barry Humphries, *Bazza Pulls It Off!*, 1971

▸ drop a clanger

to make a mistake, especially in a social context *UK, 1942*

A variation of **DROP A BOLLOCK**, based on **CLANGERS** (the testicles).

▸ drop a deuce

to defecate *US*

From the children's toilet vocabulary: **NUMBER TWO** (defecation).

- I think she's in the back dropping a deuce. — *Howard Stern Radio Show*, 24th January 2003

▸ drop a dime

to make a telephone call, especially to the police to inform on someone *US, 1966*

From the days when the price of a call from a pay phone was a dime.

- I ain't never seen so many stool pigeons in one block before in all my life. Drop a dime on you 'fore Fod can git the news. — Nathan Heard, *Howard Street*, p. 35, 1968
- There were rumors out about Milton having dropped dimes on pushers who put shit on him. — Donald Goines, *Cry Revenge*, p. 150, 1974
- He dropped a dime on you to screw me out of the six hundred grand. — Gerald Petievich, *To Live and Die in L.A.*, p. 16, 1983
- Keefe could have used the opportunity to drop the dime on Al Garcia[.] — Carl Hiaasen, *Tourist Season*, p. 143, 1986
- But listen, she can drop a dime [call the police] as quick as anybody and he's gone. — Terry Williams, *The Cocaine Kids*, p. 95, 1989
- Drop a dime? Call the cops? Don't even let anybody hear such bullshit. — *Goodfellas*, 1990
- What was the big deal about calling home? "No time to drop a dime, right?" — Richard Price, *Clockers*, p. 165, 1992
- They'll hear I dropped dime. They'll probably hear it from you. — *The Usual Suspects*, 1995

▸ drop a goolie

to make a mistake *UK, 1961*

A figurative use of **GOOLIES** (the testicles); a direct equivalent to **DROP A BOLLOCK**.

▸ drop a jewel; drop jewels

to create rap music or lyrics *US, 1991*

- Fuck droppin' a jewel[.] — Eminem (Marshall Mathers), *Just Don't Give a Fuck*, 1999

▸ drop a lug

to confront someone about their conduct; to insult *US, 1973*

- — Christina and Richard Milner, *Black Players*, p. 303, 1972

▸ drop a name

to inform *US*

- To drop a name on you. — *New Jack City*, 1990
- What do you think he'd say if he found out you dropped his name to the D.A.? — *The Usual Suspects*, 1995

▸ drop a nickel

to become involved in something *US*

- So I went over and dropped my nickel. I guess it's always a mistake to interfere with a drunk. — Raymond Chandler, *The Long Goodbye*, p. 2, 1953

▸ drop a sprog

to give birth *UK*

Combines 'drop' (to give birth, usually of an animal) with **SPROG** (a baby).

- — Nigel Foster, *The Making of a Royal Marine Commando*, 1987

▸ drop an oar in the water

to make a mistake *UK*

From rhyming slang, **OARS AND ROWLOCKS** for **BOLLOCKS**; this is an elaboration and variation of **DROP A BOLLOCK**.

- — Ray Puxley, *Fresh Rabbit*, p. 85, 1998

▸ drop beads

to unintentionally disclose your homosexuality *US*

- — *American Speech*, p. 56, Spring-Summer 1970: 'Homosexual slang'

▸ drop bottom

to set the bass levels on a car stereo system at a high level *US*

- — Chris Lewis, *The Dictionary of Playground Slang*, p. 79, 2003

▸ drop foot

to dance without restraint *JAMAICA*

- — Richard Allsopp, *Dictionary of Caribbean English Usage*, p. 204, 1996

▸ drop in it

to get someone blamed and into trouble *UK*

Euphemistic **DROP IN THE SHIT**.

▸ drop off the twig

to die *AUSTRALIA*

- I mean if, for argument's sake, I'd been awake and I really had dropped off the twig, cashed in my chips, kicked off, pegged out, found the road too weary and the hill too steep to climb — Barry Humphries, *A Nice Night's Entertainment*, 1974

▸ drop science

to explain, to educate, to make sense *US, 1992*

- "Word" was once a powerful affirmation that you were "dropping science"[.] — Nelson George, *Hip Hop America*, p. 209, 1998

▸ drop some iron

to spend money *US*

- — *Washington Post Magazine*, p. 7, 20th September 1987: 'Say wha?'
- — Vann Wesson, *Generation X Field Guide and Lexicon*, p. 58, 1997

▸ drop the bucket on

to expose someone's misdeeds; to get someone into trouble *AUSTRALIA, 1950*

The 'bucket' is a full sanitary bin, in other words, to 'put someone in the shit'.

- Publishers have been putting the hard word on me for yonks to spill the beans, tell it like it is and tip the bucket on my elitist right-wing sparring-partners[.] — Barry Humphries, *The Traveller's Tool*, p. 7, 1985

▸ drop the hammer

at the start of a drag race, to release (engage) the clutch in a sudden and forceful move *US*

- — John Lawlor, *How to Talk Car*, p. 39, 1965

▸ drop the hammer down; drop the hammer

to accelerate *US*

- — *Complete CB Slang Dictionary*, 1976
- — Peter Chippindale, *The British CB Book*, p. 154, 1981

▸ drop the hook

to arrest *US*

- It was pretty obvious that the buttons in the prowl car were about ready to drop the hook on him, so I went over there fast and took hold of his arm. — Raymond Chandler, *The Long Goodbye*, p. 6, 1953

▸ drop the kids off

to defecate *US*

- — Chris Lewis, *The Dictionary of Playground Slang*, p. 61, 2003

▸ drop the kids off at the pool

to defecate *UK*

The wide popularity of this term was reported in June 2002 on *www.LondonSlang.com*.

▸ drop them

of a woman, to readily remove her knickers as a practical necessity for sexual activity, and thus said to be symbolic of a woman's sexual availability *UK*

- Her? She's not fussy – she'll drop 'em for anyone. — Beale, 1984

▸ drop trou

as a prank, to lower your trousers, bend over and expose your buttocks to the world *US*

- — Andy Anonymous, *A Basic Guide to Campusology*, p. 8, 1966
- — John D. Bell et al., *Loosely Speaking*, p. 19, 1969

▸ drop your bundle

to lose one's composure; to go to pieces *AUSTRALIA, 1847*

- [M]um drops her bundle whenever she feels like it these days, God bless her heart. — Barry Humphries, *The Traveller's Tool*, p. 7, 1985

▸ drop your candy

to make a serious mistake *US, 1908*

- — Frederic G. Cassidy, *Dictionary of American Regional English, Volume II*, p. 206, 1991

▸ drop your guts
to fart *AUSTRALIA*
- I've broken wind, / I've dropped my guts, / Open the window please. —Ivor Biggun, *I've Parted (Misprint)*, 1978
- A typical Pickles trick, he'd sneak up behind you, then drop his guts. —Phillip Gwynne, *Deadly Unna?*, p. 179, 1998

▸ drop your handbag
to fart *UK*
A variation on **DROP YOUR GUTS**. Royal Navy slang.
- —Rick Jolly, *Jackspeak*, p. 92, 1989

▸ drop your lunch
to fart *AUSTRALIA*
- There's nothing worse than casually dropping your lunch at a business function or an extraordinary meeting of the Australian Cheese Board[.] —Barry Humphries, *The Traveller's Tool*, p. 63, 1985

drop a bombshell *verb*
to reveal a great and shocking surprise *UK*
- Ms Williams made the police statement she was advised that if she dropped a "bombshell" during the trial, she stood to make money by selling her story to the press. — *The Guardian*, 4th September 2002

drop-dead *adverb*
extremely *AUSTRALIA*
- Bondi Babe seeks love and affection from younger man. Preferrably drop dead gorgeous. — *City Hub*, p. 33, 13th November 1997
- Then suddenly – da-dah! – one of the young German ladies breaks [T]he German girls doing the tempting were such drop-dead shakeable babes that we'd have smoked heroin if we'd thought it would have helped us get into their knickers. —Ken Lukowiak, *Marijuana Time*, p. 5, 2000

drop dead!
used as a contemptuous expression of dismissal; go away! *UK, 1934*
- Wherever you go / I'll follow you / I've got your address / I'm coming for you / Why don't you drop dead? Why don't you drop dead? Why don't you drop dead? / Why don't you drop dead? Why don't you drop dead? — Space, *Drop Dead [Song]*, 1996

drop-down *noun*
in horse racing, a horse that has been moved down a class or down in claiming price *US*
- —Robert V. Rowe, *How to Win at Horse-Racing*, p. 1990, 199

drop edge of yonder *noun*
a near-death condition *US, 1939*
- Took to vomitin'. All day, all night. Hangin' on the drop edge of yonder. —William Least-Heat Moon, *Blue Highways*, p. 33, 1982

drop gun *noun*
a gun that is not registered and not capable of being traced, and thus placed by the police in the vicinity of someone whom they have shot to justify the shooting *US*
- —Carsten Stroud, *Close Pursuit*, p. 271, 1987

drop-in *noun*
1 in computing, characters added as a result of a voltage irregularity or system malfunction *US*
- —Eric S. Raymond, *The New Hacker's Dictionary*, p. 135, 1991

2 a temporary visitor *AUSTRALIA*
- Their spokespeople said they had too much to do looking after their own people to be bothered giving handouts to 'drop-ins', as they called us. —Ward McNally, *Supper at Happy Harry's*, p. 75, 1982
- There were three regulars and lots of drop-ins. —John Birmingham, *He Died With a Felafel in his Hand*, p. 142, 1994

drop in *verb*
in surfing, to start a ride on a wave already occupied by another surfer or other surfers *AUSTRALIA*
- —Nat Young, *Surfing Fundamentals*, p. 127, 1985

drop it!
stop!, especially as an injunction to stop talking or fooling *UK, 1847*

drop-kick *noun*
1 the vagina *AUSTRALIA*
Formed as an extension of rhyming slang, 'punt' for **CUNT**.
- —Ryan Aven-Bray, *Ridgey Didge Oz Jack Lang*, p. 25, 1983

2 by extension from the previous sense, a fool, especially an annoying or contemptible fool *AUSTRALIA*
- Real drop kick: Someone who is a real droob or nerd[.] —Richard Beckett, *The Dinkum Aussie Dictionary*, p. 43, 1986

3 by extension, something that is frustrating or annoying *AUSTRALIA*
- Jesus, she's a drop-kick of a thing. —Robert G. Barrett, *Davo's Little Something*, p. 37, 1992

droplifting *noun*
an act of secretly placing your own CDs in the display racks of a music retailer *UK*
- —Paul Sullivan, *Sullivan's Music Trivia*, p. 189, 2003

drop off *verb*
to go to sleep *UK, 1820*
- Anyway, the kids were exhausted, and they quickly dropped off to sleep without any apparent worries. —David Elliot Cohen, *One Year Off*, p. 182, 2001

drop-out *noun*
a person who has withdrawn from formal education or mainstream society *UK, 1930*
Usage is conventional but the company that the word keeps gives it the aura of unconventionality.
- "He's a dropout," I said roughly. "Dropout" made me think of some poor dumb-looking hoodlum wandering the streets breaking out street lights[.] —S.E. Hinton, *The Outsiders*, p. 23–24, 1967
- On many an ageing would-be drop-out's bookshelf [...] lies a yellowing copy of Protest[.] —Richard Neville, *Play Power*, p. 22, 1970

drop out *verb*
to withdraw from school, college, university or mainstream society *US, 1952*
- "Drop out" was the message both collaborators gave the audience. — *The Berkeley Barb*, p. 2, 24th June 1966
- The community's language – dropping out as opposed to climbing up – suggest vertical movement, but the real motion is lateral. —Nicholas Von Hoffman, *We Are The People Our Parents Warned Us Against*, p. 53, 1967
- Why did the hippie join the Parachute Corps? So he could keep dropping out! —Paul Laikin, *101 Hippie Jokes*, 1968
- "Drop out" means just to drop out from the games and from the things that are meaningless. —Leonard Wolfe (Editor), *Voices from the Love Generation*, p. 88, 1968
- "DROP OUT!" the yippies scream at them. —Jerry Rubin, *Do It!*, p. 115, 1970

dropper *noun*
1 a gambler who can be counted on to lose a lot of money *US*
- During his stay, hieroglyphics are secretly appended to his name on the hotel register, which catalgoue him as a "dropper" (businessman and heavy loser), "producer" (businessman), or "nonproducer" (professional gambler). —Ed Reid and Ovid Demaris, *The Green Jungle*, p. 2, 1963

2 a criminal who cashes a forged cheque *UK*
- [T]he penman, who never drops himself, has to send a minder, known as a topper, to keep an eye on the dropper[.] —Charles Raven, *Underworld Nights*, p. 81, 1956

3 a paid killer *US*
- —Joseph E. Ragen and Charles Finston, *Inside the World's Toughest Prison*, p. 797, 1962

dropper *verb*
to inject a drug intravenously *UK, 1998*
- —Mike Haskins, *Drugs*, p. 290, 2003

dropping *noun*
the criminal act of passing forged cheques *UK*
- Dropping is dodgy work. —Charles Raven, *Underworld Nights*, p. 81, 1956

dropping!
in foot-propelled scootering, a warning shout used when a jump has gone wrong *UK*
Ben Sharpe, *Scooter Crazy*, 2000, notes that: '"ARG!" works just as well though'.

drop-short *noun*
an artillery soldier *AUSTRALIA*
- 'How's the bloody drop-shorts?' jeered Lasher, grinning. —Eric Lambert, *The Veterans*, p. 170, 1954
- The 'Drop-shorts' could fire all night without disturbing anyone but the newest arrival. —Martin Cameron, *A Look at the Bright Side*, 1988

dropstick *noun*
pickpocketing *UK*
West Indian slang.
- [An 18-year old West Indian girl] talks about the London "sticksing" or "dropstick" scene [...] like a veteran. — *New Society*, 7th July 1977

dropsy *noun*
a cash bribe, or other money the taxman doesn't know about *UK, 1930*
The money is 'dropped' in the pocket or hand.
- He either had to pay up some substantial dropsy or be nicked in possession. —Charles Raven, *Underworld Nights*, p. 155, 1956
- With all the gimmes and dropsies and once we've factored in Eli's take we'll be left with a good half million. —Kevin Samson, *Outlaws*, p. 18, 2001

drop-the-hanky *noun*
a pickpocketing scheme in which the victim is distracted when an attractive woman member of the pickpocketing team drops a handkerchief or other small object which the victim stoops to recover *US*
- One setup engineering by troupes of three was called, some years back, drop the hanky. —Dev Collans with Stewart Sterling, *I was a House Detective*, p. 47, 1954

drop-top *noun*
a car with a convertible roof *US, 1973*
- Shiiit, nigga, the driveway look like some shit off the lifestyles of the Rich and Famous; a drop top Porsche, a big body Benz, two clover green Rovers. —Nikki Turner, *A Project Chick*, p. 22, 2004

drop your cocks and pull up your socks!
used for awakening a sleeping man or men *US*
A variation of **HANDS OFF COCKS – FEET IN SOCKS!**. Originally used by drill instructors to military recruits.
- Six bells and all's well. Stead as she goes. Hit the deck. Drop your cocks and grab your socks. —Ken Kesey, *One Flew Over the Cuckoo's Nest*, p. 213, 1962
- He presses his other hand against his nose and imitates the bosun's pipe. "Now, reveille, reveille, reveille!" he shouts. "Drop your cocks and grab your socks!" —Darryl Ponicsan, *The Last Detail*, p. 101, 1970
- Reveille! Drop your cocks and grab your socks! — *Full Metal Jacket*, 1987
- "COUNT TIME!" boomed from the front bars. "Drop yer coks and pull up her socks!" —Seth Morgan, *Homeboy*, p. 88, 1990

drouth *noun*
▷ see: **DROOTH**

drove *adjective*
very angry *US*
- —William K. Bentley and James M. Corbett, *Prison Slang*, p. 89, 1992

Drover's Guide *noun*
an imaginary publication that is cited as a source of rumours *AUSTRALIA, 1959*

drown *verb*
1 in oil drilling, to contaminate a well with flooding salt water *US*
- —Jerry Robertson, *Oil Slanguage*, p. 49, 1954

2 to lose heavily gambling *US*
- —John Scarne, *Scarne on Dice*, p. 466, 1974

drowning *noun*
the criminal act of gaining entry to a property with the intent to commit theft by claiming to work for a water supplier *UK*
- [P]opped out for a bit of drowning, and ended up with a couple of monkeys [£500 x 2]. —David Rowan, *A Glossary for the 90s*, p. 38, 1998

drown-proofing *noun*
in navy training, an exercise involving extended periods of treading water, especially while restrained to some degree *US*
- Next come fifteen nonstop minutes of "drown-proofing," the modern Navy version of treading water. —George Hall, *Top Gun*, p. 42, 1987
- He turned to Curran, "You wanted to watch the drownproofing, right sir?" —James B. Adair, *Navy Seals*, p. 99, 1990

drowsy high *noun*
a central nervous system despressant *UK, 1998*
From the effects of intoxication.
- —Mike Haskins, *Drugs*, p. 282, 2003

druck steaming *adjective*
drunk *UK*
What a 'druck' is or why it should be steamed is a mystery that defeats sober logic.
- — *e-cyclopaedia*, 20th March 2002

'druff *noun*
dandruff *UK*
- There were mounds of 'druff on his shoulders, and scurf clearly visible on his scalp. —Will Self, *The Sweet Smell of Psychosis*, p. 20, 1996

drug; drugg; drugged *adjective*
displeased, annoyed *US*
- I paced up and down, up and down, two steps each way, fidgety as a tiger in a thimble. I was one drugg cat. —Mezz Mezzrow, *Really the Blues*, p. 301, 1946
- M-a-a-n, I'm drug by that son of a bitch MacDoud with all his routines[.] —Jack Kerouac, *The Subterraneans*, p. 29, 1958
- —Lawrence Lipton, *The Holy Barbarians*, p. 316, 1959
- When a junkie's drugged, he's mad at somebody or something. —Clarence Cooper Jr, *The Scene*, p. 55, 1960

drug-fuck *noun*
a drug-addict, a junkie *UK*
- It's Bonnie an' fookin' Clyde except this couple are about as sexy as a dog's arse, sad drug-fooks the both of 'em. —Ben Elton, *High Society*, p. 228, 2002

drug-fucked *adjective*
incapacitated from taking drugs *AUSTRALIA*
- [A]fter all, when you're that drug-fucked, a piece of naval lint can have occult significance. — *Arena*, p. 13, 1991
- Domestic things were just intrinsic to me. Cooking and cleaning and so on. But nobody else got into it because they were all young and drug-fucked. —John Birmingham, *He Died With a Felafel in his Hand*, p. 135, 1994
- I stand up and take a piss. A long stream of urine, pissing out alcohol, water, amyl, marijuana, speed, LSD, ecstasy. Fuck, I groan, I'm drug-fucked. —Christos Tsiolkas, *Loaded*, p. 107, 1995
- DREW BARRYMORE – http://www.primenet.com/~rwilli/drew.html – it's the home page for the world's wildest drugfucked child starlet since Judy Garland[.] — *Catalog*, p. 9, 1996
- Three hundred drug-fucked and horny gay men, 200 of them visiting Americans, are invading Club Med on Queensland's Lindeman Island for six days. — *Capital Q Weekly*, p. 11, 29th March 1996
- Fuck you, yer dumb drug-fucked bitch!...jus' gimme the fucken money. — *Rants*, p. 23, 1997
- [W]hat!?! do my drugfucked eyes fool me? is that silverchair i see before me? — *Pee*, p. 10, 1998

drugged *adjective*
patently stupid *US*
- —Eric S. Raymond, *The New Hacker's Dictionary*, p. 135, 1991

druggie; druggy *noun*
a drug user, abuser or addict *US, 1966*
- There wasn't that much drug stuff then, and two of these are druggies. —George V. Higgins, *Penance for Jerry Kennedy*, p. 85, 1985
- Maybe it was a druggie out there looking for targets of opportunity. —Robert Campbell, *Juice*, p. 174, 1988
- —Ellen C. Bellone (Editor), *Dictionary of Slang*, p. 10, 1989
- I go in there to check up on some guy, they think I'm a druggie. —Elmore Leonard, *Maximum Bob*, p. 163, 1991
- It does worry me though that once you've tried dope you get the label of being "a druggy"[.] —Macfarlane, Macfarlane and Robson, *The User*, p. 16, 1996
- I suppose you don't get to hear about the ones who turned alky or druggie or hermit. — Martin King and Martin Knight, *The Naughty Nineties*, p. 137, 1999
- Down at St George's, the doors are opening at 6pm and the "druggies" that Terry and Shaun don't like are coming in[.] — *The Times Magazine*, p. 49, 24th October 2002

druggo *noun*
a drug user or addict *AUSTRALIA*
- [A]dmitting that we may have exposed ourselves to AIDS is a bit like admitting that we are a poof, or a druggo, or a slut. — *Opus*, p. 12, August 1989

drughead *noun*
a drug addict; a serious abuser of narcotics *US, 1968*
- It is set down squarely in the midst of the greatest single concentration of drunks, drugheads, whores, pimps, queers, sodomists in the hemisphere. —Walker Percy, *Lancelot*, p. 23, 1977

drug monkey *noun*
a heavy user of drugs *UK*
- Do you get bored with your drug monkey reputation? — *X-Ray*, p. 71, October 2003

drugola *noun*
1 a bribe in the form of drugs given to encourage play of a particular record on the radio *US, 1973*
- CBS was soon embroiled in something called "drugola". —Ben Fong-Torres, *Not Fade Away*, p. 150, 1999

2 bribes paid to police by drug dealers *US*

• —Jim Crotty, *How to Talk American*, p. 88, 1997

drugstore cowboy *noun*

a young man who loiters in or around a drugstore for the purpose of meeting women *US, 1923*

• Girl-watching is a sport of the ages that appeals to all ages from young drugstore cowboys to graying roues.—*Life*, p. 120, 27th October 1961
• Life was combat, and victory was not to the lazy, the timid, the slugabed, the drugstore cowboy, the libertine, the mushmouth afraid to tell pepole exactly what was on his mind[.]—Russell Baker, *Growing Up*, p. 9, 1982

drugstore dice *noun*

inexpensive shop-bought dice, not milled to casino-level tolerances *US*

• —Frank Garcia, *Marked Cards and Loaded Dice*, p. 264, 1962

drugstore handicap *noun*

in horse racing, a race in which drugs have been given to enhance performance *US, 1948*

• —David W. Maurer, *Argot of the Racetrack*, p. 25, 1951

drugstore race *noun*

in horse racing, a race in which a number of the horses involved have been drugged for enhanced or diminished performance *US*

• —Robert Saunders Dowst and Jay Craig, *Playing the Races*, p. 162, 1960

drug up *adjective*

dragged up (poorly brought up) *UK*

Deliberately illiterate to mimic its context.

• Where was you drug up?—Beale, 1984

druid *noun*

1 the promoter of a drag racing event *US*

• The term is normally used in an uncomplimentary sense by competitors who don't like a given set of rules or the way a particular meet is run.—John Lawlor, *How to Talk Car*, p. 40, 1965

2 a priest *IRELAND*

• —Brendan Behan, *Borstal Boy*, 1958

druid dust *noun*

a narcotic herb that, when smoked as a marijuana substitute, produces a gentle euphoria *UK*

Druidism is an ancient religion associated with Wales and Stonehenge in the county of Wiltshire; the latter especially is particularly popular with people who are probably marijuana smokers.

• —Alon Shulman, *The Style Bible*, p. 84, 1999

druk *verb*

to stab *SOUTH AFRICA, 1972*

• —Jean Branford, *A Dictionary of South African English*, 1978

drum *noun*

1 a place of business or residence, a house, a home, a flat, etc *UK, 1846*

• It would have been too dodgy swagging gear into Bella's drum at 3 a.m.—Charles Raven, *Underworld Nights*, p. 22, 1956
• Aristov's in Greek street, you know the drum.—Derek Raymond (Robin Cook), *The Crust on its Uppers*, p. 53, 1962
• —Angela Devlin, *Prison Patter*, p. 48, 1996
• She didn't disturb me while i was doing her drum over[.]—Danny King, *The Burglar Diaries*, p. 27, 2001

2 by extension from the previous sense, a brothel *AUSTRALIA, 1879*

• The girl said something to the drum slavey and went out with her, leaving Hilary stranded.—Norman Lindsay, *The Cousin from Fiji*, p. 187, 1945
• —Robert S. Close, *Love Me Sailor*, p. 12, 1945

3 by extension, a cell *UK, 1909*

• —John R. Armore and Joseph D. Wolfe, *Dictionary of Desperation*, p. 27, 1976
• He's in the big house for all day and night, a new fish jammed into a drum with a cribman, who acts like a gazoonie.—*San Francisco Examiner*, p. 26, 17th August 1976
• —Angela Devlin, *Prison Patter*, p. 47, 1996

4 a safe *US, 1912*

• —Joseph E. Ragen and Charles Finston, *Inside the World's Toughest Prison*, p. 797, 1962

5 reliable information; inside information *AUSTRALIA, 1915*

• Nick along and give the others the drum about it.—Robert S. Close, *With Hooves of Brass*, p. 137, 1961
• And do you have the drum about where we'll be working, and for how long?—Ray Slattery, *Mobbs' Mob*, p. 45, 1966

6 in horse racing, reliable inside information *AUSTRALIA*

• —Ned Wallish, *The Truth Dictionary of Racing Slang*, p. 24, 1989

7 the face *UK*

Rhyming slang, from 'drum 'n' bass' (an electronic music genre).

• I've got a great big spot brewing on my drum—*19*, February 2001

▸ run a drum

(of a racehorse) to run a winning race, as tipped or expected *AUSTRALIA, 1933*

Used in negative contexts.

• Wot did I tell yer! Wasn't it a put up job the last time? Couldn't run a drum in a field o' goats an' now 'e licks class company!—Raymond Spargo, *Betting Systems Analysed*, p. 44, 1933
• If 'e's with the tail-enders, 'e never run a drum.—Nino Culotta (John O'Grady), *They're A Weird Mob*, p. 76, 1957

drum *verb*

1 to steal from unoccupied premises *UK, 1925*

Probably from an earlier sense (not recorded until 1933) 'to reconnoitre for the purposes of theft by knocking – *drum*ming – on the door of a targeted premises'.

2 to inform someone about something *AUSTRALIA, 1919*

• Jesus, don't bite me, son. I was only gonna drum you.—D'Arcy Niland, *Dead Men Running*, p. 86, 1969

3 to drive a vehicle at speed *UK*

• Can you imagine drumming along the M1 and some clown does a U-turn ahead of you?—*The Observer*, p. 31, 20th December 1981

drum and fife; drummond *noun*

1 a knife *UK*

Rhyming slang.

• —Julian Franklyn, *A Dictionary of Rhyming Slang*, 1960
• —Ray Puxley, *Cockney Rabbit*, 1992

2 a wife *UK*

Rhyming slang.

• —Bodmin Dark, *Dirty Cockney Rhyming Slang*, 2003

drummed out of the Gestapo for cruelty *adjective*

unduly authoritarian, especially when applied to a senior police officer *UK*

• —*The Official Encyclopaedia of New Scotland Yard*, 1999

drummer *noun*

1 a housebreaker, especially one who steals from unoccupied premises; a confidence trickster who poses as a door-to-door salesman or similar *UK, 1856*

• Ask me who, in my opinion, is the greatest drummer of modern times[.]—Charles Raven, *Underworld Nights*, p. 31, 1956
• —Angela Devlin, *Prison Patter*, p. 48, 1996

2 a poker player who plays only with good hands or good odds favouring his hand *US*

A play on the operative adjective of **TIGHT** used to describe such a player.

• —George Percy, *The Language of Poker*, p. 31, 1988

3 a railway yard conductor *US*

• —Norman Carlisle, *The Modern Wonder Book of Trains and Railroading*, p. 262, 1946

drummie *noun*

a drum-majorette *SOUTH AFRICA, 1972*

• Drummies put their best feet forward.—*Sunday Times (South Africa)*, 19th November 2000

drumming *noun*

daylight-theft from empty premises *UK*

From **DRUM** (to steal from empty premises).

• After being caught, debabbed, and ducked in a fountain, he gave up this form of "drumming"[.]—Charles Raven, *Underworld Nights*, p. 15, 1956
• Drumming is what you might call basic burglary. You pick a dead gaff – a house you know or think is empty – sound the drum by knocking at the front door to make sure[.]—Charles Raven, *Underworld Nights*, p. 32, 1956

drumstick *noun*

a leg, especially a shapely female leg *UK, 1770*

• I dig your well-stacked drumsticks – they make me nervous, Chick! —Dan Burley, *Diggeth Thou?*, p. 34, 1959

- A sharply dressed girl, wearing high heels, had emerged from the building and was cutting diagonally across Grover Whalen Square. "Just dig them drumsticks!" —Ross Russell, *The Sound*, p. 116, 1961

d-runk *adjective*
drunk *US*
- —Connie Eble (Editor), *UNC-CH Campus Slang*, p. 3, Fall 2001

drunkalog *noun*
in twelve-step recovery programmes such as Alcoholics Anonymous, a long story recounted at a programme meeting, dwelling on the addiction and its manifestations rather than recovery *US*
- —Christopher Cavanaugh, *AA to Z*, p. 82, 1998

drunkard *noun*
a passenger train running late on a Saturday night *US*
- —Ramon Adams, *The Language of the Railroader*, p. 50, 1977

drunk as a cunt *adjective*
very drunk *UK*
Presumed to date from late C19; remembered by Beale, in 1984, as a variation of the traditional folk song 'Seven Drunken Nights': 'Oh, you're drunk, you're drunk, you stupid old cunt / You're drunk as a cunt can be'.

drunk as a lord *adjective*
being in a state of drunkenness *UK, 1796*
One of the more notable similes for 'drunk'.
- "I do believe you're drunk as a lord." I nod, don't really care if I have another drink or another line. —Darren Francis, *The Sprawl [britpulp]*, p. 304, 1999

drunk as a skunk *adjective*
very drunk *UK*
Derives not from the characteristics of a skunk but, most likely, simply from the rhyme; or possibly as a slurring of **DRUNK AS A CUNT**. Widely known.
- — *e-cyclopaedia*, 20th March 2002

drunk as a thousand dollars *adjective*
very drunk *CANADA, 1989*
- When loggers came to town to spend their stake, some indeed spent a thousand dollars along skid road in a few days of enthusiasm. —Tom Parkin, *WetCoast Words*, p. 49, 1989

drunk as Chloe *adjective*
very drunk *AUSTRALIA, 1892*
The identity of the apparently besozzled Chloe is a mystery.
- I got as Drunk as Chloe the night they closed Thurstan's, the last pub in Dundas. —Patsy Adam-Smith, *Folklore of the Australian Railwaymen*, p. 73, 1969

drunk as Cooter Brown *adjective*
very drunk *US*
- In Washington county, Arkansas, people used to say "drunker than Cooter Brown", but nobody seems to know who Cooter Brown was. —Vance Randolph and George P. Wilson, *Down in the Holler*, p. 175, 1953
- The last time she had seen Connie, the broad had been learning against the front fence of a house on 132nd Street, puking her guts out. Drunk as Cooter Brown. —Robert Deane Pharr, *Giveadamn Brown*, p. 20, 1978

drunkathon *noun*
a session of excessive drinking *UK, 2003*
- The drunkathon started on Sept. 14th at the Deutches Haus for Oktoberfest[.] — *Scat Magazine (New Orleans)*, December 2004

drunk bumps *noun*
small bumps delineating lanes on motorways and roads *US*
So named because of their role in alerting drunk drivers that they are straying out of their lane.
- —Lewis Poteet, *Car & Motorcyle Slang*, p. 74, 1992

drunken *adjective*
(used of a wink in tiddlywinks) behaving unpredictably *US*
- — *Verbatim*, p. 526, December 1977

drunken forest *noun*
in the permafrost area of northern Canada, trees tilted in many directions by natural forces and not held by their shallow root systems *CANADA*
- High winds or earth movements sometimes capsize whole areas of these unstably based trees, causing what are known as "drunken forests." — *Maclean's*, p. 92/4, 14th September 1957

drunkie *noun*
an alcoholic *UK, 1861*
- Actually, I think all addiction starts wiht soda. Every drunkie and junkie did soda first. But no one counts that. —Chris Rock, *Rock This!*, p. 62, 1997

drunkometer *noun*
any device used to measure a motorist's blood alcohol content *US*
- — *American Speech*, p. 268, December 1962: 'The language of traffic policemen'

drunk tank *noun*
a jail cell where drunk prisoners are detained *US, 1947*
- Uncle R & J Wolf and Papa spent twenty days in the drunk tank at The Dalles jail[.] —Ken Kesey, *One Flew Over the Cuckoo's Nest*, p. 274, 1962
- Drunk tank full to overflowing / Motherfuckers wall to wall / Coming twice as fast as going / Heads get big and the tank gets small. —Ken Kesey, *Last Whole Earth Catalog*, p. 234, 1971
- They stop off for a shot and a beer and can't see their way home. End up in a drunk tank. —Elmore Leonard, *Touch*, p. 62, 1977

drunk wagon *noun*
a police van used for rounding up public drunks *US*
- [T]he thought of a drunken policeman loading drunks in the drunk wagon struck him as particularly funny. —Joseph Wambaugh, *The New Centurions*, p. 298, 1970

druthers *noun*
a preference *US, 1870*
- [I]f she had her druthers, she would be there now instead of climbing toward the place that rocked her with fear[.] —Toni Morrison, *Love*, p. 160, 2003

dry *noun*
1 an instance of an actor forgetting the lines *UK, 1945*
- —Gavin Holt, *No Curtain for Cora*, 1950

2 a politician who espouses economic caution, especially a Conservative under the leadership of Margaret Thatcher *UK, 1983*
Coined as an antonym for **WET** (a middle-of-the-road politician).

▸ **on the dry**
in a state of refraining from drinking any alcohol *US*
- Jackie Gleason suffered fainting spells – and has gone "on the dry" for three months. — *San Francisco Examinaer*, p. 3 (II), 31st May 1957

Dry *noun*
▸ **the Dry**
the dry season in Australia's tropical north *AUSTRALIA, 1908*
- It was thundering then, the whole sky shattered by lightning; that hardly ever happens during the Dry —B. Wongar *Walg*, p. 123, 1983

dry *verb*
of an actor, to forget your lines during a performance *UK, 1934*
- [E]very actor has experienced the awful sensation of "drying" on stage – that moment when, inexplicably, a line or word refuses to come to hand when you need it. — *The Guardian*, 5th September 2001

dry *adjective*
1 of a heavy drinker or alcoholic, doing without alcohol, not drinking, nor under the influence of alcohol *UK*
- I'd been dry for a whole month, which had been a huge effort for me 'cos I love me pint[.] —Ben Elton, *High Society*, p. 12, 2002

2 without money *US, 1942*
- — *The Annals of the American Academy of Political and Social Sciences*, p. 124, May 1950
- —Albert H. Morehead, *The Complete Guide to Winning Poker*, p. 262, 1967
- The guys inside the counting room were all slipped in there to skim the joint dry. — *Casino*, 1995

dry *adverb*
in a simulated manner *US*
- You chump, if you had any smarts you'd have pieced it together, but they dry-humped you with a couple of quarters[.] —Edwin Torres, *Carlito's Way*, p. 49, 1975
- A few people on the ground were using the desperate infantryman's trick of dry firing their empty rifles and simulating a recoil in order to keep the approaching Ashbals ducking. —Nelson DeMille, *By the Rivers of Babylon*, p. 377, 1978
- C'mon sir. Just dry-shoot it once. —Robert Mason, *Chickenhawk*, p. 127, 1983
- One can dry hump the local roundheels without fear of infection, dry fire a pistol and spend not one day in jail. But dry snitching in prison carries the same mortal penalty as the real thing. —Seth Morgan, *Homeboy*, p. 44, 1990

dry as a dead dingo's donger *adjective*
extremely dry; extremely thirsty; parched *AUSTRALIA, 1971*
That is, as dry 'as the penis of a dead dingo' (a native dog living in arid regions).
- I really needed that, I was as dry as a dead dingo's donger. — *The Adventures of Barry McKenzie*, 1972

dry as a kookburra's kyber *adjective*
extremely dry, parched *AUSTRALIA*
- I'm dry as a kookaburra's kyber too. — Barry Humphries, *Bazza Pulls It Off!*, 1971

dry as a Pommy's towel *adjective*
extremely dry; extremely thirsty; parched *AUSTRALIA*
From the notion that English people do not wash, a stereotype long held in Australia.
- It's as dry, as he would say, as a Pommy's bath towel. — Kathy Lette, *Girls' Night Out*, p. 120, 1987

dry as a whore's cunt on Sunday morning *adjective*
extremely dry, especially of exploratory oil drillings *US*
- [T]he oilman says, "Well, that's the way it goes. Some holes got lubrication, and some is dry as a whore's cunt on Sunday morning." — William Burroughs, *Queer*, p. 45, 1985

dry balls *noun*
an ache in the testicles from sexual activity not resulting in ejaculation *BAHAMAS*
- — John A. Holm, *Dictionary of Bahamian English*, p. 67, 1982

dry bath *noun*
in prison, a strip search *UK, 1933*
- At reception, they gave him a very perfunctory searching instead of the thorough and humiliating going over, known as the "dry bath", to which the mugs were subjected. — Charles Raven, *Underworld Nights*, p. 137, 1956
- — Angela Devlin, *Prison Patter*, p. 48, 1996

dry clean *verb*
to wash your body with just a face cloth *TRINIDAD AND TOBAGO*
- — Lise Winer, *Dictionary of the English/Creole of Trinidad & Tobago*, 2003

dry clean Methodist *noun*
a Christian belonging to a church that does not practise full-immersion baptism *US, 1970*
- — Frederic G. Cassidy, *Dictionary of American Regional English, Volume II*, p. 214, 1991

dry drunk *noun*
a person who behaves like an alcoholic even though they are abstaining from drinking *US*
A term used in twelve-step recovery programmes such as Alcoholics Anonymous.
- — Christopher Cavanaugh, *AA to Z: Addictionary of the 12-Step Culture*, p. 82, 1998
- Whether George W. Bush is or was an alcoholic is not the point here. I am taking him at his word that he stopped what he termed "heavy drinking" in 1986, at age 40. The point here is that, based on Bush's recent behavior, he could very well be a "dry drunk". — *American Politics Journal*, 23rd September 2002

dry Dutch courage *noun*
drugs *US*
- — *Maledicta*, p. 54, 1986 – 1987: 'A continuation of a glossary of ethnic slurs in American English'

dry-eye *adjective*
concealing any emotional reaction *BAHAMAS*
- — John A. Holm, *Dictionary of Bahamian English*, p. 67, 1982

dry-fire; dry-snap *verb*
to practise shooting a pistol without live ammunition *US*
- Some Colloquialisms of the Handgunner — *American Speech*, p. 193, October 1957

dryfoot *noun*
in a Nova Scotia fishing village, a person who never goes fishing *CANADA*
- His hand was a bit grasping, when he sold / A little slow to open when he bought / They said he was dryfooted. — Charles Bruce, *The Mulgrave Road*, 1985
- A dryfoot is a person who talks a lot about fishing but never goes. — Lewis Poteet, *The South Shore Phrase Book*, p. 40, 1999

dry fuck *noun*
sex simulated while clothed *US, 1938*
- At best we could manage a dry fuck. And go home limping, our balls aching like sixty toothaches. — Henry Miller, *Plexus*, p. 380, 1963
- Well, Dan said, "why don't you say that you got a dry fuck and I'll say that I got bare tit. — Bob Greene, *Be True to Your School*, p. 117, 1987

dry-fuck *verb*
1 to stimulate or pantomime sexual intercourse while clothed *US, 1935*
- You could almost dryfuck, right there standing in the sawdust. — *The Berkeley Tribe*, p. 13, 5th-12th September 1969
- I lost my Frisco broad for a dame I never even dry-fucked when I had the chance. — Oscar Zeta Acosta, *The Autobiography of a Brown Buffalo*, p. 63, 1972
- Jenny and I would drive out into the country and park and neck and dry fuck through our clothes[.] — Larry Heinemann, *Close Quarters*, p. 133 – 134, 1977
- I had never seen an exotic dancer who opened her act with a brief sermon, and then dry fucked a copy of the Bible. — Dan Jenkins, *Life Its Ownself*, p. 128, 1984

2 to penetrate a vagina or rectum without benefit of lubricant *US*
- — *Maledicta*, p. 231, 1979

dry goods *noun*
clothing *US, 1851*
- We go up to her trap, and she remove the dry goods. — William Burroughs, *Naked Lunch*, p. 119, 1957

drygulch *verb*
to ambush *US, 1930*
- Even when some stage got drygulched, or an Indian shot some drunk in Kamloops or somewhere, he never associated the event with a drama someone would want to read about in Australia. — George Bowering, *Caprice*, p. 105, 1987

drygulcher *noun*
an outlaw who would hide in small canyons and ambush travellers *US, 1930*
- Drygulchers, bushwhackers, and hold-up men suffered assaults on their nerves that would send many an ordinary citizen around the bend. — George Bowering, *Caprice*, p. 124, 1988

dryhanded
inordinately proud, snobbish *US, 1947*
- After the settlement of Shelburne [NS] (1783), " Barrington began to consider itself the seat of learning and to look down its nose somewhat at the other villages, which in turn accused [it] of becoming dryhanded, too high-minded. — *"From Norfolk to the Hawk," Dalhousie Review*, 1953

dry heaves *noun*
non-productive vomiting or retching *US*
- Jimm had woken up with the dry heaves and the thought of a beer almost gave him the wet heaves[.] — William T. Vollman, *Whores for Gloria*, p. 9, 1991

dry high *noun*
marijuana *US, 1977*
- — Richard A. Spears, *The Slang and Jargon of Drugs and Drink*, p. 179, 1986
- — Mike Haskins, *Drugs*, p. 287, 2003

dry hole *noun*
a military operation based on poor intelligence and producing no results *US*
- — Gregory Clark, *Words of the Vietnam War*, p. 156, 1990

dry hoot *noun*
a joint rolled tight and not lit but sniffed *CANADA*
- He finishes rolling a joint, using the absolute minimum of paper. [It] looks taut as a stuffed sausage skin. He brings it to his lips unlit, and inhales it that way, an act he calls a dry hoot. Dry hoots are the best way to savor the flavor, he says. — Brian Preston, *Pot Planet*, p. 19, 2002

dry-hump *verb*
to simulate sexual intercourse while clothed *US, 1964*
- The girl who has let me undo her brassiere and dry-hump her at the dormitory door, grew up in this white house. — Philip Roth, *Portnoy's Complaint*, p. 248, 1969
- Sperm will not "swim" down your belly into your cunt after dry-humping to a climax. — *Screw*, p. 23, 3rd November 1969
- "D.H.T.I.C," which stood for "Dry Humpted Till I Came." — Richard Price, *The Wanderers*, p. 101, 1974
- And that broad shimmied and pranced around near-naked, jiggling her sweating little titties like someone juggling two one-pound lumps of greasy, shining hamburger, and dry-humping the air with sure and steady rhythmic thrusts of her nifty little snatch[.] — Larry Heinemann, *Paco's Story*, p. 13, 1986

- They would swing me around, with my bad haircut and plucked eyebrows, and dry hump me on the dance floor. —Sandra Bernhard, *Confessions of a Pretty Lady*, p. 66, 1988
- One can dry hump the local roundheels without fear of infection[.] —Seth Morgan, *Homeboy*, p. 44, 1990
- As we publicly dry-humped, our hormones started pumping and certain organs began to swell, including our bladders. —Anka Radakovich, *The Wild Girls Club*, p. 75, 1994
- Once, when I was being dryhnumped by some other man on the hood of a car in the alleway, Joe was mad and said, "Don't you know they're just after one thing?" —Jennifer Blowdryer, *White Trash Debutante*, p. 40, 1997
- So now it's my fault your girlfriend caught you dry-humping in a bathroom stall? — *200 Cigarettes*, 1999
- During my teenage yeras I relied on dubious behaviors known as finger-fucking, dry-humping, or pulling out, until I got my driver's license[.] —Rita Ciresi, *Pink Slip*, p. 128, 1999
- A dancer always dry-humps at least one audience member. — *Nerve*, p. 51, August-September 2000

dry lay *noun*

sexual intercourse simulated through clothing *US*

- You get a chance, grab the down-draft blonde bumping the Marine by the post there. Dry lay? Man, she'll grind it off. —Thurston Scott, *Cure it with Honey*, p. 152, 1951

dry out *verb*

1 to undergo a course of treatment designed to break dependence on alcohol *US, 1908*

- "How's the old lady?" "Dryin' out, "Malatesta said. —George V. Higgins, *The Rat on Fire*, p. 111, 1981
- I've not been patronised this much since the Queen opened the drying out ward in the Southern General. —Ian Pattison, *Rab C. Nesbitt*, 1988

2 to detoxify from heroin addiction *US*

- —Donald Louria, *Nightmare Drugs*, p. 15, 1966
- —Eugene Landy, *The Underground Dictionary*, p. 72, 1971

dry root *noun*

1 an act of simulated sexual intercourse while clothed *AUSTRALIA*

- At North Cronulla we'd progressed to dry roots. When we graduated to our new gang at Greenhills, we'd hit the big time. It was time for the spreading of the legs and the splitting up the middle. —Kathy Lette and Gabrielle Carey, *Puberty Blues*, p. 24, 1979
- Dry Root: A very basic, elementary dance step first practised outside school socials and perfected in late adolescence on doorsteps and in dark corners. —Phil Jarratt, *Sex: The Dictionary*, p. 20, 1984

2 sex without the benefit of lubrication *NEW ZEALAND*

- —David McGill, *David McGill's Complete Kiwi Slang Dictionary*, p. 43, 1998

dry-root *verb*

to simulate sexual intercourse while clothed *AUSTRALIA*

- [T]he magpies sang and the sprinkler sprinkled and the four neighbours watched their pets dry-root the furniture[.] —Gretel Killeen, *Hot Buns and Ophelia get a Bloke*, p. 30, 2000

dry rub *noun*

body contact, implicitly sexual *US*

- —Hyman E. Goldin et al., *Dictionary of American Underworld Lingo*, p. 63, 1950

dry run *noun*

1 a trip to court in which nothing happens *US*

- —Jim Crotty, *How to Talk American*, p. 54, 1997

2 a false alarm *US*

- —*American Speech*, p. 158–160, May 1959: 'Smoke jumping words'

dry shite *noun*

a boring individual *IRELAND*

- Who were they? I can't remember. A few dry shites in suits. —Joseph O'Connor, *Red Roses and Petrol*, p. 95, 1995
- 'You're only a bollix,' I said and laughed, hoping the rest of the crowd would join in. But they didn't. Silence. What a crowd of fuckin' dryshites! —Ardal O'Hanlon, *The Talk of the Town*, p. 150, 1998

dry-snap *verb*

▷ see: DRY-FIRE

dry snitch *noun*

a person who unintentionally or indirectly but intentionally betrays or informs on another *US*

- —James Harris, *A Convict's Dictionary*, p. 31, 1989

dry-snitch *verb*

to betray or inform on someone either unintentionally or indirectly but intentionally *US*

- [W]ho would happily drysnitch you off in the messhall if they saw you stealing an extra chop from the stainless-steel steamtables. —Clarence Cooper Jr, *The Farm*, p. 27, 1967
- —*Maledicta*, p. 264, Summer/Winter 1981: 'By its slang, ye shall know it: the pessimism of prison life'

dry up *noun*

to inject a drug intravenously *UK*

Probably a variation of DRAW UP.

- —Mike Haskins, *Drugs*, p. 290, 2003

dry up *verb*

to stop talking *US, 1853*

Often used as an imperative.

dry water *noun*

in Nova Scotia, an area formerly covered by water but silted in *CANADA*

- "In a few years it'll be dry water behind Warren Doane's" – a silted-up area which was formerly covered by water, caused by the building of a causeway which blocked a channel. —Lewis Poteet, *The South Shore Phrase Book*, p. 40, 1999

D/s *noun*

in sado-masochistic sex, domination and submission *US*

- Since the D/s (Dominance/submission) and B&D (bondage and discipline) crowds often incorporate dressing for pleasure as a related part of their lifestyle, it is not surprising to find that many of the posts relate to this lifestyle. —Nancy Tamosaitis, *net.sex*, p. 99, 1995

D's *noun*

Dayton tire rims *US*

- —Pamela Munro, *U.C.L.A. Slang*, p. 56, 1997
- Riding in a car with Dayton rims – skatin' on Daytons – would be 'sittin' on D's'. —Ethan Hilderbrant, *Prison Slang*, p. 164, 1998

DT *noun*

1 a police officer on a street crime beat *US*

- Jonah Perry returned to the neighborhood the night of the shooting and proclaimed, "We got a DT," street slang for "detective." —*Washington Post*, p. A1, 13th August 1985
- —Carsten Stroud, *Close Pursuit*, p. 271, 1987
- —Terry Williams, *The Cocaine Kids*, p. 136, 1989

2 heroin *UK*

- —Mike Haskins, *Drugs*, p. 283, 2003

DTK *adjective*

handsome, dressed sharply *US*

An abbreviation of 'down to kill', 'down' meaning 'ready' and 'kill' in the figurative sense.

- —*Current Slang*, p. 1, Spring 1967

d to d *adjective*

door to door *UK*

- Used to get into Bond Street in forty minutes d. to d. – not two and a quarter hours. —Henry Sloane, *Sloane's Inside Guide to Sex & Drugs & Rock 'n' Roll*, p. 55, 1985

D town *nickname*

1 Dallas, Texas *US*

- —Ethan Hilderbrant, *Prison Slang*, p. 42, 1998

2 Denver, Colorado *US*

- I can run to Denver running like this / All the way to "D" town running like this. —Sandee Shaffer Johnson, *Cadences*, p. 66, 1986

DTR *noun*

a conversation in which two people *d*efine *t*heir *r*elationship *US*

- —Connie Eble (Editor), *UNC-CH Campus Slang*, p. 2, November 2002

DTs *noun*

1 tremens, the withdrawal symptoms of an alcohol or drug addiction *US, 1857*

- If I'd acted like you do, I'd have died of tuberculosis or the d.t.s long ago. —Jim Thompson, *Roughneck*, p. 37, 1954
- Someone who smokes a few cigarettes a day is no more likely to go insane than a man who takes a few cocktails before dinner is likely to come down with the DTs. —William Burroughs, *Junky*, 1977
- —Angela Devlin, *Prison Patter*, p. 48, 1996

2 a pair of men's close-fitting and revealing nylon swimming trunks *AUSTRALIA*

Standing for DICK TOGS.

- Dick togs are also called DT's. I guess because dick togs sounds a bit rude. — *Wordmap (www.abc.net.au/wordmap)*, 2003

du *noun*
used as a term of address in male-to-male greetings *US*
An abbreviation of the already short **DUDE**.
- —Connie Eble (Editor), *UNC-CH Campus Slang*, p. 3, Fall 2000

dual *noun*
a person who is willing to play either the sadist or masochist role in a sadomasochism encounter *US*
- — *What Color is Your Handkerchief*, p. 5, 1979

dual sack time *noun*
time spent sleeping with someone *US*
- — *American Speech*, p. 310, December 1946: 'More Air Force slang'
- — *American Speech*, p. 76–79, February 1963: 'Anent "Marine Corps Slang"'

Duane Eddys *noun*
cash money *UK*
Rhyming slang for **READIES**, formed from the name of US guitarist Duane Eddy (b.1938).
- You get some nasty little Paul Anka (wanker) who's a bit short of the Duane Eddys[.] —Mervyn Stutter, *Getting Nowhere Fast*, 21st May 2004

dub *noun*
1 the last part of a marijuana cigarette that is possible to smoke *US*
- [T]ake a head of this Skunk / Twist up a big bomb of this serious dope / Smoke it down to tha dub or roach tip / So much damn resin it's startin' to drip[.] —Tone Loc, *Cheeba Cheeba*, 1989

2 a cigarette, especially when used to extend a marijuana cigarette *US*
- — *American Speech*, p. 59, Spring-Summer 1975

3 a car wheel rim *US*
Usually in the plural.
- —Connie Eble (Editor), *UNC-CH Campus Slang*, p. 2, November 2002
- Dubs, blades, shoes, sneakers, twinkies – street slang for custom wheels – are status symbols, made popular by athletes and rap stars. — *Cincinnati Enquirer*, p. 1B, 29th August 2003

4 the Western Hockey League in Canada *CANADA*
- From the initial sound of the acronym for the WHL (Western Hockey League), the organization is known as the Dub. — *Globe and Mail West*, p. 22, March 1991

5 a twenty-dollar note *US*
An abbreviation of **DOUBLE SAWBUCK**.
- —Don Wilmeth, *The Language of American Popular Entertainment*, p. 80, 1981
- —Pamela Munro, *U.C.L.A. Slang*, p. 64, 2001
- —Don R. McCreary (Editor), *Dawg Speak*, 2001
- —Rick Ayers (Editor), *Berkeley High Slang Dictionary*, p. 19, 2004

6 an incompetent and inferior person *US, 1887*
- A well known model can easily knock down a grand a week. Even dubs make $500. —Lee Mortimer, *Women Confidential*, p. 131, 1960

dub *verb*
1 to have sex with *US*
- A woman doesn't count all the miscellaneous dick: the guy she met at the club; that time she fucked Keith Sweat; the local she dubbed in Jamaica. —Chris Rock, *Rock This!*, p. 130, 1997

2 to close, to lock up *UK, 1753*
Prison use, from the obsolete sense (a key).
- [G]et up them stairs and get yourself a jug of water and then dub your door up. —Frank Norman, *Bang To Rights*, p. 14, 1958
- —Angela Devlin, *Prison Patter*, p. 48, 1996

3 to criticise, or otherwise dismiss, in speech *UK*
Teen slang.
- — Susie Dent, *The Language Report*, p. 76, 2003

Dub *nickname*
someone from Dublin *IRELAND*
- Welcome to The Joy, don't fuck with the Dubs —Howard Paul, *The Joy*, p. 44, 1996
- In the old days, when Dublin was faraway and hidden under smog and had, as its chief attraction the country's first McDonalds, hating the Dubs was an inherited thing — *Irish Times*, 31st August 2002

dube *noun*
▷ see: **DOOBIE**

dubber *noun*
a cigarette *US*
- — *American Speech*, p. 59, Spring-Summer 1975: 'Razorback slang'

dubbies *noun*
the female breasts *US*
- Christ, the dubbies on Lumper. —Richard Farina, *Been Down So Long, Looks Like Up to Me*, p. 80, 1966

dubbo *noun*
a fool *AUSTRALIA, 1973*
From the country town Dubbo, seen as a place of country bumpkins.
- —Jim Ramsay, *Cop It Sweet!*, p. 32, 1977
- The kings annoyed [the suburb Kings Cross] was not at all what the dubbos had told him. —Ryan Aven-Bray, *Ridgey Didge Oz Jack Lang*, p. 10, 1983

dub-dub-dub *noun*
the World Wide Web (www) *UK*
A spoken shortening.
- — Susie Dent, *The Language Report*, p. 30, 2003

dub dub dub *verb*
to contact or use the Internet *UK*
By ellipsis of each initial in the conventional abbreviation for World Wide Web.
- —Craig Charles, *Word for Word (BBC Radio 4)*, 19th January 2005

dubes *noun*
a central nervous system stimulant *UK*
- —Tom Hibbert, *Rockspeak!*, p. 55, 1983

dubich *noun*
a marijuana cigarette *US*
- —Jim Emerson-Cobb, *Scratching the Dragon*, April 1997

Dublin *noun*
any neighourhood populated by large numbers of Irish immigrants *US, 1963*
- —Frederic G. Cassidy, *Dictionary of American Regional English, Volume II*, p. 219, 1991

dubs *noun*
twenty dollars; something sold for twenty dollars *US*
- —Rick Ayers (Editor), *Slang Dictionary*, p. 8, 2001

Dubya *nickname*
George W. Bush, 43rd President of the US *US*
A deliberately Texan pronunciation of 'W', necessarily included in his name during the presidential campaign of 1999 and 2000 to differentiate him from his father George Bush, 41st President of the US.
- Now, let us (the Forward-thinking Motherfuckers) deliver her from Dubya's oil-pimps[.] —Brain Donor *Get Off Your Pretty Face*, 2001
- While he's now the defender of the Christian world, back in the early 70s George "Dubya" Bush was a rock-hard party God. — *Ministry*, p. 41, January 2002
- Welsh snub for Dubya[.] — *Evening Standard*, p. 10, 7th March 2003

ducat *noun*
in prison, a written order given to a prisoner for an appointment *US, 1926*
- That night after dinner, when the ducat officer passed the cell, he called "Cain," laid a ducat on the bars and passed on. The boy climbed down from the upper bunk to take the slip of paper. —Malcolm Braly, *On the Yard*, p. 246, 1967

ducats *noun*
money *US, 1866*
- You've fucked off all your ducats gambling. —Seth Morgan, *Homeboy*, p. 238, 1990
- He's single, he's 47, and he earns minor ducats for a thankless job. — *Clueless*, 1995
- C.R.E.A.M. Cash Rules Everything Around Me. It's just an old word for money. After bread and readies, but before corn and cheddar and ducats and collats. About the same time as wonga. —Diran Adebayo, *My Once Upon A Time*, p. 59, 2000
- [They] bet $400 of their own ducats against the casino point spread on five NFL games. — *The Source*, p. 102, March 2002

duchess *noun*
1 a wife *UK, 1895*
An affectionate title, adopted from 'the wife of a duke' (the highest hereditary rank of nobility), originally given to coster-mongers' wives, perhaps in relation to the coster-royalty of Pearly Kings and Queens. May be a shortened form of **DUCHESS OF FIFE**, or extended from **DUTCH** (a spouse).

2 a girlfriend *US*
- —Lou Shelly, *Hepcats Jive Dictionary*, p. 11, 1945

3 a female member of a youth gang *US*
- —Kenn "Naz" Young, *Naz's Dictionary of Teen Slang*, p. 35, 1993

4 a comfortably-off or grandly well-appointed homosexual man *UK*
- —Paul Baker, *Polari*, p. 173, 2002

duchess *verb*

to treat as a VIP *AUSTRALIA, 1956*
- This was a personal and class tragedy: the boilermaker from the bush who was duchessed, seduced into becoming a knight and thus alienated from his own kind.— *National Times*, p. 12, 31st March 1979

Duchess of Fife *noun*

a wife *UK*

Rhyming slang; often suggested as the origin of **DUTCH** (a wife) and/or **DUCHESS**. Recorded, with reference to Albert Chevalier's song, 'My Old Dutch', 1892, by Julian Franklyn, *A Dictionary of Rhyming Slang*, 1961.

Duchess of Teck; duchess *noun*

a cheque *UK*

Rhyming slang, formed from the title of Her Serene Highness Princess Victoria Mary ('Princess May') of Teck (1867–1953), queen consort of George V, or from her mother, Princess Mary Adelaide, who was entitled Duchess of Teck from 1871. The husband, **DUKE OF TECK**, serves the same purpose in slang.
- —Julian Franklyn, *A Dictionary of Rhyming Slang*, 1960

Duchess of York *noun*

pork *UK*

Rhyming slang, not recorded until after Sarah ('Fergie') Ferguson (b.1959) became Duchess of York in 1986.

duck *noun*

1 in cricket, a score of zero/nought *UK, 1868*

A shortening of the original term 'duck's egg' which derived from the shape of 0 written in the scorebook.
- —Simon Hughes, *Cricket 4*, 2001
- But then he was out for a third-ball duck as Leicestershire made a timid response [.]— *The Guardian*, 22nd May 2003

2 an unrelentingly gullible and trusting person; an odd person *US, 1848*

Prison usage.
- I have no respect for a duck who runs up to me on the yard all buddy-buddy, and then feels obliged not to sit down with me.—Eldridge Cleaver, *Soul on Ice*, p. 47, 1968
- —Paul Glover, *Words from the House of the Dead: Prison Writings from Soledad*, 1974
- —James Harris, *A Convict's Dictionary*, p. 31, 1989

3 in pool, a shot that cannot be missed or a game that cannot be lost *US*
- —Steve Rushin, *Pool Cool*, p. 12, 1990

4 an attractive target for a robbery *US*
- It was considered by hustlers a duck 'cause it was on a dark corner, there usually wasn't no peoples in sight, and the traffic was slow. —Henry Williamson, *Hustler!*, p. 155, 1965

5 a stolen car discovered by police through serendipitous checking of license plates *US*

An abbreviation of **SITTING DUCK**.
- Ducks? Ohh, I get one a week maybe. There's plenty of hot cars sitting around Hollenbeck.—Joseph Wambaugh, *The New Centurions*, p. 41, 1970

6 a portable urinal for male hospital patients *US*
- — *Maledicta*, p. 56, Summer 1980: 'Not sticks and stones, but names: more medical pejoratives'

7 a prison sentence of two years *US*

Probably from the shape of 2.
- —Charles Shafer, *Folk Speech in Texas Prisons*, p. 203, 1990

8 in a deck of playing cards, a two *US*
- —George Percy, *The Language of Poker*, p. 31, 1988

9 a surfer who lingers in the water, rarely catching a wave *US*
- —Trevor Cralle, *The Surfin'ary*, p. 32, 1991

10 an admission ticket for a paid event *US*

An abbreviation of **DUCAT**.
- —Lou Shelly, *Hepcats Jive Dictionary*, p. 11, 1945
- —Clarence Major, *Dictionary of Afro-American Slang*, p. 49, 1970

11 a firefighter *US*

New York police slang.
- —Samuel M. Katz, *Anytime Anywhere*, p. 387, 1997

12 inexpensive wine *US*

An abbreviation and then generic use of Cold Duck, a sparkling red wine that was extremely popular in the 1960s and 70s.
- —David Claerbaut, *Black Jargon in White America*, p. 63, 1972

13 used as a term of address, usually an endearment *UK, 1590*

Also used in the plural since 1936.

duck *verb*

1 to avoid *US, 1864*
- You duckin' me Dwight?— *Natural Born Killers*, 1994

2 in pool, to miss a shot or lose a game intentionally to mislead an opponent as to your true ability *US*
- —Mike Shamos, *The Illustrated Encyclopedia of Billiards*, p. 84, 1993

▸ **duck a date**

in circus and carnival usage, to fail to perform as scheduled *US*
- —Don Wilmeth, *The Language of American Popular Entertainment*, p. 81, 1981

duck and dive *verb*

to avoid or evade, especially with regard to legality or responsibility; to dodge work, to shirk; hence, to avoid regular employment but make a living nevertheless *UK, 1960*

Rhyming slang for **SKIVE** (to avoid or evade).
- Ducking and diving – and dreaming. That's Arthur.—Anthony Masters, *Minder*, p. 93, 1984
- Ducking and diving, ducking and thriving.—Terry Victor, *A Family Affair*, 1992
- Wheelin' dealin'. Duckin' divin'. Chargin' abou'.—Nick Barlay, *Curvy Lovebox*, p. 109, 1997
- He knew I was ducking and diving. Mainly diving.—Jimmy Stockin, *On The Cobbles*, p. 165, 2000

duck arse *verb*

when smoking, to wet the cigarette end with saliva *UK*

Probably a back-formation from **DUCK'S ARSE**, changing 'duck' from 'a bird' to a verb.

duckbill *noun*

an experimental 12-gauge shotgun tested by US Navy SEALS in Vietnam *US*
- —Linda Reinberg, *In the Field*, p. 69, 1991

duck bucket *noun*

in poker, a poor hand that wins a pot, especially a pair of twos *US*
- —John Vorhaus, *The Big Book of Poker Slang*, p. 15, 1996

duck butt *noun*

1 a short person *US, 1939*
- I'll also beat the living shit out of every one of your duckbutts and my teammates will help me.—Pat Conroy, *The Lords of Discipline*, p. 207, 1980

2 a hair-style popular in the early 1950s, in which the hair was tapered and curled on the nape of the neck like the feathers of a duck's tail *US*
- Judge Buchanan took issue with Von Tagen's haircut, a long, lanky affair that the judge bluntly said was called a duck butt in his mountain realm.— *San Francisco Examiner*, p. 3-', 15th March 1955

duck butter *noun*

smegma or other secretions that collect on and around the genitals *US, 1933*
- Plus, his fucksman's got a bit fist-raised dick that gotta be washed because it stays loaded with duckbutter and stinks like hell. —A.S. Jackson, *Gentleman Pimp*, p. 115, 1973

duck day *noun*

the day when a member of the US armed forces is honourably discharged *US*

An allusion to the US armed forces insignia designating honourable discharge known as the **RUPTURED DUCK**.
- — *American Speech*, p. 153, April 1946: 'GI words from the separation center and proctology ward'

duck-dive *verb*

in surfing, to push the nose of the surfboard down under a breaking wave *US*
- —Brian and Margaret Lowdon, *Competitive Surfing*, 1988

duck egg *noun*

a fool *UK*

Possibly from the cricketing term which derives from **DUCK** (zero).
- Like the duckegg I am, I'd hummed along. I always miss clues. —Jonathan Gash, *The Ten Word Game*, p. 43, 2003

duck factory *noun*
an area of marsh where ducks nest *CANADA*
• The duck factory is the name wildlife people give a southern prairie region which is the breeding ground for the majority of North America's hunted waterfowl — *Charlottetown Guardian*, p. 1/3, 18th June 1964

duck-fucker *noun*
a lazy person *US, 1986*
• That accused stated in CIC that, having passed the tests for chief and being recommended by his officers, to whom he sucks up shamelessly, especially to the XO, a notorious duck-fucker and nose-picker. — David Poyer, *The Med*, p. 258, 1988

duckhouse *noun*
▸ **one up against your duckhouse**
something to your detriment; one against you *AUSTRALIA, 1933*
• And a blooming lot of good that was, when Ma gave Minnie the sack at the end of the week on the plea that she was too young for housework – which was one up agen old Martha's duckhouse, depriving her of a kitchen minion. — Norman Lindsay, *Halfway to Anywhere*, p. 69, 1947

duckie *noun*
▹ see: DUCKY

duck out; duck out of *verb*
to avoid responsibility; to fail to attend a meeting *UK*
An elaboration of **DUCK** (to avoid).
• "Did you go last night?" "No, I ducked out" or "no, I ducked out of it". — Beale, 1984

duck plucker *noun*
used as a euphemism for 'motherfucker' *US*
• — Lanie Dills, *The Official CB Slanguage Language Dictionary*, p. 30, 1976

duck rest *noun*
a poor night's sleep *BARBADOS*
• — Frank A. Collymore, *Barbadian Dialect*, p. 42, 1965

ducks *noun*
money *US*
An abbreviation of **DUCATS**.
• — Anna Scotti and Paul Young, *Buzzwords*, p. 61, 1997

ducks and drakes *noun*
delirium tremens *AUSTRALIA, 1967*
Rhyming slang for **SHAKES**.
• — Jim Ramsay, *Cop It Sweet!*, p. 32, 1977
• — Ryan Aven-Bray, *Ridgey Didge Oz Jack Lang*, p. 24, 1983

ducks and geese *noun*
the police *AUSTRALIA, 1966*
• She was thinking of her lazy silvery moon [pimp], the ducks and geese, and the cost for the use of the drum [room] in the cracker joint [brothel] she operated from. — Ryan Aven-Bray, *Ridgey Didge Oz Jack Lang*, p. 24, 1983

duck's arse; duck's ass *noun*
1 a hairstyle popular in the early 1950s, especially among Teddy Boys; the hair was tapered and curled on the nape of the neck like the feathers of a duck's tail *UK, 1951*
Also widely known by the initials **DA**, and occasionally by the euphemistic 'duck's anatomy'.
• — Janey Ironside, *A Fashion Alphabet*, p. 191, 1968
• Long enough for a pompadour in front and a duck's ass in the back. — Piri Thomas, *Stories from El Barrio*, p. 56, 1978
• [R]adiating perfection from the crease in his duck's arse hairstyle down to the toes of his winklepicker boots. — Mark Pass, *Marc Bolan, The Sharper Word*, p. 39, 1998
• I had my hair in a duck's arse with a quiff. — Simon Napier-Bell, *Black Vinyl White Powder*, p. 10, 2001

2 a cigarette end that is over-moistened with a smoker's saliva *UK*
• I made sure my lips were dry so I wouldn't put a duck's arse on it. I took a small drag and gave the fag back to him quick. — Roddy Doyle, *Paddy Clarke Ha Ha Ha*, p. 252, 1993

3 an informant *UK*
Rhyming slang for **GRASS** (an informant), probably formed during the 1950s when the 'duck's arse' hairstyle was in fashion.
• — Ray Puxley, *Cockney Rabbit*, 1992

▸ **tighter than a duck's arse**
very drunk or drug-intoxicated *UK*
An oddly mixed metaphor.
• I was wired before I started drinking, strung out tighter than a duck's arse. — Ben Elton, *High Society*, p. 12, 2002

duck's disease; ducks' disease; duck-disease *noun*
shortness of stature, especially applied to short legs *UK, 1925*
A humorous reference to an anatomical characteristic of ducks.
• — Ryan Aven-Bray, *Ridgey Didge Oz Jack Lang*, p. 24, 1983

duck's guts *noun*
1 trouble *BARBADOS*
• If you get catch dong that, boy, you going to be in the duck's guts. — Frank A. Collymore, *Barbadian Dialect*, p. 42, 1965

2 something superlative *AUSTRALIA, 1979*
• This is the ducks guts, as we term it in Western Australia. — *Senate Hansard*, 9th November 1994

duck shoving *noun*
the passing of a problem on to another *NEW ZEALAND*
• — Louis S. Leland, *A Personal Kiwi-Yankee Dictionary*, p. 35, 1984

duck's nest *noun*
in oil drilling, a brick-lined hole under a boiler that enhances combustion *US*
• — Jerry Robertson, *Oil Slanguage*, p. 50, 1954

duck soup *noun*
an easy task; a cinch *US, 1902*
• — Lou Shelly, *Hepcats Jive Talk Dictionary*, p. 24, 1945
• I was duck soup there in that room with my back toward him and he missed. — Mickey Spillane, *One Lonely Night*, p. 130, 1951

duck suit *noun*
a brown and tan camouflage suit, not dissimilar to the suit worn by a duck hunter, issued to US special forces in Vietnam *US*
The colours were not particularly suited for Vietnam and the suits were largely rejected by the troops.
• — Gregory Clark, *Words of the Vietnam War*, p. 157, 1990

duck tail *noun*
1 a hair-style popular in the early 1950s in which a boy's hair was tapered and curled on the nape of the neck like the feathers of a duck's tail *US, 1943*
• They were held on $1,000 bail each, were forced to undergo something worse than jail: short haircuts to eliminate their long sideburns and "ducktail" coiffures. — *Life*, p. 29, 6th August 1951
• In a courtroom jam-packed with zoot suiters, the 19-year-old Ranson, who affects Hollywood-type clohtes and a duck-tail haircut, narrated events before and after he pumped five bullets from a 45 automatic[.] — *San Francisco Call Bulletin*, p. 1, 1st July 1953

2 an unruly South African youth *SOUTH AFRICA*
• The minister of justice, Charles R. Swart, who has been one of the main architects of apartheid, has hit on an ingenious soluiton for dealing with the "ducktails," as they call the criminal teddy boys out there[.] — *San Francisco News*, 23rd May 1959
• — Partridge, 1968

ducky; duckie *noun*
used as a term of address *UK, 1819*
Originally in general use, especially by women; from mid-C20, usage by men is often affected, implying homosexuality.
• SIMON: I mean lines, ducky, can you handle lines? GEORGE: I'll have a bash. — *A Hard Day's Night*, 1964
• JULIAN: Yoicks, tally-ho, ducky! SANDY: We are your actual Carnaby Hunt. — Barry Took and Marty Feldman, *Round The Horne*, 25th June 1967
• I didn't stop to ask him, ducky. — John Milne, *Alive and Kicking*, p. 26, 1998
• We knew they [gay men] spoke in squeaky voices, wore lipstick and said "ooh ducky", but none of had ever seen one. — Mark Steel, *Reasons to be Cheerful*, p. 22, 2001

ducky *adjective*
attractive, good *US, 1901*
• I could picture her ducky black body with the tiny waist and round, bucket-shaped hips. — Chester Himes, *If He Hollers Let Him Go*, p. 5, 1945

Ducky *nickname*
Le Duc Tho (1911 – 1990), North Vietnamese politician, who declined the 1973 Nobel Peace Prize which he won jointly with Dr Henry Kissinger of the US *US*
• — Linda Reinberg, *In the Field*, p. 69, 1991

duct *noun*

cocaine *US*

An abbreviation of **C-DUCT**.

- —Richard A. Spears, *The Slang and Jargon of Drugs and Drink*, p. 99, 1986
- —Mike Haskins, *Drugs*, p. 280, 2003

dud *noun*

a worthless or unsuccessful person or thing, a failure *UK, 1915*

Originally, 'an unexploded bomb or shell'.

- "Oh my God!" Gayle suddenly realised what she'd done. "Are they duds [forged bank-notes]." —Anthony Masters, *Minder*, p. 116, 1984

dud *verb*

to fool or deceive; to swindle *AUSTRALIA*

- Only good thing about the place is you can dud people who are a bit tempted to experiment. —Kevin Mackey, *The Cure*, p. 116, 1970
- —Barry Humphries, *A Nice Night's Entertainment*, p. 147, 1974
- He had been charged with dudding, that is, misrepresenting the origin, quality and value of goods he sold. —*(Sydney) Bulletin*, 26th April 1975
- 'Right there, are you, mate?' he said, and I knew immediately that I'd been dudded. —Shane Maloney, *Nice Try*, p. 75, 1998

dud *adjective*

worthless, useless, unsatisfactory *UK, 1903*

- If you think you've had a weak or a dud pill and are considering taking another, wait at least an hour. —*Mixmag*, p. 105, February 2002

dud bash *noun*

an unsatisifying sexual partner *AUSTRALIA*

- For this reason the Australian girl has the undeserved reputation of being a "dud bash". —Sue Rhodes, *Now you'll think I'm awful*, p. 21, 1967
- And even if you are the very worst dud bash, no man on earth would ever, ever notice. —Gretel Killeen, *Hot Buns and Ophelia get shipwrecked*, p. 13, 2001

dudder *noun*

a swindler; a con artist *AUSTRALIA*

- But George Danton was used to the role of dudder and he came right in. —Clive Galea, *Slipper*, p. 37, 1988

dude *noun*

1 a regular fellow *US, 1883*

In the US, the term had this vague sense in the hippie culture, and then a much more specific sense in the 1970s and 80s.

- GEORGE: A dude? What does he mean, "dude"? Dude ranch?' BILLY: A dude. WYATT: No, no. Dude means – uh – a nice guy, you know. Dude means a regular sort of person. —Peter Fonda, *Easy Rider*, p. 110, 1969
- During our stay we had all the white clientele coming from downtown and all the down black dudes and chicks too. —Babs Gonzales, *Movin' On Down De Line*, p. 9, 1975
- Look at the card, dude. —Bret Easton Ellis, *Less Than Zero*, p. 14, 1985
- One night while I was visiting with Frankie there was a massive dude named Sol there who I eventually got to know and work with. —Herbert Huncke, *Guilty of Everything*, p. 113, 1990
- I imagine the rest of the band and it is one heavenly combo – Jimi and Jim and John and Bob and Elvis – all the dudes you are into. —Francesca Lia Block, *Missing Angel Juan*, p. 277, 1993
- Who is this fucking dude? —Mark Powell, *Snap*, p. 148, 2001

2 used as a term of address, young male to young male *US, 1945*

- "Hey, dude," an older voice called out. —John Clellon Holmes, *The Horn*, p. 162, 1958
- With the nuances of pronunciation, dudes who said "dude" had no problem communicating. Pronounced "Duuhuhude" it meant "Right on, I'm into it if you are[.]" —Nina Blake, *Retrohell*, p. 120, 1997
- She's a mermaid, dude. —*American Pie*, 1999

3 a railway conductor *US*

- —Norman Carlisle, *The Modern Wonder Book of Trains and Railroading*, p. 262, 1946

dude *adjective*

well-dressed *BAHAMAS*

- —John A. Holm, *Dictionary of Bahamian English*, p. 67, 1982

Dude *nickname*

Lenny Dykstra (b.1963), a hard-playing and hard-living center fielder and leadoff hitter (1985–1996) *US*

dude up *verb*

to dress up *US, 1899*

- They were all duded up in tuxedos and patent leather so they must have made a score in New York. —Edwin Torres, *Carlito's Way*, p. 95, 1975

Dudley *noun*

a beginner gambler *US*

- —Victor H. Royer, *Casino Gamble Talk*, p. 53, 2003

Dudley Do-Right; Dudley Dogooder *noun*

the epitome of a sincere, moral, upstanding citizen, despised by those who live on the fringes of the law *US*

From a cartoon feature *Dudley Do-Right of the Mounties* first aired in 1961 as a segment on the *Rocky and Friends Show*.

- As soon as the last editorial is printed, the last speech made, and the last pulpit pounded, all the Dudley Dogooders will be the first back down here for a little fun. —Seth Morgan, *Homeboy*, p. 30, 1990

Dudley Moore; dudley *noun*

a sore, hence any kind of uncomfortable skin-condition *UK*

Rhyming slang, formed from the name of a British actor, comedian and jazz-musician, 1935–2002.

- Herpes sufferers may break out in "Dudley's"[.] —Ray Puxley, *Cockney Rabbit*, 1992

dudly; dudley *adjective*

(used of a boy) extremely boring *US*

- —Mimi Pond, *The Valley Girl's Guide to Life*, p. 55, 1982

dud root *noun*

an unsatisifying sexual partner *AUSTRALIA*

- Finally she told everyone I was a dud root and she went off with my younger brother. —Bettina Arndt, *The Australian Way of Sex*, p. 170, 1985
- —John Birmingham, *He Died With a Felafel in his Hand*, p. 26, 1994
- For now, he was content to lose himself in the SODD editor's ruminations on why he was a dud root. —Linda Jaivin, *Rock n Roll Babes from Outer Space*, p. 60, 1996

duds *noun*

1 clothing *UK, 1307*

- "I left Bakersfield with the travel-bureau car and left my gui-tar in the trunk of another one and they never showed up – gui-tar and cowboy duds[.] —Jack Kerouac, *On the Road*, p. 167, 1957
- And dressed up in those fancy duds he has (given to him by welathy summer people) he looks like a matinee idol. —Jim Thompson, *The Kill-Off*, p. 30, 1957
- I'm the coolest of studs when it comes to duds. —Dan Burley, *Diggeth Thou?*, p. 44, 1959
- I mean all the studs in fancy duds and foxy chicks togged to the bricks is gonna be there. —Ross Russell, *The Sound*, p. 218, 1961
- But the kind of duds you wear down at the garage, when you're tinkering with the scooter, or out on the field, when're you're tossing around a football, just aren't right for Saturday night. —Dick Clark, *To Goof or Not to Goof*, p. 80, 1963
- Sometimes I lay awake all night and thought about all the things I would do when I grew up, about the nice duds I'd have like a champ uptown[.] —Piri Thomas, *Down These Mean Streets*, p. 70, 1967
- I'm goin' downtown and buy me some new duds. —Nathan Heard, *Howard Street*, p. 68, 1968
- What do you think, leave our new duds in the car? —Elmore Leonard, *Out of Sight*, p. 170, 1996

2 fake drugs *UK*

From **DUD** (a worthless thing).

- —Angela Devlin, *Prison Patter*, p. 48, 1996

due *noun*

the residue left in a pipe after smoking crack cocaine *US*

- —Terry Williams, *The Cocaine Kids*, p. 136, 1989

due *adjective*

of a professional criminal, considered likely to be arrested whether or not actually responsible for the crime in question *UK*

- —Angela Devlin, *Prison Patter*, p. 48, 1996

due-back *noun*

something that is borrowed, such as a cigarette, with an expectation of a ultimate return of the favour *US*

- —*Newsweek*, p. 28, 8th October 1951

Duesie *noun*

a Duesenberg car *US*

- Most experts believe it was the finest car ever built in the U.S. The company was revived recently and a new Duesie is in production. —John Lawlor, *How to Talk Car*, p. 41, 1965

duey *noun*

▷ see: **DEWEY**

duff *noun*

the buttocks, the rump *UK, 1840*

Although first recorded in the UK, modern usage began in the US in 1939.

- Let's get off our duffs and out on the road. — *Drugstore Cowboy*, 1988
- I guess I am, but shoving paper around and sitting on my duff listening to people yammer about ways and means, instead of getting out there and doing what's got to get done, could turn me into a stone. — Robert Campbell, *In a Pig's Eye*, p. 31, 1991

▸ **up the duff**

pregnant *AUSTRALIA, 1941*

Perhaps from 'duff' (pudding).

- I don't like long haired Pommie bastards who get nice sheilas up the duff and then shoot through. — Barry Humphries, *The Wonderful World of Barry McKenzie*, p. 46, 1968
- [T]he decision of some to confine their heterosexual activity to sodomy, "because she won't get up the duff that way." — Richard Neville, *Play Power*, p. 82, 1970
- They get some girl up the duff and like the idea of being a dad. — Greg Williams, *Diamond Geezers*, p. 82, 1997
- [S]he aint up the duff again. — Sacha Baron-Cohen, *Da Gospel According to Ali G*, 2001

duff *verb*

to escape *US, 1963*

- Inside her bowels, the hot sausage and pepper on French played hell, pushing the beer, wine and juju seeds to the side so it could duff. — Steve Cannon, *Groove, Bang, and Jive Around*, p. 5–6, 1969

duff *adjective*

no good, inferior, useless *UK*

- In the ring the joey [clown] was a "drip" (useless chap) from the "gaffs" (fairgrounds) and a lot of acts were "duff"[.] — Butch Reynolds, *Broken Hearted Clown*, p. 31, 1953
- "I bought six cars last week at an auction and four of them are duff." "What do you mean duff?" "I'm sorry I mean they are no good." — Frank Norman, *Bang To Rights*, p. 112, 1958
- So Lester ends up giving one of these duff fifties to Tucker. — Dave Courtney, *Raving Lunacy*, p. 101, 2000
- 97% of "genuine antiques" are forgeries, fakes, duff, dud, Sexton Blakes, sham, lookalikes, replicates, all meaning worthless. — Jonathan Gash, *The Ten Word Game*, p. 50, 2003

duffel drag *noun*

the final morning of a soldier's service in Vietnam *US*

- For example, "four and a duffel drag" would indicate a soldier had four more days to serve and then was going home. — Linda Reinberg, *In the Field*, p. 69, 1991

duffer *noun*

1 a doltish old man *UK, 1730*

In recent times, the term has come to take on an emphasis on age.

- Right then this old duffer on the jury horns in, "How much you selilng your stock for, mister?" — Guy Owen, *The Flim-Flam Man and the Apprentice Grifter*, p. 198, 1972
- When she asked one of the old duffers why they called their beauty contest winner "Ms. Emerson," the geezer said, "Knock-knock." — Joseph Wambaugh, *Finnegan's Week*, p. 229, 1993

2 an incompetent, a person of no ability *UK, c. 1730*

Possibly from Scots *doofart* (a stupid person).

- [H]e makes much of being a bit of a duffer where computers are concerned. — *The Guardian*, 19th June 2003

Duff's Ditch *noun*

the Red River floodway, built 1962–68 when Duff Roblin was Premier *CANADA*

- The term "Duff's Ditch" was used by detractors of the project who claimed that it would never work and wasted money. Those living in Winnipeg are now very grateful for it. — Chris Thain, *Cold as a Bay Street Banker's Heart*, p. 59, 1987

duff up *verb*

to beat up, to assault someone *UK, 1961*

- It was the man from Sa Trincha, the man whom I'd duffed up earlier! — Wayne Anthony, *Spanish Highs*, p. 149, 1999

duffy *noun*

1 a spasm feigned by a drug addict in the hope of eliciting sympathy from a physician *US*

- — David Maurer and Victor Vogel, *Narcotics and Narcotic Addiction*, p. 404, 1973

2 a doltish old man *UK*

A variation of **DUFFER**.

- I gave the old duffy a swift boot in the ribs and told him to have a bit more respect in future. — Danny King, *The Bank Robber Diaries*, p. 107, 2002

duffy; duffie *verb*

to leave quickly *US*

A simpler version of **TAKE IT ON THE ARTHUR DUFFY**.

- I sometimes see it in the prison publications usually spelled "duffie" with a lower case "d." I recall reading in one prison paper the line "He duffied out of there." — *San Francisco Examiner*, p. 15, 20th March 1945

dufus *noun*

▹ see: **DOOFUS**

duggy *adjective*

dressed in style *US*

- — *Washington Post*, 14th October 1993

dugongs

the female breasts *UK*

- Most girls like you have got no tits have they? [...]I really like what you've got – socking great dugongs you can wade about in. — Henry Sloane, *Sloane's Inside Guide to Sex & Drugs & Rock 'n' Roll*, p. 48, 1985

Dugout Doug *nickname*

General Douglas MacArthur (1880–1964) of the US Army *US*

- — Frank Hailey, *Soldier Talk*, p. 46, 1982

duh *noun*

an offensive, despicable person; a clumsy person; a socially awkward person *SOUTH AFRICA, 1976*

From the expression of disgust at someone's stupidity.

- — Jean Branford, *A Dictionary of South African English*, 1978
- [Y]our name has now officially been shifted from geek, nerd or spaced out, to duh, mufar or loser, wannabe and a pile-on — *The Times of India*, 30th September 2002

duh!

used for expressing disgust at the stupidity of what has just been said *US, 1963*

A single syllable with a great deal of attitude.

- SEBASTIAN: You don't even know what it is. GRETCHEN: Duh. It's a book — *Cruel Intentions*, 1999
- "You reckon Parky nicked it?" "Dhur, I don't know, what do you reckon? Of course he fucking nicked it[."] — Danny King, *The Burglar Diaries*, p. 217, 2001
- They're going for different ones [answers]. "Duh! That's a red herring, dick-brain!" — Kevin Sampson, *Clubland*, p. 112, 2002

duji; doogie; doojie *noun*

heroin *US, 1960*

- I wasn't certain about how it was changing or what was happening, but I knew it had a lot to do with duji, heroin. — Claude Brown, *Manchild in the Promised Land*, p. 187, 1965
- He marveled dispassionately at the New Yorker's good, good doggie. — Nathan Heard, *Howard Street*, p. 174, 1968
- Yo, dig this. One pound of pure Malaysian white douge. — Cleo Odzer, *Goa Freaks*, p. 85, 1995
- The doojie's on me. — Joel Rose, *Kill Kill Faster Faster*, p. 70, 1997
- — Robert Ashton, *This Is Heroin*, p. 205, 2002

duke *noun*

1 a regular fellow; a tough guy *US, 1939*

- A limo driver by day, Lou is a regular old duke at the Melody Burlesk – one of their up-and-coming resident uncles, a young pup of fifty-one. — Josh Alan Friedman, *Tales of Times Square*, p. 29, 1986

2 poor quality tobacco issued by the State of California to prisoners *US*

Named after former California Governor Deukmejian (1983–91).

- — James Harris, *A Convict's Dictionary*, p. 31, 1989

3 in card games, a hand (of cards) *US*

- — Albert H. Morehead, *The Complete Guide to Winning Poker*, p. 262, 1967

Duke *noun*

1 a Ducati motorcycle *UK*

- — Douglas Dunford, *Motorcycle Department, Beaulieu Motor Museum*, 1979

2 a socially inept person *US*

- — Connie Eble (Editor), *UNC-CH Campus Slang*, p. 2, Spring 1983

duke *verb*

1 to fight with fists *US, 1935*

- I was going down to the A.C. on Thirty-fifth Street, learning how to duke. — Chester Himes, *If He Hollers Let Him Go*, p. 105, 1945
- Here's your chance. Come on, let's see you duke. — Ralph Ellison, *Invisible Man*, p. 368, 1947
- Me and this black kid duked it out after he said, "Let me hold a quarter." — Edwin Torres, *Carlito's Way*, p. 9, 1975
- What am I talking about? I didn't even drive tonight. You wanna duke it? Let's go. — *Tin Men*, 1987
- Oasis's attitude helps. They're still a band who choose to duke it out[.] — *Q*, p. 10, May 2002

2 to give *US*

- Well, let's try to duke out bet in again. —Joseph Wambaugh, *The Blue Knight*, p. 144, 1973
- We duked the parking lot attendant a dollar and were soon among the Friday night North Beach throng. —Bill Cardoso, *The Maltese Sangweech*, p. 202, 1984
- [T]he guy that ran the men's room would then duke you whatever the doorman had written on a note. —Herbert Huncke, *Guilty of Everything*, p. 110, 1990

3 to allow *US*

- Maybe I could convince Scarlet to duke me in with this crowd. —Stephen J. Cannell, *The Tin Collectors*, p. 260, 2001

4 to fool; to deceive *US*

- Lieutenant Finque ain't trying to duke you into the Oriental community by using you as a part time community relations officer at Japanese luncheons. —Joseph Wambaugh, *The Choirboys*, p. 92, 1975
- —Don Wilmeth, *The Language of American Popular Entertainment*, p. 81, 1981
- —Gene Sorrows, *All About Carnivals*, p. 15, 1985: 'All about sorrows'

5 to have sex *US*

- — *People Magazine*, p. 72, 19th July 1993

6 to short-change someone by palming a coin given as part of the change *US*

- —Don Wilmeth, *The Language of American Popular Entertainment*, p. 81, 1981

Duke *nickname*

1 Edwin Donald Snider (b.1926) *US*

Snider played centre field for the Brooklyn and Los Angeles Dodgers baseball teams of the 1950s and was the most powerful hitter in the Dodgers' line-up. He was more formally known as the 'Duke of Flatbush'.

- I shoot it gently, with just a flick of the wrist, at the opposing team's shortstop as he comes trotting out onto the field, and still without breaking stride, go lopin in all the way, shoulders shifting, head hanging, a touch pigeon-toed, my kneeds coming slowly up and down in an altogether brilliant imitation of The Duke. —Philip Roth, *Portnoy's Complaint*, p. 78–79, 1969

2 the film actor John Wayne, 1907–79 *US*

- [P]ilots [in the Gulf war] would "yip like a cowboy" every time they hit the enemy and the tactical sign of "Duke" (Wayne's nickname) was popular. — *The Guardian*, 17th October 2001

duke breath *noun*

bad breath *US*

- — *People Magazine*, p. 72, 19th July 1993

duked out *adjective*

dressed up *US, 1938*

- He was all duked out ina hard-boiled collar and a blue serge suit. —Jim Thompson, *Savage Night*, p. 81, 1953

Duke of Argyle *noun*

a file (a tool) *UK*

Rhyming slang.

- —Ray Puxley, *Cockney Rabbit*, 1992

Duke of Argyles; the duke *noun*

haemorrhoids *UK: SCOTLAND*

Rhyming slang for 'piles'.

- You'll get the Duke ae Argylls if ye sit on that cold waw much longer. —Michael Munro, *The Patter, Another Blast*, 1988
- I've been suffering with the Duke recently. —Bodmin Dark, *Dirty Cockney Rhyming Slang*, 2003

Duke of Kent *noun*

rent *UK, 1932*

Rhyming slang, no earlier than C20.

- I no longer had a lease there, down to not paying the duke. —Derek Raymond (Robon Cook), *The Crust on its Uppers*, p. 29, 1962

Duke of Kent *adjective*

bent (in all senses) *UK*

Rhyming slang.

- —Ray Puxley, *Cockney Rabbit*, 1992

Duke of Montrose *noun*

the nose *UK: SCOTLAND*

Glasgow rhyming slang.

- —Michael Munro, *The Patter, Another Blast*, 1988

Duke of Teck; duke *noun*

a cheque *UK*

Rhyming slang.

- —Julian Franklyn, *A Dictionary of Rhyming Slang*, 1960
- A "dodgy duke" is a rubber one. —Ray Puxley, *Cockney Rabbit*, 1992

Duke of York *noun*

1 a cork *UK, 1931*

Rhyming slang.

- —Ray Puxley, *Cockney Rabbit*, p. 54, 1992

2 talk *UK*

Rhyming slang.

- Herpes sufferers may break out in "Dudley's"[.] —Ray Puxley, *Cockney Rabbit*, 1992
- —Ray Puxley, *Cockney Rabbit*, p. 54, 1992

3 a fork *UK*

Rhyming slang.

- —Ray Puxley, *Cockney Rabbit*, 1992

duke on *verb*

to give *US*

- I was building a model of the state cap'tol. I figured when I got it done, I'd duke it on the gov'nor. —Malcolm Braly, *On the Yard*, p. 204, 1967

duker *noun*

a person inclined to fight *US*

- A few arguments, but no fights (a miracle 'cause some of these guys were dukers for days). —Edwin Torres, *After Hours*, p. 295, 1979

dukes *noun*

1 the hands; fists *US, 1859*

The singular is 'duke', or variant 'dook', which is probably rhyming slang, formed on **DUKE OF YORK** for 'forks' (the fingers).

- Slippers was a good man with his dukes. —Louis Armstrong, *Satchmo*, p. 114, 1954
- Come on Whalen, put up yr. dukes and fight! —Jack Kerouac, *Letter to Philip Whalen*, p. 542, 16th January 1956
- Then she doubled up her fists and put up her dukes and said she guessed she'd just have to teach Doyle a lesson. —Gurney Norman, *Divine Right's Trip (Last Whole Earth Catalog)*, p. 203, 1971
- He had blown into town with no 'ho. And worse, no wheels and frozen fireworks (jewelry] exploding off his dukes, necessary to cop a star 'ho. —Iceberg Slim (Robert Beck), *Airtight Willie and Me*, p. 21, 1979
- —Angela Devlin, *Prison Patter*, p. 48, 1996
- Being a bit slow and not so handy with my dukes at that point in time[.] —Kevin Sampson, *Outlaw*, p. 312, 2001

2 cut-off blue jean shorts *US*

An abbreviation of **DAISY DUKES**.

- —Connie Eble (Editor), *UNC-CH Campus Slang*, p. 3, March 1996

duke shot *noun*

any method by which a carnival game operator allows a customer to win a rigged game *US*

- —Gene Sorrows, *All About Carnivals*, p. 16, 1985: 'Terminology'

duke's mixture *noun*

1 a transracial person *US, 1961*

- Blacks, tans, cinnamons, octoroons, reds and dukes mixture, moving Artis down the street. —Fannie Flagg, *Fried Green Tomatoes at the Whistle Stop Cafe*, p. 120, 1987

2 a random conglomeration *US, 1914*

- Palo verde trees, small fuzzy cholla trees, and a duke's mixture of other desert plants were scattered among the giant saguaro cacti. —Jim Conover, *Greenhorns and Killer Mountains*, p. 206, 1999

dukey *noun*

1 a brown paper lunch bag *US*

Chicago slang.

- —Bill Reilly, *Big Al's Official Guide to Chicagoese*, p. 24, 1986

2 in the circus, a lunch prepared for circus workers on long train journeys between towns *US*

- —Joe McKennon, *Circus Lingo*, p. 31, 1980

3 in circus and carnival usage, a meal ticket or book of meal tickets *US*

- —Don Wilmeth, *The Language of American Popular Entertainment*, p. 81, 1981

▷ **see: DOOKIE**

dukey rope *noun*

a gold chain necklace *US*

- —Ellen C. Bellone (Editor), *Dictionary of Slang*, p. 10, 1989

dukey run *noun*

in the circus, a long train ride between shows *US*

- —Joe McKennon, *Circus Lingo*, p. 31, 1980

duky *noun*
an operator of a DUKW barge *ANTARCTICA, 1966*
- —Bernadette Hince, *The Antarctic Dictionary*, p. 108, 2000

dull and dowdy *adjective*
cloudy *UK*
Rhyming slang, recorded by Ray Puxley, *Cockney Rabbit*, 1992, noting that it can refer to poorly conditioned beer as well as the weather.

dull as arse *adjective*
very boring, extremely dull *UK*
- But there was nowt goin' down anywhere except cocaine, pills and vintage Dom P. Fookin' dull as arse.—Ben Elton, *High Society*, p. 119, 2002

dullsville *noun*
the epitome of a boring existence *US, 1960*
- But linguistically speaking, Disraeli is dullsville.—Kurt Vonnegut, *Welcome to the Monkey House*, p. 123, 1968

Dullsville, Ohio *noun*
anywhere other than Las Vegas *US*
- —*Washington Post*, p. B1, 17th January 1985

dumb as a mud fence *adjective*
very stupid *US*
- [M]ost actors are dumb as a mud fence.—*Uncut*, p. 74, March 2004

dumb-ass *noun*
1 a stupid person *US, 1958*
- Oh, the dumbass at the donut place put a chocolate cream filled I asked for in your box.—*Natural Born Killers*, 1994

2 stupidity *US*
- I'm what a lot of you spooks might think of as a red neck with a terminal case of the dumb-ass.—Dan Jenkins, *Semi-Tough*, p. 7, 1972

▸ **eat up with the dumb ass**
very stupid *US*
- When I saw ol' Delbert tryin' to siphon gas uphill, I knew for sure he was eat up with the dumb ass.—Ken Weaver, *Texas Crude*, p. 112, 1984

dumb-ass; dumb-assed *adjective*
stupid, foolish *US, 1957*
From the noun sense.
- [P]lay tricks on that dumb-ass cracker, the park ranger.—Howard Stern, *Miss America*, p. 430, 1995
- [I]f you're not wearing the right leather waistcoat or something, or some dumb-ass shit!—Ben Malbon, *Cool Places*, p. 270, 1998

dumb as two short planks *adjective*
used to describe someone who is very stupid *CANADA, 1989*
- Anyone cutting a board who attempts to rectify a short measure by making a similar second cut is a knothead indeed.—Tom Parkin, *WetCoast Words*, p. 50, 1989

dumbbell *noun*
a stupid person *US, 1918*
- That's a life for bums and dumbbells. Don't be a fool!—James T. Farrell, *Saturday Night*, p. 16, 1947
- I wasn't a dumbbell. I didn't let that gob grow inside my neck, week after week, in silent fear.—Philip Wylie, *Opus 21*, p. 7, 1949
- "Because I love you, dumbbell!" she cried, abandoning civility.—Max Shulman, *Anyone Got a Match?*, p. 108, 1964
- They're used to dumbbells.—Darryl Ponicsan, *The Last Detail*, p. 120, 1970

dumb blonde *noun*
a stereotypical (pehaps mythical) blonde-haired, sexually attractive woman who is not especially intelligent *US, 1936*
- The Essex girl archetype is as dated as the image of Marilyn Monroe, believes [Joanna] Pitman. "We've moved from dumb blonde to power blonde, like Hillary Clinton. Now it's possible to feel empowered as a blonde."—*The Guardian*, 25th September 2001

dumb bomb *noun*
a bomb that must be dropped accurately *US*
Back formation from 'smart bomb'.
- —Linda Reinberg, *In the Field*, p. 69, 1991

dumbbutt *noun*
a dolt *US, 1973*
- Convert the Super Dome to microwave / Tell them its a pie. The dumbbutts can't count.—Barbara Smith, *Wild Sweet Note*, p. 90, 2000

dumb cake *noun*
in Newfoundland, a cake baked and eaten by unmarried women in silence *CANADA*
- During the making, baking, and consumption of the dumb cake, no talking was permitted. Fate would grant a prophetic vision of the man who would marry the maiden.—Bill Casselman, *Canadian Food Words*, p. 34–35, 1998

dumb cluck *noun*
a fool *AUSTRALIA*
- He stands there unable to comprehend...just a big dumbcluck. —Sumner Locke Elliott, *Rusty Bugles*, p. 33, 1948
- They were things you couldn't say to a dumb cluck like Midget.—Wilda Moxham, *The Apprentice*, p. 116, 1969

dumb crooker *noun*
a social misfit *US*
- —Carol Ann Preusse, *Jargon Used by University of Texas Co-Eds*, 1963

Dumb Dora *noun*
an empty-headed woman *US, 1922*
- But I don't mind a Dumb Dora if she has looks and knows the tricks.—James T. Farrell, *The Life Adventure*, p. 180, 1947

dumb down *verb*
to simplify the content of something so that it can be understood by the general uneducated public *US, 1933*
- —*American Speech*, Winter 1988
- —Pamela Munro, *U.C.L.A. Slang*, p. 61, 1997

dumb dust *noun*
cocaine or heroin *US*
- But the idea that Buckingham Palace is a warehouse for the dumb-dust market in Candlestick Park and McDonald's and Madison Square Garden is going to be hard one to sell to anybody except Ed Meese and Jan Wenner.—Hunter S. Thompson, *Generation of Swine*, p. 95, 1986

dumbfuck; dumb-fuck *noun*
a despicable, stupid person *US, 1950*
- I already asked Toby Dumbfuck. Obvioulsy, I've interrupted.—*Romy and Michele's High School Reunion*, 1997
- Listen Rees you dumb-fuck! I don't have to ask[.]—Jack Allen, *When the Whistle Blows*, p. 240, 2000

dumbjohn *noun*
a person of no importance, especially a military cadet *US, 1951*
- We could play like back at the Point, upperclassmen hazing the Dumbjohns.—James Jones, *From Here to Eternity*, p. 113, 1951

dumbo *noun*
a dolt, a fool *US, 1932*
- Somebody later told me it was an experiment to put together a gorup of dumbos and halfwits who wouldn't question orders.—*Forrest Gump*, 1992

Dumbo *noun*
during the war in Vietnam, a C-123 US Air Force provider *US*
- [W]e and our jeeps boarded "Dumbo" choppers and headed south. —David H. Hackworth, *About Face*, p. 378, 1989

dumbshit *noun*
an imbecile *US, 1961*
- I could call first, of course, I'd call, dumbshit, ask them if they have the speakerphone.—Dave Eggers, *A Heartbreaking Work of Staggering Genius*, p. 26, 2001

dumbshit *adjective*
stupid *US, 1967*
- Am I going to be a pathetic dumbshit Addict and continue to waste myh life or am I going to say no and try to stay sober and be a decent Person.—James Frey, *A Million Little Pieces*, p. 258, 2003

dumb sock *noun*
a dolt *US, 1932*
- —Frederic G. Cassidy, *Dictionary of American Regional English, Volume II*, p. 233, 1991

dumbwad *noun*
an imbecile *US, 1978*
- Clean your loathsome bodies, dumbwads.—Pat Conroy, *The Lords of Discipline*, p. 170, 1980

dum-dum *noun*
1 a soft-core bullet that expands upon impact *UK, 1897*
- How could Jack tell a jury what it was like to have his insides ripped out by a dumdum?—Mickey Spillane, *I, The Jury*, p. 6, 1947

- The bullet went straight through the door of the car, tearing a hole the size of a small ham in the metal. It must have been a dumdum. —Derek Raymond (Robin Cook), *The Crust on its Uppers*, p. 134, 1962
- The Fox glimpsed him through the mist and pumped a dumdum that shattered Cocio's tailbone. —Iceberg Slim (Robert Beck), *Death Wish*, p. 251, 1977

2 a simpleton *US, 1937*
- Boy, what dum-dums. Don't they know what's waiting for them in the Jeresey swamps. —Piri Thomas, *Stories from El Barrio*, p. 24, 1978

3 Demerol™, a central nervous system depressant *US*
- —Inez Cardozo-Freeman, *The Joint*, p. 495, 1984

dummies *noun*

1 in horse racing, spurs approved for racing *AUSTRALIA*
- —Ned Wallish, *The Truth Dictionary of Racing Slang*, p. 24, 1989

2 imitation drugs *US*
- —Maria Hinojas, *Crews*, p. 167, 1995

dummkopf *noun*

a dolt; a fool *US, 1809*

German for 'dumb-head'.
- [T]he Germans saw that apparently whatever we said about collective responsibility we were only going to hang those dumkopfs at Nuremberg[.] —Clancy Sigal, *Going Away*, p. 213, 1961

dummy *noun*

1 a fool; a mentally retarded person *UK, 1796*
- Okay. I'm nobody's dummy. I'm everybody's dummy. I believe everything I read, see, and hear. —Lester Bangs, *Psychotic Reactions and Carburetor Dung*, p. 185, 1976
- Nobody did it better than a dummy, and it wasn't a nice thing to say but it was like that sometimes[.] —John King, *White Trash*, p. 65, 2001

2 a mute *US*
- —Joseph E. Ragen and Charles Finston, *Inside the World's Toughest Prison*, p. 797, 1962

3 a representative of a corrupt police officer in insurance fraud *UK*
- The dummy was someone known to the bogey [policeman], whom he would recommend to the assessor as having provided vital information leading to the recovery of the stolen property[.] —Charles Raven, *Underworld Nights*, p. 75, 1956

4 a feigned injury or illness *US*
- —Jay Robert Nash, *Dictionary of Crime*, p. 66, 1992

5 a substance other than narcotics sold as narcotics *US*
- —Jay Robert Nash, *Dictionary of Crime*, p. 113, 1992

6 a solitary confinement cell in prison *NEW ZEALAND*
- —David McGill, *David McGill's Complete Kiwi Slang Dictionary*, p. 41, 1998

7 a train that transports railway workers *US*
- —Norman Carlisle, *The Modern Wonder Book of Trains and Railroading*, p. 262, 1946

8 a wallet *UK*

From an earlier use as 'a pocket-book'.
- My mate took out his dumie [dummy] and took out a jacks (= a £5 note) —Frank Norman, *Bang To Rights*, p. 124, 1958

9 the penis *US*
- —Hyman E. Goldin et al., *Dictionary of American Underworld Lingo*, p. 63, 1950

▸ beat your dummy

(used of a male) to masturbate *US*
- I'll bet some of those businessmen are licking the glass and beating their dummies for all they're worth. —*Adam Film World*, p. 63–64, 1977

▸ on the dummy

quiet *US*
- I knew the punk was rank, but Jackson was crazy about him so I stayed on the dummy —Iceberg Slim (Robert Beck), *The Naked Soul of Iceberg Slim*, p. 122, 1971

dummy *verb*

to pack marijuana into a rolled cigarette butt *US*
- I used to be real slow at rolling reefers and at dummying reefers, but when I came back from Warwick I was a real pro at that. —Claude Brown, *Manchild in the Promised Land*, p. 146, 1965

dummy-chucker *noun*

a swindler who pretends to be the victim of accidents *US*
- The oranges was an item from the dummy-chuckers' workbag, a frammis of the professional accident fakers. Beaten with the fruit, a person sustained bruises far out of proportion to his actual injuries. —Jim Thompson, *The Grifters*, p. 70, 1963

dummy dust *noun*

1 phencyclidine, the recreational drug known as PCP or angel dust *US*

Recorded as a 'current PCP alias' by Ronald Linder, *PCP*, 1981.
- —*Drummer*, p. 77, 1977

2 cocaine *US*
- —Connie Eble (Editor), *UNC-CH Campus Slang*, p. 4, Spring 1992

dummy flogger *noun*

a masturbator *US*
- [T]he theater manager, who was sick and tired of dummy floggers chasing off legitimate customers, grabbed Wingnut by the scruff of the neck and dragged him right out of his seat[.] —Joseph Wambaugh, *The Secrets of Harry Bright*, p. 61, 1985

dummy oil *noun*

Demerol™, a branded central nervous system depressant *US*
- Bob has one of the cabinets open only to find Demerol (otherwise known to drug addicts as "dummy oil"). —*Drugstore Cowboy*, 1988

dummy stick *noun*

a bamboo stick used to carry baskets on each end, carried across the shoulders *US*
- This much better than toting dummy stick! —Tony Zidek, *Choi Oi*, p. 68, 1965

dummy up *verb*

to stop talking; to be quiet *US, 1928*
- I began to see the handwriting on the wall. I began to dummy up. —*San Francisco Call Bulletin*, p. A2, 10th December 1945
- A 33-year-old convict faced murder charges today for slicing off the head of another prisoner in the presence of 225 other inmates who "dummied up" to protect the slayer. —*San Francisco News*, p. 8, 15th December 1948
- I says, "You dummy up. I'll do the stealing and there ain't gonna be any pistols." —Bruce Jackson, *In the Life*, p. 99, 1972
- —David Powis, *The Signs of Crime*, 1977
- Dummy up you square ass punks. —Iceberg Slim (Robert Beck), *Airtight Willie and Me*, p. 3, 1979
- —Thomas L. Clark, *The Dictionary of Gambling and Gaming*, p. 70, 1987

dump *noun*

1 the buttocks *US*
- [L]ooking down at her while she was on her knees with her well-rounded dump propped up in the air really made a freak outta me[.] —A.S. Jackson, *Gentleman Pimp*, p. 110, 1973

2 an act of defecation *US, 1942*
- I started documenting any large or unusually shaped bowel movements. I knew I was becoming obsessive when I filmed my third monster dump of the week. —Anka Radakovich, *The Wild Girls Club*, p. 86, 1994
- I thought I could get through the job okay and have a dump after, but I was wrong. —Danny King, *The Burglar Diaries*, p. 4, 2001

3 an unpleasant place or location *US, 1899*
- Well, finally I gets back to this dump where I lives. A rotten little flat in a big old block[.] —John Peter Jones, *Feather Pluckers*, p. 9, 1964

4 in a smuggling operation, the place where the goods to be smuggled are assembled *US*
- —*American Speech*, p. 98, May 1956: 'Smugglers' argot in the Southwest'

5 a ticket returned unsold to a theatre by a ticket agency *US*
- —Don Wilmeth, *The Language of American Popular Entertainment*, p. 82, 1981

6 a large, unprocessed amount of information *US*
- —Eric S. Raymond, *The New Hacker's Dictionary*, p. 137, 1991

7 a hospital patient who is transferred from one hospital or nursing home to another *US*
- —*Maledicta*, p. 38, 1983: 'More common patient-directed pejoratives used by medical personnel'

8 a mortuary *US*

Gallows humour from the Vietnam war.
- —Linda Reinberg, *In the Field*, p. 69, 1991

9 a fall from a surfboard, usually caused by a wave's impact *US*
- —John Severson, *Modern Surfing Around the World*, p. 169, 1964

▸ take a dump

1 to defecate *US, 1942*
- Jackie will go into the bathroom and take A HEARTY, SLOPPY, SMELLY DUMP complete with foul noises and splashing toilet water. —Howard Stern, *Miss America*, p. 196, 1995
- I mean, don't you think it's time you learned to take a dump at school? —*American Pie*, 1999

2 to lose a game intentionally, especially for the purpose of taking advantage of spectator betting *US*

- So get in there tonight and take a dump, go in the tank.—Rocky Garciano (with Rowland Barber), *Somebody Up There Likes Me*, p. 255, 1955

▸ **the dumps**

melancholy *UK, 1714*

Often in phrases 'in the dumps' and 'down in the dumps'.

- When you're feeling in the dumps, / Don't be silly chumps.—Eric Idle, *Look On the Bright Side of Life (All Things Dull and Ugly)*, 1979

dump *verb*

1 to beat; to kill *US*

- "I'm just warning you to stay clear. I keep you punks from dumping (beating) each other, I'm satisfied."—*Man's Magazine*, p. 12, February 1960
- Marvin Lewis, attorney for Richard rock, one of five men indicted for murder and conspiring to murder the union official, said that "dumping" meant assaulting a man. Assistant District Attorney Walter Biubbbini argued in opposition that "dumping" is listed in lexicons of slang and criminal lingo as synonymous with "killing." —*San Francisco Chronicle*, p. 5, 27th May 1966

2 to assault *US*

- —*American Speech*, p. 194, October 1951: 'A study of reformatory argot'

3 to break off a romantic relationship with someone *AUSTRALIA*

- —Sue Rhodes, *Now you'll think I'm awful*, p. 58, 1967
- He thought she needed her head read to dump a feller like Kev in favour of a bloke like Arnie.—Wilda Moxham, *The Apprentice*, p. 90, 1969
- Sometimes, if the surf was high, really high, he'd get dumped.—Lance Peters, *The Dirty Half-Mile*, p. 52, 1979
- —Kathy Lette, *Girls' Night Out*, p. 96, 1987
- Usually this happens after he's cheated on you and it's usually because he feels real bad and is too much of a coward to tell the truth. Dump him!—*Dolly*, p. 55, 1996
- —Gretel Killeen, *Hot Buns and Ophelia get shipwrecked*, p. 74, 2001

4 to derive sexual pleasure from sadistic acts *US*

- Tricks pay a hundred dollars to dump girls. Sometimes more. I'd never take a dumping myself for less than a hundred.—John M. Murtagh and Sara Harris, *Cast the First Stone*, p. 155, 1957

5 in bowling, to release the ball with the fingers and thumb at the same time *US*

- —Lou Bellisimo, *The Bowler's Manual*, p. 107, 1969

6 to fall from a surfboard; to be battered by a wave while bodysurfing *AUSTRALIA, 1967*

- —Gary Fairmont R. Filosa II, *The Surfer's Almanac*, p. 184, 1977

7 in motorcyling, to fall to the ground with the motorcyle *US*

- —Ed Radlauer, *Motorcylopedia*, p. 18, 1973

8 in hot rodding and drag racing, to damage a component partially or completely *US*

- For example, to dump a clutch.—John Lawlor, *How to Talk Car*, p. 41, 1965

9 to lose a game intentionally, especially for the purpose of taking advantage of spectator betting *US*

- The possiblity of trial and conviction for these basketball players who took dough to dump games is protected by a statute which makes it a felony to tamper with a sport.—*San Francisco News*, p. 17, 28th February 1951
- Though all hustlers use the verb "to dump" in referring to a game that the hustler deliberately loses for the purpose of cheating spectators, hustlers vary in the object they attach to the verb.—Ned Polsky, *Hustlers, Beats, and Others*, p. 58, 1967
- —Zander Hollander and Sandy Padwe, *Basketball Lingo*, p. 31, 1971
- —Steve Rushin, *Pool Cool*, p. 12, 1990
- "She threw th' fuckin' case, went in the tank, intentionally bricked it." "You never said that before. If she dumped it, you would've told me."—Stephen J. Cannell, *The Tin Collectors*, p. 156, 2001

10 in horse racing, to bet a large amount on a horse just before a race *US*

- —David W. Maurer, *Argot of the Racetrack*, p. 25, 1951

11 to lose a large sum of money gambling in a short period *US*

- I have dumping to stiffs.—Lee Solkey, *Dummy Up and Deal*, p. 112, 1980

12 to vomit after injecting heroin or a synthetic opiate *US*

- —*Current Slang*, p. 22, Fall 1968
- —William K. Bentley and James M. Corbett, *Prison Slang*, p. 77, 1992

13 to complete an illegal drug sale by delivering the drug *US*

- —Bill Valentine, *Gang Intelligence Manual*, p. 76, 1995: 'Black street gang terminology'

▸ **dump it out**

to defecate *US*

- —Charles Shafer, *Folk Speech in Texas Prisons*, p. 203, 1990

▸ **dump the clutch**

in drag racing, to engage the clutch in a quick and forceful manner *US*

- When you dump the clutch, you do it fast and with as much power as the car can use without having something break.—Ed Radlauer, *Drag Racing Pix Dix*, p. 19, 1970

▸ **dump your load**

to ejaculate *NEW ZEALAND*

- —David McGill, *David McGill's Complete Kiwi Slang Dictionary*, p. 41, 1998

dumper *noun*

1 a toilet *UK*

- A final-reel splatterfest that took out America's current sweethearts would mean there'd be two whole reasons to see the Jen [Jennifer Lopez] and Ben [Affleck] Go Down the Dumper flick.—*The Guardian*, 8th August 2003

2 an athlete who dumps a game, intentionally losing *US*

- Reams of copy have already been written on big time basketball's latest smellero, involving enough Toledo and Bradley University cagers to make up a first string of "dumpers" and a second string of "dumpers."—*San Francisco Call Bulletin*, p. 11, 30th July 1951
- C.CV.N.Y.'s Ed Warner (right, rear) one of the dumpers, had soft job waiting on tables. [Caption]—*Life*, p. 38, 5th March 1951
- —Steve Rushin, *Pool Cool*, p. 12, 1990

3 a person who takes sexual pleasure from sadistic acts *US*

- That's what one dumper told mee. Boy, you should have heard him talking. 'Honey,' he says, 'all I want to do is beat you up a little bit and then I'll be finished.'—John M. Murtagh and Sara Harris, *Cast the First Stone*, p. 155, 1957
- I have always refused to take "dumpers," men who beat you.—Sara Harris, *The Lords of Hell*, p. 72, 1967
- —Kenn "Naz" Young, *Naz's Underground Dictionary*, p. 26, 1973

4 an uninspiring, boring experience *UK*

- —Tom Hibbert, *Rockspeak!*, p. 55, 1983

5 a large and dangerous wave that breaks suddenly *AUSTRALIA, 1920*

- —Grant W. Kuhns, *On Surfing*, p. 116, 1963
- —Bill Hornadge, *The Ugly Australian*, p. 216, 1975
- —Jim Ramsay, *Cop It Sweet!*, p. 33, 1977
- The curling, twelve foot dumpers would raise him up, hold him in breath-taking suspension and then dash him down the watery slope to the very depths.—Lance Peters, *The Dirty Half-Mile*, p. 52, 1979
- —Gretel Killeen, *Hot Buns and Ophelia get shipwrecked*, p. 74, 2001

dumpi; dumpy *noun*

the smallest size (340ml) bottle of beer *SOUTH AFRICA, 1966*

From the squat shape.

- —Penny Silva, *A Dictionary of South African English*, 1996
- —*Lonely Planet Southern Africa*, 2000

dumping *noun*

a beating in the context of sadistic sex *US*

- I don't take tricks for dumping unless I'm awful broke. Tricks pay a hundred dollars to dump girls. Sometimes more. I'd never take a dumping myself for less than a hundred.—John M. Murtagh and Sara Harris, *Cast the First Stone*, p. 155, 1957

dumping table *noun*

a blackjack table in a casino where players have been consistently winning *US*

- —Michael Dalton, *Blackjack*, p. 44, 1991

dumpling *noun*

a fool, a dunce *UK: SCOTLAND*

- I'd open for the swots in the back row, then you'd reply for the dumplings in the front.—Ian Pattison, *Rab C. Nesbitt*, 1988

dump off *verb*

(used of a casino dealer) to overpay a bet made by a confederate *US*

- —Steve Kuriscak, *Casino Talk*, p. 20, 1985

dump out *verb*

(of a casino employee) to lose intentionally as part of a scheme with a gambler or gamblers *US*

- [I]n a court of law, if a blackjack Dealer gets terribly unlucky and his table keeps losing fifteen nights in a row, there is no legal proof that he is cheating for the benefit of an "outside" man or "crossroader," that he is "dumping out."—Mario Puzo, *Inside Las Vegas*, p. 180, 1977

dumps *noun*

the female breasts *US*

- —Don R. McCreary (Editor), *Dawg Speak*, 2001

▸ **down in the dumps**
depressed, melancholy *UK, 1714*
- Sometimes it's very embarrassing when girls see me when I am blue. Down in the dumps. They think I'm normal. I don't feel normal myself. —Jason Kingsley, *Count Us In*, p. 62, 1994

dump stroke *noun*
in pool, the minuscule adjustment to a shot that a player makes when intentionally missing a shot *US*
- —Steve Rushin, *Pool Cool*, p. 12, 1990

dump truck *noun*
1 a court-appointed public defender *US*
- My dump truck wants me to cop a second degree burglary. Fuck him! —Inez Cardozo-Freeman, *The Joint*, p. 495, 1984

2 a car filled with lesbians *US*
- —*American Speech*, p. 57, Spring-Summer 1970: 'Homosexual slang'

3 a prisoner who does not hold up his end of a shared task or relationship *US*
- —James Harris, *A Convict's Dictionary*, p. 32, 1989

dumpty *noun*
a latrine *AUSTRALIA*
- I will say Grandma's pretty good sport, locking herself in dumpties and blurting out all that hot stuff at dinner. —Norman Lindsay, *The Cousin from Fiji*, p. 14, 1945
- I had visions of tramping some lonely path to an old dumpty, perched over a big hole full of spiders and wiggly things. —Mona Anderson, *Both Sides of the River*, p. 101, 1981

dumpy *adjective*
(used of waves) weak, erratic *US*
- —Michael V. Anderson, *The Bad, Rad, Not to Forget Way Cool Beach and Surf Discriptionary*, p. 6, 1988

dun *noun*
a male friend *US*
- —Connie Eble (Editor), *UNC-CH Campus Slang*, p. 4, October 2002

duncey *adjective*
stupid *TRINIDAD AND TOBAGO, 1962*
- —Lise Winer, *Dictionary of the English/Creole of Trinidad & Tobago*, 2003

duncy; duncey *adjective*
foolish, stupid *BARBADOS*
- —Frank A. Collymore, *Barbadian Dialect*, p. 42, 1965

dundus *noun*
an albino *UK*
West Indian and UK black patois.
- Easy smile to himself and hummed his version of a classic ragga rhythm: "I spy with my little eye, Grange undercover bwai, with dutty [dirty] dun-dus eye." —Karline Smith, *Moss Side Massive*, p. 226, 1994

dune coon *noun*
an Arab *US*
Very offensive.
- I was tryin' to deal with a Dune Coon the other day. —Dan Jenkins, *Life Its Ownself*, p. 92, 1984
- I convince Lavonne to see Israel before them doon coons take it back. —James Ellroy, *Hollywood Nocturnes*, p. 206, 1994
- Lord knows what vermin live in the butt of a dune coon. —*Three Kings*, 1999

duner *noun*
a person who enjoys driving dune buggies in the desert *US, 1974*
- The sand dunes about a quarter mile away make the campground a handy base for "duners." —Jackie Sheckler Finch, *The Unofficial Guide to the Best RV and Tent Campgrounds*, p. 111, 2002

dungarees *noun*
battle fatigues *US*
Marine Corps usage in World War 2 and Korea.
- Battle dress was dungarees. —William Manchester, *Goodbye, Darkness*, p. 146, 1979

dung beetle *noun*
used by bookmakers for describing a person who thrives on blather or bullshit *AUSTRALIA*
- —Ned Wallish, *The Truth Dictionary of Racing Slang*, p. 24, 1989

dunge *noun*
a dent *IRELAND*
- Bumper battered the bat against the wall hard enough to leave a permanent dunge. —Eamonn Sweeney, *Waiting for the Healer*, p. 181, 1997

dungeon *noun*
a nightclub catering to sado-masochistic fetishists *US*
- The theater of choice for many devotees of sadomasochism, or S/M, is the dungeon, a kind of specialized club catering to those with a taste for domination, bondage or submission. —James Ridgeway, *Red Light*, p. 81, 1996

dunger; dunga *noun*
the penis *NEW ZEALAND*
- —David McGill, *David McGill's Complete Kiwi Slang Dictionary*, p. 41, 1998

dungout *noun*
an utter failure *NEW ZEALAND, 1995*
- —Harry Orsman, *A Dictionary of Modern New Zealand Slang*, p. 45, 1999

dungpuncher *noun*
the male playing the active role in anal sex *AUSTRALIA*
- —Thommo, *The Dictionary of Australian Swearing and Sex Sayings*, p. 38, 1985
- —David McGill, *David McGill's Complete Kiwi Slang Dictionary*, p. 41, 1998

dung-scuffer *noun*
a cowboy *US*
A euphemism for **SHITKICKER**.
- Drawing stares at Bardelli's: Red-headed Don Imus, togged like a real dung-scuffer in Western hat, faded Levis, red bandana and pointed cowboy boots. —*San Francisco Chronicle*, p. 27, 8th March 1974

dunk *verb*
to humiliate in any context *US*
- —Connie Eble (Editor), *UNC-CH Campus Slang*, p. 4, Fall 1999

dunka *noun*
a large posterior *US*
- —Connie Eble (Editor), *UNC-CH Campus Slang*, p. 2, November 2002

Dunkirk *noun*
work *UK*
Rhyming slang.
- I'll see you later, I'm off to Dunkirk. —Ray Puxley, *Cockney Rabbit*, 1992

dunky; dunkey *noun*
a condom *UK*
- "What! You didn't shag 'er." Brad shook his head. "Why not?" "No dunkies, mate." —Colin Butts, *Is Harry on the Boat?*, p. 42, 1997
- [I] knew this bloke right he used to put one dunkey on over another cos he was paranoid about getting his girl pregnant[.] —Patrick Jones, *Unprotected Sex*, p. 211, 1999

Dunlop tyre; dunlop *noun*
a liar *UK*
Rhyming slang.
- —Ray Puxley, *Cockney Rabbit*, 1992

dunnies *noun*
a toilet block *AUSTRALIA, 1933*
- Puts the low down on a bloke, bowled out dooing a snoop on girl's dunnies. —Norman Lindsay, *Halfway to Anywhere*, p. 20, 1947
- Hand down my tweeds...fingers coiled around my python...tug, tug...dragged off by the skewer...behind the dunnies[.] —Jack Hibberd, *A Stretch of the Imagination*, p. 15, 1971
- Tracey looked us up and down. "Comin' down the dunnies for a fag?" —Kathy Lette and Gabrielle Carey, *Puberty Blues*, p. 16, 1979

dunnit?
doesn't it? *UK*
A phonetic slurring.
- Mebbe I am. Depends, dunnit? —Anthony Masters, *Minder*, p. 70, 1984
- It just depends on how clever you are, dunnit? —Shaun Ryder, *Shaun Ryder... in His Own Words*, 1996

dunno; dunna; dunnaw
don't know; I don't know *UK, 1842*
A phonetic slurring.
- I dunno, we seem to get chucked out of every place we go. —John Peter Jones, *Feather Pluckers*, p. 19, 1964
- Mazz shook his head. "Dunno. How about you, you still playing?" —John Williams, *Cardiff Dead*, p. 48, 2000

dunny *noun*
1 a toilet *AUSTRALIA, 1933*
A shortening of *dunniken*, from British dialect and cant. According to Hotten,*The Slang Dictionary*, 1859, a compound of 'danna' (excrement) and 'ken' (house). Before the age of septic tanks and flush toilets the 'dunny' was a wooden outhouse

standing far back from a dwelling. The spelling 'dunnee' seems only to have been favoured by Barry Humphries in his *Bazza MacKenzie* comic strip.

- Oh, get ripped – you wasn't here when the dunny blew up. —Sumner Locke Elliott, *Rusty Bugles*, p. 15, 1948
- This place pongs like an out back dunnee! —Barry Humphries, *The Wonderful World of Barry McKenzie*, p. 19, 1968
- He went to the dunny and sat on the seat lid and cried. —Ronald McKie, *The Mango Tree*, p. 193, 1975
- "Betty!" screamed the cook. "Take Mr Scobie to the dunny willya." —Elizabeth Jolley, *Mr Scobie's Riddle*, p. 185, 1983
- You were a bit of a smartarse when you started here. Putting a tenpenny bunger under Old Jack's backside when he sat on the dunny. —Barry Dickins, *What the dickins*, p. 86, 1985
- There was no torch available for my father because I had dropped it down the dunny the night before. —Peter Carey, *Oscar and Lucinda*, p. 4, 1988

2 the vagina *BAHAMAS*

- —John A. Holm, *Dictionary of Bahamian English*, p. 67, 1982

3 money *JAMAICA*

- —Velma Pollard, *Dread Talk*, p. 49, 2000

dunny budgie *noun*

a blowfly *AUSTRALIA*

- Keep the dunny budgies off the meat, mother! —*Wordmap (www.abc.net.au/wordmap)*, 2003

dunny can *noun*

a sanitary bin *AUSTRALIA, 1962*

- Tarzan, Tarzan, swinging on a lacker band, / Up comes Superman and kicks him in the dunny can. —Wendy Lowenstein, *Improper Play Rhymes*, p. 163, 1973

dunny cart *noun*

a vehicle for collecting sanitary bins *AUSTRALIA, 1963*

- —Jim Ramsay, *Cop It Sweet!*, p. 33, 1977
- I often watched the dunny cart from the front window. —Clive James, *Unreliable Memoirs*, p. 50, 1980

dunny diver *noun*

a plumber *NEW ZEALAND*

- —Sonya Plowman, *Great Kiwi Slang*, p. 64, 2002

dunny documents *noun*

toilet paper *AUSTRALIA*

- 'You girls were home? Didn't you hear me calling out for dunny documents?' Jake affected outrage. —Linda Jaivin, *Rock n Roll Babes from Outer Space*, p. 65, 1996

dunny man; dunnyman *noun*

a man employed to empty sanitary bins *AUSTRALIA, 1962*

- The dunnyman in his heavy loaded truck looked tired as the motor ground up the hill to the depot where the nightsoil would be buried. —David Ireland, *The Flesheaters*, p. 5, 1972
- Ever since I could remember, the dunny man had come running down the driveway once a week. —Clive James, *Unreliable Memoirs*, p. 50, 1980

dunny paper *noun*

toilet paper *AUSTRALIA*

- In the toilet cubicle, I camoflaged the seat in layers of dunny paper. —Kathy Lette, *Girls' Night Out*, p. 59, 1987

duns *noun*

money *JAMAICA, 1982*

- —Thomas H. Slone, *Rasta is Cuss*, p. 44, 2003

dupe *noun*

a duplicate *US, 1891*

- "Give me the dupe to the suite and 'Skeeter' and I will fine-tooth it while you lug her out to a restaurant or a show tonight." —Iceberg Slim (Robert Beck), *Airtight Willie and Me*, p. 177, 1979

dupe *verb*

to duplicate *US, 1912*

- So that no one will dupe this copy. —Robert Stoller and I.S. Levine, *Coming Attractions*, p. 151, 1991

duper *noun*

a duplicating machine, such as a mimeograph *US*

- —*American Speech*, p. 25, Spring 1982: 'The language of science fiction fan magazines'

duppy *noun*

a ghost *BARBADOS*

- —Frank A. Collymore, *Barbadian Dialect*, p. 42, 1965
- What's happening, rudebwai? How you so jumpy? Settle nuh, you look like a duppy fe real. —Karline Smith, *Moss Side Massive*, p. 174, 1994

duppy and the dog *noun*

a crowd made up of everyone you can think of *BARBADOS, 1980*

- —Richard Allsopp, *Dictionary of Caribbean English Usage*, p. 207, 1996

duppy tucks *noun*

clothes burnt by an iron *BARBADOS*

- —Frank A. Collymore, *Barbadian Dialect*, p. 36, 1965

Durban *noun*

marijuana from the Durban area of South Africa *SOUTH AFRICA*

- [The] lunatic Durban or dat sticky fokkin orange skunk[.] —Nick Barlay, *Curvy Lovebox*, p. 33, 1997
- "Heh." "Mighty Mite seeds." "California Girl cross Durban." "Same." —Brian Preston, *Pot Planet*, p. 232, 2002

Durban brown *noun*

brownish marijuana, said to have been grown in Natal Province, South Africa *UK*

- —Nick Brownlee, *This Is Cannabis*, p. 151, 2002

Durban poison *noun*

a variety of marijuana *SOUTH AFRICA*

- Other types include Purple Haze, Sumatran Red, Durban Poison and skunk. —Macfarlane, Macfarlane and Robson, *The User*, p. 142, 1996
- Some of the best African grasses include South African known as Durban Poison. This is a straw green colour, where as what is sold more commercially is darker green. It is sticky and smells of ammonia. —Mike Rock, *This Book*, 1999
- Tricky has bucked the trend with a general 'down' on the whole drug culture; he called his sub-label 'Durban Poison' after an especially potent brand of weed. —Harry Shapiro, *Waiting For The Man*, 1999

durn *adverb*

used as a folksy variation of 'darn' or 'darned', a euphemism for 'damned' *US*

- Just eager and anxious to go climbin around and so durn cheerful, I ain't never seen a better kid. —Jack Kerouac, *The Dharma Bums*, p. 176, 1958

durog *noun*

marijuana *US, 1977*

A variant of **DUROS**, punning on 'drug'.

- —Richard A. Spears, *The Slang and Jargon of Drugs and Drink*, p. 180, 1986
- —Mike Haskins, *Drugs*, p. 287, 2003

durong *noun*

marijuana *UK*

A variation of **DUROG** and **DUROS**.

- —Mike Haskins, *Drugs*, p. 287, 2003

duros *noun*

marijuana *US, 1971*

The Spanish masculine noun *duro* is a five-peseta coin; the anglicised plural puts a cheap price on the drug.

- —Richard A. Spears, *The Slang and Jargon of Drugs and Drink*, p. 180, 1986
- —Mike Haskins, *Drugs*, p. 287, 2003

durry *noun*

a cigarette *AUSTRALIA, 1941*

Origin unknown. It has been suggested that it is extracted from Bull *Dur*ham™, a brand of tobacco, but this is drawing a long bow indeed.

- If the durry was hanging on his chin, he had no more than a good pair and was going for a ride. If it stuck out, he had two pair or three of a kind. —Sam Weller, *Old Bastards I Have Met*, p. 77, 1979
- —Phillip Gwynne, *Deadly Unna?*, p. 119, 1998

duss *verb*

to kill *UK*

West Indian and UK black pronunciation of **DUST** (to kill).

- "They'll duss me if I say anything." "Wrong. I'm going to duss you if you don't start talking." Storm pushed the Browning into the boy's started face. —Karline Smith, *Moss Side Massive*, p. 225, 1994

dust *noun*

1 a powdered narcotic, especially cocaine or heroin *US, 1916*

- All of them, and most of the others mentioned so far in the case (plus others unmentioned but nevertheless inovlved), have dabbled in dust deals[.] —*San Francisco Examiner*, p. 23, 6th December 1948
- Do you ever get high? A walk on the wild side? Ever do dust? —*Nashville*, 1975
- He snorted dust from his diamond encrusted spoon strung on a gold chain around his neck. —Iceberg Slim (Robert Beck), *Airtight Willie and Me*, p. 171, 1979

- DEALER: Hey, man. You wanna cop some blow? / JUNKIE: Sure, watcha got? Dust, flakes or rocks? / DEALER: I got China White, Mother of Pearl...I reflect what you need. —Grandmaster Flash & The Furious Five featuring Melle Mel, *White Lines*, 1983
- Man, I don't know if it was the real thing or a fuckin' hallucination. I've been doin' dust and reds for three days now. —James Ellroy, *Blood on the Moon*, p. 110, 1984
- Cocaine is known as C, Charlie, coke, dust[.] —James Kay and Julian Cohen, *The Parents' Complete Guide to Young People and Drugs*, p. 134, 1998

2 phencyclidine, the recreational drug known as PCP or angel dust *US*
An abbreviation of **ANGEL DUST**.
- — *Drummer*, p. 77, 1977
- The carpeted lobby was littered with fallen rainbows, dexis, bennies, ludes, speed, even some dust, though it had a bad rep these days[.] —Joseph Wambaugh, *The Glitter Dome*, p. 122, 1981
- In '77 he smoked a bag of dust he bought from a dago. —*New Jack City*, 1990

3 inexpensive cigarette tobacco given free to prisoners *US*
- There were two types available – a fine powdery rolling tobacco, called "Dust," and a pipe cut which wasn't quite inferior enough to warrant a derisive nickname. —Malcolm Braly, *On the Yard*, p. 46, 1967

4 the powdered malted milk used in soda fountain malt drinks *US*
- — *American Speech*, p. 88, April 1946: 'The language of West Coast culinary workers'

5 money *UK, 1607*
- —Malachi Andrews and Paul T. Owens, *Black Language*, p. 89, 1973
- —Bill Davis, *Jawjacking*, p. 37, 1977

6 a small amount of money *TRINIDAD AND TOBAGO, 1987*
- —Lise Winer, *Dictionary of the English/Creole of Trinidad & Tobago*, 2003

7 the condition of being doomed or finished *US*
- Oh, man, we're dust! We're so history! —*Airheads*, 1994
- They're just sitting on me till they can tell her I'm dust. —Stephen J. Cannell, *The Tin Collectors*, p. 87, 2001

▸ **on the dust**
working as a refuse collector *UK*
- On the dust I worked with a great bunch of blokes[.] —Dave Courtney, *Stop the Ride I Want to Get Off*, p. 95, 1999
- I half-knew a few of the blokes he worked with on the dust (yes, he's a dustman, and he looks down on me). —Danny King, *The Burglar Diaries*, p. 50, 2001

dust *verb*

1 to beat *UK, 1612*
- [O]thers are just scared that the dad will dust you if you dust their son. —Paul Fraser and Shane Meadows, *TwentyFourSeven*, p. 15, 1997

2 to shoot; to kill *US, 1972*
- "Face down! And nothing sexy, I'll dust ya, I swear you'll die." —Seth Morgan, *Homeboy*, p. 73, 1990

3 to leave *US*
- —Lou Shelly, *Hepcats Jive Dictionary*, p. 11, 1945

4 to use and become intoxicated with phencyclidine, the recreational drug known as PCP or angel dust *US*
- —Geoffrey Froner, *Digging for Diamonds*, p. 27, 1989

5 to combine marijuana and heroin for smoking *US*
- — Sacramento Municipal Utility District, *A Glossary of Drugs and Drug Language*, 1986
- —Robert Ashton, *This Is Heroin*, p. 208, 2002

6 in horse racing, to administer a drug to a horse before a race *US*
- —David W. Maurer, *Argot of the Racetrack*, p. 25, 1951

dustbin *noun*
a gun turret *UK*
- A simple cupola, consisting of a slotted 'dustbin,' rose from the rear walls of the turret. —Bryan Perrett, *Panzerkampfwagen IV Medium Tank*, p. 5, 1990

dustbin lid; dustbin *noun*

1 a child *UK, 1960*
Rhyming slang for 'kid'; rarely, if ever, singular. May be reduced further to 'binlid'.
- There's no binlids to queer the pitch. —Kevin Sampson, *Outlaws*, p. 242, 2001

2 a Jewish person *UK*
Rhyming slang for **YID**.
- —Ronnie Barker, *Fletcher's Book of Rhyming Slang*, 1979

dust-biter *noun*
during the US war against Iraq, an infantry soldier assigned to front line duty *US*
- A dust-biter would ask the pogue if he ever set up a 'T, R, double E' – referring to an antenna – and the progue would almost always say 'Yes. —*Army*, p. 48, November 1991

dust bunny *noun*
a cluster of dust that accumulates under furniture *US, 1966*
- Sleep and Dust Bunnies[.] —*American Speech*, p. 145, Summer 1981

dust-eater *noun*
the last vehicle in a military convoy *US, 1986*
- The dust eaters in Vietnam were the rear security elements of the convoy. —Gregory Clark, *Words of the Vietnam War*, p. 158, 1990

dusted *adjective*

1 drug-intoxicated *US, 1959*
Originally of cocaine, then less and less discriminating.
- —Eugene Landy, *The Underground Dictionary*, p. 72, 1971
- Bitch, I don't sell crack, I smoke it / My brain's dusted; I'm disgusted at my habits[.] —Eminem (Marshall Mathers), *Weed Lacer (Freestyle)*, 1999
- —Mike Haskins, *Drugs*, p. 291, 2003

2 drunk *US*
- — *Current Slang*, p. 2, Summer 1966

dusted out; dusted *adjective*
under the influence of phencyclidine, the recreational drug known as PCP or angel dust *US*
- The trucker was dusted out on PCP and it was only Jane's choke hold that saved the life of a foot-beat cop who was nearly beaten to death with his own stick by the duster. —Joseph Wambaugh, *The Delta Star*, p. 10, 1983
- —Kenn "Naz" Young, *Naz's Dictionary of Teen Slang*, p. 35, 1993

duster *noun*

1 a metal device worn above the knuckles so that, when punching, it both protects the fist and lends brutal force to the blow *UK*
An abbreviation of 'knuckleduster'; from **DUST** (to beat).
- Chelsea bastard caught me with a punch. Think he must have been wearing dusters. — Martin King and Martin Knight, *The Naughty Nineties*, p. 53, 1999
- I dipped into my pockets and got a duster on each hand and then smacked the cunt driving right in the head and knocked him out[.] —Dave Courtney, *Raving Lunacy*, p. 119, 2000

2 an M-2 anti-aircraft tank armed with twin Bofars 40mm guns *US, 1969*
The tank was designed for anti-aircraft combat, but the North Vietnamese did not operate in the air, so the M-2 was used on the ground, where it was quite good at **DUSTING** (killing) enemy soldiers.
- —Linda Reinberg, *In the Field*, p. 69, 1991

3 a user of phencyclidine, the recreational drug known as PCP or angel dust *US, 1967*
- The trucker was dusted out on PCP and it was only Jane's choke hold that saved the life of a foot-beat cop who was nearly beaten to death with his own stick by the duster. —Joseph Wambaugh, *The Delta Star*, p. 10, 1983

4 in oil drilling, a hole that produces no oil *US, 1898*
It may produce salt water, but it is still dry.
- —Jerry Robertson, *Oil Slanguage*, p. 50, 1954

5 the inner door of a safe *US*
- —Vincent J. Monteleone, *Criminal Slang*, p. 77, 1949

6 the buttocks *US*
- Keep on wriggling your saucy duster and smelling sweet. —Mezz Mezzrow, *Really the Blues*, p. 199, 1946

duster *verb*
to punch someone using a knuckleduster *UK*
- So I dustered him spark out[.] —Dave Courtney, *Raving Lunacy*, p. 224, 2000

dusters *noun*
the testicles *US*
- —Dale Gordon, *The Dominion Sex Dictionary*, p. 61, 1967
- — *Maledicta*, p. 195, Winter 1980: 'A new erotic vocabulary'

dust hawk *noun*
a horse driven in sulky races *CANADA*
- I wasn't off my feed, nor hadn't lost my head neither. I wanted that dust hawk and he knew it; but I got it on him with the harness and the sulky. —Sir H. Gilbert Parker, *The World for Sale*, p. 221, 1971

dusties *noun*

old phonograph records of out-of-fashion songs *US*

- — *American Speech*, p. 154, Spring-Summer 1972: 'An approach to Black slang'

dust it *verb*

to leave hurriedly *TRINIDAD AND TOBAGO, 1990*

- — Lise Winer, *Dictionary of the English/Creole of Trinidad & Tobago*, 2003

dust of angels *noun*

phencyclidine, the recreational drug known as PCP or angel dust *US*

- — US Department of Justice, *Street Terms*, October 1994

dust-off *noun*

medical evacuation by helicopter *US, 1967*

Vietnam war usage.

- Yes, sir, what we needs just this minute is one of them medevac choppers, a dust-off, don't ya know. — Larry Heinemann, *Close Quarters*, p. 92, 1977
- I picked up a stretcher from the Dust Off ship. — Robert Mason, *Chickenhawk*, p. 174, 1983
- They'd pass out from shock and die before the dust-off medevac chopper could haul-ass out to us. — Larry Heinemann, *Paco's Story*, p. 21, 1986

dust off *verb*

1 to kill *US, 1940*

- He tried to dust me off a little while ago. — Mickey Spillane, *I, The Jury*, p. 83, 1947

2 to evacuate (the wounded) *US*

- They dusted him off to the 27th evac. — Ronald J. Glasser, *365 Days*, p. 121, 1971

3 in hot rodding and drag racing, to defeat in a race *US*

- — Fred Horsley, *The Hot Rod Handbook*, p. 209, 1965

dust puppy *noun*

a cluster of soft dust that accumulates on the floor *US, 1943*

- Kristen who couldn't bake, couldn't clean house without leaving the corners full of dustypuppies and the wallpaper smeared where her broom had brushed down cobwebs. — Wallace Stegner, *The Big Rock Candy Mountain*, p. 57, 1943
- Dust puppies tended to clump where the pipes turned, and she stopped occasionally to clean them away. — Larry Niven, *Footfall*, p. 419, 1985

dusts *noun*

brass knuckles *US*

- — Kenn "Naz" Young, *Naz's Dictionary of Teen Slang*, p. 35, 1993

dust-up *noun*

a fight; a disturbance; an engagement with an enemy *UK, 1897*

Military coinage; the image of dust raised in a physical conflict.

- Immediate cause of the dustup was the fact that Oppermann had asked City Attorney Dion R. Holm for a ruling on legality of his issuing permits for twenty-five foot lots in two new subdivisions west of Twin Peaks. — *San Francisco Examiner*, p. 16, 25th November 1950
- I hoped Channel 8 had either ignored Teddy's police dust-up or prejudiced his case. — George V. Higgins, *Penance for Jerry Kennedy*, p. 125, 1985
- [A] bit of a dust-up between King Harry and Sir Thomas a'Becket down the Old Kent Road[.] — Andrew Nickolds, *Back to Basics*, p. 163, 1994

dusty *noun*

an old person, thought to be aged 70 or more *UK*

Upper-class society use.

- — Ann Barr and Peter York, *The Official Sloane Ranger Handbook*, p. 158, 1982

dusty *adjective*

under the influence of phencyclidine, the recreational drug known as PCP or angel dust *US*

- Someone "dusty" is always dangerous, because you never know what the next puff can lead to. — Nelson George, *Hip Hop America*, p. 39, 1998

dusty and cleaning *noun*

a surgical scraping of the uterus *US*

A back formation from the technical term D & C (dilation and curetage).

dutch *noun*

▸ **in dutch**

in trouble *US, 1851*

- The door was still sealed pending further investigation and I didn't want ot get in dutch with the D.A.'s office by breaking it[.] — Mickey Spillane, *I, The Jury*, p. 56, 1947
- In such situations the bookmakers said they were "in Dutch." Hence the name "dutch book." — Toney Betts., *Across the Board*, p. 189, 1956
- When I told him about it the next day he swore he hadn't meant to get me in dutch and I believed him. — Louise Meriwether, *Daddy Was a Number Runner*, p. 97, 1970
- "I didn't want you getting in Dutch with Clara again. I thought I'd just make sure you were awake." In Dutch? You make a note to look up this expression in Partridge's dictionary of slang when you get to work. — Jay McInerney, *Bright Lights, Big City*, p. 55, 1984
- Better hurry it up. I'm in dutch with the wife. — *Raising Arizona*, 1987

Dutch *noun*

1 a spouse, especially a wife *UK, 1889*

Usually as 'old Dutch' and preceded by a possessive pronoun. Albert Chevalier (1861–1923) explained the derivation as 'old Dutch clock', likening a wife's face to a clock-face, or punning on **CLOCK** (a face). The etymology is uncertain, but often confused with **DUCHESS** (a wife) and **DUTCH PLATE** (a friend).

- There ain't a lady livin' in the land / As I'd "swop" for my dear old Dutch! — Albert Chevalier, *My Old Dutch*, 1892
- My old Dutch and I, as we sit by our Jermiah [fire] in Buckingham Palace[.] — Ronnie Barker, *Fletcher's Book of Rhyming Slang*, p. 39, 1979

2 suicide *US, 1915*

- Four years ago, she was about to do a Dutch over the Brooklyn Bridge. — Mickey Spillane, *I, The Jury*, p. 8, 1947

▷ **see:** **DOUBLE DUTCH, DUTCH PLATE**

dutch *verb*

▸ **dutch a book**

in an illegal betting operation, to accept bets with odds and in a proportion that guarantees the bookmaker will lose money regardless of the outcome that is being bet on *US, 1911*

- — David W. Maurer, *Argot of the Racetrack*, p. 25, 1951

Dutch *verb*

in hot rodding and car customising, to paint elaborate pinstripes or flames on the car body in the style of 1950s customiser Kenneth 'Von Dutch' Howard *US*

- — John Edwards, *Auto Dictionary*, p. 49, 1993

Dutch *adverb*

paying your own way *US, 1914*

- When they are eating alone or with a musician boy friend (with whom they usually go "Dutch") you'll find them at the soda fountains[.] — Jack Lait and Lee Mortimer, *New York Confidential*, p. 143, 1948
- I thought you were going to guess I wanted to go Dutch. — Philip Wylie, *Opus 21*, p. 33, 1949
- So we go dutch, and everybody eats and drinks what he wants and no hard feelings[.] — John Nichols, *The Sterile Cuckoo*, p. 91, 1965

Dutch act; Dutch route *noun*

suicide *US, 1902*

- The farewell note said she was just tired of it all, life was a bore and she was getting no place, thus the Dutch act. — Mickey Spillane, *My Gun is Quick*, p. 98, 1950
- — William K. Bentley and James M. Corbett, *Prison Slang*, p. 105, 1992

Dutch auction; Dutch sale *noun*

a mock-auction or sale where goods are sold at nominal prices; especially an auction where the price is slowly decreased until the first bid is made and the lot is sold; in a multiple lot sale the highest bidder wins the right to purchase at the lowest bid price *UK, 1859*

- Chisholm stood there, looking at Arthur. "What's this then? A Dutch auction[?]" — Anthony Masters, *Minder*, p. 133, 1984

Dutch bath *noun*

a cursory washing of the body using little water *US, 1953*

- — Frederic G. Cassidy, *Dictionary of American Regional English*, p. 241, 1985

Dutch book *noun*

in a bookmaking operation, a horse race in which the odds are such that the astute bettor can bet on any horse and win *US, 1912*

- In such situations the bookmakers said they were "in Dutch." Hence the name "dutch book." — Toney Betts., *Across the Board*, p. 189, 1956

Dutch cap *noun*

a diaphragm or pessary *US, 1950*

- — *Maledicta*, p. 200, Winter 1980: 'A new erotic vocabulary'

Dutch clock *noun*
a speed recording device on a railway engine *US*
• —Norman Carlisle, *The Modern Wonder Book of Trains and Railroading*, p. 262, 1946

Dutch courage *noun*
courage induced by drink *UK, 1826*
• [H]e was full of Dutch courage and had a breath like a distillery. —Charles Raven, *Underworld Nights*, p. 178, 1956
• "Thought you might need a bit of Dutch courage," said Dave. —Anthony Masters, *Minder*, p. 166, 1984
• For the most part Dutch courage aroused Martin's anger[.]—Wayne Anthony, *Spanish Highs*, p. 151, 1999

Dutch door action *noun*
bisexual activity *US*
• —Vann Wesson, *Generation X Field Guide and Lexicon*, p. 58, 1997

Dutch dumplings *noun*
in homosexual usage, the buttocks *US*
• — *Maledicta*, p. 54, 1986–1987: 'Continuation of a glossary of ethic slurs in American English'

Dutch fuck *noun*
the act of lighting your cigarette from one that another person is smoking *UK, 1948*
Often accompanied by the catchphrase: 'Hold it close to mine and take the draws down slowly'.

Dutch girl *noun*
in homosexual usage, a lesbian *US*
A painful pun alluding to Holland's flood control.
• — *Maledicta*, p. 54, 1986–1987: 'Continuation of a glossary of ethnic slurs in American English'

Dutchie *noun*
a Dutch person *UK*
• When he looks up again, the Dutchies have gone.—Guy Ritchie, *Lock, Stock... & Four Stolen Hooves*, p. 67, 2000

Dutch leave *noun*
an absence without permission *US, 1898*
• —Richard Lederer, *A Man of My Words*, p. 24, 2003

dutchman *noun*
1 any after-the-fact alteration of a flawed work process *US, 1859*
Discussed at great length in '"Dutchman": an on-the-job etymology', Archie Green, *American Speech*, December 1960.
• —Ramon Adams, *The Language of the Railroader*, p. 52, 1977
2 in oil drilling, the shaft of a screw that remains in a hole after the head has been sheared or twisted off *US*
• —Jerry Robertson, *Oil Slanguage*, p. 50, 1954
3 a drug dealer *US*
• —Jay Robert Nash, *Dictionary of Crime*, p. 114, 1992

Dutchman *nickname*
Norm Van Brocklin (1926–83), quarterback for the Los Angeles Rams during their glory days (1949–57) and then for the Philadelphia Eagles (1958–60) *US*

Dutchman's fart *noun*
a sea-urchin *UK*
• —D. Butcher, *Trawelermen*, 1980

Dutch Mill *nickname*
the infiltration surveillance centre at Nakhon Phonom, Thailand *US*
Sensors along routes of North Vietnamese infiltration into South Vietnam broadcast to an orbiting aircraft which relayed the signals to the US base at Nakhon Phonom, Thailand. Because of the distinctive shape of one of its antennas, the installation was called Dutch Mill.
• —Linda Reinberg, *In the Field*, p. 70, 1991

Dutch nickel *noun*
a hug or quick kiss *US, 1949*
• —Frederic G. Cassidy, *Dictionary of American Regional English, Volume II*, p. 246, 1991

Dutch oven *noun*
a prank performed by farting in a shared bed and then holding the unfortunate victim under the sheets *AUSTRALIA*
• Dutch Oven – Share bed, fart, spit in the air and yell "Ghosts".—Ryan Aven-Bray, *Ridgey Didge Oz Jack Lang*, p. 25, 1983
• This is created when someone breaks wind when in bed with someone else, then buries his partner's head beneath the sheets to enforce an appreciation of the smell.—Peter Furze, *Tailwinds*, p. 60, 1998
• —Chris Lewis, *The Dictionary of Playground Slang*, p. 79, 2003

Dutch Owl *noun*
a Dutch Owl™ cigar re-made to contain marijuana *US*
• I was instrumental in introducing Phillies Blunts to the UK [...] It was LL Cool J who taught me how to roll a Phillies. I can roll Phillies, Dutch Owls and White Owls.— *Mixmag*, p. 75, April 2003

Dutch pegs *noun*
the legs *UK, 1923*
Rhyming slang.

Dutch plate; Dutch *noun*
a friend *UK*
Rhyming slang for **MATE**; glossed as 'had some currency in the 1960s and 1970s, mainly in its shortened form' by John Ayto, *The Oxford Dictionary of Rhyming Slang*, 2002. Sometimes, and easily, confused with **DUTCH** (a spouse, especially a wife).

Dutch rod *noun*
a Luger pistol *US*
• —Vincent J. Monteleone, *Criminal Slang*, p. 77, 1949

Dutch rub *noun*
a playground torture consisting of rubbing the head of a boy restrained in a headlock with the restrainer's knuckles *US, 1930*
• The headlock; the Dutch rub, they called it then; the arm bent behind the back[.]—Elmore Leonard, *Gold Coast*, p. 179, 1980

Dutch sea wife *noun*
a simulated vagina, used for masturbation by males *US*
Collected by Peter Tamony on 22nd November, 1957, from a seafaring friend of Archie Green.

Dutch straight *noun*
in poker, a hand with five cards sequenced by twos, worth nothing but not without its beauty *US*
• —Irwin Steig, *Common Sense in Poker*, p. 184, 1963

Dutch treat *noun*
an arrangement in which each person pays their own way *US, 1887*
• The luncheons were run on a Dutch treat basis, and each woman continued to pay her dollar fee per lesson.—Jack Lait and Lee Mortimer, *Washington Confidential*, p. 138, 1951
• "But we always go Dutch treat," said I, which we did. "Look," she said, "Did you or did your not ask me out on a date?"—Max Shulman, *I was a Teen-Age Dwarf*, p. 45, 1959
• — Multicultural Management Program Fellows, *Dictionary of Cautionary Words and Phrases*, 1989
• "My treat?" "Dutch treat."—Joseph Wambaugh, *Finnegan's Week*, p. 215, 1993

Dutch uncle *noun*
a person given to pedantic lectures *UK, 1838*
• I talked like the proverbial dutch uncle to him about staying for a medical discharge but to no avail and that afternoon we watched him split.—Herbert Huncke, *The Evening Sun Turned Crimson*, p. 205, 1980

dutty *adjective*
dirty *UK*
West Indian and UK black patois pronunciation.
• Easy smiled to himself and hummed his version of a classic ragga rhythm: "I spy with my little eye, Grange undercover bwai, with dutty dun-dus [albino] eye."—Karline Smith, *Moss Side Massive*, p. 226, 1994

duty *noun*
a duty officer *US*
• The "Duty," as he is called, takes the business of waking the troops quite seriously because the sergeant of the guard is likely to appear in a minute or two later to see that everyone is out of the sack.—Martin Russ, *The Last Parallel*, p. 19, 1957

duty dog *noun*
the officer acting as prison governor when the governor is absent *UK*
• —Angela Devlin, *Prison Patter*, p. 48, 1996

duvet day *noun*
an unofficial day off work that is taken for no good reason *UK*
In August 2004 'duvet days' are being discussed as employee incentives. Recorded by the BBC on 3rd January 2001.

- If anyone in your office is audacious enough to take a duvet day this Friday, you will know what they are up to. — *The Guardian*, 13th February 2003

duw duw!

used for registering frustration, exasperation or sympathy *UK: WALES*

Pronounced 'jew jew'; a reduplication of Welsh *duw* (god) used widely, and without especial reference to its religious significance, by non-Welsh-speaking South Walians.

- Duw duw, there's a lot of bother. Me, I was born here in Ponty, Janeylove, and I have never moved. — James Hawes, *White Powder, Green Light*, p. 27, 2002

dux *adjective*

smart *FIJI*

Recorded by Jan Tent in 1993.

DV *noun*

a Cadillac Coupe de Ville car *US*

- — Edith A. Folb, *runnin' down some lines*, p. 234, 1980

dwaddle *verb*

to waste time, to dawdle *US, 1950*

- This is not time to dwaddle, his mentor said. — Flannery O'Connor, *The Violent Bear it Away*, p. 462, 1960

dwang *noun*

a short piece of timber inserted between wall studs *NEW ZEALAND*

- Fitted over the exposed wooden dwangs inside dcorrugated iron walls, it becomes hooks upon which one may hang hats. — *(Wellington) Dominion*, p. 8, 23rd July 1988

▸ in the dwang

in trouble *SOUTH AFRICA, 1994*

From Afrikaans for 'constraint'.

- Dad catch you out of bed you'll be in the dwang. — Alexandra Fuller, *Don't Let's Go to the Dogs Tonight*, p. 212, 2001

dwarf *noun*

the butt of a marijuana cigarette *US*

Crush That Dwarf, Hand Me the Pliers was a Firesign Theatre play about the life of Everyman George Tirebiter, punning, as was the fashion of the time, on marijuana use.

dweeb; dweebie *noun*

a socially inept person *US*

- But face it, you're a neo-maxi-zoom dweebie! — *The Breakfast Club*, 1985
- Everyone has a word for weenie again. The latest one I've heard is "dweeb," as in "He's a total dweeb." — *Wasington Post (reprinted from The Nation)*, p. C5, 22 December 1985
- Get out of my face you little dweeb. — *Wayne's World*, 1992
- "Let's move outta the way," Bobbie said, "before one a those dweebs hunks a bellyful on our heads." — Joseph Wambaugh, *Finnegan's Week*, p. 271, 1993
- [W]hy don't you dweebs go out and get a drink and lighten up. — Howard Stern, *Miss America*, p. 20, 1995
- Skip was a bad role model for middle America, espeically for sexually repressed, buck-toothed dweebs. — Editors of Ben is Dead, *Retrohell*, p. 173, 1997
- You're just like every other dweeb who worships Quentin Tarantino for the same reason you can't let go of the camera: because you don't know how to be a real person in real life. — *American Beauty*, 1999

dweeby *adjective*

foolish, inept, out of touch with current trends *US*

- Jeff came home trailing trails of hunger and without any of those dweeby creatures that are usually attached to him. — Hadley Irwin, *Kim/Kimi*, p. 43, 1987
- OK, I guess I *was* being dweeby. — Melanie McGrath, *Hard, Soft & Wet*, p. 123, 1998

dwell *verb*

▸ dwell the box

to be patient *UK*

- I dwelt the box for a couple of seconds at the door. — Charles Raven, *Underworld Nights*, p. 169, 1956

DWI *adjective*

poorly dressed *US*

'*D*ressed *w*ithout *i*nstructions', a play on the usual meaning of the initials, '*d*riving *w*hile *i*ntoxicated'.

- — Judi Sanders, *Da Bomb!*, p. 8, 1997

dwid *noun*

a social outcast *US*

- — Michael V. Anderson, *The Bad, Rad, Not to Forget Way Cool Beach and Surf Discriptionary*, p. 6, 1988

dwim *noun*

in computing, a command meaning '*d*o *w*hat *I* *m*ean' *US*

- — Guy L. Steele et al., *The Hacker's Dictionary*, p. 59, 1983

dwindles *noun*

the condition of an older hospital patient who is fading away *US, 1981*

- — Sally Williams, *"Strong" Words*, p. 140, 1994

dyam *adjective*

used as an intensifier *UK*

A West Indian and UK black patois variation of 'damn'.

- The paper would look dyam foolish if we printed a story about some man who claims to be licking down half of the Metropolitan Police Force. — Donald Gorgon, *Cop Killer*, p. 107, 1994

dye *noun*

▷ see: DIE

dye party *noun*

a gathering to tie-dye an assortment of clothes for personal use or sale *US*

- — David Shenk and Steve Silberman, *Skeleton Key*, p. 75, 1994

dying on its arse *adjective*

failing *UK*

The image of sitting down to wait for death and decay.

- It is going to transform that part of the city, which has lay dying on its arse for decades. — Kevin Sampson, *Outlaws*, p. 30, 2001

dyin' holy dyin'

used as a curse or oath, especially in Nova Scotia *CANADA*

Unlike a number of the maritime sacrilegious curses, this one is often used to express surprise.

- Dyin' holy dyin', but it is blowing hard outside the harbour here! — Lewis Poteet, *The South Shore Phrase Book*, p. 42, 1999

dyke; dike *noun*

1 a lesbian, especially a 'mannish', aggressive one *US, 1931*

Safely used by insiders, with caution by outsiders.

- I never saw such a crowd of dikes and faggots. — Horace McCoy, *Kiss Tomorrow Good-bye*, p. 277, 1948
- Inspector, you are acquainted with the vernacular for Lesbian, are you not – the word "dyke?" — *San Francisco Examiner*, p. 8, 5th March 1953
- I use that as an excuse (because Alice dike-like silent unpleasant and strange and likes no one) to lay the two bills on Mardou's dishes at sink[.] — Jack Kerouac, *The Subterraneans*, p. 74, 1958
- A dyke ein blue jeans, drunk and jealous, throws her bottle. — Willard Motely, *Let No Man Write My Epitaph*, p. 247, 1958
- This is not a queer bar – it is an outcast bar – Negroes and vagrant whites, heads and hypese, dikes and queens. — John Rechy, *City of Night*, p. 184, 1963
- [T]he pool-playing dykes and femmes sit at tables in one corner away from the juke-box, and the "straights" fill out the rest of the bar. — Roger Gordon, *Hollywood's Sexual Underground*, p. 18, 1966
- It's hard to spot dikes, cause sometimes we're married to them. — Lenny Bruce, *The Essential Lenny Bruce*, p. 163, 1967
- If you mean am I a dike, no. Not at all. — Gore Vidal, *Myra Breckinridge*, p. 140, 1968
- [W]e was renting hotel suites, feeding the dykes coke, and watching the show. — Edwin Torres, *Carlito's Way*, p. 80, 1975
- — Multicultural Management Program Fellows, *Dictionary of Cautionary Words and Phrases*, 1989
- I call myself a dyke so it's not too devastating when some throwback screams it at me as I'm leaving a bar at night. — *Chasing Amy*, 1997
- She's a fuckin' dyke. — Stuart Browne, *Dangerous Parking*, p. 45, 2000
- Come and TRY IT DYKE! — Jack Allen, *When the Whistle Blows*, p. 140, 2000

2 a toilet *UK, 1923*

- 'Meet you in the dyke,' Mick hissed and fled. — Russell Braddon, *The Naked Island*, p. 11, 1952
- You, Tramp, check the dikes; you Evan, have a look in the saloon bar. — Geoff Wyatt, *Saltwater Saints*, p. 58, 1969
- It's normal for you to go to the dyke fifty times a night. — Tim Winton, *That Eye, The Sky*, p. 120, 1986

3 *dipipanone*, an analgesic opiate used for recreational narcotic effect *UK*

- — Angela Devlin, *Prison Patter*, p. 48, 1996

dyke daddy *noun*

a male who prefers and seeks the friendship of lesbians *US*

- — Connie Eble (Editor), *UNC-CH Campus Slang*, p. 2, Fall 1991

dykey *adjective*
overtly lesbian, mannish *US, 1964*
- Now don't smile like that, nothing dikey has happened or will. —Gore Vidal, *Myra Breckinridge*, p. 242, 1968
- [P]arties have been getting dykier by the dance step and Red Raw on January 25 promises to be a winner. —*Lesbians on the Loose*, p. 44, 1997

dykon *noun*
a person or image seen as inspirational to lesbians *UK*
A variation on 'gay icon', combining **DYKE** (a lesbian) and 'icon' (a devotional image).
- Actress Sharon Stone has become a living dykon (dike-icon) to the "grrrrls". Other current faves include k.d.lang and Jodie Foster[.] —Alon Shulman, *The Style Bible*, p. 85, 1999

dynamite *noun*
1 powerful alcohol or drugs *US, 1919*
- Even if it's only one stick of dynamite this boy is always a sly cat. —Hal Ellson, *Duke*, p. 27, 1949
- "That was dynamite you gave me the other night, Luke," she murmured[.] —George Mandel, *Flee the Angry Strangers*, p. 120, 1952
- The good stuff, in its round cylinders of cigarettes, he stacked in one pile: dynamites. —Willard Motley, *Let No Man Write My Epitaph*, p. 107, 1958
- If you were nice to Tony, he was nice to you; he came up with dynamite when you were nice to him. —Clarence Cooper Jr, *The Scene*, p. 67, 1960
- When the two men allegedly introduced the drug into the Bay Area a short time ago, the addicts spread the word that some "real dynamite" was available, said O'Connor. —*San Francisco Examiner*, p. 17, 22nd April 1962
- Not just any connection, but a connection who deals good quality stuff – "dynamite," not "garbage." —James Mills, *The Panic in Needle Park*, p. 15, 1966
- We copped off that stud from New Yawk who came over with that dynamite every now and then. —Nathan Heard, *Howard Street*, p. 161, 1968
- "We ain't got no bigger thang goin' on than yhou 'n Zelma," he replied finally, sprawling back on the bed, the first effects of the dynamite seeping in. —Odie Hawkins, *Chicago Hustle*, p. 33, 1977
- [I]f we don't take charge of this gizmo for making dynamite out of low-grade shit, you won't be tops no more if somebody else gets hands on it. —Robert Deane Pharr, *Giveadamn Brown*, p. 208, 1978
- I asked if she could help me cop and she said she had some shit – $3.50 bags – not dynamite, but decent. —Herbert Huncke, *The Evening Sun Turned Crimson*, p. 161, 1980

2 nitroglycerin tablets prescribed to cardiac patients *US*
- —John Gould, *Maine Lingo*, p. 84, 1975

3 any amphetamine, methamphetamine or other central nervous system stimulant *US*
- National Institute on Drug Abuse— *What do they call it again?*, 1980

4 cocaine *US*
- —J.E. Schmindt, *Narcotics Lingo and Lore*, p. 54, 1959

5 a blend of heroin and cocaine *US, 1937*
- Addicts sometimes blend heroin and cocaine in a mixture called dynamite. —Harry J. Anslinger, *The Murderers*, p. 271, 1961
- —Robert Ashton, *This Is Heroin*, p. 208, 2002

6 something that is very good *US, 1902*
- Dynamnite, baby, but get your paws out of my pockets. —Richard Farina, *Been Down So Long*, p. 119, 1966
- This grass is DYNAMITE. —Doug Lang, *Freaks*, p. 109, 1973

7 in an illegal betting operation, money that one bookmaker bets with another bookmaker to cover bets that he does not want to hold *US*
- —David W. Maurer, *Argot of the Racetrack*, p. 25, 1951

8 a fight *UK*
Rhyming slang. May be abbreviated to 'dyna'.
- —Ray Puxley, *Cockney Rabbit*, 1992

dynamite *verb*
to stop a train suddenly *US*
- —Ramon Adams, *The Language of the Railroader*, p. 52, 1977

▸ **dynamite the brakes**
in trucking, to make a sudden, emergency stop *US*
- —Montie Tak, *Truck Talk*, p. 54, 1971

dynamite *adjective*
excitingly excellent *US, 1922*
- The first bite was dynamite! —Max Shulman, *Guided Tour of Campus Humor*, p. 21, 1955
- There were also some nice Playboy shots that I kept (1 dynamite fleshy configuration from Europe that gave me an erection), and all the other essentials for clerking. —Clarence Cooper Jr, *The Farm*, p. 50, 1967
- Dynamite! This is dynamite! —*King of Comedy*, 1976
- She's really a sho' 'nuff dynamite sister. —Odie Hawkins, *Chicago Hustle*, p. 222, 1977
- Coulda been a dynamite score. —Edwin Torres, *After Hours*, p. 310, 1979
- The next gig is gonna be dynamite, huge, you'll see. —*The Blues Brothers*, 1980
- It's like the Rastafarians say, you really don't need acid, because dynamite reefer makes you trip. —Stephen Gaskin, *Amazing Dope Tales*, p. 15, 1980

dyn-no-mite!
used for expressing strong approval *US*
A stock laugh-line catchphrase used by the character J.J. Evans, played by Jimmie Walker, in the 1970s situation comedy *Facts of Life*.
- Michael moved in the direction of his quarry, overtaking two small black kids in Dyn-O-Mite T-shirts. —Armistead Maupin, *Tales of the City*, p. 125, 1978

dyno *noun*
1 heroin, especially if nearly pure *US, 1969*
An abbreviation of 'dynamite'.
- —Richard A. Spears, *The Slang and Jargon of Drugs and Drink*, p. 182, 1986
- —Robert Ashton, *This Is Heroin*, p. 205, 2002
- —Mike Haskins, *Drugs*, p. 283, 2003

2 alcohol *US*
- —Joseph E. Ragen and Charles Finston, *Inside the World's Toughest Prison*, p. 798, 1962

3 a dynometer (an instrument used to measure engine power) *US, 1954*
- With the engine running, you make adjustments until the dyno shows the engine is tuned right. —Ed Radlauer, *Drag Racing Pix Dix*, p. 19, 1970

dyno *adjective*
excellent *US, 1962*
An abbreviation of **DYNAMITE**.
- —Jonathan Roberts, *How to California*, p. 168, 1984
- —Pamela Munro, *U.C.L.A. Slang*, p. 36, 1989

dyno- *prefix*
dynamic *US*
- —William Nealy, *Mountain Bike!*, p. 160, 1992

dyno-pure *noun*
especially pure heroin *UK*
An elaboration of **DYNO**.
- —Robert Ashton, *This Is Heroin*, p. 205, 2002
- —Mike Haskins, *Drugs*, p. 283, 2003

Dyson *noun*
an act of mutual oral-genital sex *UK, 2001*
Dyson™ is the brand name of a vacuum cleaner that introduced 'dual-cyclone' technology which, it is claimed, provides improved suction; 'Dyson', as a sex-act, stresses the dual-functionality of such suction. This is not the first use of a vacuum cleaner as a sexual simile: Electrolux™, another major brand, at one time used the slogan 'Nothing Sucks Like An Electrolux' which, unsurprisingly, lead to its use as an epithet for 'a fellatrix'.

Ee

E *noun*

1 MDMA, the recreational drug best known as ecstasy *UK*
Generally from the initial letter of **ECSTASY**, specifically in reference to any MDMA tablet stamped with the symbol.
- —Pulp, *Sorted for E's & Wizz*, 1995
- —Mike Haskins, *Drugs*, p. 289, 2003

2 dismissal, rejection *UK*
An abbreviation of **ELBOW**.
- [S]he's given the door. The Royal 'E'. Back on the rock-and-roll. —Andrew Nickolds, *Back to Basics*, p. 13, 1994

3 in poker, the fifth player to the left of the dealer *US*
- —George Percy, *The Language of Poker*, p. 32, 1988

E *verb*

to take MDMA, the recreational drug best known as ecstasy *UK*
From the noun use.
- [T]he lads that used to E with him regularly were E'ing the next weekend after he died. —Macfarlane, Macfarlane and Robson, *The User*, p. 69, 1996

e- *prefix*

electronic; in practice, mainly applied to communication by computer
A back formation from 'e-mail', used in such constructions as 'e-address' and 'e-government'.
- —Coustance Hale, *Wired Style*, 1996

each-way all each-way *noun*

in multiple and accumulator betting, a method of settling each-way bets by dividing the total return from one stage of a bet into equal parts to be wagered on the next stage *UK*
- —David Bennet, *Know Your Bets*, p. 34, 2001

eager beaver *noun*

an annoyingly diligent and hard-working person *US, 1943*
- The all-time eager beaver. —Philip Wylie, *Opus 21*, p. 63, 1949
- George Katz, the eager beaver that he was, was directing the unloading of those books[.[—Evan Hunter, *The Blackboard Jungle*, p. 72, 1954

eagle *noun*

▸ **the eagle flies; the eagle screams; the eagle shits**
used for expressing payday *US, 1918*
Often used with 'when'.
- It was on a Thursday, the day before the Negro payday. The eagle always flew on Friday. —Dick Gregory, *Nigger*, p. 30, 1964
- —*Current Slang*, p. 18, Summer 1970
- —Hermese E. Roberts, *The Third Ear*, 1971
- [T]he weight of four more days (and maybe five) of clock punching and lockstepping ahead of them before the eagle flies. —Donald Goines, *The Busting Out of an Ordinary Man*, p. 12, 1985

eaglebird *noun*

1 the winner of any long-odds bet, such as the double zero in roulette *US*
- —Jay Robert Nash, *Dicitonary of Crime*, p. 115, 1992

2 in horse racing, a long-shot winner that nobody has bet on *US*
- —Dan Parker, *The ABC of Horse Racing*, p. 145, 1947

eagle day *noun*

pay day *US, 1941*
On pay day, it it said that **THE EAGLE FLIES/SCREAMS**, hence this term.
- —*American Speech*, p. 55, February 1947: 'Pacific War language'

E and E *noun*

evasion and escape *US*
Korean war usage.
- One of my responsibilities was to establish an evasion-and-escape [E&E] operation across Korea to rescue downed fliers. —Joseph C. Goulden, *Korea: The Untold Story of the War*, p. 468, 1982

E and E *verb*

to avoid combat duty *US*
From the accepted 'escape and evasion'. Military use in Vietnam.
- —Linda Reinberg, *In the Field*, p. 71, 1991

E and T; ET *noun*

in craps, a one-roll bet on eleven and twelve *US, 1983*
The bet was originally known as 'E and T'; with the popularity of the film *E.T.*, the terminology quickly changed.
- —Thomas L. Clark, *The Dictionary of Gambling and Gaming*, p. 71, 1987

ear *noun*

1 a citizens' band radio antenna *US*
- —*Complete CB Slang Dictionary*, 1976
- —Peter Chippindale, *The British CB Book*, p. 154, 1981

2 a person who is not a part of the criminal underworld but who reports what he hears to those who are *US*
- —R. Frederick West, *God's Gambler*, p. 225, 1964: 'Appendix A'

3 extremely drunk *IRELAND*
- He shook his head and nearly went on his ear again. —Roddy Doyle, *The Van*, p. 83, 1991

4 a police officer *SOUTH AFRICA*
- The ears. The jacks. The tokoloshes. The police. —Peter Driscoll, *The Wilby Conspiracy*, 1973

5 on a playing card, a bent corner used by a cheat to identify the card *US*
- —Hyman E. Goldin et al., *Dictionary of American Underworld Lingo*, p. 34, 1950
- He put the ear on it. —John Scarne, *Scarne's Guide to Modern Poker*, p. 277, 1979

▸ **keep your ear to the ground; have your ear to the ground**
to be alert to whatever is happening *UK, 1920*
- I kept my ear to the ground to see if those seizures led to a drought of the drug on the streets, or a price increase, but there was no change at all. —*The Guardian*, 16th January 2002

▸ **on your ear**
easily *UK*
- [H]e'd be out in a twelve-month. He could do it on his ear. —Charles Raven, *Underworld Nights*, p. 137, 1956

ear angel *noun*

a very small, nearly invisible speaker in a television announcer's ear by which others can communicate with the announcer while on air *US*
- In his "ear angel," the director told him to go right to commercial. —Stephen Cannell, *King Con*, p. 84, 1997

earballs *noun*

listeners to commercial broadcasting *US, 1999*
- [S]eize B2B [business to business] e-tailers and re-envisioneer innovative partnerships that evolve dot-com initiatives delivering synergistic earballs to incentivize. —*The Plain English Campaign*, Winter 2002

ear banger *noun*

a person who enjoys the sound of his own voice *US, 1942*
- —Jerry Robertson, *Oil Slanguage*, p. 51, 1954

earbash *noun*

a conversation; an unwanted lecture; a tirade *AUSTRALIA, 1951*
- 'You mean,' White said, hiding his wonderment and his smile, 'that the Old Man will get you into his cabin sooner or later and have a good old earbash about school days?' —J.E. MacDonnell, *Sabotage!*, p. 51, 1964
- I got the wash of this earbash just standing at the other end. —Max Walker, *How To Tame Lions*, p. 38, 1988

earbash *verb*
to talk to someone at length; to bore someone with speech *AUSTRALIA, 1944*
- When a bloke doesn't want ter talk, yer don't earbash 'im. — Nino Culotta (John O'Grady), *They're A Weird Mob*, p. 100, 1957
- She sees young Gillian every day at school, it beats me why she's got to stay up half the night earbashing on the telephone, and you ought to hear the drivel they talk! — Barry Humphries, *A Nice Night's Entertainment*, p. 38, 1960
- After the king had earbashed them they took off for Bethlehem. — Kel Richards, *The Aussie Bible*, p. 17, 2003

earbasher *noun*
an incessant talker; a bore *AUSTRALIA, 1941*
- Real earbasher he is, always on for a yap. — Ray Lawler, *Summer of the Seventeenth Doll*, p. 48, 1957
- — Harvey E. Ward, *Down Under Without Blunder*, p. 38, 1967
- [There were] photos on the wall, the mighty Bernborough in full gallop, Les Darcy, Churchill (the footballer, not the old ear-basher), the landing at Gallipoli[.] — Frank Hardy, *The Outcasts of Foolgarah*, p. 12, 1971
- Never have ears taken such a savage punishment...the keener the fisherman, the bigger the ear-basher. — Bob Staines, *Wot a Whopper*, p. 7, 1982

ear-bashing *noun*
1 an insistent barrage of chatter; constant nagging *AUSTRALIA, 1945*
- Usually travelling in pairs, these sundowners spent so much time in each other's company that 'magging' or 'earbashing' was something that just couldn't be tolerated. — Bill Wannan, *Bullockies, Beauts and Bandicoots*, p. 72, 1960
- So I had to be carried out again, and the coppers really give me an earbashing, but I don't mind that – it's the fair dinkum bashing I don't like. — Ray Denning, *Prison Diaries*, p. 64, 1978
- If a player was bald, ginger, fat, thin, tall, short or, worst of all, ex-West Ham, he'd receive an ear-bashing for ninety non-stop minutes[.] — Martin King and Martin Knight, *The Naughty Nineties*, p. 113, 1999

2 a harsh reprimand *NEW ZEALAND*
- — Louis S. Leland, *A Personal Kiwi-Yankee Dictionary*, p. 36, 1984

ear bender *noun*
an overly talkative person *US, 1934*
- — John Scarne, *Scarne's Guide to Modern Poker*, p. 277, 1979

earbobs *noun*
large, dangling earrings *US*
- — Connie Eble (Editor), *UNC-CH Campus Slang*, p. 3, Fall 1986

ear candy *noun*
1 music that is pleasant, if not challenging *US, 1984*
- — Vann Wesson, *Generation X Field Guide and Lexicon*, p. 60, 1997

2 a platitude *US*
- — David Olive, *Business Babble*, p. 51, 1991

earcon *noun*
an artificial sound that is representative of an action or content *UK, 1988*
A contrived piece of jargon awkwardly derived from 'icon', its visual equivalent, and slowly creeping into everyday usage.
- Use earcons. Think of audible signals as icons for the ear[.] — Sheryl Lindsell-Roberts, *Technical Writing for Dummies*, p. 169, 2001

earful *noun*
a reprimand, especially when robust or lengthy *US, 1911*
- He looked at her sheepishly, expecting an earful. — Colin Butts, *Is Harry on the Boat?*, p. 137, 1997

earhole *noun*
the ear *AUSTRALIA, 1934*
By synecdoche.
- But he knew he might himself punch Ronnie in the earhole. — Geoff Wyatt, *Saltwater Saints*, p. 95, 1969
- But how was I to know you'd bend my ear'oles too[.] — Chas 'n' Dave, *Rabbit*, 1980
- I disliked him intensely and, after he had belted me over the earhole once too often, I decided to do something about it. — Rex Hunt, *Tall Tales – and True*, p. 50, 1994

▸ **on the earhole; on the ear'ole**
on the scrounge *UK*
Extends the sense of 'earhole' (whatever you can hear) to 'whatever you can pick up'.
- He wasnt a bad fella, but someone who's always on the ear'ole[.] — Lenny McLean, *The Guv'nor*, p. 137, 1998
- Coming round here on the earhole when I'm having me bath. — Martin King and Martin Knight, *The Naughty Nineties*, p. 112, 1999

earhole *verb*
1 to eavesdrop, to listen in on someone's conversation *UK*
- — Frank Norman, *Bang to Rights*, 1958

2 in motorcyle racing, to bank the motorcyle to an extreme degree in a turn, bringing the driver (and the driver's ear) close to the ground *US*
- — John Lawlor, *How to Talk Car*, p. 41, 1965

earie *noun*
▸ **on the earie**
alert, informed *US*
- Carnival owners at the annual showmen's meetings in the Sherman Hotel sent lesser known employees into the lobby 'to stay on the earie', and at regular intervals they reported all conversations heard to their boss. — Joe McKennon, *Circus Lingo*, p. 66, 1980

ear job *noun*
sexual talk on the telephone *US, 1978*
- — Steven Daly and Nalthaniel Wice, *alt.culture*, p. 182, 1995

earl *verb*
to vomit *US, 1968*
A rhyme with **HURL**.
- — Connie Eble (Editor), *UNC-CH Campus Slang*, p. 3, Spring 1987

Earls Court *noun*
salt *UK*
Rhyming slang, formed from the name of an area of west London.
- — Ray Puxley, *Cockney Rabbit*, 1992

early bath *noun*
▷ **see: EARLY SHOWER**

early bird *noun*
a word *UK, 1937*
Rhyming slang.
- — Ray Puxley, *Cockney Rabbit*, 1992

early doors *noun*
women's knickers, panties, etc *UK*
Rhyming slang for 'drawers'; probably since late C19 when 'early doors' was current for a theatrical performance and it was a time when women actually wore 'drawers'.
- She then took off her fly-be's [tights] / And dropped her early doors. — Ronnie Barker, *Fletcher's Book of Rhyming Slang*, p. 22, 1979

early doors *adjective*
early on, especially in relation to a sporting contest *UK, 1998*
Originally applied to admissions to old time music halls; now used, with almost catchphrase status, by football commentator Ron Atkinson.
- [T]hey disqualified me early doors, never even gave a fellera chance. — Jeremy Cameron, *Brown Bread in Wengen*, p. 92, 1999
- — Susie Dent, *The Language Report*, p. 53, 2003

early electic *noun*
used as a humorous description of a mix of design or decorating styles *US*
- — *Maledicta*, p. 242, Winter 1980: 'Lovely, blooming, fresh and gay: the onomastics of camp'

early foot *noun*
in horse racing, speed in the initial stages of a race *US*
- — Robert Saunders Dowst and Jay Craig, *Playing the Races*, p. 162, 1960

early morn *noun*
the erect penis *UK*
Rhyming slang for **HORN**.
- — Ray Puxley, *Cockney Rabbit*, 1992

early o'clock *noun*
shortly after an activity has started *TRINIDAD AND TOBAGO, 1983*
- — Lise Winer, *Dictionary of the English/Creole of Trinidad & Tobago*, 2003

early opener *noun*
a public hotel that opens early in the morning to cater for shift workers *AUSTRALIA*
- One of Sydney's more famous early openers, the First and Last at Circular Quay, was recently sold by Tooth to Citicentre Holdings for $1.5 million as a development site. — *Sunday Telegraph*, p. 24, 23rd August 1981

early out *noun*

1 a separation from the armed forces that is earlier than anticipated *US*

• —Linda Reinberg, *In the Field*, p. 71, 1991

2 in American casinos, an early dismissal from work due to smaller than expected numbers of gamblers *US*

• —Lee Solkey, *Dummy Up and Deal*, p. 112, 1980

early riser *noun*

a prisoner who is about to be released *UK*
Discharge from prison usually occurs early in the day.

• —Angela Devlin, *Prison Patter*, p. 48, 1996

early shopper *noun*

in horse racing, a bettor who places a bet as soon as the betting windows open *AUSTRALIA*

• —Ned Wallish, *The Truth Dictionary of Racing Slang*, p. 25, 1989

early shower; early bath *noun*

an ejection from an athletic contest *NEW ZEALAND*

• Peteone beat Porirura 2-0 but lost Pickering to an early shower after she apparently kicked an opponent. —*(Wellington) Dominion*, p. 16, 14th July 1978

ear-moll *verb*

to listen in; to eavesdrop *UK*

• I gave Sharon a bell from home – [the wife] must have been ear-molling on the extension. —Anthony Masters, *Minder*, p. 73, 1984

earn *noun*

an amount of money earned, especially earned illicitly *AUSTRALIA, 1977*

• —Jim Ramsay, *Cop It Sweet!*, p. 33, 1977
• Joe soon found that there was a nice little earn for the picking on the side in this job. —Clive Galea, *Slipper*, p. 8, 1988

earn *verb*

to make a dishonest profit *UK*

• We can all really earn on this one! —David Powis, *The Signs of Crime*, 1977

earner *noun*

1 a job that pays; something that generates income *UK, 1970*

• 'Colletti might sling big Davey,' gloated Watson with a far from pretty laugh, 'but he's a blow-in, a once-only earner for Billy.' —Clive Galea, *Slipper*, p. 66, 1988
• As a collector of antiques and other nice little earners, I am greatly appreciating the new series of For Love Or Money. —*Sun-Herald*, p. 152, 24th September 1989
• I'm afraid that little earner had gone the way of safari suits, the Fonz and Bachman Turner Overdrive. —John Birmingham, *The Tasmanian Babes Fiasco*, p. 64, 1997

2 any circumstance that criminals can turn to profitable advantage *UK*

• We are on to an earner here! —David Powis, *The Signs of Crime*, 1977

3 a member of an organised crime enterprise who produces high profits, however unpleasant his character may be *US*

• He was a money machine. A tremendous earner for these guys. —*Casino*, 1995

4 money earned, especially money from an illicit source or corrupt practice *UK*

• —G.F Newman, *Sir, You Bastard*, 1970
• Your earners is coppers' language for pay-off money. —P.B Yuill, *Hazel Plays Solomon*, 1974

earnings *noun*

proceeds from crime *SOUTH AFRICA*

• —Angus Hall, *On the Run*, 1974

ear'ole *noun*

in betting, odds of 6–4 *UK*
From the **TICK-TACK** signal used by bookmakers.

• —John McCririck, *John McCririck's World of Betting*, p. 59, 1991

ears *noun*

a citizens' band radio receiver *US, 1976*
Citizens' band radio slang; usually phrased 'put your ears on', 'have your ears on', etc.

• Break! Break! Iron Lady? You got your ears on? C'mon! —Peter Chippindale, *The British CB Book*, p. 145, 1981

▸ **be all ears**

to listen with close attention *UK, 1865*

• I am all ears in my waterside aviary[.] —*The Years Afternoon [The Guardian]*, 18th January 2003

▸ **get your ears raised**

to have your hair cut *US*

• —Jerry Robertson, *Oil Slanguage*, p. 60, 1954

▸ **have your ears flapping; keep your ears flapping**

to listen, especially to make an effort to keep up with what is going on *UK, 1984*

▸ **pull ears**

in the language of paragliding, to intentionally collapse both tips of the wing to increase speed *US*

• —Erik Fair, *California Thrill Sports*, p. 335, 1992

▸ **put the ears on**

to attempt a controlled roll of the dice *US*

• —John S. Salak, *Dictionary of Gambling*, p. 198, 1963

▸ **your ears are burning**

applied to a sensation that somebody is talking about you *UK*
Known in many variations since C14.

ear sex *noun*

a sexually-oriented telephone conversation with a person working for a telephone sex service *US*

• The idea in ear sex, not to be overly bashful about it, is that you call up and have a woman talk dirty to you while you masturbate. —Cecil Adams, *The Straight Dope*, p. 63, 1984

earth *noun*

a marijuana cigarette *BAHAMAS*

• —John A. Holm, *Dictionary of Bahamian English*, p. 68, 1982
• —Richard A. Spears, *The Slang and Jargon of Drugs and Drink*, p. 183, 1986
• —Mike Haskins, *Drugs*, p. 287, 2003

▸ **the earth**

a great expense *UK, 1924*

• [P]people looking for value for money, looking for a treat that won't cost the earth. —*The Guardian*, 1st February 2002

Eartha Kitt; eartha *noun*

1 faeces; an act of defecation; (as a plural) diarrhoea *UK, 1992*
Rhyming slang for **SHIT**, formed on the name of popular singer Eartha Kitt (b.1928).

• [C]reate the demand then market the Eartha Kitt out of it. —Andrew Nickolds, *Back to Basics*, p. 79–80, 1994
• Right, where's the paper... I'm going for an Eartha Kitt. —Caroline Aherne and Craig Cash, *The Royle Family*, 1999

2 the female breast *UK, 2001*
Rhyming slang for **TIT**.

earthless *adjective*

used as a non-profane negative intensifier *BARBADOS*

• I haven't one earhtless cent. —Frank A. Collymore, *Barbadian Dialect*, p. 43, 1965

earthly *adverb*

▸ **no earthly; not an earthly**

no chance whatever *UK, 1899*

• Cricket had its chance in the US. [...]. Now even baseball is struggling to maintain its hold against faster, less cerebral games. Cricket does not have an earthly. —*The Guardian*, 13th March 2003

earth mother; earth mama *noun*

a woman who eschews makeup, synthetic fabric and meat *US*

• —Connie Eble (Editor), *UNC-CH Campus Slang*, p. 2, Fall 1980

earth pads *noun*

shoes *US*
Teen slang.

• —Marcus Hanna Boulware, *Jive and Slang of Students in Negro Colleges*, 1947
• —*San Francisco News*, p. 6, 25th March 1958

earthshake *noun*

an earthquake *JAMAICA*

• —Peter L. Patrick, *Some Recent Jamaican Creole Words*, 2003

earth to

used as a humorous suggestion that the person named is not in touch with reality *US, 1977*

• "Earth to Brian, earth to Brian." Mary Ann coaxed him back into the here and now with a bemused smile. —Armistead Maupin, *Babycakes*, p. 114, 1984
• Earth to Alice, come in. I switched the topic of conversation to football. Try to stay in the game, honey. —Jimmy Buffett, *Tales from Margaritaville*, p. 71, 1989

- "Earth-to-Archie! You're MILES away!" "Oh, I guess I was day-dreaming." — *New Archie's Comics Digest Magazine*, October 1989
- Earth to Richie. Don't you wanna ask your new friend to join us. — Quentin Tarantino, *From Dusk Till Dawn*, p. 104, 1995

earwig *noun*

an eavesdopper; a lookout man *UK, 1950*

- — Angela Devlin, *Prison Patter*, p. 48, 1996

earwig *verb*

1 to eavesdrop *UK, 1927*
A poor pun on 'to hear'.

- — Nigel Foster, *The Making of a Royal Marine Commando*, 1987
- Sly lickle [little] Betty does be earwiggin' at keyholes. — Murphy Tom, *A Whistle in the Dark*, p. 17, 1989
- We earwig the conversations. — Martin King and Martin Knight, *The Naughty Nineties*, p. 52, 1999
- He noticed a man earwigging our conversation. "Vada the homi macaroni," he hissed. — Jake Arnott, *He Kills Coppers*, p. 52, 2001

2 to understand, to realise *UK*
Rhyming slang for **TWIG**.

- — Ray Puxley, *Cockney Rabbit*, 1992

ease *verb*

to leave *US*

- She's the bang of the ball but has to ease at midnight or be turned back into a scarecrow. — Haenigsen, *Jive's Like That*, 1947
- "Let's ease this punk," she told Leslie. — Clarence Cooper Jr, *The Scene*, p. 35, 1960

easel *noun*

a motorcycle's prop stand *UK*

- — Douglas Dunford, *Motorcycle Department, Beaulieu Motor Museum*, 1979

ease off *verb*

to urinate *UK*

- I slowly got out of bed to ease off and tidy up. — Bill Naughton, *Alfie Darling*, 1970

ease on *verb*

to leave with a parting gesture *US*

- — *American Speech*, p. 154, May 1959: 'Gator (University of Florida) slang'

ease up *verb*

to have sex *US*

- I know a couple 'a niggas that done eased up in her. — *Menace II Society*, 1993

easie; easy *noun*

a latex girdle *NEW ZEALAND*

- Later came rubberised latex girdles, sometimes call easies or roll-ons. — *New Zealand Women's Weekly*, p. 40, 24th June 1991

east and west *noun*

1 complementary doses of MDMA, the recreational drug best known as ecstasy, and amphetamine, both in powder form, inhaled via different nostrils *UK*
'East' is signified by **E** (MDMA), 'west' extends from an initialism of **WHIZZ** (amphetamine).

- So it's E up one nostril and whizz up the other. East and West, which is best. I snort hard, one after the other. — Ben Graham, *Weekday Service (Disco Biscuits)*, p. 166, 1996

2 the female breast *UK*
Or simply 'east west'.

- — *Sky Magazine*, July 2001
- [O]ne east west is so much bigger than the other. — Bodmin Dark, *Dirty Cockney Rhyming Slang*, 2003

3 the breast or the chest, hence the upper body *UK, 1923*
Rhyming slang.

4 a vest *US*
Rhyming slang; in pickpocket usage.

- — Vincent J. Monteleone, *Criminal Slang*, p. 77, 1949

East Anus *nickname*

the town of East Angus, Quebec *CANADA*

- Because it has a large paper mill which spreads an odor through the area, East Angus has the nickname East Anus. — 1977

Easter bunny *noun*

money *UK*
Rhyming slang.

- — Ray Puxley, *Fresh Rabbit*, 1998

Easter egg *noun*

1 a message hidden in a computer program's object code *US*

- — Eric S. Raymond, *The New Hacker's Dictionary*, p. 138, 1991
- Triggered by secret combinations of keystrokes, these "eggs" range from cartoons to surprise snapshots of the programmer's family. — Vann Wesson, *Generation X Field Guide and Lexicon*, p. 60, 1997

2 an icon or hidden process on the menu of a DVD that, when selected or followed, leads to hidden features *US*

- — Marc Salzman, *DVD Confidential*, 2002

3 the leg *UK*
Rhyming slang.

- — Ray Puxley, *Fresh Rabbit*, 1998

▸ **on the Easter egg**

begging, scrounging *UK: SCOTLAND*
Glasgow rhyming slang for **ON THE BEG**.

- Never mind comin roon here on the Easter egg, ya aul moocher, ye. — Michael Munro, *The Patter, Another Blast*, 1988

East Ham *adjective*

nearly mad *UK*
On the map of the London Underground East Ham is 'one stop short of Barking'; playing on **BARKING** (raving mad).

Eastie *nickname*

East Boston, Massachusetts *US*

- Across one building was strung a banner that read: "Eastie Loves the Pope." — *Washington Post*, p. A1, 2nd October 1979

East India Docks *noun*

1 any sexually transmitted infection *UK*
Rhyming slang for **POX**, formed from the name of one of the docks of east London.

- — Ray Puxley, *Cockney Rabbit*, 1992

2 socks *UK*
Rhyming slang.

- — Ray Puxley, *Fresh Rabbit*, 1998

East Jesus; East Jesus Nowhere *noun*

the outback *US, 1961*

- "East Jesus Nowhere" is near Werthaficarwee. — David Mazerolle, *LAvant tu take off, please close the lights*, p. n.p., 1993

East Jesus, Arkansas *noun*

a fictitious place, difficult to find and peopled with uneducated and poor people *US*

- — Michael Dalton Johnson, *Talking Trash with Redd Foxx*, p. 15, 1994

East Los *nickname*

east Los Angeles, California *US*

- — Dagoberto Fuentes and Jose Lopez, *Barrio Language Dictionary*, p. 57, 1974
- — Judi Sanders, *Da Bomb*, p. 5, 1997
- Since all of the Mexican Mafia's founders came from East Los [East Los Angeles], and because most of the rank and file were also from that region, they referred to themselves as Surenos, which means southerners in Spanish. — Bill Valentine, *Gangs and Their Tattoos*, p. 23, 2000

eastman *noun*

a pimp *US, 1911*

- — Vincent J. Monteleone, *Criminal Slang*, p. 77, 1949

East Overshoe *noun*

the mythical town in Maine which is the home to fools and idiots *US*

- — John Gould, *Maine Lingo*, p. 199, 1975

Eastside player *noun*

crack cocaine *US*

- — US Department of Justice, *Street Terms*, October 1994

easy *noun*

1 in craps, a point made by a combination other than a matched pair *US*
From the fuller 'easy way'.

- Sydney: Easy eight. A five and a three. Stickman: Eight. It came easy. The point. — *Hard Eight*, 1996

2 in poker, the fifth player to the left of the dealer *US*
A name based on the scheme of 1 = A, 2 = B, etc.

- — George Percy, *The Language of Poker*, p. 32, 1988

▷ **see: EASIE**

easy *verb*
to silence or kill *US*
- —Jay Robert Nash, *Dicitonary of Crime*, p. 115, 1992

easy *adjective*
1 sexually accessible *UK, 1699*
- Like any member of the town, Bill and Waldo had a tabulated list of the town's easy ladies.—Norman Lindsay, *Halfway to Anywhere*, p. 53, 1947
- [S]he wasn't a cock-teaser, a cold fish, or an easy lay[.]—Margaret Atwood, p. 29, 1977

2 having no preference when given a choice *AUSTRALIA, 1941*
- —Gavin Casey, *It's Harder for Girls*, p. 177, 1941
- Clarrie looks at me and Bob Grainger. 'What about it?' 'I'm easy,' I tell him, 'but a seven o'clock finish would do me.'—John Morrison, *Stories of the Waterfront*, p. 190, 1953
- —Jim Ramsay, *Cop It Sweet!*, p. 33, 1977

▸ **easy on the eye**
pleasing to look at; good looking, especially of women *UK, 1936*
- People will find it rather easy on the eye, it's true it's not the most difficult work.— *The Guardian*, 5th September 2003

easy
1 used as a greeting *US*
Noted in current UK use.
- —Julian Johnson, *Urban Survival*, p. 258, 2003
- —Connie Eble (Editor), *UNC-CH Campus Slang*, p. 3, Spring 2003

2 used as a warning *UK*
- —Angela Devlin, *Prison Patter*, p. 49, 1996

3 used as a farewell *US*
Hawaiian youth usage; often accompanied by a hand gesture, wiggling the hand from the wrist emphasising the thumb and little finger. Noted in current UK use.
- —Elizabeth Ball Carr, *Da Kine Talk*, p. 129, 1972
- —Julian Johnson, *Urban Survival*, p. 258, 2003

easy as ABC *adjective*
very easy *UK*
A simplicity noted by Shakespeare, 'then comes the answer like an Absey booke', 1595.
- ABC, baby, oo ooo! / 123, baby, nah nah! / Do re mi, baby, huh! / —Jackson 5 *ABC*, 1970

easy as apple pie *adjective*
very easy *AUSTRALIA*
Variation of **EASY AS PIE**.

easy as damn it *adjective*
very easy *UK, 1937*
Recorded by Partridge in the 1st edition of his *Dictionary of Slang and Unconventional English* and still familiar. Other variations noted at that time include 'easy as pissing the bed' and 'easy as shelling peas'.

easy as falling off a log; easy as rolling off a log *adjective*
very easy *US*
Mark Twain used 'easy as rolling off a log' in 1880.

easy as kiss my arse *adjective*
very easy *UK, 1937*
Recorded, with the euphemistic variation 'easy as kiss my ear', by Partridge in the 1st edition of his *Dictionary of Slang and Unconventional English*.

easy as kiss my eye *adjective*
very easy *UK*
Euphemistic variation of **EASY AS KISS MY ARSE**.

easy as pie *adjective*
very easy *US*
- Henry reckoned if we grabbed him in the side streets we could hop off with the money bag easy as pie.—John Peter Jones, *Feather Pluckers*, p. 30, 1964

easy as shaking drops off your john *adjective*
very easy *UK*
Masculine use; **JOHN THOMAS; JOHN** (the penis).

easy as winking *adjective*
very easy *UK, 1937*
- Another damnation for imagining myself among those / whose fornications came as easy as winning[.]—C.H. Sissons, *[a poem]*, 1976

easybeats *noun*
a team or opponent which is easily defeated *AUSTRALIA*
Punning on The Easybeats, an Australian 1960s rock group.
- If your prediction as to the composition of the final three is correct, Collingwood and Essendon would make a serious mistake if they regarded us as "easybeats".— *Sydney Morning Herald*, p. 22, 12th July 1990

easy chair *noun*
in a group of three or more trucks travelling on a motorway, the middle truck *US*
- —Lanie Dills, *The Official CB Slanguage Language Dictionary*, p. 30, 1976

easy go *noun*
an unstrenuous prison job *US*
- —Marlene Freedman, *Alcatraz*, 1983

easy greasy *noun*
an icy road *US*
- — *Complete CB Slang Dictionary*, 1976
- —Peter Chippindale, *The British CB Book*, p. 154, 1981

easy, greasy!
take it easy! *US*
Teen slang.
- — *American Weekly*, p. 2, 14th August 1955

Easy Hall *noun*
a notional place of great comfort and ease *BARBADOS, 1980*
Recorded by Richard Allsopp.

easy like kissing hand *adjective*
very easy *TRINIDAD AND TOBAGO*
- —Lise Winer, *Dictionary of the English/Creole of Trinidad & Tobago*, 2003

easy mark *noun*
a person who is easily persuaded *US, 1915*
- You think religion is for suckers and easy marks and mollycoddles, huh?—Richard Brooks, *Elmer Gantry*, 1960

easy meat *noun*
someone who can be seduced, or made a victim; something that is easy to achieve *UK, 1961*
The original sense is 'a sexually available woman'.
- Politically, they were easy meat. Few in the western world, women or men, would grieve to see them [the Taliban] go.— *The Guardian*, 11th December 2001

easy-peasy *adjective*
very easy, very simple *UK, 1976*
A childish reduplication of 'easy', occasionally taken further as 'easy-peasy, lemon-squeezey'.
- As soon as the whole party was on the move, we'd pepperpot [a military manoeuvre] our way back to the boats. "Easy peasy," said Stew.—Chris Ryan, *Stand By, Stand By*, p. 227, 1996
- "Easy fucking peasy." "Easy peasy Nicky. No problem."—Jeremy Cameron, *Brown Bread in Wengen*, p. 21, 1999
- [F]ucking easy-peasy, it were.—Kevin Sampson, *Outlaws*, p. 15, 2001
- The guys here have just beaten the wankers in Philadelphia and Cambridge to inventing the computer. Easy peasy.—Tony Wilson, *24 Hour Party People*, p. 146, 2002

easy rider *noun*
1 a pimp *US, 1914*
- —Robert A. Wilson, *Playboy's Book of Forbidden Words*, p. 96, 1972

2 a guitar *UK, 1949*
From an earlier use as 'a compliant sexual partner'.
- More innocently, easy rider was sometimes merely the guitar slung over the itinerant guitarist's back.—Peter Clayton and Peter Gammond, *Jazz A-Z*, p. 90, 1986

3 a type of LSD identified by a design based on the 1969 film *Easy Rider* *UK*
- —Harry Shapiro, *Recreational Drugs*, p. 266, 2004

4 cider *UK*
Rhyming slang, reducing to 'easy'.
- Give us a pinta Easy mate.— *www.LondonSlang.com*, June 2002

easy street *noun*

a comfortable, affluent situation for little expenditure of effort *US, 1897*

- Fucking easy street, it were. Didn't last all that long, though. —Kevin Sampson, *Outlaws*, p. 15, 2001

easy touch *noun*

▷ see: SOFT TOUCH

easy way *noun*

(used of an even-numbered point in craps) scored in any fashion other than a pair *US*

- —John Scarne, *Scarne on Dice*, p. 466, 1974

eat *noun*

eating *US*

- I just wanna get my eat on. — *Menace II Society*, 1993

eat *verb*

1 to perform oral sex *US, 1916*

- "Babe, I'd like to eat you," said the man in the ballet tights at Les Deux Freres. —John Rechy, *City of Night*, p. 405, 1963
- He said, "All I have to do is scarf her a few times and I get anything I want." Nuttee asked Diehl to explain the word "scarf." "To eat her box, in other words." —Richard Honeycutt, *Candy Mossler*, p. 80, 1966
- There is the type who likes to eat his woman up after you get through piling her. —Eldridge Cleaver, *Soul on Ice*, p. 170, 1968
- You know, Preach, I don't mind you fucking up my eating, but I don't want you eating up my fucking. —Roger Abrahams, *Positively Black*, p. 101, 1970
- The first time, I was perfectly calm while he lifted my dress and took down my panties and ate me. —John Warren Wells, *Tricks of the Trade*, p. 47, 1970
- Baby-san give you number one blow job, you like? Come on G.I. Me suck you guts out. Baby'san love to eat G.I. dick. — *Screw*, p. 5, 15th February 1971
- [T]he broads are like eating each other, right. —Stephen Ziplow, *The Film Maker's Guide to Pornography*, p. 90, 1977
- Gabriella shows a very pretty pussy as D.T. eats her[.] — *Adult Video*, p. 53, August/September 1986
- I once sucked a woman's pussy so hard I got a hangover. If you don't eat pussy your woman's going to be gone. She'll find someone else who will. —Chris Rock, *Rock This!*, p. 134, 1997
- Eww! You eat the cock!? —Kevin Smith, *Jay and Silent Bob Strike Back*, p. 27, 2001

2 to swallow *US*

Used especially in the context of ingesting LSD.

- [Y]our average acid-eating freak will be getting arrested for attempting to sit in the park under General Thomas' horse in Thomas Circle[.] —Raymond Mungo, *Famous Long Ago*, p. 29, 1970
- Maybe he'll smoke a little weed or eat a pill or two. —Bruce Jackson, *In the Life*, p. 107, 1972
- You eat a lot of acid, Miller, back in the hippie days? — *Repo Man*, 1984

3 (of tobacco) to chew *CANADA*

- I guess next to eatin' tobacco yer maw hates gamblin'. —W. O. Mitchell, *Jake and the Kid*, p. 135, 1961

4 to bother *US, 1892*

- He looked over at the blonde, then raised his eyebrow at me. "Any idea what's eating him?" —Rita Ciresi, *Pink Slip*, p. 323, 1999

5 to accept a monetary loss *US, 1955*

- I ate twenty-four pairs of BLue Oyster Cult tickets last time around. — *Fast Times at Ridgemont High*, 1982

▸ **be able to eat an apple through a bird cage**

to have buck teeth *AUSTRALIA*

- Geez, mate, you could eat an apple through a bird cage. —Phillip Gwynne, *Deadly Unna?*, p. 53, 1998

▸ **could eat the hind leg off a donkey**

applied to someone who is very hungry *UK, 1961*

A variation of 'eat a horse', on the model of TALK THE HIND LEG OFF A DONKEY.

▸ **eat a horse and chase the rider/jockey**

to be very hungry *AUSTRALIA*

- I'm that hungry I could eat a horse and chase the jockey. — *The Adventures of Barry McKenzie*, 1972
- Threatened with such unappetising dishes it is an advantage to be so hungry that: 'I could eat a hollow log full of green ants' (a distinctively northern New South Wales or Queensland expression), or 'I could eat a horse and chase the rider.' —Nancy Keesing, *Lily on the Dustbin*, p. 118, 1982
- Eat the horse and chase the jockey. Extreme pangs of hunger. — *The Dinkum Dictionary Of Australian English*, p. 26, 1990
- After everyone started the day well with Kinkara tea from Olive's best cups on the front verandah, Uncle Les arrived saying: 'I'm so hungry I could eat a horse and chase the rider.' —Hugh Lunn, *Fred & Olive's Blessed Lino*, p. 106, 1993

▸ **eat a shit sandwich**

to accept humiliations as punishment *UK*

A variation on EAT SHIT.

- Yeah cos what you gonna do? – Ain't gonna eat shit sandwich thass for sure. – You wanna try eatin' shit sandwich some time. Makes eatin' humble pie a lot easier. —Nick Barlay, *Curvy Lovebox*, p. 163, 1997
- Accepting an upgrade like you did last year means eating a shit sandwich from time to time[.] —Chris Ryan, *The Watchman*, p. 97, 2001

▸ **eat a stock**

to buy undesirable stock to maintain an order market in the stock *US*

- —Kathleen Odean, *High Steppers, Fallen Angels, and Lollipops*, p. 94, 1988

▸ **eat asphalt**

to crash while riding a motorcyle, bicycling, or taking part in any recreational activity on the street *US*

- He is, so don't play hockey with him unless you want to eat asphalt. — *Times Colonist (Victoria, British Columbia)*, p. A2, 15th July 2002
- But most people who use them, even top skiers, at some point eat asphalt. — *Scripps Howard News Service*, 19th September 2002

▸ **eat bad food**

to get pregnant *TRINIDAD AND TOBAGO, 1974*

- —Lise Winer, *Dictionary of the English/Creole of Trinidad & Tobago*, 2003

▸ **eat cards**

in blackjack, to draw more cards than you normally would in a given hand in order to learn more about what cards are remaining unplayed *US*

The card-eater takes a short-term loss in hope of a long-term big win.

- —Michael Dalton, *Blackjack*, p. 45, 1991

▸ **eat cheese**

to curry favour *US*

- —Mary Swift, *Campus Slang (University of Texas)*, 1968

▸ **eat concrete**

to drive on a motorway *US*

- —Montie Tak, *Truck Talk*, p. 55, 1971

▸ **eat crow**

to be forced to accept humiliation *US, 1877*

According to legend, a British Army officer tricked then forced an American to eat a crow that the latter had shot.

- [A]ll those columns saying Ii was going to fail were afraid to eat some crow. So it was up to me to celebrate my success. —Howard Stern, *Miss America*, p. 289, 1995

▸ **eat cunt**

to perform oral sex on a woman *US*

- They claim they don't like girls, but when I get to eating their cunts, they love it. —Roger Blake, *What you always wanted to know about porno-movies*, p. 244, 1972

▸ **eat dick**

to perform oral sex on a man *US*

- Instead of making him eat dick, the other prisoners kept out of his way right from the beginning. —Gerald Petievich, *Shakedown*, p. 85, 1988

▸ **eat dim sum**

to take the passive role in anal intercourse *UK*

Rhyming slang for TAKE IT UP THE BUM.

- Every time we go to bed she wants to eat dim sum. —Bodmin Dark, *Dirty Cockney Rhyming Slang*, 2003

▸ **eat dirt**

to fall on your face *US*

A literal consequence.

▸ **eat face**

to kiss in a sustained and passionate manner *US*

- —Andy Anonymous, *A Basic Guide to Campusology*, p. 8, 1966
- —Collin Baker et al., *College Undergraduate Slang Study Conducted at Brown University*, p. 112, 1968

▸ **eat for breakfast**

to vanquish, outdo, overcome *AUSTRALIA*

- [Y]ou know I eat little boys for breakfast. —Kevin Mackey, *The Cure*, p. 119, 1970
- Mr Seedy stood unperturbed, one corner of his mouth pulled up with an expression that said, I eat players like you for breakfast. —Linda Jaivin, *Rock n Roll Babes from Outer Space*, p. 139, 1996

▸ **eat from the bushy plate**
to engage in oral sex on a woman *UK*
Probably coined by comedian Sacha Baron-Cohen (b.1970); his influence on late C20 UK slang is profound.
- WHILE AT THE EARLY STAGES OF A RELASHUNSHIP U IZ PROBABLY UP FOR EATING FROM DE BUSHY PLATE. —Sacha Baron-Cohen, *Da Gospel According to Ali G*, 2001

▸ **eatin' ain't cheatin'**
used as a jocular assertion that oral sex does not rise to the level of adultery or infidelity *US*
A maxim that enjoyed sudden and massive appeal in the US during the President Clinton sex scandals.
- —Michael Dalton Johnson, *Talking Trash with Redd Foxx*, p. 56, 1994

▸ **eat it**
1 to suffer an accident, especially a fall *US*
Hawaiian youth usage.
- —Douglas Simonson, *Pidgin to da Max Hana Hou*, 1982

2 in surfing, to lose control and fall from your surfboard *US*
- You go in there, you're gonna eat it on the rocks. —*Point Break*, 1991

▸ **eat lead**
to be shot *US, 1927*
- I got news that old sidekick Dinty Colebeck had eaten lead in St. Louis. —Red Rudensky, *The Gonif*, p. 142, 1970

▸ **eat like a horse**
to have a very large appetite *UK, 1971*
- I might look like a stick insect, but I eat like a horse. —*The Observer*, 13th October 2002

▸ **eat plastic**
(used of a hospital patient) to be intubated *US*
- —Sally Williams, *"Strong" Words*, p. 133, 1994

▸ **eat pussy**
to perform oral sex on a woman *US*
- She said, "Well, little daddy, I guess you and I are through / 'cause if you can't eat this pusssy there's nothin' else you can do." —Bruce Jackson, *Get Your Ass in the Water and Swim Like Me*, p. 127, 1965
- To believe that a man couldn't eat pussy properly or a woman suck like an expert is to disbelieve in the ability of the sexes to communicate with each other[.] —Angelo d'Arcangelo, *The Homosexual Handbook*, p. 74–75, 1968
- 64. If you eat pussy you're a maniac. 65. If you eat pussy you're a moron. 66. If you eat pussy you'll become a sex fiend. 67. If you'll eat pussy you'll do anything. 68. Only guys who can't fuck eat pussy. —Gilbert Sorrentino, *Steelwork*, p. 48, 1970
- He eats pussy! I don't. Man, I won't eat pussy unless I get well paid for it. —Christina and Richard Milner, *Black Players*, p. 218, 1972
- "The absolutely most wonderful feeling I ever had was watching myself on the screen when my husband was sucking my ass and "Greedy Jim" was eating my pussy. —Roger Blake, *What you always wanted to know about porno-movies*, p. 102, 1972
- I actually experienced three climaxes during a one-hour session, all because of this incredibly adept chick who was really, but really good at eating pussy. —*Porno Films and the People who make them*, p. 177, 1973
- "Sweetheart, that's all very nice," she replies, "but if you're not going to easy pussy, you're not a dyke." —Kim Akass, *Reading Sex and the City*, p. 40, 2004

▸ **eat raw; eat raw without salt**
to defeat or destroy mercilessly *TRINIDAD AND TOBAGO*
- —Lise Winer, *Dictionary of the English/Creole of Trinidad & Tobago*, 2003

▸ **eat razor blades**
to speak harshly and offensively *BARBADOS*
Collected in 1972.

▸ **eat sausage**
to perform oral sex on a man *NEW ZEALAND, 1984*
- —Harry Orsman, *A Dictionary of Modern New Zealand Slang*, p. 46, 1999

▸ **eat shit**
1 as a condition of subservience, to do something disagreeable or humiliating *US, 1930*
May be varied to 'eat crap'.
- The upshot is I've had to eat shit and stop flogging my machines to other clubs. —Mike Hodges, *Get Carter*, p. 53, 1971
- New youth was abroad and feisty; too many five-oh incidents tolerated, too much shit eaten and now too much to prove. —Mick Farren, *Give the Anarchist a Cigarette*, p. 347, 2001

2 in surfing, to lose control of a ride and fall off your surfboard *US*
- This is a 5/6" tri-fin squash-tail thruster. You'd eat major shit on this, dude. —*Point Break*, 1991

▸ **eat someone's lunch**
to thrash; to exact revenge *US*
- —*Current Slang*, p. 4, Spring 1968

▸ **eat the cookie**
while surfing, to be pounded fiercely by a breaking wave *US*
- —Vann Wesson, *Generation X Field Guide and Lexicon*, p. 60, 1997

▸ **eat the crutch off a low-flying emu**
to be very hungry *AUSTRALIA*
- We're restaurant-mad these days and at about twelve noon most Australian executives are that hungry they could eat the crutch off a low-flying emu – no worries. —Barry Humphries, *The Traveller's Tool*, p. 78, 1985

▸ **eat the floormat**
to throw yourself to the floor of a car *US*
- [B]oth narcs ate the floormat until the Mercedes turned west on Franklin. —Joseph Wambaugh, *The Glitter Dome*, p. 77, 1981

▸ **eat the ginger**
to play the leading role in a play *US*
- —Wilfred Granville, *The Theater Dictionary*, p. 65, 1952

▸ **eat the head off, eat the face off**
to verbally abuse or attack *IRELAND*
- I've a good mind to go around there now and eat the head off the lot of them. —Bernard Share, *Slanguage*, p. 97, 2003
- He "ate" a lot of people in his time. —Bernard Share, *Slanguage*, p. 97, 2003

▸ **eat your gun**
to commit suicide by gun *US*
- —Jim Crotty, *How to Talk American*, p. 50, 1997

▸ **eat your hat**
used for expressing a certainty that such and such will not happen *UK, 1837*
Very occasionally taken literally as 'a wager against fate'.
- The EU has solemnly declared its intention to make the European economy the most competitive in the world by 2010. If it succeeds, I will eat my hat. —*The Guardian*, 8th June 2004

▸ **eat your own dog food**
to make use of whatever product or service you provide *US*
- — Susie Dent, *The Language Report*, p. 83, 2003

▸ **I could eat a baby's bum through a cane chair**
to be extremely hungry *AUSTRALIA*
- I've been suddenly that hungry I could eat a baby's bum through a cane chair. —Barry Humphries, *The Traveller's Tool*, p. 79, 1985

▸ **I could eat a scabby horse between bedrags**
I am very hungry *UK*
Used by a lorry driver quoted in *New Society*, 28th May 1981.

▸ **I could eat that; I could eat that without salt**
a catchphrase that is used of an attractive girl or young woman *UK*
An unattractive girl may inspire the opposite: 'I couldn't eat that'; on the other hand, girls wishing to express desire may use: 'he could eat me without salt'. The sense is occasionally exaggerated as: 'I could boil up her knickers and drink the gravy.'
- I couldn't eat that last one. —Pamela Branch, *The Wooden Overcoat*, 1951

ea-tay *noun*
marijuana *US, 1938*
Pig Latin for 'tea'.

eat chain!
used as an insult along the lines of 'drop dead!' *US*
An abbreviation of 'eat a chain saw!'.
- —Vann Wesson, *Generation X Field Guide and Lexicon*, p. 60, 1997

eat dick!
used as a dismissive retort *UK*
- NAPPER: Bye, Topsy. Say hello to Kute Kinte, won't you? GLORIA: (Levelly) Eat dick. —Trevor Griffiths, *Oi For England*, p. 4, 1982

eater *noun*
a person who eats marijuana *US, 2001*
- —*www.addictions.org*, 1999

eat flaming death!
used as an overblown expression of hostility *US*
- —Fireside Theater, *In the Next World, You're on your Own*, 1975

eat fuck!
used as a dismissive retort *US*
A variation of 'eat shit!'.
- A lot of people [...] call me bigheaded, conceited, loud-mouthed. Who does he think he is? To them I say EAT MUCHO FUCK! — *Ask*, p. 46, 5th May 1979

eating tobacco *noun*
chewing tobacco *US, 1901*
- The lawyer would stand in chewing away thoughtfully on his wad of "eating tobacco." — *Toronto Globe and Mail*, p. 28/9, 28th May 1959

eat me!
used as a somewhat coarse expression of defiance *US, 1962*
The taboo component is fading if not faded.
- It is usually used by the heterosexual but does not mean to fellate although its unfriendly meaning is drawn from the heterosexual's low regard for the homosexual in this sex act. — *The Guild Dictionary of Homosexual Terms*, p. 14, 1965
- WAYNE: So, uh, everybody, uh, have fun. VOICE IN THE CROWD: EAT ME! — *Wayne's World 2*, 1993
- COP #2: So, fifty years old, huh? MURTAUGH: Eat me. — *Lethal Weapon*, 1995

eat my shorts!
used as a humorous declaration of defiance *US, 1979*
- BENDER: Eat my shorts. VERNON: What was that? BENDER: Eat my shorts! — *The Breakfast Club*, 1985

eat out *verb*
to perform oral sex, usually on a woman *US, 1966*
- We had been eating each other out all afternoon — *Screw*, p. 3, 21st February 1969
- — Helen Dahlskog (Editor), *A Dictionary of Contemporary and Colloquial Usage*, p. 21, 1972
- Scarfing pussy gets great press, but most men know shit about eating out women. — *Screw*, p. 5, 12th June 1972
- It's laying hands on Marsellus Wallace's new wife in a familiar way. Is it as bad as eatin her out – no, but you're in the same fuckin' ballpark. — *Pulp Fiction*, 1994
- I lost my tolerance for the bullshit baggage that comes with eating girls out. What's the big deal? — *Chasing Amy*, 1997
- [T]he Gaiety was also able to offer its patrons the unique opportunity to eat out any member of the lunchtime strip-show at very reasonable rates. — David Peace, *Nineteen Seventy-Four*, p. 101, 1999

eats *noun*
food, a meal *UK, 1782*
- Awright yuh bastids, line up single file for eats. — Iceberg Slim (Robert Beck), *Doom Fox*, p. 54, 1978
- The eats are on me, so long as you don't eat me out of house and home. — Larry Heinemann, *Paco's Story*, p. 102, 1986

eat shit and die!
used as a powerful expression of dislike or disapproval *US*
- — Connie Eble (Editor), *UNC-CH Campus Slang*, p. 3, October 1986

eat the apple, fuck the Corps
used as a defiant yet proud curse of the marines by the marines *US*
- It was the common reaction among marines to all abrupt direction changes: "Eat the apple fuck the Corps." — Charles Anderson, *The Grunts*, p. 36, 1976
- "Eat the apple, fuck the Corps," they'd say. — Myra MacPherson, *Long Time Passing*, p. 83, 1984

eatum-up stop *noun*
a roadside restaurant or truckstop *US*
- — Lanie Dills, *The Official CB Slanguage Language Dictionary*, p. 31, 1976

eat up *verb*
(used of a wave) to overcome and knock a surfer from the surfboard *US*
- — John M. Kelly, *Surf and Sea*, p. 283, 1965

eat what you can and can what you can't
used for urging someone to be frugal and conservationist *CANADA, 1989*
- During the Depression and World War II, British Columbians were urged to preserve food for self-reliance, and so enable commercial canners to better supply the armed forces. Now the expression is "eat what you can and pop the leftovers in the freezer." — Tom Parkin, *WetCoast Words*, p. 51, 1989

eau-de-cologne *noun*
1 a telephone *UK*
Rhyming slang. Sometimes corrupted to 'the odour' or 'odie'.
- — Julian Franklyn, *A Dictionary of Rhyming Slang*, 1961

2 a woman *UK, 1937*
Rhyming slang on polari 'palone' (a woman).

e-ball *noun*
MDMA, the recreational drug best known as ecstasy *US*
- — Connie Eble (Editor), *UNC-CH Campus Slang*, p. 4, Spring 1992

Ebeneezer Goode *noun*
the personification of the culture surrounding MDMA, the recreational drug best known as ecstasy *UK, 1992→*
- He was like some garish Ebeneezer Goode, in your face the whole time, driving everybody on – on one, up for it, mad for it, top one. — Kevin Sampson, *Powder*, p. 198, 1999
- In 1992 the Shamen released "Ebeneezer Goode", about a guy who was the life and soul of the party. In the chorus the backing voices chanted "Eezer Goode" – (E's are good.) — Simon Napier-Bell, *Black Vinyl White Powder*, p. 312, 2001

e-bomb *noun*
MDMA, the recreational drug best known as ecstasy *UK*
- — Mike Haskins, *Drugs*, p. 289, 2003

E-brake *noun*
a vehicle's emergency brake *US*
- — John Cann, *The Stunt Guide*, p. 58,: 'Terms and definitions'

ecaf; eek; eke *noun*
the face *UK*
Back slang used in polari, especially in the abbreviated forms.
- Omes and palones of the jury, vada well the eek of the poor ome who stands before you. — Barry Took and Marty Feldman, *Round The Horne*, 13th March 1966
- So bona to vada / OH YOU / Your lovely eek and / Your lovely riah [hair]. — Morrisey, *Piccadilly Palare*, 1990
- [D]istract attention from the cod [bad] eke and chronic pots [teeth]. — James Gardiner, *Who's a Pretty Boy Then?*, p. 123, 1997

e-car *noun*
an electrically powered *car* *UK, 2003*
- — *Collins English Dictionary*, 2003

eccer *noun*
an abbreviation for (homework) exercise *IRELAND*
This term makes use of the suffix **-ER** which is especially common in Dublin Hiberno-English and is used at the end of abbreviated names, for example, 'Croker', for Croke Park, Headquarters Stadium of the G.A.A. (named after Archbishop Croke, d. 1902).
- I'll check their eccers every nigh', don't worry. — Roddy Doyle, *The Van*, p. 49, 1991

eccy; ec *noun*
economics *US, 1924*
- "Mama," I said. "There ain't no boys in Home Ec. The boys are in the science class." — Nora Ephron and Alice Arlon, *Silkwood*, 1983

echo *noun*
a variety of MDMA, the recreational drug best known as ecstasy *UK*
From the international phonetic alphabet, **E** (MDMA) is ECHO, also playing on the first syllable of **ECSTASY** (MDMA).
- — Angela Devlin, *Prison Patter*, p. 49, 1996

echo *verb*
to repeat what was just said *US*
- — *American Speech*, p. 62, February 1967: 'Soda-fountain, restaurant and tavern calls'

'eck-as-like
in answer to a rhetorical question, certainly not, it is very unlikely *UK*
A Yorkshire-ism, often used in bad impressions of a northern accent; not recorded, surprisingly, until 1979.
- Hare populations in many countries are waxing, which the pessimistic beagler will tell you is a bad thing. Is it 'eck as like? — *Hunting Magazine*, October 1997

ecker; ecky *noun*
MDMA, the recreational drug best known as ecstasy; a tablet of MDMA *UK*
Based on the first syllable of **ECSTASY** (MDMA).
- I'd like a Smarties tube full of eckers for me birthday. — Niall Griffiths, *Kelly + Victor*, p. 37, 2002

eckied *adjective*
intoxicated with MDMA, the recreational drug best known as ecstasy *UK*
From **ECKY; ECKIE** (ecstasy).
- Leave her alone, she's eckied oot her brain. — Michael Munro, *The Complete Patter*, p. 49, 1996

ecky; eckie *noun*
MDMA, the recreational drug best known as ecstasy; a tablet of MDMA *UK*
Plays with the first syllable.
- Mibbee see if the cunt's goat [got] any eckies, eh. — Irvine Welsh, *The State of the Party (Disco Biscuits)*, p. 33, 1995
- CALL IT... Adam, brownies, burgers, disco biscuits, doves, eckies, tulips, X[.] JUST DON'T CALL IT... MDMA – too scientific — *Drugs An Adult Guide*, p. 34, December 2001
- [B]oshing [swallowing] eccies and hoovering gak [snorting cocaine] — *Ministry*, p. 39, January 2002

ecky-becky *noun*
a poor white person *BARBADOS*
- Ecky-bekcy is a nation, true brotheration; as you touch dem, dem run at the station. — Frank A. Collymore, *Barbadian Dialect*, p. 43, 1965

ecnop *noun*
a person who lives off prostitutes' earnings, a ponce *UK*
Back slang.
- I'm not going to say it's all for the best, because we know that's a lot of pony-and-trap, but at least it's saved Iris from that dirty little ecnop, Ronny. — Charles Raven, *Underworld Nights*, p. 24, 1956

eco- *prefix*
used to signify an assocation with environmental issues *US, 1969*
An abbreviation of 'ecology/ecological'.
- Eco-aware attitudes, activities and products have become important components in late 20th-century Western counterculture. — Sarah Callard and Will Hoon, *Surfers Soulies Skinheads & Skaters*, 1996

ecofreak *noun*
a radical environmentalist *US, 1970*
- We're just a bunch of fascists, racists, terrorists, sexists, anarchists, commuinsts, Young Americans for Freedom, Democrats and just plain folksy ecofreaks. — Edward Abbey, *Hayduke Lives!*, p. 188, 1990
- Your ecofreaks take over, Blanche, every job in the state will go[.] — David Powyer, *Down to a Sunless Sea*, p. 71, 1996

eco-freako *adjective*
overly devoted to ethical ecological principles *UK*
- We didn't want it to look eco-freako. — *Woman's Hour*, 18th June 2004

ecology freak *noun*
a devoted environmentalist *US*
- The 2.2 million ecology freaks who live there [Oregon] are reminded by their Highway Division to "thank Heaven we live in God's Country." — Bill Cardoso, *The Maltese Sangweech*, p. 88, 1984

econ *noun*
economics *US*
- — Connie Eble (Editor), *UNC-CH Campus Slang*, p. 3, March 1979

econut *noun*
a zealous environmentalist *US, 1972*
- [T]he increasing number of paperbacks on "ecofiction" and man's position in the environmental crisis foretells more creations coming from the econuts. — Robert Kirk Mueller, *B uzzwords*, p. 70, 1974

ecoporn; eco-porn *noun*
aesthetically pleasing pictures of ecological subjects, especially when of no scientific or environmental value; used derisively of any advertising that praises a company's 'green' record or policies *US*
- [F]ull of sly art and eco-porn. Scenes of the Louisiana bayous, strange birds in slow-motion flight — Edward Abbey, *The Monkey Wrench Gang*, p. 236, 1985
- The peaks are of such heart-stopping beauty that you feel like tipping them after taking their picture; they are ecoporn, in virtually any pose. — Timothy Egan, *Lasso the Wind*, p. 195, 1999

ecowarrior *noun*
a person who is especially active in any political struggle or violent action against forces that are seen to threaten the environment or balance-of-nature *UK*
Formed on 'eco', a widely used abbreviation of 'ecology/ecological'. The natural enemy of the 'ecowarrior' is the 'ecoterrorist', a term first recorded in 1988.
- [A] digital, shoulder-shot, Blair Witch-style, mocumentary, shoot-em-up, yoofsploitation number based on ecowarriors[.] — James Hawes, *White Powder, Green Light*, p. 5, 2002

ecstasy *noun*
methylene-dioxymethamphetamine, MDMA, a mildly hallucinogenic empathogen and/or entactogen, a drug of empathy and touch *US*
Easily the most recognisable slang name for this widely popular recreational drug; it derives from the senses of well-being and affection felt by users. The illegal status of the drug has encouraged a great many alternative names; some are generic (**E** is probably the most widely known), and some serve as brand names. Originally synthesized by German pharmaceutical company Merck some time before 1912. Since the 1980s the drug has been inextricably linked with **RAVE** culture.
- It is called MDMA – or "Ecstasy" – and users say it has the incredible power to make people trust one another[.] — *Newsweek*, p. 96, 15th April 1985
- It is called by some Ecstasy and, like LSD, it is pyschedlic. — *ABC World News Tonight*, 17th April 1985
- Ecstasy, or MDMA, is a "designer drug," a class of substances with actions similar to banned drugs, but chemically different, allowing them to escape the law.. — *United Press International*, 28th June 1985
- On the street, its name is "ecstasy"or "Adam," which should tell how people on the street feel about it. — *Los Angeles Times*, p. 1 (Part 5), 29th March 1985
- The long-term effects of ecstasy use are are not known, although there's no shortage of guinea pigs. — Ben Osborne, *The A-Z of Club Culture*, p. 82, 1999
- [I]t seemed as though Ecstasy had been waiting for the age of intelligent machines. — Sadie Plant, *Writing on Drugs*, p. 165, 1999
- Ecstasy is both a young drug and a drug embraced by the young. — Gareth Thomas, *This Is Ecstasy*, p. 9, 2002

E'd; E-ed; E'd up; E-ed up *adjective*
intoxicated with MDMA, the recreational drug best known as ecstasy *UK*
Under the influence of **E** (ecstasy).
- E'd up and gurning at the moon. — *Sky Magazine*, p. 70, May 2001
- Still half E'd up. Buzzin. Mam wants to know why I keep huggin her all the time. — Niall Griffiths, *Kelly + Victor*, p. 35, 2002
- [E]ighty or so boys and girls, mostly E'd to the nines[.] — Tony Wilson, *24 Hour Party People*, p. 189, 2002

Eddie Grundies *noun*
underwear *UK*
A variation of **GRUNDIES**, formed from the name Eddie Grundy, a popular character in the BBC radio soap opera *The Archers*.
- — John Ayto, *The Oxford Dictionary of Rhyming Slang*, 2002

edelweiss *noun*
a type of marijuana developed in Holland *UK*
- — Nick Jones, *Spliffs*, p. 68, 2003

e-deuce *noun*
an M-14 automatic rifle *US*
- Mac humped his automatic M-14, something like a BAR, which everyone called an E-deuce. — Larry Heinemann, *Close Quarters*, p. 46, 1977

Edgar Britt; Edgar *noun*
an act of defecation *AUSTRALIA, 1969*
Rhyming slang for **SHIT**. In the plural, used for 'diarrhoea'.
- Chilla was squatted on the dunny having a Gerry Riddle and an Edgar Britt. — Frank Hardy, *The Outcasts of Foolgarah*, p. 209, 1971
- — Ryan Aven-Bray, *Ridgey Didge Oz Jack Lang*, p. 27, 1983
- — Ned Wallish, *The Truth Dictionary of Racing Slang*, 1989

Edgar Britts; Edgars *noun*
a bad mood, anxiety, fear *AUSTRALIA*
Rhyming slang for **THE SHITS**.
- You give me the Edgar Britts, sometimes. — Bruce Dawe, *Over Here, Harv!*, p. 101, 1983
- — Ned Wallish, *The Truth Dictionary of Racing Slang*, p. 25, 1989

edge *noun*

1 in gambling, a statistical advantage, usually expressed as a percentage *US*

- By the time the tax people take their bite off the top you have a 20 perecent "Edge" working against you. — Mario Puzo, *Inside Las Vegas*, p. 46, 1977
- The house edge in "even money" bets in roulette (European rules) is 1.35% — David Bennet, *Know Your Bets*, p. 34, 2001

2 antagonism; a tension arising from mutual dislike *UK*

- There is a bit or regional edge to all this. The "Redhill Crowd" are just a bit miffed about being beaten by the "Midlands Mafia". — *The Telegraph Sunday Magazine'*, 19th August 1979

3 a knife, used or intended for use as a weapon *US*

- — David Claerbaut, *Black Jargon in White America*, p. 63, 1972

4 an urban area with bars, nightclubs and prostitution *US*

- Since I was getting one vine out of every four from the three girls, my wardrobe was now twice as large as any nigger's on the edge. — A.S. Jackson, *Gentleman Pimp*, p. 32, 1973

▸ on edge

very tense, nervy, anxious *UK, 1870*

- With Brussels on edge as it awaits tomorrow's reports on fraud allegations at the EU statistics agency Eurostat, there is a whiff of blood in the air. — *The Guardian*, 22nd September 2003

▸ on the edge

in gambling, out of funds; broke *US*

- — Richard Jessup, *The Cincinnati Kid*, p. 127, 1963

Edge City *noun*

a notional place where people live on the edge of danger *US*

- — Robert J. Glessing, *The Underground Press in America*, p. 175, 1970: 'Glossary of terms used in the underground press'

edged *adjective*

angry *US*

- Like I'm just lying there next to the pool, and my lame little brother throws the car keys into the Jacuzzi, right, and now I'm edged, fer shurr! — Mary Corey and Victoria Westermark, *Fer Shurr! How to be a Valley Girl*, 1982

edge note *noun*

a fifty pound (£50) note *UK*

Prison slang, current in February 2002.

edge work *noun*

the alteration of dice by rounding off the edges to affect the roll *US*

- — *The Annals of the American Academy of Political and Social Sciences*, p. 124, May 1950

edgy *adjective*

1 nervous, irritable, tense *UK, 1837*

- Nearly every customer was male, everyone seemed slightly edgy about the whole exercise[.] — Brian Preston, *Pot Planet*, p. 89, 2002

2 leading a trend *UK*

Probably from 'cutting-edge'.

- — Susie Dent, *The Language Report*, p. 19, 2003

3 in the used car business, said of a car that needs body work *US*

- — *Esquire*, p. 118, March 1968

Edinburgh fringe *noun*

the female pubic hair; the vagina *UK, 2002*

Rhyming slang for **MINGE**.

- — *www.LondonSlang.com*, June 2002
- — Bodmin Dark, *Dirty Cockney Rhyming Slang*, 2003

Edison *noun*

in horse racing, a hand battery used illegally by a jockey to impart a shock to his horse *US*

- — Dan Parker, *The ABC of Horse Racing*, p. 145, 1947

Edison medicine *noun*

electric shock therapy *US*

Alluding to Thomas Edison, a central figure in the early history of electricity; not a common phrase, although not for lack of cleverness.

- With the Edison medicine, shootin speedballs makes me double crazy[.] — Seth Morgan, *Homeboy*, p. 77, 1990

Edmonchuk *nickname*

the city of Edmonton, Alberta *CANADA*

- Edmonchuk is a nickname for Edmonton, probably from the Ukrainian component of the population. — *Toronto Globe and Mail*, p. C6, 30th May 1998

Edmundo Ros; edmundo *noun*

a boss *UK*

Rhyming slang, formed from the name of Trinidadian band-leader Edmundo Ros (b.1910) who, from 1940, brought Latin American rhythms to Britain.

- — Ray Puxley, *Fresh Rabbit*, 1998

edna!

watch out!; be quiet! *UK, 1960*

Rhyming slang, 'Edna May', based on 'way'; originally used for 'on your way' or 'on my way', now an imperative. Based on the name of actress and singer Edna May (May Edna Pettie), 1878–1948.

- — Angela Devlin, *Prison Patter*, p. 49, 1996

Ednabopper *noun*

a fan of Dame Edna Everage *AUSTRALIA*

Coined by Barry Humphries, the man behind the Dame.

- Prince Charles, an "Ednabopper" of long standing, comes occasionally to Humphries' house in Hampstead for dinner. — John Lahr, *Dame Edna Everage and the Rise of Western Civilisation*, p. 30, 1991

Edna Everage; Edna *noun*

a drink *UK*

Rhyming slang for 'beverage'; based on the 'Housewife Superstar' character created by Australian comedian and satirist Barry Humphries (b.1934).

- Would you like an Edna? — *Antiquarian Book Review*, p. 18, June 2002

Edsel; Flying Edsel *nickname*

the US Air Force F-111 aircraft *US, 1972*

An allusion to the single greatest failure in American car manufacture.

- The result was an Edsel aircraft of monumental proportions. — John Singlaub, *Hazardous Duty*, p. 265, 1991
- Not bad for what was once called the Flying Edsel. — *Texas Monthly*, p. 14, July 1996

educated currency *noun*

in horse racing, bets placed on the basis of what is believed to be authentic, empircal tips *US*

- — David W. Maurer, *Argot of the Racetrack*, p. 26, 1951

educator *noun*

in the circus or carnival, the *Billboard* weekly newspaper *US*

- — Joe McKennon, *Circus Lingo*, p. 32, 1980

Edward *noun*

MDMA, the recreational drug best known as ecstasy *UK*

Early phonetic alphabet for **E** (predating 'E easy' and 'E echo').

- Street names [...] doves, E, Edward, essence[.] — James Kay and Julian Cohen, *The Parents' Complete Guide to Young People and Drugs*, p. 136, 1998

Edward Heath; Ted Heath; Edwards; Teds *noun*

the teeth *UK*

Rhyming slang, formed on the former UK Prime Minister, 1970–74, and Conservative Party leader, who was famously caricatured with a toothy grin.

- — *Daily Telegraph*, 17th December 1972: 'Slang It to me in rhyme'
- — Ray Puxley, *Cockney Rabbit*, 1992

eed-way *noun*

marijuana *US, 1938*

Pig Latin for **WEED**.

eejit; eedjit; idjit *noun*

an idiot *IRELAND, 1955*

Phonetic spelling of Irish pronunciation; earlier variations include 'eediot' and 'eegit'.

- "There never was any money, you old idjit," Kilroy said. "There never was any." — Troy Kennedy Martin, *Z Cars*, p. 156, 1962
- Come here, you wee eedjit! What are we going to do with you? — Kevin Sampson, *Powder*, p. 19, 1999
- [T]he only people trying to rob them were amateurs and fucking eejits. — Val McDermid, *Keeping on the Right Side of the Law*, p. 180, 1999
- [Y]ou really do think we're all a bunch of eejit culchies, don't you? — James Hawes, *Dead Long Enough*, p. 262, 2000

eek *noun*
▷ see: ECAF

eel *noun*
1 an untrustworthy or otherwise despicable person *UK*
Adapting the 'slippery character' sense to more general derogatory usage; possibly, also, a disguised reference to a **HEEL** (a dishonest, untrustworthy person).
- He's just a eel. He's a out-and-out shitbag that preys on old ladies and defenceless schoolboys.—Kevin Sampson, *Outlaws*, p. 95, 2001

2 a spy or informer *US*
- —*American Speech*, p. 98, May 1956: 'Smugglers' argot in the Southwest'

3 the penis *US, 1968*
From a perceived resemblance.
- —J.E. Lighter, *Historical Dictionary of American Slang, Volume 1*, p. 697, 1994

eels *noun*
in electric line work, insulated line hose used for covering up lines during work *US*
- —A.B. Chance Co., *Lineman's Slang Dictionary*, p. 6, 1980

eels and liquor; eels *noun*
one pound (£1) *UK*
Rhyming slang for **NICKER**, formed from the name of a classic dish of London cuisine.
- —Ray Puxley, *Cockney Rabbit*, 1992

eensy-weensy *adjective*
very small *US*
A rarely-heard variant of 'teensy-weensy'.
- C'mon. One eensy-weensy guess.—Armistead Maupin, *Tales of the City*, p. 58, 1978

eeoo-leven *noun*
in craps, an eleven *US*
- —Steve Kuriscak, *Casino Talk*, p. 21, 1985

eez *noun*
sex *BERMUDA*
- —Peter A. Smith and Fred M. Barritt, *Bermewjan Vurds*, 1985

eff; F
used as a euphemism for 'fuck' in all its different senses and parts of speech *UK, 1929*
Originally purely euphemistic, but soon a jocular replacement for **FUCK**.
- Going into a Western Union office, I sent off a telegram to Mr. Charles P. Bailey of Atlanta. It read: WHO GOT EFFED THIS TIME.—Ethel Waters, *His Eye on the Sparrow*, p. 209, 1951
- Eff them. Eff the lot of them. Us poor peepul.—Geoffrey Fletcher, *Down Among the Meths Men*, p. 79, 1966
- Earlier in his talk, Murray had said that San Francisco State was nothing more than a "nigger-producing factory," and that any black student who went along with the college program was "all effed up."—Dirkan Karagueuzian, *Blow it Up*, p. 40, 1971
- Mr. Lawson took quite strong exception. "Eff off," he said to the officer.—*San Francisco Chronicle*, p. 27, 14th March 1972
- Reeb, daybreak is on the turn. What the F you doing down here with the phone?—Iceberg Slim (Robert Beck), *Doom Fox*, p. 165, 1978
- He was drunk and he told me to eff myself. I hung up.—*San Francisco Examiner*, p. 18, 18th July 1978
- Yo! Yo! He effed you up!—*New Jack City*, 1990
- You was effing it up in Chicago when you was nine or ten and you ain't done a helluyva lot better since your ass got out here.—Odie Hawkins, *Midnight*, p. 9, 1995

eff and blind *verb*
to swear; to pepper discourse with obscenities *UK*
A combination of two euphemisms: **EFF** (**FUCK**) and **BLIND** (**BLOODY**).
- They'd eff and blind till your ear-'oles started to frizzle.—Michael Harrison, *Reported Safe Arrival*, 1943
- You've heard those street kids of three and four effing and blinding.—Chris Ryan, *Stand By, Stand By*, p. 103, 1996
- The other day I was effin' and blindin' on the phone, right, she goes, "Mummy, don't swear!"—Diran Adebayo, *My Once Upon A Time*, p. 117, 2000
- I don't see the need for the constant effing and blinding those kids get up to[.]—Kevin Sampson, *Clubland*, p. 77, 2002

eff and jeff *verb*
to swear; to pepper discourse with obscenities *UK*
A variation of **EFF AND BLIND**.
- Mind your Ps and Qs – so no effing and jeffing.—Noel Fielding and Julian Barratt, *The Mighty Boosh*, 7th June 2004

effect *noun*
▸ **in effect; in effect mode**
relaxed, in-control, unstressed *US*
- When you were "in effect" you were truly "large" [doing well].—Nelson George, *Hip Hop America*, p. 209, 1998

effed up *adjective*
used as a euphemism for 'fucked up' *US*
- Earlier in his talk, Murray had said that San Francisco State was nothing more than a "nigger-producing factory," and that any black student who went along with the college program was "all effed up."—Dirkan Karagueuzian, *Blow it Up*, p. 40, 1971

effer *noun*
a person, a fucker *UK*
- Leave the effer alone, will yer? He's pissed, that's all.—Geoffrey Fletcher, *Down Among the Meths Men*, p. 35, 1966

efficient *adjective*
▸ **get efficient**
to smoke marijuana *US*
- —Jim Emerson-Cobb, *Scratching the Dragon*, April 1997

effing; effin'; f-ing *adjective*
used as an intensifier; a euphemism for 'fucking' *UK, 1929*
- Because when you were just about my age you went through something like this. I mean one hell of a big effing overnight success. (Quoting Thomas Heggen).—*Esquire*, p. 102, November 1960
- I get so effing cross[.]—Derek Raymond (Robin Cook), *The Crust on its Uppers*, p. 22, 1962
- "That's the smallest effing set on the stage," said the camerman. "I can't get three effing machines in there."—Max Shulman, *Anyone Got a Match?*, p. 218, 1964
- Wet 'er feet, 'e did. Aw, yus, yus. Aw. Aw. The effin' scouse.—Geoffrey Fletcher, *Down Among the Meths Men*, p. 34, 1966
- I ain't an effing thicky—Ian Dury, *Billericay Dickie*, 1977
- He said the spyer was like a f-ing phantom, and he didn't know where he was.—James Ellroy, *White Jazz*, p. 184, 1992
- I want to stay here. I f'ing told you!—Mark Powell, *Snap*, p. 222, 2001
- Says no way is he coming back to work for that effin' bee.—Kevin Sampson, *Clubland*, p. 165, 2002

eff off *verb*
used as a euphemism for 'fuck off' *UK, 1945*
- We all got told to eff off when it opened up again.—Garry Bushell, *The Face*, p. 271, 2001

effort *noun*
a specific article that is not accurately named *UK, 1925*
Originally public school usage.
- I've half a mind to become one of them fuckin' feminist efforts.—*The Full Monty*, 1997
- Scalding hot tea out of a proper pot. None of them farting tin efforts[.]—Kevin Sampson, *Outlaws*, p. 227, 2001

efink *noun*
a knife *UK, 1859*
Back slang.
- —Paul Baker, *Polari*, p. 173, 2002

egad!
used as a mild oath *UK, 1673*
Possibly 'ah God'. Generally considered to be obsolete from later C19 but survives in ironic usage.
- "Egad! gasped Dec, "Was that a Luger pistol being loaded?"—*SMTV LIVE it's wicked*, p. 28, 2000

egg; green egg; wobbly egg *noun*
a capsule of branded tranquilliser Temazepam™ *UK*
From the appearance.
- —Angela Devlin, *Prison Patter*, p. 49, 1996
- Temazepam are called "green or yellow eggs", "jellies" and "jelly babies"[.]—James Kay and Julian Cohen, *The Parents' Complete Guide to Young People and Drugs*, p. 150, 1998

egg *noun*
1 a person *UK, 1864*
From 'bad egg' (a rascal).
- He knows all the good eggs in boxing and all the bad ones.—*San Francisco Call Bulletin*, p. 14, 2nd March 1948

- Besides, the Cafeteria was a popular place and the owner was a well egg who didn't deserve getting shook by a big pinch right in the middle of his rush hour. —Mickey Spillane, *Return of the Hood*, p. 79, 1964
- "Mike's a good egg. Alex is a good egg. Frankie is an awfully good egg. But who is the best egg?" "Who rattled your cage?" Alex said. "Don't ask," Mike said. —Guy Burt, *The Hole*, p. 56, 1993

2 a fool, especially an obnoxious fool *US, 1918*
Possibly derived from **YEGG** (a criminal).
- He could have a grand in his slid with most of it being one dollar bills and this egg would break a twenty just for a pack of cigarettes. —A.S. Jackson, *Gentleman Pimp*, p. 98, 1973
- "All right, you fucking egg," I tell him. "Get hold of the legs." —Ted Lewis, *Jack Carter's Law [britpulp]*, p. 52, 1974

3 a white person who associates with, and takes on, the culture of south Asians *US*
The egg, like the person described, is white on the outside but yellow on the inside.
- —Pamela Munro, *U.C.L.A. Slang*, p. 62, 1997

4 a novice surfer *AUSTRALIA*
- Remember, you are still an "egg," a surfer who is a learner, and in some cases a menace to all. —Jack Pollard, *The Australian Surfrider*, p. 21, 1963

5 a person who is trying to bet his way out of debt and, predictably, failing *AUSTRALIA*
- —Ned Wallish, *The Truth Dictionary of Racing Slang*, p. 25, 1989

6 a bookmaker who refuses a bet *AUSTRALIA*
From the bookmaker's claim 'I've already laid it'.
- —Ned Wallish, *The Truth Dictionary of Racing Slang*, p. 26, 1989

7 a railway police officer *US*
- —Ramon Adams, *The Language of the Railroader*, p. 53, 1977

8 a billiard ball *US, 1988*
- —Mike Shamos, *The Illustrated Encyclopedia of Billiards*, p. 85, 1993

9 a bomb *US*
- Disabled Bomber Dumps its 'Eggs,' Terrifies Canadians [Headline] —*San Francisco News*, p. 3, 11th November 1950

10 a theatrical failure *US*
- —Wilfred Granville, *The Theater Dictionary*, p. 25, 1952

11 crack cocaine *US*
- — US Department of Justice, *Street Terms*, October 1994

12 a short surfboard with a round tail and a round nose, extremely common in the late 1960s and early 70s *AUSTRALIA*
- —*surfresearch.com.au*

egg *verb*
to perform poorly *US*
- —Connie Eble (Editor), *UNC-CH Campus Slang*, p. 4, October 2002

egg and spoon; egg *noun*
1 a black person *UK, 1992*
Derogatory; rhyming slang for **COON**. Subject to some politically correct confusion with earlier 'good egg' (an expression of approval, hence 'good person', 1903).
- "Good egg" is deemed to be too closely associated with "egg and spoon" – rhyming slang for "coon". —*The Guardian*, p. 7, 15th May 2002

2 a procurer of prostitutes, a pimp *AUSTRALIA*
Rhyming slang for **HOON** (a pimp).
- —*The (Sydney) Bulletin*, 26th April 1975

eggbeater *noun*
1 a single rotor helicopter *US, 1936*
Coined well before the war in Korea, but used extensively by US forces in Korea.
- Known by such nicknames as "choppers," "eggbeaters," "whirly-birds," and "airedales," helicopters were flown by a single pilot and had two external pods to carry wounded. —Stanley Sandler, *The Korean War*, p. 129, 1995

2 a twin-engine training plane *US*
- —*American Speech*, p. 310, December 1946: 'More Air Force slang'

3 an oldish, not very powerful motor car *UK*
An affectionate usage, reported by Mrs C. Raab, 1981.

4 a small outboard motor for a boat *US, 1942*
- We ran across the four miles of lake under power, having brought with us a 3 h.p. Johnson. People were rude to this small machine in that land of big riverboats and 25 h.p. kickers–they called it an eggbeater and burst into laughter at the sight of it. —*Beaver*, p. 16/2, Winter 1956

5 a paddle skier *SOUTH AFRICA*
The skier sits on a small bulbous canoe and paddles into the surf using paddles. His whirring repetitive paddling motion, especially when gaining speed to catch a wave, resembles an eggbeater.

6 a bad head-over-skis fall while skiing *US*
- —*American Speech*, p. 205, October 1963: 'The language of skiers'

egg breaker *noun*
in electric line work, a guy strain insulator *US*
- —A.B. Chance Co., *Lineman's Slang Dictionary*, p. 6, 1980

egg crate *noun*
in hot rodding and car customising, a grille design with a cross hatch *US*
- —John Edwards, *Auto Dictionary*, p. 52, 1993

egg flip *noun*
in horse racing, useful information about a horse or race *AUSTRALIA, 1966*
- Rhyming slang for tip. —Ryan Aven-Bray, *Ridgey Didge Oz Jack Lang*, p. 27, 1983
- —Ned Wallish, *The Truth Dictionary of Racing Slang*, p. 26, 1989

egghead *noun*
1 an intellectual, often a scientist; a very smart person *US, 1918*
- —*American Speech*, December 1957
- Most frightening of all is the fact that American education is controlled by females and eunuchs – eggheads. —Lee Mortimer, *Women Confidential*, p. 94, 1960
- "Sure, Stew," he said, "all the eggheads are for Stevenson. But how many eggheads are there?" —*Saturday Evening Post*, p. 30, 8th September 1962
- In high school, I was an egghead who wrote poems. —Malcolm Boyd, *My Fellow Americans*, p. 144, 1970
- The "eggheads" and there were a few, had an uphill struggle. —Odie Hawkins, *Scars and Memories*, p. 159, 1987
- [Billy the Kid addressing Freud] Way to go, egghead. —*Bill and Ted's Excellent Adventure*, p. 85, 1989
- [A] Singaporean government minister, known as a bit of an egghead, got up to make a rousing speech. —*The Guardian*, 10th December 2002

2 a bald person *US, 1907*
- As for his head? It was completley bald. Clean shaven. A total egghead. —Vincent Zandri, *Godchild*, p. 249, 2000

egghead brigade *noun*
forensic scientists *UK*
Police use, from **EGGHEAD** (an intellectual, often a scientist).
- —John Wainwright, *Dig His Grave and Let Him Lie*, 1971

eggheaded *adjective*
1 intellectual yet lacking common sense *US, 1956*
- I gushed, then froze becaues I realized – too late as usualy – that I'd been too eager and too eggheaded. —Haywood Smith, *The Red Hat Club*, p. 38, 2003

2 bald *US, 1920*
- The two boys skated and stumbled to the next staircase and grabbed on, the larger one following the eggheaded one and running into him. —Richard Dry, *Leaving*, p. 370, 2002

egg in a hole *noun*
a slice of bread fried with an egg in a hole cut out of the middle *CANADA*
- "Egg in the hole" is the customary dish served during a "TacEval," an unannounced visit to a friend's home after a particularly convivial evening at the mess. Originally a naval dish, the purpose of the bread is to prevent the egg from slipping at sea. —Tom Langeste, *Words on the Wing*, p. 88, 1995

egg on your face *noun*
humiliation or embarrassment *CANADA, 1964*
- The minister for local government and the regions [...] Currently has some egg on his face, having been the chief cheerleader for elected mayors nationwide as bid to diffuse voter apathy. —*The Guardian*, 23rd October 2002

eggplant *noun*
a black person *US, 1934*
- —Jim Goad, *Jim Goad's Glossary of Northwestern Prison Slang*, December 2001

egg roll *noun*
1 an idiot *AUSTRALIA*
- Dickheads are also known as Parras, Westies, nerds, Brizzoes, Reggie Rev-Heads, veggies and egg rolls. —Phil Jarratt, *Surfing Dictionary*, p. 16, 1985

2 a beginner surfer *AUSTRALIA*
- —Trevor Cralle, *The Surfin'ary*, p. 33, 1991

eggs *noun*
the testicles *US*
• I mean, even if I whacked off your eggs, I don't think I'd really get to you. —Jack W. Thomas, *Heavy Number*, p. 162, 1976

eggshell blonde *noun*
a bald person *AUSTRALIA*
• —Jim Ramsay, *Cop It Sweet!*, p. 34, 1977
• —Thommo, *The Dictionary of Australian Swearing and Sex Sayings*, p. 38, 1985

eggsucker *noun*
1 a sycophant *US, 1838*
• My name is Vic, you little eggsucker. —Harlan Ellison, *A Boy and His Dog*, p. 971, 1969
• —Linda Reinberg, *In the Field*, p. 73, 1991
2 in electric line work, an insulated line tool formally known as a grip-all stick *US*
• —A.B. Chance Co., *Lineman's Slang Dictionary*, p. 6, 1980

egg-sucking *adjective*
despicable *US, 1845*
• This way you escape possible suspicion that you are an apple-polishing, bootlicking, egg-sucking, backscratching sycophant trying to win brownie points. —Leil Lowndes, *Talking the Winner's Way*, p. 192, 1999

eggy *adjective*
1 unpleasant, tasteless *UK*
• I started saying how generally eggy I thought it was, but, it turned out, the girls had rather enjoyed it[.] —Mike Stott, *Soldiers Talking, Cleanly*, 1978
2 annoyed, angry *UK, 1961*
Possibly a phonetic variation of 'aggravated'.
• Dis woz de work of de gods who woz well eggy at him[.] —Sacha Baron-Cohen, *Da Gospel According to Ali G*, 2001

Eglinton Toll; eglinton *noun*
the anus; by extension, the buttocks *UK: SCOTLAND*
Glasgow rhyming slang for **ARSEHOLE**, formed from an area of that city.
• Are you gauny get aff yer Eglinton an make a move? —Michael Munro, *The Patter, Another Blast*, 1988

egoboo *noun*
favourable words, praise *US*
• —*American Speech*, p. 25, Spring 1982: 'The langage of science fiction fan magazines'

Egon Ronay; egon *noun*
an act of defecation *UK*
Rhyming slang for **PONY** (**PONY AND TRAP**), imperfectly formed from the name of a celebrated food critic.
• —Ray Puxley, *Fresh Rabbit*, 1998

ego surf *verb*
to search for mentions of your name on the Internet *US*
• —Vann Wesson, *Generation X Field Guide and Lexicon*, p. 62, 1997

ego trip *noun*
any activity that is motivated by self-importance *US*
• All these people away on power trips and ego trips. I'm almost to the point of being sick of it, sick of being a Digger. —Nicholas Von Hoffman, *We Are The People Our Parents Warned Us Against*, p. 97, 1967
• Yet there is a way of integrating your own ego trip with a sense of community, with a concept of the "we." —Abbie Hoffman, *Woodstock Nation*, p. 6–7, 1969
• One big ego trip on the party of Anthony Nensley is no excuse for the creation of a film. —*Screw*, p. 7, 25th April 1969
• He said because he always wanted to see his picture on a bubblegum card. Well, me too. It's an ego trip. —Jim Bouton, *Ball Four*, p. ii, 1970
• The three most popular reasons given for appearing in porno films are money, a chance to stardom, and the old ego trip. —Stephen Ziplow, *The Film Maker's Guide to Pornography*, p. 43, 1977
• Another little ego trip for the feminists. —Monty Python, *Life of Brian*, 1979
• I want you to explain to this honkie bitch who I am and I want her to understand I won't put up with any bullshit ego trips. —Elmore Leonard, *City Primeval*, p. 9, 1980
• I feel sexy doing this. It's definitely an ego trip. It's kind of thrilling to get paid for it. —Anka Radakovich, *The Wild Girls Club*, p. 125, 1994

egregious *adjective*
very bad *US*
Conventional English rendered slang by attitude and drawn-out pronunciation.
• —*USA Today*, p. 1D, 5th August 1991: 'A sterling lexicon of the lingo'

Egypt *noun*
a neighbourhood populated largely by black people *US*
• —*Maledicta*, p. 158, 1979: 'A glossary of ethnic slurs in American English'

Egyptian *noun*
a tablet of MDMA, the recreational drug best known as ecstasy *UK*
• —Mike Haskins, *Drugs*, p. 289, 2003

Egyptian queen *noun*
in homosexual usage, an attractive black man *US*
An incorrect racial label.
• —*Maledicta*, p. 54, 1986–1987: 'A continuation of a glossary of ethnic slurs in American English'

eh
used after a positive statement without any suggestion of questioning *AUSTRALIA*
Usage after virtually every positive statement a speaker makes is characteristic of many speakers of both New Zealand and northern Australia.
• 'They must sling to the cops, eh?' commented Gabriel with a knowing wink, and the waiter grinned. —Vince Kelly, *The Bogeyman*, p. 33, 1956
• Like that, eh! —W.R. Bennett, *Wingman*, p. 70, 1961
• You have read my files, eh. —Nelson Mandela, *Long Walk to Freedom*, p. 343, 1994
• 'Hot enough for ya, is it eh? he said. Rocker was from Queensland, he said 'eh' after everything. —Phillip Gwynne, *Deadly Unna?*, p. 140, 1998
• 'Can't she see I'm on the black? Tell her I'm on me way, eh.' —Phillip Gwynne, *Deadly Unna?*, p. 158, 1998
• Thanks, eh. —*Lonely Planet Southern Africa*, 2000
• Spent a year in Brisbane. One guy up there in particular was so bad every sentence finished with 'eh'. I went home to NSW and my mate laughed at how much I used it. I must have picked it up temporarily. —*Wordmap (www.abc.net.au/wordmap)*, 2003

eh?
do you agree? *CANADA, 1945*
• It may be that in the Golden Horseshoe "eh" isn't used as extravagantly as in the rest of Canada, but here in Northern Ontario, we use it fluently. If I'm telling someone about an event, one listener will interject with "no, eh? or "Yeah. eh?" —John Keast, *in The Latest Morningside Papers*, p. 26, 1989

E-head *noun*
a habitual user of MDMA, the recreational drug best known as ecstasy *UK*
Combines **E**, the familiar shorthand for **ECSTASY** (MDMA) with **-HEAD** (a user).
• [A] crowd of nutty e-heads with their tops off[.] —Dave Haslam, *Dear Colin*, p. 158, 1999

Eiffel Tower; eiffel *noun*
1 a shower *UK*
Rhyming slang.
• —Ray Puxley, *Cockney Rabbit*, 1992
2 a good look *UK*
Rhyming slang and homophone, **EYEFUL**.
• A peeping Toms delight, an eyeful in the Eifel [sic]. —Ray Puxley, *Cockney Rabbit*, 1992
• [H]ave a tower! —*www.LondonSlang.com*, June 2002

eight *noun*
1 heroin *US*
'H' is the 8th letter of the alphabet, and there is the phonetic connection to 'H'.
• —*Providence (Rhode Island) Journal-Bulletin*, p. 6B, 4th August 1997
2 one-eighth of an ounce of a drug *US*
• If we can find somebody Jackson's been selling the eights to, we might be able to get Wells sinside to set him up for a buy[.] —Vernon E. Smith, *The Jones Men*, p. 125, 1974
3 an eight fluid ounce beer glass; a serving of beer in such a glass *AUSTRALIA*
• I call them fours, sixes, and eights. That's a very simple system. —John O'Grady, *It's Your Shout, Mate!*, p. 56, 1972
• —Maureen Brooks and Joan Ritchie, *Tassie Terms*, p. 49, 1995

eight and out *noun*
in pool, a win achieved by sinking all eight balls in a single turn *US*
• —Mike Shamos, *The Illustrated Encyclopedia of Billiards*, p. 85, 1993

eight ball *noun*

1 one eighth of an ounce *US*

- Detectives found $5,000 worth of cocaine in powdered form that had been packaged as "eightballs," or one-eighth ounces. — *The Record*, p. A40, 24th July 1988
- Had to be, Strike reasoned, because an eight ball – just three and a half grams – wouldn't be worth the risk of selling in such a public place. — Richard Price, *Clockers*, p. 110, 1992
- Tenner means one sixteenth of an ounce. One eighth is called a eightball. You ever do cringe? — Joseph Wambaugh, *Finnegan's Week*, p. 40, 1993
- Tony would [...] come in and start doing up the eight-ball he seemed invariably to have with him as a chemical security blanket. — Mick Farren, *Give the Anarchist a Cigarette*, p. 361, 2001
- Trev, there's an eight-ball of nose [cocaine] in this for you[.] — Colin Butts, *Is Harry Still on the Boat?*, p. 377, 2003

2 a discharge from the US Army for mental unfitness *US*
From the regulation AF 600–208.

- — Carl Fleischhauer, *A Glossary of Army Slang*, p. 18, 1968

3 Old English 800™ malt liquor *US*

- — Michael Small, *Break it Down*, p. 219, 1992: 'Hip-hop dictionary'
- — Connie Eble (Editor), *UNC-CH Campus Slang*, p. 11, Spring 1998

4 a dark-skinned black person *US, 1919*
The 'eightball' in billiards is black.

- — Lou Shelly, *Hepcats Jive Dictionary*, p. 11, 1945
- An eight-ball like him sweet on a high-yaller gal will find out where Hitler is buried at. — Chester Himes, *A Rage in Harlem*, p. 148, 1957

5 a conventional, staid, unsophisticated person *US*

- — Clarence Major, *Dictionary of Afro-American Slang*, p. 50, 1970

6 a mixture of crack cocaine and heroin *US*

- I'm busy crankin' off an eight-ball, dude. — Stephen J. Cannell, *The Tin Collectors*, p. 116, 2001
- — Robert Ashton, *This Is Heroin*, p. 209, 2002

▸ **behind the eight ball**
in a difficult position *US, 1932*
From a tactical disadvantage when playing pool.

eight-charge *noun*
eighty pounds of gunpowder in a satchel *US*

- Cpl. Tobias Rios, 27, of Elizabeth, N.J., rammed home an "eight-charge" – 80 pounds of black powder trussed in a canvas satchel. — *Boston Globe*, 29th January 1991

eighteen *noun*
an eighteen gallon keg of beer *AUSTRALIA, 1918*

- — Sue Rhodes, *Now you'll think I'm awful*, p. 55, 1967
- — Bill Wannan, *Folklore of the Australian Pub*, p. 8, 1972
- It's just that they have to make sure that they get rid of the eighteen of beer. — Roy Higgins and Tom Prior, *The Jockey Who Laughed*, p. 91, 1982
- — Roy Slaven (John Doyle), *Five South Coast Seasons*, p. 9, 1992

eighteen-carat *adjective*
first-class, excellent *UK, 1880*
From the 'carat' which is used to classify the weight of diamonds and other precious stones, generally considered to be a measurement of quality.

- An eighteen-carat watering hole and safe haven for some of Fulham's finest denizenry [sic]. — Andrew Nickolds, *Back to Basics*, p. 3, 1994

eighteen pence *noun*
sense, common-sense *UK, 1932*
Rhyming slang.

- Ain't you got no eighteen pence? — Ray Puxley, *Cockney Rabbit*, 1992

eighter from Decatur *noun*
in craps, a roll of eight *US*

- — *The Annals of the American Academy of Political and Social Sciences*, p. 124, May 1950
- I listened for a moment to the snapping of their fingers, their low intent voices. "Eighter from Decatur!" — Chester Himes, *Cast the First Stone*, p. 134, 1952
- "Eighter from decatur, eighter from Decatur." He tosses the dice again and loses, a four and a three. — Darryl Ponicsan, *The Last Detail*, p. 12, 1970
- I heard the cracking of dice coming from the next tent and I heard somebody say 'Eighta from Dakata. . .' It was like a godsend. — Edward Lin, *Big Julie of Vegas*, p. 119, 1974
- "Eighter from Decatur," Duffy shouted. "A winner." — Stephen Cannell, *Big Con*, p. 201, 1997

eighth *noun*
▷ see: 8TH

eight miler *noun*
a distracted driver who drives for several miles with a turn signal flashing *US*

- — Montie Tak, *Truck Talk*, p. 55, 1971

eight-pager *noun*
a small pornographic comic book that placed well-known world figures or comic book characters in erotic situations *US*

- It would be very difficult at Hanson Elementary living down probation for selling "eight-pagers." — Clancy Sigal, *Going Away*, p. 356, 1961
- The turning to "eight-pagers" – prison-made booklets consisting of crude, lewd pictures depicting both heterosexual and homosexual activity – appears to be, in effect, a securing of some sex satisfaction[.] — *New York Mattachine Newsletter*, p. 6, August 1961
- When I was in high school, those little comic sex books we called "Eight Pagers" were the vogue. — Angelo d'Arcangelo, *The Homosexual Handbook*, p. 186, 1968
- Buck was reading a copy of an eight-pager about TV's Hugh Downs and Barbara Walters and, instead of pictures about discussions, poverty, pollution and revolutions, they were heavy into orgies. — Steve Cannon, *Groove, Bang, and Jive Around*, p. 142, 1969
- [H]e becomes the victim of a moon shot by no less than Popeye himself in a famous old eight-pager[.] — Robert A. Wilson, *Playboy's Book of Forbidden Words*, p. 170, 1972

eight-six *noun*
▷ see: EIGHTY-SIX

eight-track *noun*
an eight-lane motorway *US*
A borrowing from the name of the 'eight-track' tape player popular in the 1970s.

- — Bill Davis, *Jawjacking*, p. 37, 1977

eighty *noun*
eighty dollars worth of crack cocaine *US*

- When an undercover detective asked the 50-year-old Dean what he wanted, the chamber head allegedly said he was looking to buy some "80" – street slang for $80 worth of crack cocaine. — *Los Angeles Times*, p. 1 (Part 2), 23rd July 2003

eighty-deuce *nickname*
the 82nd Airborne Division, US Army *US*

- — Linda Reinberg, *In the Field*, p. 73, 1991

eighty-eight *noun*
a piano *US, 1942*
From the 88 keys on a standard piano.

- And the gate that rocked at the eighty-eight was blowin' "How High the Moon." — William "Lord" Buckley, *The Ballad of Dan McGroo*, 1960
- "Real fine eight-eight-box, man," Red commented, brushing his sleeve over the Steinway. — Ross Russell, *The Sound*, p. 188, 1961
- — Clarence Major, *Dictionary of Afro-American Slang*, p. 50, 1970

eighty-eighter *noun*
a piano player *US, 1949*
Drawn from the number of keys on a piano.

- — Arnold Shaw, *Dictionary of American Pop/Rock*, p. 117, 1982

eighty-eights
best wishes; love and kisses *US, 1934*

- Football-player-type coats with "88" stitched onto the front (this mean's "love and kisses" in ham radio code). — *San Francisco Chronicle*, p. 17, 25th January 1966
- — Lanie Dills, *The Official CB Slanguage Language Dictionary*, p. 31, 1976

eighty-five *noun*
a girlfriend *US*

- They're threatening you with murder because Ray's wife was your eight-five. — Stephen J. Cannell, *The Tin Collectors*, p. 174, 2001

eighty niggers and two white men *nickname*
the 82nd Airborne Division, US Army *US*
During the Vietnam war, it was perceived that the 82nd Division enjoyed an above-average black population.

- — Linda Reinberg, *In the Field*, p. 73, 1991

eighty-one mike mike *noun*
an 81mm medium extended-range mortar, found in the mortar platoon of an infantry battalion *US*

- — Linda Reinberg, *In the Field*, p. 73, 1991

eighty-six; eight-six *noun*
an order barring a person from entering a bar or other establishment *US, 1943*
- I take the offender aside and warn him that another complaint will result in an eighty-six. — Helen P. Branson, *Gay Bar*, p. 88–89, 1957
- [T]wo other versions of the Eighty-Six exist. — Bill Cardoso, *The Maltese Sangweech*, p. 149, 1984

eighty-six; eight-six *verb*
to eject; to bar from entry *US, 1955*
- — Francis J. Rigney and L. Douglas Smith, *The Real Bohemia*, p. xiv, 1961
- "Shut your nelly mouth, Mary," said the Negro queen – "or I'll have you eight-sixed out of this bar[.]" — John Rechy, *City of Night*, p. 186, 1963
- Another journalist was eighty-sixed for being too sympathetic. — Hunter S. Thompson, *Hell's Angels*, p. 201, 1966
- Hey, I been eighty-sixed out of better situations'n that. — George V. Higgins, *The Rat on Fire*, p. 77, 1981
- Getting eightysixed from the methadone program was every client's nightmare. — Seth Morgan, *Homeboy*, p. 188, 1990
- He's half in the bag and nobody told him he was eight-sixed from the joint[.] — *Casino*, 1995
- The sign said: "Two Blonde Girls – 86'd". 86 is slang for throwing an undesirable out of a bar or club and permanently banning them. — Jennifer Blowdryer, *White Trash Debutante*, p. 48, 1997
- Fortunately, I had enough native intelligence not to completely eighty-six the Oxbridge [accent]. — Mick Farren, *Give the Anarchist a Cigarette*, p. 16, 2001

eina!
used as an exclamation of pain or as a cry of sympathy for someone else's pain *SOUTH AFRICA, 1913*
Pronounced 'aynah!'.
- [T]he young girl drops her load [a severed head], whereupon it shouts: Eina! (Ouch!) All the girls now throw down their meat and run home[.] — Breyten Breytenbach, *Dog Heart*, p. 151, 1999
- Roughly speaking, the chances of the vasectomised one experiencing "chronic testicular pain" – ranging from mild and intermittent discomfort to really eina most of the time[.] — *Longevity*, March 2004

Einstein *noun*
used as an ironic nickname for someone who has mastered basic logic *UK*
Albert Einstein (1878–1955) is the one modern scientist, it seems, that everyone has heard of.
- ["]What's up with you? No don't tell me, let me guess. Women's problems." "Spot on, Einstein." — Colin Butts, *Is Harry on the Boat?*, p. 106, 1997
- What, you moved out? demanded The Wop. – Thank you, Einstein, said Harry. — James Hawes, *Dead Long Enough*, p. 45, 2000

Einstein's mate *noun*
an especially unintelligent person *UK*
An ironic comparison.
- — David Powis, *The Signs of Crime*, 1977

Eisenhower *noun*
a shower *UK*
Rhyming slang, formed from the name of the 34th US President, General Dwight D. Eisenhower, 1890–1969.
- — Ray Puxley, *Cockney Rabbit*, 1992

eke *noun*
cosmetics; a room used when applying makeup *UK, 1984*
Derived from polari backslang **ECAF** (the face), and used within homosexual society.

ek sê; ek se; ekse
used as an emphatic affirmation of a statement *SOUTH AFRICA, 1959*
From Afrikaans *ek* (I) *sê* (say), probably a shortening of *ek sê vir jou* (I'm telling you).
- We are an Earth band, ek se. Cape Town has got so much history, it's where we live, love and work[.] — *Sunday Times (South Africa)*, 23rd December 2001

ekusen o'clock *noun*
in the morning *SOUTH AFRICA*
- — *Sunday Times (South Africa)*, 1st June 2003

El *noun*
an elevated railway *US, 1906*
Chicago, New York and Philadelphia are major cities with an El.
- Gene lived way out on the far end of the South Side, and it took him more than an hour to get home by the streetcar or the El. — Mezz Mezzrow, *Really the Blues*, p. 145, 1946
- [T]he so-called sophisticated set has taken over its dingy, old-fashioned saloons under the "El" with the homey Irish names[.] — Jack Lait and Lee Mortimer, *New York Confidential*, p. 61, 1948
- Right up the street under the el was an all-night hash joint, and what I needed was a couple mugs of good black java to bring me around. — Mickey Spillane, *My Gun is Quick*, p. 6, 1950
- My Brooklyn in the dream is true, becuase I often have such dreams of the vast Brooklyn, I ride on endless els[.] — Jack Kerouac, *Letter to Allen Ginsberg*, p. 417, May 1953
- He had got on the subway – there had been no subway in Chicago in the old days – and then had ridden out on the El, shooting along the express tracks, looking out at the same old deteriorating buildings of the Black Belt[.] — James T. Farrell, *Kilroy was Here*, p. 63, 1954
- The Third Avenue El screams above pillared, narrow cobbled streets[.] — Clancy Sigal, *Going Away*, p. 436, 1961
- The street all the way to the el station a block away had been spooked of people — Iceberg Slim (Robert Beck), *Death Wish*, p. 113, 1977
- So I grab my coat and hat and walk over to the El, where I get the train which takes me to the neighborhood where he's lived all these years[.] — Robert Campbell, *Cat's Meow*, p. 21, 1988

▸ **the El**
the boy's reformatory at Elmira, New York *US*
- — Hyman E. Goldin et al., *Dictionary of American Underworld Lingo*, p. 65, 1950

Elaine *noun*
MDMA, the recreational drug best known as ecstasy *UK*
A personification of the drug by elaboration of **E** (MDMA).
- — Mike Haskins, *Drugs*, p. 289, 2003

elbow *noun*
1 a dismissal or rejection *UK, 1971*
- Yeah – he's had the elbow. — Anthony Masters, *Minder*, p. 107, 1984
- Lets face it, Richmond gave me the elbow and I was happy to go to Geelong because the Cats wanted a centre half-forward. — Rex Hunt, *Tall Tales – and True*, p. 8, 1994

2 a pound (0.45kg) of marijuana *US*
A phoentic rendition of the abbreviation 'lb' (pound).
- Fay allegedly asked for an "elbo," or street slang for a pound of marijuana. — *Times Union (Albany, New York)*, p. B4, 26th July 1997
- — Nick Brownlee, *This Is Cannabis*, p. 151, 2002

3 in electric line work, an underground cable terminator *US*
- — A.B. Chance Co., *Lineman's Slang Dictionary*, p. 6, 1980

▸ **on the elbow**
freeloading, on the scrounge *UK*
Playing, perhaps, with **ON THE EARHOLE**.
- — David Powis, *The Signs of Crime*, 1977

elbow-bending *noun*
immoderate consumption of alcohol *US, 1934*
- Leave it to the 20-somethings to break in Arizona's extra hour of elbow bending. While millions of Arizonans slept, thousands of young bar warriors strapped on their beer goggles until 2 a.m. Wednesday[.] — *Arizona Republic*, p. 1B, 26th August 2004

elbow-bending *adjective*
drinking to excess *US*
- Western bands twang happily in the St. Charles Saloon as elbow-bending good old boys raise a little harmless hell. — Don W. Martin, *The Best of San Francisco*, p. 268, 2002

elbow cake *noun*
in the Gaspe region of Canada, a hot biscuit *CANADA*
- Elbow cake is mi'kmaq English – the words for bread and elbow are phonetically similar in the native language. The surface of the hot biscuit vaguely resembles the skin pattern of the human elbow. — Bill Casselman, *Canadian Food Words*, p. 169, 1998

elbow grease *noun*
hard manual labour; effort *UK, 1672*
- "I'd start with a little 'elbow grease.' " Norine looked absently around her. "Scrub the floor, you mean?" — Mary McCarthy, *The Group*, p. 140, 1963

elbow-lifting *noun*
drinking, especially as part of a drinking session *UK, 1961*
- As this was not directly attributed to his constant elbow-lifting at the aforesaid hostelry, his propensity did not result in a ban from the pub. — *www.brighton-listings.co.uk*, 21st May 2002

elbow list *noun*

a list, often notional, of despised things or persons *UK*

- —Tom Hibbert, *Rockspeak!*, p. 56, 1983

elbow-tit *verb*

to graze or strike an unknown female's breast with your elbow *US*

- Anyways, he bumps into this fat lady an' starts elbow tittin.—Richard Price, *The Wanderers*, p. 88, 1974

El Cid *noun*

LSD *UK*

A punning play on the first letter of LSD and the second syllable of 'acid' (LSD), giving the name of a legendary Spanish hero.

- —Mike Haskins, *Drugs*, p. 285, 2003

El D; LD *noun*

1 a Cadillac El Dorado car *US*

- —*Current Slang*, p. 9, Fall 1970
- —John R. Armore and Joseph D. Wolfe, *Dictionary of Desperation*, p. 28, 1976
- "[S]he was his number-one piece, never saw fresh air but what she was in the passenger seat of that big El D he drives."—John Sayles, *Union Dues*, p. 152, 1977
- "The El D. ain't no beast of burden," he muttered repeatedly.—Jim Carroll, *Forced Entries*, p. 56, 1987

2 Eldorado™ fortified wine *UK: SCOTLAND*

- —Michael Munro, *The Original Patter*, p. 23, 1985

elderberry *noun*

an older homosexual man *UK*

- —*Maledicta*, p. 222, 1979: 'Kinks and queens: linguistic and cultural aspects of the terminology for gays'

elder days *noun*

in computing, the years before 1980 *US*

A conscious borrowing from Tolkien.

- —Eric S. Raymond, *The New Hacker's Dictionary*, p. 140, 1991

el diablito *noun*

a mix of cocaine, heroin, marijuana and phencyclidine, the recreational drug known as PCP or angel dust *US, 1998*

The Spanish 'little devil' offers a more elaborate recipe than **EL DIABLO**.

- —Mike Haskins, *Drugs*, p. 283, 2003

el diablo *noun*

a mix of cocaine, heroin and marijuana *UK, 1998*

Spanish *el diablo* (the devil).

- —Mike Haskins, *Drugs*, p. 293, 2003

El Dog *noun*

a Cadillac El Dorado car *US*

- —Carl J. Banks Jr, *Banks Dictionary of the Black Ghetto Language*, 1975

electric *adjective*

1 used as a superlative; marvellous, strange, sudden *UK*

- —David Powis, *The Signs of Crime*, 1977

2 augmented with LSD *US*

- [A]s in electric banana or electric Kool-Aid (Kook-Aid spiked with LSD].[—Ruth Bronsteen, *The Hippy's Handbook*, p. 13, 1967
- I checked my bag – one Yippie film, ten copies of Fuck the System; Mao's little red book; recipes for Molotov cocktails, electric Koolaid and digger stew...—Abbie Hoffman, *Woodstock Nation*, p. 33, 1969
- —Edward R. Bloomquist, *Marijuana*, p. 339, 1971
- —Eugene Landy, *The Underground Dictionary*, p. 73, 1971

electric bookmaker *noun*

a bookmaker who is regularly shocked by the results of the events bet on *AUSTRALIA*

- —Ned Wallish, *The Truth Dictionary of Racing Slang*, p. 26, 1989

electric cure *noun*

execution by electrocution *US*

- —Hyman E. Goldin et al., *Dictionary of American Underworld Lingo*, p. 65, 1950

electrician *noun*

a person who provokes or accelerates a confrontation *US*

- —Ethan Hilderbrant, *Prison Slang*, p. 44, 1998

electric puha *noun*

marijuana, especially New Zealand-grown *NEW ZEALAND, 1989*

Puha is the Maori name for 'wild sowthistle'.

- —Harry Orsman, *A Dictionary of Modern New Zealand Slang*, p. 46–47, 1999

electrics *noun*

a vehicle's electric circuitry *UK, 1946*

- Then you hold your finger on a button and the car's electrics do everything else[.]—*The Guardian*, 29th June 2003

electric soup *noun*

1 a mixture of metholated spirits and cheap red wine *UK: SCOTLAND, 1985*

- Le soup electrique! Chateau d'paralytical!—Ian Pattison, *Rab C. Nesbitt*, 1990

2 Eldorado™, a fortified wine sold in Scotland *UK: SCOTLAND*

- Eldorado – known locally as "electric soup".—*New Society*, 10th March 1983

Electric Strawberry *nickname*

the 25th Infantry Division, US Army *US*

The Division's insignia is a green taro leaf in a red circle, suggesting a strawberry.

- —Linda Reinberg, *In the Field*, p. 73, 1991

electro- *prefix*

when applied to a musical style, involving synthesizers *UK*

As well as the examples listed as headwords, the following styles have been recorded: 'electro-baroque', 'electro-boogie', 'electro-bossa', 'electro-death', 'electro-dup', 'electro-funk', 'electro-goth' and 'electro-noir'.

- —Susie Dent, *The Language Report*, p. 43, 2003

Electrolux *noun*

a person gifted at performing oral sex on men *UK*

From the branded vacuum cleaner and its advertising boast – 'Nothing sucks like an Electrolux'.

electros *noun*

electrical equipment employed for sexual stimulation, especially when advertised by a prostitute *UK*

- —Caroline Archer, *Tart Cards*, 2003

elef *noun*

eleven; in betting, odds of 11–1 *UK*

A shortening and slovening of 'eleven'.

- —John McCririck, *John McCririck's World of Betting*, p. 59, 1991

elef a vier *noun*

in betting, odds of 11–4 *UK*

A phonetic slurring of **ELEF** (11) and 'four'.

- —John McCririck, *John McCririck's World of Betting*, p. 59, 1991

elegant *adjective*

1 (used of a homosexual male) polished, effete *US*

- Elegant – Adjective used for homosexual who prides himself on his higher social level, as regards behavior, haunts, friends, conversation, etc., in comparison with his more sordid brethren.—Anon., *The Gay Girl's Guide*, p. 8, 1949
- —Bruce Rodgers, *The Queens' Vernacular*, p. 75, 1972

2 in computing, simple yet extremely efficient *US*

- —Karla Jennings, *The Devouring Fungus*, p. 220, 1990

elegant sufficiency *noun*

used as an indication that enough has been had to eat *UK, 1984*

A jocular mocking of genteel mannners which has, perhaps, become a cliché.

elephant *noun*

1 heroin *UK*

- —Angela Devlin, *Prison Patter*, p. 49, 1996

2 marijuana *UK*

- —Mike Haskins, *Drugs*, p. 287, 2003

3 a high-ranking Naval officer *US*

US naval aviator usage.

- —*United States Naval Institute Proceedings*, p. 108, October 1986

Elephant and Castle *noun*

1 arsehole, in anatomic and figurative senses *UK, 2002*

Rhyming slang, based on an area of south London.

- —*www.LondonSlang.com*, June 2002
- —Bodmin Dark, *Dirty Cockney Rhyming Slang*, 2003

2 a parcel *UK*

Rhyming slang.

- —John Gosling, *The Ghost Squad*, 1959

elephant bag *noun*
in the usage of forest fire fighters, a large canvas bag used for dropping cargo from aeroplanes *US*
• —*American Speech*, p. 158–160, May 1959: 'Smokejumping words aero'

elephant bucks *noun*
a large amount of money *AUSTRALIA*
• He'd established a very famous bistro in Double Bay and sold it for elephant bucks a few months before he moved into our place.—John Birmingham, *He Died With a Felafel in his Hand*, p. 194, 1994
• The job paid elephant bucks.—Harrison Biscuit, *The Search for Savage Henry*, p. 17, 1995

elephant ear *noun*
in electric line work, a high-strength strain insulator *US*
• —A.B. Chance Co., *Lineman's Slang Dictionary*, p. 6, 1980

elephant gun *noun*
1 any powerful rifle *US, 1918*
• The first time I fired it, I was tensed up for a real jaw-shaking, something much worse than a .458 Winchester Magnum elephant gun.—John Plaster, *Ultimate Snipe*, p. 160, 1993
2 an M79 grenade launcher *US, 1964*
Vietnam war usage. It is a single-shot, break-open, breech-loading, shoulder-fired weapon.
• —*Solider of Fortnue*, p. 57, July 1992
3 a surfboard designed for big-wave conditions *US*
• —Grant W. Kuhns, *On Surfing*, p. 116, 1963

elephant intenstines *noun*
the cotton tubes used by the Viet Cong to carry rice in the field *US*
• —Gregory Clark, *Words of the Vietnam War*, p. 162, 1990

elephant juice *noun*
the drug etorphine, a synthetic morphine 1,000 times more potent than morphine *AUSTRALIA*
• —Ned Wallish, *The Truth Dictionary of Racing Slang*, p. 26, 1989

elephant motor *noun*
the Chrysler Hemi engine *US*
Huge displacement and power.
• —John Edwards, *Auto Dictionary*, p. 52, 1993

elephant pill *noun*
the large orange anti-malaria chloroquine-primequine pill taken once a week by US troops in Vietnam *US, 1980*
• —Linda Reinberg, *In the Field*, p. 73, 1991

Elephants' Graveyard *nickname*
the Boston Naval District headquarters *US*
• The form requested a transfer "for personal reasons" to a lackluster staff job at the Boston Naval District headquarters, "the Elephants' Graveyard" in Navy slang.—Neil Sheehan, *The Arnheiter Affair*, p. 10, 1971

elephant snot *noun*
in car repair, gasket sealant, usually referring to Permatex™ sealant, a tradmarked product *US*
• —Lewis Poteet, *Car & Motorcyle Slang*, p. 77, 1992

elephant's trunk; elephant trunk *noun*
a drunk *US*
Rhyming slang.
• A paraffin lamp, an elephant's trunk—Ian Dury, *Blackmail Man*, 1977

elephant's trunk; elephant trunk; elephant's; elephants *adjective*
drunk *UK, 1859*
Rhyming slang, influenced by the pink elephants that only drunks can see.
• He became very elephant's trunk and Mozart [drunk][.]—Ronnie Barker, *Fletcher's Book of Rhyming Slang*, p. 26, 1979

elephant tracker *noun*
a railway detective *US*
• The term originated because such detectives were jokingly said to be so bumbling that they would not be able "to track an elephant in a snow storm."—*American Speech*, p. 287, December 1968: 'Addenda to the vocabulary of railroading'

elephant tranquilizer; elephant *noun*
phencyclidine, the recreational drug known as PCP or angel dust *US, 2004*
• —Hillsborough County (Florida) Sheriff's Office, *www.hcso.tampa.fl.us*, 2005

elevator *noun*
1 in trucking, a hydraulic lift on the back of a trailer *US*
• —Montie Tak, *Truck Talk*, p. 55, 1971
2 a false cut of a deck of playing cards *US*
• —Michael Dalton, *Blackjack*, p. 45, 1991

elevator jockey *noun*
an elevator (lift) operator *US*
• When elevator jockeys aren't selling them, clerks and typists, white and dark, are.—Jack Lait and Lee Mortimer, *Washington Confidential*, p. 72, 1951
• —*American Speech*, p. 158–159, May 1960: 'The burgeoning of 'Jockey''

eleven *noun*
1 a stunningly gorgeous woman who swallows semen after oral sex *AUSTRALIA*
An elaboration of the 'perfect **TEN**'.
• —Thommo, *The Dictionary of Australian Swearing and Sex Sayings*, p. 40, 1985
2 in a deck of playing cards, a jack or knave *US*
• —John Vorhaus, *The Big Book of Poker Slang*, p. 15, 1996

eleven bang-bang *noun*
an infantry soldier *US, 1980*
11-B was the numerical MOS code assigned to an infantry soldier.
• —Linda Reinberg, *In the Field*, p. 73, 1991
• And what can they do to him? Send him to Nam? He's eleven bang-bang. Mortars. He's going to Nam all right.—Richard Seltzer, *Spit and Polish*, 1996
• His military job specialty is 11-B, or as some here call it, "11-bang-bang." In other words, Sharp is a rifleman, assigned to Company A, 2nds Brigade, 327th Infantry.—*Lexington (Kentucky) Herald Leader*, p. A1, 12th February 2003

eleven bravo *noun*
an infantry soldier *US*
• —Linda Reinberg, *In the Field*, p. 73, 1991
• And in contrast with that, 11 Bravo, there are 18 infantrymen being called and 21 infantry officers, 11 Alpha.—*Meeting of the House Armed Services Committee*, 7th July 2004

eleven bush *noun*
an infantry soldier *US, 1970*
• I began to wonder if they weren't in the market for a radio operator, but perhaps just looking for Eleven-Bushes (11-B the standard infantry MOS).—Don Ericson, *Charlie Rangers*, p. 43–44, 1989

eleven-foot pole *noun*
an imagined device for touching someone whom another would not touch with a ten-foot pole *US*
• —John Gould, *Maine Lingo*, p. 85, 1975

eleven from heaven *noun*
a roll of eleven in a craps game *US*
• "Natural eleven!" the stick man sang. "Eleven from heaven. The winner!"—Chester Himes, *A Rage in Harlem*, p. 27, 1957

elevenses *noun*
mid-morning refreshments; a mid-morning break from work, generally for refreshments but also used as an opportunity for cigarette smoking *UK, 1887*
Originally Kent dialect, extended from 'eleven o'clock'; late C19 workmen also had 'fourses'.
• I really mustn't have a drink; it's not even elevenses.—Jenny Eclair, *Camberwell Beauty*, p. 5, 2000

eleventh commandment *noun*
any rule which is seen as a mandatory guideline on a plane with the Ten Commandments *US, 1975*
A term probably coined by Ronald Reagan and applied to his adage that no Republican (except him) should disparage another Republican. Eventually applied, often jocularly, to many different situations. For example: the mythical commandment but very real criminal code – thou shalt not get caught.
• —Troy Harris, *A Booklet of Criminal Argot, Cant and Jargon*, p. 9, 1976
• —*American Speech*, Fall 1985

eleventh gear *noun*
in trucking, neutral, used for conserving fuel when coasting down a hill *US*
• —Montie Tak, *Truck Talk*, p. 55, 1971

elf *noun*
a technical market analyst *US*
• —Rachel S. Epstein and Nina Liebman, *Biz Speak*, p. 72, 1986

el fabuloso!
used for expressing strong approval *NEW ZEALAND*
• —David McGill, *David McGill's Complete Kiwi Slang Dictionary*, p. 42, 1998

el foldo *noun*
an utter, relentless collapse *US, 1943*
• Honorable mention to NBC Sports boss Dick Ebersol for pulling an El Foldo and televising all future NASCAR events on a five-second delay.— *Daily News (New York)*, p. 98, 10th October 2004

Eli *nickname*
Yale University; a Yale student; a Yale sports team *US, 1879*
• He starred for the Eli hockey, baseball, and football teams and was captain of the skaters in 1926–27.—Daniel K. Fleschner, *Bulldogs on Ice*, p. 16, 2003

Eli Lilly *noun*
morphine *US*
From the drug manufacturer's name.
• —*American Speech*, p. 87, May 1955: 'Narcotic argot along the Mexican border'

eliminate *verb*
to kill a person *UK, 1937*
Originally jocular, but no longer.
• What about would-be terrorists? These are the ones you really want to eliminate, since most of the known terrorists, being suicide bombers, have already eliminated themselves.— *The Observer*, 26th January 2003

elite *adjective*
in the world of Internet discussion groups, offering the illegal *US*
• [A]n "elite" BBS would be a BBS which features pirated software, utilities for cracking passwords, lists of stolen credit card numbers, phreak files, etc.—Andy Ihnatko, *Cyberspeak*, p. 62, 1997

Elizabeth Regina *noun*
the vagina *UK*
Rhyming slang, formed from Queen Elizabeth.
• —Bodmin Dark, *Dirty Cockney Rhyming Slang*, 2003

Elizabeth's corner *noun*
gossip *AUSTRALIA*
• —Ned Wallish, *The Truth Dictionary of Racing Slang*, p. 27, 1989

Elkie Clark *noun*
▷ **see: LK**

elk river *noun*
in poker, a hand with three tens *US, 1968*
• —Thomas L. Clark, *The Dictionary of Gambling and Gaming*, p. 73, 1987

Elky *noun*
a Chevrolet El Camino pickup truck, manufactured from 1959 until 1987 *US*
• —John Edwards, *Auto Dictionary*, p. 52, 1993

-ella *suffix*
used to feminise a noun and thus create a derogative sense *US*
• They really went over the edge, didn't they, the punkerellas.— *Ask*, p. 43, 5th May 1979

elle momo *noun*
marijuana laced with phencyclidine, the recreational drug known as PCP or angel dust *UK*
The etymology is uncertain; it looks French, sounds Spanish and is possibly a play on American 'mom'.
• —Mike Haskins, *Drugs*, p. 287, 2003

ellie *noun*
an elephant seal *ANTARCTICA, 1990*
• —Bernadette Hince, *The Antarctic Dictionary*, p. 115, 2000

Ellis Day *noun*
LSD *UK*
Almost a homophone.
• —Mike Haskins, *Drugs*, p. 285, 2003

Elly and Castle *nickname*
the Elephant and Castle district of south London *UK*
Reported by Laurie Atkinson, 1976.

Elmer *noun*
in circus and carnival usage, an unsophiscticated, gullible local *US, 1926*
• —Don Wilmeth, *The Language of American Popular Entertainment*, p. 84, 1981

El Producto *noun*
oil *US, 1980s→*
Texan.
• —Ken Weaver, *Texas Crude*, 1984

El Ropo *noun*
any cheap cigar *US, 1960*
Mock Spanish.
• "You're supposed to flush that, not smoke it," he says, eyeing a hood's El Ropo cigar.—Richard Schickel, *Clint Eastwood*, p. 397, 1996

Elsie Tanner *noun*
1 a spanner *UK*
Rhyming slang, formed from the name of a character in the television soap opera *Coronation Street*, played, from 1960 to 84, by actress Pat Phoenix, 1923–86.
• —Ray Puxley, *Cockney Rabbit*, 1992

2 a single instance or example of something *UK: SCOTLAND*
Glasgow rhyming slang for 'wanner'.
• Anither coat a emulsion on the ceilin or lee it wi an Elsie Tanner? —Michael Munro, *The Patter, Another Blast*, 1988

El Smoggo; El Stinko *nickname*
El Paso, Texas *US*
A tribute to the city's air quality.
• — *Current Slang*, p. 17, Spring 1970

el tee *noun*
a lieutenant *US, 1978*
From the abbreviation 'Lt'.
• —Linda Reinberg, *In the Field*, p. 73, 1991

elton *noun*
a toilet *UK, 1977*
A play on **JOHN** (a toilet) and musician Elton John (b.1947).
• —Chris Lewis, *The Dictionary of Playground Slang*, p. 83, 2003

Elton John; elton *noun*
deception; an act intended to trick or deceive; a tale intended to deceive *UK*
Rhyming slang for 'con', formed from the name of popular musician Sir Elton John (Reginal Kenneth Dwight) (b.1947).
• The recently knighted musician goes on record as any kind of stitch up, tuck up or take on, always as an "Elton".—Ray Puxley, *Fresh Rabbit*, 1998

elvis *noun*
LSD *UK*
• —Mike Haskins, *Drugs*, p. 285, 2003

Elvis *noun*
a poker player who is nearly broke but manages to stay in a game far longer than one would predict *US*
Like Elvis Presley, the poker player refuses to die.
• —John Vorhaus, *The Big Book of Poker Slang*, p. 15, 1996

emag *noun*
a game *UK, 1873*
Back slang.
• What a bleeding emag this is!—David Powis, *The Signs of Crime*, 1977
• —Paul Baker, *Polari*, p. 173, 2002

E-man *noun*
a police officer assigned to the Emergency Service Unit *US*
New York police slang.
• —Samuel M. Katz, *Anytime Anywhere*, p. 387, 1997: 'The extremely unofficial and completely off-the-record NYPD/ESU truck-two glossary'

embalmed *adjective*
very drunk *US, 1934*
- Oh and your mother's pickled, Evan. I mean I've seen her drunk before, but this is different: she's embalmed. —Richard Yates, *Cold Spring Harbor*, p. 156, 1986

embalmed beef *noun*
canned beef *US, 1898*
A term most strongly associated with profiteers during the Spanish–American war; mostly historical use.
- At one rally, a heckler asked him about the "embalmed beef" scandal of the Spanish war, in which (presumably Republican) suppliers foisted tainted meat off on the soldiers. —H.W. Brands, *T.R.*, p. 403, 1997

embalming fluid *noun*
phencyclidine, the recreational drug known as PCP or angel dust *US*
- —Jay Robert Nash, *Dicitonary of Crime*, p. 116, 1992
- But "embalming fluid"is an old street slang term for PCP, Lawrence said. "There is some confusion about what people are really doing," Lawrence said. — *Cincinnati Enquirer*, p. 6A, 4th December 2003

embroidery *noun*
the punctures and sores visible on an intravenous drug user's body *US*
- —David Maurer and Victor Vogel, *Narcotics and Narcotic Addiction*, p. 405, 1973

embugger *verb*
to hinder, to hamper *UK*
Military.
- [T]here seemed to be nothing embuggering them. —Andy McNab, *Immediate Action*, p. 100, 1995

embuggerance *noun*
any unforeseen hazard that complicates a proposed course of action
Originally military.
- If we could keep ourselves well maintained and free of embuggerances, the better tactically we would be. —Andy McNab, *Immediate Action*, 1995

emby *noun*
in carnival usage, a gullible player *US*
- —Gene Sorrows, *All About Carnivals*, p. 16, 1985: 'Terminology'

emcee *noun*
▷ see: MC

EM club *noun*
an enlisted men's club *US*
- We sat in the EM Club that night while he told us, smiling and laughing his little laugh[.] —Larry Heinemann, *Close Quarters*, p. 97, 1977

Eme *noun*
the Mexican Mafia, a Mexican-American prison gang *US*
From the Spanish pronunciation of the letter 'M'.
- [I]n the pen, both being members of urban barrio gangs, they automatically became members of La Eme, the socalled Mexican Mafia, and were now sworn carnales, the Hispanic term for home-boys. —Seth Morgan, *Homeboy*, p. 176, 1990
- These terms were being seen with greater frequency, thrown up as graffiti throughout Calfiornia's prisons along with the numeral 13, which signifies the letter M, or more prcisely, La eMe. —Bill Valentine, *Gangs and Their Tattoos*, p. 23, 2000

em ef *noun*
▷ see: MF

emeffing *adjective*
used as a euphemism for 'motherfucking' *US*
- Them emeffing guards is bringing it in fountain pens, selling it like hot dogs at the ball game. —Willard Motley, *Let No Man Write My Epitaph*, p. 120, 1958

Emergency *noun*
▸ **the Emergency**
World War 2 *IRELAND*
- Every day, I would catch the 5.14 home from Westland Row and bolt my tea, which in that last year of what we called the Emergency, was coarse war-time bread and a slice of over-the-ration boiled ham[.] —Hugh Leonard, *Out After Dark*, p. 83, 1989

emergency gun *noun*
an improvised method to puncture the skin and inject a drug *US*
- —David Maurer and Victor Vogel, *Narcotics and Narcotic Addiction*, p. 405, 1973

emergency handout *noun*
in prison, the consequent act of separating an imprisoned mother from her baby when, for disciplinary reasons, the parent is removed from the mother and baby unit – the baby is therefore handed out into local authority care *UK*
- —Angela Devlin, *Prison Patter*, p. 49, 1996

Emma Chisit?
how much is it? *AUSTRALIA*
The most famous and well-remembered piece of STRINE. The story goes that a visiting English writer, Monica Dickens, was autographing copies of her latest book in Sydney and a woman handed her a copy and asked in her best Australian accent 'How much is it?'. Monica Dickens took the book and wrote: 'To Emma Chisit' and signed her autograph below. This was reported in the *Sydney Morning Herald*, 30th November 1964.
- Gimmie utter martyr and an airman pickle. Emma chisit? —Afferbeck Lauder, *Let Stalk Strine*, p. 36, 1965
- There are also superlocusts [unwanted tourists] who possess several such loathsome characteristics. Typical screech-cry of such pests is 'Emma Chisett.' —Arthur Chipper, *The Aussie Swearer's Guide*, p. 41, 1972

Emma Freud *noun*
a haemorrhoid *UK, 1997*
Rhyming slang, formed from the name of journalist Emma Freud (b.1961), daughter of Sir CLEMENT FREUD, whose name serves a synonymous purpose.
- [If not for Sigmund Freud, her grandfather] Cockneys would have to think of new rhyming slang for their piles, other than "Emma Freuds". — *The Guardian*, 28th June 2002

Emma G *noun*
a machine gun *US*
A formation built on the initials MG.
- —Vincent J. Monteleone, *Criminal Slang*, p. 78, 1949

Emma Jesse *noun*
an emergency brake *US*
- —Montie Tak, *Truck Talk*, p. 56, 1971

Emmerdale Farm; emmerdale *noun*
the arm *UK*
Rhyming slang, formed from the title of a UK soap opera, broadcast since 1972, later changing its name to *Emmerdale*.
- All right if you're twisting my Emmerdale I'll have a double. —Ray Puxley, *Fresh Rabbit*, 1998

emmet *noun*
a holiday-maker or tourist in Cornwall *UK*
Derisory. *Emmet* is a dialect word for 'ant'; in Cornwall the holiday-makers obviously swarm and get everywhere.
- [T]here are even T-shirts on sale locally saying "I am not an Emmet". — *Illustrated London News*, May 1978

emptyhead *noun*
an idiot *UK*
- [H]e could have went to uni [university] if he'd've wanted. He weren't an emptyhead. —Kevin Sampson, *Outlaws*, p. 192, 2001

empty nest *noun*
a home in which the children have all grown and gone away *US, 1973*
- — *American Speech*, Fall-Winter 1971

empty suit *noun*
a person of no substance *US*
- The nastiest description of the Saints is "empty suits." — *Washington Post*, p. E5, 24th October 1980
- Bush wasn't the word-scrambling empty suit that he sometimes appeared to be in front of cameras. — *Orlando (Florida) Sentinel*, p. G3, 10th October 2004

emu; emu bobber *noun*
a person who picks up tickets at a racecourse in the hope of finding an unclaimed win *AUSTRALIA, 1966*
From the emu, a large, flightless Australian bird related to the ostrich, with long legs and a long neck, that bends to pick things off the ground.
- —Jim Ramsay, *Cop It Sweet!*, p. 34, 1977
- Emu Bobber – Fossicker after discarded betting tickets. —Ryan Aven-Bray, *Ridgey Didge Oz Jack Lang*, p. 27, 1983
- —Ned Wallish, *The Truth Dictionary of Racing Slang*, p. 27, 1989

emu bob; emu parade; emu patrol; emu stalk; emu walk *noun*

a patrol by a group of people over a certain area of ground for the purpose of searching or cleaning the area *AUSTRALIA, 1941*

- Every Monday an emu parade is organised by one of the senior teachers. — *Centralian Advocate*, p. 3, 1st July 1981

emu-bob *verb*

to pick things up off the ground, such as litter or kindling *AUSTRALIA, 1926*

- He took the heavy end of things, of course, but there were a lot of little jobs she took a hand at for a few hours, picking up the lighter sticks for burning off – emu-bobbing it's called[.] — Frank Dalby Davison, *The Wells of Beersheba*, p. 183, 1965

enchilada *noun*

▸ **the whole enchilada**

all of something *US, 1966*

Popularised in the US during the Watergate scandal of 1972–1974.

- Then Rice looked straight at the Garcias, knowing they'd go for the plan: bullshit, truth, the whole enchilada. — James Ellroy, *Suicide Hill*, p. 700, 1986
- You could've just taken the five, ten million Hindy Reno would've squeezed out of Twelvetrees for you. But no, you wanted the whole goddamn enchilada. — Robert Campbell, *Alice in La-La Land*, p. 318, 1987
- DICK: Now, if you want to sell a little bit at a time – CLARENCE: No way! The whole enchilada in one shot. — *True Romance*, 1993

end *noun*

1 the best; an extreme *UK, 1938*

- "Buster," said Red gratefully, "your timing was like the end, ya know?" — Steve Allen, *Bop Fables*, p. 49, 1955
- Nothin can touch the 47 Continental convertible. Theyre the end. — Hubert Selby Jr, *Last Exit to Brooklyn*, p. 28, 1957
- Of course, the girls think it's the end – but these are the kinds of minutes you go through when you let your hair down. — Herbert Huncke, *Guilty of Everything*, p. 145, 1990

2 a share or portion *US, 1887*

- I say I'm not waiting. I want my end. — Malcolm Braly, *On the Yard*, p. 235, 1967
- Several years ago, Beano had sent her his end of a two-month land swindle to pay for her nursing school. — Stephen Cannell, *King Con*, p. 56, 1997

3 the penis *US*

- You wanna get your end wet, call me. I got broads. — Max Shulman, *Rally Round the Flag, Boys!*, p. 190, 1957

4 money *US, 1960*

- — John R. Armore and Joseph D. Wolfe, *Dictionary of Desperation*, p. 28, 1976

▸ **get your end in**

of a man, to have sex *UK*

- It was the place in the town for getting one's end in, they said, and it was naturally very crowded. — Leslie Thomas, *The Virgin Soldiers*, 1966

▸ **the end**

something or someone that tests you to the end of your endurance *UK, 1938*

- Let me up. I've got stones digging holes in my back. You really are the absolute end. — Anne McCaffrey, *Dragonsdawn*, p. 59, 1988

endjie *noun*

▷ **see: ENTJIE**

endo *noun*

1 in mountain biking, an accident in which the cyclist is thrown over the handlebars; the course the cyclist follows in such an accident; a mountain biking trick in which the front brake is sharply applied thus forcing the back wheel to come up off the ground *US*

- We've grimaced and chuckled simultaneously at face plants [a face-first encounter with the gound], endos, biffs [a crash] and crash-landings. — *Mountain Bike Magazine's Complete Guide To Mountain Biking Skills*, p. 32, 1996

2 in motor racing, an end-over-end flip *US, 1976*

- Not everybody can do an endo but everyone who does an endo remembers it. — Ed Radlauer, *Motorcyclopedia*, p. 19, 1973

3 a backwards fall off a surfboard *US*

- — Michael V. Anderson, *The Bad, Rad, Not to Forget Way Cool Beach and Surf Discriptionary*, p. 6, 1988

4 in the television and film industry, any stunt in which a vehicle goes through the air end-over-end *US*

- — John Cann, *The Stunt Guide*, p. 58,: 'Terms and definitions'

5 marijuana *US*

- — Judi Sanders, *Da Bomb*, p. 5, 1997
- — Mike Haskins, *Drugs*, p. 287, 2003

end of

enough said, no more *UK*

End of story.

- And my body – well, my body needs more proper exercise, end of. — Kevin Sampson, *Outlaws*, p. 106, 2001

end of discussion

used as a humorous, if stock, indication that there is nothing more to be said on the subject at hand *US*

- End of discussion. We're gonna wait. — *Lethal Weapon*, 1987

end of story

used as a way to indicate that all that needs to be told has been told, all that needs to be said has been said *US*

Often jocular.

- Mrs. Mohra heard about the homicides out here and she thought I should call it in, so I called it in. End of story. — *Fargo*, 1996
- [G]row up will you -it's over end of fucking story[.] — Patrick Jones, *Unprotected Sex*, p. 240, 1999

end of the line *noun*

the absolute end, the finish of something *US, 1948*

- Is it the end of the line for cocaine? — *The Guardian*, 4th April 2002

end of the road *noun*

the finish of something *UK, 1954*

- End of the road for Thatcher's big beast. — *The Guardian*, 14th September 2001

end of watch *noun*

death *US*

- The thought of finally going end-of-watch as the result of something as relentless as lung cancer scared the crap out of Mario Villalobos. — Joseph Wambaugh, *The Delta Star*, p. 40, 1983

ends *noun*

1 money *US*

An abbreviation of **DIVIDENDS** (money).

- — Judi Sanders, *Da Bomb!*, p. 10, 1997

2 cash on hand *US*

- — Don R. McCreary (Editor), *Dawg Speak*, 2001

3 a rich customer of a prostitute *US*

- — *Maledicta*, p. 150, Summer/Winter 1986–1987: 'Sexual slang: prostitutes, pedophiles, flagellators, transvestites, and necrophiles'

4 the hair *UK*

Possibly by back-formation from 'split-ends'. Recorded in use in contemporary gay society.

- — *Attitude*, p. 60, July 2003: 'New palare lexicon'

endsville *noun*

1 the end *US, 1962*

- I hope this book will inspire other people the way I was inspired by him in my life. Endsville. — Douglas Nason and Greg Escalante, *Rat Fink*, p. 106, 2003

2 the best *US, 1957*

- [A] large buffet, always laden with endsville goodies, mostly to eat. — Terry Southern, *Riding the Lapping Tongue*, 1973

3 the worst *US*

- As a convention town, this is strictly Endsville. — Jonathan Van Meter, *The Last Good Time*, p. 200, 2003

Ene *nickname*

1 the Northern Structure prison gang *US*

Spanish for the letter 'N' used by English speakers in the American southwest.

- — Bill Valentine, *Gang Intelligence Manual*, p. 41, 1995: 'Hispanic gang terminology'

2 a member of the Nuestra Familia prison gang *US*

- — George Carpenter Baker, *Pachuco*, p. 41, January 1950
- — Bill Valentine, *Gangs and Their Tattoos*, p. 36, 2000

enema queen *noun*

a male homosexual with an enema fetish *US*

- I have found that a large percentage of my discipline cases are enema queens. — *Screw*, p. 7, 20th October 1969

Enema Sue; Enema Zoo *nickname*
New Mexico State University *US*
A cheerful play on the initials NMSU.
- — *Current Slang*, p. 17, Spring 1970

energizer *noun*
phencyclidine, the recreational drug known as PCP or angel dust *US*
- —Richard A. Spears, *The Slang and Jargon of Drugs and Drink*, p. 186, 1986

energy powder *noun*
amphetamine *UK*
- —Angela Devlin, *Prison Patter*, p. 21, 1996

enforcer *noun*
a criminal who uses violence or intimidation to enforce the will of a criminal gang *US, 1929*
- —Edward J. MacKenzie, *Street Soldier*, 2003

en fuego!
used as a humorous observation that somebody is performing very well *US*
Coined and popularised by ESPN's Dan Patrick; probably the most widely used of the ESPN-spawned catchphrases.
- —Pamela Munro, *U.C.L.A. Slang*, p. 80, 1997
- —Keith Olberman and Dan Patrick, *The Big Show*, p. 14, 1997
- —Connie Eble (Editor), *UNC-CH Campus Slang*, p. 3, April 1997

engine *noun*
▸ **on the engine**
(used of a racehorse) well in front in a race *US*
- —Igor Kushyshyn et al., *The Gambling Times Guide to Harness Racing*, p. 115, 1994

engineer *noun*
the first active participant in serial sex with a single passive partner *US*
From 'to **PULL A TRAIN**' (to engage in serial sex).
- Carolina Moon announced that she was going to take her blanket into the bushes and pull the train. "I'm first! I'm the engineer!" cried Harold Bloomguard. —Joseph Wambaugh, *The Choirboys*, p. 333, 1975

engine room *noun*
1 the forward pack on a rugby union team *NEW ZEALAND, 1998*
- —Harry Orsman, *A Dictionary of Modern New Zealand Slang*, p. 47, 1999

2 the rhythm section of a band *TRINIDAD AND TOBAGO, 1990*
- —Lise Winer, *Dictionary of the English/Creole of Trinidad & Tobago*, 2003

3 the mid-boat rowers in an eight-person racing shell *US, 1949*
- She wears a microphone attached to speakers so she can communicate with the middle of the boat, "the engine room," and the bow. — *San Francisco Chronicle*, p. D1, 16th August 2004

England *noun*
▸ **go to England**
to have a baby in secret *TRINIDAD AND TOBAGO, 1960*
- —Lise Winer, *Dictionary of the English/Creole of Trinidad & Tobago*, 2003

Englebert Humperdink; englebert *noun*
a drink *UK*
Rhyming slang, formed from the name of singer Englebert Humperdink (Gerry Dorsey) (b.1936) who came to popular fame in the mid-1960s.
- —Ray Puxley, *Fresh Rabbit*, 1998

English *noun*
in pool, spin imparted on the cue ball to affect the course of the object ball or the cue ball after striking the object ball *US, 1869*
- You had a lot of English on it. It was rolling right for the pocket. —Max Shulman, *The Zebra Derby*, p. 54, 1946
- —Mike Shamos, *The Illustrated Encyclopedia of Billiards*, p. 88, 1993

English-Channel eyes *noun*
bloodshot eyes from exposure to cigarette and/or marijuana smoke *US*
From photographs of swimmers staggering out of the water having crossed the Channel, their eyes bloodshot.
- —Connie Eble (Editor), *UNC-CH Campus Slang*, p. 3, March 1979

English method *noun*
the rubbing of the penis between the thighs of another boy or man until reaching orgasm *US*
More commonly known in the US as the 'Princeton Rub'.
- — *Maledicta*, p. 54, 1986–1987: 'A continuation of a glossary of ethnic slurs in American English'

English muffins *noun*
in homosexual usage, a boy's buttocks *US*
- — *Maledicta*, p. 54, 1986–1987: 'A continuation of a glossary of ethnic slurs in American English'

English return *noun*
dead silence after what was supposed to be a funny joke *US*
- The unlaugh, or monstrous silence; also known as the English Return. — *Everybody's Digest*, p. 21, September 1951

English vice *noun*
flagellation *US*
- — *Maledicta*, p. 237, 1979: 'Kinks and queens: linguistic and cultural aspects of the terminology for gays'

enin *noun*
nine; in betting, odds of 9–1 *UK, 1859*
Backslang.
- —John McCririck, *John McCririck's World of Betting*, p. 59, 1991

enin to rouf *noun*
in betting, odds of 9–4 *UK*
A combination of **ENIN** (nine) and **ROUF** (four) when, if used alone, each word signifies more than the number itself.
- —John McCririck, *John McCririck's World of Betting*, p. 112, 1991

enit?
don't you know? *US*
One of the very few Native American expressions used in a slangy sense by English-speaking Native Americans.
- Grandma: A good name. It means he's going to win, enit? — *Smoke Signals*, 1998

enjoy!
used as a benediction by restaurant waiters, and then mimicked in other contexts *US*
- Yeah, yeah. Enjoy. — *Casino*, 1995
- The keg's back there. Enjoy! — *American Pie*, 1999

enjoy the trip?; enjoy your trip?
a catchphrase readily delivered to anyone who stumbles or trips over something *UK*
Often phrased 'did you enjoy the trip?'; sometimes elaborated 'send a postcard next time!'.
- A later version , often heard in the 1930s, was "Did you enjoy your trip?" or simply "Enjoy your trip?" when anyone caught a toe on anything. —Christopher Fry, 1974

enlisted swine *noun*
an enlisted soldier *US, 1986*
- They don't let enlisted swine fly. What they had me doing was writing the written parts. —W.E.B. Griffin, *Speical Ops (Brotherhood of War)*, p. 76, 2001

Enoch *noun*
a coloured immigrant child *UK*
By ironic transference from Enoch Powell, 1912–98, a noted opponent of immigration into the UK. Recorded by Harré, Morgan and O'Neill, *Nicknames*, 1979, as being used by white primary-school children, but the example was surely set by a parent.

Enoch Powell; enoch *noun*
1 a towel *UK*
Rhyming slang, formed from the name of British scholar and politician, Enoch Powell 1912–98.
- A peeping Toms delight, an eyeful in the Eifel [sic]. —Ray Puxley, *Cockney Rabbit*, 1992

2 a trowel *UK*
Rhyming slang.
- —Ray Puxley, *Cockney Rabbit*, 1992

enough *noun*
▸ **can never get enough**
to be sexually insatiable *UK, 1974*

▸ have had enough
to be tipsy, drunk *UK, 1937*
A not entirely honest form of words – the implied sense is 'to have had more than enough'.

enthuse *verb*
to be enthusiastic, or create enthusiasm in others *US, 1827*
- Toby Ziegler [a character in TV drama series "The West Wing"], White House communications director, war-weary liberal enthused by the new energy of the President. — *The Observer*, 30th June 2002

entjie; endjie *noun*
a cigarette, especially the stub of a cigarette that may be saved for later; a marijuana cigarette *SOUTH AFRICA, 1946*
Formed on Afrikaans *end* (end), 'entjie' is pronounced 'ayn-chee'.
- — Partridge, *A Dictionary of the Underworld*, 1950

entreprenerd *noun*
a computer- or Internet-business entrepreneur *UK*
A play on **NERD**.
- — Susie Dent, *The Language Report*, p. 48, 2003

entry *noun*
▸ up your entry
appropriate to your taste or requirements *UK*
- This job came in that I thought would be right up your entry. —*Journal of British Photography*, 4th June 1980

envelope *noun*
1 a condom *US*
- —Roger Blake, *The American Dictionary of Sexual Terms*, p. 66, 1964

2 an aeroplane's performance limits *US*
- If that failed, McKeown would deliberately "depart" the plane (take it outside its flight envelope) as a last resort maneuver. —Robert K. Wilcox, *Scream of Eagles*, p. 140, 1990

Enzed *noun*
New Zealand *AUSTRALIA, 1915*

Enzedder *noun*
a New Zealander *AUSTRALIA, 1933*

EOT *adjective*
dead *US*
- A D.O.A. is someone who's gone E.O.T., end of tour. — *The New Yorker*, p. 35, 10th August 1998

ep *noun*
an episode *US, 1915*
A broadcasting abbreviation in wider currency.
- [T]his little ep has served as one almighty wakey-wakey[.]—Kevin Sampson, *Outlaws*, p. 63, 2001

EPA *nickname*
East Palo Alto, San Mateo County, California *US*
A black ghetto surrounded by Silicon Valley wealth.
- Curiously, the 18th Street gangsters, who have definite roots in the L.A. area, nevertheless claim norte while bangin' in EPA. —Bill Valentine, *Gangs and Their Tattoos*, p. 112, 2000

epic *adjective*
excellent, outstanding *US*
- — *USA Today*, 29 September 1983
- —Judi Sanders, *Faced and Faded, Hanging to Hurl*, p. 14, 1993

epidoddle *noun*
epidural anaesthesia *US*
- —Sally Williams, *"Strong" Words*, p. 140, 1994

eppie scoppie *noun*
a tantrum *UK*
- Fraser stormed around the compound throwing a major eppie scoppie, while even the innocent hid behind locked doors, giggling. —Andy McNab (writing of the late 1970s/early 80s), *Immediate Action*, p. 162, 1995

eppis *noun*
nothing *US*
- — *American Speech*, p. 280, December 1966: 'More carnie talk from the West Coast'

eppo *noun*
an attack, an outburst *IRELAND*
- My phone rings when we're, like, halfway through our food and it's the old man (q.v.), having an eppo as per focking usual. —Paul Howard, *Ross O'Carroll-Kelly*, p. 152, 2003

eppy *noun*
a display of temper *UK*
- Big Bawjaws'll take an eppy when he sees what wee Tony wrote on the playground. —Michael Munro, *The Patter, Another Blast*, p. 22, 1988

Eppy *nickname*
Brian Epstein (1934–67), manager of the Beatles *UK*
- No-one was allowed into the studio when [the Beatles] were recording. Even Eppy had always been encouraged to go and find something else to do. —Simon Napier-Bell, *Black Vinyl White Powder*, p. 107, 2001

eppy *adjective*
epileptic *UK, 1988*
- Jack- my God, Maddox's having an eppy fit about you. —Mo Hayder, *Birdman*, p. 376, 1999

epsilon *noun*
a very small amount *US*
- —Guy L. Steele et al., *The Hacker's Dictionary*, p. 60, 1983

EPT *nickname*
El Paso, Texas *US*
- —Dagoberto Fuentes and Jose Lopez, *Barrio Language Dictionary*, p. 60, 1974

EQ; EQs *noun*
an equalizer, the device which controls the tonal quality of domestic and professional sound-reproduction equipment *UK*
- Too much EQ trickery can sound cluttered and may distract from how cool the original tune was in the first place. —J. Hoggarth (quoting Prime Cuts), *How To Be a DJ*, p. 72, 2002

equalizer; equaliser *noun*
a gun or any object that can be used in a fight *US, 1899*
Not without irony.
- "He ain't go' do nothin' t'me, not long as I got my equalizer." He patted his stomach, where a small .22 automatic pistol was hidden[.] —Nathan Heard, *Howard Street*, p. 86–87, 1968
- Why do we have to split with him? I've got the equalizer stuck in my belt for those big muscles he's got. —Iceberg Slim (Robert Beck), *Trick Baby*, p. 164, 1969
- They'd have tactical firearm squads on every corner before you knew it. Cops with equalisers and the full backing of the popular press. —Greg Williams, *Diamond Geezers*, p. 206, 1997

equator *noun*
the waist *US*
- You dames with wide circumferences should not rumba. If you must, please don't quake below the equator. —Jack Lait and Lee Mortimer, *New York Confidential*, p. 237, 1948

equipped *adjective*
1 stylish and fashionable *US*
- —David Claerbaut, *Black Jargon in White America*, p. 63, 1972

2 armed, equipped with a weapon *UK*
- —Angela Devlin, *Prison Patter*, p. 49, 1996

'er *noun*
▷ **see: HER INDOORS**

-er; -ers *suffix*
used to create a slangy variation of a conventional, generally abridged, word *UK*
By this process, the word 'indigestion' becomes, in its simplest form, 'indigesters'; 'football' becomes **FOOTER** and 'rugby football' becomes 'rugger'. Now known as the 'Oxford -er(s)', it began at Rugby school in 1875 (*Oxford English Dictionary*), but this origin has been disputed and claimed for Harrow School. Usage migrated via Oxford University into general (upper-) middle-class slang, and Royal Navy Service.

eradication squad; 'radication squad *noun*
a unit of armed police *UK*
- You sent the 'radication squad to her house and she was killed. —Donald Gorgon, *Cop Killer*, p. 117, 1994

-erama *suffix*
▷ **see: -RAMA**

-erati *suffix*
when added to a type or cultural interest, creates a fashionable group with a common identity or interest *UK*
On the model of 'literati'; better-known uses include 'liggerati' (hangers-on), 'niggerati' (successful members of black society).

- Westminsterati, glitterati, belligerati, inconsiderati, jitterati, textaerati, chicerati. —Susie Dent, *The Language Report*, p. 17, 2003
- [S]oftware like Max allows endless permutations for creators of funny noises everywhere, and allows the Glitcherati [musicians creating the glitch electronic music] to hook up with improvisers for a spot of real time abstraction. — *BBCi*, 6th July 2003

erdie; erdy *noun*
an unimaginative, conventional person *UK*
From German *erde* (earth, the Earth, the ground).
- "Bunch of Erdies," Jagger moaned. —Anthony Scaduto, *Mick Jagger*, 1974

'ere; here
said when passing a marijuana cigarette *US, 2001*
- —Simon Worman, *Joint Smoking Rules*, 2001

erecstasy *noun*
a recreational drug cocktail of MDMA, the recreational drug best known as ecstasy, and Viagra™ (a branded drug that enables a male erection) *IRELAND*
A conflation of 'cause' and 'effect'.

erector *noun*
a semi-erect penis *UK*
- [S]ome of them sitting [on] the geezers' knees giving them erectors. —Jeremy Cameron, *Brown Bread in Wengen*, p. 115, 1999

-ereemo *suffix*
used as a meaningless appendage *UK*
Jocular, maybe just for fun.
- GAZ: Where's he gonna get a gun from round 'ere? Nah, you Stick it on then, Davereemo – I'm there. — *The Full Monty*, 1997

-er -er *suffix*
a doer (of the verb) *AUSTRALIA*
Jocular repetitious use of the agent suffix '-er'. Normally only one 'er' is used for a compound verb, thus 'wash up' becomes 'washer-up'. Then, added to both parts of the compound, 'washer-upper'. And sometimes, for comic effect, with a third '-er' added to the new compound as a whole, 'washer-upperer'. This last especially used by children.
- 'I'll say this for you,' his friend admitted, 'you're the best butterer-upper that side of the Black Stump. They swallowed it whole, the poor benighted buggers.' —J.E. MacDonnell, *Sabotage!*, p. 25, 1964
- Any stories, jokes or photos of life at the pub will be credited to your name in any publication, and the sender-inner elegible for a decent reward. —Bazza and Curly, *Betcha Wrong!*, p. 75, 1990

erie *noun*
▸ **on the erie**
engaged in eavesdropping *US*
- — *The Annals of the American Academy of Political and Social Sciences*, p. 128, May 1950
- —Joseph E. Ragen and Charles Finston, *Inside the World's Toughest Prison*, p. 810, 1962: 'Penitentiary and underworld glossary'

'er indoors *noun*
▷ **see: HER INDOORS**

E-ring *adjective*
high-ranking *US*
Military usage. Refers to the 'E-ring' of the Pentagon where high-ranking officers work.
- — Department of the Army, *Staff Officer's Guidebook*, p. 60, 1986

-erino *suffix*
used as a suffix to create humorous variants understood from their base *US, 1890s→*
- Well, Steverino, this looks like where I get off and join another trolley. —Odie Hawkins, *Great Lawd Buddha*, p. 85, 1990

erk; irk *noun*
a contemptible person *UK, 1959*
From a military use as 'a serviceman of low rank'.
- —John Ayto, *The Oxford Dictionary of Slang*, p. 225, 1998

erk!
used for expressing disgust *AUSTRALIA, 1981*
- Erk! What's that big ugly growth you've got? —Paul Vautin, *Turn It Up!*, p. 29, 1995
- Richard Grieco is baring all for Playgirl and so is Baywatch regular. —Jaason Simmons, *Girlfriend*, p. 118, 1995

erky *adjective*
mildly disgusting; unpleasant *AUSTRALIA, 1959*
From **ERK!** (an expression of mild disgust). The suggestion in the *Australian National Dictionary* (1988) that it derives from 'disparate*erk*' (a naval rating) is mere clutching at straws.

ernie *noun*
a fool, especially one who does not concentrate *US*
Snowboarders' slang.
- —Jim Humes and Sean Wagstaff, *Boarderlands*, p. 221, 1995

-eroo *suffix*
used as a meaningless embellishment; also used to intensify *US, 1931*
- —Hyman E. Goldin et al., *Dictionary of American Underworld Lingo*, p. 65, 1950
- A smasheroo she was – a real zinger. —Max Shulman, *I was a Teen-Age Dwarf*, p. 8, 1959
- My famous one-two, learned from Myron: first, excessive flattery with a grain of truth swatched in cultured nacre; then the lethal puncheroo. —Gore Vidal, *Myra Breckinridge*, p. 51, 1968
- His strategy was to slip it in while fingering her, taking advantage of the darkness to pull the old switcheroo. —Richard Price, *The Wanderers*, p. 40, 1974
- Glenn made Jack feel as he had around his stepfather – a master barroom conneroo who would afterwards deride those who always stood him a drink[.] —Earl Thompson, *Tattoo*, p. 227, 1974
- In any case, all of them are skilled enough to create a steamy anticipation throughout the audience that can only be relieved when the last piece of cloth magically unveils snatcheroo. —Josh Alan Friedman, *Tales of Times Square*, p. 9, 1986

-erooni; -eroony *suffix*
used as a decorative intensifier *US, 1966*
The epic 1960s Philadelphia radio DJ Hy Lit embellished his first name to 'Hyski-eronni'.
- The golfers are suspicious that this is another Joe Alioto zingeroony. — *San Francisco Examiner*, p. 35, 8th August 1972
- A Smasherooni! -Eliot Fremont-Smith of the Village Voice— *San Francisco Examiner*, p. 11, 21st September 1975
- "People said the same thing about 'Superstar,'" Rice says, while Webber points to 'Evita's' enormous success in England, where reviewers have called it "Another smasheroonie". — *San Francisco Chronicle*, p. 38, 3rd February 1977
- Busy schedulerooni na mean [know what I mean]. —Nick Barlay, *Curvy Lovebox*, p. 71, 1997

Eros and Cupid *adjective*
stupid *UK*
Rhyming slang.
- —Ray Puxley, *Fresh Rabbit*, 1998

erp *verb*
to vomit *US*
- —Collin Baker et al., *College Undergraduate Slang Study Conducted at Brown University*, p. 112, 1968

errie *noun*
an aeroplane *UK: SCOTLAND*
- [W]atch the erries coming in and that! —Ian Pattison, *Rab C. Nesbitt*, 1988

Errol Flynn *noun*
the chin, in senses anatomic and figurative *UK, 1961*
Rhyming slang, formed from the name of the swashbuckling film actor, 1909–59.
- "[T]ake it on the Errol" or take it like a man[.] —Ray Puxley, *Cockney Rabbit*, 1992

Erroll Flynns *noun*
spectacles *UK*
Rhyming slang for **BINS**.
- —Ray Puxley, *Cockney Rabbit*, 1992

-ers *suffix*
▷ **see: -ER**

Ervine *noun*
a police officer *US*
- —Jay Robert Nash, *Dicitonary of Crime*, p. 118, 1992

esar *noun*
▷ **see: ESRA**

esclop *noun*

a police officer *UK*

Back slang, however the 'c' is not pronounced, and the 'e' is generally omitted, thus, 'slop'. First noted by Henry Mayhew in *London Labour and the London Poor*, 1851.

- —David Powis, *The Signs of Crime*, 1977

escort service *noun*

a prostitution business operating euphemistically under the guise of providing an escort, not a prostitute *US*

- Another woman runs an "escort" service on the side, sometimes using her own mansion when her husband is gone.—Kent Smith et al., *Adult Movies*, p. 180, 1982

ese *noun*

used as a term of address to a young male; an aware, street-wise young man *US*

Border Spanish used in English conversation by Mexican-Americans.

- —George Carpenter Baker, *Pachuco*, p. 41, January 1950
- Shit, ese. I mean just one joint.—Oscar Zeta Acosta, *The Revolt of the Cockroach People*, p. 120, 1973

eskimo *noun*

in oil drilling, a worker from Alaska or Montana *US*

- —Jerry Robertson, *Oil Slanguage*, p. 51, 1954

Eskimo *noun*

a Jewish person *US*

- I have no plausible evidence as to why the perjorative code word for "Jew" was/is/became "Eskimo."—Leo Rosten, *The Joy of Yinglish*, p. 152, 1989

Eskimo ice cream *noun*

a mixture of tallow, berries and fish *CANADA*

- Eskimo Ice Cream. Melt tallow and while still warm mix well by hand. Keep adding [other ingredients] until not able to stir anymore. —*Favorite Recipes*, p. 39, 1962

Eskimo Nell; eskimo *noun*

a bell (a telephone call) *UK*

Rhyming slang, formed from the heroine of a famously bawdy ballad.

- Even though telephones don't ring any more, people are still inclined to give each other an "Eskimo".—Ray Puxley, *Fresh Rabbit*, 1998

Eskimo pie *noun*

the vagina of a frigid woman *US*

- —*Maledicta*, p. 17, Summer 1977: 'A word for it!'

Eskimo roll *noun*

a manoeuvre used by surfers to pass through a wave coming at them by rolling under their surfboard *US*

- —Gary Fairmont R. Filosa II, *The Surfer's Almanac*, p. 185, 1977

Eskimo salad *noun*

moss from a caribou stomach, prized as food by Eskimos *CANADA*

- Some Eskimo tribes even eat the half digested contents of the stomach. It is chewed-up moss and we call it Eskimo salad.—Tony Onraet, *Sixty Below*, p. 129, 1948

Eskimo sisters *noun*

women who have at some point had sex with the same man *US*

Used as the title of a 2002 play by Laline Paull.

- Their shared experience made them "Eskimo sisters," united by the fact that they had both slept with the same guy.—Anka Radakovich, *The Wild Girls Club*, p. 6, 1994

esky *noun*

a portable cooler for food and drink in the form of an insulated oblong box with a flat lid *AUSTRALIA, 1953*

Proprietary name; from '*esk*imo' with a '-y' suffix. A quintessential item of Australian suburban life.

- Every esky full of Bulimba Gold Top.—John O'Grady, *Aussie Etiket*, p. 9, 1971
- He spent four hours at the Rose Bay wharf one night catching yellowtail and putting them in a huge Esky.—Bob Staines, *Wot a Whopper*, p. 19, 1982
- [T]he only running the Dag has ever done is to the Esky during commercial breaks.—Ignatius Jones, *True Hip*, p. 32, 1990
- Mick set up two deck chairs in front of the car, just behind the boundary line. He struggled by with an enormous esky.—Phillip Gwynne, *Deadly Unna?*, p. 96, 1998

Esky *noun*

an Eskimo *US*

- —*Maledicta*, p. 156, Summer/Winter 1978: 'How to hate thy neighbor: a guide to racist maledicta'

Esky lid *noun*

a small bodyboard used for surfing *AUSTRALIA*

Used derisively.

- The big bad buzzsaw rapidly reduces the Esky lid to beanbag stuffing.—Glyn Parry, *Mosh*, p. 31, 1996

Esky lidder *noun*

a bodyboarder *AUSTRALIA*

- I HATE Esky-lidders!—Glyn Parry, *Mosh*, p. 28, 1996

esnortiar *noun*

cocaine *UK*

Of Spanish origin.

- —Mike Haskins, *Drugs*, p. 280, 2003

esong *noun*

the nose *UK*

Back slang.

- —Paul Baker, *Polari*, p. 173, 2002

esra; esrar; esar *noun*

marijuana *US, 1982*

A Turkish word now in wider usage.

- —Richard A. Spears, *The Slang and Jargon of Drugs and Drink*, p. 187, 1986
- —Mike Haskins, *Drugs*, p. 287, 2003

esroch *noun*

a horse *UK, 1859*

Back slang.

- —Ray Puxley, *Cockney Rabbit*, p. 188, 1992

essence *noun*

MDMA, the recreational drug best known as ecstasy *US*

- Street names [...] E, Edward, essence, fantasy[.]—James Kay and Julian Cohen, *The Parents' Complete Guide to Young People and Drugs*, p. 136, 1998
- —*Miramonte High School Parents Club Newsletter (Orinda, California)*, p. 1, 26th November 2001

essence *adjective*

beauty, especially when ascribed to a woman *UK*

- —Nigel Foster, *The Making of a Royal Marine Commando*, 1987

essence of magic mushrooms *noun*

psilocybin or *psilocin*, usually in powder or capsule form *UK*

- —Mike Rock, *This Book*, p. 135, 1999

Essex girl *noun*

used as a stereotype for jokes, an Essex girl is brash, vulgar, trashy, sexually available, deeply unintelligent and, allegedly, from Essex *UK*

Derogatory. Essex girl jokes such as: 'Q: What do you call an Essex girl with two brain cells? A: Pregnant' have been in circulation since the 1980s.

- If nerdy men revenge themselves by emailing truly disgusting jokes to Essex girls websites, it's pretty much their problem.—Germaine Greer, *Long Live the Essex Girl*, 5th March 2001

establishment *noun*

the dominant power in any society *UK, 1955*

- He said, break into the Establishment, and that he was about three quarters inclined to try it.—Clancy Sigal, *Going Away*, p. 243, 1961
- Here is a list of names, those who constitute the real creme de la creme of Los Angeles power and influence. This is "the establishment."—*Los Angeles Free Press*, p. 2, 22nd October 1964
- If we do our job well, we hope even to nettle that amorphous but thickhided establishment that so often nettles us.—*The Berkeley Barb*, p. 4, 31st August 1965
- This afternoon at the Straight theater I was listening to the Indians rap against the establishment[.]—Nicholas Von Hoffman, *We are the People Our Parents Warned Us Against*, p. 147, 1967
- I think they adopted the Indian because the Indian has been terribly suppressed by the establishment[.]—Leonard Wolfe (Editor), *Voices from the Love Generation*, p. 239, 1968
- His main trip is anti-Establishment, and we can beat him like a gong on that one.—Hunter S. Thompson, *Songs of the Doomed*, p. 135, 1971
- And they knew that ultimatey the establishment would love to lock me up and throw away the key until that fatal day of execution. —Bobby Seale, *A Lonely Rage*, p. 269, 1978
- It ain't nothing to rip off the man – it's all part of the Establishment.—Stephen Gaskin, *Amazing Dope Tales*, p. 69, 1980

esthole *noun*
an enthusiastic supporter of the est human growth movement *US*
An appropriate play on 'asshole'.
- Term originated from enlightening program sessions where the leader would challenge an initiate by referring to him or her as an asshole. — Editors of Ben is Dead, *Retrohell*, p. 69, 1997

estuffa *noun*
heroin *US, 1984*
From border Spanish for 'stuff' (a drug, especially heroin).
- — Richard A. Spears, *The Slang and Jargon of Drugs and Drink*, p. 187, 1986
- — Mike Haskins, *Drugs*, p. 283, 2003

ET *noun*
in drag racing, the elapsed time of a particular quarter mile sprint *US*
- We got a Deuce Coupe, a Stingray, a rail job and and XKE / We'll be the fastest the drags, man, we'll really cut some low ET's. — The Beach Boys, *Our Car Club*, 1963

▷ see: E AND T

e-tard *noun*
a person whose life has been adversely effected by excessive use of MDMA *US*
- — Pamela Munro, *U.C.L.A. Slang*, p. 65, 2001

etch-a-sketch *verb*
to manually stimulate both of a sex-partner's nipples *NEW ZEALAND*
A similar action is required to operate an Etch-a-Sketch™, a children's toy drawing machine. 'Trying to draw a smile on a woman's face by twiddling both of her nipples simultaneously' (unknown source quoted in private correspondence, 13th March 2002).

etched *adjective*
drunk *UK*
- — *e-cyclopaedia*, 20th March 2002

E Team *noun*
in the language of hang gliding, expert fliers from Lake Elsinore, California *US*
- — Erik Fair, *California Thrill Sports*, p. 328, 1992

eternal care *noun*
in hospital, intensive care *UK*
Medical slang, darkly humorous.
- — Adam T. Fox, St Mary's Hospital, London, 10th October 2002

ethanolic *noun*
a drunkard *US*
- — *Maledicta*, p. 68, Summer/Winter 1978: 'Common patient-directed pejoratives used by medical personnel'

Ethiopian paradise *noun*
in a racially segregated cinema, the balcony *US, 1900*
- — *Maledicta*, p. 168, 1979: 'A glossary of ethnic slurs in American English'

Ethy meat *noun*
a black woman as a sex object *US*
An abbreviation of 'Ethiopian', a racial rather than national label.
- — *Maledicta*, p. 52, 1986 – 1987: 'A continuation of a glossary of ethnic slurs in American English'

E-tool *noun*
an entrenching tool with an extendable telescopic handle and folding blade *US*
- Then you grab your E-tool and hit me in the foot, right here real hard, see? — Charles Anderson, *The Grunts*, p. 93, 1976
- — Linda Reinberg, *In the Field*, p. 76, 1991

e-type *noun*
a person with a professional or recreational interest in electronics *UK, 2003*
- — *Collins English Dictionary*, 2003

Euan Blair; Euan *noun*
Leicester Square *UK*
Rhyming slang, recalling an incident in July 2000 when Prime Minister Blair's 16-year-old son Euan was found 'drunk and incapable' in Leicester Square.
- But will anyone know of Euan Blair[?] — *Antiquarian Book Review*, p. 18, June 2002

euaned *adjective*
very drunk *UK*
Pronounced 'you-and'. From 6th July 2000: Prime Minister Blair's 16-year-old son was arrested for being 'drunk and incapable'.
- I got completely Euaned last night! — *www.LondonSlang.com*, June 2002

euchre *verb*
to ruin or destroy *US, 1853*
- Now how do you reckon a man would get on in this country, in this suburb, if he was euchred and had to build a mud hut somewhere[.] — Geoff Wyatt, *Saltwater Saints*, p. 87, 1969
- The hole you blew the yolk and the white out of had to be as small as possible, and the bigger it was the less the egg was worth to you, or as a swap. Sometimes you blew the whole end out of an egg, and that euchred it, of course. — T.A.G. Hungerford, *Stories From Suburban Road*, p. 66, 1983

eucy; eucy oil *noun*
eucalyptus oil *AUSTRALIA, 1977*

euphoria *noun*
a combination of mescaline, crystal methadrine and MDMA, the recreational drug best known as ecstasy *UK*
- — Mike Haskins, *Drugs*, p. 293, 2003

Europe *noun*
▸ **go Europe**
to vomit *BERMUDA*
- — Peter A. Smith and Fred M. Barritt, *Bermewjan Vurds*, 1985

Eurotrash *noun*
rich foreigners living in the US *US*
Taki Theodoracopulos popularised the term in society columns written for *Vanity Fair* and the *Spectator*.
- Stuff like crucifixes covered in reptile skin: from his hands to Eurotrash necks. — Jim Carroll, *Forced Entries*, p. 7, 1987
- So Dan booked them a moldy suite at this crumbling relic frequented, as far as she could tell, by Eurotrash with black socks and sandals. — Seth Morgan, *Homeboy*, p. 232, 1990

eva *noun*
a pill marked with E on one side and A on the obverse, sold as MDMA, the recreational drug best known as ecstasy, actually containing a mixture of MDMA and amphetamine *UK*
- — Gareth Thomas, *This Is Ecstasy*, p. 54, 2002

evac *noun*
an evacuation *US, 1954*
- For the medical evacs," Moser said, "a pilot had to come in perpendicular to the ridge. — Dandridge M. Malone, *Small Unit Leadership*, p. 107, 1983

evac *verb*
to evacuate *US, 1944*
- "I'll draw them off. Evac your people." — Eric Nylund, *First Strike*, p. 263, 2003

Eve *noun*
MDMA, the recreational drug best known as ecstasy *US*
A play on ADAM, itself almost an anagram of MDMA.
- It will be supplanted – already there is a new variation, MDE, Eve. — *Washington Post*, p. D1, 1st June 1985

evening breeze; sweet evening breeze *noun*
cheese *UK*
Rhyming slang.
- — Ray Puxley, *Cockney Rabbit*, 1992

evening glass *noun*
calm surf conditions in the evening after the afternoon wind has diminished *US*
- — Dennis Aaberg and John Milius, *Big Wednesday*, p. 209, 1978

Evening News *noun*
a bruise, especially a love-bite *UK*
Rhyming slang, formed from the title of a London evening newspaper that ceased publication in 1980.
- — Ray Puxley, *Cockney Rabbit*, 1992

even shake; fair shake; good shake *noun*
a fair deal *US, 1830*
- Early reviewing means that books don't get a fair shake[.] — *The Guardian*, 22nd September 2003

even steven; even stephen; even stevens; even stephens *adjective*
even, equal *US, 1866*
'Steven' adds nothing but the rhyme.
- Al, it seemed, had a great deal of pride. He liked to keep things even-Steven, and he didn't take nothing off no one. —Jim Thompson, *Roughneck*, p. 89, 1954
- "How would be split the take, Jake?" "Even steven, baby .... even steven." —Odie Hawkins, *The Busting Out of an Ordinary Man*, p. 75, 1985
- And, for a while at least, we were even steven on the pitch. —Martin King and Martin Knight, *The Naughty Nineties*, p. 145, 1999
- My solution of "even Stephens" is equality for Conservative and Labour[.] —Lord Randall of St. Budeaux, *Lords Hansard*, 18th May 1999
- [T]he most recent Scottish poll puts Labour and the Scottish National party (SNP) even stevens when it came to people's intentions on voting for the House of Commons[.] — *The Guardian*, 20th October 2000

everafters *noun*
consequences *UK*
- Yer can't expect to diss a big fuckin beak [cocaine] dealer without some everafters, can yer? —Niall Griffiths, *Kelly + Victor*, p. 336, 2002

everclear *noun*
cocaine *UK*
- —Nick Constable, *This is Cocaine*, p. 181, 2002
- —Mike Haskins, *Drugs*, p. 280, 2003

ever hear more!; ever see more!
used as an expression of surprise *TRINIDAD AND TOBAGO*
- —Lise Winer, *Dictionary of the English/Creole of Trinidad & Tobago*, 2003

everlastin joob-joob *noun*
a fool, an idiot; a contemptible person *UK: SCOTLAND*
Glasgow rhyming slang for **TUBE**, formed on an improbable-sounding sweet.
- Look at the mess ye're makin, ya everlastin joob-joob. —Michael Munro, *The Patter, Another Blast*, 1988

ever-loving *adjective*
used as an intensifier *US, 1919*
- "Chet, are you out of your ever-loving skull?" Joe demanded. —Franklin W. Dixon, *Danger on Vampire Trail*, p. 123, 1971

ever such *adjective*
used to describe a great or fine example *UK, 1803*
- Victorian pickle fork, ever such a pretty fork with the lovely design that the Victorian silversmiths were famous for. — *Glamorgan Antiques online catalogue*, August 2003

Everton toffee; everton *noun*
coffee *UK, 1857*
Rhyming slang.

every crab from the bush
everyone *CAYMAN ISLANDS*
- —Aarona Booker Kohlman, *Wotcha Say*, p. 28, 1985

every home should have one
a catchphrase generally applied to common objects, babies and non-material things *UK*
Thought to have been an advertising slogan in the 1920s.
- "Yeah, we want one of those [a car]," said Colly. "Every home should have one." —Ivor Drummond, *The Power of the Bug*, 1974

every man and his dog
everyone *AUSTRALIA*
- Every man and his dog was on our queue, pushing and shoving to get on. —Robert English, *Toxic Kisses*, p. 158, 1979
- —Sonya Plowman, *Great Kiwi Slang*, p. 69, 2002

every man Jack *noun*
absolutely everyone *UK, 1828*
- [T]hat's what they are: every manjack of them. Volunteers. —Mike Stott, *Soldiers Talking, Cleanly*, 1978

Every Minute Sucks *noun*
work with an Emergency Medical Service unit *US*
New York police slang; back-formation from the initials EMS.
- —Samuel M. Katz, *Anytime Anywhere*, p. 387, 1997: 'The extremely unofficial and completely off-the-record NYPD/ESU truck-two glossary'

everything-but girl *noun*
a woman who will engage in any and all sexual activity short of intercourse *US*
- —Amy Sohn, *Sex and the City*, p. 155, 2002

everything in the garden's lovely!
a catchphrase used to exclaim: all is well, all goes well *UK, 1910*
- It's not difficult to persuade ourselves that everything in the garden is lovely. — *The Guardian*, 10th March 2003

everything is everything
used for conveying that all is well when asked how things are going *US*
- —Hy Lit, *Hy Lit's Unbelievable Dictionary of Hip Words for Groovy People*, p. 14, 1968
- — *Washington Post Magazine*, p. 17, 28th June 1987: 'Say wha?'

everything's drawing
everything's going well, thank you! *US*
Nautical origins, suggesting that all sails are set and there is a following breeze.
- —Charles F. Haywood, *Yankee Dictionary*, p. 55, 1963

everything that opens and shuts *noun*
everything possible *AUSTRALIA*
- On top of all this a man's trying to run a business, but you can't win I'm telling you. When you've got a wife and family they want everything that opens and shuts. —Barry Humphries, *A Nice Night's Entertainment*, p. 38, 1960
- [caption] The mainstay of rallying; the pit crew examining everything that opens and shuts. — *West Australian*, p. 12, 7th September 1991

every which way *adverb*
in every manner or direction *US, 1824*
- [Hans] Koller favours multi-linear intricacies going every which way rather than the more orderly rhythmic march of the riff. — *The Guardian*, 6th September 2002

every which way but
in every manner or direction except the correct one *UK, 1984*
A specific refinement of **EVERY WHICH WAY**.

eve teasing *noun*
an act of a male outraging the modesty of a female in a public place by indecent speech or actual and unwanted physical contact *INDIA, 1979*
- —Paroo Nihalini, R.K. Tongue and Priya Hosali, *Indian and British English*, 1979
- A 40-year-old man was arrested from the North Campus area on Tuesday on charges of eve-teasing. The accused [...] allegedly propositioned a lady constable in plain clothes. — *Times of India*, 1st April 2004

evil *noun*
a man with a body piercing through his penis *NEW ZEALAND*
Collected during an extensive survey of New Zealand prison slang, 1996–2000.

evil *adjective*
1 mean-spirited, inconsiderate *US, 1939*
- —Pamela Munro, *U.C.L.A. Slang*, p. 62, 1997

2 excellent *UK*
- Then she pointed out which way the bleeding Champs [Elysee] got to. Then we were on it. Evil. —Jeremy Cameron, *Brown Bread in Wengen*, p. 95, 1999

3 in computing, not designed for the speaker's purpose *US*
- We thought about adding a Blue Glue interface but decided it was too evil to deal with. —Eric S. Raymond, *The New Hacker's Dictionary*, p. 146, 1991

evo *noun*
the evening *AUSTRALIA*
- —Jim Ramsay, *Cop It Sweet!*, p. 34, 1977

Ev'o'lene, the Nevada Queen *noun*
in craps, the number eleven *US*
- —Steve Kuriscak, *Casino Talk*, p. 68, 1985

ex *noun*
1 a former lover or spouse *US, 1929*
The prefix 'ex-', like those so-named, stands alone.
- Even if a man thought his ex was inadequate in bed, he should not say, "You know, I've never slept with such a dead fish." —Anka Radakovich, *The Wild Girls Club*, p. 39, 1994

2 exercise, games *UK*
- — *The Felstedian*, December 1947

3 in target shooting, a bullseye *US*
From the notion, perhaps, that 'X marks the spot'.
- — *American Speech*, p. 193, October 1957: 'Some colloquialisms of the handgunner'

4 a car's accelerator *TRINIDAD AND TOBAGO, 1971*
- —Lise Winer, *Dictionary of the English/Creole of Trinidad & Tobago*, 2003

ex!; exie!
used for expressing enthusiastic approval *UK: SCOTLAND*
Contractions of **EXCELLENT!** used by Glasgow schoolchildren.
- Ah've seen that wan. It wis pure ex!—Michael Munro, *The Complete Patter*, p. 51, 1996

exacta *noun*
in horse racing, a bet on first and second place *US*
- —John McCririck, *John McCririck's World of Betting*, p. 175, 1991

exacto!
exactly *US*
Mock Spanish.
- "You want the files but you don't want to pay." "Exacto!" said Kingsbury.—Carl Hiaasen, *Native Tongue*, p. 201, 1991

exacts *noun*
mundane, easily obtained facts about a person, gathered by an investigator *US*
- —Jim Crotty, *How to Talk American*, p. 52, 1997

excellent *adjective*
impressive, amazing *US*
Conventional English turned slang by the young. Stress is on the first syllable, which follows something close to a glottal stop; the 'l' is lazy.
- —Connie Eble (Editor), *UNC-CH Campus Slang*, p. 3, Spring 1982
- Ted, I totally have a most excellent moustache.—*Bill and Ted's Excellent Adventure*, 1989
- I live in Aurora which is a suburb of Chicago. Excellent.—*Wayne's World*, 1992

excellent!
used for expressing enthusiastic approval *US*
- TED: And that is why we need triumphant T-shirts. BILL AND TED: Excellent!—*Bill and Ted's Excellent Adventure*, 1989

excellent behaviour!
used for registering approval *UK*
- [T]hey look at your old actual *record* record collection and go, Wow, vinyl, excellent behaviour! like it was some fashion decision you cunningly made twenty years ahead of the game.—James Hawes, *Dead Long Enough*, p. 159, 2000

excess leggage *noun*
a more than usual display of a person's legs *UK*
- That's why I'm showing excess leggage.—Jo Whiley, *Glastonbury 2004*, 27th June 2004

Exchange & Mart *noun*
a prostitute *UK*
Rhyming slang for **TART**; formed from the title of a weekly publication (published every Thursday since 1868) devoted to advertisements from people wishing to buy, sell or barter the widest range of goods or services.
- —Ray Puxley, *Cockney Rabbit*, 1992

excitement *noun*
sexual intercourse; the penis *IRELAND*
- He whispers, the thing between your legs is the excitement. I don't like the other names, the dong, the prick, the dick, the langer.—Frank McCourt, *Angela's Ashes*, p. 149, 1997
- It is in the army in Germany that he has, on a regular basis, paid and unpaid, "the excitement", a Limerick euphemism for the sexual act.—Bernard Share, *Slanguage*, p. 100, 2003

ex-con *noun*
an ex-*con*vict, a former prisoner *US, 1906*
Also recorded in the UK.
- —Angela Devlin, *Prison Patter*, p. 49, 1996
- And a little spell in the can wouldn't necessarily mean the end of his career; after all, ex-cons G. Gordon Liddy, Chuck Colson and Oliver North haven't let convictions get in the way of their right-wing talk-radio gigs.—*American Prospect*, p. 9, November 2003

excruciate *verb*
to aggravate, to irritate, to anger *UK*
- You're excruciatin' me on my weddin' day you fuckhead.—Nick Barlay, *Curvy Lovebox*, p. 131, 1997

excuse-me; 'scuse-me; bo-excuse-me; ooscuse-me *noun*
an educated, middle-class person *SOUTH AFRICA, 1963*
Township slang; contemptuous.
- Awareness of social differentiation was reflected in the language of the townships, which became a biting commentary on such divisions. In Cape Town and Durban, the respectable were labelled "ooscuse-me".—William Beinart, *20th-Century South Africa*, p. 192, 2001

excuse me?
regarding a statement just made, used as an expression of disbelief, either of the content of the statement or of the fact the statement has been made at all *UK*
- "At the time, hip hop was really just Michael Jackson." Excuse me?—Patrick Neate, *Where You're At*, p. 175, 2003

excuuuuuse me!
used as a humorous admission of error *US*
Made wildly popular by comedien Steve Martin during frequent appearances on NBC's *Saturday Night Live* in the 1970s and 1980s. Repeated with referential humour.

exec *noun*
1 a corporate executive *UK, 1896*
- Various agency execs force themselves to attend a party at Morton's to check out – sorry, welcome – the new talent at Storm model agency.—*ES Magazine*, p. 39, 22nd June 2001

2 an executive military officer *US, 1898*
- "The exec up there got frostbitten, and they've asked for a replacement," said the Major.—Max Shulman, *Rally Round the Flag, Boys!*, p. 2, 1957

executive services *noun*
sexual intercourse, as distinct from masturbation, when advertised as a service offered by a prostitute *UK*
- —Caroline Archer, *Tart Cards*, 2003

exercise *verb*
▸ **exercise the ferret**
(from a male perspective) to have sex *AUSTRALIA*
- Jeez don't tell me she's expectin' me to exercise the ferret. A bastard'll have to be a flamin' contortionist!—Barry Humphries, *Bazza Pulls It Off!*, 1971

▸ **exercise the one-eyed trouser snake**
(of a male) to urinate *UK*
Based on **ONE-EYED TROUSER SNAKE** (the penis).
- Exercise The One-Eyed Trouser Snake. Shaking, I hold my tortured, terrified dick and try to pass water.—Stuart Browne, *Dangerous Parking*, p. 280, 2000

exes *noun*
1 expenses, out-of-pocket costs *UK, 1864*
Also known as 'ex's', 'exs' and 'x's'.
- I needed a few exes to help with the tape-recorders[.]—Derek Raymond (Robin Cook), *The Crust on its Uppers*, p. 81, 1962

2 six; in betting, odds of 6–1 *UK, 1951*
Backslang. Also variant 'exis'.
- —John McCririck, *John McCririck's World of Betting*, p. 59, 1991

exes and a half *noun*
in betting, odds of 13–2 *UK*
In bookmaker slang **EXES** is 6–1, here the addition of 'a half' increases the odds to 6½–1 or 13–2.
- —John McCririck, *John McCririck's World of Betting*, p. 112, 1991

exes to fere *noun*
in betting, odds of 6–4 *UK, 1937*
A combination of **EXES** (six) with a corruption of 'four'.

exes to rouf *noun*
in betting, odds of 6–4 *UK*
A combination of **EXES** (six) and **ROUF** (four) when, if used alone, each word signifies more than the number itself.
- —John McCririck, *John McCririck's World of Betting*, p. 112, 1991

exfil *noun*
*exfil*tration (the act of withdrawing troops or spies from a dangerous position) *UK*
Military.
- [G]oing to caches for more stores for the exfil.—Andy McNab, *Immediate Action*, p. 104, 1995

ex-govie *adjective*
in the Australian Captial Territory, descriptive of a dwelling, formerly owned by a government department but now privately owned *AUSTRALIA*
- Our street is a line of ex-guvvie houses.—*Canberra Times*, p. 4, 7th August 1988

exie
▷ see: EX!

exiticity *noun*
MDMA, the recreational drug best known as ecstasy *UK*
• —Mike Haskins, *Drugs*, p. 289, 2003

exo *verb*
to equip an off-road vehicle with an external safety cage *US, 1972*
From 'exoskeleton'. Collected by John Thompson of Hendersonville, North Carolina, 2004.

exo *adjective*
excellent *AUSTRALIA*
• Have I got an exo idea for this Mothers' Day. —*Bancks' Ginger Meggs in Sun-Herald*, p. 69, 13th May 1990

expat *noun*
an *expat*riate, a person from the UK living overseas *US, 1961*
• We end up in an expat bar down an alleyway not far from McDonald's[.] —Melanie McGrath, *Hard, Soft & Wet*, p. 263, 1998

expect *verb*
▸ **expect a flood**
to wear trousers that are too short *TRINIDAD AND TOBAGO, 1993*
• —Lise Winer, *Dictionary of the English/Creole of Trinidad & Tobago*, 2003

expedite *verb*
▸ **expedite into eternity**
to die *US*
• —Sally Williams, *"Strong" Words*, p. 140, 1994

expendable *adjective*
describes casualties of war whose loss is anticipated and considered acceptable as the price of success *UK, 1971*
A military and political term borrowed from accounting.
• There is a line in our time, and in every time, between those who believe that all men are created equal, and those who believe that some men, and women, and children, are expendable in the pursuit of power. —*The Guardian*, 12th September 2001

expensive care unit *noun*
a hospital's intensive care unit *US*
• —*Maledicta*, p. 32, 1988–1989: 'Medical maledicta from San Francisco'

expensive scare *noun*
in hospital, intensive care *UK*
Medical slang.
• —Adam T. Fox, St Mary's Hospital, London, 10th October 2002

experience *noun*
an experience of using LSD or mescaline *UK*
• —Home Office, *Glossary of Terms and Slang Common in Penal Establishments*, July 1978

explorers' club *noun*
a group of LSD users *US*
Another 'LSD-as-travel' metaphor.
• —John Williams, *The Drug Scene*, p. 111, 1967

expressions *noun*
profanity *BARBADOS*
• You so young and using expresssions. —Frank A. Collymore, *Barbadian Dialect*, p. 45, 1965

exsqueeze me!
excuse me! *US*
• —Lavada Durst, *The Jives of Dr. Hepcat*, p. 12, 1953

extra *noun*
1 in the coded language of the massage parlour, sex *US*
A 2002 Incident Report from the Sausalito (California) Police Department describes the activities of a massage parlour: 'The girls will try to sell you "extras." These include $200 for a nude massage, $250 for a mutual touching massage and $300 and up for oral and full service massage'.
• If the man would ask if there were any extras, you'd have to say no, because he mnight be a cop. —James Ridgeway, *Red Light*, p. 216, 1996
2 in the language surrounding the Grateful Dead, an extra ticket for that day's concert *US*
• —David Shenk and Steve Silberman, *Skeleton Key*, p. 83, 1994

extra *adverb*
very *NEW ZEALAND*
• —Sonya Plowman, *Great Kiwi Slang*, p. 69, 2002

extract *verb*
▸ **extract the michael**
to make fun of someone; to pull someone's leg; to jeer at, to deride *UK, 1984*
A 'humorous' variation of TAKE THE MICKY, probably on the model of the synonymous EXTRACT THE URINE.

▸ **extract the urine**
to make fun of someone; to pull someone's leg; to jeer at, to deride *UK, 1948*
A 'humorous' euphemistic variation of TAKE THE PISS.

extra-curricular activities *noun*
adulterous sexual play, especially sexual intercourse *UK*

eye *noun*
1 desire, an appetite *US, 1934*
• When she has "big eyes" for you – she means she "goes" for you. —Walter Winchell, *San Francisco Call-Bulletin*, p. 7, 15th January 1946
• —Babs Gonzales, *Be-Bop Dictionary and History of its Famous Stars*, p. 9, 1949
• Why don't you forget this bum and give that Betsy Bugbee a tumble? She's got big eyes for you. —Bernard Wolfe, *The Late Risers*, p. 25, 1954
• "You're out of your skull," said the papa bear, "although it does look as if somebody had eyes for the soup over there." —Steve Allen, *Bop Fables*, p. 9, 1955
• I would prefer if he didn't have eyes for her so obviously[.] —Jack Kerouac, *The Subterraneans*, p. 84, 1958
• He had big eyes for her, and each time he saw her and the other girl he started playing with an expensive brooch, looking at Alice. —Clarence Cooper Jr, *The Scene*, p. 34, 1960
• "Big eyes to scoff," Hassan said. —Ross Russell, *The Sound*, p. 15, 1961
• I thought you had such big eyes for her. —Terry Southern, *Blue Movie*, p. 97, 1970
• There are plenty of women with big eyes for me tonight. —Richard Condon, *Prizzi's Glory*, p. 187, 1988
2 a person who is not a part of the criminal underworld but who reports what he sees to those who are *US*
• —R. Frederick West, *God's Gambler*, p. 225, 1964: 'Appendix A'
3 a private detective *US, 1930*
• Listen, Propser, listen to me good, the eyes in those smooth stores have the hone for uncool threads. —Bernard Wolfe, *The Magic of Their Singing*, p. 25, 1961
4 a hand-held mirror used by a prisoner to see what is happening down their cellblock *US*
• —William K. Bentley and James M. Corbett, *Prison Slang*, p. 6, 1992
5 an automatic timing light on a drag racing track *US*
• There is a set of eyes at both the starting and finish lines. —Ed Radlauer, *Drag Racing Pix Dix*, p. 21, 1970
6 a railway track signal *US*
• —Norman Carlisle, *The Modern Wonder Book of Trains and Railroading*, p. 262, 1946
• —Ramon Adams, *The Language of the Railroader*, p. 56, 1977
7 the anus *US*
• —Charles Shafer, *Folk Speech in Texas Prisons*, p. 203, 1990

▸ **I will in my eye**
used for registering refusal *IRELAND*
• He'll bring you? He will in his eye. —Patrick McCabe, *Carn*, p. 37, 1993

▸ **my eye!; all my eye!; my eye and Betty Martin!**
used for registering disbelief *UK, 1842*
• —A P Cowie, R Mackin and I R McCaig, *Oxford Dictionary of Current Idiomatic English*, p. 393, 1983

Eye *noun*
▸ **the Eye**
1 a metal detector *US*
• When men approaching the big yard saw the Eye in operation they immediately dropped their knives, and after lock-up the guards would gather the harvest. —Malcolm Braly, *On the Yard*, p. 170, 1967
2 the US Federal Bureau of Investigation *US*
From 'FBI' to 'eye'.
• She was in her rookie year at the Eye. —Stephen Cannell, *Big Con*, p. 315, 1997

eyeball *noun*

1 a meeting between two shortwave radio operators who have only known each other over the radio *US*

- — Radio Shack, *CBer's Handy Atlas/Dictionary*, p. 23, 1976
- Unless you organise an eyeball (actually meeting another CBer face to face) [...] your handle [CB ID] is the only thing other people know about you — Peter Chippindale, *The British CB Book*, p. 15, 1981

2 a visual observation *US, 1951*

- No sign of assault or a sexual attack, but that's just my eyeball. — Robert Crais, *L.A. Requiem*, p. 41, 1999

3 the identification of a criminal by a witness to the crime *US*

- — Jay Robert Nash, *Dicitonary of Crime*, p. 118, 1992

4 a favoured child or pet *TRINIDAD AND TOBAGO, 1986*

- — Lise Winer, *Dictionary of the English/Creole of Trinidad & Tobago*, 2003

5 a truck or car headlight *US*

- — Bill Davis, *Jawjacking*, p. 38, 1977

eyeball *verb*

1 to see, to stare, to identify in a police line-up *US, 1901*

- When a john had eyeballed the parade and made his choice he would follow her upstairs, where the landlady sat at a little desk in the hall. — Milton Mezzrow, *Really the Blues*, p. 22, 1946
- The guv means you've been eyeballed by witnesses! — *The Sweeney*, p. 19, 1976
- You brought me up here to get eyeballed, didn't you? Who're those guys. You try and put me in the Plaza today – that where they're from? — Elmore Leonard, *Split Images*, p. 110, 1981

2 to stare aggressively *US*

After **EYEBALL TO EYEBALL** (descriptive of an aggressive confrontation).

- [E]ach wrestler tries to unhinge the other by eyeballing him menacingly. — Charles Danziger, *Japan For Starters*, p. 121, 1996

eyeball palace *noun*

a homosexuals' bar where there is a lot of looking and not much touching *US*

- — Guy Strait, *The Lavendar Lexicon*, 1964

eyeball queen *noun*

a male homosexual who looks but does not touch *US*

- — Guy Strait, *The Lavendar Lexicon*, 1964

eyeballs *noun*

▸ **to the eyeballs**

to the maximum of capacity, absolutely full, totally *UK, 1933*

- One night I got pilled to the eyeballs and got uptight thinking about these things[.] — Jamie Mandelkau, *Buttons*, p. 32, 1971

eyeballs, come back here!

used by a clever boy for expressing approval of a passing girl *US*

- — *American Weekly*, p. 2, 14th August 1955

eyeball to eyeball *adjective*

on the verge of a hostile confrontation *US, 1953*

A variation of conventional 'face to face'.

- "Any leadership race is as personal as you can get," Vander Jagt said. "It's eyeball to eyeball." — *Washington Post*, p. A2, 8th December 1980

eyeball-to-eyeball *adverb*

in direct, face-to-face confrontation *US, 1953*

- "She can deal eyeball-to-eyeball with anyone," says Stockman. — *Washington Post*, p. H1, 29th November 1981

eyeball van *noun*

a police van equipped for surveillance *US*

- The other vehicle, an "eyeball van" with one-way glass and surveillance equipment, was parked on Virginia Avenue[.] — Thomas Harris, *The Silence of the Lambs*, p. 102, 1988

eye black *noun*

mascara *UK*

- — Wilfred Granville, *The Theater Dictionary*, p. 69, 1952

eye bleeder *noun*

powerful, green marijuana *US*

- — Vann Wesson, *Generation X Field Guide and Lexicon*, p. 64, 1997

eye candy *noun*

an extremely attractive person, regardless of their character or intellect, regardless of their sex, regardless of their sexual orientation *US, 1984*

- — Connie Eble (Editor), *UNC-CH Campus Slang*, p. 3, March 1996
- — Jeff Fessler, *When Drag Is Not a Car Race*, p. 95, 1997

eye doctor *noun*

the active participant in anal sex *US*

From **EYE** (the anus).

- — Vincent J. Monteleone, *Criminal Slang*, p. 79, 1949
- — *Maledicta*, p. 231, 1979: 'Kinks and queens: linguistic and cultural aspects of the terminology for gays'

eye! eye!; eye-eye!

look out!; also used as a warning that a prisoner is under surveillance; or as an injunction to be vigilant *UK, 1950*

- — Angela Devlin, *Prison Patter*, p. 50, 1996

eye fiddle *noun*

an ugly person *IRELAND*

From the Irish *aghaidh fidil* (a face-mask made from coloured paper).

- She is a right eye-fiddle. — Irwin Liam, *North Munster Antiquarian Journal*, p. 84, 2000

eye-fuck *verb*

to look at with unmasked sexual intentions *US, 1916*

- I like the girl to eye-fuck the viewer. — *East Bay (Oakland, California) Express*, 18th February 2004

eyeful *noun*

a good look at something *UK, 1899*

- [P]uritan babes get an eyeful. — *The Guardian*, 9th March 1999
- [S]he was happy to give the world an eyeful. — Tom Perrotta, *Little Children*, p. 248, 2004

eye-game *verb*

to exchange flirtatious looks *TRINIDAD AND TOBAGO*

- — Lise Winer, *Dictionary of the English/Creole of Trinidad & Tobago*, 2003

eyeglasses *noun*

used as a warning by an orchestra conductor to the musicians that a particularly difficult passage is coming up *US*

- — Sherman Louis Sergel, *The Language of Show Biz*, p. 82, 1973

eye in the sky *noun*

1 surveillance stations or cameras in casinos concealed above two-way mirrors on the ceiling *US, 1961*

- The Casino Manager must use the "eye in the sky" and closed circuit television to make sure his personnel remain honest. — Mario Puzo, *Inside Las Vegas*, p. 181, 1977
- Except that here you could stand upright, follow a wide catwalk with handrails, and from both sides of it look down through one-way smoked glass at the casino floor: at the tables, the slot machines, the mass of players and strollers less than ten feet below. — Elmore Leonard, *Glitz*, p. 228–229, 1985

2 a police helicopter *US*

- — Jay Robert Nash, *Dicitonary of Crime*, p. 121, 1992

eye job *noun*

cosmetic surgery around the eyes *US*

- Maybe if enough San Diego citizens kept shooting, stabbing, bashing, and strangling one another she could get enough time-and-a-half to afford one [face-lift]. At least an eye-job, if not the whole cut-and-snip. — Joseph Wambaugh, *Floaters*, p. 137, 1996

eyelash *noun*

an act of urination *UK*

Rhyming slang for **SLASH** (urination).

- This French lager's murder on the bladder [...] I'm desperate for an eyelash. — Bernard Demsey and Kevin McNally, *Lock, Stock... & Two Sips*, p. 287, 2000

eye-opener *noun*

1 a strong drink, especially early in the morning *US, 1817*

- Tomorrow I've got enough for my eye opener of wine. — Willard Motely, *Let No Man Write My Epitaph*, p. 374, 1958
- Donnell brought Mr. Woody his eye-opener, vodka and pale dry ginger ale, half and half, two of them on a silver tray. — Elmore Leonard, *Freaky Deaky*, p. 183, 1988
- J.C. on the porch, holding a tray out. "Hey! We have an eye opener!" — James Ellroy, *White Jazz*, p. 39, 1992

2 a drug addict's first injection of the day *US*

- —J.E. Schmidt, *Narcotics Lingo and Lore*, p. 57, 1959
- To wake up without an eye opener has only happened to me twice in all the time I've been on junk. —David Maurer and Victor Vogel, *Narcotics and Narcotic Addiction*, p. 405, 1973

3 any drug that acts as a central nervous system stimulant *BAHAMAS*

- —John A. Holm, *Dictionary of Bahamian English*, p. 71, 1982
- —Richard A. Spears, *The Slang and Jargon of Drugs and Drink*, p. 188, 1986
- —Mike Haskins, *Drugs*, p. 279, 2003

4 the active participant in anal sex *US*

- —Vincent J. Monteleone, *Criminal Slang*, p. 79, 1949

eyes *noun*

▸ **keep your eyes peeled; keep your eyes skinned**

to be extra-observant *US, 1833*

'Keep your eyes skinned' predated 'peeled' by 20 years.

- Some people do it naturally, sending flowers, following up meetings, keeping their eyes skinned for any opportunity to get in with the rich and/or grand. —*Sunday Times (South Africa)*, 6th April 2003
- Fascinatingly, 12 cut-out Jordans have gone awol from Yates's Wine Lodges. Keep your eyes peeled, ladies. — *The Guardian*, 5th September 2003

▸ **the eyes**

in craps, a roll of two *US*

An abbreviation of **SNAKE EYES**.

- —Chris Fagans and David Guzman, *A Guide to Craps Lingo*, p. 6, 1999

eye's front *noun*

a contemptible fool *UK*

Rhyming slang for **CUNT**, formed from the military command 'Eyes front!'.

- —David Hillman, 15th November 1974

eyes like cod's bollocks *adjective*

protuberant eyes *UK, 1961*

eyes like piss-holes in the snow *noun*

deeply sunken or squinting eyes (whether naturally, or as a result of illness, or – most commonly – as a symptom of a hangover) *UK, 1984*

- But just off the boat, 19 with dead white skin and two scabby eyes like piss holes in the snow, I've nowhere to go. — *The Guardian*, 24th November 1999

eyes of blue *adjective*

true *UK*

Rhyming slang.

- 100% eyes of blue, stand on me. —Ray Puxley, *Cockney Rabbit*, 1992

Eyetalian *noun*

an Italian or, in the US, an Italian-American *AUSTRALIA, 1900*

- Another time I got my neck all scraped up from a bicycle chain some eye-talian wrapped around me. —Edwin Torres, *Carlito's Way*, p. 9, 1975
- I'd rather deal with an Eyetalian or a Greek than the Poms. —Sandra Jobson, *Blokes*, p. 163, 1984

Eyetalian *adjective*

Italian *UK*

A spelling that follows pronunciation.

- He wears those Eyetalian clothes, off duty, doesn't he? —Troy Kennedy Martin, *Z Cars*, p. 35, 1962

Eyetie *noun*

1 an Italian or Italian-American *US, 1919*

Originally army use in World War 1.

- I know, I done business with the frogs and eyeties before. —Terry Southern, *Blue Movie*, p. 94, 1970
- Is there any way the Eyeties could be getting the word in advance? —Roy Higgins and Tom Prior, *The Jockey Who Laughed*, p. 59, 1982
- [D]idn't matter if he got dumped on or made to look a fool by some Eye-tie. (Jackie would call them "guinea fucks" and one time DeLeon said, "Excuse me, my granddadddy was Italian," and had to listen to Jackie explain he meant these wise-guy schmucks, not your real Eyetalians. —Elmore Leonard, *Glitz*, p. 236, 1985

2 the Italian language *UK, 1925*

Derogatory, if not intentionally so.

- [D]aily doses of Eyetie housewife pulchritude via spy satellites. —Andrew Nickolds, *Back to Basics*, p. 85, 1994

Eyetie *adjective*

Italian *UK, 1925*

- —Michael Peters, *Pommie Bastard*, p. 19, 1969
- Your Eyetie wonder better watch himself, there's some real competition on the scene now. —Jenny Pausacker, *What are ya?*, p. 41, 1987

Eyetoe *noun*

1 an Italian *AUSTRALIA, 1941*

- As he got closer, we saw he was too tall to be a Pong or an Eyetoe, though there was something about him that made us think of both. —Dal Stivens, *The Scholarly Mouse*, p. 65, 1957

2 the Italian language *AUSTRALIA*

- We were too far away to hear what he was saying but it didn't sound like English to us but more like Pong yabber or Eyetoe or Dago gibberish. —Dal Stivens, *The Scholarly Mouse*, p. 65, 1957

eye trouble *noun*

1 a tendency to stare *NEW ZEALAND*

Prison usage.

- —Harry Orsman, *A Dictionary of Modern New Zealand Slang*, p. 47, 1999

2 extreme fatigue *US*

- —Montie Tak, *Truck Talk*, p. 56, 1971

eye up *verb*

to look something or someone over, especially to appraise someone as sexually desirable *UK, 1982*

- You can see the boys eyeing up the girls and comparing them. —Sheila Scraton, *Shaping Up to Womanhood*, p. 92, 1992

eye-wash *noun*

1 nonsense *UK, 1930*

- Choreographic eyewash it may be; but [Deborah] Colker's forte is not sophistication, it's showmanship. — *The Guardian*, 12th December 2003

2 intentionally deceptive words or actions *US, 1917*

- You can't trust Tommy's tells. They're all eyewash. —John Vorhaus, *The Big Book of Poker Slang*, p. 16, 1996

3 tear gas *US*

- —Jay Robert Nash, *Dicitonary of Crime*, p. 122, 1992

ey up; ey-up

used as a greeting; used as a means of directing attention to something *UK*

A northern English dialect phrase in wide use.

- Ey-up, we've got a message from some chuffer in the States. — *The Guardian*, 28th December 2002

E-Z *adjective*

easy *US*

Phonetic American spelling.

- [A]ny amateur can revel in a few minutes of E-Z listening fame. —Charles Danzigger, *Japan for Starters*, p. 108, 1996
- —Dylan Jones, *Easy!*, 1997
- —Susie Dent, *The Language Report*, p. 76, 2003

e-zine *noun*

a low-budget, self-published magazine made available over the Internet *US*

A combination of 'e-' (a prefix, denoting electronic) and **ZINE** (a **FANZINE**, a magazine for and by fans).

- Whilst the e-zine has the potential to reach a very wide audience, it does so at the loss of individuality, lacking the personal qualities of paper zines. —Marion Leonard, *Cool Places*, p. 103, 1998

Ff

F *noun*

1 **oral sex** *US, 1987*

An abbreviation of **FRENCH** used in personal advertising.

- Other turn-ons include GS [golden shower], F and S/M [sadomasochism][.] —Kevin Sampson, *Clubland*, p. 70, 2002

2 **in poker, the sixth player to the left of the dealer** *US*

- —George Percy, *The Language of Poker*, p. 33, 1988

F *adjective*

in the written shorthand of the Internet and texting, in a homosexual context, feminine *UK*

Short for **FEMME**.

- —Michelle Baker and Steven Tropiano, *Queer Facts*, p. 13, 2004

F

▷ **see: EFF**

F2F

face-to-face, in Internet or texting shorthand *UK*

- —Constance Hale, *Wired Style*, p. 69, 1996
- [A] meeting under the F2F protocol[.] —*Freelance*, August/September 2000

F-40; Lilly F-40; forty *noun*

an orange-coloured 100 mg capsule of secobarbital sodium (trade name Seconal™), a central nervous system depressant *US*

- —Donald Wesson and David Smith, *Barbiturates*, p. 122, 1977
- —Edith A. Folb, *runnin' down some lines*, p. 236, 1980

FA *noun*

▷ **see: FANNY ADAMS**

fab

very good, excellent; used for registering general approval or agreement *US*

A shortening of **FABULOUS** (very good, etc.); hugely popular usage in the 1960s, in part thanks to The Beatles. Subsequently in and out of vogue, surviving between times as irony. The cult science fiction television programme *Thunderbirds* (1964–66) used 'F.A.B.' as an acknowledgement but otherwise meaningless catchphrase; the 1999 UK re-run coincided with a vogue revival.

- And the great Kahoona. He's absolutely fab. —Frederick Kohner, *Gidget*, p. 59, 1957
- PAUL: We do, you know. We sound like us having a ball. It's fab. GIRL: Is it really fab or are you just saying that to convince yourself? —*A Hard Day's Night*, 1964
- —Carol Covington, *A Glossary of Teenage Terms*, 1965
- [P]op has the fab habit of suddenly changing its clothes, drugs and music every now and then. —John Robb, *The Nineties*, p. 148, 1999
- [T]his fab fivesome [the pop group Steps]. —*CD:UK*, p. 14, 2000
- As I sat there, getting all this fab coverage from Dolan, I began to regret having laid out the fifty on the cracker-discrimination case. —Terry Southern, *Now Dig This*, p. 145, 2001
- Email is fast and convenient and generally fab[.] —Claire Mansfield and John Mendelssohn, *Dominatrix*, p. 280, 2002

fabbo *adjective*

fabulous; excellent *AUSTRALIA*

From '*fab*ulous'.

- Sneak away from the reception early and celebrate your anniversary with your own 'bride' in a fabbo hotel. —*Sydney Morning Herald*, 12th July 2003

fabe *adjective*

very good, excellent *UK*

An affected elaboration of **FAB**.

- JULIAN: I see Danish teak everywhere. SANDY: Fabe! —Barry Took and Marty Feldman, *Round The Horne*, 21st April 1967

fabel *adjective*

very good, excellent, lovely *UK*

An elaboration of **FAB**.

- —Paul Baker, *Polari*, p. 174, 2002

faboo *adjective*

***fab*ulous** *US*

- Janine is known for her faboo media coverage, from Howard Stern to Jay Leno, and for her policy of appearing in only "girl-girl" scenes. —*The Village Voice*, 21st September 1999

fabric *noun*

clothing in general *US*

- —David Claerbaut, *Black Jargon in White America*, p. 64, 1972

fabulicious *adjective*

good and good tasting *US*

Usually used to describe a sexually appealing man.

- —Jeff Fessler, *When Drag Is Not a Car Race*, p. 82, 1997

fabulosa *adjective*

▷ **see: FANTABULOSA**

fabulous *adjective*

used as a clichéd term of praise *US*

- The standard among all gay guy exclamatory cliches. —Jeff Fessler, *When Drag Is Not a Car Race*, p. 82, 1997

face *noun*

1 **pride, self-esteem, confidence, reputation, standing** *UK, 1876*

- For a hustler in our sidewalk jungle world, "face" and "honor" were important. —Malcolm X and Alex Haley, *The Autobiography of Malcolm X*, p. 127, 1964
- He couldn't risk losing face in front of the network people. —*Mallrats*, 1995

2 **a known criminal** *US, 1944*

- "He's not a gangster, you know," said Terry, enjoying the nectarine. "He's a name – he's a face." —Anthony Masters, *Minder*, p. 4, 1984
- —Ronan Bennet, *Face*, 1997

3 **in racecourse gambling, a bettor who is believed to have useful information regarding the likely outcome of a race** *UK*

A bookmakers' usage.

- "Betting to faces" refers to the bookmaking practice of hedging the face's selection while laying other runners liberally. —David Bennet, *Know Your Bets*, p. 35, 2001

4 **a leading member of the Mod youth fashion movement** *UK*

- I'm the face, baby. Is that clear? —The High Numbers, *I'm The Face*, 1964

5 **in professional wrestling, a wrestler who is designed by the promoters to be seen by the audience as the hero** *US*

Short for **BABYFACE**.

- No word on his heel/face status. —*Herb's Wrestling Tidbits*, 18th January 1990
- Until 1982, he had always wrestled as a face, a hero. —*World of Wrestling Magazine*, p. 7, June 1999
- —*Washington Post*, p. N36, 10th March 2000: 'A wrestling glossary'

6 **a professional pool player who is well known and recognised, making it impossible for him to make a living betting unsuspecting amateurs** *US*

- —Steve Rushin, *Pool Cool*, p. 12, 1990

7 **a stranger; any person** *US, 1946*

- —Robert S. Gold, *A Jazz Lexicon*, p. 99, 1964

8 **used as a term of address** *UK, 1891*

- Later on everybody started using the expression "Face" as a greeting; you'd say "Watcha know, Face," and the answer would come back, "Nothin' to it, Face." —Mezz Mezzrow, *Really the Blues*, p. 235, 1946

9 **oral sex** *US, 1968*

- —Kenn "Naz" Young, *Naz's Underground Dictionary*, p. 28, 1973
- —Inez Cardozo-Freeman, *The Joint*, p. 495, 1984

10 **in betting, odds of 5–2** *UK*

From the **TICK-TACK** signal used by bookmakers.

- —John McCririck, *John McCririck's World of Betting*, p. 59, 1991

11 **a clock or watch** *US*

- —*Swinging Syllables*, 1959

▸ **between the face and eyes**
where a blow or shocking news hits *US*
• —John Gould, *Maine Lingo*, p. 12, 1975

▸ **feed your face; stuff your face**
to eat, especially to eat hungrily or in an ill-mannered way *UK, 1939*
• [T]ell stories around a campfire, feed your face at the cook house, sleep out on the range trail[.]—*Ponca City News (Oklahoma)*, 6th June 1997
• Monkeybone now spends most of his time feeding his face and making the beast with two backs with Julie[.]—*Washington Post*, 23rd February 2001
• Lazy fat westerners [...] stuffing their faces with pills when they should be ordering a salad.—*The Guardian*, 6th May 2004

▸ **in your face**
adversarial, confrontational *US, 1976*
• I'm special counsel for Internal Affairs, so my jurisdiction's pretty much in your face.—*A Few Good Men*, 1992
• L7 is an L.A. chick band known for their aggressive, in-your-face lyrics.—Robert Crais, *L.A. Requiem*, p. 96, 1999

▸ **off your face**
drunk or drug-intoxicated *UK*
Variation of **OFF YOUR HEAD**.
• I remember so well the days when foreign travel fulfilled with remarkable efficiency my desires to get off my face.—Howard Marks, *The Howard Marks Book of Dope Stories*, p. 112, 2001
• I'm going to have-a best time-a me bastard life. I'm off me fuckin face already, mun, I am.—Niall Griffiths, *Sheepshagger*, p. 58, 2001
• "If they are off their faces on drugs at least they will not be killing each other." Local [Bosnia] drug dealer.—*Mixmag*, p. 90, December 2001
• All that's left to do now is fire it up and get off your face.—Nick Jones, *Spliffs*, p. 101, 2003

▸ **put a face on**
to apply makeup *UK, 1946*
• Im going to shower, dress and put a face on then we can go to Mary's for a few drinks[.]—Hubert Selby Jr, *Last Exit to Brooklyn*, p. 231, 1957
• "Had to put on a new face." She smiled.—Earl Thompson, *Tattoo*, p. 644, 1974

▸ **your face and my arse**
a catchphrase response to a smoker's request, 'Have you got a match?' *UK, 1984*

face *verb*
to humiliate *US*
• —Connie Eble (Editor), *UNC-CH Campus Slang*, p. 3, Spring 1983

▸ **face the breeze**
in horse racing, to be in the position immediately behind and outside the leader *US*

face!
used as the stinging finale to a deliberate insult *US, 1979*
Youth slang.
• "You look nice today in that acid-washed jacket and those neon jelly shoes." "Thanks." "Face!"—Morgan and Ferris, *Retrohell*, p. 71, 1997

face-ache *noun*
used, generally, as a disparaging form of address *UK, 1937*
Harsher when used behind someone's back.
• [T]he vicar (old Face-ache) and the men to do the plumbing[.]—Henry Sloane, *Sloane's Inside Guide to Sex & Drugs & Rock 'n' Roll*, p. 55, 1985
• Bringing the jug-eared face-ache back to Everton is something I have been thinking about.—*The Guardian*, 15th August 2003

face as long as a wet Sunday *noun*
used for describing an expression of depression or sadness *CANADA*
• Manley had a face as long as a wet Sunday, so Experience asked, "Why?"—*Coast Guard*, p. 4, 6th June 1984

face bubble *noun*
in motorcyling, a plastic shield attached to the helmet to cover the face *US*
• —Ed Radlauer, *Motorcylopedia*, p. 21, 1973

faced *adjective*
1 drunk *US*
• —Collin Baker et al., *College Undergraduate Slang Study Conducted at Brown University*, p. 113, 1968
• Being "faced" used to mean being too stoned, short for "shit-faced"—Paul Iannone, *Retrohell*, p. 71, 1997

2 under the influence of MDMA, the recreational drug best known as ecstasy *US*
3 embarrassed, humiliated *US*
Youth slang.
• —Kenn "Naz" Young, *Naz's Dictionary of Teen Slang*, p. 39, 1993
• It was awful to get faced. It meant you looked awful in front of your friends. Example: "You look nice today in that acid-washed jacket and those neon jelly shoes." Thanks." "Face!"—Morgan and Ferris, *Retrohell*, p. 71, 1997

face-fart *verb*
to burp *NEW ZEALAND, 1982*
• —Harry Orsman, *A Dictionary of Modern New Zealand Slang*, p. 48, 1999

face-fucking *noun*
oral sex, from an active perspective *US*
• [T]he sucking and face fucking and rimming and fagging is done behind the closed doors of the individual booths[.]—Peter Sotos, *Index*, p. 23, 1996

face fungus *noun*
whiskers, men's facial hair *UK, 1907*
• MEYER: Just better put on this false beard. BARRY: How come all the face fungus doc?—Barry Humphries, *Bazza Pulls It Off!*, 1971
• The ads feature John Travolta with, yet again, silly face fungus [a goatee beard]—*The Guardian*, 23rd July 2001

face job *noun*
cosmetic surgery designed to alter your appearance *US*
• No running. No face jobs or new paper.—Richard Condon, *Prizzi's Honor*, p. 278, 1982

face lace *noun*
whiskers *US, 1927*
• —Lou Shelly, *Hepcats Jive Talk Dictionary*, p. 24, 1945

facelift *noun*
in the used car business, the procedure of turning back the miles on the mileometer (odometer) *US*
• —Anna Scotti and Paul Young, *Buzzwords*, p. 37, 1997

face like a bag of arses *noun*
an ugly face *UK*
A variation of **FACE LIKE A BAG OF SPANNERS**.
• —Chris Lewis, *The Dictionary of Playground Slang*, p. 86, 2003

face like a bag of spanners *noun*
a hard and rough face, mostly used when describing a woman *UK*
Recorded as used by a man describing his mother-in-law.
• —*The Times*, 8th May 1975

face like a bulldog *noun*
an ugly face, mostly applied to a girl or woman *UK*
Embellishments abound, such as 'face like a bulldog chewing a wasp' or 'face like a bulldog licking piss off a nettle'.
• —Chris Lewis, *The Dictionary of Playground Slang*, p. 86, 2003
• [T]he most sour-faced girl I have ever seen. She made Siouxsie Sue look like Moira Stewart and had a face, as the local [Lancashire] adage had it, like a bulldog licking piss of a nettle.—Stuart Maconie, *Cider with Roadies*, p. 111, 2003

face like a dyin' calf *noun*
a morose, sorrowful look *CANADA*
• A boy looks so sad he has a face like a dyin' calf.—Harry Bruce, *Down Home*, p. 109, 1988

face like a leper licking piss off a thistle *noun*
an ugly face, mostly applied to a girl or woman *UK*
• —Chris Lewis, *The Dictionary of Playground Slang*, p. 86, 2003

face like a slapped arse *noun*
a very miserable-looking countenance *UK*
• What's up with you... you've got a face like a slapped arse?—Caroline Aherne and Craig Cash, *The Royle Family*, 1999
• I don't want to see you walking around here with a face like a slapped arse.—Paul *The Salon*, 1st April 2003

face-off *noun*
an ejaculation of semen onto a lover's face *US*
• He gave her a face-off.—Jackie Collins, *V Graham Norton*, 29th May 2003

face-plant *noun*

a face-first fall; in snowboarding, a face-first fall into the snow *US*

- — *San Francisco Sunday Examiner & Chronicle*, p. 20, 2nd September 1984: 'Say it right'
- — Elena Garcia, *A Beginner's Guide to Zen and the Art of Snowboarding*, p. 122, 1990: 'Glossary'
- — Jim Humes and Sean Wagstaff, *Boarderlands*, p. 221, 1995
- We've grimaced and chuckled simultaneously at face plants, endos [an accident in which the cyclist flies over the handlebars], biffs [a crash] and crash-landings. — *Mountain Bike Magazine's Complete Guide To Mountain Biking Skills*, p. 32, 1996
- — Don R. McCreary (Editor), *Dawg Speak*, 2001

faces and spaces *noun*

joint consideration of equipment and personnel for the field and non-field positions *US*

- — Department of the Army, *Staff Officer's Guidebook*, p. 60, 1986

face-shot *noun*

an air-to-air guided missile *US*

- — *Army*, p. 48, November 1991

face time *noun*

time spent in a meeting or conversation with an important or influential person; time spent on television *US*

- — Eric S. Raymond, *The New Hacker's Dictionary*, p. 148, 1991
- But the general rule was that action officers didn't get much – if any – face time with admirals. So much for networking. — Richard Marcinko and John Weisman, *Rogue Warrior*, p. 190, 1992
- Speaking of which, as soon as he gets back from Russia and China, we'll get you in there for some face-time, let the two of you catch up. — *Traffic*, 2000
- Granada Reports, the local TV show which still gave Wilson face time. — Tony Wilson, *24 Hour Party People*, p. 202, 2002

face train *noun*

serial oral sex, from the point of view of the provider *US*

- A friend of mine recently came to Throb on her birthday and wanted a face train, where women sat on her face, one after another, and she serviced them. — *The Village Voice*, 11th July 2001

facety *adjective*

rude, arrogant *JAMAICA, 1943*

- MATT (white police officer): Will you please calm down? Joe Facety little nigger. — *The Guardian*, 7th June 2003

face-up massage *noun*

an erotic massage *CANADA*

An oral report from a Toronto massage parlour: 'You want oil or powder?' (Chris Coyle, 10th June 2002).

face-welly *noun*

a gas mask *UK*

Conventional 'face' combined with 'welly' (a protective rubber boot). In Royal Air Force use, 2002.

facey *adjective*

indicating criminal qualities *UK*

From FACE (a known criminal).

- They were all nice blokes but real facey fellas. It was villains wall-to-wall. — Dave Courtney, *Raving Lunacy*, p. 19, 2000

fachiva *noun*

heroin *UK*

- — Mike Haskins, *Drugs*, p. 283, 2003

facial *noun*

1 ejaculation onto a person's face *US*

Depictions of the act in pornographic films and photographs promise great pleasure to the recipient.

- And what should be this film's finest sex scene, the finale between Ashlyn and Jamie, turns out to be mainly a simple b.j. ending in a facial. — *Adult Video News*, p. 48, February 1993
- — *Adult Video News*, p. 44, August 1995
- Facials are common in porn, as most male viewers like to see cum on a woman's face. Many women don't like facials but put up with them. — Ana Loria, *1 2 3 Be A Porn Star!*, p. 100, 2000
- — Caroline Archer, *Tart Cards*, 2003

2 in rugby, an aggressive rubbing of the face of a tackled opponent *NEW ZEALAND*

- Kearney's been hammered, and he's copped a real facial. Often observed by commentators but rarely by referees. — David McGill, *David McGill's Complete Kiwi Slang Dictionary*, p. 48, 1998

facist; facistic *adjective*

descriptive of a computer program with security walls or usage policies that the speaker finds excessive *US*

- — Eric S. Raymond, *The New Hacker's Dictionary*, p. 149, 1991

facking *adjective*

used as an intensifier *UK*

A variant spelling of 'fucking' based on London Cockney pronunciation.

- "A fucking what?" "A facking Lilly the Pink [drink], you slay-agg [slag]!" — Kevin Sampson, *Outlaws*, p. 172, 2001

factoid *noun*

a fact *UK*

- [H]e insists on giving us every single factoid, nuance, personal implication and interpretation. — Patrick Neate, *Where You're At*, p. 175, 2003

factor *noun*

in horse racing, a horse who is contending for the lead in a race *US*

- — Robert Saunders Dowst and Jay Craig, *Playing the Races*, p. 162, 1960

factory *noun*

1 a police station *UK, 1891*

- The local factory will love you when I make a complaint. — *The Sweeney*, p. 17, 1976
- — Angela Devlin, *Prison Patter*, p. 51, 1996
- Putney police station on Upper Richmond was one of the capital's leading factories[.] — Duncan MacLaughlin, *The Filth*, p. 59, 2002

2 the equipment needed to inject drugs *US*

- — Eugene Landy, *The Underground Dictionary*, p. 76, 1971
- Get out the factory, the doctor is here. — David Maurer and Victor Vogel, *Narcotics and Narcotic Addiction*, p. 405, 1973
- — Inez Cardozo-Freeman, *The Joint*, p. 495, 1984

▸ **the factory**

the theatre *UK*

Jocular usage by actors.

- — William Granville, *A Dictionary of Theatrical Terms*, p. 72, 1952

factory driver *noun*

in motor racing, a driver officially representing a car manufacturer *US*

- For example, Mario Andretti competed in Grand Prix races in recent seasons as the factory driver for Ferrari. — Hal Higdon, *Finding the Groove*, p. 300, 1980

fac-U *nickname*

during the Vietnam war, the forward air controller training facility in Phan Rhang *US*

The FAC from '*f*orward *a*ir *c*ontroller', the U from '*u*niversity', and the combination from a sense of mischief.

- — Linda Reinberg, *In the Field*, p. 77, 1991

fade *noun*

1 a departure *US, 1942*

- The studs got cool and copped their fade. They left old Boptown in a perfect panic[.] — Dan Burley, *Diggeth Thou?*, p. 19, 1959

2 a black person who tries to lose his identity as a black person and to assume an identity more pleasing to the dominant white society *US*

- — Clarence Major, *Dictionary of Afro-American Slang*, p. 52, 1970

3 a white person *US*

- — Helen Dahlskog (Editor), *A Dictionary of Contemporary and Colloquial Usage*, p. 22, 1972
- — William K. Bentley and James M. Corbett, *Prison Slang*, p. 55, 1992

4 a haircut style in which the sides of the head are closely cut and the top of the head is not *US, 1989*

Also heard as a 'fadie'.

- Yo could you fix my fade? — *Boyz N The Hood*, 1990
- Look, all that Kinte cloth and zig-zag fadies and fight the power? It's fashion. — *New Jack City*, 1990
- He also had his hair molded into a sloped-back six-inch-high fade, with the words "Street" and "Smart" shaved in over his temples. — Richard Price, *Clockers*, p. 97, 1992

fade *verb*

1 to leave, to disappear *US, 1899*

- [I]t's pretty obvious that this geezer and her were planning to fade together. — Alan Hunter, *Gently Down the Stream*, 1957

- Thumper emerged from the driver's side, and the clockers faded fast. —Richard Price, *Clockers*, p. 520, 1992
- Don't fade on me now, Bear. — *Get Shorty*, 1995
- I'm about to fade out, leave Maria to do her business[.] —John Williams, *Cardiff Dead*, p. 169, 2000

2 to idle; to waste time *US*

- —Collin Baker et al., *College Undergraduate Slang Study Conducted at Brown University*, p. 113, 1968

3 to match the bet of another gambler; to bet against another gambler's success *US, 1890*

- You faded what the other man wanted to shoot – and what he often chose to shoot was the exact amount of your winnings. —Jim Thompson, *Bad Boy*, p. 368, 1953

4 to buy part of something *US*

- "That looks like a good pie, can I fade on that?" —Rick Ayers (Editor), *Berkeley High Slang Dictionary*, p. 20, 2004

5 to deal with, to handle *US*

- —Bruce Jackson, *Outside the Law*, p. 56, 1972: 'Glossary'

▸ **fade a beef**

to cause a complaint or criminal charge to be removed *US*

- He was afraid he'd be traded in to fade a meet one of them might have with the LAPD, who were notorious. —Emmett Grogan, *Final Score*, p. 23, 1976

fadeaway *noun*

in hot rodding, a design feature that blends the front fender back into the car body *US*

- —*American Speech*, p. 6, May 1954
- The idea was featured on the 1941 through 1947 Packard Clipper and later became a popular customizing technique. —John Lawlor, *How to Talk Car*, p. 44, 1965

fade away *verb*

to become quiet *US*

- —Marcus Hanna Boulware, *Jive and Slang of Students in Negro Colleges*, 1947

faded *adjective*

1 drunk *US*

- —Connie Eble (Editor), *UNC-CH Campus Slang*, p. 3, Fall 1998
- —Don R. McCreary (Editor), *Dawg Speak*, 2001

2 drug-intoxicated *US, 1998*

- —Mike Haskins, *Drugs*, p. 291, 2003

fade-out *noun*

a disappearance *US, 1918*

- We began to rehearse like mad, and walked away so chesty we would have made Miss Peacock pull a fade-out. —Mezz Mezzrow, *Really the Blues*, p. 61, 1946

faff about; faff around *verb*

to mess about; to waste time on matters of no importance *UK, 1874*

An apparent euphemism for **FUCK** but originally British dialect *faffle* with the same sense.

- Richard faffed around trying to avoid burning himself[.] —Will Self, *The Sweet Smell of Psychosis*, p. 4, 1996
- [I]t's just when my brother's on it [a video game], he says "oh you can play on it" then he just faffs about, then he goes "oh I'll have it back now", so really, he's just messing about with it. —Sara McNamee, *Cool Places*, p. 202, 1998
- Whatever you do, don't faff around[.] —Liza Cody (Editors: Stella Duffy and Lavren Henderson), *Queen of Mean [Tart Noir]*, p. 80, 2002

fag *noun*

1 a male homosexual *US, 1921*

Shortened from 'faggot'.

- But most of the pickups in Greenwich Village are those between fags and between skirted women-hunters. —Jack Lait and Lee Mortimer, *New York Confidential*, p. 69, 1948
- I knew they'd read the journals because they said, 'So you're a big fag, eh? So you like little boys, eh? —John Clellon Holmes, *John Clellon*, p. 239, 1952
- If a sucker comes up on him, he pretends to feel his leg like he was a fag. —William Burroughs, *Junkie*, p. 44, 1953
- I have $30 to my name & hope to earn some in Xmas rush baggageroom work if possible in this overcrowded frosty fag town[.] —Jack Kerouac, *Letter to Carolyn Cassady*, p. 403, 3rd December 1953
- Now all you get is chromium, drunken women, fags, hostile bartenders, anxious owners who hover around the door, worried about their leather seats and the law[.] —Jack Kerouac, *On the Road*, p. 147, 1957
- A screaming fag afraid of his own shadow. —Mickey Spillane, *Return of the Hood*, p. 95, 1964
- Oh shit, I ain't gonna screw no motherfuckin' fag. —Piri Thomas, *Down These Mean Streets*, p. 55, 1967
- I recall being surprised as he was a fag or I always thought[.] —Gore Vidal, *Myra Breckinridge*, p. 21, 1968
- A reliable, hard-working, floor-scrubbing, bill-paying fag who doesn't owe nothin' to nobody. —Mart Crowley, *The Boys in the Band*, p. 30, 1968
- Contending that all of the defendants except Bobby Seale were "fags," he told the Loyola Academy Boosters Club, "We've lost our kids in the freaking fag revolution." —J. Anthony Lukas, *The Barnyard Epithet and Other Obscenities*, p. 32, 1970
- "Heard he's a fag," says Billy. —Darryl Ponicsan, *The Last Detail*, p. 88, 1970
- That was her interpretation of a lace shirt and curly hair – we're fags. —Susan Hall, *Gentleman of Leisure*, p. 12, 1972
- "Hey, man, this is Liberace!" I look into the man's face. Sonofabitch! It is the world-famous fag. —Oscar Zeta Acosta, *The Revolt of the Cockroach People*, p. 162, 1973
- Men shouldn't feel like fags just because they want to have nice-looking bodies. [Quoting Arnold Schwarzenegger] —*Oui*, August 1977
- Pimples had a meet with a fag who – so he said – was good for a double sawbuck[.] —Herbert Huncke, *The Evening Sun Turned Crimson*, p. 50–51, 1980
- John Wayne was a fag. —*Repo Man*, 1984
- 1-2-3-4-5-6-7- Oswald was a fag. —*The Usual Suspects*, 1995
- Her next boyfriend saw my Bowie poster and started calling him a fag. —Francesca Lia Block, *Baby Be-Bop*, p. 391, 1995
- Carol, the waitress, this is Simon, the fag. —*As Good As It Gets*, 1997
- "Are you some kind of a fag band? I can't imagine a band without a drummer." "Gay," I say. "Nobody says "fag" anymore." "Whatever you want to call it. A queer's still a queer." —Darren Francis, *The Sprawl [britpulp]*, p. 300, 1999

2 a cigarette, a cigarette butt *UK, 1888*

- "Say, got a fag?" asked Buddy. "Here's a coffin nail," Phil said, talking out of the side of his mouth and extending a pack to Buddy. —James T. Farrell, *Saturday Night*, p. 28, 1947
- His eyes lit on Choo-Choo's half-smoked package of Camels on the table. "Dump out those fags," he ordered a cop, watching Sheik's reaction. —Chester Himes, *The Real Cool Killers*, p. 69, 1959
- I lays on me bed with a fag to think. —John Peter Jones, *Feather Pluckers*, p. 10, 1964
- He says he was sittin' in a cell in a Southwest jail / where he landed doin' three days for vag. / A drunk came in, his eyes lit up like a hungry pup / as I handed him a tailor-made fag. —Bruce Jackson, *Get Your Ass in the Water and Swim Like Me*, p. 82, 1966
- Perry goes to the kitchen for a glass of water, wanders away to his shared bedroom, puffing on the fag-end of his cigarette. —Odie Hawkins, *Ghetto Sketches*, p. 161, 1972
- I puffed [to smoke marijuana] before I smoked any fags. —Macfarlane, Macfarlane and Robson, *The User*, p. 1, 1996
- He sparked up a fag and sucked fitfully at it. —Kevin Sampson, *Powder*, p. 100, 1999

3 a despicable, unlikeable person *US*

No allegation of homosexuality is inherent in this usage.

- Ohmigod, I mean my fag little brother sees Jeff and goes, 'Tiffany's got her period,' and I could totally die. —Mary Corey and Victoria Westermark, *Fer Shurr! How to be a Valley Girl*, 1982
- —Connie Eble (Editor), *UNC-CH Campus Slang*, p. 3, Spring 1989

▹ see: **FAG PACKET**

fag around *verb*

(of presumptively heterosexual male friends) to joke around or engage in horseplay *US*

- —Judi Sanders, *Da Bomb*, p. 6, 1997

fag-bag *verb*

to rob a homosexual man *US*

- You're big and bad enough you can play them along and get them alone and pow! There's a couple dudes around making a living from fag-bagging but you don't last long. —John Sayles, *Union Dues*, p. 290, 1977

fag-bait *noun*

an effeminate boy or young man *US, 1974*

- He quotes a book reviewer from the New York Times who refused to review the book once it was published as referring to the book of pictures of Arnold as "fag bait." —Michael Blitz, *Why Arnold Matters*, p. 146, 2004

fag bangle *noun*

a homosexual man who accompanies a heterosexual woman *UK*

Derives from the purely decorative effect of the relationship.

- EDINA: I'll be going to the show with a gay man on my arm. PATSY: You don't need a fag bangle. —Jennifer Saunders, *Absolutely Fabulous*, 28th December 2002

fag factory *noun*

1 a place where homosexuals gather *US*

Formed on **FAG** (a homosexual).

- —Vincent J. Monteleone, *Criminal Slang*, p. 80, 1949

2 a prison, especially one with a large homosexual population *US*
- —Jay Robert Nash, *Dicitonary of Crime*, p. 123, 1992

fagged out; fagged *adjective*
exhausted *UK, 1785*
- —Collin Baker et al., *College Undergraduate Slang Study Conducted at Brown University*, p. 114, 1968
- Playing poker on a big scale demands a lot of physical stamina when a game goes twice around the clock. I noticed all the poker players I knew looked a little fagged out.—Jimmy Snyder, *Jimmy the Greek*, p. 25, 1975
- I tell you, you're looking a bit fagged.—Nicholas Blincoe, *Ardwick Green (Disco Biscuits)*, p. 10, 1996

fagging *noun*
male homosexual anal-intercourse *US*
- [T]he sucking and face fucking and rimming and fagging is done behind the closed doors of the individual booths[.]—Peter Sotos, *Index*, p. 23, 1996

faggish *adjective*
effeminate, blatantly homosexual *US*
- [L]ike maybe Gonzales the Mexican sort of bum or hanger-on sort of faggish who kept coming up to her place[.]—Jack Kerouac, *The Subterraneans*, p. 43, 1958

faggot *noun*
a male homosexual *US, 1914*
- This was the doorman I had talked to on the phone a little earlier, but on the phone he hadn't sounded like a faggot.—Horace McCoy, *Kiss Tomorrow Good-bye*, p. 276, 1948
- I never could stomach the relish with which soldiers would describe how they had stomped some faggot in a bar.—Norman Mailer, *Advertisements for Myself*, p. 223, 1954
- Let's see those knockers ... Memo to casting. Get a new monster. This one's a faggot.—Max Shulman, *Rally Round the Flag, Boys!*, p. 66, 1957
- Oh, babe, she was such a faggot! Awful.—John Rechy, *City of Night*, p. 203, 1963
- It was the first time I'd been around guys who weren't afraid of being faggots. They were faggots because they wanted to be.—Claude Brown, *Manchild in the Promised Land*, p. 146, 1965
- The talk turned way out, on faggots and their asses which, swinging from side to side, could make a girl look ridiculous, like she wasn't moving.—Piri Thomas, *Down These Mean Streets*, p. 54, 1967
- Come to think of it, you're the type that gives faggots a bad name. —Mart Crowley, *The Boys in the Band*, p. 30, 1968
- I said, "DId you know that [FBI Director J. Edgar] Hoover is a faggot – your boss?"—H. Rap Brown, *Die Nigger Die!*, p. 103, 1969
- Look, Gussie, you are dealing with the oldest faggot in the Upper Ubangi, so come off the peg.—William Burroughs, *Queer*, p. 71, 1985
- Multicultural Management Program Fellows— *Dictionary of Cautionary Words and Phrases*, 1989
- I don't know whether I walked like a man or the biggest faggot that ever came down the pike, but I did walk across that office.—Herbert Huncke, *Guilty of Everything*, p. 22, 1990
- By calling himself a faggot, he steals the thunder away from the mouthy jerks of this world who'd like to beat him to it.—*Chasing Amy*, 1997
- Sometimes he still dreamed about it, though – the way they held him down and took turns with him, calling him a faggot[.]—Francesca Lia Block, *I Was a Teenage Fairy*, p. 162, 1998

Faggot Flats *nickname*
a neighbourhood in Los Angeles, south of the Sunset Strip and north of Santa Monica Boulevard *US*
- It was an area called "Faggot Flats" by insiders because of its big homosexual population.—Vance Donovan, *High Rider*, p. 25, 1969

faggot road *noun*
a road topped with sapling bundles *CANADA*
- The Council was concerned with the building of faggot roads and bridges.—Mary Innis, *Travellers West*, p. 24, 1956

faggotry *noun*
male homosexuality; male homosexual practices *US, 1970*
- But the life-cry of that love has long since hissed away into no more than this idle and bitchy faggotry.—Thomas Pynchon, *Gravity's Rainbow*, p. 616, 1973
- The hunters in their pickup trucks were of the opinion that to vote for this woman was to vote for faggotry – and lesbianism, and socialism, and alimony, and New York.—John Irving, *The World According to Garp*, p. 484, 1978

faggot's lunch box *noun*
a jock strap; an athletic supporter *US*
- —Roger Blake, *The American Dictionary of Sexual Terms*, p. 69, 1964
- —Dale Gordon, *The Dominion Sex Dictionary*, p. 67, 1967

faggot's moll *noun*
a hetersexual woman who seeks and enjoys the company of homosexual men *US, 1969*
- Fag Hags, Fruit Flies, Faggot's Molls, is what the latter are rather unkindly called.—John Francis Hunter, *The Gay Insider*, p. 90–91, 1971

faggoty; faggotty *adjective*
obviously homosexual *US, 1927*
- It was a young man, a rather faggotty-looking character in a Volkswagen, asleep.—Robert Gover, *Here Goes Kitten*, p. 122, 1964
- It is those faggoty intellectuals who've never gotten it up themselves[.]—Oscar Zeta Acosta, *The Revolt of the Cockroach People*, p. 31, 1973

faggy *adjective*
effeminate, blatantly homosexual *US*
- That faggy guy that let me in went for the stuff.—Hal Ellson, *Duke*, p. 111, 1949
- [Y]ou could hear them all yelling, deep and terrific on the Pencey side, because practically the whole school except me was there, and scrawny and faggy on the Saxon Hall side, because the visiting team hardly ever brought many people with them.—J.D. Salinger, *Catcher in the Rye*, p. 2, 1951
- The faggy words, the determinedly masculine tone – the latter again meant to obviate the former and render it acceptable.—John Rechy, *Numbers*, p. 67, 1967
- That's too faggy for Alan to play – he wouldn't be any good at it. —Mart Crowley, *The Boys in the Band*, p. 126, 1968
- You were a faggy little leather boy with a smaller piece of stick.—Mick Jagger, *Memo to Turner*, 1970
- "You and your faggy big words," Roscoe shouted[.]—Joseph Wambaugh, *The Choirboys*, p. 166, 1975
- Robin was the name of that faggy guy who hung with him.—*Gone in 60 Seconds*, 2000
- We all got faggier by the day. You never saw a more limp-wristed bunch of sissies.—Simon Napier-Bell, *Black Vinyl White Powder*, p. 144, 2001

fag hag *noun*
1 a female cigarette smoker *US, 1944*
Teen slang, formed on **FAG** (a cigarette). Noted by a Toronto newspaper in 1946, and reported as 'obsolescent or obsolete' by Douglas Leechman, 1959. This sense of the term is long forgotten in the US but not the UK.
- —*American Speech*, p. 303, December 1955: 'Wayne University slang'

2 a woman who seeks and enjoys the company of male homosexuals *US*
Formed on **FAG** (a homosexual). At times now used with derision, at times with affection.
- —*The Guild Dictionary of Homosexual Terms*, p. 15, 1965
- The fag hag, sometimes known as a fruit fly, is a girl or woman who, although she is more than likely homosexual herself, has never admitted it.—Ruth Allison, *Lesbianism*, p. 112, 1967
- [I]t is only within the past several years that homosexual argot has developed a special term ("faghag") to refer to such a woman.—Ned Polsky, *Hustlers, Beats, and Others*, p. 129, 1967
- Freedom of speech does not consist of the right of noisy minorities, such as the Homosexual International and their front-men or camp critics and fag hags, to seize control of propagandistic areas such as clothing fashions[.]—G. Legman, *The Fake Revolt*, p. 11, 1967
- And it's unfortunate that most of the "easy" girls, the fag-hags and such, are such shanks and likely as not to be unclean[.]—Angelo d'Arcangelo, *The Homosexual Handbook*, p. 210, 1968
- It had all the types in the hustling scene: the new hustler, the aging hustler, the old queen, the fag-haf, etc.—*Screw*, p. 8–9, 24th January 1969
- Fag Hags, Fruit Flies, Faggot's Molls, is what the latter are rather unkindly called.—John Francis Hunter, *The Gay Insider*, p. 90–91, 1971
- —Connie Eble (Editor), *UNC-CH Campus Slang*, November 1976
- And for the fag-hag's castrating hatred, these men will pay them back by "adoring" them but never desiring them.—John Rechy, *The Sexual Outlaw*, p. 187, 1977
- "You are not a fag hag, Mona." "Look at the symptoms. I hang around with you, don't I / We go boogying at Buzzby's and the Endup. I'm practically a fixture at The Palms"[.]—Armistead Maupin, *Tales of the City*, p. 101, 1978
- I'd had a deadly relationship the previous summer with another media maiden who was a self-declared faghag[.]—Lester Bangs, *Psychotic Reactions and Carburetor Dung*, p. 291–292, 1979
- And the sad truth is that you'll accomplish none of that and wind up as either an even more bitter misogynist or a reverse fag hag.—*Chasing Amy*, 1997
- Carol clicked her knitting needles. "The word is fag hag."—Rita Ciresi, *Pink Slip*, p. 15, 1999
- "I'M A TOTAL FAG-HAG!" screams Kelly Osbourne.— *X-Ray*, p. 12, November 2002

fag-hater *noun*
a person with a pathological dislike for homosexuals *US*
- — *Maledicta*, p. 242, 1979: 'Kinks and Queens: linguistic and cultural aspects of the terminology for gays'

Fagin *noun*

1 a leader of thieves *US*

Formed on the character created by Charles Dickens in *Oliver Twist*, 1837.

- He was a small-time fagin who set up marks for others to score. —Emmett Grogan, *Final Score*, p. 69, 1976

2 in pool, a person who backs a player financially in his bets *US*

- —Steve Rushin, *Pool Cool*, p. 13, 1990

fag loop *noun*

a loop on the back of a man's shirt *US*

- My research shows that they are also known as locker loops and fag loops, and that they have pretty much disappeared because most men no longer hang dress shirts. —*Plain Dealer (Cleveland, Ohio)*, p. E4, 20th December 2001

fag mag *noun*

a magazine marketed to homosexuals *UK*

A compound of **FAG** (a homosexual) and **MAG** (a magazine).

- You could always just not buy any of the fag mags. —*Attitude*, p. 146, October 2003

fag moll *noun*

a woman who keeps company with homosexual men *US*

- "I've become a fag moll really," she [Loulou de la Falaise] laughs. "There's nothing more fun than fags." —*Newsweek*, 27th August 1973

fagola *noun*

a homosexual *US*

- Are you a fagola, sir? My friends and me, we got to know. —Bernard Wolfe, *The Magic of Their Singing*, p. 128, 1961

fag out *verb*

to go to bed *US*

- —Collin Baker et al., *College Undergraduate Slang Study Conducted at Brown University*, p. 114, 1968

fag packet; fag *noun*

a jacket *UK*

Rhyming slang.

- Entry into the best places is forbidden without a "fag" on. —Ray Puxley, *Cockney Rabbit*, 1992

fag roller *noun*

a criminal who preys on homosexual victims *US, 1962*

- [H]e would read in great detail how Coco Salas had been beaten almost to death by some fag-rollers in Old Havana. —Reinaldo Arenas, *The Color of Summer*, p. 369, 1990
- Some specialized as "fag rollers" and would pick up men and then rob and beat them, justifying their brutality as punishment of "fairies." —Eric C. Schneider, *Vampires, Dragons, and Egyptian Kings*, p. 134, 1999

fag show *noun*

in the circus or carnival, a performance by female impersonators *US*

- —Joe McKennon, *Circus Lingo*, p. 33, 1980

fag tag *noun*

a loop on the back of a man's shirt *US, 1980*

- —Chris Lewis, *The Dictionary of Playground Slang*, p. 86, 2003

failure to float *noun*

drowning or near drowning *US*

- —Sally Williams, *"Strong" Words*, p. 141, 1994

failure to fly

a tag applied to failed suicides *UK*

Medical slang.

- —Adam T. Fox, St Mary's Hospital, London, 10th October 2002

fainits!; fain I!; fains!; fain it!; faynights!; fainites!

used to call a playground truce *UK, 1870*

Schoolchildren's use, probably from conventional 'feign' (to pretend) hence 'to shirk', 'to evade'; often used in conjunction with a fingers-crossed gesture, the middle finger twisted over and around the forefinger, in the traditional sign of the cross, hence the call for truce may actually be a plea for sanctuary derived from conventional 'fen', corrupted from French *fend* (to forbid); note also 'forfend' (to protect) as in the phrase 'Heaven forfend'.

- As always, double fainites are exactly twice as effective. —Jonathan Blythe, *The Law of the Playground*, 2004

fainting fits; faintings *noun*

the female breasts *UK*

Rhyming slang.

- —*Daily Telegraph*, 17th December 1972: 'Slang it to me in rhyme'

faints *noun*

in the illegal production of alcohol, low-proof distillate *US*

- —David W. Maurer, *Kentucky Moonshine*, p. 115, 1974

fair *adjective*

1 (used of a gang fight) without weapons *US*

- J.J. liked it because he couldn't beat anyhbody in a fair fight, and whenever we stomped somebody, all of us stomped him. —Claude Brown, *Manchild in the Promised Land*, p. 98, 1965
- He got away from the stoop and asked, "Fair one, Gringo?" —Piri Thomas, *Down These Mean Streets*, p. 50, 1967

2 absolute; total *AUSTRALIA*

- 'I know how you feel, cobs,' he said, 'she's a fair bastard.' —J.E. Macdonnell, *Don't Gimme the Ships*, 1960

fairbank *verb*

in a gambling cheating scheme, to let a victim win at first, increasing his confidence before cheating him *US, 1961*

- —Thomas L. Clark, *The Dictionary of Gambling and Gaming*, p. 76, 1987

fair bollix *noun*

a fair deal, a just proportion *IRELAND*

Variation of **FAIR DO'S**.

- [I]f you do it in under twenty there's a fiver on top. – Fair bollix to you. Hop in so. —James Hawes, *Dead Long Enough*, p. 100, 2000

fair buck *noun*

used as a plea for fair treatment *NEW ZEALAND*

- —David McGill, *David McGill's Complete Kiwi Slang Dictionary*, p. 44, 1998

fair cow *noun*

an annoying person or circumstance *AUSTRALIA, 1904*

- 'Don't like the look of it at all,' he said more than once. 'It's a fair cow.' —Nevil Shute, *The Far Country*, p. 150, 1952
- Getting him home was a fair cow. —Patsy Adam-Smith, *Folklore of the Australian Railwaymen*, p. 116, 1969
- 'That's how it is with rich people like Tye and Squatter Fleming. They can only eat three meals a day and sleep in one bed. Can't spend all their money. Must be a fair cow.' —Frank Hardy, *Legends From Benson's Valley*, p. 146, 1972
- —Jim Ramsay, *Cop It Sweet!*, p. 34, 1977

fair crack of the whip *noun*

fair treatment, equal opportunity *AUSTRALIA, 1929*

To give someone a 'fair crack of the whip' is to deal fairly with that person.

- CHERYLENE: Perhaps you'd better draw another on on her! BARRY: Fair crack of the whip!!! It just wouldn't be natural! —Barry Humphries, *Bazza Pulls It Off!*, 1971
- It's not exactly a straightener either, fighting cancer. A fair crack of the whip don't come into it. —Dave Courtney, *Dodgy Dave's Little Black Book*, p. 173, 2001

fair crack of the whip!

be fair! *AUSTRALIA, 1924*

- Cripes – fair crack of the whip – like no – but I'll give it a burl if you really reckon my song was a bit of all right. Warbling in a night club eh? Well it's better than a poke in the eye with a burnt stick! —Barry Humphries, *The Wonderful World of Barry McKenzie*, p. 16, 1968

fair dinks *adverb*

honestly *AUSTRALIA, 1983*

- Fair dinks, I'm willing to go down fighting on this issue. —Roy Slaven (John Doyle), *Five South Coast Seasons*, p. 11, 1992

fair dinkum *adjective*

1 displaying typical Australian characteristics, such as honesty, directness, guts, sense of humour and the like *AUSTRALIA, 1937*

- 'She's fair dinkum,' said the young nurse, rather shocked. 'She's beaut.' —Jean Brooks, *The Opal Witch*, p. 71, 1967
- Any man who doesn't groove on the hump scene in *Candy* can't be fair dinkum. —Kevin Mackey, *The Cure*, p. 146, 1970
- Mick Zammit was the boss and I have never done business with a more fair-dinkum bloke, or a funnier one. —Sam Weller, *Old Bastards I Have Met*, p. 51, 1979
- 'The most fair dinkum Aussie story ever told,' Truthful Jones replied, downing the last of his beer. —Frank Hardy, *Hardy's People*, p. 33, 1986
- I'd like to invite you to the most dinky-di, ridgy didge, fair dinkum, no worries mate tournament that you could imagine. —*Australian Ultimate*, p. 7, 2003

2 real; actual *AUSTRALIA, 1937*

- Don't come the raw prawn! I only gave her a bit of a smack on the chops, we didn't get around to the fair dinkum article! —Barry Humphries, *The Wonderful World of Barry McKenzie*, p. 12, 1968

- Anyway, that second time [she went into labour] was fair dinkum, an' she had young Steve.—John O'Grady, *Aussie Etiket*, p. 15, 1971
- [T]he TV boys were organised for a more fair dinkum bit of stoush than those world championship wrestlers.—Frank Hardy, *The Outcasts of Foolgarah*, p. 71, 1971
- We were fair dinkum bush articles all right.—Kerry Cue, *Crooks, Chooks and Bloody Ratbags*, p. 210, 1983
- Like I told you, my mum was a fair-dinkum tactical genius.—Phillip Gwynne, *Deadly Unna?*, p. 105, 1998

3 serious; in earnest *AUSTRALIA, 1934*

- Are you fair dinkum?—Nino Culotta (John O'Grady), *They're A Weird Mob*, p. 57, 1957
- 'I'm going to ask the C.O. to ground me.' 'You're not fair dinkum!'—W.R. Bennett, *Night Intruder*, p. 65, 1962
- I was fair dinkum, and I only answered those things he picked on me about.—John Wynnum, *Jiggin' in the Riggin'*, p. 26, 1965
- I'm fair dinkum in saying that the bloke in charge of the cookhouse has set a standard he may find hard to maintain.—Ray Slattery, *Mobbs' Mob*, p. 21, 1966
- D'you blokes think he was fair dinkum?—Ray Slattery, *Mobbs' Mob*, p. 32, 1966
- But when they get fair dinkum it's another matter.—Sam Weller, *Old Bastards I Have Met*, p. 3, 1979
- I'm not sure those goes at me have been fair dinkum anyway.—Peter Corris, *Make Me Rich*, p. 59, 1985
- We welcome all readers, and fair dinkum drinkers, to contribute.—Bazza and Curly, *Betcha Wrong!*, p. 144, 1990
- If Brian was fair dinkum...—Shane Maloney, *Nice Try*, p. 54, 1998
- Some of the prisoners were fair dinkum with their threats, while others were full of shit[.]—William Dodson, *The Sharp End*, p. 40, 2001

4 fair; honest; equitable *AUSTRALIA*

- 'Fair dinkum shares with a bloke. I'm in this too.'—Norman Lindsay, *Halfway to Anywhere*, p. 141, 1947
- Did I ever tell you about the only fair dinkum raffle ever run in Australia?—Frank Hardy, *The Yarns of Billy Borker*, p. 13, 1965
- LEW: We can talk in the car on the way back to London. BARRY: Are you fair dinkum? I can do with the oscar [money][.]—Barry Humphries, *Bazza Pulls It Off!*, 1971
- It worked all right and the raffle was more fair dinkum than a lot of government-run ones.—Frank Hardy, *Hardy's People*, p. 167, 1986
- Ask around Australia and [...] to a man they will tell you that [Rodney] Marsh is honest and straight-talking – he is "fair dinkum".—*The Daily Telegraph*, 11th May 2003

5 true; genuine *AUSTRALIA, 1908*

- 'You're pulling my leg!' 'No. That's fair dinkum.'—John Wynnum, *Tar Dust*, p. 119, 1962
- 'It's fair dinkum, I tell yer,' Mulga M. insisted, 'he bought that big empty mansion orf of Signemup and Leavum.'—Frank Hardy, *The Outcasts of Foolgarah*, p. 200, 1971

fair dinkum *adverb*

1 honestly; really; seriously; in all truth *AUSTRALIA, 1894*

First recorded in 1881 from the dialect of north Lincolnshire (*English Dialect Dictionary*) as an excalmation equivalent to 'fair play!', in which usage it had a brief life in Australia from 1890 to 1924 (*Australian National Dictionary*).

- 'You sound like a whale that's swallowed a bellyfulla carbide, fair dinkum!' 'Get knotted,' belched Steeger.—W.R. Bennett, *Wingman*, p. 69, 1961
- Wouldn't it! I'm not in the mood now...fair dinkum you bastards are worse than a dose of arrowroot!—Barry Humphries, *The Wonderful World of Barry McKenzie*, p. 17, 1968
- Next thing in came this little old dear and, fair dinkum, she could have been a waitress at the Last Supper.—Sam Weller, *Old Bastards I Have Met*, p. 21, 1979
- So when I grabbed hold of his tail, fair dinkum, the bastard spat at me.—Sam Weller, *Old Bastards I Have Met*, p. 52, 1979
- I told yer! I can't locate me wallet! Fair dinkum! I'm not makin' it up!—Lance Peters, *The Dirty Half-Mile*, p. 119, 1979

2 totally; properly; well and truly *AUSTRALIA, 1918*

- I'm going to get drunk. Fair dinkum drunk, too. On beer.—Norman Lindsay, *Halfway to Anywhere*, p. 180, 1947
- He's fair dinkum bonkers, if you ask me.—John O'Grady, *Aussie Etiket*, p. 67, 1971
- A cabbage patch doll! Can you believe it? I am fairdinkum spewin badly.—Kylie Mole (Maryanne Fahey), *My Diary*, p. 3, 1988
- It's a fair dinkum exact repeat performance each time.—Clive Galea, *Slipper*, p. 96, 1988
- I don't believe this. I dead set, fair dinkum, don't bloody well believe it.—Robert G. Barrett, *Davo's Little Something*, p. 205, 1992
- I came to realise that life on crutches is a bummer. It's just fair dinkum like a whole new lifestyle[.]—Paul Vautin, *Turn It Up!*, p. 54, 1995

3 fairly *AUSTRALIA*

- 'Where did you get them from, then?' 'I got them fair dinkum from old Jerry Crankle workin' at the gasworks.'—Norman Lindsay, *Halfway to Anywhere*, p. 41, 1947

fair do's; fair dues

fair and just treatment *UK, 1859*

A plural of 'do' as action (deeds), sometimes confused with 'dues' (requirements) without substantially altering the sense.

- "You tell those thieves down there we mean business," the oldest voice told him. "Fair do's or fair thumps!"—*The Sweeney*, p. 13, 1976

fair enough *noun*

a homosexual *UK*

Rhyming slang for PUFF (a homosexual); probably coined as an elaboration of FAIRY (a homosexual), its reduced form.

- —Ray Puxley, *Cockney Rabbit*, 1992

fair enough!

used for expressing agreement *UK, 1926*

- —W.R. Bennett, *Wingman*, p. 14, 1961
- 'I'll give you a corrected course when we get to the Frisians.' 'Fair enough,' the pilot murmured[.]—W.R. Bennett, *Night Intruder*, p. 122, 1962
- —Paul Lesley, *PT Command*, p. 16, 1963
- I'll see what I can do to get you posted to the Yank steamer. Fair enough?—John Wynnum, *Jiggin' in the Riggin'*, p. 28, 1965
- —Frank Hardy, *The Outcasts of Foolgarah*, p. 186, 1971
- —Jim Ramsay, *Cop It Sweet!*, p. 34, 1977
- 'I think it is the right thing to give them first go this time. Peter said, 'Fair enough. Tee it up.'—Sam Weller, *Old Bastards I Have Met*, p. 50, 1979

fair fight; fair one *noun*

a fight between members of rival gangs in which weapons or at least lethal weapons are forbidden *US*

- "That's okay by us then. Do you want a fair one?" "Okay, a fair one," Tomboy said.—Hal Ellson, *Tomboy*, p. 110, 1950
- —Dale Kramer and Madeline Karr, *Teen-Age Gangs*, p. 174, 1953
- Fair one – A fist fight, without weapons, between one or more representatives of two rival gangs.—*New York Times Magazine*, p. 28, 20th October 1957
- Such as battle is usually planned as "a fair one." This means that only weapons agreed upon by the leaders are to be used.—Harrison E. Salisbury, *The Shook-up Generation*, p. 41, 1958
- "A fiar fight isn't rough," Two-Bit said. "Blades are rough. So are chains and heaters and pool sticks and rumbles. Skin fighting isn't rough."—S.E. Hinton, *The Outsiders*, p. 28, 1967
- —H. Craig Collins, *Street Gangs*, p. 221, 1979

fair fucks *noun*

credit, merit *IRELAND*

- You're a good one Brady if you think I'll fall for that he says. But fair fucks to your for trying.—Patrick McCabe, *The Butcher Boy*, p. 123, 1992

fair go *noun*

an act or instance of just treatment; a fair or reasonable opportunity *AUSTRALIA, 1904*

- FAIR GO – Just treatment.—Gilbert H. Lawson, *A Dictionary of Australian Words and Terms*, 1924
- No matter who you are, the Australian will give you a fair go.—Frank Hardy, *The Yarns of Billy Borker*, p. 80, 1965
- Yer gotta pay it, luv, or do a stretch. Yair, yer might get a nice rest in the clink, but wotta waste of time! It's not a fair go, luv.—Sue Rhodes, *And when she was bad she was popular*, p. 10, 1968
- Ar, come on, Ahmed, give the copper a fair go. They're not such bad blokes.—Alexander Buzo, *Norm and Ahmed*, p. 20, 1969
- You've always had a fair go from me and you know it.—Barry Oakley, *A Salute to the Great McCarthy*, p. 79, 1970
- You've gotta give the boys from the bush a fair go.—Alexander Buzo, *The Roy Murphy Show*, p. 122, 1970
- Give 'em a fair go, you pot-bellied old germ.—Frank Hardy, *The Outcasts of Foolgarah*, p. 71, 1971
- He recalled coming home from school one day and fighting five white kids who had ganged up on him. Suddenly an Irishwoman came out of a house and intervened, saying, 'Give the poor bugger a fair go!'—Herb Wharton, *Cattle Camp*, p. 75, 1994

fair go!

1 be fair! *AUSTRALIA, 1938*

- 'Now, fair go, mate,' said the bushman. 'That's one thing I won't allow.'—Bill Wannan, *Bullockies, Beauts and Bandicoots*, p. 117, 1960
- A bit of order, fair go, Sam, plenty of time to discuss the form for Saturday later[.]—Frank Hardy, *The Outcasts of Foolgarah*, p. 48, 1971

2 this is true! *NEW ZEALAND*

- Fair go. It really hurts. If you listen, I'll tell you why.—Phillip Wilson, *Pacific Star*, p. 8, 1976

fair go?

indeed? *NEW ZEALAND*

- Fair go? asked Jack, scenting a yarn in Sam's tone.—Barry Crump, *Hang on a Minute, Mate*, p. 149, 1961

fair go, spinner!

in the gambling game two-up, used as a call signifying that the coins are to be tossed *AUSTRALIA, 1945*

- The boxer calls, 'Come in, Spinner,' or sometimes, 'Fair go, Spinner.' —James Holledge, *The Great Australian Gamble*, p. 100, 1966

fairies *noun*

▸ **away with the fairies**

day-dreaming, possibly drug-intoxicated; mentally deranged; out of this world *NEW ZEALAND*

- —David McGill, *David McGill's Complete Kiwi Slang Dictionary*, p. 11, 1998
- Is he away with the fairies? Is he away with you —Gomez, *Las Vegas Dealer*, 1999
- A lot of the old team [...] were either away doing time, away down in Goa or away with the fairies[.] —J.J. Connolly, *Layer Cake*, p. 17, 2000
- [O]nly two could produce relatives who remembered the area pre-war. One of them was so far away with the fairies that she probably bedded down under a toadstool every night. —Liz Evans, *Barking!*, p. 187, 2001
- I did go doolally and away with the fairies for a few weeks. —Jim Drury, *Ian Dury and the Blockheads*, p. 115, 2003

fair play!

used for expressing appreciation *UK*

Probably from the Welsh *chwarae teg*, used as an expression of approval by English-speaking Welsh, and also in its literal translation (fair play).

- You do a hard job well, in my opinion. For not much reward either. Fair play to you. —John King, *White Trash*, p. 256, 2001
- But fair play to old Jay, the birds love 'im. —Ben Elton, *High Society*, p. 119, 2002

fair shake *noun*

▷ **see:** EVEN SHAKE

fair suck of the pineapple!

used for registering surprise or complaint *AUSTRALIA*

A humorous variation of **FAIR CRACK OF THE WHIP**.

- Too right, Kev! Fair suck of the pineapple!!! I got to eat a crust somehow. —Barry Humphries, *Bazza Pulls It Off!*, 1971

fair suck of the sauce bottle!

be fair! *AUSTRALIA*

- Hey, fair suck of the sauce bottle sport. It's me and Blanche doing a feature here. — *The Adventures of Barry McKenzie*, 1972

fair suck of the sauce stick *noun*

fair treatment, equal opportunity *AUSTRALIA*

- —Barry Humphries, *Bazza Pulls It Off!*, 1971

fair to middling *adjective*

average, especially in reply to an inquiry about your health or situation *UK, 1889*

- Is this massive investment in two fair-to-middling personalities a dodge[?]— *The Guardian*, 19th September 2003

fairy *noun*

1 a male homosexual *US, 1895*

- And Susie, the fag, who used to give out bum checks, the dirty fairy. —James T. Farrell, *Saturday Night*, p. 31, 1947
- There are floor shows in which most entertainers are fairies, men playing the female roles. —Jack Lait and Lee Mortimer, *New York Confidential*, p. 67, 1948
- "In the booth, with the fairies" and they all looked guardedly toward a simpering young man in a turtle neck sweater, who sat tightly squeezed between two other young men very much like him. —John Clellon Holmes, *Go*, p. 100, 1952
- I'll show you the fairies in one bar, the Lesbians in another, and then for excitement I'll take you to a bowling alley. —George Mandel, *Flee the Angry Strangers*, p. 209, 1952
- We sat at a table in the Iron Pot and Major said, "Sam, I don't like that fairy at the bar," in a loud voice. —Jack Kerouac, *On the Road*, p. 78, 1957
- I know a few fairies who own an Arts & Crafts Shoppe in the Village. —Hubert Selby Jr, *Last Exit to Brooklyn*, p. 50, 1957
- —Donald Webster Cory and John P. LeRoy, *The Homosexual and His Society*, p. 264, 1963: 'A lexicon of homosexual slang'
- Once, years ago, El Paso had been a crossroads, between the Eastcoast and the Westcoast, for the stray fairies leaving other cities for whatever restless reasons. —John Rechy, *City of Night*, p. 91, 1963
- And taking out that word and putting in the word 'homosexual' or 'fairy,' that would take away, completely, in your opinion, from this story and make it just completely another one? —Lenny Bruce, *How to Talk Dirty and Influence People*, p. 117, 1965
- [T]hey're the same old tired fairies you've seen around since the day one. —Mart Crowley, *The Boys in the Band*, p. 24, 1968
- One of our jocko things is to mince around like a fairy, which is pretty funny sometimes, especially while wearing baseball underwear. —Jim Bouton, *Ball Four*, p. 231, 1970
- All the animals come out at night. Whores, skunk pussies, buggers, queens, fairies, dopers, junkies, sick, venal. — *Taxi Driver*, 1976
- Multicultural Management Program Fellows— *Dictionary of Cautionary Words and Phrases*, 1989
- I'm a fairy too! Hey, I'm a freaking fairy too. —Francesca Lia Block, *I Was a Teenage Fairy*, p. 157, 1998

2 an avionics tradesman in the Royal Air Force *UK, 2002*

fairy dust *noun*

phencyclidine, the recreational drug known as PCP or angel dust *US*

- From the drug's perceived or imagined popularity in the gay community. —Peter Johnson, *Dictionary of Street Alcohol and Drug Terms*, p. 72, 1993

fairy hawk *noun*

a criminal who preys on homosexuals *US*

- [W]hen you have that, you have fairy hawks, muggers that specialize in gays. —Elmore Leonard, *Freaky Deaky*, p. 25, 1988

fairyland *noun*

1 any roadside park *US*

So named because of the belief that homosexuals congregate at roadside parks in search of sexual partners.

- —Montie Tak, *Truck Talk*, p. 58, 1971

2 a colour light multiple aspect gantry (a railway signal) *UK*

- —Harvey Sheppard, *Dictionary of Railway Slang*, 1970

fairy loop *noun*

a cloth loop on the back of a man's shirt *US, 1970*

- Fairy loop or fairy hook would, therefore, represent a leap from the original "fag loop." — *Plain Dealer (Cleveland, Ohio)*, p. E4, 20th December 2001

fairy powder *noun*

any powdered drug *US*

- —Jay Robert Nash, *Dicitonary of Crime*, p. 123, 1992

fairy story; fairy *noun*

Tory (Conservative); a Tory politician *UK*

Rhyming slang.

- Vote fairy[.] —Ray Puxley, *Cockney Rabbit*, 1992

fairy wand *noun*

a cigarette holder *US*

- Baby – sweetheart – would you mind retrieving her fairy-wand ... please ... for a Lady? —John Rechy, *City of Night*, p. 361, 1963

fake *noun*

1 a counterfeit thing, or a person that pretends to be something other than he or she is *UK, 1827*

- UK nuclear evidence a fake. British intelligence claims that Saddam Hussein has been trying to import uranium for a nuclear bomb are unfounded, according to UN nuclear inspectors. — *The Guardian*, 8th March 2003

2 in a magic act, a piece of equipment that has been altered for use in a trick *US*

- —Don Wilmeth, *The Language of American Popular Entertainment*, p. 88, 1981

3 a swindler; a confidence man *UK, 1884*

- He was a pretty good fake in his day[.] —A.S. Jackson, *Gentleman Pimp*, p. 134, 1973

4 a medicine dropper used by an intravenous drug user to inject the drug *US*

At times embellished as 'fakus'.

- Just get the fake out and let's fix. —David Maurer and Victor Vogel, *Narcotics and Narcotic Addiction*, p. 405, 1973

5 an erection *UK*

- —Paul Baker, *Polari*, p. 174, 2002

fake *verb*

1 to deceive *UK, 1859*

- If I was them and a man fake me like I taking them, would I believe him? —Sara Harris, *The Lords of Hell*, p. 55, 1967

2 to falsify for the purposes of deception *UK, 1851*

- Were the lunar landings faked? — *The Guardian*, 13th September 2002

3 to make, to do *UK*

- —Paul Baker, *Polari*, p. 174, 2002

4 to hit *UK, 1933*
Polari.
- I thought he was going to fake him a proper one. —Butch Reynolds, *Broken Hearted Clown*, p. 28, 1953

5 to play music by ear *US, 1926*
- —Arnold Shaw, *Dictionary of American Pop/Rock*, p. 122, 1982

▸ **fake it till you make it**
in twelve-step recovery programmes such as Alcoholics Anonymous, used as a slogan to encourage recovering addicts to modify their behaviour immediately, with their emotional recovery to follow *US*
- —Christopher Cavanaugh, *AA to Z*, p. 89, 1998

fake *adjective*
used in combination with an article to create an artificially constructed article, i.e. fake (hair) for a wig *UK*
- —Paul Baker, *Polari*, p. 174, 2002

fake bake *noun*
a suntan acquired in an indoor tanning booth *US*
- —Connie Eble (Editor), *UNC-CH Campus Slang*, p. 4, Spring 1991

fake book *noun*
a book of chords used by musicians who improvise off the basic chords *US*
- —Clarence Major, *Dictionary of Afro-American Slang*, p. 52, 1970
- I borrowed a fake-book so I could follow the chord changes, since I didn't know any of the tunes. —Frank Zappa, *The Real Frank Zappa Book*, p. 41, 1989

fake it *verb*
usually of a woman, to pretend to experience an orgasm during sexual intercourse *US*
- SALLY: Why? Most women at one time or another have faked it. HARRY: Well, they haven't faked it with me. SALLY: How do you know? —Rob Reiner, *When Harry Met Sally*, 1989

fakement *noun*
1 personal adornment such as jewellery or makeup *UK*
Extends an earlier theatrical sense as 'face-paint'.
- —Paul Baker, *Polari*, p. 174, 2002

2 a thing; used of something the name of which escapes you *UK*
- —Paul Baker, *Polari*, p. 174, 2002

fake out *verb*
to bluff, to dupe *US, 1949*
- Emerson's left end faked out the opposing halfback and dashed toward the corner of the field. —Carolyn Keene, *Nancy's Mysterious Letter*, p. 130, 1968
- I faked out one defenseman, slammed the other so hard he lost his breath[.] —Erich Segal, *Love Story*, p. 114–115, 1970
- McGuire had faked out Vernon by referring to sleights of Scott's that never existed. —David Britland, *Phantoms of the Card Table*, p. 162, 2004

fake riah; fashioned riah *noun*
a wig *UK*
A combination of **FAKE** or 'fashioned' (made/artificial) and **RIAH** (the hair).

fakes *noun*
breast implants *US*
- —Anna Scotti and Paul Young, *Buzzwords*, p. 108, 1997

fakie *noun*
1 in foot-propelled scootering, a travelling backwards manoeuvre, usually performed with only the rear wheel in contact with the ground *UK*
- —Ben Sharpe, *Scooter Crazy*, p. 40, 2000

2 in skateboarding, a travelling-backwards manoeuvre *UK*
- Andy did it pulling a fakie, no more than two feet up a ramp. —Nicholas Blincoe, *Ardwick Green (Disco Biscuits)*, p. 19, 1996

fall *noun*
an arrest and/or conviction *US, 1893*
In the US often formed as 'take a fall', in the UK 'get a fall'.
- Jack had taken a fall on a safe job and was in the Brox County jail, awaiting trial. —William Burroughs, *Junkie*, p. 33, 1953
- With the messenger picking up the money, you know, and that wino to take the fall if there was one. —Jim Thompson, *After Dark, My Sweet*, p. 120–121, 1955
- He had peddled the stuff for Treetop Coulter before he took his first fall[.] —Mickey Spillane, *Return of the Hood*, p. 105, 1964
- On her third night out she took a fall. By 9 A.M. when she faced the judge, it was evident she was a junkie[.] —Babs Gonzales, *I Paid My Dues*, p. 107, 1967
- He says that at home he has every copy of *The Realist* published up to the time of his fall. —Eldridge Cleaver, *Soul on Ice*, p. 46, 1968
- By the time he was twenty-three he had done four bits in the joint. On each fall he had been "jacked up" for either strong-arm robbery or "till tapping." —Iceberg Slim (Robert Beck), *Pimp*, p. 33, 1969
- Things continued to go along pretty rough for me until I took a fall for possession of a five dollar bag of heroin and was sentenced to six months on Rikers Island. —Herbert Huncke, *The Evening Sun Turned Crimson*, p. 57, 1980
- I've taken four falls and never ratted on anyone in my life. —Gerald Petievich, *To Live and Die in L.A.*, p. 132, 1983
- I'm the one that's gonna take the fall if this place is busted. —Terry Williams, *The Cocaine Kids*, p. 46, 1989
- If it was possible to count all the bads guys still in doing a hard fall, but have friends on the outside they could pay the judge back, we'd have to use the walls in there too. —Elmore Leonard, *Maximum Bob*, p. 89, 1991

fall *verb*
1 to be arrested *US, 1873*
- I'd heard that he was busted about 6 months after I fell, but I didn't know they'd sent him down here. —Clarence Cooper Jr, *The Farm*, p. 10, 1967
- Even if they stop us, everybody ain't got to fall. —Donald Goines, *El Dorado Red*, p. 37, 1974
- I got enough bankroll, if you fall, to raise you for murder one with a telephone call. —Iceberg Slim (Robert Beck), *Doom Fox*, p. 30, 1978

2 of police and shop detectives, to arrive *AUSTRALIA*
- Often in "the law falls (or fell)!", the police arrive or make a raid. —*(Sydney) Bulletin*, 26th April 1975

3 to come; to go *US, 1943*
- "Let's fall upsta irs," said the papa bear, "and find out what the skam is." —Steve Allen, *Bop Fables*, p. 10, 1955
- "I'll probably be packing." "Might fall by." —Richard Farina, *Been Down So Long*, p. 23, 1966
- Lar introduced him to Norman (disguised for the occasion in sweatshirt and jeans, and needing a shave) as "a poet friend of mine who just happened to fall by." —Terry Southern, *Now Dig This*, p. 242, 2001

4 to become pregnant *UK, 1722*

▸ **fall into the bottle**
to become a drunkard *US*
- Maybe if I'd talked about it when it happened I wouldn't have fallen into the bottle. —Robert Campbell, *Sweet La-La Land*, p. 40, 1990

▸ **fall off a mango tree**
to be extremely naive *TRINIDAD AND TOBAGO, 1991*
- —Lise Winer, *Dictionary of the English/Creole of Trinidad & Tobago*, 2003

▸ **fall off the roof**
to start the bleed period of the menstrual cycle *US*
- —Connie Eble (Editor), *UNC-CH Campus Slang*, March 1973

▸ **fall on the grenade**
in a social situation, to pay attention to the less attractive of a pair of friends in the hope that your friend will have success with the more attractive member of the pair *US*
- —Connie Eble (Editor), *UNC-CH Campus Slang*, p. 4, October 2002

fall about *verb*
to laugh immoderately *UK, 1967*
- It was, after all, a major part of the variety act that had audiences falling about for 50 years. —*The Guardian*, 9th November 2002

Fallbrook redhair *noun*
marijuana purportedly grown near Fallbrook, California *US*
- —Jay Robert Nash, *Dicitonary of Crime*, p. 124, 1992

fall by *verb*
to visit *US*
- Go slow, and maybe we'll fall by some surprising afternoon. —Richard Farina, *Letter to Peter Tamony*, 3rd March 1965

fall down *verb*
to fail at something *US, 1899*
- [T]he private sector completely fell down on the job, as with the railways[.] —*The Guardian*, 30th December 2003

fallenatnite *noun*
used as a mock scientific name for a stone *CANADA*
- This [B.C.] Department of Highways term describes non-precious stones found on roads throughout the province. It is similar to "leaverite" except that it should be removed. The Geotechnical Branch claims that fallenatnite comes from faults in bedrock. —Tom Parkin, *WetCoast Words*, p. 52, 1989

fallen off the back of a lorry; fell off a lorry; off the back of a lorry *adjective*

stolen (not necessarily from a vehicle) *UK*

A pretence at discretion which advertises a conspiratorial acknowledgment of an article's ill-gotten provenance; well known in the latter half of C20.

- —David Powis, *The Signs of Crime*, 1977
- —Angela Devlin, *Prison Patter*, p. 51, 1996
- [C]limb up on the lorry or open the back door to a van, roll off whatever you see and hope to find something profitable in the wreckage. "Off the back of a lorry" became a term for pilfered goods.—Brian McDonald, *Elephant Boys*, p. 37, 2000
- [P]eople naturally assume it's been nicked from a shop or a factory and don't feel as bad about handing over cash for stuff that's "fallen off the back of a lorry".—Danny King, *The Burglar Diaries*, p. 64, 2001

fall for *verb*

1 to be greatly attracted by someone or something, to fall in love with someone; in a less positive sense, to be taken in by someone or something *US, 1903*

- Paul [McCartney]'s army of female fans were still falling for him.—*The Guardian*, 31st May 2001

2 to become pregnant *UK*

'She'd been married only a couple of months when she fell for it', an army corporal's wife recorded in 1968.

fall guy *noun*

a person who is set up to be blamed for a crime *US, 1904*

From **FALL** (an arrest/a conviction).

- And the eventual opinion in police circles was that the pickpockets had created him, a fictitious fall guy, in the hope of excusing their own misdoings.—Jim Thompson, *Bad Boy*, p. 353, 1953
- They're caught right in the middle of some kind of crazy mob war they can't do a thing about and wouldn't they just love to have a fall guy handy.—Mickey Spillane, *Last Cop Out*, p. 23, 1972
- We know they used you as a patsy, a fall guy.—Edwin Torres, *Carlito's Way*, p. 122, 1975
- —Angela Devlin, *Prison Patter*, p. 51, 1996

fall in *verb*

1 to join; to stay *US*

- "Where'll you go?" "Oh, I'll fall in somewhere."—George Mandel, *Flee the Angry Strangers*, p. 51, 1952
- She said she had other plans for the evening but she would like to fall in some other time.—Herbert Huncke, *The Evening Sun Turned Crimson*, p. 51, 1980

2 in horse racing, to barely hold off challengers and win a race *AUSTRALIA*

- —Ned Wallish, *The Truth Dictionary of Racing Slang*, p. 28, 1989

fall into *verb*

to acquire by chance or without effort *US*

- [W]hen prohibition came on every piss-ant and his brother suddenly fell into big money[.]—Mezz Mezzrow, *Really the Blues*, p. 20, 1946

fall money *noun*

money placed in reserve by a criminal for use if arrested *US, 1893*

- —Franklin W. Dixon, *The Hardy Boys Detective Handbook*, p. 165, 1959

fall on *verb*

to become pregnant *UK*

- As soon at the woman realised she had "fallen on" or "got caught", she would take action [to obtain an abortion].—*New Society*, 15th July 1976

fall out *verb*

1 to be overcome with emotion *US, 1938*

- I fell out and rolled all over the floor laughing.—Chester Himes, *If He Hollers Let Him Go*, p. 2, 1945
- I almost fell out when he invited me to come along with the musicians to the Royal Garden[.]—Mezz Mezzrow, *Really the Blues*, p. 29, 1946
- She fell out when she saw my white Lincoln what I was rolling around in at the time.—Edwin Torres, *Carlito's Way*, p. 67, 1975

2 to lose consciousness due to a drug overdose *US*

- —Lawrence Lipton, *The Holy Barbarians*, p. 316, 1959

fall partner *noun*

a confederate with whom you have been arrested *US, 1969*

- So we got into the place and I told my fall partner, "Let's go, man, everything's packed."—Bruce Jackson, *Outside the Law*, p. 69, 1972

falls *noun*

▸ over the falls

said of a surfer carried over the breaking edge of a wave *US*

- —John Severson, *Modern Surfing Around the World*, p. 175, 1964

fall scratch *noun*

money set aside to cover expenses incurred in the event of an arrest *US*

- You dumb chicken-hearted bitch, whatta you think I got this ass pocket full of "fall" scratch for?—Iceberg Slim (Robert Beck), *Pimp*, p. 66, 1969

fall togs *noun*

conservative, traditional clothing worn by a seasoned criminal on trial to improve his chances with the jury or judge *US*

- —Joseph E. Ragen and Charles Finston, *Inside the World's Toughest Prison*, p. 798, 1962: 'Penitentiary and underworld glossary'

fall up *verb*

to go to *US, 1952*

- He and the cat had fallen up to Vickie's and she had turned them on.—Herbert Huncke, *The Evening Sun Turned Crimson*, p. 54, 1980

false!

used for expressing doubt about the truth of the matter just asserted *US*

- —Pamela Munro, *U.C.L.A. Slang*, p. 37, 1989

false alarm *noun*

the arm *UK*

Rhyming slang, always used in its full form to avoid confusion with 'falses' and **FALSIES** (breast enhancements).

- —Ray Puxley, *Cockney Rabbit*, 1992

falsie basket *noun*

crotch padding worn by males to project the image of a large penis *US*

- They all wear enormous falsie baskets.—William Burroughs, *Naked Lunch*, p. 135, 1957

falsies *noun*

pads that aggrandise the apparent size of a girl or woman's breasts *US, 1943*

- She had a big nose and her nails were all bitten down and bleedy-looking and she had on those damn falsies that point all over the place, but you felt sort of sorry for her.—J.D. Salinger, *Catcher in the Rye*, p. 3, 1951
- [M]ost of them wear those damn falsies that stick out all over the place and I'd rather be caught dead than be a phony about a thing like your bosom.—Frederick Kohner, *Gidget*, p. 10, 1957
- I'm bowlegged, bony-hipped, scaly, hairy, wear falsies and spew bad breath.—Robert Gover, *The Maniac Responsible*, p. 129, 1963
- Down but not out, she took up smoking and drinking and wearing falsies on account of being in love until the end of Time Immemorial with Joe Grubner[.]—John Nichols, *The Sterile Cuckoo*, p. 15, 1965
- I was really getting sick of looking at all those teensy dolls with falsies propped up in this dump.—Eve Babitz, *Eve's Hollywood*, p. 71, 1974
- If you don't make good, I'll stay up all night thinking of Arthur-Arlene's falsies.—James Ellroy, *Blood on the Moon*, p. 99, 1984

falsitude *noun*

a lie *US*

- —Don R. McCreary (Editor), *Dawg Speak*, 2001

falsy *noun*

a chipped marble *TRINIDAD AND TOBAGO*

- —Lise Winer, *Dictionary of the English/Creole of Trinidad & Tobago*, 2003

fam *noun*

1 the hand *UK, 1699*

English gypsy use.

- —Jimmy Stockin, *On The Cobbles*, p. 10, 2000

2 a family *AUSTRALIA*

Also recorded in the US.

- [H]eaps of food stalls for the fam.—*Beat*, p. 18, 9th July 1996
- —Ethan Hilderbrant, *Prison Slang*, p. 47, 1998

family *noun*

a group of prostitutes and their pimp *US*

- "Her old man got one-to-three in the joint for burglary. She wants to join our family."—Iceberg Slim (Robert Beck), *Pimp*, p. 208, 1969
- I felt deep down in my heart that I could now sit back, relax, and enjoy the silky life and get my family of four girls in order.—A.S. Jackson, *Gentleman Pimp*, p. 81–82, 1973

family *adjective*

homosexual *US*

- —Kevin Dilallo, *The Unofficial Gay Manual*, p. 240, 1994
- I just found out my boss was family ... and to think I have talked about hockey scores for the past six months to throw him off! —Jeff Fessler, *When Drag Is Not a Car Race*, p. 36, 1997
- "Also family," says Josef. "Family" means homosexual in gay slang. —Bart Luirink (translated by Loes Nas), *Moffies*, p. 118, 2000

▸ **in the family way**

pregnant *UK, 1796*

- Those who dabble in bawdy pleasures can often find themselves in the family way before long[.] — *The Guardian*, 6th April 2004

family jewels *noun*

the male genitals *US, 1922*

- The first time he saw Carl, Lee thought, "I could use that, if the family jewels weren't in pawn to Uncle Junk [heroin]." —William Burroughs, *Queer*, p. 21, 1985

family pot *noun*

in poker, a hand in which most of the players are still betting at the end of the hand *US*

- —Anthony Holden, *Big Deal*, p. 300, 1990

family reunion *noun*

in trucking, a meeting of several drivers for one company at a truck stop *US*

- —Montie Tak, *Truck Talk*, p. 58, 1971

family-style *adjective*

(used of parts in a manufacturing plant) stored together *US*

- — *American Speech*, p. 226, October 1955: 'An aircraft production dispatcher's vocabulary'

famine *noun*

a lack of availability of an addictive drug *US*

- —Jay Robert Nash, *Dicitonary of Crime*, p. 125, 1992

famous dimes *noun*

crack cocaine *US*

- —US Department of Justice, *Street Terms*, October, 1994

Famous Fourth *nickname*

the Fourth Army Division, US Army *US*

- —Linda Reinberg, *In the Field*, p. 77, 1991

famous last words

a catchphrase used as an expression of doubt regarding the certainty of whatever has just been promised *UK, 1948*

- ROSE: At chemmy it's bancos. The banks won't run. NONA: Famous last words. —Terence Rattigan, *Variation on a Theme*, 1951

fan *noun*

1 the preliminary touching of a targeted victim by a pickpocket *US*

- — *New York Times Magazine*, p. 88, 16th March 1958

2 crack cocaine *US*

- —Peter Johnson, *Dictionary of Street Alcohol and Drug Terms*, p. 72, 1993

fan *verb*

to beat; to spank *UK, 1785*

- I'm in hot enough already, and Sam'll really fan me if I get him in trouble. —Irving Shulman, *The Amboy Dukes*, p. 111, 1947

fanac *noun*

an activity for a serious fan *US*

- — *American Speech*, p. 53, Spring 1978: 'Star Trek lives: trekker slang'

fananny whacker *noun*

a person who cheats at marbles by encroaching over the shooting line *AUSTRALIA*

- —Jim Ramsay, *Cop It Sweet!*, p. 35, 1977

fananny whacking *noun*

cheating at marbles by edging your hand over the shooting line *AUSTRALIA*

- Our rules included no 'fananny wacking', fudging or cribbing. Fananny wacking is pushing your hand forward as you fire. You have to keep your hand still. —Cathy Hope, *Themes from the Playground*, p. 3, 1985

fan belt inspector *noun*

an agent of the Federal Bureau of Investigations *US*

A back formation from the initials FBI. Collected from an FBI informer in Bakersfield, California, in 1971.

- Ever since the disaster at the Branch Davidian compound in Waco, he referred to the FBI as "fan belt inspectors" because in his opinion only a bunch of dumb-ass grease monkeys could have let so many children get killed. —Larry Simmons, *Broken Seals*, p. 113, 2001

fancom *noun*

a convention put on by fans *US, 1976*

- — *American Speech*, p. 53, Spring 1978: 'Star Trek lives: trekker slang'

fancy *noun*

a man's dress shirt with a coloured pattern *US*

- —Rachel S. Epstein and Nina Liebman, *Biz Speak*, p. 80, 1986

fancy *verb*

1 to desire, to wish for, to want *UK, 1598*

- Plum eventually became the most cosmopolitan of dogs: she fancied riding in taxicabs and loved being the center of attention[.] —Shirlee Kalstone, *How to Housebreak Your Dog in 7 Days*, p. 59, 1985

2 to desire sexually; to find sexually attractive *UK*

From the more general sense, 'to desire'; the sexual shadings were evident by Shakespeare's time. It slipped into current usage towards the end of C19.

- [P]retty pictures to provoke the fancy[.] —James Shirley, *The Lady of Pleasure*, 1635
- [S]he'd known he fancied her within a few minutes of talking to him in the hospital, felt the same way herself[.] —John King, *White Trash*, p. 252, 2001

▸ **fancy the muff off; fancy the tits off; fancy the pants off**

to find a woman extremely desirable *UK*

Intensification of FANCY (to desire) by specifiying MUFF (the vagina), TIT(S) (the female breasts) or 'pants' (underwear).

- [Y]ou could sit with her and merrily admit that you fancy the pants off her and no harm meant luv. —James Hawes, *Dead Long Enough*, p. 30, 2000
- She knew me from school and I'd always fancied the muff off her. —Mark Powell, *Snap*, p. 126, 2001

▸ **fancy your chances; fancy your chance**

to presume that your charm or skill will suffice to achieve success *UK*

- Aylen he saw as a skiving bastard who fancied his chance, so he was out to needle him whenever he could. —Colin Evans, *The Heart of Standing*, 1962

▸ **fancy yourself**

to have too high an opinion of yourself (probably) *UK, 1866*

Shortened from the conventional 'fancy yourself as' or 'fancy yourself to be something'.

fancy!; fancy that!

used as an exclamation of surprise *UK, 1813*

Often as an imperative; however, when spoken disinterestedly, it may be used to quench another's excitement.

- [I]f something on the web seems too stupid to be true, it probably is. Just fancy that! — *The Guardian*, 11th August 2003

fancy boy *noun*

in poker, a draw in the hope of completing a hand that is extremeley unlikely *US*

- —Albert H. Morehead, *The Complete Guide to Winning Poker*, p. 262, 1967

fancy Dan *noun*

an elegant, conceited man *US, 1943*

- Jake was a real Fancy Dan, but he was generous with all his old friends[.] —Reginald Hill, *Pictures of Perfection*, p. 71, 1994

fancy-Dan *adjective*

pretentious *US, 1938*

- I know this is one of those fancy-Dan rooms that don't serve booze while the act is on, so set up a few bottles of the grape fast, before it's too late. —Jacqueline Susann, *Valley of the Dolls*, p. 295, 1966

fancy man *noun*

a man who lives off the earnings of a prostitute or several prostitutes; a male lover *UK, 1811*

- Many of the girls who won't service blacks have black "fancy men" waiting for them in Cadillacs when they leave the houses for a week off. —Gerald Paine, *A Bachelor's Guide to the Brothels of Nevada*, p. 92, 1978
- I'm gonna kill my baby / And blast and blast her fancy man. — Dr Feelgood, *Shotgun Blues*, 1979

fancy pants *noun*

a dandy; a pretentious, superior, self-important person *US, 1934*

- Hauser was an intellectual fancy pants who was using the labor movement merely as a springboard[.] — Clancy Sigal, *Going Away*, p. 361, 1961
- The art of pebbledashing went out of fashion a long time ago." Well, la-di-dah. Thus Miss Fancy-pants introduces Michael Landy's latest work[.] — *The Daily Telegraph*, 29th May 2004

Fancy Pants *nickname*

Anthony Joseph 'A. J.' Hoyt (b.1935), a stock car racing driver who dominated the sport in the US during the 1950s and 60s *US*

Because of Hoyt's fastidious dressing habits, alluding to a Bob Hope film of the era.

fancy woman *noun*

a kept mistress; a female lover *UK, 1812*

Often used of a man's woman friend to disapprove of an implied immorality.

- Len pushed off to Essex with his fancy woman some decades earlier. — *The Guardian*, 1st March 2003

fandabidozi!

wonderful! *UK, 1978*

A catchphrase coined by comedy double-act The Krankies; it has some (mainly ironic) currency. Seen, in 2004, as the slogan on a tee-shirt and the message on a greetings card.

fan dancer *noun*

a sexual dancer who employs a large fan in her dance *US, 1936*

A type of striptease performer, most famously exemplified by Sally Rand (real name Harriet Helen 'Hazel' Gould Beck), who popularised the style at the 1933 Chicago Century of Progress World Fair.

- [T]he strippers have finally divided themselves into three classes: "fan-dancers," who keep up the pretense of hiding their nakedness as they enlarge it. — Jack Lait and Lee Mortimer, *Chicago Confidential*, p. 158, 1950
- Sally Rand, who is still a star, and the late Faith Bacoln, are described as fan dancers, not to be confused with stripping, though many peelers do both and call themselves "exotic dancers." — Lee Mortimer, *Women Confidential*, p. 134, 1960
- — Don Wilmeth, *The Language of American Popular Entertainment*, p. 89, 1981

fandangee *adjective*

overdressed or otherwise assuming an air of superiority *TRINIDAD AND TOBAGO*

- — Lise Winer, *Dictionary of the English/Creole of Trinidad & Tobago*, 2003

faned *noun*

the editor of a single-interest fan magazine *US*

- — *American Speech*, p. 26, Spring 1982: 'The langage of science fiction fan magazines'

fanfic *noun*

further stories and adventures for characters in familiar television programmes and films written for pleasure by fans of the original, especially widespread on the Internet *US, 1998*

From '*fan fic*tion'.

- Barry Trotter and the Order of the Penis dealt with Barry's stormy puberty and fueled an ocean of inaccurately-erotic fanfic, as well as breaking all sales figures for the printed word. — Michael Gerber, *Barry Trotter and the Unauthorized Parody*, p. 112, 2001

fan fuck *noun*

a heterosexual pornographic film in which male fans of the female pornography star are selected to have sex with her *US*

- First, you join the club of the star who is hosting the "fan fuck." Then you can request an application form, fill it out, and mail it back with a photo of yourself. — Ana Loria, *1 2 3 Be A Porn Star!*, p. 66, 2000

fang *noun*

1 a bite *AUSTRALIA*

- After ordering a bottle of the local poison and prior to taking an initial fang, I noticed that certain hieroglyphics were sketched on the wrapping paper. — Martin Cameron, *A Look at the Bright Side*, 1988

2 eating *AUSTRALIA*

- Yer good on the fang, mate. — Nino Culotta (John O'Grady), *They're A Weird Mob*, p. 109, 1957
- Now, I'm big on the fang when it comes to barbecues[.] — Rex Hunt, *Tall Tales – and True*, p. 112, 1994

3 a drive taken at high speed *AUSTRALIA*

From **FANG** (to drive fast).

- If I were one of the back room boys, you wouldn't see me here before noon. I'd be down by the pool or out for a fang in the Jag. — Alexander Buzo, *Front Room Boys*, p. 20, 1970

fang *verb*

1 to drive fast *AUSTRALIA*

Said to be from Juan Fangio, 1911–95, Argentine racing car driver, but since the 'g' in Fangio is pronounced as a 'j' some question is thrown over this origin.

- Let's hop in the B and fang up to the beach. — Alexander Buzo, *Rooted*, p. 36, 1969
- Candy and Johnny, reckless young bandits in lurve, pull off a robbery with the help of two depraved men in uniform, and fang into the desert in a big car. — *Sydney Morning Herald*, 4th March 2002

2 to yell furiously *US*

- They only bumped fenders, but the drivers were really fanging each other. — *American Speech*, p. 268, December 1962: 'The language of traffic policemen'

fang down *verb*

to eat *AUSTRALIA*

- Earthlings eat animal and vegetable, ayles [aliens] fang down on mineral. — Linda Jaivin, *Rock n Roll Babes from Outer Space*, p. 84, 1996

fang man *noun*

a man who is a hearty eater *AUSTRALIA*

- Len Muller of Brisbane, noted fang man on crabs, couldn't believe his eyes while travelling down to the mouth of Cribb Island Creek[.] — Bob Staines, *Wot a Whopper*, p. 34, 1982

fangs *noun*

musical ability *US, 1958*

An outgrowth of 'chops'.

- — Robert S. Gold, *A Jazz Lexicon*, p. 101, 1964

▸ put the fangs in

to ask for a loan of money *AUSTRALIA, 1919*

- 'Putting the bite on' somebody is also 'putting the fangs in'. — John O'Grady, *Aussie English*, p. 39, 1965

fan key *noun*

the command key on a Macintosh computer *US*

From the symbol on the key, which can be seen to resemble the blades of a fan.

- — Andy Ihnatko, *Cyberspeak*, p. 69, 1997

fanner *noun*

1 a pickpocket *US*

Likely a variant of **FINGER**.

- — *The New American Mercury*, p. 707, 1950

2 a fan dancer *US*

- — Don Wilmeth, *The Language of American Popular Entertainment*, p. 88, 1981

fanners

in a child's game, pronounced to ward off another child's claim to half of something *CANADA*

The game, under the name 'halfies' or 'halvers', is listed in the *Oxford English Dictionary* as 'very old'.

- Halvers is the child's term that stakes his or her claim to half of what you have. Your only protection is to say fanners before they can say halvers. — Chris Thain, *Cold as a Bay Street Banker's Heart*, p. 80, 1987

fanny *noun*

1 the vagina *UK, 1879*

A popular female name, possibly combined with the vulvic symbolism of a fan-light (a loosely triangular opening). It is worth noting that John Cleland's *The Memoirs of Fanny Hill* features a sexually active heroine; however its publication in 1749 is about a hundred years before 'fanny' came to be used in this sense.

- The Duke reckons 'er religion 'as got side tracked and made a blow lamp of her fanny. — Robert S. Close, *Love Me Sailor*, p. 138, 1945
- 'You know, those new-fangled monthly rags, shaped like a white mouse with a tail on it. You know, the ones they shove up their fanny. — Frank Hardy, *The Outcasts of Foolgarah*, p. 149, 1971
- At least that was him off my back, or rather my fanny, for a good eighteen months. — Jenny v, *Camberwell Beauty*, p. 77, 2000
- Nice kid, that Nadia. Nice, tight, gushy fanny. — Kevin Sampson, *Outlaws*, p. 41, 2001
- — *Journal of Sex Research*, p. 146, 2001
- My fanny couldn't get wet. — *Sky Magazine*, p. 60, July 2001
- — Lise Winer, *Dictionary of the English/Creole of Trinidad & Tobago*, 2003

2 a woman objectified sexually *UK*

From the previous sense.

- "There's a group of half a dozen lads [...]" "Fanny?" "Yeah, a few bits and pieces.["] — Colin Butts, *Is Harry on the Boat?*, p. 111, 1997
- A real waste of decent fanny. — John King, *Human Punk*, p. 9, 2000
- Thought you'd still be shacked up with that fanny. What happened? — Niall Griffiths, *Kelly + Victor*, p. 43, 2002

3 the buttocks *US, 1919*

- —Gloria Thomas, *Ten Minute Trim Tummies & Shapely Fannies*, 2001

4 a story, lies *UK, 1933*

- Although a lot of this was Dutch [unintelligible language] to me at the time, my friend knew how to "tell the fanny"[.]—Butch Reynolds, *Broken Hearted Clown*, p. 31, 1953
- [He] span a fanny about how he was expecting a friend from the North[.]—Charles Raven, *Underworld Nights*, p. 37, 1956
- His name was Kenny Mac and he was the size of tuppence, but he could give some old fanny.—Lenny McLean, *The Guv'nor*, p. 79, 1998
- Lying through his teeth, he assured her that he had finished with Geraldine, that she had meant nothing to him anyway, he was just using her for sex – the usual old fanny.—Garry Bushell, *The Face*, p. 192, 2001

fanny *verb*

to talk glibly, especially to talk until a crowd has gathered *UK*
Recorded in use among market traders.

- —*John o' London's Weekly*, 4th March 1949

fanny about; fanny around *verb*

to waste time, to idle *UK, 1971*

- I fannied about deciding what to wear on top.—Jenny Eclair, *Camberwell Beauty*, p. 355, 2000
- Fuck this. Fannyin around. I finish the bottle[.]—Niall Griffiths, *Kelly + Victor*, p. 173, 2002

Fanny Adams; sweet Fanny Adams; sweet Miss Adams; sweet FA; FA; fanny *noun*

nothing at all *UK, 1914*
From the brutal and maniacal murder, on 24th August 1867, of 8-year-old Fanny Adams, at Alton in Hampshire. Parts of her body were found over several days in different parts of the rural countryside. Upset with the tinned mutton that they were being served, British sailors in 1869 began to refer to the tins as containing the butchered contents of 'Sweet Fanny Adams'. It evolved into a suggestion of 'fuck', or 'nothing', and has been used in that sense in the C20.

- MILLIGAN: Buy us a drink, Jim; go on, be a pal. TATLOR: You'll get sweet Fanny Adams; you're half cut already.—Graeme Kent, *The Queen's Corporal [Six Granada Plays]*, p. 82, 1959
- Oh, he is such a useless drip. Look at the way he hedged in bunch like that. Hell, we started out with the idea of reinstating the man and ended up doing absolutely fanny adams at all.—Geoffrey Wagner, *The Asphalt Campus*, 1963
- A bloke can sometimes do it for sweet Fanny Adams!—Barry Humphries, *Bazza Pulls It Off!*, 1971
- They got sweet FA.—David Peace, *Nineteen Seventy Four*, p. 4, 1999
- I don't believe there's a God who says, If you drink, do drugs and swear and rob houses you're not sitting on my cloud. It's all cock. It's all fanny.—*Q*, p. 100, May 2002

fanny batter *noun*

vaginal secretions *UK*

- [A] fanny batter bobsleigh.—Phil Jupitus, *Never Mind The Buzzcocks*, 14th January 2002

fannyboo *noun*

the vagina *US*
Childish elaboration of **FANNY** (the vagina).

- There's [a...] "mongo," a "pajama," "fannyboo," "mushmellow," "a ghoulie["].]—Eve Ensler, *The Vagina Monologues*, p. 6, 1998

Fanny Cradock; Fanny Craddock *noun*

a haddock *UK*
Rhyming slang, formed from the name of Fanny Cradock, 1909–94, still remembered as the intimidating (now iconic) presenter of 1950s and 60s television cookery programmes; the second version, as recorded by Ray Puxley in 1992, is a popular misspelling of her name.

fanny fart *noun*

an eruption of trapped air from the vagina, usually during sexual intercourse *AUSTRALIA*

- [S]he could also execute fanny farts.—Kathy Lette, *Girls' Night Out*, p. 58, 1987
- We do fanny farts. We can't help it.—Annie Evans, *An A-Z of Rude Health*, 18th January 2002

fanny farter *noun*

a woman who can execute fanny farts *AUSTRALIA*

- I was an apprentice fanny farter[.]—Kathy Lette, *Girls' Night Out*, p. 64, 1987

fanny-flaps *noun*

the vaginal labia *UK*

- —Chris Lewis, *The Dictionary of Playground Slang*, p. 87, 2003

Fanny Hill *noun*

a pill, especially 'the pill' (a contraceptive) *UK*
Rhyming slang, formed from the title of John Cleland's erotic novel *The Memoirs of Fanny Hill*, 1749. Presumed to be a 1960s coinage as Cleland's classic was controversially republished at the same time as the contraceptive pill was being introduced.

- —Ray Puxley, *Cockney Rabbit*, 1992

Fanny Hill *nickname*

the Los Angeles County women's jail *US*

- The Los Angeles women's jail, Sybil Brand Institute, is perched high up over the San Bernadino Freeway. The cops called it Fanny Hill.—Joseph Wambaugh, *The Glitter Dome*, p. 114, 1981

fanny lip *noun*

the vaginal lips; the *labium majora* or *minora* *UK*
A combination of **FANNY** (the vagina; the vulva) and the conventional translation of 'labium'; generally in the plural.

- Flap dancin' I call it 'cos if you're lucky they give you the full two sets of fanny lips even though they in't s'posed to[.]—Ben Elton, *High Society*, p. 119, 2002

fanny merchant *noun*

a glib talker *UK*

- It reminded him of the corpses-in-waiting you saw on the telly at Conservative Party conferences, chuckling vacantly at some fanny merchant's dismal, scripted one-liner.—Christopher Brookmyre, *Not the End of the World*, p. 96, 1998

fanny on; fanny *verb*

to talk with the intention to persuade or deceive *UK, 1949*

- Mooney had been fannying on all the time about me joining his lodge.—Jake Arnott, *He Kills Coppers*, p. 75, 2001

fanny pelmet *noun*

a very short skirt *UK*

- She'd abandoned the fanny pelmet but the sussies [suspenders] were still in place.—Kitty Churchill, *Thinking of England*, p. 119, 1995

fanny quack *noun*

a gynaecologist *UK*
A combination of **FANNY** (the vagina) and **QUACK** (a doctor).

- Down one side, down the other, then she moved her knees up and there she was waiting for me. Examined her like I was a straight up fanny quack.—Jeremy Cameron, *Brown Bread in Wengen*, p. 52, 1999

fanny rag *noun*

a sanitary towel *AUSTRALIA*

- —Thommo, *The Dictionary of Australian Swearing and Sex Sayings*, p. 42, 1985

fan on *verb*

to decline an offer *US*

- —Vann Wesson, *Generation X Field Guide and Lexicon*, p. 64, 1997

fanoogie; fenugie *noun*

during the Vietnam war, a soldier freshly arrived in Vietnam *US*
A back formation from **FNG** (**FUCKING NEW GUY**).

- —Linda Reinberg, *In the Field*, p. 78, 1991
- Franks was what the troops called a "fanoogie," abbreviated as FNG and standing for "f'ing new guy." It was a way for veterans to set themselves apart from the newcomers and to tell the new guys that they had lots to learn[.]—Tom Clancy with Fred Franks Jr, *Into the Storm*, p. 26, 1991

fantabulosa; fabulosa *adjective*

wonderful *UK*
Arch elaborations of 'fabulous'.

- SANDY: Oh fantabulosa! But I think the ceiling will have to go[.]—Barry Took and Marty Feldman, *Round The Horne*, 21st April 1967
- —Paul Baker, *Polari*, p. 174, 2002
- —*Attitude*, p. 60, July 2003: 'Old palare lexicon'

fantabulous *adjective*

very good *US, 1958*
A blend of 'fantastic' and 'fabulous'. Contemporary UK gay usage.

- —*San Francisco Examiner*, p. III-2, 22nd March 1960
- A fantabulous night to make romance / 'Neath the cover of October skies.—Van Morrison, *Moondance*, 1970
- I managed to catch a fantabulous Malay bitch named Daisy and a place to hang my hat.—Odie Hawkins, *Ghetto Sketches*, p. 84, 1972
- "Fantabulous!" squealed Connie. "How long you here for?" —Armistead Maupin, *Tales of the City*, p. 3, 1978
- —*Attitude*, p. 60, July 2003: 'New palare lexicon'

fantasia *noun*

1 a variety of MDMA, the recreational drug best known as ecstasy *UK*

- —Angela Devlin, *Prison Patter*, p. 51, 1996

2 DMT (dimethyltryptamine), a powerful but short-lasting hallucinogen *UK*

- —Harry Shapiro, *Recreational Drugs*, p. 292, 2004

fantastic *adjective*

excellent, almost excellent, very good, merely good *US, 1929*

- To come off the bench and score was fantastic, something really wonderful.—*The Guardian*, 13th June 2002

fantastic buy *noun*

in poker, a card drawn to make a strong hand in a heavily bet situation *US*

- —George Percy, *The Language of Poker*, p. 33, 1988

fantasy *noun*

the recreational drug GHB *US*

Coined, no doubt, as an attractive marketing brand; it also stresses GHB's relation to **FANTASIA** (**ECSTASY**).

- I bumped into Shaun Ryder who gave me a fantasy tablet.—John Robb, *The Nineties*, p. 149, 1999

fantidilysastic *adjective*

great *NEW ZEALAND*

A teenage invention of the 1960s.

- —David McGill, *David McGill's Complete Kiwi Slang Dictionary*, p. 44, 1998

fanzine *noun*

an inexpensively self-published magazine devoted to such topics as hobbies, music, film and politics *US, 1949*

A combination of 'fantasy' and 'magazine'; originally a magazine produced for science fiction fans but adopted by and produced by fans of any topic imaginable.

- —*American Speech*, October 1952
- —*American Speech*, p. 53, Spring 1978: 'Star Trek lives: trekker slang'
- Examples are Thunder Road (the Bruce Springsteen fanzine) and Relix (the Grateful Dead fanzine).—Jay Saporita, *Pourin' It All Out*, p. 203, 1980
- Self publication had been a method closely associated with several art movements [...] The explosion of fanzines in response to punk rock established these publications as youth culture media.—Marion Leonard, *Cool Places*, p. 103, 1998

FAQ *noun*

*f*requently *a*sked *q*uestions *US*

A real-life acquisition from the Internet, where FAQ files were created as a resource of informative and regularly updated information; gently punning on 'fact'. On-screen the acronym is both singular and plural; in speech the plural is generally indicated by the addition of an 's'.

- "So you want to do the FAQs right away?" "The what?" "The FAQs. Frequently-asked-questions." "I'm not sure if I have any questions." "Oh, OK."—Lee Child, *The Visitor*, p. 124, 2000

FAR *noun*

a hard and fast rule *US*

- They are not negotiable. Franks calls such items FARs – "flat-ass rules."—Tom Clancy, *Into the Storm*, p. 189, 1991

far and near *noun*

beer *UK*

Rhyming slang; glossed as C19, but remains a familiar term, perhaps because of its neat reversal with **NEAR AND FAR** (a bar).

- —Julian Franklyn, *A Dictionary of Rhyming Slang*, 1960
- —Ray Puxley, *Cockney Rabbit*, 1992

farang *noun*

a foreigner *US*

Vietnamese, borrowed by US soldiers.

- —Linda Reinberg, *In the Field*, p. 77, 1991

fare *noun*

a prostitute's client *UK, 1959*

Both heterosexual and homosexual usage.

- —Angela Devlin, *Prison Patter*, p. 51, 1996

fark

'fuck', in all its senses *AUSTRALIA*

The word 'fuck' as filtered through the Australian accent.

- (He continues [gardening] for a while, then stops suddenly, in pain and bent over at a fixed angle at the hips.) Faaarrk.—Jack Hibberd, *A Stretch of the Imagination*, p. 23, 1971
- 'Farkin' hell!'—David Foster, *Plumbum*, p. 56, 1983
- Fark! said the cockatoo in its cage.—Tim Winton, *Cloudstreet*, p. 133, 1991
- Experts reckon that now our bastard drought has broken, roaches will breed like buggery and we'll stand no farkin' chance.—*Picture*, 5th February 1992
- And if this year's show is anything to go by, that'll be a dead farkin' cert.—*Picture*, 7th December 1994
- Faark! (Sorry, I had to say that 'cause this word is a major part of Australian surfer's dialect.)—*Tracks*, p. 51, 1996
- Tanith, and her typewriter put this zine together, and it is so farken cool.—*Hairball Goulash*, p. 26, 1998

farm *noun*

▸ **back to the farm**

laid off due to lack of work *US*

- —Norman Carlisle, *The Modern Wonder Book of Trains and Railroading*, p. 258, 1946

farmer *noun*

an unsophisticated person *US, 1864*

- —Kenn "Naz" Young, *Naz's Underground Dictionary*, p. 28, 1973

▸ **I could eat a farmer's arse through a hedge**

used as a declaration of great hunger *UK: SCOTLAND*

- Ah could eat a farmer's arse through a hedge[.]—Michael Munro, *The Patter, Another Blast*, 1988

Farmer Giles; farmers *noun*

haemorrhoids *UK*

Rhyming slang for 'piles'. Used in Australia and the UK.

- —Mary Durack, *Keep Him My Country*, p. 351, 1955
- The late Monsewer Eddie Gray, in drag as a gypsy clairvoyant, used to invite questions from the audience... more accurately, planted Moulin Rouges – stooges – and to the query "How would you help the farmers?" he replied, "I'm a fortune-teller not a chemist."—Red Daniells, 1980
- [W]hen Mo complains bitterly in EastEnders (BBC1) about her farmers, they are not, as I thought, her farmer's onions/bunions. Rather, her farmer Giles.—*The Guardian*, p. 22, 10th June 2003

farmer's set *noun*

in dominoes, the 6–4 piece *US*

- —Dominic Armanino, *Five-up Domino Games*, p. 2, 1964

farmer tan *noun*

a suntanned face, neck and lower arms *US*

- Has one of those farmer tans. You see Buddy in the shower, his face and arms have color but his body's pure white.—Elmore Leonard, *Out of Sight*, p. 43, 1996

farm out *verb*

to delegate to another *UK*

- Klein with a scruffy young lawyer with the public defender's office who apparently had drawn the short straw when they farmed out Ernesto Cabal's case.—Carl Hiaasen, *Tourist Season*, p. 37, 1986

farmyard confetti *noun*

nonsense *AUSTRALIA, 1973*

A probable play on **BULLSHIT**; a later variation of **COW**(**YARD**) **CONFETTI** and **FLEMINGTON CONFETTI**.

far out *adjective*

1 excellent, innovative, creative, daring *US, 1954*

Originally a jazz term with an emphasis on 'experimental', and then in general use with a more general meaning.

- Yes, but I heard the group was too far out for the West Coast crowds.—*The Sound*, p. 127, 1961
- He said we gassed him, but we were too far out for the people.—Babs Gonzales, *I Paid My Dues*, p. 40, 1967
- I had never seen him before but yesterday morning Gloria Gordon (who is in my Empathy I class) told me he gave "far-out" parties[.] —Gore Vidal, *Myra Breckinridge*, p. 59, 1968
- The cat on drums, he is so far out (far in, he said last night).—*East Village Other*, 20th August 1969
- "Far out!," D.R. exclaimed. "Far out!"—Gurney Norman, *Divine Right's Trip (Last Whole Earth Catalog)*, p. 29, 1971
- What has happened to me the past couple of weeks is so weird even a far-out cat like you wouldn't believe it.—Tom Robbins, *Another Roadside Attraction*, p. 75, 1971
- People like Sinatra and Dean Martin are still considered "far out" in Vegas.—Hunter S. Thompson, *Fear and Loathing in Las Vegas*, p. 156, 1971
- I mean, friends and neighbors, I mean he [Neal Cassady] was far out, just one hell of a hero and the tales of his exploits will always be blowing around us...—*The Last Supplement to the Whole Earth Catalog*, p. 84, March 1971
- STEPHANIE: So why did you say "far out?" TONY: It sounded like "far out." It was "far out," wasn't it?—*Saturday Night Fever*, 1977

2 drug-intoxicated *US*

- I smoked three in a gas station lavatory but they did nothing. I was not at all far out, or unattached. —Clancy Sigal, *Going Away*, p. 366, 1961
- [W]hen you're a little too far out – moving your feet would be dangerous and even ungainly. —Tony Wilson, *24 Hour Party People*, p. 210, 2002

farshtinkener; fushtookanah *adjective*

stinking *US*

From German to Yiddish to American slang.

- At a dinner party, a farshtinkener anti-Semite, recounting his trip to central Africa, said, "It was wonderful. I didn't run into a single pig or Jew. —Leo Rosten, *The Joys of Yiddish*, p. 114, 1968
- David Douglas Klein, the 'Douglas' a dead giveaway you are not of my kindred blood, you farshtinkener Dutch fuck. —James Ellroy, *White Jazz*, p. 61, 1992
- I did an airtight job on that fushtookanah script[.] —Joel Rose, *Kill Kill Faster Faster*, p. 188, 1997

farsighted *adjective*

said of a restaurant waiter or waitress who is intentionally ignoring a customer signalling for service *US*

- —*Maledicta*, p. 47, 1995: 'Door whore and other New Mexico restaurant slang'

far south *noun*

Antarctica *ANTARCTICA, 1881*

- —Bernadette Hince, *The Antarctic Dictionary*, p. 125, 2000

fart *noun*

1 an anal emission of gases *UK, 1386*

From Chaucer in 1386 through to the present day.

- I'm going to hang around like a fart in a Volkswagen[.] —Ivor Biggun, *The Winker's Paradise*, 1978

2 an unlikeable, even contemptible person *UK, 1891*

- Well, Coughlin, you old fart, what you been doin? —Jack Kerouac, *The Dharma Bums*, p. 23, 1958
- This ol' fart Blastic, heh's comin' to pieces befo' my very eyes. —Ken Kesey, *One Flew Over the Cuckoo's Nest*, p. 31, 1962
- He sure was one pissed-off old fart, but he was a smart old fart too. —Mickey Spillane, *Last Cop Out*, p. 160, 1972
- Some of them old farts out three, four days a time, you don't say squat to them. —*Saturday Night Fever*, 1977
- He's got some gadgets you old farts maybe never heard of. —*Gone in 60 Seconds*, 2000

3 used as a symbol of contempt *UK, 1685*

- [T]he Minister for Public Transport does not give a fart for forest land in Leyton. —Harry Cohen, *Hansard (United Kingdom Parliament)*, 15th March 1989

▸ a fart in a windstorm

a fuss made over something unimportant *CANADA, 1963*

The *Dictionary of American Regional English* gives several variations on this phrase, including 'fart in a whirlwind', but in this form only since 1963.

- Equivalent to the widely known "mountain out of a molehill," a fuss made over something unimportant is said to be "a fart in a windstorm." —Lewis Poteet, *The South Shore Phrase Book*, p. 43, 1999

▸ like a fart in a trance

listless, distracted, indecisive *UK*

- Away oot fur gooness sake insteed a hingin aboot the hoose lik a fart in a trance. —Michael Munro, *The Original Patter*, 1985
- You've been going about like a fart in a trance for the last three months. —Tim Parks, *Shear*, p. 136, 1995
- Shooting back, he decided, beat pacing about like a fart in a trance, all hollow! —Dewey Lambdin, *Sea of Grey*, p. 23, 2002

fart *verb*

to produce an anal emission of gases, to break wind *UK, 1250*

- I've farted, I've farted, / I've made a trouser cough[.] —Ivor Biggun, *I've Parted*, 1978

▸ fart the Star-spangled Banner

to do everything that is required and more *US*

An ironic claim to super-capability, usually made in addition to a list of everything ordinarily required.

- —Peter Furze, *Tailwinds*, p. 77, 1998

▸ fart through silk

to live a life of luxury and ease *US, 1927*

- They want to wear wing-tipped shoes, fart through silk, and drive Cadillacs and BMW's. —Andrew Garrod et al., *Souls Looking Back*, p. 198, 1999

fart about *verb*

to waste time foolishly *UK, 1900*

- [A] workman might be told to stop farting about if there was something needed doing as a matter of urgency. —Peter Furze, *Tailwinds*, p. 71, 1998
- None of this fiddlin and friggin and fartin about[.] —Niall Griffiths, *Kelly + Victor*, p. 18, 2002

fart along *verb*

to dawdle *UK*

- That car in front of us holding up traffic is just farting along. —Peter Furze, *Tailwinds*, p. 71, 1998

fart around *verb*

to waste time *US, 1931*

- Just farting around like two kids sitting on a railroad track on a hot afternoon[.] —Jack Kerouac, *Letter to Neal Cassady*, p. 114, 26th August 1947
- I follow Fink into the main lobby of the station. Everybody's farting around. —Abbie Hoffman, *Revolution for the Hell of It*, p. 19, 1968
- —Collin Baker et al., *College Undergraduate Slang Study Conducted at Brown University*, p. 115, 1968
- She's got her little pajamas on and her bathrobe and we're farting around. —Leonard Shecter and William Phillips, *On the Pad*, p. 147, 1973
- "Joo peeky pany, lady?" I said, but I had blown my cool, so I stopped fartsin' around. —Edwin Torres, *After Hours*, p. 273, 1979
- Who wants to be a fuck'n forty-five-year-old rock 'n' roller farting around in front of people less than half their age? —*This is Spinal Tap*, 1984

fart arse *noun*

a fool, a useless person *UK*

Contemptuous.

- [W]e could hear them bickering all the way up the stairs: "Move it, fart arse," "Shut it, poof." —Jenny Eclair, *Camberwell Beauty*, p. 317, 2000

fart-arse *verb*

to spend time unproductively; to idle *AUSTRALIA, 1971*

- —Barry Humphries, *A Nice Night's Entertainment*, p. 158, 1974
- —Lance Peters, *The Dirty Half-Mile*, p. 128, 1979
- I'm not a Commo but my favourite hobby / Is fart-arsing around with the environment lobby. —Barry Humphries, *Les Patterson's Australia*, p. 61, 1987

fart-arse about *verb*

to waste time very foolishly *UK, 1984*

An intensification of **FART ABOUT**.

- —Peter Furze, *Tailwinds*, p. 71, 1998

fart blossom *noun*

a despicable person *US, 1938*

- I look upon it as my sacred duty to run as many of your fart blossoms out of the Marine Corps as I can. —Pat Conroy, *The Great Santini*, p. 205, 1976

fartbreath *noun*

a despicable person *US, 1974*

- Fart Breath starts talking about a trial, about this girl got gang-raped[.] —James Lee Burke, *Cimarron Rose*, p. 277, 1997

fart-catcher *noun*

a male homosexual *UK*

- Oh, bleeding hell [...] manager's a flaming pouve. A fart catcher. —John Gardner, *Madrigal*, 1967

farter *noun*

1 a person who farts *AUSTRALIA*

- Well, I was going to tell you my latest yarn 'the fantastic farter from Finnigan's Falls' but, seeing as there are ladies present I'll settle for the 'The Champion Chunderer from Cooper's Creek'[.] —Frank Hardy, *The Outcasts of Foolgarah*, p. 198, 1971
- —Kathy Lette, *Girls' Night Out*, p. 72, 1987
- Ila wasn't about to raise her children to be dirty farters and belchers. —*Sick Puppy*, p. 13, 1998

2 the anus *AUSTRALIA*

- Whatever the reason, Jeff wasn't keen to get a foot-and-a-half of fishy frot-iron up his farter. —*Picture*, p. 20, 5th February 1992

fart-face *noun*

a despicable person *US, 1938*

- Except for the fact that that old fartface flubbed up the name of Li Po by calling him by his Japanese name and all such famous twaddle, he was all right. —Jack Kerouac, *The Dharma Bums*, p. 23, 1958
- That fart face done flipflop his Whiteass lid for sure! —Robert Gover, *One Hundred Dollar Misunderstanding*, p. 170, 1961

farthead *noun*

a despicable person *US, 1962*

- "You little snipe," he said. "You arrogant little farthead!" —Eric Gabriel Lehman, *Summer's House*, p. 243, 2000

farthole *noun*
a despicable person or thing *US, 1972*
• Piece of goddamn cockpuss farthole Navy surplus bubbleshit junk. —Dan Simmons, *The Crook Factory*, p. 433, 1999

fart hook *noun*
a worthless, useless person *US, 1973*
• Monk wore the uniform of the Burdock County High School basketball team, the Bulldogs – or, as they were variously known around Needmore, with as much despair as disparagement, the Shit-heels, the Fart-hooks, and the Turd-knockers. —Ed McClanahan, *The Natural Man*, p. 10, 1983

fart in a thunderstorm *noun*
something of negligible worth or impact *UK*
• His announcement had just about as much impact on the proceedings as a fart in a thunderstorm. —Rick Jolly, *Jackspeak*, p. 104, 1989

farting *adjective*
trifling, contemptible, insubstantial *UK*
• Scalding hot tea out of a proper pot. None of them farting tin efforts where the tea leaks all over the fucking table[.] —Kevin Sampson, *Outlaws*, p. 227, 2001

farting spell *noun*
1 a moment, a pause *UK*
• —Peter Furze, *Tailwinds*, p. 74, 1998

2 a loss of temper *UK*
From the previous sense (a moment) via 'to have a moment' (to experience a short-lived change of equanimity).
• —Peter Furze, *Tailwinds*, p. 74, 1998

fart-knocker *noun*
1 a despicable person *US, 1952*
• Some no-good fart-knocker is out there beatin' up on a woman. —Dorothy Garlock, *After the Parade*, p. 291, 2000

2 an incompetent blunderer *US, 1952*
Used with humour and often affection.
• — *Maledicta*, p. 254, Summer/Winter 1981: 'Five years and 121 dirty words later'
• —Connie Eble (Editor), *UNC-CH Campus Slang*, p. 3, March 1996

fartleberries *noun*
1 haemorrhoids *UK*
From an image of faecal remnants that cling to anal hair. Royal Navy slang.
• —Rick Jolly, *Jackspeak*, p. 104, 1989

2 small pieces of faeces clinging to anal hairs *UK, 1785*
Also variant 'fart-o-berries'.
• —James McDonald, *A Dictionary of Obscenity, Taboo and Euphemism*, p. 51, 1988

farts *noun*
▸ **the farts**
an attack of flatulence *UK*
• [They] announce quite simply that they "have the farts". —Peter Furze, *Tailwinds*, p. 76, 1998

fart sack *noun*
1 a bed *US*
• —William K. Bentley and James M. Corbett, *Prison Slang*, p. 6, 1992
• —T.K. Pratt, *Oral informant in Prince Edward Island Sayings*, p. 92, 1998

2 a sleeping bag *US, 1943*
• —Carl Fleischhauer, *A Glossary of Army Slang*, p. 18, 1968
• —Jim Ramsay, *Cop It Sweet!*, p. 35, 1977
• —Judi Sanders, *Mashing and Munching in Ames*, p. 7, 1994
• —Harry Orsman and Des Hurley, *The Beaut Little Book of New Zealand Slang*, 1994

fartsucker *noun*
a despicable person *UK, 1891*
• "How about fartsuckers?" 'Not rotten enough." —Joseph Wambaugh, *The Choirboys*, p. 32, 1975

farty *adjective*
flatulence-inducing *UK*
• "She's a vegetarian," muttered Ann. "She stews beans in that. Farty beans." —Beryl Bainbridge, *Sweet William*, 1975

fascinoma *noun*
a medical case that is unusual and thus interesting *US*
• —Sally Williams, *"Strong" Words*, p. 141, 1994
• —Adam T. Fox, St Mary's Hospital, London, 10th October 2002

fascists *noun*
the police *UK*
Used by late 1980s – early 90s counterculture travellers.
• —Martin Roach, *Dr. Marten's Air Wair*, 1999: 'Glossary of travellers' terms'

fash *adjective*
fashionable *AUSTRALIA*
• It's quite fash to say that. And fash in the fash way of saying fashionable. —Kylie Mole (Maryanne Fahey), *My Diary*, p. 6, 1988

fa'sheezy
▷ see: **FO'SHEEZY**

fash hag *noun*
a follower of *fash*ion *UK*
Modelled on **FAG HAG** (a woman who seeks the company of gay men).
• [Y]ou just look like all those other "fake-revolutionary" fash hags. — *X-Ray*, p. 21, May 2003

fashion casualty *noun*
someone in the thrall of clothes-designers' more ridiculous excesses *UK*
A variation of **FASHION VICTIM**.
• A long queue was snaking out into Praed Street, plenty of dressed-up kids, a few older trendies and some outrageous fashion casualties. —Kevin Sampson, *Powder*, p. 87, 1999

fashioned riah *noun*
▷ see: **FAKE RIAH**

fashionista *noun*
someone who dictates, or is in the vanguard of, trendiness *UK*
• Unlike most fashionista babes, there's a lot more to Sophie than her job. —Chris Ryan, *The Watchman*, p. 74, 2001
• [T]he arty fashionista set are hot on her sneakers[.] —*The Times Magazine*, p. 43, 16th February 2002
• London's fashionistas clearly believe the hype. — *The Guardian*, p. 23, 1st June 2002
• Only football managers and fashionistas are allowed to wear their coats indoors. — *The Times Magazine*, p. 7, 2nd March 2002

fashion victim *noun*
someone in the thrall of fashion designers' more ridiculous excesses; often applied, loosely, to someone who is conspicuously expensively dressed *UK, 1984*
• The intrepid Fairchild weighed in annually with his IN and OUT list and his roost of the year's 'fashion victims', those ladies who dared to wear the worst of fashion. —Teri Agins, *The End of Fashion*, p. 11, 1999

fash mag *noun*
a fashion magazine *UK*
• Fellow Hoxton darling and fash-mag-folkie Beth Orton[.] — *The Times Magazine*, p. 43, 16th February 2002

fash pack *noun*
a loose categorisation of pre-eminent people in the fashion industry *UK*
Modelled on **RAT PACK** and subsequent gangs, real and imagined.
• [G]ave the catwalk-weary, fash-pack a much-needed lift[.] — *The Times Magazine*, p. 81, 24th October 2002

fast *noun*
▷ see: **FAST STUFF**

fast *adjective*
overly concerned with the affairs of others *TRINIDAD AND TOBAGO*
• —Lise Winer, *Dictionary of the English/Creole of Trinidad & Tobago*, 2003

▸ **as fast as lightning over Cuba**
very fast *CAYMAN ISLANDS*
• —Aarona Booker Kohlman, *Wotcha Say*, p. 29, 1985

▸ **faster than the mill-tails of hell**
moving very, very fast *CANADA, 1999*
• Proverbial, metaphorical way of describing speed, which owes something to the nineteenth-century waterwheels and mill-races in the rivermouths of the South Shore. —Lewis Poteet, *The South Shore Phrase Book*, p. 43, 1999

▸ **get fast**
in a criminal enterprise, to cheat a partner out of money or goods *US*
• —Carsten Stroud, *Close Pursuit*, p. 272, 1987

▸ **so fast he's goin' like greased lightnin' thru a gooseberry bush**

used for indicating great speed *CANADA, 1988*
Note the alliteration–goin', greased, gooseberry–which is often characteristic of Nova Scotia slang.

- A man moves so fast he's goin' like greased lightnin' thru' a gooseberry bush. —Harry Bruce, *Down Home*, p. 109, 1988

fast *adverb*

in gambling, betting large amounts without fear of loss *US*

- "Actually, I had won $3,400. That's how fast I was playing." (Note: "playing fast" has very little to do with speed of the game; it has to do with the willingness of the player to let her winnings pile up.) —Edward Lin, *Big Julie of Vegas*, p. 188, 1974

fast and out of place *adjective*

emphatically over-concerned with the affairs of others *TRINIDAD AND TOBAGO*

- —Lise Winer, *Dictionary of the English/Creole of Trinidad & Tobago*, 2003

fast bird *noun*

in Vietnam, a high-speed attack jet aircraft *US*

- —Linda Reinberg, *In the Field*, p. 78, 1991

fast buck *noun*

money that is easily earned, especially if done so illicitly *US, 1949*

- An entire mini-industry has flourished out of the deaths of Tupac Shakur and the Notroius B.I.G., besieging all legitimate attempts to explore possible motives or true culprits behind both murders with a barrage of conjecture and regurgitated fantasy designed to make a fast buck[.] —Jake Brown, *Ready to Die*, p. 16–17, 2004

fast burner *noun*

a person who is advancing quickly through the ranks *US, 1986*
US Air Force usage.

- —*Seattle Times*, p. A9, 12th April 1998

fast-count *verb*

to shortchange *US*

- —Vincent J. Monteleone, *Criminal Slang*, p. 81, 1949

fastened up *adjective*

imprisoned *UK*

- If you don't stop you're gonna kill me and then you'll get fastened up for life. —Lanre Fehintola, *Charlie Says...*, p. 119, 2000

fast in *noun*

1 MDMA, the recreational drug best known as ecstasy *UK*

- —Mike Haskins, *Drugs*, p. 289, 2003

2 amphetamines *UK*

- —Mike Haskins, *Drugs*, p. 279, 2003

fast lane *noun*

a lifestyle showing no regard for the future *US, 1976*

- Elizabeth noticed changes in herself that she didn't like – low self-esteem (which showed itself in poor personal grooming, excessive weight, compulsive overeating, and excessive alcohol consumption). She lived life in the fast lane. —Michio Kushi, *The Cancer Prevention Diet*, p. 145, 1993

fast-mouth *adjective*

fond of talking *TRINIDAD AND TOBAGO*

- —Lise Winer, *Dictionary of the English/Creole of Trinidad & Tobago*, 2003

fast mover *noun*

in Vietnam, a jet aircraft *US, 1972*

- —Linda Reinberg, *In the Field*, p. 79, 1991

fast one *noun*

a trick intended to deceive or defraud, usually in the phrase 'pull a fast one' *US, 1923*

- We've all heard stories about car hire companies trying to pull a fast one and add on punitive charges. —*The Guardian*, 10th June 2004

fast pill *noun*

in horse racing, a stimulant given to a horse *US*

- —Dan Parker, *The ABC of Horse Racing*, p. 145, 1947

fast sheet setup *noun*

an apartment or motel that caters to prostitutes and their customers *US*

- In addition to being a whore, she ran a fast sheet setup for a dozen whores. They tricked out of her joint. —Iceberg Slim (Robert Beck), *Pimp*, p. 271, 1969

fast shuffle *noun*

a swindle; a deceptive act *US, 1930*

- Shawn was indeed a liar (but he had to be, in his job) and an artist at the fast shuffle (again, as he had to be). —Gardner Botsford, *A Life of Privilege, Mostly*, p. 258, 2003

fast stuff; fast; go-fast *noun*

amphetamines, speed *UK*

- —Angela Devlin, *Prison Patter*, p. 21, 1996
- I wouldn't mind some Charles [cocaine] but I'm a bit skint. What about the fast stuff? —Colin Butts, *Is Harry on the Boat?*, p. 114, 1997

fast-talking Charlie *noun*

a Jewish person, or someone who is thought to be Jewish *US*

- —Edith A. Folb, *runnin' down some lines*, p. 236, 1980

fast time *noun*

daylight saving time *CANADA*

- When do we eat? Slow time. Fast time. Doctor's time. Methodist's time. When do we eat. —Robert Moon, *This is Saskatchewan*, p. 14, 1953

fat *noun*

1 an erection *AUSTRALIA, 1941*

- Bone. Fat. Horn. Hard-on. Pole. Pork sword. Stalk. —Bettina Arndt, *The Australian Way of Sex*, p. 11, 1984
- —David McGill, *David McGill's Complete Kiwi Slang Dictionary*, p. 48, 1998

2 a fattened cow or bull ready for market *AUSTRALIA, 1888*

- —Ion L. Idriess, *Over the Range*, p. 43, 1947
- There's a few more head still in the sandhills, but we pushed the biggest part, including the fats, out in time. —Wal Watkins, *Race the Lazy River*, p. 44, 1963
- —Herb Wharton, *Cattle Camp*, p. 18, 1994

3 used as a eupherism in place of 'fuck' *BERMUDA*

- —Peter A. Smith and Fred M. Barritt, *Bermewjan Vurds*, 1985

fat *adjective*

1 good *US*

- —*Newsweek*, p. 28, 8th October 1951
- —Collin Baker et al., *College Undergraduate Slang Study Conducted at Brown University*, p. 115, 1968
- —Hy Lit, *Hy Lit's Unbelievable Dictionary of Hip Words for Groovy People*, p. 14, 1968

2 wealthy *UK, 1699*

- RACINE: How'd he get so fat? MATTY: The stock market, investments, real estate. —*Body Heat*, 1980

3 (used of a fuel mixture) too rich *US*
Biker (motorcyle) usage.

4 (used of a part in a dramatic production) demanding, challenging, rewarding *US*

- —Sherman Louis Sergel, *The Language of Show Biz*, p. 85, 1973

5 when said of a military unit, over-staffed *US*
Vietnam war usage.

- Theirs was a "fat" battalion, meaning a unit at over its authorized strength. —Philip Caputo, *A Rumor of War*, p. 206, 1977

6 (ironically) slim; little *AUSTRALIA, 1938*
Especially in the phrases 'fat chance' and 'fat hopes'.

- Well, he's got fat hopes of doing that. —Sue Rhodes, *Now you'll think I'm awful*, p. 21, 1967
- Fat fucking chance of relaxing with fucking secret police driving the cabs. —Robert English, *Toxic Kisses*, p. 38, 1979
- 'Fat chance,' sneered Joe. —Lance Peters, *The Dirty Half-Mile*, p. 68, 1979

7 out of fashion, old-fashioned *UK*

- "Hippies are fat" said one 16-year old I spoke to last week. —*New Society*, 7th February 1980

fat Albert; Bert *nickname*

any exceptionally large aircraft, especially a Boeing 737, a Lockheed C-5A Galaxy or a Lockheed C-130 Hercules *US*
The Boeing 737 was first manufactured in 1967: The Lockheed C-130 was delivered into service in 1970. The first Lockheed C-5A was delivered in late 1969.

- With a length only one foot greater than its wingspan, the stubby aircraft earned the nickname, "Fat Albert." —*Nasa Facts Online*, May 1994
- The planned visit will take place on November 7th or 8th and will actually be made by an aircraft that is affectionately called "Fat Albert". The aircraft is a U.S. Air Force C-5A Galaxy, and it's called Fat Albert for a good reason. —*LeHigh Valley International Airport information booth*, 6th November 2000
- You guys ready to go flying?" the driver and co-pilot, Marine Capt. Andrew Hall, asked his flight crew waiting by the four-engine transport [a C-130 Hercules turboprop] nicknamed "Fat Albert" for their turn in the spotlight at the Miramar Air Show. —*North County Times*, 15th October 2000

fat and wide *noun*
a bride *UK*
Rhyming slang, from a playground variation of 'Here Comes the Bride'.
- —Ray Puxley, *Cockney Rabbit*, 1992

Fat Arse Brigade *noun*
collectively, the older women who support the People's National Movement party in Trinidad *TRINIDAD AND TOBAGO, 1977*
- —Lise Winer, *Dictionary of the English/Creole of Trinidad & Tobago*, 2003

fat-arsed *adjective*
broad-bottomed; hence, wealthy *UK, 1937*
- Fatso the fat-arsed wombat, the Games' unofficial mascot, is being auctioned off for charity on Olympic Aid's website.—*The Guardian*, 29th September 2000

fat ass *noun*
a fat person *US, 1931*
- ["]You call me fatso again and I'll rearrange your face." "Fatso, fat ass, lard butt, blimpo -"[.]—Janet Evanovich, *Seven Up*, p. 37, 2001

fat-ass *adjective*
of impressive dimensions *US*
- [A] fat ass J, of some bubonic chronic that made me choke[.]—Snoop Doggy Dogg, *Gin and Juice*, 1993

fatback *adjective*
lacking sophistication, rustic *US, 1934*
- "A fantastic spectacle in honor of some fatback grossero named Del Webb."—Hunter S. Thompson, *Fear and Loathing in Las Vegas*, p. 9, 1971

fat bags *noun*
crack cocaine *UK, 1998*
- —Mike Haskins, *Drugs*, p. 281, 2003

fat bastard *noun*
an overweight person *UK*
- A fat bastard like me. How could I be a popstar?—Simon Napier-Bell, *Black Vinyl White Powder*, p. 302, 2001

fat boy box *noun*
a box with enough packaged food to last several days in the wilderness *US*
- —Murry A. Taylor, *Jumping Fire*, p. 456, 2000

Fatboy Slim; Fatboy *noun*
a gym *UK, 2001*
Popney rhyming slang, based on the stage name of musician and DJ Norman Cook (b.1963). Popney was contrived for *www.music365.co.uk*, an Internet music site.

fat cat *noun*
1 a wealthy, powerful, prominent individual *US, 1925*
- The fat cats coughing up $300 a ticket give off some really good vibes. Real groovy!!!—Abbie Hoffman, *Woodstock Nation*, p. 95, 1969
- Republican fat-cat businessmen see their kids become SDS leaders. —Jerry Rubin, *Do It!*, p. 88, 1970

2 an overpaid company director *UK, 1971*
A specifically British usage of the more general US term.
- Fat cats' pay is the result of greed, not competition[.] Interchangeable CEOs use imaginary markets to inflate their salaries.—*The Guardian*, 24th December 2003

fatcha *noun*
the face *UK*
Polari, from Italian *faccia*.

fatcha *verb*
to shave, to apply cosmetics *UK*
From the noun sense as 'the face'.
- —Paul Baker, *Polari*, p. 174, 2002

fat chance *noun*
no chance at all *US, 1908*
- "It stands to reason that at least one of those Board of Education members has read Elmo Goodhue Piggrass's Thoughts of My Tranquil Hours." "Fat chance," sneered Clothilde.—Max Shulman, *The Many Loves of Dobie Gillis*, p. 7, 1951
- Personally, I feel the world would be a much better place if evey radio station played Frank's version of "My One and Only Love" at least once an hour. Fat chance!—C.D. Payne, *Youth in Revolt*, p. 8, 1993

fat city *noun*
success, wealth *US, 1964*
- And then came the war – fat city, big money even for Linkhorns. —Hunter S. Thompson, *Hell's Angels*, p. 155, 1966

Fat City *nickname*
1 Ottawa, Ontario, Canada's capital city *CANADA*
The name derives from the huge largess of taxpayer funds the city gets for museums, the Tulip Festival, the winter canal skating season, and so forth.
- Rochet Rached and the Fat City – he formed the Ottawa Blues Society.—*soundzgood.com*, 8th January 2001

2 the headquarters of the Military Assistance Command Vietnam, located in Saigon *US*
- —Linda Reinberg, *In the Field*, p. 78, 1991

fat devil *noun*
a good-looking woman *US*
- "Fat devils! Fine good-looking chicks, I mean."—Bobby Seale, *A Lonely Rage*, p. 138, 1978

fat farm *noun*
a facility where people go to lose weight through a regime of exercise and proper diet *US, 1969*
- The Golden Door! America's most sumptuous and blue-blooded fat farm! A jeweled oasis of sauna baths and facials, pedicures and manicures, dancing lessons, herbal wraps and gourmet cuisine! —Armistead Maupin, *Tales of the City*, p. 186, 1978

fat grrrls *noun*
a young, radical faction of the 'fat acceptance movement' *US*
- —Steven Daly and Nathaniel Wice, *alt.culture*, p. 79, 1995

fat guts *noun*
nuts (the fruit) *UK*
Rhyming slang, possibly deriving from an effect of over-indulgence.
- —Ray Puxley, *Cockney Rabbit*, 1992

fathead *noun*
1 a fool *US, 1842*
- I recall publicly gloating about the defeat of some of the noxious fatheads Texas used to send to Congress.—Molly Ivins, *You Got to Dance with Them What Brung You*, p. 118, 1998

2 a black person's hair style in which the hair stands out from the head *TRINIDAD AND TOBAGO*
- —Lise Winer, *Dictionary of the English/Creole of Trinidad & Tobago*, 2003

father *adjective*
excellent *BARBADOS*
- That is picture father, boy.—Frank A. Collymore, *Barbadian Dialect*, p. 47, 1965

fatherfucking *adjective*
used as a variant of 'motherfucking' *US*
- Fatherfucking cops! wont leave me! alone!—John Rechy, *City of Night*, p. 353, 1963

father's day *noun*
the day each month when fathers appear in court to make child support payments *US*
- —Malachi Andrews and Paul T. Owens, *Black Language*, p. 51, 1973

Father-Son-Holy Ghost house *noun*
a style of three-storey terraced house consisting of three rooms stacked vertically *US*
- —Claudio R. Salvucci, *The Philadelphia Dialect Dictionary*, p. 40, 1996

father's t'other end *noun*
a room built on the end of the house *CANADA, 1999*
The odd word 't'other' is a shortened form of 'the other' much used in southwestern Nova Scotia.
- —Lewis Poteet, *The South Shore Phrase Book*, p. 43, 1999

father time *noun*
1 a criminal judge who is inclined to give long sentences *US*
- —Hyman E. Goldin et al., *Dictionary of American Underworld Lingo*, p. 68, 1950

2 a prison warden *US*
- —Vincent J. Monteleone, *Criminal Slang*, p. 81, 1949

fatigue *noun*
teasing; good-natured insults *TRINIDAD AND TOBAGO, 1904*
- —Lise Winer, *Dictionary of the English/Creole of Trinidad & Tobago*, 2003

fat jabba *noun*
▷ see: JABBA

fat lip *noun*
a fist blow to the mouth *US, 1944*
- I'm warning you, Fen, break another window and you're gonna get a fat lip. — *Diner*, 1982

fat lot *noun*
(ironically) little or none *UK, 1892*
- — Barbara Baynton, *Human Toll*, p. 123, 1907
- — Gavin Casey, *It's Harder for Girls*, p. 80, 1941
- Fat lot of trouble you've taken to find out that I'm back. — Norman Lindsay, *The Cousin from Fiji*, p. 232, 1945
- — Jean Brooks, *The Opal Witch*, p. 84, 1967
- [A] fat lot of good it has done them. — *The Guardian*, 28th June 2003

fatmouth *verb*
to insult, to taunt, to tease, to trade barbs *US, 1962*
- For some reason, I got a bang outta fat mouthing with 'em. — A.S. Jackson, *Gentleman Pimp*, p. 30, 1973
- What was it he said when people got pissed off and started fat mouthin' 'im? — Donald Goines, *The Busting Out of an Ordinary Man*, p. 40, 1985

fat-mouthed *adjective*
loud-mouthed *US*
- You're a liar and a fat-mouthed scoundrel. — Ralph Ellison, *Invisible Man*, p. 402, 1952

fat one *noun*
1 a substantial marijuana cigarette *UK*
- I just shrug and roll a fat one[.] — Kevin Williamson, *Heart of the Bass (Disco Biscuits)*, p. 113, 1996
- Emyr seemed to be as stoned as ever, popping out into the deserted yard area [...] to share a fat one with the Colonel. — John Williams, *Cardiff Dead*, p. 183, 2000

2 a generous line of powdered cocaine
- Brandon [Block] chopped out a fat one behind the decks[.] — *Ministry*, p. 22, January 2002

fat pants *noun*
wide-legged trousers *TRINIDAD AND TOBAGO*
- — *www.addictions.org*, 1999

fat pappy *noun*
a large marijuana cigarette *US*
- — *www.addictions.org*, 1999

Fat Pill *noun*
(among Canadian forces personnel) a sweet snack *CANADA*
- A doughnut, cookie, slice of pie, cupcake, brownie, or any other sweet confection is a Fat Pill. "I do believe that I'll have a Fat Pill with my coffee." — Tom Langeste, *Words on the Wing*, p. 94, 1995

fat pockets *noun*
wealth *US*
- — Anna Scotti and Paul Young, *Buzzwords*, p. 61, 1997

fat rat *noun*
the US Army's five-quart collapsible water bladder *US*
- — Gregory Clark, *Words of the Vietnam War*, p. 171, 1990

fat-rat *adjective*
easy, privileged *US*
- Toward the end of his tour, he negotiated a fat-rat job off the line as a jeep driver and was thinking of extending his time in 'Nam in exchange for an early discharge. — Peter Goldman and Tony Fuller, *Charlie Company*, p. 317, 1983

fats *noun*
fatigues, the military work uniform *US*
- — Gregory Clark, *Words of the Vietnam War*, p. 171, 1990

fatso *noun*
an obese person; used as a common nickname or rude term of address for an obese person *US, 1933*
- You were sick, weren't you, fatso? If you'd stop fressing so much[.] — Lenny Bruce, *How to Talk Dirty and Influence People*, p. 145, 1965
- "You see a fatso old broad?" he shouted. — Iceberg Slim (Robert Beck), *Airtight Willie and Me*, p. 119, 1979
- "Who you calling fatso? You call me fatso again and I'll rearrange your face." "Fatso, fat ass, lard butt, blimpo -" — Janet Evanovich, *Seven Up*, p. 37, 2001

fat stuff *noun*
a fat person *US, 1926*
- "Thought you were tough, fat stuff." The remark rattled Boots. He didn't like to be called "fat stuff," "fatso," or any other name referring to his build. — Matthew F. Christopher, *Tough to Tackle*, p. 18, 1971

fat talk *noun*
excessive boasting *TRINIDAD AND TOBAGO*
- — Lise Winer, *Dictionary of the English/Creole of Trinidad & Tobago*, 2003

fatten *verb*
in poker, to increase a bet *US*
- — Irwin Steig, *Common Sense in Poker*, p. 184, 1963

fatty *noun*
1 a fat person, often as an offensive name-calling, sometimes as a nickname *UK, 1797*
- Hey fatty, it's not your fault. — *The Globe and Mail (Toronto)*, 10th July 2003

2 an extra-large marijuana cigarette *US, 1969*
Also variant 'fattie'.
- — Connie Eble (Editor), *UNC-CH Campus Slang*, p. 3, Fall 1996
- I was just – you know – smokin' a fatty. — *Jackie Brown*, 1997
- Drinking beers, beers, beers, rolling fatties, smoking blunts! — Kevin Smith, *Jay and Silent Bob Strike Back*, p. 9, 2001
- No other cop I know would sit around with some kid and bogart a fatty. — Stephen J. Cannell, *The Tin Collectors*, p. 87, 2001
- He's smoked a whole fattie of it — Brian Preston, *Pot Planet*, p. 228, 2002
- — Mike Haskins, *Drugs*, p. 291, 2003

fatty *adjective*
used of a pornographic categorisation that displays obese performers *UK*
- [A] full-on batch of fatty mags. — Kevin Sampson, *Clubland*, p. 78, 2002

fat zero; big fat zero *noun*
nothing at all, none *UK*
- [He] got a fat zero for his efforts. — *The Sweeney*, p. 50, 1976
- [F]ifteen-year-old boot boys with zero chance of a bunk-up[.] — John King, *Human Punk*, p. 105, 2000

faubourg; fauxbourg *noun*
in Quebec, a suburb or a part of a city keeping the old name; a large indoor shopping complex *CANADA*
From the French for 'false town', this term is in use in Montreal to designate the area known as the Faubourg de Melasse (where ships loaded molasses) and the Faubourg, a complex of shops and boutiques in the centre of town.
- — Walter Avis, *Dictionary of Canadianisms*, p. 252, 1967

faucet nose *noun*
the condition experienced by surfers who have water forced up their nose while being pummelled by a wave *US*
- — Trevor Cralle, *The Surfin'ary*, p. 36, 1991

faunch; fawnch *verb*
to complain vociferously *US, 1911*
- I want you to quit fawnching around this house and get out there and get your grass off my yard, 'cause it ain't gettin' anything but higher, and I ain't gettin' anything but madder. — Ken Weaver, *Texas Crude*, p. 112, 1984

fausty *adjective*
unpleasant, distasteful *US*
High school usage.
- — *Washington Post*, 23rd April 1961: 'Man, dig this jazz'

faux-hawk *noun*
a hairstyle in which a central section (running from front to back) is grown longer/higher than the hair on the rest of the head *US, 1996*
Pronounced 'fohawk'; this is a play on the 'mohawk' haircut (which this style approximates) and 'faux' (fake, artificial). Footballer and style-icon David Beckham sported the style in the summer of 2002.
- — *The Word Spy*, 5th September 2003

fauxmosexual *noun*
a homosexual who behaves in the manner of a conventional heterosexual *UK*
A compound of 'faux' (fake) and 'homosexual'; as an aural pun only the first letter is changed.
- — *Attitude*, p. 60, July 2003: 'New palare lexicon'

fav *noun*
in horse racing, the horse with the shortest odds to win a race *US*
An abbreviation of 'favourite'.
- — Robert Saunders Dowst and Jay Craig, *Playing the Races*, p. 163, 1960

fave; fav *adjective*

favourite *US, 1921*

A term with a definite teen magazine flavour.

- "Shit, Rodney, you're out of all my faves," said Shake. — Dan Jenkins, *Life Its Ownself*, p. 145, 1984
- They've been asked to open a show for new glam fave Suede. — *Rolling Stone*, p. 16, 27th May 1993
- WHAT ARE YOUR FAV TV SHOWS? — *Rated*, p. 48, June 2002

fave rave *noun*

a notably favourite person or thing, especially with relation to the creative arts *US, 1967*

- You asked me to tell you my favorite. My absolute fave rave. The one that vanquishes all the other comers. — Richard Powers, *Plowing the Dark*, p. 244, 2000

favourite; favourites *adjective*

excellent *UK, 1943*

- A great smile spreads over his face. "Oh, favourite," he says. "Fucking favourite." — Ted Lewis, *Jack Carter's Law*, p. 200, 1974

fawmy *noun*

a ring *UK*

English gypsy use, from earlier *fawny*.

- — Jimmy Stockin, *On The Cobbles*, p. 10, 2000

fawnty *noun*

a car in a poor state of repair *UK: SCOTLAND*

In Glasgow this is a humorous 'brand name'.

- He drives a Fawnty... fawin [falling] tae bits. — Michael Munro, *The Patter, Another Blast*, p. 24, 1988

fax *noun*

facts *UK, 1837*

- Just the fax, ma'am. — *Dragnet*, 1987

fay *noun*

a white Caucasian *US, 1927*

- OFAY has come to mean the white man. FAY is the faster form. — Malachi Andrews and Paul T. Owens, *Black Language*, 1973

fay *adjective*

1 homosexual *US, 1928*

- 'Now look are you going to cooperate" – three vicious diddles – "or does the ... does the Man cornhole you???" He raises a fay eyebrow. — William Burroughs, *Naked Lunch*, p. 196, 1957

2 white, Caucasian *US, 1927*

- I really went for Ray's roll on the drums; he was the first fay boy I ever heard who mastered the vital foundation of jazz music. — Mezz Mezzrow, *Really the Blues*, p. 62, 1946
- The Gay and Free Will (Headline) — *One: The Homosexual Magazine*, p. 13, August 1953
- Loboy got a fay chick sommers. — Chester Himes, *Cotton Comes to Harlem*, p. 38, 1965
- — *Current Slang*, p. 2, Fall 1966
- Couple of years ago, I just missed getting locked up myself, or maybe getting shot by a "blue." It happened on a Mardi Gras. I was walking along and looked at a "fay bitch," just a little too long. — Robert deCoy, *The Nigger Bible*, p. 234, 1967
- He was a good-looking cat so we'd have a good time at my discotheque – a lot of the fay chicks would go for his revolutionary bullshit[.] — Edwin Torres, *Carlito's Way*, p. 81, 1975
- I think Leroy thinks about fay chicks too, when he beats his meat. — Clarence Major, *All-Night Visitors*, p. 25, 1998

Fayette-Nam *nickname*

Fayetteville, North Carolina, home of Fort Bragg and the US Special Forces *US*

- — Connie Eble (Editor), *UNC-CH Campus Slang*, p. 3, Spring 1987

faygeleh *noun*

a male homosexual *US*

Yiddish, literally 'little bird'.

- Jews use faygeleh as a discreet way of describing a homosexual – especially when they might be overheard. — Leo Rosten, *The Joys of Yiddish*, p. 115, 1968
- — H. Max, *Gay (S)language*, p. 15, 1988

faynights!

▷ see: FAINITS!

faze *verb*

to surprise, to disconcert *US, 1830*

- [H]aving a tear-up down the boozer with some geezer don't really faze you any more. — Dave Courtney, *Dodgy Dave's Little Black Book*, p. 95, 2001

fazool *noun*

one dollar *US*

- Six ounces for fifteen fazools. — Vincent Patrick, *The Pope of Greenwich Village*, p. 151, 1979

f beep beep k

'fuck', in any use *INDIA*

- So while 'f beep beep k's' have not quite disappeared from betwixt the lips of the cigarette toting stand-abouts, word has it that Indo-Americanisations has invaded the realm of petty college slang. — *The Times of India*, 30th September 2002

FBI *noun*

1 *f*at, *b*lack and *i*gnorant *US*

Used in ritualistic insults.

- — Hermese E. Roberts, *The Third Ear*, 1971

2 used for describing people of East Indian origin *TRINIDAD AND TOBAGO*

An initialism for '*f*at-*b*elly *I*ndian', '*f*at-*b*ottom *I*ndian', '*f*ine *b*oned *I*ndian', or any number of similar constructions.

- — Lise Winer, *Dictionary of the English/Creole of Trinidad & Tobago*, 2003

3 an informer *UK*

Used by a Jamaican inmate in a UK prison, August 2002.

4 a Filipino *US*

An abbreviation of '*f*ull-*b*looded *I*locano'. Ilocano is a dialect spoken in the Philippines; among Hawaiian youth, the term applies to any Filipino, no matter what dialect, if any, they speak.

- — Douglas Simonson, *Pidgin to da Max Hana Hou*, 1982

F bomb *noun*

the word 'fuck', especially when used in a setting where such profanity is not expected *US*

- [Gary] Carter said he has been thrown out only twice in the majors, both times by Eric Gregg. "That was when I used to use the F-bomb." — *Newsday (New York)*, p. 146, 11th August 1988
- It's Callander's playground, where he violates listeners, airs randy prank calls, and occasionally hosts f-bomb-filled interviews with acts like Insane Clown Posse. — *Cleveland Scene*, 7th April 2004

FDAM *noun*

an occasion for ostentatious dress *CANADA*

For '*F*irst *D*ay *a*t (the) *M*arina'.

- Pronounced to rhyme with "ram," FDAM is the day when Full Nanaimo outfits appear – chintzy whitebuck shoes, white belt, polyester pants, and a blue blazer with spurious crest. — Bill Casselman, *Canadian Words*, p. 201, 1995

fear *noun*

▸ **put the fear of God into**

to terrify *UK, 1905*

- It is very threatening and intimidating. It has already put the fear of God into parents. They are just going to hear alarm bells and think, "the cost, the money, my house". — *The Guardian*, 12th May 2004

fear

in twelve-step recovery programmes such as Alcoholics Anonymous, used as an acronym for an addict's choices – *f*uck *e*verything *a*nd *r*un, or *f*ace *e*verything *a*nd *r*ecover *US*

- — Christopher Cavanaugh, *AA to Z*, p. 91, 1998

fearful *adjective*

used as general intensifier *UK, 1991*

- — John Ayton, *The Oxford Dictionary of Slang*, 1998

fearfully *adverb*

very, greatly *UK, 1835*

Dated but still familiar, especially in the works of P.G. Wodehouse.

- [Victorian anatomist, Professor Richard] Owen invented the word "dinosaur" ("fearfully great lizard"), and the South Kensington institution he founded [The Natural History Museum] has dined out, as it were, on dinosaur bones, and prehistoric animatronics, ever since. — *The Guardian*, 26th November 2001

Feargal Sharkey *noun*

a black person *UK*

Rhyming slang for DARKY, formed from the name of a (white) Irish singer born in 1958.

- — Ray Puxley, *Fresh Rabbit*, 1998

feasty *adjective*

excellent *US*

Teen slang.

- — *San Francisco News*, p. 6, 25th March 1958

feather *verb*

1 in hot rodding, to operate the accelerator in a controlled, light manner *US*

- —John Lawlor, *How to Talk Car*, p. 44, 1965

2 in horse racing, a light jockey *US*

- —David W. Maurer, *Argot of the Racetrack*, p. 26, 1951

3 in pool, to only barely glance the object ball with the cue ball *US*

- —Steve Rushin, *Pool Cool*, p. 13, 1990

feather and flip *noun*

a bed; sleep *UK, 1934*
Rhyming slang for **KIP**.

- —Ronnie Barker, *Fletcher's Book of Rhyming Slang*, 1979

featherbed *verb*

to create work rules that require employment of workers who have no real tasks or not enough real tasks to justify their pay *US, 1921*

- —*American Speech*, December 1944
- —Ramon Adams, *The Language of the Railroader*, p. 58, 1977

featherfoot *noun*

a racing car driver who uses a light touch on the throttle during turns to control the engine speed precisely *US*

- —John Edwards, *Auto Dictionary*, p. 58, 1993

feather hauler *noun*

a trucker with a light load, especially one of dry freight *US*

- —Montie Tak, *Truck Talk*, p. 58, 1971

featherhead *noun*

a superficial, silly and/or dim-witted person *US, 1868*

- They'd barricaded themselves in Jessie's room, talking conspiratorially, trashing the in crowd as conformists, shallow featherheads with no compassion.—Anne Lamott, *Crooked Little Heart*, p. 21, 1997

feather merchant *noun*

1 a civilian employee of the military; a civilian *US, 1941*

- "You do whatever you want with those cruddy feather merchants, but let's get one thing straight: they are never going to set foot on my Army post."—Max Shulman, *Rally Round the Flag, Boys!*, p. 221, 1957
- —*Current Slang*, p. 13, Fall 1967

2 a timid, conservative poker player *US*

- —Peter O. Steiner, *Thursday Night Poker*, p. 409, 1996

feather plucker *noun*

1 a sharp practitioner *UK*
Rhyming slang for 'clever **FUCKER**'.

- Bunch of feather pluckers; or so they thought, but they wasn't so clever after all.—John Peter Jones, *Feather Pluckers*, p. 126, 1964

2 an objectionable person *UK, 1961*
Rhyming slang for **FUCKER**, generally used only in a jocular or affectionate way.

- —Ray Puxley, *Cockney Rabbit*, 1992

feathers *noun*

1 a bed *US, 1899*

- What are you like in the feathers? Are you real great in the feathers, Movement? Do you do everything?—Bernard Wolfe, *The Late Risers*, p. 229, 1954
- You been three in the feathers before, ain' you?—Ross Russell, *The Sound*, p. 191, 1961
- Oh there may be girls who get a hundred to spend a whole night with a John – dinner and the theater and eight hours in the feathers. —John Warren Wells, *Tricks of the Trade*, p. 13, 1970

2 body hair, especially fine hair or pubic hair *US*

- "Is it true all them white women shows theyself mother naked?" the old bum grinned, exposing a couple of dung-colored snaggleteeth. "Mother naked!" he croaked. "They ain't even that. They done shaved off the feathers."—Chester Himes, *Come Back Charleston Blue*, p. 92, 1966
- "My, my," the Spook murmurered, "not a feather on him. Some jocker's due to score."—Malcolm Braly, *On the Yard*, p. 35, 1967
- —Inez Cardozo-Freeman, *The Joint*, p. 496, 1984
- —Lise Winer, *Dictionary of the English/Creole of Trinidad & Tobago*, 2003

3 sleep *US*

- —Ramon Adams, *The Language of the Railroader*, p. 58, 1977

4 in darts and Bingo (also House and Tombola), the number thirty-three *UK*
Also variant 'fevvers'.

- —Jack McClintock, *The Book of Darts*, p. 159, 1977
- [A]n allusion to the Cockneyism "firty-free fahsand fevvers on a frush's froat"—Beale, 1984

▸ **make the feathers fly**

to cause uproar, to disturb the status quo *US, 1825*

featherwood *noun*

a white woman *US*
Back formation from **PECKERWOOD**.

- —James Harris, *A Convict's Dictionary*, p. 32, 1989

feature *noun*

1 an act of sexual intercourse *AUSTRALIA*

- Hey, fair suck of the sauce bottle sport. It's me and Blanche doing a feature here.—*The Adventures of Barry McKenzie*, 1972

2 in carnival usage, the rigged game that a particular operator operates best *US*

- —Gene Sorrows, *All About Carnivals*, p. 16, 1985: 'Terminology'

feature *verb*

1 to have sex *AUSTRALIA, 1965*
Popularised by the Barry McKenzie cartoon strip.

- He's half shicker, Phil. If you don't come over pronto he'll be featuring with some jam tart!!!—Barry Humphries, *The Wonderful World of Barry McKenzie*, p. 30, 1968
- You know something, I reckon I could feature with this sheila!—Barry Humphries, *The Wonderful World of Barry McKenzie*, p. 18, 1968

2 to take note of, to pay attention *US*

- Feature that! Grass – tearing grass outa the lawn. Who'd ever have thought.—William Bast, *The Myth Makers [Six Granada Plays]*, p. 167, 1958

3 to approve of *US*

- "A couple of fags are running it, but they're okay." "I don't feature that."—Hal Ellson, *The Golden Spike*, p. 184, 1952
- I did not feature lying next to her in bed, watching the news next to her wrath on the small bedroom TV.—George V. Higgins, *Penance for Jerry Kennedy*, p. 125, 1985

4 to give an appearance; to look like *BARBADOS*

- —Frank A. Collymore, *Barbadian Dialect*, p. 47, 1965
- "I don't know you or your boys," I said, "but they look cool to me. They don't feature as punks."—Piri Thomas, *Down These Mean Streets*, p. 50, 1967

feature creature *noun*

a computer programmer who enjoys adding features to programs *US*

- —Eric S. Raymond, *The New Hacker's Dictionary*, p. 152, 1991

featured dancer *noun*

a sex club performer whose appearance at the club is advertised and who travels from club to club *US*

- When I was a 'house' dancer I would watch all the 'featured' dancers, most of whom were porn stars, come in and make all the money, get lines of people and get the beautiful pictures.—Ana Loria, *1 2 3 Be A Porn Star!*, p. 107, 2000

-features *noun*

used, when combined with an appropriate (generally genital) noun, as an unflattering nickname *UK*
In 1909 it was sufficient to call someone 'features'. Contemporary examples, found during a cursory search of the Internet on 8th October 2003, include 'bollock-features', 'cunt-features', 'prick-features' and 'twat-features'.

fecal freak *noun*

a person who derives sexual pleasure from eating the faeces of others *US*

- —Eugene Landy, *The Underground Dictionary*, p. 40, 1971

feck *verb*

1 to steal *IRELAND*

- Next, after a week as a part-time postman, Liamy Cleary had fecked a postal order, and it was either nine months' goal or find the mailboat fare to Holyhead.—Hugh Leonard, *Out After Dark*, p. 26, 1989

2 'fuck', in all senses and derivatives *IRELAND, 1989*
Scarcely euphemistic; widely popularised by *Father Ted*, a BBC television situation comedy, 1995–98.

- MRS. DOYLE: And what do you say to a cup? JACK: Feck off cup! —Graham Linehan and Arthur Matthews, *Father Ted*, 21st April 1995
- Ah feck off Father Murphy. You're nothing but a feckin' fecker. —Colin Murphy and Donal O'Dea, *The Book of Feckin' Irish Slang*, p. 23, 2004

fecked *adjective*

drunk *IRELAND*

A variation of **FUCKED**.

- —*e-cyclopaedia*, 20th March 2002

fed *noun*

1 an agent of the federal government *US, 1916*

- That woman was under surveillance by the feds. —Mickey Spillane, *Kiss Me Deadly*, p. 18, 1952
- He could feel trouble in the air: Sonny busted by the Feds[.] —Clarence Cooper Jr, *The Scene*, p. 12, 1960
- He then called back and told me that he and his brother felt that she was a federal agent. I thought that was incredible, but then I also thought it would be incredible if she weren't a fed. —James Simon Kunen, *The Strawberry Statement*, p. 70, 1968
- I've been working for the feds for some time. —Herbert Huncke, *Guilty of Everything*, p. 195, 1990
- You said he was a fed, some kind of federal cop. —Elmore Leonard, *Riding the Rap*, p. 189, 1995
- I like cops. I would have liked to have been a Fed myself[.] —*The Usual Suspects*, 1995

2 a police officer *AUSTRALIA, 1966*

- You want the Feds on my tail? —Wilda Moxham, *The Apprentice*, p. 35, 1969
- "Feds?" said Joey? "Maybe." "Wait here." —Garry Bushell, *The Face*, p. 27, 2001

3 a member of the Royal Air Force police *UK, 2002*

Adopted from the sense 'a member of the FBI'.

federal *adjective*

excellent *US*

- —Ben Applebaum and Derrick Pittman, *Turd Ferguson & The Sausage Party*, p. 20, 2004

federal court *noun*

a floor manager in a casino or cardroom *US*

- When the players have a disputel, they settle it in federal court. —John Vorhaus, *The Big Book of Poker Slang*, p. 16, 1996

federales *noun*

the federal government *US*

From the Spanish.

- At the time we didn't know Tait was a rat working for the federales and just waiting for an excuse to fuck up the club. —Ralph "Sonny" Barger, *Hell's Angel*, p. 233, 2000

federation *noun*

a noisy, tumultuous gathering *BARBADOS*

An allusion to the attempt in 1876 by John Pope-Hennessy to create a Confederation of the Windward Islands, which resulted in riots.

- —Frank A. Collymore, *Barbadian Dialect*, p. 47, 1965

fed ex *noun*

a person who has served time in a federal prison *US*

Punning on the name of an express delivery business.

- —Jim Crotty, *How to Talk American*, p. 352, 1997

fedlercarp!

used as a non-profane oath *US*

Used by spacecraft pilots, especially Lt Starbuck, on the US television series *Battlestar Galactica* (ABC, 1978–80), and briefly in popular speech.

fed up *adjective*

bored, disgusted, tired of, miserable *UK, 1900*

- Just fed up / That's my word[.] —Eminem (Marshall Mathers), *If I Had*, 1999
- And I was depressed enough. Or, as Mum called it, "fed up a bit". Whenever I said I was depressed she said I wasn't, I was just fed up a bit. —Mary Hooper, *(megan)2*, p. 146, 1999

fee *noun*

coffee *US*

- —John D. Bell et al., *Loosely Speaking*, p. 6, 1966

feeb *noun*

1 a person who is feeble, in spirit, mind or body *US, 1911*

- Trouble was, he was a victim of chronic anxiety – the willies, the jumps, which tended to trim off only when it was comfortably past sunset and the nine-to-five feebs had all lit out for the suburbs[.] —Bernard Wolfe, *The Late Risers*, p. 34, 1954
- —Connie Eble (Editor), *UNC-CH Campus Slang*, April 1977
- How's me faverit fuckin half-wit then eh? The world's best inbred backwoods feeb psycho mong? —Niall Griffiths, *Sheepshagger*, p. 73, 2001

2 an agent of the US Federal Bureau of Investigation (FBI); the FBI *US*

- "Feebs," he said. He put the binoculars in Carr's hands. "That's my guess." —Gerald Petievich, *The Quality of the Informant*, p. 175, 1985
- He found something from the FBI fingerprint section in Washington and held it to the light, without success; the clever Feebs used opaque envelopes. —Carl Hiaasen, *Tourist Season*, p. 238, 1986

fee-bee *noun*

in craps, a five *US, 1968*

Almost certainly a corruption of the more common **PHOEBE**.

- —Thomas L. Clark, *The Dictionary of Gambling and Gaming*, p. 78, 1987

feebie *noun*

an agent of the Federal Bureau of Investigation (FBI) *US, 1942*

- Sampson and I spent the next few hours with the Feebie technicians who were searching the apartment for anything that might give the Bureau a clue about Sara Rosen. —James Patterson, *Jack & Jill*, p. 424, 1996

feed *noun*

1 a meal, especially an excellent and lavish one *UK, 1808*

- We put on a terrific feed that night, then we went bouncing around the tablaos. —Edwin Torres, *Carlito's Way*, p. 75, 1975

2 the chords played by a jazz band during a solo *US*

- —Clarence Major, *Dictionary of Afro-American Slang*, p. 53, 1970

3 a comedian's foil *UK*

- —William Granville, *A Dictionary of Theatrical Terms*, p. 72, 1952

feed *verb*

1 in pinball, to put a coin into the machine *US*

- —Bobbye Claire Natkin and Steve Kirk, *All About Pinball*, p. 112, 1977

2 when gambling on a slot-machine, fruit machine or one-armed bandit, to put a coin or coins into the machine's slot *UK*

- In Rio's casino, a carnival salsas away in galleons sailing over your head as you mindlessly feed the slots. —*The Guardian*, 1st July 2000

3 in a jazz band, to play a chord background for a soloist *US, 1961*

- —Robert S. Gold, *A Jazz Lexicon*, p. 104, 1964

▸ **feed rice**

to speak plainly *UK*

- Feed 'em rice, Jimmy! is similar to: "Give them a piece of your mind, James!" —Rick Jolly, *Jackspeak*, 1989

▸ **feed the monkey**

to sustain a drug addiction *US*

- —William D. Alsever, *Glossary for the Establishment and Other Uptight People*, p. 9, December 1970

▸ **feed the ponies**

to bet on horse racing *US*

- —Jim Crotty, *How to Talk American*, p. 345, 1997

▸ **feed the pony**

to manually stimulate the vagina *UK*

Possibly related to *Smack the Pony*, a television comedy-sketch programme mainly written and performed by women, first broadcast in 1999.

- —*www.LondonSlang.com*, June 2002

▸ **feed the warden**

to defecate *US*

- —Reinhold Aman, *Hillary Clinton's Pen Pal*, p. 37, 1996

▸ **feed with a long spoon**

to be very careful in dealing with someone *TRINIDAD AND TOBAGO*

- —Lise Winer, *Dictionary of the English/Creole of Trinidad & Tobago*, 2003

▸ **feed your face**

to eat *US*

- —Collin Baker et al., *College Undergraduate Slang Study Conducted at Brown University*, p. 116, 1968

▸ **feed your head**

to use psychoactive drugs *US*

A phrase immortalised by Jefferson Airplane in the 1967 song 'White Rabbit', with Grace Slick's commanding vocal of 'Remember, what the door mouse said / Feed your head, feed your head'.

- We took to smoking grass in Van Cortlandt Park on upper Broadway, a nice place to feed your head[.] —Raymond Mungo, *Famous Long Ago*, p. 154, 1970

feed bag *noun*
a container of drugs *US*
- —Jay Robert Nash, *Dicitonary of Crime*, p. 126, 1992

feeder *noun*
1 a comedian's foil *UK*
- —William Granville, *A Dictionary of Theatrical Terms*, p. 72, 1952

2 a hypodermic needle and syringe *US*
- —J.E. Schmidt, *Narcotics Lingo and Lore*, p. 59, 1959

feeding time at the zoo *noun*
a period of great disorder and disruption *AUSTRALIA, 1944*
- World War II might well have been a prime attraction to the extraterrestrials, tantamount to feeding time at the zoo.—Murray Stott, *Aliens Over Antipodes*, p. 229, 1984

feel *verb*
1 to understand *US*
- "Are you feeling me?"—Connie Eble (Editor), *UNC-CH Campus Slang*, p. 3, November 2002

2 to agree with *US*
- I think the teacher is being hypocritical, do you feel me?—Rick Ayers (Editor), *Berkeley High Slang Dictionary*, p. 21, 2004

3 to approve of or enjoy *US*
- I'm definitely not feeling that shirt.—Connie Eble (Editor), *UNC-CH Campus Slang*, p. 4, Spring 2003

4 to fight with someone *UK*
Literally, 'to feel the blows of an opponent'.
- Tommy Carson, who they reckon once felt Ken Buchanan.—Jimmy Stockin, *On The Cobbles*, p. 137, 2000

▸ **feel it**
to feel good, to enjoy something *US*
- That DJ was off the hook, I was really feelin' it.—Connie Eble (Editor), *UNC-CH Campus Slang*, p. 4, Fall 2001

▸ **feel no pain**
to be drunk *US*
- —*American Speech*, p. 303, December 1955: 'Wayne University slang'
- You weren't feeling no pain either," the waitress said. "I come over to the table, I said isn't that your beeper? He didn't even hear it.—Elmore Leonard, *City Primeval*, p. 21–22, 1980
- Joey was feeling no pain by the time the car reached the city[.]—Joel Rose, *Kill Kill Faster Faster*, p. 24, 1997

feeler *noun*
1 a finger *UK, 1831*
- —Lou Shelly, *Hepcats Jive Dictionary*, p. 11, 1945

2 in poker, a small bet made for the purpose of assessing how other players are likely to bet on the hand *US*
- —Albert H. Morehead, *The Complete Guide to Winning Poker*, p. 262, 1967

3 a citizens' band radio antenna on a truck *US*
- —"Slingo", *The Official CB Slang Dictionary Handbook*, p. 23, 1976

feel fine; feel *noun*
nine, especially nine pounds (£9) *UK*
Rhyming slang.
- "Give me a feel" is a request for £9. Be careful who you ask.—Ray Puxley, *Cockney Rabbit*, 1992

feeling *noun*
marijuana *UK*
- —Mike Haskins, *Drugs*, p. 287, 2003

feeling fine *noun*
mutual, simultaneous oral sex between two people *UK*
Rhyming slang for **69**.
- —Bodmin Dark, *Dirty Cockney Rhyming Slang*, 2003

feel up *verb*
to fondle someone sexually *US, 1930*
- They would grab girls in the dark hallways in order to "feel them up."—Phyllis and Eberhard Kronhausen, *Sex Histories of American College Men*, p. 78, 1960
- Have you ever been felt up? Over the bra, under the blouse, shoes off, hoping to God your parents don't walk in?—*The Breakfast Club*, 1985
- Shirley Votypka, the first girl I ever felt up.—*Sleepless in Seattle*, 1993
- Everyone in the gypsy community knows me a Toucher, or Touch for short [...] I got the name as a tiny kid so it's got nothing to do with feeling the ladies up.—Jimmy Stockin, *On The Cobbles*, p. 117, 2000

feely; feele; feelier; fellia; feely-omi *noun*
a young man, a boy *UK, 1859*
Polari, originally with the more general sense as 'children'; from Italian *figlie* (children). A distinction is made in *Old Palare Lexicon*, where 'feele' is defined as 'a child' and 'feely omi' as 'a young man (sometimes specifically an underaged young man)'.
- [T]he feelies in Dressing Room 12.—the cast of 'Aspects of Love', Prince of Wales Theatre, *Palare (Boy Dancer Talk) for Beginners*, 1989–92
- "So sister," I polaried. "Will you take a varder [look] at the cartz [genitalia] on the feely-omi in the naf [poor taste] strides [trousers][.]—James Gardiner, *Who's a Pretty Boy Then?*, p. 123, 1997
- —*Attitude*, p. 60, July 2003: 'Old palare lexicon'

feen *verb*
to look at nude pictures *US*
- —John R. Armore and Joseph D. Wolfe, *Dictionary of Desperation*, p. 28, 1976

feep *noun*
the electronic alert sound made by a computer terminal *US*
- —*Coevolution Quarterly*, p. 30, Spring 1981: 'Computer slang'
- —Eric S. Raymond, *The New Hacker's Dictionary*, p. 152, 1991

feet *noun*
▸ **get your feet muddy**
to get into trouble, especially with the criminal law *UK*
- He got his feet muddy before he had straight work.—David Powis, *The Signs of Crime*, 1977

▸ **have two left feet**
to be clumsy when moving, especially when dancing *UK, 1915*
- "Do you dance well?" "No," the girl said shyly. "I've got two left feet. I only come to watch the others dance."—Piers Anthony, *On a Pale Horse*, p. 174, 1983

feet and yards; feet *noun*
playing cards *UK*
Rhyming slang; always plural.
- —Ray Puxley, *Cockney Rabbit*, 1992

fegary *noun*
▷ see: FIGARY

feh true *adverb*
▷ see: FE TRUE

feh!
used as a declaration of disapproval or disgust *US*
Yiddish, although the Yiddish etymology is not at all clear.
- Feh! You and your gun. Get out of here. Who needs you?—*Goodfellas*, 1990

feisty *adjective*
aggressive, spirited, lively *US, 1896*
- If you like your clubbing to be fierce and feisty, try Le Queen[.]—*The Guardian*, 18th January 2003

felch *verb*
to suck semen from another's anus and rectum *US*
- —Bruce Rodgers, *The Queens' Vernacular*, p. 80, 1972
- [P]olished eveyrthing off by protruding his tongue into Slave's rectum to felch.—Larry Kramer, *Faggots*, p. 6, 1978
- —*Maledicta*, p. 232, 1979: 'Kinks and queens'
- —*Adult Video News*, p. 44, August 1995
- Suck it out. Suck it. Pucker, pucker. When I get a mouthful of that stuff, after I felch her good, I move my hands to my mama's face. —Karen Finley, *A Different Kind of Intimacy*, p. 52, 2000

felcher squelcher *noun*
a condom intended for anal intercourse *UK*
- —David Rowan, *A Glossary for the 90s*, 1998

Felix the cat *noun*
a type of LSD *UK*
Presumably identified by an image of the cartoon hero created by Otto Messmer in 1919.
- —Mike Haskins, *Drugs*, p. 285, 2003

fellah; fella; feller *noun*
1 a male *UK*
- That chimpanzee's a fella[.]—A.S.C. Ross, *U and Non-U Revisited*, 1978

2 a man *UK*
An affected or lazy pronunciation of 'fellow'. 'Feller' since 1825; 'fellah', originally associated with affected or aristocratic speech, since 1864; 'fella' (and variations) since 1934.

- Among things a Fella does, correct grammar is not included. —Winifred Holtby, *Truth Is Not Sober*, 1931
- [Y]ou hear fellars talk about Times Square and Fifth Avenue, and Charing Cross and gay Paree. —Samuel Selvon, *The Lonely Londoners*, p. 103, 1956
- A fella ambles over and shakes Mike by the hand. —Martin King and Martin Knight, *The Naughty Nineties*, p. 65, 1999
- I just headed for this young fella I could see. —Dave Courtney, *Raving Lunacy*, p. 12, 2000

fellia *noun*
▷ see: FEELY

fell off a lorry *adjective*
▷ see: FALLEN OFF THE BACK OF A LORRY

fellowship *noun*
a group activity involving a shared vice *US*
Word play with the conventional, religious usage.
- Let's go have fellowship in the cemetery. —Connie Eble (Editor), *UNC-CH Campus Slang*, p. 3, Fall 1986

fellow traveller; fellow traveler *noun*
1 a person who sympathises with a cause without being a full-blown member of the cause *US, 1936*
Originally applied only to communist sympathisers; translated from the Russian.
- Mr. Ferguson got sprung this afternoon, no thanks to his fellow travelers. —C.D. Payne, *Youth in Revolt*, p. 299, 1993

2 a flea *UK*
- [G]ive them [meths men] six foot clearance if you are still sensitive about fellow travellers, that being the average length of a hefty flea's jump. —Geoffrey Fletcher, *Down Among the Meths Men*, p. 18, 1966

felony *noun*
a girl under the legal age of consent *US*
- —Ben Applebaum and Derrick Pittman, *Turd Ferguson & The Sausage Party*, p. 34, 2004

felony shoes *noun*
expensive training shoes *US*
Favoured by urban youth, often involved in, and more often associated with, crime.
- Most of us know them by their American handles: tennis, gym shoes, sneaks, mackerels, felony sohes, hightops or lowcuts, pussyfooters or athletic shoes. —*Washington Post*, p. B1, 18th August 1978
- These younger patrons are sensitive to the older habitues' description of them as "young turks" or "kids in felony shoes[.]" —Terry Williams, *The Cocaine Kids*, p. 102–103, 1989

felony sneakers *noun*
expensive trainers favoured by urban youth *US, 1979*
- Fifteen ghetto guerrillas wearing Pro-Ke4ds (what transit cops call "felony sneakers") swoop down on a victim, then scatter back into subway oblivion. —Josh Alan Friedman, *Tales of Times Square*, p. 51, 1986

female unit *noun*
a girlfriend *US*
A cheap imitation of 'parental unit'.
- —Connie Eble (Editor), *UNC-CH Campus Slang*, p. 3, Spring 1984

femalia *noun*
those parts of the female body that have a sexual resonance *US*
- The size of her femalia: her tits, lips and the color and feel of her underwear. —Peter Sotos, *Index*, p. 57, 1996

femdom *noun*
a *fem*ale sexual *dom*inant, a dominatrix; female domination as a sexual subculture *US, 1989*
- The front cover [of a specialist magazine] hinted at the delights inside showing pictures of three pairs of women's feet and the headlines: Ladies barefeet Nylon stockings and high-heeled shoes Femdom feet. —Kitty Churchill, *Thinking of England*, p. 156, 1995

fem grem *noun*
an unskilled female surfer *US*
An abbreviation of 'female GREMMIE'.

feminazi *noun*
a feminist *US*
A popular term with, and probably coined by, US radio entertainer Rush Limbaugh who uses the term in order to marginalise any feminist as a hardline, uncompromising man-hater.
- [A]nti-abortion activists holding placards reading "Thank You Lord for This Victory in Life" and "Feminazis Go Home." —*New York Times*, p. 1 (Metro), 4th July 1989
- —David Rowan, *A Glossary for the 90s*, p. 5, 1998
- —Connie Eble (Editor), *UNC-CH Campus Slang*, p. 4, Fall 1999

femme; fem *noun*
1 a young woman *US, 1871*
- "That depends on the fems you got here," said Phil. —James T. Farrell, *Saturday Night*, p. 46, 1947

2 in a homosexual relationship, the person who plays the passive, 'feminine' role *US, 1934*
- —Donald Webster Cory and John P. LeRoy, *The Homosexual and His Society*, p. 264, 1963: 'A lexicon of homosexual slang'
- "In bed, the difference between femme and butch disappears," they will say. "There everybody is ki-ki." —Donald Webster Cory, *The Lesbian in America*, p. 107, 1964
- A typical example of this type of fem lesbian is Geri, whose current liaison is with a "hard-dressing stomper" who calls herself Sam. —Ruth Allison, *Lesbianism*, p. 34, 1967
- In my estimation, a femme is someone, male or female, who embodies the traits, of either or both appearance or character, that we traditionally associated with femaleness. —*Taste of Latex*, p. 6, Winter 1990–1991
- Maggie was Bad Bob's sister's squeeze – the femme half of a dyke duo. —James Elroy, *Hollywood Nocturnes*, p. 287, 1994
- After I saw teenagers Tatum O'Neal and Kristy McNichol in Little Darlings (the perfect butch-femme dyke couple), I couldn't wait to – not to lose my virginity to Matt Dillon, but to have a sex slumber party with those two cuties. —*The Village Voice*, 17th June 2002

femme *adjective*
1 blatantly effeminate *US*
- Chuck the masculine cowboy and Miss Desetiny the femme queen: making it from day to park to bar to day like all the others in that ratty world of downtown L.A. —John Rechy, *City of Night*, p. 105, 1963

2 female *UK*
- Now everyone is scrambling after the femme dollar[.] —*The Times*, 2nd August 2003

femme looker *noun*
in circus and carnival usage, an attractive female *US*
- —Don Wilmeth, *The Language of American Popular Entertainment*, p. 90, 1981

femme queen *noun*
an overtly effeminate male homosexual *US*
- Occasionally the femmequeens from the 1–2–3 or Ji-Jis breeze in like wilted flowers, carried on the currents of smoke: giggling, regally scanning the bar – making studied defiant exits with great airs, grand queenly shrieks of exiled laughter. —John Rechy, *City of Night*, p. 163, 1963

femmi *adjective*
feminist *UK*
- CINDY: fuck off willya bernard manning – if someone said it was a menstrual cycle you'd try an nick it – PIP: wha – talking fucking femmi again eh cind? —Patrick Jones, *Everything Must Go*, p. 143, 2000

femmo *adjective*
feminist *AUSTRALIA*
- We were a vaguely daggy femmo rock band, sort of interesting for a minute. —Peter Wilmoth, *Glad All Over*, p. 114, 1993

fence *noun*
a person who trades in stolen goods *UK, 1698*
- They had made contact with a "fence" from Philadephia, to whom they were to turn over the swag for $150,000 in currency. —Jack Lait and Lee Mortimer, *Chicago Confidential*, p. 18, 1950
- He had been released from Riker's Island almost two months before, and had picked up a few dollars steering second-story men to a friend of his from Chicago days, a fence. —John Clellon Holmes, *John Clellon*, p. 198, 1952
- [I]t's good for a fin by any fence. —George Mandel, *Flee the Angry Strangers*, p. 312, 1952
- They had an exceptionally good fence, the owner of a real estate office, a highly respected citizen. —Clarence Cooper Jr, *The Scene*, p. 34, 1960
- Longshoremen, or fences for them, would come into the bars selling guns, cameras, perfumes, watches, and the like, stolen from the shipping docks. —Malcolm X and Alex Haley, *The Autobiography of Malcolm X*, p. 86, 1964
- He even cut me into the good drygoods thieves so that I would never get burned by fences. —Claude Brown, *Manchild in the Promised Land*, p. 167, 1965
- —Peter Laurie, *Scotland Yard*, p. 323, 1970
- Fenster and McManus have a fence set to take the stuff. —*The Usual Suspects*, 1995

▸ **go over the fence**
to escape from prison *UK*
- —Angela Devlin, *Prison Patter*, p. 58, 1996

▸ **sit on the fence**
to be impartial, neutral or waiting to see who wins *UK, 1887*
- Dad is Caribbean, / mam is a tyke, / do I sit on the fence? / Do I take sides? — *The Guardian*, 3rd May 2001

▸ **take the fence**
(used of a bookmaker) to fail to pay off a winning bet *US*
- — Dan Parker, *The ABC of Horse Racing*, p. 149, 1947

fence *verb*
1 to purchase, receive and/or store stolen goods *UK, 1610*
- Hume calms down and then he asks us how much we fenced it for. — Ted Lewis, *Jack Carter's Law*, 1974
- You start fooling around trying to fence shit like that... — Elmore Leonard, *City Primeval*, p. 18, 1980

2 to cheat on a test *US*
- — *American Speech*, p. 303, December 1955: 'Wayne University slang'

fenced *adjective*
irritated, angry *US*
- So Andrea scores another ten thousand points on Centipede and beats me, right, and then like I break a nail and I'm fenced, fer shurr. — Mary Corey and Victoria Westermark, *Fer Shurr! How to be a Valley Girl*, 1982

fence hanger *noun*
in motor racing, a spectator, usually female, who is more interested in the participants in the race than in the race itself *US*
- Fence hangers are called such because they are usually found clinging to a fence to get a better look, when they are unable to find something more substantial to cling to. — Don Alexander, *The Racer's Dictionary*, p. 25, 1980

fence painting *noun*
a scene in a pornographic film or a photograph of oral sex performed on a woman in a fashion designed to maximise the camera angle, not the woman's pleasure *US*
- Fence painting. Often totally unrealistic, but necessary for viewer coverage, so it looks as if the pussy eater is painting a fence. — *Adult Video News*, p. 44, August 1995

fence parole *noun*
a prison escape *US*
- Kool Tool suddenly clutched Joe's shirt and pointed across the Yard, crying: "Mira! Dude's goin for a fence parole!" — Seth Morgan, *Homeboy*, p. 177, 1990

fence rider *noun*
in motor racing, a driver who moves through the turns on the outside of the curve, nearest the fence *US*
- — Hal Higdon, *Finding the Groove*, p. 300, 1980

fence-to-fence *adjective*
in carnival usage, in control of all the activities in an engagement *US*
- — Gene Sorrows, *All About Carnivals*, p. 16, 1985: 'Terminology'

fencing *noun*
a trade in, or the act of dealing in, stolen property *UK*
- [A] bit of rural screwing where the fencing came unstuck[.] — Derek Raymond (Robin Cook), *The Crust on its Uppers*, p. 42, 1962

fender *noun*
a new employee *US*
Like a fender absorbing the impact of a collision, the new employee absorbs the wrath of the supervisor.
- — *American Speech*, p. 226, October 1955: 'An aircraft production dispatcher's vocabulary'

fender bender *noun*
a minor car accident *US*
- — *American Speech*, p. 268, December 1962: 'The language of traffic policemen'
- — Malachi Andrews and Paul T. Owens, *Black Language*, p. 116, 1973
- — Lewis Poteet, *Car & Motorcycle Slang*, p. 80, 1992
- DONLAN: What happened to you, Freddy? FREDDY: Oh. Little fender bender. — *Copland*, 1997

fenderhead *noun*
a dolt *US*
- Listen, you slant eyed little fenderhead, I'm tellin you she was lopin' my mule under the table. — Joseph Wambaugh, *The Choirboys*, p. 99, 1975

Fenian *noun*
an Irish catholic *UK*
From the American-Irish 'brotherhood' for the support of the revolutionary overthrow of the English government in Ireland.
- [H]ow happy he was back in the Old Regiment over in Ireland, best days of his life, Paddy bashing, fuckin Fenians and cuntin Prods as well, cos they're all shit-shovelling Micks, ain't they, all the same. — J.J. Connolly, *Layer Cake*, p. 109, 2000

fen-phen *noun*
a combination of fenfluramine and phentermine, used as a diet drug and/or central nervous system stimulant *US, 1996*
- — *American Speech*, p. 188, Summer 1997: 'Among the new words'

fenugie *noun*
▷ see: FANOOGIE

feral *noun*
a person holding strong environmentalist views and living an alternative lifestyle *AUSTRALIA, 1994*
- — John Birmingham, *He Died With a Felafel in his Hand*, p. 144, 1994
- The 'ferals', as they are known, lie at the extreme green end of the conservation movement and practice [sic] what they preach by living among and on top of the trees. — *Sun-Herald*, p. 3, 1st January 1995
- We still had our rough edges, our greatcoated winos and barefoot ferals[.] — Shane Maloney, *Nice Try*, p. 129, 1998
- '[A]n odd collection of aboriginals, neo-hippies, "ferals" (back-to-the-land types who have reverted to a semiwild state of nature, indicated usually by matted dreadlocks, permanent deep sunburns, and unkempt hippie garb)[.] — Brian Preston, *Pot Planet*, p. 92, 2002

feral *adjective*
1 aggressive; wild *AUSTRALIA*
- We took it for a few days before turning feral. We'd go, 'Yeah, yeah, yeah,' and piss off to our rooms[.] — John Birmingham, *He Died With a Felafel in his Hand*, p. 172, 1994
- Ray Denning was feisty, feral, and apparently fearless. — Donald Catchlove, *Ray Denning My Life and Time*, p. 2, 1994

2 living a low-technology, alternative, environmentally friendly lifestyle *AUSTRALIA*
- — John Birmingham, *He Died With a Felafel in his Hand*, p. 109, 1994
- Folkies still gather in vast numbers at Port Fairy in Victoria, this year some 80,000 'feral folk' turned out[.] — *Sydney Morning Herald (Spectrum)*, p. 14, 14th January 1995

ferdutzt *adjective*
(among Nova Scotians of German descent) used to describe someone who is confused *CANADA*
- Ferdutzt appears in the English conversation of Lunenburg County people to mean "confused," and derives from the German "verdutzt," vexed, chagrined. — Lewis Poteet, *The South Shore Phrase Book*, p. 45, 1999

fe real; for real *adverb*
genuine; honestly, genuinely; credibly *US, 1956*
- I don't need the bad bwai business, fe real. You always have to be sneaky with drugs[.] — Karline Smith, *Moss Side Massive*, p. 21, 1994
- No seriously, I think its a good idea. Fe real. — Donald Gorgon, *Cop Killer*, p. 21, 1994

fern *noun*
a female's pubic hair *US*
- — *Maledicta*, p. 254, Summer/Winter 1981: 'Five years and 121 dirty words later'

ferret *noun*
1 the penis *AUSTRALIA*
A celebration of the animal's talent for exploring holes.
- [T]he randy old bastard [a ghost] can't think of anything else but puttin' his phantom ferret through the furry hoop [the vagina]! — Barry Humphries, *Bazza Pulls It Off!*, 1971

2 a member of the security services engaged to 'sweep' for and remove electronic bugging devices *UK*
- — John Le Carre, *The Honourable Schoolboy*, 1977

3 a customs officer engaged in searching cargo or cabins for smuggled goods *UK, 1984*
Also called a 'ferreter'.

4 a beret *UK*
In Royal Air Force use, 2002; a deliberately poor rhyme.

▸ **give the ferret a run**
(of a male) to engage in sexual intercourse *AUSTRALIA*
Also variant 'exercise the ferret'.
- This sheila's a flamin' nut case! I haven't even exercised the ferret yet. —Barry Humphries, *The Wonderful World of Barry McKenzie*, p. 42, 1968
- [D]ip the wick, to. To feature or exercise the ferret. —Barry Humphries, *Bazza pulls it off!*, 1971
- —Jim Ramsay, *Cop It Sweet!*, p. 40, 1977
- Ferret, To give it a run: The ferret is a long, phallic animal whose sole purpose in life is to stick its length into a hole and stir up rabbits. Get the picture? —Phil Jarratt, *Sex*, p. 26, 1984

ferry dust *noun*
heroin *UK, 1998*
A play on magical 'fairy dust'.
- —Robert Ashton, *This Is Heroin*, p. 205, 2002
- —Mike Haskins, *Drugs*, p. 283, 2003

ferschlugginer *adjective*
used as a mildly profane intensifier *US, 1955*
A Yiddish term.
- I would suggest you invest in a current issue of it as a kind of test drive before you lay out $70 for the whole ferschlugginer mess. —*Atlanta (Georgia) Journal and Constitution*, p. 4P, 10th October 1999

fer shur; fur shur *adverb*
certainly *US*
A staple of the Valley Girl lexicon, often used as an exclamation.
- —Mary Corey and Victoria Westermark, *Fer Shurr! How to be a Valley Girl*, 1982
- Fere sure, fer sure / She's a Valley Girl —Moon Unit and Frank Zappa, *Valley Girl*, 1982
- Rings fur shur knew she had a career, as in like the Original Gig, though how much choice was less clear. —Seth Morgan, *Homeboy*, p. 4–5, 1990

ferstay *verb*
to understand *CANADA*
- "Ferstay" is the English rendition of the German "verstehe," and in English it is used in place of the word "understand" at the end of an explanation or a set of directions. It may be used with rising inflection for the question, "ferstay?" —Chris Thain, *Cold as a Bay Street Banker's Heart*, p. 65, 1987

fertilize *verb*
▸ **fertilize the vegetables**
to feed or medicate neurologically depressed hospital patients *US*
- —*Maledicta*, p. 118, 1984–1985: 'Milwaukee medical maledicta'

fess; fess up *verb*
to confess *US, 1840*
- [Jim] Morrison, def, does not get a pie in the face! He 'fessed up! —Lester Bangs, *Psychotic Reactions and Carburetor Dung*, p. 36, 1970
- Get 'em to fess up that it's pretty much prisons or casinos in terms of their choices for economic growth. —*Traffic*, 2000
- So even the Conservative power elites have had to fess up and admit they got high in college. —Brian Preston, *Pot Planet*, p. 127, 2002

-fest *suffix*
a gathering together of, or a concentration of, or an event celebrating the qualifying noun with which it combines *US, 1865*
Abbreviated from '*fest*ival'.
- I was always on the lookout for new records to pep up those wax-fests of ours. —Mezz Mezzrow, *Really the Blues*, p. 118, 1946
- Etc., etc., then finally disintegrating into a wild talkfest and yellfest and finally songfest with people rolling on the floor in laughter[.] —Jack Kerouac, *The Dharma Bums*, p. 23, 1958
- —*American Speech*, p. 207–213, 1981: 'Milwaukee medical maledicta'
- —*American Speech*, p. 261–264, Fall 1984: 'Another fest-icon'
- —Connie Eble (Editor), *UNC-CH Campus Slang*, p. 4, Fall 1986: 'Beerfest, buelfest, sleepfest'.
- The Gasworks. An excellent heavy metal bar. Always a babe fest. —*Wayne's World*, 1992
- What's with the screamfest? —*Airheads*, 1994
- Breaking from our gabfest, we dirty-danced to Tom Jones songs. —Anka Radakovich, *The Wild Girls Club*, 1994
- Chili Palmer. Chilly outside. Chili inside. It's a regular fuckin' chili-fest. —*Get Shorty*, 1995
- A major media opportunity [plugfest] to plug your new book mercilessly. Unless spite outdoes the puffery [...] when it becomes what the Sunday papers now call a slugfest. —David Rowan, *A Glossary for the 90s*, p. 125, 1998
- The Cannabis Cup is a huge smokefest[.] —Brian Preston, *Pot Planet*, p. 7, 2002
- Cornershop's reference-fests, however, eschew accusations of ironic posturing. —*Uncut*, p. 88, May 2002
- [S]uch right-leaning slagfests as The O'Reilly Factor[.] —*The Guardian*, 25th July 2003

festering *adverb*
exceedingly *AUSTRALIA*
A euphemism for 'fucking'.
- The Banner is a festering great jumper, but make sure you bring him down between the fences. —Roy Higgins and Tom Prior, *The Jockey Who Laughed*, p. 43, 1982

festivity *noun*
a drinking party *US*
- —*American Speech*, p. 302, December 1955: 'Wayne University slang'

festy *adjective*
disgusting; dreadful; awful *AUSTRALIA*
- —James Lambert, *The Macquarie Book of Slang*, 1996

fet *noun*
am*phet*amine *UK*
- —Angela Devlin, *Prison Patter*, p. 21, 1996

fetch *verb*
1 to deliver (a blow) *UK*
A conventional usage from C12 that slipped into the colloquial register sometime around late C19 or early C20.
- He always used to slam it and try and fetch her shins a wallop. —Ray Galton and Alan Simpson, *Hancock's Half Hour*, 22nd April 1958
- She's lost her colour now, except for the spot on the side of her face where I fetched her one. —Ted Lewis, *Jack Carter's Law*, p. 129, 1974

2 in computing, to retrieve and import a file from an Internet site to your computer *US*
- —Christian Crumlish, *The Internet Dictionary*, p. 68, 1995

fetch up *verb*
to arrive, especially to arrive eventually *US, 1858*
- He dropped out of school in his mid-teens, and duly fetched up in reform school. —*The Guardian*, 12th May 2004

fe true; for true; feh true *adverb*
honestly, truly *UK*
West Indian and UK black patois, 'for true'. Also used as an exclamation and intensifier.
- "Wha'appen, rudebwai?" Zukie said laughing. "Me never recognise yuh fe true.["] —Karline Smith, *Moss Side Massive*, p. 120, 1994

fetschpatz *noun*
(among Ontario's Mennonites) a dumpling *CANADA*
- Fetschpatzen are dumplings fried by dropping batter by the tablespoonful into hot fat and then serving with maple syrup. The name comes from German "Fett-spatz," a "lard-sparrow." —Bill Casselman, *Canadian Food Words*, p. 181, 1998

fever *noun*
1 five *US*
An intentional corruption of **FIVER**.
- On the four-part number six Otto actually sank his second putt for a bogey-five. "Fever!" Otto cried. "Gimme a fever!" "Five for Otto!" Archie said[.] —Joseph Wambaugh, *The Secrets of Harry Bright*, p. 150, 1985

2 in craps, a roll of five *US*
Sometimes embellished to 'fever in the South'.
- —*The Annals of the American Academy of Political and Social Sciences*, p. 124, May 1950

3 in a deck of playing cards, any five *US, 1951*
- —Albert H. Morehead, *The Complete Guide to Winning Poker*, p. 262, 1967

4 a $5 note *US, 1961*
- —George Percy, *The Language of Poker*, p. 34, 1988

5 an enthusiastic interest or, perhaps, mass-hysteria *UK, 1885*
- Football fever gripped even Wimbledon yesterday with all eyes focused on Lisbon and England's final Euro 2004 group match against Croatia. —*The Guardian*, 22nd June 2004

fevver clucker *noun*
used as a humorous euphemism for 'clever fuker' *NEW ZEALAND*
- —David McGill, *David McGill's Complete Kiwi Slang Dictionary*, p. 49, 1998

few *noun*
1 a few alcoholic drinks *AUSTRALIA, 1903*
- 'Pay no attention to him, Kev, he's as silly as Mawbey when he's had a few.' —Angelo Loukakis, *For the Patriarch*, p. 153, 1981

2 any short jail sentence *US*
- —Vincent J. Monteleone, *Criminal Slang*, p. 82, 1949

fews and twos *noun*
very little money *US*
- —Jack Lait and Lee Mortimer, *New York Confidential*, p. 235, 1948: 'A glossary of Harlemisms'
- —Clarence Major, *Dictionary of Afro-American Slang*, p. 53, 1970

fey *adjective*

effeminate *US*

- He arched his shoulder and made a fey grimace of imitation. —John Clellon Holmes, *Go*, p. 7, 1952
- And there was such a peculiar charm about her, such a fey-ish quality, that they never fought nor protested. —Jim Thompson, *Roughneck*, p. 136, 1954
- This is all a bit fey for my taste. —Gore Vidal, *Myra Breckinridge*, p. 61, 1968
- If he was a true pothead – and sometimes he thought that he was – this fey sixty-year-old with the flyaway hair and the old kimonos was the fiend who had led him down the garden path. —Armistead Maupin, *Babycakes*, p. 29, 1984
- Dodie called the entire group [the Bee Gees] fey in the worst of ways and proof that lightning could strike more than once in the same family. —Rita Ciresi, *Pink Slip*, p. 107, 1999

Fezzer *noun*

a Ford 'Fiesta' car *UK*

Essex use.

- —Chris Lewis, *The Dictionary of Playground Slang*, p. 88, 2003

fezzie *noun*

a festival *UK*

- [T]he next Exodus festival, which they called a Fezzie. —Brian Preston, *Pot Planet*, p. 137, 2002

FFF *verb*

to *f*ind, *f*ix and *f*inish *US*

A military axiom for dealing with the enemy; the 'fix' is 'to fix in position', while the 'finish' is 'to kill'.

- —Gregory Clark, *Words of the Vietnam War*, p. 175, 1990

FHB

*f*amily *h*old *b*ack! *AUSTRALIA*

A directive to family members to take guests into account when serving themselves.

- By that time, Mother had brewed a pot of tea and returned from the shop with the Swallows assorted cream biscuits which she passed around in the packet with that FHB (Family Hold Back) look which meant one biscuit each[.] —Kerry Cue, *Crooks, Chooks and Bloody Ratbags*, p. 21, 1983

fid *noun*

a British worker in Antarctica *ANTARCTICA, 1952*

Originally an acronym of 'Falkland Island Dependencies Survey'.

- —Bernadette Hince, *The Antarctic Dictionary*, p. 127, 2000

fiddle *noun*

1 a swindle, a deception; in later use, especially of petty-fraud *UK, 1873*

- Either this bloke in the paper is a bloody liar, or there is a fiddle going on with you people. —Joe Morgan, *Eastenders Don't Cry*, p. 90, 1994

2 a one-pound note; the sum of one pound; (collectively) money *AUSTRALIA*

- He kept on with the milk cart, enjoying the steady bank, the extra fiddle and an outdoor job where he was his own boss. —Clive Galea, *Slipper*, p. 9, 1988

3 in pickpocket usage, a coat *US, 1943*

- —Vincent J. Monteleone, *Criminal Slang*, p. 82, 1949

4 a radio *US*

- —Montie Tak, *Truck Talk*, p. 58, 1971

▸ **on the fiddle**

engaged in swindling or petty-fraud *UK, 1961*

fiddle *verb*

1 to swindle *UK, 1590*

- If I'd been in the paymaster's section, they'd have suspected I'd fiddled the books. —John Baxter, *A Pound of Paper*, p. 122, 2002

2 to falsify a personal statement of expenses, or corporate accounts and finances; to fraudulently amend examination or election results *UK, 1970*

A specialised use of the overall sense (to swindle).

- Archer's secretary denies fiddling expenses. —*The Guardian*, 7th June 2001
- On 21 July, the WorldCom corporation admitted that it had fiddled the books to the tune of $3.8bn of stockholders' money. —*The Observer*, 22nd December 2002

▸ **fiddle with yourself**

to masturbate *US*

- JOHN LENNON: I mean I suppose your first sex experience is fiddlin' with yourself. —*Screw*, p. 4, 27th June 1969

fiddle and fire *noun*

in the car sales business, a radio and heater *US*

- —*Cars*, p. 40, December 1953

fiddle bitch *verb*

to potter aimlessly *CANADA*

- —Tom Parkin, *WetCoast Words*, p. 52, 1989

fiddlededee; fiddley *noun*

an act of urination *UK*

Rhyming slang for **PEE** or **WEE**. Presumably coined with some euphemistic intent, yet 'to go for a fiddley' seems, somehow, a more ambiguous option.

- —Ray Puxley, *Cockney Rabbit*, 1992

fiddlefart around *verb*

to waste time doing little or nothing *US, 1972*

- —Pamela Munro, *U.C.L.A. Slang*, p. 63, 1997

fiddlefuck *verb*

to waste time *US, 1949*

- Boys, Grandmother was slow, but she was crippled and born blind. But you've been fiddlefuckin' around here for three hours and ain't accomplished Jack Shit. —Ken Weaver, *Texas Crude*, p. 112, 1984

fiddler *noun*

1 a bookmaker who will only take small bets *UK*

- It's cockle [10–1] with the fiddlers. —John McCririck, *John McCririck's World of Betting*, p. 110, 1991

2 a paedophile *NEW ZEALAND*

Prison usage.

- —Harry Orsman, *A Dictionary of Modern New Zealand Slang*, p. 49, 1999

fiddler's elbow *noun*

the right-angled sharp turns in country roads *CANADA*

- Narrow, curving, and unblessed with gravel, the road to Hudson's Hope has many a switchback and 'fiddler's elbow' too slippery to negotiate in wet weather. —*Beaver*, p. 18, September 1950
- —Harry Shufelt, *Along the Old Roads*, p. 40, 1965

▸ **in and out like a fiddler's elbow**

applied to anything or anyone that enters and exits a given situation with unusual rapidity; especially, of a male's enthusiastic thrusting during sexual intercourse *UK*

- A cruise down The Listening Bank, make em pay attention by waving a sawn-off around and hop it with a bag of notes, in an out like a fiddler's elbow. —Andrew Nickolds, *Back to Basics*, p. 105, 1994
- What are the Government's intentions on the proposed draft Mental Health Bill, which appears to have been in and out like a fiddler's elbow? Again, the House and people outside are keen to find out what is happening. —Andrew Stunell (Hazel Grove), *Hansard (The United Kingdom Parliament)*, 19th December 2002

fiddler's fuck *noun*

a notional item of no value *US, 1961*

- Didn't make a fiddler's fuck and all they could was to hang tough and hope the scene would break soon. —Hubert Selby, *Requiem for a Dream*, p. 183, 1978

fiddlers three; fiddlers *noun*

an act of urination *UK*

Rhyming slang for **WEE** or **PEE**, formed from the lyrics to the traditional nursery-song, 'Old King Cole'. A variant of **FIDDLEDEDEE**.

- —Ray Puxley, *Cockney Rabbit*, 1992

fiddlesticks!

used as an all-purpose cry of frustration *UK, 1600*

Considered inoffensive, however it is possibly a pun on 'penis', via 'sword', the Shakespearean 'fiddlestick', although the bawdy pun itself is not made by Shakespeare.

- "Careful, fiddlesticks!" she snapped. —Jim Thompson, *Savage Night*, p. 119, 1953
- Shit! Fuck! Fiddlesticks! Guy'd be going mad. —Kevin Sampson, *Powder*, p. 297, 1999

fiddley *noun*

a one-pound note; the sum of one pound *AUSTRALIA, 1941*

Short for **FIDDLEYDID**.

- —Jim Ramsay, *Cop It Sweet!*, p. 35, 1977

fiddleydid *noun*

a one-pound note; the sum of one pound *AUSTRALIA, 1941*

Rhyming slang for **QUID**. This lasted briefly after the introduction of decimal currency (1966), and was used to denote the comparative sum of $2.

- —Nino Culotta (John O'Grady), *They're A Weird Mob*, p. 42, 1957
- Paid a hundred thousand fiddleydids for a billiard table.—Frank Hardy, *The Yarns of Billy Borker*, p. 94, 1965
- —Jim Ramsay, *Cop It Sweet!*, p. 35, 1977

fiddly bits *noun*

chrome embellishments on a motorcyle saddle bag and seat *US*

Biker (motorcycle) usage.

fidlet *noun*

a British expeditioner recently arrived in Antarctica *ANTARCTICA, 1967*

- —Bernadette Hince, *The Antarctic Dictionary*, p. 128, 2000

fido!

used for suggesting that a group overcome an obstacle *US*

An abbreviation of '*f*uck *i*t, *d*rive *o*n'.

- —Connie Eble (Editor), *UNC-CH Campus Slang*, p. 2, November 1983
- —Linda Reinberg, *In the Field*, p. 79, 1991

fido dido *noun*

a variety of MDMA, the recreational drug best known as ecstasy *UK, 1990s*

From the borrowed image of Fido Dido, a fashionable cartoon youth of Spanish origin, imprinted into the tablet as a brand logo.

fi-do-nie *noun*

opium *US, 1954*

- —Richard A. Spears, *The Slang and Jargon of Drugs and Drink*, p. 193, 1986
- —Jay Robert Nash, *Dicitonary of Crime*, p. 128, 2003
- —Mike Haskina, *Drugs*, p. 283, 2003

field *verb*

to work as a bookmaker *AUSTRALIA*

- He had very little time to celebrate Comedy King's success for within a few minutes he was fielding on the next race.—Maurice Cavanough and Meurig Davies, *Cup Day*, p. 147, 1960
- —James Holledge, *The Great Australian Gamble*, p. 81, 1966
- Grafter Kingsley was fielding at Boolaroo races. His bank was light and when the first three favourites won, he went broke.—Frank Hardy and Athol George Mulley, *The Needy and the Greedy*, p. 37, 1975
- —Joe Andersen, *Winners Can Laugh*, p. 70, 1982
- —Clive Galea, *Slipper*, p. 64, 1988

field circus *noun*

in computing, field service *US*

- Q. How can you recognize a DEC field circus engineer with a flat tire? A: He's changing each tire to see which one is flat. Q: How can you recognize a DEC field circus engineer who is out of gas? A: He's changing each tire to see which one is flat.—Eric S. Raymond, *The New Hacker's Dictionary*, p. 154, 1991

fielder *noun*

a bookmaker *AUSTRALIA, 1936*

- Fielders Differ [heading]Book makers could not agree on an early market for the flying Handicap.—*Sydney Morning Heaarld*, 13th February 1954
- Bookmaker Harry Barrett was happy with the switch of the Randwick interstate betting ring on Saturday but it has its critics. Bookmakers operating on away events were positioned closer to the local fielders, where there was formerly a gap.—*Sydney Morning Herald*, p. 41, 26th September 1994

fielders *noun*

a rum ration carried on a field trip *AUSTRALIA, 1972*

- —Bernadette Hince, *The Antarctic Dictionary*, p. 128, 2000

field goal *noun*

in pool, a shot in which the cue ball passes between the object ball and another ball, touching neither *US*

An allusion to American football, in which a field ball is scored when the ball is kicked between the goalpost uprights.

- —Mike Shamos, *The Illustrated Encyclopedia of Billiards*, p. 93, 1993

field music *noun*

a military bugler *US*

Last used in the Korean war.

- Each infantry battalion rates a bugler or "field musik."—Martin Russ, *The Last Parallel*, p. 153, 1957
- A cleanup of barracks, no matter how long it lasted, was a field day; a neck tie was a field scarf, drummers and trumpeters were field musics.—William Manchester, *Goodbye, Darkness*, p. 146, 1979

field nigger *noun*

a black person who does not curry favour from white people and thus is afforded no degree of privilege *US*

- Professors are house niggers and students are field niggers.—Jerry Rubin, *Do It!*, p. 215, 1970
- Malcolm X extended and popularized the concept; a field nigger was more likely to become a revolutionary while the house nigger was more likely to be an Uncle Tom.—Clarence Major, *Dictionary of Afro-American Slang*, p. 53, 1970
- A term used by young Black Revolutionaries in the late 1960s as a way of identifying the slave who wasn't ready for slavery. (The term went out with the 70's, but the feeling remains.)—Malachi Andrews and Paul T. Owens, *Black Language*, p. 78, 1973

field of wheat *noun*

a street *UK, 1859*

Rhyming slang, with a deliberately ironic inversion of its original sense.

- You're only a field of wheats away from work.—*The Sweeney*, p. 6, 1976

fields *noun*

▷ **see:** STRAWBERRY FIELDS

field scarf *noun*

a necktie *US*

Marine Corps usage in World War 2 and Korea.

- A cleanup of barracks, no matter how long it lasted, was a field day; a necktie was a field scarf[.]—William Manchester, *Goodbye, Darkness*, p. 146, 1979

field-strip *verb*

1 to disassemble; to take apart *US, 1947*

- They must, as well, memorize ... how to field strip its seventeen major components at speed.—Daniel Da Cruz, *Boot*, p. 62, 1987

2 to break tobacco loose from a smoked cigarette and disperse it in the wild without leaving a trace of the cigarette *US, 1963*

- If you don't want to put the butt in your pocket because of loose tobacco, you can "field strip" it.—Mark Harvey, *The National Outdoor Leadership School's Wilderness Guide*, p. 162, 1999

fiend *noun*

1 a person who habitually or compulsively indulges in narcotics, especially morphine and cocaine *US, 1881*

Modern usage is generally ironic, except when politicians and tabloid newspapers need a headline.

2 a person who smokes marijuana when alone *UK*

Marijuana use is considered to be a communal activity hence a solo-smoker is the subject of criticism. Used ironically in this context.

3 an enthusiast *US, 1884*

From the sense as 'addict'.

- Diary of a drag fiend.—*The Guardian*, 1st September 2001

fiend *verb*

1 to cause a car to drop suddenly, almost to the ground, by use of hydraulic lifts *US*

- —Edith A. Folb, *runnin' down some lines*, p. 236, 1980

2 when arresting an unruly person, to use a choke hold *US*

- —Carsten Stroud, *Close Pursuit*, p. 271, 1987

fiendish *adjective*

excellent *US, 1900*

- —*Current Slang*, p. 23, Fall 1968
- —Carl J. Banks Jr, *Banks Dictionary of the Black Ghetto Language*, 1975

fiend on *verb*

to show off; to better *US*

- —Edith A. Folb, *runnin' down some lines*, p. 237, 1980

fierce *adjective*

very, very good *US*

- I love RuPaul. She is fierce.—Kevin Dilallo, *The Unofficial Gay Manual*, p. 240, 1994
- Gaultier's fall line is fierce!—Jeff Fessler, *When Drag Is Not a Car Race*, p. 83, 1997

fife and drum *noun*

the buttocks *UK, 1960*

- A naughty child may be threatened with having its fife and drum smacked.—Ray Puxley, *Cockney Rabbit*, 1992

fifi bag *noun*
a home-made contraption used by a masturbating male to simulate the sensation of penetration *US*
- Jail birds, cons, and other unfortunate victims of bad laws call this ingenious invention a Fifi Bag. — *Screw*, p. 23, 27th October 1969
- — *Maledicta*, p. 218, 1979: 'Kinks and queens: linguistic and cultural aspects of the terminology for gays'
- Males, bereft of female comfort, sometimes resort to a fi-fi bag, a plastic sack containing a warm, wet towel used as a vagina. — *Maledicta*, p. 265, Summer/Winter 1981
- They take orange juice cartons from the Commissary, yeah, cut em in half and stuff em with a baggie loaded with hand lotion. That's your basic fifi bag. — Seth Morgan, *Homeboy*, p. 211, 1990
- — William Bentley, *Prison Slang*, p. 63, 1992
- A Fifi towel is a homemade vagina. — Suroosh Alvi et al., *The Vice Guide*, p. 207, 2002

fifteen and two; fifteen-two *noun*
a Jewish person *US, 1984*
Rhyming slang; Partridge suggests the term originates in scoring for the card game cribbage.

fifteen fucker *noun*
a military disciplinary reprimand *US*
- Instead, each of them was reprimanded, fined $300, and given an Article 15 – an administrative punishment known within the ranks as a Fifteen Fucker – "for conduct totally unbecoming an officer." — Rick Atkinson, *The Long Gray Line*, p. 295, 1989

fifteen minutes of fame *noun*
the brief period of celebrity that Andy Warhol saw as an element of pop culture *US*
- AUSTIN: If you can become famous, everyone will have their fifteen minutes of fame, man. ANDY WARHOL: "Fifteen minutes of fame?" I'm going to use that quote and not give you any credit for that, either. — *Austin Powers*, 1997

fifth *noun*
▸ **take the fifth**
to listen to a fellow alcoholic recount their worst misdeeds without comment or judgement *US*
- You want to take the fifth with me? — Robert Campbell, *Sweet La-La Land*, p. 40, 1990

fifth gear *noun*
a state of intoxication *US*
- — *Current Slang*, p. 7, Spring 1968

Fifth Street *noun*
in seven-card stud poker, a player's third face-up card (the *fifth* card dealt to the player) *UK*
- — Dave Scharf, *Winning at Poker*, p. 235, 2003

fifty *noun*
1 a serving of beer that is half new and half old *AUSTRALIA, 1965*
A shortening of FIFTY FIFTY.
- Five schooners of fifty, thanks, love. — Frank Hardy, *The Outcasts of Foolgarah*, p. 76, 1971
- — John O'Grady, *It's Your Shout, Mate!*, p. 90, 1972

2 a .50 calibre machine gun *US*
- I wrapped my blanket around my shoulders and sat behind my fifty with my knees drawn up[.] — Larry Heinemann, *Close Quarters*, p. 201, 1977
- No-one had told him, I'm quite sincere / That a fifty will put a hole / In a Centurion's rear. — Martin Cameron, *A Look at the Bright Side*, 1988

fifty-dollar lane *noun*
in trucking, the inside passing lane *US*
A name based on the fine at the time on many motorways for truckers who used the inside lane.
- — Wayne Floyd, *Jason's Authentic Dictionary of CB Slang*, p. 14, 1976

fifty-eleven *noun*
a mythical large number *US*
- — Clarence Major, *Dictionary of Afro-American Slang*, p. 53, 1970

fifty-fifty *noun*
1 oral sex followed by anal sex *US*
Largely supplanted by HALF AND HALF.

2 in the television and film industries, a shot of two actors facing each other, each taking up half the screen *US*
- — Tony Miller and Patricia George, *Cut! Print!*, p. 73, 1977

3 a serving of beer that is half new and half old *AUSTRALIA*
- I tried 'em all – new an' old and fifty fifty an' what have you. — John O'Grady, *It's Your Shout, Mate!*, p. 44, 1972

fifty-fifty!
give me half of what you are consuming! *FIJI*
Recorded by Jan Tent.

fifty-five *noun*
in craps, a roll of two fives *US, 1974*
- — Thomas L. Clark, *The Dictionary of Gambling and Gaming*, p. 79, 1987

fifty-mission cap *noun*
a cap similar to that worn by bomber crews during World War 2 *US, 1956*
- He grinned, doffing his fifty-mission cap. — Stephen J. Cannell, *The Plan*, p. 235, 1995

fifty-one; one-fifty-one *noun*
small pieces of crack cocaine sprinkled in a tobacco or marijuana cigarette *US*
- — US Department of Justice, *Street Terms*, October 1994
- Terrence Moore is standing in the men's room in the concrete catacombs of Houlihan's Stadium, doing his business and talking about how it feels to smoke a "51" – street slang for a cocaine and marijuana cigarette. — *St. Petersburg (Florida) Times*, p. 1B, 18th May 1997

fifty PSI finger *noun*
(among Canadian armed forces personnel) a finger poked into someone's chest to emphasise a point forcefully *CANADA*
- The "fifty-p.s.i. finger" is an index finger that is jabbed angrily into another's chest, to punctuate points in an argument. The finger is said to have a pressure of about 50 pounds per square inch. — Tom Langeste, *Words on the Wing*, p. 96, 1995

fifty-two *noun*
in craps, a roll of five and two – a seven *US*
- I faded his bet / and to my regret / and watched him throw fifty-two. — Lightnin' Rod, *Hustlers Convention*, p. 58, 1973

fifty-two/twenty club *noun*
US military veterans who were entitled to benefits of $20 a week for a year after World War 2, making a life of bohemian leisure possible *US, 1946*
- — *American Speech*, February 1949
- My reason for going to the Veteran's Administration was the 52–20 Club. The Government gave all ex-GIs $20 a week for a year or until you could find a job. — Lenny Bruce, *How to Talk Dirty and Influence People*, p. 27, 1965
- Mac ran around with all the 52–20 madmen in Papa Joe's[.] — Gilbert Sorrentino, *Steelwork*, p. 73, 1970

fig *noun*
1 hardly anything at all *UK, 1400*
- "But a fig to them all!" cried Linden-Evarts, breaking into Jefferson's reverie. — Max Shulman, *Anyone Got a Match?*, p. 69, 1964

2 an effeminate male *US*
An amelioration of FAG.
- — *San Francisco Examiner: People*, p. 8, 27th October 1963: 'What a "Z"! The astonishing private language of Bay Area teenagers'

3 (of chewing tobacco) a plug *CANADA, 1862*
- All I can offer you right now is a chaw off my fig o'tobacco. — Thomas Raddall, *The Wings of Night*, p. 78, 1956

figary; fegary *noun*
a fanciful mood; stylish clothing; whimsical ideas or notions; an impulsive decision *IRELAND*
- I strummed the strings, rising to a gradual crescendo. In the end it was so loud that all the boys turned to investigate this sudden fegary. — Billy Roche, *Tumbling Down*, p. 9, 1984

figging *adjective*
used as a euphemism for the intensifying 'fucking' *US*
- Hope of Chateau-roux is worth a figging king's ransom to Philip and the Pope. — Katherine Sutcliffe, *Hope and Glory*, p. 66–67, 1999

Fightertown USA *nickname*
the Miramar Naval Air Station, Miramar, California *US*
- They were beginning to call the base "Fightertown," as the U.S. military increased its readiness in response to the growing war in Southeast Asia. — Robert K. Wilcox, *Scream of Eagles*, p. 15, 1990

fighting drunk *adjective*
in a state of drunken intoxication that prompts aggressive behaviour *UK, 1937*
Also used as a noun.
- I get called to people who are fighting drunk and I inject them to calm them down. This is not an easy job. — *The Guardian*, 13th August 2002

fighting fifth *noun*
any sexually transmitted infection *UK*
Rhyming slang for 'syph' (syphilis).
- —Ray Puxley, *Cockney Rabbit*, 1992

Fighting Hannah *nickname*
the USS Hancock *US*
An aircraft carrier that saw service in World War 2 and Vietnam.
- Fightin' Hannah Has Proud Record [Headline] —*Treasure Island Digest*, p. 7, 27th October 1945

Fighting Irish *nickname*
the athletes of Notre Dame University *US*
- —Howard B. Bonham, *Football Lingo*, p. 18, 1962
- He escaped by being an all-American linebacker for the fighting Irish[.] —Jimmy Buffett, *Tales from Margaritaville*, p. 67, 1989

fighting lager *noun*
a lager of more than average strength *UK*
- Any brand of lager that is lower in alcohol than a "fighting lager". —Andrew Holmes, *Sleb*, p. 150, 2002

Fightlink *nickname*
a Dublin night bus *IRELAND*
- I think about heading for a Fightlink, roysh [right], but I end up hitting Cocoon on my focking sweeney. —Paul Howard, *Ross O'Carroll-Kelly*, p. 175, 2003

figjam *noun*
a boastful person *AUSTRALIA*
- [F]igjam – f@#k im good, just ask me. It is referred to those who think they're the best. Example: that guy over there is such a figjam. Comments: It is used by teens, it is rude. You dont want to be called a figjam! —*KID (Kids Internet Dictionary)*, 1996
- The open advocate of their own creativity is quickly given a place in the pecking order along with the rest of the 'tall poppies, the figjams, the big-noters, the ambitious crawlers, the trouble-makers, the stirrers and the nerds'. —Murray Cree, *Troublesome Pathways*, 2000

figjam!
stop boasting! *AUSTRALIA*
- —Susan Kurosawa, *Teenspeak*, p. 30, 1996

figmo; fuigmo *noun*
fuck it, got my orders; fuck you, I got my orders *US, 1957*
Korean and then Vietnam war usage. Descriptive of a somewhat defiant attitude. The sanitised version is FIGMOH: 'finally I got my orders home!'.
- —*American Speech*, p. 121, 2nd May 1960: 'Korean bamboo english'
- —*Current Slange*, p. 13, Fall 1967
- It was very hard to get figmo people to do a job well. They were just plain complacent. So what are the factors thta lead pilots to become figmo? —R. Randall Padfield, *Flying in Adverse Conditions*, p. 245, 1994

figmo chart *noun*
a record which a soldier kept of the number of days remaining until he was rotated home from Korea or, later, Vietnam *US*
- —*True*, p. 81, August 1966
- —Carl Fleischhauer, *A Glossary of Army Slang*, p. 19, 1968

fig-skin family *noun*
distant relatives whom you rarely see *TRINIDAD AND TOBAGO, 1999*
- —Lise Winer, *Dictionary of the English/Creole of Trinidad & Tobago*, 2003

figure *noun*
a number to be bet upon in an illegal lottery or numbers game *US*
- For two weeks the runner tried to stall his customers but one night they found him with his throat cut and since that day I have never played another "figure." —Babs Gonzales, *I Paid My Dues*, p. 7, 1967

figure *verb*
▸ **it figures; that figures**
it is reasonable or understandable; it works out as expected *US, 1952*
A figurative use of the arithmetic sense.
- Well, it figures. Women, in my experience, are pushovers for fashion. —*The Observer*, 8th December 2002

figure of eight it *verb*
(a notional action) to tighten the vagina *UK*
- Blimey you'd 'ave to figure of eight it to get any pleasure from it! —*www.LondonSlang.com*, June 2002

figures *noun*
an illegal lottery in which winners are those who have bet on a number chosen by some random method *US*
Best known as 'the numbers' or 'policy racket'.
- Every year for the next five, he opened another restaurant chain to his empire, while all the time dabbling in the figures (Numbers game). —Babs Gonzales, *I Paid My Dues*, p. 83, 1967

fiji *noun*
a member of the Phi Delta Gamma college fraternity *US, 1963*
- He invited even the youngest midshipmen to the FIJI house for parties. —*The Virginian-Pilot*, p. A1, 6th November 1994

Fila cunt's trainer *noun*
a Fila™ sport shoe *UK*
An aural pun on 'feeler', current in UK prisons in August 2002.

file *noun*
a pickpocket *UK, 1665*
- —Vincent J. Monteleone, *Criminal Slang*, p. 83, 1949
- —Joseph E. Ragen and Charles Finston, *Inside the World's Toughest Prison*, p. 798, 1962: 'Penitentiary and underworld glossary'

file *verb*
1 to throw away *US*
Office irony.
- —Connie Eble (Editor), *UNC-CH Campus Slang*, p. 2, Fall 1982

2 to dress up *US*
An abbreviation of 'profile'.
- —Connie Eble (Editor), *UNC-CH Campus Slang*, p. 3, Spring 1989

file 13 *noun*
an office waste-paper basket *US, 1942*

file 17 *noun*
the rubbish (trash) *US*
- —Delbertt W.Hamilton, *American Speech*, February 1989: 'Pacific war language'

filet *noun*
an attractive female *US*
- —Pamela Munro, *U.C.L.A. Slang*, p. 38, 1989

filiome *noun*
a young man, especially an underage participant in homosexual sex *UK*
A combination of **FEELY** (a boy) and **OMEE** (a man).
- —Paul Baker, *Polari*, p. 174, 2002

fill *verb*
▸ **fill a blanket**
to roll a cigarette *US*
- —Vincent J. Monteleone, *Criminal Slang*, p. 83, 1949

▸ **fill the bill**
to fulfil requirements, to meet the need *US, 1880*
- If you enjoy a lively nightlife, the area all around the Bund will fill the bill. —*The Guardian*, 24th February 2003

▸ **fill your boots**
1 to do whatever it is you want very much to do, but are hesitating over *CANADA*
This is a Nova Scotia encouraging injunction. It has been suggested that it derives from either the pursuit of fish while wearing high-top wading boots or the effect on the bowels of extreme enjoyment after restraint.
- —Lewis Poteet, *The South Shore Phrase Book*, p. 45, 1999

2 to have as much of something as you want or need; to do some activity to its limit *UK*
- —Susie Dent, *The Language Report*, p. 81, 2003

filled *adjective*
1 (used of a woman) shapely *US*
- —Judi Sanders, *Da Bomb!*, p. 10, 1997

2 of a car's body, repaired with glass fibre *UK*
- —*Woman's Own*, 28th February 1968

filled-in *adjective*
pregnant *AUSTRALIA, 1955*

filler pig *noun*
in a carnival, a woman hired to entertain customers outside a side show before the featured talent appears *US*
- —*American Speeche*, p. 308–309, December 1960: 'Carnival talk'

fillet *noun*
cocaine *US*
A metaphor alluding to the drug's high cost and status.
- —Peter Johnson, *Dictionary of Street Alcohol and Drug Terms*, p. 74, 1993

fillet of cod; fillet *noun*
an unpleasant individual *UK*
Rhyming slang for **SOD** (a contemptible man).
- Cheeky little fillet of cod. What she needed was a good smack on the Kingdom come [the bottom]. —Ronnie Barker, *Fletcher's Book of Rhyming Slang*, p. 43, 1979

fillet of plaice; fillet *noun*
a face; the face *UK*
Rhyming slang.
- —Ray Puxley, *Cockney Rabbit*, 1992

fill in *verb*
1 to temporarily replace someone at work *US, 1930*
- This is Janine [...] she said, She's filling in for Maggie. - Welcome Janine filler-in-for-Maggie, he said[.]—Jane Rogers, *Lucky*, p. 15, 1999

2 to beat up *UK, 1948*
- I had been filled in a few times[.]—Andy McNab, *Immediate Action*, p. 48, 1995
- He's right, Brad. Filling Mario in won't achieve anything. —Colin Butts, *Is Harry on the Boat?*, p. 188, 1997

3 to make pregnant *AUSTRALIA, 1955*
- 'I told that Maudie bitch of mine,' he said. 'I warned her. "Watch yourself," I said. "You get yourself filled in and that's the end of you."' —Olaf Ruhen, *Naked Under Capricorn*, p. 96, 1958

fillings *noun*
loose tobacco *US*
- —Hyman E. Goldin et al., *Dictionary of American Underworld Lingo*, p. 69, 1950

Fillmore *noun*
a potent mixture of alcoholic beverages *US*
- Sidney Hil, 24, says he stayed wasted on "Fillmores" - street slang for a mixture of Olde English, St. Ides, gin and orange juice - before hitting bottom and coming to Recovery House. —*San Francisco Chronicle*, p. A19, 3rd June 1993

fills *noun*
dice which have been weighted for cheating *US*
- —*The Annals of the American Academy of Political and Social Sciences*, p. 124, May 1950

fillum; filum *noun*
a motion picture *AUSTRALIA, 1932*
Representing a widely decried but nonetheless common enough Australian pronunciation of 'film' with two syllables.
- Saw a beaut fillum the other day. —Sue Rhodes, *Now you'll think I'm awful*, p. 71, 1967
- —Barry Humphries, *A Nice Night's Entertainment*, p. 183, 1978
- [T]he arse has dropped out of the Australian fillum industry. —*The Traveller's Tool*, p. 19, 1985
- Not in this fucking movie, by the way. Oh no, kidder - in this filum I'm a lad that's got a tiny little dick. —Kevin Sampson, *Clubland*, p. 32, 2002

fill up *verb*
in poker, to complete a desired hand by drawing cards *US*
- —*American Speech*, p. 98, May 1951

filly *noun*
1 a young woman *UK, 1614*
- [S]ome of his I.W.W. constiuents would probably kick over the traces if they saw the highfalutin' fillies he runs with in Washington. —Jack Lait and Lee Mortimer, *Washington Confidential*, p. 87, 1951
- Seriously, I wish I had Super Bowl seats for every time I had some filly just come up and start talking to me without the slightest provocation. —*Sex, Lies and Videotape*, 1989
- Maybe there were some decent fillies on your flight. —Colin Butts, *Is Harry on the Boat?*, p. 61, 1997
- I prefer to take a filly back to Sanderson Acres[.]—Kevin Sampson, *Clubland*, p. 104, 2002

2 in poker, a hand consisting of three of the same suit and a pair *US*
Conventionally known as a 'full house'.
- —*American Speech*, p. 98, May 1951

filly *adjective*
pretty *UK*
- —Paul Baker, *Polari*, p. 174, 2002

film *noun*
underwear *FIJI*
Recorded by Jan Tent in 1992.

filth *noun*
1 the police; the CID *UK, 1967*
- —Tom Hibbert, *Rockspeak!*, p. 60, 1983
- "We went to Jimmy South's funeral." "So did all the crooks in London." "Thanks." "And half the filth." —Anthony Masters, *Minder*, p. 165, 1984
- Told him to go away before she called the filth. —Greg Williams, *Diamond Geezers*, p. 13, 1997
- At least when you're caught by the filth, it's just business. —Danny King, *The Burglar Diaries*, p. 78, 2001
- And how much of my cocaine has gone up that big fat Filth [police] bugle of yourn? —Garry Bushell, *The Face*, p. 88, 2001
- I had no idea then that the CID are actually known as "The Filth" within police ranks[.]—Duncan MacLaughlin, *The Filth*, p. 48, 2002

2 a very attractive person *US*
- —Anna Scotti and Paul Young, *Buzzwords*, p. 19, 1997

filth *adjective*
great; excellent; brilliant *AUSTRALIA*
- My lounge room, changed forever. Someone's filth imagination has done the decorating. Reg Mombassa oils fill HDTV flatscreens. —Glyn Parry, *Mosh*, p. 32, 1996

filthiness *noun*
the bleed period of the menstrual cycle *BAHAMAS*
- —John A. Holm, *Dictionary of Bahamian English*, p. 75, 1982

filth merchant *noun*
a man driven by his sexual appetites *UK*
- He's a proper filth merchant as well; he'll shag anything with a pulse, and actually the pulse is optional. —Dave Courtney, *Dodgy Dave's Little Black Book*, p. 82, 2001

filthy *noun*
a look of disdain *IRELAND*
- [E]veryone else on the flight gives us, like, total filthies, and we're talking totally here. We sit down, roysh [right], and then a minute later we're in the air and knocking back the beers again. —Paul Howard, *Ross O'Carroll-Kelly*, p. 45, 2003

filthy *adjective*
1 excessive, especially unpleasantly so *UK, 1733*
- His harshness, his domineering ways, his filthy temper. —*The Observer*, 21st October 2001

2 upset, extremely angry *AUSTRALIA*
- He realised that even though he was filthy on the world and screaming inside he was going to have to be a little more polite to people as time went by[.]—Robert G. Barrett, *Davo's Little Something*, p. 98, 1992
- Don't they get disappointed and filthy? —Paul Vautin, *Turn It Up!*, p. 58, 1995

3 great; excellent; brilliant *AUSTRALIA*
- 'Filthy waves,' agreed Bodge. 'Classic.' —Kathy Lette, *Girls' Night Out*, p. 188, 1987

4 attractive, fashionable, stylish *US*
- —*People Magazine*, p. 73, 19th July 1993
- —Linda Meyer, *Teenspeak*, p. 29, 1994
- —Anna Scotti and Paul Young, *Buzzwords: L.A. Freshspeak*, p. 19, 1997

filthy dirty *adjective*
very dirty *UK, 1843*
The narrow usage of **FILTHY** as an intensifier; also duplicating the conventional senses of 'filthy' and 'dirty' has caused this cliché to verge on hyphenated single-word status.
- Dave with his socks down over his shoes and his trousers splitting and his shirt filthy dirty. —*The Guardian*, 28th November 2002

filthy great *adjective*
very large *UK*
The narrow usage of **FILTHY** as an intensifier; here also the play on synonymous 'dirty' has caused this cliché to verge on hyphenated single-word status.
- There was a filthy great crab biting me on the tit! Naturally, I ran screaming to the men's room. —Phillip Scott, *Gay Resort Murder Shock*, 2003

Filthy McNasty *noun*
a dirty, rude person *US*
- —John D. Bell et al., *Loosely Speaking*, p. 8, 1969

filthy rich *adjective*

very wealthy *UK, 1940*

The narrow usage of **FILTHY** as an intensifier has caused this cliché to verge on hyphenated single-word status.

- Call me a mentalist, call me filthy rich, call me white trash. But call me middle-class, and you immediately identify yourself as a sad wanker who is obviously looking for a punch up the bracket. — *The Guardian*, 12th April 2002

filum *noun*

▷ **see:** FILLUM

fimps *noun*

in craps, a roll of two fives *US, 1968*

- — Thomas L. Clark, *The Dictionary of Gambling and Gaming*, p. 79, 1987

fin *noun*

1 a five-pound or five-dollar note *UK, 1868*

- That's what they give him a fin for, to buy with'n Lukey. — George Mandel, *Flee the Angry Strangers*, p. 244, 1952
- I drank all day in a wild poolhall-bar-restaurant-saloon two-part joint, also got burned for a fin (Mexican, 5 pesos, 60 cents) by a connection. — Jack Kerouac, *Letter to Neal and Carolyn Cassady*, p. 359, 27th May 1952
- Maybe he had a morning's work in the produce market, unloading fruit crates, or maybe he touched one of his old pals for a fin. — Rocky Garciano (with Rowland Barber), *Somebody Up There Likes Me*, p. 10, 1955
- He was a kid trying to get a fin or a sawbuck a day to keep his habit up. — Willard Motely, *Let No Man Write My Epitaph*, p. 369, 1958
- So he pressed a fin into her palm. — William "Lord" Buckley, *The Bad-Rapping of the Marquis de Sade*, 1960
- "How 'bout it, my mannnnn?" he called out to elijah above the clatter of the balls being racked, "shoot one for a fin?" — Odie Hawkins, *Chicago Hustle*, p. 85, 1977

2 a five-year prison sentence *UK, 1925*

- — Joseph E. Ragen and Charles Finston, *Inside the World's Toughest Prison*, p. 798, 1962: 'Penitentiary and underworld glossary'
- I said, "It isn't a little trouble. Under the 'Max' I could get a 'fin.'" — Iceberg Slim (Robert Beck), *Pimp*, p. 46, 1969

3 a US Navy diver who is not qualified for SCUBA diving *US*

Vietnam war usage.

- — Linda Reinberg, *In the Field*, p. 80, 1991

finagle *verb*

to obtain in a manipulative manner *US, 1922*

- They spent what remained of their honeymoon on deck, learning how to finagle their way through Ellis Island. — Jeffrey Eugenides, *Middlesex*, p. 73, 2002

final *noun*

the moment in a confidence swindle when the victim is left to discover his loss *US*

- Folks, black con men call this the final. — Iceberg Slim (Robert Beck), *Trick Baby*, p. 124, 1969

final curtain *noun*

in carnival usage, death *US*

The obituary section in the *Amusement Business* magazine is named 'Final Curtain'.

- — Gene Sorrows, *All About Carnivals*, p. 16, 1985: 'terminology'

finale-hopper *noun*

a young man who goes to a dance without a partner, cutting in on another's partner at the end of the evening in the hope of leaving the dance with her *US, 1922*

- Petted and indulged by the old man, Julio grows up into a sleek-haired finale hopper who tangos sinuously[.] — S.J. Perlman, *Most of the Most of S.J. Perlman*, p. 546, 1958

final gallop *noun*

the hastening pace of lovemaking that climaxes at orgasm *UK*

- — Bill Naughton, *Alfie Darling*, 1970

financial *adjective*

having ready cash; solvent *AUSTRALIA, 1899*

finders keepers

said to signify that the person who finds an object is entitled to keep it *UK, 1856*

First recorded as 'findee keepee, lossee seekee' in a 1825 *Gloss of North Country Words*. The full phrase, known by every UK and US child, is 'Finders, keepers / losers, weepers'.

- "They play finders-keepers, baby." — Richard Farina, *Been Down So Long*, p. 234, 1966

find them, fool them, fuck them, forget them

used as a formula for male relationships with females *US*

The earliest form is 'find, feel, fuck and forget'; also known as the 'four F method'. Mutliple variants exist.

- "Find 'em, fool 'em, fuck 'em, and fort 'em," he was often heard to say[.] — Larry McMurtry, *The Last Picture Show*, p. 103, 1966
- PEGGY GRAVEL: Go ahead, feel her up! Just like you did to me! Find em, feel em, fuck em, forget em...is THAT your new motto?? GRIZELDA BROWN: Zip that gaping hole of a mouth up, Peggy, before I plug it up with my fist. PEGGY GRAVEL: You're just like all the rest of the common dykes in this town! — John Wters, *Desperae Living*, 1977

fine *adjective*

1 sexually attractive *US, 1944*

- He's so fine (doo-lang-doo-lang-doo-lang) / Wish he were mine (doo-lang-doo-lang-doo-lang) — The Chiffons, *He's So Fine*, 1963
- Damn, you looking good. You're fucking fine. You're a fine-looking woman. — Chris Rock, *Rock This!*, p. 185, 1997

2 in twelve-step recovery programmes such as Alcoholics Anonymous, *f*ucked-up, *i*nsecure, *n*eurotic and *e*motional *US*

- — Christopher Cavanaugh, *AA to Z*, p. 93, 1998

▸ **fine as May wine**

excellent *US*

- I met chicks who were fine as May wine, and cats who were hip to all happenings. — Malcolm X and Alex Haley, *The Autobiography of Malcolm X*, p. 56, 1964

fine *adverb*

▸ **cut fine; run fine**

to succeed by a very narrow margin *UK, 1871*

- I left the office for a flight to Ireland (there's nothing like cutting it fine). — *The Guardian*, 21st February 2002

fine and dandy *noun*

brandy *UK*

Rhyming slang.

- — Jack Jones (Ed.), *Rhyming Cockney Slang*, 1971

fine and dandy *adjective*

splendid, excellent *US, 1910*

- Nice moves, very stylish; made the prosecutor look like a high-school football coach. Sent from the man? Andre nodding, pleased. Fine of fine and dandy, man. — Elmore Leonard, *Gold Coast*, p. 27, 1980
- Everything I do is fine and dandy to you, Miss Celie she say. — Alice Walker, *The Color Purple*, p. 57, 1982

fine how-d' ya do *noun*

a dillema, a problem *US*

- Jay was talking to a police captain and some detectives. "Ain't this a fine how-d'ya-do?" he said glumly. — Mezz Mezzrow, *Really the Blues*, p. 290, 1946

finest *noun*

the police *US, 1914*

Used with irony, alluding to the popular phrase identifying a city's policemen as 'the city's finest citizens'. In 1875, New York began to claim it had the 'finest police force in the world', a phrase borrowed from the claim of General Joseph Hooker during the US Civil War that he commanded 'the finest army on the planet'. In the early C20, New York began to refer to its fire department as 'the bravest' and the police simply as 'the finest'.

- Those two representatives of New York's finest stared at me as though I had two heads. — Mezz Mezzrow, *Really the Blues*, p. 301, 1946
- "You mean," I said sarcastically, "that the Finest haven't got one single unsolved murder on their hands?" — Mickey Spillane, *One Lonely Night*, p. 65, 1951
- I've been one of this city's finest for six years and I've never shot anybody once, not even accidentally. — Clarence Cooper Jr, *The Scene*, p. 51, 1960
- And two of Berkeley's finest marched Mario Savio off from amidst a crowd of demonstrators. — *Berkeley Barb*, p. 3, 2nd December 1966
- And then it was our turn and sure enough, in charged four of the finest, with expressions of rage such as I have never seen. — Terry Southern, *Now Dig This: The Unspeakable Writings of Terry Southern 1950–1995*, p. 126, November 1968
- I took another sip of coffee and turned around to check her out and saw two of New York's finest coming in the slammer. — A.S. Jackson, *Gentleman Pimp*, p. 151, 1973
- New York's finest, Chiodo thought. The phrase covered a lot of ground. — Charles Whited, *Chiodo*, p. 147, 1973
- 'I thought the Finest were my friends,' Francis said. — Robert Deane Pharr, *Giveadamn Brown*, p. 21, 1978

- "Oh, Jesus Christ!" whined Seymour, pushing his stocky way through the crowd of New York's finest to sit on the edge of his desk. —Clarence Major, *All-Night Visitors*, p. 195, 1998

finest kind *noun*

the very best *US*

- —Connie Eble (Editor), *UNC-CH Campus Slang*, p. 3, March 1981

fine stuff *noun*

marijuana that has been cleaned and trimmed, also marijuana in general *US, 1955*

- —Richard A. Spears, *The Slang and Jargon of Drugs and Drink*, p. 193, 1986
- —Mike Haskins, *Drugs*, p. 287, 2003

fine thing *noun*

a sexually attractive female *IRELAND*

- If the rest of her is as good as her lungs she'll be a fine thing when she grows up. —Roddy Doyle, *The Van*, p. 90, 1991

fine tuner *noun*

in car repair, a sledge hammer *US*

Facetious.

- —Lewis Poteet, *Car & Motorcyle Slang*, p. 81, 1992

fine up *verb*

(of weather) to improve *CANADA, 1990*

- In Prince Edward Island, "fine up" means clearing weather. — *New Maritimes*, p. 29, March-April 1990

fine weather *noun*

a pretty girl *US*

- —Marcus Hanna Boulware, *Jive and Slang of Students in Negro Colleges*, 1947

f-ing *adjective*

▷ **see:** EFFING

fingee *noun*

a new member of personnel, especially one who is not wished for or welcomed *US, 1990*

Derived, loosely, from 'fucking new guy'.

- —Bernadette Hince, *The Antarctic Dictionary*, p. 128, 2000

finger *noun*

1 a gesture of contempt, the index finger raised from a fist with the palm inwards as the hand jerks upward suggesting an intimate destination *US, 1961*

Often accompanied with an invitation to 'spin on it', **TWIST!** or the elliptical 'oliver!' (**OLIVER TWIST!**).

- To give the finger to man like Flint Granite was, of course, reprehensible[.] —Max Shulman, *Anyone Got a Match?*, p. 25, 1964
- [S]he says something rude that I can't hear and Julian gives her the finger. —Bret Easton Ellis, *Less Than Zero*, p. 178, 1985
- But he felt the other boys' eyes on him and flipped the finger anyhow. —Jess Mowry, *Way Past Cool*, p. 20, 1992
- She's giving us the finger. —J.J. Connolly, *Know Your Enemy [britpulp]*, p. 155,1999

2 an unpopular individual *UK*

Metropolitan Police slang.

- —Peter Laurie, *Scotland Yard*, p. 323, 1970

3 a pickpocket *UK, 1925*

- [S]he started two timing him with the biggest grass in the whole smoke [London], a finger known as Harry the Thief. —Charles Raven, *Underworld Nights*, p. 107, 1956

4 a marijuana cigarette *UK*

From the shape.

- —Mike Haskins, *Drugs*, p. 287, 2003

5 an individual banana in a bunch *CAYMAN ISLANDS*

- —Aarona Booker Kohlman, *Wotcha Say*, p. 23, 1985

6 a citizens' band radio antenna *US*

- —*Dictionary of CB Lingo*, p. 65, 1976: 'Elementary electronics'

▸ **get your finger out; pull your finger out; take your finger out; pull it out**

to stop time-wasting and start doing something useful *UK*

Often used as a semi-exclamatory injunction. Probably 'out from up your arse', but there is no need to say so.

- MILLIGAN: Cor blimey, where's the fire? BELL: Get your finger out then. —Graeme Kent, *The Queen's Corporal [Six Granada Plays]*, p. 87, 1959
- 'They have been working me too hard here. I'm looking for the easy life.' He grinned again. 'Ha-ha, now you'll have to take your finger out, won't you, Golden Boy?' —George Johnston, *My Brother Jack*, p. 312, 1964
- Get you finger out. Rufe, get cracking and none of your backchat. —Wilda Moxham, *The Apprentice*, p. 44, 1969
- I come pounding up, say, "Pull it out, for cheese cake" [Christ's sake]. —Nicholas Blincoe, *The Beautiful Beaten-up Irish Boy of the Arndale Centre*, p. 11, 1998

▸ **have your finger up your arse**

to be doing nothing *UK*

- Leave the probabtion officer with his finger up his arse; and good luck. —John Peter Jones, *Feather Pluckers*, p. 74, 1964

▸ **lift a finger; move a finger**

to make the slightest effort, usually applied in a negative sense to a lack of effort *UK, 1936*

- They wouldn't even lift a finger to save their own grandmothers from the Ravenous Bugblatter Beast of Traal. —Douglas Adams, *The Hitchhiker's Guide to the Galaxy*, 1979
- Do you think for a moment I should lift a finger to help her? —Iain Pears, *An Instance of the Fingerpost*, p. 85, 1998

▸ **on the finger**

on credit *US*

- —Swen A. Larsen, *American Speech*, p. 97, May 1951: 'The vocabulary of poker'
- —Albert H. Morehead, *The Complete Guide to Winning Poker*, p. 262, 1967
- —David M. Hayano, *Poker Faces*, p. 185, 1982

▸ **put the finger on**

to identify; to name; to inform on somebody *US, 1924*

- —Angela Devlin, *Prison Patter*, p. 51, 1996

▸ **put your finger on**

to identify or explain exactly *UK*

- Perhaps it the idea that hip hop is "just about good music", because it's always been about more than that for me; even if I can't quite put my finger on exactly what I mean. —Patrick Neate, *Where You're At*, p. 43, 2003

finger *verb*

1 to identify; to name; to inform upon somebody *US, 1930*

- Magoo could finger us. He's the pusher which the junkies get their charge from him. Me, I only take the money; but Magoo talks, they come'n get us. —George Mandel, *Flee the Angry Strangers*, p. 253, 1952
- Some kid I had helped out fingered me. —Herbert Huncke, *Guilty of Everything*, p. 82–83, 1990
- The Hungarians were going to buy the one guy that could finger Soze for them. — *The Usual Suspects*, 1995
- —Angela Devlin, *Prison Patter*, p. 51, 1996

2 to digitally stimulate/explore the vagina as a part of sexual foreplay *UK*

- [W]e'd love to knob every single one of them, except the pigs, or at least finger them, or get inside their bras[.] —John King, *Human Punk*, p. 30, 2000

finger and ring *adjective*

very close *TRINIDAD AND TOBAGO*

- —Lise Winer, *Dictionary of the English/Creole of Trinidad & Tobago*, 2003

finger and thumb; finger *noun*

1 a mother *UK*

- My old finger's getting on a bit[.] —Ray Puxley, *Cockney Rabbit*, 1992

2 a companion, a friend *UK, 1961*

Rhyming slang for **CHUM**.

3 a drum *UK*

Rhyming slang.

- —Ray Puxley, *Cockney Rabbit*, 1992

4 the buttocks *UK*

Rhyming slang for **BUM**.

- [P]eople still say they've a Randolph (Scott=spot) on their finger and thumb[.] —*Antiquarian Book Review*, p. 18, June 2002

5 rum *UK, 1851*

- —Ray Puxley, *Cockney Rabbit*, 1992

finger artist *noun*

a lesbian *US*

- —Clarence Major, *Dictionary of Afro-American Slang*, p. 53, 1970

fingerbang *verb*

to insert a finger or fingers into a partner's vagina or rectum for their sexual pleasure *US*

- I mean I've sucked some titties and finger banged a couple of hunnies but I never stuck it in. — *Boyz N The Hood*, 1990
- I'm gonna finger-fuck her tight little asshole! Finger-bang ... and tea-bag my balls ... in her mouth! —Kevin Smith, *Jay and Silent Bob Strike Back*, p. 50, 2001

finger bowl faggot *noun*

a wealthy, ostentatious, homosexual male *US*

- In this rarified area, johns are not johns but cuff link faggots or queens, an expression derived from their tendency to wear extravagant looking jewelry. They are also called "finger bowl faggots." — Antony James, *America's Homosexual Underground*, p. 29, 1965

finger cot *noun*

a latex covering used by a doctor on his finger when examining a rectum or vagina *US*

- — *American Speech*, p. 201, Fall-Winter 1973: 'The language of nursing'

finger flip *verb*

in skateboarding, to perform a jump during which the board moves laterally through 360° *UK*

- The new friend was a dab hand at "finger flipping" – that's jumping so you flick the board over with your feet and land on it the right way round. Fingers have nothing to do with it. — *The Times*, p. 16, 26th April 2003

fingerfuck *noun*

the manual stimulation of another's vagina or anus *US*

- — Eugene Landy, *The Underground Dictionary*, p. 77, 1971

fingerfuck *verb*

to insert a finger or fingers into a partner's vagina or rectum *UK, 1793*

Plain-speaking former US President Lyndon Johnson (1963–1969) was said to have said 'Richard Milhouse Nixon has done for the United States of America what pantyhose did for finger-fucking'.

- I was a guest at Aly Khan's for dinner, when you were still back in Newark, New Jersey, finger-fucking your little Jewish girl friend. — Philip Roth, *Portnoy's Complaint*, p. 239, 1969
- No humping-like movements, or finger-fucking or clit chatting with their fingertips. — *Screw*, p. 5, 24th January 1969
- Eugenie and I used to neck and fingerfuck-fuck at the "show" at night. — John Francis Hunter, *The Gay Insider*, p. 143, 1971
- [T]hen a little lesbian 69, some fingerfucking, vibrators, and who knows what else — Roger Blake, *What you always wanted to know about porno-shops*, p. 7, 1972
- "Who taught you to kiss like that, Cousin Alldean?" "Yes, as a matter of fact, he did." "He fingerfuck you too?" — Earl Thompson, *Tattoo*, p. 475, 1974
- At this moment she hated his mechanical finger-fucking that had, after all, done nothing for her that she couldn't have done for herself. — Iceberg Slim (Robert Beck), *Death Wish*, p. 20, 1977
- His finger-fucking talents were obviously driving her crazy, because her entire body began to move spasmodically. — *Adam Film World*, p. 54, August 1978
- [T]he butch I thought was "straight" but wanted to be finger-fucked while getting blown[.] — Peter Sotos, *Index*, p. 6, 1996
- I'm gonna finger-fuck her tight little asshole! Finger-bang ... and tea-bag my balls ... in her mouth! — Kevin Smith, *Jay and Silent Bob Strike Back*, p. 50, 2001

finger-fucker *noun*

a person who finger fucks *US*

- Up here in the airways, down there on the ground, you're the best finger-fucker around. — Steve Cannon, *Groove, Bang, and Jive Around*, p. 131, 1969

finger horse *noun*

in horse racing, the favourite *US*

- — *Argot of the Racetrack*, p. 26, 1951

finger in the pie *noun*

an involvement in an activity, especially a share in the profits of something *UK, 1659*

- Even established developers have to keep their fingers in the pies to make sure that everything turns out correctly[.] — R. Dodge Woodson, *Be a Successful Residential Land Developer*, p. 84, 2000

finger job *noun*

1 digital stimulation of the vagina or anus *US, 1963*

- — Eugene Landy, *The Underground Dictionary*, p. 77, 1971

2 an act of betrayal *US*

- "No, it wasn't exactly a finger job. What she did was sit at the bar, keeping an eye on the guy." — Elmore Leonard, *Mr. Majestyk*, p. 62, 1974

finger lid *noun*

marijuana *UK*

- — Mike Haskins, *Drugs*, p. 287, 2003

finger line *noun*

a line-up in which crime victims or witnesses attempt to identify the criminal(s) *US*

- — Troy Harris, *A Booklet of Criminal Argot, Cant and Jargon*, p. 10, 1976

finger louse *noun*

a police informer *US*

- — *American Speech*, p. 98, May 1956: 'Smugglers' argot in the southwest'

finger man; fingerman *noun*

1 a person who provides criminals with inside information to aid a robbery or other crime *US, 1930*

- These are finger men for the hold-up gangs, who scrape up acquaintances with the girls, then lift their house-keys from their purses. — Jack Lait and Lee Mortimer, *Chicago Confidential*, p. 70, 1950
- It is hard to prove anything on a finger man – one who studies the habits of someone who wears valuable jewels publicly and tips off the thieves at the opportune time for robbery or holdup[.] — Robert Sylvester, *No Cover Charge*, p. 241, 1956
- Our finger man is a junkie punk. — Iceberg Slim (Robert Beck), *Pimp*, p. 252, 1969

2 a professional killer *US, 1930*

- George P. Harding, a 39-year-old gunman and underworld fingerman, was shot to death by Joe Nesline[.] — Jack Lait and Lee Mortimer, *Washington Confidential*, p. 129, 1951

finger poker *noun*

a game of poker bet on credit *US*

- — *American Speech*, p. 98, May 1951
- — Albert H. Morehead, *The Complete Guide to Winning Poker*, p. 262, 1967

fingerprint *noun*

in poker, a player's signature move *US*

- Albert always raises Big Maxx in early position. It's his fingerprint. — John Vorhaus, *The Big Book of Poker Slang*, p. 16, 1996

fingerprint *verb*

in trucking, to manually unload a trailer *US*

- — Montie Tak, *Truck Talk*, p. 59, 1971

finger-puppet audition *noun*

an act of masturbation *UK*

- — Chris Lewis, *The Dictionary of Playground Slang*, p. 90, 2003

fingers *noun*

a piano player *US*

- — Kenn "Naz" Young, *Naz's Underground Dictionary*, p. 28, 1973

▸ **have your fingers in the till**

to steal from your employer or place of work *UK, 1974*

- And I also urgently need a saleswoman who knows her job and hasn't got her fingers in the till all the time. — Cornelia Funke and Oliver Latsch, *The Thief Lord*, p. 328, 2001

▸ **the fingers**

a gesture (the forefinger and the middle finger are extended to form a V shape, the palm turned in towards the gesturer) that is used to insult or otherwise cause offence, especially when made in conjunction with threatening or abusive language e.g. 'fuck off!' or 'up yours!' with which the sign may be considered synonymous *UK*

- [T]he entire top deck of a 610 bus had turned to gawp and give me the fingers – that's "fingers" as in Kes and Harvey Smith, not the "finger" as in bratty Americans[.] — Stuart Maconie, *Cider with Roadies*, p. 105, 2003

Fingers *nickname*

used as a pickpocket's nickname *US*

- — Vincent J. Monteleone, *Criminal Slang*, p. 83, 1949
- — John Gosling, *The Gost Squad*, 1959
- — Angela Devlin, *Prison Patter*, p. 51, 1996

fingers crossed!

used for expressing hope *UK, 1924*

Describes the action – the middle finger twisted over and around the forefinger – that doesn't always accompany the words. A basic prayer, representing the sign of the cross, although the Christian God is mostly forgotten in familiar and superstitious usage. The gesture, but not the term, may also accompany the swearing of an oath, or represent friendship and sexual contact.

- "Wish me luck," smiled Guy [...] "Fingers crossed, boys..." — Kevin Sampson, *Powder*, p. 39–40, 1999

finger sheet *noun*
in horse racing, a publication giving the entries and odds for a day's races *US*
• — *Argot of the Racetrack*, p. 26, 1951

fingersmith *noun*
1 a pickpocket *UK, 1823*
• — *The New American Mercury*, p. 707, 1950
2 a thief *BARBADOS*
• — Frank A. Collymore, *Barbadian Dialect*, p. 47, 1965

fingers to fingers
used as an oath and pledge *US*
The original pledge was heard on the US television comedy *The Life of Riley* (NBC, 1949–58); the full pledge, used by the Brooklyn Patriots of Los Angeles fraternal group, was 'Fingers to fingers, toes to toes, if I break this pact, break my nose'. On the comedy *The Honeymooners* (CBS, 1955–56), the toast version used by the fraternal order of Raccoons was 'Fingers to fingers, thumbs to thumbs, watch out below, here she comes'.

fingertip *noun*
in the car sales business, power steering *US*
• — *Cars*, p. 40, December 1953

fingertips *noun*
someone adept at masturbating others *US*
• — Charles Shafer, *Folk Speech in Texas Prisons*, p. 204, 1990

finger-walk *verb*
with one hand, to roll a coin over and through the knuckles *US*
• Red removed a half-dollar-size gambling chip from his pocket and tried to make it finger-walk on the back of his hand. — Gerald Petievich, *Money Men*, p. 26, 1981

finger wave *noun*
1 a digital examination of the rectum, either as part of an prostate examination or a drug search *US, 1962*
• Have you ever gone to the doctor for a finger wave? — Angelo d'Arcangelo, *The Homosexual Handbook*, p. 83, 1968
• When they check out cells we always have to take it [a mascara pencil] and stick it up our butt so we can hide it. They never give us a finger wave here [anal inspection], it's against the rules. — Bruce Jackson, *In the Life*, p. 400, 1972
• — David Maurer and Victor Vogel, *Narcotics and Narcotic Addiction*, p. 409, 1973
• — *Maledicta*, p. 56, Summer 1980: 'Not sticks and stones, but names: more medical pejoratives'
• Jack, walking into the house with his glass, heard Cullen say, "... give it the old finger wave," but didn't hear what Harby thought about it. — Elmore Leonard, *Bandits*, p. 261, 1987
2 a gesture with the middle finger, usually interpreted to mean 'fuck you!' *US*
• — Porter Bibb, *CB Bible*, p. 93, 1976

fingy *noun*
a new arrival in Antarctica *ANTARCTICA*
A pronunciation of **FNG** or **FUCKING NEW GUY**.
• — *Cool Antarctica*, 2003: 'Antarctic slang'

finif *noun*
1 a five-dollar note *US, 1859*
From the Yiddish *finif* (five).
• Widely used in colloquial English, especially by sports fans, gamblers, Broadway types, nightclub habitues, and newspaper columnists, who memorialize these gaudy provinces of diversion. — Leo Rosten, *The Joys of Yiddish*, p. 117, 1968
• Ray saw plenty of people he knew, but nobody he could tap for a finnif or a sawbuck. — Robert Campbell, *Juice*, p. 11, 1988
2 a prison sentence of five years *US, 1904*
• — Vincent J. Monteleone, *Criminal Slang*, p. 84, 1949
3 in dice games, a five on one die *US*
• — *The Annals of the American Academy of Political and Social Sciences*, p. 124, May 1950

finish *verb*
▸ **finish on the chinstrap**
in horse racing, to win a race easily under restraint *US*
• — David W. Maurer, *Argot of the Racetrack*, p. 26, 1951

finishing school *noun*
a reformatory for juvenile delinquents *US*
• — Troy Harris, *A Booklet of Criminal Argot, Cant and Jargon*, p. 10, 1976

finito
the end, no more *UK*
Italian *finito* (finished). The elaboration 'finito, Benito' adds an Italian name – thus stressing the word's Italian origin.
• A right to the head and then a cut up his ribs like a sword, and it was goodnight nurse, finito. Thanks for coming and fuck off! — Jimmy Stockin, *On The Cobbles*, p. 162, 2000
• [O]ut of my fucking hair for good. Finito, by the way. — Kevin Sampson, *Outlaws*, p. 255, 2001
• We find him, you chop him – finito, end of story. — Chris Ryan, *The Watchman*, p. 140–141, 2001

fink *noun*
1 an informer *US, 1902*
• He looks like a dirty fink to me. A first-class enameled fink! — Ralph Ellison, *Invisible Man*, p. 219, 1947
• They never go into detail, they say here's the name of the fink, do him. — Elmore Leonard, *Glitz*, p. 179, 1985
• Don't you know you're working with one of the biggest finks in the city? — Herbert Huncke, *Guilty of Everything*, p. 195, 1990
2 a non-union job or worker *US, 1917*
• "With all your education, you can't even keep a fink job driving a taxicab," Ruth screamed. — James T. Farrell, *Ruth and Bertram*, p. 95, 1955
3 in circus and carnival usage, a broken piece of merchandise *US*
• — Don Wilmeth, *The Language of American Popular Entertainment*, p. 91, 1981

fink *verb*
to inform on *US, 1925*
• Doolie will fink if he has to. — William Burroughs, *Junkie*, p. 56, 1953

fink-and-fort it *adjective*
used of a London working-class accent *UK*
A phonetic representation of 'think and thought it'.
• He was a working-class boy, educated at a grammar school where even the teachers took the piss out of his "fink-and-fort it" council house accent. — Garry Bushell, *The Face*, p. 4, 2001

fink book *noun*
the record of a longshoreman's or seafarer's employment *US, 1934*
The books were used by employers to punish labour activists and enforce non-union conditions in the workplace.
• Seafarers, longshoremen, and allies in other trade unions assembled, not far from the fink hall, to burn their hated fink books. — Archie Green, *Torching the Fink Books and Other Essays on Vernacular Culture*, p. 178, 2001

fink out *verb*
to betray; to inform *US, 1962*
• Took part in a payroll hesit and got finked out. — Elmore Leonard, *Mr. Paradise*, p. 122, 2004

finky *adjective*
disloyal, cowardly *US, 1948*
• "It would serve the finky bastard right," said the fat, gruff colonel. — Joseph Heller, *Catch 22*, p. 441, 1955

Finlay Quaye *adjective*
homosexual *UK*
Rhyming slang for 'gay', formed from the name of a singer who enjoyed notable success in the late 1990s.
• — Bodmin Dark, *Dirty Cockney Rhyming Slang*, 2003

finny *adjective*
(used of a hand or foot) deformed *BARBADOS*
• — Frank A. Collymore, *Barbadian Dialect*, p. 47, 1965
• — Lise Winer, *Dictionary of the English/Creole of Trinidad & Tobago*, 2003

Finsbury Park *noun*
an *arc* light *UK*
Rhyming slang, formed from the name of an area of north London.
• — Ray Puxley, *Cockney Rabbit*, 1992

finski *noun*
a five-dollar note *US, 1952*
• — Ralph de Sola, *Crime Dictionary*, p. 52, 1982

fin-up *noun*
a prison sentence of five years to life *US*
• — Frank Prewitt and Francis Schaeffer, *Vacaville Vocabulary*, 1961–1962

FIP *noun*
a scene in a pornographic film or a photograph of a man pretending to ejaculate inside a vagina or rectum *US*
An initialism for '*f*ake *i*nternal *p*op-shot'; used in softcore pornography.
- — *Adult Video News*, p. 44, August 1995

fir *noun*
marijuana *US, 1984*
- — Richard A. Spears, *The Slang and Jargon of Drugs and Drink*, p. 194, 1986
- — Mike Haskins, *Drugs*, p. 287, 2003

fire *noun*
1 matches or a cigarette lighter *US, 1959*
- — Judi Sanders, *Mashing and Munching in Ames*, p. 7, 1994

2 a detonator *UK*
- When the keyhole is threequarters full [with gelignite] you insert the "fire"[.] — Charles Raven, *Underworld Nights*, p. 28, 1956

3 a sexually transmitted infection *NORFOLK ISLAND*
- — Beryl Nobbs Palmer, *A Dictionary of Norfolk Words and Usages*, p. 14, 1992

4 a combination of crack cocaine and methamphetamine *UK, 1998*
- — Mike Haskins, *Drugs*, p. 293, 2003

5 a running car engine *US*
Usually in the context of a comment such as 'your fire went out' when a motorist shuts off his engine.
- — *American Speech*, p. 268, December 1962: 'The language of traffic policemen'

6 a car heater *NEW ZEALAND*
- — David McGill, *David McGill's Complete Kiwi Slang Dictionary*, p. 49, 1998

▸ **I wouldn't spit on him (her) if he (she) was on fire; I wouldn't piss on him if he was on fire**
I detest him (her) *UK*
- I wouldn't spit on a copper if he was on fire. — *British Journal of Photography*, 1st June 1979

▸ **on fire**
(used of a homosexual) patently, obviously *US*
As in **FLAMING**.
- — Kevin Dilallo, *The Unofficial Gay Manual*, p. 243, 1994

fire *verb*
1 to light up a cigarette or a marijuana cigarette *US*
Literally 'to apply a flame'.
- While I fired a cig he called an extension number and was connected. — Mickey Spillane, *My Gun is Quick*, p. 13, 1950
- I fired a cigarette, — Diran Abedayo, *My Once Upon A Time*, p. 149, 2000
- All that's left to do now is fire it up and get off your face. — Nick Jones, *Spliffs*, p. 101, 2003

2 (of a mechanical device) to start up *US*
Also 'fire up' as a variant.
- MICHAEL scarpers. JAMIE tries to fire the engine again. — Chris Baker and Andrew Day, *Lock, Stock... & One Big Bullock*, p. 350, 2000

3 to inject a drug intravenously *US, 1936*
- — David Maurer and Victor Vogel, *Narcotics and Narcotic Addiction*, p. 406, 1973
- Ever fire when you were in the joint? — Joseph Wambaugh, *The Blue Knight*, p. 30, 1973

4 to dismiss from employment *US, 1887*
A pun on 'discharge'.
- Tory gay rights rebel was fired by pager. — *The Guardian*, 4th December 1999

5 to destroy by arson *US*
- So bad he'd fire his hotels if he could collect on them. — Jim Thompson, *The Kill-Off*, p. 27, 1957

6 to ejaculate *UK, 1891*
- The last time that Hans fired too early in the motel room, the sneering groupie said, "You better start carrying two jizz rags." — Joseph Wambaugh, *The Delta Star*, p. 105, 1983

7 to play a sport exceedingly well; to be 'on fire' *AUSTRALIA*
- — Jim Ramsay, *Cop It Sweet!*, p. 35, 1977

▸ **fire a leak**
to urinate *TRINIDAD AND TOBAGO*
- — Lise Winer, *Dictionary of the English/Creole of Trinidad & Tobago*, 2003

▸ **fire one**
to have a drink *BARBADOS*
- — Frank A. Collymore, *Barbadian Dialect*, p. 48, 1965

▸ **fire the acid**
to drink rum *JAMAICA*
Recorded by Richard Allsopp.

▸ **fire the ack-ack gun**
to smoke a cigarette dipped in a heroin solution *US*
- — Richard Lingeman, *Drugs from A to Z*, p. 78, 1969

fire alarms *noun*
arms (weaponry); the *arms* *UK*
Rhyming slang.
- — Ray Puxley, *Cockney Rabbit*, 1992

fire-and-forget *adjective*
(used of a missile) guided automatically *US*
- — *American Speech*, p. 389, Winter 1991: 'Among the new words'

fire away *verb*
to commence, to start *UK, 1775*
Generally as imperative or invitation.
- www.insults.net, has a plentiful supply of Shakespearean insults. Just choose your play and fire away. — *The Guardian*, 18th May 2000

fireball *noun*
1 an extremely energetic person *US, 1949*
- Children who were once seens as "bundles of energy," "day-dreamers," or "fireballs," are now considered "hyperactive," "dis-tractible," and "impulsive." — Thomas Armstrong, *The Myth of the A.D.D. Child*, p. 4, 1995

2 in pinball, a ball that leaves play without scoring any points *US*
- — Bobbye Claire Natkin and Steve Kirk, *All About Pinball*, p. 112, 1977

3 a tracer bullet *US*
- — *American Speech*, p. 268, December 1962: 'The language of traffic policemen'

4 a short but intense use of artillery in the Vietnam war *US*
- — Linda Reinberg, *In the Field*, p. 81, 1991

fire bomber *noun*
an aircraft for fighting fire *CANADA*
- Tools used for forest firefighting range from rolls of toilet paper to the spectacular new fire bombers, mobile water tankers. — *Canada Month*, p. 42/1, 6th October 1961

firebug *noun*
1 an arsonist; a person with a pathological love of fire *US, 1872*
- You are going to catch all the firebugs and make everybody safe in their beds. — George V. Higgins, *The Rat on Fire*, p. 7, 1981
- Jesus Bernal yearned to abandon Skip Wiley's circus and rejoin his old gang of dedicated extortionists, bombers, and firebugs. — Carl Hiaasen, *Tourist Season*, p. 135, 1986

2 in poker, a player who bets and plays in a reckless fashion *US*
- — John Vorhaus, *The Big Book of Poker Slang*, p. 16, 1996

fireburner *noun*
a zealot *US*
- I like to have me a little bitty young lawyer, a fire-burner. — Bruce Jackson, *Outside the Law*, p. 130, 1972

firecan *noun*
a type of radar system in a military aircraft *US*
- Arranged in a circle around a "Firecan" radar, these 85-millimeter guns spat shells at Rasimus one gun at a time in a circular pattern. — John Darrell Sherwood, *Fast Movers*, p. 57, 1999
- "I got a Firecan in search mode." A Firecan was an old AAA radar. — Richard Herman, *The Last Phoenix*, p. 385, 2002

firecracker *noun*
a secret fragmentation artillery shell used on an experimental basis in Vietnam *US*
The formal name was Controlled Fragmentation Munition, or CoFraM.
- — Linda Reinberg, *In the Field*, p. 81, 1991

fired *adjective*
excited, eager, sexually aroused *US*
- — Collin Baker et al., *College Undergraduate Slang Study Conducted at Brown University*, p. 117, 1968

fired up *adjective*
enthusiastic
- Few things gave him pleasure. He could not get fired up. Clothes, maybe. — Kevin Sampson, *Powder*, p. 33, 1999

fire; fire-ie *noun*
▷ see: FIREY

fire-eater *noun*
a ferociously brave person *US, 1808*
- I don't deal blackjack so good, hobbled like this, but I maintain I'm a fire-eater in a stud game.—Ken Kesey, *One Flew Over The Cuckoo's Nest*, p. 232, 1962

fire engine *noun*
corned beef served in a tomato sauce over white rice *BAHAMAS*
- —John A. Holm, *Dictionary of Bahamian English*, p. 76, 1982

firefighter cute *adjective*
describes an attractive young man *US*
Teenspeak, post-11th September 2001 – the day firefighters became 'American heroes'.
- Girls might say a boy is "firefighter cute" instead of the more common "hottie".—*The Washington Post*, 19th March 2002

firefly *noun*
a helicopter equipped with a powerful search light, usually teamed with several gunships in the Vietnam war *US*
- —Linda Reinberg, *In the Field*, p. 81, 1991

fire in the hole!
1 used as a warning that an explosive is about to be detonated *US*
- Fire in the hole!—*Platoon*, 1986
- —Linda Reinberg, *In the Field*, p. 81, 1991

2 in the illegal production of alcohol, used as a warning of approaching law enforcement officials *US*
- Adapted from the coal mines, where it is used to indicate that the fuse has been lit and a powder charge is about to explode.—David W. Maurer, *Kentucky Moonshine*, p. 118, 1974

fire into *verb*
to approach with an intent to seduce *UK*
- Right, well you fire intae him n ah'll fire intae his mate.—Irvine Welsh, *The State of the Party (Disco Biscuits)*, p. 55, 1995
- [He] found what he wanted, a gang of Geordie birds going on their holidays. He shamelessly fired into them [...], found out where they were going and bought a ticket to Malaga.—J.J. Connolly, *Know Your Enemy [britpulp]*, p. 162, 1999

fireless cooker *noun*
a gas chamber *US*
- The gas chamber – or, as the prisoners call it, "the fireless cooker" – has only two seats.—*San Francisco Chronicle*, p. 27, 30th September 1962

fireman *noun*
in a group smoking marijuana from a pipe, the second person to smoke *SOUTH AFRICA*
- The fireman lights two matches held together, scrapes off the sulphur and holds it to the pipe for the person "busting" it. For his troubles, the fireman gets the next hit.—*Surfrikan Slang*, 2004

fireman's *noun*
horse races *AUSTRALIA*
Rhyming slang, from 'fireman's braces'.
- —Ned Wallish, *The Truth Dictionary of Racing Slang*, p. 29, 1989

fireman's hose; fireman's *noun*
the nose *UK*
Rhyming slang.
- Don't pick your fireman's you'll go bandy.—Ray Puxley, *Cockney Rabbit*, 1992

fire on *verb*
1 to excite sexually *US*
- Girls with long legs fire me on.—*Screw*, p. 5, 7th March 1969

2 to punch someone *US*
- —Malachi Andrews and Paul T. Owens, *Black Language*, p. 77, 1973

fire pie *noun*
a red-headed woman's pubic hair and vulva *US*
- —Chris Lewis, *The Dictionary of Playground Slang*, p. 90, 2003

fireplace *noun*
in hot rodding, the grille on the front of a car *US*
- —*Good Housekeeping*, p. 143, September 1958: 'Hot-rod terms for teen-age girls'
- —Tom MacPherson, *Dragging and Driving*, p. 138, 1960

fireproof *adjective*
invulnerable *UK, 1984*
- [G]oin' on like he was the fuckin' Old Bill [police] or something, as if he was fire proof.—Lanre Fehintola, *Charlie Says...*, p. 130, 2000

fire-rage *noun*
an argument *BARBADOS*
- —Frank A. Collymore, *Barbadian Dialect*, p. 48, 1965

fire track *noun*
an armoured personnel carrier or tank equipped with a flame-thrower *US*
- —Linda Reinberg, *In the Field*, p. 81, 1991

fire up *verb*
1 to light a pipe, a cigar or a cigarette *UK, 1890*

2 to light and smoke a marijuana cigarette *US, 1962*

3 to inject drugs *UK*
- —Angela Devlin, *Prison Patter*, p. 52, 1996

4 to enthuse *UK, 1986*
- Vibing off the aforementioned Sam Selvon, another writer to fire me up[.]—Paolo Hewitt, *The Sharper Word*, p. 119, 1999

firewater *noun*
1 strong alcohol *US, 1817*
A term associated with Native Americans, often pronounced with an ambiguous accent approximating an accent used by Indian actors in old cowboy films.
- If you can't do without your firewater, consult the ticket agent before boarding the train.—Jack Lait and Lee Mortimer, *New York Confidential*, p. 198, 1948
- [Y]ou've been shooting it out with cattle rustlers and train robbers who have been dynamiting the new railroad trestles and selling firewater to the Injuns.—Bernard Wolfe, *The Late Risers*, p. 163, 1954
- Will you just look at the Big chief slug down on that firewater!—Ken Kesey, *One Flew Over the Cuckoo's Nest*, p. 227, 1962
- Firewater brings out the real browness of this buffalo.—Oscar Zeta Acosta, *The Autobiography of a Brown Buffalo*, p. 36, 1972
- Firewater, Tonto? Is that what you-—*48 Hours*, 1982
- I got to leave that firewater alone, and just stick with reefer.—Odie Hawkins, *Men Friends*, p. 145, 1989

2 GBL, a drug that is nearly identical in molecular structure to the recreational drug GHB *US*
- Another case inovlved a 14-year-old Bernalillo County boy whose heart rate slowed after drinking bright red "Firewater."—*Santa Fe New Mexican*, p. A1, 29th January 1999
- —*Sky Magazine*, July 2001

3 spruce beer and also, phosphorescence in salt water *CANADA*
- When fishing for albacore or tuna, at night, when there is a glow of phosphorescence about the moving fish, the men call it firewater. —Helen Creighton, *Lunenburg County*, p. 110, 1950
- Some made moccasins and snowshoes, other spruce beer, the original firewater.—*Canada Month*, p. 27/3, January 1962

fireworks *noun*
1 a great disturbance; dramatic excitement *UK, 1889*

2 an exchange of gunfire *US, 1864*
- —Joseph E. Ragen and Charles Finston, *Inside the World's Toughest Prison*, p. 799, 1962: 'Penitentiary and underworld glossary'

3 a police car with flashing lights *US*
- —*Complete CB Slang Dictionary*, 1976
- —Peter Chippindale, *The British CB Book*, p. 154, 1981

4 roadside flares warning motorists of an accident or other problem ahead *US*
- —*American Speech*, p. 268, December 1962: 'The language of traffic policemen'

firey; fire-ie; firee *noun*
a firefighter, especially of bushfires *AUSTRALIA, 1996*
- The flame rushed up the gully towards the homes and the smoke was so thick you could only see up to two metres in front of you. The fireys are real heroes.—*Herald Sun*, p. 2, 2nd January 2002

firing line *noun*
▸ **in the firing line**
in danger of dismissal from employment *UK, 1961*
- TV chiefs in the firing line.—*The Guardian*, 28th March 2002

firm *noun*

1 a gang of football hooligans *UK*
A business-like self-description, adopted from professional criminals.
- Chelsea also made up the bulk of the England mob that had become a powerful magnet to firm members up and down the country. — Martin King and Martin Knight, *The Naughty Nineties*, p. 47, 1999

2 a criminal gang *UK*
From the conventional sense as a 'business'.
- Even before we was a firm, we was a tidy little crew. — Kevin Sampson, *Outlaws*, p. 19, 2001

3 a squad of detectives, especially a close-knit group *UK*
A humorous adoption of the 'criminal gang' sense.
- — David Powis, *The Signs of Crime*, 1977

4 a criminal set-up between a police officer or officers, especially CID, and a criminal gang *UK*
- — G.F Newman, *Sir, You Bastard*, 1970

▸ **on the firm**
as a constant arrangement, steadily *UK*
- So we started seeing each other on the firm and everything is rosy for a couple or three months. — Danny King, *The Burglar Diaries*, p. 29, 2001

▸ **the firm**
the British royal family *UK*
Monarchy seen as a business is a notion very much in tune with the ethics of the late 1980s.
- [Diana, Princess of Wales] was an outcast from the family she called "the firm". — Mark Steel, *Reasons to be Cheerful*, p. 251, 2001

firm up *verb*
to form into a gang *UK*
- [T]he people firmed up, moved as a crew[.] — Lanre Fehintola, *Charlie Says...*, p. 130, 2000

first aid *noun*

1 a *blade* (as a weapon); a razor *blade* *UK*
Rhyming slang; inspired, according to Ray Puxley, *Cockney Rabbit*, 1992, by the catchphrase threat: 'Can your wife [or mum] do first aid? Well get her to stitch this up'.

2 a small shop that sells, amongst other commodities, patent medicines *BARBADOS*
- — Frank A. Collymore, *Barbadian Dialect*, p. 48, 1965

first aid kit; first aid *noun*
the female breast *UK*
Rhyming slang for **TIT**; usually plural.
- — Ray Puxley, *Cockney Rabbit*, 1992

first base *noun*

1 in teenage categorisation of sexual activity, a level of foreplay, most commonly referring to kissing *US, 1928*
The exact degree varies by region and even by school.
- Anyhow, you're just saying that 'cause you're jealous and can't get to first base with Lucky. — Hal Ellson, *Tomboy*, p. 76, 1950
- Maybe I don't like the idea of another guy making time with Fay when I've never been able to get to first base. — Jim Thompson, *After Dark, My Sweet*, p. 31, 1955
- They've all tried. Nobody's got to first base. — *M*A*S*H*, 1970
- "Hell," says Larry, "we aren't even gonna get to first base, I bet." — Darryl Ponicsan, *The Last Detail*, p. 121, 1970

2 in blackjack played in American casinos, the seat immediately to the dealer's left *US*
- — Steve Kuriscak, *Casino Talk*, p. 23, 1985

first cab off the rank *noun*
the first in a series *AUSTRALIA, 1966*
- — Arthur Chipper, *The Aussie Swearer's Guide*, p. 32, 1972
- — Jim Ramsay, *Cop It Sweet!*, p. 35, 1977
- It was unanimously decided there and then that when I wrote 'Publican Bastards I Have Met', McLean had to be first cab off the rank. — Sam Weller, *Old Bastards I Have Met*, p. 14, 1979

first call *noun*
in Antarctica, the first ship to arrive at the South Pole each season *ANTARCTICA*
- — *Cool Antarctica*, 2003: 'Antarctic slang'

first class *adjective*
extremely good *UK, 1879*
- Britain has 'no first-class university' left now. — *The Guardian*, 22nd December 2002

first dollar *noun*
in television and film making, the first money generated after release *US*
- — Ralph S. Singleton, *Filmaker's Dictionary*, p. 64, 1990

first drop *noun*
in cricket, the 3rd position in the order of batting *UK, 1960*
- — Keith Foley, *A Dictionary of Cricketing Terminology*, p. 136, 1998

First Fleeter *noun*
a person, or a descendant of a person, who arrived on the first fleet of ships to bring British colonists to Australia in 1788 *AUSTRALIA, 1826*
A great deal of pride is associated with this lineage in Australia.
- Descendants of the original First Fleeters and pioneers will wear the clothes at a parade in Sydney, with 40 of the latest Zegna garments. — *The Sun*, p. 9, 4th April 1988

first horse *nickname*
the First Cavalry Division, US Army *US*
- — Carl Fleischhauer, *A Glossary of Army Slang*, p. 19, 1968

first Louie *noun*
a first lieutenant *US*
- — Linda Reinberg, *In the Field*, p. 81, 1991

first off
as a beginning *US, 1880*
- First off, as an expat, let me welcome you to England. — *The Guardian*, 18th November 2003

first-of-May *noun*

1 an inexperienced worker *US, 1961*
A circus word, based on the start of the circus season.
- "Some of the fellows in the shop laugh about you behind your back. Know what they call you? 'First of May.' That's an old carnival term for someone who comes out in the spring but doesn't last through the winter. They don't think you have the stuff to stick[.] — Earl Thompson, *Tattoo*, p. 573, 1974
- More common certainly than having some first-of-May, fucking-new-guy rookie triage medic sit there picking at a millions slivers of shrapnel with a manicure scissors, a magnifying glass, and a bottle of hydrogen peroxide. — Larry Heinemann, *Paco's Story*, p. 51, 1986

2 a newcomer to a circus or carnival *US, 1926*
- — Joe McKennon, *Circus Lingo*, p. 34, 1980

First of the First *noun*
the First Battalion of the First Regiment, US Marine Corps *US*
Korean war usage.
- So the "First of the First" was rested and scrappy when they moved north through darkness and a swirling snowstorm at two o'clock on the morning of December 8. — Joseph C. Goulden, *Korea*, p. 376, 1982
- I witnessed the fighting from the vantage point of Company Commander, H&S Company, 1st Battalion, 1st Marines – which we called "the 1st of the 1st of the 1st." — William B. Hopkins, *One Bugle No Drums*, p. x, 1986

first pig *noun*
a first sergeant, the most senior non-commissioned officer in the US Army *US, 1975*
- — Linda Reinberg, *In the Field*, p. 81, 1991

first reader *noun*
a railway conductor's trainbook *US*
- — Norman Carlisle, *The Modern Wonder Book of Trains and Railroading*, p. 262, 1946

first sergeant *noun*
your wife *US*
- — Wayne Floyd, *Jason's Authentic Dictionary of CB Slang*, p. 16, 1976

first shirt *noun*
a first sergeant in the US Army *US, 1969*
- Secondly, gunnies have enough rank that few people screw with them, and they do not have to be an asshole like the first shirt (sergeant) to get the job done. — John Culbertson, *A Sniper in the Arizona*, p. 104, 1999

first sleeve *noun*
a first sergeant *US*
- — *American Speech*, p. 227, October 1956: 'More United States Air Force slang'
- — Carl Fleischhauer, *A Glossary of Army Slang*, p. 19, 1968

first soldier *noun*

a first sergeant in the US Army *US, 1946*

- Now first sergeants are renowned in the army for being the "Top Kick," the "First Soldier," the senior NCO in the unit, and usually he's the toughest man in the company. —Larry Gwin, *Baptism (A Vietnam Memoir)*, p. 74, 1999

first suck of the sauce bottle *noun*

first in a queue *AUSTRALIA*

- I want first suck of the sauce bottle or I'll flamin' drop you! —Barry Humphries, *Bazza Pulls It Off!*, 1971

first today and last tomorrow

in horse racing, said of an inconsistent performer *US*

- —David W. Maurer, *Argot of the Racetrack*, p. 26, 1951

fish *noun*

1 the vagina *UK, 1891*

- Other verb forms are: eat fish and chew the fish. —G. Legman, *The Language of Homsexuality*, p. 1165, 1941

2 a woman, usually heterosexual *UK, 1891*

- —Anon., *The Gay Girl's Guide*, p. 9, 1949
- —Donald Webster Cory and John P. LeRoy, *The Homosexual and His Society*, p. 264, 1963: 'A lexicon of homosexual slang'
- But a jealous bartender, who Knows, tells three sailors who want to make it with her that shes not a fish, shes a fruit[.] —John Rechy, *City of Night*, p. 118, 1963
- —*Fact*, p. 26, January-February 1965
- I know that women are referred to as "fish" in fag-lang. But that's defamation. —Angelo d'Arcangelo, *The Homosexual Handbook*, p. 210, 1968
- JANET: Oh, Brad. *Oh, Janet.* Brad my darling *Janet, my fish.* —Sal Piro and Michael Hess, *The Official 'Rocky Horror Picture Show' Audience Participation Guide*, p. 37, 1991

3 a male homosexual *JAMAICA*

Collected in a UK prison, August 2002.

4 a prisoner who has recently arrived in prison *US, 1864*

- Word buzzed through the grapevine about the new "fish"[.] —Mezz Mezzrow, *Really the Blues*, p. 10, 1946
- Bud was between romances, the Parole Board having sent his previous inamorata out several weeks prior to the time Sam showed up in his group of 'fish.' —*New York Mattachine Newsletter*, p. 6, July 1961
- As a "fish" (prison slang for a new inmate) at Charlestown, I was physically miserable and as evil-tempered as a snake, being suddenly without drugs. —Malcolm X and Alex Haley, *The Autobiography of Malcolm X*, p. 152, 1964
- All "fish" new cons were housed here to be given a thorough medical check out and classification before being assigned to work details out in "population." —Iceberg Slim (Robert Beck), *Pimp*, p. 50, 1969
- "Dont touch it, fish," warned the fumigator, using the handle for new prisoners. —Seth Morgan, *Homeboy*, p. 167, 1990
- —Angela Devlin, *Prison Patter*, p. 52, 1996

5 a lover *NORFOLK ISLAND*

- —Beryl Nobbs Palmer, *A Dictionary of Norfolk Words and Usages*, p. 14, 1992

6 a person *UK, 1722*

Always suffixed to an adjective.

- Sophie has not provided the safe harbour that this poor fish [Prince Edward] needs. —*The Guardian*, 1st October 2001
- He is, on the face of it, a cold fish. —*The Observer*, 21st July 2002

7 a fool *UK*

- How we gonna find out where he lives, you fish? —*Dog Eat Dog*, 2000

8 a heavy drinker *US*

- —Judi Sanders, *Cal Poly Slang*, p. 4, 1990

9 a drug addict who supports his habit by pimping *US*

- —*American Speech*, p. 87, May 1955: 'Narcotic argot along the Mexican border'

10 in poker, an unskilled player who is a likely victim of a skilled professional *US*

- —Peter O. Steiner, *Thursday Night Poker*, p. 411, 1996

11 in on-line poker, the weakest player in the game

- —*FHM*, p. 147, June 2003

12 in cricket, a weak batsman *TRINIDAD AND TOBAGO, 1990*

- —Lise Winer, *Dictionary of the English/Creole of Trinidad & Tobago*, 2003

13 a poor chess player *US*

- —*American Speech*, p. 233, Autumn-Winter 1971: 'Checkschmuck! The slang of the chess player'

14 in oil drilling, any object inadvertently dropped down a well *US*

- —Jerry Robertson, *Oil Slanguage*, p. 54, 1954

15 a Plymouth Baracuda car *US*

- —Wayne Floyd, *Jason's Authentic Dictionary of CB Slang*, p. 16, 1976

16 a torpedo *US*

- —*American Speech*, p. 38, February 1948: 'Talking under water: speech in submarines'

17 a dollar *US*

- —Hyman E. Goldin et al., *Dictionary of American Underworld Lingo*, p. 70, 1950
- The clients of the Carne Organization were charged a minimum, of one hundred fish per diem and they expected service in their homes. —Raymond Chandler, *The Long Goodbye*, p. 97, 1953

18 in electric line work, a glass strain insulator *US*

- —A.B. Chance Co., *Lineman's Slang Dictionary*, p. 7, 1980

▸ **have other fish to fry; have bigger fish to fry**

to have other business, or other things to do or achieve *UK, 1660*

- You're not that important, kid. They got bigger fish to fry. —Derek Bickerton, *Payroll*, p. 76, 1959
- Clearly, the talented and the impassioned have other fish to fry. —*New Statesman*, 31st January 2000
- Teams with bigger fish to fry leave room for flounders— *The Guardian*, 8th March 2003

fish *verb*

1 to dance in a slow and sexual manner, moving the body but not the feet *US*

- "Something slow and sweet so we can fish." The music came on, and he took her in the close, tight embrace of the dance[.] —Hal Ellson, *The Golden Spike*, p. 28, 1952
- You ever dance fish, West? —Evan Hunter, *The Blackboard Jungle*, p. 159, 1954
- We fished real close and felt each other up. —Piri Thomas, *Down These Mean Streets*, p. 223, 1969
- —Kenn "Naz" Young, *Naz's Underground Dictionary*, p. 29, 1973

2 in gin, to discard in a manner that is designed to lure a desired card from an opponent *US*

- —Irwin Steig, *Play Gin to Win*, p. 138,

3 in poker, to stay with a bad hand in the hope of drawing the only card that can possibly make the hand a good one *US*

- —Victor H. Royer, *Casino Gamble Talk*, p. 57, 2003

4 to use a prison's plumbing system to pass a note from cell to cell *US*

- [F]ishing (passing messages from one cell to another by flushing a line attached to a kite down the toilet, to be retrieved by another inmate housed in another cell[.] —Bill Valentine, *Gangs and Their Tattoos*, p. 38, 2000

▸ **fish for food**

to gossip *US*

- —Marcus Hanna Boulware, *Jive and Slang of Students in Negro Colleges*, 1947

▸ **fish on the half-line**

in the Maritime Provinces, to fish for half of the catch as wages *CANADA*

- In return for his investment the factory owner received one-half of the season's catch from each boat. This was referred to as "fishing half-line." —J. Clinton Morrison, *Along the North Shore*, p. 70, 1983

▸ **fish or cut bait; fish, cut bait or go ashore**

make up your mind! *US, 1860*

The shorter, two-option phrase is more popular today than the longer original.

- —Charles F. Haywood, *Yankee Dictionary*, p. 59, 1963

fish

used as a euphemism for 'fuck', a cry of despair, surprise, rage, resignation; an abbreviated euphemism for 'fuck off', a cry of disbelief *UK*

Often lingering on the 'f' before pronouncing the 'ish' so that a disguised intention is made obvious.

- Don't you feel ready to conquer the globe? / Oh fish —Ian Dury, *Jack Shit George*, 1998
- —Paik Choo, *The Coxford Singlish Dictionary*, p. 37, 2002

fish and chip; fish *noun*

1 the *lip*; *lip* (impudence) *UK*

Rhyming slang.

- —Ray Puxley, *Cockney Rabbit*, 1992

2 a gratuity *UK*

Rhyming slang for 'tip'.

- —Ray Puxley, *Cockney Rabbit*, 1992

fish and chips *noun*
in poker, a group of unskilled players with a lot of money to lose *US*
- —John Vorhaus, *The Big Book of Poker Slang*, p. 17, 1996

fish and shrimp *noun*
a pimp *US, 1935*
Rhyming slang.
- —Vincent J. Monteleone, *Criminal Slang*, p. 84, 1949
- —Bodmin Dark, *Dirty Cockney Rhyming Slang*, 2003

fish and tank *noun*
a bank *UK*
Rhyming slang.
- —Ray Puxley, *Fresh Rabbit*, 1998

fishbelly *noun*
a white person *US, 1985*
- "Heavenly days," I said, "talk about ethnic stereotyping." "You go on back to Boston, fishbelly, and stay there and don't come near my lady again." —Robert Parker, *Taming a Seahorse*, p. 39, 1986

fishbite *noun*
the condition that exists when someone pulls your trousers or underpants forcefully upward, forming a wedge between buttock cheeks *US*
- —*American Speech*, Fall 1990

fishbowl *noun*
1 a room in HMP Wormwood Scrubs where prisoners meet their visitors *UK*
- Prisoners say it is like being in a goldfish bowl. —Angela Devlin, *Prison Patter*, p. 52, 1996

2 the area in a prison where newly arrived prisoners are housed *US*
- —Jay Robert Nash, *Dicitonary of Crime*, p. 131, 1992

fish bull *noun*
a new and young prison guard *US*
- —Inez Cardozo-Freeman, *The Joint*, p. 496, 1984

fish-burner *noun*
a sled dog *US, 1967*
An extension of the early C20 'hay-burner' (horse).
- —Russell Tabbert, *Dictionary of Alaskan English*, p. 205, 1991

fish cake *noun*
five dollars *US*
- —Steve Kuriscak, *Casino Talk*, p. 23, 1985

fishcunt *noun*
used by adolescent boys as a derisory term for any girl of similar maturity *UK*
Describes an olfactory and physical difference between the genders.
- You FUCKIN' SPUNKERS. Wankaaaahs. – FISHCUNTS. Bitches. Then they all take deep breaths an' start chantin' the same thing at each other. —Nick Barlay, *Curvy Lovebox*, p. 45, 1997

fish-eater *noun*
a Roman Catholic *US*
From the largely forgotten practice of abstaining from eating meat on Fridays.
- — *Maledicta*, p. 124, Summer 1980: 'Racial and ethnic slurs: regional awareness and variations'

fisherman's daughter; fisherman's *noun*
water *UK, 1888*
Rhyming slang. One of several terms that have 'daughter' as the common (dispensible) element.
- Shortened to "a drop of fisherman's" this is an old accompaniment of scotch. —Ray Puxley, *Cockney Rabbit*, 1992

fisherman's dinner *noun*
a steak *CANADA*
- As listed on menus of restaurants in fishing ports, [fisherman's dinner] always means a steak. For some reason, many fishermen hate eating their catch. —Tom Parkin, *WetCoast Words*, p. 53, 1989

fish eye *noun*
an expressionless stare *US, 1941*
From the appearance.
- I gets a big charge going in there with these two birds, seeing people give me the fish eye, thinking what's this herbert doing in our boozer[.] —John Peter Jones, *Feather Pluckers*, p. 43, 1964

fish eyes *noun*
tapioca *US, 1918*
- Compare what other people are eating to gross things their food looks like. Examples: tapioca pudding – fish eyes. —Matt Groening, *Bart Simpson's Guide to Life*, p. 24, 1993

fish fingers *noun*
said of fingers that have been used to stimulate a woman's vagina *AUSTRALIA*
- — Thommo, *The Dictionary of Australian Swearing and Sex Sayings*, p. 45, 1985

fish frighteners *noun*
a pair of men's close-fitting and revealing nylon swimming trunks *AUSTRALIA*
- Don't make me go water skiing with dad today, he's got his fish frighteners out. — *Wordmap (www.abc.net.au/wordmap)*, 2003

fish gallery *noun*
the area in a prison where newly arrived prisoners are kept *US*
- —Joseph E. Ragen and Charles Finston, *Inside the World's Toughest Prison*, p. 799, 1962: 'Penitentiary and underworld glossary'

fishhead *noun*
a person from Southeast Asia *US, 1971*
- I can hear what they are saying but all I can think of is pig, white, guinea, spic, hebe, motherfucker, nigger, donkey, mick, fishhead. —Dennis Smith, *Report from ENgine Co. 82*, p. 62, 1972

fish-hook *noun*
1 in a deck of playing cards, any seven *US*
- —Albert H. Morehead, *The Complete Guide to Winning Poker*, p. 262, 1967

2 in a deck of playing cards, a jack or knave *US*
- —Jim Glenn, *Programmed Poker*, p. 156, 1981z

fish-hooks *noun*
problems *NEW ZEALAND*
- —Sonya Plowman, *Great Kiwi Slang*, p. 73, 2002

fishies *noun*
MDMA, the recreational drug best known as ecstasy *US*
- The drug Ecstasy was called fishies or double stacks, according to the affidavit. — *Orlando Sentinel*, p. B2, 17th August 2002

fishing expedition *noun*
a litigation tactic of requesting a broad range of probably irrelevant information in the hope of discovering something helpful *US, 1874*
- Lawyers in major fraud cases were warned today by an old Bailey judge not to go on "fishing expeditions" which were forbidden by law and an abuse of the court process. —*Press Association Limited*, 14th December 1993
- I was wondering why so many judges accuse – there is no other word – why they accuse lawyers of going on fishing expeditions. — *The Lawyers Weekly*, 8th July 1994

fishing pole *noun*
any contrivance fashioned to pass or retrieve items from cell to cell *US*
- — AFSCME Local 3963, *The Correctional Officer's Guide to Prison Slang*, 2001

fish line *noun*
in a prison, a string used to pull objects from one cell to another *US*
- —James Harris, *A Convict's Dictionary*, p. 32, 1989

fishmonger *noun*
a lesbian *UK*
Conventionally 'one who deals in fish' (*Oxford English Dictionary*), playing on **FISH** (the vagina).
- — *www.LondonSlang.com*, June 2002

fish 'n' chip mob *noun*
anyone who is considered socially wanting due to lack of breeding or hereditary privilege *UK*
Patronising upper-class usage; originally military for any regiment considered socially inferior.
- —Ann Barr and Peter York, *The Official Sloane Ranger Handbook*, p. 91, 1982

fisho *noun*

an angler *AUSTRALIA, 1971*

- —Frank Hardy, *The Outcasts of Foolgarah*, p. 241, 1971
- The fishos were told their tackle would be returned to them at their local police station on the payment of a small fine.—Bob Staines, *Wot a Whopper*, p. 45, 1982
- —Frank Hardy, *Hardy's People*, p. 63, 1986

fish queen *noun*

a homosexual male who spends a great deal of time in the company of heterosexual women *US, 1941*

- Fish-Queen – Properly a "cunt-sucker", but in general usage applied to any homosexual who makes a point of bringing women with him[.]—Anon, *The Gay Girl's Guide*, p. 9, 1949
- —*The Lavendar Lexicon*, 1st June 1964

fish scale *noun*

crack cocaine *US*

From the appearance.

- The kids out here don't know a flake from a fish – if you asked them what fishscale is, they wouldn't know. [Fishscale is high-grade cocaine powder with few rock-like chunks.'—Terry Williams, *The Cocaine Kids*, p. 41, 1989
- —Mike Haskins, *Drugs*, p. 281, 2003

fish scales *noun*

cocaine *US*

- The wiretaps recorded a primer of street slang for powder cocaine: white lady, white fingers, soft, fish scales and sand.—*Orlando Sentinel*, p. B2, 17th August 2002

fishskin *noun*

a condom *US, 1936*

- In my memory the image of him standing by the car and holding up that transparent sack of rubber or fishskin was the finale – CURTAIN.—Mary McCarthy, *How I Grew*, p. 80–81, 1987

fishtail *verb*

to cause the rear of an aeroplane or car to swerve from side to side *US, 1927*

- I wrenched the wheel over, felt the rear end start to slide, brought it out with a splash of power and almost ran up the side of the cliff as the car fishtailed.—Mickey Spillane, *Kiss Me Deadly*, p. 7, 1952
- [W]hen his hand came out empty he began fishtailing across three lanes of highway.—Richard Price, *Clockers*, p. 517, 1992
- The boys had almost reached the lower corner when the cop car skidded around the intersection behind them, fishtailed, recovered sloppily[.]—Jess Mowry, *Way Past Cool*, p. 15, 1992

fish tank *noun*

1 a holding cell for newly arrived prisoners *US*

A wonderful pun with independently formed terms.

- —Don Dempsey, *American Speech*, p. 269, December 1962: 'The language of traffic policemen'
- —Inez Cardozo-Freeman, *The Joint*, p. 496, 1984

2 a bus *UK*

- —Peter Chippindale, *The British CB Book*, p. 154, 1981

fish wife *noun*

a married male homosexual's wife *US*

- —Eugene Landy, *The Underground Dictionary*, p. 78, 1971

fishy *adjective*

inducing suspicion *US, 1840*

- We didn't catch you with the goods tonight, but ... if we ever do catch anything fishy goin' on in here, we're gonna bust the bunch o' ya. —Odie Hawkins, *Ghetto Sketches*, p. 36, 1972
- I am not suggesting the News Of The World was guilty of entrapment [...] but there was something fishy about its story nevertheless.—*The Guardian*, p. 7, 1st June 2002

fist city *noun*

a physical fight *US, 1930*

- Jump down Jackson if you want to go to fist city you can naturally take off.—Lavada Durst, *The Jives of Dr. Hepcat*, p. 1, 1953

fister *noun*

a person who inserts their hand into another's vagina or rectum for sexual gratification *US*

- An old-school fister, Bert's into getting high on pot and poppers and stuffing gobs of Crisco, whereas I am into endorphin highs and a nice, thick water-based lubricant—*The Village Voice*, 2nd November 1999

fist fuck; fist *verb*

to insert your lubricated fist into a partner's rectum or vagina, leading to sexual pleasure for both *US*

- —Bruce Rodgers, *The Queens' Vernacular*, p. 81, 1972
- "Please sir. I've never been fisted." "Just shut your fucking mouth, asshole."—*Drummer*, p. 55, 1977
- —*What Color is Your Handkerchief*, p. 5, 1979
- —*Maledicta*, p. 231–232, 1979: 'Kinks and queens: linguistic and cultural aspects of the terminology for gays'
- Then he asked if she'd ever been fisted.—Anka Radakovich, *The Wild Girls Club*, p. 165, 1994
- I remember once I was being fisted by Sebastian Cabot – but here's where the story gets interesting.—*Austin Powers*, 1999
- Fist-fucked by grief...—Rita Ciresi, *Pink Slip*, p. 22, 1999
- I was tied screaming to her bed, before she greased her arm with cream an fist-fucked me.—Niall Griffiths, *Kelly + Victor*, p. 107, 2002

fist-fucker *noun*

1 a practitioner of fist fucking *US, 1972*

- Another ugly extreme of S & M is the burgeoning of a "group" calling itself the F.F.A. (Fist Fuckers of America).—John Rechy, *The Sexual Outlaw*, p. 256, 1977

2 a frequent, obsessive masturbator *US, 1962*

- I feel plumb sorry for you poor Wichita fistfuckers, bein deperived of growin up without an ole cow, sheep er sow er somethin.—Earl Thompson, *Tattoo*, p. 133, 1974

fist-fucking; fisting *noun*

1 the practice of inserting the hand (and part of the arm) into a partner's anus (or vagina) for the sexual pleasure of all involved *US, 1972*

Predominantly gay usage but also found in heterosexual practice.

- —*Maledicta*, p. 163, Summer/Winter 1986–1987: 'Sexual slang: prostitutes, pedophiles, flagellators, transvestites, and necrophiles'
- Fisting, incest and anal sex. We shelve it under Viking interest. —Melanie McGrath, *Hard, Soft & Wet*, p. 192, 1998
- KYLE'S MOTHER: "What is 'fisting'? CARTMAN'S MOTHER: That's when the fist is inserted into the anus or vagina for sexual pleasure. —*South Park*, 1999

2 masturbation *UK, 1891*

- FIST FUCKING! [Headline]—*Screw*, p. 11, 1st September 1969

fist it!

be quiet! *US*

- —Linda Meyer, *Teenspeak!*, p. 31, 1994

fist sandwich *noun*

a punch in the mouth *US, 1982*

- Bronk offers Artie a fist sandiwch.—Joe Bob Briggs, *Joe Bob Goes to the Drive-In*, p. 47, 1987

fit *noun*

1 the equipment needed to inject a drug *US, 1959*

A shortened form of OUTFIT. Also recorded in England.

- I'm waiting for you to finish cleaning your fit and get away from the basin, so I can use mine.—Clarence Cooper Jr, *The Scene*, p. 249, 1960
- I don't know what they had planned, but they sure was making a fit. —Joseph Wambaugh, *The Blue Knight*, p. 30, 1973
- —William K. Bentley and James M. Corbett, *Prison Slang*, p. 80, 1992
- —Angela Devlin, *Prison Patter*, p. 52, 1996

2 an outfit of clothing *US*

- —David Claerbaut, *Black Jargon in White America*, p. 64, 1972
- —Connie Eble (Editor), *UNC-CH Campus Slang*, p. 7, Spring 1994

▸ **have a fit; have forty fits**

to lose your temper, to become very angry *UK, 1877*

- Father would have forty fits if she were let loose in the old house. —Carola Dunn, *Mistletoe and Murder*, p. 52, 2002
- The poor Puritans would have had a fit on April 9, with bells and crosses and copes and unbleached candles burning in daylight and a Roman cardinal standing in the chancel.—*The Daily Telegraph*, 13th April 2002

fit; fit up; fix up *verb*

to ensure that someone is convicted of a criminal charge, often by nefarious means; to frame *AUSTRALIA, 1882*

- I'll bet you ten-to-one you don't fit me with this.—James Holledge, *The Call-girl in Australia*, p. 87, 1964
- —Frank Hardy, *The Outcasts of Foolgarah*, p. 220, 1971
- —Jim Ramsay, *Cop It Sweet!*, p. 35, 1977
- —Ryan Aven-Bray, *Ridgey Didge Oz Jack Lang*, p. 28, 1983
- Oh sure, there's a chance that JB is as guilty as sin, but there is the 0.003 probability that he's been fitted up[.]—Roy Slaven (John Doyle), *Five South Coast Seasons*, p. 150, 1992

▸ **fit where they touch; fits where it touches**
applied to loose or ill-fitting clothes *UK, 1932*

▸ **to fit just like a smack on the lips**
(of a raincoat) to be the perfect size *CANADA, 1988*
- On the South Shore [of Nova Scotia] a raincoat fits just like a smack on the lips. — Harry Bruce, *Down Home*, p. 108, 1988

fit *adjective*
sexually attractive *UK*
Originally a black term, now in wider usage; coinage is obviously informed by the conventional sense as 'healthy'.
- Do you ever look at other girls? [...] Sometimes, if they're really fit. — *SMTV LIVE it's wicked*, p. 24, 2000
- THOU SHALT NOT COMMIT ADULTERY (UNLESS SHE IZ REALLY FIT). — Sacha Baron-Cohen, *Da Gospel According to Ali G*, 2001
- Yeah, yeah like I said, you are really fit / But, my gosh, don't you just know it? — Mike Skinner, *Fit But You Know It*, 2004

▸ **are you fit?**
are you ready? *UK, 1984*

fit and spasm *noun*
an orgasm *UK*
Rhyming slang, formed on appropriate imagery.
- I can never tell when she has a fit and spasm. — Bodmin Dark, *Dirty Cockney Rhyming Slang*, 2003

fit as a fiddle *adjective*
in good health or condition *UK, 1616*
- Kathleen Grundy, 81, fit as a fiddle and a tireless worker on behalf of the elderly[.] — *The Guardian*, 1st February 2000

fitbin *noun*
the vagina *UK, 2001*
- — *Sky Magazine*, July 2001

fit fanny *noun*
a sexually attractive woman or women *UK*
- There's some fit fanny here this year. — Colin Butts, *Is Harry Still on the Boat?*, p. 25, 2003

FITH *adjective*
demented, stupid *AUSTRALIA*
From '*f*ucked *i*n *t*he *h*ead'.
- — *Maledicta*, p. 92, 1986–1987: 'Australian maledicta'

fitness *noun*
sexually attractive young women *UK*
From FIT (sexually attractive).
- [T]he young security guard was more interested in the amount of "fitness" coming to the dance. — Karline Smith, *Moss Side Massive*, p. 97–98, 1994

fit 'n' furry *adjective*
used as a description of a hirsute, sexually attractive man *UK*
- Drooling over the fabulously fit 'n' furry Rive Gauche model does make you wonder how we started adoring baldy-bods in the first place. — *Attitude*, p. 80, October 2003

fitted *adjective*
1 falsely incriminated *UK*
- "Or what?" I said. "Or you'll find yourself well fitted. You know the score, we know the score[.] — Lenny McLean, *The Guv'nor*, p. 78, 1998

2 well-dressed *US*
- — *San Francisco Chronicle*, p. E5, 10th August 2003
- — Rick Ayers (Editor), *Berkeley High Slang Dictionary*, p. 21, 2004

fit to *adjective*
at the point of doing something; likely to do something *UK, 1585*
- And somewhere, far away, William Forster is laughing fit to bust. — *The Guardian*, 12th May 2003

fit to be tied *adjective*
very angry, furious *US, 1894*
- And now I was going to keep her waiting. I was fit to be tied. — Claire Mansfield and John Mendelssohn, *Dominatrix*, p. 120, 2002

five *noun*
1 a slap of the hand in greeting *US, 1959*
- They exchange fives and remain in the window, checking out the mid-afternoon scene. — Odie Hawkins, *Ghetto Sketches*, p. 111, 1972

2 five pounds *UK*
- "Ya got five?" she asked. — Frank Skinner, *Frank Skinner*, p. 214, 2001

3 an amphetamine tablet *US*
- — US Department of Justice, *Street Terms*, August 1993

4 a five-year prison sentence *UK*
- — Frank Norman, *Bang to Rights*, 1958

5 Chanel No. 5™ perfume *US*
- I don't care if the world buys Opium until it comes to an end; I'm gonna always have me some 5. — Odie Hawkins, *Lost Angeles*, p. 188, 1994

▸ **come and take five**
to make a short visit *GRENADA, 1976*
Recorded by Richard Allsopp.

▸ **get your five**
to attain the highest rank in the Canadian civil service *CANADA*
- And he'd "got his five," as they said, the top civil service pay scale EX-5. He had reason to feel pleased with himself. — Robert MacNeil, *The Voyage*, p. 2, 1995

▸ **give five**
to shake hands or to slap hands in a greeting *US, 1935*
- "Hyuh, Larry, give me five.' Larry refuses the outstretched hand. — Darryl Ponicsan, *The Last Detail*, p. 60, 1970
- Murphy leaned forward to give his partner five. "Right on, brother! Right on!" — Odie Hawkins, *Chicago Hustle*, p. 98–99, 1977
- I had it because a week later Chillie gave me five [a stylized hand slap] and the coke was in his hand. — Terry Williams, *The Cocaine Kids*, p. 78, 1989
- No jive, gimme five. — Editors of Ben is Dead, *Retrohell*, p. 202, 1997

▸ **take five**
to take a short break *US, 1929*
- Following any personal or professional ordeal while on duty at the Clinic, it was the practice of the young nurses to 'take five,' as they expressed it, in Nurses Rest rooms. — Terry Southern, *Flash and Filigree*, p. 61, 1958
- [T]hey have to rest after every joke. Take five. Have a cuppa. — Nick Barlay, *Curvy Lovebox*, p. 33, 1997

five and dime *noun*
in poker, a hand with a five and a ten and three other unpaired cards in between *US, 1968*
- — Thomas L. Clark, *The Dictionary of Gambling and Gaming*, p. 80, 1987

five and two *noun*
used as a formula for the services of a prostitute – her fee and the room fee *US*
- He lies back in the chaise and shuts his eyes and sees all the whorehouses, all the bar hookers he's had – the five and two's: five for the girl and two for the room. — Darryl Ponicsan, *The Last Detail*, p. 126, 1970

five-by-five; five-by *adverb*
loud and clear *US, 1954*
- "This is Rattlesnake one. Read you five by. How me? Over." "This is Rattlesnake two. Read you five by." — James N. Rowe, *Five Years to Freedom*, p. 22, 1971
- Lima Charlie and five-square mean the same thing as five by five. — *Atlanta (Georgia) Journal-Constitution*, p. 2D, 26th April 2002

five by two *noun*
a Jewish person *AUSTRALIA*
- — John Meredith, *Learn to talk Old Jack Lang*, p. 24, 1984

five-card Charlie *noun*
in casino blackjack games, a bonus paid to a player who draws three cards and still has a total count of 21 or less *US*
- — Frank Scoblete, *Best Blackjack*, p. 261, 1996

five-cent paper *noun*
five dollars' worth of a drug *US*
- — Eugene Landy, *The Underground Dictionary*, p. 78, 1971

five-digit disco *noun*
an act of female masturbation *UK*
- — Michelle Baker and Steven Tropiano, *Queer Facts*, p. 46, 2004

five finger *noun*
a thief, especially a pickpocket *US, 1932*
- — Ralph de Sola, *Crime Dictionary*, p. 52, 1982

five-finger *verb*
to shoplift *US, 1919*
- We've five-fingered most of the action figure aisle. — *Airheads*, 1994

five-finger discount *noun*
theft by shoplifting *US, 1966*
- —*Current Slang*, p. 7, Summer 1969
- I folded the note and put it in Lefty's grungy backpack (veteran of countless shoplifting capers and itself acquired through a past five-finiger discount).—C.D. Payne, *Youth in Revolt*, p. 67, 1993

five-fingered chequebook *noun*
acquisition by shoplifting *NEW ZEALAND*
- —Harry Orsman and Des Hurley, *The Beaut Little Book of New Zealand Slang*, 1994

five-fingered Mary *noun*
a man's hand as the means of masturbation *US, 1971*
- Poor bastards, they can't get a woman from one month to the next, and so it's five-fingered Mary and her horny-palmed sister in their hammock each night.—Christopher Peachment, *Caravaggio*, p. 171, 2002

five-fingered widow *noun*
(of a male) the hand as a masturbatory tool; masturbation *UK, 1977*
- [T]he rest of us were spending more time with the five-fingered widow than girls of our own age.—John King, *Human Punk*, p. 147, 2000

five fingers *noun*
a five-year prison sentence *US*
- —Jay Robert Nash, *Dicitonary of Crime*, p. 131, 1992

five hundred club *noun*
the notional association of all those who have been in Antarctica for more than 500 consecutive days *ANTARCTICA*
- —*Cool Antarctica*, 2003: 'Antarctic slang'

five-knuckle shuffle *noun*
masturbation *US*
- —Helen Dahlskog (Editor), *A Dictionary of Contemporary and Colloquial Usage*, p. 23, 1972
- —Connie Eble (Editor), *UNC-CH Campus Slang*, p. 7, Fall 1987
- Copperknob doing a five knuckle shuffle in the loo[.]—Jack Allen, *When the Whistle Blows*, p. 105, 2000

five-K rig *noun*
a 5000 watt public address system *UK*
- —Bob Young and Micky Moody, *The Language of Rock 'n' Roll*, p. 44, 1985

five-o *noun*
fifty *US*
- That big five-o would have pretty well covered a high-stepping evening on the town with the nifty Mike Hammer secretary.—Terry Southern, *Now Dig This*, p. 145, 2001

five o'clock follies *noun*
during the Vietnam war, the daily military press briefings *US, 1966*
- He resolved to meander by MACV headquarters later in the day, perhaps in time for the famous Five O'clock Follies, the chest-thumping press briefing that so amused the collected media cynics every afternoon.—Lucian K. Truscott, *Army Blue*, p. 89, 1989
- In the view of correspondents who reported from Vietnam, it is considerably less useful than the much-satirized "Five O'Clock Follies," the daily briefing in Saigon, because far fewer facts are made available.—*New York Times*, p. A9, 4th February 1991

five o'clock shadow *noun*
fast-growing, dark facial whiskers, which give the appearance of needing a shave by late in the afternoon *US, 1937*
President Richard Nixon was known and ridiculed for his.
- I shaved then. We are all afraid of Five O'clock Shadow.—Philip Wylie, *Opus 21*, p. 76, 1949
- I told his burly man with the five-o'clock shadow next to me that I had been to a reunion of some of my old clubhouse friends.—Clancy Sigal, *Going Away*, p. 358, 1961
- Still, his perpetual five o'clock shadow remains zit-free, so he has no real reason for complaint.—C.D. Payne, *Youth in Revolt*, p. 179–180, 1993

five of clubs *noun*
the fist *US, 1947*
Often used in constructions such as 'I dealt him the five of clubs'.
- —Ken Weaver, *Texas Crude*, p. 55, 1984
- —Michael Dalton Johnson, *Talking Trash with Redd Foxx*, p. 98, 1994

five-oh *noun*
the police; a police officer *US, 1983*
From *Hawaii Five-O*, a police television series that aired from September 1968 to April 1980, featuring an elite four-man police unit.
- Yo! Y! You 5-0. This dude is a cop! A cop!—*New Jack City*, 1990
- The best he could do was to get somebody to spot them sneaking into a building from the rear, yell out "Five-oh" so nobody did anything stupid.—Richard Price, *Clockers*, p. 4, 1992
- New youth was abroad and feisty; too many five-oh incidents tolerated, to much shit eaten and now too much to prove.—Mick Farren, *Give the Anarchist a Cigarette*, p. 347, 2001

five on the sly; five on the soul side *noun*
a mutual slapping of palms as an 'inside' greeting *US*
- —Edith A. Folb, *runnin' down some lines*, p. 240, 1980

five-pinner *noun*
a bowler in a five-pin game *CANADA*
- An estimated 1,000,000 Canadian players are engaged in five-pin bowling as this truly native Canadian game gets into full swing on some 7,000 alleys across the country.—*Kingston Whig-Standard*, p. 42/5, 10th October 1957
- I don't know whether you've noticed, but the five pinners, once complete rulers of the local picture, are facing a real challenge from the ten pinners and with good reason.—*Calgary Herald*, p. 16/1, 23rd January 1964

five-pound word *noun*
any profanity *BAHAMAS*
From the fine that one might receive for using profanity.
- —John A. Holm, *Dictionary of Bahamian English*, p. 78, 1982

fiver *noun*
1 a five-pound or five-dollar note *US, 1843*
- This is going to cost you about a fiver.—Willie Fennell, *Dexter Gets The Point*, p. 114, 1961
- I can't be takin no all night fer one fast fiver, so I start in playin roun wiff his lil ol pecker.—Robert Gover, *One Hundred Dollar Misunderstanding*, p. 21, 1961
- Reggie got out of the car and walked up the highway and gave the cop a ten-spot, and all the way to Detroit Reggie and One-Eye argued, I mean vehemently, about whether we could have gotten away with only a fiver.—Clancy Sigal, *Going Away*, p. 156, 1961
- Rialto handed him a folded fiver. "Quit while you're ahead."—Robert Campbell, *Alice in La-La Land*, p. 276, 1987
- Prostitutes; ten quid for it, a fiver for a hand job.—Irish Jack, *History, The Sharper Word*, p. 31, 1998
- He said we all had to bring a tenner in next week, and from then on it was going to be a fiver a week subs[.]—Kevin Sampson, *Powder*, p. 142, 1999

2 in craps, the number five *US*
- —Steve Kuriscak, *Casino Talk*, p. 68, 1985

fiver-finger *noun*
money *UK*
Derived from shoplifting and pickpocketing.
- —Angela Devlin, *Prison Patter*, p. 52, 1996

fiver, fiver, racetrack driver *noun*
in craps, the number five *US*
- —Steve Kuriscak, *Casino Talk*, p. 68, 1985

fives *noun*
1 dice that have been altered to have two fives, the second five being where one would expect to find a two *US*
Used in combination with DEUCES, likely to produce a seven, an important number in the game of craps.
- —John Scarne, *Scarne on Dice*, p. 466, 1974

2 the fifth landing or floor level in a prison *UK*
- —Angela Devlin, *Prison Patter*, p. 52, 1996

3 the fingers *US*
- —Kenn "Naz" Young, *Naz's Underground Dictionary*, p. 29, 1973

fives!
used to reserve your seat as you briefly leave the room *US*
The promise inherent is to be right back – in, let's say, *five* minutes.
- —Connie Eble (Editor), *UNC-CH Campus Slang*, p. 3, Fall 1996

fives-a-pair *noun*
fifty-five miles an hour *US*
The near-universal speed limit on US roads from the mid-1970s until the early 90s.
- —Radio Shack, *CBer's Handy Atlas/Dictionary*, p. 24, 1976

fives artist *noun*
an expert at a shortchanging scheme using a five-dollar note *US*
- My fives artist woul d have skipped the show immediately and gone in quest of another sucker. —Jim Thompson, *Bad Boy*, p. 351, 1953

five-six-seven *noun*
collectively, Chevrolets manufactured in 1955, 1956 or 1957 *US*
Five-six-seven clubs exist in several North American cities, dedicated to the restoration and preservation of 1955, 1956 and 1957 Chevrolets, Corvettes, Pontiacs and Chevrolet and GMC trucks.
- —John Edwards, *Auto Dictionary*, p. 60, 1993

five-spot *noun*
1 a five-dollar note *US, 1892*
- If I had a five-spot or a ten, they always knew that I was good for it. —Herbert Huncke, *Guilty of Everything*, p. 189, 1990

2 a five-pound note *UK, 1984*
Adopted directly from the previous sense.

3 a prison sentence of five years *US, 1901*
- —Vincent J. Monteleone, *Criminal Slang*, p. 84, 1949
- A felony. It rates up to a five-spot in Quentin. —Raymond Chandler, *The Long Goodbye*, p. 53, 1953
- —Bruce Jackson, *Outside the Law*, p. 57, 1972: 'Glossary'
- I'll take a five-spot and go on down. A five-spot does this for him: on his record, it shows that he really did get a conviction, and that is all that ever really matters. —Bruce Jackson, *Outside the Law*, p. 135, 1972

five-square *adverb*
loud and clear *US, 1956*
- Lima Charlie and five-square mean the same thing as five by five. —*Atlanta (Georgia) Journal-Constitution*, p. 2D, 26th April 2002

five thousand
▷ **see:** 5000

five to four *adjective*
sure, certain *UK*
Rhyming slang.
- Are you five to four? —Ray Puxley, *Cockney Rabbit*, 1992

five-to-lifers *noun*
a pair of shoes issued to prisoners by the state *US*
Purported to last at least five years.
- —James Harris, *A Convict's Dictionary*, p. 32, 1989

five to two *noun*
a Jewish person *UK, 1932*
Rhyming slang for 'Jew'.
- [S]marmy five to two, thought the Dean, oops, no anti-semitism intended, but it just wasn't a good idea to have a family of Jews so prominent in the Party in a country like Australia. —Frank Hardy, *The Outcasts of Foolgarah*, p. 155, 1971

five twenty-nine *noun*
a jail sentence of one day less than six months *US*
The maximum sentence for a misdemeanor charge in some jursidictions.
- So Mike spent at least half of his time on the Island doing "five-twenty-nine" for jostling. —William Burroughs, *Junkie*, p. 26, 1953

five watter *noun*
▷ **see:** 5 WATTER

five-way *noun*
a powdered-drug cocktail of cocaine, heroin, flunitrazepam and methamphetamine ingested nasally whilst also drinking alcohol *UK*
Probably applies to any mix of five recreational stimulants.
- —Robert Ashton, *This Is Heroin*, p. 209, 2002

five will get you ten
used for an expression of confidence in the assertion that follows *US*
- GIANT: Five will get you ten he's with Jeanne. —*Mo' Better Blues*, 1990

fivezies *noun*
in poker, a pair of fives *US*
- —George Percy, *The Language of Poker*, p. 35, 1988

fix *noun*
1 an injection of a drug, especially heroin *US, 1936*
- How about a fix? How about a fix, man? —John Clellon Holmes, *Go*, p. 7, 1952
- "Angel will give me a fix," he told himself. "He'll have the stuff." —Hal Ellson, *The Golden Spike*, p. 3, 1952
- Life telescopes down to junk, one fix and looking forward to the next[.] —William Burroughs, *Junkie*, p. 35, 1953
- Do we take a fix here? —John D. McDonald, *The Neon Jungle*, p. 48, 1953
- I saw the best minds of my generation destroyed by madness, starving hysterical naked, / dragging themselves through the negro streets at dawn looking for an angry fix[.] —Allen Ginsberg, *Howl*, 1956
- Suddenly he grew tired and quiet and went in the house and disappeared in the bathroom for his pre-lunch fix. —Jack Kerouac, *On the Road*, p. 151–152, 1957
- He would have to have a fix soon. —Clarence Cooper Jr, *The Scene*, p. 12, 1960
- Half an hour ago I gave myself a fix. —Alexander Trocchi, *Cain's Book*, 1960
- You're going to see someone who's promised to give you a fix. —Douglas Rutherford, *The Creeping Flesh*, p. 181, 1963
- I need a fix 'cause I'm going down. —John Lennon and Paul McCartney, *Happiness is a Warm Gun*, 1969
- They turned out to be fairly decent – even arranging to get me a fix later when I began getting really sick. —Herbert Huncke, *The Evening Sun Turned Crimson*, p. 93, 1980

2 by extension, what a person craves or needs *US*
- I guess in a way Angel Juan is my fix and I've been jonesing for him. —Francesca Lia Block, *Missing Angel Juan*, p. 332, 1993

3 an illegal arrangement *US*
- You might buy one guy and you might put the fix in for two, but not four. —Horace McCoy, *Kiss Tomorrow Good-bye*, p. 263, 1948
- I told her where to meet me, a hotel on West forty-seventh where the fix was in strong. —Jim Thompson, *Savage Night*, p. 52, 1953

4 a well-thought-out plan with criminal intent *AUSTRALIA*
- —*(Sydney) Bulletin*, 26th April 1975

5 trouble, a difficult position *US, 1834*
- In a fix over funding? —*The Guardian*, 4th November 2003

6 in the slang of pool players, proper position for the next shot or shots *US*
- —Roger D. Abrahams, *Deep Down in the Jungle*, p. 261, 1970

▸ **get a fix on**
to make a plan of action *US*
- These people also are habitually "getting a fix" on things, a phrase presumably borrowed from navigation. If one of these boys is in a muddle as to how he and the girl friend are going to spend the evening, he says, "Let's get a fix on this evening." —*Philadelphia Evening Bulletin*, 11th October 1955

fix *verb*
1 to inject or otherwise ingest a drug, especially heroin *US, 1936*
- Trials have been held, with girls in bobbysox and sweaters testifying in childish voices to the sickening details of "blasting pot" (smoking marijuana) and fixing (use of heroin). —*San Francisco Call-Bulletin*, p. 23, 19th August 1953
- At times, after we had fixed and blown some pot, with a sleek thrust of my own soul, a thrust of empathy, I used to find myself identifying with him. —Alexander Trocchi, *Cain's Book*, p. 75, 1960
- Then they fixed up. I found out later it was heroin. —Henry Williamson, *Hustler!*, p. 67, 1965
- I had fixed only a short time before being arrested so that it wasn't until the following day that the real misery began. —Herbert Huncke, *The Evening Sun Turned Crimson*, p. 154–155, 1980
- Goddamnit, Bob, what you got to fix in the car for? —*Drugstore Cowboy*, 1988
- As for her health, Kitty hadn't fixed for twelve days. —Seth Morgan, *Homeboy*, p. 135, 1990

2 to prepare *US, 1725*
- I go first to the Guildhall Square, a coffee bar called Verrechia's to see some mates, Harry and Splif to get fixed for pills for the evening. —Ian Hebditch, *Weekend*, *The Sharper Word*, p. 132, 1969

3 (with connotations of coercion or violence) to deal with someone, or settle a situation, or exact revenge *UK, 1961*

4 to falsely incriminate *US, 1790*
Also variant 'fix up'.
- —Angela Devlin, *Prison Patter*, p. 52, 1996

5 to neuter (an animal), to castrate *US*
- She said its name was Featherfoot, and that it was a boy but she had had it fixed. —Lawrence Block, *No Score [The Affairs of Chip Harrison Omnibus]*, p. 99, 1970

6 to have sex *FIJI*
Jan Tent recorded the following usage in 1992: 'His sister a no good fuck-around. She fixes plenty boys'.

▸ fix your bones
to use drugs, especially while suffering withdrawal pains *US*
- —William K. Bentley and James M. Corbett, *Prison Slang*, p. 72, 1992

▸ fix your pipe
in the usage of counterculturalists associated with the Rainbow Nation gatherings, to give someone marijuana *US*
- —Jim Crotty, *How to Talk American*, p. 288, 1997

fixed *adjective*
situated *US*
- How are ya fixed for moonlight ? / How are ya fixed for stars? / How are you fixed for kissin' ? / While we listen to soft guitars?—Frank Sinatra and Keely Smith, 1958

fixer *noun*
1 a person who can solve problems informally *US*
- When you want a lawyer, you don't want a trial lawyer, you want a fixer. You don't care how good he is in a courtroom, you want to fix it; you don't want to go to trial.—Bruce Jackson, *Outside the Law*, p. 130, 1972

2 a person who takes care of legal problems encountered by a circus or carnival *US, 1900*
- —Joe McKennon, *Circus Lingo*, p. 34, 1980

3 an agent working for the police *UK*
- —Angela Devlin, *Prison Patter*, p. 52, 1996

fixing to *verb*
preparing to (do something); about to (do something) *US*
- —Hermese E. Roberts, *The Third Ear*, 1971

fixit *noun*
a criminal enterprise in which cars are given new identities *UK*
- She said you operated a fixit [..] you know, stolen cars repainted and given bastardised parts and a new license number!—Richard Allen, *Boot Boys*, 1972

fix or repair daily *noun*
a Ford truck; any Ford vehicle *US*
A back formation from the initials FORD. Reported as contemporary UK motor trade slang by a car salesman, 4th August 2004.
- —Montie Tak, *Truck Talk*, p. 60, 1971

fix up *verb*
to arrange a (romantic) introduction and meeting on someone else's behalf *US, 1930*
- [F]eeling in love and magnanimous I decided to fix him up with Ellen.—*The Observer*, 27th July 2003

▷ **see:** FIT; FIT UP

fizgig; fizzgig *noun*
a police informer *AUSTRALIA, 1895*
Also spelt with 'ph'.
- FIZGIG – Police informer.—Gilbert H. Lawson, *A Dictionary of Australian Words and Terms*, 1924
- —George Blaikie, *Remember Smith's Weekly?*, p. 219, 1950
- No cop could get within spying range of the sly-grog shop, and any phizgig or pimp would soon finish up in hospital.—Vince Kelly, *The Bogeyman*, p. 111, 1956
- —Jim Ramsay, *Cop It Sweet!*, p. 36, 1977
- —Ryan Aven-Bray, *Ridgey Didge Oz Jack Lang*, p. 39, 1983
- I was after the fizzgig prick in front of her. I wasn't chasing her.—Clive Galea, *Slipper*, p. 89, 1988

fizgig; fizzgig *verb*
to work as an informer *AUSTRALIA*
- Just a line on Catchpole – who he's fizzgigging for at the moment. —Peter Corris, *Make Me Rich*, p. 37, 1985

fizz *noun*
any sparkling wine *UK, 1864*
- Most cheap fizz is produced by cuve close (or 'Charmat' or 'tank' method).—Tom Stevenson, *Tom Stevenson's Champagne & Sparkling Wine Guide*, p. 1, 2002

fizzed *adjective*
gently drunk *UK*
- I wasn't drunk, just slightly fizzed.—Wayne Anthony, *Spanish Highs*, p. 146, 1999

fizzer *noun*
1 a failure; a dud *AUSTRALIA, 1957*
From the sense as 'a dud firework.'
- —Jim Ramsay, *Cop It Sweet!*, p. 36, 1977
- The plain fact was that nobody wanted a fizzer.—John Bryson, *Evil Angels*, p. 418, 1985
- [Y]ou know its a fizzer when the champion interstate import who 'cost a packet' is finally cleared and he 'can't get a kick'.—Ivor Limb, *Footy's No Joke!*, p. 31, 1986

2 in the military, a charge of misconduct *UK, 1935*
- —John W. Mussell, *The Token Book of Militarisms*, p. 1995, 29

3 a police informer *AUSTRALIA, 1943*
From FIZGIG.
- —Ryan Aven-Bray, *Ridgey Didge Oz Jack Lang*, p. 28, 1983

4 the face *UK: SCOTLAND*
A variation of PHIZOG used in Glasgow.
- What's up wi your fizzer?—Michael Munro, *The Complete Patter*, p. 55, 1996

fizzler *noun*
a failure *NEW ZEALAND*
- —Louis S. Leland, *A Personal Kiwi-Yankee Dictionary*, p. 40, 1984

fizzog *noun*
▷ **see:** PHIZOG

fizzy boat *noun*
a small but loud motorboat *NEW ZEALAND*
- —David McGill, *David McGill's Complete Kiwi Slang Dictionary*, p. 50, 1998

flab *noun*
fat, flabbiness, obesity *UK, 1923*
- But in the countryside, and in particularly the poorer centre and south of Italy, flab is more acceptable.—*The Guardian*, 4th September 2003

flabbergast *verb*
to astound, to utterly confuse *UK, 1772*
- When I went to California I was flabbergasted to learn that smoking was banned in restaurants and bars. It was like some freaky joke.—*The Guardian*, 8th July 2003

▸ my flabber is gasted; never has my flabber been so gasted
I am astounded or astonished *UK, 1984*
Jocular phrases formed on the verb FLABBERGAST (to astound). The second form is particularly associated with British comedian Frankie Howerd, 1917–92.

flabby labby *noun*
unusually pronounced vaginal labia *US*
- —Chris Lewis, *The Dictionary of Playground Slang*, p. 90, 2003

flack *noun*
a publicist; a spokesperson *US, 1939*
- Obviously, Eisner wrote the letter himself – no PR flack in his right mind would've sent out such hyperbolic twaddle.—Carl Hiaasen, *Team Rodent*, p. 41, 1998

fladanked *adjective*
drug-intoxicated *US*
- —*Maybeck High School Yearbook (Berkeley, California)*, p. 28, 1997

fladge; flage *noun*
flagellation *UK, 1948*
- —*Maledicta*, p. 237, 1979: 'Kinks and queens: linguistic and cultural aspects of the terminology for gays'

flag *noun*
1 a criminal gang's lookout *US*
- —Vincent J. Monteleone, *Criminal Slang*, p. 85, 1949

2 while injecting a drug into a vein, the flow of blood up into the syringe, indicating that the vein has been pierced *US*
- —Geoffrey Froner, *Digging for Diamonds*, p. 29, 1989

3 in computing, a variable that has two values *US*
- —Eric S. Raymond, *The New Hacker's Dictionary*, p. 157, 1991

4 in gambling, a wager of 23 bets consisting of four selections *UK*
- —David Bennet, *Know Your Bets*, p. 38, 2001

5 the grade 'F' *US*
- —Collin Baker et al., *College Undergraduate Slang Study Conducted at Brown University*, p. 117, 1968

6 the ground floor of a tiered prison cellblock *US*
- —William K. Bentley and James M. Corbett, *Prison Slang*, p. 7, 1992

7 a one-pound note *AUSTRALIA*
- —Ned Wallish, *The Truth Dictionary of Racing Slang*, p. 29, 1989

▸ **have your flag in port**
to experience the bleed period of the menstrual cycle *US*
• After the end of the month rolls around and that bitch's flag jump back in port / then keep every inch a your natural prick right down her pricksucken throat. — Bruce Jackson, *Get Your Ass in the Water and Swim Like Me*, p. 129, 1966

▸ **the flag is up; the red flag is up**
experiencing the bleed period of the menstrual cycle *US*
• — *Maledicta*, p. 197, Winter 1980: 'A new erotic vocabulary'
• — Karen Houppert, *The Curse*, 1999

flag *verb*
1 to label or categorise someone *US*
• — William K. Bentley and James M. Corbett, *Prison Slang*, p. 32, 1992
2 in the military, to make an entry on a soldier's record which will prevent further promotion *US*
• Wilson was authorized to order Colonel James D. Kiersey, chief of staff at Fort Benning, to "flag" Calley's record, an Army procedure freezing any promotion or transfer for a soldier. — Seymour M. Hersh, *My Lai 4*, p. 120, 1970
3 to give a student in college a notification of academic deficiency *US*
• — *American Speech*, p. 76–77, February 1968: 'Some notes on flunk notes'
4 to display or wear prominently (a handkerchief or other symbol of sexual taste) *US, 1896*
• If you wear (or "flag") a hankie on the right, you're a bottom; on the left, a top. — *The Village Voice*, 17th–23rd November 2002
5 to wear an article of clothing signifying gang membership *US*
• — *American Speech*, p. 391, Winter 1995: 'Among the new words'
6 to arrest *US, 1927*
• They got me up tight, and you know that ain't right / In fact, they even flagged me wrong. — Dennis Wepman et al., *The Life*, p. 62, 1976
• — John R. Armore and Joseph D. Wolfe, *Dictionary of Desperation*, p. 29, 1976
7 to fail (a test or course) *US*
• — *Time*, p. 57, 1st January 1965: 'Students: the slang bag'
8 to skip, as in missing a class *US*
• — Vann Wesson, *Generation X Field Guide and Lexicon*, p. 66, 1997

flag country *noun*
in the US Navy, the area where an admiral works *US*
• Climbing the ladders up to Flag Country, as the area where the admiral and his staff worked and lived (lurked would be a better word, Boyle thought) was torture. — Gerry Carroll, *North S*A*R*, p. 32, 1991

flag day *noun*
the bleed period of the menstrual cycle *US*
• — Collin Baker et al., *College Undergraduate Slang Study Conducted at Brown University*, p. 117, 1968

flag football *noun*
a friendly, non-competitive game of poker *US*
In the US, flag football is played with a tame set of rules which forbid most of the physical contact associated with the game.
• — John Vorhaus, *The Big Book of Poker Slang*, p. 17, 1996

flagging *adjective*
said of a woman experiencing the bleed period of her menstrual cycle *US*
• — *American Speech*, p. 298, December 1954: 'The vernacular of menstruation'

flag-off *noun*
a commencement *INDIA*
• Several leaders were present for the flag-off ceremony here. — *Times of India*, 10th March 2004

flag off *verb*
to start, to commence *INDIA*
From the use of a flag to signal the start of a race.
• The yatra [journey] took off on a musical note with singer Kailash rendering Bharat chamak raha hai song. Venkaiah Naidu flagged-off the yatra. — *Times of India*, 10th March 2004

flagpole *noun*
the erect penis *US, 1922*
Especially in the phrase 'properly saluting the flagpole' (oral sex).
• — Erica Orloff and JoAnn Baker, *Dirty Little Secrets*, p. 83, 2001

flags *noun*
▸ **have the flags out**
to experience the bleed period of the menstrual cycle *AUSTRALIA*
• If you've got the flags out flamin' say so[.] — Barry Humphries, *The Wonderful World of Barry McKenzie*, p. 22, 1968
• — Barry Humphries, *The Traveller's Tool*, p. 25, 1985

flag's up!
in circus and carnival usage, used for conveying that a meal is ready *US*
• — Don Wilmeth, *The Language of American Popular Entertainment*, p. 93, 1981

flag unfurled *noun*
the world *UK*
Rhyming slang, replacing the earlier sense (man of the world).
• — Ray Puxley, *Cockney Rabbit*, 1992

flag up *verb*
to draw attention to, to advertise *UK*
• Ferry is here to flag up the arrival of Frantic, the first Brian Ferry album in seven years[.] — *Q*, p. 13, May 2002

flag-waver *noun*
1 a rousing, patriotic song or performance *US, 1937*
• John Oatis went out on a dark siding behind a tin baling-shed and my engine, with all the flag-wavers and brass bands, boiled on toward dawn. — Ray Bradbury, *Bradbury Stories*, p. 655, 2003
2 in horse racing, a horse that flicks its tail up and down while racing *US*
• — David W. Maurer, *Argot of the Racetrack*, p. 28, 1951

flah *verb*
to have sexual intercourse *IRELAND*
The word appears to be most commonly used in Cork.
• [E]verybody wondered if he was having an affair with her or, as it was put, "Would you say Bert is flaain' that Protestant Lady?" — Bernard Share, *Slanguage*, p. 107, 2003

flahulach *adjective*
generous *IRELAND*
• He is a flahulach man. — *Dail Eirean (Parliamentary Debates)*, 31st May 1967
• — Colin Murphy and Donal O'Dea, *The Book of Feckin' Irish Slang*, p. 24, 2004

flail *verb*
to surf awkwardly *US*
• — *Surfing*, p. 43, 14th March 1990

flak *noun*
abuse, criticism *US, 1963*
From the original sense (anti-aircraft fire).
• But there was some heavy flak from the manager and we had to satisfy ourselves with the shots of Marsha on the staircase. — Fred Baker, *Events*, p. 11, 1970
• Clinton gets too much flack. Every move he makes, his enemies are right up his ass. — Chris Rock, *Rock This!*, p. 192, 1997

flake *noun*
1 cocaine *US, 1961*
• — John B. Williams, *Narcotics and Hallucinogenics*, p. 111, 1967
• To read you your rights! When was the last time you bought a quarter of flake? Empty your purse on the desk! — Joseph Wambaugh, *Finnegan's Week*, p. 113, 1993
• — Angela Devlin, *Prison Patter*, p. 52, 1996
• [A] narcotic selection box: top quality Peruvian flake, California Ecstasy and Caribbean smoke [marijuana]. — Wayne Anthony, *Spanish Highs*, p. 67, 1999
• — Nick Constable, *This is Cocaine*, p. 181, 2002
2 the shavings off a solid mass of crack cocaine *US*
• DEALER: Hey, man. You wanna cop some blow? / JUNKIE: Sure, watcha got? Dust, flakes or rocks? / DEALER: I got China White, Mother of Pearl...I reflect what you need. — Grandmaster Flash & The Furious Five featuring Melle Mel, *White Lines*, 1983
• There is also disagreement on how much of a kilo should be "flake off the rock" as opposed to the more valued crystalline form. — Terry Williams, *The Cocaine Kids*, p. 35, 1989
3 an unreliable, unstable person *US, 1959*
• Tops among the baseball flakes is Phil Linz, Philadelphia Phillie infielder formerly with the New York Yankees. — Zander Hollander, *Baseball Lingo*, p. 53, 1967
• There is no bigger flake in organized baseball than Drabowski. — Jim Bouton, *Ball Four*, p. 148, 1970
• I thought I'd met all the flakes in my courtroom. Saturday they found a snake in my mailbox. — Elmore Leonard, *Maximum Bob*, p. 218, 1991

- Harp must be fucking desperate if he's listening to you two flakes. — *Point Break*, 1991
- You're a flake, man, you don't care about this band. — *Airheads*, 1994
- She was an emotional flake. A dangerous woman — Ben Elton, *High Society*, p. 201, 2002

4 the planting of evidence on a suspected criminal *US*
- Thus we have the flake, which is planting evidence by a policeman upon a – what can he be called? Suspect? Victim? — Leonard Shecter and William Phillips, *On the Pad*, p. 115, 1973

5 in the Maritime Provinces, a wooden rack for drying fish *CANADA*
- In L'Anse-A-Beaufils [Quebec] you will still see the cod drying on the flakes, instead of being fast-frozen and packed in fancy plastic bags. — *Toronto Globe and Mail*, p. 19/8, 25th July 1963

flake *verb*

1 to plant evidence on a suspected criminal *US*
- They were rather casual about this, sometimes flaking bookmakers with numbers slips or numbers runners with bookmaking records, a practice which infuriated the gamblers more than being arrested. — *The Knapp Commission Report on Police Corruption*, p. 83, 1972
- Serpico would see a plainclothesman count the plays carried by someone he had searched, and when the number fell short of the required hundred, "flake" his prisoner – add additional plays to make up the difference. — Peter Maas, *Serpico*, p. 113, 1973
- — Angela Devlin, *Prison Patter*, p. 52, 1996

2 to fall asleep; to pass out *US*
Often used as the variant 'flake out'.
- Q: What will you do until then? A: I'm gonna flake out. Q: What? A: Pat the pad, sack out, lay in the sun — Max Shulman, *Guided Tour of Campus Humor*, p. 106, 1955
- He was just about conscious until we got him back to the mess; then he flaked out. — Graeme Kent, *The Queen's Corporal [Six Granada Plays]*, p. 103, 1959
- — Robert George Reisner, *The Jazz Titans*, p. 155, 1960
- After a particularly hectic party at a newspaper office she flaked out and slept the night on the chief sub's table. — Sue Rhodes, *Now you'll think I'm awful*, p. 100, 1967
- Do youse reckon I could flake at your dump for the arvo? — Barry Humphries, *The Wonderful World of Barry McKenzie*, p. 58, 1968
- Twenty minutes later he flakes and they lead him into the back of Sutton's junk and amp carting van. — Kevin Mackey, *The Cure*, p. 4, 1970
- — Louis S. Leland, *A Personal Kiwi-Yankee Dictionary*, p. 40, 1984

flake artist *noun*

a police officer inclined to plant evidence on a suspected criminal *US*
- But Otto Oberman, that flake artist, fucked it up for me. — Leonard Shecter and William Phillips, *On the Pad*, p. 118, 1973

flaked *adjective*

unconscious *US, 1959*
A shortening of **FLAKED OUT**.
- Lew Silver, a well known artistic four by two [Jew], who, at the time of writing, is pretty flaked[.] — Barry Humphries, *Bazza Pulls It Off!*, 1971

flaked out *adjective*

exhausted, unconscious *US, 1958*
- — *American Speech*, p. 155, May 1959: 'Gator (University of Florida) slang'

flake of corn *noun*

an erection (of the penis) *UK*
Rhymng slang for **HORN**.
- — Ray Puxley, *Cockney Rabbit*, 1992

flake off *verb*

to go away *US*
- "Chuckles with you?" she hooted. "Oh, flake off, little man!" — Max Shulman, *Rally Round the Flag, Boys!*, p. 58, 1957

flake off and die, dude!

used as an all-purpose insult *US*
- — Michael V. Anderson, *The Bad, Rad, Not to Forget Way Cool Beach and Surf Discriptionary*, p. 7, 1988

flake out *verb*

to collapse *UK, 1942*
- I'm gonna settle in the first pub and flake out on the deck there and just pour the stuff right down my flamin' throat! — J.E. MacDonnell, *Don't Gimme the Ships*, p. 98, 1960
- — W.R. Bennett, *Wingman*, p. 71, 1961

flakers *adjective*

1 drunk to the point of passing out *NEW ZEALAND*
- 'Anybody seen Charlie?' 'In the rubbity this afto. He's probably flakers.' — Nel Hillard, *The Power and the Dream*, p. 166, 1978

2 tired, exhausted *UK*
- — Nigel Foster, *The Making of a Royal Marine Commando*, 1987

flakie *noun*

▶ **take a flakie; throw a flakie**

to have a fit of temper *UK: SCOTLAND*
Glasgow slang.
- The gaffer [boss]'s gauny [going to] take a flakie when he sees this isny finished yet. — Michael Munro, *The Patter, Another Blast*, p. 24, 1988

flak shack *noun*

a military hospital or hospital ward where soldiers suffering from war-related psychological problems are treated *US, 1944*
- Before we established "flak shacks" for their rehabilitation, it was a very real problem. — Ian Hawkins, *B-17s over Berlin*, p. 260, 1990
- [F]light crews were given a week of rest and recuperation at various rest homes, sometimes known as flak shacks, that were operated by the Red Cross. — Tim Russert, *Bigg Russ and Me*, p. 14, 2004

flak trap *noun*

a tactic used by the North Vietnamese in which anti-aircraft fire is withheld from the area of a downed US aircraft until the rescue aircraft get near *US*
- — Linda Reinberg, *In the Field*, p. 82, 1991

flaky *adjective*

inattentive, distracted, unreliable *US, 1959*
Partridge suggested a connection between the adjective and cocaine, which was 'flaky' in nature.
- — Zander Hollander, *Baseball Lingo*, p. 53, 1967
- But if I begin to sense that she won't because she's flaky or immature, then I try to get as much money as I can before she blows. — Susan Hall, *Gentleman of Leisure*, p. 8, 1972
- "She's a good kid, but flaky." "Well, nobody says you got to talk to 'em." — Elmore Leonard, *Split Images*, p. 175, 1981
- He's flaky, but you might want to question him. — Robert Crais, *L.A. Requiem*, p. 74, 1999
- If you're a flatliner (a person with a flat mobile phone battery), you're flaky. — *The Times Magazine*, 21st June 2003

flam *noun*

a deceptive front *UK, 1632*
- — Eugene Landy, *The Underground Dictionary*, p. 79, 1971

flam *verb*

to swindle, to fool, to deceive *UK, 1637*
- — Charles Shafer, *Folk Speech in Texas Prisons*, p. 204, 1990

flamage *noun*

incendiary rhetoric used in a computer posting or Internet discussion group *US*
- — Eric S. Raymond, *The New Hacker's Dictionary*, p. 158, 1991

flame *noun*

1 a cigarette lighter *US*
- — Judi Sanders, *Mashing and Munching in Ames*, p. 7, 1994

2 an insulting or aggressive e-mail or Internet discussion group posting *US*
The collective noun is **FLAMAGE**.
- — Guy L. Steele et al., *The Hacker's Dictionary*, p. 65, 1983

flame *verb*

to post insulting personal attacks on others posting messages on an Internet bulletin board or in an Internet discussion group, or to send an insulting personal attack by e-mail *US*
From an earlier sense of simply 'insulting', in the absence of any computer technology.
- — *Coevolution Quarterly*, p. 31, Spring 1981: 'Computer slang'
- — Guy L. Steele et al., *The Hacker's Dictionary*, p. 65, 1983
- A newbie with the nerve to post in alt.sex.bondage, without taking the time to lurk (read, not post) for several weeks, can expect to be flamed to blackened perfection. — Nancy Tamosaitis, *net.sex*, p. 75, 1995
- — Connie Eble (Editor), *UNC-CH Campus Slang*, p. 4, April 1995

flamebait *noun*

a message posted in an Internet discussion group for the express purpose of soliciting insulting messages *US*
- One person will post flamebait. Idiots take the bait. — Nancy Tamosaitis, *net.sex*, p. 113, 1995

flame bath *noun*

the dropping of 55 gallon drums of combustible liquids from a utility helicopter, followed by flares that ignite the fuel *US*

- Company A, 25th Aviation Battalion (Little Bear) – CS and Flame Bath drops, resupply and MEDEVAC. — Department of the Army, *Combat After Action Interview Report, 18th Military History Detachment, 25th Infantry Division*, 31st January 1970

flame cooking *noun*

the process of smoking freebase cocaine by placing the pipe over a flame

- —Nick Constable, *This is Cocaine*, p. 182, 2002

flamefest *noun*

a protracted exchange of insulting and inflammatory messages on an Internet discussion group *US*

- —Christian Crumlish, *The Internet Dictionary*, p. 71, 1995

flame-out *noun*

1 in hot rodding and motor racing, a complete failure of the ignition system while the car is operating *US*

- When a flame-out occurs, the engine stops dead, even though the vehicle may be travelling at a very high speed. —John Lawlor, *How to Talk Car*, p. 46, 1965

2 an empty petrol tank *US*

- — *San Francisco Examiner*, p. III-2, 22nd March 1960

flamer *noun*

1 a blatant and conspicuous homosexual *US*

- The three young boys sitting together on one side of the booth were flamers, with big Windsor knots in their gaudy ties and shirt collars four sizes too big[.] —Horace McCoy, *Kiss Tomorrow Good-bye*, p. 278, 1948
- —Collin Baker et al., *College Undergraduate Slang Study Conducted at Brown University*, p. 118, 1968
- I thought I smelled smoke – here comes that huge flamer Dennis. —Jeff Fessler, *When Drag Is Not a Car Race*, p. 8, 1997

2 an alcoholic drink which is set on fire in the glass (after the flames have been extinguished, the fumes are inhaled before the drink is swallowed); an alcoholic drink which is set alight in the drinker's mouth in the hope that swallowing puts the flame out *UK*

- Ben, 24, says: "Flamers make your head go a bit doolally – it feels like it won't fit through doors!" — *Sky Magazine*, p. 89, May 2001

3 an Internet user who posts vitriolic, insulting messages in Internet discussion groups *US*

- —Guy L. Steele et al., *The Hacker's Dictionary*, p. 65, 1983
- A flamer is an incendiary on-liner who delights in inciting trouble by chiming in whenever possible with derisive commentary. —Nancy Tamosaitis, *net.sex*, p. 5, 1995

4 a pistol *US*

- —Anna Scotti and Paul Young, *Buzzwords*, p. 133, 1997

flamethrower *noun*

1 in hot rodding and drag racing, an ignition system that has been greatly enhanced *US*

- — *Good Housekeeping*, p. 143, September 1958: 'Hot-rod terms for teen-age girls'

2 a diesel truck with flames showing on the smokestack from an incorrect fuel-to-air ratio *US*

- —Montie Tak, *Truck Talk*, p. 61, 1971

3 a cigarette dressed with cocaine and heroin *UK, 1998*

- —Robert Ashton, *This Is Heroin*, p. 209, 2002

flame war *noun*

a virulent exchange of insulting messages in an Internet discussion group *US*

- Given the raunchiness of the subject matter, the posts are generally rather civil, and flame wars are few and far between. —Nancy Tamosaitis, *net.sex*, p. 115, 1995

flaming *adjective*

1 (used of a homosexual) patently, obviously *US, 1941*

- Most used in the term flaming queen, a homosexual who attempts thus to attract attention and drum up trade. —G. Legman, *The Language of Homsexuality*, p. 1165–1166, 1941
- Why would anybody want to go to bed with a flaming little sissy like you? —Mart Crowley, *The Boys in the Band*, p. 159, 1968
- These were the flaming swishes of his prison days; "Bernice" and "Joan." —Odie Hawkins, *Midnight*, p. 159, 1995
- If she were a lesbian, she'd be a FLAMING lesbian. She'd be out and quite vocal about it. —Howard Stern, *Miss America*, p. 178, 1995
- For all I know, all five members could be flaming homos who are good at playing breeders. — *The Village Voice*, 25th July 2000

2 used as an intensifier *UK, 1895*

- I forgot to shut that flamin' door. —Arthur Upfield, *Bony and the Mouse*, p. 49, 1959
- This place is like a flamin' mortuary. —Graeme Kent, *The Queen's Corporal [Six Granada Plays]*, p. 88, 1959
- I'm no flaming quitter. —Wal Watkins, *Race the Lazy River*, p. 54, 1963
- You an' yer flamin' dope! Four bloody boxes I ate, an' all for nothin'. —Walter Gill, *Petermann Journey*, p. 14, 1968
- Flaming asshole —Collin Baker et al., *College Undergraduate Slang Study Conducted at Brown University*, p. 118, 1968
- —Eugene Landy, *The Underground Dictionary*, p. 79, 1971
- "What a prick," Bob says. "What a flaming prick." —Ted Lewis, *Jack Carter's Law*, p. 49, 1974
- I'm just his flamin' dog.' Except Mr Ridge didn't say 'flaming' he was supposed to have said that other word 'fucking' which neither Bern nor Henry dared say out loud. —Barney Roberts, *Where's Morning Gone?*, p. 102, 1987

flaming asshole *noun*

a truly despicable person *US, 1968*

- —John D. Bell et al., *Loosely Speaking*, p. 2, 1969
- "Mr. Gitche is a flaming asshole." "Hardly a professional evaluation, Robbins." "Oh no? I thought you Freudians were really big on assholes." —Tom Robbins, *Even Cowgirls Get the Blues*, p. 240, 1976
- I was a flaming asshole. —Howard Stern, *Private Parts*, p. 100, 1994
- What a flaming asshole you are. I don't even know why we're talking. —Carl Hiaasen, *Basket Case*, p. 314, 2002

flaming coffin *nickname*

a DH-4 bomber aircraft *US, 1919*

- We were given de Havilland DH-4s to fly, known as "flaming coffins," and Curtiss JN-4 "Jennys." —James Doolittle, *I Could Never Be So Lucky Again*, p. 57, 1991
- Airmen had become "pawns," forced to fly antiquated biplanes like the De Havilland DH-4, which they nicknamed "the flaming coffin" because they claimed it easily cuaght fire when it crashed. —Douglas C. Waller, *A Question of Loyalty*, p. 20, 2004

flaming end *noun*

a remarkable and pleasing thing or person *UK*

- —Tom Hibbert, *Rockspeak!*, p. 61, 1983

flaming fury *noun*

a toilet built over a deep pit in the ground, the contents of which are periodically set alight *AUSTRALIA, 1960*

flaming hell!

used for registering surprise, anger, amazement, etc *UK*

A euphemism for **FUCKING HELL!** rather than a literal elaboration of 'hell'.

flaming Nora!

used as a euphemistic replacement for 'flaming hell!' *UK*

Coined for the racial tension situation comedy *Love Thy Neighbour*, 1972–76. The *Coronation Street* character Jack Duckworth, since 1979, also uses the television-friendly term, hence its wider currency.

- "Flaming Nora!" Jack Smethurst's racist white proletarian socialist would exclaim when confounded yet again by Rudolph T Walker's aspirant black Tory. —Stuart Jeffries, *Mrs Slocombe's Pussy*, p. 104, 2000

flaming onion *nickname*

the Ordnance Corps of the US Army *US, 1944*

From the flaming grenade insignia.

- —Linda Reinberg, *In the Field*, p. 83, 1991

flaming piss pot *nickname*

the Ordnance Corps of the US Army *US, 1980*

From the flaming grenade insignia.

- —Linda Reinberg, *In the Field*, p. 83, 1991

flaming well *adverb*

damned well *AUSTRALIA*

- She's broken down – and if that wasn't enough we're flamin' well bogged[.] —D'Arcy Niland, *The Shiralee*, p. 73, 1955
- You can just go flamin well without for that. —Ray Lawler, *Summer of the Seventeenth Doll*, p. 34, 1957
- —Ray Slattery, *Mobbs' Mob*, p. 18, 1966
- How am I flamin' well going to get back to Earls Court I haven't got a blessed razoo! —Barry Humphries, *The Wonderful World of Barry McKenzie*, p. 13, 1968

Flanagan & Allen; flanagan *noun*
a *gallon* (of motor fuel) *UK*
Rhyming slang, formed from the names of music hall comedians Bud Flanagan, 1896–1968, and Chesney Allen, 1894–1982, who worked together as a double act and as part of the Crazy Gang.
- —Ray Puxley, *Cockney Rabbit*, 1992

flange *noun*
1 the vagina *AUSTRALIA*
- [Q] What do you do to keep fit? [A] Shake tits and suck flange. —*Lesbians on the Loose*, p. 15, 1996
- 'Female Flange'—Sacha Baron-Cohen, *Da Gospel According to Ali G*, 2001
- —Paul Baker, *Polari*, p. 175, 2002

2 the outer lips of the vagina *AUSTRALIA*
- —Thommo, *The Dictionary of Australian Swearing and Sex Sayings*, p. 47, 1985

flange *verb*
to walk along *UK*
- —Paul Baker, *Polari*, p. 175, 2002

flange-head *noun*
a Chinese person *US*
- —*American Speech*, p. 30, February 1949: 'A.V.G. lingo'

flanger *noun*
in target shooting, a shot that strikes outside a close group of shots on the target *US*
- —*American Speech*, p. 193, October 1957: 'Some colloquialisms of the handgunner'

flanker *noun*
a trick, a swindle, a doublecross *UK, 1923*
Originally military; usually as 'do/play/pull/work a flanker'.
- Pull a flanker an' you know what you'll get.—Nick Barlay, *Curvy Lovebox*, p. 140, 1997

flannel *noun*
empty and pretentious talk *UK, 1927*
- Kept on giving me the old flannel there about all the artists what they knew[.]—John Peter Jones, *Feather Pluckers*, p. 40, 1964
- I find myself thinking "Sounds like a lot of flannel," before pushing the unkind thought away.—Duncan MacLaughlin, *The Filth*, p. 78, 2002

flannel *verb*
to flatter; to deceive *UK, 1941*
- "You're asking me to shut the shop, Regan. If I talk I'm finished." "Don't flannel me! You're paying protection and can name the extortionist!"—*The Sweeney*, p. 41, 1976

flannelmouth *noun*
a loudmouth; an insincere, silver-tongued talker *US, 1881*
- I don't ever want to hear some Dallas flannelmouth compare the Cowboys of today – or any other day – to the "perfect" Dolphins of that era.—Bert Sugar, *I Hate the Dallas Cowboys*, p. 157, 1997

flannel-mouthed *adjective*
thick-tongued, especially as the result of drinking to excess *US*
- —Sherman Louis Sergel, *The Language of Show Biz*, p. 87, 1973

flannel panel *noun*
in a magazine, a list of who did what in that edition *UK*
- On its credit list (the journalists had told him it was called a "flannel panel") he saw both their names, under features editor and advertising manager.—Andrew Holmes, *Sleb*, p. 205, 2002

flannie *noun*
a flannelette shirt *AUSTRALIA*
- From upper-class art directors to flannie-clad band members..the Wadaiko Ichiro Drummers certainly spread their appeal about.—*Beat*, p. 31, 3rd August 1996

flanno *noun*
a flannelette shirt *AUSTRALIA, 1996*
- A doomie is usually someone who resides in public-housing, perpetually unemployed, smoke in mouth, bad haircut, wears flannos and black jeans[.]—*Wordmap (www.abc.net.au/wordmap)*, 2003

flanno *adjective*
made from flannelette *AUSTRALIA*
- Cronulla was in a time warp of flanno shirts, desert boots and panel vans.—Kathy Lette, *Girls' Night Out*, p. 187, 1987

flap *noun*
1 a disturbance or crisis *UK, 1916*
- "I say, old boy, what's all the flap about?" he exclaimed, legs apart and putting a match to his pipe.—J.E. Johnson, *Wing Leader*, p. 28, 1956
- I suggested informally, when the Korean flap started in 1950, that we go north immediately with incendiaries and delete four or five of the largest towns[.]—Curtis E. LeMay with MacKinlay Kantor, *Mission with LeMay*, p. 382, 1965
- Over the course of a year, Nesbit had seen both Blevins and Gomez in action during a number of crises, or "flaps."—Richard Herman Jr, *The Warbirds*, p. 24, 1989

2 the vaginal lips; the *labia majora* or *minora* *UK*
Although there is some evidence of 'flap' meaning 'the vagina' in C17, it is long obsolete; this sense is a shortening of the synonymous **PISS FLAPS**.
- Flap dancin' I call it [lap dancing] 'cos if you're lucky they give you the full two sets of fanny lips even though they in't s'posed to[.]—Ben Elton, *High Society*, p. 119, 2002

3 the mouth *AUSTRALIA*
- Oh button your flap!—J.E. MacDonnell, *Don't Gimme the Ships*, p. 150, 1960

4 the ear *UK*
As a plural it is often the nickname for men with large ears.
- —David Powis, *The Signs of Crime*, 1977

5 strands of hair that a semi-bald man may cultivate and style to lay over his naked pate *UK*
- —Ray Puxley, *Cockney Rabbit*, p. 201, 1992

6 a cheque *AUSTRALIA, 1955*
Underworld and prison use.
- *[F]lap*, blank cheque leaf[.]—*Parramatta Jail Glossary*, p. 1, 1972
- —Ryan Aven-Bray, *Ridgey Didge Oz Jack Lang*, p. 28, 1983

flap *verb*
1 to be agitated; to panic, to dither *UK, 1912*
- Sometimes I'd come back at four in the morning and my mum would be flapping.—Andy McNab, *Immediate Action*, p. 8, 1995

2 while surfing, to make awkward flapping arm motions trying to gain your balance *US*
- —Trevor Cralle, *The Surfin'ary*, p. 38, 1991

▸ **flap skin**
to have sex *US*
- [N]ow that I wanna flap some skins Brandi ain't down for it even if I wear a jim hat.—*Boyz N The Hood*, 1990

flapdoodle *noun*
nonsense *UK, 1833*
- Why waste space with repeated choruses [...] or any of that flapdoodle?—Lester Bangs, *Psychotic Reactions and Carburetor Dung*, p. 115, 1973
- I asked him what he was doing on my wharf, and he gave me a crate of flapdoodle about lookin' for a dog.—John Gould, *Maine Lingo*, p. 96, 1975
- He'd suffered through these flapdoodle attempts at intimidation by official omniscience before.—Seth Morgan, *Homeboy*, p. 49, 1990

flapjacked *adjective*
drunk *US*
- —Connie Eble (Editor), *UNC-CH Campus Slang*, p. 4, October 2002

flapjaw *noun*
a person who talks incessantly *US, 1950*
- "Well, flapjaw, what now?" Boo asked herself, sitting again.—Max Shulman, *Anyone Got a Match?*, p. 252, 1964

flapper *noun*
1 the penis in a flaccid state *US*
- —*Maledicta*, p. 195, Winter 1980: 'A new erotic vocabulary'

2 the ear *US, 1933*
- To his thinkin, what they don't know they can't buzz in the narcops' wide flappers.—Bernard Wolfe, *The Magic of Their Singing*, p. 77, 1961

3 a radio antenna *US*
- —Wayne Floyd, *Jason's Authentic Dictionary of CB Slang*, p. 16, 1976

flapper steak *noun*
a pig's ear sandwich *US*
- —Marcus Hanna Boulware, *Jive and Slang of Students in Negro Colleges*, 1947

flapper track *nickname*
an unofficial greyhound race track often used so that dogs could get a 'kill' to sharpen their appetites before an official race *IRELAND*
- You can forget about taking my dogs to a Flapper Track – for a kill or anything else.—Wesley Burrows, *The Riordans A Personal History*, p. 12, 1977

flapping track *noun*

a small, unlicensed dog racing track *UK*

- —David Powis, *The Signs of Crime*, 1977

flaps *noun*

the female breasts *US*

- Their secondary sex characteristics are simply too conspicuous to pass without insult, and we were unmerciful towards them: tits, boobs, knockers, jugs, bubbies, bazooms, lungs, flaps and hooters we called them, and there was no way to be polite about it. —*Screw*, p. 6, 3rd January 1972

flare *noun*

a type of scratch (a manipulation of a record to create a musical effect) that cuts out the middle of a sample *US*
Named for DJ Flare who invented the move in the late 1980s.

- Yeah, a chirp sounds like: chig-chig, chig-chig, whereas a flare sounds like: dibbet, dibbet, dibbet – it doubles it with only one click! —J. Hoggarth (quoting DJ Olsen), *How To Be a DJ*, p. 95, 2002

flared *adjective*

1 drunk *CANADA*

- When I take enough liquor to reach the point you're talking about, I know I'm flared. —P. Wylie, *They Both Were Naked*, 1965

2 angry *US*

- —Kenn "Naz" Young, *Naz's Dictionary of Teen Slang*, p. 42, 1993

flare kicker *noun*

the crew member who operates an airship's flare dispenser *US*

- When it was secure, one of the other guys climbed onto the door to take his place as the flare kicker while another stood by with a flare in his hand ready to put it in the chute when the pilot called for it. — SamC130, *First Flight Up North (1966)*, 1997

flares *noun*

flared trousers *US, 1964*

- [T]he only saving grace of flares was political: in the early seventies, you really could get into trouble at school or work for wearing them. —James Hawes, *Dead Long Enough*, p. 150, 2000
- [Manchester in the early 1990s] had a thriving music and club scene, many of its inhabitants could get away with wearing flares and tie-dye shirts[.] — *The Observer*, 7th July 2002

flash *noun*

1 a sudden onset of drug-induced effects *US, 1946*

- When a man fixes he is turned on almost instantaneously ... you can speak of a flash, a tinily murmured orgasm in the bloodstream, in the central nervous system. —Alexander Trocchi, *Cain's Book*, p. 33 – 34, 1960
- He's gonna get a flash, let me tell you. —Richard Farina, *Been Down So Long*, p. 115, 1966
- Cocaine and bombitas are both stimulants and combined with heroin, a depressant, they produce an electrifying "rush" or "flash" far more pleasurable to the addict than heroin alone. —James Mills, *The Panic in Needle Park*, p. 36, 1966
- His last flash had been all about time, it had taken him down the passageway to the very door of the rose garden, but as he was about to go in the flash had started to wear off. —Gurney Norman, *Divine Right's Trip (Last Whole Earth Catalog)*, p. 123, 1971
- Effects of cocaine and to a lesser extent methedrine. —Home Office, *Glossary of Terms and Slang Common in Penal Establishments*, July 1978
- No, Bob, really, this is good stuff, clears right up in the spoon, no residue, hair-raising flash. — *Drugstore Cowboy*, 1988

2 LSD *US*

- —US Department of Justice, *Street Terms*, October 1994
- Street names [...] dots, drops, flash, Gorbachovs[.] —James Kay and Julian Cohen, *The Parents' Complete Guide to Young People and Drugs*, p. 141, 1998

3 any central nervous system stimulant *UK*

- —Tom Hibbert, *Rockspeak!*, p. 61, 1983

4 illicitly distilled alcohol *UK*
Used by British expatriates in Saudi Arabia.

- —J.B Smith of Bath, 1981

5 a revelation; an epiphany; a satori *US, 1924*

- You can get flashes all kinds of ways. I got a flash once when my parachute didn't open. — *Whole Earth Catalog*, p. 116, 1971

6 in a striptease show, the stripper's entrance onto the stage *US*

- In succession as the Flash or entrance; the Parade or march across the stage, in full costume; the Tease or increasing removal of wearing apparel; and the limactic Strip or denuding down to the G-String[.] — *Saturday Review of Literature*, p. 28, 18th August 1945: 'Take em off!'

7 a large number of small-denomination banknotes with a large-denomination note showing, giving the impression of a great deal of money *UK*

- —Angela Devlin, *Prison Patter*, p. 52, 1996

8 inexpensive, showy jewellery *US, 1927*

- Everybody in both worlds kissed your ass black and blue if you had flash and front. —Iceberg Slim (Robert Beck), *Pimp*, p. 118, 1969

9 an inexpensive carnival prize that is so appealing that people will spend great sums trying to win it *US, 1927*

- Blue had dismantled the wheel and taken the flash dolls and stuffed animals off the back wall when the dapper hoodlums finished their counting. —Iceberg Slim (Robert Beck), *Trick Baby*, p. 98, 1969
- —Joe McKennon, *Circus Lingo*, p. 35, 1980
- —Gene Sorrows, *All About Carnivals*, p. 16, 1985: 'Terminology'

10 a suit of clothes *US*

- —Hyman E. Goldin et al., *Dictionary of American Underworld Lingo*, p. 71, 1950

11 the appearance of wealth or success *US*

- The money's just for flash. You spend as little as you have to and bring the rest back. —Joseph Wambaugh, *The Choirboys*, p. 252, 1975

12 a know-all *UK*
Used in borstals and detention centres.

- —Home Office, *Glossary of Terms and Slang Common in Penal Establishments*, July 1978

13 in horse racing, a last-minute change in odds *US*

- —David W. Maurer, *Argot of the Racetrack*, p. 28, 1951

▸ **bit of flash**

ostentation, a superficial show *UK*

- [H]e likes to put on a bit of flash, so he goes swimming up and down the King's Road in his Chevvy convertible[.] —Derek Raymond (Robin Cook), *The Crust on its Uppers*, p. 23, 1962

flash *verb*

1 to exhibit as naked a part or parts of the body that are usually clothed *UK, 1893*

- She would also "flash" – that is, at one or two appropriate moments she would remove her G string and present herself to the audience naked as a jaybird. — *Eros*, p. 30, Spring 1962
- [W]hen you go off to do something so very simple as exchanging money for goods, it isn't necessary to flash your snatch at everyone this side of the horizon. —Philip Roth, *Portnoy's Complaint*, p. 242, 1969
- In N.Y.C. topless is O.K. but total nudity is out but on some nights the girls do flash a raw pussy. — *Screw*, p. 9, 18th April 1969
- Strippers were subject to arrest if they showed their pubic hair or "flashed." —Marilyn Salutin, *The Sexual Scene*, p. 172, June 1971
- The monisher [woman]'s flashing her strides [knickers, panties]. —Patrick O'Shaughnessy, *Market Traders Slang*, 1979
- And every year, a coed would have to flash at least one cop by lifting her T-shirt to reveal her address written across her tits. —Joseph Wambaugh, *Fugitive Nights*, p. 133, 1992
- Occasionally, a stripper would "flash," that is, pull her G-string down for a tantalizing second or two. —Marilyn Suriani Futterman, *Dancing Naked in the Material World*, p. 125, 1992
- In fact, flashing can be much smore sleazy than nude dancing. —James Ridgeway, *Red Light*, p. 149, 1996

2 to show off *UK, 1754*

- Silky's off flashing with the other guys and trying to cop girls. —Susan Hall, *Gentleman of Leisure*, p. 174, 1972
- They wouldn't miss the opportunity to flash at something like this fight. —Vernon E. Smith, *The Jones Men*, p. 151, 1974
- "Oh, you see him in the neighborhood every now 'n then, flashin', ... he don't want nobody to know where he's stayin'," Taco added. —Donald Goines, *The Busting Out of an Ordinary Man*, p. 74, 1985

3 to show *UK, 1754*

- [G]et to a bar or someplace, flash a few of your folds [money] [...] and you'll get all the ladies you can deal with -—Diran Adebayo, *My Once Upon A Time*, p. 9, 2000

4 to display official credentials *UK*

- "Police," Regan replied, flashing his warrant card.— *The Sweeney*, p. 30, 1976

5 while dealing blackjack in a casino, to briefly and unintentionally expose the down card *US*

- Bill says I'm flashing my hole card, but I can't see how I could be. —Lee Solkey, *Dummy Up and Deal*, p. 113, 1980

6 to display prizes in a carnival game in order to attract customers *US*

- — *American Speech*, p. 280, December 1966: 'More Carnie Talk from the West Coast'

7 to vomit *US*

- —Collin Baker et al., *College Undergraduate Slang Study Conducted at Brown University*, p. 118, 1968

8 to vomit after injecting heroin or while withdrawing from heroin use *US*

- I gave her a hypodermic. She "flashed" – to use the slang expression; barely made it to the sink before she started vomiting.—Jim Thompson, *The Kill-Off*, p. 41–42, 1957
- —David Maurer and Victor Vogel, *Narcotics and Narcotic Addiction*, p. 406, 1973

9 to inhale glue or industrial solvents for the psychoactive effect *US*

- —William D. Alsever, *Glossary for the Establishment and Other Uptight People*, p. 11, December 1970

10 to remember an event from the past in a sudden and powerful manner *US*

An abbreviation of 'flashback'.

- He wondereed if the canyons at night would make him flash to Nam.—Joseph Wambaugh, *Lines and Shadows*, p. 41, 1984

11 to break light bulbs in their sockets, either as an act of vandalism or prepatory to a crime *US*

- —Dale Kramer and Madeline Karr, *Teen-Age Gangs*, p. 175, 1953

12 to commit a social gaffe *US*

- —Carol Ann Preusse, *Jargon Used by University of Texas Co-Eds*, 1963

▸ **flash a brown**

to drop your trousers and expose your buttocks *NEW ZEALAND*

- —David McGill, *David McGill's Complete Kiwi Slang Dictionary*, p. 50, 1998

▸ **flash a joint**

to display prizes in a carnival game *US*

- To "flash the joint" means to put up the prizes for display at any of the give-away (or gambling) games[.]—E.E. Steck, *A Brief Examination of an Esoteric Folk*, p. 8, 1968

▸ **flash the ash**

used as a demand that someone offer a cigarette *UK, 1984*

A variation of **CRASH THE ASH**; probably arose in the 1950s but now rare.

▸ **flash the cash**

to spend some money; to offer payment *UK*

- [F]lash the cash, give him enough for a good bit of the old wacky baccy and who knows.—J.J. Connolly, *Know Your Enemy [britpulp]*, p. 149, 1999

▸ **flash the gallery; flash the range**

in prison, to use a small mirror to watch out for approaching guards while conducting some prohibited activity in your cell *US*

- —*Maledicta*, p. 267, Summer/Winter 1981: 'By its slang, ye shall know it: the pessimism of prison life'

▸ **flash the hash**

to vomit *US*

- —*American Speech*, p. 194, October 1965: 'Notes on campus vocabulary, 1964'
- —Collin Baker et al., *College Undergraduate Slang Study Conducted at Brown University*, p. 118, 1968
- —Michael Dalton Johnson, *Talking Trash with Redd Foxx*, p. 47, 1994

▸ **flash your ass**

to commit a social gaffe *US*

- —Fred Hester, *Slang on the 40 Acres*, p. 10, 1968

flash *adjective*

1 ostentatious, showy *UK, 1785*

- They think we are cocky, flash and cowardly.— Martin King and Martin Knight, *The Naughty Nineties*, p. 151, 1999
- I went through a very flash phase when the first cheques came in. I bought a hot tub and a brand new BMW.—Paul Godfrey, *The Guardian*, 16th August 2003

2 impudent, cheeky *UK*

- Have six moon [a six-month prison sentence] for being flash.—Sean McConville, *The State of the Language*, 1980

flashback *noun*

a relapse into a hallucinatory drug experience long after the effect of the drug has worn off *US*

- —Edward R. Bloomquist, *Marijuana*, p. 339, 1971
- —Home Office, *Glossary of Terms and Slang Common in Penal Establishments*, July 1978
- The myth of the flashback was widely promoted by the media and government as one of the severe dangers of LSD.—Cam Cloud, *The Little Book of Acid*, p. 18, 1999

flash-bang *noun*

an explosive device designed to deafen and blind without otherwise injuring *US*

- A couple more of his peoiple are being treated for severe concussion. It was determined they got in the way of a flash-bang.—Elmore Leonard, *Be Cool*, p. 245, 1999

flash cash *noun*

a large, ostentatious bankroll *US*

- At least until I got the bread to lay down on a far-out ride (maybe a vintage Rolls, fur-trimmed) B.R. (flash cash) and threads to dazzle and lure whores[.]—Iceberg Slim (Robert Beck), *Airtight Willie and Me*, p. 4, 1979

flash cloth *noun*

colourful draping used in a carnival concession *US*

- —Gene Sorrows, *All About Carnivals*, p. 17, 1985: 'Terminology'

flash dough *noun*

counterfeit money *US*

- —Vincent J. Monteleone, *Criminal Slang*, p. 85, 1949

flasher *noun*

1 a person with a psychopathological need to expose his or her genitals *US, 1962*

- You know those guys in the park, the flashers?—Lenny Bruce, *The Essential Lenny Bruce*, p. 157, 1967
- The patients include an introverted neurotic with a penchant for the one-liner, a psychosomatically blind muscle man (who believes masturbation has done it to him), a jealous lesbian, a couple of transvestites, a flasher, and others.—Kent Smith et al., *Adult Movies*, p. 163, 1982
- The guy could be a crackhead, a psychopath, a flasher, a junkie[.] —*Sleepless in Seattle*, 1993
- I had my first encounter with a Japanese flasher.—Josie Dew, *The Sun In My Eyes*, p. 293, 2001
- Someone who saw him with his dick out thought he was a flasher. —Duncan MacLaughlin, *The Filth*, p. 64, 2002

2 a casino dealer who inadvertently reveals his down card *US*

- —Michael Dalton, *Blackjack*, p. 48, 1991

flash flood *noun*

in poker, a sudden sequence of good cards *US*

- —John Vorhaus, *The Big Book of Poker Slang*, p. 17, 1996

flash Harry *noun*

an ostentatiously or expensively accoutred man *UK*

The character of Flash Harry created by George Cole (b.1925) in the *St Trinians* films (mid-1950s–mid-60s) is, perhaps, the most widely known popular usage – adding a shading of criminality to the meaning; Sir Malcolm Sargent (1895–1967), a conductor noted for his elegance and showmanship, is remembered by the nickname Flash Harry.

- [T]hey'd bin to this and that party with all sorts of flash Harrys.—John Peter Jones, *Feather Pluckers*, p. 40, 1964

flash house *noun*

a room, apartment or house where amphetamine addicts gather to inject the drug *US*

- —William D. Alsever, *Glossary for the Establishment and Other Uptight People*, p. 11, December 1970

flash mob *noun*

a large crowd that materialises in a public place to perform a scripted action for several minutes before dissolving *US*

- They probably don't realize it, but they've just witnessed San Francisco's second "flash mob," a phenomenon that was born in New York and is spreading across the United States and Europe with the speed of an Internet virus.— *San Francisco Chronicle*, p. D1, 11th August 2003
- Once there, participants in flash mobs, the compulsively deconstructed geek-chic game of the summer, briefly perform some collective activity, then flee.— *New York Times*, p. WK5, 17th August 2003
- In recent weeks, New Yorkers have been using forwarded e-mails to coordinate "flash mobs," or not-so-random crowds that appear and dissipate within a matter of minutes.— *Chicago Tribune*, 11th July 2003
- Organizing a "flash mob" basically involves e-mailing a bunch of people with instructions to show up at a certain place for a few moments, then disappear.— *Ventura County (California) Star*, 1st July 2003

flash-mob *verb*

to take part in a flash mob *UK*

- — *The Times*, p. 5, 12th June 2004

flash mobber *noun*

a participant in a flash mob *US*

- Flash mobbers make no apollogies for their lack of political mission, but stake a claim to significance nonetheless.— *New York Times*, p. WK5, 17th August 2003

flash money *noun*
money, especially in a bankroll, intended for impressing, not spending *US*
- He had retrieved it and arrested Big Dog, taking him to the detectives who, since Big Dog was a pimp, and had a five-page rap sheet, decided to book him for robbery, impound his car, and book his roll of flash money as evidence. —Joseph Wambaugh, *The New Centurions*, p. 223, 1970

flash on *verb*
to think about with great intensity and focus *US*
- —Lewis Yablonsky, *The Hippie Trip*, p. 367, 1968: 'Glossary'

flash paper *noun*
paper that dissolves completely and quickly when exposed to water *US*
- You mean like flash paper? I've heard of that. —Joseph Wambaugh, *The Blue Knight*, p. 195, 1973
- You won't find the bottom line for the Super Bowl only on the scoreboard. Some of it will be scrawled hastily on flash paper by bookies across the country. —*Chicago Tribune*, p. C11, 24th January 1987
- They had been printed on flash paper, which bookies used to keep their betting records. Victoria had scooped them up on her way to the bathroom and dropped them in the toilet. —Stephen Cannell, *Big Con*, p. 384, 1997
- The most important rule; Listen to Johnson or you're gone quicker than flash paper. —*Fresno (California) Bee*, p. D1, 13th July 2003

flash roll *noun*
a large number of small-denomination banknotes with a large-denomination note showing, giving the impression of a great deal of money *US*
- Neil unfolded and fanned out the rest of the bundle. It was mostly fives and tens, maybe adding up to another hundred, two hundreds bucks at most. "You take the five, all I've got left is a flash roll." —Robert Campbell, *Alice in La-La Land*, p. 21, 1987

flash trash *noun*
a gaudy, cheap woman *US*
- She wears a black motorcyle jacket, a very short skirt, stiletto heels. Her hair is up. Her make-up is severe. In the darkness, in the shadows, she looks about 19. A hot 19. A hot flash-trash 19. —*Basic Instinct*, 1992

flash up *verb*
in circus and carnival usage, to add embellishments to a piece of clothing *US*
- —Don Wilmeth, *The Language of American Popular Entertainment*, p. 95, 1981

flat *noun*
1 a flat area for spectators in the centre of a racecourse *AUSTRALIA, 1846*
- Eventually, he got a licence to make a book on the flat at Flemington racecourse. —Frank Hardy, *The Yarns of Billy Borker*, p. 102, 1965

2 in an illegal number gambling lottery, a bet that two digits will appear in the winning number *US*
- —*American Speech*, p. 191, October 1949

3 a police officer *UK*
Probably a shortening of **FLATFOOT**.
- The meths men themselves are a distinct race from the well-heeled West End alcoholics and drug takers; a flat, to them, is just another word for policeman. —Geoffrey Fletcher, *Down Among the Meths Men*, p. 9, 1966

4 good quality tobacco, as opposed to prison issue tobacco *AUSTRALIA, 1902*

5 a case of beer containing 24 bottles *CANADA*
- —Emily *An American's Guide to Canada*, p. 3, 10th November 2001

6 a conventional, law-abiding, boring person *UK, 1753*
- —Lou Shelly, *Hepcats Jive Dictionary*, p. 11, 1945

7 a smooth-sided subway (underground) carriage that lends itself to graffiti art *US*
- —Jim Crotty, *How to Talk American*, p. 141, 1997

8 a credit card *UK*
- —David Powis, *The Signs of Crime*, 1977

Flat *noun*
the season of flat horse racing *UK, 1937*
- [T]he exuberance, the informality, of National Hunt racing made it more attractive to the Queen Mother than the starched collar of the Flat. —*The Observer*, 31st March 2002

flat *adjective*
1 without money, broke *AFGHANISTAN, 1832*
A shortening of 'flat broke'.
- "Well, if I'd had the dough to play on Red Pepper this afternoon, I'd be swimming in good nature," Dopey said. "Me too. I was flat." —James T. Farrell, *Saturday Night*, p. 28, 1947
- Book-me, who was doubling with me, said he was flat and I had to pay him off myself. —Chester Himes, *Cast the First Stone*, p. 66, 1952
- But man, I ain't been working. I'm flat. —Ross Russell, *The Sound*, p. 135, 1961
- "Now I ain't flat," said the beat-up cat / 'We're traveling boosters, you know." —Dennis Wepman et al., *The Life*, p. 55, 1976
- You would have done better to catch some of the other guys in the parking lot. I'm almost flat, buddy. —James Ellroy, *Brown's Requiem*, p. 211, 1981

2 (of a prison sentence) full, unqualified *US*
- So the minute the pop comes, one of the guys that was out in front during all this, he offered a ten-flat [ten-year sentence]. —Bruce Jackson, *In the Life*, p. 170, 1972
- Those were the good ole days of the indeterminate sentence. Mayhem's a flat four now. —Seth Morgan, *Homeboy*, p. 150, 1990

3 (used of a bet) unvarying in amount *US*
- —Jerry L. Patterson, *Blackjack*, p. 20, 1978

▸ **that's flat; and that's flat**
used for emphasis or for concluding a preceding remark *UK*
An early usage (late C16) can be found in act 1, scene 3 of Shakespeare's *Henry IV Part 1*.

flat *adverb*
completely *US*
- Deek had scored them a room and gotten them flat puking drunk that night[.] —Jess Mowry, *Way Past Cool*, p. 40, 1992

flat-ass *adverb*
absolutely *US, 1964*
- Say something about my family and I will flatass stretch you out! —Ken Weaver, *Texas Crude*, p. 112, 1984

flat-ass calm *noun*
in lobstering, the condition of the sea when there are no waves and no wind *US*
- —Kendall Merriam, *The Illustrated Dictionary of Lobstering*, p. 38, 1978

flat-back *verb*
to engage in prostitution *US, 1967*
From the image of a prostitute having sex lying on her back.
- [I]t's some deadend hype turin all her flatbackin money inta shit. —Robert Gover, *JC Saves*, p. 16, 1968
- She can 'flat-back' and so long as she keeps breathing you can get some scratch. —Iceberg Slim (Robert Beck), *Pimp*, p. 105, 1969
- But to me, at this stage of my life, I didn't want anything but a flat-backing whore. —Donald Goines, *Whoreson*, p. 134, 1972
- [W]hen push comes to shove, it is easier to rob than to flatback. —Gail Sheehy, *Hustling*, p. 95, 1973
- She stripped down to her panties and then remembered that Jimmy was not flatbacking her and stood confused for a second[.] —William T. Vollman, *Whores for Gloria*, p. 132, 1991

flat-back; flat-bottom *adjective*
possessing modest buttocks *TRINIDAD AND TOBAGO, 1971*
- —Lise Winer, *Dictionary of the English/Creole of Trinidad & Tobago*, 2003

flatbacker *noun*
a prostitute of an undiscerning nature *US, 1969*
- I wasn't scoring a big buck from the streets with one flat-backer. —Iceberg Slim (Robert Beck), *Airtight Willie and Me*, p. 47, 1979

flat blue; flat; blue flat *noun*
a tablet of LSD *US*
- —Eugene Landy, *The Underground Dictionary*, p. 79, 1971
- —Richard A. Spears, *The Slang and Jargon of Drugs and Drink*, p. 197, 1986
- —Mike Haskins, *Drugs*, p. 285, 2003

flatcatcher *noun*
in horse racing, a horse that looks the part but evades actual achievement *UK*
- —Rita Cannon, *Let's Go Racing*, p. 71, 1948

flat-chat *adverb*
as fast as one can go *AUSTRALIA, 1981*
- Me brain is going flat-chat and I can't keep still. —Tim Winton, *That eye, the sky*, p. 146, 1986

flat chunks *noun*
a combination of crack cocaine and benzocaine *UK, 1998*
- —Mike Haskins, *Drugs*, p. 293, 2003

flat dog *noun*
bologna *US*
- —Charles Shafer, *Folk Speech in Texas Prisons*, p. 204, 1990

flatfoot *verb*
1 a police officer, especially one assigned on foot patrol *US, 1912*
- That dumb flatfoot, Tracy, will beat us up.—Chester Gould, *Dick Tracy Meets the Night Crawler*, p. 160, 1945
- All day long we haunted the Western Union office, looking over our shoulders to see if that flatfoot was trailing us[.]—Mezz Mezzrow, *Really the Blues*, p. 131, 1946
- I'll bet you a sandwich against a marriage license he's got a flatfoot downstairs covering every exit in the place[.]—Mickey Spillane, *I, The Jury*, p. 15, 1947
- The flatfoots busted him down last night with a load – he's in the Tombs.—Hal Ellson, *The Golden Spike*, p. 232, 1952
- But the subway is moving. "So long flatfoot!" I yell[.]—William Burroughs, *Naked Lunch*, p. 2, 1957
- Everything about him from the armful of gold hash stripes to the box-toed custom-made shoes said "flatfoot."—Chester Himes, *The Real Cool Killers*, p. 39, 1959
- He could remember when he'd made more arrests than all the other flatfoots combined.—Clarence Cooper Jr, *The Scene*, p. 111, 1960
- How can anyone compare a good girl like Tilly with a mob of droobs and flat-feet?—George Blaikie, *Remember Smith's Weekly?*, p. 218, 1966
- —Angela Devlin, *Prison Patter*, p. 52, 1996
- [T]he Cadet School at Hendon actually did produce a flatfoot who represented his country at the race-walking event in the 1992 Olympics[.]—Duncan MacLaughlin, *The Filth*, p. 53, 2002

2 to walk *US*
- I say that you niggers better flat-foot it on back home.—Joseph Nazel, *Black Cop*, p. 98, 1974

flatfooted *adjective*
unprepared, unready, not 'on your toes' *US, 1908*
- In the battle for 'hearts and minds', the propaganda war, the West has been caught flat-footed by bin Laden's use of videotaped interviews[.]— *The Observer*, 14th October 2001

flat fuck *noun*
sex without loss of semen *US*
- — *Maledicta*, p. 132, Summer/Winter 1982: 'Dyke diction: the language of lesbians'

flat-hat *verb*
to fly very close to the ground at a high speed *US, 1939*
- "Roger that, Boss," said Slim, as he felt his juices flowing. "Did yo uhear that, Sundance? We've got our flat-hatting license!"—William M. La Barge and Robert Lawrence, *Sweetwater Gunslinger 201*, p. 79, 1983

flat joint; flat store *noun*
an illegal gambling operation where players are cheated as a matter of course *US, 1914*
- — *American Speech*, p. 308–309, December 1960: 'Carnival talk'
- Folks, we play short on the flat-joint.—Iceberg Slim (Robert Beck), *Trick Baby*, p. 111, 1969
- —Gene Sorrows, *All About Carnivals*, p. 17, 1985: 'Terminology'
- —Thomas L. Clark, *The Dictionary of Gambling and Gaming*, p. 82, 1987

flatkey *noun*
a fifty-five miles an hour speed limit *US*
A term borrowed from shortwave radio users (to depress the transmit switch) by citizens' band radio users, and then applied to the nearly universal road speed limit implemented in the US after the oil embargo of the early 1970s.
- —Porter Bibb, *CB Bible*, p. 93, 1976

flatline *verb*
to die *US, 1981*
An allusion to the flat line on a medical monitoring device that indicates death.
- They knew that Shelby was vibrating from having done a teener of go-fast, and that he'd chill pretty soon. Or else he'd flat-line, and they wouldn't mind that either.—Joseph Wambaugh, *Finnegan's Week*, p. 235, 1993
- Tories can read polls as well as anyone else, and we know that we continue to flatline.— *The Guardian*, 25th January 2002
- [G]ot Ketamine for the nutters (oh, that'll make you flatline).—Julian Johnson, *Urban Survival*, p. 170, 2003

flatliner *noun*
1 a dead person; a dead thing *US*
From **FLATLINE** (to die). *Flatliners* is a 1990 film by Joel Schumacher in which five medical students experiment with the line between life and death.
- — *Business Solutions*, February 1998: 'Bringing a flatliner back to life.'
- [W]hen Elliott declares his love for the creature, why, the flatliner bounces back from the dead[.]— *The Guardian*, 15th March 2002

2 a mobile phone user who allows the phone's batteries to run down *UK*
A Manchester youth usage, from the sense 'a dead person', possibly, here, specificially 'brain dead'.
- If you're a flatliner, your flaky.— *The Times Magazine*, 21st June 2003

3 in poker, an unskilled and uninspired player *US*
The moral equivalent of 'brain dead'.
- —John Vorhaus, *The Big Book of Poker Slang*, p. 17, 1996

4 4-methylthioamphetamine, the recreational drug best known as 4-MTA *UK*
- —Harry Shapiro, *Recreational Drugs*, p. 254, 2004

flat-out *adjective*
absolute, complete *US, 1959*
- It was an absolute flat-out fabrication.—Janet Evanovich, *Seven Up*, p. 63, 2001

flat-out *adverb*
as fast as possible *AUSTRALIA, 1941*
- Everyone's flat out just at the moment[.]—Eric Lambert, *The Veterans*, 64 1954
- If they've unloaded a full cargo then they'll have worked flat-out to finish by dark[.]—J.E. MacDonnell, *Sabotage!*, p. 31, 1964
- —Patsy Adam-Smith, *Folklore of the Australian Railwaymen*, p. 150, 1969
- [T]he car was going flat out, and the fleet of irate husbands was in hot pursuit.— *Alvin Purple*, p. 116, 1974
- Machines, bodies, and brains worked flat out, spurred on by an impatient deadline and an irate editor.—Kerry Cue, *Crooks, Chooks and Bloody Ratbags*, p. 95, 1983
- —Herb Wharton, *Cattle Camp*, p. 120, 1994

flat out like a lizard drinking *adjective*
going or working as fast as possible *AUSTRALIA, 1935*

flat passer *noun*
shaved dice used in cheating schemes *US*
- Then I started using flat passers; they're basically shaved dice so the four, five, nine, and ten turn up more frequently.—Stephen Cannell, *Big Con*, p. 215, 1997

flatroofer *noun*
in the Maritime Provinces, a fishing boat with a reduced sailing rig for winter *CANADA*
- In wintertime we sends 'em down and we sails as a flatroofer–nawthin' but the four lowers–winter rig we calls it.—Frederick Wallace, *Roving Fisherman*, p. 28, 1955

flats *noun*
1 the lowest tier of cells in a prison *US*
- —John R. Armore and Joseph D. Wolfe, *Dictionary of Desperation*, p. 29, 1976

2 dice, the surfaces of which have been altered for cheating *US*
- — *The Annals of the American Academy of Political and Social Sciences*, p. 124, May 1950

flat-spot *verb*
(used of a car for sale) to remain in one spot without being driven or even moved *US*
- —Lewis Poteet, *Car & Motorcyle Slang*, p. 127, 1992

flat-stick *adjective*
very busy; at top speed *NEW ZEALAND*
- 'We are flat stick on Friday night and I refuse to turn this business away,' he said.— *(Wellington) Evening Post*, 20th August 1972

flat-strap *adverb*
as fast as possible *AUSTRALIA*
- Within twenty-minutes I had a team geared up and heading for Tweed Heads, flat strap on a blue-light run.—William Dodson, *The Sharp End*, p. 258, 2001

flatten out *verb*
to serve a prison sentence completely *US*
- —John R. Armore and Joseph D. Wolfe, *Dictionary of Desperation*, p. 29, 1976
- Man I only got to flatten out six years in prison and I'll be out.—Inez Cardozo-Freeman, *The Joint*, p. 497, 1984

flattie *noun*
1 a flat tyre *AUSTRALIA*
- He give me an hand an' puts the flatty and the jack back in the boot for me[.]—John O'Grady, *Aussie Etiket*, p. 20, 1971
- —David McGill, *David McGill's Complete Kiwi Slang Dictionary*, p. 44, 1998

2 a flat-heeled shoe, as distinguished from the high-heeled variety *UK*
Also as variant 'flat'.
- —John Boswell, *Lost Girl*, 1959
- My own superior, on being confronted with the glad news that I'd worn a raincoat and flatties to the ball of the year congratulated me heartily and advised me to turn up, next time, in paint-stained jeans.—Sue Rhodes, *Now you'll think I'm awful*, p. 135, 1967

flat tire *noun*

1 a shoe that has been forced off a person's heel by someone walking behind them *US*

2 a sagging breast *US*
- —Anna Scotti and Paul Young, *Buzzwords*, p. 108, 1997

flattop *noun*

an aircraft carrier *US, 1942*
- With the U.S. flattops busy pursuing the decoy, two Japanese battleship groups would close on Leyte from the north and south[.]—James D. Hornfischer, *The Last Stand of the Tin Can Sailors*, p. 3, 2004

flatty *noun*

1 a member of an audience *UK, 1933*
Gently derogatory; extended by circus showmen from the (probably) now obsolete sense 'a rustic, an unitiated person', first recorded by John Camden Hotten in 1859.
- The flatties thought my antics were all part of the game and laughed well[.]—Butch Reynolds, *Broken Hearted Clown*, p. 17, 1953
- [F]latties [...] men (especially those who make up an audience).—Paul Baker, *Polari*, p. 175, 2002

2 a person who works in a flat joint (an illegal gambling operation where players are cheated as a matter of course) *US*
- Flatties are considered, even among carnival performers, as common thieves and unlike the performers who give the marks something for their money.—Don Wilmeth, *The Language of American Popular Entertainment*, p. 95, 1981
- —Gene Sorrows, *All About Carnivals*, p. 17, 1985: 'Terminology'

3 a uniformed police officer or a plain-clothes officer who is recognisable as a foot-patrol officer *US, 1866*
A variation of **FLATFOOT**.

4 a flat-bottomed boat *AUSTRALIA, 1934*
- Jamaica was breathing heavily with the effort of rowing the flattie against the tide.—Kylie Tennant, *Lost Haven*, p. 32, 1946

5 a flathead fish *AUSTRALIA, 1962*
- It took time and the winch broke down twice, but I finally got it in and it was the biggest flattie you've ever seen.—Bob Staines, *Wot a Whopper*, p. 10, 1982
- —Phillip Gwynne, *Deadly Unna?*, p. 47, 1998

flat wheel *noun*

a person with a limp *US*
- —Ramon Adams, *The Language of the Railroader*, p. 61, 1977

flatworker *noun*

a burglar who specialises in flats (apartments) *UK*
- —Angela Devlin, *Prison Patter*, p. 52, 1996

flava *noun*

style, especially when unique *US, 1982*
Also with more conventionally spelt variants, 'flavor' and 'flavour'.
- Blue [...] loved gangsta rap. Fluxy preferred to have a little more flavour in his ear.—Karline Smith, *Moss Side Massive*, p. 2, 1994
- [C]ome hear the brand new flava in / Ya ear...—Craig Mack, *Flava In Ya Ear*, 1994
- I got all kinda flavors; I got styles that I didn't even start doin' yet. —*A2Z (quoting KRS-One, 1992)*, p. 36, 1995

flavor *noun*

1 in computing, a type or variety *US*
- —Guy L. Steele et al., *The Hacker's Dictionary*, p. 65, 1983

2 cocaine *US*
- —Bill Valentine, *Gang Intelligence Manual*, p. 75, 1995: 'Black street gang terminology'

flavorful *adjective*

in computing, pleasing *US*
- —Eric S. Raymond, *The New Hacker's Dictionary*, p. 160, 1991

flavor of the month; flavour of the month *noun*

the latest, short-lived trend or fashion or relationship *US, 1946*
Derisory, even contemptuous; originally conceived as a marketing strategy for ice-cream.
- —*Slang Bag 93 (University of Toronto)*, p. 2, Winter 1993
- It's like your flavor of the month, and then it suddenly changes. —*Boston Globe*, 17th March 2002
- Ron Atkinson, former manager of the town's football club, was no longer flavour of the month.—*The Guardian*, 28th April 2004

flavor of the week; flavour of the week *noun*

the latest, short-lived trend or fashion or relationship *US*
- —Don R. McCreary (Editor), *Dawg Speak*, 2001
- Widespread Panic create explosive, energetic music that shuns the need to pander to rock's flavour of the week and, instead, goes straight to the ears of eager fans.—*Wandsworth (London) Guardian*, 14th February 2002

flawless *adjective*

1 flawed *US*
- —Connie Eble (Editor), *UNC-CH Campus Slang*, p. 3, Spring 1982
- Flawless apartment, Sydney. Have you named the cockroaches yet?', p.83. 1997.—Jeff Fessler, *When Drag Is Not a Car Race*, p. 83, 1997

2 handsome *US*
- —Bruce Rodgers, *The Queens' Vernacular*, p. 82, 1972

flea *noun*

1 someone who has refused to pay a debt *AUSTRALIA*
- —Ned Wallish, *The Truth Dictionary of Racing Slang*, p. 30, 1989

2 in American casinos, a gambler who places very small bets *US*
- —Steve Kuriscak, *Casino Talk*, p. 24, 1985

3 in the car sales business, a customer determined to spend a small amount of money but buy an excellent car *US*
- —*Cars*, p. 40, December 1953

4 in a hospital, an internist *US*
- —Sally Williams, *"Strong" Words*, p. 142, 1994

flea and louse *noun*

1 a house, especially one that is run down or unsalubrious *UK, 1859*
Rhyming slang.
- —Ray Puxley, *Cockney Rabbit*, 1992

2 a brothel, a whore house *UK*
Rhyming slang.
- I used to go to the flea and louse every weekend.—Bodmin Dark, *Dirty Cockney Rhyming Slang*, 2003

fleabag *noun*

1 a low-cost, run-down motel, room, boarding house or apartment *US, 1924*
- The five bucks they ask, plus three dollars for a room in a handy flea-bag, should be reported to the Better Business Bureau[.]—Jack Lait and Lee Mortimer, *Washington Confidential*, p. 32, 1951
- [H]e fled after he saw, he swore, a red ribbon tired across the open commode, fled to a Fifth Street fleabag.—Clancy Sigal, *Going Away*, p. 206, 1961
- "There's two more," Morty admitted mournfully, "but they're complete flea bags, Sid!"—Terry Southern, *Blue Movie*, p. 66, 1970
- They were working in the room next to his in that fucking fleabag hotel and that hole in the wall came from a slug[.]—Mickey Spillane, *Last Cop Out*, p. 96, 1975
- Two of them dirty niggers carried her out to the back door of the flea bag across the street.—Iceberg Slim (Robert Beck), *Long White Con*, p. 164, 1977
- Some damn tribe of withered old bitches doesn't want us to terminate that fleabag hotel. All because Glenn Miller and his band once took a shit there.—*Heathers*, 1988

2 a person dressed in old or dirty clothes; a smelly person *UK*
- —Chris Lewis, *The Dictionary of Playground Slang*, p. 91, 2003

3 a drug user *CANADA*
- —Marcel Danesi, *Cool: The Signs and Meanings of Adolescence*, p. 58, 1994

4 a dishonest, disreputable carnival *US*
- —Joe McKennon, *Circus Lingo*, p. 35, 1980

fleabag *verb*

to nag *UK*
Rhyming slang.
- —Ray Puxley, *Cockney Rabbit*, 1992

fleapit *noun*

a shabby cinema *UK, 1937*
- Our days were filled with reading esoterica novels in the control room, going to the 42nd Street flea-pit movies, running off pornography to ease our boredom, and playing poker.—Clancy Sigal, *Going Away*, p. 468, 1961
- Knocking back a free night at the flea-pit too.—Barry Humphries, *Bazza Pulls It Off!*, 1971
- There was a flea-pit cinema called the Rialto near the Blue Anchor market area of Bermondsey.—Brian McDonald, *Elephant Boys*, p. 235, 2000

flea powder *noun*
weak and/or diluted heroin *US, 1956*
- —*American Speech*, p. 87, May 1955: 'Narcotic argot along the Mexican border'
- —Peter Johnson, *Dictionary of Street Alcohol and Drug Terms*, p. 75, 1993
- —Angela Devlin, *Prison Patter*, p. 52, 1996
- —Robert Ashton, *This Is Heroin*, p. 209, 2002

fleas and itches *noun*
motion pictures *AUSTRALIA, 1967*
Rhyming slang.
- —Jim Ramsay, *Cop It Sweet!*, p. 36, 1977
- —Ryan Aven-Bray, *Ridgey Didge Oz Jack Lang*, p. 28, 1983

fleas and lice *noun*
ice *UK*
Rhyming slang.
- —Ray Puxley, *Cockney Rabbit*, 1992

flea track *noun*
a parting in the hair *NEW ZEALAND*
- —David McGill, *David McGill's Complete Kiwi Slang Dictionary*, p. 44, 1998

flea trap *noun*
an inexpensive, shoddy hotel or boarding house *US, 1942*
- The Spanish Trail Inn didn't offer luxury accomodations, but it was far better than some of the flea traps Angie had frequented in her time.—J.A. Jance, *Desert Heart*, p. 237, 1993

fleder deder *noun*
a handicap *JAMAICA*

Flemington confetti *noun*
nonsense *AUSTRALIA, 1941*
A probable play on **BULLSHIT**; after the Flemington stockyards.

flesh *noun*
an actor who appears on stage *US*
- —Don Wilmeth, *The Language of American Popular Entertainment*, p. 96, 1981

flesh *adjective*
in the music industry, appearing and performing live *US*
- There are scores of men and women infesting every radio station and theater where "flesh" performances still remain.—Jack Lait and Lee Mortimer, *New York Confidential*, p. 32, 1948

flesh agent *noun*
a talent agent *US*
- How do the old flesh agents tell an old stripper when she's ready to be put out to pasture? "You just stop booking her," says Anthony.—Josh Alan Friedman, *Tales of Times Square*, p. 42, 1986

flesh-coloured highlights *noun*
baldness *UK, 2001*
Jocular.

flesh market *noun*
an area where prostitution and other sex businesses thrive *US*
- In La-La Land the premier hole in the wall was Nifty Shiftie's, at the top end of Hollywood, just out of the flesh market.—Robert Campbell, *Alice in La-La Land*, p. 251, 1987

fleshmeet *noun*
a *meet*ing in the *flesh* of on-line correspondents *US, 1996*
- FLESHMEET. Not nearly as messy as it sounds, this is just one of the names given in online discussions to a meeting under the F2F protocol (face-to-face). And we're having one, in collaboration with NUJ Central London Branch[.]—*Freelance*, August/September 2000

flesh peddler *noun*
an entertainer's business manager or agent *US, 1935*
- Outside of San Francisco, most rock managers were just flesh peddlers; the last thing they cared about was the music.—Alice Echols, *Scars of Sweet Paradise*, p. 172, 1999

flesh pit *noun*
a bar or nightclub where people come in search of sexual partners *US*
- [A]nd then McGarr talking later, at the Luau, a Beverly Hills flesh pit, about how he could remember when Farmer was a radical and it scared him to see how far he'd drifted from the front lines.—Hunter S. Thompson, *Songs of the Doomed*, 1991

fleshpot *noun*
a brothel *US*
- Men on leave find they save a half-hour on their way to the fleshpots by getting off at Wilson Avenue.—Jack Lait and Lee Mortimer, *Chicago Confidential*, p. 67, 1950
- In Illinois, this means being shipped to fleshpots in Chicago, Peoria, Calumet city or Cairo.—Lee Mortimer, *Women Confidential*, p. 144, 1960
- Amanda's papa refused to take his pubescent daughter into the Parisian fleshpots, but he did point them out to her from the window of a taxi.—Tom Robbins, *Another Roadside Attraction*, p. 47, 1971
- Here, then, are some devious path ways to Manhattan's fleshpots.—Bernhardt J. Hurwood, *The Sensuous New York*, p. 86, 1973

flesh torpedo *noun*
the erect penis *UK*
- —Richard Herring, *Talking Cock*, p. 30, 2003

fleshy flute *noun*
the penis *US*
Especially in the phrase 'playing a tune on the fleshy flute' (oral sex).
- —Erica Orloff and JoAnn Baker, *Dirty Little Secrets*, p. 83, 2001

flex *noun*
cocaine *UK*
- —Mike Haskins, *Drugs*, p. 280, 2003

flex *verb*
1 to display power by a show of strength *US*
From 'to flex your muscles'.
- Saw the police and they rolled right past me / No flexin' / Didn't even look in a nigga's direction as I ran / The intersection[.]—Ice Cube, *It Was a Good Day*, 1993

2 to leave *US*
- —*Washingnton Post*, 14th October 1993
- —Vann Wesson, *Generation X Field Guide and Lexicon*, p. 66, 1997

flex *adjective*
flexible *US*
- —Judi Sanders, *Kickin' like Chicken with the Couch Commander*, p. 9, 1992

flexi-flyer *noun*
in drag racing, a racing car with a long wheelbase with built-in flexibility to keep the wheels on the tracks *US, 1960s*
- —Lyle K. Engel, *The Complete Book of Fuel and Gas Dragsters*, p. 151, 1968

flick *noun*
1 a film *UK, 1926*
- [O]ne time roadie and part-time pimp, horror flick fanatic, and failed steel guitarist[.]—Doug Lang, *Freaks*, p. 20, 1973
- The only drag is that since they really made it, they never gave me any gigs in their flicks even when they are powerful enough to order the casting director to.—Babs Gonzales, *Movin' On Down De Line*, p. 60, 1975
- French flick uses hoary European art house premise, ie, and older, richer daddy gets involved with a gorgeous but debt ridden young babe.—*Sydney City Hub*, p. 12, 4th April 1996
- A black porno flick is the sorriest thing on earth. No actors, no actresses, just a bunch of people sitting in a hotel room waiting for somebody to yell, "Action."—Chris Rock, *Rock This!*, p. 26, 1997
- But put that bad boy in a flick, every motherfucker out there want one.—*Jackie Brown*, 1997
- Many of the flicks looked like the kind of stuff that always filled the lower shelves at the video store[.]—Christopher Brookmyre, *Not the End of the World*, p. 17, 1998
- The flick depicts an ambivalent protagonist undercover as a contestant at the Miss USA pageant.—*Sydney Scope Magazine*, p. 22, 2001

2 a photograph *US, 1962*
- It was a helluva price to pay for having a white woman's flick in my wallet.—Odie Hawkins, *Scars and Memories*, p. 54, 1987

3 rejection; dismissal *AUSTRALIA, 1982*
Short for **FLICK PASS**.
- —Ivor Limb, *Footy's No Joke!*, p. 42, 1986
- So the guys gave this young groupie type of person the flick.—Kathy Lette, *Girls' Night Out*, p. 22, 1987
- Nuthin' will get you the flick faster than fallin' in love.—Kathy Lette, *Girls' Night Out*, p. 23, 1987
- —John Birmingham, *He Died With a Felafel in his Hand*, p. 98, 1994
- —Rex Hunt, *Tall Tales – and True*, p. 95, 1994
- I'd already decided to give Steve the flick and I wasn't much interested in listening to him bicker with his father.—Shane Maloney, *Nice Try*, p. 277, 1998

flick *verb*

1 to reject *AUSTRALIA*

- There had been plenty of women at the club who fancied him, but he had politely turned them away until lately. Now Joe seemed less keen to flick them. —Clive Galea, *Slipper*, p. 93, 1988

2 to turn back or alter a car's mileometer (odometer) to increase resale value *NEW ZEALAND, 1991*

- —Harry Orsman, *A Dictionary of Modern New Zealand Slang*, p. 51, 1999

▸ **flick your bean**

(of a woman) to masturbate *UK*

Fairly conventional use of 'flick' (to move with the fingers) applied to **BEAN** (the clitoris).

- The scenes with her flicking her bean are fucking good, by the way. —Kevin Sampson, *Outlaws*, p. 228, 2001

▸ **flick your Bic**

in trucking, to tap your brakes at night signalling to another driver *US*

A borrowing from advertising for Bic™ cigarette lighters.

- —Wayne Floyd, *Jason's Authentic Dictionary of CB Slang*, p. 16, 1976

▸ **flick your switch**

to sexually excite you *UK*

A play on **TURN ON** (to thrill).

- What should a chap be doing in bed then, to flick your switch? —*FHM*, p. 50, June 2003

▸ **flick your wick**

to speed up, to hurry up *NEW ZEALAND*

- —Sonya Plowman, *Great Kiwi Slang*, p. 75, 2002

▸ **flick yourself off**

of a woman, to masturbate *UK*

From the small movements necessary to manipulate the clitoris.

- The finger with which a woman flicks herself off. —*Roger's Profanisaurus*, p. 78, 2002

flicker *noun*

a film *US, 1926*

- —Lou Shelly, *Hepcats Jive Dictionary*, p. 11, 1945
- —Marcus Hanna Boulware, *Jive and Slang of Students in Negro Colleges*, 1947
- I spoke about leaving for the last roundup in the ranch house up yonder, an idea I got from a Johnny Mack Brown cowboy flicker. —Piri Thomas, *Down These Mean Streets*, p. 15, 1967

flick pass *noun*

rejection; dismissal *AUSTRALIA, 1983*

Rhyming slang for 'arse'. A 'flick pass' is a type of open-handed pass made in Australian Rules football.

- Anyway, the bloke who got the low scores made sure we got the flick pass. —Kathy Lette, *Girls' Night Out*, p. 27, 1987
- I could only see big trouble for myself if I didn't give them the flick pass. —Clive Galea, *Slipper*, p. 155, 1988

flicks *noun*

the cinema *UK, 1927*

- Well, wot about comin' ter the flicks? —Nino Culotta (John O'Grady), *They're A Weird Mob*, p. 132, 1957
- —D.E. Charlwood, *All the Green Year*, p. 63, 1965
- —Ward McNally, *Supper at Happy Harry's*, p. 78, 1982
- —Kerry Cue, *Crooks, Chooks and Bloody Ratbags*, p. 71, 1983
- I think Derek [Malcolm] and me would be hard pushed to ever pick a Saturday night out at the flicks together. —*The Guardian*, 18th January 2001

flid *noun*

used as term of playground abuse *UK*

Derives from thalidomide, pronounced 'flidomide'.

- One fourth-year boy referred to another as a "flid". —*New Society*, 31st January 1980
- —Chris Lewis, *The Dictionary of Playground Slang*, p. 92, 2003

flier *noun*

1 in sports, a very fast start; in cricket, a swift rate of scoring at the beginning of a match *UK, 1984*

A shortening of conventional 'flying start', usually in the phrase 'off to a flier'.

- Trust Tebbutt to get Tuscan off to a flier. —*The Observer*, 1st June 2003

2 in target shooting, a shot that strikes outside a close group of shots on the target *US*

- —*American Speech*, p. 193, October 1957: 'Some colloquialisms of the handgunner'

3 a prisoner who commits suicide by jumping or is murdered by being thrown from the top tier of a prison *US, 1942*

- —John R. Armore and Joseph D. Wolfe, *Dictionary of Desperation*, p. 29, 1976

▸ **take a flier**

to leave *US, 1914*

- Remembers his mama stopped slaving in white folk's mansions . . . took a flyer in show biz ... exotic dancer[.] —Iceberg Slim (Robert Beck), *Long White Con*, p. 25, 1977

flies *noun*

▸ **and no flies**

used to aver the honesty of the statement to which it is appended *UK, 1851*

- —Paul Baker, *Polari*, p. 162, 2002

▸ **no flies on you**

nothing at all wrong or amiss with you *AUSTRALIA, 1845*

- —Leonard Mann, *Flesh in Armour*, p. 200, 1932
- No flies on Gary, mate, you mark my words. —Alexander Buzo, *Norm and Ahmed*, p. 16, 1969
- —Ward McNally, *Supper at Happy Harry's*, p. 18, 1982

flight attendant *noun*

a security guard at a rock concert, usually large and muscular, stationed at the barricades near the stage *US*

- —Jim Crotty, *How to Talk American*, p. 219, 1997

flight deck *noun*

the female breasts *UK*

- Lovely flight deck she's got! —Posy Simmonds, *True Love*, 1981

flightie *noun*

a person who has relocated to the Highlands of Scotland from the urban realities of England in search of a rural dream *UK: SCOTLAND*

Derogatory. Probably from the verb 'to take flight'.

- It's all a far cry from socially-diverse Leicestershire, and the Dobsons were shocked when a newspaper report referred to them as "flighties"[.] —*Radio Times*, p. 36, 27th November 2004

flight lieutenant Biggles *noun*

giggles *UK*

Rhyming slang, based (although wrongly ranked) on the flying-ace hero created by W.E. Johns in 1932.

- I had a bad case of the Flight Lieutenants. —*www.LondonSlang.com*, June 2002

flight lustre *noun*

a mythical substance for which new recruits in the Canadian Air Force are sent to search *CANADA*

- "Flight Lustre" [during 1950s and '60s] was one of many useful but mythical substances that have caused embarrassment to apprentices. Others include Propwash, Relative Bearing Grease, Skyhook. —Tom Langeste, *Words on the Wing*, p. 104, 1995

flight skins *noun*

military flight pay *US, 1945*

- I was also paid air crew flight pay, or "flight skins," for an additioanl $50 a month. —Don Hoover, *The Road to 311 No. York St.*, p. 146, 2003

flight time *noun*

in motor racing, the elapsed time a car unintentionally spends in the air, usually upside down *US*

Grim humour.

- —Don Alexander, *The Racer's Dictionary*, p. 27, 1980

flik *noun*

a song from which the lyrics have been changed for humorous consumption by science fiction fans *US*

- —Eric S. Raymond, *The New Hacker's Dictionary*, p. 155, 1991

flim *noun*

a five-pound note; the sum of £5 *UK, 1870*

Originally an abbreviation of 'flimsy', adjective and obsolete noun use for the early, large white banknotes.

- You can give me a flim for the introduction. —Charles Raven, *Underworld Nights*, p. 90, 1956
- [G]iving him two and a half pound out of a flim. —Kevin Sampson, *Outlaws*, p. 119, 2001
- Thinks he's a fuckin hero of the people cos he once gave a flim to Shelter. —Niall Griffiths, *Kelly + Victor*, p. 316, 2002

flimflam *noun*

1 nonsense, pretentious or deceptive nonsense *UK*

In conventional use until late C19.

- [Cat Power] has transcended the faddishness of music trends to remain a true voice among so much flimflam. —*X-Ray*, p. 23, August 2003

2 a swindle involving a supposedly lost wallet supposedly found on the ground near the victim *US*

- This is one of the oldest of the confidence games; and was called "pigeon-trapping" in years gone by, but is usually called the flim-flam these days. —W.M. Tucker, *The Change Raisers*, p. 24, 1960

flimflam *verb*

to shortchange, to swindle *US, 1881*

- Then I wouldn't have to flimflam poor crazy Zelda any more, and I would tell her the whole hideous truth. —Max Shulman, *I was a Teen-Age Dwarf*, p. 121, 1959
- He said, "Blue, I'll die and go to the bottomless pits of hell before I let you flimflam me out of my two grand." —Iceberg Slim (Robert Beck), *Trick Baby*, p. 33, 1969
- He had been up in Harlem flimflamming a colored woman preacher out of $935 and thought he would take a little vacation. —*The Life & Loves of Mr. Jiveass Nigger*, p. 15, 1969
- After all these years of flimflamming, it's time to get real. —Odie Hawkins, *Great Lawd Buddha*, p. 196, 1990

flimflam man *noun*

a confidence swindler *US*

- Everyone in Hollywood is a phony, a fruit, or a flim-flam man, a partner had warned him. —Joseph Wambaugh, *The New Centurions*, p. 151, 1970

flimflammer *noun*

a swindler who engages in the flim-flam swindle (a swindle involving a supposedly lost wallet supposedly found on the ground near the victim) *US*

- The flim-flammer often goes to a bank or a bus station in order to spot a victim with a fat billfold. —W.M. Tucker, *The Change Raisers*, p. 24, 1960
- There's lesbians, masochists, hypes, whores, flim flammers, paddy hustlers, hugger muggers, ex-cons of all descriptions, and anybody else with a kink of some kind or other. —Joseph Wambaugh, *The New Centurions*, p. 174, 1970

flimp *verb*

to cheat, to swindle; in betting, to underpay or offer bets at below the odds *UK, 1925*

From an earlier sense of 'theft by snatching'; ultimately from west Flemish *flimpe* (knock, slap in the face).

- I bet you've flimped on every flipping tickle we've had[.] —Charles Raven, *Underworld Nights*, p. 185, 1956
- —John McCririck, *John McCririck's World of Betting*, p. 60, 1991

flimsy *noun*

any order written on thin, onion skin paper *UK, 1889*

The orders were written on 'flimsy' paper, hence the nounification of the adjective.

- —Norman Carlisle, *The Modern Wonder Book of Trains and Railroading*, p. 263, 1946
- —*American Speech*, p. 226, October 1955: 'An aircraft production dispatcher's vocabulary'

fling *noun*

a limited period devoted to self-indulgent pleasures, especially sexual; a short-lived sexual liaison *UK, 1827*

- Mum – cried in the kitchen as she heard about the latest fling. —Mark Powell, *Snap*, p. 8–8, 2001

fling *verb*

▸ **fling a dummy**

to die suddenly *UK*

- He flung a dummy yeah, He flung a dummy, / He kicked the bucket – he just passed away (brown bread). —Viv Stanshall, *Flung a Dummy*, 1981

▸ **fling baby**

to undergo an abortion *TRINIDAD AND TOBAGO*

- —Lise Winer, *Dictionary of the English/Creole of Trinidad & Tobago*, 2003

flinger *noun*

1 an impulsive poker player who is inclined to raise bets without regard to the quality of his hand *US*

- —George Percy, *The Language of Poker*, p. 35, 1988

2 in target shooting, a shot that strikes outside a close group of shots on the target *US*

- —*American Speech*, p. 193, October 1957: 'Some colloquialisms of the handgunner'

fling-wing *noun*

a helicopter *US*

- —Linda Reinberg, *In the Field*, p. 83, 1991

Flintstones *nickname*

1 the UK armed forces *US*

The cartoon television series *The Flintstones* depicted a stone-age world in which C20 technology is comically replaced by prehistoric ingenuity. As a nickname used by the US military it reflects the outdated 'prehistoric' equipment and shortages of everyday supplies that force the UK forces to improvise and scrounge.

- —*Evening Standard*, p. 6, 7th March 2003: 'Why the Yanks call us the Flintstones'

2 a variety of LSD *UK*

Identified by a picture of the cartoon characters the Flintstones, created by William Hanna and Joseph Barbera in 1966; sometimes shortened to 'flints'.

- —Angela Devlin, *Prison Patter*, p. 52, 1996

flip *noun*

1 a condition of mental instability *US, 1953*

- [S]he'd walk down the street in her flip and actually feel the electric contact with other human beings[.] —Jack Kerouac, *The Subterraneans*, p. 29, 1958

2 a person who has lost touch with reality *US*

- Just frantic people, all of us. Just flips. —George Mandel, *Flee the Angry Strangers*, p. 373, 1952

3 an LSD experience *US*

- —Jay Robert Nash, *Dicitonary of Crime*, p. 134, 1992

4 in trucking, a return trip *US*

- Enjoyed the modulation, good buddy, catch you on the flip. —Lanie Dills, *The Official CB Slanguage Language Dictionary*, p. 33, 1976

5 a male homosexual who plays the passive role in sex *US*

- —William K. Bentley and James M. Corbett, *Prison Slang*, p. 49, 1992

6 a police informer *US*

- Then some little junker flip bitch oh-deed. —Malcolm Braly, *On the Yard*, p. 28, 1967
- The flip's name is Francisc Kingsbury. —Carl Hiaasen, *Native Tongue*, p. 313, 1991

Flip *noun*

a Filipino *US, 1931*

- —Multicultural Management Program Fellows, *Dictionary of Cautionary Words and Phrases*, 1989
- —Judi Sanders, *Da Bomb*, p. 6, 1997

flip *verb*

1 to become very angry or agitated; to go temporarily crazy *US, 1950*

- Wigged? Christ, it looks like he flipped. —Thurston Scott, *Cure it with Honey*, p. 57, 1951
- "You look like some other cat." "Baby," said the wolf, "you're flippin'!" —Steve Allen, *Bop Fables*, p. 46, 1955
- Whereas if you goof (the ugliest word in Hip), if you lapse back into being a frightened stupid child, or if you flip, if you lose your control[.]' —Norman Mailer, *Advertisements for Myself*, p. 351, 1957
- [P]erhaps some day he would flip and kill one of them. —Hubert Selby Jr, *Last Exit to Brooklyn*, p. 215, 1957
- [S]he's having therapy, has apparently very seriously flipped only very recently[.] —Jack Kerouac, *The Subterraneans*, p. 11, 1958
- Well, he's flipping,' said Jean looking after him, 'flipping right out of his skull. —Terry Southern, *Flash and Filigree*, p. 151, 1958
- That he's getting married has her flipped. —Philip Roth, *Goodbye, Columbus*, p. 47, 1958
- Now I was fighting for my life. They must have thought that I'd flipped, the way I was coming back on them. —Jamie Mandelkau, *Buttons*, p. 24, 1971
- Hey, what the hell's with you Tony, you flipping out? —*Saturday Night Fever*, 1977
- Hey, turkey. What the hell you doing out there praying your behind off. You done flipped or something? —Piri Thomas, *Stories from El Barrio*, p. 38, 1978
- The first time she wore it was right after Mark smoked grass at home, had an allergic reaction and flipped out. —Sandra Bernhard, *Confessions of a Pretty Lady*, p. 50, 1988
- PCP is alright but it's dangerous gear [...] I can imagine fucking flipping out on it. —Shaun Ryder, *Shaun Ryder... in His Own Words*, 1988
- She was a very nervous and high-strung person and it flipped her out at the time, not so that she bcame a hospital case, but it did cause her to become frigid. —Herbert Huncke, *Guilty of Everything*, p. 16, 1990
- I'm not going to do what you think I'm going to do, which is flip out. —*Jerry Maguire*, 1996

2 to become enthusiastic and excited *US, 1950*

- She was as ugly as a pan of worms, but when I saw those sandwiches with the crusts cut off, boy, I flipped! —Max Shulman, *I was a Teen-Age Dwarf*, p. 59, 1959
- They all came in to congratulate me. The whole campus flipped. —Dick Gregory, *Nigger*, p. 92, 1964
- She really flipped over you. —Hunter S. Thompson, *Fear and Loathing in Las Vegas*, p. 124, 1971

3 to induce a betrayal *US, 1980*

- You don't see what that motherfucker's doing? How he's trying to flip you, turn you against me? — Elmore Leonard, *Be Cool*, p. 230, 1999

4 to betray; to inform on *US*

- You don't have to larceny me – I won't flip on you. I'll never flip on nobody again. — Clarence Cooper Jr, *The Scene*, p. 14, 1960
- They wanted me to flip on the guy who had sold the stuff to me. — Henry Williamson, *Hustler!*, p. 138, 1965

5 to gesture *UK*

As used in **FLIP THE BIRD** (to raise the middle finger).

- I just flipped off President George / I'm going to dizz knee land. — Dada *Dizz Knee Land*, 1992
- Also rubbing your eye or scratching your ear with your middle finger is a good way to flip off an authority figure without getting caught. — Editors of Ben is Dead, *Retrohell*, 1997
- But when she saw the billboard of Ashley, lying prone and twisted like an accident victim, she could not resist flipping it off[.] — Francesca Lia Block, *I Was a Teenage Fairy*, 1998
- Horns blew, She flipped them off. — Robert Crais, *L.A. Requiem*, 1999
- [He] was flipping gang signs with four others in similar colours. — Diran Adebayo, *My Once Upon A Time*, p. 58, 2000

6 the railways, to step aboard a moving train *US*

- — Ramon Adams, *The Language of the Railroader*, p. 62, 1977

▸ flip a bitch

to make a u-turn *US*

- — Connie Eble (Editor), *UNC-CH Campus Slang*, p. 3, Fall 2000

▸ flip a trick

(of a prostitute) to have sex with a customer *US*

Far less common than to 'turn' a **TRICK**.

- She was scratching and nodding and flipping car tricks at Sunset and La Brea when I got back to L.A. two months later. — Iceberg Slim (Robert Beck), *Airtight Willie and Me*, p. 169, 1979

▸ flip the bird

to gesture in derision with a raised middle finger *US, 1968*

- Did he flip her the bird again? — Armistead Maupin, *Tales of the City*, p. 344, 1978
- I just flip 'em the bird / And keep goin', I don't take shit from no-one[.] — Eminem (Marshall Mathers), *Criminal*, 2000

▸ flip the bishop

(of a male) to masturbate *UK*

Plays on **FLIP** as a euphemistic **FUCK** and, conventionally, as a 'manipulation'. A variation of **BASH THE BISHOP** (to masturbate).

▸ flip the bone

to extend the middle finger in a rude gesture of defiance *US*

- [A]ll Jeff did was flip the bone at his old man which is a very dirty way of telling somebody where to get off. — Frederick Kohner, *Gidget*, p. 48, 1957

▸ flip the grip

to shake hands *US*

- — Lou Shelly, *Hepcats Jive Talk Dictionary*, p. 24, 1945

▸ flip the lip

to talk *US*

- And she is always flippin' the lip about him bein' such a weary Willie, the citizens of the burg, even the hepcats, mark him solid. — Haenigsen, *Jive's Like That*, 1947

▸ flip your gut

to evoke sympathy or sadness *US*

- — Jim Crotty, *How to Talk American*, p. 352, 1997

▸ flip your lid; flipflop your lid

to lose emotional control *US*

- That fart face done flipflop his Whiteass lid for sure! — Robert Gover, *One Hundred Dollar Misunderstanding*, p. 170, 1961
- He finally flipped his lid. He walked around with a bible in his hands, would come up to you and ask, "What did you say?" — Herbert Huncke, *Guilty of Everything*, p. 178, 1990

▸ flip your stick

to move your penis during an all-cavity strip search *US*

- — Gary K. Farlow, *Prison-ese*, p. 21, 2002

▸ flip your wig

to lose your mental composure *US*

- Nate took away her emotional security and she flipped her wig and snuck into the locker room and hacked up his athletic equipment. — Max Shulman, *I was a Teen-Age Dwarf*, p. 33, 1959

flip *adjective*

pleasant, fashionable, popular *US*

- — *American Speech*, p. 302, December 1955: 'Wayne university slang'

flip

euphemistic replacement for some noun and most verb senses of 'fuck' *UK*

The last citation is a re-working of **FUCK THIS FOR A GAME OF SOLDIERS**.

- Why the hell can't you do as you're told. Flip you, you flipper. — Charles Raven, *Underworld Nights*, p. 18, 1956
- Well, flip me! The frau herself. — William Best, *The Myth Makers (Six Granada Plays)*, 1958
- Flip this for a game of toy soldiers. — Graeme Kent, *The Queen's Corporal [Six Granada Plays]*, p. 94, 1959

flip act *noun*

feigned insanity *US*

- Jimmy was trying to beat the rap by pulling a flip act. He was good. He told me to go crazy and I'd beat the chair. — Piri Thomas, *Down These Mean Streets*, p. 243, 1967

flipflap *noun*

in circus usage, a back handspring *US*

- — Don Wilmeth, *The Language of American Popular Entertainment*, p. 96, 1981

flipflop *noun*

1 a sandal that is not bound to the foot, usually worn around a swimming pool *US, 1970*

From the sound made when walking on concrete.

- Blew out my flip flop, stepped on a pop-top / Cut my heel, had to cruise on back home. — Jimmy Buffett, *Margaritaville*, 1977
- She will take black spikes or Capezios or even foam-rubber flip-flops. — Hunter S. Thompson, *A Generation of Swine*, p. 109, 28 April 1986
- The dozen or so trustees who had run of the place and were walking around in T-shirts, drawstring gym pants and rubber flip-flops. — Richard Price, *Clockers*, p. 96, 1992
- "If my nine wasn't drying out,I" Fortney said to the lifeguards, "I'd blast you moondoggies right outta your flip-flops." — Joseph Wambaugh, *Floaters*, p. 83, 1996
- [T]he Hunk of the Week competition, in which half-cut men in football shirts and flip-flops had to prove their worth[.] — Iain Aitch, *A Fete Worse Than Death*, p. 286, 2003

2 a return journey *US*

- We'll catch you on the flip-flop. — C.W. McCall, *Convoy*, 1976
- [C]atch you on the flip-flop[.] — Peter Chippindale, *The British CB Book*, p. 153, 1981

3 a traffic lane designed for turning around *US*

Detroit usage.

- — Jim Crotty, *How to Talk American*, p. 76, 1997

4 (used of two homosexuals) a reversal of sexual roles *US*

- It's hard to tell who's doing what. You'd be surprised. Some of it that you would swear is strictly aggressive type is what they call flip-flop. — Bruce Jackson, *In the Life*, p. 393, 1972

flip-flop *verb*

1 to change positions on a political issue or issues in response to changing public opinion *US*

- A day after a top administration official announced the National Office of AIDS Poilicy had become obsolete, President Bush flipflopped and said he was keeping the office open. — *San Francisco Chronicle*, p. A3, 8th February 2001
- In just the last few weeks, for example, the Bush administration flip-flopped on a campaign promise to limit carbon-dioxide emissions[.] — *Daily Sun*, 31st March 2001
- The Bush Administration has flip-flopped on North Korea. — *Time Magazine*, p. 38, 28th October 2002
- She said President Bush had flipflopped on America's global role: "For a man who said it was not our job to police the world, he seems to be pretty at ease with this." — *USA Today*, p. 12A, 21st March 2003
- I could tick off five or six things on which George W. Bush is a flip-flopper, on enormously important issues: Homeland Security Department, 9/11 Commission, abortion itself, George W. Bush flip-flopped. — *News from CNN*, 5th November 2004

2 (used of two homosexuals) to reverse sexual roles after sexual satisfaction is achieved by the active partner *US*

- Many snide remarks would be passed to the effect that they were most probably 'flipflopping,' another way of saying that they were interchanging their roles in the sex act. — *New York Mattachine Newsletter*, p. 7, July 1961

3 to have sex with both men and women *US*

- — William K. Bentley and James M. Corbett, *Prison Slang*, p. 59, 1992

flip-flopping *noun*

changing positions on an issue or issues *US*

- But his flip-flopping from con to pro on Federal aid to New York could hurt him in a September primary race[.] — *Newsweek*, p. 25, 12th January 1976

flip off!
go away!; used as a euphemistic replacement for 'fuck off!' *UK*
- Here is a pony for any inconvenience you may have been caused. Now flip off. —Charles Raven, *Underworld Nights*, p. 39, 1956

flipped *adjective*
smart, attractive *US*
- You're really flipped – aren't you. — *Rebel Without a Cause*, 1955

flipper *noun*
1 the hand *UK, 1812*
- Reach out to the clerk, shake his flipper, and say, "Hi ya, glad to see you again." —Jack Lait and Lee Mortimer, *New York Confidential*, p. 201, 1948

2 to a lineman in American football, the forearm *US*
- —Zander Hollander and Paul Zimmerman, *Football Lingo*, p. 45, 1967

3 the ear *US, 1905*
- —Lou Shelly, *Hepcats Jive Dictionary*, p. 11, 1945

4 a temporary partial denture used to mask the absence of a single tooth or several teeth, especially with child actors *US*
Technically known as a 'stayplate', it flips in and out of the child's mouth.

5 a friend *UK*
- And somehow that was the moment she became my best flipper. From that time on I truly loved her. —Adrian Reid, *Confessions of a Hitch-Hiker*, 1970

6 a criminal who informs on friends and associates to reduce his own sentence or to completely avoid charges *US*
- —Jim Crotty, *How to Talk American*, p. 51, 1997

7 in the television and film industries, a section of set that can be easily replaced *UK*
- —Oswald Skilbeck, *ABC of Film and TV Working Terms*, p. 55, 1960

8 the game of pinball *US*
- —Connie Eble (Editor), *UNC-CH Campus Slang*, March 1974

9 in hot rodding, a hubcap *US*
- — *Good Housekeeping*, p. 143, September 1958: 'Hot-rod terms for teen-age girls'
- —Tom MacPherson, *Dragging and Driving*, p. 138, 1960

10 a turn signal in a truck or car *US*
- — *Dictionary of CB Lingo*, p. 66, 1976: 'Elementary electronics'

flippers *noun*
anchovies *US*
- — *Maledicta*, p. 12, 1996: 'Domino's pizza jargon'

flipping *adjective*
used as an intensifier *UK, 1911*
Since about 1940 the commonest of all euphemisms for **FUCKING** in the UK, as in the common exclamation of disgust 'Flipping 'eck!' (fucking hell!), often used unwitting of the term it disguises.
- I don't flipping well know— *Seven Days To Noon*, 1950
- [W]hen the bogies were about to search him on some very hot sus, he swallowed a flipping great sapphire and diamond star pendant[.] —Charles Raven, *Underworld Nights*, p. 9, 1956
- You'd have to do your nut to start knocking flippin' armoured cars around, I'll tell you, mate. —Derek Bickerton, *Payroll*, p. 32, 1959
- My old man don't earn much / In fact he's flippin' skint. —Lonnie Donegan, *My Old Man's a Dustman*, 1960
- A big man alongside her roared in pain: 'Take the stick outer my flippin eye; Ain't no call to stick it in my flippin' eye.' —Sutton Woodfield, *A for Artemis*, p. 121, 1960
- Well, up him, I'll pinch the flipping tank and I'll show Con how I can drive. —Bluey, *Bush Contractors*, p. 177, 1975
- I'm not a flipping thicky. —Ian Dury, *Billericay Dickie*, 1977
- Ah, you're flippin' nuts. — *Repo Man [televised version]*, 1984
- Use your flippin' nod [head]. —Diran Abedayo, *My Once Upon A Time*, p. 272, 2000

flippy *adjective*
eccentric, crazy *US, 1965*
- Everyone knew his mother and father were flippy. —Richard Price, *The Wanderers*, p. 33, 1974

flip-side *noun*
1 the reverse side of a vinyl record *US*
From the action of flipping the disc over.

2 the opposite of something *US, 1967*
A figurative application of the earlier sense as 'the reverse side of a record'.
- The flip-side is that the easy-going punter on holiday can quickly harden[.] —Wayne Anthony, *Spanish Highs*, p. 4, 1999

▸ **on the flip-side**
later on *US*
- —Connie Eble (Editor), *UNC-CH Campus Slang*, p. 4, October 2002

flip top *noun*
1 the top of a canned food or beverage that peels open without resort to an opening device *US, 1955*
- I ripped the flip top off another one. —Oscar Zeta Acosta, *The Autobiography of a Brown Buffalo*, p. 169, 1972

2 a truck cab that tilts up to expose the engine *US*
- —Montie Tak, *Truck Talk*, p. 61, 1971

flip-wreck *noun*
a habitual masturbator *AUSTRALIA, 1950*
Referring to the supposed damaging effects of masturbation.
- One can be called a 'Flip-wreck' if one is an over-enthusiastic onanist. —Bettina Arndt, *The Australian Way of Sex*, p. 12, 1985

flit *noun*
1 an effeminate homosexual male *US, 1935*
- —G. Legman, *The Language of Homsexuality*, p. 1166, 1941
- The other end of the bar was full of flits. They weren't too flitty-looking – I mean they didn't have their hair too long or anything – but you could tell they were flits anyway. —J.D. Salinger, *Catcher in the Rye*, p. 142, 1951
- Still, when this assistant prop man, crew-cut kid, flit, floppy wrists and pursy lips, what they called rough trade, a real camp, when he'd begun stroking Biff's elbows and saying how gone he was on him, Biff hadn't come down with the immediate kyawkyaws. —Bernard Wolfe, *The Late Risers*, p. 202, 1954
- The reason she married Oscar in the first place was that she had been bored silly with the flits and lushs of cafe society. —Max Shulman, *Rally Round the Flag, Boys!*, p. 72, 1957
- "Has he been married?" "I bet he has been. He's not flit." "Flit?" "Stands for faggot." —Frederick Kohner, *Gidget*, p. 115, 1957
- —Collin Baker et al., *College Undergraduate Slang Study Conducted at Brown University*, p. 119, 1968

2 a discreet and hurried departure to avoid debts *UK, 1952*
Probably from **MOONLIGHT FLIT**.
- [I]f, for some weird and wonderful reason, you decide to do a flit, I can trace you —Ross Thomas, *Out on the Rim*, p. 86, 2003

3 any insecticide in a spray can *TRINIDAD AND TOBAGO, 1993*
A generic use, from the trade name of an insecticide.
- —Lise Winer, *Dictionary of the English/Creole of Trinidad & Tobago*, 2003

flitters *noun*
tatters *IRELAND*
- It was common knowledge that Englishwomen, their morals in flitters from six years of war, were coming to Ireland to eat farm eggs and butter, unrationed steaks and any young Irishmen they might find. —Hugh Leonard, *Out After Dark*, p. 97, 1989
- Our regional policy has been described as being in flitters. — Mr Deenihan, *House of the Oireachtas Parliamentary Debates*, 25th February 1999

fliv *verb*
in circus and carnival usage, to fail or to perform poorly *US, 1917*
- —Don Wilmeth, *The Language of American Popular Entertainment*, p. 96, 1981

flivver *noun*
an old, worn car, especially a Ford car *US, 1910*
The term was, by the early 1980s, chiefly associated with the early model Ford cars, and had thus become historical.
- The hustlers would be waiting in flivvers to haul people with gunny sacks home. —Iceberg Slim (Robert Beck), *The Naked Soul of Iceberg Slim*, p. 97, 1971

flix *noun*
photographs *US*
Possibly a variation of **FLICKS** (the cinema).
- YOU GOT SOME FAT FLIX? Send only top-quality photos to the address below. — *The Source*, p. 90, March 2002

flixy *adjective*
easy *FIJI*
Recorded by Jan Tent in 1994.

FLK *noun*
a strange-looking child; a *f*unny-*l*ooking *k*id *US, 1961*
Recorded in an article about medical slang in British (3 London and 1 Cambridge) hospitals.
- — *Maledicta*, p. 117, 1984 – 1985: 'Milwaukee medical maledicta'
- — *Ethics and Behaviour*, August 2003

flo *noun*

1 a variety of marijuana

- The motivational high produced by Flo is quite unique, the flavor is like Nepalese Temple Hash. — *Seedbank*, 2001

2 a young person *CANADA*

- Floune is a conflation of "flo" - Quebec street slang for "kid" - and "cloune," French for clown. — *Washington Times*, p. E1, 23rd October 1991

float *noun*

1 a sum of money kept in a cash register, or otherwise provided, to meet the basic operational needs of a business *UK, 1902*

2 a customer's down payment, treated by the salesman collecting it as a short-term loan *US*

- — *American Speech*, p. 309–310, Winter 1980: 'More jargon of car salesmen'

3 a tyre *US*

- — *Dictionary of CB Lingo*, p. 66, 1976: 'Elementary electronics'

4 military duty onboard a ship *US*
Vietnam war US Marines usage.

- — Linda Reinberg, *In the Field*, p. 83, 1991

float *verb*

1 in the gambling game two-up, to toss the coins so that they only give the appearance of spinning *AUSTRALIA, 1945*

- The coins were not spinning at all. They were being floated - that is, they were wobbling enough to give the impression that they were turning over but, in fact, the heads were remaining upwards during the time the coins were in the air[.] — Joe Andersen, *Winners Can Laugh*, p. 51, 1982

2 to eat after extensive drinking *UK*

- — Tom Hibbert, *Rockspeak!*, p. 63, 1983

▸ **float a log**
to defecate *UK*

- — Bob Young and Micky Moody, *The Language of Rock 'n' Roll*, p. 44, 1985

▸ **float a sausage to the seaside**
to defecate into a sewage system *UK*
The phrase may have originated in the comic *Viz*.

- — *www.LondonSlang.com*, June 2002

▸ **float dice**
to drop dice suspected of having been weighted into a glass of water to see if they roll over on one side *US*

- If you're winning too much, he'll also float the dice. — Stephen Cannell, *King Con*, p. 136, 1997

▸ **float the gears**
to shift gears without using the clutch *US*

- — Lawrence Teeman, *Consumer Guide Good Buddy's CB Dictionary*, p. 53, 1976

▸ **float your boat**
to please; to make happy *US*

- — Connie Eble (Editor), *UNC-CH Campus Slang*, p. 3, Fall 1984
- [L]et us know which new bands are floating your boat the most. — *Kerrang!*, p. 3, 1st December 2001
- [W]e have to defend the rights of homosexuals to nail each other's gonads to planks of wood if that's what floats their boat. — Christopher Brookmyre, *The Sacred Art of Stealing*, p. 244, 2002

floater *noun*

1 a corpse found floating in a body of water *US, 1890*

- We pulled a floater out of the Quabbin Reservoir a couple years ago, one of the Mackling gang[.] — George V. Higgins, *The Judgment of Deke Hunter*, p. 7, 1976
- Floater comes up at Waterworks Park, makes your fucking day. — Elmore Leonard, *Split Images*, p. 65–66, 1981
- Valentine wouldn't soon forget the floater call. — Thomas Larry Adcock, *Precinct 19*, p. 17, 1984
- "What is it, son?" "A floater!" Andy exclaimed. Garcia felt a sour knotting in his gut. Living with a homicide cop had given Donna's youngsters a gruesome vocabulary. — Carl Hiaasen, *Strip Tease*, p. 99–100, 1993
- Another floater. The water was warm enough for the bacteria to have cooked fast, and after several days methane gas had brought it bobbing to the surface, bobbing lazily against the rocks. — Joseph Wambaugh, *Floaters*, p. 147, 1996

2 a particle of food floating in a bottled drink (having been washed into the bottle as it was being drunk from) *UK: SCOTLAND*

- Okay, ye can get a slug but don't gie us any a yer floaters. — Michael Munro, *The Patter, Another Blast*, p. 24, 1988

3 in circus and carnival usage, a slice of imitation fruit floating on the top of imitation fruit juice *US*

- — Don Wilmeth, *The Language of American Popular Entertainment*, p. 96, 1981

4 a meat pie served with pea gravy *AUSTRALIA, 1915*

- South Australians, especially during their short winters, are fond of a thing called a 'floater'. — John O'Grady, *Aussie Etiket*, p. 61, 1971

5 the recreational drug methaqualone, best known as Quaaludes™ *US*

- SOUTHERN: [C]hicks love Quaaludes - makes them less self-conscious, I suppose, about fucking. The druggist says it's a great favorite with hookers. With students and hookers. They must have something in common. BURROUGHS: Intense pain. SOUTHERN: They call them "floaters" - I guess they float above the pain. — Victor Bockris, *The Howard Marks Book of Dope Stories*, p. 35, 1997

6 a person who is temporarily assigned to one job or another™ *US, 1909*

- I want you as a floater between agencies. — Jame Ellroy, *Suicide Hill*, p. 666, 1986

7 a migratory worker *US, 1859*

- Don't want any floaters, anyway. This is a home-town paper for home-town people. — Jim Thompson, *Roughneck*, p. 113, 1954

8 a person who is a poor credit risk because of constantly changing employment *US*

- — *American Speech*, p. 312, Autumn-Winter 1975: 'The jargon of car salesmen'

9 an early release from jail, usually with an order to leave town immediately *US, 1914*

- Father was released on a "floater" and came for me with chastisement and shame flooding his florid features. — Neal Cassady, *The First Third*, p. 123, 1971

10 a river-rafting enthusiast *US*

- — Jim Crotty, *How to Talk American*, p. 213, 1997

11 in the language of wind surfing, a sailboard that can support the weight of a person in the water *US*

- — Frank Fox, *A Beginner's Guide to Zen and the Art of Windsurfing*, p. 151, 1985: 'A short dictionary of wind surfing terms'

12 a big, buoyant surfboard *US*

- — John Severson, *Modern Surfing Around the World*, p. 169, 1964

13 a pinball machine which is nearly level, lacking the playfield pitch needed for a good game *US*
The fact that the playfield is nearly level makes it seem as if the ball floats on the playfield.

- — Bobbye Claire Natkin and Steve Kirk, *All About Pinball*, p. 112, 1977

14 in the gambling game two-up, a coin which does not spin properly and so is illegal *AUSTRALIA, 1944*

15 in the television and film industries, a section of set that can be easily replaced *UK*

- — Oswald Skilbeck, *ABC of Film and TV Working Terms*, p. 55, 1960

16 a mistake *UK, 1913*

- Not just a floater [a mistake] but a real old-fashioned clangeroo. — Terence Rattigan in introduction to Mander and Mitchenson, *Theatrical Companion to Coward*, 1957

floaters *noun*
spots before the eyes *UK*

- — *Weekend*, 21st May 1969

floaties *noun*
(used by surfers) faeces floating in the sea *US*

- — Trevor Cralle, *The Surfin'ary*, p. 39, 1991

floating *adjective*

1 moving; not settled in a definite place *US*
Almost always applied to an illegal crap game that moves from location to location.

- Clean-up or no, there usually are more floating crap-games, illegal bookies and after-hour spots in Prince Georges than there are in Reno, where all such things are legal. — Jack Lait and Lee Mortimer, *Washington Confidential*, p. 66, 1951
- Up in the Bronx, a Negro held up some Italian racketeers in a floating crap game. — Malcolm X and Alex Haley, *The Autobiography of Malcolm X*, p. 124, 1964
- What do you think they was doing down there, having a floating crap game? — Robert Campbell, *Junkyard Dog*, p. 65, 1986

2 drunk or marijuana-intoxicated *US, 1938*

- — Richard McKenna, *The Sand Pebbles*, 1962

floating chrome *noun*

a commerical truck embellished with a lot of extra chrome *US*

- — Montie Tak, *Truck Talk*, p. 62, 1971

floating shotgun *noun*

a rocket-armed landing craft *US*

Korean war usage.

- "Floating shotguns," someone in the invasion fleet called these vessels (LSMRs, for landing ships, medium rocket). — Joseph C. Goulden, *Korea*, p. 210, 1982

float-out *noun*

a jail sentence suspended contingent upon the criminal leaving town *US*

- This here one don't fall off that luv an ack like a lady she gonna get a floatout. — Robert Gover, *JC Saves*, p. 18, 1968

floats *noun*

dice that have been hollowed out to affect their balance *US*

Because most dice used in casinos are now transparent, the practice and term are almost obsolete.

- — *The Annals of the American Academy of Political and Social Sciences*, p. 125, May 1950

flob *verb*

to spit *UK*

Noted at a time when punks showed appreciation of their musical heroes by expectorating at the stage.

- — *New Society*, 6th October 1977

flock *noun*

a group of unskilled poker players *US*

- — John Vorhaus, *The Big Book of Poker Slang*, p. 17, 1996

flockatoon *noun*

in Quebec's Gaspe area, an event at which people get happily drunk *CANADA*

- A "flockatoon" is a happy drunken event, to celebrate the finishing of a big job, for example. It may come from an Acadian word, "flocatoun," which means "home-made beer." — Lewis Poteet, *Talking Country*, p. 39, 1992

flog *noun*

1 a prostitute *AUSTRALIA*

- [H]e thought of the uncouth, common, broken down sluts who had featured momentarily at the studio in their careers and were destined to end up as cheap flogs in the brothels on the waterfront that catered to Goanese Indian seamen[.] — Len Riley, *The Kings Cross Racket*, p. 106, 1967

2 an act of male masturbation *AUSTRALIA*

- Having a flog, or flogging yourself. — Bettina Arndt, *The Australian Way of Sex*, p. 12, 1985

flog *verb*

1 to endorse, to promote, to sell *US, 1983*

- I hadn't got any idea what time it was, because I'd flogged me watch the day before. — John Peter Jones, *Feather Pluckers*, p. 54, 1964
- [H]e flogged some drills to a bloke. — *The Sweeney*, p. 50, 1976
- Hymie used to print and sell his own tip sheet titled Gift Horses at Bay Meadows until cataracts sealed the dapper little horse savant within a white waxen world and he was reduced to flogging forms. — Seth Morgan, *Homeboy*, p. 58, 1990
- — *Times Educational Supplement*, p. 43, 6th July 2001: 'Eminem and Del Boy flog skills on the market'
- By owning the Blue Jays and Sportsnet, considered a smaller sports channel compared with rival TSN, that gives (Rogers) a great platform to showcase their team, which also means that you have a captive audience which you can then flog to advertisers[.] — *Calgary Sun*, p. 45, 7th July 2001

2 to sell, especially illicitly *AUSTRALIA*

- And about using illegal mesh to kill undersized fish to flog to the shops for fish cakes — John O'Grady, *Gone Fishin'*, p. 25, 1962
- They're all past masters at flogging the Australian gimmick[.] — Barry Humphries, *A Nice Night's Entertainment*, p. 73, 1962

3 to steal *AUSTRALIA, 1962*

- I'm sorry I couldn't ring but some arsehole flogged the fucking phone. — Martin Cameron, *A Look at the Bright Side*, 1988
- She legs it to the playground equipment in case I try to flog her flagon. — Glyn Parry, *Mosh*, p. 49, 1996

4 to go with much effort *UK, 1925*

- — John Ayto, *The Oxford Dictionary of Slang*, p. 378, 1998

5 to have sex *BAHAMAS*

- — John A. Holm, *Dictionary of Bahamian English*, p. 78, 1982

6 in drag racing, hot rodding and motor racing, to push the car to its limit or beyond *US*

- — John Edwards, *Auto Dictionary*, p. 62, 1993

▸ **flog a dead horse**

to work hard to little or no purpose *UK, 1872*

- The Republicans rule the roost in the US, while the EU is dominated by the right. This begs the question: are those centre-left leaders who remain flogging a dead horse? — *The Guardian*, 25th April 2003

▸ **flog the bishop**

(of a male) to masturbate *US*

A variation on **BASH THE BISHOP** (to masturbate) using conventional 'flog' (to beat); note the synonymous 'flog your donkey' and 'flog your mutton' were coined at around the same time.

- Spanking the monkey. Flogging the bishop. Choking the chicken. Jerking the gherkin. — *American Beauty*, 1999
- Another way to say "the boy is masturbating" [...] Flogging the bishop[.] — Erica Orloff and JoAnn Baker, *Dirty Little Secrets*, p. 65, 2001

▸ **flog the infidel**

(of a male) to masturbate *US*

Probably a play on 'ity'.

- Another way to say "the boy is masturbating" [...] Flogging the infidel[.] — Erica Orloff and JoAnn Baker, *Dirty Little Secrets*, p. 65, 2001

▸ **flog your chops**

to wear yourself out *AUSTRALIA*

- — Alex Buzo, *Norm and Ahmed*, 1968

▸ **flog your dong**

(used of a male) to masturbate *US*

- Meanwhile, every Tom, Dick and Dick outside is trying to flog my dong. — *Airheads*, 1994

▸ **flog your dummy**

(used of a male) to masturbate *US, 1922*

- [W]hen I left I told him not to flog his damn dummy too much[.] — Jack Kerouac, *The Dharma Bums*, p. 178, 1958
- What if he blabs to the Daily News? ASST HUMAN OPP'Y COMMISH FLOGS DUMMY. — Philip Roth, *Portnoy's Complaint*, p. 197, 1969
- Then he confesses that when he was little he flogged his dummy maybe a thousand times and didn't tell the priest in confession. — Joseph Wambaugh, *Lines and Shadows*, p. 129, 1984

▸ **flog your guts out**

to wear yourself out *UK*

- In fact the pair of them were flogging their guts out for as much as they could have got from National Assistance for the asking. — Derek Bickerton, *Payroll*, p. 29, 1959

flogged *adjective*

drug-intoxicated *US*

- — Vincent J. Monteleone, *Criminal Slang*, p. 89, 1949

flogging *adjective*

damned *AUSTRALIA*

Used as an intensifier. A euphemism for **FUCKING**.

- 'Cripes, this floggin' rain'd make you cry, wouldn't it? Can't the duddy weather office give us a bit of a change?' — D'Arcy Niland, *The Shiralee*, p. 122, 1955

flog off *verb*

to leave *NEW ZEALAND*

- — David McGill, *David McGill's Complete Kiwi Slang Dictionary*, p. 46, 1998

flog on *verb*

to surf the Internet for masturbatory inspiration *NEW ZEALAND, 2002*

Puns 'flog', the root verb of many terms for masturbation, with 'log on', IT jargon for connecting to the Internet.

flo is coming to town

used as a code phrase for the bleed period of the menstrual cycle *US*

- — Amy Sohn, *Sex and the City*, p. 155, 2002

flood *verb*

1 to experience the bleed period of the menstrual cycle, used especially of a heavy flow *US, 1942*

- We always jokingly refer to it as "flooding" and our pads or tampons as "sandbags." — a contributor, *The Museum of Menstruation and Women's Health*, May 2001

2 (used of professional wrestlers) to rush into the ring or arena in large numbers *US*

- All the faces (Pillman, Biff Wlington, Owen Hart, Bruce Hart etc.) flooded the ring and poured champagne over Benoit and Chris did a great victory interview. — *Herb's Wrestling Tidbits*, 20th August 1992

3 to wear trousers that don't reach the shoes *US*

- — *Columbia Missourian*, p. 1A, 19th October 1998

floodgates *noun*

▶ **floodgates open up**

to commence the bleed period of the menstrual cycle *US*

- We always jokingly refer to it as "flooding" and our pads or tampons as "sandbags." The first day, our "floodgates open up". —a contributor, *The Museum of Menstruation and Women's Health*, May 2001

floods *noun*

long trousers that are too short or shorts that are too long *US*

- —Douglas Simonson, *Pidgin to da Max Hana Hou*, 1982
- —Lise Winer, *Dictionary of the English/Creole of Trinidad & Tobago*, 2003

flooey *adverb*

awry *US, 1905*

- Why not go over and help Nelson run the lot? Something's going flooey over there. —John Updike, *Rabbit at Rest*, p. 171, 1990

flookum *noun*

in circus and carnival usage, an artificially flavoured and coloured 'fruit' drink; the syrup used to make the drink *US*

- —Raymond Oliver, *American Speech*, p. 280, December 1966: 'More carnie talk from the west coast
- —Don Wilmeth, *The Language of American Popular Entertainment*, p. 96, 1981

floor *noun*

used as a figurative or notional description of the place where out-of-work workers wait for a job referral at a union hiring hall *US*

- I went to Local 802 to look for work. With the war over, the union floor was crowded with recently discharged GIs, good musicians anxious to reidentify themselves as saxophonists in name bands. —Larry Rivers, *What Did I Do?*, p. 37, 1992

▶ **on the floor**

poor *UK*

Rhyming slang; also serves as a metaphor.

- —Julian Franklyn, *A Dictionary of Rhyming Slang*, 1960
- —Ray Puxley, *Cockney Rabbit*, 1992

▶ **take off the floor**

to remove a prostitute from service in a brothel *US*

- The price for removing a girl from service, "taking her off the floor," as they say, is one hundred fifty bucks. —Gerald Paine, *A Bachelor's Guide to the Brothels of Nevada*, p. 112, 1978

floor *verb*

1 to confound, to puzzle *UK*

- The sequence of non-sequiturs floored me. —*The Guardian*, 14th May 2003

2 to push a vehicle's accelerator to the floorboard *US, 1953*

- But the guy got the Mustang started, jammed it into reverse, and floored it. —Joseph Wambaugh, *Fire Lover*, p. 35, 2002

floor box *noun*

in hot rodding, a car with a manual transmission *US*

- — Fremont Drag Strip, *Guide to Drag Racing*, 1960

floorburners *noun*

shoes *US*

- —David Claerbaut, *Black Jargon in White America*, p. 64, 1972

floor lamp *noun*

a woman actor with good looks but not blessed with acting ability *US*

- —Sherman Louis Sergel, *The Language of Show Biz*, p. 88, 1973

floor liner *noun*

the vagina *UK*

Rhyming slang.

- —Bodmin Dark, *Dirty Cockney Rhyming Slang*, 2003

floor-pop *noun*

in the car sales business, a customer who walks into the showroom *US*

- I got this floor-pop who's looking for a roller but I can't use the OA for the DP on his old sled – I'd take him to the mouse house but he has no sticks. —*San Francisco Chronicle*, p. 2-1, 31st October 1966

floor whore *noun*

an aggressive retail salesperson *US*

- Just above the baitfish are the "floor whores," salespeople who have survived by learning to pounce on the first person who walks in cold, without making an appointment. —Remar Sutton, *Don't Get Taken Every Time*, p. 46, 2001

floor work *noun*

in a strip or sex show, movements made on the floor simulating sexual intercourse, offering strategic and gripping views as the dancer moves her legs *US*

- Meanwhile, back at the strip show, I knew that according to all true Christian standards nudity in itself was certainly not lewd, but burlesque – with its "subtle" charades of grabbing, "floor work," pulling and touching – was lewd. —Lenny Bruce, *How to Talk Dirty and Influence People*, p. 53, 1965
- If strippers choose a face that is shy, it is because they want their "floor work" (crouching or lying on the floor and simulating intercourse) and "dirty work" ("flashing" and spreading their legs) to remind the audience of demure girls. —Marilyn Salutin, *The Sexual Scene*, p. 173, June 1971
- Great girl. Oh, and remember, Nick likes floorwork. —George Paul Csicsery (Editor), *The Sex Industry*, p. 116, 1973
- The five-day Pure Talent School allowed Burana to polish her 'floor work' skills on the dance stage – skills that Burana forthrightly acknowledges she lacked in the early years of her career – and refine her 'pole work. —*Denver Post*, p. E1, 10th October 2001

flooze *noun*

a woman or girl *US, 1952*

- The flooze down in Florida had tired of his mooching and sent him packing northward. —Ben Hamper, *Rivethead*, p. 21, 1991

floozie; floozy; floosie; floosy *noun*

a woman, especially one with few sexual inhibitions; a prostitute *US, 1902*

- [T]hey were all wobbling around the floor with their floozies, so durnk they could hardly stand. —Mezz Mezzrow, *Really the Blues*, p. 183, 1946
- [S]ome say there are at least ten thousand floozies actively in full-time business at this moment. —Jack Lait and Lee Mortimer, *Washington Confidential*, p. 22, 1951
- And do not think that it is the abode, the stomping ground, of only the pimp, sharpie, and floozy set. —John D. McDonald, *The Neon Jungle*, p. 6, 1953
- You floozie. You must've been born with larceny between the legs. —Bernard Wolfe, *The Late Risers*, p. 10-11, 1954
- A woman that wasn't my wife?" I said. "A youthful mistake? A floozy? —Jim Thompson, *The Nothing Man*, p. 183, 1954
- Fraser's cut would have kept him in floozies for a few months at least. —Charles Raven, *Underworld Nights*, p. 76, 1956
- You going with that little Mexican floozy? —Jack Kerouac, *On the Road*, p. 101, 1957
- You poor sap, that old stale floozie would marry ajigaboo if he was making big dough. —Iceberg Slim (Robert Beck), *Death Wish*, p. 213, 1977
- My parents are in an uproar over Paul. He's moved some floozie in with him up in the studio over the garage. —C.D. Payne, *Youth in Revolt*, p. 254, 1993

flop *noun*

1 a place to spend the night *US, 1910*

- [H]e himself is completely conscious not only of the old barbershop and the old B movie and bouncing his tennis ball downtown streets of Denver and the bum flops and poolhalls. —Jack Kerouac, *Letter to Carl Solomon*, p. 329, 27th December 1951
- I decided to grab a bite before I scouted up a flop for the night[.] —Robert Edmond Alter, *Carny Kill*, p. 12, 1966
- [A]nd a regretful return to the monotonous rounds of one-nighter, or at most, bi-monthly, exchange of flops[.] —Neal Cassady, *The First Third*, p. 133, 1971
- I tailspinned down to Tijuana, found a flop and a bottle of drugstore hop, and went prowling for Maggie Cordova. —James Ellroy, *Hollywood Nocturnes*, p. 291, 1994

2 a house or garage where criminals escaping from the scene of a crime can safely hide themselves or store weapons, tools and stolen property, thus leaving their own homes uncompromised *UK*

- —David Powis, *The Signs of Crime*, 1977
- —Angela Devlin, *Prison Patter*, p. 52, 1996

3 a drunk sleeping in public *US, 1949*

- A sleeping lush – known as a "flop" in the trade – attracts a hierarchy of scavengers. —William Burroughs, *Junkie*, p. 43, 1953

4 a complete, dismal failure *US, 1919*

- "Just another flop," he said to nobody in particular. —Robert Sylvester, *No Cover Charge*, p. 74, 1956
- He enjoyed a succession of resounding flops, and each night he came home screaming like a wounded thing. —Max Shulman, *Anyone Got a Match?*, p. 62, 1964
- Clare Short, the international development secretary, reopened the controversy on Thursday night when she dismissed the [Millennium] dome as a "disaster" and a "flop" —*The Guardian*, 23rd September 2000

5 a demotion *US*
- Once the flop is in the record only the heaviest of hooks – the PC or the mayor himself – could ever restore the policeman to his previous eminence. —Leonard Shecter and William Phillips, *On the Pad*, p. 171, 1973

6 the denial of a release on parole by a prison parole board *US, 1944*
- I been to the parole board and they hit me with a year flop. —A.S. Jackson, *Gentleman Pimp*, p. 130, 1973

7 an arrest, conviction and/or imposition of a prison sentence *US, 1904*
- He act like he knows ... That man ever took a flop there people would pass him around, everybody have a piece. —Elmore Leonard, *Stick*, p. 99, 1983

8 in hold 'em poker, the first three cards dealt face-up in the centre of the table *US*
- —Anthony Holden, *Big Deal*, p. 300, 1990

9 in a dice game, a roll of the dice *US*
- —Frank Garcia, *Marked Cards and Loaded Dice*, p. 262, 1962

10 the ear *US*
- —Lou Shelly, *Hepcats Jive Dictionary*, p. 11, 1945

flop *verb*

1 to reside temporarily; to stay overnight *US, 1907*
- We rushed into a phone booth and called the Cumberland Hotel, at 54th and Broadway, where we knew the whole gang was flopping. —Mezz Mezzrow, *Really the Blues*, p. 173, 1946
- You ever flop into some cat's pad? —Evan Hunter, *The Blackboard Jungle*, p. 1954, 1954
- Whenever I and the mob finished with our night's work, I would find me the nearest hole and crawl in it and flop. —Rocky Garciano (with Rowland Barber), *Somebody Up There Likes Me*, p. 68, 1955
- Charlotte, we got no place to flop tonighht. Could you give us a floor? —Darryl Ponicsan, *The Last Detail*, p. 91, 1970
- A nice old guy didn't have a dime and never hurt nobody, gets shot in the back while he's floppin' in a doorway on Seventh Avenue, and you call it a tough break! —Emmett Grogan, *Final Score*, p. 5, 1976
- About a week or so after Bryden and I had been flopping she showed up with a 1,000-dollar check. —Herbert Huncke, *Guilty of Everything*, p. 169, 1990

2 to go to sleep *UK, 1936*
- [W]aiting for householders to flop. —Charles Raven, *Underworld Nights*, p. 68, 1956

3 to fail completely *US, 1900*
- Your plan flopped, boss. —Chester Gould, *Dick Tracy Meets the Night Crawler*, p. 89, 1945
- Whenever they flopped, I sank way down in the dumps. —James T. Farrell, *The Ain't the Men They Used to Be*, p. 81, 1955
- Why Blair's missionary message flopped with African leaders. — *The Observer*, 8th September 2002

4 in police work, to demote in rank or assignment *US*
- — *New York Times*, 15th February 1970
- Serpico was resigned to the fact that he would be transferred back – "flopped," a cop would say – to the uniformed force sooner or later. —Peter Maas, *Serpico*, p. 97, 1973
- The reason it was a mistake is that Martin, who was subsequently flopped out of the bureau for seeking the help of Hugh Mulligan, bookmaker, loan shark, fixer, in getting a Police Department promotion, fell in love with the place. —Leonard Shecter and William Phillips, *On the Pad*, p. 134, 1973
- In those days, one big collar and you were in the Detective Bureau. But now they flop you for nothing. —Edwin Torres, *Q & A*, p. 17, 1977

5 in bar dice games, to shake the dice in the dice cup and then roll them onto a surface *US*
- —Jester Smith, *Games They Play in San Francisco*, p. 104, 1971

flop box *noun*

a hotel room, a bedroom, lodgings *US*

A variation of **FLOP** (a place to sleep).
- — *Complete CB Slang Dictionary*, 1976
- —Peter Chippindale, *The British CB Book*, p. 154, 1981

flophouse *noun*

1 an inexpensive, shoddy, tattered, dirty place to stay, catering to transients *US, 1909*
- He was not living in a flophouse this time – he lived in a Park Avenue hotel at $4.50 per day. —Jack Kerouac, *Letter to Allen Ginsberg*, p. 91, 23rd August 1945
- Sweet dreams, all you flophouse grads. —Mezz Mezzrow, *Really the Blues*, p. 317, 1946
- Sandwiched between them are hockshops and the flophouses where homeless hobos rent a clean bed for two bits[.] —Jack Lait and Lee Mortimer, *New York Confidential*, p. 62, 1948
- They were three noisy blocks, filled with pawn-shops, second-hand stores, pool-rooms, bail-bond brokers, beer joints, sidewalk hamburger stands, flop-houses, oil stations and narrow, messy parking lots[.] —Horace McCoy, *Kiss Tomorrow Good-bye*, p. 177, 1948
- The guy would do anything for a few bucks, no quesitons asked, and the suitcase would be delivered to him at this flophouse he lived in. —Jim Thompson, *After Dark, My Sweet*, p. 103, 1955
- It looked like something that had been dragged out of the storeroom in an Egyptian flophouse. —Tom Robbins, *Another Roadside Attraction*, p. 246, 1971
- No home, twenty-five cents a night in a flophouse. —Bobby Seale, *A Lonely Rage*, p. 295, 1978
- The Buckingham was a ten-story flophouse across from the Dempsy Greyhound station. —Richard Price, *Clockers*, p. 222, 1992
- It's not a flop house. It's basic and simple. That doesn't make it a flop house. —Quentin Tarantino, *From Dusk Till Dawn*, p. 42, 1995
- Fuckin flophouse. We're still short on the rent. — *Kids*, 1995

2 a brakevan (caboose) *US*
- —Ramon Adams, *The Language of the Railroader*, p. 62, 1977

flop joint *noun*

a flophouse *US, 1928*
- But now, thank heaven if you get in a flop joint. —Jack Lait and Lee Mortimer, *New York Confidential*, p. 201–202, 1948
- For example, two of the ladies pick up some joker at a sleazy bar and end up having a threesome in his flop-joint apartment. —Kent Smith et al., *Adult Movies*, p. 180, 1982

flop on *noun*

the penis that has become flaccid when an erection is to be preferred *UK*
- [A]bout ten minutes into it I got a flop on. —Richard Herring, *Talking Cock*, p. 168, 2003

flopper *noun*

1 the arm *US*
- —Lou Shelly, *Hepcats Jive Dictionary*, p. 11, 1945

2 a person who feigns having been struck by a car in hope of collecting insurance payments from the driver *US*
- —Ralph de Sola, *Crime Dictionary*, p. 53, 1982

3 a modified stock car in which the entire fiberglass body lifts from the front to gain access to the engine and driver seat *US*
- —John Edwards, *Auto Dictionary*, p. 62, 1993

flopperoo *noun*

a failure *US, 1931*
- —Lou Shelly, *Hepcats Jive Dictionary*, p. 11, 1945

flopper-stopper *noun*

a brassiere *AUSTRALIA, 1984*

Jocular.

flopping *adjective*

damned *AUSTRALIA*

Used as an intensifier. A euphemism for **FUCKING**.
- 'You can come in,' said Tom, surprisingly, 'but you're not going to cart so much as a dead match outside of this floppin' house.' —Geoff Wyatt, *Saltwater Saints*, p. 48, 1969

floppy *noun*

a black person *SOUTH AFRICA, 1978*

An insulting term that is likely to have been military slang in Rhodesia.

flop sweat *noun*

a panic associated with the possibility of failure, whether or not actual perspiration is involved *US, 1966*
- "Flop sweat," they call it in the theater. Many capable, decent people are so frightened of failure that they won't even try for success. —Harvey Reese, *How to License Your Million Dollar Idea*, p. 183, 2002

floptrips *noun*

in a game of on-line poker, a three-of-a-kind after the flop (the initial deal of three cards)
- — *FHM*, p. 147, June 2003

Florida Hilton *nickname*

the federal prison camp at Eglin Air Force Base, Eglin, Florida *US*
- The place where the Watergate burglars spent much of their time in confinement is a white collar prison dubbed "The Florida Hilton." — *San Francisco Chronicle*, p. 6, 19th March 1974

Florida snow *noun*

cocaine *US*
- From Florida's standing as the major entry point for cocaine into the US. —US Department of Justice, *Street Terms*, August 1994
- —Nick Constable, *This is Cocaine*, p. 181, 2002

floss *noun*

1 cotton candy *US*

The spun sugar is known as 'candy floss' in the UK but not known as such in the US, making what would be a simple UK abbreviated form to be a piece of slang in the US.

- —*American Speech*, p. 308–309, December 1960: 'Carnival talk'
- —Joe McKennon, *Circus Lingo*, p. 35, 1980

2 a thong-backed bikini bottom *US*

- —Trevor Cralle, *The Surfin'ary*, p. 39, 1991

floss *verb*

1 to behave with ostentatious style and flair *US*

- A fear of muhfucka flossin' (mackin' or showing off) too hard.—*Hip-Hop Connection*, p. 22, July 2002

2 to show off *US*

- Just because you have a new car, you don't have to floss.—Connie Eble (Editor), *UNC-CH Campus Slang*, p. 3, Spring 1999

3 to wear expensive clothes and jewels *UK*

Used by urban black youths.

- The Queen is always flossin'.—*Live*, p. 38, Winter 2004

flossie *noun*

a homosexual male *UK*

- Either of those two flossies with you?—Ted Lewis, *Jack Carter's Law*, p. 111, 1974

flossing *adjective*

excellent *US*

- —Connie Eble (Editor), *UNC-CH Campus Slang*, p. 2, Spring 2001

flossy *adjective*

1 in circus and carnival usage, showy *US, 1895*

- —Don Wilmeth, *The Language of American Popular Entertainment*, p. 97, 1981

2 excellent *US*

- —Rick Ayers (Editor), *Berkeley High Slang Dictionary*, p. 21, 2004

flotsam *noun*

new or unskilled surfers in the water *BARBADOS*

- —Gary Fairmont R. Filosa II, *The Surfer's Almanac*, p. 185, 1977

flotty *noun*

a hat that, by the inclusion of a little cork in a zippered pocket, is designed to float *SOUTH AFRICA*

- —*Lonely Planet Southern Africa*, 2000

flounder *noun*

a native of Newfoundland *US*

- —Vincent J. Monteleone, *Criminal Slang*, p. 88, 1949

flounder and dab *noun*

a taxi *UK, 1865*

Rhyming slang for 'taxi-cab'; generally abbreviated to 'flounder'.

- —Peter Laurie, *Scotland Yard*, p. 323, 1970

flour mixer *noun*

1 a Gentile woman *UK*

Rhyming slang for 'shixa' (**SHIKSE**); employed by Jewish Cockneys.

2 a female shop assistant or domestic worker *UK*

A nuance of the rhyming slang for a 'Gentile woman'.

- —David Powis, *The Signs of Crime*, 1977

3 an inoffensive man, especially one who is a clerk *UK*

Extended from the previous senses which are specifically of a woman.

- —David Powis, *The Signs of Crime*, 1977

flow *noun*

1 the style in which a rap artist creates lyrics and/or performs *US*

'Flow' is a verb used to express a quality of conventional poetry.

- All these other females are there trying to flow and everyone can't do it.—*A2Z [quoting Smooth, 1993]*, p. 36, 1995
- —Alex Ogg, *The Hip Hop Years*, p. 209, 1999

2 money *US*

An abbreviation of the conventional 'cash flow'.

- —Pamela Munro, *U.C.L.A. Slang*, p. 65, 1997
- —*Ebony Magazine*, p. 156, August 2000: 'How to talk to the new generation'

flower *noun*

1 a male homosexual *US*

- —Hal Ellson, *Duke*, p. viii, 1949: 'Partial glossary of gang terminology'

2 marijuana *UK, 1998*

- —Mike Haskins, *Drugs*, p. 287, 2003

3 in poker, a hand made up of cards of the same suit *US*

Conventionally known as a 'flush'.

- —George Percy, *The Language of Poker*, p. 36, 1988

flower-bed *verb*

to drive a truck with the right wheels on the hard shoulder of the road, kicking up dust *US*

- —*American Speech*, p. 204, Fall 1969: 'Truck driver's jargon'

flower child *noun*

a participant in a 1960s youth movement promoting peace and love *US, 1967*

Flower children used marijuana (**FLOWER**) and other drugs as an expression of their culture, and distributed ordinary flowers as symbols of their beliefs. In its first usage 'flower children' meant 'marijuana users'; the media adopted the more openly cultivated flowers as the image to sell.

- In London in 1967, every Friday night until dawn, shimmering flower children [...] tripped inside a monstrous basement or queued outside[.]—Richard Neville, *Play Power*, p. 30, 1970

flowered up *adjective*

intoxicated on drugs, especially marijuana, possibly MDMA, the recreational drug best known as ecstasy *UK*

- Flowered up having their video banned by the BBC for being too pro-drug—Harry Shapiro, *Waiting For The Man*, 1999

flower flipping *noun*

MDMA, the recreational drug best known as ecstasy *UK*

- —Mike Haskins, *Drugs*, p. 289, 2003

flower key *noun*

in computing, the comma key on a Macintosh computer *US*

- —Eric S. Raymond, *The New Hacker's Dictionary*, p. 160, 1991

flower patch *noun*

a woman's vulva and pubic hair *US*

- If they get into long skirts, they got a slit up the front almost to the flower patch, and their tits is fallin' out of the tops of their blouses.—Robert Campbell, *In La-La Land We Trust*, p. 180, 1986

flower pot *noun*

1 an inexpensive, poorly made helmet *US*

Biker (motorcyle) usage.

2 a cot *UK*

Rhyming slang.

- —Ray Puxley, *Cockney Rabbit*, 1992

3 in electric line work, a pad-mount transformer *US*

- —A.B. Chance Co., *Lineman's Slang Dictionary*, p. 7, 1980

flower pot *adjective*

hot, especially in the context of a hot (severe) reprimand *UK*

Rhyming slang.

- To "cop a flower pot" is to "cop it hot"[.]—Ray Puxley, *Cockney Rabbit*, 1992

flower power *noun*

the amorphous creed or philosophy of the hippie movement, based on drugs, sex, music, non-violence and a rejection of all things material *US*

- Flower power. The power of love and peace; term and concept were originated in San Francisco.—Ruth Bronsteen, *The Hippy's Handbook*, p. 13, 1967
- Flower Power Sucks!—Frank Zappa, *Absolutely Free*, 1968

flower-power suit *noun*

a camouflaged combat-suit *UK, 1984*

An army term. 'Make love not war' shot through with irony.

flowers; monthly flowers *noun*

the bleed period of the menstrual cycle *UK*

From Latin *fluor* (to flow) via French *fleurs* (flowers); in conventional usage from C15 to mid-C19.

- I've got my flowers.—*The Museum of Menstruation and Women's Health*, April 2002

flowers and frolics *noun*
the testicles *UK*
Rhyming slang for **BOLLOCKS**, recorded as Anglo-Irish.
- —Julian Franklyn, *A Dictionary of Rhyming Slang*, 1960

flower sign *noun*
fresh *flowers* by a hospital patient's bed seen by medical staff as a *sign* that the patient has a supportive family *UK*
- —Adam T. Fox, St Mary's Hospital, London, 10th October 2002

flowers of spring *noun*
used condoms in a sewage system *US*
- In the old days, a Dept. of Public Works veteran tells me, they used to overflow with those rubbery objects euphemistically termed "the flowers of spring," but as he observes, "I guess nobody uses those things any longer." —*San Francisco Chronicle*, p. 23, 19th January 1973

flower tops *noun*
marijuana *US, 1969*
From the most potent part of the plant.
- —Richard A. Spears, *The Slang and Jargon of Drugs and Drink*, p. 199, 1986
- —Mike Haskins, *Drugs*, p. 287, 2003

flowery dell; flowery *noun*
1 a room, lodgings, accommodation *UK*
Rhyming slang for 'cell'.
- —Paul Baker, *Polari*, p. 175, 2002

2 a prison cell *UK, 1925*
Rhyming slang.
- [Y]ou can help P.O. Ferris get a Condemned Flowey Dell ready[.] —Charles Raven, *Underworld Nights*, p. 106, 1956
- —Angela Devlin, *Prison Patter*, p. 52, 1996

flox; floxy *noun*
a homosexual man *UK*
A variation of 'moxy'.
- —*Attitude*, p. 60, July 2003: 'New palare lexicon'

floxen *noun*
a group of homosexual men *UK*
The plural of 'flox', recorded in contemporary gay usage.
- —*Attitude*, p. 60, July 2003: 'New palare lexicon'

flu; 'flu *noun*
influenza *UK, 1839*
A colloquial shortening.
- Jack Urquhart still has the flu[.] —*The Guardian*, 19th November 2002

flub *verb*
to botch *US, 1916*
- Except for the fact that that old fartface flubbed up the name of Li Po by calling him by his Japanese name and all such famous twaddle, he was all right. —Jack Kerouac, *The Dharma Bums*, p. 23, 1958
- —*Dobie Gillis Teenage Slanguage Dictionary*, 1962

▸ **flub the dub**
to masturbate *US, 1922*
- —*American Speech*, p. 238, October 1946: 'World War II slang of maladjustment'

flubadub *noun*
a fool *US, 1975*
From the name of a puppet on the *Howdy Doody Show*.
- [H]ost Gena Davis can't help but be better informed than perennial flubadub Joan Rivers. —*Houston Chronicle*, p. 8, 14th March 1999

flube tube *noun*
a cardboard tube filled with scented cloth that masks the smell of exhaled marijuana smoke *US*
- —Chris Lewis, *The Dictionary of Playground Slang*, p. 216, 2003

flue *noun*
1 a room *US*
- And most of the flues [rooms] around have a open light bulb which hide up nothing from view so he wants the lights turned off. —Christina and Richard Milner, *Black Players*, p. 117, 1972

2 a confidence swindle involving money in an envelope; the envelope used in the swindle *US*
- Ordinarily we used the flue as a short con game on barkeeps and small businessmen in the small towns surrounding the city. —Iceberg Slim (Robert Beck), *Trick Baby*, p. 27, 1969
- —M. Allen Henderson, *How Con Games Work*, p. 220, 1985: 'Glossary'

3 a prison warder *UK*
Rhyming slang for **SCREW** (a prison warder).
- —Angela Devlin, *Prison Patter*, p. 52, 1996

4 the stomach *US*
- I woke up frisky and frolicsome as a two-year-old, lined my flue with some fine chocolate and brioche dished by this gay old lady[.] —Mezz Mezzrow, *Really the Blues*, p. 191-', 1946

fluey *adjective*
characteristic of, or characterised by, influenza *UK*
Reported by Albert Petch, 1969.
- I was pleased to finish [the London Marathon] because I had been feeling fluey all week so I just wanted to get round! —Angellica Bell, *Newsround*, 14th April 2002

fluff *noun*
1 a woman, especially an attractive woman of no further consequence than her sexual availability *UK, 1903*
Usually construed with 'a bit of' or 'a piece of'. Combines the sense as 'pubic hair', with an image of 'fluff' as something of no consequence. Not kind.
- [T]he girl was strictly an Arkansas slick chick, a rife, loose, teenage fluff[.] —Chester Himes, *If He Hollers Let Him Go*, p. 74, 1945
- Until I sat down and looked in the mirror behind the shelves of pie segments, I didn't notice the fluff sitting off to one side at a table. —Mickey Spillane, *My Gun is Quick*, p. 6, 1950
- Also, he hadn't mentioned that he had no job and no prospects and that almost his last dollar had gone into paying the check at The Dancers for a bit of high class fluff[.] —Raymond Chandler, *The Long Goodbye*, p. 5, 1953
- For another, you can't for the life of you recall this excited bit of fluff who seems so delighted to see you again. —Dev Collans with Stewart Sterling, *I was a House Detective*, p. 15, 1954
- What do you think I am? A little bit of fluff? —Alexander Baron, *A Bit of Happiness [Six Granada Plays]*, p. 213, 1959
- Okay, okay, if you guys want to let this fluff get away, it's up to you. —Donald Goines, *Daddy Cool*, p. 155, 1974
- Falling for some little ass-shaker, cute little minldless fluff who probably didn't wear a bra and said "groovy" and "cool" and smoked pot. —Elmore Leonard, *52 Pick-up*, p. 41, 1974
- The wire thing Vicksburg Kid, and his fluff, junoesque Rita, finally showed to break up the cat game. —Iceberg Slim (Robert Beck), *Long White Con*, p. 19, 1977

2 the female pubic hair *UK*
An otherwise obsolete usage that survives in the term **BIT OF FLUFF**.

3 an effeminate lesbian *US*
- But now the fluff, maybe she's been in there three or four days and her habits just coming down on her and she wants to get a little something on. —Bruce Jackson, *In the Life*, p. 118, 1972

4 to a homosexual who practises sado-masochism, a homosexual of simpler tastes *US*
- —Wayne Dynes, *Homolexis*, p. 123, 1985

5 a mistake in the delivery of theatrical lines, also in broadcasting; a minor mistake when playing music *UK, 1891*
Originally 'lines imperfectly learned'.
- —Arnold Shaw, *Dictionary of American Pop/Rock*, p. 130, 1982

6 in the television and film industries, a flubbed line of dialogue *UK*
- —Oswald Skilbeck, *ABC of Film and TV Working Terms*, p. 56, 1960

fluff *verb*
1 to perform oral sex on a male pornography performer who is about to be filmed so that he will enter the scene with a full erection *US*
- Even though the term "fluffing" is used a lot on the set, I have never actually been on a shoot where someone was paid for this service. —Stephen Ziplow, *The Film Maker's Guide to Pornography*, p. 85, 1977
- They want help, they want fluffing. Hey, I'm sorry but I don't get off on getting a guy ready to go. —Anthony Petkovich, *The X Factory*, p. 99, 1997
- The Houston 500 gang bang actually produced a spinoff video entitled The Fluff Girls of the Houston 500 – so maybe "fluffing" is coming back. —Ana Loria, *1 2 3 Be A Porn Star!*, p. 31, 2000

2 to make a mistake in a theatrical performance, such as by mispronouncing or muddling words; likewise in broadcasting; also in musical performance, by playing the wrong note, etc *UK, 1884*
- She was fluffing her lines – something unimaginable in her days of health[.] —*The Guardian*, 18th December 1999

3 to fart *NEW ZEALAND, 1944*
Juvenile origins in New Zealand schoolboy 'fluffing contests' and US 'laying a fluffy'. Possibly from UK dialect *fluff* (a slight explosion), or 'fluff' (a mistake). UK usage is nursery and childish.
- —Peter Furze, *Tailwinds*, p. 87, 1998
- —Harry Orsman, *A Dictionary of Modern New Zealand Slang*, p. 51, 1999

4 to ignore; to discard *US, 1959*
- —Robert S. Gold, *A Jazz Lexicon*, p. 110, 1964

5 to fail (an examination) *US*
- —*American Speech*, p. 303, December 1955: 'Wayne University slang'

fluff and buff *noun*
a fluff-dried battle dress utility uniform with buff-polished boots, the standard uniform of the US Airborne *US*
- —Hans Halberstadt, *Airborne*, p. 130, 1988: 'Abridged dictionary of airborne terms'
- —Linda Reinberg, *In the Field*, p. 84, 1991

fluffed *adjective*
1 drunk *UK*
From the theatrical FLUFF (to slip, to make an error) and obsolete 'fluffer' (a drunk, an actor who is likely to forget lines).

2 cocaine-intoxicated *UK*
A new use for the previous sense.
- James hoovered his line [of cocaine] in one, languorous draught and exhaled with satisfaction. "Ah! Very nice. Mmmm. Consider me suitably fluffed."—Kevin Sampson, *Powder*, p. 87, 1999

fluffer *noun*
in the making of a pornographic film, a person employed to bring the on-camera male performers to a state of sexual readiness *US*
Extension of the conventional sense of 'fluff' (to make fuller or plumper).
- A fluffer is a girl who is hired to play with the men while they're off-camera so that they can keep their erections and stay in a state of readiness.—Stephen Ziplow, *The Film Maker's Guide to Pornography*, p. 85, 1977
- "No fluffers," screamed someone – the rule sheet strictly forbade it.—Josh Alan Friedman, *Tales of Times Square*, p. 94, 1986
- Fluffers are off-screen technicians whose job it is to make sure that the male stars remain at full stretch.—Kitty Churchill, *Thinking of England*, p. 164, 1995
- Older lingo referring to the days when an extra babe was hired just to be the FLUFFER. She gave blow jobs to male actors to keep them up during transitions in sex scenes[.]—*Adult Video News*, p. 48, August 1995
- At the end of these two lines are fluffers who suck off the bum steers, makin' 'em hard for Jasmin (at least that's the theory).—Anthony Petkovich, *The X Factory*, p. 189, 1997
- "Fluffers," or young women who offer fellatio to the male talent to prepare them for a sex scene, are mainly a thing of the past.—Ana Loria, *1 2 3 Be A Porn Star!*, p. 31, 2000
- All porn movie sets have a "fluffer" – a girl who administers oral sex to the actors between shots to keep them standing to attention.—*Sky Magazine*, p. 88, July 2001

fluff girl *noun*
a fluffer *US*
- In the old days, you used to have fluff girls on the set who kept the guys worked up in between.—Robert Stoller and I.S. Levine, *Coming Attractions*, p. 55, 1991

fluffie; fluffy *noun*
an anti-globalisation activist with a belief in peaceful protest *UK*
- —*The Guardian*, 14th April 2001: 'Fluffies on the run as spikies win battle of the streets'

fluff off *verb*
1 to dismiss, to reject *US, 1944*
- But the old man is dead now and his son fluffed me off.—Babs Gonzales, *Movin' On Down De Line*, p. 132, 1975

2 to evade work or duty *US, 1962*
- If you persist in thinking about fluffing off, I'll come over there and pinch a nerve that will electrify you with pain.—Odie Hawkins, *Lost Angeles*, p. 16, 1994

fluff stuff; fluffy stuff *noun*
snow *US*
- —*Complete CB Slang Dictionary*, 1976
- —Peter Chippindale, *The British CB Book*, p. 154, 1981

fluffy *adjective*
1 light-hearted, non-serious *UK*
- Norman wants to know what kind of audience it is – heavy or fluffy? —Dave Haslam, *Adventures of the Wheels of Steel*, p. 98, 2001

2 in the theatre, unsure of your lines *UK*
- —William Granville, *A Dictionary of Theatrical Terms*, p. 78, 1952

fluid *noun*
whisky *US, 1843*
- —James T. Farrell, *Saturday Night*, 1947
- "Say, have you boys any fluid? Another drink and I'll be just rarin' to go, and any mother's sonofabtich can just try and get tough with me," Red Murphy said.—James T. Farrell, *Saturday Night*, p. 38, 1947

fluids and electrolytes conference *noun*
used in a hospital as humorous code for a drinking party to be held on hospital grounds *US*
- —*Maledicta*, p. 33, 1988–1989: 'Medical maledicta from San Francisco'

fluke *noun*
a stroke of luck, an accident *UK, 1857*
In the game of billiards, a 'fluke' is a 'lucky shot'.
- Turns out it was a dead fluke me getting nicked [arrested] the way I did.—John Peter Jones, *Feather Pluckers*, p. 57, 1964
- [T]he fluke of memory: which bits I remember. Flukes.—Mike Stott, *Soldiers Talking, Cleanly*, 1978
- —Keith Foley, *A Dictionary of Cricketing Terminology*, p. 142, 1998

fluke *verb*
to do a thing well by accident *UK, 1860*
- Roger takes over and flukes a yellow in off the black[.]—Niall Griffiths, *Sheepshagger*, p. 165, 2001
- Celtic [football club] fluked it[.]—*The Observer*, 18th May 2003

fluked out *adjective*
drug-intoxicated *US*
- You're real fluked out, Dinch; take it easy, be cool.—George Mandel, *Flee the Angry Strangers*, p. 131, 1952

fluke out *verb*
to become drug-intoxicated *US*
- Then she slides off the bed, her big body toppling over sideways. She has fluked out.—Willard Motley, *Let No Man Write My Epitaph*, p. 160, 1958

fluking iron *noun*
in fencing, an épée *UK*
A derisory term, suggesting that FLUKE (luck) rather than skill is required when engaging with such weapons.
- —E.D. Morton, *Martini A-Z of Fencing*, 1988

fluky; flukey *adjective*
more by luck than design *AUSTRALIA, 1867*
- Change things a bit and life would never have happened. This looks suspiciously flukey, but it can be readily explained by the multi-verse.—*The Guardian*, 23rd September 2003

flummox *verb*
to perplex, to confuse *US, 1834*
- [H]e half forgot the words to "It's So Easy" but was the cunt flummoxed? Was he fuck.—Kevin Sampson, *Clubland*, p. 198, 2002
- The British flummox other nationalities with a self-effacing vocabulary and a tendency for false modesty[.]—*The Guardian*, 31st March 2003

flummy dumm *noun*
in Newfoundland, a hunters' and trappers' bread *CANADA*
- "Flummy dumm" is a quick trappers' bread, cooked either on a stick or around the stovepipe; hence it is also known as funnel bun, funnel cake, or stove cake.—Bill Casselman, *Canadian Food Words*, p. 40–41, 1988

flunk *noun*
a locked and fortified compartment within a safe *US, 1928*
- —Hyman E. Goldin et al., *Dictionary of American Underworld Lingo*, p. 72, 1950

flunk *verb*
to completely and irrevocably fail an examination *US, 1837*
- Rats given a synthetic cannabinoid – an active component of marijuana – flunked the test.—*The Guardian*, 12th June 2003
- Derrick Turnbow became the first major leaguer publicly identified as testing positive for a banned steroid when he flunked a drug test during a U.S. Olympic training camp.—*San Francisco Chronicle*, 6th January 2004

flunkey and lackey *noun*
a Pakistani; any Asian or Afro-Asian immigrant; loosely, any native of the Indian subcontinent *UK*
Rhyming slang for PAKI.
- —Ray Puxley, *Cockney Rabbit*, 1992

flunk out *verb*
to leave an educational establishment as a result of failing your examinations *US, 1920*
- They are 17, 18, 19 years old: rich, aimless, white boys and girls who have flunked out of high school with nothing to do all day but hang out at the mall[.]—*The Guardian*, 1st March 2002

flunky *noun*

a person assigned to assist, to perform menial jobs *UK, 1855*
In the US, originally a work camp waiter or assistant cook, and usually not quite as harsh as Partridge's 'parasite' or 'toady'.
- [A]ll I could do around his people was to be a flunkey and get kicked in the mouth. —Chester Himes, *If He Hollers Let Him Go*, p. 89, 1945
- The flunky recognized my voice from last night and was a little more polite. —Mickey Spillane, *One Lonely Night*, p. 72, 1951
- The flunkies (waiters) rushed more food to the table, refills of the original dishes. —Jim Thompson, *Bad Boy*, p. 392, 1953
- One stud got juiced and played the flunky, to a very surprised old Brazilian monkey. —Dan Burley, *Diggeth Thou?*, p. 17, 1959
- I had two or three flunkies after I'd been there for a month. —Claude Brown, *Manchild in the Promised Land*, p. 144, 1965
- A West Indian messman – Issac was his name – had told me never to take shit from anybody on board or I'd become a flunky. —Piri Thomas, *Down These Mean Streets*, p. 191, 1967
- He was saying that the administration man he was working with was a "kirk too, or flunky, or whatever." —James Simon Kunen, *The Strawberry Statement*, p. 140, 1968

flunky *verb*

to work as a low-level assistant *US*
- All he did now was drink cheap wine and flunky for anyone who'd give a dime to help him along toward the forty-nine cents it cost to buy a pint. —Nathan Heard, *Howard Street*, p. 50, 1968
- Twenty years ago he hung out and flunkied in the joints around Thirty-Ninth and Cottage Grove. —Iceberg Slim (Robert Beck), *Trick Baby*, p. 42, 1969

flurry *noun*

a flourish *BARBADOS*
- —Frank A. Collymore, *Barbadian Dialect*, p. 50, 1965

flush *verb*

1 to draw blood back into a syringe *UK*
Drug users' term.
- —Home Office, *Glossary of Terms and Slang Common in Penal Establishments*, July 1978

2 to leave work *US*
- —Eric S. Raymond, *The New Hacker's Dictionary*, p. 160, 1991

3 to fail (a test or course) *US, 1964*
- —*Time*, p. 57, 1st January 1965: 'Students: the slang bag'

▸ **flush the john**

in a casino, to play slot machines *US, 1979*
- —Thomas L. Clark, *The Dictionary of Gambling and Gaming*, p. 82, 1987

flush *adjective*

having plenty of money, especially as an exception to the rule *UK, 1603*
- [T]he various ticket prices are displayed slightly more clearly, and if you're feeling flush, the first class fares are shown too. —*The Guardian*, 11th May 2002

flush bucket *noun*

in motor racing, a carburettor that feeds the engine more of the air/fuel mixture than it can use *US*
- —John Edwards, *Auto Dictionary*, p. 62, 1993

flute *noun*

1 the penis *UK, 1671*
Plays on the shape, informed by oral sex. Variations include 'flesh flute', 'living flute', **ONE-HOLED FLUTE**, **SILENT FLUTE**, **SKIN FLUTE**; also **PINK OBOE**; the sense compares with Romany *haboia* (a hautboy, an early oboe). In the *Dictionary of Shakespeare's Sexual Puns and Their Significance*, 1984, Frankie Rubinstein discovers examples in *A Midsummer Night's Dream*, 1600 (or earlier) and *Anthony and Cleopatra*,1606–7, of Shakespeare punning on 'flute' as 'penis'. In more general usage in the C18.

2 a soda bottle filled with alcoholic drink *US, 1971*
- Patrolman Phillips testified that it was not uncommon for policemen assigned to a radio car to pick up a "flute" – a Coke bottle filled with liquor – which they would deliver to the station house. —*The Knapp Commission Report on Police Corruption*, p. 172, 1972
- It was responsible for bringing sandwiches and beer to the station house's administrative and clerical personnel, and "flutes" – Coca-Cola bottles filled with liquor supplied by bars in the precinct – to the lieutenants and sergeants. —Peter Maas, *Serpico*, p. 60, 1973
- Cop calls the station house and the sergeant says, pickup a flute for the lieutenant. —Leonard Shecter and William Phillips, *On the Pad*, p. 94, 1973
- Hanrahan would send a patrolman out to a nearby bar for what he called a "flute" – a Coke bottle filled with gin. —Vincent Patrick, *The Pope of Greenwich Village*, p. 114, 1979

3 a car radio *NEW ZEALAND*
From the language of car sales.
- —David McGill, *David McGill's Complete Kiwi Slang Dictionary*, p. 49, 1998

flute around *verb*

to waste time, to be unresolved in action *IRELAND*
- Are yiz [you] getting out or what? I've a bleedin living to make. Stop fluting around and tell me where yiz are wanting to go. —Paul Howard, *The Joy*, p. 140, 1996

flute player *noun*

a person who performs oral sex on a man *US, 1916*
- —*Maledicta*, p. 231, 1979: 'Kinks and queens: linguistic and cultural aspects of the terminology for gays'

fluter *noun*

a male homosexual *US*
- —Joseph E. Ragen and Charles Finston, *Inside the World's Toughest Prison*, p. 799, 1962: 'Penitentiary and underworld glossary'
- —*Maledicta*, p. 16, Summer 1977: 'A word for it!'

fluthered *adjective*

completely drunk *IRELAND*
- Georgie. . . 'if Wexford don't win that match on Sunday I'll be fluthered drunk comin' home on that bus. —Roche Billy, *Poor Beast in the Rain*, p. 73, 1992
- Come on, I'll get you home. You're fluthered. —Eamonn Sweeney, *Waiting for the Healer*, p. 296, 1997

flutter *noun*

a small bet *UK, 1874*
Originally meant 'a good try'.
- Around 70 per cent of adults in Britain like a flutter and some twenty million do the pools[.] —John McCririck, *John McCririck's World of Betting*, p. 26, 1991

flutter bum *noun*

a good-looking and popular boy *US*
Teen slang.
- —*American Weekly*, p. 2, 14th August 1955

flutter-finger *noun*

in the usage of youthful model road racers (slot car racers), a person who fluctuates speed constantly *US*
- —Phantom Surfers, *The Exciting Sounds of Model Road Racing (Album cover)*, 1997

fly *noun*

an attempt; a try *AUSTRALIA, 1915*
Usually in the phrase 'give something a fly'.
- Oh well, no harm in giving it a fly. —Wilda Moxham, *The Apprentice*, p. 29, 1969
- —Jim Ramsay, *Cop It Sweet!*, p. 36, 1977

▸ **on the fly**

on the railways, said of a moving train that is boarded *US*
- —Ramon Adams, *The Language of the Railroader*, p. 104, 1977
- We waited till they linked up the various cars and gave the highball and then we caught it on the fly. —Herbert Huncke, *Guilty of Everything*, p. 39, 1990

fly *verb*

1 to act cautiously *US*
- —Miss Cone, *The Slang Dictionary (Hawthorne High School)*, 1965

2 to sneak a look *JAMAICA*
- —Peter L. Patrick, *Some Recent Jamaican Creole Words*, 2003

▸ **be flying it**

to do extremely well, to make great progress *IRELAND*
Used in the present participle only.
- I heard you're flying it beyond. —Eamonn Sweeney, *Waiting for the Healer*, p. 60, 1997

▸ **fly a desk**

of an aircraft pilot, to work in air traffic administration *UK*
Originally military.
- —Paul Brickhill, *The Dambusters*, 1951
- He watched the world rush toward him, blue and green and beautiful. The hell with it, he thought. Flying a desk would never be like this. —Nora Roberts, *Time and Again*, 2001

▸ **fly aeroplane**

to stand up *SINGAPORE*
- —Paik Choo, *The Coxford Singlish Dictionary*, p. 37, 2002

▸ fly a kite
1 to tentatively reveal an idea as a test of public opinion *UK, 1937*
2 to pass a worthless cheque *UK, 1927*
3 in prison, to write a letter; especially to smuggle correspondence in or out of prison *US, 1960*

▸ fly by the seat of your pants
to attempt any unfamiliar task and improve as you continue *UK, 1960*
From aircraft pilots' original use as 'to fly by instinct'.
- People think I'm a bit sharp and that I'm flying by the seat of my pants. — *The Observer*, 24th August 2003

▸ fly in ever decreasing circles until he disappears up his own asshole
(among Canadian military personnel) to exhibit much ineffective activity while being anxious *CANADA*
- "To fly in ever-decreasing circles until [one] disappears up his own asshole", in the Canadian Forces, describes a person who is overcome with indecision and worry but who expresses it through unfocussed, though vigorous, activity. — Tom Langeste, *Words on the Wing*, p. 106, 1995

▸ flying low
to have one's trouser fly unbuttoned or unzipped *CANADA*
- "Flying low": a verbal signal to someone that his fly is down. — Tom Parkin, *WetCoast Words*, p. 55, 1989

▸ fly light
to work through a meal break *US*
- — Norman Carlisle, *The Modern Wonder Book of Trains and Railroading*, p. 263, 1946

▸ fly low
1 to drive (a truck) at a very high speed *US*
- — Montie Tak, *Truck Talk*, p. 62, 1971

2 to act cautiously *US*
- — Miss Cone, *The Slang Dictionary (Hawthorne High School)*, 1965

▸ fly Mexican Airlines; fly Mexican Airways
to smoke marijuana and experience euphoric effects *US, 1972*
FLYING (experiencing the effects of drugs) plus Mexico which has long been considered a major source of fine quality cannabis such as **ACAPULCO GOLD**.
- — Richard A. Spears, *The Slang and Jargon of Drugs and Drink*, p. 201, 1986
- — Mike Haskins, *Drugs*, p. 290, 2003

▸ fly off the handle
to lose your temper; to lose self-control *US, 1843*
- Anthony Eden [...] flew off the handle on hearing of Nasser's takeover at Suez. — *The Guardian*, 15th February 2003

▸ fly right
to behave in a manner appropriate to the situation *US*
- — Inez Cardozo-Freeman, *The Joint*, p. 467, 1984

▸ fly the bean flag
to be experiencing the bleed period of the menstrual cycle *US, 1954*
- — J. E. Lighter, *Historical Dictionary of American Slang, Volume 1*, p. 113, 1994

▸ fly the flag
to appeal a conviction in hope of a reduced sentence *AUSTRALIA*
- — *(Sydney) Bulletin*, 26th April 1975

▸ fly the kite
to defraud, to cheat, especially by passing a fraudulent cheque or by obtaining and dishonouring a credit arrangement *UK*
- "They all knock me," says Tony. "knocking" is the same as "flying the kite," meaning spinning the credit line out and out. — Tom Wolfe, *The Pump House Gang*, p. 199, 1968

▸ fly the mail
to drive (a truck) very fast *US*
- — *American Speech*, p. 273, December 1961: 'Northwest truck drivers' language'

▸ fly the red flag
to experience the bleed period of the menstrual cycle *US*
- — *American Speech*, p. 298, December 1954: 'The vernacular of menstruation'
- — Collin Baker et al., *College Undergraduate Slang Study Conducted at Brown University*, p. 119, 1968

▸ fly the rod
to gesture with the middle finger, roughly conveying 'fuck you!' *US*
- — Collin Baker et al., *College Undergraduate Slang Study Conducted at Brown University*, p. 119, 1968

▸ flying without a licence
of a male, having an undone trouser fly *UK, 1977*
Generally juvenile.

fly *adjective*
1 good, pleasing, fashionable *US, 1879*
A term which has enjoyed three bursts of popularity – in the swing jazz era of the late 1930s, the emergence of black exploitation films in the early 1970s and with the explosion of hip-hop culture in the 1980s.
- — Lou Shelly, *Hepcats Jive Talk Dictionary*, p. 24, 1945
- In fact, the smooth, know-it-all act I put on was so strong that a lot of the girls took me for a bigtime pimp. Marcelle must have figured me for a fly cat goo, and her curiousity was aroused. — Mezz Mezzrow, *Really the Blues*, p. 23, 1946
- They were something fly – suede with the wet look on top of suede and heels. — Susan Hall, *Gentleman of Leisure*, p. 49, 1972
- I'm runnin' round with these fly broads from 111th Street and Fifth Avenue. — Edwin Torres, *Carlito's Way*, p. 11, 1975
- And his fabulous sky was broke so fly / That the city had it banned. — Dennis Wepman et al., *The Life*, p. 48, 1976
- — Connie Eble (Editor), *UNC-CH Campus Slang*, p. 3, Fall 1984
- This is some fly shit, huh? Like some James Cagney, George Raft-type shit. — *New Jack City*, 1990
- I remember when attractive women were simply "fly" and great records were "da joint." — Nelson George, *Hip Hop America*, p. 209, 1998
- But whatever I'm wearing, I like to be looking fly. — *Style*, p. 96, July 2001

2 cunning, devious; artful, knowing *UK*
From Scottish dialect *fly* (sly; smart).

3 cunningly discreet *UK*
A slight variation of the previous sense.
- He'd be off to the storeroom for a refill and a fly fag [cigarette], or maybe just a wank if he was out of snout. — Christopher Brookmyre, *Boiling a Frog*, p. 341, 2000

4 in the youth trend for 'souped-up' motor-scootering, daring, dangerous, clever *UK*
- The boy looks over his shoulder to see if his mates – four other boys on bikes – are following, but more importantly, to check they saw his "fly" manoeuvres. — *The Independent Magazine*, p. 17, 28th August 2004

5 aware of what is going on; wise to criminal ways *AUSTRALIA, 1882*
- FLY – Wide awake; smart. — Gilbert H. Lawson, *A Dictionary of Australian Words and Terms*, 1924
- Come on. You're not too fly not to know what they are. — John Wynnum, *Tar Dust*, p. 18, 1962
- [W]hen the gang attempted to inveigle the black down to the 'pub', they saw that he was too fly for them. — Bill Wannan, *Folklore of the Australian Pub*, p. 41, 1972

6 unreliable; dishonest *TRINIDAD AND TOBAGO*
- — Lise Winer, *Dictionary of the English/Creole of Trinidad & Tobago*, 2003

flybait *noun*
1 an unattractive girl *US*
- "She's not my type." "Me neither. To me, she's flybait." — Haenigsen, *Jive's Like That*, 1947

2 a corpse *US*
- — Jay Robert Nash, *Dicitonary of Crime*, p. 134, 1992

fly baker; fly bravo *verb*
to experience the bleed period of the menstrual cycle *US*
In the phonetic alphabet from 1941 – 56 'baker' was given for 'B', from 1956 to date 'bravo' is used; in naval signalling to fly the flag representing 'B' means 'I am taking on, carrying or discharging dangerous goods'; a large red flag is flown.
- — Karen Houppert, *The Curse*, 1999
- — *The Museum of Menstruation and Women's Health*, May 2001

fly ball *noun*
in handball, a shot played off the front wall before it hits the ground *US*
- — Paul Haber, *Inside Handball*, p. 65, 1970: 'Glossary'

fly beer *noun*
in the Maritime Provinces, beer of potatoes and hop yeast, and molasses or sugar and water *CANADA*
- There was the Widow Whinney, she sold ale and cockaninny / She sold whiskey, gin and fly-beer[.] — Alan Mills, *Songs of the Maritimes*, p. 5/1, 1959

fly-blown *adjective*
broke; penniless *AUSTRALIA, 1853*

- And what is that that I hear? You follow the girls? What? Gossip Angelo, you, the fair, the flyblown, following the girls! — Eve Langley, *The Pea-Pickers*, 1958
- — Jim Ramsay, *Cop It Sweet!*, p. 36, 1977
- The fly-blown tramps Nor'-West of Bourke To stations far Out Back[.] — Keith Garvey, *Absolutely Australian*, p. 22, 1979
- — David McGill, *David McGill's Complete Kiwi Slang Dictionary*, p. 50, 1998

flybog *noun*

jam *AUSTRALIA, 1920*

- — Jim Ramsay, *Cop It Sweet!*, p. 36, 1977

flyboy *noun*

1 a military aviator *US, 1937*

- — *American Speech*, February 1951
- The flyboys're apeshit. — William Wilson, *The LBJ Brigade*, p. 77, 1966
- From an elevation of 200 feet or so, and in a gray overcast, a helicopter came buzzing back and forth. Stokely Carmichael of Snick had quipped over the microphone, "CIA's flyboys." — Sidney Bernard, *This Way to the Apocalypse*, p. 33, 1967
- Them goddamn Navy fly-boys always thought they were hot shit, but the surface Navy is the Navy. — Jimmy Buffett, *Tales from Margaritaville*, p. 132, 1989

2 in drag racing, a hobbyist who confines their passion to weekend racing *US*

Punning on the 1940s 'aviator' sense of the term.

- — John Lawlor, *How to Talk Car*, p. 46, 1965
- — Lyle K. Engel, *The Complete Book of Fuel and Gas Dragsters*, p. 151, 1968

fly-by *noun*

a missile that misses its target and does no damage *US*

- A seventh Scud was what battalion commander Lt. Col Leroy Neel called a "flyby," falling harmlessly into the Pesian Gulf. — *Missourian*, p. 5A, 22nd January 1991

fly-by-night *noun*

a person who is drunk *UK*

Rhyming slang for **TIGHT** (tipsy).

- — Ray Puxley, *Cockney Rabbit*, 1992

fly-by-night *adjective*

unreliable; likely to disappear *US, 1914*

- They was a fly-by-night bunch, I think. — Mickey Spillane, *My Gun is Quick*, p. 138, 1950

fly-by-nights; fly-be's *noun*

tights *UK*

- She then took off her fly-be's / And dropped her early doors [drawers]. — Ronnie Barker, *Fletcher's Book of Rhyming Slang*, p. 22, 1979

fly cemetery *noun*

a currant pudding *UK*

- — *New Society*, 22nd August 1963

fly chick *noun*

an attractive woman *US*

- — Lou Shelly, *Hepcats Jive Talk Dictionary*, p. 24, 1945

flyer *noun*

1 a chance, a gamble, a risk *US*

Originally a financial speculation. Also spelt 'flier'.

- I could've just took a flyer and that, could've done a runner and hoped for the best. — Kevin Sampson, *Outlaws*, p. 256, 2001

2 a conversational line used to start conversation when seeking a sexual encounter *US*

- Flyers – opening statements; ice-breakers used when cruising. — Bruce Rodgers, *The Queens' Vernacular*, p. 83, 1972

3 a person who threatens to or has jumped to his death *US*

- — *Maledicta*, p. 180, Summer/Winter 1986–1987: 'Sexual slang: prostitutes, pedophiles, flagellators, transvestites, and necrophiles'

fly-fishing position *noun*

in fencing, an unconventional guard position used by some épéeists *UK*

From the image of a fisherman casting.

- — E.D. Morton, *Martini A-Z of Fencing*, 1988

fly-fly boy *noun*

a military aviator *US, 1949*

- When my Army unit went to Vietnam in 1966, the Navy took us there in a troop ship and kept our supplies coming. When our bases came under attack, the"fly-fly boys" of the Air Force lent their support. — *Richmond (Virginia) Times Dispatch*, p. A16, 13th June 2002

fly gee *noun*

in circus and carnival usage, a clever, sarcastic, sophisticated man with a flexible approach to the truth *US*

- — Don Wilmeth, *The Language of American Popular Entertainment*, p. 97, 1981

fly girl *noun*

an attractive, sexually alluring young woman *US*

- — Connie Eble (Editor), *UNC-CH Campus Slang*, p. 4, Fall 1986
- — Ellen C. Bellone (Editor), *Dictionary of Slang*, p. 10, 1989
- I see they are mini flygirls with skin like a dark pony's velvetness. — Francesca Lia Block, *Missing Angel Juan*, p. 303, 1993
- In the ad for this line two fly girls are sitting in a hot tub talking on the phone. — Anka Radakovich, *The Wild Girls Club*, p. 56, 1994

fly-in *noun*

an extravagent party for homosexual men in which men fly in to the party from all parts of the country *US*

- The realtor nodded. "We did a fly-in togther once. Gamma Mu." He tossed out the name like bait, Michael noticed, as if everyone had heard of the national gay millionaires' fraternity. — Armistead Maupin, *Further Tales of the City*, p. 7, 1982

flying *adjective*

1 experiencing the euphoric or mind-altering effects of a drug *US, 1942*

A shortened form of 'flying high' or 'flying in the clouds'.

- — Richard A. Spears, *The Slang and Jargon of Drugs and Drink*, p. 200, 1986
- — Angela Devlin, *Prison Patter*, p. 52, 1996
- — Mike Haskins, *Drugs*, p. 291, 2003

2 making great progress, doing exceedingly well *IRELAND*

- They leaned right over to me and in a soft top secret voice said how's your mother Francie? Oh I says she's flying… — Patrick McCabe, *The Butcher Boy*, p. 14, 1992

3 in poker, full, as in a full house *US*

- — Albert H. Morehead, *The Complete Guide to Winning Poker*, p. 263, 1967

flying a *noun*

an extremely obnoxious person *US*

The 'a' is usually understood as **ASSHOLE**.

- — Collin Baker et al., *College Undergraduate Slang Study Conducted at Brown University*, p. 120, 1968

flying arse *noun*

nothing at all, the very least amount *UK*

A variation of **FLYING FUCK**.

- The majority of celebrities that go to these parties don't give a flying arse about the music. — *Mixmag*, p. 36, February 2002

flying banana *nickname*

1 a military transport helicopter, especially the Piasecki HRP *US, 1950*

- In August, HMX-1 receivd the Piasecki HRP-i. Nicknamed the "Flying Banana" due to its shape, the twin-rotor aircraft had a payload of 900 pounds at a speed of 100 miles per hour. — Jon T. Hoffman, *USMC*, p. 428, 2002

2 an H-21 helicopter *US, 1957*

Vietnam war usage with variant 'banana'.

- "I see banana smoke" the AC radios and the bird banks slightly left dropping quickly then levels and aims for the LZ. — John M. Del Vecchio, *The 13th Valley*, p. 632, 1982
- The helicopter the Army had sent to Vietnam, the H-21 Shawnee, was an ungainly-looking machine of Korean War vintage, shaped like a fat bent pipe with large rotors fore and aft and appropriately named the Flying Banana by its crew. — Neil Sheehan, *A Bright Shining Lie*, p. 74, 1988

flying boxcar *nickname*

a transport aircraft, especially a C-119 *US, 1918*

- Santa Claus headed north driving a sleigh, in the shape of a C-119 Flying Boxcar, from 435 (Transport) Squadron at Namao, Alberta. — *Arctic Spotter*, p. 4, January 1958
- — Linda Reinberg, *In the Field*, p. 84, 1991

flying brick *noun*

any heavy aircraft that is difficult to control *US, 1944*

- The pilots called it the "flying brick" – heavy, with no engines, gliding in on delta-wing slivers. — Tess Gerritsen, *Gravity*, p. 195, 1999

flying brickyard *nickname*

the Orbiter Space Shuttle *US*

A derisory reference to the 34,000 heat resistant tiles designed to protect the craft during re-entry to the earth's atmosphere;

construction began in 1975, and the first mission was flown in 1983.

- —John Horton, *The Grub Street Dictionary of International Aircraft Nicknames*, p. 23, 1994

flying carpet *noun*
a livery taxi *US*
New York police slang; an allusion to the large number of immigrant drivers.

- —Samuel M. Katz, *Anytime Anywhere*, p. 388, 1997: 'The extremely unofficial and completely off-the-record NYPD/ESU truck-two glossary''

flying coffin *noun*
any dangerous aircraft, such as a glider used by paratroopers *US, 1918*
A reference to the gliders' vulnerability to artillery.

- —*American Speech*, p. 310, December 1946: 'More air force slang'

flying douche *noun*
▸ **take a flying douche**
used as an intense expression of 'go to hell' *US*

- How can a guy stand aside twiddling his planagos, and watch his bosom buddy take a flying douche?—John Nichols, *The Sterile Cuckoo*, p. 88, 1965

flying duck
used for all senses of 'fuck' *UK*
Rhyming slang.

- —Ray Puxley, *Cockney Rabbit*, 1992

flying Dutchman *noun*
a drug dealer *US*

- —Jay Robert Nash, *Dicitonary of Crime*, p. 136, 1992

Flying Edsel *nickname*
▹ see: EDSEL

flying firetruck *noun*
nothing, the very least amount *UK*
A barely euphemistic variation of FLYING FUCK.

- I couldn't give a flying firetruck about your reputation.—*Redcap*, 7th January 2003

flying flapjack *nickname*
the XF5 U-1 experimental military hovering aircraft *US, 1973*

- [T]he United States Navy was working on its own version: a prop-driven, circular machine, the XF5U-1, otherwise known as the "flying flapjack."—Curt Sutherly, *UFO Mysteries*, p. 4, 2001

flying fox *noun*
a device for crossing or transporting goods across rivers, ravines, or the like *AUSTRALIA, 1901*

- The platoon commander will take you down the river where you will do river crossings on various flying foxes.—Martin Cameron, *A Look at the Bright Side*, 1988

flying fuck *noun*
nothing at all, the very least amount *US, 1946*
Usually couched in the negative.

- John Simon is trying to tell us that a flying f— is less offensive than to say between you and I. (Quoting Leon Botsein).—*San Francisco Examiner*, p. 22, 12th November 1979
- Well, I don't give a flying fuck what you think!—*Reservoir Dogs*, 1992
- You're a bad person with an ugly heart, and we don't give a flying fuck what you think.—*Romy and Michele's High School Reunion*, 1997
- [W]ho gave a flying fuck if you weren't in tune or on the beat?—Dave Courtney, *Raving Lunacy*, p. 70, 2000

▸ **take a flying fuck**
get lost! *US*

- "And you can go pack your feeete in a cement block," she imagined she was saying to her father, "and take a flying fuck to the moon."—Richard Condon, *Prizzi's Money*, p. 197, 1994

flying fuckland *noun*
a fantasy world; used for registering disbelief *UK*

- When in flyin' fuckland 'ave you driven two-tonners?—Bernard Dempsey and Kevin McNally, *Lock, Stock ... & Two Hundred Smoking Kalashnikovs*, p. 110, 2000

flying gas station; gas station in the sky *nickname*
a KC-135 aircraft used for inflight refuelling of jet aircraft *US*

- —Linda Reinberg, *In the Field*, p. 84, 1991

Flying Horsemen *nickname*
during the war in Vietnam, the First Air Cavalry Division *US*
An elite reconnaissance troop.

- Throckmorton made a few calls, and the next thing we knew the "Flying Horsemen" 1st Air Cav came galloping to the rescue.—David H. Hackworth, *About Face*, p. 471, 1989

flying Jenny *noun*
a US Army shortwave radar set *US*

- —*American Speech*, p. 153, April 1947: 'Radar slang terms'

flying lesson *noun*
1 the reported US and South Vietnamese practice of pushing suspected Viet Cong or captured North Vietnamese soldiers from helicopters to their death *US*

- —Linda Reinberg, *In the Field*, p. 84, 1991

2 the act of throwing a prisoner or guard off a high tier in a prison cellblock *US*

- —William K. Bentley and James M. Corbett, *Prison Slang*, p. 90, 1992

flying orders *noun*
instructions given to a truck driver by a dispatcher *US*

- —Montie Tak, *Truck Talk*, p. 62, 1971

flying Oscar *nickname*
a Boeing-Vertol CH-47 helicopter, the US Army's prime cargo helicopter in Vietnam *US*
So named because of the likeness to an Oscar Meyer™ hotdog.

- —Linda Reinberg, *In the Field*, p. 84, 1991

flying pasty *noun*
excrement, wrapped and thrown from a prison window *UK*
Defined by Francis Grose in *Dictionary of the Vulgar Tongue*, 3rd edition, 1796, as 'Sirreverence wrapped in paper and thrown over a neighbour's wall'. The term survives where modern sanitation is not easily available.

- —Angela Devlin, *Prison Patter*, p. 52, 1996
- BRUMMIE: If you gotter 'ave a dump in the night you do a flyin' pasty. BACON: A flyin' what? IRONBAR: Flyin' pasty. Shit on a piece of paper, wrap it up, bung it out the window. You'll stink the whole drum out else.—Chris Baker and Andrew Day, *Lock, Stock... & A Good Slopping Out*, p. 411, 2000

flying prostitute *nickname*
a B-26 bomber aircraft *US, 1943*
Like the lady of the night, the B-26 had no means of visible support.

- —*American Speech*, p. 310, December 1946: 'More air force slang'

flying saucer *noun*
a morning glory seed, thought to have psychoactive properties *US*

- —Eugene Landy, *The Underground Dictionary*, p. 81, 1971

flying saucer cap *noun*
a military service cap *US, 1971*

- Standing in the light from the streetlight was The Fist in his courtroom blazer and flying saucer cap.—Jimmy Breslin, *I Don't Want to go to Jail*, p. 340, 2001

flying sheep's dick *noun*
nothing at all, the very least amount *UK*

- I couldn't give a flying sheep's dick about music, jingly jangly bollocks.—Shaun Ryder, *Shaun Ryder... in His Own Words*, 1992

flying sixty-nine *noun*
mutual and simultaneous oral sex *UK, 1984*
A variation of SOIXANTE-NEUF.

flying squad *noun*
a fast-moving, versatile group *US*

- He alerted the flying squad and phoned the warden, who authorized an emergency count.—Malcolm Braly, *On the Yard*, p. 198, 1967

flying telephone pole; telephone pole *nickname*
a surface-to-air missile, especially an SA-2 *US, 1977*
Vietnam war usage.

- He glanced down and saw two SAMS lifting, dust and dirt swirling behind the 35-foot "telephone poles."—Robert Kowilcox, *Scteam of Eagles*, p. 221, 1990
- The strike force was speeding over green jungle, which was high enough to avoid small arms fire, but low enough to be safe from any surface-to-air missiles (SAMS), the deadly "flying telephone poles" that would later put so many American flyers in North V—Robert K. Wilcox, *Scream of Eagles*, p. 17, 1990

• No SAMS came at him. It seemed that absolutely everyone else had seen the front end of one of those deadly "telephone poles". — Gerry Carroll, *North S*A*R*, p. 15, 1991

flying ten *noun*
a ten-dollar advance on pay given to a soldier when newly assigned to a base *US, 1956*
• — Carl Fleischhauer, *A Glossary of Army Slang*, p. 19, 1968

Flying Tiger Air Force *noun*
a collection of American mercenaries who flew air raids in support of Chiang Kai-shek's losing effort on mainland China *US*
• Several years earlier the CIA had taken control of General Clair Chennault's old "Flying Tiger" air force from the Second World War – American mercenaries and regulars who fought for Chiang Kaishek against the Communists[.] — Joseph C. Goulden, *Korea*, p. 470, 1982

flying triangle *noun*
LSD *UK*
• — Mike Haskins, *Drugs*, p. 285, 2003

flying twenty-five *noun*
a pay advance in the military *US, 1956*
• Recruits were given a pay advance, the so-called flying twenty-five, with which they purchased toilet articles and brass and shoe polish. — James Ebert, *A Life in a Year*, p. 28, 1993

flying wedge *noun*
a group of people in a wedge-shaped formation, advancing rapidly into a crowd *US*
A practice and term used by police, security workers and American football players.
• Thirty cops formed a flying wedge to drive us off. — Jerry Rubin, *Do It!*, p. 33, 1970

fly in the ointment *noun*
anything that spoils the perfection of a finished article *UK, 1833*
Of biblical inspiration (Ecclesiastes 10:1).
• To invite a third party to portray the portraying is to add another risk to a fragile situation; to be victims not so much of a fly on the wall but a fly in the ointment. — *The Guardian*, 14th January 2004

fly in the sky *noun*
an aircraft, especially a police helicopter *US*
• — *Complete CB Slang Dictionary*, 1976
• — Peter Chippindale, *The British CB Book*, p. 154, 1981

Flynn
▸ **in like Flynn**
1 easily, quickly, without effort *US, 1945*
Originally a reference to the legendary sexual exploits of actor Errol Flynn.
• Then I'm golden, man. I go ape. I'm in like Flynn. — Max Shulman, *Guided Tour of Campus Humor*, p. 106, 1955
• "Well, how'd you make out?" "In like Flynn, Louie." — Piri Thomas, *Down These Mean Streets*, p. 102, 1967
• Mention my name to the bloke on the door and you'll be in like the proverbial Flynn. — Alexander Buzo, *Norm and Ahmed*, p. 24, 1969
• [S]pill a glass of vino on your fly. Look helpless and let her mop it up with her serviette. If she takes her time you could find a simple way of making her task harder and I'd reckon you'll be in like Flynn within half an hour. — Barry Humphries, *The Traveller's Tool*, p. 52, 1985
• So when Her Majesty's favourite film-maker Dickie Attenborough is off making "Chaplin 2 – The Holborn Empire Strikes Back' or some such, I shall be in like flynn[.] — Andrew Nickolds, *Back to Basics*, p. 17, 1994
• If we win we'll be in like Flynn,' he said. — Phillip Gwynne, *Deadly Unna?*, p. 59, 1998
2 in poker, said of a player who bets before it is his turn *US*
• — *American Speech*, p. 99, May 1951

fly-over *noun*
the inability of a mail plane in rural Alaska to land and deliver mail *US*
• Also in Southeastern the weather is so bad many times that the residents suffer what is known as a "fly-over." That is the weather is so bad the planes can't land. — Mark Wheeler, *Half Baked Alaska*, p. 41, 1972

fly's eyes *noun*
the testicles semi-exposed through tight pants *AUSTRALIA, 2000*
It can also refer to the act of a male exposing his testicles by pulling his underwear tightly between them with the object of terrorising people with the spectacle.
• Change your pants – I can see your fly's eyes in those ones. — *Wordmap (www.abc.net.au/wordmap)*, 2003

flyspeck *noun*
Tasmania *AUSTRALIA, 1966*
A reference to the size of Tasmania relative to mainland Australia.
• — Maureen Brooks and Joan Ritchie, *Tassie Terms*, p. 53, 1995

flyspeck 3 *noun*
any miniscule, unreadable font *US*
• — Eric S. Raymond, *The New Hacker's Dictionary*, p. 162, 1991

fly-trap *noun*
the mouth *UK, 1795*
• Nobody calls Larry Haugen 'Larry'; they call him 'Fly Trap,' as in 'Shut your fly trap for a change. — Shawn Wong, *American Knees*, p. 130, 1995

fnarr! fnarr!
used for expressing amusement at a double entendre *UK*
A rote catchphrase response that, for a while, threatened to replace actual laughter with young people.
• — *Roger's Profanisaurus*, December 1997

FNF *noun*
used by prison officers to categorise prisoners who are held as a result of a Friday night altercation *UK*
An initialism of '*F*riday *n*ight *f*racas'.
• — Angela Devlin, *Prison Patter*, p. 52, 1996

FNG *noun*
a newly arrived soldier in Vietnam *US, 1966*
A '*f*ucking *n*ew *g*uy'.
• The FNG was usually avoided and shunned b y others in the unit for fear of his making a serious mistake or having an accident that could affect others. Because soldiers were often transferred individually into units, being an FNG was particularly lonely — Linda Reinberg, *In the Field*, p. 84, 1991

fnudger *noun*
a person who cheats at marbles by advancing over the shooting line *AUSTRALIA, 1974*
Perhaps an alteration of 'fudge'.
• — Jim Ramsay, *Cop It Sweet!*, p. 38, 1977

FOAD
used as shorthand in Internet discussion groups and text message to mean '*f*uck *o*ff *a*nd *d*ie' *US*
• — Gabrielle Mander, *WAN2TLK? ltl bk of txt msgs*, p. 44, 2002

FOAF *noun*
a *f*riend *o*f *a* *f*riend *US*
The most common source for an urban legend or other apocryphal story.
• — Eric S. Raymond, *The New Hacker's Dictionary*, p. 162, 1991

foaklies *noun*
inexpensive imitations of Oakley™ sunglasses *US*
• — Connie Eble (Editor), *UNC-CH Campus Slang*, p. 4, November 2003

foam *noun*
beer *US, 1908*
• [S]ome raggedy kid on the Corner who hasn't got the price of admission to see the stage show at the Apollo or a deuce of blips to buy himself a glass of foam. — Mezz Mezzrow, *Really the Blues*, p. 333, 1946

foamer *noun*
1 a railway fan whose love for railways is obsessive *US*
• The most widely used term is foamer, which may have been used first by Amtrak employees to refer to rail fans who grew so excited when looking at trains they seemed to be rabid. Another theory holds that this term was adapted from the acronym FOMITE, which stood for "fanatically obnoxious mentally incompetent train enthusiast". — Randy Kennedy, *Subwayland*, p. 18–19, 2004
2 a glass of beer *US*
• — *Swinging Syllables*, 1959

foamie *noun*
a surfboard made from polyurethane *US*
• — John M. Kelly, *Surf and Sea*, p. 285, 1965
• After school the break in front of the village is packed with kids riding pieces of marine ply. Standing up, doing back flips and angling across the foamies. — *Tracks*, p. 63, October 1992

foaming at the mouth *adjective*
very angry *UK, 1961*
From a symptom of utter madness.
- And, why do you not keep a photocopy of the changes you marked all the way through the copy-edited manuscript so that when it goes missing for days in the post there is no need to start foaming at the mouth? — *The Guardian*, 17th June 2003

foamy *noun*
a glass of beer *US*
- — *Esquire*, p. 180, June 1983

foamy cleanser *noun*
in hold 'em poker, an ace and a jack as the first two cards dealt to a particular player *US, 1981*
Building on the synonymous **AJAX**, a branded cleaner and obvious homophonic leap from 'ace-jack'.

fob *noun*
a Samoan *NEW ZEALAND*
- — David McGill, *David McGill's Complete Kiwi Slang Dictionary*, p. 46, 1998

FOB *noun*
a foreign exchange student; an international student *US*
- — Connie Eble (Editor), *UNC-CH Campus Slang*, p. 2, Fall 1993

FOB *adjective*
1 lazy, inefficient; *f*lat *o*n his *b*ehind *US*
- — *American Speech*, p. 226, October 1955: 'An aircraft production dispatcher's vocabulary'

2 *f*resh *o*ff the *b*oat *US*
An initialism usually applied to recent immigrants, but in the usage of Hawaiian youth applied to visitors to the islands.
- — Douglas Simonson, *Pidgin to da Max*, 1981

focker *noun*
a fucker (in all senses) *UK: NORTHERN IRELAND*
Filtered through a Northern Ireland accent.
- I said out, yer focker. Now! — Chris Ryan, *The Watchman*, p. 2, 2001

focus *noun*
vision, eyesight *US*
- — Marcus Hanna Boulware, *Jive and Slang of Students in Negro Colleges*, 1947

FOD *noun*
*f*oreign *o*bject *d*amage to an aircraft *US*
- "We police the the flight deck for anything lying around that might cause an aircraft to FOD-out." "Foreign object damage," Carmen said. "I guess something that might get sucked into the jet engine." — Elmore Leonard, *Killshot*, p. 90, 1989

foeitog!; foei tog!
used as an exclamation of pity or sympathy, and as a cry of 'shame!' *SOUTH AFRICA, 1910*
An Afrikaans term, *foei* (shame) *tog* (nevertheless), that has some currency among speakers of South African English.

fog *noun*
1 a person who is profoundly out of touch with current trends and his social peers *US*
- — *Concord (New Hampshire) Monitor*, p. 17, 23rd August 1983: 'Slang slinging: an intense and awesome guide to prep school slanguage'

2 steam *US*
- — Jerry Robertson, *Oil Slanguage*, p. 55, 1954

fog *verb*
to shoot and kill someone *US, 1913*
- — Lou Shelly, *Hepcats Jive Dictionary*, p. 11, 1945

fog and mist; foggy *noun*
drunk *UK*
Rhyming slang for **PISSED**.
- — Ray Puxley, *Cockney Rabbit*, 1992

fogey *noun*
an increase in military pay *US, 1878*
- Typically, every two years, military members receive a years-of-service, or fogey, pay raise. — P.J. Budahn, *Military Money Guide*, p. 7, 1996

foggy *adjective*
▸ **haven't the foggiest**
to be unclear in your mind *UK, 1917*
With ellipsis of idea or notion.
- [N]ational rail inquiries haven't the foggiest about what's doing. — *The Guardian*, 15th January 2002

fogscoffer *noun*
a rainbow appearing in a fog about to dissipate *CANADA*
- With the calms come fog bows – the "fog-eaters" of the Eskimos, or "fog-scoffers," resembling a rainbow in the fog, mainly made up of thick, grey fog. On some days, this arch will revolve completely around an observer as the sun turns in the sky. — *North*, p. 11/1, March-April 1963

fogy; fogey *noun*
an old person with out-dated ideas and values *UK, 1720*
- What on earth had possessed Father to send him as P.G. to these old fogies? — Douglas Rutherford, *The Creeping Flesh*, p. 11, 1963
- Then all the fogies had a good snuffle and cackle, and Bobbie found herself with three Bacardis and two more brandies, compliments of the geezer gang. — Joseph Wambaugh, *Finnegan's Week*, p. 229, 1993
- He's a really cool guy. I hope I'm doing shit like this when I'm a fogey. — Francesca Lia Block, *I Was a Teenage Fairy*, p. 88, 1998

fogy; fogey *adjective*
old-fashioned, or unusual *UK*
Recorded in use among Leicestershire teenagers.
- Oh Mum, what a fogey pair of shoes! — D. and R. McPheely and Paul Beale, 1984

foil *noun*
1 a quantity of illegal drugs wrapped in aluminium foil *AUSTRALIA*
- They found some old fits and foils and left it at that. — John Birmingham, *He Died With a Felafel in his Hand*, p. 213, 1994

2 heroin *UK*
- — Mike Haskins, *Drugs*, p. 283, 2003

▸ **put on the foil**
in hockey, to apply tinfoil layers (illegally) under the gloves to increase the impact of punches in fights *CANADA*
- The Hanson brothers put on the foil, goons as they are. — *Slap Shot*, 1977

foilhead *noun*
a person with highlighted hair *US*
- — Don R. McCreary (Editor), *Dawg Speak*, 2001

fokkin *adjective*
used as an intensifier *UK*
A variant spelling of 'fucking' based on Irish pronunciation.
- Er, look, just give us your fokkin money. Again. — *[Caption to a cartoon of Sir Bob Geldof] The Guardian*, p. 5, 28th May 2003

fold *noun*
money *UK*
- [F]lash a few of your folds and maybe one of those flowers you're so keen on, and you'll get all the ladies you can deal with. — Diran Adebayo, *My Once Upon A Time*, p. 9, 2000
- — Don R. McCreary (Editor), *Dawg Speak*, 2001

fold *verb*
1 to fail, to cease to be operational, used of a business venture or theatrical production *UK, 1928*
- Earlier this year, the UK's favourite flying saucer fanzine, UFO Magazine, folded due to declining sales. — *The Guardian*, 14th June 2004

2 in poker, to withdraw from a hand, forfeiting your bet *US*
- — Irwin Steig, *Common Sense in Poker*, p. 184, 1963

▸ **fold hands**
to stop working *TRINIDAD AND TOBAGO*
- — Lise Winer, *Dictionary of the English/Creole of Trinidad & Tobago*, 2003

folded *noun*
drunk *US*
- — Anna Scotti and Paul Young, *Buzzwords*, p. 133, 1997

folding; folding stuff; folding green *noun*
paper money, hence money *US, 1930*
- Just put this hunk of folding back in your saddlebag and forget you ever met me. — Raymond Chandler, *The Little Sister*, p. 38, 1949
- I'll do anything for a but of folding stuff[.] — Barry Humphries, *Bazz Pulls It Off!*, 1971
- Readers of discernment (by which I mean those of you who handed over the folding stuff [...]). — Andrew Nickolds, *Back to Basics*, 1994
- You're in above the neck, son. You owe me folding, plus the juice. — Greg Williams, *Diamond Geezers*, p. 10, 1997
- [W]e're dressed like fuckin' prices and we're holding the folding to back it up. — J.J. Connolly, *Know Your Enemy*, p. 151, 1999

- We are about to extend a considerable outlay of foldin'. I'd appreciate a bit of attention. —Bernard Dempsey and Kevin McNally, *Lock, Stock ... & Two Hundred Smoking Kalashnikovs*, p. 109, 2000

folding lettuce *noun*
money, paper money *US, 1958*
A lesser variant of FOLDING STUFF.

Folex *noun*
an inexpensive imitation of a Rolex™ wristwatch *US*
- —Connie Eble (Editor), *UNC-CH Campus Slang*, p. 4, November 2003

folkie *noun*
a folk singer or musician; a folk music enthusiast *US, 1966*
From the 1960s; a 'folknik' was an untalented traveller on the same bandwagon.
- [A] decided majority of the rising bands were composed of ex-folkies[.] —Lester Bangs, *Psychotic Reactions and Carburetor Dung*, p. 41, 1970
- As early as 1962 he was a dope-smoking folkie living communally. —Barney Hoskyns, *Waiting For The Sun*, p. 142, 1996
- [F]lash-mag-folkie Beth Orton[.]— *The Times Magazine*, p. 43, 16th February 2002

folknik *noun*
a member of the folk music counterculture of the 1950s and 60s *US, 1958*
- "All the folkniks were running around the schmucky coffeehouses," said Young, "and the nightclub owners were giving people folk music – and booze." —David Hajdu, *Positively 4th Street*, p. 48, 2001

folks *noun*
a group of your friends *US*
- — *Maybeck High School Yearbook (Berkeley, California)*, p. 28, 1997
- — *San Jose Mercury News*, 11th May 1999

follies *noun*
the Quarter Sessions *UK, 1950*
An ironic comparison between justice and vaudeville. The Courts Act 1971 replaced the Quarter Sessions with the Crown Courts.
- —Angela Devlin, *Prison Patter*, p. 53, 1996

follow-cat *noun*
a person who imitates others *TRINIDAD AND TOBAGO, 1982*
- —Lise Winer, *Dictionary of the English/Creole of Trinidad & Tobago*, 2003

follow-pattern *adjective*
copied, derivative, imitative *BARBADOS*
- —Frank A. Collymore, *Barbadian Dialect*, p. 50, 1965

follow through *verb*
to accidentally defecate at the conclusion of a fart *UK*
- — *Roger's Profanisaurus*, December 1997
- Colm lifts one arse cheek an lets out a loud fart which tirns into a gurgle an ee looks terrified for a moment before ee leaps up an sprints bow-legged to thuh bog yelling: – SHITE! Av follered fuckin through! —Niall Griffiths, *Grits*, p. 17, 2000
- [T]he sudden movement made me follow through and I shat myself. — *Loaded*, p. 18, June 2003

follow your nose!
a catchphrase addressed to a person seeking directions *UK, 1664*
- Feeling hungry? Just follow your nose. — *The Guardian*, 7th January 2001

follytricks *noun*
politics *JAMAICA*
- —Thomas H. Slone, *Rasta is Cuss*, p. 47, 2003

FoMoCo *nickname*
the Ford Motor Company *US*
- I had talked to the FoMoCo boss the night before[.] —Hunter S. Thompson, *Fear and Loathing in Las Vegas*, p. 40, 1971

fond of her mother; good to her mother *adjective*
homosexual *UK*
A euphemism based on a stereotype.
- —the cast of 'Aspects of Love', Prince of Wales Theatre, *Palare (Boy Dancer Talk) for Beginners*, 1989–92

f-one-j-one *noun*
Fiji *AUSTRALIA*
- —James Lambert, *The Macquarie Book of Slang*, 1996

fong *noun*
1 any alcoholic beverage *NEW ZEALAND*
- On the odd occassion he wouldn't front up in the morning. I always assumed it was because he'd attacked the fong (booze) the night before. — *(Aukland) Metro*, p. 47, September 1985
- —David McGill, *David McGill's Complete Kiwi Slang Dictionary*, p. 46, 1998

2 a kick *IRELAND*
With variant 'fon'.
- We found him! Petey gave him four good raps on the poll with his knuckles and one frightful fon in the behind and couldn't wake him. —John B. Keane, *The Man from Clare*, p. 76, 1962
- I'll give you a fong up in the hole. —Denis O'Shaughnessy, *Stories of Limerick*, p. 67, 2002

fonged *adjective*
very drunk *NEW ZEALAND*
- It occurred to him that Harry was fonged already. —Phillip Wilson, *Outcasts*, p. 50, 1965
- —David McGill, *David McGill's Complete Kiwi Slang Dictionary*, p. 46, 1998

fonk *noun*
a male homosexual *BAHAMAS*
- —John A. Holm, *Dictionary of Bahamian English*, p. 79, 1982

foo *noun*
in computing, used as an arbitrary, temporary name for something *US*
- —Guy L. Steele et al., *The Hacker's Dictionary*, p. 66, 1983

food *noun*
bullets *UK*
- —Dave Courtney, *Dodgy Dave's Little Black Book*, p. 7, 2001

foodaholic *noun*
a compulsive eater *US, 1965*
- We couldn't possibly wear the same size. She was massive. She was probably some foodaholic who stuffed her face day and night. —Cherie Bennett, *Life in the Fat Lane*, p. 123, 1998

food boat *noun*
in prison, a financial alliance between several prisoners to pay for food *UK*
- —Angela Devlin, *Prison Patter*, p. 53, 1996

food chain *noun*
a pecking order or hierachy *US*
- She joined the usual gaggle of overworked pack journalism bodies who, at the bottom of the food chain, are at the back of the plane, having to file every hour to their radio stations or TV outlets or newspaper editors,as each alleged sensation breaks out. — *Edmonton Sun*, p. 11, 7th March 1998

food coma *noun*
the drowsiness often experienced after eating too much *US*
- —Connie Eble (Editor), *UNC-CH Campus Slang*, p. 3, Spring 1987

foodie *noun*
a person who has a passionate interest in the latest trends in gourmet food *UK, 1982*
- —Rachel S. Epstein and Nina Liebman, *Biz Speak*, p. 88, 1986
- Foodies are also overfed, which makes them cranky and jaded. — *New York Times Magazine*, p. 53, 29 July 2001

food stamps *noun*
in poker, a player's cash reserved for household expenses pressed into action after he has lost his betting money *US*
- —John Vorhaus, *The Big Book of Poker Slang*, p. 18, 1996

foof *noun*
the breast *UK*
Usually in the plural.
- —Paul Baker, *Polari*, p. 175, 2002
- — *Attitude*, p. 60, July 2003: 'Old palare lexicon'

foofoo *noun*
1 the vagina *UK, 1998*
- Nonsense slang referred to vague, inoffensive terms that had little or no meanings in standard English: terms like biff, foo-foo, minky and winkie in FGTs [female genital terms], and chod, dongce, spondoolies, and winks in MGTs [male genital terms]. — *Journal of Sex Research*, p. 146, 2001

2 a prissy or girlish man *US, 1848*
- Fortney shaved closer than usual that afternoon. He even splashed on a little foo-foo cologne. —Joseph Wambaugh, *Floaters*, p. 170, 1996

3 cologne, perfume *US, 1928*

- Keep cleaners, perfumes, deodorants, and any other foofoo stuff locked up. —Sandra Hardin Gookin, *Parenting for Dummies*, p. 224, 2002

4 something that is purely decorative without adding functional value *US*

- — *United States Naval Institute Proceedings*, p. 108, October 1986

foofoo dust; foofoo stuff; foofoo *noun*

1 heroin *US, 1998*

- —Robert Ashton, *This Is Heroin*, p. 205, 2002

2 cocaine *UK*

- —Nick Constable, *This is Cocaine*, p. 181, 2002

3 talcum powder *UK, 1962*

Also called 'foo stuff' and 'foofoo powder'.

- Pusser's [pusser] foo foo is a foot and body powder issued in tropical zones[.] —Rick Jolly, *Jackspeak*, p. 114, 1989

foo gas; phou gas *noun*

an explosive mixture in a buried steel drum serving as a defence around the perimeter of a military base *US, 1978*

- —Shelby L. Stanton, *Vietnam Ordre of Battle*, p. 356, 1981

fook

'fuck' in all senses and forms *UK*

A phonetic rendering of accented English.

- I've got fook all on me. —Shaun Ryder, *Shaun Ryder... in His Own Words*, 1997
- God, fookin'ell, what a mess, baby. — *The Guardian*, p. 6, 28th June 2004

fool *noun*

used as a term of address, sometimes suggesting foolishness and sometimes not *US*

- Shit, King, it ain't d-e-r-e man, it's d-e-a-r, and Sara don't have no two r's in it, fool. — *Platoon*, 1986

fool *adjective*

silly, foolish; often a pejorative intensifier *UK*

In conventional use from C13 to late C19. Now especially used in the US, often in the phrase 'that fool thing'.

- Some refuse to kill even when it's necessary to protect the innocent, and others are itching to blast anyone at odds with U.S. foreign policy (whatever that fool thing is from one moment to the next). — *Salt Lake Tribune*, 8th March 2003

fool around *verb*

to have a casual sexual relationship *US, 1937*

fool file *noun*

the mythical library of the stupidest things ever said *US*

- —Eric S. Raymond, *The New Hacker's Dictionary*, p. 164, 1991

fool-fool *noun*

a simple-minded fool *JAMAICA*

By reduplication.

- "Listen Jackie," he said in mock patois with a smile, "any fool-fool come trouble you, tell dem they better not ramp wid yuh[."] —Donald Gorgon, *Cop Killer*, p. 79, 1994

foolio *noun*

a fool; a social outcast *US*

- And to all you youngsters out there, acting like little 'foolios' that think this can't happen to you, think again! — *Los Angeles Timser*, p. B1, 6th December 1994
- —Pamela Munro, *U.C.L.A. Slang*, p. 66, 1997
- —Rick Ayers (Editor), *Berkeley High Slang Dictionary*, p. 22, 2004

foolish powder *noun*

heroin; cocaine; any powdered drug *US, 1930*

- —Robert Ashton, *This Is Heroin*, p. 205, 2002
- —Mike Haskins, *Drugs*, p. 280, 2003

fool killer *noun*

a notional creature called upon to dispose of fools *US, 1853*

- It was the kind of crowd that would have made the Fool Killer lower his club and shake his head and walk away, frustrated by the magnitude of the opportunity. —Tom Wolfe, *The Right Stuff*, p. 246, 1979

fools seldom differ

used as a derogatory retort to the catchphrase 'great minds think alike' *UK*

- — Partridge, *A Dictionary of Catchphrases*, 1977

foont *noun*

▷ **see:** FUNT

foop *noun*

▸ **one swell foop**

used as a humorous reversal of 'one fell swoop' *US, 1972*

- "It's being done in one swell foop." Mutters another: "And that's frequently how it comes out!" — *Forbes*, p. 84, 12th November 1979
- Diane has finally gone from the bargain basement to the penthouse, in one swell foop. (I'm partial to spoonerisms.) —Haywood Smith, *The Red Hat Club*, p. 246, 2003

foop *verb*

to have sex *BARBADOS*

Recorded by Richard Allsopp.

fooper *noun*

a homosexual male *US*

Apparently back-slang of **POOF**.

- — *American Speech*, p. 59, Spring-Summer 1975: 'Razorback slang'

foops *noun*

a fart *TRINIDAD AND TOBAGO*

- —Lise Winer, *Dictionary of the English/Creole of Trinidad & Tobago*, 2003

foot *noun*

▸ **on the one foot in front of the other caper**

on the run *UK*

- Arthur's on the run – well and truly on the one foot in front of the other caper. —Anthony Masters, *Minder*, p. 170, 1984

▸ **put your foot in it**

to do or say something tactless, to blunder *UK, 1823*

foot *verb*

to run fast *US*

- "[F]oot it, Sonny! Foot it!" I said, "Like, what's wrong, man?" He said, "Run!"[.] —Claude Brown, *Manchild in the Promised Land*, p. 131, 1965

football *noun*

1 a tablet of Dilaudid™, a central nervous system depressant manufactured by the Knoll Pharmaceutical Company *US*

- So I had some footballs, some Dilaudid. I think it's a full grain. I gave this girl some. She got mad because I broke a football in two; she wanted the whole thing. —Bruce Jackson, *Outside the Law*, p. 107, 1972
- Supposed to put you to sleep tough. I think he called them footballs. —Emmett Grogan, *Final Score*, p. 81, 1976

2 a tablet of dextroamphetamine sulphate and amphetamine sulphate (trade name Diphetamine™), a central nervous system stimulant *US*

- —Donald Louria, *Nightmare Drugs*, p. 28, 1966

3 a simple musical accompaniment used when a performer is ad libbing *US*

- The orchestrator will cooperate by scoring the orchestra on one note (a whole note) in each bar. A whole note looks like a very small football. —Sherman Louis Sergel, *The Language of Show Biz*, p. 90, 1973

4 the briefcase carrying the communication equipment that enables the president of the US to launch a nuclear attack *US, 1968*

- They carry the "football," a briefcase that contains reference documents that outline U.S. strategic attack options, communications instructions, and the codewords that the President would use to authorize the release of nuclear weapons[.] —Michael K. Bohn, *Nerve Center*, p. 50, 2003

football team *noun*

a very sparse moustache *UK, 1984*

There are eleven men – or hairs – on each side. The UK version of Australia's cricket team.

foot burner *noun*

a walking plough *US*

- — *American Speech*, p. 269, December 1958: 'Ranching terms from eastern Washington'

footer *noun*

the game of football (soccer) *UK*

An early example of the Oxford University **-ER**, a slangifying process.

footie; footy *noun*

1 the game of football (soccer) *UK, 1940*

- We could go see a footie game? — *The Full Monty*, 1997

- He wished the embarrassing fashion among bands for pretending to be into "the footie" would die a natural death. —Kevin Sampson, *Sampson*, p. 97, 1999

2 the game of rugby union *NEW ZEALAND*
- —David McGill, *David McGill's Complete Kiwi Slang Dictionary*, p. 51, 1998

3 a football *AUSTRALIA*
- Do ya wanna kick a footy?—Kerry Cue, *Crooks, Chooks and Bloody Ratbags*, p. 193, 1983

4 a pedestrian police surveillance operative *UK*
- The footies [...] have radioed in. —Duncan MacLaughlin, *The Filth*, p. 185, 2002

foot-in-mouth disease *noun*
the tendency to say that which ought not to be said *US, 1968*
- Attentive listening is the best antidote for foot-in-mouth disease. —Jo-Ellan Dimitrius, *Put Your Best Foot Forward*, p. 226, 2000

foot it *verb*
to walk, especially a considerable distance *US, 1972*
Originally US black.
- He was footing it along a mutilated walkway[.]—Greg Williams, *Diamond Geezers*, p. 8, 1997

foot on the till *noun*
in horse racing, used for describing the position of a horse that is racing well *AUSTRALIA*
- —Ned Wallish, *The Truth Dictionary of Racing Slang*, p. 30, 1989

footpounder *noun*
an infantry soldier *US, 1986*
- —Linda Reinberg, *In the Field*, p. 85, 1991

footprint *noun*
the portion of a tyre that contacts the track *US*
- Footprint – Surface area of racing tire which actually makes contact with ground—Jerry Miller, *Fast Company*, p. 176, 1972

footrest *noun*
an accelerator pedal *US*
- —*Complete CB Slang Dictionary*, 1976
- —Peter Chippindale, *The British CB Book*, p. 154, 1981

foots *noun*
theatrical footlights *US, 1919*
- —Wilfred Granville, *The Theater Dictionary*, p. 75, 1952

footsack!
go away! *SOUTH AFRICA, 1855*
An anglicised pronunciation of Afrikaans *voetsek* (a curt command to a dog, offensive when applied to a person).

footsie *noun*
foot-to-foot contact, usually out of sight such as under a restaurant table *US, 1944*
- His wife, who was the quiet type, sat playing footsie with Pancho under the table. —Steve Cannon, *Groove, Bang, and Jive Around*, p. 131–132, 1969

footwarmer *noun*
1 a linear amplifier for a citizens' band radio *US*
- —Warren Smith, *Warren's Smith's Authentic Dictionary of CB*, p. 38, 1976

2 a walking plough *CANADA*
- Afterwards we broke 20 acres of gumbo with the John Deere "foot warmer." —*Ghost Pine*, p. 61, 1954

foozle *noun*
in golf, a mis-hit shot *UK: SCOTLAND, 1869*
- —Peter Davies, *Davies' Dictionary of Golfing Terms*, 1980

for Africa *adverb*
hugely, in large amounts, greatly *SOUTH AFRICA, 1970*
- —Jean Branford, *A Dictionary of South African English*, 1978
- Go ahead and indulge – there'll be juice for Africa! —*Cosmopolitan (South Africa)*, August 1991

for-and-aft cap *noun*
a military garrison cap *UK, 1940*
- After that he correctly adjusted his fore-and-aft cap, then glanced around until he spotted Dillon, whereupon he waved cheerfully. —W.E.B. Griffin, *Close Combat*, p. 266, 1993

for a start-off *noun*
to begin with *UK*
- CORP: I want to know. For a start-off – what were you in the nick for last time?—Clive Exton, *No Fixed Abode [Six Granada Plays]*, p. 122, 1959

forbidden fruit *noun*
a youthful, attractive male who is under the age of legal consent *US*
Homosexual usage.
- —*Maledicta*, p. 220, 1979: 'Kinks and queens: linguistic and cultural aspects of the terminology for gays'

force *noun*
in stage magic, any method of ensuring that a particular card (or other object) is chosen *UK*
- Glide Force, Double Cut Force, Dribble Force, Spread Cull Force, 20 Count Force, etc—*Card Trick Central*, 2003

▸ **the force**
the police *UK, 1868*

for cheese cake!
used for registering anger or surprise *UK*
Euphemism and rhyming slang, **FOR CHRIST'S SAKE!**, varied as an assonant pun 'for Jesus' sake!'.
- I come pounding up, say, "Pull it out, for cheese cake."—Nicholas Blincoe, *The Beautiful Beaten-up Irish Boy of the Arndale Centre*, p. 11, 1998

for Christ's sake!
used as an expletive, if not employed as a prayer *UK*
Recorded in conventional use since late C14; as an expletive since 1944.
- "You don't go down with the first punch, for Christ's sake," said the actor Bryan Brown. —*The Guardian*, 8th November 1999

for crying out loud!
used for registering anger, irritation, surprise, astonishment, etc *UK*
Probably a euphemistic replacement of **FOR CHRIST'S SAKE!**.
- Pull it off, for crying out loud! Just pull it off!—Stuart Jeffries, *Mrs Slocombe's Pussy*, p. 66, 2000

for days *adjective*
to a great degree *US*
- "He get hair fo' days!"—Douglas Simonson, *Pidgin to da Max*, 1981
- That guy has arms for days. —Kevin Dilallo, *The Unofficial Gay Manual*, p. 240, 1994

for days!
1 that's the truth! *US*
- —*Current Slang*, p. 24, Fall 1968

2 used for expressing amazement *US*
- —*American Speech*, p. 57, Spring-Summer 1970: 'Homosexual slang'

fore-and-after hat *noun*
a military garrison cap *US, 1931*
- Roy Barksdale advised that they had a lifeboat mounted on a truck bed and an admiral's uniform, complete with fore and aft hat. —James Dolittle, *I Could Never Be So Lucky Again*, p. 101, 1991

foreground *verb*
to assign a high priority to a task *US*
- If your presentation is due next week, I guess I'd better foreground writing up the design document. —Eric S. Raymond, *The New Hacker's Dictionary*, p. 165–166, 1991

forehand *adjective*
(used of surfing) facing the wave *AUSTRALIA*
- —Nat Young, *Surfing Fundamentals*, p. 127, 1985

foreign *adjective*
(used of a betting chip) from another casino *US*
- —Thomas F. Hughes, *Dealing Casino Blackjack*, p. 72, 1982

foreigner *noun*
an illicit employment using the time and materials of your legitimate employer; any work done while claiming unemployment benefit *UK, 1943*
- We just lost our life savin's doing a foreigner for two con artists. —Alan Bleasdale, *Boys From the Blackstuff*, 1982

for England *adverb*

(to perform an everyday action) to an extravagant degree *UK*

- [H]e and his girlfriend took turns at sleeping for England—Wayne Anthony, *Spanish Highs*, p. 91, 1999

forever and a day *noun*

an indefinite but considerable length of time *UK, 1984*

An intensification of 'for ever'.

forever-forever

used as a motto by the Black Guerrilla Family prison gang *US*

- The 415 motto is "Forever-Forever." This term is used to close the oath and to open and close serious business meetings.—Bill Valentine, *Gangs and Their Tattoos*, p. 19, 2000

for fake

used as a sarcastic reply when asked 'for real?' *US*

- —Connie Eble (Editor), *UNC-CH Campus Slang*, p. 4, November 2003

for free *adjective*

free, gratis *US, 1942*

The 'for' is redundant.

- [T]his weekend families are so welcome that under-16s get in for free.—*The Guardian*, 23rd July 2002

forget it!

don't worry about it! *US, 1903*

- The condition of the shirts will reflect in their value. "If it looks worn or faded in any kind of way, forget it," says Mr Boelhouwer.—*The Guardian*, 22nd February 2003

for God's sake!

used as an expletive, if not employed as a prayer *UK*

In conventional use by 1300; as an expletive it is widely recorded since 1932.

- [An] eccentric soundtrack of 1960s British invasion hits (The Creation! Unit 4 + 2! Chad and Jeremy, for God's sake!).—*New Statesman*, 23rd August 1999

for goodness' sake!

▷ see: GOODNESS' SAKE!

for it *verb*

to be due for punishment; to be in immediate trouble *UK, 1925*

fork *verb*

1 used as a euphemism for 'to fuck' *US*

- How could I tell her I had already let more than a dozen boys fork me by the time I was eighteen?—Rita Ciresi, *Pink Slip*, p. 11, 1999

2 to ride (a horse) *US, 1882*

- "Can you fork a bronc?" "What?" "Can you sit a horse, man?"—George Bowering, *Caprice*, p. 238, 1987

fork and knife *noun*

1 life *UK, 1934*

Rhyming slang, generally used in the phrases 'not on your fork and knife' and 'never in your fork and knife'.

- —Ray Puxley, *Cockney Rabbit*, 1992

2 a wife *UK, 1937*

Rhyming slang.

forked *adjective*

in computing, unacceptably slow or dysfunctional *US*

Probably a euphemism for **FUCKED**.

- —Eric S. Raymond, *The New Hacker's Dictionary*, p. 166, 1991

forked-tongued *adjective*

duplicitous *US*

Ascribing stereotypical snake-like qualities; best remembered (although possibly apocryphal) from cowboy films in the phrase 'white man speak with forked tongue'.

- "What a forked-tongued phoney you are," I told him, "coming here and trying to put the arm on me for the Mafia.—Harry J. Anslinger, *The Murderers*, p. 238, 1961

forklift *noun*

in poker, a substantial win *US*

- —John Vorhaus, *The Big Book of Poker Slang*, p. 18, 1996

fork out *verb*

to pay *UK, 1831*

- [T]hrow such thrifty instincts to the wind and fork out for a brand new model[.]—*The Observer*, 9th May 2004

fork over *verb*

to hand over *UK, 1820*

- This landlady would hand out a metal check and a towel to the girl, while the customer forked over two bucks.—Mezz Mezzrow, *Really the Blues*, p. 22–23, 1946

forks *noun*

the fingers *UK, 1812*

Originally a pickpocket's term.

- —Lou Shelly, *Hepcats Jive Dictionary*, p. 11, 1945

form *noun*

1 a criminal record *UK*

- [I]n the course of chewing the fat we told each other all about our form.—Charles Raven, *Underworld Nights*, p. 148, 1956
- You can get at least a five and maybe even a neves for getting captured with a shooter especially if you've got a bit of form with you.—Frank Norman, *Bang to Rights*, 1958
- —Peter Laurie, *Scotland Yard*, 1970
- "Has he got form?" "Any former?"—Angela Devlin, *Prison Patter*, p. 53, 1996
- He's got form for mugging an old granny outside her own home[.] —Greg Williams, *Diamond Geezers*, p. 43, 1997

2 a person's character or true nature *AUSTRALIA, 1944*

- It's no use trying to keep up that haughty air any longer with us. We've got her form now, all right.—Robert S. Close, *With Hooves of Brass*, p. 81, 1961

3 the situation, organisation or position *UK, 1948*

- Excuse our embarrassing naivety, but what's the form?—*The Guardian*, 13th August 2003

4 women viewed as sexual prospects *US, 1953*

- He turned to Guido, an expert on the local form. 'Guido, who's that girl in the black and white dress with,' he almost gulped, 'those fantastic legs?'—Clive Galea, *Slipper*, p. 13, 1988

5 high spirits *UK, 1877*

Generally used with 'in' as, for instance, 'he's in form tonight'.

6 luck *AUSTRALIA*

From 'form' as 'a record of a racehorse's past performance'.

- This same bird started pumpin' Toggle and me about getting something on the cheap. How'd you like their rotten form, eh? —John Wynnum, *Tar Dust*, p. 77, 1962
- 'What's the chance of picking up a cab this time of day?' 'Knowing my form, not so hot.'—John Wynnum, *Jiggin' in the Riggin'*, p. 36, 1965
- How's his flamin' form!—Ray Slattery, *Mobbs' Mob*, p. 121, 1966

formal *adjective*

▸ **go formal**

to wear a clean flannel shirt *US*

- —Jim Crotty, *How to Talk American*, p. 310, 1997

formerly known as

known as *US, 1993*

A wildly popular construction after recording artist Prince announced in 1993 that he had changed his name to The Artist Formerly Known as Prince.

- "The person you are addressing," the Educated One corrected, is "the Writer Formerly Known as the Columnist."—*The Cattanooga Times*, p. B5, 11 February 1997
- The Once-Proud Franchise Formerly Known as the Bears was outscored 38-0 in the second half, giving up more points in a half than a Once-Proud Franchise Formerly Known as the Bears ever has.—*Chicago Tribune*, p. C1, 20th November 1997

for mossies *adverb*

for no special reason, for amusement *SOUTH AFRICA, 1973*

- —Penny Silva, *A Dictionary of South African English*, 1996

form player *noun*

in horse racing, someone who bets based on information found in a racing form *US*

- —Tom Ainslie, *Ainslie's Complete Guide to Thoroughbred Racing*, p. 331, 1976

formula one *noun*

a hammerhead shark *AUSTRALIA*

Used by surfers.

- —Trevor Cralle, *The Surfin'ary*, p. 41, 1991

for Pete's sake!

euphemistic for 'God's sake!' *UK, 1924*

- This is Wayne Anthony, for Pete's sake!—Wayne Anthony, *Spanish Highs*, p. 90, 1999

for real *adverb*
▷ see: FE REAL

for real?
used for expressing surprise and perhaps doubt *US*
• —Connie Eble (Editor), *UNC-CH Campus Slang*, p. 3, Fall 1995

Forrest Gump; forrest *noun*
1 an act of defecation *UK*
Rhyming slang for DUMP formed from the title of a 1994 Oscar-winning film and its eponymous leading character.
• [T]o go for a "Forrest" is to squeeze one out.—Ray Puxley, *Fresh Rabbit*, 1998

2 an unpleasant place or location *UK*
Rhyming slang for DUMP.
• —Ray Puxley, *Fresh Rabbit*, 1998

for Ron
for later *on* *UK*
Punning on a diminutive of the name Ronald.
• I realised that it would probly be a wise move on my part to put it [a marijuana joint] out for "Ron".—Ken Lukowiak, *Marijuana Time*, p. 207, 2000

for shame!
used as a humorous admission that you have been cleverly ridiculed *US*
• —*American Speech*, p. 275, December 1963: 'American Indian student slang'

for sure!
used as an enthusiastic, stylish affirmation *US*
• BRIDESMAID 2: Look at all the holes in the lapel! AXEL: For sure!—*The Deer Hunter*, 1978
• —Connie Eble (Editor), *UNC-CH Campus Slang*, p. 3, Spring 1983

Forsyte Saga *noun*
lager *UK*
Rhyming slang, after the 1970s television dramatisation of the series of novels by John Galsworthy (1867–1933).
• I will have to go and pour him a large Forsyte Saga to keep him quiet.—Ronnie Barker, *Fletcher's Book of Rhyming Slang*, p. 39, 1979

Fort Apache *nickname*
the police station in the 41st precinct, New York *US, 1976*
An allusion to the American West and the wild, lawless character of the neighbourhood.
• —Ralph de Sola, *Crime Dictionary*, p. 54, 1982

Fort Bushy *noun*
the vulva and female pubic hair *US, 1961*
• —Dale Gordon, *The Dominion Sex Dictionary*, p. 71, 1967

Fort Fucker *nickname*
Fort Rucker, Alabama *US*
Home of the US Army Aviation Center for both fixed wing and helicopter training.
• —Linda Reinberg, *In the Field*, p. 86, 1991

Fort Fumble *nickname*
the Canadian National Defence Headquarters in Ottawa *CANADA*
• Fort Fumble came particularly to refer to NDHQ's Building 155, the home of the Director-General of Aerospace Engineering and Maintenance. In the US [the term] refers to the Pentagon.—Tom Langeste, *Words on the Wing*, p. 110, 1995

Forth Bridge job *noun*
anything needing constant amendment, or renewal or updating *UK, 1984*
An allusion to the job of painting the Forth Bridge – the painters are reputed to start again at the other end as soon as they have finished the job.

Fort Head *nickname*
Fort Hood, a US Army installation *US, 1968*
From the preponderance of drug use there during the Vietnam war.
• Soon, similar problems cropped up at home. Fort Hood, Texas, became known as Fort Head[.]—Rick Atkinson, *The Long Gray Line*, p. 367, 1989

for the love of Mike!
used for registering exasperation, disbelief, surprise, exaltation, etc *UK*
A euphemism 'for the love of Christ' or, possibly, 'Moses'.
• O'Mally is a cheerful Irish boaster, who makes Bell laugh and never strays from his side. O'MALLY: For the love of mike. Did you see those legs she had on her? BELL: I saw them.—Graeme Kent, *The Queen's Corporal [Six Granada Plays]*, p. 87, 1959

for the love of Pete!
used for registering exasperation, disbelief, surprise, exaltation, etc *US*
A euphemistic 'for the love of God'; probably American Irish Roman Catholic origins; a variation of FOR PETE'S SAKE!, on the model of FOR THE LOVE OF MIKE!.

forthwith *noun*
an order to a police officer to report immediately *US*
• —*New York Times Magazine*, p. 88, 16th March 1958

Fort Knox *noun*
in shuffleboard, a number that is well hidden or guarded *US*
• —Omero C. Catan, *Secrets of Shuffleboard Strategy*, p. 66, 1967: 'Glossary of terms'

Fort Liquordale *nickname*
Fort Lauderdale, Flordia *US*
A nickname earned from the invasion of heavy-drinking college students each spring.
• —Ralph de Sola, *Crime Dictionary*, p. 199, 1982

Fort Lost in the Woods *nickname*
Fort Leonard Wood, Missouri *US, 1974*
• —Linda Reinberg, *In the Field*, p. 85, 1991
• Basic Training was at Fort Leonard Wood, Missouri. Sometimes referred to as Fort Lost-in-the-Woods or Little Korea, the post was isolated in the Missouri Ozarks.—George E. Dooley, *Battle for the Central Highlands*, p. 11, 2000

Fortnum & Mason; fortnum *noun*
a basin *UK*
Rhyming slang, formed on the name of a London department store.
• —Ray Puxley, *Fresh Rabbit*, 1998

fortnum cut *noun*
a short back and sides haircut, mockingly called a basin cut or a pudding-basin cut *UK*
Formed from rhyming slang for FORTNUM & MASON (a basin).
• —Ray Puxley, *Fresh Rabbit*, 1998

Fort Piss *nickname*
Fort Bliss, Texas *US*
Home to the US Army Air Defense Artillery Center.
• —Linda Reinberg, *In the Field*, p. 86, 1991

Fort Pricks *nickname*
Fort Dix, New Jersey *US, 1974*
A major training, mobilisation and deployment centre. The scene of frequent demonstrations against the Vietnam war.
• —Linda Reinberg, *In the Field*, p. 86, 1991

Fort Puke *nickname*
Fort Polk, Louisiana *US, 1974*
Home to the JRT Operations Group, the 2nd Armored Cavalry Regiment, the 519th Military Police Battalion and the Warrior Brigade.
• —Linda Reinberg, *In the Field*, p. 86, 1991

Fortrash *noun*
the FORTRAN computer language *US*
• —Eric S. Raymond, *The New Hacker's Dictionary*, p. 166, 1991

for true *adverb*
▷ see: FE TRUE

Fort Screw Us *nickname*
Fort Lewis, Washington *US*
Home of the I Corps.
• —Linda Reinberg, *In the Field*, p. 86, 1991

Fort Smell *nickname*
Fort Sill, Oklahoma *US*
The primary field artillery training facility during the conflict in Vietnam.
• —Linda Reinberg, *In the Field*, p. 86, 1991

Fort Turd *nickname*
Fort Ord, Monterey, California *US*
• —Linda Reinberg, *In the Field*, p. 86, 1991

fortune cookie *noun*
1 an aphorism or joke that appears on a computer screen when a user logs in *US*
• —Eric S. Raymond, *The New Hacker's Dictionary*, p. 166, 1991
2 in poker, a bet made without having seen all of your cards *US*
• —John Vorhaus, *The Big Book of Poker Slang*, p. 19, 1996

fortuni *adjective*
gorgeous *UK*
• —Paul Baker, *Polari*, p. 175, 2002

Fort Useless *nickname*
Fort Eustis, Virginia *US, 1974*
Home to the US Army Transportation School, with training in rail, marine, amphibious operations and other modes of transportation.
• —Linda Reinberg, *In the Field*, p. 86, 1991

forty *noun*
▷ see: F-40

forty-deuce *nickname*
42nd Street, New York *US*
• [E]specially in New York's Forty-Deuce area around Times Square and Eight Avenue hustler havens. —*Maledicta*, p. 156, Summer/Winter 1986–1987: 'Sexual slang: prostitutes, pedophiles, flagellators, transvestites, and necrophiles'
• Tonight we find that place, right on Forty-deuce itself, between Seventh and Sixth. —Jim Carroll, *Forced Entries*, p. 7–8, 1987
• This being New York, of course, there are plenty of curmudgeons around who bewail the death of the old sleazy Forty Deuce with its porn shops, XXX cinemas, and ragged street people. —Holly Hughes, *Frommer's New York City with Kids*,, p. 187, 2003

forty-fin *noun*
a millipede *BAHAMAS*
• —John A. Holm, *Dictionary of Bahamian English*, p. 81, 1982

forty-four *noun*
a whore *UK*
Rhyming slang.
• —Bodmin Dark, *Dirty Cockney Rhyming Slang*, 2003

forty-going-north *adjective*
leaving or moving quickly *US*
• —*Washington Post*, p. C5, 7th November 1993

fortyleg *noun*
a centipede *BARBADOS*
• —Frank A. Collymore, *Barbadian Dialect*, p. 51, 1965

forty-miler *noun*
a new and inexperienced carnival worker or one who never travels far from home with the carnival *US, 1935*
• —Gene Sorrows, *All About Carnivals*, p. 17, 1985: 'Terminology'

forty-niner *noun*
a cocaine user *US*
An allusion to the gold rush of 1849, with cocaine serving as 'gold dust'.
• —Jay Robert Nash, *Dicitonary of Crime*, p. 138, 1992

forty-pounder *noun*
a 40 ounce bottle of alcohol *CANADA*
• In Canada, a 40-ounce bottle of liquor is known as a forty-pounder. —*Toronto Globe and Mail*, p. C6, 30th May 1998

forty-rod *noun*
strong, cheap whisky *US, 1861*
• It [hootchinoo] was sometimes referred to as Forty-Rod Whisky because it was supposed to kill a man at that distance. —Pierre Berton, *Klondike*, p. 23, 1958

Forty Thieves *noun*
the mostly white, all wealthy shop owners on Front Street, Hamilton, Bermuda *BERMUDA*
• —Peter A. Smith and Fred M. Barritt, *Bermewjan Vurds*, 1985

forty-three *verb*
to keep apart from the main prison community for 'safety of self or others' *UK*
• He was forty-threed. —Angela Devlin, *Prison Patter*, p. 53, 1996

forty-weight *noun*
1 strong coffee *US*
Inviting a comparison with motor oil.
• —Wayne Floyd, *Jason's Authentic Dictionary of CB Slang*, p. 32, 1976
2 beer, especially Iron City™ *US*
• —*Dictionary of CB Lingo*, p. 67, 1976: 'Elementary electronics'

forty winks *noun*
a nap, a short sleep *UK, 1872*
• Dyer – accused of taking forty winks to such cost during defeat at the Nou Camp – was as bright as anyone as he made a supercharged dash into the box[.] —*The Guardian*, 15th December 2002

forward *noun*
any amphetamine or other central nervous system stimulant *US*
• —J. L. Simmons and Barry Winograd, *It's Happening*, p. 170, 1966: 'glossary'

FOS *adjective*
full of shit, literally or figuratively *US*
• —*Maledicta*, p. 68, Summer/Winter 1978: 'Common patient-directed pejoratives used by medical personnel'

fo' sheezy; fo' sheazy; fa' sheezy; fo' sho sho
certainly *US*
• Still packing fo sho / Yeezy Weezy off of the heezy fo sheezy / Cruise with the top off of the 'Ghini[.] —Lil Wayne, *Fo Sheezy*, 1999
• Fa sheezy my neezy keep my arm so greasy / Can't leave rap alone the game needs me[.] —Jay Z, *to the Izzo*, 2001
• —Connie Eble (Editor), *UNC-CH Campus Slang*, p. 4, October 2002

fo' shizzle
▷ see: SHIZZLE

fossick *verb*
1 to search for gold in abandoned mines or mining refuse *AUSTRALIA, 1852*
From the British dialect of Cornwall.
• Gold had got into Joe's blood, mate. He fossicked around for ten years, but did no good. —Frank Hardy, *The Yarns of Billy Borker*, p. 145, 1965
2 to rummage about in searching for something *AUSTRALIA, 1855*
• Davo looked up from his rolling every now and then to see more than the usual number of customers fossicking through the cabinets[.] —Robert G. Barrett, *Davo's Little Something*, p. 102, 1992
3 to poke about a place *AUSTRALIA, 1941*
• She enjoys fishing, travelling over the old tracks and fossicking across the outback. —Herb Wharton, *Cattle Camp*, p. 147, 1994

fossicker *noun*
a person who fossicks *AUSTRALIA, 1852*
• The diggings had been a sanctuary to them from infant days, their legal property by right of usage, since no one used them but a few old fossickers and Chinamen[.] —Norman Lindsay, *Halfway to Anywhere*, p. 175, 1947

fossil *noun*
1 an old person with outmoded ideas and values *US, 1952*
• [H]e didn't know how to tell her that the oldest fossil in the joint wasn't fifteen years his senior. —Joseph Wambaugh, *Finnegan's Week*, p. 230, 1993
2 a parent *US*
• "Cause it'll be my eighteenth birthday, and the fossils promised to buy me a Harley if I pass math." —Max Shulman, *Rally Round the Flag, Boys!*, p. 59, 1957
3 in computing, a feature that is retained after it is no longer needed in order to preserve compatibility *US*
• —Eric S. Raymond, *The New Hacker's Dictionary*, p. 166, 1991

fother mucker *noun*
used euphemistically for 'motherfucker' in all senses *US*
A Spoonerism; noted in 2004; in the Brite Bar in New York it is possible to buy a 'Fother Mucker' cocktail.
• —Chris Lewis, *The Dictionary of Playground Slang*, p. 93, 2003

fotog *noun*
▷ **see:** PHOTOG

fougasse *noun*
napalm-thickened petrol, used in an improvised flame-thrower *US*
Korean and Vietnam war usage.
- Right in front of the triple concertina we had 55-gallon drums cut in half and filled with fougasse – a sort of napalm mixture. — Eric Hammel, *Khe Sanh: Siege in the Clouds*, p. 146, 1989

foul *adjective*
unpleasant, unfriendly *US*
Conventional English rendered slang with attitude.
- The people at this school are so incredibly foul. — *Ten Things I Hate About You*, 1999

foulball *noun*
a despised person *US, 1925*
- I got snaky last night on Waley's bum gin, and some big foulball of a dick came along. — James T. Farrell, *Saturday Night*, p. 28, 1947
- [T]o be honest, there wasn't anyone much interested in a foul ball like me – except FDA. — Max Shulman, *Anyone Got a Match?*, p. 230, 1964

fouler *noun*
a very bad mood *IRELAND*
- [H]e turns around to me and asks where JP is tonight. I'm like, 'He's still in a fouler with me.' — Paul Howard, *Ross O'Carroll-Kelly*, p. 193, 2003

foul-up *noun*
an instance of something being botched or ruined *US, 1943*
- Chads are gone, but Florida faces new voting foul-up fears[.] — *The Guardian*, 18th April 2004

foul up *verb*
to botch, to ruin *US, 1942*
- Thou hadst a chance to be beautiful, yet thou hadst fouled it up. — Bel Kaufman, *Up the Down Staircase*, p. 145, 1964

found-in *noun*
a person arrested for patronising an illegal bar or gambling club *CANADA*
- Found-ins from a raided Toronto gambling club are taken by paddy wagon to face charges. — *Maclean's*, p. 18/1, 26th March 1960
- R.C.M.P. had raided the house about a week earlier [and] seized a quantity of liquor and questioned the "guests" who had been there at the time of the raid. Names of the "found-ins" were not disclosed to the court. — *News of the North*, p. 3, 2nd May 1963

fountains of Rome *noun*
in homosexual usage, urinals in a public toilet *US*
- — *Maledicta*, p. 60, 1986–1987: 'A continuation of a glossary of ethnic slurs in American English'

four *noun*
1 a capsule of Empirin™ with codeine, designed for pain relief but abused by users of central nervous system depressants and opiates *US*
- — Walter L. Way, *The Drug Scene*, p. 108, 1977

2 a four ounce glass of beer *AUSTRALIA*
- What do we call them? Fours, sixes and eights. — John O'Grady, *It's Your Shout, Mate!*, p. 56, 1972

3 yes; an affirmative *US, 1976*
Also writen as '4.' An abbreviation of the conventional citizens' band radio code 10–4.
- That's a four for sure. — Peter Chippindale, *The British CB Book*, p. 155, 1981

four-banger *noun*
a four-cylinder engine *US, 1953*
- The 36-horse four-banger idled easily as the wind whistled louder and louder through the seams of the sliding windows. — Drew Kampion, *The Lost Coast*, p. 3, 2004

four-be-two *noun*
a prison warder *UK*
Rhyming slang for SCREW.
- — Angela Devlin, *Prison Patter*, p. 53, 1996

four bits *noun*
a fifty-year prison sentence *US*
- — Charles Shafer, *Folk Speech in Texas Prisons*, p. 204, 1990
- — Ethan Hilderbrant, *Prison Slang*, p. 51, 1998

four-by *noun*
a prison warder *AUSTRALIA*
- — Ryan Aven-Bray, *Ridgey Didge Oz Jack Lang*, p. 28, 1983

four-by-four *noun*
1 a vehicle with four wheels and four-wheel drive *US*
- — John Edwards, *Auto Dictionary*, p. 64, 1993

2 a whore *UK*
Rhyming slang.
- — Bodmin Dark, *Dirty Cockney Rhyming Slang*, 2003

four by too's *noun*
in twelve-step recovery programmes such as Alcoholics Anonymous, used for describing why recovering addicts don't attend programme meetings – too busy, too tired, too lazy or too drunk *US*
A play on 'two-by-four', the dimensions of the most common timber used in construction.
- — Christopher Cavanaugh, *AA to Z*, p. 99, 1998

four by two *noun*
1 a Jewish person *UK, 1936*
Rhyming slang, originally military. Variants include 'four by', 'fourby' and 'four-he' – but 'three by two', a civilian variation, is now obsolete.
- Lew Silver, a well known artistic four by two, who, at the time of writing, is pretty flaked[.] — Barry Humphries, *Bazza Pulls It Off!*, 1971
- Excuse the lack of etiquette, but what's your name? Mort? Mort Lazarus. (To himself) A four-by-two. — Jack Hibberd, *A Stretch of the Imagination*, p. 9, 1971
- Hang on a sec you silly dag while I square off this four-by-two. — *The Adventures of Barry McKenzie*, 1972
- [A] rich four-by-twoish merchant. — Ronnie Barker, *Fletcher's Book of Rhyming Slang*, p. 27, 1979

2 a prison warder *AUSTRALIA*
Rhyming slang for SCREW.
- When they were in a good mood they called us 'screws', 'four-by-twos' or 'boss'[.] — William Dodson, *The Sharp End*, p. 11, 2001

four-color glossies *noun*
any literature that contains some useful information but which emphasises style over substance *US*
- Often applied as an indication of superficiality even when the material is printed on ordinary paper in black and white. Four-color glossy manuals are never useful for finding a problem. — Eric S. Raymond, *The New Hacker's Dictionary*, p. 167, 1991

four-cornered *adjective*
caught in the commission of a crime *US*
- — William K. Bentley and James M. Corbett, *Prison Slang*, p. 92, 1992

four-deuce *noun*
an M-30 4.2 inch heavy mortar *US*
Vietnam war usage.
- — Carl Fleischhauer, *A Glossary of Army Slang*, p. 20, 1968
- The Viet Cong were maintaining their usual invisibility – but the four-deuces would at least suppress the VC rifle fire. — Phil Caputo, *A Rumor of War*, p. 281, 1977
- — Gregory Clark, *Words of the Vietnam War*, p. 298, 1990

fourex fever *noun*
a state of drunkenness caused by XXXX™ lager *AUSTRALIA*
- That night I sat on the beach succumbing to Fourex fever, and planning our southern route to escape. — Richard Neville writing in 'HQ Magazine', 1991, *Out Of My Mind*, p. 91, 1996

four-eyed *adjective*
wearing glasses *US, 1878*
- Tryin' to shop us, eh, you four-eyed git! — Charles Raven, *Underworld Nights*, p. 18, 1956
- He's got scoliosis and a clubfoot but the guy's an engineer, he pulls down seventy-five thousand a year, and that four-eyed fuck never cracked a schoolbook in his life. — Richard Price, *Clockers*, p. 523, 1992

four-eyes *noun*
a person who wears glasses *US, 1865*
- Even the so-called nice guys / Called us four-eyes. — Lenny Bruce, *The Essential Lenny Bruce*, p. 127, 1967
- One a tall tennis-anyone type, the other a bespectacled mouse type. I opted for Minnie Four-Eyes. — Erich Segal, *Love Story*, p. 2, 1970

• Four eyes. People with glasses give me a peculiar feeling. —Darryl Ponicsan, *The Last Detail*, p. 121, 1970
• —Connie Eble (Editor), *UNC-CH Campus Slang*, November 1976

four five *noun*
a .45 calibre handgun *US*
• —Ann Lawson, *Kids & Gangs*, p. 56, 1994: 'Common African-American gang slang/phrases'

fourflusher *noun*
a liar, a fraud *US, 1904*
• Mooches, fags, fourflushers, stool pigeons, bums – unwilling to work, unable to steal, always short of money, always whining for credit. —William Burroughs, *Junkie*, p. 54, 1954

four f's *noun*
used as a jocular if cynical approach to male relationships with women – find them, feel them, fuck them, forget them *US, 1942*
A pun on 4F draft status, which meant that a man was physically unfit to serve.
• —Roger Blake, *The American Dictionary of Sexual Terms*, p. 76, 1964
• —Dale Gordon, *The Dominion Sex Dictionary*, p. 71, 1967
• —Robert A. Wilson, *Playboy's Book of Forbidden Words*, p. 110, 1972
• —Kenn "Naz" Young, *Naz's Underground Dictionary*, p. 65, 1973

four-laner *noun*
a truck driver who prefers large interstate motorways *US*
• —Montie Tak, *Truck Talk*, p. 64, 1971

four-letter man *noun*
1 an unpleasant person *US, 1923*
Euphemistic disguise for the letters *s h i t* or *c u n t*.
• —*Maledicta*, p. 13, Summer 1977: 'A word for it!'
• —Ann Barr and Peter York, *The Official Sloane Ranger Handbook*, p. 158, 1982
2 a male homosexual *US*
• —Vincent J. Monteleone, *Criminal Slang*, p. 90, 1949

four-letter word *noun*
a profanity, especially although not always one with four letters, and usually the word 'fuck' *US, 1936*
• —*American Speech*, April 1949
• —*American Speech*, May 1950

four-lunger *noun*
a four-cylinder engine *US*
• —Montie Tak, *Truck Talk*, p. 64, 1971

four-o-four *adjective*
▷ **see:** 404

four-one-one *noun*
▷ **see:** 411

four-on-the-floor *noun*
1 a car with a four-speed transmission with the gear shift mounted on the floor *US*
• —Lyle K. Engel, *The Complete Book of Fuel and Gas Dragsters*, p. 151, 1968
2 use of the bass drum on every beat, especially in disco music *US*
Playing on the automotive term.
• —Walter Hurst and Donn Delson, *Delson's Dictionary of Radio & Record Industry Terms*, p. 54, 1980
• But then with a disco style beat of "four on the floor" the whole place starts to jump and jive. —Jack Allen, *When the Whistle Blows*, p. 134, 2000

fourpenny dark *noun*
cheap wine *AUSTRALIA, 1955*
• You can recognise them by their habit of calling for a bottle of plonk, bombo, or steam, or for a glass of fourpenny dark. —Cyril Pearl, *So, you want to be an Australian*, p. 44, 1959
• —Arthur Chipper, *The Aussie Swearer's Guide*, p. 67, 1972

four percent *noun*
a mild beer that was for a time sold in the west *CANADA*
• Under the general term liquor we have "Old Alky" for whiskey, and "four per-cent" for a milder variety of beer. —*Alberta Historical Review*, p. 16/1, Autumn 1962

four plus *adverb*
to the utmost degree *US, 1961*
• That accident is four plus drunk. I can't get a decent history from him. —*American Speech*, p. 145–148, May 1961: 'The spoken language of medicine; argot, slang, cant'

fours *noun*
1 in poker, four of a kind *US*
• —Albert H. Morehead, *The Complete Guide to Winning Poker*, p. 263, 1967
2 the fourth landing or floor level in a prison *UK*
• —Angela Devlin, *Prison Patter*, p. 53, 1996

fours and dors *noun*
a combination of number four codeine tablets and Doriden™ sleeping pills, which produces an opiate-like effect on the user *US*
• —Geoffrey Froner, *Digging for Diamonds*, p. 30, 1989

four-square *noun*
in new car sales, the work sheet used by a sales representative *US*
• —*Doctor's Review*, August 1989

four-star *adjective*
excellent *US, 1935*
From a common rating system used with hotels, restaurants and the like.
• She had already made up her mind she'd have a lousy time, and besides, there was a four-star film on the telly later than night. —Jane Moore, *Fourplay*, p. 54, 2001

four-s time *noun*
the time before going out on the town; in the armed services, the pre-liberty period *US*
The s's are 'shit, shave, shower and shine'.

four-striper *noun*
a captain in the US Navy *US, 1914*
• Temporary or not, I was a four-striper. And I had clout. —Richard Marcinko, *Rogue Warrior*, p. 334, 1992

fourteen *noun*
1 an M-14 rifle *US*
• They made us switch to the M-16 during our tour. I liked the fourteens much better. —Al Santoli, *To Bear Any Burden*, p. 106, 1985
2 the Grumman F-14 Tomcat, a long-range strike-fighter aircraft *US*
Vietnam war usage.
• "You using your 14's for escort?" "Of course." The Grmann F-14 Tomcat was the best fighter craft in the world. —Nelson DeMille, *By the Rivers of Babylon*, p. 25, 1978

fourteen and two *noun*
a typical punishment of 14 days restricted to barracks with two hours of extra duty each day *US*
Punishment imposed under Article 15 of the Uniform Code of Military Justice for minor misconduct by military members.
• —Linda Reinberg, *In the Field*, p. 87, 1991

fourteener *noun*
any one of the 54 peaks over 14,000 feet in the Colorado Rocky Mountains *US*
• —Jim Crotty, *How to Talk American*, p. 210, 1997

Fourteen Feathers *noun*
Thunderbird™ wine *US*
On account of the 14 feathers on the label's bird.

four-tens *noun*
a work schedule of four ten-hour days a week *US, 1979*
A schedule that became popular in the US in the late 1970s and early 80s, keeping the basic 40-hour workweek but creating an additional 52 days a year off work.
• —*American Speech*, Spring 1982

fourth of July *noun*
a tie *UK, 1931*
Rhyming slang.

four to the floor *adjective*
1 in music, a four-bar beat; describes most modern dance music *UK*
• From techno, came trance, with its wobbly and bleepy noises, pounding four-to-the-floor bass line, uplifting and climactic snare-drum roll and some oligatory cheesy sci-fi flick sample thrown in. —J. Hoggarth, *How To Be a DJ*, p. 10, 2002

2 falling-down drunk *UK*
Suggesting the drunkard is possibly a musician and is probably on 'all fours'.
- — *e-cyclopaedia*, 20th March 2002

four-trey, the country way *noun*
a roll of seven in a craps game *US*
- 'Four-trey, the country way,' the stick man san, raking in the dice. 'Seven! The loser!' — Chester Himes, *A Rage in Harlem*, p. 26, 1957

four-twenty *noun*
1 marijuana *US*
Also written as '420'. False etymologies abound; the term was coined by teenagers in Marin County, California, and does not refer to any police code.
- With the cocaine kangarooing me, and this booby-trapped nest of low-life suckers I stumbled into I had more than a frantic yearning for maybe four-twenty at the Haven. — Iceberg Slim (Robert Beck), *Pimp*, p. 143, 1969
- "Four-twenty" – once an obscure Bay Area term for pot – is showing up nationally in the advertisements and business names of concert promoters, travel agencies, even high-tech companies. — *Los Angeles Times*, 20th April 2002

2 any time that is considered the appropriate time to smoke marijuana *US*
Also written as '4:20'. Coinage is credited to California students in the 1970s then, via the scene surrounding the Grateful Dead into wider usage.
- — Steven Wishnia, *The Cannabis Companion*, p. 151, 2004

four-twenty man *noun*
▷ **see:** 420 MAN

four-way *noun*
a mixture of four drugs, usually psychedelics and stimulants *US*
- — Jay Robert Nash, *Dicitonary of Crime*, p. 138, 1992

four-way *adjective*
willing to engage in four types of sexual activity, the exact nature of which depends upon the person described and the context *US*
- I was taught early that suffering is inevitable and necessary for an aspiring pimp, pickpocket or con man and even just a nigger compelled to become a four-way whore for the Establishment. — Iceberg Slim (Robert Beck), *The Naked Soul of Iceberg Slim*, p. 17–18, 1971
- A racehorse goes four ways. She gets tricked two ways. She eats the person up and also – actually, she does anything a man wants, that's what she does, she's all the way around. — Bruce Jackson, *In the Life*, p. 181, 1972

four-wheeler *noun*
1 in trucking, a passenger car *US*
- — Ed and Ruth Radlauer, *Truck Tech Talk*, p. 26, 1986

2 a nominal Christian, originally specifically a Catholic, who only goes to church for his or her baptism, marriage and funeral *UK*
Shorter form of 'four-wheel Christian'. The four wheels are, in turn, on a pram, a wedding-car and a hearse.
- — *Universe*, 28th February 1969

four wheel skid *noun*
▷ **see:** FRONT WHEEL SKID

four-year lesbian *noun*
a woman who takes lesbian lovers in college, planning to return to the safer waters of heterosexuality after graduation from college *US*
- — Steven Daly and Nalthaniel Wice, *alt.culture*, p. 138, 1995

four zero *adjective*
40 years old *UK*
This entry stands as an example of all variations from 20 to 90.
- [H]e's about four zero so he's leaving it late. — J.J. Connolly, *Layer Cake*, p. 18, 2000

fox *noun*
1 a beautiful woman or girl *US, 1961*
- Since there were two Negro colleges near his town, why not cut out all the old time "handkerchief head waitress" and recruit all young college "foxes". — Babs Gonzales, *I Paid My Dues*, p. 83, 1967
- Name's Dee-Dee. She a fox, too. I think Jimmy strung out behind her. — Nathan Heard, *Howard Street*, p. 63, 1968
- Your sister is really turning into a fox. — *Fast Times at Ridgemont High*, 1982

2 in poker, the sixth player to the left of the dealer *US*
- — George Percy, *The Language of Poker*, p. 33, 1988

fox *verb*
1 to follow; to spy on *NEW ZEALAND, 1905*
- 'We're being followed,' he said. 'Peter Herlihy. He's foxing us.' — Bill Pearson, *Coal Flat*, p. 153, 1963

2 to slaughter a horse for fox food *CANADA*
- "Ya, well, father," said Seamus on a more solemn note, ""we have ta fox that old mare, she's gettin' old and snappy". — Allan Morrison, *A Giant Among Friends*, p. 61, 1980

fox and badger *noun*
the penis *UK*
Rhyming slang for **TADGER**.
- — Bodmin Dark, *Dirty Cockney Rhyming Slang*, 2003

fox and hound *noun*
a *round* of drinks *UK*
Rhyming slang, formed on the name of a pub.
- Whose fox and hound is it? — Ray Puxley, *Cockney Rabbit*, 1992

Fox Charlie Charlie; Friendly Candy Company *nickname*
the Federal Communications Commission *US*
- Back formations from the agency's initials. Sorry, guys and beavers, but the world's greatest fun machine has got a few rules and regulations that we must all abide by, or the folks at the Friendly Candy Company may come and take our toys away. — Wayne Floyd, *Jason's Authentic Dictionary of CB Slang*, p. 17, 1976

foxcore *noun*
rock music played by women *UK*
- — Susie Dent, *The Language Report*, p. 42, 2003

fox hunter *noun*
an Englishman *AUSTRALIA*
- — Ned Wallish, *The Truth Dictionary of Racing Slang*, p. 30, 1989

foxie *noun*
1 an attractive girl *US*
- — H. Craig Collins, *Street Gangs*, p. 222, 1979

2 a fox terrier *AUSTRALIA, 1906*
- Mother isn't certain how a Dane and an Alsatian would mix with two Australian foxies. — Barry Humphries, *A Nice Night's Entertainment*, p. 8, 1956
- — Patsy Adam-Smith, *Folklore of the Australian Railwaymen*, p. 156, 1969

foxtress *noun*
a beautiful woman or girl *UK*
- Bubbly Welsh foxtress[.] — *Q*, p. 84, July 2005

foxtrot yankee!
fuck you! *US*
From the military phonetic alphabet – FY.
- — Linda Reinberg, *In the Field*, p. 87, 1991

foxy *adjective*
attractive, beautiful *US, 1895*
Usually but not always applied to a woman.
- We members of the viper school were making music that was real foxy, all lit up with inspiration and her mammy. — Mezz Mezzrow, *Really the Blues*, p. 94, 1946
- I mean all the studs in fancy duds and foxy chicks togged to the bricks is gonna be there. — Ross Russell, *The Sound*, p. 218, 1961
- Now, I see you on down on the scene. / Oh, Foxy . . .! / You make me wanna get up and scream! / Foxy . . .[.] — Jimi Hendrix, *Foxy Lady*, 1968
- George looked and saw a very foxy Danish girl sitting down. — Cecil Brown, *The Life & Loves of Mr. Jiveass Nigger*, p. 113, 1969
- He went on to say that "she was a foxy little thing" and "better than your average piece of ass." — Elmore Leonard, *City Primeval*, p. 8, 1980
- Offensive description of a woman's physical appearance. — Multicultural Management Program Fellows, *Dictionary of Cautionary Words and Phrases*, 1989
- You're the foxiest bitch I've ever known. — *Boogie Nights*, 1997

frabjous *adjective*
joyous, wonderful *UK, 1872*
A nonsense word coined by Lewis Carroll (C.L. Dodgson), and used vaguely in various contextual senses.
- "Face In A Cloud" [by Audio Bullys] is pure 60s mod given a frabjous nu-skool twist[.] — *Bang*, p. 77, May 2003

fracture *verb*

to have a strong, favourable effect upon someone *US, 1946*

- "You fracture me," she said.—Max Shulman, *The Many Loves of Dobie Gillis*, p. 123, 1951
- —Robert George Reisner, *The Jazz Titans*, p. 155, 1960

fractured *adjective*

drunk *US, 1953*

- They had already annihihlated kegs of beer and started to get fractured on Gallo wine.—Frederick Kohner, *Gidget*, p. 123, 1957
- —Eugene Landy, *The Underground Dictionary*, p. 81, 1971

frag *noun*

1 a *frag*mentation hand grenade or bomb *US, 1943*

- —Helen Dahlskog (Editor), *A Dictionary of Contemporary and Colloquial Usage*, p. 25, 1972
- You peep through that skinny-ass embrasure with your M-16 on full rock and roll, a double armful of fragmentation grenades – frags we called them[.]—Larry Heinemann, *Paco's Story*, p. 10, 1986
- We got two men need attention here. Police up your extra ammo and frags.—*Platoon*, 1986

2 a *frag*ment from a bullet or artillery shell *US, 1966*

- "They got frags from the woman and two good ones from Gujy, the casing intact..."—Elmore Leonard, *City Primeval*, p. 60, 1980

3 a *frag*mentary order *US, 1962*

- Major Henri (Pete) Mallet, the 3rd Brigade operations officer, flew in with a half-page "frag" from Colonel Brown.—Harold G. Moore, *We Were Soldiers Once ... And Young*, p. 56, 1992

frag *verb*

1 to kill a fellow soldier, usually an officer and usually with a fragmentation grenade *US, 1970*

A term coined in Vietnam to describe a practice that became common if not widespread in Vietnam.

- Don't "frag" that cute little Second Lieutenant – fuck the daylights out of him!—*Screw*, p. 11, 21st June 1971
- —Helen Dahlskog (Editor), *A Dictionary of Contemporary and Colloquial Usage*, p. 25, 1972
- [O]thers in prisons for fragging officers who ordered them about[.]—Emmett Grogan, *Ringolevio*, p. 231, 1972
- And there's a rumor about fragging! Someone heard some policemen talking about bombing a watch commander!—Joseph Wambaugh, *The Choirboys*, p. 209, 1975
- "To frag," said Gianni. A spirited demonstration of lack of confidence in or respect for a leader. From the Latin, Fragmentation grenade.—John Sayles, *Union Dues*, p. 249, 1977
- Seems to me he got himself fragged.—*Apocalypse Now*, 1979
- I say we frag the fucker.—*Platoon*, 1986
- He had been convicted of being an accessory to murder for having held open a hooch door while another Marine threw in a fragmentation grenade and killed their company commander. It was a time when "fragging" had become a new and frightening threat[.]—*Providence (Rhode Island) Journal-Bulletin*, p. 1E, 20th April 2000

2 by extension, to score a 'kill' over another player in video and computer games, especially Quake™ *US*

- After that I blew him to bits with a rocket launcher. But then he fragged me several times in succession.—*BBC News Online*, 19th November 2002

3 to dispatch by a fragmentary order *US, 1967*

- The Marines arranged for a special helicopter (or "fragged a chopper," as we used to call it) to take him in and out of Khe Sanh one afternoon.—Michael Herr, *Dispatches*, p. 223, 1977

4 in motor racing, to cause an engine to explode, sending pieces of motor through the engine block *US*

- —Lewis Poteet, *Car & Motorcyle Slang*, p. 88, 1992

fragged-out *adjective*

over-stressed *UK*

Military, from US military abbreviation of 'fragmentary/fragmentation'.

- [V]engeful, careworn wives, fragged-out blokes worrying about money and their families' security from dawn to dusk[.]—Chris Ryan, *The Watchman*, p. 149, 2001

fraggle *noun*

1 in prison, a mentally ill inmate *UK*

A Fraggle is a television puppet character from Jim Henson's *Fraggle Rock*, 1983–87; this excerpt from the theme lyric may well explain the derivation: 'Dance your cares away, / Worry's for another day [...] Let the Fraggles play'. Jim Henson also created *The Muppets* which also serve as models for the slow-witted.

- —Angela Devlin, *Prison Patter*, p. 53, 1996
- [S]houting out of their cell windows, cursing the disturbed man. "Shut the fuck up, you fraggle." "Quiet, you nutter."—Erwin James, *The Guardian*, 31st August 2000: 'a life inside'

2 (among Canadian Forces personnel) an avionics technician *CANADA*

- A "fraggle" is an avionics technician. The term is borrowed from the CBC television series of the 1980s, *Fraggle Rock*. Fraggles were creatures of uncommon idleness, who lived in their own, most unusual world.—Tom Langeste, *Words on the Wing*, p. 112, 1995

fraggle juice *noun*

in prison, medication given to mentally ill inmates *UK*

- —Angela Devlin, *Prison Patter*, p. 53, 1996

Fraggle Rock *noun*

1 a section of a prison dedicated to psychiatric criminal care *UK*

- —Angela Devlin, *Prison Patter*, p. 53, 1996

2 (among Canadian Air Force personnel) the Air Command Headquarters in Winnipeg *CANADA*

- "Fraggle Rock," like all headquarters, is viewed as a place where all sorts of amazing and inexplicable things occur. "I hear that you'll be spending the next three years at Fraggle Rock!"—Tom Langeste, *Words on the Wing*, p. 112, 1995

frag list *noun*

a frag order *US*

Vietnam war usage.

- I just wanted to hit them harder than the frag list allowed.—Stephen Coonts, *Flight of the Intruder*, p. 358, 1986

frag order *noun*

an order setting the day's specific military objectives *US*

Shortened 'fragmentation order'. Vietnam war usage.

- Some frag order, Jack through, as he tried to decipher the long message detailing the targets for the wing's next mission.—Richard Herman, *The Warbirds*, p. 266, 1989

fraho; frajo *noun*

marijuana *US*

Originally a 'cigarette' or 'marijuana cigarette'.

- —*American Speech*, p. 25, February 1952: 'Teen-age hophead jargon'
- —Richard A. Spears, *The Slang and Jargon of Drugs and Drink*, p. 204, 1986
- —Mike Haskins, *Drugs*, p. 287, 2003

'fraid so

I'm afraid so *US*

Often answered with ''fraid not'.

- "And Michael Landon?" "'Fraid so," Al Garcia said.—Carl Hiaasen, *Tourist Season*, p. 196, 1986
- Is there much more? 'Fraid so.—*The Guardian*, 17th February 2003

fraidy cat *noun*

a cowardly person *UK, 1910*

- "Timmy's a fraidy-cat," Lex called. "What a stupid jerk," Tim said.—Michael Crichton, *Jurassic Park*, p. 237, 1990

frail *noun*

a woman *US, 1899*

- [L]eaning over to brush some crumbs off the table, he'd bump up against some pretty young frail with his rear end and send her flying.—Mezz Mezzrow, *Really the Blues*, p. 85, 1946
- It is lined with walls of men waiting for the frails to come out of the bars, strip dives, and burlesque houses.—Jack Lait and Lee Mortimer, *Washington Confidential*, p. 268, 1951
- And the Frail was named Stella, a fraud Cinderella, out trying to trick any citified Hick[.]—Dan Burley, *Diggeth Thou?*, p. 47, 1959
- I'm hip to the ways you pimps try to play / And the lugs you drop on a frail.—Dennis Wepman et al., *The Life*, p. 86, 1976
- Willie Poe got his papa's inky skin. He got his French mama's features and silky hair. The combination is got the frails so creamy between the legs they can't walk for running to catch Willie Poe.—Iceberg Slim (Robert Beck), *Death Wish*, p. 112, 1977

frak!

used as a non-profane oath *US*

Used by spacecraft pilots, especially Lt Starbuck on the US television series *Battlestar Galactica* (ABC, 1978–80), and briefly in popular speech.

frame *noun*

1 the general circumstance, especially of a crime *UK, 1970*

Conventionally a frame fits the picture; figuratively applied.

- Scotland Yard works on informers, and if you go in the frame for something, you get picked up and fitted up[.] — *The Listener*, 8th March 1979
- Vince wanted to be top do now that Gavin was out of the frame. — Danny King, *The Bank Robber Diaries*, p. 63, 2002

2 the body *US*

- Some poontang to cradle my lonesome frame. — George Mandel, *Flee the Angry Strangers*, p. 59, 1952
- I left the tavern, returned to the dormitory, and put my miserable frame ito the sack. — Max Shulman, *Guided Tour of Campus Humor*, p. 60, 1955

▸ **in the frame**

under suspicion of involvement in a crime that is being investigated *UK*

- — Angela Devlin, *Prison Patter*, p. 65, 1996

frame *verb*

to incriminate a person by contriving false evidence *US, 1899*

- I never od nothin' wrong but every time I get the blame / I been framed! — Cheech Marin and Tommy Chong, *Framed*, 1976
- — Angela Devlin, *Prison Patter*, p. 53, 1996

frame dame *noun*

an attractive and sexually active, if not too bright, girl *US, 1979*

- — Kenn "Naz" Young, *Naz's Dictionary of Teen Slang*, p. 44, 1993

frame job *noun*

a conspiracy, especially one where blame for a misdeed is placed on someone *US, 1973*

- "Assuming a frame job and murder, where is Lee's body?" Sam asked neutrally. — Elizabeth Lowell, *The Color of Death*, p. 79, 2004

framer *noun*

a bed *US*

- — Kenn "Naz" Young, *Naz's Underground Dictionary*, p. 30, 1973

frames *noun*

eyeglasses *US*

- — David Claerbaut, *Black Jargon in White America*, p. 64, 1972

frame-up; frame *noun*

manufactured evidence that is intended to incriminate *US, 1908*

- In 1996 another opposition leader, the Reverend Ndabaningi Sithole, also alleged a frame-up after being being convicted of plotting to kill Mr Mugabe. — *The Guardian*, 3rd February 2003

frammis *noun*

a commotion *US*

- Probably a dozen people saw that little frammis this morning. — Jim Thompson, *A Swell-Looking Babe*, p. 69, 1954

France *noun*

used as a euphemistic subsitute for 'hell' *BARBADOS*

- — Frank A. Collymore, *Barbadian Dialect*, p. 51, 1965
- 'What the France you think you doing?' — Lise Winer, *Dictionary of the English/Creole of Trinidad & Tobago*, 2003

France and Spain; frarny *noun*

rain *UK, 1931*

Rhyming slang.

Francis Drake *noun*

a brake *UK*

Rhyming slang, formed on the name of celebrated circumnavigator and national hero Sir Francis Drake, 1540–96.

- — Ray Puxley, *Cockney Rabbit*, 1992

franger *noun*

a condom *AUSTRALIA, 1981*

Perhaps an alteration of **FRENCH LETTER** and the **-ER** suffix.

- Ever conscious of the dreaded clap, one said to the other 'Have you got a franger on you?' — Martin Cameron, *A Look at the Bright Side*, 1988
- — Ignatius Jones, *The 1992 True Hip Manual*, p. 188, 1992
- — Roy Slaven (John Doyle), *Five South Coast Seasons*, p. 107, 1992
- It was frangers a-go-go when the glitterati turned out for a big AIDS fundraising bash... — *People*, p. 11, 16th December 1992
- Yup, Thai body sliding is the most fun a bloke can have in Queensland without breaking the law, wearing a franger or worrying bout the bastard AIDS virus. — *Picture*, p. 5, 5th February 1992
- Mucky Michael Hales, 38, learned to recognise the various wrappers used to ship the blow-up dolls, vibrators, frangers and porn he was supposed to deliver! — *People*, p. 65, 5th July 1999

frangler *noun*

a condom *AUSTRALIA*

- — James McDonald, *A Dictionary of Obscenity, Taboo and Euphemism*, p. 29, 1988

Franglish *noun*

French and English mixed or blended in the same sentence *CANADA*

- As they say in Franglais – that curious French-English mixture popular among newly "bilingual" English-speaking Montrealers these days – la preuve is in le pudding. — *Calgary Herald*, p. 5/4, 2nd January 1964
- Not even Franglish — *Calgary Herald*, p. 4/1 (Headline), 2nd January 1964

frank *noun*

a *frank*furter, a hot dog *US, 1925*

- We had a farewell meal of franks and beans in a Seventh Avenue Riker's[.] — Jack Kerouac, *On the Road*, p. 9, 1957
- I'm at the supermarket, I bought a pack of franks. — Chris Rock, *Rock This!*, p. 164, 1997

Frank and Pat *noun*

talk *UK*

Rhyming slang for 'chat', based on long-running characters Frank Butcher (from 1987) and Pat Evans (from 1986) in BBC television soap opera *EastEnders*.

- Do you ever stop your Frank and Pat? — *www.LondonSlang.com*, June 2002

Franken- *prefix*

in combination with a noun denotes a freakish, genetically modified or ugly form of that thing *US*

After Mary Shelly's 1818 novel *Frankenstein* but from the images provided by C20 Hollywood.

- If they want to sell us Frankenfood, perhaps it's time to gather the villagers, light some torches and head to the castle. [Letter to the Editor] — *New York Times*, p. A24, 16th June 1992
- An Atlanta chef is leading the charge against "Frankenfood" – genetically altered foods that are expected on store shelves soon. — *Atlanta Constitution*, p. G2, 16th October 1992
- Some editors chart an easy course in dubbing anything to do with GM produce "Frankenfood". — *The Guardian*, 7th June 2002
- Hello Kitty or Frankenpet? — *San Francisco Chronicle*, 20th April 2004

Frankie Boy *nickname*

Frank Sinatra, American singer (1915–1998) *US*

- The latest casino owner in Las Vegas to embark on the hearts-and-flowers route is Francis Albert Sinatra, better known as The Leader, The General, The Dago, The Pope, and Frankie Boy. — Ed Reid and Ovid Demaris, *The Green Felt Jungle*, p. 74, 1963

Frankie Dettori *noun*

a *story*; the facts or circumstance *UK*

Rhyming slang, formed from the name of the champion jockey (b.1970).

- What's the Frankie Dettori (sp?) on Feelin' Carter? — Andrew Holmes, *Sleb*, p. 83, 2002

Frankie Fraser; frankie *noun*

a razor *UK*

Rhyming slang, formed from the name of 'Mad' Frankie Fraser (b.1923), an ex-gangster with a reputation for violence and a celebrity profile.

- Football? No, but see him go to work with his cosh, or his Frankie, now that's when he was a player. — Garry Bushell, *The Face*, p. 33, 2001

Frankie Howerd; frankie *noun*

a coward *UK*

Rhyming slang, formed from the name of a popular comedian, 1917–92.

- — Ray Puxley, *Cockney Rabbit*, 1992

Frankie Laine; frankie *noun*

a toilet *chain* (to flush the lavatory); hence a handle that operates a cistern *UK*

Rhyming slang, formed from the name of a popular American singer (b.1913).

- Even though this apparatus [a chain] has become a rarity in modern toilets people still "pull the Frankie". — Ray Puxley, *Cockney Rabbit*, 1992

Frankie Vaughan; frankie *noun*

1 pornography *UK*

Rhyming slang for **PORN**; formed from the name of Liverpool-born singer and actor Frankie Vaughan (b.1928). Also used as an adjective.

- Could have been watching Frankie Vaughan on the telly and giving herself a scratch [masturbating]. — Ian Dury, *This is What We Find*, 1979

- He's fucking potty about films [...] Always going on about the plot and that, supporting roles and all that carry-on. Even with the Frankies. —Kevin Sampson, *Outlaws*, p. 227, 2001
- Telling you man, the Frankie Vaughan and the Viagra is worth more to me these days than a few keys of smack [heroin]. —Kevin Sampson, *Clubland*, p. 76, 2002

2 a prawn *UK*
Rhyming slang, formed from the name of a popular British singer, 1928–99.
- —Ray Puxley, *Cockney Rabbit*, 1992

Frankie Vaughno *noun*
pornography *UK*
An extension of the original rhyming slang for **PORN**, to match **PORNO**.
- [T]he lads start going on about the Frankie Vaughno. —Kevin Sampson, *Clubland*, p. 104, 2002

frantic *adjective*
exciting, thrilling *US, 1934*
- —Lou Shelly, *Hepcats Jive Dictionary*, p. 11, 1945
- Monkey Pollack was a frantic cat, small, tough, and game as they make them. —Mezz Mezzrow, *Really the Blues*, p. 69, 1946
- —*Newsweek*, p. 28, 8th October 1951
- —*Dobie Gillis Teenage Slanguage Dictionary*, 1962
- Shorty would take me to groovy, frantic scenes in different chicks' and cats' pads, where with the lights and juke down mellow, everybody blew gage and juiced back and jumped. —Malcolm X and Alex Haley, *The Autobiography of Malcolm X*, p. 56, 1964

frap *verb*
to whip *US, 1894*
- —Charles Shafer, *Folk Speech in Texas Prisons*, p. 204, 1990

frapping *adjective*
used as a euphemism for 'fucking' in its different senses *US, 1968*
- I can't say that I think too much of your frapping Chemlites, John. —James H. Kyle, *The Guts to Try*, p. 343, 1995

frarny *noun*
▷ **see:** FRANCE AND SPAIN

Fraser and Nash; Frazer-Nash *noun*
an act of urination *UK, 1974*
Rhyming slang for **SLASH** (a urination); from Frazer-Nash, a sports car manufacturer until 1939.
- Fraser and Nash, pony and trap. —Ian Dury, *Blackmail Man*, 1977
- —Ray Puxley, *Fresh Rabbit*, 1998

frat *noun*
a college fraternity *US, 1895*
- Alpha Cholera is a darn swell frat and it's loads of fun. —Max Shulman, *The Zebra Derby*, p. 64, 1946
- I've completely neglected to mention – it was the weekend of the big frat formal. —Robert Gover, *One Hundred Dollar Misunderstanding*, p. 9, 1961
- The "misunderstanding" develops when James C. Holland, having been badgered into it by some of his frat brothers, goes to "this Negro ill-repute house." —Terry Southern, *Now Dig This*, p. 201, 17th November 1962
- They were blocking the sidewalk and encouraging a frat brother to do a semi-striptease for the benefit of a coed hanging out the window of a restaurant overhead. —Joseph Wambaugh, *Finnegan's Week*, p. 279, 1993

frat around *verb*
to idle, to gossip instead of studying *US*
- —Carol Ann Preusse, *Jargon Used by University of Texas Co-Eds*, 1963

fratastic *adjective*
displaying characteristics associated with college fraternities *US*
- —Connie Eble (Editor), *UNC-CH Campus Slang*, p. 4, November 2003

frat dick *noun*
a borish member of a college fraternity *US*
- —Pamela Munro, *U.C.L.A. Slang*, p. 40, 1989

fraternity brother *noun*
a fellow prisoner *US*
- —Vincent J. Monteleone, *Criminal Slang*, p. 90, 1949

frat mattress *noun*
a girl who is sexually attracted to and available for college fraternity boys *US*
- —Connie Eble (Editor), *UNC-CH Campus Slang*, p. 2, Spring 2001

frat rat *noun*
an obnoxious, aggressive, arrogant example of a college fraternity member *US, 1958*
- —Collin Baker et al., *College Undergraduate Slang Study Conducted at Brown University*, p. 121, 1968

frat tuck *noun*
a shirt worn tucked into the trousers in the front but hanging loose in the back *US*
- —Don R. McCreary (Editor), *Dawg Speak*, 2001

fratty *adjective*
characteristic of college fraternity behaviour, style or language *US*
- —Connie Eble (Editor), *UNC-CH Campus Slang*, p. 4, Spring 2003

fratty bagger *noun*
a stereotypical fraternity member who dresses, talks and lives the part to a fault *US*
- —Connie Eble (Editor), *UNC-CH Campus Slang*, March 1973

frau *noun*
a wife *UK, 1821*
A jocular borrowing from German.
- Most of it revolves around Desi Arnaz and his frau, Lucille Ball, who have developed a sock new act. —Bart Andrews, *I Love Lucy Book*, p. 13, 1985

frazzle-assed *adjective*
worn out *US*
- I don't give a fuck for them, see? Not a single, goddarn solitary frazzle-assed fuck. —James Jones, *From Here to Eternity*, p. 397, 1951

frazzled *adjective*
1 confused *US, 1883*
- I'm getting plumb frazzled out of my wits. —Jim Thompson, *Pop. 1280*, p. 19, 1964

2 drunk *US, 1906*
- —Ramon Adams, *The Language of the Railroader*, p. 64, 1977

freak *noun*
1 a person with strong sexual desires, often fetishistic *US, 1922*
- O, a lovely club I know on 72nd street thats just filled with freaks like you. —Hubert Selby Jr, *Last Exit to Brooklyn*, p. 193, 1957
- Say, there was asshole shellackers and shitpackers / and freaks who drunk blood from a menstruatin' womb. —Bruce Jackson, *Get Your Ass in the Water and Swim Like Me*, p. 146, 1964
- How'd you figure it was a freak, Chilly? —Malcolm Braly, *On the Yard*, p. 88, 1967
- KAREN: You know, I'm kind of a freak myself. BILLY: Ha. I never really thought of myself as a freak. But I love to freak. —Peter Fonda, *Easy Rider*, p. 156, 1969
- They don't want their wives to know they're cold freaks," she explains. "They bring their sex hang-ups to us. —George Paul Csicsery (Editor), *The Sex Industry*, p. 9, 1973
- That girl is pretty wild now / The girl's a super freak / The kind of girl you read about / In New-wave magazines —Rick James, *Super Freak*, 1981
- This girl's a freak! You can fuck 'her in the ass, fuck 'er in the mouth. Rough stuff, too. She's a freak for it. —*True Romance*, 1993
- Women want a man to think he's got a good woman, but they don't want him to think he's got a freak. Their solution: ration the pussy. —Chris Rock, *Rock This!*, p. 129–130, 1997

2 a devotee, an enthusiast *US, 1895*
- It seems like a pose, or even a perversion – and maybe it is, but to bike freaks it is very real. —Hunter S. Thompson, *Hell's Angels*, p. 94, 1966
- He is divorced from his wife and has an 18-year-old boy who, he says, with an approving grin, "is a science freak with honors out of Erasmus High. —Sidney Bernard, *This Way to the Apocalypse*, p. 39, 1966
- [F]reak referred to styles and obsessions, as in "Stewart Brand is an Indian freak" or "the zodiac – that's her freak[.]" —Tom Wolfe, *The Electric Kool-Aid Acid Test*, p. 10, 1968
- —*American Speech*, p. 306–307, Winter 1969: 'Freak compounds for argot freaks'
- He was the co-editor with S.I. Hayakawa of ETC., the magazine put out by those word freaks. —Oscar Zeta Acosta, *The Autobiography of a Brown Buffalo*, p. 100, 1972
- The man had been a tile-freak. —Ed Sanders, *Tales of Beatnik Glory*, p. 91, 1975
- The 2.2 million ecology freaks who live there [Oregon] are reminded by their Highway Division to "thank Heaven we live in God's Country." —Bill Cardoso, *The Maltese Sangweech*, p. 88, 1984
- All thae [those] fitness freaks[.] —Ian Pattison, *Rab C. Nesbitt*, 1988
- They were degenerate gamblers, coke freaks. —*Casino*, 1995

3 a member of the 1960s counterculture *US, 1960*
Originally a disparaging negative, turned around and used in a positive, complimentary sense. Widely used from the mid-1960s; hurled as abuse at the original hippies, the term was adopted by

them and turned back on the critics by the self-confessed 'freaks' with an ability to **FREAK OUT** themselves and others.

- [F]reak referred ... just to heads in costume. It wasn't a negative word. —Tom Wolfe, *The Electric Kool-Aid Acid Test*, p. 10, 1968
- They are the fringe whites ... outcasts ... worse than being a Negro or Puerto Rican. Assistant Chief Inspector Joseph McLaughjlin, boss of Manhattan South detectives, is tempted to send all these freaks to Hell. —*The Digger Papers*, p. 12, August 1968
- Anyway, I was struck by the distance between me and those street freaks. —Hunter S. Thompson, *Songs of the Doomed*, p. 119, 16th February 1969
- The university became a fortress surrounded by our foreign culture, longhaired, dopesmoking, barefooted freeks who were using state-owned university property as a playground. —Jerry Rubin, *Do It!*, p. 26, 1970
- I feel like letting my freak flag fly. —David Crosby, *Almost Cut My Hair*, 1970
- [Y]our average acid-eating freak will be getting arrested for attempting to sit in the park under General Thomas' horse in Thomas Circle[.] —Raymond Mungo, *Famous Long Ago*, p. 29, 1970
- Freak: The accepted word for those who are hip. —*Screw*, p. 7, 12th October 1970
- Which goes to show how much I knew about freaks in those days. —Gurney Norman, *Divine Right's Trip (Last Whole Earth Catalog)*, p. 9, 1971
- Let's have around for these freaks and these soldiers. —Joni Mitchell, *Carey*, 1971
- Typical freaks, huh? —Cheech Marin and Tommy Chong, *Santa Calus and his Old Lady*, 1971
- What I mean by a FREAK is somebody who – well, everyone knows what it means, don't they? —Doug Lang, *Freaks*, p. 12, 1973
- "Go to India," someone told me. 'That's where the Freaks live." —Cleo Odzer, *Goa Freaks*, p. 13, 1995
- It's home sweet home to some sweet arse freaks. —Ian Dury, *Itinerant Child*, 1998
- I dozed off and was woke up by all these scary freaks and beefy gaylords, E'd up and gurning at the moon. —*Sky Magazine*, p. 70, May 2001

4 a habitual drug user
Usually suffixed to a defining drug.

- [W]hen Roger Daltrey sand "My Generation" with the stutter of a pill freak, it made The Who the figureheads of the Mod movement. —Simon Napier-Bell, *Black Vinyl White Powder*, p. 72, 2001

5 used as a term of endearment *US*
Teen slang.

- —*Look*, p. 88, 10th August 1954

6 a dance with strong suggestions of sexual movement, first popular as a 1975 disco dance and then again in the late 1990s and early 2000s *US*
Used with 'the' unless used as a verb.

- Freak: 1) Also known as free-style. The latest and possibly the greatest form of disco dancing. —Bruce Pollack, *The Disco Handbook*, p. 6, 1979
- Freak, The/La Freak/The Freaky Deaky: A 1975 disco dance often done in lines with movements like the Mashed Potato, the Shimmy, and the Twist of the 1960s and the Dirty Boogie of the 1950s. The dancer leads with the hips, but there is a lot of body touch[.] —Mari Helen Schultz, *May I Have This Dance?*, p. 38, 1986
- The latest version of dirty dancing is called "freaking" and while it's been a mainstay at high school dances and teen parties for the last five years, now the moves are getting hotter and kids as young as 12 are doing them. —*San Francisco Chronicle*, p. A23, 3rd June 2001

7 a nonsensical novelty song *US*

- All crazy songs which make no sense are "freaks." —Jack Lait and Lee Mortimer, *New York Confidential*, p. 33, 1948

8 a wrestler whose huge size is obviously the result of the use of anabolic steroids *US*

- The WWF has just shown old clips of UW, reminding people of the steroid freak that existed in the WWF years ago. —*Herb's Wrestling Tidbits*, 28th March 1996

9 in poker, a wild card, which may be played as a card of any value *US, 1949*

- —Albert H. Morehead, *The Complete Guide to Winning Poker*, p. 263, 1967

▸ **get your freak out**
to enjoy a sexual perversion *US*

- The price is seventy five dollars a fuck, gentlemen, you gittin your freak on or what? —*Kill Bill*, 2003

freak *verb*
to panic *US, 1964*

- I'm going to freak. I'm going to freak. I have to freak. I will freak. I must freak. I am freaking, and that's official. —Nicholas Von Hoffman, *We are the People Our Parents Warned Us Against*, p. 149, 1967
- The liberals try to get everyone freaked at Wallace so we won't notice that they do precisely what he advocates... —Jerry Rubin, *Do It!*, p. 145, 1970
- I said for her to be there alone and you freaked! —*Ferris Buehler's Day Off*, 1986
- Al right, I'm, freaking too. But they tell you to stay calm. —*Jerry Maguire*, 1996

freak *adjective*

1 in jazz, unorthodox *US, 1955*

- —Robert S. Gold, *A Jazz Lexicon*, p. 112, 1964

2 attractive *US*

- —Linda Meyer, *Teenspeak!*, p. 29, 1994

freaked *adjective*
disturbed, unsettled, nervous

- I've brawled, lived and loved my way through this freaked decade. —John Robb, *The Nineties*, p. 2, 1999

freak house *noun*

1 an abandoned building used as a temporary residence for drug addicts who have been evicted from their own dwelling *US*

- —Mark S. Fleisher, *Beggars & Thieves*, p. 289, 1995: 'glossary'

2 a room, apartment or house where amphetamine addicts gather to inject the drug *US*

- —William D. Alsever, *Glossary for the Establishment and Other Uptight People*, p. 11, December 1970

freaking *adjective*
used as an intensifier where 'fucking' is to be avoided *US, 1928*

- And nobody is even lapsing into the oldpub system either, that business where you work your gourds off all day and then sink into the foamy quicksand of the freaking public house at night[.] —Tom Wolfe, *The Pump House Gang*, p. 81, 1968
- The real vision, the real freaking flash, was just like the reality, only looped to replay without end. —Lester Bangs, *Psychotic Reactions and Carburetor Dung*, p. 11, 1971
- "Freakin' fruit," said Fuzzy, pulling off the wide-brimmed hat and throwing back his long blond hair. —Joseph Wambaugh, *The Blue Knight*, p. 137, 1973
- On top of being a freaking pig, you gotta add insult to injury. —Piri Thomas, *Stories from El Barrio*, p. 87, 1978
- A goddamn, almost bona fide, freaking Christmas miracle? —Joseph Wambaugh, *Lines and Shadows*, p. 98, 1984
- I'm a fairy too! Hey, I'm a freaking fairy too. —Francesca Lia Block, *I Was a Teenage Fairy*, p. 157, 1998
- What's your freakin' problem, anyway? —*200 Cigarettes*, 1999
- Rah! Who'd have freakin' thought it? I was a blackhead with connections. —Diran Abedayo, *My Once Upon A Time*, p. 183, 2000

freaking A!
used as a euphemism for 'fucking A!' in expressing surprise *US*

- —Connie Eble (Editor), *UNC-CH Campus Slang*, p. 4, October 2002

freakish *adjective*
sexually perverted *US, 1929*

- Shug say, Wellsah, and I thought it was only whitefolks do freakish things like that. —Alice Walker, *The Color Purple*, p. 112, 1989

freak jacket *noun*
a reputation for unconventional sexual interests *US*

- Maybe you can ease from under the freak jacket you've been carrying. —Malcolm Braly, *On the Yard*, p. 32, 1967

freaknasty *noun*
a sexually active woman who shares her activity with multiple partners *US*

- —Don R. McCreary (Editor), *Dawg Speak*, 2001

freaknik *noun*
a mass celebration of black students in the streets of Atlanta, Georgia, during college spring break *US, 1992*

- 'Freaknik' festivities have come to the streets of Atlanta, as the 16th annual Black College Spring Break turns the town into a party. —*San Francisco Sunday Examiner and Chronicle*, p. A17, 19th April 1998

freako *noun*
a weirdo; a sexual deviant; a habitual drug-user *US, 1963*

- [T]he quack doctor who services every freako and housewife on Woodward Ave. threw me out of his offices. —Lester Bangs, *Psychotic Reactions and Carburetor Dung*, p. 172, 1975

freak off *verb*

1 to have sex, especially with vigour and without restraint *US*
An extremely subjective verb, perhaps referring to homosexual sex, perhaps to oral sex, perhaps to heterosexual anal sex.

- I love to freak off, but get strung out? That's something else. —Malcolm Braly, *On the Yard*, p. 326, 1967

- Hey, let's all go up my room, get high an freak off. —Robert Gover, *JC Saves*, p. 17, 1968
- Pepper is a rotten freak broad. You ain't the only stud she freaks off with. I could name a half dozen who ride her. —Iceberg Slim (Robert Beck), *Pimp*, p. 67, 1969
- Tenderloin Tim and his lady "were like married," according to Queenie, "but sometimes he would let her freak off with another woman." —Christina and Richard Milner, *Black Players*, p. 156, 1972
- Grace was a sadist, one of the maddest / Who'd freak off in the good Lord's face. —Dennis Wepman et al., *The Life*, p. 109, 1976
- —Edith A. Folb, *runnin' down some lines*, p. 238, 1980

2 to go, to leave *US*

- [N]o one minds if you freak-off to Katmandu for a few days, or years. —Richard Neville, *Play Power*, p. 265,1970

freak-out *noun*

1 a celebratory event, a gathering together of counterculturists to enjoy music and drugs *US*

A response to the critics who called them 'freaks', via **FREAK OUT** (to panic).

- These curious way-out events, simulating drug ecstasies, which are known as "freak-outs", in which girls writhe and shriek and young men roll themselves naked in paint or jelly —*Daily Express*, 2nd March 1967
- Those public freakouts which were initiated and promoted by the Underground itself were genuinely permissive[.] —Richard Neville, *Play Power*, p. 33, 1970
- The Hog Farm Freakout at NYU, March 1969, which took place the evening of the first day of shooting on Events. —Fred Baker, *Events*, p. 11, 1970
- [They] were enjoying the sort of bacchanalian freakout usually the preserve of mushied-up drongos invading Stonehenge for the Solstice. —Kevin Sampson, *Powder*, p. 27, 1999

2 an uninhibited sexual exhibition *US*

- "Man, these motherfuckers have this restaurant, a Greek restaurant and jack if a chick wants a workout, I mean a freakout, that's where they go. These Greeks work in teams, man. They fuck the chick between the toes, in the nose, and shit like that." —Cecil Brown, *The Life & Loves of Mr. Jiveass Nigger*, p. 148, 1969

3 a temporary loss of sanity and control while under the influence of a psychoactive drug *UK, 1966*

- Besides the freak-out in the bathroom they are expecting a psychiatrist to look at Bob. —Joan Didion, *Slouching Toward Bethlehem*, p. 108, 1967

4 a complete panic and loss of control *US*

- Mothers and little kids dropped their picnic baskets and fled when they saw the signs. Near freakout. —Jerry Rubin, *Do It!*, p. 38, 1970
- I did think I'd just tell Hugh that I wanted to sleep with this guy. He freaked out. Total freak-out! Said he thought we were an item! —Sally Cline, *Couples*, p. 136, 1998

5 a member of the 1960s counterculture *UK*

- Vogue and whiskey upper-class freak-outs who orbited around Paul Getty's holiday house[.] —Richard Neville, *Play Power*, p. 234, 1970

freak out *verb*

1 to lose sanity while under the influence of LSD or another hallucinogen *US*

- Freaking out is erratic behavior resulting from a bum trip. —Nicholas Von Hoffman, *We Are The People Our Parents Warned Us Against*, p. 225, 1967
- —Joe David Brown (Editor), *The Hippies*, p. 218, 1967: 'Glossary of hippie terms'
- Anybody who could take LSD for the first time and go through all that without freaking out… —Tom Wolfe, *The Electric Kool-Aid Acid Test*, p. 207, 1968
- Sometimes that gets tested on acid – when somebody freaks out. —Leonard Wolfe (Editor), *Voices from the Love Generation*, p. 33, 1968
- [Y]ou can go out into the country free so you can straighten your head out or freak out among true friends. —*The Digger Papers*, p. 3, August 1968
- No, I haven't freaked out. —Tom Robbins, *Another Roadside Attraction*, p. 77, 1971
- A lot of folks who are freaking out in hospitals, people who got taken to hospitals for acid, had real bad trips after they got to the hospital[.] —Stephen Gaskin, *Amazing Dope Tales*, p. 48, 1980

2 to panic *US, 1964*

- —Joe David Brown (Editor), *The Hippies*, p. 218, 1967: 'Glossary of hippie terms'
- The liberals try to get everyone freaked at Wallace so we won't notice that they do precisely what he advocates. —Jerry Rubin, *Do It!*, p. 145, 1970
- MARSELLUS; No fuckin' shit she'll freak. —*Pulp Fiction*, 1994

3 to make someone feel unsettled, astonished or bizarre *US, 1964*

- I mean, I like it and everything, it just doesn't freak me out. —*Sex, Lies and Videotape*, 1989
- Why don't you man? Too freaked out? —Francesca Lia Block, *Cherokee Bat*, p. 209, 1992

4 to snap under intolerable pressure *UK*

- [The 3 racing-drivers] have all punched marshals at one time or another, which Hunt calls "freaking-out". —*Now!*, 2nd November 1979

5 to behave in a crazed manner as a response to an emotional stimulus *US, 1966*

- —Angela Devlin, *Prison Patter*, p. 53, 1996
- I'd just tell Hugh that I wanted to sleep with this guy. He freaked out. Total freak-out! —Sally Cline, *Couples*, p. 136, 1998

freak show *noun*

a fetishistic sexual performance *US*

- Court documents state that 50 patrons were watching 25 strippers inside a red, one-story building where West Lanvale Street dead-ends into a fenced-in industrial complex. Sources familiar with the investigation said the event was advertised as a "Freak Show. —*Baltimore Sun*, p. 1B, 30th May 2001

freak trick *noun*

a prostitute's customer who pays for unusual sex *US*

- —Eugene Landy, *The Underground Dictionary*, p. 82, 1971

freaky *noun*

a habitual drug user *UK*

- —*Punch*, 22nd October 1969

freaky *adjective*

1 odd, bizarre *US, 1895*

- —Hy Lit, *Hy Lit's Unbelievable Dictionary of Hip Words for Groovy People*, p. 16, 1968
- The Be-in: a new medium of human relations. A magnet drawing together all the freaky, hip, unhappy, young, happy, curious, criminal, gentle, alienated, weird, frustrated, far-out, artistic, lonely, lovely people to the same place at the same time. —Jerry Rubin, *Do It!*, p. 56, 1970
- Oh, you see lots of freaky stuff in a cab. Especially when the moon's out. —*Taxi Driver*, 1976

2 sexually deviant *UK*

- —David Powis, *The Signs of Crime*, 1977

3 characteristic of the 1960s counterculture *US*

- The freaky, zoned-out style being developed on the misty slopes of the Haight had still made few inroads into intense, political Berkeley. —J. Anthony Lukas, *Don't Shoot – We Are Your Children*, p. 386, 1971
- Maybe they didn't like my freaky clothes. —Cleo Odzer, *Goa Freaks*, p. 103, 1995

▸ **get freaky**

to have sex *US*

- —Connie Eble (Editor), *UNC-CH Campus Slang*, p. 3, March 1996

freaky-deaky *adjective*

acting without restraint, especially in a sexual way *US*

- Originally a disco/funk style of music and dance.That's where Spinks has been for more than a month, in the woods of Michigan conditioning himself relentlessly, stripping every ounce of fat off and renouncing those old "freaky deaky" ways of his wherein he often could be found liberally enjoying the wine and young ladies. —*United Press International*, 11th June 1981
- —Rick Ayers (Editor), *Berkeley High Slang Dictionary*, p. 22, 2004

freckle *noun*

the anus *AUSTRALIA, 1967*

Popularised by the Barry McKenzie cartoon strip.

- You can put it up your freckle if you don't flamin' like it, you Ikey bastard!' —Barry Humphries, *The Wonderful World of Barry McKenzie*, p. 56, 1968
- —Jim Ramsay, *Cop it Sweet*, p. 37, 1977

freckle-puncher *noun*

a male homosexual *AUSTRALIA, 1968*

- Bugger me if the first pom I meet turns out to be a freckle !!!puncher!!!. —Barry Humbphris, *Bazza Pulls Its Off!*, 1971
- 'For an awful minute, you think you've turned freckle-puncher.' —Kathy Lette, *Girls' Night Out*, p. 83, 1987

Fred Astaire *noun*

1 a chair *UK*

Rhyming slang.

- — Susie Dent, *The Language Report*, p. 98, 2003

2 a hair *UK*

Rhyming slang, formed on the name of the American entertainer, 1899–1987.

- —Ray Puxley, *Cockney Rabbit*, 1992

freddy *noun*

an amphetamine tablet, especially a capsule of ephedrine *US*

- —Jay Robert Nash, *Dictionary of Crime*, p. 138, 1992
- —*Providence (Rhode Island) Journal-Bulletin*, p. 6B, 4th August 1997: 'Doctors must know the narcolexicon'

Freddy Fraternity *noun*
a stereotypical college fraternity member who looks, dresses, talks and lives the part *US*
• "Suzi Sorority" and "Freddie Fraternity," if they ever existed, are not quite as clean or wholesome as might appear at first glance. — *Maledicta*, p. 133, 1995

Fred Nerk; Fred Nerks *noun*
used as a name for an unknown person *AUSTRALIA*
• I feel I could surely be forgiven for being unaware that Fred Nerks plays for Woop Woop or wherever. — Sue Rhodes, *Now you'll think I'm awful*, p. 84, 1967
• That looks like the float which belongs to Fred Nerk, the horse trainer. — Roy Higgins and Tom Prior, *The Jockey Who Laughed*, p. 76, 1982

Fred's *nickname*
Fortnum & Mason, an upmarket grocers and department store in Piccadilly, London *UK*
Upper-class society usage.
• — Ann Barr and Peter York, *The Official Sloane Ranger Handbook*, p. 158, 1982

Fred's out
used as a warning that you have farted *US*
• — Connie Eble (Editor), *UNC-CH Campus Slang*, March 1973

free *noun*
the world outside prison *US, 1966*
• USA Today: Do you have any special advice or words to inmates when they leave the prison? HAMBRICK: Yes, I tell them that, "If I see you again, may it be in the free." — *USA Today*, p. 11A, 5th December 1988

free *verb*
▸ **free the tadpoles**
of a male, to masturbate *UK*
• — *Roger's Profanisaurus*, p. 14, October 1999
• — Chris Lewis, *The Dictionary of Playground Slang*, p. 94, 2003

free *adjective*
unaffected by any conventional values *US*
A critical if vague word from the 1960s counterculture.
• During the convention I wore a sign that said free on it. — Nicholas Von Hoffman, *We Are The People Our Parents Warned Us Against*, p. 131, 1967
• All the petty bullshit things that before kept us apart vanished and for the first time we were free. — *East Village Other*, 20th August 1969

freeball *verb*
(used of a male) to dress without underwear *US*
• — Anna Scotti and Paul Young, *Buzzwords*, p. 104, 1997
• — Pamela Munro, *U.C.L.A. Slang*, p. 70, 2001

freebase *noun*
nearly pure cocaine alkaloid which can be obtained from powdered cocaine hydrochloride and is then burnt and inhaled *US*
• They were smoking free base, also known as the "white tornado" – the form of cocaine favored by those beyond the nasal stage of evolution. — *Hi Life*, p. 78, 1979
• CAROLINE: What is this, like freebase? SETH: Not like. It is. — *Traffic*, 2000
• — Nick Constable, *This is Cocaine*, p. 182, 2002

freebase *verb*
to remove the impurities from cocaine to advance and heighten the effect *US, 1980*
By ellipsis from 'free the base'.
• Besides, the idiot uses a blowtorch to freebase. — Bret Easton Ellis, *Less Than Zero*, p. 81, 1985
• John found a coke connection and started free-basing – smoking a purified form of cocaine. — Cleo Odzer, *Goa Freaks*, p. 261, 1995
• — Angela Devlin, *Prison Patter*, p. 53, 1996

free baser *noun*
a user of freebase cocaine *US*
• [M]ost free basers in North America smoke either through a fire base pipe or off foil[.] — *Hi Life*, p. 78, 1979

freebie; freeby *noun*
something that is given away at no cost *US, 1928*
• Maybe it was because the meal was a freebie and didn't cost me anything but a song – or I should say, a hymn. — Louis Armstrong, *Satchmo*, p. 92, 1954
• [T]his place is sold out. Freebies are rife[.] — Lester Bangs, *Psychotic Reactions and Carburetor Dung*, p. 209, 1977
• You copping two bills a week and freebie skag to shoot. — Iceberg Slim (Robert Beck), *Airtight Willie and Me*, p. 173, 1979
• Awww, what the fuck you tryin' to pull, Rudy!? All you wanna do is take a freebie on our backs. — Donald Goines, *The Busting Out of an Ordinary Man*, p. 31, 1985
• The son of a bitch never paid me. The first time in my life I didn't ask for it up front, that's what happens. I go, 'Hey, come on, man, I don't give freebies.' He says it was for fun, like I get laid on my day off. — Elmore Leonard, *Maximum Bob*, p. 238, 1991
• Hanging round us all the time and getting freebies. — Lanre Fehintola, *Charlie Says...*, p. 23, 2000

freebie *adjective*
free of charge *US*
• [I]t's the brakeman who throws freebie passengers off[.] — Mezz Mezzrow, *Really the Blues*, p. 256, 1946
• The clubhouse here is kind of cramped and the Yankees would probably sneer at it, but there's a soda fountain – Coca-Cola, root beer, 7-Up, cold, on tap, freebie. — Jim Bouton, *Ball Four*, p. 14, 1970
• [H]e had received no end of crank calls from women wanting freebie obscene phonecalls. — Kitty Churchill, *Thinking of England*, p. 162, 1995

freeco *noun*
something of value given away for free *TRINIDAD AND TOBAGO, 1985*
• — Lise Winer, *Dictionary of the English/Creole of Trinidad & Tobago*, 2003

freedom bird *noun*
an aeroplane bringing troops back to the US from Vietnam *US, 1971*
• Sitting in foxholes that night watching the moon, watching shooting stars and sipping the new clean water, the Freedom Bird and the World didn't look like lies anymore[.] — Charles Anderson, *The Grunts*, p. 77, 1976
• [E]ven as the freedom birds began flying the first 25,000 boys home in June, Charlie Company and scores of line outfits like it were obliged to linger behind[.] — Peter Goldman and Tony Fuller, *Charlie Company*, p. 122, 1983

freeganism *noun*
a political/ecological philosophy of consuming food and drink that is past its use-by or sell-by date and would, therefore, otherwise be thrown away *US*
A combination of 'free' and 'veganism'.
• Freeganism is rooted in a political philosophy that condemns over-consumption and waste in Amreican society. — *Sacramento Bee*, p. E1, 27th May 2003
• An unwritten rule of freeganism is that you leave enough for people who genuinely need the food. — *The Observer*, 23rd November 2003

free, gratis and for nothing *adjective*
costing nothing *UK, 1841*
Tautological.
• No [political] party ever offered such a cornucopia of naked bribes to the voter, all absolutely free, gratis and for nothing. — *The Guardian*, 10th August 2003

free green peppers *noun*
a sneeze by a food preparer *US*
Limited usage, but clever.
• — *Maledicta*, p. 12, 1996: 'Domino's pizza jargon'

free it up *verb*
to disclose information *US*
• — Anna Scotti and Paul Young, *Buzzwords*, p. 63, 1997

freelancer *noun*
a prostitute unattached to either pimp or brothel *US*
• Freelancers operate out of their own apartments, which are usually, like those of madams, located in good buildings in the better neighborhoods. — Bernhardt J. Hurwood, *The Sensuous New York*, p. 17, 1973
• In addition to the freelancers who swiveled past him, rimming their bloddy red lips with lascivious tongues, there were ladies of the windows. — Odie Hawkins, *Great Lawd Buddha*, p. 181, 1990

freeload *verb*
to cadge; to subsist at other people's expense *US, 1942*
• I couldn't freeload off her anymore. She was beginning a whole new life, I was just grateful for the time she let me stay with her. — Christy Canyon, *Lights, Camera, Sex!*, p. 205, 2003

freeloader *noun*
a person who manages to eat, drink and socialise at the expense of others *US, 1936*
• Tell him you don't like freeloaders, either, especially that roommate you had in college who never lifted a finger to pickup a damn thing. — Michael Moore, *Dude, Where's My County?*, p. 188, 2003

• I am not going to allow a few freeloaders to ride on the back of hundreds of thousands of law-abiding citizens. — *The Guardian*, 19th February 2003

free lunch *noun*
used as a symbol of something that is provided freely *US, 1949*
• It is said that there's no such thing as a free lunch. But the universe is the ultimate free lunch. — Stephen Hawking, *A Brief History of Time*, p. 134, 1996

freeman *noun*
▸ **on the freeman's**
gratis, for free *UK*
• Booze on the freeman's you hear what I'm saying? — Jeremy Cameron, *Brown Bread in Wengen*, p. 204, 1999

freeness *noun*
1 an open-invitation party *TRINIDAD AND TOBAGO, 1948*
• — Lise Winer, *Dictionary of the English/Creole of Trinidad & Tobago*, 2003
2 a free event *BARBADOS*
• — Frank A. Collymore, *Barbadian Dialect*, p. 51, 1965

Freep *nickname*
the Los Angeles *Free Press*; the Detroit *Free Press* *US*
• — Eugene Landy, *The Underground Dictionary*, p. 83, 1971
• Back at the Trop, Meisner and the boys remained one step above panhandling by selling copies of "the Freep," the Los Angeles Free Press, an alternative weekly newspaper, on the streets of Sunset Boulevard. — Marc Eliot, *To the Limit*, p. 31, 1998
• Clem Grogan was standing with his arms around the ten- or eleven-year-old daughter of a Freep staffer (unbeknownst to her mother), chanting "There is no good, there is no evil." — Ed Sanders, *The Family*, p. 324, 2002

free pass to bankruptcy *noun*
a credit card *US*
• — Montie Tak, *Truck Talk*, p. 65, 1971

free ride *noun*
1 used as a metaphor for attaining something without effort or cost *US, 1899*
• I wanted the free ride and I wanted to be paid in my own coin[.] — John D. MacDonald, *Free Fall in Crimson*, p. 174, 1981
2 in poker, the right to stay in a hand without further betting, most commonly because the player has bet his entire bankroll on the hand *US*
• — Irwin Steig, *Common Sense in Poker*, p. 184, 1963
3 an orientation flight on a military aircraft *US*
• The IP who came to our table would take the four of us on our orientation flight, the only "free ride" in the course. — Robert Mason, *Chickenhawk*, p. 29, 1983

free-rider *noun*
a motorcyclist who shares a gang's philosophy but does not formally join the gang *US*
• — Paladin Press, *Inside Look at Outlaw Motorcyle Gangs*, p. 35, 1992

Free Shoes University *noun*
Florida State University *US*
A back formation from the initials FSU, playing on the role of athletics and the sponsorship of athletics by a major shoe company at the university.
• Speaking – or in this case thinking – of football, I then wondered, "Who will win the NCAA football title next year?" The Nebraska Cornthuggers (sorry, Huskers) or the Free Shoes University (FSU) Seminoles, or, if you prefer, Free Shirts University. — *The Daily Illini*, p. 1, 5th May 2000

freeside *adjective*
outside prison *US, 1960*
• And I wished I could stop thinking about the free side. The free side – dig that! In the beginning I'd said "outside"; now I said "free side" just like a con. — Piri Thomas, *Down These Mean Streets*, p. 254, 1967

freestyle *noun*
heterosexual intercourse *UK*
• I need a good charver, a bitta freestyle, a good bunk-up. — J.J. Connolly, *Layer Cake*, p. 211, 2000

freestyle *verb*
to improvise and perform a rap lyric, often a capella *US*
• My record is mainly a freestyle album. — *A2Z [quoting Shaquille O'Neal, 1994]*, p. 37, 1995

freeware *noun*
computer software provided free of charge *US*
• A number of electronic bulletin boards offer "freeeware"of various sorts for the cost of copying the program. — *Christian Science Monitor*, p. 17, 22nd March 1983
• Cybersurfers are used to getting things for free online. They regularly download shareware or freeware programs. — Greg Holden, *Starting an Online Business for Dummies*, p. 48, 2002

freeway *noun*
in a prison dormitory, the aisle through the centre of the room *US*
Alluding to the constant foot traffic.
• — Reinhold Aman, *Hillary Clinton's Pen Pal*, p. 38, 1996

freeway surfer *noun*
a person who embraces the mannerisms of surfing, owns the equipment needed to surf, but who chooses to watch from the safety of the car *US*
• — Mitch McKissick, *Surf Lingo*, 1987

free, white and 21 *adjective*
possessing free will and able to exercise self-determination *US*
• "I'm free, white and twenty-one", she said. — Raymond Chandler, *The Little Sister*, p. 75, 1949
• "You don't care what I do, do you?" she cried out. "You're free, white, and twenty-one," Bert answered. — James T. Farrell, *Ruth and Bertram*, p. 105, 1955
• From what I hear they were all free, white and twenty-one. They knew what they were getting into. They were big boys. — George V. Higgins, *The Friends of Eddie Doyle*, p. 200–201, 1971
• She was free, white and nearly twenty-one. She thought she had nothing to fear from the police. — Charles W. Moore, *A Brick for Mister Jones*, p. 172, 1975

free world *noun*
life outside prison *US, 1960*
• — Bruce Jackson, *Outside the Law*, p. 57, 1972: 'Glossary'

free-world *adjective*
civilian; from outside prison *US*
• These are boneroo free-world shoes. — Malcolm Braly, *On the Yard*, p. 140, 1967
• One day a week a free-world dentist comes in to do the major work. — Bruce Jackson, *Outside the Law*, p. 159, 1972

free-world gal *noun*
a male prisoner who practised homosexuality before entering prison *US*
• A free-world gal, she's not going to mess with any of them rums anyway. — Bruce Jackson, *Outside the Law*, p. 173, 1972
• — Charles Shafer, *Folk Speech in Texas Prisons*, p. 204, 1990

free-world punk *noun*
a male prisoner who engaged in homosexual sex before prison *US*
• We classify them two ways: penitentiary punk and free-world punk. — Bruce Jackson, *Outside the Law*, p. 176, 1972

freeze *noun*
1 cocaine *US*
From the numbing, cooling effect.
• — R.C Garrett et al., *The Coke Book*, p. 200, 1984
2 a small amount of cocaine placed on the tongue *US*
• They snort a bit, "take a freeze" (place a pinch of cocaine on the tongue], chat another minute or two, then go in to see Chillie. — Terry Williams, *The Cocaine Kids*, p. 29, 1989
3 a rejection of affection *US, 1942*
Colder than the proverbial 'cold shoulder'.
• For nights that seemed like years the Duykes had given Frank the freeze. — Irving Shulman, *The Amboy Dukes*, p. 188, 1947
• She gave me the big freeze when I said hello that day, though. — J.D. Salinger, *Catcher in the Rye*, p. 77, 1951

freeze *verb*
1 to stop moving completely *UK, 1848*
• Tony and Ray, into Miami street life and dope busts. Freeze, motherfuckers. Do you ever say that? He said, I think I have. — Elmore Leonard, *Maximum Bob*, p. 97, 1991
2 in draw poker, to decline the opportunity to discard and draw any new cards *US, 1971*
• — Thomas L. Clark, *The Dictionary of Gambling and Gaming*, p. 85, 1987

▸ **freeze your nose**

to use cocaine *US*

From the drug's numbing effect on mucuous membranes.

- But almost all I know like to sniff coke – they call it freezing their noses. — Bruce Jackson, *Outside the Law*, 1972

▸ **freeze your nuts**

to be extremely cold *UK*

- I was camping in Derbyshire – gas camper, fucking cold, freezing my nuts[.] — *Uncut*, p. 36, July 2001

freeze-out *noun*

a poker game in which all participants must play until they lose all their money or win all the other players' money *US*

- Nick and Ryan, it developed, had been in a poker game in Las Vegas, a 250,000-dollar freeze-out. — Jimmy Snyder, *Jimmy the Greek*, p. 197, 1975

freezer *noun*

in poker, an early call made even as other players continue to raise their bets *US*

- — Albert H. Morehead, *The Complete Guide to Winning Poker*, p. 263, 1967

▸ **the freezer**

Antarctica *ANTARCTICA, 1993*

- — Bernadette Hince, *The Antarctic Dictionary*, p. 136, 2000

freeze up *verb*

to become paralysed with fear *US*

An occupational hazard of those who work high above the ground.

- "You can see he isn't doing nothing but standing there," the raising-gang foreman said. "He's froze-up. He wouldn't stand there like that if he wasn't froze-up. Would he?" — Elmore Leonard, *Killshot*, p. 140, 1989

freight *noun*

the cost of something, especially a bribe *US*

- — Hyman E. Goldin et al., *Dictionary of American Underworld Lingo*, p. 74, 1950

▸ **pull freight**

on the railways, to quit a job *US*

- — Ramon Adams, *The Language of the Railroader*, p. 118, 1977

freight train *noun*

a wave breaking powerfully in perfect formation *US*

- — Mitch McKissick, *Surf Lingo*, 1987

French *noun*

1 oral sex, especially on a man *US, 1916*

- I say, Yoo-hoo, pitty baby, you wanna lil french? Haff an haff? How about jes a straight? I say, Twenty berries an you alla roun the mothahfuggin worl'. — Robert Gover, *One Hundred Dollar Misunderstanding*, p. 21, 1961
- "[I]f he just wants a straight fuck or a straight French, then I say, "Why don't you spend a little extra, and we have a good time?" — John Warren Wells, *Tricks of the Trade*, p. 63, 1970
- And it was so funny, because they would describe you as 'Greek, active/passive; French, active/passive- – French being blow jobs and Greek being fucked. — James Ridgeway, *Red Light*, p. 222, 1996
- Neither she or Marie talked of "French" (i.e. oral sex) being in demand with Dublin men. — Fiona Pitt-Kethley, *Red Light Districts of the World*, p. 36, 2000

2 an open-mouthed, French kiss *US*

- "Yes," I said grimly, "a French kiss, he tried for French." — Terry Southern, *Now Dig This*, p. 220, 1978

3 profanity *US, 1865*

- Pardon my French but you're an asshole! — *Ferris Buehler's Day Off*, 1986
- And I said yeah, walked straight into the fucking twilight zone. Pardon my French. — Carl Hiaasen, *Skin Tight*, p. 115, 1989

▸ **excuse my French!; pardon my French!**

employed as an apology for a use of spoken language which may cause offence *UK, 1936*

Often used in a cursory manner or with insincerity. The original intention, presumably, was to allow the apologee the pretence not to have understood a 'foreign' word; now the apology is a cliché which merely acknowledges an inappropriate use of robust unconventional English.

- [M]oody perfume, sunglasses, snide Polo, cheap fucking tat, excuse my French. — Greg Williams, *Diamond Geezers*, p. 135, 1997
- He's got the biggest fuckin' – pardon my French – biggest pad you've never heard of. — Diran Adebayo, *My Once Upon A Time*, p. 63, 2000
- She will, pardon my French, get laid[.] — *The Guardian*, 24th January 2003

French *verb*

1 to perform oral sex *US, 1923*

G. Legman wrote in 1941 that 'The term derives from the popular and not entirely erroneous belief that the practice is very common in France'.

- — Donald Webster Cory and John P. LeRoy, *The Homosexual and His Society*, p. 264, 1963: 'A lexicon of homosexual slang'
- All I needed to do was to French just one. She then passed on the word to the others. — *Screw*, p. 5, 7th March 1969
- Here, again, is an advantage of Frenching. If a man's not hard, you can't have intercourse with him, but you can suck him. — John Warren Wells, *Tricks of the Trade*, p. 27, 1970
- You see, grown up men like to get laid and they like to get Frenched, but they don't like to get jerked off. — Delle Brehan, *Kicks is Kicks*, p. 59, 1970
- "I thought I Frenched him to death," she said. "Oh, mercy." "You may have Frenched him into a coma," I told her. — Lawrence Block, *Chip Harrison Scores Again*, p. 222, 1971

2 to French kiss; to kiss with open lips and exploratory tongues *US, 1955*

- Dr. Sommers narrated as the two Frenched, fondled, and took a bubble bath[.] — Anka Radakovich, *The Wild Girls Club*, p. 114, 1994
- I can't believe you let him French you! — *200 Cigarettes*, 1999

3 in drag racing and hot rodding, to fit the bonnet (hood) over the headlights to create the apperance of recessed headlights *US*

- — Olney Ross, *Kings of the Drag Strip*, p. 186, 1968

French blue *noun*

a manufactured combination of tranquillizer (methaqualone) and stimulant (amphetamine) taken recreationally *UK, 1964*

- I see Harry and get my tabs from him – thirty "French" Blues at sixpence a time. — Ian Hebditch, *Weekend*, *The Sharper Word*, p. 133, 1969
- — Eugene Landy, *The Underground Dictionary*, p. 83, 1971
- — Carl Chambers and Richard Heakman, *Employee Drug Abuse*, p. 205, 1972
- Drug pushers; sixpence each for French Blues, a shilling for a Roaring Twenty — Irish Jack (writing of the 1960s), *History*, *The Sharper Word*, p. 31, 1998
- I'd taken about half a dozen French Blues and I was in no mood for these shipyard wankers. — Stuart Browne, *Dangerous Parking*, p. 2, 2000
- [W]e were all speeding out of our heads – French blues[.] — Simon Napier-Bell, *Black Vinyl White Powder*, p. 167, 2001

French bull-hook *noun*

a deceptive explanation *BAHAMAS*

- — John A. Holm, *Dictionary of Bahamian English*, p. 82, 1982

French date *noun*

oral sex performed on a man by a prositute *US*

- At the hotel, if it's a straight date it's usually $10, and a French date, a blow job, is $20. — Bruce Jackson, *Outside the Law*, p. 186, 1972

French deck *noun*

a deck of cards decorated with art ranging from naughty and nude to pornographic *US, 1963*

- At the end of 1966, he bought thirteen of the old machines, offering fifty-fifty splits to the several existing bookshops whose most extreme material were under-the-counter nudist volumes, girlie playing cards (French Decks), and Times Square standards[.] — Josh Alan Friedman, *Tales of Times Square*, p. 74–75, 1986

French dip *noun*

precoital vaginal secretions *US*

- — *Maledicta*, p. 55, 1986–1987: 'A continuation of a glossary of ethnic slurs in American English'.

French dressing *noun*

semen *US*

An allusion to **FRENCH** (oral sex).

- — *Maledicta*, p. 55, 1986–1987: 'A continuation of a glossary of ethnic slurs in American English'.

French Embassy *noun*

a premises of the Young Men's Christian Association *US*

An allusion to the association between the YMCA and homosexual men who enjoy **FRENCH** (oral sex).

- "They don't call this Y the French Embassy for nothing," the merchant marine laughs. — John Rechy, *City of Night*, p. 25, 1963
- — *Maledicta*, p. 218, 1979: 'Kinks and queens: linguistic and cultural aspects of the terminology for gays'.

French fits *noun*

delirium tremens *US*

Possibly combines a conventional fit of the **SHAKES** with an allusion to the stereotypical French characteristic of shrugging.

- Too much dope for the time. I was having the French fits coming out of it. — Raymond Chandler, *Farewell My Lovely*, p. 131, 1940

French fries *noun*

1 3 inch sticks of crack cocaine with ridged edges *US*

- —Peter Johnson, *Dictionary of Street Alcohol and Drug Terms*, p. 77, 1993
- —Mike Haskins, *Drugs*, p. 281, 2003

2 the thighs *UK*

Rhyming slang.

- I can thrust downwards, which is that bit easier on the old French fries.—Kevin Sampson, *Clubland*, p. 133, 2002

French harp *noun*

a harmonica *US, 1983*

- [T]he French harp was given to him by a "colored shoeshine boy" he met in a barbershop.—Joe Klein, *Woody Guthrie*, p. 27, 1980

Frenchie *noun*

a light-skinned person; an unlikeable person *SAINT KITTS AND NEVIS*

Recorded by Richard Allsopp.

▷ see also: FRENCHY

French inhale *verb*

to draw cigarette smoke into the mouth and then allow it to drift out and upwards for inhalation through the nose *US, 1957*

The French credit is presumably to signal how sophisticated such technique is thought to be.

- She lifts up her sunglasses and then French-inhales while she stares at Mrs. Williams' hair.—Rebecca Wells, *Little Altars Everywhere*, p. 87, 1992
- —Chris Lewis, *The Dictionary of Playground Slang*, p. 119, 2003

French joint *noun*

an over-sized, conical marijuana cigarette *US*

- —Jim Emerson-Cobb, *Scratching the Dragon*, April 1997

French kiss *noun*

1 a kiss with the mouths open and tongues adventuring *UK*

With variant 'Frenchie'.

- What about a Frenchie?—*RI:SE*, 27th October 2003

2 an act of urination; urination *UK*

Rhyming slang for **PISS**.

- —Ray Puxley, *Cockney Rabbit*, 1992

French kiss *verb*

to kiss with the mouth open and the tongue active *US, 1918*

- One of the boys had a lot of experience with girls, and he told me about French or tongue kissing[.]—Phyllis and Eberhard Kronhausen, *Sex Histories of American College Men*, p. 124, 1960

French lay *noun*

oral sex *US*

- All the sex is extra. How about a French lay? / (But, but, my massage!) Well, here goes my pay.—*Screw*, p. 7, 15th May 1972

French leave *noun*

a departure without intimation; flight *UK, 1771*

- —Lou Shelly, *Hepcats Jive Talk Dictionary*, p. 45, 1945
- There was one night when some of my previous fellow officers went out to deliver a piece of paper to a guy that took French leave from the prison and I was ordered to join them[.]—George V. Higgins, *The Rat on Fire*, p. 4, 1981

French lessons *noun*

oral sex *US*

- —Robert J. Glessing, *The Underground Press in America*, p. 176, 1970: 'Glossary of terms used in the underground press'
- Instead of soliciting passing males, the hookers of London remained out of sight, if not out of mind, advertising their services on discreetly euphemistic postcards in the windows of local newsagents. "French Lessons", "Large Chest for Sale", "Stocks and Bonds", "Remedial Discipline by Stern Governess" – the oblique side of obvious, with a local phone number.—Mick Farren, *Give the Anarchist a Cigarette*, 2001

French letter *noun*

a condom *UK, 1856*

In the mid-C20 so common in use as to be almost conventional, however usage inevitably diminished with the advent of the contraceptive pill. In post-AIDS society 'French letter' is now just one among hundreds of newer slang terms for the condom. Unusual variations are 'American', 'Italian' or 'Spanish' letters. The French repaid the compliment with *capote alglaise* (a condom), literally an English hooded cape, which abbreviates as *capote*; interestingly, when 'French letter' is abbreviated the nationality remains and it becomes a **FRENCHY** or a **FRENCHIE**.

- "Do you sell French letters?" he whispered at last. "We sell contraceptives, certainly," I answered coolly, hoping that my contempt for his slang terms was well demonstrated.—Petra Christian, *The Sexploiters*, p. 45, 1973

French loaf *noun*

four *UK, 1974*

Rhyming slang, on back slang 'rofe' (**RUOF**).

- —Ray Puxley, *Cockney Rabbit*, 1992

Frenchman's acre

an arpent or since the 1970s, a hectare, French measures of land *CANADA*

- Like the "jag," this unit of measure is said to be "bigger when they buy, smaller when they sell." The suspicion [of English people] arises from the confusion created by the use of French terms and measures. An arpent is 0.84 of an acre.—Lewis Poteet, *Talking Country*, p. 40–41, 1992

French massage *noun*

oral sex *AUSTRALIA*

- —Thommo, *The Dictionary of Australian Swearing and Sex Sayings*, p. 49, 1985

French postcard *noun*

a photographic postcard depicting anything ranging from simple female nudity to full-blown sexual activity *US, 1926*

- "I thought you had some French postcards," Rick said jokingly.—Evan Hunter, *The Blackboard Jungle*, p. 179, 1954
- —*Maledicta*, p. 159, 1979: 'A glossary of ethnic slurs in American English'

French safe *noun*

a condom *US, 1870*

- "French safes" (meaning condoms), they were uncharitably called.—Robert MacNeil, *Looking for My Country*, p. 33, 2003

French screwdriver *noun*

a hammer *US*

- —*Maledicta*, p. 55, 1986–1987: 'A continuation of a glossary of ethnic slurs in American English'

French tickler *noun*

a condom with external protrusions marketed as giving pleasure to the wearer's partner *US, 1916*

- I was heading out the door when he called after me, "And don't come back without French ticklers."—*Eros*, p. 39, Autumn 162
- Our catalog will display various articles of leather designed for the bondage-minded person, plus various specialty items, i.e., dildoes, french ticklers and other items.—Michael Leigh, *The Velvet Underground*, p. 70, 1963
- Because of the uncertain legal status of the real French tickler in this country, I have been unable to find a U.S. manufacturer or distributor who sells them openly.—Roger Blake, *The Stimulators*, p. 177, 1968
- Did you know 95% of the men in the U.S. have at one time or another heard of French Ticklers? [Advertisement]—*Screw*, p. n.p., 21st February 1969
- He hits another. "A French tickler." He continues to hit the lockers.—Darryl Ponicsan, *The Last Detail*, p. 6, 1970
- [T]here were scabby bumps on them as satisfying to the touch as the pleasure-dots on a french tickler[.]—William T. Vollman, *Whores for Gloria*, p. 85, 1991

French trick *noun*

oral sex performed by a prostitute *US*

- A quick French trick for $10 and if they wanted to stand up and perform the act, it was $20.—Bruce Jackson, *In the Life*, p. 389, 1972

French wank *noun*

an act of sexual gratification in which the penis is rubbed between a female partner's breasts *UK*

- —*Roger's Profanisaurus*, p. 11, December 1997

Frenchy; Frenchie *noun*

1 a French or French Canadian person, often as a nickname *UK, 1883*

- [Y]ou gotta give these Frenchies some credit—Christopher Brookmyre, *The Sacred Art of Stealing*, p. 283, 2002
- [Mouse] Morris left of his own accord at 15 to join Frenchie Nicholson's stable near Cheltenham.—*The Observer*, 7th April 2002

2 a fundamentally honest gambler who will cheat occasionally if the right opportunity arises *US, 1961*

- —Thomas L. Clark, *The Dictionary of Gambling and Gaming*, p. 85, 1987

3 a condom *UK*

A familiar shortening of **FRENCH LETTER**.

4 an act of oral-genital sex *US*

- —John M. Murtagh and Sara Harris, *Cast the First Stone*, p. 259, 1957: 'Glossary'
- Okay, but only a quick Frenchie. Give me the hundred.—Edwin Torres, *Q & A*, p. 169, 1977

Frenchy; Frenchie *adjective*

French *UK, 1883*

- [T]he huge investment of national pride in this defiantly Frenchy invention.—*The Guardian*, 17th October 2000

freq; freak *noun*

a radio frequency *US, 1969*

- —Gregory Clark, *Words of the Vietnam War*, p. 422, 1990

frequency *noun*

a level of understanding *US, 1959*

- We are tuning in to one another more and more, and finding, to our communal delight, that we are all on the same frequency!—Sue Ellen Cooper, *The Red Hat Society*, p. 89, 2004

frequently outwitted by inanimate objects *adjective*

extremely incompetent *US*

US naval aviator usage.

- —*United States Naval Institute Proceedings*, p. 108, October 1986

fresca *noun*

an affectionate pat on the head *US*

From the film *Caddy Shack*.

- —Connie Eble (Editor), *UNC-CH Campus Slang*, p. 3, Spring 1984

fresh *verb*

to flatter *US*

- All the Kids would rap, charm (talk to), or game to impress girlfriends; hang it up (insult) or fresh (compliment) male friends by using special words.—Terry Williams, *The Cocaine Kids*, p. 90, 1989

fresh *adjective*

1 good, sharp, stylish *US*

Possibly shortened from 'We're fresh out the pack / so you gotta stay back, / we got one Puerto Rican / and the rest are black', an early 1980s signature routine by Grand Wizard Theodore and the Fantastic 5 MCs.

- —Bradley Elfman, *Breakdancing*, p. 40, 1984
- —Connie Eble (Editor), *UNC-CH Campus Slang*, p. 3, Fall 1984
- It must be a secret place to keep the squares out and let the hip, fresh and chill crowds in.—Terry Williams, *The Cocaine Kids*, p. 97, 1989
- —*The Fresh Prince of Bel Air*, 1990
- [E]verything, from laceless sneakers to baseball caps worn sideways, was "fresh".—Nelson George, *Hip Hop America*, p. 209, 1998
- Lookin' fresh tonight, Pussy-Kat.—*Ten Things I Have About You*, 1999

2 impudent *US, 1845*

Possibly from German *frech* (impudent).

3 bad smelling *BARBADOS*

- —Frank A. Collymore, *Barbadian Dialect*, p. 51, 1965
- —Lise Winer, *Dictionary of the English/Creole of Trinidad & Tobago*, 2003

fresh and sweet *adjective*

very recently released from jail *US*

- —Ralph de Sola, *Crime Dictionary*, p. 55, 1982

freshener *noun*

any alcoholic drink *US*

- "Fresheners," Nancy said. "Tighteners and fresheners. Sometimes drinkees or martin-eyes."—Elmore Leonard, *The Big Bounce*, p. 88, 1969

freshen up *verb*

to clean, to smarten, to revive *UK, 1937*

An example of a conventional term, 'freshen', being made colloquial by the addition of an unnecessary adverb.

- I'd head back to the hotel to freshen up, then go for dinner with friends[.]—*The Guardian*, 6th September 2003

fresher *noun*

a university freshman *UK, 1882*

- Freshers expect £7,000 bill.—*The Guardian*, 13th August 2003

fresh-fucked *adjective*

energised and happy, whether the result of recent sex or not *US*

- —Michael Dalton Johnson, *Talking Trash with Redd Foxx*, p. 69, 1994

freshie *noun*

a freshwater crocodile *AUSTRALIA, 1964*

freshies *noun*

1 in snowboarding, the first tracks in virgin snow *US*

- Whoever hikes the ridge first gets the freshies.—Jim Humes and Sean Wagstaff, *Boarderlands*, p. 221, 1995

2 fresh fruit and vegetables *ANTARCTICA, 1990*

- —Bernadette Hince, *The Antarctic Dictionary*, p. 136, 2000
- —*Cool Antarctica*, 2003: 'Antarctic slang'

fresh meat *noun*

1 a person, especially a virgin, seen merely as a object for sexual conquest *UK, 1896*

- Freshmen know they're fresh meat for senior guys.—Rosalind Wiseman, *Queen Bees and Wannabes*, p. 286, 2002

2 a newly arrived soldier *US, 1908*

Also referred to as 'new meat'.

- Well I'll be dipped in shit – new meat!—*Platoon*, 1986
- —Linda Reinberg, *In the Field*, p. 89, 1991

fresh money *noun*

in horse racing, the cash actually brought to the track and bet on a given day *US*

- —Dan Parker, *The ABC of Horse Racing*, p. 146, 1947
- —Bob and Barbara Freeman, *Wanta Bet? A Study of the Pari-Mutuels System in the United States*, p. 290, 1982

fresh-water American; fresh-water Yankee *noun*

a person who has never been to the US but speaks with an American accent and embraces other American mannerisms *TRINIDAD AND TOBAGO, 1961*

- —Lise Winer, *Dictionary of the English/Creole of Trinidad & Tobago*, 2003

fress *verb*

1 to eat greedily or to excess *US*

From the German for 'devour'.

- —Leo Rosten, *The Joys of Yiddish*, p. 120, 1968
- We're still doing OK on the fressing front.—*San Francisco Chronicle*, 21st October 1987

2 to engage as the active partner in oral sex *US, 1998*

From the sense 'to eat greedily'.

fret *adjective*

enthusiastic; excellent *IRELAND*

- He's a fret for football.—Terence Dolan, *A Dictionary of Hiberno-English*, p. 114, 1999
- The film was a fret.—Terence Dolan, *A Dictionary of Hiberno-English*, p. 114, 1999

Freud squad *noun*

psychiatrists *UK*

Doctors' slang, punning on 'fraud squad'. Recorded in an article about medical slang in British (3 London and 1 Cambridge) hospitals.

- —*Ethics and Behaviour*, August 2003

Friar Tuck; friar; friar's

used for all noun, verb and expletive senses of 'fuck' *UK*

Rhyming slang, often in phrases like 'not give a friar's', from the name of Robin Hood's band of merry men. Friar Tuck is also the source of a popular Spoonerism.

- College Harry was on the back seat, cursing like Friar Tuck on a wet Wednesday[.]—Charles Raven, *Underworld Nights*, p. 38, 1956
- "D'you want a Friar Tuck?" The stock answer was "I'd sooner fry a sausage."—Ray Puxley, *Cockney Rabbit*, p. 67, 1992

Friar Tucked *adjective*

thwarted *UK*

Rhyming slang for **FUCKED**.

- —Michael Munro, *The Complete Patter*, 1996

frick and frack *noun*

the testicles *US*

- —Edith A. Folb, *runnin' down some lines*, p. 238, 1980

fricko *noun*

a chicken stew *CANADA*

- The fricot, or fricko, a favourite dish, is made by frying chicken with pork, adding shallots, diced potatoes, and a thickened batter.—Aubin Arsenault, *Memoirs of the Hon A.E.Arsenault*, p. 5, 1951

friction *noun*
a match *TRINIDAD AND TOBAGO, 1953*
- —Frank A. Collymore, *Barbadian Dialect*, p. 51, 1965
- —Lise Winer, *Dictionary of the English/Creole of Trinidad & Tobago*, 2003

Friday car; Friday afternoon car *noun*
a car that is constantly going wrong; hence anything that is imperfect may be prefixed by Friday or Friday afternoon *UK*
From the notion that car-factory workers may skimp on the last shift of the week.
- —Peter Dickinson, *One Foot in the Grave*, 1979

fridge *noun*
1 a refrigerator *US, 1926*
- Do you like the kitchen? There's an enormous fridge, and they give you all your silver.—Richard Farina, *Been Down So Long*, p. 20, 1966
- It's nice to meet you all. There's Cokes in the fridge.—*Bill and Ted's Excellent Adventure*, 1989
- They'd bug my sisters, look for porno tapes in my dad's closet, raid our fridge.—*Chasing Amy*, 1997

2 (usually of a woman) a person who is sexually unresponsive *US, 1996*
A play on 'frigid'.
- Either she's a dyke or a fridge[.]—Kevin Sampson, *Clubland*, p. 138, 2002

fried *adjective*
1 drunk or drug-intoxicated *US, 1923*
- —Lou Shelly, *Hepcats Jive Dictionary*, p. 11, 1945
- —*News Chronicle*, 22nd May 1958: 'Fugitives from Fowler'
- —*Current Slang*, p. 3, Spring 1967
- —Collin Baker et al., *College Undergraduate Slang Study Conducted at Brown University*, p. 121, 1968
- "A customer comes out," Frank said, "Absolutely fried."—Elmore Leonard, *Swag*, p. 67, 1976
- [H]e and Aunt Helen drove down from San Francisco high on peyote all night and snowed up at our front door the next morning fried out of their minds.—Eve Babitz, *L.A. Woman*, p. 66, 1982
- On Saturday night, Shelby lost most of his in a biker's bar in National City, too fried on crystal meth to be gambling on a game of pool, but doing it nonetheless.—Joseph Wambaugh, *Finnegan's Week*, p. 137, 1993
- It is one thing to spark up a dubie and get laced at parties, but it is quite another to be fried all day.—*Clueless*, 1995

2 mentally exhausted *US, 1980*
- —Connie Eble (Editor), *UNC-CH Campus Slang*, p. 2, Fall 1982

3 in computing, not working because of a complete hardware failure *US*
- —Guy L. Steele, *Coevolution Quarterly*, p. 31, Spring 1981: 'Computer slang'

4 sunburnt *US*
- —Connie Eble (Editor), *UNC-CH Campus Slang*, p. 3, Spring 1989

fried, dried, and swept aside *adjective*
said of bleached hair that suggests straw *US*
- —Anna Scotti and Paul Young, *Buzzwords*, p. 104, 1997

fried, dyed, combed (swooped) to the side *adjective*
used as a description of a black person's hair that has been chemically straightened *US*
- —Edith A. Folb, *runnin' down some lines*, p. 238, 1980

fried egg *noun*
the insignia of the US Military Academy *US, 1908*
- —Lou Shelly, *Hepcats Jive Talk Dictionary*, p. 45, 1945

fried eggs *noun*
small female breasts *UK*
- "Do you fancy that Kate Moss?" "Naaaah! Tits like fried eggs". —*Roger's Profanisaurus*, p. 11, December 1997

friend *noun*
in poker, any card that improves a hand *US*
- —George Percy, *The Language of Poker*, p. 37, 1988

▸ **have a friend visiting**
to experience the bleed period of the menstrual cycle *UK, 1889*
- —Collin Baker et al., *College Undergraduate Slang Study Conducted at Brown University*, p. 121, 1968

friend *verb*
1 to engage in sexual foreplay *CANADA*
Reported in Toronto as a term used by Trinidadian teens.
- They were friendin' in the Corvette.—Jack Chambers (Editor), *Slang Bag 93 (University of Toronto)*, p. 3, Winter 1993

2 to have sex; to take part in a romantic relationship *TRINIDAD AND TOBAGO, 1971*
- —Lise Winer, *Dictionary of the English/Creole of Trinidad & Tobago*, 2003

friendly *adjective*
used as a coded euphemism for 'passive' in sadomasochistic sex *US*
- —*Maledicta*, p. 164, Summer/Winter 1986-1987: 'Sexual slang: prostitutes, pedophiles, flagellators, transvestites, and necrophiles'

Friendly Candy Company *nickname*
▹ **see:** FOX CHARLIE CHARLIE

Friendly City *nickname*
Port Elizabeth, South Africa *SOUTH AFRICA, 1951*
- Friendly City lets its hair down for a good cause.—*Sunday Times (South Africa)*, 15th June 2003

friend of Dorothy *noun*
a homosexual *AUSTRALIA*
Thought to be from the Judy Garland character in *The Wizard of Oz*; Garland is a gay icon.
- Judy Garland had become a cult figure in the gay community and her role as Dorothy in The Wizard of Oz was held in highest esteem. To be a 'friend of Dorothy' was the way these people referred to themsleves.—Clive Galea, *Slipper*, p. 152, 1988
- Roehm was a well known Friend of Dorothy and was becoming a bit of an embarrassment to the resolutely hetero Fuehrer.—Ignatius Jones, *The 1992 True Hip Manual*, p. 118, 1992
- —Jack Chambers (Editor), *Slang Bag 93 (University of Toronto)*, p. 1, Winter 1993
- —Kevin Dilallo, *The Unofficial Gay Manual*, p. 240, 1994
- FRIENDS OF DOROTHY TRAVELS Have Shoes Will Travel Australia's first 24 hour Gay owned and operated travel service[.]—*Capital Q Weekly*, p. 18, 18th March 1994
- He's a disco-dancing, Oscar Wilde-reading, Streis and ticket-holding friend of Dorothy.—*Clueless*, 1995
- [T]he lager, sweat and jism stained grey cobbles of Manchester's Canal Street – but there are more Friends of Dorothy than you can shake a stick at[.]—Andrew Fraser, *Attitude*, p. 34, October 2003

friend of Pedro *noun*
someone in possession of cocaine *UK*
PEDRO (cocaine) has lots of friends.
- [A]re you a friend of Pedro?" "Not too close, just at the moment. Sorry."—Kevin Sampson, *Powder*, p. 87, 1999

friends *verb*
to court *BARBADOS*
Used only in the present participle.
- [T]hey been friendsing a long time.—Frank A. Collymore, *Barbadian Dialect*, p. 51, 1965

fries *noun*
pieces of crack cocaine *US*
Shortened from **FRENCH FRIES**.
- —US Department of Justice, *Street Terms*, October 1994

frig *noun*
▸ **give a frig; care a frig**
to care, to be concerned – usually in a negative context *UK, 1955*
- I don't give a frig about Sinnott's heredity.—Mary McCarthy, *A Charmed Life*, p. 64, 1954
- "What about my poor meadows?" "You wouldn't care a frig."—John McGahern, *By the Lake*, p. 125, 2002

frig *verb*
1 to masturbate *UK, 1598*
- The joy-juice flies as these girls suck, frig their clits, and ready their assholes for cock.—*Adult Video*, p. 66, August/September 1986

2 to digitally stimulate/explore the vagina as a part of sexual foreplay *UK*
A nuance of the sense 'to masturbate'.
- —Chris Lewis, *The Dictionary of Playground Slang*, p. 94, 2003

3 to dawdle or waste time *US*
- A Maine lady of unimpeachable gentility once described her late husband as nervous and ill at ease in plublic, and said he would sit "frigging with his necktie."—John Gould, *Maine Lingo*, p. 102, 1975

frig
used now as a euphemism for 'fuck' in all its senses *UK, 1879*
- I know she frigs around so why should he get sore about it?—Hal Ellson, *Duke*, p. 125, 1949

- Yeah, that's a gone coat, but frig it, where's the water? — Hal Ellson, *The Golden Spike*, p. 138, 1952
- He uses frig all over the place, and he doesn't even know what he's saying. If a girl uses that word, she knows damn well what she's saying, and you can chalk up another roll in the hay. — Evan Hunter, *The Blackboard Jungle*, p. 146, 1954
- [M]ost of the time they jealous and afraid the new one become you head chick, the one you frig more often. — Sara Harris, *The Lords of Hell*, p. 48, 1967
- I might have known I'd land up shit creek friggin' around with a spooky push like youse lot!! — Barry Humphries, *Bazza Pulls It Off!*, 1971
- And another one, Roberet B–, told me that her brother started frigging her, so she believes that's why she turned out. — Bruce Jackson, *In the Life*, p. 326, 1972
- Maureen pokes me in the side and says, "The frig was that?" — Nicholas Blincoe, *The Beautiful Beaten-up Irish Boy of the Arndale Centre*, p. 1, 1998

frig about *verb*

to waste time doing little or nothing *UK, 1933*

- None of this fiddlin and friggin and fartin about[.] — Niall Griffiths, *Kelly + Victor*, p. 18, 2002

frigger *noun*

used as a euphemism for 'fucker' *IRELAND*

- An old man at the bar interrupted a comment from his wife to say: "We're strangers here, we don't know anything," before adding "They're friggers, anyway, all the trouble they brought around Clonaslee." — *Irish Times*, 22nd June 1996

frigging *adjective*

1 damned *AUSTRALIA*

- Ah, he hasn't got the sense of a friggin' flea. — Sumner Locke Elliott, *Rusty Bugles*, p. 25, 1948
- This corner's alive with frigging coppers. — Criena Rohan, *The Delinquents*, p. 123, 1962
- Yore friggin' luck! A reverind's come for yer. And Mrs Reverind too. Hope yer know how to behave fuckin' grateful. — Thomas Keneally, *The Chant of Jimmie Blacksmith*, p. 13, 1972
- Jimmy looked up at him. 'Stupid friggin' squarehead...want to look what you're doin'...' — James McQueen, *Uphill Runner*, p. 123, 1984
- 'How much longer?' asked the small man. 'We've been in this frigging hole for three weeks already.' — James McQueen, *Uphill Runner*, p. 120, 1984
- [T]hink I'm gunna friggin' puke! — *Sick Puppy Comix*, p. 6, 1998

2 used as a euphemism for 'fucking', usually as an intensifier *UK, 1893*

With variant 'fricking'.

- Mine wants to marry the boss-'s daugther – a frigging eight-day wonder! — Ralph Ellison, *Invisible Man*, p. 221, 1947
- "And some friggen class it is," he mumbled. — Evan Hunter, *The Blackboard Jungle*, p. 143, 1954
- What with the frigging cop butting in, I have to go all the way down to Seventh Street to clip a bag of coal[.] — Rocky Garciano (with Rowland Barber), *Somebody Up There Likes Me*, p. 50, 1955
- It don't make a damn frigging difference whether you're in The Place or hiking up Matterhorn, it's all the same old void, boy. — Jack Kerouac, *The Dharma Bums*, p. 45, 1958
- "No friggin' record company!" Royo exclaimed angrily. — Ross Russell, *The Sound*, p. 165, 1961
- Especially when a bunch of friggin' Texans got together to kill the Indian agent and scare the bands off the Brazos. — Clancy Sigal, *Going Away*, p. 108, 1961
- [I]t's getting so I can't install the simplest frigging component but what I need a bracer. — Ken Kesey, *One Flew Over the Cuckoo's Nest*, p. 55, 1962
- I know my orders are going to be for some damn tin can and I'm gonna wind up on the friggin deck force. — Darryl Ponicsan, *The Last Detail*, p. 4, 1970
- Purcell's got a friggin' ape in here! — Tom Robbins, *Another Roadside Attraction*, p. 31, 1971
- The friggin' inspectors almost fell off their chairs! — Gerald Petievich, *Money Men*, p. 45, 1981
- That's hard frickin' work. — *Airheads*, 1994
- I got a hard-on just filling the frigging thing out. — Anka Radakovich, *The Wild Girls Club*, p. 24, 1994
- I have one simple request – sharks with friggin' laser beams attached to their heads, and it can't be done? — *Austin Powers*, 1997
- "Till you at least eleven years old you turn round and you say bleedin' or friggin', right? Got that? No fuckin'?" "Got it Dad. Noreen this friggin' stew's bleedin' ace[.] — Jeremy Cameron, *Brown Bread in Wengen*, p. 139, 1999
- Frickin' scared, but okay. — Stephen J. Cannell, *The Tin Collectors*, p. 325, 2001
- I just couldn't deal with another frigging person that day. — *The Guardian*, 11th September 2002
- Wake up pricks, we're all fricking late. — *X-Ray*, p. 29, June 2003

frigging *adverb*

damned well *AUSTRALIA*

- You ought to hear Molly play that. Aw, Christ it's friggin' lovely. — Sumner Locke Elliott, *Rusty Bugles*, p. 42, 1948

-frigging- *infix*

damned *AUSTRALIA*

- 'Paris, France,' Grossman breathed. 'Aw, come on!' Fielding scoffed. 'Paris friggin' France! Big deal!' — Morris Lurie, *Seven Books for Grossman*, p. 43, 1983
- And yes, we may well learn the sorry truth about the legendary Mars Bar incident in which police a-friggin'-llegedly burst into Keef Richard's UK home Redlands and found Marianne feeding Mick a Mars Bar. — *Picture*, p. 55, 5th February 1992
- I'll drink anythin put in front of me tonight, anyfrigginthing. — Niall Griffiths, *Kelly + Victor*, p. 54, 2002

frigging hell!

used for registering surprise, anger, amazement *UK*

Euphemism for FUCKING HELL!.

- Chrissie is halfway under [a fence] and stuck. CHRISSIE: Friggin' hell. — Alan Bleasdale, *Boys From The Blackstuff*, 1982

frigging in the rigging

wasting time idling when on duty *AUSTRALIA*

From a bawdy ballad.

- The first mate's name was Wiggun, / by God, he had a big 'un, / We bashed his cock / with a lump of rock, / for friggin' in the riggin'. — 'S. Hogbotel & S. ffuckes', *Snatches & Lays*, p. 87, 1962
- Chorus: Oh it's friggin' in the riggin', / It's friggin' in the riggin', / It's friggin' in the riggin', / And there's fuck all else to do. — Dorothy Hewett, *The Chapel Perilous*, p. 44, 1972
- Rodney and Sid drank whiskey in the street and, arms round each other, sang 'Friggin in the Rigging'. Then they embraced each other on the nature strip. — Ross Fitzgerald, *All About Anthrax*, p. 15, 1987

fright *noun*

an ugly person *UK, 1832*

- Betsy looked a fright. The bloom was gone from her cheeks[.] — Sylvia Plath, *The Bell Jar*, p. 43, 1971

▸ he (she) wouldn't give you a fright on a dark night

said of a person with a reputation for meanness *UK*

Glasgow use.

- — Michael Munro, *The Patter, Another Blast*, 1988

frightener *noun*

a scare *UK*

- I'd been terrified [...] but once I got over the first frightener I sort of liked it. — L.J. Cunliffe, *Having It Away*, 1965

frighteners *noun*

▸ put the frighteners on

to scare someone *UK, 1958*

- Another factor is the perceived need to "put the frighteners" on London every so often by raising the threat of exclusion [from the EU]. — *The Guardian*, 19th May 2000

frightful *adjective*

used as a general-purpose intensifier *UK, 1752*

- [T]he many attempts to find a peaceful solution to the frightful mess that resulted[.] — *The Guardian*, 6th April 2002

frightfully *adverb*

very, extremely *UK, 1809*

- Just look at Harold Wilson, or John Major. One frightfully clever, the other frightfully decent. — *The Guardian*, 5th February 2003

frigidaire *noun*

a sexually frigid woman *US*

An allusion to the refrigerator brand.

- — Vincent J. Monteleone, *Criminal Slang*, p. 91, 1949

frig off *verb*

to go away, to leave *US, 1961*

Often in the imperative.

- He gave me the look. "Frig off," I said. "Bite me," he whispered. — Sheree Fitch, *One More Step*, p. 22, 2002

frig up *verb*

to botch, to ruin *US, 1933*

- Sometimes it does an even better job when the person in charge isn't there to frig it up[.] — Stephen King, *Dolores Claiborne*, p. 62, 1993

frillies *noun*

women's underclothing, especially insubstantial 'feminine' garments *UK, 1937*

- [W]here to buy those last-minute frillies (answer: it doesn't really matter because 38% of French women take them back anyway). — *The Guardian*, 14th February 2002

fringe *noun*
thin strips of material attached to the G-string worn by a striptease dancer *US*
- —Don Wilmeth, *The Language of American Popular Entertainment*, p. 97, 1981

fringe *verb*
to get something from somebody else by imposing on their hospitality or generosity *US*
- —Marcus Hanna Boulware, *Jive and Slang of Students in Negro Colleges*, 1947

fringes *noun*
the eyes *US*
- —Marcus Hanna Boulware, *Jive and Slang of Students in Negro Colleges*, 1947

fringie *noun*
a person on the fringes of a gang, not a hardcore member *US, 1966*
- —Jennifer Blowdryer, *Modern English*, p. 61, 1985

frios *noun*
marijuana mixed with phencyclidine, the recreational drug known as PCP or angel dust *UK, 1998*
- —Mike Haskins, *Drugs*, p. 293, 2003

frip *adjective*
lousy *US*
Youth usage.
- —*Time*, 3rd October 1949

frisbee *noun*
1 a biscuit from an army c-ration *US*
- —Linda Reinberg, *In the Field*, p. 89, 1991

2 an agent of the Federal Bureau of Investigations *US*
- —Kenn "Naz" Young, *Naz's Dictionary of Teen Slang*, p. 45, 1993

'Frisco *nickname*
San Francisco, California *US, 1849*
Never used by San Franciscans, and a sure sign of a tourist.
- "I was up there once," I said. "I like Frisco, it's a good city."—Chester Himes, *If He Hollers Let Him Go*, p. 41, 1945
- In which case, if you came to Frisco, I could still see you and Allen, but couldn't ship out.—Jack Kerouac, *Letter to Neal Cassady*, p. 114, 26th August 1947
- Washington's Chinatown is neither as large as Frisco's, as colorful as New York's, nor as odoriferous as Boston's.—Jack Lait and Lee Mortimer, *Washington Confidential*, p. 57, 1951
- Hell, I could get a farm someplace, maybe out near Frisco with Hart Kennedy.—John Clellon Holmes, *Go*, p. 51, 1952
- We wished each other luck. We would meet in Frisco.—Jack Kerouac, *On the Road*, p. 57, 1957
- She had me out to Frisco for two weeks over the New Year's holidays.—Babs Gonzales, *Movin' On Down De Line*, p. 148, 1975
- In the seat next to her, an aggressive sailor made inane conversation about "Frisco," boring her with endless details about his tour of duty on Treasure Island.—Armistead Maupin, *Tales of the City*, p. 197, 1978
- Folks who live here think it's hokey to call it Frisco.—Seth Morgan, *Homeboy*, p. 383, 1990
- The term "Frisco," for so long a nickname non grata in these parts, is making a comeback as mysterious as those random, unclaimed single socks on the folding table.—*San Francisco Chronicle*, p. D1, 14th October 2003

Frisco speedball; Frisco special; San Francisco bomb *noun*
a combination of cocaine, heroin and LSD *US, 1969*
Up, down and out – all at once; a combination of a SPEEDBALL (cocaine and heroin) with the drug that made FRISCO (San Francisco) psychedelic.
- —Carl D. Chambers and Richard D. Heckman, *Employee Drug Abuse*, p. 205, 1972
- —Robert Ashton, *This Is Heroin*, p. 209, 2002
- —Mike Haskins, *Drugs*, p. 293, 2003

frisk *verb*
1 to search the person for illicit goods *UK, 1789*
- —Angela Devlin, *Prison Patter*, p. 53, 1996
- We were frisked and had our placards taken off us.—*The Guardian*, 21st February 2003

2 to laugh *UK*
- —Angela Devlin, *Prison Patter*, p. 53, 1996

frisker *noun*
a pickpocket *UK, 1802*
- —Ralph de Sola, *Crime Dictionary*, p. 55, 1982

frisky *noun*
cocaine *US*
- —Richard A. Spears, *The Slang and Jargon of Drugs and Drink*, p. 206, 1986

frisky *adjective*
sexually aroused *US*
- —Anna Scotti and Paul Young, *Buzzwords*, p. 19, 1997

frisky powder *noun*
cocaine *US*
- —*American Speech*, p. 87, May 1955: 'Narcotic argot along the Mexican border'

frit *noun*
in Quebec, a French fried potato *CANADA*
- The special is hamburger, all dressed, with french fried. The "fried" becomes a noun [not] an adjective, and it's assumed you know they're talking about frits, a term that's known enough as the name of a fast food chain, and used in English jingles.—*The Downtowner*, p. 3, 7th May 1986

Frito *noun*
a woman who is sexually expert *US*
A pun on the Frito Lay company name – a 'good lay'.
- —*Current Slang*, p. 14, Fall 1967

fritterware *noun*
computer software that is seductive to users, consumes time and adds little to functionality *US*
- —Eric S. Raymond, *The New Hacker's Dictionary*, p. 168, 1991

fritz *noun*
▸ **on the fritz**
broken *US, 1902*
- Even though the air conditioning in Dad's Beamer was on the fritz, he made us ride over with the windows up so the other motorists wouldn't think he didn't have any.—C.D. Payne, *Youth in Revolt*, p. 14, 1977
- His car's been on the fritz and he borrowed a Cadillac from someone.—Janet Evanovich, *Seven Up*, p. 43, 2001

Fritz *noun*
a German *UK, 1915*

fritz *verb*
to break *US, 1918*
- [S]omething fritzed the gates. Goddamn things closed on the Rolls before it was through.—Robert Campbell, *In La-La Land We Trust*, p. 49, 1986

friznaughti *adjective*
drug-intoxicated *US*
- I got me a dubie and I'ma get friznaughti tonight—*A2Z, the Book of Rap and Hip-Hip Slang*, 1995

frizzle *adjective*
very cold *NORFOLK ISLAND*
- —Beryl Nobbs Palmer, *A Dictionary of Norfolk Words and Usages*, p. 15, 1992

'fro *noun*
a bushy Afro hair style *US*
- —*Current Slang*, p. 7, Fall 1970
- I don't know how anybody could've recognized us, you especially with that 'fro.—Elmore Leonard, *Freaky Deaky*, p. 35, 1988

frob *noun*
any small object *US*
- —Eric S. Raymond, *The New Hacker's Dictionary*, p. 168, 1991

frob *verb*
to manipulate dials or settings *US, 1983*
- When I questioned our local computer wizard about what she meant when she said she was going to frob my workstation, she gave me this tutorial on hackerese.—Steven Pinker, *The Language Instinct*, p. 163, 1994

frobnicate *verb*
to manipulate dials or settings *US, 1983*
- —Gilbert Held, *The Complete Cyberspace Reference*, p. 6, 1994

frobnitz *noun*
any device the name of which is unknown, escapes the speaker's mind or is not relevant *US*
- —Eric S. Raymond, *The New Hacker's Dictionary*, p. 169, 1991

frock *noun*
women's clothing; a theatrical costume *UK*
- —Paul Baker, *Polari*, p. 175, 2002

frock *verb*
to decorate as a military officer *US*
From the C19 sense of 'investing with priestly office'.

- The message announced tersely that Lieutenant Commander Robert A. Toland, III. USNR, had been "frocked" as a commander, USNR, which gave him the right to wear the three gold stripes of a commander[.]—Tom Clancy, *Red Storm Rising*, p. 124, 1986
- Regardless of the H's and I's on my fitreps, I'd finally been frocked for captain in February 1985.—Richard Marcinko and John Weisman, *Rogue Warrior*, p. 284, 1992

frock and frill *noun*
a *chill*, a cold *UK*
Rhyming slang.
- —Ray Puxley, *Cockney Rabbit*, 1992

frock billong lallies *noun*
trousers *UK*
A combination of Tok Pisin, a Melanesian pidgin, *billong* (belong) and polari **FROCK** (clothing) and **LALLY** (the leg).
- —Paul Baker, *Polari*, p. 175, 2002

froffy *adjective*
poor and shabby looking *BARBADOS*
Recorded by Richard Allsopp.

frog *noun*
1 a social outcast *US*
- Frog originally meant a first semester freshman, but this use is becoming archaic. Its use today is usually derisive or derogatory. —Fred Hester, *Slang on the 40 Acres*, p. 6, 1968

2 a promiscuous girl *US*
- —Bill Valentine, *Gang Intelligence Manual*, p. 76, 1995: 'Black street gang terminology'

3 a French Canadian *CANADA*
- I hope the Canadians [sic] or Frogs as you call them, beat the hell out of your Hogtown heroes."—*Toronto Globe and Mail*, p. 23/8, 14th April 1966

4 a condom *AUSTRALIA, 1952*
Probably as a play on **FRENCH LETTER** or **FRENCHY** (a condom).
- Got some frogs under the bed, have you?—Alexander Buzo, *Rooted*, p. 90, 1969
- —Jim Ramsay, *Cop It Sweet!*, p. 37, 1977

5 the French language *UK, 1955*
- "You speak kraut [German]?" says Mike. [...] "Frog?" he pursued gamely. "Well up to frog. And Spanish. Good. Some Eyetie [Italian]."—Derek Raymond (Robin Cook), *The Crust on its Uppers*, p. 46, 1962
- You're the only one whose Frog is good enough for this, sir.—Craig Thomas, *Wolfsbane*, 1978

6 one dollar *US*
- —Frank Garcia, *Marked Cards and Loaded Dice*, p. 262, 1962

Frog *noun*
a person from France *UK, 1778*
Like all the 'frog' terms for the French, it refers to the eating of frogs.
- You went the distance for the fab frog poet.—Terry Southern, *Now Dig This*, p. 232, 1989
- This was the same Frog who threatened to phone the consulate every time he got stopped for ripping around Mission Bay like a Paris cabbie in one of those dopey little Citroens, fit only for delivery of car bombs by neurotic Arabs.—Joseph Wambaugh, *Floaters*, p. 2, 1996
- [T]he sustained tradition of sense derangement among decadent frogs of the so-called Quality-Lit crowd!—Victor Bockris, *With William Burroughs [The Howard Marks Book of Dope Stories]*, p. 35, 1997
- [T]he Yanks, Frogs, Ruskies, Chinese, Indians and every other cunt who's now got the bomb[.]—Danny King, *The Bank Robber Diaries*, p. 186, 2002

frog *verb*
to fail (a test or exam) *US*
- —Mary Swift, *Campus Slang (University of Texas)*, 1968

Frog *adjective*
French *US, 1910*
Unkind.
- Back to Chicago we drove that very night to prepare for our grand tour of the Continent, Danny coaching us in the Frog lingo all the way home so we could gab with the parlay-voo's when we landed in good old Paree.—Mezz Mezzrow, *Really the Blues*, p. 129, 1946
- I hope I don't get a rash or anything. I hear these Frog sheilahs are riddled with whatever it is!!!—Barry Humphries, *Bazza Pulls It Off!*, 1971
- I suppose the Frog movie must be over by now.—C.D. Payne, *Youth in Revolt*, p. 403, 1993

frog!
used for expressing disgust *US*
- —Eric S. Raymond, *The New Hacker's Dictionary*, p. 169, 1991

frog and toad; frog *noun*
the road *UK, 1859*
Rhyming slang.
- —Duke Tritton, *Learn to talk Old Jack Lang*, p. 12, 1905
- We'll have one for the frog and toad.—Frank Hardy, *The Outcasts of Foolgarah*, p. 26, 1971
- —Jim Ramsay, *Cop It Sweet!*, p. 37, 1977
- I met a bird one evening / As I walked down the frog[.]—Ronnie Barker, *Fletcher's Book of Rhyming Slang*, p. 21, 1979
- I nearly 'ad a seizure, / When I clocked 'im in the frog.—Viv Stanshall, *Ginger Geezer*, 1981
- —Ryan Aven-Bray, *Ridgey Didge Oz Jack Lang*, p. 28, 1983

frog-choker *noun*
a heavy rain *CANADA*
- —Bill Casselman, *Canadian Sayings*, p. 151, 2002

frogeater *noun*
a French person; a French-Canadian *US, 1812*
This term, highly derogatory along with 'Frog', has passed out of use, not adapted like 'Pepper' from 'Pepsi', and in any case could be more aptly applied to the Acadians of Louisiana, who are fond of frog-legs from the bayous.
- They frightened the Frenchmen, and so we won the battle of the Alma for the frogeaters, with nothing but our bayonets.—M. Constantin-Weyer, *The Half-Breed*, p. 40, 1954

frogeyed sprite *noun*
an Austin-Healy Sprite *UK*
- —Lewis Poteet, *Car & Motorcyle Slang*, p. 40, 1992

Froggie; Froggy *noun*
1 France *UK*
- [W]e needed fresh finance for that trip to Froggie.—Jeremy Cameron, *Brown Bread in Wengen*, p. 81, 1999

2 a person from France *US, 1870s*
- The Froggie scampered across the boatyard to the fence, yelling, "No! You shall not to fo-toe le keel!"—Joseph Wambaugh, *Floaters*, p. 2, 1996

froggy *adjective*
1 aggressive *US, 1939*
- There were a couple of other guys in the group that might get froggy if someone leaped[.]—Joseph Wambaugh, *The Blue Knight*, p. 68, 1973
- —Edith A. Folb, *runnin' down some lines*, p. 238, 1980

2 used to describe a dry mouth after smoking marijuana *UK*
Probably from the phrase 'frog in the throat' (hoarse).
- —Nick Brownlee, *This Is Cannabis*, p. 152, 2002

Froggy; Froggie *adjective*
French *UK, 1872*
- Mr Hoon looked flustered by all these attacks on our froggie friends.—*The Guardian*, 20th March 2001

frog hair *noun*
a very short distance *US, 1958*
- He'd jump all over the stage swiping wildly at the air, come within a frog hair of splatting his fist in to the chafing dish a dozen times[.] —Katherine Dunn, *Greek Love*, p. 250, 1989

frogman *noun*
a diver equipped with air tanks *UK, 1945*
- You'll never be a SEAL unless you first become a frogman.—Dick Couch, *The Warrior Elite*, p. 29, 2001

frog-march; frog's march *verb*
to push someone forward holding them by their collar and the seat of their trousers *UK, 1884*
- I wonder what the cop would think if I began jumping with glee and yelling: "Frog's march him! For God's sake, frog's march him!"—Terry Southern, *Now Dig This*, p. 158, 1972
- Gripping Archie under the arm, the undercover cop frogmarched him to the end of the causeway and down the steep steps to Kearny Street.—Seth Morgan, *Homeboy*, p. 205, 1990

frog salad *noun*
in carnival usage, any performance that features scantily clad women *US*
- —Don Wilmeth, *The Language of American Popular Entertainment*, p. 101, 1981

frog show *noun*
a dance performance that features scantily clad women *US*
- It is an old joke in the United States that whenever there is a great "leg piece," sometimes called a "frog salad" (i.e., a ballet with unusual opportunities for studying anatomy), the front seats are invariably filled with veteran roues.—Sherman Louis Sergel, *The Language of Show Biz*, p. 15, 1973

frogskin *noun*

1 money; paper money; a one-dollar note *US, 1902*

- Why couldn't it be me up there in that crazy pad with my mitt out for all those frog skins? —Iceberg Slim (Robert Beck), *Pimp*, p. 135, 1969
- "Frog skin" was based on the colour of the one-dollar bill; this term, where still in use, will have to go when the one-dollar bill gives way to the one-dollar coin. —Chris Thain, *Cold as a Bay Street Banker's Heart*, p. 68, 1987

2 a condom *NEW ZEALAND*

- —David McGill, *David McGill's Complete Kiwi Slang Dictionary*, p. 46, 1998

frogskins *noun*

a wetsuit and other cold-water garments *US*

- —Trevor Cralle, *The Surfin'ary*, p. 42, 1991

frog-spawn *noun*

tapioca pudding *UK*

One of the joys of a public school education.

- —F. Spencer Chapman, *The Jungle is Neutral*, 1949

frogsticker *noun*

a knife *US*

- "Lee-roy," the Kingfish says, icy, "put that damn frog-sticker away." —Guy Owen, *The Flim-Flam Man and the Apprentice Grifter*, p. 113, 1972

frog-strangler *noun*

a torrential downpour *US, 1942*

- Now I really understood what the phrases "coming down in buckets," "raining in sheets," and "frog strangler" meant. —Frank E. Walton, *Once They Were Eagles*, p. 31, 1986

frog-walk *verb*

to forcefully carry somebody face-down *US, 1960*

- Bernard B. O'Hare, of course, was the young man who had captured me at the end of the war, who had frog-walked me through the death camp at Ohrdruf[.] —Kurt Vonnegut, *Mother Night*, p. 61, 1966

frolic *noun*

a New Brunswick work bee and party *CANADA*

- All bees provided entertainment and social intercourse as well as hard work. On that account they were usually called "frolics" in New Brunswick. —Edwin Guillet, *Pioneer Days in Upper Canada*, p. 120, 1964
- In New Brunswick, a "frolic" is always a cooperative effort crossed with a party. It might be a barn raising or quilting bee, but it always meant work mixed with music, food, and friends. —*cbc4kids.ca*, 15th June 2002

from arsehole to breakfast time

all the time, all the way *UK, 1984*

- STARLING: What have you taken? JIG: Not a brass fart. We'll be here from arsehole to breakfast-time at this rate. —Rod Wooden, *Smoke and Moby Dick*, 1996
- They'd give him fuckin therapy from arsehole to breakfast time[.] —J.J. Connolly, *Layer Cake*, p. 37, 2000

from away *adjective*

from any place other than the area of the eastern Canadian coast speaker's own local region or town *CANADA*

Exactly opposite of 'from around here', this term is flexible in application and odd in that the object of the preposition is a word not ordinarily used in the noun position.

- The outer limit of "away" is not always fixed at the world, but may be, in minority usage, North America or the rest of Canada only. People from Ontario are especially said to be "from away." —*Atlantic Provinces Linguistic Association Proceedings*, 1985

from here to there without a pair

in poker, used for describing a hand of sequenced cards *US*

Conventionally known as a 'straight'.

- —*American Speech*, p. 98, May 1951

frompy *adjective*

unattractive *US*

- —Jack Lait and Lee Mortimer, *New York Confidential*, p. 235, 1948: 'A glossary of Harlemisms'

from way downtown – bang

used as a humorous comment on a witty remark, a correct answer or other verbal victory *US*

Coined by ESPN's Keith Olberman to describe three-point shots in basketball.

- —Keith Olberman and Dan Patrick, *The Big Show*, p. 14, 1997

frone *noun*

an ugly woman *US*

- —Marcus Hanna Boulware, *Jive and Slang of Students in Negro Colleges*, 1947

frone *adjective*

terrible *UK*

- Anything very bad might also be called "frone" or "sad." —*Woman's Digest*, p. 40, September 1945

front *noun*

1 a person's public appearance; stylish clothing *US, 1899*

- A European charm of manner and a slight Scandinavian accent completed his front. —William Burroughs, *Junkie*, p. 43, 1953
- Joe, you have a short, some fronts, and a fine ticker too. —Bruce Jackson, *Get Your Ass in the Water and Swim Like Me*, p. 91, 1964
- I layed off for another four months, but I was able to keep up a front by doing weekends in "Jersey" and "Connecticut". —Babs Gonzales, *I Paid My Dues*, p. 61, 1967
- Everybody in both worlds kissed your ass black and blue if you had flash and front. —Iceberg Slim (Robert Beck), *Pimp*, p. 118, 1969
- Despite his four years in The Life, Mojo has not yet been able to get his "front" together[.] —Christina and Richard Milner, *Black Players*, p. 146, 1972
- The whole thing happened because we both were consumed by the desire to get a top-notch front that would cause us to be two of the youngest major-league mack men in the city of Detroit. —A.S. Jackson, *Gentleman Pimp*, p. 59, 1973

2 the genitals; sex *BAHAMAS*

- —John A. Holm, *Dictionary of Bahamian English*, p. 82, 1982

3 the beginning *US*

Especially in the phrase 'from the front'.

- —Lawrence Lipton, *The Holy Barbarians*, p. 316, 1959

▸ **at the front**

used of a drug that is taken before another *UK*

- —Home Office, *Glossary of Terms and Slang Common in Penal Establishments*, July 1978

▸ **more front than Selfridges/Harrods/Buckingham Palace/Albert Hall/Brighton/Brighton beach/ Woolworths/Myers**

audaciousness; impudence *UK*

Puns 'front' (cheek) with the exceptional frontage of Selfridges, a very large department store in Oxford Street; Harrods is another impressive London shop; Buckingham Palace is the Queen's official London residence; the Albert Hall is a major concert venue; and Brighton is a seaside resort on the south coast – 'front' in this instance abbreviated from 'seafront'. In Australia, Myers is a large department store in Melbourne.

- Does she take me for a mug or what? She's got more front than Selfridges —Frank Norman, *Bang To Rights*, p. 65, 1958
- [Parking] slap under a no-parking sign ... more front than Buckingham Palace. —Derek Raymond (Robin Cook), *The Crust on its Uppers*, p. 23, 1962
- I shouldn't speak ill of the living but he's a cheeky bugger – always has been – more front on him than Myers —Barry Humphries, *A Nice Night's Entertainment*, p. 165, 1978
- Terry steered Justin away from the shop. "You've got more front than the Albert Hall," he told him. —Anthony Masters, *Minder*, p. 4, 1984
- [W]e both had as much front as Woolworths. —Mark Pass, *Marc Bolan, The Sharper Word*, p. 43, 1992

▸ **out front**

owing someone who has extended goods to you for payment later *US*

- People be telling him nobody be staying out front for too long. —Terry Williams, *The Cocaine Kids*, p. 44, 1989

▸ **the front**

the main road or street within the area of a Teddy Boy gang's influence *UK*

- —*The Observer*, 1st March 1959

▸ **up front**

in advance *US, 1970*

- "I want the five up front," Joe Loop said, "or Nick can do the guy himself." —Elmore Leonard, *Be Cool*, p. 127, 1999

Front *noun*

▸ **the Front**

1 Piccadilly, as an area of homosexual commerce and prostitution *UK*

- —*Evening Standard*, 20–24th July 1964: 'London's hidden problems'

2 Oxford Street, London *UK*

- —David Powis, *The Signs of Crime*, 1977

front *verb*

1 in jazz or popular music, to be a band leader, or lead singer of a band *US, 1936*

- [Jonathan] Maitland plays the guitar while the delightfully named Jackie Collins fronts the band on vocals. — *The Guardian*, 1st February 2002

2 to lie; to project a false image of yourself *US*

- — *Washington Post*, 14th October 1993

3 to show up; to make an appearance *AUSTRALIA, 1968*

- [T]hey'd call the cops if I fronted[.] — Kevin Mackey, *The Cure*, p. 7, 1970
- It took Phil two days to pluck up the guts to front, but he walked in and mum met him with a cheerful 'Hello, Phil'. — Sam Weller, *Old Bastards I Have Met*, p. 115, 1979
- — Kathy Lette, *Girls' Night Out*, p. 31, 1987

4 to confront someone *AUSTRALIA, 1945*

- — Peter Corris, *Make Me Rich*, p. 37, 1985
- I had been there and done that myself and so justice was tempered with mercy; 'Will you front the Boss? or would you perhaps volunteer for some extra duty time in which you can repent of your sinfulness.' — Martin Cameron, *A Look at the Bright Side*, 1988

5 to appear before a court *AUSTRALIA, 1941*

- He fronted on three busts. — (Prisoner) 35 *The Argot*, 1950

6 to provide something of value to someone with the expectation of being paid later *US*

- Various terms are employed to describe this: suppliers may say they give cocaine "on credit" or as a "loan" to distributors; at all levels, it is called "fronting." — Terry Williams, *The Cocaine Kids*, p. 34, 1989

7 to back down from a physical confrontation *US*

- — Carsten Stroud, *Close Pursuit*, p. 272, 1987

8 to pretend, to fake *US*

- So don't front like you don't know what my name is[.] — Akinyele *Checkmate*, 1993

▸ **front an air biscuit**

to pretend innocence of generating a guilty fart *UK*

- — *The A-Z of Rude Health*, 18th January 2002

▸ **front it**

to face up to a difficult problem or situation; hence, to leave a Vulnerable Prisoners' Unit and return to the main prison *UK*

- — Angela Devlin, *Prison Patter*, p. 53, 1996

front and back *noun*

a sack, the sack *UK*

Rhyming slang.

- — Bodmin Dark, *Dirty Cockney Rhyming Slang*, 2003

front bottom *noun*

the vulva and vagina *UK*

- I've subsequently been told of a man in Japan who can facilitate a woman's orgasm merely by hovering his hands over her front bottom. — *The Sunday Times*, 26th October 2003

front botty; front bum *noun*

the vagina *AUSTRALIA*

- — Lenie Johansen, *The Dinkum Dictionary*, 1988
- — David McGill, *David McGill's Complete Kiwi Slang Dictionary*, p. 125, 1998
- So although Phallus did not see Hot Buns' breasts he did see her front botty[.] — Gretel Killeen, *Hot Buns and Ophelia get a Bloke*, p. 18, 2000
- Abjection was invoked in various ways: through reference to dirtiness (e.g., front bum, dirt box), uncooked (bloody?) meat (e.g., meat seat, chopped liver), vaginal secretions of all types (e.g., slushing fuck pit, the snail trail), smell (e.g. smelly hole, stench trench), and wounds (e.g., gash, gaping axe wound). — *Journal of Sex Research*, p. 146, 2001
- Take your mother to the doctor's cos her front bum's wrecked. — Goldie Coloured Chain, *Your Mother's Got a Penis*, 2004

front bumpers *noun*

the female breast *UK*

An elaboration of **BUMPER**.

- Rits's fabulous front bumpers. — Petra Christian, *The Sexploiters*, p. 102, 1973

front door *noun*

1 the vagina *UK, 1890*

As opposed to the **BACK DOOR** (the rectum).

- Though advised Dale to get laid tonight; be his last shot at some front-door lovin'. Dale wouldn't talk about it. — Elmore Leonard, *Maximum Bob*, p. 200, 1991

2 the leading vehicle in a convoy of citizens' band radio users *US, 1975*

- Yeah, we definitely got the front door, good buddy. — C.W. McCall, *Convoy*, 1976
- — Peter Chippindale, *The British CB Book*, p. 154, 1981

front doormat *noun*

a woman's pubic hair *UK*

- — *Maledicta*, p. 183, Winter 1980: 'A new erotic vocabulary'

fronter *noun*

1 an inexperienced swindler working on a scam by telephone who makes the initial call to potential victims *US*

- — Kathleen Odean, *High Steppers, Fallen Angels, and Lollipops*, p. 132, 1988

2 a person who appears to be something he is not and who does not deliver on promised action *US*

- — *Newsday*, p. B2, 11th October 1997

front line *noun*

an urban area where a resident, in a mainly black community may come into conflict with an adjacent white community or with the laws of white society *UK*

West Indian and UK black.

- — Eddy Grant *Living on the Front Line and The Front Line Symphony*, 1978
- I read the papers on account of somethin' 'bout the front line [Brixton] gonna be in 'em most days and usually not too complimentary. — Ben Elton, *High Society*, p. 110, 2002

front-liner *noun*

a person in a youth gang who is capable of murder *US*

- — Bill Valentine, *Gang Intelligence Manual*, p. 110, 1995: 'Jamaican gang terminology'

frontload *verb*

to drink at home before going out for a night of drinking on the town *US*

- — Connie Eble (Editor), *UNC-CH Campus Slang*, p. 4, Fall 1999

front-loading *noun*

a technique for observing the dealer's down card in casino blackjack as the dealer tips the card up to slide it under his up card *US*

- — Michael Dalton, *Blackjack*, p. 49, 1991

front man *noun*

someone who is employed to cover for a criminal operation by posing as the legitimate owner/leader or by acting as spokesperson *US, 1934*

- — Angela Devlin, *Prison Patter*, p. 53, 1996

front money *noun*

1 money paid in advance for the purchase of drugs *US, 1978*

- "I need front money for the first load of snow," Mona said. — Gerald Petievich, *The Quality of the Informant*, p. 6, 1985
- — Angela Devlin, *Prison Patter*, p. 53, 1996

2 money needed to start a venture *US, 1925*

- "Here's some of the front money," he said. "Bet you thought I was gonna try and use your maxed-out Visa card." — Stephen Cannell, *King Con*, p. 110, 1997

front off *verb*

1 to place yourself in a highly visible position *US*

- "Yeah, you! You go." "Why me? Why do I have to front myself off when it's my idea?" — Clarence Cooper Jr, *The Scene*, p. 61, 1960

2 to sell drugs on credit *US*

- — Mark S. Fleisher, *Beggars & Thieves*, p. 289, 1995: 'Glossary'

front porch *noun*

in poker, the earliest position in a hand *US*

- — John Vorhaus, *The Big Book of Poker Slang*, p. 19, 1996

front-running *noun*

to support a person or team only when they are doing well *US*

- Front running is not limited to coaches. — Jim Bouton, *Ball Four*, p. 157, 1970

fronts *noun*

legitimate, square, unaltered dice *US*

- — *The Annals of the American Academy of Political and Social Sciences*, p. 125, May 1950

▷ **see: GOLD FRONTS**

front street *noun*

▸ **put on front street**

to inform on, to betray *US*

- — Bill Valentine, *Gang Intelligence Manual*, 1995: 'Black street gang terminology'

Front Street *noun*

▸ **on Front Street; on front street**

in the open; in public *US*

• —William K. Bentley and James M. Corbett, *PrisonSlang*, p. 32, 1992
• I'll never tell Mary anything again. She always puts my business on Front Street. —Connie Eble (Editor), *UNC-CH Campus Slang*, p. 3, November 2002

front up *verb*

to appear in *front* of; to con*front* *AUSTRALIA, 1945*

• [W]e fronted them up and they bottled out[.] —John King, *Human Punk*, p. 133, 2000

front wedgy *noun*

the condition that exists when a tight-fitting pair of trousers, shorts, bathing suit or other garment forms a wedge between a woman's labia, accentuating their shape *US*

The **WEDGY** brought around to the front of the body.

front wheel skid; four wheel skid; four-wheeler *noun*

a Jewish person *UK, 1943*

Rhyming slang for **YID**. Noted as 'intentionally more offensive than five-to-two' by Red Daniells, 1980.

• —David Powis, *The Signs of Crime*, 1977
• —*www.LondonSlang.com*, June 2002

front yard *noun*

in trucking, the road ahead of you *US*

• —Bill Davis, *Jawjacking*, p. 43, 1977

frosh *noun*

a freshman (first year student), either in high school or college *US, 1915*

• I'm glad I use Dial whenever I wash / I've used it to clean me since I was a frosh. —Max Shulman, *Guided Tour of Campus Humor*, p. 49, 1955
• The upperclassmen were vastly impressed that a couple of frosh could make themselves so much at home in so short a time with such apparent ease[.] —John Nichols, *The Sterile Cuckoo*, p. 49, 1965
• —Connie Eble (Editor), *UNC-CH Campus Slang*, p. 4, Spring 1982

frost *verb*

to anger *US, 1895*

Often in combination with a body part.

• What was frosting her ass was the fact that he was queering her pitch. —Robert Campbell, *Alice in La-La Land*, p. 245, 1987

▸ **frost your balls**

to anger *US*

• The kid's only been here two months and they make him foreman. Doesn't that frost your balls? —Michael Dalton Johnson, *Talking Trash with Redd Foxx*, p. 128, 1994

frost boil *noun*

the irregular road surface caused by frost heave *CANADA*

• Frost boils are those queasy-to-drive-over bumps on a paved road caused by the expanding of moisture in the pavement during freezing weather. Spring repair of frost boils is a feature of Canadian municipal road maintenance. —Bill Casselman, *Canadian Words*, p. 192, 1995

frosted *adjective*

angry *US, 1956*

• —Vann Wesson, *Generation X Field Guide and Lexicon*, p. 70, 1997

frosted face *noun*

the photographic depiction of a woman's face covered with semen *US*

American heterosexual pornography has long shown a fascination for ejaculations on a woman's face. In the late 1990s, this fascination expanded to embrace the depiction of multiple ejaculations on a woman's face. Any Internet search engine will uncover dozens of sites boasting 'frosted faces', a term that puns on the branded cereal 'Frosted Flakes' while inviting a visual comparison with the cereal's sugar glaze.

frost freak *noun*

a person who inhales freon, a refrigerant, for its intoxicating effect *US*

• —William D. Alsever, *Glossary for the Establishment and Other Uptight People*, p. 12, December 1970

frosty *noun*

a cold beer *US, 1961*

• I learned, with the advent of the "Bennie God" to make an acceptable "bennie machine" out of aluminum foil, and use it on the flat back porch every afternoon during the spring semester to "catch a few rays" while downing some frosties. —John Nichols, *The Sterile Cuckoo*, p. 60, 1965
• —*American Speech*, p. 59, Spring-Summer 1975: 'Razorback Slang'

frosty *adjective*

cool, calm, collected *US*

• Stay frosty. Relax. That's the way to do this job. —Joseph Wambaugh, *The New Centurions*, p. 77, 1970
• Come on, let's stay frosty here, Ray. —Stephen J. Cannell, *The Tin Collectors*, p. 8, 2001

frot *verb*

to rub against another person for sexual stimulation, usually surreptitiously *UK*

• These transvestites, nymphos, junkies are in hell. They frot and turn on – take drugs – to give them the illusion of living[.] —*The Observer*, 11th February 1973

froth *noun*

in horse racing, a double *AUSTRALIA*

Rhyming slang from 'froth and bubble' to 'double'.

• —Ned Wallish, *The Truth Dictionary of Racing Slang*, p. 30, 1989

froth *verb*

to engage in an abusive verbal attack *UK*

• —Dave Courtney, *Dodgy Dave's Little Black Book*, p. 7, 2001

froth and bubble *noun*

trouble *AUSTRALIA, 1955*

Rhyming slang.

• Take this Lady Godiva [£5] for your froth and bubble. —Ronnie Barker, *Fletcher's Book of Rhyming Slang*, p. 27, 1979

frothing *adjective*

(used of a party) populated by many girls *US*

• —Surf Punks, *Oh No! Not Them Again!*, 1988

froudacity *noun*

lying about something you know nothing about *TRINIDAD AND TOBAGO, 1967*

A blending of 'audacity' and 'fraudulence'.

• —Lise Winer, *Dictionary of the English/Creole of Trinidad & Tobago*, 2003

frou-frou *adjective*

fussy, overly fancy *US, 1940s*

• Tell me the truth. Is that what you want in a girl – chic-chi, frou-frou, fancy clothes, permanet waves? —Max Shulman, *The Many Loves of Dobie Gillis*, p. 64, 1951

frown *noun*

lemon syrup or fresh lemon added to a coca-cola *US*

• —*American Speech*, p. 88, April 1946: 'The language of West Coast culinary workers'

frowney; frowney face *noun*

the emoticon depicting a frown – :(*US*

• —Eric S. Raymond, *The New Hacker's Dictionary*, p. 169, 1991

froyo *noun*

frozen yogurt *US*

• —Pamla Munro, *U.C.L.A. Slang*, p. 40, 1998
• —*Columbia Missourian*, p. 8A, 19th October 1998

froze *adjective*

1 cocaine-intoxicated *US*

Evocative of the C18 meaning of the word as 'drunk'.

• But I did manage to cop on her that if she liked to get froze, to get in touch. I left her with my phone number, and knowing bitches, they all like a little coke now and then. —Donald Goines, *Never Die Alone*, p. 157, 1974

2 frozen *UK, 1590*

• My nose is froze and my toes is froze —*101 Dalmations*, 1961

frozen *adjective*

1 excellent *US*

Teen slang.

• —*Look*, p. 88, 10th August 1954

2 dull, lacking action *NEW ZEALAND*

• —David McGill, *David McGill's Complete Kiwi Slang Dictionary*, p. 46, 1998

3 in pool, directly touching (a ball or the rail of the table) *US*

• The cue ball was nearly frozen to the top rail. —Walter Tevis, *The Color of Money*, p. 57, 1984
• —Steve Rushin, *Pool Cool*, p. 13, 1990

frozen chosen *noun*
the people who work in Antarctica *US, 1997*
- —Bernadette Hince, *The Antarctic Dictionary*, p. 137, 2000

frozen Chosin *nickname*
the Chanjin Reservoir, identified on Japanese maps as the Chosin Reservoir, scene of heroic military action by the US Marine Corps in the winter of 1950–51 *US, 1952*
- The Chinese indeed ran X Corps out of "Frozen Chosin" but at a price that effectively took its Ninth Army Group out of the war for crucial weeks.—Joseph Goulden, *Korea*, p. 381, 1982

frozen custard *noun*
the vagina of a frigid woman *US*
- —*Maledicta*, p. 17, Summer 1977: 'A word for it!'

frozen fireworks *noun*
jewellery *US*
- He had blown into town with no 'ho. And worse, no wheels and frozen fireworks exploding off his dukes, necessary to cop a star 'ho.—Iceberg Slim (Robert Beck), *Airtight Willie and Me*, p. 21, 1979

frozen mitt *noun*
1 a rejection; a brush off *UK, 1915*
A variant of 'cold shoulder'.
- You can have the usual break-down – but don't get off your bike, If she hands you out the frozen mitt and says she'd rather hike. You can plead and say its springtime, when even lizards mate, But you can't get any further if she won't co-operate.—K. Grant, *It's 'ard to go wrong in the suburbs*, p. 19, 1940
- She'd give a bloke the frozen mit if he tried a bear-up.—Norman Lindsay, *Halfway to Anywhere*, p. 52, 1947

2 an intentionally unwelcoming reception *UK, 1903*
With 'icy mitt' as a variant.

frug *verb*
to dance *UK*
Originally a fashionable dance which was contrived and flourished briefly in the mid-1960s. Its re-emergence is as an ironic generic for all non-specific dancing.
- [S]potting Pat McIntosh down the front, frugging with a gang of Alternate kids, [he] went to join the scrummage.—Kevin Sampson, *Powder*, p. 352, 1999

fruit *noun*
1 a homosexual, especially an obviously homosexual male person *US, 1900*
- She walked with a swagger and he minced his way to the sidewalk holding on to her arm. Fruit.—Mickey Spillane, *I, The Jury*, p. 70, 1947
- [T]old us about conditions there, how when girls go fruit they put em in cottages alone, all girls go fruit, black girls go fruit for mexican girls.—Jack Kerouac, *Letter to John Clellon Holmes*, p. 338, 8th February 1952
- "He's a panhandler and a fruit. A disgrace to the Jewish race." —William Burroughs, *Junkie*, p. 68, 1953
- He asked Vinnie, laughing and slapping him on the shoulder, who that fruit was that was with them the other night and Vinnie told him she was just one of the queens from uptown, one a Georgetts friends.—Hubert Selby Jr, *Last Exit to Brooklyn*, p. 168–169, 1957
- It was an uninviting prospect. The old fruit must be forty.—Mary McCarthy, *The Group*, p. 89, 1963
- And malehustlers ("fruithustlers"/"studhustlers": the various names for the masculine hustlers looking for lonely fruits to score from[.] —John Rechy, *City of Night*, p. 100, 1963
- Enclosed please find cine script by yrs truly and a crafty old fruit. —Terry Southern, *Now Ddig This*, p. 49, 1964
- "Why there are some guys – some guys I know right at school – who'll sell their ass to some fruit for twenty bucks, just because they're too lazy to get a job."—Gore Vidal, *Myra Breckinridge*, p. 149, 1968
- The nuns, he explained as cavalierly as possible, were "some crazy friends of Mona's." And, yes, they were men. "Fruits?"—Armistead Maupin, *Tales of the City*, p. 268, 1978
- This twisted old fruit here tells me that you have fucked up my reservations.—*This is Spinal Tap*, 1984
- Hey, fruit alert!—*Bull Durham*, 1988
- —Multicultural Management Program Fellows, *Dictionary of Cautionary Words and Phrases*, 1989
- —Angela Devlin, *Prison Patter*, p. 54, 1996
- What were once quaintly called fruits. These days you could be upfront about being gay[.]—Stewart Home, *Sex Kick [britpulp]*, p. 224, 1999

2 an eccentric or even mentally unstable person *US, 1959*
A shortening of **FRUITCAKE**.

▸**do your fruit**
to go mad; to lose your temper *UK*
Probably suggested by **BANANAS** (crazy, mad); recorded by Jack Slater, 1978.

fruitbait *noun*
a man who attracts the attention of other men *US*
- Nick, always a man of few words, said "Siddown, fruitbait."—Joseph Wambaugh, *The Blue Knight*, p. 140, 1973

fruit basket *noun*
the male genitalia when offered to view from behind *US, 2001*
Strong homosexual overtones: **BASKET** (the male genitals) combined with **FRUIT** (a homosexual).
- Fruit basket for Russell Woodman!—David Duchovny, *Evolution*, 2001

fruitbat *noun*
a crazy person *AUSTRALIA*
- Jaco Pastorius, bass legend and utter fruitbat, is beaten to death trying to get into a Miami nightclub.—Ignatius Jones, *The 1992 True Hip Manual*, p. 166, 1992

fruit boot *noun*
1 a style of shoe popular in the 1950s and 60s, ankle-high suede shoes with crepe rubber soles conventionally known as 'desert boots' *US*
English mods embraced desert boots made by Clarks of England, and their popularity spread to the US, where they were labelled 'fruit boots' because of their perceived popularity with perceived homosexuals.
- —Guy Strait, *The Lavendar Lexicon*, 1st June 1964
- Then he sat down and took off his fruitboots and socks, and wiggled his toes in the cool air.—John Nichols, *The Sterile Cuckoo*, p. 71, 1965
- —*Esquire*, p. 180, June 1983

2 an in-line skater *UK*
Derogatory.
- —Ben Sharpe, *Scooter Crazy*, p. 40, 2000

fruitcake *noun*
1 an eccentric or even mentally unstable person *US, 1942*
- —*American Speech*, p. 238, October 1946: 'World War II slang of maladjustment'
- Easy, feller, easy. She's a fruitcake.—Mickey Spillane, *Kiss Me Deadly*, p. 7, 1952
- Hey you, Blondie, you like fruitcake kids like that?—Ken Kesey, *One Flew Over the Cuckoo's Nest*, p. 230, 1962
- —*American Speech*, Fall-Winter 1976
- United fruitcake outlet.—*Repo Man*, 1984
- People are starting to hate you, I mean, really hate you. Not just the usual fruitcakes, either.—Carl Hiaasen, *Tourist Season*, p. 25, 1986
- —Angela Devlin, *Prison Patter*, p. 54, 1996
- KNIGHTY: Here comes Lieutenant Darcy Fruitcake the Fifth. MEGGY: He's off his head, man.—Paul Fraser and Shane Meadows, *TwentyFourSeven*, p. 12, 1997

2 a blatantly homosexual man *US, 1960*
- I'd dress up like a fruitcake and stroll through the park, you know, asking for it.—Elmore Leonard, *Freaky Deaky*, p. 25, 1988
- The facist fruitcake gasped when he saw the handcuffs securing the Tender Trap's door handles.—Seth Morgan, *Homeboy*, p. 67, 1990
- "We're calling that fruitcake display of yours strike one," he announced.—C.D. Payne, *Youth in Revolt*, p. 165, 1993
- —Angela Devlin, *Prison Patter*, p. 54, 1996

fruit cupper *noun*
an amateur racing car driver, especially in sports car races *US*
- The term derives from the small cups often awarded as trophies in such competition.—John Edwards, *Auto Dictionary*, p. 66, 1993

fruiter *noun*
a homosexual *US, 1918*
- No one yells 'fruiter' faster'n an undercover fruiter.—Malcolm Braly, *On the Yard*, p. 31, 1967
- —Inez Cardozo-Freeman, *The Joint*, p. 498, 1994

fruit fly *noun*
a heterosexual woman who befriends homosexual men *US*
- —*The Guild Dictionary of Homosexual Terms*, p. 17, 1965
- The fag hag, sometimes known as a fruit fly, is a girl or woman who, although she is more than likely homosexual herself, has never admitted it.—Ruth Allison, *Lesbianism*, p. 112, 1967
- Fag Hags, Fruit Flies, Faggot's Molls, is what the latter are rather unkindly called.—John Francis Hunter, *The Gay Insider*, p. 90–91, 1971

fruit for the sideboard *noun*
unexpected financial gain *AUSTRALIA*
- —Ned Wallish, *The Truth Dictionary of Racing Slang*, p. 31, 1989

fruit fuzz *noun*

a police officer assigned to an anti-homosexual vice operation *US*

- — *Maledicta*, p. 234, 1979: 'Kinks and queens: linguistic and cultural aspects of the terminology for gays'.

fruit hustler *noun*

a homosexual prostitute; a criminal who preys on homosexual victims *US, 1959*

- And malehustlers ("fruithustlers"/"studhustlers": the various names for the masculine hustlers looking for lonely fruits to score from[.] —John Rechy, *City of Night*, p. 100, 1963
- I'd remember the contemptuous look on the cold hearted fruit hustler's face as he patted my twenty dollar bill in his pocket. —Iceberg Slim (Robert Beck), *Mama Black Widow*, p. 23, 1969
- I stopped by the arcade and saw a big muscle-bound fruit hustler standing there. —Joseph Wambaugh, *The Blue Knight*, p. 26, 1973
- He looked more like a rock musician or a high-priced fruit hustler; sensitive in an arrogant way. —James Ellroy, *Brown's Requiem*, p. 107, 1981

fruiting *noun*

promiscuous behaviour *US*

- — *Maledicta*, p. 131, Summer/Winter 1982: 'Dyke diction: the language of lesbians'

fruit jacket *noun*

a prison record identifying a person as a homosexual *US*

- Not wanting a fruit jacket, he agreed. —James Ellroy, *Suicide Hill*, p. 584, 1986

fruitliner *noun*

a White Freightliner truck *US*

- —Montie Tak, *Truck Talk*, p. 66, 1971

fruit loop *noun*

1 an effeminate homosexual man *US, 1989*

An elaboration of **FRUIT**, from the brand name of a popular breakfast cereal.

- Silly little fruitloop woke me up this mawnin all excited. —Seth Morgan, *Homeboy*, p. 16, 1990

2 a psychiatric patient *US*

- —Sally Williams, *"Strong" Words*, p. 136, 1994

3 the cloth loop on the back of a man's shirt *US*

- Collecting fruit loops is in. These are the tiny tabs from the backs of ivy league shirts. — *San Francisco Examiner*, p. 17, 17th June 1966

fruit on the sideboard; fruit for the sideboard *noun*

something easily obtained *AUSTRALIA, 1953*

James Holledge claims this originated with the famous Sydney bookmaker Andy Kerr.

- Kerr started the now well-worn cliché: 'More fruit for the sideboard.' It was a famous trademark expression he shouted when taking a bet from a mug punter on a horse he personally felt had no chance in the race. —James Holledge, *The Great Australian Gamble*, p. 88, 1966
- Some of our blokes were easy pickings for those bastards. Fruit on the sideboard. —Alexander Buzo, *Norm and Ahmed*, p. 8, 1969

fruit pinch *noun*

an arrest of a homosexual man *US*

- 'Let's go over to the park and bust a quick fruit or two,' said Ranatti. We haven't made a fruit pinch for a few days. —Joseph Wambaugh, *The New Centurions*, p. 186, 1970

fruit ranch *noun*

a mental hospital or a psychiatric ward *US*

- — *Maledicta*, p. 117, 1984–1985: 'Milwaukee medical maledicta'
- —Sally Williams, *"Strong Words"*, p. 142, 1994

fruit roll *noun*

the violent robbing of a homosexual *US*

- I didn't think the defense counsel was succeeding too well in trying to minimize the thing as just another fruitroll[.] —Joseph Wambaugh, *The Blue Knight*, p. 164, 1973

fruit salad *noun*

1 a display of military medals *UK, 1943*

- —Lou Shelly, *Hepcats Jive Talk Dictionary*, p. 24, 1945
- — *American Speech*, p. 55, February 1947: 'Pacific war language'

2 a pooled mix of different types of pills contributed by several people and then consumed randomly *US, 1969*

- —William D. Alsever, *Glossary for the Establishment and Other Uptight People*, p. 12, December 1970
- — *Current Slang*, p. 12, Spring 1971

3 a group of stroke patients who cannot care for themselves *US*

- — *Maledicta*, p. 68, Summer/Winter 1978: 'Common patient-directed pejoratives used by medical personnel'

4 a person of mixed race *FIJI*

Recorded by Jan Tent in 1992.

▸ **do the fruit salad**

to expose your genitals in public *US*

- Flashing, or as they say in California, "doing the fruit salad," is also curious because one almost has to ask why, out of all the sexual deviations, somebody would choose this. —Anka Radakovich, *The Wild Girls Club*, p. 12–13, 1994

fruit show *noun*

a display in which a prostitute will stimulate and masturbate herself utilising any of a variety of fruits or vegetables, especially when advertised as a service *UK*

- —Caroline Archer, *Tart Cards*, 2003

fruit tank *noun*

a jail cell reserved for homosexual prisoners *US*

- Gloria la Marr says there's some queen down in the fruit tank who tricked with your boy Bozwell. —Joseph Wambaugh, *The Glitter Dome*, p. 157, 1981
- Trusties wearing slit-bottomed khakis listlessly pushing brooms down the corridor, a group of them standing outside the fruit tank, cooing at the drag queens inside. —James Ellroy, *Suicide Hill*, p. 575, 1986

fruity *adjective*

1 of language or content, very rich or strong; sexually suggestive; amorous *UK, 1900*

- The story goes that Shane [Warne] meant to send a few fruity suggestions to a barmaid[.] — *The Guardian*, 30th August 2003

2 obviously homosexual *US, 1940*

- As soon as he could decently do so he took me into his private office, which was lavishly furnished and interiorly decorated in Alfred's own inimitably fruity way. —Clancy Sigal, *Going Away*, p. 386, 1961
- He saw himself as a fruity little Lord Fauntleroy jiggling around on a gilded stage. —Albert Goldman, *Freak Show*, p. 54, 1968
- She keeps telling me how much I'd love it [drama] but I don't know – it seems so damned gay and fruity or something[.] —Beatrice Sparks (writing as 'Anonymous'), *Jay's Journal*, p. 81, 1979
- Al wouldn't be caught dead in platform shoes. He thinks they're fruity and the Bee Gees are too. —Rita Ciresi, *Pink Slip*, p. 107, 1999

frumpy *adjective*

poorly dressed, rumpled, messy *US*

- —Marcus Hanna Boulware, *Jive and Slang of Students in Negro Colleges*, 1947
- —Don R. McCreary (Editor), *Dawg Speak*, 2001

frups *noun*

a fart *TRINIDAD AND TOBAGO, 1987*

- —Lise Winer, *Dictionary of the English/Creole of Trinidad & Tobago*, 2003

frupse *noun*

nothing at all *BARBADOS*

Something that is 'not worth a frupse' is 'worthless'.

- —Frank A. Collymore, *Barbadian Dialect*, p. 52, 1965

fruta *noun*

a homosexual *US*

A literal application of Spanish to English slang.

- —Judi Sanders, *Da Bomb*, p. 6, 1997

fry *noun*

1 crack cocaine *US*

- — US Department of Justice, *Street Terms*, October 1994

2 crack cocaine, especially mixed with embalming fluid or LSD *US, 1998*

Probably from 'fry your brains' but the presence of embalming fluid in this potentially lethal mixture suggests **FRY** (to execute by electrocution).

- —Mike Haskins, *Drugs*, p. 293, 2003

3 marijuana mixed with embalming fluid or LSD *UK*

- —Mike Haskins, *Drugs*, p. 293, 2003

4 LSD *US*

- —Jay Robert Nash, *Dicitonary of Crime*, p. 141, 1992

5 a car accident in which an occupant or occupants of the car are burnt *US*

- — *American Speech*, p. 269, December 1962: 'The language of traffic policemen'

fry *verb*

1 to put to death by electrocution *US, 1928*

- You don't know what it feels like, waitin' in your cell to find out if you goin' to fry or not. —Mezz Mezzrow, *Really the Blues*, p. 267, 1946

- If they don't fly, they'll fry," the professor said — Chester Himes, *The Real Cool Killers*, p. 85, 1959
- For he was one of the mob who was caught on a job / and the state said he must fry. — Bruce Jackson, *Get Your Ass in the Water and Swim Like Me*, p. 82, 1966
- Well, they fried Tough Tony last night / The man who didn't know the meaning of fright. — Dennis Wepman et al., *The Life*, p. 117, 1976
- Swell. And the punctual guy fries in the chair for rape. — C.D. Payne, *Youth in Revolt*, p. 36, 1993
- You sonofabitch! You're gonna fry! — *Something About Mary*, 1998
- In 1966, Ronald Reagan was elected governor of California, promising to punish the mouthy students acting up in Berkeley and to fry the inmates on San Quentin's death row. — Peter Coyote, *Sleeping Where I Fall*, p. 116, 1998
- Move 'em to Texas, fry 'em up — *Traffic*, 2000

2 in computing, to fail completely *US*

- — Guy L. Steele et al., *The Hacker's Dictionary*, p. 69, 1983

3 to use and be under the influence of LSD *US*

- — *People Magazine*, p. 72, 19th July 1993
- — Linda Meyar, *Teenspeak*, p. 31, 1994

4 of a drug, to destroy or impair the mind by extreme intoxication; of a drug-user, to experience the consequences of LSD *US*

- Unfortunately, by the time Brian was recording these songs his mind had really been fried by acid. — Barney Hoskyns, *Waiting For The Sun*, p. 127–128, 1996

5 to alter the mind irreparably *US, 1972*

- [T]he [Rolling] Stones and feedback and Trout Mask Replica [by Captain Beefheart]. All these were milestones, each one fried my brain a little further[.] — Lester Bangs, *Psychotic Reactions and Carburetor Dung*, p. 12, 1971

6 to straighten your hair, chemically or with heat *US*

- — Lou Shelly, *Hepcats Jive Dictionary*, p. 11, 1945
- You ain't had your hair fried, is you boy? Where'd you get them pretty waves. — Mezz Mezzrow, *Really the Blues*, p. 115, 1946
- — Jack Lait and Lee Mortimer, *New York Confidential*, p. 235, 1948: 'A glossary of Harlemisms'
- I mean, she went to the beauty shop to have her hair fried, oiled, curled, or straightened to make it look like Lady Clairol[.] — Clarence Major, *All-Night Visitors*, p. 65, 1998

7 in motor racing, to overheat (an engine or component) *US*

- — John Edwards, *Auto Dictionary*, p. 66, 1993

fry daddy *noun*

a marijuana and crack cocaine cigarette *US*

- — Geoffrey Froner, *Digging for Diamonds*, p. 30, 1989
- — US Department of Justice, *Street Terms*, October 1994
- — Mike Haskins, *Drugs*, p. 293, 2003

frying size *noun*

said of children of elementry school age *US*

- — Jerry Robertson, *Oil Slanguage*, p. 56, 1954

fry stick *noun*

a marijuana cigarette laced with embalming fluid or phencyclidine, the recreational drug known as PCP or angel dust *UK*

- — Mike Haskins, *Drugs*, p. 287, 2003

fry-up *noun*

a quickly cooked collation of any foodstuffs prepared by frying *UK, 1967*

- [W]e had fry-ups at anytime and all times of the day and night. — Johnny Speight, *It Stands to Reason*, p. 67, 1973

FTA

fuck the army *US*

A popular sentiment shared by those both in and not in the army during the Vietnam war. Country Joe McDonald of 'Look's Like I'm Fixin' To Die Rag' fame, took an anti-war show named 'FTA!' on the road to GI coffee houses in 1971.

- — Carl Fleischhauer, *A Glossary of Army Slang*, p. 20, 1968
- — Linda Reinberg, *In the Field*, p. 89, 1991

FTW

used as a defiant stance against everything – *fuck the world* *US, 1972*

- "Fuck the World" (FTW) is their motto and arrogant attitude by which this sub-culture attains its goals and objectives. — Paladin Press, *Inside Look at Outlaw Motorcyle Gangs*, p. 14, 1992
- — Bill Valentine, *Gangs and Their Tattoos*, p. x, 2000
- He noted that Jessie had several tattoos, including one on his right arm that said "FTW" (it was noted that that stood for "Fuck the World"). — Mara Leveritt, *Devil's Knot*, p. 76, 2002

FUBAR *adjective*

1 used as an expression of disgust because a situation is fucked up beyond all recognition *US, 1944*

Of the many military acronyms with a prominent 'F' coined during World War 2, one of the few to survive.

- "Not only profanity has crept into your speech," she said, "but also the peculiar jargon of the Army." "Snafu," I said, "tarfu, fubar, and weft." — Max Shulman, *The Zebra Derby*, p. 174, 1946
- In 1993 he [Brandon Block] ran a Sunday night [club] "FUBAR" (Fucked Up Beyond All Recognition). — Dave Haslam, *Adventures of the Wheels of Steel*, p. 115, 2001

2 drunk *US, 1985*

A sense created by using 'fucked up' to mean 'drunk', not 'botched. '

- — Connie Eble (Editor), *UNC-CH Campus Slang*, p. 2, Fall 1991

fuck *noun*

1 the act of sex *UK, 1675*

- I ain't had a fuck in ages & no new girl (except whores) since 1945. — Neal Cassady, *The First Third*, p. 197, 1950
- [H]e has absolutely no ambition except to get a fuck every night. — Henry Miller, *Tropic of Cancer*, p. 85, 1961
- I've always believed that the reason I couldn't lock her down was because she didn't like my fuck. So a bit of me always felt I was one premier performance away from sorting this situation. — Diran Abedayo, *My Once Upon A Time*, p. 208, 2000

2 a person objectified as a sex-partner *UK, 1874*

- Too much – you hang onto her 'cause she's a good fuck / Too much – cherry cheesecake and shooting up — Viv Albertine (the Slits), *So Tough*, 1979
- Even if I was the fastest fuck in the east, which I was. — Larry Rivers, *What Did I Do?*, p. 49, 1992

3 a despicable or hapless person *UK, 1927*

- "That evil little fuck is so guilty that I should probably kill him myself, on general principles." — Hunter S. Thompson, *Fear and Loathing in Las Vegas*, p. 125, 1971
- Give ya some cash, get that Scagnetti fuck off your back, and we'll be talking to ya. — *Reservoir Dogs*, 1992
- Okay you freshmen fucks, listen up. — *Dased and Confused*, 1993
- [A]s though the world owed the stupid wee fuck a living. — Irvine Welsh, *The State of the Party (Disco Biscuits)*, p. 61, 1995
- Take it all. Take it, you fuck. Take it, you bitch. Take it you cocksucker. Take it. — Joel Rose, *Kill Kill Faster Faster*, p. 79, 1997
- We'll drag the fat fuck out the back way. Accept no offers of help. — Kevin Sampson, *Powder*, p. 31, 1999
- It all started getting crazy when Charlie Magoo was having a beer in one of the Porterville bars and some fuck in the bar said something stupid to him. — Ralph Sonny Barger, *Hell's Angerl*, p. 150, 2000
- Not what I've heard, you lying fuck! — Mark Powell, *Snap*, p. 68, 2001

4 used for intensifying *US, 1934*

Often construed with 'the'.

- Get the fuck out of the way! Are you blind?! — Ruth Butler, *Cool Places*, p. 88, 1998
- Where the fuck you been, Kingy? — Martin King and Martin Knight, *The Naughty Nineties*, p. 32, 1999
- Now how the fuck am I supposed to get out of debt? — Emnem (Marshall Mathers), *Still Don't Give a Fuck*, 1999
- [H]e was infuriated by her laughter. "Fucks so funny?" "Nothing," said Tyra, her face falling now. — John Willams, *Crdiff Dead*, p. 69, 2000
- Hell's Angels killed it [the spirit of peace and love] off at Altamont. Their Brit counterparts like to pin it on the violence and confusion at the Isle of Wight pop festival. Others cited the deaths of Jimi, Jim, Janis and Brian. Get the fuck out of here! Nothing died except people. — Mick Farren, *Give the Anarchist a Cigarette*, p. 234, 2001
- What in the name of fuck does a bird like that see in that scruffy get? — Niall Griffiths, *Kelly + Victor*, p. 79, 2002

5 an extreme *UK, 1928*

- He was a great lad, Beano, and a fuck of a drummer. — Kevin Sampson, *Powder*, p. 73, 1999
- [S]he used to live on fucking sunbeds and all, Debbi, and she used to wax herself to fuck. There was not a trace of hair on that girl. — Kevin Sampson, *Outlaws*, p. 101, 2001

6 something of no value *UK, 1790*

- I don't give a fuck any more what's behind me, or what's ahead of me. — Henry Miller, *Tropic of Cancer*, p. 50, 1961
- Why should they give a fuck? — Mario Puzo, *Inside Las Vegas*, p. 145, 1977
- If it ain't stiff it ain't worth a fuck. — *the slogan of Stiff Records*, 1977
- Pumpkin: Just like banks, these places are insured. The managers don't give a fuck, they're just tryin' to get ya out the door before you start pluggin' diners. — *Pulp Fiction*, 1994

▸ **and fuck**
and so on, etc *UK*
• —Brain Donor *Peace Love & Fuck*, 2002

▸ **as fuck**
an intensifier, used in combination with an adjective *UK*
Other examples include: 'heavy as fuck', 'daft as fuck', 'queer as fuck', etc.
• [T]ight as fuck harmonies and great guitar shapes.— John Robb, *The Nineties*, p. 130, 1999
• This reinvention of the Madchester foursome's funky-as-fuck classic— *Sky Magazine*, p. 7, May 2001
• So, fame. Curse, or cool as fuck? Cool as fuck. No, curse. Tell you what, it's a curse. But it's a pretty cool-as-fuck curse.—Andrew Holmes, *Sleb*, p. 109, 2002

▸ **for fuck's sake!; fuck sake!**
used as a register of exasperation or impatience *US, 1961*
• "Oh for fuck's sake," says Maurice, getting up and catching his medallion on the edge of the booth's narrow table.—Ted Lewis, *Jack Carter's Law*, p. 23, 1974
• Okay, okay, don't fuckin go on, fuck sake, Gene.—J.J. Connolly, *Layer Cake*, p. 46, 2000
• I mean murder! For fuck's sake! How they could ever have thought they'd be able to get us on that one, mun... fucking beyond, mun, aye[.]—Niall Griffiths, *Sheepshagger*, p. 238, 2001
• When you're busy in a restaurant there's no time for pleasantries so when my girlfriend asked what I wanted the menu changed to I shouted 'For fuck's sake just put lamb'.— *The Observer*, 21st April 2001

▸ **like fuck**
like hell; very much *UK*
• [T]he cheeks of my arse began to sting like fuck.—Martin King and Martin Knight, *The Naughty Nineties*, p. 34, 1999

▸ **running fuck at a rolling doughnut**
an extremely difficult manoeuvre or operation *UK*
• [of air-to-air refuelling] It's like taking a running fuck at a doughnut. —Robert Prest, *Phantom*, 1979

fuck *verb*
1 to have sex *UK, 1500*
• I've met a lot of girls out here, and at least two of them are anxious for me to fuck them, but I never get around to it.—Jack Kerouac, *Letter to Neal Cassady*, p. 127, 13th September 1947
• I've heard that until you've fucked on cocaine you just haven't fucked.—Herbert Huncke, *Guilty of Everything*, p. 8, 1990
• "Fucking" is not limited to penetration, Banky. For me it describes any sex when it's not totally about love.— *Chasing Amy*, 1997

2 to damage beyond repair *UK, 1775*
• Before we left the cafe Ginger made a phone call to Harley Pete and said, "I'm going to fuck you."—Jamie Mandelkau, *Buttons*, p. 31, 1971

3 used as an intense verb of abuse *UK, 1915*
• Fuck him seventy eight times. Fuck the literateurs too. Fuck the whole lot.—Jack Kerouac, *Letter to Neal Cassady*, p. 175, 8th December 1948

4 to confound *AUSTRALIA*
• Why the fuck do spunky sheilas fuck up their bods and put them fucken rings/studs/shrapnel through their bellybuttons? Fucks me, but I wish they wouldn't do it.— *Picture*, p. 86, 22nd July 1998

▸ **be fucked in the car**
to have had something done to you that you did not deserve *CANADA*
Reported by a correspondent from the Royal Military College of Canada, 1969.

▸ **couldn't organise a fuck in a brothel**
used of an inefficient person *UK, 1961*

▸ **do you fuck!; will you fuck!**
used as a strong and disapproving denial: no you did not, no you will not *UK, 1961*

▸ **fuck a duck**
to shirk, to avoid work *US, 1977*
Vietnam war usage.
• Jonesy raised his head from his rucksack, where he was taking one of his famous naps – fucking the duck, we called it – and stage-whispered right back[.]—Larry Heinemann, *Paco's Story*, p. 6, 1986

▸ **fuck anything that moves**
applied to a person's rampant sexuality *UK, 1977*
The variations of this catchphrase are manifold, all formed on 'fuck anything' – *with* 'a hole', 'a crack', 'a cock', 'a dick', 'a vagina', 'hair on it', 'breasts', 'tits', 'a heart beat', 'a pulse' etc.; *that moves on* 'two legs'.
• If you're a man, you'd better act like one, / Develop your muscles, use your prick like a gun. / Fuck anything that moves, but never pay the price, / Steal, fuck, slaughter, that's their advice.—Crass, *Big Man, Big M.A.N.*, 1979

▸ **fuck in the ass**
to victimise; to force into submission *US*
Figurative.
• You ever get fucked in the ass by a wiseguy?—Howard Stern, *Miss America*, p. 429, 1995
• When all the time he was simply fuckin' us all in the arse.—Lanre Fehintola, *Charlie Says...*, p. 130, 2000

▸ **fuck the arse off**
to have exceptionally vigorous sex *UK*
Applied to conventional sexual intercourse; despite the use of 'arse', anal sex is neither included or precluded. Usage is generally something of a boast.
• [H]e will fuck the arse off her tonight, he thinks, he will shag her senseless, screw her daft[.]—Niall Griffiths, *Grits*, p. 53, 2000

▸ **fuck the dog**
to idle instead of working *US, 1935*
• — *Maledicta*, p. 284, 1984–1985

▸ **fuck the fucking fuckers**
used for expressing contempt and defiance of and towards just about everyone *US*
• — *Maledicta*, p. 170, Winter 1980: 'A brief survey of some unofficial prosigns used by the United States Armed Forces'

▸ **fuck them if they can't take a joke**
during the Vietnam war, used as a cynically humorous retort when things went wrong *US*
Multiple variants.
• — *Maledicta*, p. 170, Winter 1980: 'A brief survey of some unofficial prosigns used by the United States Armed Forces'
• "We're not going on any wild-goose chase in those boonies tonight and get mortared for three hours like the last time. Fuick him if he can't take a joke."—Lucian K. Truscott, *Army Blue*, p. 11, 1989
• If not, well, screw the camel drivers if they can't take a joke. —T.E. Cruise, *Wings of Gold III*, p. 362, 1989

▸ **fuck up the arse**
to betray *UK*
Combines **FUCK** (to damage) with 'up the arse', which makes it personal.
• [T]hey're double into this because it's a cross [doublecross]. It's the old guard getting fucked up the arse and I know they're going to be bang into that.—Kevin Sampson, *Outlaws*, p. 253, 2001

▸ **fuck your fist**
to masturbate *US*
• But therefore I was not Samson, so I fucked my fist once more / but I taken good aim and shot it – through this keyhole in the door.—Bruce Jackson, *Get Your Ass in the Water and Swim Like Me*, p. 222, 1966
• Fuck Your Fist with Me [Headline]— *Partner Magazine*, p. 27, December 1980

▸ **fuck you very much!**
used as a humorous expression of defiance *US*
• — *Maledicta*, p. 170, Winter 1980: 'A brief survey of some unofficial prosigns used by the United States Armed Forces'
• Good luck to the first team and fuck you very much.—Joseph Wambaugh, *The Glitter Dome*, p. 41, 1981
• I told him Arnie thought I sounded like Teresa Brewer. 'No,' he said, 'more like the Bee Gees.' 'Well, fuck you very much.'—Armistead Maupin, *Maybe the Moon*, p. 64, 1992

▸ **who do you have to fuck?**
used as an impatient enquiry: who do I have to persuade?, who is responsible for something? how can I do or get something? *US*
Probably hyperbolic.
• Who do you have to fuck to get a drink around here?—Mart Crowley, *Boys in the Band*, p. 48, 1968
• Who do I have to fuck to get a waffle?—Terrance McNally, *Frankie and Johnny*, 1991
• Reilly proved them all wrong by becoming so omnipresent he admits to once thinking, "Who do I have to fuck to get off TV?"— *The Village Voice*, 15th October 2001

▸ **will I fuck!**
used as an expression of strong disagreement *UK, 1961*
Often applied in the third person: 'will he fuck!', 'will they fuck!'.

fuck *adjective*

▸ **a fuck sight**

a lot *UK*

- I know what's out there and it's a fuck sight better than this shithole. —Mark Powell, *Snap*, p. 186, 2001

fuck!

used as a simple exclamation *UK, 1929*

- Fuck, I said, you're playing some goddam part, only it's to the wrong audience. —Clancy Sigal, *Going Away*, p. 265, 1961

▸ **is it fuck!**

used as an emphatic negative *UK, 1984*

fuck

used to create a non-specific type within a recognisable form *UK*

Dismissive.

- The best thing he'd ever done was give up on that Man in the Iron Mask fuckology. —Roddy Doyle, *The Van*, 1991
- [P]sychology, sociology, theology and every fuckin other sort of fuckology[.] —J.J. Connolly, *Layer Cake*, p. 40, 2000
- But these cunts think "ah an obvious case of socio-bollocko fuckism caused by a disillusioned shit"[.]l —Mark Perry, *Sniffin' Glue [a compilation of 12 issues of the late 1970s fanzine]*, p. 336, 2000

fuckable *adjective*

sexually appealling *UK, 1891*

- —Collin Baker et al., *College Undergraduate Slang Study Conducted at Brown University*, p. 122, 1968
- 'Don't think that sticking your boobs out and trying to look fuckable will help. Remember you're in a rock band. It's not "fuck me!" its "fuck you!"' Simon Napier-Bell quoting. —Chrissie Hynde, *In Black Vinyl White Powder*, p. 168, 2001
- They look alright." "Are they fuckable? ... Are they fuckable, or what?. —Dr Dre, *Baar One*, 2001

fuck about; fuck around *verb*

to play the fool, to waste time; to make a mess of; to inconvenience *UK, 1922*

- —Brendan Behan, *Borstal Boy*, 1958
- So we fucked around Wahoo until dark[.] —Neal Cassady, *The First Third*, p. 218, 30 August 1965
- Well, I fucked around and didn't take a job as a barber in his shop, so he hit me for my house key. —A.S. Jackson, *Gentleman Pimp*, p. 20, 1973
- We fucked around with theh vents trying to get in because neither of us had a tool. —Herbert Huncke, *Guilty of Everything*, p. 45, 1990
- Cunt should be fucking grateful he's got a fucking job, by the way – fucking fucking about with his paymasters and that. —Kevin Sampson, *Outlaws*, p. 212, 2001

fuck-a-doodle-doo!

used as an ironic exclamation of delight *UK*

- — *Four Weddings and a Funeral*, 1994
- — *Shaun of the Dead*, 2004

fuck a duck!

used for registering surprise *UK, 1940s*

- Well fuck a duck. Ain't seen your ugly mugs round 'ere lately. —Chris Baker and Andrew Day, *Lock, Stock... & a Fist Full of Jack and Jills*, p. 162, 2000

fuckaholic *noun*

a person obsessed with sex *US, 1981*

- I used to think that you did, and now you're just a regular fuckaholic! —Kevin E. Young, *Ghett OH Luv*, p. 138, 2004

fuck all; fuckall *noun*

nothing, nothing at all *UK, 1918*

- The Monkees had windows in their house, we had fuck all. —Shaun Ryder, *Shaun Ryder... in His Own Words*, 1990
- We ken nowt, we ken fuck all... nane ay us ken fuck all[.] —Irvine Welsh, *The State of the Party (Disco Biscuits)*, p. 37, 1995
- In their own way, I suppose, everyone does, with fuckall effect. —Richard Neville writing in 'Oz', 1972, *Out Of My Mind*, 1996
- They were white-bread, all-American boys in all but one critical degree, which is that they didn't care fuck-all about material wealth. —Peter Coyote, *Sleeping Where I Fall*, p. 133, 1998
- I've had it with going here, there and everywhere and walking miles for fuckall. —Martin KIng and Martin Knight, *The Naughty Nineties*, 1999

fuck almighty!

used in despair when others may call upon God *UK*

Euphemistic use of **FUCK** for what might otherwise border on blasphemy.

- Fuck almighty, do I have to tell you everything? —*Sky Magazine*, p. 129, July 2001

fuck and blind *verb*

to swear *UK*

A frank variation of **EFF AND BLIND**.

- [T]he key seems to jam and he fucks and blinds and eventually Peter pushes him out of the way and the key turns first time. —Ted Lewis, *Jack Carter's Law*, p. 148, 1974

fuck-around *noun*

1 a promiscuous person *FIJI*

Recorded by Jan Tent in 1992.

2 a young street ruffian *FIJI, 1984*

Recorded by Jan Tent in 1993.

fuck-arse around *verb*

to play the fool, to waste time; to make a mess of; to inconvenience *UK*

- [A]in't gonna be generally fuck-arsing around[.] —J.J. Connolly, *Layer Cake*, p. 10, 2000

fuckass *noun*

a despicable person *UK, 1960*

- Don't touch me, you fuckass, I'll kill you with my bare hands. —Gregg Easterbrook, *The Here and Now*, p. 133, 2002

fuckass *adjective*

despicable *US, 1961*

- Any man'd leave it layin around's a fuckass soldier anyway. —James Jones, *The Thin Red Line*, p. 21, 1962

fuckathon *noun*

an extended bout of sex *US, 1968*

- How could he confess to her that he had been on a fuckathon. —John M. Del Vecchio, *The 13th Valley*, p. 336, 1982

fuckbag *noun*

a despicable person *US*

- They were, undoubtedly, rancid Welsh fuckbags like himself. —Robert McLiam Wilson, *Ripley Bogle*, p. 8, 1989

fuck book *noun*

a sexually explicit book, usually heavily illustrated *US, 1944*

- —Carl Fleischhauer, *A Glossary of Army Slang*, p. 20, 1968
- Fuckbooks, in the space of about three years in this country, have become so numerous that it is not within the scope of any one reader to even thumb through them all, let alone read them —*Screw*, p. 13, 7th February 1969
- —Robert A. Wilson, *Playboy's Book of Forbidden Words*, p. 117, 1972
- A Barney Google fuck book. Barney's cock like a whole bologna, radiating ee-lectric squiggles and flecking great airndrops of jiss as he galled at and rammed the thing into the cartoon women with equally electric cunts that looked like toothless mouths. —Earl Thompson, *Tattoo*, p. 25, 1974
- I got two letters from Jenny and the two fuck books, the ones with yellow covers, I had sent for back in December. —Larry Heinemann, *Close Quarters*, p. 259, 1977
- People will drop names on you you've never heard of 'cause you haven't read shit but fuck books. —Odie Hawkins, *Midnight*, p. 90, 1995
- I'm back in the lockup and this, this has turned from a fuck book into the sad, sad story of Joey One-Way. —Joel Rose, *Kill Kill Faster Faster*, p. 193, 1997

fuckboy *noun*

a young man as the object of homosexual desire *US, 1971*

- In prison, the convicts who are sexually assaulted are the sissies, the effeminate, and they are called "punks" or "fuckboys." —Fox Butterfield, *All God's Children*, p. 289, 1996

fuckbrain *noun*

an idiot *UK*

A variation of the equally derisory **FUCKWIT**.

- Just guys innit. Just guys is all. – Guys... fuckbrains. —Nick Barlay, *Curvy Lovebox*, p. 111, 1997

fuck buddy *noun*

a friend who is also a sex companion *US, 1972*

- While we were looking the whore spots over, we ran into an old fuck buddy of mine. We pulled up on her and after a few minutes of rapping she slid her big tasty ass in the car. —A.S. Jackson, *Gentleman Pimp*, p. 71, 1973

fucked *adjective*

1 ruined, spoiled, potentially doomed *UK, 1955*

- We're all fucked. I'm fucked. You're fucked. The whole department is fucked. It's the biggest cock-up ever. We're all completely fucked. — *The Times*, 2nd March 2002

2 extremely weary, exhausted *UK, 1984*

- Yir up fir an ooir then yir fucked.—Irvine Welsh, *The State of the Party (Disco Biscuits)*, p. 33, 1995

3 drunk or drug-intoxicated *US, 1965*

- And with tunes bouncing round off the walls and attacking you on every side you didn't even need to be fucked on acid to enter another dimension.—Dave Courtney, *Raving Lunacy*, p. 40, 2000
- [B]attered s**tfaced f**cked messed up[.]—Stuart Walton, *Out of It*, cover, 2001

4 insane, crazy, senseless *US, 1970*

- They wanted to believe that [Crosby, Stills, Nash and Young] were actually spokesmen for today's society. That's fucked. But it's more naive than fucked.]', p.185. 1997.—Jabberrock quoting Graham Nash, 1997
- No, it was not that she did not give a fuck; but she fucked if she was going to show it.—James Hawes, *Dead Long Enough*, p. 137, 2000

fucked if I can

it is very unlikely that I will be able to do something *UK*

- A younger man can see the sense in Records of Achievement, Key Stage 4, Attainment Target 8 [...] Caleb is fucked if he can.—Jack Allen, *When the Whistle Blows*, p. 16, 2000

fucked off *adjective*

1 fed up, disgruntled, annoyed, angry *UK*

Since the 1940s.

- I get pissed off at times when my mates are off to play badminton or something and I can't, but I get more fucked off when there's something I can do[.]—Ruth Butler, *Cool Places*, p. 92, 1998
- [E]ven as he was realising this and ready to be thoroughly fucked off, Maggie was smiling back at him[.]—John Williams, *Cardiff Dead*, p. 67, 2000
- The thing about Terry is, as well, that he gets really fucked off with you if you don't believe him.—Danny King, *The Burglar Diaries*, p. 112, 2001

2 having been told to fuck off or to have been on the receiving end of a similar injunction or intimation *UK*

- If you try posing you're going to get fucked off but you know, it's pretty obvious where I'm coming from – middle class Asian, London[.]—Ben Malbon, *Cool Places*, p. 278, 1998

fucked up *adjective*

1 drunk or drug-intoxicated *US, 1944*

- "Were you that drunk?" "I was pretty fucked up, yes."—Doug Lang, *Freaks*, p. 16, 1973
- I'm not even fuckin' joking with you, don't you be bringing some fucked up pooh-but to my house.—*Pulp Fiction*, 1994
- Check this out. You get a baby's bottle, right? Fill it up with high-test gasoline and a week-old lima bean. Let it sit overnight. Suck it all down. Man, you'll get fucked up!—Chris Rock, *Rock This!*, p. 79, 1997
- [O]ut witha boys arseholed ratarsed fucked up[.]—Patrick Jones, *Unprotected Sex*, p. 255, 1999
- "You reeally believeElivis was fucked-up? I was now on the defensive" High as a kite.—Mick Farren, *Give the Anarchist a Cigarette*, p. 391, 2001

2 mentally unstable; depressed; anguished; spoiled *UK, 1939*

- I hear he is like completely fucked up.—Bret Easton Ellis, *Less Than Zero*, p. 17, 1985
- "I guess I'm just a sad, fucked-up fashion victim," says Daniel. —Melanie McGrath, *Hard, Soft & Wet*, p. 108, 1998
- The relationship between genius and being fucked up.—Tony Wilson, *24 Hour Party People*, p. 76, 2002
- [I]n my fucked-up country and in my fucked-up part of the world (the Middle East)[.]—*The Guardian*, p. 6, 28th June 2004

3 despicable *US, 1945*

- Suddenly one of the cats near the door we had entered through spoke up, looking contemptuously at me, saying "you are fucked up man. —Herbert Huncke, *The Evening Sun Turned Crimson*, p. 134, 1980

4 ruined, spoiled, broken *US*

- It was back in the time of nineteen hundred and two / I had a fucked-up deck a cards and I didn't know what to do.—Bruce Jackson, *Get Your Ass in the Water and Swim Like Me*, p. 46, 1965

fucked-upness *noun*

a depressed or ruined condition *UK*

- [I]f it [a penis] is on the front of some lying bastard then it just contributes to the general fucked-upness of your life.—Richard Herring, *Talking Cock*, p. 285, 2003

fucken *adjective*

used as a general intensifier *UK*

A variant spelling of **FUCKING**.

- "That's it! That's fucken it! That's the noise!" "Is it fuck!"—Kevin Sampson, *Outlaws*, p. 165, 2001
- "Allan," he says then, "just listen to the fucken records and get back to me."—*Uncut*, p. 35, November 2003

fucker *noun*

1 a man, a spirited person *UK, 1893*

Often used affectionately or derisively; not generally a term of abuse unless combined with an appropriate adjective e.g. 'dirty', 'miserable', etc.

- Like a cross between Terry Waite and Brutus from the Popeye cartoons. One big fucker.—Martin King and Martin Knight, *The Naughty Nineties*, p. 32, 1999
- Like there must be strings holding this fucker up{.]—Tony Wilson, *24 Hour Party People*, p. 20, 2002

2 a contemptible person *UK, 1890*

- "Is the fucker alone?" Scum runs in packs.—Marc 'Animal' MacYoung, *Street E&E*, p. 38, 1993
- "The fucker [Henry Kissinger] doesn't perform surgery or make house cals, does he?" [Quoting President George H. W. Bush]—Kitty Kelley, *The Family*, p. 350, 2004

3 a nuisance, an awkward thing *US, 1945*

- [T]he wind still whipped me raw as I stood at the door, juggling handshakes and a cigarette that had been a fucker to light.—David Peace, *Nineteen Seventy-Four*, p. 8, 1999

fuckery *noun*

1 oppression; the inherent corruption of a dominant society *US*

- That wasn't any act of God. That was an act of pure fuckery.—Stephen King, *The Stand*, p. 702, 1978
- —Thomas H. Slone, *Rasta is Cuss*, p. 48, 2003

2 things, concepts *US*

- Thety're always inventing some fuckery fifty years ahead of everyone else.—Brian Preston, *Pot Planet*, p. 240, 2002

▸ **like fuckery**

vigorously *UK*

- I've always fought like fuckery, put my liberty on the line daily, to avoid ending up in one of those houses down there[.]—J.J. Connolly, *Layer Cake*, p. 69, 2000

fuckface *noun*

an offensive or despicable person *US, 1945*

- Laugh away fuckface. That picture is going to be on the cover of every major newspaper in two days time.—*Repo Man*, 1984
- The chemist found himself changing places with the little fuck-face[.]—Joseph Wambaugh, *The Secrets of Harry Bright*, p. 68, 1985
- Hey, fuckface. Give me that.—Cleo Odzer, *Goa Freaks*, p. 264, 1995
- What? What are you gonna do, fuck-face?—Paul Fraser and Shane Meadows, *TwentyFourSeven*, p. 100, 1997
- You comin' to the party tongiht, Ozzie, you fuckface?—*American Pie*, 1999

fuckfaced *noun*

despicable, ugly *US, 1940*

- YOU TELL THAT FUCKING DICKBRAIN TO STICK HER UP HIS AGEING ASSHOLE, YOU FUCKFACED WASP.—Richard E. Grant, *With Nails*, p. 161, 1999

fuck-features *noun*

a contemptible person *AUSTRALIA*

- We were, but fuck-features here changed his mind.—David Williamson, *Juggler's Three*, p. 126, 1972

fuck film; fuck flick *noun*

a pornographic film *US*

- Well, you were talking to me in bed about making fuck films.—Fred Baker, *Events*, p. 50, 1970
- '69's Best & Worst Fuckfilm Fare (Headline)—*Screw*, p. 14, 19th January 1970
- Floods the screen with banal Pat Rocco films from Hollywood, but now and then shows a homoerotic winner like Man and Man, a full-length fun fuck film that will have you aghast and horny.—John Francis Hunter, *The Gay Insider*, p. 147, 1971
- I was waiting tables, cleaning theaters, driving taxis, and I said, "Fuck all this shit, I can make more money doing fuck films."—Stephen Ziplow, *The Film Maker's Guide to Pornography*, p. 150, 1977
- Nobody is making fuck films in New York," he says, "because all the actresses are living in LA.—James Ridgeway, *Red Light*, p. 44, 1996

fuckhead *noun*

used as an all-purpose insulting term of address or descriptive noun for a despicable, stupid person *US, 1966*

- —Collin Baker et al., *College Undergraduate Slang Study Conducted at Brown University*, p. 123, 1968
- A week later I received a letter from some fuck head called "Lon" of Research and man, like this jasper really poured the shit out thick. —*Screw*, p. 13, 27th June 1969
- That's right. Call Daddy, fuckhead!—Jack W. Thomas, *Heavy Number*, p. 105, 1976
- Come on, fuckhead!—*Saturday Night Fever*, 1977

- Paul is looking at me, giggling. "Simonon you fuckhead -" I begin[.] —Lester Bangs, *Psychotic Reactions and Carburetor Dung*, p. 236, 1977
- Get out of there you fuckheads. Move! Move! — *Platoon*, 1986
- They, Jeff. Them. The fuckheads who run the universe. —Armistead Maupin, *Maybe the Moon*, p. 163, 1992
- FABIAN: Shut up fuck head! I hate that Mongoloid voice. — *Pulp Fiction*, 1994
- Move it, fuckhead. —Colin Butts, *Is Harry on the Boat?*, p. 9, 1997
- Your present, fuckhead. Open it. — *200 Cigarettes*, 1999
- Lock the gate on these fuckheads. — *Almost Famous*, 2000

fuckhole *noun*

the vagina *UK, 1893*

- —Dale Gordon, *The Dominion Sex Dictionary*, p. 73, 1967
- — *Maledicta*, p. 131, Summer/Winter 1982: 'Dyke diction: the language of lesbians'.
- Four young wannabe sex stars get their nearly cherry fuckholes stretched, slammed, and jizzed on by big-dicked professional porn studs in the latest installment of this raunchy, hot series. — Penthouse Magazine, *The Penthouse Erotic Video Guide*, p. 232, 2003

fuckie-fuckie *noun*

sex *US*

Vietnam war usage.

- I didn't want any of that "Say hey, slopehead, fuckie-fuckie?" —Larry Heinemann, *Close Quarters*, p. 176, 1977

fucking *noun*

sexual intercourse *UK, 1568*

Well known but, aside from macho bragging and fantasising, kept safely between the sheets in a book or a bedroom; however in 1996, advertising the title of Mark Ravenhill's successful play, *Shopping and Fucking*, challenged and, perhaps, changed some media taboos.

- —Mark Ravenhill, *Shopping and Fucking*, 1996
- [D]iscover how to see in the forms of fucking, sucking, licking, and masturbating the transcendental formlessness of the Absolute[.] —David Ramsdale, *Red Hot Tantra*, p. 22, 2004

-fucking- *infix*

used as an intensifier *US, 1921*

One of the very few infix intensifiers used in the US or UK.

- Somebody better be careful, he gets himself infuckingvolved. —Richard Farina, *Been Down So Long*, p. 79, 1966
- Tony was delighted. "Fan-fucking-tastic!" —Terry Southern, *Blue Movie*, p. 95, 1970
- Suddenly she was smiling, and there was genuine cheer in her voice. "Far fucking out." —Gurney Norman, *Divine Right's Trip (Last Whole Earth Catalog)*, p. 159, 1971
- Brand-fucking-new guns. —George V. Higgins, *The Friends of Eddie Doyle*, p. 5, 1971
- Well, he's not going to find the answer to anything over in Su-fucking-matra. —Dan Jenkins, *Semi-Tough*, p. 176, 1972
- She said to herself, Un-fucking-real, went inside to the bar and made him another drink and one for herself. —Elmore Leonard, *Switch*, p. 123, 1978
- — *Maledicta*, p. 142–143, Summer 1980: 'Fucking INsertions'
- You gonna love the Nam, man, for-fucking-ever. — *Platoon*, 1986
- In front of Jane fucking Pauley? —Carl Hiaasen, *Tourist Season*, p. 196, 1986
- The fairy fucking godmother said it. Out-fucking-standing! — *Full Metal Jacket*, 1987
- How Rooski swore he cased the place, guaranfuckenteed the chink pharmacists went home at six. —Seth Morgan, *Homeboy*, p. 21, 1990
- Hardy-fucking-har. What did he say? — *Reservoir Dogs*, 1992
- Good work, my brothers. Fan-fucking-tastic! — *Natural Born Killers*, 1994
- Somebody call 9 fucking 1-1. — *Get Shorty*, 1995
- Well, boo-fucking-hoo. — *Jerry Maguire*, 1996
- What a shock – "Not fucking likely!". — *Chasing Amy*, 1997
- Do you realize that in 1997 some women still don't give head? Ninety-fucking-seven. —Chris Rock, *Rock This!*, p. 133, 1997
- Far out. Far fuckin' out. — *The Big Lebowski*, 1998
- I'm the Marsha fucking Brady of the upper East Side and sometimes I want to kill myself for it. — *Cruel Intentions*, 1999
- "No fucking duh," I said. —Rita Ciresi, *Pink Slip*, p. 14, 1999
- Well, fuck me for not curling up on the sofa with a TV remote, a pension plan and a Pot-fucking-Noodle! —Dave Courtney, *Raving Lunacy*, p. 70, 2000
- Un-fucking-believable. —Kevin Smith, *Jay and Silent Bob Strike Back*, p. 78, 2001
- Ianto wrecked a house in a morning. When he went doofuckinlally. —Niall Griffiths, *Sheepshagger*, p. 55, 2001
- I've got no chance whatso-fuckin-ever of hearing[.] —Niall Griffiths, *Kelly + Victor*, p. 12, 2002
- [W]e have a balcony balustrade made of shaped QE-fucking-2 mahogany[.] —Tony Wilson, *24 Hour Party People*, p. 140, 2002

fucking

used as an attention-getting intensifier *US, 1857*

- I am King fucking MONTEZUMA, that's who, and this is the coin of my kingdom. —Richard Farina, *Been Down So Long*, p. 32, 1966
- Brad, I really fuckin' hate McDonald's, man. — *Fast Times at Ridgemont High*, 1982
- I fucking saw that you little sack of shit. — *Dazed and Confused*, 1993
- You're fucking twenty minutes late. What the fuck is that. — *The Big Lebowski*, 1998
- Oh. Well, hey, well done. Fucking artistic, actually. —Audrey Niffenegger, *The Time Traveler's Wife*, p. 137, 2003
- 'Malcolm [McLaren] arrested on the 'God Save the Queen' Jubilee boat trip, manhandled by police and shouting 'you fucking fascist bastards'[.]' — *The Observer*, 21st March 2004

fucking A!

used as an expression of surprise, approval or dismay *US, 1947*

- Schoons thought this was the fuckin'-A twitty-bird funniest thing the Regals (Himself) had ever heard[.] —John Nichols, *The Sterile Cuckoo*, p. 66, 1965
- FUCKIN' AY!! [Cartoon caption]. — *East Village Other*, p. 14, 18th October 1968
- Or if somebody said, "Are you taking Louise to the dance," you had to say, "Fuckin' ay I am." —Jim Bouton, *Ball Four*, p. 361, 1970
- Fuacking-ay-John Dity-Bag well-told I don't. —Darryl Ponicsan, *The Last Detail*, p. 171, 1970
- "You fuckin' A-right!" Jimmy snapped. —Nathan Heard, *Howard Street*, p. 72, 1973
- It's just HAHAHAHA ... ridiculous ... HAHAHAHA, you know what I mean. Fucking A! Oh! There was only one good-looking chick. — *Ask*, p. 45, 5th May 1979
- Fucking A! — *Platoon*, 1986
- BODHI: You want the ultimate thrill, you gotta be willing to pay the ultimate price. NATHANIEL: Fucking A! — *Point Break*, 1991
- So Jimmy and Code Six went back a long way. Fucking A! —William T. Vollman, *Whores for Gloria*, p. 37, 1991
- Fucking A it worked, that 's what I'am talkin' about! — *Pulp Fiction*, 1994
- Sydney: It works. John: Fuckin' A it does. — *Hard Eight*, 1997
- Fuckin' A! — *The Big Lebowski*, 1998

fucking Ada!

used for registering annoyance, frustration, etc *UK, 1962*

- Tell me tomorrow don't bother me now / Fucking Ada, fucking Ada / Fucking Ada, fucking Ada[.] —Ian Dury, *Fucking Ada*, 1980
- [M]ostly I just wanted shout, "Fucking Ada, it's Robin Cook [UK Foreign Secretary] on the phone. —Mark Steel, *Reasons to be Cheerful*, p. 242, 2001

fucking arseholes!

used as an exclamation of surprise, anger, amazement *UK*

A standard intensification of **ARSEHOLES!**; often lazily or deliberately reduced to **'KIN' ARSE'OLES**.

fucking hell!

used as an exclamation of surprise, anger, amazement *UK*

An intensification of **HELL**. Often lazily or deliberately reduced to **'KIN' 'ELL** or run together as a single word.

- So where the fucking hell have you been? —Ted Lewis, *Jack Carter's Law*, p. 5, 1974
- They just kept walking over and catching your eye and, fuckinell, I'm telling you, there is some tott [attractive women] out there! —Kevin Sampson, *Powder*, p. 20, 1999
- I remember when I first saw the rave scene and thought, Fucking hell! —Dave Courtney, *Raving Lunacy*, p. 6, 2000
- Fucking hell, Don said [...] Look at that. —John King, *White Trash*, p. 58, 2001

fucking machine *noun*

a lustful lover *AUSTRALIA*

- 'Whatever you say, you big, hard-boned, hairy-chested fucking machine,' Fanny agreed sentimentally. —Frank Hardy, *The Outcasts of Foolgarah*, p. 108, 1971
- You don't want a man. You want some idolised fucking machine. —Dorothy Hewett, *The Chapel Perilous*, p. 75, 1972

fucking new guy *noun*

a recent arrival to combat *US*

A key term and key concept in Vietnam.

- Then he looked over at me. "Who's the fucken new guy?" —Larry Heinemann, *Close Quarters*, p. 34, 1977
- More common certainly than having some first-of-May, fucking-new-guy rookie triage medic sit there picking at a million slivers of shrapnel with a manicure scissors. —Larry Heinemann, *Paco's Story*, p. 51, 1986

fucking well *adverb*

used for emphasis *UK, 1922*

- In America they [householders] can beat you up and fucking do whatever they fucking-well like[.] —Danny King, *The Burglar Diaries*, p. 205, 2001

fuck-in-law *noun*

someone who has had sex with someone you have had sex with *US*

Leading to a punning exploration of the 'sex degrees of separation' between people.

- —Steven Daly and Nalthaniel Wice, *alt.culture*, p. 79, 1995
- —Alon Shulman, *The Style Bible*, p. 99, 1999

fuck it!

used as a general declaration of rejection or dimissal; may also imply resignation to a situation *UK*

Fuck KKKanada! *verb*

in Quebec, used for denigrating the Canadian confederacy *CANADA, 2002*

fuck knows *noun*

an uncertain measure of time *UK*

Clipped from 'fuck knows how long'.

- I'm headin' to my place for the first time in fuck knows. —Nick Barlay, *Curvy Lovebox*, p. 87, 1997

fuck knuckle *noun*

an annoying or despicable person; an idiot; a jerk *AUSTRALIA*

- 'You been knockin' stuff off, ay! Righto, righto, put it back.' 'Already paid for 'em,' Kevin tried to say as Mawbey entered the shop from the workroom 'Ask Mawbey.' 'You stay outa this fucknuckle!' – he turned on Mawbey who looked as if he was having a heart attack. —Angelo Loukakis, *For the Patriarch*, p. 155, 1981
- Joey: Hey, fucknuckle. Johnny: What's that?. —John Patrick Shanley, *Beggars in the House of Plenty*, 1981
- —Thommo *The Dictionary of Australian Swearing and Sex Sayings*, p. 53, 1985
- Come on dickhead, get that shit out of there! Today, fuck knuckle! —*Rants*, p. 41, 1997
- I have one comment for all you churchy fuck knuckles – get a dog up ya! —*URL: nerc2.nerc.com/~aharvey/hitlist.html*, 1997
- It's been such a long time since I've been to the beach, I've forgotten what an oily, muscle-headed, fuck-knuckle looks like. —*Sick Puppy Comix*, p. 5, 1997
- Frankie Knuckles ain't worth a damn / Here in fuckknuckle buck's night mini-bus land. —*www.geocities.com/~victimsoftism/news.htm*, 1998
- —Harry Orsman, *A Dictionary of Modern New Zealand Slang*, p. 53, 1999

fuck load *noun*

a considerable quantity *US*

- "Him and Marty pulled a righteous fuckin' fuckloda of burglaries together." —James Ellroy, *The Big Nowhere*, p. 80, 1988
- See, there's always been millions of people – between about five and ten million they say – that smoke puff. [...] That's a fuck load of people waiting for something to come along. —Dave Courtney, *Raving Lunacy*, p. 51, 2000
- I wanted his attention so badly and drnak fuckloads ot impress him, and tried so hard to be an outlaw. —Margaret Cho, *I'm the One That I Want*, p. 179, 2001

fuck machine *noun*

a very active sexual partner *US*

- MR BROWN: The pain is reminding the fuck machine what it was like to be a virgin. —*Reservoir Dogs*, 1992
- I don't know how much longer I can take it, being abused by this powerful little fuck machine. —Simon Sheppard, *Hotter Than Hell*, p. 160, 2001

fuck-me *adjective*

extremely sexually suggestive *US, 1974*

- There was a time when no self-respecting queen could be ignorant of Carmen Miranda's hats, Joan Crawford's ankle-strap wedgies (called fuck-me shoes). —*Maledicta*, p. 237, Winter 1980
- —Pamela Munro, *U.C.L.A. Slang*, p. 41, 1988
- She wore blood-red lipstick, gold hoop earrings, a white miniskirt, fuck-me pumps and a sleeveless salmon blouse. —Carl Hiaasen, *Strip Tease*, p. 285, 1993
- I know I'm better than what I've been doing the last ten years, walking around in a tank top and fuck-me pumps waiting till it's time to scream. —*Get Shorty*, 1995
- I think Ginger pictured Lady Larue in that mental institution in her fuck me stripper shoes and a huge blonde wig[.] —Jennifer Blowdryer, *White Trash Debutante*, p. 67, 1997
- Cindy C wearing nothing but a pink fuck-me swimsuit[.] —Greg Williams, *Diamond Geezers*, p. 15, 1997
- I stuffed my stocking-clad feet into four-inch fuck-me pumps. —Janet Evanovitch, *High Five*, 1999
- Expensive, sluttish clothes. Fuck-me shoes. I'm into her. —Kevin Sampson, *Outlaws*, p. 151, 2001
- —Connie Eble (Editor), *UNC-CH Campus Slang*, p. 4, Fall 2001

fuck me!

used for registering disbelief, despair, surprise, satisfaction *UK, 1929*

Often used in a wry or semi-humorous manner; since the 1950s usage is likely to provoke the rejoinders 'not now' or 'later' or 'no thanks', etc. Also used in many combinations and elaborations, all with same sense. Often ironic.

- HEATHER CHANDLER: Fuck me gently with a chainsaw. Do I look like Mother Theresa? —*Heathers*, 1988
- "Fuck me," muttered Francis Kingsburgy. —Carl Hiaasen, *Native Tongue*, p. 144, 1991
- I'd be sitting there, eating hamburgers, thinking, fuck me, that's a good life.', 1996. —Shaun Ryder, *Shaun Ryder... in His Own Words*, 1996
- Twenty years [imprisonment] for bringing over some puff! Fuck me. —Dave Courtney, *Raving Lunacy*, p. 6, 1998
- Well, fuck me! —*200 Cigarettes*, 1999
- "Well, fuck me, who let you out?" I laugh. —Danny King, *The Burglar Diaries*, p. 37, 2001
- Fuck me stiff! Near fuckin shat me trousers then! —Niall Griffiths, *Sheepshagger*, p. 85, 2001
- "Fuck me blind and call me Susie," Peralta said. —Jon Talton, *Concrete Desert*, p. 9, 2001
- [T]wo lines [of cocaine], an snort. Fuck me stiff this is strong. —Niall Griffiths, *Kelly + Victor*, p. 320, 2002

fuck me blue!

used as an elaborate variant of 'fuck me!' *US*

- I've told them and told them to get the hell out once we've made our goddamn move. Fuck me blue! —*Drugstore Cowboy*, 1988

fuck me harder!

used as an elborate and graphic expression of frustration *US*

- —Eric S. Raymond, *The New Hacker's Dictionary*, p. 170, 1991

fuck-me's *noun*

very tight, form-fitting trousers on a man *US*

- —Bruce Rodgers, *The Queens' Vernacular*, p. 53, 1972

fuck movie *noun*

a pornographic film *US*

- "I got some fuck-movies at home," the man tries to entice him[.] —John Rechy, *Numbers*, p. 105, 1967
- May be should get it all out front and show fuck movies in Time's Square. —*Screw*, p. 16, 23rd May 1969
- "We made a few fuck movies," says brother Art [Mitchell]. —Kenneth Turan and Stephen E. Zito, *Sinema*, p. 167, 1974

fuck no

used as an emphatic negative

- A replenishable landlord? Fuck no! —Lester Bangs, *Psychotic Reactions and Carburetor Dung*, p. 286, 1979
- Wasn't that leading the march thing a '60s attitude? "Fuck no. Hell![""] —*Ask*, p. 45, 28th March 1981

fucknut *noun*

a contemptible person *US*

- First they draft all the fucknuts who flunk out of school, and then they take the douchebags who bring home report cards like this. —Peter Farrelly, *Outside Providence*, p. 68, 1988
- You think I'd go away for shooting a fucknut like you? —Tom Corcoran, *Gumbo Limbo*, p. 217, 1999
- I bask now in the fantasy that I could actually feel happy and festive and self-respectful about being a testosterone-possessed fucknut. —Rob Brezsny, *Televisionary Oracle*, p. 45, 2000
- [H]e asked me what kind of fucknut I was[.] —Jill Davis, *Girls' Poker Night*, p. 208, 2002

fucko *noun*

used as a jocular if derisive term of address *US, 1973*

- Hey! Fucko! You want something? —*Goodfellas*, 1990
- McMANUS: What truck? VOICE: The truck with the guns, fucko. —*The Usual Suspects*, 1995
- "Yeah, right, fucko," J.W. said under his breath after he raised his window. —Ralph "Sonny" Barger, *Dead in 5 Heartbeats*, p. 288, 2003

fuck of a *noun*

a considerable or notable quantity or example of something *US, 1928*

- "Yes, a lot." "A fuck of a lot actually." "Yes. A hell of a fuck of a lot." "Yes." —Malcolm Pryce, *Aberystwyth Mon Amour*, p. 230, 2001
- One fuck of a party. —Niall Griffiths, *Kelly + Victor*, p. 26, 2002

fuck-off *noun*

1 a person who shirks their responsibility and duty *US, 1947*

- Diggers are more politically oriented but at the same time bigger fuckoffs. —Elmore Leonard, *Revolution for the Hell of It*, p. 26, 1968

2 a truant *UK*

- From fifteen years to sixteen nobody knew what to do with the crazies. The nutters,slow-learners, school phobics, headbangers, disaffected youth, fuck-offs, lowlife scumbags. Call them what you want. —Jack Allen, *When the Whistle Blows*, p. 36, 2000

fuck off *verb*

1 used for dismissing a foolish statement *UK*

- "Here listen," Chgarlie says. "That ain't right. You said all I had to do was 'phone her. You said all..." "Oh, fuck off Charlie. We know you're stupid but not that fucking stupid." —Ted Lewis, *Jack Carter's Law*, p. 98, 1974
- "Here, you'd better fuck off hadn't you." "Yeah." —David Peace, *Nineteen Seventy-Four*, p. 6, 1999
- Dude, anybody who doesn't think Terrance and Phillip is funny can fuck off anyways. —*South Park*, 1999
- I can't stand being near him anymore and fuck off home. —Danny King, *The Burglar Diaries*, p. 119, 2001

2 to treat someone as unworthy of respect or notice *US, 1962*

- [T]hey fucked us off, straight up and down. They were just crooks. —Alex Ogg, *The Hip Hop Years [quoting Rodney C of the Funky Four]*, p. 64, 1999
- Fighting and arguing and fucking people off is real. —*Q*, p. 97, May 2002

3 to postpone, to cancel *UK*

- Says he'll fuck everything off and come down for the weekend[.] —Kevin Sampson, *Clubland*, p. 103, 2002

fuck-off *adjective*

1 obvious, unmissable *UK*

- [Y]ou told me not to put any pants on – walking down stairs like John bastard Wayne I was – like sum huge fuckoff secret. —Patrick Jones, *Unprotected Sex*, p. 210, 1999
- We did blatant, fuck-off, "Here we are, come and get us!" style advertising. —Dave Courtney, *Raving Lunacy*, p. 29, 2000
- There's Mercs, Lexus, Beamers, Mitzis, all kinds of fuck-off four wheel drives and that – pure quality, la. —Kevin Sampson, *Clubland*, p. 2, 2002
- Huge fook-off bastards wi' hands like hams[.] —Ben Elton, *High Society*, p. 217, 2002

2 describes an attitude of not caring for the opinions of others *UK*

- [T]his is the coolest, the best, the baddest, the most f***-off collection of fiction around. —*britpulp*, back cover, 1999
- Raving was like rock, psychedelia and punk all rolled up into one big fuck-off party. —Dave Courtney, *Raving Lunacy*, p. 38, 2000
- [A] punishing cup of fuck-off strength espresso. —Stuart Browne, *Dangerous Parking*, p. 346, 2000

3 incompetent *US, 1953*

- [A] fuckoff group like Deep Purple[.] —Lester Bangs, *Psychotic Reactions and Carburetor Dung*, p. 47, 1970

fuck off and die!

go away – and don't come back! *UK*

An emphatic variation of **FUCK OFF**. Abbreviated for text messaging as **FOAD**.

- Half a minute of that [a singing audition] and Mazz waved to Emyr to stop and told the bloke to fuck off and die. —John Williams, *Cardiff Dead*, p. 22, 2000
- [F]*** off and die[.] —*a TXT BK*, 2001

fuckola

used as an embellished 'fuck' in any of its senses *US*

- Fuck me! Fuckola, man. —*The Big Lebowski*, 1998

fuck over *verb*

to treat another person with contempt or cruelty in any way; to mistreat, to hurt emotionally or physically, to betray, to victimise, to cheat *US, 1961*

- Get smart and I'll fuck you over – sayeth the Lord. —Frank Zappa, *The Real Frank Zappa Book*, p. 298, 1989
- [A]lways getting banged up [imprisoned] or fucked over. —Shaun Ryder, *Shaun Ryder... in His Own Words*, 1991
- MR. BLONDE: It's about a girl who is very vulnerable and she's been fucked over a few times. —*Reservoir Dogs*, 1992
- [O]ut-thought, outflanked and just plain fucked over. —Kevin Sampson, *Clubland*, p. 13, 2002

fuck pad *noun*

a room, apartment or house maintained for the purpose of sexual liaisons *US*

- When I walk into his combination office and fuck pad I see this little jive broad from Howard or Tuskegee. —Babs Gonzales, *Movin' On Down De Line*, p. 36, 1975
- A young white peeper spotted roof-prowling fuck-pad motels, jazz clubs. —James Ellroy, *White Jazz*, p. 46, 1992

fuckpole *noun*

the penis *US*

- She had two rusty nuts that swung from her butt / and a fuck-pole longer than mine. —Bruce Jackson, *Get Your Ass in the Water and Swim Like Me*, p. 159, 1966
- The verse, what I could recall, moved him, and he would idly play with what he called his "fuck-pole," but in no provocative way. —Gore Vidal, *Palimpsest*, p. 94, 1995

fuckries *noun*

trouble; wrongs *UK*

West Indian and UK black patois.

- I suppose you are proud of all the fuckries you've caused by having Fluxy shot? —Karline Smith, *Moss Side Massive*, p. 240, 1994
- Is pure fuckries going on for black people in this country, you know. —Donald Gorgon, *Cop Killer*, p. 14–15, 1994

fucks!

used as an expression of anger, frustration or resignation *UK: WALES*

An elaboration of **FUCK!**.

- What, an get me bastard hands torn open? Fucks. Still give yew a nasty rip, this little fucker would. —Niall Griffiths, *Sheepshagger*, p. 36, 2001

fucksome *adjective*

sexually desirable *UK, 1937*

fuck spider!

used for expressing extreme frustration *SINGAPORE*

- —Paik Choo, *The Coxford Singlish Dictionary*, p. 37, 2002

fuck stick *noun*

1 the penis *US, 1976*

Used by Saigon prostitutes during the Vietnam war, adopted by US soldiers.

- My pistol is like my fuck-stick. Don't go nowhere without it. —Edwin Torres, *Q & A*, p. 195, 1977
- "Oh, baby," she moaned, "listen to your white slut's pussy talking to your big black fuck stick!" —Penthouse Magazine, *Letters to Penthouse XVIII*, p. 220, 2003
- The idea of me having some kind of manhood mania, fuckstick fixation or penile preoccupation is palpable poppycock. —Richard Herring, *Talking Cock*, p. 1, 2003

2 a despicable person *US, 1958*

- Do you love this place, fuckstick? —Pat Controy, *The Lords of Discipline*, p. 164, 1980

fuck-struck *noun*

infatuated or obsessed with someone because of their ability in sex *US, 1966*

- I was duly fuck-struck as I waved him off[.] —Julian Barnes, *Love, etc.*, p. 67, 2000

fuck that for a lark!; fuck this for a lark!

no chance!; used as an emphatic dismissal of any activity or notion that you have no wish to subscribe to *UK*

- But then it turned out one of them was queer! Fuck that for a lark. —Mark Steel, *Reasons to be Cheerful*, p. 22, 2001
- Then I sees two tablets and I thinks fuck that for a lark and I necks the pair a them. —Kevin Sampson, *Clubland*, p. 156, 2002
- Fuck this for a lark. I am not a quiz show host, nor was ever meant to be. —Tony Wilson, *24 Hour Party People*, 2002

fuck the bourgeoisie

used as a slogan by the hippie counterculture *UK*

The first time many young people heard of the bourgeoisie.

- [D]uring London's October '68 anti-Vietnam demonstration, a spontaneous mixed chorus of "Fuck the bourgeoisie" aggravated the hostility of the onlooking staff. —Richard Neville, *Play Power*, p. 79, 1970

fuck this for a game of soldiers!; fuck that for a game of soldiers!

used as an emphatic dismissal of any activity or notion that you have no wish to subscribe to *UK, 1979*

A military variation of earlier 'fuck that for a game of skittles'; in turn an elaboration of 'fuck that'.

- SELF PITY KILLS says the slogan. Yes, well, fuck that for a game of soldiers. —Stuart Browne, *Dangerous Parking*, p. 321, 2000
- Fuck that for a game of toy soldiers, he'd thought. —Jake Arnott, *He Kills Coppers*, p. 35, 2001

fuck truck *noun*

any car, truck or van used for sexual encounters *AUSTRALIA*

- Sydney: Guy 22 bi, 8" with surf fuck truk [sic.] wants singles, couples for weekend trips up coast or quickies, enjoys adultery. —*Guy*, p. 16, 21st April 1974
- —David McGill, *David McGill's Complete Kiwi Slang Dictionary*, p. 51, 1998

fuck-up *noun*

a chronic, bungling, dismal failure (person or thing) *US, 1944*

- [F]ixed the plug fuck-up there & roared. —Neal Cassady, *The First Third*, p. 218, 1965
- We nonstudent fuck-ups say, "Excuse me, student. Did you know the sun is shining?" —Jerry Rubin, *Do It!*, p. 209, 1970
- Despite Hippy Pimp's fondness for the flourishes of the Aquarian Age, among most pimps the consensus is that "only the fuck-ups fall into the hippy bag[.]" —Christina and Richard Milner, *Black Players*, p. 167, 1972
- But if you were a fuck-up you made the cemetery gang, and were known as a "ghoul." —Herbert Huncke, *Guilty of Everything*, p. 47, 1990
- He was a serious fuck-up. I'm glad the son-of-a-bitch is dead. —*Slacker*, 1992
- You weren't abused, you aren't stupid, and as far as I can tell, you're only slightly psychotic – so what is it that you're such a fuck-up? —*Ten Things I Hate About You*, 1999
- I don't want another bollock. No fuck-ups. —Mark Powell, *Snap*, p. 91X, 2001

fuck up *verb*

1 to spoil, to destroy *UK, 1916*

- Let me tell you about this machine, a real dream; whether or not turned nitemare – the best truck I ever fucked up. —Neal Cassady, *The First Third*, p. 207, ugust 1965
- He sliced a painting in two? Did you fuck up a painting that night? —Gilbert Sorrentino, *Steelwork*, p. 21, 1970
- They fuck you up, your mum and dad [...] They were fucked up in their turn[.] —Philip Larkin, *This Be The Verse*, 1974
- Fuck it. They're dead. No big fucking deal. Move on." " – 's dead." "Fucking – fucked up. He's dead." "He shouldn't have fucked up. He wouldn't be fucking dead." —Jonathan Shay, *Achilles in Vietnam*, p. 38, 1995
- Let's go and fuck 'em up! —Kevin Sampson, *Powder*, p. 254, 1999
- The thing is, once you've been raving you can't do any other dance. It fucks you up that way. —Dave Courtney, *Raving Lunacy*, p. 7, 2000
- We battled long and hard for about a year, and it wasn't pretty. Oakland and Frisco Hell's Angels would fuck each other up at every chance. —Ralph "Sonny" Barger, *Hell's Angel*, p. 148, 2000
- Graham Taylor, Graham Taylor. Thanks for fucking-up the Wolves [Wolverhampton Wanderers FC]. Thanks for fu-u-u-cking-up the Wolves. —Frank Skinner, *Frank Skinner*, p. 117, 2001

2 to make a mistake *US, 1945*

- He says he remembers all the little ways he fucked up when he built your place. —Richard Russo, *Straight Man*, p. 38, 1998

3 to fail dismally *US*

- So you fuck up and you know what. —Darryl Ponicsan, *The Last Detail*, p. 21, 1970
- Andy [Warhol] gave me the freedom to fuck up. — *The Guardian*, 13th February 2002

4 to cause drink or drug intoxication, especially if extreme *UK*

- As long as it fucks you up, it's good for you. —Richard Neville, *Play Power*, p. 304, 1970

fuckwad *noun*

1 the semen ejaculated at orgasm *UK*

- It happens all the ime – you shoot a big fuckwad and bust some small blood vessel or other. —Stuart Browne, *Dangerous Parking*, p. 244, 2000

2 a contemptible fool; a despicable person; used as a general purpose pejorative *US, 1974*

The negative suffix '-wad' intensified.

- Why don't you just go piss up a rope, fuckwad. —*Drugstore Cowboy*, 1988
- YOU PRETENTIOUS CUNTING FUCKWAD! —Stuart Browne, *Dangerous Parking*, p. 77, 2000

fuckwit *noun*

an annoying or despicable person; a fool; an idiot *AUSTRALIA*

A blend of ***FUCK*** and ***NITWIT*** or ***HALF-WIT***.

- GIBBO: [Jacko hurls a stapling machine at Gibbo, who ducks.] Ooh, temper! Well, ta-ta for now, fuckwit. —Alexander Buzo, *The Front Room Boys*, p. 89, 1968
- Of course they do, you fuckwit. They're all rotten. —Suzy Jarratt, *Permissive Australia*, p. 142, 1970
- You're the bloody dregs. There's no bloody doubt about it. I've seen some cowardly fuckwits hiding behind their uniforms in my time but without a doubt you're the bottom of the bloody barrel. —David Williamson, *The Removalists*, p. 101, 1972
- YOU STUPID BLOODY FUCKWIT. IT'S AN ENEMA PIPE! GET THE STINKING THING OUT OF HERE BEFORE I RAM IT UP YOUR ARSE AND OUT THROUGH YOU DICKHEAD THROAT. —*Ribald*, p. 24, 31st July 1975
- I say piss him off and other foreign fuckwits. —*Ribald*, p. 7, 13th November 1975
- I was reading June letters when I saw Boon, from Cronulla. I would just like to say Bart sounds like a fuckwit, but you're wrong about the '20 upwards riding a shark bickie'. How old is Ben Severson, Mike Stewart (eight time world champ) and Eppo? —*Tracks*, p. 13, 1992
- You don't know for sure, but you're gonna act like a fuckwit anyway. —*Sydney Star Observer*, p. 33, 8th April 1994
- You get in my face, talking pure shit, / crapping on how you live for the pit. / Piss in my pocket, like you know the lot, / a fuckwit like you thinks two foot is hot! —*Tracks*, p. 15, 1996
- I felt like a royal fuckwit re-entering the house for the mull. —*Rants*, p. 27, 1997
- —David McGill, *David McGill's Complete Kiwi Slang Dictionary*, p. 46, 1998
- [Y]ou cloth-eared brainless overpaid legal fuckwit. —Mark Steel, *Reasons to be Cheerful*, p. 103, 2001
- London society was peopled almost entirely by fuckwits. —Chris Ryan, *The Watchman*, p. 152, 2001
- [H]im and Tommy Maguire; two brainless fuckwits together. —Niall Griffiths, *Kelly + Victor*, p. 45, 2002
- Although on that occasion he'd been "a fuckwit", he considered himself something of an expert on pot. —Brian Preston, *Pot Planet*, p. 91, 2002
- Two coked-up fookwits[.] —Ben Elton, *High Society*, p. 21, 2002

fuckwit *adjective*

stupid *UK*

- [S]ometimes shamed by my fellow men for their fuckwit behaviour. —Richard Herring, *Talking Cock*, p. 276, 2003

fuck with *verb*

1 to meddle with; to interfere with; to play around with *UK*

- [Ecstasy] transformed the way we thought, dressed, accessed music and it changed the way we fucked with our minds and bodies. —John Robb, *The Nineties*, p. 55, 1999
- Queen's had the sort of decor that was already lairy enough to fuck with your brain —Dave Courtney, *Raving Lunacy*, p. 11, 2000

2 to impress *US*

- [T]he level of perfection that he [Dr Dre] works at is amazing. Fuckin' with the best producer in hip-hop music, I had to be more on point. —Eminem (Marshall Mathers), *Angry Blonde*, p. 4, 2001

fuck-wittage *noun*

a state of stupidity *UK, mid-1990s*

- [H]er theory on the Richard situation: 'Emotional fuck-wittage', which is spreading like wildfire among men over thirty. —Helen Fielding, *Bridget Jones's Diary*, 1996

fuckwitted *adjective*

idiotic *AUSTRALIA*

- You two-timing, fuck-witted mongrel of a slut! Open up or I'll stuff you with a fist full of broken glass! —Jack Hibberd, *A Stretch of the Imagination*, p. 40, 1971
- The tautologous 'fuckwitted drongo' loses no impact from the repeptition. It is applied most satisfactorily to persons in high office, such as prime ministers. Beats me how that fuckwitted drongo can't see that the country is going down the gurgler. If his arse was on fire, he'd think it was a hot north wind. — *University of South Australia, student's essays on slang*, 1993
- —David McGill, *David McGill's Complete Kiwi Slang Dictionary*, p. 46, 1998
- [T]he thriving neo-Nazi scene is a) fuckwitted pub rock and b) has been in disarray[.] — *Uncut*, p. 5, May 2001

fucky *adjective*

1 trendy, sexy, stylish *UK*

- The lovely people as Nottingham's fuckiest disco, Home Taping is Killing Music, have printed up a sack of badges promoting their fab night. — *Bang*, p. 23, August 2003

2 lustfully erotic *AUSTRALIA*

- What was a sweet fucky marriage but the sublimation of orgies never undertaken? — *Australian Playboy*, p. 136, 1989

3 used as an intensifier, replacing 'fucking' *UK*

- Fucky dingnuts and bastardy cunt-holes. —Jenny Eclair, *Camberwell Beauty*, p. 208, 2000

fucky-fucky sauce *noun*

semen *US*

- Most of the guy's load hits her chin but she gets some of the fucky-fucky sauce down. — *Screw*, p. 15, 6th November 1972

fuck you!

used contemptuously as an expression of disdain, dismissal or disbelief *UK*

- [A]ll we got were a few anti-establishment fuck-yous. —Naomi Klein, *No Logo*, p. 82, 2001
- Coke was the "fuck-you" drug. You didn't give a damn what other people thought. —Simon Napier-Bell, *Black Vinyl White Powder*, p. 144, 2001

fuck you and the horse you rode in on!

used as an emphatic and insulting rejection *US*

- Eddie Coyle smiled. "Fuck you, lady," he said, "and the horse you rode in on." —George V. Higgins, *The Friends of Eddie Doyle*, p. 108, 1971
- —*Maledicta*, p. 170, Winter 1980: 'A brief survey of some unofficial prosigns used by the United States Armed Forces'

fuck-you lizard *noun*

a Vietnamese Tokay gecko lizard *US*

US soldiers in Vietnam thought that the gecko's call sounded as if the gecko was saying 'fuck you'. In polite company, the lizard was called an 'insulting lizard'.

- A 2nd Brigade chaplains' assistant is trying to put his outdoorsman's skills to work on a somewhat embarrassing problem at the 4th Inf. Div.'s Highlander Chapel. The nemesis in this case was the infamous Vietnamese "insulting Lizard" who lurks in every nook and cranny. —*Pacific Stars and Stripes*, 15th May 1970
- —Linda Reinberg, *In the Field*, p. 90, 1991

fuck-your-buddy week *noun*

a notional designation of the present week, explaining rude behaviour by your superiors *US, 1960*

- "What is this," Bruce snarled, "Fuck-You-Buddy Week?" —Paul Krassner, *Confessions of a Raving, Unconfined Nut*, p. 247, 1993

fuck yourself!; go and fuck yourself!

used as an expression of dismissal *UK, 1879*

- "I've got the Chairman of the Governors with me!" "He can go and fuck himself as well!" —Jack Allen, *When the Whistle Blows*, p. 206, 2000
- "Fuck yourself," said the man [US Vice President Dick Cheney] who is a heartbeat from the presidency. —*Washington Post*, p. A4, 25th June 2004

fuck you sideways!

used contemptuously as an expression of disdain or dismissal *UK*

An intensification of FUCK YOU!.

- Well, fuck you, Sandra. Fuck you fucking sideways. —Garry Bushell, *The Face*, p. 119, 2001

fucky-sucky *noun*

a combination of oral and vaginal sex *US*

- You likee me? You likee fuckee-suckee? —Earl Thompson, *Tattoo*, p. 336, 1974

fucky-sucky *verb*

to engage in oral and then vaginal sex *US*

- The bottom line is how many can you fucky-sucky. —James Ridgeway, *Red Light*, p. 204, 1996

FUD *noun*

uncertainty and doubt *US*

- The FUD factor is popularly used to explain why IBM sold so many mainframes. That middle manager couldn't understand the features of all the different systems, and ultimately decided that nobody ever got fired for buying an IBM. —Andy Ihnatko, *Cyberspeak*, p. 77–78, 1997

fuddle-duddle!

used as a euphemism for 'fuck off' *CANADA*

Said by Canadian Prime Minister Pierre Trudeau in the House of Commons, 16th February 1971.

- —*Maledicta*, p. 182–183, 1979: 'Canadian slurs, ethnic and other'
- He had been caught in the House silently mouthing a four-letter word. But outside the house he told the press he'd said "fuddle-duddle." As one Parliament wag remarked, "The PM wants to be obscene and not heard." —Bill Casselman, *Canadian Words*, p. 146–147, 1995

fuddy *noun*

an old-fashioned person *US*

An abbreviation of FUDDY-DUDDY.

- Well, here's my point, Eleanor: the girls are cooped in here the whole day with all old sick fuddies – then a young man pops up! —Terry Southern, *Flash and Filigree*, p. 57, 1958

fuddy-dud *noun*

an old-fashioned, inhibited, conventional person *US, 1904*

- But my wife thinks it's the other way; call me a fuddy-dud, but I must admit I don't consider it fitting for my wife to tell me what to do in bed. —John M. Murtagh and Sara Harris, *Cast the First Stone*, p. 166, 1957
- Come on, don't be a fuddy dud. We'll have a party. You and me. —Jill Smolinski, p. 220, 2002

fuddy-duddy *noun*

a fussy, old-fashioned, narrow-minded person *US, 1904*

- Father is a fuddy duddy! —Haenigsen, *Jive's Like That*, 1947
- It was part of his graft to look, dress, and act like a benevolent old fuddy-duddy. —Charles Raven, *Underworld Nights*, p. 200, 1956
- Britain is still in the grips of some particularly dotty censorship legislation. The fuddy duddies are bound to give in sooner or later[.] —Barry Humphries, *Bazza Pulls It Off!*, 1971
- Aw, it's O.K., Alice. Christ, we're not a couple of old fuddy-duddies. I remember what I was like at Mike's age. —Armistead Maupin, *Tales of the City*, p. 263, 1978
- What would an old fuddy-uddy like me know about the fashions of young women? —Robert Campbell, *Sweet La-La Land*, p. 221, 1990

fuddy-duddy *adjective*

fussy, old-fashioned, narrow-minded *US, 1907*

- They thought England still too fuddy-duddy and conservative. —Richard Barnes, *Mods*, p. 24, 1979

fudge *noun*

▷ see: MAGIC FUDGE

fudge *verb*

to cheat *US*

- Perhaps he has been fudging on his tax returns. —Raymond Chandler, *Playback*, p. 83, 1958
- —Collin Baker et al., *College Undergraduate Slang Study Conducted at Brown University*, p. 123, 1968

fudge

used as a euphemism for 'fuck' *UK, 1766*

Based on the opening sound (as is 'sugar' for 'shit').

- "Fudge," I said. "Land o'Goshen, heck, tarnation, crim-a-nentlies." —Max Shulman, *The Zebra Derby*, p. 174, 1946
- Twenty fudging bucks would put a gang of relief in sight for my personal smog. —Bernard Wolfe, *The Late Risers*, p. 5, 1954
- ["E]verything will be just like it always was. Oh, fudge." "What?" "Nothing. It doesn't matter." —Darren Francis, *The Sprawl [britpulp]*, p. 313, 1999

fudge factor *noun*

an allowance made for possible error in estimating the time, material or money needed for a job *US, 1962*

- —John Edwards, *Auto Dictionary*, p. 66, 1993

fudge nudger *noun*

someone who engages in anal sex, especially a male homosexual *UK*

- —Chris Lewis, *The Dictionary of Playground Slang*, p. 95, 2003

fudgepacker *noun*

a gay man *US, 1985*

Someone who packs 'fudge' (excrement), thus a graphic description of a participant in anal intercourse.

- Well, yeah – J. M. Barrie was a fudgepacker from way back, and clearly some of that forbiddenness sneaks into every version. —Nicholson Baker, *Vox*, p. 36, 1992
- —Connie Eble (Editor), *UNC-CH Campus Slang*, p. 3, Spring 1993
- You wanna celebrate because some fudgepacker that you date has been elected the first queer President of the United States —*As Good As It Gets*, 1997
- Can you imagine the humiliation your father's going to feel when he finds our his pride and joy is a fudgepacker! —*Cruel Intentions*, 1999
- [A] fully confirmed fudge-packing pillow-biter. —Jenny Eclair, *Camberwell Beauty*, p. 193, 2000

fudger *noun*

a planespotter who claims greater success than is true *UK*

- I also found out that a "fudger" is someone who claims to have seen aeroplanes that they haven't, just so they can cross the numbers off in their book to finish classes of aircraft. —Iain Aitch, *A Fete Worse Than Death*, p. 73, 2003

fuel *noun*

1 cocaine *US*

- But clearly you are not the only person in here to take on fuel. Lots of sniffing going on in the stalls. —Jay McInerney, *Bright Lights, Big City*, p. 5, 1984

2 marijuana *US*

- —Peter Johnson, *Dictionary of Street Alcohol and Drug Terms*, p. 78, 1993

3 marijuana adulterated with psychoactive chemicals *US*

- —Jay Robert Nash, *Dicitonary of Crime*, p. 141, 1992

fueled *adjective*

very drunk *US*

- —Connie Eble (Editor), *UNC-CH Campus Slang*, p. 3, Fall 1997

fueler *noun*

a drag racing car that does not use petrol as fuel *US*

- —Ed Radlauer, *Drag Racing Pix Dix*, p. 23, 1970

fuel-tank justice *noun*
a fistfight to settle a dispute at work *US*
This type of conflict resolution often took place behind a fuel tank, near the work location but out of sight, usually after work. Reported by a union business agent, Vacaville, California, 2001.

fuel up *verb*
to eat quickly *US*
• —Eric S. Raymond, *The New Hacker's Dictionary*, p. 171, 1991

fuete *noun*
a hypodermic needle *US, 1973*
From Cuban Spanish *fuete* (a whip).
• —Richard A. Spears, *The Slang and Jargon of Drugs and Drink*, p. 208, 1986
• —Mike Haskins, *Drugs*, p. 292, 2003

FUFA
an army deserter during the Vietnam war – *f*ed *u*p with the *f*ucking *a*rmy *US*
• —Gregory Clark, *Words of the Vietnam War*, p. 140, 1990

fufnick *noun*
in the car sales business, a car part or mechanism that has been altered in appearance but not in substance *US*
• Like low mileage on a car ten years old. In this case the speedometer is a "fufnick." —*Cars*, p. 40, December 1953

fufu *noun*
1 an eccentric person; a crazy person *CAYMAN ISLANDS*
• —Aarona Booker Kohlman, *Wotcha Say*, p. 25, 1985
2 a homosexual *US*
• —Judi Sanders, *Faced and Faded, Hanging to Hurl*, p. 16, 1993

fug
used as a euphemism for 'fuck' in all its variant uses and derivatives *US*
• I mean have a real flower of something and not just the usually American middleclass fuggup with appearances. —Jack Kerouac, *The Dharma Bums*, p. 161, 1958
• I don't know jes where the fug he think he is at. —Robert Gover, *One Hundred Dollar Misunderstanding*, p. 21, 1961
• Ah, what the fug, held others; it's only a game, it's not sacred. —Bill Cardoso, *The Maltese Sangweech*, p. 141, 1984
• There are five people in this fuggin' band that have got no problems! —Shaun Ryder, *Shaun Ryder... in His Own Words*, 1993
• Marrying music and poetry, the New York band [The Fugs, 1960s US rock band] lifted a mock expletive Norman Mailer had utilized frequently in his 1948 war novel, 'The Naked and the Dead' in place of the f-word. —Simon Warner, *Rockspeak!*, p. 34, 1996

Fugawi *noun*
a mythical tribe or people, so named because after years of wandering they asked, 'Where the fuck are we?' *US*
Military origins.
• In the 1/18th, the Fugawi Award went to the company or individual staff officer responsible for the biggest snafu or screwup of the week. —David H. Hackworth, *About Face*, p. 364, 1989

fugazi *adjective*
crazy *US*
Coined during the Vietnam war.
• —Linda Reinberg, *In the Field*, p. 90, 1991

fugazzi *adjective*
wrong *UK*
A disguising of **FUCK** and, possibly, **ARSE**.
• If it all went fugazzi it would have been because he'd been negligent[.] —Christopher Brookmyre, *The Sacred Art of Stealing*, p. 216, 2002

fugging *adverb*
used as a euphemism for the intensifier 'fucking' *US*
• And if I was in the way that was just too fuggin' bad. —Gerald Petievich, *To Die in Beverly Hills*, p. 185, 1983

fugly *noun*
an extremely ugly person *AUSTRALIA*
• Fugly – An extremely ugly woman. A blending of 'fucking' and 'ugly' to describe the woman. —*More Than Mere Bravo*, 1970
• Wanna furgle an old fugly for a fortune? —*Picture*, p. 19, 5th February 1992

fugly *adjective*
very ugly *US, 1984*
A blending of **FUCKING** (or 'funky') and 'ugly'.
• —Connie Eble (Editor), *UNC-CH Campus Slang*, p. 4, Fall 1988
• —Eric S. Raymond, *The New Hacker's Dictionary*, p. 171, 1991
• The catch is that the bloke in question is friggin' ancient, fugly as sin and, worse still, he's a South African! —*Picture*, p. 18, 5th February 1992
• —Jack Chambers (Editor), *Slang Bag 93 (University of Toronto)*, p. 3, Winter 1993
• Her face dropped when she saw that the mingle consisted of our group plus ten fugly women and two cute guys[.] —Anka Radakovich, *The Wild Girls Club*, p. 72, 1994

fuigmo *noun*
▷ **see: FIGMO**

full *adjective*
1 drunk *US, 1844*
• Another pub? Too early to get full. —Eric Lambert, *The Veterans*, p. 18, 1954
• —Joseph E. Ragen and Charles Finston, *Inside the World's Toughest Prison*, p. 800, 1962: 'Penitentiary and underworld glossary'
• —Connie Eble (Editor), *UNC-CH Campus Slang*, p. 4, Spring 1990
2 heavily drugged *UK*
A shortening of 'full of drugs'.
• — Home Office, *Glossary of Terms and Slang Common in Penal Establishments*, July 1978
3 pregnant *TRINIDAD AND TOBAGO, 1976*
• —Lise Winer, *Dictionary of the English/Creole of Trinidad & Tobago*, 2003

full as a bull's bum *adjective*
extremely full *AUSTRALIA*
• A bloke'd have to be full as a bull's bum to come to that! —Barry Humphries, *Bazza Pulls It Off!*, 1971

full as a fairy's phone book *adjective*
extremely full; very drunk *AUSTRALIA*
Alluding to the allegedly inherent fickle nature of homosexual males.
• I've had a couple of drinks as a matter of fact – who hasn't, for Christ's sake? To tell you the truth, I'm as full as a fairy's phone book. —Barry Humphries, *A Nice Night's Entertainment*, p. 181, 1978

full as a family jerry *adjective*
completely full *AUSTRALIA*
• There was less unanimity, however, about 'full as a family jerry' (or po). In some families this refers only to insobriety, in others always to being well fed, but some families use it in either sense. —Nancy Keesing, *Lily on the Dustbin*, p. 185, 1982
• Jerry (that's me driver, and he's aptly named – he's always full. I once said, 'Jerry you're that full your place is under the bed.'). — Barry Humphries, *The Traveller's Tool*, p. 125, 1985

full as a family po *adjective*
extremely full; very drunk *AUSTRALIA*
• 'Full as a goog' must be nearly as venerable and long-lived as 'full as a family po'. —Nancy Keesing, *Lily on the Dustbin*, p. 140, 1982

full as a goog *adjective*
extremely full; very drunk *AUSTRALIA, 1941*
• —Dymphna Cusack, *Picnic Races*, p. 22, 1962
• Never stopped till they filled him full as a goog with tranquillizers. —Dymphna Cusack, *Picnic Races*, p. 107, 1962
• —Arthur Chipper, *The Aussie Swearer's Guide*, p. 52, 1972
• —Jim Ramsay, *Cop It Sweet!*, p. 38, 1977

full as a pommie complaint box *adjective*
extremely full; very drunk *AUSTRALIA*
• It's true that from time to time, due to pressure of work and jet-lag, I've been known to get as full as a pommie complaint box[.] — Barry Humphries, *The Traveller's Tool*, p. 71, 1985

full as a state school *adjective*
extremely full; very drunk *AUSTRALIA, 1945*
• You've got to have a steady hand on the wheel, and last time he arrived plastered to the eyeballs, full as a State school. —Criena Rohan, *Down by the Dockside*, p. 212, 1963
• Hold yer horses – any more of that [an alcoholic drink] and you'll end up as full as a state school! —Barry Humphries, *Bazza Pulls It Off!*, 1971

full as a teddy bear *adjective*
to be very drunk *CANADA*
• —T. K. Pratt, *Oral informants in Prince Edward Island Sayings*, p. 90, 1998

full as a tick *adjective*
extremely full; very drunk *AUSTRALIA, 1892*
• 'Blithered.' 'Stonkered.' 'Full as a tick.' These synonyms for intoxication expressed a sense of immense achievement, mangnificent in its humour. —Norman Lindsay, *Halfway to Anywhere*, p. 186, 1947

full-auto *adjective*

(used of a firearm) fully automatic *US*

- There be them big dudes with their full-auto Uzis, an go bailin warp-seven cause Gordy gots the balls to shoot back with this! — Jess Mowry, *Way Past Cool*, 1992

full belt *adverb*

at top speed *AUSTRALIA, 1901*

- Away you go again full belt and presently stop again at another similar box at which there is a stockman waiting to send a telegram. — Patsy Adam-Smith, *Folklore of the Australian Railwaymen*, p. 298, 1969

full-bird colonel *noun*

▷ see: BIRD COLONEL

full bottle *noun*

full speed or maximum volume *UK*

A Londoners' term.

- Screeching away at full bottle. — *British Journal of Photography*, 8th July 1977

full bull *noun*

a colonel in the US Army *US, 1962*

- A full bull earned maybe twenty-three thousand in retirement pay; she earned that every six months, and she was just getting going. — Walter Boyne Steven Thompson, *The Wild Blue*, p. 487, 1986

full chart *noun*

a sale with maximised profit realised from financing the sale *US*

- — *American Speech*, p. 309–310, Winter 1980: 'More jargon of car salesmen'

full dress *adjective*

of a motorcyle, fully equipped and accessorised *US*

- A full dress machine might have saddlebags, double seat, extra lights, radio, fairings, windshield, cargo box, stereo tape player, air conditioning – doesn't every motorcyle have air conditioning? — Ed Radlauer, *Motorcylopedia*, p. 26, 1973

full dresser *noun*

a factory stock Harley Davidson Electra-Glide motorcyle with every possible accessory *US*

Biker (motorcyle) usage.

- As opposed to choppers, "full dressers" are motorcyles that keep all of the original manufacturer's pieces on, plus they add accessories[.] — Ralph "Sonny" Barger, *Hell's Angel*, p. 57, 2000

full eek *noun*

a face that is fully made-up *UK*

- — Paul Baker, *Polari*, p. 175, 2002

full French *noun*

oral sex performed on a man until he ejaculates *US*

- Before you walk a trick you must give half and half or full french for the minimum price. — George Paul Csicsery (Editor), *The Sex Industry*, p. 48, 1973
- Blowjob to orgasm? They call it "full French" here. — Gerald Paine, *A Bachelor's Guide to the Brothels of Nevada*, p. 15, 1978

full Greek *noun*

in pinball, a shot up and then back down a lane with a scoring device, scoring twice *US*

- — Bobbye Claire Natkin and Steve Kirk, *All About Pinball*, p. 112, 1977

full guns *adverb*

to the maximum *US*

- At any rate, I'm glad to hear everything's going full guns. — Jack Kerouac, *Letter to Caroline Kerouac Blake*, p. 132, 25th September 1947

full hand *noun*

said of a person infected with multiple sexually transmitted diseases *US*

- — Roger Blake, *The American Dictionary of Sexual Terms*, p. 81, 1964

full harva *noun*

anal intercourse *UK*

- Anal intercourse was referred to as the full harva. — Paul Baker, *Polari*, p. 163, 2002

full hit *noun*

everything *UK*

- Dool brings the brekkies [breakfasts] over. Full hit, bacon, sausages, plum tomatoes [etc]. — Kevin Sampson, *Outlaws*, p. 227, 2001

full house *noun*

1 a combination of several non-existent diseases *US*

- Soldiers at a port of embarkation have been told in detail about the foregoing ailments and then told: 'If you get a full house, you might just as well stay over there'. — *American Speech*, p. 305, December 1947: 'Imaginary diseases in army and navy parlance'

2 said of a person infected with both gonorrhea and syphilis *US*

- — *Maledicta*, p. 228, Summer/Winter 1981: 'Sex and the single soldier'

3 a state in which a person is infested with more than one form of parasite, such as head and body lice *UK*

- — David Powis, *The Signs of Crime*, 1977

4 in drag racing and hot rodding, a highly modified engine *US*

- — *Hot Rod Magazine*, p. 13, November 1948: 'Racing jargon'
- — *Good Housekeeping*, p. 143, September 1958: 'Hot-rod terms for teen-age girls'
- — Lyle K. Engel, *The Complete Book of Fuel and Gas Dragsters*, p. 151, 1968
- — Phantom Surfers, *The Exciting Sounds of Model Road Racing (Album cover)*, 1997

full house and no flush *noun*

the situation in which all available latrines are occupied *US*

- — *American Speech*, p. 55, February 1947: 'Pacific war language'

full house mouse *noun*

in hot rodding, a small car with a fully modified engine *US*

- A souped Volkswagen for example, is a full house mouse. — John Lawlor, *How to Talk Car*, p. 50, 1965

full monty; full monte; monte *noun*

everything required within a given context *UK*

Usage widely popularised by the success of the film *The Full Monty*, 1997. Three plausible etymologies are well rehearsed: from the nickname 'Monty', given to Field Marshall Montgomery, 1st Viscount of Alamein (1887–1976); the card game called Spanish Monte or Monte Bank; an abbreviation of Montague Burton, a high street menswear and tailoring company, retailers of a complete suit of clothing.

- GAZ: Well... er, this lot go all the way. Don't they, lads? DAVE: You what? LOUISE: The full monty? You lot? Hellfire, that would be worth a look. — *The Full Monty*, 1997
- [B]ades and rice flails and baseball bats, the monte. — Jeremy Cameron, *Brown Bread in Wengen*, p. 231, 1999
- Goes back to when I had my first hole. First proper goose and that, the full monty. — Kevin Sampson, *Clubland*, p. 84, 2002

full moon *noun*

1 a woman's menstrual period *US*

- — *American Speech*, p. 298, December 1954: 'The vernacular of menstruation'

2 buttocks of the large variety *US*

- — Anna Scotti and Paul Young, *Buzzwords*, p. 13, 1997

3 a large slice of peyote cactus *US*

- — William D. Alsever, *Glossary for the Establishment and Other Uptight People*, p. 12, December 1970

Full Nanaimo *noun*

a garish dress outfit simulating official naval attire *CANADA*

- Frequently seen at formal ceremonies during the 1970s, this code of bad dress is attributed to Nanaimo [BC], but various yachting cities use it to degrade competitors. White buck shoes, white patent leather belt, polyester pants, phony crest blazer. — Tom Parkin, *WetCoast Words*, p. 56, 1989

full of beans *adjective*

vigorous, energetic, in high spirits, full of life *UK, 1854*

- I had just done my first stretch at the Scrubs and was feeling full of beans. — Charles Raven, *Underworld Nights*, p. 158, 1956
- "You seem full of beans," said Brad. "What did you get up to last night?" — Colin Butts, *Is Harry on the Boat?*, p. 90, 1997
- [Louby-Lou] had been lying in the nursery rocking chair as stuffed with straw as Andy and Teddy were full of beans. — Stuart Jeffries, *Mrs Slocombe's Pussy*, p. 19, 2000

full of gob *adjective*

talkative; too talkative *UK*

- [W]e were cocky young upstarts who knew it all and were, as one put it succinctly, "full of gob". — Duncan MacLaughlin, *The Filth*, p. 67, 2002

full of run *adjective*

(used of a racehorse) in good racing form *US*

- — David W. Maurer, *Argot of the Racetrack*, p. 30, 1951

full of shit *adjective*

(of a person) deliberately or congenitally stupid, misleading or misinformed *US*

- "Mothers are full of shit,"Miss Lee observed and took off her leather coat. —John Kenedy Toole, *A Confederacy of Dunces*, p. 24, 1980
- I know people will read this and say, "Aww, he's full of shit[.]" —Howard Stern, *Miss America*, p. 129, 1995
- No, fuck B.Jay, he's full of shit. —Lanre Fehintola, *Charlie Says...*, p. 23, 2000

full of yourself *adjective*

conceited, self-involved *UK, 1866*

- Every journalist who is not too stupid or too full of himself to notice what is going on knows that what he does is morally indefensible. —Janet Malcolm, *Reading Chekhov*, 2001

full-on *adjective*

maximum, complete, absolute, very *US, 1970*

- —Jonathan Roberts, *How to California*, p. 168, 1984
- Course, if they come, it with their screamer full on, just like now. —Jess Mowry, *Way Past Cool*, p. 15, 1992
- No, she's a full-on Monet. —*Clueless*, 1995
- Which made every whack, clump, kick and butt seem even worse because you got the full on sound effect. —Dave Courtney, *Stop the Ride I Want to Get Off*, p. 218, 1999
- She's wearing about a ton too much of that full-on beige face powder. —Kevin Sampson, *Outlaws*, p. 239, 2001

full out *adverb*

completely, intensely *US, 1918*

- —Leonard Wolfe (Editor), *Voices from the Love Generation*, p. 278, 1968

full personal *noun*

sexual intercourse, as distinct from masturbation, when advertised as a service offered by a prostitute *UK*

- —Caroline Archer, *Tart Cards*, 2003

full sails *adverb*

in trucking, driving at top speed with the wind behind you *US*

- —Wayne Floyd, *Jason's Authentic Dictionary of CB Slang*, p. 17, 1976

full screw *noun*

a corporal in the army *UK*

- Each of us full screws was responsible for between twelve and fifteen recruits. —Andy McNab, *Immediate Action*, p. 46, 1995

full service *noun*

in the coded language of massage parlours, sexual intercourse *US*

A 2002 Incident Report from the Sausalito (California) Police Department describes the activities at a local massage parlour as follows: 'Only a few girls will do full service (sexual intercourse) and oral (oral copulation) massages'.

full stop; full stop – end of story

a catchphrase used as a firm signal that a matter is at an end *UK, 1976*

Verbalised punctuation, exactly matching US use of 'period'.

- The prime minister's official spokesman said "there were no plans to end the right-to-buy. Full stop. Period. End of story." Well, we all know that with John Prescott there aren't many full stops. —*The Guardian*, 8th October 2002

full-timer *noun*

a person who lives in a recreational vehicle all year *US*

- —Jim Crotty, *How to Talk American*, p. 39, 1997

full tit *noun*

an all-out effort *NEW ZEALAND*

- —David McGill, *David McGill's Complete Kiwi Slang Dictionary*, p. 47, 1998

full tub *noun*

in poker, a hand consisting of three cards of the same rank and a pair *US*

Conventionally known as a 'full house'.

- —George Percy, *The Language of Poker*, p. 38, 1988

full up to dolly's wax

replete with food; entirely full *AUSTRALIA, 1945*

- However, everyone was full up to dolly's wax and I was absolutely stonkered[.] —Barry Humphries, *A Nice Night's Entertainment*, p. 85, 1965
- Referring to dolls which were formerly made with wax heads. —Maureen Brooks and Joan Ritchie, *Tassie Terms*, p. 55, 1995

full weight *noun*

a package of drugs that weighs as much as it is claimed to weigh *US*

- [A]nd sold full weights – or at least never bitched that Ty packed full weights. —Jess Mowry, *Way Past Cool*, p. 30, 1992

fully *adverb*

very *US*

- —Mimi Pond, *The Valley Girl's Guide to Life*, p. 55, 1982
- If they threw a party, the chances are it would be "fully geeking." —*New York Times*, 12th April 1987

fuma d'Angola; fumo d'Angola *noun*

marijuana *US, 1969*

Portuguese, meaning 'smoke of Angola'.

- —Richard A. Spears, *The Slang and Jargon of Drugs and Drink*, p. 209, 1986
- —Mike Haskins, *Drugs*, p. 287, 2003

fumble *verb*

in college, to do poorly and receive a notification of academic deficiency *US*

- —*American Speech*, p. 76–77, February 1968: 'Some notes on flunk notes'

fumble fingers *noun*

clumsy hands *US*

- I figure it's because there are people who might not agree with such a violent way of making a protest, but who do not want the perpetrator – who did not mean to hurt anyone, just a building – to go to jail for having fumble fingers. —Robert Campbell, *Junkyard Dog*, p. 120, 1986

fumed-up *adjective*

marijuana-intoxicated *UK*

- Carboot Soul [by Nightmares on Wax] and it's lazy, fumed-up charms will win you over lickety-split. —*Ministry*, May 2002

fumigate *verb*

to take an enema before or after anal sex *US*

- —Bruce Rodgers, *The Queens' Vernacular*, p. 91, 1972

fummydiddle *verb*

to waste time or to bungle *US*

- —John Gould, *Maine Lingo*, p. 103, 1975

fun *noun*

a grain of opium *US*

- They'd give you a tin that was a little smaller than a tin of salve, and it weighed exactly twelve "fun." —Jeremy Larner and Ralph Tefferteller, *The Addict in the Street*, p. 159, 1964

fun *verb*

to tease, to joke *US*

- "Damn, boy," he said, "we's only funnin' with you-all." —Piri Thomas, *Down These Mean Streets*, p. 162, 1967

fun *adjective*

amusing, interesting, light-hearted *US, 1950*

- Castro clone moustaches and Burton "fun" shirts seemed to be the order of the day[.] —Kitty Churchill, *Thinking of England*, p. 45, 1995
- I had such a fun time working with the cast and crew[.] —*The Guardian*, 27th January 2000
- I didn't take much persuading, it seemed like a fun thing to do. —*The Observer*, 2nd September 2001

fun and frolics *noun*

the testicles

Rhyming slang for **BOLLOCKS**, recorded as Anglo-Irish.

- —Julian Franklyn, *A Dictionary of Rhyming Slang*, 1960

fun and games *noun*

1 a (very) agreeable time; love-making, petting and/or sexual intercourse *UK, 1961*

The second sense is, of course, a specialisation of the first.

2 ironically, a disagreeable time; a brush with an enemy *UK, 1948*

Originally navy, when the enemy was at sea.

- She had taken off her cloak which was stained by the fun and games with the hearse. —Martin Waddell, *Otley*, p. 35, 1966

fun bags *noun*

the female breasts *US, 1965*

- Every time her instructor let himself be thrown, he did a number on her fun bags you wouldn't believe. —Jack W. Thomas, *Heavy Number*, p. 1, 1976
- —Judi Sanders, *Cal Poly Slang*, p. 4, 1990
- —J.R. Schwartz, *The Official Guide to the Best Cat Houses in Nevada*, p. 165, 1993: 'Sex glossary'

fun book *noun*

a collection of discount coupons given to guests by casinos *US*

- —Michael Dalton, *Blackjack*, p. 49, 1991

fun box *noun*

in skateboarding and foot-propelled scootering, any manufactured obstacle (usually made of wood) that provides varying configurations of ramps and surfaces for the boarder to employ *US, 1992*

- —Ben Sharpe, *Scooter Crazy*, p. 40, 2000
- That's a fun box, shaped like a mountain with a flat top and a grind rail.— *The Times*, p. 16, 26th April 2003

funch *noun*

sex during lunch *US*

- Baths vary in character, from the Wall Street Sauna, where businessmen go to get their rocks off during the lunch hour (it's called "funch"), to the Beacon[.]— *The Village Voice*, 27th September 1976

Fun City *nickname*

New York *US, 1966*

Coined by Mayor John Lindsay in 1965.

- Remember Fun City? That's what New York was called when it had a glamorous mayor named Lindsay who seemed destined for even higher officer, maybe the White House.— *Washington Post*, p. A2, 19th August 1979
- Meanwhile, the phrase "Fun City" became something of a sick joke[.]—Robert A. M. Stern, *New York 1960*, p. 32, 1995

fundage *noun*

money *US*

- —Judi Sanders, *Faced and Faded, Hanging to Hurl*, p. 16, 1993

fundie; fundi; fundy *noun*

1 of religious faith, fundamentalist; a fundamentalist, especially a Christian fundamentalist but also applied in non-religious uses *UK, 1982*

- One contributor accuses a fellow group member of "just the sort of thing a fundie [fundamentalist Christian] does as the opening barrage for an assault on Evolution"[.]—David Porter, *Internet Culture*, p. 192, 1997
- —Harry Orsman, *A Dictionary of Modern New Zealand Slang*, p. 53, 1999
- Mo was no fundie, but distrusted technology. Man-stuff, she called it.—Eugene Byrne, *Bagged 'n' Tagged [Witpunk]*, p. 160, 2003

2 an expert, a teacher *SOUTH AFRICA, 1937*

- Yes if you are a music fundi, this jazz legend brings orgasm to your ears.— *Sunday Times (South Africa)*, 24th June 2000

funeral *noun*

▸ **it's your funeral; your funeral**

it's of no concern to me (regardless of what the business, circumstance or situation that is being referred to is) *US, 1895*

- "I'll risk it," Clark said. Tillie shrugged. "Your funeral."—Cherie Bennett, *See No Evil*, p. 147, 2002

funeral train *noun*

a long line of cars whose progress is impeded by one slow driver who refuses to pull over and let them pass *US*

- — *American Speech*, p. 269, December 1962: 'The language of traffic policemen'

fun factor *noun*

the ratio of a car's power to its weight *US*

- A light car with a moderately powerful engine can be as much fun as a more powerful, heavier car.—Lewis Poteet, *Car & Motorcyle Slang*, p. 90, 1992

fungee; fungy *noun*

a fruit dumpling or a deep-dish blueberry pie *CANADA*

- They never made blueberries into a fungy, as Mrs. Canaan did–they just stewed them.—Ernest Buckler, *The Mountain and the Valley*, p. 48, 1952
- Apparently the same dish (blueberry grunt) is called Fungy, Fungee, in Yarmouth County.— *Dutch Oven*, p. 28, 1953

fungoo!

fuck you! *US, 1942*

Often accompanied by graphic body language.

- Union placard shakers – Chick Vecchio facing them off – the stiff-arm fungoo up close.—James Ellroy, *White Jazz*, p. 58, 1992

fun hog *noun*

an obsessed enthusiast of thrill sports *US*

- —William Nealy, *Mountain Bike!*, p. 161, 1992: 'Bikespeak'

funk *noun*

1 a strong human smell; the smell of human sexual activity *US, 1917*

- Better to suffocate, he reasoned, than to die from an overload of funk.—Donald Goines, *White Man's Justice, Black Man's Grief*, p. 20, 1973

2 semen; smegma *US*

- They had fried shit choplets and hot funk custard / Drank spit out of cocktail glasses and used afterbirth for mustard.—Dennis Wepman et al., *The Life*, p. 112, 1976

3 a genre of dance music that combines soul, blues, gospel and jazz with irresistible beats and rhythms *US, 1958*

From the sense as 'the smell of sex'.

- If you ain't reggae for it..funk out! / No-one knocking at your door? / Overpowered by funk? Funk out!—The Clash 1982
- Ambassadors of Funk went out to conquer America and the world. —Alan Shulman, *The Style Bible*, p. 99, 1999
- "I was lucky enough to be the one who created real funk [...]," says James Brown, who, as the godfather of funk, should know.—Ben Osborne, *The A-Z of Club Culture*, p. 102, 1999

4 a depressed state of mind *UK, 1820*

- He fell into a black funk, then snatched the record off the turntable and shattered it with the hammer he kept in the tool box under the kitchen sink.—Armistead Maupin, *Further Tales of the City*, p. 39, 1982
- Lefty came over in a blue funk. His sister heard on the grapevine about his penile eccentricity and told his parents.—C.D. Payne, *Youth in Revolt*, p. 12, 1993

funk; funk it *verb*

to lose your nerve, to have your courage or determination give way *UK, 1857*

- Ulster Unionist leader Mr Trimble said exclusion of Sinn Fein would have been "fair and just" but Mr Reid had "funked it" and chosen to suspend the institutions out of fear of the IRA abandoning its ceasefire altogether.— *The Guardian*, 15th October 2002

funk!

used for expressing anger or disgust *US*

- —Carol Ann Preusse, *Jargon Used by University of Texas Co-Eds*, 1963

funked out *adjective*

drug-intoxicated *US*

- —Eugene Landy, *The Underground Dictionary*, p. 84, 1971

funki dred *noun*

a young blackman who wears his hair in dreadlocks as a part of his fashionable style – not as a profession of Rastafarianism *UK, 1990s*

Deliberate misspellings of **FUNKY** (fashionable) and 'dread' (a dreadlock wearer).

- The doorman looked at the young funki dred. He was sure he'd seen the face before.—Karline Smith, *Moss Side Massive*, p. 98, 1994

funk out *verb*

to become exhausted *BAHAMAS*

- —John A. Holm, *Dictionary of Bahamian English*, p. 83, 1982

funky *adjective*

1 sexual in a primal sense, earthy *US, 1954*

- It was dark in here and loud, the sound cranked way up, but he liked it, the heavy beat, the girls' funky moves as they belted the lyrics, each holding a mike.—Elmore Leonard, *Be Cool*, p. 52, 1999

2 bad, distasteful, dirty, smelly *US*

- Long underwear that looked like the housing project of some gophers on a fresh air kick, about ten sizes too big and five quarts of creosote too funky.—Mezz Mezzrow, *Really the Blues*, p. 33, 1946
- The shop will be open from eight to eight and she'll be setting and washing peoples' funky hair.—Susan Hall, *Gentleman of Leisure*, p. 158, 1972
- It smells like a funky fanny.—Lisa Jewell, *Labia Lobelia [Tart Noir]*, p. 247, 2002

3 earthy, fundamental, emotional, and when applied to music, characterised by blues tonalities *US, 1954*

- She didn't want to dance to the blues, the gut bucket, the funky songs.—Dick Gregory, *Nigger*, p. 60, 1964
- On the other hand one does not want to arrive "poormouthing it"in some outrageous turtleneck and West Eight Street bell-jean combination, as if one is "funky" and of "the people."—Tom Wolfe, *Radical Chic & Mau-Mauing the Flak Catchers*, p. 13, 1970
- The place was musty with cigar smoke and sherry, funky in the Black jazz man's sense of the word.—Odie Hawkins, *The Life and Times of Chester Simmons*, p. 30, 1991

4 fashionable *US, 1969*

- [F]unky boots[.] — *SMTV LIVE it's wicked*, p. 19, 2000

5 in computing, descriptive of a feature that works imperfectly but not poorly enough to justify the time and expense to correct it *US*

- The Intel i860's exception handling is extraordinary funky. — Eric S. Raymond, *The New Hacker's Dictionary*, p. 171, 1991

Funky Fourth *nickname*

the Fourth Army Division *US*

- — Linda Reinberg, *In the Field*, p. 90, 1991

funky-fresh *adjective*

fashionable, stylish *US, 1982*

- Scott and Kris were a funky-fresh brand of b-boy – they waved the culture's contradictions in your face like a dare. — Alan Light, *The Vibe History of Hip-Hop*, p. 148, 1999

funky yellow *noun*

a variety of LSD *UK*

- — Angela Devlin, *Prison Patter*, p. 54, 1996

funny *adjective*

1 homosexual *US*

- — Anthony Romeo, *The Language of Gangs*, p. 18, 4th December 1962

2 odd, strange; hence, unwell *UK*

- She makes me feel funny – like when we climbed rope in gym class. — Dana Carvey, *Wayne's World*, 1991

funny bomb *noun*

a fragmenting explosive *US*

Army use.

- — Linda Reinberg, *In the Field*, p. 90, 1991

funny bone *noun*

the extremity of the *humerus*, specifically that part of the elbow over which the ulnar nerve passes; a notional part of the body that is stimulated by comedy *UK, 1840*

A pun on 'humerus' and 'humorous', stressing the funny-peculiar sensation that is felt when the nerve is struck.

- With each joke an area of the volunteer's pre-frontal cortex lit up, revealing the brain's "funny bone", so to speak. — *The Guardian*, 4th October 2002

funny book *noun*

1 a pornographic book or magazine *US*

- — Len Buckwalter, *CB Radio*, p. 106, 1976

2 in trucking, a driver's daily log book *US*

- — Wayne Floyd, *Jason's Authentic Dictionary of CB Slang*, p. 17, 1976

funny boy *noun*

a male homosexual *US*

- Next to loneliness the biggest problem the trucker encounters on the highway is the "queer," the lollipop artist, the funny boys. They harrass a trucker unmercifully. — Gwyneth A. "Dandalion" Seese, *Tijuana Bear in a Smoke 'Um Up Taxi*, p. 75, 1977

funny bunny *noun*

an eccentric *US, 1966*

- Abominating the cops, crooks, scavengers and funny-bunnies of the twentieth century, he abandons civilization and takes the family to live in the Honduran jungle. — Paul Theroux, *The Great Railway Bazaar*, 1975

funny business *noun*

dishonest enterprises, criminal activities *UK, 1891*

- The last thing I wanted was to get mixed up in any funny business. — Charles Raven, *Underworld Nights*, p. 132, 1956

funny car *noun*

1 in the language of car salesmen, a small car, especially a foreign-made car *US*

- — *American Speech*, p. 312, Autumn-Winter 1975: 'The jargon of car salesmen'

2 in drag racing, a car with a drag racing chassis and engine covered with a fiberglass replica of a conventional car body *US, 1960s*

- — John Edwards, *Auto Dictionary*, p. 67, 1993

funny cigarette *noun*

a marijuana cigarette *US, 1949*

- He looked for new faces standing around on corners and talked to them, and told them he didn't like funny cigarettes or worse sold on his beat and that he had a good memory for faces. — W.E.B. Griffin, *The Murderers*, p. 304, 1994
- They stepped off that plane and put on funny suits, and bought funny cigarettes, and found very young blond girls. — Peter Biskind, *Easy Riders, Raging Bulls*, p. 56, 1998
- Well, the Rock is standing there staring at Stone Cold Steve Austin like he's got three heads, thinking What kind of fuinny cigarettes have you been smoking? — Rock, *The Rock Says*, p. 231, 2000
- What kind of funny cigarettes have you been smoking? What kind of Texas Moonshine have you been pouring down your esophagus? — Rock, *The Rock Says*, p. 231, 2000

funny fag *noun*

a marijuana cigarette *UK*

Formed on **FAG** (a cigarette).

- You can let the coppers have a drag on your funny fag while we're there. — John Milne, *Alive and Kicking*, p. 12, 1998

funny farm *noun*

a hospital for the mentally ill *US, 1959*

- I said, "Not too well. She's on a funny farm." — Iceberg Slim (Robert Beck), *Trick Baby*, p. 173, 1969
- On a Michigan funny farm there are three inmates, each of whom believes he is Jesus Christ. — Tom Robbins, *Another Roadside Attraction*, p. 269, 1971
- The only obstacle is they're shipping me out to the funny farm in four days. — *Natural Born Killers*, 1994
- Dave 1 was well on the road to the funny farm. — Andy McNab, *Immediate Action*, p. 289, 1995
- — Angela Devlin, *Prison Patter*, p. 54, 1996

Funny Farm Express *nickname*

in trucking, a Frozen Foods Express truck *US*

A back formation from the company's initials.

- — Wayne Floyd, *Jason's Authentic Dictionary of CB Slang*, p. 17, 1976

funny five minutes *noun*

a temporary aberration *UK*

- [H]e was hastily demoted, in an email just three minutes later, to "a Liberal Democrat on the committee". Perhaps regular Lib Dem education supremo Phil Willis was having a funny five minutes. — *The Guardian*, 2nd March 2004

funny ha-ha; ha-ha funny *adjective*

amusing, inviting of laughter, as opposed to 'funny' in the sense of peculiar *UK, 1938*

From the oft-cited contrast of **FUNNY PECULIAR** and 'funny ha-ha' by British novelist and dramatist Ian Hay.

- "That bird gives me the creeps. He's funny. Not ha ha funny, but koo koo funny." — Iceberg Slim (Robert Beck), *Mama Black Widow*, p. 33, 1969

funny kine *adjective*

strange, unexpected, abnormal *US*

Hawaiian youth usage.

- Oh, he ac' real funny kine. — Douglas Simonson, *Pidgin to da Max*, 1981

funny money *noun*

1 counterfeit or play currency *US, 1938*

- I tore open the bandana! It was a dummy loaded with funny-money. — Iceberg Slim (Robert Beck), *Airtight Willie and Me*, p. 16, 1979
- I will show you my ten grand buy money before you show me the funny money. — Gerald Petievich, *Money Men*, p. 5, 1981
- Tom was a Geordie whose speciality was funny money[.] — Duncan MacLaughlin, *The Filth*, p. 148, 2002

2 during the Vietnam war, military payment certificates *US*

The certificates were handed out to the military instead of currency to prevent black market use of the US dollar. Denominations of the certificates ranged from five cents to 20 dollars.

- — *Time*, p. 34, 19th December 1965
- — Carl Fleischhauer, *A Glossary of Army Slang*, p. 20, 1968
- The boy was counting MPC, Military Payment Certirficates, GI funny money, which he stuffed into the pockets of his shorts. — Larry Heinemann, *Close Quarters*, p. 40, 1977

3 any foreign currency *UK, 1984*

A resolutely English coinage, disregarding Scottish notes and sneering at the Euro.

4 the scrip issued in Alberta by the Canadian Social Credit party, which advocated free credit and monetary reform; the party became known as the 'funny-money party' *CANADA*

- Solon Low, provincial treasurer in Alberta's first Social Credit Government, later leader of the "funny-money" party's national

representation in Parliament, returned to Raymond High School. — *Time (Canadian edition)*, p. 3, 15th September 1958
- Real Caouette [advocated] the Aberhart free credit or funny-money policies in Quebec. — *Toronto Globe and Mail*, p. 7, 28th February 1963

5 promotional coupons issued by casinos to match money bets *US*
- —Victor H. Royer, *Casino Gamble Talk*, p. 57, 2003

funnyosity *noun*
a *funny*-peculiar curi*osity* *UK*
By elision.
- [I]f you've reached the age of fifty-five and you can't tell the difference between a filly and a colt – you're a funnyosity, that's what you are in your own language – a funnyosity. —Troy Kennedy Martin, *Z Cars*, p. 47, 1962

funny papers *noun*
1 LSD *UK*
A reference to the cartoon images printed on, or simply the effect of, LSD impregnated blotting paper.
- —Angela Devlin, *Prison Patter*, p. 54, 1996

2 topographical maps *US, 1980*
Vietnam war usage; a tad cynical about the accuracy of the military's maps.
- "It must been a Montegnard ville, but it's collapsed and there's new growth over it all. Over." "Any indication of it on your funny papers? Over." "Negative that." —John M. Del Vecchio, *The 13th Valley*, p. 464, 1982

3 building plans *US*
- "You got funny papers?" "Funny papers? "Plans." —Robert Campbell, *Nibbled to Death by Ducks*, p. 79, 1989

funny peculiar *adjective*
funny in the sense of peculiar, as opposed to 'funny ha-ha' (amusing) *UK, 1938*
- Alan Pardew saw the funny side – funny peculiar, that is. — *The Guardian*, 24th February 2003

funny puff *noun*
a marijuana cigarette *US*
- —Warren Smith, *Warren's Smith's Authentic Dictionary of CB*, p. 39, 1976

funny valentine *noun*
a tablet of Dexedrine™, a central nervous system stimulant *US*
A reference to the tablet's heart shape.
- Still popular among the non-psychedlics are the "funny valentines," so called because of their heart shape. —Roger Gordon, *Hollywood's Sexual Underground*, p. 58, 1966

funny ward *noun*
a hospital ward reserved for the mentally ill *US, 1963*
- Once again, Lilah's husband had been summoned to the 'funny' ward at City General. —Marci Blackman, *Po Man's Child*, p. 6, 1999

funny water *noun*
any alcoholic beverage *US, 1974*
- Don Nickles admonished me to stop drinking whatever funny water I had found. —James M. Jeffords, *An Independent Man*, p. 271, 2003

funster *noun*
a joker; a person who reminds you how much fun we are having *US*
The name of a model of Chrysler outboard boat and given a nod in 'Tenement Funster', a song composed by Roger Taylor and recorded by Queen in 1974.
- To succeed in this society of professed funsters a man must be on the make. —Bill Cardoso, *The Maltese Sangweech*, p. 115, 1984

funsy-wunsy *noun*
sex *US*
- And when he wants funsy-wunsy / Pray, what do you give him? I give him the gate! —Cole Porter, *Ladies-in-Waiting*, 1956
- Please, Izzy, we are mature adults. We don't have to refer to it as funsy-wunsy anymore. It's perfectly acceptable to call it whoopie. — *Secret Lives of the Sexists*, 1981

funsy-wunsy *adjective*
fun, cute *US*
- [M]ostly the cameras just observed 'a lot of things that really go down on a tour that are not cute or funsy-wunsy.' —David Downing, *A Dreamer of Pictures*, p. 195, 1995

funt; foont; pfund *noun*
a pound (£); money *UK, 1857*
From German *pfund* pronounced 'foont' and Yiddish *funt*, incorporated into parleyaree and thence polari.
- [A]nyway I'd forgotten my pfund, hadn't I[?] —cast of 'Aspects of Love', Prince of Wales Theatre, *Palare (Boy Dancer Talk) for Beginners*, 1989–92
- —Paul Baker, *Polari*, p. 175, 2002

fun tickets *noun*
money *US*
- Can't make happy hour, Bro. I'm all out of fun tickets. —Vann Wesson, *Generation X Field Guide and Lexicon*, p. 70, 1997

funzine *noun*
a purportedly humorous single-interest fan magazine *US*
- — *American Speech*, p. 26, Spring 1982: 'The langage of science fiction fan magazines'

fur *noun*
1 the female pubic hair; a woman as a sex object *US*
Contemporary use mainly in **FURBURGER**, **FUR PIE**, etc.
- Nothin to do now but smoke unless they knows some place else to buy some fur. —Warren Miller, *The Cool World*, p. 121, 1959
- — *Maledicta*, p. 131, Summer/Winter 1982: 'Dyke diction: the language of lesbians'
- Oohh, I saw a bit of fur then! —Danny King, *The Burglar Diaries*, p. 221, 2001

2 a woman's hairpiece *US*
- —David Claerbaut, *Black Jargon in White America*, p. 65, 1972

▸ **make the fur fly**
to cause uproar, to disturb the status quo *US, 1814*
- Making the fur fly[.] —Jacksonville Jaguars and Carolina Panthers, *The Sporting News*, 18th March 1996

furball *noun*
an aerial dogfight involving several planes *US, 1983*
- During furball, close-in dogfighting, the Vector-A system remained off, and the fighter's original equipment gun sight was used to aim its brace of 20-millimeter cannons. —T.E. Cruise, *Wings of Gold III*, p. 354, 1989
- — *Army*, p. 48, November 1991
- — *American Speech*, p. 390, Winter 1991: 'Among the new words'

fur beef *noun*
a prison sentence for rape *US*
- —John R. Armore and Joseph D. Wolfe, *Dictionary of Desperation*, p. 30, 1976

furburger *noun*
the vagina, especially as an object of oral pleasure-giving; a woman as a sex object *US*
A term that is especially popular with Internet pornographers.
- I found it not at all disagreeable to mix up a few "tinis sours, or stumplifters" in a milk jug, jump into a "flip-top motivatin' unit," and "flazz off" in search of "furburgers." —John Nichols, *The Sterile Cuckoo*, p. 60, 1965
- — *American Speed*, p. 228, October 1967: 'Some special terms used in a University of Connecticut men's dormitory'
- If youse get jack [bored] of stropping the Mulligan and feel like spearing the bearded clam [having sexual intercourse] or tucking into a nice fur-burger, tell the tart you love her! —Barry Humphries, *Bazza Pulls It Off!*, 1971
- —Eugene Landy, *The Underground Dictionary*, p. 85, 1971
- —Robert A. Wilson, *Playboy's Book of Forbidden Words*, p. 118, 1972
- — *American Speech*, p. 59, Spring-Summer 1975: 'Razorback slang'
- —Pamela Munro, *U.C.L.A. Slang*, p. 68, 1997
- —Erica Orloff and JoAnn Baker, *Dirty Little Secrets*, p. 91, 2001

fur coat and no knickers
applied to someone whose surface rectitude masks a less than respectable morality *UK*
- —Mike Harding, *Fur Coat and No Knickers*, 1980
- Forum [a 'swingers' club] members, it said, tended to be above average in status (I think the expression is "all fur coat and no knicker") and, as a consequence, tried to avoid scandal. —Kitty Churchill, *Thinking of England*, p. 131, 1995
- Kettners really is all fur coat and no knickers. It has the aspect of the grandest of establishments (a lustre only emphasised by its champagne bar) yet the menu of a pizzeria. —Jay Rayner, *The Observer*, 28th July 2002

fur cup *noun*
the vagina *US*
- —John D. Bell et al., *Loosely Speaking*, p. 9, 1966
- Why the Fur Cup is Not Just an Inside-Out Cock (Headline) — *Screw*, p. 9, 8th December 1969

▸ **drink of the fur cup**
to perform oral sex on a woman *US*
- —John D. Bell et al., *Loosely Speaking*, p. 9, 1966

furious fifties *noun*
the latitutes of 50 to 59 degrees south *ANTARCTICA, 1906*
- —Bernadette Hince, *The Antarctic Dictionary*, p. 139, 2000

furkid *noun*
a pet whose owner makes much of it *CANADA*
- My girlfriend, who has acres of children, calls pets "furkids," in honour of the mad people who pay creepy tribute to their deceased furry offspring on deranged Web sites.— *Toronto Globe and Mail*, p. F3, 6th July 2002

furlough baby *noun*
a baby born after a serviceman's brief visit home *CANADA*
- A "furlough baby" is a child born as a consequence of a military or navy man's home visit during World War II.—Tom Parkin, *WetCoast Words*, p. 56, 1989

furnace and organ *noun*
a car radio and heater *US*
- — Chrysler Corporation, *Of Anchors, Bezels, Pots and Scorchers*, September 1959

furniture *noun*
a rifle's or a similar weapon's stock *UK*
- There was a torch mounted under the Armalite, held on with bits of masking tape on the furniture.—Andy McNab, *Immediate Action*, p. 37, 1995

furphy *noun*
1 a rumour *AUSTRALIA, 1915*
A similar semantic development can be seen with **SCUTTLEBUTT**. Rarely 'furfy'.
- It is then the 'furphy' manufacturer will come into his own. He will issue special editions daily, each one contradicting the 'dinkum oil' contained in the predecessor.— *Kia Ora Coo-ee*, p. 17, 15th September 1918
- FURPHY – Wild rumour.—Gilbert H. Lawson, *A Dictionary of Australian Words and Terms*, 1924
- —Leonard Mann, *Flesh in Armour*, p. 177, 1932
- 'Or d'you think all the sheilas believe that furfy about matloes bein' built like lower-deck booms?'—J.E. MacDonnell, *Don't Gimme the Ships*, p. 139, 1960
- —Dymphna Cusack, *Picnic Races*, p. 23, 1962
- A stage company with girls, coming to Finnschafen? It isn't just another of your silly furphies?—Ray Slattery, *Mobbs' Mob*, p. 26, 1966
- —Jim Ramsay, *Cop It Sweet!*, p. 38, 1977
- —Barry Humphries, *A Nice Night's Entertainment*, p. 188, 1981
- —Clive Galea, *Slipper*, p. 96, 1988

2 an iron water cart *AUSTRALIA, 1938*
From the name of a manufacturer of such carts.
- Lying there in my bed I'd hear the rattle of kereosene tins, buckets, tin dishes, even the rumble of a horse-drawn furphy, the little iron tank on wheels.—Patsy Adam-Smith, *Folklore of the Australian Railwaymen*, p. 25, 1969

fur pie *noun*
the vulva and pubic hair *US, 1934*
- Candy lay back again with a sigh, closed-eyed, hands joined behind her head, and Grindle resumed his fondling of her sweet-dripping little fur-pie.—Terry Southern, *Candy*, p. 207, 1958
- His face is maybe twelve inches from Sabrina's fur pie, and the guy is fucking snoring.—Carl Hiaasen, *Strip Tease*, p. 19, 1993
- Lee is mistaken for Dweller by Devon Shore, who is as fresh-faced a slice of fur pie you're likely to see in this kinky a video.— Penthouse Magazine, *The Penthouse Erotic Video Guide*, p. 29, 2003

furra *noun*
heroin *UK*
- —Robert Ashton, *This Is Heroin*, p. 205, 2002
- —Mike Haskins, *Drugs*, p. 283, 2003

furry folds *noun*
the vagina *US*
- —Erica Orloff and JoAnn Baker, *Dirty Little Secrets*, p. 71, 2001

furry hoop *noun*
the vagina *AUSTRALIA*
- [T]he randy old bastard [a ghost] can't think of anything else but puttin' his phantom ferret [the penis] through the furry hoop!—Barry Humphries, *Bazza Pulls It Off!*, 1971

furry letterbox *noun*
the vagina *UK*
- Women's genitalia were represented as (potential) containers (e.g., bucket, box, hair goblet), places to put things in (e.g., furry letterbox, disk drive, socket, slot), containers for semen (e.g., gism pot, spunk bin, honey pot), and containers for the penis/sex (e.g., willy warmer, wank shaft, shagbox).— *Journal of Sex Research*, p. 146, 2001

furry monkey *noun*
the vagina *UK*
- Do you wanna have a look at my furry monkey?—Daisy Donovan, *The 11 o'Clock Show*, 1999

fur shur *adverb*
▷ **see: FER SHUR**

further *noun*
▸ **in the further**
in the future *US*
Used when saying goodbye.
- Catch you on the FURTHA.—Malachi Andrews and Paul T. Owens, *Black Language*, p. 76, 1973

further *adverb*
▸ **have it further back**
to know a lot and share that knowledge in talk *CANADA*
- Said of "old fellers that knowed everything" around the [Nova Scotia] LaHave Islands General Store: they had it further back, and wove their experience into their talk.— *Journal of American Folklore*, p. 334, October-December 1972: 'The LaHave Island General Store'

furthermucker *noun*
used as a humorous euphemism for 'motherfucker' *US, 1965*
- He beats everybody in the place once on the pool table and circles around to the first boy he beat and says to him, "Rack 'em up, furthermucker."—Padgett Powell, *Aliens of Affection*, p. 187, 1998

fur tongue *noun*
a sycophant or toady *US*
- — *Maledicta*, p. 16, Summer 1977: 'A word for it!'

fur-trapper *noun*
a thief who distracts hotel guests in the lobby or at the hotel desk long enough to steal their furs *US*
- The fur-trappers were older and bolder.—Dev Collans with Stewart Sterling, *I was a House Detective*, p. 97, 1954

fusebox *noun*
the head *US, 1946*
- —Kenn "Naz" Young, *Naz's Underground Dictionary*, p. 30, 1973

fuselighter *noun*
an artillery soldier *US*
- —Hans Halberstadt, *Airborne*, p. 130, 1988: 'Abridged dictionary of airborne terms'
- —Linda Reinberg, *In the Field*, p. 90, 1991

fushtookanah *adjective*
▷ **see: FARSHTINKENER**

fuss *noun*
▸ **don't make a fuss**
a bus *UK*
Rhyming slang.
- —Julian Franklyn, *A Dictionary of Rhyming Slang*, 1960

fuss *verb*
used as a euphemistic replacement for 'fuck' *US*
- "POK. Fuss you, sisser," Glenn said, drawing himself up.—Earl Thompson, *Tattoo*, p. 59, 1974

fuss-arse *noun*
a fussy person *UK, 1961*
In 2003, usage appears to be mainly limited to south and southwest Wales.

fuss-box *noun*
a finicky, fussy person *UK, 1901*
- —Frank A. Collymore, *Barbadian Dialect*, p. 52, 1965

fussbudget *noun*
a chronic worrier *US, 1904*
- Old Janson is a fussbudget.—Mary McCarthy, *The Group*, p. 326, 1963

fussed *adjective*

▸ **not fussed**

unconcerned *UK, 1988*

- "We are not fussed where they come from," said Sir Ken [Morrison], "but primarily they are coming from Safeway and Sainsbury's." — *The Guardian*, 19th September 2003

fusspot *noun*

a very fussy person *UK, 1921*

A combination of 'fuss', as an indicator of the dominant characteristic, and **-POT** (a person).

- [H]er mother with her middle-class fuss pot idea was coming over to visit them for tea. — Troy Kennedy Martin, *Z Cars*, p. 25, 1962
- Call me a fusspot, but I don't see why the fire-fighting equipment couldn't have gone in the dressing table. — *The Guardian*, 2nd April 2002

fussy *adjective*

finicky *UK*

- I am not now, nor have ever been, what one might describe as a fussy eater[.] — *The Observer*, 14th April 2002

▸ **not fussy**

not especially keen; unconcerned *CANADA, 1984*

- £250,000+ for something more sizeable, though you can get bargains if you're not fussy about location or period details. — *The Guardian*, 11th November 2003

▸ **not that fussy about**

having an aversion to something, not liking it *CANADA*

- The Department of Highways was not that fussy about the slightly lower reaches of the road, either, and there were always petitions demanding "better service for the tax dollar." — Alistair MacLeod, *Island*, p. 274, 2000

futz around *verb*

to waste time; to tinker with no results *US, 1930*

- So I'm futzing around with her new kitten while she's making tea. — Robert Stoller and I.S. Levine, *Coming Attractions*, p. 78, 1991

futz up *verb*

used as a euphemism for 'fuck up', meaning to bungle *US, 1947*

- The deal was futzed up enough as it was, and it didn't make sense. — Jim Thompson, *The Nothing Man*, p. 282, 1954

fuzz *noun*

1 a police officer; the police *US, 1929*

- [H]e told me Fuzz is hangin by his house. — George Mandel, *Flee the Angry Strangers*, p. 167, 1952
- By the way they knocked he knew it was the fuzz[.] — Alexander Trocchi, *Cain's Book*, p. 235, 1960
- — Chris Farlowe, *Buzz with the Fuzz*, 1964
- I used to try Central Park, but the fuzz there thought I was a nut and almost booked me for disturbing the peace. — Nat Hentoff, *Jazz Country*, p. 114, 1965
- Fuzz, man, they want to bust you, they bust you, doesn't matter what the charges, that's the whole fuzz syndrome right there. — Richard Farina, *Been Down So Long*, p. 64, 1966
- But Bible told me he never was busted and never expect to be. "The fuzz can't touch me, man," he say. — Sara Harris, *The Lords of Hell*, p. 12, 1967
- All of us was taking off a joint, and the fuzz busted down on us and shot Dirty Red and Tim. — Donald Goines, *Dopefiend*, p. 154, 1971
- Hey, watch it, fuzz ahead. — *American Graffiti*, 1973
- The fuzz told his partner that it was just a family beef. — A.S. Jackson, *Gentleman Pimp*, p. 152, 1973
- "He's fuzz!" a sharper, older voice said from behind the spot. "Inspector Regan," Jack said, playing it by ear. — *The Sweeney*, p. 13, 1976
- Wasn't that like a cop? Didn't trust the local fuzz, had to come here and see for himself. — Elmore Leonard, *Glitz*, p. 100, 1985

2 the pubic hair, usually on a female *US*

- — *Maledicta*, p. 254, Summer/Winter 1981: 'Five years and 121 dirty words later'
- JAMIE: Two words, three effs [fuck off]. She's got to be a Velcro [lesbian]? LEE: All bets're off if she likes fuzz on fuzz. — Bernard Dempsey and Kevin McNally, *Lock, Stock ... & Two Hundred Smoking Kalashnikovs*, p. 100, 2000

fuzz *verb*

to shuffle (a deck of playing cards) by simultaneously drawing cards from the bottom and top of the deck *US*

- — Albert H. Morehead, *The Complete Guide to Winning Poker*, p. 264, 1967

fuzzball *noun*

a fart *UK*

Generally phrased in the manner of 'someone dropped a fuzzball' and 'who's made the fuzzballs?'.

- — Patrick O'Shaughnessy, *Market Traders' Slang*, 1979

fuzz box *noun*

in electric line work, a noise-producing voltage tester *US*

- — A.B. Chance Co., *Lineman's Slang Dictionary*, p. 7, 1980

fuzzburger *noun*

the vagina as an object of oral pleasure-giving *US*

- — *American Speed*, p. 228, October 1967: 'Some special terms used in a University of Connecticut men's dormitory'

fuzz-buster *noun*

an electronic radar-detection device *US*

- — Wayne Floyd, *Jason's Authentic Dictionary of CB Slang*, p. 17, 1976

fuzzed *adjective*

drug-intoxicated *US*

- I was so fuzzed on White Horse, dexedrine, Miltown and the rages of brain music which beat with alternating triumph and despondency inside my head that my legs and arms felt encased in frozen concrete. — Clancy Sigal, *Going Away*, p. 400, 1961

fuzzie *noun*

a girl or young woman *US*

- Get ride of the fuzzies. We got something to talk about. — Elmore Leonard, *52 Pick-up*, p. 131, 1974

fuzz one; fuzz two; fuzz three *noun*

used as a rating system by US forces in Vietnam for the films shown on base; the system rated films on the amount of pubic hair shown *US*

The more, the better.

- — Gregory Clark, *Words of the Vietnam War*, p. 21–22, 1990

fuzz-spotter *noun*

a rear view mirror *UK*

From **FUZZ** (the police).

- — Douglas Dunford, *Motorcycle Department, Beaulieu Motor Museum*, 1979

fuzztail *noun*

a horse *US*

- — *American Speech*, p. 270, December 1958: 'Ranching terms from eastern Washington'

fuzzy *noun*

1 in horse racing, a horse that is seen as certain to win a race *US*

- — Toney Betts, *Across the Board*, 1956

2 in a deck of playing cards, the joker *US*

- — George Percy, *The Language of Poker*, p. 38, 1988

fuzzy-wuzzy *noun*

1 any black or dark-skinned native of a foreign land *UK, 1892*

A soldier's term, originally of a Sudanese warrior, widened to include all of Africa and islands such as Fiji. Now offensive and disdainful.

- He might as well have been the king of the Fuzzy-Wuzzies, or any other of the inconsequential outlanders that civilized people have looked down their noses at throughout history. — Thomas Cahill, *How the Irish Saved Civilization*, p. 30, 1995

2 (during World War 2) a native of Papua New Guinea *AUSTRALIA, 1942*

- From time to time he gets some leave and this bright yellow man appears (Nan says it's the pills he takes) and gives me some souvenirs, like the bayonet of a dead Japanese soldier or a pair of stone knives made by the Fuzzy-Wuzzies. — Phillip Adams, *The Unspeakable Adams*, p. 2, 1977

3 a dust ball *US*

- The windows hadn't been washed in months, and the rooms were full of dust and fuzzy-wuzzies. — Irving Shulman, *The Amboy Dukes*, p. 24, 1947

fuzzy-wuzzy angel *noun*

(during World War 2) a native of Papua New Guinea who gave assistance to Australian service personnel *AUSTRALIA, 1942*

- The production of the film 'Angels of War', a saga of the part played by Papua New Guineans in the fight against the Nipponese in the last war, has seen a spate of references to the "Fuzzy-Wuzzy Angels" who oftimes brought succour to Australians. — *Canberra Times*, p. 19, 28th April 1982

fwefen *noun*

the vagina *TRINIDAD AND TOBAGO*

- — Lise Winer, *Dictionary of the English/Creole of Trinidad & Tobago*, 2003

fwoarrrgh!

▹ **see: PHWOAR!**

f-word *noun*

1 the word 'fuck' *US*

The intent is to specify one word, out of thousands that begin with 'f,' that the speaker will not use.

- Pressed by Mr. Kuntsler, all she would say was: "Every other word was that 'f' word." — J. Anthony Lukas, *The Barnyard Epithet and Other Obscenities*, p. 29, 1970
- — *American Speech*, Winter 1988
- The infamous f-word, a designation which came into my consciousness several years ago from my children, now seems to have achieved a kind of respectability among adults discussing questions of obscenity. — *Maledicta*, p. 9, 1988 – 1989
- I'd use the F word but Ice Cube got the copyright[.] — MC Serch, *Mic Tecniques*, 1991
- You know. The 'F' word. — Carl Hiaasen, *Native Tongue*, p. 13, 1991
- And he sure liked to say the "F" word alot. "F..." this, and "F..." that. And everytime he said the "F" word all of them people, for some reason, would cheer. — *Forrest Gump*, 1992
- Let me help you Bashful, did it involve the F-word? — *Pulp Fiction*, 1994
- MR. GARRISON: Eric! Did you just say the "F" word? CARTMAN: Fragile? KYLE: No, he's talking about fuck, dude. You can't say fuck in front of Mr. Garrison. — *South Park*, 1999
- [T]hey all used the F-word with the same regularity: as a comma (f'ckin'), for definition (fackin'), or for emphasis (far-kin), and they all looked the same. — Andrew Holmes, *Sleb*, p. 150, 2002
- The F-word and the MF-word. — *The Times Magazine*, p. 43, 16th February 2002

2 fusion (of musical genres) *UK*

In music such fusion is viewed with great trepidation, stressed here by its deliberate confusion with 'fuck'.

- Necmi Calvi does the f-word with Turkish sounds and Western dance beats. — *Songlines*, p. 52, July/August 2002

FYA

used as Internet shorthand to mean '*f*or *y*our *a*musement' *US*

- — Andy Ihnatko, *Cyberspeak*, p. 78, 1997

FYI

used in computer message shorthand to mean '*f*or *y*our *i*nformation' *US*

- — Eric S. Raymond, *The New Hacker's Dictionary*, p. 342, 1991

Gg

G *noun*

1 one thousand dollars; one thousand pounds; one thousand *US, 1928*
From **GRAND**.
- She needs doctors and nurses and a place to live and something to eat for maybe years. Take six or seven gees for that… —Horace McCoy, *Kiss Tomorrow Good-bye*, p. 62, 1948
- I'll even take care of the babe's ten g's out of my end. —Jim Thompson, *A Swell-Looking Babe*, p. 80, 1954
- Everything is going to be O.K. then, maybe next year sometime, when I retire from the ring with several Gs in my kick. —Rocky Garciano (with Rowland Barber), *Somebody Up There Likes Me*, p. 261, 1955
- Gonzalo's regular tip for headwaiters and bandleaders was a "G." —Lee Mortimer, *Women Confidential*, p. 79, 1960
- Suppose you had killed him for $75,000 – would that have been worth it? Ain't no bartender got 75 gees, I answered. —Piri Thomas, *Down These Mean Streets*, p. 219, 1967
- I got to kick this habit you conned me into. I won't give you any headaches. You got to loan me that "G." —Iceberg Slim (Robert Beck), *Pimp*, p. 101, 1969
- And where'd the Church get the 50 G in the first place? — *The Bad Lieutenant*, 1992
- [T]he dangling of a £35g carrot would speed the process[.] —Tony Wilson, *24 Hour Party People*, 2002

2 a gram *UK*
Used mainly in a drug context.
- Course the pukin's fuck all to do with the two gees o' whizz [speed] he does for breakfast. An' an E on top. —Nick Barlay, *Curvy Lovebox*, p. 25, 1997
- [W]hen they said a line they meant half a g for starters. —James Hawes, *White Powder, Green Light*, p. 37, 2002

3 one grain (of a narcotic) *US*
- — *Mr.*, p. 9, April 1966: 'The hippie's lexicon'

4 a generic manufactured cigarette *US*
- —William K. Bentley and James M. Corbett, *Prison Slang*, 1992

5 a gang member *US, 1990*
- [T]he small army of junior G's. —Karline Smith, *Moss Side Massive*, p. 8, 1994

6 a close friend *US, 1989*
- —James Haskins, *The Story of Hip-Hop*, p. 137, 2000

7 a girlfriend *US, 1991*
- —James Haskins, *The Story of Hip-Hop*, p. 137, 2000

8 a G-string *US*
- For a long time, all you can get is belly dancers willing to strip down to their G's. —Robert Campbell, *Boneyards*, p. 191, 1992

<g>

used as Internet shorthand to mean 'grin' conveying amusement *US*
A higher level of amusement may be signalled by a greater number of g's.
- —Andy Ihnatko, *Cyberspeak*, p. 83–84, 1997

g' *adjective*

good, especially in g'day, g'night, g'morning *UK, 1961*

gaar *noun*

the buttocks *TRINIDAD AND TOBAGO, 1987*
- —Lise Winer, *Dictionary of the English/Creole of Trinidad & Tobago*, 2003

gab *noun*

unimportant conversation *UK, 1790*
- 'Give it to me,' said Frost, 'and cut that hipster gab. It's making me sick.' —Terry Southern, *Flash and Filigree*, p. 145, 1958

gabacho; gavacho *noun*

a white person *US*
Derogatory border Spanish used in English conversation by Mexican-Americans.
- —George Carpenter Baker, *Pachuco*, p. 41, 1950
- — *Current Slang*, p. 18, Spring 1970
- —Dagoberto Fuentes and Jose Lopez, *Barrio Language Dictionary*, p. 69, 1974
- — Multicultural Management Program Fellows, *Dictionary of Cautionary Words and Phrases*, 1989

gabalash *verb*

(of quilting) to lash the quilt into the frame with big stitches, so that the precise, tiny stitches of the quilting design itself may be done *CANADA*
The word may derive from blending the two words 'gab' and 'lash', as the quilting sessions are also occasions for talk.
- I can't gabalash it unless you pass me the big needle. —Lewis Poteet, *The South Shore Phrase Book "You're just gabalashing it!"*, p. 50, 1999

gabber *noun*

any central nervous system stimulant *US*
- The pills are actually nothing but rounded bits of plastic with a yellow dust of pure meth. One simply takes thirty or so of these little gabbers, leaving them in their little pill bottle. —Jim Carroll, *Forced Entries*, p. 29, 1987

gabbleguts *noun*

a talkative person *AUSTRALIA, 1966*
- —Arthur Chipper, *The Aussie Swearer's Guide*, p. 65, 1972

gabby bench *noun*

a bench favoured by idle talkers *BAHAMAS*
- —John A. Holm, *Dictionary of Bahamian English*, p. 84, 1982

gabbyguts *noun*

a talkative person *AUSTRALIA*
- You were a bit of a gabbyguts, Bowen. —Wilda Moxham, *The Apprentice*, p. 16, 1969

Gabby Hayes hat *noun*

the field hat worn by US soldiers in Vietnam *US*
Likened to the narrow brim and low crown of the hat worn by the US Western film star Gabby Hayes.
- I dress and gather up my forty-five web belt and Gabby Hayes bush hat. —Larry Heinemann, *Close Quarters*, p. 134, 1977
- — *Maledicta*, p. 260, Summer/Winter 1982: 'Viet-Speak'
- —Linda Reinberg, *In the Field*, p. 91, 1991

gabfest *noun*

a group talk, usually about gossip or trivial matters *US, 1897*
- Jane DePugh to Sandra Giles – pitch-girl for Mark C. Blome Tires, semi-regular on Tom Duggan's TV gabfest. —James Ellroy, *Hollywood Nocturnes*, p. 104, 1994

gabins *noun*

money *TRINIDAD AND TOBAGO*
- —Lise Winer, *Dictionary of the English/Creole of Trinidad & Tobago*, 2003

Gabriel *nickname*

a prisoner who plays the chapel organ *UK, 1950*
- —Angela Devlin, *Prison Patter*, p. 55, 1996

gabs *noun*

trousers made of *gab*ardine (a twill-woven cloth) *UK*
- TONY: (groans) Me whipcord gabs. Ruined! —Ray Galton and Alan Simpson, *Hancock's Half Hour*, 14th June 1955

gack *noun*

1 cocaine *UK*
- [W]e do a couple more dabs of gak from Nood's bag. —Nick Barlay, *Curvy Lovebox*, 1997
- What'd you get for a key of gack, eh? What's that go for? —Kevin Samson, *Outlaws*, p. 18, 2001
- As the Seventies roll around and gak takes over, suddenly Jung can't trust anyone —Simon Lewis, *Uncut*, June 2001
- Checks hooter for gak build-up in the mirror.', p.7. — *Ministry*, January 2002

2 a despised person *US*
- —Vann Wesson, *Generation X Field Guide and Lexicon*, p. 72, 1997

gack *verb*
in poker, to fold holding a hand that would have won had the player stayed in the game *US*
• —John Vorhaus, *The Big Book of Poker Slang*, p. 19, 1996

gack-blowing *noun*
the process of anally ingesting cocaine *UK*
• —Nick Constable, *This is Cocaine*, p. 182, 2002

gacked *adjective*
cocaine-intoxicated *UK*
• —Mike Haskins, *Drugs*, p. 291, 2003

gack-nag; gak-nag *noun*
a cocaine user *UK*
• [T]he previously cuddly [Jason] Donovan was outed as a gak-nag of near unparallelled proportions. —*Ministry*, p. 41, January 2002

gack scab *noun*
a crusting of damaged mucous membrane that forms around the nostrils as the result of inhaling cocaine *UK*
Combines GACK (cocaine) with conventional 'scab'.
• He watched the systematic trickles water the gack scabs around James's nostrils without judgement[.] —Kevin Sampson, *Powder*, p. 218, 1999

gad *noun*
in horse racing, the whip used by jockeys *US*
• —Tom Ainslie, *Ainslie's Complete Guide to Thoroughbred Racing*, p. 331, 1976

gadabout *noun*
a Lada car *UK*
Citizens' band radio slang.
• —Peter Chippindale, *The British CB Book*, p. 161, 1981

Gadaffi *noun*
the NAAFI (Navy, Army and Air Force Institutes) *UK*
In Royal Air Force use, 2002; rhyming slang, based on the name of Lybian leader Colonel Moammar el Gadaffi.

gad daigs!
used for expressing surprise *BAHAMAS*
• Well, gad daigs! The gal look good, eh? —John A. Holm, *Dictionary of Bahamian English*, p. 84, 1982

gadget *noun*
1 used as a general term for any cheating device used in a card game *US*
• —George Percy, *The Language of Poker*, p. 38, 1988
2 in poker, any special rule applied to a game using wild cards *US*
• —Albert H. Morehead, *The Complete Guide to Winning Poker*, p. 264, 1967
3 a G-string or similar female article of clothing *US*
• —Joe McKennon, *Circus Lingo*, p. 38, 1980
4 a US Air Force cadet *US, 1944*
• —*American Speech*, p. 310, December 1946: 'More Air Force Slang'

gadgie *noun*
a man *UK: SCOTLAND*
Noted as 'an idiot or fool' by Micheal Munro, *The Patter*, 1985.
• [Irvine] Welsh, not so rock'n'roll, more of a peace'n'quiet gadgie these days. —*The Scotsman*, 1st August 2003

gaff *noun*
1 a location *UK*
• Keith had visited the Balearics a few years previously and didn't rate the gaff. —Wayne Anthony, *Spanish Highs*, p. 2, 1999
2 a place of residence; home; a shop or other place of business *UK, 1932*
• You had a drink in a boozer down the Nile with Freddie Stokes, then you went round to his gaff —Frank Norman, *Bang To Rights*, p. 122, 1958
• When he's in London he leaps in and out of the bath at Rome Street, S.W.3, our gaff[.] —Derek Raymond (Robin Cook), *The Crust on its Uppers*, p. 23, 1962
• As I left the gaff, Fordy was cheerily bidding farewell to our hosts. —Martin King and Martin Knight, *The Naughty Nineties*, p. 107, 1999
3 a prison cell *UK*
A narrower sense of 'a place of residence'.
• —Angela Devlin, *Prison Patter*, p. 55, 1996
4 a fair or fairground; a place of public amusement *UK, 1753*
Circus.
• In the ring the joey [clown] was a "drip" (useless chap) from the "gaffs" (fairgrounds). —Butch Reynolds, *Broken Hearted Clown*, p. 31, 1953
5 a cheating device *US, 1893*
• —Frank Garcia, *Marked Cards and Loaded Dice*, p. 262, 1962
• There are fellows who laugh when they use the gaff / To take a sucker's dough. —Dennis Wepman et al., *The Life*, p. 162, 1976
• On the midway, he learned the art of "cake cutting," or shortchanging customers, using "sticks" – carnies posing as customers pretending to win a big prize – and "gaffs" – concealed devices such as magnets used to ensure that the house always won. —Kim Rich, *Johnny's Girl*, p. 37, 1993
6 a device used to hide the shape of a male transvestite's penis *US*
• Another device is the "gaff," a cradle, usually made of canvas or denim, to which elastic hoops are attached. The gaff is pulled up tight at the crotch, the effect being to flatten the genitals[.] —George Paul Csicsery (Editor), *The Sex Industry*, p. 74, 1973

gaff *verb*
1 to fix or rig a device *US, 1934*
• Say a mark is right beside you in the joint. Blue is gonna gaff that wheel on your number and heave you a heavy cop to excite the mark. —Iceberg Slim (Robert Beck), *Trick Baby*, p. 93, 1969
2 to cheat *UK, 1811*
• —Lou Shelly, *Hepcats Jive Dictionary*, p. 11, 1945
3 to talk aimlessly and pleasantly *TRINIDAD AND TOBAGO, 1994*
• —Lise Winer, *Dictionary of the English/Creole of Trinidad & Tobago*, 2003

gaffer *noun*
1 used as a form of address *UK: ENGLAND, 1748*
A loose variation of 'gaffer' as 'boss' or 'old man', usually showing respect.
• ALF: All I want is to do what's right. CARDWICK: Look, Gaffer, there's good causes and there's bad causes. —John O'Toole, *The Bush and the Tree [Six Granada Plays]*, p. 35, 1960
2 an employer, a boss, a foreman *UK, 1659*
• I told the gaffer that yer'd probly be interested. —Niall Griffiths, *Kelly + Victor*, p. 141, 2002
3 a senior electrician in a film unit *US*
• —Raymond Spottiswoode, *The Focal Encyclopedia of Film and Television Techniques*, 1969
4 on the railways, a track crew supervisor *US*
• —Ramon Adams, *The Language of the Railroader*, p. 66, 1977
5 in motorcyle racing, a leader of a racing team *US*
• —John Lawlor, *How to Talk Car*, p. 53, 1965
6 in circus and carnival usage, a manager *US*
• —Don Wilmeth, *The Language of American Popular Entertainment*, p. 105, 1981

gaffle *noun*
in street gambling, a protocol under which the winner shares his winnings with other players *US*
• —*American Speech*, p. 406, Winter 1997: 'Among the new words'

gaffle *verb*
1 to steal *US, 1900*
• —Vincent J. Monteleone, *Criminal Slang*, p. 93, 1949
• Go in and gaffle the money and run to one of your aunt's cribs[.] —Eminem Marshall Mathers, *Guilty Conscience*, 1999
2 to arrest; to catch *US, 1954*
• I heard they had you gaffled. The goon squad. Someone said they marched you right across the yard. —Malcolm Braly, *On the Yard*, 1967
• Far as she was concerned, the feds who gaffled him up were angels of mercy. —Seth Morgan, *Homeboy*, p. 49, 1990
• Besides, the way we got gaffled up by the sheriff's at the muthafucka? —*Menace II Society*, 1993
3 to cheat, to swindle, to defraud *US*
• —Ethan Hilderbrant, *Prison Slang*, 1998

gaffs *noun*
dice that have been altered for cheating *US*
• —*The Annals of the American Academy of Political and Social Sciences*, p. 125, May 1950

gaff shot *noun*
in pool, an elaborate shot, especially an illegal one *US, 1985*
• —Mike Shamos, *The Illustrated Encyclopedia of Billiards*, p. 106, 1993

gaffus *noun*

a hypodermic syringe and needle, especially when improvised *US, 1967*

- —Richard A. Spears, *The Slang and Jargon of Drugs and Drink*, p. 208, 1986
- —Mike Haskins, *Drugs*, p. 292, 2003

gafu *noun*

a collosal mistake *NEW ZEALAND*

A '*g*od *a*lmighty *f*uck-*u*p'.

- —David McGill, *David McGill's Complete Kiwi Slang Dictionary*, p. 53, 1998

gag *noun*

1 a manner of doing something, a practice *US, 1890*

- John McEnroe used that gag in every successful tennis match.—Joseph Wambaugh, *Finnegan's Week*, p. 110, 1993

2 in the television and film industries, a stunt *US*

- —John Cann, *The Stunt Guide*, p. 59,: 'Terms and definitions'
- [He would] watch movies on cable TV, cars burning in flames, stunt men being shot off of high places – see if he could recognize the work, or how it was done if it was a new gag[.]—Elmore Leonard, *Freaky Deaky*, p. 179, 1988

3 any artifice employed by a beggar to elicit sympathy *US*

- —Joseph E. Ragen and Charles Finston, *Inside the World's Toughest Prison*, p. 800, 1962: 'Penitentiary and underworld glossary

4 an event or activity contrived to provide amusement or excitement *UK*

- —Angela Devlin, *Prison Patter*, p. 55, 1996

5 an indefinite prison sentence *US*

- —*New York Times Magazine*, p. 88, 16th March 1958

6 a small group of close friends *US*

- —Judi Sanders, *Mashing and Munching in Ames*, p. 8, 1994

7 a quick use of cocaine *US*

- —Anna Scotti and Paul Young, *Buzzwords*, p. 130, 1997

8 in craps, a bet that the shooter will make his even-numbered point in pairs *US*

- —*The Annals of the American Academy of Political and Social Sciences*, p. 125, May 1950

gag *verb*

to panic in the face of a great challenge *US*

- —Michael V. Anderson, *The Bad, Rad, Not to Forget Way Cool Beach and Surf Discriptionary*, p. 7, 1988

gaga *adjective*

1 infatuated, silly *UK, 1917*

- "I'm gaga with curiousity. Tell us," Kate said.—James T. Farrell, *Saturday Night*, p. 21, 1947
- "Maybe the debs can't do the job as well as the regulars, but they don't go ga-ga when they see a DePuyster," he said.—Jack Lait and Lee Mortimer, *New York Confidential*, p. 52, 1948
- I do what I know they want, make believe I'm ga-ga over them. —John M. Murtagh and Sara Harris, *Cast the First Stone*, p. 165, 1957
- You think he's gonna go ga-ga over this one before he checks her out?—Robert Campbell, *Alice in La-La Land*, p. 166, 1987

2 mad, especially as a result of senility *UK, 1920*

- His grandfather must be ga-ga to think up such a crazy fucking thing..—Richard Condon, *Prizzi's Glory*, 1988
- For how much of his presidency was Reagan gaga?—*The Observer*, p. 61, 21st March 1993
- Rumour had it she [a little old lady] went gaga. Started swearing every time she opened her mouth[.]—Jenny Eclair, *Camberwell Beauty*, p. 37, 2000
- [T]he dependably gaga Charlton Heston[.]—John Patterson, *The Guardian*, 25th July 2003

gag-awful *adjective*

horrible *US*

- —Connie Eble (Editor), *UNC-CH Campus Slang*, p. 3, Fall 1981

gage *noun*

1 marijuana *US, 1934*

Also variants 'gauge' and 'gages'.

- I passed a stick of gauge around for the other boys to smoke[.]—Mezz Mezzrow, *Really the Blues*, p. 72, 1946
- It's only gauge he's on, a little jive. Marijuana ain't no habit like heroin.—George Mandel, *Flee the Angry Strangers*, p. 20, 1948
- Three teenage boys had a fifteen-year-old girl inside, all blowing gage.—Chester Himes, *A Rage in Harlem*, 1957
- That gage done got me into more trouble now than I can get out of. —Chester Himes, *The Real Cool Killers*, p. 49, 1959
- Shorty would take me to groovy, frantic scenes in different chicks' and cats' pads, where with the lights and juke down mellow, everybody blew gage and juiced back and jumped.—Malcolm X and Alex Haley, *'The Autobiography of Malcolm X*, 1964
- I could not see how they were more justified in drinking than I was in blowing the gage.—Eldridge Cleaver, *Soul on Ice*, p. 4, 1968
- The lion let out with a mighty rage / Like a young cocksucker blowing his gauge.—Anonymous ("Arthur"), *Shine and the Titanic; The Signifying Monkey; Stackolee*, p. 1, 1971
- I mentioned knowing a pot connection who might be around although I hadn't seen him since getting out of jail – that I liked smoking pot – we called it gauge or tea in those days[.]—Herbert Huncke, *The Evening Sun Turned Crimson*, p. 81, 1980
- I passed a stick of gage around for the other boys to smoke and we started a set.—Harry Shapiro, *Waiting For The Man*, 1999
- —Mike Haskins, *Drugs*, p. 287, 2003

2 alcohol, especially whisky *US, 1932*

- —Lou Shelly, *Hepcats Jive Dictionary*, p. 11, 1945

▸ **get a gage up**

to smoke a marijuana cigarette *UK, 1998*

- —Mike Haskins, *Drugs*, p. 290, 2003

gage butt *noun*

a marijuana fashioned cigarette *US, 1938*

- —Ernest L. Abel, *A Marijuana Dictionary*, p. 41, 1982

gaged *adjective*

drug-intoxicated *US, 1932*

- Jodie was gaged on heroin and kept snapping that knife open and shut and looking at me as if he'd like to cut my throat.—Chester Himes, *A Rage in Harlem*, p. 225, 1957

gage out; guage out *verb*

to become, or be, sleepy as a result of marijuana intoxication *UK*

- [W]e'd mong and guage out.—Macfarlane, Macfarlane and Robson, *The User*, p. 92, 1996

gagers; gaggers *noun*

methcathinone *US, 1998*

- —US Office of National Drug Control Policy *Drug Facts*, February 2003

gagged *adjective*

disgusted *US*

- —Collin Baker et al., *College Undergraduate Slang Study Conducted at Brown University*, p. 123, 1968

gagging *adjective*

desperately craving something, such as a cigarette, a drink or sex *UK, 1997*

- The woman's name was Samantha and although I didn't wish to judge a book by its cover, when the cover said Razzle, I had to agree. Samantha was gagging for it.—Kitty Churchil, *Thinking of England*, 1995
- Most of them [...] were "gagging for a bit of Regimental pipe".—Chris Ryan, *The Watchman*, 2001
- Scuse me, everybody, but I'm gagging for it.—Ben Elton, *High Society*, 2002
- But is he posh [in possession of drugs]? – He'd bloody better be, I'm gagging. – Mmmm.—James Hawes, *White Powder, Green Light*, p. 205, 2002
- Now, shall we go to the bar and get a drink? I'm gagging.—Colin Butts, *Is Harry Still on the Boat?*, p. 293, 2003

gagging for a blagging *adjective*

used of banks, etc, that exhibit poor security *UK*

A combination of GAGGING (desperate for something) and BLAGGING (a robbery with violence).

- Trevor also planned and carried out armed heists on various security vans that deliberately invited robbery by their provocative habit of driving to the same banks and building societies at the same time every week. That, said Trev, meant they were just[.]—Garry Bushell, *The Face*, p. 79, 2001

gaggle *noun*

a formation of several military aircraft flying the same mission *US, 1942*

- —*American Speech*, p. 118, May 1963: 'Air refueling words'

gaggler *noun*

1 MDMA, the recreational drug best known as ecstasy *UK*

- —Mike Haskins, *Drugs*, p. 289, 2003

2 amphetamines *UK*

- —Mike Haskins, *Drugs*, p. 279, 2003

gag me!; gag me with a spoon!

used for expressing disgust *US*

A quintessential Valley Girl expression of disgust.

- He like sits there and like plays with all his rings / And he like flirts with all the guys in the class / It's like totally disgusting / I'm like so sure / It's like BARF ME OUT / Gag me with a spoon!—Moon Unit and Frank Zappa, *Valley Girl*, 1982
- —Connie Eble (Editor), *UNC-CH Campus Slang*, p. 2, Fall 1982

gagster *noun*
a comedian *UK, 1935*
- The gagster and his girl staggered out of the place and reported in at the nearest hospital[.] — Robert Sylvester, *No Cover Charge:*, p. 205, 1956

Gainesburger *noun*
in the military, canned beef patties *US*
Alluding to a dog food product. Vietnam war usage.
- "Gainesburgers," said Banjo. We had named the army's canned ground beef patties, served in gravy, after the dog food. — Robert Mason, *Chickenhawk*, p. 81, 1983

Gainesville green *noun*
marijuana grown in or near Gainesville, Florida *US, 1976*
- — *American Speech*, Winter 1982

gak-nag *noun*
▷ see: GACK-NAG

gal *noun*
a woman or a girl *UK, 1795*
This gal is a woman with a chequered history: 'Cockney for girl', 1824, but then the pronunciation worked its way up the social ladder until, by about 1840, it was quite upper-class. From around 1850 a 'gal' was a 'servant girl' or a 'harlot', and from about 1860, a 'sweetheart' as used by Albert Chevalier in *My Old Dutch*, 1893. The current sense is recorded in US jazz and jive circles from the 1930s. By the turn of the millennium, having passed through respectability once again, 'gal' was patronising or kitsch, and rarely found without 'guys'.
- She's a dear good old gal, I'll tell yer all about 'er[.] — Albert Chevalier, *My Old Dutch*, 1893
- No hooch, no gals, no nothing. — Raymond Chandler, *Farewell My Lovely*, p. 5, 1940
- Gators, Guys and Gals. You have been initiated to the lingo of the hep people. — Lavada Durst, *The Jives of Dr. Hepcat*, 1953
- Lucky's my best friend but he ain't no gal — Robin Miller and George Haimsohn, *Dames At Sea*, 1968
- Welcome Couples, Single Gals and Single Guys! Meet Real People Who Want Sex With You Now! — *Internet advertisement*, 2001

galactic *adjective*
great, wonderful, amazing *US*
- One of the boys says it was cool. Another says it was galactic. — Melanie McGrath, *Hard, Soft & Wet*, p. 22, 1998

galah *noun*
a fool *AUSTRALIA, 1938*
From the name of an endemic Australian cockatoo, commonly kept as a cage bird, and able to be coaxed into antic behaviour. The name of the bird comes from the Australian Aboriginal language Yuwaalaraay.
- The big galah might be silly enough to blab it around the mill[.] — Robert S. Close, *With Hooves of Brass*, p. 41, 1961
- Jeez, those two galahs really put the wind up me! — Barry Humphries, *The Wonderful World of Barry McKenzie*, p. 11, 1968
- It'll be a ripsnorter of a tournie, and you'd be a galah if you missed it. — *Australian Ultimate*, p. 7, 2003

galba *noun*
the penis *TRINIDAD AND TOBAGO*
- — Lise Winer, *Dictionary of the English/Creole of Trinidad & Tobago*, 2003

gal block *noun*
a section of a prison reserved for blatantly homosexual prisoners *US*
- One night they was here and everybody in the gal block knew about it and he called me out. — Bruce Jackson, *In the Life*, p. 398, 1972

gal-boy *noun*
an effeminate young man *US*
- You willing to fight anybody wants you as their gal-boy? — Elmore Leonard, *Bandits*, p. 144, 1987

galf *noun*
a girlfriend *US*
A reduction of 'galfriend'.
- My ex-galf'd got mad at me[.] — Lester Bangs, *Psychotic Reactions and Carburetor Dung*, p. 288, 1979

Galilee stompers *noun*
in homosexual usage, sandals *US*
- — *Maledicta*, p. 56, 1986 – 1987: 'A continuation of a glossary of ethnic slurs in American English'

gall *noun*
effrontery, impudence *US, 1882*
- Hip-hop labels are rarely known for their subtlety, but few would have the gall to interrupt an album by their biggest female singer with an ad for a forthcoming album by a different artist[.] — *The Guardian*, 20th June 2003

gallery 13 *noun*
a prison graveyard *US*
- — Ralph de Sola, *Crime Dictionary*, p. 56, 1982
- — William K. Bentley and James M. Corbett, *Prison Slang*, 1992

gallery god *noun*
a threatre-goer who sits in the uppermost balcony *US*
- During the early part of my career as a theater fan I was a "gallery god." All gallery seats were unreserved. — *San Francisco Examiner*, p. 21, 12th August 1947

gallon *noun*
a container for liquid, without regard to the precise volume *FIJI*
Recorded by Jan Tent in 1993.

gallop *verb*
▸ **gallop the lizard**
(of a male) to masturbate *AUSTRALIA*
- They're lucky if they've got the energy to buy Playboy and gallop the lizard. — Barry Humphries, *The Traveller's Tool*, p. 61, 1985
- Yeah, you've really got him gallopin' the lizard. — Kathy Lette, *Girls' Night Out*, p. 167, 1987

galloper *noun*
a racehorse *AUSTRALIA, 1960*
- — Maurice Cavanough and Meurig Davies, *Cup Day*, p. 14, 1960
- — James Holledge, *The Great Australian Gamble*, p. 23, 1966
- Thereafter, although he always had one or two gallopers in his stables, he was primarily a punter. — James Holledge, *The Great Australian Gamble*, p. 53, 1966
- A well-performed city galloper had been entrered, under a false name, in a mediocre field, in a minor race, at a country course. — Roy Higgins and Tom Prior, *The Jockey Who Laughed*, p. 38, 1982
- — Joe Andersen, *Winners Can Laugh*, p. 81, 1982

galloping *adjective*
worsening *UK, 1785*
- The soldier had died a few hours after he came into the hospital on the fourth day; he had had galloping pneumonia. — Norman Mailer, *The Naked and the Dead*, p. 371, 1950

galloping bones *noun*
dice *US, 1920*
- Kate and I were right at home with all those little clicking wheels and felt tables and galloping bones and slot machines. — Albert Murray, *Godd Morning Blues*, p. 364, 1985

galloping dandruff *noun*
body lice *US, 1920*
- No point in sending squad cars screaming around the countryside if granny's demise had been by galloping dandruff and not the hand of a desperate ruffian. — Keith McCarthy, *A Feast of Carrion*, p. 22, 2003

galloping dominoes *noun*
dice *US, 1918*
- — Thomas L. Clark, *The Dictionary of Gambling and Gaming*, p. 88, 1987

galloping horse *noun*
heroin *US, 1959*
An elaboration of **HORSE** (heroin).
- — Richard A. Spears, *The Slang and Jargon of Drugs and Drink*, p. 212, 1986
- — Robert Ashton, *This Is Heroin*, p. 205, 2002
- — Mike Haskins, *Drugs*, p. 284, 2003

gallops *noun*
horse racing *AUSTRALIA, 1950*
- It was the same at the gallops. — Wilda Moxham, *The Apprentice*, p. 84, 1969
- Abie and Asher, two addicts of the gallops, met on the way home from Randwick races. — Frank Hardy and Athol George Mulley, *The Needy and the Greedy*, p. 67, 1975
- — Roy Higgins and Tom Prior, *The Jockey Who Laughed*, p. 85, 1982
- I thought you more a gallops man. — Frank Hardy, *Hardy's People*, p. 157, 1986

gallup *noun*
heroin *UK*
Building on the **HORSE** image.
- — Robert Ashton, *This Is Heroin*, p. 205, 2002
- — Mike Haskins, *Drugs*, p. 284, 2003

gallus; gallows *adjective*

attractive, wonderful; self-confident, quick-witted, brave, ostentatious, nonchalant; also used as an intensifier *UK, 1789*

A phonetic slurring of 'gallows', suggesting 'fit for the gallows' and thus 'wicked' – a very early example of 'bad' means 'good'. In the US from the 1840s to 1940s.

- Pure gallus, so they are. — Ian Pattison, *Rab C. Nesbitt*, 1988
- We are the people meant we are the people. It was just a gallus affirmation of being happy with who you were, and good luck to anyone who felt that way. — Christopher Brookmyre, *The Sacred Art of Stealing*, p. 338, 2002

galoot; galloot *noun*

a man, especially if hulking, stupid, boorish, foolish, clumsy or otherwise objectionable *UK, 1818*

Possibly from Dutch *gelubt* (a eunuch).

- Go on, you galoot, it's about time we got into our togs. — Norman Lindsay, *The Cousin from Fiji*, p. 263, 1945
- The goose thereafter laid up a storm, and Jack, who was no astute galoot, went on a toot with a local beaut, bought himself a zooty suit and still had a little loot to boot. — Steve Allen, *Bop Fables*, p. 66–68, 1955
- I don't want verite, you crazy galoot, I want poetry! — Terry Southern, *Now Dig This*, p. 11, 1986
- Look how pleased he is to see YT [me], the big galloot. — Kevin Sampson, *Outlaws*, p. 5, 2001

gal pal *noun*

1 a woman's female friend *US*

- Angela was not only married, she was a friend of Maria's. Needless to say, it created a bit of tension between gal pals. — Erica Orloff and JoAnn Baker, *Dirty Little Secrets*, p. 141, 2001

2 a female friend of a male homosexual *US*

- — Bruce Rodgers, *The Queens' Vernacular*, p. 92, 1977

gal tank *noun*

a holding cell in a jail reserved for homosexual prisoners *US*

- There's punks all over the place in the gal tank. — Bruce Jackson, *In the Life*, p. 399, 1972

galvanise *noun*

sheets of corrugated iron *BARBADOS*

- The house is roofed with galvanise. — Frank A. Collymore, *Barbadian Dialect*, p. 52, 1965

galvo *noun*

galvanised iron *AUSTRALIA, 1945*

Iron corrugated sheets are a common building material in rural Australia.

- But just as often I prefer to listen to the wind in the trees or the rain on the galvo. — Phillip Adams, *The Unspeakable Adams*, p. 3, 1977

gam *noun*

1 the leg *UK, 1785*

Originally applied to a crippled leg, later to a woman's leg.

- For the rest of her career in Hollywood, while her gams are still straight and her figure otherwise, she'll pose cheesecake for fan-mags and Sunday sheets[.] — Jack Lait and Lee Mortimer, *New York Confidential*, p. 145, 1946
- Those gams. Next to her, Diedrick is a pellagra case. — Bernard Wolfe, *The Late Risers*, p. 143, 1954
- A flash of the harlequin's crotch-zinging legs reminded him of Rachel's gams. — Iceberg Slim (Robert Beck), *Death Wish*, p. 113, 1977
- Beats looking at Bonny Prince Charles's skinny gams under a kilt. — Rita Ciresi, *Pink Slip*, p. 50, 1999
- "Has anybody ever told you," he asked, "that you have a really gorgeous set of gams?" — Claire Mansfield and John Mendelssohn, *Dominatrix*, p. 78, 2002

2 an act of oral sex *UK*

Also variant 'gambo'.

- I heard a prostitute in Malaya, 1954, on being asked her charge, say, "I no fuck. I holiday. But, I give you gam for ten bucks." — Beale, 1984
- [She] starts giving us a gam. — Kevin Sampson, *Outlaws*, p. 217, 2001

gam *verb*

1 to pretend *IRELAND*

- Them are the ones that gam on not to know you when they meet you. — Murphy Tom, *A Whistle in the Dark*, p. 13, 1989

2 to boast *US*

- — Clarence Major, *Dictionary of Afro-American Slang*, p. 57, 1970

3 to perform oral sex *UK*

- — Paul Baker, *Polari*, p. 175, 2002

gamahuche *noun*

an act of oral sex *UK, 1865*

Possibly a combination of Scots dialect words *gam* (gum, mouth) and *roosh* (rush), hence a 'rushing into the mouth'; more likely from French *gamahucher* which shares the same sense.

- [S]he always did it with her men, and said they were made for it; it's what they call gamahuching, the French pleasure. — William Gibson, *The Difference Engine*, p. 236, 1991
- Sitting there, he's watched himself on the editing machine fall out of bed and out of focus, go limp in a stockyard, sneeze in the middle of a gamahuche[.] — Robert Coover, *The Adventures of Lucky Pierre*, p. 120, 2002
- Gamahuche? Sure. All of my girlfriends here are in the lust business. There's not much I haven't heard of. — Michelle Black, *The Second Glass of Absinthe*, p. 77, 2003

gambage *noun*

showing off *TRINIDAD AND TOBAGO, 1940*

- — Lise Winer, *Dictionary of the English/Creole of Trinidad & Tobago*, 2003

Gamble and Procter; gamble *noun*

a doctor *UK*

Rhyming slang, formed on a reversal of the pharmaceutical company Procter and Gamble.

- — Ray Puxley, *Fresh Rabbit*, 1998

gambler's bankroll; gambler's roll *noun*

a bankroll consisting of a large-denomination note on the outside of a number of small-denomination notes *US*

- Whistler took out his gambler's roll. A fifty was on top. You'd think he was carrying big money if you didn't know the rest was ones with maybe a couple of fives. — Robert Campbell, *In La-La Land We Trust*, p. 96, 1986

game *noun*

1 an athlete's style and ability *US*

- — Connie Eble (Editor), *UNC-CH Campus Slang*, p. 3, Fall 1997
- You like Kobe's game? I do. — *Gone in 60 Seconds*, 2000

2 a person's style, visual and oral *US*

- Now the monkey had practiced his game till it was sharp as glass / And keep in his heart he knew he could kick the baboon's ass. — Dennis Wepman et al., *The Life*, p. 31, 1976
- You look at any dude out here got a real strong game together like I do, it's cause they got theyself a strong lady like this one. — John Sayles, *Union Dues*, p. 183, 1977

3 a conventional attitude *UK*

A counterculture concept that refuses to accept non-drop-out society as anything more than a game with unnecessary rules.

- — Burton H. Wolfe, *The Hippies*, 1967

4 a criminal activity; crime as a profession *UK, 1739*

- Once these guys got hip to themselves and went into the bootlegging game, big money started to show up. — Mezz Mezzrow, *Really the Blues*, p. 20, 1946
- This game's too risky for the small amount of dough we get out of it. — Vince Kelly, *The Bogeyman*, p. 20, 1956
- I couldn't wait to get out the game and get into the media lark. — Dave Courtney, *Dodgy Dave's Little Black Book*, p. 20, 2001

5 business *AUSTRALIA, 1877*

- 'She's a cow of a game,' said Tom. — Gavin Casey, *It's Harder for Girls*, p. 164, 1941
- — Dominic Healy, *A Voyage to Venus*, p. 128, 1943
- Yer look a bit posh ter me for this game. — Nino Culotta (John O'Grady), *They're A Weird Mob*, p. 35, 1957

6 an attempt to con *US*

- Bart, I know when I hear it. You're trying to hustle me for two grand. — Charles W. Moore, *A Brick for Mister Jones*, p. 142, 1975

7 sex appeal *US*

- — Connie Eble (Editor), *UNC-CH Campus Slang*, p. 5, Fall 1999

8 an interest in the opposite sex *US*

- "You got game?" continued Cochrane. "You can play some ball?" — *The Observer*, p. 19, 18th March 2001

9 a romantic or sexual relationship outside your primary relationship *UK*

Synonymous with **PLAY AROUND**; also, 'game' has strong sexual overtones, as in **ON THE GAME** (engaged in prostitution).

- I began to have a strong sus that Billie was having games although I was still getting letters and she was still coming to see me every month. — Frank Norman, *Bang To Rights*, p. 44, 1958

▸ give the game away
to cease doing something; to abandon; to give up *AUSTRALIA, 1953*
- He hid his face in his arms, trembling. 'Let him be, Lash,' I whispered. 'He's given the game away.' — Eric Lambert, *The Veterans*, p. 129, 1954
- If I couldn't run two homes on ten thousand quid I'd give the game away. — John Morrison, *Stories of the Waterfront*, p. 28, 1962
- — Jim Ramsay, *Cop It Sweet!*, p. 40, 1977

▸ on the game
to be working as a prostitute *UK, 1898*
- His old woman who was a brass on the game down the Baze. — Frank Norman, *Bang To Rights*, p. 8, 1958
- When I first went on the game, it seemed to me that I was meeting a gallery of widely various and interesting people. — Anonymous *Streetwalker*, p. 14, 1959
- [T]he eldest daughter is on the game and has three kids by different fathers[.] — Martin King and Martin Knight, *The Naughty Nineties*, p. 137, 1999

▸ out of the game
married, engaged or dating only one person *US*
- — Don R. McCreary (Editor), *Dawg Speak*, 2001

▸ run a game
to fool, to swindle *US, 1940*
- Jinx had a pretty long run, then he tried to run a game on a friend of mine. Shakedown. So much per week 'cause I'm bad. — Edwin Torres, *Carlito's Way*, p. 15, 1975
- Oh, so you trying run that game, huh? — *Boyz N The Hood*, 1990

▸ the game
the business of prostitution *UK, 1898*
- Probably this was her way of letting me know that she would be available if I would give up the game. — Donald Goines, *Whoreson*, p. 137, 1972
- Pimps often call themselves "the players" and their profession "The Game[.]" — Christina and Richard Milner, *Black Players*, p. 10, 1972
- The game is deep. In being a mack, you're supposedly the supreme being of man. — Susan Hall, *Gentleman of Leisure*, p. 39, 1972
- You see, my dear reader, I lived true to the code of the game. — A.S. Jackson, *Gentleman Pimp*, p. 156, 1973
- — Angela Devlin, *Prison Patter*, p. 55, 1996

Game *noun*

▸ the Game
the criminal lifestyle *US*
- Well it's all the same, 'cause it's all in the Game / As I dug when I set out to play. — Dennis Wepman et al., *The Life*, p. 59, 1976

game *verb*

1 to deceive, to mislead, to trick *US, 1963*
- I have the vague hope that he's "gaming," playing the con, for the heartless white folks for some personal benefit or advantage. — Iceberg Slim (Robert Beck), *The Naked Soul of Iceberg Slim*, p. 19, 1971
- Obviously you do not know that you are in the presence of a superior jailhouse intellect that does not enjoy being gamed. — James Ellroy, *Suicide Hill*, p. 576, 1986

2 to flirt; to woo *US*
- Cause I'm gamin' on a female that's gamin' on me — NWA *I Ain't Tha 1*, 1988
- You think you gaming on 'em and they the ones that gaming you. — *Boyz N The Hood*, 1990

game!
used for expressing that enough is enough *US*
- — Anna Scotti and Paul Young, *Buzzwords*, p. 63, 1997

game as a pissant *adjective*
very courageous *AUSTRALIA, 1944*
- To be classified 'game as a pissant' is to be praised very highly indeed. — John O'Grady, *Aussie English*, p. 68, 1965

game face *noun*
in sports, a serious expression and demeanour reflecting complete concentration on the competition at hand *US*
Now used outside of sports, extended to any serious situation.
- I guess I'm up early because this is Friday and it will be our last serious work-out of the week. I believe I'm getting my game-face on. — Dan Jenkins, *Semi-Tough*, p. 90, 1972

gameless *adjective*
unskilled *US*
- — Connie Eble (Editor), *UNC-CH Campus Slang*, p. 2, November 1983

game of nap *noun*

1 a cap *UK*
Rhyming slang, from the card game.
- You'd better take your game of nap and Aunt Ella [umbrella]. — *The Sweeney*, p. 9, 1976

2 an act of defecation *UK*
Rhyming slang for **CRAP**.
- Sorry I'm late, I was having a game of nap. — Ray Puxley, *Cockney Rabbit*, 1992

game over!
used for expressing that enough is enough *US*
- — Anna Scotti and Paul Young, *Buzzwords*, p. 63, 1997

gamer *noun*

1 a video game or role-playing game enthusiast *US*
- Wars are declared at home, in library basements and in hotel rooms in weekends, where gamers stockpile cases of beer and munchies and barricade themselves against the world. — *Washington Post*, p. 3 (Weekend), 14th October 1977
- — Connie Eble (Editor), *UNC-CH Campus Slang*, p. 4, November 2003

2 an athlete who can always be counted on for a gritty, all-out effort *US*
- She [Chris Evert] doesn't say anything because she doesn't like to have any excuses. She's a gamer. — *Washingotn Post*, p. C1, 9th September 1977
- But he [Rob DiMaio] is, the Bruins believe, a gamer. — *The Boston Globe*, p. D3, 3rd October 1996

3 a person engaged in swindles and hustles as a way of life *US*
- All of New Yorks biggest gamers saw a bitch whip this cat's ass and she didn't come on the scene for weeks. — Babs Gonzales, *Movin' On Down De Line*, p. 45, 1975

game refuge *noun*
any institution where traffic violators who are under pursuit are free from further pursuit once they pass the gates *US*
- — *American Speech*, p. 267, December 1962: 'The language of traffic policemen'

games and sports; games *noun*
warts *UK*
Rhyming slang.
- [L]ooks like I've got a bad dose of games. — Bodmin Dark, *Dirty Cockney Rhyming Slang*, 2003

gamey eye *noun*
a tendency to flirt *IRELAND*
- You've a gamey eye. I've seen you in action often enough. — Joseph O'Connor, *Red Roses and Petrol*, p. 9, 1995

gamma delta iota *noun*
a college student who is not a fraternity or sorority member; a notional fraternity or sorority comprised of students who don't belong to fraternites or sororities *US*
A back formation from **GDI** (god damn independent).
- I got around fifteen desirable pledges to quit the three major sororities and form our own, GDI- Gamma Delta Iota or God Damn Independents. — Leorge Tanenbaum, *Slut! Growing Up Female with a Bad Reputation*, p. 61, 2000
- [T]hey so dictated the terms of student life that the Gamma Delta Iota movement began. — Murray Sperber, *Beer and Circus*, p. 4, 2001

gammon *noun*
one microgram *US*
The unit of measurement for LSD doses, even in the non-metric US.
- — Richard Lingeman, *Drugs from A to Z*, p. 81, 1969

gammon rasher *noun*
a superlative thing *UK*
Rhyming slang for **SMASHER**.
- "Ennit a gammon rasher!" is used in appreciation of almost anything. — Dave Hillman, 1974

gammy *adjective*

1 inferior, of low quality *UK*
As in 'gammy gear' (inferior goods).
- — Patrick O'Shaughnessy, *Market Traders' Slang*, 1979

2 lame *UK, 1879*
- [C]rusty ex-servicemen of the "No, dash it, leave me behind, I've got a gammy leg, I'll only slow you down" variety,[.] — *The Guardian*, 27th February 2003

gammy chant *noun*
a bad situation *IRELAND*
- How come you don't have your car home with you? – Bagged. Bagged and banned. Another six months to go...That's bad now, Paul. It's a gammy chant. — Eamonn Sweeney, *Waiting for the Healer*, p. 50, 1997

gamoosh *noun*

a fellow, usually not referring to a winner in the zero-sum game of life *US*

- "There's Bill Ray. Happy-go-lucky gamoosh, ain't he," Sam's Man said. — Robert Campbell, *Juice*, p. 16, 1988

gamot *noun*

heroin; morphine *UK, 1998*

- — Mike Haskins, *Drugs*, p. 284, 2003

gander *noun*

a look *US, 1914*

- I just had a gander at the notice-board. — J.E. MacDonnell, *Don't Gimme the Ships*, p. 136, 1960
- Let's have a gander under that plaster. — Barry Oakley, *A Salute to the Great McCarthy*, p. 152, 1970

▸ **cop a gander**

to look at, especially with discretion *US*

- — Hyman E. Goldin et al., *Dictionary of American Underworld Lingo*, p. 49, 1950

▸ **get your gander up**

to become annoyed or angry *UK*

A variation, probably by mis-hearing, of **DANDER**.

- [I]f there's one thing that gets my gander up, it people who say breeze block walls are just as good as thermalite walls[.] — Danny King, *The Bank Robber Diaries*, p. 31–32, 2002

Gandhi's flipflop *noun*

used in similes as an example of extreme dryness *UK*

Mahatma Gandhi, 1869–1948, wore sandals.

- Are you gonna make a brew or what? I've got a throat like Ghandi's flip-flop. — Caroline Aherne and Craig Cash, *The Royle Family*, 1999

gandies *noun*

underwear *US*

- — *Current Slang*, p. 7, Winter 1970

G and T *noun*

gin and tonic *UK, 1966*

Initialism.

- A new entry in the Top Ten of bar standards – just above a JD and Coke and just behind a G&T — *GQ*, p. 68, July 2001

gandy *noun*

in Newfoundland, a pancake *CANADA*

- I'd have dumplings every day for dinner, and candy afterward, and gandies with lassy coady. — Harold Horwood, *Tomorrow Will Be Sunday*, p. 24, 1966

gandy dancer *noun*

1 a railway track worker *US, 1918*

Ramon Adams asserts in *The Language of the Railroader* that he was 'so called from the Gandy Manufacturing Company of Chicago, which made many of the tools used by the section gangs'.

- — Norman Carlisle, *The Modern Wonder Book of Trains and Railroading*, p. 263, 1946
- A few yards down from me, on the inside of the marshaling grounds, were a bunch of railroad men, a bit above the gandy-dancer class (they were engine drivers and coal heavers and points men). — Clancy Sigal, *Going Away*, p. 144, 1961
- I had worked that winter in the mountains of Mofo, Georgia, slugging it out as a gandy dancer, a man who pounds twelve-inch spikes with a fifteen-pound sledge. — Oscar Zeta Acosta, *The Revolt of the Cockroach People*, p. 22, 1973

2 a road worker *US*

- — Wayne Floyd, *Jason's Authentic Dictionary of CB Slang*, p. 17, 1976

3 in trucking, a tractor trailer that weaves back and forth on the road *US*

- — Montie Tak, *Truck Talk*, p. 69, 1971

gandy gang *noun*

on the railways, a crew of track workers *US*

- — Ramon Adams, *The Language of the Railroader*, p. 66, 1977

ganef *noun*

▷ see: **GONNIF**

gang *noun*

1 a work crew *US*

Still heard on occasion, but largely replaced with the standard English 'crew'.

- I'm finished at Standard Federal. They want to put me on the detail gang, plumbing up. I said no way, I'm a connector… — Elmore Leonard, *Killshot*, p. 44, 1989

2 a person's social group *UK, 1945*

From earlier conventional senses.

3 a great many *US, 1811*

- We spent a gang of mornings after that trying to learn the number[.] — Mezz Mezzrow, *Really the Blues*, p. 13, 1946

4 marijuana *BAHAMAS*

- — John A. Holm, *Dictionary of Bahamian English*, p. 85, 1982

gang *verb*

to engage in serial, consecutive sex, homosexual or heterosexual, especially to engage in multiple rape *UK*

A shortened **GANG-BANG**.

- We'll [...] gang her[.] — Richard Allen, *Boot Boys*, 1972

gangbang *noun*

1 successive, serial copulation between a single person and multiple partners *US, 1945*

- — Vincent J. Monteleone, *Criminal Slang*, p. 94, 1949
- Sometimes he [Jack Kerouac] lapses into pages of terrifying gibberish that sound like a tape recording of a gang bang with everybody full of pod, juice and bennies all at once. — *The Nation*, p. 161, 23 February 1957
- "Now that you're here, what do you plan to do?" "We were thinking along the lines of a gang-bang," Schoons said[.] — John Nichols, *The Sterile Cuckoo*, p. 69, 1965
- [R]eturnees from the gangbang were still popping in with regularity[.] — Robert Gover, *Poorboy at the Party*, p. 118, 1966
- With luck, he'll get off with nothing more than a few fights, broken glasses or a loud and public sex rally involving anything from indecent exposure to a gang-bang in one of the booths. — Hunter S. Thompson, *Hell's Angels*, p. 116, 1967
- There ain't nothing like a gang bang to blow away your blues. — The Sensational Alex Harvey Band, *Gang Bang*, 1973
- Tara Alexander, the heroine of the night, successfully balled, sucked, and jerked off eight-two strange men and her husband for a gang-bang total of eighty-three. — Josh Alan Friedman, *Tales of Times Square*, p. 89, 1986
- She did her first gangbang in I Can't Believe I Did The Whole Team! — *Cult Movies No. 17*, p. 47, 1996
- Gang bangs used to happen all the time. — Ralph "Sonny" Barger, *Hell's Angel*, p. 99, 2000
- [U]sually refering to one woman with more than three blokes. "We met up with Naomi last night and had a fantastic gang bang." — *Sky Magazine*, p. 73, July 2001

2 an orgy at which several couples have sex *US*

Described as 'depraved' by David Powis, *The Signs of Crime*, 1977, who draws the distinction between this sense and that of multiple rape.

- Sometimes these small rooms, cubby holes really, entertain as many as a dozen homosexuals engaging in what is called a gang-bang. — Antony James, *America's Homosexual Underground*, p. 62–63, 1965

3 a cluster of reporters descending on a public figure with microphones, cameras, notepads and shouted questions *US*

Sometimes shortened to 'bang' or the variant 'major bang'. Collected from a CNN producer, May 2001.

4 a social gathering *UK*

A humorously ironic use of the orgiastic sense.

- [S]ay, a garden party or a vicarage fete – "a real gang-bang". — David Powis, *The Signs of Crime*, 1977

5 a group of friends talking together on citizens' band radio *US*

- — Bill Davis, *Jawjacking*, p. 43, 1977

6 a television writing session involving multiple writers *US*

- — Anna Scotti and Paul Young, *Buzzwords*, p. 4, 1997

7 the utilisation of a large number of computer programmers to create a product in a short period of time *US*

- Though there have been memorable gang bangs (e.g., that over-the-weekend assembler port mentioned in Steven Levy's Hackers), most are perpetrated by large companies trying to meet deadlines and produce enormous buggy masses of code[.] — Eric S. Raymond, *The New Hacker's Dictionary*, p. 172–173, 1991

8 a fight between youth gangs *US, 1967*

- — Hermese E. Roberts, *The Third Ear*, 1971
- The last man standing won a nominal prize that hardly compensated for the broken teeth and fractured bones resulting from these gang bangs. — Nelson George, *Hip Hop America*, p. vii, 1998

gangbang *verb*

1 to engage in successive, serial copulation with multiple partners *US, 1949*

Also in figurative use.

- I used to do it myself, but these pre-verts would want to gang-bang your broad. —Edwin Torres, *Carlito's Way*, p. 12, 1975
- She got fucked up on Chivas Regal and gang-banged the dudes who didn't bring dates, which was very polite of her. —Larry Heinemann, *Close Quarters*, p. 132, 1977
- Gang-bang the slags! A fuckin line-up! —Irvine Welsh, *The State of the Party (Disco Biscuits)*, p. 53, 1995
- [T]his was the eighties, when the unions were being murdered in the press and the bosses lining up to gang-bang organised Labour. —John King, *Human Punk*, p. 149, 2000

2 to be an active part of a gang; to battle another gang *US, 1968*

- Homies all standin around, just hangin / Some dope-dealin, some gang-bangin —NWA *Gangsta Gangsta*, 1988
- We were a tagging crew [graffiti artists] and we would do gang banging [fight with other crews over wall turf] and other shit like that. —Terry Williams, *The Cocaine Kids*, p. 60, 1989
- It's the environment the kids live in. This kid may not be gangbanging and that's the problem with the cops. —Tim Lucas, *Cool Places*, p. 155, 1998

gangbanger *noun*

a youth gang member *US, 1969*

- —David Claerbaut, *Black Jargon in White America*, p. 65, 1972
- A lot of cops think that the kids are gangbangers. We know they're not, and the cops assume they're gangbangers because of the way they dress. —Tim Lucas, *Cool Places*, p. 155, 1998
- [L]ooked at a wallboard of photos taken of deceased gangbangers lying shot to death in the street, some of them with tubes sticking out of them, the tubes meant to save their lives but too late. —Elmore Leonard, *Be Cool*, p. 30, 1999

gangbuster *noun*

a zealous, energetic police official or prosecutor who targets organised crime *US, 1936*

- Ever since Tom Dewey, every damn prosecutor in the country's been playing gangbusters, figuring they put enough Mafia skells in jail they could get to be president or some damn thing. —Robert K. Tannenbaum, *Immoral Certainty*, p. 57, 1991

gangbusters *noun*

▸ **like gangbusters**

aggressively, with force *US, 1940*

- But I'm a player and I'm gonna conquer some young fine fox and come back like gang busters. —Iceberg Slim (Robert Beck), *The Naked Soul of Iceberg Slim*, p. 125, 1971
- He's coming after you, like gangbusters. Special task force. —Edwin Torres, *After Hours*, p. 434, 1979

gang cheats *noun*

two or more people working as confederates in a cheating scheme *US*

- —George Percy, *The Language of Poker*, p. 39, 1988

gange *noun*

marijuana *US, 1971*

A shortening of **GANJA** (marijuana).

- —Mike Haskins, *Drugs*, p. 287, 2003

gang-fuck *noun*

an uncoordinated mess *UK*

- If we started losing contact, it would all go to a gang fuck. —Andy McNab (writing of the late 1970s/early 80s), *Immediate Action*, p. 230, 1995

gang-fuck *verb*

to engage in serial, consecutive sex, homosexual or hetereosexual *US, 1916*

- —G. Legman, *The Language of Homsexuality*, p. 1166, 1941
- These cops will go fifty bucks a head to beat her into submission and then gang-fuck her. —Hunter S. Thompson, *Fear and Loathing in Las Vegas*, p. 114, 1971

gangie *noun*

serial sex between one person and multiple partners, consensual or not *NEW ZEALAND*

- What is a 'gangie' or 'gangbang'? – A gang of jokers on to one girl. It could be rape, but might not be. I took it as a rape. —*Truth*, p. 7, 30th March 1971

gangplank *noun*

a bridge *US*

- —*Complete CB Slang Dictionary*, 1976
- —Peter Chippindale, *The British CB Book*, p. 155, 1981

gangplank fever *noun*

in the military, a fear of transfer to an assignment overseas *US, 1945*

- —*American Speech*, p. 238, October 1946: 'World War II slang of maladjustment'

gang-shag *noun*

successive, serial copulation between a single person and multiple partners *US, 1927*

- "Gang shag" was a term I had heard before. But I had never managed to believe in the reality of it until I became an actual witness to such an affair. —Artie Shaw, *The Troble with Cinderlla*, p. 161, 1952
- In Bryant Park, just behind the public library one night recently, a girl was reported to have been assaulted by a whole gang of boys who took turns on her in what has become known in the psycopathic fringe as a "gang shag." —*Esquire*, p. 112, September 1954
- There is the sexual ambivalence in the gang's exclusion of girls from its activities and then suddenly forcing some luckless girl to submit to the gang "shag," or "lineup," where each member of the gang waits his turn for sexual relations with the female[.] —Herbert Block and Arthur Neiderhoffer, *The Gang*, p. 104, 1958
- —Lawrence Lipton, *The Holy Barbarians*, p. 316, 1959
- The gangshag is a homosexual project? Interesting. —Bernard Wolfe, *The Magic of Their Singing*, p. 167, 1961
- If a good gang-shag has any advantage over any other sort of sexual performance, it seems to me to be its indifference to and rather neutralizing effect upon emotional love. —Angelo d'Arcangelo, *The Homosexual Handbook*, p. 116, 1968

gang-splash *noun*

serial sex between one person and multiple partners, heterosexual or homosexual, consensual or not *AUSTRALIA*

- It's a line up. It's a group of males having intercourse with a girl or girls one after the other. Isn't that what happened? Yes – but I wouldn't call that a gang splash[.] —*Truth*, p. 7, 30th March 1971

gangsta *noun*

a young black member of a (criminal) gang *US*

A deliberate respelling of 'gangster'.

- 200 gun crimes had been reported, most of which were drug related and involved young black gangsta youth – "Yardies", as they liked to call themselves – both as perpetrators and victims. —Lanre Fehintola, *Charlie Says...*, p. 53, 2000

gangsta *adjective*

good, exciting *US*

Hip-hop.

- Well, "gangsta" is a slang word that we use when something is hot, or something is good, like "Wow, that's gangsta!" —*Ministry*, p. 65, October 2002

gangsta-lette *noun*

a female gang member *US*

- See, I was the kinda gansta-lette would take a bullet fo' my set. —*Rolling Stone*, p. 86, 12 April 2001

gangstamuthafucka *noun*

a gangster, especially one who is considered powerful *UK*

An intensification of **GANGSTA**.

- They look at the car an' think no way is mista gangstamuthafucka gonna drive it. —Nick Barlay, *Curvy Lovebox*, p. 84, 1997

gangsta rap; g-rap *noun*

a rap music genre characterised by explicit sex and violence which, it is claimed, reflects black urban existence *US, 1992*

Combines **GANGSTA** or 'g' (a black urban anti-hero) with **RAP** (a musical style).

- Blue, like a lot of youths his age, loved gangsta rap. —Karline Smith, *Moss Side Massive*, p. 2, 1994
- The post-NWA careers of Ice Cube, Eazy E and Dr Dre would dominate gangsta rap in their own differing ways. —John Robb, *The NIneties*, p. 241, 1999

gangsta rapper *noun*

a rap artist who reflects on the black urban experience in an explicitly sexual and violent manner *US*

GANGSTA RAP has been an influential music genre since the late 1980s.

- The pioneer gangster rapper who attempts to enliven his audience by shouting, "All the people with AIDS keep quiiii-et." —*Los Angeles Times*, p. 56 (Calendar), 3rd June 1990
- Some regard Philadelphia's Schooly D as the original gangsta rapper, but the genre was fully inaugerated in Ice-t's 1987 album Rhyme Pays. —Steven Daly and Nalthaniel Wice, *alt.culture*, p. 87, 1995
- The lyrics are so lewd and violent they would make even gangsta-rappers blush[.] —*The Times Magazine*, p. 12, 23rd February 2002

gangster *noun*

1 marijuana *US*

Promotes the outlaw self-image enjoyed by smokers of the illegal substance; possibly playing on **GANJA**.

- Just go on and smoke that gangster and be real cool. Drink that juice and smoke that gangster and keep them needles outta your arm. —Clarence Cooper Jr, *The Scene*, p. 219, 1960
- His eyes were glazed. He was sucking a stick of "gangster." —Iceberg Slim (Robert Beck), *Pimp*, p. 96–97, 1967
- —Mike Haskins, *Drugs*, p. 287, 2003

2 a cigarette *US*

- —David Claerbaut, *Black Jargon in White America*, p. 65, 1972

gangster bitch *noun*

a female who associates with youth gang members *US*

- —Don R. McCreary (Editor), *Dawg Speak*, 2001

gangster doors *noun*

any four-door sedan *US*

- —Edith A. Folb, *runnin' down some lines*, p. 238, 1980

gangster lean *noun*

1 a style of driving a car in which the driver leans towards the right side of the car, leaning on an arm rest, steering with the left hand; by extension, a slouching walk or posture *US*

- Only your head is visible from the outside. Oh, and while you're at it lean to the right, put your left hand on the steering wheel and be even more cool. That's called leaning. —Malachi Andrews and Paul T. Owens, *Black Language*, p. 84, 1973
- —Edith A. Folb, *runnin' down some lines*, p. 245, 1980
- Diamonds in the back, sunroof top / diggin the scene with the gangster lean. — Massive Attack, *Be Thankful for What You've Got*, 1991
- Then with his book bag over his shoulder, he did a gangsta lean into the building. —Stephen J. Cannell, *The Tin Collectors*, p. 38, 2001

2 a car with hydraulic shock aborbers that are set to leave the car higher on one side than the other *US*

- Diamonds in the back, sunroof top / diggin the scene with the gangster lean. — Massive Attack, *Be Thankful for What You've Got*, 1991
- —Judi Sanders, *Mashing and Munching in Ames*, p. 8, 1994

gangster pill *noun*

any barbiturate or other central nervous system depressant *US*

- — US Department of Justice, *Street Terms*, August 1994

gangster whitewalls *noun*

showy, flashy, whitewalled tyres *US*

- Though you may not drive a great big Cadillac / Gangster whitewalls, TV antennas in the back. —Curtis Mayfield, *Just Be Thankful (For What You've Got)*, 1972
- Elijah had added gangster whitewalls and now he was on the scene, stylin' for the people who could really dig such things. —Odie Hawkins, *Chicago Hustle*, p. 147, 1977
- He put gangster whitewall tires on his ride and cruised through Cavalier Manor hawking drugs and supervising the guys working for him. —Nathan McCall, *Makes Me Wanna Holler*, p. 124, 1994

gang-up *noun*

serial sex between multiple active participants and a single passive one *US*

- This is the gang-up. Men like that put you to sleep with their drops. Then one man after another goes in and takes you. Then these men go all over town next day and boast of what they've done to you. —Ethel Waters, *His Eye is on the Sparrow*, p. 101, 1951

gangy *noun*

a close friend; a fellow member of a clique *US*

Hawaiian youth usage.

- —Douglas Simonson, *Pidgin to da Max Hana Hou*, 1982

ganja *noun*

1 marijuana, notably from Jamaica *JAMAICA*

Hindi word for 'cannabis', possibly derived from **BHANG** and adopted around 1920 by 'Anglo-Indian drug addicts'; by 1970 the UK Home Office 'could ascribe it to West Indians'. Celebrated in song by, among many others, Clancy Eccles, 'Ganja Free', 1972 and Leslie Butler, 'Ashanti Ganja Dub', 1975. With many spelling variations including 'ganj', 'ganjah', 'ganjuh' and 'ganga'.

- —Clancy Eccles, *Ganja Free*, 1972
- [T]he Busaccas can have the franchise to sell the hard shit and the Hispanics cann sell the speed and ganja. —Richard Condon, *Prizzi's Glory*, p. 166, 1988
- Got us a little Rasta mon here. Peace, love, an ganja. —Jess Mowry, *Way Past Cool*, p. 18, 1992
- He remembers an uncle getting "so mean on ganja, he kills his girlfriend." —*People*, p. 77, 23rd May 1994
- "Yeah, feeling good, huh?" Louis said, getting close, the man's face. "You like that ganja." —Elmore Leonard, *Riding the Rap*, p. 131, 1995
- Most Rastas have no interest in violent action – and with such a devotion to consuming vast quantities of the very finest sinsemilla ganja in chalices, chillums or spliffs the size of ice cream cones, how could it be otherwise? —Harry Shapiro, *Waiting For The Man*, 1999

2 the white establishment *US*

- —James Haskins, *The Story of Hip-Hop*, p. 139, 2000

ganja *adjective*

white-skinned *US*

- —James Haskins, *The Story of Hip-Hop*, p. 139, 2000

gank *noun*

1 marijuana *US*

- —Ellen C. Bellone (Editor), *Dictionary of Slang*, p. 11, 1989

2 a substance sold as an illegal drug that is actually fake *US*

- Before Pitman tests it, however, he says he figures it's "gank". —*Union Leader*, p. 1, 1st August 1994
- [P]olice checked it out and found Smith in possessoin of the gank, which Dallavia said is a wax or soap substance that sometimes can be passed off as crack. — *Buffalo (New York) News*, p. 5B, 19th January 1999

gank *verb*

1 to steal *US*

- —Connie Eble (Editor), *UNC-CH Campus Slang*, p. 3, Fall 1996
- —*Columbia Missourian*, p. 1A, 19th October 1998

2 in Internet game-playing, to 'kill' a player, especially unfairly *UK*

Also used as a noun.

- What a gank! — *You and Yours*, 30th April 2003

ganky *adjective*

ugly, repulsive *IRELAND*

- —Colin Murphy and Donal O'Dea, *The Book of Feckin' Irish Slang*, p. 28, 2004

gaol-bait, gaol-bird *nouns*

▷ **see:** JAILBAIT, JAILBIRD

GAP *noun*

the Great American Public *US, 1965*

- Already traffic streamed through Tahyer Gate as the GAP – the Great American Public – poured onto the reservation for the parade and the football game. —Rick Atkinson, *The Long Gray Line*, p. 57, 1989

gap *verb*

to watch, to witness a crime *US*

- —Vincent J. Monteleone, *Criminal Slang*, p. 94, 1949

▸ **gap your axe**

to annoy *NEW ZEALAND*

- As foretelling the future of a young pup is impossible, one of those you put in someone else's hands could easily go on to win a major title – and wouldn't that gap your axe! —John Gordon, *Three Sheep & A Dog*, p. 56, 1998

gape *noun*

a completley relaxed, distended anus *US*

A term used by anal sex fetishists, especially on the Internet.

- In the adult industry, the post-fucking state of openness of an ass which you refer to is called "the gape," as in the popular vid series "Planet of the Gapes." People write to me about seeing the gape in porn videos all the time, but usually it's in fear. —Tristan Taormino, *puckerup.com*, 1999

gape *verb*

to idle, to wander *US*

- —John D. Bell et al., *Loosely Speaking*, p. 9, 1966

gaper *noun*

1 a dolt *US*

An abbreviation of **GAPING ASSHOLE**.

- —John D. Bell et al., *Loosely Speaking*, p. 9, 1966

2 a novice skier, or a non-skier watching others ski *US*

- —Judi Sanders, *Cal Poly Slang*, p. 4, 1990

3 a mirror *US, 1931*

- —Clarence Major, *Dictionary of Afro-American Slang*, p. 57, 1970

gaper-block *noun*
a traffic problem created by motorists slowing down to gawk at an accident *US*
- —Don Dempsey, *American Speech*, p. 269, December 1962: 'The language of traffic policemen'
- —Helen Dahlskog (Editor), *A Dictionary of Contemporary and Colloquial Usage*, p. 26, 1972
- In St. Louis, one such policeman has invented (apparently) a term for the traffic-jam caused by drivers slowing down to gawk at an accident or incident: gaper-block. —*Verbatim*, p. 627, May 1978

gaping and flaming *adjective*
(used of a party) wild, rowdy, fun *US*
- —Collin Baker et al., *College Undergraduate Slang Study Conducted at Brown University*, p. 124, 1968

gaping asshole *noun*
a dolt *US*
- —John D. Bell et al., *Loosely Speaking*, p. 9, 1966

gap it *verb*
to make a quick exit *SOUTH AFRICA*
- —*Lonely Planet Southern Africa*, 2000

GAPO *noun*
used as an abbreviation of *g*orilla *a*rm*p*it *o*dour *US*
- —*Current Slang*, p. 4, Spring 1967

gaposis *noun*
a notional disease involving a gap of any kind *US, 1942*
- Go one step further and pull the tape tighter to prevent "gaposis" of the neckline and force the lapel to roll. —Pati Palmer, *Easy, Easier, Easiest Tailoring*, p. 54, 1977

gap out *verb*
to daydream and miss something for lack of attention *CANADA*
- —Jack Chambers (Editor), *Slang Bag 93 (University of Toronto)*, p. 3, Winter 1993

gapper *noun*
a mirror *US, 1934*
Prisoner usage to describe a mirror used to watch for approaching guards as the prisoners do something which they ought not to do.
- —Troy Harris, *A Booklet of Criminal Argot, Cant and Jargon*, p. 12, 1976

gappings *noun*
a salary *US, 1955*
- —Robert S. Gold, *A Jazz Lexicon*, p. 119, 1964

gap up *verb*
to fill capsules with a powdered narcotic *US*
- —Eugene Landy, *The Underground Dictionary*, p. 86, 1971

gar *noun*
1 a black person *US, 1962*
An abbreiviation of **NIGGER**.
- —Eugene Landy, *The Underground Dictionary*, p. 86, 1971

2 marijuana rolled in ci*gar* leaf *US*
- —Mike Haskins, *Drugs*, p. 287, 2003

gar *adjective*
excellent, pleasing *US*
- —Kenn "Naz" Young, *Naz's Dictionary of Teen Slang*, p. 47, 1993

garage *noun*
a subset of a criminal organisation *US*
- Rocco was from another garage – but a boss-type. —Edwin Torres, *Carlito's Way*, p. 21, 1975

garage action *noun*
a legal action for libel (usually against a newspaper) brought by the police on their own behalf *UK*
The damages awarded are often substantial enough to buy a new garage for the police officer's home.

garage band *noun*
an amateur rock group with a basic, three-chord approach to music *US, 1977*
From the custom of practising in the garage at the home of the parents of a band member.
- Zehn Archar came from Baltimore. They represent the ultimate garage band. Actually, the insertion of the second letter of the alphabet smack in the middle of the garage would give a better inkling of their performance Wednesday. —*Washington Post*, p. C5, 21st July 1978
- Like the time Joe and his garage band won the "Battle of the Bands" at El Monte Legion Stadium. —James Ellroy, *Suicide Hill*, p. 597, 1986
- Girlfriends come and go faster than bass players in a garage band, but guy friends are forever. —*Wayne's World 2*, 1993
- Telling him they were kids, a garage band, not very good – if he happened to notice. —Elmore Leonard, *Be Cool*, p. 61, 1999

garage man's companion *noun*
a truck manufactured by General Motors Corporation *US*
A back formation from the initials GMC.
- —Montie Tak, *Truck Talk*, p. 69, 1971

garans!
certainly *US*
Hawaiian youth usage; shortened from 'guaranteed'.
- —Douglas Simonson, *Pidgin to da Max*, 1981

garbage *noun*
1 anything of poor quality or little or no worth; nonsense *UK, 1592*
From the sense as 'refuse'.
- The man was talking garbage. Willy Fowler knew this because he was an experimental nuclear physicist and nobody could do what the man, Fred Hoyle, was claiming[.] —*The Guardian*, 13th March 2003

2 heroin; low quality heroin *US, 1962*
- Tony never had anything but garbage, you know that, and I'll put him right out of business." —James Mills, *The Panic in Needle Park*, p. 41, 1966
- Just stay away from the garbage. You know what I mean. —*Goodfellas*, 1990
- —Robert Ashton, *This Is Heroin*, p. 209, 2002

3 farm produce *US*
- —Wayne Floyd, *Jason's Authentic Dictionary of CB Slang*, p. 17, 1976

4 any and all food, usually low in protein and high in carbohydrate, not in a bodybuilder's diet *US*
- —*American Speech*, p. 199, Fall 1984: 'The language of bodybuilding'

5 cocktail garnishes *US*
- I was mesmerized watching them at the service bar as they called in their drink orders and dredged the fruit containers for cocktail garnishes. (I remember we had called it "garbage.") —Kathryn Leigh Scott, *The Bunny Years*, 1998

6 in hot rodding, a surfeit of accessories unrelated to the car's performance *US*
- Garbage – Unnecessary gadgets, equipment and chrome on car —Fremont Drag Strip, *Guide to Drag Racing*, 1960

7 in poker, the cards that have been discarded *US*
- —Albert H. Morehead, *The Complete Guide to Winning Poker*, p. 264, 1967

garbage barge *noun*
a tuna fish sandwich *US*
- —*Maledicta*, p. 284, 1984–1985: 'Food names'

garbage down *verb*
to eat quickly *US*
- —*American Speech*, p. 154, May 1959: 'Gator (University of Florida) slang'

garbage dump *noun*
the California State Prison at San Quentin *US*
- —Jay Robert Nash, *Dicitonary of Crime*, p. 144, 1992

garbage guts *noun*
a glutton *AUSTRALIA*
- —Jim Ramsay, *Cop It Sweet!*, p. 38, 1977

garbage hauler *noun*
a truck driver hauling fruit or vegetables *US*
- —Montie Tak, *Truck Talk*, p. 69, 1971

garbage head *noun*
an addict who will use any substance available *US*
A term used in twelve-step recovery programmes such as Alcoholics Anonymous.
- —William D. Alsever, *Glossary for the Establishment and Other Uptight People*, p. 12, December 1970
- —Christopher Cavanaugh, *AA to Z*, p. 99, 1998

garbage in – garbage out
a catchphrase employed as an admonition to computer users: if you program mistakes into a computer then an output of rubbish will surely result *US*
- Well, you know the old saying about garbage in, garbage out. If wrong assumptions go in, wrong predictions come out. — *Forbes*, p. 71, 15th July 1976

garbage mouth *noun*
a person who regularly uses profanity *US, 1970*
- — Peter Chippindale, *The British CB Book*, p. 155, 1981

garbage rock *noun*
crack cocaine, especially of inferior quality *UK, 1998*
- — Mike Haskins, *Drugs*, p. 281, 2003

garbage shot *noun*
in pool, a shot made with luck, not with skill *US, 1979*
- — Mike Shamos, *The Illustrated Encyclopedia of Billiards*, p. 108, 1993

garbage stand *noun*
in circus and carnival usage, a novelty concession *US*
- — Don Wilmeth, *The Language of American Popular Entertainment*, p. 106, 1981

garbage time *noun*
the minutes at the end of an athletic contest when the outcome is not in doubt and substitute players are used freely by either or both teams; games at the end of a season when a team's record is such that a win or loss will not make a difference and substitute players are freely used *US*
- — Zander Hollander and Sandy Padwe, *Basketball Lingo*, p. 47, 1971
- Here's how good the Dolphins' defense was when the game was in the balance, before garbage time. — *South Florida Sun-Sentinel*, 10th September 2001

garbage up *verb*
1 to eat *US*
- — *American Speech*, p. 303, December 1955: 'Wayne University slang'

2 in bodybuilding, to eat food that is not in your regular diet *US*
- — *American Speech*, p. 199, Fall 1984: 'The language of bodybuilding'

garbage wagon *noun*
a standard Harley-Davidson motorcyle *US*
The term came from those who stripped the Harley of all the 'garbage' they didn't want, keeping only the functional necessities.
- The Angels refer to standard 774s as "garbage wagons," and Bylaw Number 11 of the charter is a put-down in the grand manner: "An Angel cannot wear the colors while riding on a garbage wagon with a non-Angel." — Hunter S. Thompson, *Hell's Angels*, p. 97, 1966
- The street term for full dressers is "garbage wagons," and in the old days you'd never catch a Hell's Angel on one of them. — Ralph "Sonny" Barger, *Hell's Angel*, p. 58, 2000

garbanzos *noun*
the female breasts *US, 1982*
- H&S sales, based in College Point, Queens, N.Y., is the premiere manufacturer and distributor of "big breast oriented material" – videotapes and magazines fixated on woman with gigantic knockers, huge garbzanos[.] — *Adult Video*, p. 47, August/September 1986

garbo *noun*
1 a rubbish collector *AUSTRALIA, 1953*
- Even a Garbo is entitled to his more than one enchanted evening[.] — Frank Hardy, *The Outcasts of Foolgarah*, p. 16, 1971
- — Arthur Chipper, *The Aussie Swearer's Guide*, p. 44, 1972
- Still, I'd have loved to have finished that little item before the garbos chucked it on the back of their truck. — Barry Humphries, *A Nice Night's Entertainment*, p. 165, 1978

2 a rubbish bin *AUSTRALIA*
- Mouche lathered up one armpit in silence, retrieved a discarded razor from the garbo and carved her way through the foam. — Kathy Lette, *Girls' Night Out*, p. 109, 1987

garbologist *noun*
a rubbish collector *AUSTRALIA*
- No, sir, old Jasper got in there amongst it all, tipping and throwing everything that came his way, then coming back to the dump and sifting for all the – extras that made it worth his while to be a garbologist. — Ricki Francis, *Hotel Kings X*, p. 48, 1973

garburator *noun*
a garbage disposal unit mounted in the sink *CANADA*
- The name garburator perhaps comes from combining "garbage" and either "carburetor" or "incinerator." — *Toronto Globe and Mail*, p. C6, 30th May 1998

garden *noun*
1 a woman's pubic hair *US*
- — *Maledicta*, p. 131, Summer/Winter 1982: 'Dyke diction: the language of lesbians'

2 a railway yard *US*
- — Norman Carlisle, *The Modern Wonder Book of Trains and Railroading*, p. 263, 1946

Gardena miracle *noun*
in a game of poker, a good hand drawn after a poor dealt hand *US*
Gardena is a city near Los Angeles where poker rooms are legal.
- — David M. Hayano, *Poker Faces*, p. 186, 1982

gardener *noun*
1 a bookmaker who extends his prices beyond his competitors *AUSTRALIA*
- — Ned Wallish, *The Truth Dictionary of Racing Slang*, p. 32, 1989

2 in pool, a betting player who wins *US*
- — Steve Rushin, *Pool Cool*, p. 14, 1990

garden gate *noun*
1 eight pounds, £8 *UK*
At times abbreviated to 'eight'.
- — Ray Puxley, *Cockney Rabbit*, p. 69, 1992
- — John Ayto, *The Oxford Dictionary of Rhyming Slang*, p. 281, 2002

2 a magistrate *UK, 1859*
Rhyming slang.
- — D.W.Maurer with Sidney J.Baker, *Australian Rhyming Argot in the American Underworld*, 1944

garden gate *verb*
to perform oral sex on a woman *UK*
Rhyming slang for **PLATE** (to engage in oral sex). Recorded in August 2002.

garden gnome *noun*
a comb *UK*
Rhyming slang.
- — Ray Puxley, *Cockney Rabbit*, 1992

garden plant; garden *noun*
an Aunt *UK*
Rhyming slang, used only in the third person.
- — Ray Puxley, *Cockney Rabbit*, 1992

garden punk *noun*
a male homosexual *BAHAMAS*
- — John A. Holm, *Dictionary of Bahamian English*, p. 85, 1982

garden tool *noun*
a promiscuous girl or woman *US*
Alluding, of course, to a 'hoe'.
- — Connie Eble (Editor), *UNC-CH Campus Slang*, p. 4, November 1990

Gareth Gate *verb*
to masturbate *UK*
Rhyming slang, inspired by the name of pop singer Gareth Gates (b.1984) who came to fame in 2002.
- — Bodmin Dark, *Dirty Cockney Rhyming Slang*, 2003

Gareth Hunt *noun*
an unpleasant or despicable person *UK*
Rhyming slang, formed on the name of a well known London-born actor (b.1943).

gargle *noun*
alcoholic drink *AUSTRALIA*
- The gargle has ruined many a good man. — Frank Hardy, *The Yarns of Billy Borker*, p. 36, 1965
- The barman didn't give me a second look, which was okay from the point of view of me getting served with the gargle and me being underage... — Lee Dunne, *Goodbye to the Hill*, p. 50, 1966
- Another six bags to go then we'll take 'em to the bottle yard and repair to the local for a well-earned gargle. — Frank Hardy, *The Outcasts of Foolgarah*, p. 1, 1971
- From the second I saw him coming through the gate back on to the wing, I knew he was gargled. He couldn't walk straight. — Howard Paul, *The Joy*, p. 23, 1996
- A point in favour of drink. If you've a gang of gargle in you the hay can be hit without wondering...if you're going to snuff it. — Eamonn Sweeney, *Waiting for the Healer*, p. 85, 1997

- —Sonya Plowman, *Great Kiwi Slang*, p. 79, 2002
- [B]ut dis [this] kinda shit happens every time we go out. I go te de [to the] jacks, or to get the gargles in[.]—Donal Ruane, *Tales in a rear view mirror*, p. 171, 2003

gark *noun*
a scratch *NEW ZEALAND*
- —David McGill, *David McGill's Complete Kiwi Slang Dictionary*, p. 53, 1998

garlo *noun*
a police officer *UK*
English gypsy use.
- The garlos only ever come onto the site mob-handed.—Jimmy Stockin, *On The Cobbles*, p. 30, 2000

garm *noun*
clothing; an item of clothing *UK*
An abbreviation of 'garment'; current in the black community.
- Look at the pair of you. Your garms are wacked. You're a dog's dinner.—Nick Barlay, *Curvy Lovebox*, p. 60, 1997
- Haven't they got any decent garms in the outback?—Diran Abedayo, *My Once Upon A Time*, p. 66, 2000

garmed up *adjective*
fashionably or smartly dressed *UK*
- Steff's garmed up for a disco inferno.—Nick Barlay, *Curvy Lovebox*, p. 141, 1997

gar-mouth *verb*
to issue threats which cannot and will not be implemented *US*
In honour of the 'gar', a fish of the pike family with long jaws – a big mouth.
- "I'll knock your ass up so high you'll have to climb a stepladder to shit!" is a classic gar-mouth line.—Ken Weaver, *Texas Crude*, p. 55, 1984

garn!
go on! *AUSTRALIA, 1911*
- Garn, there's stacks o' room! Bring yer tart erlong an' 'ave a spin! —Norman Lindsay, *Comic Art of Norman Lindsay*, p. 185, 1914
- Said "Scat" to a cat and "Garn" to a dog.—Wilda Moxham, *The Apprentice*, p. 3, 1969
- Ar garn! He's head and shoulders above any other full-back playing football.—Alexander Buzo, *The Roy Murphy Show*, p. 120, 1970

garnish *noun*
cash *US*
- Candy, markers, ammo, liners, stocking stuffer, sweetener, garnish, and pledges are all terms for cash.—Henry Hill and Byron Schreckengost, *A Good Fella's Guide to New York*, p. 123, 2003

garnot *noun*
heroin *UK*
- —Robert Ashton, *This Is Heroin*, p. 205, 2002

Garrison finish *noun*
in horse racing, a sprinting finish by a horse that has lagged back until the final moment *US, 1890*
- —David W. Maurer, *Argot of the Racetrack*, p. 30, 1951

garrity *adjective*
madly over-excited *UK*
Presumably after someone who exhibited such characteristics; possibly Freddie Garrity (b.1940), prancing and dancing lead singer of Freddie & The Dreamers, a 1960s pop group from Manchester.
- Chelsea miss one and the Millwall players and fans go garrity. — Martin King and Martin Knight, *The Naughty Nineties*, p. 127, 1999

Gary Ablett *noun*
a tablet, especially of MDMA, the recreational drug best known as ecstasy *AUSTRALIA, 1992*
Rhyming slang, ironically based on Australian Rules Football player Gary Ablett whose career was marred by a controversial involvement with drink and drugs. The etymology is confused by Liverpool FC player Gary Ablett.
- —Angela Devlin, *Prison Patter*, p. 55, 1996

Gary Cooper *noun*
in craps, a roll of 12 *US, 1983*
From Cooper's starring role in the Western film *High Noon*.
- —Thomas L. Clark, *The Dictionary of Gambling and Gaming*, p. 90, 1987

Gary Glitter *noun*
the anus; a lavatory *UK*
Rhyming slang for **SHITTER**. The original 1980s use for entertainer Gary Glitter (Paul Francis Gadd b.1944), as inspiration for a rhyming slang term was as 'bitter' (beer), however in the mid-90s allegations of under-age sex changed the public's perception and Gary Glitter became an **ARSEHOLE** or was associated with toilets. In 1999 he was found innocent of charges concerning under-age sex but convicted and imprisoned for downloading porn from the Internet. Unlike much rhyming slang this is generally used in full, if only to avoid confusion with **GARY LINEKER** (vinegar).
- I can't miss it. There's a big chunk of chopped tomato right in the middle of her Gary Glitter.—Kevin Sampson, *Outlaws*, p. 166, 2001

Gary Lineker *noun*
vinegar *UK*
Imprecise rhyming slang, based on the name of Gary Lineker (b.1960), a popular footballer and television personality. Walkers Crisps, whose advertising he is closely associated with, introduced a 'Salt and Lineker' flavour after this slang term was in circulation.
- —Ray Puxley, *Fresh Rabbit*, 1998

Gary Player; Gary *noun*
an 'all-*dayer*' event *UK*
Rhyming slang, based on the name of South African golfer Gary Player (b.1936).
- —*Antiquarian Book Review*, p. 18, June 2002

gas *noun*
1 a pleasing and/or amusing experience or situation *US, 1953*
A jazz term that slipped into mainstream youth slang.
- "Wasn't that a gas!" Zaida cried, breathless[.]—Ross Russell, *The Sound*, p. 13, 1961
- I stayed there a month with Phineas Newborn's great trio and it was a gas every night.—Babs Gonzales, *I Paid My Dues*, p. 139, 1967
- We panhandled a few cigarettes, which is really a gas.—Abbie Hoffman, *Revolution for the Hell of It*, p. 34, 1968
- But it's alright now / In fact, it's a gas.—Mick Jagger and Keith Richard (The Rolling Stones), *Jumping Jack Flash*, 1968
- You're a gas, Myra.—Gore Vidal, *Myra Breckinridge*, p. 103, 1968
- It would have been a gas for me to sit on a pillow beneath the womb of Baldwin's typewriter and catch each newborn page as it entered this world of ours.—Eldridge Cleaver, *Soul on Ice*, p. 97, 1968
- This is a gas! Too bad nobody'll believe it.—*King of Comedy*, 1976
- When people say, "Look, dirty filthy hippies," you know, I think what a fucking gas.—Paul E. Willis, *Profane Culture*, p. 93, 1978
- Next, you handy-dandy AR-15 by Colt. *** We got 'em, everybody thought, oh, man, this here's a gas on full automatic.—Elmore Leonard, *Bandits*, p. 267, 1987
- Look at the get-up of him. It's gas, isn't it?—(Dolan) Joseph O'Connor, *Red Roses and Petrol*, p. 38, 1995
- That's the way I'd like to be in the world, a gas man—Frank McCourt, *Angela's Ashes*, p. 146, 1997

2 anabolic steroids *US*
The term drew national attention in the US on 14th July 1994, when Terry Bollea (aka Hulk Hogan) testified in criminal proceedings against wrestling promoter Vince McMahon in Uniondale, New York. Asked if he had heard any slang for steroids, Bollea/Hogan answered 'Juice. Gas'.
- "If you're going to get big naturally, then that's what you need to do, and not on gas, because it does have the side effects and I just choose not to deal with that." [interviewing 2 Cold Scorpio]—*Wrestling Flyer*, 1st January 1994
- You had a team of guys who were 6'4" tall and 240 pounds when they were dry; however, they went on the gas and went from 240 to 280. —Jeff Archer, *Theater in a Squared Circle*, p. 117, 1999

3 batteries *US*
From the radio as **CAR** metaphor.
- —Gary K. Farlow, *Prison-ese*, p. 23, 2002

4 money *SOUTH AFRICA*
- —Gary Fairmont R. Filosa II, *The Surfer's Almanac*, p. 186, 1977

5 in pool, momentum or force *US*
- —Mike Shamos, *The Illustrated Encyclopedia of Billiards*, p. 108, 1993

▶ **cut the gas**
to stop talking *US*
- Cut the gas has replaced shut up.—*Newsweek*, 8th October 1951

▶ **take gas**
to be knocked from a surfboard by a wave; to fall from a skateboard *US*
- —*Paradise of the Pacific*, p. 27, October 1963
- —John Severson, *Modern Surfing Around the World*, p. 183, 1964

- Takin' gas in a bush takes a lotta nerve. —Jan Berry and Dean Torrance, *Sidewalk Surfin'*, 1964
- —Hy Lit, *Hy Lit's Unbelievable Dictionary of Hip Words for Groovy People*, p. 39, 1968

▸ **take the gas**

to lose your composure *US*

- It seems Lloyd's of London has finally "taken the gas." That's a golfing term for a player who chokes up or "swallows the olive." —*San Francisco Examiner*, p. 6, 5th February 1961

gas *verb*

1 to talk idly; to chatter *US, 1847*

The 'gas' is hot air.

- Twice he stopped to gas with some character and I made like I was interested in a menu pasted on the window of a joint. —Mickey Spillane, *My Gun is Quick*, p. 70, 1950
- Quit gassing and start working —John M. Murtagh and Sara Harris, *Cost the First Stone*, 1957
- We gassed a while and the husband asked me, half in joke, whether I wanted to go out toThe Dalles with them. —Clancy Sigal, *Going Away*, p. 86, 1961
- Poor old Henry and me and a few of the boys was standing outside Bert's, just gassing, when this pair of rubber-heelers comes goosestepping round the corner. —John Peter Jones, *Feather Pluckers*, p. 7, 1964

2 to tease, to joke, to kid *US, 1847*

- ALF: Now she doesn't care. D'ye know – I'm gassing! —John O'Toole, *The Bush and the Tree [Six Granada Plays]*, p. 31, 1960
- In six months, Satin? You ain't gassing me, baby? —Sara Harris, *The Lords of Hell*, p. 49, 1967

3 to please, to excite *US, 1941*

- Just the same the game gassed me. —Louis Armstrong, *Satchmo*, p. 123, 1954
- Things were "cool" and cool things "gassed" the initiates and anything that was particularly cool was "crazy." —Robert Sylvester, *No Cover Charge*, p. 287, 1956
- He said he gassed him, but we were too far out for the people. —Babs Gonzales, *I Paid My Dues*, p. 40, 1967

4 to inhale glue or any volatile solvent for the intoxicating effect *US*

- —William D. Alsever, *Glossary for the Establishment and Other Uptight People*, p. 13, December 1970

5 to straighten (hair) with chemicals and heat *US*

- —Lavada Durst, *The Jives of Dr. Hepcat*, p. 12, 1953
- You could tell that he was a pimping motherfucker by the way his hair was gassed. —Bruce Jackson, *Get Your Ass in the Water and Swim Like Me*, p. 162, 1965
- Those two pimps? That style is just called a process, some call it a marcel. Old-time policemen might refer to it as gassed hair[.] —Joseph Wambaugh, *The New Centurions*, p. 66, 1970

gasbag *noun*

a very talkative individual, a boaster, a person of too many words *US, 1862*

- And you implied that I was a gasbag, a do-nothing liberal. —Mort Sahl, *Heartland*, p. 138, 1976

gas-cooker *verb*

to catch out; to put in a difficult position; to trick or delude *UK: SCOTLAND*

Glasgow rhyming slang for **SNOOKER**.

- If that last nut'll no shift we'll be gas-cookered. —Michael Munro, *The Patter, Another Blast*, 1988

gaseech *noun*

a face *UK*

- Usually employed when attacking a custard-curdling gaseech[.] —Ray Puxley, *Cockney Rabbit*, 1992

gas 'em stop *noun*

a petrol station *US*

- —*Complete CB Slang Dictionary*, p. 7, 1976

gas factor *noun*

(among Canadian forces personnel) a measure of a person's commitment to a project *CANADA*

The initials represent '*give a shit*'.

- "Gas Factor" is a mythical, but nonetheless useful gauge for describing one's interest or devotion to the task at hand. —Tom Langeste, *Words on the Wing*, p. 113, 1995

gas gun *noun*

a large-bore shotgun loaded with tear-gas cannisters *US*

- —*American Speech*, p. 269, December 1962: 'The language of traffic policemen'

gas-guzzler *noun*

a motor vehicle that demands immoderate quantities of fuel, either by design or in consequence of a driver's excessive demands *US, 1973*

- —Peter Chippindale, *The British CB Book*, p. 155, 1981
- Sandy-haired yobbos with a big gas guzzler throbbing in the car park. —Robert Drewe, *The Bodysurfers*, p. 115, 1983
- They continued churning out heavy, often unreliable gaz-guzzlers (an Americanism of 1969) in overmanned factories that were massively uncompetitive compared with the lean manufacturing techniques of the Japanese. —Bill Bryson, *Made in America*, p. 346, 1994

gash *noun*

1 the vagina; sex with a woman; a woman as a sex object *US, 1866*

- At first Connie paid for this fancy gash. —Bernard Wolfe, *The Late Risers*, p. 48, 1954
- A fucking veritable GASH – a great slit between the legs lookin more like murder than anything else. —Jack Kerouac, *Letter to Allen Ginsberg*, p. 499, 14th July 1955
- I screw the old gash. —William Burroughs, *Naked Lunch*, p. 40, 1957
- Not a bad-looking gash, and she really likes Teddy. —George V. Higgins, *The Judgment of Deke Hunter*, p. 57, 1976
- Son, for ya survivin' ya gotta git it solid in ya noggin all gash is the same, hairy or bald, tight or loose[.] —Iceberg Slim (Robert Beck), *Doom Fox*, p. 230, 1978
- —Joe McKennon, *Circus Lingo*, p. 38, 1980
- Some grimacing ugly, Richard decided, coldly presenting her dry gash to the balding as he took off his trench coat[.] —Will Self, *The Sweet Smell of Psychosis*, p. 3–4, 1996
- [H]e slung 50p in Monique's pot and leered, "I'll make it a quid when I've seen your gash[.]" —Garry Bushell, *The Face*, p. 127, 2001

2 a male homosexual who is sexually passive *US*

- —Hyman E. Goldin et al., *Dictionary of American Underworld Lingo*, p. 77, 1950

3 refuse *ANTARCTICA, 1958*

A British contribution to South Pole slang.

- —Bernadette Hince, *The Antarctic Dictionary*, p. 142, 2000
- Many bases have a gash-rota whereby each member in turn is gashman for the day. This means that they help in the kitchen with the menial tasks, wash-up, deal with the gas – rubbish/garbage and generally carry out various base house-keeping duties. —*Cool Antarctica*, 2003: 'Antarctic slang'

4 a second helping of food *AUSTRALIA, 1943*

- [A] second helping or "back-up" became "gash". —Rohan D. Rivett, *Behind Bamboo*, p. 212, 1946

5 marijuana *US*

- —Richard A. Spears, *The Slang and Jargon of Drugs and Drink*, p. 213, 1986
- —Mike Haskins, *Drugs*, p. 287, 2003

gash *verb*

to have sex *US*

- —Pamela Munro, *U.C.L.A. Slang*, p. 41, 1989

gash *adjective*

useless, of poor quality *UK*

Extended from the sense 'superfluous'.

- Fuckin 'ell, la, you Italians may be gash in the sack, but yer fucking quick when it comes to catching on. —Colin Butts, *Is Harry on the Boat?*, p. 24, 1997

gas-head *noun*

1 an abuser of industrial solvents for their psychoactive effects *UK*

- We all tried solvents, but none of us were serious "gas heads". —Macfarlane, Macfarlane and Robson, *The User*, p. 60, 1996

2 a person with chemically straightened hair *US*

- —*Current Slang*, p. 25, Fall 1968
- —David Claerbaut, *Black Jargon in White America*, p. 65, 1972

gash hound *noun*

a man who is obsessed with women *US*

- "How can you stand this gash hound?" Wolf asked Mosca, his voice deliberately quiet, insulting. "He's had so many dames sitting on his head, his brain's gone soft." —Mario Puzo, *The Dark Arena*, p. 138, 1955
- —Joseph E. Ragen and Charles Finston, *Inside the World's Toughest Prison*, p. 800, 1962: 'Penitentiary and underworld glossary'
- "I told you he was a gash hound," Clete said. —James L. Burke, *A Stained White Radiance*, p. 82, 1992
- They're all gash-hounds in New Hampshire, but California is a different story, eh? —Hunter S. Thompson, *Better Than Sex*, p. 111, 19th August 1992
- "I noticed," said Karras. "Sure you did," said Recevo. "Gash-hound like you." —George P. Pelecanos, *The Big Blowdown*, p. 58, 1996

gasket *noun*

1 any improvised seal between the end of a dropper and the hub of a needle *US*

- —William D. Alsever, *Glossary for the Establishment and Other Uptight People*, p. 19, December 1970

2 a doughnut *US, 1942*

- —Ramon Adams, *The Language of the Railroader*, p. 67, 1977

gasket jint; gasket *noun*

a pint, especially of beer *UK: SCOTLAND*

Glasgow rhyming slang, formed on the local pronunciation of 'joint'.

- [W]e'll nick oot fur a couple a gaskets.—Michael Munro, *The Patter, Another Blast*, 1988

gasoline!

in oil drilling, used as a shouted warning that a boss is approaching *US*

- —Jerry Robertson, *Oil Slanguage*, p. 57, 1954

gasoline alley *noun*

in motor racing, the area at the race track where race teams repair and prepare cars for the race *US*

- —John Lawlor, *How to Talk Car*, p. 53, 1965
- I met him at around midnight first week of May, 1958, in "Gasoline Alley." I was working late in the garage area at Indy.—Henry "Smokey" Yunick, *Best Damn Garage in Town*, p. 287, 2003

gasp and grunt; grunt *noun*

the vagina; a woman or women sexually objectified *UK*

Rhyming slang for **CUNT**.

- —Julian Franklyn, *A Dictionary of Rhyming Slang*, 1961

gas-passer *noun*

an anaesthetist *US*

- —*American Speech*, p. 145–148, May 1961: 'The spoken language of medicine; argot, slang, cant'
- So find the gas-passer and tell him to premedicate the patient. —*M*A*S*H*, 1970

gasper *noun*

1 a cigarette *UK, 1914*

Descriptive of the respiratory effect of tobacco-smoking. Originally military slang for an inferior cigarette, popularised in World War 1, in wider usage by 1930. Concurrently, from about 1914, any cigarette.

- And that's what the so-called Surgeon General has going for him – a black hat: cigarettes. Coffin nails, gaspers – a black hat if ever there was one.—Max Shulman, *Anyone Got a Match?*, p. 42, 1964

2 a marijuana cigarette *US, 1984*

From the earlier sense (cigarette).

- —Richard A. Spears, *The Slang and Jargon of Drugs and Drink*, p. 213, 1986
- —Mike Haskins, *Drugs*, p. 287, 2003

3 something that is astonishing *US*

- "You know what that's from?" – and he looks out at everyone and hesitates before laying this gasper on them – "That's from the Declaration of Independence."—Tom Wolfe, *Radical Chic & Mau-Mauing the Flak Catchers*, p. 24, 1970

4 in typography, an exclamation mark (!) *UK*

- [K]nown in the newspaper world as a screamer, a gasper, a startler or (sorry) a dog's cock.—Lynne Truss, *Eats, Shoots and Leaves*, p. 136, 2003

Gaspers *nickname*

the Asper family of Winnipeg, Manitoba, socially, culturally and politically prominent *CANADA*

- As boss of Southam, he did not blink when the publisher of his Windsor Star backed the NDP – a principle the Gaspers, of Winnipeg, do not understand. He initiated the Southam Fellowships at the University of Toronto, a project the Gaspers have killed.—*Toronto Globe and Mail*, p. A2, 18th May 2002

gasper stick *noun*

a marijuana cigarette *UK, 1998*

- —Mike Haskins, *Drugs*, p. 287, 2003

Gaspe steak *noun*

fried bologna *CANADA*

- —Bill Casselman, *Canadian Food Words*, p. 169, 1998

gas pump jock *noun*

in the days before self-service, a petrol station attendant *US*

- Warming the seats on any given night we might see the likes of someone's Uncle Jack, a contingent of elevator operators, a randy row of young gas-pump jocks from Queens[.]—Josh Alan Friedman, *Tales of Times Square*, p. 15, 1986

gas queen *noun*

a male homosexual who patronises young male prostitutes working on the street *US*

- —Jim Crotty, *How to Talk American*, p. 160, 1997

gassed *adjective*

1 tipsy, drunk *US, 1919*

World War 1 military use from the stupefying effects of gas; then, its origins soon forgotten, just another synonym for 'drunk'.

- Let's go over to Beer Can Boulevard and get gassed!—Max Shulman, *Rally Round the Flag, Boys!*, p. 173, 1957
- They play the juke box circuit and get gassed on beer, but New York has few such emporiums and even beer is expensive.—Lee Mortimer, *Women Confidential*, p. 41, 1960
- As far as they knew, all they did in port was visit around the Spanish-speaking sections and get gassed up.—Mickey Spillane, *Me, Hood!*, p. 47, 1963
- —*Current Slang*, p. 3, Fall 1966
- —Collin Baker et al., *College Undergraduate Slang Study Conducted at Brown University*, p. 124, 1968
- Couldn't find us a bottle of that bubbly [champagne] everyone's gassed on?—Kevin Sampson, *Powder*, p. 22, 1999

2 describes a drug that is considered to be terrific or very enjoyable, used especially of marijuana, *US*

- Jim, this jive you got is gassed[.]—Mezz Mezzrow, 1946, *quoted in 'Waiting For The Man' by Harry Shapiro*, 1999

gasser *noun*

1 something wonderful, very exceptional; extraordinarily successful *US, 1944*

- —*Time Magazine*, p. 92, 20th January 1947: 'Dicty Dictionary'
- He got this great Mexican shit, man. It's a gasser.—Bernard Wolfe, *The Late Risers*, p. 168, 1954
- "Yeah," said the wolf. "It's a gasser."—Steve Allen, *Bop Fables*, p. 44, 1955
- And it's a gasser, if I say so myself.—Max Shulman, *I was a Teen-Age Dwarf*, p. 13, 1959
- But the last set was a gasser. They really came on then, man!—Ross Russell, *The Sound*, p. 14, 1961

2 a cigarette *AUSTRALIA, 1984*

Partidge suggests 'perhaps a slovening of the synonym **GASPER**'; a darker etymology reflecting the cough-inducing and life-shortening properties of tobacco is also possible.

3 an anaesthetist *UK*

Medical slang. Often teamed with surgeons as 'gassers and **SLASHERS**'.

- —Adam T. Fox, St Mary's Hospital, London, 10th October 2002

4 in drag racing, a car that only uses petrol for fuel *US*

- —Fred Horsley, *The Hot Rod Handbook*, p. 209, 1965: 'Hot talk – a glossary of hot rod terms'
- Some drag rules say that gassers must use pump gas, which is just like the gasoline you buy in a station.—Ed Radlauer, *Drag Racing Pix Dix*, p. 25, 1970

5 in oil drilling, a well that produces no oil *US*

- —Jerry Robertson, *Oil Slanguage*, p. 57, 1954

gas station in the sky *nickname*

▷ **see: FLYING GAS STATION**

gassy *adjective*

excellent, pleasant, humorous *US*

- Always used to show up at the parties with some gassy thing, a gopher snake or a white mouse or some gassy thing like that in his pocket? —Ken Kesey, *One Flew Over the Cuckoo's Nest*, p. 218, 1962
- —Eugene Landy, *The Underground Dictionary*, p. 87, 1971

Gastown *noun*

now a section of downtown Vancouver, named after a Victorian-era saloonkeeper *CANADA*

- Gas Town. (From Captain John "Gassy Jack" Deighton, builder of a hotel and saloon on Burrard Inlet, 1867.—Robert Hamilton, *Canadian Quotations*, p. 37, 1952

gastro *noun*

gastroenteritis *AUSTRALIA, 1975*

- Pat Hill's battalion had been in Vietnam about five days when Pat and a lot of mates came down with gastro and diarrhoea due to change in water, food and climate.—Martin Cameron, *A Look at the Bright Side*, 1988

gat *noun*

1 a gun, especially a pistol; in the Royal Air Force, a rifle *US, 1897*

- We're just curious why a couple of hard guys like you two weren't carrying your gats. —Irving Shulman, *The Amboy Dukes*, p. 164, 1947
- As she came out, two men slipped from the front seat, and as one opened the door the other, with his hand inside his coat at his armpit where he carried his gat, looked up and down the block. —Jack Lait and Lee Mortimer, *New York Confidential*, p. 17, 1948
- "Five hundred plus the gat?" I asked. He looked down at it rather absently. Then he dropped it into his pocket. —Raymond Chandler, *The Long Goodbye*, p. 21, 1953
- Pullin' gats for fun[.] —*C.R.E.A.M.*, 1994
- —Angela Devlin, *Prison Patter*, p. 55, 1996

2 the anus *SOUTH AFRICA, 1968*
From Afrikaans (a hole).

gat *verb*

to shoot *US*

- Oh shit somebody gonna get gatted! —*Boyz N The Hood*, 1990

gat-creeper *noun*

a sycophant *SOUTH AFRICA, 1985*
From Afrikaans *gat* (hole), hence **GAT** (the anus), and *kruiper* (creeper).

gate *noun*

1 a jazz musician; hence a fashionable man *US, 1936*
A pun on 'swinging' (swing gate, abbreviated from **GATOR**).

- And the gate that rocked at the eighty-eight was blowin' "How High the Moon." —William "Lord" Buckley, *The Ballad of Dan McGroo*, 1960

2 used as a term of address among jazz lovers of the 1930s and 40s *US, 1936*

- Friends are addressed as gate or slot, verbal shorthand for gatemouth and slotmouth, which are inner-circle racial jokes to begin with[.] —Mezz Mezzrow, *Really the Blues*, p. 220, 1946

3 a young person *US, 1936*

- —Lou Shelly, *Hepcats Jive Dictionary*, p. 11, 1945

4 release from prison *US*

- So to even the score, they gave the rat four / when he should have got the gate. —Bruce Jackson, *Get Your Ass in the Water and Swim Like Me*, p. 82,

5 a vein into which a drug is injected *US*

- —Richard A. Spears, *The Slang and Jargon of Drugs and Drink*, p. 214, 1986

6 the mouth *US, 1936*

- She's just big-gatin', boss, tryna run up de price. —Chester Himes, *Cotton Comes to Harlem*, p. 38, 1965

gate *verb*

in private dice games, to stop the dice while rolling, either as a superstition or to check for cheating *US*

- —John S. Salak, *Dictionary of Gambling*, p. 109, 1963

-gate *suffix*

used as an embellishment of a noun or name to suggest a far-reaching political scandal *US, 1973*
From the Watergate scandal that consumed and ultimately destroyed the Nixon presidency between 1972 (the burglary) and 1974 (the resignation from office).

- —*American Speech*, Fall 1978
- —*American Speech*, Summer 1984
- What impressions do people get when a term like "Shawinigate" is reported? Do they assume it merely means allegations of wrong-doing? Or does the word itself suggest unethical behavior and a cover-up? —*CBC News Online*, 10th April 2001
- The toilet incident at Glastonbury, when they [Manic Street Preachers] brought a private loo along, artfully dubbed "Crappergate" by one magazine, made them look like preening rock stars, not the post-punk revolutionaries that they once claimed to be. —*The Independent*, 25th January 2002
- Clark details the 'terrible, personal toll' of Casinogate. The charges stem from allegations that he improperly assisted a casino license application by a former friend and neighbour, who also gave [him] a good deal on home renovations. —*Toronto Globe and Mail*, p. A9, 29th June 2002
- Camillagate [for Camilla Parker-Bowles], Cheriegate [for Cherie Blair]. Monicagate [for Monica Lewinsky], Campbellgate [for Alastair Campbell]. —Susie Dent, *The Language Report*, p. 17, 2003
- Nipplegate: Janet Jackson's revealing moment at the Super Bowl. —*The Guardian*, picture caption, 14th February 2004

gate-crash *verb*

to achieve entrance to a place, or an event such as a party, without proper credentials or an invitation *US, 1922*

- The 'comedy terrorist' who gatecrashed Prince William's 21st birthday party may have zero talent for jokes or impersonation. —*The Guardian*, 25th June 2003

gate-crasher *noun*

a person who achieves entrance to a place, or an event such as a party, without proper credentials or an invitation *US, 1927*

- Since then the party has been made gatecrasher-proof. —*The Observer*, 4th November 2001

gate-crashing *noun*

the act of achieving entrance to a place, or an event such as a party, without proper credentials or an invitation *US, 1927*

- Royal gatecrashing: what's the crime? —*Law in Action*, 27th July 2003

gate fever *noun*

the anxiety suffered by prisoners as they approach their release date *UK*

- —Frank Norman, *Bang to Rights*, 1958
- —John R. Armore and Joseph D. Wolfe, *Dictionary of Desperation*, p. 30, 1976
- —Home Office, *Glossary of Terms and Slang Common in Penal Establishments*, 1978
- —Harry Orsman, *A Dictionary of Modern New Zealand Slang*, p. 54, 1999
- "Maybe what you got is a big old dose of what's called gate fever in reverse." "Gate fever?" "When guys are comin to the end of a bitta bird they start panicking, getting anxious, cos they can see the end. You're sweatin about gettin captured." —J.J. Connolly, *Layer Cake*, p. 90, 2000

gate happy *adjective*

(of prisoners) being exuberant or excited at the approach of a release date *UK*

- —Angela Devlin, *Prison Patter*, p. 55, 1996

gate jaw *noun*

in trucking, a driver who monopolises conversation on the citizens' band radio *US*

- —Wayne Floyd, *Jason's Authentic Dictionary of CB Slang*, p. 17, 1976

gatekeeper *noun*

a person who introduces another to a first LSD experience *US*

- —John Williams, *The Drug Scene*, p. 112, 1967

gate money *noun*

the cash given to a prisoner upon release from prison *US, 1931*

- [H]e signed his parole papers and was issued a hundred dollars in gate money. —Seth Morgan, *Homeboy*, p. 388, 1990
- Foley came out with his fifty dollars gate money and took a bus to L.A. where Buddy was waiting for him in a car he'd boosted for the occasion. —Elmore Leonard, *Out of Sight*, p. 25, 1996
- The career burglar had previously lived in the Crenshaw area and the Inland Empire, but he had only $200 in "gate" money and needed a quick place to shower and sleep. —*Los Angeles Times*, p. 1, 30th November 2002

gatemouth *noun*

a gossip *US, 1944*

- —Clarence Major, *Dictionary of Afro-American Slang*, p. 57, 1970

Gatemouth *nickname*

jazz trumpeter Louis Armstrong (1901 – 1971) *US, 1936*

- [I]t marked the first time Old Gatemouth ever put his scatting on wax. —Mezz Mezzrow, *Really the Blues*, p. 119, 1946

gates *noun*

1 used as a term of address, male-to-male, usually collegial *US, 1936*

- Then I said to him, "Gates leave your vibes, aint no need to set them up every night." —Babs Gonzales, *Movin' On Down De Line*, p. 69, 1975

2 marijuana *US, 1966*

- —Ernest L. Abel, *A Marijuana Dictionary*, p. 42, 1982

3 a house *BERMUDA*

- —Peter A. Smith and Fred M. Barritt, *Bermewjan Vurds*, 1985

Gateshead *noun*

▸ **get out at Gateshead**

during sex, to withdraw the penis from the vagina just before ejaculation, to practise *coitus interruptus* *UK*

- Since the nineteenth century, natives of Newcastle-upon-Tyne have described the procedure alliteratively as getting out at Gateshead. —*Times Literary Supplement*, 4th December 1970

gates of Rome *noun*
home *UK, 1960*
Rhyming slang.
- Be it ever so humble there's no place like your "gates of Rome". —Ray Puxley, *Cockney Rabbit*, 1992

gate to heaven; jade gate *noun*
the vagina *US*
Notable for what seems to be the first slang uses of 'gate' as 'vagina' – not for the sub-'Perfumed Garden'-style of metaphorical imagery.
- —Erica Orloff and JoAnn Baker, *Dirty Little Secrets*, p. 71, 2001

Gateway to the South *noun*
Balham, a district in south London *UK*
An ironic title, coined in the early 1960s for a satirical 'travelogue' 'Balham – Gateway to the South' written by Frank Muir and performed by Peter Sellers.
- —David Powis, *The Signs of Crime*, 1977

gatey *adjective*
of prisoners, suffering anxiety as the date of release from prison approaches *UK*
- —Frank Norman, *Encounter*, 1959

gather *noun*
a police officer *UK*
- There's about twenty fuckin' gathers running around the gaff now, some of them have got shooters[.] —J.J. Connolly, *Know Your Enemy [britpulp]*, p. 157, 1999

gather *verb*
to arrest *AUSTRALIA*
Usually as the passive 'be gathered'.

Gatnick *noun*
London *Gatwick* airport *UK*
A pun on **NICK** (to steal), based on the reputation of the baggage handlers.
- I was working at Gatwick (or GatNICK) Airport[.] —Martin King and Martin Knight, *The Naughty Nineties*, p. 104, 1999

gato *noun*
heroin *US, 1980*
Spanish *gato* (a cat).
- —Richard A. Spears, *The Slang and Jargon of Drugs and Drink*, p. 214, 1986
- —Mike Haskins, *Drugs*, p. 284, 2003

gator *noun*
1 an alligator *US, 1844*
- Crocs are meaner, more aggressive. Gators get fat and lazy. —Carl Hiaasen, *Tourist Season*, p. 115, 1986
- One of the deputies said, "Well, it's a fact, gators love dog." —Elmore Leonard, *Maximum Bob*, p. 74, 1991

2 an all-purpose male form of address *US, 1944*
Originally a Negro abbreviation of 'alligator'; in the 1930s it was adopted into **JIVE** (black/jazz slang) as an equivalent of **CAT** (a man); *gato* is a 'male cat' in Spanish. Eventually rock 'n' roll spread the word and it died out.
- The little number will pull you dead to the kerb. Gators she is a panic. —Lavada Durst, *The Jives of Dr. Hepcat*, 1953
- See you later alligator, / After 'while, crocodile. —(Robert Guidry) Bill Haley and His Comets, *See You Later Alligator*, 1956

3 a swing jazz enthusiast *US, 1944*
An abbreviation of **ALLIGATOR**.
- —Lou Shelly, *Hepcats Jive Dictionary*, p. 11, 1945

Gator *nickname*
Ron Guidry (b.1950), one of the best pitchers to ever play for the New York Yankees (1975–88) *US*
Guidry came from Louisiana, a state with swamps that are home to alligators.

gator boy; gator girl *noun*
a member of the Seminole Indian tribe *US*
- —*American Speech*, p. 271, December 1963: 'American Indian student slang'

gator grip *noun*
in television and film making, a clamp used to attach lights *US*
An abbreviation of 'alligator grip', from the resemblance to an alligator's jaws.
- —Ira Konigsberg, *The Complete Film Dictionary*, p. 141, 1987

gatted *adjective*
drunk *UK*
- —*e-cyclopaedia*, 20th March 2002

gatter *noun*
a drink; alcohol, especially beer *UK, 1841*
English gypsy use.
- —Jimmy Stockin, *On The Cobbles*, p. 10, 2000

gattered *adjective*
drunk *UK*
Possibly a variation of **GUTTERED**.
- —Pete Brown, *Man Walks into a Pub*, 2003

gauching *adjective*
used to describe the glazed-eyed, open-mouthed state of an intoxicated drug taker *UK*
- —Angela Devlin, *Prison Patter*, p. 55, 1996

gauge *noun*
a shotgun *US*
- —Kenn "Naz" Young, *Naz's Dictionary of Teen Slang*, p. 48, 1993
- —*Los Angeles Times*, p. B1, 19th December 1994
- —Bill Valentine, *Gang Intelligence Manual*, p. 76, 1995: 'Black street gang terminology'

gavacho *noun*
▷ see: **GABACHO**

gavel and wig; gavel *verb*
to probe your eye or your anus in order to relieve an irritation *UK*
Rhyming slang for **TWIG**.
- [H]aving a good old gavel. —Ray Puxley, *Cockney Rabbit*, 1992

gavvers *noun*
the police *UK*
English gypsy and underworld use.
- It's going off, I thought, maybe the gavvers are here again making themselves busy. —Jimmy Stockin, *On The Cobbles*, p. 29, 2000
- —Dave Courtney, *Dodgy Dave's Little Black Book*, p. 9, 2001

gawd; gaw; gor *noun*
god *UK, 1877*
Phonetic spelling of Cockney pronunciation, subsequently treated as almost euphemistic.
- Gawd stone me! What's the matter now? —Clive Exton, *No Fixed Abode [Six Granada Plays]*, p. 118, 1959
- JOHN: Gaw, it's depressing in here, isn't it? —*A Hard Day's Night*, 1964
- Gawd, we might have had to deliver that baby ourselves. —Mary Hooper, *(megan)2*, p. 39, 1999

Gawd forbid; Gawd fer bid *noun*
▷ see: **GOD FORBID**

gawd love-a-duck!; cor love-a-duck!
used as a mild expression of shock or surprise *UK, 1984*
A variation of **LORD LOVE-A-DUCK!**.

gawjo *noun*
▷ see: **GORGER**

gawk *noun*
in circus and carnival usage, a local who loiters as the show is assembled or taken down *US*
- —Don Wilmeth, *The Language of American Popular Entertainment*, p. 107, 1981

gay *noun*
a homosexual *US, 1953*
- An Perry – he's a gay – June found him layin on the road one night about a week ago. —Robert Gover, *Here Goes Kitten*, p. 154, 1964
- —Collin Baker et al., *College Undergraduate Slang Study Conducted at Brown University*, p. 124, 1968
- Gay: The acceptable term for homosexuals, male or female. —*Screw*, p. 7, 12th October 1970
- —Ellen C. Bellone (Editor), *Dictionary of Slang*, 1989

gay *adjective*
1 homosexual *US, 1933*
- Not all who call their flats in Greenwich Village "studios" are queer. Not all New York's queer (or, as they say it, "gay") people live in Greenwich Village. —Jack Lait and Lee Mortimer, *New York Confidential*, p. 65, 1948
- The only word used by homosexuals with reference to themselves, their friends, their haunts, etc. —Anon., *The Gay Girl's Guide*, p. 10, 1949
- Anyway, what's so special about being gay except a lot of heartaches and headaches? Heteros don't brag about the novels and paintings they've produced because they go to bed with the opposite sex. —*One: The Homosexual Magazine*, p. 19, February 1953

- Now you see, I always thought that being gay was about the most iconoclastic, minority thing there was.—Bernard Wolfe, *The Late Risers*, p. 213, 1954
- [T]ook pride in being a homosexual by feeling intellectually and esthetically superior to those (especially women) who weren't gay. —Hubert Selby Jr, *Last Exit to Brooklyn*, p. 39, 1957
- Back in the days when I was first in the navy, I didn't know a gay guy from a straight guy.—Willard Motely, *Let No Man Write My Epitaph*, p. 210, 1958
- They wanted to know if I knew what "gay" meant. I said sure – happy, fun, jolly.—Ann Aldrich (Marijane Meaker), *We, Too Must Love*, 1958
- [T]he champ would throw the next fight in a gay or effeminate manner[.]—Terry Southern, *The Magic Christian*, p. 59, 1959
- Eve was so beautiful and open to love – but she chose to seek satisfaction inside her own sex.—Joan Ellis, *Gay Girl*, 1962
- The theater is one of the gayest in New York. Late at night, men stand leaning along the stairways, waiting.—John Rechy, *City of Night*, p. 45, 1963
- I went back downstairs, got a scared glance from the gay boy at the desk and went outside to the drugstore on the corner[.]—Mickey Spillane, *Return of the Hood*, p. 97, 1964
- And eventually she found out like she wasn't gay.—James Mills, *The Panic in Needle Park*, p. 55, 1966
- "Rubber" was "gay" but he weighed two hundred pounds and was so rough that he got any "guy" he had eyes for.—Babs Gonzales, *I Paid My Dues*, p. 53, 1967
- They started over to the M&M to join the gay set.—Nathan Heard, *Howard Street*, p. 224, 1968
- Also met other gay cats, had many talks with them.—Jefferson Polard and Valsie Alison, *The Records of the San Francisco Sexual Freedom League*, 1971
- The gay boy had been pressing Phil to go below with him and making various remarks full of suggestive sexual connotation[.]—Herbert Huncke, *The Evening Sun Turned Crimson*, p. 101, 1980
- Yes, maybe Hoover and top aid Clyde Tolson had a gay thing going on.—*Florida Today (Brevard County, Florida)*, 24th October 1999

2 catering to or patronised by homosexuals *US*

- "I heard from a girl friend it was a gay place." "What does the word 'gay' mean to you?" asked Falvery. Her head still averted, she said, "Homosexual." "Does the word 'gay' refer to the premises?" "Yes." —*San Francisco News*, p. 1, 20th December 1954
- I own a homosexual bar. In the nomenclature of the homosexual, it is called a Gay Bar.—Helen P. Branson, *Gay Bar*, p. 23, 1957
- Advertising itself as the "the world's first gay sacramental church", the Beloved Disciple Parish of the American Orthodox Church of the United States celebrates the most ancient Western Christian Mass. —John Francis Hunter, *The Gay Insider*, p. 169, 1971
- He ain't got no girls no more. He's sinking down. He goes to gay bars and throws champagne bottles against the wall.—Susan Hall, *Gentleman of Leisure*, p. 54, 1972

3 bad, stupid, out of style *US, 1978*

General pejorative in juvenile use; a reversal of the politically correct norm much as 'good' is **BAD** and **WICKED** is 'good'.

- —Connie Eble (Editor), *UNC-CH Campus Slang*, p. 3, Spring 1987
- —Pamela Munro, *U.C.L.A. Slang*, p. 41, 1989
- But for really up-to-the-minute types, gay doesn't mean homosexual any more, and it certainly doesn't mean bright and jolly. It's now uncool, unattractive, drab, kitsch – mauve lino with metal green wallpaper, a Boston haircut, doing the Mashed Potato to John Denver records – you get the idea.—*Manly Daily*, 31st August 1991
- —Kenn "Naz" Young, *Naz's Dictionary of Teen Slang*, p. 48, 1993
- Man, that shit was so gay – fucking eighties style.—Kevin Smith, *Jay and Silent Bob Strike Back*, p. 10, 2001
- School is gay!—*Mixmag*, p. 146, June 2003

gay 90s *noun*

US Treasury 3.5% bonds issued in 1958, due to return in 1990 *US*

- —*American Speech*, p. 196, October 1960: 'Corporate nicknames in the stock market'

gay and frisky *noun*

whisky *UK, 1919*

Rhyming slang.

- —Ray Puxley, *Cockney Rabbit*, 1992

gay and hearty *noun*

a party *AUSTRALIA*

Rhyming slang.

- We're going to have a bit of a gay and hearty.—Geoff Wyatt, *Saltwater Saints*, p. 44, 1969

gay as a French horn *adjective*

undoubtedly homosexual *UK*

- "What about Dale Winton?" "Gay!" shouted Marco. "Gay as a French horn."—Garry Bushell, *The Face*, p. 136, 2001

gay-ass *adjective*

extremely out of fashion *CANADA*

- When I say the word party, I don't mean your fucking twelve-year-old nephew's gay-ass birthday bash.—Suroosh Alvi et al., *The Vice Guide*, p. 156, 2002

gay bar *noun*

a bar catering to a homosexual clientele *US*

- At that time it was a gay bar – that means a bar where homosexuals go – and he could do us a lot of good or a lot of harm.—*San Francisco News*, p. 13, 14th October 1953
- I own a homosexual bar. In the nomenclature of the homosexual, it is called a Gay Bar.—Helen P. Branson, *Gay Bar*, p. 23, 1957
- In that shadowed world of dim bars characterized by nervous gestures, furtive looks, masked Loneliness – the World of the Gay Bars[.]—John Rechy, *City of Night*, p. 197, 1963
- —Florida Legislative Investigation Committee (Johns Committee), *Homosexuality and Citizenship in Florida*, 1964: 'Glossary of homosexual terms and deviate acts'
- A man who spends long evenings in a "gay bar" hoping to "cruise" what he knows is going to be a one-night stand cannot fulfill his office functions the next morning.—Antony James, *America's Homosexual Underground*, p. 59, 1965
- This is one reason why the gay bars flourishing all over the United States attract even the more respectable deviates.—Joe David Brown, *Sex in the '60s*, p. 69, 1968
- She had entered a gay bar and taken a seat beside him.—Angelo d'Arcangelo, *The Homosexual Handbook*, p. 21, 1968
- When we first "came out" we spent many happy and exciting times in gay bars from one coast to the other.—*Screw*, p. 8, 24th November 1969
- —*New York Times*, p. 1, 24th August 1972
- "A few years ago," says Herb, "it became chic to go to gay bars to see us – like socialites going to Harlem in the 20s."—*Washington Post*, p. M9, 13th January 1980
- Going to a gay bar, having a gay roommate off-base, marching in a gay parade, that's associational behavior. That is not against the policy.—*Washington Times*, p. A19, 21st February 2000

gay bashing *noun*

violent beatings targeted on homosexuals *US*

- [P]ink warnings posted, GAY BASHING BEWARE[.]—Joel Rose, *Kill Kill Faster Faster*, p. 112, 1997

gay boy *noun*

a homosexual male, especially one who is flamboyant and young *US, 1945*

- —Elisabeth Lambert, *The Sleeping House Party*, 1951
- She shoulders some of the little gay boys out of her way, in contempt.—Willard Motely, *Let No Man Write My Epitaph*, p. 248, 1958
- "Each year – new hustlers, new queens, new – ..." she hesitated, " – new gay boys just out for kicks[.]"—John Rechy, *City of Night*, p. 330, 1963

gaycat *verb*

to have a good, carefree time *US, 1924*

- I wasn't working then and didn't have much money left to gaycat with, but I couldn't refuse to light my friends up.—Mezz Mezzrow, *Really the Blues*, p. 215, 1946

gay chicken *noun*

a young homosexual male *US*

- —J.D. Mercer, *They Walk in Shadow*, p. 564, 1959: 'Slang vocabulary'

gaydar; gadar *noun*

the perceived or real ability of one homosexual to sense intuitively that another person is homosexual *US, 1982*

- —Connie Eble (Editor), *UNC-CH Campus Slang*, p. 4, April 1995
- I may not have – a new expression I read several times in the Blade in the last few weeks – the best gaydar around.—William Leap, *Word's Out*, p. 52, 1996
- After he [Lou Pearlman] chose 25 semifinalists, he hugged these boys he didn't even know a little too much for my gaydar.—*The Village Voice*, 25th July 2000
- Ex boyfs [boyfriends] on gaydar.—*Attitude*, p. 12, October 2003

gayer *noun*

a homosexual *UK*

An elaboration of **GAY**.

- I think the chances of global fame finding that little gayer are now fairly slim.—*Attitude*, p. 146, October 2003

gay for pay *adjective*

said of a heterosexual man who portrays a homosexual man in a film or other theatrical performance *US*

- "Gay-for-pay" performers – proclaimed heterosexual men who slide up the Kinsey Scale when the money is right – are discussed and dissed as well.—*Variety*, p. 96, 23rd June 1997

- Gay-for-pay (straight actor in gay roles, straight men in gay porn) is commonplace in Hollywood movies and in pornography, so why not with politicians?— *SF Weekly*, 9th July 2003
- Dylan McDermott is going gay – for pay. McDermott, the ex-"The Practice" star, has signed on to play Will's love interest on "Will & Grace" for an episode airing Oct. 30.— *Chicago Tribune*, p. 44, 18th September 2003

gay ghetto *noun*
a section of a city largely inhabited by openly homosexual men *US*
Probably coined by Martin Levine, who wrote 'Gay Ghetto', published in *Journal of Homosexuality*, Volume 4 (1979). Examples include Greenwich Village and Chelsea in New York, the North Side in Chicago and the Castro in San Francisco. Unlike all other ghettos, they are affluent.
- When one thinks of gay ghettos across the country, his mind leaps to the Pansy Patch of West Hollywood[.]—John Francis Hunter, *The Gay Insider*, p. 172, 1971

gay gordon *noun*
a traffic warden *UK*
Rhyming slang, probably formed from the Gay Gordons, a traditional Scottish dance.
- —Ray Puxley, *Cockney Rabbit*, 1992

gaylord *noun*
a homosexual man *UK*
An elaboration of **GAY** via a somewhat obscure male forename; introduced to the UK, and possibly coined by, comedian Sacha Baron-Cohen (b.1970).
- Phyzical Heducation iz probly responible for making more gaylords in dis country dan any other thing (apart maybe from house music).
—Sacha Baron-Cohen, *Da Gospel According to Ali G*, 2001
- —[S]cary freaks and beefy gaylords Jack, *Sky Magazine*, May 2001

gayly *adverb*
in a manner that is recognised as obviously homosexual *UK*
- Jane oversaw him getting in on Paul Salmon's friend's guest list, and watched him plunge, gaily and gayly, into the unknown crowd[.]
—James Hawes, *White Powder, Green Light*, p. 221, 2002

gay-marry *verb*
to commit to a lifelong relationship with someone of the same sex *US*
- —Rita Ciresi, *Pink Slip*, 1999
- Maybe you should just get gay-married to somebody.—Rita Ciresi, *Pink Slip*, p. 42, 1999

gaymo *noun*
used as an insult by very young children *UK*
- —Jonathan Blyth, *The Law of the Playground*, p. 68, 2004

gayola; gay-ola *noun*
extortion of homosexuals by the police *US, 1960*
- The existence of these laws also affords constant opportunities for balckmail and for shakedowns by real or phony cops, a practice known as "gayola."—Joe David Brown, *Sex in the '60s*, p. 73, 1968
- Investigators from the State Franchise Tax Board have joined the hue & cry in the "gayola" quiz here.— *San Francisco Examiner*, p. 1 (II), 15th May 1970
- [I]n the late Fifties it was the "Gay-ola" affair, involving pay-offs to city authorities.—John Francis Hunter, *The Gay Insider*, p. 196, 1971

Gay Paree *noun*
▷ **see:** PAREE

gay plague *noun*
AIDS *US*
This term, with overtones of pious hate and biblical retribution, spread the misconception that the AIDS epidemic was exclusively reserved for 'ungodly' homosexuals.
- The mystery sickness gets the name "gay plague" because 75 percent of the victims are homosexuals.— *United Press International*, 26th June 1982

gay radar *noun*
the ability to recognise a homosexual *AUSTRALIA*
- So we'd say these brutal things which he'd pick up on his sophisticated gay radar.—John Birmingham, *He Died With a Felafel in his Hand*, p. 15, 1994

gay-tastic *adjective*
especially wonderful or fabulous in a way that appeals to homosexuals *US*
- [O]ne of the show's totally gay-tastic spectacles[.]— *Blender*, p. 166, September 2004

gay 'til graduation *adjective*
temporarily or situationally homosexual or bisexual *US*
- —Connie Eble (Editor), *UNC-CH Campus Slang*, p. 3, March 1996

gay white way *noun*
▷ **see:** GREAT WHITE WAY

Gaza II *noun*
Concordia University, Montreal, formed of Sir George and Loyola Universities in 1974 *CANADA*
- The fallout from the Sept. 9 clash between pro-Palestinian and pro-Israeli students at Concordia–The message coming from Jewish donors, they said, is this: "We're not supporting Gaza II."— *Montreal Gazette*, p. A8, 26th September 2002

gazebbies *noun*
the female breasts *US*
Vietnam war usage.
- Gazebbies!! Ga-za-beys – most always plural – but not in dictionary!—Tony Zidek, *Choi Oi*, p. 95, 1965

gazelle *noun*
▸ **in a gazelle**
feeling good *CANADA*
Teen slang, reported by a Toronto newspaper in 1946, and reported as 'obsolescent or obsolete' by Douglas Leechman, 1959.

gazillion *noun*
a very large, if indefinite, number *US*
- Suddenly, Daddy had a case that had to be solved right away, so some clerks and Josh came to help go through a gazillion depositions.
— *Clueless*, 1995

gazongas *noun*
the female breasts *US, 1978*
- —Judi Sanders, *Faced and Faded, Hanging to Hurl*, p. 16, 1993

gazook *noun*
1 a loud lout *US, 1901*
- The head gazook made me rent a tie.—Larry Heinemann, *Close Quarters*, p. 190, 1977
- It was that long-haired gazook in Chinatown.—Henry Miller, *Moloch*, p. 39, 1992

2 a boy *US*
- —Vincent J. Monteleone, *Criminal Slang*, p. 95, 1949

gazookus *noun*
in carnival usage, a genuine article *US, 1924*
- —Don Wilmeth, *The Language of American Popular Entertainment*, p. 107, 1981

gazoony *noun*
1 a fellow, especially a low-life *US, 1914*
- "The gazooney bother you much, Frannie?" Jinni said.—Bernard Wolfe, *The Late Risers*, p. 130, 1954
- —Joe McKennon, *Circus Lingo*, p. 38, 1980
- "That's enough for some gazoony out on the pavement to cut your throat and drink your blood," Whistler said.—Robert Campbell, *Alice in La-La Land*, p. 21, 1987

2 a manual labourer in a carnival *US*
- — *American Speech*, p. 281, December 1966: 'More carnie talk from the West Coast'

3 the passive participant in anal sex *US, 1918*
- —G. Legman, *The Language of Homsexuality*, p. 1167, 1941
- —Dale Gordon, *The Dominion Sex Dictionary*, p. 75, 1967
- He's in the big house for all day and night, a new fish jammed into a drum with a cribman, who acts like a gazoonie.— *San Francisco Examiner*, p. 26, 17th August 1976

gazoozie *verb*
to swindle *US*
- —Jay Robert Nash, *Dicitonary of Crime*, p. 146, 1992

gazump *verb*
1 to raise the selling-price of a property after agreeing the terms of sale; hence to outbid an agreed sale *UK, 1971*
A specialisation of the sense 'to swindle'.

- The network fears the net could gazump it by offering video to the US audience before NBC gets round to its "live" package. — *The Guardian*, 14th September 2000
- "I was gazumped," she said. "I was really upset about it. I knew it went on, but I never thought it would happen to me." — *The Observer*, 14th April 2002

2 to swindle *UK, 1928*

- I watched two homies [men] gazumping the joskins [country bumpkins][.] — Butch Reynolds, *Broken Hearted Clown*, p. 61, 1954
- — Jay Robert Nash, *Dicitonary of Crime*, p. 146, 1992

gazumping *noun*

the act of raising the selling-price of a property after agreeing the terms of sale; hence, outbidding an agreed sale *UK, 1971*
From the verb **GAZUMP**.

- Gazumping sweeps Britain. — *The Observer*, 14th April 2002

gazunder *noun*

a chamberpot *AUSTRALIA, 1981*
Also variant 'guzunder'.

- [G]azunder – Any of us who suffer nocturnal incontinence knows what this little item is. It's a potty and it 'gazunder' the bed! — John Blackman, *The Aussie Slang Dictionary*, 1990

gazunder *verb*

of a house-owner or a swindler, to reduce the selling price of a property, especially shortly before exchange of contracts, with a threat that the sale must go through on the new terms *UK, 1988*
A play on **GAZUMP**.

GB *noun*

1 sex between one person and multiple, sequential partners *US*
An abbreviation of **GANG BANG**.

- There was some debate between my chief advisers and myself, regarding the need to devote an entire chapter to the G.B. – gangbang, that is. — Larry Townsend, *The Leatherman's Handbook*, p. 201, 1972

2 any barbiturate or central nervous system depressant *US*
An abbreviation of **GOOFBALL**.

- He was high on barbiturates, goofballs, GB's. — James Mills, *The Panic in Needle Park*, p. 27, 1966
- — Donald Wesson and David Smith, *Barbiturates*, 1977

3 goodbye *US*

- — Lou Shelly, *Hepcats Jive Dictionary*, p. 11, 1945

GBH *noun*

1 the criminal charges of *g*rievous *b*odily *h*arm and malicious wounding; the act of causing serious injury *UK, 1949*
Initialism.

- [H]e was doing a three [years sentence] there [HMP Pentonville] for g.b.h.[.] — Derek Raymond (Robin Cook), *The Crust on its Uppers*, p. 41, 1962
- — Angela Devlin, *Prison Patter*, p. 55, 1996

2 the recreational drug GHB *UK*
A jumbling of the letters in GHB gives an abbreviation for **GRIEVOUS BODILY HARM**.

- — Angela Devlin, *Prison Patter*, p. 56, 1996
- By May 1994 200 people has [sic] been hospitalised in the UK after using GBH and there has been one reported death. — Ben Osborne, *The A-Z of Club Culture*, p. 110, 1999

GBH of the brain *noun*

the activity of studying *UK*
From **GBH** (physical assault and damage).

- — Angela Devlin, *Prison Patter*, 1996

GBH of the eardrums *noun*

loud music *UK*
From **GBH** (physical assault and damage).

- — Angela Devlin, *Prison Patter*, p. 56, 1996

GBH of the earhole; GBH of the ear *noun*

a verbal assault *UK*
Extended from the criminal offence of **GBH** (*g*rievous *b*odily *h*arm). Usually jocular.

- I'm working on contracts, tickets – getting GBH of the earhole from Soldier. — Anthony Masters, *Minder*, p. 28, 1984
- I hadn't told her I was meeting Mark because I wasn't up to the GBH of the ear that I knew I'd get. — Mary Hooper, *(megan)2*, 1999

G bit *noun*

a prison sentence to a federal penitentiary *US*

- — Hyman E. Goldin et al., *Dictionary of American Underworld Lingo*, p. 77, 1950

g'bye

goodbye *UK, 1925*

- G'bye to g'days. A Blighty-bound Patrick Barkham reflects on the good – and the not so good – aspects of life in Australia — *The Guardian*, 25th March 2002

G-car *noun*

a federal law enforcement agency car *US*

- True guided the G-car through stop-and-go airport traffic, across the Sepulveda bridge, and onto Century Boulevard. — Gerald Petievich, *One-Shot Deal*, p. 204, 1981

GCM!

used as an expression of frustration or wonder *SOUTH AFRICA, 1984*
An initialism of 'God, Christ, Moses'.

g'day; gooday; gidday

hello! *AUSTRALIA, 1928*
An extremely common, and now iconic, Australian greeting.

- Oh. G'day, Pearl. Come on in. — Ray Lawler, *Summer of the Seventeenth Doll*, p. 37, 1957
- 'G'day,' said the Italian, with his ingratiating smile. — Jean Brooks, *The Opal Witch*, p. 89, 1967
- 'Dad. This is Bruce. Bruce, my father.' 'Gidday Mr Vickers. Gettin' heaps?' — Kathy Lette and Gabrielle Carey, *Puberty Blues*, p. 54, 1979
- The mob was surprised to see Jesus and ran up to say "G'day." — Kel Richards, *The Aussie Bible*, p. 48, 2003

GDI *noun*

a college student who is not a fraternity or sorority member, a *g*od-*d*amn *i*ndependent *US*

- — Andy Anonymous, *A Basic Guide to Campusology*, p. 11, 1966
- — Pamela Munro, *U.C.L.A. Slang*, p. 42, 1989
- GDI is what the dormies call themselves. People who aren't in frat or sorority houses. — Jeffrey Wilds Deaver, *The Lessons of her Death*, p. 23, 1993
- Even though I'm not in a sorority – I am a GDI (God Damn Independent) – I still dance at every set. — April Sinclair, *Ain't Gonna Be the Same Fool Twice*, p. 39–40, 1996

G-dog *noun*

a good friend *US*

- — *Columbia Missourian*, p. 1A, 19th October 1998

GE *noun*

the electric chair *US*
Homage to General Electric.

- — Charles Shafer, *Folk Speech in Texas Prisons*, p. 205, 1990

gear *noun*

1 marijuana; heroin; drugs in general *US, 1954*

- Cannabis Sativia is better known to us by its Spanish-Mexican name, Marijuana. Or pot, grass, weed, dope, gear, Kiwi green. — R. Rose, *New Zealand Green*, p. 5, 1976
- — Liz Cutland, *Kick Heroin*, 1985
- It takes a hell of a long time to come when you are on gear and it was great when the chick didn't know you were stoned. — Shaun Ryder, *Shaun Ryder... in His Own Words*, 1996
- — Angela Devlin, *Prison Patter*, p. 56, 1996
- [S]o strung out on all that free gear that they couldn't be bothered. — Dave Courtney, *Stop the Ride I Want to Get Off*, p. 271, 1999
- [T]hey have caught me a couple of times before actually digging [injecting] gear [heroin]. — Lanre Fehintola, *Charlie Says...*, p. 20, 2000
- [T]hey do smoke gear after all[.] — *Skymail, Sky Magazine*, p. 11, May 2001
- — Robert Ashton, *This Is Heroin*, p. 206, 2002

2 anything, especially anything illicit, intentionally undefined *AUSTRALIA*
Included in the 'Australian Underworld Terms Current in 1975' appendix to the 8th edition of Partridge's *Dictionary of Slang and Unconventional English* with the notation 'peculiarly Australian cant'.

3 the equipment and paraphanalia associated with drug use, especially syringes, etc *UK*

- — Angela Devlin, *Prison Patter*, p. 56, 1996

4 stolen goods *UK*

- It would have been too dodgy swagging gear into Bella's drum at 3 a.m. — Charles Raven, *Underworld Nights*, p. 22, 1956
- It's nothing silly, it's just a bit of gear I knock out to a few reliable fellas. — Danny King, *The Burglar Diaries*, p. 31, 2001

5 stuff, things *UK, 1415*

- The hitch-hiker hoisted his gear in and stuffed it on the floor. — Gurney Norman, *Divine Right's Trip (Last Whole Earth Catalog)*, p. 11, 1971

6 clothes *AUSTRALIA, 1970*
Recorded in the US in *Newsday*, 11th October 1997.
- Do you think she should be played by a girl who strips at every orgy in town and expects to be fucked the instant her gear's off? — *Janie Stagestruck*, p. 101, 1972
- — Roy Slaven (John Doyle), *Five South Coast Seasons*, p. 124, 1992

7 (of a woman) the obvious physical attributes *US*
Extended from the purely genital sense.
- "Wonder gear," it developed, is an attractive girl, in Navy lingo[.] — *San Francisco News*, 14th October 1953
- So, obviously, is Joey Heatherton. Her gear is mobile, shapely and slender. — *San Francisco Examiner*, p. 19, 14th Janauy 1965
- You'll be [...] having a smoke and a laugh with the lads, clocking the gear on the little honeys in the queue[.] — Kevin Sampson, *Outlaws*, p. 66, 2001

8 a homosexual *US*
- A couple of gears own it; they dress in drag. — Bruce Jackson, *Outside the Law*, p. 113, 1972

▸ **get your arse into gear; get your ass into gear**
to stop idling, to apply yourself to an activity, to start doing something useful *US, 1914*
- I'm not gonna stand around here when I got to get my ass in gear tomorrow morning[.] — George V. Higgins, *The Judgment of Deke Hunter*, p. 50, 1976
- She tells – no, commands – Edgar to get his arse into gear, fast. — *Sunday Times (South Africa)*, 15th June 2003

gear *adjective*
very good, outstanding *UK, 1951*
Brought to the world by the Beatles, dropped from fashionable use in the mid-1960s; revived in the UK, later C20, and continues in ironic use.
- JOHN [LENNON] touches the costume on one actor. JOHN: (to actor) Gear costume! ACTOR: (eyeing him) Swap? — *A Hard Day's Night*, 1964
- — J. R. Friss, *A Dictionary of Teenage Slang (Mt. Diablo High)*, 1964
- "No. We never expected anything like this – it was really fear." "Gear?" "Fab," he explained, translating quickly from his native Beatle-ese, "you know – really great." — *Life*, p. 34, 21st February 1964
- — John Lawlor, *How to Talk Car*, p. 53, 1965
- — Fritz Spiegl, *Lern Yerself Scouse*, 1966

gear bonger; gear banger *noun*
a poor driver, especially one who crashes the gears *US, 1971*
- — *Complete CB Slang Dictionary*, 1976
- — Peter Chippindale, *The British CB Book*, p. 155, 1981

gear-box *noun*
the vagina *UK*
A survival and technological updating of obsolete 'gear '(the vagina), used in East Anglia, notably Suffolk. Reported by F. Leech, 1972.

gear down *verb*
to dress up *BARBADOS*
- — Frank A. Collymore, *Barbadian Dialect*, p. 52, 1965

geared *adjective*
available for homosexual relations *US, 1935*
- — *New York Mattachine Newsletter*, p. 6, June 1961: 'Sex deviation in a prison community'

geared up *adjective*
dressed up *UK*
Also used of motorcyclists in full protective wear.
- — Patrick O'Shaughnessy, *Market Traders' Slang*, 1979

gear (for something) *adjective*
obsessed with, fanatic about *US*
- — Bruce Jackson, *Outside the Law*, p. 57, 1972: 'Glossary'

gear head *noun*
in mountain biking, a bicycle mechanic *US*
- — William Nealy, *Mountain Bike!*, p. 162, 1992: 'Bikespeak'

gear jammer *noun*
a truck driver who has a difficult time shifting gears, especially one who is constantly clashing the gears as he shifts *US, 1929*
- — Montie Tak, *Truck Talk*, p. 71, 1971

gear-lever *noun*
the penis *UK*
Historically 'gear' has meant both male and female genitals so the derivation here is ambiguous. Remembered by Beale as the term used by UK National Servicemen (National Service ran from 1946–60).
- — B.S Johnson (Editor), *All Bull*, 1973

gears *noun*
the testicles *US*
- About the only part of an old pig we don't eat is his pizlum. That's his auger. But we did eat the other part of his male self – we call them his gears. Some will stay away from those things. — Earl Conrad, *Rock Bottom*, p. 246, 1952

geaze *noun*
▷ see: **GEEZE**

gedanken *adjective*
in computing, impractical or poorly designed *US*
From the German for 'thought'.
- A gedanken thesis is usually marked by an obvious lack of intuition about what is programmable and what is not, and about what does and does not constitute a clear specificaton of an algorithm. — Guy L. Steele et al., *The Hacker's Dictionary*, p. 71, 1983

gedunk *noun*

1 ice-cream, sweets, potato crisps and other junk food; the ship store where junk food can be bought *US, 1927*
A US Navy term. One theory is that 'geedunk' is the sound made by a vending machine when it disposes a soft drink in the cup.
- — Linda Reinberg, *In the Field*, p. 92, 1991

2 a place where sweets and snacks are sold *US, 1956*
Variant spellings exist, such as 'gedonk'.
- Maybe they have a gedonk there where he can get some candy, I don't know. — Darryl Ponicsan, *The Last Detail*, p. 167, 1970

gedunk truck *noun*
a catering truck *US*
Probably mock German.
- It begins with a catering truck, like hundreds that ply San Diego work sites. Yes, but this is no ordinary roach coach, ptomaine wagon or gedunk truck. — *Los Angeles Times*, p. 1, 8th July 1992

gee *noun*

1 a man, a fellow *US, 1907*
- From the first letter of 'guy'; sometimes spelling 'ghee'. To some people you're a wrong gee. — Raymond Chandler, *The Long Goodbye*, 1953
- Well, it took you gees long enough to get here. [Steve Canyon comic strip] — *San Francisco Examiner*, 17th September 1954
- We was the gees on the first bench and what we said was law. — Hubert Selby Jr, *Last Exit to Brooklyn*, p. 43, 1957
- After all, I'm not a heavy gee. — Iceberg Slim (Robert Beck), *Trick Baby*, p. 14, 1969
- Plenty of big ghees have been my clients, guys like Larry. — Edwin Torres, *Q & A*, p. 137, 1977
- He was one of six Mafia ghees in my conspiracy trial in 1970. — Edwin Torres, *After Hours*, p. 159, 1979

2 opium; heroin *US, 1938*
Possibly a respelling of the initial letter of a number of synonyms, or from Hindi *ghee* (butter), or playing on the sense as **HORSE** (heroin).
- — Richard A. Spears, *The Slang and Jargon of Drugs and Drink*, p. 214, 1986
- — Mike Haskins, *Drugs*, p. 284, 2003

3 $1,000 *US, 1936*
From the first letter of **GRAND** ($1,000).

4 a piece of praise *UK*
Possibly from the verb sense 'to encourage'.
- "I told him in this country we have the toughest street fighter I have ever seen. No-one is a match for this Lenny McLean." I said, "Now, that's a lovely gee, but you didn't ask me down here to tell me that, I know." — Lenny McLean, *The Guv'nor*, p. 144, 1998

5 a market trader's or circus entertainer's assistant who is discreetly positioned in the crowd to incite responses *UK, 1934*
- [A] circus man who sits in the audience and pretends to be one of the flatties is called a "gee". — Butch Reynolds, *Broken Hearted Clown*, p. 32, 1953

6 a strong, respected, manipulative prisoner *US*
- A 'gee' is not necessarily the most formidable physical specimen of his group. He may achieve his position by virtue of superior craftiness in 'making connections' or 'pulling deals. — *American Speech*, p. 194, October 1951: 'A study of reformatory argot'

7 any device used to secure a needle to an eye dropper as part of an improvised mechanism to inject drugs *US*

- You hold the needle on by tearing the edge of a dollar bill and wrapping it around the small end of the dropper. You call that the 'G'. — Clarence Cooper Jr, *The Scene*, p. 82, 1960
- They pulled out two spikes, laid out two hypes / And rolled some one-dollar-bill gees. — Dennis Wepman et al., *The Life*, p. 56, 1976

8 the vagina *IRELAND*

The term gives rise to the 'gee bag' condom, 'missed by a gee hair' (a near miss or accident) and the expression 'do ya the gee' said by a boy to a girl and meaning 'do you have sex'.

- But he'd had to keep feeling them up and down from her knees up to her gee after she'd said that... — Roddy Doyle, *The Van*, p. 65, 1991
- And I thought, gee is certainly something that gobshite knows all about. — Joseph O'Connor, *Red Roses and Petrol*, p. 7, 1995

9 a horse *UK, 1879*

gee *verb*

1 to encourage, to incite *UK, 1932*

From the commands to a horse: 'gee up!'.

- I was in the thick of it as usual, geeing everyone along. — Dave Courtney, *Stop the Ride I Want to Get Off*, p. 59, 1999

2 to inform *UK*

From the initial letter of **GRASS** (to inform).

- — Angela Devlin, *Prison Patter*, p. 56, 1996

gee!; jee!

an exclamation used for expressing surprise, astonishment or shock *US, 1895*

Probably a euphemism for 'Jesus!'; later use is often ironic.

- Gee, Officer Krupke, / We're down on our knees, / 'Cause no one wants a fella with a social disease. / Gee, Officer Krupke, / What are we to do! / Gee, Officer Krupke, / Krup you! — Stephen Sondheim, *Gee, Officer Krupke!*, 1957

geech *noun*

money *US*

- — Hy Lit, *Hy Lit's Unbelievable Dictionary of Hip Words for Groovy People*, p. 17, 1968

geechee *noun*

an uneducated, rural black person, especially one who is not easily understood *US, 1905*

- One of the funniest things I ever heard was mac spieling in Yiddish, because he spoke it with a thick Southern drawl, piling on more "you-alls" than a Geechee senator. — Mezz Mezzrow, *Really the Blues*, p. 70, 1946
- Thought you might be one of those salt-water Gitchies. — Earl Conrad, *Rock Bottom*, p. 98, 1952
- Daddy was a Geechee so we had rice every day. — Louise Meriwether, *Daddy Was a Number Runner*, p. 99, 1970
- Decatur said, "The black geechie with the wavy moss." — Iceberg Slim (Robert Beck), *Death Wish*, p. 112, 1977
- And it's right on time too, because I got them three geechee boys from Delaware coming back. — Richard Price, *Clockers*, p. 520, 1992
- Gullah people, known as Geechee in Georgia and Florida, occupied the Lowcountry coast from the Cape Fear River in North Carolina to the St. John's River in northern Florida. — *Post and Courier (Charleston, South Carolina*, p. 2C, 18th December 2003

geed up *adjective*

excited *UK, 1932*

Influenced by the meaning as 'drug-intoxicated' but actually from **GEE** (to encourage).

- We're ready for him, we're geed up. — Nicholas Blincoe, *The Beautiful Beaten-up Irish Boy of the Arndale Centre*, p. 10, 1998

gee'd up *adjective*

1 drug-intoxicated *US, 1936*

Originally of opium (**GEE**), gradually less discriminating.

- — *American Speech*, p. 25, February 1952: 'Teen-Age hophead jargon'

2 dressed in clothing associated with youth gangs *US*

- — Bill Valentine, *Gang Intelligence Manual*, p. 76, 1995: 'Black street gang terminology'

geedus *noun*

in circus and carnival usage, money *US*

- — Don Wilmeth, *The Language of American Popular Entertainment*, p. 107, 1981

gee-eyed *adjective*

completely drunk *IRELAND*

- I'm at the bor, roysh [right], shooting some pool with Christian, two o'clock in the day and the two of us gee-eyed. — Paul Howard, *The Teenage Dirtbag Years*, p. 55, 2001

gee-gees *noun*

1 horse races *AUSTRALIA, 1963*

Singular 'gee gee' is a '(race)horse' and 'the gee gees' means 'horse racing' – both of which are used in the UK from 1869.

- 'Easy seeing you don't go to the gee-gees.' 'What's that got to do with it?' — Frank Hardy, *The Yarns of Billy Borker*, p. 48, 1965
- — James Holledge, *The Great Australian Gamble*, p. 139, 1966
- — Lance Peters, *The Dirty Half-Mile*, p. 39, 1979
- [H]e's been pissing away his readies on the gee gees[.] — Greg Williams, *Diamond Geezers*, 1997

2 veterinary drugs *IRELAND*

- But if Squirrel had gone to drama classes instead of spending his evenings casing gaffs, perfecting handbrake turns in stolen cars and developing an unhealthy appetite for palf and gee-gees, then he might have been up there on the screen himself. — Howard Paul, *The Joy*, p. 103, 1996

gee head *noun*

a frequent Paregoric user *US*

- — William D. Alsever, *Glossary for the Establishment and Other Uptight People*, p. 24, December 1970
- — Eugene Landy, *The Underground Dictionary*, p. 87, 1971

geek *noun*

1 a carnival freak, usually an alcoholic or drug addict, who would sit and crawl in his own excrement and occasionally bite the heads off snakes and chickens *US, 1928*

Perhaps from German *gucken* (to peep, to look) or synonymous German slang or dialect *kieken*.

- — William Gresham, *Nightmare Alley*, 1946
- My mother said, "So nice meeting you," but my old man just stared at him like he was a geek out of sideshow. — Frederick Kohner, *Gidget*, p. 92, 1957
- They're used by the rummies who swamp up the lot and by the alk-paralyzed geek. — Robert Edmond Alter, *Carny Kill*, p. 8, 1966
- [H]e knew the india-rubber man – the fat woman – the bearded lady – the sword swallower – the snake charmer – geeks – midgets[.] — Herbert Huncke, *The Evening Sun Turned Crimson*, p. 37, 1980
- The geek, virtually non-existent today, was considered a freak, usually a fake, who performed sensationally disgusting acts that normal people would not. — Don B Wilmeth, *The Language of American Popular Entertainment*, p. 107, 1981
- [A] story [...] about the rise of a carny conman and his subsequent descent into geekdom. — Paul Duncan, *Noir Fiction*, p. 48–49, 2000

2 a student whose devotion to study excludes all other interests or society; someone who is considered too studious; someone obsessed with computers *US*

Pejorative.

- — Edith A. Folb, *runnin' down some lines*, p. 239, 1980
- — Connie Eble (Editor), *UNC-CH Campus Slang*, p. 2, Fall 1982
- Joe Stumpy Pepys, great, great, uh, tall blond geek with glasses. — *This is Spinal Tap*, 1984
- Do I look like Mother Theresa? If I did, I probably wouldn't mind talking to the Geek Squad. — *Heathers*, 1988
- You ought to ditch the two geeks you're in the car with now and get in with us. — *Dazed and Confused*, 1993
- Oh, God, he is such a geek. — *Romy and Michele's High School Reunion*, 1997
- Geeks know how sad they are, but they don't care. Being sad is a badge of geek strength and endurance. The transformation of computer buffs from lonely bedroom moles to triumphant geeks is one of the late twentieth century's existential glories. — Melanie McGrath, *Hard, Soft & Wet*, p. 162, 1998
- Ronald, e-mail's for geeks and pedophiles. — *Cruel Intentions*, 1999

3 an offensive, despicable person; a clumsy person; a socially awkward person *UK, 1876*

- The only answer he got was "I"ll lay a baseball bat on you, you underage geek." — Bernard Wolfe, *The Late Risers*, p. 5, 1954
- — *American Weekly*, p. 2, 14th August 1955
- [A]s opposed to the "frustration" of fat-assed American geeks safe at home worrying over whether to have bacon, ham, or sausage with their grade-A eggs in the morning[.] — Eldridge Cleaver, *Soul on Ice*, p. 18, 1968
- Here's this poor geek living in a world of convertibles zipping past him on the highways all the time, and he's never even ridden in one. — Hunter S. Thompson, *Fear and Loathing in Las Vegas*, p. 17, 1971
- [T]heir mothers apparently won't let em watch the whole movie out there in the city of geeks and weirdos. — Joe Bob Briggs, *Joe Bob Goes to the Drive-In*, p. 67, 1987

4 a prostitute's customer with fetishistic desires *US*

- — *Washington Post*, p. C5, 7th November 1993

5 an awkward skateboarder or a pedestrian who gets in the way *US*

- — Albert Cassorla, *The Skateboarder's Bible*, p. 200, 1976

6 crack cocaine mixed with marijuana *UK, 1998*

- —Mike Haskins, *Drugs*, p. 293, 2003

7 a look; a peek *AUSTRALIA, 1966*

- —Jim Ramsay, *Cop It Sweet!*, p. 39, 1977
- Now she's smoking a Mahawat and every time she leans forward to place the bets, two rows of onlookers stretch for a geek at her tits. —Robert English, *Toxic Kisses*, p. 3, 1979
- —Roy Slaven (John Doyle), *Five South Coast Seasons*, p. 135, 1992

geek *verb*

1 to display severe anxiety when coming off cocaine intoxication *US*

- —*Washington Post*, p. C5, 7th November 1993
- —Mark S. Fleisher, *Beggars & Thieves*, p. 289, 1995: 'Glossary'

2 to act foolish *US*

- —*Columbia Missourian*, p. 1A, 19th October 1998

3 to look, watch, peer *AUSTRALIA, 1966*

From Cornish dialect.

- That's all we need. A team of moonfaces geeking at us through the window all afternoon. —Robert G. Barrett, *Davo's Little Something*, p. 53, 1992
- —David McGill, *David McGill's Complete Kiwi Slang Dictionary*, 1998

geek-a-mo *noun*

a geek *US*

- —Trevor Cralle, *The Surfin'ary*, p. 43, 1991

geeked *adjective*

1 in a psychotic state induced by continuous use of amphetamine or methamphetamine *US*

- Last Saturday I did a sixteenth of speed and was totally geeked. —Geoffrey Froner, *Digging for Diamonds*, p. 31, 1989

2 sexually aroused while under the influence of a central nervous system stimulant *US*

- Geeked means to be so hungry for sex that your tongue hangs down to your feet. —Geoffrey Froner, *Digging for Diamonds*, p. 31, 1989

3 marijuana-intoxicated *US*

- Tyrone says he still gets "geeked" – street slang for being high on marijuana[.] —*Milwaukee Journal Sentinel*, p. 1A, 17th March 2002

4 jittery, childishly excited *US, 1984*

- I'm so geeked because you're here. —Graham Norton (to Deborah Harry), *V Graham Norton*, 17th May 2002

geeked out *adjective*

unordinary; injured *US*

- —Connie Eble (Editor), *UNC-CH Campus Slang*, p. 5, October 2002

geeker *noun*

1 a user of crack cocaine *US*

- Indeed, some students said crack smokers they see on the streets – known here as "geekers" – are mostly in their 30s and are objects of ridicule. "We all make fun of geekers". —*Washington Post*, p. A1, 2nd April 1990

2 a starer *AUSTRALIA*

- There's a gasp from most of the geekers which could mean anything. —Robert English, *Toxic Kisses*, p. 4, 1979

geekerati *noun*

an elite grouping of people involved in information technology *US, 2000*

- Malda, his best friend Jeff Bates (also 23) and a passel of buddies run Slashdot.org, a four-year-old site on the Web that has become required reading for the geekerati. —*Washington Post*, p. C1, 10th May 2000
- [A] gaggle of media and geekerati attended the event and, well, much fun was had by all[.] —*Austin Chronicle*, 11th June 2004

geeker rental *noun*

a car stolen by a crack cocaine addict who then trades use of the car for drugs *US*

- Many car thefts are "geeker rentals," said Assistant Prosecutor Paul Scarsella. That's street slang for a crack addict who steals a vehicle and rents it out in exchange for drugs, he said. —*Columbus (Ohio) Dispatch*, p. 1A, 7th January 2002

geeking *adjective*

inept; unfashionable; awkward *US*

- If they threw a party, the chances are it would be "fully geeking." —*New York Times*, 12th April 1987

geekish *adjective*

obsessed with computers; socially inept *US*

- His first film part was in Class, playing Rob Lowe's geekish buddy who ends up bedding Lowe's mother, Jacqueline Bisset. —*Toronto Star*, p. F12, 8th March 1986
- I ended up with this cult of geekish friends —Melanie McGrath, *Hard, Soft & Wet*, p. 173, 1998
- "Where's the little geeky guy?" Benny asked. "Isn't he hanging out with you anymore?" —Janet Evanovich, *Seven Up*, p. 98, 2001

geek out *verb*

to enter a highly technical mode which is too difficult to explain *US*

- Pardon me while I geek out for a moment. —Eric S. Raymond, *The New Hacker's Dictionary*, p. 175, 1991

geek-o-zoid *noun*

a student whose devotion to study excludes all other interests or society, hence an unpopular student; someone who is considered too studious; someone obsessed with computers *UK*

An elaboration of **GEEK**.

- "He's a spod-boy," she said, over coffee in the kitchen of their communal Chiswick flat. "He's got all the right clothes, but you take them off and he's a geek-o-zoid underneath." —Andrew Holmes, *Sleb*, p. 169, 2002

geeksploitation *noun*

an act, or general policy, of taking profitable advantage of the enthusiasm and willingness to work of young computer programmers; also used of entertainment designed to appeal to the technologically obsessed *US*

A combination of **GEEK** (a studious-type or IT obsessive) and 'exploitation'.

- Forget "geeksploitation," says Suck, it's the nicely-suited money folks who are losing here. —*Saint Paul (Minnesota) Pioneer Press*, p. 1E, 21st October 1996
- Of course, not everyone talks this way. Complaining about "geeksploitation" may fly in Silicon Valley, but probably not in an accounting firm or a department store[.] —*Hannibal Courier-Post*, 28th February 1998

geekster *noun*

a geek *US*

- —Trevor Cralle, *The Surfin'ary*, p. 43, 1991

geeky *adjective*

socially inept; overly involved with computers *US, 1981*

- People are just a little bit "geeky," but they mind their own business in great little Spanish houses off Moorpark. —Sandra Bernhard, *Confessions of a Pretty Lady*, p. 117, 1988
- Kia (T. Wendy McMillan) sets her up with geeky granola-type Ely (V.S. Brodie). —*Vogue*, p. 91, June 1994
- Her first role was the geeky best friend in Adventures in Babysitting. —*Mademoisell*, p. 68, June 1994
- "Where's the little geeky guy?" Benny asked. —Janet Evanovich, *Seven Up*, p. 98, 2001

gees *noun*

horse racing *UK*

- Won it on the gees. —Derek Bickerton, *Payroll*, p. 119, 1959

geeser *noun*

a small amount of an illegal drug *US*

- —*American Speech*, p. 25, February 1952: 'Teen-age hophead jargon'

geet *noun*

a dollar *US*

- [T]he same can be said of pert Dorothy Shay, who is so hot at the b-o these days that she isn't required to do any feudin', fussin' or fightin' to land the same bundle of geets. —*Capital News from Hollywood*, p. 2, November 1947

geets *noun*

money *US*

- —Babs Gonzales, *Be-Bop Dictionary and History of its Famous Stars*, p. 9, 1949
- —Robert George Reisner, *The Jazz Titans*, 1960

geetus *noun*

money *US, 1926*

- The geetis taken in from that source couldn't possibly keep anything but bush baseball alive. —*San Francisco Call-Bulletin*, p. 17, 2nd May 1947
- Anselms testified thatonce Dahl came to him for a $100 advance, and another time walked up and said, "Where's the geitus?" —*San Francisco Call-Bulletin*, p. 4, 2nd February 1950

- So now Floyd is not fighting for his health, or his title, or for geetus. — *San Francisco Chronicle*, p. 39, 4th July 1963
- "I got enough geetus that I don't have to live up here if I don't want," he said all at once. — Robert Edmond Alter, *Carny Kill*, p. 41, 1966
- Pay me back when your Chi Town lawyer unties the geeters your father left you from the I.R.S. — Iceberg Slim (Robert Beck), *Doom Fox*, p. 91, 1978

gee-up *noun*

1 an act or instance of stirring *AUSTRALIA*
- — Paul Vautin, *Turn It Up!*, p. 144, 1995
- Yeah, good gee up mate, did Mummy tell you what to ask for? — Paul Vautin, *Turn It Up!*, p. 148, 1995

2 a swindler's confederate who leads others to spend their money *AUSTRALIA, c.1899*
- Well, he has advertised a colt by Tomahawk out of one of his shit mares and all the usual gee-ups are in place and there is a giant con underway. — Clive Galea, *Slipper*, 1988

gee up *verb*

1 to motivate; to encourage *AUSTRALIA, 1955*
- I'll get them to keep geeing up in their columns in the Telegraph and the Sun. — Clive Galea, *Slipper*, 1988
- Yeah, well, all you lot were geeing him up, giving it this, giving it that. I knew he wouldn't be able to go the distance... — *The Observer*, 4th November 2001
- That didn't stop national rural manager Colin Dick from geeing up the troops who assembled in cosmopolitan Wellington. — *Sunday Star-Times*, p. D16, 17th August 2003

2 to tease *UK*
- — Tom Hibbert, *Rockspeak!*, p. 71, 1983

gee whiz!

used for registering shock, surprise, disappointment or for emphasis *US, 1876*
Elaboration of **GEE!**.
- I'd had a deadly relationship the previous summer with another media maiden who was a self-declared faghag so gee whiz I didn't mean to be prejudiced[.] — Lester Bangs, *Psychotic Reactions and Carburetor Dung*, p. 291–292, 1979

gee willikers!

used as a mock oath *US, 1851*
There are countless variants.
- She screwed her mouth sideways. Gee willikers was it dry. — Seth Morgan, *Homeboy*, p. 274, 1990

geez *noun*

1 a friend *UK*
- — Julian Johnson, *Urban Survival*, p. 258, 2003

2 a look *AUSTRALIA, 1981*
A variant of **GEEK**.

geez!

▷ see: **JEEZ!**

geeze; geaze; greaze *noun*

heroin; an injection of heroin; narcotics *US, 1967*
- The greaze is nice / and at a decent price — Lightnin' Rod, *Hustlers Convention*, p. 15, 1973
- "I could use a little geeze right now," Pelon says. — Oscar Zeta Acosta, *The Revolt of the Cockroach People*, p. 124, 1973
- — Inez Cardozo-Freeman, *The Joint*, 1984

geeze; geaze *verb*

to inject by hypodermic needle *US, 1966*
- See, before I geeze, I always clean the area where I'm going to do it with alcohol. — Nicholas Von Hoffman, *We are the People Our Parents Warned Us Against*, p. 153, 1967
- Sell me and Clearhead a dime paper and we can geeze in one of the pads in the abandoned building down the block. — Emmett Grogan, *Ringolevio*, p. 43, 1972
- We had just finished geazin' / when the bitches started teasin' / for us to split and lay. — Lightnin' Rod, *Hustlers Convention*, p. 16, 1973
- I'll stop geezing while we're at war, man. — Oscar Zeta Acosta, *The Revolt of the Cockroach People*, p. 125, 1973
- Still think about geezing when you're inside? — Joseph Wambaugh, *The Blue Knight*, p. 29, 1973
- I'm clean, Officers. I got me a nice little job, and I got me Nalline test results that prove I don't geez no more. — James Ellroy, *White Jazz*, p. 70, 1992

geezer *noun*

1 a man *UK, 1885*
Possibly from Basque *giza* (a man), picked up by Wellington's soldiers during the Peninsular War (1808–14); alternatively it may derive from C15 English dialect *guiser* (a mummer). Variant spellings include 'geyser' and the abbreviated 'geez'.
- Last week down our alley come a toff, / Nice old geezer with a nasty cough — Albert Chevalier, *Wot Cher! or Knocked 'em in the Old Kent Road*, 1891
- He is a dark, middle-sized, middle-aged geezer with an ugly, oh but definitely ugly, kisser [face][.] — Charles Raven, *Underworld Nights*, p. 9, 1956
- I turned and saw a fellow who I had never seen before in my life. He was a big geezer. — Frank Norman, *Bang To Rights*, p. 18, 1958
- Anyway, you're being finished at the Art School for some suave international geyser with handmade shoes. — Peter Nichols, *Promenade [Six Granada Plays]*, p. 50, 1959
- That smart old geezer owned buildings, dry cleaning stores, groceries, you name it. — Edwin Torres, *Carlito's Way*, 1975
- — Vivian Stanshall, *Ginger Geezer*, 1981
- He was a right lovely geezer but, like so many people, he was shy. — Dave Courtney, *Raving Lunacy*, p. 74, 2000
- Discipline maketh the geez — Roots Manuva, *Witness (One Hope)*, 2001

2 an old person, somewhat infirm *UK, 1885*
An objectionable reference to a senior citizen.
- They look like harmless old geezers. — Chester Gould, *Dick Tracy Meets the Night Crawler*, p. 31, 1945
- That smart old geezer owned buildings, dry cleaning stores, groceries, you name it. — Edwin Torres, *Carlito's Way*, p. 28, 1975
- — Multicultural Management Program Fellows, *Dictionary of Cautionary Words and Phrases*, 1989
- When she asked one of the old duffers why they called their beauty contest winner "Miss Emerson," the geezer said, "Knock-knock." — Joseph Wambaugh, *Finnegan's Week*, p. 229, 1993
- Why don't you geezers take your game over to the park. — *Get Shorty*, 1995
- Even a dumb geezer should know that emergency automatically pulls up your name. — *As Good As It Gets*, 1997

3 a fellow-prisoner *UK*
- — Frank Norman, *Bang to Rights*, 1958

4 a man who is easily duped *UK*
- — Frank Norman, *Encounter*, 1959

5 a young manual worker who lives with his parents and spends his disposable income on leisure and pleasure *UK*
Created by a research company as a sociological label for commercial and marketing purposes; a specialised variation.
- Ten ways to tell if your a Geezer. — *The Observer*, 8th June 2003

6 an intravenous drug user *US*
Sometimes spelled 'geazer' from the variant verb spelling.
- See, before I geeze, I always clean the area where I'm going to do it with alcohol. You won't see most geezers doing that, but look at my veins, clean, good, not sore, nothin'. — Nicholas Von Hoffman, *We are the People Our Parents Warned Us Against*, p. 153, 1967
- Every geezer in Soho knew what went down with Matt[.] — Emmett Grogan, *Ringolevio*, p. 203, 1972

7 a small amount of a drug *US*
- — Eugene Landy, *The Underground Dictionary*, p. 87, 1971

geezerbird; geezerchick *noun*

a young-woman characterised by her behaviour and positive involvement in activites (drinking, swearing, sport, etc) stereotypically enjoyed by males *UK*
Combines **GEEZER** (a man) with a less-than-politically correct term for a 'young woman'.
- Sara Cox has come a long way since her Girlie Show geezer-chick days [...] This Sara Cox bears little resemblance to the brassy, leggy, curvaceous, expletive-not-deleted "geezerbird" of popular mythology. — *The Times Magazine*, p. 17, 15th June 2002

geezo *noun*

1 a hardened prison inmate *US*
- He wished he could be a hot geezo like the big-time con he once heard about who yelled when sentenced to 20 years: "That's a cinch, Judge; I can do that standing on my head!" — *San Francisco Chronicle*, p. 10, 27th May 1951
- — *American Speech*, p. 100, May 1956: 'Smugglers' argot in the Southwest'

2 an armed robbery *US*
- And what he did along the way was become a drug dealer and a geezo artist just like the people he was supposed to lock up. — *Chicago Sun-Times*, p. 19, 12th April 2001

gefuffle *noun*

▷ see: **CURFUFFLE**

geggie; gegg *noun*

the mouth *UK: SCOTLAND*
Glaswegian use.
- Just shut your geggie, pal. — Michael Munro, *The Original Patter*, 1985

gehuncle *noun*

a cripple *US*

- Ah, what was that gehuncle going for?—Bernard Wolfe, *The Late Risers*, p. 169, 1954

gel *noun*

1 a girl *UK*

With a hard 'g'.

- You wan those two gels?—Graham Greene, *Travels With My Aunt*, p. 69, 1969

2 dynamite used for opening a safe *US*

- —Bruce Jackson, *Outside the Law*, p. 57, 1972: 'Glossary'

3 a socially inept person *US*

- —Trevor Cralle, *The Surfin'ary*, p. 43, 1991

gelly; jelly *noun*

gelignite *AUSTRALIA, 1941*

- I got a case of gelly down here, and a detonator and fuse all set for a match.—Arthur Upfield, *Bony and the Mouse*, p. 188, 1959
- [S]et him to work screwing [burgling] – send him out with a pound of jelly, dets [detonators], or a dodgy twirl [key][.]—Derek Raymond (Robin Cook), *The Crust on its Uppers*, 1962
- While the crow was still stunned, Harold tied a stick of 'gelly' to it. —Bob Staines, *Wot a Whopper*, p. 36, 1982

gelt; geld *noun*

money *UK, 1529*

Originally conventional English, then out of favour, then back as slang. German, Dutch and Yiddish claims on its origin.

- How is he to collect all this gelt?—Charles Raven, *Underworld Nights*, p. 52, 1956
- She still ignored the drunks figuring somebody with gelt would popup.—Hubert Selby Jr, *Last Exit to Brooklyn*, p. 120, 1957
- Mickey Cohen is Skidsville, U.S.A., and he needs moolah, gelt, the old cashola.—James Ellroy, *White Jazz*, p. 7, 1992
- "AWB". It stands not for the rightwing grouping but "Almal Wil Baklei" (Everyone wants to fight). "Over geld (money)," he laughs. —*Sunday Times (South Africa)*, 21st June 2000
- —Paul Baker, *Polari*, p. 175, 2002

gen *noun*

information *UK, 1940*

Originally military, possibly deriving from the phrase 'for the *gen*eral information of all ranks'.

gen; gen up *verb*

to learn; to inform, to brief *UK, 1943*

After the noun.

- Even more reason then, to make sure you gen up on Eddie [Izzard] trivia[.]—*The Guardian*, 11th September 2000

gendarme *noun*

a police officer *UK, 1906*

Adopted directly from the French *gendarme*.

- [T]he Garners, a traditional tribe, steer clear of gendarmes – let them protect them who need protecting.—Mark Powell, *Snap*, p. 12, 2001

gender bender *noun*

a person with an ambiguous or androgynous sexual identity, or with asexual identity divergent from their biological sex *UK*

- The cult hallows ambiguous sexuality: Mr David Bowie, the rock star "gender bender", is a key hero.—*The Economist*, p. 48, 27th December 1980
- Pop's leading gender bender argued that his putting on a happy face is really not so odd.—*People*, p. 44, 18th June 1984
- I shoulda put Boy George between those two gender benders.—Joseph Wambaugh, *The Secrets of Harry Bright*, p. 115, 1985

gender mender *noun*

a computer cable with either two male or two female connectors *US*

- —Eric S. Raymond, *The New Hacker's Dictionary*, p. 175, 1991

general *noun*

a railway yardmaster *US*

- —Norman Carlisle, *The Modern Wonder Book of Trains and Railroading*, p. 263, 1946

General *noun*

▸ **The General**

1 Frank Sinatra, American singer (1915–1998) *US*

- The latest casino owner in Las Vegas to embark on the hearts-and-flowers route is Francis Albert Sinatra, better known as The Leader, The General, The Dago, The Pope, and Frankie Boy.—Ed Reid and Ovid Demaris, *The Green Felt Jungle*, p. 74, 1963

2 Ireland's most famous criminal, Martin Cahill *IRELAND*

- Martin Cahill, Tango One, the General, Public Enemy Number One, did not conform to the psychological profile of a criminal mind.—Paul Williams, *The General*, p. 14, 1995

General Booth *noun*

a tooth *UK*

Rhyming slang, formed from the name of William Booth, 1829–1912, the founder of the Salvation Army.

- —Ray Puxley, *Cockney Rabbit*, 1992

general election *noun*

an erection *UK*

Rhyming slang, the source of many jokes about standing members, even if we only get one every four or five years.

- —Ray Puxley, *Cockney Rabbit*, 1992

general mess of crap *noun*

a truck manufactured by General Motors Corporation *US*

A humorous back formation from the initials GMC.

- —Montie Tak, *Truck Talk*, p. 71, 1971

General Smuts; generals *noun*

the testicles *UK*

Rhyming slang for **NUTS**, formed from the name of a South African statesman, 1870–1950.

- —Ray Puxley, *Cockney Rabbit*, 1992

General Westhisface

US Army General William Westmoreland *US*

Not particularly kind.

- Do not have the gunge. When the Army wants you to have it, it will be issued to you. Signed, General Westhisface—Larry Heinemann, *Close Quarters*, p. 272, 1977

Generation X; Gen X *noun*

the marketing category that defines people born between the late 1950s and mid-70s *US, 1965*

Originally the title of a sociological book by Charles Hamblett and Jane Deverson, 1965; moved beyond jargon when adopted as the name of a UK punk band in the mid-1970s; in 1991 Douglas Coupland employed it to describe a new generation; usage is now almost conventional. Generation Y does not appear to have caught on.

Generation Xer; Gen-Xer; Xer; X *noun*

in marketing terms, someone born between the late 1950s and mid-70s, seen as well educated but without direction *US, late 1970s*

- What kind of people are Xs?—Paul Fussell, *Class*, 1984
- [I]nformation about Xers, Generation Y and twenty-somethings was suddenly a most precious commodity[.]—Naomi Klein, *No Logo*, p. 71, 2001

Generation XL *noun*

a (notional) sociological group of children, teenagers or young adults who are clinically obese *UK*

A play on **GENERATION X** and XL, the retail abbreviation for 'extra large'.

- —Susie Dent, *The Language Report*, p. 13, 2003

generic *adjective*

stupid, dull, boring *US*

- —Connie Eble (Editor), *UNC-CH Campus Slang*, p. 5, Spring 1988
- —Vann Wesson, *Generation X Field Guide and Lexicon*, p. 76, 1997

geni-ass *noun*

a smart and diligent student *US*

A play on 'genius'.

- —Collin Baker et al., *College Undergraduate Slang Study Conducted at Brown University*, p. 124, 1968

genius *noun*

1 a person skilled at performing oral sex *US*

A pun based on **HEAD** (oral sex).

- —Connie Eble (Editor), *UNC-CH Campus Slang*, p. 3, November 2002

2 in computing, an obvious or easily guessed password *US*

- —Karla Jennings, *The Devouring Fungus*, p. 220, 1990

genny; jenny *noun*

a *gen*erator *UK*

- —Alan Hunter, *Gently by the Shore*, 1956
- —Len Deighton, *Bomber*, 1970

gent *noun*

1 a good man, an honourable man, a man who is admired *UK, 1987*
From '*gent*leman' and characteristics generously ascribed to the stereotype.
- We had been seeing each other for a while and he was a real gent, and totally respected me and my decision to wait. — *The Guardian*, 13th February 2004

2 a man with pretentions to class or status *UK, 1605*
Used in a derisory context.
- The Powers That Be. The quiet gents on the fifth floor. — Mike Stott, *Soldiers Talking, Cleanly*, 1978

3 money *UK, 1859*
Survives as a variant of **GELT** (money) but, in fact, derives not from German *gelt* but French *argent* (silver; money); original use was especially of silver coins.
- — Paul Baker, *Polari*, p. 175, 2002

4 a maggot used as fishing bait *AUSTRALIA*
- 'What ya up to?' 'Bottling up some gents, young'un. Why don't ya come over and give me a hand?' — Phillip Gwynne, *Deadly Unna?*, p. 44, 1998

gentleman jockey *noun*
in horse racing, an amateur jockey, especially in a steeple-chase event *US*
- — Dan Parker, *The ABC of Horse Racing*, p. 146, 1947

gentleman of leisure *noun*
a pimp *US*
- — Kenn "Naz" Young, *Naz's Underground Dictionary*, p. 31, 1973

gentleman's call *noun*
in pool, an understanding that a shot need not be called if it is obvious *US, 1992*
- — Mike Shamos, *The Illustrated Encyclopedia of Billiards*, p. 108, 1993

gentleman's fever *noun*
a sexually transmitted infection *BAHAMAS*
- — John A. Holm, *Dictionary of Bahamian English*, p. 86, 1982

gentlemen's relish *noun*
sperm *UK*
- — *www.LondonSlang.com*, June 2002

gents *noun*
a gentlemen's public convenience *US, 1960*
- [He] got up and made for the gents and I followed him. — Malcolm Pryce, *Aberystwyth Mon Amour*, p. 24, 2001

gen up *verb*
▷ see: **GEN**

Gen X, Gen Xer *nouns*
▷ see: **GENERATION X, GENERATION XER**

Geoff Hurst; geoff *noun*

1 a *first* class honours degree *UK, 1998*
Rhyming slang, based on the name of Geoff Hurst (b.1941), the only footballer to have scored a hat-trick in a World Cup final.
- — Ray Puxley, *Fresh Rabbit*, p. 42, 1998

2 a thirst *UK*
Rhyming slang, formed on the name of the only footballer to have scored a hat-trick in a World Cup final.
- Not to mention callinig for more sherbets [drinks] because the biscuits had given 'em a right Geoff Hurst. — Andrew Nickolds, *Back to Basics*, p. 93, 1994

3 urination *UK*
Rhyming slang.
- Footballer Geoff (Hurst=burst or urination) may not be too pleased. — *Antiquarian Book Review*, p. 18, June 2002

Geoffrey Chaucer *noun*
a saucer *UK*
Rhyming slang, formed on the name of the great English poet, who lived from about 1343 to 1400, and who, fittingly, used slang in his rhyme.
- — Ray Puxley, *Cockney Rabbit*, 1992

geog; geoggers *noun*
*geog*raphy, especially as a subject of study *UK, 1940*
- Even pupils in the Anglo-Chinese schools of Hong Kong talk of chem – and math, geog, phiz, etc. — Beale, 1984
- [W]ho's that tall girl doing geoggers? — Ben Elton and Rik Mayall, *The Young Ones*, 8th May 1984

geologist *noun*
a physician who considers his patients to be as intelligent as a rock *US*
- — *Maledicta*, p. 68, Summer/Winter 1978: 'Common patient-directed pejoratives used by medical personnel'

George *noun*

1 a gambler who tips the dealer or places bets in the dealer's name *US*
- Sitting there with people that are Georges, which means a good toker, you want them to win – even though you're a house person. — Edward Lin, *Big Julie of Vegas*, p. 210, 1974
- — Lee Solkey, *Dummy Up and Deal*, p. 114, 1980

2 in American casinos, a skilled and lucky gambler *US*
- — Steve Kuriscak, *Casino Talk*, p. 27, 1985

3 used as a term of address for any Pullman porter *US, 1939*
- — J. Herbert Lund, *Herb's Hot Box of Railraod Slang*, p. 8, 1975

4 an act of defecation *UK*
A euphemism by personification, but why a George should be so honoured is not recorded.
- Bowles, I'm going to have my Morning George now ... Bowles, always have your George in the morning. — John Winton, *We Joined the Navy*, 1959

▸ **call it George**
to agree that a matter is settled *GUYANA*
Collected in 1962.

George *adjective*
excellent *US, 1930*
- "She's real George all the way," one teen-ager remarked. — *Newsweek*, p. 28, 8th October 1951
- Ginny got the sticks and the horse. She says they're both real george. — John D. McDonald, *The Neon Jungle*, p. 44, 1953
- — James Harris, *A Convict's Dictionary*, p. 32, 1989

George and Ringo *noun*
bingo *UK*
Rhyming slang, formed from the names of two of the Beatles, George Harrison and Ringo Starr, and probably not heard since the Beatles broke up.
- — Ray Puxley, *Cockney Rabbit*, 1992

George and Zippy *adjective*
(of weather) cold, chilly *UK, 2002*
Rhyming slang for **NIPPY**, based on two of the puppet characters in long-running Thames television children's programme *Rainbow* (from 1972).
- — *www.LondonSlang.com*, June 2002
- — Bodmin Dark, *Dirty Cockney Rhyming Slang*, 2003

George Bernard Shaw; George Bernard *noun*
a door *UK*
Rhyming slang, formed from the name of the Irish playwright, 1856–1950.
- — Ray Puxley, *Cockney Rabbit*, 1992

George Blake *noun*
a snake *UK*
Rhyming slang, formed from the name of a notorious British security and intelligence operative who spied for the KGB from 1944–61.
- — Ray Puxley, *Cockney Rabbit*, 1992

George Martin *noun*
farting *UK*
Rhyming slang, formed from the name of orchestral arranger and producer Sir George Martin (b.1926).
- — Bodmin Dark, *Dirty Cockney Rhyming Slang*, 2003

George Melly *noun*
the belly, a paunch *UK*
Rhyming slang, formed from the name of the jazz singer and surrealist (b.1937) whose shape echoes the sense.
- — Ray Puxley, *Cockney Rabbit*, 1992

George Michael; George *verb*
to cycle *UK, 2001*
Popney rhyming slang, based on popular singer George Michael (b.1963). Popney was originally contrived for *www.music365.co.uk*, an Internet music site; this is one of several terms that caught on.

George Raft *noun*
1 a draught *UK*
Rhyming slang, formed on the name of US film actor George Raft (1895–1980).
- I am a continual George Raft. —Ronnie Barker, *Fletcher's Book of Rhyming Slang*, p. 26, 1979

2 hard work *UK*
Rhyming slang for **GRAFT**.
- —Ray Puxley, *Cockney Rabbit*, 1992

George Smack; George *noun*
heroin *US, 1967*
- —Richard A. Spears, *The Slang and Jargon of Drugs and Drink*, p. 216, 1986
- —Robert Ashton, *This Is Heroin*, p. 206, 2002
- —Mike Haskins, *Drugs*, p. 284, 2003

George Spelvin *noun*
used in a theatre programme as a fictitious name for an actor *US, 1908*
- —Sherman Louis Sergel, *The Language of Show Biz*, p. 96, 1973

George the Third *noun*
1 a bird *UK*
Rhyming slang, recorded as an alternative to **RICHARD THE THIRD**.
- —Julian Franklyn, *A Dictionary of Rhyming Slang*, 1961

2 a lump of excrement *UK*
Rhyming slang for **TURD**.
- —Ray Puxley, *Cockney Rabbit*, 1992

George W. *noun*
a person with an inflated sense of self-worth *US*
An unkind allusion to US President George W. Bush.
- —Don R. McCreary (Editor), *Dawg Speak*, 2001

Georgia; Georgie *verb*
to cheat, to swindle; (of a prostitute) to have sex with a customer without collecting the fee *US*
Especially used in the context of prostitution.
- One of the girls georged him, just for kicks, just to see if he was as good a producer as a braggart. —Clarence Cooper Jr, *The Scene*, p. 31, 1960
- She ain't got no man. She's a "come" freak. She's 'Georgied' three bullshit pimps since she got here a month ago. —Iceberg Slim (Robert Beck), *Pimp*, p. 79, 1969
- She started to come, jerked his head forward, and made him georgia her some more. —Steve Cannon, *Groove, Bang, and Jive Around*, p. 8, 1969
- What I wanted was for a white whore to hit on me to spend some money with her, that way I'd have a chance to "georgia" her out of some cock. —Donald Goines, *Whoreson*, p. 203, 1972
- Don't let no bitch georgia you. Don't fuck a bitch 'til the bread is right. In short, Little Willie, sell that dick! —A.S. Jackson, *Gentleman Pimp*, p. 27, 1973

Georgia buggy *noun*
a wheelbarrow *US, 1918*
- Rolling those "Georgia buggies" was a killing job. —Chester Himes, *Cast the First Stone*, p. 32, 1952

Georgia ham *noun*
a watermelon *US*
- —Hermese E. Roberts, *The Third Ear*, 1971
- —*American Speech*, p. 153, Spring-Summer 1972: 'An approach to Black slang'

Georgia homeboy *noun*
the recreational drug GHB *US, 1993*
A disguise for the initials **GHB**.
- —*American Speech*, p. 84, Spring 1995: 'Among the new words'

Georgia night rider *noun*
a trucker who drives at night in the hope of avoiding police *US*
- —Warren Smith, *Warren's Smith's Authentic Dictionary of CB*, p. 40, 1976

Georgia overdrive *noun*
coasting down a hill with the car or truck in neutral *US*
- I got me ten forward gears and a sweet Georgia overdrive[.] —Dave Dudley, *Six Days on the Road*, 1963
- —Montie Tak, *Truck Talk*, p. 71, 1971

Georgia scuffle *noun*
1 a swindle which fails because the intended victim is not smart enough to be swindled *US*
- —Jay Robert Nash, *Dicitonary of Crime*, p. 146, 1992

2 in carnival usage, rough handling of an extremely naive customer in a swindle *US*
- —Hyman E. Goldin et al., *Dictionary of American Underworld Lingo*, p. 78, 1950

Georgie Best *noun*
1 a pest, especially a drunken pest *UK*
Rhyming slang, reflecting footballer George Best's fall from grace to alcoholism.
- —Ray Puxley, *Cockney Rabbit*, 1992

2 the female breast *UK*
Rhyming slang.
- —Bodmin Dark, *Dirty Cockney Rhyming Slang*, 2003

▸ **be my Georgie Best!**
do as you wish; you are welcome to have whatever has been asked for *UK*
Rhyming slang for 'be my guest', formed on the name of Irish footballer George Best (b.1946).
- — Partridge, *A Dictionary of Catchphrases*, p. 28, 1977

ger *verb*
get *UK, 1895*
A slovenly pronunciation that occurs when the following word commences with a vowel, in uses such as 'ger along'.

gerbil around *verb*
in car repair, to work at a somewhat frantic pace in an effort to hide the fact that the problem at hand, or car repair in general, is too difficult *US*
- —Lewis Poteet, *Car & Motorcyle Slang*, p. 92, 1992

gercha!, gerdoying!, geremoff!
▷ **see: GERTCHA!, KERDOING!, GET 'EM OFF!**

geriatrick *noun*
an older homosexual man as a one-time sex-partner *UK*
- — *Maledicta*, p. 222, 1979: 'Kinks and queens: linguistic and cultural aspects of the terminology for gays'

germ *noun*
1 a German *UK, 1915*
- —Thomas H. Slone, *Rasta is Cuss*, p. 48, 2003

2 a despised person *US, 1942*
- —*San Francisco Examiner*, p. III-2, 22nd March 1960
- —Ned Wallish, *The Truth Dictionary of Racing Slang*, p. 32, 1989

Germaine Greer *noun*
a glass of beer *AUSTRALIA*
Rhyming slang, formed from the name of an Australian feminist and academic who has become a media personality (b.1939).
- We washed down the meal with Germaine Greers and Donald Ducked on the Rory O'Moore. —Kathy Lette, *Girls' Night Out*, p. 170, 1987
- —Ray Puxley, *Fresh Rabbit*, 1998

German *noun*
(used by prisoners) a prison officer *UK*
A hangover from World War 2 when the Germans were the enemy.
- —Angela Devlin, *Prison Patter*, p. 56, 1996

German band *noun*
the hand *UK*
Rhyming slang.
- —Ronnie Barker, *Fletcher's Book of Rhyming Slang*, p. 8, 1979

Germans *noun*
drug dealers from the Dominican Republic as perceived by African-American drug dealers competing for the same market – the enemy *US*
- —Terry Williams, *Crackhouse*, p. 148, 1992

germs *noun*
gentlemen, as a form of address *UK*
A jocular slurring, especially in the pairing 'Ladeez and Germs'.

Geronimo *noun*

1 an alcoholic drink mixed with a barbiturate *US*
A dangerous cross reaction.
- —William D. Alsever, *Glossary for the Establishment and Other Uptight People*, p. 12, December 1970
- —Donald Wesson and David Smith, *Barbiturates*, p. 122, 1977

2 a barbiturate *US*
- When we lifted her up, out of her pocket spilled about fifity geronimos. —Herbert Huncke, *Guilty of Everything*, p. 193, 1990

Geronimo!

used as a cry of triumphant discovery *UK*
From an earlier use as a US military war cry; ultimately from the soubriquet of the Apache leader Goyathlay, 1829–1909.
- "I couldn't take my eyes off the Kilburns [rock group 'Kilburn and the High Roads']," says [Dave] Robinson, recalling the sighting. "I thought, 'Geronimo!'" —Will Birch, *No Sleep Till Canvey Island*, p. 146, 2003

gerook; gerooked *adjective*

drug- or alcohol-intoxicated *SOUTH AFRICA, 1970*
From Afrikaans for 'cured/smoked'.
- —Penny Silva, *A Dictionary of South African English*, 1996

gerraway!

▷ **see:** GET AWAY

gerrick *noun*

piece of rolled up silver foil used as a filter in marijuana pipes *SOUTH AFRICA*
The 'gerrick' is made by laying out a piece of foil (usually from a cigarette box), or thin cardboard (usually from the same box) into a square, rolling it up, bending it into a circle and wedging it into the bottom of a bottleneck pipe to keep the marijuana from falling out when the smoke is sucked in.
- —*Surfrikan Slang*, 2003

gerry *nickname*

an old person *NEW ZEALAND*
An abbreviation of 'geriatric'.
- —David McGill, *David McGill's Complete Kiwi Slang Dictionary*, p. 53, 1998

Gerry *nickname*

▷ **see:** JERRY

gert *noun*

great *UK*
A C14 dialect word that is widely familiar.
- What are you doing wi' them, you gert bugger? —*The Full Monty*, 1997

gertcha!; gercha!; gertcher!

I don't believe you!; used for registering disbelief *UK, 1937*
An alteration of 'get away!'; immortalised in song by Chas and Dave, 1979.

Gertie Gitana; Gertie *noun*

a banana *UK*
Rhyming slang, based on the name of music hall entertainer Gertie Gitana, 1888–1957; originating in the first decade of C20 with her name replacing the refrain 'Have a banana' in the song 'Let's All Go Down the Strand'. Still in use.
- I'll have a Gertie[.] —*Antiquarian Book Review*, p. 18, June 2002

gert stonkers *noun*

large female breasts *AUSTRALIA*
- —James McDonald, *A Dictionary of Obscenity, Taboo and Euphemism*, p. 61, 1988

Gestapo *noun*

1 the police *UK, 1941*
Originally used of the military police during World War 2 in a (presumably) jocular allusion to the German Secret Police of the Third Reich. Often used with 'the'.
- CIB3 are the old bill [police]'s internal Gestapo, out to catch wrong'uns. —J.J. Connolly, *Layer Cake*, p. 234, 2000

2 uniformed personnel (such as bus inspectors) or others (such as teachers) who enjoy the little power of their authority *UK*
Reported by Albert E. Petch, 1969.

3 the motorcycle officers of the Metropolitan police traffic division *UK*
Police use (especially the Metropolitan Police Drugs Squad); probably inspired by the jackboots and black breeches uniform. Noted as 'c.1970'.
- —*The Official Encyclopaedia of New Scotland Yard*, 1999
- If you really wanted to make his day, you could have called in the Gestapo[.] —Duncan MacLaughlin, *The Filth*, p. 87, 2002

get *noun*

▷ **see:** GIT

get *verb*

1 to understand, to appreciate *US, 1892*
- Not everyone "gets" her [Princess Superstar] though. "I've been pretty lucky, the press understand the irony and the humour[.] —*The Times Magazine*, p. 45, 16th February 2002

2 to worry, to vex, to annoy *US, 1867*
- But what gets me [...] is the mix of anarchic spirits and low crime rates, adult debauchery and kiddy fun, pert bodies and carnival queens old enough to be your granny[.] —*The Guardian*, 12th January 2003

3 to enthral, to appeal to, to affect emotionally, to obsess *UK, 1913*
- It gets me every time. Worrying about something else distracts me. —*The Guardian*, 9th July 2003

4 to obtain sexual intercourse *AUSTRALIA*
- Morning, Col. Getting any? —Alexander Buzo, *The Roy Murphy Show*, p. 103, 1970
- What does God do when he/she needs to 'get a bit'? Call upon the devil? —Gretel Killeen, *Hot Buns and Ophelia get shipwrecked*, p. 89, 2001

▸ **get amongst**

to perform some task or take part enthusiastically *AUSTRALIA, 1970*
- One local identity decided he would get amongst them and, armed with a very thick line and live mullet, he heaved it out with all his might. —Bob Staines, *Wot a Whopper*, p. 56, 1982
- Apart from that, quite a few Queenslanders have been doing the traditional winter bolt to Indo to get amongst some tropical juice. —*Tracks*, p. 137, October 1992

▸ **get any; get anything; get enough; get a little bit**

to have sex *US*
- I'm getting enough, and the only thing I wish is that I could stay at Park for about three more years. —James T. Farrell, *Saturday Night*, p. 36, 1947
- Outside of the football team and the basketball team, there were only a few going steady who were getting any. [Interview with Walt Grove] —*Playboy*, p. 130, May 1963
- "Gettin' any lately?" [Cartoon caption] —*East Village Other*, p. 14, 18th October 1968
- And another thing. Every time me and my old lady try to get a little bit / You come 'round here with that roaring shit. —Anonymous ("Arthur"), *Shine and the Titanic; The Signifying Monkey; Stackolee*, p. 1, 1971
- And she's not getting anything? Jesus, she must be dying. —Elmore Leonard, *Gold Coast*, p. 19, 1980
- How come when you're nineteen you can't get any? [Note from Joe Bob: I just went to ask the editor if I can explain what "get any" means and he said no sireee, Joe Bob.] —Joe Bob Briggs, *Joe Bob Goes to the Drive-In*, p. 27, 1987
- He has to make up for his mom not getting any. —*As Good As It Gets*, 1997

▸ **get it**

1 to be punished, especially physically *UK, 1851*
- I would usually hide under the porch until it came time to "get it." "You just wait till your father comes, then you're really gonna get it." —Lenny Bruce, *How to Talk Dirty and Influence People*, p. 2, 1965

2 to be killed *US*
- —R. Frederick West, *God's Gambler*, p. 226, 1964: 'Appendix A'
- The wife of one of their people got it. —Richard Condon, *Prizzi's Honor*, p. 237, 1982

3 to become infected with a sexually transmitted infection *UK, 1937*

▸ **get it in one**

to understand immediately *UK, 1942*
- HELENA: So ... you think I can do it better. (Reese smiles at her. She's got it in one.) You know, Detective, that sounds a lot like entrapment. —Hans Tobeason, *Birds of Prey*, 19th February 2003

▸ **get it on**

1 to have sex *US, 1970*
- And if you feel, like I feel baby / Come on, oh come on / Let's get it on. —Marvin Gaye, *Let's Get It On*, 1973
- DJ's who wanted to get it on with Lynn would give her a sleepy look in a hang-out bar and say, "You want to get it?" —Elmore Leonard, *Touch*, p. 23, 1977

- Hey, don't you think a hair stylist's got any interest in gettin' it on? — *48 Hours*, 1982
- I don't have a real relationship right now, so when I'm not making a film, I ain't getting it on at all. — *Adult Video*, p. 9, August/September 1986

2 to fight *US, 1959*

- I would back out then because I was tight with both clicks and couldn't take sides when they'd get it on. — Edwin Torres, *Carlito's Way*, p. 25, 1975

3 to join battle *US*

US Marines usage in Vietnam.

- — Linda Reinberg, *In the Field*, p. 92, 1991

▸get it up

to achieve an erection *US, 1943*

- Feivel couldn't get it up with splints. — Irving Shulman, *The Amboy Dukes*, p. 53, 1947
- Well the Buyer comes to look more and more like a junky. He can't drink. He can't get it up. His teeth fall out. — William Burroughs, *Naked Lunch*, p. 15, 1957
- I'm surprised you could even get it up – look at the way you sweating now. — James Baldwin, *Blues for Mister Charlie*, p. 101, 1964
- I got to be the one that gets it up first. — *Drugstore Cowboy*, 1988
- Lindwood gamely gave in, and then was disappointed when he couldn't get it up. I barely noticed[.] — Jennifer Blowdryer, *White Trash Debutante*, p. 82, 1997
- [B]loke's got a problem getting it up 'cause he's taking too many Es. — John Williams, *Cardiff Dead*, p. 188, 2000

▸get some

to have sex *US*

- So he goes to England and all his pals are getting some but he stays true to his wife, and he goes to Paris and all his pals are getting some, but he stays true to his wife. — Darryl Ponicsan, *The Last Detail*, p. 15, 1970

▸get well

to make money *US*

- This way we hit the cops where it hurts and get well in the meantime. — *The Usual Suspects*, 1995

▸get wet

to kill someone using a knife or bayonet *US*

- — Linda Reinberg, *In the Field*, p. 92, 1991

▸get with

to have sex with *UK*

- Even if a bloke was hot for me, there was no way I would get with him unless he came with a medical. — Kathy Lette, *Girls' Night Out*, p. 71, 1987
- Found out why Dino dropped me! He has been getting wif someone else. — Kylie Mole (Maryanne Fahey), *My Diary*, p. 109, 1988
- I've wanted to get with her for a while now. — *Kids*, 1995
- I tried to get with her for four years, without much success. Then I went on "The Joan Rivers Show." It was my first TV break. Right away she slept with me. — Chris Rock, *Rock This!*, p. 126, 1997

▸get with the program

to start to behave in a responsible manner *US*

A generally figurative application of the recovery programmes promoted by Alcoholics Anonymous, Gamblers Anonymous, etc.; usually as an injunction.

- — Connie Eble (Editor), *UNC-CH Campus Slang*, p. 3, Spring 1983
- They tell her to get real and get with the programme. — Karline Smith, *Letters to Andy Cole*, p. 140, 1998

▸get with the words!

explain yourself! *US*

- — Miss Cone, *The Slang Dictionary (Hawthorne High School)*, 1965

▸get you!; get him!; get her!

1 (with an emphatic stress on the pronoun) used to deflate a conceited male ego or to imply an unmasculine oversensitivity or homosexuality *UK*

- ETHEL: Aren't you men drinking? TONY: No. 'Tis but a small sacrifice for such charming company. HERMIONE: Ooh blimey, get him! — Ray Galton and Alan Simpson, *Hancock's Half Hour*, 22nd April 1958
- — *A Glossary for Our Times (News Chronicle)*, 22nd and 23rd May 1958
- "I don't care how many winners you get – I can't strike up a relationship with you." "Get him!" put in Terry, but Arthur ignored the comment. — Anthony Masters, *Minder*, p. 98, 1984
- That's getting on me wick. Stop it now or I'll break yewer fuckin fingers, Ianto boy. Danny and Llyr do the "wooooo, get him" noises[.] — Niall Griffiths, *Sheepshagger*, p. 59, 2001

2 used for expressing disbelief at what has just been said *US*

Homosexual.

- — Anon, *The Gay Girl's Guide*, p. 10, 1949

▸get your arse to an anchor

sit down! *CANADA*

Adapted from nautical (likely fisherman) usage, this phrase came ashore for general purposes.

- It was an order from a skipper of a small boat, to someone who may be making the boat unstable. It means "sit down and keep still!" — Danny Bower, 1978

▸get your end away

to have sex *UK, 1975*

- If it moved [in Ponder's End, an area north of London], someone shagged it[...] Talk about getting your Ponder's End away! — Duncan MacLaughlin, *The Filth*, p. 153–154, 2002

▸get your kit off!

used as ribald encouragement to undress *UK*

- September Song [Andreson/Weill], the sentiments of which pretty much amount to "Get your kit off, I'll be croaking soon!" — *The Guardian*, 2nd October 1999

▸get your leather

to have sex *CANADA*

- Males in Pictou, NS who get laid say they "got their leather." — *"In Which...." in Matrix*, p. 45, Fall 1985

▸get your own back

to get revenge *UK, 1910*

- Dickens, for example, got his own back on Richard Bentley, the publisher who diddled him in his early career, by naming the wife-beating sadist in Great Expectations Bentley Drummle. — *The Guardian*, 28th July 2003

▸get yours

to get the punishment you deserve *US, 1905*

- "He'll get his some day," I said. — Chester Himes, *Cast the First Stone*, p. 124, 1952
- I read that The Enforcer got his finally, with a .32 Smith & Wesson and a .38 Colt, in the barbershop of the Park Sheraton Hotel in New York City[.] — Clancy Sigal, *Going Away*, p. 472, 1961

▸get your skates on

to hurry up *UK, 1895*

Often as an imperative. Originally military.

- Right, then, you lot, get your skates on 'cos it's beach party time. — Colin Butts, *Is Harry on the Boat?*, p. 51, 1997

▸get your skin

to have sex *CANADA*

- "Getting your skin" is said of a young male to describe sexual intercourse. — Lewis Poteet, *The South Shore Phrase Book*, p. 101, 1999

get!; git!

go!; go away! *US, 1884*

- "You spill a word to the cops," he hissed, "and they'll be serving you up next week in the cheap restaurants as force-meat balls. Now git." — Douglas Rutherford, *The Creeping Flesh*, p. 203, 1963
- Y'll have a sore arse if you're not off it an' up those stairs. Now go on, git! — Alan Bleasdale, *Boys From the Blackstuff*, 1982

get a black dog up you!

go to hell! *AUSTRALIA*

- This famous telegram, which should have read something like 'Get a black dog up ya!', was, in the finest traditions of Cricket, couched in much more civil terms. —
- — Ignatius Jones, *The 1992 True Hip Manual*, p. 159, 1992

get above yourself *verb*

to become conceited, arrogant *UK, 1923*

- They'd say, "It's a bit of a waste of time really." Or they'd say, "You're getting above yourself, my girl!" — Sally Cline, *Couples*, p. 157, 1998

get across *verb*

to make yourself (or your subject) understood *US, 1913*

- Tories failing to get message across before key local election test[.] — *The Guardian*, 8th March 2003

get a dog up you

go to hell! *AUSTRALIA, 1996*

- Down one side of the page is the slang and down the other are Nick's translations, so Molly can learn. So far he's got: 1. Grouse Mate – very good. 2. How's it hangin'? – how are you? 3. Get a dog up ya – get f——d. 4. Fair dinkum – true. — *Sun-Herald (Sunday Life)*, p. 6, 17th May 1998

get a grip!

control yourself! *US*

- — Connie Eble (Editor), *UNC-CH Campus Slang*, p. 3, Fall 1982
- Get a fuckin grip, Victor, yer losing it. — Niall Griffiths, *Kelly + Victor*, p. 129, 2002

get a life!

used to tease someone who is revealing a lack of grounding in reality or who is too obsessed with something *US*

- Jesus, Ann, get a life. I just asked what he looked like. — *Sex, Lies and Videotape*, 1989
- — Connie Eble (Editor), *UNC-CH Campus Slang*, p. 3, Fall 1989
- — Eric S. Raymond, *The New Hacker's Dictionary*, p. 176, 1991
- — Jack Chambers (Editor), *Slang Bag 93 (University of Toronto)*, p. 3, Winter 1993
- DONNY ASTRICKY: You ever notice how it [the show 'Dukes of Hazard'] had a different interior every week? That bugged me. MIRROR MAN: Three words. Get A Life. — *Gone in 60 Seconds*, 2000

get along!

used for registering incredulity *UK*

Similar to the later 'get away!'.

get along with you!

go away! be quiet! *UK, 1837*

get a roll of stamps and mail it in

used as a humorous comment on a lack of effort *US*

Coined by ESPN's Keith Olberman to describe 'a lackluster effort on the part of a player or team'.

- — Keith Olberman and Dan Patrick, *The Big Show*, p. 15, 1997

get a room!

used for discouraging public displays of affection *US*

- OK, Mini-Me, why don't you and the laser get a frickin' room. — *Austin Powers*, 1999

get at *verb*

1 to attack verbally, to tease *UK, 1891*

- Don't get narky (annoyed). I'm not friggin gettin at yer or anythin. — Niall Griffiths, *Kelly + Victor*, p. 229, 2002

2 to mean, to imply a meaning *US, 1899*

- [O]bserve the reality of what Camus was getting at in his discussion of the myth of Sisyphus. — *The Observer*, 6th July 2003

get at it *verb*

to tease someone, to make a fool of someone *UK*

- You see I did this on purpose just to get her at it. — Frank Norman, *Bang to Rights*, 1958

getaway *noun*

the last morning of a military tour of duty *US*

- — Carl Fleischhauer, *A Glossary of Army Slang*, p. 21, 1968

get away!; gerraway!

don't talk nonsense!; don't flatter! *UK, 1848*

In 2002 a travel company used the slogan 'Get away' in a television advertising campaign, punning the conventional sense (to escape, to go on holiday) with an exclamation of disbelief that such holidays could be so cheap.

- "It's on the beat where you keep your peace," Percy Twentyman roared. "Gerraway, Sarge." — Troy Kennedy Martin, *Z Cars*, p. 41, 1962

getaway day *noun*

in horse racing, the last day of a racing meet *US*

- — Mel Heimer, *Inside Racing*, p. 211, 1962

get-back *noun*

an act of revenge *US*

- Those guys got some get-backs coming for what they done to Johnny last week. — Inez Cardozo-Freeman, *The Joint*, p. 499, 1984
- You do to me and I do to you. Get-back. — Robert Campbell, *Nibbled to Death by Ducks*, p. 248, 1989
- — Gary K. Farlow, *Prison-ese*, p. 23, 2002

get bent!

used as an exclamation of defiance, roughly along the lines of 'go to hell!' *US*

- We also talked about the expressions we used in high school. Things like "Get bent," which was meant to put a guy down. — Jim Bouton, *Ball Four*, p. 361, 1970
- — *Esquire*, p. 180, June 1983

getcha vine *noun*

a thorny vine found in the jungles of Vietnam *US*

- — Gregory Clark, *Words of the Vietnam War*, p. 552, 1990

get down *verb*

1 to depress *UK, 1930*

- Tina wants her doctor to prescribe pills for depression. "It really gets me down being shut in so much with the kids," she says. — *The Guardian*, 24th May 2000

2 in sports betting, to place a bet *US*

- By the way, ask him what the odds are on the Giants? I want to get down for a hundred. — Edward Lin, *Big Julie of Vegas*, p. 99, 1974
- I seen a couple of guys I know, had a couple of pops, got something down on it. — John Sayles, *Union Dues*, p. 24, 1977
- — *Bay Sports Review*, p. 8, November 1991

3 to be a part of, or to relate to *UK*

- New Labour was sniffed at for trying to "get down with the kids". — John Robb, *The Nineties*, p. 154, 1999

get-down time; git-down time *noun*

the time of day or night when a prostitute starts working *US*

- As the "git-down" time neared, the women complained about having to go to work on public transportation rather than in a car. — Christina and Richard Milner, *Black Players*, p. 149, 1972
- Get-down time in the Combat Zone and Inez was waiting to draw first blood. — John Sayles, *Union Dues*, p. 180, 1977

get down to it *verb*

to begin to work with serious application, sometimes used of sexual activity *US, 1937*

- I told him to roll his sleeves up and get down to it. — *The Observer*, 11th November 2001

get-'em-off *noun*

an exit ramp; a motorway exit *US*

- — *Complete CB Slang Dictionary*, 1976
- — Peter Chippindale, *The British CB Book*, p. 155, 1981

get 'em off!; geremoff!

used as a jocular imperative to strip *UK*

- [A stag party's] appearance inside the pub was announced by an erupting roar of women screaming "Geremoff!" and "Phwoar!" — Iain Aitch, *A Fete Worse Than Death*, p. 165, 2003

geters *noun*

money *US*

- — Carl J. Banks Jr, *Banks Dictionary of the Black Ghetto Language*, 1975

get-go; git-go; gitty up *noun*

the very start *US, 1966*

- — Stewart L. Tubbs and Sylvia Moss, *Human Communication*, p. 121, 1974
- I want it be understood from the git-go that this is my plan[.] — Odie Hawkins, *The Busting Out of an Ordinary Man*, p. 170, 1985
- Everything about the Irish cop was a threat, right up front, Leddy thought. Right from git-go. — Robert Campbell, *Boneyards*, p. 49, 1992
- I just find out the nigger stealing me blind since the gitty-up. — Richard Price, *Clockers*, p. 67, 1992
- Joey know from the git-go. — Joel Rose, *Kill Kill Faster Faster*, p. 76, 1997

get-hard *adjective*

sexually arousing to men *UK*

- [T]art called Salome does a get-hard dance for Herod, he grants her a fairy-tale wish, she plumps for the head of John the Bap. — Ken Lukowiak, *Marijuana Time*, p. 83, 2000

get her!

used as a comment on someone's over-reaction *UK*

Combined with a pronoun, such as **GET HIM!**, **GET YOU!**; often delivered with a sneer.

- — Paul Baker, *Fantabulosa*, 2002
- Oooh, get 'er! The US rap beef continues to pile up like some crazy hip hop butcher's shop gone mental[.] — *Jockey Slut*, p. 5, August 2003

get-high *noun*

crack cocaine *US*

- I hooked you up for that last get-high. — *New Jack City*, 1990
- She says, "I was by Darius' house, and he said y'all just left. You got any get-high?" — Chris Rock, *Rock This!*, p. 74, 1997

get in; get-in *verb*

of a staged-entertainment, to bring in and set up staging and technical equipment *UK*

The reverse (to deconstruct and entirely remove staging equipment) is 'get out'. Also used as nouns.

- Special rates of pay for "Getting In" and "Getting Out" were established in the awards of theatrical employees unions. — Valantyne Napier, *Glossary of Terms Used in Variety, Vaudeville, Revue & Pantomime 1880–1960*, 1996
- What a vibe the "get-in" is. — Ben Elton, *High Society*, p. 216, 2002

get-in Betty *noun*

a crowbar used by burglars *US*

- We had a pretty good bunch of O'Sullivans, a torch man, a mechanic, a jigger and a hard-shell biscuit who'd been with a gopher mob. We crashed with a get-in betty. — *The New American Mercury*, p. 709, 1950

get into *verb*

to come to know and like *UK*

- The more I got into Davey, the more I felt I loved him and depended him. — Jenny Fabian and Johnny Byrne, *Groupie*, 1968

get-it-on *adjective*

vigorous, energetic in approach *US*

- [S]uch get-it-on frontrunners in the Heavy sets as Grand Funk[.] — Lester Bangs, *Psychotic Reactions and Carburetor Dung*, p. 31, 1970

get knotted!

used for expressing contempt *UK*

Usage was frozen in time and soon considered archaic. Later use is marked with irony.

- I shall show my contempt by going down the polling booth, taking my form, crossing both their names out and writing "Get knotted" in. — Ray Galton and Alan Simpson, *Hancock's Half Hour*, 23rd March 1958
- You sound like a whale that's swallowed a bellyfulla carbide, fair dinkum!' 'Get knotted,' belched Steeger. — W.R. Bennett, *Wingman*, p. 69, 1961
- So I tells him to get knotted and this chinless twit don't have any idea what he's talking about. — John Peter Jones, *Feather Pluckers*, p. 52, 1964
- PAUL: Eh. I thought you were looking after the old man. RINGO: (with simple dignity) Get knotted! — *A Hard Day's Night*, 1964
- Prior snarled, "Get knotted," and made a run for the door. — *The Sweeney*, p. 32, 1976
- Get knotted. What a fantastic expression. Nobody outside a seventies British sitcom ever said "Get knotted". — Stuart Jeffries, *Mrs Slocombe's Pussy*, p. 103, 2000
- "Get knotted," groaned Ant[.] — *SM:tv LIVE it's wicked*, p. 27, 2000

get lost!

used as a contemptuous imperative of dismissal *US, 1902*

get off *verb*

1 to form an initial liaison with someone sexually attractive, especially with a view to greater intimacy *UK, 1925*

- I heard that one of our Sergeants had been sniffing around, you know – trying to get off with her. — Clive Exton, *No Fixed Abode [Six Granada Plays]*, p. 123, 1959
- "How did you get on with them birds you had on Saturday?" In fact Banrey and Ginger hadn't got on at all. Or got off. — John Burke and Stuart Douglass, *The Boys*, p. 100, 1962

2 to achieve sexual climax *US, 1867*

- Annie got off on her own fingers while describing exactly what it felt like to her ex-husband on the telephone[.] — Doug Lang, *Freaks*, p. 30, 1973
- Harry Reems made a reputation as one of those rare people with "the ability to always get it off." — Kenneth Turan and Stephen E. Zito, *Sinema*, p. 182, 1974
- Q: "She can't get off" – "getting off" meaning in this context what? A: "Getting off" in this context indicates that she has trouble achieving an orgasm. MR. JUSTICE MOCATTA: She has what? A: She has trouble achieving an orgasm, a sexual climax. — Frank Zappa, *The Real Frank Zappa Book*, p. 136–137, 1989
- They're just tapes that he makes so he can sit around and get off. — *Sex, Lies and Videotape*, 1989
- There's come all over the sheets – he got off before he got offed. — *Basic Instinct*, 1992
- [N]ot wanting to hurt her feelings by just paying up and getting off. — Kevin Sampson, *Powder*, p. 56, 1999
- I mean, it's sex, okay? It's two people – in a bed – getting off! It's not some ethereal thing out there to embrace humanity. — *200 Cigarettes*, 1999
- Oh, that's where you have sex for a really long time and don't get off. — *The Village Voice*, 30th January 2001

3 to use a drug; to feel the effects of a drug *US, 1952*

- We got a free bag, and he asked me if I ever got off before. — Jeremy Larner and Ralph Tefferteller, *The Addict in the Street*, p. 210, 1964
- When he has finally injected the heroin (he calls it "shooting up," "taking off," "getting off"), he may or may not go on a "nod" – his eyelids heavy, his mind wandering pleasantly[.] — James Mills, *The Panic in Needle Park*, p. 15, 1966
- "How many mikes?" Papa All wanted to know. "Ahh, I dunno. They'll get ya off." — Nicholas Von Hoffman, *We Are The People Our Parents Warned Us Against*, p. 26, 1967
- That woman knew he hadn't got off since six this evening, and it was close to eleven now. — Nathan Heard, *Howard Street*, p. 15, 1968
- And this would get the reindeer off, man? — Cheech Marin and Tommy Chong, *Santa Calus and his Old Lady*, 1971
- Man, I am so fucking messed up and ripped! I got off on the first hit, man!? — John Rechy, *The Fourth Angel*, p. 32, 1972

4 by extension, to take pleasure from *US, 1952*

- Well, I don't know if you knew this, but half the girls in this place are take-home whores anyway, they get off on shit like that. — *Hard Eight*, 1996

5 to crash while riding a motorcyle *US*

Sacracastic and euphemistic biker (motorcyle) usage.

get off!; get off it!

used as an register of impatience or incredulity *UK, 1969*

get-off house *noun*

a place where you can both purchase and inject heroin *US*

- He points out two empty units as "get-off houses"- $10 for the drug, $2 for a needle, $2 for use of the premises. — *St. Petersburg (Florida) Times*, p. 1D, 14th January 1990
- — Robert Ashton, *This Is Heroin*, p. 209, 2002
- — *Detroit News*, p. 5D, 20th September 2002

get off on *verb*

to greatly enjoy something *UK, 1973*

After **GET OFF** (to achieve sexual climax).

- Sometimes I get in a real talkative mood – but not very often. I get off on hearing other people's voices. — *The Guardian*, 23rd January 2004

get off the stove, I'm ridin' the range tonight!

used for expressing enthusiasm about an upcoming date *US*

- — *Philadelphia Evening Bulletin*, 11th November 1951

get on *verb*

1 of people, to agree, to co-exist *UK, 1816*

Often with a modifying adverb. Conventional English is 'get along'.

- To be up front and honest. And you have to get on with each other. — *Sunday Times (South Africa)*, 4th August 2002
- I get on well with young people and I'd like to help them. — *The Guardian*, 5th November 2002
- Arnie [Arnold Schwarzenegger] and [Warren] Buffett got on like a house on fire, one thing led to another, and now Buffett will advise Arnie on all things economic if the former Mr Universe is elected. — *The Observer*, 17th August 2003

2 to become elderly *UK, 1885*

- Even though he is getting on, he [Malaysian prime minister, Mahathir Mohamad, age 76] is still robust and could call an election early next year. — *The Guardian*, 26th June 2002

3 to use drugs *US*

- You wanna get on? I got some pot stashed by the subway. — George Mandel, *Flee the Angry Strangers*, p. 26, 1952

4 to have *US*

- TRE: Say, pop, can I get on one of those stamps? FURIOUS: If you mean can you have one, yes. — *Boyz N The Hood*, 1990

get-out *noun*

1 an escape, an excuse, an evasion *UK, 1899*

- In truth, politicians are to blame for the blameworthy actions (and inactions) of private and public sector managers alike. This truth is unfortunate because it gives managers a get-out (like blaming bloody and bloody-minded unions in the pre-Thatcher era) — *The Observer*, 21st September 2003

2 to the extreme *US, 1838*

- We've passed the danger mark and I'm pleased as all get-out! — Gore Vidal, *Myra Breckinridge*, p. 258, 1968

get out *verb*

(used of a bettor) to recoup earlier losses *US*

- — David W. Maurer, *Argot of the Racetrack*, p. 31, 1951

get out of here!

used for expressing disbelief at what has just been said *US*

- SMOKER: I ask the kid how come nobody called the manager, and he says it happens twice a week, sometimes more. RANDAL: Get out of here. SMOKER: I kid you not. — *Clerks*, 1994

get out of here, Mary!

used for expressing doubt *US*

- Say Wha? — *Washington Post Magazine*, p. 16, 26th December 1987

get out of it!

used for expressing a lack of belief in what has just been said *UK, 1984*

get outta here!; get the fuck outta here!

used as an expression of complete disbelief *US*

Established as a potent catchphrase by Eddie Murphy in *Beverly Hills Cop* (1984).

- — Connie Eble (Editor), *UNC-CH Campus Slang*, p. 3, Spring 1993

get-over *noun*

success through fraud *US*

- People don't look at show business as a job. They think it's the ultimate get-over. The ultimate "you got lucky." — Chris Rock, *Rock This!*, p. 83, 1997

get over *verb*

to take advantage of someone, making yourself look good at their expense *US*

- — *Maledicta*, p. 266, Summer/Winter 1981: 'By its slang, ye shall know it: the pessimism of prison life'

▸ cannot get over

to be astounded *UK, 1899*

- I can't get over how far you can see over there. — *The Guardian*, 25th March 2004

▸ get over on

to seduce *US*

- I was switching gears ... forget about being a conceited asshole ... I was now trying to get over on her. — Jim Carroll, *Forced Entries*, p. 52, 1987

get over it!

used as a suggestion that the hearer move on from the issue that is dominating the moment *US*

- — Kevin Dilallo, *The Unofficial Gay Manual*, p. 240, 1994
- "You want ... this... don't you?" Get over it. Get used to it. — Christopher Brookmyre, *Boiling a Frog*, p. 11, 2000

get over you!

used in order to deflate a person's excessive sense of importance *US*

- — Jeff Fessler, *When Drag Is Not a Car Race*, p. 83, 1997

get real *verb*

to face the facts *US*

Often as an imperative.

- They tell her get real and get with the programme. — Karline Smith, *Letters to Andy Cole*, p. 140, 1998
- Get real, you plank [idiot]. — Martin King and Martin Knight, *The Naughty Nineties*, p. 117, 1999

get real!

used for expressing scorn at that which has just been said *US*

- — Connie Eble (Editor), *UNC-CH Campus Slang*, p. 3, Fall 1982
- How many people in this state been executed in the last thirty years? One, maybe? Two? Get real! — Joseph Wambaugh, *Floaters*, p. 169, 1996
- Get real, you plank [idiot]. — Martin King and Martin Knight, *The Naughty Nineties*, p. 117, 1999

get round *verb*

to circumvent *US, 1849*

- Labour's policy of all-women short lists [...] had been ruled out following a legal challenge, but twinning got round the legal difficulties[.] — *The Guardian*, 9th May 2003

get shagged!

used as a general expression of disbelief or contempt *UK*

- Gerald? Go get shagged – he'd tell every bugger – we'd be laffed out of Sheffield. — *The Full Monty*, 1997

get some *verb*

to kill enemy soldiers *US*

- [T]he grunts back on the perimeter looked at each other and grinned – "Get some, Man, oh get some!" — Charles Anderson, *The Grunts*, p. 131, 1976
- — Linda Reinberg, *In the Field*, p. 92, 1991

get stuffed!

used as a general expression of disbelief or contempt *UK, 1952*

- ERIC: No shooters. Cyril said no shooters, you stupid bastard. PETER: Get stuffed. — Mike Hodges, *Get Carter*, p. 62, 1971

getting any?

used as a male-to-male greeting *US*

Instantly jocular due to the inquiry as to the other's sex life.

- It read: "Gittin' any? Hee-hee." — Terry Southern, *Candy*, p. 211, 1958
- COWBOY: Been getting any? JOKER: Only your sister. — *Full Metal Jacket*, 1987

getting on *adjective*

(of time) late; growing late *UK*

- It's getting on now, and people start drifting away. — John King, *Human Punk*, p. 52, 2000

get to *verb*

to annoy someone *US, 1961*

- He's a nice old duffer, who still occasionally buys the Morning Star when the Guardian gets too strident for him. But this gets to me. — *New Statesman*, 21st January 2002

get-up *noun*

1 an outfit or costume *UK, 1847*

- DeDe was wearing a Hermes scarf on her head and oversized sunglasses. Mary Ann was reminded of Jackie O's old shopping get-up for Greece. — Armistead Maupin, *Further Tales of the City*, p. 147, 1982
- His get-up consisted of a black lacy teddy with no underwear and a visible penis. — Anka Radakovich, *The Wild Girls Club*, p. 225, 1994
- Fuck only knows who the geezer in the golfing get up was. — J.J. Connolly, *Know Your Enemy [britpulp]*, p. 151, 1999

2 manufactured evidence that is intended to incriminate *UK*

- I can't really get annoyed when the police have a get-up against Harry. — Peter Crookston, *Villain*, 1967

3 a piece of criminal trickery, an elaborate deceit *UK*

- — G.F. Newman, *Sir, You Bastard*, 1970

4 the last morning of a jail sentence or term of military service *US*

- "A getup and coffee," Little Junior said. — Clarence Cooper Jr, *The Farm*, p. 88, 1967
- — *Maledicta*, p. 267, Summer/Winter 1981: 'By its slang, ye shall know it: the pessimism of prison life'

get up *verb*

1 to be released from prison *US*

- When does she get up? — Clarence Cooper Jr, *The Farm*, p. 37, 1967
- The old man shook his head and walked away. "I should have remembered you're gettin' up in the morning," he answered over his shoulder. — Donald Goines, *Black Gangster*, p. 12, 1977

2 to succeed in painting your graffiti tag in a public place *US*

- — Linda Meyer, *Teenspeak!*, p. 30, 1994
- "If you can get up on a heaven, then the other taggers coming by, like the ones from Miami especially, they can see your tag," he says. — *New Times Broward-Palm Beach (Florida)*, 12th December 2002

3 to win; to succeed *AUSTRALIA, 1904*

- — Maurice Cavanough and Meurig Davies, *Cup Day*, p. 227, 1960
- — Joe Andersen, *Winners Can Laugh*, p. 215, 1982
- — Joe Brown, *Just for the Record*, p. 135, 1984
- You wouldn't believe it, St Kilda got up and won. — Rex Hunt, *Tall Tales – and True*, p. 134, 1994

4 to cause a racehorse to win *AUSTRALIA*

- In a bustling finish, Dale got Shiny Star up to score by a nose from the favourite. — Wilda Moxham, *The Apprentice*, p. 72, 1969

get-up-and-go *noun*

vigour, energy, drive *US, 1907*

Earlier variations from which this derives are 'get-up' and 'get-up-and-get'. In 1984, Beale recorded the pun 'My get up and go just got up and went'.

- But that get-up-and-go optimism seems to have served the US pretty well down the years[.] — *The Guardian*, 10th April 2003

get up off of *verb*

to concede something of importance or value *US*

- I finally had to get up off of two hundred dollars. — William Burroughs, *Queer*, p. 9, 1985

G force!

used as an expression of enthusiastic assent *US*

From a Japanese comic strip.

- — Connie Eble (Editor), *UNC-CH Campus Slang*, p. 3, Fall 1987

GFE; girl friend experience *noun*

a dinner date followed by sex as a service offered by a prostitute *UK*

- A dinner 'date' costs upwards of £500, known in the trade as the GFE, or 'Girl Friend Experience'. — *The Times*, 16th April 2005

GFY

go fuck yourself US

Used when discretion suggests avoiding the word 'fuck'.

- — Carsten Stroud, *Close Pursuit*, p. 272, 1987

GG *noun*

in transexual usage, a *g*enuine or *g*enetic *g*irl *US*

- — *Maledicta*, p. 173, Summer/Winter 1986–1987: 'Sexual slang: prostitutes, pedophiles, flagellators, transvestites, and necrophiles'

GH *noun*
General Hospital, a popular television daytime drama *US*
• —Connie Eble (Editor), *UNC-CH Campus Slang*, p. 3, March 1981

Ghan *noun*
an Afghan *AUSTRALIA, 1911*
In outback Australia this referred to the numerous immigrants from Afghanistan and nearby regions who came to work in the desert regions as camel-drivers. Not used to refer to recent migrants from Afghanistan.
• They used to say there was a dip of the 'Ghan in her, coming as she did from Tibooburra.—Dymphna Cusack, *Picnic Races*, p. 217, 1962
• The Ghan was hopping mad and this stirred the S.M. up.—Patsy Adam-Smith, *Folklore of the Australian Railwaymen*, p. 208, 1969

ghana *noun*
marijuana *UK, 1989*
Possibly a variant spelling of **GANJA** (Jamaican marijuana) although current usage doesn't acknowledge this etymology nor specify an alternative, such as marijuana from Ghana.
• —Mike Haskins, *Drugs*, p. 287, 2003

ghar *noun*
the buttocks *TRINIDAD AND TOBAGO, 1976*
From the Hindi for 'donkey'.
• —Lise Winer, *Dictionary of the English/Creole of Trinidad & Tobago*, 2003

GHB *noun*
a pharmaceutical anaesthetic used as a recreational drug *US, 1990*
Gamma hydroxybutyrate is a foul tasting liquid, invented in the 1960s by Dr Henri Laborit, who swore by its powers as an aphrodisiac. The drug has been marketed as an anaesthetic and a health supplement, but it is a heightened sense of touch, sustained erections and longer orgasms that make it popular with 'up-for-it clubbers'.
• —*American Speech*, p. 84, Spring 1995: 'Among the new words'
• —Angela Devlin, *Prison Patter*, p. 56, 1996
• GHB is said to increase sensuality and can lead to great sex.—Simon Napier-Bell, *Black Vinyl White Powder*, p. 329, 2001
• And although losing your inhibitions may lead to the shag of the century, it can get you into potentially dangerous situations – hence GHB being dubbed a "date rape" drug.—*Sky Magazine*, p. 76, July 2001

gheid *noun*
a Paregoric user *US*
• —Eugene Landy, *The Underground Dictionary*, p. 87, 1971

gherao *verb*
in India and Pakistan, to surround someone and not allow him or her to go from an office, desk, etc, as a demonstration against that person *INDIA, 1967*
From Hindi *gherna* (to surround, to beseige).
• Students yesterday gheraoed the Vice-Chancellor of Krishnapur University.—Paroo Nihalini, R.K. Tongue and Priya Hosali, *Indian and British English*, 1979
• Medical college principal gheraoed.—*The Times of India*, 20th February 2000
• DSP [Deputy Superintendent of Police] gheraoed "for helping pimp".—*Tribune (India)*, 22nd November 2002

gherkin *noun*
the penis, especially a small penis *US*
A variation of 'pickle' (the penis), especially in the phrase **JERK THE GHERKIN** (to masturbate).
• —Amy Sohn, *Sex and the City*, p. 155, 2002

ghetto *noun*
the anus *US*
• Nearly in tears, he bent over and fairly begged me to penetrate his ghetto.—Richard Frank, *A Study of Sex in Prison*, p. 36, 1973

ghetto *adjective*
inferior, shoddy, bad *US*
• —Connie Eble (Editor), *UNC-CH Campus Slang*, p. 5, April 1995
• —*Columbia Missourian*, p. 1A, 19th October 1998
• We were so wasted we passed out. / I got that gnarly sunburn, it was so ghetto[.]—Me First and the Gimmes Gimmes, *End of the Road*, 2003

ghetto- *prefix*
used to qualify an adjective as being in the style of black culture *US*
Has positive connotations when used by the black community but can be patronising and derogatory.
• The sight of this outrageously flamboyant, ghetto-fab machine perked me up considerably[.]—*ES Magazine*, p. 3, 22nd June 2001

ghetto bird *noun*
a police helicopter, especially one flying at night with a bright spotlight *US*
• Police and media helicopters, known in south-central Los Angeles as ghetto birds, saw nothing but calm.—*CNN News*, 17th April 1993
• —*Ebony Magazine*, p. 156, August 2000: 'How to talk to the new generation'

ghetto blaster; ghetto box *noun*
a large, portable radio and tape player; a portable music system *US, 1981*
Described as 'offensive because it is culture specific and stereotypical' by the Multicultural Management Program Fellows, *Dictionary of Cautionary Words and Phrases*, 1989.
• That sucker's the fifth thief I seen this morning with brand new ghetto blasters glued to his fuckin ears.—Joseph Wambaugh, *The Delta Star*, p. 22, 1983
• —Connie Eble (Editor), *UNC-CH Campus Slang*, Spring 1983
• Out in the bus lane, a kid in a Blessed Mother High School sweatshirt turns down the volume on his ghetto-blaster.—Jay McInerney, *Bright Lights, Big City*, p. s, 1984
• They have no ghetto blasters, no rap or funk tracks to dance to, which makes them an a cappella dance troupe.—Josh Alan Friedman, *Tales of Times Square*, p. 55, 1986
• [W]atching some street kids with shaved heads huddling around a ghetto blaster as if it were a fire.—Francesca Lia Block, *Witch Baby*, p. 143, 1991
• There were fewer gunfights, usually, but more music from the hundreds of ghetto blasters, each of them seemingly tuned to a different station.—Odie Hawkins, *Amazing Grace*, p. 14, 1993
• Now he went to talk to a man who prepared cafe Cuabno and smoked Cohiba panatelas listening to Radio Mambi on his ghetto box[.]—Elmore Leonard, *Out of Sight*, p. 108, 1996

ghetto bootie *noun*
large buttocks *US*
• —Don R. McCreary (Editor), *Dawg Speak*, 2001

ghetto fabulous *adjective*
ostentatious, exemplifying the style of the black hip-hop community *US*
• Founded by Andre Harrell, it merged the softer approach of rhythm and blues with the hard edge of hip-hop to create what Mr. Harrell called "New Jack Swing" – or, as he describes it, "high-style urban black life a.k.a. ghetto fabulous."—*New York Times*, p. 4 (Section 13), 14th January 1996
• In the "gettin' jiggy with it," ghetto fabulous '90s, it's all about flexing the strength of hip hop's newfound pop status.—Vibe Magazine, *The Vibe History of Hip Hop*, p. 278, 1999
• —Don R. McCreary (Editor), *Dawg Speak*, 2001
• Puffy's "Ghetto fabulous" entourage preferred monographed shirts —*The Observer*, p. 19, 18th March 2001
• —Connie Eble (Editor), *UNC-CH Campus Slang*, p. 4, November 2003

ghetto lullaby *noun*
inner-city nightime noises – sirens, gunfire, helicopters, etc *US*
• I ain't raisin no family down here. The ghetto lullaby puttin' my kids to sleep. Copters and shit flyin' by all night.—*Menace II Society*, 1993

ghetto rags *noun*
clothing typical of the inner-city ghetto *US*
• When you go downtown, y'all wear your ghetto rags ... see ... Don't go down there with your Italian silk jerseys on and your brown suede and green alligator shoes and your Harry Belafonte shirts.—Tom Wolfe, *Radical Chic & Mau-Mauing the Flak Catchers*, p. 99, 1970

ghetto sled *noun*
a large, luxury car *US*
• —Vann Wesson, *Generation X Field Guide and Lexicon*, p. 78, 1997

ghetto star *noun*
a youth gang leader *US*
• His years there would galvanize his legend on the streets as a "ghetto star," but they would also eventually propel him toward a renunciation of gang life[.]—*New York Times*, p. C27, 23rd July 1993
• —Bill Valentine, *Gang Intelligence Manual*, p. 76, 1995: 'Black street gang terminology'

'Ghini *noun*
a Lambourghini car *US*
A hip-hop abbreviation and aspiration.
• Still packing fo sho / Yeezy Weezy off of the heezy fo sheezy / Cruise with the top off of the 'Ghini[.]—Lil Wayne, *Fo Sheezy*, 1999

ghost *noun*

1 a faint, secondary duplicate video image in a television signal, caused by the mixing of the primary signal and a delayed version of the same signal *US, 1942*

- —*American Speech*, February 1951
- Life in this great pretzel center is distinguished by the worst television reception enjoyed by any metropolitan American city – not even barring blast-furnacy Pittsburgh, runner-up for ghosts, blizzards, fade-outs and other visual blah.—*San Francisco News*, p. 21, 22nd May 1952

2 a blank stop on a casino slot machine *US*

- —Frank Scoblete, *Guerrilla Gambling*, p. 310, 1993

3 in poker, a player who frequently absents himself from the table *US*

- —John Vorhaus, *The Big Book of Poker Slang*, p. 20, 1996

4 LSD *US*

Usually used with 'the'.

- —John Williams, *The Drug Scene*, p. 112, 1967

▸ **do a ghost**

to leave quickly *US*

- —Bill Valentine, *Gang Intelligence Manual*, p. 75, 1995: 'Black street gang terminology'

▸ **when the ghost walks**

in oil drilling, pay day *US*

- —Jerry Robertson, *Oil Slanguage*, p. 59, 1954

ghost *verb*

1 to transfer a prisoner from one prison to another at night after the prison has been secured *US*

- —Ralph de Sola, *Crime Dictionary*, p. 57, 1982
- —William K. Bentley and James M. Corbett, *Prison Slang*, p. 10, 1992
- —Angela Devlin, *Prison Patter*, p. 57, 1996
- Come out [of solitary confinement] after two days, fight again, more chokey. I was up and down like a bride's nightie until we were ghosted off to the seaside.—Lenny McLean, *The Guv'nor*, p. 42, 1998

2 to vanish *US*

- Their skulls won't let 'em believe a Nigger was clever enough to ghost outta here.—Iceberg Slim (Robert Beck), *Pimp*, p. 265, 1969

3 to relax, especially while evading duty *US, 1982*

Military use.

- —Linda Reinberg, *In the Field*, p. 93, 1991

ghost battalion *noun*

during the Vietnam war, the First Battallion, Ninth Marines *US*

So named because of the large number of casualties suffered at Con Thien and Khe Sanh.

- —Linda Reinberg, *In the Field*, p. 93, 1991

ghostbust *noun*

to search in an obsessive and compulsive way for small particles of crack cocaine *US*

- —Terry Williams, *Crackhouse*, p. 148, 1992
- —Nick Constable, *This is Cocaine*, p. 182, 2002

ghosted *adjective*

out of sight *UK*

- He decided to get ghosted and indicated left at Stepney Green tube station.—Donald Gorgon, *Cop Killer*, p. 151, 1994

ghost hand *noun*

in poker, a hand or part of a hand that is dealt to the same player twice in a row *US*

- —George Percy, *The Language of Poker*, p. 39, 1988

ghost town *noun*

▸ **send to ghost town**

to transfer a prisoner without warning *UK*

- —Angela Devlin, *Prison Patter*, p. 102, 1996

ghost train *noun*

▸ **on the ghost train**

used of a prisoner who is being moved without warning from one prison to another overnight *UK*

From **GHOST** (to transfer overnight).

- —Angela Devlin, *Prison Patter*, p. 82, 1996

ghost-walking day *noun*

in circus and carnival usage, payday *US*

- —Don Wilmeth, *The Language of American Popular Entertainment*, p. 110, 1981

ghoulie *noun*

the vagina *US*

Something frightening that lurks in the dark.

- There's [a...] a "pajama," "fannyboo," "mushmellow," "a ghoulie," "possible," "tamale[".]—Eve Ensler, *The Vagina Monologues*, p. 6, 1998

ghoulie *adjective*

ghoulish *US*

- "Who was that ghoulie guy?" I ask the Bat Man back at the apartment.—Francesca Lia Block, *Missing Angel Juan*, p. 341, 1993

GI *noun*

1 an enlisted soldier in the US Army *US, 1939*

- The slang expression "GI" has been barred for the Army public relations officers. They'll have to refer to a soldier as a soldier.—*The Milwaukee Star*, 28th June 1951

2 an American Indian who has abandoned his indigenous culture and language in favour of mainstream American culture; a *g*overnment *I*ndian *US*

- —*American Speech*, p. 272, December 1963: 'American Indian student slang'

GI *verb*

1 to clean thoroughly *US, 1944*

- At night, he would bring the dings their chow, G.I. their cells and stroll the catwalk exchanging words with them through the bars.—James Ellroy, *Suicide Hill*, p. 585, 1986

2 to strip *US*

- Jackie nervously G.I.ed his cigarette[.]—Nathan Heard, *Howard Street*, p. 208, 1968

Gianluca Vialli; gianluca *noun*

cocaine *UK, 1998*

Rhyming slang for **CHARLIE** (cocaine); based on the name of Gianluca Vialli (b.1964), a famous Italian football player and manager.

- CALL IT... Basuco, gianluca, blow, percy, lady, toot, white[.] JUST DON'T CALL IT... Charlie – too Eighties—*Drugs An Adult Guide*, p. 34, December 2001

gib *noun*

a man's buttocks *US*

- Looked at Whistler's thigh and asked the white mugger if he liked "gibs," which the mugger said he liked all right when there was nothing else available.—Robert Campbell, *In La-La Land We Trust*, p. 112, 1986

GIB *noun*

the back seat member of the crew on a fighter aircraft *US, 1967*

An initialism for '*g*uy *i*n *b*ack'.

- —Linda Reinberg, *In the Field*, p. 93, 1991

GIB *adjective*

skilled in sex *US, 1977*

An initialism for '*g*ood *i*n *b*ed'.

- —Kevin DiLallo, *The Unofficial Gay Manual*, p. 218, 1988

Gib *nickname*

*Gib*raltar *UK, 1822*

- [T]he Rock Hotel, Gibraltar's finest, which displays the signatures of a rich mix of celebrity guests on its lounge menu: Prince Andrew, Sean Connery, Errol Flynn, Jimmy Young (Jimmy is very big in Gib).—*The Guardian*, 11th February 2002

gibber *noun*

a small stone used for throwing *AUSTRALIA, 1902*

From the extinct Australian Aboriginal language Dharug (Sydney region). Originally, since 1833 (*Australian National Dictionary*), referring to 'large boulders', it has undergone a reduction in size over the decades. As a technical term of geologists it refers to smallish stones of dark reddish chaceldony that litter the surface of large areas of the arid inland. Colloquially it is used of any rock, stone or pebble suitable for throwing.

- Her face was red and polished like a gibber.—Arthur Upfield, *Bony and the Mouse*, p. 21, 1959
- —Jim Ramsay, *Cop It Sweet!*, p. 39, 1977
- The inquisition over, Connie strolled through the kitchen, looked into the laundromat where her father was bulling a few hefty housewives, went outside and kicked every gibber in the backyard, then locked herself in the lavatory and cried.—Paul Radley, *Jack Rivers and Me*, p. 10, 1981

gibbled *adjective*
(of a machine) broken down *CANADA*
• [D]escriptive of equipment that has malfunctioned– they say it is "gibbled"[.] —Tom Parkin, *WetCoast Words*, p. 58, 1989

gibbs *noun*
the lips *US*
• —Charles Shafer, *Folk Speech in Texas Prisons*, p. 205, 1990

gib-gib *noun*
used for mocking another's laughter *TRINIDAD AND TOBAGO, 1994*
From an advertisement for Gibbons Chicken Ration.
• —Lise Winer, *Dictionary of the English/Creole of Trinidad & Tobago*, 2003

giblet *noun*
a stupid, foolish or inept person *US*
Playing on a turkey image.
• And it is a heatbreak to be sitting waiting for the truck and the giblet comes out and drives it away. —*Repo Man*, 1984

giblets *noun*
1 the female gentalia *UK*
• —Chris Lewis, *The Dictionary of Playground Slang*, p. 100, 2003
2 showy chrome accessories on a motorcyle *US*
Biker (motorcycle) usage.

gibroni *noun*
▷ see: JOBRONI

Gibson girl *noun*
an emergency radio used when a military aircraft is shot down over a body of water *US, 1943*
• —*American Speech*, p. 310, December 1946: 'More Air Force slang'

gick *noun*
excrement *IRELAND*
• If I did a gick in me pants he'd kill me! —Roddy Doyle, *Paddy Clarke Ha Ha Ha*, p. 1, 1993

gick *verb*
to defecate *IRELAND*
• I was gicking meself [sic] 'cos, as well as me own bit of robbin, the supermarket had been hit by a couple of armed robberies. —Howard Paul, *The Joy*, p. 44, 1996

gidday
▷ see: G'DAY

giddy *noun*
a tourist, especially on a package holiday *UK*
Used by holiday reps.
• Finish your drink an' let's leave all these giddies an' go an' 'ave a proper night out. —Colin Butts, *Is Harry on the Boat?*, p. 123, 1997

giddyap; giddyup *noun*
the beginning; the inception *US, 1974*
• He told us right from the giddyap what he was willing to put into acquisiton of the siding property. —George V. Higgins, *Penance for Jerry Kennedy*, p. 25, 1985

giddy as a kipper *adjective*
dizzy *UK*
A 'giddy kipper', although not in this sense, has been a feature of English slang since the late C19.
• What've you given me mam, she's gone giddy as a kipper. —Caroline Aherne and Craig Cash, *The Royle Family*, 1999

giddy goat *noun*
in horse racing, the totalisator *AUSTRALIA*
Rhyming slang from 'tote'.
• —Ned Wallish, *The Truth Dictionary of Racing Slang*, p. 1, 1989

gif *noun*
an aircraft pilot *US, 1945*
From the initials of '*g*uys *i*n the *f*ront seat'. Reported by Royal Air Force Squadron Leader G.D. Wilson, 1984.

giffed *adjective*
drunk *UK*
• —Pete Brown, *Man Walks into a Pub*, 2003

giffer *noun*
a pickpocket *US*
• —Vincent J. Monteleone, *Criminal Slang*, p. 97, 1949

gift *noun*
in a sex club, used as a coded euphemism for payment for special services *US*
• And it's hers because this is a girl who wakes up, comes to work, and hustles. "Do you have a gift for me?" "Do you want some company?" —Anthony Petkovich, *The X Factory*, p. 40, 1997

▸ the gift
the bleed period of the menstrual cycle *US*
• I say "I'm gifted" when I'm having it, or "I have not received my gift yet" when not. —a contributor *The Museum of Menstruation and Women's Health*, April 2001

▸ the gift that keeps giving
a sexually transmitted disease *US*
• —Connie Eble (Editor), *UNC-CH Campus Slang*, p. 5, March 1986

gifted *adjective*
experiencing the bleed period of the menstrual cycle *US*

gift of the sun; gift of the sun god *noun*
cocaine *UK, 1998*
• —Nick Constable, *This is Cocaine*, p. 181, 2002
• —Mike Haskins, *Drugs*, p. 280, 2003

gig *noun*
1 a musical performance or concert *US, 1926*
Originally musicians' slang for an engagement at a single venue.
• We'll put the band back together, do a few gigs, we get some bread. —*The Blues Brothers*, 1980
• We got that gig in L.A., we'll just leave a little early. —*Boys on the Side*, 1995
• You'd look for punks who'd driven up to a gig in cars or, the best, punks whose Mom had dropped them off. —Susan Ruddick, *Cool Places*, p. 354, 1998
2 a job *US, 1908*
• What's your gig in all this? —*Ten Things I Hate About You*, 1999
3 a party *US, 1954*
• Let's get that sneaky pete [wine] and have us a gig. —Harrison E. Salisbury, *The Shook-up Generation*, p. 29, 1958
• —Malachi Andrews and Paul T. Owens, *Black Language*, p. 55, 1973
4 a prison or jail sentence *US*
• I saved him a gig for a shirttail hanging out on an IG inspection. —Larry Heinemann, *Close Quarters*, p. 133, 1977
• He was at FPC doing a gig for fraud, I think credit cards. —Elmore Leonard, *Out of Sight*, p. 57, 1996
5 a police informer *AUSTRALIA, 1953*
A clipping of **FIZGIG**.
• Okay Bobby, but keep your voice down, plenty of gigs are enjoying your discomfort. —Clive Galea, *Slipper*, p. 220, 1988
6 a busybody *AUSTRALIA, 1944*
• It was always on the cards that he could end up with a bit of swish if he got sprung being a gig. —Ryan Aven-Bray, *Ridgey Didge Oz Jack Lang*, p. 10, 1983
7 a person who stands out because they look foolish; a fool *AUSTRALIA, 1943*
In pre-C20 British slang and dialect.
• 'Yeah, well you should know all about gigs, Davo,' smiled Kathy. 'Being one yourself.' —Robert G. Barrett, *Davo's Little Something*, p. 10, 1992
8 the vagina *US*
• —Dale Gordon, *The Dominion Sex Dictionary*, p. 76, 1967
9 a look; a peek *AUSTRALIA, 1924*
• Have a gig at this. —John O'Grady, *Aussie English*, p. 42, 1965
10 a demerit or other indication of failure *US*
• —Carl Fleischhauer, *A Glossary of Army Slang*, p. 21, 1968
11 in an illegal number gambling lottery, a bet that a specific three-digit number will be drawn *US, 1846*
• —*American Speech*, p. 191, October 1949
• It's the prospect of the big payoff that hooks them. A dime played on a gig that hits brings eight-six dollars. A buck on a lucky gig or bet pays eight hundred and sixty dollars. —Iceberg Slim (Robert Beck), *Mama Black Widow*, p. 97, 1969
12 in harness racing, a sulky *US*

gig *verb*
1 to work; to have a job *US, 1939*
• "There's a lot of bread to be made gigging right around here in Roxbury," Shorty explained to me. —Malcolm X and Alex Haley, *The Autobiography of Malcolm X*, p. 45, 1964

- So like what, a cat with heart is gonna gig in some shoulder-pad factory? — Edwin Torres, *Carlito's Way*, p. 144, 1975
- Some of us had even copped white girls and after we finished gigging we'd go in and let the white girls order then we'd eat out the same plate with them. — Babs Gonzales, *Movin' On Down De Line*, p. 3, 1975
- He doesn't gig in the store any more. — Iceberg Slim (Robert Beck), *Doom Fox*, p. 132, 1978

2 of a musician or group of musicians, to play an engagement or a series of engagements *UK, 1939*

- Oh, he played good, I'm hip, but he never gigged a hundred towns, and worked a dozen bands, and been a bum[.] — John Clellon Holmes, *The Horn*, p. 85, 1958
- I hipped him to the club where she'd be gigging and tole him she'd be starting to work tomorrow night — A.S. Jackson, *Gentleman Pimp*, p. 161, 1973
- When we gigged in America we got a great response[.] — *Croyden Guardian*, 29th July 2004

3 to go out to bars, clubs and/or parties *US*

- — *Ebony Magazine*, p. 156, August 2000: 'How to talk to the new generation'

4 to look or stare; to take a peek *AUSTRALIA, 1959*

- Jim was craning his neck out the window to try and see what everyone was trying to gig at. — Bluey *Bush Contractors*, p. 372, 1975

5 to tease *AUSTRALIA*

- Rufe was only gigging him for Chrissake, just for something to do. — Wilda Moxham, *The Apprentice*, p. 113, 1969

6 in carnival usage, to win all of a player's money in a single transaction *US*

- The step by step process of beating a player is considered a work of art and a good agent prides himself with this skill, therefore the practice of GIGGING is frowned upon by these professionals. — Gene Sorrows, *All About Carnivals*, p. 18, 1985

gigging *noun*

teasing *AUSTRALIA*

- The Scot and the Englishman both got their fair share of gigging. — George Blaikie, *Remember Smith's Weekly?*, p. 104, 1966

giggle and titter; giggle *noun*

bitter (beer) *UK*

- — Ray Puxley, *Cockney Rabbit*, 1992

giggle band *noun*

the decorative hemmed edge at the top of a stocking *UK*

Get beyond that and you're laughing.

giggle bin *noun*

an institution for containment and care of the mentally disturbed *UK*

- I reckon they'll chuck him in the giggle bin and throw away the key[.] — John Peter Jones, *Feather Pluckers*, p. 55, 1964

giggle factory *noun*

an insane asylum *AUSTRALIA*

- This bloke's a flamin' ratbag! He ought to be doing time in a giggle factory!! — Barry Humphries, *The Wonderful World of Barry McKenzie*, p. 25, 1968

giggle house *noun*

an insane asylum *AUSTRALIA, 1919*

giggle juice *noun*

alcohol *US, 1939*

- — Judi Sanders, *Kickin' like Chicken with the Couch Commander*, p. 10, 1992

giggler *noun*

a scene in a pornographic film involving sex with two women *US*

From the **GIRL-GIRL** designation. Recorded in an interview of Jim Holliday, 12th June 1987.

giggles; good giggles *noun*

marijuana *US*

- — Richard A. Spears, *The Slang and Jargon of Drugs and Drink*, p. 219, 1986
- — Mike Haskins, *Drugs*, p. 287, 2003

giggle smoke *noun*

marijuana; a marijuana cigarette *US, 1952*

- — Richard A. Spears, *The Slang and Jargon of Drugs and Drink*, p. 219, 1986
- — Mike Haskins, *Drugs*, p. 287, 2003

gigglesoup *noun*

any alcoholic beverage *US*

- I guess they both reasoned my pardner was still stewed from the Kingfish's gigglesoup. — Guy Owen, *The Flim-Flam Man and the Apprentice Grifter*, p. 116, 1972

giggle water *noun*

alcohol, especially champagne *US, 1926*

giggle weed *noun*

marijuana *US, 1937*

From the definite effect **WEED** has on your sense of humour. Foreshadowed in 'New Giggle Drug Puts Discord in City Orchestras', *The Chicago Tribune*, 1st July 1928, but not recorded until 1951.

- — Richard A. Spears, *The Slang and Jargon of Drugs and Drink*, p. 219, 1986
- — Mike Haskins, *Drugs*, p. 287, 2003

giggling academy *noun*

a mental hospital *US, 1949*

- Wolfe winked at Bob again. Bob eyed him as if he had just escaped from the Bellevue Giggling Academy. — Bill Fitzhugh, *Pest Control*, p. 124, 1996

giggly *adjective*

very good *UK*

Probably from the euphoric reaction to marijuana. West Indian and UK black use, recorded in August 2002.

giggy; gigi *noun*

the anus and rectum *US, 1953*

- — *Maledicta*, p. 15, 1977: 'A word for it!'
- Whereas Roland, who had the world by the giggy at the present time, had a piss-poor view of the ocean down a street and between some apartments. — Elmore Leonard, *Gold Coast*, p. 130, 1980

GI gin *noun*

cough syrup *US, 1964*

- I reached into the pocket of my loose jungle fatigues for the bottle of GI gin. A good slug of this 80 proof terpin hydrate elixir guarantees an hour free of coughing. — Robin Moore, *The Green Berets*, p. 170, 1965
- The guys had showed me how to drink GI gin – cough syrup with codeine – a nasty high but a powerful buzz[.] — Art Neville, *The Brothers*, p. 81, 2000

gig-lamps; gigs *noun*

spectacles, eye-glasses *UK, 1853*

From the lights placed to each side of a 'gig' (a light carriage); 'headlights' (glasses), a later coinage, reflects similar inspiration.

- Blind as fuck and all. The lenses on the cunt's gigs are about a foor thick. — Kevin sampson, *Outlaws*, p. 164, 2001

GIGO

in computing, used as a reminder that output is only as good as input (*g*arbage *in*, *g*arbage *o*ut) *US, 1964*

- — Robert Kirk Mueller, *Buzzwords*, p. 87, 1974
- — Karla Jennings, *The Devouring Fungus*, p. 220, 1990

gig shot *noun*

in carnival usage, the method used by an operator to win all of a player's money in a single transaction *US*

- — Gene Sorrows, *All About Carnivals*, p. 18, 1985: 'Terminology'

gig wagon *noun*

transportation used by a rock band during a concert tour *UK*

- — Bob Young and Micky Moody, *The Language of Rock 'n' Roll*, p. 48, 1985

GI Joe *noun*

a quintessential American soldier *US, 1935*

A term fuelled by a cartoon in the 1940s, a Robert Mitchum movie in 1945 and a line of toys starting in 1964.

- Charlie Company was a "grunt" unit; its men were the foot soldiers, the "GI Joes," who understood they were to take orders, not question them. — Seymour Hersh, *My Lai 4*, p. 18, 1970

gildy *adjective*

fancy, ornate *UK*

- A tart in gildy clobber[.] — Paul Baker, *Polari*, p. 175, 2002

gilf *noun*
a sexually appealing mature woman *US*
A variation of **MILF** (a sexually appealing mother) and **DILF** (a sexually appealing father); an acronym of 'grandma I'd like to fuck'.
• —Chris Lewis, *The Dictionary of Playground Slang*, p. 148, 2003

gil-gil *noun*
used for mocking another's laughter *TRINIDAD AND TOBAGO, 1993*
• —Lise Winer, *Dictionary of the English/Creole of Trinidad & Tobago*, 2003

gilhooley *noun*
in motor racing on an oval track, a spin *US*
• —John Lawlor, *How to Talk Car*, p. 55, 1965

gill; gills *noun*
in circus and carnival usage, a customer, especially a gullible one *US*
• —Don Wilmeth, *The Language of American Popular Entertainment*, p. 111, 1981

Gillie Potters *noun*
1 pig's trotters *UK*
Rhyming slang; formed from the name of British comedian, an early star of BBC radio, Gillie Potter, 1887–1975. Reported by Red Daniells, 1980.
2 the feet *UK*
Rhyming slang for **TROTTERS**; formed from the name of British comedian, an early star of BBC radio, Gillie Potter, 1887–1975. Reported by Red Daniells, 1980.

gillie suit *noun*
camouflaged uniforms used by the US Army Special Forces *US*
Gulf war usage.
• —*American Speech*, p. 87, Spirng 1992: 'Gulf War words supplement'

Gilligan *noun*
a hapless, socially inept person *US*
From *Gilligan's Island* television programme, in which Gilligan was a hapless, socially inept person.
• —Trevor Cralle, *The Surfin'ary*, p. 44, 1991

Gilligan hitch *noun*
any and every method to bind with a chain or tie with a rope *US, 1919*

gillion *noun*
ten to the ninth power; untold millions *US*
• —Eric S. Raymond, *The New Hacker's Dictionary*, p. 177, 1991
• Okay, we all know it's a gemstone and was there lurking in the ground these gillion years[.]—Jonathan Gash, *The Ten Word Game*, p. 21, 2003

gillopy *noun*
▷ see: **JALLOPY**

gilly *noun*
1 a member of an audience, especially a woman *UK, 1933*
Theatrical and circus.
• [F]latties [...] men (especially those who make up an audience). The female equivalent in gillies.—Paul Baker, *Polari*, p. 175, 2002
2 a man, especially a gullible rustic *US, 1882*
Market traders and English gypsy use, from the previous sense as 'a member of a circus audience'.
• —Jimmy Stockin, *On The Cobbles*, p. 10, 2000

gilly-galloo *noun*
in circus and carnival usage, an outsider *US*
• —Don Wilmeth, *The Language of American Popular Entertainment*, p. 112, 1981

gils!
used for expressing pleasant surprise *US*
• —Connie Eble (Editor), *UNC-CH Campus Slang*, p. 5, October 2002

gilt *noun*
money *UK, 1708*
Derives from German *gelt* (gold) and conventional 'gilt' (silverplate).
• He started telling me how he con[n]ed all this gilt off the old dear. —Frank Norman, *Bang To Rights*, p. 108, 1958
• [W]hen the establishment Mafioso realise how much gilt, paper, cashish, wonga, wedge, corn, cutter, loot, spondos, dollar, readies, shillings, folding, dough, money is on offer[.]—J.J. Connolly, *Layer Cake*, p. 94, 2000

G.I. marbles *noun*
dice *US*
Because of the love for dice games displayed by American soldiers, especially during World War 2.
• —*The Annals of the American Academy of Political and Social Sciences*, p. 125, May 1950

Gimli glider *noun*
a Boeing 737 which ran out of petrol and glided to a safe landing in Gimli, Manitoba; later, any car that has run out of petrol *CANADA*
The incident happened because of a confusion between metric and English ways of measuring petrol during the fill-up. One of the pilots had been a glider pilot.

gimme *noun*
1 a request or demand for money *UK*
From 'give me'.
• With all the gimmes and dropsies and once we've factored in Eli's take we'll be left with a good half million.—Kevin Sampson, *Outlaws*, p. 18, 2001
2 an easy victory or accomplishment *US, 1986*
• He was one of the city's biggest hijackers. Clothes. Razor blades. Booze. Cigarettes. Shrimp and lobsters were the best. They went fast. And almost all of them were gimmie's.—*Goodfellas*, 1990
3 a pistol *US*
• A "gimme" is a pistol – because they're often seen in the hands of somebody saying "gimme your money."—*Los Angeles Times*, p. B1, 19th December 1994
4 in pool, a shot that cannot be missed or a game that cannot be lost *US*
• —Steve Rushin, *Pool Cool*, p. 14, 1990

gimme *verb*
used for 'give me' *US, 1883*
A lazy phonetic abbreviation.
• If I don't get some shelter / Yeah, I'm gonna fade away—The Rolling Stones *Gimme Shelter*, 1969
• Gimme gimme gimme a man after midnight / Take me through the darkness to the break of the day—Abba, *Gimme Gimme Gimme (A Man After Midnight)*, 1979
• Gimme the tune. Do I like this tune?—Frank Zappa, *The Real Frank Zappa Book*, p. 141, 1989
• —UK TV series *Gimme Gimme Gimme*, 1999–2000

gimme five *noun*
a mutual hand-slapping used as greeting or to signify mutual respect *UK*
From the phrase 'give me your hand'; 'gimme' (give me) 'five' (fingers, hence hand).
• They slapped hands, cackling. "Whoops!" smiled Wheezer. "What?" "That was a bit London, wasn't it? The gimme five."—Kevin Sampson, *Powder*, p. 97–98, 1999

gimmel *noun*
in betting, odds of 3–1 *UK*
Probably coined by a Jewish bookmaker with a sense of humour, from *gimel* (the Hebrew letter which, in Judaic teaching, symbolises a rich man running after a poor man) which, in turn, derives from Hebrew *gemul* (the giving of reward and punishment).
• —John McCririck, *John McCririck's World of Betting*, p. 112, 1991

gimmes *noun*
a selfishly acquisitive characteristic *US, 1918*
• If you can convince a kid with a bad case of the gimmes to squirrel a little away, you've won the biggest battle.—Lynn O'Shaughnessy, *The Investing Bible*, p. 434, 2001

gimmick *noun*
1 a gadget, an ingenious device or contrivance such as may be used in crime and magic to deceive or distract, or commercially, especially in the entertainment industry, to attract publicity and attention *US, 1926*
'You Gotta Get a Gimmick', Stephen Sondheim, 1959, is a song performed by striptease artistes demonstrating their ingenious methods of standing out from the crowd.
2 characteristics such as costume, haircut or entrance music that collectively make a professional wrestler stand out as a unique marketable commodity *US*

- What a gimmick they had! Lord Blearas, with his pageboy haircut and monocle, seemed to be constantly looking down his nose. Holmes, his manager, was impeccably upper class, with black bowler hat and walking stick. They never failed to rile a crowd. —Ted Lewin, *I Was a Teenage Professional Wresiter*, p. 22, 1993
- A gimmick may be owned by a wrestler or by a promoter; at Gleason's one afternoon the rumor circulated that the Undertaker gimmick was purchased by the WWF for $75,000. —Sharon Mazer, *Professional Wrestling*, p. 48, 1998
- Alex's new gimmick is that he requests the audience to be completely silent during the match so he can concentrate. — *Herb's Wrestling Tidbits*, 14th November 1998
- "There's one more thing we need to know," Vince declared. "I need to know that you're completely comfortable with your gimmick (costume)." —Mick Foley, *Mankind*, p. 373, 1999
- — *Washington Post*, p. N36, 10th March 2000: 'A wrestling glossary'

3 the actual device used to rig a carnival game *US*
- The device used to gaff a game is the "gimmick" and is not to be confused with something one might pick up at the dime-store. —E.E. Steck, *A Brief Examination of an Esoteric Folk*, p. 9, 1968

4 in poker, a special set of rules for a game *US*
- —George Percy, *The Language of Poker*, p. 39, 1988

gimmick *verb*

to rig for a result *US, 1922*
- So he fix up two ropes – one gimmicked to stretch, the other the real McCoy. —William Burroughs, *Naked Lunch*, p. 79–80, 1957
- Jake Roberts vs. Sting in a "Spin the Wheel, Make the Deal" match, where Sting will apparently spin a gimmicked wheel to determine which type of match takes place. —Herb Kunze, *Herb's Wrestling Tidbits*, 10th September 1992

gimmicks *noun*

the equipment needed to inject drugs *US, 1967*
- —Richard Horman and Allan Fox, *Drug Awareness*, p. 466, 1970
- —Eugene Landy, *The Underground Dictionary*, p. 89, 1971
- He had his gimmicks with him, and he began his regular procedure of turning on. —Emmett Grogan, *Ringolevio*, p. 55, 1972

gimmie *noun*

marijuana and crack cocaine mixed together for smoking in a cigarette *US*
- — US Department of Justice, *Street Terms*, October 1994

gimp *noun*

1 a limp; a cripple *US, 1925*
- Leo wasn't there – probably out chasing missing persons, the birdbrain – but the gimp officer manager, Gil Lazarro, was at his desk. —Bernard Wolfe, *The Late Risers*, p. 4, 1954
- Just another ugly refugee from the Love Generation, some doom-struck gimp who couldn't handle the pressure. —Hunter S. Thompson, *Fear and Loathing in Las Vegas*, p. 63, 1971
- This juror walks with a gimp, he's mad at the world. —Edwin Torres, *Carlito's Way*, p. 126, 1975
- Hi, gimp. Luckiest thing ever happened to you. —Dan Jenkins, *Life Its Ownself*, p. 41, 1984
- Well, goddamn, the gimp caught me – at the same time slouching more and sliding out of the chair. —Larry Heinemann, *Paco's Story*, p. 148–149, 1986
- What I want to know is, who's the gimp? — *The Usual Suspects*, 1995

2 an incompetent or weak person *US, 1924*
- —Linda Reinberg, *In the Field*, p. 93, 1991
- Henry, with his pustulating skin and the carbuncles on his neck and his diminutive chin is not just "gross" but a "gimp" and a "retard" and a "mong". —Jenny Eclair, *Camberwell Beauty*, p. 153, 2000

3 a sexual submissive who seeks satisfaction in dehumanising, fully including fetish clothing and crippling bondage *US*

A specialisation of the previous senses made very familiar by Quentin Tarantino, *Pulp Fiction*, 1993 – the film featured a masked-creature (taking his pleasure at the hands of a dominatrix) known only as 'the gimp'.
- "Simon must have had a screw loose," chomped Fry, pulling an ill-fitting gimp mask over his flabby features. "And he will be punished." — *The Guardian*, 22nd September 2003

gimper; gimpster *noun*

a cripple *US, 1974*
- "Before I go get the gimper," said the rent-a-cop, pinching harder, "how about you telling me some portion of the truth." —Carl Hiaasen, *Native Tongue*, p. 73, 1991

gimp out *verb*

to panic in the face of great challenge *US*
- —Michael V. Anderson, *The Bad, Rad, Not to Forget Way Cool Beach and Surf Discriptionary*, p. 7, 1988

gimpy *noun*

a (long-haired) member of the counterculture, a hippy *UK*
- They're building a motorway in Leytonstone. All those gimpys up in trees demonstrating. —John Milne, *Alive and Kicking*, p. 168, 1998

gimpy *adjective*

1 crippled; handicapped *US, 1929*
- Like for you, hey, you don't want to have a gimpy leg no more. —Michael Chabon, *The Amazing Adventures of Kavalier & Clay*, p. 145, 2000
- Buckner nearly ruined his career. The gimpy left ankle caused him to put excessive weight on his right leg, which led to a series of debilitating injuries. —Jeff Pearlman, *TheBadGuys Won!*, p. 208, 2004

2 inferior *US*
- [T]hey could grow up to drink and eat and fuck gimpy. —Gilbert Sorrentino, *Steelwork*, p. 147, 1970
- —Connie Eble (Editor), *UNC-CH Campus Slang*, p. 5, October 2002

gims *noun*

the eyes *US*
- —Lou Shelly, *Hepcats Jive Dictionary*, p. 12, 1945

gin *noun*

1 a black prostitute *US*
- —Joseph E. Ragen and Charles Finston, *Inside the World's Toughest Prison*, p. 800, 1962: 'Penitentiary and underworld glossary'

2 an Aboriginal female *AUSTRALIA*
- — Thommo, *The Dictionary of Australian Swearing and Sex Sayings*, p. 58, 1985

3 cocaine *US*
- —Donald Louria, *The Drug Scene*, p. 190, 1971
- —Nick Constable, *This is Cocaine*, p. 181, 2002

4 a street fight between youth gangs *US*
- —Kenn "Naz" Young, *Naz's Dictionary of Teen Slang*, p. 49, 1993

gin *verb*

1 (used of a woman) to have sex *US*
- Now my deadliest blow came when the whore / Took sick and couldn't gin. —Dennis Wepman et al., *The Life*, p. 84, 1976

2 to fight *US*
- —David Claerbaut, *Black Jargon in White America*, p. 66, 1972

gin and Jaguar bird *noun*

a wealthy, usually married, woman from the upper-class districts surrounding London, especially Surrey, regarded as a worthwhile target for sexual adventuring *UK*

A **BIRD** (a woman) who lives in the 'gin and Jaguar belt'.
- —David Powis, *The Signs of Crime*, 1977

ginch *noun*

1 the vagina *US*
- Thinks that it's a cinch / To get up in my ginch / And if you got the inch / Then I'll treat you like a prince— Peaches, *The Inch*, 2003

2 a woman; a woman as a sex object *US, 1936*
- Of the thirty or so outlaws at the El Adobe on a weekend night, less than half would take the trouble to walk across the parking lot for a go at whatever ginch is available. —Hunter S. Thompson, *Hell's Angels*, p. 193, 1966
- Jesus Christ, a cop can't afford that kind of ginch. —George V. Higgins, *The Rat on Fire*, p. 114, 1981
- I got a half-decent lead on a ginch Maggie used to whore with[.] —James Ellroy, *Hollywood Nocturnes*, p. 274, 1994

ginchy *adjective*

1 fashionable, attractive, pleasing *US, 1959*
- —Dobie Gillis, *Teenage Slanguage Dictionary*, 1962
- "Everything groovy?" Janice yelled up at me. "Ginchy," I called back, and went into my apartment. —Harlan Ellison, *The Resurgence of Miss Ankle-Strap Wedgie*, p. 624, 1968

2 sharp-witted, clever, shrewd *UK*

A sarcastic variation of the sense as 'attractive'.
- Gee, that's kinda ginchy. This disc has three different sleeves so you can have your favourite Broster on the cover[!] — *NME*, June 1988

giner *noun*

the vagina *US*
- —Connie Eble (Editor), *UNC-CH Campus Slang*, p. 3, April 2004

gin flat *noun*

an apartment where alcohol is served illegally to a paying not-so public *US*
- We have already referred to the gin-flats in Black Town, where home-made gin – raw ethyl alcohol flavored with juniper and sometimes diluted with apple cider – is sold. —Jack Lait and Lee Mortimer, *Washington Confidential*, p. 130, 1951

ging *noun*

a handheld catapult; a slingshot *AUSTRALIA, 1903*

- Conkey firmly renounced all pretensions to fortune's favours. 'I knocked a robin with my ging last week, so my luck's out,' he said. —Norman Lindsay, *Saturdee*, p. 82, 1934
- [Taken] as reprisal for Waldo's filching of one pair of new ging rubbers from Bulljo. —Norman Lindsay, *Halfway to Anywhere*, p. 146, 1947
- —Jim Ramsay, *Cop It Sweet!*, p. 39, 1977

ginger *noun*

1 a sandy- or red-haired person; often as a nickname *UK, 1885*
Originally (1785) used of a cock with reddish plumage.

- Ginger Geezer. An Appreciation [of Vivian Stanshall]. —*The Guardian*, 8th March 1995

2 the backside *AUSTRALIA, 1967*
From **GINGER ALE**.

- 'Yeh, and the legal-eagles are on our ginger.' —Frank Hardy, *The Outcasts of Foolgarah*, p. 76, 1971

3 a prostitute who steals from her clients *AUSTRALIA*
Also 'ginger girl' and 'gingerer'.

- —Sidney J. Baker, *Australia Speaks*, 1953

▸ **on the ginger**

(of prostitutes) working at gingering their clients *AUSTRALIA*

- They went into partnership on the ginger. —Lance Peters, *The Dirty Half-Mile*, p. 164, 1979

ginger ale; ginger *noun*

1 jail *UK*
Rhyming slang.

- The ginger's full of gingers [homosexuals]. —Ray Puxley, *Cockney Rabbit*, 1992

2 bail *NEW ZEALAND, 1963*
Rhyming slang.

- —Harry Orsman, *A Dictionary of Modern New Zealand Slang*, p. 56, 1999

3 the backside *AUSTRALIA, 1967*
Rhyming slang for **TAIL**.

- —Jim Ramsay, *Cop It Sweet!*, p. 40, 1977
- —Ryan Aven-Bray, *Ridgey Didge Oz Jack Lang*, p. 29, 1983

ginger beer; ginger *noun*

1 a homosexual man *UK, 1959*
Rhyming slang for **QUEER**.

- [T]his dirty old ginger beer started looking at me. —John Peter Jones, *Feather Pluckers*, p. 12, 1964
- [A] rude boy called Tailor / Cried out "Hello Sailor" / And something about ginger beer. —Ivor Biggun, *The Charabanc Trip*, 1978
- Didn't get himself a portion. He ain't a ginger, is he? —Greg Williams, *Diamond Geezers*, p. 120, 1997

2 a member of the Royal Australian Engineers *AUSTRALIA, 1941*
Rhyming slang for 'engineer'.

- —Ryan Aven-Bray, *Ridgey Didge Oz Jack Lang*, p. 29, 1983

ginger beer; ginger *adjective*

homosexual *UK*
Rhyming slang for **QUEER**.

- I made sure he copped it big-time. And I gave him an extra one for being ginger. —Dave Courtney, *Stop the Ride I Want to Get Off*, p. 73, 1999

gingering *verb*

(of a prostitute or accomplice) stealing from a client's clothing *AUSTRALIA, 1944*

- "[G]ingering" or robbing prospective clients was considered low taste, but after all, the man was a copper —Kylie Tennant, *The Joyful Condemned*, 1953
- Gingering was done by two whores in concert. —Lance Peters, *The Dirty Half-Mile*, p. 164, 1979

ginger minger; ginger minge; ginge minge *noun*

a person who has (it is presumed) naturally ginger pubic hair *UK*

- "What's a minge?", "Ginger minge" (a nickname given to a red-haired female member of the staff), "Ginger minger", and so on. —Peter Woods and Martyn Hammersley, *Gender and Ethnicity in Schools*, p. 88, 1993
- —Chris Lewis, *The Dictionary of Playground Slang*, p. 101, 2003

ginger pop *noun*

1 a police officer *UK*
Rhyming slang for **COP**.

- —Ray Puxley, *Cockney Rabbit*, 1992

2 ginger beer *UK, 1827*

- I'll be there in shorts and a t-shirt, a bag of sausage rolls and wine gums in one hand, and a stone bottle of ginger pop in the other! —*The Guardian*, 8th December 2000

gingersnaps *noun*

▸ **(have had) too many gingersnaps last night**

to have had too much alcohol to drink *CANADA*

- —T. K. Pratt, *Oral Informant in Prince Edward Island Sayings*, p. 90, 1998

ginger-top *noun*

a redhead *UK*
From **GINGER**.

- Five-ten, nicely-sized medium-to-large bristols, hips crying out to have your hands round them, an immaculate pair of legs going all the way up to where it matters and a ginger-top at that, Jimbo. Even you must fancy that[.] —John Milne, *Alive and Kicking*, p. 53, 1998

ginhead *noun*

a habitual drinker of gin *US, 1927*

- [T]here was plenty of these gin heads about[.] —Frank Norman, *Bang To Rights*, p. 120, 1958

gin jockey *noun*

a white man who cohabits with an Aboriginal woman *AUSTRALIA*

- He hated the ignominy of capitulating to a harlot, and a black one at that. Macauley, the gin-jockey, they could say. —D'Arcy Niland, *The Shiralee*, p. 121, 1955
- Ah, he's a gin jockey too, is he? Young bastard. —Randolph Stow, *Tourmaline*, p. 68, 1963
- — Thommo, *The Dictionary of Australian Swearing and Sex Sayings*, p. 58, 1985

gink *noun*

1 a naive rustic; a dolt *US, 1906*

- —Vincent J. Monteleone, *Criminal Slang*, p. 98, 1949
- I got them running around the block night making a gink of myself for the other stables to see. —Wilda Moxham, *The Apprentice*, p. 122, 1969
- See thae [those] ginks, they get right up my onions [irritate], so they dae. —Ian Pattison, *Rab C. Nesbitt*, 1988

2 a look; a peek *AUSTRALIA*
Perhaps a nasalised variant of **GEEK**.

- The glare stung my eyes like hot fat, but for the mate's benefit I kept staring so that he could get a gink at me wide awake. —Robert S. Close, *Love Me Sailor*, p. 227, 1945
- Get a gink at that chin, mates! —Robert S. Close, *With Hooves of Brass*, p. 121, 1961

3 an unpleasant smell *UK: SCOTLAND*

- There's some gink in that changin room. —Michael Munro, *The Patter, Another Blast*, p. 27, 1988

gink *verb*

to give off an unpleasant smell *UK: SCOTLAND*

- These denims a mine are ginkin. —Michael Munro, *The Patter, Another Blast*, p. 27, 1988

ginky *adjective*

out of style *US*

- — *Current Slang*, p. 7, Winter 1969

gin mill *noun*

a bar *US, 1866*
The term has shed most of its unsavoury connotations of the past and is now generally jocular.

- Look, to most whites the ginmills of Harlem mean only one thing, the underworld. —Mezz Mezzrow, *Really the Blues*, p. 228, 1946
- At three-thirty the word went out in the back of a gin mill off Forty-second and Third. —Mickey Spillane, *Kiss Me Deadly*, p. 56, 1952
- [T]hese are mostly ginmills featuring bootleg and the white liquor called King Kong. —Robert Sylvester, *No Cover Charge*, p. 67–68, 1956
- Our flop was as small as this trailer, and we ate at this gin mill every night, because you got free seconds on the cold cuts. —James Ellroy, *White Jazz*, p. 321, 1992
- When they got to Fin's favorite gin mill they were lucky to grab a parking space only half a block away. —Joseph Wambaugh, *Finnegan's Week*, p. 226, 1993

ginned *adjective*

drunk *US, 1900*

- —Joseph E. Ragen and Charles Finston, *Inside the World's Toughest Prison*, p. 801, 1962: 'Penitentiary and underworld glossary'

ginny barn *noun*
a prison for females or a section of prison reserved for females *US*
• But the most fascinating thing about the ward: the women's section, the Ginnybarn, was situated a mere 100 feet from the UT unit[.] —Clarence Cooper Jr, *The Farm*, p. 22, 1967

ginola *adjective*
supremely attractive *UK*
A tribute to the good-looking French footballer David Ginola (b.1967); recorded in use in contemporary gay society.
• —*Attitude*, p. 60, July 2003: 'New palare lexicon'

ginormous *adjective*
very large *UK, 1962*
Pronounced '*jye*-normous'.
• The prices were ginormous. —Adrian Reid, *The Confessions of a Hitch-Hiker*, 1970

gin's piss *noun*
poor quality or weak beer *AUSTRALIA*
From 'gin' meaning 'a female Australian Aboriginal'; from the extinct Australian Aboriginal language Dharug (Sydney region).
• Yeah, but you come from England. That's gin's piss country. —John O'Grady, *It's Your Shout, Mate!*, p. 43, 1972

ginzo *noun*
an Italian-American or Italian *US, 1931*
Offensive. Probably a derivative of **GUINEA**.
• —Helen Dahlskog (Editor), *A Dictionary of Contemporary and Colloquial Usage*, p. 27, 1972
• A crazy ginso with a horseshoe up his ass. Suspicious of his own mother. —Edwin Torres, *Carlito's Way*, p. 56, 1975
• Well don't you let the ghinzos know that. —John Sayles, *Union Dues*, p. 232, 1977
• "This isn't back when we were kids, beating up on the yids and ginzos," Pat said. —Robert Campbell, *Juice*, p. 171, 1988

Giorgio Armani; giorgio *noun*
a sandwich *UK*
Rhyming slang for 'sarnie', formed from the name of the Italian fashion designer (b.1934).
• —Ray Puxley, *Fresh Rabbit*, 1998

gip *noun*
▷ see: **GYP**

gip-gip *noun*
used for mocking another's laughter *TRINIDAD AND TOBAGO, 1997*
• —Lise Winer, *Dictionary of the English/Creole of Trinidad & Tobago*, 2003

gipsy's ginger *noun*
human excrement found out of doors *UK, 1984*
From a characteristic colour of excrement combined with a denigratory stereotype of gipsy life.

gippo *noun*
▷ see: **GYPO**

gipsy's kiss; gipsey's *noun*
an act of urination *UK*
Rhyming slang for **PISS**.
• I need a gipsy's. —Jack Dash (an ex-docker from London), 1979

gipsy's warning; gipsy's *noun*
1 a sinister warning, a final warning, a warning of immediate reprisal *UK, 1918*
Negative stereotyping.
• If we'd had a bad day, we'd get a "gypsy's warning", The sergeant major would say, "The following people, come and see me [...] You didn't do very well yesterday. This is a gypsy's.; you'd better sort your shit out, because next time you'll be gone. —Andy McNab, *Immediate Action*, p. 64, 1995

2 morning *UK*
Rhyming slang.
• —Julian Franklyn, *A Dictionary of Rhyming Slang*, 1960

giraffe *noun*
a *half* ounce, especially of drugs *UK*
Rhyming slang.
• —Nick Jones, *Spliffs*, p. 251, 2003

girdle *noun*
1 a waistband *UK*
Recorded in use in contemporary gay society.
• —*Attitude*, p. 60, July 2003: 'New palare lexicon'

2 an over-the-shoulder car seat belt *US*
• —*American Speech*, p. 269, December 1962: 'The language of traffic policemen'

3 in motor racing, the main support for the engine *US*
• —John Edwards, *Auto Dictionary*, p. 69, 1993

girl *noun*
1 cocaine *US, 1953*
• Leslie thought of copping – four girls and four boys. A speed-ball. —Clarence Cooper Jr, *The Scene*, p. 36, 1960
• She had taught me to snort "girl," and almost always when I came to her pad, there would be thing sparkling rows of crystal cocaine on the glass top of the cocktail table. —Iceberg Slim (Robert Beck), *Pimp*, p. 61, 1969
• After the well wishes were over, we rapped, we smoked, and we took a toot of boy and girl. —A.S. Jackson, *Gentleman Pimp*, p. 70, 1973
• Dig, my man, how about dropping off two spoons of boy, and a hundred dollar bag of girl. —Donald Goines, *El Dorado Red*, p. 69, 1974
• From Timbuctoo to London Dell / They toasted the best girl in town. —Dennis Wepman et al., *The Life*, p. 105, 1976
• [W]ish I had some more coke ... that was some nice girl Monkeydude had. Maybe Nick'll have some. —Odie Hawkins, *Chicago Hustle*, p. 15, 1977
• —Angela Devlin, *Prison Patter*, p. 57, 1996

2 crack cocaine *UK*
• —Mike Haskins, *Drugs*, p. 281, 2003

3 heroin *US, 1981*
• —Richard A. Spears, *The Slang and Jargon of Drugs and Drink*, p. 221, 1986
• —Robert Ashton, *This Is Heroin*, p. 206, 2002
• —Mike Haskins, *Drugs*, p. 284, 2003

4 a lesbian *US*
A term used by lesbians.
• But you know, she's got that "back off" thing goin' on so I just assumed that she was one of the girls. —*Boys on the Side*, 1995

5 a homosexual male, especially an effeminate one *US, 1912*
• —G. Legman, *The Language of Homsexuality*, p. 1167, 1941
• —Bruce Rodgers, *The Queens' Vernacular*, p. 96, 1972
• Real girl is used to refer to someone who's not a girl (i.e homosexual man) or a drag queen in the Polari sense. —Paul Baker, *Polari*, p. 188, 2002

6 (especially in sporting contexts) an effeminate male *AUSTRALIA*
• Football supporters also like to call them 'gutless wonders', 'fairies', 'cream puffs' or 'girls'. —Ivor Limb, *Footy's No Joke!*, p. 57, 1986

7 in a deck of playing cards, a queen *US*
• —Albert H. Morehead, *The Complete Guide to Winning Poker*, p. 264, 1967

girl and boy *noun*
a toy *UK*
Rhyming slang.
• —Ray Puxley, *Cockney Rabbit*, 1992

girl-deb *noun*
a girl who spends time with a boy's youth gang, whether or not she is a gang member's girlfriend *US*
• And all the change we could beat out of our girl-debs. —Piri Thomas, *Down These Mean Streets*, p. 18, 1967

girlf *noun*
a girlfriend *UK*
• [T]he best way to get over an ex girlf. Try not to pick anyone who looks too much like her[.] —*BBCi*, 25th May 2003

Girl Friday *noun*
a young woman who is very useful to have about the place as an assistant *US, 1940*
From Defoe's tale of Robinson Crusoe and his Man Friday.
• —*American Speech*, p. 299, December 1955: "Mimeo Minnie,' 'Sadie, the office secretary,' and other women Office workers in America'
• There is a small office-supply company on Market Street. The sales manager needs a Girl Friday. —Armistead Maupin, *Tales of the City*, p. 25, 1978

girlfriend *noun*
1 a male homosexual's lover or friend *US*
• I got them wholesale from a girl friend of mine, Bill S., who ran one of those head parlors off Broadway. —Antony James, *America's Homosexual Underground*, p. 133, 1965
• He hoped for early release, but got in trouble, injured a hack and shanked some cons for picking on his girlfriend – a cute guy he'd see once in a while now in West Hollywood – and had to do six years straight up, no time off. —Elmore Leonard, *Be Cool*, p. 175, 1999

2 used as an affectionate term of address for a friend or acquaintance *US*

- You're gonna knock 'em dead, girlfriend. — Stephen Cannell, *King Con*, p. 17, 1997

3 cocaine *US, 1979*

An elaboration of **GIRL** (cocaine).

- — Richard A. Spears, *The Slang and Jargon of Drugs and Drink*, p. 221, 1986
- — Mike Haskins, *Drugs*, p. 280, 2003

girl friend experience *noun*

▷ see: **GFE**

girl-girl *noun*

a scene in a pornographic film, or an entire pornographic film, involving two women *US*

- "Girl-girl" has always been a thriving subgenre in porno. — Ana Loria, *1 2 3 Be A Porn Star!*, p. 101, 2000

girl-girl *adjective*

in pornography, involving two women *US*

- Say you're shooting a girl-girl hard-core and you want to shoot an extreme close-up of one girl masturbating another with her finger. — *Porno Films and the People who make them*, p. 101, 1973
- Janine is known for her faboo media coverage, from Howard Stern to Jay Leno, and for her policy of appearing in only "girl-girl" scenes. — *The Village Voice*, 21st September 1999

girlie *noun*

a young woman *UK, 1860*

Patronising and derisory.

- I always knew, you know, about his girlies. — Jenny Eclair, *Camberwell Beauty*, p. 186, 2000

girlie *adjective*

mildly pornographic, featuring naked women but not sexual activity *US, 1921*

Mainly in use from the mid-1950s.

- In girlie magazines, nudity stops only at the mons Veneris – and sometimes not even there. — Joe David Brown, *Sex in the '60s*, p. 14, 1968
- The legally produced "girlie" books and magazines of former years never showed the exposed sex organs or the nude female breasts. — Roger Blake, *What you always wanted to know about porno-shops*, p. 16, 1972
- It was produced and directed by the managing editor of a bona fide girlie magazine, but the film is more of an adult male fantasy about the skin-magazine business. — Kent Smith et al., *Adult Movies*, p. 51, 1982
- At the end of 1966, he bought thirteen of the old machines, offering fifty-fifty splits to the several existing bookshops whose most extreme material were under-the-counter nudist volumes, girlie playing cards (French Decks), and Times Square standards[.] — Josh Alan Friedman, *Tales of Times Square*, p. 74–75, 1986
- "I was the east coast rep for one of the biggest distributors of girlie magazines in the country, and as I sold magazines to wholesalers I began to notice that big boob material was always a consistant seller[.] — *Adult Video*, p. 47, August/September 1986
- All the stuff, about the police and the Communist Party being right wing and not gawking at girlie calendars, I could take that. — Mark Steel, *Reasons to be Cheerful*, p. 105, 2001

girlie bar *noun*

a drinking place at which 'hostesses' are available *US*

- At first, only the girlie bars let it all hang out. — *The Advocate*, p. 13, 31st March – 13th April 1971
- — *New Society*, 17th January 1980

girlie film *noun*

a film featuring naked women but no sexual activity *US*

- Is he making nudies? girlie films? stag films? — *Porno Films and the People who make them*, p. 18, 1973
- Back in the neolithic days of 1969, most sex theaters were running loops of ten-minute girlie films. — George Paul Csicsery (Editor), *The Sex Industry*, p. 165, 1973

girlie magazine *noun*

a commercial publication that features many pictures of naked women *US*

The sex industry sells 'girlies' not 'women'.

- It was produced and directed by the managing editor of a bona fide girlie magazine, but the film is more of an adult male fantasy about the skin-magazine business. — Kent Smith et al., *Adult Movies*, p. 51, 1982
- [T]he dresser was cluttered with scraps of paper, a model of the starship Enterprise, girlie magazines, food-encrusted dishes and mugs. — Janet Evanovich, *Seven Up*, p. 51, 2001

girls *noun*

a woman's breasts *US*

From the television situation comedy *Anything but Love* (1989–92), in which the character played by Jamie Lee Curtis proudly nicknamed her breasts 'the girls'.

- — Pamela Munro, *U.C.L.A. Slang*, p. 121, 2001

girls and boys *noun*

noise *UK*

Rhyming slang.

- — Ray Puxley, *Cockney Rabbit*, 1992

girl's blouse *noun*

an effeminate male *AUSTRALIA, 1996*

- Your efforts to appear tough are being hampered by the fact that you're a sissy girl's blouse who packs cucumber sandwiches for lunch. — *Large*, p. 58, 2002
- — Sonya Plowman, *Great Kiwi Slang*, p. 81, 2002

girls in blue *noun*

female police officers *AUSTRALIA*

- Not that I can be too disparaging about the boys and girls in blue. — Shane Maloney, *Nice Try*, p. 310, 1998

girls' school *noun*

a reformatory for female juvenile offenders *US*

- — Ralph de Sola, *Crime Dictionary*, p. 57, 1982

girl's week *noun*

the bleed period of the menstrual cycle *US*

- — Don R. McCreary (Editor), *Dawg Speak*, 2001

girl thing *noun*

1 a problem or subject best understood by females *US*

- — Connie Eble (Editor), *UNC-CH Campus Slang*, p. 4, Spring 1992

2 the various hygiene steps taken by a female pornography performer before a sex scene *US*

Also called 'girl stuff'.

- — *Adult Video News*, p. 48, August 1995
- "You do your girl thing and then you go out and they start to shoot you." (Quoting Jill Kelly) — Ana Loria, *1 2 3 Be A Porn Star!*, p. 27, 2000

girly-girl *noun*

1 a stereotypically feminine female *US*

- — Connie Eble (Editor), *UNC-CH Campus Slang*, p. 3, Fall 1991

2 a female friend *US*

- — *Newsday*, p. B2, 11th October 1997

3 a tampon *US*

- — Connie Eble (Editor), *UNC-CH Campus Slang*, p. 5, Fall 1999

giro *noun*

1 a fraud perpetrated on the social security system whereby a Giro cheque benefits payment is signed and cashed by someone other than, but with the connivance of, the intended payee who then reports the cheque as lost and waits for a duplicate payment *UK*

- — Angela Devlin, *Prison Patter*, p. 57, 1996

2 a social security/benefits cheque *UK, 1981*

An abbreviation of 'Giro cheque'.

- — Angela Devlin, *Prison Patter*, p. 57, 1996

GI's; GI shits *noun*

diarrhoea *US, 1944*

- — Helen Dahlskog (Editor), *A Dictionary of Contemporary and Colloquial Usage*, p. 27, 1972
- Cures heartburn, jungle rot, the Gee-fucken-Eyes, all them things. — Larry Heinemann, *Close Quarters*, p. 26, 1977
- Every last man on KP has a job to do, even the guy who boils the water to keep us from getting the GI shits! — Martin Blumenson, *Patton*, p. 222, 1985

GI shower *noun*

a military hazing or punishment in which a group of soldiers forcibly clean a dirty peer with wire brushes *US, 1956*

- DAWSON: Sir, a marine has refused to bathe on a regular basis. The men in his squad would give him a G.I. shower. KAFFEE: What's that? DAWSON: Scrub brushes, brillo pads, steel wool. — *A Few Good Men*, 1992
- These men got a GI shower. A number of us would stirp them and drag their nude bodies to the shower. They were forced to lather with carbolic soap, and we then scrubbed them with the stiff bristle scrub brushes that we used on the floor. — Robert W. Black, *A Ranger Born*, p. 27, 2002

gism; gissum *noun*
▷ see: JIZZ

gismo *noun*
▷ see: GIZMO

gism pot *noun*
the vagina *UK*
- Women's genitalia were represented as (potential) containers (e.g., bucket, box, hair goblet), places to put things in (e.g., furry letterbox, disk drive, socket, slot), containers for semen (e.g., gism pot, spunk bin, honey pot), and containers for the penis/sex (e.g., willy warmer, wank shaft, shagbox)—*Journal of Sex Research*, p. 146, 2001

gissa
▷ see: GIZZA

git; get *noun*
an objectionable individual; an idiot *UK, 1940*
'Get' was conventional English from the C14 to C18, meaning 'a child', 'one of his get' (one of his begetting); hence a useful synonym for **BASTARD**. Usage is now mainly in northwest England. 'Git' is a mispronunciation.
- [Y]ou and me and one or two more like that skiving git Jim Taylor[.] —Graeme Kent, *The Queen's Corporal [Six Granada Plays]*, p. 82, 1959
- One of the coppers, a sandy-haired git, with freckles[.]—John Peter Jones, *Feather Pluckers*, p. 14, 1964
- You soft get.—Alan Bleasdale, *Boys From the Blackstuff*, 1982
- [T]hat stunted little get and his phoney strung-out water hymns, Twat!—Kevin Sampson, *Powder*, 1999

gitbox *noun*
a guitar *US, 1937*
- I got a soft spot for any guy who'll go out to meet Judgment Day packed up with a battered old git-box and as much hay as he can carry.—Mezz Mezzrow, *Really the Blues*, p. 169, 1946
- Scat Man Crothers, as zany as they come, plucks his gitbox and hums like a hummingbird.—*Capitol News*, p. 15, March 1949

git-down time *noun*
▷ see: GET-DOWN TIME

gite *noun*
a bed and breakfast *CANADA*
In Quebec, even anglophones know and use 'gite', but it is often accompanied by 'bed and breakfast' so tourists from the US are not confused: Le Gite Park Ave., Bed and Breakfast. Au Gite Olympique is located on a major street in Montreal.
- At the gite you will also receive most publicities.—*www.saraphina.com (visitors holiday information)*, 21st May 2002

git-faced *adjective*
having an objectionable countenance *UK*
- Loud, git-faced, embarrassing[.]—James Hawes, *Dead Long Enough*, p. 80, 2000

git-fiddle *noun*
a guitar *US, 1935*
A decidedly rural term.
- "Ah brought muh git-fiddle." He slung his gorgeously decorated guitar around his neck.—Max Shulman, *Rally Round the Flag, Boys!*, p. 229, 1957
- That Chet Atkins can make that gitfiddle stand up and talk, can't he?—Ken Weaver, *Texas Crude*, p. 113, 1984

Gitmo *nickname*
the US naval base at Guantanamo Bay, Cuba *US, 1959*
- Arrive at Gitmo at 2 plus 36. On arrival Guantanamo Bay, you will be further briefed on specific missions and targets[.]—Pat Conroy, *The Great Santini*, p. 227, 1976
- We took off in April '65 with our first stop in Guantanamo Bay, Cuba. "Gitmo."—Ed Kugler, *Dead Center*, p. 16, 1999
- They would have skinned Clinton alive and thrown what was left of his carcass in Gitmo.—Michael Moore, *Dude, Where's My Country?*, p. 11, 2003

gitty up *noun*
▷ see: GET-GO

G-Ivan *noun*
a Russian enlisted soldier *US*
- —*American Speech*, p. 74, February 1946: 'Some words of war and peace from 1945'

give *noun*
inside information *UK*
- In the case of bullion robberies criminals usually rely on inside information – or "gives" as they are known.—*Now!*, 3rd April 1980

give *verb*
1 used as an imperative: to tell a secret *UK, 1956*
- —John Ayto, *The Oxford Dictionary of Slang*, p. 316, 1998

2 to consent to have sex *US, 1935*
- That's the problem with men: we always think we can buy sex. "If I take her here she'll give me some. If I buy her this she'll give me some." Nothing gets you nothing.—Chris Rock, *Rock This!*, p. 124, 1997

3 to have sex with a woman *UK*
- I gave it her.—Bill Naughton, *Alfie Darling*, 1970

▸**give a fuck**
to care, to be concerned *US*
Often in the negative.
- Treated us like decent people and that – they gave a fuck about us, know what I mean.—Kevin Sampson, *Outlaws*, p. 269, 2001

▸**give good X; give great X**
to be notable for the noun that follows *US, 1971*
On the original model of **GIVE HEAD** (to perform oral sex).
- They had style, they had grace / Rita Hayworth gave good face[.] —Madonna, *Vogue*, 1990
- Robbie Williams gives good concert.—Frank Skinner, *Frank Skinner*, p. 65, 2001
- She always gives good arrival.—*The Guardian*, 14th November 2003

▸**give her tarpaper**
to work very hard *US*
Used in Michigan's Upper Peninsula.

▸**give it**
1 to behave in the manner of whatever noun or adjective follows *UK*
- Nana don't half give it some of that. (GESTURING WITH HIS HAND THAT SHE TALKS TOO MUCH)—Caroline Aherne and Craig Cash, *The Royle Family*, 1999
- Dont think me pie and mash [flash, showy] for giving it Jack the biscuit [a show-off]—private correspondence with a prison inmate, *HMP Blunden, Suffolk*, January 2002

2 either by speech or action, to make your attitude to someone or something obvious *UK*
- But there would be people around me who would be giving it, "I just dropped my tenth E".—Macfarlane, Macfarlane and Robson, *The User*, p. 104, 1996

▸**give it all that**
to brag, to show off *UK*
- —David Powis, *The Signs of Crime*, 1977

▸**give it away**
to engage in sex without pay; to engage in sex promiscuously *US*
- She looked as if she might have worked half those years in a cat house, and if she hadn't she must have given a lot of it away.—Chester Himes, *If He Hollers Let Him Go*, p. 19, 1945

▸**give it some**
to put a great deal of effort into something *UK*
Possibly abbreviated from 'give it some wellie'.
- Cor, you were giving it some this morning weren't you? You started off in the bedroom and ended up in the kitchen!—Mark Steel, *Reasons to be Cheerful*, p. 176, 2001

▸**give it the nifty fifty**
(used of a male) to masturbate *US*
- One of the chaplains found that out the hard way, when he was caught in his cabin one afternoon with a girlie magazine in one hand and his wife's best friend in the other. In the Marines such a practice is known as 'giving it the nifty fifty.'—Robert McGowan and Jeremy Hands, *Don't Cry For Me Sergeant-Major*, p. 42, 1983

▸**give it the off**
to go, to leave *UK*
- Come on, Russell, let's give it the off.—Greg Williams, *Diamond Geezers*, p. 50, 1997

▸**give it to**
to copulate with *US*
- A couple punks tore up the place and then gave it to the nuns but good.—*The Bad Lieutenant*, 1992

▸**give it up**
to applaud *US, 1990*
Often as an imperative to an audience.
- —Connie Eble (Editor), *UNC-CH Campus Slang*, p. 4, Spring 1998
- I gotta give it up to y'all for showing love to [hip-hop artists] Mobb Deep.—*The Source*, p. 42, March 2002

▸ give Jack his jacket
to give credit where credit is due *BARBADOS*
Recorded by Richard Allsopp in Barbados in 1975.
- —Lise Winer, *Dictionary of the English/Creole of Trinidad & Tobago*, 2003

▸ give laugh for pea soup
to bring gossip or interesting news when you visit, hoping for a meal in exchange *JAMAICA, 1977*
Recorded by Richard Allsopp.

▸ give leather
to thrust forcefully while having sex *TRINIDAD AND TOBAGO*
- —Lise Winer, *Dictionary of the English/Creole of Trinidad & Tobago*, 2003

▸ give me a break; gimme a break
used as an expression of dismay at that which has just been said *US*
Ubiquitous in the 1990s.
- "It's just navy, Mom," Bobbie had insisted. "Gimme a break!"—Joseph Wambaugh, *Finnegan's Week*, p. 26, 1993

▸ give skin
to slap hands in greeting *US*
- He nearly dropped the powder can. "My homeboy! Man, gimme some skin! I'm from Lansing."—Malcolm X and Alex Haley, *The Autobiography of Malcolm X*, p. 44, 1964

▸ give someone one
to have sex with someone *UK*
- "Do you want one, Jack. Eh, Audrey, why don't you give him one?" He almost falls off the settee, he's laughing so hard. "No thanks," I say to Audrey, looking her straight in the eye, "I had one before I came here."—Ted Lewis, *Jack Carter's Law*, p. 16, 1974
- I've asked around my political colleagues and peer group, and every bloke I've talked to says he never gives his wife one without first asking if she's awake.—Barry Humphries, *The Traveller's Tool*, p. 21, 1985
- I'd still giver her one, okay.—Ian Pattison, *Rab C. Nesbitt*, 1988
- Thrusting away with their hips as they tickled the flippers [of a pinball machine], like they were giving it one.—Jake Arnott, *He Kills Coppers*, p. 33, 2001
- [T]he delights of sucking cocaine off his cock in between giving her one in as many positions as he could manage.—Garry Bushell, *The Face*, p. 111, 2001
- Fine, go round there, give her one and be all lovey dovey with her. —Danny King, *The Burglar Diaries*, p. 115, 2001
- [I] thumbed the G-string from between her tanned golden arse cheeks and gave her one from behind.—Ben Elton, *High Society*, p. 21, 2002

▸ give the office
to signal or give information *UK, 1804*
- The boss almost shook his wig off giving me the office from behind a post[.]—Mezz Mezzrow, *Really the Blues*, p. 178, 1946
- We keep this up much longer we're a cinch to give 'em the office. —Horace McCoy, *Kiss Tomorrow Good-bye*, p. 242, 1948

▸ give the skins
to have sex with someone *US*
- So you gonna give me the skins or what?—*Boyz N The Hood*, 1990

▸ give two fucks
to care, to be concerned *US*
An elaboration of **GIVE A FUCK**, and usually in the negative.
- I don't give two fucks about what's behind all this[.]—Ted Lewis, *Jack Carter's Law [britpulp]*, p. 43, 1974

▸ give up as a bad job
to abandon something that has no prospect of success *UK, 1862*
- My boyfriend, who before he met me was a regular square-eyes, has more or less given it up as a bad job these days[.]—*The Guardian*, 6th October 2001

▸ give what for
to beat, to thrash, to scold *UK, 1873*
Derives, apparently, from an exchange in which a person threatened with punishment asked 'What for?' and received the formulaic answer 'I'll give you what for'.

▸ give wings
to inject someone else with heroin or to teach them to inject themselves *US*
- —Donald Louria, *The Drug Scene*, p. 190, 1968
- [H]e knew he was going to join the hyp class and become a full-out junkie now that he had given himself his wings – his first mainline fix.—Emmett Grogan, *Ringolevio*, p. 40, 1972
- He gave me my wings, that dirty rat fuck / He thought he was slick, charging a buck.—Dennis Wepman et al., *The Life*, p. 171, 1976
- —Robert Ashton, *This Is Heroin*, p. 209, 2002

▸ give you hell
to deal with you in a harsh or severe manner *UK, 1851*
- As Mr Jones and his colleagues left for a further meeting with Gordon Brown, the chancellor, pensioners at the rally shouted "give him hell".—*The Guardian*, 8th November 2000

▸ give you the reds
to anger *US*
Teen slang.
- —*Newsweek*, p. 28, 8th October 1951

▸ give you your hat
to release from prison *US*
- Well, baby, I got busted, just like that / So I hope this toast helps you when they give you your hat.—Dennis Wepman et al., *The Life*, p. 53, 1976

▸ give your right ball/testicle for
to give everything for *AUSTRALIA*
- I have got a horse and I'd give my right ball to train it for the right owner.—Clive Galea, *Slipper*, p. 35, 1988

give-and-get *noun*
a bet *UK*
Rhyming slang.
- —Ray Puxley, *Fresh Rabbit*, 1998

give-and-take *noun*
a cake *UK*
Rhyming slang.
- —Julian Franklyn, *A Dictionary of Rhyming Slang*, 1960

give-a-shit lobe *noun*
the frontal lobe of the brain *US*
If shot in the frontal lobe, the patient rarely cares about anything.
- —Gregory Clark, *Words of the Vietnam War*, p. 201, 1990

give-away *noun*
a revelation or betrayal, either deliberate or inadvertent *US, 1882*
- "My name's Vaz." Mikey looked at Vaz's name tag. "Yeah, I know. That's the thing with badges, always a bit of a give-away.—Colin Butts, *Is Harry Still on the Boat?*, p. 82, 2003

give away *verb*
to cease doing something; to give up *AUSTRALIA, 1944*
- 'Want to give it away, Billy?' 'No, it's been chewing at my gut for too long. I've got to do it.'—Ward McNally, *Supper at Happy Harry's*, p. 85, 1982

give over!
stop it! *UK, 1984*
- Listen, Frank doesn't fancy me and I don't fancy him, alright, so bloody give over.—*The Full Monty*, 1997

giz *noun*
the vagina *US, 1975*
- [H]is mouth was dry as Rose Bird's giz[.]—Joseph Wambaugh, *The Delta Star*, p. 127, 1983

giz!
give me; give us *UK*
A slurring of 'give us', where 'us' is often used for 'me'.
- "I'll lend you twenty rips [pounds]" [...] "Giz fifty."—Kevin Sampson, *Powder*, p. 83, 1999

gizmo; gismo *noun*
a gadget, device or contraption, the exact name of which is forgotten by, or unimportant to, the speaker *US, 1942*
- Now we're getting down to where the rubber meets the road. Identification! That's the gizomo!—Max Shulman, *Rally Round the Flag, Boys!*, p. 182, 1957
- It had to be a compressed air gizmo.—Iceberg Slim (Robert Beck), *Pimp*, p. 143, 1969
- And, I gotta admit, the MCC is a fancy building with a lot of electronic gadgets and gismos.—Edwin Torres, *After Hours*, p. 158, 1979

gizmo *verb*
to outfit with a device *US*
- The limo back seat is gizmoed, and I copped Jake's hundred and twenty grand in 'queer' and the valises.—Iceberg Slim (Robert Beck), *Long White Con*, p. 212, 1977

gizz *verb*
to gaze *UK*
- So you spent the morning gizzing at bits of capurtle [a woman as a sex object) in flouncy dresses.—Douglas Clark, *Premeditated Murder*, 1975

gizza; gissa
used for making a demand *UK*
Phonetic compound of 'give us [me] a'. 'Gizza job' became a catchphrase in the mass-unemployment circumstances of the early 1980s.
- Gizza job, go on, gizzit ... gizza go, go on. I could do that. You only have to walk straight. I can walk straight, go on, gizza job, go on, gizza go. — Alan Bleasdale, *The Boy's from the Blackstuff*, 1982
- Gizza tenner an' they're yours. — Donald Gorgon, *Cop Killer*, p. 67, 1994
- I know where you live. So gizza job or the Labrador gets it. — Val McDermid, *Keeping on the Right Side of the Law*, p. 183, 1999

gizzard *noun*
250 or 300 dollars *AUSTRALIA*
An allusion to a 'monkey' ($500), with the gizzard being the guts of the monkey.
- — Ned Wallish, *The Truth Dictionary of Racing Slang*, p. 33, 1989

gizzit *noun*
a looted item *UK*
Short for 'give us it'; used by the military in the 1982 Falklands war.
- — *The Times*, 4th September 1982

gizzuts *noun*
guts, courage *US*
- — *The Bell (Paducah Tilghman High School)*, p. 8–9, 17th December 1993: 'Tilghmanism: the concealed langage of the hallway'

GJ *noun*
grand *jury* *US*
- LAGONDA: Fuck the GJ. You're Superboy. You saved what six black babies? That shit plays. — *Copland*, 1997

G-joint *noun*
1 a federal penitentiary *US*
- — Jay Robert Nash, *Dicitonary of Crime*, p. 150, 1992

2 a crooked carnival game *US, 1946*
'G' is for 'gaffed' (rigged).
- — Lindsay E. Smith and Bruce A. Walstad, *Keeping Carnies Honest*, p. 42–43, 1990: 'Glossary'

GLA *noun*
a car theft; grand *l*arceny *a*utomobile *US*
- Then get the ten latest GLA's off the hot sheet. — Charles Whited, *Chiodo*, p. 27, 1973

glacines *noun*
heroin *UK, 1998*
Possibly a misspelling of 'glassine', a material used to make bags in which the drug may be supplied.
- — Robert Ashton, *This Is Heroin*, p. 206, 2002
- — Mike Haskins, *Drugs*, p. 284, 2003

glacio *noun*
a glaciologist *UK, 1985*
- — Bernadette Hince, *The Antarctic Dictionary*, p. 147, 2000

glad *noun*
a *glad*iolus; a cut gladiolus flower *AUSTRALIA*
- Now, most of the other invalids get glads or carnies so Beryl said Valda must have really put her thinking cap on. — Barry Humphries, *A Nice Night's Entertainment*, p. 110, 1968

glad bag *noun*
1 a body bag, used to cover corpses *US, 1983*
Coined in Vietnam; still in use in the Gulf war and after.
- — Linda Reinberg, *In the Field*, p. 93, 1991

2 a condom *UK*
- — David Rowan, *A Glossary for the 90s*, 1998

gladdy; gladdie *noun*
a *glad*iolus; a cut gladiolus flower *AUSTRALIA, 1947*
- Gladdies are very funny flowers in their private lives incidentally, and that is a horticultural horror story I'll be telling you later whether you like it or not. — Edna Everage (Barry Humphries), *My Gorgeous Life*, p. 7, 1989

glad eye *noun*
a come-hither look *US, 1903*
- Getting excited because a newspaper seller had given her the glad eye? — Marian Keyes, *Sushie for Beginners*, p. 103, 2003

glad hand *noun*
1 a welcome, rousing if not always sincere *US, 1873*
- They sure gave me the glad-hand when they laid their peepers on my new car. — Mezz Mezzrow, *Really the Blues*, p. 88, 1946

2 on the railways, the metal air hose coupling between carriages *US*
The interlocking connectors vaguely resemble hands clasped in a handshake.
- "Glad Hands" are used on all the trains / So air won't suffer parting pains. — J. Herbert Lund, *Herb's Hot Box of Railraod Slang*, p. 104, 1975

glad-hand *verb*
to greet with profuse, if insincere, enthusiasm *US, 1895*
Often found in the context of politicians.
- All they can do is go around all the time, glad-handing people and acting like jerks, and nobody remember them five minutes after they see them. — George V. Higgins, *The Judgment of Deke Hunter*, p. 17, 1976
- After a moment of glad-handing and stowing my AWOL bag and settling in, Stepik arrived. — Larry Heinemann, *Close Quarters*, p. 123, 1977
- Baby Jewels gladhanding politicos, grabassing showgirls, squeezed into nightclub booths with minor celebrities, lolling in his box at Candlestick Park. — Seth Morgan, *Homeboy*, p. 29, 1990
- Then Bob Bix, glad-handing president of the senior class, introduced the queen's court in ascending order of beauty, popularity, and personality. — C.D. Payne, *Youth in Revolt*, p. 437, 1993

glad-handing *adjective*
insincere and false *US*
- His glad-handing, varsity chumminess was totally alien and therefore suspect[.] — Donna Tartt, *Secret History*, p. 49, 1992
- [O]ut of all of them glad-handing no-marks – I would've put my shirt on him being here. — Kevin Sampson, *Outlaws*, p. 225, 2001

gladiator school *noun*
a violent prison *US*
- — *Maledicta*, p. 266, Summer/Winter 1981: 'By its slang, ye shall know it: the pessimism of prison life'
- The judge recanted his sentence suspension and hit him with five years in the California Youth Authority Facility at Soledad – the "Baby Joint" and "Gladiator School." — James Elroy, *Suicide Hill*, p. 580, 1986
- Not that it matters. Joints all the same, gladiator schools. — Seth Morgan, *Homeboy*, p. 161, 1990
- Gladiator schools breed gang members because fighting and criminal activities are the primary lessons learned there. — William Bentley, *Prison Slang*, p. 4, 1992

glad lad *noun*
an attractive male *US*
- — *Yank*, p. 18, 24th March 1945

glad-on *noun*
an erection *UK*
A happy variation of **HARD-ON** (an erection).
- Sight of that Britannia always, always gives myself half a glad-on. — Kevin Sampson, *Outlaws*, p. 6, 2001

glad plaid *noun*
a bright plaid pattern *US*
Mexican-American youth (Pachuco) usage in the American southwest.
- — *Common Ground*, p. 81, Summer 1947

glad rag *noun*
a piece of cloth saturated with glue or an industrial solvent, used for recreational inhaling *US*
- — Eugene Landy, *The Underground Dictionary*, p. 89, 1971
- — Ralph de Sola, *Crime Dictionary*, p. 5758, 1982

glad rags *noun*
your best clothes *US, 1899*
- The handbags and the gladrags / That your poor old Grandad had to sweat to buy you. — Mike D'Abo, *Handbags and Gladrags*, 1964
- — Hy Lit, *Hy Lit's Unbelievable Dictionary of Hip Words for Groovy People*, p. 18, 1968

glad stuff *noun*
any hard drug; cocaine, heroin, morphine, opium *US, 1953*
- — Mike Haskins, *Drugs*, p. 280, 2003

glad we could get together
used as a humorous farewell *US*
A catchphrase television sign-off by John Cameron Swayze on NBC in the 1950s. Repeated with referential humour.

glaiket *adjective*
foolish; having a foolish appearance *UK, 1985*
From an earlier sense as 'inattentive to duty'.
- Are you deaf as well as glaiket? — Ian Pattison, *Rab C. Nesbitt*, 1988

glam *noun*
glamour *US, 1937*

glam; glam up *verb*
to dress more smartly *UK, 1937*
- And the three of us had glammed up a bit. Just in case. — Mary Hooper, *(megan)2*, p. 168, 1999

glam *adjective*
1 glamorous *UK*
- Her name's Maxine. She's rather glam, isn't she? — John Winton, *All The Nice Girls*, 1964

2 flamboyant, especially in dress and appearance *US*
- A few glam drag queens in miniskirts and high heels are strutting in the shadows cooing and hollering. — Francesca Lia Block, *Missing Angel Juan*, p. 345, 1993
- They've been asked to open a show for new glam fave Suede. — *Rolling Stone*, p. 16, 27th May 1993
- Leitch and Skye are in the midst of cutting their first album with their glam-rock band, Nancy Boy[.] — *Vogue*, p. 86, June 1994

glamazon *noun*
a beautiful, well-muscled woman
A compound of 'glamour' and 'Amazon'.
- I've heard you described as a "glamazon" [...] A glamourous Amazonian! Well, it's true that people used to think I was a man. — *Gwen Stefani interviewed in Q*, p. 98, December 2001

glammed-up *adjective*
dressed or presented in a glamorous manner *UK, 1924*
- [S]ome glammed-up babe escaping the nine to five[.] — Dave Courtney, *Raving Lunacy*, p. 93, 2000

glamor boy *noun*
a US Air Force flier *US*
- — *American Speech*, p. 310, December 1946: 'More Air Force slang'

glamor-puss; glamour-puss *noun*
a sexually attractive person, especially one who has enhanced a natural beauty with artificial glamour *US, 1941*
- Hey, hey, glamorpuss. I'm sorry. — *Rebel Without a Cause*, 1955
- [A]n endless succession of glamourpusses in figure-hugging gleaming leather and latex and PVC. — Claire Mansfield and John Mendelssohn, *Dominatrix*, p. 10, 2002

glamottle *noun*
a 13 ounce bottle of Budweiser™ beer *US, 1948*
Budweiser advertised that it was a 'glass that holds more than a bottle', which is corrupted here.
- — *American Speech*, p. 62, February 1967: 'Soda-fountain, restaurant and tavern calls'

glamour *noun*
a sexually attractive female *AUSTRALIA, 1983*
- One of the Qantas staff, a glamour, made her way over to us. — Paul Vautin, *Turn It Up!*, p. 214, 1995

Glamour-don't *noun*
a huge fashion mistake *CANADA*
From a fashion 'do's and don'ts' column in *Glamour Magazine*.
- — Jack Chambers (Editor), *Slang Bag 93 (University of Toronto)*, p. 3, Winter 1993

glamour groovie *noun*
a fashion-conscious person *US*
- Once upon a time in Switzerland there was a glamour groovie named William Tell. — Haenigsen, *Jive's Like That*, 1947

G-land *noun*
Grajagan, Indonesia *US*
A surfing destination.
- — Trevor Cralle, *The Surfin'ary*, p. 43, 1991

glare glasses; glares *noun*
sunglasses *INDIA*
- You must wear glare glasses here in the summer. — Paroo Nihalini, R.K. Tongue and Priya Hosali, *Indian and British English*, 1979

glark *verb*
to decipher a meaning from context *US*
- The System III manuals are pretty poor, but you can generally glark the meaning from context. — Eric S. Raymond, *The New Hacker's Dictionary*, p. 177, 1991

Glasgow grin; Glesga grin *noun*
a slash or slash-scar on the face *UK: SCOTLAND*
- Let's see whit the Cockney wide boy looks lik wi a Glesga grin. — Michael Munro, *The Patter, Another Blast*, p. 27, 1988

Glasgow kiss; Glesga kiss *noun*
a head butt to your opponent's face *UK*
- — Michael Munro, *The Patter, Another Blast*, p. 27, 1988
- The slap hurt. Rick's instinctive reaction was to give her a Glasgow kiss. — Colin Butts, *Is Harry on the Boat?*, p. 272, 1997
- "[W]here do you stand on the Glasgow Kiss?" "Glasgow Kiss? I ain't never heard of that." "I thought not." — Christopher Brookmyre, *Not the End of the World*, p. 378, 1998

Glasgow nod; Glesga nod *noun*
a head butt to your opponent's face *UK: SCOTLAND*
- Never mind arguin wi the diddy [fool] – gie um the Glesga nod. — Michael Munro, *The Patter, Another Blast*, p. 27, 1988

Glasgow Ranger; glasgow *noun*
a stranger *UK*
Rhyming slang, formed from Glasgow Rangers football club; recorded as an underworld term.
- — Ray Puxley, *Cockney Rabbit*, 1992

glass *noun*
1 amphetamine powder; methamphetamine powder *UK, 1998*
- — Mike Haskins, *Drugs*, p. 279, 2003

2 heroin *UK*
- — Mike Haskins, *Drugs*, p. 284, 2003

3 a hypodermic syringe *US, 1942*
- — Robert Ashton, *This Is Heroin*, p. 209, 2002
- — Mike Haskins, *Drugs*, p. 292, 2003

4 a shop window *US*
- This usually occurred about one o'clock in the morning, and did not happen again until six, when a patrolman was required to check all the "glass" – shop windows – in his post. — Peter Maas, *Serpico*, p. 63, 1973

5 a five ounce glass of beer *AUSTRALIA*
- — John O'Grady, *It's Your Shout, Mate!*, p. 14, 1972
- A glass is five ounces, a middy is seven ounces, an' a pot's ten. — John O'Grady, *It's Your Shout, Mate!*, p. 15, 1972

6 a smooth water surface *US*
- Like to finish up operations early and fly down to Vung Tau for the evening glass. — *Apocalypse Now*, 1979

7 a diamond *US, 1918*
- — Vincent J. Monteleone, *Criminal Slang*, p. 100, 1949

8 in drag racing and hot rodding, fibreglass, used to reduce weight *US*
- — Olney Ross, *Kings of the Drag Strip*, p. 187, 1968

▷ **see:** GLASS OF WATER

glass *verb*
1 to attack someone's face using a glass or bottle as a weapon *UK, 1936*
- Well, the next thing we ken is thit the specky cunt's glassed Tam, cut the side of hes face open. — Irvine Welsh, *The State of the Party (Disco Biscuits)*, p. 33, 1995
- — Angela Devlin, *Prison Patter*, p. 57, 1996
- He did six months for glassing some bloke[.] — John King, *Human Punk*, p. 52, 2000
- I have to slap his hand away or knee him in the balls or glass his stupid fuckin grid [face]. — Niall Griffiths, *Kelly + Victor*, p. 289, 2002

2 in hot rodding, to repair a car body with lead compound or fibreglass *US*
- — Tom MacPherson, *Dragging and Driving*, p. 139, 1960

glassbottle *noun*
pieces of broken glass set into the top of a wall *TRINIDAD AND TOBAGO, 1920*
- — Frank A. Collymore, *Barbadian Dialect*, p. 53, 1965
- — Lise Winer, *Dictionary of the English/Creole of Trinidad & Tobago*, 2003

glass ceiling *noun*
a notional barrier to personal advancement, especially in the employment prospects of a woman, a disabled person or anyone from an ethnic minority *US, 1984*
'You can't see it but you know it's there' – or 'the sky's the limit'.

- — *American Speech*, Summer 1990
- The City, the financial world, in those days was almost exclusively male and even now the glass ceiling is much lower in the City than most professions. — Sally Cline [quoting Denis Healey], *Couples*, p. 344, 1998

glass chandelier *noun*
homosexual; a homosexual *UK*
Rhyming slang for **QUEER**.
- Give him a stage and he starts acting like a glass chandelier. — Bodmin Dark, *Dirty Cockney Rhyming Slang*, 2003

glass cheque *noun*
a bottle with a deposit on it *UK: SCOTLAND*
- Gie's that glass cheque till Ah run out tae the ice-cream man. — Michael Munro, *The Patter, Another Blast*, p. 27, 1988

glass chin *noun*
a window built in the area immediately below and slightly behind the nose of a bomber *US*
- An Antonov AN-12 Cub, all right, with a glass chin for the navigator to peer out of. — Stephen Coonts, *Final Flight*, p. 369, 1988

glass dick *noun*
a pipe used to smoke crack cocaine *US*
- — Mark S. Fleisher, *Beggars & Thieves*, p. 289, 1995: 'Glossary'
- [B]ut he always been one boned-out nigga, spen' way too much time suckin' da glass dick. — Stephen Cannell, *King Con*, p. 50, 1997

glass diet *noun*
an addiction to crack cocaine *US*
- — Jim Crotty, *How to Talk American*, p. 90, 1997

glass gun *noun*
a hypodermic syringe and needle *US, 1949*
- — Richard A. Spears, *The Slang and Jargon of Drugs and Drink*, p. 222, 1986
- — Mike Haskins, *Drugs*, p. 292, 2003

glass house *noun*
1 a guard room, detention barracks or military prison *UK, 1931*
From the glass-roofed North Camp military prison in Aldershot.
2 in prison, a detention cell or cells *UK*
- — Angela Devlin, *Prison Patter*, p. 57, 1996

3 in surfing, a smooth ride inside the hollow of a wave *US*
- — Mitch McKissick, *Surf Lingo*, 1987

Glass House *nickname*
the Parker Center police headquarters in Los Angeles *US*
- [T]he vice grabs her and off she goes in a very real coach to the glasshouse[.] — John Rechy, *City of Night*, p. 104, 1963
- They call it the Glass House because the block-square building looks like solid glass, a cute architectural trick. — Oscar Zeta Acosta, *The Revolt of the Cockroach People*, p. 51, 1973
- "I'm not drunk," he repeated all the way to the Glass House[.] — Joseph Wambaugh, *The Blue Knight*, p. 46, 1973

glassie *noun*
a clear glass marble *AUSTRALIA, 1934*
- 'Give yer a game of alleys, glassies up,' challenged Pigeon. — Norman Lindsay, *Saturdee*, p. 124, 1934
- The ones that came out of lemonade bottles were known as Glassies too. — Cathy Hope, *Themes from the Playground*, p. 3, 1985

glass itch *noun*
irritation of the skin by fibreglass dust *US*
Surfing usage.
- — Dennis Aaberg and John Milius, *Big Wednesday*, p. 209, 1978

glass jaw *noun*
a weak jaw in the context of boxing or fighting *US*
- I didn't think it as right I should hit a guy hard who played on the violin like Golden Boy. But he had a glass jaw. — Rocky Garciano (with Rowland Barber), *Somebody Up There Likes Me*, p. 271, 1955

glass of beer *noun*
the ear *UK*
Rhyming slang.
- — Julian Franklyn, *A Dictionary of Rhyming Slang*, 1961

glass of plonk *noun*
the nose *UK*
Rhyming slang for **CONK**.
- — Ray Puxley, *Cockney Rabbit*, 1992

glass of water; glass *noun*
a quarter of an ounce (seven grams) of cocaine *UK*
Rhyming slang for **QUARTER**. Recorded in August 2002.

glass pack *noun*
in hot rodding, a muffler that has been stuffed with fibreglass, increasing the roar of the engine *US*
- — Tom MacPherson, *Dragging and Driving*, p. 139, 1960

glass work *noun*
in poker, the use of a small mirror or other refective surface to cheat *US, 1968*
- — Thomas L. Clark, *The Dictionary of Gambling and Gaming*, p. 91, 1987

glassy *adjective*
(used of an ocean condition) smooth, not choppy *US*
- — Grant W. Kuhns, *On Surfing*, p. 117, 1963

Glasto *noun*
the *Glasto*nbury Festival; to a lesser extent, the town of Glastonbury *UK*
The festival began in 1970 when it was known as The Glastonbury Fayre. The earliest references to the event as 'Glasto' seem to be late 1990s.
- WIN! A DJ SET AT GLASTO! — *Mixmag*, front cover, June 2003
- t's their first Glasto, and they are in shock. — *The Guardian*, p. 2, 28th June 2004

glaze *verb*
to daydream *NEW ZEALAND*
- — David McGill, *David McGill's Complete Kiwi Slang Dictionary*, p. 55, 1998

glazed *adjective*
drunk *US*
- — Helen Dahlskog (Editor), *A Dictionary of Contemporary and Colloquial Usage*, p. 27, 1972

glazey doughnut *noun*
the residue of vaginal secretions ringing a cunnilinguist's mouth *UK*
- — *www.LondonSlang.com*, June 2002

gleam *verb*
▸ **gleam the tube**
(of a female) to masturbate *US*
- Another way to say "the girl is masturbating" [...] Gleaming the tube[.] — Erica Orloff and JoAnn Baker, *Dirty Little Secrets*, p. 67, 2001

gleamer *noun*
any reflective surface used by the dealer for cheating in a card game *US, 1969*
- — Thomas L. Clark, *The Dictionary of Gambling and Gaming*, p. 91, 1987

gleaming *adjective*
excellent *US*
- — Judi Sanders, *Da Bomb!*, p. 13, 1997

gleek *noun*
in poker, three of a kind *US*
- — Albert H. Morehead, *The Complete Guide to Winning Poker*, p. 264, 1967

gleesome threesome *noun*
group sex with three participants *AUSTRALIA*
- OZZIE: I don't want to come betwen youse and bazza or anything like that. SUKI: You mean a gleesome threesome. Don't come the raw prawn with me Ozzie[.] — Barry Humphries, *Bazza Pulls It Off!*, 1971

Glen Hoddle; Glen *noun*
an objective achieved with ease; in sport, an easy win or simple victory *UK*
Rhyming slang for 'doddle', based on the name of footballer and former England coach Glen Hoddle.
- — *Antiquarian Book Review*, p. 18, June 2002

Glesga grin, Glesga kiss, Glesga nod *nouns*
▹ **see:** GLASGOW GRIN, GLASGOW KISS, GLASGOW NOD

glider *noun*
▹ **see:** GUIDER

glide time *noun*
a flexible work schedule *NEW ZEALAND*
- You look as if you spent the night there. Isn't that carrying glide-time to excess? — Roger Hall, *Glide Time*, p. 14, 1977

glifty *verb*
to steal *US*
- —Jerry Robertson, *Oil Slanguage*, p. 59, 1954

glim *noun*
1 a light *UK, 1676*
- —Lou Shelly, *Hepcats Jive Dictionary*, p. 12, 1945
- He ganders glims up in the steeple! — Haenigsen, *Jive's Like That*, 1947

2 the eye *UK, 1789*
- —Vincent J. Monteleone, *Criminal Slang*, p. 101, 1949

3 a railway lantern *US*
- —Norman Carlisle, *The Modern Wonder Book of Trains and Railroading*, p. 263, 1946

glim *verb*
to see *US, 1912*
- Yeh Rocky, just to 'glim' him and you know he's rough, but what in the Hell cut his box off? — Iceberg Slim (Robert Beck), *Pimp*, p. 51, 1969

glimmer *noun*
1 a light *UK, 1566*
- A paper bag was wrapped around the overhead glimmer to curb the brightness[.] — Mezz Mezzrow, *Really the Blues*, p. 117, 1946

2 any reflective surface used by a dealer to cheat in a game of cards *US*
- —Frank Garcia, *Marked Cards and Loaded Dice*, p. 262, 1962
- —Thomas L. Clark, *The Dictionary of Gambling and Gaming*, p. 91, 1987

Glimmer Man *nickname*
a man appointed by the Gas Company during World War 2 to inspect homes for any contravention of the rationing of gas *IRELAND*
- [T]he Gas Company sent out inspectors to ensure that the gas was not being used during off-period. These inspectors became known as the Glimmer Men. — Éamonn Mac Thomáis, *Gur Cake and Coal Blocks*, p. 120, 1976

glimmers *noun*
the eyes or eyeglasses *UK, 1814*
- —Hyman E. Goldin et al., *Dictionary of American Underworld Lingo*, p. 82, 1950

glimmer twins *nickname*
Mick Jagger and Keith Richard of The Rolling Stones *UK, 1968*
A self-given nickname, apparently – according to Keith Richard – in response to the question 'Who ARE you? What's it all about? Come on, give us a clue. Just give us a glimmer'.

glimp *verb*
to peer, to peep *UK*
Military; an abbreviation of 'glimpse' (to see briefly).
- —Nigel Foster, *The Making of a Royal Marine Commando*, 1987

gliss around *verb*
to make small talk *US*
- — *Time Magazine*, p. 92, 20th January 1947: 'Dicty Dictionary'

glitch *noun*
a malfunction *US, 1962*
From the Yiddish for 'slip'. Heard on BBC television, 20th October 1965.
- —Guy L. Steele, *Coevolution Quarterly*, p. 31, Spring 1981: "Computer Slang'

glitching *noun*
a temporary or intermittent loss of control (of a radio-controlled aircraft) when interference from another signal occurs *UK*
- — *Glitching on the Beacon (New Society)*, 20th September 1979

glitter *noun*
salt *US*
- — *Maledicta*, p. 267, Summer/Winter 1981: 'By its slang, ye shall know it: the pessimism of prison life'

glitter fairy *noun*
a style-conscious, effeminate homosexual man *US*
Usually derogatory.
- I get a lotta calls. Collegiate types. Lotta guys get sick of the glitter fairies in this town. —Armistead Maupin, *Tales of the City*, p. 114, 1978

glittergal *noun*
in circus and carnival usage, a female performer *US*
- —Louis M. Ackerman, *American Speech*, p. 308–309, December 1960: 'Carnival Talk'
- —Don Wilmeth, *The Language of American Popular Entertainment*, p. 112, 1981

glitter gulch *noun*
downtown Las Vegas, Nevada *US, 1953*
- The commercial center of Las Vegas is Glitter Gulch, the two blocks of Fremont Street which comprise the most concentrated gambling complex in the world. — Ed Reid and Ovid Demaris, *The Green Jungle*, p. 3, 1963
- "Glitter Gulch," as some call it, was the brightest main drag I'd ever seen anywhere. — *Screw*, p. 7, 7th March 1969
- —Thomas L. Clark, *The Dictionary of Gambling and Gaming*, p. 91, 1987

glitz *noun*
superficial glamour, especially as applied in show-business *US, 1977*
- I was not deceived by the glitz of his chameleonlike story[.] — Katherine Neville, *The Eight*, p. 233, 1988

glitzy *adjective*
ostentatious, gaudy, especially with a sense of tawdry show-business glamour; often applied to something that glitters *US, 1966*
- In North Beach you had the glitzy strip palaces like Carol Doda's with her famous bust outlined on the marquee. — Jeffrey Eugenides, *Middlesex*, p. 482, 2002

GLM *noun*
(in doctors' shorthand) *g*ood *l*ooking *m*um *UK*
Recorded in an article about medical slang in British (3 London and 1 Cambridge) hospitals.
- — *Ethics and Behaviour*, August 2003

glo *noun*
crack cocaine *US*
- — US Department of Justice, *Street Terms*, October 1994

glob *noun*
expectorated sputum *US*
- — *Maledicta*, p. 32, 1988–1989: 'Medical maledicta from San Francisco'

globber *noun*
an expectoration *US*
- Maybe we could cough a phlegm globber in it or something. — *Heathers*, 1988

globes *noun*
the female breasts *US, 1889*
- "I resent that," said Sheila Gomez, glancing at the little crucifix that dangled its gold-skinned heels above her globes. — Tom Robbins, *Jitterbug Perfume*, p. 57, 1984
- —Pamela Munro, *U.C.L.A. Slang*, p. 43, 1989

globetrotter *noun*
a heroin addict who contacts many heroin dealers in search of the best heroin *US*
- —William D. Alsever, *Glossary for the Establishment and Other Uptight People*, p. 13, December 1970

globule *noun*
a contemptible person *UK*
- Ya wee globule yi! — Ian Pattison, *Rab C. Nesbitt*, 1988

glom *verb*
1 to steal, to snatch, to grab *US, 1897*
Scots dialect *glam*, *glaum* (to clutch or grasp).
- "Hell, he ain't there," the big one said. "Somebody must of glommed him off.["] — Raymond Chandler, *Farewell My Lovely*, p. 125, 1940
- They shoulda iced him as soon as he come out and glommed the money – they take this mafia shit too serious. — Edwin Torres, *Carlito's Way*, p. 52, 1975
- [C]ut the coke with some of the bennies I glom from the narco guys[.] — James Ellroy, *Blood on the Moon*, p. 172, 1984
- [M]eanwhile running around glomming anything on the island of Manhattan wasn't nailed down. — Vincent Patrick, *Family Business*, p. 37, 1985

2 to attach to, to seize upon, to grab hold of for oneself *US, 1972*
- I knew my asshole brothers were going to come up with something like this when I tell them what I glommed on to. — Robert Campbell, *Juice*, p. 154, 1988
- [M]ore and more cells glommed together (no one said this book is scientific), and life forms got bigger[.] — Erica Orloff and JoAnn Baker, *Dirty Little Secrets*, p. 1, 2001

3 to eat hastily *US*
- —Charles Shafer, *Folk Speech in Texas Prisons*, p. 205, 1990

gloom note *noun*
in college, a notification of academic deficiency *US*
- — *American Speech*, p. 76–77, February 1968: 'Some notes on flunk notes'

gloots *noun*
▷ **see:** GLUTES

glop *verb*

1 to drink noisily; to drink quickly; to slurp *UK*
Derives from 'glop' (a viscous liquid), probably as a mispronunciation of 'gulp'.
- —Nigel Foster, *The Making of a Royal Marine Commando*, 1987

2 to pour or apply with gusto *US*
- Poor Renee, the last of the true believers, glopped the stuff on her thighs for three weeks and got nothing for her troubles but a nasty rash. —Armistead Maupin, *Maybe the Moon*, p. 14, 1992

glophead *noun*
a habitual drunk *UK*
Combines **GLOP** (to drink) with **-HEAD** (a user).
- —Nigel Foster, *The Making of a Royal Marine Commando*, 1987

glopper *noun*
someone who is unfashionably dressed *UK*
Used among foot-propelled scooter-riders.
- —Ben Sharpe, *Scooter Crazy*, p. 40, 2000

Gloria Gaynors *noun*
trainers *UK*
Rhyming slang, formed from the name of soul singer Gloria Gaynor (b.1949).
- —Ray Puxley, *Fresh Rabbit*, 1998

Gloria Soames *noun*
glorious homes *AUSTRALIA, 1965*
- In the background, Nob Hill itself reached for the stars, a square mile of prime real estate in every borrowed shape and size, ranch style, split level, Regency, contemporary modern, old English, no Australian style to speak of because the only things ever invented here were the boomerang and the Australian crawl, but Gloria Soames all[.] —Frank Hardy, *The Outcasts of Foolgarah*, p. 189, 1971

glory *noun*
on the railways, an accidental death *US*
- —Norman Carlisle, *The Modern Wonder Book of Trains and Railroading*, p. 263, 1946

▸ **get the glory**
while in prison, to become religious – a state of being that may well outlast the prison sentence *UK, 1950*
- —Angela Devlin, *Prison Patter*, p. 56, 1996

glory be *noun*
tea (the beverage or the meal) *UK*
Rhyming slang.
- Wash your hands your glory be's on the table. —Ray Puxley, *Fresh Rabbit*, 1998

glory be!
used as an expression of delight or astonishment *UK, 1893*
Shortened from 'Glory be to God!' but often having to do without God in spirit as well as word.

glory card *noun*
a licence from the Federal Communications Commission to operate a citizens' band radio *US*
- —Wayne Floyd, *Jason's Authentic Dictionary of CB Slang*, p. 17, 1976

glory fit *noun*
an exhibition of religious emotional frenzy *CANADA*
- He had not the religion of some of the outport Newfoundlanders who were subject to "glory fits" and loud repentances. —Will Bird, *Sunrise for Peter*, p. 5, 1946

glory hole *noun*

1 a hole between private video booths in a pornography arcade or between stalls in a public toilets, designed for anonymous sex between men *US*
- Glory-hole – Phallic size hole in partition between toilet booths. Sometimes used for a mere peep-hole. — Anon., *The Gay Girl's Guide*, p. 10, 1949
- The boy looks into Mugwump eyes blank as obsidian mirrors, pools of black blood, glory holes in a toilet wall closing on the Last Erection. —William Burroughs, *Naked Lunch*, p. 75, 1957
- Some reports have been received that police themselves have cut the so-called "glory holes" in booth partitions which invite the curiosity of the man who believes himself to be in privacy. — *Mattachine Review*, p. 7, November 1961
- Why are they named "glory-holes"? Possibly because of the glorious sexual release of being blown, standing with your erect prick stuck through it and being sucked off by a warm, hot mouth on the other side. — *Screw*, p. 5, 19th March 1971
- Confusing all the rest of us so sometimes we're supposed to grab the guys at the glory holes, and it's a goddamned outrage all the dirty stuff that's going on[.] —George V. Higgins, *The Judgment of Deke Hunter*, p. 99, 1976
- "And each one has a hole in the wall, about three feet from the floor." "The optimum height," I said helpfully. "That's the glory hole," Robin crowed, always eager to display his state of degeneracy. —Tony Fennelly, *The Glory Hole Murders*, p. 13, 1985
- The peep show has lost its popularity. The buddy window, glory hole. —James Ridgeway, *Red Light*, p. 212, 1996

2 any unpleasant place or situation *NEW ZEALAND, 1951*
- —Harry Orsman, *A Dictionary of Modern New Zealand Slang*, p. 56, 1999

3 any room or cupboard where oddments are stored *UK, 1984*

4 the officer's sleeping quarters on a navy ship *US, 1889*
- Shaking, he rose from the chair, shut the window, and hobbled into the glory-hole that had been his father's bedroom. —Emmett Grogan, *Final Score*, p. 43, 1976

5 a clear spot in an otherwise cloudy sky through which a fighter aircraft can reach its target *US*
- —Linda Reinberg, *In the Field*, p. 94, 1991

glory hour *noun*
the hour between noon and 1pm on Sundays, the only hour of the day when drinking is permitted in pubs *FALKLAND ISLANDS (MALVINAS), 1982*
- —Bernadette Hince, *The Antarctic Dictionary*, p. 147, 2000

glory seeds *noun*
seeds of the morning glory plant, eaten for their psychoactive properties *US*
- —Jay Robert Nash, *Dicitonary of Crime*, p. 151, 1992

glory wagon *noun*
a brakevan (caboose) *US*
- —Ramon Adams, *The Language of the Railroader*, p. 68, 1977

gloss *noun*
a shine *US*
- I looked down at my "Stomps" [shoes]. They could stand a gloss all right. —Iceberg Slim (Robert Beck), *Pimp*, p. 118, 1969

glossy *noun*

1 a photograph *US, 1931*
- — *Swinging Syllables*, 1959

2 a 'glossy' magazine, a copy of a 'glossy' magazine *US, 1945*
- [A] woman's glossy that she'll skim through... then bin. — *The FHM Little Book of Bloke*, p. 69, June 2003

glove *noun*
a condom *US, 1958*
Leading to the safe-sex slogan 'No glove, no love'.
- Lundgren talks about condoms ("No glove, no love" is a popular class mnemonic), and abortion is presented as a fact of life. — *Time Magazine*, p. 54, 24th November 1986
- —Pamela Munro, *U.C.L.A. Slang*, p. 76, 2001
- The gift shop offers "No Glove, No Love" coffee mugs and "In Rubber We Trust" key chains and T-shirts[.] — *USA Today*, p. 1D, 12th July 2004

glove *verb*
to examine a prisoner's rectum for contraband *US*
- I've got it stashed. If they don't glove [examine the rectum] me, I'm through. —Bruce Jackson, *In the Life*, p. 223, 1972

gloves *noun*

▸ **the gloves are off; take the gloves off**
used for expressing a commitment to action without compromise, compassion or hesitation *UK*
- Right, he thought. Gloves off. Let's cock, lock and rock. —Chris Ryan, *The Watchman*, p. 347, 2001

glovework *noun*
in cricket, a wicketkeeper's skill or performance *UK, 1996*
- —Keith Foley, *A Dictionary of Cricketing Terminology*, p. 157, 1998

glow *noun*
a pleasant, warming sense of intoxication *US, 1942*
- I think I'll get a glow on. —Willard Motely, *Let No Man Write My Epitaph*, p. 279, 1958

- He had a right good glow on, old Boxcar[.] — Guy Owen, *The Flim-Flam Man and the Apprentice Grifter*, p. 115, 1972
- Lynn didn't fail to notice that Breda was getting a glow. — Joseph Wambaugh, *Fugitive Nights*, p. 146, 1992

glub *noun*
a slob or lazy person *NEW ZEALAND*
Used widely since the 1980s.

glub out *verb*
to idle; to relax completely *NEW ZEALAND*
Common since the 1980s.

glue *noun*
1 semen *UK*
- [I] go in a corner and clean up the glue the best I can. — John King, *Human Punk*, p. 108, 2000

2 the residue produced during heroin manufacture *US*
- — Jay Robert Nash, *Dicitonary of Crime*, p. 151, 1992

3 in computing, any interface protocol *US*
- — Eric S. Raymond, *The New Hacker's Dictionary*, p. 180, 1991

4 a police detective *US*
- But no one knows why a "broadman" is a crooked card-player or why "glues" are detectives. — *The New American Mercury*, p. 708, 1950

▸ **do glue**
to sniff glue for the psychoactive effect *UK*
- — Angela Devlin, *Prison Patter*, p. 57, 1996

glued *adjective*
drunk *US, 1957*
- — Collin Baker et al., *College Undergraduate Slang Study Conducted at Brown University*, p. 126, 1968

glued up *adjective*
intoxicated as a result of solvent abuse, especially glue-sniffing *UK*
- Some of them might be drunk or glued up or whatever[.] — Kevin Sampson, *Outlaws*, p. 244, 2001

glue gun *noun*
a weapon which fires a hardening resin to paralyse the human target *UK*
- The SAS recently began training with "glue guns" that fire a web of resin from a gun-mounted aerosol. — *The Observer*, p. 13, 18th March 2001

gluehead *noun*
a person who inhales glue or any volatile solvent for the intoxicating effect *US*
- "[H]e's a glue head." "Any port in a storm." — Joseph Wambaugh, *The New Centurions*, p. 258, 1970
- — William D. Alsever, *Glossary for the Establishment and Other Uptight People*, p. 13, December 1970
- The city let the Pagoda rot and punks and drunks and whores and glue-heads started getting up inside of it, doing things that made the paint peel. — *Sun (Baltimore)*, p. 9 (Sunday Magazine0, 10th July 1994
- Sometimes we pure caved in with the giggles, specially the glueheads in the company[.] — Kevin Sampson, *Outlaws*, p. 8, 2001
- Mama's Pride walked into the sound of Gregg playing with a backup band made up of, as Liston remembers, "local glue-head losers." — *Riverfront Times (St. Louis)*, 17th December 2003

gluepot *noun*
1 the vagina *UK*
Rhyming slang for **TWAT**, combined, perhaps, with allusive imagery.
- — Ray Puxley, *Cockney Rabbit*, 1992

2 a racehorse that performs very, very poorly *US, 1924*
- — *San Francisco Call-Bulletin*, p. 16, 2nd April 1947

3 in cricket, a wicket with a 'sticky' surface (caused by the sun drying wet turf) *UK*
- — Michael Rundell, *The Dictionary of Cricket*, p. 100, 1985
- — Keith Foley, *A Dictionary of Cricketing Terminology*, p. 157, 1998

gluer *noun*
a person who sniffs model glue for the psychoactive effect *US*
- — Ralph de Sola, *Crime Dictionary*, p. 58, 1982

gluey *noun*
a person who inhales glue or any volatile solvent for the intoxicating effect *US, 1967*
- — William D. Alsever, *Glossary for the Establishment and Other Uptight People*, p. 13, December 1970

glug *noun*
a swallow, a mouthful, a swig of a drink *US*
Echoic.
- [R]ight in the middle of a glug of champagne at some jet-set hot spot. — Lester Bangs, *Psychotic Reactions and Carburetor Dung*, p. 13, 1971

glutes; gloots *noun*
the gluteus maximus muscles (the three large muscles in the buttocks) *US, 1984*
- — Judi Sanders, *Faced and Faded, Hanging to Hurl*, p. 17, 1993
- — Anna Scotti and Paul Young, *Buzzwords*, p. 108, 1997
- So how're those gloots of yours doin'? Are they good and hard right now? — Kevin Sampson, *Powder*, p. 348, 1999

g-ma *noun*
grandmother *US*
- — Judi Sanders, *Da Bomb*, p. 18, 1997

GMFU; GMBU *noun*
a situation of organisational choas
Initialism of '*g*rand *m*ilitary *f*uck *u*p' or '*g*rand *m*ilitary *b*alls *u*p'; probably since World War 2.
- — Ann Barr and Peter York, *The Official Sloane Ranger Handbook*, p. 158, 1982

GMOF *noun*
a grossly obese hospital patient *US*
A '*g*reat *m*ass *o*f *f*lesh'.
- — *Maledicta*, p. 35, 1988–1989: 'More Milawukee medical maledicta'

GMT *noun*
time to clean out the refrigerator *CANADA*
Back formation from the Greenwich standard, abbreviating here '*g*reen *m*eat *t*ime'.
- — *Toronto Globe and Mail*, p. D12, 3rd August 2002

gnarlatious *adjective*
extremely impressive *US*
- — Trevor Cralle, *The Surfin'ary*, p. 45, 1991

gnarly *adjective*
1 treacherous, challenging *US*
Originally surfer slang applied to waves and surf conditions, and then broadened to an all-purpose adjective.
- — Gary Fairmont R. Filosa II, *The Surfer's Almanac*, p. 186, 1977
- "None of those gnarly grease-burgers and NO OKI DOGS!" Duck said. — Francesca Lia Block, *weetzie bat*, p. 62, 1989
- I remember that day – gnarly fucking ass! — *Break Point*, 1991
- Gnarly. Synonym for hairy, scary or sick. — Jim Humes and Sean Wagstaff, *Boarderlands*, p. 222, 1995
- Creator of a gnarly incestual sicko freak scene read by every preteen girl I hung out with[.] — Editors of Ben is Dead, *Retrohell*, p. 5, 1997

2 bad, disgusting *US, 1978*
- — Connie Eble (Editor), *UNC-CH Campus Slang*, p. 5, Fall 1985
- FEMALE STONER IN ARMY JACKET: I heard it was really gnarly. She sucked down a bowl of multi-purpose deodorizing disinfectant then she smashed. — *Heathers*, 1988
- Don't go soft on me now, you gnarly old fart. — Carl Hiaasen, *Basket Case*, p. 325, 2002
- We were so wasted we passed out. / I got that gnarly sunburn, it was so ghetto[.] — Me First and the Gimmes Gimmes, *End of the Road*, 2003

3 excellent *US, 1982*
An absolute reversal of the original sense, used amongst foot-propelled scooter-riders.
- — Ben Sharpe, *Scooter Crazy*, p. 40, 2000
- That was gnarly, dude, like really bodacious. — John Nichols, *The Voice of the Butterfly*, p. 159, 2001

gnashers *noun*
the teeth *NEW ZEALAND*
- — Louis S. Leland, *A Personal Kiwi-Yankee Dictionary*, p. 46, 1984
- I'll just brush me gnashers[.] — Kevin Sampson, *Powder*, p. 311, 1999

gnat bites *noun*
small female breasts *UK*
- My breasts are small / They always have been / Gnat bites / Peas on a drum / 28B / is how they've been described[.] — Mary Longford, *Body Language*, 1980

gnat-brain *noun*
an idiot *UK*
- Wilson and Erasmus turned away from gnat-brain[.] — Tony Wilson, *24 Hour Party People*, p. 47, 2002

gnat's *noun*

something very small *UK*

A reduction of, or a suggestion of, many terms including: 'gnat's arse', 'gnat's chuff' and 'gnat's whiskers'; in such uses as 'within a gnat's' and 'tight as a gnat's arse', etc.

- We were a gnat's away from getting Harry Hill this year[.]— *The Guardian*, 5th December 2001

gnat's blood *noun*

tea purchased from a railway canteen or refreshment bar *UK*

- —Frank McKenna, *A Glossary of Railwaymen's Talk*, 1970

gnat's eyelash *noun*

a very small distance *US, 1937*

The variant bodyparts are seemingly infinite, with 'eyelash' as the earliest recorded.

- It doesn't matter a gnat's gear box to me.—Graeme Kent, *The Queen's Corporal [Six Granada Plays]*, p. 93, 1959
- —Richard Scholl, *Running Press Glossary of Baseball Language*, p. 38, 1977
- They have those calculations down to a gnat's eyelash.—*Florida Today*, p. 4, 1st February 2003

gnat's piss *noun*

a weak beverage such as tea or beer *UK, 1984*

gnawing *noun*

kissing *NEW ZEALAND*

- We did some gnawing, that was it. She didn't want to go any further.—David McGill, *David McGill's Complete Kiwi Slang Dictionary*, p. 50, 1998

gnawing-the-nana *noun*

oral sex on a man *AUSTRALIA*

- [S]he's not that struck – as yet – on gnawing-the-nana!!!—Barry Humphries, *Bazza Pulls It Off!*, 1971

gnome *noun*

a socially inept outcast *US*

- —*Time Magazine*, p. 46, 24th August 1959

G-note *noun*

a $1000 note *US, 1930*

- —Frank Garcia, *Marked Cards and Loaded Dice*, p. 262, 1962
- —Don Wilmeth, *The Language of American Popular Entertainment*, p. 104, 1981

go *noun*

1 a turn at something; an attempt *UK, 1825*

- You'll have a go, will you, friend?—D'Arcy Niland, *The Shiralee*, p. 102, 1955
- If we had plenty of wickets in hand, then we would certainly 'give it a go.—Richie Benaud, *Spin me a Spinner*, p. 150, 1963
- Popular documentary writer, Jimmy Holledge, surveys our favourite mania..."Have a go, mate!"—Ricki Francis, *The Kings Cross Racket*, p. 128, 1967
- A lack of public spirit. Nobody seems to be prepared to have a go, these days.—Ted Lewis, *Jack Carter's Law*, p. 203, 1974
- You had better give them a go.—Sam Weller, *Old Bastards I Have Met*, p. 21, 1979
- Surely, at this crucial time in our nation's history, a large newspaper like yours should try to encourage and rally Australians to have a go[.]—*Herald*, p. 6, 7th May 1990
- Browse the town's small galleries and non-naff gift shops. Have a go at a 10-pin bowling alley right next door.—*The Guardian*, 26th January 2002

2 an opportunity *AUSTRALIA*

- 'Here's a go!' called Jeffries.—John Wynnum, *Jiggin' in the Riggin'*, p. 80, 1965

3 a fair chance *AUSTRALIA, 1937*

Commonly used in the phrase 'give someone a go'.

- I've got no chance of getting a go here.—Ray Denning, *Prison Diaries*, p. 108, 1979

4 an attack *AUSTRALIA*

- Why don't yuh get out and have a go at me?—William Dick, *A Bunch of Ratbags*, p. 239, 1965
- I'm not sure those go's at me have been fair dinkum anyway.—Peter Corris, *Make Me Rich*, p. 59, 1985

5 a look *AUSTRALIA, 1930*

- Have a go at this Dave. It's nearly pure silver ore.—Bluey *Bush Contractors*, p. 377, 1975

6 a preference *AUSTRALIA*

- He doesn't drink milk. Water is his go.—Bert Newton, *Bert!*, p. 168, 1977
- I don't know what the story is Joe but she can only be bad news for you as I know love for sale was never your go.—Clive Galea, *Slipper*, p. 138, 1988

7 approval, agreement *US, 1878*

- But Sheldon Gurtz and Kitty Feldman were the people who would stay with Rita's Limo Stop if the network gave it a "go" and "ordered thirteen [episodes].—Dan Jenkins, *Life Its Ownself*, p. 156, 1984
- One day in August 1997, Matheson called Heather's office. "I've got great news," he said. "It's a go."—*Readers Digest (Canada)*, 29th October 2003

8 high-spirits, vigour, energy, as a human characteristic *UK, 1825*

Originally, and still, applied to horses.

9 used of a busy period or energetic activity *UK, 1965*

- Revolution? It's all go on the western front.—*The Guardian*, 8th February 2003

10 a fight, especially a prize-fight; an argument *US, 1890*

- They should ban the bloody women like they did in the old days. Then there'd be some fuckin' goes.—Peter Corris, *Make Me Rich*, p. 105, 1985

11 an event *AUSTRALIA*

- It was the third race on the programme that was the big go – a welter handicap with some well-known animals from the city competing.—Robert English, *Toxic Kisses*, p. 156, 1979

12 a drag race event *US*

- —*American Speech*, p. 98, May 1954
- —John Lawlor, *How to Talk Car*, p. 19, 1965

13 amphetamines *UK*

From the 'get up and go' nature of the drug's effects.

- —Mike Haskins, *Drugs*, p. 279, 2003

14 MDMA, the recreational drug best known as ecstasy *UK*

- —Mike Haskins, *Drugs*, p. 289, 2003

15 a goanna *AUSTRALIA, 1904*

'Goanna' is the Guyana Indian name for 'lizard', attached here to the monitor lizard.

▸ **from the word go**

from the very start *US, 1838*

From the starting of a race.

- [I]t tells you everything about sex from the word go.—Peter Cook, *Not Only But Also*, 1966
- Dame Wendy Hiller, who has died aged 90, was stage-struck from the word go.—*The Guardian*, 16th May 2003

▸ **have a go at**

to criticise *UK, 1977*

From the sense 'to attack'.

- It's 'have a go at Tottenham' time but we're not the only club not signing players.—*The Guardian*, 1st August 2002

▸ **make a go of it**

to make a success of something *US, 1877*

- I'd like to see you make a go of it.—Kylie Tennant, *The Honey Flow*, p. 89, 1956
- I really felt when I came out I was going to make a go of it without crime.—*The Guardian*, 2nd February 2001

go *verb*

1 when reporting a conversation, to say *US, 1942*

A thoroughly annoying quotative device found as early as 1942, favoured by teenagers in the 1970s and 80s.

- —Miss Cone, *The Slang Dictionary (Hawthorne High School)*, 1965
- So I said, "What's your name?" And she goes, "My name's Sandra."—Leonard Wolfe (Editor), *Voices from the Love Generation*, p. 171, 1968
- I go, 'Wait a minute. What about all these people here?' The William Morris guy goes, 'Did I invite them? Check with us first, doll, before you make any plans.'—Elmore Leonard, *Touch*, p. 29–30, 1977
- He [Roman Polanski] showed me a Vogue Magazine that he had done and he said, "Would you like me to take your pictures?" And I went, "Yes."—*Testimony of Samantha Jane Gailey to Los Angeles County Grand Jury*, 24th March 1977
- —Connie Eble (Editor), *UNC-CH Campus Slang*, p. 3, November 1983
- I went, "Oh, I always see my boyfriend at the weekend," and he went, "well, that's that, I s'pose."—Jenny Pausacker, *What are ya?*, p. 42, 1987
- Mum went to me that Dino went to her to go to me that he isn't wif Amanda anymore.—Kylie Mole (Maryanne Fahey), *My Diary*, p. 124, 1988
- I'm going, "Why do I keep ending up back in this business?"—Robert Stoller and I.S. Levine, *Coming Attractions*, p. 102, 1991
- The professor announced a twenty page paper due in two days, and I'm going 'No way'.—Connie Eble (Editor), *UNC-CH Campus Slang*, p. 4, Spring 1992
- We took it for a few days before turning feral. We'd go, 'Yeah, yeah, yeah,' and piss off to our rooms[.]—John Birmingham, *He Died With a Felafel in his Hand*, p. 172, 1994
- He saw the Jimi poster in my room and goes, 'That nigger looks like he's got a mouth full of cum.'—Francesca Lia Block, *Baby Be-Bop*, p. 391, 1995
- He goes "Hey, quit hassling me cause I don't speak French or whatever," and the other guy goes something in Paris talk, and I go, "Um, just back off," and he goes "Get out" and I go "Make me."—*Austin Powers*, 1997

- He looks into the camera and goes, "Hi! I'm Glenn." —Dave Courtney, *Raving Lunacy*, p. 139, 2000
- You listen to that, you go, "Wow, they went a long way, didn't they? —Peter Noone, *Uncut*, p. 47, July 2001

2 to take on the mannerisms and customs of a place or group of people *US, 1917*
- Andy Warhol has "gone Hollywood." —*The Advocate*, p. 13, October 1967
- Assuring his friends back at Dartmouth that even though he'd gone to Hollywood, he had not gone Hollywood. —Eve Babitz, *Eve's Hollywood*, p. 177, 1974

3 to find acceptable, to wish for, to enjoy *UK*
Especially, and usually, when applied to food or drink.
- "I'll bet you could go a cup of tea, Sonny," I asked. —Caddie, *A Sydney Barmaid*, 1953
- 'Yer could go a feed, couldn' yer?' —Nino Culotta (John O'Grady), *They're A Weird Mob*, p. 46, 1957
- Gees, I could go a beer. —Nino Culotta (John O'Grady), *They're A Weird Mob*, p. 126, 1957

4 to urinate; to defecate *UK, 1926*
Probably a shortening of 'go to the toilet', now a euphemism.
- [H]e wished he'd had the sense to go before he got in the truck. —Derek Bickerton, *Payroll*, p. 50, 1959
- I'd only just "been" five minutes or so before his arrival. —*The Guardian*, 25th May 2000: 'A life inside'

5 to attack physically; to fight *AUSTRALIA, 1924*
- I was itching to go him. —Robert S. Close, *Love Me Sailor*, p. 149, 1945
- 'You bloke go all right,' one of them said, 'that was a bloody good fight.' —Clive Galea, *Slipper*, p. 151, 1988

6 to race *US*
- You know, a guy goes up to another guy's car and looks it up and down like it has gangrene or something, and he says: 'You wanna go? —Tom Wolfe, *The Kandy-Kolored Tangerine-Flake Streamline Baby*, p. 88, 1965

7 to become (of a politician or political constituency) *US, 1937*
- Newark, a Labour seat for almost 30 years, went Tory, too, dispatching another junior minister. —*The Guardian*, 4th May 1979

8 in a casino, to earn in tips *US*
- What did we go last night? —Lee Solkey, *Dummy Up and Deal*, p. 114, 1980

9 to weigh *US*
- Built like one of those giant Samoans you saw, this one going at least two-sixty in his tanktop, a do-rag down on his eyebrows, thick black hair to his huge shoulders. —Elmore Leonard, *Be Cool*, p. 58, 1999

10 of a telephone, to ring *UK*
- Eight in the morning, the phone's gone, it's Gene. —J.J. Connolly, *Layer Cake*, p. 85, 2000

▸ go all the way
to have sexual intercourse *US, 1924*
- If a girl goes all the way, a boy doesn't have to find out. —Frederick Kohner, *Gidget*, p. 71, 1957
- My buddy saw a girl just once (last May 10th) and he said they went all the way. —*San Francisco Chronicle*, p. 13, 24th December 1957
- There was a point at which I felt the dangers of our sexual relationship going "all the way" too soon. —Phyllis and Eberhard Kronhausen, *Sex Histories of American College Men*, p. 118, 1960
- A week before he was moving we went all the way. I think about him all the time and feel lost without him. —*San Francisco Examiner*, p. 9, 7th October 1961
- He was going to take advantage of me! He was going to go all the way. . . ! —John Nichols, *The Sterile Cuckoo*, p. 170, 1965
- The younger and more naive kids were sure Duane went all the way[.] —Larry McMurtry, *The Last Picture Show*, p. 63, 1966
- I would be insulted if my Mom gave me the pill. That's like saying she doesn't care if I went all the way. —*San Francisco Chronincle*, p. 39, 24th October 1968
- She said she was so horny she might go all the way! —Richard Price, *The Wanderers*, p. 25, 1974
- About three months ago one thing led to another and before we knew it, Hall and I went all the way. —*San Francisco Examiner & Chronicle Sundy Scene*, p. 6, 14th April 1974
- A: I would say that this song is not specifically about sex. Q: Well, we have agreed that the title "Would You Go All The Way?" means "Would you have sexual intercourse?" —Frank Zappa, *The Real Frank Zappa Book*, p. 132, 1989
- She was in love, but she couldn't "go all the way." —Kathryn Leigh Scott, *The Bunny Years*, p. 51, 1998

▸ go Alzheimers
to forget *UK*
Public awareness of Alzheimer's confuses the disease with the premature senile dementia it causes.
- There's a boat waiting at Tilbury. We slap him on it and we go Alzheimers on the whole business. —Bernard Demspey and Kevin McNally, *Lock, Stock... & Two Sips*, p. 319, 2000

▸ go bent
1 to become dishonest *UK*
From **BENT** (crooked).
- [T]hey were going to make Bobby go bent, and there were so many bent trade union officials[.] —*Uncut*, p. 6, February 2002

2 (of a police witness) to retract a statement or renege on an undertaking *UK*
The implication is that the witness is behaving in a criminal manner, **BENT**.
- —Peter Laurie, *Scotland Yard*, p. 320, 1970

▸ go big, go fat
to achieve substantial height or distance in snowboarding *US*
- —Jim Humes and Sean Wagstaff, *Boarderlands*, p. 222, 1995

▸ go down the rabbit hole
to use drugs *CANADA*
An allusion to Lewis Carroll and *Alice in Wonderland*.
- —Jack Chambers (Editor), *Slang Bag 93 (University of Toronto)*, p. 3, Winter 1993

▸ go for a burton
1 to to be killed in an air crash *UK, 1941*
Military slang of uncertain etymology.

2 to be destroyed or ruined, to be forgotten *UK, 1957*
- Their attendance soon went for a Burton[.] —Danny King, *The Burglar Diaries*, p. 150, 2001

▸ go great guns
to do very well, to prosper *UK, 1913*
- Chelsea could go great guns if they get a top striker or Jimmy-Floyd Hasselbaink finds his old form. —*The Guardian*, 15th August 2003

▸ go off like a two-bob rocket
to lose your temper in a very unsubtle way *UK: SCOTLAND*
- All Ah says wis "How's yer love life?" an he goes aff lik a two-bob rocket!" —Michael Munro, *The Complete Patter*, 1996

▸ go on
to talk at length *UK, 1822*
- The government is always going on about giving people choice[.] —*The Guardian*, 26th January 2004

▸ go over jackass hill
to be a teenager *CANADA*
- [He's] "going over jackass jill" is a Hereford, Quebec way to say that a young man is a teenager. —Lewis Poteet, *Talking Country*, p. 46, 1992

▸ go over the wall
1 to secretly depart from anywhere you are duty-bound to be *US, 1933*
Applies to escape from prison and the wider world.
- The [Holy] communion IS our smokescreen [...] no cunt is going to expect us to be going over the wall Sunday of all days. —Kevin Sampson, *Outlaws*, p. 232, 2001

2 to go to prison *UK, 1917*
- [H]e went over the wall at Leicester about ten years ago. —*The Sweeney*, p. 29, 1976

▸ go some
1 to fight *US*
- —Joan Fontaine et al., *Dictionary of Black Slang*, 1968

2 to go well, to proceed with notable vigour *US, 1911*
- He edges it and Cork takes a very smart catch at slip. It was going some! What a superb early breakthrough for England! —*The Guardian*, 6th September 2002

▸ go south
1 to deteriorate; to break *US*
- Once we got to SoCal, my transmission went south too. —Ralph "Sonny" Barger, *Hell's Angel*, p. 30, 2000

2 in a gambling cheating scheme, to take dice or money off the gaming table *US*
- "Time to go south," Duffy said. —Stephen Cannell, *Big Con*, p. 197, 1997

▸ go through the card
to cover everything that is available in a given circumstance *UK*
Originally a horse racing term.
- Blokes and birds, birds and blokes, birds and birds, even, well, blokes and blokes, and ... I mean, they really did go though the card. —Mike Stott, *Soldiers Talking, Cleanly*, 1978

▸ **go to bat**
to stand trial *US*
A baseball metaphor.
- I went up to bat on the sale first. —Henry Williamson, *Hustler!*, p. 141, 1965
- "He went to bat for wasting [killing] three of 'em, but he beat those raps." —Iceberg Slim (Robert Beck), *Airtight Willie and Me*, p. 94, 1979

▸ **go to ground**
to go into hiding *US*
- Of course that's where Rooski would go to ground[.] —Seth Morgan, *Homeboy*, p. 60, 1990

▸ **go to higher game**
to launch a legitimate business after a period in an underworld enterprise *US*
- They never have been able to get enough money together to retire or go on to higher game[.] —Christina and Richard Milner, *Black Players*, p. 157, 1972

▸ **go to New Norfolk**
to be crazy *AUSTRALIA, 1988*
A reference to the asylum located in New Norfolk.
- —Maureen Brooks and Joan Ritchie, *Tassie Terms*, p. 58, 1995

▸ **go to the wall**
to exert yourself at all costs without regard to the consequences *US*
- —John R. Armore and Joseph D. Wolfe, *Dictionary of Desperation*, p. 31, 1976

▸ **go up fool's hill**
to be a teenager *CANADA*
- [In Shelburne, NS] a person "going up fool's hill" is typically fifteen to eighteen years old. —Lewis Poteet, *The South Shore Phrase Book*, p. 52, 1999

▸ **go upside someone's head**
to hit someone on the head *US*
- If she hollers cop, all you do is bop – her by going up side her head with your fist hard as lead! —Dan Burley, *Diggeth Thou?*, p. 5, 1959
- He as ready to go up side her head (beat her) when she threw $2,200 on the bed. —Babs Gonzales, *I Paid My Dues*, p. 97, 1967

▸ **go west on you**
to fail, to let you down *CANADA*
- To go west on you is to say "to let you down in a major way," as, for example, an engine that breaks. —Lewis Poteet, *The South Shore Phrase Book*, p. 53, 1999

▸ **go with the flow**
to acquiesce *US, 1977*
- All the teachers said people in your situation should just go with the flow for a while. Wendy looked at her sandwich, trying to imagine what it would mean to go with the flow. —Joyce Maynard, *The Usual Rules*, p. 77, 2003

▸ **not go much on**
to not like much *AUSTRALIA, 1932*
- 'Boys', she said, 'never go much on kissun. That is', she said, 'they will, but up to a point. It is funny.' —Patrick White, *The Tree of Man*, p. 120, 1955
- —Patsy Adam-Smith, *Folklore of the Australian Railwaymen*, p. 160, 1969

go!
used for expressing approval and encouraging further effort *US*
- Therefore one finds words like go, and make it, and with it, and swing: "Go with its sense that after hours or days or months or years of monotony, boredom, and depression one has finally had one's chance[.] —Norman Mailer, *Advertisements for Myself*, p. 350, 1957

go-ahead *adjective*
progressive; anxious to succeed *US, 1840*
- They are a very go-ahead nation and are working hard to improve their economy and what is taking place out there. —G Trumper, *Hansard (Canada)*, 9th October 2002

go ahead, make my day
used to summon defiance *US*
From the film character Dirty Harry played by Clint Eastwood. US President Ronald Reagan used the line in a speech to the American Business Conference in March 1985: 'I have only one thing to say to the tax increasers. Go ahead – make my day!'. He liked the line so much that he repeated it in a speech at his 83rd birthday in 1994.
- Like that line Dirty Harry said in that picture, 'Make my day.' The writer who wrote that line didn't think it up. He heard it somewhere. I heard it a long time before Dirty Harry said it. But he said it and then a hundred million people said… —Robert Campbell, *Juice*, p. 213, 1988

go-ahead man *noun*
in horse racing, a person working with someone selling 'inside' information on the horses and races *US*
- —Mel Heimer, *Inside Racing*, p. 211, 1962

go-aheads *noun*
thong sandals *US*
- —*American Speech*, p. 288, December 1962: 'Marine corps slang'

goalie *noun*
1 a goal-keeper *UK*
In football and ice hockey; first recorded in the modern spelling in 1957 – as 'goalee', known since 1921.
- [H]e had a goalie's intuition of the conditions of space[.] —*The Guardian*, 21st August 2002

2 the clitoris *US*
- —Robert A. Wilson, *Playboy's Book of Forbidden Words*, p. 124, 1972

go and fuck yourself!
▷ see: FUCK YOURSELF!

goanna *noun*
a piano *AUSTRALIA, 1918*
Rhyming slang for 'pianna', a variant pronunciation.
- He went out in a boat with his mate in the middle of the night, grabbed the grand goanna and lowered it down in a lifeboat[.] —Frank Hardy, *The Yarns of Billy Borker*, p. 39, 1965

goat *noun*
1 a person responsible for a failure or loss, especially a player in an atheltic contest *US, 1894*
A short form of 'scapegoat'.
- It was in the 1963 Series that he lost a throw from third base in the shirts of the crowd and was the goat of the game. —Jim Bouton, *Ball Four*, p. 313, 1970

2 in horse racing, a poor-performing racehorse *AUSTRALIA, 1941*
- "Best hoop in the country, the old Darb." "I seen 'im ride goats. Cooky too." "Cooky don't take on too many goats. Sharp as a tack, Cooky." —Nino Culotta (John O'Grady), *They're A Weird Mob*, p. 72, 1957
- —Robert Saunders Dowst and Jay Craig, *Playing the Races: A Guide to the American Tracks*, p. 163, 1960

3 a fool *UK, 1879*
Often, and originally, in the phrase 'act the goat'.
- She could have poisoned me. What a bloody ratbag – a fully qualified goat. —John Wynnum, *Jiggin' in the Riggin'*, p. 116, 1965
- —Louis S. Leland, *A Personal Kiwi-Yankee Dictionary*, p. 7, 1984

4 in motor racing, a Dodge car *US*
- The term derives from the ram once used as a trade mark by Dodge. —John Lawlor, *How to Talk Car*, p. 55, 1965

5 in hot rodding, an old car *US*
- —*Hot Rod Magazine*, p. 13, November 1948: 'Racing jargon'

6 an engine used in a railway yard *US*
- —Norman Carlisle, *The Modern Wonder Book of Trains and Railroading*, p. 263, 1946

7 a goatee *US, 1956*
- —Judi Sanders, *Da Bomb!*, p. 13, 1997

▸ **get your goat**
to succeed in making someone lose their temper *US, 1904*
- Got his goat properly, I can tell you, way I offered him out on the spot. —Norman Lindsay, *Halfway to Anywhere*, p. 200, 1947
- [H]e went with a woman once who kept acting like she couldn't remember his name right and calling him Hooligan just to get his goat. —Ken Kesey, *One Flew Over the Cuckoo's Nest*, p. 44, 1962

goat boater *noun*
a surfer who uses a surfboard/canoe hybrid craft
Mainly derogatory. Reported by a correspondent who surfs in West Wales, September 2002.

goat fuck *noun*
a colossal, confused mess *US, 1971*
- —Linda Reinberg, *In the Field*, p. 94, 1991
- This op is a Larry Bailey goatfuck – we're gonna come up dry. I can't see six feet in front of me. —Richard Marcinko and John Weisman, *Rogue Warrior*, p. 96, 1992
- Bush would never say no to a friend, so then they'd have the Free world's Leader-to-be in a YR goat fuck. —Richard Ben Cramer, *What It Takes*, p. 1020, 1993
- What a goat-fuck that turned out to be. We're all lucky a nuclear war didn't break out. —Dale Brown, *Air Battle Force*, p. 154, 2003

goat hair *noun*
illegally manufactured alcoholic drink *US*
- —Roger D. Abrahams, *Deep Down in the Jungle*, p. 261, 1970

goat head *noun*
in electric line work, an angle-iron punch *US*
- —A.B. Chance Co., *Lineman's Slang Dictionary*, p. 8, 1980

goat heaven *noun*
bliss *BARBADOS*
- —Frank A. Collymore, *Barbadian Dialect*, p. 54, 1965

goat knee *noun*
a callous, especially one on the head from carrying heavy loads *BARBADOS*
- —Frank A. Collymore, *Barbadian Dialect*, p. 53, 1965

goat land *noun*
in oil drilling, non-productive land *US*
- —Jerry Robertson, *Oil Slanguage*, p. 59, 1954

goat locker *noun*
in the US Navy, the kitchen and dining hall reserved for officers *US, 1990*
- We knew why he'd done it; if he hadn't, he would have taken grief in the chief's goat locker, so to keep the peace he reamed us out. —Richard Marcinko and John Weisman, *Rogue Warrior*, p. 55, 1992

goat mouth; goat bite *noun*
a curse; bad luck *TRINIDAD AND TOBAGO, 1827*
- —Lise Winer, *Dictionary of the English/Creole of Trinidad & Tobago*, 2003

goat pasture *noun*
any worthless land sold as part of a confidence swindle *US*
- —M. Allen Henderson, *How Con Games Work*, p. 220, 1985: 'Glossary'

goat rope *noun*
a rumour *US*
Gulf war usage.
- —*American Speech*, p. 390, Winter 1991: 'Among the new words'

goat screw *noun*
a disorganised, confusing situation *US*
- —Hans Halberstadt, *Airborne*, p. 130, 1988: 'Abridged dictionary of airborne terms'
- The op was a classic goat-screw. —Gary Stubblefield, *Inside the US Navy Seals*, p. 139, 1995

goat track *noun*
a rough, winding hill road *NEW ZEALAND*
- Locals call the road a goat track, partly becauses it is tight and winding in places[.] —*Dominion Post*, p. A5, 11th December 2002

go away *verb*
to be sent to jail or prison *US*
- That's what happens when you go away. We're on our own. —*Goodfellas*, 1990
- They bring him to trial he's going away. —Elmore Leonard, *Riding the Rap*, p. 107, 1995

go-away gear *noun*
a truck's highest gear *US*
- —Montie Tak, *Truck Talk*, p. 74, 1971

gob *noun*
1 the mouth *UK, 1550*
Originally Scots and northern English dialect.
- Down the disco you pull some bird / She gives you oral in the bog / Next thing you know her ex comes up / and smacks you in the gob —Stewart Home, *Sex Kick [britpulp]*, p. 229, 1999
- I took a big gob full of beer[.] —David Peace, *Nineteen Seventy-Four*, p. 181, 1999
- [G]ormless and open-gobbed, she would sit for long periods [...] saying and doing nothing. —Stuart Jeffries, *Mrs Slocombe's Pussy*, p. xix, 2000

2 a slimey lump or clot, especially of spittle *UK*
In conventional use until early C19.
- [T]he old man coughing and spitting in the wash basin [...] I goes in there in the morning and sees the gob hanging in the plug hole. —John Peter Jones, *Feather Pluckers*, p. 10, 1964

gob *verb*
1 to spit *UK, 1872*
- —Albertos y Lost Trios Paranoias, *Gobbing on Life*, 1977
- There is, however, one other aspect of audience appreciation which ain't nearly so cute: gobbing. —Lester Bangs, *Psychotic Reactions and Carburetor Dung*, p. 230, 1977
- —Kenn "Naz" Young, *Naz's Dictionary of Teen Slang*, p. 50, 1993
- The original punk gobs into the fog below. —Glyn Parry, *Mosh*, p. 12, 1996
- Orright man, he says gobbin' out the window, let's do some work. —Nick Barlay, *Curvy Lovebox*, p. 34, 1997
- He gobbed on the photo[.] —Kevin Sampson, *Powder*, p. 5, 1999
- Dave gobbing at me, a great big greeny landing on my right boot[.] —John King, *Human Punk*, p. 108, 2000

2 to eat *UK*
- We sat back sipping our teas clocking Slip gobbing his apples. —Jeremy Cameron, *Brown Bread in Wengen*, p. 114, 1999

go back on *verb*
to break a promise or a trust *UK, 1859*

gobbie *adjective*
▷ see: **GOBBY**

gobble *noun*
an act of oral sex *UK, 1984*
- There's a um, you know, like an etiquette in the sack, see. They like a good gobble first. —Kathy Lette, *Girls' Night Out*, p. 22, 1987
- Donny old bean! What a nite. Michelle J gave me a gobble. Details later. —Christopher Brookmyre, *The Sacred Art of Stealing*, p. 121, 2002

gobble *verb*
1 to perform oral sex on a man *US*
- Hell, I'd rather let some score do a little gobbling on my joint than spend all day cleaning some guy's latrine. —Johnny Shearer, *The Male Hustler*, p. 16, 1966
- "She gobbles about twenty joints a night," said Ranatti. —Joseph Wambaugh, *The New Centurions*, p. 182, 1970
- This sort is so anxious to gobble a joint that he doesn't even take his own pants off. —*Screw*, p. 12, 13th July 1970
- [He found] photographs (including portraits of the Pope and Sneed Hearn and a series of pornographic pictures of two men and two women upping, gobbling and generally carrying on regardless), tampons, fish hooks and abundance of soiled pages of the Foolgarah Distorter. —Frank Hardy, *The Outcasts of Foolgarah*, p. 175, 1971
- He clutched her ears as she gobbled, [...] jammed himself hard into her head. —Kevin Sampson, *Powder*, p. 61, 1999

2 to talk *US*
- —Marcus Hanna Boulware, *Jive and Slang of Students in Negro Colleges*, 1947

3 in drag racing, to achieve very high speeds *US*
- —John Lawlor, *How to Talk Car*, p. 55, 1965

▸ **gobble the goop**
to perform oral sex on a man *US, 1918*
- —G. Legman, *The Language of Homsexuality*, p. 1167, 1941
- —Roger Blake, *The American Dictionary of Sexual Terms*, p. 88, 1964
- [S]he got right down in broad daylight standin outside the car, me layin back in the seat and gobbled the goop. —Earl Thompson, *Tattoo*, p. 225, 1974

gobble alley *noun*
the upper balcony in a cinema favoured by homosexuals *US*
- In Chicago, they're called "Gobble Alley." In Los Angeles, some studs refer to the balconies as the "Last Chance." —Johnny Shearer, *The Male Hustler*, p. 77, 1966

gobble down *verb*
in computing, to obtain *US*
- —Guy L. Steele et al., *The Hacker's Dictionary*, p. 73, 1983

gobbledygook *noun*
dense, pompous and unintelligible jargon *US, 1944*
- —*American Speech*, October 1945
- —*American Speech*, October 1947
- Why do you bother going through this legal gobbledegook? —Robert Campbell, *Juice*, p. 264, 1988

gobble hole *noun*
in pinball, a hole near the centre of the playing field which takes a ball from play while scoring a large number of points *US*
- —Edward Trapunski, *Special When Lit*, p. 153, 1979

gobble off *verb*
to perform oral sex on a man *UK*
A more complete elaboration of **GOBBLE**.
- She takes a gulp of [...] Diet Coke – holds it in her mouth, then gobbles you off. —*The FHM Little Book of Bloke*, p. 24, June 2003

gobbler *noun*
a hospital patient with petty complaints *US*
- —*Maledicta*, p. 56, Summer 1980: 'Not sticks and stones, but names: more medical pejoratives'

gobbling irons *noun*
a knife, fork and spoon *UK*
A trawlermen's term.
• —W. Mitford, *Lovely She Goes*, 1969

gobbling rods *noun*
a knife, fork and spoon *UK*
Gulf war usage.
• —*American Speech*, p. 390, Winter 1991: 'Among the new words'

gobbo *adjective*
stupid *UK*
• [A] battle with some gobbo boss over not enough pay[.]—Niall Griffiths, *Kelly + Victor*, p. 208, 2002

gobby *noun*
a small lump of dried nasal mucus *UK*
• [H]is struggle with the gobby continues[.]—Jack Allen, *When the Whistle Blows*, p. 61, 2000

gobby; gobbie *adjective*
loquacious, too talkative; impudent *UK*
• Don't get fucking gobbie with me, you crow, or I'll fucking drop you.—Ken Lukowiak, *A Soldier's Song*, p. 78, 1993
• We've got you down as gobby. Just listen to what people have to say and take it in. And don't gob off.—Andy McNab, *Immediate Action*, p. 108, 1995
• [Y]er mates were bein all loud and gobby but you were just sittin there[.]—Niall Griffiths, *Kelly + Victor*, p. 16, 2002

gobdaw *noun*
1 an ordinary fool *IRELAND*
• 'What kind of gobdaws are yous,' he said, 'to be made eejits (idiots) of be [sic] the English?'—Hugh Leonard, *Out After Dark*, p. 30, 1989
• [I]t was OK to have any and every self appointed and self opinionated gobdaw in the country telling us how they had brought about the good times and the good times would never end.—*Western People*, 20th November 2002

2 a dolt, a gullible person *IRELAND*
• Every second gobdaw can tell in detail how Saddam has gassed the Kurds, has goosed the Shiites—*Western People*, 19th March 2003

go between *noun*
a cow gate *CANADA*
• A "go between" is simply two posts set so close together that, while a person can go between them, cattle cannot.—Chris Thain, *Cold as a Bay Street Banker's Heart*, p. 73, 1987

gobgrabbing *noun*
in prison, the practice of trying to *grab* and steal drugs concealed in someone's *gob* (the mouth) *UK*
• —Angela Devlin, *Prison Patter*, p. 57, 1996

goblet of jam *noun*
marijuana *US, 1969*
From the direct translation from Arabic *m'juni akbar* (a hashish-based confection).
• —Richard A. Spears, *The Slang and Jargon of Drugs and Drink*, p. 223, 1986
• —Mike Haskins, *Drugs*, p. 287, 2003

gob off *verb*
to talk loudly or too much *UK*
• We've got you down as gobby. Just listen to what people have to say and take it in. And don't gob off.—Andy McNab, *Immediate Action*, p. 108, 1995
• Thoughtful and quiet among his loud and sparky mates, gobbin off thee [sic] are, showin off, like[.]—Niall Griffiths, *Kelly + Victor*, p. 163, 2002

gobs *noun*
1 a great deal of *US, 1839*
In the C16, a 'gob' or 'gubbe' referred specifically to a 'great deal of money' or a 'large mouthful of fatty meat'. By World War 2, the term had acquired this broader meaning, as evidenced by the title of Johnny Viney's 1943 wartime humorous novel *Sailors are Gobs of Fun, Hattie*.
• And every time the train stopped, Cole would hop off and buy gobs of candy and cold drinks and cookies and everything else he could lay hands on.—Jim Thompson, *The Grifters*, p. 79, 1963
• —Collin Baker et al., *College Undergraduate Slang Study Conducted at Brown University*, p. 126, 1968
• They have washed, gobs of people in front of me, alongside me, behind me, and I'm still standin'.—Edwin Torres, *After Hours*, p. 335, 1979

2 in a hospital, gynaecology *UK*
Rhymed on the model of **OBS** (obstetrics).
• —Adam T. Fox, St Mary's Hospital, London, 10th October 2002

gobshite *noun*
a fool; an unpleasant person *UK: ENGLAND*
Combines **GOB** (the mouth) and **SHITE** (rubbish), hence 'someone who talks rubbish': the subsequent, more abusive sense depends on the phonetic ugliness of the word.
• He replied that he did not want to see any gobshite of an editor; he wanted the boss man.—Hugh Leonard, *Out After Dark*, p. 30, 1989
• Come 'ead [ahead] – look at us then, you gobshite! [...] Do you want bollocks [trouble]? Little cunt!—Kevin Sampson, *Outlaws*, p. 3, 2001

gobsmack *noun*
a shock that renders you speechless *UK*
A back-formation from the verb.
• Once we had recovered from our collective gobsmack, everyone descended on Todd[.]—*The Guardian*, 7th June 2001: 'A life inside'

gobsmacked *adjective*
being speechless or lost for words as the result of amazement or shock *UK*
Adopted from northern dialect; silence is the suggested result of a 'smack' (hit) in the **GOB** (mouth).
• "I'm totally gobsmacked," she said girlishly.—Greg Williams, *Diamond Geezers*, p. 76, 1997
• We were just ... absolutely gobsmacked, mate.—Dave Courtney, *Raving Lunacy*, p. 35, 2000
• Roger McClay said he would be 'gobsmacked' if CYF's most senior social worker had the time to help out a minister part-time.—*Dominion Post*, p. 1, 17th July 2003

gobsmacking *adjective*
shocking *UK*
• The double standards of these politicians is just gobsmacking!—Ben Elton, *High Society*, p. 56, 2002

gobsmackingly *adverb*
surprisingly *NEW ZEALAND*
• John Tamihere says the wananga [college] is 'gobsmackingly great' at the level it is pitching at, with tutors who are 'highly evangelical and energetic'.—*Sunday Star-Times*, p. C5, 17th August 2003

gobstopper *noun*
1 a large ball-shaped sweet that reveals layers of colour as sucking diminishes its size *UK*
Combines **GOB** (the mouth) with the effect of a large sweet.

2 the penis *UK*
Rhyming slang for **CHOPPER** rejoicing in puns of size and sweetness.
• —Ray Puxley, *Cockney Rabbit*, 1992

gobstoppers *noun*
the testicles *UK*
From **GOBSTOPPER** (a ball-shaped sweet).
• —*A–Z of Rude Health*, 11th January 2002

gobstruck *adjective*
very surprised *UK, 1988*
From **GOB** (the mouth) and 'struck' (hit).
• Whenever we uncover something they should have told us, it's as if they're gobstruck that we hadn't already known it.—Val McDermid, *A Place of Execution*, p. 182, 1999

go button *noun*
a car's accelerator *US*
• —John Edwards, *Auto Dictionary*, p. 70, 1993

goby *noun*
a middleman in a criminal enterprise *UK, 1970*
From 'go-between'.
• You're going to have to be the goby on this one.—Jake Arnott, *He Kills Coppers*, p. 257, 2001

go-by *noun*
a passing by *US*
• I wasn't going in. I was going to give it the go-by but I don't see anybody inside so I went in and ordered a coke.—Hal Ellson, *Duke*, p. 145, 1949

go-by-the-wall *noun*

a cornerboy *IRELAND*

- Never mind about it being a sin: that's Canon McGough's department. No, what concerns me is that it turns fine lads into contemptible weaklings: cowardly go-by-the-walls. — Hugh Leonard, *Out After Dark*, p. 71, 1989

God *noun*

General Lewis Walt, commander of the US Marine forces in Vietnam from May 1965 to May 1967 *US*

- — Linda Reinberg, *In the Field*, p. 94, 1991

God Almighty *noun*

a woman's nightdress, a 'nightie' *UK*

Rhyming slang.

- A repeatedly postponed event is said to be on and off like a bride's God Almighty. — Ray Puxley, *Fresh Rabbit*, 1998

God-awful *adjective*

terrible, dreadful *US, 1897*

'God' as the intensifier of all that is bad.

- [T]he lead singer's twerpy attempts at Doctor John-ish mumbo-jumbo [...] were godawful. — Lester Bangs, *Psychotic Reactions and Carburetor Dung*, p. 98, 1972
- Christ! How many more of these fucking god-awful evenings do I have to endure before I can get into your knickers? — Danny King, *The Burglar Diaries*, p. 29, 2001

God bless you *noun*

used as a mnemonic device in snooker for remembering the correct spotting of ball colours – green, brown, yellow *US*

- — Mike Shamos, *The Illustrated Encyclopedia of Billiards*, p. 109, 1993

God-botherer; God-pesterer *noun*

an immoderately religious individual *UK, 1937*

- CARTER: He's a cricketer. REGAN: Yeah, I was coming to that. And a pound to a penny he's a God-botherer. CARTER: Well, with his size, you see, his prayers don't have to go far. — *The Sweeney*, 4th October 1976
- However, as far as the God-botherers were concerned, the deposit off a crate of ginger bottles would be too much of an outlay if it was spent on something they disapproved of. — Christopher Brookmyre, *The Sacred Art of Stealing*, p. 336, 2002

God Calls Me God *noun*

a GCMG (Grand Commander of St Michael and St George) *UK, 1961*

A pun elaborated on the initials; used by civil servants demonstrating a jocular familiarity with the honour.

- BERNARD WOOLLEY: Of course in the service, CMG stands for Call Me God. And KCMG for Kindly Call Me God. JIM HACKER: What does GCMG stand for? BERNARD WOOLLEY: God Calls Me God. — Anthony Jay and Jonathan Lynn, *Yes Minister ('Doing the Honours')*, 2nd March 1981

God damn *noun*

jam (the preseve) *UK*

Rhyming slang.

- — Ray Puxley, *Cockney Rabbit*, 1992
- — Ray Puxley, *Fresh Rabbit*, 1998

-goddamn- *infix*

used as an intensifier *US*

- This is the most, baby. I mean abso-goddamn-lute most! — Nathan Heard, *Howard Street*, p. 68, 1968
- You fuck up in a firefight and I guaran-goddamned-tee you, a trip out of the bush – in a bodybag. — *Platoon*, 1986
- If it isn't, ces't-la-goddamn-guerre. — James Ellroy, *Hollywood Nocturnes*, p. 60–61, 1994
- This is ri-goddamn-diculous. — *Austin Powers*, 1999

godfather *noun*

in horse racing, someone who provides financial assistance to a financially failing operation *AUSTRALIA*

- — Ned Wallish, *The Truth Dictionary of Racing Slang*, p. 33, 1989

God forbid; Gawd forbid; Gawd fer bid *noun*

1 a child *UK, 1909*

Rhyming slang for **KID**.

- My old Dutch [a spouse] and I, as we sit by our Jermiah [fire] in Buckingham Palace, with our Gawd fer bids by our side[.] — Ronnie Barker, *Fletcher's Book of Rhyming Slang*, p. 39, 1979
- — *Maledicta*, p. 151, Summer/Winter 1986–1987: 'Sexual slang: prostitutes, pedophiles, flagellators, transvestites, and necrophiles'

2 a Jewish person *UK, 1960*

Rhyming slang for **YID**.

- — Ray Puxley, *Cockney Rabbit*, 1992

Godfrey *noun*

used in oaths in place of 'God' *US*

- No by Godfrey, I won't take it to the office. — Max Shulman, *I was a Teen-Age Dwarf*, p. 108, 1959
- By Godfrey and Godfrey Mighty! are the commonest ways to use Godfrey. — John Gould, *Maine Lingo*, p. 111, 1975

God hates a coward

in poker, used for luring a reluctant bettor to bet *US*

- — *American Speech*, p. 99, May 1951

godhead *adjective*

excellent at playing Internet games *UK*

Possibly an elaboration of 'good'.

- He's so godhead. — *You and Yours*, 30th April 2003

godiva *noun*

▷ see: **LADY GODIVA**

God love her *noun*

a mother *UK*

Rhyming slang, reported by David Hillman, 1974.

go down *verb*

1 to happen *US, 1946*

- There's not that much truth going down in the straight world. — Leonard Wolfe (Editor), *Voices from the Love Generation*, p. 33, 1968
- Number one contender for the middleweight crown / Had no idea what kinda shit was about to go down. — Bob Dylan, *Hurricane*, 1975
- Just think, if we had known what was going to go down, we would have been a lot less careful and maybe I would have your child now. — Odie Hawkins, *The Busting Out of an Ordinary Man*, p. 11, 1985
- I always figured if a bust ever went down I'd be the guy they'd come for. — Herbert Huncke, *Guilty of Everything*, p. 195, 1990
- Me and Mr. Orange jumped in the car and Mr. Brown floored it. After that, I don't know what went down. — *Reservoir Dogs*, 1992
- What's goin' down, son? — *Basic Instinct*, 1992
- But there was nowt goin' down anywhere except cocaine, pills and vintage Dom P. — Ben Elton, *High Society*, p. 119, 2002

2 to be arrested and/or imprisoned *UK, 1906*

- Vito, Lilo, Big John, Chin, everybody went down. — Edwin Torres, *Carlito's Way*, p. 46, 1975
- They're makin' me bankrupt. I'll go down before you[.] — Alan Bleasdale, *Boys From the Blackstuff*, 1982
- Your boys are going down. I can't stop it anymore. — *A Few Good Men*, 1992
- [S]ometimes literally meaning down the court steps. — Angela Devlin, *Prison Patter*, p. 57, 1996
- [T]he reason they're frightened of getting caught is that they don't want to go down and "lose their freedom". — Danny King, *The Burglar Diaries*, p. 18, 2001

3 while working as a police officer in a patrol car, to park and sleep *US*

- As a rookie cop, Serpico was also introduced to the fine art of "cooping," or sleeping on duty, a time-honored police practice that in other cities goes under such names as "huddling" and "going down." — Peter Maas, *Serpico*, p. 63, 1973

go-down man *noun*

in an illegal betting operation, the employee designated to identify himself as the operator in the event of a police raid, accepting risk in place of the actual operator *US*

- — David W. Maurer, *Argot of the Racetrack*, p. 32, 1951

go down on; go down; go down south *verb*

to perform oral sex *US, 1914*

- — Donald Webster Cory and John P. LeRoy, *The Homosexual and His Society*, p. 264, 1963: 'A lexicon of homosexual slang'
- I remembered – and I felt that strange, numb, helpless, cold fear when you realize you cant change the past – the first time someone had gone down on me in a public restroom. — John Rechy, *City of Night*, p. 381, 1963
- I'd held in reserve the bit of going down on him, because as a fag if there was anything that would turn him on, that was it. — Robert Leslie, *Confessions of a Lesbian Prostitute*, p. 55, 1965
- [W]here they lucked up and busted 1 guy going down on another. — Clarence Cooper Jr, *The Farm*, p. 52, 1967
- I wonder where he is now and what sweet young thing he's going down on. — John Warren Wells, *Tricks of the Trade*, p. 47–48, 1970
- There's one thing she always hated, it's going down on me. — George V. Higgins, *The Friends of Eddie Doyle*, p. 43, 1971
- Inside, the man goes down on Jim. — John Rechy, *The Sexual Outlaw*, p. 197, 1977
- Q Then what happened? A And then he [Roman Polanski] went down and he started performing cuddliness. Q What does that mean? A It means he went down on me or he placed his mouth on my vagina. — *Testimony of Samantha Jane Gailey to Los Angeles County Grand Jury*, 24th March 1977

- I simply had to stay in L.A. and learn how to go down on him. —Eve Babitz, *L.A. Woman*, p. 11, 1982
- It means that if we get busted the nice, bright-eyed prosecutors are going to describe prison to you, tell you about the two-hundred-pound diesel with a smelly snatch who's going to share your cell and how you'll have to go down on half the guards[.] —Vincent Patrick, *Family Business*, p. 69, 1985
- He goes down on Tantala and eats her cunt with a tongue-movement that is at once very funny and extremely hot. —*Adult Video*, p. 29, August/September 1986
- Does he go down on you? —*Sex, Lies and Videotape*, 1989
- If you went down on a horse, you'd tell me, right? —*South Park*, 1999
- [W]hat would I need to do? Go down on Satan, maybe? Go down on you? —Christopher Brookmyre, *Boiling a Frog*, p. 162, 2000

go downtown *verb*

to have sex *US*

Coined for US television comedy *Seinfeld*, 1993–98.

- —Susie Dent, *The Language Report*, 2003

God-pesterer *noun*

▷ see: GOD-BOTHERER

God save the Queens *noun*

green vegetables, especially cabbage *UK*

Rhyming slang for 'greens'.

- —Ray Puxley, *Cockney Rabbit*, 1992

God's flesh *noun*

1 psilocybin, a hallucinogenic mushroom *US*

- —William D. Alsever, *Glossary for the Establishment and Other Uptight People*, p. 26, December 1970

2 LSD *UK*

- —Mike Haskins, *Drugs*, p. 285, 2003

God's gift to women; God's gift *noun*

of a man, a great lover

A familiar idiom, also used in other contexts as 'God's gift to something or someone'; generally heavily ironic.

- You think you're God's gift / You're a liar / I wouldn't piss on you / If you were on fire —Chumbawumba *Mouthful*, 1994

God's honest truth *noun*

the absolute truth *UK*

- It's the God's honest truth I'm telling you, Johnny. —Derek Bickerton, *Payroll*, p. 126, 1959

God shop *noun*

a church *US*

- "God-Shop" for "Church" —*American Speech*, p. 234, October 1965

God-size *adjective*

very, very large *US*

- — *Current Slang*, p. 7, Summer 1968

God slot *noun*

a regular position in a television or radio broadcast schedule given over to religious programmes *UK, 1972*

- From the G-spot to a God slot: Cosmo discovers religion[.] —*Daily Telegraph*, 30th November 2003

God's medicine; God's own medicine *noun*

morphine; opium *US, 1925*

- —Angela Devlin, *Prison Patter*, p. 57, 1996
- —Mike Haskins, *Drugs*, p. 274, 2003

God squad *noun*

1 church authorities; evangelical enthusiasts *US, 1965*

- —Stephen H. Dill (Editor), *Current Slang*, p. 7, Summer 1968
- [Y]ou been watching fucking songs of praise or summat mun [man] – all fucking godsquad alloffafucking sudden -—Patrick Jones, *Unprotected Sex*, p. 221, 1999
- Someone else had knobbed his wife, he'd been arrested, fired, jailed and stabbed, and now he was about to pucker up to the God Squad. —Christopher Brookmyre, *Boiling a Frog*, p. 327, 2000

2 the US military Chaplains Corps *US, 1965*

- [T]his member of the general's "God squad" was actually going to hump with them, share the merciless heat with them. —Charles Anderson, *The Grunts*, p. 53, 1976
- —Gregory Clark, *Words of the Vietnam War*, p. 202, 1990

God's waiting room *noun*

a nursing home; a rest home *US*

- — *Maledicta*, p. 32, 1988–1989: 'Medical maledicta from San Francisco'

goer *noun*

1 a proposition that seems a likely success *AUSTRALIA*

- All the rage. Just think of it – Magic Mountain waterbeds. A goer. What can be more relaxing than sleeping on a ton and a half of water? —*Alvin Purple*, p. 30, 1974
- —Jim Ramsay, *Cop It Sweet!*, p. 40, 1977
- —Frank Ross, *Dead Runner*, 1977
- What a goer his sexual dysfunction treatments were. —B. Selkie, *Lime Juice*, p. 36, 1995
- Without [actress, Kathryn] Hunter at its centre this [production of Richard III would not be a goer. But she carries all before her. —*The Guardian*, 13th June 2003

2 an enthusiastic participant in sexual activity *UK, 1984*

- He wanted to know if you're a goer. —Caroline Aherne and Craig Cash, *The Royle Family*, 1999

3 in hot rodding, a fast car *US*

- —*American Speech*, p. 97, May 1954

4 a person with get-up-and-go *AUSTRALIA*

- You'd have to agree that for seventy she's a real goer. —Kerry Cue, *Crooks, Chooks and Bloody Ratbags*, p. 208, 1983

5 a horse being honestly ridden to win *AUSTRALIA, 1966*

- To the experienced eye, it wasn't too difficult to spot the dead'n or the goer on the unregistered tracks. —Joe Andersen, *Winners Can Laugh*, p. 66, 1982

go-fast *noun*

any amphetamine or other central nervous system stimulant *US*

- I can let you have a quarter a go-fast for twenny bucks. This special sale can't be repeated. —Joseph Wambaugh, *Finnegan's Week*, p. 138, 1993

go-faster *noun*

any amphetamine or other central nervous system stimulant *US*

- —Richard A. Spears, *The Slang and Jargon of Drugs and Drink*, p. 223, 1986

gofer; gopher; go-for *noun*

1 a low-level assistant who typically runs petty errands *US, 1930*

He or she *goes* for this and *goes* for that.

- Some gopher forgot to lock the gate. —Raymond Chandler, *The Long Goodbye*, p. 105, 1953
- Now, I'm the son's go-for. —Iceberg Slim (Robert Beck), *Long White Con*, p. 180, 1977
- Presently employed as chauffeur, bodyguard, and gofer to Lorenzo "Pesh" Franconi. —Edwin Torres, *Q & A*, p. 37, 1977
- Of course I'm just a gopher but that's cool. —Beatrice Sparks (writing as 'Anonymous'), *Jay's Journal*, p. 90, 1979
- She had just been promoted to stage manager from "broadcast associate," which used to be called "production assistant," or "PAS," or more to the point, "go-fer." —Dan Jenkins, *Life Its Ownself*, p. 186, 1984
- The "gopher" shook his head, puzzled, unaccustomed to the ways of sharp black prophets. —Donald Goines, *The Busting Out of an Ordinary Man*, p. 157, 1985
- The journalists, subs, production people, secretaries, designers and gofers who tenanted this stunted maze[.] —Will Self, *The Sweet Smell of Psychosis*, p. 33, 1996
- Slaughter's go-for. He's a bit younger than me. —John Milne, *Alive and Kicking*, p. 217, 1998
- "Say in the paper this Chili Palmer used to be a wiseguy." "He was a gofer, a hired hand." —Elmore Leonard, *Be Cool*, p. 109, 1999
- You, you are just the fuckin' gofer anyway son. You're only the Joey as they say at your end of the business. —J.J. Connolly, *Know Your Enemy [britpulp]*, p. 158, 1999
- I became Spencer's gofer, his Joey, and worked a twenty-four-hour shift[.] —Lanre Fehintola, *Charlie Says...*, p. 64, 2000

2 in the military, a special team assigned with the task of bypassing normal channels to acquire needed supplies *US*

- —Gregory Clark, *Words of the Vietnam War*, p. 279, 1990

gofer *verb*

to act as an assistant and errand-runner *UK*

From the noun.

- [H]e'd gophered at Ronnie Scott's, the crucial British home of modern jazz[.] —Mick Farren, *Give the Anarchist a Cigarette*, p. 18, 2001

goffer *noun*

1 a cold drink of mineral water or lemonade *AUSTRALIA, 1945*

Derives from drinks manufacturer Goffe & Sons Ltd.

- —Nigel Foster, *The Making of a Royal Marine Commando*, 1987

2 a wave washing inboard *UK*

- —Nigel Foster, *The Making of a Royal Marine Commando*, 1987

3 a punch, a blow *UK*

- Graham called out "Hop him, give him a goffer" [...] I then received a blow on my left shoulder. — *Session papers of the Central Criminal Court*, 11th February 1886
- — Nigel Foster, *The Making of a Royal Marine Commando*, 1987

4 a salute *AUSTRALIA*

- Also sometimes used in reference to a salute. ie "chuck a goffer" = to give a salute. — *Wordmap (www.abc.net.au/wordmap)*, 2003

go for *verb*

1 to attack with words (spoken or written) or with physical force *UK, 1880*

- Fat Tony was waiting there, and all three of them now went for him at once. When he eventually got home, his father beat him for being so late back from school. — *The Guardian*, 25th November 2000

2 to pay for *US*

- I would have gone for the funeral, but he had insurance. — Edwin Torres, *Carlito's Way*, p. 74, 1975

go for it!

used as a general exhortation *US, 1978*

- CARRIE: Make a wish, Daddy. RIANNE: Go for it, Dad. — *Lethal Weapon*, 1987

go forth and multiply!

go away! *UK*

Genesis 1:28 provides this archly euphemistic variation of 'fuck off!'.

- Fenton and Hank led our guests out the front door and released them. "Go forth and multiply," Fenton said. — James Patterson, *The Beach House*, p. 342, 2002

go for the gusto!

used as an exhortation to take risks and live life fully *US*

From a slogan for Schlitz beer; often used ironically.

- It was an 89–69 Seam play, when you go for the gusto. — *Milwaukee Journal*, p. 3C, 7th November 1988

gog *noun*

a person from North Wales *UK: WALES*

From Welsh *gogledd* (north).

- I'm not having him kept out of all the decent jobs by a bunch of bloody Gogs. – Gogs? – Northerners. – Oh yes, I remember. The Gogs. The ones that talk through their noses. — James Hawes, *White Powder, Green Light*, p. 31, 2002
- Can you understand the 'gogs'? Last week an MP from North Wales, Martyn Jones, said that the Caernarfon accent was difficult to understand. — *Hacio*, 6th March 2003

go-getter *noun*

a very active, enterprising person *US, 1910*

- All women want the go-getter. The conqueror. But after he's made the conquest they get mad because he won't stick around — Chris Rock, *Rock This!*, p. 125, 1997
- Wolfie was a real go-getter, a right little money maker — Dave Courtney, *Raving Lunacy*, p. 13, 2000

gogga *noun*

1 something frightening, monstrous or unwanted, especially in a political or business context *SOUTH AFRICA, 1934*

From the sense as 'an insect'.

- The equity gogga will simply fall asleep and we will all get on with the business of business. — *Sunday Times (South Africa)*, 17th November 2002

2 any insect *SOUTH AFRICA, 1905*

A generic term, from Khoikhoi *xo-xon* via Afrikaans.

- An impulse made me reach for my watchmaker's eye-glass; I slipped it into one eye and zoomed in on the little gogga. — Athol Fugard, *Notebooks*, p. 227, 1983

3 a germ, a disease *SOUTH AFRICA*

- It's unfit for human consumption being full of goggas that begin with a B. — Athol Fugard, *Blood Knot*, 1963

goggatjie; gogga *noun*

used as a term of endearment *SOUTH AFRICA, 1972*

From Afrikaans for 'little insect'.

- Yes, frightened me to death, you terrible old goggatjie you! — Laurens Van Der Post, *A Far-Off Place*, p. 131, 1974

goggle *verb*

▸ **goggle the horizon**

used by motorcylists to mean a number of things, most commonly to keep an eye out *US*

goggle box *noun*

a television *UK, 1959*

Conventional 'goggle' (to stare) elaborates viewers' response to the box (television).

goggler *noun*

a male homosexual *US*

- — Robert J. Glessing, *The Underground Press in America*, p. 176, 1970: 'Glossary of terms used in the underground press'

goggles *noun*

spectacles *UK, 1871*

From the conventional sense (spectacles for eye-protection).

- — Janey Ironside, *A Fashion Alphabet*, p. 119, 1968

Gogland *nickname*

North Wales *UK: WALES*

From Welsh *gogledd* (north).

- [I]t's a four hour drive to Gogland, give them Anglesey and Gwynedd and good fucking luck to them[.] — James Hawes, *White Powder, Green Light*, p. 57, 2002

go-go *noun*

a discotheque; a venue for erotic-dance performance *US*

- — Smokey Robinson & The Miracles, *Going to a Go-Go*, 1965
- You're just between engagements. Like between Swan Lane and the go-go and Marrakesh. — Anthony Masters, *Minder*, p. 161, 1984

go-go *adjective*

associated with a discotheque *UK, 1960s*

A very big word for a very few years.

- He had gone to a go-go bar to meet a buddy of his, had one beer, that's all, while he was waiting, minding his own business and this go-go whore came up to his table and starting giving him a private dance he never asked for. — Elmore Leonard, *Maximum Bob*, p. 1, 1991

go-go bird *noun*

a CH-47 transport helicopter fitted with window-mounted machine guns and used as a gunship *US*

Not a successful experiment.

- — Linda Reinberg, *In the Field*, p. 94, 1991

go-go boy *noun*

an attractive, usually homosexual, young man who is a paid dancer at a nightclub or bar *US*

- Thus the phenomenon of the orgy bars with their nude go-go boys is likely to persist. — John Francis Hunter, *The Gay Insider*, p. 11, 1971
- The Honey bucket, the little Hollywood bar that made the break-through with nude go-go boys early last year, has officially given up on nude dancers, at least for the time being. — *The Advocates*, p. 13, 31st March–13th April 1971
- It's a really dreadful experience. I mean, the go-go boys in strip joints here. — James Ridgeway, *Red Light*, p. 160, 1996

go-go dancer *noun*

a paid dancer at a nightclub *US*

- Many go-go dancers come to Come Again to buy G-strings and costumes[.] — James Ridgeway, *Red Light*, p. 122, 1996

go-go dancing *noun*

dancing for pay at a nightclub in a cage or platform above the patrons *US*

- While my father had been seeing Tammy, my mother was under contract, go-go-dancing at a club in Kodiak. — Kim Rich, *Johnny's Girl*, p. 84, 1993

go-go juice; go juice *noun*

petrol; diesel *US*

- — *Complete CB Slang Dictionary*, 1976
- — Peter Chippindale, *The British CB Book*, p. 155, 1981

go home

used as a humorous farewell *US*

A catchphrase television sign-off on *The Tracey Ullman Show* (Fox, 1987–90). Repeated with referential humour.

gohong *noun*

during the Korean war, food or chow *US, 1951*

From the Korean word for 'rice' applied by American soldiers to food in general.

- — *The Baltimore Sun*, 24th June 1951

goie *noun*

a central nervous system stimulant such as Dexedrine™ or Benzedrine™ *US*

- —Robert George Reisner, *The Jazz Titans*, p. 157, 1960

go-in *noun*

a fight *AUSTRALIA, 1900*

- [T]he Horse was still smarting from his go-in with Chip Monk[.]—Ray Slattery, *Mobbs' Mob*, p. 47, 1966

going!

used for encouraging another's action *US*

Hawaiian youth usage.

- "Should I tank dis beer o' wot?" "Going, brah, going!"—Douglas Simonson, *Pidgin to da Max Hana Hou*, 1982

going home gear *noun*

a truck's highest gear *US*

- —Montie Tak, *Truck Talk*, p. 74, 1971

going-over *noun*

1 a beating; a verbal assault *US, 1942*

- [S]natching the more troublesome educationalists from the audience and giving them a good going over.—*The Guardian*, 25th June 2002

2 a detailed inspection, a search *US, 1919*

- [G]ive the place a good going over before it is prepared for spring. —*The Observer*, 15th July 2001

goings-on *noun*

behaviour or proceedings *UK, 1775*

Usually with a pejorative implication.

- I imagine that my Cherokee forebears' remote ancestors probably left behind some nasty goings-on in Siberia.—*The Guardian*, 20th February 2003

goitre *noun*

a large quantity of banknotes, usually folded into a trouser pocket *UK*

From the unsightly bulge.

- —David Powis, *The Signs of Crime*, 1977

go-juice *noun*

alcohol (liquor) *US*

- —Collin Baker et al., *College Undergraduate Slang Study Conducted at Brown University*, p. 126, 1968

go jump in the creek

go away!, be off with you! *AUSTRALIA*

- You go an' jump in the creek, Bill Gimbal.—Norman Lindsay, *Halfway to Anywhere*, p. 156, 1947

GOK

God only knows *UK*

An informal medical acronym.

- GOK That's God Only Knows, one of the secret codes doctors use[.] —*Daily Mail*, 9th August 2003

gold *noun*

1 money *US, 1940*

- A lot of the guys who hung around were squares who worked for their gold, more gamblers than gangsters[.]—Milton Mezzrow, *Really the Blues*, p. 20, 1946
- I got back all right with all the gold and gave it to Juan. He threw me the twenty[.]—Hal Ellson, *Duke*, p. 73, 1949
- Just give me the gold.—Ross Russell, *The Sound*, p. 93, 1961
- —*Mr.*, p. 9, April 1966: 'The hippie's lexicon'

2 used generically for jewellery, especially goods that are traded illicitly *UK*

- This is when Matty was on his feet, buying and selling gold.—Lanre Fehintola, *Charlie Says...*, p. 73, 2000

3 a type of bet in an illegal lottery *US*

- He played the money row, lucky lady, happy days, true love, sun gonna shine, gold, silver, diamonds, dollars and whiskey.—Chester Himes, *A Rage in Harlem*, p. 23, 1957

4 potent marijuana *US*

Often combined with a place name for the formation of place plus colour.

- Claude asks me if I want to smoke some gold and lays a joint on me – I take it and put in on Billy.—*The Digger Papers*, p. 10, August 1968

5 in drag racing and hot rodding, a trophy or prize *US*

- —Lyle K. Engel, *The Complete Book of Fuel and Gas Dragsters*, p. 151, 1968

golda *noun*

a Jewish homosexual *SOUTH AFRICA*

Gay slang, formed on the name Golda and originating among Cape coloureds.

- —Bart Luirink (translated by Loes Nas), *Moffies: Gay Life in Southern Africa*, p. 150, 2000

Goldberg *noun*

used as a stereotype of a Jewish merchant *US*

- This was the first time I'd ever heard "Goldberg" used this way. I said, "Who's Goldberg?" "You know, Mr. JHew. That's the cat who runs the garment center."—Claude Brown, *Manchild in the Promised Land*, p. 295, 1965
- Making money off of women just as high as making it off doing Goldberg's dirty work in some damn dress factory downtown.—Sara Harris, *The Lords of Hell*, p. 136, 1967
- —Christina and Richard Milner, *Black Players*, p. 301, 1972
- At least three different poems and articles that have some mention of 'offing Goldberg' or 'wasting the kikes'.—John Sayles, *Union Dues*, p. 154, 1977
- —Edith A. Folb, *runnin' down some lines*, p. 240, 1980

goldbrick *noun*

a person who shuns work or duty *US, 1918*

- —Lou Shelly, *Hepcats Jive Talk Dictionary*, p. 45, 1945
- Jack, the plumber I was assigned to, was a prize goldbrick, a man who saw no virtue in work whatsoever.—Jim Thompson, *Bad Boy*, p. 338, 1953

goldbrick *verb*

to avoid a work detail *US, 1918*

- Just the thought of marching around all afternoon while they sweated their asses off made me feel sort of inferior, a gold-bricking weakling.—Mezz Mezzrow, *Really the Blues*, p. 321, 1946
- Goldbricking cocksuckers. Where's a man without his Nubians? —William Burroughs, *Naked Lunch*, p. 151, 1957
- —Gregory Clark, *Words of the Vietnam War*, p. 202, 1990

goldbricker *noun*

a swindler *US, 1902*

- I've seen a lot of spinals, Dude, and this guy is a fake. A fucking goldbricker.—*The Big Lebowski*, 1998

goldbug *noun*

a person who buys and hoards gold *US*

- The two old geezers were goldbugs from Spring Street in Los Angeles.—Joseph Wambaugh, *The Glitter Dome*, p. 88, 1981

gold buttons *noun*

a conductor on a train *US*

- —Ramon Adams, *The Language of the Railroader*, p. 69, 1977

Gold Coast *nickname*

1 a high-rise, high-rent district on Lakeshore Drive bordering Lake Michigan in northern Chicago, Illinois *US*

- Smooth adventurers set up swank apartments on the chi chi North Side gold Coast[.]—Jack Lait and Lee Mortimer, *Chicago Confidential*, p. z, 1950
- This is the Gold Coast. This the beautiful woman, Chicago.—Willard Motley, *Let No Man Write My Epitaph*, p. 167, 1958
- Behind me, the outline of the wealthy Gold Coast: luxurious apartments glistening goldenly in the sun[.]—John Rechy, *City of Night*, p. 293, 1963
- Alex lived on the Gold Coast of Chicago, and the night I drove out there the police stopped me three times along the way.—Dick Gregory, *Nigger*, p. 145, 1964
- And there were quite a few whites from Chicago's gold coast soaking up the rich nigger atmosphere.—Iceberg Slim (Robert Beck), *Trick Baby*, p. 193, 1969
- I found the Gold Coast lifestyle incredible.—Odie Hawkins, *Scars and Memories*, p. 34, 1987
- —Laurence Urdang, *Names and Nicknames of Places and Things*, p. 109, 1987
- It was one of the boundary lines of the old Gold Coast.—Herbert Huncke, *Guilty of Everything*, p. 28, 1990

2 an area in Harlem, New York, where police bribes are common and lucrative *US*

- At the time of the investigation, certain precincts in Harlem, for instance, comprised what police officers called "the Gold Coast" because they contained so many payoff-prone activities[.]—*The Knapp Commission Report on Police Corruption*, p. 67, 1972

3 the Atlantic coast of South Florida *US*

- Money is cheap on the Gold Coast, and there is a lot of it floating around.—Hunter S. Thompson, *Songs of the Doomed*, p. 193, 1983
- He's got the entire Gold Coast terrified, your venerable newspaper included.—Carl Hiaasen, *Tourist Season*, p. 191, 1986

4 a stretch along the east coast of Queensland, Australia, noted for extraordinarily good surfing *AUSTRALIA*

- —Trevor Cralle, *The Surfin'ary*, p. 46, 1991

gold-digger *noun*
someone who pursues another romantically because of their wealth *US, 1916*
Glossed as: 'used to characterize women as pedators of men' by the Multicultural Management Program Fellows, *Dictionary of Cautionary Words and Phrases*, 1989.
- I shambled out of the dormitory, cursing her for a heartless golddigger and myself for an idiot. — Max Shulman, *The Many Loves of Dobie Gillis*, p. 56, 1951
- Who the fuck wants a gold-digger around. — Edwin Torres, *After Hours*, p. 297, 1979
- Stacy Donovan shines as an empty-headed golddigger[.] — *Adult Video*, p. 80, August/September 1986
- As Erin grew older, she accepted the fact that her mother was a restless gold digger who would never be happy[.] — Carl Hiaasen, *Strip Tease*, p. 26, 1993

gold-digging *adjective*
engaged in the romantic pursuit of a wealthy lover *US, 1994*
- [M]ore than a few shady-looking fellas and gold-digging birds. — Wayne Anthony, *Spanish Highs*, p. 183, 1999

gold dust *noun*
1 cocaine *US*
Extends **DUST** (playing on the expense).
- — Joseph E. Ragen and Charles Finston, *Inside the World's Toughest Prison*, p. 801, 1962: 'Penitentiary and underworld glossary'
- Street names [...] dust, gold dust, lady[.] — James Kay and Julian Cohen, *The Parents' Complete Guide to Young People and Drugs*, p. 134, 1998

2 heroin *UK*
- — Angela Devlin, *Prison Patter*, p. 57, 1996

Gold Dust Twins *nickname*
Timothy Leary and Dick Alpert, LSD pioneers *US*
- I first took acid because the Gold Dust Twins, Tim Leary and Dick Alpert, had so thoroughly nurtured my trust. — *The Last Supplement to the Whole Earth Catalog*, p. 66, March 1971

golden *noun*
marijuana *UK*
From the colour of the leaf.
- — Mike Haskins, *Drugs*, p. 287, 2003

golden *adjective*
successful, excellent, charmed *US, 1958*
- — *Current Slang*, p. 4, Spring 1967
- — *USA Today*, 29th September 1983
- Once we get airplay we're golden. — *Airheads*, 1994

golden arm *noun*
in craps, a player with a long streak of good luck rolling the dice *US*
- — Frank Scoblete, *Guerrilla Gambling*, p. 310, 1993

golden BB
the bullet or anti-aircraft round that hits you *US, 1969*
- Unfortunately it was the "Golden BB," the lucky shot, the aircrews often joked about, and it struck the LOX bottle under Johnny Nelson's seat in the pit. — Richard Herman Jr, *The Warbirds*, p. 258, 1989
- So far, it seemed that he had avoided the "Golden BB," the one lucky round that would bring him down. — Gerry Carroll, *North S*A*R*, p. 207, 1991

golden bollocks *noun*
a lucky man *UK, 1984*
- Never hardly give us the time of day when she was with aul' golden bollocks. — Kevin Sampson, *Clubland*, p. 165, 2002

golden boy *noun*
1 a favoured male *AUSTRALIA*
- Where previously they'd liked her, because golden boy had told them she was divorced, now, suddenly they hated her guts. — Sue Rhodes, *Now you'll think I'm awful*, p. 48, 1967
- Among the university students in our intake, Wokka Clark was undoubtedly the golden boy. — Clive James, *Unreliable Memoirs*, p. 144, 1980

2 in homosexual usage, a handsome young man at his sexual prime *US*
- — *Male Swinger Number 3*, p. 45, 1981: 'The complete gay dictionary'

golden brown *noun*
heroin *UK*
An elaboration of **BROWN** (heroin).
- — The Stranglers *Golden Brown*, 1981
- What do you think it is, little girl? It's heroin, that's for sure, golden brown, like in the song. — Ben Elton, *High Society*, p. 58, 2002

golden bullet *noun*
the bullet or anti-aircraft round that hits your combat plane *US*
- Since then, the main danger has been what the pilots call the golden bullet. "That's the aimed or unaimed bullet that you run into because there are so many bullets,," said a lieutenant colonel named Greg. — *Washington Times*, p. B4, 23rd January 1991

golden chair!
used to reserve your seat as you briefly leave the room *US*
- — Connie Eble (Editor), *UNC-CH Campus Slang*, p. 3, Fall 1996

golden crescent *noun*
an area in Afghanistan, Iran and Pakistan where heroin is produced *US*
- — Jay Robert Nash, *Dicitonary of Crime*, p. 152, 1992

golden doughnut *noun*
the vagina *AUSTRALIA, 1972*

golden dragon *noun*
LSD *UK*
- — Mike Haskins, *Drugs*, p. 285, 2003

golden flow *noun*
the urine test given to US soldiers upon their return to the US from Vietnam *US*
- — Linda Reinberg, *In the Field*, p. 94, 1991

golden ghetto *verb*
a large, comfortable US Army divisional base camp in South Vietnam *US*
A term used with derision by the marines.
- — Gregory Clark, *Words of the Vietnam War*, p. 203, 1990

golden girl *noun*
1 a favoured woman *AUSTRALIA*
- It seems the golden girl has been forced back into recording by, one hardly dares mention it,money — *Sunday Herald Sun*, p. 105, 12th July 1992

2 high quality cocaine *US*
- — Edith A. Folb, *runnin' down some lines*, p. 240, 1980

3 heroin *US*
- — US Department of Justice, *Street Terms*, October 1994
- — Robert Ashton, *This Is Heroin*, p. 206, 2002

Golden Girls *nickname*
the women's track team from the Bahamas at the 2000 Olympics *US*
- Here's the team from the Bahamas including Debbie Ferguson, one of the vets of this event as well as the Olympic Games. — *NBC Olympic Coverage*, 26th August 2004

golden glow *noun*
a luminous daub used by card cheats to mark cards *US*
- — George Percy, *The Language of Poker*, p. 49, 1988

golden leaf *noun*
1 marijuana of excellent quality *US, 1925*
Possibly descriptive of the plant's appearance, as well as the value placed upon it.
- "Man, this is some golden-leaf I brought up from New Orleans, it'll make you feel good, take a puff." — Mezz Mezzrow, *Really the Blues*, p. 51, 1946

2 a marijuana cigarette *UK*
- — Mike Haskins, *Drugs*, p. 291, 2003

golden mile *noun*
the area west of McGill in central Montreal, characterised by large stone mansions *CANADA*
- [Stephen Leacock]'s success allowed him to become a Victorian gentleman with a Montreal home in the golden mile and a summer residence on Lake Simcoe. Leacock relished his position in the Anglo-Canadian establishment. — *Montreal Gazette*, p. J4, 22nd June 2002

golden ointment *noun*
a large win in betting; money *AUSTRALIA*
- — Ned Wallish, *The Truth Dictionary of Racing Slang*, p. 34, 1989

golden oldie *noun*
1 a song from the past that is still popular, especially a rock and roll song from the 1950s or 60s *US, 1966*
- I'll do three golden oldies for every one I want to play[.] — Elmore Leonard, *Glitz*, p. 73, 1985

2 by extension, anything that can be categorised in a nostalgic context *UK*
After the old songs a radio DJ announces.
- Teenagers moved trendily from designer drugs, like ecstasy, to golden oldies, like pot and pep pills. — Simon Napier-Bell, *Black Vinyl White Powder*, p. 333, 2001

golden shower *noun*
a shared act of urine fetishism; the act of urination by one person on another for sexual gratification *US, 1943*
- — Dale Gordon, *The Dominion Sex Dictionary*, p. 78, 1967
- I couldn't believe that "golden shower" sequence in Sensations! (Letter to Editor) — *Adam Film Quarterly*, p. 77, October 1976
- Another large percentage of the pictures have to do with urination or, as we call them, "golden showers." — Stephen Ziplow, *The Film Maker's Guide to Pornography*, p. 14, 1977
- I can take about an hour on the tower of power / as long as I get a little golden shower — Frank Zappa, *Bobby Brown Goes Down*, 1979
- No golden showers for me!" (Quoting Tina Russell). — *Adam Film World*, p. 18, January 1980
- Golden showers is a source of humiliation, punishment, and reward. — *Women in Command*, p. 10, 1983
- An extreme form of humiliation involves receiving the dominant partner's urine on the masochist's body. This practice, sometimes called "golden showers," is described by Scott (1983) as "the ultimate insult." — Roy F. Baumeister, *Masochism and the Self*, p. 159–160, 1989
- And he would like for me to give 'im golden showers. He liked for me to drink like a sixpack of beer and then after about a good hour then he'd want me to piss all in his mouth[.] — William T. Vollman, *Whores for Gloria*, p. 54, 1991
- Fuck for about an hour, now she want a golden shower — Luke & The Notorious BIG, *Bust a Nut*, 1993
- Lately a lot of people have made it pretty trendy to do water sports or golden shower kind of things. — Anthony Petkovich, *The X Factory*, p. 129, 1997
- At one table sat a uniform fetishist, a submissive man into cross dressing, a gay male couple who like public sex and golden showers[.] — *The Village Voice*, 24th November 1999

▸ **couldn't organise a urine sample in a golden shower**
used of an inefficient person or organisation *UK*
A later variation of '...**PISS-UP IN A BREWERY**' and '...**COCK-UP IN A BROTHEL**'.
- This is to certify: Mr Elephant Testicle and his entire Ministry COULDN'T ORGANISE A URINE SAMPLE IN A GOLDEN SHOWER. — *The Guardian*, p. 24, 28th June 2005

golden shower queen *noun*
a male homosexual who derives sexual pleasure from being urinated upon *US*
- — Florida Legislative Investigation Committee (Johns Committee), *Homosexuality and Citizenship in Florida*, 1964: 'Glossary of homosexual terms and deviate acts'
- Yes, there are those who like to be peed on (Golden Shower Queens, they were once known as)[.] — John Francis Hunter, *The Gay Insider*, p. 190, 1971

golden spike *noun*
a hypodermic needle *US*
- — *American Speech*, p. 87, May 1955: 'Narcotic argot along the mexican border'

golden T *nickname*
in New York, Fifth Avenue from 47th Street north to 57th Street, and 57th Street between Madison and Sixth Avenues *US*
- — *The New York Times*, p. B1, 13th July 1989

golden time; golden hours *noun*
in the entertainment industry, time worked at a premium overtime rate *US*
- Christ, may, it's seven-ten Saturday night – that's one hour and forty minutes of golden time! — Terry Southern, *Blue Movie*, p. 187, 1970
- — Sherman Louis Sergel, *The Language of Show Biz*, p. 98, 1973
- But we were pushing golden time, where the rates triple, and that hadn't been budgeted. — Robert Stoller and I.S. Levine, *Coming Attractions*, p. 82, 1991

golden triangle *noun*
an area in Burma, Laos and Thailand where heroin is produced *US*
- — Jay Robert Nash, *Dicitonary of Crime*, p. 152, 1992

goldfinger *noun*
synthetic heroin *US*
- — Jay Robert Nash, *Dicitonary of Crime*, p. 153, 1992

goldfish *noun*
a strain of marijuana, also known as 'orange bud' *UK*
- It's this orange bud, man. No wonder they call it goldfish. It knackers your memory. — Ed Allen and Johnny Vaughan, *'Orrible*, 10th September 2001

goldfish *verb*
to mouth words, to talk without being heard *US*
Imitative of a goldfish.
- [C]ops goldfishing to reporters[.] — Chris Niles, *Revenge is the Best Revenge [Tart Noir]*, p. 15, 2002

goldfish bowl *noun*
a jail's interrogation room *US*
- — *American Speech*, p. 269, December 1962: 'The language of traffic policemen'

goldfishing *noun*
the behaviour of visitors being shown around a prison *UK*
From the similarity to a naturally wide-eyed, open-mouthed goldfish.
- — Angela Devlin, *Prison Patter*, p. 57, 1996

gold fronts; fronts *noun*
ornamental dental work *US*
- Why get gold fronts? — *The Source*, January 1994
- He now had a bandana tied around his head, a mouthful of gold fronts, and slouched as moodily as his crutches would let him[.] — Diran Adebayo, *My Once Upon A Time*, p. 58, 2000
- Fronts have diminished in popularity since their heyday in '94 but they never disappeared. — *The Source*, p. 64, March 2002

Goldie Hawn *noun*
a prawn *UK*
Rhyming slang, formed from the name of the US film actress (b.1945).
- — Ray Puxley, *Fresh Rabbit*, 1998

Goldilocks *noun*
a sexually transmitted infection *UK*
Rhyming slang for **POX**, caught from a fairytale heroine – 'Who's been sleeping in my bed?'.
- — Ray Puxley, *Fresh Rabbit*, 1998

gold Lebanese; gold leb *noun*
▷ see: **LEBANESE GOLD**

gold mine *noun*
an establishment that sells alcohol illegally, by the drink *US*
- Shot-house operators run informal (and illegal) taverns in their own homes (shot-house operators are often women). The houses go by other names too; gold mine, good-time house, blind tiger, shine parlor, or juicejoint. — Burgess Laughlin, *Job Opportunities in the Black Market*, p. 10–9, 1978

gold nuggets *noun*
in dominoes, the 5–5 piece *US*
- — Dominic Armanino, *Dominoes*, p. 17, 1959

gold ring *noun*
(of playing cards) a king *UK*
Rhyming slang, also used of monarchy but, at the time of writing in 2003, there is no current application.
- — Ray Puxley, *Cockney Rabbit*, 1992

gold room *noun*
a room in the Pentagon where the Joint Chiefs and Staff meet with the Operations Deputies *US*
- — Department of the Army, *Staff Officer's Guidebook*, p. 67, 1986

gold rush *noun*
1 the frantic searching for jewellery or coins that follows a shift in the slope of a beach, exposing lost articles *US*
- — Ken Suiso and Rell Sunn, *A Guide to Beach Survival*, p. 70, 1986

2 in hold 'em poker, a hand consisting of a four and a nine *US*
An allusion to the California gold rush of 1849.
- — John Vorhaus, *The Big Book of Poker Slang*, p. 20, 1996

gold seal *noun*
good quality marijuana *UK*
- — Angela Devlin, *Prison Patter*, p. 57, 1996

gold star *noun*
marijuana *UK, 1998*
- — Mike Haskins, *Drugs*, p. 287, 2003

gold-star lesbian *noun*
a lesbian who has never had sex with a man and intends that she never will *UK*
- — Michelle Baker and Steven Tropiano, *Queer Facts*, p. 200, 2004

Goldstein *noun*
a Jewish person *US*
- —Edith A. Folb, *runnin' down some lines*, p. 240, 1980

gold watch *noun*
Scotch whisky *UK, 1992*
Rhyming slang, always given full measure.
- —Ray Puxley, *Cockney Rabbit*, 1992
- I've got a parcel of export gold watch, forty foot of it.—Garry Bushell, *The Face*, p. 152, 2001

golfball *noun*
1 crack cocaine; a large piece of crack cocaine *US*
- —US Department of Justice, *Street Terms*, October 1994

2 any central nervous system despressant *UK, 1998*
- —Mike Haskins, *Drugs*, p. 282, 2003

3 a changeable sphere with 88 different characters used on IBM Selectric typewriters *US*
- —Eric S. Raymond, *The New Hacker's Dictionary*, p. 181, 1991

golfballs *noun*
1 dice *US*
- —Frank Garcia, *Marked Cards and Loaded Dice*, p. 262, 1962

2 LSD *UK*
- —Mike Haskins, *Drugs*, p. 285, 2003

golfballs and bullets *noun*
a US Army c-rations meal of meatballs and beans *US*
- —Linda Reinberg, *In the Field*, p. 94, 1991

Golf Course *nickname*
Camp Radcliff, base camp for the Fourth Infantry Division near An Khe, South Vietnam *US*
Named for a large helicopter airfield with low-cut grass.
- —*Life*, p. 33, 25th February 1966
- —Carl Fleiscnnauer, *A Glossary of Army Slang*, p. 22, 1968
- The Golf Course, the heliport cleared of all its trees, stood out against the green. Golf Course control, Preacher eight-seven-niner, five miles east for landing instructions.—Robert Mason, *Chickenawk*, p. 72, 1983
- There were bases like An Khe with its famous Golf Course, with tons of troops and hundreds of tons of hardware, but the VC were all around them.—Dennis Marvicsin and Jerold Greenfield, *Maverick*, p. 89, 1990
- —Linda Reinberg, *In the Field*, p. 95, 1991

goliath *noun*
a multiple bet, gambling on eight horses, combining 247 bets in a specific pattern *UK*
- —John McCririck, *John McCririck's World of Betting*, p. 45, 1991
- —David Bennet, *Know Your Bets*, p. 47, 2001

gollies *noun*
▸ **the gollies**
dog racing *UK*
From rhyming slang; for **GOLLIWOG** (a dog).
- —Ray Puxley, *Cockney Rabbit*, 1992

golliwog *noun*
1 a dog, especially a greyhound *UK*
Rhyming slang, may be abbreviated to 'gollie'.
- —Ray Puxley, *Cockney Rabbit*, 1992

2 fog *UK*
Rhyming slang, often reduced to 'golly'.
- —Ray Puxley, *Fresh Rabbit*, 1998

golliwoggy; golly *adjective*
foggy *UK*
- [Y]ou've either got your eyes closed or it's "bloody golly".—Ray Puxley, *Fresh Rabbit*, 1998

gollop *verb*
to eat hurriedly and with great gusto *UK, 1937*
A variation of conventional 'gulp'.
- Don't gollop yer food or I'll mash yer!—Chris Lewis, *The Dictionary of Playground Slang*, p. 103, 2003

golly *noun*
1 a black person *UK*
A shortening of 'golliwog'.
- —Brian Fairborn, *Good Luck, Mister Cain*, 1976

2 any person of non-white ethnicity; a native of the Indian subcontinent; an Arab *UK*
A play on **WOG** via 'golliwog' (a negroid doll).
- For the average Tommy [British soldier], black or white, any local, be he Arab, Indian, or Somali, is a "Golly"[.]—*The Observer*, 11th June 1967

3 a gob of phlegm or mucus *AUSTRALIA, 1938*
Origin unknown. The *English Dialect Dictionary* records 'golls' as 'mucus dripping from a child's nose' as current in East Anglia in the mid-C19, but 'golly' is probably an independant formation.
- Come to think of it, them oysters looked more like the chef had puked up a dozen king sized green gollies!—Barry Humphries, *The Wonderful World of Barry McKenzie*, p. 58, 1968
- —Jim Ramsay, *Cop It Sweet!*, p. 40, 1977

4 a half gallon jar of beer *NEW ZEALAND*
- —Harry Orsman, *A Dictionary of Modern New Zealand Slang*, p. 57, 1999

golly *verb*
to expectorate *AUSTRALIA, 1978*

golly!
used for registering surprise, shock, etc *UK, 1775*
Euphemistic variation on 'God', which evokes a childish innocence.
- Maybe his customers' cellars did leak a bit, but, by golly, when a fellow has been living, say, on 68th Street, it sure made him feel mighty proud[.]—Max Shulman, *Rally Round the Flag, Boys!*, p. 51, 1957
- "Golly, what'll they think of next?" articles [...] stories in which wide-eyed music writers discussed rap[.]—*The Source*, p. 80, March 2002

gollyer *noun*
a gob of spittle *IRELAND*
- He shot a big gollyer out the window—Lee Dunne, *Goodbye to the Hill*, p. 27, 1966

golly gee, Buffalo Bob
used for expressing mock astonishment *US*
- —John D. Bell et al., *Loosely Speaking*, p. Appendix, 1969

golpe *noun*
heroin *US, 1980*
From Spanish *golpe* (a blow, a shot).
- —Richard A. Spears, *The Slang and Jargon of Drugs and Drink*, p. 225, 1986
- —Robert Ashton, *This Is Heroin*, p. 206, 2002
- —Mike Haskins, *Drugs*, p. 284, 2003

gom *noun*
a foolish, awkward person; a simpleton; an idiot *IRELAND*
- I saw this drunken hairy-looking gom come bounding and staggering out into the road[.]—Joseph O'Connor, *The Irish Male at Home and Abroad*, p. 55, 1996

GOM *noun*
morphine; opium *UK*
An initialism of **GOD'S OWN MEDICINE**.
- —Angela Devlin, *Prison Patter*, p. 57, 1996
- —Mike Haskins, *Drugs*, p. 274, 2003

goma; guma *noun*
heroin *US, 1967*
Possibly an elaboration of **GOM**.
- —Richard A. Spears, *The Slang and Jargon of Drugs and Drink*, p. 225, 1986
- —Mike Haskins, *Drugs*, p. 284, 2003

gomer *noun*
1 a US Marine, especially a clumsy trainee *US, 1984*
Terminology used with affectionate derision by the US Army during the Vietnam war. From the television show *Gomer Pyle*, which is not a completely flattering image of the marines.
- —*American Speech*, Summer 1989
- —Linda Reinberg, *In the Field*, p. 95, 1991

2 a repulsive, non-compliant hospital patient *US, 1993*
From the plea – '*g*et *o*ut of *m*y *e*mergency *r*oom!'.
- —Sally Williams, *"Strong" Words*, p. 143, 1994

go-minh money *noun*
compensation payment to Vietnamese civilians by the US military for accidental losses resulting from military actions *US*
From the Vietnamese for 'extract yourself from a predicament'.
- —Gregory Clark, *Words of the Vietnam War*, p. 208, 1990

gommed up *adjective*

dirty *US*

• —Sam McCool, *Pittsburghese*, p. 13, 1982

gommie *noun*

a silly person *CANADA, 1990*

• — *New Maritimes*, p. 29, March-April 1990

gomtor; gom *noun*

an uncouth person, especially when applied to an Afrikaner *SOUTH AFRICA, 1970*

From Afrikaans *gomtor* (a lout).

• —Jean Branford, *A Dictionary of South African English*, 1978

gon *noun*

a *gon*dola train carriage *US, 1934*

• —Norman Carlisle, *The Modern Wonder Book of Trains and Railroading*, p. 263, 1946
• Both the little bum and I, after unsuccessful attempts to huddle on the cold steel in wraparounds, got up and paced back and forth and jumped and flapped arms at each our end of the gon. —Jack Kerouac, *The Dharma Bums*, p. 5, 1958

gonad alert *noun*

▷ see: NAD ALERT

gondola *noun*

heroin *UK*

• —Mike Haskins, *Drugs*, p. 284, 2003

gone *adjective*

1 superlative, profoundly in touch with current trends *US, 1946*

Nellie Lutcher's 1947 recording of 'He's a Real Gone Guy' did as much as anything to introduce the term into the language.

• "That's Bop language!" he laughed and handed me a Bop dictionary which translates the slang used by "real gone Boppers." —*San Francisco Examiner*, p. Pictorial Review, 3rd December 1948
• They were all good records: Frankie Lane, Sarah Vaughn, Billy Eckstein, all gone, good singers. They were goners. —Hal Ellson, *Duke*, p. 105, 1949
• I had a pad on tenth street living with a gone little chick from Newark. —Jack Kerouac, *Letter to Neal Cassady*, p. 234, 6 October 1950
• Isn't this wild, isn't this crazy, ain't this gone, this sure is! —William "Lord" Buckley, *Nero*, 1951
• I'll pay. I'm a real gone guy. Don't I trade with you a lot? —Hal Ellson, *The Golden Spike*, p. 170, 1952
• Mary selected some gone numbers and beat on the table with the expression of a masturbating idiot. —William Burroughs, *Junkie*, p. 29, 1953
• "Your grandma," he said, "is gone." "I'm hip," said Red. "She is the swingin'est, but let's take it from the top again." —Steve Allen, *Bop Fables*, p. 47, 1955
• "But this is only after you and I, dear Carlo, go to Texas, dig Old Bull Lee, the gone cat I've never met[.]" —Jack Kerouac, *On the Road*, p. 48, 1957
• Man, he's the gonest!" one of the fellows said. —Willard Motely, *Let No Man Write My Epitaph*, p. 363, 1958
• "Crazy, man, crazy," spieled his pal, one eye lamping a real gone gal. —Dan Burley, *Diggeth Thou?*, p. 18, 1959
• They say this French chick is real gone. —Ross Russell, *The Sound*, p. 183, 1961
• [A]n she is hot for a new one, so watch out, man – but if you ain't got a pad, you can always make it at Destinee's – it's like a gone mission, man! —John Rechy, *City of Night*, p. 102, 1963
• He looked like one the real-gone cats with his signifying-walk[.] —Chester Himes, *Cotton to Haariem*, 1965
• I was gonna get a gone high ... a gone high ... a gone high. —Piri Thomas, *Down These Mean Streets*, p. 58, 1967
• I'm gonna be a real gone cat / Then I won't want you. —Dave Bartholomew et al., *I'm Gonna Be a Wheel Someday*, 1999

2 drunk or drug-intoxicated *US, 1933*

• You know. Drunk stewed, clobbered, gone, liquored up, oiled, stoned, in the bag. —Max Shulman, *Guided Tour of Campus Humor*, p. 106, 1955
• —Connie Eble (Editor), *UNC-CH Campus Slang*, p. 5, April 1995
• —Angela Devlin, *Prison Patter*, p. 58, 1996

3 completely destitute and physically ruined because of crack cocaine addiction *US*

• — US Department of Justice, *Street Terms*, October 1994

4 infatuated *US*

• Dig Number one: being gone on a boy is more important than having a boy gone on you. —Frederick Kohner, *Gidget*, p. 103, 1957

5 pregnant *AUSTRALIA*

• Didn't you notice it? She's five months gone. —Norman Lindsay, *The Cousin from Fiji*, p. 105, 1945
• Papa, she's fixing your favorite dinner, macaroni and cheese, short ribs, yams and homemade biscuits. And even when she's eight months gone. —Iceberg Slim (Robert Beck), *Doom Fox*, p. 246, 1978

6 caught *AUSTRALIA*

• We're dodging down a lane when we run slap bang into a provost. "We're gone," I says to myself. —Eric Lambert, *The Veterans*, p. 13, 1954

goneburger *noun*

anything that is redundant or finished *NEW ZEALAND*

• A Christchurch based State-owned enterprise in the meat industry will be investigated for compiling a hit list, known as the 'goneburger' list of nearly 100 staff it wanted to cull. —*Evening Post*, p. 2, 5th October 2000

gone case *noun*

a hopeless cause *SINGAPORE*

• —Paik Choo, *The Coxford Singlish Dictionary*, p. 40, 2002

goner *noun*

1 someone who has died or is unavoidably doomed to die very soon *UK, 1847*

From 'gone' as a euphemism for 'dead'.

• Syphilis Joe will be a goner by this time. —Geoffrey Fletcher, *Down Among the Meths Men*, p. 15, 1966
• Strike me lucky, I reckon I'm a gonna!!! —Barry Humphries, *Bazza Pulls It Off!*, 1971
• "Fuck. I think this one's a gonner," was the Sergeant's verdict[.] —Donald Gorgon, *Cop Killer*, p. 8, 1994

2 someone who is doomed to failure *US*

• That does it. The goddamn F.B.I. We're goners. —Darryl Ponicsan, *The Last Detail*, p. 159, 1970

3 a person who excels *US*

• They were all good records: Frankie Lane, Sarah Vaughn, Billy Eckstein, all gone, good singers. They were goners. —Hal Ellson, *Duke*, p. 105, 1949

gone to bed *adjective*

dead *UK*

• Old Sid has gone to bed and he ain't getting up. —Ray Puxley, *Cockney Rabbit*, 1992

gone to Gowings *adjective*

well and truly gone *AUSTRALIA*

From an advertising campaign for Gowing Bros, a Sydney department store. Used as an intensifier of 'gone', especially for slang senses of 'gone'.

• GONE TO GOWINGS: pec[uliar to] Sydney. Hopelessly beaten or outclassed. —Jim Ramsay, *Cop It Sweet!*, p. 40, 1977

gone to hell *adjective*

utterly ruined *UK, 1984*

• Bush and his cronies stole the election, and everything since has gone to hell'. — *The Guardian*, 11th April 2003

gone up *adjective*

drunk or drug-intoxicated *US*

• —William D. Alsever, *Glossary for the Establishment and Other Uptight People*, p. 15, December 1970

gong *noun*

1 a military medal or decoration *UK, 1921*

• V.C. [the Victoria Cross] or no V.C. Trouble is you've let that flippin' gong make you into a martyr. —Graeme Kent, *The Queen's Corporal [Six Granada Plays]*, p. 98, 1959
• —Linda Reinberg, *In the Field*, p. 95, 1991

2 a medal *UK, 1945*

• Johnstone was among those to collect a gong[.] — *The Guardian*, 11th October 1999

3 opium; heroin *US, 1936*

• —Richard A. Spears, *The Slang and Jargon of Drugs and Drink*, p. 225, 1986
• —Mike Haskins, *Drugs*, p. 284, 2003

4 marijuana *US, 1977*

• —Richard A. Spears, *The Slang and Jargon of Drugs and Drink*, p. 225, 1986
• —Mike Haskins, *Drugs*, p. 287, 2003

5 a gun *US*

• —Bill Valentine, *Gang Intelligence Manual*, p. 110, 1995: 'Jamaican gang terminology'.

gong down *verb*

to ring the alarm bell on a police car as a signal to another motorist to stop *UK*

Early police cars were fitted with bell-shaped gongs. During the 1930s and 40s the police patrolling in cars were known as 'gongers'.

• [A]ll-of-a-sudden the odd gongs him down[.] —Frank Norman, *Bang To Rights*, p. 123, 1958

gonies *noun*

the testicles *US*

A diminutive of 'gonads'.

- "And if I'm permitted to state one more fact," says Mule, "my goddam gonies are frozen." — Darryl Ponicsan, *The Last Detail*, p. 132, 1970

gonj *noun*

marijuana *UK*

- — Mike Haskins, *Drugs*, p. 287, 2003

gonk *noun*

1 a prostitute's client *UK*

A contemptuous term used by prostitutes, deriving, perhaps, from a type of humanoid doll.

- — David Powis, *The Signs of Crime*, 1977

2 a fool, an idiot *UK*

Teen slang.

- — Susie Dent, *The Language Report*, p. 76, 2003

gonk *verb*

1 to sleep *UK*

- — Nigel Foster, *The Making of a Royal Marine Commando*, 1987
- Among the New Word., p.390. ter 1991. — John Algeo and Adele Algeo, *American Speech*, p. 390, 1991

2 to lie *US*

- — Eric S. Raymond, *The New Hacker's Dictionary*, p. 182, 1991

gonna; gunna; gunner; gonner *verb*

going to *US, 1913*

Slovenly pronunciation.

- We're not gonna take it, / Never did and never will. — Pete Townshend, *We're Not Going To Take It*, 1969
- If you're gunna get wiped out, well, might as well get wiped out with a few sounds in your head[.] — Mike Stott, *Soldiers Talking, Cleanly*, 1978
- LEE: We're auditioning ero'ic dancers. JAMIE: We ain't gunner 'ave strippers in 'ere! — Guy Ritchie et al., *Lock, Stock... & Four Stolen Hooves*, p. 5, 2000
- There're kiddies gonner be playing around here in a minute. — Niall Griffiths, *Sheepshagger*, p. 195, 2000

gonnabe *noun*

a wannabe (someone with ambition) who has a realistic chance of achieving the goal *US*

- There are about 70,000 gang members, including "wannabes" and "gonnabes," the prepubescent boys awaiting initiation[.] — *New York Times*, p. 30 (Section 6), 22nd May 1988
- First used by Liam Gallagher of Oasis who [...] remarked that "Has-beens shouldn't give awards to gonna-bees". — Alon Shulman, *The Style Bible*, p. 107, 1999
- For [Maggie] Gyllenhaal, it's a star-making turn, one which shunt her alongside brother Jake as a sure-fire gonnabe. — *Uncut*, p. 124, June 2003

gonnif; gonif; ganef *noun*

a thief; a crook *UK, 1839*

Yiddish from Hebrew. Depending on the tone, can range from laudatory to disdainful.

- The little bulb-nosed goneff who used to play clarinet and had three fingers and his teeth shot out at Omaha Beach[.] — Clancy Sigal, *Going Away*, p. 352, 1961
- Then New York with Jimmy Walker – a heavy gonif, a master gonif, man. — Lenny Bruce, *The Essential Lenny Bruce*, p. 57, 1967
- — *American Speech*, p. 145–151, Spring-Summer 1975: 'Yiddish ganef: its family and friends'
- I'm on the floor in the back of a car with somebody's shoe on my neck before I know what hits me. It's a black shoe, well-polished and with a pointy toe. A dancer's shoe. A gonif's shoe. A shoe which belongs to a man who knows how to damage a man's ribs with a kick. — Robert Campbell, *Junkyard Dog*, p. 126, 1986

go-no-go *noun*

the point on a runway where a pilot taking off must decide whether to abort a take-off or to take off *US*

- — *American Speech*, p. 118, May 1963: 'Air refueling words'

gonski *adjective*

gone *UK*

- Meanwhile, Sid's going waffling on in my ear'ole about some old bollocks but really the canister [the head]'s gonski. — J.J. Connolly, *Layer Cake*, p. 77, 2000

gonzo *noun*

cocaine *UK*

- — Angela Devlin, *Prison Patter*, p. 58, 1996

gonzo *adjective*

crazed; having a bizarre style *US*

Although coinage is credited to US journalist and author Bill Cardoso, close friend and partner in adventure with the late Hunter S. Thompson, the dust jacket to Cardoso's collected essays claims only that he is 'the writer who inspired Dr Hunter S. Thompson to coin the phrase "Gonzo journalism"'. Thompson first used the term in print and the term is irrevocably linked with him in the US.

- [T]here was no avoiding the stench of twisted humor that hovered around the idea of a gonzo journalist in the grip of a potentially terminal drug episode being invited to cover the National District Attorneys' Conference on Narcotics and Dangerous Drugs. — Hunter S. Thompson, *Fear and Loathing in Las Vegas*, p. 80, 1971
- This myth of street wisdom as the ultimate enlightenment is already a tired chic cliche of so-called gonzo journalism, and Wolfe, who both "created" and wrote this program, hasn't sparked new life into it. — *Washington Post*, p. B7, 10th January 1977
- — *American Speech*, p. 73–75, Spring 1983
- — Bill Cardoso, *The Maltese Sangweech*, 1984
- [H]e knew it was either tend to business or go gonzo[.] — James Ellroy, *Suicide Hill*, p. 695, 1986
- I mean, Hunter Thompson's whole "gonzo" oevre is right there in something like your "Twirling at Old Miss" and a few others. — Terry Southern, *Now Dig This*, p. 5, 1986
- The mother tried to save the kid, but the Reaper turned gonzo and knifed her in the stomach. — Joe Bob Briggs, *Joe Bob Goes to the Drive-In*, p. 13, 1987
- Soon enough, other porn directors caught on and his style of filming was dubbed "Gonzo." — Ana Loria, *1 2 3 Be A Porn Star!*, p. 119, 2000
- "She was gonzo," Lula said. "Made no sense at all. Never seen her so mad." — Janet Evanovich, *Seven Up*, p. 158, 2001
- Gonzo chef! Surly and sexy! Outlaw in the kitchen! — *The New York Times*, 8th January 2002

gonzoid *adjective*

crazed; having a bizarre style *US*

- Those gonzoid things are applicable to rock and roll. The intensity, the aggression, the uninhibitedness, the audacity, the cockiness, the sex, those are the things. — *Ask*, p. 41, 5th May 1979

Gonzo the great; gonzo *noun*

a state of drunkenness *UK*

Rhyming slang for 'a state', formed on a popular puppet character in television's *The Muppet Show*, from 1976, and subsequent Muppet films.

- You was in a right Gonzo you last night. — Ray Puxley, *Fresh Rabbit*, 1998

goo *noun*

1 any semi-liquid or viscous stuff, especially of an unknown origin *US, 1903*

- On the wall was more of his goo, with the plaster cracked from where the bullet entered. — Mickey Spillane, *I, The Jury*, p. 76, 1947
- And just how many of these chicks make enough to pay eight a month for a sleeping room and take all their meals in restaurants and buy clothes and lots of frigging goo to smear on the faces that the good Lord gave 'em... — Jim Thompson, *The Grifters*, p. 14, 1963
- Only the bombs of flaming hot goo entered the villages where the little people lived. — Oscar Zeta Acosta, *The Revolt of the Cockroach People*, p. 175, 1973

2 a look *IRELAND*

- Every couple of seconds when you thought you were going to get a goo at her knickers, she pulled down her skirt at the sides. — Roddy Doyle, *The Van*, p. 263, 1991

▸ **give with the goo**

to explain fully *CANADA*

Teen slang, reported by a Toronto newspaper in 1946, and reported as 'obsolescent or obsolete' by Douglas Leechman, 1959.

goob *noun*

1 a large facial blemish *US*

- — *Verbatim*, p. 280, May 1976

2 methcathinone *US, 1998*

- — US Office of National Drug Control Policy, *Drug Facts*, February 2003

goober *noun*

in the usage of young street racers, anyone who drives a car with an automatic transmission *US*

- The cop was a Goober, street slang for some fool who runs with an automatic transmission[.] — *Los Angeles Times*, p. A1, 6th June 2003

gooby *noun*
a gob of spit or phlegm *NEW ZEALAND*
- Goobie's? I had never seen it spelled. It meant spit. Sometimes it meant something worse, vis-a-vis nose. — David McGill, *The G'day Country*, p. 20, 1985

gooch *noun*
an inept, unaware person *US*
- — Warren Smith, *Warren's Smith's Authentic Dictionary of CB*, p. 41, 1976

gooch-eyed *adjective*
blind in one eye *US*
- I said, "I don't want to meet that gooch-eyed bitch. — Bruce Jackson, *In the Life*, p. 74, 1972

good *adjective*
▸ **come good**
of people, to rise to or surpass expectations; of things, to work out well or better than expected *UK, 1892*
- I did a bit of smoodging to the wife of the pub owner in town, and she came good. — John Cleary, *The Climate of Courage*, 1954
- Outsiders come good for Megson. — *The Guardian*, 2nd December 2002

▸ **have it good; have it so good**
to be possessed of (many) advantages *US, 1946*
- Let us be frank about it: most of our people have never had it so good. — Harold Macmillan, 20th July 1957

good *adverb*
▸ **make good**
in poker, to match another player's increased bet *US*
- — Albert H. Morehead, *The Complete Guide to Winning Poker*, p. 268, 1967

good and *adverb*
absolutely, completely, properly *UK, 1885*
- [T]he Israeli leader simply restated his position. His troops would leave when they were good and ready. — *The Guardian*, 13th April 2002

good and plenty *noun*
heroin *US*
Playing with a trademarked sweet confection name.
- — US Department of Justice, *Street Terms*, October 1994

good and proper *adverb*
to the greatest degree, completely *UK, 1928*
- Jimmy has been done good and proper and he's weighed up twenty-five years against appearing for the Queen. Against us. — Ted Lewis, *Jack Carter's Law*, p. 16, 1974

gooday
▷ see: G'DAY

good buddy *noun*
used as a term of address *US, 1956*
A term that enjoyed meteor-like ascendancy in popularity with the citizens' band radio craze that swept the US in 1976. Still used with jocular irony.
- — Wayne Floyd, *Jason's Authentic Dictionary of CB Slang*, p. 17, 1976

good butt *noun*
a marijuana cigarette *US, 1960*
- — Richard A. Spears, *The Slang and Jargon of Drugs and Drink*, p. 226, 1986
- — Mike Haskins, *Drugs*, p. 287, 2003

Good-bye Girls *nickname*
the 2004 US women's Olympic soccer team *UK*
An acknowledgement of the fact that many of the team members were playing in their final competition.
- The Goodbye Girls won. Of course they won. They had to win[.] — *Philadelphia Inquirer*, 27th August 2004

good-bye, kids
used as a humorous farewell *US*
On the final episode of the children's television classic *Howdy Doody Show* (NBC, 1947–60), these final words were uttered by Clarabell the Clown, who for 14 years had not spoken. Repeated with referential humour.

good-bye kiss *noun*
the repurchase at a premium of stock by a target company from the company attempting a takeover *US*
- — Kathleen Odean, *High Steppers, Fallen Angels, and Lollipops*, p. 117, 1988

good chute *noun*
a successful ejection of pilot and crew from a downed US aircraft *US*
- — Gregory Clark, *Words of the Vietnam War*, p. 203, 1990

good cop *noun*
in a pair of police, the partner who plays the sympathetic, understanding role during an interrogation *US*
- Rourke, who's got a very sweet face and disposition, plays the good cop but between the two, if I had to face it out or duke it out, I'd rather go up against O'Shea than Rourke any day of the week. — Robert Campbell, *In a Pig's Eye*, p. 23, 1991

good cop, bad cop *noun*
a police interrogation method in which one interrogator plays the role of a hardliner, while the other plays the role of a sympathetic friend *US*
- Bitsy looked at Canaan sidelong, suspicious that they were going to play the good-cop-bad-cop game on him. — Robert Campbell, *Sweet La-La Land*, p. 189, 1990

goodee!
▷ see: GOODY!

goodfella *noun*
a gangster *US*
Brought into mainstream use by the 1989 film *Goodfellas*.
- — Susie Dent, *The Language Report*, p. 146, 2003

good few *noun*
a fair number *US, 1828*
- There have been a good few wars in our time, but none like Iraq War Two. — *The Guardian*, 26th August 2003

good for *adjective*
having sufficient money or credit to pay the specified requirement *UK, 1937*

good for you!
used as a register of approval of something achieved or said by the person addressed or spoken of *UK, 1861*
- "Last week on my only day off I went out and bought a set of dumbbells." Good for him. — *The Guardian*, 21st August 2003

good fuck!
used for registering surprise *UK*
- Oh good fuck there's Kelly wavin at me. — Niall Griffiths, *Kelly + Victor*, p. 67, 2002

good fun *noun*
a great deal of fun *US*
Hawaiian youth usage.
- — Douglas Simonson, *Pidgin to da Max*, 1981

good giggles *noun*
▷ see: GIGGLES

good gravy!
used as an utterly unprofane exclamation *US*
- Good gravy, I've never seen anything that came close to this. — Iceberg Slim (Robert Beck), *The Naked Soul of Iceberg Slim*, p. 65–66, 1971
- Good gravy, why are people so boring? — Eugene Boe (Compiler), *The Wit & Wisdom of Archie Bunker*, p. 28, 1971

good grief!
used as an all-purpose expression of surprise, anger, disappointment, dismay *US, 1937*
Given great popularity in the 1960s by Charles Schultz's *Peanuts* comic strip.
- "Good Grief," cried Candy, in a very odd voice, "it's Daddy!" pushing her hands violently against the gardner's chest. "It's Daddy!" — Terry Southern, *Candy*, p. 41, 1958

good guts *noun*
correct and pertinent information *AUSTRALIA*
- Just givin' yer the good guts, that's all. Just lettin' yer know wot yer lettin' yerself in for. — Nino Culotta (John O'Grady), *They're A Weird Mob*, p. 61, 1957
- If I could get another pinpoint, then check my chart, I could give you the good guts[.] — W.R. Bennett, *Target Turin*, p. 53, 1962

good H *noun*
heroin *UK*
An elaboration of H (heroin), possibly playing on the conventional exclamation 'good heavens!'.
- — Robert Ashton, *This Is Heroin*, p. 206, 2002

good hands
used in farewell *BAHAMAS*
• —John A. Holm, *Dictionary of Bahamian English*, p. 90, 1982

good hitter *noun*
in pool, an excellent cue stick *US*
• "Hitter" is never used in reference to a poor stick, so the only time you'll hear someone speak of a "bad hitter" is in a predominantly black poolroom, where the expression is synonymous with "good hitter." —Steve Rushin, *Pool Cool*, p. 14, 1990

good horse *noun*
heroin *UK*
A playful elaboration of **HORSE** (heroin).
• —Robert Ashton, *This Is Heroin*, p. 206, 2002

goodie *noun*
1 a valuable possession *UK*
• Now it's about this point when normally you would be getting jacked of all your goodies. —Julian Johnson, *Urban Survival*, p. 21, 2003

2 something that is special and good *US*
• I'll go for the goodies, but I can't compete with my brains or family or education, so I do it with my balls. —Edwin Torres, *Carlito's Way*, p. 42, 1975
• Well, you can either take your goodies home and get high, or, you can stay at The Enterprise. —*New Jack City*, 1990
• Chester, this is your agent, how ya' doing – great. Looks like we got a goodie for you! —Odie Hawkins, *Lost Angeles*, p. 103, 1994

3 a person on the side of right, especially in works of fiction *US, 1873*
• The question uppermost in my mind was whether Tam and her monsters were baddies or goodies. —Martin Waddell, *Otley*, p. 29, 1966

4 extra parts or equipment for a car, enhancing its performance and/or embellishing its appearance *US, 1954*
• —Levette J. Davidson, *American Speech*, p. 305, 1956: 'Hot-rodders' jargon again'
• Well the engine compartment's filled with all chrome goodies / In my no-go showboat. —The Beach Boys, *No-Go Showboat*, 1963

5 in poker, a card that improves a hand *US*
• —Irv Roddy, *Friday Night Poker*, p. 218, 1961

6 an ambush or mechanical ambush *US*
• —Linda Reinberg, *In the Field*, p. 95, 1991

goodie and baddie; goodie *noun*
an Irish person *UK*
Rhyming slang for **PADDY**.
• —Ray Puxley, *Cockney Rabbit*, 1992

goodied up *adjective*
(used of a truck) embellished with lights, chrome and other accessories *US*
• —Montie Tak, *Truck Talk*, p. 75, 1971

goodies *noun*
1 the vagina *US, 1959*
• —Edith A. Folb, *runnin' down some lines*, p. 240, 1980

2 the female breasts *US*
• God you wouldn't believe it what some of them around the house, showing you the goodies, boy, some of them just asking for it. —Elmore Leonard, *The Big Bounce*, p. 111, 1969

good looks *noun*
employment documents *UK: SCOTLAND*
Rhyming slang for **BOOKS**.
• Carry on like this an ye'll be gettin yer good looks. —Michael Munro, *The Patter, Another Blast*, 1988

good man Friday *noun*
a pimp *US*
• But I would never take a girl if I knew she had a Good Man Friday, more commonly known as a pimp. —Polly Adler, *A House is Not a Home*, p. 132, 1953

goodness!; goodness me!
used as a mild expletive, or register of shock, surprise, etc *UK, 1704*

goodness gracious!; goodness gracious me!
used as a mild expletive, or register of shock, surprise, etc *UK, 1840*
In 1960 Peter Sellers, in the character of an Indian doctor, recorded a successful comedy duet entitled 'Goodness Gracious Me' with Sophia Loren (written by Herbert Kretzmer); the old exclamation soon had catchphrase status. In 1996, four British-Indian comedians, adopted the term as the ironic title for a radio comedy series, subsequently a television success. Now this term, the earliest recorded usage of which is by Charles Dickens, is considered by many to be a part of the stereotypical Indian vocabulary.
• Let's face it, we all knew what a woman's breasts looked like, so we didn't need anything like this to goodness gracious, she really was rather beautiful, wasn't she? —Christopher Brookmyre, *The Sacred Art of Stealing*, p. 362, 2002

goodness only knows!
used as a mild declaration of ignorance; used of something beyond your knowledge or experience *UK, 1819*
• Goodness only knows what morale must be like in the Leeds camp but, even if they can scrape together eleven players, I can't see them getting anything out of this one. —*The Guardian*, 31st January 2003

goodness' sake!; for goodness' sake!
used as a mild register of exasperation or impatience *UK, 1613*
The earliest use was in reference to the goodness of God.
• Yes, I know DH Lawrence was brought up there [Eastwood, Nottinghamshire], but for goodness sake spare me the blue-plaque nostalgia-industry blah. —*The Guardian*, 29th October 2003

Good night Chet. Good night David.
used as a humorous exchange of farewells *US*
The signature sign-off of television news anchors Chet Huntley and David Brinkley in the 1960s. Repeated with referential humour.

goodnight kiss *noun*
an act of urination; urination *UK*
Rhyming slang for **PISS**.
• —Ray Puxley, *Cockney Rabbit*, 1992

good-night nurse *noun*
a smoker's last cigarette of the night before going to sleep *US*
• —John Fahs, *Cigarette Confidential*, p. 301, 1996: 'Glossary'

goodnight, nurse
used for indicating the end or the finish of an activity *UK*
• A right to the head and then a cut up his ribs like a sword, and it was goodnight nurse, finito. Thanks for coming and fuck off! —Jimmy Stockin, *On The Cobbles*, p. 162, 2000

good numbers
(used in citizens' band radio transmissions) best wishes, regards *US*
• —*Complete CB Slang Dictionary*, 1976
• —Peter Chippindale, *The British CB Book*, p. 155, 1981

good-oh; good-o; goodoh; goodo *adjective*
very good; all right; well; in good health *AUSTRALIA, 1905*
• "Tastes good-oh, eh?" "I couldn't hurt the kid's feelings so I ate it, and it was goodo." —Duke Tritton, *Learn to talk Old Jack Lang*, p. 12, 1905
• GOODO – All right. —Gilbert H. Lawson, *A Dictionary of Australian Words and Terms*, 1924

good-oh; good-o; goodoh; goodo *adverb*
well; satisfactorily; all right *AUSTRALIA, 1920*
• They'll go goodo with the cackleberries. —D'Arcy Niland, *The Shiralee*, p. 33, 1955
• I got on good-ho with the lot of 'em. —Arthur Upfield, *Bony and the Mouse*, p. 51, 1959

good-oh!; good-o!; goodoh!; goodo!
1 terrific!, well done! *AUSTRALIA, 1904*
• Bloody good-oh!' roared the Electrical Officer. —John Wynnum, *Tar Dust*, p. 12, 1962

2 all right!, okay! *AUSTRALIA, 1918*
• 'Good-oh, Mrs. Grosnik,' replied Pierre. —Geoffrey Tolhurst, *Flat 4 Kings Cross*, p. 42, 1963
• 'Goodoh,' agreed Muldoon. —John Wynnum, *Jiggin' in the Riggin'*, p. 57, 1965

good oil *noun*
correct and pertinent information *AUSTRALIA, 1916*
• I don't know anyone in this dump who can give me the good oil. —Barry Humphries, *The Wonderful World of Barry McKenzie*, p. 3, 1968
• Mobil – A racecourse tipster who promises you that he has the good oil for the next race. —Taffy Davies, *Australian Nicknames*, 1977
• He started talking to them, and gave them the good oil on a whole lot of things. —Kel Richards, *The Aussie Bible*, p. 41, 2003

good old *adjective*

1 used as an affectionate (occasionally derisive) modifier of a term of reference or address *UK, 1821*
- That is close on a quarter of a billion in two years – most of it to good old Gordon Brown. — *The Times*, 3rd October 2003

2 familiar; used for expressing commendation or approval *UK, 1898*
- If you don't laugh, you've never enjoyed good old British pantomime. — *The Guardian*, 10th August 1989

good old boy *verb*

a white male from the southern US who embraces the values of his region and race *US*
- E.J. was a good old boy. — Clancy Sigal, *Going Away*, p. 83, 1961

good on you

used in farewell *US*
- — Anna Scotti and Paul Young, *Buzzwords: L.A. Freshspeak*, p. 64, 1997

good on you!

well done!, good for you! *AUSTRALIA, 1907*
- Good on yer, Lil. Everybody'll be with yer. — Vince Kelly, *The Bogeyman*, p. 40, 1956
- 'Know where it is? Top of Hawker Hill? Behind Blue Miller's place.' 'I know.' 'Good on you.' — Jean Brooks, *The Opal Witch*, p. 11, 1967
- 'If they do, they shut up about it.' 'Good on them. Why don't we do that?' — Beverley Farmer, *Milk*, p. 120, 1983
- With a big grin, and a voice that could rattle windows, she said: 'Good onya Mary! You beaut!'. — Kel Richaaards, *The Aussie Bible*, p. 10, 2003

good people *noun*

a person who can be trusted and counted on *US, 1891*
- — Hyman E. Goldin et al., *Dictionary of American Underworld Lingo*, p. 84, 1950
- That's all right, kid, you're good people. — Willard Motely, *Let No Man Write My Epitaph*, p. 243, 1958
- J.I. and Jukey say you're good people. — Morton Cooper, *High School Confidential*, p. 112, 1958
- God only knows what he's writin, but he's good people. — Hunter S. Thompson, *Hell's Angels*, p. 242, 1966
- Chilly tended to like and trust men who had solid reputations behind the walls, those who were known as good people, and it was two such men that he approached. — Malcolm Braly, *On the Yard*, p. 234, 1967
- Kesey was a stud who was just as tough as they [the Hells Angels] were. He had just been busted for marijuana, which certified him as Good People in the Angels' eyes. — Tom Wolfe, *The Electric Kool-Aid Acid Test*, p. 150, 1968
- Kenny could see that he was good people and a likable dude and he was smart and had a quick-witted way which made you laugh. — Emmett Grogan, *Ringolevio*, p. 136, 1972
- The guy he works for his good people. — Peter Maas, *Serpico*, p. 165, 1973
- She was good people. Her trouble was she was waitin' on some guy to solve her problem. — Edwin Torres, *After Hours*, p. 280, 1979
- I think you're good people – come on – let's go somewhere and light up the joint. — Herbert Huncke, *The Evening Sun Turned Crimson*, p. 73, 1980
- Understand, if Dick didn't assure me you're good people I'd just tell ya, none of your fuckin' business. — *True Romance*, 1993

good plan!

used as a humorous expression of approval *US*
- — Connie Eble (Editor), *UNC-CH Campus Slang*, p. 3, Fall 1981

goods *noun*

1 the genuine article, the real thing; exactly who or what is required *US, 1899*
- Silly stunts prove you're The Goods. — Ann Barr and Peter York, *The Official Sloane Ranger Handbook*, p. 95, 1982
- [I]f Mel hadn't of come across with the goods when she did. — Danny King, *The Burglar Diaries*, p. 29, 2001
- [T]he party has delivered the goods to the vast majority of Chinese people and will continue to do so. — *The Guardian*, 11th November 2002
- [H]uge pressure was put on the intelligence agencies [...] to come up with the goods required to start a war[.] — *The Observer*, 8th June 2003

2 positive evidence of guilt *US, 1900*
- They had the goods on me, all right, and there was nothing I could do about it. — Clancy Sigal, *Going Away*, p. 214, 1961
- He's got the goods on me!. — Angela Devlin, *Prison Patter*, p. 58, 1996

3 any drug *US*
- — Eugene Landy, *The Underground Dictionary*, p. 91, 1971

4 yourself, especially areas of intimate contact *UK*
- Hey, get your paws off the goods, pal. — Ian Pattison, *Rab C. Nesbitt*, 1988

▸ the goods

an attractive person *UK*
- She's the goods. — Beale, 1984

good shake *noun*

▷ see: EVEN SHAKE

good ship venus; good ship *noun*

the penis *UK*

Rhyming slang.
- — Ray Puxley, *Cockney Rabbit*, 1992

good show!; jolly good show!

used as an expression of delight *UK, 1940*
- A Burberry fashion PR event brought on a gruelling attack of bad Sloane Ranger accents – "Lashings of lemonade!"; "Jolly good show!", etc. — *Listener (New Zealand)*, 9th April 2004

good sort *noun*

a sexually attractive woman *AUSTRALIA, 1944*
- A bit of beer, eh? A few good sorts? Meet a few of your mates? — Eric Lambert, *The Veterans*, p. 65, 1954
- That he could hang off until he went back to Erica and get sweet again with the good sort he had known there. — Robert S. Close, *With Hooves of Brass*, p. 113, 1961
- They say that Ray's brains are in his balls and that young stud tries on every good sort that comes into the place. — Clive Galea, *Slipper*, p. 115, 1988
- Hey while I'm on the subject of good sorts. How's your sister these days? — Robert G. Barrett, *Davo's Little Something*, p. 26, 1992
- She's often a 'good sort', but maybe she's a bit of a 'slut'. 'You can tell if she wants a start,' the Sydney-based rugby league player said. — *Sydney Morning Herald*, 22nd March 2003

good stuff *noun*

among criminals, a respected criminal *UK*
- — Dave Courtney, *Dodgy Dave's Little Black Book*, p. 9, 2001

good style *adverb*

excellently *UK*
- There's all sorts of Judies in there [...] all hanging round the lads, showing out for them good style. — Kevin Sampson, *Outlaws*, p. 249, 2001

good thing *noun*

1 a lucrative opportunity *AUSTRALIA*
- 'There's always a good thing in machinery spares.' Toggle gave a knowing wink. — John Wynnum, *Tar Dust*, p. 25, 1962

2 a sucker; someone who is easily tricked *US, 1909*
- "Man," Cowboy said, "didn't I just see you with a bottle 'bout an hour ago? What you think I am – a good thing or somethin'?" — Nathan Heard, *Howard Street*, p. 53, 1968

3 a horse that is tipped to win *AUSTRALIA, 1877*
- — David W. Maurer, *Argot of the Racetrack*, p. 32, 1951
- How come the stable backed your mount, boy, and your friends weren't told he was a damn good thing? — Wilda Moxham, *The Apprentice*, p. 78, 1969

4 a good thing *US*

Made slang by attitude and tone. A signature line of Martha Stewart on her television show *Martha Stewart Living Television*, first aired in 1993. Repeated with referential humour.

▸ like a good thing

in an active, pleasing or exciting way *IRELAND*
- [A]nd take another slug out of me cup of hooch. It's murder. I'm buzzing like a good thing here[.] — Paul Howard, *The Joy*, p. 153, 1996

good thinking!

used as a register of approval for an excellent idea or good suggestion, or ironically in the case of a bad or obvious suggestion *UK, 1968*

good time *noun*

1 a period of incarceration that does not destroy the prisoner's spirit *US*
- In the Joint I always get in top shape; no coke, no pot, no pussy, so you work out. I always do good time. — Edwin Torres, *Carlito's Way*, p. 41, 1975

2 a reduction of a prison sentence for good behaviour in jail *US*
- "I've already taken sixty days of your good-time, Monroe," he said. — Chester Himes, *Cast the First Stone*, p. 298, 1952
- Now I never got in no fights, 'cause on construction you could box all you wanted to, and wouldn't lose no good time. — Henry Williamson, *Hustler!*, p. 70, 1965
- Sonja is short – I'd be very drugged if she lost goodtime about some dyke production. — Clarence Cooper Jr, *The Farm*, p. 169, 1967
- I was released after twenty-one months. I got three months "good time" for good conduct. — Iceberg Slim (Robert Beck), *Pimp*, p. 75, 1969

- You'll get solitary confinement, and you'll lose your good time, more than eight years, and your last chances for parole. —Red Rudensky, *The Gonif*, p. 17, 1970
- I got a pencil and paper down and figured my good time, and I wouldn't have but about two and a half years to do if I can get it all back. —Bruce Jackson, *In the Life*, p. 322, 1972

3 time that counts towards a soldier's military commitment *US*

- It's considered good time if you are in a medical facility even if you spend your whole tour there – the Army simply counts it as Vietnam time. —Ronald J. Glasser, *365 Days*, p. 7, 1971

▸ **the original good time that was had by all**

used of a sexually promiscuous woman *US, 1981*

A twist of the clichéd catchphrase 'a good time was had by all', coined by US film actress Bette Davis, 1908–89. The original catchphrase is credited to poet Stevie Smith, who acquired it for use as a title from the reportage of parish magazines.

good-time house *noun*

an establishment that sells alcohol illegally, especially by the drink *US*

- Shot-house operators run informal (and illegal) taverns in their own homes (shot-house operators are often women). The houses go by other names too; gold mine, good-time house, blind tiger, shine parlor, or juicejoint. —Burgess Laughlin, *Job Opportunities in the Black Market*, p. 10–9, 1978

good to go *adjective*

prepared to start a mission *US*

Airborne slang in Vietnam, quickly absorbed into the non-military mainstream.

- —Linda Reinberg, *In the Field*, p. 95, 1991
- —Connie Eble (Editor), *UNC-CH Campus Slang*, p. 3, Fall 1993

good to her mother *adjective*

▷ see: FOND OF HER MOTHER

good to me!

used for expressing self-praise *US*

- —Connie Eble (Editor), *UNC-CH Campus Slang*, October 1972

good wood *noun*

a dependable, trustworthy white prisoner *US*

Derived from PECKERWOOD.

- —James Harris, *A Convict's Dictionary*, p. 33, 1989

goody!; goodee!

used as an expression of delight *UK, 1796*

Childish; often reduplicated in excitement.

- So you met someone who set you back on your heels / Goody, goody / You met someone and now you know how it feels / Goody, goody —Frankie Lymon & The Teenagers, *Goody, Goody*, 1957
- "Would you like something to drink?" "Oh, goodee," Livvy slips into her baby talk and claps her hands[.] —Glen Huser, *Touch of the Clown*, p. 32, 1999

goody drawer *noun*

any drawer in a bedroom containing contraceptives, lubricants or sex toys *US*

- —Amy Sohn, *Sex and the City*, p. 155, 2002

goody-goody *noun*

1 an excessively good person *UK, 1871*

Usually uttered with some degree of derision.

- Because you shouldn't get mad. (Says the goody-goody). —Elmore Leonard, *Switch*, p. 56, 1978
- While preserving a goodie goodie image I frequently did a whole bunch of stuff. —Odie Hawkins, *Scars and Memories*, p. 154, 1987

2 marijuana *UK*

From the exclamation of delight.

- —Mike Haskins, *Drugs*, p. 287, 2003

goody-goody *adjective*

(of children) too well-behaved; (of adults) hypocritically or sentimentally pious *UK, 1871*

- They're not goody-goody Willies, but they stick to their jobs, and they all seem to be getting somewhere. —James T. Farrell, *Saturday Night*, p. 13, 1947
- To us, those goody-goody people who worked shitty jobs for bum paychecks, who took the subway to work every day and worried about their bills, were dead. —*Goodfellas*, 1990
- A goody-goody kid tries to deliver a message to the headmaster but runs into the school herberts[.] —Martin King and Martin Knight, *The Naughty Nineties*, p. 150, 1999

goody gumdrops; goody goody gumdrops; goody gumdrop

used as an expression of delight; often ironic in later use *UK, 1959*

- —The 1910 Fruitgum Company, *Goody Goody Gumdrops*, 1969
- Around closing time, I nodded at Azar. "Well, goody gumdrop," he said. —Tim O'Brien, *The Things They Carried*, p. 206, 1990
- What's this? Goody gumdrops – a recess while Joe Dirtbag buys time to find a conveyance form that every person in the courtroom knows doesn't exist. —Douglas Coupland, *Hey Nostradamus!*, p. 200, 2003

goody two-shoes *noun*

a person of excessive virtue *US, 1934*

- Oh, stop with the goodytwoshoes bit. It's a war out there. —Seth Morgan, *Homeboy*, p. 108, 1990
- Ramona Spelling in high school was a traditional version of Miss Goodie Two Shoes. —Odie Hawkins, *Black Chicago*, p. 139, 1992
- "Good," said Sheeni. "I hoped you'd say that. I was worried you might be a bit of a Goody Two-Shoes." "Hardly," I said. "I'm in a state of permanent open revolt around here." —C.D. Payne, *Youth in Revolt*, p. 87, 1993
- Are you shitting me – Mr. Good Two Shoes? He was like a fucking eagle scout. —*Something About Mary*, 1998
- Don't play the goody-two-shoes with me, Mr Slag. I know where your willy's been. —Jenny Eclair, *Camberwell Beauty*, p. 346, 2000

gooey *noun*

in computing, a graphic user interface (GUI) such as windows and icons *US*

- —Steven Daly and Nalthaniel Wice, *alt.culture*, p. 140, 1995

gooey *adjective*

1 viscous or semi-viscous *US, 1903*

- TILLEY: It so happens I haven't been to this restaurant before. I don't know how they do their eggs. . . If they're over easy and they're gooey, I'm not happy with it. —*Tin Men*, 1987
- These buds are the gooiest, most resin-soaked things I've ever seen[.] —Brian Preston, *Pot Planet*, p. 96, 2002

2 excessively sentimental *UK, 1935*

- Nobody goes all gooey over a character like me[.] —Raymond Chandler, *Playback*, p. 105, 1958
- Both were of the gooey sentimental type, dripping with sickly sweetness, but the latter was a real dilly. —Jim Thompson, *The Grifters*, p. 32, 1963

gooey ball *noun*

any sticky confection made with marijuana or hashish *US*

- —Rick Ayers (Editor), *Slang Dictionary*, p. 10, 2001

gooey louey *noun*

a second lieutenant in the US Army *US*

- —Linda Reinberg, *In the Field*, p. 95, 1991

goof *noun*

1 an alcoholic beverage *US, 1964*

Found only in Ontario, this term may have derived from GOOFBALL (a barbiturate drug).

- "Here comes that old juicehead, Tiger, luggin a jug of goof." ["his paper-bagged bottle of $1.40 4 Aces port"]. "What's that you've got, your weekend supply of goof?" ["a coupla bottles of sherry I got for old Wilbur, my star boarder."] —Hugh Garner, *The Intruders*, p. 1, 3–25, 1976

2 a barbiturate *US, 1944*

An abbreviation of GOOFBALL.

- Hell, no, man, none of that goof fo rme! —John Clellon Holmes, *Go*, p. 101, 1952
- People's first introduction to things like goofs and speed was by way of newspapers. —Herbert Huncke, *Guilty of Everything*, p. 9, 1990

3 a frequent marijuana smoker *US*

- —Hyman E. Goldin et al., *Dictionary of American Underworld Lingo*, p. 84, 1950

4 a silly, soft or stupid person *US, 1916*

- It was just bad look. He'd simply caught a goof, and goofs couldn't be figured. —Jim Thompson, *The Grifters*, p. 7, 1963

5 a joke, a prank *US, 1958*

- Is it you & Tiny's personal goof, or really what you all want? —*The Berkeley Barb*, p. 2, 19th November 1965
- I went to my room and decided to call a Trustee, more for a goof. —James Simon Kunen, *The Strawberry Statement*, p. 164, 1968

6 a swim *SOUTH AFRICA*

- Let's go for a goof. —*Surfrikan Slang*, 2004

goof *verb*

1 to botch, to ruin *US*

- But we goofed our stuff! — Hal Ellson, *The Golden Spike*, p. 32, 1952
- [T]he cool little pig goofed altogether and at the last possible minute built himself a real blue-lights shack out of clarinet reeds and scotch tape. — Steve Allen, *Bop Fables*, p. 21, 1955
- Whereas if you goof (the ugliest word in Hip), if you lapse back into being a frightened stupid child, or if you flip, if you lose your control[.] — Norman Mailer, *Advertisements for Myself*, p. 351, 1957
- Or maybe it started when he goofed on the Bertha Travis set-up[.] — Clarence Cooper Jr, *The Scene*, p. 21, 1960
- "The gig wasn't that easy to put together," Zaida said. "Red, promise me you won't goof it, this time." — Ross Russell, *The Sound*, p. 44, 1961
- She can rattle a pimp into goofing his whole game. — Iceberg Slim (Robert Beck), *Pimp*, p. 159, 1969

2 to tease, to joke *US, 1931*

- It never occurs to you that life is serious and there are people trying to make something decent out of it instead of just goofing all the time. — Jack Kerouac, *On the Road*, p. 194, 1957
- Yo Thumper, man, I was goofin', I was goofin'. — Richard Price, *Clockers*, p. 36, 1992

3 to give yourself away to the police *UK*

- — Home Office, *Glossary of Terms and Slang Common in Penal Establishments*, 1978

4 to spoil an injection of a narcotic, during either preparation or application *UK*

- — Home Office, *Glossary of Terms and Slang Common in Penal Establishments*, 1978

5 to smoke marijuana *US*

- — William D. Alsever, *Glossary for the Establishment and Other Uptight People*, p. 20, December 1970

6 to enter what appears to be a near coma as a result of drug intoxication *US, 1951*

- He was, in the junkies' word, "goofing." — James Mills, *The Panic in Needle Park*, p. 27, 1966
- I was goofing so bad, I couldn't hold my head up and just kept going into my nod. — Piri Thomas, *Down These Mean Streets*, p. 205, 1967

goof around *verb*

to pass time enjoyably but unproductively *US, 1931*

- Dean and I goofed around San Francisco in this manner until I got my next GI check and got ready to go back home. — Jack Kerouac, *On the Road*, p. 177, 1957
- [W]e had time to go over to the drugstore in the shopping center and goof around. — S.E. Hinton, *The Outsiders*, p. 20, 1967
- MEL GIBSON Said he was goofing around all his life anyway, so he thought he might as well get paid for it. — Aubrey Dillon-Malone, *I Was a Fugitive from a Hollywood Trivia Factory*, p. 4, 1999

goofball *noun*

1 a barbiturate used for non-medicinal purposes *US, 1939*

- Much more potent is a sleeping pill or "goofball" dissolved in a glass of beer. — Jack Lait and Lee Mortimer, *Chicago Confidential*, p. 148, 1950
- Nembutals are the prostitutes' favorite. Among initiates they are known as goof balls, or nemmies. — Jack Lait and Lee Mortimer, *Washington Confidential*, p. 117, 1951
- [O]f course I can't sleep, I want free goofballs. — Jack Kerouac, *Letter to Neal Cassady*, p. 325, 31st August 1951
- Lots of jive and goofballs, maybe a couple caps of Horse. — George Mandel, *Flee the Angry Strangers*, p. 56, 1952
- But he was always high on something – weed, benzedrine, or knocked out of his mind on "goof balls." — William Burroughs, *Junkie*, p. 26, 1953
- He gave me the address of a guy that peddles goof balls, though, but kee-rist, who wants to get hungup that way? — John Clellon Holmes, *Go*, p. 101, 1953
- Five-grain amytal. Goofballs. Tricky stuff. — Jim Thompson, *Savage Night*, p. 39, 1953
- [W]e have a pretty complete exhibit of the little pills downtown. Bluejays, redbirds, yellow jackets, goofballs, and all the rest of the list. — Raymond Chandler, *The Long Goodbye*, p. 230, 1953
- That night Marylou took everything in the books; she took tea, goofballs, benny, liquor, and even asked Old Bull for a shot of M[.] — Jack Kerouac, *On the Road*, p. 148, 1957
- "Don't goof with no goof-balls," Juan remembered Seldom Seen telling him once. "You goof with them and pretty soon you're riding the Horse." — Willard Motley, *Let No Man Write My Epitaph*, p. 87, 1958
- I've got some goofballs and we can get a bottle of cough syrup. — Alexander Trocchi, *Cain's Book*, p. 79, 1960
- Maybe if I picked up some goof balls from that drugstore? — Ross Russell, *The Sound*, p. 239, 1961
- He was high on barbiturates, goofballs, GB's. — James Mills, *The Panic in Needle Park*, p. 27, 1966
- "Doc," Wanger said. "Look, Doc, how about a goofball?" — Malcolm Braly, *On the Yard*, p. 59, 1967
- I encountered a young man named Joe who had been introduced to me as a connection for practically anything – pot, goofballs, amphetamine pills of various kinds and heroin. — Herbert Huncke, *The Evening Sun Turned Crimson*, p. 131, 1980

2 a mixture of heroin and cocaine *US, 1969*

- — Robert Ashton, *This Is Heroin*, p. 209, 2002
- — Mike Haskins, *Drugs*, p. 293, 2003

3 a habitual smoker of marijuana *SOUTH AFRICA*

- Pete is such a goofball. He's always pulling goofed actions — *Surfrikan Slang*, 2004

4 a silly and/or dim-witted person *US, 1944*

- Hey, goofball, are you listening to me? — Robert Gover, *Poorboy at the Party*, p. 91, 1966
- He had pinned his grandiose hope of redemption on his last homemade bomb, only to see it claim the wrong victim, some goofball news reporter. — Carl Hiaasen, *Tourist Season*, p. 294, 1986

goof butt; goof-butt; goofy butt *noun*

a marijuana cigarette *US, 1938*

A combination of GOOF (a marijuana smoker) and BUTT (a cigarette).

- And marijuana has legal standing, so the next time some fifteen-year-old sucks a goof butt and walks through a glass patio slider, me and the other old hippie selling nickel bags are defendants in a gigantic class-action lawsuit[.] — Mike Gray, *Busted*, p. 194, 2002
- — Mike Haskins, *Drugs*, p. 291, 2003

goofed; goofed up; goofed-up *adjective*

1 wrong *US*

- Any sound concept of living is goofed-up. — George Mandel, *Flee the Angry Strangers*, p. 3, 1952

2 experiencing the effects of drugs, especially barbiturates or marijuana; drunk *US, 1944*

- I guess I just wanted them for myself to get goofed a little. — Hal Ellson, *Duke*, p. 3, 1949
- — William D. Alsever, *Glossary for the Establishment and Other Uptight People*, December 1970
- [T]hese guys ain't gay, they're goofed up[.] — Lester Bangs, *Psychotic Reactions and Carburetor Dung*, p. 101, 1972
- — Home Office, *Glossary of Terms and Slang Common in Penal Establishments*, 1978

goofer *noun*

1 a barbiturate capsule, especially glutethimide *US, 1969*

- — Walter L. Way, *The Drug Scene: Help or Hang-up?*, p. 109, 1977
- — Richard A. Spears, *The Slang and Jargon of Drugs and Drink*, p. 227, 1986
- — Mike Haskins, *Drugs*, p. 282, 2003

2 someone who toys with recreational drugs *UK, 1998*

3 a person who regularly uses drugs in pill form *US, 1952*

- — Eugene Landy, *The Underground Dictionary*, p. 92, 1971

4 a homosexual male prostitute who assumes the active role in sex *US, 1941*

- — G. Legman, *The Language of Homosexuality*, p. 1167, 1941
- — *Male Swinger Number 3*, p. 45, 1981: 'The complete gay dictionary'

goofer dust *noun*

a barbiturate *US*

- And that blood was loaded with the goofer dust. — Jim Thompson, *The Nothing Man*, p. 282, 1954

go off *verb*

1 to happen, occur *UK, 1804*

- On such an evening, you know the classes were great, you feel elated the presentations went off as planned. — *The Guardian*, 29th January 2002

2 of a fight, to happen, to start *UK*

- Message to all Chelsea fans! Millwall at Parsons Green and it's going off. — Martin King and Martin Knight, *The Naughty Nineties*, p. 129, 1999
- "Get much trouble here?" we asked, incredulous. "Yeah, it goes off all the time 'ere, mate," came the disinterested reply. — Wayne Anthony, *Spanish Highs*, p. 3, 1999
- Jeez, it's all going off! — *Ministry*, p. 7, October 2002

3 to vehemently display anger *AUSTRALIA*

- 'Debbie! Sue!' Cheryl called out to us. 'Come here! What'd Bishop say? Did he go off?' she asked us. — Kathy Lette and Carey Gabrielle, *Puberty Blues*, p. 16, 1979
- — Ivor Limb, *Footy's No Joke!*, p. 55, 1986
- And mum goes right off at us. — Kylie Mole (Maryanne Fahey), *My Diary*, p. 40, 1988

4 to cease to like something or someone *UK, 1934*

- I think she just went off people. She didn't like them in our life, judging her life. — *The Guardian*, 20th May 2001

5 to fall asleep *UK, 1887*
- [S]he patted his fingers, let air out through her mouth, and went off to sleep thinking about blasting caps[.] — *The Guardian*, 2nd August 2000

6 to ejaculate *UK, 1866*
- One man who wanted to go off using my rear end, when I told him I would not allow this, sneered, "You think it's a perversion, don't you?" — Sara Harris, *The Lords of Hell*, p. 72, 1967

7 to give birth *AUSTRALIA*
- I had her dug out, and some forming up, and Steve comes to me an' says his missus is about ready to go off, an' would I keep an eye on her in case she had to go while he was at work. — John O'Grady, *Aussie Etiket*, p. 14, 1971

8 to turn out; to come off *AUSTRALIA, 1867*
- The breakfast went off good too. — Frank Hardy, *Hardy's People*, p. 198, 1986

9 to perform brilliantly *AUSTRALIA*
- 'Shit, she went off.' 'That's hot.' — Kathy Lette, *Girls' Night Out*, p. 195, 1987

10 to behave extravagantly; to go all out *AUSTRALIA*
- So anyway, anniversary night and I've gone off. The sensational dinner, booked a swanky hotel and had a blinder. — Paul Vautin, *Turn It Up!*, p. 126, 1995

11 to defecate *TRINIDAD AND TOBAGO, 1973*
- — Lise Winer, *Dictionary of the English/Creole of Trinidad & Tobago*, 2003

12 to pass peak condition; to deteriorate in freshness *UK*
- I'd like to go [die] just when I'm going off, you know what I mean, when the crowd's catching me up[.] — Paul E Willis, *Profane Culture*, p. 27, 1978

13 to be raided by authorities *AUSTRALIA, 1941*
- [T]he S.P. man and the man or woman who sells a few drinks under the lap are fair game for the pimp. The one's who don't go off have to pay. — Vince Kelly, *The Bogeyman*, p. 99, 1956
- The Sari Club, however, goes off. — *Sun-Herald (Sunday Life)*, p. 10, 17th May 1998

14 to make a noise *UK*
An extension of 'go off' (to start).
- "[L]ounging around on a farm listening to the cows go off." "Go off where?" "Go off. You know, like car alarms." — Melanie McGrath, *Hard, Soft & Wet*, p. 97, 1998

15 (of a party or nightclub venue) to be thoroughly exciting and enjoyable *AUSTRALIA, 1993*

16 (of a prize) to be awarded *AUSTRALIA*
- Three passes at the target and twenty points to qualify for the finals with big cash prizes and a brand new superseded Toyota sedan to go off. — Alexander Buzo, *The Roy Murphy Show*, p. 112, 1970

17 (of a woman) to engage in sexual intercourse *AUSTRALIA*
- Oh, I know the one you mean. She's last year's number, worth getting on to, too. She likes to go off, but only if her back's on damp wet sand. — Len Riley, *The Kings Cross Racket*, p. 34, 1967
- Hey, I tell you what I do remember, the night Susan went off. — Alexander Buzo, *Rooted*, p. 85, 1969

18 in motor racing, to suffer a diminution of performance, either because of a handling problem or driver fatigue *US*
- — Don Alexander, *The Racer's Dictionary*, p. 28, 1980

19 (of a racehorse whose true abilities have been kept secret) to be raced to win *AUSTRALIA, 1936*
- I had been touting this thing for months, and here it was ready to 'go off', and what hope had I of being in at the kill? — James Holledge, *The Great Australian Gamble*, p. 41, 1966

go off on one *verb*
to lose your temper *UK*
- Russell was finding it difficult to bite his tongue when Ron went off on one. — Greg Williams, *Diamond Geezers*, p. 74, 1997

goofies *noun*
1 a swimming bath *SOUTH AFRICA, 1970*
Children's slang.
- — Penny Silva, *A Dictionary of South African English*, 1996

2 LSD *US*
- — Don R. McCreary (Editor), *Dawg Speak*, 2001

goof-off *noun*
a lazy person *US, 1945*
- Somewhere along the line, the pack decided that Al Gore was a sanctimonious, graspy exaggerator running against a likeable if dim-witted goof-off. — Al Franken, *Lies*, p. 40, 2003

goof off *verb*
to waste time, to idle *US, 1943*
- Honey, you can sit the next set out in the back yard if you promise not to goof off and get lost. — Steve Allen, *Bop Fables*, p. 4, 1955
- I stay loose. I hit the flicks, goof off a little, quaff a few brews with the boys. — Max Shulman, *Guided Tour of Campus Humor*, p. 105, 1955
- "Yes, I think so," said the dark-haired girl, then added with a frown: "Unless they're goofing off. We've had a lot of goofing off lately – especially among the boys." — Terry Southern, *Candy*, p. 179, 1958
- The doctors said I was a malingerer. I said I only liked regular sex. Then I found out they meant I was goofin' off. Okay. — Edwin Torres, *After Hours*, p. 360, 1979
- You could go down on the corner and pick up on any of those Puerto Rican kids you've seen goofing off and they could give you a rundown on that scene that would put me to shame. — Herbert Huncke, *Guilty of Everything*, p. 9, 1990

goof on *verb*
to joke about, to make fun of *US, 1956*
- I first started goofing on Michael Jackson when he started showing up in the tabloids[.] — Howard Stern, *Miss America*, p. 61, 1995

goof-up *noun*
a blunder, an error of judgement *US, 1956*
- I made a goof-up. She took it the wrong way. — Richard Francis, *The Rialto*, p. 96, 1999

goofus *noun*
1 a fool *US, 1917*
- [H]er mother and goofus of a 7th grade brother[.] — Lester Bangs, *Psychotic Reactions and Carburetor Dung*, p. 59, 1971

2 in circus and carnival usage, an extremely gullible customer who demonstrates great potential as a victim *US*
- — Don Wilmeth, *The Language of American Popular Entertainment*, p. 116, 1981

goofy *noun*
1 a fool, especially as a form of address *UK*
Goofy is the name of the foolish dog in Walt Disney's Mickey Mouse cartoons.
- You should hear me playing the solo in Saturday Night at the Duckpond. No, goofy, it's a song not a pub. — Jonathan Aitken, *The Young Meteors*, 1967

2 a skateboarder who skates with the right foot to the front *UK*
- — Fabrice le Mao, *Skateboarding*, p. 91, 2004

goofy *adjective*
gawky, clumsy, foolish, eccentric *US, 1919*
- In high school he had planned to be one, but most guys thought that artists were goofy, and he couldn't stand being laughed at as an artist. — James T. Farrell, *Saturday Night*, p. 25, 1947
- I'd like to check around Portland and Hood River and The Dalles to see if there's any of the guys I used to know back in the village who haven't drunk themselves goofy. — Ken Kesey, *One Flew Over the Cuckoo's Nest*, p. 311, 1962
- That's what makes you so goofy, banging her so much. — Jim Thompson, *Pop. 1280*, p. 191, 1964
- He was sitting on a bench in the park filming anyone goofy who walked by. — Anka Radakovich, *The Wild Girls Club*, p. 95, 1994
- There is a seriously goofy man behind this. — *As Good As It Gets*, 1997
- "I'm the oldest and my mom and dad are like these goofy kids, so I haven't had much experience with that," he said. — Francesca Lia Block, *I Was a Teenage Fairy*, p. 95, 1998
- Mooner is like a goofy stray kitten[.] — Janet Evanovich, *Seven Up*, p. 25, 2001

-goofy *suffix*
mentally imbalanced as a result of the precedent activity *US*
- I said, "Blue, what did you mean about Dirty Red going con goofy?" — Iceberg Slim (Robert Beck), *Trick Baby*, p. 125, 1969

goofy butt *noun*
▷ see: GOOF BUTT

goofy foot *noun*
a surfer who surfs with the right foot forward *AUSTRALIA, 1962*
Most surfers surf with their left foot forward.
- — Grant W. Kuhns, *On Surfing*, p. 117, 1963
- — *Paradise of the Pacific*, p. 27, October 1963
- I'm Bill Kilgore. I'm a goofy foot. — *Apocalypse Now*, 1979

goofy footed *adjective*
in foot-propelled scootering, used of someone who rides with the left foot behind the right *UK*
From surfing.
- — Ben Sharpe, *Scooter Crazy*, p. 40, 2000

goofy's *noun*
LSD *UK*
- —Mike Haskins, *Drugs*, p. 285, 2003

goog *noun*
an egg *AUSTRALIA, 1941*
Shortening of **GOOGIE**.
- —Jim Ramsay, *Cop It Sweet!*, p. 41, 1977
- I can't remember if you use a goog or not. Maybe you do.—Barry Dickins, *What the Dickins*, p. 42, 1985

googan *noun*
in pool, someone who plays for fun *US*
- —Steve Rushin, *Pool Cool*, p. 14, 1990

googie *noun*
an egg *AUSTRALIA, 1903*
From Gaelic.
- Hey, Beryl, I said, take a look at this. This googie's empty.—Barry Humphries, *A Nice Night's Entertainment*, p. 113, 1968
- —Barry Humphries, *A Nice Night's Entertainment*, p. 207, 1981
- —Harry Orsman and Des Hurley, *The Beaut Little Book of New Zealand Slang*, 1994

google; google hut *noun*
an egg-shaped, fibreglass field hut *ANTARCTICA, 1992*
- —Bernadette Hince, *The Antarctic Dictionary*, p. 149, 2000

google *verb*
to search for something on the Internet by means of a search engine; to check a person's credentials by investigating websites that contain that person's name *US*
A generic use of Google™ (a leading Internet search engine).
- Eggers is owner of probably the most Googled name out there right now.—*Dener Post*, p. L-02, 10th September 2000
- The most popular application is to Google a potential date.—*Telegraph Herald (Dubuqe, Iowa)*, p. E1, 14th January 2001

Google bomb *noun*
an effort to create a great number of Internet pages with links to a specific website so that it achieves a position near the top of a *Google* search directory for seemingly unrelated words *US*
Google™ is an Internet search engine.
- Mathes' original Google Bomb remains the classic of the genre. It's pretty funny to see your friend come up in Google as the No. 1 talentless hack in the whole world.—*Slate Magazine*, 23rd March 2002
- The first Google bomb was created by Adam Mathes in 2001. He exploited Google's page ranking system to return a friend's website when the words "talentless hack" were used as a search term [...] the Google bomb found its target.—*The Guardian*, 10th July 2003

Google bombing *noun*
the deliberate creation of a great number of Internet pages with links to a specific website with an intent that the website achieves a position near the top of a *Google* search directory for seemingly unrelated words *US*
Google™ is an Internet search engine.
- Mathes even invented a name for his joke: Google Bombing.—*Slate Magazine*, 23rd March 2002
- [T]he widely publicised cases of "Google bombing". One example: if you search for "miserable failure", the first result is: Biography of President George W Bush.—*The Guardian*, 1st April 2004

google box *noun*
television *NEW ZEALAND*
- —Louis S. Leland, *A Personal Kiwi-Yankee Dictionary*, p. 47, 1984

googlewhack *noun*
among Internet users, the result of a search for any webpage that, uniquely, contains a combination of two randomly chosen words and is therefore indexed by the search-engine *Google* as '1 of 1' *US, 2002*
- It started when I received an e-mail from a stranger telling me that I was a googlewhack. I didn't know what a googlewhack was. Now I do.—Dave Gorman on his stageshow, *Dave Gorman's Googlewhack Adventure*, 2003

googlewhack *verb*
among Internet users, to search for any webpage that, uniquely, contains a combination of two randomly chosen words and is therefore indexed by the search-engine *Google* as '1 of 1' *US*
A back-formation from **GOOGLEWHACKING**.
- Have you Googlewhacked lately?—Janet Kornblum, *USA Today*, 30th January 2002

googlewhacking *noun*
among Internet users, a popular craze for searching for any webpage that, uniquely, contains a combination of two randomly chosen words and is therefore indexed by the search-engine *Google* as '1 of 1' *US, 2002*
Coinage is credited to Gary Stock, Chief Innovation Officer and Technical Compass of a company in Kalamazoo, Michigan, who discovered and named this 'compelling' time-wasting activity.

googly *noun*
an awkward question *AUSTRALIA, 1942*
A figurative use of the cricketing sense.

goo-goo eyes *noun*
romantic glances *US, 1897*
- [T]he oldest of the 8 urchins, a good-looking blonde about 17 or so has discontinued the goo-goo eyes & has gone to the show with boy friend[.]—Neal Cassady, *The First Third*, p. 213, 1965

googs *noun*
in circus and carnival usage, eyeglasses *US, 1924*
A corruption of 'goggles'.
- —Joe McKennon, *Circus Lingo*, p. 40, 1980
- —Don Wilmeth, *The Language of American Popular Entertainment*, p. 116, 1981

goo guard *noun*
on a truck, a mudflap *US*
- —Montie Tak, *Truck Talk*, p. 75, 1971

gooi *noun*
a brief sexual liaison *SOUTH AFRICA*
Punning **FLING** on the verb **GOOI** (to fling).
- —Jean Branford, *A Dictionary of South African English*, 1978

gooi *verb*
to give; to put; to throw, to fling; to drop; etc *SOUTH AFRICA*
From Afrikaans for 'to fling'.
- When a gang is on the jon there is always a lookout [...] who will "gooi a canary" [whistle] if he should sight a diener or "Transvaler".—*Cape Times*, 23rd May 1946
- They're just opening the cockpit window, shouting, "hey Josiah, gooi [put in] petrol", and then blasting off in the direction of Antartica[.] —*Sunday Times (South Africa)*, 7th September 2003

gook *noun*
1 a Vietnamese, especially if an enemy of the US; a person from the Far East, especially a Filipino, Japanese or Korean; any dark-skinned foreigner *US, 1919*
A derogatory term, too all-encompassing to be directly racist but deeply xenophobic. Coined by the US military; the Korean and Vietnam wars gave the word a worldwide familiarity (if not currency). Etymology is uncertain, but many believe 'gook' is Korean for 'person'.
- —*American Speech*, p. 55, February 1947: 'Pacific War language'
- "Hey, you," Brody shrieked at the Filipinos ahead, "hey, you Gooks, take off those shirts. You want to get us ambushed?"—Norman Mailer, *Advertisements for Myself*, p. 137, 1951
- She probably only wore a look which I took to be "frightened," and which may just have been her habitual absent-minded gook-stare[.]—Jack Kerouac, *Letter to Neal Cassady*, p. 277, 3rd January 1951
- When arrested for sodomy in Indonesia, Clem said to the examining magistrate: "Tain't as if it was being queer. After all they's only Gooks."—William Burroughs, *Naked Lunch*, p. 158, 1957
- —*American Speech*, p. 120, May 1960: 'Korean bamboo English'
- Before she finished hers, a sleek-looking gook in sharp duds came over and without looking at me asked her to dance.—Mickey Spillane, *Me, Hood!*, p. 62, 1963
- "We've been stomping from one village to the next. Flushing out them gooks."—*The Berkeley Barb*, p. 3, 3rd December 1965
- Kill 'em, kill'em, strafe those gook creeps!—The Fugs, *Kill for Peace*, 1966
- Years later when the dudes are fat, middle-aged men they get together and reminisce about all the "gooks" they killed[.]—H. Rap Brown, *Die Nigger Die!*, p. 39, 1969
- But that's a fucking Viet Cong flag they've got there! We're at war with those gooks, for Chrissake!—Terry Southern, *Blue Movie*, p. 212, 1970
- They figure what's another gook more or less.—Darryl Ponicsan, *The Last Detail*, p. 34, 1970
- But he didn't think of it as hurting a person. It was justs a gook and they were not people, you know.—John Kerry, *The New Soldier*, p. 60, 1971
- The gook was waiting, lying on the gorund, no more than two meters from the door.—Ronald J. Glasser, *365 Days*, p. 6, 1971
- The artillery dudes and straight-leg grunts and the gooks was doin' it hand to hand.—Larry Heinemann, *Close Quarters*, p. 29, 1977

- He was A.R.V.N. patrols and had one a them little cocky gook asshole Lieutenants. — *Apocalypse Now*, 1979
- "The word 'gooks.' Does this mean the enemy? Or civilians? Or both?" Farley seemed glad someone posed an easy question. "Gooks could be both." — Nelson DeMille, *Word of Honor*, p. 414, 1985
- Nixon went half-mad with rage at the very idea of such a thing, much less the televised reality of a few dozen gooks in black pajamas actually fired weapons into the U.S. Embassy compound. — Hunter S. Thompson, *Songs of the Doomed*, p. 238, 1985
- I learned early that "Gook," meaning any North Korean soldier, and UTA, "up to the ass," meaning abundance, were the most frequently used expressions in conversation. — William B. Hopkins, *One Bugle No Drums*, p. 41, 1986
- Y'hear the story the gooks is putting chemicals in the grass so's we become pacifists so's we don' fight. — *Platoon*, 1986
- One day while crawling through the jungle trees / Sam shot a gook right in the knees. — Sandee Shaffer Johnson, *Cadences*, p. 140, 1986
- Oh, there are some soldiers thought Code Six as he watched, soldiers like Jimmy and I were, fighting the fucking GOOKS and SLANTS and SLOPES, soldiers trotting single file across a smoking field. — William T. Vollman, *Whores for Gloria*, p. 36, 1991

2 the Vietnamese language; any Asian language *US*

- Bozwell was with a dink the night Violet met him and they talked a few words of gook. — Joseph Wambaugh, *The Glitter Dome*, p. 157, 1981

3 an unspecified, unidentified, unpleasant, viscous substance *US, 1942*
Sometimes spelt 'guck'.

- [T]his kind of gas has a great deal of O-Octane gook in it[.] — Jack Kerouac, *On the Road*, p. 209, 1957
- I never want to be stuck with some hag with gook falling off her face and me taking it. — *Ask*, p. 65, 21st April 1979
- You messed up the wall the last time – all that guck you slicked your hair down with. — Elmore Leonard, *City Primeval*, p. 84, 1980

4 the recreational drug GHB *US*

- Investigators say GHB is a powerful drug that also goes by the nicknames of Gook, Easy Lay, Gamma 10 and Liquid X. — *The Houston Chronicle*, p. 17, 10th September 1996

gook *adjective*
Vietnamese *US*

- What's the name of the goddamn village – Vin Drin Drop or Lopu; damn gook names all sound the same. — *Apocalypse Now*, 1979

gooker *noun*
in hot rodding, a car with many cheap accessories but no performance enhancements that would qualify it as a hot rod *US*

- — Fred Horsley, *The Hot Rod Handbook*, p. 209, 1965: 'Hot talk – a glossary of hot rod terms'

gook sore *noun*
any skin infection suffered by a US soldier in Vietnam *US, 1989*

- — Linda Reinberg, *In the Field*, p. 95, 1991
- As well, most of the grunts had scars on their legs and arms called "Gook sores." — John Culbertson, *Operation Tuscaloosa*, p. 41, 1997

Gookville *noun*
a neighbourhood, hamlet or city occupied by Vietnamese people *US, 1967*

- You guys just marched right through the middle of Gookville like you was comin down the middle a Main Street. — John M. Del Vecchio, *The 13th Valley*, p. 394, 1982
- [T]hose girls – the short tails of their high-school uniform blouses loose around their hips – remind him of the Viet girls at the hand-laundry whorehouse at Ham Lom (Gookville, we called it), across the road from fire Base Harriette. — Larry Heinemann, *Paco's Story*, p. 86, 1986

gook wagon *noun*
in hot rodding, a car with many cheap accessories but no performance enhancements that would qualify it as a hot rod *US, 1953*

- — Fred Horsley, *The Hot Rod Handbook*, p. 209, 1965: 'Hot talk – a glossary of hot rod terms'

goola *noun*
a piano *US, 1944*

- — Robert S. Gold, *A Jazz Lexicon*, p. 128, 1964

goolie *adjective*
black *UK*

- — Paul Baker, *Polari*, p. 176, 2002

goolie ogle fakes *noun*
sunglasses *UK*
A combination of **GOOLIE** (black), **OGLE** (the eye) and **FAKE** (a manufactured article).

- — Paul Baker, *Polari*, p. 176, 2002

goolies *noun*
the testicles *UK, 1937*
Originally military, from Hindi *gooli* (a pellet), in phrases such as 'Beecham Sahib's goolis' for 'Beechams pills', and so punning on **PILLS** (the testicles). Usually in the plural, except in phrases like **DROP A GOOLIE/DROP A BOLLOCK** (make a mistake).

- — James McDonald, *A Dictionary of Obscenity, Taboo and Euphemism*, p. 7, 1988
- Thursday, 11 February [1993] Teresa Gorman [...] knows exactly what should be done with rapists: "Cut off their goolies!" — Gyles Brandreth, *Breaking the Code*, p. 158, 1999

gooly; gooley *noun*
a small stone suitable for throwing *AUSTRALIA, 1924*
Probably from an Australian Aboriginal language. The usual derivation from Hindi *goli* (ball) and 'bullet' is at best farfetched.

- GOOLEY – A stone. — Gilbert H. Lawson, *A Dictionary of Australian Words and Terms*, 1924
- Someone's been bunging goolies through her window. — Ruth Park, *The Harp In The South*, p. 37, 1948
- — Jim Ramsay, *Cop It Sweet!*, p. 41, 1977

goom *noun*
methylated spirits used as a drink by alcoholics *AUSTRALIA, 1967*
Probably an alteration of a word from an Australian Aboriginal language.

- — Jim Ramsay, *Cop It Sweet!*, p. 41, 1977
- BARRIE: You got some hid? MALLIE: What? BARRIE: Goom, liquor. You got it hid? — Thomas Keneally, *Bullie's House*, p. 61, 1981
- — Ryan Aven-Bray, *Ridgey Didge Oz Jack Lang*, p. 29, 1983

goombah *noun*
a loyal male friend; an Italian-American *US*
Italian-American. Sometimes used in a loosely derogatory tone.

- "I will beat this Giambra," he insists, "and prove Italty still produces fine fighters. It's hard to see how he can be proved wrong. Joey is a goombah, too! — *Coshocton (Ohio) Tribune*, p. 8, 2nd December 1954
- He was a mean, cruel, brutal heavyweight of a goomba who would just as soon have strangled you as look at you[.] — Emmett Grogan, *Ringolevio*, p. 96, 1972
- "Hey, goombah," he said, "you ain't your cheery self tonight." — Charles Whited, *Chiodo*, p. 143, 1973
- Brigante. Where'd you get that name? Goombah? — Edwin Torres, *After Hours*, p. 162, 1979
- He's my goombah, Charlie. I still call him uncle. — Vincent Patrick, *The Pope of Greenwich Village*, p. 104, 1979
- Pachoulo stared at Phila for a minute as though wondering what the hell that was supposed to mean, then he grinned his toad's grin and said, "Hey, goomba." — Robert Campbell, *Juice*, p. 168, 1988
- [H]e got into a beef with some old goombah down at Benny's Lounge over his vedeo games. — Richard Price, *Clockers*, p. 381, 1992
- [Johnny] Rotten spotted me from across the crowded room and started in my direction with a couple of spikey-haired goombahs in tow. — Mick Farren, *Give the Anarchist a Cigarette*, p. 371, 2001

goomie *noun*
a derelict alcoholic who drinks methylated spirits *AUSTRALIA, 1973*

goon *noun*
1 a unintelligent or slow-witted person *US, 1921*
From Alice the Goon, a character in the comic strip *Thimble Theatre* (1919), via a large and stupid character known as 'the goon' in Elzie Segar's comic strip *Popeye the Sailor* (1935–38), which popularised the word and introduced it to the UK. Originally English dialect *gooney* (a simpleton), possibly from Middle English *gonen* (to gape) and Old English *ganian* (to gape, to yawn). UK usage from the 1950s is influenced by *The Goon Show*, a surreal BBC radio – subsequently television – comedy with a cast of fools.

- "I'll clout you again, you goon," Frank drew back his fast, but Black Benny held him — Irving Shulman, *The Amboy Dukes*, p. 49, 1947
- Tightened them, rather, against the multimillion goons who would as soon sell all of liberty down any creek as their own two-big integrity. — Philip Wylie, *Opus 21*, p. 148, 1949
- I mean, that could have been really nice, only the goon that played the Playboy spoiled any fun it might have been. — J.D. Salinger, *Franny and Zooey*, p. 28–29, 1961
- Now all the poor goons were staggering into the heads and sicking their hearts out. — Derek Raymond (Robin Cook), *The Crust on its Uppers*, p. 128, 1962

- The goons grab the girl and take off in Sparky's car. —Carl Hiaasen, *Tourist Season*, p. 11, 1986
- Not good enough for one of the fucking goons, mind you. —Kevin Sampson, *Outlaws*, p. 50, 2001

2 a clownish person, especially one with a surreal, wild and zany sense of humour *UK*
From *The Goon Show*, a BBC radio comedy series first broadcast in 1951.

- Mr Campion [...] was very easy to talk to with those long clown lines in his pale face, a natural goon, born rather too early [she] suspected. —Margery Allingham, *The China Governess*, 1963

3 a hired thug *US, 1938*
A broadening of the original sense.

- He had told them they were a pair of stupid goons who had got their training in violence on the New York police force and had been "broken" for extortion or sheer witlessness. —Mary McCarthy, *The Group*, p. 137, 1963
- Ron could rustle up a goon squad within minutes if he really needed it. —Greg Williams, *Diamond Geezers*, p. 55, 1997

4 a partisan on either side of a labour dispute hired to perpetrate violence *US, 1938*

- Travis was a rough character who had lost an eye last year, or the year before, when a bunch of Steelworker Union goons broke into a radio station from which he was broadcasting in Alabama. —Clancy Sigal, *Going Away*, p. 123, 1961
- I'll teach those union goons to destroy other people's property! —C.D. Payne, *Youth in Revolt*, p. 296, 1993

5 a North Korean soldier *US*

- —*American Speech*, p. 120, May 1960: 'Korean bamboo English'

6 cheap wine *AUSTRALIA*

- For a cheap night out stuff a goonbag down your pants and smuggle it into a club, unzip your fly for easy access to the nozzle and offer to replace your mates' empty with a nice glass of goon. — *Wordmap (www.abc.net.au/wordmap)*, 2003

7 a flagon of cheap wine *AUSTRALIA, 1982*
It has been suggested that this comes from 'flagoon', a jocular pronunciation of 'flagon', but this is not supported by any evidence.

- And cheap because none of the wine he reviewed ever cost more than ten bucks a bottle. In fact very few even came within cooee of that, mostly tapering off at five or six bucks per four litre 'goon.' — *The Tasmanian Babes Fiasco*, p. 86, 1997

8 phencyclidine, the recreational drug known as PCP or angel dust *US*

- —*Drummer*, p. 77, 1977
- —Ronald Linder, *PCP: The Devil's Dust*, p. 9, 1981
- —US Department of Justice, *Street Terms*, October 1994

9 a gooney-bird (a C-47A Skytrain plane) *US, 1937*

- I haven't logged more than twenty hours of piston-engine time in the last four years, and only a little of that was in a Goon. —Walter Boyne and Steven Thompson, *The Wild Blue*, p. 212, 1986

go on!
used as an expression of surprise, incredulity or derision *UK, 1916*

goonbag; goonsack *noun*
the plastic bladder from inside a cardboard wine box *AUSTRALIA*

- The use I know for goonbag is usually in "goonbag soccer" – the game you play by blowing up the empty goonbag and drunkenly kicking it about. — *Wordmap (www.abc.net.au/wordmap)*, 2003
- 'Goon' comes in a 'goonsack' (i.e. the "bladder") or also called a 'goonbag'. — *Wordmap (www.abc.net.au/wordmap)*, 2003

goonboards; goonieboards *noun*
short, homemade skis *US*

- —*American Speech*, p. 206, October 1963: 'The language of skiers'

goon boy *noun*
a socially inept, unpopular person *US*

- —*American Speech*, p. 302, December 1955: 'Wayne University slang'

goonda *noun*
a hooligan; a street-rough *INDIA, 1926*
Directly from Hindi.

- And it was that potent combination of racial and religious hatred that provided the breeding ground for the electoral politics of the British National party, on the one hand, and the goonda politics of the National Front, on the other – and provoked the recent uprisings of young Asians. — *The Guardian*, 17th August 2001

goondaism *noun*
hooliganism *India*
Hindi *goondah* anglicised with '-ism'.

- —Paroo Nihalini, R.K. Tongue and Priya Hosali, *Indian and British English*, 1979
- How long are we going to mortgage our conscience to unabashed gimmickry and goondaism? — *Tribune (India)*, 24th April 2001

goon dust *noun*
phencyclidine, the recreational drug known as PCP or angel dust *US*

- —*Q Magazine*, p. 75, February 2001

gooned out *adjective*
under the influence of a drug *US, 1968*

- I think he's gooned out most a the time. On ludes or something. —Joseph Wambaugh, *The Delta Star*, p. 17, 1983

gooner *noun*
a North Vietnamese soldier *US, 1969*

- —Linda Reinberg, *In the Field*, p. 95, 1991
- Be advised that you have two groups of gooners aproaching your pos, one from the north and one form the west. —B.H. Norton, *Force Recon Diary, 1969*, p. 108, 1991
- These men were chopper pilots who had reenlisted for their second or third tours of duty in Vietnam. Their war had been reduced to gooks, dinks, slant-eyes, and gooners. —Ted Bartimus, *Warn Torn*, p. 257, 2002

gooney; goonie *noun*
a communist Chinese soldier; a North Korean soldier *US*

- People began yelling all sorts of cheerful things: "Get down!" "Goonies!" (Chinese). —Martin Russ, *The Last Parallel*, p. 140, 1957
- —*American Speech*, p. 120, May 1960: 'Korean bamboo English'

gooney bird *noun*
1 a C-47A Skytrain plane, also known as a DC-3, most commonly used to transport people and cargo, but also used as a bomber and fighter *US, 1942*

- She was known affectionately as the "Gooney Bird," "Dak," and "Dizzy Three" to the men who flew her during World War II. —*San Francisco Chronicle*, p. 60, 18th January 1975
- These craft were affectionately known as "Gooney Birds" to the American fighting men, "Dakotas" to the British soldiers, and DC-3s to most civilians. —Ian Padden, *U.S. Air COmmando*, p. 6, 1985
- Weather like this makes we wish to hell I'd never told them I could fly Gooney Birds. —Walter Boyne and Steven Thompson, *The Wild Blue*, p. 212, 1986

2 a foolish or dim-witted person *US, 1956*

- That's shroud music, boy, that's goony-bird music. —John Clellon Holmes, *The Horn*, p. 67, 1958
- Strike stayed mute, glancing over at Futon doing the gooney bird. —Richard Price, *Clockers*, p. 13, 1992

goonie party; goon party *noun*
a backyard party at which goonbags of different wines are hung on a rotary clothesline which is then spun so that fate decides what you will drink next *AUSTRALIA*

- Goonie parties eventuated amongst the bored and impoverished, where multiple goonbags were hung on the hillshoist in the backyard. — *Wordmap (www.abc.net.au/wordmap)*, 2003

goon squad *noun*
a group of prison guards who use force to quash individual or group rebellions *US*

- [B]ut somebody called out the GoonSquad, who, all 4, look exactly what they're called. —Clarence Cooper Jr, *The Farm*, p. 139, 1967
- In less than a minute the door flew open and three guards entered on the double. "The goon squad," Nunn whispered to Manning. —Malcolm Braly, *On the Yard*, p. 34, 1967

goon stand *noun*
in the television and film industries, a large stand for supporting large equipment or devices *US*

- —Tony Miller and Patricia George, *Cut! Print!*, p. 83, 1977

goony *adjective*
silly, doltish *US, 1939*

- "And, man, oh, man," he clucked suddenly, "am I lushed. I'm goony." —John Clellon Holmes, *The Horn*, p. 55, 1958
- You know, one good thing about having Hovely up there, he's too goony to be scared. —Jim Bouton, *Ball Four*, p. 246, 1970

goonyland *noun*
territory controlled by the North Korean Army and/or Chinese troops during the Korean war *US*
- The words "goonie" and "goonyland" are used exclusively around here. —Martin Russ, *The Last Parallel*, p. 286, 1957
- — *American Speech*, p. 120, May 1960: 'Korean bamboo English'

goop *noun*
1 any sticky, viscid, unpleasant substance the exact chemical composition of which is unknown *US, 1918*
- Skink said, "I got some goop if want it. Great stuff." —Carl Hiaasen, *Native Tongue*, p. 155, 1991
- I bet your toxic goop got dumped in T.J. —Joseph Wambaugh, *Finnegan's Week*, p. 144, 1993

2 the chemical jelly used in incendiary bombs *US, 1944*
- — *American Speech*, p. 74, February 1946: 'Some words of war and peace from 1945'

3 liquid resin used in surfacing surfboards *US*
- —John M. Kelly, *Surf and Sea*, p. 286, 1965

4 the recreational drug GHB *US*
- Gamma-hydroxybutyrate (GBH, Goop), flunitrazepam (Roofies) and ketamine (SPecial K) are new additions to a long list of substances that have often been encountered in these settings. — *Testimony of Terrance Woodworth to the United States Congress*, 11th March 1999

5 a fool *US, 1915*
- "You goop," said her brother. "That pamphlet was written for slum women; by a Vassar graduate, I bet." —Mary McCarthy, *The Group*, p. 229, 1963

gooper *noun*
lung phlegm *US*
- Hey, fella, go and spit your goopers in the gutter, not on my property. —Joseph Wambaugh, *The Black Marble*, p. 264, 1978

goop gobbler *noun*
a person who enjoys and/or excels at performing oral sex on men *US*
- — *Male Swinger Number 3*, p. 45, 1981: 'The complete gay dictionary'

go or blow
used to describe a situation in car repair or motor racing where an engine will either perform very well or self-destruct *US*
- —Lewis Poteet, *Car & Motorcyle Slang*, p. 94, 1992

goori *noun*
a poorly performing racehorse *NEW ZEALAND*
From an early sense of the word, a corrupted form of the Maori *kuri* (dog).

goose *noun*
1 a socially inept, out-of-fashion person *US*
- —Collin Baker et al., *College Undergraduate Slang Study Conducted at Brown University*, p. 126, 1968

2 in poker, an unskilled player who is a likely victim of a skilled professional *US*
- —Peter O. Steiner, *Thursday Night Poker*, p. 412, 1996

3 a shop assistant *AUSTRALIA*
Especially in shoplifters' use.
- — *The (Sydney) Bulletin*, 26th April 1975

4 an act of copulation *UK, 1893*
Rhyming slang for 'goose and duck', **FUCK**.
- Goes back to when I had my first hole. First proper goose and all that. —Kevin Sampson, *Clubland*, p. 84, 2002

5 in television and film making, the truck carrying the cameras and sound equipment *US*
- —Ralph S. Singleton, *Filmaker's Dictionary*, p. 76, 1990

6 a girlfriend, a woman *SOUTH AFRICA, 1974*
From an earlier English use. Also variant 'goosie'.
- [H]e teased another young goosie but returned to glance at her[.] —Zoe Wicomb, *David's Story*, 2001

goose *verb*
1 to jab or poke someone, especially between the buttock cheeks *US, 1906*
- Henri Cru and I rushed out with our clubs, gun and flashlights, laughing like hell and goosing each other on the way[.] —Jack Kerouac, *Letter to Neal Cassady*, p. 114, 26th August 1947
- He was always saying, "Try this for size," and then he'd goose the hell out of you while you were going down the corridor. —J.D. Salinger, *Catcher in the Rye*, p. 143, 1951
- And whoops and slaps his leg and gooses Billy with his thumb till I think Billy will fall in a dead faint from blushing and grinning. —Ken Kesey, *One Flew Over the Cuckoo's Nest*, p. 99, 1962

2 by extension, to urge into action *US, 1934*
- Keyes goosed his little MG convertible across the causeway and made it to the motel in eighteen minutes flat. —Carl Hiaasen, *Tourist Season*, p. 33, 1986

goose and duck; goose *noun*
a trifle, something of no value *UK*
Rhyming slang for **FUCK**.
- I don't give a goose what she thinks[.] —Bodmin Dark, *Dirty Cockney Rhyming Slang*, 2003

goose and duck; goose *verb*
to have sex *IRELAND, 1944*
Rhyming slang for **FUCK**, also used to create euphemistic expletives.
- "Goose off", "Goose me", "Goosing hell", etc. —Ray Puxley, *Cockney Rabbit*, 1992
- The photographer had obviously gone for the just-goosed or just-about-to-be-goosed look cos her hair was designer messy[.] —J.J. Connolly, *Layer Cake*, p. 59, 2000

gooseberry *noun*
a person whose presence interferes with the relationship, especially romance, of two other people *UK, 1837*
- Andy, this isn't official I hope? A drink with an old friend is one thing but if this is turning into an inter-rogation, I want my solicitor playing gooseberry. —Reginald Hill, *On Beulah Height*, p. 236, 1998
- PRs sitting in on interviews can be a real drag. Playing gooseberry, they sour that special one- to-one relationship that's at the heart of a good interview. —Sally Adams, *Interviewing for Journalists*, p. 146, 2001

gooseberry ranch *noun*
a rural brothel *US, 1930*
- —R. Frederick West, *God's Gambler*, p. 226, 1964: 'Appendix A'

gooseberry tart *noun*
1 the heart *UK, 1937*
Rhyming slang.
- —Ray Puxley, *Fresh Rabbit*, 1998

2 a fart *UK*
Rhyming slang.
- Whichever way you drop it, it's a "gooseberry". —Ray Puxley, *Fresh Rabbit*, 1998

goosed *adjective*
drunk *US, 1979*
- — *e-cyclopaedia*, 20th March 2002

goosed moose *noun*
in hot rodding and car customising, a car with a front that is substantially lower than its rear *US*
- —John Edwards, *Auto Dictionary*, p. 70, 1993

goose egg *noun*
1 zero; nothing *US, 1866*
Originally baseball slang.
- The 4/23 F.I.s and the snitch feedback are goose-egg. —James Ellroy, *Because the Night*, p. 336, 1984
- The more homicides a prison successfully prosecutes, the sexier a warden's bonuses and prettier his commendations. My string of goose eggs makes me look soft, Mel. —Seth Morgan, *Homeboy*, p. 215, 1990
- A real heavy investigation. Zilch. Goose egg. — *Basic Instinct*, 1992

2 a swollen bump *US, 1953*
- Jesus, that's gonna be a goose egg. Hang on ... I've got some alcohol and Band-Aids in my travel kit. —Armistead Maupin, *Babycakes*, p. 170, 1984

3 an oval cylindrical polystyrene float used in fishing *CANADA*
- —Lewis Poteet, *The South Shore Phrase Book*, p. 53, 1999

goose eye *noun*
in the illegal production of alcohol, a perfect formation of bubbles on the meniscus of the product, indicating 100 proof *US*
- —David W. Maurer, *Kentucky Moonshine*, p. 119, 1974

goose flare *noun*
a type of runway flare used in wartime Canada *CANADA*
- "Goose flares" were like a teakettle with a great long neck on them and filled with kerosene and a wick. —James Williams, *The Plan*, p. 87, 1984

goose grease *noun*
KY jelly, a lubricant *US*
• — *Maledicta*, p. 117, 1984–1985: 'Milwaukee medical maledicta'

goose juice *noun*
powerful sedative medication given to mental patients *US*
• Besides, I can sell that goose juice on the street, make a few bucks and serve law and order by keeping the Negro element sedated. — James Ellroy, *Suicide Hill*, p. 584, 1986

goose's neck; goose's *noun*
a cheque *UK, 1961*
• — Ned Wallish, *The Truth Dictionary of Racing Slang*, p. 34, 1989

Goose Village *nickname*
the Victoriatown area of waterfront Montreal *CANADA*
• Goose Village was a warren of row housing across the canal from Griffintown. Victoriatown's nickname was Goose Village probably because of the wild geese that visited the marshy ground. — *Montreal Gazette*, p. A6, 24th June 2002

goosey *adjective*
jumpy, wary, nervous *US, 1906*
• I have to pay Dawn. She called, she's getting goosey. — Elmore Leonard, *Riding the Rap*, p. 206, 1996

goosie *noun*
in male homosexual relations, the passive or 'female' rôle *SOUTH AFRICA, 1965*
Prison slang.
• — Penny Silva, *A Dictionary of South African English*, 1996

gooter *noun*
penis *IRELAND*
• When Dawn turned to get her glass off the bar Jimmy Sr. got his hand in under his gooter and yanked it into an upright position – and Anne Marie was looking at him. — Roddy Doyle, *The Van*, p. 268, 1991

goot-n-tight *adjective*
▷ see: GUDENTIGHT

go-out *noun*
a surfing session *US*
• — Surf Punks, *Oh No! Not Them Again!*, 1988

go out *verb*
1 to die, especially from a drug overdose *US*
• — Jim Crotty, *How to Talk American*, p. 88, 1997
2 to suffer a relapse while participating in a twelve-step recovery programme such as Alcoholics Anonymous *US*
• — Christopher Cavanaugh, *AA to Z*, p. 101, 1998

go over *verb*
to paint over another's graffiti with your art *US*
• — Jim Crotty, *How to Talk American*, p. 141, 1997

Gopaul luck not Seepaul luck
used for expressing that one man's good fortune is not another's *TRINIDAD AND TOBAGO, 1990*
• — Lise Winer, *Dictionary of the English/Creole of Trinidad & Tobago*, 2003

go pedal *noun*
an accelerator pedal *UK*
• He took his anger out on the road and stomped the go pedal to the floor. The speedo needle moved up to 80 mph[.] — Donald Gorgon, *Cop Killer*, p. 173, 1994

gopher *noun*
1 a person who is easily swindled, who 'goes for' the pitch *US*
• — *American Speech*, p. 150–151, May 1959: 'Notes on the cant of the telephone confidence man'
2 a poker player who plays with a high degree of optimism *US*
So named because of the player's willingness to 'go for' a draw in almost any situation.
• — John Vorhaus, *The Big Book of Poker Slang*, p. 20, 1996
3 a criminal who tunnels into a business to rob it *US, 1928*
• — Vincent J. Monteleone, *Criminal Slang*, p. 105, 1949
▷ see: GOFER

go-pill *noun*
any amphetamine or other central nervous system stimulant *US, 1957*
• I gave her two "go" pills and took her to the street for the cut into Phyllis and Ophelia. — Iceberg Slim (Robert Beck), *Pimp*, p. 213, 1969
• — Richard A. Spears, *The Slang and Jargon of Drugs and Drink*, p. 228, 1986

gopping *adjective*
dirty *UK*
Gulf war usage.
• — *American Speech*, p. 390, Winter 1991: 'Among the new words'

gor *noun*
▷ see: GAWD

gora *noun*
a white person *INDIA*
• — R.E. Hawkins, *Coomon Indian Words in English*, 1984
• — *Times Educational Supplement*, 31st March 2004

Gorbachoff!
used as a blessing when someone sneezes *US*
Possibly related to 'gesundheit!'.
• — Connie Eble (Editor), *UNC-CH Campus Slang*, p. 4, November 1990

gorbie *noun*
a stupid tourist *CANADA*
This term is also reported in use, with the same meaning, at Mont Tremblant ski resort in Quebec.
• Gorbie is an impolite term used in the national parks for tourists who ask questions such as "How much does that mountain weigh?" and "What's the white stuff on top of that peak?" and "What do the animals do at night?" — Tom Parkin, *WetCoast Words*, p. 60, 1989

gorblimey *adjective*
stereotypically (parodically) Cockney *UK*
• To rock in cockney always seemed to conjure a perky gorblimey factor, the musical equivalent of Barbara Windsor[.] — Mick Farren, *Give the Anarchist a Cigarette*, p. 372, 2001

gorblimey!
▷ see: COR BLIMEY!

Gorby blots; Gorbacher *noun*
a type of blotter LSD popular in the early 1990s *US*
The blotters were illustrated with the face of Mikhail Gorbachev, hence the 'Gorby'.
• — David Shenk and Steve Silberman, *Skeleton Key*, p. 116, 1994
• Street names [...] dots, drop, flash, Gorbachovs, hawk[.] — James Kay and Julian Cohen, *The Parents' Complete Guide to Young People and Drugs*, 1998

Gordon and Gotch; gordon *noun*
a watch *UK, 1960*
Rhyming slang, formed from the name of a long-gone book-dealing company based in Plaistow, east London.
• — Ray Puxley, *Cockney Rabbit*, 1992

Gordon Bank *noun*
an act of masturbation *UK*
Rhyming slang, formed from football goalkeeper Gordon Banks (b.1937).
• — Bodmin Dark, *Dirty Cockney Rhyming Slang*, 2003

Gordon Bennett!
used as a mild expletive *UK, 1984*
Probably an alteration of 'gorblimey!'.
• Gordon Bennett, that's how it currently is in cutting-edge reformation Wales. — *The Observer*, 2nd February 2003

gorge *noun*
in circus and carnival usage, food *US*
• — Don Wilmeth, *The Language of American Popular Entertainment*, p. 116, 1981

gorge *adjective*
used for expressing approbation *UK*
A shortening of 'gorgeous'.
• This island is gorge, amazing, triff... total paradise. — Colin Butts, *Is Harry Still on the Boat?*, p. 144, 2003

gorgeous *adjective*
used for expressing approbation *US, 1883*
• [River Phoenix] was an incredible person and so different from anybody, everybody. And that's gorgeous. That's beautiful. — *The Guardian*, 28th March 2002

gorger; gorgia; gawjo *noun*
a non-gypsy, anyone who is not a part of the travelling community *UK, 1900*
English gypsy use.
• Travellers, gorgers, hard men, monied men – they were all here. —Jimmy Stockin, *On The Cobbles*, p. 34, 2000

gorgon *noun*
a ruthless leader or bully *JAMAICA*
• —Velma Pollard, *Dread Talk*, p. 43, 2000

goric *noun*
1 a paregoric, an opiate-based medicinal syrup *US*
• —Ralph de Sola, *Crime Dictionary*, p. 58, 1982
2 opium; heroin *US, 1977*
From 'pare*goric*' (a medicine that assuages pain).
• —Richard A. Spears, *The Slang and Jargon of Drugs and Drink*, p. 228, 1986
• —Mike Haskins, *Drugs*, p. 284, 2003

gorilla *noun*
1 a criminal who relies on brute strength and force *US, 1861*
• People started saying that he was a gorilla, that he was going around shaking down people, shaking down numbers controllers and cats who were dealing drugs. —Claude Brown, *Manchild in the Promised Land*, p. 213, 1965
• [E]verybody joined in, even the door gorillas. —Jake Arnott, *He Kills Coppers*, p. 21, 2001
2 a prisoner who obtains what he wants by force *US*
• In the argot of the inmates, an individual who takes what he wants from others by force is known as a gorilla. —Gresham M. Sykes, *The Society of Captives*, p. 91, 1958
3 in the entertainment industry, a technical member of a film crew *US*
• It is classic Hollywood protocol that the actors be quartered separately from the technicians ("apes" or "gorillas," as they are affectionately called[.] —Terry Southern, *Blue Movie*, p. 66, 1970
4 in the music industry, a very popular bestselling song *US*
• —Arnold Shaw, *Dictionary of American Pop/Rock*, p. 143, 1982
5 one thousand dollars *AUSTRALIA*
Building on 'monkey' ($500).
• —Ned Wallish, *The Truth Dictionary of Racing Slang*, p. 34, 1989

gorilla *verb*
to manhandle, to beat *US, 1922*
• "Daddy, what happens now. Maybe 'Poison' will come back and gorilla me." —Iceberg Slim (Robert Beck), *Pimp*, p. 239, 1969
• I'd travel for blocks to duke with a cat that would try to gorilla a friend. —Edwin Torres, *Carlito's Way*, p. 14, 1975

gorilla dust *noun*
intimidating bluffing *US*
• Perot called other issues brought up by GM "gorilla dust," referring to the way gorillas throw dust at their opponents to distract them during a fight. —*Associated Press*, 8th December 1986
• He said his competitors were creating "gorilla dust." —*The State (Columbia, South Carolina)*, p. A1, 21st May 2004

gorilla-grip *verb*
in skateboarding, to jump holding the ends of the board with the toes *US*
• —Laura Torbet, *The Complete Book of Skateboarding*, p. 105, 1976

gorilla pill *noun*
a barbiturate capsule or other central nervous system depressant *US*
• —Richard Lingeman, *Drugs from A to Z*, p. 86, 1969

gorilla pimp *noun*
a brutish pimp who relies heavily on violence to control the prostitutes who work for him *US*
• One who uses brutality and threats is a gorilla pimp or hard Mack. —Christina and Richard Milner, *Black Players*, p. 35, 1972
• The Red Velvet Turtle was the 430 Club without sawdust on the floor, Pitts Pub, without the "Brutality Booth" where the gorilla pimps used to go and slug their women in the chops. —Odie Hawkins, *Men Friends*, p. 108, 1989

gorilla salad *noun*
thick pubic hair *US*
• —*Male Swinger Number 3*, p. 45, 1981: 'The complete gay dictionary'

gork *noun*
1 a patient with severe mental deficiences *US, 1964*
• —*Maledicta*, p. 68, Summer/Winter 1978: 'Common patient-directed pejoratives used by medical personnel'
2 a fool; a contemptible person *US, 1970*
• The man was thick bodied, his glasses like Coke-bottle bottoms; he looked like the gork that Mr. Fielding was. —Caroline B. Cooney, *Driver's Ed*, p. 147, 1994
• Of course they were staring at me. I'm a six foot-five gork. —Howard Stern, *Miss America*, p. 101, 1995

gorked *adjective*
stupefied from anesthetic *US*
• —*American Speech*, p. 205, Fall-Winter 1973: 'The language of nursing'

gorm *verb*
to bungle; to act awkwardly *US*
• —John Gould, *Maine Lingo*, p. 114, 1975

gorm!
used for expressing surprise *TRINIDAD AND TOBAGO, 1997*
• —Lise Winer, *Dictionary of the English/Creole of Trinidad & Tobago*, 2003

gormless *adjective*
foolish *NEW ZEALAND*
• Any man who thinks and reads beyond the immediate requirements of getting a good job is a fool – 'wet', 'gormless', dilberry' etc. —*Landfall*, p. 221, 1952

gorp *noun*
1 a complete social outcast *US*
• —*Verbatim*, p. 280, May 1976
2 a snack of nuts and dried fruit favoured by hikers *US*
From '*g*ood *o*ld *r*aisins and *p*eanuts'.
• —Eric S. Raymond, *The New Hacker's Dictionary*, p. 182, 1991

gorsoon *noun*
a young male *IRELAND*
• Partnering Fergal at midfield in that win was Seamus O'Neill. In stark contrast to Fergal however, Seamus is just 18 years old, a gorsoon. —*Irish Examiner*, 1st August 2001

go-see *noun*
in modelling, a visual 'interview' *US*
• The really big ones will invite you to their studios for an interview (in modelling jargon such an appointment is euphemistically known as a "go-see"). —*Screw*, p. 11, 15 December 1969

Gosford dog *noun*
a person of Mediterranean background *AUSTRALIA*
Rhyming slang for **WOG**. From Gosford, a satellite city of Sydney which has a greyhound racing track.
• Some Australians attached to the Victorian challenge were less than fulsome, too, in their praise of the Italian crew, to whom they referred as "Gosfords" – you know, Gosford dogs, wogs. —*Sun-Herald*, p. 34, 31st July 1983

gosh
used in expressions of surprise, frustration *UK, 1757*
A euphemistic 'God'.
• Yeah, yeah like I said, you are really fit / But, my gosh, don't you just know it? —Mike Skinner, *Fit But You Know It*, 2004

gosh-darned; gosh-derned; gosh-danged *adjective*
used as a mild intensifier *US*
A euphemistic replacement for 'God-damned'.
• King Crimson, and Genesis are still amazing and revelatory today. Especially deserve respect for being do gosh-darned happy, positive, and goal-oriented. —Brian Doherty, *Retrohell*, p. 165, 1997

go-slow *noun*
a deliberate slowing of production by workers as a type of industrial action *AUSTRALIA, 1917*
• No go-slows or stop-work meetings. No one works to regulations or goes on strike. —Phillip Adams, *The Unspeakable Adams*, p. 17, 1977

gospel true *adjective*
entirely true *AUSTRALIA, 1957*
• Probably few of the countless anecdotes published under the 'Unofficial History of the A.I.F.' were gospel true. —George Blaikie, *Remember Smith's Weekly?*, p. 161, 1966

gospel truth *noun*
sincerely the truth *AUSTRALIA, 1902*
• I was the toast of Tobruk, and that's the gospel truth. —Alexander Buzo, *Norm and Ahmed*, p. 10, 1969

goss *noun*
gossip *NEW ZEALAND, 1985*
• Let's hear the goss! — *Flatball News*, p. 10, 1993
• — Harry Orsman, *A Dictionary of Modern New Zealand Slang*, p. 58, 1999
• Gemma nearly choked on an ice cube. "Wow! That is big goss." — Ben Elton, *High Society*, p. 249, 2002

got *verb*
▸ **have got on**
to possess evidence against someone *UK, 1928*
• Why do you ignore all the evidence from Norway, Scotland and Ireland? What is it that the fish farmers have got on you guys anyway? How much did they donate to your campaign and that of the party? — Raif Mair, *CKNW (Canada)*, 12th July 2001

gotcha *noun*
in computing, a misfeature that generates mistakes *US*
• — Eric S. Raymond, *The New Hacker's Dictionary*, p. 183, 1991

gotcha!
1 used as a humorous exclamation of a verbal conquest of some sort *UK, 1932*
Often used as the gloating afterword when a practical joke is played. On 2nd May 1982, during the Falklands war, the Argentine ship Belgrano was torpedoed by the Royal Navy as she sailed away from the exclusion zone. At least 386 lives were lost. The Sun newspaper printed the notorious, gloating one-word headline: 'GOTCHA'. Also used in triumph when a capture or victory has been achieved. In the Royal Air Force it is a 'Snatch raid in which air-crew are taken for unannounced survival training' (Strong and Hart Davis, *Fighter Pilot*, 1981).
• Gotcha. Can't win. Don't try. — John Swartzwelder, *The Simpsons*, 1992
• Okay, gotcha. What did you think I was going to ask? — *As Good As It Gets*, 1997
• He groped for his jeans and worked his fingers into the tiny hip pocket. Aha! Gotcha, you boundah! — Kevin Sampson, *Powder*, p. 128, 1999
• I saw him look over and then look away. Gotcha! — Dave Courtney, *Raving Lunacy*, p. 95, 2000
• Then the General Belgrano was torpedoed, 340 Argentine sailors were drowned, and the nation rejoiced. Gotcha. You sick bastards. — Mark Steel, *Reasons to be Cheerful*, p. 127, 2001

2 used for registering an understanding of what someone has said *UK, 1966*
A slovening of '[I] got you'.
• — John Ayto, *The Oxford Dictionary of Slang*, p. 297, 1998

gotchie *noun*
1 a security guard or park keeper *IRELAND*
• [U]p to St. Patrick's park to pick flowers and run like Herb Elliot until you made it to Naller...Sure the old groundsmen or gotchies hadn't a chance. — Bernard Share, *Slanguage*, p. 134, 2003

2 a schoolboy prank, especially around Niagara Falls, Ontario, in which the victim's underpants are pulled up between his buttock cheeks *CANADA*
The research of Professor J. K. Chambers of the University of Toronto has revealed a striking difference in the nicknaming of this act: in the US, it is called a 'wedgie', but in the Canada, a 'gotchie', which both comes from 'gotch' for 'underpants' (with Hungarian and eastern European source words) and is a pun.

goth *noun*
a member of a youth fashion cult, characterised by a dark, sepulchral appearance and stark white and black makeup *UK, 1984*
Inspired by C19 *goth*ic-romance images of vampires, this dress sense is allied to a style of rock music also called 'goth'.
• — Connie Eble (Editor), *UNC-CH Campus Slang*, p. 5, Spring 1992
• — Tony Thorne, *Fads, Fashions & Cults*, p. 98, 1993
• The goth sees all this and is shaking with rage. Her face is glowing red so much that you can see it under the white schlep [make-up]. — J.J. Connolly, *Know Your Enemy [britpulp]*, p. 155, 1999

Gotham *noun*
New York City *US, 1807*
Alluding to a mythical village inhabited by wise fools.
• I hadn't believed we would leave Gotham, even after the New Jersey stadium was under construction. — Dan Jenkins, *Life Its Ownself*, p. 17, 1984

gothoid *adjective*
recognisably goth in fashion *UK*
• Pick up Kerrang! and you're visually assaulted by fantastically garish groups [...] gothoid intensities, punkers, skayecore baggied up adrenaline junkies[.] — John Robb, *The Nineties*, p. 234, 1999

go through *verb*
1 to leave hurriedly; to decamp *AUSTRALIA, 1944*
• You should have seen X going through. I was left dizzy by his eddy. — Rohan D. Rivett, *Behind Bamboo*, p. 282, 1946

2 (of a man) to have sex with a woman *AUSTRALIA*
• He's been through half the female population of Sydney. — Sue Rhodes, *Now you'll think I'm awful*, p. 43, 1967
• Hey dude, we're going to get Leigh pissed and all go through her. — *Aussie Post*, p. 47, 29th August 1998

got it!
used for urging another surfer not to catch this wave, which you claim as yours *US*
• — Trevor Cralle, *The Surfin'ary*, p. 46, 1991

go-to-godamn *adjective*
damned *US*
• I'll be go-to-goddam if a police car didn't draw up next to me near 66th Street. — Clancy Sigal, *Going Away*, p. 435, 1961

Go to Hell *nickname*
Go Dau Ha, home to a US Naval Advanced Base from 1969 to 71, close to the Cambodian border on the Vam Co Dong River, South Viethnam *US*
• The road continued through Go Dau Ha, which everyone, of course, referred to as "Go to Hell." — Dennis Marvicsin and Jerold Greenfield, *Maverick*, p. 225, 1990

go-to-hell rag *noun*
a neckerchief worn by an infantry soldier *US*
• — Linda Reinberg, *In the Field*, p. 94, 1991

go-to-whoa *noun*
in horse racing, the entire length of a race *AUSTRALIA*
• Usually he talked from go to whoa: what was the matter? — David Ireland, *The Unknown Industrial Prisoner*, p. 54, 1971
• — Ned Wallish, *The Truth Dictionary of Racing Slang*, p. 5, 1989

gotta like that!
used for expressing approval, genuine or ironic *US*
• — Connie Eble (Editor), *UNC-CH Campus Slang*, p. 4, Spring 1987

got you covered!
I understand! *US*
• — *American Speech*, p. 303, December 1955: 'Wayne University slang'

gouch *noun*
a period of drug-induced exhaustion *UK*
• I'm just on a gouch, that's all. I wish you'd leave me alone! — Lanre Fehintola, *Charlie Says...*, p. 95, 2000

gouge *verb*
to surf expertly and stylishly *US*
Applied to a ride on a wave.
• — *Surfing*, p. 43, 14th March 1990

Gouge and Screw Tax *noun*
▷ **see:** GRAB AND STEAL TAX

gouger *noun*
an aggressive lout *IRELAND*
• The more embittered view all offenders as "gougers" who should be locked up for as long as possible. — *Irish Times*, 6th May 1997
• I was...mugged last week on my way back from the post office by two gougers after my pension. — Donal Ruane, *Tales in a rear view mirror*, p. 81, 2003

goulash *noun*
1 an illegal cardroom that is open 24 hours a day *US*
• To give himself something to do, he had roused himself, at last, to invest in one of the local Goulashes, Goulash being a generic term for the round-the-clock, never-closing card houses that had been springing up around New York[.] — Edward Lin, *Big Julie of Vegas*, p. 12–13, 1974

2 in prison, a meat stew of any description *UK*
• — Angela Devlin, *Prison Patter*, p. 58, 1996

3 in electric line work, any insulating compound *US*
• — A.B. Chance Co., *Lineman's Slang Dictionary*, p. 8, 1980

go up *verb*

1 to be sentenced to prison; to be sent to prison *US, 1872*

- One that went up for murder – he was an Army Sergeant. —*Apocalypse Now*, 1979
- Louis was letting it become "we" to get next to Bobby and know what he was thinking, and because they were both in the life and had done state time, Bobby for shooting a man Bobby said pulled a gun on him instead of paying what he owed and went up on a manslaughter plea deal. —Elmore Leonard, *Riding the Rap*, p. 54, 1995

2 while acting, to miss your cue or forget a line *US*

- —Sherman Louis Sergel, *The Language of Show Biz*, p. 107, 1973
- —Don Wilmeth, *The Language of American Popular Entertainment*, p. 115, 1981

gourd *noun*

the head *UK, 1829*

- "Sure," said Sid, "nothing that a kick in the gourd won't fix," and he raised his foot to deliver a simulated stomp on the face of the fallen Rex. —Terry Southern, *Blue Movie*, p. 35, 1970

▸ bored out of your gourd

extremely bored *US*

The rhyme on **GOURD** (the head) intensifies 'bored'.

- I'm bored out of my gourd[.] —Eminem (Marshall Mathers), *Cum On Everybody*, 1999

▸ out of your gourd

1 extremely drug-intoxicated *US*

Substitutes **GOURD** (a head) in synonymous 'out of your head'.

- He'd come in in his mohair suit and his attache case, trying to play electronics executive, but he'd be stoned outa his gourd. —Nicholas Von Hoffman, *We Are The People Our Parents Warned Us Against*, p. 157, 1967
- And he was stoned out of his fucking gourd! —James Ellroy, *White Jazz*, p. 177, 1992
- I had just dropped enough acid to get four people stoned out of their gourd. —Howard Stern, *Miss America*, p. 97, 1995
- [T]his teenage dope dealer who's doing the best impression of someone completely out of their gourd that Mazz has ever seen of film. —John Williams, *Cardiff Dead*, p. 188, 2000

2 crazy *US, 1963*

- Chester! Are you outta your fuckin' gourd! You think we're gonna bite ourselves in the ass? —Odie Hawkins, *Lost Angeles*, p. 63, 1994

gourd guard *noun*

in drag racing, a crash helmet *US*

- —Lyle K. Engel, *The Complete Book of Fuel and Gas Dragsters*, p. 151, 1968

gourmet ghetto *noun*

north Berkeley, California; any neighbourhood featuring speciality food shops and gourmet restaurants *US*

Originally applied to a two-block stretch of Shattuck Avenue between Cedar Street and Rose Street in Berkeley.

- The geographic focus of the new sensibility is a broad, sunny section of Shattuck AVenue dubbed "the gourmet ghetto." At its center, guarded only by a modest redwood fence and a narrow, shaded courtyard, is Chez Panisse[.] —*Newsweek*, p. 42, 22nd August 1983
- And I also destroyed half of Berkeley's gourmet ghetto. —C.D. Payne, *Youth in Revolt*, p. 158, 1993
- [Y]ou'll find everything from Marczyk's burger blowouts to happy out specials at restaurants and coffeehouses up and down what Marczyk calls Denver's "gourmet ghetto." —*Denver Westword*, 31st July 2003

gov *noun*

a prison *governor* *UK*

- —Angela Devlin, *Prison Patter*, p. 58, 1996

govern *verb*

to play the active role in sex, sadomasochistic or not *US*

- —*American Speech*, p. 19, Spring 1985: 'The language of singles bars'

government artist *noun*

an unemployed person in receipt of state benefits *UK*

From a joke, heard in the high unemployment of the 1980s. A popular choice of occupation still, if questionnaires are to be believed.

- My solution to this problem, which is not only restricted to this area, is to utilise the labour of 'Government artists' – dole drawers[.] —*Western Daily Press (Bristol)*, p. 12, 15th February 2003
- Presumably she's heard the old one about someone calling him/herself a "Government Artist"? And why? Becaues he/she draws the dole. —*Grimsby Evening Telegraph*, p. 16, 20th February 2004

government-inspected meat *noun*

1 a soldier or sailor *US*

Homosexual usage.

- —Clarence Major, *Dictionary of Afro-American Slang*, p. 61, 1970

2 a soldier as the object of a homosexual's sexual desire *US*

- —*Male Swinger Number 3*, p. 45, 1981: 'The complete gay dictionary'

government jewellery *noun*

restraints worn on prisoners' bodies to restrict movement *CANADA*

- Government jewellery means the old ball and chain, leg shackles, handcuffs, or whatever other restraints law enforcement officers may use. Wearing government jewellery means being in prison. —Chris Thain, *Cold as a Bay Street Banker's Heart*, p. 75, 1987

government job *noun*

poor craftmanship *US*

- —Robert O. Bowen, *An Alaskan Dictionary*, p. 16, 1965

government juice *noun*

water *US*

- —Lise Winer, *Dictionary of the English/Creole of Trinidad & Tobago*, 2003

Government Racing Car

a car of the Gendarmerie Royale du Canada, the French name for the Mounties *CANADA*

Back formation from the initials GRC.

- GEORGE DEW: "Where I grew up (rural Alberta) we understood that the other abbreviation on their vehicles – GRC – stood for 'Government Racing Car'". —*Toronto Globe and Mail*, p. D12, 4th August 2002

governor *noun*

1 an acknowledged expert *UK*

- Artistic dirty pictures [...] Time was, you used to be the governor at tasteful nudity without whiskers. —*Journal of British Photography*, 4th January 1980

2 an employer, a superior *UK, 1802*

governor's *noun*

a prison governor's adjudication or ruling *UK*

- —Angela Devlin, *Prison Patter*, p. 58, 1996

gov'nor *noun*

▷ see: **GUV'NOR**

gow *noun*

1 a drug, especially opium *US, 1922*

- [W]hite women learned where they could get a "belt," a "jolt," or a "gow." —Jack Lait and Lee Mortimer, *New York Confidential*, p. 103–104, 1948

2 sauce *US*

- [I]t was some of that gow you smear all over our good state food. —Malcolm Braly, *On the Yard*, p. 221, 1967

3 herring roe *CANADA*

- Gow is a legal Canadian export. The name is a rough Englishing of a Japanese word that signifies "little eggs." It is [herring] eggs spawned on a small piece of seaweed. —Bill Casselman, *Canadian Food Words*, p. 267–268, 1998

gowed up *adjective*

drunk *CANADA*

- Ralph Kappel, gowed up on the wine he'd bought that morning with a lone ten-dollar bill from an old lady's purse he'd snatched the night before on Dundas, made his way along Carlton Street in the 9 p.m. darkness. —Hugh Garner, *The Intruders*, p. 314, 1977

go west *verb*

to be spoiled or ruined; to die *UK, 1925*

- The KGB, Smersh, the ballistic missiles trained on London – they had all gone west with the evil empire. —*The Daily Telegraph*, 15th September 2003

gowhead *noun*

a drug addict *US*

- Juicemen are too smart to lend money to people with habits like booze and skag, though sometimes an alkie or a gow-head in a three-piece suit puts one over on them. —Robert Campbell, *Juice*, p. 21, 1988

go-with-the-flow *adjective*

easy going, relaxed

After the phrasal verb 'go with the flow'.

- [T]he most go-with-the-flow person I've ever met. —*Kerrang!*, p. 12, 3rd November 2001

gow job *noun*

used in the 1940s to describe what in the 50s would be called a hot rod *US, 1941*

- —John Edwards, *Auto Dictionary*, p. 70, 1993

gowster *noun*

a drug addict or heavy drug user *US, 1936*

- Reefer-smokers are called "gowsters." —Jack Lait and Lee Mortimer, *New York Confidential*, p. 104, 1948
- "This pretty 'gowster' is sure pimping his ass off," I thought. —Iceberg Slim (Robert Beck), *Pimp*, p. 129, 1969
- Listening to the developing roar of the crowd as the horses headed into the stretch, and the old gowster's tall, sad story of what the old days used to be like was exciting, disturbing, interesting. —Odie Hawkins, *Chicago Hustle*, p. 151, 1977

goy *noun*

a Gentile *UK, 1841*

Yiddish.

- They're holy things and I want no part of them. You couldn't be expected to know, being a goy. —Charles Raven, *Underworld Nights*, p. 166, 1956
- He worships me because I'm a goy. —Mary McCarthy, *The Group*, p. 344, 1963
- I like to talk Yiddish in front of him, especially if there are goy cops in hearing distance. —Abbie Hoffman, *Revolution for the Hell of It*, p. 18, 1968
- He drank – of course, not whiskey like a goy, but mineral oil and milk of magnesia[.] —Philip Roth, *Portnoy's Complaint*, p. 3, 1969
- If a goy told it, you'd get all bent out of shape- —Rita Ciresi, *Pink Slip*, p. 191, 1999

goyish; goyische *adjective*

Gentile *US*

- It doesn't matter even if you're Catholic; if you live in New York you're Jewish. If you live in Butte, Montana, you're going to be goyish even if you're Jewish. —Lenny Bruce, *How to Talk Dirty and Influence People*, p. 5, 1965
- [E]very spring they sent him and my mother for a hotsy-totsy free weekend in Atlantic City, to a fancy goyische hotel no less. —Philip Roth, *Portnoy's Complaint*, p. 5, 1969
- The carol playing in the background, "Rudolph the Red-Nosed Reindeer," seemed loud and ridiculous, and I listened to it – and resented the way he made me hear it – through Strauss's ears, as tacky and goyish. —Rita Ciresi, *Pink Slip*, p. 328, 1999

gozohomey bird *noun*

an aircraft that returns you home *UK*

In Royal Air Force use, 2002.

gozz *noun*

gossip *UK*

- — *New Society*, 10th March 1983

GP *noun*

a *g*eneral *p*rinciple *US, 1944*

- Sometimes they would stop you on just G-P, or give you a bullshit ticket just so they could try and tear up your car on the pretext of searching for drugs. —Donald Goines, *Whoreson*, p. 211, 1972
- — *Ethics and Behaviour*, April 2003

GPO

(in doctors' shorthand) *g*ood for *p*arts *o*nly *UK*

Recorded in an article about medical slang in British (3 London and 1 Cambridge) hospitals.

- — *Ethics and Behaviour*, April 2003

GR8 *adjective*

in text messaging, great

A variant spelling; one of several constructions in which a syllable pronounced 'ate' is replaced by the homophone 'eight'.

- Gr8 result for charity. — *The Guardian*, 31st July 2002

gra *noun*

appetite; desire *IRELAND*

The Hiberno-English word for 'love, liking, affection'.

- She'd a terrible gra for the booze, good God, when I think, she'd suck the amontillado out of a dishcloth, the same poor girl. —Joseph O'Connor, *Red Roses and Petrol*, p. 11, 1995

grab *noun*

1 an arrest *UK, 1753*

- —Angela Devlin, *Prison Patter*, p. 58, 1996

2 a person who has been arrested *US*

- Strike sat tight, just watched as Crunch stepped out and escorted his grab to the rear of the Fury. —Richard Price, *Clockers*, p. 9, 1992

grab *verb*

1 to capture your imagination and attention *UK, 1966*

- Then one day, it just grabbed me. I finally understood what it is all about. From then on, I have been trying to get people to touch the trees. — *Wandsworth Guardian*, 26th August 2004

2 to impress *US*

- —William D. Alsever, *Glossary for the Establishment and Other Uptight People*, p. 13, December 1970

3 to arrest *UK, 1753*

- —Angela Devlin, *Prison Patter*, p. 58, 1996

4 in horse racing, to win a race with a long shot *US*

- —David W. Maurer, *Argot of the Racetrack*, p. 33, 1951

▸ **grab a dab**

to engage in male-on-male rape *US*

- —Charles Shafer, *Folk Speech in Texas Prisons*, p. 205, 1990

▸ **grab air**

to apply a truck's brakes *US*

- —Montie Tak, *Truck Talk*, p. 76, 1971

▸ **grab sack**

to muster courage *US*

- —Connie Eble (Editor), *UNC-CH Campus Slang*, p. 5, Fall 1999

▸ **grab the apple**

to seize tightly on the saddle horn while riding a bucking animal *CANADA*

- Grabbing the apple is to grab hold of the saddle horn when riding a bucking horse, one way in which a rider can "pull leather" and, when done in saddle bronc riding, it is grounds for disqualification. —Chris Thain, *Cold as a Bay Street Banker's Heart*, p. 75, 1987

▸ **up for grabs**

available, especially if suddenly or recently so *US, 1928*

- Well, she thought he was up for grabs. It's different if you're going back with him. —Mary Hooper, *(megan)2*, p. 36, 1999

grab-a-granny *noun*

used to describe an event where you can meet mature women *UK*

- Up in Frankie's it's grab a granny night where all the married crumpet goes for a bit of excitement. — *The Guardian*, 3rd January 1987
- As a dashing lieutenant on service in Germany he was the champion of his regiment's annual Grab-a-Granny contest, where young subalterns vie to race off the oldest and ugliest fraulein. — *Sun Herald (Sydney)*, p. 140, 17th July 1988
- Younger men [...] would go there to meet the divorcees. It was known locally as Grab-a-Granny night. —Frank Skinner, *Frank Skinner*, p. 88, 2001

grabalishus *adjective*

greedy *BAHAMAS*

- —Patricia Clinton-Meicholas, *More Talkin' Bahamian*, p. 53, 1995

grab all, lose all

used for expressing the dangers of greed *TRINIDAD AND TOBAGO*

- —Lise Winer, *Dictionary of the English/Creole of Trinidad & Tobago*, 2003

grab and snatch *noun*

the Goods and Services Tax (GST) *NEW ZEALAND*

- —David McGill, *David McGill's Complete Kiwi Slang Dictionary*, p. 58, 1998

Grab and Steal Tax; Gouge and Screw Tax *noun*

the Canadian Goods and Services Tax *CANADA*

A back formation on the initials GST.

- 7% that goes on top of just about every purchase (in addition to the provincial sales taxes). The current Prime Minister, Jean Chretien, got elected partly because he promised to get rid of this tax, and then promptly didn't. —Emily *An American's Guide to Canada*, p. 6, 10th November 2001

grab-ass *noun*

horseplay *US, 1947*

- —Carl Fleischhauer, *A Glossary of Army Slang*, p. 22, 1968
- That don't mean you should play grab-ass for five days before showing up at Portsmouth. —Darryl Ponicsan, *The Last Detail*, p. 21, 1970
- He quit all grabass in the barracks, pursued his job and studied with new purpose[.] —Earl Thompson, *Tattoo*, p. 651, 1974
- When the pace of the action was broken by periods like this, we sometimes compensated by indulging in what the army called "grab-ass." —Robert Mason, *Chickenhawk*, p. 289, 1983

grab-ass *verb*

to engage in physical horseplay *US*

- Shoving and grab-assing with each other, and braying like a bunch of mules. —Jim Thompson, *Savage Night*, p. 75, 1953
- They'll fuck around and fart around and grab-ass around, and jack that thing up so's it'll be some horse's ass of a hero's statue. —Larry Heinemann, *Paco's Story*, p. 157, 1986

grab bag *noun*

1 a loose assortment of anything *US, 1879*
From a lucky dip offered at US fairs.
- [A] grab-bag of talent including Busted and art-rockers Goldfrapp[.] — *The Guardian*, 13th January 2004

2 a pooled mix of different types of pills contributed by several people and then consumed randomly *US*
- —William D. Alsever, *Glossary for the Establishment and Other Uptight People*, p. 12, December 1970

3 the theft of a suitcase or briefcase accomplished by placing a look-alike bag near the bag to be stolen and then picking up and leaving with the bag to be stolen; the suitcase or briefcase stolen in such a theft *US*
- He looked at the grab bag closely. Nice grained leather, expensive make.—Odie Hawkins, *Chicago Hustle*, p. 28, 1977
- Elijah sometimes felt like the only man in the world when he did the grab bag ... because it was as though everyone knew what he was doing...—Odie Hawkins, *Chicago Hustle*, p. 27, 1977

4 a lunch box or lunch bag *US*
- —Jerry Robertson, *Oil Slanguage*, p. 60, 1954

5 a bag of equipment prepared for grabbing in the event of an emergency *UK*
- [H]e swam under the wreckage to pull out a liferaft from the well of the forward cabin, before returning underwater to find an emergency "grab-bag" containing a satellite telephone, spare batteries, torches and flares.— *The Times*, 10th August 2004

grabber *noun*

1 the hand *UK, 1859*
- She held those chopsticks in her grabbers with her arms raised in front of her.—Mezz Mezzrow, *Really the Blues*, p. 102, ' 1946

2 a surfer who ignores surfing etiquette and catches rides on waves 'owned' by other surfers *US*
- —Trevor Cralle, *The Surfin'ary*, p. 46, 1991

3 a story that captures the imagination *US, 1966*
- Read it. It's a grabber.—*Get Shorty*, 1995

4 a shame; a pity *US*
- —William J. Bradley, *CB Fact Book and Language Dictionary*, p. 16, 1977

5 a railway conductor *US, 1931*
- —Ramon Adams, *The Language of the Railroader*, p. 70, 1977

grabble *verb*

to grab violently *UK, 1781*
- —Lise Winer, *Dictionary of the English/Creole of Trinidad & Tobago*, 2003

grabby *adjective*

1 attention-grabbing *UK*
- I wouldn't feel comfortable about being grabby, but there are times when I would put myself first, yes.— *The Guardian*, 9th June 1998

2 greedy, grasping, selfish *UK, 1953*

grab-iron *noun*

a handle on the side of a goods wagon *US*
- The hand holds on the side of freight cars and known as "Grab Irons" and are used in conjunction with the still step in boarding a freight car.—J. Herbert Lund, *Herb's Hot Box of Railraod Slang*, p. 148, 1975

grab joint *noun*

an eating concession in a circus or carnival *US, 1904*
- —Sherman Louis Sergel, *The Language of Show Biz*, p. 99, 1973
- —Joe McKennon, *Circus Lingo*, p. 41, 1980
- —Gene Sorrows, *All About Carnivals*, p. 18, 1985: 'Terminology'

grad *noun*

1 an amphetamine tablet or other central nervous stimulant *US, 1977*
- —Richard A. Spears, *The Slang and Jargon of Drugs and Drink*, p. 230, 1986

2 an ex-convict *US*
- —Hyman E. Goldin et al., *Dictionary of American Underworld Lingo*, p. 86, 1950

3 a *grad*uate *US, 1871*
- Sweet dreams, all you flophouse grads.—Mezz Mezzrow, *Really the Blues*, p. 317, 1946

grade *noun*

▸ **make the grade**

to achieve a required standard *US, 1908*
- Twenty-four beaches in England made the grade, up one on last year.— *The Guardian*, 31st May 2000

grade-grubber *noun*

a student whose only goal is to get good grades *US*
- —John D. Bell et al., *Loosely Speaking*, p. 9, 1966

graduate *noun*

an ex-convict *US*
- —Vincent J. Monteleone, *Criminal Slang*, p. 106, 1949

graduate *verb*

1 to complete a prison sentence *US*
A construction built on the jocular 'college' as 'jail'.
- —Lou Shelly, *Hepcats Jive Dictionary*, p. 12, 1945

2 to be cured of a sexually transmitted infection *US*
- — *American Speech*, p. 31, February 1949: 'A.V.G. lingo'

3 to begin using more powerful drugs, or to stop taking drugs completely *US*
- —Jay Robert Nash, *Dictionary of Crime*, p. 155, 1992

4 (used of a racehorse) to win a race for the first time *US*
- —Tom Ainslie, *Ainslie's Complete Guide to Thoroughbred Racing*, p. 332, 1976

grad wrecks *noun*

the Graduate Records Examinations *US*
The standardised testing given to undergraduate students seeking admission to graduate school in the US.
- —John D. Bell et al., *Loosely Speaking*, p. 10, 1966

graf *noun*

1 graffiti *US*
- —Jim Crotty, *How to Talk American*, p. 141, 1997
- To distance themselves from rap's negative perceptions, those involved in the underground scene promote its four elements: MC-ing, DJ-ing (what DJ's do), graf (graffiti) art and break dancing. — *Orange County (California) Register*, p. F7, 24th March 2000
- [A] bona-fide graf-based comic, within The Source's very pages. —Carlito Rodriguez, *The Source*, p. 36, March 2002

2 a paragraph *US*
- Never mind that, just read the last three grafs.—Carl Hiaasen, *Native Tongue*, p. 41, 1991

graffer *noun*

a graffiti artist who produces complete works, not just a stylised signature *US*
- Graffiti artists, or "graffers," operate in many British towns.— *The Guardian*, p. E18, 10th May 1993
- —Jim Crotty, *How to Talk American*, p. 141, 1997

graf-head *noun*

a graffiti artist *UK, 1998*
- If you live, breathe, piss, and shit hip-hop culture, you'll feel at home hanging out at Oaklandish, checking out its weekly series and live music happenings – to maybe just collecting wildstyle hieroglyphs from local graf-heads in your black book.— *East Bay Express (Oakland, California)*, 5th May 2004

graft *noun*

1 personal and financial advantage as the result of dishonest or unethical business or political practice, especially bribery and patronage; corporate corruption in general *US, 1901*
- But, of course, if you need to build a dam where a camp like that ought to be – to make some graft and pay off your political army or something – why, that's different!— *Mr Smith Goes to Washington*, 1939

2 any kind of work, especially hard work *UK, 1859*
- I've been out of graft for months; and now this is the best I can do. They've made a bit of work repairing the roads and fillin' the drain down Riley Street.—Frank Hardy, *Power Without Glory*, p. 60, 1950
- [I]t was heavy "graft" (work) and very little "denari" [money][.]—Butch Reynolds, *Broken Hearted Clown*, p. 30, 1953
- [G]et back to graft put[t]ing the cane about[.]—Frank Norman, *Bang To Rights*, p. 58, 1958

graft *verb*

1 to work hard *UK, 1859*
- We'd been grafting hard for twenty hours.—William Dodson, *The Sharp End*, p. xv, 2001
- James Last box sets came to those who grafted.—Mark Steel, *Reasons to be Cheerful*, p. 4, 2001

2 to labour at criminal enterprises *UK, 1859*
- I thought we agreed not to graft again for another three weeks. —Charles Raven, *Underworld Nights*, p. 22, 1956
- —Angela Devlin, *Prison Patter*, p. 58, 1996

grafter *noun*

1 a hard worker *AUSTRALIA, 1891*

- She was hard to please, rather a "nark" as he put it, and easily "needled" (annoyed), but a "clever dona" (good girl) and a "grafter" (worker). —Butch Reynolds, *Broken Hearted Clown*, p. 29, 1953
- You will? Thanks a mill, Norm. You're a real little grafter. —Barry Humphries, *A Nice Night's Entertainment*, p. 186, 1981

2 among market traders, a market trader *UK*

- —Patrick O'Shaughnessy, *Market Traders' Slang*, 1979

3 a thief, a crook, a swindler *US, 1866*

- [N]ipped off on a plane with Anzac Jack, a dead [very] young grafter, leaving a whole load of angst behind. —Derek Raymond (Robin Cook), *The Crust on its Uppers*, p. 20, 1962

4 a criminal who identifies opportunities for other thieves *UK*

- —Piers Paul Read, *The Train Robbers*, 1978

graf-write *verb*

to write or draw in the style of graffiti *US*

- "Underground Vandal" puts Freestyle up front in a song that finds him representing the best underground rappers by graf-writing their names on walls throughout New York City. —*Denver Westword*, 20th April 2000

graf-writing *noun*

the act of *graffiti*-ing *US*

- Banksy is one of the most explosive artists in the British graf-writing squadron. —*The Face*, p. 146, June 2001
- And the graf-writing element can be compared to the hieroglyphics of ancient Egypt. —*Black Parenting Today*, p. 15, 30th June 2001

grain *noun*

a heavy drinker *US*

- —*American Speech*, p. 276, December 1963: 'American Indian student slang'

grain and drain train *noun*

solitary confinement *US*

- Twenty days on the grain and drain train for Andy down there in solitary. —Stephen King, *Different Seasons*, p. 66, 1982

grains *noun*

semen; sperm *TRINIDAD AND TOBAGO*

- —Lise Winer, *Dictionary of the English/Creole of Trinidad & Tobago*, 2003

grammie *noun*

a tape deck, especially one mounted in the dashboard of a truck or car *US*

- —Elementary Electronics, *Dictionary of CB Lingo*, p. 71, 1976

grammy *noun*

one gram (of a drug) *US*

- —Jay Robert Nash, *Dictionary of Crime*, p. 156, 1992

gramp; gramps; grampa *noun*

a grandfather; also used as an address for an old man *UK, 1898*

A slurring of GRANDPA.

- Grandpa. Here Gramp. Wake up a minute. —Clive Exton, *No Fixed Abode [Six Granada Plays]*, p. 120, 1959
- I'm real crook on [displeased with] youse gramps!!! —Barry Humphries, *Bazza Pulls It Off!*, 1971

gran *noun*

a grandmother, especially as a form of address *UK, 1863*

Childish or affectionate shortening.

- [Y]our old gran had a flat top cart there, used to sell salt fish[.] —Alan Bleasdale, *Boys From the Blackstuff*, 1982
- [W]atch your language in front in front of your gran[.] —Danny King, *The Burglar Diaries*, p. 12, 2001

grand *noun*

a unit of 1,000, usually applied to US dollars or the pound sterling *US, 1915*

- [C]onning some old dear out of a few grand. —Frank Norman, *Bang To Rights*, p. 108, 1958
- A fin [five dollars] for a number-five cap. A sixteenth [of an ounce] for a 'C' [one hundred dollars]. A piece [ounce] for a grand. —Iceberg Slim (Robert Beck), *Pimp*, p. 128, 1969
- A.J: How much? Lucas: Nine grand! —*Empire Records*, 1985
- We weren't doing jumps any higher than twelve grand, the maximum height we could go without oxygen. —Andy McNab, *Immediate Action*, p. 147, 1995

grand bag *noun*

in homosexual usage, a large scrotum *US*

- —*Male Swinger Number 3*, p. 45, 1981: 'The complete gay dictionary'

grand canyon *noun*

in homosexual usage, a loose anus and rectum *US*

- —*Male Swinger Number 3*, p. 45, 1981: 'The complete gay dictionary'

grand charge *noun*

an empty threat or boast *TRINIDAD AND TOBAGO, 1973*

- —Lise Winer, *Dictionary of the English/Creole of Trinidad & Tobago*, 2003

grand dad *noun*

a grandfather *UK, 1819*

- Clean those shoes, my lad. You're not at your Grand-dad's now. The holiday's over. —Alexander Baron, *A Bit of Happiness [Six Granada Plays]*, p. 203, 1959
- Fucking hell, he's old – he looks like my granddad. —Simon Napier-Bell, *Black Vinyl White Powder*, p. 11, 2001

grand duchess *noun*

a hetersexual woman who enjoys the company of homosexual men *US*

- —*American Speech*, p. 57, Spring-Summer 1970: 'Homosexual slang'

grandfather clock *noun*

the penis *UK*

Rhyming slang for COCK, often paired with POLISH AND GLOSS (to masturbate).

- She wouldn't go all the way but she didn't mind polishing my Grandfather Clock. —Ray Puxley, *Cockney Rabbit*, 1992

grandma *noun*

1 the bleed period of the menstrual cycle *US, 1929*

- Grandma's here. —Karen Houppert, *The Curse*, 1999

2 an older homosexual man *US*

- —Roger Blake, *The American Dictionary of Sexual Terms*, p. 91, 1964

Grandma *noun*

the lowest gear in a truck or car *US, 1941*

The lowest gear is the slowest gear, hence the reference to grandmother.

- —Mary Elting, *Trucks at Work*, 1946
- Put it where Grandpa put it: in Grandma. —Ken Weaver, *Texas Crude*, p. 9, 1984

grandma's peepers *noun*

in dominoes, the 1–1 piece *US*

- —Dominic Armanino, *Dominoes*, p. 17, 1959

grandpa *noun*

a grandfather; also used as an affectionate form of address to an old man *UK, 1848*

An abbreviation of 'grandpapa'.

- Grandpa. Here Gramp. Wake up a minute. —Clive Exton, *No Fixed Abode [Six Granada Plays]*, p. 120, 1959
- Jesus, grandpa, don't you ever think to cut your toenails? —Stuart Jeffries, *Mrs Slocombe's Pussy*, p. 216, 2000

grandpappy *noun*

grandfather *US*

- We even had a couple of grandpappys drawing pensions from the Spanish American War. —Chester Himes, *Cast the First Stone*, p. 183, 1952

grandpa's dozen *noun*

a twelve-pack of inexpensive beer *US*

- —Judi Sanders, *Mashing and Munching in Ames*, p. 9, 1994

grandstand *noun*

a large handicap weight for a racehorse *AUSTRALIA*

- [M]ost experts had dismissed him from calculations because he had the 'grandstand' of 10 stone 9lbs. on his back. —James Holledge, *The Great Australian Gamble*, p. 141, 1966
- 'You stupid mug!' one of the battlers said to the jockey. 'Our horse will have to carry the grandstand next start.' —Frank Hardy and Athol George Mulley, *The Needy and the Greedy*, p. 47, 1975

grandstand *verb*

to perform in a flashy manner, with an eye towards audience perception rather than the level of performance *US, 1900*

- He had made us learn strategy all over again, made us promise to lay off the grandstanding. —Dick Gregory, *Nigger*, p. 70, 1964
- Why didn't you call in for backup instead of makin' a grandstand play. —*48 Hours*, 1982
- BLEEK: Shadow, when are you gonna stop grandstanding? SHADOW: The people eat it up. —*Mo' Better Blues*, 1990

granfer *noun*

a grandfather *UK*

A slurring of 'grandfather'.

- GRANDPA: That's the first new pair of shoes I've had in years that is. I don't think they're bad. LOFTY: They're all right, Granfer. — Clive Exton, *No Fixed Abode [Six Granada Plays]*, p. 129, 1959

granite boulder *noun*

the shoulder *UK*

Rhyming slang.

- — Ray Puxley, *Cockney Rabbit*, 1992

grannie grunt; old grannie *noun*

an annoying person *UK*

Rhyming slang for **CUNT** (an idiot).

- [A]n "old Grannie" refers to someone who is annoyingly sensible or "old womanish". The slow driver that you cannot overtake, for example[.] — Ray Puxley, *Cockney Rabbit*, 1992

grannies *noun*

the bleed period of the menstrual cycle *US, 1929*

- Ive got the grannies. — Karen Houppert, *The Curse*, 1999

grannie's wrinkles; grannies *noun*

winkles (seafood) *UK*

Rhyming slang.

- — Ray Puxley, *Cockney Rabbit*, 1992

granny *noun*

1 grandmother *UK, 1698*

- I got a jug of rotgut your granny left behind. — C.D. Payne, *Youth in Revolt*, p. 389, 1993

2 an old woman *UK, 1699*

Extended from the previous sense.

- US anti-war grannies face justice[.] — *www.news.bbc.co.uk*, 23rd July 2005

3 the bleed period of the menstrual cycle *US, 1929*

- [A] funny term my grandmother (who is 73) uses. She calls menstruation 'granny,' and it was used by the women in her family. — a contributor, *The Museum of Menstruation and Women's Health*, August 2001

4 a bungled knot; anything that has been bungled *US*

- — John Gould, *Maine Lingo*, p. 115, 1975

5 the quality of pride *UK, 1851*

Defined by Henry Mayhew in 1851 as 'the conceit of superior knowledge'. Derives from the idiomatic phrase 'teach your grandmother to suck eggs', in which 'granny' (an abbreviation of grandmother) represents anyone wiser than you.

- You wait here like good boys and we'll be back to beat the fucking granny out the lot of you. — Martin King and Martin Knight, *The Naughty Nineties*, p. 49, 1999

6 an apple of the Granny Smith variety *AUSTRALIA, 1944*

- I pop in a fresh slice of granny every day and I've just given his swing a wipe and his mirror a bit of a lick and a promise in case he gets lonely. — Barry Humphries, *A Nice Night's Entertainment*, p. 131, 1971
- — Barry Humphries, *A Nice Night's Entertainment*, p. 207, 1981

granny-dumping *noun*

the convenient removal of elderly relatives from family responsibility to permanent hospital or nursing-home care *UK*

- Delegates also expressed their concern about 'granny dumping'. — *The Times*, 8th April 1987
- [T]he plan [for overseas Japanese retirement colonies] died a natural death because an incensed public viewed it as a form of "granny-dumping"[.] — Charles Danziger, *Japan for Starters*, p. 129, 1996

granny farm *noun*

a care home or estate for elderly residents *UK*

From 'granny' (generic old woman). An ironic coinage reflecting UK society's apparent treatment of the elderly as so much livestock to be managed by others.

- [T]he old, segregated from the family and its rejuvenating frictions, are dying in lonely discomfort in rip-off Granny-Farms. — *The Guardian*, 9th January 1988

granny gear *noun*

1 tranquillizers and anti-depressants, such as Valium™, Prozac™ and Rohipnol™ *UK*

Drugs intended for **GRANNY** (an old woman), or intended to slow you down which is a stereotypical characteristic of a grandmother.

2 a car, truck or bicycle's lowest gear; in a four-wheel drive vehicle, the lowest gear combined with the lowest range in the transfer case *US*

- — John Edwards, *Auto Dictionary*, p. 71, 1993
- Go ahead-downshift into a 24 x 32-tooth granny gear, stand up and pound the pedals. — *Mountain Bike Magazine's Complete Guide To Mountain Biking Skills*, p. 61, 1996

granny jazzer *noun*

used as a euphemism for 'motherfucker' *US*

- — *Maledicta*, p. 11, Summer 1977: 'A word for it!'

granny panties *noun*

large, cotton underpants *US*

- — Connie Eble (Editor), *UNC-CH Campus Slang*, p. 5, Spring 1991

granny rag *noun*

a red flag used for indicating an oversized load on a truck *US*

- — Montie Tak, *Truck Talk*, p. 77, 1971

granny's here for a visit

experiencing the bleed period of the menstrual cycle *US*

- — Collin Baker et al., *College Undergraduate Slang Study Conducted at Brown University*, p. 129, 1968

granola *noun*

a throw-back to the hippie counterculture of the 1960s *US*

- — Connie Eble (Editor), *UNC-CH Campus Slang*, p. 3, Fall 1982
- Kia (T. Wendy McMillan) sets her up with geeky granola-type Ely (V.S. Brodie). — *Vogue*, p. 91, June 1994
- Welcome to Padua High School, your typical urban-suburban high school in Portland, Oregon. Smarties, Skids, Preppies, Granolas, Loners, Lovers, the In and the Out Crowd rub sleep out of their eyes and head for the main building. — *Ten Things I Hate About You*, 1999

Grant *noun*

a fifty-dollar note *US*

From the engraving of Ulysses S. Grant, a distinguished general and less-than-distinguished president, on the note.

- With shaking fingers she showed Bernie two new crisp fifty-dollar bills tucked into the lining of her glove. New bills always seemed to have such a lovely pale green color, apple-green. "Real U.S. Grants, baby," she told him[.] — Ross Russell, *The Sound*, p. 181, 1961
- "I see you again," Slick had told her, "it better be behind a pile of dead Presidents. Take a load of Jacksons and Grants get you off my shit list, girl." — John Sayles, *Union Dues*, p. 181, 1977
- There were twenty fifty-dollar bills. Nice new crisp U.S. Grants. — James Ellroy, *Brown's Requiem*, p. 42, 1981

g-rap *noun*

▷ **see: GANGSTA RAP**

grape *noun*

1 wine *US, 1898*

Often used in the plural.

- I don't conk out on grape! — Dan Burley, *Diggeth Thou?*, p. 34, 1959
- If they saw him he'd be forced to share it with them, just as they were when he caught one of them with the groovy grape. — Nathan Heard, *Howard Street*, p. 54, 1968
- He was just a Deep South chump driven to the grape by the confusion and disappointment of a big city. — Iceberg Slim (Robert Beck), *Trick Baby*, p. 42, 1969
- The wine bottle, the reefer, or Jesus. A taste of grape, the weed or the cross. — H. Rap Brown, *Die Nigger Die!*, p. 17, 1969
- There's a wine store, baby; let's chip in and get a couple bottles of grapes. — Donald Goines, *Dopefiend*, p. 95, 1971
- We took another bottle of the beautiful grape with us. — Odie Hawkins, *Scars and Memories*, p. 176, 1987
- Dot Parker was no stranger to the grape[.] — Terry Southern, *Now Dig This*, p. 206, 2001

2 gossip *US, 1864*

A shortening of **GRAPEVINE** (the source of gossip).

- — Don R. McCreary (Editor), *Dawg Speak*, 2001

3 in the language of car salesmen, a promising potential customer *US*

Like the grape, the customer is 'ripe for picking'.

- — *American Speech*, p. 312, Autumn-Winter 1975: 'The jargon of car salesmen'

4 a member of a flight deck refuelling crew *US, 1986*

- The "grapes," the puple-shirted members of a refueling crew, hauled out a heavy hose from the catwalk alongside the flight deck[.] — Gerry Carroll, *North S*A*R*, p. 170, 1991
- — *Seattle Times*, p. A9, 12th April 1998: 'Grunts, squids not grunting from the same dictionary'

grapefruit league *noun*

in baseball, a notional league of the teams that conduct spring training in Florida *US, 1929*

- —Richard Scholl, *Running Press Glossary of Baseball Language*, p. 39, 1977
- Tom Hamilton, Mike Hegan and Matt Underwood will do the first three games of the Grapefruit League season on March 5, 6 and 7[.] — *Plain Dealer*, p. D6, 21st January 2004

grapefruits *noun*

large female breasts *US*

- —Roger Blake, *The American Dictionary of Sexual Terms*, p. 91, 1964
- —Dale Gordon, *The Dominion Sex Dictionary*, p. 79, 1967

grape parfait *noun*

LSD *US, 1977*

From the purple hue of the drug.

- —Richard A. Spears, *The Slang and Jargon of Drugs and Drink*, p. 231, 1986
- —Mike Haskins, *Drugs*, p. 285, 2003

graper *noun*

in oil drilling, a sycophantic worker *US*

- —Jerry Robertson, *Oil Slanguage*, p. 61, 1954

grapes *noun*

1 the testicles *US*

- Tried to kick him in the grapes, at least. Not sure if I connected. —George V. Higgins, *Penance for Jerry Kennedy*, p. 227, 1985

2 the female breasts *US*

- —Edith A. Folb, *runnin' down some lines*, p. 240, 1980

3 haemorrhoids *NEW ZEALAND*

- —David McGill, *David McGill's Complete Kiwi Slang Dictionary*, p. 58, 1998

4 a percent sign (%) on a computer keyboard *US*

- —Eric S. Raymond, *The New Hacker's Dictionary*, p. 39, 1991

grapes of wrath *noun*

wine *US*

- —Marcus Hanna Boulware, *Jive and Slang of Students in Negro Colleges*, 1947

grapevine *noun*

1 a network of rumour or gossip; the mysterious source of rumours *US, 1862*

- Word buzzed through the grapevine about the new "fish"[.] —Mezz Mezzrow, *Really the Blues*, p. 10, 1946
- How should I know? The grapevine don't come from one guy. —Mickey Spillane, *My Gun is Quick*, p. 38, 1950
- She realizes it wasn't grapevine magic that tipped Baptiste to her mother's visit. —Iceberg Slim (Robert Beck), *Doom Fox*, p. 99, 1978

2 a line, especially a washing line *UK*

Rhyming slang, often shortened to 'grape'.

- —Ray Puxley, *Cockney Rabbit*, 1992

graph *noun*

an autograph *US*

- At poety readings at the 92nd Street Y, they usually managed to hang out backstage grabbing the 'graphs, man. —Ed Sanders, *Tales of Beatnik Glory*, p. 21, 1975

grappler *noun*

a wrestler *US*

More of a fan word than an insider's word, but heard.

- If he was to be considered the best grappler ever, he would have to join the WWF and beat the likes of the Ultimate Warrior and Hulk Hogan. — *Herb's Wrestling Tidbits*, 12th July 1990

grass *noun*

1 an informer *UK, 1932*

Rhyming slang for 'hopper', **COPPER** (a policeman), but see also the 2000 citation.

- I haven't got any time for grasses, but if people can't be barons with out going around punching little geezers up in the air. They deserve a capture. —Frank Norman, *Bang To Rights*, p. 19, 1958
- I'm no fuckin' grass. Right? —Cath Staincliffe, *Trainers*, p. 55, 1999
- "There's an informer on the spur, lads!" he proclaimed, pointing towards the cell where Grady was installing his few intact possessions. "Ssssss," came the reply in chorus. (An informer in prison is known as a grass from the phrase "snake in the grass".) — *The Guardian*, 30th March 2000

2 marijuana *US, 1943*

The term of choice during the 1960s and 70s.

- Don't nobody come up thataway when he picks up on some good grass. —Mezz Mezzrow, *Really the Blues*, p. 213, 1946
- At one time or another I have winked at marijuana (and don't call it tea or reefers or grass or weed or by any other romantic euphemism); I have never been other than disgusted by heroin and its users. — *Metronone*, p. 34, September 1951
- But I never blew up a joint in the folks' apartment the whole time I was on pot – that's grass, you know; you know, marijuana. I really never did. —David Hulburd, *H is For Heroin*, p. 47, 1952
- Their hunger for "grass," or marijuana, and H was unquenchable; to keep themselves in "junk," they forged prescription blanks, encouraged robbery, sold their furniture, drove all the way to Mexico for supplies, and borrowed from their parents. —*Saturday Review*, 21st June 1952
- "Movement," Solly said, "how's about stashing a couple ounces for me? This new grass doublebanks me." —Bernard Wolfe, *The Late Risers*, p. 84, 1954
- Marijuana has names like weed, grass, tea, Mary Jane, and gage, but usually it is called pot. — *New York Times*, p. 27, 21st March 1966
- WYATT: No, man – this is grass. GEORGE: You – you mean marijuana? WYATT: Yeah. —Peter Fonda, *Easy Rider*, p. 121, 1969
- Acid, booze, and ass / Needles, guns, and grass / Lots of laughs, lots of laughs. —Joni Mitchell, *Blue*, 1971
- Grass gets you through times of no money better than money gets you through times of no grass. —Stephen Gaskin, *Amazing Dope Tales*, p. 90, 1980

3 hair, especially a crew cut *AUSTRALIA, 1919*

- —Lou Shelly, *Hepcats Jive Dictionary*, p. 12, 1945

4 a woman's pubic hair *US*

- —Roger Blake, *The American Dictionary of Sexual Terms*, p. 91, 1964
- — *Maledicta*, p. 131, Summer/Winter 1982: 'Dyke diction: the language of lesbians'

▸ **have more grass than Kew Gardens**

used of a person who is known as a regular police informer *UK*

- "You can depend on me, Arthur." "You? You've got more grass than Kew Gardens." "Me, Arthur? Never. On my mother's eyesight." "She's dead." —Anthony Masters, *Minder*, p. 167, 1984

▸ **out to grass**

retired from work; hence no longer in use *UK*

An image of old horses put out to grass. Noted by Albert Petch, 1969.

- You may have an impeccable body of qualifications, but if the cheekbones fail to come up to scratch, then you're out on your ear. And if you are beautiful but 30-plus, then you're out to grass anyway. — *New Statesman*, 1st May 2000

grass *verb*

1 to inform; to betray *UK, 1936*

From **GRASS** (an informer). Also variant 'grass up'.

- Anyhow, it was a dirty trick grassing his pals. —James Curtis, *The Gilt Kid*, 1936
- Grassed on me, he did," I said morosely. (Note: Grass is English thief slang for inform.) —William Burroughs, *Naked Lunch*, p. 2, 1957
- [T]hey could have got out of it if they had grassed their mates[.] —Frank Norman, *Bang To Rights*, p. 70, 1958
- Once Fatty started grassing he couldn't stop! — *The Sweeney*, p. 19, 1976
- You grassed up the Kingston blag to the Sweeney. — *Terry Victor, 'A Family Affair*, 1993
- — *The Official Encyclopaedia of New Scotland Yard'*, *Appendix six*, 1999
- You're not going to grass us up, are yer? —Cath Staincliffe, *Trainers*, p. 55, 1999
- It's very hard to grass someone up if you know them well. —Dave Courtney, *Raving Lunacy*, p. 7, 2000

2 to engage in sexual intimacy *CANADA*

- We went grassin' up on skin hill. —Lewis Poteet, *The South Shore Phrase Book*, p. 53, 1999

3 to defeat; to beat *US*

- —Connie Eble (Editor), *UNC-CH Campus Slang*, p. 3, November 2002

grassback *noun*

a promiscuous girl *US*

- — *Current Slang*, p. 7, Winter 1969

grass bottle *noun*

pieces of broken bottle glass *TRINIDAD AND TOBAGO*

- —Lise Winer, *Dictionary of the English/Creole of Trinidad & Tobago*, 2003

grass castle *noun*

a large dwelling owned by someone believed to have made their fortune dealing in marijuana *AUSTRALIA*

- That bloke's must have 'worked' hard to build himself a Grass Castle! — *Wordmap (www.abc.net.au/wordmap)*, 2003

grass colt *noun*
an illegitimate child *CANADA, 1990*
'It's like a colt born out on the pasture, where no one sees it, rather than at home in the barn', from *Dictionary of Prince Edward Island* (in *New Maritimes*, p. 29, March–April 1990).

grassed up *adjective*
in lobstering, covered with slime *US*
• —Kendall Merriam, *The Illustrated Dictionary of Lobstering*, p. 42, 1978

grasser *noun*
an informer *UK, 1957*

grass fight *noun*
a hard fought argument or fight *AUSTRALIA*
• Of course, this did not stop the Melbournians and the Sydneyites having the occasional argument, slanging match or grass fight over such fundamental issues as beer, race horses and football.—Frank Hardy, *Hardy's People*, p. 63, 1986

grass-fighter *noun*
a tough and willing brawler *AUSTRALIA, 1951*
• But his shuffling gait was deceptive: he was as lithe and agile as a buck deer and a tough grass fighter.—Frank Hardy, *Legends From Benson's Valley*, p. 2, 1963

grasshead *noun*
a habitual marijuana smoker *US*
• Laughing like a grasshead now, she made another determined lunge and this time successfully caught her hands around the wheel, forcing Tony to swerve into the rod on their right.—Morton Cooper, *High School Confidential*, p. 89, 1958
• There's me, bouncing about, full of pills, full of everything I could get my hands on ... and there's Pete [Townshend], very serious, never laughing, always cool, a grasshead—Keith Moon, *Waiting For The Man*, 1999

grasshopper *noun*
1 a tourist *AUSTRALIA, 1955*
• Us locals live up here all year long and try to keep our beach safe from all you Briso and Grasshopper pricks[.]—Sandra Jobson, *Blokes*, p. 66, 1984

2 a customer who inspects one line of goods after another without buying anything *UK*
• —Patrick O'Shaughnessy, *Market Traders' Slang*, 1979

3 a type of clutch on a motorcyle *US*
• We rebuilt the clutch and bought new discs and a chain for it, then took the clutch cover, the "grasshopper" (a spring-loaded assist for a manual clutch), the tool kit, the headlight, and a few more odds and ends to be chromed.—Peter Coyote, *Sleeping Where I Fall*, p. 109, 1998

4 a police officer; a police informer *UK*
Rhyming slang for **COPPER** (policeman). Rarely heard, but as familiar as **GRASS** (an informer).

5 marijuana *UK*
• —Mike Haskins, *Drugs*, p. 287, 2003

6 in electric line work, an open-link cutout *US*
• —A.B. Chance Co., *Lineman's Slang Dictionary*, p. 8, 1980

Grasshopper *noun*
used as a humorous form of address to someone being instructed in cod-philosophical truths
From the US television series *Kung-Fu*, 1972–75.
• Look hard enough at the past, Grasshopper, and you will find the seeds that become tomorrow's mighty acorns.—Andrew Nickolds, *Back to Basics*, p. 175, 1994
• He has the air of wisdom and good humour of a guru: I half expect him to start calling me Grasshopper.—*The Guardian*, 24th July 1999

grass in the park *noun*
an informer *UK*
Rhyming slang for **NARK**, and a development of **GRASS** (informer).

grass palace *noun*
a house bought with profits from the commercial cultivation of marijuana *AUSTRALIA*
• The Nimbin hippies made money and built grass palaces[.]—Brian Preston, *Pot Planet*, p. 91, 2002

grass sandwich *noun*
a child born of a sexual union in the outdoors *CANADA*
• [In] Prince Edward Island, a term is used to describe children born of "grassing" [sexual intercourse outdoors]: a grass sandwich.—Lewis Poteet, *The South Shore Phrase Book*, p. 53, 1999

grass stains *noun*
green discoloration on the fingers of a person who has been handling marijuana *US*
• —Simon Worman, *Joint Smoking Rules*, 2001

grass-widow *noun*
a wife who is temporarily apart from her husband *UK, 1846*
Originally, mainly Anglo-Indian in use.
• —Snoo Wilson, *Grass Widow*, 1983

grass-widower *noun*
a husband who is temporarily apart from his wife *US, 1862*
• US Ambassador Edward Walker [...] who has been a grass widower since presenting his credentials in December 1997, will soon have his marital status fully restored. His wife, Wendy, who remained in Cairo [...] is now about to join him permanently.—*Jerusalem Post*, 25th May 1999

grassy ass!
thank you *US*
An intentionally butchered *gracias*.
• —Connie Eble (Editor), *UNC-CH Campus Slang*, p. 4, November 1990

grata *noun*
marijuana *UK, 1998*
• —Mike Haskins, *Drugs*, p. 287, 2003

Grauniad *noun*
▸ **the Grauniad**
the *Guardian* newspaper *UK*
An anagram, coined in the mid- to late 1970s by satirical magazine *Private Eye*. Despite the improvement in spell-check technology the nickname remains widely popular.
• [The] Guardian newspaper, celebrated for it's lousy typesetting, can henceforth never escape being, "The Grauniad".—*Sunday Telegraph*, 18th February 1979
• [B]y saying that St James' Park is in London (nr Home Office), not Newcastle – you are obviously a North London Grauniad journo [.] —*The Guardian*, 5th September 2003

gravalicious *adjective*
greedy, avaricious *JAMAICA*
• —Wailing Souls, *Bredda Bravalicious*, 1979
• Dem a rum-a-come – come-a wid a gravalicious.—Bob Marley, *Hypocrites*, 1992
• —Paul Sullivan, *Sullivan's Music Trivia*, p. 35, 2003

grave *noun*
a work shift at night, usually starting at or after midnight *US*
An abbreviation of **GRAVEYARD SHIFT**.
• —Lee Solkey, *Dummy Up and Deal*, p. 114, 1980

gravedigger *noun*
1 in the dice game crown and anchor, a spade *UK, 1961*
Of naval origin.

2 in circus usage, a hyena *US*
• —Don Wilmeth, *The Language of American Popular Entertainment*, p. 56, 1981

gravedodger *noun*
an old person *UK*
• The air hostesses were in great demand, having to explain to the grave-dodgers just what the fuck the Captain was on about.—Dean Cavanagh, *Mile High Meltdown (Disco Biscuits)*, p. 210, 1996

gravel *noun*
1 an air-delivered mine introduced by the US in Vietnam *US*
Formally known as an XM42 mine dispensing system.
• Gravel was a little Marquis de Sade touch introduced in the Vietnam War. A tiny, innocent looking explosive about the size of a lemon, it was a mine released in large numbers from low-flying aircraft. —William C. Anderson, *Bat-21*, p. 20, 1980

2 crack cocaine *US*
• —US Department of Justice, *Street Terms*, October 1994
• Crack is known as base, freebase, gravel, ice, rock and wash.—James Kay and Julian Cohen, *The Parents' Complete Guide to Young People and Drugs*, p. 134, 1998

gravel agitator *noun*
an infantry soldier *US, 1898*
• —*American Speech*, p. 55, February 1947: 'Pacific war language'
• We used to call non-pilots, Ground Pounders, Paddle Feet, Gravel Agitators, Grunts.—Charlie Cooper, *Tuskegee's Heroes*, p. 3, 2001

gravel and grit *noun*
faeces *UK*
Rhyming slang for **SHIT**.
• —Bodmin Dark, *Dirty Cockney Rhyming Slang*, 2003

gravel cruncher *noun*
a non-flying officer in the US Air Force *US, 1929*
• —*American Speech*, p. 310, December 1946: 'More air force slang'
• You're not bad for a gravel cruncher, Captain. —Pat Conroy, *The Great Santini*, p. 408, 1976
• Those damned gravelcrunchers back at the base already had their lunch, and by the time we land the chow hall will be closed. —Chuck Yeager, *Yeager*, p. 66, 1985

gravel-crusher *noun*
an infantry soldier *US, 1918*
• —Linda Reinberg, *In the Field*, p. 96, 1991

gravel puncher *noun*
a solitary miner using antiquated equipment *CANADA*
• Hard long work might have paid me a dollar a day, which was what the few remaining gravel punchers managed to gross on some of the better bars upriver. —V. Angier, *At Home in the Woods*, p. 197, 1951

gravel rash *noun*
scraped skin and cuts resulting from a motorcyle accident *US*
• —Lewis Poteet, *Car & Motorcyle Slang*, p. 95, 1992

grave-nudger *noun*
from the perspective of youth, an older person *UK: SCOTLAND*
• You should stick tae the over-30s nights alang wi aw the other grave-nudgers. —Michael Munro, *The Patter, Another Blast*, p. 29, 1988

graveyard *noun*
the area of a beach where waves break *US*
• —John M. Kelly, *Surf and Sea*, p. 280, 1965

graveyard shift; graveyard tour; graveyard watch *noun*
a work schedule that begins very late at night and lasts until the morning shift begins, traditionally from midnight until 8am *US, 1907*
• —Norman Carlisle, *The Modern Wonder Book of Trains and Railroading*, p. 263, 1946
• —Jerry Robertson, *Oil Slanguage*, p. 61, 1954
• JIMMIE: Now she's workin' the graveyard shift at the hospital. —*Pulp Fiction*, 1994

graveyard spiral *noun*
a downward spiral of an aeroplane from which recovery is nearly impossible and as a result of which impact with the ground is inevitable *US*
• He may think he is flying level, when actually he is turning and descending steeply in what airmen call "the graveyard spiral." —Neil Sheehan, *A Bright Shining Lie*, p. 787, 1988
• Gunfighter One watched the MiG nose over, then disappear through the clouds in a classic graveyard spiral. —Joe Weber, *Defcon One*, p. 250, 1989

gravity check *noun*
in footbag, the bag dropping to the ground *US*
• —Jim Crotty, *How to Talk American*, p. 122, 1997

gravy *noun*
1 money, especially money that is easily and/or illegally obtained *US, 1930*
• We were in the gravy once more[.] —Mezz Mezzrow, *Really the Blues*, p. 131, 1946
• On this gravy you pay a maximum 26 percent tax,not the full graduated scale. —Bernard Wolfe, *The Late Risers*, p. 71, 1954
• And what does Christ think of the easy-money boys who do none of the work and take all of the gravy? —Budd Schulberg, *On the Waterfront*, 1954
• "You getting all the gravy?" —Ross Russell, *The Sound*, p. 189, 1961
• "And all that gravy you'd be missing." "Right on! And all that unsopped up gravy". —Odie Hawkins, *The Busting Out of an Ordinary Man*, p. 156, 1985

2 an unexpected benefit *US, 1910*
• A big turnover is the gravy for these guesthouses. —Jack Lait and Lee Mortimer, *Washington Confidential*, p. 68, 1951
• After this it's all gravy. I've done it for five innings and nobody could ask for more. —Jim Bouton, *Ball Four*, p. 315, 1970

3 in poker and other games that are bet on, winnings *US*
• —Albert H. Morehead, *The Complete Guide to Winning Poker*, p. 264, 1967

4 any sexual emission, male or female *UK, 1796*
• Going down for the gravy [oral sex]. —Jack Slater, 1978

5 blood *UK*
• You reckon inside some geezer's Judge Dread [head] they got to have a load of gravy. Not this geezer's. —Jeremy Cameron, *Brown Bread in Wengen*, p. 4–5, 1999

6 a mixture of blood and drug solution in a syringe *US*
Perhaps from 'gravy' as 'blood' in C19 boxing slang.
• Addicts call this "shooting gravy" "Because that's what it is – right? Cooked blood?" —James Mills, *The Panic in Needle Park*, p. 78, 1966
• —Edward R. Bloomquist, *Marijuana*, p. 341, 1971
• —Richard A. Spears, *The Slang and Jargon of Drugs and Drink*, p. 232, 1986
• —Mike Haskins, *Drugs*, p. 284, 2003

7 sexual innuendo or bawdiness when used to enliven a dull script *UK*
A pun on **SAUCE** (impudence).
• Put some gravy on it – make it saucy! —*an unnamed BBC Radio programme*, 13th September 1973

8 a prison sentence *UK, 1950*
Especially in the phrase **DISH OUT THE GRAVY** (to sentence harshly).
• —Angela Devlin, *Prison Patter*, p. 58, 1996

9 pasta sauce *US, 1976*
Mid-Atlantic Italian-American usage.
• —Claudio R. Salvucci, *The Philadelphia Dialect Dictionary*, p. 43, 1996

▸ **clear gravy**
an unexpected bonus or profit *US*
An embellishment of the more common **GRAVY**.
• —John Gould, *Maine Lingo*, p. 52, 1975

gravy *adjective*
all right *US*
• —Connie Eble (Editor), *UNC-CH Campus Slang*, p. 5, October 2002

gravy
used for expressing approval *UK*
• — Susie Dent, *The Language Report*, p. 75, 2003

gravy hauler *noun*
a truck driver who will only drive high-paying jobs *US*
• —Montie Tak, *Truck Talk*, p. 77, 1971

gravy run *noun*
on the railways, a short and easy trip *US*
• —Ramon Adams, *The Language of the Railroader*, p. 71, 1977

gravy strokes *noun*
during sex, the climactic thrusts prior to male ejaculation *NEW ZEALAND*
Presumably from **GRAVY** (any sexual emission: semen).
• —Chris Lewis, *The Dictionary of Playground Slang*, p. 105, 2003

gravy train *noun*
a money-making opportunity, a generous situation *US, 1914*
• Ten per cent and I furnish the car! You think this is a gravy train you're riding? —Horace McCoy, *Kiss Tomorrow Good-bye*, p. 46, 1948
• Graft's the new gravy train so the silly things have climbed aboard[.] —Derek Raymond (Robin Cook), *The Crust on its Uppers*, p. 22, 1962
• You're upset that you're missing the gravy train? —*Airheads*, 1994
• Mercenary little bitch knew a good gravy train when she was riding one. —Danny King, *The Bank Robber Diaries*, p. 24, 2002

gray *noun*
1 a white person *US, 1944*
• You know, I've spent a lot of time wondering what it is you spades have and us grays are looking for? —Ross Russell, *The Sound*, p. 101, 1961
• Thus, for a time, the most common term for whites in Negro parlance was "gray." —Roger Abrahams, *Positively Black*, p. 32, 1970

2 a white betting token usually worth one dollar *US, 1983*
• —Thomas L. Clark, *The Dictionary of Gambling and Gaming*, p. 93, 1987

3 a police officer *US*
• A gray – A Nigrite name reserved for police or law enforcement officers. —Robert deCoy, *The Nigger Bible*, p. 28, 1967

gray *adjective*
white, Caucasian *US, 1944*
Derogatory.
• Say, chief, what's that gray boy doing in yo' job? —Chester Himes, *If He Hollers Let Him Go*, p. 102, 1945
• I came up to the cab, and he had two gray bitches in it. —Claude Brown, *Manchild in the Promised Land*, p. 163, 1965

- GRAY BOY – A Nigrite name for a Caucasian male. — Robert deCoy, *The Nigger Bible*, p. 31, 1967
- "What about that gray girl in San Jose who had your nose wide open?" — Eldridge Cleaver, *Soul on Ice*, p. 9, 1968
- This was one little black girl you gray boys wouldn't get a chance to play out of a million. — Donald Goines, *Whoreson*, p. 256, 1972
- Baby, it's a hip little supper club on Third Avenue and a lotta actors are the tricks and most of the girls are gray and classy and the bread is long. — A.S. Jackson, *Gentleman Pimp*, p. 161, 1973

gray area *noun*

in motor racing, the portion of the track immediately above the quickest line around the track *US*

- — Hal Higdon, *Finding the Groove*, p. 301, 1980

Graybar hotel; Graybar Motel *noun*

a jail or prison *US, 1970*

- "Pardon me, Officers," said the Greek, who certainly didn't want to share accommodations at the graybar hotel with a Turk. — Joseph Wambaugh, *The Glitter Dome*, p. 66, 1981
- At California's newest Graybar Hotel, the Centinela State Prison in Imperial County, a search is a search. — *Los Angeles Times*, p. A3, 1st April 1994
- — *Los Angeles Times*, 19th October 1994
- So for a six-month stint in the "graybar hotel," an inmate could rack up a $12,000 tab. — *Salt Lake Tribune*, p. C2, 31st January 2003

grayboy *noun*

a white male *US, 1951*

- I had copped him a lawyer / a grayboy named Sawyer. — Lightnin' Rod, *Hustlers Convention*, p. 12, 1973
- A gray boy called him a "savage" once, Leroy drove a maiming fist between his eyes. — Clarence Major, *All-Night Visitors*, p. 27, 1998

gray cat *noun*

a white male *US*

- Das why I call you up, on account'a you was tryin' t'splash on dem guinea gray cats. — Stephen Cannell, *Big Con*, p. 49–50, 1997

gray eye *noun*

a work shift that starts in the middle of the night *US*

- — Ramon Adams, *The Language of the Railroader*, p. 71, 1977

gray matter *noun*

brains, thus intelligence *US, 1899*

- I'm gonna make him think his grey matter depends on it. — *Natural Born Killers*, 1994

grays on trays *noun*

adult snowboarders *US*

Noted in the UK by Susie Dent, *The Language Report*, 2003.

- Derisively called "the grays on trays" by a Gen-Xer riding a ski-lift last year, the group of eight has proudly adopted the name. — *Plain Dealer (Cleveland, Ohio)*, p. 3J, 9th February 1997
- Grays on trays: Your parents on snowboards. — *Rock River Times (Illinois)*, 21st April 2004

grayspace *noun*

the brain *US*

- — *American Speech*, p. 27, Spring 1982: 'The langage of science fiction fan magazines'

Graystone College *noun*

a jail or prison *US, 1933*

- — Vincent J. Monteleone, *Criminal Slang*, p. 106, 1949
- "Graystone College, they call it," the coach announced. *** "It's real name is Saint Cloud State Penitentiary," the coach added. — Will Weaver, *Hard Ball*, p. 26, 1998

graze *noun*

1 in cricket, time spent fielding in a quiet area of the out field *UK, 1997*

2 food, a meal *SOUTH AFRICA*

- What's for graze mom? — *Surfrikan Slang*, 2004

graze *verb*

1 to pay only superficial attention to any television channel, preferring instead to flick from one programme to another *US*

- The term goes beyond television to the whole diversity of newspapers, Internet pages, magazine sections, etc, that surround us. As the Washingto Post put it, "random grazing is in". — David Rowan, *A Glossary for the 90s*, p. 105, 1998

2 (used of an amphetamine user) to search obsessively in a carpet for pieces of amphetamine or methamphetamine *US*

- — Geoffrey Froner, *Digging for Diamonds*, p. 33, 1989

grease *noun*

1 any lubricant used in anal sex *US*

- — Donald Webster Cory and John P. LeRoy, *The Homosexual and His Society*, p. 264, 1963: 'A lexicon of homosexual slang'
- — *The Guild Dictionary of Homosexual Terms*, p. 19, 1965
- — *Male Swinger Number 3*, p. 45, 1981: 'The complete gay dictionary'

2 any hair cream *BAHAMAS*

- — John A. Holm, *Dictionary of Bahamian English*, p. 93, 1982

3 nitroglycerin *US*

- — Vincent J. Monteleone, *Criminal Slang*, p. 106, 1949
- If you really want to get good as a touch man, you got to study grease and explosives for a couple of years. — Red Rudensky, *The Gonif*, p. 80, 1970

4 in trucking, ice or snow *US*

- — Wayne Floyd, *Jason's Authentic Dictionary of CB Slang*, p. 18, 1976

5 food, especially US Army c-rations *US*

- — Linda Reinberg, *In the Field*, p. 96, 1991
- — E.M.Flangn Jr *Army*, p. 48, 1991

6 a young, urban tough *US*

An abbreviation of **GREASER**.

- I'm a grease, same as Dally. — S.E. Hinton, *The Outsiders*, p. 25, 1967

7 a black person *US*

- — Hermese E. Roberts, *The Third Ear*, 1971

8 in pool, extreme spin imparted on the cue ball to affect the course of the object ball or the cue ball after striking the object ball *US*

- — Mike Shamos, *The Illustrated Encyclopedia of Billiards*, p. 110, 1993

9 a bribe *UK, 1823*

- There were clerks who took the grease and clerks who did not, and this man was a taker. — Charles Whited, *Chiodo*, p. 244, 1973

10 butter *UK, 1788*

A shorter form of 'axle-grease'.

- — Lou Shelly, *Hepcats Jive Dictionary*, p. 12, 1945

▸ **shoot the grease**

to make the initial approach in a confidence swindle *US*

- — Bill Reilly, *Big Al's Official Guide to Chicagoese*, p. 51, 1982

grease *verb*

1 to shoot or kill *US, 1964*

Vietnam war usage.

- "I ain't killing MacGreever just to grease some fucking Lieutenant Colonel." — Ronald J. Glasser, *365 Days*, p. 160, 1971
- He was runnin' around outside yellin' 'Troi Oi! Troi Oi! (Oh God) "and then Crowe greased him and he didn't do no more yellin. — Philip Caputo, *A Rumor of War*, p. 302, 1977
- You'll come out now or we grease you on the spot. — Alfred Coppel, *The Apocalypse Brigade*, p. 245, 1981
- What would I do if you got greased? I'd be a rifleman again. — Nelson DeMille, *Word of Honor*, p. 129, 1985
- They greased half the 4th platoon and Lieutenant Stennett's brand-new radioman, and we greased so many of them it wasn't even funny. — Larry Heinemann, *Paco's Story*, p. 7, 1986
- The A-gunner's brains blew all over him. His squad was getting greased. — John Skipp and Craig Spector, *The Scream*, p. 99, 1988
- I'm gonna grease somebody in here I swear to God! — *Airheads*, 1994

2 to bribe or otherwise favourably induce others to act as desired *UK, 1528*

- [T]hey needed fifty dollars each to grease the right guy. — Babs Gonzales, *I Paid My Dues*, p. 73–84, 1967
- "Her old man is doing a lot of greasing in the district." — Iceberg Slim (Robert Beck), *Pimp*, p. 253, 1969
- [J]udges who could be greased and judges who could not. — Charles Whited, *Chiodo*, p. 243, 1973
- — Angela Devlin, *Prison Patter*, p. 59, 1996

3 to eat *US*

- — Inez Cordosa Freeman, *The Joint*, p. 502, 1984

4 to use nitroglycerin to break into a safe *US*

- — Vincent J. Monteleone, *Criminal Slang*, p. 106, 1949

5 to barely pass a course in school or college *US*

- — *Time Magazine*, p. 46, 24th August 1959

▸ **grease heel**

to run away quickly *TRINIDAD AND TOBAGO, 1939*

- — Lise Winer, *Dictionary of the English/Creole of Trinidad & Tobago*, 2003

▸ **grease someone's palm**
to persuade by bribery *UK, 1807*
- If you grease his palm, he'll sit you down by the mock waterfall and tell you his life story. —Josh Alan Friedman, *Tales of Times Square*, p. 58, 1986
- [A]n informer called Joe Bloggs whose palm needed to be greased[.] —Duncan MacLaughlin, *The Filth*, p. 115, 2002

▸ **grease the skids**
to facilitate something, especially by extra legal means *US*
- If you need me to grease the skids obtaining the various licenses and permits, all you got to do is say the word. —Robert Campbell, *Nibbled to Death by Ducks*, p. 275, 1989

▸ **grease the tracks**
to be hit by a train *US*
- —Ramon Adams, *The Language of the Railroader*, p. 71, 1977

▸ **grease the weasel**
to have sex (from the male perspective) *US*
- —Chris Lewis, *The Dictionary of Playground Slang*, p. 105, 2003

▸ **grease your chops**
to eat *US*
- [T]here wasn't a gas-meter between them all, and they couldn't remember when they'd greased their chops last. —Mezz Mezzrow, *Really the Blues*, p. 177, 1946
- —Paul Glover, *Words from the House of the Dead*, 1974

greaseball *noun*
1 a person of Latin-American or Mediterranean extraction *US, 1922*
A derogatory generic derived from a swarthy complexion.
- —*American Speech*, p. 306, December 1964: 'Lingua cosa nostra'
- Three kikes, one guinea, one greaseball. —Lenny Bruce, *The Essential Lenny Bruce*, p. 11, 1967
- The second time around she was standing with some monster guinea with a leather jacket and no teeth. She pointed at Buddy. The big greaseball lumbered over to the car[.] —Richard Price, *The Wanderers*, p. 186, 1974
- All he did, he said sorta under his breath, he said "greaseballs, fucking spicdicks" – and they laid into him. —*Saturday Night Fever*, 1977
- It was among the Italians. It was real greaseball shit. —*Goodfellas*, 1990
- Now, these old greaseballs might not look it, but believe me, these are the guys who secretly controlled Las Vegas. —*Casino*, 1995

2 an odious, unappealing, unattractive person *US, 1917*
Derives from racist usage.
- The greaseball on the floor was awake now, but he wasn't looking at me. —Mickey Spillane, *My Gun is Quick*, p. 10, 1950
- I'll pay you when I'm good and ready, you dirty leech. Until then, stay out of my way. God, what a greaseball. —Bernard Wolfe, *The Late Risers*, p. 10, 1954
- [S]ome greaseball zillionaire in a sta-prest suit[.] —Melanie McGrath, *Hard, Soft & Wet*, p. 42, 1998

3 a railway mechanic *US*
- —Ramon Adams, *The Language of the Railroader*, p. 71, 1977

4 in circus and carnival usage, a food concession stand *US*
- —Don Wilmeth, *The Language of American Popular Entertainment*, p. 117, 1981

greaseburger *noun*
a despicable person *US*
- "He is such a greasburger!" Duck told Dirk. —Francesca Lia Block, *Witch Baby*, p. 107, 1991

greased *adjective*
drunk *US, 1928*
- —Pete Brown, *Man Walks into a Pub*, 2003

grease for peace
used as a humorous farewell *US*
A catchphrase television sign-off on the *Sha Na Na* programme (1971–81). Repeated with referential humour.

grease gun *noun*
the US Army's M-3 submachine gun *US*
Based on **GREASE** (to kill).
- They carry a shotgun, a .38 caliber pistol and .45 caliber semiautomatic rifle – known in the military as a grease gun. —Bill Cardoso, *The Maltese Sangweech*, p. 4, 1984
- Gotta grease gun, K-Bar by his side / These are the weapons that he lives by. —Sandee Shaffer Johnson, *Cadences*, p. 98, 1986
- —Linda Reinberg, *In the Field*, p. 96, 1991

grease-hand *noun*
a bribe *TRINIDAD AND TOBAGO, 1966*
- —Lise Winer, *Dictionary of the English/Creole of Trinidad & Tobago*, 2003

grease it!
in playground basketball, used as a cry to encourage a ball tottering on the rim of the hoop to fall through for a score *US*
- —Chuck Wielgus and Alexander Wolff, *The In-Your-Face Basketball Book*, p. 44, 1980

grease man *noun*
a criminal with expertise in using explosives to open safes *US*
- Since I was considered one of the top grease men in the country, it was natural that I would be contacted. —Red Rudensky, *The Gonif*, p. 7, 1970

grease money *noun*
a bribe *TRINIDAD AND TOBAGO, 1987*
- —Lise Winer, *Dictionary of the English/Creole of Trinidad & Tobago*, 2003

grease monkey *noun*
1 a car or aeroplane mechanic *US, 1928*
- —Lou Shelly, *Hepcats Jive Talk Dictionary*, p. 46, 1945
- Well, Winfred, grease monkeys get a good union wage with fringe benefits and a pension plan[.] —Max Shulman, *I was a Teen-Age Dwarf*, p. 80, 1959
- —Tom MacPherson, *Dragging and Driving*, p. 139, 1960
- Me an' the Chief here locked horns with two greasemonkeys. —Ken Kesey, *One Flew Over the Cuckoo's Nest*, p. 264, 1962
- A free greasemonkey with otherwise clean habits is looking for garage space in which to practice his trade. —*The Digger Papers*, p. 20, August 1968
- "Everyone assumes he was a grase monkey. But at twenty years old he was a first lieutenant. He flew a P-Forty-seven." —Elmore Leonard, *52 Pick-up*, p. 88, 1974
- Maybe, just maybe, he'd won himself a date, this middle-aged grease monkey in shining armor, who would steal Kandi Barbour from the Dire Straits. —Josh Alan Friedman, *Tales of Times Square*, p. 12, 1986

2 in oil drilling, a worker who lubricates equipment *US*
- —Jerry Robertson, *Oil Slanguage*, p. 61, 1954

grease orchard *noun*
an oil field *US*
- —Jerry Robertson, *Oil Slanguage*, p. 62, 1954

grease out *verb*
to enjoy good luck *US*
- —Charles Shafer, *Folk Speech in Texas Prisons*, p. 205, 1990

grease pit *noun*
a low-quality, low-price restaurant *US*
- What the hell would I do with that grease pit? —Quentin Tarantino, *From Dusk Till Dawn*, p. 3, 1995

greaser *noun*
1 a Mexican or any Latin American *US, 1836*
Offensive.
- J. Geils explains greaser culture. —Lester Bangs, *Psychotic Reactions and Carburetor Dung*, p. 142, 1973
- Then she begins to explain about some greasers, "sort of like the Black Panters," who are kicking up dust in East L.A. —Oscar Zeta Acosta, *The Revolt of the Cockroach People*, p. 25, 1973
- I do not look down on niggers, kikes, wops or greasers. Here you are all equally worthless. —*Full Metal Jacket*, 1987
- [H]e's going by the name Edward Mallon, but you could tell by looking at him he was a greaser. Excuse me, I mean a Latin. I have to watch that. —Elmore Leonard, *Killshot*, p. 182, 1989
- — Multicultural Management Program Fellows, *Dictionary of Cautionary Words and Phrases*, 1989

2 a motorcycle gang member *UK*
The collective noun is 'grease'.
- This gang was ordinary grease, or what most people called Rockers. —Jamie Mandelkau, *Buttons*, p. 21, 1971
- The boys were in the typical style of the motor-bike boy, or "rocker", or "greaser". —Paul E Willis, *Profane Culture*, p. 11, 1978
- Gangs of mods and their rivals, the rockers, who these days call themselves "greasers" or "bikers". —*Loughborough Echo*, 28th September 1979
- [T]he fighting between mods, rockers, skinheads, Pakistanis, suedeheads, Hell's angels, boot boys, greasers, Teds, punks, soulboys, rockabillies, rude boys, casuals and every other shade of herbert going[.] —John King, *Human Punk*, p. 295, 2000

3 a hamburger, especially one from a fast-food restaurant *US*
- —Bill Reilly, *Big Al's Official Guide to Chicagoese*, p. 28, 1982

4 a young, poor tough *US*
- —J. R. Friss, *A Dictionary of Teenage Slang (Mt. Diablo High)*, 1964
- I am a greaser and most of my neighborhood rarely bothers to get a haircut. —S.E. Hinton, *The Outsiders*, p. 5, 1967

- The greasers seemed to be attending a non-stop party to which I was not invited, and I quickly decided that even if I couldn't sniff glue and drunk-drive with them, at least I could entertain. —Jennifer Blowdryer, *White Trash Debutante*, p. 11, 1997

5 a slimey lump or clot of spittle and mucus *UK: SCOTLAND*
- Some clatty [dirty] article's gobbed a great big greaser on this windy [window]. —Michael Munro, *The Patter, Another Blast*, p. 29, 1988

6 a submachine gun, especially the M-3 or M3A-1 submachine gun *US*
- —Linda Reinberg, *In the Field*, p. 96, 1991

7 a Teddy Boy *UK*
Greased hair was an important part of 1950s fashion.

grease up *verb*
to lubricate the anus, especially in order to smuggle contraband within the body *UK*
- —Angela Devlin, *Prison Patter*, p. 59, 1996

greasies *noun*
take-away food, especially fish and chips *NEW ZEALAND*
- Across the road from Joe's, a gang of callow youths eat their greasies and swig rudely from bottles of beer. —Robert Williams, *Skin Deepe*, p. 131, 1979

greasy *noun*
a shearer *AUSTRALIA, 1939*

greasy *adjective*
having an insincere and ingratiating manner *UK, 1848*
- Their greasy lawyer did everything but admit it. —Peter Straub, *The Hellfire Club*, p. 109, 1996

greasy eyeball *noun*
a foul or menacing look *AUSTRALIA*
- —James Lambert, *The Macquarie Book of Slang*, 1996

greasy luck *adjective*
good luck *US*
A whaling expression that persisted after whaling in New England.
- —Charles F. Haywood, *Yankee Dictionary*, p. 71, 1963

greasy spoon *noun*
an inexpensive and all-round low-brow restaurant *US, 1912*
- They duck out for smokes at the same time, have their crullers and java in the same lunchrooms or greasy spoons. —Jack Lait and Lee Mortimer, *New York Confidential*, p. 142, 1948
- I find myself eating at some greasy spoon next to a liquor store and talking to the most embittered cluck this side of the Continental Divide. —Clancy Sigal, *Going Away*, p. 134, 1961
- [I]t would have gone under because the people seemed to prefer a little greasy-spoon joint down the street from their place. —Nathan Heard, *Howard Street*, p. 83, 1968
- Tonight I got a date to lay a cute hashslinger that works in the greasy spoon around the corner. —Iceberg Slim (Robert Beck), *Trick Baby*, p. 219, 1969
- Annie's Restaurant was a small, greasy spoon diner located on Alvarado, off Wilshire in downtown Los Angeles. —Donald Goines, *Kenyatta's Last Hit*, p. 117, 1975
- Henry lunches with the lads, in a restaurant, pub or a specially treasured working-class caff ("greasy' spoon"). —Ann Barr and Peter York, *The Official Sloane Ranger Handbook*, p. 117, 1982
- I bought an afternoon edition of the evening paper, went to a Greasy spoon for a cup of tea and a bit of quiet. —John Milne, *Alive and Kicking*, p. 97, 1998

great *adjective*
very skilled *UK, 1784*
- Pete [Sampras] was great at blocking everything out and Tim [Henman] isn't as disciplined. —*The Guardian*, 1st June 2004

great action!
used as an expression of happy approval *US*
- —Connie Eble (Editor), *UNC-CH Campus Slang*, p. 3, Fall 1980

great army *noun*
in horse racing, the body of regular bettors *AUSTRALIA*
- —Ned Wallish, *The Truth Dictionary of Racing Slang*, p. 35, 1989

Great Australian Adjective *noun*
the word 'bloody' used as an intensifier *AUSTRALIA, 1897*
This had an extremely high frequency amongst many speakers, especially formerly, though now it has lost much ground to **FUCKING**.
- The main charge against the Aussie swearer is that he is unimaginative and too closely chained to the Great Australian Adjective[.] —Harvey E. Ward, *Down Under Without Blunder*, p. 13, 1967
- And although you may not be accustomed to using the word 'bloody' and 'bastard' so early in the morning, you remember that bloody is the 'great Australian adjective', and that bastard is a 'term of endearment'. —John O'Grady, *Aussie Etiket*, p. 50, 1971
- —Arthur Chipper, *The Aussie Swearer's Guide*, 1972
- —Ignatius Jones, *The 1992 True Hip Manual*, p. 158, 1992

great balls of fire!
used as a mockingly profane expression of surprise *US*
Found in *Gone With The Wind* (1939) but made famous by Jerry Lee Lewis in his 1957 hit song written by Jack Hammer and Otis Blackwell.
- "Great balls of fire, don't make me go now!" I cried. —Max Shulman, *The Many Loves of Dobie Gillis*, p. 120, 1951
- Too much love drives a man insane / You broke my will, but what a thrill / Goodness, gracious, great balls of fire!" —Jerry Lee Lewis, *Great Balls of Fire*, 1957

great big *adjective*
intensifies the merely big *UK, 1857*
- This great big fuss ensued and I had to speak to people on their mobiles and all sorts. —*The Guardian*, 9th August 2002

great Caesar's ghost!
used as a non-profane oath *US*
The non-profane outburst of the *Metropolis Daily Planet* editor, Perry White, on *The Adventures of Superman* (1951–1957). Repeated with referential humour.

great divide *noun*
the labia *US*
From the nickname of the continental divide, where north American rivers flow either east or west. Perhaps best known from its usage in the erotic poem 'The Ballad of Eskimo Nell': 'She dropped her garments one by one / With an air of conscious pride / And as he stood in her womanhood / He saw the Great Divide'.
- —*Maledicta*, p. 185, Winter 1980: 'A new erotic vocabulary'

Great Runes *noun*
in computing, text displayed in UPPER CASE ONLY *US*
A legacy of the teletype.
- —Eric S. Raymond, *The New Hacker's Dictionary*, p. 183, 1991

great Scott!
used for registering exasperation or surprise; also as an oath *UK, 1885*
- TONY: Sorry to let you down like that. BILL: But great scott man, you scored two hundred and seventy-three. —Ray Galton and Alan Simpson, *Hancock's Half Hour*, 13th January 1957

great stuff *noun*
anything excellent *UK, 1934*
- A woman told us she had decided not to vote Labour because of John Prescott. "We don't want people like that in power." "Great stuff, great stuff!" said Boris [Johnson]. —*The Guardian*, 1st June 2001

great unwashed *noun*
▸ **the great unwashed**
1 the proletariat *UK, 1937*
Originally derisive and jocular, now somewhat snobbish, but familiarity breeds unthinking colloquialisms.
- [The] mildly preposterous the crass assumption that the great unwashed were also unread. —*Ther Guardian*, 11th November 2000

2 hippies *UK*
At the time, no doubt, this was seen as a literal description of long-haired counterculturists.
- —David Powis, *The Signs of Crime*, 1977

great white chief *noun*
▷ see: **BIG WHITE CHIEF**

great white combine *noun*
a prairie hailstorm *CANADA*
- The hailstorm, so destructive to crops, is named aptly when it comes just as the crop is ready for harvest and the summer's work is lost to the great white combine. —Chris Thain, *Cold as a Bay Street Banker's Heart*, p. 76, 1987

great white father *noun*
any unpopular authority figure *US*
- —*American Speech*, p. 272, December 1963: 'American Indian student slang'

great white hope *noun*
crack cocaine *UK*
Used with 'the'.
- —Mike Haskins, *Drugs*, p. 282, 2003

great white light *noun*
LSD *US*
- —Richard Alpert and Sidney Cohen, *LSD*, 1966

great white way; gay white way *noun*
Broadway and the theatre district of New York *US, 1901*
- The color line along the Great White Way wasn't broken, exactly, but it sure got dented some, during the weeks we blew our lumps down there.—Mezz Mezzrow, *Really the Blues*, p. 286, 1946
- The few who stayed, and the tourists, stayed to the Gay White Way, as they used to name it, clubbing, bar hopping, or taking in a show. —Mickey Spillane, *Return of the Hood*, p. 80, 1964
- With my second [pay check] I decided to hit the Great White Way and see what all the fun was about.—Antony James, *America's Homosexual Underground*, p. 113, 1965
- Gazing from Broadway and 42nd toward Macy's at 34th, one saw The Great White Way, the main drag of vaudeville and musical comedy theaters, the medium of the day.—Josh Alan Friedman, *Tales of Times Square*, p. 48, 1986

great white whale *noun*
cocaine *UK*
An exaggeration and romantic allusion based on the colour of cocaine.

greaze *noun*
▷ see: GEEZE

greaze *verb*
to eat *US*
- —Collin Baker et al., *College Undergraduate Slang Study Conducted at Brown University*, p. 129, 1968

grebo; greebo *noun*
a member of a British youth cult that flourished in the mid- to late 1980s; grebos/greboes are characterised as being intentionally unkempt and categorised as rock and heavy metal music enthusiasts *UK: ENGLAND, 1987*
Adapted from **GREASER** (a youth subculture), perhaps influenced by 'greb' (an insult).
- —Pop Will Eat Itself *Oh Grebo I Think I Love You*, 1988
- The grebos, the crusties and the goths / And the only living boy in New Cross—Carter USM *The Only Living Boy in New Cross*, 1992
- [T]he chance to poke fun at smelly greboes was too good to miss. —*Radio Times*, p. 8, 30th March 2002

greedy-guts *noun*
a glutton; a person (ocassionally, thing) driven by greed or appetite *UK, 1550*
'Greedy gut' is the earlier form.
- [S]ome people are greedy gutses, aren't they. Ain't you got enough yet?—Derek Bickerton, *Payroll*, p. 125, 1959

greedy pig *noun*
used by card sharps of a victim *UK*
- —David Powis, *The Signs of Crime*, 1977

greefa; grifa; griff; griffa; griffo *noun*
marijuana *US, 1931*
Originally border Spanish used in English conversation by Mexican-Americans.
- Grefa was kid-stuff to me, but opium meant dope and I was really scared of it.—Mezz Mezzrow, *Really the Blues*, p. 98, 1946
- —George Carpenter Baker, *Pachuco*, p. 41, January 1950
- Tea. Grifa. Yesca. Marijuana. Whatever you want to call it.—Thurston Scott, *Cure it with Honey*, p. 4, 1951
- —Mike Haskins, *Drugs*, p. 287, 2003

Greek *noun*
1 unintelligible language *UK, 1600*
- "What about stelfactiznide chloride?" "What? Now you're talking Greek to me."—James Ellroy, *White Jazz*, p. 44, 1992

2 anal sex; a practitioner of anal sex *US*
- —Dale Gordon, *The Dominion Sex Dictionary*, 1967

3 a male homosexual, especially the active partner in anal sex *US, 1938*

4 in pinball, a shot up a lane with a scoring device with sufficient force to activiate the scoring device *US*
- —Bobbye Claire Natkin and Steve Kirk, *All About Pinball*, p. 112, 1977

Greek *adjective*
(of sex) anal *US, 1934*
- —Dale Gordon, *The Dominion Sex Dictionary*, p. 79, 1967
- They'll give a beating, they'll take a beating, they'll go Greek – and all for the same fifteen, or twenty, or whatever it is.—John Warren Wells, *Tricks of the Trade*, p. 24, 1970
- —Helen Dahlskog (Editor), *A Dictionary of Contemporary and Colloquial Usage*, p. 28, 1972
- The film's raunchiest scene takes place in the kitchen, where C.J. Laing engages in "water sports" and "Greek" coupling.—Kent Smith et al., *Adult Movies*, p. 31, 1982
- And it was so funny, because they would describe you as 'Greek, active/passive; French, active/passive- – French being blow jobs and Greek being fucked.—James Ridgeway, *Red Light*, p. 222, 1996

Greek culture; Greek style; Greek way *noun*
anal sex *US*
- —Dale Gordon, *The Dominion Sex Dictionary*, p. 79, 1967
- —Robert A. Wilson, *Playboy's Book of Forbidden Words*, p. 129, 1972
- —Helen Dahlskog (Editor), *A Dictionary of Contemporary and Colloquial Usage*, p. 28, 1972
- Of course there are requests, especially again from the older men, for the around-the-world trip – the Greek style – and those requests in general. [Quoting Xaviera]—*Screw*, p. 6, 6th March 1972

Greek lightning *noun*
arson financed by the owner of a failing business *US*
In Chicago, Greeks enjoy the reputation of being arsonists. Chicago residents cite a rule of Three Ns – 'never give matches to a Greek, whiskey to an Irishman, or power to a Polack'.
- —Bill Reilly, *Big Al's Official Guide to Chicagoese*, p. 28, 1982

Greek massage *noun*
anal sex *AUSTRALIA*
- — Thommo, *The Dictionary of Australian Swearing and Sex Sayings*, p. 61, 1985

Greek rodeo *noun*
anal sex between men *US*
- Holding on with both hands, we bounced through the night. The Greek Rodeo!—Angelo d'Arcangelo, *The Homosexual Handbook*, p. 79, 1968

Greek's *noun*
a small cafe or milkbar *AUSTRALIA, 1946*
Post-World War 2 migrants from southern Europe commonly opened such businesses, though they were not, of course, all Greek.
- Then round the town, swooping up the rest of the crowd, out to the Greek's for the fish to barbecue, then across to the Wasteland – a desolate spot among sand-dunes where the men set about lighting a huge fire.—Coralie Rees, *Spinifex Walkabout*, p. 29, 1953

Greek shift *noun*
in card trickery, a method of repositioning a card *US*
- —*Card Trick Central*, 2003

Greek shot *noun*
in dice games, a controlled roll with a controlled result *US*
- —Frank Garcia, *Marked Cards and Loaded Dice*, p. 262, 1962
- "In the old days, I used to skip- roll the dice," he said as he worked. "Perfected my Greek shot. That's a controlled roll where the dice hit the rail one on top of the other so the bottom cube doesn't roll over."—Stephen Cannell, *Big Con*, p. 215, 1997

Greek shuffle *noun*
in card trickery, a cut of the deck that leaves the cards in the same order as before the cut *US*
- —*Card Trick Central*, 2003

green *noun*
1 money *US, 1898*
From the green colour of paper currency in the US.
- With a pocketful of green I was digging the scene the other bright[.] —Dan Burley, *Diggeth Thou?*, p. 36, 1959
- How 'bout it, pal – got a taste for the easy green?—Terry Southern, *The Magic Christian*, p. 15, 1959
- Yeah, my old man had a lot of green.—Clarence Cooper Jr, *The Scene*, p. 250, 1960
- He wasn't all that big and she had plenty of baby oil going in the way of lubricant and if he wanted to lay out all that green for a real piece of ass, he was the customer and the customer was always right.—Mickey Spillane, *Last Cop Out*, p. 49, 1972

- These were fifteen-thousand-a-year guys – not paying with plastic, either: hard-earned green. — Vincent Patrick, *The Pope of Greenwich Village*, p. 13, 1979
- JOSH: It's about the green. MOE: It's about da money. — *Mo' Better Blues*, 1990

2 in American casinos, a $25 chip *US*
- — Steve Kuriscak, *Casino Talk*, p. 28, 1985

3 marijuana, especially with a low resin count *US*
- Threw green down the toilet, getting ready to visit you. — Jack Kerouac, *Letter to Allen Ginsberg*, p. 512, 1st, 6th September 1955
- [H]e got hold of some bad green, as it's called in the trade – green, uncured marijuana, quite by mistake, and smoked too much of it. — Jack Kerouac, *On the Road*, p. 184, 1957
- Royo had left Los Angeles with a kilo of long Mexican green, lately smuggled across the border at Tijuana. — Ross Russell, *The Sound*, p. 86, 1961
- Billy got some light green, Whoreson, while Eddie's smoke is good, it's got a lot of sticks and stuff in it. — Donald Goines, *Whoreson*, p. 130, 1972

4 phencyclidine, the recreational drug known as PCP or angel dust *US*
From the practice of sprinkling the drug on parsley or mint.
- — Ronald linder, *PCP*, p. 9, 1981

5 the recreational drug ketamine *US*
From the drug's natural green colour.
- — Richard A. Spears, *The Slang and Jargon of Drugs and Drink*, p. 233, 1986

6 mucus *UK*
- [He] opens up a little sidewindow dredgin' up green from his lungs. — Nick Barlay, *Curvy Lovebox*, p. 33, 1997

7 the felt surface of a pool table *US*
- — Steve Rushin, *Pool Cool*, p. 15, 1990

8 a stage, especially in the phrase 'see you on the green' *UK, 1931*
All that remains in current use of theatrical rhyming slang 'green gage'.

9 an unbroken wave *US*
- — John Severson, *Modern Surfing Around the World*, p. 169, 1964

10 a green capsule containing drugs, especially a central nervous system stimulant *US, 1966*
Also variant 'greenie'.
- Or he'll say, "How fabulous are greenies? (The answer is very. Greenies are pep pills – dextroamphetamine sulpahte – and a lot of baseball players couldn't function without them.) — Jim Bouton, *Ball Four*, p. 80, 1970
- — Mike Haskins, *Drugs*, p. 279, 2003

11 a supporter of conservation politics *UK*
- — *New Society*, 22nd July 1982

▸ **in the green**
flying with all instruments recording safe conditions *US*
- — *American Speech*, p. 119, May 1963: 'Air refueling words'.

green *adjective*

▸ **not as green as you are cabbage-looking**
more intelligent than you look *UK, 1931*
Jocular.
- I will admit, albeit reluctantly, that the C.I.D. are not always as green as they're cabbage-looking, — Charkes Raven, *Underworld Nights*, p. 95, 1956
- I'm not as green as I'm cabbage-looking," announced James, propos of nothing in particular[.] — Redmond O'Hanlon, *Into the Heart of Borneo*, 1985

greena *noun*
marijuana *UK*
- — The New Initiatives Project, *The Grass aint always Greena [a report of a Drug Education Programme]*, April 1998

green about the gills *adjective*
ill, nauseous, sickly-pale *UK, 1949*
- She looks all green about the gills. What have you done to her? — Catherine Coulter, *Mad Jack*, p. 68, 1999

green and black *noun*
a capsule of Librium, a central nervous system depressant *US*
- — Jay Robert Nash, *Dictionary of Crime*, p. 156, 1992

green and brussel; greens and brussels *noun*
a muscle; muscles *UK*
Rhyming slang.
- — Ray Puxley, *Cockney Rabbit*, 1992

green and friendly *noun*
a prison-issue phone card *UK*
- — Angela Devlin, *Prison Patter*, p. 59, 1996

green-and-white *noun*
a green and white police car *US*
- Gary watched a green-and-white creeping toward them from the far end of the house, coming past sabal palms, dipping over the uneven ground in low gear. — Elmore Leonard, *Maximum Bob*, p. 78, 1991

green apple quick-step *noun*
diarrhoea *US*
- — Michael Dalton Johnson, *Talking Trash with Redd Foxx*, p. 47, 1994

green around the gills *adjective*
giving an appearance of being about to vomit *US*
- Kind of green around the gills. Claimed he felt all right, felt fine. — George V. Higgins, *Penance for Jerry Kennedy*, p. 267, 1985

greenback *noun*

1 a one-dollar note *US, 1862*
- The only relic of their brief courtship is a postcard photograph of them taken in Las Vegas in 1956 at the Horseshoe Club and Casino in front of the club's landmark, a giant horeshoe containing a million dollars in greenbacks. — Kim Rich, *Johnny's Girl*, p. 26, 1993

2 a one-pound note *UK, 1961*
A green-coloured banknote, first issued in 1917, the colour remained despite diminishing size and value, except for the period 1940–48 when it was blue, until 1988 when it ceased to be legal tender. Sometimes shortened to 'greenie'.
- [A] brutal lunge at the greenies in your wallet. — *Time Out*, 9th May 1980

3 an Australian one-pound note *AUSTRALIA, 1919*
Fell out of use after the introduction of decimal currency in 1966.
- He slid one of the greenbacks across to Bruno[.] — Wilda Moxham, *The Apprentice*, p. 34, 1969

4 in surfing, a swell that has not broken *US*
- — Grant W. Kuhns, *On Surfing*, p. 117, 1963

5 an implement for re-railing a train carriage or engine *US*
- — Norman Carlisle, *The Modern Wonder Book of Trains and Railroading*, p. 263, 1946

green baggy *noun*
the cap worn by Australian test cricketers *AUSTRALIA*
- [He is a] New South Wales cricketing all-rounder who may have got the nod once or twice to wear the green baggy. — Roy Slaven (John Doyle), *Five South Coast Seasons*, p. 169, 1992

green bait *noun*
a cash bonus paid to US soldiers who re-enlisted during the Vietnam war *US*
- — Linda Reinberg, *In the Field*, p. 96, 1991

green bean *noun*
in South Africa, a township municipal police officer *SOUTH AFRICA, 1987*
Derisory; from the colour of the uniform.
- — Penny Silva, *A Dictionary of South African English*, 1996

green bud; green buds *noun*
marijuana *US, 1981*
From the colour of the plant.
- — Richard A. Spears, *The Slang and Jargon of Drugs and Drink*, p. 234, 1986
- — Mike Haskins, *Drugs*, p. 287, 2003

green burger *noun*
a blend of amphetamine and caffeine marketed as MDMA, the recreational drug best known as ecstasy *UK*
- — Macfarlane, Macfarlane and Robson, *The User*, p. 74, 1996

green can *noun*
a can of Victoria Bitter™ beer *AUSTRALIA*
- We use Green can in Halls Creek, WA to mean a VB. — *Wordmap (www.abc.net.au/wordmap)*, 2003

green cart *noun*
an imaginary vehicle used to take people to an asylum for the insane *AUSTRALIA, 1935*
- He wants to look out, they'll be sending the green cart for him next. — Nancy Keesing, *Lily on the Dustb*, p. 164, 1982

green door *noun*
the door leading to an execution chamber *US*
- When we reach the green door, I happen to look in / I didn't mind the silence, but the lights were so goddamn dim. —Dennis Wepman et al., *The Life*, p. 119, 1976

green double dome *noun*
▷ see: DOUBLE DOME

green dragon *noun*
1 LSD enhanced with botanical drugs from plants such as Deadly Nightshade or Jimsonweed *US*
- —William D. Alsever, *Glossary for the Establishment and Other Uptight People*, p. 3, December 1970

2 any barbiturate or other central nervous system depressant *US, 1971*
- —US Department of Justice, *Street Terms*, August 1994

3 heroin *US*
- —Charles Shafer, *Folk Speech in Texas Prisons*, p. 205, 1990

4 the M-113 armoured personnel carrier *US*
The primary armoured tracked personnel carrier used by the US forces in Vietnam.
- —Linda Reinberg, *In the Field*, p. 97, 1991

green drinking voucher, green egg *nouns*
▷ see: DRINKING VOUCHER, EGG

greenery *noun*
marijuana *US*
Collected from a college student in Chicago, Illinois, 2001.

green eye *noun*
on the railways, a clear signal *US*
- —Norman Carlisle, *The Modern Wonder Book of Trains and Railroading*, p. 263, 1946

green eyes *noun*
jealousy, envy *US*
- "You got green eyes," Liz said, taking no offense. "You wish you had what I had." —Hal Ellson, *Tomboy*, p. 28, 1950

green fairy *noun*
absinthe, a French gin *UK*
- After being banned for a century, the 70 per cent proof French loopy juice, aka The Green Fairy, has become a UK staple — *Sky Magazine*, p. 88, May 2001

greenfly *noun*
used as a collective noun for Army Intelligence Corps personnel *UK, 1984*
From the bright green beret they adopted in the mid-1970s.

green folding; folding green *noun*
paper money *UK*
- —Don Wilmeth, *The Language of American Popular Entertainment*, p. 118, 1981
- You see – apart from that – you've got twenty notes of folding green in the bin [pocket]. —Anthony Masters, *Minder*, p. 113, 1984

green frog *noun*
a central nervous system despressant *UK, 1998*
- —Mike Haskins, *Drugs*, p. 282, 2003

greengages; greens *noun*
wages *UK, 1932*
Rhyming slang.
- I'll be getting me greengages today. — *The Sweeney*, p. 6, 1976
- —Ray Puxley, *Cockney Rabbit*, 1992

green game *noun*
in a casino, a game with a mininum bet of $25 (the green betting token) *US, 1983*
- —Thomas L. Clark, *The Dictionary of Gambling and Gaming*, p. 94, 1987

green goblin *noun*
absinthe, a French gin *UK*
From private correspondence with a rock group whose management prefer to remain anonymous. Named after the arch-enemy of Spiderman.

green goddess *noun*
1 marijuana *US, 1938*
From the colour of the leaf and the elation it inspires; several ancient religions worshipped a green goddess.
- —Richard A. Spears, *The Slang and Jargon of Drugs and Drink*, p. 234, 1986
- —Mike Haskins, *Drugs*, p. 287, 2003

2 an emergency firefighting vehicle that is made available (for operation by the military) when regular firefighters and their fire engines are out of service *UK*
First came into the public vocabulary during the 1977 strike by Fire Brigade officers.
- Red goddesses, fire engines used for training and held in reserve by local authorities, joined the emergency fleet of green goddesses yesterday to cover for the second round of the firefighters' strike. — *The Guardian*, 23rd November 2002

green gold *noun*
cocaine *UK*
- —Mike Haskins, *Drugs*, p. 280, 2003

green goods *noun*
counterfeit money *US*
- —Vincent J. Monteleone, *Criminal Slang*, p. 107, 1949

green grolly *noun*
a deposit of phlegm *UK*
Abbreviates as 'grolly'. Schoolboy and military use.
- —Rick Jolly, *Jackspeak*, 1989

greenhorn *noun*
a person recently arrived in the city or recently immigrated to a new country *UK, 1753*
- For mutual protection and to insure against loneliness in an alien land, greenhorns usually gather together. —Jack Lait and Lee Mortimer, *Chicago Confidential*, p. 71, 1950
- Better to have a father who drank and chased women or no father at all, than to have someone like this – a runt who didn't even seem like a man, a real greenhorn[.] —Hal Ellson, *The Golden Spike*, p. 84, 1952

green hornet *noun*
a capsule combining a central nervous stimulant and a central nervous system depressant *US, 1942*
- There were also green and brown capsules, known to pill heads as green hornets. —Roger Gordon, *Hollywood's Sexual Underground*, p. 55, 1966

greenhouse *noun*
1 a small room or enclosed space where marijuana is being smoked *US*
- —Pamela Munro, *U.C.L.A. Slang*, p. 77, 2001

2 in surfing, a smooth ride inside the hollow of a wave *US*
- —Mitch McKissick, *Surf Lingo*, 1987

3 in hot rodding and car customising, the upper part of the car body *US*
- —John Edwards, *Auto Dictionary*, p. 71, 1993

green ice *noun*
emeralds *US*
- —Hyman E. Goldin et al., *Dictionary of American Underworld Lingo*, p. 87, 1950

greenie *noun*
1 any paper money *UK*
- [They] build (not buy) each other a drink and pay for it with greenies, crispies, lottery tickets, drinking vouchers. —Ann Barr and Peter York, *The Official Sloane Ranger Handbook*, p. 117, 1982
- —George Percy, *The Language of Poker*, p. 41, 1988

2 a one-pound note *UK*
From the colour of the note.
- [A] brutal lunge at the greenies in your wallet. — *Time Out*, 9th May 1980

3 an Australian one-pound note *AUSTRALIA*
Shortening of GREENBACK.
- [C]ome again? I'd need a stack of greenies before I flashed the old feller on T.V. —Barry Humphries, *The Wonderful World of Barry McKenzie*, p. 46, 1968

4 a gob of thick nasal mucus and catarrhal matter *UK*
From the colour.
- Dave gobbing at me, a great big greeny landing on my right boot[.] —John King, *Human Punk*, p. 108, 2000
- Just spit, not a big fuckin greenie! —Niall Griffiths, *Kelly + Victor*, p. 267, 2002

5 a speeding ticket *US*

- —Warren Smith, *Warren's Smith's Authentic Dictionary of CB*, p. 42, 1976
- In Los Angeles, they are known as "greenies," after the color of the copy of the citation that the officer keeps.—*Los Angeles Times*, p. B8, 19th December 1994
- Shouldn't you guyis be parked on a corner somewhere, writing greenies?—Stephen J. Cannell, *The Tin Collectors*, p. 74, 2001

6 a conservationist *AUSTRALIA, 1973*

From 'green ban' (a ban imposed for environmental reasons).

- Greenies can be seen buried up to their necks in the ground or manacled to earthmoving equipment.—*The Dinkum Dictionary Of Australian English*, p. 33, 1990

7 an ocean wave, especially a large breaking wave suitable for surfing *AUSTRALIA*

- The surf was fantastic. You should have seen those greenies.—Barry Humphries, *A Nice Night's Entertainment*, p. 77, 1964
- —Nigel Foster, *The Making of a Royal Marine Commando*, 1987

greenie in a bottle *noun*

a bottle of beer *AUSTRALIA*

- —Trevor Cralle, *The Surfin'ary*, p. 9, 1991

green ink *noun*

time spent in aerial combat *US*

- [I]t was decided that it was time for him to get some combat decorations on his chest and in his record, and some green ink, signifying combat flight time.—Gerry Carroll, *North S*A*R*, p. 139, 1991

green-ink brigade *noun*

collectively, people who write cranky or abusive (often illegible) letters *UK*

Derives from the notion that only a person who disdains conventional standards could possibly be ill mannered enough to write in green ink – or, sometimes, green crayon.

- [R]evealing an email address does not mean a politician will be swamped with missives from the green ink brigade.—*The Guardian*, 31st October 2001

green light *noun*

in prison, permission to kill *US*

- To reinforce their goal of becoming the most feared gang in San Quentin, the AB, which numbered around 100 members, put out the green light [open season to hit] on all blacks[.]—Bill Valentine, *Gangs and Their Tattoos*, p. 6, 2000

green-light *verb*

to give approval *UK*

In traffic signalling, the green light means 'go'.

- Some mad fellas come round and mashed [beat] us without green-lighting it with yourself, Johnny.—Kevin Sampson, *Outlaws*, p. 76, 2001

green-light *adjective*

approved *UK*

After the verb sense.

- [The] project is deffo going ahead. One hundred per cent green-light jobbie.—Kevin Sampson, *Outlaws*, p. 91, 2001

green machine *noun*

1 the US Army *US, 1969*

Vietnam war usage.

- "The Green Machine," as the American soldier had come to so aptly name the Army of this war, had demanded and been given 841,264 draftees by Christmas 1967[.]—Neil Sheehan, *A Bright Shining Lie*, p. 717, 1988

2 a computer built to military specifications for field use *US*

- —Eric S. Raymond, *The New Hacker's Dictionary*, p. 185, 1991

green man *noun*

1 marijuana *US*

To 'see the green man' is to smoke or buy marijuana.

- —Jim Emerson-Cobb, *Scratching the Dragon*, April 1997

2 a bottle of Ballantine™ ale *US*

- "The Regs'll take a grasshacker (lawnmower) and the fuzz (head) off a little green man (Ballantine Ale)," Schoons said.—John Nichols, *The Sterile Cuckoo*, p. 66, 1965

green meanie *noun*

any green amphetamine or barbiturate capsule *US, 1981*

- —Richard A. Spears, *The Slang and Jargon of Drugs and Drink*, p. 234, 1986

green micro *noun*

a type of LSD *UK*

- —Angela Devlin, *Prison Patter*, p. 59, 1996

Green Onion *noun*

a Montreal parking violation officer *CANADA*

- Best events of the last ten years: Green Onions getting caught for parking stickers.—*Montreal Mirror*, 1999
- Parking infractions are monitored by city employees in reddish-orange cars, who wear green uniforms and are known as Green Onions.—*Montreal.com*, 2002

greenout *noun*

the joy felt on seeing and smelling plants after an extended stay on Antarctica *ANTARCTICA*

- —*Cool Antarctica*, 2003: 'Antarctic slang'

green paint *noun*

marijuana *UK*

- —Mike Haskins, *Drugs*, p. 287, 2003

green paper *noun*

money *US*

- "I knew there was something funny about it," bellowed a delighted Willie Nebille Jr as he thrust his hand deep into a pile of the green paper.—*Washington Post*, p. A1, 29th July 1979
- —Bill Valentine, *Gang Intelligence Manual*, p. 130, 1995: 'Asian street gang terminology'
- Bill Gates is rich beyond measure because we all agree that his green paper and the numbers in his account ledgers mean something.—*Rockford (Illinois) Register*, p. 19D, 5th January 2004

green pastures *noun*

high earnings for railwaymen; bonus payments; overtime *UK*

- —Frank McKenna, *A Glossary of Railwaymen's Talk*, 1970

greenpea *noun*

a novice *US, 1912*

- —Anna Scotti and Paul Young, *Buzzwords*, p. 38, 1997

green penguin *noun*

a variety of LSD *UK*

- —Angela Devlin, *Prison Patter*, p. 59, 1996

green queen *noun*

a male homosexual who takes pleasure in outdoor sex in public parks *US*

- —*Male Swinger Number 3*, p. 45, 1981: 'The complete gay dictionary'

green room *noun*

1 in surfing, a smooth ride inside the hollow of a wave *US*

- —Mitch McKissick, *Surf Lingo*, 1987
- —Judi Sanders, *Don't Dog by Do, Dude!*, p. 14, 1991

2 an execution chamber *US*

- A cheap ploy to avoid the green room at San Quentin that isn't going to work.—James Ellroy, *Brown's Requiem*, p. 206, 1981

greens *noun*

1 currency notes *US, 1904*

The colour of money.

- Where'd you get all that green stuff?—Hal Ellson, *Duke*, p. 74, 1949
- Now why would you wanna pay two hunnerd sweet greens to get you white ass laughed at, Crazee Motherfucker?—Stuart Browne, *Dangerous Parking*, p. 189, 2000

2 marijuana

From the colour and after **GREEN** (marijuana), possibly informed by the vegetable sense and the UK expression of maternal care 'eat your greens, they're good for you'.

- [H]is good hand manoeuvred the greens with a deftness born of necessity[.]—Diran Abedayo, *My Once Upon A Time*, p. 21, 2000

3 green vegetables, especially cabbage and salad *UK, 1725*

- You don't need a doctor, or a journalist, to tell you to stop smoking, drink moderately, eat your greens, and get regular exercise.—*The Guardian*, 16th September 2003

4 loose green clothing worn by hospital employees, especially in operating theatres *US*

- I'd stand around in my greens and my surgical shower cap, hair all tucked up underneath, looking like a goon[.]—Sandra Bernhard, *Confessions of a Pretty Lady*, p. 56, 1988

5 the green US Army dress uniform *US*

- —Carl Fleischhauer, *A Glossary of Army Slang*, p. 23, 1968

6 sexual activity *UK, 1888*

- He was getting a very bad case of the accumulated greens over Gillian.—*The Guardian*, 14th February 1983

▷ **see: GREENGAGES**

greens and beans *noun*

basic groceries *US*

- I was going to be forced to get out into the streets, back into all that dripping drama, for the sake of some greens and beans. —Odie Hawkins, *Lost Angeles*, p. 146, 1994

greenseed *noun*

a US soldier freshly arrived in Vietnam *US, 1988*

- I've had ten telexes from San Francisco this week about some Greenseed who must be someone's nephew. —Danielle Steel, *Message from Nam*, p. 193, 1990
- —Linda Reinberg, *In the Field*, p. 97, 1991

greens fee *noun*

the amount charged by a pool room to play pool *US*

Punning on a conventional term found in golf, alluding to **GREEN** (the surface of a pool table).

- —Steve Rushin, *Pool Cool*, p. 15, 1990

green shield stamps *noun*

money *UK*

A variation on **GREENSTAMPS**; Green Shield Stamps were a sales promotional scheme popular in the 1960s and 70s.

- —Peter Chippindale, *The British CB Book*, p. 155, 1981

green single dome *noun*

▷ see: **DOUBLE DOME**

green slime *noun*

green peppers *US*

Limited usage, but clever.

- —*Maledicta*, p. 13, 1996: 'Domino's pizza jargon'

green snow; green tea *noun*

phencyclidine, the recreational drug known as PCP or angel dust *US*

The colour reference is to the parsley or mint on which the drug is often sprinkled.

- —Richard A. Spears, *The Slang and Jargon of Drugs and Drink*, p. 235, 1986

greenstamp *noun*

a traffic ticket for speeding *US, 1975*

- —Wayne Floyd, *Jason's Authentic Dictionary of CB Slang*, p. 18, 1976

greenstamps *noun*

in trucking, money *US, 1956*

- —Wayne Floyd, *Jason's Authentic Dictionary of CB Slang*, p. 18, 1976
- —Peter Chippindale, *The British CB Book*, p. 155, 1981

green stuff *noun*

currency notes *US, 1887*

- Where'd you get all that green stuff? —Hal Ellson, *Duke*, p. 74, 1949

green teen *noun*

an environmentally conscious young person *US*

- —Steven Daly and Nalthaniel Wice, *alt.culture*, p. 95, 1995

green thumb *noun*

in pool, the ability to make money playing for wagers *US*

- —Steve Rushin, *Pool Cool*, p. 15, 1990

green-to-green *adjective*

running smoothly, without problem *US*

Nautical origins – ships following the rules of navigation.

- —John Gould, *Maine Lingo*, p. 116, 1975

green triangle *noun*

a variety of MDMA, the recreational drug best known as ecstasy *UK*

From the colour of the tablet and the embossed motif.

- Green-triangle pills containing only DXM (dextromethorphan, a drug that cause audio hallucinations). —Gareth Thomas, *This Is Ecstasy*, p. 81, 2002

green 'un *noun*

a one-pound note *UK*

- It's thirty quid in green 'uns on the night[.] —Trevor Griffiths, *Oi For England*, p. 21, 1982

greenwash *noun*

a pretended concern for ecological matters *UK, 2003*

A play on 'whitewash' (a covering-up of faults), possibly also on **EYE-WASH** (something that is intended to conceal; nonsense).

green wedge *noun*

LSD *US, 1975*

- —Richard A. Spears, *The Slang and Jargon of Drugs and Drink*, p. 235, 1986
- —Mike Haskins, *Drugs*, p. 285, 2003

green womb *noun*

the inside of a hollow breaking wave *US*

- —Trevor Cralle, *The Surfin'ary*, p. 47, 1991

green worms *noun*

the undulating green lines on a radar screen *US*

- —*American Speech*, p. 153, April 1947: 'Radar slang terms'

green yoke *noun*

a young inexperienced horse *UK*

- Don't worry about me. It is just some green yoke I'm giving a run around for Fred Winter. —Stan Mellow, 25th November 1969

greet *verb*

▸ **greet the judge**

in horse racing, to win a race *AUSTRALIA*

- —Ned Wallish, *The Truth Dictionary of Racing Slang*, p. 35, 1989

greeter; greta *noun*

marijuana *US, 1952*

- —Richard A. Spears, *The Slang and Jargon of Drugs and Drink*, p. 235, 1986
- —Mike Haskins, *Drugs*, p. 287, 2003

Gregory Peck; gregory *noun*

1 a cheque *AUSTRALIA*

Rhyming slang, formed on the name of film actor Gregory Peck, 1916–2003.

- —Ryan Aven-Bray, *Ridgey Didge Oz Jack Lang*, p. 29, 1983
- —John Blackman, *The Aussie Slang Dictionary*, p. 42, 1990
- [H]aving to write a gregory for the tax man! —Andrew Nickolds, *Back to Basics*, p. 13, 1994

2 the neck *AUSTRALIA, 1966*

Also known in the UK, especially after use in mid-1970s BBC television's *Porridge*.

- —*The (Sydney) Bulletin*, 26th April 1975
- Many years before a slapsie driver had him lumbered for chundering down the back of the driver's Gregory Peck. —Ryan Aven-Bray, *Ridgey Didge Oz Jack Lang*, p. 10, 1983

Gregory Pecks; gregories *noun*

spectacles *UK: SCOTLAND*

Rhyming slang for **SPECS**, formed from the name of film actor Gregory Peck, 1916–2003.

- —Michael Munro, *The Original Patter*, 1985

grem *noun*

an unskilled skateboarder; generally, anyone who is maladroit at anything *UK, 1978*

Teen slang; probably a shortening of **GREMMIE**.

gremlin *noun*

1 a mysterious spirit that haunts aircraft, deluding pilots; hence, any mechanical fault *UK, 1929*

Originally Royal Air Force slang.

- Just last week a new batch of complaints had flooded in concerning a potentially life-threatening in-flight malfunction of the variable-sweep swing wing. Gold couldn't account for the gremlins. —T.E. Cruise, *Wings of Gold III: The Hot Pilots*, p. 324, 1989
- The bald guy's pilot must have figured that something very bad had happened, because he jumped back in his Cessna and took off, mechanical gremlins and all[.] —Joseph Wambaugh, *Fugitive Nights*, p. 37, 1992

2 an inexperienced surfer who does not respect surfer etiquette *US, 1961*

- One who, due to objectionable actions both in and out of the water, causes public surfing bans and the closing of private beaches to all surfers. —Grant W. Kuhns, *On Surfing*, p. 117, 1963

gremmie *noun*

1 an unpopular, unfashionable person *US, 1962*

- —*Current Slang*, p. 3, Fall 1966

2 an unskilled surfing or skateboarding novice *AUSTRALIA, 1962*

- —Jack Pollard, *The Australian Surfrider*, p. 18, 1963
- —Albert Cassorla, *The Skateboarder's Bible*, p. 200, 1976

3 marijuana and crack cocaine mixed for smoking in a cigarette *US*

- —Geoffrey Froner, *Digging for Diamonds*, p. 33, 1989

grette *noun*
a cigarette *US*
• — *Current Slang*, p. 3, Winter 1966

Greville Starkey *noun*
a black person *UK*
Rhyming slang for **DARKY**, formed from the name of the English jockey and Derby winner (b.1939). Noted as predating synonymous **FEARGAL SHARKEY**.
• — Ray Puxley, *Fresh Rabbit*, 1998

grey *noun*
in a mixed race couple, the other partner *BERMUDA*
• — Peter A. Smith and Fred M. Barritt, *Bermewjan Vurds*, 1985

grey *adjective*
a middle-aged, conventionally minded, conservatively dressed person in the eyes and vocabulary of the counter-culture *UK*
• — *The Observer*, 3rd December 1967

grey death *noun*
insipid prison stew *AUSTRALIA, 1967*
• — Jim Ramsay, *Cop It Sweet!*, p. 42, 1977
• — Ryan Aven-Bray, *Ridgey Didge Oz Jack Lang*, p. 29, 1983

greyer *noun*
someone dull who perpetuates dullness *UK*
• I was not answerable to some greyer of a boss who would take delight in making your life a misery. — Paolo Hewitt, *Heaven's Promise*, p. 120, 1999

grey ghost *noun*
a parking inspector in Victoria, New South Wales and Western Australian *AUSTRALIA, 1967*
From the colour of the uniform.
• If you get bushed in the city ask a policeman, or a grey ghost. — *The Dinkum Dictionary Of Australian English*, p. 13, 1990

grey goose *noun*
a grey California Department of Corrections bus used for transporting prisoners *US*
An allusion to the Greyhound bus line.
• — Paul Glover, *Words from the House of the Dead*, 1974

greyhound *noun*
a very short skirt *UK*
A pun on (pubic) hair.
• [L]ook at the greyhound on that bird! — *www.LondonSlang.com*, June 2002
• [O]nly an inch from the hare. — *unknown source quoted in private correspondence*, 13th March 2002
• — Chris Lewis, *The Dictionary of Playground Slang*, p. 106, 2003

Greyhound *noun*
an M-8 armoured car *US*
World War 2 vintage, used at the beginning of the Vietnam war by the Army of the Republic of Vietnam.
• — Gregory Clark, *Words of the Vietnam War*, p. 296, 1990

greyhound *verb*
(used of a black person) to pursue a white person in the hopes of a romantic or sexual relationship *US*
From **GREY MAN** (a white person).
• — David Claerbaut, *Black Jargon in White America*, p. 67, 1972

greylist *verb*
to hold a person under consideration for blacklisting *CANADA*
• Hollywood once had a notorious blacklist of political radicals; today it has a greylist of 'oldies'. — *The Globe and Mail (Canada)*, 16th December 2002

grey man *noun*
1 a white man *UK, 1984*
Black slang.
2 a dull, boring undergraduate *UK, 1960*
Oxford and Cambridge students' term.

grey mare *noun*
a bus or train fare *UK*
Rhyming slang.
• — Ray Puxley, *Cockney Rabbit*, 1992

grey shield *noun*
LSD *UK*
• — Mike Haskins, *Drugs*, p. 285, 2003

grice; gricer *noun*
a locomotive (train) spotter *UK*
Trainspotters' slang.
• — *Steam Railway*, April and June 1982

grice *verb*
to practise trainspotting *UK*
Trainspotters' slang.
• — *Steam Railway*, April and June 1982

grick *noun*
a Greek immigrant or Greek-American *US*
• And those given a name were stuck with it forever: Svade, Svenska, Lugan, Schnapps, Moishe, Stosh, Henie, Mockie, Guinea, Canuck, Bohunk, Pork-dodger, Limey, Greaseball, Krauthead, Dutchie, Squarehead, Grick, Mick, Paddy, Goombah, Polski, Dago, Hunkie, Wop and Frog. — *San Francisco Examiner*, p. A15, 28th July 1997

grid *noun*
1 the face *UK*
• It's not often that you manage to get the time to give your grid a proper fucking scrape [shave]. — Kevin Sampson, *Outlaws*, p. 85, 2001
• Look at yer grid. Can't take yer friggin beams away from her, lar. — Niall Griffiths, *Kelly + Victor*, p. 147, 2002

2 the female breast *US*
• — Kenn "Naz" Young, *Naz's Dictionary of Teen Slang*, p. 53, 1993

3 a bicycle *AUSTRALIA, 1927*
• Other kids swept past on junky grids, pulling wheelies and skids in the dirt[.] — Tim Winton, *Cloudstreet*, p. 84, 1991

G-ride *noun*
1 a stolen car *US*
• — Jennifer Blowdryer, *Modern English*, p. 61, 1985
• — *Los Angeles Times*, p. B8, 19th December 1994

2 a rebuilt, customised vintage car with a suspension system that allows the body to be lifted and lowered *US*
• — Anna Scotti and Paul Young, *Buzzwords*, p. 39, 1997
• G-ride (street slang for a nice car). — *Tulsa (Oklahoma) World*, p. A5, 13th April 2003

gridley grinder *noun*
on Prince Edward Island, a bad storm *CANADA*
• "A gridley grinder is a hell of a storm." "Sounded like a grinder." "Here comes a gridley grinder." — T. K. Pratt, *oral citations from Dictionary of Prince Edward Island English*, p. 69, 1988

grief *noun*
trouble, problems *US, 1897*
Originally in the phrase **COME TO GRIEF** (to get into trouble, to fail).
• The flag had scarcely fallen than [sic] the grief commenced. — *The Sportsman*, 28th February 1891
• There's always going to be grief[.] — Kevin Sampson, *Outlaws*, p. 66, 2001

▸ **give someone grief**
to tease; to criticise *US*
• — Collin Baker et al., *College Undergraduate Slang Study Conducted at Brown University*, p. 125, 1968

grief *verb*
to trouble someone *UK*
• Look, star. Just take the money and hurry up. They never grief you for ID, so shoosh your noise. — Julian Johnson, *Urban Survival*, p. 268, 2003

griefer *noun*
an Internet game player who tries to spoil the fun of other players by harassing them *UK*
Someone who creates **GRIEF** (trouble).
• — *You and Yours*, 30th April 2003

griever *noun*
a union spokesman on a contract grievance committee *US*
• — Norman Carlisle, *The Modern Wonder Book of Trains and Railroading*, p. 263, 1946

grievous bodily harm *noun*
the recreational drug GHB *US, 1993*
Extended from the punning **GBH**.
• — *American Speech*, p. 84, Spring 1995: 'Among the new words'
• GHB has been marketed as a liquid or powder and has been sold on the street under names such as Grevious Bodily Harm, Georgia Home Boy, Liquid Ecstasy, Liqiud X, Liquid E, GHB, GBH, Soap, Scoop, Easy Lay, Salty Water, G-Riffick, [and] Cherry Menth. — *Morbidity and Morality Weekly Report*, p. 281, 4th April 1997

grifa; griff *noun*
▷ see: GREEFA

g-riffick *noun*
the recreational drug GHB *US*
A combination of the 'g' of **GHB** and 'terrific'.
• GHB has been marketed as a liquid or powder and has been sold on the street under names such as Grevious Bodily Harm, Georgia Home Boy, Liquid Ecstasy, Liqiud X, Liquid E, GHB, GBH, Soap, Scoop, Easy Lay, Salty Water, G-Riffick, [and] Cherry Menth.—*Morbidity and Morality Weekly Report*, p. 281, 4th April 1997

grifter *noun*
1 a person who makes their living by confidence swindles, especially short cons *US, 1915*
Widely familiar from Jim Thompson's 1990 novel and film adaptation, *The Grifters*.
• Its 200 yards are lined almost unbrokenly by cheap hotels and rooming-houses sheltering all manner of strange characters: retired vaudevillians, down-and-out horse players, dope fiends, grifters and grafters[.]—Jack Lait and Lee Mortimer, *New York Confidential*, p. 13, 1948
• I don't want you messing with the grifters around here.—George Mandel, *Flee the Angry Strangers*, p. 52, 1952
• In town, Kid's woman, Rita, the fledgling grifter in the minor role of Lance Wellington's Baroness sister, stood impatiently on the front porch of the mob's museum-mansion set-up in a secluded area of the city.—Iceberg Slim (Robert Beck), *Long White Con*, p. 125, 1977

2 in horse racing, a bettor who makes small, conservative bets *US*
• —David W. Maurer, *Argot of the Racetrack*, p. 33, 1951

grig *verb*
to annoy, to tease *IRELAND*
From the Irish *griog*.
• Stop grigging her.—Irwin Liam, *North Munster Antiquarian Journal*, p. 84, 2000

grill *noun*
1 a person of Mediterranean background *AUSTRALIA, 1957*
Post-World War 2 migrants from southern Europe commonly opened businesses selling fried or grilled food.
• —Jim Ramsay, *Cop It Sweet!*, p. 42, 1977
• What would you know? You're nothing but a bloody grill?—*Wordmap (www.abc.net.au/wordmap)*, 2003

2 a motor accident in which an occupant or occupants of the car are burnt *US*
• —*American Speech*, p. 269, December 1962: 'The language of traffic policemen'

3 the bars or mesh of a prison cell *US*
• —William K. Bentley and James M. Corbett, *Prison Slang*, p. 7, 1992

grille *noun*
the teeth *US*
• —Jim Goad, *Jim Goad's Glossary of Northwestern Prison Slang*, December 2001

griller *noun*
a verbal assault, a roasting, especially when given by the authorities *AUSTRALIA*
• —*The (Sydney) Bulletin*, 26th April 1975

▸ **to put on the griller**
to assault verbally *AUSTRALIA*
Mostly in the passive sense.
• —*The (Sydney) Bulletin*, 26th April 1975

grime *noun*
a modern music genre focused on lyrical and aural interpretation of an inner-city environment and street-culture that combines the musical influences of hip-hop and UK garage with the practical low-budget, do-it-yourself spirit of punk rock and reggae sound-systems *UK*
So-named, apparently, to acknowledge the music's origins in the grimey urban sprawl.
• It won't buy a Bel Air mansion, but there are no middle men: a big grime hit can sell 5,000[.]—*Mojo*, p. 56, November 2004

grimmy *noun*
1 a middle-aged woman *UK*
• [T]he grimmies are grateful.—Diana Winsor, *Red on Wight*, 1972

2 marijuana *UK*
• —Mike Haskins, *Drugs*, p. 287, 2003

Grimsby Docks *noun*
socks *UK*
Rhyming slang, formed from a location on the northeast coast of England.
• —Ray Puxley, *Fresh Rabbit*, 1998

grimy *adjective*
1 rude; uncouth *US*
• She called your boyfriend while you were in the room? That was grimy.—Connie Eble (Editor), *UNC-CH Campus Slang*, p. 3, November 2002

2 excellent *UK*
• —Susie Dent, *Larpers and Shroomers*, p. 72, 2004

grin *noun*
1 a good and amusing situation *US, 1966*
• —Connie Eble (Editor), *UNC-CH Campus Slang*, March 1973

2 used as Internet shorthand to mean 'your message amused me' *US*
• —Andy Ihnatko, *Cyberspeak*, p. 83–84, 1997

grinch *noun*
a bad-tempered person whose negative attitude depresses others *US, 2003*
Adopted from the characteristics of the Grinch, a mean-spirited character created by Dr Seuss (Theodor Seuss Geisel) in the novel *How The Grinch Stole Christmas*, 1957, and subsequently played by Jim Carrey in the 2000 film version.

grinchy *adjective*
unpleasant, distasteful, bad *US*
High school usage.
• —*Washington Post*, 23rd April 1961: 'Man, dig this jazz'

grind *noun*
1 sexual intercourse; an act of sexual intercourse *UK, 1870*
• That thoroughfare, once the home of a dozen proud theaters, including the New Amsterdam of red plush and wonderful memories, is now devoted to "grind" movie houses[.]—Jack Lait and Lee Mortimer, *New York Confidential*, p. 30, 1948
• Yeah, well, she got knocked up. At a grind session.—Evan Hunter, *The Blackboard Jungle*, p. 158, 1954
• His dick hurt too much for even the most erotic of dreams. A grind was a grind and he could still tell the difference[.]—Donald Gorgon, *Cop Killer*, p. 164, 1994

2 in a striptease or other sexual dance, a rotating movement of the hips, pelvis and genitals *US, 1931*
• A lot of white vocalists, even some with the big name bands today, are either as stiff as a stuffed owl or else they go through more wringing and twisting than a shake dancer, doing grinds a bumps all over the place[.]—Mezz Mezzrow, *Really the Blues*, p. 27, 1946
• She hummed to herself, trying out words: "I'm out of my cast at last, and rarin' for some darin'..." Bump on "rarin'," grind on "darin'." —Bernard Wolfe, *The Late Risers*, p. 292, 1954
• Traditional stripping involves several dance movements, including the bump, the grind, and the "hootchy-kootchy."—Marilyn Suriani Futterman, *Dancing Naked in the Material World*, p. 126, 1992

3 hard, dull, routine, monotonous work; work in general *UK, 1851*
Originally with special emphasis on academic work; now more general and often construed as 'the grind' or 'the daily grind'.
• This was not a cosy night at the opera [...] back to the grind in the morning, and that's that.—Richard Neville, *Play Power*, p. 64, 1970
• The terror of facing their daily grind "straight" was unimaginable. —Lanre Fehintola, *Charlie Says...*, p. 170, 2000

4 a serious, dedicated, diligent student *US, 1889*
• But mummy didn't want any daughter of hers turning into a grind. —John M. Murtagh and Sara Harris, *Cast the First Stone*, p. 35, 1957
• —*Wesleyan Alumnus*, p. 29, Spring 1981
• Finally he settles on Donna Horowtiz, Beth Shields, and Sally Burdett, grinds who remain until after dark each day in the Chem Lab[.] —James Ellroy, *Because the Night*, p. 519, 1984

5 in the used car business, a concerted assault of negotiation with a potential customer *US*
• "You want fifteen hunner dollars ... I'll go twleve," he said, beginning the familiar dance that used-car barkers call "the grind."—Stephen Cannell, *King Con*, p. 30, 1997

6 a style of hard rock appealing to the truly disaffected, featuring a fast, grinding tempo, bleak lyrics and relentlessly loud and distorted guitars *US*
Also known as 'grindcore'.
• Well, it's not exactly speed or thrash or grunge or grind.—*Airheads*, 1994

grind *verb*

1 to have sex *UK, 1647*
- I'm busy grindin' so you can't come in. —Mezz Mezzrow, *Really the Blues*, p. 45, 1946
- She said, "Well, you know, daddy, you know you can find a grinder any time that can grind a while." —Bruce Jackson, *Get Your Ass in the Water and Swim Like Me*, p. 127, 1966
- I can find a grinder any time, that can grind for a while / But tonight I want my love done the Hollywood style. —Roger Abrahams, *Positively Black*, p. 95, 1970
- —Edith A. Folb, *runnin' down some lines*, p. 240, 1980
- The overpowering rapture of just grinding gently with her, without compassion[.] —Clarence Major, *All-Night Visitors*, p. 4, 1998

2 in a striptease or other sexual dance, to rotate the hips, pelvis, and genitals in a sensual manner *US, 1928*
- Dancing boys strip-tease with intestines, women stick severed genitals in their cunts, grind, bump, and flick it at the man of their choice. —William Burroughs, *Naked Lunch*, p. 37–38, 1957
- You can pull all the stops out / Till they call the cops out / Grind your behind till you're banned. —Stephen Sondheim, *You Gotta Get a Gimmick*, 1960

3 to study hard *US*
- I'm completely faked out in my two departmentals, but I'll be damned if I'll grind. —Max Shulman, *Guided Tour of Campus Humor*, p. 105, 1955
- — *Wesleyan Alumnus*, p. 29, Spring 1981

4 in computing, to format code so that it looks attractive *US*
- —Guy L. Steele et al., *The Hacker's Dictionary*, p. 74, 1983

5 to eat *US*
Hawaiian youth usage.
- —Douglas Simonson, *Pidgin to da Max*, 1981
- Students there [Hawaii] do not eat, they "grind." —*New York Times*, 12th April 1987

6 to call out and invite patrons to enter a performance *US*
- For a game, however, the operator usually grinds for his own tip, but he also has help. —E.E. Steck, *A Brief Examination of an Esoteric Folk*, p. 9, 1968

▸ **grind your ass**
to annoy *US*
- His negative attitude really grinds my ass. —Connie Eble (Editor), *UNC-CH Campus Slang*, p. 4, March 1996

grindage *noun*
food *US*
- —Connie Eble (Editor), *UNC-CH Campus Slang*, p. 4, November 1990
- —Jack Chambers (Editor), *Slang Bag 93 (University of Toronto)*, p. 3, Winter 1993

grinder *noun*

1 a sexual partner *US*
- She said, "Well, you know, daddy, you know you can find a grinder any time that can grind a while." —Bruce Jackson, *Get Your Ass in the Water and Swim Like Me*, p. 127, 1966
- I can find a grinder any time, that can grind for a while / But tonight I want my love done the Hollywood style. —Roger Abrahams, *Positively Black*, p. 95, 1970
- Precious Percy, the pimp, the ladies' good time grinder and weak spot finder. —Odie Hawkins, *Chicago Hustle*, p. 35, 1977

2 a striptease artist *US*
- [T]he strippers have finally divided themselves into three classes: "fan-dancers," who keep up the pretense of hiding their nakedness as they enlarge it; "grinders," also known as bumpers and belly dancers, who feature undulations and various wiggles and squirms[.] —Jack Lait and Lee Mortimer, *Chicago Confidential*, p. 158, 1950
- This was Times Square's aristocratic era, before Prohibition, before honky-tonk emerged out of the Depression, a twenty-five year epoch, before the grand theaters of 42nd Street, converted to B-movie grinders. —Josh Alan Friedman, *Tales of Times Square*, p. 47, 1986

3 a person who calls out and invites patrons to enter a performance *US*
- The man standing in front of a "freak store" talking interminably is a "grind man" or "grinder." —E.E. Steck, *A Brief Examination of an Esoteric Folk*, p. 9, 1968
- —Joe McKennon, *Circus Lingo*, p. 42, 1980

4 a pornographic film with poor production values and little plot or dialogue, just poorly filmed sex *US*
- —*Adult Video News*, p. 48, August 1995

5 the drill field in an armed forces training camp *US*
- —*American Speech*, p. 76–79, February 1963: 'Marine corps slang'

6 in competition sailing, a person who in tandem operates a winch-like device to raise a large sail very quickly *US*
- Next Thursday we can say we're grinders with Team Dennis Conner. —Joseph Wambaugh, *Floaters*, p. 56, 1996

grinders *noun*
the teeth *UK, 1676*
- Hey, there, old buddy, what's my chance of gettin' some toothpaste for brushin' my grinders? —Ken Kesey, *One Flew Over the Cuckoo's Nest*, p. 90, 1962

grind film *noun*
a pornographic film, usually with crude production values and no plot or character development *US*
- Just keep that crumpled sepia 1947 grind film in the basement and enjoy it next time one of your friends gets married. —Stephen Ziplow, *The Film Maker's Guide to Pornography*, p. 12, 1977

grind house *noun*
a theatre exhibiting continuous shows or films of a sexual or violent nature *US, 1929*
- Past the souvenir shops, past the grind houses where the fags hang out[.] — *Rogue for Men*, p. 46, June 1956
- Their budgets seldom exceed one hundred thousand dollars, which can be recouped in a string of rather shady movie "grind" houses scattered across the country. —Michael Milner, *Sex on Celluloid*, p. 18, 1964
- If it's raining I have to work the theaters and grind-houses, and it's dark in there so the most I can expect is five dollars for a movie job. —Johnny Shearer, *The Male Hustler*, p. 72, 1966
- Ain't another grind house in the big apple that can match that. — *Screw*, p. 7, 12th January 1970
- The grind houses proclaim their programs in the most explicit terms, glaring posters promote the attractions of topless go-go-dancer joints. —Bernhardt J. Hurwood, *The Sensuous New York*, p. 21, 1973
- [S]ome of them are movies I used to take three-hour bus rides to see at all-night grindhouses and revival theatres[.] —Quentin Tarantino, *Uncut*, p. 66, November 2003

grinding *adjective*
(used of surf conditions) powerful, breaking consistently *US*
- —Mitch McKissick, *Surf Lingo*, 1987

grind joint *noun*
a casino dominated by slot machines and low-limit tables *US*
- —Michael Dalton, *Blackjack*, p. 52, 1991

grind man *noun*
a person who calls out and invites patrons to enter a performance *US*
- The man standing in front of a "freak store" talking interminably is a "grind man" or "grinder." —E.E. Steck, *A Brief Examination of an Esoteric Folk*, p. 9, 1968

grinds; grines *noun*
food *US*
- —Douglas Simonson, *Pidgin to da Max*, 1981
- —Jim Humes and Sean Wagstaff, *Boarderlands*, p. 222, 1995

▸ **get your grinds**
to have sex *US*
- —John D. Bell et al., *Loosely Speaking*, p. 10, 1966

grind show *noun*
a carnival attraction that relies on a relentless patter to attract customers inside *US, 1927*
- —Gene Sorrows, *All About Carnivals*, p. 18, 1985: 'Terminology'
- Of course there were the cheapies and grind shows and old theatre houses fallen to movie status. —Lawrence J. Quirk, *Bob Hope*, p. 17, 2000

grind store *noun*
an illegal gambling operation where players are cheated as a matter of course *US*
- —Gene Sorrows, *All About Carnivals*, p. 18, 1985: 'Terminology'

grine *noun*
sexual intercourse; an act of sexual intercourse *JAMAICA*
A variation of **GRIND**.
- —Glen Adams & The Hippy Boys, *I Want a Grine*, 1970

grine *verb*
to have sex *JAMAICA*
A variation of **GRIND**.
- Look when we used to grine / wooh! / You and I —Charlie Ace, *Grine Grine*, 1971

gringo *noun*
among Latinos in the US, a white person *US, 1849*
The source of considerable false etymology based on the marching song 'Green grow the rushes, o'. Often used with a lack of affection.

- I almost liked the big gringo.—Piri Thomas, *Down These Mean Streets*, p. 215, 1967
- It is unimportant that I poisoned brothers in Panama with the gringo's venomous Christ-shit.—Oscar Zeta Acosta, *The Revolt of the Cockroach People*, p. 47, 1973
- — Multicultural Management Program Fellows, *Dictionary of Cautionary Words and Phrases*, 1989
- Abel knew that a real driver would be a gringo, not a former "Rodino" like himself, who felt lucky to have such a job.—Joseph Wambaugh, *Finnegan's Week*, p. 39, 1993

gringo gallop *noun*
diarrhoea suffered by tourists in Mexico or Latin America *US*
- [T]hey admit that, like most Americans, they suffered a three-day gastric upset described by a variety of names like the Gringo Gallop and Montezuma's revenge.—*Washington Post, Times Herald*, p. AW8, 24th January 1960

grinner *noun*
a rock which just shows above the ground *CANADA*
- Grinners are just sitting there with their little circular edge grinning at you.—Chris Thain, *Cold as a Bay Street Banker's Heart*, p. 76–77, 1987

grins and shakes *noun*
a tour of a military facility or a visit to the troops *US*
- —Linda Reinberg, *In the Field*, p. 97, 1991

grip *noun*
1 a small suitcase *US, 1879*
A shortened form of 'gripsack'.
- I drove my car down the alley in back of his uplace and he lowered his grips into the rumble seat with the aid of a clothesline[.]—Mezz Mezzrow, *Really the Blues*, p. 129, 1946
- I got clean, put my riding habit in a grip and went to Artie's beat up wheel and pulled around in front of Robin's place and parked. —A.S. Jackson, *Gentleman Pimp*, p. 110, 1973

2 money *US*
- —*Washington Post*, 14th October 1993

3 a large amount *US*
- —Judi Sanders, *Da Bomb!*, p. 13, 1997
- —Jim Goad, *Jim Goad's Glossary of Northwestern Prison Slang*, December 2001

4 a photograph *ANTARCTICA*
- —*Cool Antarctica*, 2003: 'Antarctic slang'

▸ **get a grip**
to get control of your emotions and actions *US, 1971*
- BRIDGET: Eric, will you please get a grip? ERIC: Fine, I've got a grip! Now I want an explanation!—*200 Cigarettes*, 1999
- The arts council was warned to "get a grip" last night as a report revealed that 13 of the 15 main lottery-funded building projects it backed were over-budget.—*The Guardian*, 2nd May 2003

grip *verb*
1 to arrest *UK*
- Fuckin awful tha would be aye, trine t'stey on-a streyt like an get fuckin gripped with a multi-pack a fuckin Hula Hoops up me fuckin jumper.—Niall Griffiths, *Grits*, p. 60, 2000

2 to flatter and curry favour with those in power *US*
- —*Maledicta*, p. 264, Summer/Winter 1981: 'By its slang, ye shall know it: the pessimism of prison life'

3 to masturbate *US*
- —Eugene Landy, *The Underground Dictionary*, p. 93, 1971

▸ **grip your shit**
to satisfy your requirements *UK*
- 2RGJ [2nd battalion Royal Green Jackets] were now a mechanized battalion, which didn't grip my shit at all.—Andy McNab, *Immediate Action*, p. 50, 1995

gripe *noun*
a complaint *US, 1918*
- In cases where your gripe is aimed at a bank or an insurer, for example, you should be able to deal with the complaint yourself without the services of a lawyer.—*The Guardian*, 16th February 2002

gripe *verb*
to moan, to complain *US, 1928*
- Most of them felt compelled to speak, as seeing me [a pregnant woman] had made them realise how ridiculous they were for complaining and griping about the heat.—*The Guardian*, 10th August 2003

gripester *noun*
in prison, a chronic complainer *US*
- —Joseph E. Ragen and Charles Finston, *Inside the World's Toughest Prison*, p. 802, 1962: 'Penitentiary and underworld glossary'

griping *noun*
complaints; the act of complaining *US, 1945*
- But amidst the kowtowing, the griping and the diffidence, surely there must be some endearing traits to British office life?—*The Guardian*, 31st March 2003

grip off *verb*
to annoy *UK*
Used among bird-watchers, usually as 'gripped off'.
- If you miss a rarity a fellow twitcher sees, you are gripped off.—*New Society*, 17th November 1977

grippers *noun*
men's underpants *US*
- —Connie Eble (Editor), *UNC-CH Campus Slang*, p. 4, April 1985

grips *noun*
1 a porter on a passenger train *US*
- —Ramon Adams, *The Language of the Railroader*, p. 72, 1977

2 running shoes *US*
- —Connie Eble (Editor), *UNC-CH Campus Slang*, p. 3, Fall 1991

▸ **come to grips**
to get control of your emotions and actions *UK*
- You don't abuse your house guests, Phoebe. It's not on. I mean come to grips.—Ian Pattison, *Rab C. Nesbitt*, 1988

gripy *adjective*
miserable *US*
- Well, we all laid around in that fleabag-with-room-service for a couple of gripy weeks[.[—Mezz Mezzrow, *Really the Blues*, p. 177–178, 1946

gristle *noun*
the penis *UK, 1665*
A relatively obscure term, but well understood when adopted as a confrontational name by 1980s thrash metal pioneers Throbbing Gristle.

grit *noun*
1 spirit, stamina, courage, especially if enduring *US, 1825*
- —Marguerite Roberts, *True Grit*, 1969
- Carry On Katie [a racehorse] proved that she has grit as well as abundant talent in the Group One Cheveley Park Stakes at New-market yesterday[.]—*The Guardian*, 3rd October 2003

2 a member of the Canadian Liberal Party *CANADA*
- Clear grit was an adjectival phrase that meant stubborn. The Clear Grits merged with the Liberal Party. And Liberals today still bear their nickname, the Grits.—Bill Casselman, *Canadian Words*, p. 147, 1995

3 a narrow-minded if not reactionary person *US*
- —*Washington Evemning Star and Daily News (Teen Weekender)*, p. 12, 2nd December 1972: 'For adults: solid slang'

4 a stereotypical rural, southern white *US*
- —Connie Eble (Editor), *UNC-CH Campus Slang*, October 1972

5 food *US, 1959*
- [B]esides she got some good grit waiting for me.—Piri Thomas, *Down These Mean Streets*, p. 139, 1967

6 crack cocaine *US*
Another rock metaphor, based on the drug's appearance.
- —US Department of Justice, *Street Terms*, October 1994

7 a cigarette *US*
- —Judi Sanders, *Cal Poly Slang*, p. 5, 1990

grit *verb*
to eat *US*
- —Collin Baker et al., *College Undergraduate Slang Study Conducted at Brown University*, p. 130, 1968

gritch *verb*
a complaint *US*
- —Guy L. Steele et al., *The Hacker's Dictionary*, p. 74, 1983

grizzle *verb*
to sleep *US*
- —Anna Scotti and Paul Young, *Buzzwords*, p. 64, 1997

grizzle-guts; grizzly-guts *noun*
a tearful, whining person *UK, 1937*
From the verb 'to grizzle'.

groan *noun*
a standup bass fiddle *US*
- —Lou Shelly, *Hepcats Jive Dictionary*, p. 12, 1945

groaner *noun*
a foghorn with a prolonged monotone *US*
- —Jim Crotty, *How to Talk American*, p. 174, 1997

groats *noun*
the epitome of unpleasant *US*
- I guess they had to do it, especially after dad became suspicious and found out what I'd been doing with the caps. It's the groats! —Beatrice Sparks (writing as 'Anonymous'), *Jay's Journal*, p. 32, 1979

groceries *noun*
1 the genitals, breasts and/or buttocks, especially as money-earning features *US, 1965*
- —Dale Gordon, *The Dominion Sex Dictionary*, p. 79, 1967
- —H. Max, *Gay (S)language*, p. 18, 1988

2 crack cocaine *US*
A sad euphemism.
- — US Department of Justice, *Street Terms*, October 1994

3 in horse racing, horse feed *US*
- —David W. Maurer, *Argot of the Racetrack*, p. 33, 1951

grocer's shop *noun*
an Italian *UK*
Rhyming slang for **WOP**.
- —Ronnie Barner, *Fletcher's Book of Rhyming Slang*, 1979

grocery boy *noun*
a heroin addict who is craving food *US*
- —David Maurer and Victor Vogel, *Narcotics and Narcotic Addiction*, p. 412, 1973
- —Richard A. Spears, *The Slang and Jargon of Drugs and Drink*, p. 235, 1986

grocery French *noun*
a barely passable command of the Quebec French language *CANADA*
- Grocery french is a term for limited competence in the language. —Laurel Doucette, *Cultural Retention and Demographic Change*, p. 36, 1980

grocery getter *noun*
a car for everyday use *US*
- —John Edwards, *Auto Dictionary*, p. 71, 1993

grock *noun*
a fool *UK*
Probably after Adrien Wettach, 1888–1959, the Swiss clown named Grock, who was inducted in the Clown Hall of Fame in 1992.
- What I've got for the big grock today is a really vile dog-sex movie[.] —Kevin Sampson, *Clubland*, p. 78, 2002

G-rock *noun*
cocaine; a one gram rock of crack cocaine *UK, 1998*
- —Mike Haskins, *Drugs*, p. 280, 2003

grockle *noun*
1 a tourist *UK, 1964*
Disparaging; sometimes shortened to 'grock'. Grock was the professional clown-name of Charles Adrien Wettach (1880–1959), hence 'grockle' is probably intended to represent a tourist as a clown; however not abbreviated until the 1990s.
- It was too weird to be brawling with grocks in the middle of Amsterdam in the middle of a Friday afternoon[.] —Kevin Sampson, *Powder*, p. 315, 1999

2 a social inferior *UK*
Disparaging, upper-class usage; acquired from the sense as 'tourist'.
- A grockle is a mixture of an oik and an incompetent. —Ann Barr and Peter York, *The Official Sloane Ranger Handbook*, p. 91, 1982

grockly *adjective*
common, inferior *UK*
Used by upper-class youths, from **GROCKLE** (a social inferior).
- —Ann Barr and Peter York, *The Official Sloane Ranger Handbook*, p. 91, 1982

grody *noun*
a dirty, homeless hospital patient infested with lice *US*
- — *Maledicta*, p. 15, 1984–1985: 'A medical Christmas song'

grody; groady; groaty *adjective*
messy, unkempt, disgusting *US*
- —Carol Ann Preusse, *Jargon Used by University of Texas Co-Eds*, 1963
- —Andy Anonymous, *A Basic Guide to Campusology*, p. 12, 1966
- — *San Francisco Examiner*, p. 17, 17th June 1966: 'Teen slanguage: real shark'
- — *Current Slang*, p. 2, Summer 1966
- —Helen Dahlskog (Editor), *A Dictionary of Contemporary and Colloquial Usage*, p. 29, 1972
- I'm sitting there, and like this crispo waitress serves me hot tea in a Styrofoam cup, right, and it's like so grody, the Styrofoam is melting in the tea, like barf me out! —Mary Corey and Victoria Westermark, *Fer Shurr! How to be a Valley Girl*, 1982
- And the lady like goes, oh my God, your toenails are like so GRODY. —Moon Unit and Frank Zappa, *Valley Girl*, 1982
- —Connie Eble (Editor), *UNC-CH Campus Slang*, p. 3, Spring 1983

grody to the max *adjective*
extremely disgusting *US*
- Like all the stuff like sticks to the plate / And it's like, it's like somebody elses food, y'know / And it's like GRODY / GRODY TO THE MAX. —Moon Unit and Frank Zappa, *Valley Girl*, 1982
- —Connie Eble (Editor), *UNC-CH Campus Slang*, p. 4, Fall 1984

groendakkies *noun*
a mental hospital *SOUTH AFRICA*
From Afrikaans for 'green roofs'.
- —Jean Branford, *A Dictionary of South African English*, p. 52, 1978

grog *noun*
1 an alcoholic drink, especially beer *US, 1805*
- They say it takes fourteen days to get grog out of your system. —Les Such, *A Yen for Yokohama*, p. 30, 1963
- Wanna come down the beach for five minutes and have a few grogs with your old mates? —William Dick, *A Bunch of Ratbags*, p. 267, 1965
- 'Ya wanna grog?' he invited me. —Sue Rhodes, *Now you'll think I'm awful*, p. 83, 1967
- 'I think you better come up and have a grog with us,' Evan said[.] —Geoff Wyatt, *Saltwater Saints*, p. 77, 1969
- Davo got stuck into the grog, didn't he? —Alexander Buzo, *Rooted*, p. 30, 1969
- Better grab me grog and shoot through [go][.] —Barry Humphries, *Bazza Pulls It Off!*, 1971
- He had spent a lot on grog and prostitutes[.] —Petru Popescu, *The Last Wave*, p. 49, 1977

2 a clot of spittle *UK: SCOTLAND*
Glasgow slang.
- —Michael Munro, *The Original Patter*, p. 30, 1985

▸ on the grog
drinking steadily; taking part in a drinking session; binge drinking *AUSTRALIA, 1946*
- —Alexander Buzo, *Norm and Ahmed*, p. 25, 1969
- —Alexander Buzo, *Rooted*, p. 44, 1969
- Eventually I saved some money and decided to head home, but I only got as far as Swan Hill and then I got on the grog. —Herb Wharton, *Cattle Camp*, p. 35, 1994

grog *verb*
1 to drink alcohol *US, 1824*
- That's one of the drawbacks of this flamin' night racket – interferes with a bloke's grogging. —W.R. Bennett, *Night Intruder*, p. 73, 1962
- They boys were grogging – this is thirsty country up here with a constant over the century heat in summer and a week at a time over 110 degrees. —Patsy Adam-Smith, *Folklore of the Australian Railwaymen*, p. 87, 1969
- When you spend too much at the hotel drinking, you are in fact 'grogging on'! —John Blackman, *The Aussie Slang Dictionary*, p. 42, 1990

2 to spit *UK: SCOTLAND*
Glasgow slang.
- Which wan a you ratbags grogged oan ma jaikit [jacket]. —Michael Munro, *The Original Patter*, p. 30, 1985

grogan *noun*
a piece of excrement; a turd *AUSTRALIA, 1980*
- I have hermetically sealed a selection of my best grogans at the rock bottom price of just $49.95 (plus postage and handling) but you had better get in quick as I am running out of All Bran. — *www.wf.com.au/interviews/ichoke.html*, 2002

grog artist *noun*
a heavy drinker *AUSTRALIA, 1965*
- Mr d'Abbs would not have credited that an ignorant working man, a grog-artist at that, would behave in such a way. —Peter Carey, *Oscar and Lucinda*, p. 273, 1988

grog boss *noun*
a person serving alcohol at a work party *CANADA*
- During the day the "gros-boss" dealt out plenty of refreshment from a pail, while a couple of meals were served. —Edwin Guillet, *Upper Canada*, p. 137, 1964

grog-doped *adjective*
intoxicated by kava, a herbal beverage made from the root of the tropical shrub *piper methysticum* *FIJI*
- One grog-doped husband discovered the real narcotic effect of grog one weekend after he asked his wife to make coconut chutney. —*Fiji Times*, 9th April 1992
- More and more wives are leaving grog-doped husbands who cannot perform in bed, it has been claimed. —*Daily Post*, p. 1, 26th April 1996

groggery *noun*
a disreputable bar *US, 1822*
- Eighth Street runs into Sailors' Row proper, a line of groggeries and lunch-rooms that hit bottom. —Jack Lait and Lee Mortimer, *Washington Confidential*, p. 33, 1951

grogging *noun*
drinking alcohol; boozing *AUSTRALIA*
- That's one of the drawbacks of this flamin' night racket – interferes with a bloke's grogging. —W.R. Bennett, *Night Intruder*, p. 73, 1962

grogging-on *noun*
drinking heartily, or to excess *AUSTRALIA*
- Gambling and grogging-on were the initial mainstays. —Lance Peters, *The Dirty Half-Mile*, p. 305, 1979

groggy *noun*
a person who drinks to excess *FIJI*
- Many experienced groggies are of the opinoin that Sitveni Rbauka's coup were less bloody (not bloodless as his propaganda ministry keeps trying to convince everyone) only because the whole bally country was too grog-doped to do anything about it! —*Daily Post*, p. 9, 8th August 1994

groggy *adjective*
weak, unsteady, faint *UK, 1828*
From conventional 'groggy' (drunk).
- I felt distinctly groggy. Bloody worn out, just watching. —Mike Stott, *Soldiers Talking, Cleanly*, 1978

grog-on *noun*
a drinking session or party *AUSTRALIA*
- [H]e had to put the others to the test: an invitation to a grog-on outcast's celebration from a man just out of jail and labelled a lout, hooligan, agitator and Communist[.] —Frank Hardy, *The Outcasts of Foolgarah*, p. 183, 1971

grog on *verb*
to take part in a drinking session; to drink steadily and heavily *AUSTRALIA, 1951*
- According to Banjo this Cassidy grogged on terribly[.] —George Blaikie, *Remember Smith's Weekly?*, p. 158, 1966
- —Sandra Jobson, *Blokes*, p. 56, 1984
- When you spend too much at the hotel drinking, you are in fact 'grogging on'! —John Blackman, *The Aussie Slang Dictionary*, p. 42, 1990

grog session *noun*
an extended kava drinking session *FIJI*
Kava is a tranquillity-inducing beverage made from the root of a tropical shrub. Recorded by Jan Tent in 1995.
- "One only has to read the newspapers, or listen to discussions over a grog sessoin to realise how many broken families we have," Ratu Penaia said. —*Fiji Times*, 19th April 1991

grog shanty *noun*
a roughly constructed building selling alcohol *AUSTRALIA, 1895*
- —Bill Wannan, *Folklore of the Australian Pub*, p. 14, 1972
- Young Joe Flick walked into the bar of a grog shanty near Turnoff Lagoon, kept by a man and wife by the name of Cashman. —Herb Wharton, *Cattle Camp*, p. 40, 1994

grog shop *noun*
1 an off-licence (liquor store) *AUSTRALIA, 1799*
- The sprawling collection of humpies, stores and grog shops was called Stawell[.] —James Holledge, *The Great Australian Gamble*, p. 112, 1966

2 a cheap tavern *UK*
- Along the muddy alley at the side of the station was a block of grog-shops[.] —Jack Lait and Lee Mortimer, *Chicago Confidential*, p. 58–59, 1950

grog swiper *noun*
an intemperate kava drinker *FIJI*
Kava, made from the root of a tropical shurb, induces tranquillity.
- The grog swipers had to put an end to their grog sessions as they were required to attend the early services of Resurrection Day. —*The Daily Post*, p. 11, 25th May 1996

grog-up *noun*
a drinking session or party *AUSTRALIA, 1959*

grog up *verb*
to drink heavily and steadily *AUSTRALIA*
- It's the kid who never sees men grogging up who takes to it when he grows up. —Alan Marshall, *I Can Jump Puddles*, p. 178, 1955

groid *noun*
a black person *US, 1972*
A shortened 'negroid'.
- —Connie Eble (Editor), *UNC-CH Campus Slang*, March 1973

groin; groyne; growne *noun*
a ring *UK, 1931*
- The lot, tiara, ear-rings, pearls, diamond necklace, emerald collar, bracelets and groins (rings), was insured for £75,000. —Charles Raven, *Underworld Nights*, p. 16, 1956
- Doesn't really go with her big tattooed navvy marts which she waves around a lot to show off her groins[.] —James Gardiner, *Who's a Pretty Boy Then?*, p. 123, 1997
- —Paul Baker, *Polari*, p. 177, 2002

groinage *noun*
jewellery *UK*
From **GROIN** (a ring).
- —Paul Baker, *Polari*, p. 177, 2002
- —*Attitude*, p. 60, July 2003: 'Old palare lexicon'

groinplant *noun*
in mountain biking, an unintended and painful contact between the bicycle and your groin *US*
- —William Nealy, *Mountain Bike!*, p. 161, 1992: 'Bikespeak'

groin-throb *noun*
someone, of either sex, who is the object of sexual lust
A play on the more romantic 'heart-throb'.
- David Lee Roth, whose spangled-rooster, Jim-Dandy-as-Captain-America antics made him an instant groupie groin-throb. —Barney Hoskyns, *Waiting For The Sun*, p. 296, 1996

grok *verb*
to understand, to appreciate *US*
Coined by Robert Heinlein (1907–88) for the science-fiction novel *Stranger in a Strange Land*, 1961; adopted into semi-mystical use by the counterculture.
- —Steve Salaets, *Ye Olde Hiptionary*, 1970
- Some of my early grokkings while I was tripping had been on the nature of relativity. —Stephen Gaskin, *Amazing Dope Tales*, p. 197, 1980
- —Guy L. Steele et al., *The Hacker's Dictionary*, p. 74, 1983
- In other words, it was established that the [Smothers] Brothers could do what they wanted, but so could the network. In other words, grok Catch-22. —Bill Cardoso, *The Maltese Sangweech*, p. 237, 1984
- Hard Drugs: Like I said, at first no one grokked how hard they were. —Amy Wallace, *Retrohell*, p. 61, 1997
- I groked the fullness of my role in the cosmos and didn't like what I discovered. —Mick Farren, *Give the Anarchist a Cigarette*, p. 24, 2001

grolly *noun*
an unpleasant thing *UK*
Ascribes the attributes of a **GREEN GROLLY**, often abbreviated as 'grolly' (a lump of phlegm) to any given object.
- —Nigel Foster, *The Making of a Royal Marine Commando*, 1987

grom *noun*
a beginner surfer *US*
An abbreviation of **GROMMET**.
- —*Surfing*, p. 43, 14 March 1990
- The white water is barely visible but the sound of surf is enough to lure any half-stoked grom to the shore. —*Tracks*, p. 65, October 1992

grommet *noun*
1 a novice surfer, especially one with a cheeky attitude *AUSTRALIA, 1981*
- —Nat Young, *Surfing Fundamentals*, p. 127, 1985
- But for a grommet who got his first head job from a thirteen-year-old when he was ten, intimidation is a thing of the past. —*Tracks*, p. 82, October 1985

- Waxheads on L plates or just daggy types who get gravel rash on the knees trying to ingratiate themselves into the big gangs are 'Grommitts' — *Sydney Morning Herald*, p. 7, 3rd January 1987
- I hear she's a hot grommet. Better than you, maybe. — Tim Winton, *Lockie Leonard: Scumbuster*, p. 106, 1993

2 by extension, a zealous novice in other sports *US*
Recorded in use by skateboarders by Dan Maley, *Macon Telegraph and News*, p. 9A, 18th June 1989. Applied to scooter-riders by Ben Sharpe, *Scooter Crazy*, p. 40, 2000.

- Grommets [...] The beginners' hill is almost untouched by high-speed skiers and boarders. — Jim Humes and Sean Wagstaff, *Boarderlands*, p. 138, 1995

3 a kid *AUSTRALIA*

- He folds up the letter, and details a couple of little grommets to carry the equalisers, and the camera 'Rachel' was carrying. — Dirk Flinthart, *Brotherly Love*, p. 33, 1995

4 the anus *UK, 1889*

- — Robert S. Close, *Love Me Sailor*, p. 4, 1945
- What the hell are you standing there with your finger in your grommet for mister? — Robert S. Close, *Love Me Sailor*, p. 158, 1945
- — Robert S. Close, *Love Me Sailor*, p. 221, 1945

gromp *verb*
in tiddlywinks, to move a pile of winks as a whole onto another wink or pile of winks *US*

- — *Verbatim: The Language Quarterly*, p. 526, December 1977

gronk *noun*
an unattractive woman *UK*

- — Nigel Foster, *The Making of a Royal Marine Commando*, 1987

gronk *verb*
in computing, to shut down and restart a computer whose operation has been suspended *US*
A term popularised by Johnny Hart in his *B.C.* newspaper comic strip.

- — Guy L. Steele, *Coevolution Quarterly*, p. 31, Spring 1981: 'Computer slang'
- — Eric S. Raymond, *The New Hacker's Dictionary*, p. 187, 1991

groom *verb*
to attract children into sexual activity *UK*
A euphemism that hides a sinister practice.

- — Angela Devlin, *Prison Patter*, p. 59, 1996
- An award-winning NSPCC project is trying to stop paedophiles 'grooming' children - even from behind prison bars — *The Guardian*, p. 4, 4th April 2001
- [J]ust as monkeys groom each other in preparation for mating, "adults intent on sexually abusing children first set in motion instinctual processes that will help them pacify their targets". — *The Guardian*, p. 9, 11th February 2003

groove *noun*

1 the prevailing mood *UK*

- If you just stand at the side of the room waiting for the perfect track to come on, you'll be waiting all night so you have to try to get into the groove pretty quick. — Ben Malbon, *Cool Places*, p. 272, 1998

2 a routine; the regular way of doing something *UK, 1984*

- Then an old friend strolled by and told him, "You're standing too far from the ball," and, hey presto, he was back in the groove. — *The Guardian*, 29th August 2003

3 a profound pleasure, a true joy *US, 1946*

- It's your special groove; you can be away from the world with your special lanuage and special pleasures. — George Mandel, *Flee the Angry Strangers*, p. 341, 1952
- "Aren't they a groove," she was saying, "they're so funny." — Terry Southern, *Candy*, p. 139, 1958
- JOY: You really enjoyed it, huh? RYAN: It was a groove, it really was a groove, yeh. — Fred Baker, *Events*, p. 118, 1970
- It's a groove if we decided to be Mr. or Mrs. Clean. — Jack W. Thomas, *Heavy Number*, p. 29, 1976
- Charlie was kind of a groove in many ways, an intelligent dude. — Stephen Gaskin, *Amazing Dope Tales*, p. 79, 1980

4 (of music) an aesthetic pleasure in tune with the zeitgeist *US*

- Music where 'the groove is right' or that 'has the groove' suggests that it is both of quality and up to date. — Simon Warner, *Rockspeak!*, p. 286, 1996

5 a rhythm *UK*

- Hep-cast are at it, the jive is on, they're in a groove. — William Sansom, *A Public for Jive [The Public's Progress]*, p. 58, 1947

6 the act of dancing *UK*

- [W]e loafed for a bit, had a bit of a groove when it starts kicking off. — Ben Malbon, *Cool Places*, p. 272, 1998

▸ **in the groove**
totally involved, at that moment, with making or enjoying music *US, 1932*
Originally used in jazz but has been applied to most subequent modern music forms.

- Like most jazz expressions, referred first to players, and only later to fans. When the player suddenly hit his real stride, so that he improvised brilliantly and effortlessly, he was "in the groove". — *The Observer*, 16th September 1956

groove *verb*

1 to enjoy *US, 1950*

- Word had gone out that this was going to be a head-knocking run anyway, and the idea of having a writer in too didn't groove anybody. — Hunter S. Thompson, *Hell's Angels*, p. 116, 1966
- I get up and shave with Grayson Kirk's razor, use his toothpaste, splash on his after-shave, grooving on it all. — James Simon Kunen, *The Strawberry Statement*, p. 34, 1968
- How can a guy really groove on cunt unless he has one? — Angelo d'Arcangelo, *The Homosexual Handbook*, p. 74, 1968
- I began to think of myself as some sort of lean and hungry Pierre Sal, as I grooved there with Dave Delinger[.] — Terry Southern, *Now Dig This*, 1968
- I groove on Hollywood movies – even bad ones. — Jerry Rubin, *Do It!*, p. 12, 1970
- "Most of us have too many friends outside that we groove on," she insisted. — Malcolm Boyd, *My Fellow Americans*, p. 147, 1970
- And they used to sit around and groove all the time, y'know. — Cheech Marin and Tommy Chong, *Santa Calus and his Old Lady*, 1971
- [J]oking and vibing and grooving[.] — *Uncut*, p. 44, May 2001

2 to please, to make happy *US*

- This enabled him to get enough morphine to keep "grooved" for several weeks. — John Clellon Holmes, *Go*, p. 198, 1952

3 to make good progress, to co-operate *UK*

- — *The Observer*, 3rd December 1967

4 to have sex *US*

- [H]ere was a man who could do a lot of good, who had the bread to support her bee and give her almost face value for the goods she pulled, all for a little grooving. — Clarence Cooper Jr, *The Scene*, p. 34, 1960

5 to be relaxed and happy *US*

- — Adrian Reid, *The Confessions of a Hitch-Hiker*, 1970

groover *noun*
a drug user who enjoys psychedelic accessories to his drug experience *US*

- — Eugene Landy, *The Underground Dictionary*, p. 93, 1971

groovily *adverb*
pleasantly *UK*

- Funky, conga-led grooves gel groovily with a slick arrangement. — *Ministry*, p. 97, January 2002

groovy *adjective*

1 very good, pleasing *US, 1937*
The word enjoyed two periods of great popularity, first in the early 1940s and then in the mid- to late 1960s, where it caught on both in the mainstream and in hip circles. Since then, it has become a signature word for mocking the attitudes and fashions of the 1960s.

- "You sound groovy," I said[.] — Chester Himes, *If He Hollers Let Him Go*, p. 161, 1945
- He'd light up and get real high, and when he was groovy as a ten-cent movie he'd begin to play the blues on a beat-up guitar. — Mezz Mezzrow, *Really the Blues*, p. 51–52, 1946
- "You like the groovy music on the juke?" Barrelhouse said. — Ralph Ellison, *Invisible Man*, p. 425, 1947
- — Arnold Shaw, *Lingo of Tin-Pan Alley*, p. 12, 1950
- "I pitched a no-hit game last summer," said Georgie. "Hey, groovy," said Sally. — Max Shulman, *The Many Loves of Dobie Gillis*, p. 83, 1951
- Cats say things are really groovy down on the Street. — Ross Russell, *The Sound*, p. 94, 1961
- It's not a big motocycle / Just a groovy little motorbike — The Beach Boys, *Little Honda*, 1964
- Shorty would take me to groovy, frantic scenes in different chicks' and cats' pads, where with the lights and juke down mellow, everybody blew gage and juiced back and jumped. — Malcolm X and Alex Haley, *The Autobiography of Malcolm X*, p. 56, 1964
- So split for Athens, Mykonos, someplace groovy. — Richard Farina, *Been Down So Long*, p. 111, 1966
- Wild thing / you make everything / groovy — The Troggs, *Wild Thing*, 1966
- Wouldn't you agree / baby you and me / We've got a groovy kind of love. — Wayne Fontana and the Mindbenders, *A Groovy Kind of Love*, 1966
- Just kickin' down the cobble stones / Looking for fun and feelin' groovy[.] — Simon and Garfunkel, *The 59th Street Bridge Song (Feelin' Groovy)*, 1967

- [A]nd then it's quickly followed by some broad telling you how groovy some gasoline is and how you can get laid practically as much as you want if you use it. —James Simon Kunen, *The Strawberry Statement*, p. 67, 1968
- It's really very groovy to take her to a movie / Where we make it in the balcony. —The Fugs, *Slum Goddess*, 1968
- Everything groovy. Everything with style ... must be first class. —*The Digger Papers*, p. 15, August 1968
- You know what we ought to do, man? The first thing – go and get us a groovy dinner. —Peter Fonda, *Easy Rider*, p. 55, 1969
- It's only midnight. If her parties are anything like they used to be, things are getting groovy about now. —Iceberg Slim (Robert Beck), *Mama Black Widow*, p. 27, 1969
- So many groovy heads are here that we could certainly figure out a way to survive. —*East Village Other*, 20th August 1969
- It's goovy to be carnal. —Richard Neville, *Play Power*, p. 74, 1970
- If she could have believed that he was over there at the picnic table grooving on the food freak simply because he was stoned on acid and everything he saw and heard seemed groovy, it would have been one thing. —Gurney Norman, *Divine Right's Trip (Last Whole Earth Catalog)*, p. 87, 1971
- Jim was groovy with me but he had an odd way of taking care of his business. —A.S. Jackson, *Gentleman Pimp*, p. 98, 1973
- That's why right now is a very groovy time, man. —*Austin Powers*, 1997

2 sexually attractive *UK*

A nuance of the sense as 'pleasing'.

- —*The Observer*, 3rd December 1967

3 profoundly out-of-style *US*

- —Connie Eble (Editor), *UNC-CH Campus Slang*, p. 3, Spring 1983

4 used to describe the effects of amphetamine *UK*

Drug-users (no-one else could be so subjective).

- —Home Office, *Glossary of Terms and Slang Common in Penal Establishments*, 1978

grope *noun*

an act of sexual fondling, especially when such fondling is the entire compass of the sexual contact *US, 1946*

- Her face warn't up to much but she were good fer a grope. —Alan Titchmarsh, *Trowell and Error*, p. 126, 2002

▸ **come the grope**

to feel up sexually *AUSTRALIA*

- [W]ho do you think made up the story about Sneed coming the old grope on Liza Minnelli? —Frank Hardy, *The Outcasts of Foolgarah*, p. 191, 1971
- If he'd come the grope with Aunty Edna, the Pope's a Jew. —*The Adventures of Barry McKenzie*, 1972

▸ **go the grope**

to feel up sexually *AUSTRALIA*

- [T]he soldier started to go the grope on me, so I woke Kath and said "Do your own dirty work". —Criena Rohan, *The Delinquents*, p. 62, 1962
- So we steamed to the huts to go the grope with some little raving bunny. —Barry Humphries, *A Nice Night's Entertainment*, p. 80, 1964
- —Frank Hardy, *The Outcasts of Foolgarah*, p. 16, 1971
- —Jim Ramsay, *Cop It Sweet!*, p. 41, 1977

grope *verb*

to grab or caress someone's genitals, usually in an impersonal manner *UK, 1380*

- —Guy Strait, *The Lavendar Lexicon*, 1964

Groper *nickname*

a non-Aboriginal native or resident of Western Australia, especially a descendant of an early settler *AUSTRALIA, 1899*

A shortening of **SANDGROPER**.

Groperland *noun*

the state of Western Australia *AUSTRALIA, 1900*

- —Jim Ramsay, *Cop It Sweet!*, p. 42, 1977

gross *adjective*

disgusting *US, 1959*

- —Andy Anonymous, *A Basic Guide to Campusology*, p. 12, 1966
- —*Kiss*, 1969: 'Groupie glossary'
- His conversation was soon loaded with "brew" and "beevo," with talk of "hometown honeys" and things being "gross." —John Sayles, *Union Dues*, p. 278, 1977
- He's like so GROSS / He like sits there and like plays with all his rings / And he like flirts with all the guys in the class / It's like totally disgusting. —Moon Unit and Frank Zappa, *Valley Girl*, 1982
- "My mom went out with this gross trucker guy once," Pup told him. —Francesca Lia Block, *Baby Be-Bop*, p. 391, 1995
- Gross. I hate it when my mom does that. —*American Beauty*, 1999
- [S]he didn't act as if there was anything gross about it at all. —Mary Hooper, *(megan)2*, p. 119, 1999
- Yuck. Ick. Gross! —Janet Evanovich, *Seven Up*, p. 55, 2001

gross-out *noun*

a disgusting thing *US, 1968*

- [A] stunning abundance of cultural riches, silly delights, and cathartic gross-outs. —Wendy Mogel, *The Blessing of a Skinned Knee*, p. 89, 2001

gross out *verb*

to disgust, to shock *US, 1965*

From **GROSS** (disgusting).

- —Collin Baker et al., *College Undergraduate Slang Study Conducted at Brown University*, p. 130, 1968
- I had a "gross-out contest" (what the fuck is a "gross-out contest"?) with Captain Beefheart and we both ate shit on stage. —Frank Zappa, *The Real Frank Zappa Book*, p. 14, 1989

Grosvenor Squares *noun*

flared trousers, flares *UK*

Rhyming slang.

- —Ray Puxley, *Cockney Rabbit*, 1992

grot *noun*

1 dirt, filth *UK, 1971*

By back-formation from **GROTTY**.

- The search is on for the grimmest, most fly-tipped, burnt-car littered, supermarket trolley infested stretch of grot in Britain. —*The Guardian*, 17th September 2003

2 a filthy person *AUSTRALIA, 1985*

- When it came to personal hygiene, the crims were no different from the rest of society – some of them were squeaky clean and others were filthy grots. —William Dodson, *The Sharp End*, p. 23, 2001

3 a toilet *NEW ZEALAND*

- Lots of lily-arsed bastards who dont know whether to stand or squat when they go to the grot. —Greg McGee, *Foreskin's Lament*, p. 76, 1981

grotbag; grot-bag; grot *noun*

an unpleasantly dirty person *UK: SCOTLAND*

A combination of **GROT** (dirt), with the suffix **-BAG** (personifies an unpleasant quality). Glasgow use.

- —Michael Munro, *The Patter, Another Blast*, p. 29, 1988

grot-hole *noun*

in caving and pot-holing, a small cave that leads nowhere and is difficult to manoeuvre in *UK*

- —David Morrison of Wessex Cave Club, 29th February 2004

grots *noun*

in caving and pot-holing, any (well used) clothing *UK*

- Dry grots are used for digging. "It's only a dry grots trip". —David Morrison of Wessex Cave Club, 29th February 2004

grotty; grot; grotbags *adjective*

unattractive, inferior *UK*

- SIMON: Now, you'll like these. You really "dig" them. They're "fab" and all the other pimply hyperboles. GEORGE: I wouldn't be seen dead in them. They're dead grotty. SIMON: Grotty? GEORGE: Yeah, grotesque. —*A Hard Day's Night*, 1964
- Unpleasant, disorganised. Younger Sloanes' word. —Ann Barr and Peter York, *The Official Sloane Ranger Handbook*, p. 158, 1982
- [B]ear to be led by my ring-laden hand – all grotty, second-hand cast-offs from Ratners[.] —John McCririck, *John McCririck's World of Betting*, p. 9, 1991
- [George Harrison]'s other memorable achievement was to speak the line which gave us the word "grotty". "Alun Owen made that up," he protested recently, "I didn't". —*Uncut*, p. 45, February 2002

grouch *noun*

an ill-tempered person *US, 1900*

- She was a grouch. She didn't seem afraid of him or even care he was here. —Elmore Leonard, *Glitz*, p. 188, 1985

grouch bag *noun*

literally, a small bag hidden on the person with emergency funds in it; figuratively, a wallet or a person's supply of money *US, 1908*

- "How's the grouch bag holding?" he asked. "All right. I've got a few bucks." —Robert Edmond Alter, *Carny Kill*, p. 8, 1966
- —Joe McKennon, *Circus Lingo*, p. 42, 1980

Groucho Marx; groucho *noun*

an electrician *UK*

Rhyming slang for **SPARKS**, formed from the name of the American comedian, 1890–1977.

ground *noun*

an area of operation or influence *UK*

In police use.

- Putney station was my ground – we don't call it "manor" or "patch"[.] —Duncan MacLaughlin, *The Filth*, p. 58, 2002

▸ **back on the ground; on the ground**

freed from prison *US*

- —Ralph de Sola, *Crime Dictionary*, p. 107, 1982
- —William K. Bentley and James M. Corbett, *Prison Slang*, p. 108, 1992

▸ **on the ground**

in horse racing, said of a jockey serving a suspension *US*

- —Tom Ainslie, *Ainslie's Complete Guide to Thoroughbred Racing*, p. 335, 1976

ground *verb*

to punish a child by refusing to let them leave the house for any social events *US, 1950*

- So I said, "What's the deal, Uncle Jeff? In wartime you want to be a pacifist and in peacetime you want to be a solider. It took, you twenty years to figure out you don't believe in anything?" Grounded. Just like that. Two weeks. —*Ferris Buehler's Day Off*, 1986
- What are you going to do, ground me? —*American Beauty*, 1999

ground apple *noun*

a brick *US*

- —Lou Shelly, *Hepcats Jive Talk Dictionary*, p. 25, 1945

ground clouds *noun*

fog *US*

- —Wayne Floyd, *Jason's Authentic Dictionary of CB Slang*, p. 18, 1976
- —Peter Chippindale, *The British CB Book*, p. 155, 1981

ground control *noun*

a person who guides another through an LSD experience *US*

Another LSD-as-travel metaphor.

- —John Williams, *The Drug Scene*, p. 112, 1967
- It was the only trip where I had somebody who acted as a guide or a ground control. —Stephen Gaskin, *Amazing Dope Tales*, p. 86, 1980

grounder *noun*

a crime that does not demand much effort by the police to solve *US, 1984*

- —Carsten Stroud, *Close Pursuit*, p. 272, 1987
- They pulled in sixty, seventy, most of them grounders, somebody doing his wife or his best friend, the occasional fag stabbing, although the solve rate was slipping a little. —Richard Price, *Clockers*, p. 99, 1992
- [H]e and Shane had shared a few easy grounders back when Shane was still working uniform in Southwest. —Stephen J. Cannell, *The Tin Collectors*, p. 15, 2001

ground floor *noun*

▸ **in on the ground floor**

in at the early stages of a project, trend, technical development, etc *US, 1864*

Generally phrased 'get in on', 'let in on' and 'be in on'.

- [S]alespeople ring up and verbally bludgeon them into parting with cash – usually with the line that the investor is getting in "on the ground floor" and by insisting they hand over cash immediately or lose out on the "opportunity" altogether. —*The Guardian*, 3rd May 2003

ground gripper *nickname*

a Hawker Siddeley 'Trident' aircraft *US*

Introduced into service in 1964.

groundhog *noun*

1 in the language of parachuting, anyone who has not parachuted *US*

- —Dan Poynter, *Parachuting*, p. 170, 1978: 'The language of parachuting'

2 a railway brakeman *US, 1926*

- —Norman Carlisle, *The Modern Wonder Book of Trains and Railroading*, p. 263, 1946

ground joker *noun*

any non-flying personnel in the Air Force *US*

- —*American Speech*, p. 310, December 1946: 'More air force slang'

groundlark *noun*

a bookmaker who illegally conducts business at a horse race track *AUSTRALIA*

- —Ned Wallish, *The Truth Dictionary of Racing Slang*, p. 35, 1989

groundman *noun*

in a group of friends taking LSD or another hallucinogen, a person who does not take the drug and helps those who do navigate their experience *UK*

- —Tom Hibbert, *Rockspeak!*, p. 78, 1983

ground-pounder *noun*

a member of the infantry *US, 1942*

Coined in World War 2, and used in every war since.

- —*Current Slang*, p. 16, Fall 1967
- "Lose pilots in combat" was a groundpounder's euphemism for "We won't need pilots anymore." —Walter Boyne and Steven Thompson, *The Wild Blue*, p. 413, 1986
- [U]nlike so many of his fellow ground pounders, numbers had a personal meaning for him ever since they had lost Tom Gomez. —Richard Herman, *The Warbirds*, p. 351, 1989
- Some "ground pounders" wearing "chocolate chip cookie cammies" even talk of an "Adopt-a-Pilot" campaign and cheer when the jets roar overhead. —*Houston Chronicle*, p. 15, 24th January 1991
- I'm beginning to feel like a groundpounder. Sure will feel good to feel that old prop pulling you along again. —Calvin L. Christman et al., *Lost in the Victory*, p. 62, 1998

groundscore *verb*

to find something of value, real or perceived, on the ground *US*

- —Jim Crotty, *How to Talk American*, p. 145, 1997

ground-sluice *verb*

to shoot at a bird on the ground *CANADA*

- Ground-sluicin' in Nova Scotia is to shoot at a bird on the ground rather than, in true sporting fashion, on the wing. The expression teasingly suggests that the inexpert hunter is actually digging a ditch with his bullet. —Lewis Poteet, *The South Shore Phrase Book*, p. 54, 1999

groundsman *noun*

an assistant to a bookmaker who collects bets and pays off winners *AUSTRALIA*

- —Ned Wallish, *The Truth Dictionary of Racing Slang*, p. 35, 1989

ground-trog *verb*

in caving and pot-holing, to search the surface for cave entrances *US*

- —David Morrison of Wessex Cave Club, 29th February 2004

ground week *noun*

the first week of US Army airborne parachute training *US*

- —Linda Reinberg, *In the Field*, p. 98, 1991

ground zero *noun*

1 the centre of action *US*

From the lingo of atomic weapons, literally meaning 'the ground where a bomb explodes'.

- "Ground zero," said Heff, shaking out his soaking jacket. —Richard Farina, *Been Down So Long*, p. 112, 1966

2 a back-to-basics condition from which a recommencement or restructuring may be developed *UK, 2001*

Figurative, from sense as a 'centre of targeted destruction'.

- Radio 1 embarked on a ground zero policy in the 1990s, recreating itself as a yoof [...] station for 15- to 24-year olds[.] —*The Sunday Times*, p. 13, 23rd June 2002

3 an untidy bedroom *US*

Described in *The Times*, 23rd March 2002, as 'teenspeak' and 'an example of post-Sept 11[2001] "terror humour"'.

- Their bedrooms are "ground zero." Translation? A total mess. —*The Washington Post*, 19th March 2002

group grope *noun*

1 group therapy *US*

In 1984, Beale noted: 'By ca. 1974 the term was being applied, in the UK, to the use of group-working in psychotherapy, where the mutual "groping" is mental rather than physical'.

- In the 1960s the United States saw the growth of a number of group-therapy cults which introduced into their procedures various rituals of mass-touching. These "group-gropes", as they were called[.] —Desmond Morris, *Man-Watching*, 1977

2 sex involving more than two people *US*

- I remember the first group grope I went to was with some guy and his girl friend. —Nicholas Von Hoffman, *We Are The People Our Parents Warned Us Against*, p. 183, 1967
- —*American Speech*, p. 57, Spring-Summer 1970: 'Homosexual slang'
- —Eugene Landy, *The Underground Dictionary*, p. 93, 1971

- — *Maledicta*, p. 232, 1979: 'Kinks and queens: linguistic and cultural aspects of the terminology for gays'
- Kind of gal Alyssa is, you don't think she's been in the middle of an all-girl group grope?— *Chasing Amy*, 1997

groupie; groupy *noun*

1 a girl who trades her sexual availability to rock groups and musicians in exchange for hanger-on status *US*

- They're called Groupies and can be found on the Sunset Strip in Los Angeles, on Macdougal Street around the Night Owl Cafe, or on Carnaby Street in London. The run of the mill Groupie has long blonde hair and heavily made-up eyes.— *The Berkeley Barb*, p. 5, 2nd September 1966
- — *Kiss*, 1969: 'Groupie glossary'
- Like a groupie who gets her hots not from being fucked by a rock star but from the image of herself getting fucked by a star[.]— *Screw*, p. 8, 24th November 1969
- —Eugene Landy, *The Underground Dictionary*, p. 93, 1971
- The little blonde groupie with the film crew! You think he sodomized her?—Hunter S. Thompson, *Fear and Loathing in Las Vegas*, p. 54, 1971
- Gertrude the Groupie was a rock 'n roll fan who stood by the stage door.—Shel Silverstein, *Roland The Roadie And Gertrude The Groupie*, 1973
- There you will rub shoulders with freaks, groupies, and liberated types of assorted colors, sizes, and styles.—Bernhardt J. Hurwood, *The Sensuous New York*, p. 34, 1973
- That night I was twenty-three and a daughter of Hollywood, alive with groupie fervor, wanting to fuck my way through rock'n'roll[.]—Eve Babitz, *L.A. Woman*, p. 15, 1982
- Knopfler weighs in as a heavier catch on the groupie fish scale[.] —Josh Alan Friedman, *Tales of Times Square*, p. 11, 1986
- The really famous groupies were extremely tough and unpleasant. —Nick Kent, *quoted in Waiting For The Sun*, p. 262, 1996
- Of all the vairous shatterlings of the candy-asssed world of glam rock, perhaps none is still as interesting as groupies.— Editors of Ben is Dead, *Retrohell*, p. 84, 1997
- PENNY: "Groupies" sleep with rock stars because they want to be near someone famous. We are here because of the music. We are Band Aids.— *Almost Famous*, 2000

2 a follower or hobbyist devoted to a pre-eminent person within a given field, or to a genre or subject type *US, 1967*

An extension of the previous sense, this usage is not restricted to rock groups or music, nor is there a suggestion that sex is a prerequisite; the tone may be derogatory, jocular or ironic.

- "Any station groupies with tits that big?" pondered Lieutenant Grimsley[.]—Joseph Wambaugh, *The Choirboys*, p. 370, 1975
- After two productions at the National Theatre ("I'm a Peter Hall groupie") the parts are more important than the place.— *Sunday Telegraph*, 1st July 1979
- A thrilled female De Lorean trial groupie jostled her way through the wedge of TV cameramen and news photographers to a better vantage point to proclaim, "Yeah, John!"— *United Press International*, 17th August 1984
- A younger generation knows her as the witch in "Rosemary's Baby," for which she won an Academy Award; the funeral groupie in "Harold and Maude"[.]— *New York Times*, p. 28, 11th November 1984
- She wondered if cop groupies out at the Polo Lounge would go for Gary Hammond or think he was impersonating a police officer. —Elmore Leonard, *Maximum Bob*, p. 88, 1991

Group of One; G1 *noun*

the United States *CANADA*

- In the rarefied atmosphere of summit planning, they know right away what you mean when you say G1. What else would the Group of One be but the United States? In effect, G1 is short for unilateralism–the recurring US practice of charting its own course.— *Toronto Globe and Mail*, p. A15, 21st June 2002

grouse *noun*

1 a grumble; a cause for complaint *UK, 1917*

- Can the Governing Council help to solve Iraqis' main grouse: the lack of security?— *The Economist*, 17th July 2003

2 a good thing; something of the best quality *AUSTRALIA*

- GROUSE – Something good.—Gilbert H. Lawson, *A Dictionary of Australian Words and Terms*, 1924
- 'How'd it go, mate?' he asked his son as they leaned their backs up against a pillar and stared across the sea. 'The grouse, Pop!'—Colleen McCullough, *Tim*, p. 38, 1975
- —Jim Ramsay, *Cop It Sweet!*, p. 42, 1977
- That's my rat's tail – it's the grouse.—Robert G. Barrett, *Davo's Little Something*, p. 23, 1992

grouse *verb*

to grumble *UK, 1885*

- [W]aking up at dawn, hungry, with rough voices and puffy eyes, grousing about who is responsible for getting them lost in the woods.— *The Guardian*, 28th July 1999

grouse *adjective*

great; excellent; top quality *AUSTRALIA, 1924*

Origin unknown. Commonly intensified as 'extra grouse'.

- [M]rs. Fondant Savorie looked extra grouse today.—Sutton Woodfield, *A for Artemis*, p. 35, 1960
- Remember the time we got 50 grand and caught a plane up to Surfers' and had a grouse time?—Kevin Mackey, *The Cure*, p. 100, 1970
- 'Private Russell you really make a slack baggy-arse soldier.' Russell replied, 'Yes sir, but I would make a grouse civilian.'—Martin Cameron, *A Look at the Bright Side*, 1988
- —David McGill, *A Dictionary of Kiwi Slang*, 1988

grouser *noun*

a complainer *UK, 1885*

From the verb **GROUSE**.

grouter *noun*

▸ **come in on the grouter**

to gain a fortuitous and unfair advantage, especially by appearing at an opportune time *AUSTRALIA, 1902*

The origin of this term is unknown, although one might conjecture that since grouting is the last task in a tiling job, to come in on the grouter would be to arrive when there is no work left to be done.

- This joker reckons he was in Tobruk, but I'm a wake-up to him. Probably come in on the grouter and bludged in a base job somewhere or other.—Lawson Glassop, *We Were The Rats*, p. 273, 1944
- —Jim Ramsay, *Cop It Sweet!*, p. 66, 1977

grovel *verb*

1 in computing, to work with great diligence but without visible success *US*

- —Guy L. Steele, *Coevolution Quarterly*, p. 31, Spring 1981: 'Computer slang'
- The file scavenger has been grovling through the file directories for ten minutes now.—Guy L. Steele et al., *The Hacker's Dictionary*, p. 75, 1983

2 to ride a wave even as it runs out of force *US*

- — *Surfing*, p. 43, 14th March 1990

Grover *noun*

a one-thousand dollar note; one thousand dollars *US*

From the portrait of US President Grover Cleveland on the notes, first issued in 1928.

- It was nothing Big Ed couldn't handle with Grovers.—Dan Jenkins, *Life Its Ownself*, p. 163, 1984

grow *verb*

▸ **grow your own**

to promote an enlisted man to a non-commissioned officer vacancy in a unit; to promote from within *US*

- —Gregory Clark, *Words of the Vietnam War*, p. 210, 1990

growed-up truck *noun*

an eighteen wheeled over-the-road truck *US*

- —Warren Smith, *Warren's Smith's Authentic Dictionary of CB*, p. 43, 1976

growl *verb*

▸ **growl at the badger**

to engage in oral sex on a woman, especially noisily *UK*

- —Chris Donald, *Roger's Profanisaurus*, p. 38, 1998
- —Chris Lewis, *The Dictionary of Playground Slang*, p. 108, 2003

growl and grunt; growl *noun*

the vulva and vagina *AUSTRALIA, 1941*

Rhyming slang for **CUNT**.

- —Dale Gordon, *The Dominion Sex Dictionary*, p. 79, 1967
- —Robert A. Wilson, *Playboy's Book of Forbidden Words*, p. 130, 1972
- —Jim Ramsay, *Cop It Sweet!*, p. 42, 1977
- —Ryan Aven-Bray, *Ridgey Didge Oz Jack Lang*, p. 29, 1983

growler *noun*

1 a bowel movement *US*

- —Judi Sanders, *Faced and Faded, Hanging to Hurl*, p. 18, 1993

2 a fart *UK*

- —Bodmin Dark, *Dirty Cockney Rhyming Slang*, p. 18, 2003

3 in the language of barbershop quartets, a strident bass singer *US*

- — *American Speech*, p. 298, Autumn-Winter 1975: 'The jargon of barbershop'

4 the lowest gear in a truck *US*

- —Montie Tak, *Truck Talk*, p. 78, 1971

5 a largely submerged iceberg *ANTARCTICA, 1912*
- We began to strike growlers with the regularity of a radio frequency. —Jennie Darlington and Jane McIlvaine, *My Antarctic Honeymoon*, p. 125, 1956
- —Bernadette Hince, *The Antarctic Dictionary*, p. 161, 2000

6 the vagina *AUSTRALIA, 1988*
- Dana's growler in *PlayBoy* in 1989 — *People*, p. 2, 5th July 1999

7 a prison cell used for solitary confinement *US*
- —Inez Cardozo-Freeman, *The Joint*, p. 502, 1984

8 beer, the dregs of a cask *IRELAND*
- He first put on his bowler, then he buttoned up his trousers, And he whistled for a growler and he said 'My men, Take me up to Monto, Monto, Monto....' — *Take Me Up to Monto*, 1999

9 a wrestler *US*
- —Lou Shelly, *Hepcats Jive Dictionary*, p. 12, 1945

10 a hotel's activity log *US*
- In the indictments lodged against bellboys in the hotel "growler," the rough equivalent of a ship's log, one word appeared over and over – caught. —Jim Thompson, *Bad Boy*, p. 356, 1953

11 a beer can *US*
- —Vincent J. Monteleone, *Criminal Slang*, p. 108, 1949

growne; groyne *noun*
▷ see: **GROIN**

grub *noun*

1 food; provisions of food *UK, 1659*
- Well, we'll have better grub than this. Don't you worry. —James T. Farrell, *The Life Adventure*, p. 186, 1947
- You'll need taxi fare and grub money, plus what the guy will ask. —Mickey Spillane, *My Gun is Quick*, p. 128, 1950
- No more worries about rotten grub. —Frank Norman, *Bang To Rights*, p. 157, 1958
- Got him some baby grub. — *Raising Arizona*, 1987

2 bullets *UK*
From the previous sense.
- —Dave Courtney, *Dodgy Dave's Little Black Book*, p. 7, 2001

3 an inferior, lowly person *UK, 1845*
- —Miss Cone, *The Slang Dictionary (Hawthorne High School)*, 1965

grub *verb*

1 to kiss with passion *US*
- —Carol Ann Preusse, *Jargon Used by University of Texas Co-Eds*, 1963
- —Connie Eble (Editor), *UNC-CH Campus Slang*, p. 3, March 1981

2 to engage in sexual foreplay *US*
- — *Verbatim*, p. 280, May 1976

grubber *noun*

1 a disgusting person *US, 1941*
- — *American Speech*, p. 60, Spring-Summer 1975: 'Razorback slang'
- I don't want to be a grubber. A hustler. A parasite. —Cleo Odzer, *Goa Freaks*, p. 39, 1995

2 in cricket, a ball bowled underarm *UK, 1837*
Also variant 'grub'.
- [I]n 1981, Aussie captain, Greg Chappel, ordered his brother, Trevor, to bowl underarm. The resulting "grubber" won Australia the match and caused a sporting outcry. — *FHM*, p. 151, June 2003

grubbies *noun*
old, worn comfortable clothes *US*
- —John D. Bell et al., *Loosely Speaking*, p. 10, 1966
- They wore cutoffs and jeans and grubbies of all kinds. —Joseph Wambaugh, *The Delta Star*, p. 217, 1983

grubby *noun*
a young male summer resident of a camp on a Canadian lake *CANADA*
- They're just a crowd of indistinguishable, usually grimy young boys who have to be fed three times a day, whose crusts and crumbs and rinds have to be cleaned up afterwards. The counsellors call them Grubbies. —Margaret Atwood, *The New Oxford Book of Canadian Stories*, p. 254, 1997

grubby *adjective*
not neat, not clean *US*
- —Carol Covington, *A Glossary of Teenage Terms*, 1965

grubs *noun*
old, worn and comfortable clothes *US*
- — *Current Slang*, p. 4, Winter 1966

grudge-fuck *verb*
to have sex out of spite or anger *US*
- To avenge the crack about Joe, she grudgefucked Dan. —Seth Morgan, *Homeboy*, p. 171, 1990

gruesome and gory *noun*
the penis *UK*
Rhyming slang for **COREY**.
- —Ray Puxley, *Cockney Rabbit*, 1992

gruesome twosome *noun*
a couple who date steadily *US, 1941*
- — *American Speech*, p. 303, December 1955: 'Wayne university slang'
- The gruesome twosome. That's been going on since 1948 when they graduated from Bryn Mawr. —Rita Mae Brown, *Rubyfruit Jungle*, p. 165, 1973
- We became the gruesome twosome. The pair that everyone wanted at parties because we were so entertaining together. Always high on life, on each other. —Jane Green, *Straight Talking*, p. 40, 2003

Grumann Greyhound *noun*
the C-2A aircraft *US*
Manufactured by Grumann, a twin engine, prop-driven plane used by the US Navy to transport troops (hence the 'Greyhound' as an allusion to the bus company) or cargo.
- —Linda Reinberg, *In the Field*, p. 98, 1991

grumble and grunt; grumble *noun*
the vagina; hence women objectified sexually *UK, 1938*
Rhyming slang for **CUNT**.
- —Ray Puxley, *Cockney Rabbit*, 1992
- It's a well-known thing – the more I bevvy [drink], the more I has to find me some grumble. —Kevin Sampson, *Outlaws*, p. 186, 2001

grumble and mutter *noun*
a bet *UK*
Rhyming slang for **FLUTTER**.
- —Ray Puxley, *Cockney Rabbit*, 1992

grume *noun*
a filthy, decrepit patient in a hospital casualty department *US*
- — *Journal of American Folklore*, p. 568–581, January–March 1978: 'The gomer'

grummet *noun*
a woman, or women, objectified sexually *UK*
From earlier senses, now lost, as 'the vagina' and 'sexual intercourse'.
- [T]wo lovely bits of grummet. —Patrick Campbell, *Come Here Till I Tell You*, 1960

grump *noun*
an ill-tempered person *UK, 1900*
- Well, I'll tell you about it if you want – you grump. —Leif Enger, *Peace Like a River*, p. 67, 2001

grumpus-back *noun*
a gruff, churlish person *BARBADOS*
- —Frank A. Collymore, *Barbadian Dialect*, p. 56, 1965

grundies; grunds *noun*
underpants *AUSTRALIA*
Short for **REG GRUNDIES**.
- —Arthur Delbridge, *Aussie Talk*, p. 149, 1984

grundy *adjective*
medicore *US*
- Some feel he is "real crazy" (fine), but others find him "just grundy" (not good, not bad). — *Look*, p. 49, 24th November 1959

grunge *noun*

1 unpleasant dirt or filth *US, 1965*
- I blew tons of grunge from my nose, with more to follow. —Wayne Anthony, *Spanish Highs*, p. 48, 1999

2 a rock music genre *US*
From the previous sense, abstractly applied to the 'dirty' guitar sound; it is occasionally recorded from the mid-1960s but until Nirvana and other Seattle-based US groups came to prominence in the early 90s 'grunge' was not a genre.
- What do they sound like? Great! Grunge noise and mystikal studio abstractions[.] —Lester Bangs, *Psychotic Reactions and Carburetor Dung*, p. 102, 1972
- Grunge – America's answer to Punk Rock – described both a new generation of loud, guitar-orientated rock music and the attitudes of its exponents. —Sarah Callard and Will Hoon, *Surfers Soulies Skinheads & Skaters*, 1996

- [Nirvana's] influence didn't impact straight away, it took a couple of years to filter through, but by 1992 grunge had totally destroyed the LA cock rock scene. —John Robb, *The Nineties*, p. 227, 1999
- Grunge [...] became the first angry trend in white music for ten years to achieve mass popularity. —Mark Steel, *Reasons to be Cheerful*, p. 232, 2001

3 a style of loose-fitting, layered clothes favoured by fans of the grunge music scene *US*

- But even the grunge-wear could not dull the brilliant polished-mineral black of his eyes[.] —Francesca Lia Block, *I Was a Teenage Fairy*, p. 73, 1998
- By '92 there were high-fashion grunge catwalks[.] —John Robb, *The Nineties*, p. 227, 1999

4 an obnoxious, graceless person *US*

- —Collin Baker et al., *College Undergraduate Slang Study Conducted at Brown University*, p. 131, 1968

grungejumper *noun*

used as a euphemism for 'motherfucker' *US*

- I picked him out real careful, ya grungejumper! —Jack Kerouac, *The Dharma Bums*, p. 145, 1958

grungie *noun*

1 a filthy or disgusting person *UK*

- Ten years ago you had the grungies up at the top [of the street][.] —Jenny Eclair, *Camberwell Beauty*, p. 36, 2000

2 a post-hippie youth in rebellion *US*
Also spelt 'grungy'.

- —Connie Eble (Editor), *UNC-CH Campus Slang*, p. 4, Spring 1982

grungy *adjective*

filthy, dirty, unpleasant, untidy *US, 1965*
Of **GRUNGE** (an unpleasant substance); however contemporary use also refers to the deliberately messy fashion associated with **GRUNGE** music.

- —*Current Slang*, p. 4, Winter 1966
- Fine and professional, yet intensely driving and almost grungy [...], it was truly exciting music[.] —Lester Bangs, *Psychotic Reactions and Carburetor Dung*, p. 17, 1971
- I went to the University of Miami three years, majored in psychology, and I worked as a stripper for three years in topless bars in Miami, but not the grungy joints. —Elmore Leonard, *Pronto*, p. 332–323, 1993
- He's dressed in old tie-dyes and army surplus, and he looks like something out of one of those peace convoys, all grungy[.] —J.J. Connolly, *Know Your Enemy [britpulp]*, p. 147, 1999
- She told me that she's relieved herself in a motorway services loo on the way because Portaloos reminded her too much of work – ie, grungy rock festivals. —*ES Magazine*, p. 3, 22nd June 2001

grunt *noun*

1 a member of the US Marine Corps *US, 1968*

- Listen, us guys are goddam saints compared to the grunts. —Darryl Ponicsan, *The Last Detail*, p. 15, 1970
- —*Current Slang*, p. 16, Summer 1970
- Having served in Korea as a dogface grunt, he knew a lifer when he saw one. —Joseph Wambaugh, *Finnegan's Week*, p. 27, 1993

2 An infantry soldier, especially but not necessarily a marine *US, 1962*
An important piece of slang in the Vietnam war.

- —*Time*, p. 34, 10th December 1965
- Charlie Company was a "grunt" unit; its men were the foot soldiers, the "GI Joes," who understood they were to take orders, not question them. —Seymour Hersh, *My Lai 4*, p. 18, 1970
- No, just medics and grunts. —Ronald J. Glasser, *365 Days*, p. 29, 1971
- They call them grunts, you know, the guys from the bush in Nam, and they're supposed to be the gungiest mothers around. —Charles Anderson, *The Grunts*, p. 15, 1976
- I heard some grunt rolled a grenade in his tent. —*Apocalypse Now*, 1979
- Now according to some people, folks do not want to hear about Alpha Company – us grunts – busting jungle and busting cherries from Landing Zone Skator-Gator to Scat Man Do[.] —Larry Heinemann, *Paco's Story*, p. 5, 1986
- Grunts walk hard and they walk far / In Artillery we ride by car. —Sandee Shaffer Johnson, *Cadences*, p. 80, 1986
- Grunts who give half their pay to buy gooks toothbrushes and deodorants – winning of hearts and minds, okay? —*Full Metal Jacket*, 1987
- Marine riflemen, the "grunts" as they called themselves in these Vietnam years, do not depend for air support on the vagaries of the Air Force or on the regular Navy planes from the carriers. —Neil Sheehan, *A Bright Shining Lie*, p. 537, 1988

3 a menial, unskilled worker *US, 1970*

- I found in my kitchen cabinet a monstrous rodent chewing himself blue in the race on a Brillo pad, causing me to bag Brooklyn and my grunt job in publishing and move out to the 'burbs. —Rita Cirtesi, *Pink Slip*, p. 1, 1999

4 an electrician or electrical lineman's assistant *US, 1926*
Some power companies in the US have tried to prohibit use of the term to describe the helper position; in general, linemen have perceived this attempt as political correctness carried to an absurd extreme and have continued calling their helpers 'grunts'.

- —Lou Shelly, *Hepcats Jive Talk Dictionary*, p. 46, 1945

5 a railway engineer *US, 1939*

- —Norman Carlisle, *The Modern Wonder Book of Trains and Railroading*, p. 264, 1946

6 in mountain biking, a steep and challenging incline *US*

- There's a boulder on one of my local singletrack grunts that sticks up about hub-high. I tried it three times, then filed it under "dismount and walk"[.] —*Mountain Bike Magazine's Complete Guide To Mountain Biking Skills*, p. 53, 1996

7 power *NEW ZEALAND*

- —David McGill, *David McGill's Complete Kiwi Slang Dictionary*, p. 58, 1998

8 marijuana *US*

- —Peter Johnson, *Dictionary of Street Alcohol and Drug Terms*, p. 86, 1993

▷ **see:** GASP AND GRUNT

grunt *verb*

to eat *US*

- —Collin Baker et al., *College Undergraduate Slang Study Conducted at Brown University*, p. 131, 1968
- —Michael Dalton Johnson, *Talking Trash with Redd Foxx*, p. 44, 1994

grunt-and-squeal jockey *noun*

a truck driver who hauls cattle or pigs *US*

- —Montie Tak, *Truck Talk*, p. 78, 1971

grunter *noun*

1 a bed *NEW ZEALAND*

- —Louis S. Leland, *A Personal Kiwi-Yankee Dictionary*, p. 89, 1984

2 a foghorn with two tones *US*

- —Jim Crotty, *How to Talk American*, p. 174, 1997

grunts *noun*

food *US*

- —Collin Baker et al., *College Undergraduate Slang Study Conducted at Brown University*, p. 131, 1968
- —Dennis Aaberg and John Milius, *Big Wednesday*, p. 209, 1978

grunt-tight *adjective*

(used of a bolt) tightened by feel rather than by measured torque *US*

- —Lewis Poteet, *Car & Motorcyle Slang*, p. 97, 1992

grush *noun*

a mad scramble of boys to get a coin or some similar gift thrown at them; a present given to people outside a church after a wedding *IRELAND*

- Me pal Whacker said that the altar boys got a grush of money all to themselves. —?monn MacThom?, *Gur Cake and Coal Blocks*, p. 37, 1976

gruts *noun*

underpants *NEW ZEALAND*

- —David McGill, *David McGill's Complete Kiwi Slang Dictionary*, p. 59, 1998

gry; gryer *noun*

a horse *UK*
Romany.

- —Patrick O'Shaughnessy, *Lore and Language*, January 1978

GS *noun*

a shared act of urine fetishism; the act of urination by one person on another for sexual gratification *US*
Used in personal advertising; an abbreviation of **GOLDEN SHOWER**.

- —*What Color is Your Handkerchief*, p. 6, 1979
- Other turn-ons include GS, F [French] and S/M [sadomasochism] —Kevin Sampson, *Clubland*, p. 70, 2002

GSD *noun*

an Alsatian *UK*
Initialism of *G*erman *S*hepherd *D*og, the original breed name, which was changed by the UK Kennel Club after World War 1 for reasons of political sensitivity.

- Home visit made to discuss problem of GSD barking continuously through the day. —*internal report by local authority dog warden*, August 2002

G shot *noun*
an injection of a small amount of a drug while in search of a larger amount *US*
- —Jay Robert Nash, *Dictionary of Crime*, p. 159, 1992

G-star *noun*
a youth gang member *US*
- —Bill Valentine, *Gang Intelligence Manual*, p. 76, 1995: 'Black street gang terminology'

G-string *noun*
1 a small patch of cloth passed between a woman's legs and supported by a waist cord, providing a snatch of modesty for a dancer *US, 1936*
A slight variation on the word 'gee-string' used in the late C19 to describe the loin cloth worn by various indigengous peoples.
- Take 'Em Off! — *Saturay Review of Literature*, p. 28, 18 August 1945
- One or two Oasis girls strip completely, without G-strings, plaster or anything on. —Jack Lait and Lee Mortimer, *Washington Confidential*, p. 264, 1951
- She knew they would take her clothes off and see the red spangled G string she was wearing. —Hubert Selby Jr, *Last Exit to Brooklyn*, p. 49, 1957
- G-strings like phosphorescent badges etched across the thighs; spread legs radiating their unfulfilled invitation[.] —John Rechy, *City of Night*, p. 297, 1963
- The 6–3 votes allows local or state governments to require that dancers wear at least pasties and a G-string so long as everyone else also is forbidden to appear naked in public. — *Washington Post*, 30th March 2000

2 a BMW Series 3 car *SOUTH AFRICA*
Scamto youth street slang (South African townships).
- — *The Times*, 12th February 2005

GTA *noun*
the criminal charge of grand theft, auto *US*
The punch-line of an oft-repeated joke: 'What do you call four [ethnic minority of choice at the moment] in a brand new Cadillac?'.
- "For GTA once," Shelby said. ""Drove a hot Porsche for six months 'fore they nailed me." —Joseph Wambaugh, *Finnegan's Week*, p. 40, 1993

GTG
used as shorthand in Internet discussion groups and text messages to mean *'got to go' US*
- —Gabrielle Mander, *WAN2TLK? ltl bk of txt msgs*, p. 45, 2002

G thing *noun*
a subject matter best understood by young urban gangsters *US*
- —Connie Eble (Editor), *UNC-CH Campus Slang*, p. 4, Spring 1994

G-top *noun*
a tent or trailer in a carnival reserved exclusively for carnival employees *US*
Employees can drink and gamble out of sight of the public and police.
- —Joe McKennon, *Circus Lingo*, p. 42, 1980
- —Gene Sorrows, *All About Carnivals*, p. 18, 1985: 'Terminology'

guage out *verb*
▷ see: GAGE OUT

Guardianista *noun*
a liberal, politically-correct person *UK*
Intended as derogatory; from the stereotype that is, allegedly, a reader of the *Guardian* newspaper and combined with left-wing Nicaraguan revolutionaries the Sandinistas.
- Asylum-seekers "sponging" off the country's welfare system are among his [Sun columnist, Richard Littlejohn] regular targets, as are do-gooder "Guardianistas", and Cherie Blair, who has been branded "the Wicked Witch" and actually controls the country. — *The Guardian*, 31st January 2003

Guat *noun*
a *Guat*amalan *UK*
- The kids didn't care if we were Guats or Brits[.] —Andy McNab, *Immediate Action*, p. 211, 1995

Guatamala dirt dobbers *noun*
sandals *US*
- — *Current Slang*, p. 18, Spring 1970

guava *noun*
1 an upwardly mobile young adult *SOUTH AFRICA, 1989*
An acronym for 'grown up and very ambitious' or 'growing up and very ambitious'.
- —Penny Silva, *A Dictionary of South African English*, 1996

2 the buttocks, the backside *SOUTH AFRICA, 1975*
Especially in the phrase 'on your guava'.
- —Penny Silva, *A Dictionary of South African English*, 1996

guava *adjective*
very good, superlative *US*
- —Trevor Cralle, *The Surfin'ary*, p. 48, 1991
- Guava tunes, kid. — *Empire Records*, 1995

guava days; gauva season; guava times *noun*
difficult times *TRINIDAD AND TOBAGO, 1979*
- —Lise Winer, *Dictionary of the English/Creole of Trinidad & Tobago*, 2003

gub *verb*
to hit in the mouth; to defeat *UK: SCOTLAND, 1985*
From 'gub' (the mouth).
- Sometimes they [women] need a right good gubbing and other times they need romance, know? —Ian Pattison, *Rab C. Nesbitt*, 1988

gubbins *noun*
used as a replacement for any single or plural noun that the user cannot or does not wish to specify *UK, 1944*
- [F]itting two bedrooms, two shower/toilets, kitchen and saloon, never mind her engine and other technical gubbins into a space 12 metres by 3.5 metres is a tall order. — *The Guardian*, 1st June 2003

gubbish *noun*
in computing, nonsense *US*
A blend of 'garbage' and 'rubbish'.
- —Guy L. Steele et al., *The Hacker's Dictionary*, p. 75, 1983

Gucci *adjective*
stylish, especially cleverly so *UK*
From the high-profile fashion brand.
- There was a torch mounted under the Armalite, held on with bits of masking tape on the furniture (stock). I thought, that's quite Gucci, I wouldn't mind one of those. —Andy McNab, *Immediate Action*, p. 27, 1995

gucky *noun*
Gucci, a fashion-design label *UK*
Upper-class society usage; a deliberate and jocular mispronunciation of a favourite brand.
- Gucci (makes you feel the opposite of sick). [see: gucky] —Ann Barr and Peter York, *The Official Sloane Ranger Handbook*, p. 158, 1982

gucky *adjective*
sickening *UK*
Upper-class society use.
- —Ann Barr and Peter York, *The Official Sloane Ranger Handbook*, p. 158, 1982

gudentight; goot-n-tight *adjective*
tight, especially in a sexual context *US*
A mock German or Dutch construction.
- Goot-n-tight! Annette's sister. —Steve Cannon, *Groove, Bang, and Jive Around*, p. 45, 1969

guernsey *noun*
▸ **get a guernsey**
to be selected for something, such as a team, job, award or the like *AUSTRALIA, 1918*
Originally 'to be picked for a football team', from 'guernsey' as 'a top worn by football players'.
- Allen could only get a 'guernsey' in the Fifth Test and the bulk of the off spinning was borne by the versatile Titmus. —Richie Benaud, *Spin me a Spinner*, p. 20, 1963
- —Jim Ramsay, *Cop It Sweet!*, p. 43, 1977
- [E]very neurotic fear from hair loss to irreparable burn scars gets a guernsey. — *Beat*, p. 31, 9th July 1996

▸ **give a guernsey**
to select someone *AUSTRALIA*
- Must've been bloody frustrating, Mark, being given a guernsey you didn't want. —W.R. Bennett, *Target Turin*, p. 104, 1962

guess *noun*
▸ **by guess and by God**
a casual form of nautical navigation *US*
- —Hans Halberstadt, *USCG: Always Ready*, p. 128, 1986: 'Glossary'

▸ **miss your guess**
to be mistaken *US, 1921*
- Else I miss my guess, he will chop their heads before supper. — Michael Crichton, *Timeline*, p. 273, 2000

▸ **your guess is as good as mine**
a catchphrase used to describe a situation where neither party knows the facts *CANADA, 1939*
- Finally, if hackers are so smart, how come Stanley is so dumb? Your guess is as good as mine. — *The Guardian*, 21st July 2001

guessing stick *noun*
a slide rule *US, 1941*
- — Jerry Robertson, *Oil Slanguage*, p. 62, 1954

guessing tubes *noun*
a stethoscope *UK*
Medical slang.
- — Adam T. Fox, St Mary's Hospital, London, 10th October 2002

guesstimate; guestimate *noun*
a rough calculation *US, 1934*
Part 'guess', part 'estimate'.
- The official guesstimate of the cost of drug addiction [in Britain] is somewhere between £10bn and £18bn a year – mostly in crime and its consequences. — *The Guardian*, 23rd April 2003

guest *noun*
a prisoner *US*
Used in combinations such as 'guest of the city', 'guest of the governor' or 'guest of the nation'.
- — Ralph de Sola, *Crime Dictionary*, p. 60, 1982

guest star *noun*
a last-minute replacement to take the place of someone who has cancelled a date *US*
- — Amy Sohn, *Sex and the City*, p. 155, 2002

guff *noun*
1 foolish nonsense, usually spoken or sung *US, 1888*
From 'guff' (empty talk), later usage informed by the sense of 'a fart', punning and adding a noxious element to **HOT AIR** (nonsense).
- "Don't take any guff from these swine," I said as he slammed the phone down. — Hunter S. Thompson, *Fear and Loathing in Las Vegas*, p. 12, 1971
- All Ragga [music genre with violent and sexist lyrics] was the same kinda guff with a digital edge instead of using established dub plates. — John Robb, *The Nineties*, p. 180, 1999
- [H]e doesn't believe in any of his religious kitschy crap and his guff about the strong-walled mansions of the dead[.] — James Hawes, *Dead Long Enough*, p. 83, 2000
- [A]ll that guff about a prisoner one phone call (usually to his lawyer) was just that – so much guff. — Duncan MacLaughlin, *The Filth*, p. 97, 2002

2 back-talk, verbal resistance *US, 1879*
- Just because I went to college don't make me take any guff from a nit like you. — Raymond Chandler, *The Long Goodbye*, p. 35, 1953
- You can tell the colonel your phone's been out of order if he gives you any guff. — Jim Thompson, *The Nothing Man*, p. 202, 1954

3 a fart *UK, 1998*
Probably from the sense 'nonsense', thus a play on **HOT AIR**.
- — *An A-Z of Rude Health*, 18th January 2002
- You blame a guff on a dog. — *The FHM Little Book of Bloke*, p. 27, June 2003

guff *verb*
1 to fart *UK*
Probably from **GUFF** (nonsense), hence a play on **HOT AIR**.
- — *Roger's Profanisaurus*, p. 13, December 1997
- Phew!!! Who guffed? — *SMTV LIVE it's wicked*, p. 6, 2000
- — *An A-Z of Rude Health*, 18th January 2002

2 to eat and drink greedily *INDIA*
- — Paroo Nihalini, R.K. Tongue and Priya Hosali, *Indian and British English*, 1979

3 to anger and prepare to fight *TRINIDAD AND TOBAGO*
- — Lise Winer, *Dictionary of the English/Creole of Trinidad & Tobago*, 2003

guggle *noun*
the throat, the gullet *US*
- [P]lastic models of everything from your guggle to your zatch [genitals]. — Barbara and William Conable, *How to Learn the Alexander Technique*, p. 96, 1991

guide *noun*
a person who monitors the LSD experience of another, helping them through bad moments and caring for their physical needs *US*
- He gazes at the lights coming through the window as a guide comforted a friend. — Richard Alpert and Sidney Cohen, *LSD*, p. 116, 1966
- It was the only trip where I had somebody who acted as a guide or a ground control. — Stephen Gaskin, *Amazing Dope Tales*, p. 86, 1980

guider; glider *noun*
a children's makeshift vehicle, typically constructed of a soapbox and pram-wheels *UK, 1979*

guido *noun*
an Italian or Italian-American, especially a macho one *US*
Disparaging.
- — Connie Eble (Editor), *UNC-CH Campus Slang*, p. 5, Spring 1988
- Guido's of the world unite. — *New Jack City*, 1990
- In the locker rooms of the Eighteenth District Station and around the cop bars, he called Italians guidos or wops, Poles polacks, Bohemians hunkies, Mexicans spicks or greasers, and African-Americans niggers or darkies. — Robert Campbell, *Boneyards*, p. 10, 1992
- Al Dante was the ultimate in guido. — Rita Cirtesi, *Pink Slip*, p. 2, 1999

guillotine *noun*
the lip of a wave crashing down on a surfer's head *US*
- — Trevor Cralle, *The Surfin'ary*, p. 48, 1991

guilt trip *noun*
an effort to make someone else feel guilty *US, 1972*
- And how dare you try to lay a guilt trip on me about it – in public, no less! — *Chasing Amy*, p. 99, 1997

guilt-trip *verb*
to attempt to make someone feel guilty *US*
- I have a lot of trouble with gay activists who try to guilt-trip people into doing something when they don't know the consequences. — *AM Cycle*, 27th July 1977
- I mighta known. You've got a black belt in guilt-tripping. — Joseph Wambaugh, *Finnegan's Week*, p. 244, 1993

guinea *noun*
1 an Italian or Italian-American *US, 1890*
- How do you think he feels about you guineas [referring to Pureto Ricans] coming into Brownsville and marking up our shuls? — Irving Shulman, *The Amboy Dukes*, p. 47, 1947
- "The agent's a goddam guinea, just like the owner," Red charged. — Ross Russell, *The Sound*, p. 144, 1961
- I wouldn't be a guinea on a motherfucking bet. — Piri Thomas, *Down These Mean Streets*, p. 30, 1967
- Know he would stand in the ghinny corner of the yard with his boss, Pete Amadeo[.] — Edwin Torres, *After Hours*, p. 159, 1979
- Slow husky voice with that South Philly street guinea accent, that tought-guy shit they learned when they were kids. — Elmore Leonard, *Glitz*, p. 137, 1985
- This little guinea fuck. Someday he's gonna be a boss. — *Goodfellas*, 1990
- He cetainly didn't need to worry about tripping and spraying fizz on my highly unprofessional outfit: a pair of cutoffs and a man's white V-neck T-shirt that Dodie procalimed was the equivalent of a neon sign that said guinea. — Rita Ciresi, *Pink Slip*, p. 39, 1999

2 in horse racing, a horse groom *US*
- — Mel Heimer, *Inside Racing*, p. 211, 1962

Guinea football *noun*
a homemade bomb *US, 1918*
- — Hyman E. Goldin et al., *Dictionary of American Underworld Lingo*, p. 87, 1950

guinea people *noun*
Jamaicans with a strong sense of African identity *JAMAICA*
- — Peter L. Patrick, *Some Recent Jamaican Creole Words*, 2003

guinea pig *noun*
1 a person used as the subject of an experiment *US, 1920*
- [I]nmates from both Hart's and Riker's were being shipped over to King's County Hospital, where they were being used as guinea-pigs by some city doctors to find out what the score was with marihuana. — Mezz Mezzrow, *Really the Blues*, p. 317, 1946

2 a wig *UK*
Rhyming slang.
- — Ray Puxley, *Fresh Rabbit*, 1998

guinea red *noun*
cheap Italian red wine *US, 1933*
Offensive because of the national slur.
• "What's the matter? You think I can't talk?" Felita said. "I ain't a pair of shoes or a jug of guinea red." —Robert Campbell, *Alice in La-La Land*, p. 276, 1987

Guineatown *noun*
a neighbourhood dominated by Italian-Americans and/or Italian immigrants *US*
• He left his own car back in Guineatown. —Richard Price, *Clockers*, p. 248, 1992

guiver *noun*
▷ see: GUYVER

gulch *noun*
on Prince Edward Island, junk food or unappetising food *CANADA*
• That gulch was the worst food I ever tasted. —T. K. Pratt, *oral citation from The Dictionary of Prince Edward Island English*, p. 70, 1988

gulch *verb*
to engage in sexual intimacy in the outdoors *CANADA*
• A Newfoundland way to say "grassin" is "gulching," suggesting the comparatively more rugged landscape teenagers on the Rock have to [engage in sexual] play in. —George Patterson, *Dialect of Newfoundland in Explorations in Canadian Folklore*, p. 68, 1985

gullwing *noun*
a car body style in which the passenger doors are hinged at the top and open upwards *US*
• —John Edwards, *Auto Dictionary*, p. 72, 1993

gully *noun*
in cricket, a fielding position that covers the gap between slip and cover point *UK, 1920*
Derives from a conventional 'gully' (a gap).
• Adam Gilchrist on 14, is dropped by Craig White at gully. —*The Guardian*, 24th July 2001

gully *adjective*
1 inferior; not up to expectations *US*
• —Connie Eble (Editor), *UNC-CH Campus Slang*, p. 5, October 2002

2 excellent *UK*
A reversal of the earlier sense on the **BAD** is 'good' principle; used by urban black youths.
• Thierry Henry is gully. —*Live*, p. 39, Winter 2004

gully-gut *noun*
a glutton *UK, 1542*
• —Malachi Andrews and Paul T. Owens, *Black Language*, p. 99, 1973

gully monkey *noun*
a person lacking intelligence and class *TRINIDAD AND TOBAGO*
• —Lise Winer, *Dictionary of the English/Creole of Trinidad & Tobago*, 2003

guluptious *adjective*
big and awkward *TRINIDAD AND TOBAGO*
• —Lise Winer, *Dictionary of the English/Creole of Trinidad & Tobago*, 2003

gum *noun*
1 crude, unrefined opium *US*
• —*American Speech*, p. 100, May 1956: 'Smugglers' argot in the southwest'
• —Richard A. Spears, *The Slang and Jargon of Drugs and Drink*, p. 237, 1986
• —Mike Haskins, *Drugs*, p. 284, 2003

2 MDMA, the recreational drug best known as ecstasy *UK*
• —Mike Haskins, *Drugs*, p. 289, 2003

3 in pool, a cushion *US*
Cushions were once fashioned with rubber gum.
• —Mike Shamos, *The Illustrated Encyclopedia of Billiards*, p. 111, 1993

guma *noun*
▷ see: GOMA

gumball *noun*
1 the flashing coloured lights on a police car *US, 1971*
• —Helen Dahlskog (Editor), *A Dictionary of Contemporary and Colloquial Usage*, p. 29, 1972
• [A]nd if the guy didn't sideswipe some cars and pile up he'd be on him before he hit Woodward, nail him with the gumballs flashing blue and siren turned up to high yelp. —Elmore Leonard, *Switch*, p. 150, 1978
• A lone gumball sits perched atop the passenger side of the roof. —*Menace II Society*, 1993
• [T]he amateur photographer turned on the patrol boat's gumball-blue light and hit them with a few siren yelps. —Joseph Wambaugh, *Floaters*, p. 3, 1996

2 in stock car racing, a soft tyre used for extra traction in qualifying heats but, because it wears out so quickly, not in races *US*
• —John Lawlor, *How to Talk Car*, p. 57, 1965
• They even had special tires for qualifying, soft tires, called "gumballs," they wouldn't last more than ten times around the track in a race, but for qualifying, which is generally three laps, they are great, because they hold tight on the corners. —Tom Wolfe, *The Kandy-Kolored Tangerine-Flake Streamline Baby*, p. 137, 1965

3 heroin *UK*
• —Mike Haskins, *Drugs*, p. 284, 2003

gumball *verb*
to activate the flashing coloured lights on a police car *US*
• Within five minutes, there were a dozen police cars blocking the street, their red and blue lights gumballing in all directions. —Joseph Wambaugh, *The Delta Star*, p. 114, 1983

gum-beat *verb*
to talk, to chat *US, 1942*
• Like practically all jazz disciplines they really came to listen, not to dance or gumbeat around the table. —Mezz Mezzrow, *Really the Blues*, p. 77, 1946

gumbies *noun*
black tennis shoes *US*
• —*Current Slang*, p. 6, Spring 1969

gumbo *noun*
1 in horse racing, thick mud *US*
• —Dan Parker, *The ABC of Horse Racing*, p. 146, 1947

2 in oil drilling, any viscuous or sticky formation encountered in drilling *US*
• —Jerry Robertson, *Oil Slanguage*, p. 62, 1954

gum boot *noun*
a condom *NEW ZEALAND*
• —Sonya Plowman, *Great Kiwi Slang*, p. 85, 2002

gumbooter *noun*
a dairy farmer *NEW ZEALAND*
• I love webfoot for a Taranaki farmer, who is also known as a gumbooter or herringboner. —*Dominion Post*, p. C6, 22nd November 2002

gumby *noun*
in computing, an inconsequential but highly visible display of stupidity *US*
A borrowing from Monty Phython.
• —Eric S. Raymond, *The New Hacker's Dictionary*, p. 188, 1991

gumdrop *noun*
a capsule of secobarbital, a central nervous system depressant; any drug in capsule form *US*
• —Edith A. Folb, *runnin' down some lines*, p. 241, 1980

gum it *verb*
to perform oral sex on a woman *US*
• —Eugene Landy, *The Underground Dictionary*, p. 94, 1971

gummer *noun*
a gumboot, a Wellington boot *UK, 1984*

gummi *noun*
rubber as a fetish *UK*
From German *gummi* (rubber). In London in 2003 there was a specialist club called Gummi.

gummy *noun*
a gumboot or Wellington boot *NEW ZEALAND*
• Some people were paying money to biff [throw] gummies down the main street. Yesterday was Taihape Gumboot Day, the day when the world gumboot throwing record is annually under threat. —*(Wellington) Dominion*, p. 19, April 1995

gummy *adjective*
old, in poor condition *AUSTRALIA*
From Australian *gummy* (a sheep that has lost its teeth).
• I met an Aussie called Laith who wheeled broadside on a bit of a bashed-up bicycle [...] "Jesus," he said, "this is a real gummy bike, mate." —Josie Dew, *The Sun In My Eyes*, p. 285, 2001

gump *noun*

1 a passive homosexual man *US*

- — *Maledicta*, p. 265, Summer/Winter 1981: 'By its slang, ye shall know It: the pessimism of prison life'
- — Reinhold Aman, *Hillary Clinton's Pen Pal: A Guide to Life and Lingo in Federal Prison*, 1996

2 a chicken (of the foul persuasion) *US*

- — Don Wilmeth, *The Language of American Popular Entertainment*, p. 121, 1981

gump stump *noun*

the rectum *US*

- We got time up the gump stump, we're on per diem, let's just check the hell into a hotel and catch the early train tomorrow morning. — Darryl Ponicsan, *The Last Detail*, p. 41, 1970

gumption *noun*

common sense, shrewdness; initiative, application, determination *UK, 1719*

- [T]hey have neither the guts nor gumption to rise to the occasion when the pressure is really on [.] — *The Guardian*, 8th December 2002

gums *noun*

overshoes *US*

- — Claudio R. Salvucci, *The Philadelphia Dialect Dictionary*, p. 43, 1996

▸ **flap your gums; beat your gums; beat up your gums**

to talk *US, 1955*

- I am not flappin' my gums for dental exercise – I am trying to make a point 'ere. — Bernard Demsey and Kevin McNally *Lock, Stock... & Two Sips*, p. 291, 2000

▸ **give your gums a rest**

to stop talking *US*

- You'd think the Republicans might give their gums a rest now that they have a ferociously rightwing president[.] — *The Guardian*, 25th July 2003

gumshoe *noun*

a private investigator or detective *US, 1908*

- We were in the gravy once more, and we looked that gumshoe square in the eye again. — Mezz Mezzrow, *Really the Blues*, p. 131, 1946
- I thought you'd be out of that uniform by now, doing gumshoe work. — Horace McCoy, *Kiss Tomorrow Good-bye*, p. 189, 1948
- That's why I'm upset to find out that you think that I've been a detective with this club, a gumshoe. — Jim Bouton, *Ball Four*, p. 258, 1970
- This kid, looks like a girl, is a private eye. A shamus. A gumshoe. — Robert Campbell, *Alice in La-La Land*, p. 202, 1987

gumsucker *noun*

a non-Aboriginal inhabitant of the state of Victoria *AUSTRALIA, 1840*

Referring to the habit of chewing *gum* 'the sap of various native Australian trees (gumtrees)'. Now mainly historical.

- I should add that your thoroughbred gumsucker never speaks without apostrophising his 'oath' and interlarding his diction with the crimsonest of adjectives. — Russel Ward, *The Australian Legend*, p. 66, 1966
- — Jim Ramsay, *Cop It Sweet!*, p. 43, 1977

gum tree *noun*

▸ **up a gum tree**

in trouble; in a hopeless situation *AUSTRALIA, 1851*

- [Y]ou'll suddenly wake up one bright morning to find he's slipped a swiftie over you, has the whole game sewn up, and all you slow-coaches up a gum tree telling the crows he can't do it. — Dymphna Cusack, *Picnic Races*, 1962
- In the army we have only two trees: pine trees and bushy trees. Unless you want to find yourself up a gum tree, bear that in mind! — Graham McInnes, *Humping My Bluey*, p. 81, 1966

gum tree mail *noun*

a non-official mail service in which a letter to be posted is stuck in a cleft stick and passed to the driver or guard of a train passing through a remote area *AUSTRALIA*

- A stockman stands in the middle of the track frantically waving a stick. His horse is tethered to a nearby bush. This is the first of many occasions upon which you will see how the 'gum tree mail' operates. — Patsy Adam-Smith, *Folklore of the Australian Railwaymen*, p. 278, 1969

gum up *verb*

▸ **gum up the works**

to interfere and so spoil things *US, 1932*

- Depopulate. Get rid of people. They gum up the works — *The Guardian*, 6th September 1998

gun *noun*

1 a hired gunman *US, 1920*

- — R. Frederick West, *God's Gambler*, p. 226, 1964: 'Appendix A'
- She said the two guns who had guarded the truck were known as Four-Four and Freddy[.] — Chester Himes, *Cotton Comes to Harlem*, p. 85, 1965

2 an expert at some occupation, especially shearing *AUSTRALIA, 1897*

- — Jim Ramsay, *Cop It Sweet!*, p. 43, 1977
- I've never seen anything like it. He was a gun, all right, Blue. He used that big blade the way a surgeon uses a scalpel. — James McQueen, *Uphill Runner*, p. 14, 1984

3 a pickpocket *US*

- It was on that Sixth Street to Market, between Central Avenue and Plum / that's the worst old place in ragtown for a shuckman or gun. — Bruce Jackson, *Get Your Ass in the Water and Swim Like Me*, p. 85, 1965

4 a hypodermic needle and syringe *US, 1899*

- Said, "Let's have a party, have some fun / for God's sake, fellas, don't forget the gun / 'cause man, I want some two in one." — Bruce Jackson, *Get Your Ass in the Water and Swim Like Me*, p. 149, 1964
- I emptied the dropper. I pulled out the gun. — Iceberg Slim (Robert Beck), *Pimp*, p. 183, 1969

5 the upper arm; the bicep muscle *US*

- — Malachi Andrews and Paul T. Owens, *Black Language*, p. 79, 1973
- — James Harris, *A Convict's Dictionary*, 1989
- — Connie Eble (Editor), *UNC-CH Campus Slang*, p. 3, Fall 1998

6 the penis *UK, 1675*

- This is my rifle / This is my gun / One's for fightin' / One's for fun. — *Screw*, p. 16, 11th January 1971
- — Anon., *King Smut's Wet Dreams Interpreted*, 1978

7 any instrument used for tattooing *US*

- — James Harris, *A Convict's Dictionary*, 1989

8 an electric guitar *US*

From the symbolic actions of guitarists like Jimi Hendrix (1942–70) who stressed the metaphor when he recorded the song 'Machine Gun' in 1969.

- "That's a nice gun, man," said the leering voice of some long-haired clown — Sean Hutchinson, *Crying Out Loud*, p. 176, 1988

9 a brass horn *US*

- — Robert George Reisner, *The Jazz Titans*, 1960

10 a large surfboard used for big-wave conditions *US*

- — D.S. Halacy, *Surfer!*, p. 215, 1965

11 in the language of wind surfing, a sailboard that is moderately long and tapered at the rear *US*

- — Frank Fox, *A Beginner's Guide to Zen and the Art of Windsurfing*, p. 151, 1985: 'A short dictionary of wind surfing terms'

12 in horse racing, a complete effort by a jockey *US*

- — Tom Ainslie, *Ainslie's Complete Guide to Thoroughbred Racing*, p. 332, 1976

13 on the railways, a track torpedo used to warn an engineer of danger ahead *US*

- — J. Herbert Lund, *Herb's Hot Box of Railraod Slang*, p. 160, 1975

14 any signal that a quarter of a football game has ended *US*

- — Howard Arthur and Alvin Ebeling, *The Falcon Illustrated Football Dictionary*, p. 39, 1971

▸ **on the gun**

engaged in crime as a profession *US*

- — *The New American Mercury*, p. 710, 1950

▸ **under the gun**

1 (used of a prison) under armed guard *US*

- — Gary K. Farlow, *Prison-ese*, p. 77, 2002

2 in poker, said of the player who must act first in a given situation *US*

- — Oswald Jacoby, *Oswald Jacoby on Poker*, p. 142, 1947

gun *verb*

1 to accelerate a vehicle or rev its engine *US, 1920*

- "Hang on! We're off," and Francine gunned the hot motor and burned rubber as she peeled away from the parking lot. — Vance Donovan, *High Rider*, p. 38, 1969
- Gerry Burtonshaw gunned his engine, pulled round a lumbering lorry and came alongside the speeding Jaguar. — *The Sweeney*, p. 53, 1976

2 to inject a drug intravenously *UK*

- — Mike Haskins, *Drugs*, p. 290, 2003

3 to look over, to examine *UK, 1812*

- Al always showed up surrounded by a gang of trigger men – they sat in a corner, very gay and noisy but gunning the whole situation out of the corners of their eyes. —Mezz Mezzrow, *Really the Blues*, p. 63, 1946
- "Why are you gunning me?" Chllly asked. —Malcolm Braly, *On the Yard*, p. 244, 1967

4 to attack verbally *UK*

- —Susie Dent, *The Language Report*, p. 76, 2003

5 in computing, to use a computer's force-quit feature to close a malfunctioning program *US*

- Some idiot left a useless background program running, soaking up half the cycles. So I gunned it. —Guy L. Steele et al., *The Hacker's Dictionary*, p. 75, 1983

▸ **gun it**

(of a vehicle) to travel at top speed *US*

From earlier, now conventional sense of 'gun' (to run an engine at full power).

- —*Complete CB Slang Dictionary*, 1976
- —Peter Chippindale, *The British CB Book*, p. 155, 1981

gun *adjective*

1 excellent *NEW ZEALAND*

- —David McGill, *David McGill's Complete Kiwi Slang Dictionary*, p. 53, 1998

2 expert *AUSTRALIA, 1916*

- Mr Flood is one of about 12 gun shearers – men who can shear 200 sheep on a good day – in Tasmania. —*Sunday Tasmanian*, p. 23, 1st October 1989

gun and bomb *noun*

a condom *UK*

Rhyming slang; the plural is 'guns and bombs'.

- —Bodmin Dark, *Dirty Cockney Rhyming Slang*, 2003

gun and rifle club *noun*

an inner-city hospital's casualty department *US*

- —*Maledicta*, p. 68, Summer/Winter 1978: 'Common patient-directed pejoratives used by medical personnel'

gun ape *noun*

an artillery soldier *US, 1988*

- —Linda Reinberg, *In the Field*, p. 99, 1991

gun belt *noun*

the American defence industry *US*

- —David Olive, *Business Babble*, p. 75, 1991

gunboats *noun*

large, heavy shoes *US, 1862*

- Hobnailed, high-topped gunboats weighing about ten pounds each, with one-inch soles as flexible as a petrified tree. —Mezz Mezzrow, *Really the Blues*, p. 33, 1946

gun-bull *noun*

an armed prison guard *US, 1928*

- High on the north block wall he glimpsed a gun bull[.] —Malcolm Braly, *On the Yard*, p. 4, 1967
- —Marlene Freedman, *Alcatraz*, 1983

gun bunny *noun*

an artilleryman *US, 1980*

- —Hans Halberstadt, *Airborne*, p. 130, 1988: 'Abridged dictionary of airborne terms'
- And because gun bunnies are too dumb to navigate, you're doing the navigating and scouting[.]. —Michael Takiff, *Brave Men, Gentle Heroes*, p. 59, 2003

Gunchester *nickname*

Manchester *UK*

- The machetes and cutlasses of old had been swapped for more sophisticated weaponry, and they didn't care you got caught up in the cross fire [...] No wonder Manchester had acquired the nickname "Gunchester". —Karline Smith, *Moss Side Massive*, p. 215, 1994

gun down *verb*

(used of a male) to masturbate while looking directly at somebody else *US*

- They say John got caught on the third shift gunnin' down the C.O. —Gary K. Farlow, *Prison-ese*, p. 27, 2002

gunfighter seat *noun*

in a public place, a seat with the back against the wall, overlooking the room *US*

From the caution exercised by gunfighters in the West.

- Tommy had the gunfighter seat, with his back to the wall so he could scope out the hot-looking talent coming up from the pool. —Stephen Cannell, *Big Con*, p. 206, 1997

gun for *verb*

to be on the lookout for with the intent of hurting or killing *US, 1878*

- This cat, Eddie Carter, who was gunning for Kelsey, had heard about Jim. —Claude Brown, *Manchild in the Promised Land*, p. 217, 1965

gun from the gate *noun*

in horse racing, a racehorse that starts races quickly *US*

- —David W. Maurer, *Argot of the Racetrack*, p. 33, 1951

gunga din *noun*

used to address a man with a perceived Indian or Asian ethnicity *UK*

Racist, derogatory; a stereotypical appellation from the poem 'Gunga Din', Rudyard Kipling, 1897: 'Of all them black-faced crew/ The finest man I knew / Was our regimental *bhisti* [a water-carrier], Gunga Din'.

- "Oi, gunga din. I want a car to Woodford," was his opening remark to Sanjay, the cab firm's owner. —Donald Gorgon, *Cop Killer*, p. 24, 1994

Gunga Din; gunga *noun*

the chin *UK*

Rhyming slang, formed from Rudyard Kupling's 'The finest man I knew / Was our regimental bhisti, Gunga Din'.

- —Ray Puxley, *Cockney Rabbit*, 1992

gunge *noun*

1 an (unidentifiable or disgusting) viscid substance; general filth *UK, 1965*

- It was all very well that his 3rd Street apartment, a quarter-hour trudge from Washington Square Park, probably set for all time the outer parameters of gunge. —Ed Sanders, *Tales of Beatnik Glory*, p. 80, 1975
- Sauce or gravy or mud. —Ann Barr and Peter York, *The Official Sloane Ranger Handbook*, p. 158, 1982

2 rubbish, nonsense *UK*

- "Oh, I'm so pleased!" she carolled. "Weren't you on the Oceana cruise to Venice...?" and similar gunge. —Jonathan Gash, *The Ten Word Game*, p. 72, 2003

3 any tropical skin disease affecting the crotch area of a US soldier in Vietnam *US*

- [Rule] 5. Do not get the gunge. When the Army wants you to have it, it will be issued to you. —Larry Heinemann, *Close Quarters*, p. 272, 1977
- —Linda Reinberg, *In the Field*, p. 99, 1991

gunge; gunge up *verb*

in a general sense, to make filthy; more narrowly, to deliberately swamp someone with a viscous mess (humorously known as 'gunge') *UK, 1976*

- [O]ne of the teachers had been 'gunged' (to raise money for charity)[.] —Michael J. Reiss, *Understanding Science Lessons*, p. 74, 2000

gunged up; gungey; gungy *adjective*

filthy, sticky; clogged with filth, especially with an unidentifiable or disgusting viscid substance *UK, 1962*

From GUNGE.

- "Don't ever try and tell me that children prefer a chlorinated swimming pool to salty water," says reader Julia Carruthers. "They adore the gungy mess, nasty bits of seaweed to squeal over, drinks that spill and don't matter[.]" —*The Guardian*, 6th September 2003

gungeon; gunja; gunjeh; gunga *noun*

marijuana, especially from Jamaica *US, 1944*

A corruption of GANJA. Used to describe the most potent grade of marijuana in the 1940s.

- R.S.V.P., and bring your own gunja. —Mezz Mezzrow, *Really the Blues*, p. 128, 1946
- [A]nd the top grade, the "gungeon," which produces a voluptuous "bang," bringing as high as a dollar[.] —Jack Lait, *New York Confidential*, p. 118, 1948
- [T]he best marijuana cigarettes to be had were made of the gunja and kisca that merchant sailors smuggled in from Africa and Persia. —Malcolm X and Alex Haley, *The Autobiography of Malcolm X*, p. 86, 1964
- I flew all the way to Jamaica to get you this gunja. —Snoop Doggy Dogg, *A Day in the Life of Snoop Doogy Dog [cover art]*, 1993
- —Angela Devlin, *Prison Patter*, p. 55, 1996
- —Mike Haskins, *Drugs*, p. 287, 2003

gung-ho *adjective*
dedicated, spirited, enthusiastic *US, 1942*
Originally coined as a slogan understood to mean 'Work together!' by the US Marines during World War 2, then embraced as an adjective.
- [H]e's all gung-ho about current events and I'm passing political science and want to keep passing. — Robert Gover, *One Hundred Dollar Misunderstanding*, p. 97, 1961
- There was the FBI in heavy numbers guarding the National Security and all that other gung-ho shit. — Abbie Hoffman, *Woodstock Nation*, p. 56, 1969
- Nat says you were a gung ho guy in uniform, Al, always up in the squad room, asking questions, y' know. — Edwin Torres, *Q & A*, p. 154, 1977
- Semper fi, do or die! / Gung ho, gung ho, gung ho! — *Full Metal Jacket*, 1987
- Now Neal was a hard guy to get to know intimately because he lived very much within himself, as gung-ho as he was. — Herbert Huncke, *Guilty of Everything*, p. 94, 1990
- [T]heir [the UK Labour Party's] gung-ho record during the Falklands War. — Mark Steel, *Reasons to be Cheerful*, p. 129, 2001

gungun *noun*
marijuana variously claimed to be from Africa, Jamaica or Mexico *UK, 1998*
From **GUNGEON** (marijuana).
- — Mike Haskins, *Drugs*, p. 287, 2003

gungy; gungi *adjective*
enthusiastic, spirited, brave *US, 1961*
Formed from **GUNG-HO**.
- If someone is "gungi," he's all right, it's good to have him on our side, he's afraid of nothing, he never gets tired[.]" — Charles Anderson, *The Grunts*, p. 29, 1976

gun hand *noun*
in racquetball, the hand with which a player holds the racquet *US*
- — Dick Squires, *The Other Racquet Sports*, p. 221, 1971: 'Glossary'

gunk *noun*
1 an unidentified and unpleasant substance *US, 1938*
- She wanted – repeat wanted – yours truly to drive this gangster's Imperial, just take it out for a spin, I suppose, and blow the gunk out of its huge engine. — Robert Gover, *One Hundred Dollar Misunderstanding*, p. 142, 1961
- [T]here's a thingamajig they can put on the projector that'll cut through that gunk like Bruce Lee's foot through Velveeta cheese. — Joe Bob Briggs, *Joe Bob Goes to the Drive-In*, p. 9, 1987
- You just get them all covered with gunk on the next load. — C.D. Payne, *Youth in Revolt*, p. 291, 1993

2 a thick liquid *UK*
Originally the brand name for a chemical cleaner.
- What's that gunk you're drinking? That's like a strawberry milkshake, is it, but flat? Full of chemicals I bet. — Simon Lewis, *In The Box [britpulp]*, p. 127, 1999

3 any industrial solvent inhaled for its psychoactive effect *US*
- — Ralph de Sola, *Crime Dictionary*, p. 60, 1982

gun moll *noun*
a female gangster *US, 1908*
- "You thought any about becoming a gun moll?" I asked. — Max Shulman, *The Many Loves of Dobie Gillis*, p. 9, 1951
- Don't worry, I'm not a gun moll. — Jack Kerouac, *On the Road*, p. 121, 1957

gun-mouth pants *noun*
men's trousers with straight, tapered legs *TRINIDAD AND TOBAGO, 1937*
- — Lise Winer, *Dictionary of the English/Creole of Trinidad & Tobago*, 2003

gunna *noun*
a procrastinator *AUSTRALIA*
- There are two types of people that own utes. People who do things, like tradesmen, and people who think they are going to do something, who are planning to do something. They are called 'gunnas'. — *Sydney Morning Herald*, p. 8s, 29th June 1996

gunna *verb*
▷ **see:** GONNA

gunna
going to *AUSTRALIA, 1944*
- Gunna stay for a cuppa? — Jon Cleary, *Justin Bayard*, p. 172, 1955
- Thought yer might like the list ter know who's gunna be there. — Dymphna Cusack, *Picnic Races*, p. 18, 1962

gunner *noun*
1 a person with sexual expertise and experience *US*
- I suppose she's a real gunner; bangs away, huh? — John Nichols, *The Sterile Cuckoo*, p. 88, 1965
- — Collin Baker et al., *College Undergraduate Slang Study Conducted at Brown University*, p. 132, 1968

2 in poker, the player with the best hand or who plays his hand as if it were the best hand *US*
- — *American Speech*, p. 99, May 1951

3 the person shooting the dice in craps *US, 1930*
- He never paid back loans, would stand at the edges of a crap game and bet his dime or quarter on the gunner if he was on a hot roll. — Gilbert Sorrentino, *Steelwork*, p. 156, 1970

4 a student who takes competition to an aggressive level *US*
- — Sally Williams, *"Strong" Words*, p. 145, 1994

gunners *noun*
braces (suspenders) *US*
- — Vincent J. Monteleone, *Criminal Slang*, p. 109, 1949

gunnif *noun*
a thief, a crook *UK*
A variation of **GONNIF**.
- [H]ousebreakin, warehouses, terrorising the local market traders, nicking anything, a right pair of gunnifs we were. — J.J. Connolly, *Layer Cake*, p. 53, 2000

gunny *noun*
1 a US Marine Corps gunnery sergeant *US*
- The gunny called the platoon sergeants and assigned each of the newcomers. — Charles Anderson, *The Grunts*, p. 106, 1976

2 a door gunner on an airship, or a crew member of a gunship *US, 1980*
- A door gunner's best friend was his hatch M-60, which many gunnies took to calling Hog-60's[.] — Jack Hawkins, *Chopper One #2*, p. 27, 1987

3 a gun enthusiast *US*
- — *American Speech*, p. 193, October 1957: 'Some colloquialisms of the handgunner'

4 potent marijuana *US, 1970*
- I don't know where my head was, behind that jive wine and that bad gunny. — Odie Hawkins, *Ghetto Sketches*, p. 119, 1972

gun pet *noun*
a parapet fortified to protect artillery *US*
- The "gun pets" were circular and large enough to allow the gun and its tail to be rotated full circle. — Greg Clark, *Words of the Vietnam War*, p. 391, 1990

gunpowder *noun*
▷ **see:** CHINESE GUNPOWDER

guns *noun*
1 a helicopter gunship *US*
Used by the US Army Aero Weapons Platoon in Vietnam.
- — Gregory Clark, *Words of the Vietnam War*, p. 212, 1990

2 to marines in Vietnam, a weapons squad or platoon *US*
- — Gregory Clark, *Words of the Vietnam War*, p. 213, 1990

3 the fists *US*
- — *Maledicta*, p. 266, Summer/Winter 1981: 'By its slang, ye shall know it: the pessimism of prison life'

gunsack *noun*
thick, heavy female thighs *TRINIDAD AND TOBAGO*
- — Lise Winer, *Dictionary of the English/Creole of Trinidad & Tobago*, 2003

gunsel *noun*
1 a young homosexual man *US, 1918*
- But punishment varies in almost all prisons and sometimes both"wolf" and "gunsel" are "sent to the hole." — *Ebony*, p. 82, July 1951
- I'm talking to you, gunsel. — Chester Himes, *Cast the First Stone*, p. 13, 1952
- The term gunsel is derived from the heyday of safe crackers when it referred to a criminal who specialized in this form of thievery and was accompanied by a youthful apprentice. — *New York Mattachine Newsletter*, p. 6, June 1961
- — Paul Glover, *Words from the House of the Dead: Prison Writings from Soledad*, 1974
- But not matter what, Dio must be snuffed. Him and his fucking gunsel. — Gerald Petievich, *Money Men*, p. 148, 1981
- "So why was this gunsel so runny-mouthed with you?" "I was doing him and he had the idea him talking about doing you would arouse me to greater efforts, if you know what I mean!" — Robert Campbell, *Boneyards*, p. 249, 1992

2 a thug *US, 1943*

- We shot out under the electric horshoe and the big gunsel in the front seat made a sharp right turn onto the highway back to Oakland. —Thurston Scott, *Cure it with Honey*, p. 120, 1951
- A gunsel, he thought immediately, using the term they applied to any kind on the make for trouble or a reputation as a hard rock. —Malcolm Braly, *On the Yard*, p. 243, 1967
- It was Arnold's gunsel. —Joseph Wambaugh, *The Black Marble*, p. 381, 1978

gunship *noun*

1 in the Metropolitan Police, a Flying Squad car when firearms are being carried *UK*

- — *The Official Encyclopaedia of New Scotland Yard*, 1999

2 in the Metropolitan Police, an Armed Response Vehicle *UK*

- — *The Official Encyclopaedia of New Scotland Yard*, 1999

3 a van used in a drive-by shooting *US*

- The vans they go around in? They call 'em gunships. Drive by a house and spray it up with an Uzi. —Elmore Leonard, *Freaky Deaky*, p. 129, 1988

gun-shot *noun*

a single measure of chilled After Shock™ cinnamon or peppermint liqueur imbibed through a straw in a single action *UK*

- Widespread use of drugs means we're happy turning the bar into a chemistry set. People are creating their own mixes and methods (gun-shots, snorting or mouthwashing anyone?)— *Sky Magazine*, p. 88, May 2001

gunslinger *noun*

a chronic masturbator *US*

- —Gary K. Farlow, *Prison-ese*, p. 27, 2002

gunsmith *noun*

an experienced pickpocket who trains novice pickpockets *US, 1934*

- —Vincent J. Monteleone, *Criminal Slang*, p. 110, 1949

gun talk *noun*

tough, threatening talk *TRINIDAD AND TOBAGO*

- —Lise Winer, *Dictionary of the English/Creole of Trinidad & Tobago*, 2003

guntz *noun*

the whole lot, the whole way *UK*

Adopted from Yiddish, ultimately German *das Ganze* (all of it).

- This time I went the guntz and blag[g]ed her for a grand. —Frank Norman, *Bang To Rights*, p. 113, 1958

gun up *verb*

to prepare to fight, either with fists or weapons *US*

- — *Maledicta*, p. 266, Summer/Winter 1981: 'By its slang, ye shall know it: the pessimism of prison life'

guppies *noun*

anchovies *US*

Limited usage, but clever.

- — *Maledicta*, p. 13, 1996: 'Domino's pizza jargon'

guppy *noun*

1 an individual who is socially categorised as a *g*ay *u*pwardly mobile *p*rofessional *UK, 1984*

A blend of **GAY** and **YUPPIE**.

- Pop over to this friendly, guppie kind of hangout for two-for-one happy "hour" (2pm to 8pm daily). — *Lonely Planet Florida*, p. 273, 2003

2 a navy diver who is not SCUBA qualified *US*

- —Linda Reinberg, *In the Field*, p. 100, 1991

3 a heavy drinker *US*

From **FISH**.

- —Judi Sanders, *Don't Dog by Do, Dude!*, p. 14, 1991

gur *noun*

▸ **on the gur**

of a child, sleeping roughly *IRELAND*

- And far too many boys and girls today are out on gur (sleeping rough in the streets or parks), but we as chisellers only made threats of going on the gur. We always seemed to change our minds at night-time. —Éamonn MacThomáis, *Gur Cake and Coal Blocks*, p. 101, 1976

gurner *noun*

a person intoxicated by MDMA, the recreational drug best known as ecstasy *UK*

From the similarity between the distorted faces pulled by **ECSTASY** users and the ugly faces deliberately pulled by gurners in traditional gurning competitions.

- Brendan on the sofa gurning for England[.] —Dave Courtney, *Raving Lunacy*, p. 107, 2000
- E'd up and gurning at the moon— *Sky Magazine*, p. 70, May 2001

gurning *noun*

the effect of tightened facial muscles as a result of taking MDMA, the recreational drug best known as ecstasy *UK*

From the conventional sense when the facial distortion is both voluntary and humorous.

- [U]sers find themselves grinding their teeth ("gurning") and licking their lips. —Macfarlane, Macfarlane and Robson, *The User*, p. 75, 1996

gurrier *noun*

a lout, a ruffian *IRELAND*

- —Colin Murphy and Donal O'Dea, *The Book of Feckin' Irish Slang*, p. 34, 2004

guru *noun*

an expert *US*

- My man is a bowling guru. —Connie Eble (Editor), *UNC-CH Campus Slang*, p. 4, Fall 1986

guru you!

used as a humorous euphemism for 'screw you' *US*

- —Eugene Landy, *The Underground Dictionary*, p. 94, 1971

gush *verb*

1 to express yourself in an over-effusive or sentimental manner *UK, 1864*

- "He looked as if he'd been a Real [Madird] player all his life," gushed the pages of As. It appears Beckham has found his niche. — *The Guardian*, 18th September 2003

2 in professional wrestling, to bleed *US*

- Steve Armstrong gushes. — *Herb's Wrestling Tidbits*, 19th October 1992

gusset *noun*

the vagina *UK*

Conventionally, a 'gusset' is a piece of material that reinforces clothing, particularly at the crotch and hence in this sense by association of location.

- With one hand the artist guided his shaft into her welcoming gusset. —Stewart Home, *Sex Kick [britpulp]*, p. 219, 1999

gussy up *verb*

to dress up *US, 1952*

- They were gussied up to look like sensible townandcountry doggers. —Seth Morgan, *Homeboy*, p. 268, 1990
- The documentarist in Hodges didn't want to gussy up this milieu: rain and neon could have drained it of malignancy[.] —Graham Fuller, *Brute Force*, p. 85, 2001

gusto *noun*

money *US, 1984*

- To have gangster style you have to get "getting paid" – making so much gusto (money) until it's goofy. —Nelson George (quoting Teddy Riley, 1988), *Hip Hop America*, p. 166, 1998

gut *noun*

1 a school course that requires little effort *US, 1916*

- I've had two guts all lined up, but they backfired. —Max Shulman, *Guided Tour of Campus Humor*, p. 105, 1955
- Couple of guys in the house took that one-o-one course for their science requirement, said it was a real gut. —Richard Farina, *Been Down So Long*, p. 35, 1966
- —Collin Baker et al., *College Undergraduate Slang Study Conducted at Brown University*, p. 132, 1968
- [T]here's a good proportion of air heads and space cadets in those courses, too. — *Wesleyan Alumnus*, p. 29, Spring 1981

2 a main street through town *US*

- — *Current Slang*, p. 4, Spring 1968

3 the belly, the stomach *UK, 1362*

- Sgt Felipe Vega, from the same unit, said he felt ' kicked in the gut, slapped in the face' because his return from Iraq had been delayed[.]— *Daily Telegraph*, 21st July 2003

4 an air hose on a brake system *US*

- —Norman Carlisle, *The Modern Wonder Book of Trains and Railroading*, p. 264, 1946

5 in electric line work, insulated rubber hose used on 5kV line *US*
- — A.B. Chance Co., *Lineman's Slang Dictionary*, p. 8, 1980

gut *verb*
in hot rodding, to remove all but the bare essentials from a car's interior *US*
- — *Good Housekeeping*, p. 143, September 1958: 'Hot-rod terms for teen-age girls'

gut bag *noun*
a plastic bag containing frozen food, the exact identity of which is not clear *US*
- — *American Speech*, p. 205–209, Summer 1991: 'The language of smokejumping – again'

gut-barge *verb*
to use your beer-belly to bump into another's in an informal trial of strength *UK*
- O'Donnell's is the sort of after-hours joint where bouncers go to gut-barge each other between sets. — Liza Cody, *Queen of Mean [Tart Noir]*, p. 75, 2002

gut bomb *noun*
any greasy, tasty, heavy food, especially a greasy hamburger *US*
- — *Current Slang*, p. 6, Spring 1968
- Rodeo riders are credited with naming "gut bombs." The suspicion is that the tough old Brahma bull that disappeared off the circuit after one too many crowhops has ended giving the cowboys new pains as part of the many gut bombs they put away. — Chris Thain, *Cold as a Bay Street Banker's Heart*, p. 78, 1987
- After the movie last night, the two of them had stayed in the wardroom and waited for the stewards to open up the "Mid-rats" line, the midnight snack service where officers could purchase the infamous "gut bombs." These were double cheeseburgers topped with nearly everything that science was still atttempting to classify. — Gerry Carroll, *North S*A*R*, p. 193, 1991

gut bucket *noun*
1 an earthy style of jazz music combining elements of ragtime and blues *US, 1929*
A 'gutbucket' was a cheap saloon from the name given to a bucket placed beneath a barrel of gin to catch and recycle leakages. The musicians in these type of places played for tips, and the style of music they played there became known as 'gutbucket'.
- People want gut bucket orchestras ... the hip liquor toter wants sensational noise — Frederic Ramsay Junior, *Chicago Documentary*, p. 28, 1944
- We sopped up a lot of learning at Capone's University of Gutbucket Arts. — Mezz Mezzrow, *Really the Blues*, p. 62, 1946
- She didn't want to dance to the blues, the gut bucket, the funky songs. — Dick Gregory, *Nigger*, p. 60, 1964
- [L]ots of people still care about getdown gutbucket rock 'n' roll passionately[.] — Lester Bangs, *Psychotic Reactions and Carburetor Dung*, p. 69, 1971

2 a rough and rowdy bar with rough and rowdy patrons *US, 1970*
- I mean, like sho' nuff groovy gut bucket Black. — Odie Hawkins, *Great Lawd Buddha*, p. 29, 1990

3 a fish bait boat; by extension a messy space of any kind *US*
- — John Gould, *Maine Lingo*, p. 119, 1975

gut card *noun*
in gin, a card that completes a broken sequence *US*
- — Irwin Steig, *Play Gin to Win*, p. 140,

gut check *noun*
a test of courage or determination *US*
- — Fred Hester, *Slang on the 40 Acres*, p. 15, 1968

gutful; gutsful *noun*
too much of something *UK, 1900*
- Even Peter Beattie [premier of Queensland, Australia) prefaced last week's attack on Americanisms by declaring that he'd "had a gutful". — *The Guardian*, 17th March 2003

gut hopper *noun*
a student who moves from one easy course to another *US*
- I'm nont gut hopper, but this term is the worst. — Max Shulman, *Guided Tour of Campus Humor*, p. 105, 1955

gut issue *noun*
the one most important issue in a discussion *US*
- — Department of the Army, *Staff Officer's Guidebook*, p. 61, 1986

gutless *adjective*
1 cowardly, lacking determination *US, 1900*
- Get up, you gutless little bugger. — Geoff Brown, *I Want What I Want*, p. 76, 1966

2 used to describe an extreme of quality: either very good or very bad *UK*
- — Paul Baker, *Polari*, p. 177, 2002

gutless wonder *noun*
an outstanding coward *US, 1900*
- [H]e began to curse the shire engineer and the road gang responsible for the upkeep of this by-blow of a road, a set of wool-brained gutless wonders, none of whem worked an ounce of fat off their carcasses in a month. — Kylie Tennant, *The Honey Flow*, p. 58, 1956
- You can't run away! Fight, you gutless wonder! — Barry Oakley, *A Salute to the Great McCarthy*, p. 113, 1970
- — Peter Corris, *Make Me Rich*, p. 142, 1985
- — Ivor Limb, *Footy's No Joke!*, p. 57, 1986
- Copernicus was a gutless wonder who is only remembered because he was indisputably a world-shaking genius. — Ignatius Jones, *The 1992 True Hip Manual*, p. 36, 1992
- — Phillip Gwynne, *Deadly Unna?*, p. 9, 1998

gutrage *noun*
a visceral anger *US*
- And there was this one big barrel-chested man-mountain with a bad eye for everybody who was standing at the bar chasing down his bourbon with beer – in some silent gutrage over God-only-knows-what in particular. — Robert Gover, *Poorboy at the Party*, p. 105, 1966

gut reamer *noun*
the active participant in anal sex *US*
- — Joseph E. Ragen and Charles Finston, *Inside the World's Toughest Prison*, p. 802, 1962: 'Penitentiary and underworld glossary'

gut-ripper *noun*
an antipersonnel grenade that explodes at waist level *US*
- These hit the ground, jump into the air and explode at about stomach level. Gut rippers, they are called, the scourge of infantrymen. — *Boston Globe*, 29th January 1991

guts *noun*
1 the stomach; the general area of the stomach and intestines *UK, 1393*
Standard English from late C14; slipped into unconventional usage early in C19.
- I was dead charlie and the little fairies were having a right game in my guts. — Frank Norman, *Bang To Rights*, p. 49, 1958

2 the essentials, the important part, the inner and real meaning *UK, 1663*
- I think there is material here we can work with, but it is a bit of a muddle and needs a lot more clarity in the guts of it in terms of what is new/old. — *The Guardian*, 25th September 2003

3 the pulp and membrane inside a fruit *TRINIDAD AND TOBAGO, 1990*
- — Lise Winer, *Dictionary of the English/Creole of Trinidad & Tobago*, 2003

4 the interior of a car *US*
- — *American Speech*, p. 312, Autumn-Winter 1975: 'The jargon of car salesmen'

5 information *AUSTRALIA, 1919*
- But by God I was going to get the guts about Ernie if I choked her. — Robert S. Close, *Love Me Sailor*, p. 258, 1945
- — Nino Culotta (John O'Grady), *They're A Weird Mob*, p. 157, 1957
- — Jim Ramsay, *Cop It Sweet!*, p. 43, 1977

6 courage *US, 1891*
- A couple of drinks'll give us some guts. — Irving Shulman, *The Amboy Dukes*, p. 77, 1947
- Jesus had guts! He wasn't afraid of the whole Roman army. — Richard Brooks, *Elmer Gantry*, 1960
- CARTER: You shit. You didn't have the guts to do it yourself, did you? — Mike Hodges, *Get Carter*, p. 65, 1971

7 in the gambling game two-up, the bets placed with the spinner of the coins *AUSTRALIA, 1941*
- The 'guts' is sometimes called the 'centre'. It is the money wagered by each player who takes a turn in the actual spinning of the coins, and also the amounts put in by other players to cover him. — James Holledge, *The Great Australian Gamble*, p. 100, 1966

▸ **have your guts for garters**
used for expressing a level of personal threat *UK, 1933*
An idea that has been in circulation since about 1592. Hyperbolical, but none the less real for all that.
- [T]he universities will be outraged on principle, not to mention the Royal Society. It'll go totally barmy. Have my guts for garters, too. It can't believe we're even discussing this. — *The Guardian*, 8th October 2003

guts and butts doc *noun*
a gastroneterologist *US*
- —Sally Williams, *"Strong" Words*, p. 145, 1994

gut sausage *noun*
a poor man's meal: cornmeal and suet in an intestine *CANADA*
- Take a big gut with all fat on. Now wash good. Turn inside out and scrape and wash good again. Tie with string every little ways. Dry and smoke over camp fire. Sure good for eat. —Gwen Lewis, *Buckskin Cookery II*, p. 30, 1958

gutser *noun*
1 a person who eats a great deal *NEW ZEALAND*
- —David McGill, *David McGill's Complete Kiwi Slang Dictionary*, p. 53, 1998

2 a heavy fall *AUSTRALIA, 1918*
Usually in the phrase 'come a gutser'. Variants include 'gutzer' and 'gusta'.
- That slacked the chain. Prindy took a flying leap over the ledge. He probably wouldn't have heard Coon-Coon yell, 'You treacherous little bastard!' With both chains tautening, what began as a dive ended with a gutser. —Xavier Herbert, *Poor Fellow My Country*, p. 978, 1975
- If you're planning to spring any sort of gutzer here tonight, your missus'll be the first to get it! —Lance Peters, *The Dirty Half-Mile*, p. 289, 1979
- —Lance Peters, *The Dirty Half-Mile*, p. 151, 1979
- Patrick said that if they come a gutsa, the money is there to render assistance, and if no one is injured the money jackpots. —Roy Slaven (John Doyle), *Five South Coast Seasons*, p. 68, 1992

▸**come a gutser**
to come undone; to fail miserably *AUSTRALIA, 1918*
- Anyhow, if the little tart what gave me the info about Annie's place connects me with any reprisal againster her bludger, then all our plans will have come a gutzer! —Lance Peters, *The Dirty Half-Mile*, p. 151, 1979
- He thinks the horse is doped. But after the race we'll see what a good judge he is. Christ I hope he comes a gutser. —Clive Galea, *Slipper*, p. 212, 1988

gut shot *noun*
1 a bullet wound in the stomach, painful and often fatal *US*
- —Jay Robert Nash, *Dictionary of Crime*, p. 161, 1992

2 in poker, a drawn card that completes an inside straight *US*
- —*American Speech*, p. 97, May 1951: 'The vocabulary of poker'
- If the player (with queens) wins the pot, they are "ladies"; but if he loses the pot, they are "whores." —Albert H. Morehead, *The Complete Guide to Winning Poker*, p. 264, 1967

gutsiness *noun*
courage *UK, 1959*
- The game was in the balance throughout but it was Monty [golfer Colin Montgomerie]'s excellence with the long irons and gutsiness over mid-range putts which saw the Europeans home. —*The Guardian*, 26th September 1999

gutslider *noun*
a bodyboarder *SOUTH AFRICA*
A term of derision when used by surfers.

guts like calabash *noun*
extreme courage *TRINIDAD AND TOBAGO, 1991*
- —Lise Winer, *Dictionary of the English/Creole of Trinidad & Tobago*, 2003

gutsy; guts *noun*
an overweight or obese person *UK, 1596*
A nickname and derogatory term of abuse; 'gutsy' is a mid- to late C20 variation of 'guts'.
- "Enjoy your tea, tubs?", "Ready for Saturday, gutsy?" —Martin King and Martin Knight, *The Naughty Nineties*, p. 46, 1999

gutsy *adjective*
1 courageous *UK, 1893*
- TILLEY: Look, we can be scientific from now to doomsday, but we gotta be gutsy and go for the big one. —*Tin Men*, 1987

2 of music, heartfelt, spirited *UK, 1984*
- [A] mixed batch of songs in which their gutsy vocals are sometimes swamped by over-production and clattering percussion. —*The Guardian*, 25th October 2002

gutted *adjective*
being bitterly disappointed; used to describe a depressed, empty feeling *UK, 1981*
Derives, possibly, from the image of a gutted fish or similar; how much emptier could you feel?
- —Angela Devlin, *Prison Patter*, p. 59, 1996
- [T]hey'll be gutted to be turned away after coming all that way. —Irvine Welsh, *The Naughty Nineties*, p. 13, 1999
- MOON: Y'know I'm missing out on a shag 'ere? LEE: Gutted for yer. —Bernard Demspey and Kevin McNally, *Lock, Stock... & Two Sips*, p. 313, 2000
- I still feel gutted to this day at how Mark's life was ended. —Jimmy Stockin, *On The Cobbles*, p. 172, 2000
- Oh well boo-fucking-hoo, I'm all fucking gutted for them[.] —Danny King, *The Burglar Diaries*, p. 190, 2001

gutter *noun*
a vein, especially a prominent one suitable for drug injection *US*
- —US Department of Justice, *Street Terms*, October 1994

gutter ball *noun*
in pool, a shot in which the cue ball falls into a pocket *US*
Homage to bowling.
- —Mike Shamos, *The Illustrated Encyclopedia of Billiards*, p. 111, 1993

gutter bunny *noun*
a commuter who bicycles to work *US*
Mountain bikers' slang.
- They're called "gutter bunnies." They're the cyclists you seek cranking along the snowbanks every morning in January, huffing home sweating bullets in August, and pedaling off to work, come rain, shine and everything in between. —*Saint Paul (Minnesota) Pioneer Press*, p. 1D, 9th May 1996
- —*The Word Spy*, 21st September 1997

guttered *adjective*
drunk *UK: SCOTLAND*
Used in Inverness.
- —*e-cyclopaedia*, 20th March 2002

gutter glitter *noun*
cocaine *UK*
- —Mike Haskins, *Drugs*, p. 280, 2003

gutter junkie; gutter hype *noun*
a drug-addict reduced by the circumstances of addiction to living in the streets or, at best, using inferior drugs *US, 1936*
A combination of **JUNKIE** (an addict) or **HYPE** (an addict) with 'gutter' representing the lowest point achievable.
- —Richard A. Spears, *The Slang and Jargon of Drugs and Drink*, p. 239, 1986
- —Mike Haskins, *Drugs*, p. 292, 2003

gutter slut *noun*
a sexually promiscuous woman *UK*
- When we bone these gutter-sluts [...] we don't respect them or even think of them as proper people with mums and dads and feelings and shit. —Colin Butts, *Is Harry Still on the Boat?*, p. 257, 2003

guttersnipe *noun*
a despicable low-bred individual *IRELAND*
- Accused of calling Deputy McManus a "pro-abortionist", Mr Roche was labelled "a thug", "a slithering political lizard" and a "gutter-snipe" by opposition politicians amid ugly scenes in Leinster House. —*Irish Examiner*, 2nd December 2003

gutter wear *noun*
fashionably shabby clothing *US*
- —*Washington Post Magazine*, p. 21, 21st August 1988: 'Say wha?'

gutty *noun*
an unpleasant person *IRELAND*
- We shared secrets and even a bed for years, talking confidentially of penknives and 'gutties', canvas runners with little air vents on the side that you could wear under the covers without fear of getting smelly feet. —Ardal O'Hanlon, *The Talk of the Town*, p. 232, 1998

guv *noun*
an informal style of address to a male of superior status *UK, 1890*
Short for 'governor' and **GUV'NOR**.
- That's great, guv. That'll keep the slags guessing. —Martin King and Martin Knight, *The Naughty Nineties*, p. 223, 1999
- "Where we picking up from, guv?" "Downing Street," said Michael. —Gyles Brandreth, *Breaking the Code*, p. 3, 1999
- "But that's past Wigmore Street, guv." I hate being called Guv. I want to reach through the open partition and whack him in the fucking teeth. —Stuart Browne, *Dangerous Parking*, p. 45, 2000

guv'nor; guvnor; gov'nor *noun*
1 a boss *UK*
Reduced from 'governor'.
- Just remember, I'm the Guv'nor. —Troy Kennedy Martin, *The Italian Jon [uncut script]*, 1969

- What's he want, gov'nor? A miracle-maker or a routine investigation? — *The Sweeney*, p. 51, 1976
- [T]he best guv'nor for a doorman to work for[.] — Dave Courtney, *Raving Lunacy*, p. 10, 2000

2 the landlord of a public house *UK*
Originally a lazy reduction of 'governor'.

- [N]one of the others are in the Duke of York as planned. The guvnor has told Ally that the police had instructed him to close[.] — Martin King and Martin Knight, *The Naughty Nineties*, p. 32, 1999

guy *noun*
a man or a boy; a general form of address; in the plural it can be used of and to men, women or a mixed grouping *US, 1847*

- Guys and gals, it knocks me out to be able to elucidate — Lavada Durst, *The Jives of Dr. Hepcat*, 1953
- Then in flies a guy that's all dressed up just like the Union Jack — Mick Jagger and Keith Richard, *Get Off Of My Cloud*, 1965
- I appreciate that us guys, at our age [16], need some kind of escape in our lives[.] — Macfarlane, Macfarlane and Robson, *The User*, p. 13, 1996
- Guys, uh, what exactly does third base feel like? — Paul Herz, *American Pie*, 1999

guyed out *adjective*
drunk *US*
An allusion to the tightness achieved through guy wires.

- — Sherman Louis Sergel, *The Language of Show Biz*, p. 100, 1973

guy-magnet *noun*
a person who is attractive to men *AUSTRALIA*

- Are you a guy-magnet or do you scare 'em more than that shirt their Gran bought them for Christmas? — *Dolly*, p. 64, 1996

guy thing *noun*
a problem or subject best understood by males *US*

- — Connie Eble (Editor), *UNC-CH Campus Slang*, p. 4, Spring 1992

guyver; guiver *noun*
insincere talk; pretence *AUSTRALIA, 1864*

- GUYVER – Pretence. — Gilbert H. Lawson, *A Dictionary of Australian Words and Terms*, 1924
- Lotta jumped-up blow-ins putting on more guyver than the Governor's wife. — Dymphna Cusack, *Picnic Races*, p. 19, 1962

guzzle-and-grab *noun*
eat and drink, with an emphasis on fast, low-brow food and alcohol *US*

- A favorite after-work guzzle-and-grab spot is the Cafe of All Nations[.] — Jack Lait and Lee Mortimer, *Washington Confidential*, p. 78, 1951

guzzled *adjective*
drunk *US, 1939*

- — Pete Brown, *Man Walks into a Pub*, 2003

guzzle guts *noun*
a glutton or a heavy drinker *UK, 1959*

- — Iona Archibald Opie, *The Lore and Language of Schoolchildren*, p. 167, 1959

gwaai; gwai; gwa *noun*
tobacco; a cigarette *SOUTH AFRICA*
From the Zulu *ugwayi* (tobacco).

- — Jean Branford, *A Dictionary of South African English*, p. 82, 1978

gwaffed *adjective*
drug-intoxicated *SOUTH AFRICA*

gwan *verb*
happening, going on
A patois slurring of 'going on'.

- [M]ore time is needed when you don't want the "other" man to understand wha' ah gwan [going on], seen? — Donald Gorgon, *Cop Killer*, p. 99, 1994

gwarr; gwarry; gwat *noun*
the vagina *SOUTH AFRICA*

- The woman in that sleazy bar gripped her gwat. — *Surfrikan Slang*, 2004

GWB
the *G*eorge *W*ashington *B*ridge *US*
It crosses the Hudson River between upper Manhattan and Fort Lee, New Jersey.

- Radio Voice Over: ... and out top story – a hero cop jumps off the GWB after two African-American minors, reportedly unarmed, are shot in a pre-dawn gunfight on the bridge. — *Copland*, 1997

gweep *noun*
an overworked computer programmer *US*

- — Karla Jennings, *The Devouring Fungus*, p. 220, 1990

G-wheel *noun*
in a carnival, a game wheel that has been rigged for cheating *US*
'G' is for 'gaffed' (rigged).

- — Lindsay E. Smith and Bruce A. Walstad, *Keeping Carnies Honest*, p. 42–43, 1990: 'Glossary'

gyac
*g*od *y*ou're *a* *c*unt; *g*ive *y*ou *a* *c*lue *UK, 2003*
An initialism. Pronounced as if retching.

gyal *noun*
a girl; girls
A phonetic variation.

- [D]at's how me feel when me spy dem nice-nice gyal up Dalston way. — Donald Gorgon, *Cop Killer*, p. 112, 1994
- He reckoned that too many gyal, ah too quick to drop dem panty. — Donald Gorgon, *Cop Killer*, p. 112–113, 1994

gyke *noun*
a gynaecologist *UK, 1984*
Used among middle-class women, especially in hospital. Noted as a 1950s usage, but not recorded until 1984.

gym bunny *noun*
someone who makes regular use of a gymnasium *UK*

- Are you still a gym bunny? I'm still pretty good at doing aerobics and step classes. — *FHM Bionic*, p. 83, December 2001

gymhead *noun*
someone who exercises obsessively and therefore spends a great deal of time in a gymnasium *UK*
A combination of 'gym' (a gymnasium) and **-HEAD** (a user).

- [H]alf looks as if he's on the steggies [steroids] and that, bit of a gymhead. — Kevin Sampson, *Clubland*, p. 101, 2002

gym queen *noun*
a man who spends a great deal of time at a gym *US*

- And Genre's going after the white boy, gym queen, partyboys who don't really want to read too much. — *San Francisco Examinier*, p. C19, 4th December 1994
- [S]o too is the gym queen: a thing that needs to be exhaustively manicured and viewed publicly in a little diorama-box, with a proud groomer next to it[.] — *San Francisco Examiner*, p. C19, 22nd August 1997
- There are some deficiencies that the gym queens definitely don't have. — Suroosh Alvi et al., *The Vice Guide*, p. 272, 2002
- — Connie Eble (Editor), *UNC-CH Campus Slang*, p. 5, Spring 2003

gym rat *noun*
an exercise fanatic *US, 1978*

- In a grim twist that could fit into one of his songs, in the past year Zevon has been a gym rat ("I was working out more than Vin Diesel," he says) and assumed that his shortness of breath and the tightness in his chest were side effects of his regimen. — *Los Angeles Times*, 13th September 2002

gymslip training *noun*
the process of instructing, and conditioning the behaviour of a transvestite who wishes to be treated as an adolescent girl, especially when used in a dominant prostitute's advertising matter *UK*

- — Caroline Archer, *Tart Cards*, 2003

gynae; gyno *noun*
gynaecology; a gynaecologist *UK, 1933*

- Eventually had to call gynae myself on a public telephone[.] — Henry Sloane, *Sloane's Inside Guide to Sex & Drugs & Rock 'n' Roll*, p. 93, 1985
- — Jeremy Cameron, *Brown Bread in Wengen*, p. 52, 1999

gynie *noun*
a gynaecological examination *UK*

- Faced with explaining away a nappy rash at my next gynie, I wrote off to Miss Prim. — Kitty Churchill, *Thinking of England*, p. 64, 1995

gyno; gynae *noun*
a gynaecologist *AUSTRALIA, 1967*

- No, it'll be another false alarm. Another furphy. That gyno of hers is trying to put the wind up me, that's all. — Barry Humphries, *A Nice Night's Entertainment*, p. 188, 1981
- — Barry Humphries, *The Traveller's Tool*, p. 107, 1985

- Examined her like I was a straight up fanny quack. "Excuse me," I goes, "I am a qualified gyno and I got to make an urgent inspection." —Jeremy Cameron, *Brown Bread in Wengen*, 1999

gyno shot *noun*
a close-up scene in a pornographic film or a photograph showing a woman's genitals *US*
- — *Adult Video News*, p. 48, August 1995

gyp; gip *noun*
1 someone or something that is considered a cheat; someone who does not honour debts and obligations *US, 1859*
Abbreviated from 'gypsy'; an unconsidered racial slur. Also spelt 'gip'.
- These gyps (and there are plenty of them still operating) prey on the vanity of out-of-town visitors[.] —Dev Collans with Stewart Sterling, *I was a House Detective*, p. 135, 1954
- Before Bissel can apply his breakthrough on a global scale [in the movie 'I Was a Teenage Werewolf'], though, the ungrateful punk tears his throat out. Regular Freudian gyp. — *Uncut*, p. 22, February 2002

2 in horse racing, someone who owns only a few horses *US, 1938*
An abbreviation of 'gypsy'; not derogatory.
- —Mel Heimer, *Inside Racing*, p. 211, 1962

3 in oil drilling, gypsum *US*
- —Jerry Robertson, *Oil Slanguage*, p. 63, 1954

4 pain, actual or figurative *UK, 1910*
Also 'jyp'.
- He'd hurt his back parachuting a few months before, and it was still giving him gyp. —Chris Ryan, *Stand By, Stand By*, p. 94, 1996
- I've a dishwasher – Hotpoint – on the blink, making noises, generally playing up and giving me gyp. —Jenny Eclair, *Camberwell Beauty*, p. 209, 2000

gyp; gip *verb*
to cheat (someone), to swindle *US, 1880*
- VOICE: I'm going to shoot. Don't move, eh? AGENT: No, that thing – VOICE: I've been gypped – AGENT: But, listen, that money —Harry J. Anslinger (US Commissioner of Narcotics), *The Murderers*, p. 153, 1961
- They got to be going to a white fish market, that's gon by gypping them. —Claude Brown, *Manchild in the Promised Land*, p. 339, 1965
- — Multicultural Management Program Fellows, *Dictionary of Cautionary Words and Phrases*, 1989
- Now I'm the one gettin' gyped. — *Pulp Fiction*, 1994
- What, does he think Nunez gipped him because he wasn't scared enough? Nunez gipped him because Allesandro was bein' cheap. —Christopher Brookmyre, *The Sacred Art of Stealing*, p. 10, 2002

gypo; gyppo; jippo; gippo; gyppy; gypper *noun*
a gypsy; gypsy *UK, 1916*
Derogatory, casually racist.
- There's a difference, you see, between white rats and 'orrible, squirmy, scumbag, gyppo rats that run about in fields and live in sewage farms. —Shaun Ryder, *Shaun Ryder... in His Own Words*, 1989
- [B]uying single roses for the trouble from gyppos with baskets. —Andrew Nickolds, *Back to Basics*, p. 85, 1994
- "You interested in the Romany Way?" "What?" "White vans and gyppos?" "Where?" —David Peace, *Nineteen Seventy-Four*, p. 44, 1999
- You all seen they gypos tryin' to cheat me[.] —Chris Baker and Andrew Day, *Lock, Stock... & One Big Bullock*, p. 354, 2000
- You see some gyppo site and there's filth everywhere, ain't there? —Jake Arnott, *He Kills Coppers*, p. 177, 2001

gypo-bashing *noun*
racially motivated physical attacks on gypsies *UK*
On the model of **PAKI-BASHING** (attacks on Pakistanis and other Asians).
- [N]o groups took up "gypo-bashing", or shouted abuse across the street to them. —Jimmy Stockin, *On The Cobbles*, p. 15, 2000

gyppo *noun*
an avoidance or shirking of a duty; a shirker *SOUTH AFRICA, 1978*
From gypsy or Egyptian via military slang.
- —Penny Silva, *A Dictionary of South African English*, 1996

gyppo *verb*
to dodge an unpleasant responsibility, to shirk a duty; to avoid something *SOUTH AFRICA, 1971*
From gypsy or Egyptian via military slang.
- —Penny Silva, *A Dictionary of South African English*, 1996

gyppo *adjective*
small-time *CANADA*
- This office did offer me the usual dime a dozen jobs selling thingamajigs door-to-door on commission for the gyppo firms. — *Vancouver Sun*, p. 4–5, 26 May 1959
- I been a bull goose catskinner for every gyppo logging operation in the Northwest[.] —Ken Kesey, *One Flew Over the Cuckoo's Nest*, p. 19, 1962

gyppo's dog *noun*
used as a standard of skinniness *UK*
Based on a stereotypical image of a gypsy's dog.
- You're built like a gyppo's dog, all prick and bones. —Frank Skinner, *Frank Skinner*, p. 118, 2001

gyppy *adjective*
painful; annoying (causing a figurative pain) *UK*
- Well, we can't be doing with gyppy dishwashers. —Jenny Eclair, *Camberwell Beauty*, p. 209, 2000

gypsy *noun*
1 in circus and carnival usage, an undependable employee, especially a drunk *US*
- —Don Wilmeth, *The Language of American Popular Entertainment*, p. 122, 1981

2 in trucking, an owner-operator who works independently *US*
- —Mary Elting, *Trucks at Work*, 1946

gypsy *adjective*
1 unlicensed, unregulated, usually owned by the operator *US*
Most often applied to a taxicab or truck, although originally to a racehorse owner/jockey.
- There are five half-mile tracks in Maryland, which run almost all year with unknown plugs and has-beens, raced by "Gypsy" horsemen. —Jack Lait and Lee Mortimer, *Washington Confidential*, p. 273, 1951
- I see this gypsy cab doubeparked in front of the club. —Edwin Torres, *After Hours*, p. 263, 1979
- "Gypsy cab" drivers who have stopped to drink beer and snort a little perico talk near the barbershop[.] —Terry Williams, *The Cocaine Kids*, p. 24, 1989

2 meddling, nosy, officious *BARBADOS*
- Why don't you mind your own business? You too damn gypsy. —Frank A. Collymore, *Barbadian Dialect*, p. 56, 1965

gypsy bankroll *noun*
a roll of money in which the top several notes are real large-denomination notes and the rest are counterfeit, plain paper or small-denomination notes *US*
- It's a fucking gypsy bankroll! The hundreds are counterfeit! —Gerald Petievich, *Money Men*, p. 89, 1981

gyrene *noun*
a US Marine *US, 1894*
- Despite a Navy directive to cut it out, Navy pilots remain "Airedales" and Marines are still "Gyrenes." — *New York Times Magazine*, p. 17, 5th June 1955
- "Jist some nudie gy-rene," Gibson Hand said. —Joseph Wambaugh, *The Glitter Dome*, p. 170, 1981

gyro; gyro wanker *noun*
a surfer who constantly flaps his arms to gain balance on the surfboard *US*
- —Trevor Cralle, *The Surfin'ary*, p. 49, 1991

gyve *noun*
a marijuana cigarette *US, 1938*
This archly ironic reference to marijuana addiction uses an almost obsolete standard English word meaning 'shackles and fetters' whilst punning on **JIVE**.
- —Richard A. Spears, *The Slang and Jargon of Drugs and Drink*, p. 240, 1986
- —Mike Haskins, *Drugs*, p. 287, 2003

Hh

H *noun*

heroin *US, 1926*

- More specifically, it was classified as M, C, and H – Mary, Charlie, and Harry – which stood for morphine, cocaine, and heroin. —William J. Spillard and Pence James, *Needle in a Haystack*, p. 147–148, 1945
- Maybe he's got his H down there. —Hal Ellson, *The Golden Spike*, p. 5, 1952
- You never was on 'H', was you? Great, one time; crazy! —George Mandel, *Flee the Angry Strangers*, p. 56, 1952
- Herman came back from his thirty-day cure on Riker's Island and introduced me to a peddler who was pushing Mexican H on 103rd and Broadway. —William Burroughs, *Junkie*, p. 40, 1953
- It's not like H or M. Nothing like that! —Ross Russell, *The Sound*, p. 22, 1961
- Whenever eight kilos of H gets away from its handlers, there's some hell waiting for somebody. —Mickey Spillane, *Me, Hood!*, p. 71, 1963
- Pinky's got the habit. He's on H. —Chester Himes, *Come Back Charleston Blue*, p. 22, 1966
- "Snort, man," Waneko said. "It's H." —Piri Thomas, *Down These Mean Streets*, p. 110, 1967
- I tried hard to be like him, so I got hooked on 'H.' —Iceberg Slim (Robert Beck), *Pimp*, p. 99, 1969
- When you're married to H you're married for life[.] —Savoy Brown *Needle and Spoon*, 1970

▸ the H

Houston, Texas *US*

- —Ethan Hilderbrant, *Prison Slang*, p. 127, 1998

H-17 *noun*

in casino blackjack gambling, a rule that the dealer must draw a card if he has a 17 made with an ace counting 11 points *US*

The 'h' is for HIT.

- —Frank Scoblete, *Best Blackjack*, p. 263, 1996

H8 *verb*

in text messaging, hate *UK*

A variant spelling; one of several constructions in which a syllable pronounced 'ate' is replaced by the homophone 'eight'.

- Txting and the h8 it causes are nothing new[.] —*The Guardian*, 2nd July 2002

hab *noun*

a habitual criminal *US*

- —Marlena Kay Nelson, *Rookies to Roaches*, p. 7, 1963

habdabs *noun*

▷ see: ABDABS

habit *noun*

an addiction to any drug *UK, 1881*

- —Angela Devlin, *Prison Patter*, p. 59, 1996

habitual *noun*

▸ the habitual

a criminal charge alleging habitual criminal status *US*

- They filed the habitual on me and I jumped bond. —Bruce Jackson, *In the Life*, p. 85, 1972

ha-bloody-ha!

▷ see: HA-FUCKING-HA!

Habra Dabra and the crew *noun*

any random representatives of the populace *BARBADOS*

The functional equivalent of 'Tom, Dick and Harry'.

- —Frank A. Collymore, *Barbadian Dialect*, p. 57, 1965

hache *noun*

heroin *US*

The Spanish pronunciation of the letter 'h'.

- —*American Speech*, p. 87, May 1955: 'Narcotic argot along the Mexican border'
- —Richard A. Spears, *The Slang and Jargon of Drugs and Drink*, p. 241, 1986
- —Robert Ashton, *This Is Heroin*, p. 206, 2002
- —Mike Haskins, *Drugs*, p. 284, 2003

hachi; hodgy *noun*

the penis *US, 1954*

- But "eat a hodgy" must have been nationwide, because Norm was saying "eat a hodgy" out on the coast while I was saying it in Bloom Township High in Chicago Heights. —Jim Bouton, *Ball Four*, p. 361, 1970

hack *noun*

1 a journalist, a reporter *UK, 1810*

- [O]ne of the few hacks to sue and to have been sued[.] —John McCririck, *John McCririck's World of Betting*, p. 70, 1991
- [W]e want a proper writer to do our story. Not some twopenny-halfpenny hack. —Jake Arnott, *He Kills Coppers*, p. 110, 2001

2 a prison guard *US, 1914*

- The boy sneered. "It's the goddamn hack." —Clarence Cooper Jr, *The Scene*, p. 224, 1960
- He killed a hack, and they had to send him to Materwann. —Claude Brown, *Manchild in the Promised Land*, p. 370, 1965
- "Just put one blanket down and cover yourself with the other," said the hack who led me in. —Piri Thomas, *Down These Mean Streets*, p. 243, 1967
- The van went through the gates manned by rock-faced "hacks" carrying scoped, high-powered rifles. —Iceberg Slim (Robert Beck), *Pimp*, p. 49, 1969
- At that moment the hack motioned for me to leave, so I told Willie I had to split. —A.S. Jackson, *Gentleman Pimp*, p. 62–63, 1973
- He smelled up the joint something awful and the hacks used to die. —*Goodfellas*, 1990

3 a solution to a computer problem; an impressive and demanding piece of computer work *US*

- —*Co-Evolution Quarterly*, p. 31, Spring 1981: 'Computer slang'
- —Eric S. Raymond, *The New Hacker's Dictionary*, p. 189, 1991
- [A] palindromic music composition was considered a good hack (thus making Haydn, with his Palindrome Symphony, an honorary hacker). —Katie Hafner and John Markoff, *quoted in Wired Style*, p. 70, 1996

4 in computing, a quick, often temporary, fix of a problem *US*

- —Guy L. Steele et al., *The Hacker's Dictionary*, p. 75, 1983

5 a single act of unlawfully invading and exploring another's computer system by remote means *US, 1983*

- The information was the trophy – the proof of the hack. —Kevin Mitnick, *The Secret History of Hacking*, 22nd July 2001

6 an opportunist *UK*

Used at Oxford University.

- Some who seeks to make his way by joining all the right groups, attending the best parties, and being elected or appointed to the morst prestigious post. In short he is what I would call a chancer. —*The Guardian*, 23rd April 1980

7 a taxi *US, 1928*

- We took a bath together and after we were done I called a hack to take Satin to her gig. —A.S. Jackson, *Gentleman Pimp*, p. 110, 1973
- Billy Ray was still waiting to get discovered, driving a hack meanwhile, when he wasn't trying to get an angle on girls in thin dresses standing at bus stops with the sun behind them. —Robert Campbell, *Juice*, p. 3, 1988

8 a hot rod *US*

- —*Good Housekeeping*, p. 143, September 1958: 'Hot-rod terms for teen-age girls'

9 a brakevan (caboose) *US, 1916*

- —Norman Carlisle, *The Modern Wonder Book of Trains and Railroading*, p. 264, 1946

10 a game of Hacky Sack *US*

- —Anna Scotti and Paul Young, *Buzzwords*, p. 65, 1997

hack *verb*

1 to tolerate, endure, survive *US, 1952*

Usually used with 'it'.

- The reason I couldn't hack it was I really didn't want to write a thesis. —Gurney Norman, *Divine Right's Trip (Last Whole Earth Catalog)*, p. 107, 1971
- Anyway," Elvin said, "here's this boy has to do a mandatory twenty-five on a life sentence and he's, I mean, depressed, doesn't think he can hack it. —Elmore Leoanrd, *Maximum Bob*, p. 50, 1991
- Much as I can hack a few nights in the cells, I really don't fancy straight porridge [prison time]. —Danny King, *The Burglar Diaries*, p. 235, 2001

2 to bother, to annoy *US, 1893*
- You know, people have been stealing his riffs for all these years. That's one of the things that hacks him up so bad[.] —Ross Russell, *The Sound*, p. 177, 1961
- That hacks me off. —Frank Skinner, *Frank Skinner*, p. 84, 2001

3 to unlawfully invade and explore another's computer system by remote means *US, 1983*

4 to investigate the possibilities of a computer purely for the pleasures of discovery; to create new possibilities for a computer bit without commercial consideration *US*
- Hacking [...] exploring the boundaries of computing experiments – even if they didn't own it. — *The Secret History of Hacking*, 22nd July 2001

5 to work with a computer *US*
- — *Co-Evolution Quarterly*, p. 31, Spring 1981: 'Computer slang'
- —Guy L. Steele et al., *The Hacker's Dictionary*, p. 76, 1983

6 to drive a taxi *US, 1903*
- These are used by men who hack in their spare time, such as policemen, chauffeurs, and government employees, who act as cabbies for four or five hours a day. —Jack Lait and Lee Mortimer, *Washington Confidential*, p. 289, 1951
- I went back to hacking for Yellow Cab, which was my first experience as a Negro[.] —Clancy Sigal, *Going Away*, p. 473, 1961
- Who else would hack through South Bronx or Harlem at night? — *Taxi Driver*, 1976

7 to play with a hackysack beanbag *US*
- —Connie Eble (Editor), *UNC-CH Campus Slang*, p. 3, Fall 1995

▸ **hack butts**
to smoke cigarettes *CANADA*
- —Jack Chambers (Editor), *Slang Bag 93 (University of Toronto)*, p. 3, Winter 1993

▸ **hack it**
to cope with, to accomplish *US, 1952*
- That is our mission and you are either going to hack it or pack it. —Lewis John Carlino, *The Great Santini*, 1979
- [Ronnie] Biggs just couldn't hack it any more. —Erwin James, *The Guardian*, 10th May 2001: 'A life inside'
- Sack it off [reject it] if ye can't hack it. —Niall Griffiths, *Kelly + Victor*, p. 143, 2002
- You'll have to handle whatever all by your lonesome. Hope you can hack it. — *The Trinidad Guardian*, 1st November 2003

hack around; hack off; hack *verb*
to waste time, usually in a context where time should not be wasted *US, 1888*
- —Collin Baker et al., *College Undergraduate Slang Study Conducted at Brown University*, p. 132, 1968
- I got to stop hacking around, is all. —George V. Higgins, *The Friends of Eddie Doyle*, p. 33, 1971

hack driver *noun*
in horse racing, a jockey *US*
- —David W. Maurer, *Argot of the Racetrack*, p. 33, 1951

hacked; hacked off *adjective*
annoyed *US, 1936*
- —Robert S. Gold, *A Jazz Lexicon*, p. 135, 1964
- Our front door is always unlocked in case one of the boys is hacked off at his parents and needs a place to lay over and cool off. —S.E. Hinton, *The Outsiders*, p. 93, 1967
- —Eugene Landy, *The Underground Dictionary*, p. 95, 1971
- Smiles was hacked off and had been meaning to tell me why[.] —John King, *Human Punk*, p. 184, 2000

hacker *noun*

1 a person who uses their computer expertise in any effort to breach security walls and gain entry to secure sites *US, 1963*
- —Guy L. Steele et al., *The Hacker's Dictionary*, p. 79, 1983

2 a person with a profound appreciation and affection for computers and programming *US*
- — *Co-Evolution Quarterly*, p. 31, Spring 1981: 'Computer slang'
- —Guy L. Steele et al., *The Hacker's Dictionary*, p. 79, 1983

3 an expert in any field *US*
- —Guy L. Steele et al., *The Hacker's Dictionary*, p. 79, 1983

4 a taxi driver *BAHAMAS*
- —John A. Holm, *Dictionary of Bahamian English*, p. 97, 1982

hackette *noun*
a female journalist *UK, 1984*
Patronising.
- Well, nobody apart from the odd feminist hackette but no one gives a shit what they think. —Shaun Ryder, *Shaun Ryder... in His Own Words*, 1990

hackie *noun*
a carriage or taxi driver *US, 1899*
- Bell-boys and hackies can steer you to anything. —Jack Lait and Lee Mortimer, *Washington Confidential*, p. 270, 1951

hack mode *noun*
while working on or with a computer, a state of complete focus and concentration *US*
- —Eric S. Raymond, *The New Hacker's Dictionary*, p. 190, 1991

Hackney Wick *noun*
a penis *UK*
Rhyming slang for **PRICK**. Hackney Wick is an area of east London, located considerably closer to the source of Cockney rhyming slang than the more popular synonym **HAMPTON WICK**.

hacktivist *noun*
a cultural activist and skilled computer-user who invades a corporate website to leave subversive messages *UK*
- The real-world jammers have been joined by a global network of on-line "hacktivists" who carry out their raids on the Internet. —Naomi Klein, *No Logo*, p. 282, 2001

hacky sack *noun*
a beanbag used in a game in which a circle of players try to keep the bag from hitting the ground without using their hands *US*
A trademarked product that has lent its name to a game and to rival products.
- — *American Speech*, Summer 1989

haddock and cod; haddock *noun*
used as a general pejorative, a sod *UK, 1962*
Rhyming slang.
- The stuff that half the haddocks you see around are wearing I was wearing year ago. —Mark Pass, *Marc Bolan, The Sharper Word*, p. 45, 1992

had-it *noun*
a person who was formerly successful *UK*
- Even Cliff Richard and Adam Faith were still on his mind. "I suppose they're had-its in a way but they've done something.["] —Mark Pass, *Marc Bolan, The Sharper Word*, p. 46, 1992

had-it *adjective*
exhausted; completely worn out *US*
Hawaiian youth usage.
- —Douglas Simonson, *Pidgin to da Max*, 1981

haemorrhoid; hemorrhoid *noun*
an irritation, an annoying person *UK*
An excruciating pun on 'pain in the arse'.
- "Hemmorrhoids?" "Everybody uses that." —Joseph Wambaugh, *The Choirboys*, 1975
- Dining alone with Keith Floyd / Is something we all should avoid. / Everything's fine / Till he gets to the wine, / And then he's a right haemorrhoid. — *I'm Sorry I Haven't a Clue, the Official Limerick Collection*, 1998

haffie *noun*
▷ **see: HALF-JACK**

ha-fucking-ha!; ha-bloody-ha!; ha-di-fucking-ha!; hardy fuckin' ha, ha!
used as a jeering response to unfunny jokes; and to dismiss impossible suggestions *UK, 1976*
- [He had] been forced to endure a string of remarks about "not being so full of shit anymore". Ha ha fucking ha. At least he was alive to endure them[.] —Christopher Brookmyre, *Boiling a Frog*, p. 296, 2000
- [I] was to meet him outside King's Cross Train Station in twenty minutes. Well, hardy fuckin' ha, ha. —Lanre Fehintola, *Charlie Says...*, p. 103, 2000

hag *verb*
to annoy, to bother *BARBADOS*
- —Frank A. Collymore, *Barbadian Dialect*, p. 57, 1965

hagged out *adjective*

1 exhausted *US*
- —Collin Baker et al., *College Undergraduate Slang Study Conducted at Brown University*, p. 133, 1968

2 (of a woman) ugly *US*
From 'hag' (an unattractive woman), possibly punning on **SHAGGED; SHAGGED OUT** (tired).

• Legendary US shock jock, Howard Stern has blasted Paul McCartney's late wife Linda, calling her "annoying" and "hagged out". — *Music 365 – Rock News*, 25th July 2001

Haggis McBagpipe *nickname*

British Columbia radio and television personality Jack Webster *CANADA*

• This West Coast media personality has been called a lot of things which one wouldn't dare to say to his face. "The Mouth that Roared" is mild compared to the Scottish slang insulting nicknames. — Tom Parkin, *WetCoast Words*, p. 151, 1989

ha-ha *noun*

a glass of beer; beer *US*

• — Connie Eble (Editor), *UNC-CH Campus Slang*, p. 4, March 1979

ha-ha bird; ha-ha pigeon *noun*

a kookaburra, a well-known Australian bird *AUSTRALIA, 1938*

From its call which resembles human laughter.

• They shot and cooked kangaroos, even shot 'Ha-Ha birds' and magpies until I stopped them. — Patsy Adam-Smith, *Folklore of the Australian Railwaymen*, p. 128, 1969

• Italians working on the Snowy River scheme called the kookaburra, or 'laughing jackass', 'Ha-ha Pigeon'. — Nancy Keesing, *Lily on the Dustbin*, p. 149, 1982

ha-ha-funny *adjective*

▷ see: FUNNY HA-HA

Haight *noun*

▸ **the Haight**

the Haight-Ashbury neighbourhood of San Francisco *US*

• The fog came every day and destroyed the sunshine, and then the Haight was left to itself. — Nicholas Von Hoffman, *We Are The People Our Parents Warned Us Against*, p. 9, 1967

• I came to the Haight in the beginning of 1966. — Leonard Wolfe (Editor), *Voices from the Love Generation*, p. 100, 1968

Haight-Ashbury *nickname*

a neighbourhood in San Francisco, the epicentre of the hippie movement in the mid- to late 1960s *US*

From the intersection of Haight and Ashbury Streets. More recently referred to simply as **THE HAIGHT**.

• — Laurence Urdang, *Names and Nicknames of Places and Things*, p. 119, 1987

hail *noun*

1 crack cocaine *US*

Based on the drug's resemblance to pieces of hail.

• — US Department of Justice, *Street Terms*, October 1994

2 in soda fountain usage, ice *US, 1935*

• — *American Speech*, p. 88, April 1946: 'The language of West Coast culinary workers'

hailer *noun*

in the television and film industries, a bullhorn *US*

• — Tony Miller and Patricia George, *Cut! Print!*, p. 85, 1977

Hail Mary *noun*

1 a last-minute, low-probability manoeuvre *US*

• But what the hell, why not try? I flung a Hail Mary to the shortest end I'd ever seen, the producer they had assigned to me/my project, a neurotic little bastard named Teddy. — Odie Hawkins, *Lost Angeles*, p. 61, 1994

• McVeigh's lawyers, she said, were "in a Hail Mary situation, not by their own doing but by the government's control of the timetable." — *Contra Costa Times*, p. A24, 8th June 2001

2 in poker, a poor hand that a player holds into high betting in the hope that other players are bluffing and have even worse hands *US*

• — John Vorhaus, *The Big Book of Poker Slang*, p. 21, 1996

hail smiling morn *noun*

the erect penis, an erection *UK*

Rhyming slang for **HORN**.

• — Red Daniells, 1980

haim *noun*

▷ see: HAME

haint; hain't

a have-not; to have not *UK*

Verb and noun. A vulgar contraction.

• [A]sk just what sort of Irish churchwebbed haints Van Morrison might be the product of. — Lester Bangs, *Psychotic Reactions and Carburetor Dung*, p. 21, 1971

hair *noun*

1 courage *US, 1959*

• — J. R. Friss, *A Dictionary of Teenage Slang (Mt. Diablo High)*, 1964

• — John M. Kelly, *Surf and Sea*, p. 286, 1965

• — *American Speech*, p. 194, October 1965: 'Notes on campus vocabulary, 1964'

• You never would have worked up the hair to hit on her, but she came right up and started talking to you. — Jay McInerney, *Bright Lights, Big City*, p. 69, 1984

2 in computing, intricacy *US*

• — Guy L. Steele, *Coevolution Quarterly*, p. 31, Spring 1981: 'Computer Slang'

• — Guy L. Steele et al., *The Hacker's Dictionary*, p. 80, 1983

▸ **get in your hair**

to annoy or irritate *US*

• I'm gonna wash that man right out of my hair. — Oscar Hammerstein II, *South Pacific*, 1949

• [T]wo years having the time of your life and not getting in people's hair. — Graeme Kent, *The Queen's Corporal [Six Granada Plays]*, p. 85, 1959

▸ **let down your hair**

to behave in a (more than usually) uninhibited manner *US, 1933*

• [T]his is the school's once-a-year chance to let its hair down but we don't want anyone letting their hair down too much, do we now? Controlled fun is what we're about. — *The Guardian*, 7th December 2003

▸ **put hair on your chest; put hairs on your chest**

a quality ascribed to an alcoholic drink or, when encouraging a child to eat, used of food (especially crusts and brussel sprouts); also applied more broadly to robust or challenging questions of aesthetic taste or preference *UK, 1964*

• It's good to push him a little bit, and besides, getting up at five o'clock'll put hair on your chest. — Lloyd Garver, *'The Route of All Evil' (Home Improvement episode 87)*, January 1995

• It's a rip roaring punk song which does nothing but puts hair on your chest and fire in your head. — *www.bbc.co.uk/manchester*, 5th February 2003

• Mike returned, carrying two brimming pints of bitter – girls didn't bother with halves, I noticed, watching Max drain her froth-scummed glass – and plonked one down in front of me. 'This'll put hairs on your chest.' I sipped it, even though I didn't like the stuff[.] — Kate Lock, *Dangerous Love*, 2005

▸ **tear your hair; tear your hair out**

to behave in a highly agitated manner, especially as a result of worry *UK, 1606*

• Now he [Tony Blair] is said by those round him to be 'tearing his hair' out at the lack of impact his party has had on the SNP over the past year. — *The Guardian*, 7th April 1999

▸ **wear your hair out against the head of the bed; wear your hair out on the bedhead**

to go bald *UK, 1961*

A jocular explanation.

hairbag *noun*

a veteran police officer *US, 1958*

• — *New York Times Magazine*, p. 88, 16th March 1958

• — *New York Times*, 15th February 1970

hairbagger *noun*

an experienced police officer *US, 1958*

• They'll probably put you on patrol with some hairbagger. — Charles Whited, *Chiodo*, p. 45, 1973

hairball *noun*

1 an obnoxious, borish person, especially when drunk *US*

• She glanced at the two hairballs in leather jackets[.] — Joseph Wambaugh, *The Glitter Dome*, p. 144, 1981

• — Pamela Munro, *U.C.L.A. Slang*, p. 46, 1989

2 a large, powerful wave *US, 1981*

• — Trevor Cralle, *The Surfin'ary*, p. 49, 1991

hairball! *adjective*

terrifying! *US*

• [G]lamorous Malibu types fleeing the bush fires [...], "hey, dude, get in the station wagon. Those flames are like totally hairball!" — David Rowan, *A Glossary for the 90s*, p. 190, 1998

hairblower *noun*

a severe telling-off, a scolding *UK*

• He'll be giving the team a hairblower after that. — *Champions League Live*, 26th November 2002

hairburger *noun*

the vulva, especially in the context of oral sex *US*

• — Eugene Landy, *The Underground Dictionary*, p. 96, 1971

hair burner; hair bender *noun*
a hair stylist *US*
- —Guy Strait, *The Lavendar Lexicon*, 1 June 1964
- — *Male Swinger Number 3*, p. 45, 1981: 'The complete gay dictionary'

haircut *noun*
1 a short prison sentence *UK, 1950*
From the short period of time between haircuts. 'Barnet cut' is the rhyming slang equivalent.
- —Paul Tempest, *Lag's Lexicon*, p. 9, 1950
- — *Delinquently Yours*, February 1959
- —Angela Devlin, *Prison Patter*, p. 59, 1996

2 a lowering of the true mileometer (odometer) reading of a motor vehicle to increase its resale value *NEW ZEALAND*
- Normally when speedos are illegally tampered with, the odometer is deftly wound back. In some shadier parts of the trade, this technique is known as 'giving the car a haircut.' — *AA Motoring Today*, p. 9, April 1990

3 marijuana *UK*
- —Mike Haskins, *Drugs*, p. 287, 2003

4 a sore on a man's penis as the result of a sexually transmitted infection *TRINIDAD AND TOBAGO*
From the popular belief that the sore was caused by a woman's pubic hair.
- —Lise Winer, *Dictionary of the English/Creole of Trinidad & Tobago*, 2003

haircut *adjective*
describes an image of fashionability that is without deeper significance *UK*
- I'm twenty-two, playing with this fucking eighties haircut band, and the first thing I want to do is go to Coney Island. —John Williams, *Cardiff Dead*, p. 120, 2000

hairdresser *noun*
a homosexual *UK*
From the presumption that all hairdressers are gay.
- He's a hairdresser! He's a hairdresser! — *drunken office workers taunting a fellow-worker at a Christmas party in Marlborough, Wiltshire*, 21st December 2001

hair-dry *adjective*
without getting your hair wet *US*
- I paddled out hair dry. —Trevor Cralle, *The Surfin'ary*, p. 49, 1991

haired up *adjective*
angry *US*
From a dog's bristling back when angry.
- —John Gould, *Maine Lingo*, p. 122, 1975

hair fairy *noun*
a homosexual male with an extravagent hairdo *US*
- —Guy Strait, *The Lavendar Lexicon*, 1 June 1964
- "Swish" bars for the effeminates and "hair fairies" with their careful coiffures. —Joe David Brown, *Sex in the '60s*, p. 70, 1968
- That is as unrepresentative of the spectrum of lesbians as the male "hairy fairy" or "queen" is of the male homosexual population. — *San Francisco Chronicle*, p. 22, 30th June 1969
- During this period of homosexuality all the girls relate that they were 'hair fairies." That is, they would wear their hair long and tease it. —George Paul Csicsery (Editor), *The Sex Industry*, p. 67, 1973
- There was a not-so-well-known incident that happened three years before Stonewall when young San Francisco drag queens, "hair fairies" and hustlers, fed up with police harassment, rioted at Compton's Cafeteria at the corner of Turk and Taylor STreets. — *San Francisco Chronicle*, p. 8 (Datebook), 22nd June 2001

hair in the gate *noun*
in television and film making, any foreign object in the camera gate *US*
- —Ralph S. Singleton, *Filmaker's Dictionary*, p. 79, 1990

hair pie *noun*
1 the vulva; oral sex performed on a woman *US, 1938*
Also spelt 'hare' pie or 'hairy' pie.
- —Dale Gordon, *The Dominion Sex Dictionary*, p. 81, 1967
- Billie digs Harlow's cuisine. Goes big for hair pie... —Sidney Bernard, *This Way to the Apocalypse*, p. 173, 1967
- —Eugene Landy, *The Underground Dictionary*, p. 96, 1971
- Eating the old hare pie and tucking into a nice fresh furburger. —Barry Humphries, *Bazza Pulls It Off!*, 1971
- —Ruth Todasco et al., *The Intelligent Woman's Guide to Dirty Words*, p. 25, 1973
- Are you accusin' me of bein' a hair-pie man, Nathan? —Edwin Torres, *Q & A*, p. 155, 1977
- You won't believe it when I tell you I haven't seen the old hair pie in twenty-seven years. —Elmore Leonard, *Bandits*, p. 281, 1987
- —Ethan Hilderbrant, *Prison Slang*, p. 59, 1998
- It's not as if he hasn't had his fingers in enough hairy pies in his time. Hairy pie, hairy pie[.] —Jenny Eclair, *Camberwell Beauty*, p. 353, 2000

2 a pizza with an errant hair embedded in it *US*
Limited usage, but clever.
- — *Maledicta*, p. 13, 1996: 'Domino's pizza jargon'

hairpins *noun*
homosexual code phrases inserted casually into a conversation, trolling for a response *US, 1950*
- — Florida Legislative Investigation Committee (Johns Committee), *Homosexuality and Citizenship in Florida*, 1964: 'Glossary of homosexual terms and deviate acts'
- Keep your hairpins up, dearies. There's a 'straight' inside. —Antony James, *America's Homosexual Underground*, p. 142, 1965
- —Dale Gordon, *The Dominion Sex Dictionary*, p. 61, 1967
- —Robert A. Wilson, *Playboy's Book of Forbidden Words*, p. 95, 1972

hairtree *noun*
a man who wears his hair long and styled as a fashion statement *US*
- Labels like Geffen moved in to sweep every pretty-boy hairtree, some of whom were just unemployed actors on Harleys. —Barney Hoskyns, *Waiting For The Sun*, p. 326, 1996

hair-trunk *noun*
in horse racing, a bad-looking horse that performs poorly *UK*
- —Rita Cannon, *Let's Go Racing*, p. 72, 1948

hairy *noun*
1 a long-haired, bearded individual *UK*
- — *The Observer*, 13th June 1976

2 a former non-commissioned officer training to become an officer *UK*
Military.
- —Colin Strong and Duff Hart-Davis, *Fighter Pilot*, 1981

3 a young woman with a reputation for sluttishness *UK: SCOTLAND*
Glasgow slang.
- What are ye runnin about wi that wee hairy for? —Michael Munro, *The Original Patter*, p. 31, 1985

4 heroin *US*
A phonetic distortion of **HARRY**.
- —David Maurer and Victor Vogel, *Narcotics and Narcotic Addiction*, p. 413, 1973
- —Robert Ashton, *This Is Heroin*, p. 206, 2002

hairy *adjective*
1 dangerous; scary (especially if thrilling) *US, 1945*
- [A] pudgy white kid immersed in a sea of blacks, eyes wide as [James] Brown tore the place up. "It was a little hairy, " he [Billy Joel] remembers, "but Brown blew me away." —Jay Saporita, *Pourin' It All Out*, p. 25, 1980
- In later years, my job has taken me to some hairy locales; not hairy in the Sandy Gall/John Pilger sense, as in Gaza Strip or Grozhny. But certainly as hairy as the urban West gets, such as the Reeperbahn, the Chicago Housing project of Cabrini Green or Moss Side. —Stuart Maconie, *Cider with Roadies*, p. 109, 2003

2 bad, difficult, undesirable *UK, 1848*
A popular term in C19, resurrected in later C20 youth usage.
- — *Time*, 3rd October 1949
- —Grant W. Kuhns, *On Surfing*, p. 117, 1963
- —J. R. Friss, *A Dictionary of Teenage Slang (Mt. Diablo High)*, 1964
- It got a little hairy at the end when we drove him to the bus, however. —Erich Segal, *Love Story*, p. 74, 1970
- It's cool. I'll handle the hairy ones. Most of the time they're just trying to get your attention. —Armistead Maupin, *Tales of the City*, p. 155, 1978
- I mean it's hairy – they got some pretty heavy ordnance, boy. — *Apocalypse Now*, 1979
- It all got a bit hairy at school. They chucked me out. —Mary Hooper, *(megan)2*, p. 170, 1999

3 in computing, complicated *US*
- —Guy L. Steele et al., *The Hacker's Dictionary*, p. 80, 1983

4 good, impressive *US*
- In teen-age jargon, he is still "the hairiest" (the coolest, the greatest). — *Look*, p. 49, 24th November 1959
- —J. R. Friss, *A Dictionary of Teenage Slang (Mt. Diablo High)*, 1964

hairy-arse; hairy-arsed *adjective*
describes a thuggish, insensitive brute *UK*
- A bird wouldn't want some hairy-arse doorman looking through her handbag. —Dave Courtney, *Dodgy Dave's Little Black Book*, p. 198, 2001

hairyback; hairy *noun*
an Afrikaner *SOUTH AFRICA, 1970*
Derogatory.
- —Jean Branford, *A Dictionary of South African English*, 1978

hairy bank *noun*
a prostitute's vagina *GUYANA*
Collected by Richard Allsopp.

hairy belly *noun*
in dominoes, the 6–6 piece *US*
- —Dominic Armanino, *Dominoes*, p. 17, 1959

hairy chequebook *noun*
the vagina, as used for payment in kind instead of money *AUSTRALIA*
- —James Lambert, *The Macquarie Book of Slang*, 1996

hairy clam *noun*
the vagina *UK*
An almost subtle combination of **FISH** and visual imagery.
- [F]uck off back to Lesbos – to live out the rest of their Dyke Days diving for the hairy clam in the clear blue waters of the Aegean. —Stuart Browne, *Dangerous Parking*, p. 358, 2000
- 'At least I don't eat fur burgers like some people I know.' 'You gobble the hairy clam,' Chicky said. 'So does Andy.'—*Granata 80*, p. 191, Winter 2002

hairy eyeball *noun*
a hostile stare *US*
Deriving, perhaps, from the eyelashes that mask the eye.
- And there was this young one with him from Finland, with tits on her like she was deformed or something, and he was giving her the hairy eyeball, you know.—Joseph O'Connor, *Red Roses and Petrol*, p. 7, 1995
- —Susie Dent, *The Language Report*, p. 81, 2003
- —Chris Lewis, *The Dictionary of Playground Slang*, p. 111, 2003

hairy fairy *adjective*
of a man, effeminate to some degree *UK*
A pun on **AIRY-FAIRY** (delicate, insubstantial) and **FAIRY** (a homosexual man).

hairy goat *noun*
a racehorse that is a slow runner or poor performer *AUSTRALIA, 1933*
- I thought I'd backed everything in me day from elephant-beetles when I was a kid to fighting cocks in the jungle and hairy goats what some jokers call horses, but I never nowhere knew no one come at backin' rats.—Dymphna Cusack, *Picnic Races*, p. 116, 1962
- 'A bloody hairy goat' was how they described him to Fred.—Joe Andersen, *Winners Can Laugh*, p. 81, 1982

hairy goblet *noun*
the vagina *UK*
- Women's genitalia were represented as (potential) containers (e.g., bucket, box, hair goblet), places to put things in (e.g., furry letterbox, disk drive, socket, slot), containers for semen (e.g., gism pot, spunk bin, honey pot), and containers for the penis/sex (e.g., willy warmer, wank shaft, shagbox).—*Journal of Sex Research*, p. 146, 2001

hairy growler *noun*
the vagina *UK*
- The female genitalia were represented as places from which people/things never return (e.g., the Bermuda triangle) or get sucked into (e.g., the black hole, electrolux), hidden dangers (e.g., squirrel trap), and warnings of danger (e.g., hairy growler, bomb doors).—*Journal of Sex Research*, p. 146, 2001

hairy leg *noun*
1 a man *UK*
CItizens' band radio slang.
- —Peter Chippindale, *The British CB Book*, p. 155, 1981

2 a railway fettler *AUSTRALIA*
- —Patsy Adam-Smith, *Folklore of the Australian Railwaymen*, p. 254, 1969

hairy maclary *noun*
a female who invites sexual foreplay but stops short of intercourse *NEW ZEALAND*
- —David McGill, *David McGill's Complete Kiwi Slang Dictionary*, p. 60, 1998

ha-ja *noun*
▷ see: **HALF-JACK**

hale and hearty *adjective*
a party *UK*
Rhyming slang.
- —Ray Puxley, *Cockney Rabbit*, 1992

Hale and Pace; hale *noun*
the face *UK*
Rhyming slang, from comedy double act Gareth Hale and Norman Pace.
- When you're stoking the fire you don't worry about the Hale! —*www.LondonSlang.com*, June 2002
- —Bodmin Dark, *Dirty Cockney Rhyming Slang*, 2003

half *noun*
1 used colloquially as an elliptical noun when the original noun is omitted, especially of a half pint (of beer) *UK, 1937*
- If your 'and one for yourself' offer is accepted, the publican or bar staff will say 'Thank you, I'll have a half (or whatever)' and add the price of their chosen drink to the total cost of your order.—Social Issues Research Centre, *Passport to the Pub*, 3rd April 2005

2 a child travelling at half-fare *UK, 1961*
- One and a half to the lightship please.—*Evening Star (Ipswich)*, 2nd September 2003

half *adverb*
1 used to strengthen any action *UK*
- I can half lead the cunts round the world and they still wouldn't find YT [me].—Kevin Sampson, *Outlaws*, p. 251, 2001

2 used to reverse what is being said, which is usually formed as a negative, and thus stress the intention, i.e. 'not half bad' is pretty good *UK, 1583*
- He's a top lad, our Paul, but 'e don't 'alf talk some fookin' toss sometimes.—Shaun Ryder, *Shaun Ryder... in His Own Words*, 1990

half a bar *noun*
until 1971, ten shillings; post-decimalisation, fifty pence *UK, 1911*
- —David Powis, *The Signs of Crime*, 1977

half a C *noun*
fifty dollars *US*
A shortened allusion to $100 as a 'C-note'.
- Look my man, when you was in my town, you ate free at my joint, misused my hospitality and left town owing my "Mom" fifty dollars. You don't have to have a drink with me, but I'll take the 'half a C' for Moms.—Babs Gonzales, *I Paid My Dues*, p. 88, 1967

half a case *noun*
fifty cents *US*
- —Hyman E. Goldin et al., *Dictionary of American Underworld Lingo*, p. 90, 1950

half a chip *noun*
sixpence, a sixpenny bit *UK*
- —Paul Tempest, *Lag's Lexicon*, 1950

half a cock *noun*
five pounds (£5) *UK*
Based on rhyming slang **COCKLE AND HEN** (ten).
- —Paul Tempest, *Lag's Lexicon*, 1950

half a crack *noun*
a half-crown coin, half-a-crown, two shillings and sixpence *UK, 1933*
A coin and coinage that paid the price of decimalisation in 1971.

half a dollar *noun*
1 a prison sentence of 50 years *US*
- —Charles Shafer, *Folk Speech in Texas Prisons*, p. 205, 1990

2 a half-crown coin; two shillings and sixpence *UK, 1916*
Pre-decimalisation, that is pre-1971, a half-crown coin was valued at two shillings and sixpence (12½p), and, presumably, at the point of coinage, a pound was worth approximately four US dollars.

half a football field *noun*
fifty crystals of crack cocaine *UK, 2001*
Collected from a correspondent who should know better.

half-a-man *noun*
a short person *US*
- The labels were cruel: Gimp, Limpy–go-fetch, Crip, Lift-one-drag one, etc. Pint, Half-a-man, Peewee, Shorty, Lardass, Pork, Blubber, Belly, Blimp. Nuke-knob, Skinhead, Baldy. Four-eyes, Specs, Coke bottles.—*San Francisco Examiner*, p. A15, 28th July 1997

half a mo *noun*

a very short but vaguely defined time *UK, 1896*

A shortening of 'half a moment'.

- Cor blimey, Jimmy, half a mo – look you, up the canny apples and pears, like, bah gum. I'm terribly sorry. Aren't there just too many faux regional accents in that first barking sentence? — *The Guardian*, 12th December 2000

half and half *noun*

1 oral sex on a man followed by vaginal intercourse *US, 1937*

- I say, Yoo-hoo, pitty baby, you wanna lil french? Haff an haff? How about jes a straight? I say, Twenty berries an you alla roun the mothahfuggin worl'. — Robert Gover, *One Hundred Dollar Misunderstanding*, p. 21, 1961
- [A] lot of them will want half-and-half, starting with a blow job and finishing off with straight intercourse. — John Warren Wells, *Tricks of the Trade*, p. 19, 1970
- She frowned and said impatiently, "Well, how about spending a fin with me for a half-and-half?" — Iceberg Slim (Robert Beck), *The Naked Soul of Iceberg Slim*, p. 116, 1971
- Lou asked Cissy, "You going to give me a half and half, baby?" She could feel his strong fingers pressing into her upper arm. — Hugh Garner, *The Intruders*, p. 41, 1976
- Half-and-half still costs you more than straight, so if you need the girl's mouth on your dingus to get you up it will set you back a total of thirty dollars[.] — Gerald Paine, *A Bachelor's Guide to the Brothels of Nevada*, p. 26, 1978
- What do you think? Half-and-half for fifty dollars. — Elmore Leonard, *Cat Chaser*, p. 139, 1982
- When Nicole came into the kitchen she was naked except for her red shirt. -You want a half-and-half? she said. — William T. Vollman, *Whores for Gloria*, p. 14, 1991
- A friendly little half-and-half before you go away, Dawn? — Joseph Wambaugh, *Floaters*, p. 68, 1996

2 a hermophrodite *US, 1935*

- — Joe McKennon, *Circus Lingo*, p. 44, 1980

3 a pint drink comprising equal measures of two different beers *UK, 1909*

- — Oscar A. Mendelsohn, *The Dictionary of Drink and Drinking*, p. 159, 1966

half and half *adjective*

1 mediocre *TRINIDAD AND TOBAGO, 1958*

- — Lise Winer, *Dictionary of the English/Creole of Trinidad & Tobago*, 2003

2 bisexual *US*

- — *American Speech*, p. 60, Spring-Summer 1975: 'Razorback slang'

half a nicker *noun*

1 pre-decimalisation, ten shillings; after 1971, fifty pence *UK, 1895*

From **NICKER** (one pound).

2 a vicar *UK, 1974*

Rhyming slang. Also variant 'half-nicker man'.

half-apple *noun*

in television and film making, a standard-sized crate used for raising objects or people, half as high as a standard 'apple' *US*

- — Ralph S. Singleton, *Filmaker's Dictionary*, p. 79, 1990

half-assed; half-arsed *adjective*

1 inferior, unsatisfactory, incompetent *US, 1865*

- East St. Louis, for example, was a half-assed gangster town. — Herbert Huncke, *Guilty of Everything*, p. 38, 1990
- Lisa, if you don't like your job you don't strike. You just go in every day, and do it really half-assed. That's the American way. — *The Observer*, 20th April 2003

2 incomplete, not serious, half-hearted *US, 1933*

- They got a bang out of things, though – in a half-assed way, of course. — J.D. Salinger, *Catcher in the Rye*, p. 6, 1951
- We're talking about murder, man, not a little half-assed assault. — Elmore Leonard, *City Primeval*, p. 59, 1980

half a stretch *noun*

1 a six-month prison sentence *UK, 1950*

From 'stretch' (a year's sentence).

- — Angela Devlin, *Prison Patter*, p. 59, 1996

2 gambling odds of 6–1 *UK, 1984*

half a yard *noun*

fifty dollars *US, 1961*

- — Gene Sorrows, *All About Carnivals*, p. 19, 1985: 'Terminology'
- — Thomas L. Clark, *The Dictionary of Gambling and Gaming*, p. 95, 1987

half-baked *adjective*

intellectually deficient *UK, 1855*

Dialect.

- Blair blames union dinosaurs and half-baked employers. — *The Guardian*, 23rd November 2002

half-chat *noun*

a half-caste *UK, 1909*

Also used in Australia.

- I'm an Anglo-Indian – a half-chat, a chillicracker, a blackie-white – the first is the polite term – the other's are what they [the full-whites] call us behind our backs. — Berkely Mather, *The Memsahib*, 1977

half-cock *noun*

▸ **at half-cock**

not fully prepared or ready *UK*

- House of Lords reform is at half cock. — *The Guardian*, 14th August 2000

▸ **go off at half-cock**

generally, to start without being ready; in sex, to ejaculate prematurely or without being fully erect *UK, 1904*

A variation of **HALF-COCKED**.

half-cock *adjective*

ill-considered; inferior *UK*

- [T]he half-cock selection of artists for this year's Turner prize, — *The Guardian*, 6th November 2002

half-cocked *adjective*

1 not fully capable; not completely thought out; unfinished; incomplete *US, 1833*

Derives from the mechanism of a gun.

- You know, we're not going into that thing half-cocked. I made a thorough survey of the consumer situation before I laid my plans. — Max Shulman, *The Zebra Derby*, p. 54, 1946
- But I wasn't rushing off half-cocked. — Malcolm X and Alex Haley, *The Autobiography of Malcolm X*, p. 140, 1964
- [A] half-cocked ponce[.] — Ian Dury, *Blackmail Man*, 1977

2 drunk *AUSTRALIA, early C19*

▸ **go off half-cocked**

generally, to start without being ready; in sex, to ejaculate prematurely or without being fully erect *UK, 1809*

After the action of a gun.

- I don't want them going off half cocked and fucking things up even more. — Ted Lewis, *Jack Carter's Law*, p. 64, 1974

half colonel *noun*

a lieutenant-colonel *US, 1956*

- "What's the SAS commanded by?" "A half colonel." "Well, we'll use a full colonel." — Charlie A. Beckwith, *Delta Force*, p. 109, 1983
- Scovell rose from major to half-colonel for what he achieved there. He finished up as Major-General Sir George Scovell, Lieutenant-Governor of Sandhurst. — *The Guardian*, 15th September 2001

half-cut *adjective*

drunk *UK, 1893*

- Scotty had turned up at the meet half cut[.] — Charles Raven, *Underworld Nights*, p. 30, 1956
- MILLIGAN: Buy us a drink, Jim; go on, be a pal. TAYLOR: You'll get sweet Fanny Adams [nothing]; you're half cut already. — Graeme Kent, *The Queen's Corporal [Six Granada Plays]*, p. 82, 1959
- — John A. Holm, *Dictionary of Bahamian English*, p. 98, 1982

half-cuts *noun*

trainers (sneakers) *BARBADOS*

Collected by Richard Allsopp.

halfers *noun*

▸ **go halfers; go haufers**

to share equally between two parties *UK: SCOTLAND*

- Me 'n the wee brother's gaun [going] haufers on a motor. — Michael Munro, *The Original Patter*, p. 31, 1985

half-fried *adjective*

of eggs, fried on one side only *INDIA*

The Indian-English equivalent to **SUNNY SIDE UP**.

- — Paroo Nihalini, R.K. Tongue and Priya Hosali, *Indian and British English*, 1979

half G *noun*

a half-gallon jar of alcohol *NEW ZEALAND*

- Real hard case that joker. Yah should seen him knocking back those half Gs. — Tim Shadbolt, *Bullshit and Jellybeans*, p. 85, 1971

half-gone *adjective*
half-drunk *UK, 1925*

half-half *adjective*
mediocre *FIJI*
Recorded by Jan Tent in 1996.

half-hearty *adjective*
of medicore health, recovering from an illness but not completely recovered *BARBADOS*
- —Frank A. Collymore, *Barbadian Dialect*, p. 57, 1965

half-het *noun*
a bisexual *US*
- [Quoting correspondence to *The San Francisco Bay Times* in April 1991] Suspected bisexuals ("half-hets") were asked to take a loyalty oath.—Marjorie Garber, *Vice Versa*, p. 53, 1995

half hour *noun*
a short prison sentence *UK*
A little bravado in this prisoner's exaggeration. Collected in private correspondence, January 2002.

halfie *noun*
a half-caste person *AUSTRALIA, 1945*
- But when he suggested that unmarried mothers of 'halfies' should have the same rights to a maintenance allowance from the presumed father as their white-skinned sisters in a similar predicament, they dug in their heels.—Dymphna Cusack, *Picnic Races*, p. 92, 1962
- The half-caste is a halfie or yeller-feller.—Sidney J. Baker, *The Australian Language*, p. 324, 1966

half-inch *verb*
to steal; to arrest *UK, 1925*
Rhyming slang for **PINCH** (to steal or to arrest).
- —Jim Ramsay, *Cop It Sweet*, p. 43, 1977
- —Angela Devlin, *Prison Patter*, p. 59, 1996
- [T]his art gallery was turned over and a shit-load of paintings were half-inched.—Danny King, *The Burglar Diaries*, p. 193, 2001

half-iron *noun*
a heterosexual or bisexual man who associates with homosexuals *UK*
From 'iron' (a homosexual male).
- —Paul Tempest, *Lag's Lexicon*, 1950
- —Angela Devlin, *Prison Patter*, p. 59, 1996

half-jack; ha-ja; haffie *noun*
a half-bottle (375 ml) of spirits *SOUTH AFRICA, 1953*
- —Jean Branford, *A Dictionary of South African English*, 1978

half-load *noun*
fifteen packets of heroin *US*
- —Kenn "Naz" Young, *Naz's Underground Dictionary*, p. 35, 1973
- —Robert Ashton, *This Is Heroin*, p. 209, 2002

half-man *noun*
a kneeboarder, or a surfer who rides without standing *US*
- —Trevor Cralle, *The Surfin'ary*, p. 49, 1991

half-mast *adjective*
1 (used of a penis) partially but not completey erect *US*
- —Robert A. Wilson, *Playboy's Book of Forbidden Words*, p. 134, 1972
- — Anon., *King Smut's Wet Dreams Interpreted*, 1978

2 partially lowered *US, 1871*
- My fly is at half mast; my hands look shaky.—James Ellroy, *Hollywood Nocturnes*, p. 6, 1994

half of marge *noun*
a police sergeant *UK*
Rhyming slang for **SARGE**, formed from a measure of margarine.
- —Ray Puxley, *Fresh Rabbit*, 1998

half-ounce *verb*
to cheat *UK, 1960*
- Anyone thick enough to try to find the lady deserves to be "half ounced".—Ray Puxley, *Cockney Rabbit*, 1992

half-ounce deal *noun*
in prison, a trade that swaps a half ounce of tobacco for a single marijuana cigarette *UK*
- —Angela Devlin, *Prison Patter*, p. 59, 1996

half ounce of baccy *noun*
a Pakistani, especially a Pakistani child *UK*
An elaboration (perhaps a reduction) of **OUNCE OF BACCY** (**PAKI**).
- —Ray Puxley, *Cockney Rabbit*, 1992

half ouncer *noun*
a physically intimidating individual employed to control the clients of any establishment, usually of a premises offering entertainment, e.g. pub, club, concert venue, music festival, etc; a 'chucker-out'; door-security *UK*
Rhyming slang for **BOUNCER**, with a degree of irony.
- —Ray Puxley, *Cockney Rabbit*, 1992

half past six *adjective*
incompetent *SINGAPORE*
A sexual reference, with the hands of the clock indicating impotence.
- —Paik Choo, *The Coxford Singlish Dictionary*, p. 44, 2002

half past two *noun*
a Jewish person *UK*
Rhyming slang.
- —Julian Franklyn, *A Dictionary of Rhyming Slang*, 1960

halfpenny dip; ha'penny dip; ha'penny *noun*
1 a sleep *UK*
Rhyming slang for **KIP**.
- Steaming in his ha'penny when he ought to be doing a bit of George Raft [work].—Red Daniells, 1980
- [T]o "have a ha'penny" is to be asleep.—Ray Puxley, *Cockney Rabbit*, 1992

2 a ship *UK*
Rhyming slang.
- —Julian Franklyn, *A Dictionary of Rhyming Slang*, 1961
- [U]sed by London dockers when London had docks.—Ray Puxley, *Cockney Rabbit*, 1992

halfpenny stamp; ha'penny *noun*
a tramp *UK*
Rhyming slang.
- —Ray Puxley, *Cockney Rabbit*, 1992

half-pick duck *noun*
an incomplete account *TRINIDAD AND TOBAGO, 1975*
- —Lise Winer, *Dictionary of the English/Creole of Trinidad & Tobago*, 2003

half-pie *adjective*
half-hearted *AUSTRALIA, 1941*
- —Jim Ramsay, *Cop It Sweet!*, p. 43, 1977
- There it was again. A barely disguised half-pie shot at Joe.—Clive Galea, *Slipper*, p. 114, 1988

half-pie *adverb*
not fully *AUSTRALIA*
- I reckon they'd half-pie know who it is too.—Robert G. Barrett, *Davo's Little Something*, p. 238, 1992
- I got half-pie interested then but do you reckon I could crack it for a chat? Nah.—Paul Vautin, *Turn It Up!*, p. 80, 1995

half piece *noun*
14g (½ oz) of a powdered drug, especially heroin *US, 1938*
- —Robert Ashton, *This Is Heroin*, p. 209, 2002

half-pint *noun*
a short person *US, 1876*
From the non-metric measure of volume.
- "Say, Melvin, who is that half-pint con with the magazine?" Joe asks, to halt Melvin.—Iceberg Slim (Robert Beck), *Doom Fox*, p. 220, 1978

half-pipe *noun*
a trough in a snow slope used for aerial manoeuvres in snowboarding *US*
- —Doug Werner, *Snowboarders Start-Up*, p. 112, 1993: 'Glossary'

half-power *noun*
a worker working with a hangover *US*
- —A.B. Chance Co., *Lineman's Slang Dictionary*, p. 8, 1980

half-rack *noun*
in the US, half a case of beer (12 bottles or cans); in Canada, a six-pack of beer *US*
- —Jim Crotty, *How to Talk American*, p. 310, 1997

half-scooped; hauf-scooped *adjective*

tipsy *UK: SCOTLAND*

- On yer bike, you. Ye're no turnin up hauf-scooped tae take me oot. —Michael Munro, *The Patter, Another Blast*, p. 31, 1988

half-seas-over *adjective*

half-drunk *UK, 1700*

- Hey, what's up – are you feeling a half seas over shipmate? —Barry Humphries, *Bazza Pulls It Off!*, 1971
- They are "up the monument" or "half seas over"; they are "on a bender", "out of it" or "off their tits". —Peter Ackroyd, *London The Biography*, p. 359, 2000

half-sheet *noun*

a punishment, usually a fine, received by a prison warder *UK, 1950*

This generalised term derives from the half-sheet of blank paper that an officer is given to explain his conduct.

- [M]ake sure no one had it away. Which if it did happen would cost some one half a sheet. —Frank Norman, *Bang To Rights*, p. 39, 1958

half smart *adjective*

stupid *US, 1927*

- —Ned Wallish, *The Truth Dictionary of Racing Slang*, p. 36, 1989

half-soaked *adjective*

moderately competent *UK*

- I think it's important to realise that any half-soaked fucker with a bit of luck can end up strolling down red carpets[.] —Frank Skinner, *Frank Skinner*, p. 36, 2001

half stamp *noun*

a tramp *UK, 1984*

Rhyming slang.

half-step *verb*

to make a half-hearted, insincere effort *US*

- —Richard McAlister, *Rapper's Handbook*, p. 1, 1990
- —William K. Bentley and James M. Corbett, *Prison Slang*, p. 15, 1992
- —Mark S. Fleisher, *Beggars & Thieves*, p. 289, 1995: 'Glossary'

half-stepper *noun*

a person who does things half way and cannot be counted on *US*

- —*Maledicta*, p. 265, Summer/Winter 1981: 'By its slang, ye shall know it: the pessimism of prison life'

half tanked *adjective*

mildy drunk *AUSTRALIA*

- And Chilla was randy, as was usual when he was half tanked or worried, which was most of the time these days[.] —Frank Hardy, *The Outcasts of Foolgarah*, p. 114, 1971

half track *noun*

crack cocaine *UK, 1998*

Rhyming slang.

- —Mike Haskins, *Drugs*, p. 281, 2003

half-wit *noun*

a stupid fool *UK, 1755*

- Optimistic Conservatives have concluded [...] that Britain will now follow America in electing a rightwing half-wit who no one can quite believe got the job. —*The Guardian*, 31st March 2001

half your luck

you're so lucky! *AUSTRALIA, 1933*

Elliptical for 'I wish I had half your luck'.

- 'I'll be glad to get on that plane this afternoon,' Judith said with feeling. Sancha sighed. 'Half your luck.' —Blanche d'Alpuget, *Turtle Beach*, p. 284, 1981

halibut head *noun*

to the indigenous peoples of Alaska, a white person *US*

- —Robert O. Bowen, *An Alaskan Dictionary*, p. 17, 1965

halter *noun*

a necktie *US*

- —*San Francisco Examiner*, p. III-2, 22nd March 1960

halvsies *noun*

1 half a share of something that is to be divided *US, 1927*

Variants include 'halfsies' and 'halfies'.

- The blackjack Dealer goes "halfies" with a player who is also a friend of his. —Mario Puzo, *Inside Las Vegas*, p. 224, 1977
- Just figured you wanted halfies. —Piri Thomas, *Stories from El Barrio*, p. 87, 1978
- Maybe we'll go halfsies on a keg. —Carl Hiaasen, *Native Tongue*, p. 401, 1991

2 mutual oral sex performed simultaneously *US*

- —*American Speech*, p. 19, Spring 1985: 'The language of singles bars'

ham *noun*

1 an amateur shortwave radio operator and enthusiast *US, 1919*

- A civilian Navy employee working on Siapan yesterday was expressing gratitude for two radio hams who put him in indirect contact with members of his family in Richmond. —*San Francisco Examiner*, p. 27, 27th March 1947
- Heathrow air traffic controllers are searching for a radio ham in the Windsor area who could unwittingly be triggering the crash warning system on planes approaching the airport. —*The Guardian*, 27th March 2003

2 theatrical antics *US, 1930*

- The afternoon will be pure ham. —Oscar Zeta Acosta, *The Revolt of the Cockroach People*, p. 95, 1973

3 in circus and carnival usage, food or a meal *US*

- —Don Wilmeth, *The Language of American Popular Entertainment*, p. 123, 1981

4 any type of alcoholic drink *US*

- —Vann Wesson, *Generation X Field Guide and Lexicon*, p. 86, 1997

5 a member of the armed forces in complete dress uniform *US*

- —Linda Reinberg, *In the Field*, p. 101, 1991

6 overtime *UK*

- —Frank McKenna, *A Glossary of Railwaymen's Talk*, 1970

ham *verb*

1 to over-act, to be an inferior actor *US, 1930*

- [Warren] Mitchell is in his element as Solomon, bent-backed, hamming furiously, his caterpillar eyebrows doing a whole separate show of their own[.] —*The Guardian*, 10th September 2003

2 to walk *US*

- —Joseph E. Ragen and Charles Finston, *Inside the World's Toughest Prison*, p. 802, 1962: 'Penitentiary and underworld glossary'

▸ **ham it up**

to behave theatrically, to exaggerate *US, 1955*

- [Actor, David Jason] was always a bit prone to ham it up. —*The Observer*, 23rd December 2001

ham actor; ham actress; ham *noun*

an unsubtle actor *US, 1881*

- [Michael] Caine is O'Malley, an ageing ham actor playing Richard III in an absurd Nazi-era staging. —*The Guardian*, 16th May 2003

ham and beef *noun*

a *chief* prison warder *UK*

Rhyming slang.

ham and egg; ham *noun*

the leg *UK, 1932*

Rhyming slang.

- Usually employed in relation to the shapely female variety. —Ray Puxley, *Cockney Rabbit*, 1992

ham-and-egger *noun*

1 in professional wrestling, a wrestler whose regular role is to lose to help the careers of others *US*

A slight variation on the boxing original.

- Naively, I expected to be furnished with the vital statistics of every wrestler, including the unknown ham and eggers who got pounded by the stars for TV. —Larry Nelson and Jim Jones, *Strangehold*, p. 42, 1999

2 in oil drilling, an operator who has suffered loss after loss and is now burdened with poor credit *US*

- —Jerry Robertson, *Oil Slanguage*, p. 63, 1954

3 an inconsequential person who has achieved little *US*

- 'Who is this jerk?' I say. 'Why is he on this? Little ham-and-egger here, everybody knows him.' —George V. Higgins, *Penance for Jerry Kennedy*, p. 234, 1985

ham and egging *verb*

a general system or understanding that allows different members of a sports team to achieve best performances at complementary times *US, 1997*

- — Susie Dent, *The Language Report*, p. 52, 2003

ham and eggs cap *noun*

▷ see: SCRAMBLED EGGS CAP

hambone *noun*

1 a male striptease act *AUSTRALIA*
A popular male display in the 1960s.
- [A]nd then Phil did this king hambone on the kitchen table and ran round the house in the raw ripping the gear off all the birds[.] — Martin Sharp, *Oz*, 1964
- Hambones, unfortunately are not restricted to parties. I have seen similar performances in top class restaurants and at society balls. — Sue Rhodes, *Now you'll think I'm awful*, p. 57, 1967

2 a trombone *US, 1934*
- — Lou Shelly, *Hepcats Jive Dictionary*, p. 12, 1945

3 a telephone *UK*
Rhyming slang.
- — Ray Puxley, *Cockney Rabbit*, 1992

4 a black prisoner *US*
- — James Harris, *A Convict's Dictionary*, p. 29, 1989

hamburger *noun*
a socially inept outcast *US, 1949*
High school usage.
- — *Washington Post*, 23rd April 1961: 'Man, did this jazz'

hamburger helper *noun*

1 crack cocaine *US*
The drug bears some resemblance to a brand name food product.
- — US Department of Justice, *Street Terms*, October 1994

2 a linear amplifier for a citizens' band radio *US*
- — Lanie Dills, *The Official CB Slanguage Language Dictionary*, p. 38, 1976

Hamburger Hill *nickname*
Dong Ap Bia Mountain, in South Vietnam close to the Laos border *US*
Taken at great cost by the US Marines in battle in May 1969, and then quietly abandoned a week later. Of marginal tactical importance and ultimately symbolic of the lack of military vision.
- But during the first five hours of Hamburger Hill, fifteen medics were hit, ten were killed. — Ronald J. Glasser, *365 Days*, p. 41, 1971
- — Linda Reinberg, *In the Field*, p. 101, 1991

hamburger home *noun*
a boarding house used by oil field workers *US*
- — Jerry Robertson, *Oil Slanguage*, p. 92, 1954

hame; haim; haym *noun*
a job, especially a menial or unpleasant one *US, 1941*
- A haim is a job, but junkies don't bother with 'em. — Clarence Cooper Jr, *The Scene*, p. 55, 1960
- His bread (money) had dwindled by this time and he knew that he had to cop him a haym (job). — Babs Gonzales, *I Paid My Dues*, p. 95, 1967

hamfat *noun*
an amateur performer *US, 1911*
- Around the poolroom I defended the guys I felt were my real brothers, the colored musicians who made music that sent me, not a lot of beat-up old hamfats who sang and played a commercial excuse for the real thing. — Mezz Mezzrow, *Really the Blues*, p. 49, 1946

hamhock circuit *noun*
a tour of black bars and nightclubs *US*
- B.B. has been out here twenty years playing the ham-hock circuit. — Babs Gonzales, *Movin' On Down De Line*, p. 105, 1975

Hamilton *noun*
a ten-dollar note *US, 1948*
From the engraving of Alexander Hamilton on the note.
- Having counted ten Hamiltons out of the corner of her eye, and knowing what good times they would buy, Lacy was about to do as requested[.] — Robert Campbell, *In La-La Land We Trust*, p. 1, 1986

hammed *adjective*
drunk *US*
- — Pamela Munro, *U.C.L.A. Slang*, p. 75, 1997

hammer *noun*

1 the penis *US*
- — Dale Gordon, *The Dominion Sex Dictionary*, p. 81, 1967

2 a handgun *US*
- Hours after the shootng death of graduate student AL-Moez Alimohamed, two of his alleged teen-age killers reportedly sat in jail laughing and singing."Yo, I got my hammer," Ollie "Homicide" Taylor, 15, and Anthony Archer, 15, rapped through their laughter. — *Times-Picayune (New Orleans)*, p. A11, 2nd October 1994

3 heroin *NEW ZEALAND, 1982*
- They just seem to think that they are ordinary people selling hammer (as they call heroin). — Frank Hardy, *Hardy's People*, p. 105, 1986
- — Harry Orsman, *A Dictionary of Modern New Zealand Slang*, p. 63, 1999
- "Then some cunt in Sydney had the bright idea that the hippies might get tired of smoking their own shit, and they might like the hammer." "The hammer?" "Heroin." — Brian Preston, *Pot Planet*, p. 91, 2002
- — Mike Haskins, *Drugs*, p. 284, 2003

4 an attractive girl or young woman *US, 1970*
- — David Claerbaut, *Black Jargon in White America*, p. 67, 1972
- — *American Speech*, p. 154, Spring-Summer 1972: 'An approach to Black slang'

5 a pizza with ham topping *US*
- — *Maledicta*, p. 13, 1996: 'Domino's pizza jargon'

6 an accelerator pedal *US, 1974*
Citizens' band radio slang, often as 'back off the hammer' (to slow down) and 'put the hammer down' (to accelerate).
- I says "Pigpen, this here's Rubber Duck / And I'm about to put the hammer down. — C.W. McCall, *Convoy*, 1976
- Put the hammer down and I didn't let her up until I hit Ludlow. — George V. Higgins, *The Rat on Fire*, p. 106, 1981

7 in shuffleboard, the eighth and final shot *US*
- — Omero C. Catan, *Secrets of Shuffleboard Strategy*, p. 67, 1967: 'Glossary of terms'

8 in bar dice games, the player who wins the chance to play first *US*
- — Jester Smith, *Games They Play in San Francisco*, p. 104, 1971

▸ on your hammer

1 following close behind; tailing *AUSTRALIA, 1942*
From **HAMMER AND NAIL**. Erroneously said by Baker (*The Australian Language*, 1945) to be from 'hammer and tack' for 'track', but 'to be on someone's track' is not idiomatic.
- Wonder why he didn't try and pull round on our hammer, skip? — W.R. Bennett, *Night Intruder*, p. 33, 1962
- If we c'n toss this joker sitting on our hammer. — W.R. Bennett, *Night Intruder*, p. 68, 1962
- There's a bloody night-fighter right on that bloke's hammer! — W.R. Bennett, *Night Intruder*, p. 117, 1962

2 badgering *AUSTRALIA*
From **HAMMER AND TACK**.
- The child was on his hammer from the moment he woke. She pestered him impatiently. — D'Arcy Niland, *The Shiralee*, p. 37, 1955
- I'll keep on Pauline Fraser's hammer[.] — Stuart Mills, *Wives and Lovers*, p. 114, 1976

▸ put the hammer on
to press someone for something *IRELAND*
- He called for a large bottle and paid for it, which led me to presume that he must have put the hammer on Johnny for a few quid. — Billy Roche, *Tumbling Down*, p. 12, 1984

hammer *verb*

1 to drive a vehicle at maximum speed *AUSTRALIA*
- Talking of cars, Paddy and I were really belting it along the big new Middlesex motorway the other week, gave her the gun and bunged her up to ninety and we hammered her the whole way[.] — Barry Humphries, *A Nice Night's Entertainment*, p. 42, 1960

2 to inflict a resounding defeat *UK, 1948*
- Australia gets hammered by the All Blacks in Saturday night's semi-final in Sydney, and loses its coveted World Cup. — *The Belfast Telegraph*, 13th November 2003

3 to beat up *UK, 1973*
- [H]e'd come out of his house and fuckin' beat him up. Hammer him. — Shaun Ryder, *Shaun Ryder... in His Own Words*, 1986

4 to stretch physical limits *UK*
- I've done extra weights, hammered myself, I have – but I do feel fantastic. — Kevin Sampson, *Clubland*, p. 209, 2002

▸ get hammered

1 while surfing, to be knocked from your surfboard and violently thrashed by the surf *US*
- — Michael V. Anderson, *The Bad, Rad, Not to Forget Way Cool Beach and Surf Discriptionary*, p. 6, 1988

2 in mountain biking, to experience a violent accident *US*
- — William Nealy, *Mountain Bike!*, p. 161, 1992: 'Bikespeak'

hammer and discus *noun*
facial hair, whiskers *UK*
Rhyming slang.

hammer and nail; hammer *verb*
to follow, to tail *UK*
Rhyming slang.
- —Julian Franklyn, *A Dictionary of Rhyming Slang*, 1961

hammer and tack *noun*
the back *AUSTRALIA*
Rhyming slang.
- —Jim Ramsay, *Cop It Sweet!*, p. 43, 1977
- —Ryan Aven-Bray, *Ridgey Didge Oz Jack Lang*, p. 31, 1983

hammer and tongs *adverb*
energetically; vigorously, strongly; violently *UK, 1708*
From the vigorous use a blacksmith makes of these tools.
- Frankie's going hammer and tongs with his latest squeeze [girlfriend]. — *The Guardian*, 25th May 2002

hammer-blowed *adjective*
drunk *UK*
- — *e-cyclopaedia*, 20th March 2002

hammered *adjective*
drunk *US, 1960*
- —Collin Baker et al., *College Undergraduate Slang Study Conducted at Brown University*, p. 133, 1968
- "Fin!" she cried suddenly. "I got a flash for you. We're hammered. Smashed. Fried. Tanked." —Joseph Wambaugh, *Finnegan's Week*, p. 157, 1993
- NANA: Looking forward to the wedding, Dave? DAVE: Oh aye, big style. I can't wait. I'll be hammered by eight. —Caroline Aherne and Craig Cash, *The Royle Family*, 1999
- [F]irst we hammered out a peace treaty, then we all got hammered and laughed about the end of the war. —Ralph "Sonny" Barger, *Hell's Angel*, p. 149, 2000
- [H]ammered, blitzed, mashed, off-your-tits[.] —Stuart Walton, *Out of It*, cover, 2001

hammerhead *noun*
one of several kinds of inferior horse *US, 1941*
- Well, you have seen her horse. Most cowboy's horses are sorry-looking beasts, bang-tails, hammer-heads, scruffy animals with questionable parentage. Then there is that black she is riding. —George Bowering, *Caprice*, p. 195, 1987

hammerheading *noun*
an act of taking a recreational drug cocktail of MDMA, the recreational drug best known as ecstasy, and Viagra™ (a branded drug that enables a male erection) *UK*
From the after-effect of a throbbing headache.

hammering *noun*
a defeat, a significant defeat; a beating *UK, 1900*
- Independent reporters not embedded with UK and US military units were taking a "hammering". — *The Guardian*, 9th April 2003

hammer man *noun*
a male of considerable sexual prowess *IRELAND*
Related to the expression 'going at it hammer and tongs' to describe highly energetic sexual activity.
- He's some hammer-man, he must have scooby-dooed half of Abbeytown. —Eamonn Sweeney, *Waiting for the Healer*, p. 182, 1997

hammers *noun*
the female thighs *US*
- —Edith A. Folb, *runnin' down some lines*, p. 241, 1980

hammer-slammer *noun*
an airframe technician *US*
US Army usage.
- — *Seattle Times*, p. A9, 12th April 1998: 'Grunts, squids not grunting from the same dictionary'

hammer time *noun*
a decisive point; the time to launch a military attack *US*
Adapted from a catchphrase attached, in the late 1980s, to California rapper MC Hammer.
- But make no mistake, when the president says go, look out, it's hammer time, OK? It is hammer time. —Vice Admiral Timothy Keating, Commander, US 5th Fleet, *CNN*, 19th March 2003

hammock *noun*
a sanitary towel *UK*
Generally used by young males, often in the jocular formula: 'hammock for a bleeding lazy cunt'.
- —Chris Lewis, *The Dictionary of Playground Slang*, p. 111, 2003

hammock for two *noun*
a brassiere *US*
- — *American Speech*, p. 273, December 1963: 'American Indian student slang'

hammock season *noun*
the bleed period of the menstrual cycle *SOUTH AFRICA*
The image of a sanitary towel as a **WEE HAMMOCK** or 'mouse's hammock'.
- — *The Museum of Menstruation and Women's Health*, January 2001

hammy; hammie *noun*
a hamstring *AUSTRALIA*
- Unfortunately, once you've 'done a hammy' it never seems to be quite the same. —Ivor Limb, *Footy's No Joke!*, p. 39, 1986
- You can quickly get over a pulled hammy, a dickey calf or even a stiff Achilles. — *Evening Post*, p. 30, 5th February 2002

hammy *adjective*
melodramatic, theatrical *US, 1899*
- A little at a time at first, hammy gestures, a few mugging expressions. —Evan Hunter, *The Blackboard Jungle*, p. 122, 1954

ham patch *noun*
a telephone connection enabled by shortwave radio *ANTARCTICA*
- —Carnegie Mellon Astrophysics Peterson Group, *Antarctic Vocabulary*, 19th September 1997

Hampden roar *noun*
the state of affairs, the current situation *UK: SCOTLAND*
Rhyming slang for **THE SCORE**, formed from 'Scotland's National Stadium' and the roar of a football crowd.
- What's the Hampden roar? —Michael Munro, *The Original Patter*, 1985

Hampstead Heath; hampsteads; ampstids; hamps *noun*
the teeth *UK, 1887*
Rhyming slang, from a rural area of north London.
- [T]he rot had set in something horrible with her hampsteads and scotches [the legs], not to mention the boat [the face]. —Derek Raymond (Robin Cook), *The Crust on its Uppers*, p. 34, 1962
- [B]efore the invention of false hampsteads when everyone spoke funny. —Andrew Nickolds, *Back to Basics*, p. 53, 1994

Hampton Court; hampton *noun*
salt *UK*
Rhyming slang, formed on a historic Surrey location. Recorded, with a warning not to confuse it with **HAMPTON WICK** (the penis) by Ray Puxley, *Cockney Rabbit*, 1992.

Hampton Wick; Hampton; Wick *noun*
1 a penis *UK*
Rhyming slang for **PRICK** (the penis), after a suburb of London. A polite euphemism in its reduced forms.
- —Julian Franklyn, *A Dictionary of Rhyming Slang*, 1960
- He gets on me wick. — *Uncut*, p. 92, June 2001
- [N]ot much blood comes in and out so your hampton remains small. —Richard Herring, *Talking Cock*, p. 157, 2003

2 a fool *UK*
Rhyming slang for **PRICK** (general term of offence).
- I'm the Blackmail Man / Hampton Wick—Ian Dury, *Blackmail Man*, 1977

ham sandwich *noun*
language *UK: SCOTLAND*
Glasgow rhyming slang; this is a convincing rhyme in the appropriate accent.
- Just keep the ham sangwidge respectable in front a ma aul dear, eh? —Michael Munro, *The Patter, Another Blast*, 1988

ham shank *noun*
1 an American *UK*
Rhyming slang for **YANK**. Recorded by Julian Franklyn, *A Dictionary of Rhyming Slang*, 1961, as a World War 2 Merchant Navy coinage to describe American ships or men, subsequently adopted by the Americans.
- —Mark McShane, *The Straight and Crooked*, 1960

2 a bank *UK*
Rhyming slang.
- [I]t's the parlous state of your average High Street ham-shank. —Andrew Nickolds, *Back to Basics*, p. 51, 1994

3 an act of masturbation *UK*
Rhyming slang for **WANK**.
- —John Ayto, *The Oxford Dictionary of Rhyming Slang*, 2002

ham stealer *noun*
a thief who steals to eat, rather than for profit *US*
- Now he's known as Greasy Wheeler, the boss ham stealer. —Dennis Wepman et al., *The Life*, p. 78, 1976

hamster *noun*
a discrete piece of computer code that does what it is supposed to do well *US*
- The image is of a hamster happily spinning its exercise wheel. —Eric S. Raymond, *The New Hacker's Dictionary*, p. 194, 1991

hamster crab; crab *noun*
a type of scratch (a manipulation of a record to create a musical effect) *UK*
Derives from the crab-like movements of the DJ's fingers; 'hamster' is a reference to the hamster switch.
- [W]e are going to describe this in the hamster position (known as hamster crab) as opposed to normal crab. —J. Hoggarth (quoting DJ Olsen), *How To Be a DJ*, p. 96, 2002

hamster-style *noun*
a method of manipulating record turntables in which the priorities are reversed *UK*
DJ jargon; on a sound mixer the hamster switch is a crossfader reverse switch, so named for the 'BulletProof Scratch Hamsters' who are credited with its invention in the mid-1990s.
- I think it's easier to get your head round hamster-style than normal. —J. Hoggarth (quoting Precise), *How To Be a DJ*, p. 89, 2002

Hancock *verb*
to sign *US, 1967*
A shortened version of **JOHN HANCOCK**. From his admirable signature on the Declaration of Independence.
- I'm gonna stick him up for a hundred grand before I Hancock a fucking contract. —Iceberg Slim (Robert Beck), *Long White Con*, p. 180, 1977

hand *noun*
five; in betting, odds of 5 – 1 *UK*
From the **TICK-TACK**five; signal used by bookmakers.
- —John McCririck, *John McCririck's World of Betting*, p. 60, 1991

▸ **do it with one hand tied behind your back**
to do something very easily *UK, 1984*
- Fulham won with one hand tied behind their backs. —*The Guardian*, 9th December 2002

▸ **hand has no hair**
used for expressing a willingness to accept money in the present situation *TRINIDAD AND TOBAGO, 1982*
- —Lise Winer, *Dictionary of the English/Creole of Trinidad & Tobago*, 2003

hand *verb*

▸ **hand it to**
to admit the superiority of someone or something *US, 1914*
- But you have to hand it to the Trots – they can still produce huge numbers of identical hand held placards on the latest "ishoo" apparently overnight. —*The Guardian*, 25th September 2000

HAND
in text messaging, *have a nice day* *UK, 2003*

hand and a half *noun*
in betting, odds of 11 – 2 *UK*
In bookmaker slang **HAND** is 5 – 1, here the addition of a 'half' increases the odds to 5½ – 1 or 11 – 2.
- —John McCririck, *John McCririck's World of Betting*, p. 112, 1991

hand and fist *adjective*
drunk *UK*
Rhyming slang, always used in full, for **PISSED**.
- —Ray Puxley, *Cockney Rabbit*, 1992

H and B *adjective*
sexually aroused; *hot and bothered* *US*
- —Collin Baker et al., *College Undergraduate Slang Study Conducted at Brown University*, p. 132, 1968

handbag *noun*

1 an attractive male escort for a woman at a social engagement *AUSTRALIA*
- And every true bitch knows the value to her social standing, of the type of men best described as 'handbags'. They're lovely to look at, beautifully dressed and totally brainless. —Sue Rhodes, *Now you'll think I'm awful*, p. 70, 1967
- —Sue Rhodes, *And when she was bad she was popular*, p. 15, 1968
- You're training me to become your human handbag that you can take on your arm to premieres and dinner parties. —Kathy Lette, *Girls' Night Out*, p. 181, 1987
- Like the time she described James Packer as a 'handbag', something that apparently made him unhappy. —*Sydney Morning Herald (Good Weekend)*, p. 17, 22nd June 1996

2 a male homosexual *AUSTRALIA*
- According to all the reputable sources, his Greatness was not only the conqueror of the known world and then some, but also a Screaming Handbag. —Ignatius Jones, *The 1992 True Hip Manual*, p. 94, 1992

3 money *UK, 1984*
Also variant 'hambag'.
- —Paul Baker, *Polari*, p. 177, 2002
- —*Attitude*, p. 60, July 2003: 'New palare lexicon'

handbag-positive *adjective*
applied to a confused and disoriented patient, lying in a hospital bed, clutching their handbag or purse *UK*
A jocular medical condition.
- —Adam T. Fox, St Mary's Hospital, London, 10th October 2002

handbags *noun*
a minor verbal or physical disagreement, especially on a sports pitch *UK*
- — Susie Dent, *The Language Report*, p. 52, 2003

Handbags *nickname*
second battalion, Royal Green Jackets *UK*
- —Andy McNab, *Immediate Action*, p. 17, 1995

handbags at dawn
a minor verbal or physical disagreement *UK*
- "Our solicitors are now going to study the programme and we will then decide what action to take." Handbags at dawn this morning, then. —*The Guardian*, 17th October 2003

handbags at ten paces
a conflict that, despite its potential for violent confrontation, comes to nothing more than posturing *UK*
The number of paces may vary.
- Then a scuffle broke out between Brentford's Bates and Albion's Bradely. 'Handbags at 10 paces,' said Bobby Gould, Albion's manager, with a glint in his eye. —*The Guardian*, 21st October 1991
- At the crossroads it's handbags at thirty paces, with the police firmly implanted in the middle of the two mobs. —Martin King and Martin Knight, *The Naughty Nineties*, p. 66, 1999
- Mind you, it wasn't much more explosive than handbags at 30 paces. —*Sunday Mirror*, p. 55, 31st January 1999
- — Susie Dent, *The Language Report*, p. 81, 2003

handball *verb*
to insert your lubricated hand into your partner's rectum or vagina, providing sexual pleasure for both *US*
- —*What Color is Your Handkerchief*, p. 5, 1979
- —Wayne Dynes, *Homolexis*, p. 64, 1985

handballing *noun*
the insertion of a hand and fist into a person's rectum or vagina for sexual gratification *US*
- Anal fisting, also known as handballing, is the gradual process of putting your hand (and for very experienced players, sometimes your forearm) inside someone's ass. —*The Village Voice*, 2nd November 1999

hand bomb *verb*
to throw a just-caught salmon using both hands *CANADA*
- "Hand bombing" is, in British Columbia commercial fishing, to pitch fresh salmon using both hands. Troll-caught fish must not be handled carelessly by the tail, or with tools, to avoid marking the skin, as these fish are often sold whole. —Tom Parkin, *WetCoast Words*, p. 66, 1989

handbook *noun*
a bookmaker who operates on the street, without the benefit of a fixed office *US*
- Like all handbooks though, he was scared of plain-clothes vice-cops but completely ignored uniformed policemen. —Joseph Wambaugh, *The Blue Knight*, p. 47, 1973

handbrake *noun*

a wife or girlfriend, seen as preventing a man from having a good time *AUSTRALIA*

- —Eric Spilstead, *The Great Aussie Slang Book*, p. 10, 1998

handbrakie *noun*

a handbrake turn *AUSTRALIA*

- —James Lambert, *The Macquarie Book of Slang*, 1996

H and C *noun*

a mixture of *h*eroin *and* *c*ocaine *US, 1971*

A play on 'hot and cold', shown on taps as H and C.

- — US Department of Justice, *Street Terms*, October 1994
- —Angela Devlin, *Prison Patter*, p. 59, 1996
- —Robert Ashton, *This Is Heroin*, p. 209, 2002

hand cannon *noun*

a large pistol *US, 1929*

Used for effect, quaintly old-fashioned.

- VINCENT: Why the fuck didn't you tell us about that guy in the bathroom? Slip your mind? Forget he was in there with a goddamn hand cannon?— *Pulp Fiction*, 1994

handcuff *noun*

an engagement or wedding ring *US, 1926*

- —Marcus Hanna Boulware, *Jive and Slang of Students in Negro Colleges*, 1947
- —Vincent J. Monteleone, *Criminal Slang*, p. 112, 1949

handcuffed *adjective*

married *US*

- —Lou Shelly, *Hepcats Jive Dictionary*, p. 12, 1945

hand-doodle *noun*

to masturbate *US*

- Bab, the most beautiful Jew ever to come out of Fex, took exception to all this hand-doodling. But I maintained that masturbation is an end in itself.—Angelo d'Arcangelo, *The Homosexual Handbook*, p. 88, 1968

H and E *noun*

high explosives *US*

- Pressed into the ground, Mayfield saw the shadow pass by, heard the same deafening roar, and this time the incredible explosions of H and E.—Ronald J. Glasser, *365 Days*, p. 34, 1971

-handed *suffix*

denotes the specific or general size of a gang when combined with a unit of measurement, e.g. two-, ten-, mob-handed *UK*

- "They're here!" they gasped, almost disbelievingly. "How many?" "Forty-handed at least."— Martin King and Martin Knight, *The Naughty Nineties*, p. 199, 1999
- [R]eal villains and gangsters don't consider themselves villains and gangsters, and don't go around "firm-handed" showing they are hard.—Dave Courtney, *Stop the Ride I Want to Get Off*, p. 4, 1999

hand fuck *verb*

to insert your lubricated fist into a partner's rectum or vagina, leading to sexual pleasure for both *US*

- — *What Color is Your Handkerchief*, p. 5, 1979

handful *noun*

1 a troublesome person who is difficult to control; something difficult to control *UK, 1887*

- Until recently, when it became a bit of a handful and they gave it away, Frank Bonner and his family had a pet dog – a beagle.— *The Guardian*, 18th August 2000

2 a prison sentence of five years *US, 1930*

- —Hyman E. Goldin et al., *Dictionary of American Underworld Lingo*, p. 90, 1950
- —Angela Devlin, *Prison Patter*, p. 60, 1996

3 in a restaurant or soda fountain, five *US*

- — *American Speech*, p. 62, February 1967: 'Soda-fountain, restaurant and tavern calls'

4 in racing, five *UK, 1937*

As high as you can count on one hand. To win by 'a couple of handfuls' is to win by ten lengths.

5 five pounds (£5) *UK, 1961*

6 gambling odds of 5 – 1, especially among bookmakers *UK, 1984*

▸ **have a handful**

to fondle a woman's breasts, buttocks or genitals *UK*

- —David Powis, *The Signs of Crime*, 1977

hand gallop *noun*

an act of male masturbation *US*

- In Lewisburg he used to tell me he was saving it up, no hand-gallops for him[.]—George V. Higgins, *The Friends of Eddie Doyle*, p. 43, 1971

hand grenaded *adjective*

(used of a racing car engine) exploded and damaged *US*

- —Don Alexander, *The Racer's Dictionary*, p. 30, 1980

handicap *noun*

a sexually transmitted infection, especially gonorrhoea *UK*

Rhyming slang for **CLAP**.

- —Ray Puxley, *Cockney Rabbit*, 1992

handicap chase; handicap *noun*

a face, especially an ugly face *UK*

Rhyming slang.

- Look at the handicap on that poor sod.—Ray Puxley, *Cockney Rabbit*, 1992

handie *noun*

an act of manual masturbation *AUSTRALIA*

From **HAND JOB**.

- Do you think that when I'm old and smelly like Dick I'll be giving deros handies for a beer?—Helen Barnes, *The Crypt Orchid*, p. 37, 1994

handies *noun*

fondling of hands by lovers *AUSTRALIA, 1915*

handing out *noun*

in prison, the act of separating an imprisoned mother from her baby (subject to disciplinary exceptions the parent and child may spend up to eighteen months in a mother and baby unit) *UK*

- —Angela Devlin, *Prison Patter*, p. 60, 1996

hand jig; hand gig *noun*

masturbation *US*

- —Joseph E. Ragen and Charles Finston, *Inside the World's Toughest Prison*, p. 802, 1962: 'Penitentiary and underworld glossary'
- You know most of the punks, they don't take it in the ass at all. They just give hand-jigs or they'll give blowjobs.—Bruce Jackson, *In the Life*, p. 399, 1972
- — *Male Swinger Number 3*, p. 45, 1981: 'The complete gay dictionary'
- —Charles Shafer, *Folk Speech in Texas Prisons*, p. 205, 1990

hand jive *noun*

1 a rhythmic pattern of hand-movements performed to music as a substitute for more usual forms of dance; hence, obscure hand signals *US, 1958*

- —Johnny Otis, *Willie and the Hand Jive*, 1958
- Hand-jive high-fives are all very well if conducted by 7ft larger-than-life basketball players.— *The Guardian*, 24th October 2003

2 an act of masturbating a male *UK*

- I did the hand jive to stop him whining all night.—Chris Lewis, *The Dictionary of Playground Slang*, p. 111, 2003

hand job *noun*

1 manual stimulation of another's genitals *US, 1937*

- —Donald Webster Cory and John P. LeRoy, *The Homosexual and His Society*, p. 264, 1963: 'A lexicon of homosexual slang'
- The handjob is so basic it is like reading and writing.—*Screw*, 6th October 1969
- At Caesar's Retreat, Larry Kleinman was offered a "topless hand job" for $25.—George Paul Csicsery (Editor), *The Sex Industry*, p. 103, 1973
- C carved it in with a nail the night she gave him his first hand job in Big Playground.—Richard Price, *The Wanderers*, p. 5, 1974
- Fourteen, I think. Yeah, fourteen. But I was giving hand jobs before that.—Elmore Leonard, *Switch*, p. 114, 1978
- I ain't had so much as a hand job in a week and I gotta work overtime!—Joseph Wambaugh, *The Glitter Dome*, p. 170, 1981
- Despite their assertion that go-go is only a bit of "good clean fun," many strip-club owners tolerate – or even encourage – prostitution (or "side work," as the dancers call it): a blow job or hand job outside in the parking lot[.]—James Ridgeway, *Red Light*, p. 204, 1996
- I had to give all the guys in the service department hand jobs.— *Romy and Michele's High School Reunion*, 1997
- Give you a hand-job for a fiver, eh?— *The Full Monty*, 1997
- Everything about you is in it. The blow jobs. The hand jobs.— *Cruel Intentions*, 1999
- Basically, my first three hand-jobs were literally dry-runs[.]—Frank Skinner, *Frank Skinner*, p. 198, 2001

2 in trucking, cargo that must be hand-loaded *US*

- —Montie Tak, *Truck Talk*, p. 80, 1971

hand-job *verb*
to masturbate another person *US, 1969*
- In other words, she'd be blowing, fucking, and handjobbing four guys simultaneously, an act that would make her Queen of the Gang-Bang. —Josh Alan Friedman, *Tales of Times Square*, p. 90, 1986

handkerchief head *noun*
a black person *US, 1942*
- "Swamp Guinea," shot back Ray Barrett. "Han'kerchief Head," said Ricky Leopoldi. —Richard Price, *The Wanderers*, p. 160, 1974

handle *noun*
1 a name, a nickname *US, 1837*
- That place never did have a name – we forgot to think one up ahead of time, and after our gala opening we never had time to hang a handle on it. —Mezz Mezzrow, *Really the Blues*, p. 86, 1946
- You had room for all the rest. First name, middle name, last – the whole damned handle. —Jim Thompson, *A Swell-Looking Babe*, p. 85, 1954
- Two of them go as Morgan and Walker. I don't know the slim stud's handle. —Chester Himes, *A Rage in Harlem*, p. 74, 1957
- [T]hey even had the class to pick one of the most righteous handles of all time: the Troggs. —Lester Bangs, *Psychotic Reactions and Carburetor Dung*, p. 53, 1971
- Here's what a guy who goes by the chick-magnet Net handle of "Wampa-One" thinks about Bluntman and Chronic. —Kevin Smith, *Jay and Silent Bob Strike Back*, p. 20, 2001

2 a self-titled identity used on citizens' band radio *US, 1974*
- There are no rules about choosing a handle. —Peter Chippindale, *The British CB Book*, p. 14, 1981

3 a big nose *US, 1750*
- —Lou Shelly, *Hepcats Jive Dictionary*, p. 12, 1945

4 a glass of beer served in a 10 fluid ounce glass with a handle *AUSTRALIA, 1943*
- No schooners here, George, but I guess a handle will do the job. They're about the same size, I'm told. ... These aren't schooner size, mate... They're about the size of a middy. —M.J. Burton, *Bush Pub*, p. 148, 1978

5 a half-pint glass of beer *NEW ZEALAND*
- —Harry Orsman and Des Hurley, *The Beaut Little Book of New Zealand Slang*, 1994

6 in horse racing, the total amount bet, either on a given race or an entire season *US*
- —David W. Maurer, *Argot of the Racetrack*, p. 34, 1951

▸ **get a handle on**
to gain a means of comprehending or controlling someone or something *US, 1972*
- In the last four months I've started to get a handle on it and I can see that it really does work. — *The Guardian*, 26th May 2004

handle *verb*
to stay in control *US*
Hawaiian youth usage as an intransitive verb.
- Oh, wow, man, I too loaded! I cannot handle! —Douglas Simonson, *Pidgin to da Max*, 1981

▸ **handle swollen goods**
(of a male) to masturbate *UK*
Punning a criminal activity: 'to handle stolen goods'.
- Saturday night poses, broken noses, wanks (handling swollen goods)[.] —Mark Powell, *Snap*, p. 224, 2001

handler *noun*
1 a drug dealer who deals in large quantities to retail-level sellers *US*
- —Dale Kramer and Madeline Karr, *Teen-Age Gangs*, p. 175, 1953

2 in drag racing, a driver *US*
- —Lyle K. Engel, *The Complete Book of Fuel and Gas Dragsters*, p. 151, 1968

handles *noun*
in basketball, ball-handling skill *US*
- —Judi Sanders, *Da Bomb!*, p. 14, 1997

handle-slammer *noun*
a person who manipulates the handles of a slot machine that is in need of repair, forcing the machine to pay out regardless of the spin *US*
- —J. Edward Allen, *The Basics of Winning Slots*, p. 57, 1984

hand like a foot *noun*
in card games, a very bad hand of cards *UK*
A pun that was previously used of poor handwriting. Currently in popular use at Internet sites devoted to poker.
- — *Sunday Times*, 15th July 1956

handmade *noun*
1 a large penis *US*
An allusion to the belief that excessive masturbation will produce a larger-than-average penis.
- —Dale Gordon, *The Dominion Sex Dictionary*, p. 81, 1967

2 a hand-rolled cigarette *US*
- I don't know what smoking handmades has to do with horse races[.] —Robert Campbell, *The Cat's Meow*, p. 50, 1988

hand mucker *noun*
in gambling, a cheat who switches cards *US*
- —John Scarne, *Scarne's Guide to Modern Poker*, p. 280, 1979
- Besides dice tats and 7UPS, there were volumes for nail nickers and crimpers (card markers), hand muckers and mit men (card switchers), as well as card counters and shiner players. —Stephen Cannell, *Big Con*, p. 143, 1997

handout *noun*
in prison, the act of giving a prisoner's property to a visitor for removal *UK*
- —Angela Devlin, *Prison Patter*, p. 60, 1996

hand over fist *adverb*
very quickly, especially applied to making or losing money *UK, 1888*
- Railtrack was losing money hand over fist, especially after the Hatfield train crash in October 2000[.] — *The Guardian*, 27th June 2002

hand queen *noun*
a male homosexual who favours masturbating his partner *US*
- —Roger Blake, *The American Dictionary of Sexual Terms*, p. 94, 1964

hand-reared *adjective*
endowed with a large penis *UK, 1961*
A reference to masturbation, presumably with the suggestion that such manipulation promotes growth.

hand relief *noun*
masturbation in the context of a hand-massage – a sexual service offered in some massage parlours *UK*
- VIP massage: massage with hand relief. —Caroline Archer, *Tart Cards*, 2003

hand ride *noun*
in horse racing, a race run without using a whip *US*
- —Les Conklin, *Payday at the Races*, p. 205, 1974

hand-rolled *noun*
a marijuana cigarette *US*
Mildly euphemistic, and thus mildly humorous.
- You want a hand-rolled? —Elmore Leonard, *Switch*, p. 169, 1978

hands *noun*
▸ **put your hands up**
to confess, especially to admit to a crime *UK*
The universal gesture of surrender. The singular 'put your hand up' seems unlikely; it smacks of a schoolchild seeking attention.
- —Peter Laurie, *Scotland Yard*, p. 326, 1970
- He put his hands up = he surrendered or he admitted to all the crimes put to him. —David Powis, *The Signs of Crime*, 1977
- —Angela Devlin, *Prison Patter*, p. 93, 1996

hands and feet *noun*
meat *UK*
Rhyming slang.
- —Ray Puxley, *Cockney Rabbit*, 1992

hands and heels *adjective*
in horse racing, used for describing a ride in which the jockey did not use his whip *AUSTRALIA*
- —Ned Wallish, *The Truth Dictionary of Racing Slang*, p. 36, 1989

handshake *noun*
1 the synchronisation mechanism of two computers or two programs *US*
- —Eric S. Raymond, *The New Hacker's Dictionary*, p. 195, 1991

2 to engage in mutual masturbation *US*
- Mutual masturbation, or "hand-shaking," however, presents a different situation and would seem to constitute a perverted act. — *New York Mattachine Newsletter*, p. 7, June 1961

hand shandy; handy shandy *noun*
an act of male masturbation *UK*
- Babies be bollocksed. Nowadays it's a quick hand-shandy in a test-tube and you're out the door, mate. — *The Full Monty*, 1997
- With prostitutes it's favours offered, usually a blowjob or hand shandy. — Duncan MacLaughlin, *The Filth*, p. 81, 2002
- Something new had to be coined to cover getting stocious on Bailey's and giving the new Financial Services Advisor a hand-shandy[.] — Christopher Brookmyre, *The Sacred Art of Stealing*, p. 71, 2002
- You can have a hand job – a handy shandy is fine. — Phil Hammond, *An A to Z of Rude Health*, 25th January 2002
- — Chris Lewis, *The Dictionary of Playground Slang*, p. 112, 2003

hand shoe *noun*
a glove *US*
- — Ramon Adams, *The Language of the Railroader*, p. 74, 1977

hands off cocks – feet in socks!; hands off your cocks and pull up your socks!; hands off cocks – on with socks!; hands off cocks, on socks!
used for awakening sleeping men *UK, 1984*
Military. Remembered from national service.

handsome!
excellent, first-rate; used for registering approval *UK*
- "Bust a left, Russ," instructed Ron[...] "What here?" questioned Russell. "Handsome." — Greg Williams, *Diamond Geezers*, p. 47, 1997

hand thing *noun*
the act of masturbating a man *US*
A variation of **HAND-JOB**.
- Twenty [dollars] for a hand thing. You go into overtime if you take all day. — Janet Evanovich, *Seven Up*, p. 94, 2001

hand-to-gland combat *noun*
an act of masturbation, especially if conducted with vigour *AUSTRALIA*
A pun on 'hand-to-hand combat'.
- — Chris Lewis, *The Dictionary of Playground Slang*, p. 112, 2003

hand tools *noun*
lockpicks, screwdrivers and other tools used by burglars *US*
- — Ralph de Sola, *Crime Dictionary*, p. 61, 1982

hand to rouf *noun*
in betting, odds of 5–4 *UK*
A combination of **HAND** (five) and **ROUF** (four) when, if used alone, each word signifies more than the number itself.
- — John McCririck, *John McCririck's World of Betting*, p. 112, 1991

hand up *verb*
to incriminate *UK*
- In fact he felt the full force of the law after repeatedly refusing to turn Queen's and hand up me, Vince and Sid. — Danny King, *The Bank Robber Diaries*, p. 56, 2002

handwave *verb*
to oversimplify or give a cursory explanation of a complicated point *US*
- — Guy L. Steele, *Coevolution Quarterly*, p. 31, Spring 1981: 'Computer Slang'
- If someone starts a sentence with "Clearly..." or "Obviously..." or "It is self-evident that...," you can be sure he is about to handwave. — Guy L. Steele et al., *The Hacker's Dictionary*, p. 81, 1983

handy *noun*
among antique dealers, an antique small enough to conceal in the palm of the hand *UK*
- He bought a few handies off me[.] — Jonathan Gash, *The Ten Word Game*, p. 137, 2003

handy *adjective*
good at fighting *UK*
- Ron needed people who could be a bit handy, who could put it about a bit[.] — Greg Williams, *Diamond Geezers*, p. 95, 1997

hane *adjective*
disgusting *US*
An abbreviation of **HEINOUS**.
- — *Washington Post*, 14th October 1993

hang *noun*
1 a little bit *UK, 1861*
Used as a euphemism for 'damn'; always in the negative.
- Mike, you're too damned big and tough to give a hang what people say. — Mickey Spillane, *One Lonely Night*, p. 15, 1951
- Shoot, my old man don't give a hang whether I'm in jail or dead in a car wreck or drunk in the gutter. — S.E. Hinton, *The Outsiders*, p. 78, 1967

2 used as a euphemism for 'hell' *SOUTH AFRICA, 1960*
- — Penny Silva, *A Dictionary of South African English*, 1996
- — David McGill, *David McGill's Complete Kiwi Slang Dictionary*, p. 54, 1998

3 a person who regularly spends time in one place, or around people and places that are in some way associated *US*
- He was never really a hang at the scene, you wouldn't see him in the clubs. — David Anderle, *quoted in Waiting For The Sun*, p. 124, 1996

4 a job *US, 1950*
- — Clarence Major, *Dictionary of Afro-American Slang*, p. 64, 1970
- — Hermese E. Roberts, *The Third Ear*, 1971

▸ **get the hang of**
to learn how to do something *US, 1847*
- I can drive pretty good [...] Got the hang of it when I was doing this job as a vanboy. — John Peter Jones, *Feather Pluckers*, p. 38, 1964

▸ **give a hang; care a hang**
to care, to be concerned – usually in a negative context *UK, 1861*
- I don't give a hang what he does / As long as he does what he likes! — Oscar Hammerstein, II, *Soliloquy [Carousel]*, 1945
- [T]hey did not care a hang for the "socialist ministers"[.] — P. D. Uspenskii, *In Search of the Miraculous*, 1949
- I don't give a hang about women[.] — Witi Ihimaera, *The Whale Rider*, p. 72, 1987

hang *verb*
1 to make a turn while driving a car *US, 1967*
- — *Current Slang*, p. 6, Spring 1968
- Quick. Hang a right! — *American Graffiti*, 1973
- Bobby nudged him out of his reverie. "Hang a right." — James Ellroy, *Suicide Hill*, p. 600, 1986
- A white Mercedes sedan with clear windows and two men inside hung a left in front of our car. — *The Observer*, 27th July 2003

2 to turn, especially but not exclusively applied to driving a vehicle *US, 1967*
Usually in the phrase 'hang a left/right' (to make a left/right turn).
- — Peter Chippindale, *The British CB Book*, p. 155, 1981

3 to tolerate, to keep up with *US*
- He looks down at me frowning like, How can this will-o'-the-wisp white child think she can hang with this? — Francesca Lia Block, *Missing Angel Juan*, p. 330, 1993

4 used for registering annoyance, impatience, etc *UK, 1392*
From the sense 'to execute by hanging'.
- Oh well, hang the expense. It has to be Chateau D'Yquem 1990[.] — *The Guardian*, 4th December 2002

5 to idle *US, 1941*
- — *Newsweek*, p. 28, 8th October 1951
- The other two always hang. — *Break Point*, 1991
- You know. It's boring with just my mom to hang with. — Francesca Lia Block, *I Was a Teenage Fairy*, p. 128, 1998

6 (used of a computer program) to wait in suspension for something that will not occur *US*
- — Guy L. Steele et al., *The Hacker's Dictionary*, p. 82, 1983

▸ **hang crepe**
in a hospital, to manage a patient's expectations by leading them to expect the very worst *US*
- — Sally Williams, *"Strong" Words*, p. 145, 1994

▸ **hang five**
to surf with five toes extended over the front edge of the board *US*
- — Grant W. Kuhns, *On Surfing*, p. 117, 1963

▸ **hang hard**
to suffer a hangover *US*
- — Connie Eble (Editor), *UNC-CH Campus Slang*, p. 4, March 1996

▸ **hang heels**
to surf with your heels extended backwards over the tail of the surfboard *US*
- — Gary Fairmont R. Filosa II, *The Surfer's Almanac*, p. 187, 1977

▸ **hang her alongside awhile before we heist her aboard**
(of an idea or plan) to urge someone to think about it before we do anything *CANADA*
- "Hang her alongside" is another version of "tow it alongside" in Nova Scotia, to suggest that an idea or project needs to be considered before being put into action. —Lewis Poteet, *The South Shore Phrase Book*, p. 55, 1992

▸ **hang it up**
1 to insult *US*
- All the Kids would rap, charm (talk to), or game to impress girlfriends; hang it up (insult) or fresh (compliment) male friends by using special words. —Terry Williams, *The Cocaine Kids*, p. 90, 1989

2 to stop talking; to shut up *US*
- —*San Francisco Examiner: People*, p. 8, 27 October 1963: 'What a "Z"! The astonishing private language of Bay Area teenagers'

3 to retire *US, 1936*
Or 'hang them up'.
- I quit. Hit my dinger and hang 'em up. —*Bull Durham*, 1988

▸ **hang loose**
to do little and to do it without angst *US, 1955*
- Reading over the Book I'm giving the impression that I'm hanging loose and bemused and don't overly care about anything. —James Simon Kunen, *The Strawberry Statement*, p. 110, 1968

▸ **hang on the iron**
to put snow chains on a truck's tyres *US*
- —*American Speech*, p. 273, December 1961: 'Northwest truck drivers' language'

▸ **hang on the leg**
(used of a prisoner) to associate and curry favour with prison authorities *US*
- —William K. Bentley and James M. Corbett, *Prison Slang*, p. 32, 1992

▸ **hang on the wall**
(used of a groupie) to loiter at a rock and roll club in the hopes of making contact with a musician *US*
- —*Kiss*, 1969: 'Groupie glossary'

▸ **hang one on**
to punch *AUSTRALIA*
- Can't you leave a man in peace for awhile? Bloody good mind to hang one on ya. —J. Gaby, *The Restless Waterfront*, p. 171, 1974

▸ **hang paper**
1 to pass counterfeit money *US*
- I've hung a little paper, not much, there's no excitement in it. —Elmore Leonard, *Swag*, p. 14, 1976
- Better call bunco-forgery. The Czech's trying to hang bad paper. —Joseph Wambaugh, *The Delta Star*, p. 91, 1983
- But when I was hanging paper, I never scored from him. —Gerald Petievich, *The Quality of the Informant*, p. 54, 1985

2 to pass cheques with fraudulent intent *UK*
- —Angela Devlin, *Prison Patter*, p. 60, 1996

▸ **hang ten**
to surf with all the toes of both feet extended over the front of the board *US*
- —Grant W. Kuhns, *On Surfing*, p. 117, 1963

▸ **hang tight**
to stay put, to stay resolved *US, 1947*
- This is Ian with you. Hang tight, we'll be back with you after these messages. —*Airheads*, 1994

▸ **hang up your jock**
to quit or retire *US*
- "Either hang up our jocks and admit he's untouchable or be slicker than he is," Chance said. —Gerald Petievich, *To Live and Die in L.A.*, p. 123, 1983

▸ **hang your hat**
to live, to reside *US*
- —Marvin Gaye, *Wherever I Lay My Hat (That's My Home)*, 1969
- Look, I've got to get a hold of Frank and see where I'm hanging my hat. —*As Good As It Gets*, 1997

▸ **hang your own**
in circus and carnival usage, to brag *US*
A metaphor derived from the image of the braggart hanging posters advertising himself.
- —Don Wilmeth, *The Language of American Popular Entertainment*, p. 125, 1981

hang about *verb*
to loiter, to hesitate, to haunt *UK, 1892*
- At night he hung around the estate's parade of shops and, as his mother says, "got in with the wrong people". —*The Guardian*, 20th April 2000
- Nobody in Gowan Avenue had "described, let alone identified the defendant or anyone else hanging about near No 29 in the vital 30 minutes or so before her death", Mr Mansfield said. —*The Guardian*, 15th June 2001

hang about!
used for demanding a pause in an activity *UK, 1974*
Always imperative, sometimes used to indicate that the speaker has suddenly understood something.

hangar *noun*
in trucking, a garage *US*
- —Wayne Floyd, *Jason's Authentic Dictionary of CB Slang*, p. 18, 1976

hangar-flying *noun*
a group conversation among combat pilots, reliving combat missions *US, 1918*
- —Gregory Clark, *Words of the Vietnam War*, p. 217, 1990

Hangar Lane *noun*
a nuisance, an annoyance, a frustration, an irritation *UK*
Rhyming slang for **PAIN**, formed from the name of a traffic-junction on London's North Circular road, probably coined by a driver in a jam.
- —Ray Puxley, *Cockney Rabbit*, 1992

hang around *verb*
to idle, to pass time aimlessly, to socialise *US, 1830*
- Students started hanging around nonstudent tables, and forgetting to go to their classes. —Jerry Rubin, *Do It!*, p. 25, 1970
- FREDDY: He says I should just hang around my apartment and wait for a phone call. —*Reservoir Dogs*, 1992
- I been hangin' around this town on the corner / I been bummin' around this old town for way too long. —Counting Crows, *Hanging Around*, 2000

hangar queen *noun*
an aircraft that spends an inordinate amount of time being repaired *US, 1943*
- —*American Speech*, p. 228, October 1956: 'More United States Air Force slang'

hangashore; angishore *noun*
a person who does not go out fishing and thus is regarded as lazy *CANADA*
Originally from the Irish word *aindeiseoir* (a wretch), this word was adapted by folk etymology to apply to the fishing culture of Atlantic Canada.
- [A]ngishore, also hangashore. Someone who didn't want to fish. —T. K. Pratt, *Field Survey II for Dictionary of Prince Edward Island English*, p. 5, 1988

hangcher *noun*
a handkerchief *TRISTAN DA CUNHA, 1963*
- —Bernadette Hince, *The Antarctic Dictionary*, p. 163, 2000

hang-down *noun*
the penis *US*
- Get some stinky on your hang down[.] —Erica Orloff and JoAnn Baker, *Dirty Little Secrets*, p. 88, 2001

hanged up *adjective*
drug-intoxicated *US*
- Any time you want to get hanged up, let me know. I got connections. —Hal Ellson, *Duke*, p. 34, 1949

hanger *noun*
1 a piece of paper currency that has not fallen all the way through the slot on a casino table where cash is dropped *US*
- —Lee Solkey, *Dummy Up and Deal*, p. 114, 1980

2 in pool, a ball that is at rest right at the edge of a pocket *US, 1937*
- —Steve Rushin, *Pool Cool*, p. 15, 1990

3 a handgun cartridge that fails to detonate immediately after being struck by the firing pin *US*
- —*American Speech*, p. 193, October 1957: 'Some colloquialisms of the handgunner'

4 a handbag with a strap *US*
- —Hyman E. Goldin et al., *Dictionary of American Underworld Lingo*, p. 90, 1950

hang-gut *noun*
a paunchy stomach *BAHAMAS*
- —John A. Holm, *Dictionary of Bahamian English*, p. 99, 1982

hanging *adjective*
1 of inferior quality *UK*
- The Guinness is friggin hanging in this upper bar[.] —Niall Griffiths, *Kelly + Victor*, p. 13, 2002

2 drunk; exhausted *UK*
- —*e-cyclopaedia*, 20th March 2002

hanging bacon *noun*
the outer labia of the vagina *UK*
- —*www.LondonSlang.com*, June 2002

hanging Johnny *noun*
the penis in a flaccid state *US*
- —*Maledicta*, p. 195, Winter 1980: 'A new erotic vocabulary'

Hanging Sam *noun*
General Samuel T. Williams of the US Army *US*
Williams fought Pancho Villa in Mexico, and then in World War 1, World War 2, Korea and Vietnam.
- Beginning in 1955, the U.S. Military Aid and Assistance Group under the command of General "Hanging Sam" Williams and General Lionel C. McGarr dismantled the small, mobile units of the French-trained army[.[—Francis FitzGerald, *Fire in the Lake*, p. 121, 1972

hang it!; hang it all!
used for registering annoyance, irritation or despair *UK, 1703*
- Hang it all, everyone in his early twenties can't be dead[.] —R.F. Delderfield, *To Serve Them All My Days*, p. 45, 1997

hangman *noun*
a difficult person *NEW ZEALAND*
- —Sonya Plowman, *Great Kiwi Slang*, p. 88, 2002

hangnail *noun*
a slow-moving person, a dawdler, especially a slow driver *UK*
Rhyming slang for 'snail', from the characteristics of the creature.
- —Ray Puxley, *Fresh Rabbit*, 1998

hang on *verb*
1 to wait; to wait while using a telephone *UK*
Often used in the imperative.
- Hang on a minute, Vale. May I say something, sir? —Graeme Kent, *The Queen's Corporal [Six Granada Plays]*, p. 106, 1959
- —The Supremes *You Keep Me Hangin' On*, 1966
- Hey! Hang on, fellas! We're falling out with each other in our first proper meeting. —Kevin Sampson, *Powder*, p. 52, 1999

2 to make a criminal charge against *US*
- He'd been pushing for five years, and they couldn't hang one on him. —William Burroughs, *Naked Lunch*, p. 211, 1957

hangout *noun*
a place where people gather to socialise *US, 1892*
At times a negative connotation.
- That had become our hangout, when we weren't jamming at The Deuces[.] —Mezz Mezzrow, *Really the Blues*, p. 159, 1946
- One of the most colorful and successful of the Swing Street hangouts opened in 1938 in a former stable in West 51st Street].] —Robert Sylvester, *No Cover Charge*, p. 81, 1956
- Kathy knew him slightly from the Polo Lounge, an after-work hangout off Military Trail, but had never seen Gary Hammond there. —Elmore Leonard, *Maximum Bob*, p. 88, 1991
- You know. Rest areas are homosexual hangouts. —*Something About Mary*, 1998

hang out *verb*
1 to spend time with someone, usually a friend or friends *US, 1867*
- Jim Morrison used to sit outside my door when I lived in Laurel Canyon, wanting to hang out with me. —Arthur Lee, *quoted in Waiting For The Sun*, p. 124, 1969
- I was double leery when I left her because I knew "hang out" was New York white hippie argot for you know what. —Iceberg Slim (Robert Beck), *Death Wish*, p. 9, 1977

2 to monitor a citizens' band radio channel *US*
- —*Complete CB Slang Dictionary*, 1976
- —Peter Chippindale, *The British CB Book*, p. 155, 1981

hangtime *noun*
time spent waiting for something to happen *US*
- —Connie Eble (Editor), *UNC-CH Campus Slang*, p. 5, Spring 1991

hang tough!
used for expressing support when departing *US*
- —Judi Sanders, *Cal Poly Slang*, p. 5, 1990

hangup; hang-up *noun*
1 an emotional problem, neurosis or inhibition *US, 1952*
- "And what about all these maniac hangups you've got – secretly, mind you, but got all the same – with Morality and Conduct, and like that?" "Hangups?" "This whole neurotic syndrome about love." —Richard Farina, *Been Down So Long*, p. 109, 1966
- Max is telling me how he lives free of all the old middle-class Freudian hang-ups. —Joan Didion, *Slouching Toward Bethlehem*, p. 97, 1967
- Cassady brought in a Scandanavian-style blonde who was always talking about hangups. Everybody had hangups. —Tom Wolfe, *The Electric Kool-Aid Acid Test*, p. 118, 1968
- I was always treated in terms of goals I was achieving. I'd retained that. Which is a hangup. —Leonard Wolfe (Editor), *Voices from the Love Generation*, p. 63, 1968
- You will still have most of your sexual and emotional hang-ups and maybe a few new ones. The hang-ups of the people you will meet may be worse. —Richard Neville, *Play Power*, p. 84, 1970
- And she had a tremendous hang-up of going out and turning a date with another man, because she felt that her body belonged to me. —Christina and Richard Milner, *Black Players*, p. 93, 1972
- They didn't have any hang-ups about jealousy either[.] —Dave Courtney, *Raving Lunacy*, p. 111, 2000

2 in foot-propelled scootering, a seizing-up of a wheel during the performance of a trick *UK*
- —Ben Sharpe, *Scooter Crazy*, p. 40, 2000

hang up *verb*
1 when combined with an article symbolic of a trade, profession or sport, to retire from that field of endeavour *UK*
'Hang up your fiddle', which carries the generalised sense of retiring, is first recorded in 1833, however the current wide use may well owe its generation to Western films, particularly the cliché of an aged or disabled gun-fighter hanging up his guns. Of modern variations 'Hang up (one's) tits' is recorded of a retiring female impersonator in 1984. In 2003 a brief search of contemporary sources reveals a hairdresser hanging up his scissors, a judge hanging up the wig and robe, a Malayan who has hung up his Kalashnikov, a chef who hangs up his toque and white jacket, and a war correspondent who has hung up her flak jacket; jockeys hang up their silks, boxers hang up their gloves, sumo wrestlers hang up their loinclothes, etc.
- Michael Flatley may have hung up his dancing shoes, but the Irish dance phenomenon is still clackety-clacking its way unchecked around the globe[.] —*The Guardian*, 25th September 1999
- Experts wonder if Lindros should hang up the skates. —*Canadian Press*, 14th March 2000
- It's four years since Eric Cantona hung up his boots and went into movies. —*The Observer*, 6th May 2001
- Gretzky's younger brother wonders whether it's time to hang up the skates – because he and his wife are raising three young children, and have had enough of moving from city to city. —*espn.go.com*, 5th April 2002
- Sebastian Coe, now Lord Coe, was elected as a Conservative MP after he hung up his spikes[.] —*The Guardian*, 4th February 2003

2 in a prayer group, to pray last *US*
If 'to pray first' is to **DIAL**, then it is only logical that 'to pray last' is 'to hang up'.
- —Connie Eble (Editor), *UNC-CH Campus Slang*, p. 3, November 1990

▸ **hang up a shingle**
to go into business for yourself *US*
- You hang up a shingle. I know some people who will throw work your way. —Stephen Cannell, *King Con*, p. 90, 1997

hanhich *noun*
hashish *UK*
Probably a misspelling of 'hashish'.
- —Mike Haskins, *Drugs*, p. 287, 2003

hank *noun*
▸ **take your hank**
to masturbate *US*
- If taking your hank could destroy someone, I'd of been boiled down to a grease spot years ago. —Malcolm Braly, *On the Yard*, p. 209, 1967

hank book *noun*
a pornographic book or magazine *US*
- —Paul Glover, *Words from the House of the Dead*, 1974

hank freak *noun*

a person obsessed with masturbating *US*

- [N]ightly the hank freak would read of one coupling after another while he masturbated. — Malcolm Braly, *On the Yard*, p. 152, 1967

Hank Marvin *adjective*

very hungry *UK, 1998*

Rhyming slang for 'starving'; based on the name of popular guitarist Hank Marvin (b.1941).

- [T]he booze and the sea air had left us all Hank Marvin. — Martin King and Martin Knight, *The Naughty Nineties*, p. 104, 1999
- I hope you've left your knickers off cos I'm Hank Marvin. — Garry Bushell, *The Face*, p. 121, 2001

hankty *adjective*

suspicious *US*

- He stopped into Lewis' place where all the boys was having fun / Brock got kind of hankty and he felt for his gun. — Bruce Jackson, *Get Your Ass in the Water and Swim Like Me*, p. 56, 1966
- I don't know if she was hankty [suspicious] or what, because she handed the syrup in, in a cup, and kept her hand on the grill. — Bruce Jackson, *In the Life*, p. 115, 1972

hanky; hankie *noun*

a handkerchief; a tissue (often qualified as a paper hankie) *UK, 1895*

In the US a childish shortening, used for effect; virtually conventional in the UK.

- I put your hankies in here. [She indicates a drawer of the chest of drawers] They're all ironed. — Alexander Baron, *A Bit of Happiness [Six Granada Plays]*, p. 211, 1959
- I once shoved that stuff up me conk [nose] and me hankie turned brown. — Barry Humphries, *Bazza Pulls It Off!*, 1971
- Not the way Richie, bleeding all over himself, kept moaning, saying to him, "Bird, you have a hanky? Man, I'm cut bad." — Elmore Leonard, *Killshot*, p. 69, 1989
- Not even if you hear a thud from inside my home and a week later there's a smell from in there that can only come from a decaying body and you have to hold a hanky against your face because the stench is so thick[.] — *As Good As It Gets*, 1997
- [W]e ring 999 and give it the old hanky over the mouth routine. — Danny King, *The Burglar Diaries*, p. 72, 2001

hanky code; hankie code *noun*

a designation of a person's sexual preferences, signalled by the colour of the handkerchief and the pocket in which it is worn *US*

- Though the hanky code was originated by gay men, it has been adopted by cruising lesbians and bi's. — *Taste of Latex*, p. 24, Winter 1990–1991
- To make matters worse, after we've spent years figuring out an entire, ever expanding hanky code of fun things to do, now we hear about 'safe sex.' — Cindy Patton, *Fatal Advice*, p. 92, 1996
- [T]he authors recount "apocryphal tales of all-male square dances, where the man dancing the woman's part wore a red bandanna on his arm – the precursor of the modern hanky code." — *San Francisco Chronicle*, p. 1 (Sunday Review), 14th April 1996
- Adopted by dykes and straights, the kinky hankie code was created by gay leathermen in the early days of s/m culture as a way to communicate about sex. — *The Village Voice*, 17th–23rd November 2002

hanky pank *noun*

a carnival game in which the customer is allowed to win small, inexpensive prizes *US*

- So even though a player usually wins every time, there is still some HANKY PANK as to the size of the prize. — Gene Sorrows, *All About Carnivals*, p. 19, 1985

hankypank *adjective*

(used of a carnival game) inexpensive *US*

- — *American Speech*, p. 235, October 1950: 'The argot of outdoor boob traps'

hanky-panky; hankie-pankie *noun*

1 trickery, mischief, especially of a sexual nature *UK, 1841*

- As long as our guests are quiet about it, we'll put up with a little hanky-panky. — Jim Thompson, *A Swell-Looking Babe*, p. 1, 1954
- He imprisoned her in a tower in rags, and on her sixteenth birthday, the King decided to make any hankie-pankie impossible. — Iceberg Slim (Robert Beck), *Long White Con*, p. 41, 1977
- Before I get too cranky, you better like / hanky-panky (hanky-panky) / Nothing like a good spanky (good spanky). — Madonna, *Hanky Panky*, 1990
- "It's the sexual hankypanky the board frowns on most," he explained. — Seth Morgan, *Homeboy*, p. 308, 1990
- I'd sure hate to tape any hanky-panky through somebody's bedroom window, but I said I'd do the job and I will. — Joseph Wambaugh, *Fugitive Nights*, p. 161, 1992
- [T]hree things are taboo: sex, alcohol and tattoos! So no hanky-panky, no visiting the local pubs, and no graffiti on your bodies. — Duncan MacLaughlin, *The Filth*, p. 51, 2002

2 a boyfriend *UK*

Teen slang.

- — Susie Dent, *The Language Report*, p. 76, 2003

Hannibal Lecter *noun*

a ticket inspector *UK*

Rhyming slang, formed from the name of a fictional serial killer who caught the popular imagination, created in 1981 by author Thomas Harris and portrayed on film in 1986 by Brian Cox, and, most famously, by Anthony Hopkins from 1992.

- — Ray Puxley, *Fresh Rabbit*, 1998

Hanoi Hannah *noun*

a composite character on Radio Hanoi who broadcast during the Vietnam war with a target audience of US troops and a goal of lessening troop morale *US*

- — Gregory Clark, *Words of the Vietnam War*, p. 218, 1990

Hanoi Hilton *nickname*

a North Vietnamese prisoner of war camp, formally known as the Hoa Lo Prison (1964–1973) *US*

The title of a 1987 film starring Michael Moriarty and Jeffrey Jones as US prisoners of war trying to survive in the camp.

- The only facility North Vietnamese have taken newsmen to visit is one wryly known among American Pilots as the "Hanoi Hilton." — *New York Times*, p. 16, 24th November 1970
- Which was when the instructor said, "Well, smart-asses, that's how we did it at the Hanoi Hilton." — John Weisman, *Soar: A Black Ops Mission*, p. 46, 2003
- When cruelly exploiting Cindy's brief addiction to prescription painkillers didn't work, they [President George W. Bush's operatives] said McCain was crazy – too long at the Hanoi Hilton as a POW. — John W. Dean, *Worse Than Watergate*, p. 4, 2004

hanyak *noun*

a smokeable methamphetamine *UK, 1998*

- — Mike Haskins, *Drugs*, p. 279, 2003

hap *noun*

1 an event or activity *US*

An abbreviation of 'happening'; usually found in questions such as 'What's the hap?'.

- — Eugene Landy, *The Underground Dictionary*, p. 98, 1971

2 a bite; a mouthful *SOUTH AFRICA*

Directly from Afrikaans.

- Give me a hap of your apple. — Jean Branford, *A Dictionary of South African English*, p. 85, 1978

hapas capas *noun*

a writ of *habeas corpus* *US*

- — Hyman E. Goldin et al., *Dictionary of American Underworld Lingo*, p. 91, 1950

ha'penny *noun*

the female genitals *UK, C20*

From the small value halfpenny coin.

▷ **see:** HALFPENNY DIP, HALFPENNY STAMP

ha'porth *noun*

a small or negligible measure of something (cost, potency, wit, etc) *UK*

A colloquial contraction of 'halfpennyworth' that orginally, surely, suggested greater value and less contempt.

- Such an effective controlled revelation marred by a ha'porth of sensationalism. — *The Times*, 10th March 1976
- [H]ow [...] a regional government or assembly would make a ha'porth of difference? — Mr Robert Key, *Hansard (United Kingdom Parliament)*, 6th December 1991

ha'p'orth; haporth; apeth *noun*

a fool *UK*

A contraction of 'halfpennyworth' signifying something of little value; gently contemptuous and usually qualified as 'daft ha'porth', 'silly apeth', etc.

- Silly apeth gave her a car for her birthday. — Richard Francis, *The Rialto*, p. 93, 1999

happen *verb*

to be successful *US, 1949*

- [Roger] Federer has blown two break points, it's all happening in Gstaad. Again — *The Observer*, 13th July 2003

happening *noun*

1 an unstructured event built around music, drugs and a strong sense of bonding *US, 1959*

- In Japan, the Gutai group started off the current wave of happenings in the early 1950s with an art show in the sky (balloons, kites, etc. from the roof of a department store). — *Los Angeles Free Press*, p. 6, 19th February 1965
- — J. L. Simmons and Barry Winograd, *It's Happening*, p. 170, 1966: 'glossary'
- Balls, Happenings, Theatre, Dance, and spontaneous experiments in joy. — *The Digger Papers*, p. 15, August 1968
- One Saturday night Danny and I stepped outside to discover that our block was the scene of a massive happening. — Ann Fettamen, *Trashing*, p. 29, 1970
- We simply told them we wanted to have a "happening," which they assumed would be something like the colorful street fairs the Artists' Liberation Front had been sponsoring, and agreed to let us use their building. — Peter Coyote, *Sleeping Where I Fall*, p. 77, 1998

2 a party at which there is much drinking; a booze-up *AUSTRALIA*

- Not political parties (though they could be called that) but grog parties, dings, chevoos, happenings, piss-ups. — Frank Hardy, *The Outcasts of Foolgarah*, p. 181, 1971
- The basic requirements of a good 'happening' were: an ample supply of 'Blue' or 'Green' (Vic. or Foster's beer), the sappers, and someone fool enough to let it happen in his tent[.] — Martin Cameron, *A Look at the Bright Side*, 1988

happening *adjective*

modern, fashionable, chic *US, 1977*

In common with many words that define the times, 'happening' is now deeply unfashionable, surviving in irony and the vocabularies of those who were there when it was 'happening'.

- — Connie Eble (Editor), *UNC-CH Campus Slang*, p. 3, Fall 1982
- [H]e looks like he's "happening." We'll make him an A&R man[.] — Frank Zappa, *The Real Frank Zappa Book*, p. 204, 1989
- — Trevor Cralle, *The Surfin'ary*, p. 50, 1991

▸ **it's all happening!**

used when more than one thing happens at the same time; used of a general state of excitement *UK, 1976*

- Manchester United have just equalised. It's all happening oop north. — *The Guardian*, 18th September 2002

happily *adverb*

in computing, operating without awareness of an important fact *US*

- The program continues to run, happily unaware that its output is going to /dev/null. — Eric S. Raymond, *The New Hacker's Dictionary*, p. 196, 1991

happiness *noun*

MDMA, the recreational drug best known as ecstasy *UK*

- Ecstasy is "disco biscuits" and "happiness", heroin is "death trip". — Robert Ashton, *This Is Heroin*, p. 55, 2002

happy *noun*

a variety of MDMA, the recreational drug best known as ecstasy *UK*

- — Angela Devlin, *Prison Patter*, p. 60, 1996

happy *adjective*

slightly drunk *UK, 1770*

▸ **are you happy in your work?**

asked, ironically, of someone engaged in dirty or dangerous work *UK, 1943*

Originally military, in the form 'are you happy in the Service?'.

-happy *suffix*

mentally unbalanced or obsessed in the manner denoted by earlier or current circumstances, or impending fate, as affixed *US, 1931*

Originally military, from HAPPY (slightly drunk); thus 'bomb-happy' (nerves shattered by exposure to imminent death or mutilation), 'demob-happy' (obsessed by *demobilisation*, release from service).

- He's a bit of a nut case, paddy field-happy, you know. It's a wonder we haven't all gone round the bend [mad][.] — Graeme Kent, *The Queen's Corporal [Six Grandada Plays]*, p. 83–84, 1959

happy as a pig in shit *adjective*

extremely happy *AUSTRALIA*

- 'No, it's not true, Jennifer is as happy as a pig in the proverbial and we get on like a house on fire,' he told Spotlight. — *Herald Sun*, p. 46, 1991
- Chuck was happy as a pig in shit. — *Sick Puppy*, p. 13, 1998

happy as Larry *adjective*

extremely happy *AUSTRALIA, 1905*

Just exactly who the proverbially happy Larry was is one of those snippets of information lost in time.

- 'Happy?' she smiled. 'Happy as Larry,' he confirmed. — John Wynnum, *Tar Dust*, p. 91, 1962
- As a kid I was as happy as Larry, and I've got a mate called Larry and he is fucking happy, let me tell you. — Dave Courtney, *Stop the Ride I Want to Get Off*, p. 14, 1999

happy bag *noun*

a holdall in which an armed robber carries the equipment of his trade *UK*

- [A]nd sure enough there was what we were looking for: a happy bag. — Duncan MacLaughlin, *The Filth*, p. 113, 2002

happy bunny *noun*

1 a person who is very contented *UK*

Childish imagery, originally business jargon.

- I'd just had a blinding time, danced all night, said hello to hundreds of people I didn't know and gone home a fucking happy bunny. — Dave Courtney, *Raving Lunacy*, p. 17, 2000

2 a contented worker, or team member *UK*

A late C20 usage that probably originated as office jargon. Usually with a negative sense: 'not a happy bunny'.

happy camper *noun*

used as a humorous description of a contented person *US, 1981*

Often said with sarcasm or used in the negative.

- Time for luncheon, happy campers. — George V. Higgins, *Penance for Jerry Kennedy*, p. 168, 1985
- — Connie Eble (Editor), *UNC-CH Campus Slang*, p. 5, Fall 1985
- Vice President Dan Quayle, in an exchange of letters with American Samoa's representative in Congress, has sought to clear up his puzzling reference to Samoans as "happy campers." — *Baltimore Sun*, 16th May 1989
- Well, as you know, she didn't get admission in medical school. I am sure she is not a happy camper right now. — *The Hindu*, p. 26, 28th October 1997
- Flo was not a happy camper. — Erica Orloff and JoAnn Baker, *Dirty Little Secrets*, p. 155, 2001

happy cigarette *noun*

a marijuana cigarette *US, 1982*

- — Richard A. Spears, *The Slang and Jargon of Drugs and Drink*, p. 245, 1986
- — Mike Haskins, *Drugs*, p. 287, 2003

happy-clappy *adjective*

filled with spiritual joy, sometimes applied to Christians but rarely in the conventional Church *UK*

- In an ideal world this would still be the AFFM's parking lot, but Happy Clappies he could live with. — Christopher Brookmyre, *Not the End of the World*, p. 21, 1998
- I was a bit doubtful about the occasional wish that [Bob] Dylan would stop his moaning and become some kind of happy-clappy hippie mystic. — *Uncut*, p. 5, July 2001

happy day *noun*

a mixture of bottled strong ale and draught beer *UK: SCOTLAND*

- What's up wi your fizzer? Gie's a pint a heavy, barman ... naw, make it a happy day. Ah could do wi wan. — Michael Munro, *The Complete Patter*, p. 70, 1996

happy days *noun*

1 a type of bet in an illegal numbers game lottery *US*

- He played the money row, lucky lady, happy days, true love, sun gonna shine, gold, silver, diamonds, dollars and whiskey. — Chester Himes, *A Rage in Harlem*, p. 23, 1957

2 breadfruit *BARBADOS*

- — Frank A. Collymore, *Barbadian Dialect*, p. 57, 1965

happy drug *noun*

MDMA, the recreational drug best known as ecstasy *UK*

- — Mike Haskins, *Drugs*, p. 289, 2003

happy dust *noun*

cocaine, morphine or any powdered mind-altering drug *US, 1922*

Imparts a sense of retro, not unlike WACKY BACCY (marijuana). The term of choice for cocaine in George Gerswhin's *Porgy and Bess*.

- — *American Speech*, p. 26, February 1952: 'Teen-age hophead jargon'
- "Sportin' Life," said Mona. "Happy dust. This stuff is an American institution." — Armistead Maupin, *Tales of the City*, p. 46, 1978
- — R.C. Garrett et al., *The Coke Book*, p. 200, 1984
- — Nick Constable, *This is Cocaine*, p. 181, 2002

happy fag *noun*

a marijuana cigarette *UK*

- They used to throw the old happy fags at me in India. — Phil Tufnell, *They Think It's All Over*, 8th February 2002

happy gas *noun*

nitrous oxide, laughing gas *AUSTRALIA*

- Dental sedation comes in many forms, but the most commonly used is relative analgesia or "happy gas." It is a light flow of nitrous oxide in oxygen. — *Courier-Mail (Brisbane)*, 9th May 1986

happy hacking

used as a farewell *US*

- — *Co-Evolution Quarterly*, p. 32, Spring 1981
- — Guy L. Steele et al., *The Hacker's Dictionary*, p. 76, 1983

happy happy joy joy

used as a humorous, often sarcastic, celebratory remark *US*

First heard in the *Ren and Stimpy* cartoon (1991 – 1995), and then popularised with a broader audience by Keith Olberman on ESPN.

- — Keith Olberman and Dan Patrick, *The Big Show*, p. 17, 1997

happy herb *noun*

marijuana *UK, 1998*

- Queen Elizabeth gladly accepts a "kind" bouquet of marijuana buds (left) from legalization advocate Colin Davies (above) whose efforts to loosen her royal highness' view on the happy herb were snuffed by her pot-poaching chauffeur. [Caption] — *New York Post*, p. 3, 15th October 2000

happy hour *noun*

a period of time in the late afternoon when a bar serves free snacks and drinks at reduced prices *US, 1959*

- He knew he shouldn't mix the drug with the happy-hour booze, but what the hell, George Bush took them and hadn't expired yet. — Joseph Wambaugh, *Finnegan's Week*, p. 108, 1993

happy hours *noun*

flowers *UK*

Rhyming slang.

- — Julian Franklyn, *A Dictionary of Rhyming Slang*, 1960

happy little Vegemite *noun*

a happy person, especially a child *AUSTRALIA*

From an advertising jingle for Vegemite™, a yeast-based spread popular in Australia.

- If you're keen to introduce the happy little vegemites in your life to the joys of ' theatre-going ', you should get them off to see The Marvellous Adventures of Tyl . — *Sydney Morning Herald (Metro)*, p. 5, 8th January 1988
- Whatever it was, rotund funnyman Barry Humphries was not at all a happy little Vegemite when he visited one of Melbourne's "in" restaurants, Orexis, in Brunswick St, Fitzroy, on Logies' eve. — *Herald*, p. 10, 12th March 1990

happy meal *noun*

a mixture of chemical stimulants and depressants *UK*

A Happy Meal is more usually a product of McDonalds™ fast-food restaurants.

- Ecstasy dealers have taken to branding their tablets with famous logos: there is Big Mac E, Purple Nike Swirl E, X-Files E, and a mixture of uppers and downers called a "Happy Meal" — Naomi Klein, *No Logo*, p. 297, 2001

happy pie *noun*

the vagina *US*

- [G]roping under skirts between bare, plump young thighs, getting a finger or two in someone's happy pie. — Earl Thompson, *Tattoo*, p. 156, 1974

happy pill *noun*

1 an amphetamine or other central nervous system stimulant *UK, 1956*

- They upped her dose of happy pills. — Jeremy Cameron, *Brown Bread in Wengen*, p. 227, 1999

2 a Prozac™ tablet *UK*

- CALL IT... Spikers, prozie JUST DON'T CALL IT... The "happy" pill — *Drugs An Adult Guide*, p. 35, December 2001

3 a tablet of MDMA, the recreational drug best known as ecstasy *UK*

- — Mike Haskins, *Drugs*, p. 289, 2003

happy powder *noun*

cocaine *UK, 1998*

- — Mike Haskins, *Drugs*, p. 280, 2003

happy Sally *noun*

strong, homemade whisky *US*

- Masters of moonshine prided themselves in their ancient, father-to-son receipes and the white lightning, blue John, red eye, happy Sally, and stumphole whiskey they made, Smith said. — *Chicago Tribune*, p. C-1, 15th January 1986
- It is called corn liquor, white lightning, sugar whiskey, skully cracker, popskull, bush whiskey, stump, stumphole, 'splo, ruckus juice, radiator whiskey, rotgut, sugarhead, block and tackle, wildcat, panther's breath, tiger's sweat, Sweet spirits of cats a-fighting, alley bourbon, city gin, cool water, happy Sally, deep shaft, jump steady, old horsey, stingo, blue John, red eye, pine top, buckeye bark whiskey and see seven stars. — *Star Tribune (Minneapolis)*, p. 19F, 31st January 1999

happy shop *noun*

an off-licence (liquor store) *US*

- — *American Speech*, p. 153, Spring-Summer 1972: 'An approach to Black slang'

happy slapping *noun*

an apparently motiveless violent attack on a randomly chosen innocent person while the incident is filmed by an accomplice; or such attacks collectively; or the teenage craze for such attacks *UK*

- Concern over rise of 'happy slapping' craze[:] Fad of filming violent attacks on mobile phones spreads[.] — *The Guardian*, 26th April 2005

happy stick *noun*

a marijuana cigarette enhanced with phencyclidine, the recreational drug known as PCP or angel dust *US*

- While the Detroit house scene was relatively drug-free, in Chicago it was different. Cannabis was often dipped in angel dust to create 'happy sticks'; poppers, cocaine and LSD were all popular — Harry Shapiro, *Waiting For The Man*, 1999

happy trails *noun*

cocaine *US*

From the cowboy song known by those who came of age in the US in the 1950s and 60s.

- — Peter Johnson, *Dictionary of Street Alcohol and Drug Terms*, p. 89, 1993

happy trails

used as a farewell *US*

A catchphrase television sign-off sung on *The Roy Rogers Show* (NBC, 1951 – 57). Repeated with referential humour.

happy valley *noun*

the cleft between the buttock cheeks *US, 1970s*

- — Bruce Rodgers, *The Queens' Vernacular*, p. 103, 1972

Happy Valley *nickname*

the Vinh Thanh Valley, during the war a dangerous area northeast of An Khe, South Vietnam *US*

- The mission we had been assigned was simple: an early-morning flight over the An Khe pass toward Qui Hnon; a left turn up between two skinny ridges into Vinh Thanh Valley, known to us as Happy Valley[.] — Robert Mason, *Chickenhawk*, p. 95, 1983

haps *noun*

the latest; something that is popular *US, 1961*

Often heard as 'the haps'.

- — Andy Anonymous, *A Basic Guide to Campusology*, p. 13, 1966
- — Connie Eble (Editor), *UNC-CH Campus Slang*, p. 5, Fall 1990

harami *noun*

a shrewd or cunning person; used as a term of abuse it may carry the same sense as 'bastard' *INDIA*

From Urdu *haram* (that which is sacred), hence Urdu *harami* (a rogue). Collected by Chris Lewis, with anecdotal evidence that it has been used in the UK since the 1960s. Current in Pakistan and Indian street slang, as is the equivalent but more abusive Urdu term *haramzada* (a son of wickedness; a **BASTARD**).

- Man you know what? David is a harami! — Chris Lewis, *The Dictionary of Playground Slang*, p. 112, 2003

harass *verb*

to flirt *TRINIDAD AND TOBAGO*

- — Lise Winer, *Dictionary of the English/Creole of Trinidad & Tobago*, 2003

Harbour City *nickname*

Sydney *AUSTRALIA*

- In some respects they may even have the racket better organised than in the harbour city. — James Holledge, *The Call-girl in Australia*, p. 124, 1964
- I'm thinking of journeying to the Harbour city. — Kevin McKay, *The Cure*, p. 128, 1970

harbour light; harbour *adjective*

right *UK, 1961*

Rhyming slang.

- If everything is all right it is referred to as "all harbour light" and often "all harbour". — Ray Puxley, *Cockney Rabbit*, 1992

hard *noun*

1 an erection *US*

- What good are the fancy ties and the fine siuts if you can't get a hard on any more? — Henry Miller, *Tropic of Cancer*, p. 116, 1961
- — Helen Dahlskog (Editor), *A Dictionary of Contemporary and Colloquial Usage*, p. 30, 1972
- He lifts his blanket and he's lying there with a hard. — Herbert Huncke, *Guilty of Everything*, p. 48, 1990

2 hardcore sexual material *US*

- I put in parts of Ohio where they don't run hard, and it ran 6 weeks in one theater. — Stephen Ziplow, *The Film Maker's Guide to Pornography*, p. 78, 1977

3 an addictive drug *NEW ZEALAND*

- I sometimes held hard, it was difficult not to slip into the habit of selling a bit of pethl, morph., opium tincture and so on. — Greg Newbold, p. 15, 1982

4 coins *US*

- — Hyman E. Goldin et al., *Dictionary of American Underworld Lingo*, p. 91, 1950

hard *adjective*

1 of drinks, intoxicating, spiritous, 'strong' *US, 1789*

- Look, mister, we serve hard drinks in here for men who want to get drunk fast. — *USA Today*, 17th January 2000

2 (used of drugs) powerfully addictive *US, 1955*

- I read him the riot law – if I find out you're using hard shit I'm gonna pull your tongue out yo' ass, etc. — Edwin Torres, *Carlito's Way*, p. 73, 1975
- The hard-stuff trade is dead. — Edwin Torres, *After Hours*, p. 247, 1979
- Hard drugs were for running away from life, for altering your mind or searching your soul – heroin, morphine and barbiturates. Acid lay somewhere between soft and hard. — Simon Napier-Bell, *Black Vinyl White Powder*, p. 124, 2001

3 fine, excellent *US*

- — Jack Lait and Lee Mortimer, *New York Confidential*, p. 235, 1948: 'A Glossary of Harlemisms.'
- I was givin' him some balls off too, but their game was not as hard as mine! — Henry Williamson, *Hustler!*, p. 128, 1965
- — Judi Sanders, *Da Bomb*, p. 7, 1997

4 muscular, toned *US*

- — Judi Sanders, *Cal Poly Slang*, p. 5, 1990

5 of rock music, serious, uncompromising, with a strong rhythmic force *US*

First heard in the late 1960s.

- The big hook of Sunshine Of Your Love is a grinding, instantly memorable hard-rock riff, stuttering between two notes before hellishly descending for a few more, then rising in an upward squiggle. — *The Guardian*, 31st January 2004

6 of rave music, relentlessly rhythmic *UK*

- Then we got a beer and headed for one of the "harder" rooms where we loafed for a bit, had a bit of a groove when it starts kicking off. — Ben Malbon, *Cool Places*, p. 272, 1998

7 of pornographic material, descriptive of anything that is more explicit than society finds generally acceptable *UK*

A flexible standard depending on where you are.

- Erika's repressed emotional life is displaced not merely into her specialist passion for Schubert and Schumann, but into a taste for hard porn. — *The Guardian*, 15th May 2001

8 in craps, a point made with a matching pair *US, 1930*

A bet on a 'hard' number means that the only combination that will win is a pair. Often used in the phrase 'the hard way'.

- With equal ease, I could quote the Roman lyric poet, Catullus, or the odds against making four the hard way. — Jim Thompson, *Roughneck*, p. 2, 1954
- It was hot and dry, and they pay 10 to 1 on eight the hard way. — Max Shulman, *Rally Round the Flag, Boys!*, p. 187, 1957
- Two thousand dollar hard eight. — *Hard Eight*, 1996

9 (used of straightened hair) heavily greased *US*

- — Clarence Major, *Dictionary of Afro-American Slang*, p. 64, 1970

10 in blackjack, said of a hand without an ace or with an ace and a value of 12 or higher *US*

- — Jerry L. Patterson, *Blackjack*, p. 19, 1978

11 (used of a theatre ticket) reserved for a specific seat *US*

- — Sherman Louis Sergel, *The Language of Show Biz*, p. 104, 1973

hard *adverb*

▸ **go hard**

to engage in gunfire *US*

- Trainum and Garrett were looking for robbers who "went hard" – street slang for gunplay – and started shooting when they lost control[.] — *Washington Post*, p. W14, 2nd May 2003

hard ankle *noun*

a working man, especially a trucker *US*

- — Warren Smith, *Warren's Smith's Authentic Dictionary of CB*, p. 44, 1976

hard-arsed; hard-ass; hard-assed *adjective*

uncompromising, unyielding, tough, stubborn *UK, 1903*

- The original Oakland Angels were hard-ass brawlers[.] — Hunter S. Thompson, *Hell's Angels*, p. 131, 1966
- I still had a pile of complaints to deal with from a bunch of hard-arsed punters[.] — Lanre Fehintola, *Charlie Says...*, p. 162, 2000

hard ask *noun*

a difficult challenge *NEW ZEALAND*

- As they are fond of saying in league commentaries, it could be a hard ask. — *Sunday Star-Times*, p. C3, 22nd October 2000

hard-ass *noun*

a strict, unforgiving, unrelenting person *US, 1966*

- I bet you played the hardasss, didn't you. Show 'em no fucking mercy. — Elmore Leonard, *Freaky Deaky*, p. 276, 1988
- I'm always talking to them and playing with them, but Silent Bob won't join in. He's a fucking hard-ass. — *Mallrats*, 1995
- You were a hard ass and you took his dad out, Sydney. — *Hard Eight*, 1996
- She had proved herself to be less of a hard-ass than I first imagined. — Rita Ciresi, *Pink Slip*, p. 41, 1999

hard-ass *verb*

1 to endure a difficult situation *US*

- You did it the easiest way you could and hard-assed the difference. — Malcolm Braly, *On the Yard*, p. 10, 1967

2 to treat harshly *US*

- Do you think we're gonna stand here and be hard-assed because some dude in Norfolk forgot to endorse our orders? — Darryl Ponicsan, *The Last Detail*, p. 143, 1970

hard at it *adjective*

very busy, especially when engaged on a particular task *UK, 1749*

- We've been hard at it since mid-July in what was the toughest build-up to any season that any one of us can remember. — *The Guardian*, 2nd September 2002

hardback *adjective*

old *JAMAICA*

- The 6–3 votes allows local or state governments to require that dancers wear at least pasties and a G-string so long as everyone else also is for bidden to appear naked in public. — *Washington Post*, 30th March 2000
- — Peter Patrick, *Some Recent Jamaican Creole Words*, 2003

hardball *noun*

1 competition or conflict with no holds barred *US, 1972*

- This guy's looking to play tit-for-tat. That's not my game. I'm gonna play hardball. — *Tin Men*, 1987
- It's a hardball world, son. We've got to keep our heads until this peace craze blows over. — *Full Metal Jacket*, 1987

2 crack cocaine *UK*

- — Mike Haskins, *Drugs*, p. 282, 2003

hardballer *noun*

a person who competes or pursues an interest with an intense focus and little thought as to the consequences *US*

- Chief of Police Kolender, true to his word, did come to Southern Division to reassure Manny's men of what a hell of a bunch of gutsy hardballers they really were[.] — Joseph Wambaugh, *Lines and Shadows*, p. 294, 1984

hardbelly *noun*

a teenage girl or young woman *US*

Biker (motorcyle) usage.

- "There was no confusin' her with the other hardbellies [slim biker chix] at the bar," the article says. [Quoting an article in the November 1987 issue of Outlaw Biker]. — *Washington Post*, p. W5, 3rd January 1988

hard bit *noun*

a prison sentence that is especially difficult to serve

- — Angela Devlin, *Prison Patter*, p. 60, 1996

hard-boiled *adjective*

callous, cynical, emotionally uninvolved, tough; describing the characteristics of macho tough guys in 'hard-boiled' pulp fiction *US, 1904*

Figurative usage of the solid properties of hard-boiled eggs, or clothing vigorously boiled in starch; applied by Mark Twain (1835–1910) to refer to rigid rules of grammar (1886); in the early 1900s it applied to hard or stiff clothing; by 1918 it was being used to describe a person who stuck rigidly to the rules; from which the current sense evolved.

- Raymond Chandler (1888–1959) was the writer who changed the Hard-Boiled protagonist, and most influenced all subsequent Hard-Boiled writers. — Paul Duncan, *Noir Fiction*, p. 10, 2000

hardboot *noun*

a person from Kentucky *US, 1923*

- — Dan Parker, *The ABC of Horse Racing*, p. 146, 1947

hard candy *noun*

1 heroin *US, 1970*

- — Richard A. Spears, *The Slang and Jargon of Drugs and Drink*, p. 246, 1986
- — Robert Ashton, *This Is Heroin*, p. 206, 2002
- — Mike Haskins, *Drugs*, p. 284, 2003

2 a person who has been identified for revenge by a prison gang *US*

- — Anna Scotti and Paul Young, *Buzzwords*, p. 135, 1997

hard-case *noun*

a hardened, tough person *US, 1836*

- She was a bit of a hard case and likes to be different. — Dal Stivens, *Jimmy Brockett*, p. 175, 1951
- You think your [sic] a real hard case don't you? — Frank Norman, *Bang To Rights*, p. 58, 1958
- Before the era of the psycho-analyst a tough boss was a 'rugged individualist' and an eccentric character was a 'hard case'. — Bill Wannan, *Bullockies, Beauts and Bandicoots*, p. 43, 1960
- A hard-case bastard, that whippet,' Buffalo Bill said. 'He seemed okay.' 'He is, but he's a hard case all the same. — Ivan Agnew, *Loner*, p. 67, 1974
- Well, one day one of his mates at work, a bit of a hard case, said: 'What are you worrying about? You've got plenty of money; why don't you employ someone to do your worrying for you?' — Frank Hardy, *Hardy's People*, p. 29, 1986
- He's a hard case alright. You can't help but like him though. — Robert G. Barrett, *Davo's Little Something*, p. 197, 1992

hard-case *adjective*

eccentric, unconventional *NEW ZEALAND*

- Complete with a long whip and a hardcase old straw hat, the 'bullocky' looked the part. — Barry Crump, *Bastards I Have Met*, p. 59, 1971

hard cat *noun*

a well-dressed, popular male *US*

- — *Time Magazine*, p. 46, 24th August 1959

hard-charge *verb*

in car racing, to drive aggressively *US*

- The opposite of stroking it is "hard-charging." — Tom Wolfe, *The Kandy-Kolored Tangerine-Flake Streamline Baby*, p. 156, 1965

hard chaw *noun*

a thug *IRELAND*

- Of all the characters, Begbie was the most realistic and the scariest, the quintessential psychopath, the hardest hard chaw on the estate, a man who would glass you as soon as he'd shake your hand. — *Sunday Business Post*, 23rd January 2003

hard cheddar *adjective*

bad luck *UK, 1931*

- — Ivan Bracklin and William Fitzgerald, *All About Darts*, p. 98, 1975

hard cheese *noun*

bad luck *UK, 1876*

Often said in commiseration.

- In a different interest rate environment, this might be a straightforward case of hard cheese. — *The Guardian*, 11th October 2003

hardcore *noun*

1 amyl nitrite *UK*

Perhaps from 'hardcore' as a grade of pornography because of the drug's reputation as a sexual relaxant.

- — Angela Devlin, *Prison Patter*, p. 60, 1996

2 a regular soldier of the North Vietnamese Army or the Viet Cong *US*

- — Linda Reinberg, *In the Field: The Words of the Vietnam War*, p. 102, 1991

hardcore *adjective*

1 of pornography, graphic, explicit *US*

The gradations between **SOFTCORE** and 'hardcore' vary over time and place; in general, the erect penis, penetration and ejaculation are the hallmarks of hardcore pornography.

- In hard-core pornography," Aileen said, "the man's core is hard." "That's an old gag," Gregor said. "Professional humor," she said. — Lawrence Block, *No Score [The Affairs of Chip Harrison Omnibus]*, p. 62, 1970
- Like the little girl who posed shyly in a nudist magazine and then graduated into hardcore porn, most are totally anonymous. — *Associated Press, PM cycle*, 14th April 1977

2 extreme *US*

- — Connie Eble (Editor), *UNC-CH Campus Slang*, p. 4, Fall 1997

hardcore *adverb*

extremeley *US*

- — Connie Eble (Editor), *UNC-CH Campus Slang*, p. 4, Fall 1997

hard cut *adjective*

rough, tough, hard-living *CANADA*

- The gold fields to the north were ajump with hard cut miners. — Alan Fry, *Ranch on the Cariboo*, p. 39, 1962

hard-doer; hard doer *noun*

a person who struggles valiantly against difficulties *AUSTRALIA, 1910*

Literally, a person who 'does it hard'. A term of approbation.

- He had to pierce the veil that shielded the action in one hundred aboriginal minds, then quickly assemble the fact by his aboriginal knowledge, aided by a wide local geography and knowledge of hard-doer outside blacks and of their country. — Ion L. Idriess, *Over the Range*, p. 195, 1947
- 'Hard doer, ain't he?' grumbled the council staff[.] — Arthur Upfield, *Bony and the Mouse*, p. 69, 1959
- Among his mates was a slow-speaking hard-doer named Jack Stevens and his amusingly drawled utterances caused many a laugh at Renballa pub. — Bill Wannan, *Bullockies, Beauts and Bandicoots*, p. 40, 1960
- — Patsy Adam-Smith, *Folklore of the Australian Railwaymen*, p. 252, 1969

hard dresser *noun*

an aggressive, 'mannish' lesbian *US*

- Known variously as a bull, a stomper, a bad butch, a hard dresser, a truck driver, a diesel dyke, a bull dagger and a half dozen other soubriquets, she is the one who, according to most homosexual girls, gives lesbians a bad name. — Ruth Allison, *Lesbianism*, p. 125, 1967

hard-earned *noun*

money, especially that identified as earnings

- I don't have to tell you what kind of treat you're in for if you fork over your hard-earned[.] — Lester Bangs, *Psychotic Reactions and Carburetor Dung*, p. 152, 1975
- [H]anding over a wedge of hard-earned in return for a catering-size bag of barbecue flavoured snacks. — Andrew Nickolds, *Back to Basics*, p. 59, 1994

hard-ears *noun*

said of a stubborn person *TRINIDAD AND TOBAGO*

- — Lise Winer, *Dictionary of the English/Creole of Trinidad & Tobago*, 2003

har-de-har-har

used as a vocalisation mocking laughter *US*

- "I drive you ape, and you just don't trust yourself with me, that's what it is." "Har-de-har-har!" replied Comfort. — Max Shulman, *Rally Round the Flag, Boys!*, p. 58, 1957

hardfist *noun*

a violence-prone, tough person *CANADA*

- Among the "hardfists" of the wilderness he had been a good companion. — Edgar Collard, *Yesterdays*, p. 38, 1955

hard graft *noun*

hard work *AUSTRALIA, 1873*

- [E]veryone [was] combining hard graft with as much of the picnic spirit as urgency of labour allowed. — Frank Dalby Davison, *The Wells of Beersheba*, p. 106, 1965

hard-grafting *adjective*
hard-working *AUSTRALIA*
- The real heros of the bush weren't the young larrikins who became outlaws, but hard-grafting 'ringers' of the sheds[.] — Bill Wannan, *Folklore of the Australian Pub*, p. 58, 1972

hard guy *noun*
a serious, violent criminal *US, 1916*
- Such veteran hard guys as are still extant differ as to what contretemps the Dutchman and The Mick's brother involved themselves. — Robert Sylvester, *No Cover Charge*, p. 60, 1956

hard hat *noun*
an elite, full-time Viet Cong soldier *US, 1965*
- Named from the metal helmets they wore, not worn by guerilla fighters. The advisors tended to group both together, calling them "hard hats" because they wore turtle-shaped sun helmets, an imitation of the colonial sun helment that one saw in Lipingesque movies of British India on late-night television[.] — Neil Sheehan, *A Bright Shining Lie*, p. 66, 1988
- — Linda Reinberg, *In the Field*, p. 102, 1991

hard head *noun*
a criminal who uses explosives to break into safes *US*
- — Vincent J. Monteleone, *Criminal Slang*, p. 112, 1949

hard hit *noun*
an act of defecation *UK*
Rhyming slang for **SHIT**, especially in the phrase 'go for a hard hit'.
- — Jack Slater, 1978

Hard John *noun*
1 an agent of the Federal Bureau of Investigation (FBI) *US*
- — Lou Shelly, *Hepcats Jive Talk Dictionary*, p. 25, 1945

2 a tough, uncompromising person *US*
- [T]he "hard Johns" from the federal narcotics bureau had invaded this most neighborly of neighborhoods[.] — Ross Russell, *The Sound*, p. 219, 1961

hard knock *adjective*
toughened by life *US*
Having been through the **SCHOOL OF HARD KNOCKS**.
- It's the Hard-Knock Life — Martin Charnin, *Annie*, 1977
- I get talking to the guy next me. Mancunian hard knock: two ear studs; powder bue eyes[.] — Pete McCarthy, *McCarthy's Bar*, p. 18, 2000

hard labour *noun*
a neighbour *UK*
Rhyming slang.
- — Ray Puxley, *Cockney Rabbit*, 1992

hard leg *noun*
an experienced, cynical prostitute *US, 1967*
- — Kenn "Naz" Young, *Naz's Underground Dictionary*, p. 35, 1973

hard line *noun*
crack cocaine *UK, 1998*
- — Mike Haskins, *Drugs*, p. 282, 2003

hard lines *noun*
bad luck *UK, 1824*
Probably of nautical origins. Often said in commiseration.

hard-look *verb*
to stare at aggressively *US*
- — Ann Lawson, *Kids & Gangs*, p. 55, 1994: 'Common Mexican gang slang/phrases'

hard mack *noun*
a brutish pimp who relies on force and the threat of force to control his prostitutes *US*
- One who uses brutality and threats is a gorilla pimp or hard Mack. — Christina and Richard Milner, *Black Players*, p. 35, 1972

hard man *noun*
1 a professional thug; a person not afraid of violent action *US*
- [S]treet-corner society has a typology of its own denizens, pointing not only to H"hard men" or "gorillas"[.] — Roger Abrahams, *Positively Black*, p. 85, 1970
- He said, "So you think of yourself as a bit of a hardman?" "Oh, very much so," I said. — Dave Courtney, *Raving Lunacy*, p. 121, 2000
- Movie hard man [Charles] Bronson dies at 81. — *The Guardian*, 2nd September 2003

2 an uncompromising politician or businessman *UK, 1976*
- IDS [Iain Duncan Smith] Hard Man Act Fails To Convince. — *Sunday Herald (Scotland)*, 12th October 2003

hard money *noun*
cash *US*
- A lot of times it's not too much – you'd be surprised how small an amount they can open on – but as long as they're handling hard money, you're going to get some. — Bruce Jackson, *Outside the Law*, p. 104, 1972

hard-mouth *verb*
to threaten or disparage *TRINIDAD AND TOBAGO, 1960*
- — Lise Winer, *Dictionary of the English/Creole of Trinidad & Tobago*, 2003

hard nail *noun*
a hypodermic needle *US*
- — *American Speech*, p. 87, May 1955: 'Narcotic argot along the Mexican border'

hard-nosed *adjective*
stubborn, uncompromising *US, 1927*
- [T]he campaign, created by the respected ad agency Mother and featuring a businessman who takes a hard-nosed business approach so seriously he wears a false metal nose, was "very irritating". — *The Guardian*, 13th May 2003

hard nut *noun*
a dangerous foe; a tough individual; a difficult challenge *US, 1884*
Clipped from 'a hard nut to crack'.
- The SPG were like the SAS of the police, a renowned bunch of hardnuts. — Dave Courtney, *Raving Lunacy*, p. 31, 2000
- I was going to get this hardnut who was twice my size. — Brian McDonald, *Elephant Boys*, p. 206, 2000
- [O]ne snag: her boyfriend was a Teddy boy who was known as the local hardnut. — Jimmy Stockin, *On The Cobbles*, p. 73, 2000

hard nut to crack *noun*
▷ see: TOUGH NUT

hard of hearing *adjective*
undisciplined, disobedient *TRINIDAD AND TOBAGO, 1973*
- — Lise Winer, *Dictionary of the English/Creole of Trinidad & Tobago*, 2003

hard-on *noun*
1 the erect penis; an erection *US, 1888*
- I got immediately a hardon, told Bob, ordered him in fact to drive to the woods. — Jack Kerouac, *Letter to Neal Cassady*, p. 298, 10th January 1951
- One incident which I recall rather vividly was my first understanding of the slang expression "hard-on," which I got from another boy in the sixth grade. — Phyllis and Eberhard Kronhausen, *Sex Histories of American College Men*, p. 77, 1960
- One looks forward to being buried with a hard-on. — Angelo d'Arcangelo, *The Homosexual Handbook*, 1968
- [H]e had only to hear or speak in her Southern hue, or make the slightest reference to that blessed place he knew so well, and he would get a hard-on. — Cecil Brown, *The Life & Loves of Mr. Jiveass Nigger*, p. 40, 1969
- Sometimes, though, I'd go home afterwards, after having had a hard-on for four hours of making out on the floor and in the bleachers, but without creaming, and it really gave you a sore dick. — *The Berkeley Tribe*, p. 13, 5th-12th September 1969
- You know, I think there are a lot of women that would be glad to have a young, straight male making a pretty good living beside them in bed with a hard on. — *Sex, Lies and Videotape*, 1989
- It's not so cool to leave me with a hard-on. — *Boogie Nights*, 1997
- And she's getting more relaxed and more flirty, I'm getting a hard-on. And I know where I'm going with this hard-on. — Kevin Sampson, *Outlaws*, p. 102, 2001

2 a grudge *US, 1931*
- Just that you got a hard on for ofays. — Ross Russell, *The Sound*, p. 91, 1961
- There's a lot you don't know about, like the old man's old lady having a hard-on for him. — Darryl Ponicsan, *The Last Detail*, p. 94, 1970
- He knows I'm a cop, of course, and he knows I'm a federal cop, so he's got to figure I got a hard-on for Panthers. — George V. Higgins, *The Friends of Eddie Doyle*, p. 29, 1971
- God has a hard-on for marines because we kill everything we see! — *Full Metal Jacket*, 1987

3 a stubborn, bellgerent person *US, 1968*
- Nah, not now, all those hard-ons around. I'll wait. — *Raging Bull*, 1980
- I'm saying it's a way to do it," Bobby said, sounding like a hard-on, a man who thought he was always right. — Elmore Leonard, *Riding the Rap*, p. 56, 1995
- You don't want to act like a hard-on. You're standing there in your undies. You know what I'm saying? — *Get Shorty*, 1995
- Look, I don't wanna be a hard-on about this, and I know it wasn't your fault, but I just thought it was fair to tell you that Gene and I will be submitting this to the League[.] — *The Big Lebowski*, 1998

4 a prized possession; something to be desired *UK*
Derives from the sense as 'an erection', via the idea that inanimate objects can be **SEXY** (desirable).
- If we decide to reissue it on CD in a year's time, when the band are huge, none of the ten thousand who buy the EP will complain. It just adds value to their red-vinyl hard-on. It's like having "Anarchy" on EMI. —Kevin Sampson, *Powder*, p. 66, 1999

5 a desire for *US, 1971*
- You got some hardon for Cokes, kid – I like em, Sprenger said. —Gilbert Sorrentino, *Steelwork*, p. 21, 1970

hard on *adjective*
addicted to *BAHAMAS*
- —John A. Holm, *Dictionary of Bahamian English*, p. 100, 1982

hard one *noun*
in necrophile usage, a corpse that has stiffened with rigor mortis *US*
- —*Maledicta*, p. 180, Summer/Winter 1986–1987: 'Sexual slang: prostitutes, pedophiles, flagellators, transvestites, and necrophiles'

hard pimp *noun*
a pimp who relies on violence and the threat of violence to control his prostitutes *US*
- I then went to Dian and got her gun because he was a hard pimp and just might not accept this kinda shit. —A.S. Jackson, *Gentleman Pimp*, p. 143, 1973

hard-pushed *adjective*
in difficulties, especially financial *UK, 1834*
- [N]ew graduates can find themselves hard-pushed to repay the money quickly. — *The Observer*, 28th September 2003

hard rice *noun*
during the Vietnam war, weapons and ammunition *US*
- It probably belonged to Air America and was making a hard rice drop, as munitions were called, to the Meo tribesmen in the mountains around the Plaines Des Jars. —Barry Sadler, *Casca #14: The Phoenix*, p. 37, 1985

hard rock *noun*
crack cocaine *UK, 1998*
An elaboration of **ROCK**.
- —Mike Haskins, *Drugs*, p. 282, 2003

hardshell Baptist; hard-shell Baptist *noun*
a member of the Primitive Baptist Church, or any other rigidly orthodox Baptist *US, 1838*
- Bill Hill's ex-wife, Barbararose, who was a hard-shell Baptist out of Nashville, where there were 686 different Fundamentalist churches, had called the whole Uni-Faith setup "a mockery in the eyes of God." —Elmore Leonard, *Touch*, p. 90, 1977

hard shells *noun*
powerfully addictive drugs, such as heroin, morphine and cocaine *US*
- —Robert George Reisner, *The Jazz Titans*, p. 157, 1960

hard, soft and wet
denotes all that is necessary to operate a computer *UK*
- The title, Hard, Soft and Wet is shorthand for hardware, software and wetware, wetware being us. —Melanie McGrath, *Hard, Soft & Wet*, p. 296, 1998

hard sports *noun*
sadomasochistic sex-play involving defecation, especially when it is offered as a service in a prostitute's advertising *UK*
- —Caroline Archer, *Tart Cards*, 2003

hard spot *noun*
an ambush using tanks or other armour as part of the ambush *US*
- —Linda Reinberg, *In the Field*, p. 102, 1991

hard stuff *noun*
1 alcoholic drink other than beer or wine *AUSTRALIA, 1832*
- Hard stuff must be bought at liquor stores and taken out. —Jack Lait and Lee Mortimer, *Washington Confidential*, p. 69, 1951
- "I normally don't touch the hard stuff, but damn, look at those prices," says Billy. Above the mirror behind the bar is a line of signs listing the kinds of whiskey that can be had, two shorts for forty-five cents. —Darryl Ponicsan, *The Last Detail*, p. 70, 1970

2 addictive drugs such as heroin or cocaine *US*
- After they become habituated to them, they are forced to seek the more expensive reefers or go to "hard stuff" – cocaine and heroin. —Jack Lait and Lee Mortimer, *Chicago Confidential*, p. 148, 1950
- They were using hard stuff so I cut out fast. —Babs Gonzales, *Movin' On Down De Line*, p. 117, 1975
- —Angela Devlin, *Prison Patter*, p. 60, 1996
- —Robert Ashton, *This Is Heroin*, p. 206, 2002

3 coins *US, 1788*
- —Hyman E. Goldin et al., *Dictionary of American Underworld Lingo*, p. 91, 1950

hardtail *noun*
a motorcyle with no rear shock absorbers *US*
- —Paladin Press, *Inside Look at Outlaw Motorcyle Gangs*, p. 36, 1992

hard time *noun*
a long prison sentence, whether in absolute terms or relative to the crime or relative to the prisoner's ability to survive *US, 1927*
- Manning did hard time and the time was hard on him. —Malcolm Braly, *On the Yard*, p. 172, 1967
- Besides, if you ain't dead, you'll be doing one hell of a lot of hard time. —Mickey Spillane, *Last Cop Out*, p. 168, 1972
- Another was doing time up state. Long hard time for murder one. —Joseph Nazel, *Black Cop*, p. 76, 1974
- He would bet they had put in some hard time at Raiford or maybe a federal lockup. They wore pass-the-time tattoos on their arms, the coarse designs of prison artists. —Elmore Leonard, *Split Images*, p. 197, 1981
- JODIE: He got two years back inside for that. FREDDY: Goddamn, that's hard time. —*Reservoir Dogs*, 1992

hard-timer *noun*
a prisoner serving a long sentence *US, 1986*
- These boys were fish and Foley as a celebrity hard-timer who'd robbed more banks than they'd been in to cash a check. —Elmore Leonard, *Out of Sight*, p. 10, 1996

hard up *adjective*
1 in want of money, impoverished *UK, 1818*
- Hard-up police have to hitch ride. —*The Guardian*, 24th June 2003

2 in need of something specified *UK, 1840*
- [W]hat Dallas isn't is hard up for attractive women. —*Dallas Observer*, 15th June 2000

hardware *noun*
1 weapons, usually guns *US, 1865*
- The Copiens, the Socialistics, the Bachelors, the Comanches – all bad motherfuckers – these were the gangs that started using hardware. —Edwin Torres, *Carlito's Way*, p. 8, 1975
- I got to pick up my hardware from my room, then we can pull up. —Donale Goines, *Black Gangster*, p. 44, 1977
- He bolted reflexively, but stopped when he realized it was hardware digging into his backside. —James Ellroy, *Brown's Requiem*, p. 211, 1981

2 ostentatious jewellery *US, 1939*
- —Lou Shelly, *Hepcats Jive Dictionary*, p. 12, 1945

3 silverware *US*
- —Joseph E. Ragen and Charles Finston, *Inside the World's Toughest Prison*, p. 802, 1962: 'Penitentiary and underworld glossary'

4 any medal or trophy awarded in a competition *US, 1921*
- —*American Speech*, p. 206, October 1963: 'The language of skiers'

hardware shop *noun*
a homosexual male brothel *UK*
- —*Maledicta*, p. 144, Summer/Winter 1986–1987: 'Sexual slang: prostitutes, pedophiles, flagellators, transvestites, and necrophiles'

hardware store *noun*
a poker game in which players generally bet based on the value of their hands and do not bluff *US*
An allusion to the True Value chain of hardware stores in the US.
- —John Vorhaus, *The Big Book of Poker Slang*, p. 21, 1996

hard word *noun*
▸ put the hard word on
1 to ask someone for sexual intercourse *AUSTRALIA, 1936*
- Girls like Gertie Sparks and Polly Tanner would give a bloke the frozen mit if he tried to do a line with them – let alone have the audacity to put the hard word on them. —Norman Lindsay, *Halfway to Anywhere*, p. 57, 1947
- At seventeen, I became a student at Melbourne University, where pretty soon I had the 'hard word' put on me. —Wendy Bacon, *Uni Sex*, p. 45, 1972
- Went out with Nigel. He put the hard word on me. But I said no because I didn't want to be unfaithful to John. —John Birmingham, *He Died With a Felafel in his Hand*, p. 101, 1994

2 to make a fervent request *AUSTRALIA, 1918*

- Publishers have been putting the hard word on me for yonks to spill the beans[.] — Barry Humphries, *The Traveller's Tool*, p. 7, 1985

hard yakka; hard yacker *noun*

hard work *AUSTRALIA, 1888*

- Ut's hard yacker. Diggin' foundations. — Nino Culotta (John O'Grady), *They're A Weird Mob*, p. 29, 1957
- The old man come up the hard way but his kids'll always have plenty others to do the hard yakka. — Mary Durack, *Kings in Grass Castles*, p. 167, 1959
- — Dymphna Cusack, *Picnic Races*, p. 138, 1962
- — Harvey E. Ward, *Down Under Without Blunder*, p. 40, 1967

hard yard *noun*

a difficult challenge *NEW ZEALAND*

- Cindy was there to show that perfection is within our grasp if we're prepared to do the hard yards. — *Evening Post*, p. 8, 5th September 2000

hard yards *noun*

exacting work *AUSTRALIA*

Originally a sporting metaphor.

- The bottom line was that if they were prepared to put aside their egos and do the hard yards, we could step up to the next level and mould a half-decent outfit. — William Dodson, *The Sharp End*, p. 249, 2001
- I will die, just as the Bible predicted. But it will be hard yards for my betrayer. — Kel Richards, *The Aussie Bible*, p. 63, 2003

hardy fuckin' ha, ha!

▷ see: HA-FUCKING-HA!

hare and hound *noun*

a round of drinks *UK*

Rhyming slang; a variation of **FOX AND HOUND**.

- — Ray Puxley, *Cockney Rabbit*, 1992

hare-and-hound race *noun*

a long motorcyle race in the desert *US*

- A single rider, the "hare," is sent out before the event to mark an irregular course... Then the contestants, the "hounds," are allowed to chase after the "hare" and find his trail. — John Lawlor, *How to Talk Car*, p. 59, 1965
- — Ed Radlauer, *Motorcylopedia*, p. 29, 1973

haricot bean; haricot *noun*

a male homosexual *AUSTRALIA*

Rhyming slang for **QUEEN**.

- Who's this haricot? — Barry Humphries, *Bazza Pulls It Off!*, 1971

Harlem credit card *noun*

a siphon used for stealing pertrol from parked cars *US*

- — *Maledicta*, p. 168, 1979: 'A glossary of ethnic slurs in American English'

Harlem handshake *noun*

a series of hand-to-hand manoeuvres that combine into an idiosyncratic handshake *US*

Harlem, New York, is a centre of the black community and figuratively used to emphasise stereotypical and negative black characteristics.

- "Cool." And he gives me a complex Harlem handshake which loses me halfway through. — Stuart Browne, *Dangerous Parking*, p. 41, 2000

Harlem heater *noun*

any improvised source of heat, such as leaving an oven door open to heat the room *US*

New York police slang.

- — Samuel M. Katz, *Anytime Anywhere*, p. 387, 1997: 'The extremely uofficial and completely off-the-record NYPD/ESU truck-two glossary'

Harlem sunset *noun*

the blood-red line on freshly razor-slashed skin *US, 1940*

Harlem, New York, is a centre of the black community and figuratively used to emphasise negative black characteristics; here, combined with an allusion to 'blood red sunsets', the suggestion is that only black people get into razor fights.

- But don't come limping back here with an armload of bloody doctor bills if she carves a Harlem sunset in your face with a pealhandled straight razor. — Scott Rubin, *National Lampoon's Big Book of Love*, p. 9, 2004
- Chicago overcoats, Harlem sunsets, a jorum of skee, a chippie with boss getaway sticks, giving a canary the Broderick... — Tim Dorsey, *Cadillac Beach*, p. 258, 2004

Harlem taxi *noun*

a large, luxury car painted in an extravagant colour *US*

- — *American Speech*, p. 269, December 1962: 'The language of traffic policemen'

Harlem tennis *noun*

the game of craps *US, 1983*

- — Thomas L. Clark, *The Dictionary of Gambling and Gaming*, p. 97, 1987

Harlem toothpick *noun*

a pocket knife; a switchblade *US, 1944*

- — Lou Shelly, *Hepcats Jive Talk Dictionary*, p. 25, 1945
- — *Rhythm and Blues*, p. 28, June 1955
- — Clarence Major, *Dictionary of Afro-American Slang*, p. 64, 1970

Harley wrench *noun*

a hammer *US*

Humorous biker (motorcyle) usage, suggesting a low degree of sophistication among motorcyle mechanics. Recorded in *www.mattsphotos.com/bikerslang*.

harmonic *noun*

Indian *tonic* water *UK*

Rhyming slang.

- Now – what was it? Vera [gin] and Harmonic for the lady – and an orange juice for you. — Anthony Masters, *Minder*, p. 16, 1984

harm reducer *noun*

marijuana *UK*

A reference to the claim that smoking tobacco mixed with marijuana will cause less harm than unadulterated tobacco.

- — Mike Haskins, *Drugs*, p. 287, 2003

harness *noun*

1 reinforcement on the outside of a safe *US*

- — Vincent J. Monteleone, *Criminal Slang*, p. 113, 1949

2 a uniform *US, 1853*

- — Norman Carlisle, *The Modern Wonder Book of Trains and Railroading*, p. 264, 1946

3 the leather clothing worn by some motorcyle riders and embraced as a fashion statement by others *US*

- — Kenn "Naz" Young, *Naz's Dictionary of Teen Slang*, p. 56, 1993

harness *adjective*

uniformed *US, 1903*

- In two minutes a squad car pulled up to the curb and a pair of harness bulls jumped out. — Mickey Spillane, *My Gun is Quick*, p. 10, 1950
- They hurried to join the group of harness cops converging on the fighters. — Chester Himes, *A Rage in Harlem*, p. x, 1957
- A tough-faced harness bull clomped into the arcade and handed Ferris a shoebox[.] — Robert Edmond Alter, *Carny Kill*, p. 31, 1966
- With all the harness bulls from the local precinct who're never supposed to go near the place standing round us in a circle jerk, smiling their jive asses off. — Emmett Grogan, *Final Score*, p. 70, 1976
- I was in a schoolyard, fer chrissake, maybe five, ten minutes, when these two cops from the 86th precinct bum-rap me! Can you imagine? Two dumb harness-bulls run me in for 'loitering with sexual intent.' — Terry Southern, *Now Dig This*, p. 146, 2001

harness rack *noun*

an old horse *CANADA*

- The old or otherwise decrepit horse, which is no longer any good for work, is nothing but a harness rack. — Chris Thain, *Cold as a Bay Street Banker's Heart*, p. 80, 1987

Harold Lloyd; harold *noun*

celluloid (as a housebreaking tool) *UK*

Rhyming slang, formed from the name of the legendary silent film comedian, 1893–1971.

- — John Gosling, *The Ghost Squad*, 1959

Harold Macmillan; 'arold *noun*

a villain *UK*

Rhyming slang, formed from the name of a British prime minister (1957–63) and statesman, 1894–1986.

- — Ray Puxley, *Cockney Rabbit*, 1992

Harold Pinter; 'arold *noun*

a splinter *UK*

Rhyming slang, formed from the name of a playwright (b.1930). Harold Pinter's literary style inspired the adjective 'Pinteresque' to describe terse dialogue laden with pauses.

- — Ray Puxley, *Cockney Rabbit*, 1992

harolds *noun*
knickers *AUSTRALIA*
Probably rhyming slang, from **HARRY TAGGS** – shortened to Harry, thus Harold.
- I reckon she would've dropped her harolds[.] —Barry Humphries, *Bazza Pulls It Off!*, 1971

harp *noun*
1 a harmonica *US, 1887*
- Singing Elmore James tunes and blowing the harp for us down here. — *The Blues Brothers*, 1980

2 an Irish-American or an Irish person *US, 1898*
- He viewed such casual insults as signs of good fellowship, the easy, rude, irrevent ways of family, fellow soldiers, brothers-in-combat, laughing when they called him a harp or a cat-lick. —Robert Campbell, *Boneyards*, p. 10, 1992

harpic *adjective*
mad, crazy, eccentric *UK*
A play on **ROUND THE BEND** (mad) and branded toilet cleaner Harpic's advertising slogan 'cleans round the bend'. It is interesting to note that a cocktail of blue curacoa, kahlua, vodka and lemonade is named Harpic – probably not just for the colour. Also used as a nickname.

harpist *noun*
a harmonica player *UK*
From **HARP** (a harmonica).
- "My Boy Lollipop," which showcased the guitar of Skatalite Ernest Ranglin and an unsung harpist from Jimmy Powell and Five Dimensions. —Timothy White, *Catch a Fire*, 1993

harpoon *noun*
a needle used to inject drugs intravenously, especially a hollow needle used in an improvised contraption *US, 1938*
- —David Maurer and Victor Vogel, *Narcotics and Narcotic Addiction*, p. 413, 1973

Harris tweed *noun*
amphetamine *UK*
Rhyming slang for **SPEED**.
- —Tom Hibbert, *Rockspeak!*, p. 80, 1983

Harry *noun*
heroin *US, 1954*
Giving an personal identity and disguise to **H** (heroin).
- More specifically, it was classified as M, C, and H – Mary, Charlie, and Harry – which stood for morphine, cocaine, and heroin. —William J. Spillard and Pence James, *Needle in a Haystack*, p. 147–148, 1945
- —Richard Lingeman, *Drugs from A to Z*, p. 83, 1969
- —Eugene Landy, *The Underground Dictionary*, p. 99, 1971
- —Angela Devlin, *Prison Patter*, p. 60, 1996
- —Robert Ashton, *This Is Heroin*, p. 206, 2002

Harry-big-button *noun*
any cheap electrical appliance characterised by unfashionable design, especially large control knobs *UK*
- The stereo's a bit Harry-big-button. — *www.LondonSlang.com*, June 2002

harry-carry *noun*
suicide *UK*
From Japanese *hara-kiri* (ritual suicide by disembowelment).
- —Angela Devlin, *Prison Patter*, p. 60, 1996

Harry Freemans *noun*
anything that is free *UK*
Royal Navy, from obsolete 'drink at freeman's quay' (to drink at another's expense).
- —Wilfred Granville, *A Dictionary of Sailors' Slang*, 1962

Harry Hill *noun*
a tablet of MDMA, the recreational drug best known as ecstasy *UK*
Rhyming slang for 'pill'; based on the name of UK comedian Harry Hill (b.1964).
- Despite often being referred to as Harry Hills, the big-collared comedian has never been linked with the drug. — *FHM Bionic*, p. 11, December 2001

Harry Hoof *noun*
a male homosexual *UK: SCOTLAND*
Glasgow rhyming slang for **POOF**.
- —Michael Munro, *The Original Patter*, 1985

Harry Huggins *noun*
a fool, an idiot, often with an implication that the fool is a victim (and a fool to be so) *UK*
Rhyming slang for **MUGGINS** (an idiot).
- If you get caught who'll cop a bollocking? Harry Huggins here. —Ray Puxley, *Cockney Rabbit*, 1992

Harry James *noun*
the nose *UK*
A pun on 'trumpet', connected to band leader and trumpet player Harry James (1916–83).
- [T]here is plenty of dust floating about in the air, which gets in your north and south and up your Harry James[.] —Frank Norman, *Bang To Rights*, p. 29, 1958

Harry Lauder *noun*
a prison warder *UK, 1961*
Rhyming slang, formed from the name of the Scottish comedian and singer, Sir Harry Lauder, 1870–1950.
- —Ray Puxley, *Cockney Rabbit*, 1992

Harry Lime *noun*
time *UK, 1972*
Rhyming slang, formed from the name of the character played by Orson Welles in the 1950 film *The Third Man*.
- What's the Harry Lime? —Ray Puxley, *Cockney Rabbit*, 1992

Harry Monk; harry *noun*
semen *UK, 1992*
Rhyming slang for **SPUNK**; generally reduced.
- ["]Was she as dirty as she looked?" "Can't really remember. Plenty of Harry on the boat [the face], though." —Colin Butts, *Is Harry on the Boat?*, p. 89, 1997
- [H]er brand new Schott top was splattered with Harry's semen – or Harry's Harry[.] —Garry Bushell, *The Face*, p. 172, 2001
- That? It's me 'Arry, mate. I've been collecting it for years. —Duncan MacLaughlin, *The Filth*, p. 92, 2002

Harry Selby *noun*
used in a theatre programme as a fictitious name for an actor *US*
Less common than **GEORGE SPELVIN**, but serving the same purpose.
- —Sherman Louis Sergel, *The Language of Show Biz*, p. 96, 1973

Harry Tagg *noun*
bag *UK*
Rhyming slang; theatrical. Current in 1960.

Harry Taggs; harolds *noun*
trousers *UK*
Rhyming slang for 'bags' (trousers).
- —Ray Puxley, *Cockney Rabbit*, 1992

Harry Tate *noun*
1 eight pounds (£8) *UK*
Rhyming slang, formed from the stage name of musical hall performer Ronald Hutchinson, 1872–1940.
- —Ray Puxley, *Cockney Rabbit*, 1992

2 a plate *UK*
Rhyming slang, formed from the stage name of musical hall performer Ronald Hutchinson, 1872–1940.
- —Ray Puxley, *Cockney Rabbit*, 1992

3 a first officer in the Merchant Navy *UK*
Rhyming slang for 'mate'.
- —Julian Franklyn, *A Dictionary of Rhyming Slang*, 1961

4 a confusion; an attack of nerves; an emotional state *UK, 1932*
Rhyming slang for 'state'.
- —Ray Puxley, *Cockney Rabbit*, 1992

Harry Tate *adjective*
late *UK, 1960*
Rhyming slang, formed from the stage name of musical hall performer Ronald Hutchinson, 1872–1940.
- Look at the time. It'll be too bleeding Harry to go in a minute. —Ray Puxley, *Cockney Rabbit*, 1992

Harry Tates *noun*
branded cigarettes, Player's 'Weights' *UK*
Rhyming slang, reported by David Hillman, 1974.

Harry, Tom and Dick *adjective*
▷ **see:** TOM AND DICK

Harry Wragg; Harry Rag; harry *noun*
a cigarette *UK*
Rhyming slang for **FAG** (a cigarette), formed on the name of jockey Harry Wragg, 1902–85.
- Harry Rag, Harry Rag, / Do anything just to get a Harry Rag, / And he curses himself for the life he's led, / And rolls himself a Harry Rag and puts himself to bed. —The Kinks, *Harry Rag*, 1967
- —John Fahs, *Cigarette Confidential*, p. 301, 1996: 'Glossary'

Harry X-ers
with Harry preceding and -ers suffixed, a personified variation of an adjective or adverb *UK, 1925*
Mainly nautical, in applications such as 'Harry Nuders' (naked).

harsh *noun*
marijuana, hashish *UK*
Probably a play on the pronunciation of **HASH** (hashish) but may well refer to the quality.
- —Mike Haskins, *Drugs*, p. 287, 2003

harsh *verb*
to criticise or disparage *US*
- —Connie Eble (Editor), *UNC-CH Campus Slang*, p. 5, Spring 1988
- —*People Magazine*, p. 72, 19th July 1993

▸ **harsh a mellow**
to ruin a calm situation *US*
- —Jim Crotty, *How to Talk American*, p. 162, 1997

harsh *adjective*
1 disagreeable, forbidding, severe *US, 1984*
Conventional English rendered slang by the young.
- —Connie Eble (Editor), *UNC-CH Campus Slang*, p. 4, Fall 1987
- Mr. Hall was way harsh! He gave me a C minus. —*Clueless*, 1995
- You're really harsh, man. —Kenneth Lonergan, *This is Our Youth*, p. 44, 2000

2 in motor racing, bumpy and rough *US*
- —Don Alexander, *The Racer's Dictionary*, p. 30, 1980

Hart, Schaffner and Marx *noun*
in poker, three jacks *US*
An allusion to a men's clothing manufacturer.
- —George Percy, *The Language of Poker*, p. 42, 1988

harum-scarum *adjective*
reckless, careless *UK, 1751*
- This nutty storyline allows [Ron] Howard to insert some midnight car chases and harum scarum shootouts into the film. —*The Guardian*, 16th February 2002

harum-scarum *adverb*
recklessly, wildly *UK, 1691*
- She left her weeding, uprooted shoots scattered harum-scarum across the dirt, and hurried to the toolshed. —Donna Tartt, *The Little Friend*, p. 288, 2002

harva *noun*
▷ **see:** ARVA

harvest moon; harvest *noun*
a black person *UK*
Rhyming slang for **COON**.

Harvey Nichol *noun*
a predicament *UK, 1932*
Rhyming slang for **PICKLE**, formed from the name of London department store Harvey Nichols.

Harvey Nichols *noun*
pickles, savoury condiments *UK*
Rhyming slang, formed from the name of a London department store.
- —Julian Franklyn, *A Dictionary of Rhyming Slang*, 1960

Harvey Nicks; Harvey Nic's *nickname*
Harvey Nichols, a fashionable department store *UK, 1991*
- I caught sight of my backview trying something on in Harvey Nic's. —Jennifer Saunders, *Absolutely Fabulous*, p. 124, 1992
- Yesterday, Harvey Nicks opened in Edinburgh, and next year will expand its operation in Birmingham, where it already has a small outlet. —*The Guardian*, 16th August 2002

Harvey Smith *noun*
a v-sign as an insulting gesture *UK*
Following an incident on 15th August 1971 when show-jumper Harvey Smith used the gesture at the British Jumping Derby and as a result was disqualified (a decision subsequently overturned); his spontaneous action swiftly became part of UK folklore.
- It was no longer the "two fingers" gesture, or the "up yours" – it was now simply "The Harvey Smith"[...] Many a lady will, in future, be relieved of the necessity of making a certain unladylike gesture by simply saying instead: "A Harvey Smith to you". —Desmond Morris, *Gestures*, p. 236, 1979

Harvey Wallbanger *noun*
any unsafe, reckless and/or drunk driver *US*
- —Lawrence Teeman, *Consumer Guide Good Buddy's CB Dictionary*, p. 61, 1976
- —Peter Chippindale, *The British CB Book*, p. 155, 1981

has *noun*
hashish *UK, 1998*
An abbreviated variation of **HASH**.
- —Mike Haskins, *Drugs*, p. 287, 2003

has-been *noun*
a person whose best days and greatest achievements are in the past *UK, 1606*
- [N]ow they say that he was just a bag of wind, a guy with a big mouth, a punch-drunk pug, a has-been. —Irving Shulman, *The Amboy Dukes*, p. 57, 1947
- James Mason wading into the sundown on account of being a has-been and all. —Frederick Kohner, *Gidget*, p. 4, 1957
- Some guy might boast about how he is going to get out next time and stay out, and some will put him down by saying he'll soon be back, playing marbles like a hasbeen[.] —Eldridge Cleaver, *Soul on Ice*, p. 43, 1968
- Who says Toots never talks to has-beens? —Jim Bouton, *Ball Four*, p. 97, 1970
- [I]ncreasingly bitter old washed-up hasbeen.. —Lester Bangs, *Psychotic Reactions and Carburetor Dung*, p. 377, 1981
- The first four were aging has-beens and never-weres. They were so grateful for this one more job ... that their biggest worry was not to lose control and piss all over their master's leg. —Robert Campbell, *Alice in La-La Land*, p. 195, 1987
- Oh I was a singer in a big band but now I'm a has-been so I need to get my head back in a magazine. —Shaun Ryder, *Shaun Ryder... in His Own Words*, 1994

has beens *noun*
green vegetables, especially cabbage *UK, 1984*
Rhyming slang for **GREENS**.
- —Ray Puxley, *Cockney Rabbit*, 1992

hasbian *noun*
a former lesbian; a woman who took lesbian lovers in college, but who reverted to heterosexuality after graduation from college *US*
- —Steven Daly and Nalthaniel Wice, *alt.culture*, p. 138, 1995

hash *noun*
1 hashish (cannabis resin or pollen) *US, 1948*
Variant spellings include 'hashi', 'hashis' and 'haschi'. Derived from the Arabic word for 'herb' or 'grass', as though it were the herb 'par excellence' (Sadie Plant, *Writing On Drugs*, 1999).
- 'And a little hash,' added Jean-baby. 'There was a little hashish in the can, too.' —Terry Southern, *Flash and Filigree*, p. 121, 1958
- All hashes are capable of producing great guffaws. —Mike Rock, *This Book*, 1999
- He'd done what you usually only see in those films with Hollywood party scenes: he'd filled five glass fruit bowls full of grass, weed, hash, Charlie and whizz[.] —Dave Courtney, *Raving Lunacy*, p. 63, 2000
- I kept in my pocket a chunk of hash, the hard brown resin of the female cannabis plant, much easier to carry around than a bag full of grass. —Simon Napier-Bell, *Black Vinyl White Powder*, p. 3, 2001

2 a number sign (#) on a computer keyboard *US*
- —Eric S. Raymond, *The New Hacker's Dictionary*, p. 39, 1991

▸ **make a hash**
to spoil, to make a mess of something *UK, 1833*
- The government has made a hash of free nursing care, and is trying to find someone to blame[.] —*The Guardian*, 1st June 2002

hash *verb*
to serve alcoholic drink that is not the brand claimed *US*
- Some asshole wants a Chivas sour, charge him for it but pour Chivas. And whatever the label says is what's going to be in the bottle. No hashing. —Vincent Patrick, *The Pope of Greenwich Village*, p. 150, 1979

hash and trash *noun*
background noise during a citizens' band radio transmission *US*
- —Wayne Floyd, *Jason's Authentic Dictionary of CB Slang*, p. 18, 1976

Hashbury *nickname*
the Haight-Ashbury neigbourhood of San Francisco *US*
A blending of the two street names and an allusion to the drug-using propensities of the area's residents.
- Colloquial for Haight-Ashbury (hippy central in S.F.).—Ruth Bronsteen, *The Hippy's Handbook*, p. 14, 1967
- —*American Speech*, Winter 1982

hashcake *noun*
a confection that has marijuana or hashish as a major ingredient *UK*
- Bits uv cheese an onion an stuff are tryin tih slither up the hair towards er face, but that could just be thuh hashcake.—Niall Griffiths, *Grits*, p. 18, 2000

hash cannon *noun*
a device for smoking marijuana or hashish, used to force smoke deep into the lungs *US, 1970*
- —Ernest L. Abel, *A Marijuana Dictionary*, p. 48, 1982

hasher *noun*
a waitress in an inexpensive restaurant *US, 1908*
- —Ramon Adams, *The Language of the Railroader*, p. 75, 1977

hash girl *noun*
▷ see: HESH GIRL

hash head *noun*
a frequent smoker of hashish *US*
- You bloody hash-heads, get out of here!—William Burroughs, *Naked Lunch*, p. 92, 1957

hash house *noun*
a restaurant that serves inexpensive, simply prepared food, catering to working men *US, 1868*
- I called the Globe office from a hash house down the street.—Mickey Spillane, *One Lonely Night*, p. 23, 1951
- It was a hash house run by a Greek, Mike Manos, and he was nice. —Willard Motley, *Let No Man Write My Epitaph*, p. 43, 1958
- Just after Santa Barbara, I walked into a drive-in hash house.—Clancy Sigal, *Going Away*, p. 63, 1961

hash joint *noun*
a hash house *US, 1895*
- Right up the street under the el was an all-night hash joint, and what I needed was a couple mugs of good black java to bring me around. —Mickey Spillane, *My Gun is Quick*, p. 6, 1950

hash out *verb*
to discuss until an issue is resolved *US*
- We'd hash it out sowly and she'd be pacified.—Howard Stern, *Miss America*, p. 168, 1995

hashover *noun*
a general feeling of lethargy or malaise following marijuana use *UK*
A play on 'hangover' and HASH (marijuana).
- —Angela Devlin, *Prison Patter*, p. 60, 1996

hash-puppy *noun*
a dog trained to sniff-out marijuana
A play on Hush Puppies™, US branded footware, introduced in 1958.
- In Israel trained "hash-puppies" will sniff you out[.]—Richard Neville, *Play Power*, p. 139, 1970

hash-slinger *noun*
a waitress or cook *US, 1868*
- "Yes, boys, you'll meet the higher brand of hash slingers here," Jack said.—James T. Farrell, *Saturday Night*, p. 46, 1947
- Tonight I got a date to lay a cute hashslinger that works in the greasy spoon around the corner.—Iceberg Slim (Robert Beck), *Trick Baby*, p. 219, 1969

hassle *noun*
a problem, trouble, harrassment *US, 1946*
- He's Mrs. Jenks' boy; what's the hassle?—George Mandel, *Flee the Angry Strangers*, p. 56, 1952
- And like after all these hassles out here Red will have big eyes to blow as soon as he hits the Apple.—Ross Russell, *The Sound*, p. 96, 1961
- —J. L. Simmons and Barry Winograd, *It's Happening*, p. 170, 1966: 'glossary'
- He saw her through the mirror, but he didn't feel like going through a hassle about whatever was bothering her[.]—Nathan Heard, *Howard Street*, p. 195, 1968
- What's the hassle babe?—*Airheads*, 1994
- I've had hassle from the old bill [police] myself[.]—Mark Steel, *Reasons to be Cheerful*, p. 2, 2001

hassle *verb*
1 to harass, annoy *US, 1959*
- The nightclub acts haven't been paid in so long that they're hassling with me and with each other.—Dick Gregory, *Nigger*, p. 118, 1964
- Almost everyday I get hassled. Illegally hassled. Unlawfully hassled. —Susan Hall, *Gentleman of Leisure*, p. 12, 1972
- Widows and divorcees don't get ... what's Mona's word? ... hassled. We don't get hassled as much as single girls.—Armistead Maupin, *Tales of the City*, p. 49, 1978
- Try obeyin' the law once in a while and I won't have to hassle you. —*48 Hours*, 1982
- Anywhere else in the country, I was a bookie, a gambler, always lookin' over my shoulder, hassled by cops, day and night.—*Casino*, 1995

2 to engage in mock plane-to-plane aerial combat *US, 1979*
- Those jets were fighting – hassling – he was sure of it. He banked his jet, and accelerated toward them.—Robert K. Wilcox, *Scream of Eagles*, p. 3, 1990

hasta la bye-bye
goodbye *US*
Intentionally butchered Spanish.
- —Connie Eble (Editor), *UNC-CH Campus Slang*, p. 1, Spring 1990

hasta la vista, baby!
see you later! *US*
Popularised by Tone Loc in his 1989 rap hit 'Wild Thing'.
- —Connie Eble (Editor), *UNC-CH Campus Slang*, p. 5, November 1990

hasta lumbago
used as a humorous farewell *US*
An intentional corruption of the Spanish *hasta luego* (until later).
- "I'll see you in the morning." "Hasta lumbago."—Edwin Torres, *Q & A*, p. 30, 1977

hat *noun*
1 in drag racing, a crash helmet *US*
- —Lyle K. Engel, *The Complete Book of Fuel and Gas Dragsters*, p. 151, 1968

2 a condom *US*
- —Judi Sanders, *Kickin' like Chicken with the Couch Commander*, p. 11, 1992
- Well I hope you wore a hat.—*Menace II Society*, 1993
- —Connie Eble (Editor), *UNC-CH Campus Slang*, p. 3, Spring 1993

3 a woman *US, 1963*
- —Robert S. Gold, *A Jazz Lexicon*, p. 140, 1964

4 on the railways, an incompetent worker *US*
- —Ramon Adams, *The Language of the Railroader*, p. 75, 1977

5 a US Marines drill instructor *US*
- —Linda Reinberg, *In the Field*, p. 102, 1991

6 twenty-five dollars *US*
- For the price of a "hat," which is to say $25, one of the clerical men he knew there introduced him to a clerk in division.—Leonard Shecter and William Phillips, *On the Pad*, p. 32, 1973

7 anything bought with a bribe, used as code for a bribe *US*
- "Here," he said lazily, "get yourself a hat." A "hat" was a code word for a bonus above regularly scheduled payoffs.—Peter Maas, *Serpico*, p. 158, 1973
- We got some rules that go along with giving you this hat.—Stephen J. Cannell, *The Tin Collectors*, p. 246, 2001

8 the up-arrow or caret key (^) on a computer keyboard *US*
- —Eric S. Raymond, *The New Hacker's Dictionary*, p. 40, 1991

9 a dose of LSD *US*
- —US Department of Justice, *Street Terms*, October 1994

10 in pinball, a piece of plastic that indicates a value when lit *US*
Conventionally known as a 'playfield insert'.
- —Bobbye Claire Natkin and Steve Kirk, *All About Pinball*, p. 113, 1977

▸**get hat**
to leave *US, 1966*
- The wise thing for you to do would be to get hat. And not be found in this area again, you dig?—Joseph Nazel, *Black Cop*, p. 155, 1974

▸ **in the hat**

marked for murder by a prison gang *US*

- State and federal authorities confirmed last week that the man called 'the most dangerous man in California' in the wake of Diane Whipple's brutal death in January 2001 has been marked for assassination – or "placed in the hat," in the parlance of the white supremacist gang. — *San Francisco Chronicle*, p. C1, 28th October 2003

▸ **throw your hat in first**

to test out a situation before taking part *AUSTRALIA, 1953*

- It was Fay McFee again, declaring in her brassy contralto that she supposed she ought to throw her hat in first, but didn't have one. — Xavier Herbert, *Poor Fellow My Country*, p. 343, 1975

▸ **wear more than one hat; wear several hats**

to simultaneously hold more than one post, or position of responsibility *UK, 1984*

- Many change projects require you to wear more than one hat. — Daryl R. Conner, *Managing at the Speed of Change*, 1993

hat and coat *noun*

a boat, especially a refrigerated cargo ship *UK*

Rhyming slang.

- — Ray Puxley, *Cockney Rabbit*, 1992

hat and feather; hatton *noun*

weather *UK*

Rhyming slang.

- When's this poxy hat and feather gonna clear up? — Ray Puxley, *Cockney Rabbit*, 1992

hat and scarf *noun*

a bath *UK*

Rhyming slang, with Cockney pronunciation.

- — Ray Puxley, *Cockney Rabbit*, 1992

hatch *noun*

1 the vagina *US*

- — Dale Gordon, *The Dominion Sex Dictionary*, p. 82, 1967

2 the mouth *US*

- — Hy Lit, *Hy Lit's Unbelievable Dictionary of Hip Words for Groovy People*, p. 49, 1968

hatch *verb*

▸ **hatch it**

to forget about something *US*

- — Joan Fontaine et al., *Dictionary of Black Slang*, 1968

hatchery *noun*

a psychiatric ward or mental institution *US*

- — Sally Williams, *"Strong" Words*, p. 137, 1994

hatchet job *noun*

an unwarranted and harshly critical attack on someone's or something's reputation *UK, 1944*

- [Martin] Amis survives hatchet job on day of the long knives for other star writers[.] — *The Guardian*, 16th August 2003

hatchet man *noun*

1 a person who is called upon to perform distasteful tasks *US, 1937*

From the literal image of a paid assassin armed with a hatchet; sometimes abbreviated to a simple 'hatchet'.

- Some years earlier this man had been a "hatchet" – paid executioner – for the Hip Sing Tong. — Harry J. Anslinger (US Commissioner of Narcotics), *The Murderers*, p. 123, 1961
- He's Butcher Knife Brown's ace runner and hatchet man since Brown has got elderly and half-blind. — Iceberg Slim (Robert Beck), *Trick Baby*, p. 305, 1969
- One of the meanings of 'hatchet man' is someone who is hired by a company to bring about changes which the employees may not like. — *The Hindu*, 27th March 2001

2 a physically aggressive athlete, especially one who is tasked with roughing up an opponent *US*

- — Zander Hollander and Sandy Padwe, *Basketball Lingo*, p. 54, 1971
- — Bill Shefski, *Running Press Glossary of Football Language*, p. 54, 1978

hatchintan *noun*

a gypsy site *UK*

English gypsy use, from Romany *hatsh* (stop, rest).

- — Jimmy Stockin, *On The Cobbles*, p. 10, 2000

hatch, match and dispatch; hatches, matches, dispatches; hatched, matched, dispatched *noun*

newspaper announcements of births, marriages and deaths *UK, 1937*

A neat summation of life, originally applied by journalists to such newspaper columns; later recognised by church authorities as the times when most people are prepared to be part of a service or congregation.

- Hatch, match and dispatch. More deaths than births were recorded in Scotland in 1999[.] — *BBC News (Scotland)*, 20th July 2000
- HATCHES, MATCHES & DISPATCHES RETURN TO GATEHOUSE — Dumfries and Galloway Council, 24th June 2003

hatch, match, and dispatch *verb*

(of a local preacher), to carry a person through life's big events *CANADA*

- Lennoxville [Quebec] proverbial clergyman job description. This one adds baptism to two duties in another. — Lewi Poteet, *Talking Country*, p. 43–44, 1992

hate *verb*

used in the phrase 'hate to say' as a substitute for 'have' *US*

- Did you see their house? I hate to say that ours is bigger[.] — Maggie Balistreri, *The Evasion-English Dictionary*, p. 38, 2003

▸ **hate your guts**

to hate you intensely *UK, 1918*

- "He hates the Fascists." He hesitated. "Know who else hates their guts? Luciano.["] — Harry J. Anslinger (US Commissioner of Narcotics), *The Murderers*, p. 104, 1961
- Jimmy hates your fucking guts, Charlie. — Ted Lewis, *Jack Carter's Law*, p. 52, 1974

hated *adjective*

1 bad, unpleasant *US*

- — Connie Eble (Editor), *UNC-CH Campus Slang*, p. 3, Fall 1989

2 (used of a girl) beautiful beyond imagination *US*

Usually as 'hated **BETTY**'.

- — Surf Punks, *Oh No! Not Them Again! (liner notes)*, 1988

hater *noun*

a jealous or envious person *US*

- — Connie Eble (Editor), *UNC-CH Campus Slang*, p. 5, Fall 2001

hater juice *noun*

derogatory speech *US*

- — Connie Eble (Editor), *UNC-CH Campus Slang*, p. 5, Spring 2003

hating life *adjective*

depressed *US*

- — Connie Eble (Editor), *UNC-CH Campus Slang*, p. 5, Spring 1989

hatless tap dance *noun*

(among Canadian Forces personnel) the march into the Commanding Officer's office to face a charge *CANADA*

- The "Hatless Tap-Dance" is a "charge parade," that is, the process of formally marching in a servicemember charged with a service offence, to a hearing before the Commanding Officer. — Tom Langeste, *Words on the Wing*, p. 138–139, 1995

hat out; hat up *verb*

to leave *US, 1970*

- — David Claerbaut, *Black Jargon in White America*, p. 68, 1972
- I had scrounged up 'bout $600,000 worth o' diamonds, some really good 'n some really bad, and I was gettin' ready to hat up. — Odie Hawkins, *The Busting Out of an Ordinary Man*, p. 89, 1985

hats *noun*

LSD *UK, 1998*

- — Mike Haskins, *Drugs*, p. 285, 2003

hats off

congratulations *UK*

An imperative variation of 'take your hat off to'; when hats were everyday wear the action would echo the words or make their use unnecessary.

- Hats off to Jack. — David Peace, *Nineteen Seventy-Four*, p. 99, 1999

hatstand *adjective*

mad, crazy *UK*

From the cartoon character 'Roger Irrelevant: he's completely hatstand' in the comic *Viz*.

- — Susie Dent, *The Language Report*, p. 13, 2003

hatter *noun*

1 a solitary worker in a rural or remote area, especially one who suffers from social phobia *AUSTRALIA, 1853*
Originally applied to miners who worked their claims without a partner. Possibly from the phrase 'your hat covers your family' (you are alone in the world), though no doubt the concept of the 'mad hatter' must have had an influence. Now only historical.
- Sorenson also knew a boundary-rider hatter named Jack-the-Rager who had a habit of reciting poems in a strident voice when he was alone by his fire at night. — Bill Wannan, *Bullockies, Beauts and Bandicoots*, p. 78, 1960
- These solitary men are usually known as hatters. Some of them go under the name of death adder men, for it is reckoned they will bite your head off if spoken to before noon. — Jock Marshall and Russell Drysdale, *Journey Among Men*, p. 56, 1962

2 a homosexual man *UK, 1984*
From **BROWN-HATTER** (a gay man).

Hattie Jacques; Hatties *noun*

tremens, the shakes *UK*
Rhyming slang, based on the name of actress and comedienne Hattie Jacques (1924–80).
- After that booze up I 'ad a bad case of the Hatties. — *www.LondonSlang.com*, June 2002
- — Bodmin Dark, *Dirty Cockney Rhyming Slang*, 2003

hatton *noun*

▷ see: **HAT AND FEATHER**

hat trick *noun*

three consecutive successes, usually in a sporting context; three linked events *UK, 1909*
Originally and conventionally a cricketing term, recorded to mark the bowling of three wickets with consecutive balls; achieving this phenomenal feat entitled the sportsman to a new hat from his club, hence 'hat trick'. Subsequently adopted by other sports for lesser feats of three, such as three goals scored in a football match (which may well not be rewarded with a hat).
- [M]utterings he overheard suggested the [violent] incidents were related, he made a nervous bet with himself that day three wouldn't witness a hat-trick, and was proved right. — Christopher Brookmyre, *Boiling a Frog*, p. 42, 2000

hatty *adjective*

used to describe the qualities of an elaborate hat *UK*
- [G]irls couldn't possibly go to races without really hatty hats[.] — Derek Bickerton, *Payroll*, p. 38, 1959

hat up!

used for urging departure *US*
- — Hermese E. Roberts, *The Third Ear*, 1971

haud the bus!

▷ see: **HOLD THE BUS!**

hauf-scooped *adjective*

▷ see: **HALF-SCOOPED**

haul *noun*

the proceeds of a crime or business operation *US*
- — Hyman E. Goldin et al., *Dictionary of American Underworld Lingo*, p. 92, 1950

haul *verb*

▸ **haul ass**

to go swiftly *US, 1918*
- [T]he aptly named Fuzz, a hefty British Columbian, who's famous for greeting every new environment with "Let's haul ass outa here"[.] — Richard Neville, *Play Power*, p. 211, 1970
- So let's haul ass, Sergeant. — *M*A*S*H*, 1970
- "Now haul ass," he says, "and pray God I never see you two brought in here." — Darryl Ponicsan, *The Last Detail*, p. 143, 1970
- Told Sweeney, forget the landloard and haul ass to Bristol. — George V. Higgins, *The Rat on Fire*, p. 182, 1981
- Mr. Hall, I was surfing the crimson wave. I had to haul ass to the ladies'. — *Clueless*, 1995
- Fine, Greg. That's just fine. Now will you kindly haul arse. — Wilbur Smith, *Cry Wolf*, p. 136, 2001

▸ **haul butt**

to move quickly *US*
- — Collin Baker et al., *College Undergraduate Slang Study Conducted at Brown University*, p. 134, 1968

▸ **haul coal**

(used of a white person) to have sex with a black person *US*
- Some of the relationships in here are interracial, about 25 percent. The whites say, "Okay, if you wanna haul coal." — Bruce Jackson, *In the Life*, p. 359, 1972

▸ **haul over the coals**

to give a stern reprimand to someone *UK, 1795*
- I got hauled over the coals by our esteemed advisor. — Cynthia Voigt, *The Runner*, p. 197, 1997

▸ **haul the mail**

1 in trucking, to drive faster to make up for lost time *US*
- — Montie Tak, *Truck Talk*, p. 81, 1971

2 in hot rodding and drag racing, to perform at the highest potential *US*
- — John Edwards, *Auto Dictionary*, p. 74, 1993

hauler *noun*

1 in the usage of youthful model road racers (slot car racers), a fast model road car *US*
- — Phantom Surfers, *The Exciting Sounds of Model Road Racing (Album cover)*, 1997

2 a very fast drag racing car *US, 1960s to 70s*
- — John Radlauer, *Drag Racing Pix Dix*, p. 26, 1970

haurangi *adjective*

drunk *NEW ZEALAND*
- She's getting around with a mob like this – haurangi half the time. — Noel Hilliard, *Maoria Girl*, p. 101, 1960

have *verb*

1 to have sex with someone *UK, 1594*
- Don't you know that he's married, and that he's had more women than you can count? — Juan Rulfo (translated by Josephine Sacabo), *Pedro Paramo*, 1994

2 to believe something, to accept *UK*
- I'll tell him I've got the number off've Misty the other night when she was trying to get through to him. He'll have that. And I'll tell him I thought I was being followed. He'll have that and all, too. — Kevin Sampson, *Outlaws*, p. 255, 2001

3 to outwit, to cheat, to deceive *UK, 1805*

▸ **have a no**

I don't have *US*
Korean war usage from Japanese pidgin; a supply officer's perfect answer to a requisition for supplies not in stock.
- — *The Baltimore Sun*, 24th June 1951

▸ **have a pop at**

to attack, especially verbally *UK*
A variation of 'have a pop at' (to try) adopting a different sense of 'pop' (to hit).
- [Y]ou're in no position to have a pop at us. — *Kerrang!*, p. 8, 3rd November 2001

▸ **have got 'em; have got 'em bad**

to have the *delirium tremens*, to have a fit of nerves or depression or 'the blues' *UK, 1893*
- Yes that's what makes me feel so sad people / Oh, and today I got 'em bad. — B.B King, *Got 'em Bad*, 1956

▸ **have got it bad; have got it badly**

to have fallen in love or to be infatuated *UK, 1911*
- She wants me / Like poison ivy / Needs me / Like a hole in the head / Everyone can see she's got it bad. — Elvis Presley, *The Lady Loves Me*, 1983

▸ **have had it**

1 to be faced with an unavoidable prospect of defeat or ruin; to be defeated, to be ruined; to be dead or to have been killed *UK, 1941*
- Jimmy Green spotted some 'nasty looking pillboxes along the coast'. One looked particularly lethal. 'If there's anybody in there,' Green thought, 'We've had it'. — *The Observer*, 1st June 2003

2 to have had more than enough of; to be sick and tired of *UK, 1984*
- Waiting for him to give us the word. Waiting to start off. I've had waiting. — Derek Bickerton, *Payroll*, p. 42, 1959
- I've had it with going here, there and everywhere and walking miles for fuck all. — Martin King and Martin Knight, *The Naughty Nineties*, p. 123, 1999

▸ **have had it up to here**
to have had more than enough of; to be sick and tired of *UK, 1984*
An elaboration of **HAVE HAD IT**; here accompanied with a gesture that indicates the neck or the top of the head.

▸ **have it**
to fight *UK*
- [N]ewspaper pundits who get all stiff and moist over biographies of bare-knuckle fighters often turn a bit squeamish at the thought of two mobs having it in public streets with not a purse in sight for the victor. —Irvine Welsh, *The Naughty Nineties*, p. 9, 1999

▸ **have it away**
1 to escape from imprisonment or arrest; to get away *UK, 1958*
- [T]he PO [Prison Officer] who was in charge of the escort that was going to take us and look after us and make sure no one had it away. —Frank Norman, *Bang To Rights*, p. 39, 1958
- [T]he infantry went home with drums beating six months ago, the sappers have packed up, even the chinkies [Chinese] have had it away[.] —Graeme Kent, *The Queen's Corporal [Six Granada Plays]*, p. 82, 1959
- —Angela Devlin, *Prison Patter*, p. 61, 1996

2 to steal *UK*
- They thought they'd had it away with a Belgian juggernaut and there were six Old Bill sitting in the back. —Anthony Masters, *Minder*, p. 59, 1984

▸ **have it in for**
to bear a grudge against; to wish to harm *UK, 1840s*
- [W]ith things as they are now Bell and O'Mally have got it in for you and I don't blame them either. Coming in here you're just asking for trouble. —Graeme Kent, *The Queen's Corporal [Six Granada Plays]*, p. 86, 1959

▸ **have it made; have got it made**
to be on the point of succeeding; to be faced with no (more) obstacles; to have it easy *US, 1955*
- Bartenders got it made. Drugs, sex, money, connections – an endless supply coming across the bar. — *The Guardian*, 23rd January 1999

▸ **have it off**
1 to have sex *UK, 1937*
- They walk in, have it off with me, say 'Ta' and then stroll out again, nice and simple with no complications. Like buying a packet of fags. — *Flame*, p. 11, 1972
- Let me put it another way – were you and Billy havitng it off on the side. —Anthony Masters, *Minder*, p. 74, 1984
- [P]ictures of the Spice Girls having it off with each other[.] —Danny King, *The Burglar Diaries*, p. 58, 2001

2 to succeed in a criminal enterprise *UK, 1936*
- [T]hey pulled off some lovely jobs. They had been having it off very nicely for some months[.] —Charles Raven, *Underworld Nights*, p. 46, 1956

▸ **have it on your dancers**
to escape; to run away *UK*
An elaboration of **HAVE IT ON YOUR TOES**.

▸ **have it on your toes; have it away on your toes**
to escape; to run away *UK, 1958*
- [H]e had been transfer[e]d because he had had it on his toes, and was out for about three months before he had got captured. —Frank Norman, *Bang To Rights*, p. 102, 1958
- —Angela Devlin, *Prison Patter*, p. 61, 1996
- Everyone else had it away on their toes when Maltese Mickey died. —John Milne, *Alive and Kicking*, p. 52, 1998

▸ **have one in the departure lounge**
to feel the urgent need to defecate *UK*
- — *www.LondonSlang.com*, June 2002

▸ **have yourself**
to indulge yourself or provide yourself with something *US, 1929*
- ["T]hirty min-utes?" "Make it an hour and you have yourself a deal." "An hour, then." Dora retreated to her room[.] —Maureen Tan, *A.K.A. Jane*, p. 80, 1999

have-a-go *adjective*
describes a person who bravely attempts to prevent a crime; intrepid *UK, 1971*
- Have-a-go hero saves the Brits. — *BBC News*, 16th February 1999
- Have-a-go father praised. — *The Guardian*, 29th January 2003

have a good one
goodbye *US*
Slightly cooler than urging someone to 'have a good day'.
- —Jonathan Roberts, *How to California*, p. 168, 1984
- —Connie Eble (Editor), *UNC-CH Campus Slang*, p. 5, Spring 1989
- DANTE: Thanks. Have a good one. — *Clerks*, 1994

have an apple!
get lost, forget it, calm down *CANADA*
- A night-watchman came along and yelled at Mary, asking if she wanted to knock the lights over. "Oh, have an apple!" Mary yelled back at him. —Morley Callaghan, *Stories*, p. 240, 1959

have been!
I'll see you later! *US*
Youth usage.
- — *Time*, 3rd October 1949

have legs *verb*
of an abstract, to have the ability to progress *UK, 1999*
Media jargon that has seeped into wider usage.
- Are you sure this idea has legs? —Stewart Home, *Sex Kick [britpulp]*, p. 202, 1999

have off *verb*
1 to steal from *UK*
- He invested in some tables and chairs for outside and someone's had 'em off. — *ID*, 1994
- [H]ordes of tourists and trippers [...] from all over the world, expressly to be had off. By us. —Kevin Sampson, *Outlaws*, p. 7, 2001

2 to use without respect *UK*
A variation of the previous sense.
- We're getting misquoted! [...] The press are having us off good style! —Kevin Sampson, *Powder*, p. 227, 1999

3 to defeat, to overthrow, to supplant *UK*
- [A] younger lad will walk up to you and pure have you off [...] Pop [kill] you. Zap [shoot] you in the leg. Knock you out if you're lucky. —Kevin Sampson, *Outlaws*, p. 66, 2001

have on *verb*
to take up a challenge; to accept an invitation to fight or compete *AUSTRALIA, 1941*
- Stu watched them go, then said, "Looks like he's gonna have you on, Math." —Simon French, *Hey Phantom Singlet*, p. 31, 1975

have you been?
have you used the lavatory? *UK, 1969*
Euphemistic.

have you ever wanted a bindi?
used with humour to accompany a threatened knuckle blow to a companion's forehead *UK*
A catchphrase that offers a red mark in the centre of the forehead; heard in use 16th January 2003 and reported as having been in circulation for 'a couple of years'.

Hawaiian *noun*
1 very potent marijuana cultivated in Hawaii *US*

2 a marijuana cigarette *UK*
- —Mike Haskins, *Drugs*, p. 291, 2003

Hawaiian black *noun*
a dark leafed marijuana from Hawaii
- —Mike Haskins, *Drugs*, p. 287, 2003

Hawaiian disease *noun*
sexual abstinence due to an absence of women *US*
An allusion to the mythical illness 'lakanuki' (lack of sex).
- "Granddaddy says she is suffering from some terrible old maid's Hawaiian disease." "Oh really? What?" "Something called lackanoo-kie," she said perfectly straight and with no recognizable humor. —Shirley MacLaine, *It's All in the Playing*, p. 139, 1987

Hawaiian head *noun*
a strain of marijuana, known elsewhere as New Zealand green, Thai Buddha or Tasmanian tiger *US*
- [A] strain that had once been called Thai Buddha, then went to Hawaii for a while and came back with the name Hawaiian Head. —Brian Preston, *Pot Planet*, p. 97, 2002

Hawaiian homegrown hay *noun*
a marijuana grown in Hawaii *UK*
- —Mike Haskins, *Drugs*, p. 287, 2003

Hawaiian number *noun*
any elaborate production number in a show or film *US*
- The derivation seems to stem from those old technicolor movie musicals in which there cropped up every so often elaborate, complicated, costly, and essentially inane production numbers of a

"Hawaiian" or "Polynesian' genre.—Sherman Louis Sergel, *The Language of Show Biz*, p. 105, 1973

Hawaiian sunshine *noun*

LSD *US, 1982*

- —Richard A. Spears, *The Slang and Jargon of Drugs and Drink*, p. 252, 1986
- —Mike Haskins, *Drugs*, p. 285, 2003

haw-eater *noun*

an Ontarian from Manitoulin Island *CANADA*

- Their local word for themselves comes from [the fact that] they like hawberries, the dark-red fruit of a hawthorn common in northern Ontario.—Bill Casselman, *Canadian Food Words*, p. 182, 1998

hawg *noun*

a large motorcyle, especially a Harley-Davidson *US*

- Thirty or so hawgs are parked in front, many of their owners (One Percenters, as they're known) pissing into the night highway.—Bill Cardoso, *The Maltese Sangweech*, p. 243, 1984

hawk *noun*

1 LSD *US*

May be used with 'the'.

- —Donald Louria, *Nightmare Drugs*, p. 45, 1966
- Street names [...] Gorbachovs, hawk, L, lightning flash[.]—James Kay and Julian Cohen, *The Parents' Complete Guide to Young People and Drugs*, p. 141, 1998

2 a lookout *US*

- —*American Speech*, p. 98, May 1956: 'Smugglers' argot in the southwest'

3 any cold night wind *US, 1946*

Often with 'the'.

- —Connie Eble (Editor), *UNC-CH Campus Slang*, p. 4, Spring 1982
- As if on cue, the ramp behind Evans began to open, letting in the cold night air, known to the paratroopers as "the Hawk."—Harold Coyle, *Sword Point*, p. 83, 1988
- Paratroopers call it "The Hawk," a piercing chill that cuts through the flesh to the bone with a talon-like grip.—*Washington Times*, 30th January 1991

Hawk *noun*

▸ **the Hawk**

a strong wind that blows off Lake Michigan across Chicago, Illinois *US, 1946*

- It wasn't bad at all in the summer, that wind, but in the winter it was gruesome. The Hawk, it was called ironically. Lou Rawls sings about it, calls it a giant razor blade.—Odie Hawkins, *Black Casanova*, p. 119, 1984
- The wind Chicagoans called the Hawk flew over the empty lots, the eyeless windows, flying low, talons scraping the big painted plate-glass windows, prying into doorways where derelicts sought shelter, chattering in rage down the alleys.—Robert Campbell, *Boneyards*, p. 184, 1992
- I'm wearing no coat against the frontline urgency of the Hawk of Lake Michigan.—Clarence Major, *All-Night Visitors*, p. 142, 1998

hawk *verb*

1 to expectorate sputum *US*

- —*Maledicta*, p. 32, 1988–1989: 'Medical maledicta from San Francisco'

2 to watch closely, to check out *US, 1886*

- All I have to do is pull around the corner where nobody can hawk the license plate.—Clarence Cooper Jr, *The Scene*, p. 61, 1960
- Yeah, she looked at me like I was duck under glass and I hawked her likewise.—A.S. Jackson, *Gentleman Pimp*, p. 77, 1973
- I'm hawkin' the three guys at the pool table, but all I see is cue-sticks.—Elmore Leonard, *After Hours*, p. 170, 1979
- He'd been brought in there the time he was picked up for hawking a queer and released when the queer wouldn't identify him.—Elmore Leonard, *City Primeval*, p. 19, 1980

3 to make an aggressive romantic approach *US*

- —Kenn "Naz" Young, *Naz's Dictionary of Teen Slang*, p. 56, 1993

▸ **hawk the fork**

(of a woman) to work as a prostitute *AUSTRALIA*

- Daughter hawking the fork in Honkers, dirty little bitch.—Barry Humphries, *A Nice Night's Entertainment*, p. 170, 1978

▸ **hawk your mutton**

to work as a prostitute *UK*

- [T]he old man used to have a soft spot for this Moira when she was on street corners 'awkin' the mutton.—Bernard Demsey and Kevin McNally, *Lock, Stock... & Two Sips*, p. 288, 2000

Hawk *nickname*

Coleman Hawkins, a leading jazz saxophonist of the 1920s and 1930s *US*

- He presented Dizzy, Hawk, Yardbird, Sarah and many others in concert back in "43".—Babs Gonzales, *Be-Bop Dictionary and History of its Famous Stars*, p. 12, 1949
- When Hawk was the 'King of the Street' he used to come home through Central Park in his Caddy.—Babs Gonzales, *Movin' On Down De Line*, p. 76, 1975

hawker *noun*

expectorated sputum *US, 1974*

- —*Maledicta*, p. 32, 1988–1989: 'Medical maledicta from San Francisco'

Hawkesbury Rivers *noun*

the shivers *AUSTRALIA, 1941*

From the name of a river in New South Wales.

- —Ryan Aven-Bray, *Ridgey Didge Oz Jack Lang*, p. 31, 1983

hawk-eye *verb*

to watch closely *US*

- I had agreed to hawk-eye (from my modest pad down the hall) and occupy the suite during prime burglar time.—Iceberg Slim (Robert Beck), *Airtight Willie and Me*, p. 47, 1979

hawkins *noun*

cold weather *US, 1934*

An embellishment and personification of **HAWK**.

- —Marcus Hanna Boulware, *Jive and Slang of Students in Negro Colleges*, 1947

hawkshaw *noun*

a detective *US, 1888*

From the name of a detective in the 1863 play *The Ticket of Leave Man* by Tom Taylor, and later and more relevantly from the comic strip *Hawkshaw the Detective*, drawn by Gus Mager (1913–22, 1931–48). In UK West Indian use.

- —Vincent J. Monteleone, *Criminal Slang*, p. 114, 1949
- —David Powis, *The Signs of Crime*, 1977
- —Ralph de Sola, *Crime Dictionary*, p. 62, 1982

hawkshaw *verb*

to snoop, to inquire *US*

- When the German censor came hawkshawing around to see what Hughes was doing on his program, he was shown a record labeled La Tristesse de St. Louis[.]—Mezz Mezzrow, *Really the Blues*, p. 195, 1946

haw maws *noun*

the testicles *UK: SCOTLAND*

Glasgow rhyming slang for **BAWS** (**BALLS**), from a cry to attract your mother's attention.

- Ooyah, right in the haw maws!—Michael Munro, *The Patter, Another Blast*, 1988

hay *noun*

1 a bed, either in the context of sleep or of sex *US, 1903*

- The difference was that the one named Al had the reputation of being great in the hay.—Norman Mailer, *Advertisements for Myself*, p. 392, 1950
- In the good old days, the consecrated left-wingers used to go to the Soviet Embassy, where they proved their party loyalty by getting in the hay with the men from Moscow.—Jack Lait and Lee Mortimer, *Washington Confidential*, p. 152, 1951
- My wife says I'm a bastard, but she still likes me in the hay.—Mary McCarthy, *The Group*, p. 48, 1963
- We ate on the run and ran back for the hay.—Antony James, *America's Homosexual Underground*, p. 115, 1965

2 marijuana *US, 1934*

A play on **GRASS**.

- At the Mexican's we could at least get loaded on good hay[.]—Mezz Mezzrow, *Really the Blues*, p. 164, 1946
- The boys had roughed him up pretty badly bringing him in and now, what with the hay and all, he was a regular wild man.—Jim Thompson, *The Killer Inside*, p. 37, 1952
- Be a living doll, will you, and go in the other room and see can you contact this lad to bring up some hay?—Bernard Wolfe, *The Late Risers*, p. 203, 1954
- —Angela Devlin, *Prison Patter*, p. 61, 1996
- —Mike Haskins, *Drugs*, p. 287, 2003

3 money *AUSTRALIA, 1939*

- —John Scarne, *Scarne on Dice*, p. 470, 1974

hayburner *noun*

a horse, especially a poor-performing racehorse *US, 1904*

- —Robert Saunders Dowst and Jay Craig, *Playing the Races*, p. 164, 1960
- I reckon His Honour has three hay-burners in work. No hope of paying for their feed far as I can see. Pity, since you've been strapping two of them, Persian Pat and Beehive.—Wilda Moxham, *The Apprentice*, p. 31, 1969

hay butt *noun*

a marijuana cigarette *US, 1942*

- —Richard A. Spears, *The Slang and Jargon of Drugs and Drink*, p. 253, 1986
- —Mike Haskins, *Drugs*, p. 287, 2003

hayed up *adjective*

marijuana-intoxicated *US*

- A Mexican pipeliner had got all hayed up on marijuana and stabbed another Mexican to death. —Jim Thompson, *The Killer Inside*, p. 37, 1952

hay head *noun*

a marijuana user *US, 1942*

- —*American Speech*, p. 87, May 1955: 'Narcotic argot along the Mexican border'

haym *noun*

▷ see: HAME

haymaker *noun*

1 a powerful fist blow to the head *US, 1902*

- BRAD casually sets himself, then delivers the most powerful right haymaker in the history of cinema. —Terry Southern, *Now Dig This*, p. 96, 1967
- Felix lashed back with a haymaker, right off the ghetto streets. —Piri Thomas, *Stories from El Barrio*, p. 138, 1978
- The black fighter had just landed a haymaker on the white fighter who was even now reeling across the ring on legs of jelly. —Anthony Masters, *Minder*, p. 3, 1984
- Come on, you pup, you're up against Gerry O'Byrne!' and laid the fellow out with an almighty haymaker in the breadbasket. —Aidan Higgins, *Donkey's Years*, p. 149, 1995

2 in cricket, a batsman's powerful but reckless shot *UK, 1954*

- —Keith Foley, *A Dictionary of Cricketing Terminology*, p. 171, 1998

haymaking *verb*

in cricket, powerful but reckless batting *UK, 1986*

- —Keith Foley, *A Dictionary of Cricketing Terminology*, p. 171, 1998

hayo *noun*

cocaine *US*

From a Caribbean name for the coca plant.

- —R.C. Garrett et al., *The Coke Book*, p. 200, 1984

hayron *noun*

heroin *UK*

Possibly a deliberately perverse pronunciation.

- —Mike Haskins, *Drugs*, p. 284, 2003

hayseed *noun*

a rustic or country yokel *US, 1851*

Strongly suggests a high degree of unsophistication.

- [A] hayseed from Jersey who went on to great heights in the glamor field as a teacher of modeling, a radio commentator and a fashion editor, before hitting the diplomatic set. —Lee Mortimer, *Women Confidential*, p. 133, 1960
- Cocaine, my dear hayseed, is the most expensive high there is. —Iceberg Slim (Robert Beck), *Trick Baby*, p. 167, 1969
- Looks like a hayseed bank and, tell you the truth, it is a hayseed bank. —*Raising Arizona*, 1987

hay shaker *noun*

a farmer *US, 1924*

- —Chris Thain, *Cold as a Bay Street Banker's Heart*, p. 81, 1987

haystack *noun*

the back, the rear *UK*

Rhyming slang. 'Going round the haystack' is noted as a possible euphemism for paying a visit to a toilet.

- —Julian Franklyn, *A Dictionary of Rhyming Slang*, 1960
- [T]radesman's round the haystack. —Ray Puxley, *Cockney Rabbit*, 1992

hay wagon *noun*

a brakevan (caboose) *US*

- —Ramon Adams, *The Language of the Railroader*, p. 75, 1977

haywire *adjective*

out of control; crazy; in wild disorder; chaotic *US, 1920*

The image of wire on a bale of hay that flails wildly when cut.

- —Collin Baker et al., *College Undergraduate Slang Study Conducted at Brown University*, p. 135, 1968
- [I]t was love gone hellacious and haywire. —Joel Rose, *Kill Kill Faster Faster*, p. 125, 1997
- [A] split second before it's all gone haywire [...] This is the bit in the movie where it all goes into slow motion. —J.J. Connolly, *Know Your Enemy [britpulp]*, p. 157, 1999

haze *noun*

1 LSD *US*

A shortened form of **PURPLE HAZE**.

- —US Department of Justice, *Street Terms*, October 1994

2 a variety of marijuana

- [T]he Real McCoy, which is a Haze-Skunk cross[.] —Brian Preston, *Pot Planet*, p. 232, 2002

haze *verb*

to bully, insult and ridicule a homosexual *UK*

A specialised nuance of the conventional sense (to punish, to bully).

- —David Powis, *The Signs of Crime*, 1977

hazed *adjective*

drug-intoxicated *US*

- —Pamela Munro, *U.C.L.A. Slang*, p. 80, 2001

Hazel *noun*

heroin *US, 1949*

Abbreviated **WITCH HAZEL** (heroin), and subsequently disguised as 'Aunt Hazel'.

- —J.E. Schmidt, *Narcotics Lingo and Lore*, p. 8, 1959
- —Robert Ashton, *This Is Heroin*, p. 206, 2002

haz-mat *noun*

hazardous material *US*

- The danger and helplessness of not knowing what to do that day resulted in formation of a "Haz Mat" unit[.] —*United Press International, BC cycle*, 11th September 1983

HBI *noun*

*h*ouse *b*reaking *i*mplements *UK, 1950*

Initialism.

- —Angela Devlin, *Prison Patter*, p. 61, 1996

H bomb *noun*

heroin mixed with MDMA, the recreational drug best known as ecstasy *UK*

Extended from **H** (heroin), playing on the devastating power of a nuclear weapon.

- —Robert Ashton, *This Is Heroin*, p. 209, 2002

H cap *noun*

a capsule of heroin *US*

- —Gilda and Melvin Berger, *Drug Abuse A-Z*, p. 73, 1990

he; him *noun*

the penis *UK*

A derivation immemorial.

- Abby puts her hand under the table, then gives him a squeeze. —Bill Naughton, *Alfie Darling*, 1970

head *noun*

1 a member of the counterculture, usually involving drugs *US*

- And that South American ring-ding with his sequined rodeo shirt, they couldn't be heads. —Richard Farina, *Been Down So Long*, p. 114, 1966
- A night club on the Sunset Strip called The Trip was obviously a gathering place for heads. —Lawrence Schiller (Introduction) to Richard Alpert and Sidney Cohen, *LSD*, p. 8, 1966
- Trouble is, heads don't take care of themselves. —Nicholas Von Hoffman, *We Are The People Our Parents Warned Us Against*, p. 211, 1967
- Anyway, just a couple of weeks before, the heads had held their first big "be-in" in Golden Gate Park, at the foot of the hill leading up into Haight-Ashbury, in mock observation of the day LSD became illegal in California. —Tom Wolfe, *The Electric Kool-Aid Acid Test*, p. 10, 1968
- What are heads interested in? They're interested in color, clothes, in dope, they're interested in lots of fresh fruit, and good natural foods[.] —Leonard Wolfe (Editor), *Voices from the Love Generation*, p. 12, 1968
- A few thousand of the absolutely most together and peaceful and loving and beautiful heads in the world are gathered in a grand tribal new beginning. —*East Village Other*, 20th August 1969
- [H]undreds of itinerant heads had freaked out on acid punch[.] —Richard Neville, *Play Power*, p. 232, 1970
- So, if heads on the land are responsible to their environment and its inhabitants (and not all of them are), then potential opponents at the barricades may have second thoughts. —*The Last Supplement to the Whole Earth Catalog*, p. 90, March 1971

2 a habitual user of drugs *US, 1953*

In the Vietnam war, the term differentiated between a person who smoked marijuana and a **JUICER** who abused alcohol.

- What you have to do is make a couple new heads. —John M. Murtagh and Sara Harris, *Cast the First Stone*, p. 45, 1957

- I mean everyone's a head – you know, just everyone! —John Clellon Holmes, *The Horn*, p. 107, 1958
- This is not a queer bar – it is an outcast bar – Negroes and vagrant whites, heads and hypes, dikes and queens. —John Rechy, *City of Night*, p. 184, 1963
- Take hippies and straights, heads and narcos, put them together for 36 hours – under a church roof. —*Berkeley Barb*, p. 3, 25th February 1967
- He was a friend of the sergeant's. They were the 'juicers' [alcohol drinkers] and I was the 'head' [pot smoker]. —Myra MacPherson, *Long Time Passing*, p. 398, 1984

3 a state of drug intoxication *US*

- Chico shot up immediately, but there was no real kick in the drug. Still, it got him a "head" and made him feel better. —Hal Ellson, *The Golden Spike*, p. 194, 1952
- Have you been using smack?" "Yeah. I've been using smack [...] It's an unbelievable head, man. THE best. Inbelievable. —Doug Lang, *Freaks*, p. 119–120, 1973

4 enough marijuana to fashion a single cigarette *UK*

- —Angela Devlin, *Prison Patter*, p. 61, 1996

5 a fan of hip-hop music *US*

- Dead Prez [a hip-hop group] left so much conflict amongst heads, it was hectic. —Patrick Neate, *Where You're At*, p. 89, 2003

6 a respected graffiti artist *US*

- —Jim Crotty, *How to Talk American*, p. 141, 1997

7 a familiarising term used to address both sexes, but more generally male *IRELAND*

Head can also be used to designate certain groups, for example, a 'D4 [Dublin 4] head' is a post southside person, not necessarily living in the D4 postcode.

- Clinger, head, how're they hangin'? —Eamonn Sweeney, *Waiting for the Healer*, p. 39, 1997

8 oral sex *US, 1941*

- Say, "Do you think you could teach me to deal, rob, and steal, beat some poor lame for his bread / turn a trick or suck dick in case I could sell some head?" —Bruce Jackson, *Get Your Ass in the Water and Swim Like Me*, p. 90, 1964
- [Y]ou were talking so brave and so sweet, / Giving me head on the unmade bed. —Leonard Cohen, *Chelsea Hotel*, 1968
- Excuse me, mademoiselle, to give you some head. —Steve Cannon, *Groove, Bang, and Jive Around*, p. 108, 1969
- Connie probably takes Raymond's little peanut of a cock between her brittle chapped lips and then scrapes her ugly decayed teeth up and down on it while asshole Raymond thinks he's getting the best head on the East Coast. —John Waters, *Pink Flamingos*, p. 59, 1972
- (Quoting Linda Lovelace) Just from guys saying that I was, like, the best, that I gave the best head they ever had. —*Screw*, p. 4, 9th October 1972
- Hey, now, you know it's funny you should ask that, because I would say, pound-for-pound, she gives about the best head in the city. —Terry Southern, *Now Dig This*, p. 33, 1975
- Let's see – the best head is Tina Russell. (Quoting Harry Reems). —*Adam Film Quarterly*, p. 77, December 1975
- You can get some cunt, asshole, or head / As long as you got the motherfucking bread. —Dennis Wepman et al., *The Life*, p. 128, 1976
- C'mon over and give me head while I'm passed out. —Lester Bangs, *Psychotic Reactions and Carburetor Dung*, p. 218, 1977
- Kiki had some real dynamite head. The best head on Eighth Avenue. —Robert Deane Pharr, *Giveadamn Brown*, p. 51, 1978
- I liked head and let him give it to me as frequently as it could be arranged. —Herbert Huncke, *The Evening Sun Turned Crimson*, p. 26, 1980
- But you're such a hunk / So full of spunk / I'll give you / Head / Til you're burning up. —Prince *Head*, 1980
- I love to give head. I love to make a guy come with my mouth. —*Adult Video*, p. 10, August/September 1986
- She gives great head. She really gets down and does this. —Robert Stoller and I.S. Levine, *Coming Attractions*, p. 131, 1991
- Back in those days, to discuss or request or demand the giving or getting of a blow job, you had to use the word "head," e.g., "She gave me head" or "I gave her head" or "Gee, I'd like some head." —Larry Rivers, *What Did I Do?*, p. 57, 1992
- But what happens when you get in the car, and you don't make with the head? Don't they kick your ass to the curb? —Kevin Smith, *Jay and Silent Bob Strike Back*, p. 26, 2001

9 the penis *TRINIDAD AND TOBAGO*

- —Lise Winer, *Dictionary of the English/Creole of Trinidad & Tobago*, 2003

10 a talking head *US*

With this shortened form, a good expert guest on a television or radio show becomes 'good head'.

11 deception *TRINIDAD AND TOBAGO, 1993*

- —Lise Winer, *Dictionary of the English/Creole of Trinidad & Tobago*, 2003

12 a crime victim *US*

- —Carsten Stroud, *Close Pursuit*, p. 272, 1987

13 a toilet *US, 1942*

- It seems Edith (bah) arrived at the bus depot early & while waiting for Patricia, feeling sleepy, retired to the head to sleep on a sofa. —Neal Cassady, *The First Third*, p. 190, 7th March 1947
- [F]inally Wallenstein going to the head for a leak[.] —Jack Kerouac, *The Subterraneans*, p. 77, 1958

14 music played without a musical score *US*

- The music they were turning out, thanks to Bix's head arrangements, was ten years ahead of its time. —Mezz Mezzrow, *Really the Blues*, p. 79, 1946
- But maybe if we do a whole set of heads, old ones- —John Clellon Holmes, *The Horn*, p. 193, 1958
- Our whole book is made up of heads. —Ross Russell, *The Sound*, p. 58, 1961

15 a railway worker *US*

- —Linda Niemann, *Boomer*, p. 251, 1990

▸ bite your head off; snap your head off

to attack verbally, especially as a disproportionate response *UK, 1984*

- Alright, alright, don't bite me bloody head off. I didn't say a word. —Niall Griffiths, *Kelly + Victor*, p. 292, 2002

▸ do it standing on your head; do on your head

to achieve with ease *UK, 1896*

- We'll both give it the large [brag] and talk a load of bollocks [nonsense] about how we'll do it standing on our heads. —Danny King, *The Burglar Diaries*, p. 241–242, 2001

▸ do your head in

to emotionally overload, confuse and make stressed *UK*

- It's the tablets girl. They do your head in. —Alan Bleasdale, *Boys From the Blackstuff*, 1982
- Doin' my head in, I tell you. —Cath Staincliffe, *Trainers*, p. 55, 1999
- Mam, will you go and get rid of that nobhead I'm marrying... it's doing my head in, this. —Caroline Aherne and Craig Cash, *The Royle Family*, 1999
- Yeah, the bouncing sound was the thing that done your head in most. —Dave Courtney, *Raving Lunacy*, p. 39, 2000
- The city had been doing all our heads in, he had proclaimed[.] —Diran Abedayo, *My Once Upon A Time*, p. 33, 2000
- [O]ne thing pure guaranteed to do my head in is selfish driving. —Kevin Sampson, *Outlaws*, p. 2, 2001

▸ get your head down; get your head down to it

to plead guilty *AUSTRALIA*

From bending the head in unspoken affirmative.

- —*The (Sydney) Bulletin*, 26th April 1975

▸ give head

to perform oral sex *US, 1956*

- You can't see too much, but in the dark light you can make out a per 18-year-old McCarthy supporter (Mancy MacKay?), giving the finest head to old Rip[.] —*Screw*, p. 21, 10th November 1969
- "Spit," Ophelia concluded, "that's the whole trick to giving head. Just spit." —Eve Babitz, *L.A. Woman*, p. 16, 1982

▸ have a head like a sieve

to be very forgetful *UK, 1984*

- Don't ask me for any names. I've got a head like a sieve. —Lee Harris, *Murder in Hell's Kitchen*, p. 55, 2003

▸ have your head screwed; have your head screwed on right; have your head screwed on the right way

to be shrewd and businesslike, to have a practical intelligence *UK, 1821*

- I haven't made my mind up whether I'll vote for him, but he has his head screwed on. He would do a good job. —*The Guardian*, 2nd October, 1999

▸ have your head up your ass

stupid, unaware, uninformed *US, 1944*

- That desk clerk's got his head up his ass – the man never left. —Elmore Leonard, *Bandits*, p. 145, 1987
- [I]f only he'd taken his head out of his arse long enough to hear her. —Christopher Brookmyre, *Boiling a Frog*, p. 4, 2000
- I still fuckin reckon tho that yew all had yewer heads up yewer arses. A little bit of fuckin awareness like, that's all was fuckin needed. —Niall Griffiths, *Sheepshagger*, p. 94, 2001

▸ need to have your head read

to have ridiculous ideas *AUSTRALIA, 1938*

That is, 'you need to see a psychiatrist'.

- Jimmy's gettin' married next Saturdy. Wants 'is 'ead read. —Nino Culotta (John O'Grady), *They're A Weird Mob*, p. 50, 1957
- —Harvey E. Ward, *Down Under Without Blunder*, p. 10, 1967
- That bloody umpire needs 'is 'ead read. —Sue Rhodes, *Now you'll think I'm awful*, p. 83, 1967
- —Wilda Moxham, *The Apprentice*, p. 32, 1969

▸ **off your head**
in a state of mental confusion; drug-intoxicated *UK*
The latter meaning dates from the 1960s and the distinction between the two senses may be blurred.
- [T]he people that had obviously just come out of a club and were stoned or completely off their heads. —Dave Courtney, *Stop the Ride I Want to Get Off*, p. 127, 1999
- I got proper fucking off my cake, I did. Right off my head. —Dave Courtney, *Raving Lunacy*, p. 152, 2000

▸ **on your head**
in motor racing, flipped (of a race car) *US*
- —Don Alexander, *The Racer's Dictionary*, p. 45, 1980

▸ **out of your head**
in a state of drug or drink intoxication *UK*
When combined with a mental or emotional state, the sense varies: 'with grief', 'with worry', etc.
- —Angela Devlin, *Prison Patter*, 1996
- So that left me on me own, out of me 'ead and still randy as 'ell. —Ben Elton, *High Society*, 2002

▸ **pull your head in**
to mind one's own business *AUSTRALIA, 1944*
- Yer big, stupid galah! Fercrysake pull yer bloody 'ead in and keep climbing. —Robert S. Close, *With Hooves of Brass*, p. 91, 1961

▸ **put the head on; stick the head on**
to head-butt an opponent's face *UK: SCOTLAND, 1985*
- Boab went an stuck the heid oan the bouncer. —Michael Munro, *The Patter, Another Blast*, p. 31, 1988

▸ **you'd forget your head if it wasn't screwed on**
a catchphrase addressed to (or, in the third person, of) an absent-minded person *UK, 1979*
Variations are mainly concerned with the method of fixing: 'if it wasn't attached', '...tied on', '...stuck on', '...jammed on', etc.
- You'd forget your head if it wasn't stuck on your shoulders. —*North County Times (California)*, 13th May 2001

▸ **you need your head examined; you want your head examining**
a catchphrase addressed to someone who has said or done something stupid *US, 1942*
Originally, 'you want your head read' but it adapted as fashion and technique moved from phrenology to psychiatry.
- "You can't seriously -" "Oh yes... Why not?" Howard snorted. "You need your head examined." "Perhaps. But it doesn't alter the facts." —Francis Clifford, *The Blind Side*, 1971
- It may not just be Saddam who needs his head examined. —*The Guardian*, 14th November 2002

head *verb*
1 to leave *US*
- —Connie Eble (Editor), *UNC-CH Campus Slang*, p. 5, Spring 2003

2 to carry (something) on your head *BARBADOS*
- —Frank A. Collymore, *Barbadian Dialect*, p. 57, 1965

-head *suffix*
a habitual user of the indicated substance; hence an enthusiast, a fan *US, 1953*
- Now get your ass in the bathroom and wash your mouth out. I want you to kill that fuckin' odor. Where I'm gettin' ready to take you, I don't want the people to think I brought a juice head along with me. —Donald Goines, *Daddy Cool*, p. 95–96, 1974
- Florence and I both didn't want to be invaded by amphets heads. —Herbert Huncke, *The Evening Sun Turned Crimson*, p. 174, 1980
- "I'm Department of Corrections," Kathy said. "What are you?" A rockhead for one thing, no doubt lights popping in his brain. —Elmore Leonard, *Maximum Bob*, p. 65, 1991

headache *noun*
1 your spouse *US, 1933*
- —Lou Shelly, *Hepcats Jive Dictionary*, p. 12, 1945
- Always some John Family or silk moll with bookoo toadskins playing around with a yuk who'll ante to keep the knockdown from the bundleman or headache. —*The New American Mercury*, p. 708, 1950

2 a journalist *US*
Gulf war usage.
- —*American Speech*, p. 391, Winter 1991: 'Among the new words'

headache!
used as a warning in various industries that an object has been accidentally dropped from a height and that those working below should immediately take care *US, 1944*
- —Jerry Robertson, *Oil Slanguage*, p. 65, 1954
- —A.B. Chance Co., *Lineman's Slang Dictionary*, p. 9, 1980

headache bar *noun*
a steel bar welded onto a bulldozer or other piece of heavy equipment to protect the operator from branches or other sources of potential head injury *US*
- —Gregory Clark, *Words of the Vietnam War*, p. 222, 1990

headache Mary *noun*
low grade marijuana *US*
- Also known as doodley-squat, salt and pepper, and "male twigs," this female-impersonator a/k/a Headache Mary is sometimes advertised as "good commercial"[.] —*Hi Life*, p. 15, 1979

headache rack *noun*
the grill at the rear of a truck cab designed to protect the driver and any passengers from injury if the load should shift forward due to a sudden stop *US, 1969*
- —Montie Tak, *Truck Talk*, p. 81, 1971
- —John Edwards, *Auto Dictionary*, p. 74, 1993

headache stick *noun*
a police nightstick *US, 1919*
- Hold your piechopper, "don't vip another vop" or I'll take my headache stick and "massage your top." —Lavada Durst, *The Jives of Dr. Hepcat*, p. 9, 1953
- —Clarence Major, *Dictionary of Afro-American Slang*, p. 80, 1970
- The other guy was busy trying to kick in some kid's ribs and he didn't notice Kenny take the headache-stick away from his partner, but he heard the sound it made when Kenny crushed in the side of his friend's face with it. —Emmett Grogan, *Ringolevio*, p. 160, 1972
- Jim Garrison and John Ed Cothran admire a stick tapered like a baesball bat (called a "headache stick" by Southern police) days before a riot after James Meredith's attempt to intergrate the University of Mississippi in 1962. —*San Francisco Chronicle*, p. M1, 6th April 2003

head-and-a-half *noun*
an intellectual person *AUSTRALIA*
- Anyone with intellectual leanings is called a 'Head-and-a-half'. —*Sydney Morning Herald*, p. 7, 3rd January 1987

head artist *noun*
a person skilled at giving oral sex *US*
- —*Maledicta*, p. 231, 1979: 'Kinks and queens: linguistic and cultural aspects of the terminology for gays'

head-bang *verb*
to jerk your head up and down to add to the enjoyment of fast music *US*
Collected from fans of heavy metal music by Seamus O'Reilly, January 1995.

headbanger *noun*
1 a violent psychotic *UK, 1983*
- Footballers are used to head-bangers[.] —Alan Bleasdale, *Boys From the Blackstuff*, 1982
- TOOTHLESS: Can't be that headbanger, can it? [...] FRANKIE: Too mad. —Chris Baker and Andrew Day, *Lock, Stock... & a Good Slopping Out*, p. 407, 2000
- The place was full of headbangers[.] —Jimmy Stockin, *On The Cobbles*, p. 131, 2000
- [H]e became a right fuckin headbanger, a complete fuckin head-the-ball[.] —J.J. Connolly, *Layer Cake*, p. 36, 2000

2 a devotee of heavy metal music *US, 1979*
- In England devoted heavy-metal fans, called "headbangers" or "punters," often crowd the stage, flailing away on imaginary guitars[.] —*Washington Post*, p. G1, 13th July 1980
- —Connie Eble (Editor), *UNC-CH Campus Slang*, p. 6, Spring 1988
- —Ellen C. Bellone (Editor), *Dictionary of Slang*, p. 13, 1989
- [H]ead-banger was re-cast to give Eddie Garrity a working name [Ed Banger and the Nosebleeds]. The link between placing your ear next to a speaker stack and getting a nosebleed was also made. —Simon Warner, *Rockspeak!*, p. 15, 1996

3 a prisoner who bangs his head against walls, doors, etc *UK*
- —Angela Devlin, *Prison Patter*, p. 61, 1996

headbin *noun*

a crazy, unstable person *IRELAND*

- McNab is a 45-year-old mammy's boy with a name for being the local "loo-la" and a "headbin of the highest order". — *Sunday Business Post*, 20th August 2001

head case *noun*

an emotionally troubled or mentally disturbed person *UK, 1966*

- "Eddie, he's a head case," says Parillo, waving back. — Josh Alan Friedman, *Tales of Times Square*, p. 138, 1986
- The bottom line is neither of us are going to get her if we don't do something about that headcase she's with now. — *Something About Mary*, 1998
- [E]ven Khan, a headcase Paki [Pakistani] who doesn't mind kicking some knocked-out kid's brains in. — John King, *Human Punk*, p. 59, 2000
- I usher her towards the front door. "You're a fucking headcase, out." — Danny King, *The Burglar Diaries*, p. 25, 2001

head cheese *noun*

smegma in a male *US, 1941*

- I gasped so hard up my nose the head cheese locked into place and he let me breathe, still holding my hair. — Jack Fritscher, *Stand By Your Man*, p. 150, 1999

head chick *noun*

the dominant and favoured prostitute among a group of prostitutes working for a pimp *US*

- [T]hey are their "head chicks" instead of just one or another of their "barnyard hens." — John M. Murtagh and Sara Harris, *Cast the First Stone*, p. 10, 1957

head-cook and bottle-washer *noun*

a person who does all the work *UK, 1876*

Humorous. Originally 'bottle-washer' carried the same meaning with or without the head-cook's help. The British adaptation of the earlier US **CHIEF COOK AND BOTTLE WASHER**.

head cunt *noun*

the mouth (as an object of sexual penetration) *US*

- [H]is gums are bleeding or he has herpes or a cold sore inside that head cunt. — Peter Sotos, *Index*, p. 11, 1996

head dab *noun*

in mountain biking, a face-first fall *US*

- — William Nealy, *Mountain Bike!*, p. 160, 1992: 'Bikespeak'

head down and arse up

working busily *AUSTRALIA*

- I kept their heads down and their arses up. — Robert S. Close, *Love Me Sailor*, p. 108, 1945
- He is a 'head down and arse up player.' — Ivor Limb, *Footy's No Joke!*, p. 40, 1986

head drugs *noun*

amphetamines *UK, 1998*

- — Mike Haskins, *Drugs*, p. 279, 2003

head 'em *verb*

1 to take part in the gambling game two-up *AUSTRALIA, 1902*

- The expense to Thomas was enormous, but it was more than covered by the two shillings ... collected by his boxer from each spinner who 'headed 'em'. — Vince Kelly, *The Bogeyman*, p. 167, 1956

2 in the game two-up, to throw a pair of heads *AUSTRALIA, 1925*

- They hit the ground, and from every throat (if they are the same) comes the cry: 'He's headed 'em,' or 'He's tailed 'em.' — James Holledge, *The Great Australian Gamble*, p. 101, 1966

header *noun*

1 a head-first dive *UK, 1849*

- [H]e took a header out of a patrol car and got clean away. — Charles Raven, *Underworld Nights*, p. 32, 1956
- I almost took a header as I came out into the dusky haze of early morning. — Jim Thompson, *Pop. 1280*, p. 10, 1964

2 oral sex *US, 1976*

An embellishment of the more common **HEAD**.

- — Mary Corey and Victoria Westermark, *Fer Shurr! How to be a Valley Girl*, 1982

3 in hot rodding, a type of exhaust manifold that improves engine performance *US*

- — *Hot Rod Magazine*, p. 13, November 1948: 'Racing jargon'

head faggot *noun*

a male homosexual with an appetite for performing oral sex *US*

- [H]e'll suck on your dick just like every other head faggot will. — Peter Sotos, *Index*, p. 30, 1996

head-faking *adjective*

stimulating, exciting *UK*

- — Tom Hibbert, *Rockspeak!*, p. 81, 1983

headfit *noun*

an uncontrolled outburst of temper *UK*

- Errol takes a headfit. Screams at the top of his voice. "What the fuck you on about man? No way!" — Jack Allen, *When the Whistle Blows*, p. 50, 2000

head fuck *noun*

1 a state of mental confusion *UK*

- [When using MDMA] You get this "head fuck" when you feel it come on[.] — Macfarlane, Macfarlane and Robson, *The User*, p. 67, 1996
- Hearing the monumental "Complete Control" by The Clash on Radio One sent him into a total head fuck. — John Robb, *The Nineties*, p. 144, 1999
- Eh, I know what it's like the first time inside [prison]. Bit of a head fuck. — Chris Baker and Andrew Day, *Lock, Stock... & A Good Slopping Out*, p. 412, 2000

2 something that deliberately confuses or misleads *UK*

- I'm not sure I will forgive you for sharing that one, de Xavia. That's a headfuck if ever I heard one. — Christopher Brookmyre, *The Sacred Art of Stealing*, p. 345, 2002

headfuck *adjective*

confusing, misleading, especially when deliberately so *UK*

- Erm, what's that? – Bottle of whiskey, like you said. – Yeh, exactly, whiskey, not povo headfuck cheap piss like that. — Niall Griffiths, *Sheepshagger*, p. 184, 2001
- The headfuck climax, however, is confusing and distracting[.] — *Uncut*, p. 160, October 2002

head game *noun*

a psychological ploy *US, 1979*

- But I realized I was just playing head games, justifying an escape because of my stage fright. — Jim Carroll, *Forced Entries*, p. 62, 1987
- I think a gauntlet has been thrown doon, regardless of whatever headgames he's trying to play. — Christopher Brookmyre, *The Sacred Art of Stealing*, p. 345, 2002

head gasket *noun*

a condom *US, 1964*

Conventionally, 'a mechanical seal', with a further pun on **HEAD** (an act of oral sex).

- — David Rowan, *A Glossary for the 90s*, 1998

head gee *noun*

a prison warden *US*

- — John R. Armore and Joseph D. Wolfe, *Dictionary of Desperation*, p. 32, 1976

head-hunt *verb*

in boxing, to try to hit the opponent in the head *US, 1960*

- Sometime I rubbed resin on my gloves between rounds so I could fuck – so I would waste the guy's eyes when I went head-hunting. — James Ellroy, *Suicide Hill*, p. 781, 1986

headhunter *noun*

1 a person who recruits others for specific jobs with specific firms, especially professionals and executives *US, 1960*

- "My father would never take a job I found for him. It would violate his competitive Type A standards." "You're probably right," said Sheeni. "OK. I'll pretend to be a headhunter and I'll call him up." — C.D. Payne, *Youth in Revolt*, p. 99, 1993

2 a psychiatrist *US*

- "Ah, fuck off you lousy bums. What do you know about death?" I scream at my two head-hunters. — Oscar Zeta Acosta, *The Autobiography of a Brown Buffalo*, p. 134, 1972

3 an oral sex enthusiast *US*

- Head-hunters, cannibals and kid-fruits are fellators[.] — *New York Mattachine Newsletter*, p. 6, June 1961
- Hidden safely behind anthropological images of Amazonian tribes hunting enemy skulls for religious and decorative purposes, as the initiated of the jazz world knew, were the real headhunters, hip guys constantly seeking to receive or administer blow jobs. — Larry Rivers, *What Did I Do?*, p. 57, 1992

4 a homosexual male *US*

- — Charles Shafer, *Folk Speech in Texas Prisons*, p. 206, 1990

5 a police officer assigned to investigate complaints of misconduct by other police *US, 1965*

- I wonder if Lieutenant Grimsely and all them IAD headhunters get a finder's fee when they nail a cop. — Joseph Wambaugh, *The Choirboys*, p. 155–156, 1975

6 a paid killer *US*

- —Ralph de Sola, *Crime Dictionary*, p. 62, 1982

7 a female who trades sex for money or drugs *US*

- —Bill Valentine, *Gang Intelligence Manual*, p. 76, 1995: 'Black street gang terminology'

head job *noun*

an act of oral sex *US*

- —Donald Webster Cory and John P. LeRoy, *The Homosexual and His Society*, p. 264, 1963: 'A lexicon of homosexual slang'
- Most guys would rather have head jobs and that's a lot easier for her.—Joseph Wambaugh, *The New Centurions*, p. 182, 1970
- —Eugene Landy, *The Underground Dictionary*, p. 100, 1971
- The kind who wore a wig and took a man to a back booth and gave him a head job for $10 and a bottle of champagne[.]—Dan Jenkins, *Dead Solid Perfect*, p. 168, 1986

head-job *verb*

to shoot in the head *UK*

- Typical, he thought I wanted to take him away and head-job him. —Ken Lukowiak, *A Soldier's Song*, p. 48, 1993
- The players saw him, must have thought there was something wriggly, went and got their weapons and head-jobbed him.—Andy McNab, *Immediate Action*, p. 281, 1995

head jockey *noun*

a practicioner of oral sex on a woman *US*

- —Eugene Landy, *The Underground Dictionary*, 1971

headless chicken *noun*

used as the object of comparison for something or someone acting without rhyme or reason *AUSTRALIA, 1957*

- Without him we're like a headless chook.—V.H. Lloyd, *Hidden Enemy*, p. 142, 1957
- Louis forgot her crushed foot and rushed round the room like a headless chook, getting nowhere, retracting her steps and getting nowhere again.—Lance Peters, *The Dirty Half-Mile*, p. 38, 1979
- TV people were rushing round like headless chooks.—Peterq Robb, *Pig's Blood and other fluids*, p. 109, 1999
- —Kel Richards, *The Aussie Bible*, p. 42, 2003

headlights *noun*

1 the female breasts *US*

- With a pair of the biggest female headlights you ever saw pointing right at it.—Barry Oakley, *A Salute to the Great McCarthy*, p. 182, 1970
- —Malachi Andrews and Paul T. Owens, *Black Language*, p. 112, 1973
- During a [radio] show on breasts, Infinity was fined because I said: "Boobs, xonkers, headlights, watermelons, sweater puppies, pointers, knockers, jugs, tatas – these are some of the words to describe women's breasts'.—Howard Stern, *Miss America*, p. 441, 1995
- —Gary K. Farlow, *Prison-ese*, p. 29, 2002

2 the female nipples when obviously erect although masked by clothing *CANADA*

A more narrowly focused meaning from the previous sense.

- —Chris Lewis, *The Dictionary of Playground Slang*, p. 112, 2003

3 large jewels, especially diamonds *US, 1899*

- —Lou Shelly, *Hepcats Jive Dictionary*, p. 12, 1945

4 LSD *US*

- —US Deparment of Justice, *Street Terms*, October 1994

head like an unplayable lie *noun*

an ugly person *AUSTRALIA*

- Very unattractive, with a head like an unplayable lie and a sense of humour that wouldn't have got a laugh on a wharf.—Paul Vautin, *Turn It Up!*, p. 131, 1995

head like a robber's dog *noun*

an unattractive person *AUSTRALIA*

- Every single thing Tich stood up in had been found in garbage cans, from the football boots without laces and the football socks, one red, the other blue and white, to the green-peaked baseball cap on his robber's dog head[.]—Frank Hardy, *The Outcasts of Foolgarah*, p. 2, 1971
- She had a north and south full of broken tatts and a loaf of bread like a robber's dog.—Ryan Aven-Bray, *Ridgey Didge Oz Jack Lang*, p. 14, 1983

head motherfucker in charge *noun*

the leader of an enterprise *US*

- —Connie Eble (Editor), *UNC-CH Campus Slang*, p. 3, Spring 2001

head nigger in charge *noun*

the leader of an enterprise *US*

- —*Maledicta*, p. 159, Summer/Winter 1978: 'How to hate thy neighbor: a guide to racist maledicta'
- Finally, it dawned on one of those superduper crackers that I was actually the Head Nigger in Charge.—Odie Hawkins, *The Busting Out of an Ordinary Man*, p. 90, 1985
- —Connie Eble (Editor), *UNC-CH Campus Slang*, p. 3, Spring 2001

head on *adverb*

in gambling games such as twenty-one, playing directly against the dealer without other players *US*

- Thorp claims he could bust the sate of Nevada in eighty days "if the casinos did not cheat him, if he could play head on (alone against a delaer) for eight hours a day[.]"—Ed Reid and Ovid Demaris, *The Green Felt Jungle*, p. 207, 1963

head over heels *adjective*

deeply, completely (especially in descriptions of love) *UK*

By ellipsis from the cliché 'fall head over heels in love'.

- About halfway through the season he fell head over heels with a client[.]—Colin Butts, *Is Harry Still on the Boat?*, p. 78, 2003

head over turkey *adverb*

upside down; head over heels *AUSTRALIA, 1915*

- Well, before I quieten her, I knock Sir Frederick Salisbury, or whatever his name is, head over turkey into a clump of peacocks[.]—Alan Marshall, *I Can Jump Puddles*, p. 51, 1955

head phones *noun*

a stethoscope *US*

- —*American Speech*, p. 152–154, Summer 1982: 'More on nursing terms'

head plant *noun*

to fall face first while snowboarding *US*

- —Doug Werner, *Snowboarders Start-Up*, p. 113, 1993: 'Glossary'

headquarters puke *noun*

a member of the military assigned to the rear echelon staff *US*

Gulf war usage.

- —*American Speech*, p. 87, Spirng 1992: 'Gulf war words supplement'

head rag *noun*

a bandana or piece of cloth worn with straightened or processed hair *US*

- Sapphire usually sleeps with a head rag.—Carolyn Greene, *70 Soul Secrets of Sapphire*, p. 24, 1973

heads and heels *noun*

a youthful, sexually inexperienced male who is the object of an older homosexual's desire *US*

The suggestion is that you have to lift the inexperienced boy by his head and heels to get him into position for sex.

- —*Maledicta*, p. 221, 1979: 'Kinks and queens: linguistic and cultural aspects of the terminology for gays'

heads down *adjective*

in computing, so focused on a task as to be ignorant of all else *US*

- —Eric S. Raymond, *The New Hacker's Dictionary*, p. 197, 1991

head serang; head sherang *noun*

the person in charge *AUSTRALIA, 1918*

From Anglo-Indian *serang* (a captain of a native Indian vessel), from Persian.

- I'll go down and see the head serang.—D'Arcy Niland, *The Shiralee*, p. 123, 1955
- The head sherangs wrote nasty little notes to the lower bosses every time they saw it, and the little bosses protested as reasonably as they could to the office staff[.]—David Ireland, *The Unknown Industrial Prisoner*, p. 36, 1971

head shed *noun*

a military headquarters *US, 1963*

Vietnam war usage.

- —Carl Fleischhauer, *A Glossary of Army Slang*, p. 24, 1968
- The head shed has decided that you're going to have to make like Charley Tuna.—William C. Anderson, *Bat 21*, p. 126, 1980
- [T]he head-shed wanted some experienced observer to get a good look[.]—Chris Ryan, *Stand By, Stand By*, p. 93, 1996

head shop *noun*

a shop that retails drug paraphernalia, incense, posters, lights and other products and services associated with drug use *US*

- —Joe David Brown (Editor), *The Hippies*, p. 218, 1967: 'Glossary of hippie terms'
- The head shop is the liquor store of the hippies. Most often it is a small airless place, with a locked-in scent not unlike that of burning tapioca. Carries a thousand items for the head-hippie fraternity, from

Tarot cards to paper wrappers for tea. —Sidney Bernard, *This Way to the Apocalypse*, p. 58, 1968
- Head shop motto: The customer is always wrong – unless he's stoned. —Richard Neville, *Play Power*, p. 263, 1970
- On a corner I found a headshop. Goa Freaks loved gadgets, and at the start of each season they fussed over the latest inventions brought from the West. —Cleo Odzer, *Goa Freaks*, p. 193, 1995
- Lee became a staunch supporter of law reform and still runs a 'head shop' in London's Portobello Road which the police have tried unsuccessfully to close down under the Drug Trafficking Act which bans the sale of drug paraphernalia. —Harry Shapiro, *Waiting For The Man*, 1999
- I was coming out of my third Head shop on my Peachtree search when I saw him[.] —Stuart Browne, *Dangerous Parking*, p. 81–82, 2000

headshrinker *noun*

a pyschiatrist or other therapist *US, 1950*
- GENE: You know if the boy ever talked to a psychiatrist? PLATO: Head-shrinker? —*Rebel Without a Cause*, 1955
- So take him to a headshrinker. —Stephen Sondheim, *West Side Story*, 1957
- Remember when my old lady took me to New York to see this head-shrinker? —Max Shulman, *Rally Round the Flag, Boys!*, p. 127, 1957
- I once discussed this problem with Larry who is my sister's husband and a professional headshrinker. —Frederick Kohner, *Gidget*, p. 11, 1957
- Go first to a headshrinker. Andy and me went last year and he said we ought to leave Mama, remember, Andy? —Clancy Sigal, *Going Away*, p. 11, 1961
- —*American Speech*, p. 145–148, May 1961: 'The spoken language of medicine; argot, slang, cant'
- "You sound like a damn headshrinker," I hit at him. —John Rechy, *City of Night*, p. 379, 1963
- I knew we were on the way to a headshrinker – the Army psychiatrist. —Malcolm X and Alex Haley, *The Autobiography of Malcolm X*, p. 106, 1964
- Mom and Dad are sending me to a headshrinker beginning next Monday. —Anonymous, *Go Ask Alice*, p. 92, 1971
- But, frankly, pal, I think you'd better go see a headshrinker. —Charles Whited, *Chiodo*, p. 62, 1973

head shrinking *noun*

the practice of psychiatry *US*
- I gotta impress the old quack what does the head shrinking. —John Peter Jones, *Feather Pluckers*, p. 63, 1964

heads I win, tails you lose

however a situation is resolved I cannot lose *UK, 1832*

Mocking the principle that a toss of a coin normally offers a choice of winner.
- [T]hat was the Brit establishment for you – heads they win, tails you lose. —Chris Ryan, *The Watchman*, p. 126, 2001

heads-up *adjective*

1 clever, alert *US, 1934*

From the earlier sense as 'wide-awake'.
- —Zander Hollander, *Baseball Lingo*, p. 64, 1967
- And the Gillian thing wasn't the only heads-up brainfucker that Gretton came up with. —Tony Wilson, *24 Hour Party People*, p. 108, 2002

2 in motor racing, said of a competition with no handicap *US*
- —John Edwards, *Auto Dictionary*, p. 75, 1993

heads-up *adverb*

(of a game of pool) with no handicaps in effect *US*
- —Mike Shamos, *The Illustrated Encyclopedia of Billiards*, p. 114, 1993

head-the-ball *noun*

a crazy person *UK*
- [H]e became a right fuckin headbanger, a complete fuckin head-the-ball[.] —J.J. Connolly, *Layer Cake*, p. 36, 2000
- Fuckin knob-end. Fuckin head-the-ball yew are[.] —Niall Griffiths, *Sheepshagger*, p. 249, 2001
- I Just know Some things I am convinced of: 'The Last Time Ever I Saw your Face" performed by Roberta Flack is the best love song of all time; Patsy McGowan is a head-the-ball; Frank Galligan is a great writer. —*Donegal Times*, March 2001
- And I want someone on to Interpol to see if these heidthebaws have hit anywhere else. —Christopher Brookmyre, *The Sacred Art of Stealing*, p. 205, 2002

head time *noun*

an opportunity to think *UK*
- He was too wired about the market itself being a success to have any head-time left for worrying about what was happening to the delegates[.] —Christopher Brookmyre, *Not the End of the World*, p. 17, 1998

head-up *adjective*

straightforward, direct *US*
- We don't use no weapons, no razors or nothin', it's just a head-up fight, and sometimes I come out all covered in knots and bruises. —*Rolling Stone*, p. 85, 12th April 2001

heal *verb*

▸ **heal with steal**

to perform surgery *US*
- —Sally Williams, *"Strong" Words*, p. 146, 1994

healthy *adjective*

1 (used of a girl) well built *US*
- —*Current Slang*, p. 8, Winter 1970

2 large, excellent *UK, 1937*
- [T]he kind of spring in his stride that only a healthy bank balance can give a man. —T.F Banks, *The Thief Taker*, p. 89, 2002

heap *noun*

1 a car, especially an old and run-down car *US, 1921*
- What did he do, call from the front gate or the filling station where I left my heap? —Mickey Spillane, *I, The Jury*, p. 20, 1947
- He and two of his pals lifted a heap and busted into a gas station. —John D. McDonald, *The Neon Jungle*, p. 31, 1953
- We just zeroed three kids in a heap. Crest Drive and Observatory. —*Rebel Without a Cause*, 1955
- "See that toe?" he said as he gunned the heap to eighty and passed everybody on the road. —Jack Kerouac, *On the Road*, p. 79, 1957
- We're gonna leave this heap in a parking lot and get one the cops don't know about. —*Jackie Brown*, 1997

2 a slovenly woman, usually preceded by an adjective *UK, 1806*

Originally dialect.

3 a large number, a great deal *UK, 1661*
- Impressive start on a heap of social problems. —*The Guardian*, 26th November 2002
- Others will have new money, and heaps of it, in need of a home out of the taxman's reach. —*The Guardian*, 18th October 2003

heap *adjective*

very *US*

A crude borrowing of the speech of native American Indians as portrayed by pulp fiction and film screenwriters.
- J.L.'s the heap big kingpin around the joint, I gather. —Morton Cooper, *High School Confidential*, p. 22, 1958

heap of coke; heap *noun*

a man *UK, 1851*

Rhyming slang for **BLOKE**.
- —Ray Puxley, *Cockney Rabbit*, 1992

heap of shit *noun*

a mechanical item that is old, unreliable or broken *UK*
- [S]he had this heap of shit to get fixed. Anna kicked the dish-washer shut. —Jenny Eclair, *Camberwell Beauty*, p. 209, 2000

heaps *noun*

▸ **give someone heaps**

to chastise, denigrate or attack someone unrestrainedly *AUSTRALIA, 1978*
- In an outback pub, the drinkers were giving heaps to a fella named Macquarie: he was a thief, a wife starver, a cattle duffer, a pisspot, a liar and a cheat. You name any sin in the book and Macquarie had committed it, according to these blokes. —Frank Hardy, *Hardy's People*, p. 175, 1986

hear *verb*

to understand *US*
- —Kenn "Naz" Young, *Naz's Underground Dictionary*, p. 36, 1973

hearse *noun*

a brakevan (caboose) *US, 1930*
- —Ramon Adams, *The Language of the Railroader*, p. 76, 1977

heart *noun*

1 physical courage, especially as displayed in the commission of a crime *US, 1937*
- He had great skill and daring – what junkies call "heart." —James Mills, *The Panic in Needle Park*, p. 21, 1966
- I gotta admit he's got a lot of heart – I meaen besides being a nut. —Piri Thomas, *Stories from El Barrio*, p. 100, 1978
- —William K. Bentley and James M. Corbett, *Prison Slang*, p. 32, 1992

2 an amphetamine capsule, especially dextroamphetamine sulphate (trade name Dexedrine™) *US, 1965*
From the shape of the tablet.
- Maltese is wantin' hearts as well as munney. —Geoffrey Fletcher, *Down Among the Meths Men*, p. 32, 1966
- —Edward R. Bloomquist, *Marijuana*, p. 160, 1968
- I suspect she knows a little about drugs, because she's given me hearts a couple of times when I've been really low. —Anonymous, *Go Ask Alice*, p. 53, 1971
- —Mike Haskins, *Drugs*, p. 279, 2003

▸ my heart bleeds for you; my heart bleeds
faux-sympathy, used ironically for expressing bitterness or jealousy *US*
- My heart bleeds for the poverty of those who guard the wealthiest city in the world. —E.V. Cunningham, *Samantha*, 1968
- Oh yeah. Tough job. Put together a buyer and a seller and make millions. My heart bleeds for you, Brother. Let me tell you about tough jobs. —Stephen W. Frey, *The Vulture Fund*, p. 89, 1997
- There are hundreds of professionals in Britain who are genuinely out of work, so you could have found one or two with more heart-rending tales. Ian Nolan, holidaying in Florida every year? My heart bleeds. —*The Observer*, 2nd February 2003

▸ put the heart crossways
to shock *IRELAND*
- Johnny, it's just lovely to see you, son. You put the heart crossways in me. —Joseph O'Connor, *Red Roses and Petrol*, p. 38, 1995

heartbeat *noun*
1 any of several signals produced by a computer or software *US*
- —Eric S. Raymond, *The New Hacker's Dictionary*, p. 197, 1991

2 a short measure of time *US, 1985*
- —Hans Halberstadt, *Airborne*, p. 130, 1988: 'Abridged dictionary of airborne terms'

Heartbreak Hill *nickname*
a challenging hill at approximately mile 20 of the Boston Marathon *US*
- —Louis Phillips and Burnham Holmes, *The Complete Book of Sports Nicknames*, p. 214, 1998

heartburn palace *noun*
a roadside restaurant that features greasy food *US*
- —Montie Tak, *Truck Talk*, p. 82, 1971

heart check *noun*
a test of courage *US*
- —Mark S. Fleisher, *Beggars & Thieves*, p. 288, 1995: 'Glossary'

heart check!
I defy you!; I dare you!; I challenge you! *US*
- —Jim Goad, *Jim Goad's Glossary of Northwestern Prison Slang*, December 2001

heartface *noun*
a form of address used by some homosexual men *UK*
- JULIAN: Now how can we help you visage de coeur? SANDY: That's French for heartface! —Barry Took and Marty Feldman, *Round The Horne*, May 1968
- A mere powder compact's throw from here heartface. —Emma Hindley, *Storm in a Teacup*, 1993

heart scald *noun*
a troublesome individual *IRELAND*
- They had an old rip of a mother-in-law who was a heart scald, but they were saintly in all their dealings with her and would give her pedicures, ignore all her grizzling and ingratitude and take her out for long spins in the wheelchair or whatever. —*Irish Times*, 24th January 1998

hearts of oak; hearts *adjective*
penniless *UK, 1934*
Rhyming slang for **BROKE**.
- —Ray Puxley, *Cockney Rabbit*, 1992

heart starter *noun*
an alcoholic drink taken upon waking *AUSTRALIA, 1975*
- He crashed about seven o'clock one night and woke up again at one, hit himself with the bottle of beer he had beside his bed for a heart-starter, then got the walkabouts. —Sam Weller, *Old Bastards I Have Met*, p. 129, 1979

heartthrob *noun*
a very attractive man *US, 1926*
- —Donald F. Reuter, *Heartthrob*, 1998

heat *noun*
1 pressure, stress *US, 1929*
- Fruit Jar had been sitting pretty with no heat on him and a swell income, and The Man had hauled him in on something that could be very hot. —Jim Thompson, *Savage Night*, p. 61, 1953
- We even started drinking at the Sinners Club because it had a back door and a window we could get out of. I mean the heat was on, man. We were hurtin. —Hunter S. Thompson, *Hell's Angels*, p. 28, 1966
- We take married heat, kid heat, boss heat, car heat, bank heat, credit heat, political heat, IRS heat, health heat, appliance heat, and every other kind of heat you can think of. —Dan Jenkins, *Life Its Ownself*, p. 132, 1984
- The problem was, Nicky was not only bringing heat on himserlf, but on me too. The FBI watched every move he made. —*Casino*, 1995

2 the police *US, 1931*
- The heat was on something fierce. —Edwin Torres, *Carlito's Way*, p. 71, 1975
- Generally, whores are not a good deal. They attract heat, and most of them will talk. —William Burroughs, *Junkie*, p. 53, 1953
- Last night I pinned the heat, I see them. They were sitting there. —Lenny Bruce, *The Essential Lenny Bruce*, p. 202, 1967
- I hear it's a very good scene there. Not much heat, beautiful people, no speed freaks, and righteous dope. —Nicholas Von Hoffman, *We Are The People Our Parents Warned Us Against*, p. 47, 1967
- They split threatening an ambulance and, for all we know, the Heat, so everybody settles down again with "Come on baby" going very strong. —*The Digger Papers*, p. 10, August 1968
- Was the 'heat' chasing you or something? —Iceberg Slim (Robert Beck), *Pimp*, p. 116, 1969
- This part of town, they'll make us for heat the second we walk in. —*48 Hours*, 1982
- I took one look at him and said, "Jesus Christ, get him out of here, man. This guy is heat." —Herbert Huncke, *Guilty of Everything*, p. 69, 1990
- I wasted most of it with your brother and his crew, who not only lost what pitiful few they managed to boost, but also alerted the heat as to our endeavor. —*Gone in 60 Seconds*, 2000

3 intense police interest or pressure following a crime *US, 1928*
- —Angela Devlin, *Prison Patter*, p. 61, 1996

4 a firearm *US, 1926*
- "Man, you oughta seen old Fuss-face scratching for his heat," one of them said, jubilantly. —Chester Himes, *Cast the First Stone*, p. 33, 1952
- We both reached for our heat at the same time[.] —Babs Gonzales, *I Paid My Dues*, p. 43, 1967
- "What kinda heat you got?" Benny's eyes glittered a little in the shadows as he recited the pieces in his artillery. —Odie Hawkins, *Chicago Hustle*, p. 39, 1977

5 crowd or audience reaction *US*
An entertainment industry term embraced by professional wrestling.
- [B]uilding a hysterical crowd up to a climax is called "heat." —Pappy Boyington, *Baa Baa Black Sheep*, p. 375, 1958
- —*Los Angeles Times Magazine*, 6th August 1995: 'Palm latitutdes: L.A. speak'
- These things will all still happen, but the idea is if they are "illegal" they will draw more heat when they happen behind the referee's back. —*Herb's Wrestling Tidbits*, 18th June 1997
- On the indy scene, when you want to get heat, you pick out a small group of fans and work on them. —*Raw Magazine*, p. 49, September 2000

6 popularity, audience appeal *US, late 1970s*
- You know, head down to L.A., get some gigs going, get the heat happening. —*Boys on the Side*, 1995

7 in roller derby, a fight, be it scripted or spontaneous, staged or real *US*
- —Keith Coppage, *Roller Derby to Rollerjam*, 1999

8 in pinball, the part of the pinball machine that rises as a panel in the front of the machine *US*
Conventionally known as the 'lightbox'.
- —Bobbye Claire Natkin and Steve Kirk, *All About Pinball*, p. 113, 1977

9 the ultimate, the best *US*
- —Connie Eble (Editor), *UNC-CH Campus Slang*, p. 5, Fall 1985

10 a dildo *US*
- [I]f she's packin' heat (wielding a dildo), which you know they imagine she is, well, there you have it. —*The Village Voice*, 5th October 1999

▸ on heat
of a woman, sexually aroused *UK, 1937*
Correctly used of animals.

▸ take the heat
to sunbathe *US*
- —Collin Baker et al., *College Undergraduate Slang Study Conducted at Brown University*, p. 135, 1968

▸ **take the heat off; take heat off**
to relieve the pressure on someone *UK*
- The aim is that the escorts take the heat off the bombers by engaging the CAP [combat air patrol] fighters. —Robert Prest, *F4 Phantom; a Pilot's Story*, 1979
- [T]he best lead in the case, and the best hope for taking the heat off Scott, seemed to go bust[.] —Michael Fleeman, *Laci*, p. 55, 2003
- [I]t's the father's way of taking heat off their daughter. It's not your fault, sweetheart, it's the caddy's[.] —Rick Reilly, *Who's Your Caddy?*, p. 233, 2003

heated hell *noun*
the worst of the worst *US*
- —Lou Shelly, *Hepcats Jive Talk Dictionary*, p. 26, 1945

heater *noun*
1 a revolver *US, 1926*
The term smacks of gangster films.
- I'll say what it takes to make you point that heater someplace else. —Mickey Spillane, *Kiss Me Deadly*, p. 50, 1952
- "Man, if I had my heater I bet I could shoot that sergeant down there dead bewteen the eyes," he said. —Chester Himes, *The Real Cool Killers*, p. 49, 1959
- When he came in I cold cocked him with an iron pipe and took the heater, a grand in foreskin and the dope out of his pockets. —Iceberg Slim (Robert Beck), *Mama Black Widow*, p. 100, 1969
- —Angela Devlin, *Prison Patter*, p. 61, 1996

2 a linear amplifier for a citizens' band radio *US*
- You might also be interested to know that while Uncle Charlie permits Class B transmissions up to 150 miles, you'd need one cotton pickin heater to do it. —*Complete CB Slang Dictionary*, p. 2, 1976

3 a good-looking boy *US*
- —Connie Eble (Editor), *UNC-CH Campus Slang*, p. 3, Spring 1993

4 an excellent thing *US*
- —Connie Eble (Editor), *UNC-CH Campus Slang*, p. 5, Spring 2003

5 in poker, a period of good luck for one player *UK*
- "Paul sure got on a heater last night." You will also hear that a player is "hot," meaning that he is on a heater. —Dave Scharf, *Winning at Poker*, p. 236, 2003

6 a large cigar *US, 1918*
- —Lou Shelly, *Hepcats Jive Dictionary*, p. 12, 1945
- He went back to the terrace puffing on the big heater. —Richard Condon, *Prizzi's Honor*, p. 84, 1982

7 a cigarette *US*
- —*Merriam-Webster's Hot Words on Campus Marketing Survey '93*, p. 2, 13th October 1993

▸ **take a heater**
to defecate *US*
- —Don R. McCreary (Editor), *Dawg Speak*, 2001

heater and cooler *noun*
a shot of whisky and a glass of beer *US*
- —Bill Reilly, *Big Al's Official Guide to Chicagoese*, p. 28, 1982

heating food *noun*
any food thought to enhance sexual strength and passion *INDIA*
A euphemism of social and spiritual significance. Those seeking a godly and contemplative life (and, according to custom, all women, especially widows) should stick to 'cooling foods'.
- —Nigel Hankin, *Hanklyn-Janklin*, 2003

heat magnet *noun*
anything that draws the attention of the authorities *CANADA*
Based on **HEAT** (the police).
- DJ Nitro, who constantly wears the guaranteed heat magnet of a tight wool cap pulled low to the top of his wraparound shades, annnounces, "I got searched twice just leaving my country[.]" —Brian Preston, *Pot Planet*, p. 243, 2002

heat station *noun*
a police station *US*
From **HEAT** (the police).
- [T]he driver says have you been clipped or raped lady? – and: I will take you to the heat station. —John Rechy, *City of Night*, p. 118, 1963

heaty *adjective*
under police surveillance or the subject of police interest *US*
- It is enforced only in that the proprietor sometimes may ask players to keep payoffs out of sight – not to toss the money on the table after the game – if the room is currently "heaty," e.g., if an arrest as recently been made there. —Ned Polsky, *Hustlers, Beats, and Others*, p. 48, 1967

heave *noun*
an ejection, a dismissal *UK: SCOTLAND*
Used in the construction 'give someone (or something) the heave'.
- —Michael Munro, *The Original Patter*, p. 32, 1985

heave *verb*
to vomit *US, 1832*
- —Collin Baker et al., *College Undergraduate Slang Study Conducted at Brown University*, p. 135, 1968
- —Helen Dahlskog (Editor), *A Dictionary of Contemporary and Colloquial Usage*, p. 31, 1972
- —Connie Eble (Editor), *UNC-CH Campus Slang*, p. 5, April 1995

heave-ho *noun*
an ejection, a dismissal *US, 1932*
- —Parke Cummings, *Dictionary of Baseball*, p. 27, 1950
- The gambling was unorganized – the syndicate boys who tried to move in got the fast heave-ho. —Jim Thompson, *Roughneck*, p. 142, 1954
- Like Billy, he has fourteen years in and he can't give them any opportunity to give him the heave-ho before he puts in his twenty and gets a pension. —Darryl Ponicsan, *The Last Detail*, p. 13, 1970
- One pitch earlier, St. Louis manager Whitey Herzog got the heave-ho from home plate umpire Don Denkinger for protesting a call in Andujar's defense. [Caption] —*Chicago Tribune*, 28th October 1985
- She wanted him out. Warren got the heave-ho. —Howard Stern, *Miss America*, p. 178, 1995
- Ralphy was just about to give her the heave-ho. —John Milne, *Alive and Kicking*, p. 220, 1998
- [Liberace] reeked with the kind of emetic language that can only make grown men long for a quiet corner, an aspidistra, a handkerchief and the old heave-ho. —*The Guardian*, 12th August 2000
- Clemens is one of the few players even to have been ejected from a playoff game, getting the heave-ho from a 1990 game in Oakland by plate umpire Terry Cooney for abusive language while arguing balls and strikes. —*Chicago Tribune*, p. 1C, 23rd October 2003

heaven *noun*
1 seven or eleven *UK*
Rhyming slang, used by dice gamblers.
- —Julian Franklyn, *A Dictionary of Rhyming Slang*, 1961

2 cocaine *UK*
- —Nick Constable, *This is Cocaine*, p. 181, 2002

3 heroin *UK*
- —Mike Haskins, *Drugs*, p. 284, 2003

4 a billboard in the language of graffiti artists *US*
- "We're, like, riding bikes down the highway and looking for heavens," Dems says, using the graffiti slang for billboards. "If we see a nice heaven that hasn't been hit yet, we'll leave our bikes to the side, climb up, and hit it". —*new Times Broward-Palm Beach (Florida)*, 12th December 2002

heaven and hell; heaven *verb*
to give off a bad smell *UK*
Rhyming slang.
- [T]hat "don't half heaven!" —Ray Puxley, *Cockney Rabbit*, 1992

heaven dust; heavenly dust; heaven flour *noun*
any powdered drug; cocaine; heroin *US, 1933*
Perhaps a positive alternative to **HELL DUST**.
- —Robert Ashton, *This Is Heroin*, p. 206, 2002
- —Mike Haskins, *Drugs*, p. 284, 2003

heavenly blue; heavenly sunshine *noun*
LSD *US, 1977*
- —Richard A. Spears, *The Slang and Jargon of Drugs and Drink*, p. 255, 1986
- —Mike Haskins, *Drugs*, p. 285, 2003

heavenly blues *noun*
morning glory seeds as a psychoactive agent *US*
- —Ralph de Sola, *Crime Dictionary*, p. 63, 1982

heaven on a stick *noun*
a very good thing *US*
- —Connie Eble (Editor), *UNC-CH Campus Slang*, p. 4, Spring 1990

heavens above *noun*
love *UK*
- —Julian Franklyn, *A Dictionary of Rhyming Slang*, 1961
- —Ray Puxley, *Cockney Rabbit*, 1992

heaven sent *noun*

MDMA, the recreational drug best known as ecstasy *UK*

- —Angela Devlin, *Prison Patter*, p. 61, 1996

heavens to Betsy!

used as a register of shock, surprise, etc *US, 1940*

Charles Earle Funk researched and failed to discover the etymology of this phrase for *Heavens to Betsy!*, 1955; he believed that the phrase is certainly mid-C19 but was unable to discover its usage before 1940.

heavens to Murgatroyd!

used as a register of shock, surprise, etc *US*

A variation of **HEAVENS TO BETSY!**; popularised by Hanna Barbera's animated lion Snagglepuss, from 1959; also credited to US comedian Red Skelton, 1913–97. The identity of Murgatroyd is a mystery.

heaves and squirts *noun*

symptoms of heroin withdrawal *US*

A rather graphic way of describing vomiting and diarrhoea.

- —David Maurer and Victor Vogel, *Narcotics and Narcotic Addiction*, p. 414, 1973

heavies *noun*

large waves *US, 1961*

Always in the plural.

- — *Paradise of the Pacific*, p. 27, October 1963
- —John Severson, *Modern Surfing Around the World*, p. 171, 1964

▸ **the heavies**

serious newpapers, as opposed to the tabloid press *UK, 1950*

- [T]he Glasgow Herald, one of the heavies among regional papers. — *The Guardian*, 2nd September 2003

heaviosity *noun*

a quality of some (drug-inspired) heavy rock music *US*

- So how does he [Billy Squier] describe the main quality of his tunes? "Heaviosity." — *People*, p. 131, 28th December 1981
- Compulsory sex. Synchronised drug-taking. Maximum heaviosity. All in the name of art... — *Mojo*, April 1997
- This album is the real rock deal; the heaviosity of AC/DC spliced with the sassiness of L7[.] — *X-Ray*, p. 21, May 2003
- If you are going to talk to a band such as the Warlocks about, like, psychedelia and heavyosity, where better than the skunk [a type of marijuana] of Europe [Amsterdam]? The Warlocks are even more unhappy talking about drugs than they are about heavyosity. — *X-Ray*, November 2003

heavy *noun*

1 an experienced criminal who relies on violence and force *US, 1930*

- Not that her word wouldn't be plenty against us, a bellboy and three heavies, but there's a lot more than that. —Jim Thompson, *A Swell-Looking Babe*, p. 69, 1954
- —Angela Devlin, *Prison Patter*, p. 61, 1996

2 armed robbery; an armed robber *US*

- —Hyman E. Goldin et al., *Dictionary of American Underworld Lingo*, p. 93, 1950
- —Angela Devlin, *Prison Patter*, p. 61, 1996

3 sexually aroused, especially if aggressively so *UK*

A sense used by prostitutes.

- He was getting heavy, and I'm trying to get myself together to split from this car. — *Time Out*, 30th May 1980

4 a physically intimidating prison officer brought in to deal with rioting prisoners *UK*

- —Angela Devlin, *Prison Patter*, p. 61, 1996

5 a lesbian prison officer *UK*

- —Angela Devlin, *Prison Patter*, p. 61, 1996

6 in the television and film industries, an antagonist *US, 1926*

- —Tony Miller and Patricia George, *Cut! Print!*, p. 86, 1977

7 an officer *US*

Vietnam war coinage.

- Them fucking heavies back in their air-conditioned bunkers at Quang Tri just sit there drinking beer and throwing darts at the map. —Charles Anderson, *The Grunts*, p. 43, 1976
- The "heavies" – CAG, the squadron C.O's, Capt. Andrews, and the staff – had been watching closely for signs of deterioration. —Gerry Carroll, *North S*A*R*, p. 192–193, 1991

8 an important person *US, 1925*

- Some of the heavies in the mob have hit the mattress, the big names are surrounding themselves with soldiers and a few have dropped out of sight entirely. —Mickey Spillane, *Last Cop Out*, p. 84, 1972

9 heroin *US*

- —Edward R. Bloomquist, *Marijuana*, p. 342, 1971

10 a potent dose or a potent drug or both *US*

- Don't give her no heavy, Rick. We've got work to do tonight. —*Drugstore Cowboy*, 1988

11 medium gravity beer *UK: SCOTLAND*

Not to be confused with **WEE HEAVY** (a barley wine).

- Confusingly, "heavy" is usually light in colour, whereas "light" is dark. —Brian Glover, *CAMRA Dictionary of Beer*, 1985
- Avignon is like late-summer Edinburgh, though inevitably there is less chance of finding a really good pint of heavy. — *The Guardian*, 25th May 2002

12 a large aircraft *AUSTRALIA*

- Not big enough to be one of our heavies, skip. —W.R. Bennett, *Night Intruder*, p. 126, 1962

13 an aircraft carrier *US*

- Under my command, during a naval maneuver in European waters, we picked up what we thought was a "heavy," or aircraft carrier, on our sonar. —William R. Anderson and Clay Blair, *Nautilus 90 North*, p. 37, 1959

heavy *verb*

1 to threaten with violence; to menace *UK*

- A brief [solicitor] offering me readies [cash] to go round and heavy the kind of toerags I'd gladly sort out as a favour? —Val McDermid, *Keeping on the Right Side of the Law*, p. 185, 1999

2 to harass, threaten or victimise someone; to coerce someone threateningly *AUSTRALIA, 1974*

- It is not the first time the public has heard of its politicians being heavied by some of the business elite. — *West Australian*, p. 13, 12th July 1991

heavy *adjective*

1 very serious, very intense *US, 1963*

- "I got a new album. Three electronic sitars and a buzuki." "Is it good?" "I don't know yet. It's heavy, I'll tell you that." —Nat Hentoff, *I'm really dragged but nothing gets me down*, p. 10, 1968
- I learned enough shit from it, though, that maybe it wasn't such a bummer after all. All I can say is, man, I took a heavy trip! —Abbie Hoffman, *Woodstock Nation*, p. 5, 1969
- Heavy! Eaten by some squirrels. — *Annie Hall*, 1977
- "Far out" carried a lot of weight in the countercultural vocabulary – it was a "heavy" term. —Sean Hutchinson, *Crying Out Loud*, p. 177, 1988
- Death. It's so incredibly heavy, it's like so much heavier than like ninety-five percent of the shit you deal with in the average day that constitutes your supposed life. —Kenneth Lonergan, *This is Our Youth*, p. 118, 2000
- Norman wants to know what kind of audience it is – heavy or fluffy? —Dave Haslam, *Adventures of the Wheels of Steel*, p. 98, 2001

2 wonderful, excellent *US*

- Just the funkiest, heaviest set of girls [...] and complete with outstanding new back-up band. — *Melody Maker*, 8th July 1972
- —Julian Johnson, *Urban Survival*, p. 258, 2003

3 (of drugs) addictive *US, 1959*

- But its subject matter, ranging as it does from heavy drugs to transvestism and sodomy, will seem bold enough to many or most people. — *New York Times*, p. 5 (Section 2), 10th June 1984
- The music they played was unmistakeably heavy and the group did heavy drugs to go with it. —Simon Napier-Bell, *Black Vinyl White Powder*, p. 78, 2001

4 violent, inclined to use violence *US, 1902*

- And I was just as determined not to become a suicidal stickup artist or other "heavy" hustler. —Iceberg Slim (Robert Beck), *The Naked Soul of Iceberg Slim*, p. 26, 1971
- And when the revolution did get heavy, they would not know our methods nor would they have the stamina to even move to fight white racists. —Bobby Seale, *A Lonely Rage*, 1978
- I know you have been cool, but then this penis stepped in and had to get all heavy. — *Airheads*, 1994

▸ **get heavy**

to study *US*

- — *American Speech*, p. 303, December 1955: 'Wayne University slang'

heavy!

used for expressing approval *UK*

- — Susie Dent, *The Language Report*, p. 75, 2003

heavy A *noun*
an assistant drill instructor, US Marine Corps *US*
- Starting as Third Hat with a platoon on graduato in, whatever his rank, the D.I. can look forward to promotion after one or two series to Heavy A, and after several more, to senior drill instructor. —Daniel Da Cruz, *Boot*, p. 71, 1987

heavy Chevy *noun*
a Chevrolet with a big block engine *US*
- —Lewis Poteet, *Car & Motorcyle Slang*, p. 102, 1992

heavy closer *noun*
in a swindle, a person who makes the final deal with the victim *US*
- They were the "heavy closers" – psychological intimidation specialists who sized up weaknesses on the follow-up calls and made the sucker sign. —James Ellroy, *Suicide Hill*, p. 596, 1986

heavy cream *noun*
a hefty, large-breasted woman *US*
- —Robert George Reisner, *The Jazz Titans*, p. 158, 1960

heavy-duty *adjective*
serious, intense *US, 1935*
- Heavy duty shit, Augie. Heavy duty. —James Ellroy, *Brown's Requiem*, p. 171, 1981
- —Tom Hibbert, *Rockspeak!*, p. 83, 1983
- The moanin' 'bou' each other an' the heavy duty politics like they was warlords carvin' empires[.] —Nick Barlay, *Curvy Lovebox*, p. 13, 1997

heavy-fisted *adjective*
said of a gambling house operative who takes more than the appropriate share of the winnings of a poker game for the house share *US*
- —*American Speech*, p. 99, May 1951

heavy-footed *adjective*
pregnant *UK: NORTHERN IRELAND*
- —C. I. Macafee, *A Concise Ulster Dictionary*, p. 169, 1996

heavy hammer *noun*
any powerful pain medication *US*
- —Sally Williams, *"Strong" Words*, p. 146, 1994

heavy handbag *noun*
a rich (homosexual) boyfriend *UK*
From **HANDBAG** (money); recorded in use in contemporary gay society.
- —*Attitude*, p. 60, July 2003: 'New palare lexicon'

heavy-handed *adjective*
used of a person who pours alcoholic drinks too generously, or mixes alcoholic drinks at too great a strength *UK, 1971*
From the conventional sense (clumsy).

heavy hitter *noun*
a person with a deserved reputation for violence *US, 1970*
A baseball metaphor.
- But his uncle was a made-guy, a lieutenant with the Mulberry Street crew – a heavy hitter[.] —Edwin Torres, *Carlito's Way*, p. 21–22, 1975
- His guy walks and the other two heavy hitters have to convey their sympathies to their clients. —George V. Higgins, *The Judgment of Deke Hunter*, p. 240, 1976
- Because we start out, all we see are heavy hitters, all your suspects. —Elmore Leonard, *Glitz*, p. 252, 1985

heavy lifter *noun*
a dangerous, tough person *US*
- You'll be slappin' skin with the heavy lifters from south of Hawthorn. —Stephen J. Cannell, *The Tin Collectors*, p. a, 2001

heavy manners *noun*
any form of authoritarian control or discipline experienced by black individuals or communities *UK*
- [W]hen Kingston is under "heavy manners", they have a curfew or call out the army. —Mike Pawka, *www.niceup.com/patois*, 2001
- Later, when they had her under manners, Edwards [a policeman] teased her[.] —Karline Smith, *Moss Side Massive*, p. 171, 1994

heavy metal; HM; metal *noun*
a music genre, characterised by loud amplification, the primacy of electric guitars and simple, powerful – if occasionally lumbering – rhythmic patterns *US*
The origin may be in military and munitions terminology but the popular and probable etymology is as follows: 'The term heavy metal was originally coined by Beat novelist William Burroughs in his *Naked Lunch*, reintroduced into the pop vocabulary by Steppenwolf in their hit 'Born to Be Wild' ('heavy metal thunder') and subsequently redefined by rock critic Lester Bangs in the heavy metal fan magazine *Creem*.' (*Rolling Stone Encyclopaedia of Rock & Roll*, 1983). In fact, William Burroughs wrote of Uranium Willie, the Heavy Metal Kid, in *Nova Express*, 1946, 13 years before *Naked Lunch* was published. Lester Bangs was writing about the Yardbirds. In later use 'metal' takes over as the preferred abbreviation, creating a subtle differentiation understood by fans of heavy music.
- The Progidy's crossover from being a rave act to a metal act has been one of the important points of the decade. —John Robb, *The Nineties*, p. 229, 1999
- John Entwhistle [bass guitarist with the Who] once said "I'm only interested in heavy metal when it's me who's playing it. I suppose it's a bit like smelling your own fart." —Simon Napier-Bell, *Black Vinyl White Powder*, p. 115, 2001

heavy metaler *noun*
a musician or fan of heavy metal music *US*
- [Y]our child is showing signs of becoming [...] a heavy metaler[.] —Frank Zappa, *The Real Frank Zappa Book*, p. 290, 1989
- Heavy metallers were so clueless it was difficult to like anything about them, regardless of their occasional hook. —Ju-Ji Yamasuki, *Retrohell*, p. 95, 1997

heavy mob *noun*
1 a criminal gang that relies on violence; a gang involved in large scale crimes *UK, 1944*
- —Angela Devlin, *Prison Patter*, p. 61, 1996

2 the Metropolitan Police Flying Squad *UK*
- —*The Official Encyclopaedia of New Scotland Yard*, 1999

3 physically intimidating prison officers brought in to deal with rioting prisoners *UK*
- —Angela Devlin, *Prison Patter*, p. 61, 1996

heavy paint-work passers *noun*
in a dice cheating scheme, dice that have been altered by drilling the spots and filling them with heavy metallic paint *US*
- —John S. Salak, *Dictionary of Gambling*, p. 121, 1963

heavy petting *noun*
mutual sexual caressing that stops shy of full intercourse *UK, 1960*
- I should stop. Spare you the counting of the number of fingers a boy managed to fit up inside his girl, a lad's heavy petting before coming back to "make us all sniff his fingers to show he'd been there". —*The Guardian*, 29th March 2003

heavy roller *noun*
a very important person *US*
- Word of advice to Heavy Rollers: a peacock today, a featherduster tomorrow. —Robert Kirk Mueller, *Buzzwords*, p. 91, 1974

heavy strings *noun*
useful and powerful connections *BAHAMAS*
- —John A. Holm, *Dictionary of Bahamian English*, p. 102, 1982

heavy thumb *noun*
in the usage of youthful model road racers (slot car racers), a fast, reckless racer *US*
- — Phantom Surfers, *The Exciting Sounds of Model Road Racing (Album cover)*, 1997

heavyweight Jones *noun*
a drug dealer who sells drugs in a manner calculated to lead his customers to addiction *US*
- —Eugene Landy, *The Underground Dictionary*, p. 101, 1971

heavy wizardry *noun*
in computing, designs or code that demand a specialised and deep practical understanding *US*
- Writing device drivers is heavy wizardry; so is interfacing to X without a toolkit. —Eric S. Raymond, *The New Hacker's Dictionary*, p. 198, 1991

heavy worker *noun*
a criminal who specialises in breaking into safes *US*
- —Vincent J. Monteleone, *Criminal Slang*, p. 115, 1949

Hebe; Heeb *noun*

a Jewish person *US, 1926*

Derogatory.

- Most of the famous and up-and-coming performers of the day – Ted Lewis, Sophie Tucker, Benny Davis, Eddie Cantor, Dolly Kay, Al Jolson (they even gave him the title of "The Jazz Singer") – were heebs[.] —Mezz Mezzrow, *Really the Blues*, p. 49, 1946
- "Who's that Hebe doctor?" Livia said loudly before Krankeit was well out the door. —Terry Southern, *Candy*, p. 113, 1958
- And wasn't it just last month I got a plaque for racial tolerance from them Hebes at B'Nai B'rith? —Max Shulman, *Anyone Got a Match?*, p. 51, 1964
- "You're the only one giving me trouble today," he growled, "so we'll make it special, you Heeb son-of-a-bitch." —Red Rudensky, *The Gonif*, p. 3, 1970
- His first name is John and those Hebes don't name their kids John. —Eugene Boe (Compiler), *The Wit & Wisdom of Archie Bunker*, p. 46, 1971
- And wops 'n micks 'n slopes 'n spics 'n spooks are on my list / And there's one little Hebe from the heart of Texas – is there anyone I missed? —Kinky Friedman, *They Ain't Jews Like Jesus Anymore*, 1974
- The fuckin' Hebes are taking over. —Edwin Torres, *Q & A*, p. 119, 1977
- BRIAN: I'm not a Roman, Mum, and I never will be! I'm a Kike! A Yid! A Hebe! A Hook-nose! I'm Kosher, Mum! I'm a Red Sea Pedestrian, and proud of it! —Monty Python, *Life of Brian*, 1979
- He punches some Hebe – Murray something or other. The biggest bagel face in the precinct, and Lawlor belts him. —Vincent Patrick, *The Pope of Greenwich Village*, p. 112, 1979
- "They're Hebes, I guess you can tell." "You shouldn't use a word like that," I says. "It's an insult". "Not when a Jew says it. It's like a black calling another black a motherfucker." —Robert Campbell, *Junkyard Dog*, p. 44, 1986
- A million times I wanted to yell in his fuckin' ear: "This is Las Vegas! We're supposed to be out here robbin', you dumb fucking Hebe!" —*Casino*, 1995

Hebrew hoppers *noun*

sandals *US*

From the images of Jesus Christ wearing sandals.

- —*Current Slang*, p. 19, Spring 1970

heck *noun*

used as a euphemistic alternative to 'hell' *UK, 1887*

Originally dialect; often exclamatory.

- CHERYLENE: Oh, Bazza LOOK!!! BARRY: Shit a brick! ChERYLENE: Aw, heck! —Barry Humphries, *Bazza Pulls It Off!*, 1971
- If the guy farted everyone wondered what the heck it meant[.] —*Ask*, p. 55, 19th December 1981
- I thought what the heck! I'm sufficiently old, it doesn't matter if he says "No"! —Sally Cline, *Couples*, p. 78, 1998

hecka *adverb*

very *US*

A euphemised **HELLA**.

- —Pamela Munro, *U.C.L.A. Slang*, p. 48, 1989

heck-city *adverb*

very *US*

- —Rick Ayers (Editor), *Berkeley High Slang Dictionary*, p. 24, 2004

heckety-heck *noun*

used as a euphemistic alternative to 'hell' *UK*

- But it seems like it's coming to a head at last – then we might figure out what the heckety-heck's going on. —*Mojo*, p. 19, September 2003

hecksa *adverb*

very *US*

- —Rick Ayers (Editor), *Berkeley High Slang Dictionary*, p. 24, 2004

heck you!

used as a euphemistic replacement for 'fuck you!' *FIJI*

Recorded by Jan Tent in 1996.

hectic *adjective*

1 (used of a wave) fairly treacherous *US*

- —Surf Punks, *Oh No! Not Them Again! (liner notes)*, 1988

2 extreme, outrageous (often applied to gruesome or gory acts); good *SOUTH AFRICA*

Teen and youth slang, noted by *Sunday Times* (South Africa), 1st June 2003.

- —Julian Johnson, *Urban Survival*, p. 258, 2003

hector!

used as a euphemism for 'heck', itself a euphemism for 'hell' *US*

- —Miss Cone, *The Slang Dictionary (Hawthorne High School)*, 1965

H'ed *adjective*

addicted to heroin *US*

- —Vann Wesson, *Generation X Field Guide and Lexicon*, p. 88, 1997

hedgehog *noun*

any non-white person; a native of the Indian subcontinent; an Arab; any (non-English) foreigner *UK*

Rhyming slang for **WOG**.

- [T]he xenophobe who maintains that all "hedgehogs" start at Calais. —Ray Puxley, *Cockney Rabbit*, 1992

hedge hopper *noun*

a crop dusting pilot *US*

- —Jerry Robertson, *Oil Slanguage*, p. 65, 1954

hedge monkey *noun*

a member of the counterculture travellers' community *UK*

Derogatory.

- "That'll teach the fucking hedge monkeys a lesson," I heard one [police] officer say. —Jake Arnott, *He Kills Coppers*, p. 302, 2001

hedge mumper *noun*

a tramp *UK*

An elaboration of 'mumper' (a tramp). English gypsy use.

- —Jimmy Stockin, *On The Cobbles*, p. 10, 2000

H-E-double toothpicks!; H-E-double hockey sticks!

hell! *US*

Youth slang, euphemistically spelt out.

- 7344 on the calculator. —Editors of Ben is Dead, *Retrohell*, p. 94, 1997

heeb *noun*

a jittery sensation, a fearful feeling *UK*

An abbreviation of **HEEBIE JEEBIES**.

- "I think stopping gives him the heeb," [...] "The what?" "The heeb, the vibe. The heeb and the vibe. The fear, you know." —Matthew De Abaitua, *Inbetween (Disco Biscuits)*, p. 242, 1996

Heeb *noun*

▷ see: **HEBE**

heebie-jeebies *noun*

1 the jitters, a sense of anxiety *US, 1923*

Thought to have been coined by US cartoonist Billy DeBeck (1890–1942) for the comic strip *Barney Google*.

- The apartment was so quiet that it gave her the heebie-jeebies. —James T. Farrell, *Ruth and Bertram*, p. 113, 1955
- I was still sitting in my chair getting the cold heeby-jeebies and trying to figure out my exit line. —Martin Waddell, *Otley*, p. 133–134, 1966
- "Them niggers shouting and talking in them spooky tongues gives me the heebie jeebies and the hives." —Iceberg Slim (Robert Beck), *Doom Fox*, p. 56, 1978

2 *delirium tremens* *US, 1926*

- PINK ELEPHANT: Och come on, Rab. Use your imagination. I'm the heebie jeebies! —Ian Pattison, *Rab C. Nesbitt*, 1988

3 symptoms of withdrawal from an addictive drug *US*

- The thing is, I'm still fighting back the heebie-jeebies from this drop in my dose of mojo juice [methadone]. —Jim Carroll, *Forced Entries*, p. 144, 1987

heebies *noun*

jitters *US, 1926*

- There was a conspiracy in Manhattan, headed by him, to give all Windy City musicians the heeblies until they were ready to be bugged. —Mezz Mezzrow, *Really the Blues*, p. 181, 1946

Heeeeere's Johnny......

used as a humorous introduction *US*

The drawn-out introduction of US late-night talk show host Johnny Carson by sidekick Ed McMahon from 1962 until 1992. Widely repeated, with variations and referential humour.

- "You ever watch Johnny Carson, the way they do it? You say, 'And now ... heeeeeere's Brad!" —Elmore Leonard, *Gold Coast*, p. 51, 1980

hee-haw *noun*

1 loud and braying laughter *UK, 1843*

- [A]in't but four of us out here but I bet y'all see a whole bunch o' niggers hangin' 'round outside a poolroom, heehawin' 'n wastin' time. —Odie Hawkins, *Chicago Hustle*, p. 6, 1977

2 nothing of any worth, zero *UK*

The value of a donkey's bray.

- His Eminence was going to tell the Monsignor precisely hee-haw. —Christopher Brookmyre, *Boiling a Frog*, p. 130, 2000

heel *noun*

1 a dishonourable or untrustworthy individual *US, 1914*

- So you reckon I'm being a heel do youse.—Barry Humphries, *Bazza Pulls It Off!*, 1971

2 in professional wrestling, a wrestler designed by the promoters to be seen by the audience as a villain *US*

- For examples: wrestle is "work"; fall is "going over"; "finish" is the routine just before the deciding fall; hero is "baby face"; villain is "heel."—Pappy Boyington, *Baa Baa Black Sheep*, p. 375, 1958
- "It's rough out there," panted television's Mr. T., who joined good-guy wrestling champion Hulk Hogan in stomping two heels in a tag-team grudge match.—*Associated Press*, 31st March 1985
- "Heel" is the name given to wrestlers that blatantly break the rules, thus becoming the object of the fans' hatred.—Pat Barrett, *Everybody Down There Hates Me*, p. 221, 1990
- Types of heels: the rulebreaker, the underhanded fop, the interfering manager, the nasty foreigner, the diabolic brat, the disloyal sibling, the braggart, the evolutionary throwback.—*Herb's Wrestling Tidbits*, 28th September 1995
- Gorgeous George was a heel with heat. His flaunting, taunting performances provoked loud, exuberant expressions of apparently homophobic antipathy in the audience.—Sharon Mazer, *Professional Wrestling*, p. 94, 1998
- —Dallas Hudgens, *Washington Post*, p. 36, 10th March 2000: 'A Wrestling Glossary'

3 by extension, any figure in the wrestling business designed by the promoters to be disliked by the fans *US*

- He was riding on this moment of fame in his local gigs, where he would appear as heel manager "Big Daddy Money Bucks"[.]—Sharon Mazer, *Professional Wrestling*, p. 161, 1998
- When Smoky began an interpromotional feud with the USWA, Brian had finally gotten a chance to wrestle, and as a vicious heel referee turned wrestler, was finally able to truly showcase his talents.—Mick Foley, *Herb's Wrestling Tidbits*, p. 301, 1999
- He is still a superb heel announcer, yet his sharp edge has been honed, and at times he almost comes across as a normal guy.—Jeff Archer, *Theater in a Squared Circle*, p. 36, 1999

heel *verb*

to leave without paying a bill *US*

- We managed to heel that motel before they could give us the bill.—*American Speech*, p. 281, December 1966: 'More Carnie Talk from the West Coast'
- —Joe McKennon, *Circus Lingo*, p. 46, 1980

heel-and-toe *verb*

to run away quickly *CANADA, 1870*

- You a heel-and-toe boy? A grifter?—Evan Hunter, *The Blackboard Jungle*, p. 160, 1954

heeled *adjective*

1 armed *US, 1866*

- I nudged him with the gun, ran my hand over his pockets and beltline to make sure he wasn't heeled[.]—Mickey Spillane, *Return of the Hood*, p. 107, 1964
- "I'd feel a hell of a lot better if I was heeled," Grave Digger confessed.—Chester Himes, *Come Back Charleston Blue*, p. 84, 1966
- "This private-eye fucker – is he gonna be heeled?" Ronnie broke a swizzle stick in half. "Always. Waxman buys him a gun permit from a judge every year."—Gerald Petievich, *Money Men*, p. 82, 1981

2 provided with funds *US, 1873*

- —Joseph E. Ragen and Charles Finston, *Inside the World's Toughest Prison*, p. 803, 1962: 'Penitentiary and underworld glossary'

3 in possession of drugs *US*

- —William D. Alsever, *Glossary for the Establishment and Other Uptight People*, p. 15, December 1970

heeler *noun*

1 a political party worker who does readily what is ordered *US, 1876*

- "Judges," she said, "are all political heelers or they would not be judges."—Margaret Stewart, *Ask No Quarter*, p. 268, 1959

2 an opportunistic sneak thief *US, 1931*

- —Inez Cardozo-Freeman, *The Joint*, p. 504, 1984

3 in poker, an unmatched card retained in a player's hand when drawing *US*

- —Albert H. Morehead, *The Complete Guide to Winning Poker*, p. 264, 1967

heelie *noun*

in skateboarding, a manoeuvre in which the rider elevates the rear wheels of the board while riding forward on the front wheels *US*

- —Laura Torbet, *The Complete Book of Skateboarding*, p. 106, 1976

heelish *adjective*

in professional wrestling, villainous *US*

- Owen Hart broke his heelish character to praise his father for raising great kids.—*Herb's Wrestling Tidbits*, 24th October 1996

heel list *noun*

a list of persons unwelcome as guests at a hotel *US*

- So his name was entered on the "heel list" – a catalogue of undesirables – and he ceased to be a guest.—Jim Thompson, *Bad Boy*, p. 358, 1953

heesh *noun*

hashish *US*

- —Ralph de Sola, *Crime Dictionary*, p. 63, 1982

heeze *noun*

hashish *CANADA*

- —Suroosh Alvi et al., *The Vice Guide*, p. 102, 2002

heezie *noun*

▸ **off the heezie; off the heezie for skeezie**

awesome *US*

Coined by rapper Snoop Doggy Dogg.

- —Connie Eble (Editor), *UNC-CH Campus Slang*, p. 7, Fall 2001

heezy *noun*

▸ **off the heezy**

wonderful, cool, amazing *US*

A hip-hop variation of 'off the hook'.

- Still packing fo sho / Yeezy Weezy off of the heezy fo sheezy / Cruise with the top off of the 'Ghini[.]—Lil Wayne, *Fo Sheezy*, 1999

Hef *nickname*

Hugh Hefner (b.1926), founding publisher of *Playboy* magazine, which first appeared in December 1953 *US*

- Look, Hef, while I've got you -—Tom Wolfe, *The Pump House Gang*, p. 49, 1968

hefty *noun*

in circus and carnival usage, a performer in a strong-man act *US*

- —Don Wilmeth, *The Language of American Popular Entertainment*, p. 128, 1981

hefty *adjective*

1 well-funded at the moment *US*

Teen slang.

- —*San Francisco News*, p. 6, 25th March 1958

2 intense *AUSTRALIA*

- "It's hefty there, man," he says. "I became friends with this prostitute; she was a smackhead."—*The Guardian*, p. 12, 26th February 2002

he-girl *noun*

a person with mixed sexual physiology, usually the genitals of a male and surgically augmented breasts *US*

- —*www.adultquarter.com/blossary.html*, January 2004: 'Glossary of adult Internet terms'

hehe

in a game of on-line poker, used for acknowledging luck in winning a hand

- —*FHM*, p. 147, June 2003

Heidi *noun*

a young woman with back-to-the-earth, 1960s values and fashion sense, especially one with pigtails *US*

- —Don R. McCreary (Editor), *Dawg Speak*, 2001

heifer *noun*

a stocky girl or woman *US, 1835*

An insult, if not a fighting word.

- No, I'm talking about that old light-skin heifer that's always comin' around here to see your daddy.—Claude Brown, *Manchild in the Promised Land*, p. 383, 1965
- —Connie Eble (Editor), *UNC-CH Campus Slang*, p. 3, October 1986
- I feel like such a heifer. I had two bowls of Special K, three peices of turkey bacon, a handful of popcorn, five peanut butter M&M's, and like three pieces of licorice.—*Clueless*, 1995
- 'No, mon, the only Fatty I know is my mother-in-law who is 22 stone.' 'Geez a big fat heifer, eh,' I laughed.—Paul Vautin, *Turn It Up!*, p. 179, 1995

heifer dust *noun*

nonsense *US, 1927*

A euphemism for **BULLSHIT**.

- —William D. Alsever, *Glossary for the Establishment and Other Uptight People*, p. 14, December 1970
- "Heifer dust" is a more polite way of saying bull shit.—Chris Thain, *Cold as a Bay Street Banker's Heart*, p. 82, 1987

heifer paddock *noun*

a girls' school *AUSTRALIA, 1885*

- —Jim Ramsay, *Cop It Sweet!*, p. 45, 1977

heigh-ho!

used as a signal of enthusiasm *US, 1930s to 50s*

- "Let us taste all the joys that this great city as to offer." "Heigh-ho," she replied airily and linked her pretty arm in mine.—Max Shulman, *The Many Loves of Dobie Gillis*, p. 28, 1951

height *noun*

▸ **from a great height**

used to intensify the infliction of punishment or suffering *UK, 1961*

Always preceded with the passive sense of a verb combined with 'on', e.g. 'come down on'.

- Yet somehow I'm feeling that the fuzz [the police] have got a trap here. Like I just take another step forward and I shall be dropped on from a great height.—Alan Hunter, *Gently in Trees*, 1974
- 'You cannot quote me – a word out of place and I get crapped on from a very great height,' said one academic.—*The Observer*, 3rd September 2000
- I always knew that as soon as there was any controversy, any chink in my armour that I was going to be dropped on from a great height. —*Croydon Guardian*, 28th June 2001
- And I want to help you sort out whoever's trying to shit on you from a great height.—Judith Cutler, *Power on Her Own*, p. 86, 2003
- [H]ow to keep smiling when you're being shat on from a great height. We all need to know how to do that.—Guy Browning, *Innervation*, 2003
- Labour has not run Waltham Forest well for years but what is unprecedented is the severity of the treatment handed out by the Labour party to someone who knew what the problems were and was making an effort to get on top of them, whether or not he was being successful. He has been jumped on from a great height.—*The Guardian*, 28th July 2003

heing and sheing *noun*

sex *US*

- —Kenn "Naz" Young, *Naz's Dictionary of Teen Slang*, p. 57, 1993

heinie; heiny *noun*

▷ see: HINEY

Heinie *noun*

a German; German *US, 1904*

- Later – when lists of Nazis were released – we saw many of these stolid heinies on record.—Jack Lait and Lee Mortimer, *New York Confidential*, p. 81, 1948
- I remember a booby trap they set on a Heinie general's car once. —Mickey Spillane, *Kiss Me Deadly*, p. 79, 1952

Heinies *noun*

Heineken™ beer *US*

- —Lillian Glass with Richard Liebmann-Smith, *How to Deprogram Your Valley Girl*, p. 27, 1982

heinous *adjective*

offensive, unpleasant *US, 1982*

Conventional English elevated to slang by attitude.

- —Connie Eble (Editor), *UNC-CH Campus Slang*, p. 5, March 1986
- We are in danger of flunking most heinously tomorrow, Ted.—*Bill and Ted's Excellent Adventure*, 1989
- I believe "heinous bitch" is the term used most often.—*Ten Things I Hate About You*, 1999

Heinz *noun*

a multiple bet, combining 57 bets *UK, 1983*

Based on the advertising slogan for, and synonymous with, the products of the food company H.J. Heinz. A 'super heinz' combines 120 bets.

- The Canadian, also known as a Super Yankee, combines five Heinz 57 varieties – get it?—John McCririck, *John McCririck's World of Betting*, p. 45, 1991

heir and a spare

two sons, in the context of a male line of succession; hence, one and a spare of anything *UK*

Used as a minimum breeding requirement by powerful and privileged families whose bloodline justifies their inheritance, applied especially to monarchies.

- I realise I've forgotten my notebook. As there's always an heir and a spare in the car, I dash out to fetch it.—*Daily Telegraph*, 26th July 2003
- Former butler Paul Burrell wrote in a new chapter added to his best-selling book, A Royal Duty, that Diana held the view that she had been "sold to the Royal Family" to produce "an heir and a spare".—*The Scotsman*, 28th May 2004

heist *noun*

a theft or robbery *US*

- Punks shooting up a delicatessen on their first heist.—Emmett Grogan, *Final Score*, p. 68, 1976

heist *verb*

1 to accept; when used in the negative, to reject a story or idea as untruthful or fanciful *CANADA*

- "I couldn't heist that one" means "I couldn't believe that one," said of a story too farfetched or fanciful. "Heist" is of course a version of "hoist," and comes from fishing.—Lewis Poteet, *The South Shore Phrase Book*, p. 57, 1999

2 to steal, especially to shoplift *UK, 1815*

There are enough Hollywood heist films to make a genre. Also spelt 'hyste'.

- I gotta hyste a fish market tonight.—George Mandel, *Flee the Angry Strangers*, p. 387, 1952
- We traced it to a group heisted from an armory in Illinois.—Mickey Spillane, *Kiss Me Deadly*, p. 109, 1952
- Until finally I heisted a gold watch off one of the girl dancers in the show[.]—Ross Russell, *The Sound*, p. 195, 1961
- If you're heisted, the worst thing is not to have any money on you[.] —Jimmy Snyder, *Jimmy the Greek*, p. 63, 1975
- [O]ld dude drives to Richmond to heist some cigs.—Janet Evanovich, *Seven Up*, p. 56, 2001

heister *noun*

a thief or robber *UK, 1865*

From the earlier 'hoister'.

- I described the two heisters as well as I could.—Jimmy Snyder, *Jimmy the Greek*, p. 67, 1975
- "Jungle" John Lembeck, white male, age thirty-four, two-time convicted strong-arm heister, lived in a bungalow court on Serrano just off the Boulevard.—James Ellroy, *Hollywood Nocturnes*, p. 188, 1994

Helen *noun*

heroin *US, 1971*

Giving an identity and disguise to H (heroin).

- —US Department of Justice, *Street Terms*, October 1994
- —Robert Ashton, *This Is Heroin*, p. 206, 2002

heli *noun*

a *heli*copter *US*

- If a friend has been on a heli trip, they will be saying heli-this, heli-that all season long.—Jim Humes and Sean Wagstaff, *Boarderlands*, p. 222, 1995

helicopter *noun*

1 in skateboarding, a manoeuvre in which the rider jumps off the board, turns in the air and then lands on the board *US*

- —Albert Cassorla, *The Skateboarder's Bible*, p. 200, 1976

2 a Chinese-educated person *SINGAPORE*

- —Paik Choo, *The Coxford Singlish Dictionary*, p. 46, 2002

helicopter view *noun*

a non-detailed overview *CANADA*

- Jargon may help managers give staff a helicopter view of their blue sky ideas, but many mask their own ignorance and one in five office workers don't understand it[.]—*Financial Post (Canada)*, 16th February 2000

hell *noun*

1 used widely in oaths, and to reinforce imprecations, and questions (often rhetorical) of impatience and irritation *UK, 1596*

- The men of D company were discussing the question of why in hell they had had no beer, or at least soda, for a whole month when I arrived on their hill.—*The Guardian*, 9th March 1971
- Where the hell's the high school?—Billie Letts, *Where the Heart is*, p. 42, 1998
- They didn't care about math. Who the hell could remember this stuff when they were at 25,000 feet?—Robert Coram, *Boyd: The Fighter Pilot Who Changed the Art of War*, 2002
- I wish I could find what the hell I was put on this earth to do. —Po Bronson, *What Should I Do with My Life*, 2002

2 crack cocaine *UK*

- —Mike Haskins, *Drugs*, p. 282, 2003

▸ for the hell of it; for the sheer hell of it; just for the hell of it
simply for the pleasure or experience of doing something; also applied to reckless behaviour *UK, 1934*
- [I]t would be a bit casual if it just ran a referendum for the hell of it. — *The Observer*, 1st June 2003

▸ from hell
used for intensifying *US, 1965*
Humorous, hyperbolic.
- We were ushers from hell. Nobody smoked in our section. — Connie Eble (Editor), *UNC-CH Campus Slang*, p. 4, Spring 1989
- "I know, Lacey," I said. "They're the all-time Parents from Hell." — C.D. Payne, *Youth in Revolt*, p. 256, 1993

▸ get the hell out; get the hell out of here (or somewhere)
to leave, usually with some haste *US*
- Then they heard the North Vietnamese shout: "It's something like la-ri, la-ri, it means let's get the hell out of here." — *The Guardian*, 9th March 1971

▸ hell out of
when combined with a verb of violent action, such as knock, punch, thump, etc, to treat a person extremely roughly *IRELAND, 1922*
- Presumably the President [George W. Bush]'s Prayer, unlike the Lord's, wastes no breath on forgiveness, but urges the faithful to bomb the hell out of those towel-heads, Amen! — *The Observer*, 23rd September 2001

▸ play hell with; play merry hell with
to cause severe trouble for someone or something *UK, 1803*
- And it was going to play merry hell with schemes of revenge. — Jane Feather, *Velvet*, 1994
- The acceleration played hell with the Chief's inner ear. — Eric Nylund, *First Strike*, p. 45, 2003

▸ to hell
intensely, when combined with a wish or hope *UK, 1891*
- I hope to hell my present shrink can help me work this out[.] — Anna Holmes, *Hell Hath No Fury*, p. 96, 2002

▸ to hell with it!
used for registering or reinforcing dismissal *UK, 1929*
- Maybe the fact that she's more methodical I find trying, but never enough to say "to hell with it". — Sally Cline, *Couples*, p. 65, 1998

▸ will I hell!
used as an expression of strong disagreement *UK, 1931*
Often applied in the third person: 'will he hell!' or 'will they hell!'.

hella *adverb*
extremely *US*
- — Judi Sanders, *Kickin' like Chicken with the Couch Commander*, p. 11, 1992
- For an all-purpose superlative, use "hella" as in "He's hella fine,"(he's good-looking) or "that test was hella-hard." — *San Francisco Chronicle*, p. A9, 17th November 1992
- I bet he makes hella money. — *Kids*, 1995
- — Connie Eble (Editor), *UNC-CH Campus Slang*, p. 3, Fall 1998

hellacious *adjective*
especially nasty or difficult *US, 1929*
- — Collin Baker et al., *College Undergraduate Slang Study Conducted at Brown University*, p. 136, 1968
- I struck Frank Robinson out on four absolutely hellacious knuckle-balls[.] — Jim Bouton, *Ball Four*, p. 169, 1970
- [I]t was love gone hellacious and haywire. — Joel Rose, *Kill Kill Faster Faster*, p. 125, 1997

hell and gone; hell-and-gone *noun*
a far-distant place or point in time *US, 1938*
- The ignoramus has been shooting up churches from here to hell-and-gone. Now he speaks of respect. — Audie Murphy, *Hell and Back*, p. 23, 1949
- [T]hey'd be able to stymie the cops-who could search to hell and gone and find no hard evidence[.] — Elizabeth Sims, *Holy Hell*, p. 128, 2002

hell-bent *adjective*
recklessly determined *US, 1835*
- To get drunk, doped up and ride hell bent and carefree[.] — Jamie Mandelkau quoting Ken Kesey, *Buttons*, p. 154, 1971
- I've tried dragging him into the bedroom and he performs reluctantly but next time is hell bent in getting me in the water. — *Attitude*, p. 146, October 2003

hellcat *noun*
a wild, fierce woman *UK, 1605*
- Now it might not look like it, but lemme tell you something. She's a hellcat. — *Raising Arizona*, 1987

hell dust *noun*
any powdered drug; heroin; morphine *US, 1953*
- — Robert Ashton, *This Is Heroin*, p. 206, 2002

heller *noun*
a wild, uninhibited party *US*
- — *American Speech*, p. 61, Spring-Summer 1975: 'Razorback slang'

hellery *noun*
trouble, mischief, bad behaviour *CANADA*
- For years I have craftily awaiting the chance to write a column about women's brassieres, just for the (wink!wink!) hellery of it. — *Toronto Globe and Mail*, p. 31/8, 17th February 1965

hell-fire!
used as a register of exasperation, frustration, anger, etc *UK*
- Nathan! Hell-fire, what you doing out here, kid? — *The Full Monty*, 1997

hell-for-stout *adjective*
very strong *US*
- — Jerry Robertson, *Oil Slanguage*, p. 65, 1954

hell-hole *noun*
1 a horrible, infernal place *UK, 1882*
- Bay Ridge ain't the worst part of Brooklyn, you know. It ain't like a hellhole. — *Saturday Night Fever*, 1977
- I'm even talking hellholes where the warden's as hard as a bar of iron. — *Natural Born Killers*, 1994

2 in a combat helicopter, an approximately 34 inch square opening in the floor, used for emergencies and roping down to and up from the ground *US, 1976*
- They had tried to sabotage the ship, I guess, because they had spent the time slashing the seats to ribbons, smearing shit on the instruments, piling dirt into the cockpit and cramming sticks down the hell hole. — Robert Mason, *Chickenhawk*, p. 84, 1983

hellifying *adjective*
used as an adjectival intensifier *US*
- Legs is what a man looks for, not faces, and you got one hellifying pair of legs. — Gail Sheehy, *Hustling*, p. 55, 1973

hellish *adjective*
1 unpleasant, difficult *UK, 1569*
- It would prove to be a hellish campaign. — Bill Bryson, *A Short History of Nearly Everything*, p. 158, 2003

2 used as a positive intensifier; excellent *UK: ENGLAND*
- I'll tell yew who's got some hellish good brown [heroin], tho[.] — Niall Griffiths, *Sheepshagger*, p. 167, 2001
- Darren has just got a Grifter bike. You should see it, it's ellish. — Chris Lewis, *The Dictionary of Playground Slang*, p. 113, 2003

hellish *adverb*
used as a pejorative intensifier *UK, 1768*
- But it can get amortized in some hellish expensive equipment. — Mr Gantefoer, *Public Hearing: Agriculture and Food, Canadian Legislature'*, 4th January 1999

hellishing; hellishun *adverb*
used as an intensifier *AUSTRALIA, 1931*
An elaboration of HELLISH (an intensifier) on the model of FUCKING, SODDING, etc.
- I'll be hellishing popular if I send it home drunk. — KEri Hulme, *The Bone People*, p. 30, 1983

hello!
used for signalling disbelief when said as if speaking to someone slow-witted *US, 1985*
- Hello! That was a stop sign! — *Clueless*, 1995
- ROBIN: Jane's gay? HOLLY: Like, hello? You didn't know? — *Boys on the Side*, 1995
- — Connie Eble (Editor), *UNC-CH Campus Slang*, p. 5, April 1995
- Well, hello. What rubbish is he talking now? — Simon Lewis, *In The Box [britpulp]*, p. 131, 1999
- I mean, hello. You've barely even spoken to me for months. — *American Beauty*, 1999
- "Rule One. All the staff calls me Moby. OK?" Like, hello! STAFF? — Kevin Sampson, *Clubland*, p. 35, 2002

hell of *adverb*
extremely *US*
A reverse correction of the corrupted HELLA.
- "That is hell of cool," said Pup. — Francesca Lia Block, *Baby Be-Bop*, p. 391, 1995

hell of a *adjective*

an extreme, good or great example of something *UK, 1776*

May be preceded with 'a', 'the' or 'one'.

- Hell of a boy, Ianto, wasn't he. – Hell of a boy's right, aye—Niall Griffiths, *Sheepshagger*, p. 1, 2001
- He notes too that after the "hell of a fuss" broadcasters made in trying to get cameras into the Commons, footage of Parliament now forms only tiny clips in news reports.— *BBC News*, 27th May 2002
- Miserly markets mean a hell of a deficit headache.— *The Observer*, 16th February 2003
- No one owes us anything and it's going to be one hell of a struggle to win one on Sunday.— *The Guardian*, 28th March 2003

Hell Pass Hole *nickname*

El Paso, Texas *US*

- — *Current Slang*, p. 19, Spring 1970

hellride *noun*

in mountain biking, any bad trail or bad ride *US*

- —William Nealy, *Mountain Bike!*, p. 161, 1992: 'Bikespeak'

hell's bells

used as a mild oath *UK, 1832*

- Hell's bells, green nail polish?—Hal Ellson, *Summer Street*, p. 23, 1953
- So that's how you work this democratic bullshit – hell's bells!—Ken Kesey, *One Flew Over the Cuckoo's Nest*, p. 135, 1962
- "What's the latest in these art robberies, Jack?" "Hell's bells, we've got nothing to go on!"— *The Sweeney*, p. 55, 1976
- Hells Bells! Don't stop now sugar.— *Natural Born Killers*, 1994

hell's half acre *noun*

during the Vietnam war, an area just north of Cu Chi, dominated if not controlled by the Viet Cong *US*

- —Linda Reinberg, *In the Field*, p. 104, 1991

hell to breakfast *noun*

here to there, all over *US, 1930*

- —John Gould, *Maine Lingo*, p. 130, 1975

helluva

hell of a *US, 1910*

- There's going to be a helluva reward. You could use some bread, I assume...— *The Sweeney*, p. 50, 1976
- Anyway, he gave me a helluva quote.—Carl Hiaasen, *Tourist Season*, p. 201, 1986
- Sorry I'm late back, darlin. But there was a helluva queue in Prestos.—Ian Pattison, *Rab C. Nesbitt*, 1988

hell week *noun*

a period of extreme harassment, especially of new recruits to a college fraternity by their older fraternity brothers *US, 1930*

- Had it really been eighteen years – Christ, half his life! – since Nelson Schwab had cornered him during Hell Week at the Deke House to impart the privileged information that "Puff" was really an underground parable about – no shit – smoking marijuana?—Armistead Maupin, *Further Tales of the City*, p. 38, 1982

helmet *noun*

1 the head of the circumcised penis *US*

From the similarity in shape to a World War 2 German Army helmet.

- You get bored you might amuse yourselves by betting quarters whether the next guy in will be a helmet or an anteater.—Joseph Wambaugh, *The New Centurions*, p. 262, 1970

2 a uniformed police constable *UK*

- You're not a helmet anymore.—Duncan MacLaughlin, *The Filth*, p. 114, 2002

helo *noun*

a helicopter *US, 1965*

- — *Cool Antarctica*, 2003: 'Antarctic slang'
- "Captain Harper" (who had been listening to the radio chatter on the bridge) burst into CIC and asked me who was that person talking to the helos with that great voice."—Douglas Brinkley, *Tour of Duty*, p. 86, 2004

helo *adjective*

none *CANADA*

- "Mebbeso," Charlie went on, "helo chicamun stop I come back," meaning that he might return broke.—R.D. Symons, *Many Trails*, p. 74, 1963

helpcat *noun*

a tutor; a student assistant *US*

A punning allusion to **HEP CAT**.

- — *American Speech*, p. 303, December 1955: 'Wayne University slang'

helper *noun*

any amphetamine or other central nervous system stimulant *US, 1963*

- —Montie Tak, *Truck Talk*, p. 82, 1971
- —Richard A. Spears, *The Slang and Jargon of Drugs and Drink*, p. 257, 1986

helter skelter *noun*

a shelter *UK*

Originally a World War 2 coinage for an 'air raid shelter'. Noted as still in occasional use as a 'bus shelter'.

- —Ray Puxley, *Cockney Rabbit*, 1992

helter-skelter *adverb*

in defiance of order; pell-mell *UK, 1593*

- Playfully they would toss furniture helter-skelter and break china. —Jack Lait and Lee Mortimer, *Washington Confidential*, p. 121, 1951
- In 1939 the business offices of the Tatum Cigarette Company were jammed, helter-skelter, in odd corners of the factory and the warehouse.—Max Shulman, *Anyone Got a Match?*, p. 92, 1964

he-man *noun*

an especially virile or overtly masculine man, a masterful man *US, 1832*

- He may not fit into the Hollywood he-man mould, but John C Reilly has carved a cosy niche for himself playing sensitive souls[.]— *The Guardian*, 11th March 2000

hem and haw *verb*

to stutter, to hestitate while beginning a sentence *UK, 1786*

- Finally, after a convincing game of hem and haw and my almost tearful pleas for him to reveal his secret desires *** he would blurt out that he would give her one hundred dollars and die happy if he could see her fabulous body unadorned.—Iceberg Slim (Robert Beck), *The Naked Soul of Iceberg Slim*, p. 65, 1971
- [Diary entry 11th March 1996] Listening to him hemming and hawing (oh so reasonably) it's clear as crystal we're going to have weeks of debilitating shilly-shallying[.]—Gyles Brandreth, *Breaking the Code*, p. 388, 1999

hemorrhoid *noun*

a despised person *US, 1969*

▷ see: **HAEMORRHOID**

hemp *noun*

marijuana *US, 1883*

- [H]e pulled out a cigarette and puffed on it, imitating a cat pulling on some hemp.—Mezz Mezzrow, *Really the Blues*, p. 298, 1946
- When the bang of the hemp wears off, cocaine is the only thing that can take its place.—Jack Lait and Lee Mortimer, *Washington Confidential*, p. 117, 1951
- Now, smoking hemp, she let out the laughter she'd choked back with food.—George Mandel, *Flee the Angry Strangers*, p. 130, 1952
- Of the equatorial sun splashing over the matted Tehuantepec country, and of fields of hemp switching to Caribbean breezes[.] —Bernard Wolfe, *The Late Risers*, p. 6, 1954
- And when he wasn't digging their fine silouettes, he wa busy peddling filtered hemp cigarettes.—Dan Burley, *Diggeth Thou?*, p. 22, 1959
- This Harrison was a stooge for the big liquor interests. The hemp was starting to take over.—Ross Russell, *The Sound*, p. 23, 1961
- As we sat there gaily blowing on our hemp / I whispered, "Rose, darling, let me be your pimp."—Dennis Wepman et al., *The Life*, p. 39, 1976
- Your "people" are white, suburban high school boys who smoke too much hemp.— *Ten Things I Hate About You*, 1999

hempen fever *noun*

execution by hanging *UK, 1785*

- —Vincent J. Monteleone, *Criminal Slang*, p. 116, 1949

hemp head *noun*

a frequent user of marijuana *US*

- It goes on and on like that, until we became morally certain that it had been written by some hemp-head[.]—Stephen Gaskin, *Amazing Dope Tales*, p. 161, 1980

hempster *noun*

anyone involved in the business of retailing hemp *UK*

From **HEMP** (marijuana) and conventional, perfectly legal 'hemp'.

- [W]e are all involved in hemp, and we are hempsters.—Brian Preston, *Pot Planet*, p. 129, 2002

hempty *noun*

leaves from the hemp plant *CANADA*

- He has a tea made from the prefloral leaves of the crop in this hemp field. "Hempty," he calls it.—Brian Preston, *Pot Planet*, p. 223, 2002

hen *noun*

1 a woman *UK, 1626*

- He sent drinks and a forced smile down to the sitting hens and waved goodby[.] —Nathan Heard, *Howard Street*, p. 164, 1968
- She turned and smiled and entered the hen's room. —A.S. Jackson, *Gentleman Pimp*, p. 100, 1973

2 used for informally addressing a woman; also, as an endearment *UK: SCOTLAND, 1626*

- Hey, hen. I'm helpless. Fancy mothering me? —Ian Pattison, *Rab C. Nesbitt*, 1988
- Sorry to shatter your illusions, hen, but it's time you woke up[.] —Christopher Brookmyre, *Boiling a Frog*, p. 157, 2000

3 a flamboyant feminine male homosexual *TRINIDAD AND TOBAGO, 1985*

- —Lise Winer, *Dictionary of the English/Creole of Trinidad & Tobago*, 2003

4 in a deck of playing cards, a queen *US*

- —George Percy, *The Language of Poker*, p. 43, 1988

5 the Sea Knight military helicopter *US*

A term used by reconnaissance troops in Vietnam.

- —Linda Reinberg, *In the Field*, p. 105, 1991

hen apple *noun*

an egg *US, 1938*

- I'll wager he never went hunting for diamonds in hen apples again anytime soon. —Guy Owen, *The Flim-Flam Man and the Apprentice Grifter*, p. 163, 1972

hen fruit *noun*

an egg *US, 1854*

- I never saw a man look so hard-down disappointed in hen fruit before. "What's wrong with them eggs, mister?" —Guy Owen, *The Flim-Flam Man and the Apprentice Grifter*, p. 157, 1972

Henley regatta *noun*

a conversation *UK*

Rhyming slang for **NATTER**, formed from the famous sporting event.

- [H]e's waiting for his dinner and she's having a "Henley" with the woman next door. —Ray Puxley, *Fresh Rabbit*, 1998

hen mill *noun*

a women's jail or prison *US*

- We arraign you tomorrow on this evidence, we hold trial two weeks from now – next month you're doing twenty to life in the hen mill. —Clarence Cooper Jr, *The Scene*, p. 113, 1960

Henny; Hen' *noun*

Hennessy™ cognac *UK*

- Tired of always giving in when this bottle of Henny wins[.] —Eminem (Marshall Mathers), *If I Had*, 1999
- We used to mix Hen' with Bacardi Dark / and when it kicks in, you can hardly talk[.] —Eminem (Marshall Mathers), *Drug Ballad*, 2000

henny penny *noun*

a female player in a low-stakes game of poker *US*

- —George Percy, *The Language of Poker*, p. 43, 1988

henpecked *adjective*

ruled by a domineering woman *UK, c. 1680*

The surviving form of the original verb 'hen-peck'.

- [I]t's hard to distinguish between the women, or between their symmetrically henpecked husbands. —*The Observer*, 4th February 2001

hen pen *noun*

a women's prison *US*

- —William K. Bentley and James M. Corbett, *Prison Slang*, p. 4, 1992

henry *noun*

an eighth of an ounce (three and a half grams) of a drug, especially marijuana or cocaine *UK, 1998*

Cutting **HENRY THE EIGHTH** down to size.

- A mate bells me to borrow money. I got two henries and a dealer to pay. —The Streets (Mike Skinner), *It's Too Late*, 2002

Henry *noun*

1 any Ford Motor Company car or engine *US, 1917*

- —Lyle K. Engel, *The Complete Book of Fuel and Gas Dragsters*, p. 151, 1968

2 heroin *US*

From 'heroin' to **H** to Henry.

- All that good Henry and Charley. When you shoot Henry and Charley, you can smell it going in. —William Burroughs, *Junkie*, p. 84, 1953
- He got up, dressed, we took a few more toots of Christine and Henry (pineapple) and split. —A.S. Jackson, *Gentleman Pimp*, p. 71, 1973
- —Liz Cutland, *Kick Heroin*, p. 107, 1985
- —Angela Devlin, *Prison Patter*, p. 61, 1996
- —Robert Ashton, *This Is Heroin*, p. 206, 2002

Henry Fonda *noun*

a *Honda* 90 motorcycle *UK*

Rhyming slang, used by (prospective) London taxi drivers; the Honda 90 is the machine of preference when they **DO THE KNOWLEDGE**.

- —Ray Puxley, *Fresh Rabbit*, 1998

Henry IV *noun*

the human immunodeficiency virus *US*

- —Don R. McCreary (Editor), *Dawg Speak*, 2001

Henry the Eighth *noun*

eight grams of cocaine *US*

- —Peter Johnson, *Dictionary of Street Alcohol and Drug Terms*, p. 91, 1993

Henry the Fourth *noun*

four grams of cocaine *US*

- —Peter Johnson, *Dictionary of Street Alcohol and Drug Terms*, p. 91, 1993

Henry the Third *noun*

a piece of excrement *AUSTRALIA*

Rhyming slang for **TURD**.

- [E]ach shovel was flat on the concrete and was decorated with a huge Henry the Third. —David Ireland, *The Unknown Industrial Prisoner*, p. 286, 1971
- —Ryan Aven-Bray, *Ridgey Didge Oz Jack Lang*, p. 31, 1983

Henry was here *noun*

the bleed period of the menstrual cycle *UK: WALES*

- When I was in school we used to say "Henry was here," as only a man could cause such pain and inconvenience. —a contributor *The Museum of Menstruation and Women's Health*, December 2000

hen's night *noun*

a woman-only pre-wedding party held for the bride-to-be *AUSTRALIA, 1994*

The counterpart of the **BUCK'S PARTY**.

- Private function. Hen's night. Chicks only. —Shane Maloney, *Nice Try*, p. 198, 1998

hen's teeth *noun*

the epitome of that which is exceedingly rare *AUSTRALIA, 1965*

- Patsy had won herself a bursary. This was a great accomplishment, for they were as scarce as hens' teeth. —Hesba Brinsmead, *Longtime Dreaming*, p. 98, 1982

hentai *adjective*

overtly pornographic *JAPAN*

A Japanese term, usually applied to a style of Japanese animation; one of only a few Japanese terms to have worked its way into unconventional English usage, thanks to pornographic websites on the Internet.

- Dubbed "hentai" (hen-tye, literally "pervert"), these titles boast buxom beauties, sex-ninjas and schoolgirl-molesting demons, and are often cited in sensationalized news reports as the bizarre underbelly of Japanese animation. —*The Sun (Baltimore)*, p. 1H, 14th April 1996
- She quickly insinuatess herself into a sensitive negotiation with a Japanese animation company that specializes in CBI pornography, a particularly explicit kind known as hentai. —*Tulsa (Oklahoma) World*, p. S4, 21st November 2003

hep *noun*

hepatitis *US, 1967*

- The Communications Company printed up a thing about serum hep, that lays it out there, that lays the information out[.] —Leonard Wolfe (Editor), *Voices from the Love Generation*, p. 135, 1968
- It ain't been too busy a year, but maybe that's cause I was zonked with the hep for three months... —Abbie Hoffman, *Woodstock Nation*, p. 11, 1969
- —Walter Way, *The Drug Scene*, p. 110, 1977

hep *adjective*

1 aware *US, 1903*

- While she'd been hep to the play, it had only been curiosity on her part. —Chester Himes, *If He Hollers Let Him Go*, p. 170, 1945
- As the days rolled on I commenced getting hep to the jive. —Louis Armstrong, *Satchmo: My Life in New Orleans*, p. 192, 1954
- [L]ike I'd never heard anywhere and which bore resemblance to Bartok modern chords but were hep wise to bop[.] —Jack Kerouac, *The Subterraneans*, p. 67, 1958

- I guess all of you already know just about what I'm going to say, but you're not really hep to what the rewards are going to be. — Donald Goines, *Black Gangster*, p. 25, 1977

2 in step with the latest fashion, latest music and latest slang *US, 1942*

- Walters didn't want to open a typical New York cafe, appealing to the "smart" set and the heavy spenders and the "hep" crowd. — Robert Sylvester, *No Cover Charge*, p. 28, 1956

hepatic rounds *noun*

used in a hospital as a humorous code for a drinking party to be held on hospital grounds *US*

- — *Maledicta*, p. 33, 1988–1989: 'Medical maledicta from San Francisco'

hepatitis roll *noun*

a meat and salad roll *AUSTRALIA*

Used by Australian troops during the Vietnam conflict to refer to such rolls commonly sold by street vendors, and reputed to be the cause of gastrointestinal and other complaints.

- My new companion left me for a while then returned to sit beside me and gave me a 'hepatitis roll!!!' — Martin Cameron, *A Look at the Bright Side*, 1988

Hepburn's Hussars *noun*

a special police force organised by Ontario Premier Mitch Hepburn to deal with an Oshawa car workers' strike *CANADA*

- A body of police was specially organised for the occasion on military lines, "Hepburn's Hussars," as they were dubbed. — A.R.M. Lower, *Colony to Nation*, p. 525, 1946

hep cat; hepped cat *noun*

a fan of jazz or swing music; a stylish and fashionable man *US, 1938*

- All the hip cats on the corner / They don't look so sharp no mo' — Jimmy Witherspoon, *Skid Row Blues*, 1947
- — Lavada Durst, *The Jives of Dr. Hepcat*, 1953
- The customers were the hepped-cats who lived by their wits – smooth Harlem hustlers with shiny straightened hair, dressed in luried elegance, along with their tightly draped queens, chorus girls and models[.] — Chester Himes, *A Rage in Harlem*, p. 88, 1957
- Swaggering, hepcat, ala Hollywood leading many type. — Robert Gover, *The Maniac Responsible*, p. 82, 1963

heppo *noun*

hepatitis *AUSTRALIA*

- [T]hey had diagnosed a touch of the old heppo and kept him in for a few more weeks. — Kathy Lette, *Girls' Night Out*, p. 98, 1987

heppo roll *noun*

a hepatitis roll *AUSTRALIA*

- A particular delicacy offered for sale by the culinary street peddler was a meat and salad roll commonly called the 'heppo' roll. An innocent purchaser, would, no doubt, contract hepatitis and/or the 'poo and spew' syndrome amoebic dysentry [sic]. — Martin Cameron, *A Look at the Bright Side*, 1988
- The unit vehicle arrived and the big mouthed driver saw the sight of 'the man', veteran of the Japanese beer halls, upholder of young soldiers' moral standards and there he sat eating his Heppo Roll and cuddled up to him in sympathy, what must have been the oldest street walker in Vung Tau. — Martin Cameron, *A Look at the Bright Side*, 1988
- Patronized mainly by the more well to do locals only seldom did one find any GI's or fellow Aussie's enjoying the reasonably priced cold local brew and very fresh 'heppo roll's'. — *users.mildura.net.au/users/marshall/raaf/dropinn.htm*, 2003

hep square *noun*

a person who lives a conventional life but has some awareness of unconventional lifestyles *US*

- There's another thing. You have kind of a "hep square" we call them. A hep square is a person that knows a little bit of what's going on. — Bruce Jackson, *Outside the Law*, p. 145, 1972

her *noun*

cocaine *US, 1981*

- — Nick Constable, *This is Cocaine*, p. 181, 2002

Hera *noun*

heroin *UK*

Disguising 'heroin' with the name of a Greek goddess.

- — Robert Ashton, *This Is Heroin*, p. 206, 2002
- — Mike Haskins, *Drugs*, p. 284, 2003

herb *noun*

marijuana *US*

Celebrated in song by Sly & the Revolutionaries, 'Herb', 1979.

- "You been smokin' herb at Two Day's!" Hip accused. — Nathan Heard, *Howard Street*, p. 98, 1968
- A herbsman is a righteous mon who enjoy the sweetness of the earth and the fullness thereof. Him just smoke herb like the bible say, and commit no crime. — Bob Marley, 1975
- I can see him doing it, stoned on his herb. — Elmore Leonard, *Swag*, p. 142, 1976
- A pocket full of money and head full of herb / A Cadillac coupe parked at the curb. — Dennis Wepman et al., *The Life*, p. 31, 1976
- [H]e was stoked to the gills, having scored some primo Jamaican herb off a busboy at the hotel. — Carl Hiaasen, *Tourist Season*, p. 169, 1986
- We nibbled empanadas, sipped fruit juices, and smoked herb as we laughed and talked as though we had known each other all our lives. — Odie Hawkins, *Lost Angeles*, p. 176, 1994
- Lloyd spun a U-turn and headed to Brixton to score some herb. — Donald Gorgon, *Cop Killer*, p. 29, 1994
- Gets some of his herb at his mama's nursing home, from one of them Rasta fellas work there. — Elmore Leonard, *Riding the Rap*, p. 131, 1995
- You think he's got any herb? — *Kids*, 1995

▸ **cry herb; call herb**

to vomit *AUSTRALIA*

Echoic.

- Well, you've heard a bloke having a good chunder, saying "Herb... Heeeeerb... Heeeerb!" Calling for Herb, see, that's one of the many euphemisms for vomit. — Frank Hardy, *Billy Borker Rides Again*, 1967
- — Barry Humphries, *Bazza Pulls It Off!*, 1971 CRY RUTH

herb *verb*

to assault a weak person *US*

- — Maria Hinojas, *Crews*, p. 167, 1995: 'Glossary'

herbal *adjective*

pertaining to marijuana *US*

- I could really use some sort of a herbal refreshment. — *Clueless*, 1995
- Leon lit a herbal cigarette and blew smoke out of the open window. — John Milne, *Alive and Kicking*, p. 12, 1998

herbal bliss *noun*

MDMA, the recreational drug best known as ecstasy *UK*

- — Mike Haskins, *Drugs*, p. 289, 2003

herbal ecstasy *noun*

a substance that is not restricted by drug control legislation and is claimed to be a natural substitute for MDMA *UK*

- Herbal ecstasy has been sold freely at raves, clubs, concerts, and festivals. — Harry Shapiro, *Recreational Drugs*, p. 330, 2004

herbals *noun*

marijuana *US*

- — Lois Stavsky et al., *A2Z*, p. 47, 1995

herb and a' *noun*

marijuana and alcohol *US, 1980s*

A lazy clipping of **HERB AND AL**.

Herb and Al; Herbie and Al *noun*

marijuana and alcohol *US, 1981*

- — Richard A. Spears, *The Slang and Jargon of Drugs and Drink*, p. 229, 1986
- — Mike Haskins, *Drugs*, p. 287, 2003

herbert *noun*

1 a mischievous child or youth *UK*

Quite often heard as 'little herbert'.

- [T]he school herberts queuing outside the study for the cane. — Martin King and Martin Knight, *The Naughty Nineties*, p. 150, 1999
- Us gypsy boys were drinking with the local herberts. — Jimmy Stockin, *On The Cobbles*, p. 108, 2000

2 a harmless youth; a ridiculous man *UK, 1960*

An extension of the previous sense.

- She said, "Sod off, Scruffy 'erbert." — Tom Wolfe, *The Noonday Underground*, p. 67, 1968
- [H]e was a fuckin' spotty herbert student for fuck's sake. — J.J. Connolly, *Know Your Enemy [britpulp]*, p. 139, 1999
- [M]echanised Old Bill [police] too heavy and slow to catch these scruffy skin-and-bone herberts[.] — John King, *White Trash*, p. 3, 2001

3 a man in a specified field of endeavour *UK*

- All great men keep diaries. Pepys, Boswell, Shaw, all we literary herberts. — Ray Galton and Alan Simpson, *Hancock's Half Hour*, 30th December 1956

Herbie *noun*

in Antarctica, a powerful blizzard *ANTARCTICA, 1987*

- — Bernadette Hince, *The Antarctic Dictionary*, p. 167, 2000
- — *Cool Antarctica*, 2003: 'Antarctic slang'

Herbie Alley *noun*

the passage between Black Island and White Island, through which fast-moving Antarctic blizzards develop *ANTARCTICA*

- —Ethan Dicks, *English, as She is Spoke at McMurdo*, 2003

Herbie Hides *noun*

trousers *UK*

Rhyming slang for **STRIDES**, formed from the name of Nigerian heavyweight boxer Henry Hide (b.1971).

- —Ray Puxley, *Fresh Rabbit*, 1998

herbs *noun*

1 marijuana *UK*

- Yeah, man. No problem. I'll have the herbs.—Ken Lukowiak, *Marijuana Time*, p. 202, 2000

2 (of a motor engine) power *AUSTRALIA*

- It's pretty hot on herbs, but that bus of his is certainly a phenomenal little performer.—Barry Humphries, *A Nice Nights Entertainment*, p. 42, 1960
- The bloke on the throttle was a real showman. He was giving it plenty of herbs[.]—Sam Weller, *Old Bastards I Have Met*, p. 9, 1979

herbsman *noun*

a marijuana smoker *JAMAICA*

Used as a song title by King Stitt and Andy Capp, 'Herbsman', 1970.

- A herbsman is a righteous mon who enjoys the sweetness of the earth and the fullness thereof. Him just smoke herb like the bible say, and commit no crime.—*Jabberrock [quoting Bob Marley, 1975]*, p. 211, 1997

Herc; Herk; Herky Bird *noun*

the Hercules C-130 medium cargo transport aircraft manufactured by Lockheed *US, 1980*

The primary transport aircraft used for US military forces in Vietnam.

- —Gregory Clark, *Words of the Vietnam War*, p. 78, 1990
- —Linda Reinberg, *In the Field*, p. 104, 1991
- The first production C-130, often called the "Herky Bird," made its first flight on 7 April 1955."—Fred J. Pushies, *U.S. Air Forces Special Ops*, p. 41, 2000

hercules *noun*

especially potent phencyclidine, the recreational drug known as PCP or angel dust *US, 1981*

- —Richard A. Spears, *The Slang and Jargon of Drugs and Drink*, p. 257, 1986

herd *noun*

1 a packet of Camel™ cigarettes *US*

- —Lou Shelly, *Hepcats Jive Dictionary*, p. 12, 1945

2 a quantity of something *IRELAND*

- How many have yeh? Jimmy Sr asked him. – Ask no questions, compadre, said Bertie. – Not tha' many. A small herd.—Roddy Doyle, *The Van*, p. 107, 1991

Herd *noun*

▸ **The Herd**

the 173rd Airborne Brigade, US Army *US*

The first major US combat unit sent to Vietnam.

- —Linda Reinberg, *In the Field*, p. 104, 1991

herd *verb*

in hot rodding, to drive (a hot rod) *US, 1933*

- —Fred Horsley, *The Hot Rod Handbook*, p. 210, 1965: 'Hot talk – a glossary of hot rod terms'

herder *noun*

1 a prison guard assigned to a prison yard *US*

- —William K. Bentley and James M. Corbett, *Prison Slang*, p. 96, 1992

2 in horse racing, a jockey or horse that forces the other horses to bunch up behind it *US*

- —David W. Maurer, *Argot of the Racetrack*, p. 35, 1951

3 on the railways, a yard pointsman *US, 1930*

- —Linda Niemann, *Boomer*, p. 250, 1990

here

▷ see: **'ERE**

here and there *noun*

a chair *UK*

Rhyming slang, always used in full.

- —Ray Puxley, *Cockney Rabbit*, 1992

here's how

used as a toast *UK, 1896*

- Lilli raised her glass. "Chin-chin." "Here's how." We drank.—Douglas Rutherford, *The Creeping Flesh*, p. 43, 1963

here we go; here we go again

used for registering resignation at the commencement of an anticipated, predictable or otherwise undesirable event *UK, 1954*

- "Here we go," I thought. But the contagious fear that usually spreads through the crowd on these occasions was missing.—Mark Steel, *Reasons to be Cheerful*, p. 201, 2001

her indoors; 'er indoors; 'er *noun*

the wife of the user *UK*

Coined for television comedy drama series *The Minder*, 1979–94.

- Terry found himself continually attending the invalid, bringing him all kind of goods and watched cycinally by 'er indoors.—Anthony Masters, *Minder*, p. 91, 1984
- I'd better make sure 'er is up that day.—Andrew Nickolds, *Back to Basics*, p. 4, 1994
- —Angela Devlin, *Prison Patter*, p. 49, 1996
- Edward leans in lowerin' his voice but lickin' his lips like here comes a jokey secret. '...'er indoors might not approve.—Nick Barlay, *Curvy Lovebox*, p. 71, 1997
- [I]n Minder, for instance, we never see 'Er Indoors, that is to say Arthur Daley's wife[.]—Stuart Jeffries, *Mrs Slocombe's Pussy*, p. 115, 2000
- [T]here is a long tradition in the English working-class of the gentle giant of a husband giving in to Her Indoors for the sake of a quiet life.—*The Guardian*, p. 3, 12th June 2003

Herk; Herky Bird *noun*

▷ see: **HERC**

Herman Fink *noun*

ink *UK*

Rhyming slang.

- —Julian Franklyn, *A Dictionary of Rhyming Slang*, 1960

Herman the German *noun*

the penis *US*

- —Connie Eble (Editor), *UNC-CH Campus Slang*, p. 3, Fall 1991

hermit *noun*

a poker player wearing headphones during play *US*

- —John Vorhaus, *The Big Book of Poker Slang*, p. 22, 1996

hero *noun*

1 heroin *US*

- —H.J. Ainslinger, *The Traffic in Narcotics*, p. 310, 1953
- —Eugene Landy, *The Underground Dictionary*, p. 101, 1971
- —US Department of Justice, *Street Terms*, October 1994
- —Robert Ashton, *This Is Heroin*, p. 206, 2002

2 a surfer whose opinion of his own skills exceeds his actual skills *US*

- —John Blair, *The Illustrated Discography of Surf Music 1961–1965*, p. 123, 1985

hero gear *noun*

enemy paraphernalia taken from the battlefield *US*

- I swap the pastry to the troops for 'hero gear' (battle souveniers) and I swap the hero gear to the swabbies for pogey bait (candy).—Russell Davis, *Marine at War*, p. 172, 1961

heroina *noun*

heroin *US*

- —US Department of Justice, *Street Terms*, October 1994

herone *noun*

heroin *UK, 1998*

- —Mike Haskins, *Drugs*, p. 284, 2003

hero of the underworld *noun*

heroin *US*

An elaboration of **HERO** (heroin).

- —Richard A. Spears, *The Slang and Jargon of Drugs and Drink*, p. 257, 1986
- —Mike Haskins, *Drugs*, p. 284, 2003

herox *noun*

4-bromo-2,5-dimethoxyphenethylaimine, a mild hallucinogen *US*

- Shulgin recommends taking 2C-B "at or just before" recovery from an ecstasy trip.—Steven Daly and Nalthaniel Wice, *alt.culture*, p. 256, 1995

herring and kipper; herring *noun*
a striptease dancer *UK*
Rhyming slang for STRIPPER.
- No, I don't want to see some old herring taking her clothes off.—Ray Puxley, *Cockney Rabbit*, 1992

herringboner *noun*
a dairy farmer *NEW ZEALAND*
- I love webfoot for a Taranaki farmer, who is also known as a gumbooter or herringboner.—*Dominion Post*, p. C6, 22nd November 2002

herring choker *noun*
1 a person from New Brunswick or elsewhere in the Canadian Maritime Provinces *US, 1899*
- "We'll go someplace, and you'll get custard pie, and then you'll cut the damned thing up and pour vinegar on the plate and let it all soak through the crust. I know you herring-chokers."—George V. Higgins, *The Judgment of Deke Hunter*, p. 169, 1976
- A "herring-choker" is a Maritimer, especially from New Brunswick, where the rivers run thick with spring herring (alewives).—*cbc4kids.ca*, 15th June 2002

2 a Scandanavian *US, 1936*
- —Vincent J. Monteleone, *Criminal Slang*, p. 117, 1949
- Hear that herring chokers? You Norskis may need some supplements if you are eating the Standard American Diet.—Lendon Smith, *Happiness is a Healthy Life*, p. 89, 1992

herring snapper *noun*
a Scandanavian *US, 1930*
- —Vincent J. Monteleone, *Criminal Slang*, p. 117, 1949

herself *noun*
a wife, your wife, a female partner *IRELAND*
- [M]y father said: 'C'mere to me.' He looked towards the house. 'You're to say nothin' to herself, do you mind me?'[.]—Hugh Leonard, *Out After Dark*, p. 32, 1989
- But anyway, when I got home that night Herself was sprawled on the sofa watching television.—Joseph O'Connor, *The Irish Male at Home and Abroad*, p. 132, 1996

Hershey Highway *noun*
the rectum *US, 1973*
- —Pamela Munro, *U.C.L.A. Slang*, p. 71, 1989
- Then she taught me how to drive the Hershey highway and she masturbated her own clitoris until we both collapsed together in a wave of orgasms.—Harold Robbins, *The Predators*, p. 196, 1998

Hershey road *noun*
the rectum *US, 1974*
- There's been so much stick pussy shoved up that Hershey road they could rent it out for a convention center.—Seth Morgan, *Homeboy*, p. 179, 1990

Hershey squirts *noun*
diarrhoea *US, 1972*
A joking if unpleasant allusion to Hershey™ chocolate.
- Damn. I got Hereshey squirts in my shorts.—Joseph Wambaugh, *The Secrets of Harry Bright*, p. 54, 1985
- —Pamela Munro, *U.C.L.A. Slang*, p. 49, 1989
- As for her health, Kitty hadn't fixed for twelve days but still had the geewillies and was running to the bathroom every fifteen minutes with the Hershey squirts.—Seth Morgan, *Homeboy*, p. 135, 1990
- —Michael Dalton Johnson, *Talking Trash with Redd Foxx*, p. 45, 1994
- It's oddly comforting to discover that all-girl rock bands would contract "the Hershey squirts" while drinking their way through Europe and Japan.—*SF Weekly*, 3rd July 1996

he-she *noun*
a man living as a woman, either as a transvestite or transexual; an effeminate male *US, 1871*
- England is the homo's paradise where he'she's are proud members of society.—Lee Mortimer, *Women Confidential*, p. 186, 1960
- —Collin Baker et al., *College Undergraduate Slang Study Conducted at Brown University*, p. 135, 1968
- A he-she across the way giving someone a show.—Paul Glover, *Words from the House of the Dead*, 1974
- Jimmy said don't snitch on me boys I'm just a he-she and now let me hide this wig away and go get some ACTION.—William T. Vollman, *Whores for Gloria*, p. 115, 1991
- You didn't show me the photograph before you showed Kendicott and that fat he-she the photograph.—Robert Campbell, *Boneyards*, p. 175, 1992

hesher; heshen; hesh *noun*
a fan of heavy metal music *US*
- [S]toner blacklight parties in his room with the scraggly hesher chicks.—Editors of Ben is Dead, *Retrohell*, p. 95, 1997

hesh girl; hash girl *noun*
a prostitute who works in cheap drinking establishments *SOUTH AFRICA, 1973*
Urban and township slang.
- —Penny Silva, *A Dictionary of South African English*, 1996

he shoots! he scores!
used for celebrating a minor accomplishment *US*
From the television programme *Saturday Night Live*.
- —Connie Eble (Editor), *UNC-CH Campus Slang*, p. 9, Spring 1991

hesitation marks *noun*
scars on the inner wrist from failed suicide attempts *US*
- —Bruce Rodgers, *The Queens' Vernacular*, p. 163, 1972
- And he has hesitaiton marks on the forearm – little cuts to test out the blad while he thought about it.—Lee Seldes, *The Legacy of Mark Rothko*, p. 109, 1996

hessle *noun*
heroin *UK, 1998*
- —Robert Ashton, *This Is Heroin*, p. 206, 2002
- —Mike Haskins, *Drugs*, p. 284, 2003

het *adjective*
*het*erosexual *US*
- —Bruce Rodgers, *The Queens' Vernacular*, p. 190, 1972
- —*Radio Times*, 21st February 1976
- —Jim Crotty, *How to Talk American*, p. 136, 1997
- [A]lthough he himself was what the Americans would term "absolutely het", he found himself in the curious position of fancying the transvestite before him[.]—Fiona Pitt-Kethley, *Red Light Districts of the World*, p. 49, 2000

hetboy *noun*
a *het*erosexual male *US*
Internet shorthand.
- —Christian Crumlish, *The Internet Dictionary*, p. 88, 1995

heter *noun*
a *heter*osexual *UK*
- —*The Guardian*, 23rd March 1980

hetero *noun*
a *hetero*sexual *UK, 1933*
- Anyway, what's so special about being gay except a lot of heartaches and headaches? Heteros don't brag about the novels and paintings they've produced because they go to bed with the opposite sex.—*One: The Homosexual Magazine*, p. 19, February 1953
- In Big D, do as the heteros do.—Phil Andros (Samuel M. Steward), *Stud*, p. 89, 1966
- Did they make it with each other at all, or was it strictly hetero? —Jefferson Poland and Valerie Alison, *The Records of the San Francisco Sexual Freedom League*, p. 27, 1971
- A little more enlightened about their own captivity, cognizant of their Augustinian heritage, the heteros there have lived on a somewhat egalitarian bass with the homosexuals.—John Francis Hunter, *The Gay Insider*, p. 263, 1971
- Did you ask him if it was a hetero porn flick?—Joseph Wambaugh, *The Glitter Dome*, p. 199, 1981
- We figured that twenty heteros would probably talk about baseball, boobs, and the guy in Virginia whose wife cut his penis off.—Anka Radakovich, *The Wild Girls Club*, p. 164, 1994

hetgirl *noun*
a *het*erosexual female *US*
Internet shorthand.
- —Christian Crumlish, *The Internet Dictionary*, p. 88, 1995

het up; all het up *adjective*
excited *US, 1909*
From a dialect variation of 'heated' or 'heated up'.
- When they were not getting all het up, the Italians produced some of their best rugby of the season[.]—*The Guardian*, 25th March 2002

hex *noun*
a number sign (#) on a computer keyboard *US*
- —Eric S. Raymond, *The New Hacker's Dictionary*, p. 39, 1991

hexy *noun*
hexamine (a solid fuel provided in small blocks) *UK*
Military.
- [W]e sat down and got a hexy burner going for a brew.—Andy McNab, *Immediate Action*, p. 92, 1995

hey

used as a discourse break that raises emphasis or focus *US, 1974*

- Up until that point, Pennzoil had been arguing that, hey, they are reasonable people, the court in Texas is reasonable and they don't need any Federal action. — *New York Times*, p. 20, 13th January 1986

hey?

1 pardon? *SOUTH AFRICA, 1961*

Used alone or as the introduction to a question that is formed using a standard interrogative.

- — Jean Branford, *A Dictionary of South African English*, p. 89, 1978

2 used at the end of a question for emphasis or as a means of demanding a response *SOUTH AFRICA, 1969*

- — Jean Branford, *A Dictionary of South African English*, p. 88, 1978

hey-diddle-diddle *noun*

a swindle, a deception *UK: SCOTLAND*

Rhyming slang for **FIDDLE**.

- He was caught at the hey-diddle-diddle with the books. — Michael Munro, *The Patter, Another Blast*, 1988

hey-hey *noun*

a good time *US*

- "A little hey-hey" – a good time. — *Washington Post*, p. B1, 17th January 1985

hey now

1 used as a greeting *US, 1946*

- A group of zoot-suiters greted me in passing, "Hey now, daddy-o," they called. "Hew now!" "Hey now!" I said. — Ralph Ellison, *Invisible Man*, p. 485, 1947
- The "Hello!' that says you're on the bus. From the chorus of "iko Iko." — David Shenk and Steve Silberman, *Skeleton Key*, p. 143, 1994

2 used for getting attention *US*

- Hey now! Why's the air conditioning on when it's freezing outside? — Connie Eble (Editor), *UNC-CH Campus Slang*, p. 5, Fall 1987

hey-presto!

a command used by stage magicians; hence, used for registering a sudden or surprising transformation; cynically used for 'as if by magic' when a predictable change occurs *UK, 1731*

- When the truck came back again it ran over my dope (great song title that) and hey presto! It was flatter. — Ken Lukowiak, *Marijuana Time*, p. 142, 2000
- All the kids laughed and hey-presto, the poor bastard's still stuck with the tag [nickname] more than twenty years later. — Danny King, *The Burglar Diaries*, p. 148, 2001

hey rube *noun*

a fight between swindlers of any sort and their victims *US, 1900*

- Whether an event is a close call or a "hey rube" depends not so much on what is detected or suspected as on the reactions of the audience and the ability of the hustlers to cool out the other players. — Robert C. Prus and C.R.D. Sharper, *Road Hustler*, p. 114, 1977

hey, rube!

used as an insider request for help in a fight *US, 1900*

Originally and principally an expression used in the circus and carnivals.

- Early day circus troupers may have used the cry "hey rube", but during my twenty five years on the road with the larger circuses and carnivals, I have never heard it used one time. — Joe McKennon, *Circus Lingo*, p. 46, 1980
- "You better git your friend outta here right quick sonny, 'cause if I have to pull a 'Hey, Rube,' you boys will be in more trouble than you ever thought was possible." — Terry Southern, *Texas Summer*, p. 110, 1991

hey-you *noun*

an uncouth or insolent person *UK: SCOTLAND*

From the signature conversational gambit employed by such people.

- Ah'm no too happy wi that crowd she's in wi at school. That wan she brought hame the day wis a right wee hey-you. — Michael Munro, *The Patter, Another Blast*, p. 32, 1988

HFH

used as a jaded abbreviation of a jaded 'ho-fucking-hum' *US*

- "What is this?" she said, finally. "An H.F.H. good-bye?" — Joseph Wambaugh, *The Golden Orange*, p. 153, 1990

H-head *noun*

a habitual user of heroin *UK*

- "He's a lush-head, an acid-head, a pill-head, an H-head", etc. It was almost as if the hippy really was just his head[.] — Paul E Willis, *Profane Culture*, p. 109, 1978

HHOJ; HHOK

used in computer message shorthand to mean '*h*a-*h*a *o*nly *j*oking' or '*h*a-*h*a *o*nly *k*idding' *US*

- — Eric S. Raymond, *The New Hacker's Dictionary*, p. 342, 1991

hi-ball *noun*

a central nervous system stimulant, especially dextroamphetamine (trade name Dexamyl™) *US*

- — Eugene Landy, *The Underground Dictionary*, p. 65, 1971

hibber de hoy *noun*

▷ see: HOBBER DE HOY

hiccup *noun*

a fault in administration, an interruption to any smooth-running procedure *UK, 1974*

- "This is a great club but the financial situation is not good and we're going through a hiccup," said Hart. — *The Guardian*, 1st August 2001

hiccup *verb*

in computing when transferring data, to inadvertently skip some data or send some data twice *US*

- — Christian Crumlish, *The Internet Dictionary*, p. 88, 1995

hick *noun*

an unsophisticated, simple person from the far rural reaches *UK, 1565*

A familiar form of 'Richard'. Now chiefly US use.

- He decided that they'd have to try and get a quick lead over these hicks. — James T. Farrell, *Tournament Star*, p. 69, 1946
- In the old days, a chorus salary of 50 or 60 bucks a week seemed like a million to hicks in the sticks, and parental opposition was not too oppressive. — Jack Lait and Lee Mortimer, *New York Confidential*, p. 141, 1948
- It's about a hick ... a hick like you, if you please. — Robert Rossen, *All the King's Men*, 1949
- You'll find more porn per square inch in hick towns than in any big city on God's green earth. — Max Shulman, *Rally Round the Flag, Boys!*, p. 158, 1957
- If someone had hung a sign, "HICK," around my neck, I couldn't have looked much more obvious. — Malcolm X and Alex Haley, *The Autobiography of Malcolm X*, p. 34, 1964
- I have seen the hicks point in awe at the out of state tags on the cars that line the street of Walnut Avenue on the first Saturday in May of each year. — A.S. Jackson, *Gentleman Pimp*, p. 188, 1973
- He lived off the hicks from out in the sticks / He was a master of the long-shoe game. — Dennis Wepman et al., *The Life*, p. 86, 1976
- JOE: She used to be a regular on Hee-Haw. You know that country show with all those fuckin' hicks. — *Reservoir Dogs*, 1992

hickey *noun*

1 a bruise on the skin caused by a partner's mouth during foreplay; a suction kiss *US, 1942*

- — Donald Webster Cory and John P. LeRoy, *The Homosexual and His Society*, p. 264, 1963: 'A lexicon of homosexual slang'
- — *The Guild Dictionary of Homosexual Terms*, p. 21, 1965
- My best girl friend was always showing off the hickeys on her stomach. — Jefferson Poland and Valerie Alison, *The Records of the San Francisco Sexual Freedom League*, p. 112, 1971
- Hickeys. They were fun to give but a curse to receive [...] And if my parents asked what the hell that was, the answer was always that the faithful curling iron burned me (again). — Editors of Ben is Dead, *Retrohell*, p. 95, 1997

2 a favourable film review *US*

- — Anna Scotti and Paul Young, *Buzzwords*, p. 5, 1997

3 in dominoes, a type of side bet *US, 1981*

- — Thomas L. Clark, *The Dictionary of Gambling and Gaming*, p. 99, 1987

4 in pool, a rule infraction *US, 1992*

- — Mike Shamos, *The Illustrated Encyclopedia of Billiards*, p. 115, 1993

Hickey *noun*

a notional province where there are no manners or courtesy *BARBADOS*

- Where you come form? The Hickey? — Frank A. Collymore, *Barbadian Dialect*, p. 59, 1965

hickory dickory dock; hickory dickory *noun*

a clock *UK*

Rhyming slang; an elaboration of **DICKORY DOCK**, from the nursery rhyme which continues 'A mouse ran up the clock'.

- — Ray Puxley, *Fresh Rabbit*, 1998

hiddy *adjective*

1 drunk *US*

- —Pamela Munro, *U.C.L.A. Slang*, p. 49, 1989

2 hideous *US*

- —*Surfing*, p. 43, 14th March 1990

hide *noun*

1 the human skin *UK, 1607*

- [Y]ou'll never toss and turn again in a Bowery scratchpad, digging the lice and chinches out of your hide. —Mezz Mezzrow, *Really the Blues*, p. 317, 1946

2 impudence; effrontery; cheek *AUSTRALIA, 1902*

- He had deliberately held that outfit to wear himself in the fashion parade. "The hide of him!" she exclaimed. —Kylie Tennant, *Lost Haven*, p. 302, 1946

3 a wallet *US, 1932*

- So he hands over his hide, better'n a hundred in it, and I tell him some door to go knock on and splits. —Malcolm Braly, *On the Yard*, p. 25, 1967
- There's the cool old shot at the busy bus stop / Scanning on a hide. —Dennis Wepman et al., *The Life*, p. 162, 1976

4 a horse *US, 1934*

- —*American Speech*, p. 270, December 1958: 'Ranching terms from eastern Washington'

5 in hot rodding, a tyre *US*

- —Tom MacPherson, *Dragging and Driving*, p. 139, 1960

hide *verb*

▸ hide the salami

to have sex *US, 1983*

'Sausage' as 'penis' imagery; a variation of the earlier HIDE-THE-WEENIE.

- Then Candy Kane goes solo as she takes on a hunky study who seems gratefully awestruck at the abundance of flesh Candy presents, and who shows his gratitude by promptly hiding the salami deep inside Candy's spectacular cleavage. —*Adult Video*, p. 54, August/September 1986
- Lets play some serious hide the salami. —Seth Morgan, *Homeboy*, p. 156, 1990
- We might as well play hide the salami, said Jack. —William T. Vollman, *Whores for Gloria*, p. 69, 1991
- Now that I'm dating but not yet playing hide-the-salami, I wanted to further my adult education[.] —Anka Radakovich, *The Wild Girls Club*, p. 110, 1994
- We whipped the doors open and came face-to-face with Ronald DeChooch playing hide-the-salami with the clerical help. —Janet Evanovich, *Seven Up*, p. 212, 2001
- Another way to say "intercourse" [...] Hiding the salami[.] —Erica Orloff and JoAnn Baker, *Dirty Little Secrets*, p. 63, 2001

hide and seek *noun*

impudence *UK*

Rhyming slang for 'cheek'.

- You've got some hide and seek, you have! —Ray Puxley, *Cockney Rabbit*, 1992

hideaway *noun*

a pocket *US*

- —Lou Shelly, *Hepcats Jive Dictionary*, p. 12, 1945
- —Clarence Major, *Dictionary of Afro-American Slang*, p. 65, 1970

hi-de-hi

a greeting, answered by 'ho-de-ho' *UK, 1941*

First recorded during World War 2; adopted by Jimmy Perry and David Croft as the title (and catchphrase) of a television situation comedy set in a 1950s holiday camp (BBC, 1980–88); the call and response greeting is still heard, but often ironic.

hideola *adjective*

ugly *UK*

A variation of conventional 'hideous'.

- [A]ll the hideola pallones [women] in cod [bad] drag [clothes]. —the cast of 'Aspects of Love', Prince of Wales Theatre, *Palare (Boy Dancer Talk) for Beginners*, 1989–92

hides *noun*

drums *UK*

Jazz slang.

- Skins [...] Not much used in jazz circles , where 'hides' is preferred. —Peter Clayton and Peter Gammond, *Jazz A-Z*, p. 219, 1986

hide-the-baloney *noun*

sexual intercourse *US*

- Man, wouldn't I love to play hide the baloney with that. —Charles Whited, *Chiodo*, p. 224, 1973

hide-the-sausage *noun*

sexual intercourse *AUSTRALIA*

- [A] swift game of hide the sausage in the back stalls [of a cinema]. —Barry Humphries, *Bazza Pulls It Off!*, 1971

hide-the-weenie *noun*

sexual intercourse *US*

- He must have flipped because he has a heart-to-heart with his mother about how he's been playing hide-the-weenie with his tutor. —Angelo d'Arcangelo, *The Homosexual Handbook*, p. 230, 1968

hidey *noun*

the children's game hide and seek *AUSTRALIA, 1957*

- Her son was asleep. When he woke he thought Mummy was playing hidey. —Beverley Farmer, *Milk*, p. 58, 1983
- I grew up in the lower north of South Aust. We always played 'hidey', but we occasionally referred to it as 'hide and seek', never 'hide and go seek'. —*Wordmap (www.abc.net.au/wordmap)*, 2003

hi diddle diddle *noun*

1 middle, especially the middle of a dart board *UK*

Rhyming slang.

- Nearest to the "hi diddle diddle" throws first. —Ray Puxley, *Cockney Rabbit*, 1992

2 a swindle, a deception *UK*

- [O]n the hi diddle diddle. —Ray Puxley, *Cockney Rabbit*, 1992

3 a violin, a fiddle *UK*

Rhyming slang.

- —Ray Puxley, *Fresh Rabbit*, 1998

hiding *noun*

a beating; a heavy defeat *UK, 1809*

- Phil Mansfield, defending, said that when [Shawn] Gladding's [9-year-old] son had come home a second time saying he had got "a hiding", his father walked to the school getting more and more worked up as he went. —*The Guardian*, 10th July 2002

hiding to nothing *noun*

▸ on a hiding to nothing

faced with a situation in which any outcome is unfavourable *UK, 1905*

- I mean, I know we're on a hiding to nothing but I don't fancy lying down on my back with my legs in the air like a naughty dog. —Ted Lewis, *Jack Carter's Law*, p. 178, 1974

hids *adjective*

lacking fashion sense *US*

An abbreviation of the conventional 'hideous'.

- —Connie Eble (Editor), *UNC-CH Campus Slang*, p. 4, November 2002

hidy-hole; hidey-hole *noun*

a hiding place *UK, 1817*

- Having lost his favourite hidey-hole – the greenhouse – to his grandfather's disgusting plant collection, Daniel becomes justifiably suspicious about what exactly is going on in there[.] —*The Guardian*, 9th October 2001
- They've lived in their hidy hole, which they built themselves, for about six years. —*The Observer*, 26th May 2002

hidy-ho, neighbor

used as a humorous greeting *US*

A catchphrase salutation from the US television comedy *Home Improvements* (ABC, 1991–99). Repeated with referential humour.

hifalutin *adjective*

▷ see: HIGHFALUTIN

higgledy-piggledy *adjective*

in a confused jumble *UK, 1598*

Probably derived as a rhyming elaboration of the disordered huddle in which pigs exist.

- Wired up in pure Heath Robinson fashion, which is an old English phrase that I think means higgledy-piggledy (which is an even older English phrase). —Tony Wilson, *24 Hour Party People*, p. 145, 2002

high *noun*

1 the sensation produced by consuming drugs or alcohol *US, 1944*

- Not a whiskey high, I could tell it was something else. —Malcolm X and Alex Haley, *The Autobiography of Malcolm X*, p. 129, 1964
- I take the stuff because I did the high, that's all. —James Mills, *The Panic in Needle Park*, p. 102, 1966

• My high was on full blast and I stretched out in the back seat and studied the passing scenes. — Piri Thomas, *Down These Mean Streets*, p. 231, 1967
• The first high is always the best high. After that, you're just trying to get back to the original feeling. — Chris Rock, *Rock This!*, p. 61, 1997
• The local Afghan Kabul Hash produces a "spiritual rather than a splatter high," in the words of a user. — Mike Rock, *This Book*, 1999

2 a sense of exhilaration, unrelated to drugs *US, 1970*
• My acceptance was an incredible high not only for me but for the whole Frisco Chapter. — Jamie Mandelkau, *Buttons*, p. 80, 1971
• The high I get at 2001, just dancing, not just being the best. I wanta get, have, that high someplace else in my life, ya know what I mean. — *Saturday Night Fever*, 1977

High *noun*
Miller High Life™ beer *US*
• — *American Speech*, p. 62, February 1967: 'Soda-fountain, restaurant and tavern calls'

high *adjective*
1 drunk or drug-intoxicated *UK, 1627*
• [He] seldom touched anything stronger than brown ale. I've only known him get high twice. — Charles Raven, *Underworld Nights*, p. 85, 1956
• I wish you could have seen him, pleasantly "high" with drinks, take his seat with dignity[.] — Malcolm X and Alex Haley, *The Autobiography of Malcolm X*, p. 89, 1964
• I drank more Scotch but this time with ice and water, not wanting to get too high. — Sara Harris, *The Lords of Hell*, p. 185, 1967

2 under the influence of a drug, especially marijuana *US, 1931*
• He'd light up and get real high[.] — Mezz Mezzrow, *Really the Blues*, p. 51, 1946
• "You're smoking too many of them," Larry said. "You're high now." — Irving Shulman, *The Amboy Dukes*, p. 99, 1947
• Sure, man, that cat's real high on tea! Look at those big, starin eyes. Get that! — John Clellon Holmes, *Go*, p. 100, 1952
• We get some frantic kicks out of that wheel when we're high. — William Burroughs, *Junkie*, p. 28, 1953
• Jumpsteady always keyed himself up high on dope when he worked. — Malcolm X and Alex Haley, *The Autobiography of Malcolm X*, p. 90, 1964
• I did not for one minute think that anything was wrong with getting high. — Eldridge Cleaver, *Soul on Ice*, p. 4, 1968
• And almost immediately a rumor swept the land that butterfly eggs would get you high. — Tom Robbins, *Another Roadside Attraction*, p. 8, 1971
• My cousin Kendall from Indiana, he got high once and you know, he started eating like really weird foods. — *The Breakfast Club*, 1985
• Getting high is about experiencing reality from a different level[.] — Mike Rock, *This Book*, 1999

3 bad-smelling *TRINIDAD AND TOBAGO, 1935*
• — Lise Winer, *Dictionary of the English/Creole of Trinidad & Tobago*, 2003

▸ **at high warble**
angry, especially without justification *US*
Naval aviator usage.
• — *United States Naval Institute Proceedings*, p. 108, October 1986

high and light *adjective*
pleasantly drug-intoxicated *US*
• — *American Speech*, p. 26, February 1952: 'Teen-age hophead jargon'

high and mighty; high-and-mighty *adjective*
arrogant, imperious *UK, 1825*
• I must be in truth high-and-mighty to consider that he should think me any different to the hundreds of girls there[.] — Anonymous *Streetwalker*, p. 44, 1959
• [T]hese words, written in a most high-and-mighty hand[.] — *The Guardian*, 3rd June 2002

high and tight *noun*
a man's haircut in which the sides of the head are shaved and a quarter-inch of hair is left on top *US*
A military term for a military haircut.
• — Hans Halberstadt, *Airborne*, p. 130, 1988: 'Abridged dictionary of airborne terms'
• After that, they'd been checked into a recruit barracks, issued uniforms, and herded through a thirty-second haircut that left eahc recruit "high and tight." — Ian Douglas, *LUna Marine*, p. 127, 1990
• — Linda Reinberg, *In the Field*, p. 105, 1991

high as a kite *adjective*
very drunk or drug-intoxicated *US, 1939*
Rhyming slang for **TIGHT** (drunk); a clever elaboration of **HIGH**.
• Percy was higher than a kite. — Charles Raven, *Underworld Nights*, p. 85, 1956
• They get high as a kite on this dangerous stuff. — Harry J. Anslinger, *The Murderers*, p. 231, 1961
• Caleb is getting more and more excited. High as a kite if truth were told. The wonderful feeling of Horse [heroin] in his head. — Jack Allen, *When the Whistle Blows*, p. 142, 2000

high-ass *adjective*
haughty; arrogant *US, 1931*
• Hey Odessa, ain't you never comin back an see us no more? You gone highass? — Robert Gover, *JC Saves*, p. 116, 1968

highball *noun*
1 in the used car business, a knowingly inflated price *US*
• A salesman will often pitch a high ball at a cusotmer's trade-in, knowing he can bust it later. — Peter Mann, *How to Buy a Used Car Without Getting Gypped*, p. 192, 1975

2 a signal to a train engineer to increase speed *US, 1897*
• I hid in the weeds until highball, got on again, and slept then all night long flying down the unbelievable coast[.] — Jack Kerouac, *The Dharma Bums*, p. 93, 1958

3 a glass of milk *US*
• — *American Speech*, p. 88, April 1946: 'The language of West Coast culinary workers'

highball *verb*
1 to travel fast *US, 1912*
• As they highballed it southbound without lights or siren, Lloyd told the cops he was flagged for the October class at the academy[.] — James Ellroy, *Blood on the Moon*, p. 32, 1984

2 to see *US*
Probably playing on **EYEBALL**.
• I didnt know that old squarejohn highballed the trick and I continued on the play. — Bruce Jackson, *Get Your Ass in the Water and Swim Like Me*, p. 85, 1965

high beams *noun*
1 erect nipples on a woman's breasts seen through a garment *US*
• — Connie Eble (Editor), *UNC-CH Campus Slang*, p. 5, Fall 1986

2 the wide open eyes of a person under the influence of crack cocaine *US*
• — US Department of Justice, *Street Terms*, October 1994
• — David Rowan, *A Glossary for the 90s*, 1998

high bountious *adjective*
very bad-smelling *TRINIDAD AND TOBAGO*
• — Lise Winer, *Dictionary of the English/Creole of Trinidad & Tobago*, 2003

highboy *noun*
in hot rodding, a coupe, sedan or roadster that sits on top of the frame rails at stock height, that has not been lowered *US*
• — Lyle K. Engel, *The Complete Book of Fuel and Gas Dragsters*, p. 152, 1968

highbrow *noun*
a person of superior intellectual quality or interests; a person who affects interests that imply an intellectual superiority *US, 1907*
• — Lawrence W. Levine, *Highbrow/Lowbrow*, 1990

highbrow *adjective*
of superior intellectual quality or interest *UK, 1884*
• TV arts 'too highbrow' says BBC producer. — *The Guardian*, 14th April 2003

high-brown *adjective*
of mixed black and white heritage *US, 1915*
Originally white usage, then adopted by African-Americans.
• Slug Mason looked at the high-brown singer[.] — James Farrell, *Studs Lonigan*, 1938

high camp *noun*
an ostenatious, highly mannered style *US*
A refined variation of **CAMP**.

high cap *verb*
to brag, to banter, to gossip *US*
• — Charles Shafer, *Folk Speech in Texas Prisons*, p. 206, 1990

high diver *noun*
a person who enjoys or excels at performing oral sex on women *US*
A construction built on the image of going down.
• — *Male Swinger Number 3*, p. 46, 1981: 'The complete gay dictionary'

high drag *noun*
elaborate female clothing worn by a man *US*
- I went to this straight party in High Drag (and I mean High, honey – gown, stockings, ostrich plumes in my flaming hair)[.] — John Rechy, *City of Night*, p. 103, 1963
- — Guy Strait, *The Lavendar Lexicon*, 1st June 1964

higher-higher *noun*
the upper echelons of military command *US*
- — Linda Reinberg, *In the Field*, p. 105, 1991

highfalutin; hifalutin *adjective*
absurdly pompous, snobbish *US, 1839*
Probably an elaboration of 'high-flown' or similar; 'highfaluting' (the 'g' is optional) was originally hyphenated which lends strength to this etymology. Yiddish *hifelufelem* (ostentatious, self-glorifying) is also possible.
- [S]ome of his I.W.W. constiuents would probably kick over the traces if they saw the highfalutin' fillies he runs with in Washington. — Jack Lait and Lee Mortimer, *Washington Confidential*, p. 87, 1951
- He wondered if they understood any of the high-falutin' language therein[.] — Evan Hunter, *The Blackboard Jungle*, p. 86, 1954
- Her old man was one of those highfalutin Nigger doctors. — Iceberg Slim (Robert Beck), *Trick Baby*, p. 102, 1969
- Food at Pont is not quite as hifalutin as that other Conran fave, Bibendum. — *ES Magazine*, p. 43, 22nd June 2001

high five *noun*
1 a greeting or sign of approval accomplished by slapping open palms with arms extended above head-level *US*
The greeting and term originated in sports but quickly spread.
- Aguirre gave him a high five that came straight from his toes, then shuffled to the bench, grabbed Coach Ray Meyer and bearhugged him[.] — *Washington Post*, p. D11, 28th December 1980
- The Montrealers exchanged "high fives," low fives" and "sidearm fives." — *Washingotn Post*, p. D1, 15th September 1980
- How does a blonde do a high five? — *Sleepless in Seattle*, 1993

2 HIV *US*
A construction based on an abbreviation of 'high' to 'hi' and conversion of 'V' to the Roman numeral five.
- — *Oprah Winfrey Show*, 2nd October 2003

high five *verb*
to raise your open hand above your head and slap it against the open hand of someone else *US, 1981*
- The woof chorus went through the roof, everybody high-fiving, bopping in glee. — Richard Price, *Clockers*, p. 203, 1992
- The fielders and two-eighths of the ground high-fived and jigged merrily. — Diran Abedayo, *My Once Upon A Time*, p. 224, 2000

high fur *noun*
the refuelling of a hovering helicopter *US*
- This technique is known as "Helicopter In-Flight Refueling" or, HIFR, pronounced "High-fur." — Gerry Carroll, *North S*A*R*, p. 76, 1991

high grade *noun*
marijuana *UK*
Recorded by a Jamaican inmate of a UK prison, August 2002.

high hard one *noun*
forceful sex *US*
- Here she is at her quintessential best, laying virtually still for sex scene after sex scene, even as she gives blow-jobs, gets her cunt swabbed, or lifts her legs for the high hard one. — *Adult Video*, p. 72, August/September 1986
- What I want you to do is close your eyes and remember, remember the last time ol' Mickey gave you the high hard one. — *Natural Born Killers*, 1994

high hat *noun*
opium *US, 1896*
From an earlier sense (a large opium pill).
- — Angela Devlin, *Prison Patter*, p. 61, 1996

high-hat; high-hatted *adjective*
snobbish, superior, supercilious *US, 1924*
- [T]he local pig sheriff stormed in and got all high hatted and hotted up about us being there. — Jamie Mandelkau, *Buttons*, p. 84, 1971

high-heel boy *noun*
a paratrooper *US*
- — *American Speech*, p. 319, October/December 1948: 'Slang of the American paratrooper'

high holy *noun*
in the usage of counterculturalists associated with the Rainbow Nation gatherings, an older, experienced member of the counterculture *US*
Often used with a degree of irony and lack of reverence.
- — Jim Crotty, *How to Talk American*, p. 289, 1997

high horse *noun*
a position of arrogant superiority *US*
- But the thing about California is this: everybody is on their high horse trying to imitate Eastern high society[.] — Jack Kerouac, *Letter to Caroline Kerouac Blake*, p. 131, 25th September 1947

high iron *noun*
the main line of a railway *US, 1930*
- — Ramon Adams, *The Language of the Railroader*, p. 78, 1977

high-jive *verb*
to tease, to taunt, to belittle *US, 1938*
- Dinch, they'll highjive you till you get hooked with them. — George Mandel, *Flee the Angry Strangers*, p. 26, 1952

high jump *noun*
a court higher than a local magistrate's *AUSTRALIA, 1944*
- — Ryan Aven-Bray, *Ridgey Didge Oz Jack Lang*, p. 31, 1983

▸ be for the high jump
1 to be faced with a severe official reprimand or punishment *UK, 1919*
Of military origin. With variations 'be up for the high jump' and 'be in for the high jump'.
- [Y]ou've done it this time and I'll see you go for the high jump. — John Wynnum, *Tar Dust*, p. 67, 1962
- I think I'm for the high-jump when I get back on Thursday. — *The Guardian*, 8th April 2003

2 to be engaged to be married *IRELAND*
- STAPLER: What about him? CONWAY: He's for the high jump that's what about him. — Billy Roche, *The Wexford Trilogy (A Handful of Stars)*, p. 11, 1992

highland fling *noun*
to sing *UK*
Rhyming slang, credited to a 1950s recording by Billy Cotton and Alan Breeze.
- — Ray Puxley, *Cockney Rabbit*, 1992

highlighter *noun*
a political leader or spokesman among prisoners *US*
- — John R. Armore and Joseph D. Wolfe, *Dictionary of Desperation*, p. 33, 1976

highly *adverb*
used as an intensifier with an attitude *US*
- As in: highly nonoptional, the worst possible way to do something; highly nontrivial, either impossible or requiring a major research project; highly nonlinear, completely erratic and unpredictable[.] — Eric S. Raymond, *The New Hacker's Dictionary*, p. 200, 1991

highly illogical *adjective*
illogical *US*
A signature line of the Vulcan Dr Spock on the first incarnation of *Star Trek* (NBC, 1966–69). Repeated with referential humour.

high maintenance *adjective*
(used of a person) requiring a great deal of attention and/or money; needy *US*
- There are two kinds of women: high maintenance and low maintenance. — *When Harry Met Sally*, 1989
- — Connie Eble (Editor), *UNC-CH Campus Slang*, p. 3, Fall 1990
- I have a high-maintenance selling painter coming through. — *As Good As It Gets*, 1997

highness *noun*
▸ her highness; his highness
your spouse *UK, 1961*
Affectionately ironic.

high noon *noun*
1 in craps, a roll of twelve *US, 1982*
- — Thomas L. Clark, *The Dictionary of Gambling and Gaming*, p. 99, 1987

2 a spoon *UK*
Rhyming slang, formed from the title of the 1952 film.
- — Ray Puxley, *Cockney Rabbit*, 1992

high-nose *verb*
to snub; to ignore *US*
• You know I wouldn't high-nose you, Allie.—Jim Thompson, *Roughneck*, p. 116, 1954

high number *noun*
an especially fashionable member of the Mod youth fashion movement *UK*
• [...] considering changing their name to The Who before deciding on The High Numbers [...] The phrase "high numbers" was itself part of Mod parlance: to be a high number was to be notably hip.—Andrew Motion, *The Lamberts*, 1986

high octane *adjective*
caffeinated *US, 1995*
Borrowing from the language of car fuel for application to the world of coffee drinks and, to a lesser extent, soft drinks.
• —Connie Eble (Editor), *UNC-CH Campus Slang*, p. 4, Fall 1996

high off the hog *adverb*
prosperously *US*
• I love the goddam navy. I get three squares a day, a pad to lie down on, roof over my head, tuxedo to wear. We're living high off the hog.—Darryl Ponicsan, *The Last Detail*, p. 33, 1970
• I was livin' high off the hog, so it didn't really matter.—Odie Hawkins, *Ghetto Sketches*, p. 91, 1972

high play *noun*
showy spending designed to impress *US*
• —Bruce Jackson, *Outside the Law*, p. 58, 1972: 'Glossary'

high pockets *noun*
said of a tall, thin man *US, 1912*
• —Jerry Robertson, *Oil Slanguage*, p. 66, 1954

high puller *noun*
a devoted player of casino slot machines, especially those with higher bets and higher payouts *US*
A play on the term **HIGH ROLLER**.
• [T]he slot players, the "high pullers" at the dollar machines; only the crap shooters animated.—Elmore Leonard, *Glitz*, p. 228, 1985

high-rider *noun*
a car or truck that has been structurally altered to ride very high; a person who drives such a car or truck *US*
• "So this lame hi-rider like guns his Datsun pickup in the parking lot, right, and like he runs over this blitzed hodad's foot."—Mary Corey, *Fer Shurr: How to be a Valley Girl*, 1982
• —Jim Crotty, *How to Talk American*, p. 36, 1997

high-riders *noun*
trousers worn above the waist *US*
• —Carl J. Banks Jr, *Banks Dictionary of the Black Ghetto Language*, 1975

highroll *verb*
to spend freely and to live fast *US*
• When you're highrollin' in the bread you're bound to be out there jumpin' come midnight every night.—Edwin Torres, *Carlito's Way*, p. 30, 1975

high roller *noun*
1 a gambler who makes large bets and spends freely *US, 1881*
• And when Sinatra opened in Vegas, the high rollers gathered, along with the not so high rollers who enjoyed rubbing elbows with the rich.—Donald Goines, *Kenyatta's Last Hit*, p. 204, 1975
• [T]op-hatting his way around race meetings, sipping fine wines with the high rollers.—Diran Abedayo, *My Once Upon A Time*, p. 33, 2000

2 in television and film making, a large, tall, three-legged light stand *US*
• —Ralph S. Singleton, *Filmaker's Dictionary*, p. 81, 1990

high rolling *adjective*
materially successful *US, 1890*
From **HIGH ROLLER** (a big spender).
• But for the moment he was high rollin', and that was a fact!—Karline Smith, *Moss Side Massive*, p. 2, 1994

highs *noun*
in pool, the striped balls numbered 9 to 15 *US*
• —Steve Rushin, *Pool Cool*, p. 15, 1990

high school Harriet *noun*
a high school girl who is dating a college boy *US*
• —*Current Slang*, p. 3, Fall 1966

high-school Harry *noun*
an immature college male; a typical high school student *US*
• —*Time Magazine*, p. 46, 24th August 1959
• —Collin Baker et al., *College Undergraduate Slang Study Conducted at Brown University*, p. 137, 1968

high school horse *noun*
in horse racing, a racehorse that seems to win only when the odds are very high *US*
Based on the humorous suggestion that the horse is so smart it can read the posted odds.
• —David W. Maurer, *Argot of the Racetrack*, p. 35, 1951

high shots *noun*
in the illegal production of alcohol, liquor that exceeds 100 proof *US*
• —David W. Maurer, *Kentucky Moonshine*, p. 119, 1974

high side *noun*
1 the outside of a curve in a road *US*
• We've all been over the high side, baby. You know what that is? It's when your bike starts sliding when you steam into a curve at seventy or eighty.—Hunter S. Thompson, *Hell's Angels*, p. 98, 1966

2 in craps, the numbers over 7 *US*
• —*The Annals of the American Academy of Political and Social Sciences*, p. 126, May 1950

high-side *verb*
to show off *US, 1965*
• So call yourself lucky and knock off the highsiding.—Malcolm Braly, *On the Yard*, p. 249, 1967
• They walking in fours and kicking in doors; dropping Reds and busting heads; drinking wine and committing crime, shooting and looting; high-siding and low-riding[].]—Eldridge Cleaver, *Soul on Ice*, p. 27, 1968
• A boss player may occasionally indulge in stylin' and high sidin' matches as a Black cultural ritual for the fun of it[.]—Christina and Richard Milner, *Black Players*, p. 105, 1972
• —Mark S. Fleisher, *Beggars & Thieves*, p. 289, 1995: 'Glossary'

high speed, low drag *adjective*
competent, reliable, dependable *US*
Vietnam war usage.
• —Linda Reinberg, *In the Field*, p. 105, 1991

high sphincter tone *noun*
said of a person with a high degree of inhibition and a conservative nature *US*
• —Sally Williams, *"Strong" Words*, p. 146, 1994

high spot *noun*
the outstanding part or feature of something *UK, 1926*
• The week's high spot was our trip to see the Jungfrau, the region's greatest peak.—*The Guardian*, 29th January 2000

high stepper *noun*
pepper *UK*
Rhyming slang.
• —Ray Puxley, *Cockney Rabbit*, 1992

hightail *verb*
to move very quickly *US, 1919*
Almost always used with 'it'.
• [S]uddenly his pet ferret rushed out and bit an elegant teacup queer on the ankle and everybody hightailed it out the door[.]—Jack Kerouac, *On the Road*, p. 144, 1957
• So I got back in the car and hightailed it out of Cheyenne[.]—Clancy Sigal, *Going Away*, p. 169, 1961
• Next he hightails to Angie's to apologize for being pigheaded last night.—Lester Bangs, *Psychotic Reactions and Carburetor Dung*, p. 125, 1973
• We'll be putting all this junk on a truck Saturday mornin', hightailin' it to the land of saddidy niggers.—Odie Hawkins, *The Busting Out of an Ordinary Man*, p. 144, 1985

high tea *noun*
a social gathering of male homosexuals *US*
• —*Male Swinger Number 3*, p. 46, 1981: 'The complete gay dictionary'

high tide *noun*
the bleed period of the menstrual cycle *US*
• —*Current Slang*, p. 8, Winter 1970
• Cause the moon is full and look out baby / I'm at high tide [...] I've got a hundred and five fever / and it's high tide—Laurie Anderson, *Beautiful Red Dress*, 1989

high-up *noun*

a person of high rank or importance *UK, 1929*

- Once again the party high-ups look controlling and hard[.]— *The Guardian*, 24th October 2001

high waist *noun*

vigorous sex *TRINIDAD AND TOBAGO*

The 'high' suggests the woman's ability to lift the man up from below during sex.

- —Lise Winer, *Dictionary of the English/Creole of Trinidad & Tobago*, 2003

high-waist *adjective*

(used of a woman) skilled at sex *TRINIDAD AND TOBAGO*

- —Lise Winer, *Dictionary of the English/Creole of Trinidad & Tobago*, 2003

high wall job *noun*

a burglary that requires climbing *UK*

- —Angela Devlin, *Prison Patter*, p. 61, 1996

high-waters *noun*

long trousers that are too short or short trousers that are too long *US*

- — *Current Slang*, p. 6, Winter 1971
- —Douglas Simonson, *Pidgin to da Max Hana Hou*, 1982

highway princess *noun*

a prostitute, especially one who works at truck stops *US*

- — *Complete CB Slang Dictionary*, 1976
- —Wayne Floyd, *Jason's Authentic Dictionary of CB Slang*, p. 23, 1976
- —Peter Chippindale, *The British CB Book*, p. 155, 1981

highway salute *noun*

a gesture with the middle finger meaning 'fuck you' *US*

- —Bill Davis, *Jawjacking*, p. 51, 1977

highway surfer *noun*

a person who adapts the mannerisms of surfers, buys the equipment, but never seems to get out of the car into the water *US*

- — *Paradise of the Pacific*, p. 27, October 1963
- —John Severson, *Modern Surfing Around the World*, p. 171, 1964

high, wide and handsome; high, wide and fancy *adjective*

excellent; first-rate *US*

The title of a 1937 musical/romance film starring James Burke.

- "I'm stepping out, high, wide and fancy with something better than Clara Bow," Phil said.—James T. Farrell, *Saturday Night*, p. 21, 1947
- Jake married her after he left here and moved to New York – after he was riding high, wide and handsome.—Jim Thompson, *Savage Night*, p. 4, 1953
- We were going high and wide and handsome over on 6th Street. —Herbert Huncke, *Guilty of Everything*, p. 154, 1990

high wine *noun*

a mixture of alcohol and flavoured water *CANADA*

- "Mucha high wine," he said, using Alexander Henry's term for it "Firewater."—Vardis Fisher, *Pemmican*, p. 18, 1957

high yellow; high yaller; high yella *noun*

a light-skinned black person, especially female; a Creole; a mulatto *US, 1923*

'Objectionable when referring to lighter-colored black persons' according to *Dictionary of Cautionary Words and Phrases*, 1989.

- The high yellow and the tall coal black next to me were giving me nasty looks[.]—Mickey Spillane, *I, The Jury*, p. 43, 1947
- On'y hiyellas leff is Flow an Francine, so I spect this mothah gonna go up wiff Flow.—Robert Gover, *One Hundred Dollar Misunderstanding*, p. 19, 1961

high yellow; high yaller; high yella *adjective*

light-skinned *US*

- A high-yella woman, with a knife scar going along the whole length of her cheek and trying to repeat itself further down on her chin, her skirt hiked up[.]—Willard Motley, *Let No Man Write My Epitaph*, p. 90, 1958
- He couldn't stay away from the high-yellow whores with their big asses and bitch-dog sexual antics.—Iceberg Slim (Robert Beck), *Pimp*, 1969
- [H]e was twenty years older than Mrs. Edwards and should have known better than to marry a high-yaller hot-blooded Creole from New Orleans.—Louise Meriwether, *Daddy Was a Number Runner*, p. 56, 1970
- [T]heir daughter, Charlotte, is high yella, it puzzles me[.]—Clarence Major, *All-Night Visitors*, p. 18, 1998

hijinks; hijinx *noun*

an act or acts of self-indulgent frivolity *US*

An altered spelling of conventional 'high jinks'.

- Anyone with a real life doesn't have time for computer hijinks. —Howard Stern, *Miss America*, p. 12, 1995

hijo de la chingada *noun*

son of a fucked woman *US*

Border Spanish used in English conversation by Mexican-Americans; highly insulting.

- —Dagoberto Fuentes and Jose Lopez, *Barrio Language Dictionary*, p. 75, 1974

hike *verb*

to insult in a competitive, quasi-friendly spirit, especially by reference to your opponent's family *US*

- There are many different terms for playing the dozens, including "bagging, capping, cracking, dissing, hiking, joning, ranking, ribbing, serving, signifying, slipping, sounding and snapping".—James Haskins, *The Story of Hip-Hop*, p. 54, 2000

hiker *noun*

a prison officer whose duty is to be anywhere in the prison when required *UK*

- —Angela Devlin, *Prison Patter*, p. 61, 1996

hike up *verb*

1 of clothes, to work out of position or to drag into place *US, 1873*

- I got her to the floor and hiked up her clothes[.]—Paul Theroux, *The Stranger at the Palazzo d'Oro*, 2003

2 to raise prices *US*

- Eligibility for free treatments is being eroded and existing charges hiked up.— *The Guardian*, 9th July 2003

Hilda Handcuffs; Hilda *noun*

a police officer; the police *UK*

An example of **CAMP** trans-gender assignment, in this case an assonant play on handcuffs as stereotypical police equipment.

- —the cast of 'Aspects of Love', Prince of Wales Theatre, *Palare (Boy Dancer Talk) for Beginners*, 1989–92

hill *noun*

▸ **go over the hill**

to desert military duty; to escape from prison *US, 1912*

- I hoped they would understand that I wasn't going what they called it – "over the hill" – because I was yellow or wanted to dog a fight. —Rocky Garciano (with Rowland Barber), *Somebody Up There Likes Me*, p. 188, 1955
- You know, a couple of years ago, and this was in Norfolk too, a lieutenant supply officer lifted six thou and went over the hill.—Darryl Ponicsan, *The Last Detail*, p. 30, 1970
- [T]he other half dozen sick cons nearby knew we were going over the hill.—Red Rudensky, *The Gonif*, p. 14, 1970
- It was made up neat the way I learned it in the army, before I got in a hassel with a Yankee sergeant and went over the hill just five weeks before I was to be discharged.—Guy Owen, *The Flim-Flam Man and the Apprentice Grifter*, p. 4, 1972

▸ **on the hill**

in pool, needing only one more score to win *US*

- —Mike Shamos, *The Illustrated Encyclopedia of Billiards*, p. 161, 1993

▸ **over the hill**

past your prime *US, 1950*

- At least it won't break my heart, Alexander Monet turning out to be an over-the-hill asshole.—Elmore Leonard, *Be Cool*, p. 311, 1999
- [H]ard cases, headcases, nutters, headbutters, over-the-hill boxers[.] —Dave Courtney, *Stop the Ride I Want to Get Off*, p. 195, 1999
- Now you're over the hill at 42[.]— *The Observer*, 3rd March 2002

Hill *noun*

▸ **the Hill**

Parliament Hill in Ottawa *CANADA*

- Mr. Cassels said it was one thing for a person to argue in court that he was immune from arrest on the Hill, but wondered if this could be pleaded afterwards.— *Kingston Whig-Standard*, p. 34/6, 3rd March 1965

hill and dale *noun*

a tale, of the type told by a confidence trickster *UK*

Rhyming slang.

- —Jim Phelan, *The Underworld*, 1953

hillbilly *adjective*

chilly *UK: SCOTLAND*

Glasgow rhyming slang.

- Better take yer jaiket [jacket] – it's turned a bit hillbilly.—Michael Munro, *The Original Patter*, 1985

hillbilly chrome *noun*

aluminium paint *US*

- —Montie Tak, *Truck Talk*, p. 83, 1971

hillbilly craps *noun*
craps played on the sidewalk or otherwise as a private game *US*
- — *The Annals of the American Academy of Political and Social Sciences*, p. 126, May 1950

hillbilly hell *noun*
used as an embellished, intensified 'hell' *US*
- He'll have a hillbilly hell of a time every making captain. — Darryl Ponicsan, *The Last Detail*, p. 146, 1970

hillbilly heroin *noun*
the synthetic opiate oxycodone used recreationally *US*
When dissolved in water and injected, or crushed and inhaled, it has a similar effect to heroin.The drug's popularity in the rural Appalachian Mountains region led to the 'hillbilly' reference. It came to the forefront of the American national conscious in late 2003 when radio entertainer Rush Limbaugh was reported to be addicted to OxyContin™.
- Who's on it? It's known as hillbilly heroin and it's fanbase is in the US' poorest hick states like West Virginia and Kentucky. — *Mixmag*, p. 38, December 2001
- Many in Appalachia call OxyContin "Hillbilly heroin." Its abuse may not have started in the mountains, but it exploded in Appalachia. — *The Houston Chronicle*, 1st July 2001
- A few months ago, OxyContin abuse was considered a regional problem and confined to areas from the nation's population centers. — *The New York Times Magazine*, p. 35, 29th July 2001
- In this part of West Virginia, and the neighbouring hill continues of Virginia and Kentucky, they call it "hillbilly heroin" or "poor man's heroin." — *The Guardian Unlimited*, 25th June 2001
- In one missive, Limbaugh pushed Cline to get more "little blues" – code for OxyContin, the powerful narcotic nicknamed hillbilly heroin, she said. — *(New York) Daily News*, 2nd October 2003

hillbilly operahouse *noun*
a truck with a radio *US*
- — Montie Tak, *Truck Talk*, p. 83, 1971

hillbilly special *noun*
a truck manufactured by General Motors Corporation *US*
- — Montie Tak, *Truck Talk*, p. 83, 1971

Hill Fights *noun*
a series of battles in the vicinity of Khe Sanh, South Vietnam, in April and May 1967 *US*
- Ten days after Westmoreland's boast, on April 24, 1967, a five-man Marine forward observer party from Khe Sanh was ambushed in a grove of bamboo on Hill 861 northwest of the airstrip. One Marine survived. The first and cruelest struggle at Khe Sanh, the "Hill Fights" began. — Neil Sheehan, *A Bright Shining Lie*, p. 643, 1988

hill game *noun*
in pool, a situation where either player can win with a single pocket *US*
- — Mike Shamos, *The Illustrated Encyclopedia of Billiards*, p. 117, 1993

hillman hunter; hillman *noun*
a client or customer of any service that has little respect for the clients and customers *UK*
Rhyming slang, formed from the name of a 1970s car.
- — Ray Puxley, *Cockney Rabbit*, 1992

hillybin *noun*
a lesbian *NEW ZEALAND, 1973*
- — Harry Orsman, *A Dictionary of Modern New Zealand Slang*, p. 65, 1999

Hilton *noun*
a camp where firefighters fighting a forest fire sleep *US*
- — *American Speech*, p. 205–209, Summer 1991: 'The language of smokejumping – again'

him *noun*
heroin *US*
- — Richard Lingeman, *Drugs from A to Z*, p. 109, 1969
- — Robert Ashton, *This Is Heroin*, p. 206, 2002

▷ **see:** HE

Himalaya gold; Himalaya *noun*
a potent marijuana with yellow hairs on a pale green bud *UK*
A hybrid plant cultivated in the 1990s, not in the Himalayas but with genetic antecedents in Nepal and South India; the naming is, perhaps, also an ironic reference to the highest physical location on planet earth.
- — Nick Jones, *Spliffs*, p. 69, 2003

himbo *noun*
a man objectified by his good looks and presumed lack of intellectual qualities; a man who trades on this image; a gigolo *US*
Plays on contemporary use of BIMBO (a beautiful and available young woman – if you are a rich older man).
- Sex was commonplace, from a Melanie Griffith look-alike stuffed into her gown like salami in spandex to the macho himbo who strutted the Croisette wearing a 16-foot python like a stole around his shoulders and neck. — *Washington Post*, p. F1, 29th May 1988
- Musclebound hunks were transformed into the newest sex symbol archetype; the himbo. — Steven Daly and Nalthaniel Wice, *alt.culture*, p. 104, 1995
- — David Rowan, *A Glossary for the 90s*, p. 7, 1998

Hinckley; Hinkley *noun*
phencyclidine, the recreational drug known as PCP or angel dust *US*
- This summer, one brand of PCP is available as "Hinckley" (referring to John W. Hinckley Jr., who shot President Reagan) or "the Keys to St. E's" – both references to the "craziness" induced by the drug. — *Washington Post*, p. B1, 29th July 1984
- — US Department of Justice, *Street Terms*, October 1994

hincty *adjective*
conceited, vain, arrogant *US, 1924*
- I had to cut loose some way, to turn my back once and for all on that hincty, killjoy world of my sister's and move over to Bessie Smith's world body and soul. — Mezz Mezzrow, *Really the Blues*, p. 54, 1946
- Handsome queer boys who had come to Hollywood to be cowboys walked around, wetting their eyebrows with hincty fingertip. — Jack Kerouac, *On the Road*, p. 86, 1957
- Hincty little ofay is Harlemese for snotty little white girl. — John M. Murtagh and Sara Harris, *Cast the First Stone*, p. 14, 1957
- "So quit making like one of these hincty arrangers and let Bernie-oh op the writing bit." — Ross Russell, *The Sound*, p. 65, 1961
- Obviously these people come from Tucson or Albuquerque or one of those hincty adobe towns. — Tom Wolfe, *The Pump House Gang*, p. 15, 1968
- Man, I'm hip you pretty and pimping a zillion. But helly, you don't have to go hincty on ugly ass Railhead. — Iceberg Slim (Robert Beck), *Mama Black Widow*, p. 226, 1969
- Connie had studied the head of the hinkty-seeming black bitch at the wheel of the Jag and hadn't liked what she read. — Robert Deane Pharr, *Giveadamn Brown*, p. 120, 1978

hind claw *noun*
a means of support secondary to your job *BARBADOS*
- If I lose my job, I have no hind claw likeyou, you know. — Frank A. Collymore, *Barbadian Dialect*, p. 59, 1965

hind hook *noun*
the rear brakeman on a freight train *US*
- — Norman Carlisle, *The Modern Wonder Book of Trains and Railroading*, p. 264, 1946

hind tit *noun*
▸ **on the hind tit; suck the hind tit**
to be last in order or standing *US, 1940*
- — Charles F. Haywood, *Yankee Dictionary*, p. 113, 1963
- Way the college business is going these days, wherever I went I'd be hind tit to a bunch of deans. — Max Shulman, *Anyone Got a Match?*, p. 65, 1964
- He's got another year before he goes to bat again, and therefore naturally he is sucking every minority and majority hind tit he can find. — George V. Higgins, *The Rat on Fire*, p. 5, 1981
- I guess Jerry Lee'd be suckin' hind tit in a Van Cliburn competition, but I like his playin' just fine. — Ken Weaver, *Texas Crude*, p. 129, 1984
- Purdue and Ray, twenty-five years younger than the other two cronies, were still around. Still sucking hind tit. — Robert Campbell, *Juice*, p. 3, 1988

Hindu shuffle *noun*
in card trickery, a technique that will keep a card or several cards on the bottom of the deck *UK*
- The Hindu shuffle must be done in a rapid and smooth fashion in order for the force to work. — *Card Trick Central*, 2003

hiney; heiny; heinie *noun*
the buttocks *US, 1921*
- Mat car is fast, my teeth're shiney / I tell all the girls they can kiss my heinie[.] — Frank Zappa, *Bobby Brown Goes Down*, 1979
- He turned me over sos I couldn't [resist], got my heinie up in the air and my face presssed down in the bedspread. — Elmore Leonard, *Freaky Deaky*, p. 81, 1988
- ROBIN: He does have a nice heiny. JANE: Heiny? What is he, two years old? He has a nice heiny? — *Boys on the Side*, 1995

hinge *noun*
the elbow *US*
- —Lou Shelly, *Hepcats Jive Dictionary*, p. 12, 1945

hinges *noun*
▸ **off your hinges**
mentally unhinged, crazy *UK*
Word play; as 'off the hinges' from 1611 to mid-C19 .
- [I]nterviewing entertainers who were off their hinges, or at the hot centre of stardom. —Paul Morley, *Ask*, p. 128, 1986

Hinglish *noun*
a hybrid language formed of Hindi and English; also applied to an informal blending of Punjabi and English *UK*
- A further Hinglish exchange resolved that it made common sense to allow us to sit in the 100 rupee seats[.] —Phil Long, *BBCi*, 5th December 2001

hinked up *adjective*
suspicious, afraid *US*
- You seem a little hinked up. —*Gone in 60 Seconds*, 2000
- The passenger, a 23-year-old citizen of Yemen, wa "acting very strangely, and the flight attendants got real hinked up," said FBI Agent LaRae Quy. —*San Francisco Chronicle*, p. B4, 4th August 2004

hinky *adjective*
1 nervous, anxious *US, 1956*
- They make you hinky. What's their secret? you always wonder. —Joseph Wambaugh, *The New Centurions*, p. 127, 1970
- My aide thought he looked hinky and coup-wise, so he kept an eye on him. —James Ellroy, *Because the Night*, p. 484, 1984
- I think it's too hinky for a crackpot. —Carl Hiaasen, *Tourist Season*, p. 54, 1986
- [A]round the time Carlisle got hinky, J.C. told Dudley that Stemmons was acting crazy[.] —James Ellroy, *White Jazz*, p. 304, 1992
- You seem a little hinked up. —*Gone in 60 Seconds*, 2000

2 suspicious *US, 1975*
- [H]e didn't want him getting jumpy enough to switch seats and bail if he thought there anything hinky about the deal. —Christopher Brookmyre, *The Sacred Art of Stealing*, p. 20, 2002

hinky-dee *noun*
a form of comedic song *US*
- In his dressing room, Byrnie, who was trouping with his old man, Eddie Foy, and all his six brothers, jotted down what in trouper's parlance is called a "hinky dee" – one short verse and many short choruses, each with a comedy punch-lline. —*San Francisco Call-Bulletin*, p. 15, 18th August 1949

hinky-dinky *adjective*
small-time, second class, outmoded *US, 1967*
A cousin of the more famous **RINKY-DINK**.
- What are we doing sitting here boiling our balls off for some hinky-dinky little bootleg tape operation? —Robert Campbell, *Juice*, p. 5, 1988

hip *noun*
1 a member of the 1960s counterculture *US*
- The burned hips leave and Teddybear turns back to lecture. —Nicholas Von Hoffman, *We Are The People Our Parents Warned Us Against*, p. 45, 1967

2 a heroin addict *US*
- Ike explained to me that the Mexican government issued permits to hips allowing them a definite quantity of morphine per month at whole sale prices. —William Burroughs, *Junkie*, p. 103, 1953

3 the buttocks *BAHAMAS*
- —John A. Holm, *Dictionary of Bahamian English*, p. 103, 1982

hip *verb*
1 to explain, to bring up to date, to inform *US, 1932*
- And I was going to be a musician, a Negro musisican, hipping the world about the blues the way only Negroes can. —Mezz Mezzrow, *Really the Blues*, p. 18, 1946
- He got no horse to lend me, but he hips me about Tony and I'm headin for a score. —George Mandel, *Flee the Angry Strangers*, p. 313, 1952
- Al Sublette is the boy who could hip you on all the latest, especially if he has enuf money to stock his phone with records. —Jack Kerouac, *Letter to Philip Whalen*, p. 548, 7th February 1956
- He called in his flunkies and hipped 'em real good[.] —Dan Burley, *Diggeth Thou?*, p. 25, 1959
- [A] good spirit – Norman Mailer all over again – comes along and hips them to the fact[.] —Cecil Brown, *The Life & Loves of Mr. Jiveass Nigger*, p. 56, 1969
- Hip me to what happened! —A.S. Jackson, *Gentleman Pimp*, p. 27, 1973
- How about if I come with you and you hip me? —Bobby Seale, *A Lonely Rage*, p. 65, 1978

2 to figure out, to become aware *US*
- Trouble is too many guys get wasted before they hip up. Shame on them. —Edwin Torres, *Carlito's Way*, p. 77, 1975

▸ **hip to all happenings**
profoundly aware of the latest trends and happenings *US*
- I met chicks who were fine as May wine, and cats who were hip to all happenings. —Malcolm X and Alex Haley, *The Autobiography of Malcolm X*, p. 56, 1964

▸ **hip your ship**
to let you know *US*
- —Lavada Durst, *The Jives of Dr. Hepcat*, p. 12, 1953

hip *adjective*
1 knowing, understanding *US, 1902*
- [O]r else they were slinking criminals like Elmot Hassel, with that hip sneer[.] —Jack Kerouac, *On the Road*, p. 10, 1957
- They are hip without being slick, they are intelligent without being corny, they are intellectual as hell and know all about Pound without being pretentious or talking too much about it, they are very quiet, they are very Christlike. —Jack Kerouac, *The Subterraneans*, p. 1, 1958
- And these children threw around swear words I'd never heard before, even, and slang expressisons that were just as new to me, such as stud and cat and chick and cool and hip. —Malcolm X and Alex Haley, *The Autobiography of Malcolm X*, p. 43, 1964
- The Diggers are hip to property. —*The Digger Papers*, p. 3, August 1968
- But the PLP's squeals grow weaker and weaker as the people are now hip to their slimy snakelike TACTICS. —*The Black Panter*, p. 9, 2nd August 1969
- Parents are generally pretty hip to the fever scams. —*Ferris Buehler's Day Off*, 1986
- ALABAMA: That's a long time. CLARENCE: I'm hip. —*True Romance*, 1993

2 in style, fashionable, admired *US, 1944*
- It was a world of dingy backstairs "pads," Times Sqaure cafeterias, bebop joints, night-long wanderings, meetings on street corners, hitchhiking, a myriad of "hip" bars all over the city, and the streets themselves. —John Clellon Holmes, *Go*, p. 37, 1952
- One is Hip or one is Square (the alternative which each new generation coming into American life is beginning to feel), on is a rebel or one conforms[.] —Norman Mailer, *Advertisements for Myself*, p. 339, 1957
- Why do you come here? Because it's hip to come on as if jazz meant something to you? —Nat Hentoff, *Jazz Country*, p. 97, 1965
- I didn't know Johnny D. before I went to Wiltwyck, but he was about the hippest cat on Eighth AVenue, the slickest nigger in the neighborhood. —Claude Brown, *Manchild in the Promised Land*, p. 108, 1965
- Well, everybody's saying / that hell's the hippest way to go / Well I don't think so[.] —Joni Mitchell, *Blue*, 1971
- "I'm not hip," he [Meat;oaf] gloats, "and I'm glad. Because I hate hip. Hip doesn't last. I was never hip. It's not my style." —*Ask*, p. 53, 19th December 1981
- Now do you think she would prefer laidback Jim, or cool, hip Jim? —*American Pie*, 1999

hip cat *noun*
a fan of jazz or swing music; a stylish and fashionable man *US, 1947*
- All the hip cats on the corner / They don't look so sharp no mo —Jimmy Witherspoon, *Skid Row Blues*,
- —Lavada Durst, *The Jives of Dr. Hepcat*, 1953

hipe *verb*
in a cheating scheme in a game of cards, to restore a deck to its original position after a cheating move *US*
- —Frank Garcia, *Marked Cards and Loaded Dice*, p. 264, 1962

hip-flinger *noun*
a dancer in any type of overtly sexual dance *US*
- —Don Wilmeth, *The Language of American Popular Entertainment*, p. 131, 1981

hip-hop *noun*
used as a loose categorisation of (initially) black urban youth culture, encompassing breakdancing, graffiti art, DJing and rap music; used as an umbrella for any music, especially dance and rap music, that falls within the general style; any fashion or style that is defined by association with the culture *US, 1982*
Combining **HIP** (fashionable) and **HOP** (dance); like **ROCK 'N' ROLL** before it, 'hip-hop' is an American phenomenon that has had a worldwide impact.
- Hip-hop/Gang-bang? Talk-slop/School-thang? —Eugene D Redmond, *Boyz In Search of Their Soular System*, 1993
- I have watched him slip effortlessly from hip-hop street patter to a Brooks Brothers accent —Lawrence Block, *Even the Wicked*, p. 2, 1997

- Hip hop is nothing, however, if not resilient. While snubbed by high-brow critics, graffiti art found new followers in cutting-edge circles. —Nelson George, *Hip Hop America*, p. 12, 1998
- AFRIKA BAMBAATAA: On our flyers we used to say, "Come to the hip hop jam this, or the be bop jam that". [...] MICHAEL HOLMAN: Everyone picked it up from [Grandmaster Flash MC] Cowboy – "the hip, a hippy, a hippy hop, you don't stop". —Alex Ogg, *The Hip Hop Years*, p. 29, 1999
- My core audience, my hip-hop audience, is black and white, Asian and Hispanic[.] —Russell Simmons, *Life and Def*, p. 5, 2001
- Once considered a fly-by-night trend, the street-savvy movement known as hip-hop has exploded into mainstream culture. —Rob Cohen and David Wollock, *Etiquette for Outlaws*, p. 180, 2001
- [W]aiting to see, yet again, the popular hip-hop film Beat Street, which had drawn the unusually large crowd. —Darrin Keith Bastfield, *Back in the Day*, p. 37, 2002
- A popular Uptown fast-talkin' jock, DJ Hollywood, coins the term "hip-hop" in '74. —*The Source*, p. 135, March 2002
- [F]arm kids go to school dressed like New York City street rappers and talk using hip-hop slang. —Dan Kimball, *The Emerging Church*, p. 57, 2003

hip hop daisy age *noun*

an early 1990s fashion in hip-hop culture that approximated the 'peace and love' attitudes of the hippie movement *UK*

- [A]cts like De La Soul seemed to have made the so-called "hip hop daisy age" credible[.] —Patrick Neate, *Where You're At*, p. 49, 2003

hip kick *noun*

the rear pocket on a pair of trousers *US*

- —Don Wilmeth, *The Language of American Popular Entertainment*, p. 131, 1981

hipky-dripky *noun*

mischief *US*

- Now my mother and father gave each other a look because they knew that Mrs. Spencer was up to some hipky-dripky. —Max Shulman, *I was a Teen-Age Dwarf*, p. 62, 1959

hi-po *adjective*

in motor racing, high performance *US*

- —John Edwards, *Auto Dictionary*, p. 77, 1993

hipped *adjective*

1 aware of, knowledgeable of *US, 1920*

- —Marcus Hanna Boulware, *Jive and Slang of Students in Negro Colleges*, 1947

2 carrying a gun *US, 1920*

- All you boys were hipped except you and Frank. What's the matter? Get scared after Mr. Bannon was knocked off? —Irving Shulman, *The Amboy Dukes*, p. 163, 1947

hipped to the tip *adjective*

aware of everything *US*

- —Marcus Hanna Boulware, *Jive and Slang of Students in Negro Colleges*, 1947

hipper *noun*

a large, swollen bruise on the hip *UK*

Noted as a sports injury suffered by foot-propelled scooter-riders.

- —Ben Sharpe, *Scooter Crazy*, p. 40, 2000

hippie; hippy *noun*

a follower of jazz and the jazz scene who strives to be hip *US, 1952*

- Lot of these hippies here is still in high school. —Ross Russell, *The Sound*, p. 86, 1961
- For example, the hippies in his circle peppered all their choppy, laconic sentences with the word "like[.]" —Bernarde Wolfe, *The Magic of Their Singing*, p. 125, 1961
- A few of the white men around Harlem, younger ones whom we called "hippies," acted more Negro than Negroes. —Malcolm X and Alex Haley, *The Autobiography of Malcolm X*, p. 94, 1964
- The jazz musicians liked me. I was the only hippy around. —Lenny Bruce, *How to Talk Dirty and Influence People*, p. 93, 1965
- If it is true, like some of the hippies say, that Fred has been trying to be white all his life – and I'm not sure it is – that's because of me. —Nat Hentoff, *Jazz Country*, p. 94, 1965
- The young broad with the hippy just in front of me turned her head back toward me. —Iceberg Slim (Robert Beck), *Trick Baby*, p. 86, 1969

hippie crack *noun*

nitrous oxide *US*

A substance of abuse favoured by hippies and neo-hippies, seductive if not addictive.

- The gas, also referred to as "hippie crack," is sold at such parties – or "underground raves" – for 43 to $5 a balloonful, those familiar with the parties said. —*Los Angeles Times*, p. A1, 7th March 1992
- —Judi Sanders, *Da Bomb*, p. 8, 1997
- WHIPPITS: OTherwise known as "hippie crack" or "dessert crack." Either way, it's the best high a thirteen-year-old can get. —Suroosh Alvi et al., *The Vice Guide*, p. 20, 2002

hipping *noun*

a nappy (diaper) or sanitary towel *TRINIDAD AND TOBAGO*

- —Lise Winer, *Dictionary of the English/Creole of Trinidad & Tobago*, 2003

hippo *noun*

an armoured personnel carrier used by the South African police *SOUTH AFRICA*

- —Penny Silva, *A Dictionary of South African English*, 1996

Hippo *noun*

any theatre called the Hippodrome *UK, 1937*

An affectionate shortening of an actor's place of work, such as, in Britain, the Birmingham Hippo, the Bristol Hippo, and, in the US, the Baltimore Hippo.

hip pocket *noun*

a truck's glove compartment *US*

- —"Slingo", *The Official CB Slang Dictionary Handbook*, p. 32, 1976

hippy *adjective*

1 full-hipped *US*

- He never stopped to wonder why Grace Anderson, the prettiest, the ripest, the hippiest young hussy on Lomax Street had consent henceforth to share her daily bread and nightly bed with the homeliest man in the city[.] —Clarence Cooper Jr, *Black*, p. 179, 1963

2 mentally dulled by years of imprisonment *US*

- —Hyman E. Goldin et al., *Dictionary of American Underworld Lingo*, p. 96, 1950

hippy-dippy *noun*

a hippy or hippie, in either sense *US*

Derogatory.

- A pair of hippy-dippys came into the car. —Iceberg Slim (Robert Beck), *Trick Baby*, p. 86, 1969

hippy-dippy *adjective*

used to describe the 'peace and love' philosophy of the hippy movement *US*

- He couldn't stand the hippy-dippy voice any longer[.] —Clarence Cooper Jr, *The Scene*, p. 220, 1960
- In an out-of-style hippydippy strut he went into the bedroom. —Clarence Major, *All-Night Visitors*, p. 112, 1998
- A benevolent feeling towards the world that [John] Lennon was feeling is encapsulated in this song ["Rain"]. Obviously it's hippy-dippy – "I'm cool and turned on, you squares should get turned on too"[.] —*Uncut*, p. 54, July 2001
- My parents were a bit hippy-dippy, she says, not for the first time in her life. —Lisa Jewell, *Labia Lobelia [Tart Noir]*, p. 236, 2002

hippy hill *nickname*

a hill in Golden Gate Park, San Francisco, between the Stanyan Street entrance and Dinosaur Valley *US*

- There were about three hundred on Hippy Hill as the song from the Psychedlic Shop reverberated and the sitting people expelled their breath to make the slow sound of the god-centering ommmmmmm. —Nicholas Von Hoffman, *We Are The People Our Parents Warned Us Against*, p. 89, 1967

hippytitis *noun*

hepatitis *UK*

- Laughingly dubbed "hippytitis" by Consular officials. —Richard Neville, *Play Power*, p. 212, 1970

hippy-trippy *adjective*

psychedelic *UK*

A rhyming combination of the counterculture and the effects of drugs.

- A plethora of hustlers oozed from the woodwork promoting every imaginable fly-by-night scheme involving hippy-trippy, peace 'n' love garbage. —Mick Farren, *Give the Anarchist a Cigarette*, p. 124, 2001

hippy witch *noun*

a girl who 30 years later still dresses in the styles popular with the late 1960s counterculture *US*

- —Vann Wesson, *Generation X Field Guide and Lexicon*, p. 90, 1997

hip-square *noun*

a conventional person who at moments adopts the drapings of the jazz lifestyle without fully embracing it *US*

- At each new knock on the door the callers would be screened to keep out such undesirables as squares, fuzz, and hip-squares. —Ross Russell, *The Sound*, p. 109, 1961

hipster *noun*

1 a devotee of jazz and the jazz lifestyle *US, 1940*

- They too wore dark glasses, their hats were set high upon their heads, the brims turned down. A couple of hipsters, I thought, just as they spoke. —Ralph Ellison, *Invisible Man*, p. 484, 1947
- Well, she kept yelling across the room to some hipster, 'How about a fix!' —John Clellon Holmes, *Go*, p. 7, 1952
- I learned the new hipster vocabulary. —William Burroughs, *Junkie*, p. 120, 1953
- We saw a horrible sight in the bar: a white hipster fairy had come in wearing a Hawaiian shirt and was asking the big drummer if he could sit in. —Jack Kerouac, *On the Road*, p. 200, 1957
- 'Give it to me,' said Frost, 'and cut that hipster gab. It's making me sick.' —Terry Southern, *Flash and Filigree*, p. 145, 1958
- Hipster came first as a word – it was used at least as long ago as 1951 or 1952, and was mentioned in the New Directions blurb on Chandler Brossard's Who Walk in Darkness. —Norman Mailer, *Advertisements for Myself*, p. 372, 1959
- It was 'round bout midnight, hipster time, a magic hour in the cool world, when things got around to taking place, if they were gong to happen at all. —Ross Russell, *The Sound*, p. 31, 1961
- I took three of those twenty-five-cent sepia-toned, while-you-wait pictures of myself, posed the way "hipsters" wearing their zoots would "cool it"[.] —Malcolm X and Alex Haley, *The Autobiography of Malcolm X*, p. 52, 1964
- I will be out of touch. I am 39 and already I can't relate to Fabian. There's nothing sadder than an old hipster. —Lenny Bruce, *How to Talk Dirty and Influence People*, p. 35, 1965
- As soon as it appeared, the hipsters and hipstrixes started arriving in droves, loping or skulking up the stone stairs to the beat of the music gyrating from within. —Francesca Lia Block, *I Was a Teenage Fairy*, p. 70, 1998

2 a person at the stylish edge of fashionable *US*

A contemporary variation.

- One who possesses tastes, social attitudes, and opinions deemed cool by the cool. —Robert Lanham, *The Hipster Handbook*, p. 8, 2002

hipsway *noun*

dismissal *UK: SCOTLAND*

- After all the love I've splattered on yi, all these years, you're giving me the hipsway! Is that it? —Ian Pattison, *Rab C. Nesbitt*, 1988

hir

used as a gender-neutral third-person singular pronoun *US*

- Any programmer worth hir salt knows that Hawaiian Punch is the best system for delivering the most sugar and caffeine within the shortest amount of time. —Andy Ihnatko, *Cyberspeak*, p. 92, 1997

hirsute *adjective*

in computing, complicated *US*

Used as a jocular synonym for 'hairy'.

- —Guy L. Steele et al., *The Hacker's Dictionary*, p. 82, 1983

hi-si *noun*

high society *US*

- She's real hi-si, see, and if word ever got out about this, she'd be ruined with the Four Hundred. —Max Shulman, *Rally Round the Flag, Boys!*, p. 172, 1957

his lordship *noun*

used ironically of a male who is perceived to behave in a manner that is somehow above his status *UK, 1961*

Derisive.

hiss *noun*

to hike rapidly *NEW ZEALAND*

- It is not surprising that is hillmen and hillwomen should hiss along, that hissers and little hissers should flourish, and that little hisser should sometimes be used as a term of approbation. —*Tararua Tramper*, p. 29, September 1958

hissy-fit; hissy *noun*

a tantrum *US*

- There are detractors as you know / Who like to slam a movie star like me / They have to throw a hissy fit / At someone else's hit[.] —Gerard Alessandrini, *A Spoonful of Julie [Forbidden Broadway Strikes Back!]*, 1997
- Nell [McAndrew] has severely disappointed her majesty's armed forces stationed in Iraq by allegedly throwing a "hissy-fit" about her accommodation on a VIP army base in Iraq[.] —*The Guardian*, 18th December 2003

history *noun*

1 the condition of being doomed or finished *US, 1978*

- Monday morning you're history. I'll tell everyone about tonight. —*Heathers*, 1988
- The boss is sellin the business, and as soon as the new owner shows up, we're history. —Joseph Wambaugh, *Finnegan's Week*, p. 127, 1993
- Oh, man, we're dust! We're so history! —*Airheads*, 1994
- I mean, the guy is history as far as I'm concerned. History. —*Casino*, 1995
- If he said what he is alleged to have said, he is history as an England rugby player. —*Daily Mail*, 25th May 1999

2 in a swindle, the background on a victim, people likely to be encountered, a location or event *US*

- —Robert C. Prus and C.R.D. Sharper, *Road Hustler*, p. 170, 1977: 'Glossary of terms'

history sheeter *noun*

a person with a criminal record *INDIA*

- —Susie Dent, *The Language Report*, p. 127, 2003
- A notorious history-sheeter and vehicle lifter Syed Aziz Mehmood alias Javeed was found stabbed to death[.] —*Times of India*, 15th March 2004

hit *noun*

1 a single inhalation of marijuana, hashish, crack cocaine or any drug's smoke *US, 1952*

- If somebody hands you a joint and you don't take a hit off of it, it's like sticking out your hand and not having someone shake it. —Leonard Wolfe (Editor), *Voices from the Love Generation*, p. 241, 1968
- Man, I am so fucking messed up and ripped! I got off on the first hit, man!? —John Rechy, *The Fourth Angel*, p. 32, 1972
- You're gonna have to put some gum around of the base of that if you want to get a good hit, man. —*Dazed and Confused*, 1993
- A hit off it and you was messed up for the rest of the night[.] —*The Source*, p. 42, April 1994
- Barbie shrugged, took a big hit of the joint and handed it to Griffin[.] —Francesca Lia Block, *I Was a Teenage Fairy*, p. 94, 1998
- I want to have sex and do a hit right as we're coming. —*Traffic*, 2000

2 a dose of a drug *US, 1952*

- The only concern she had at the moment was whether or not she could get a hit. —Donald Goines, *Dopefiend*, p. 9, 1971
- Musicians getting a quick hit while [the police] are out of the way —A. Stuart, *The Bikers*, 1972
- They used to deal acid, while on acid. Big deals, gram deals, thousands of hits. —Stephen Gaskin, *Amazing Dope Tales*, p. 5, 1980
- When Masterrap missed an appointment with his girlfrined he came back to the apartment and said he wanted a "hit" because the girl was "messing him around. —Terry Williams, *The Cocaine Kids*, p. 48, 1989
- Lorna finally took two hits and told me I looked like an Orange Elephant. —Jennifer Blowdryer, *White Trash Debutante*, p. 37, 1997
- Single hits or small clusters of them are sold on the retail level to individual trippers. —Cam Cloud, *The Little Book of Acid*, p. 34, 1999

3 an intravenous injection of a drug, usually heroin *UK*

- —Angela Devlin, *Prison Patter*, p. 62, 1996
- I'd just got back from London with an ounce of gear [heroin] in my pocket, so I was dying for a hit. —Lanre Fehintola, *Charlie Says...*, p. 20, 2000

4 a meeting with a drug dealer and a drug user *US*

- —*American Speech*, p. 26, February 1952: 'Teen-age hophead jargon'

5 in the eastern US in the early 1990s, prescription medication with codeine *US*

- —Peter Johnson, *Dictionary of Street Alcohol and Drug Terms*, p. 93, 1993
- JAY: I got hits, hash, weed, and later on I'll have 'shrooms. We take cash or stolen MasterCard and Visa. —*Clerks*, 1994

6 a marijuana cigarette *UK*

- —Mike Haskins, *Drugs*, p. 287, 2003

7 a tablet of MDMA, the recreational drug best known as ecstasy *UK*

- I sit in my cell in New Hampshire State Prison, USA, serving an eight-20-year sentence for conspiracy to possess ecstasy (7,000 hits). Conspiracy! —*Mixmag*, p. 7, June 2003

8 a deliberate inhalation of solvent fumes, such as glue sniffing *UK*

- [They] take deep, practised hits from a white, plastic supermarket bag[.] —*Time Out*, 8th January 1982

9 a blast of euphoria, joy, excitement *US*

Figurative use of a drug term.

- Another is elation, the hit that comes when you've brought it off, an argument or whatever. —*The Last Supplement to the Whole Earth Catalog*, p. 23, March 1971

10 the electronic registration of a visit to a website *US*

- As proof, he mentioned the experience on Valentine's Day, when his firm's "build a car" application was noted as the "Cool Site of the Day" and received more than 10,000 hits on its WebSite server. —*Computerworld*, p. 53, 29th May 1995

- Hits are a common measure of the popularity of a Web site, though more sophisticated measures are evolving. — *Wired Style*, 1996

11 a planned murder *US, 1950*
- They're having a gang war and he got assigned by the Brooklyn mob to make the hit. — Chester Himes, *The Real Cool Killers*, p. 47, 1959
- So far the cops can't find anybody who heard a damn thing and whoever pulled off the hits must be either an expert at disguise or different guys altogether. — Mickey Spillane, *Last Cop Out*, p. 11, 1972
- Hits never bothered him. It was business. — *Goodfellas*, 1990
- There were no drugs on that boat. It was a hit. — *The Usual Suspects*, 1995
- Mrs. Ayala, is it true your husband has ordered a hit on Eduardo Ruiz? — *Traffic*, 2000

12 an arrest *US*
- — Kenn "Naz" Young, *Naz's Underground Dictionary*, p. 36, 1973

13 a winning bet in an illegal lottery *UK, 1818*
- With the odds at six hundred to one, a penny hit won $6, a dollar won $600, and so on. — Malcolm X and Alex Haley, *The Autobiography of Malcolm X*, p. 84, 1964
- Once he got the club over Pepper's head, he would force her to sneak in phony "hit" slips against the policy wheel. — Iceberg Slim (Robert Beck), *Pimp*, p. 69, 1969
- Them's my last two dollars, Francie, so you bring me back a hit tonight, you hear? — Louise Meriwether, *Daddy Was a Number Runner*, p. 14, 1970
- [H]is small bankroll couldn't stand a hit for over five hundred dollars. — Donald Goines, *El Dorado Red*, p. 26, 1974
- [H]e'd stake people who needed money, helped a whole lot of people and he always paid his hits, no hedging. — Edwin Torres, *Carlito's Way*, p. 28–29, 1975

14 in blackjack, a card that a player requests from the dealer to add to his hand *US*
- — Lee Solkey, *Dummy Up and Deal*, p. 114, 1980

15 in snowboarding, a snow jump *CANADA*
- — Mike Fabbro, *Snowboarding*, p. 94, 1996: 'Glossary'

▸ **on hit**
excellent *US*
- — Vann Wesson, *Generation X Field Guide and Lexicon*, p. 124, 1997

hit *verb*

1 to inject drugs into a vein *US, 1949*
- If one of them was nervous and he couldn't hit himself, if he would asks me I would hit him myself. I hit a lot of guys in my day. — Jeremy Larner and Ralph Tefferteller, *The Addict in the Street*, p. 37, 1964
- But the trouble began when I ranked my hand / And stopped blowing and started to hit. — Dennis Wepman et al., *The Life*, p. 84, 1976
- Arnie gave her stuff and asked me to hit her. — Herbert Huncke, *The Evening Sun Turned Crimson*, p. 173, 1980

2 to take an inhalation of marijuana smoke *US, 1952*
- — Richard A. Spears, *The Slang and Jargon of Drugs and Drink*, p. 261, 1986
- — Mike Haskins, *Drugs*, p. 290, 2003

3 to smoke (marijuana) *US*
- You hit a stick and you're gay. — Hal Ellson, *Duke*, p. 3, 1949

4 to guess correctly the day's number in an illegal lottery *US*
- Here I been playing for years and the first drop of the bucket you hits for that kinda money. — Ralph Ellison, *Invisible Man*, p. 325, 1947
- He said as soon as he hit a number, he would use the winnings to organize his band. — Malcolm X and Alex Haley, *The Autobiography of Malcolm X*, p. 45, 1964
- And when people hit, they would give you some. — Claude Brown, *Manchild in the Promised Land*, p. 191, 1965
- He allowed his clients to pay him in weekly installments since few people in the Ward ever had five hundred dollars at one time, unless they hit the numbers, stole it, or inherited it via some insurance firm. — Nathan Heard, *Howard Street*, p. 29, 1968
- He'd been lucky then because nobody ever hit on him for over fifty cents. — Donald Gaines, *El Dorado Red*, p. 26, 1974
- It's an everyday grind for that rice and grits / A constant watch for that number that never hits. — Dennis Wepman et al., *The Life*, p. 164, 1976
- Bed-Stuy is the kind of neighborhood where the only people with money are drug dealers; people who hit the daily number; and people who got hit by cars, sued, and got paid. — Chris Rock, *Rock This!*, p. 41, 1997

5 to kill in a planned, professional manner *US, 1949*
- There is no doubt, however, that The Mick's brother was "hit." In hood talk, when you are hit, you are killed dead. Completely dead. — Robert Sylvester, *No Cover Charge*, p. 60, 1956
- They hit the Polack two years ago, it's nothing concerns me. — George V. Higgins, *The Friends of Eddie Doyle*, p. 100, 1971
- "Who hit him?" "Outta town talent. It was a specialist kind of job." — Richard Condon, *Prizzi's Honor*, p. 20, 1982
- Even if he survives the trial without going insane or being hit like Lee Harvey Oswald by his own people, he will be better off marrying a Miskito Indian or even a fat young boy from some cannibal tribe in Ecuador than crawling out of the courtroom[.] — Hunter S. Thompson, *Generation of Swine*, p. 169, 13th October 1986

6 to rob *US*
- "What'd he hit?" asks Mule. "The commissary store." — Darryl Ponicsan, *The Last Detail*, p. 17, 1970
- The store had never been hit and naturally this permitted a laxity of surveillance. — Red Rudensky, *The Gonif*, p. 7, 1970

7 to cover with graffiti *US*
- — Jim Crotty, *How to Talk American*, p. 141, 1997

8 to visit, to go to a place *US*
- I've gotta hit the bathroom. — *Mallrats*, 1995

9 to serve a drink *US, 1932*
- Jack paused, touching his glass. "Why don't you hit it one more time." — Elmore Leonard, *Bandits*, p. 20, 1987

10 to ask for something, especially money *US, 1894*
- And no, Steve, you're not going to hit me for the royalties. — Tony Wilson, *24 Hour Party People*, p. 6, 2002

11 to telephone someone with a mobile phone *US*
- — Connie Eble (Editor), *UNC-CH Campus Slang*, p. 4, November 2002

12 to win *TRINIDAD AND TOBAGO*
From cricket.
- — Lise Winer, *Dictionary of the English/Creole of Trinidad & Tobago*, 2003

13 to have sex *US*
- — Rick Ayers (Editor), *Berkeley High Slang Dictionary*, p. 26, 2004

▸ **be hit with a bit**
to be sentenced to prison *US*
From **BIT** (a prison sentence).
- — Frank Prewitt and Francis Schaeffer, *Vacaville Vocabulary*, 1961–1962

▸ **can't hit the bull in the arse with a scoop shovel**
to be physically or mentally useless *CANADA*
'This expression describes someone who is totally uncoordinated. As this involves both a broad weapon and a broad target it refers not to poor marksmanship, but rather to a total inability to act in a coordinated manner.' Chris Thain, *Cold as a Bay Street Banker's Heart*, 1987.

▸ **hit a hurdle**
to die; to suffer a severe setback *AUSTRALIA*
- — Ned Wallish, *The Truth Dictionary of Racing Slang*, p. 38, 1989

▸ **hit a lick**
to commit a robbery *US*
- Jones and Stark approached him and asked him if he wanted to go "hit a lick at the old folks' home." — *Tampa (Florida) Tribune*, p. 1, 4th January 2001

▸ **hit daylight**
to be released from prison *US*
- He'll tell you that if there's one thing in the world I hate to do, it's lock up a man who's just hit daylight. — Gerald Petievich, *Shakedown*, p. 91, 1988

▸ **hit for six**
to demolish another's argument, proposal or plan *UK, 1937*
A figurative use of a cricketing term.
- Rivals hit for six as cricket giants merge — *The Guardian*, 24th February 2003

▸ **hit in the seat**
an act of anal intercourse *US*
- — John R. Armore and Joseph D. Wolfe, *Dictionary of Desperation*, p. 33, 1976

▸ **hit it**
to leave *US, 1930*
- No, we're gonna be hittin' it. I'll take care of the check. — *Reservoir Dogs*, 1992
- Clarence says we gotta be hittin' it. — *True Romance*, 1993

▸ **hit it a lick; hit it**
in poker, to raise a bet *US*
- — George Percy, *The Language of Poker*, p. 44, 1988

▸ **hit it off**
to take a mutual liking to someone *UK, 1780*
- [Donald] Sutherland was originally hired to play the eccentric, antique-dealing hypnotist which is now [Derek] Jacobi's part, but Sutherland and [Kenneth] Branagh didn't hit it off. — *The Guardian*, 17th October 1991

▸ **hit it up**
to strike up an acquaintance *US*
- You gotta be awful who you hit it up with, is what I always say, and you can't be too particular, neither. — *It Happened One Night*, 1934

▸ hit on the hip
to page electronically *US*
• —Connie Eble (Editor), *UNC-CH Campus Slang*, p. 4, March 1996

▸ hit the books
to study hard *US*
• —Collin Baker et al., *College Undergraduate Slang Study Conducted at Brown University*, p. 137, 1968
• Hey look, Paps, really. I've got to hit the books this semester. I'm carrying eighteen hours and I'm on pro.—Richard Farina, *Been Down So Long*, p. 26, 1996

▸ hit the bottle
to bleach your hair blonde *US*
Teen slang, punning on a term associated with drinking.
• —*American Weekly*, p. 2, 14th August 1955

▸ hit the breeze
to leave *NEW ZEALAND*
• I stayed awake until the first crack of dawn, when I hit the breeze, never to return.—Ivan Agnew, *Loner*, p. 70, 1974

▸ hit the bricks
to work on the street *US*
• Can't you recall telling me when I first hit the bricks to 'always use a safety?'—A.S. Jackson, *Gentleman Pimp*, p. 45, 1973

▸ hit the bucket
to drink very heavily *UK: SCOTLAND*
A humorous variation on 'hit the bottle' (to drink heavily).
• I got her this box of sweeties afore I hit the bucket on Monday there.—Ian Pattison, *Rab C. Nesbitt*, 1988

▸ hit the burner
to draw upon all of your inner resources and stamina *US*
US naval aviator usage.
• —*United States Naval Institute Proceedings*, p. 108, October 1986

▸ hit the ceiling
to become very angry *US, 1914*
• I phoned Kamel from a pay booth on the plaza to let him know I'd be gone a few days. He hit the ceiling. "Are you mad?" he cried over the fuzzy line.—Katherine Neville, *The Eight*, p. 419, 1988

▸ hit the cinders
to jump or fall from a moving train *US*
• —Ramon Adams, *The Language of the Railroader*, p. 79, 1977

▸ hit the deck
1 to fall or throw yourself to the ground *US, 1925*
• Then I saw all black and the last thing I remember is hitting the deck.—*A Few Good Men*, 1992
• There was the sound of gunfire and everyone hit the deck or started running for the door – it was frightening.—*The Guardian*, 2nd November 2001

2 to land a plane *UK, 1943*

3 to get out of bed *UK, 1918*
Often as an imperative.

4 to go to bed *UK, 1935*

▸ hit the dex
to work as a DJ *UK*
Fashionable spelling for (record) 'decks', combined with a vague play on other senses of **HIT THE DECK**.
• Instead of Smashie and Nicey playing discs, Pete Tong and Fatboy Slim were "hitting the dex"[.]—*The Sunday Times*, p. 13, 23rd June 2002

▸ hit the Dixie
to stop idling and start doing something *BAHAMAS*
• —John A. Holm, *Dictionary of Bahamian English*, p. 104, 1982

▸ hit the gravel; hit the grit
to fall from a moving train *US*
• —Norman Carlisle, *The Modern Wonder Book of Trains and Railroading*, p. 264, 1946

▸ hit the hay
to go to bed *US, 1912*
Originally used by tramps; anglicised in 1929 by Conan Doyle.
• He said he guessed he was pretty shot and thought he'd hit the hay.—Ken Kesey, *One Flew Over the Cuckoo's Nest*, p. 243, 1962
• I can crack a fat [get an erection] with a flamin' skinful [drunk]. Let's hit the hay!!!—Barry Humphries, *Bazza Pulls It Off!*, 1971

▸ hit the hop
to use drugs, especially heroin or opium *US*
• Maybe you've taken a couple of raps for hitting the hop over there[.]—Douglas Rutherford, *The Creeping Flesh*, p. 103, 1963

▸ hit the jackpot
to have great success or good fortune, especially when unexpected or beyond your expectations *US*
A figurative application of 'jackpot', a poker term applied generally to any gambling prize. Known worldwide in its variant forms: 'crack' (favoured in Australia), 'hit', 'strike' or 'win'.
• And the Beatles won the jackpot. They toured the world in luxury, meeting people of power and influence.—Simon Napier-Bell, *Black Vinyl White Powder*, p. 51, 2001

▸ hit the mainline
to inject a drug intravenously *US, 1950*
A combination of **HIT** (to inject) and **MAINLINE** (a vein).
• —Richard A. Spears, *The Slang and Jargon of Drugs and Drink*, p. 263, 1986
• —Mike Haskins, *Drugs*, p. 290, 2003

▸ hit the moon
to reach the highest plateau of a drug experience *US*
• —Eugene Landy, *The Underground Dictionary*, p. 104, 1971

▸ hit the needle
to inject a drug intravenously *US, 1950*
A combination of **HIT** (to inject) and the means of delivery.
• —Richard A. Spears, *The Slang and Jargon of Drugs and Drink*, p. 263, 1986
• —Mike Haskins, *Drugs*, p. 290, 2003

▸ hit the pipe
to smoke crack cocaine *US*
• They had some argument out in the parking lot. Looked like she was hitting the pipe.—Richard Price, *Clockers*, p. 197, 1992
• I [Coolio] hit the pipe again and felt a head rush. Next thing I knew I was hooked.—*The Source*, p. 74, October 1994
• People against drugs say it all starts with beer. ADDICT: "Ahh, man. I'm hitting the pipe. Can't fuck with that beer no more."—Chris Rock, *Rock This!*, p. 62, 1997

▸ hit the pit
1 to inject a drug into the armpit *UK, 1998*
A combination of **HIT** (to inject) and **PIT** (the armpit).
• —Mike Haskins, *Drugs*, p. 290, 2003

2 to be incarcerated *US*
• —William K Bentley and James M. Corbett, *Prison Slang*, 1992

▸ hit the post
in the language of radio disc jockeys, to talk during the introduction of a song, completing your thought just before the song's vocal begins *US*
• —Jim Crotty, *How to Talk American*, p. 219, 1997

▸ hit the prone
to throw yourself to the ground *US*
• The three of us hit the prone and waited, then looked behind us to see two troopers from the new seven-six half pushing, half carrying a VC.—Larry Heinemann, *Close Quarters*, p. 65, 1977

▸ hit the road; hit the trail
to go; to commence or recommence a journey *US, 1899*
• All right, pal. Hit the road.—Max Shulman, *Anyone Got a Match?*, p. 87, 1964
• We hit the road right after breakfast.—C.D. Payne, *Youth in Revolt*, p. 19, 1993
• I braced myself against the raging onslaught of the unsympathetic elements, zipped up my jacket and hit the flooded road.—Josie Dew, *The Sun In My Eyes*, p. 292, 2001

▸ hit the roof
to be, or to become very angry; to exhibit that anger *UK, 1925*
• His plan was to shack up with some fat girlfriend of his, piping [smoking crack cocaine] and bonking the night away, whilst I did all the work. I hit the roof!—Lanre Fehintola, *Charlie Says...*, p. 160, 2000

▸ hit the sack
to go to bed, to go to sleep *US, 1912*
• He gets between the sheets and tells me I better hit the sack myself[.]—Ken Kesey, *One Flew Over the Cuckoo's Nest*, p. 81, 1962
• Every night I hit the sack / Oh my aching Airborne back!—Sandee Shaffer Johnson, *Cadences*, p. 19, 1986
• I want to get back to see you before you hit the sack.—Mark Powell, *Snap*, p. 81, 2001

▸ hit the sauce
to drink alcohol *US*
• As a result, I hit the sauce uncharacteristically hard that day.—Elissa Stein and Kevin Leslie, *Chunks*, p. 26, 1997

▸ **hit the sewer**
to inject heroin or another drug intravenously *US*
- —David Maurer and Victor Vogel, *Narcotics and Narcotic Addiction*, p. 415, 1973

▸ **hit the silk**
in card games, to withdraw from or end a game or hand *US*
From the military slang for bailing out of an aircraft by parachute (silk).
- I was lucky that I had Uncle Kenneth to take me to all the football games I wanted to see, and to teach me how to run the six ball in snooker and that the best thing to do in gin was hit the silk when you got ten or under. —Dan Jenkins, *Semi-Tough*, p. 50, 1972

▸ **hit the skids**
to deteriorate *US*
- She began to hit the skids harder. —Willard Motely, *Let No Man Write My Epitaph*, p. 275, 1958

▸ **hit the slab**
to be killed *US*
- —Hyman E. Goldin et al., *Dictionary of American Underworld Lingo*, p. 96, 1950

▸ **hit the toe**
to depart; to decamp *AUSTRALIA, 1983*
- —Ryan Aven-Bray, *Ridgey Didge Oz Jack Lang*, p. 31, 1983
- Come on, Houdini, let's cop his tip, get the girls and hit the toe. —Clive Galea, *Slipper*, p. 108, 1988

▸ **hit the wall**
to reach a point of exhaustion beyond which lesser athletes will fail to continue, especially of long-distance and marathon runners *US, 1982*
- Believe what you've read about "hitting the wall." — *Washington Post*, p. G7, 18th August 1977
- Among marathoners, hitting the wall is the term for what happens when your body runs out of glycogen. Any runner who's hit the wall during a previous race will know to take in between three and ten energy gels on a marathon. — *CNN*, 31st October 2001
- [A] red faced fortysomething man struggling against the demons of lactic acid and the marathon 'wall'. — *The Observer*, 19th January 2003

▸ **hit with a check**
to discharge from employment and pay off owed wages *US*
- —Jerry Robertson, *Oil Slanguage*, p. 94, 1954

▸ **hit your marks**
in television and film making, to move to the proper place at the proper time in a scene *US*
- —Ralph S. Singleton, *Filmaker's Dictionary*, p. 81, 1990

hit and get *verb*
to rob one place and then hurry to rob somewhere else *UK*
- —Angela Devlin, *Prison Patter*, p. 62, 1996

hit and miss; hit or miss *noun*
1 a kiss *UK, 1933*
Rhyming slang, 'hit me', which evolves to 'kiss me', to 'kiss'. Sometimes abbreviated to 'hit'.
- —Ray Puxley, *Cockney Rabbit*, 1992

2 urine; alcoholic drink or (when used with 'the'), drinking or a session of drinking *AUSTRALIA*
Rhyming slang for **PISS** (and **ON THE PISS**). Noted in the US by Maurer and Baker, 1944, as 'of Australian antecedence'.
- —Julian Franklyn, *A Dictionary of Rhyming Slang*, 1960
- One can go "for a" or "on the hit and miss". —Ray Puxley, *Cockney Rabbit*, 1992

hit and run *noun*
1 a betting technique, in which a player places a single bet and withdraws from the game if he wins *US, 1950*
- —Thomas L. Clark, *The Dictionary of Gambling and Gaming*, p. 101, 1987

2 the sun *UK*
Rhyming slang.
- —Ray Puxley, *Fresh Rabbit*, 1998

hit and run *verb*
1 in casino blackjack, to enter a game when the count is advantageous to the players, to play a few games and then to move to another table *US*
- —Michael Dalton, *Blackjack*, p. 54, 1991

2 in poker, to play for a short time, win heavily and quit the game *US*
- —David M. Hayano, *Poker Faces*, p. 186, 1982

hit and run *adjective*
1 (used of entertainment engagements) in one city one night, another city the next *US*
- They had a lot of "hit and run" jobs, as the musicians called them in those days, which meant that they would close one day in, say, Orlando, Florida, and have to open up the next night in Vancouver. —Mort Sahl, *Heartland*, p. 57, 1976

2 swindled *UK*
Rhyming slang for 'done' (**DO**).
- —Ray Puxley, *Cockney Rabbit*, 1992

hit-and-split *noun*
a quick air attack followed by a quick retreat *US*
- He pressed closer now, deciding to use his gun and do a hit-and-split followed by a reattack. —Richard Herman Jr, *Firebreak*, p. 393, 1991

hitch *noun*
1 a period of duty or service *US, 1905*
- Another hitch in prison and you'll be put away for life. —Jack Kerouac, *On the Road*, p. 257, 1957
- Three hitches of four years each. —Darryl Ponicsan, *The Last Detail*, p. 2, 1970
- Yes, but how many ex-baton twirlers with only high school, two seasons with a religious revival show, and a nine-year hitch in a rodeo trailer made twenty grand a year and expenses? —Elmore Leonard, *Touch*, p. 25, 1977

2 a jail sentence *US*
- Well, I sent here a kite by my cellmate / the boy who just finished his hitch and was free. —Bruce Jackson, *Get Your Ass in the Water and Swim Like Me*, p. 116, 1964
- I did three hitches in Leavenworth and I did a ten-year bit here, and now I've got life here. —Bruce Jackson, *In the Life*, p. 97, 1972

hitch *verb*
to hitchhike *US, 1929*
A colloquial shortening.
- Okay, I asked msyelf – now, now, are you sorry you hitched? —James Simon Kunen, *The Strawberry Statement*, p. 82, 1968

▸ **hitch up the reindeers; hitch up the reindeer**
to inhale powdered cocaine *US*
Punning variously on **SNOW** (cocaine) and **SLEIGH RIDE** (the use of cocaine).
- —Richard A. Spears, *The Slang and Jargon of Drugs and Drink*, p. 261, 1986
- —Mike Haskins, *Drugs*, p. 291, 2003

Hitch *nickname*
Alfred Hitchcock (1899–1980), television and film director *US*
- Please don't come in. Hitch doesn't like you. —Mort Sahl, *Heartland*, p. 67, 1976

hitched *adjective*
married *US, 1857*
- It's all legit. Totally legit. We're hitched. —Nick Barlay, *Curvy Lovebox*, p. 127, 1997

hitchhiker *noun*
a commerical message played at the end of a radio programme *US*
- —Walter Hurst and Donn Delson, *Delson's Dictionary of Radio & Record Industry Terms*, 1980

hitch up *verb*
to marry, to partner *US, 1902*
Figurative application of a conventional 'hitch' (a knot).
- I feel sorry for Stell havin' to hitch up with the king of the screwheads. —Nick Barlay, *Curvy Lovebox*, p. 80, 1997

hit kiss *noun*
the exchange of crack cocaine smoke from one user to another through a kiss *US*
- Another example is the "hit kiss" ritual: after inhaling deeply, basers literally "kiss" – put their lips together and exhale the smoke into each other's mouths. —Terry Williams, *The Cocaine Kids*, p. 108, 1989

Hitler's drug *noun*
paramethoxyamphetamine, PMA
The drug was originally created during World War 2 by Hitler's chemists with the intention of enabling Nazi soldiers to fight around the clock. In 1999 the *Observer* reported fears of the drug's arrival in UK clubs.

hit list *noun*

a list of targets for retaliation, either physical or otherwise *US, 1972*

- — *American Speech*, Spring 1980

hit man *noun*

a professional killer *US, 1963*

- But I thought Scalisi was pretty much of a hit man, didn't do much of anything else. —George V. Higgins, *The Friends of Eddie Doyle*, p. 99, 1971
- "We have hit men like that," Shelby reminded him. —Mickey Spillane, *Last Cop Out*, p. 10, 1972
- None of us is about to deal face-to-face with a couple of guinea hit men. —Vincent Patrick, *The Pope of Greenwich Village*, p. 205, 1979
- — *American Speech*, Spring 1980
- I got him up in my motel room and he told me he was a hit man. He murdered people for a living. —William T. Vollman, *Whores for Gloria*, p. 91, 1991
- I've already solved it. I've hired a hit man. — *Sleepless in Seattle*, 1993
- He's a psycho-cokehead hitman. — *Traffic*, 2000

hit on *verb*

to flirt; to proposition *US, 1954*

- [H]e took her to dinner, never mentioned it again, took her home, didn't hit on her in any way. —Terry Southern, *Now Dig This*, p. 19, 1981

hit or miss *verb*

▷ see: HIT AND MISS

hit or sit *verb*

used for describing a player's two choices in blackjack or twenty-one – draw another card or not *US*

- Who's got five bucks they want to lose? You hit or you sit[.] —Ken Kesey, *One Flew Over the Cuckoo's Nest*, p. 120, 1962

hits *noun*

1 LSD *UK, 1998*

- —Mike Haskins, *Drugs*, p. 285, 2003

2 a pair of dice that have been altered so that they will not roll a total of seven *US*

- —Frank Garcia, *Marked Cards and Loaded Dice*, p. 262, 1962

hitsville *noun*

success *UK*

Used on the normally staid *BBC Light Programme*, 30th June 1963.

- —The Clash *Hitsville UK*, 1980

hit team *noun*

during the Vietnam conflict, a small unit of trained scouts sent on a mission to kill the enemy *US, 1987*

- —Linda Reinberg, *In the Field*, p. 106, 1991

hitter *noun*

1 a hired killer *US, 1959*

- He had put a group together in Miami, all hitters, all veterans of the Batista wars, all hungry. —Edwin Torres, *Carlito's Way*, p. 59, 1975
- A hitter from back East but he worked out here a few years back. — *48 Hours*, 1982
- And the woman was a contract hitter. —Richard Condon, *Prizzi's Honor*, p. 88, 1982
- Then the guy who sent the hitter gets hit, the macaronis are shooting each other, and it's hard to tell who's on whose side. —Elmore Leonard, *Glitz*, p. 108, 1985
- That's what this hitter is, a moonlighting prison guard. —Seth Morgan, *Homeboy*, p. 97, 1990
- Tiny stars placed on the arm in any fashion indicate that the wearer is a hitter (also known as a "cleaner" or "torpedo"). —Bill Valentine, *Gangs and Their Tattoos*, p. 36, 2000

2 a crack cocaine pipe designed for a single inhalation *US, 2001*

- — *www.addictions.org*, 1999

hit the hay *verb*

to smoke marijuana *US, 1942*

- —Richard A. Spears, *The Slang and Jargon of Drugs and Drink*, p. 262, 1986
- —Mike Haskins, *Drugs*, p. 290, 2003

hittin' *adjective*

excellent *US*

- For example, after a session Sambro is hungry, and when given a steaming hot bowl of home-cooked beans, he takes a bite and exclaims, "Dude! These bens are hittin'!" —Trevor Cralle, *The Surfin'ary*, p. 53, 1991

hitting; hittin' *adjective*

tasty *US*

- —Kenn "Naz" Young, *Naz's Dictionary of Teen Slang*, p. 59, 1993

hitting fluid *noun*

heroin *US*

- 'Mother Coco,' I says, 'I gotta get some hitting fluid.' —Richard Frank, *A Study of Sex in Prison*, p. 26, 1973

hit up *verb*

1 to inject a drug intravenously *US, 1969*

- —Richard A. Spears, *The Slang and Jargon of Drugs and Drink*, p. 262, 1986
- We'll go out later, soon as you've hit me up. Oh yes, that is fucking fantastic[.] —Ben Elton, *High Society*, p. 79, 2002
- —Mike Haskins, *Drugs*, p. 290, 2003

2 to ask for something *AUSTRALIA*

- [T]ry to hit them up for money[.] —Susan Ruddick, *Cool Places*, p. 354, 1998

3 to go to *US*

- We're about to hit up the library for some studying. —Connie Eble (Editor), *UNC-CH Campus Slang*, p. 5, October 2002

hiya

used as a casual greeting *UK, 1940*

- For a while, those who had never liked her [Margaret Thatcher] would greet each other with a perky "hiya", in the way that strangers say "good morning" on the first sunny day of spring. —Mark Steel, *Reasons to be Cheerful*, p. 196, 2001

hiya-butty-bay; hiya-butt-bay *noun*

Trecco Bay, Porthcawl in south Wales *UK: WALES*

In 1947 mining was nationalised and subsequent working practices meant that entire communities relocated to the seaside resort of Porthcawl for 'miners' fortnight'. The friendly greeting 'hiya, butty' (hello, friend) filled the air. The style of holidays changed in the 1960s, but the term is still in limited circulation.

hiya kids

used as a humorous greeting *US*

The signature greeting used on the children's television programme *Ed's Gang* (later *Andy's Gang*) (1951–58). Repeated with referential humour.

hizzie *nickname*

the room, apartment or house where someone lives *US*

- —Connie Eble (Editor), *UNC-CH Campus Slang*, p. 5, October 2002

Hizzoner *nickname*

used as a jocular reference to a mayor, especially Richard J. Daley, mayor of Chicago from 1955 until his death in 1976 *US, 1882*

A slurred 'his honor'.

- Cause in the latest Pigs-vs.-Panthers tilt Fred and Brother Mark Clark were sidelined permanently by the heavy hand of Fate and the even heavier hand of Hizzonner Richard Daley's finest. —John Sayles, *Union Dues*, p. 276, 1977
- Delvin says, "It's time for new blood in this party, especially now that Hizzoner – God rest his soul – Richard J. Daly's kid, is sitting in the mayor's office." —Robert Campbell, *In a Pig's Eye*, p. 4, 1991
- Amidst the full-court media blitz, a succession of polls found New Yorkers – including presumably more conservative up-staters – siding nearly 2–1 with the museum against Hizzoner." — *Religion in the News*, Fall 1999
- A buffet of cliches, Franklin's piece invokes Ed Koch, better known as Hizzoner, subway buskers, cabbies who drive too fast, the intolerable condition of public schools, the majesty of Central Park and the New York Public Library and the tension between Manhattan's haves and have-nots. — *Jewish World Review*, 24th February 1999
- Hizzoner's Digs. "Why are you taking this tour?" I ask the young guy behind me as we await our walk-through of Getty House, Los Angeles' official mayoral residence. — *LA Weekly*, 6th-12th April 2001
- Atkins widow fumes at Hizzoner's 'fat' joke. The widow of Dr. Robert Atkins went on national television Friday to demand that New York Mayor Michael Bloomberg apologize for calling the late diet guru "fat." — *Commerical Appeal (Memphis, Tennessee)*, p. A13, 24th January 2004

HK *nickname*

Hong Kong *UK*

Current among the UK Chinese population.

- And they're always fascinated about what's going on in H.K. —David Parker, *Cool Places*, p. 72, 1998

HM *noun*

▷ see: HEAVY METAL

HMCS

*h*ow *m*y *c*ompanion *s*nores CANADA

A jocular back formation from HCMS (Her Majesty's Canadian Ship).

- On the HCMS, how my companion snores, oft in the stilly night. — *Toronto Globe and Mail*, p. D12, 3rd August 2002

HMFIC *noun*

a commanding officer, or *h*ead *m*otherfucker *i*n *c*harge US

- — *The Retired Officer Magazine*, p. 39, January 1993

HNIC *noun*

the leader of an enterprise, the *h*ead *n*igger *i*n *c*harge US, 1972

- — Malachi Andrews and Paul T. Owens, *Black Language*, p. 81, 1973
- I see you the HNIC, (head Negro in charge) and I know if anybody can make it happen, you can. — Nikki Turner, *A Project Chick*, p. 82, 2004

ho; hoe *noun*

1 a sexually available woman; a woman who may be considered sexually available; a prostitute US, 1959

Originally black usage, from the southern US pronunciation of 'whore'; now widespread through the influence of rap music.

- Aaw, 'ho', I's jus' kiddin' witcha. — Nathan Heard, *Howard Street*, p. 86, 1968
- — Joan Fontaine et al., *Dictionary of Black Slang*, 1968
- Aw, man, white ho's are dumb. — Cecil Brown, *The Life & Loves of Mr. Jiveass Nigger*, p. 146, 1969
- "These hos out here think they hos; they ain't hos." She said, "You don't learn how to be aho, you be born aho. And I was born a ho." — Christina and Richard Milner, *Black Players*, p. 233, 1972
- She turned on the waterworks to cop her license to do me but I was immune to ho tears. — Iceberg Slim (Robert Beck), *Long White Con*, 1977
- "You two 'ho's still pushing your meth?'; she said conversationally. — Robert Deane Pharr, *Giveadamn Brown*, 1978
- — Edith A Folb, *runnin' down some lines*, 1980
- [T]hat hoe was hot, the first piece of pussy that I ever got[.] — Geto Boys *Gangster of Love*, 1990
- Let these ladies eat. Hoes gotta eat too. — *Boyz N The Hood*, 1990
- My dad's been captured by a ho. — *Sleepless in Seattle*, 1993
- I just wanted to come and see for myself what hos you both are. — Francesca Lia Block, *I Was a Teenage Fairy*, p. 105, 1998
- If a girl was labeled a hoe, a skeezer, or a freak by other students, no one seemed willing to defend her. — Nelson George, *Hip Hop America*, p. 177, 1998

2 a woman US, 1959

A weakened variation of the previous sense.

- Them ho's had bodies like goddesses, and knew it too. — *Menace II Society*, 1993
- Drugs and gang violence. Women casually described as bitches and hos. Uzis. Glocks. — *The Times Magazine*, p. 43, 16th February 2002

3 a weak or effeminate man US

- "Fuck you, hoe." "Don't call me that." "What? Hoe!" — Two Fingers, *Puff (Disco Biscuits)*, p. 220, 1996

ho; hoe *verb*

to work as a prostitute US

- But then some again treat them nice, but my cousin even treats his wife like a dog and she's Black, but she got out there and hoed for him. — Christina and Richard Milner, *Black Players*, p. 233, 1972
- I said if you gonna be hoeing [whoring] for a rap you ain't nothing but a dog bitch anyway. — Terry Williams, *The Cocaine Kids*, p. 87, 1989

HO *verb*

to withhold more than your share of something US

An initialism of '*h*old *o*ut'.

- — Hyman E. Goldin et al., *Dictionary of American Underworld Lingo*, p. 98, 1950

hoaching; hotchin *adjective*

full, teeming, crowded UK: SCOTLAND, 1911

- The joint's hoaching with media. — Ian Pattison, *Rab C. Nesbitt*, 1988
- These cases are hoachin' with serious money, sir[.] — Christopher Brookmyre, *The Sacred Art of Stealing*, p. 396, 2002

hoachy *adjective*

exceedingly lucky, fortunate UK: SCOTLAND

- — Michael Munro, *The Original Patter*, p. 35, 1985

hoagons *noun*

the female breasts US

- — Collin Baker et al., *College Undergraduate Slang Study Conducted at Brown University*, p. 137, 1968

ho, babe

used as a student-to-student greeting US

- — *American Speech*, p. 154, May 1959: 'Gator (University of Florida) slang'

hobber de hoy; hibber de hoy *noun*

an adolescent boy, especially a hooligan UK

Recorded as rhyming slang by Ray Puxley, *Cockney Rabbit*, 1992; but probably directly from 'hobbledehoy', first recorded in 1540, which, excepting the nuance of hooliganism, is synonymous; 'hobbledehoy', however, is unlikely to be rhyming slang as the earliest explicit reference to rhyming slang does not appear until about 300 years later in John Camden Hotten's *The Slang Dictionary*, 1859.

ho-bitch *noun*

a female who has earned a complete lack of respect US

Used on those special occasions when just **BITCH** or just **HO** is just not enough.

- — Judi Sanders, *Da Bomb*, p. 8, 1997

hobnail *verb*

to walk NEW ZEALAND

- We hobnailed our way round the height. — Ross McMillan, *Country Bloke*, p. 229, 2000

hobnail express *noun*

travel by walking US, 1918

- How am I going to get to town? By hobnail express, of course. — Ian Sinclair, *Boot in the Stirrup*, p. 55, 1973
- — Harry Orsman, *A Dictionary of Modern New Zealand Slang*, p. 65, 1999

hobo *noun*

1 a vagrant US, 1885

Uncertainly derived from 'hoeboy' (a migrant agricultural labourer) or the exclamation 'Ho boy!' (used by mail carriers).

- His father was a wine hobo. They hopped freights together. — Jack Kerouac, *Letter to Carroll Brown*, 9th May 1961
- I didn't quite look like a stage hobo about to die of destitution. — Edwin Lefevere, *Reminiscences of a Stock Operator*, 1994

2 in trucking, a tractor trailer that is moved from one terminal to another US

- — Montie Tak, *Truck Talk*, p. 83, 1971

3 a homing bomb, one with a targeting capability US

- But six months earlier, in May 1973, a 2,000 "Hobo" (Homing Bomb) had obliterated a bridge just north of Hanoi which had withstood repeated onslaughts of conventional bombs. — James W. Canan, *The Superwarriors*, p. 311, 1975

hobo bet *noun*

in craps, a bet on the number twelve US

From the number's association with boxcars.

- — Steve Kuriscak, *Casino Talk*, p. 31, 1985

hobo cocktail *noun*

a glass of water US

- — Marcus Hanna Boulware, *Jive and Slang of Students in Negro Colleges*, 1947
- — Clarence Major, *Dictionary of Afro-American Slang*, p. 66, 1970

hobosexual *noun*

a person who is sexually active with several partners in a short period of time US

- — *American Speech*, p. 19, Spring 1985: 'The language of singles bars'

Hobo Woods *noun*

an area in South Vietnam which was a major staging area for the North Vietnamese to launch attacks on Saigon or Cu Chi City US

- Did myself a tour with the 173rd Airborneski! Iron fucking Triangle, Hobo Woods, the Bo Loi Woods. — Larry Heinemann, *Paco's Story*, p. 152, 1986

Hobson's choice; hobsons *noun*

1 the only option that is offered and, therefore, no choice at all UK, 1649

Widely claimed, since 1712, to derive from Tobias Hobson, who hired out horses, and is reputed to have compelled his customers to take whichever horse happened to be next in line, or go without; however, 'Hodgson's choise' is recorded in 1617.

- Whose interests come first: their club or the game at large? That has given them Hobson's Choice. — *The Observer*, 3rd November 2002

2 the voice UK, 1937

Rhyming slang.

- Her hobsons, low and husky / Made my newingtons go numb. — Ronnie Barker, *Fletcher's Book of Rhyming Slang*, p. 21, 1979

Ho Chi Minh Motel *noun*

a rest house used by the Viet Cong along a trail or route *US*

• He outlined, with a map and a pointer, the objective: a reported Vietcong rest house on a route traversing the area. "The Ho Chi Minh motel," someone said, a used but still popular joke, —David Halberstam, *One Very Hot Day*, p. 8, 1967

Ho Chi Minh sandals *noun*

slip-on sandals made from the treads of discarded tyres, designed and worn by the Viet Cong during the Vietnam war *US*

• [G]oing through the gear, snatching up the silver belt buckles with the embossed star and the little pouches of smoke and the cash, the Ho Chi Minch tire-track sandals and letters from home[.]—Larry Heinemann, *Close Quarters*, p. 239, 1977
• He wore Ho Chi Minh sandals, khaki shorts and shirt and a pith helmet.—John Del Vecchio, *The 13th Valley*, p. 266, 1982
• [T]he only remedy for which was to pull the sufferer out of the field and make him wear flip-flops (a.k.a. Ho Chi Minh sandals) until his feet dried out.—David H. Hackworth, *About Face*, p. 477, 1989

Ho Chi Minh's curse *noun*

diarrhoea *US*

An existing formation of 'somebody's curse' adapted in Vietnam.

• —Linda Reinberg, *In the Field*, p. 106, 1991

Ho Chi Minh Trail *noun*

Route 209 in northeast Pennsylvania *US*

• —Gwyneth A. "Dandalion" Seese, *Tijuana Bear in a Smoke 'Um Up Taxi*, p. 14, 1977

hock *noun*

1 the male who takes the active role in homosexual intercourse *AUSTRALIA, 1944*

Origin unknown. Ted Hartley in his glossary of prison slang (1944) says that 'hocks' can mean 'feet', and is therefore in some way related to the term **HORSE'S HOOF**. Simes, in his *Dictionary of Australian Underworld Slang* (1993), suggests that 'hock' is 'feeble' and rhyming slang for 'cock'. Neither of these is overwhelmingly convincing.

• —Julian Franklyn, *A Dictionary of Rhyming Slang*, 1961
• Hocks give it. And Cats take it.—Kathy Lette, *Girls' Night Out*, p. 174, 1987
• Neither of us fell for the "arse bandit" routine, being both ugly enough and tough enough to not have to worry about any hocks fancying us.—Clive Galea, *Slipper*, p. 86, 1988

2 the foot *UK, 1785*

• —Lou Shelly, *Hepcats Jive Dictionary*, p. 12, 1945

▸ **in hock**

1 in debt, especially to a pawnbroker *US, 1883*

• What's the kid in hock for so far?—*The Hustler*, 1961
• [T]he suit didn't fit either one of them but they figured they might be able to get it in hock.—Herbert Huncke, *Guilty of Everything*, p. 3, 1990

2 in prison *US, 1859*

• —Lou Shelly, *Hepcats Jive Talk Dictionary*, p. 26, 1945

hock *verb*

1 to pawn *US, 1878*

• And even when the old firm's going a bit unsteady morries never hock their gold kettles [pocket watches][.]—Derek Raymond (Robin Cook), *The Crust on its Uppers*, p. 21, 1962
• They were hungry. I dunno. They didn't want to hock the Host, they wanted to hock that golden chalice.—*The Bad Lieutenant*, 1992

2 to clear the throat of phlegm *US, 1992*

From a confusion with conventional 'hawk'.

• He hocked such a huge looie that I had a spiderweb of saliva running from my dark glasses onto my hair.—Howard Stern, *Miss America*, p. 340, 1995

3 to nag *US*

From the Yiddish.

• She hocks me nice. But it's still hocking.—Clancy Sigal, *Going Away*, p. 18, 1961
• Stop already hocking us to be good! hocking us to be nice! Just leave us alone.—Philip Roth, *Portnoy's Complaint*, p. 136, 1969

hockey box; hock *noun*

a male homosexual prostitute *AUSTRALIA*

• —Thommo, *The Dictionary of Australian Swearing and Sex Sayings*, p. 67, 1985

hockey hair

a hair style: the hair is worn short at the front and long at the back *CANADA*

Better known, perhaps, as a **MULLET**.

• —Ben Sharpe, *Scooter Crazy*, p. 41, 2000

hockeystick *noun*

a mutton chop *NEW ZEALAND*

• The musterer's breakfast consisted of a couple of mutton chops (known as 'hockey sticks').—John Martin, *The Forgotten Worker*, p. 63, 1990
• They could eat hockeysticks or 365s, which town-dwellers know as mutton chops.—*NZWords*, 2nd August 2001

hock shop *noun*

a pawnbroker's shop *UK, 1871*

• I bought some in a hock shop.—Preston Sturges, *Hail the Conquering Hero*, 1944
• Below this intersection, for a third of a mile, is a Skid Row as low and lousy as any in the country, with the usual in the way of flop houses, flea circuses, hock shops, tattoo parlors[.]—Jack Lait and Lee Mortimer, *Chicago Confidential*, p. 14, 1950

hocus *noun*

a solution of heroin that has been heated and is ready to inject *US*

• —John B. Williams, *Narcotics and Hallucinogenics*, p. 113, 1967

hocus *verb*

to alter legitimate dice for cheating purposes *US*

• —*The Annals of the American Academy of Political and Social Sciences*, p. 126, May 1950

hocus pocus; hocus *noun*

cocaine, heroine, morphine or opium; also marijuana *UK, 1938*

Best remembered as a stage magician's incantation, but claimed to be a mocking corruption of *hoc est corpus* (this is the body); originally, 1650–1720, 'a juggler/a conjuror'; it was in circulation during the C19 and into the C20 in the sense of 'criminal deception/shady trickery'; in 1821 as 'to stupefy with alcohol' (for the purposes of robbery) and hence 'hocus' became 'a drugged liquor' from as early as 1725 and well into the C19 served as an adjective meaning 'intoxicated'. All these meanings condensed into a catalogue of hard drugs during the C20; 'marijuana' joined the list in the 1980s.

• —Mike Haskins, *Drugs*, p. 287, 2003

hodad *noun*

a non-surfer who associates with surfers and poses as a surfer *US, 1961*

• —Jack Pollard, *The Australian Surfrider*, p. 16, 1963
• —*Paradise of the Pacific*, p. 27, October 1963
• —J. R. Friss, *A Dictionary of Teenage Slang (Mt. Diablo High)*, 1964
• —Mary Corey and Victoria Westermark, *Fer Shurr! How to be a Valley Girl*, 1982

hoddie *noun*

a labourer working for a bricklayer *AUSTRALIA, 1952*

hodgy *noun*

▷ **see: HACHI**

hod of shit *noun*

a great deal of trouble *US*

• Looks to us like our old friend Lieutenant Billy is getting himself into a hod of shit the Lord couldn't save him from.—George V. Higgins, *The Rat on Fire*, p. 113, 1981

hoe *noun*

a fellow black man, usually in context of sexual bragging *US*

From **HOMEBOY** (close friend), punning on 'hero'.

• The Super Hoe is loose in your section / And he's armed with a powerful erection—Boogie Down Productions *Super Hoe*, 1987
• —Funkdoobiest, *Superhoes*, 1995
• —Sadat X Fat Joe & Diamond D, *Nasty Hoes*, 1996

▷ **see: HO**

hoedown *noun*

a street fight between youth gangs *US*

• —Kenn "Naz" Young, *Naz's Dictionary of Teen Slang*, p. 59, 1993

hoe in *verb*

to attack physically and with vigour *NEW ZEALAND*

• —Sonya Plowman, *Great Kiwi Slang*, p. 90, 2002

hoe into *verb*

to attack a task with vigour, especially the eating of a meal *AUSTRALIA, 1935*

• Shepherd 'hoed' into them in fine style for some valuable runs. —Richie Benaud, *Spin me a Spinner*, p. 105, 1963
• [S]he cut me a slice of opulent-looking cream cake, and I began to hoe steadily into it.—*Alvin Purple*, p. 21, 1974

• The kids were hoeing into peanut butter sangas and the missus produced chicken rolls and hot coffee for us. —Paul Vautin, *Turn It Up!*, p. 91, 1995

hoffing *noun*

a fight, especially between youth gangs *US*

• —Hermese E. Roberts, *The Third Ear: A Black Glossary*, 1971

hog *noun*

1 a powerful motorcyle, especially a large Harley-Davidson motorcyle *US, 1965*

• [E]ven the Angel version of the hog – which is anything but stock – can't run with the newest and best production models without extensive alterations and a very savvy rider. —Hunter S. Thompson, *Hell's Angels*, p. 95, 1966
• Across the flats of Southern California hustles a big mean hog. Ape bars, twin exhausts, chrome on everything except the rubber, this Harley is doing a ton and still hot to trot. —*Time*, p. 103, 9th September 1966
• "We'll have one hundred Hell's Angels on their hogs escort the Stones into Golden Gate Park," Grogan was quoted as saying. —Ralph "Sonny" Barger, *Hell's Angel*, p. 160, 2000
• Holy crap. This isn't just a dumb-ass bike. This is a hog. —Janet Evanovitch, *Seven Up*, p. 170, 2001

2 a utility helicopter equipped with rockets and machine guns *US*

• —Linda Reinberg, *In the Field*, p. 107, 1991

3 a Cadillac or other large luxury car *US*

• Did those oldhead mackmen who hung out at the Garden Bar think they were the only ones who could drive Hogs? —Clarence Cooper Jr, *The Scene*, p. 68, 1960
• There were ten "hogs" (Cadillacs) double parked and the big number men were operating out of every joint like they had a license. —Babs Gonzales, *I Paid My Dues*, p. 94, 1967
• I thought, "I sure gotta hurry and get my ass into a 'Hog' at least. I'll cop a Duesenberg in maybe a year." —Iceberg Slim (Robert Beck), *Pimp*, p. 128, 1969
• Sweet Peter Deeder, notoroius body peddler, ghetto entrepreneur, lounges casually against the front fender of his burgundy-colored hog[.] —Odie Hawkins, *Ghetto Sketches*, p. 12, 1972
• After five months of getting major league bread I copped me a brand new hog just like my man's. —A.S. Jackson, *Gentleman Pimp*, p. 102, 1973
• Fortunately our hog was fast / an' we had a full tank of gas. —Lightnin' Rod, *Hustlers Convention*, p. 106, 1973
• One evening Huey and a close friend named Weasel and I sat in my hog in front of my house, drinking and killing a second sick-pack of malt liquor[.] —Bobby Seale, *A Lonely Rage*, p. 187, 1978

4 the penis *US*

• —Collin Baker et al., *College Undergraduate Slang Study Conducted at Brown University*, p. 137, 1968
• [S]he snuggled right up to them guys and said to them: 'Come on, fellas, take me out in the woods and stick your big black hogs in my mouth and fuck me about twelve times[.] —George V. Higgins, *The Judgment of Deke Hunter*, p. 41, 1976

5 a police officer *US, 1970*

A variation on **PIG** (a police officer).

• As I was saying, while in my quest for the honest buck, this fat hog runs into me and calls me a fireplace pimp. —*Screw*, p. 3, 7th February 1969
• The Hogs, spits Bobby. The trio scan for the fire exit and clatter through a single door. —Mark Powell, *Snap*, p. 87, 2001

6 a US Marine Corps recruit during basic training *US, 1968*

Contemptuous.

• Okay, hogs, I've listened to you bellyache about moving to this new town. This said bellyaching will end as of 0859 hours[.] —Lewis John Carlino, *The Great Santini*, 1979

7 a leader; a strong personality *US*

• —James Harris, *A Convict's Dictionary*, 1989

8 a drug addict who requires large doses to sustain his habit *US*

• —*American Speech*, p. 26, February 1952: 'Teen-age hophead jargon'

9 heroin *US*

• Baker was the central figure in Metro's massive 'Operation Boss Hog' (Hog is street slang for heroin) in 1983[.] —*Las Vegas Review-Journal*, p. 1B, 10th September 2000

10 marijuana *US*

A term apparently coined by US soliders during the conflict in Vietnam, drawn from '*h*ash, *o*, *g*rass'.

11 phencyclidine, the recreational drug known as PCP or angel dust *US*

• —Eugene Landy, *The Underground Dictionary*, p. 104, 1971

12 a strong sedative, trade name Benaceyzine™ *US*

• —Walter L. Way, *The Drug Scene*, 1977

13 a computer program that uses a high degree of a computer's resources *US*

• —Eric S. Raymond, *The New Hacker's Dictionary*, p. 201, 1991

▸ **beat the hog**

(used of a male) to masturbate *US*

• No, I think they go home and beat the hog over them, is what I think. —George V. Higgins, *The Friends of Eddie Doyle*, p. 173, 1971

▸ **hog is pork**

there is no difference between the two alternatives being discussed *TRINIDAD AND TOBAGO*

• —Lise Winer, *Dictionary of the English/Creole of Trinidad & Tobago*, 2003

▸ **on the hog**

homosexual *US*

• —John R Armore and Joseph D. Wolfe, *Dictionary of Desperation*, 1976

hog *verb*

1 to speak rudely *TRINIDAD AND TOBAGO*

• —Lise Winer, *Dictionary of the English/Creole of Trinidad & Tobago*, 2003

2 to rape *US*

• This boy that I was with, him and this other boy hogged this Mexican that wasn't a punk. They threw him in the shitter and took all his good time. —Bruce Jackson, *In the Life*, p. 397, 1972

3 in high-low poker, to declare for both high and low *US*

• —Peter O. Steiner, *Thursday Night Poker*, p. 412, 1996

Hog-60 *noun*

an M-60 machine gun *US*

Each squad in Vietnam was assigned an M-60, the army's general purpose machine gun which entered the service in the 1950s. It was designed to be lightweight (23 pounds) and easy to carry. It produced a low 'grunting' sound and thus the porcine allusions.

• A door gunner's best friend was his hatch M-60, which many gunnies took to calling Hog-60's, though the old-timers complained a hog was a gunship and not just a small piece of the gunship's armament; but the younger hot dogs refused to listen[.] —Jack Hawkins, *Chopper One #2*, p. 27, 1987

Hogan's Alley *nickname*

the Riviera Country Club, Pacific Palisades, California *US*

Hogan enjoyed great success there, especially in 1947 and 48.

• —Michael Corcoran, *The Golf Dictionary*, p. 102, 1997

hog board *noun*

a bulletin board where soldiers post pictures of their families and girlfriends *US, 1974*

Marine usage in Vietnam.

• [C]lear the "hog board" of pictures of sweethearts and parents. —Daniel De Cruz, *Boot*, p. 96, 1987
• —Linda Reinberg, *In the Field*, p. 107, 1991

hog eye; hogger; hoghead; hogineer; hog jerk; hog jockey *noun*

a railway engineer *US*

• —Ramon Adams, *The Language of the Railroader*, p. 80, 1977

hog fuel *noun*

sawdust and bark produced by sawmills, burnt to generate steam for electricity *CANADA, 1989*

• The process is called hogging, possibly from the sound of the machine used to cut chunks in sizes small enough for easy ignition. —Tom Parkin, *WetCoast Words*, p. 69, 1989

hogging *noun*

a romantic interest in heavy people *US*

• —Ben Applebaum and Derrick Pittman, *Turd Ferguson & The Sausage Party*, p. 30, 2004

hog jaws *noun*

a special plough blade fitted to a D7E bulldozer, or Rome Plow, for use in land clearing operations in Vietnam *US*

• —Linda Reinberg, *In the Field*, p. 107, 1991

hog-leg; hog leg *noun*

1 an oversized handgun *US, 1919*

• Mr. Packard slaps his hogleg pistol. —Guy Owen, *The Flim-Flam Man and the Apprentice Grifter*, p. 13, 1972
• [A]nd the girl from the News would see it as his Dodge city pose: the daguerotype peace officer, now packing a snub-nosed .38 Smith with rubberbands around the grip instead of a hogleg .44. —Elmore Leonard, *City Primeval*, p. 35, 1980

- Spencer was holding a hog leg in his hand, the long shiny barrel pointed in his companion's direction. Loop hadn't even known that the Yankee had a hand-gun. — George Bowering, *Caprice*, 1987
- Counting the cylinder and grip, the shiny revolver is about 15 inches long and weighs seven pounds. It is, as they as, a real hogleg. — *Dallas Morning News*, p. 1A, 16th April 1995
- It's already legal in our state to strap on a hogleg; in fact, the firearms industry is free to think up new and stylish ways women and men could accessorize their Pradas and Armanis with big iron and leather. — *Santa Fe New Mexican*, p. A-7, 15th March 2001

2 a large marijuana cigarette *US*

- — Jim Emerson-Cobb, *Scratching the Dragon*, Apri 1997
- — Connie Eble (Editor), *UNC-CH Campus Slang*, p. 5, Spring 1998
- — Nick Brownlee, *This Is Cannabis*, 2002

hog liver *noun*

in electric line work, a flat porcelain guy strain insulator *US*

- — A.B. Chance Co., *Lineman's Slang Dictionary*, p. 9, 1980

hogman *noun*

a criminal who silences alarms while a crime is committed *UK*

- — Angela Devlin, *Prison Patter*, p. 62, 1996

hogmaster; hogmauler *noun*

a railway engineer *US*

- — Ramon Adams, *The Language of the Railroader*, p. 80, 1977

hog out *verb*

in motor mechanics, to enlarge an engine's openings or passages *US*

- — John Edwards, *Auto Dictionary*, p. 77, 1993

hog pen *noun*

a prison guards' control room *US*

- — Inez Cardozo-Freeman, *The Joint*, 1984

hog-tie *verb*

to bind the hands and feet *US, 1894*

- And if I ever catch ya whackin' in here again I'm gonna hog-tie ya! — Mike Judge and Joe Stillman, *Beavis and Butt-Head Do America*, p. 85, 1997

Hogtown *nickname*

Toronto *CANADA*

Nicknamed for the early C20 growth of farmer's markets and slaughterhouses, Toronto has also continued to be known as **TORONTO THE GOOD**.

- A decade later, he was Toronto-bound. He'd scarcely arrived in Hog Town, however, when he started to angle for jobs on newspapers in the Maritimes. — Harry Bruce, *Movin' East*, p. 2, 1985

hog up *verb*

to address with a lack of respect *BARBADOS*

- — Frank A. Collymore, *Barbadian Dialect*, p. 59, 1965

hog wallow *noun*

the slot used as a sighting plane on the topstrap of a Colt or Smith and Wesson pistol *US*

- — *American Speech*, p. 193, October 1957: 'Some colloquialisms of the handgunner'

hogwash *noun*

nonsense *US, 1882*

- Sure, you can sit down at night and read about the hogwash they hand out. — Mickey Spillane, *One Lonely Night*, p. 79, 1951

hog whimpering *adjective*

very drunk *UK*

- — Tom Hibbert, *Rockspeak!*, p. 85, 1983

hoha *noun*

a fuss *NEW ZEALAND*

- After a while the hoha dies down — Keri Hulme, *The Bone People*, p. 18, 1983

hoha *adjective*

weary *NEW ZEALAND*

- I get so hoha [wear] with all the negativity around. — *Dominion*, p. B5, 21st March 2003

ho-ho *noun*

a fat teenage girl *US*

- — Mary Corey and Victoria Westermark, *Fer Shurr! How to be a Valley Girl*, 1982

hoick *verb*

1 to spit *AUSTRALIA, 1941*

- He was hoeing into his Big Charlie [bubblegum] an inch at a time, giving it a good 25 crunches on either side of the mouth, blowing a bubble and then hoicking. — Paul Vautin, *Turn It Up!*, p. 22, 1995
- Just fuckin automatic like to hoik up before I spit. — Niall Griffiths, *Kelly + Victor*, 2002

2 to throw or chuck; to loft *AUSTRALIA*

- Between interstices of traveller palm an oiled wonder-boy was hoicking his board to the water. — Thea Astley, *The Acolyte*, p. 14, 1972
- I smashed my way to 70-odd in about half a dozen overs and when I got served a short one I hoicked it away high over mid wicket. — Paul Vautin, *Turn It Up!*, p. 69, 1995

3 to raise, to hoist *UK, 1898*

Sometimes spelt 'hoik'.

- They got two planks of wood and turned it into a cross. They tied him on, hoiked it up and left him hanging there. — Andy McNab, *Immediate Action*, p. 278, 1995
- A woman being pestered by an overswaddled toddler hoicked him up over the barrier and set him down in the men's area[.] — *The Observer*, 2nd February 2003

hoicked-up *adjective*

raised, especially artificially lifted *UK*

- The honey-limbed lovelies are out on the razzle in a blur of high heels, faux-Vuitton handbags, and hoicked-up bosoms. — *The Guardian*, 16th August 2003

hoi polloi *noun*

the common people; the unwashed masses *UK, 1822*

- [I]n Chicago, horny-handed, wilted hoi polloi are seen in lobbies of such swell hotels as the Ambassador and Drake in shirt-sleeves. — Jack Lait and Lee Mortimer, *Washington Confidential*, p. 4, 1951
- Not to mention, they carried germs after contact with the hoi polloi[.] — Guy Owen, *The Flim-Flam Man and the Apprentice Grifter*, p. 197, 1972
- "These aren't for you – these are for workers, civilians, the hoi polloi. This is work." Arthur made the word "work" sound like an obscenity. — Anthony Masters, *Minder*, p. 8, 1984

hoist *noun*

▸ **on the hoist**

engaged in shoplifting *UK*

- My old woman's still out on the hoist now and she's a bleeding good earner. — Frank Norman, *Bang To Rights*, p. 58, 1958

hoist *verb*

1 to drink (an alcoholic beverage) *UK*

- — Tom Hibbert, *Rockspeak!*, p. 86, 1983

2 to rob with guns *US, 1928*

- What are you going to do, man? Hoist it? — *Dazed and Confused*, 1993

3 to shoplift *UK*

- [T]hey make us look like clucking junkies hoisting down Oxford Street[.] — J.J. Connolly, *Layer Cake*, p. 93, 2000

hoister *noun*

1 a shoplifter; a pickpocket *UK, 1790*

- Most of the lady grafters I have met have been hoisters[.] — Charles Raven, *Underworld Nights*, p. 20, 1956

2 in circus and carnival usage, a ferris wheel *US*

- — Don Wilmeth, *The Language of American Popular Entertainment*, p. 131, 1981

hoisting *noun*

shoplifting *UK, 1936*

- — Angela Devlin, *Prison Patter*, p. 62, 1996

hoisting bloomers *noun*

a capacious undergarment used by shoplifters *UK*

- [T]urnover is limited to how much gear they can stow inside their hoisting bloomers. — Charles Raven, *Underworld Nights*, p. 20, 1956

hoity-toity *adjective*

snobbish, haughty, assuming, uppish *UK, 1720*

Directly from the earlier form 'highty-tighty'.

- The prime spot for a pick-up (if you're not hoity-toity) is the Central Park Mall[.] — Jack Lait and Lee Mortimer, *New York Confidential*, p. 115, 1948
- The San Remo crowd was there, virtually hanging from the rafters; the queers and phonies and hoity-toities. — Clancy Sigal, *Going Away*, p. 405, 1961
- That good-looking thing traveling with the hoity-toity blonde? — Armistead Maupin, *Further Tales of the City*, p. 222, 1982
- '[diary entry 11th November 1993] [T]oday's postbag contains a hoity-toity letter from one of my activists. — Gyles Brandreth, *Breaking the Code*, 1999
- [H]e lives in a posh snob hoity-toity house! — Ben Elton, *High Society*, p. 140, 2002

Ho Jo's *nickname*

a Howard Johnson restaurant *US*

A fixture along US motorways in the 1950s and 60s.

- [G]reet me at the hangar and whisk me off to a Jo-Jo's for a shake and fries. —John Nichols, *The Sterile Cuckoo*, p. 33, 1965

hokey; hoky; hokie *adjective*

sentimental; mawkish; in poor taste *US, 1927*

- "What is all this?" asked Polly, indicating the hokey Polynesian motif. —Max Shulman, *Anyone Got a Match?*, p. 115, 1964

hokey cokey *noun*

karaoke *UK*

Rhyming slang for a modern singalong entertainment enjoyed after a few drinks formed from the name of a song and dance that used to be enjoyed after a few drinks.

- —Ray Puxley, *Fresh Rabbit*, 1998

hokey-pokey *noun*

1 sexual intercourse *UK*

A play both on **POKE** (to have sex) and the childrens' song and dance, the 'hokey cokey'.

- —Tom Hibbert, *Rockspeak!*, p. 120, 1983

2 in circus and carnival usage, any shoddy, inexpensive merchandise *US*

- —Don Wilmeth, *The Language of American Popular Entertainment*, p. 132, 1981

hokum *noun*

nonsense *US, 1921*

- The outfit, the syndicate wanted us dead? It had to be hokum. —Iceberg Slim (Robert Beck), *Trick Baby*, p. 15, 1969

hold *noun*

in casino gambling, the amount of money bet that is retained by the casino *US*

- A table should win 20 percent of the drop. This 20 percent is called a "hold." —Mario Puzo, *Inside Las Vegas*, p. 187, 1977

▸ **in the hold**

hidden in a pocket or elsewhere on the body *US*

- You still got a dollar in the hold? —Bernard Wolfe, *The Magic of Their Singing*, p. 39, 1961

hold *verb*

1 to be in possession of drugs *US, 1935*

- —*American Speech*, p. 24, February 1952: 'Teen-age hophead jargon'
- This character's holding, but he won't turn loose of any. —William Burroughs, *Junkie*, p. 29, 1953
- And once, during those early visits down there, she was holding. —Willard Motley, *Let No Man Write My Epitaph*, p. 147, 1958
- Which reminds me. Are you holding? —Morton Cooper, *High School Confidential*, p. 69, 1958
- Don't jump the light, baby, mother's holding, you know. —Ross Russell, *The Sound*, p. 15, 1961
- "We gotta take her to her pad before the fuzz busts her." In an even more hysterical voice: "Shes holding-" —John Rechy, *City of Night*, p. 317, 1963
- "What are you holding?" "Oh, man," Danny said in disgust, "we're not junkies. We're musicians, man." —Nat Hentoff, *Jazz Country*, p. 129, 1965
- I'm afraid to go to my pad, 'cause I think some of these cats in here know what I'm holding. —Nicholas Von Hoffman, *We Are The People Our Parents Warned Us Against*, p. 37, 1967
- That wasn't even my stuff, I was holding it for a friend, man. —Cheech Marin and Tommy Chong, *Framed*, 1976
- For some reason, every dope fiend in the area could tell if you were holding. —*Drugstore Cowboy*, 1988
- I'm tellin ya ... Say, you holdin that dandy candy? —Seth Morgan, *Homeboy*, p. 17, 1990
- We fucked around until we found somebody who was holding. —Herbert Huncke, *Guilty of Everything*, p. 196, 1990
- The kid groaned to his feet – definitely holding, Rocco decided – and limped to the car. —Richard Price, *Clockers*, p. 34, 1992
- [W]earing our most freakish costumes, which was about as intelligent as carrying a sign on our backs that read "Search Me, I'm Holding". —Mick Farren, *Give the Anarchist a Cigarette*, 2001

2 to be in possession of money *US*

- I've got a thousand dollars on me. I'm afraid to go to my pad, 'cause I think some of these cats in here know what I'm holding. —Nicholas Von Hoffman, *We Are The People Our Parents Warned Us Against*, p. 37, 1967
- That means he came back, again and again. And since he wasn't the type to be holding, he avoided paying his tabs. —Leonard Shecter and William Phillips, *On the Pad*, p. 134, 1973
- —Don Wilmeth, *The Language of American Popular Entertainment*, 1981

▸ **get hold of**

to have sex with someone *UK*

- —Susie Dent, *The Language Report*, p. 76, 2003

▸ **hold court**

to get in a shoot-out with police *US*

- Are you out of your fuckin' mind? We ain't got no reason to hold court. —Donald Goines, *El Dorado Red*, p. 36–37, 1974

▸ **hold feet to the fire**

to apply great pressure and demand results *UK*

- John Major today pledged to use face-to-face talks with Sinn Fein to "hold feet to the fire" over the republican commitment to peace. —*Press Association Newsfile*, 4th May 1995
- When we ask readers what they like about InfoWorld, one of the most common answers is that we hold vendors' feet to the fire. —*InfoWorld*, p. 69, 1st September 1997

▸ **hold no brief for**

not to support or actively sympathise with someone *UK, 1918*

- I hold no brief for the Taliban, but I also hold no brief for an approach to politics which consists of demonising your opponents[.] —*The Guardian*, 11th December 2001

▸ **hold the bag**

to take the blame *US*

- Your son, unfortunately, is holding the bag. —Vincent Patrick, *Family Business*, p. 247, 1985

▸ **hold the fort; mind the fort**

to manage temporarily in an absentee's stead *UK, 1870*

- Do you want to stay here, mind the fort? —Ian Rankin, *The Falls*, p. 92, 2001

▸ **hold your dick**

to do nothing; to wait idly *UK*

- Sat outside holding his dick, first there as usual. —Kevin Sampson, *Outlaws*, p. 4, 2001

▸ **hold your mud**

to stand up to pressure and adversity *US, 1966*

- "It gets cold under those bridges." "So you couldn't hold your mud?" —Malcolm Braly, *On the Yard*, p. 31, 1967
- —*Current Slang*, p. 30, Fall 1968
- —Paul Glover, *Words from the House of the Dead*, 1974
- He's in his forties, he's a high roller, and for a long time he beat the hell out of us. You've got to respect the guy for that. And plus he held his mud. —James Mills, *The Underground Empire*, p. 539, 1986
- Just remember, homeboy. Do your own time, hold your own mud. —Seth Morgan, *Homeboy*, p. 151, 1990

▸ **hold your mug**

to keep a secret *US*

- —William D. Alsever, *Glossary for the Establishment and Other Uptight People*, p. 15, December 1970

hold down *verb*

1 to maintain (a position of employment) *US, 1896*

- [T]he Conservative MP had to look after four young children for a week and hold down two jobs to make his £70 budget stretch[.] —*The Guardian*, 16th October 2003

2 to control (a block or neighbourhood) *US*

Youth gang usage.

- —Jennifer Blowdryer, *Modern English*, p. 64, 1985

holder *noun*

a prisoner, usually not a gang member, entrusted with storing drugs controlled by a prison gang *US*

- —William K Bentley and James M. Corbett, *Prison Slang*, 1992

holding *adjective*

in possession of ready cash *AUSTRALIA, 1922*

- HOLDIN' – Possessing money. —Gilbert H. Lawson, *A Dictionary of Australian Words and Terms*, 1924
- 'How're you holding?' He was looking me straight in the eyes. Almost belligerently, as if it were a fighting question. 'We'll get by, Bo. There's only myself and the wife.' —John Morrison, *Stories of the Waterfront*, p. 33, 1962

holding ground *noun*

a position, literally or figuratively, where you can weather adversity *US*

From the nautical term for an area where the sea bottom provides a firm hold for anchors.

- —Charles F. Haywood, *Yankee Dictionary*, p. 79, 1963

holding pen *noun*

1 a cell in a local jail where prisoners are held when they first arrive, pending a decision on whether criminal charges will be filed against them or not *US*

- "Where is Leo this fine afternoon," Roscommon said. "In the holding pen," Carbone said. —George V. Higgins, *The Rat on Fire*, p. 182, 1981

2 a boarding school *NEW ZEALAND*
- Boarding-school masters would refer to the colleges as 'holding pens' for high country children who (like sheep) would be sure to return to their patch. —Michelle Dominy, *Calling the Station Home*, p. 196, 2001

holding tank *noun*
a cell at a local jail where the recently arrested are held before being processed *US*
- You're in a large holding tank; you sign in, go stand in front of another gate. —Odie Hawkins, *Lost Angeles*, p. 159, 1994

hold-it *noun*
a gratuitous television view of a pretty girl or woman, usually a spectator at a sporting event *US*
- They do this a lot, they told me, and they call it "hooking a barracuda," or a "honey shot," or, as a matter of fact, a "hold it." —Dan Jenkins, *Dead Solid Perfect*, p. 152, 1986

hold out on *verb*
to refuse to give something, often information *US, 1907*
- America has been the only country to hold out on granting access to drugs to the poorest countries, such as Botswana[.] —*The Guardian*, 8th September 2003

hold paddock *noun*
a retirement home *NEW ZEALAND*
- Waiting for God's writers are running out of ideas, credible with in the setting, a home for old people, a holding paddock as I have heard it described. —*Tablet*, p. 18, 5th June 1994

hold the bus!; haud the bus!
slow down!; wait a minute! *UK: SCOTLAND*
- Here, haud the bus. Yer shirt tail's hanging oot. —Michael Munro, *The Patter, Another Blast*, 1988

hold the phone!
wait a minute! *US*
- Now, hold the phone, counselor, you ain't talkin' to no Eighty Avenue pimp here. —Edwin Torres, *Carlito's Way*, p. 127, 1975

hold with *verb*
to agree with or approve of something or someone *UK, 1895*
- As a (lapsed) catholic Manchester United fan, I can assure Mr Bott that the Mancunian United fans (which there are quite a few of us) do not hold with the religious bigotry shown in Glasgow. —*The Guardian*, 26th July 2000

hold your horses *verb*
used imperatively to urge inaction *US, 1844*
- Hold yer horses – any more of that [an alcoholoc drink] and you'll end up as full as a state school [drunk]! —Barry Humphries, *Bazza Pulls It Off!*, 1971

hole *noun*
1 the vagina; sex with a woman; a woman; women *UK, 1592*
- "Snatch," "hole," "kooze, "slash," "pussy" and "crack" were other terms referring variously to women's genitals, to women as individuals, or to women as a species. —*Screw*, p. 5, 3rd January 1972
- —Edith A. Folb, *runnin' down some lines*, p. 242, 1980
- Goes back to when I had my first hole. First proper gooose and all that. —Kevin Sampson, *Clubland*, p. 84, 2002

2 the anus *UK, 1607*
- [S]tick this f'ing pitchfork up your hole[.] —Graham Linehan and Arthur Matthews, *And God Created Women (Father Ted, Series 1, Episode 5)*, 1995

3 the mouth *US, 1865*
- Shut your hole about my old man. —Irving Shulman, *The Amboy Dukes*, p. 26, 1947
- Aw, shut your big hole! —George Mandel, *Flee the Angry Strangers*, p. 247, 1952
- Shut your hole, Mae; youre swishing so much youre going to make a hurricane[.] —John Rechy, *City of Night*, p. 203, 1963
- [H]e's a goddam nigger-lover ... now, jest shut your hole an' git on over yonder an' check them leg-irons. —Terry Southern, *Texas Summer*, p. 75, 1991

4 a passive, promiscuous, unattached lesbian *US*
- —William K Bentley and James M. Corbett, *Prison Slang*, 1992

5 in prison, a cell designed for solitary confinement *UK, 1535*
Always with 'the'.
- Filth is an important part of hole therapy. —Clarence Cooper Jr, *The Farm*, p. 79, 1967
- When I asked for books to read in this particular hole, a trustee brought me a list from which to make selections. —Eldridge Cleaver, *Soul on Ice*, p. 34, 1968
- So they throwed us in the hole. —Bruce Jackson, *In the Life*, p. 116, 1972
- Zuzu said we was only playing, but they gave me thirty days in the hole. —Edwin Torres, *Carlito's Way*, p. 46, 1975
- "I want this punk in the hole," the black guard breathed heavily, tired by his bloody workout. —Bobby Seale, *A Lonely Rage*, p. 258, 1978
- Next thing I know I'm in the hole. Solitary confinement. —*Raging Bull*, 1980

6 an undesirable place; a place that is dirty or disordered *UK, 1876*
- I tell the Feds I am SO not sharing a cell with him, or with the guy from The Commitments, roysh [right], and they put me in one by myself and it's a bit of a hole. —Paul Howard, *The Teenage Dirtbag Years*, p. 39, 2001

7 any place where a supply of illegal drugs is hidden *US*
- "The homies talking about getting back the 'hole,' so if you see it on fire, don't trip (panic)." A "hole" is street slang for a place where drugs are stashed. —*Los Angeles Times*, p. B3, 27th May 1993

8 a monetary or social difficulty, a mess, a scrape *UK, 1760*
- [Y]ou don't have to be too near the Welsh camp to know that Graham Henry is in a bit of a hole. —*The Observer*, 18th November 2001
- Organisers in a hole over state of Shinnecock[.] —*The Guardian*, 22nd June 2004

9 the subway (underground) *US, 1933*
- —*New York Times Magazine*, p. 88, 16th March 1958
- That's why there was so much fury when they were taken out of "the hole" and replaced by Transit Authority cops. —Leonard Shecter and William Phillips, *On the Pad*, p. 159, 1973

10 a mine *US*
- Had a big one back in '68, up to Farmington. One of Consolidation's holes. —John Sayles, *Union Dues*, p. 158, 1977

11 on the railways, a passing track *US*
- —Norman Carlisle, *The Modern Wonder Book of Trains and Railroading*, p. 264, 1946

12 in trucking, a position in the gear box *US*
- —Montie Tak, *Truck Talk*, p. 84, 1971

13 a tobacco cigarette *US*
- —Eugene Landy, *The Underground Dictionary*, p. 67, 1971

14 in drag racing, the starting line *US*
- In a race, the first driver off the starting line is first out of the hole. —Ed Radlauer, *Drag Racing Pix Dix*, p. 28, 1970

▸ **after his hole; after his end**
of a man, to be seeking sex with a woman *UK, 1961*
From **HOLE** (the vagina) or **END** (the penis).

▸ **get your hole**
to have sexual intercourse *IRELAND*
- Actually getting his hole wasn't what he was after at all – he just wanted to know if he could get his hole. —Roddy Doyle, *The Van*, p. 256, 1991

▸ **go in the hole**
to fall from a pole, tower, rig or building under construction *US*
- If you had to fall, he told her, try to do it inside the structure, because they decked in every other floor as they bolted up. But either way, falling inside or out, it was called "going in the hole." —Elmore Leonard, *Killshot*, p. 35, 1989

▸ **in the hole**
in police usage, hiding and avoiding work *US*
- He was telling me things he probably told his young partners during lonely hours after two a.m. when you're fighting to keep awake or when you're 'in the hole' trying to hide your radio car, in some alley where you can doze uncomfortably for an hour, but you never really rest. —Joseph Wambaugh, *The Blue Knight*, p. 92, 1973

hole bit *noun*
while in prison, a sentence to solitary confinement *US*
- That's enough to get you a holebit in any joint. —Clarence Cooper Jr, *The Farm*, p. 78, 1967

hole card *noun*
1 in stud poker, a card dealt face-down *US*
- —Albert H. Morehead, *The Complete Guide to Winning Poker*, p. 265, 1967

2 a resource in reserve *US, 1926*
- I also know that if I give up that gun it's a probation violation vis-a-fucking-vis harboring contraband items. You know what a 'hole card' is? —James Ellroy, *White Jazz*, p. 73, 1992

3 the key to a person's character *US*
From the game of stud poker, in which a 'hole card' is a card dealt face-down.

- People peeped your hole card then, knew where you were at. —Nathan Heard, *Howard Street*, p. 181, 1968
- I've seen him damn near every day and I wasn't hip to his hole card. —A.S. Jackson, *Gentleman Pimp*, p. 104, 1973
- —Stewart L. Tubbs and Sylvia Moss, *Human Communication*, p. 121, 1974
- I thought you were a mackman, a master at the Game; But I peeped your hole card, you're a funny-time lame. —Dennis Wepman et al., *The Life*, p. 39, 1976
- I regarded him flatly and said, "Yeah, you did. Now I know your hole card." —Peter Coyote, *Sleeping Where I Fall*, p. 313, 1998

hole-in-one *noun*
sexual intercourse on a first date *US*
A puerile golf metaphor.
- —Robert A. Wilson, *Playboy's Book of Forbidden Words*, p. 140, 1972

hole in the ground; hole *noun*
a pound *UK*
Rhyming slang.
- —Ray Puxley, *Cockney Rabbit*, 1992

hole in the head *noun*
the epitome of something that is not needed at all *US, 1951*
From Yiddish.
- The Vatican needs this like a hole in the head.— *The Guardian*, 13th December 2000
- "I'm not necessarily against the Olympics," said Claire Shulman, the Queens borough president, "but New York City needs the Olympics like a hole in the head." — *The Observer*, 18th May 2003

hole in the wall *noun*
1 an automated cash machine *UK, 1985*
- [H]e needed to draw out some cash. He went to the hole in the wall, then showed me his balance. —Sally Cline, *Couples*, p. 198, 1998
- If we did [robbed] cashpoints [...] we could be the hole-in-the-wall gang. —Cath Staincliffe, *Trainers*, p. 59, 1999
- But hey, that hole in the wall's darned handy. —*Evening Post*, 5th May 2001

2 in trucking, a tunnel *US*
- —Wayne Floyd, *Jason's Authentic Dictionary of CB Slang*, p. 18, 1976
- —Peter Chippindale, *The British CB Book*, 1981

hole olie *noun*
in stud poker, a card dealt face-down *US*
A jocular embellishment of **HOLE CARD**.
- —Albert H. Morehead, *The Complete Guide to Winning Poker*, p. 265, 1967

holes *noun*
▸ **the holes**
a location, such as a public lavatory, where men may have anonymous sex with each other by means of holes bored between private cubicles *UK*
- At the holes – better than the fake baths that barely exist or the tea room pop-ups or faggot bars[.] —Peter Sotos, *Index*, p. 12, 1996

hole shot *noun*
in drag racing, the art of starting at the first possible moment without incurring a foul for starting too soon *US*
- Many a driver has won over a faster car because he could pull hole shots. —Ed Radlauer, *Drag Racing Pix Dix*, p. 28, 1970

holetime *noun*
solitary confinement in prison *US*
- doing holetime. —Clarence Cooper Jr, *The Farm*, p. 81, 1967

hole to bowl *noun*
the path taken during defecation on a toilet *US*
- Annette belched, grunted and farted; the turds said SWOOSH and shot from hole to bowl. —Steve Cannon, *Groove, Bang, and Jive Around*, p. 6, 1969

hole up *verb*
to hide *UK, 1875*
- Last night a small group of up to 40 volunteers were still holed up in a house in the corner of the castle's rambling compound. —*The Guardian*, 27th November 2001

holey dollar *noun*
a Spanish dollar with a hole punched in the centre *CANADA*
- In order to prevent the citizens from taking the coins off the Island to areas where the exchange rate was higher, the authorities punched out the centre. The punched out disc was used as a shilling while the outer rim retained the 5s. Halifax value. —*Commercial Letter*, p. 6/2, January 1963
- The Holey Dollar is now a rare collector's item. —H.C. Taylor, *Canadian Coins*, p. 19, 1964

-holic *suffix*
▹ see: **-AHOLIC**

holiday *noun*
in horse racing, the term of a suspension from competing *AUSTRALIA*
- —Ned Wallish, *The Truth Dictionary of Racing Slang*, p. 38, 1989

Holiday Inn *noun*
any large US base camp in Vietnam where field troops would stand down for several days before returning to combat in the field *US*
- —Gregory Clark, *Words of the Vietnam War*, p. 233, 1986

HOLLAND
written on an envelope, or at the foot of a lover's letter as lovers' code for '*h*ere *o*ur *l*ove *l*ies *a*nd *n*ever *d*ies' or '*h*ope *o*ur *l*ove *l*asts *a*nd *n*ever *d*ies' *UK, 1984*
Widely known, and well used by servicemen; now a part of the coded vocabulary of texting.
- —Andrew John with Stephen Blake, *The Total TxtMsg Dictionary*, p. 137, 2001

holler *verb*
to talk *US*
- — *Milwaukee Journal-Sentinel*, 5th March 2001

holler *adjective*
stylish *US*
- Them holler drapes Vann wears out in front of his band is just too much, man. —Ross Russell, *The Sound*, p. 109, 1961

holler and hoot *verb*
to engage in an abusive verbal attack *UK*
- —Dave Courtney, *Dodgy Dave's Little Black Book*, p. 7, 2001

holler and shout *noun*
a German *UK*
Rhyming slang for **KRAUT**.
- —Ray Puxley, *Cockney Rabbit*, 1992

holler boys holler; holler boys *noun*
a collar *UK*
Old rhyming slang, originally 'holloa boys', 'holloa', from a chant used on Guy Fawkes night, with a use dating back to the time of the detachable collar. Modern use is reduced to the first two elements and often without the 'h'.
- —Julian Franklyn, *A Dictionary of Rhyming Slang*, 1960

holli *noun*
a marijuana cigarette which is placed in a pipe for smoking *US*
- — *www.addictions.org*, 2001

holliers; hollyers *noun*
holidays, vacation *IRELAND*
- He couldn't wait to get up and out in the mornings, like a fuckin' kid on his summer holliers. —Roddy Doyle, *The Van*, p. 86, 1991
- Unfamiliar faces like, maybes on their hollyers[.] —Niall Griffiths, *Kelly + Victor*, p. 56, 2002

hollow leg *noun*
a characteristic ascribed to someone who is able to eat or drink in great quantities *US*
- For him, alcohol acted as a stimulant, putting him in a euphoric state, and he developed a high capacity for it – a "hollow leg," as it is often called. He could drink large quantities because of the way his body processed alcohol. —Charlotte S. Kasl, *Many Roads One Journey*, p. 128, 1992

Hollyweird *nickname*
Hollywood, California *US*
- Playing on the at times bizarre nature of the city. John Wayne (of Hollyweird) doing the La Vie En Rose sector with a big party; Wayne, Women & Song. — *Nevada State Journal*, 8th February 1953
- We're going to Hollyweird, homeboys, he said. —James Ellroy, *Suicide Hill*, p. 722, 1986

Hollywood *noun*
1 used as a teasing term of address for someone whose clothes and mannerisms suggest a high level of showmanship *US*
- —Malachi Andrews and Paul T. Owens, *Black Language*, p. 86, 1973

2 a dramatic outburst *NEW ZEALAND*
- The accused shouted and argued with the police for the benefit of his friends. 'In other words, you did a Holllywood,' said Judge Gilbert. — *Evening Post*, p. 5, 9th March 1983

3 a feigned injury *NEW ZEALAND*
- He accuses players of pulling Hollywoods. 'Sometimes, players have even feigned injury just for a few minutes spell'. — *Truth*, p. 37, 18th July 1972

4 in hot rodding, an extravagent, ostentatious exhuast system *US*
- — *Good Housekeeping*, p. 143, September 1958: 'Hot-rod terms for teen-age girls'
- — Tom MacPherson, *Dragging and Driving*, p. 139, 1960

Hollywood glider *noun*
the B-17 Flying Fortress *US*
The B-17 appeared frequently in films.
- — *American Speech*, p. 310, December 1946: 'More Air Force slang'

Hollywood no *noun*
an answer of 'no' implicit in the failure to return a phone call *US*
- Confused because the production executive hot in pursuit of your screenplay last week isn't returning your calls this week? Well, meet the Hollywood "no." "Hollywood is the most masterful town in regard to saying 'no' without saying 'no'." — *Los Angeles Times*, p. 19 (Calendar), 16th August 1992

Hollywoods *noun*
dark glasses *US*
- — Andy Anonymous, *A Basic Guide to Campusology*, p. 14, 1966

Hollywood shower *noun*
in Antarctica, a shower that exceeds the two-minute showers permitted by military authorities *ANTARCTICA*
- — *Cool Antarctica*, 2003: 'Antarctic slang'

Hollywood stop *noun*
a rolling stop at a traffic signal or a stop sign *US, 1986*
- — Jeffrey McQuain, *Never Enough Words*, p. 54, 1999

Holmes *noun*
used as a term of address from male-to-male *US*
Playing on the term 'homes'.
- Look here, Holmes, you got to dig yo'self. — Edwin Torres, *Carlito's Way*, p. 21, 1975
- I think they just got out the cop car, Holmes. — *Menace II Society*, 1993

hols *noun*
*hol*idays (both singular and plural), a vacation *UK, 1905*
- Too bad you couldn't get home for the hols. — Derek Bickerton, *Payroll*, p. 31, 1959
- And finally, have you considered keeping your hols intact by taking sick leave on the big day instead? — *Sydney Morning Herald*, 12th July 2003

Holstein *noun*
a police car *US*
An allusion to the black and white markings of the cow and a police car.
- — *American Speech*, p. 273, December 1961: 'Northwest truck drivers' language'
- — Wayne Floyd, *Jason's Authentic Dictionary of CB Slang*, p. 19, 1976

holy *adjective*
great, extreme
- PW: How about the bike? JOE: Yes, give it holy stick down the road. — Paul E. Willis, *Profane Culture*, p. 75, 1978

holy cats!
used for registering surprise, shock or alarm *US*
- Holy cats! Look at you. You look just like that singer. — Janet Evanovich, *Seven Up*, p. 257, 2001

holy chain lightning!
used as a mild oath in Nova Scotia *CANADA*
- — Harry Bruce, *Down Home*, p. 107, 1988

holy city *noun*
in poker, a high-value hand *US*
- — George Percy, *The Language of Poker*, p. 44, 1988

holy cow!
used as a mild oath, expressing surprise *US, 1927*
Popularised by baseball radio announcers Harry Caray and Phil Rizzuto.
- "And then and there he assaulted the widow four times, you should excuse the expression." "Holy cow!" whistled Nebbice. "Four times!" — Max Shulman, *The Zebra Derby*, p. 79, 1946
- James McParlan II. Junior. James McParlan. Holy Cow. — Clancy Sigal, *Going Away*, p. 179, 1961
- Holy cow! — *Lethal Weapon*, 1987

holy crap!
used for registering surprise *US*
A variation of **HOLY SHIT**.
- Our mouths all dropped open. And we all made the sign of the cross. "Holy crap," Carolli said. "You shot Jesus. That's gonna take a lot of Hail Marys." — Janet Evanovich, *Seven Up*, p. 88, 2001

Holyfield *noun*
fine quality marijuana
A neat pun using the name of three-time world heavyweight champion boxer Evander 'Real Deal' Holyfield (b.1962); here 'holy' implies 'the purest' and combines with a 'field (of grass)', and Holyfield's nickname 'Real Deal' guarantees the quality.
- [H]e'd sold some nastiness [inferior drugs] instead of the Holyfield[.] — Diran Adebayo, *My Once Upon A Time*, p. 20, 2000

Holyfield's ear; 'olyfields *noun*
a year *UK*
Rhyming slang, formed in honour of boxer Evander Holyfield, whose ear was bitten by his opponent Mike Tyson during a 1997 world heavyweight title fight.
- — Ray Puxley, *Fresh Rabbit*, 1998

holy fuck!
used for registering shock or surprise *US*
- — *Rambo, First Blood*, 1982

holy ghost *noun*
1 the corpse of a person who has died from gunshot wounds *US*
- — *Maledicta*, p. 180, Summer/Winter 1986–1987: 'Sexual slang: prostitutes, pedophiles, flagellators, transvestites, and necrophiles'

2 a coast *UK: SCOTLAND*
Glasgow rhyming slang.
- Fancy a wee run doon the holy ghost if it's nice the morra? — Michael Munro, *The Patter, Another Blast*, 1988

3 in racing, the starting post or the winning post *UK, 1932*
Rhyming slang.
- The runners are at the holy. — Ray Puxley, *Cockney Rabbit*, 1992

4 toast *UK*
Rhyming slang.
- — Julian Franklyn, *A Dictionary of Rhyming Slang*, 1960
- [A] slice of holy. — Ray Puxley, *Cockney Rabbit*, 1992

holy guacamole!
used satirically as a register of shock or surprise *UK*
'Guacamole' is pronounced to rhyme with 'holy'.
- — *Loaded*, p. 30, June 2003

Holy Joe *noun*
any religious leader *US, 1864*
The term suggests a lack of sincerity.
- — Jerry Robertson, *Oil Slanguage*, p. 66, 1954
- I tried, of course to enlist Jeff as a fellow conspirator but he was the most violent Holy Joe of the bunch. — Frederick Kohner, *Gidget*, p. 80, 1957
- — R. Frederick West, *God's Gambler*, p. 226, 1964: 'Appendix A'

Holy Lands *noun*
an area of central Belfast *UK: NORTHERN IRELAND*
Named for its principal arteries: Damascus Street, Jerusulam Street and Canterbury Street.
- [H]e set up a small-scale business selling pills and blow in Central Belfast's "Holy Lands".] — Chris Ryan, *The Watchman*, p. 4, 2001

holy man!
used as a powerful exclamation *US*
Michigan Upper Peninsula usage.
- — *www.ring.com/yooper/glossary.htm*,

holy moley!
used as an all-purpose exclamation *US*
Jocular and lighthearted.
- Holy moley, Batman, what do we have here? — Mick Farren, *Give the Anarchist a Cigarette*, p. 71–72, 2001

holy moo cow!
used as an expression of complete surprise *US*
A jocular embellishment of the more common **HOLY COW!**
- — Collin Baker et al., *College Undergraduate Slang Study Conducted at Brown University*, p. 138, 1968

holy nail *noun*
bail *UK*
Rhyming slang.
• —Ray Puxley, *Cockney Rabbit*, 1992

holy of holies *noun*
1 the vagina *US*
A crude pun on **HOLE**.
• JULES: Look, maybe your method of massage differs from mine, but touchin' his lady's feet, and stickin' your tongue in her holyiest of holyies, ain't the same ballpark, ain't the same league, ain't even the same fuckin' sport.—*Pulp Fiction*, 1994
2 any inner sanctum *US*
• And their cash flows from the tables to our boxes, through the cage and into the most sacred room in the casino, the place where they add up all the money, the holy of holies, the count room.—*Casino*, 1995

holy oil *noun*
an oil applied to the skin or clothing in the belief that it will bring the bettor luck in an illegal number gambling lottery, *US*
• —*American Speech*, p. 192, October 1949

holy old mackinaw!
used as a curse *CANADA, 1988*
• [T]hese were curse-word combinations I'd never heard before: the milder "holy old mackinaw"[.]—Harry Bruce, *Down Home*, p. 107, 1988

holy old snappin' arseholes!
used as an oath in Nova Scotia with allusions to both the lobster and fear *CANADA*
• I could detect the Maritimer in the crowd just by listening to the talk: holy old snappin' arseholes.—Harry Bruce, *Down Home*, p. 106–107, 1988

holy olie *noun*
in stud poker, the hole card *US*
• —*American Speech*, p. 99, May 1951: 'The vocabulary of poker'

holy shit
used for registering astonishment *US*
• "You said you only know how to jump out of them." "Holy shit." —Robert Ludlum, *The Bourne Supremacy*, p. 499, 1986
• "Who's his sister? Do I know her?" "Estelle Colucci. Benny Colucci's wife." Holy shit. "Small world."—Janet Evanovich, *Seven Up*, p. 81, 2001

holy show *adjective*
an embarrassment, a ridiculous sight *IRELAND*
• 'No, we'll check it afterwards,' I said, not wanting to make a holy show of myself counting out money in front of her.—Billy Roche, *Tumbling Down*, p. 22, 1984
• I was a holy show altogether with my skirt at half mast.—*Limerick Leader*, 14th July 2001

holy smoke *noun*
branded soft drink Coca-Cola™, Coke™ *UK*
Rhyming slang, originally used of the solid fuel.
• —Ray Puxley, *Cockney Rabbit*, 1992

holy smoke!
used as an exclamation of surprise and wonder *UK, 1892*
• Holy smokes, goddamn and all ye falling candles of heaven smash[!]—Jack Kerouac, *The Dharma Bums*, p. 94, 1958

holy snappin'!
used as a curse or oath *CANADA, 1982*
• "Holy snappin'," said Denny. "No harm tryin', anyways."—Silver Donald Cameron, *The Baitchopper*, p. 50, 1982

holy Toledo!
used for registering surprise *US*
A little bit of Holy Toledo goes a long way. A trademark of Milo Hamilton, radio broadcaster for the Houston Astros baseball team, and often used by Skipper, the son of Jungle Jim on *Jungle Jim* (1955).
• "Holy Toledo!" said Petey reverently. He plunged his hands into the racoon coat and then his face. "Holy Toledo!" he repeated fifteen or twenty times.—Max Shulman, *The Many Loves of Dobie Gillis*, p. 42, 1951

holy war *noun*
a debate among computer enthusiasts about a question which has no objective answer *US*
• The characteristic that distinguishes holy wars from normal technical disputes is that in a holy war most of the participants spend their time trying to pass off personal value choices and cultural attachments as objective technical evaluations.—Eric S. Raymond, *The New Hacker's Dictionary*, p. 201, 1991

holy water *noun*
1 official approval *US*
US naval aviator usage; to give such approval is to 'sprinkle holy water'.
• —*United States Naval Institute Proceedings*, p. 108, October 1986
2 a daughter *UK*
Rhyming slang.
• —Ray Puxley, *Cockney Rabbit*, 1992

holy weed *noun*
marijuana *US, 2001*
• —Simon Worman, *Joint Smoking Rules*, 2001

holy week *noun*
the bleed period of a woman's menstrual cycle *US*
• —Roger Blake, *The American Dictionary of Sexual Terms*, p. 98, 1964
• —Robert A. Wilson, *Playboy's Book of Forbidden Words*, p. 140, 1972

holy whistlin' frig!
used as a curse in Nova Scotia *CANADA, 1988*
• [T]he milder "holy whistlin' frig" (it was only the politer guys who used the euphemism "frig.")—Harry Bruce, *Down Home*, p. 107, 1988

hom *verb*
▸ **hom it up**
to flaunt your homosexuality *UK*
Substitutes an abbreviation of 'homosexual' for **CAMP** (affected) in 'camp it up' (to flaunt affectation).
• Dead camp and that, mind you, but I don't mind all that – mincing and homming it up and that.—Kevin Sampson, *Outlaws*, p. 222, 2001

hombre *noun*
1 a man *US, 1846*
Spanish *hombre* (a man), spread worldwide by Hollywood Westerns such as *Hombre*, 1967, starring Paul Newman.
• At one point the battalion XO, Major Charles Brown, took me aside to tell me Colonel Locke was one mean hombre, the worst-tempered, toughest guy he'd ever worked for.—David H. Hackworth, *About Face*, p. 233, 1989
2 a male friend *UK*
Adapted from the previous sense; this usage possibly informed by a phonetic similarity to **HOMEBOY** (a close friend).
• He's not that thrilled about [...] having to let on in front of his Yardie hombres, but he says all right anyway.—Kevin Sampson, *Outlaws*, p. 137–138, 2001
3 heroin *US, 1998*
From Spanish *hombre* (a man).
• —Robert Ashton, *This Is Heroin*, p. 206, 2002
• —Mike Haskins, *Drugs*, p. 284, 2003

home *noun*
1 a very close male friend *US, 1944*
An abbreviation of **HOMEBOY**.
• You know you fuck with me you got the whole population of homes on your untainted ass.—Elmore Leonard, *Riding the Rap*, p. 55, 1995
2 the vein into which an intravenous drug user injects a drug *US*
• —David Maurer and Victor Vogel, *Narcotics and Narcotic Addiction*, p. 415, 1973

▸ **at home in the going**
in horse racing, said of a horse that is running a track that complements the horse's skills and preferences *US*
• —David W. Maurer, *Argot of the Racetrack*, p. 11, 1951

▸ **go home**
to be released from prison *US*
• [O]ne of the blocks of numbers that made up the new year was the date on which he would leave the prison – "go home" was the universal expression[.]—Malcolm Braly, *On the Yard*, p. 160, 1967

▸ **send home**
to sentence to prison *US*
• He'd be sporting shanks like a human porcupine before he was processed through Receiving and Release the next time he was sent home.—Seth Morgan, *Homeboy*, p. 44, 1990

Home *nickname*
England or Great Britain *AUSTRALIA, 1808*
As used by C18–19 colonists this is par for the course, and that their direct descendants would use this also is hardly surprising, however, this locution remained in common use (in speech, if not

by self-conscious writers) well into C20 and only began to die out in the 1970s. Now it is very much a thing of the past.
- My father always referred to England as 'Home'; in fact England was 'Home' to most of our friends. — D.E. Charlwood, *All the Green Year*, p. 5, 1965
- When they go Home (to England) by ship; many Australians cross the Great Australian Bight, go green, and chunder. — Arthur Chipper, *The Aussie Swearer's Guide*, 1972

home and dry *adjective*
safe and sound; having accomplished an arduous task *UK, 1930*
- If the American elections were to be won on complexions, Al Gore would be home and dry. — *The Guardian*, 14th November 2000

home and hosed *adjective*
1 (of a racehorse) expected to win *AUSTRALIA*
- A trainer was telling his mate about his horse, a maiden called Lunch. 'It's in the first tomorrow, and it is home and hosed. It will open in the betting at 25/1. Get on early.' — Frank Hardy and Athol George Mulley, *The Needy and the Greedy*, p. 82, 1975
- — Ned Wallish, *The Truth Dictionary of Racing Slang*, 1989

2 all finished and done with *AUSTRALIA, 1945*
Said of a task that is easily accomplished.
- You'll be home and hosed in no time. — Alexander Buzo, *Rooted*, p. 70, 1969

homebake *noun*
morphine or heroin extracted from codeine compounds *NEW ZEALAND*
- 'In New Zealand we make or own. It isn't heroin, it's something called homebake, which is usually produced from medicines used for legitimate purposes,' executive director Sally Jackman says. — *Dominion*, p. 9, 12th April 2002

homebaker *noun*
a person who illegally manufactures drugs *NEW ZEALAND*
- Homebakers usually sell by the millilitre. That amount is considered to be a 'hit'. — *Evening Post*, p. 19, 5th April 1986

home base; home run *noun*
in the teenage categorisation of sexual activity, sexual intercourse *US, 1963*
- Why bother with first base? I'd go right the home run. — *M*A*S*H*, 1970
- "Did you at least get to home base?" "Who knows. I couldn't tell with that lousy condom." — C.D. Payne, *Youth in Revolt*, p. 157, 1993

home box *noun*
a computer enthusiast's own computer *US*
- Yeah? Well, my home box runs a full 4.2 BSD, so there! — Eric S. Raymond, *The New Hacker's Dictionary*, p. 201, 1991

homeboy *noun*
a very close male friend, often but not always from the same neighbourhood *US, 1899*
- He nearly dropped the powder can. "My homeboy! Man, gimme some skin! I'm from Lansing. — Malcolm X and Alex Haley, *The Autobiography of Malcolm X*, p. 44, 1964
- Don't put on a brave act with me, home-boy. — Piri Thomas, *Down These Mean Streets*, p. 114, 1967
- — *Amerian Speech*, p. 238–239, October 1967: 'Slang at a negro college: "homeboy"'
- Home boy, them Brothers is taking care of Business! — Eldridge Cleaver, *Soul on Ice*, p. 26, 1968
- Like, "you my homeboy, and the dude who ain't from around here, he ain't one of us." — H. Rap Brown, *Die Nigger Die!*, p. 16, 1969
- What was it all about, home boy? — Vernon E. Smith, *The Jones Men*, p. 61, 1974
- A homeboy was someone you trusted more than money, and Joe trusted Rigoletto less than himself. — Seth Morgan, *Homeboy*, p. 13, 1990
- You say it, homeboy. — Jess Mowry, *Way Past Cool*, p. 22, 1992
- Listen up man, me an' my homeboy are in some serious shit. — *Pulp Fiction*, 1994

home cooking *noun*
sex with your spouse *US*
- — Roger Blake, *The American Dictionary of Sexual Terms*, p. 98, 1964
- — Dale Gordon, *The Dominion Sex Dictionary*, p. 83, 1967

homee *noun*
▷ see: OMEE

home ec *noun*
home economics, in which the theory and practice of homemaking are studied *US, 1899*
- Nobody but a queer would teach home ec anyway. — Larry McMurtry, *The Last Picture Show*, p. 59, 1966
- MRS. CHASEN: What are you studying? CANDY: Poli sci. With a home ec minor. — *Harold and Maude*, 1971

home-ec-y *adjective*
(used of a girl) conventional, out of touch with current fashions, styles and trends *US*
- — *Current Slang*, p. 19, Spring 1970

homee-palone *noun*
▷ see: OMEE-PALONE

homegirl *noun*
a very close female friend, usually from the same neighbourhood, gang or faction of a gang; usually applied to a black girl *US, 1934*
- You really playin with power there, homegirl! — Jess Mowry, *Way Past Cool*, p. 28, 1992
- The white home-girl ebonics had vanished now. — Francesca Lia Block, *I Was a Teenage Fairy*, p. 78, 1998
- I just called my homegirl, Amber, just before you got here, and she was talkin' crazy about how she was gonna kill herself and how I should get her funeral clothes together. — *Rolling Stone*, p. 80, 12th April 2001

homegrown *noun*
marijuana, cultivated locally *US, 1974*
- [S]moking my way through a biscuit tin of wicked home grown. — Lanre Fehintola, *Charlie Says...*, p. 114, 2000

homeguard *noun*
a local worker, as contrasted with a travelling or migratory worker; a local resident *US, 1903*
- — Norman Carlisle, *The Modern Wonder Book of Trains and Railroading*, p. 264, 1946
- We both know it's never a good idea to play for [swindle] a home guard. — Iceberg Slim (Robert Beck), *Trick Baby*, p. 36, 1969

homemade *noun*
1 a cigarette rolled by hand from loose tobacco *US*
- [F]ellow who would take the news of the Apocalypse with corrugated eyes and two fingers rolling a homemade and a drawleed "Ay-uh." — Bernard Wolfe, *The Late Risers*, p. 162, 1954

2 a home-made pistol *US*
- Well, one thing, he can make as pretty a home-made as you want. — Hal Ellson, *Duke*, p. 75, 1949

home on the range *noun*
change *AUSTRALIA*
Rhyming slang.
- — Ned Wallish, *The Truth Dictionary of Racing Slang*, p. 38, 1989

home on the range *adjective*
strange *UK*
Rhyming slang, formed from the title of a well-known cowboy anthem (actually, the official song of the state of Kansas).
- — Ray Puxley, *Fresh Rabbit*, 1998

home plate *noun*
an aeroplane's home base or carrier *US*
- While there's a break here we'd like to run out and get some gas from our home plate. — Gerry Carroll, *North S*A*R*, p. 75, 1991

home port *noun*
a trucker's residence *US*
Jocular use.
- — Lanie Dills, *The Official CB Slanguage Language Dictionary*, p. 40, 1976

homer *noun*
1 a job done privately by a tradesman outside of his regular employment *UK: SCOTLAND*
Glasgow slang.
- Ah'll get that done for ye cheaper than that. Ah know a wee sparkie [electrician] that does homers. — Michael Munro, *The Complete Patter*, p. 77, 1996

2 a wound sufficiently serious to require treatment away from the theatre of war *AUSTRALIA, 1945*

3 a referee or sports official who favours the home team *US, 1888*
- — Zander Hollander and Sandy Padwe, *Basketball Lingo*, p. 56, 1971

Homer *noun*
any Iraqi soldier *US*
Gulf war usage; an allusion to the doltish Homer Simpson of television cartoon fame.
- — *American Speech*, p. 391, Winter 1991: 'Among the new words'

homers *noun*
home-brewed beer *AUSTRALIA, 1970*
A gift to the slang of the South Pole from its Australian visitors.
- —Bernadette Hince, *The Antarctic Dictionary*, p. 168, 2000

home run *noun*
the journey of a circus from the final engagement of the season to the winter quarters *US*
- —Joe McKennon, *Circus Lingo*, p. 4649, 1980

▷ see: HOME BASE

▸ **hit a home run**
to have sex *US*
- Another way to say "intercourse" [...] Hitting a home run[.]—Erica Orloff and JoAnn Baker, *Dirty Little Secrets*, p. 63, 2001

homerunner *noun*
an artillery shell that hits its target directly *US*
- —Linda Reinberg, *In the Field*, p. 107, 1991

homes *noun*
used as a term of address, usually establishing comrade status *US, 1971*
- MARSELLUS: I'm gonna call a coupla pipe-hittin' niggers who'll go to work on homes here with a pair of pliers and a blow torch.—*Pulp Fiction*, 1994

home skillet *noun*
a close friend *US*
- —*Merriam-Webster's Hot Words on Campus Marketing Survey '93*, p. 2, 13th October 1993

homeslice *noun*
1 a close friend *US, 1984*
- A good friend is a homeslice, dog or, simply, G.—*Chicago Tribune*, p. C7, 9th January 1994
- —Ethan Hilderbrant, *Prison Slang*, 1998
- "They're my brown brothers. My home slice."—Stephen J. Cannell, *The Tin Collectors*, p. 36, 2001

2 a prisoner from your home city *US*
- —William K Bentley and James M. Corbett, *Prison Slang*, 1992

homesteader *noun*
1 an American who had been in Vietnam for more than a few years *US*
- Some homesteaders stayed in Vietnam for up to 10 years and raised families there.—Linda Reinberg, *In the Field*, p. 107, 1991

2 a person who is dating one person steadily *US*
High school usage.
- —*Washington Post*, 23rd April 1961: 'Man, dig this jazz'

Homesteader's Bible *noun*
the Eaton department store catalogue *CANADA*
- The homesteader's bible was not the big family Bible that had been carried carefully all the way from the "go back land" to this new home. It was the mail-order catalogue-from T. Eaton, for prairie homesteaders. Also known as the wish book.—Chris Thain, *Cold as a Bay Street Banker's Heart*, p. 84–85, 1987

homesteader's fiddle *noun*
a cross-cut saw *CANADA*
- The monotonous swish of the crosscut saw, which, away down south in the Peace River country, I had some to know as "the homesteader's fiddle."—R.M. Patterson, *The Dangerous River*, p. 174, 1954

home sweet home *noun*
in circus and carnival usage, the final performance of a season *US*
- —Don Wilmeth, *The Language of American Popular Entertainment*, p. 132, 1981

hometown honey *noun*
a college student's date from their hometown *US*
- —Collin Baker et al., *College Undergraduate Slang Study Conducted at Brown University*, p. 138, 1968
- His conversation with soon loaded with "brew" and "beevo," with talk of "hometown honeys" and things being "gross."—John Sayles, *Union Dues*, p. 278, 1977
- Is Brtiney Spears lovesick? Two weeks after the pop tart married and then dumped a hometown honey in Las Vegas, photos have emerged of her leaving a hospital.—*Daily News (New York)*, p. 3, 18th January 2004

home twenty *noun*
a person's home town *US*
From citizens' band radio code in which '20' means 'location'.
- —Wayne Floyd, *Jason's Authentic Dictionary of CB Slang*, p. 19, 1976

homework *noun*
foreplay *US*
- —Kenn "Naz" Young, *Naz's Dictionary of Teen Slang*, p. 59, 1993

▸ **bit of homework; piece of homework**
a person objectified sexually *UK, 1945*
- —John Ayto, *Oxford Dictionary of Slang*, p. 71, 1998

homewrecker *noun*
a person whose affair with a married person leads to divorce, especially when there are children involved *US*
- Oh, he was nice, of course, and she did like him, but she wasn't a homewrecker.—Nathan Heard, *Howard Street*, p. 113, 1968
- They say you banged that little homewrecker right on Leery's pool table, Dilford.—Joseph Wambaugh, *The Delta Star*, p. 137, 1983
- "You don't think she's better-looking than your average home-wrecker?" I said.—Dan Jenkins, *Life Its Ownself*, p. 230, 1984
- Shocked, Mom flew off the handle and called Joanie a "home wrecker." Joanie got livid and said, "Oh, really? I understand your last boyfriend didn't exactly qualify as bachelor of the month!" —C.D. Payne, *Youth in Revolt*, p. 77, 1993
- Contrast that with Henry "Homewrecker" Hyde's dismissing revelations of his extramarital dalliance with a married mother of three as a "youth indiscretion" committed when he was in his 40s and you get an idea of how the debate has deteriorated.—*Sunday Gazette Mail (Charleston, West Virgnina)*, p. 8B, 11th October 1998

homey; homie *noun*
a male from your neighbourhood; a close male friend; a fellow youth gang member *US, 1944*
- —Lou Shelly, *Hepcats Jive Dictionary*, p. 12, 1945
- —Hyman E. Goldin et al., *Dictionary of American Underworld Lingo*, p. 100, 1950
- —Frank Prewitt and Francis Schaeffer, *Vacaville Vocabulary*, 1961–1962
- [D]ragging along some of his Washington homies, including 1 special loudmouth named Barry Guyse.—Clarence Cooper Jr, *The Farm*, p. 87, 1967
- Hey homie, it's all his fault.—Paul Glover, *Words from the House of the Dead*, 1974
- I moved back to my small pad and ran into a homey of mine, James Moody.—Babs Gonzales, *Movin' On Down De Line*, p. 19, 1975
- That's my lady homey. Her name's Brandi.—*Boyz N The Hood*, 1990
- Way cool blood, homey.—Jess Mowry, *Way Past Cool*, p. 9, 1992
- Called up the homies and I'm askin' y'all / Which park are y'all playing basketball[.]—Ice Cube, *It Was a Good Day*, 1993
- [Y]our Kru, or your Massive, your Thugs, or Bredrins; Dawgs, Homies, your Clique, or your Posse.—Julian Johnson, *Urban Survival*, p. 264, 2003

▷ see: OMEE

homey, don't play dat!
don't say that! *US*
A catchphrase from the television programme *In Living Color*.
- —Connie Eble (Editor), *UNC-CH Campus Slang*, p. 5, November 1990

homi *noun*
▷ see: OMEE

homicide *noun*
heroin or cocaine mixed with prescription drugs, such as scopolamine or strychnine *UK, 1998*
- —Robert Ashton, *This Is Heroin*, p. 209, 2002

homie *noun*
a homosexual *US*
- —Charles Shafer, *Folk Speech in Texas Prisons*, p. 206, 1990

homing pigeon *noun*
the US armed forces insignia designating honourable discharge *US*
- —*American Speech*, p. 153, April 1946: 'GI words from the separation center and proctology ward'

homintern *noun*
an aggressive, loyal homosexual subculture *US*
A term coined by W.H. Auden, punning on the Marxist 'comintern' or Communist International.
- The notion that the arts are dominated by a kind of homosexual Mafia – or "Homintern," as it has been called – is sometimes exaggereated, particularly by spiteful failures looking for scape-goats.—Joe David Brown, *Sex in the '60s*, p. 67, 1968

homo *noun*
1 a homosexual, especially a male homosexual *US, 1922*
- One corner of 52nd and Sixth Avenue is particularly obnoxious, a hangout for prostitutes and homos, dark and light.—Jack Lait and Lee Mortimer, *New York Confidential*, p. 45, 1948
- Soon as he opened that door I see he's a homo, a fag.—Hal Ellson, *Duke*, p. 110, 1949

- It is also the hustlers' bar – the boys who make a living among the sad old homos of the Eight Avenue night. —Jack Kerouac, *On the Road*, p. 131, 1957
- —Donald Webster Cory and John P. LeRoy, *The Homosexual and His Society*, p. 264, 1963: 'A lexicon of homosexual slang'
- Makes you think homos are suckers for punishment, right? —John Francis Hunter, *The Gay Insider*, p. 78, 1971
- The local homos threw a lovely little potluck brunch for us in Antelope Park. —Armistead Maupin, *Further Tales of the City*, p. 128, 1982
- Comedian Chevy Chase says he was only kidding when he limp wristedly referred to Cary Grant as a "homo" and "what a gal" on a TV talk show[.] —*San Francisco Examiner*, p. 11, 1st September 1982
- That doesn't mean he was a homo, Miller. —*Repo Man*, 1984
- [T]he proposed site was a mecca for homos who wanted to get quick blowjobs. —Howard Stern, *Miss America*, p. 460, 1995

2 used as an insulting term of address to someone who is not homosexual *US*

- God you are terrible. Okay, homo, I hope you are ready to take the agonizing, bitter humiliation of defeat. —*Dazed and Confused*, 1993

homogrips *noun*

sideburns *NEW ZEALAND*

- —David McGill, *David McGill's Complete Kiwi Slang Dictionary*, p. 64, 1998

homo-hater *noun*

a person with a pathological dislike for homosexuals *US*

- —*Maledicta*, p. 242, 1979: 'Kinks and queens: linguistic and cultural aspects of the terminology for gays'

homo heaven *noun*

1 a public area where homosexuals congregate in hopes of quick sex *US*

- Central Park has certain sections known as homo heavens. —Antony James, *America's Homosexual Underground*, p. 60, 1965

2 the upper balcony in a theatre patronised by homosexual men *US*

- —Johnny Shearer, *The Male Hustler*, p. 72, 1966

homosexual adapter *noun*

a computer cable with either two male or two female connectors (that connect two male connectors) *US*

- —Eric S. Raymond, *The New Hacker's Dictionary*, p. 175, 1991

hon *noun*

used as a term of endearment *US, 1906*

A shortened 'honey'. Fiercely claimed by Baltimore, Maryland, as a Baltimore-coinage.

- I'm sorry I brought it up, hon. —Irving Shulman, *The Amboy Dukes*, p. 175, 1947
- "What's the answer, hon?" Guide had asked, dreading the answer. —Max Shulman, *Rally Round the Flag, Boys!*, p. 223, 1957
- How you bin, hon? —Jean Brooks, *The Opal Witch*, 1967
- Take me to the party hon. —Kevin Mackey, *The Cure*, 1970
- A player brings in a lot of cash, hon, we have to look at it impartially, only as money, nothing else. —Elmore Leonard, *Glitz*, p. 153, 1985
- Thank you, hon. How's Fargo? —*Fargo*, 1996
- Teddy, hon, are you okay? —*Something About Mary*, 1998

hon bun *noun*

used as a term of endearment *US, 1940s*

A shortened 'honey bunny'.

- I want you clear-headed, hon bun. —Elmore Leonard, *City Primeval*, p. 54, 1980

honcho *noun*

a boss, a big-shot *US*

From the Japanese term for 'a group or squad leader'.

- This prisoner is the "honcho," or group headman, in the POW stockade. —*Coshocton (Ohio) Tribune*, 1st September 1945
- "Okay, Buddy," says the chief, "you're the honcho." —Darryl Ponicsan, *The Last Detail*, p. 20, 1970
- The broad blew up, ran downtown and put the squeal on the Palladium to her boss, an assistant D.A. name of Kuh who was already into being one of Hogan's main honchos. —Edwin Torres, *Carlito's Way*, p. 26, 1975
- We called the few tough aggressive pilots 'honchos' and the rest 'students'. —Walter Boyne and Steven Thompson, *The Wild Blue*, p. 172, 1986
- Ito-san was the head honcho, the big cheese, the number one Tomodachi[.] —Rhiannon Paice, *Too Late for the Festival*, p. 27, 1999

Honda rice *noun*

IR8, a high-yielding variety of rice introduced in Vietnam in the 1960s, doubling rice production yields *US*

- They used to call it "Honda rice" in the Delta because everybody earned enough money to buy a Honda motorbike by raising a second or third crop per year. —Al Santoli, *To Bear Any Burden*, p. 203, 1985

hondo *noun*

1 an attractive, popular male *US*

- —Levi Straus & Company, *Campus Slang*, January 1986

2 a zealous enthusiast *US*

- —*Current Slang*, p. 6, Summer 1968

honest *noun*

cherry syrup added to a soda fountain drink *US*

From the American legend of George Washington's honesty when asked as a child if he cut down a cherry tree.

- —*American Speech*, p. 88, April 1946: 'The language of West Coast culinary workers'

honest *adjective*

(used of a drug) relatively pure and undiluted *US*

- —William D. Alsever, *Glossary for the Establishment and Other Uptight People*, p. 16, December 1970

honest!

I am speaking the truth!; I do mean it! *UK, 1937*

A shortening of 'honestly'.

- [T]oo astonishing to be true. But it is true. Honest. —Jane Bryant Quinn, *Making the Most of Your Money*, 1997

Honest Abe *noun*

General Creighton Williams Abrams, Jr (1914–1974) *US*

Abrams succeeded General Westmoreland as US commander in Vietnam, where he championed the Vietnamisation of the war.

- —Linda Reinberg, *In the Field*, p. 107, 1991

honest brakeman *adjective*

a person who engages in petty theft at work but not grand theft *CANADA*

From the faint praise – 'he worked for the railroad for thirty years and never stole a boxcar'.

- —Bill Casselman, *Canadian Sayings*, p. 128, 2002

honest injun'

used as a pledge of complete honesty *US, 1851*

- He held up his hand like a Boy Scout. "Honest injun. You didn't miss a thing." —Armistead Maupin, *Further Tales of the City*, p. 217, 1982
- "Don't blame me. I kept my word." "Right." "Honest Injun." —Rita Ciresi, *Pink Slip*, p. 323, 1999
- "Honest Injun?" I can't believe what a pushover you are. —Kevin Smith, *Jay and Silent Bob Strike Back*, p. 38, 2001

honest John *noun*

1 a decent, upstanding, law-abiding citizen *US, 1884*

- [Y]ou long-suffering, honest Johns[.] —Charles Raven, *Underworld Nights*, p. 36, 1956
- He put on his best honest-John smile, and held out the license, being helpful. —Donald Goines, *White Man's Justice, Black Man's Grief*, p. 13, 1973

2 in a shoplifting operation, an honest-looking confederate who distracts the store personnel *US*

- It stated an "Honest John" is a person used to divert the attention of a clerk while an accomplice dips into the cash register. —*San Francisco Examiner*, p. 6, 22nd February 1974

honest kine?

is that right? *US*

Hawaiian youth usage.

- —Douglas Simonson, *Pidgin to da Max*, 1981

honestly!

used as an expression of disgust, exasperation, unpleasant surprise, etc *UK, 1966*

- We ate at midnight, after the girls had insisted we cook the damn stuff rather than argue about it and spill wine over each other for three hours. Well, honestly. Men. —*The Observer*, 13th July 2003

honest reader *noun*

a playing card with an unintentional imperfection that enables an observant player to identify it in another player's hand *US*

- —George Percy, *The Language of Poker*, p. 45, 1988

honest squeeze *noun*

a cherry squeeze soda fountain drink *US*

An allusion to the George Washington myth involving the cutting down of a cherry tree.

- —*American Speech*, p. 232, October 1952: 'The argot of soda jerks'

honest-to-God; honest-to-goodness *adjective*
true, genuine, thorough, honest; truly, genuinely, thoroughly, honestly *US, 1913*
- [H]igh school football, barbecue cuisine, backyard auto-repair, the Dallas Cowboys, and honest-to-God Republicanism. — *The Guardian*, 29th August 2003

honey *noun*
1 a sexually attractive young woman *US, 1930*
Sometimes spelled 'hunny'.
- Yeah, and there's two swingin' honeys for every guy. — Jan Berry and Dean Torrance, *Surf City*, 1963
- Officer Peters is not the first man who took a look at some young honey and decided he might like to try a little of that. — George V. Higgins, *The Rat on Fire*, p. 88, 1981
- I mean I've sucked some titties and finger banged a couple of hunnies but I never stuck it in. — *Boyz N The Hood*, 1990
- You'll be [...] clocking the gear on the little honeys in the queue. — Kevin Sampson, *Outlaws*, p. 66, 2001

2 a female surfer or a male surfer's girlfriend *US*
- — Rob Burt, *Surf City, Drag City*, 1986

3 a sexually desirable person *UK: SCOTLAND, 1985*
- That yin thinks he's God's gift, an he's no honey either. — Michael Munro, *The Complete Patter*, p. 77, 1996

4 an 'effeminate' lesbian *US*
- — Anon., *King Smut's Wet Dreams Interpreted*, 1978

5 used as a term of affectionate address *UK, 1350*
- Gimme a fag, honey, said Beth[.] — Geoffrey Fletcher, *Down Among the Meths Men*, p. 38, 1966

6 anything considered pleasing, attractive, effective, etc *US, 1888*
- That's a honey of an anklet you're wearing, Mrs Dietrichson. — Fred McMurray, *Double Indemnity*, p. 49, 1944

▷ **see:** POT OF HONEY

honey bear *noun*
a policewoman *US*
Extended from **BEAR** (police).
- — *Complete CB Slang Dictionary*, 1976
- — Peter Chippindale, *The British CB Book*, p. 156, 1981

honey blunt *noun*
marijuana rolled in the outer leaves of a cigar which are then sealed with honey *US*
- — Mike Haskins, *Drugs*, p. 287, 2003

honey box *noun*
the vagina *US*
- Ain't none of 'em my bitch unless I got my cock in her honey box. — Cecil Brown, *The Life & Loves of Mr. Jiveass Nigger*, p. 143, 1969

honey bucket *noun*
1 a portable toilet *US*
- — Porter Bibb, *CB Bible*, p. 96, 1976

2 a chamberpot *US, 1931*
- — Mike Doogan, *How to Speak Alaskan*, p. 34, 1993

3 a truck used to empty septic tanks *US*
- — Montie Tak, *Truck Talk*, p. 84, 1971

honey cart *noun*
a vehicle hauling human excrement; a portable toilet *US, 1929*
- — *American Speech*, p. 118, May 1960: 'Korean bamboo English'

honey dip *noun*
an attractive woman, especially one with a light brown skin colour *US*
- — *Washington Post*, 14th October 1993
- — *Ebony Magazine*, p. 156, August 2000: "How to talk to the new generation"

honey dipper *noun*
the driver of a truck that drains septic tanks *US, 1961*
- — Montie Tak, *Truck Talk*, p. 84, 1971

honey dipping *noun*
vaginal secretions *US*
- — Vincent J. Monteleone, *Criminal Slang*, p. 121, 1949

honeyfuck *verb*
to have sex with a Lolita-aged nymphet *US*
- — Dale Gordon, *The Dominion Sex Dictionary*, p. 85, 1967

honey, I'm home!
used for humorously announcing an entrance *US*
From the *Dick Van Dyke Show* (1961–66), a centrepiece in the golden age of the situation comedy on US television.
- Honey! I'm home! — *Drugstore Cowboy*, 1988
- Honey, I'm home! — *Natural Born Killers*, 1994

honeyman *noun*
a procurer of prostitutes; a man who makes his living off the earnings of prositutes *US*
- — Ralph de Sola, *Crime Dictionary*, 1982
- — *Maledicta*, p. 148, Summer/Winter 1986–1987: 'Sexual slang: prostitutes, pedophiles, flagellators, transvestites, and necrophiles'

honeymoon *noun*
1 sex *US*
Used by prostitutes in Southeast Asia during the Vietnam war.
- Dropped a hundred-thirty last night, on the same broad, and all he got outa the deal was a steam bath. She wouldn't go honeymoon with him. — Charles Anderson, *The Grunts*, p. 19, 1976

2 the early period in a drug addiction *US*
- — *American Speech*, p. 27, February 1952: 'Teen-age hophead jargon'
- — Angela Devlin, *Prison Patter*, p. 62, 1996

3 the first few hands played by a new player in a poker game *US*
- — John Vorhaus, *The Big Book of Poker Slang*, p. 22, 1996

honey oil *noun*
the recreational drug ketamine *US*
- — US Department of Justice, *Street Terms*, October 1994

honey perrs *noun*
stairs *UK: SCOTLAND*
Glasgow rhyming slang, formed on a street-vendors cry for 'sweet pears'.
- Ah'm away up the honey perrs. — Michael Munro, *The Complete Patter*, 1996

honeypot *noun*
1 the vagina *US*
Recorded as rhyming slang for **TWAT** (the vagina). It certainly rhymes, but must surely be influenced – if not inspired – by senses that are conventional, figurative and slang. Found once in the UK in 1719, and then in general slang usage with 'candy'.
- Now I am inserting the member," he explained, as he parted the tender quavering lips of the pink honeypot and allowed his stout member to be drawn slowly into the seething thermal pudding of the darling girl. — Terry Southern, *Candy*, p. 208, 1958
- You can bite the lips of the honey pot a little, but very gently[.] — Angelo d'Arcangelo, *The Homosexual Handbook*, 1968
- [A]ll he wanted was a fast duck of the dick in and out of Franny's Zen-immaculate honeypot in the back seat. — Lester Bangs, *Psychotic Reactions and Carburetor Dung*, 1971
- — Ray Puxley, *Cockney Rabbit*, 1992
- Meanwhile, she sits astride me, easing her honeypot down around the throbbing upstanding round rod. — Clarence Major, *All-Night Visitors*, p. 7, 1998

2 in male homosexual usage, the anus and rectum *US*
- — *Male Swinger Number 3*, p. 46, 1981: 'The complete gay dictionary'

3 a chamber pot *US*
- Sitting on "honeypots" on a lawn, half-Japanese children receive toilet training. — *Ebony*, p. 20, July 1954

4 in Maine, a muddy hole in the road *US*
- — John Gould, *Maine Lingo*, p. 135, 1975

honey shot *noun*
a gratuitous television view of a pretty girl or woman, usually a spectator at a sporting event *US, 1968*
- — *American Speech*, Spring-Summer 1973
- They do this a lot, they told me, and they call it "hooking a barracuda," or a "honey shot," or, as a matter of fact, a "hold it." — Dan Jenkins, *Dead Solid Perfect*, p. 152, 1986

honeytrap *noun*
the seduction by a sexually attractive person of a politican or other prominent figure into dishonest or indiscreet behaviour *NEW ZEALAND*
Used in conversation since the early 1990s.

honey-uck *verb*
to have sex in a slow, affectionate manner *US*
- — Roger Blake, *The American Dictionary of Sexual Terms*, p. 101, 1964

honey wagon *noun*

1 a vehicle hauling human excrement; a portable toilet *US, 1923*
- —John T. Algeo, *American Speech*, May 1960: 'Korean bamboo English'

2 a truck hauling beer *US*
- —Lanie Dills, *The Official CB Slanguage Language Dictionary*, p. 40, 1976

3 a catering truck *US*
- We just started gabbing outside the honey wagon one day.—Armistead Maupin, *Maybe the Moon*, p. 33, 1992

Hongcouver *nickname*

the city of Vancouver, British Columbia, Canada *CANADA*
- The nickname "Hongcouver" alludes to the large number of immigrants during the 1990s from Oriental countries, especially Hong Kong.—*peak/sfu.ca*, 9th May 2002

Hong Kong *verb*

to be odiferous *UK*

Rhyming slang for **PONG**.
- —Ray Puxley, *Cockney Rabbit*, 1992

Hong Kong *adjective*

wrong *UK*

Rhyming slang.
- It seemed like a good idea but it's all gone Hong Kong.—Ray Puxley, *Fresh Rabbit*, 1998

hong-yen *noun*

heroin, originally in pill form *US, 1949*
- —Richard A. Spears, *The Slang and Jargon of Drugs and Drink*, p. 266, 1986
- —Robert Ashton, *This Is Heroin*, 2002
- —Mike Haskins, *Drugs*, p. 284, 2003

honk *noun*

pleasure; enjoyment *US, 1964*
- My boyfriend and I do it at least once a day, generally oftener, but ever now and then he gets a honk out of watching one of his friends throw it to me.—*Screw*, p. 16, 16th May 1969

honk *verb*

1 to moan, to complain *UK*

A military usage.
- [H]e used to sit next to me honking about the state of the food.—Andy McNab, *Immediate Action*, p. 27, 1995

2 to vomit *UK, 1967*
- If you need to honk, honk into this.—*Wayne's World*, 1992
- [T]hey were both honking and spewing bits of carrot down the back of your neck.—Jenny Eclair, *Camberwell Beauty*, p. 49, 2000

3 to fart

Also used as a noun. From the noise of geese – low-flying geese may be offered as an excuse – or 'honk' (to smell).
- —Peter Furze, *Tailwinds*, p. 105, 1998

4 to smell badly *AUSTRALIA*
- —Jim Ramsay, *Cop It Sweet!*, 1977
- —Connie Eble (Editor), *UNC-CH Campus Slang*, p. 4, November 2003

5 to inhale drugs, originally through the nose *US, 1968*
- [T]he slight scratching-sounds of bankers writing checks and cocaine honked through ivory straws on yachts.—Ed Sanders, *Tales of Beatnik Glory*, p. 92, 1975
- Stephane, honking great lungfuls from a hash-pipe, is understandably monosyllabic[.]—*Ministry*, p. 49, October 2002

6 when flying an aeroplane or helicopter, to pull, to jerk, to yank *US, 1946*
- Richards "honked" back on the controls, powering the helicopter up into an arc, hoping to escape into one of the scud clouds.—Neil Sheehan, *A Bright Shining Lie*, p. 774, 1988

7 in drag racing, to defeat *US*
- —John Edwards, *Auto Dictionary*, p. 78, 1993

▸**honk your horn**

to grab a man's penis *US*
- "She groped you, huh, Rosso?" "Honest to God, she honked my horn," said Ranatti, raising a rather stubby right hand heavenward. "Gave it two toots with a thumb and forefinger before I laid the iron on her wrists."—Joseph Wambaugh, *The New Centurions*, p. 175-176, 1970

▸**honk your lot**

to vomit *UK*

An elaboration of **HONK**.
- The girl lights a cigarette, unaware that Hume's about to honk his lot.—Ted Lewis, *Jack Carter's Law*, p. 70, 1974

honked *adjective*

drunk *UK*

Of military origin.
- —John Winton, *We Joined the Navy*, 1959
- —Ralph de Sola, *Crime Dictionary*, p. 65, 1982

honked off *adjective*

angry *US, 1958*
- I never seen a man get so honked off over losin' a pool game.—Ken Weaver, *Texas Crude*, p. 114, 1984

honker *noun*

1 the penis *US*
- That honker of yours was as ready for me as mine was ready for your slick butt.—James Harper, *Homo Laws in all 50 States*, p. 36, 1968

2 the nose *US, 1942*
- Elvin and Dale had to wait before the door was opened by a stocky little guy Elvin judged to be light-skinned colored, except he had a big honker on him and maybe was trying to pass.—Elmore Leonard, *Maximum Bob*, p. 60, 1991

3 expectorated sputum *US, 1981*
- —*Maledicta*, p. 32, 1988-1989: 'Medical maledicta from San Francisco'

4 a goose *US, 1841*
- "Canada honkers up there," Papa says, squinting up.—Ken Kesey, *One Flew Over the Cuckoo's Nest*, p. 91, 1962

5 a large and powerful wave *US*
- —Trevor Cralle, *The Surfin'ary*, p. 54, 1991

6 in drag racing, a fast stock car *US*
- —Olney Ross, *Kings of the Drag Strip*, p. 187, 1968

honkers *noun*

drunk *UK*

Perhaps deriving from **HONK** (to vomit) as a side-effect of drunkenness. Used in the military for 'very drunk'.
- —*News Chronicle*, 22nd May 1958

Honkers *nickname*

Hong Kong *UK, 1984*

Military, especially used by officers.
- [B]een away, down China way, Honkers.—J.J. Connolly, *Layer Cake*, p. 103, 2000

honking *adjective*

1 very smelly; of inferior quality *UK: SCOTLAND*
- That picture [film] was honkin.—Michael Munro, *The Original Patter*, p. 35, 1985

2 very large *US*
- —Connie Eble (Editor), *UNC-CH Campus Slang*, p. 5, April 1995

honk on *verb*

in the usage of youthful model road racers (slot car racers), to race fast *US*
- — Phantom Surfers, *The Exciting Sounds of Model Road Racing (Album cover)*, 1997

honky; honkie; honkey *noun*

a white person *US, 1946*

Usually not said with kindness, especially when used to describe a member of the white ruling class.
- Damning Lyndon Johnson for sending "honky cracker federal troops into Negro communities to kill black people," [H. Rap] Brown called the President "a wild mad dog, an outlaw from Texas."—*Time*, p. 17, 4th August 1967
- He [Stokely Carmichael] shrills at the whole pantheon of American heroes, from Christopher Columbus ("a dumb honky") through George Washington ("a honky who had slaves") and Abe Lincoln ("another honkey").—*Newsweek*, p. 27, 15th May 1967
- The honkie that tried to kill me, with an unregistered, loaded pistol, was held only three hours and released on $300 bail.—Abbie Hoffman, *Revolution for the Hell of It*, p. 187, 1968
- They couldn't care less about the old, stiffassed honkies who don't like their new dances[.]—Eldridge Cleaver, *Soul on Ice*, p. 81, 1968
- [N]o honky, liberal, bleeding heart, guilt-ridden advocates of justice, but first-class case-winners[.]—*The Digger Papers*, p. 15, August 1968
- The residents of this ghetto housing project clearly show us that guerilla warfare is the key: Their uprising put six honkies out of commission, only one brother was injured, and no black people were killed.—*The Black Panther*, p. 9, 4th May 1968
- A HONKEY VISITS THE LOWER EAST SIDE AND MAKES A DAMN FOOL OF HISSELF!! [Cartoon caption]—*East Village Other*, p. 9, 18th October 1968

- But what do you think these people are but honkies? —Cecil Brown, *The Life & Loves of Mr. Jiveass Nigger*, p. 119, 1969
- You come back here and kill one racist, red-necked honkey camel-breathed peckerwood who's been misusing you and your people all your life and that's murder. —H. Rap Brown, *Die Nigger Die!*, p. 38, 1969
- [S]he only played around with honkies. —Darryl Ponicsan, *The Last Detail*, p. 124, 1970
- '[The MC5 – a rock group] have demonstrated to the honkies that anything they do to fuck with us will be exposed to their children. You don't need to get rid of all the honkies, you just rob them of their replacements and let their breed atrophy and die out[.] —Richard Neville, *Play Power*, p. 107, 1970
- WE got two honkies out there dressed like Hasidic diamond merchants. — *The Blues Brothers*, 1980
- Now, I'm a white dude, a honky, in a black man's building, in a black man's neighborhood. —Herbert Huncke, *Guilty of Everything*, p. 3, 1990
- You fucking racist motherfucking honky asshole. —Howard Stern, *Miss America*, p. 170, 1995
- He looked at me and said, "You gonna die honkey!" —Eminem (Marshall Mathers), *Brain Damage*, 1999

Honky *noun*

a person from Hong Kong *AUSTRALIA*

- Joyce and Steven were so-called since birth. "Have to speak English and be English to get on in world. No use being Honkies," Lian Choo said. — *www.masscom.com.au/archipelago/shortstories/worlds.html*, 2003

honky nut *noun*

in Western Australia, a large gumnut (the hard, dried, inedible fruit of a eucalyptus tree) *AUSTRALIA*

- My bum cracks honky nuts. —Glyn Parry, *Mosh*, p. 34, 1996

honky-tonk *noun*

a saloon, dance-hall or gambling-house *US, 1894*

Also used as an adjective.

- It's the honky tonk women / Gimme, gimme, gimme the honky tonk blues. —Jagger/Richards *Country Honk / Honky Tonk Woman*, 1969
- We did meet, and we drove out to a couple of honky-tonks. —Herbert Huncke, *Guilty of Everything*, p. 88, 1990

honourable member for Fuckinghamshire *noun*

the penis *UK*

Jocular.

- [T]he amazing truth about the Honourable Member for Fuckinghamshire —Richard Herring, *Talking Cock*, p. 23, 2003

hoo-ah!

used for expressing enthusiastic approval *US*

- The soldier had been digging foxholes for two days. "Hoo-ah!" he yelled, repeating the signature call of the American Forces. — *Houston Post*, 28th February 1991
- — *American Speech*, p. 391, Winter 1991: 'Among the new words'

hoobly goobly *noun*

nonsense *US*

- — *American Speech*, p. 228, October 1956: 'More United States Air Force slang'

hooch; hootch *noun*

1 alcohol *US, 1915*

- Most through trains carry clubs cars, in which excellent hooch is sold at moderate prices. —Jack Lait and Lee Mortimer, *New York Confidential*, p. 198, 1946
- [T]his morning they all had the shakes and rattles real bad, whether from hootch or some kind of white stuff. —Mezz Mezzrow, *Really the Blues*, p. 304, 1946
- He's got himself all jammed up with some floozy and a bottle of hooch. —Raymond Chandler, *The Little Sister*, p. 13, 1949
- He used to drink a bottle of hootch a day and I suppose the New York people thought he was a weak link in their security chain. —Clancy Sigal, *Going Away*, p. 36, 1961
- Mama frowned and scolded, "Bunny, why yu mixin' cansur with hooch? Yu gonna' die." —Iceberg Slim (Robert Beck), *Mama Black Widow*, p. 72, 1969
- Alright – bring on the free hootch! — *Chasing Amy*, 1997

2 a peasant hut; a small, improvised shelter *US, 1952*

Korean and then Vietnam war usage.

- —Carl Fleischhauer, *A Glossary of Army Slang*, p. 25–26, 1968
- Folks do not want to hear about the night at Fire Base Hariette – down the way from LZ Skator-Gator, and within earshot of a ragtag bunch of mud-and-thatch hooches everyone called Gookville – when the whole company, except for one guy, got killed. —Larry Heinemann, *Paco's Story*, p. 13–14, 1986
- I went up to Darla's hootch and banged on the door. No answer. —Elmore Leonard, *Bandits*, p. 338, 1987
- For example, any building from a wattle hut to a modern frame structure was called a "hootch," a derivative of a Japanese word for "house," uchi. —Neil Sheehan, *A Bright Shining Lie*, p. 555, 1988
- The hooches were still up, and we were envious of the relative comfort the Marines on Khe Sanh base seemed to have. —Eric Hammel, *Khe Sanh: Siege in the Clouds*, p. 100, 1989
- Next thing I know I'm naked in bed in a nootch. — *Forrest Gump*, 1992

3 marijuana *US, 1972*

Sometimes variant 'hoochie'.

- —Richard A. Spears, *The Slang and Jargon of Drugs and Drink*, p. 266, 1986
- —Mike Haskins, *Drugs*, p. 287, 2003

hooch dog *noun*

a marijuana cigarette *US*

- —Connie Eble (Editor), *UNC-CH Campus Slang*, p. 4, October 1986

hooched-up *adjective*

drunk *US, 1922*

From **HOOCH** (an alcoholic drink; also, in the UK, a brand name alcoholic drink popular with young drinkers).

- Everywhere you look there's little posses of hooched-up schoolies [schoolchildren] and shop girls[.] —Kevin Sampson, *Outlaws*, p. 112, 2001

hooch girl *noun*

a young Vietnamese woman who worked as a maid or did laundry for US troops *US, 1981*

- —Linda Reinberg, *In the Field*, p. 108, 1991
- [T]he hooch girl, woh cleaned up and took care of the laundry, stopped in her work, shook her broom at me, and started yelling, "You go kill VC! Numba fucking ten." —Paul Young, *First Recon – Second to None*, p. 195, 1992

hooch-head *noun*

a drunkard *US*

- I done tole you," he said to Mickey, "not to rent them goddamned rooms on the top floor to them Kong-cookin' hootchhead son-of-a-bitches. —Mezz Mezzrow, *Really the Blues*, p. 250, 1946

hoochie *noun*

in British Columbia fishing, a soft plastic lure with tentacles *CANADA*

- The "hoochie," made to imitate a squid, comes in psychedelic colours and were originally named hootchy-kootchies for their resemblance to Polynesian girls in grass skirts. First used by commercial trollers: what else would they dream of, all alone at sea —Tom Parkin, *WetCoast Words*, p. 69–70, 1989

▷ **see: HOOTCHIE**

hoochy koochy *noun*

a sexually suggestive dance *US, 1895*

- Sol Bloom, as an entrepreneur at the Chicago World's Fair, celebrating the 400th anniversary of the discovery of America, presented "Little Egypt" in a series of contortions while she stayed on her feet, known as the "hoochy koochy." —Jack Lait and Lee Mortimer, *Chicago Confidential*, p. 157, 1950
- But we forgot that and headed straight for North Clark Street, after a spin in the Loop, to see the hootchy-kootchy joints and hear the bop. — Jack, *On the Road*, p. 138, 1957
- [S]top to watch the hoochiekoo dancer, whose name is Carmelita[.] —Lester Bangs, *Psychotic Reactions and Carburetor Dung*, p. 124, 1973

hood *noun*

1 a neighbourhood, especially in an urban ghetto *US, 1967*

- The fire never goes out on the steam .. in the 'hood. —Odie Hawkins, *Ghetto Sketches*, p. 75, 1972
- They either don't know, don't show, and don't care what be going on in the hood. — *Boyz N The Hood*, 1990
- Hood they got no better'n ours. —Jess Mowry, *Way Past Cool*, p. 14, 1992
- When cocaine got too expensive for the 'hood, crack was invented. —Chris Rock, *Rock This*, p. 68, 1997
- [C]rack first began ripping through the 'hood in the mid-80s[.] — *The Source*, p. 74, March 2002

2 a rough street youth; a criminal *US, 1880*

A shortened 'hoodlum'.

- [T]he people he'd worked with were just lowdown grafting hoods[.] —Derek Raymond (Robin Cook), *The Crust on its Uppers*, p. 57, 1962
- When I was thirteen, I was considered a hood, even though I didn't hang out with any hoodish people." —Nicholas Von Hoffman, *We Are The People Our Parents Warned Us Against*, p. 56, 1967
- You know you walk around like you're Mr. Cool or Mr. Wisdom but you're not ... you're just an old hood. — *Hard Eight*, 1996

3 the penis *JAMAICA, 1995*

West Indian and UK black usage. Collected from a UK prisoner in May 2002.

4 the chest *US*

- —James Harris, *A Convict's Dictionary*, p. 33, 1989

5 heroin *UK*

- —Mike Haskins, *Drugs*, p. 284, 2003

6 a 12 ounce bottle of beer *US*

- —*American Speech*, p. 62, February 1967: 'Soda-fountain, restaurant and tavern calls'

▸ under the hood

literally, flying by instrumentation; figuratively, operating without knowing exactly what is going on *US*

- —*American Speech*, p. 229, October 1956: 'More United States Air Force slang'

hoodie *noun*

a sweatshirt or jacket with a hood *US, 1993*

- —Maria Hinojas, *Crews*, p. 167, 1995: 'Glossary'

hoodish *adjective*

tough, criminal *US*

- When I was thirteen, I was considered a hood, even though I didn't hang out with any hoodish people."—Nicholas Von Hoffman, *We Are The People Our Parents Warned Us Against*, p. 56, 1967

hood lifter *noun*

a motor mechanic *US*

- —Montie Tak, *Truck Talk*, p. 84, 1971

hoodlum *noun*

a ruffian, a gangster, especially if dangerous *US, 1871*

Probably from a printing error on a reversal of Muldoon (a known gangster's name), thus 'noodlum', hence 'hoodlum'; of other folk-etymologies only a gang-cry of 'huddle 'em!' is moderately convincing.

- The hoodlum Frankie defaulted on his bail, slipped out of the country with his wife and family and fled to Italy.—Harry J. Anslinger, *The Murderers*, p. 239, 1961

hoodoo *noun*

an outcropping of rock in desolate western Canadian land *US, 1879*

- She might have looked for a while at the grey hoodoos that stood in a line below the crest on the other side of the valley.—George Bowering, *Caprice*, p. 67, 1987

hoodrat *noun*

1 a tough youth who prowls the streets of his inner-city neighbourhood, in search of trouble and fun *US*

- —Judi Sanders, *Da Bomb*, p. 15, 1997

2 a promiscuous girl *US*

- —Pamela Munro, *U.C.L.A. Slang*, p. 78, 1997
- —Connie Eble (Editor), *UNC-CH Campus Slang*, p. 6, Fall 1999
- Talk about how you wanna get back with that tramp and how you forgive that hoodrat broad/dickhead.—*Hip-Hop Connection*, p. 22, July 2002

hooer; hoor *noun*

a whore *AUSTRALIA, 1952*

Representing a spelling pronunciation of 'whore'. This came to be a general term of abuse and was applied not only to women, but also to men.

- I only want what's mine. That hooer. I don't take that treatment from no one.—D'Arcy Niland, *Dead Men Running*, p. 74, 1969
- 'Cunnin' hoor, ain't he?' Harry said. 'If I'd paid her a compliment like that she'd have reckoned I was drunk or somethin'.'—M.J. Burton, *Bush Pub*, p. 155, 1978
- Tryin' to get these little black hoors out in the open.—M.J. Burton, *Bush Pub*, p. 92, 1978
- 'Bloody old hooer,' Jimmy said, 'I'd have dough in the bank if it wasn't for her!'—T.A.G. Hungerford, *Stories From Suburban Road*, p. 162, 1983

hooer lure *noun*

aftershave lotion *CANADA*

Given the crudeness of typical hockey player talk, the word 'hooer' may refer to any woman, not just a prostitute.

- One of the Saskatchewan players rerferred to aftershave lotion as "hooer lure."—*Globe and Mail West*, p. 23, March 1991

hooey *noun*

1 nonsense *US, 1912*

- Maybe this brother-and-sister stuff was just hooey, just like everything else.—James T. Farrell, *Saturday Night*, p. 19, 1947
- If Duffy wants a seven, he pulls the ace from this side, the six from the other, and holds 'em for a minute, doing some player hooey to stall long enough for the gas to warm up and turn solid.—Stephen Cannell, *King Con*, p. 138, 1997

2 a rope wrapped around three feet of an animal, secured with a half hitch *CANADA*

- When you watch the calf-roping at the rodeo you watch the cowboy rope and throw the calf, and then secure it with a hooey.—Chris Thain, *Cold as a Bay Street Banker's Heart*, p. 86, 1987

hoof *noun*

1 a foot or shoe *UK, 1598*

- —*Current Slang*, p. 10, Summer 1969

2 a sea turtle's flipper *CAYMAN ISLANDS*

- The flipper of the turtle is called the "hoof."—Aarona Booker Kohlman, *Wotcha Say*, p. 22, 1985

▸ on the hoof

1 working as a prostitute on the streets *US*

- She had no sense of it anymore, no idea of who the plainclothes might be, how fast the track was, whether she still had the heart to keep up her game out on the hoof.—John Sayles, *Union Dues*, p. 180, 1977

2 on the spot, spontaneously *US*

From the literal sense of the term, applied to cattle or swine, meaning 'alive'.

- I just made that up on the hoof.—Richard Price, *Clockers*, p. 270, 1992

▸ the hoof

dismissal from employment; expulsion *UK*

- I got the hoof, man. The sack, the chop, the proverbial bullet.—Doug Lang, *Freaks*, p. 89, 1973

hoof *verb*

1 to dance *US, 1916*

- The highly paid babes who pose for the photographers are prettier but dumber than their sisters who hoof in the choruses.—Jack Lait and Lee Mortimer, *New York Confidential*, p. 134, 1948
- [A]ll propped up by the copper wages of streetsinging, coffeehouse hoofing, bit parts in transient flicks, and the going rate for what I choose to call High Adventure.—Richard Farina, *Long Time Coming and A Long Time Gone*, p. 37, 1969

2 to walk *UK, 1641*

- Meanwhile, the goat takes off down West Street. Guess he didn't want to get locked up. We hoofed too—Edwin Torres, *After Hours*, p. 231, 1979
- If Bermondsey kids want to swim now they have to hoof-it to Rotherhithe.—John Milne, *Alive and Kicking*, p. 205, 1998

hoof and toof *noun*

foot and mouth disease *UK, 2001*

Farmers' use.

hoofer *noun*

a professional dancer, especially a tap dancer *US, 1916*

- Once a good friend of mine, a fine hoofer who was having trouble getting bookings, ran up to that tree[.]—Mezz Mezzrow, *Really the Blues*, p. 208, 1946
- A friend of ours, a newspaperman, was married to a red-headed hoofer in a Broadway night club.—Jack Lait and Lee Mortimer, *New York Confidential*, p. 127, 1948
- Clem and Jody, two oldtime vaudeville hoofers, cope out as Russian agents[.]—William Burroughs, *Naked Lunch*, p. 158, 1957
- The hoofer had originally bought it from a drag queen she worked with at the Greenwich Village Inn when they had straight acts.—Lenny Bruce, *How to Talk Dirty and Influence People*, p. 33, 1965
- Jerry's gawking at that near-nekkid hoofer lady[.]—Lester Bangs, *Psychotic Reactions and Carburetor Dung*, p. 124, 1973
- Making direct eye contact, he matches them step for step, dancing along, belly abounce, a real hoofer.—Josh Alan Friedman, *Tales of Times Square*, p. 55, 1986

hoofprint *noun*

footprints that could be identified as or surmised to be made by Viet Cong or North Vietnamese soldiers *US*

- "Well, the usual stuff: strung-out commo wire, spider holes – those are gook-size foxholes – smothered cooking fires – hoofprints – what we called hoofprints: fresh VC sandal prints; they made their sandals out of old tires. And North Vietnamese Army boots – actually black sneckers.—Nelson DeMille, *Word of Honor*, p. 131, 1989

hoof up *verb*

to sniff up, to inhale through the nose, to snort *UK*

Possibly from a mispronunciation of **HOOVER**.

- [T]he majority of their evening will have been spent hoofing up coke in the bogs[.]—*Ministry*, p. 7, January 2002

hoo-ha *noun*

a fuss or commotion; nonsense *UK, 1931*

- —Louis S. Leland, *A Personal Kiwi-Yankee Dictionary*, p. 52, 1984
- I think it's a lot of hoo-ha.—Jeffrey Eugenides, *Middlesex*, p. 362, 2002

hoo-haw *noun*

a fight, a dispute *CANADA*

• Yesterday it was tables the participants were concerned about. Today there was a hoo-haw about chairs. — *Toronto Globe and Mail*, p. 17, 13th May 1959

hoo-ing and ha-ing *noun*

a commotion, the making of a fuss *UK*

From the noun **HOO-HA**.

• Once all the hoo-ing and ha-ing was over [...] we reached the part of the proceedings that really mattered. — Ken Lukowiak, *Marijuana Time*, p. 254, 2000

hook *noun*

1 in a pickpocket team, the confederate who actually makes the theft *UK, 1863*

• — Hyman E. Goldin et al., *Dictionary of American Underworld Lingo*, p. 100, 1950
• It is understood by the police that a "bump man" or a "hook" does not operate at the Garden under the code long agreed upon between the stadium and the artistes. — Robert Sylvester, *No Cover Charge*, p. 286, 1956
• Most often, the thieves work in teams. In police parlance, the "stall" distracts the victim while the "hook" takes the merchandise. — *The New York Times*, p. B1, 13 July 1989

2 a thief *UK, 1863*

Originally applied specifically to a pickpocket.

• Of all the highly specialised hooks, and there are very many, in the various branches of the distribution industry[.] — Charles Raven, *Underworld Nights*, p. 10, 1956

3 a shoplifter *UK, 1961*

4 a finger, the hand *UK, 1829*

Usually used in the plural.

• — Lou Shelly, *Hepcats Jive Dictionary*, p. 12, 1945
• The skinny was that bohemian chicks couldn't keep their hooks off soulful, lonely sailors. — Darryl Ponicsan, *The Last Detail*, p. 75, 1970
• Now get your goddamn hooks off the blanket. — Gerald Petievich, *Money Men*, p. 48, 1981

5 a key or lockpick *US*

• Red, we need some hooks and need them quick. We've got a blast going in two weeks[.] — Red Rudensky, *The Gonif*, p. 47, 1970

6 in the used car business, a person who reverses the mileometer (odometer) to reduce the mileage shown *US*

• — Lewis Poteet, *Car & Motorcyle Slang*, p. 105, 1992

7 a person who strives to be that which he is not *US*

• — James Harris, *A Convict's Dictionary*, p. 39, 1989

8 a prostitute *US, 1918*

A shortened **HOOKER**.

• This was a thing where we got a few friends and a few light hooks to come in, get drunk, take naked, and have what we called an Eastern Regional Eat-Off. — Dan Jenkins, *Semi-Tough*, p. 64, 1972
• The rich are the worst tippers, hooks are lousy. — *Taxi Driver*, 1976

9 a contact in the police department with influence *US*

• There was an uneasy break in the dialogue until Inspector Sachson said, as if it were a perfectly sound explanation, that the man had a "hook" – an influential contact in the department. — Peter Maas, *Serpico*, p. 247, 1973

10 a superior with influence and the ability to protect *US*

New York police slang.

• — Samuel M. Katz, *Anytime Anywhere*, p. 388, 1997: 'The extremely unofficial and completely off-the-record NYPD/ESU truck-two glossary'

11 a telphone or telephone call *US*

• — *American Speech*, p. 61, Spring-Summer 1975: 'Razorback slang'

12 a CH-47 Chinook helicopter *US*

Vietnam war usage.

• — Carl Fleischhauer, *A Glossary of Army Slang*, p. 26, 1968

13 a railway demolition crane *US*

• — Norman Carlisle, *The Modern Wonder Book of Trains and Railroading*, p. 264, 1946

14 a razor *US*

• — Joseph E. Ragen and Charles Finston, *Inside the World's Toughest Prison*, p. 803, 1962: 'Penitentiary and underworld glossary'

15 the concave part of a wave *US*

• — Grant W. Kuhns, *On Surfing*, p. 117, 1963

16 a chevron insignia *US*

• — *American Speech*, p. 55, February 1947: 'Pacific war language'

17 the grade 'C' *US*

• — Collin Baker et al., *College Undergraduate Slang Study Conducted at Brown University*, p. 138, 1968

18 a feature in a computer or computer program designed to facilitate later changes or enhancements *US*

• — Eric S. Raymond, *The New Hacker's Dictionary*, p. 201, 1991

19 in a confidence swindle, the stage in the swindle when the victim is fully committed to the scheme *US*

• He was approaching that stage in his tale that black grifters call the hook. — Iceberg Slim (Robert Beck), *Trick Baby*, p. 55, 1969

20 in pointspreads established by bookmakers in sports betting, half a point *US*

• — *Bay Sports Review*, p. 8, November 1991

21 in a deck of playing cards, a jack or knave *US*

• — Irv Roddy, *Friday Night Poker*, p. 218, 1961

▸ **off the hook**

1 out of a difficult or embarrassing situation *UK, 1864*

• Sex offenders let off the hook[.] Thousands escape with cautions because police cannot cope with the flood of child porn offences[.] — *The Observer*, 28th September 2003

2 amazing, excellent *US*

• — Connie Eble (Editor), *UNC-CH Campus Slang*, p. 5, Spring 1999
• — *Sunday Times (South Africa)*, 1st June 2003

▸ **on the hook**

1 in debt *US, 1957*

• A shaky guy ... but on the hook for enough money the can't say no to anyone. — Gerald Petievich, *One-Shot Deal*, p. 193–194, 1981
• I'm on the hook for seventeen thousand dollars. — Brian Preston, *Pot Planet*, p. 232, 2002

2 in love *US*

Teen slang

• — *Newsweek*, p. 28, 8th October 1951

3 being towed by a tow truck *UK*

• — *British Road Services Magazine*, December 1951
• — Lewis Poteet, *Car & Motorcyle Slang*, p. 105, 1992

4 skipping school *US, 1906*

• For three and a half hours they sat in the Paramount balcony with the two high school babes who were also on the hook. — Irving Shulman, *The Amboy Dukes*, p. 29, 1947

hook *verb*

1 to addict *US, 1922*

• I knew that the first shot could not hook you physically. — Jeremy Larner and Ralph Tefferteller, *The Addict in the Street*, p. 53, 1964
• — Angela Devlin, *Prison Patter*, p. 62, 1996

2 to inject by hypodermic needle *US*

• "You've been hooking that spot so much it's about to get infected," he said, pointing to a needle welt. — William Burroughs, *Junkie*, p. 81, 1953

3 to snare in a swindle *UK, 1730*

• First time in ten years I ever saw Minnesota Fats hooked, really hooked. — *The Hustler*, 1961

4 to steal *US*

• — *American Speech*, p. 194, October 1951: 'A study of reformatory argot'

5 to take, but not necessarily to steal *UK*

• — *The Felstedian*, December 1947

6 to engage in prostitution *US, 1959*

• She was hooking when I met her. So I didn't go for that at all. 'Cause I never made it with a hooker before. — James Mills, *The Panic in Needle Park*, p. 56, 1966
• While girls all over the room were murmuring, 'What's she talking about?' one of the tougher, older Bunnies bellowed, 'Hooking!' — Kathryn Leigh Scott, *The Bunny Years*, p. 138, 1998

7 to ride a racehorse so that it will lose *AUSTRALIA*

• Sam hooked the horse at his next start and Jack again cleaned up, then rode him to a close win at Bellbird[.] — Joe Andersen, *Winners Can Laugh*, p. 149, 1982
• We know Watson and Robertson have bribed you to stop it just like you hooked that one yesterday. — Clive Galea, *Slipper*, p. 199, 1988

8 in trucking, to shift gears *US*

Most often heard as 'hook 'er into high'.

• — Montie Tak, *Truck Talk*, p. 84, 1971

9 to arrest *US, 1928*

• It's life if you get hooked with it and you can't really do much of anything with it except fight a war, maybe. — George V. Higgins, *The Friends of Eddie Doyle*, p. 8, 1971

• He knew what he was going to do, but it was a felony and he didn't think he should confide in her, for fear she'd hook him upon the spot. —Stephen J. Cannell, *The Tin Collectors*, p. 262, 2001

▸ **hook a barracuda**
to locate and show a gratuitous television view of a pretty girl or woman, usually a spectator at a sporting event *US*
• They do this a lot, they told me, and they call it "hooking a barracuda," or a "honey shot," or, as a matter of fact, a "hold it." —Dan Jenkins, *Dead Solid Perfect*, p. 152, 1986

hook and book *verb*
to handcuff and arrest a criminal suspect *US*
• —*Los Angeles Times*, p. B8, 19th December 1994

hook and bullet crowd *noun*
hunters and recreational fishermen, collectively as a lobbying force *US*
• Since 1976, that constituency is no longer just the hook-and-bullet crowd that the department still seems to believe it is. —*St. Louis Post-Dispatch*, p. 2C, 27th September 1990
• In the next few weeks, the Bush and Kerry camps will be rolling out their over what is often called the "hook and bullet" crowd. —*Washington Post*, p. A4, 28th June 2004

hooked *adjective*
1 addicted to drugs *US, 1922*
Originally a transitive verb – the drug hooking the person – but that formation is long forgotten in the US.
• They had a terrible contempt for guys on the "white stuff" – heroin, morphine, and cocaine, all drugs that you took with a hypodermic needle – and they told me how when you got hooked on it you got afraid of water[.] —Mezz Mezzrow, *Really the Blues*, p. 238, 1946
• Is it junk? Are you hooked, Diane? —George Mandel, *Flee the Angry Strangers*, p. 285, 1952
• When you are hooked, the effects of a shot are not dramatic. —William Burroughs, *Junkie*, p. 55, 1953
• GEORGE: Oh, no, no, no, no. I – I – I couldn't do that. I mean, I've got enough problems with the – the booze and all. I mean I – I can't afford to get hooked. WYATT: Oh, no – you won't get hooked. —*Easy Rider*, p. 122, 1969
• I tried hard to be like him, so I got hooked on 'H.' —Iceberg Slim (Robert Beck), *Pimp*, p. 99, 1969
• I had been using cocaine every day and using horse every day, so you can understand how I didn't know I was hooked. —A.S. Jackson, *Gentleman Pimp*, p. 86, 1973
• Only a skag high ain't but good the first few times out, then you hooked, all they gotta do is reel you in, by the crotch now, and squeeze till you cough up another five dollars for a bag. —Edwin Torres, *Carlito's Way*, p. 10, 1975
• Meanwhile Vickie had gotten hooked on junk. —Herbert Huncke, *The Evening Sun Turned Crimson*, p. 55, 1980

2 'addicted' to anything non-addictive *UK, 1984*
• Practically all of us, at some point in our lives, have been hooked on dairy beverages like milk, chocolate milk, and milk shakes. —Marilyn Diamond, *American Vegetarian*, 1990
• —*Hooked on Golf*, 1994

3 obsessed by an activity or a person *UK*
Figurative application of the sense 'addicted to drugs'.
• —Royal Philharmonic Orchestra, *Hooked on Classics [a series of recordings]*, 1980s
• It showed that the right music, the right people and the right chemicals could create an amazing party ... for fuck's sake, who wouldn't be hooked? —John Robb, *The Nineties*, p. 49, 1999

4 taken care of *US*
• I called about our airplane tickets and we're hooked. —Connie Eble (Editor), *UNC-CH Campus Slang*, p. 4, Fall 1989

5 put together or arranged well *US*
• —Connie Eble (Editor), *UNC-CH Campus Slang*, p. 5, October 2002

6 (of a shot in pool) obstructed *US, 1979*
• —Mike Shamos, *The Illustrated Encyclopedia of Billiards*, p. 117, 1993

hooker *noun*
1 a prostitute *US, 1845*
Probably derives from the conventional sense of 'hook' (to lure); possibly reinforced by now obsolete slang: 'hook' (to rob); and with reference to Corlear's Hook, popularly The Hook, an area of New York City known for prostitution.
• Who's going to take the word of a five-buck hooker against Elmer Gantry[.] —Richard Brooks, *Elmer Gantry*, 1960
• "'Cause like every hooker I've ever met – I've never made it with a hooker before." —James Mills, *The Panic in Needle Park*, p. 51, 1966
• They walked down a back alley and into a punter getting a Bill Clinton [fellatio] from a hooker. —Stewart Home, *Sex Kick [britpulp]*, p. 214, 1999

2 in a deck of playing cards, a queen *US*
An evolved form of the more common **WHORE**.
• —Albert H. Morehead, *The Complete Guide to Winning Poker*, p. 265, 1967

3 a towing truck *US*
• —Connie Eble (Editor), *UNC-CH Campus Slang*, p. 3, April 1978

4 a shunter (a locomotive used for moving train carriages around a shunting yard) *UK*
Railwaymen's term.
• —Harvey Sheppard, *Dictionary of Railway Slang*, 1970

5 on a moped, a modified exhaust pipe *BERMUDA*
• —Peter A. Smith and Fred M. Barritt, *Bermewjan Vurds*, 1985

6 the hand *US*
A variant of the more common **HOOK**.
• He then threw his deuce of hookers high and a big black cloud dropped from the sky. —Dan Burley, *Diggeth Thou?*, p. 28, 1959

7 a strong alcoholic drink *UK, 1833*
• [T]houghtfully sipping another hooker of scotch, Angela began to wonder whether her ethics might not be misplaced. —Max Shulman, *Rally Round the Flag, Boys!*, p. 72, 1957
• I learned later he was loaded to his ears on seconal and pot – at this point – tossing off double hookers of straight whiskey. —Herbert Huncke, *The Evening Sun Turned Crimson*, p. 44, 1980

8 a cigarette *US*
Teen slang.
• —*Newsweek*, p. 28, 8th October 1951

hooknose *noun*
a Jewish person *US, 1867*
Offensive, based on a stereotyped racial characteristic.
• BRIAN: I'm not a Roman, Mum, and I never will be! I'm a Kike! A Yid! A Hebe! A Hook-nose! I'm Kosher, Mum! I'm a Red Sea Pedestrian, and proud of it! —Monty Python, *Life of Brian*, 1979

hook-off-the-nail *noun*
clothing bought off the rack, ready to wear *BAHAMAS*
• —John A. Holm, *Dictionary of Bahamian English*, p. 105, 1982

hooks *noun*
in electric and telephone line work, climbing irons *US*
• —A.B. Chance Co., *Lineman's Slang Dictionary*, p. 9, 1980

hook shop *noun*
a brothel *US, 1889*
From **HOOKER** (prostitute).
• And he never comes back, Mr. Dillon, he's damned well told that it ain't necessary, because this is a hotel not a hook shop. —Jim Thompson, *The Grifters*, p. 15, 1963

hook up *verb*
1 to meet someone; to meet someone and have sex *US, 1986*
• —Connie Eble (Editor), *UNC-CH Campus Slang*, p. 6, Spring 1988
• Jonathan'll take you out and show you what you wanna see, then we can all hook up for lunch. —*A Few Good Men*, 1992
• Like I care about your shit. May'be I'll hook up myself. —*Chasing Amy*, 1997
• You know, like, if we hook up tonight, tomorrow I'll just be some girl you go telling all your friends about. —*American Pie*, 1999
• He's already called me to hook up. —*Cruel Intentions*, 1999

2 to work in partnership *US*
• Many punks "hook up" in protective pairing relationships, staying with one jocker in exchange for protection. —*Corrections Today*, p. 100, December 1996

3 to arm yourself *US*
• The three men were hooked up and wore their guns police style. —A.S. Jackson, *Gentleman Pimp*, p. 123, 1973

4 in drag racing and motor racing, to achieve maximum traction *US*
• —Don Alexander, *The Racer's Dictionary*, p. 31, 1980

5 to provide *US*
• Na man, c'mon, hook me up just this once. —*Menace II Society*, 1993

hooky; hookey *adjective*
criminal, stolen, counterfeit *UK*
Plays on **BENT**.
• People say the last fight was hooky. —Anthony Masters, *Minder*, p. 26, 1984
• [A]s hookey as planting actual evidence on a suspect. —Jake Arnott, *He Kills Coppers*, p. 13, 2001
• [B]e wary of touts and hooky tickets. —*X-Ray*, p. 48, June 2003

hooky bob *verb*
in icy winter conditions, to grab the bumper of a passing car and use your feet as skis as you are pulled along *US*
- —Jim Crotty, *How to Talk American*, p. 215, 1997

hooley *noun*
an especially lively party *IRELAND, 1877*
- —Louis S. Leland, *A Personal Kiwi-Yankee Dictionary*, p. 52, 1984
- [I]t's Chinese New Year starting tomorrer. We could start the hooley today, don't yer think?—Niall Griffiths, *Kelly + Victor*, p. 143, 2002

hoolie *noun*
a *hooligan* *UK*
- We were hoolies, homos and just plain hedonists.—Gavin Hills, *White Burger Danny (Disco Biscuits)*, p. 72, 1996
- [T]hat's the lot your hoolie mates were out and about with. —J.J. Connolly, *Layer Cake*, p. 126, 2000

hooligan *noun*
in motor racing on a dirt track, a consolation race *US*
- Cars which failed to qualify for the main event rate together in the holligan, which is usually held just before the main.—John Lawlor, *How to Talk Car*, p. 62, 1965

hooly-dooly; hooley-dooley
wow! *AUSTRALIA*
- The Sydney Opera House is finished, paid for, costs less than originally estimated, is officially opened, functions perfectly, has unlimited parking space, has 'house full' signs out every night, and is making an enormous profit – 'Hooly-dooly.'—John O'Grady, *Aussie English*, p. 46, 1965
- Hooley-dooley, that was no dolphin.—Tim Winton, *Lockie Leonard*, p. 5, 1997

hoon *noun*
1 a man who lives off the earnings of prostitutes; a pimp *AUSTRALIA, 1949*
- 'E's a hoon! A weak mug that bludges his money off weak molls!!—Jim McNeil, *The Chocolate Frog*, p. 48, 1973
- Bill thought we should follow the girls. 'We can be hoons, mate!' he laughed. 'A couple of Terry toons.—Max Williams, *Dingo*, p. 59, 1980
- Maybe not,' she said, 'but it won't help Sara to team up with you end up with a hoon like yours...' I stopped the exchange when I asked what a hoon was. Margaret said, 'You know...those bastards who live off you, make you work hard and take all your money.'—Sara Francis, *Sara: Her own story of her life and times in Australia's red-light world*, p. 83, 1984

2 a loud ignorant lout; a hooligan *AUSTRALIA, 1938*
Origin unknown.
- The Real Bush-pig is the female counterpart and proper companion for the Male Hoon.—Ignatius Jones, *True Hip*, p. 124, 1990
- A carful of hoons revved by in a purple Valiant. 'Oi!' one shouted out the window.—Linda Jaivin, *Rock n Roll Babes from Outer Space*, p. 82, 1996

3 a person who drives recklessly *AUSTRALIA, 1985*
- Susie's a bit of a hoon when she drives, and the car was hooked up great and we were really fanging it down that road.—*Dolly*, p. 69, July 1989
- I was in no mood to allow a hoon to get away with this type of driving.—Rex Hunt, *Tall Tales – and True*, p. 106, 1994
- The hoon in his dented Valiant Charger scereches around the corner[.]—Glyn Parry, *Mosh*, p. 109, 1996

4 a trip in a motor vehicle taken for the pleasure of, especially fast, driving *AUSTRALIA*
- —James Lambert, *The Macquarie Book of Slang*, 1996

hoon *verb*
to drive recklessly *AUSTRALIA*
- Now there was a man who knew his limitations at the wheel. No mad hooning about all over the countryside for him.—*The Mercury*, p. 8, 8th July 1992

hoonah light *noun*
in the pornography industry, a light used to illuminate the genitals of the performers *US*
- —*Adult Video News*, p. 50, October 1995

hoondom *noun*
an assemblage of louts *NEW ZEALAND*
- On display was a wide range of these Wellingtonians – louts, larrikins, lunks, lummoxes, yahoos – the creme de la creme of hoondom. —*(Wellington) Dominion*, p. 1, 24th March 1983

hoonered *adjective*
drunk *UK*
- —Pete Brown, *Man Walks into a Pub*, 2003

hooning *noun*
loutish behaviour *NEW ZEALAND*
- The sons (and daughters) of the middle classes, they are less professional in their hooning.—*Listener*, p. 12, 20th December 1986

hoonish *adjective*
loutish *NEW ZEALAND*
- A lot of hoonish summer behaviour may be the very result of biorhythmical and biochemical imbalances.—*Listener*, p. 70, 5th November 1970

hoonmobile *noun*
a lout-driven car *NEW ZEALAND*
- I wasn't sure whether to be flattered or outraged by the stares from the rear windows of the hoonmobiles.—*(Wellington) Dominion*, p. 10, 16th January 1993

hoop *noun*
1 in criminal circles, a finger-ring *US, 1856*
Conventional English for three centuries, and then ascended to criminal slang.
- —Vincent J. Monteleone, *Criminal Slang*, p. 121, 1949
- That's a twenty-five ... maybe even thirty-gee ($30,000) hoop, and you miss the point?—Iceberg Slim (Robert Beck), *Death Wish*, p. 93, 1977

2 the rectum as a place to hide prison contraband *US*
- He's gone to the hoop with it.—James Harris, *A Convict's Dictionary*, p. 34, 1989

3 a jockey *AUSTRALIA, 1941*
- Best hoop in the country, the old Darb.—Nino Culotta (John O'Grady), *They're A Weird Mob*, p. 72, 1957
- He knew the set-up: lawns smooth as the baize on a baccarat table; flowers thick as wreaths on Benny the crim's coffin; scads of humans dying to part with their money; rafts of thoroughbreds turned out beautiful as rich men's babies; flocks of hoops gaudy as parrots in a tropical jungle.—Wilda Moxham, *The Apprentice*, p. 13, 1969
- From the commonly worn silk shirts with hoops of colour.—Ned Wallish, *The Truth Dictionary of Racing Slang*, p. 39, 1989

hoopdee *noun*
a new, late-model car *US*
- —Eugene Landy, *The Underground Dictionary*, p. 105, 1971

hooped *adjective*
drunk *NEW ZEALAND*
- —David McGill, *David McGill's Complete Kiwi Slang Dictionary*, p. 58, 1998

hoopie *noun*
a bicycling enthusiast who spends more time and effort buying equipment and clothing than actually bicycling *US*
- —Anna Scotti and Paul Young, *Buzzwords*, p. 112, 1997

hoopla *noun*
a commotion *US, 1877*
Originally, the cry associated with the fairground game of tossing hoops over blocks.
- "As Americans like to say, there was much hoopla about nothing," [George] Michael said about the lyrics in his song.—*New York Daily News*, 11th March 1988

hoople *noun*
a fool, a dolt *US, 1928*
- That's some hoople goin' to pick up his girl.—Charles Whited, *Chiodo*, p. 123, 1973
- Are you a comedian or something? He says no, I'm serious, it's a good blanket. The guy's a Hoople.—Leonard Shecter and William Phillips, *On the Pad*, p. 215, 1973
- There was so many lawyers they was stumbling all over one another, bunch of hooples.—Edwin Torres, *Carlito's Way*, p. 125, 1975

hoople head *noun*
an idiot *US*
- He still sounds like a fucking hoople head half the time.—Vincent Patrick, *Family Business*, p. 54, 1985

hoop rod *noun*
a car *US*
Formed from **HOT ROD** and **HOOPTY**.
- —Don R. McCreary (Editor), *Dawg Speak*, 2001

hoops *noun*
handcuffs *US*
- —Vincent J. Monteleone, *Criminal Slang*, p. 121, 1949

hoop snake *noun*

a mythical snake that holds its own tail and rolls *AUSTRALIA*

A tale told to impress and frighten gullible visitors. An early example of the story (though not the term itself) can be found in J.S. James, *The Vagabond Papers*, 1877.

- Hoop snakes also exist in Tasmania but, to my knowledge, are limited to the north-west coast near Sisters Beach. The Tasmanian ones are quite specialised in that they live in sand dunes and use the sloping sand to gain the momentum they need to roll down. — *Wordmap (www.abc.net.au/wordmap)*, 2003

hoopsy-coopsy *adjective*

drunk *NEW ZEALAND*

- And this plonk have the kick alright and soon the coot got very hoopsy-coopsy. — W. N. McCallum, *The Half-Gallon Jar*, p. 27, 1962

hoopty *noun*

a run-down, shoddy car *US, 1970*

- — *Los Angeles Times*, p. II-6, 11th August 1986
- — Connie Eble (Editor), *UNC-CH Campus Slang*, p. 3, Spring 1993
- — *Newsday*, p. B2, 11th October 1997

hoor; hure *noun*

a whore *UK*

Variant early spellings from C14 and C15, surviving in current Irish slang.

hoo-raw *noun*

a fight, a dispute *CANADA*

- Pretty soon Canada will have a "Social Register," although not without considerable hoo-raw and the odd "exposure" about its founders. — *Grande Prairie, Alta Herald-Tribune*, p. 2–5, 21st February 1958

hooray *noun*

good news *UK*

- [T]he other bit of hooray that the truck fraternity have been telling me[.] — *Radio 4 News*, 14th April 1983

hooray

goodbye *AUSTRALIA, 1898*

- Well, hooray, Roo, I'll see you tomorrer. — Ray Lawler, *Summer of the Seventeenth Doll*, p. 69, 1957

hooray Henry; hooray *noun*

a male of the upper-classes who exhibits a superior or anti-social manner *UK, 1959*

Coined as 'Hoorah Henry' by Damon Runyon in the story *Tight Shoes*, 1936; mainly UK usage.

- The three hoorays sit down but the mob still look at them suspiciously. — Troy Kennedy Martin, *The Italian Job [uncut script]*, 1969
- Hooray Henrys are the tip of the Sloane iceberg, visible and audible for miles. — Ann Barr and Peter York, *The Official Sloane Ranger Handbook*, p. 118, 1982
- [U]sing the Hooray's own weight and momentum, he threw him hard on to his back. — Chris Ryan, *The Watchman*, p. 155, 2001
- They gave the job I was hoping for to some hooray with a degree. — Claire Mansfield and John Mendelssohn, *Dominatrix*, p. 268, 2002

hooride *verb*

in a group, to berate and humiliate someone *US*

- — *Maybeck High School Yearbook (Berkeley, California)*, p. 29, 1997
- — Rick Ayers (Editor), *Berkeley High Slang Dictionary*, p. 11, 2001

hooroo

goodbye *AUSTRALIA, 1906*

- Hoo roo Bazza! You randy of bastard. — Barry Humphries, *The Wonderful World of Barry McKenzie*, p. 10, 1968
- GARY: See you tomorrow. BENTLEY: Hoo roo. — Alexander Buzo, *Rooted*, p. 70, 1969
- Then he said 'Hooroo' and I left to take the seven camels back the 350 miles by meself. — Patsy Adam-Smith, *Folklore of the Australian Railwaymen*, p. 175, 1969

hooroos *noun*

phlegm *NORFOLK ISLAND*

- — Beryl Nobbs Palmer, *A Dictionary of Norfolk Words and Usages*, p. 20, 1992

hoor's melt; whore's melt; whoor's melt *noun*

a contemptible person *IRELAND, 1961*

Combines **HOOR** (a prostitute, perhaps implying no more than a female) with 'melt' (spawn, offspring); alternatively 'melt' may derive from Old English *milte* (the spleen) or as a dialect word for 'the tongue'.

- 'An' sure God is good, and the whoor's melt won't have a minute's luck. — Hugh Leonard, *Out After Dark*, p. 108, 1989
- I swear that hoor's melt Fitzpatrick is right about one thing[.] — James Hawes, *Dead Long Enough*, p. 262, 2000

hoose *noun*

in poker, a hand consisting of three cards of the same rank and a pair *US*

Known conventionally as a 'full house'.

- — *American Speech*, p. 99, May 1951

hoose *verb*

to bowl with speed and force *BARBADOS*

- — Frank A. Collymore, *Barbadian Dialect*, p. 59, 1965

hoosegow *noun*

a jail or prison *US, 1908*

A corruption of the Spanish *juzgado* (court or tribunal).

- [I]t would be the happiest day of my life if I can find out she really wasn't married to him and put her in the damned hoosegow for fraud[.] — Gore Vidal, *Myra Breckinridge*, p. 82–83, 1968
- "If they catch you, they'll put you in the hoosegow," He'd tell us[.] — Oscar Zeta Acosta, *The Autobiography of a Brown Buffalo*, p. 79, 1972
- The hit just ordered on the hooker in the hoosegow proved that. — Seth Morgan, *Homeboy*, p. 98, 1990
- This kid got his load on, staggered out of there with his piece like he's in Tombstone Arizona and now he's in the hoosegow — Richard Price, *Clockers*, p. 382, 1992

hoosie Fraser *noun*

▷ see: HOUSE OF FRASER

hoot *noun*

1 a cause for laughter *US, 1942*

A bit old-fashioned, often used in a sarcastic or condescending tone.

- Anna suggested they lunch at the Washington Square Bar & Grill. "It's a hoot," she laughed over the phone. — Armistead Maupin, *Tales of the City*, p. 74, 1978
- You're a hoot and a half, Gino. Really a fuckin riot. — Seth Morgan, *Homeboy*, p. 188, 1990
- I remember sitting in front of the makeup mirror in the Bunny dressing room, carefully gluing on three pairs of false eyelashes, and laughing so much. Everything about being a bunny was a hoot! — Kathryn Leigh Scott, *The Bunny Years*, p. 143, 1998
- The rain fell steadily while a razor-sharp wind cut me to the core [...] Summer in Hokkaido: what a hoot! — Josie Dew, *The Sun In My Eyes*, p. 264, 2001

2 an inhalation of marijuana *CANADA*

- [H]e hands the chillum to Paris, who takes a long hoot and over-inhales, as is so easy to do with a bong or a chillum. — Brian Preston, *Pot Planet*, p. 94, 2002

3 a little bit *US, 1878*

Generally used in phrases that have a negative intent, such as 'not give a hoot', 'not care two hoots', etc.

- "I don't give a hoot. They don't have the right to say those things." — Mickey Spillane, *One Lonely Night*, p. 30, 1951
- I couldn't give a hoot about my bollocks[.] — *FHM*, p. 31, June 2003
- The MoD [Ministry of Defence] are again ill-prepared [for war] and don't care a hoot about the lads on the ground willing to lay down their life. — *Evening Standard*, p. 6, 7th March 2003

4 money *AUSTRALIA, 1881*

- — Jim Ramsay, *Cop It Sweet!*, p. 46, 1977
- — Ryan Aven-Bray, *Ridgey Didge Oz Jack Lang*, p. 31, 1983

Hoot *noun*

a member of the Hutterian Brethren *US*

The Hutterites are an Anabaptist group that believe in communal living; they are found in rural areas of the Canadian prairies and the American states of Montana, Washington, North Dakota and Minnesota.

- — Jim Crotty, *How to Talk American*, p. 215, 1997

hootch *noun*

▷ see: HOOCH

hootched *adjective*

drunk *US*

- — Kenn "Naz" Young, *Naz's Dictionary of Teen Slang*, p. 60, 1993

hootchie; hoochie; hootchy mama *noun*

a young woman, especially when easily available for sex *US*

- I wanted to get over with one of the hootchies over there. — *Boyz N The Hood*, 1990
- — Connie Eble (Editor), *UNC-CH Campus Slang*, p. 5, April 1995

- Rap made slang aimed at women like "skeezer," "hootchie," "chickhead," and the ubiquitous "bitch"[.] — Nelson George, *Hip Hop America*, p. 186, 1998

hootchie-coo *noun*

sex *US*

- Y'all gonna do the hootchie-coo? — *Boyz N The Hood*, 1990

hootchy-kootchy; hootchie-coochie *noun*

a sexually attractive person *US*

- He was such a hoochie-coochie she didn't know what to do. — Steve Cannon, *Groove, Bang, and Jive Around*, p. 139, 1969

hootenananny *noun*

in oil drilling, any complicated piece of equipment that the speaker cannot identify by name *US, 1928*

- — Jerry Robertson, *Oil Slanguage*, p. 66, 1954

hooter *noun*

1 the nose *UK, 1958*

In senses both actual and figurative; from the trumpeting noise emitted when blown.

- Some nosey fucking busybody poking their hooter in where it wasn't needed. — Greg Williams, *Diamond Geezers*, p. 64, 1997
- I guess she's afraid of getting smacked in the shnaz. Can't blame 'er. Quite a hooter on her already. — Anthony Petkovich, *The X Factory*, p. 193, 1997
- In one session I'd been known to blow a grand's worth of trumpet up my noble hooter. — Wayne Anthony, *Spanish Highs*, p. 46, 1999

2 cocaine *US*

The drug is sniffed up the **HOOTER** (nose).

- — Joel Homer, *Jargon*, p. 197, 1979

3 a large marijuana cigarette *US, 1986*

- Enuff bud to keep tha whole party high on / I might get ill and roll an 8th in one hooter. — Tone *Cheeba Cheeba*, 1989
- — Jim Emerson-Cobb, *Scratching the Dragon*, April 1997

4 a party *US*

- — Dennis Aaberg and John Milius, *Big Wednesday*, p. 208, 1978

5 a toilet *NEW ZEALAND, 1968*

- — Harry Orsman, *A Dictionary of Modern New Zealand Slang*, p. 68, 1999

hooters *noun*

female breasts *US*

- Their secondary sex characteristics are simply too conspicuous to pass without insult, and we were unmerciful towards them: tits, boobs, knockers, jugs, bubbies, bazooms, lungs, flaps and hooters we called them, and there was no way to be polite about it. — *Screw*, p. 6, 3th January 1972
- But below the neck is an odd set of hooters that leave some in confusion as she treats the old boys with flashes of them by her second song. — Josh Alan Friedman, *Tales of Times Square*, p. 11, 1986
- She thrust out her chest when she said it, and he had to admit she had pretty nice hooters. — Joseph Wambaugh, *Finnegan's Week*, p. 170, 1993
- Playing with Ken or Barbie made it even more confusing because neither had genitals of any kind, even though Barbie had perky hooters. — Anka Radakovich, *The Wild Girls Club*, 1994

hootie mac *noun*

marijuana *US*

- — Connie Eble (Editor), *UNC-CH Campus Slang*, p. 3, Fall 1996

hooting *noun*

in surfing, shouts that compliment the quality of a wave or a ride on the wave *US*

- — Brian and Margaret Lowdon, *Competitive Surfing*, 1988

hoover *noun*

1 any vacuum cleaner *UK*

A widely used generic, from Hoover, a manufacturer of brand name vacuum cleaners since 1908.

- [T]hey perished under Mum's slippers or up the Hoover. — Martin King and Martin Knight, *The Naughty Nineties*, p. 64, 1999

2 the nose *UK*

- — Tom Hibbert, *Rockspeak!*, p. 87, 1983

hoover *verb*

1 to clean with a vacuum cleaner *UK, 1939*

A generic, almost *the* generic, from Hoover™ vacuum cleaners.

- Some chance of that [a lie-in] with 'er indoors 'oovering round the bed. — Anthony Masters, *Minder*, p. 67, 1984

2 to suck out, to remove by suction *AUSTRALIA*

- "I've thought of having this bit", Dame Edna touches the wattles under her chin, "Hoovered out, you know... What they do is make a little hole in your chin... and they suck out a kind of horrible sausage of fat." — John Lahr, *Dame Edna Everage and the Rise of Western Civilisation*, p. 10–11, 1991

3 to extract; to draw out *US*

- David Macklin had hoovered us for thousands to insure Mack would be a rich widow if I checked out back when we were young and stupid. — George V. Higgins, *Penance for Jerry Kennedy*, p. 14, 1985

4 to inhale drugs *US, 1982*

From the similarity to a 'hoover' (a vacuum cleaner) cleaning up dust.

- Whenever there are dances to be danced, drugs to be hoovered, women to be allagashed. — Jay McInerney, *Bright Lights, Big City*, p. 44, 1984
- James hoovered his line [of cocaine] in one, languorous draught[.] — Kevin Sampson, *Powder*, p. 87, 1999
- You hoovered up some silly dust back in the club, entered a K-hole and don't know what happened. — *Mixmag*, p. 142, June 2003

5 to eat or drink greedily *US, 1986*

From the similarity to a 'hoover' (a vacuum cleaner)'s indiscriminate method of swallowing anything in its path.

- — Connie Eble (Editor), *UNC-CH Campus Slang*, p. 6, Spring 1988

6 to perform oral sex on a man *UK*

From the supposed similarity to a 'hoover' (a vacuum cleaner)'s suction.

- Fancy a quick hoover d'amour? — compiled by the cast of 'Aspects of Love', Prince of Wales Theatre, *Palare (Boy Dancer Talk) for Beginners*, 1989–92

7 to perform an abortion *US*

An allusion to the branded vacuum cleaner.

- — *Oprah Winfrey Show*, 2nd October 2003

hoover d'amour *noun*

an act of oral sex on a man *UK*

From the supposed similarity to a vacuum cleaner's suction, lent romance by the French 'of love'.

- Fancy a quick hoover d'amour? — the cast of 'Aspects of Love', Prince of Wales Theatre, *Palare (Boy Dancer Talk) for Beginners*, 1989–92

hoozy *adjective*

absent-minded *US*

- — Connie Eble (Editor), *UNC-CH Campus Slang*, p. 4, November 2003

hop *noun*

1 a narcotic – opium, morphine or heroin *US, 1886*

- Over and over he kept heating this small hunk of hop, rolling it on the thumb of his left hand until it was compact and looked like a tight little wad of cotton. — Mezz Mezzrow, *Really the Blues*, p. 98, 1946
- — James T. Farrell, *Saturday Night*, p. 38, 1947
- "We go up dark stairways to get a gun punk with a skinful of hop and sometimes we don't get all the way up, and our wives wait dinner that night and all the other nights. — Raymond Chandler, *The Little Sister*, p. 218, 1949
- There was no hop behind his pupils so he was a classy workman being paid by an employer who knew what the score was. — Mickey Spillane, *Kiss Me Deadly*, p. 44, 1952
- I wasn't high on the hop; I was high on withdrawal tone-up. — William Burroughs, *Junkie*, p. 108, 1953
- "Not perfume, honey, hop," she said. And when I still didn't get it, "Opium, don't you know?" — Polly Adler, *A House is Not a Home*, p. 35, 1953
- They jumped from the sticks to St. Louis, and when he wasn't dead drunk he was shooting himself full of hop. — Jim Thompson, *The Grifters*, p. 82, 1963

2 a dance, a party *UK, 1731*

- Tonight I got a date with a Sigma, a keen babe, for a hop at the Shoreland Hotel. — James T. Farrell, *Saturday Night*, p. 35, 1947
- Some characters tap the female college alumnae lists for recent graduates resident in Washington, then pick names at random and phone with an invitation to a Yale or Princeton hop which never seems to come off. — Jack Lait and Lee Mortimer, *Washington Confidential*, p. 89, 1951

3 in handball, a ball which breaks to the left or right after rebounding off the front wall *US*

- — Peter Tyson and Mort Leve, *Handball*, p. 68, 1972: 'Glossary of handball terms'

4 in craps, a one-roll bet on the next roll *US*

- — Thomas L. Clark, *The Dictionary of Gambling*, p. 103, 1987

▸ on the hop
playing truant *UK*
- [M]y cousin, Tony McLean, and me were on the hop from school. —Lenny McLean, *The Guv'nor*, p. 6, 1998

hop *verb*
1 to work as a car hop at a drive-in restaurant where customers are served in their cars *US*
- She wore lots of cheap wigs, waited tables or hopped cars, was truly hung, might chew gum, posed for pictures, and got most of her fun in groups. —Dan Jenkins, *Semi-Tough*, p. 72, 1972

2 to go, to travel *UK, 1923*
- When lack of nightlife begins to grate, hop over to Rhodes Town. —*The Observer*, 16th November 2003

3 to flee or escape *US*
- —Hyman E. Goldin et al., *Dictionary of American Underworld Lingo*, p. 101, 1950

4 in horse racing, to administer an illegal drug to a horse, either a stimulant or a depressant *US*
- —Tom Ainslie, *Ainslie's Complete Guide to Thoroughbred Racing*, p. 333, 1976

▸ hop 'n pop
in the language of parachuting, to pull the ripcord within three seconds of clearing the aircraft *US*
- —Dan Poynter, *Parachuting*, p. 167, 1978: 'The language of parachuting'

▸ hop a hole
(used of a ball in pinball) to fall into and then keep moving out of an ejecting hole because of high velocity *US*
- —Bobbye Claire Natkin and Steve Kirk, *All About Pinball*, p. 113, 1977

▸ hop bells
to work in a hotel as a bell hop *US, 1942*
- I formerly hopped bells with him. —Jim Thompson, *Bad Boy*, p. 365, 1953
- Why I juggled a tray in a New York cafe / and I hopped hotel bells in Chi. —Bruce Jackson, *Get Your Ass in the Water and Swim Like Me*, p. 72, 1962

▸ hop in for your chop
to take your share *AUSTRALIA*
- Hop in for your chop. Make 'em give you everything you're entitled to. —Eric Lambert, *The Veterans*, p. 16, 1954

▸ hop into the horsecollar
(from a male perspective) to have sex *AUSTRALIA*
From **HORSECOLLAR** (the vagina).
- To "hop into the horsecollar" is to engage in a form of romantic dalliance[.] —Barry Humphries, *Bazza Pulls It Off!*, 1971

▸ hop it; 'oppit
to depart, especially to depart quickly *UK, 1910*
- Well, we hangs about for ages and I reckons we ought to 'oppit, and we was just about to go off when we sees them coming. —John Peter Jones, *Feather Pluckers*, p. 19, 1964

▸ hop the train
to ride the subway (underground) without paying the fare *US*
- —Maria Hinojas, *Crews*, p. 167, 1995: 'Glossary'

hop-and-drop *noun*
1 a stylised walk *TRINIDAD AND TOBAGO, 1951*
- A man's style of walking in which a slow precise lowered step is followed by a fast short rising bouncing step and a pause. —Lise Winer, *Dictionary of the English/Creole of Trinidad & Tobago*, 2003

2 a limp *BARBADOS*
- —Frank A. Collymore, *Barbadian Dialect*, p. 60, 1965

hop and pop *verb*
to wake up and spring into action *US*
- —*Seattle Times*, p. A9, 12th April 1998: 'Grunts, squids not grunting from the same dictionary'

hopdog *noun*
an opium addict *US*
- —Mezz Mezzrow, *Really the Blues*, p. 94, 1946

hope *noun*
▸ not a hope in hell!
not a chance!, not a hope! *UK, 1923*
- There was not a sniff of what was coming, not a hope in hell. —*The Guardian*, 12th September 2001

hopeless *adjective*
incompetent *UK, 1922*
- He was a charming reprobate, and absolutely hopeless when it came to telling the truth. —*The Guardian*, 22nd September 2000

hope-to-die *noun*
your spouse or romantic partner *US*
- —Eugene Landy, *The Underground Dictionary*, p. 105, 1971

hop gun *noun*
a syringe used by intravenous drug users *US*
- —Vincent J. Monteleone, *Criminal Slang*, p. 122, 1949

hophead *noun*
1 an opium addict, or, less precisely and more commonly, a user of marijuana or other drug *US, 1901*
- Dope fiends are full of nice little rules and regulations like that; Emily Post could write a book just on hophead etiquette. —Mezz Mezzrow, *Really the Blues*, p. 99, 1946
- "He's becoming a regular hophead," Benny said. —Irving Shulman, *The Amboy Dukes*, p. 99, 1947
- If I was one of them hop-heads I'd go get a sniff and a rod and blow your goddamn guts out. —Mickey Spillane, *My Gun is Quick*, p. 38, 1950
- Tell a hophead he shouldn't take dope. —Jim Thompson, *The Killer Inside*, p. 126, 1952
- It is, of course, thoroughly unfair to blame Parker for all the young hopheads who came along in his wake. —Robert Sylvester, *No Cover Charge*, p. 285, 1956
- Some knew him as a man, others thought he was a hophead Sister. —Chester Himes, *A Rage in Harlem*, p. 49, 1957
- I always knew she was a hop-hop-head with no more morals than a hound-bitch in heat. —Truman Capote, *Breakfast at Tiffany's*, p. 95, 1958
- HOP HEAD: Say now – this one's a real sassy lassie. PAT: You're drunk. HOP HEAD: Drunk? [Giggles] Yeah, that's it – drunk. Man, what a cube. —William Bast, *The Myth Makers [Six Granada Plays]*, p. 176, 1958
- Chenault had the look of a hophead, ready to turn on. —Hunter S. Thompson, *Songs of the Doomed*, p. 96, 1962
- A junkie, a dope addict, a hop-head, a mainliner – a dope fiend! —James Baldwin, *Blues for Mister Charlie*, p. 45, 1964
- New Mexico, man, I finally found him, right where every hophead in the country figured he'd be. —Richard Farina, *Been Down So Long*, p. 60, 1966
- But you went hophead and blew the bread / Now you're talking that stable shit. —Dennis Wepman et al., *The Life*, p. 86, 1976
- Goddamn – this looks like an opium den. You guys hopheads? —Herbert Huncke, *The Evening Sun Turned Crimson*, p. 100, 1980

2 a heavy drinker *AUSTRALIA, 1957*
- I was right on the point of going across and flattening hophead there and then but I didn't want to end in jail or get my face messed round till I'd seen you. —Criena Rohan, *Down by the Dockside*, p. 228, 1963

3 in horse racing, a horse that only performs well when under the influence of a stimulant *US*
- —Dan Parker, *The ABC of Horse Racing*, p. 146, 1947
- —David W. Maurer, *Argot of the Racetrack*, p. 36, 1951

hop in *verb*
to begin in earnest, especially the eating of a meal *AUSTRALIA, 1939*
- 'Hop in, sport!' someone told me, indicating the tray, and while I was hopping in someone else poured me a mug of tea. —Eric Lambert, *The Veterans*, p. 188, 1954
- I don't suppose another table in Australia has more on it than ours so hop in boys and enjoy yourselves. —Patsy Adam-Smith, *Folklore of the Australian Railwaymen*, p. 139, 1969

hop into *verb*
to attack a person, task, meal, etc, with vigour *AUSTRALIA*
- Did you see young Ernie hopping into Christenson? —Robert S. Close, *Love Me Sailor*, 1945
- On Christmas Eve they picked the lock on the den door and hopped into the lot. —Barry Humphries, *A Nice Night's Entertainment*, p. 39, 1960
- I hopped right into everything put in front of me, particularly the delicious grilled meat. —Rex Hunt, *Tall Tales – and True*, p. 11, 1994

hop it!; hoppit!
go away! *UK, 1914*
Used as an injunction, exclamation or both.
- "Where'd you get that tie?" "Mercer's. Now hop it, Billy, will you. —John Burke and Stuart Douglass, *The Boys*, p. 83, 1962
- They walks over to us and says, "Come on you lot, 'oppit. Get out quick." —John Peter Jones, *Feather Pluckers*, p. 14, 1964

hop it and scram; hop it *noun*
ham *UK*
Rhyming slang.
- —Ray Puxley, *Cockney Rabbit*, 1992

hop off *verb*
to launch an attack *US, 1918*
- When that shit hops off at that A&P market, no telling who the police will end up bustin. —Donald Goines, *Black Gangster*, p. 150, 1977

hop out *verb*
to crash (an aeroplane) *US*
• — *American Speech*, p. 123, Summer 1986: 'The language of naval fighter pilots'

hop-pad *noun*
an opium den *US*
• That was the name we gave to a little old six-foot square coal bin down in the cellar of Mike's tenement that we cleaned out and converted into our hop-pad. — Mezz Mezzrow, *Really the Blues*, p. 245, 1946

hopped; hopped up *adjective*
under the influence of drugs *US, 1918*
• Some guys were so hopped on on tea they were rocking on their heels. — Irving Shulman, *The Amboy Dukes*, p. 52, 1947
• At first I thought she was hopped up. Then I saw it wasn't dope. It was fear. — Thurston Scott, *Cure it with Honey*, p. 6, 1951
• He was hopped up and crazy. — Jim Thompson, *The Killer Inside*, p. 37, 1952
• He drove out north to a tea pad where everybody was already hopped up. — Willard Motley, *Let No Man Write My Epitaph*, p. 109, 1958
• I was hopped up when they took me in. — Douglas Rutherford, *The Creeping Flesh*, p. 141, 1963
• It took a good three seconds before his hopped up mind realized the full implications of what he was seeing[.] — Mickey Spillane, *Return of the Hood*, p. 91, 1964
• My friend F. used to say in his hopped up fashion: We've got to learn to stop bravely at the surface. — Leonard Cohen, *Beautiful Losers*, p. 4, 1966
• Hopped to the gills, the gunman stalked forward on the balls of his feet to place another slug in the absolutely motionless body[.] — Chester Himes, *Come Back Charleston Blue*, p. 87, 1966
• Johnny turns the radio on, hoping for one of those miraculously lunatic stations that spew out the blessedly mesmerizing wailing of young groups with lovely names, the hopped-up disc jockeys making bad jokes[.] — John Rechy, *Numbers*, p. 11, 1967

hopped up *adjective*
(used of a car) modified to increase the engine performance *US, 1941*
• When it flew by us, I turned the other way/The guy in the Mercury had nothin' to say/For it was kid in a hopped up Model A.' — George Wilson (performed by Arkie Shibley and His Mountain Dew Boys), *Hot Rod Race*, 1950

hopper *noun*
1 a kangaroo or wallaby *AUSTRALIA, 1879*
• [O]ne day I potted one of the hoppers for dog feed. — Bill Wannan, *Bullockies, Beauts and Bandicoots*, p. 112, 1960

2 a car shock absorber *US*
• — *Current Slang*, p. 19, Spring 1970

hopper fill heist *noun*
an attempt to defraud a casino by sitting at a slot machine with a winning combination showing that has paid off partially but requires additional coins to be added to complete the payoff *US*
• I even know a few individuals who have been caught attempting a hopper fill heist. — Charles W. Lund, *Robbing the One-Armed Bandits*, p. 121, 1999

hoppers *noun*
trainers (sneakers) *ANTIGUA AND BARBUDA*
Collected by Richard Allsopp.

hopping *adjective*
extremely busy *IRELAND*
• Sunday night of the October bank holiday weekend and the streets are hopping. — Donal Ruane, *Tales in a Rearview Mirror*, p. 95, 2003

hopping John *noun*
a stew made of boiled pig's feet, black-eye peas and rice *US, 1838*
• "Ain't nothin' but hoppin' john," Goldy said. 'I like hoppin' john, all right," Jacksosn replied. — Chester Himes, *A Rage in Harlem*, p. 53, 1957

hopping mad *adjective*
very angry *US, 1675*
• Jack Schitt and the Brontë Federation are hopping mad over the damage to the book. — Jasper Fforde, *The Eyre Affair*, p. 358, 2001

hopping pot; hopping *noun*
the lot *UK*
Rhyming slang.
• So they charges 'im with the hoppin'-pot: causing obstruction on the carriage way, causing obstruction to foot-passengers, trading without a licence, resisting the police – the lot! — Julian Franklyn, *A Dictionary of Rhyming Slang*, 1961
• "That's your hopping," means "That's you[r] lot, there's no more." — Ray Puxley, *Cockney Rabbit*, 1992

hoppit!
▷ see: HOP IT!

hoppo-bump *verb*
to bump into another for fun *AUSTRALIA*
From the name of a child's game in which players hop on one leg and bump into each other.
• The boys were hoppo-bumping each other, acting the goat, while the girls maintained an air of superior indifference. — Shane Maloney, *Nice Try*, p. 263, 1998

hops *noun*
beer *US, 1902*
• My own taste for the hops is very powerful, and I had no intention of spending a beerless weekend in the withering sun. — Hunter S. Thompson, *Hell's Angels*, p. 141, 1966
• I haven't hit the hops for a couple of weeks. — Alexander Buzo, *Rooted*, p. 63, 1969
• — David Claerbaut, *Black Jargon in White America*, p. 68, 1972

▸ **on the hops**
on a drinking binge *AUSTRALIA, 1930*
• When Gus was on the hops he'd smash everything in sight[.] — Wilda Moxham, *The Apprentice*, p. 25, 1969
• — Alexander Buzo, *Norm and Ahmed*, p. 24, 1969
• — Patsy Adam-Smith, *Folklore of the Australian Railwaymen*, p. 25, 1969

hopscotch *noun*
a watch *UK*
Rhyming slang, formed from the name of a traditional children's game.

hopscotcher *noun*
a carnival worker who moves from one carnival to another *US*
• — *American Speech*, p. 281, December 1966: 'More carnie talk from the west coast'

hop squad *noun*
a narcotics squad within a police department *US*
• — Jack Webb, *The Badge*, p. 221, 1958

hop stop *noun*
in pinball, a brief release of an extended flipper to prevent a ball from rolling up off the end *US*
• — Bobbye Claire Natkin and Steve Kirk, *All About Pinball*, p. 113, 1977

hoptoad *verb*
on the railways, to derail *US*
• — Norman Carlisle, *The Modern Wonder Book of Trains and Railroading*, p. 264, 1946

hoptoads *noun*
any dice altered for cheating *US*
• — *The Annals of the American Academy of Political and Social Sciences*, p. 126, May 1950

hop up *verb*
in hot rodding, to increase the power of an engine *US, 1942*
• When it flew by us, I turned the other way/The guy in the Murcury had nothin' to say/For it was kid in a hopped up Model A. — George Wilson (performed by Arkie Shibley and His Mountain Dew Boys), *Hot Rod Race*, 1950
• — John Lawlor, *How to Talk Car*, p. 63, 1965
• Thousands of kids are getting hold of cars and either hopping them up for speed or customizing them to some extent, ususally a little of both. — Tom Wolfe, *The Kandy-Kolored Tangerine-Flake Streamline Baby*, p. 80, 1965

horizontal *adjective*
asleep *US*
• — Connie Eble (Editor), *UNC-CH Campus Slang*, p. 5, Spring 1991

▸ **get horizontal**
to sleep *US*
• — *Complete CB Slang Dictionary*, 1976
• — Peter Chippindale, *The British CB Book*, p. 155, 1981

horizontal bop *noun*
sexual intercourse *US*
• Whether he [George Washington] and Sally [Fairfax] ever did the horizontal bop has remained a point of speculation for historians[.] — Erica Orloff and JoAnn Baker, *Dirty Little Secrets*, p. 139, 2001

horizontal exercise *noun*
sexual intercourse *US, 1918*
• "Everybody here," she wrote to one of her friends, "is busy talking about breaking new records, getting drunk and keepin up with their horizontal exercise." — Lauren Kessler, *The Happy Bottom Riding Club*, p. 61, 2000

- "I'm not quite so young as I used to be," Leino said at some point that morning when, after several days of horizontal exercises, he failed to rise to the occasion. —Harry Turtledove, *Rulers of the Darkness*, p. 321, 2002

horizontal folk-dancing *noun*

sexual intercourse; lovemaking *AUSTRALIA*

- I mean, I don't mind him demeaning his own species in the quest for the sale of more meat by getting that idiot Keegan and his horizontal folk-dancing partner to wobble about in a shop window[.] —Roy Slaven (John Doyle), *Five South Coast Seasons*, p. 143, 1992
- But it had less to do with his stated aim of building a series of world class private gardens than his desire to get in some world class horizontal folk dancing with Hoover's soon to be ex-wife, Samantha. —Harrison Biscuit, *The Search for Savage Henry*, p. 74, 1995

horizontal gymnastics *noun*

sexual intercourse *UK*

- [A] ruse to get me on my own so she could tell me yet more about her horizontal gymnastics with Sleaze Paul! —*The Guardian*, p. 9, 28th November 2001: 'Teenage Kicks'

horizontal lubricant *adjective*

any alcoholic drink or drinks, especially in the adjectival phrase 'nicely irrigated with horizontal lubricant' *UK*

- —*e-cyclopaedia*, 20th March 2002

horizontal manoeuvres *noun*

sexual intercourse *UK*

Military origins.

- Then there were all the inter-battalion horizonal manoeuvres. As soon as a battalion was away over the water, all the singlies were straight over to check out the wives. —Andy McNab, *Immediate Action*, p. 51, 1995

horizontal refreshment *noun*

sexual intercourse *UK, 1889*

- [H]e would go to China Town, to further indulge his hankering for horizontal refreshment and whiskey. —H. M. Jacks, *Not All Wanderers Are Lost*, p. 63, 2003

horizontal rumble *noun*

sexual intercourse *US*

- Nice ass on her. And big blonde hair to her shoulders. Kind of woman he used to chase down for a horizontal rumble. —Christopher Cook, *Robbers*, p. 256, 2000

hork *verb*

to spit; hence to vomit *US*

Variation of conventional 'hawk' (to clear your throat).

- He [a dog] paused for a second and horked up a mixture of cardboard box and shrimp chow mein. —Janet Evanovich, *Seven Up*, p. 152, 2001

Horlicks *noun*

a mess *UK*

Originally, upper-class society usage of a brand name; Horlicks™ is a malted food drink. Usage here is probably inspired by the salacious possibilities of the separated syllables 'whore licks' and a vague assonance to 'bollocks', as in 'make a bollocks of' (to mess up).

- [M]ake a Horlicks of it. —Ann Barr and Peter York, *The Official Sloane Ranger Handbook*, p. 158, 1982
- I'm sorry I made such a complete horlicks of the competition. —Mark Durden-Smith, *Rise*, 26th November 2002
- Its contents were accurate but because its sources had not been made clear, it made it "a complete Horlicks", he [Foreign Secretary Jack Straw] said. —*The Independent*, 25th June 2003

horn *noun*

1 the penis; the erect penis; lust *UK, 1594*

- I could pole-vault to the bathroom on my own horn there. —George V. Higgins, *Penance for Jerry Kennedy*, p. 157, 1985
- [S]he gives him the horn in a big way. —Kevin Williamson, *Heart of the Bass (Disco Biscuits)*, p. 113, 1996
- This mullarkey gives me the horn. —Bernard Demspey and Kevin McNally *Lock, Stock... & Two Sips*, p. 310, 2000

2 adultery *TRINIDAD AND TOBAGO, 1857*

- —Lise Winer, *Dictionary of the English/Creole of Trinidad & Tobago*, 2003

3 the nose *UK, 1823*

- —Lou Shelly, *Hepcats Jive Dictionary*, p. 12, 1945

4 any implement used for snorting powdered narcotics *US*

- They snorted sparkling rows of cocaine with a mother-of-pearl horn. —Iceberg Slim (Robert Beck), *Long White Con*, p. 97, 1977

5 a pipe used to smoke crack cocaine *US*

- —US Department of Justice, *Street Terms*, October 1994

6 the telephone *US, 1941*

- —*Current Slang*, p. 5, Summer 1967
- Right away Claude is on the horn talking here and there. —*The Digger Papers*, p. 10, August 1968

7 a trumpet; hence any brass or wind instrument; occasionally a piano *UK, 1966*

Jazz slang.

- Horn seems to be more frequently encountered on the backs of record sleeves and in magazine articles than in conversation. —Peter Clayton and Peter Gammond, *Jazz A-Z*, p. 119, 1986
- —John Ayto, *The Oxford Dictionary of Slang*, p. 350, 1998

▸ **around the horn**

1 the oral stimulation of all parts of a partner's body *US*

In the UK, *Round the Horne* was an innuendo-driven radio comedy originally broadcast from 1965–69.

- She was a three-way wench, played Jasper in a pinch / And took 'em around the horn. —Dennis Wepman et al., *The Life*, p. 81, 1976

2 from one location to another, in quick succession *US, 1942*

- That's why they've been sending me around the horn. In the past eighteen months I've been stationed in Detroit, Providence, Miami, and now Los Angeles. —Gerald Petievich, *One-Shot Deal*, p. 205, 1981

3 in craps, a single-roll bet on the 2, 3, 11 and 12 *US*

- —Frank Garcia, *Marked Cards and Loaded Dice*, p. 250, 1962

4 in baseball, around the infield positions *US, 1956*

After an out made at first base, if there are no runners on base the defensive team typically throws the ball 'around the horn'.

- You throw the ball around the horn – catcher to first baseman to shortstop to second baseman to third baseman – after an infield out and you do it with a lot of elan. —Jim Bouton, *Ball Four*, p. 276, 1970

▸ **put the horns on; put horns on**

1 to cuckold *UK*

After the traditional sign of a cuckold.

- It would be fun to put horns on Dennis. Ah, but what a risk! —Derek Bickerton, *Payroll*, p. 87, 1959
- In the joint, you stay up-to-date on everything – things you wouldn't know on the street you know right away inside. Whose old lady ain't putting the horns on who. —Edwin Torres, *Carlito's Way*, p. 49, 1975

2 (used of a superstitious gambler) to engage in a personal ritual designed to break a streak of bad luck *US, 1949*

- —George Percy, *The Language of Poker*, p. 72, 1988

horn *verb*

1 to inhale (a drug) through the nose *US, 1967*

- —Richard Horman and Allan Fox, *Drug Awareness*, p. 467, 1970
- I been hornin' coke all evenin', I'd hate to mess that up with anything else. —Odie Hawkins, *Chicago Hustle*, p. 201, 1977
- Before closing time I hit on her and she goes for the 'horn-a-little-coke-at-my-place' act.' —Gerald Petievich, *To Die in Beverly Hills*, p. 93, 1983
- I've held off the bonecrushers two days, rationing that stuff up my nose – horned the last just an hour ago. —Seth Morgan, *Homeboy*, p. 49, 1990
- —Nick Constable, *This is Cocaine*, p. 182, 2002
- —Robert Ashton, *This Is Heroin*, p. 209, 2002

2 to commit adultery *TRINIDAD AND TOBAGO, 1973*

- —Lise Winer, *Dictionary of the English/Creole of Trinidad & Tobago*, 2003

hornbag *noun*

a sexually attractive or highly sexed person *AUSTRALIA*

- Of course I love you, horn-bag. Just get up here, pronto, or I'll start without ya. —Barry Humphries, *A Nice Night's Entertainment*, p. 189, 1981
- In fact, if you were lying where I am, looking up the leather mini of the spunky little hornbag who's typing this out, I doubt if you'd be in a literary frame of mind either. —*The Traveller's Tool*, p. 7, 1985
- Heroine fwooar-a-minute hornbag crutch-rubbing Madonna's landed a new fillum role. —*Picture*, p. 55, 5th February 1992
- A hornbag Zulu witch is brewing up a storm in Adelaide[.] —*People*, p. 52, 5th February 1992
- So lie back and gawp, gaze, gape and goggle to your heart's content as hordes of heroic hornbags dance before your eyes. —*People*, p. 8, 30th March 1994

horndog *noun*

a person who is obsessed with sex *US, 1984*

- "I'm a horn-dog," I say. "I'm into some pretty kinky stuff to be honest." —Marty Beckerman, *Death to All Cheerleaders*, p. 24, 2000

horner man; horner woman *noun*

an adulterer *TRINIDAD AND TOBAGO, 1990*

- —Lise Winer, *Dictionary of the English/Creole of Trinidad & Tobago*, 2003

horn in *verb*

to intrude upon, to interfere *US, 1911*

- It's a nice fantasy that I could have horned in on the greatest poet of my time. — *The Guardian*, 4th July 2003

horning *noun*

heroin *UK, 1998*

- — Mike Haskins, *Drugs*, p. 284, 2003

horn movie *noun*

a pornographic film *US*

- — *American Speed*, p. 228, October 1967: 'Some special terms used in a University of Connecticut men's dormitory'

horn pill *noun*

an (allegedly) aphrodisiac tablet for men *UK, 1961*

Claimed to give the **HORN** (an erection).

hornrim *noun*

an intellectual *US*

- Derisive implications are due to the fact that the hornrims tend to get bogged down in the technology of fact-gathering and lose sight of the realities of advertising and the real-life marketplace. — Robert Kirk Mueller, *Buzzwords*, p. 93, 1974

horny *adjective*

1 desiring sex *US, 1826*

- Those girls in juvenile were horny as they could be. — Willard Motley, *Let No Man Write My Epitaph*, p. 20, 1958
- I know this because when I was pregnant I was able to ball anyone and I was never more horny. — Jefferson Poland and Valerie Alison, *The Records of the San Francisco Sexual Freedom League*, p. 103, 1971
- That creep's not a friend of mine, he's just horny. — *American Graffiti*, 1973
- What we know for sure, he's pretty horny for a guy his age, almost sixty. — Elmore Leonard, *Maximum Bob*, p. 8, 1991
- You'd get horny too if all you ever got to look at were grasshoppers and ants and toads. — Francesca Lia Block, *I Was a Teenage Fairy*, p. 60, 1998
- The sexiest raves we ever did were the ones at the holiday camps. They were the horniest. — Dave Courtney, *Raving Lunacy*, p. 226, 2000

2 of an erotic or pornographic image, sexually stimulating *UK, 1984*

From the **HORN** (the erect penis) that results.

▸ **sleep horny**

to go to bed naked (and be sensually aware of it) *UK*

- — Philip Callow, *Going to the Moon*, 1968

horny man *noun*

a federal law enforcement official *US*

A euphemistic allusion to the devil by those engaged in the illegal production of alcohol.

- — David W. Maurer, *Kentucky Moonshine*, p. 119, 1974

horny-mone *noun*

the substance that drives a cow to mate, to go into heat *CANADA*

A humorous corruption of 'hormone'.

- "Hornymones," they say, are what makes a cow "breachy," or restless to mate. — Lewis Poteet, *Talking Country*, p. 45, 1992

horny porny *noun*

pornography *US*

- — *Male Swinger Number 3*, p. 46, 1981: 'The Complete gay dictionary'

horny weed *noun*

▷ **see: PORN WEED**

horrendous *adjective*

terrible *US*

A blend of the conventional 'horrible' and 'stupendous'.

- — Collin Baker et al., *College Undergraduate Slang Study Conducted at Brown University*, p. 139, 1968
- You can get those Thai mail-order brides on the internet now. The postage must be fucking horrendous. — Dave Courtney, *Dodgy Dave's Little Black Book*, p. 34, 2001

Horrids *nickname*

Harrods department store in Knightsbridge, west London *UK*

Jocular usage, mainly by those who can't afford to shop there; the word play is enhanced by class sensitivities as 'horrid' is considered part of a socially superior vocabulary.

- These people who shop at "Horrids" and holiday in gites in the Perigord and use French phrases for emphasis. — *The Independent*, p. 11, 20th April 1996

horrie *noun*

a large and dangerous wave that breaks suddenly *AUSTRALIA*

- He thinks he has the take-off spot pegged, but almost immediately, feels the drag of a horrie, and knows he is caught inside[.] — *Sydney Morning Herald*, 15th March 2003

horries *noun*

1 *delirium tremens*; the ill-effects of drinking or drug-taking *SOUTH AFRICA, 1959*

From 'horror'.

- — Jean Branford, *A Dictionary of South African English*, 1978

2 a phobia, a horror of something *SOUTH AFRICA, 1971*

From 'horror'.

- — Penny Silva, *A Dictionary of South African English*, 1996

horror *noun*

1 a mischievous person, especially when addressed to a child *UK, 1819*

- Why do pop stars' kids grow up to be precocious little horrors? — *The Guardian*, 5th May 2004

2 an extremely unattractive woman who is seen as a sex object, especially one who is ravaged by age *UK*

- Go for a horror, any fucking day of the week. — Kevin Sampson, *Clubland*, p. 65, 2002

horror *adjective*

great, wonderful *UK*

A contraction of **HORRORSHOW**.

- That track [piece of music] was horror. — *The Big Breakfast*, 23rd July 2001

horrors *noun*

1 sickness associated with withdrawal from alcohol or drug addiction *US, 1839*

Noted specifically of withdrawal from amphetamines or heroin.

- I'm not staying, Sticks. I got the horrors. — George Mandel, *Flee the Angry Strangers*, p. 377, 1952
- — Home Office, *Glossary of Terms and Slang Common in Penal Establishments*, July 1978
- — Angela Devlin, *Prison Patter*, p. 63, 1996

2 the bleed period of the menstrual cycle *UK*

Schoolgirl use.

- — Douglas Clark, *Golden Rain*, 1980

3 acute psychosis caused by amphetamines *UK*

- — Home Office, *Glossary of Terms and Slang Common in Penal Establishments*, July 1978

horrorshow *adjective*

great, wonderful *UK, 1961*

Ultimately from Russian *khorosho* (good); coined by Anthony Burgess (1917–93) for the novel *A Clockwork Orange*, 1962. Adopted in US teen slang in the 1990s.

- Good. Real Horrorshow. Initiative comes to those that wait. I've taught you well my little droogies. — Stanley Kubrick after Anthony Burgess, *A Clockwork Orange*, 1971

hors d'oeuvre *noun*

drugs in capsule form *US*

- — Edith A. Folb, *runnin' down some lines*, p. 242, 1980

horse *noun*

1 heroin *US, 1950*

- Paddy's on Horse, that don' mean I got to. — George Mandel, *Flee the Angry Strangers*, p. 26, 1948
- Somebody is pushing horse and tea again. — John D. McDonald, *The Neon Jungle*, p. 32, 1953
- "As long as Red gets pure Horse and enough of it he can keep it under control," Hassan assured him. — Ross Russell, *The Sound*, p. 143, 1961
- Do you want this horse for yourself? — Douglas Rutherford, *The Creeping Flesh*, p. 102, 1963
- He was a cheap hood from the east side who did errands for the Stipetto brothers and lived off the white Horse he peddled around the neighborhood. — Mickey Spillane, *Return of the Hood*, p. 88, 1964
- Horse was a new thing, not only in our neighborhood but in Brooklyn, the Bronx, and everyplace I went, uptown and downtown. It was like horse had just taken over. — Claude Brown, *Manchild in the Promised Land*, p. 103, 1965
- He was sitting on the small of her back as he opened the box. Inside was a blycerin suppository filled with Motherball's uncut horse. — Richard Farina, *Been Down So Long*, p. 266, 1966

- Ain't nothing a greater blast than 'horse.' It's your privilege to wake up slow if you want. 'Horse' is what puts the ice in a pimp's game. —Iceberg Slim (Robert Beck), *Pimp*, p. 131, 1969
- I seen the horse play with them junkies like a cat with a rubber mouse. —Edwin Torres, *Carlito's Way*, p. 11, 1975
- He thought it was boss when he shot that horse / He thought he was being hip. —Dennis Wepman et al., *The Life*, p. 97, 1976
- Dylanologist A.J.Weberman insists that every time Dylan writes about horses, it is an allusion to heroin[.] —Jay Saporita, *Pourin' It All Out*, p. 61, 1980
- Elise asked me if had any horse and Ed said he would like just a small taste of the amphets —Herbert Huncke, *The Evening Sun Turned Crimson*, 1980
- For the horse you've grown much fonder / Than for me[.] —Alice in Chains *God Smack*, 1992
- Caleb is getting more and more excited. High as a kite if truth were told. The wonderful feeling of Horse in his head. —Jack Allen, *When the Whistle Blows*, p. 142, 2000

2 a casual girlfriend *UK*
Probably from a play on' whores'.
- —Wilfred Granville, *A Dictionary of Sailors' Slang*, 1962

3 a prostitute *US*
An evolution of the **STABLE** (a group of prositutes).
- But not for that new horse. I wouldn't give her one of my tricks if she stood on her head. —John M. Murtagh and Sara Harris, *Cast the First Stone*, p. 114, 1957

4 a prostitute's customer *SOUTH AFRICA, 1946*
Used by prostitutes.

5 a large man *US*
- —Marcus Hanna Boulware, *Jive and Slang of Students in Negro Colleges*, 1947

6 an affectionate male term of address *IRELAND*
- Howiya goin horse? Are ye well? —Ruane Donal, *Tales in a Rearview Mirror*, p. 187, 2003

7 in circus and carnival usage, one thousand dollars *US*
- —Don Wilmeth, *The Language of American Popular Entertainment*, p. 134, 1981

8 a person who smuggles contraband into prison *US*
- —*Maledicta*, p. 264, Summer/Winter 1981: 'By its slang, ye shall know it: the pessimism of prison life'

9 in bar dice games, a turn of rolling the dice *US*
- Boss is won by the player who wins two of three horses (hands). —Gil Jacobs, *The World's Best Dice Games*, p. 196, 1976

10 a poker player with a reputation for stinginess *US*
- —George Percy, *The Language of Poker*, p. 45, 1988

11 a Ford Mustang car *US*
- —Lanie Dills, *The Official CB Slanguage Language Dictionary*, p. 40, 1976

12 in television and film making, a stand that holds film reels while the film is fed through a viewer *US*
- —Ralph S. Singleton, *Filmaker's Dictionary*, p. 82, 1990

13 a knife or improvised sharp instrument *US*
- —Kenn "Naz" Young, *Naz's Underground Dictionary*, p. 37, 1973

horse *verb*

1 to thrash, to defeat absolutely *UK: SCOTLAND*
- I'm watching us [Glasgow Rangers] getting horsed at Love Street. —Christopher Brookmyre, *The Sacred Art of Stealing*, p. 56, 2002

2 to ruin, to destroy *UK: SCOTLAND*
Extended from the previous sense.
- You could end up horsing this for all of us because of a girl you don't even know. —Christopher Brookmyre, *The Sacred Art of Stealing*, p. 215, 2002

horse and buggy; horse and wagon *noun*
heroin and the equipment needed to prepare and inject it *US*
- —Inez Cardozo-Freeman, *The Joint*, p. 506, 1984

horse and carriage *noun*
a garage *UK*
Rhyming slang (the rhyme is accurate when spoken in a London accent).
- —Ray Puxley, *Cockney Rabbit*, 1992

horse and cart; horse *verb*

1 to start *UK*
- A mocking remark to a motorist having ignition problems was "Won't horse and cart? Get a horse and cart?" —Ray Puxley, *Cockney Rabbit*, 1992

2 to fart *UK*
Rhyming slang; reduced to its first element, usually in the past tense. ' "orsed" and "'orsin'" give the past and present participles of the verb' (David Hillman, 1974).
- What dirty swine's horse & carted? —Ray Puxley, *Cockney Rabbit*, p. 88, 1992
- London market traders are likely to say that someone has "horsed"[.] —Peter Furze, *Tailwinds*, p. 105, 1998

horse and trap *noun*

1 an act of defecation *UK*
Rhyming slang for **CRAP**, a rarer form of **PONY AND TRAP**.
- —Julian Franklyn, *A Dictionary of Rhyming Slang*, 1961

2 gonorrhoea *UK, 1961*
Rhyming slang for **CLAP**.
- —Ray Puxley, *Cockney Rabbit*, 1992

horse and trough *noun*
a cough *UK*
Rhyming slang.
- —Ray Puxley, *Cockney Rabbit*, 1992

horse around; horse about *verb*
to fool around *US, 1900*
- If we were working we wouldn't 'a been cuttin' classes and horsing around and we wouldn't be sittin' here now. —Irving Shulman, *The Amboy Dukes*, p. 106, 1947
- Gimme Foley and quit horsing around. —George V. Higgins, *The Friends of Eddie Doyle*, p. 107, 1971
- [A] ten-year-old who for most of the time horsed about with his friends in the deep end. —Andrew Taylor, *The Four Last Things*, p. 103, 1997

horse ass *noun*
anything at all; nothing *BAHAMAS*
- —John A. Holm, *Dictionary of Bahamian English*, p. 106, 1982

horse bite *noun*
heroin *UK*
An elaboration of **HORSE** (heroin).
- —Robert Ashton, *This Is Heroin*, p. 206, 2002
- —Mike Haskins, *Drugs*, p. 284, 2003

horse blanket *noun*
a filming technique employed to soften faces *US*
- —Anna Scotti and Paul Young, *Buzzwords*, p. 5, 1997

horse box *noun*
a control station in a Townsend Thorenson ferry/ship's engine room that contains the engine controls, alarms, etc *UK*
Used by ferry crews. Reported by John Malon, 1979.

horsecock *noun*

1 a sausage *US, 1942*
- The sandwiches were thick slices of bologna sausage (reviled as "horsecock" by sailors and marines) on bread plastered with artificial butter. —I.J. Galantin, *Take Her Deep!*, p. 133, 1987

2 a wooden club *US*
- You can take your hand off the horsecock you're holding under the bar. —Darryl Ponicsan, *The Last Detail*, p. 39, 1970

3 in oil drilling, a nipple used to connect hoses *US*
- —Jerry Robertson, *Oil Slanguage*, p. 67, 1954

horsecollar *noun*

1 a rescue sling lowered from a hovering helicopter to the ground or sea below *US, 1969*
- The crewmen in the back dropped the rescue sling, or "horse collar," to the survivor and watched as he put it around his back. —Gerry Carroll, *North S*A*R*, p. 89, 1991

2 the vagina, especially large or distended external female genitals *US*
The shape provides a simile.
- —Michael Dalton Johnson, *Talking Trash with Redd Foxx*, p. 62, 1994

3 in an athletic contest, a failure to score *US, 1907*
- —Parke Cummings, *Dictionary of Baseball*, p. 29, 1950
- Yet horse collars were never hung on an opponent by a team trying to out-score its basketball team. —*Spokesman Review (Spokane, Washington)*, p. C4, 3rd October 2002

4 in hot rodding, the grille from an Edsel car, popular for customising other cars *US*
- —John Lawlor, *How to Talk Car*, p. 63, 1965

horsed *adjective*
heroin-intoxicated *UK*
From **HORSE** (heroin).
- [A] negro called Mr. Jaggers comes on really horsed and steps into a routine with a few cartwheels[.] —Derek Raymond (Robin Cook), *The Crust on its Uppers*, p. 56, 1962

horse doofers; horses doovers *noun*
hors d'oevres *UK*
Jocular mispronunciations.
- [B]iggest flippin' meal you ever saw; lobsters an' oysters, an' horses doofers, then a nice bit o' smoked salmon [...] an' a whacking great slice of Stilton; real ripe. —Derek Bickerton, *Payroll*, p. 45, 1959
- Of course, the men soon retired to the rear patio and talk turned to the recent strike amid the colored lights, the multi-colored umbrellas, the palm trees, the scotches and the caviar horses doovers. —Frank Hardy, *The Outcasts of Foolgarah*, p. 191, 1971

horsefeathers *noun*
nonsense *US, 1927*
A transparent euphemism for **HORSESHIT**.
- Oh, horse feathers! I just can't believe that about your father. —Iceberg Slim (Robert Beck), *Doom Fox*, p. 146, 1978

horse feed *noun*
in circus and carnival usage, poor business *US*
- —Don Wilmeth, *The Language of American Popular Entertainment*, p. 134, 1981

horsefuck *verb*
to have sex from behind and with great vim *US*
- I'd like to break her open like a shotgun and horsefuck her. —Joseph Wambaugh, *The Blue Knight*, p. 96, 1973

horsehead *noun*
1 an amphetamine *US, 1971*
- —Richard A. Spears, *The Slang and Jargon of Drugs and Drink*, p. 271, 1986
- —Mike Haskins, *Drugs*, p. 279, 2003

2 a heroin user *US, 1952*
A straightforward combination of **HORSE** (heroin) and **-HEAD** (a user).
- They knew he was on drugs, a real horsehead who hit the main. —Hal Ellson, *The Golden Spike*, p. 68, 1952

horse heart *noun*
a tablet of Dexedrine™, a trade name for dextroamphetamine sulphate, a central nervous system stimulant *US*
- —Walter L. Way, *The Drug Scene*, p. 110, 1977

horse hockey!
used for expressing disapproval *US, 1964*
A signature line of Colonel Sherman Potter on *M*A*S*H* (CBS, 1972–83). Repeated with referential humour.
- Horse hockey, Counselor. You can't be that drunk. —Austin Davis, *Shoveling Smoke*, p. 146, 2003

horse-holder *noun*
an assistant to a high-ranking military officer *US, 1982*
- — Department of the Army, *Staff Officer's Guidebook*, p. 61, 1986

horse off *verb*
to allow horses to graze in a field, thus ruining it for cows until the crop grows back *CANADA*
- Land that is horsed off has been grazed down by horses until it is no good, until it recovers, for the grazing of cattle. —Chris Thain, *Cold as a Bay Street Banker's Heart*, p. 86, 1987

horse piddle *noun*
hospital *UK*
Word play masquerading as rhyming slang.
- —Ray Puxley, *Cockney Rabbit*, 1992

horse pill *noun*
the large, orange anti-malarial pill (chloroquine-primaquine) taken once a week by US troops in Vietnam *US*
- —Gregory Clark, *Words of the Vietnam War*, p. 100, 1990

horse piss *noun*
cheap alcoholic drink, or a brand you don't drink *US, 1970*
- They were inveterate gamblers and accomplished scroungers, who drank hair tonic in preference to post exchange beer ("horse piss")[.] —William Manchester, *Goodbye, Darkness*, p. 132, 1980
- Here's ten dollars for a case of beer and don't come back with any of that horse piss you brought last time. When I say beer I mean beer. —Ken Weaver, *Texas Crude*, p. 59, 1984

horse radish *noun*
heroin *US*
- — *Providence (Rhode Island) Journal-Bulletin*, p. 6B, 4th August 1997: 'Doctors must know the narcolexicon'

horse room *noun*
an illegal betting operation where bets can be placed and collected on horse races *US*
- Northside shopping street, with usual quota of horse rooms, taverens, and dope peddlers at principal corners. —Jack Lait and Lee Mortimer, *Chicago Confidential*, p. 289, 1950
- — *Life*, p. 39, 19th May 1952
- A week from now half the horse rooms in Brooklyn, for example, will be out of bussiness and the people will be held on high bail. —Richard Condon, *Prizzi's Honor*, p. 216, 1982

horse's *noun*
a male homosexual *AUSTRALIA, 1960*
Shortening of **HORSE'S HOOF**.

horses *noun*
dice that have been altered for cheating by omitting key losing combinations *US*
- —R. Frederick West, *God's Gambler*, p. 226, 1964: 'Appendix A'

horse's arse; horse's ass *noun*
a person who is not liked or trusted; an idiot; someone deserving of a generally abusive epithet *UK, 1865*
- [I]t still couldn't be worth making a horse's ass of yourself[.] —Lawrence Block, *No Score [The Affairs of Chip Harrison Omnibus]*, p. 151, 1970
- [T]he trial was even worse. More of a pantomime, really, but with more horses' arses than usual. —Dave Courtney, *Raving Lunacy*, p. 34, 2000

horses doovers *noun*
▷ **see: HORSE DOOFERS**

horseshit; horseshite *noun*
nonsense *US, 1923*
- For Christs sake dont give us any of that horseshit. —Hubert Selby Jr, *Last Exit to Brooklyn*, p. 113, 1957
- Horseshit. I look like hell. —Carl Hiaasen, *Tourist Season*, p. 228, 1986
- Wha'm I talkin'? Hebrew Hindi Horseshit wha'? I'm talkin' pure no shit. —Nick Barlay, *Curvy Lovebox*, p. 137, 1997
- But the thing is, Ben, that's horseshite. —James Hawes, *Dead Long Enough*, p. 214, 2000
- One experienced [US] adminstration source described this view as "horse shit"[.] — *The Guardian*, p. 3, 26th February 2002

horseshit *verb*
to deceive, to tease *US*
In the nature of **BULLSHIT**.
- Don't try to horse-shit me, buster. You ain't even half-way smart enough. —Jim Thompson, *A Swell-Looking Babe*, p. 85, 1954

Horseshit Man *noun*
Ho Chi Minh *US*
A phonetic approximation used by troops in Vietnam.
- —Linda Reinberg, *In the Field*, p. 108, 1991

horse's hoof; horses *noun*
a male homosexual *AUSTRALIA, 1944*
Rhyming slang for **POOF**.
- —Julian Franklyn, *A Dictionary of Rhyming Slang*, 1960
- So I reckon it's about time we went up and had a word with all the horse's hoofs. —Robert G. Barrett, *Davo's Little Something*, p. 238, 1992

horsespot *noun*
the vagina *US*
- There's [a...] "wee wee," "horsespot," "nappy dugout," mongo[".] —Eve Ensler, *The Vagina Monologues*, p. 6, 1998

horse-to-horse *adjective*
in a direct comparison or competition *US*
- Get rodded up. Horse-to-horse we can muscle that mob out of the grift. —Hyman E. Goldin et al., *Dictionary of American Underworld Lingo*, p. 102, 1950

horticulturalist *noun*
in pool, a player who wins money betting *US*
- —Steve Rushin, *Pool Cool*, p. 16, 1990

HO's *noun*
hangers-on attached to a rock band *UK*
- —Bob Young and Micky Moody, *The Language of Rock 'n' Roll*, p. 54, 1985

hose *noun*

the penis *US, 1928*

- Im goin' to the toilet, to let some water out of this fine hose of mine, and when I come out I don't wanna see yo' lazy, triflin' ass nowhere in sight.—Odie Hawkins, *Chicago Hustle*, p. 34, 1977
- He'd been bragging about what a hose he had.—Robert Campbell, *Sweet La-La Land*, p. 200, 1990
- Jasmin sucks hose as if she's being intubated with anaesthesia (and on the verge of nodding off).—Anthony Petkovich, *The X Factory*, p. 192, 1997

hose *verb*

1 to copulate, vaginally or anally *US, 1935*

- Hose – To pedicate. *** These terms are also used heterosexually of the copulation of a man with a woman, e.g. to give her a (good) hosing.—G. Legman, *The Language of Homsexuality*, p. 1169, 1941
- —Collin Baker et al., *College Undergraduate Slang Study Conducted at Brown University*, p. 139, 1968
- GARY: So you're a big mover with Diane, are you? BENTLEY: Practically home and hosed.—Alexander Buzo, *Rooted*, 1969
- —Connie Eble (Editor), *UNC-CH Campus Slang*, April 1977

2 to shoot with an automatic weapon *UK, 1917*

Sometimes heard as the more elaborate 'hosepipe'.

- There was no time for accurate, steady ranging if I was to save my pilot, so allowing plenty of lead, I 'hosepiped' the 190 with a long continuous burst.—J. E. Johnson, *Wing Leader*, p. 228, 1956
- Their fire on the Rangers did not last long, as they were dealt a shattering blow when a Spectre effectively "hosed" them down with 20-mm and 40-mm fire.—Ian Padden, *U.S. Air Commando*, p. 131, 1985

3 to swindle; to cheat *US, 1940*

- —Connie Eble (Editor), *UNC-CH Campus Slang*, April 1977

4 to laugh vigorously *SOUTH AFRICA*

- He was hosing himself when he fell in the pool.—*Surfrikan Slang*, 2004

▸ **hose yourself**

to get drunk *AUSTRALIA*

- When Les came to town he really hosed himself.—Sam Weller, *Old Bastards I Have Met*, p. 129, 1979

hosebag *noun*

a prostitute or promiscuous woman *US, 1978*

A conventional 'bag', punning on **BAG** (a promiscuous woman), is a container for a **HOSE** (penis).

- —Connie Eble (Editor), *UNC-CH Campus Slang*, p. 4, March 1981
- Every time he looked at his wrist he thought about that junkie hosebag and wondered if he should get a blood test.—Joseph Wambaugh, *Finnegan's Week*, p. 41, 1993
- I just wasted an hour seducing this hosebag and she has a fucking headache?—Howard Stern, *Miss America*, p. 17, 1995

hosed *adjective*

drunk *US*

- —Connie Eble (Editor), *UNC-CH Campus Slang*, p. 3, Fall 1987
- The parents aren't home, and the boy hosting is as "hosed" as his guests. The teens are chugging cheap beer, coolers, and vodka – drinking to get crazy, crawling drunk.—*Toronto Globe and Mail*, p. F4, 22nd June 2002

hose down *verb*

to rain heavily *NEW ZEALAND*

- By nightfall it was hosing down. No fire tonight, no billy-tea.—Barry Crump, *Bushwoman*, p. 18, 1995

hose in *verb*

to win handily *NEW ZEALAND*

- —David McGill, *David McGill's Complete Kiwi Slang Dictionary*, p. 58, 1998

hose job *noun*

1 oral sex on a man *US, 1978*

- Looks like the hooker was doing a hose job on one of the truckers up at the market.—Carsten Stroud, *Close Pursuit*, p. 33, 1987
- There was an extensive trade in quick hose jobs for businessmen on the way home.—Robert K. Tannenbaum, *Reversible Error*, p. 71, 1992

2 a bad situation; a situation in which you are cheated or swindled *US*

- Everybody was having such a good time in 'flower-power-land' they didn't realize what kind of hose job they were getting.—Frank Zappa, *The Real Frank Zappa Book*, p. 83, 1989

hose off *verb*

to annoy or make angry *NEW ZEALAND*

- People in those damned cloth caps waving rattles. Couldn't go it at all. Hosed me off completely.—Gordon Slatter, *A Gun in My Hand*, p. 98, 1959

hoser *noun*

1 an uncouth, dim person *CANADA*

Popularised by Bob and Doug McKenzie's 'Great White North' television skit.

- For parents puzzled by talk of hosers and such, Rick Moranis explained in a telephone interview from Edmonton, where the show is taped, that "a hoser is what you call your brother when your folks won't let you swear."—*Toronto Star*, p. A4, 2nd November 1981
- —Connie Eble (Editor), *UNC-CH Campus Slang*, p. 5, Spring 1982
- One foursome of Calgary hosers sports specially made Olympic-style red and white athletic jackets[.]—Brian Preston, *Pot Planet*, p. 243, 2002
- But there he was – Canada's quintessential hoser – giving interviews on the fourth floor of an office tower on Bloor Street. In Alaska, he got a 21-chainsaw salute on a recent visit.—*Toronto Globe and Mail*, p. R1, 3rd April 2002

2 a male with sexual experience and expertise *US*

- —Collin Baker et al., *College Undergraduate Slang Study Conducted at Brown University*, p. 139, 1968

hosing *verb*

to beat *US*

- You guys are really giving us a hosing. Why don't you let us alone? —Irving Shulman, *The Amboy Dukes*, p. 166, 1947

hoska *noun*

▷ **see: MAHOSKA**

hospital *noun*

1 jail *US*

An unabashed euphemism.

- —*American Speech*, p. 150–151, May 1959: 'Notes on the cant of the telephone confidence man'

2 in a smuggling operation, the place where the smuggled goods are picked up *US*

- —*American Speech*, p. 100, May 1956: 'Smugglers' argot in the southwest'

hospital hold *noun*

an unsafe grip on a tool *US, 1983*

- —Ken Weaver, *Texas Crude*, p. 94, 1984

hospital pass *noun*

1 the responsibility for a controversial project or task *US, 2003*

Such a responsibility will inevitably draw down painful and wounding criticism. Derives from an American football usage.

2 in team sports, a dangerously made pass which allows the opposition a good chance at defence *AUSTRALIA*

So called because of the risk of injury to the receiver.

- Occasionally he served some terrible hospital passes to his enthusiastic young team-mates, but this didn't seem to worry him much.—*Centralian Advocate*, p. 40, 3rd October 1984

hoss *noun*

1 used as a term of address, man to man *US, 1834*

- "Howdy, hoss," said Opie genially. "Have a snort." He extended a bottle of whisky to Private Roger Litwhiler.—Max Shulman, *Rally Round the Flag, Boys!*, p. 261, 1957

2 heroin *US*

In colloquial US speech, 'hoss' is a shortened form of **HORSE** (heroin).

- She went back in her purse and wrapped her fingers about her hoss.—Clarence Cooper Jr, *The Scene*, p. 36, 1960
- "Hoss was his Boss." He had chippied around and gotten hooked. —Iceberg Slim (Robert Beck), *Pimp*, p. 63, 1969

hossie *noun*

a hospital *AUSTRALIA*

- [S]tick me straight into hossie with all them other dirty bastards. —Barry Humphries, *Bazza Pulls It Off!*, 1971

hostess *noun*

a prostitute *US*

- She was now a "hostess" in a combination whore house-blind pig[.] —Jim Thompson, *Roughneck*, p. 89, 1954

hostess with the mostest *noun*

a good hostess *US*

An apparently irresisitable reduplication in the US, going 'host with the most' one better.

- I had heard stories about "My Sister Eileen" and the "Hostess With the Mostest"[.]—Red Rudensky, *The Gonif*, p. 159, 1970
- I invited them. Me and the hosetess with the mostest.—Robert Deane Pharr, *Giveadamn Brown*, p. 21, 1978
- Yes, Bobbi Flekman, the hostess with the mostest.—*This is Spinal Tap*, 1984

hostie *noun*

an air hostess *AUSTRALIA, 1960*

- So I got this Qantas hostie up into me sheilah [woman] trap and uncoiled the old one eyed trouser snake.—Barry Humphries, *Bazza Pulls It Off!*, 1971
- When TAA had a new hostie on board the boys used to play all sorts of tricks on them.—Sam Weller, *Old Bastards I Have Met*, p. 90, 1979
- —Barry Humphries, *A Nice Night's Entertainment*, p. 186, 1981
- —Barry Humphries, *The Traveller's Tool*, p. 27, 1985
- —Paul Vautin, *Turn It Up!*, p. 152, 1995
- —David McGill, *David McGill's Complete Kiwi Slang Dictionary*, p. 65, 1998

hostile *adverb*

▸ **go hostile**

to lose your temper *NEW ZEALAND*

- —David McGill, *David McGill's Complete Kiwi Slang Dictionary*, p. 51, 1998

hostile!

used for expressing strong approval *US*

Collected from fans of heavy metal music by Seamus O'Reilly, January 1995.

hostilish *adjective*

arrogant, haughty, condescending *TRINIDAD AND TOBAGO, 1960*

- —Lise Winer, *Dictionary of the English/Creole of Trinidad & Tobago*, 2003

hot *noun*

a hot meal *US, 1926*

- For a day's work, each youth is paid 50 cents plus earning his room and board, or "three hots and a cot," as one youth described it.—*New York Times*, p. 51, 28th September 1969
- Real beds. Sheets once a week. Three hots a day. Round-eyed pussy, reasonable.—Larry Heinemann, *Close Quarters*, p. 270, 1977
- Three hots a day, white sheets, dem pretty white nurses give you blowjobs too you pay them enough.—*Platoon*, 1986

hot *adjective*

1 stolen *US, 1924*

- One night, we were cruising about and just happened to drive by a lot where I'd parked a hot car some months before, in the summer. —Neal Cassady, *The First Third*, p. 194, 3rd July 1949
- And even a detailed account of the summer I spent in Denver two years ago, when Hart and I drove hot cars up into the mountains. —John Clellon Holmes, *Go*, p. 239, 1952
- "What about this hot-car ring?" said the man with the pipe[.]—William Burroughs, *Junkie*, p. 87, 1953
- A guy that bought hot cars and wrecked them for their parts.—Jim Thompson, *After Dark, My Sweet*, p. 85, 1955
- "Don't be daft, if it is the bogeys [police] how can they touch us?" "With two hot motors round the back? Who are you kidding?"—Derek Bickerton, *Payroll*, p. 43, 1959
- He still had some hot goods Marsha Lee had stashed in his closet, though[.]—Clarence Cooper Jr, *The Scene*, p. 68, 1960
- You could walk into one or another room in the house and get a hot fur coat, a good camera, fine perfume, anything from hot women to hot cars[.]—Malcolm X and Alex Haley, *The Autobiography of Malcolm X*, p. 90–91, 1964
- A brand new gun that sells for a hundred and ten bucks if you buy it legally and maybe twenty hot, but no less.—Mickey Spillane, *Last Cop Out*, p. 57, 1972
- Few prisoners in the antiquated stone jail spend more than a week as guests of the county and the charge usually is hot checks.—Jan Hutson, *The Chicken Ranch*, p. 6, 1980
- LAGARTO: This car is hot. MARLENE: What do you mean? Stolen? —*Repo Man*, 1984
- We also gotta get rid of all those cars. It looks like Sam's hot car lot outside.—*Reservoir Dogs*, 1992

2 wanted by the police *US, 1928*

- Don't laugh so loud, Buster. I'm hot – I busted out.—George Mandel, *Flee the Angry Strangers*, p. 121, 1952
- Even if I wasn't actually what was called "hot," I was now going to be under surveillance[.]—Malcolm X and Alex Haley, *The Autobiography of Malcolm X*, p. 97, 1964
- I soon got hot and the police were looking for me all over town. —A.S. Jackson, *Gentleman Pimp*, p. 96, 1973

3 suspect *UK*

- —Angela Devlin, *Prison Patter*, p. 63, 1996

4 dangerous for criminal activity *UK, 1618*

- "That neighborhood is too hot," he said loudly.—William Burroughs, *Junkie*, p. 79, 1953
- "Man, I told you before I don't want you all coming to turn on here," Lou said to Geo. "This pad's getting too hot."—Alexander Trocchi, *Cain's Book*, p. 166, 1960

5 dangerous to other criminals because of co-operation with the police *US*

- "He was hot," Veal said, explaining that "hot" was street slang for cooperating with police. "The word was out, he had to go, too." —*Washington Post*, p. C1, 14th December 2003

6 under enemy fire *US, 1864*

Although a critical term in the Vietnam war, it was coined not there, but in the US Civil War 100 years earlier.

- One of the helicopter's pilots had reported that the LZ was "hot," that is, Viet Cong were waiting below.—Seymour Hersh, *My Lai 4*, p. 45, 1970
- Night ain't the best time to go in hot.—Ronald J. Glasser, *365 Days*, p. 109, 1971
- We're down, Eagle Thrust – we're hit. We got a hot L.Z. here. —*Apocalypse Now*, 1979
- It was what they called a hot LZ, a landing zone swarming with enemy troops and alive with sniper fire from the moment they set down[.] —Peter Goldman and Tony Fuller, *Charlie Company*, p. 69, 1983

7 (used of a weapons system) activated, armed *US, 1962*

- He watched his weapons indicators go green, signifying that his ordinance was "hot."—T.E. Cruice, *Wings of Gold III*, p. 196, 1989
- Maverick pulls up, makes a quick turn, takes all the weapons off safe, "going hot" and they throw everything that gunship carries right into the exact middle of the camp.—Dennis Marvicsin and Jerold Greenfield, *Maverick*, p. 136, 1990

8 poisoned *UK*

- Hot heroin – poisoned heroin[.]—Robert Ashton, *This Is Heroin*, p. 209, 2002

9 good *US*

- Stroudsburg wasn't such a hot school anyway[.]—Darryl Ponicsan, *The Last Detail*, p. 10, 1970

10 excellent; used for describing music or musicians that create excitement *US, 1866*

- [A]in't that boy hot!—Frederic Ramsey Junior, *Chicago Documentary*, p. 31, 1944
- WAYNE: What do you think of Mickey and Mallory? CHUCK: Hot. JEFF: Hot. STEVE: Totally hot.—*Natural Born Killers*, 1994
- "I never had any intention of disappearing," he [rapper, Too Short] says now, "that's why I appeared on all the hottest shit"—*Hip-Hop Connection*, p. 35, March 2001

11 (used of jazz) traditional and spirited, as opposed to modern *US, 1924*

- When we talked about a musician who played hot, we would say he could swing or he couldn't swing, meaning what kind of effect did he have on the band.—Mezz Mezzrow, *Really the Blues*, p. 142, 1946

12 popular *US*

- I had lunch with him a couple of weeks ago. A real schnorrer, but sort of likeable, and apparently he's hot over there right now.—J.D. Salinger, *Franny and Zooey*, p. 136–137, 1961
- We's so much hotter now. Bob Marley, Jimi Hendrix, Jim Morrison, Elvis.—Francesca Lia Block, *Cherokee Bat*, p. 232, 1992

13 sexual, sensuous *US, 1931*

- Don't try to get too hot with a girl in public, or you'll wind up with the cold shoulder.—Jack Lait and Lee Mortimer, *New York Confidential*, p. 222, 1948
- Winston's, the greatest nightclub on earth (also the hottest) in Clifford Street[.]—Derek Raymond (Robin Cook), *The Crust on its Uppers*, p. 26, 1962
- [I] even had my special favourites that always got me hotter while there were others I always avoided.—Lester Bangs, *Psychotic Reactions and Carburetor Dung*, p. 334, 1980

14 (used of a striptease dance) very sexual *US*

- A stripper who can maximize the quantity of bumps and grinds she can do during the chorus of a popular song is known in the profession as working 'hot'.—William Green, *Strippers and Coochers*, p. 165, 1977

15 attractive, good-looking *US*

- He was hot, wasn't he?—*Fast Times at Ridgemont High*, 1982

16 angry *UK, 1225*

- MR. WHITE: Joe, trust me on this, you've made a mistake. He's a good kid. I understand you're hot, you're super-fuckin' pissed.—*Reservoir Dogs*, 1992

17 brief, quick *US*

- He may have been hip to his hop, but the muta made him fly right for a hot minute.—Mezz Mezzrow, *Really the Blues*, p. 96, 1946

18 in sports betting, generating heavy betting; favoured *UK, 1882*

- This judge bets college games through a buddy of his, a lawyer. All Southeast Conference. He lays it on the hot side, the favorite, every time.—Elmore Leonard, *Pronto*, p. 9, 1993

19 (used of a set in the television and film industries) fully prepared for filming *US*

- —Tony Miller and Patricia George, *Cut! Print!*, p. 88, 1977
- —Ralph S. Singleton, *Filmaker's Dictionary*, p. 82, 1990

20 drunk *BERMUDA*

- —Peter A. Smith and Fred M. Barritt, *Bermewjan Vurds*, 1985

▸ **hot as Mapp's mill-yard**

very hot *BARBADOS*

- —Frank A. Collymore, *Barbadian Dialect*, p. 71, 1965

hot air *noun*

spoken nonsense, inconsequential speech, meaningless words *US, 1873*

- Canada's promise is more hot air[.]— *The Guardian*, 23rd September 2002

hot and bothered *adjective*

sexually aroused *UK, 1821*

- —Collin Baker et al., *College Undergraduate Slang Study Conducted at Brown University*, p. 139, 1968

hot and cold *noun*

1 heroin and cocaine combined for injection *US*

Based on the initials.

- —William D. Alsever, *Glossary for the Establishment and Other Uptight People*, p. 14, December 1970
- —Richard A. Spears, *The Slang and Jargon of Drugs and Drink*, p. 271, 1986

2 gold *UK*

Rhyming slang, often reduced to its first element.

- —Julian Franklyn, *A Dictionary of Rhyming Slang*, 1961

hot and heavy *adjective*

passionate *US*

- — *Current Slang*, p. 14, Spring 1971

hot and stuck *adjective*

said of a player who is losing badly in a game of poker *US*

- —David M. Hayano, *Poker Faces*, p. 186, 1982

hot-arsed *adjective*

feeling an urgent sexual desire, lustful *UK, 1683*

- No hot-arsed Latin lovely tucked away at all? Don't answer that.—John Le Carre, *The Tailor of Panama*, p. 340, 1996

hot ass *noun*

a tin kettle with a large bottom *CANADA*

- If one wanted boiling water in a hurry for a cup of tea, one used what were called "quicks" or "hot asses," made of tin. Water boiled very quickly in these kettles, which had large bottoms that fitted the hole of the stove when the lid was removed.—Florence Barbour, *Memories of Life in the Labrador and on Newfoundland*, p. 94, 1973
- People also call such a kettle a flat-arsed kettle.—Bill Casselman, *Canadian Words*, p. 72, 1995

hot bed *noun*

a motel room rented without following proper registration procedures and rented more than once a day; a room in a cheap boarding house *US, 1940*

- —Lou Shelly, *Hepcats Jive Talk Dictionary*, p. 26, 1945
- "They're hot-bed hotels," Maria Elena explains. "They make believe they're renting to you for the night, but they know they ain't."—John M. Murtagh and Sara Harris, *Cast the First Stone*, p. 6, 1957
- Or you can wait till I talk to Dawn Coyote about how you rented her a hot bed tonight. Again.—Joseph Wambaugh, *Floaters*, p. 39, 1996

hot beef injection *noun*

▷ **see: BEEF INJECTION**

hot box *noun*

1 a sexually excited vagina; a sexually excited female *US*

- —Roger Blake, *The American Dictionary of Sexual Terms*, p. 103, 1964

2 a prison cell used for solitary confinement *US*

- —Marlene Freedman, *Alcatraz*, 1983

3 a small room or enclosed space where marijuana is being smoked *US*

- —Pamela Munro, *U.C.L.A. Slang*, p. 84, 2001

hot boy *noun*

a thief known to the authorities *BAHAMAS*

- —John A. Holm, *Dictionary of Bahamian English*, p. 106, 1982

hot-bunk *verb*

to sleep in turns or rotation on a bunk or in a sleeping bag *US, 1945*

- Rather than Folk rolling up his sleeping bag and Bannon rolling out another, they hot bunked with Bannon using Folk's sleeping bag tonight. It was a normal practice in a tactical environment.—Harold Coyle, *Team Yankee*, p. 86, 1987

hot buns *noun*

a male homosexual *US*

- —Charles Shafer, *Folk Speech in Texas Prisons*, p. 206, 1990

hot cakes *noun*

1 phencyclidine, the recreational drug known as PCP or angel dust *US*

- — US Depratment of Justice, *Street Terms*, October 1994

2 crack cocaine *UK, 1998*

An elaboration of **CAKES**.

- —Mike Haskins, *Drugs*, p. 282, 2003

hot carl *noun*

▷ **see: HOT KARL**

hot chair *noun*

the electric chair; death by electrocution in an electric chair *US, 1926*

- —Joseph E. Ragen and Charles Finston, *Inside the World's Toughest Prison*, p. 804, 1962: 'Penitentiary and underworld glossary'

hot check *noun*

a forged cheque or one intentionally drawn with insufficient funds to cover payment *US*

- I read a few years ago that in Dallas they lost $1,740,000 in hot checks in the first three months of the year and it was way down. —Bruce Jackson, *Outside the Law*, p. 80, 1972

hotchin *adjective*

▷ **see: HOACHING**

hot chrome *noun*

a car that appeals to girls *US*

- — *American Speech*, p. 101, May 1954

hot cross bun *noun*

1 a gun *UK*

Rhyming slang.

- Only really used for comic effect. Hard to imagine a security guard threatened by the words, "Don't move, there's a hot cross bun aimed at your head."—Ray Puxley, *Cockney Rabbit*, 1992

2 the sun *UK*

Ryming slang.

- —Ray Puxley, *Cockney Rabbit*, 1992

3 son *UK, 1931*

Rhyming slang.

- —Ray Puxley, *Cockney Rabbit*, 1992

4 run, as in 'on the run' from the police *UK*

Rhyming slang. Sometimes simply 'hot cross'.

- —Julian Franklyn, *A Dictionary of Rhyming Slang*, 1960

hot damn!; hot dang!; hot diggity damn!; hot damn and double damn!

used for registering pleasure, astonishment; occasionally anger *US, 1933*

- And she was dripping more diamonds than the fucking windows at Harry Winston. Hot damn and double damn.—Katy Munger, *The Man [Tart Noir]*, p. 154, 2002

hot damn, Vietnam!

used for expressing surprise, shock or dismay *US*

'Vietnam' is lengthened to three syllables.

- Busted for stealing some fucking meat! "Hot damn, Vietnam!" as the man said.—Emmett Grogan, *Ringolevio*, p. 341, 1972

hot deck *noun*

logs piled up for immediate loading *CANADA*

British Columbia logging usage.

- —John Gough, *The Story of British Columbia*, p. 185, 1952

hot diggety!; hot diggety dog!; hot diggety doggity!; hot diggity dog!

used for registering pleasure or astonishment *US, 1923*

Compounding, and linking **HOT DAMN!** and **HOT DOG!**.

- I stand at a major crossroads with an expression that says: "Hot diggety! I love this crazy old town!"—Stuart Jeffries, *Mrs Slocombe's Pussy*, p. 215, 2000

hot dinner *noun*

1 used as a measure when claiming greater experience of an activity than either that of someone else or a notional average *UK*

- WATSON: Sergeant Milligan, how many times have you been drunk in your life? [Laughter] MILLIGAN: More times than you've 'ad 'ot dinners. [Further laughter] — Graeme Kent, *The Queen's Corporal [Six Granada Plays]*, p. 105, 1959

2 a winner *UK*

Rhyming slang.

- — Ray Puxley, *Cockney Rabbit*, 1992

hot dog *noun*

1 a frankfurter or other spiced sausage served in a bread-roll *US, 1894*

The term arose at Yale University in 1894 and was quickly embraced by students at other colleges. Past suggestions that the term arose at New York's Polo Grounds have been disproved by US slang lexicographers Barry Popik and Gerald Cohen.

2 a skilled and cocky person defined as much by their cockiness as their skill *US, 1894*

- Jessie Luker is a hot dog from Alcorn A&M who's got hands on him like snowshoes. — Dan Jenkins, *Semi-Tough*, p. 92, 1972
- You might be more of a team player and a little less of a hot dog on this one, Jack. — *48 Hours*, 1982
- [T]his pilot was a hot dog, and good. — Joseph Wambaugh, *Lines and Shadows*, p. 321, 1984

3 a police officer *US*

- While kids in Northwest refer to police as "one-time," Northeast teenagers call them "bo-deen" or "hot dog," and in Southeast they're "po-pos" or good old "feds." — *Washington Post*, p. A1, 20th August 2001

4 a pornographic book or magazine *US*

- — Paul Glover, *Words from the House of the Dead*, 1974

hot dog *verb*

to perform in a flashy manner that displays your skill *US, 1961*

Surfing slang in wider usage.

- Asian kids – especially his – were not as prone to the schizophrenic hot dogging of their cola-fuelled, burger-bred white classmates. — Greg Williams, *Diamond Geezers*, p. 130, 1997

hot-dog *adjective*

given to showing off *US, 1923*

- Kathy looked over to see one of his bodyguards from TAC in the doorway: a young, hot-dog cop named Wesley, blond hair down on his forehead. — Elmore Leonard, *Maximum Bob*, p. 217, 1991

hot dog!

used for registering delight, pleasure or approval *US, 1906*

hotdog book *noun*

a book used for stimulating sexual interest while masturbating *US*

- Most of these boooks were L and L's, derived from Lewd and Lascivious Conduct, hotdog books heavy with sex, and they were always in demand. — Malcolm Braly, *On the Yard*, p. 152, 1967

hot dogger *noun*

an expert surfer *US*

- — *Paradise of the Pacific*, p. 27, October 1963

hot dope *noun*

heroin *UK, 1998*

A combination of **HOT** (excellent) and **DOPE** (drugs).

- — Robert Ashton, *This Is Heroin*, p. 206, 2002
- — Mike Haskins, *Drugs*, p. 284, 2003

hot dose *noun*

a fatal injection of a narcotic that has been adulterated with a poison *US*

- I had a private doctor do another autopsy. He said they gave her a hot dose. — *Casino*, 1995

hotel *noun*

a jail *US, 1845*

- — John R. Armore and Joseph D. Wolfe, *Dictionary of Desperation*, p. 34, 1976

hotel barber *noun*

a thief who steals from hotel rooms *AUSTRALIA, 1895*

- Hotel barber: a transient who lives by robbing hotel guests. — Thirty-Five *The Argot*, 1950

hotel parental *noun*

your parents' house *UK*

Many parents complain that their house is treated as a hotel; this youth coinage confirms parental suspicions.

- — Alon Shulman, *The Style Bible*, p. 121, 1999
- Hotel parental: The place to go when you need to be in bed, have clothes laundered, dry out or just generally recharge. — *Sunday Herald Sun (Melbourne)*, p. 22, 16th January 2000

hotels *noun*

in bar dice games, a roll from the cup in which some dice are stacked on top of others, invalidating the roll *US*

- — Gil Jacobs, *The World's Best Dice Games*, p. 201, 1976

hot fish yoghurt *noun*

semen *UK*

- [L]ean over him to change gear and get all that hot fish yoghurt in her hair. — Garry Bushell, *The Face*, p. 172, 2001

hotfoot *noun*

a prank in which a matchbook is lit and inserted into an unsuspecting victim's shoe *US, 1934*

- [T]he sight of Max Baer, the former heavyweight champ, crawling under tables sticking lighted matches in the shoes of friends or acquaintances – in short, applying the infuriating "hot foot" which is now blessedly out of fashion – was one of the truly hilarious comedy bits in all history. — Robert Sylvester, *No Cover Charge*, p. 103–104, 1956
- One of the great hot-foots (hot feets?) of all time was administered to Joe Pepitone by Phil Linz. — Jim Bouton, *Ball Four*, p. 118, 1970

hotfoot *verb*

to move quickly *US, 1896*

- I hotfooted it outside and back to my car[.] — James Ellroy, *Brown's Requiem*, p. 32, 1981
- He smiled at me and hotfooted it out to the street. — James Ellroy, *Because the Night*, p. 397, 1984
- The cops began hotfooting it down Darwin Way and they started feeling like pollos. — Joseph Wambaugh, *Lines and Shadows*, p. 61, 1984

hot footer *noun*

somebody who is in a perpetual hurry *US*

- — Norman Carlisle, *The Modern Wonder Book of Trains and Railroading*, p. 264, 1946

hot fudgey *noun*

a savoury piece of gossip *US*

- — Michael Dalton Johnson, *Talking Trash with Redd Foxx*, p. 136, 1994

hot-fuel *verb*

to fuel an aircraft while the engine is running *US*

- [T]heir roaring Phantoms "hot fueling": taking on gas as fast as they burned it, in order to be "topped off" when they were launched. — Robert K. Wilcox, *Scream of Eagles*, p. 228, 1990

hot funky *noun*

a sexually attractive, sexually available woman *US*

- — Kenn "Naz" Young, *Naz's Dictionary of Teen Slang*, p. 61, 1993

hot hay *noun*

marijuana *US*

- — *American Speech*, p. 27, February 1952: 'Teen-age hophead jargon'

hot-hot *adjective*

very hot, very spicy *INDIA*

Intensification by reduplication.

- I like hot-hot curries. — Paroo Nihalini, R.K. Tongue and Priya Hosali, *Indian and British English*, 1979

hothouse *noun*

the vagina *US*

- — Erica Orloff and JoAnn Baker, *Dirty Little Secrets*, p. 91, 2001

hot karl; hot carl *noun*

an act of defecating on a sexual partner; an act of defecating on a person who is asleep; an act of hitting someone with a sock full of human excrement *US*

In Chicago, the comedy troupe Hot Karl have been in existence since 1999; a humorous reference to scatalogical practice is inferred but not confirmed. The earliest unequivocal usage is on the Internet in 2002. In 2004 a white rapper called Hot Karl is noted; also tee-shirts with the image of a pile of steaming faeces and the slogan 'hot carl'.

- — *www.popbitch.com*, 18th December 2004

Hotlanta *nickname*

Atlanta, Georgia *US*

• —Wayne Floyd, *Jason's Authentic Dictionary of CB Slang*, p. 46, 1976

hot-lap *verb*

in motor racing, to drive around the track fast before a race or qualifying run starts, testing the car's performance *US*

• —Hal Higdon, *Finding the Groove*, p. 302, 1973

hot lead *noun*

bullets *US*

• —Vincent J. Monteleone, *Criminal Slang*, p. 123, 1949

hot-lot *verb*

to move quickly; to hurry *US*

• But he almost didn't get a chance to buy one because, as he was saying his farewells to Truman, two police patrol cars came hhot-lotting it up to the front of the house. —Emmett Grogan, *Ringolevio*, p. 207, 1972

hot mix *noun*

in trucking, hot asphalt being transported to a construction site *US*

• —Montie Tak, *Truck Talk*, p. 85, 1971

hot mouth *noun*

a tendency to speak without editing *TRINIDAD AND TOBAGO, 1988*

• —Lise Winer, *Dictionary of the English/Creole of Trinidad & Tobago*, 2003

hotness *noun*

something good or desirable *US*

• Those shoes are hotness. —Connie Eble (Editor), *UNC-CH Campus Slang*, p. 5, October 2002

▸ **the hotness**

an excellent example of something *US*

• —Connie Eble (Editor), *UNC-CH Campus Slang*, p. 5, Spring 2003

hot-nose *verb*

in aerial combat, to approach from behind and below, rising up in front of and ahead of the target plane *US*

• Another trick was 'hot-nosing.' From a hidden approach underneath, a plane would pull up right in front of you. —Robert K. Wilcox, *Scream of Eagles*, p. 156, 1990

hotnot *noun*

a black person *SOUTH AFRICA, 1846*

Offensive, insulting; from Hottentot (an indigenous people of South Africa).

• "Don't just stand there, help me!" I scream. "You damned hotnot, it's all your fault, you and your whore!" —J.M. Coetzee, *In the Heart of the Country*, p. 91, 1977

hot nuts *noun*

intense male sexual desire *US, 1935*

• —Robert A. Wilson, *Playboy's Book of Forbidden Words*, p. 142, 1972

hot pants *noun*

1 sexual desire *US, 1929*

• If she ever got hot pants, it wasn't for her husband. —Raymond Chandler, *The Long Goodbye*, p. 285, 1953
• I've still got hot pants for her, if you want to call that love. —Mary McCarthy, *The Group*, p. 48, 1963
• "Youve got the hot-pants – and youll pay for it – just like I do – because you have to!" he lashed. —John Rechy, *City of Night*, p. 166, 1963
• He'll think I have hot pants. —Elmore Leonard, *The Big Bounce*, p. 178, 1969
• When a woman's glands is actin' up and she can't control certain urges – they say she's got hot pants! Same as the meathead there. Hot toursers, hot pants, same thing! —Eugene Boe (Compiler), *The Wit & Wisdom of Archie Bunker*, p. 153, 1971
• I'm not going to screw it up just because you people got hot pants. —George V. Higgins, *The Friends of Eddie Doyle*, p. 74, 1971
• Squeezed it harder than he had ever squeezed any hot-pants cheerleader in his daddy's old Pontiac. —Tom Robbins, *Another Roadside Attraction*, p. 223, 1971
• "Damn, baby," Roman exclaimed, "it seems as if all the bitches got hot pants for you, Prince." —Donald Goines, *Black Gangster*, p. 23, 1977

2 tight, skimpy shorts as a (surprisingly enduring) fashion item *UK, 1970*

Deriving, no doubt, from the sexual sense.

• You wear them hot pants, they're out of style. —Rod Stewart, *You're Insane*, 1977
• Kylie Minogue, clearly no doormat, owes her resurgence to a pair of gold hot pants that directed attention to her fetishised bottom rather than her less-than-spectacular voice. —*The Guardian*, 4th August 2003

hot peas *noun*

the knees *UK*

Glasgow rhyming slang.

• —Michael Munro, *The Patter, Another Blast*, 1988

hot peckers *noun*

hot peppers *US*

Limited usage, but clever.

• —*Maledicta*, p. 14, 1996: 'Domino's pizza jargon'

hot pee; hot piss *noun*

a pressing desire to urinate *TRINIDAD AND TOBAGO, 1990*

• —Lise Winer, *Dictionary of the English/Creole of Trinidad & Tobago*, 2003

hot-pillow *adjective*

said of a hotel or motel that rents rooms for sexual liaisons for cash, without registering the guests using the room *US, 1954*

• Until after World War II, the tourist court was considered the poor cousin of the hotel – a place which catered to the 'hot pillow trade,' to use J. Edgar Hoover's eloquent phrase. —*Washington Post*, p. 1 (Weekend), 12th January 1979
• Many of Hoover's "dens of vice" were once decent places that, unable to keep up, turned to the "hot pillow trade." —Kenneth T. Jackson, *Crabgrass Frontier*, p. 254, 1985
• Doohan could hardly keep from telling the man that the beautiful woman everyone was admiring was the woman who spent time with him in a certain hot-pillow motel at least once a week, sometimes more. —Robert Campbell, *Juice*, p. 221, 1988

hot pit *noun*

in motor racing, the area where a pit crew works on a car during a race *US*

• The "hot pits," an area designated for team members and their management, are separated from the action on the pit road by the pit wall. —Roger Horotwitz, *Boys and their Toys*, p. 231, 2001

hot plate *noun*

the electric chair; execution by electrocution *US*

• —Vincent J. Monteleone, *Criminal Slang*, p. 124, 1949

hot-plate hamster *noun*

a prison officer who eats food intended for prisoners *UK*

• —Angela Devlin, *Prison Patter*, p. 63, 1996

hot poop *noun*

the latest information *UK*

Combines **HOT** (quick) and **POOP** (news).

• My guys in the States were calling her the Spymaster and she was passing on their hot poop. —David H. Hackworth, *Hazardous Duty*, p. 229, 1996

hot pot *noun*

1 in poker, a large amount of money bet on a hand *US*

• —George Percy, *The Language of Poker*, p. 45, 1988

2 in horse racing, a favourite *AUSTRALIA, 1904*

• He found out what it was like to lose on a hotpot. —Wilda Moxham, *The Apprentice*, p. 97, 1969
• [Y]our ex-jockey had some very bad luck on a hot pot at Canterbury yesterday. —Clive Galea, *Slipper*, p. 197, 1988

hot potato *noun*

a waiter, especially an efficient one *UK*

Cockney rhyming slang, pronounced 'pertatah' ('waitah').

• —Julian Franklyn, *A Dictionary of Rhyming Slang*, 1960
• —Ray Puxley, *Cockney Rabbit*, 1992

hot potato *verb*

to prioritise or juggle priorities *NEW ZEALAND*

• The day's other theme was the hot-potatoing of correctional factilities. —*Dominion*, p. 2, 2rd May 2001

hot ringer *noun*

a burglar alarm that advises police that an armed robbery is in progress *US*

• He had accepted a call on a "hot ringer" in Southwest. A Hoover Street jewelry store was being robbed. It was a "There Now" call. —Stephen J. Cannell, *The Tin Collectors*, p. 110, 2001

hot rock *noun*

a person who through dress or manner strives to be noticed *US, 1945*

• —*American Speech*, p. 228, October 1956: 'More United States Air Force slang'

hot rod *noun*
a car modified for speed and, sometimes, flashy looks *US, 1945*
- There kids have cars, and "hot rod" races are common. —Jack Lait and Lee Mortimer, *Washington Confidential*, p. 122, 1951
- He was around at the side of the station when I drove in, doing something to the motor of his hot rod. —Jim Thompson, *The Killer Inside*, p. 56, 1952
- Mom keeps bawling Pop out because he drives the new station wagon like a hot-rod kid[.] —Bernard Wolfe, *The Late Risers*, p. 300, 1954
- A hotrod kid came by with his scarf flying. —Jack Kerouac, *On the Road*, p. 15, 1957
- You're going to start tending to business and stop running around with those hot-rod Romeos. —Max Shulman, *Rally Round the Flag, Boys!*, p. 48, 1957

hot rod *verb*
to masturbate *US*
- —Eugene Landy, *The Underground Dictionary*, p. 106, 1971

hot roller *noun*
a stolen car that is being driven *US*
- "How about rollers?" asked Serge. "How many hot cars do you get rolling?" "Hot rollers? Oh, maybe one a month." —Joseph Wambaugh, *The New Centurions*, p. 42, 1970
- — *Los Angeles Times*, p. B8, 19th December 1994

hots *noun*
1 sexual desire, intense interest *US, 1947*
- You ain't in love with Angela. You just got a case of the hots, that's all. —Max Shulman, *Rally Round the Flag, Boys!*, p. 190, 1957
- They think I have a secret hot for her. —Clancy Sigal, *Going Away*, p. 409, 1961
- She gave him the hots in the worst way and there was nothing he could do about that, but he still enjoyed being near her. —Vance Donovan, *High Rider*, p. 21, 1969
- And besides, she doesn't even have the hots for me. —Darryl Ponicsan, *The Last Detail*, p. 113, 1970
- The bastard's got the hots for some Hun. —Barry Humphries, *Bazz Pulls It Off!*, 1971
- What the hell does she need with some half-assed lover who's got the hots for tile bathrooms? —Armistead Maupin, *Tales of the City*, p. 255, 1978
- I had the hots for Joe Perry, I followed them around on tour and partied with them[.] —Elmore Leonard, *Be Cool*, p. 92, 1999
- He's a total asshole and he's got the hots for my friend Angela and it's disgusting. —*American Beauty*, 1999
- She probably got the hots so bad for those hunks she rode Al Dante like a horse for days after. —Rita Ciresi, *Pink Slip*, p. 50, 1999
- I remember hearing the chorus from S-Express. "Got the hots for you. I got the hots for you"[.] —Wayne Anthony, *Spanish Highs*, p. 2, 1999
- "I think Stephanie's got the hots for someone else," Grandma said. —Janet Evanovich, *Seven Up*, p. 19, 2001

2 electric hair curlers *US*
- — *American Speech*, p. 61, Spring-Summer 1975: 'Razorback slang'

hot seat *noun*
1 the position of responsibility, especially if the situation attracts critical attention *UK, 1942*
- Although nobody is accusing him [Romano Prodi] of misconduct, he finds himself in the hot seat. — *The Daily Telegraph*, 19th July 2003

2 the electric chair; death by electrocution in the electric chair *US, 1925*
- And if either of you are tapped for the hot seat, you'd do a lot better by letting Pat pick you up. —Mickey Spillane, *I, The Jury*, p. 19, 1947
- His buttocks, in creased midnight-blue trousers, for the hot seat. —Willard Motley, *Let No Man Write My Epitaph*, p. 164, 1958
- Why risk sudden death or the hot seat just for a moment of playing the big shot. —Chester Himes, *The Real Cool Killers*, p. 137, 1959
- I could've got life or the hot seat for what I did. —A.S. Jackson, *Gentleman Pimp*, p. 130, 1973

hot seat game *noun*
a swindle in which all the players in a game except the victim are confederates *US*
- —Lindsay E. Smith and Bruce A. Walstad, *Sting Shift*, p. 116, 1989: 'Glossary'

hot sheet *noun*
a list of cars reported as stolen *US, 1926*
- "How often you pick up a sitting dick?" asked Serge, to change the subject, checking a license plate against the numbers on the hot sheet. —Joseph Wambaugh, *The New Centurions*, p. 41, 1970
- Then get the ten latest GLA's off the hot sheet. —Charles Whited, *Chiodo*, p. 27, 1973

hot-sheet *adjective*
said of a motel or hotel that rents rooms for sexual liaisons for cash, without registering the guests using the room *US*
- Lang returned briefly to his job loading trucks, until one night when he picked up another prostitute at a bar and they slipped into a "hot-sheet" hotel. — *Newsweek*, p. 89, 7th November 1977
- I've got peeper reports nailed at my burglary location and all over the Southside – hot-sheet motels and jazz clubs. —James Ellroy, *White Jazz*, p. 51, 1992

hot shit *noun*
an exceptionally good person or thing *US, 1960*
- —Collin Baker et al., *College Undergraduate Slang Study Conducted at Brown University*, p. 140, 1968
- Goddamn New York teams, think they're hot shit. — *Diner*, 1982

hot-shit *adjective*
exciting; fashionable *US, 1962*
- Then some hot-shit doctor comes in and revives them. —Jim Carroll, *Forced Entries*, p. 52, 1987
- [O]ne of the hot-shit writers, maybe the hottest-shit writer of them all[.] —Joel Rose, *Kill Kill Faster Faster*, p. 105, 1997

hotshot *noun*
1 an adulterated dose of a drug that is designed to be fatal when injected *US, 1936*
- — *American Speech*, p. 27, February 1952: 'Teen-age hophead jargon'
- New York detectives assigned to the Narcotics Squad are convinced that he died of what the trade calls "a hot shot" – heroin or cocaine purposely mixed with rat poison. —Robert Sylvester, *No Cover Charge*, p. 47, 1956
- "I can tell you in confidence he is due for a hot shot." (Note: This is a cap of poison junk sold to addicts for liquidation purposes. Often given to informers. Usually the hot shot is strychnine since it tastes and looks like junk.) —William Burroughs, *Naked Lunch*, p. 2, 1957
- If some hypo finds out that another hypo is a stool pigeon they give him what is called a hot shot. —Willard Motley, *Let No Man Write My Epitaph*, p. 151, 1958
- "We thought at first it was an overdose, but all you had to do was look in the kid's face to see it was a hot shot." "A hot shot?" Donald Halsted said. "An injection of poison." —Clarence Cooper Jr, *The Scene*, p. 29, 1960
- That creepin' bastard Fink! Het gets so much for what they call 'makin' a case' ... someone's goin to slip him a hotshot... —Alexander Trocchi, *Cain's Book*, p. 243, 1960
- Addicts call this type of hotshot a "ten-cent pistol" because the poison costs a dime but is as effective as a gun. —James Mills, *The Panic in Needle Park*, p. 39, 1966
- He wasn't the type, but he kept trying until he ran the "Gorilla" game on a dope dealer's broad and was set up for a "hot shot." —Iceberg Slim (Robert Beck), *Pimp*, p. 41, 1969
- The coroner says she O.D.'d on smack. She wasn't murdered – unless somebody gave her a hotshot on purpose. —Gerald Petievich, *Money Men*, p. 94, 1981

2 a gun shot fired after an emergency call to police *US*
- — *Los Angeles Times*, p. B8, 19th December 1994

3 an electric cattle prod *US*
- —John Cann, *The Stunt Guide*, p. 60,: 'Terms and definitions'

4 execution by electrocution in the electric chair *US*
- — *American Speech*, p. 155, May 1951: 'Hermann Collitz and the language of the underworld'

5 a flashy, successful person whose self-esteem is perhaps excessive *US, 1927*
- If you're such a hotshot patriot, why didn't you reenlist? —Max Shulman, *Rally Round the Flag, Boys!*, p. 115, 1957

hot spike *noun*
a dose of a drug that has been adulterated and produces serious injury or death when injected *US*
- I'm gonna dig you out of whatever trash heap you're hidin' in and stick a hot spike in your ass! —Joseph Nazel, *Black Cop*, p. 145, 1974

hot spot *noun*
in oil drilling, an area that has indications of a productive field *US*
- [I]f we get what is known as a 'hot spot' or a 'bright spot' on our computer graphs, we notify the company and then they spend a lot of money to develop the potenetial field, put in pies and cisterns. —Stephen Cannell, *Big Con*, p. 263, 1997

hot squat *noun*
the electric chair; execution by electrocution *US, 1928*
- If you smear her all over the papers as a number-one candidate for the hot squat you and me are going to have it out. — Mickey Spillane, *I, The Jury*, p. 22, 1947
- — Vincent J. Monteleone, *Criminal Slang*, p. 125, 1949

hot stepper *noun*
a fugitive from justice *JAMAICA, 1982*
- — Thomas H. Slone, *Rasta is Cuss*, p. 50, 2003

hotstick *noun*
a marijuana cigarette *US, 1957*
- — Richard A. Spears, *The Slang and Jargon of Drugs and Drink*, p. 271, 1986
- — Mike Haskins, *Drugs*, p. 287, 2003

hot stove *adjective*
said of a discussion of sports between periods in games *CANADA*
- Things we have missed may be mulled over in Hot Stove sessions which are as old and popular as the sport of hockey itself. — *Hockey Canada*, p. 12/2, November 1962

hot stuff *noun*
1 promotional literature produced as part of a telephone sales swindle *US*
- Anyone who succumbs to a sales pitch – due to the hot stuff or a phone call – becomes, in the yaks' slang, a mooch. — Kathleen Odean, *High Steppers, Fallen Angels, and Lollipops*, p. 132, 1988

2 illegal whisky *US, 1840*
- Nellie I'll get a cup o' tea for you. Morisheen An' I'll put a lacer o' the hot stuff in it. — John B. Keane, *The Man from Clare*, p. 72, 1962

3 coffee *US*
- — Bill Davis, *Jawjacking*, p. 53, 1977

4 napalm *US*
- — Gregory Clark, *Words of the Vietnam War*, p. 340, 1990

hotsy-totsy; hotsy *noun*
an attractive young woman *US, 1928*
- "This is your mother you're talking to and not one of your little hotsy-totsies." "Hotsy-totsies!" — Walker Percy, *The Movie Goer*, p. 155, 1960

hotsy-totsy *adjective*
fancy *US, 1926*
- [E]very spring, in the fullness of their benevolence, they sent him and my mother for a hotsy-totsy free weekend in Atlantic City. — Philip Roth, *Portnoy's Complaint*, p. 5, 1969
- [T]he ace air traffic controller in Pushing Tin, who baffles his colleagues by getting the hotsy-totsy girl. — *The Guardian*, 14th May 2001

hottentots *noun*
the buttocks *US*
- A white soldier, his shirttail out behind, his cunt cap crosswise on his dome, staggered along happily, held up by a chunky black whore with an enormous Hottentot can[.] — Earl Thompson, *Tattoo*, p. 121, 1974
- — *Maledicta*, p. 52, 1986–1987: 'A continuation of a glossary of ethnic slurs in American English'

hotter *noun*
a thrill-seeking criminal who drives stolen high-performance cars *UK*
- The "hotters" of Blackbird Leys prepared for another night of violence yesterday as they boasted of their terrifying exploits behind the wheels of stolen high-performance cars. — *The Independent*, 3rd September 1991
- You should see the way the hotters dodge between the police vans. — *The Guardian*, 4th September 1991

hotter than Dutch love *adjective*
very hot *US, 1950*
- [W]idowers teasing that the weather was hotter than Dutch love. — Mary Potter Engel, *A Woman of Salt*, p. 40, 2001

hot ticket *noun*
something that is extremely popular and in demand *US, 1978*
- Rings 'n' Things also has stores in hot-ticket towns like Vegas, Reno, and Atlantic City. — Stephen Cannell, *King Con*, p. 113, 1997

hottie *noun*
1 a celebrity *NEW ZEALAND*
- If you have the misfortune to date someone who moves in a circle of hotties, you're in big trouble. — *Sunday Star-Times*, p. D2, 30th June 2002

2 an attractive, sexually appealing young person *US, 1991*
- — Connie Eble (Editor), *UNC-CH Campus Slang*, p. 5, Spring 1994
- You guys are so pathetic. I'm gonna find myself a little hottie. — *American Pie*, 1999
- We see him rolling around in the sheets with some hottie[.] — *The Village Voice*, 6th February 2001

3 a great wave or surfer *US*
- — Trevor Cralle, *The Surfin'ary*, p. 55, 1991

4 a black person, especially of the Khoikhoi race *SOUTH AFRICA, 1970*
May be insulting or affectionate; from Hottentot (an indigenous people of South Africa).
- — Penny Silva, *A Dictionary of South African English*, 1996

hotting *noun*
the thrill-seeking activity of stealing and driving stolen high-performance cars *UK*
- — John Ayto, *Oxford Dictionary of Slang*, p. 99, 1998

hot toddy *noun*
the body *UK*
Rhyming slang.
- — Ray Puxley, *Cockney Rabbit*, 1992

hot tot *noun*
a very attractive young woman *UK*
A comination of **HOT** (sexually attractive) and a variation of **TOTTY** (a sexually attractive woman).
- None of them could mistake the hot tots and each promised to try their luck when they next came into sight. — Wayne Anthony, *Spanish Highs*, p. 157, 1999

hot to trot *adjective*
ready and eager for sexual activity *US, 1951*
Extended from **HOT** (sexually eager, passionate).
- Here he is hot to trot and suddenly stricken by a flash that's a surefire dong-wilter. — Lester Bangs, *Psychotic Reactions and Carburetor Dung*, p. 77, 1971
- So, it got to be too much for him, and he got himself this hot-to-trot bimbo, and it turns out – he was talking about it, in detail – there wasn't anything she couldn't do, wouldn't do or didn't want done. — George V. Higgins, *The Judgment of Deke Hunter*, p. 131, 1976
- Hot to trot, make any man's eyes pop[.] — Salt 'N' Pepa *Let's Talk About Sex*, 1991
- I said to myself a while ago that Loretta was looking for trouble. She was real hot to trot. — Janet Evanovich, *Seven Up*, p. 17, 2001

hotty; hottie *noun*
a hot water bottle *UK, 1947*
- My mother gave her hottie a realistic hug and flapped it over her shoulder, beating it savagely. — Edna Everage (Barry Humphries), *My Gorgeous Life*, p. 52, 1989
- We went to bed with a hottie, under wool blankets and an eiderdown. — *Listener*, p. 10, 22nd September 2001

hot up *verb*
1 to become increasingly lively or exciting *UK, 1923*
- [T]hings are hotting up for Christopher Nolan[.] — *The Times Magazine*, p. 10, 2nd March 2002

2 to identify, or point the finger of suspicion at someone to the police *UK*
- — Angela Devlin, *Prison Patter*, p. 63, 1996

3 to increase the power, speed and performance (of a car) *UK, 1928*
- Many people think that a rodder is a character who spends all his time hotting up his roadster. — *Hot Rod Comics*, June 1952

hot walker *noun*
in horse racing, a groom who walks a horse after a race, letting it cool down *US*
- — Tom Ainslie, *Ainslie's Complete Guide to Thoroughbred Racing*, p. 333, 1976

hot water *noun*
a state of trouble, a difficult situation *UK, 1537*
- US bank in hot water after telling clients to pull out of unionised firms. — *The Guardian*, 21st November 2002

hot wire *noun*
a linear amplifier for a citizens' band radio *US*
- — Porter Bibb, *CB Bible*, p. 96, 1976

hot-wire *verb*
to bypass a car's ignition system and start the car by cutting and connecting wires under the dashboard *US, 1954*
- We'll just steal it right back. All right? Now, you get some wire. We need, oh, about a foot. We can hot-wire it.—*American Graffiti*, 1973
- [W]e intend to have Peter Wolf explaining how to hotwire a car[.] —Lester Bangs, *Psychotic Reactions and Carburetor Dung*, p. 142, 1974
- If a blast came, I then planned, in five minutes I could hot-wire and steal a car[.]—Bobby Seale, *A Lonely Rage*, p. 64, 1978
- Never broke into a car. Never hot-wried a car.—*Repo Man*, 1984
- I'll hotwire it. Car theft is my Vato speciality.—Stephen J. Cannell, *The Tin Collectors*, p. 326, 2001

hot with two t's *adjective*
extremely sexy *US*
- —Connie Eble (Editor), *UNC-CH Campus Slang*, p. 4, Spring 2000

hot ziggedy!; hot ziggetty!; hot ziggity!; hot ziggety damn!
used for registering pleasure or astonishment; occasionally anger *US*
A variation of **HOT DIGGETY!**.
- Stoll's speech was punctuated by a parade of exclamations – "Hot ziggity!" and "Holy smokes!"[.]—Katie Hafner and John Markoff, *CYBERPUNK*, p. 169, 1995
- Well, hot ziggetty, a holiday for me. What have we got going here? —Mary Robinson, *Tell Me*, p. 135, 2002
- [W]orrying whether even mental sex with a stepmother wasn't incest? And you off with the cousins? Hot damn. "Hot ziggety damn," Bert says[.]—Hortense Calisher, *Sunday Jews*, p. 352, 2002
- Hot ziggedy! He settled into the melancholy mood saturated with evil and intrigue[.]—Vincent O. Carter and Herbert R. Lottman, *Such Sweet Thunder*, p. 374, 2003

hou-bro *noun*
a fellow fraternity member *US*
An abbreivation of 'house brother'.
- [S]ometimes longed for the uncomplicated life of lacrosse and rugby and hou-bro beevo parties, of happily hugging the toilet all night long with your barf buddies after draining a half-keg for no special occasion?—John Sayles, *Union Dues*, p. 279, 1977

hound *noun*
1 a person who is obsessed with the preceding combining noun *US, 1911*
Not, as the definition might suggest, a grammarian.
- Tall, slender, with regular features, dark and personable, Legs was a night club hound, even owned some himself.—Jack Lait and Lee Mortimer, *New York Confidential*, p. 160, 1948
- But he knew all about Estes Kefauver whom he described as a publicity hound.—Clancy Sigal, *Going Away*, p. 160, 1961
- For a minute or two, he was completely unable to think of what he could possibly say to her that would not make him sound like a cock hound[.]—Cecil Brown, *The Life & Loves of Mr. Jiveass Nigger*, p. 68, 1969
- I was a big pussy-hound. Ain't changed much either.—Edwin Torres, *Carlito's Way*, p. 12, 1975
- Once upstairs in the Melody lobby, Raven is instantly surrounded by admirers and tit hounds.—Josh Alan Friedman, *Tales of Times Square*, p. 23, 1986

2 an unattractive woman *UK*
A variation of **DOG**.
- Yi should see some of the hounds he's had by the way, doll.—Ian Pattison, *Rab C. Nesbitt*, 1988

3 a Greyhound bus *US, 1959*
- —*Swinging Syllables*, 1959
- —Montie Tak, *Truck Talk*, p. 86, 1971

hound dog *noun*
an air-to-ground missile *US*
- —Linda Reinberg, *In the Field*, p. 109, 1991

hound-dog *verb*
to track down, to follow, to find *US*
- Bud and I were sent to hound-dog them on the way, in the direction I saw them take.—Clarence Major, *All-Night Visitors*, p. 39, 1998

house *noun*
1 a prisoner's cell or the area immediately surrounding the prisoner's bed in a dorimitory-style room *US, 1970*
- "I think I'll head back to my house to read," he said.—Seth Morgan, *Homeboy*, p. 257, 1990
- This is one of the most important aspects of prison life as a person's house is his home, his solitude, where he achieves his privacy. —William Bentley, *Prison Slang*, p. 7, 1992
- —Reinhold Aman, *Hillary Clinton's Pen Pal*, p. 43, 1996

2 a police station *US, 1909*
- "How come we're taking this guy to the house?" Chiodo asked his partner.—Charles Whited, *Chiodo*, p. 47, 1973

3 in poker, a hand consisting of three cards of the same rank and a pair *US*
An abbreviation of the conventional 'full house'.
- —Anthony Holden, *Big Deal*, p. 301, 1990

▷ **see: HOUSE MUSIC**

▸ **go under the house**
to perform oral sex on a woman *US*
- —*Male Swinger Number 3*, p. 45, 1981: 'The complete gay dictionary'

▸ **in the house**
1 here and now, present, currently *US*
- —Judi Sanders, *Faced and Faded, Hanging to Hurl*, p. 22, 1993
- —*Merriam-Webster's Hot Words on Campus Marketing Survey '93*, p. 3, 13th October 1993
- The music changes. All Saints in the house.—Karline Smith, *Letters to Andy Cole*, p. 139, 1998

2 popular, stylish *US*
- —Connie Eble (Editor), *UNC-CH Campus Slang*, p. 5, Spring 1994

▸ **mind your house**
watch your back, be careful *IRELAND*
Often used in sports matches: when a player has the ball a team mate will shout 'mind your house' if an opponent is coming up behind him.
- The Circuit Court heard, yesterday, that on December 21 1998, Sgt Kevin McHugh, of Mary St Garda Station, was told by Keane to "mind your house" when he served him an appeal notice.—*Limerick Leader*, 31st July 1999

▸ **on the house**
paid for by management of the establishment *US, 1889*
- They flew him up from Miami in their private jet, comped the room, meals, everything. If you can afford to lose a hundred grand, Vincent, it's all on the house.—Elmore Leonard, *Glitz*, p. 129, 1985
- On the house.—*Empire Records*, 1995

▸ **the house**
the New York House of Detention for female prisoners *US*
- "She just got out of the house," Helen said, meaning the Women's House of Detention in Greenwich Village.—James Mills, *The Panic in Needle Park*, p. 33, 1966

house *verb*
1 to steal *US*
- —Ellen C. Bellone (Editor), *Dictionary of Slang*, p. 14, 1989

2 to carry contraband, such as a weapon or drugs *US*
- —Anna Scotti and Paul Young, *Buzzwords*, p. 136, 1997

house *adjective*
casual, verging on sloppy *US*
- —Judi Sanders, *Faced and Faded, Hanging to Hurl*, p. 21, 1993

house ape *noun*
a child *US*
- A bunch a blue-eyed spad house apes inta the bargain.—Robert Gover, *JC Saves*, p. 127, 1968

house ball *noun*
in pinball, a ball that leaves play without having scored any points *US*
- —Bobbye Claire Natkin and Steve Kirk, *All About Pinball*, p. 113, 1977

housecat *noun*
a soldier not assigned to combat duty *US*
Vietnam war usage.
- I spent two and a half days at the Tan Son Nhut Air Base, explaining about my brother and the emergency leave to a running variety of housecats behind the ticket counter [.]—Larry Heinemann, *Close Quarters*, p. 118, 1977

housed *adjective*
drunk *US*
- —Connie Eble (Editor), *UNC-CH Campus Slang*, p. 5, April 1997

house dancer *noun*
a sex club dancer who regularly appears at one club *US*
- When I was a 'house' dancer I would watch all the 'featured' dancers, most of whom were porn stars, come in and make all the money, get lines of people and get the beautiful pictures.—Ana Loria, *1 2 3 Be A Porn Star!*, p. 107, 2000

house dick *noun*
a private detective working for a hotel or other establishment *US*
- The "security officer" (refined designation for a house dick) of one of the oldest and most famous hotels in Washington, near the White House, was recently fired because he ran a shakedown racket[.] —Jack Lait and Lee Mortimer, *Washington Confidential*, p. 285–286, 1951
- Are you going peacefully, or do I call the house dick? —Max Shulman, *Anyone Got a Match?*, p. 197, 1964
- I picked her up, and carried her into the dining room, oblivious even of the house dick. —Red Rudensky, *The Gonif*, p. 114, 1970

house fee *noun*
the amount charged for entering a crack house *US*
- —Terry Williams, *Crackhouse*, p. 149, 1992

house girl *noun*
1 a prostitute working in a brothel *US*
- After the call-girls come the house-girls. Houses today are not the elaborate affairs that they used to be. —John M. Murtagh and Sara Harris, *Cast the First Stone*, p. 2, 1957

2 in a sex club, a local dancer who regularly works at the club, as distinguished from pornography stars who make limited engagements at the club *US*
- The DJ, the manager, the owner, all such 'interested' parties basically didn't want a headline dancer making them look bad in front of the house girls. —Anthony Petkovich, *The X Factory*, p. 37, 1997

house guru *noun*
▷ see: HOUSE WIZARD

housekeeper *noun*
in prison, the passive, weaker partner in a relationship who is subservient to his dominant partner's needs and wants *US*
- Prison ain't that bad, you get the hang of it… find yourself some buddies, a little housekeeper to take care of your wants… —Elmore Leonard, *Maximum Bob*, p. 197, 1991

housemaid's knee *noun*
1 a sea, the sea *UK*
Rhyming slang.
- [I]n the Royal soup and gravy, afloat on the high housemaid's knees[.] —Ronnie Barker, *Fletcher's Book of Rhyming Slang*, p. 39, 1979

2 a key *UK*
Rhyming slang.
- [A] bunch of "housemaids". —Ray Puxley, *Cockney Rabbit*, 1992

housemaid's knees *noun*
the condition caused by Osgood-Schlatter disease, calcium deposits on the lower outside quadrant of the knee *US*
- —William Desmond Nelson, *Surfing*, p. 226, 1973

houseman *noun*
the best regular player in a pool hall *US*
- —Steve Rushin, *Pool Cool*, p. 16, 1990

house mother *noun*
a madame in a brothel *US*
- —*Maledicta*, p. 150, Summer/Winter 1986–1987: 'Sexual slang: prostitutes, pedophiles, flagellators, transvestites, and necrophiles'

house mouse *noun*
1 a prisoner who takes or accepts responsibility for cleaning a prison cell, dormitory or common room *US*
- —James Harris, *A Convict's Dictionary*, p. 33, 1989

2 in Antarctica, support personnel assigned to the base, especially someone assigned to domestic duties *ANTARCTICA, 1958*
- —Bernadette Hince, *The Antarctic Dictionary*, p. 169, 2000
- —*Cool Antarctica*, 2003: 'Antarctic slang'

3 an American soldier who explored Viet Cong tunnels *US*
- Every company had what they called their 'house mouse,' who was usually the smallest guy in the bunch. —*The Houston Chronicle*, 27th October 1989

4 during the Vietnam war, a Vietnamese maid or mistress *US*
- —Linda Reinberg, *In the Field*, p. 109, 1991

house music; house *noun*
an umbrella genre for much contemporary dance music with strong repetitive rhythms – in 4/4 time, generally between 115 and 135 beats per minute *UK, 1986*
The name derives from the Ware*house* Club in Chicago where the music originated in the mid-1980s.
- House music? I couldn't even begin to tell you what House is. You have to go to the clubs and see how people react when they hear it. —Mo Bean, *Let's Go Clubbing*, p. 104, 1998

house nigger; house nigga *noun*
a black person who curries favour from white people and in return is given some small degree of privilege *US, 1968*
An updated 'house slave'.
- Professors are house niggers and students are field niggers. —Jerry Rubin, *Do It!*, p. 215, 1970
- Malcolm X extended and popularized the concept; a field nigger was more likely to become a revolutionary while the house nigger was more likely to be an Uncle Tom. —Clarence Major, *Dictionary of Afro-American Slang*, p. 53, 1970
- He remembers his father as a head-screatching, foot-shuffling odd-job boy who aspired to be a house nigger. —Darryl Ponicsan, *The Last Detail*, p. 13, 1970
- Uncle Tom is a HOUSE NIGGER. —Malachi Andrews and Paul T. Owens, *Black Language*, p. 78, 1973
- Van was doing a Tom act that would've put any old time house nigger to utter shame. —Odie Hawkins, *Scars and Memories*, p. 158, 1987
- [A]ll he got from the community, his community, was […] a lot of abuse about being an "Uncle Tom", a "house nigga", a "coconut". He had heard it all. —Karline Smith, *Moss Side Massive*, p. 181, 1994
- Then how come Nick says yeah, you're his house-nigga. —Elmore Leonard, *Be Cool*, p. 126, 1999

house nut *noun*
in the cinema business, the weekly operating expenses of the cinema *US*
- —Ralph S. Singleton, *Filmaker's Dictionary*, p. 83, 1990

House of Commons *noun*
an outdoor toilet *CANADA*
- Right across western Canada, the "house of commons" is the biffey. Now that should tell you something about the way westerners feel about the goings-on in Ottawa. —Chris Thain, *Cold as a Bay Street Banker's Heart*, p. 86, 1987

House of D *nickname*
the New York Women's House of Detention, Greenwich Avenue *US, 1964*
- —Clarence Major, *Dictionary of Afro-American Slang*, p. 67, 1970
- "The House of D" as it was unaffectionately nicknamed, stood on a trianglar block in the heart of Greenwich Village. —Karla Jay, *Tales of the Lavendar Menace*, p. 103, 1999

house of dark shadows *noun*
any building that is occupied, or thought to be occupied, by Viet Cong *US*
- —Linda Reinberg, *In the Field*, p. 109, 1991

House of Do Right *nickname*
the New York City jail *US*
- They gave up and then I was sent to the Tombs, the House of Do-Right, on 125 White Street, to await some kinda trial. —Piri Thomas, *Down These Mean Streets*, p. 243, 1967

House of Fraser; hoosie Fraser; howser *noun*
a razor, especially as a weapon *UK*
Rhyming slang, formed from the name of a retailing chain.
- —Ray Puxley, *Cockney Rabbit*, 1992
- —Michael Munro, *The Complete Patter*, 1996

house of intake *noun*
a restaurant *US*
A term coined by writers of the Coneheads skits on *Saturday Night Live* in the late 1970s, featuring three Remulakian aliens who lived quiet and normal lives in the suburbs of New Jersey. Most of the Remulakian phrases were too forced for everyday slang, such as 'molten lactate extract of hooved animals' for 'melted cheese', but a few such as this were temporarily in vogue.

house of joy *noun*
a brothel *US*
- It is difficult and dangerous to fall in with streetwalkers on the avenues, and next to impossible to locate a gambling den or a house of joy. —Jack Lait and Lee Mortimer, *New York Confidential*, p. 206, 1948

House of Lords *noun*
corduroy trousers *UK*
Rhyming slang for CORDS.
- —Ray Puxley, *Cockney Rabbit*, 1992

house of wax *noun*
a prison *US*

- I hit the old edge and saw a lotta my old pals who all gave me the usual bullshit niggers give a guy when he's justy outta the house of wax. —A.S. Jackson, *Gentleman Pimp*, p. 69, 1973

house piece *noun*
a gift of a dose of crack cocaine, given to the owner of a crack house in appreciation for the use of the premises *US*
- —Terry Williams, *Crackhouse*, p. 149, 1992

houseplant *noun*
a person who never leaves the home *US, 1917*
- —Judi Sanders, *Don't Dog by Do, Dude!*, p. 17, 1991

houser *noun*
1 a person who is part of the club music and party set *US*
- Houser: the members of this clique assigned great value to house music and to the dance club scene connected with it. —Marcel Danesi, *Cool*, p. 56–57, 1994
- —Judi Sanders, *Da Bomb*, p. 8, 1997

2 a group of close friends *US*
- —Kenn "Naz" Young, *Naz's Dictionary of Teen Slang*, p. 61, 1993

house-stoy *noun*
(among Nova Scotians of German descent) a wedding present *CANADA*
- The Lunenburg County NS "house-stoy," "wedding present," derives from the German "aussteuer," "dowry." —Murray Emeneau, *Canadian English*, p. 34–39, 1975

House that Ruth Built *nickname*
Yankee Stadium, Bronx, New York *US*
The stadium opened in 1923 at the height of Ruth's career.
- —Louis Phillips and Burnham Holmes, *The Complete Book of Sports Nicknames*, p. 214, 1998

housewife *noun*
an elementary sewing kit *UK*
- —Carl Fleischhauer, *A Glossary of Army Slang*, p. 26, 1968
- —Linda Reinberg, *In the Field*, p. 109, 1991

housewives' choice *noun*
voice *UK*
Rhyming slang, formed from the title of a record request programme broadcast on the *BBC Light Programme*, 1946–67.
- —Ray Puxley, *Cockney Rabbit*, 1992

house wizard; house guru *noun*
the technical expert in a business or organisation *US*
- A really effective house wizard can have influence out of all proportion to his/her ostensible rank and still not have to wear a suit. —Eric S. Raymond, *The New Hacker's Dictionary*, p. 203, 1991

house-wrecker *noun*
in surfing, a large and powerful wave *US*
- —Dennis Aaberg and John Milius, *Big Wednesday*, p. 209, 1978

housey housey *adjective*
itchy *UK*
Rhyming slang for 'lousy' (lice-ridden, hence itchy). Formed from the name of one of Bingo's variations.
- —Ray Puxley, *Cockney Rabbit*, 1992

Hovis *noun*
the head of a brown-skinned person *UK*
A refinement of the rhyming slang **LOAF OF BREAD** (the head); Hovis™ is a well-known brand of *brown* bread.
- —Ray Puxley, *Fresh Rabbit*, p. 101, 1998

Howard Johnsons *noun*
an outdoor street food vendor in Vietnam during the war *US*
From the name of a roadside restaurant which at the time of the Vietnam war was immensely popular in the US.
- All over Saigon you find conveniently located protable food vendors affectionately dubbed "Howard Johnsons" by the GI. —Tony Zidek, *Choi Oi*, p. 32, 1965

Howard's Way *adjective*
homosexual *UK*
Rhyming slang, from the title of a BBC television drama series, 1985–90.
- —Bodmin Dark, *Dirty Cockney Rhyming Slang*, 2003

how are you going
how are you? *AUSTRALIA, 1930*
Used as a greeting.
- He walked over to her and slapped her playfully on the backside. "How are you going?" —Wal Watkins, *Andamooka*, p. 79, 1971

how bad is that?
that's great! *US*
- —*Time*, p. 56, 1st January 1965: 'Students: the slang bag'

how can I tell?
used in prison to question the truth of that which has just been said *US*
- —William K. Bentley and James M. Corbett, *Prison Slang*, p. 46, 1992

how come?
why *US, 1848*
- "How come her parents didn't show?" the woman continued, lowering her voice, —Mary McCarthy, *The Group*, p. 22, 1963
- How come all the face fugus [whiskers] doc? —Barry Humphries, *Bazza Pulls It Off!*, 1971
- "How come?" He loved that. How come? —Joseph Wambaugh, *Finnegan's Week*, p. 205, 1993

how cool is that!
used for expressing delight *US*
- —Connie Eble (Editor), *UNC-CH Campus Slang*, p. 6, Fall 1999

how-de-do; how-d'ye-do *noun*
a shoe *UK*
Rhyming slang.
- She then began removing / Her full-length almond rock [dress], / Revealing size nine how-de do's / Which gave me quite a shock. —Ronnie Barker, *Fletcher's Book of Rhyming Slang*, p. 21, 1979

how-do-you-do; how-d'ye-do *noun*
a fuss, a noisy difficulty, an embarrassing or awkward problem *UK, 1835*
Rhyming slang for 'stew'.
- I was in a right old how d'ye do. —Ray Puxley, *Cockney Rabbit*, 1992

how do you like me now? *noun*
crack cocaine *UK, 1998*
- —Mike Haskins, *Drugs*, p. 282, 2003

howdy-do; howdy
used as a friendly greeting *US*
A reduction of 'how d'ye do' (1697).
- [Robert Plant] really gives them nothing, not even a good-natured "Howdy-do"[.] —Lester Bangs, *Psychotic Reactions and Carburetor Dung*, p. 34, 1970
- What they spoke and how they spoke it [...] How they turned round and said howdy. —Jeremy Cameron, *Brown Bread in Wengen*, p. 154, 1999

Howdy Doody *noun*
an unspecified chemical agent used in Vietnam *US*
- I've found out that those other men were drenched by a chemical spray we called Howdy Doogy – because it made you stiffen up and jerk like you were hanging on strings. —Robert R. McCammon, *Blue World*, p. 81, 1991

how goes it?
used as a greeting *US*
- Easy now, stick to vernaculars: "Hello there, Gorzy, how goes it?" —Richard Farina, *Been Down So Long*, p. 34, 1966

how high is a Chinaman?
used as a catchphrase reply to an unanswerable, or stupid, question *UK*
From a children's pun that How Hi *is* a Chinaman.
- — Partridge, *A Dictionary of Catchphrases*, 1977
- — *The Today Programme*, 18th November 2003

howie *noun*
a howitzer, field artillery *US*
- —Gregory Clark, *Words of the Vietnam War*, p. 237, 1990

howk *verb*
to dig, to excavate *UK: SCOTLAND, 1911*
- A miner howks coal, a potato-picker howks tatties, and logically enough a nose-picker howks his nose. —Michael Munro, *The Original Patter*, p. 35, 1985
- Howk up the swally [drink], pronto, big man! —Ian Pattison, *Rab C. Nesbitt*, 1988

howl *noun*

a source of great amusement *US, 1930*

- [W]ouldn't that have been a howl?—Mary McCarthy, *The Group*, p. 95, 1963

howl *verb*

▸ **howl at the moon**

to experience the bleed period of the menstrual cycle *US*

- [W]hen we're 'howlin' at the moon,' since we all menstruate on a lunar cycle, or even are 'due for the sweatlodge,' since that too happens on a lunar basis.—a contributor *The Museum of Menstruation and Women's Health*, May 2001

howler *noun*

1 a glaring mistake *UK, 1885*

- There's a real "howler," as Herb Caen would say, at the beginning of Ralph B. Sipper's review of the two new Henry Miller biographies. [Letter to the Editor]—*San Francisco Chronicle*, p. 5 (Sunday Review), 30th June 1991

2 a child *UK*

- The ideal deb [...] will raise a few children (howlers or kiddi-winks)[.] —Peter York, *Style Wars*, 1980

howling *adjective*

1 drunk *UK*

- —*e-cyclopaedia*, 20th March 2002

2 very smelly *UK*

- His boots were howlin so Ah slung them out in the close.—Michael Munro, *The Patter, Another Blast*, p. 33, 1988

3 superlative *UK, 1865*

- "Oh, dig that howling Cadillac!" Zaida cried ecstatically.—Ross Russell, *The Sound*, p. 15, 1961

howling fifties *noun*

the latitutes of 50 to 59 degrees south *ANTARCTICA, 1962*

- —Bernadette Hince, *The Antarctic Dictionary*, p. 170, 2000

Howling Mad Smith *nickname*

General Holland M. Smith, US Marine Corps *US*

The NBC action series *A-Team* (1983–87) featured a character named Captain H. M. 'Howlin' Mad' Murdock, played by Dwight Schultz, presumably named after General Smith.

- Brig. Gen. Holland M. "Howling Mad" Smith, the father of amphibiuous warfare, who was to lead the way across the Pacific and watch the men of the Corps raise the Stars and stripes over Mount Suribachi on Iwo Jima.—Neil Sheehan, *A Bright Shining Lie*, p. 295, 1988

how much?

what do you mean? *UK, 1852*

- "Says he's a nice fellow, likes hurting people, knocks girls about, sticks knives in people. An emotional pauper." "How much?" "That's college chat for a right bastard."—Laurence Henderson, *With Intent*, 1968

how rude!

used for expressing disgust *US*

A catchphrase from the television programme *Full House*.

- —Connie Eble (Editor), *UNC-CH Campus Slang*, p. 5, Spring 1990

▷ **see:** RUDE!

howser *noun*

▷ **see:** HOUSE OF FRASER

how's hacking?

used as a greeting *US*

- —*Co-Evolution Quarterly*, p. 32, Spring 1981
- —Guy L. Steele et al., *The Hacker's Dictionary*, p. 76, 1983

how's it going?

used as a greeting *US, 1944*

- "How's it going?" I said. "All right thanks," he said.—*The Guardian*, 8th May 2003
- G'day mate. How's it going?—*Australian Ultimate*, p. 7, October 2003

how's it hanging?

used as a greeting, usually male-to-male *US*

Sometimes testicularly inclusive and increased to 'they'.

- Gennaro! How's she hangin'?—Richard Price, *The Wanderers*, p. 36, 1974
- Timbo,' said Jake. 'How's it hanging, mate?'—Linda Jaivin, *Rock n Roll Babes from Outer Space*, p. 146, 1996
- Bobby comes by, cuffs him on the head. How they hanging?—Joel Rose, *Kill Kill Faster Faster*, p. 186, 1997
- We got all that "Hey, man, how they hanging?" crap out of the way[.]—Lenny McLean, *The Guv'nor*, p. 68, 1998
- [W]ho always inexplicably greeted her with the gender-inappropriate phrase, hey, how's it hanging?—Rita Ciresi, *Pink Slip*, p. 363, 1999

how-so?

how is that so? *US*

Found in the C14, but not a complete path to the current usage.

- "But this is different." "And I ask you how-so?"—Elmore Leonard, *Gold Coast*, p. 75, 1980

how's tricks?

used as a friendly greeting *UK, 1904*

Probably from the terminology of card games but may also have had nautical origins.

- [She] said the things she always said: "How's tricks?" and "Can't complain" and "Bye now."—Jean Potts, *An Affair of the Heart*, 1970
- Watcha Bex, how's tricks?—Danny King, *The Burglar Diaries*, p. 106, 2001

how sweet it is!

used for expressing pleasure *US*

One of comedian Jackie Gleason's several signature lines, often used on *The Jackie Gleason Show* (CBS, 1952–70). Repeated with obviously referential humour.

how's your arse for lovebites?

used as a greeting between young men *UK: SCOTLAND*

- —Michael Munro, *The Complete Patter*, 1996

how's-your-father *noun*

1 any act of sexual intimacy from petting to intercourse; non-conventional sexual behaviour *UK, 1931*

Originally from the music halls, 'how's your father' or 'howsyer-father' was an all-purpose catchphrase, a euphemism for any-thing; subsequent usage, especially in the services during World War 2 mainly narrowed the sense to 'a sexual dalliance'.

- PETE: [T]he chapter ends in three dots. DUD: What do those three dots mean, Pete? PETE: Well, in [Neville] Shute's hands, three dots can mean anything. DUD: How's your father, perhaps?—Peter Cook, *Not Only But Also*, 1966
- I ain't to fuckin' SP'd up [informed] on all that howsyourfather[.] —Jeremy Cameron, *Brown Bread in Wengen*, p. 26, 1999
- So suddenly it's knickers off and 'ow's your father. All four of 'em are at me!—Ben Elton, *High Society*, p. 226, 2002
- Fact is, Jessie, I've met punters that liked 'em dead, oh yeah, snuff muff. It happens, baby, don't think it don't. Necrohowsyourfather. —Ben Elton, *High Society*, p. 314, 2002

2 any activity or business that is complicated or annoying, a fuss *UK*

Rhyming slang for 'palaver'.

- [A] right old how's your father.—Ray Puxley, *Fresh Rabbit*, 1998

3 a fight *NEW ZEALAND*

- —Sonya Plowman, *Great Kiwi Slang*, p. 92, 2002

4 cocaine *UK*

- I gotta nice bitta how's-your-father. Come over and meet me there. —J.J. Connolly, *Layer Cake*, p. 212, 2000

how's your love life?; how's your sex life?

used as a greeting, often flirtatious *UK, 1969*

- —Eddie Kendricks, *How's Your Love Life Baby? (Song Title)*, 1978

how's your mind?

are you mad? *SOUTH AFRICA*

Generally asked in exasperation or irritation.

- —*Surfrikan Slang*, 2004

how X can you get?

used of someone who has a more than average measure of a specified quality *US, 1951*

- I ask you, how stupid can you get?—*The Times*, 6th September 2003

howzat?

how's that? *UK, 1961*

Often heard as a cricketer's appeal to the umpire.

- Howzat for progress?—*The Guardian*, 9th July 2003

howzit?

used as a greeting *US*

In South Africa, the usual reply is: 'No, fine', which actually means 'Yes, I am fine' (the word 'no' is often taken to mean 'yes'); an Afrikaner might reply: 'Ja, well, no fine'.

- —Hyman E. Goldin et al., *Dictionary of American Underworld Lingo*, p. 104, 1950
- —Douglas Simonson, *Pidgin to da Max*, 1981
- The cops pull up and say howzit.—Rian Malan, *My Traitor's Heart*, p. 205, 1990

hoy *verb*
to throw *AUSTRALIA*
- He punctured the can with the pig-stabber end of his pocket knife, swallowed the beer and hoyed the empty can far out into the water. —David Ireland, *The Unknown Industrial Prisoner*, p. 125, 1971

hozzo *noun*
a large and dangerous wave *AUSTRALIA*
From 'horrible', with '-o' suffix.
- They whooped and hollered as I emerged from the hozzo. —Kathy Lette, *Girls' Night Out*, p. 188, 1987

hozzo *adjective*
(of a wave or surfing conditions) large, powerful and dangerous *AUSTRALIA*
- She pulled into that hozzo tube. —Kathy Lette, *Girls' Night Out*, p. 195, 1987

hozzy; ozzy; ozzie *noun*
a hospital *UK*
- I come round not in the hozzy but in the back of a cab[.] —Kevin Sampson, *Outlaws*, p. 119, 2001
- His missus is still in thee [sic] ozzy with the baby[.] —Niall Griffiths, *Kelly + Victor*, p. 116, 2002

HP *noun*
a man *UK*
Gay slang; an initialism of polari **HOMEE-PALONE** (a man).
- —Paul Baker, *Polari*, p. 177, 2002

HRN *noun*
heroin *US, 1959*
Whilst this looks like an acronym it is simply 'heroin' devowelled.
- —Richard A. Spears, *The Slang and Jargon of Drugs and Drink*, p. 273, 1986
- —Robert Ashton, *This Is Heroin*, p. 206, 2002
- —Mike Haskins, *Drugs*, p. 284, 2003

HTH *noun*
a spouse or lover who is waiting for you back home *US*
An abbreviation of '*h*ome*t*own *h*oney'.
- —Kenn "Naz" Young, *Naz's Dictionary of Teen Slang*, p. 55, 1993

hubba *noun*
crack cocaine *US, 1988*
- —Geoffrey Froner, *Digging for Diamonds*, p. 36, 1989
- —William T. Vollman, *Whores for Gloria*, p. 139, 1991
- —Mike Haskins, *Drugs*, p. 282, 2003

hubba-hubba!
used for expressing enthusiastic appreciation of a good-looking woman *US, 1941*
- —*Chicago Tribune ("Harold the Teen" comic)*, 24th March 1945
- Legs: Like Shirley Maclaine's, but longer. Hubba, hubba! —*The Guardian*, 26th February 2002

hubba, I am back *noun*
crack cocaine *UK, 1998*
Rhyming slang.
- —Mike Haskins, *Drugs*, p. 282, 2003

hubba pigeon *noun*
a crack cocaine addict who searches for bits of crack cocaine on the ground *US*
- —Bill Valentine, *Gang Intelligence Manual*, p. 77, 1995: 'Black street gang terminology'
- Some long-term users are also plagued by the constant sense that they can see bits of crack on the ground, causing them to try frantically to pick them up. In New York City, such obsessed addicts are called "hubba pigeons" because their hunched-over bodies resemble pigeons pecking for food[.] —*New Times Los Angeles*, 19th September 1996

hubbly-bubbly *noun*
a water pipe used for smoking marijuana, hashish or crack cocaine *US*
- —William D. Alsever, *Glossary for the Establishment and Other Uptight People*, p. 16, December 1970
- We managed to get it [a small fire] out though, with the water from the hubbly-bubbly. —Macfarlane, Macfarlane and Robson, *The User*, p. 89, 1996

hubboo *adjective*
pregnant *NORFOLK ISLAND*
- —Beryl Nobbs Palmer, *A Dictionary of Norfolk Words and Usages*, p. 21, 1992

hubby; hubbie *noun*
a husband *UK, 1688*
Often used in a sardonic sense.
- Hey girls, hubby's gonna strike it rich, so bye-bye now, I'm moving to the suburbs. —Max Shulman, *Guided Tour of Campus Humor*, p. 40, 1955
- What she didn't know was that I had been having an affair with her hubby for a long time[.] —Jefferson Poland and Valerie Alison, *The Records of the San Francisco Sexual Freedom League*, p. 56, 1971
- Quiet bedroom in the afternoon, hubby's off building houses —Elmore Leonard, *Switch*, p. 106, 1978
- Fortunately, Mom lives in one of the crime capitals of America, so her dim new hubby-cop is unlikely to suspect an inside job. —C.D. Payne, *Youth in Revolt*, p. 199, 1993
- [P]ick up the kids from school, go out for a meal with hubby. —Greg Williams, *Diamond Geezers*, p. 104, 1997
- [S]he reveals to him that her former hubbie [...] is still connected[.] —Duncan MacLaughlin, *The Filth*, p. 193, 2002

hubcap *noun*
1 an important person *US*
Playing on **WHEEL** (a very important person).
- —Robert George Reisner, *The Jazz Titans*, p. 158, 1960

2 a person whose sense of importance outweights his actual importance *US*
- —*Newsweek*, 8th October 1951

huck *verb*
in snowboarding, to launch yourself into the air *US*
- —Jim Humes and Sean Wagstaff, *Boarderlands*, p. 222, 1995

huckery *adjective*
ugly *NEW ZEALAND*
Often used to describe a woman or 'moll'.
- Jools looking pretty huckery in dun frock and plastic sandals. —*(Wellington) Dominion*, p. 27, 25th March 1993

huckle *verb*
to be bundled into a place; to be thrown out; to arrest *UK: SCOTLAND*
- When he started shoutin' and swearin' the bouncers huckled him out. —Michael Munro, *The Original Patter*, p. 36, 1985
- I've got a warrant here! Sixteen charges for non-payment of fines. You're bliddy huckled! —Ian Pattison, *Rab C. Nesbitt*, 1988
- A glance out of the window confirmed two police cars in the street below. Huckling shortly ensued. —Christopher Brookmyre, *Boiling a Frog*, p. 252, 2000

hudda *noun*
a police officer; the police *US*
- While the literal translation of the shirt is the police code for homicide ("187") followed by gang slang for police ("hudda"), many Valley police, school officials and gang experts see it another way: "Murder a Cop." —*Los Angeles Times*, p. B3, 13th May 1993

huddle *verb*
while working as a police officer in a patrol car, to park and sleep *US*
- As a rookie cop, Serpico was also introduced to the fine art of "cooping," or sleeping on duty, a time-honored police practice that in other cites goes under such names as "huddling" and "going down." —Peter Maas, *Serpico*, p. 63, 1973

huddy
keep left (of a horse) *CANADA*
- He does not know the origin of most of these terms, but he tells me that "huddy" means "keep left" [i.e. to the left side of a horse]. —*Beaver*, p. 28/2, Autumn 1957

hudge *verb*
in pinball, to apply physical force to a machine to affect the trajectory of the ball without activating the tilt mechanism *US*
- —Bobbye Claire Natkin and Steve Kirk, *All About Pinball*, p. 113, 1977

huevon *noun*
a very lazy person *US*
Border Spanish used in English conversation by Mexican-Americans; from the image of the man who is so lazy that his testicles (**HUEVOS**) grow large.
- —Dagoberto Fuentes and Jose Lopez, *Barrio Language Dictionary*, p. 76, 1974

huevos *noun*
1 the testicles; courage *US*
Border Spanish used in English conversation by Mexican-Americans; literally 'eggs'.
- —Dagoberto Fuentes and Jose Lopez, *Barrio Language Dictionary*, p. 76, 1974
- At one of their impromptu Barf parties Manny guzzled five shots of mescal in one minute to show them how big his huevos were. —Joseph Wambaugh, *Lines and Shadows*, p. 150, 1984

2 waves *US*
Spanish for 'eggs', but a near-homophone for 'waves', hence the play.
• —Trevor Cralle, *The Surfin'ary*, p. 55, 1991

3 a variety of Morrocan hashish *SPAIN*
From Spanish for 'eggs', named for its shape and texture.
• Like virtually all the hashish in Spain, huevos comes from the Rif mountains.—Nick Jones, *Spliffs*, p. 86, 2003

huey *noun*
▷ see: HUGHIE

Huey *nickname*
a Bell utility military helicopter *US, 1962*
• Yeah – fishing village – helicopters over there. Hueys, lots of 'em. —*Apocalypse Now*, 1979
• We lined up with our beltkit and bergens and clambered aboard the Hueys that were going to take us in.—Andy McNab (writing of the late 1970s/early 80s), *Immediate Action*, p. 90, 1995

Huey shuffle *noun*
a common hesitation in the flight pattern by an inexperienced helicopter pilot *US*
• I overcontrolled the pedals, making the tail wag back and forth. This was a common reaction to the sensitive controls, and was called the "Huey shuffle."—Robert Mason, *Chickenhawk*, p. 44, 1983

huff *verb*
1 to inhale household or industrial chemicals for recreational purposes *US, 1969*
• —William D. Alsever, *Glossary for the Establishment and Other Uptight People*, p. 11, December 1970
• The brothers were among seven young men who repeatedly "huffed" or inhaled lacquer thinner to get a brief "high" as part of a small group of huffers in the Tampa Area.—*San Francisco Examiner*, p. 25, 19th November 1974
• Others commonly amuse themselves by inhaling assorted materials such as glue, gasoline and Lysol. Here they call it "huffing."—*Los Angeles Times*, p. 10 (Magazine), 15th June 1986
• Huffing is usually an activity for the young, whose access to other dugs is limited, or for desperate types who'll take any high they can find.—Vann Wesson, *Generation X Field Guide and Lexicon*, p. 92, 1997
• Huffing is street slang for inhaling chemicals such as cleaning fluids, glue and paint to get high, and it's on the rise in Texas.—*Austin (Texas) American-Statesman*, p. A6, 8th March 1999

2 to steal *TRINIDAD AND TOBAGO, 1990*
• —Lise Winer, *Dictionary of the English/Creole of Trinidad & Tobago*, 2003

huff and puff *noun*
a state of high anger *TRINIDAD AND TOBAGO, 1978*
• —Lise Winer, *Dictionary of the English/Creole of Trinidad & Tobago*, 2003

huff and puff *verb*
to breathe heavily *UK, 1890*
From the childhood tale of *The Three Little Pigs*.
• [A]nd the guys out by the volleyball net, huffing and puffing in twelve-year-old Madras bermudas their wave have let out at least twice[.]—Armistead Maupin, *Tales of the City*, p. 245, 1978

huffer *noun*
1 an act of oral sex on a man *US*
Probably a mistaken understanding of **HUMMER**.
• Afterwards, she explained that little extras could be provided for a "tip" – $15 for a "huffer," the quaint idiom for oral sex.—*San Francisco Examiner*, p. 6, 15th January 1973

2 a person who inhales household or industrial chemicals for recreational purposes *US*
• —*Current Slang*, p. 8, Winter 1969
• The brothers were among seven young men who repeatedly "huffed" or inhaled lacquer thinner to get a brief "high" as part of a small group of huffers in the Tampa Area.—*San Francisco Examiner*, p. 25, 19th November 1974

3 in drag racing and hot rodding, a supercharger *US*
• —Engle Lyle, *The Complete Book of Fuel and Gas Dragsters*, p. 152, 1968

hug *verb*
▸ **hug the bowl**
to vomit *US*
• —Pamela Munro, *U.C.L.A. Slang*, p. 79, 1997

hug and slug *noun*
(among Canadian Forces members) any place where girls or fights are to be found *CANADA*
• "Hug and Slug" is a generic term for any bar where "action" is to be found, be it amorous or pugilistic.—Tom Langeste, *Words on the Wing*, p. 144, 1995

hug drug *noun*
MDMA, the recreational drug best known as ecstasy *UK*
From the affectionate feelings roused by the drug.
• —Angela Devlin, *Prison Patter*, p. 63, 1996
• [A] kind of winters night, mug-of-Horlick's feeling, "the hug drug". —Simon Napier-Bell, *Black Vinyl White Powder*, p. 296, 2001
• — *Miramonte High School Parents Club Newsletter (Orinda, California)*, p. 1, 26th November 2001
• —Mike Haskins, *Drugs*, p. 289, 2003

hugger-mugger *noun*
1 chaos *US*
• —Helen Dahlskog (Editor), *A Dictionary of Contemporary and Colloquial Usage*, p. 32, 1972

2 a prostitute who beats and robs customers or who serves as a decoy for someone who beats and robs the customer *US*
• There's lesbians, masochists, hypes, whores, flim flammers, paddy hustlers, hugger muggers, ex-cons of all descriptions, and anybody else with a kink of some kind or other.—Joseph Wambaugh, *The New Centurions*, p. 174, 1970
• I took away the first stud's revolver easier than I could disarm a fourteen-year-old hugger-mugger in D.C.—James Patterson, *Kiss the Girls*, p. 334, 1995

huggie *noun*
a styrofoam or plastic cylinder that slips over a beer can, serving as insulation *US*
• —Connie Eble (Editor), *UNC-CH Campus Slang*, p. 5, Fall 2000

hugging *adjective*
bad, crazy *US*
• —*Newsday*, p. B2, 11th October 1997

huggy *adjective*
given to hugging; hence, sensitive and caring *US*
• I am a huggy person, I don't mind being touched, but not in this way – it was far too personal.—Diana Ross, *BBC News*, 22nd September 1999

huggy-bear *noun*
prolonged hugging and kissing *US, 1964*
• —*Time*, p. 57, 1st January 1965: 'Students: the slang bag'

hughie; huey *noun*
an act of vomiting *UK: SCOTLAND, 1985*
A joke was told of a person calling out the name of television presenter Hughie Green, 1920–1997; it was, in fact, the cry of someone vomiting after drinking green Chartreuse.
• Ah think Ah've got that disease where ye stuff yer face then have a right good huey.—Michael Munro, *The Complete Patter*, p. 79, 1996

Hughie; Hughey; Huey *noun*
a supposed rain god *AUSTRALIA, 1912*
Used in the phrase 'send her/it down Hughie!', said when the rains first appear after a dry spell or the dry season. The earliest instance of this is from the *Bulletin*, 3rd December 1912, where it is stated that it referred to a Mr Huie 'an amateur meteorologist who had luck in prohpesying rain'. This story has not been verified and would probably carry more force if it weren't for the fact that Hughie sounds more like a first name than a surname, and also in light of the variants that have from time to time cropped up, such as 'send her down Steve!' and 'send her down David!'.
• Within a few yards of the veranda he stopped and lifted a haggard face and a clenched fist to the sky, and shouted, "Send it down! Send it down, Hughie!"—Frank Dalby Davison, *The Wells of Beersheba*, p. 301, 1965

hughie; huey *verb*
to vomit *UK: SCOTLAND*
Echoic of the involuntary vocal accompaniment to the action.
• Watch yer feet, sumdy's hueyed on the steps.—Michael Munro, *The Original Patter*, p. 36, 1985

hugs and kisses; hugs; ugs *noun*
a wife *UK*
Rhyming slang for **MISSUS**.
• Hardly complimentary to refer to a wife as "the ugs" but it is meant to be.—Ray Puxley, *Cockney Rabbit*, 1992

huh-huh-huh; huh-huh-huh-huh
used as a representation of unspirited laughter *US*
Caricatured as the smirking laugh of teenage heavy metal fans in the animated television series *Beavis and Butthead*, MTV, 1993–97.
- Saul Bellow [...] laughs his special, slow and knowing sort of huh-huh-huh laugh that is to punctuate the rest of the afternoon. — *The Guardian*, 10th September 1997
- It's Radiohead, isn't it? What do you say to these people? Except, perhaps, 'this is pretty cool, huh huh huh...' — *The Observer*, 1st October 2000

hulk *noun*
an unusually large bodybuilder *US*
- — *Maledicta*, p. 234, Winter 1980: '"Lovely, blooming, fresh and gay": The onomastics of camp'
- — *American Speech*, p. 200, Fall 1984: 'The language of bodybuilding'

hulking *adjective*
large, especially of an unwieldy mass *UK, 1698*
- Stallone obviously thought he was up to the task being the hulking mound of talentless muscle that he doubtless is. — *The Guardian*, 20th December 2001

hull *noun*
an empty pistol cartridge case *US*
- — *American Speech*, p. 193, October 1957: 'Some colloquialisms of the handgunner'

hullabaloo *noun*
a loud noise; an uproar; confusion *UK, 1762*
- I got to thinking about that part afterwards, when all the hullabloo broke loose. — Jim Thompson, *After Dark, My Sweet*, p. 40, 1955
- They would remember the hullabaloo raised by the murders of Vivian Gordon, Dot King, and such. — Robert Sylvester, *No Cover Charge*, p. 17, 1956
- The last time you had a client that turned informer, you withdrew from the case and made a big hullabaloo that jeopardized our case. — Edwin Torres, *After Hours*, p. 182, 1979

hulloo *noun*
a completely inconsequential person *NORFOLK ISLAND*
- — Beryl Nobbs Palmer, *A Dictionary of Norfolk Words and Usages*, p. 21, 1992

hully-gully *adjective*
stylish, especially in a Rastafarian sense *BAHAMAS, 1973*
- — John A. Holm, *Dictionary of Bahamian English*, p. 107, 1982

hum *verb*
1 to be busy, to be crowded; to be lively *US, 1887*
- Ten past nine and already the place was humming. People rushed past, hurrying nowhere with great purpose. — Will Ferguson, *Happiness*, 2002

2 to have an unpleasant odour, to stink *UK, 1902*
- All the same, your patter is humming. And I mean that in a constructive way. — Ian Pattison, *Rab C. Nesbitt*, 1988

human sea *noun*
an infantry tactic of the North Korean Army, of swarming enemy positions in overwhelming numbers *US*
- The North Korean "Human Sea" attacks were also new to the G.I.'s – new and frightening. — Don Lawson, *The United States in the Korean War*, p. 35, 1964

humble *noun*
a false criminal accusation or charge *US, 1940*
- It was a jive tip, but there were a whole lot of cats up there on humbles. — Claude Brown, *Manchild in the Promised Land*, p. 142, 1965

Humbolt green *noun*
marijuana *UK*
This should, perhaps, be 'Humboldt green', indicating the county in northern California in which this green-leafed marijuana plant originates.
- — Mike Haskins, *Drugs*, p. 287, 2003

humbug *noun*
1 false or trumped-up criminal charges *US*
- My oldy lady didn't say nothin' to the dude, man. He gave her a case on a humbug. — Christina and Richard Milner, *Black Players*, p. 302, 1972
- "Sheee-it, this is a humbug, we ain't done nothin'," said the procurer. — Joseph Wambaugh, *The Blue Knight*, p. 205, 1973
- The FBI arrested my wife on a humbug ... something about a fraud. It's a nothing deal. — Gerald Petievich, *Shakedown*, p. 177, 1988
- Not surprisingly, Dennis insists that the whole murder case was a humbug, anyway. — *St. Louis Post-Dispatch*, p. D1, 2nd December 2001

2 a fight, especially between youth gangs *US, 1962*
- — Hermese E. Roberts, *The Third Ear*, 1971

humbug *verb*
1 to fight *US, 1968*
- — David Claerbaut, *Black Jargon in White America*, p. 69, 1972

2 to interfere with, to bother *TRINIDAD AND TOBAGO, 1904*
- — Frank A. Collymore, *Barbadian Dialect*, p. 61, 1965
- — Lise Winer, *Dictionary of the English/Creole of Trinidad & Tobago*, 2003

humdinger *noun*
a remarkable thing or person *US, 1905*
- One was a humdinger about a gal that meets a detective in a big city. — Mickey Spillane, *I, The Jury*, p. 39, 1947
- Not too skinny, she's not too fat / She's a real humdinger and I like it like that. — Mitch Ryder, *Devil with the Blue Dress*, 1966
- I want to make me last one for the night a real humdinger[.] — Barry Humphries, *Bazza Pulls It Off!*, 1971
- ANNIE: It was really great! ALVY: Oh, humdinger. — *Annie Hall*, 1977

hum job *noun*
oral sex performed on a male *US, 1964*
- A hum-job is the same as a blow-job however in this case the blower hums a tune, preferably a patriotic one, bringing the blowee off. — *Screw*, p. 9, 29th December 1969
- About a year ago – no, two years ago – there was this big craze for what was called a 'hum job.' — John Warren Wells, *Tricks of the Trade*, p. 26, 1970
- Can be by putting another testicles in one's mouth and humming, causing a pleasurable sensation. — Eugene Landy, *The Underground Dictionary*, p. 106, 1971

hummel *noun*
the hair *UK*
English gypsy use.
- — Jimmy Stockin, *On The Cobbles*, p. 10, 2000

hummer *noun*
1 an act of oral sex performed on a man *US, 1971*
- Did you check that poony out? I could parlay this into a hummer at least! — *Airheads*, 1994
- Paulie Shore optimistically called them 'hummer days.' His idea, apparently, was that when she was 'closed for business' his girlfriend should keep him happy with a 'hummer,' his term for a blow-job. — a contributor *The Museum of Menstruation and Women's Health*, April 2001

2 an exceptionally good thing *UK, 1681*
- Marvelous little section of life in ultra fast lane, absolutely on a hummer. — Odie Hawkins, *Scars and Memories*, p. 56–57, 1987

3 an arrest for something the person did not do; an arrest for a minor violation that leads to more serious charges *US, 1932*
- — Francis J. Rigney and L. Douglas Smith, *The Real Bohemia*, p. xv, 1961
- "You know the lieutenant doesn't want any hummer pinches." "Aw, it was no hummer, Jake," said Simeone. — Joseph Wambaugh, *The New Centurions*, p. 175, 1970
- I got busted on a hummer, something like that, my first day in. — Odie Hawkins, *Ghetto Sketches*, p. 123, 1972

4 a minor mistake *US, 1959*
- — Robert S. Gold, *A Jazz Lexicon*, p. 154, 1964

5 a joke, a prank *US*
- — Charles Shafer, *Folk Speech in Texas Prisons*, p. 207, 1990

6 the Grumman E-2, an early warning aircraft *US*
Given the official nickname 'Hawkeye', it was instantly renamed by the troops.
- The Hawkeye early warning aircraft, nicknamed "Hummer," had just informed him of unidentified "bogies" approaching the battle group. — Joe Weber, *Defcon One*, p. 3, 1989
- It is nearly impossible to flip on a TV set without seeing one – the new workhouse of the ground trooper nicknamed the Hummer. — *Washington Times*, p. G4, 22nd February 1991

7 an army weapons carrier *US, 1983*
The official designation is a High Mobility Multipurpose Wheeled Vehicle. The slang is easier.
- He drove the camouflaged High Mobility Multipurpose Wheeled Vehicle (or "Hummer") through Washington streets as he was chased by several patrol cars. — Chuck Shepherd, *News of the Weird*, p. 124, 1989

hummer days *noun*
(from a male perspective) the bleed period of the menstrual cycle *US*
- Paulie Shore optimistically called them 'hummer days.' His idea, apparently, was that when she was 'closed for business' his girlfriend should keep him happy with a 'hummer,' his term for a blow-job. — a contributor, *The Museum of Menstruation and Women's Health*, April 2001

hummingbird ass *noun*

used for suggesting that a person lacks the courage to back up his taunts *US*

- —Richard Scholl, *Running Press Glossary of Baseball Language*, p. 44, 1977
- Sometimes he let his alligator mouth override his hummingbird ass.—*Star Tribune (Minneapolis)*, p. 1B, 16th January 2003

humongous; humungous *adjective*

very large *US, 1968*

- —Collin Baker et al., *College Undergraduate Slang Study Conducted at Brown University*, p. 141, 1968
- —Stephen H. Dill (Editor), *Current Slang*, p. 7, Spring 1969
- Brereton explained that the "shoebox sized" container of salt that he took from what he described as the "humongous" salt pile was for the base of his driveway.—*Washington Post*, p. C16, 18th January 1977
- Not humongous titties but nice pointy ones.—Carl Hiaasen, *Skin Tight*, p. 297, 1989
- Big Lurleen was just that, humongous.—Seth Morgan, *Homeboy*, p. 83, 1990
- "I bet they got humongous cocks." "Fooot-long hot dogs." "Monster dongs."—Paul Russell, *The Salt Point*, p. 8, 1990
- I'm allergic to bees. I get a humungous rash.—*Wayne's World 2*, 1993
- How come you're carrying that humongous suitcase around?—Jeffrey Eugenides, *Middlesex*, p. 469, 2002

hump *noun*

1 a fit of sulks, a bad mood, depression *UK, 1873*

- So I says to this Jill bird, "Here, d'you screw?" Just to get her hump up, like. But she never batted and eyelid[.]—John Peter Jones, *Feather Pluckers*, p. 44, 1964
- —Angela Devlin, *Prison Patter*, p. 63, 1996
- Oi! Frankie! I know you've got the hump.—Greg Williams, *Diamond Geezers*, p. 57, 1997

2 an offensive or despicable person *US, 1963*

- Didya hear what them humps in Congress did? They voted a special tax bill for themselves so that they don't have to pay any more taxes.—William Cavnitz, *One Police Plaza*, p. 337, 1984

3 a dolt, a dull person *US, 1963*

- The hump pleads guilty, off he goes.—Leonard Shecter and William Phillips, *On the Pad*, p. 84, 1973
- You fuckin' hump – we went to question you, you stumbled, fell against me.—Edwin Torres, *Carlito's Way*, p. 73, 1975
- "Anyway," Garcia said, "this hump Bloodworth says he heard there's some connection between Bellamy and Sparky Harper."—Carl Hiaasen, *Tourist Season*, p. 89, 1986
- Which doesn't seem too likely with those Armenian humps holed up with Fed surveillance outside their house.—James Ellroy, *White Jazz*, p. 257, 1992

4 an act of sexual intercourse *US, 1918*

- I took his twenty and I took him to bed, and we had our little hump, and he got his twenty dollars' worth.—John Warren Wells, *Tricks of the Trade*, p. 50, 1970
- If you are the dumper, make this last hump so enjoyable that your ex will forget how much he hates your guts.—Anka Radakovich, *The Wild Girls Club*, p. 41, 1994

5 a Camel™ cigarette *US*

- —James Harris, *A Convict's Dictionary*, p. 33, 1989

6 a bridge *UK*

Citizens' band radio slang.

- —Peter Chippindale, *The British CB Book*, p. 156, 1981

7 the air route over the Himilaya Mountains during World War 2 *US, 1942*

- Civilian pilots were the first to fly the "hump" missions that kept the Chinese army linked to its U.S. supply bases in China.—*Insight*, p. 39, 17th April 1989

8 the middle section of a prison sentence *US*

- —Joseph E. Ragen and Charles Finston, *Inside the World's Toughest Prison*, p. 804, 1962: 'Penitentiary and underworld glossary'

9 a large wave *US*

Surfer usage.

- When you graduate from Malibu you move down to San Onofre or Tressle where the real big humps come blasting in.—Frederick Kohner, *Gidget*, p. 4, 1957
- —Grant W. Kuhns, *On Surfing*, p. 118, 1963

10 a military combat patrol *US, 1971*

Recorded in Australia in the C19, but not again until the US war in Vietnam.

- The first day's hump was to be of moderate length, 6000 meters, or six "clicks," and there was a road most of the way so it should have been easy, a skate.—Charles Anderson, *The Grunts*, p. 35, 1976
- You 'bush in this area near that ol' Buddhist temple we passed on the hump in.—*Platoon*, 1986

11 a lookout during a crime *US*

- —Vincent J. Monteleone, *Criminal Slang*, p. 126, 1949

12 in circus usage, a camel *US, 1926*

- —Don Wilmeth, *The Language of American Popular Entertainment*, p. 136, 1981

▸ **over the hump**

while gambling, having won enough to be gambling now with the house's money *US*

- —*The Annals of the American Academy of Political and Social Sciences*, p. 128, May 1950

hump *verb*

1 to have sex *UK, 1785*

- Them I hump her for kicks.—William Burroughs, *Naked Lunch*, p. 119, 1957
- HORSING ON THE FLOOR! HUMPING UNDER THE BED! GROUSING IN THE GOODIE!—Terry Southern, *Candy*, p. 82–83, 1958
- What's the idea of humping Virgil?—Max Shulman, *Anyone Got a Match?*, p. 253, 1964
- Did you get any action? Did you slam it to her? Did you stick her? Did you hump her? Did you run it down her throat? Did you jam it up her ass? Did you shoot your wad?—*Screw*, p. 6, 29th May 1972
- I could have been tucked up between clean sheets humping Audrey by now.—Ted Lewis, *Jack Carter's Law*, p. 5, 1974
- It'll be great, because all those Ph.D.s are in there, you know, like, discussing models of alienation and we'll be in here quietly humping.—*Annie Hall*, 1977
- In six-and-a-half years of marriage, she had humped almost everything she could get her hands on.—Hunter S. Thompson, *Songs of the Doomed*, p. 195, 1983

2 to carry, to lug, to march *AUSTRALIA, 1851*

An essential word to US soldiers in Vietnam.

- He nodded to Sid, who came over, humping a bag of groceries.—Jean Brooks, *The Opal Witch*, p. 9, 1967
- 'Pick out what you want,' says Noel. 'The rest I'm going to dump. There's a fire very close handy, it won't be far to hump.'—Patsy Adam-Smith, *Folklore of the Australian Railwaymen*, p. 228, 1969
- Some of them, too, have been humping it like that for days, if not weeks.—Ronald J. Glasser, *365 Days*, p. 4, 1971
- My college years receded, and it seemed as if I had spent almost all my life humping a too heavy pack beneath a too hot sun down a road that was too long.—Philip Caputo, *A Rumor of War*, p. 18, 1977
- Us grunts – busting jungle and busting cherries from Landing Zone Skator-Gator to Scat Man Do (where that is), humping and hauling ass all the way.—Larry Heinemann, *Paco's Story*, p. 5, 1986
- You're humping way too much, troop, don't need half this shit.—*Platoon*, 1986
- You had to pick the transmission up in your two hands – hones to God, you pick up this fucker weighing close to two hundred pounds – hump it over to the engine and run it on to the shaft.—Elmore Leonard, *Out of Sight*, p. 231, 1996

3 to earn money working as a prostitute *US*

- Satin and Nell were doing their thing together in grand style and Satin was doing her humping bit at night.—A.S. Jackson, *Gentleman Pimp*, p. 101, 1973
- Back in the days when bad girls humped good bread into my pockets, con man, Airtight Willie and pimp ... me ... lay in a double bunk cell on a tier in Chicago Cook's County Jail.—Iceberg Slim (Robert Beck), *Airtight Willie and Me*, p. 3, 1979

4 in trucking, to drive fast *US*

- —Elementary Electronics, *Dictionary of CB Lingo*, p. 78, 1976

▸ **hump it**

in poker, to raise the maximum bet allowed *US*

- —George Percy, *The Language of Poker*, p. 46, 1988

▸ **hump like a camel**

to engage in sexual intercourse with great physical enthusiasm *US*

- Without you jokers were kicking the door in, she was humping like a camel.—Lawrence Block, *No Score [The Affairs of Chip Harrison Omnibus]*, p. 123, 1970

▸ **hump the dog**

to waste time completely *US*

Similar construction to the synonymous 'fuck the dog'.

- "Meanwhile," Roland said, "we're sitting here humping the dog, huh?"—Elmore Leonard, *Gold Coast*, p. 50, 1980

▸ **hump your bluey/drum/swag**

to carry one's belongings in a swag while seeking work on foot *AUSTRALIA, 1851*

- [W]ould the old man change his ideas and go out on the track, humping his bluey, or would he be just the same, looking around for a bit of property work?—Jon Cleary, *The Long Shadow*, p. 147, 1949
- It's the tale of those two mates who had been humping their blueys out Back-o'-Bourke for months.—Bill Wannan, *Bullockies, Beauts and Bandicoots*, p. 51, 1960

hump-and-jump *adjective*
(of a job) physically demanding and fast-paced *US*
- Most likely those of us with seniority will be put back in some hump-and-jump job and those of us that don't will be down on the relief line. —John Sayles, *Union Dues*, p. 41, 1977

hump and thump *noun*
cardiovascular resuscitation *US*
- —Sally Williams, *"Strong" Words*, p. 147, 1994

humpback job *noun*
a local freight train *US*
- So called because the conductor spends much time in the caboose bending over his wheel reports. —Norman Carlisle, *The Modern Wonder Book of Trains and Railroading*, p. 264, 1946

hump date *noun*
during the Vietnam war, the date when half of a soldier's tour of duty in Vietnam is completed *US*
- Most everyone has a short-timers calendar of some sort after he had reached the hump date signifying half his tour is completed. —Tony Zidek, *Choi Oi*, p. 124, 1965

hump day *noun*
Wednesday *US, 1955*
Visualised as a hill, the peak or hump of the work week or school week is Wednesday.
- —Judi Sanders, *Mashing and Munching in Ames*, p. 10, 1994

humper *noun*
1 a member of a rock band's crew who carries heavy items *UK*
- —Bob Young and Micky Moody, *The Language of Rock 'n' Roll*, p. 61, 1985

2 a large and unbroken wave *US*
- —Gary Fairmont R. Filosa II, *The Surfer's Almanac*, p. 187, 1977

3 in motor racing, a slick drag racing tyre that has been grooved for use on a dirt track *US*
- —Don Alexander, *The Racer's Dictionary*, p. 31, 1980

hump-hump *verb*
to have sex *US*
A mock pidgin.
- Where'd they teach you to talk like this, some Panama City "Sailor want to hump-hump" bar? —*As Good As It Gets*, 1997

hump night *noun*
Wednesday night *US*
- —*American Speech*, p. 226, October 1955: 'An aircraft production dispatcher's vocabulary'
- —*Current Slang*, p. 4, Winter 1966

hump rat *noun*
a railway yard brakeman *US*
- —*American Speech*, p. 287, December 1968: 'Addenda to the vocabulary of railroading'

humpty dumpty *noun*
an extreme reaction to MDMA, the recreational drug best known as ecstasy *UK*
A probable reference to the fate of the nursery rhyme character.
- I had what is termed a "Humpty Dumpty". —Macfarlane, Macfarlane and Robson, *The User*, p. 67, 1996

Humpty Dumpty language *noun*
any word or vocabulary given an unusual or eccentric sense by the user *UK*
Derives from *Through the Looking Glass and What Alice Found There* by Lewis Carroll (Charles Dodgson), 1871: '"When I use a word," Humpty Dumpty said, in rather a scornful tone, "it means just what I choose it to mean – neither more nor less."'
- Unfortunately Forth is a Humpty Dumpty language, where you define words to mean exactly what you want them to mean. —*The Guardian*, 26th July 1984
- The Humpty Dumpty language demonstrates that. Redefining a problem is not the same as solving it. It merely allows the perceived problem to be used to justify a predetermined answer. —*Durango Herald*, 5th May 2004

humpy *noun*
a makeshift dwelling *AUSTRALIA, 1846*
Originally used of a temporary shelter made by Aboriginals; from the Australian Aboriginal language Yagara (Brisbane region).
- It was a new humpy of bark and saplings, quaintly impressive of white man's defiance of the wild. —Ion L. Idriess, *Over the Range*, p. 79, 1947
- You ever see that photo of Lionel Rose as a kid, barefoot beside a tin humpy? —Shane Maloney, *Nice Try*, p. 102, 1998

humpy *adjective*
handsome, sexy *US*
Homosexual usage.
- Myself, I like looking at pictures of peole doing it, and I prefer it when the people involved are men. Humpy men. —Angelo d'Arcangelo, *The Homosexual Handbook*, p. 183, 1968
- Humpy young longhairs; students with shining evening faces; Puerto Ricans fighting machismo, with wives at home[.] —John Francis Hunter, *The Gay Insider*, p. 137, 1971
- —*Maledicta*, p. 232, 1979: 'Kinks and queens: linguistic and cultural aspects of the terminology for gays'
- —Wayne Dynes, *Homolexis*, p. 69, 1985

humpy-bump *verb*
to have sex *US*
- I didn't know if you had to humpy-bump for a job or just know him. —Edward Lin, *Big Julie of Vegas*, p. 209, 1974

humungous *adjective*
▷ see: HUMONGOUS

hun *noun*
one hundred dollars; a one hundred dollar note *US, 1895*
- —Christina and Richard Milner, *Black Players*, p. 296, 1972

Hun *noun*
1 a German; a person of German descent *UK, 1900*
As German troops set sail for China on 27th July 1900, Wilhelm II urged them to fight 'just as the Huns a thousand years ago'. The name stuck. It was the main pejorative for the enemy in World War 2.
- That sonofabitch Joe Asbach is a hun from outside the district. —Robert Campbell, *Junkyard Dog*, p. 37, 1986

2 a Protestant *UK: SCOTLAND*
- —Michael Munro, *The Complete Patter*, 1996

hunch *noun*
an intuition or premonition *US, 1888*
Now verging on conventional.
- The Revenue, going on nothing more than a hunch, can decide that your income is far bigger. —*The Guardian*, 15th February 2003

hunch *verb*
to bring someone up to date; to inform *US*
- I hunched him to the fact that I had left my girl with his piece on the edge and asked her to break her in to the action. —A.S. Jackson, *Gentleman Pimp*, p. 98, 1973

hundoe *noun*
one hundred dollars *US*
- —Pamela Munro, *U.C.L.A. Slang*, p. 31, 2001

hundred-mile coffee *noun*
strong coffee *US*
So named because it is strong enough to keep a trucker awake to drive one hundred miles.
- —Montie Tak, *Truck Talk*, p. 86, 1971
- Now, how's about giving me some of that hundred-mile coffee of yours. —Emmett Grogan, *Final Score*, p. 80, 1976

hundred to eight *noun*
a plate *UK*
Rhyming slang, formed from bookmaker's odds.
- [T]hat's all it is, an "old hundred to eight". But as soon as it gets smashed it becomes an antique. —Ray Puxley, *Fresh Rabbit*, 1998

hundred to thirty *adjective*
dirty *UK*
Reported by David Hillman, 1974.

hung *adjective*
1 endowed with a large penis *UK, 1600*
Shakespeare punned with the term 400 years ago.
- —Donald Webster Cory and John P. LeRoy, *The Homosexual and His Society*, p. 264, 1963: 'A lexicon of homosexual slang'
- Heard these little coons are hung like horses[.] —Dick Gregory, *Nigger*, p. 10, 1964
- From a certain unevenly rounded thickness at the crotch of his blue jeans, it is safe to assume that he is marvelously hung. —Gore Vidal, *Myra Breckinridge*, p. 31, 1968

- Robbie leaned forward in his chair, toward the television set. "He's not hung at all." Sounding surprised. "I thought he was supposed to be hung." —Elmore Leonard, *Split Images*, p. 211, 1981
- The men are lean and hung, and the women look like they like to do naughty and even dirty things. — *Adult Video*, p. 29, August/September 1986
- All men are "hung". —Fiona Pitt-Kethley, *Red Light Districts of the World*, p. 12, 2000

2 fascinated or obsessed with *US*

- I remember the red air and the sadness – "the strange red afternoon light" Wolfe also was hung on – with peculiar eternity-dream vividness[.] —Jack Kerouac, *Letter to Neal Cassady*, 28th December 1950
- Mike didn't mind because, although he didn't play anything himself, he had a lot of records and he was almost as hung on jazz as I was. —Nat Hentoff, *Jazz Country*, p. 8, 1965

3 (used of a computer program) suspended, waiting for something that will not happen *US*

- —Guy L. Steele et al., *The Hacker's Dictionary*, p. 82, 1983

hung like a cashew

blessed with a small penis *UK*

From the late 1990s.

hung like a hamster

blessed with a small penis *US*

- Brad Pitt has been posing naked for a magazine only days after telling The Sun that he was "hung like a hamster". — *Sunday Times*, 9th May 2004

hung like a jack donkey; hung like a donkey

endowed with an impressively large penis *UK*

- "'E's 'ung like a fucking donkey." "Oh, please, tell me you're joking." —Colin Butts, *Is Harry on the Boat?*, p. 142, 1997

hung like a pimple

blessed with a small penis *US*

- I didn't want this new associate seeing that I was hung like a PIMPLE. —Howard Stern, *Miss America*, p. 180, 1995

hung over *adjective*

suffering from the after-effects of having drunk too much alcohol *US, 1942*

Derives from 'hangover'.

- I didn't think Japanese corporations tolerated inefficiencies like hung-over employees. — *The Guardian*, 27th December 2002

hungries *noun*

the craving for food that follows the smoking of marijuana *US*

- —William D. Alsever, *Glossary for the Establishment and Other Uptight People*, p. 6, December 1970

hungry *adjective*

stingy; mean *AUSTRALIA, 1855*

hung up *adjective*

1 obsessed, infatuated *US, 1950*

- Not to get hung up on the effects of this vision, let me tell you what it was. —Jack Kerouac, *Letter to Neal Cassady*, 28th December 1950
- And then everyone got so hungup on themselves. —John Clellon Holmes, *Go*, p. 8, 1952
- "You getting hung up on that chick, or something?" he asked me. —John Rechy, *City of Night*, p. 158, 1963
- A white man will come to the Negro club, so hung up in this race problem, so nervous and afraid of the neighborhood and the people that anything the comic says to relieve his tension will absolutely knock him out. —Dick Gregory, *Nigger*, p. 131, 1964
- Here is tangible evidence that a boy is really a man who not only can get money, but get it from a girl who is all "hung up" on him and will do anything to keep his attention. —Christina and Richard Milner, *Black Players*, p. 141, 1972
- [I]t was like a fucking river, I was "tripping" like fuck, and it was beautiful, you know, I got really hung up on the piss. —Paul E Willis, *Profane Culture*, p. 142, 1978
- Yeah, you can really get hung up on them. — *Apocalypse Now*, 1979
- I'm not hung up on you. I'm in love with you. — *Manhattan*, 1979

2 addicted *US, 1950*

- I was just about eighteen, you know, and I got hung up on the habit myself. —John Clellon Holmes, *Go*, p. 122, 1952

3 of a drug-addict who is unable to get drugs, depressed, let down, disappointed *US, 1948*

A nuance of the previous sense.

- —Home Office, *Glossary of Terms and Slang Common in Penal Establishments*, 1978

4 inhibited, neurotic *US, 1952*

- —J. L. Simmons and Barry Winograd, *It's Happening*, p. 171, 1966: 'glossary'
- Yeah, listen, uh, are you ....? ARE YOU HUNG UP? —Frank Zappa, *Are You Hung Up?*, 1968

5 while surfing, caught along the steep wall of a wave and unable to pull out *US*

- —Grant W. Kuhns, *On Surfing*, p. 118, 1963

hungus *adjective*

in computing, extremely large *US*

- — *Co-Evolution Quarterly*, p. 32, Spring 1981
- —Eric S. Raymond, *The New Hacker's Dictionary*, p. 204, 1991

hunk *noun*

a good-looking, muscular boy or man *US*

- —Lou Shelly, *Hepcats Jive Talk Dictionary*, p. 13, 1945
- — *Current Slang*, p. 3, Summer 1966
- — *Verbatim*, p. 280, May 1976
- Cherry Dilday said to mention that the Biller is a hunk. —Joe Bob Briggs, *Joe Bob Goes to the Drive-In*, p. 42, 1987
- Starlets as mermaids, Hollywood hunks covered with leaves, politicians as circus performers. —Francesca Lia Block, *I Was a Teenage Fairy*, p. 147, 1998

hunka chunka *noun*

sexual intercourse *US*

- [A]t the age of 64, Paul Theroux has decided what he's really interested in is 'hunka chunka' – people getting it on. — *Esquire*, p. 25, July 2005

hunkin *adjective*

enormous *US*

- —Judi Sanders, *Da Bomb!*, p. 15, 1997

hunky; hunkie *noun*

1 a white person *US, 1959*

Derogatory.

- The night before I had let a hunky called Big John have a dollar's worth of chips in the poker game for a monkey which he had carved from a peach seed[.] —Chester Himes, *Cast the First Stone*, p. 66, 1952
- He said, "I'm going to buy this building and turn this into a Nigger bar. I'm going to bar all you laughing hunkies." —Iceberg Slim (Robert Beck), *Trick Baby*, p. 149, 1969
- Farvel hunky motherfuckers. —Cecil Brown, *The Life & Loves of Mr. Jiveass Nigger*, p. 88, 1969
- [W]hat did they care about a handful of red-neck religious-nut hunkies[.] —Terry Southern, *Blue Movie*, p. 15, 1970
- Dem hunkies couldn't care less if a nigger was born on Mars. —J. Ashton Brathwaithe, *Niggers – This is Canada*, p. 24, 1971
- I guess every hunkie in the neighborhood must've called the po-lice soon as they saw us walkin' down the street. —Odie Hawkins, *Ghetto Sketches*, p. 119–120, 1972

2 an Eastern European; a Slav; a Hungarian *US, 1909*

Disparaging, but usually more illustrative of the speaker's lack of geographic knowledge.

- Those hunkies were lush crazy and could they drink. —Mezz Mezzrow, *Really the Blues*, p. 71, 1946
- She'd been teaching sixth-grade Polacks and Hunkies so long that she thought she could treat everybody as if they were one of her sixth-grade pupils. —James T. Farrell, *Saturday Night*, p. 9, 1947
- He played the line with a cigarette dangling out of his Hunky mouth. —Clancy Sigal, *Going Away*, p. 52, 1961
- Right, why should we get behind some hunkie we don't even know? —John Sayles, *Union Dues*, p. 38, 1977
- In the locker rooms of the Eighteenth District Station and around the cop bars, he called Italians guidos or wops, Poles polacks, Bohemians hunkies, Mexicans spicks or greasers, and African-Americans niggers or darkies. —Robert Campbell, *Boneyards*, p. 10, 1992

hunky *adjective*

attractive, muscular *US*

- —Bruce Rodgers, *The Queens' Vernacular*, p. 110, 1972
- Several years ago, while I was on holiday with several girlfriends, tucked away at a seaside Florida bar, the hunky bartender poured us all vodka shots "on the house," and asked if we wanted to "party after closing." "Define 'party,'" was my retort. —Nancy Tamosaitis, *net.sex*, p. 123, 1995

hunky dory *adjective*

satisfactory, fine *US, 1861*

- I was doing the easiest time I ever did. Everything was hunky-dory. —Chester Himes, *Cast the First Stone*, p. 112, 1952
- I saw the man once, and that's all it took for me to see he was a wrong number, but I kept my peace because you acted like everything was hunky-dory. —Robert Campbell, *Boneyards*, p. 224, 1992
- JORY: Go home, Freddy, Everything's hunky dory. — *Copland*, 1997
- You fall in love with me and want a romantic relationship, nothing changes for you with the exception of feeling honky-dory all the time. — *Chasing Amy*, 1997
- [S]he's married this guy who was a salesman and everything's normal and hunky-dory[.] — *The Guardian*, p. 5, 26th February 2002

hunt *noun*

▸ **in the hunt**

in contention *AUSTRALIA*

- Means 'e wasn't in the hunt. — Nino Culotta (John O'Grady), *They're A Weird Mob*, p. 75, 1957
- When he sat for his examinations for umpiring, Jack Ryder and all the experts tried to trick him but they weren't in the hunt. — Frank Hardy, *The Yarns of Billy Borker*, p. 35, 1965

hunt *verb*

to chase off, away or to somewhere *AUSTRALIA, 1917*

- An' listen to our Mary tryin' to 'unt us 'ome, Granny, without nothin'. — Barbara Baynton, *Toohey's Party*, p. 103, 1917
- With old Ben off the stage at last, Meaty O'Donnell was hunted on to it for a recitation[.] — Norman Lindsay, *Halfway to Anywhere*, p. 218, 1947

▸ **hunt owls**

to drive at night with your full headlight beams on, blinding oncoming traffic *US*

- — *American Speech*, p. 269, December 1962: 'The language of traffic policemen'

▸ **hunt rabbits**

in a game of poker, to go through the cards that were not played after a hand is finished in search of what might have been *US*

- — *American Speech*, p. 100, May 1951: 'The vocabulary of poker'

▸ **hunt the great white whale**

to search for a source of cocaine *UK*

The **GREAT WHITE WHALE** is a literary allusion to Moby Dick, the classic novel by Herman Melville (1819–91), and a play on the colour and power of cocaine. Collected in correspondence, 2000.

hunter *noun*

1 a pickpocket *US*

- — Vincent J. Monteleone, *Criminal Slang*, p. 126, 1949

2 cocaine *UK*

- — Mike Haskins, *Drugs*, p. 280, 2003

hunt for Red October *noun*

the bleed period of the menstrual cycle *US*

Elaboration of 'red' – the colour of blood – by adoption of the title of a novel by Tom Clancy, and subsequent film.

- — *The Museum of Menstruation and Women's Health*, October 2000

hunting license *noun*

an assignment given by a prison gang to kill someone *US*

- — William K. Bentley and James M. Corbett, *Prison Slang*, p. 94, 1992

huntsabber *noun*

a hunt saboteur *UK*

- — Brain Donor *Huntsabbers' Ball*, 2001

hunty-hunty *adjective*

(of a woman) used to describe a husband-hunter or a 'manhunter' *UK*

Reduplication of the woman's essential quality. West Indian, hence UK black.

- If she too chatty-chatty [gossipy], me nah interested. If she too hunty-hunty, me nah interested. — Diran Adebayo, *My Once Upon A Time*, p. 21, 2000

huppie *noun*

an individual socially categorised as an *H*ispanic *u*rban *p*rofessional or *H*ispanic *u*pwardly mobile *p*rofessional *US, 1986*

On the familiar model of **YUPPIE** (*y*oung *u*pwardly mobile *p*rofessional).

- Jose Delgado, who is an administrator for the Latino Theatre Lab at LATC, said he relates to Rodriguez's vignette about the burned-out Chicano activist who becomes a "huppie" (Hispanic yuppie) in the 1980s. — *Los Angeles Times*, p. 6-1, 1st September 1989
- — *The Word Spy*, 25th September 1999

hurdy *noun*

a dance hall girl *CANADA*

- Nothing indicates that the Hurdies were anything more than dancers. — Gordon Elliott, *Quesnel*, p. 30, 1958

hurl *noun*

an act of vomiting; vomit *AUSTRALIA*

- Calling for Herb, see, that's one of the many euphemisms for vomit, others include spue, burp, hurl, the big spit, the long spit, throw, the whip o'will, the technicolour laugh and, in Queensland, the chuckle. — Frank Hardy, *Billy Borker Rides Again*, 1967
- [T]he bloke's drained the dragon [urinated] a few times and had a couple of hurls[.] — Barry Humphries, *Bazza Pulls It Off!*, 1971

hurl *verb*

to vomit *AUSTRALIA, 1964*

- Now I've had liquid laughs in bars / And I've hurled from moving cars / And I've chucked where and when it suited me. — Barry Humphries, *The Wonderful World of Barry McKenzie*, p. 15, 1968
- Whatever you do, don't hurl. — *Wayne's World 2*, 1993

hurler *noun*

a person who suffers from bulimia nervosa *US*

- Well, from her figure and her appetite, I'm guessing she's either got a bowel disorder or we've got a hurler on our hands. — *Something About Mary*, 1998

hurly-burly *adjective*

confusing, tumultuous *UK, 1596*

- It as the bellboy who was always in closest contact with this hurly-burly world, a world always populated by strangers of unknown background and unpredictable behavior. — Jim Thompson, *Bad Boy*, p. 356, 1953

hurrah *noun*

in a big store confidence swindle, the stage of the swindle when the victim is fully duped *US*

- "The Hurrah," Beano explained to Victoria, "is that point in the confidence game where the mark has completely committed himself. From this point forward there's no way he's going to pull out." — Stephen Cannell, *Big Con*, p. 339, 1997

hurricane deck *noun*

the back of a bucking bronco *US, 1862*

- He'd been athletic and the hurricane deck came to him like a football does to the city youth. — Alan Fry, *The Ranch on the Cariboo*, p. 163, 1962

hurricane ham *noun*

conch *BAHAMAS*

- — John A. Holm, *Dictionary of Bahamian English*, p. 108, 1982

hurricane lamp; hurricane *noun*

a *tramp*, a vagrant *UK*

Rhyming slang.

- — Ray Puxley, *Fresh Rabbit*, 1998

hurricane lamp job *noun*

in horse racing, a horse that finishes last by a great distance *AUSTRALIA*

The horse is so far back that it is joked that a hurricane lamp is needed to find it.

- — Ned Wallish, *The Truth Dictionary of Racing Slang*, p. 39, 1989

hurricane on a ten-cent piece *noun*

a wife furious with her husband *CANADA*

- "She's a hurricane on a ten-cent piece" is said of a wife angry with her husband. It is a peppy saying from the rural interior of British Columbia, and is in St. Pierre's 1966 novel "Breaking Smith's Quarter Horse." — Bill Casselman, *Canadian Words*, p. 200–201, 1995

hurry-come *adjective*

done with haste and without care *TRINIDAD AND TOBAGO, 1987*

- — Lise Winer, *Dictionary of the English/Creole of Trinidad & Tobago*, 2003

hurry-on *noun*

a quickening of pace *AUSTRALIA*

- Sweetheart, if you don't get a hurry-on and polish those shoes, you'll be late for school. — Kerry Cue, *Crooks, Chooks and Bloody Ratbags*, p. 134, 1983

hurry-up *noun*

1 a hurry, speed *UK*

Since the 1960s.

- Then they whipped him down to the nick [police station] on the hurry-up. — Derek Raymond (Robin Cook), *The Crust on its Uppers*, p. 47, 1962

2 a request for a quickening of pace *AUSTRALIA, 1916*

- Go-slow funerals get a hurry-up — *Sunday Tasmanian*, p. 19, 1st October 1989
- Naturally then, when Joe walked out in the gathering gloom to open the batting, it was obvious he was going to get a bit of hurry-up from the Scarborough bowlers. — Rod Marsh, *Two For The Road*, p. 48, 1992

hurryup wagon *noun*

a police van *US, 1893*

- — Claudio R. Salvucci, *The Philadelphia Dialect Dictionary*, p. 45, 1996

hurt *noun*

▸ **put the hurt on**

to inflict pain *UK*

- The cops were out to put the hurt on as many of the opposition as they could. —Mick Farren, *Give the Anarchist a Cigarette*, p. 350, 2001

hurt *verb*

to crave a drug *UK*

- —Angela Devlin, *Prison Patter*, p. 63, 1996

hurt *adjective*

undesireable, unattractive, inept *US, 1973*

- —Connie Eble (Editor), *UNC-CH Campus Slang*, p. 4, Fall 1980
- —Ellen C. Bellone (Editor), *Dictionary of Slang*, p. 14, 1989

hurting *adjective*

inferior; not up to expectations *US*

- —Connie Eble (Editor), *UNC-CH Campus Slang*, p. 5, October 2002

hurt me!

used for expressing extreme pleasure or displeasure *US*

- —Connie Eble (Editor), *UNC-CH Campus Slang*, p. 3, November 1983

hurve *verb*

to move quickly; to hurry *AUSTRALIA*

- —Tom Hibbert, *Rockspeak!*, p. 88, 1983

hus *noun*

▹ see: HUSS

husband *noun*

in a homosexual relationship (male or female), the more aggressive and domineering partner *US, 1941*

- —Donald Webster Cory and John P. LeRoy, *The Homosexual and His Society*, p. 264, 1963: 'A lexicon of homosexual slang'
- The world of queens and malehustlers and what they thrive on, the queens being technically men but no one thinks of them that way – always "she"[.] —John Rechy, *City of Night*, p. 105, 1963
- —*Male Swinger Number 3*, p. 46, 1981: 'The complete gay dictionary'
- —Paul Baker, *Polari*, p. 177, 2002

husband and wife; husband *noun*

a knife *UK*

Rhyming slang.

- —Ray Puxley, *Cockney Rabbit*, 1992

hush *noun*

silence *UK, 1976*

- A little bit of hush is called for on Noise Action Day[.]— *The Sutton Guardian*, 10th May 2002

hush-em *noun*

a silencer attached to a handgun *US*

- —Vincent J. Monteleone, *Criminal Slang*, p. 126, 1949

hush-hush *adjective*

secret *UK, 1916*

Reduplicated 'hush' (to be quiet); military origins.

- "Hush-hush all the way, Mr. Regan," Kelly said. "Crikey, nobody knows who did the blag..." —*The Sweeney*, p. 50, 1976
- FIREBUG: Dead cert? LEE: Oh yeah. Well, y'know, hush-hush an' all that. —Guy Ritchie et al., *Lock, Stock... & Four Stolen Hooves*, p. 25, 2000

hush money *noun*

a bribe paid to obtain silence *UK, 1709*

- [A] former sweetheart of gambler Attilio Acalotti charged she had seen hush-money slipped to three cops. —Jack Lait and Lee Mortimer, *Washington Confidential*, p. 225, 1951
- "In hindsight, I can see why it has the appearance of 'hush money.' Perhaps I should have handled this situation differently." (Quoting Archbishop Rembver G. Weakland) —*Milwaukee Sentinel Journal*, p. 5A, 1st June 2002

hush puppy *noun*

1 a Smith and Wesson 9 mm pistol; the silencer attached to the pistol *US*

Carried by US Navy SEALS. So named, the legend goes, because of its use in killing guard dogs.

- Factory-modified. They call it a Hush-Puppy. —Elmore Leonard, *Cat Chaser*, p. 247, 1982
- —Linda Reinberg, *In the Field*, p. 110, 1991
- I carried a 9mm pistol with a hush-puppy – silencer – and my M16, with lots of extra ammo. —Richard Marcinko and John Weisman, *Rogue Warrior*, p. 129, 1992

2 a yuppie (a *y*oung *u*pwardly mobile *p*rofessional) *UK*

Rhyming slang, formed from a footwear-manufacturer's brand name.

- —Ray Puxley, *Cockney Rabbit*, 1992

hush-puppy *adjective*

(used of jazz) old-fashioned, conventional *US*

- Yah, what's this 'alabam' written up here? I ain't gonna play none of that hush-puppy jazz. —John Clellon Holmes, *The Horn*, p. 134, 1958

husk *verb*

to undress *US*

- —Lou Shelly, *Hepcats Jive Talk Dictionary*, p. 13, 1945

Husky *noun*

in trucking, a Brockway truck *US*

From the company logo.

- —Wayne Floyd, *Jason's Authentic Dictionary of CB Slang*, p. 19, 1976

huss; hus; huz *noun*

a favour *US*

Vietnam war usage, especially by marines.

- —Eugene Landy, *The Underground Dictionary*, p. 63, 1971
- If they gotta put down their cold beer for five minutes to cut somebody a hus they won't do it. —Charles Anderson, *The Grunts*, p. 29, 1976
- —Connie Eble (Editor), *UNC-CH Campus Slang*, November 1976

hustle *noun*

1 an illegal enterprise, especially one involving swindling *US, 1943*

- Pickin' pockets, why that's a hustle for a lame. —Bruce Jackson, *Get Your Ass in the Water and Swim Like Me*, p. 66, 1964
- Even though he was only twenty-three years old, he'd gotten big time without a hustle. —Claude Brown, *Manchild in the Promised Land*, p. 214, 1965
- He introduced me to the sweetest "hustle" I'd ran into. —Babs Gonzales, *I Paid My Dues*, p. 73, 1967
- Get into a hustle that pays on account of he don't have a trade, only a rich mama forgot who he is. —Elmore Leonard, *Riding the Rap*, p. 54, 1995

2 effort, exertion, desire *US, 1898*

- There are times you have to show hustle, even if it's false. —Jim Bouton, *Ball Four*, p. 16, 1970

▸ **on the hustle**

engaged in a career of swindling *US*

- The Bates family is sort of well known. There are three thousand of them. Most of the family is on the hustle. —Stephen Cannell, *King Con*, p. 91, 1997

hustle *verb*

1 to engage in prostitution *US, 1895*

- All right, she was a hustler, but she wasn't hustling for me and I did her a favor. —Mickey Spillane, *My Gun is Quick*, p. 13–14, 1950
- Many of the white women who solicit on the streets are young; it takes some time for these girls, fresh off the farms, to get the nerve to hustle in high-class hotels. —Jack Lait and Lee Mortimer, *Washington Confidential*, p. 23, 1951
- Like me, he was there almost every night; and like me, too, he was, I knew, hustling. —John Rechy, *City of Night*, p. 40, 1963
- Sandy hustled in Hollywood for a time before finding San Francisco, and he compared the police control of male prostitution. —*KFRC radio, San Francisco*, 8th November 1965: 'The Market Street proposition'
- In Philadelphia we found the place to hustle was Rittenhouse Square and Fairmount Park. —Johnny Shearer, *The Male Hustler*, p. 141–142, 1966
- The idea of hustling was not a new one to Ina. —Vance Donovan, *High Rider*, p. 47, 1969
- She told me she had been doing quite well – until but recently working as a model – doking a little hustling on the side[.] —Herbert Huncke, *The Evening Sun Turned Crimson*, p. 58, 1980
- Margo goes out and hustles a couple nights a week and that's the only money they've got coming in. —Elmore Leonard, *Split Images*, p. 90, 1981
- He put his chick out on the street even though she didn't like to hustle. —Herbert Huncke, *Guilty of Everything*, p. 186, 1990

2 to obtain after a diligent effort, especially one using unorthodox, if not illegal, means *US, 1840*

- I came to New York to start Liberty House in the West Village, which I designed, hustled the bread for, painted, and got sore fingers banging in the nails. —Abbie Hoffman, *Revolution for the Hell of It*, p. 200, 1968
- —Lise Winer, *Dictionary of the English/Creole of Trinidad & Tobago*, 2003

3 to beg, to cadge *US, 1902*

Used by beggars and tramps.

- He hustles a deutschmark off the G.I.s, then disappears to the bar. —*New Society*, 31st January 1980

4 to flirt; to make a sexual advance *TRINIDAD AND TOBAGO*

- —Lise Winer, *Dictionary of the English/Creole of Trinidad & Tobago*, 2003

hustler *noun*

1 a prostitute, especially a male homosexual *US, 1924*

- All right, she was a hustler, but she wasn't hustling for me and I did her a favor. —Mickey Spillane, *My Gun is Quick*, p. 13–14, 1950
- You go around telling people I'm a hustler and I'll break your skinny head. —George Mandel, *Flee the Angry Strangers*, p. 243, 1952
- [S]he would not have me hold her arm for fear people of the street here would think her a hustler[.] —Jack Kerouac, *The Subterraneans*, p. 68, 1958
- [B]oth those girls are workin' shimmy dancers and hustlers I know from Portland. —Ken Kesey, *One Flew Over the Cuckoo's Nest*, p. 210, 1962
- —Donald Webster Cory and John P. LeRoy, *The Homosexual and His Society*, p. 265, 1963: 'A lexicon of homosexual slang'
- And I would discover that to many of the street people a hustler became more attractive in direct relation to his seeming insensitivity – his "toughness." —John Rechy, *City of Night*, p. 37, 1963
- Making it with a "hustler" or a "piece of trade" fills this need when everything else has failed. —Antony James, *America's Homosexual Underground*, p. 14, 1965
- You can find no end of hustlers that are male prostitutes. —*KFRC radio, San Francisco*, 8th November 1965: 'The Market Street proposition'
- The folklore of the hustler's world has legendary stories of hustlers who supposedly made the scene with a big-time producer, satisfied the old auntie and ended up as a big star. —Johnny Shearer, *The Male Hustler*, p. 141, 1966
- It was Myron who observed in 1964 that all of the male hustlers were supporting Goldwater for President. —Gore Vidal, *Myra Breckinridge*, p. 43, 1968
- Male prostitutes are currently called "hustlers." —Angelo d'Arcangelo, *The Homosexual Handbook*, p. 27, 1968
- I'm not like the average hustler you'd meet. —Mart Crowley, *The Boys in the Band*, p. 177, 1968
- It had all the types in the hustling scene: the new hustler, the aging hustler, the old queen, the fag-haf, etc. —*Screw*, p. 8–9, 24th January 1969
- There'd usually be a couple of chicks, maybe a few good-looking hustlers from the Square, a friend of mine – a car thief – and a partner or two. —Herbert Huncke, *Guilty of Everything*, p. 84, 1990

2 a drug pusher *UK*

- —Angela Devlin, *Prison Patter*, p. 63, 1996

3 a person who makes his living by playing pool for wagers, feigning a skill level below his true level to secure bets *US*

- The poolroom hustler makes his living by betting against his opponents in different types of pool or billiard games, and as part of the playing and betting process he engages in various deceitful practices. —Ned Polsky, *Hustlers, Beats, and Others*, p. 41, 1967

4 a person who lives by his charm and wits, dishonest but usually not violent *US, 1896*

- Call Roy Bartholomew Beavers what you will, he never represented himself – unless it suited his immediate plans – as anything other than he was: a hustler. —Clarence Cooper Jr, *Black*, p. 233, 1963

hustler's row *noun*

any outdoor area where prostitutes loiter in search of customers *UK*

- There are a few women who come down into hustler's row occasionally. —Johnny Shearer, *The Male Hustler*, p. 72, 1966

hustling *noun*

1 the practice of dealing drugs *UK*

- He told me once that this was the first hustling he'd been involved in where he didn't feel the need to rip off something for himself. —Lanre Fehintola, *Charlie Says...*, p. 16, 2000

2 prostitution *UK*

- —David Powis, *The Signs of Crime*, 1977

hustling gal *noun*

a prostitute *US*

- Later that same year Harry Tennisen was killed by a hustling gal of the honky-tonks called Sister Pop. —Louis Armstrong, *Satchmo*, p. 91, 1954
- You take a lot of people, a lot of thieves, they have a hustling gal working for them and she's alway in and out of jail. —Bruce Jackson, *Outside the Law*, p. 137, 1972

hut *noun*

1 a house *US*

- Are we going to your hut tonight? —Ellen C. Bellone (Editor), *Dictionary of Slang*, p. 14, 1989

2 a jail cell *US*

- —Vincent J. Monteleone, *Criminal Slang*, p. 127, 1949

3 a brakevan (caboose) *US*

- —Norman Carlisle, *The Modern Wonder Book of Trains and Railroading*, p. 265, 1946

hutch *noun*

1 a domicile, be it a room, apartment or house *US*

- What to other people is a "pad" is called a "hutch" in surfing circles – most properly if it is the beach bunny's own apartment[.] —Roger Gordon, *Hollywood's Sexual Underground*, p. 144, 1966
- Shiela's hutch was on the top floor. —Robert Campbell, *In La-La Land We Trust*, p. 129, 1986

2 a prison *US*

- —*American Speech*, p. 100, May 1956: 'Smugglers' argot in the Southwest'

hutzelsup *noun*

(among Nova Scotians of German descent) a confused mess *CANADA*

- "It's a real hutzelsup" to mean a mess, in Lunenburg County, derives from a soup made of "hutzel," German for dried apple or dried pear. —Lewis Poteet, *The South Shore Phrase Book*, p. 61, 1999

huz *noun*

▷ **see: HUSS**

Hyack *noun*

in British Columbia, a volunteer fireman *CANADA*

The term, from a Chinook jargon word, is preserved in the Honorable Hyack Battery of New Westminster, BC.

- (Caption) Men of the Ancient and Honourable Hyack Battery firing their 88th annual Royal Salute. —*Weekend Magazine*, p. 34, 16th May 1959

hyak *verb*

in British Columbia, to hasten *CANADA*

The term comes from Chinook jargon.

- The firemen were called by the name used to describe them by the Indians – hyack, meaning "hurry up." —*Weekend Magazine*, p. 34/1, 16th May 1959

hyas *adverb*

big, large, very *CANADA*

- This evening we pitch off. We leave hyas quick – in half a pipe. —William Mowery, *Tales of the Mounted Police*, p. 53, 1953

hyas tyee *noun*

a great chief, an important person *CANADA*

A combination of two Chinook jargon words, **HYAS** and *tyee* (chief, king).

- Tom Hastie told me his employer, Co.. Evey, was a hyass tyee (Mighty Chief). —*Beaver*, p. 44, Summer 1956

hybolic *adjective*

pompous, wordy, bombastic *US*

Hawaiian youth usage.

- —Elizabeth Ball Carr, *Da Kine Talk*, p. 134, 1972

hybrid *noun*

in the car sales business, used as a euphemism for a car that has at least some parts that do not belong *US*

- —*Cars*, p. 40, December 1953

Hyde Park *noun*

1 an actor's mark *UK*

Rhyming slang, from the film world.

- —*Daily Telegraph*, 17th December 1972: 'Slang It to me in rhyme'

2 an informer *UK*

Rhyming slang for **NARK**.

- —Ray Puxley, *Cockney Rabbit*, 1992

hydraulic *noun*

in drag racing, a massive engine failure resulting from fuel failing to ignite within a cylinder *US*

- —*geocities.com/racerday/glossary.html*,

hydraulic *adjective*

inclined to steal *AUSTRALIA*

Like a hydraulic jack, he will 'lift' anything.

- —Ned Wallish, *The Truth Dictionary of Racing Slang*, p. 39, 1989

hydraulics *noun*

bollocks, in all senses *UK*

Euphemistic rhyming slang.

- What a load of hydraulics. —Ray Puxley, *Fresh Rabbit*, 1998

hydro *noun*

1 marijuana which is grown *hydro*ponically *US*

- Nugs is a word of marijuana. Other words include: buds, mota, chocolate tai, skunk, bunk, swag, hydro, dank, wando and crypt. —*Riverside (California) Press Enterprise*, p. D1, 8th May 1996

- What happen to the hydro Thai? —Nick Barlay, *Curvy Lovebox*, p. 33, 1997
- Barbarella never smoked, insisting that grass, hash and hydro had no effect on her. —Wayne Anthony, *Spanish Highs*, p. 72, 1999
- That shit was hydro, man. —Stephen J. Cannell, *The Tin Collectors*, p. 35, 2001
- —Mike Haskins, *Drugs*, p. 288, 2003

2 MDMA, the recreational drug best known as ecstasy *UK*
Probably from the dehydration experienced by users of the drug.
- —Mike Haskins, *Drugs*, p. 289, 2003

3 amphetamines *UK*
- —Mike Haskins, *Drugs*, p. 279, 2003

4 electric power generated by the flow of water *CANADA*
- The B.C. government has introduced safety valve legislation in case its hydro laws are repudiated by the courts. —*Victoria Daily Times*, p. 18/1, 8th February 1964

hydroponic *noun*
marijuana that is cultivated hydroponically *US*
The soilless culture of cannabis results in plants that are up to ten time as potent as those grown outdoors.
- Two weeks ago when I was writin' this rhyme / I had some hydroponic, Boy that shit was fine —Tone Loc, *Cheeba Cheeba*, 1989
- One of them was dealing some good hydroponic before, like, in-a techno tent. —Niall Griffiths, *Sheepshagger*, p. 73, 2001

hyiu *adjective*
great, many, much, very *CANADA*
The word is adapted into English from Chinook jargon.
- "Gee!" he added. "I bet they make hiyu potlatch tonight!" —*Islander*, p. 6/1, 27th February 1966

hyke *noun*
1 codeine *US*
From the brand name Hycodan™.
- —*Providence (Rhode Island) Journal-Bulletin*, p. 6B, 4th August 1997: "Doctors must know the narcolexicon"

2 hydrocodone, a synthetic codeine *US*
- —William D. Alsever, *Glossary for the Establishment and Other Uptight People*, p. 16, December 1970

Hymie *noun*
a Jewish male *US, 1973*
Like Mick (for Mickey) as a label for the Irish, Hymie is a shortened Hyman. Not used kindly.
- Had he stayed there in Ismailiya, man his size, he'd be loading ships 'stead of wearing a $400 sharkskin suit, pearl gray, and working for this little Hymie fool. —Elmore Leonard, *Glitz*, p. 137, 1985
- —Multicultural Management Program Fellows, *Dictionary of Cautionary Words and Phrases*, 1989

hype *noun*
1 a syringe *US, 1910*
- They pulled out two spikes, laid out two hypes / And rolled some one-dollar-bill gees. —Dennis Wepman et al., *The Life*, p. 56, 1976
- On the wall alongside Randy's head was a starburst of rust-brown dots where someone had booted the blood from their hype. —Richard Price, *Clockers*, p. 232, 1992

2 a needle-using drug addict *US, 1924*
- This is not a queer bar – it is an outcast bar – Negroes and vagrant whites, heads and hypes, dikes and queens. —John Rechy, *City of Night*, p. 184, 1963
- The one thing that broke me out of the big bind in the restaurant winds up in a hype's pocket and I'm worse off than I ever was. —Mickey Spillane, *Return of the Hood*, p. 88, 1964
- He's a hype but he is very down with the current scene. —Eldridge Cleaver, *Soul on Ice (letter dated 19th September, 1965)*, p. 46, 1968
- He was a 'hype' even then. —Iceberg Slim (Robert Beck), *Pimp*, p. 99, 1969
- I discovered I was working someone else's territory, or when I was held up at knife point and told to give up my junk or get cut, or the various hypes I'd be subjected to. —Herbert Huncke, *The Evening Sun Turned Crimson*, p. 138, 1980
- A bunch of strung-out hypes and stick-up men. —*Gone in 60 Seconds*, 2000

3 a frequent user of marijuana *US*
Use of the term 'addict' is controversial in the context of marijuana users, but the suggestion here is that the person has let marijuana control his life.
- —Connie Eble (Editor), *UNC-CH Campus Slang*, p. 4, Spring 1999

4 exaggeration, nonsense *US, 1938*
- But that Danny laid down a super hype, and blow my nose and call me Snorty if we didn't wind up with him giving notice to the Goldkette office[.] —Mezz Mezzrow, *Really the Blues*, p. 129, 1946
- They pick up on each bopster's hype just like a simple child. —Dan Burley, *Diggeth Thou?*, p. 34, 1959

5 deception; an act of deception; something intended to stimulate sales, etc *US, 1955*
- Most PR hypes are crass, and the Poor Little Rich Girl hype is the crassest of the lot. —*New Society*, 20th December 1979

6 a swindle or cheat *US*
- —Joe McKennon, *Circus Lingo*, p. 50, 1980

▸ **put the hype on**
to raise prices because of demand without regard to fairness of the price *US*
- —Joe McKennon, *Circus Lingo*, p. 73, 1980

hype *verb*
1 to lie, to swindle *US, 1914*
- I'd be the last guy in the world to try and hype a Pachuco. —Thurston Scott, *Cure it with Honey*, p. 33, 1951
- No hustler could have it known that he'd been "hyped," meaning outsmarted or made a fool of. —Malcolm X and Alex Haley, *The Autobiography of Malcolm X*, p. 127, 1964

2 to stimulate interest or sales *US, 1942*
- Traditionally, the methods they [the record industry] used were called hyping rather than cheating. —Simon Napier-Bell, *Black Vinyl White Powder*, p. 324, 2001

hype *adjective*
excellent *US*
- —Connie Eble (Editor), *UNC-CH Campus Slang*, p. 4, November 2002

hyped up *adjective*
stimulated or excited, especially if by artificial means *US, 1946*
- I was so hyped up I couldn't sit still. —Mezz Mezzrow, *Really the Blues*, p. 54, 1946
- I was so hyped up that anything that moved was a threat. —Andy McNab, *Immediate Action*, p. 41, 1995
- [H]e was a machine, a tennis-playing, treadmill-slogging, weightlifting, hyped-up, over-motivated, ultra-competitive, third millennium shithead. —Kevin Sampson, *Powder*, p. 218, 1999

hype guy *noun*
in circus and carnival usage, a short-change swindler *US*
- —Don Wilmeth, *The Language of American Popular Entertainment*, p. 137, 1981

hype marks *noun*
scars and sores on a drug addict's body indicating intravenous drug use *US*
- [T]he tall one is wearing a long-sleeved shirt buttoned at the cuff. To hide his hype marks, of course. —Joseph Wambaugh, *The Blue Knight*, p. 9, 1973

hyper *noun*
1 in circus and carnival usage, a short-change swindler *US*
- —Don Wilmeth, *The Language of American Popular Entertainment*, p. 137, 1981

2 a person employed to stimulate music sales in an attempt to influence the pop charts
- [O]ne songwriter has offered a £10,000 reward for information on hypers. —David Rowan, *A Glossary for the 90s*, p. 106, 1998

hyper *adjective*
emotionally stressed *US, 1942*
Abbreviated and adapted from 'hyperactive'.
- [S]he'd become more mellow, less hyper in the short time she'd worked with Guy. —Kevin Sampson, *Powder*, p. 71, 1999
- [H]e doesn't like the same stuff as I do – he goes all hyper. —Mary Hooper, *(megan)2*, p. 175, 1999

hyper- *prefix*
extremely *UK, 1984*
- I've met some hyper interesting people[.] —Andrew Blake, *Living Through Pop*, p. 136, 1999

hype stick *noun*
a hypodermic syringe *US, 1933*
- —Vincent J. Monteleone, *Criminal Slang*, p. 127, 1949
- —Richard A. Spears, *The Slang and Jargon of Drugs and Drink*, p. 275, 1986
- —Mike Haskins, *Drugs*, p. 292, 2003

hype tank *noun*
a jail holding cell reserved for drug addicts *US*
- They put me in the hype tank, I guess, because they saw the tracks (from hypodermic needles) on my arms. —*San Francisco News Call-Bulletin*, p. 3, 17th February 1964

hypo *noun*

1 a hypodermic syringe *US, 1905*

- You dissolve all the tablets – five grains – and fill the barrel of the hypo. —Philip Wylie, *Opus 21*, p. 67, 1949
- Alone in a cobwebby studio with Buster's promise to stay away by day, and a three-cap hyp ready to go[.] —George Mandel, *Flee the Angry Strangers*, p. 279, 1952
- A few minutes later a nurse came in with a hypo. —William Burroughs, *Junkie*, p. 91, 1953
- I want four caps and a hypo. —John D. McDonald, *The Neon Jungle*, p. 75, 1953
- Mayflower grimaces as Baby June takes the hypo from Bam and hits him, expertly in the neck. —Odie Hawkins, *Ghetto Sketches*, p. 128, 1972
- Shoot me up / Every damn day / With a hypo full of love —Alabama 3 *Hypo Full of Love*, 1997

2 a needle-using drug addict *US, 1904*

- If some hypo finds out that another hypo is a stool pigeon they give him what is called a hot shot. —Willard Motley, *Let No Man Write My Epitaph*, p. 151, 1958

3 a swindle *US*

- If you don't know who to get it from they pull a lot of hypos on you. —Hal Ellson, *Duke*, p. 3, 1949

Hy-town *nickname*

Hyannis, Massachusetts *US*

- "Nobody messes with Hy-town," Delancey cooed, using the street slang nickname for the town. —*Boston Globe*, p. B1, 19th June 1998

Ii

I ain't even tryin' to hear you!
I am not listening *US*
• — *The Bell (Paducah Tilghman High School)*, p. 8–9, 17th December 1993: 'Tilghmanism: the concealed langage of the hallway'

I ain't here to brag
used for demonstrating that the speaker understands that he is bragging *US*
A paralipsis of the first order. Many grammatical variants exist, as well as the simpler, 'Not to brag'.

I am a Ranger. We live for the One, we die for the One.
used with humour as an affirmation of support *US*
The motto of the interplanetary police on the US science fiction television programme *Babylon* (1994–98).

I am Canadian *noun*
a drink made with fruit juice, Quebec maple syrup and whisky or Molson Canadian beer *CANADA*
• Mapleberry Original is a carbonated fruit drink with just a touch of Quebec maple syrup. Try adding a shot of Canadian Club or Southern Comfort. With Molson Canadian beer, it's half and half. They've dubbed this drink the I am Canadian. — *Toronto Globe and Mail*, p. L4, 3rd August 2002

I am so sure!
used for expressing strong doubt about what has just been said *US*
• — Mimi Pond, *The Valley Girl's Guide to Life*, p. 59, 1982

I and I *noun*
used in the military as a jocular substitute for the official 'R and R' (rest and recreation) *US*
An abbreviation of '*i*ntercourse *and i*ntoxication', the main activities during rest and recreation.
• — *American Speech*, p. 121, May 1960: 'Korean bamboo English'
• [M]en going to Japan turned R&R into the great debauch that came to be known as I&I – intercourse and intoxication. — T.R. Fehrenbach, *This Kind of War*, p. 347, 1963
• Soldier always call it I and I, which mean 'intercourse and intoxication. — Walter J. Sheldon, *Gold Bait*, p. 31, 1973

I believe you but thousands wouldn't
a catchphrase retort that is used to express doubt or, at best, reserve judgement about the veracity of the person being addressed *UK, 1927*
This phrase exists in a number of minor variations, and is so well known that 'I believe you but!' carries the full sense.
• "It's the God's honest truth I'm telling you, Johnny." Mellors stood frowning down at him for a moment. Then he said. "All right, kid; I'll believe you but thousands wouldn't. Now sleep it off." — Derek Bickerton, *Payroll*, p. 126, 1959

I bet!; I'll bet!
I am certain *UK, 1939*
Elliptical for 'I bet you did' or 'do' or 'did'; often derisive or ironic.

Ibiza Hilton *noun*
the police station of the Guardia Civil Ibiza *SPAIN*
An ironic reference to the international Hilton hotel chain.
• The pills were sent for analysis by a laboratory, and Roy was driven to the legendary "Ibiza Hilton" – yeah, the local nick! — Wayne Anthony, *Spanish Highs*, p. 184, 1999

IBM *noun*
1 a smart, diligent student *US*
• — *San Francisco Examiner*, p. III-2, 22nd March 1960
2 a member of an organised crime family; an *I*talian *b*usiness-*m*an *US*
• — Jim Crotty, *How to Talk American*, p. 50, 1997

IBM discount *noun*
a price increase *US*
• — Eric S. Raymond, *The New Hacker's Dictionary*, p. 206, 1991

iboga *noun*
1 amphetamines *UK*
A reference to the African shrub *tabernathe iboga* and *ibogaine*, a natural stimulant that is compounded therefrom.
• — Mike Haskins, *Drugs*, p. 279, 2003
2 MDMA, the recreational drug best known as ecstasy *UK*
• — Mike Haskins, *Drugs*, p. 289, 2003

IC *noun*
during the Vietnam war, an innocent civilian *US*
• The people appeared to be civlians, "ICs or good actors." Simcox remarked, "Yeah, I have seen a real innocent civilian since I left San Francisco." — Nelson DeMille, *Word of Honor*, p. 125, 1985

I can catch *noun*
the US Interstate Commerce Commission *US*
A back formation from the agency initials: ICC.
• — Montie Tak, *Truck Talk*, p. 87, 1971

I can read his lips, and he's not praying
used as a humorous comment on a profanity *US*
Popularised by ESPN's Keith Olberman.
• — Keith Olberman and Dan Patrick, *The Big Show*, p. 19, 1997

I can't fight that!
used by a clever boy for expressing approval of a girl who has just passed by *US*
• — *American Weekly*, p. 2, 14th August 1955

I can't HEAR you!
used as a humorous solitiction of more enthusiastic support *US*
A signature line of marine drill instructor Vince Carter on the television situation comedy *Gomer Pyle, USMC* (CBS, 1964–69). Repeated with referential humour.

I can't take you anywhere
used as a humorous, if stock, tease of someone who has commited a faux pas *US*
• I can't take you anywhere. — *Natural Born Killers*, 1994

ice *noun*
1 diamonds *UK, 1905*
• They came by the dozens, loaded down with ice like it was rock candy[.] — Mezz Mezzrow, *Really the Blues*, p. 91, 1946
• It's nothing hot like you think. No ice. No emerald pendants. — Raymond Chandler, *The Little Sister*, p. 41, 1949
• She was going to wear all her ice, every stone of it. — Charles Raven, *Underworld Nights*, p. 16, 1956
• I knew that Jerry was Chicago's top hot-ice dealer. — Iceberg Slim (Robert Beck), *Trick Baby*, p. 18, 1969
• This promised to be a healthy bundle, since this was no ordinary ice mark. — Red Rudensky, *The Gonif*, p. 6, 1970
• Can you move the ice afterwards? I don't know nobody who can move ice. — *Reservoir Dogs*, 1992
2 cocaine, especially in blocks *US, 1971*
• Don't get me wrong; there is some herb you know, but no rocks, no heroin or ice that I could spot. — Odie Hawkins, *Midnight*, p. 123, 1995
3 smokeable amphetamine or methamphetamine *US*
• It is most likely that ice is simply methamphetamine that is being marketed with an exciting new image. — Geoffrey Froner, *Digging for Diamonds*, p. 37, 1989
• [A]s crack is to cocaine, so ice is to speed (methamphetamine) – the drug in a smokable, more potent crystal form. — Steven Daly and Nalthaniel Wice, *alt.culture*, p. 109, 1995

- Sort of a cross between smack, E and ice. You've got to smoke it in a little pipe. —Will Self, *The Sweet Smell of Psychosis*, p. 39, 1996
- On an average night, I binge Es or ice with amyl nitrite, followed by tranx and spliffs. —Macfarlane, Macfarlane and Robson, *The User*, p. 91, 1996
- Smoked in its crystalline form, speed is known as ice and produces an explosive and fucked up high, lasting for hours. —John Robb, *The Nineties*, p. 60, 1999

4 heroin *US*

- I was dancing with Wren at Max's tonight ("Sympathy for the Devil"), waiting for my man (who happens to be a woman) to show with the ice[.] —Jim Carroll, *Forced Entries*, p. 24, 1987

5 protection money paid by a business to criminals or by criminals to the police *US, 1887*

- —*The Annals of the American Academy of Political and Social Sciences*, p. 126, May 1950
- —*Life*, p. 39, 19th May 1952
- Poilcemen assigned the posts the whores patrolled. Their "ice" was $1.40 a week per girl. —Lee Mortimer, *Women Confidential*, p. 178, 1960
- The ice has got to stop for you, today. —Richard Condon, *Prizzi's Honor*, p. 217, 1982

6 a pay-off, a bribe; an added charge *US*

- The cat gets ICE for hard to get seats for the World Series games. —Hy Lit, *Hy Lit's Unbelievable Dictionary of Hip Words for Groovy People*, p. 23, 1968

7 the difference between the listed price and the price actually paid for theatre tickets for a very popular show *US*

- —Sherman Louis Sergel, *The Language of Show Biz*, p. 111, 1973

8 in poker, a stacked deck *US*

- —Albert H. Morehead, *The Complete Guide to Winning Poker*, p. 265, 1967

9 solitary confinement in prison *US*

- I was on to her and we got in a fight and i went to ice [solitary]. —Bruce Jackson, *In the Life*, p. 408, 1972
- —Charles Shafer, *Folk Speech in Texas Prisons*, p. 207, 1990

10 any computer program designed as a system security scheme *US*

- —Christian Crumlish, *The Internet Dictionary*, p. 92, 1995

▸ on ice

incarcerated *US, 1931*

- —Ralph de Sola, *Crime Dictionary*, p. 106, 1982
- —William K. Bentley and James M. Corbett, *Prison Slang*, p. 28, 1992
- —*Detroit News*, p. 5D, 20th September 2002

▸ on the ice

(of a racehorse) being secretly, and illicitly, kept from running to win *AUSTRALIA*

- 'The others are on the ice,' it was now his turn to whisper. Oxenham was openly incredulous. 'That's rubbish,' he said. 'Someone's having you on. How could you possibly be certain they're all dead?' —James Holledge, *The Great Australian Gamble*, p. 82, 1966

Ice *noun*

▸ the Ice

Antarctica *ANTARCTICA, 1834*

- Jan and Scotty are lucky; they get to take tomorrow's flight in a C-5 Galaxy – the largest of all the aircraft that fly to the ice. —Warren Herrick, *A Year on Ice*, p. 22, 1997
- —Bernadette Hince, *The Antarctic Dictionary*, p. 173, 2000
- —*Cool Antarctica*, 2003: 'Antarctic slang'

ICE *noun*

in-car entertainment, especially audio equipment *UK*

- —Julian Johnson, *Urban Survival*, p. 200, 2003

ice *verb*

1 to kill *US, 1941*

- Word was he had already iced some greaseball in the Bronx whose bail had dropped too low. —Edwin Torres, *Carlito's Way*, p. 22, 1975
- And in making my exit, I iced a cop / 'Cause the motherfucker shot at me when I wouldn't stop. —Dennis Wepman et al., *The Life*, p. 118, 1976
- I was in the news media and I was charged with "icing," as the prisoners say, a supsected agent of the CIA or FBI. —Bobby Seale, *A Lonely Rage*, p. 269, 1978
- [H]is father had been unable to figure out any other way to ice Little Phil Terrone, the heaviest shit and boo dealer in the North Bronx. —Richard Condon, *Prizzi's Honor*, p. 4, 1982
- Manny whispered in English, "If they draw, ice them." —Joseph Wambaugh, *Lines and Shadows*, p. 310, 1984
- It's them Brennan shitehawks that's getting iced. —Kevin Sampson, *Clubland*, p. 246, 2002

2 to place in solitary confinement *US, 1933*

- —Clarence Major, *Dictionary of Afro-American Slang*, p. 69, 1970

3 to ignore with a vengeance *US, 1932*

- —Connie Eble (Editor), *UNC-CH Campus Slang*, p. 4, Fall 1987

4 to give up; to stop *US, 1962*

- And this time, I want you to ice the rubber and let him get a shot of pure honey. —A.S. Jackson, *Gentleman Pimp*, p. 47, 1973

5 to reject; to stand up *US*

- —Pamela Munro, *U.C.L.A. Slang*, p. 80, 1997

▸ ice it

1 to stop doing something *US*

- —Stewart L. Tubbs and Sylvia Moss, *Human Communication*, p. 121, 1974

2 to forget something *US*

- —*San Francisco Examiner*, p. III-2, 22nd March 1960

iceberg *noun*

1 an emotionally cold person, especially a woman *UK, 1840*

- I run into a dame – not a bad looker, either – but boy, was she an iceberg! —*It Happened One Night*, 1934

2 a sexually frigid woman *US*

- —Vincent J. Monteleone, *Criminal Slang*, p. 127, 1949

iceberg act *noun*

unfriendly treatment *US*

- —Lavada Durst, *The Jives of Dr. Hepcat*, p. 12, 1953

ice blink *noun*

a whitish glow on the horizon or on clouds caused by light reflecting off ice *CANADA*

- In arctic or subarctic waters an experienced mariner can often predict massive sea ice long before it is visible, by noticing the "ice-blink." —Bill Casselman, *Canadian Words*, p. 140, 1995

ice-block *noun*

an ice confection on a stick *AUSTRALIA, 1948*

- [K]ids from the other mills along the track would be already down at the store, eating all the ice-blocks. —Robert S. Close, *With Hooves of Brass*, p. 39, 1961

icebox *noun*

1 a morgue *US, 1928*

- —Troy Harris, *A Booklet of Criminal Argot, Cant and Jargon*, p. 16, 1976

2 a jail or prison *US, 1938*

An extension of the more common **COOLER** (jail).

- He also makes good and with my fond help he has so far stayed out of the icebox. —Raymond Chandler, *The Long Goodbye*, p. 100, 1953

ice cold *noun*

a chilled beer *AUSTRALIA*

- Once you've wrapped yourself around a few ice colds you'll feel as though all your birthdays have come at once! —Barry Humphries, *The Wonderful World of Barry McKenzie*, p. 28, 1968

ice cold *adjective*

rude *US*

- —Connie Eble (Editor), *UNC-CH Campus Slang*, p. 3, Fall 1990

ice cream *noun*

a white child; white children *UK*

Used defensively by children of different hues.

- —Rom Harre, Jane Morgan and Christopher O'Neill, *Nicknames*, 1979

ice-cream freezer; ice-cream *noun*

a man *UK*

Rhyming slang for **GEEZER**.

- [T]hat's not to say I've got much sympathy for most of the ice-creams I was at school with[.] —Derek Raymond (Robin Cook), *The Crust on its Uppers*, 1962
- "Oh, 'im." "Who's 'im?" "Justin something. Right ice-cream." —Anthony Masters, *Minder*, p. 16, 1984

ice cream habit *noun*

the irregular consumption of drugs by an occasional user *US*

'Ice-cream eater' and 'ice-creamer' are obsolete slang terms for an irregular user of opium, an earlier application (late C19 to the 1930s) based on the notion that ice-cream is an occasional pleasure and not an every day diet.

- —Richard Horman and Allan Fox, *Drug Awareness*, p. 468, 1970

ice-cream man *noun*

a drug dealer, especially one selling opiates *US*

- —*American Speech*, p. 27, February 1952: 'Teen-age hophead jargon'
- —William D. Alsever, *Glossary for the Establishment and Other Uptight People*, p. 26, December 1970

ice cream truck *noun*

▸ **and the ice cream truck you rode in on!**

used to extend and emphasise an absolute rejection *US*

• [Of Bob Dylan] in context, one could screw bel canto and the ice-cream truck it road in on. —Mick Farren, *Give the Anarchist a Cigarette*, p. 46, 2001

ice cube *noun*

crack cocaine *US*

• —US Department of Justice, *Street Terms*, October 1994

iced *adjective*

drunk, drug-intoxicated *US*

• "Sylvia dead drunk, paralyzed, spifflicated, iced to the eyebrows," I said harshly. —Raymond Chandler, *The Long Goodbye*, p. 25, 1953

iced down *adjective*

wearing many diamonds *US*

• —Ethan Hilderbrant, *Prison Slang*, p. 68, 1998

iced out *noun*

wearing a great deal of diamond-bearing jewellery *US*

• —Connie Eble (Editor), *UNC-CH Campus Slang*, p. 5, Fall 2000

ice down *verb*

to completely cover with graffiti *US*

• —Jim Crotty, *How to Talk American*, p. 141, 1997

icehouse *noun*

a jewellery store *US*

From **ICE** (a diamond).

• —Vincent J. Monteleone, *Criminal Slang*, p. 127, 1949

Icelandic Air Force *noun*

(around Gimli, Manitoba) flocks of pelicans *CANADA*

• Gimli, with its large Icelandic population, calls the large pelican population "the Icelandic Air Force." Once there was a large Air Force training base there, but now it only caters to out-of-fuel Air Canada flights. —Chris Thain, *Cold as a Bay Street Banker's Heart*, p. 88, 1987

ice luge *noun*

a block of ice used in a drinking game in which a shot of vodka, tequila or other alcoholic drink is poured down the ice into the drinker's mouth *US*

• —Don R. McCreary (Editor), *Dawg Speak*, 2001

iceman *noun*

1 a person who bribes a government official or otherwise 'fixes' difficult situations *US*

From **ICE** (a bribe).

• —Don Wilmeth, *The Language of American Popular Entertainment*, p. 139, 1981

2 in horse racing, a jockey who rides without using the whip or vigorous kicks *AUSTRALIA*

• —Ned Wallish, *The Truth Dictionary of Racing Slang*, p. 40, 1989

3 a mechanic who works on truck refrigeration units *US*

• —Montie Tak, *Truck Talk*, p. 88, 1971

ice money *noun*

money used to bribe *US*

• The operation worked well provided that when he was raided, his case went before a judge, who, like some of the beat cops, was paid off with so-called ice money. —Kim Rich, *Johnny's Girl*, p. 142, 1993

ice pack *noun*

high quality marijuana *US*

• —Eugene Landy, *The Underground Dictionary*, p. 108, 1971

ice palace *noun*

1 a jewellery store *US*

• —*American Speech*, p. 99, May 1956: 'Smugglers' argot in the Southwest'

2 a hockey rink *CANADA*

• Robertson should have an attraction tonight at the ancient Whitehall ice palace that should be well worth taking in. —*Winnipeg Free Press*, p. n.p., 14th January 1955

ice widow *noun*

a woman whose husband is in Antarctica *NEW ZEALAND, 1971*

• —Bernadette Hince, *The Antarctic Dictionary*, p. 187, 2000

-icide *suffix*

▷ **see: -CIDE**

icing *noun*

cocaine *US*

• —R.C. Garrett et al., *The Coke Book*, p. 200, 1984

• —Nick Constable, *This is Cocaine*, p. 181, 2002

ick *noun*

1 any unpleasant sticky substance *UK*

• I knuckle the crusted ick out of me eyes[.] —Niall Griffiths, *Kelly + Victor*, p. 24, 2002

2 in the language surrounding the Grateful Dead, a bacterial or viral infection that quickly spreads among those following the band on tour *US*

Always with 'the'.

• —David Shenk and Steve Silberman, *Skeleton Key*, p. 155, 1994

3 a social outcast *US, 1942*

• I had to accept him, as there's a special college ruling that you can't refuse a date with one of them. He's an ick anyhow. —Max Shulman, *Guided Tour of Campus Humor*, p. 72, 1955

ick *adjective*

mawkishly sentimental, hence unpalatable *US*

An abbreviation of **ICKY**.

• "Yuck. Ick. Gross!" I grabbed the flowers and tried to throw them away[.] —Janet Evanovich, *Seven Up*, p. 55, 2001

ickies *noun*

foreign money of any type *UK*

Royal Navy usage, possibly a variation of **ACKER** (money). One 'ickie' equals one hundred **KLEBBIES**.

• How many ickies do you get to the pound in this place? —Rick Jolly, *Jackspeak*, p. 148, 1989

ickle *adjective*

little *UK, 1864*

A small child's pronunciation employed archly by those old enough to know better.

• "Hand me a tissue," she said, "an wait while I have an ickle blub." —Liza Cody, *Queen of Mean [Tart Noir]*, p. 76, 2002

• But who would want to do that to an ickle cow? —*The Guardian*, 28th October 2003

icky *noun*

a rich person *US*

• Jackson if you are tamping the stroll pinning the fly chicks and the ickies as they fall from their gone castles on all cuts and stems[.] —Lavada Durst, *The Jives of Dr. Hepcat*, p. 3, 1953

icky *adjective*

1 unattractive, distasteful *US, 1929*

First found in jazz to describe oversweet music other than jazz, then migrated into general use with the more general meaning.

• With all your high and mighty scorn for all icky, longhair, corn! — Haenigsen, *Jive's Like That*, 1947

• After class, however, she confessed to me that she thought Mr. Obispo was icky. —Max Shulman, *The Many Loves of Dobie Gillis*, p. 97–98, 1951

• But if she doesn't turn in a tip for every hat, she loses her job on grounds she swiped the money or she is so stupid or icky that she gets stiffed. —Jack Lait and Lee Mortimer, *Washington Confidential*, p. 282, 1951

• It was one of those icky desert winds we call the Santa Ana[.] —Frederick Kohner, *Gidget*, p. 124, 1957

• For six rigorous days, she had driven her body to its limits, rising at six forty-five to flop about the countryside in a pale pink sweatsuit, her face stripped of makeup, her hair drab and icky in a thick coat of Vaseline. —Armistead Maupin, *Tales of the City*, p. 196, 1978

• Your true feelings were too gross and icky for you to face. —*Heathers*, 1988

• Some part of me is not comfortable with myself, my own sexuality; I'm still icky about it somewhere inside. —Robert Stoller and I.S. Levine, *Coming Attractions*, p. 102, 1991

• [T]his brand new spanking blender is icky with goop. —Simon Lewis, *In The Box*, p. 131, 1999

2 unwell *UK, 1939*

Probably from baby-talk variations of 'sick' or 'sickly'.

• My stomach felt icky, like I might throw up. —Sue Monk Kidd, *The Secret Life of Bees*, p. 174, 2002

3 overly sentimental, especially of music or of a taste in music *US, 1929*

Originally from jazz.

• There's a cheesy dance floor in the bar, so it's icky, old-fashioned music. —Leslie O'Kane, *Death of a PTA Goddess*, p. 239, 2002

icky-poo *adjective*
unwell *UK, 1920*
Baby-talk variation of 'sick' or 'sickly'.
- Publisher's Weekly dismissed [Jonathan Livingston] Seagull as "a wispy little fable," with prose that "gets a mite too icky poo for comfort." — Bruce J. Schulman, *The Seventies*, p. 79, 2001

ICL
used as shorthand in Internet discussion groups and text messaging to mean '*i*n *C*hristian *l*ove' *US*
- — Gabrielle Mander, *WAN2TLK? ltl bk of txt msgs*, p. 46, 2002

I could cure the plague
used by a woman to describe her condition when experiencing the bleed period of the menstrual cycle *US*
- — *The Museum of Menstruation and Women's Health*, November 2000

I could just scream!
used as an expression of frustration *US*
A signature line of Captain Wallace B. Binghamton on the television comedy *McCahle's Navy* (ABC, 1962–66). Repeated with referential humour.

icy-pole *noun*
an ice confection on a stick *AUSTRALIA, 1932*
Generic use of a trademark term.
- The odd icy-pole vendor or shoe-shine tot got through. But not for long. — B. Selkie, *Lime Juice*, p. 31, 1995

ID *noun*
an identity card or other means of identification *US, 1941*
- You got an I.D. for the liquor? — *American Graffiti*, 1973
- Stephie, we got money and we got fake ID's. — *200 Cigarettes*, 1999

ID *verb*
to identify someone *US, 1944*
Derives from the noun uses as 'identification/identity'.
- [I]t ain't really a fair way of IDing someone is it – pointing at them in a cell? The second copper changed stories and said that the defendants had been ID'd at the time of arrest[.] — Dave Courtney, *Raving Lunacy*, p. 34–35, 2000

idea hamster; ideas hamster *noun*
a person who is employed to generate new ideas *UK*
- Part of what I'm supposed to do is to bring in these people they call 'idea hamsters'. They talk absolute shite for two hours and it's exhausting but out of that you still get three minutes of very interesting ideas. — *The Independent*, 13th February 2001

identity *noun*
a noted person; an odd or interesting person *AUSTRALIA, 1874*
- There was a widely told tradition about these parts that years ago an old identity from Rhyndaston named Mrs Delany had taken off her red flannel petticoat and waved it to stop a train when a bridge had been washed away[.] — Patsy Adam-Smith, *Folklore of the Australian Railwaymen*, p. 195, 1969
- Consider, for instance, the adventures of Yossal, a well-known Melbourne race-track identity who never seems to pick the winners that count. — Roy Higgins and Tom Prior, *The Jockey Who Laughed*, p. 40, 1982
- One local identity decided he would get amongst them and, armed with a very thick line and live mullet, he heaved it out with all his might. — Bob Staines, *Wot a Whopper*, p. 56, 1982
- I had another run-in with a local identity when I was a kid at Mordialloc. — Rex Hunt, *Tall Tales – and True*, p. 50, 1994

idi *adjective*
cruel *UK*
Probably after Ugandan dictator Idi Amin, 1925(?)-2003; recorded in use in contemporary gay society.
- — *Attitude*, p. 60, July 2003: 'New palare lexicon'

idiot blocks *noun*
options placed at the end of a staffing paper designed to allow the reader simply to tick the option which describes his decision *US*
- — Department of the Army, *Staff Officer's Guidebook*, p. 61, 1986

idiot board *noun*
in television, an out-of-camera board on which a performer's lines are displayed *UK, 1952*
- "I USUALLY... KEEP THAT INFORMATION... VERY CLOSE... TO MY CHEST," she read carefully from the idiot board just left of camera. — *The Guardian*, 25th September 2003

idiot box *noun*
1 the television *US, 1955*
- I get tired of the idiot box. — Antony James, *America's Homosexual Underground*, p. 137, 1965
- — Collin Baker et al., *College Undergraduate Slang Study Conducted at Brown University*, p. 142, 1968
- If you were to take your eyeballs and ears out of that idiot box for a hot minute and pay attention to... — Odie Hawkins, *Ghetto Sketches*, p. 152, 1972
- "Don doesn't care much for TV." "Know what I call it, I call it the Idiot Box," Tonay smiled. — Tony Wilson, *24 Hour Party People*, p. 55, 2002

2 an automatic car transmission *US*
- — John Edwards, *Auto Dictionary*, p. 81, 1993

idiot card *noun*
in the television and film industries, a poster board with the dialogue written in large letters for actors to read *US, 1957*
- — Tony Miller and Patricia George, *Cut! Print!*, p. 89, 1977

idiot-head *noun*
a stupid person *AUSTRALIA*
Used by young children.
- Wot do you want, idiot-head? — Kylie Mole (Maryanne Fahey), *My Diary*, p. 44, 1988

idiot juice *noun*
any alcoholic beverage brewed in prison, especially a nutmeg/water mixture *US, 1974*
- — Ralph de Sola, *Crime Dictionary*, p. 69, 1982
- — William K. Bentley and James M. Corbett, *Prison Slang*, p. 70, 1992

idiot light *noun*
in a car, a warning light on the dashboard in place of a gauge *US, 1968*
- — John Edwards, *Auto Dictionary*, p. 81, 1993
- — Judi Sanders, *Mashing and Munching in Ames*, p. 10, 1994

idiot pill *noun*
a barbiturate or central nervous system depressant *US, 1953*
- — Donald Wesson and David Smith, *Barbiturates*, p. 122, 1977

idiot's delight *noun*
in dominoes, the 5-0 piece *US*
- — Dominic Armanino, *Dominoes*, p. 16, 1959

idiot spoon *noun*
a shovel *US, 1947*
- — Jerry Robertson, *Oil Slanguage*, p. 69, 1954

idiot stick *noun*
1 a small carved copy of a totem pole *CANADA*
- The talented carver has to choose between volume production of low-priced souvenir [totem] poles (called by some idiot "idiot sticks") and works of high quality which must be sold at high prices — Wilson Duff, *Indian History of British Columbia*, p. 83, 1964
- An "idiot stick," a tiny carved replica of a totem pole, sold in the tourist trade, is not made by northwest BC natives. — Tom Parkin, *WetCoast Words*, p. 73, 1989

2 a shovel *US, 1930*
- An idiot-stick needs no brains to manipulate it – only muscle! — Vincent J. Monteleone, *Criminal Slang*, p. 127, 1949
- — *American Speech*, p. 273, December 1954: 'Fire terms: additional words and definitions'

3 a digging bar *US*
- — A.B. Chance Co., *Lineman's Slang Dictionary*, p. 10, 1980

idjit *noun*
▷ see: EEJIT

I don't think so
used as a humorous rejection of the sentiment that has been expressed *US*
- Can Amerika absorb smoke-ins, fuck-ins, liberated zones, what have you, inside its borders? I don't think soooo. — Abbie Hoffman, *Woodstock Nation*, p. 97, 1969
- It looks like they just fell out of bed and put on some baggy pants, and take their greasy hair – ew! – and cover it up with a backwards cap and like, we're expected to swoon? I don't think so. — *Clueless*, 1995

I don't want to know
used as refusal to accept unwelcome news or facts *UK*
- I have heard all that before and I just don't want to know. — Anthony Phelps, *I Couldn't Care Less*, 1946

idren *noun*
friend; friends *UK*
West Indian, Rastafarian and UK black patois for 'brethren' (brothers), with religious and political overtones.
- What happen to your idren? —Karline Smith, *Moss Side Massive*, p. 211, 1994

idyat bwai *noun*
a fool *UK*
West Indian patois (idiot boy).
- So am I a cunt? Or am I an idyat bwai? Tough choice. —Nick Barlay, *Curvy Lovebox*, p. 81, 1997

if bet *noun*
in horse racing, a bet that is made contingent upon winning a bet in an earlier race *US*
- —Walter Steigleman, *Horseracing*, p. 274, 1947

if cash *noun*
in gambling, a type of conditional bet: an instruction to re-invest all or part of a winning return on another bet *UK*
- —David Bennet, *Know Your Bets*, p. 26, 2001

iffiness *noun*
a quality of unreliability, subject to doubt *UK*
From IFFY.
- [I]n spite of the cunt not being able to hide his iffiness[.] —Kevin Sampson, *Outlaws*, p. 305, 2001

iffy *adjective*
1 tenuous, uncertain *US, 1937*
- Though I doubt that, being a visitor with an iffy passport. —Elmore Leonard, *Bandits*, p. 197, 1987
- I thought the brakes were getting a bit iffy and that's why I was travelling behind[.] —Roy Slaven (John Doyle), *Five South Coast Seasons*, p. 74, 1992
- His English is a bit iffy, but he's learning fast[.] —John King, *Human Punk*, p. 29, 2000

2 dangerous, risky *UK*
Extends from the previous sense.
- [H]e tries to get it across that they never ran. It just half got a bit iffy for a minute. —Kevin Sampson, *Outlaws*, p. 174, 2001
- I ain't taking my money through some iffy council estate neither[.] —Garry Bushell, *The Face*, p. 12, 2001

if I'm lying, I'm dying
I am telling the truth *US*
There are multiple reduplicative variations.
- "If I'm lyin, I'm flyin." "If you're lyin, you're fryin," the Weasel corrected him. "If you're lying, your dyin," the Ferret corrected them both[.] —Joseph Wambaugh, *The Glitter Dome*, p. 71, 1981
- BB: He's bluffing. CHEESE: If I'm lying, I'm dying. CARLY: I'm out. —*Tin Men*, 1987
- Oh, yes, trust me, Grum. They will be 19 and 0. If I'm lying, I'm dying. —*The Denver Post*, p. D1, 14th November 2003

If it ain't broke, don't fix it.
used as a humorous suggestion to leave well enough alone *US*
- "If it ain't broke, don't fix it" is the attitude of players and fans. —*Financial Times*, p. 6, 15th February 1990
- Taking an if it ain't broke, don't fix it attitude, NCUA Chairman Roger W. Jepsen said the agency already provides several forums for credit unions[.] —*NCUA Watch*, p. 1, 25th October 1993

if it isn't
(used as an acknowledgement of someone) it is *US, 1951*
- "Well – if it isn't Justin James," Terry said sourly. —Anthony Masters, *Minder*, p. 3-178, 1984

if it's too loud, you're too old
used for dismissing complaints of loudness at rock concerts *US*
A saying attributed to Kiss. Collected from fans of heavy metal music by Seamus O'Reilly, January 1995.

if-lose; if-win *noun*
in gambling, a type of conditional bet: a bet is required only if the prior selection loses/wins or is a non-runner *UK*
- —David Bennet, *Know Your Bets*, p. 26, 2001

ifs, ands or buts *noun*
conditions, contingencies, exceptions *US*
- Tonight, Boogie. No ifs-ands-or-buts. —*Diner*, 1982

if they back up the truck
used in the entertainment industry for expressing a recognition that if the offer is lucrative enough, the actor speaking will accept the role despite its dramatic limitations *US*
The phrase conjures up the image of a truck full of bags of money backing up the driveway to be emptied. Collected in Los Angeles, June 2001.

if ya wonders, then ya is
used in twelve-step recovery programmes such as Alcoholics Anonymous as a judgement on those who stop to wonder if they might be an addict *US*
- —Christopher Cavanaugh, *AA to Z*, p. 109, 1998

if you say so
used for indicating (grudgingly, or to placate) acceptance of what has been said *UK, 1956*
- "Glory at last!" If you say so. —*The Guardian*, 3rd April 2003

ig *verb*
to ignore *US, 1946*
- —Jack Lait and Lee Mortimer, *New York Confidential*, p. 235, 1948: 'A glossary of Harlemisms'

iggie *noun*
a feigned ignorance *US, 1961*
Circus and carnival usage. Often used in the phrase 'give them the iggie'.
- —Don Wilmeth, *The Language of American Popular Entertainment*, p. 139, 1981

igloo *noun*
a one-hundred-dollar note *AUSTRALIA*
From the resemblance between '100' and 'loo'.
- —Ned Wallish, *The Truth Dictionary of Racing Slang*, p. 40, 1989

ign'ant *adjective*
ignorant *US*
- THE IGN'ANT DIY ACTIVITY OF THE MONTH – REMEMBER KIDS, DON'T TRY THIS AT HOME... —*Hip-Hop Connection*, p. 22, July 2002

ignorant *adjective*
▸ **make ignorant**
to make angry *UK*
A south London term.
- —David Powis, *The Signs of Crime*, 1977

ignorant end *noun*
in poker, the low card in a five-card sequence *US*
- —Anthony Holden, *Big Deal*, p. 301, 1990

ignorant oil *noun*
alcohol, especially cheap and potent alcohol *US, 1954*
- The last time I'd seen him he was downing a quarter of "ignorant oil" a day in Paris. —Babs Gonzales, *I Paid My Dues*, p. 144, 1967
- —David Claerbaut, *Black Jargon in White America*, p. 69, 1972
- That's pennant fver for you. And ignorant oil. —Bill Cardoso, *The Maltese Sangweech*, p. 152, 1984

ignorant spoon *noun*
in oil drilling, a shovel *US*
- —Jerry Robertson, *Oil Slanguage*, p. 69, 1954

ignuts *noun*
an ignorant fool *US, 1934*
- It's always freebies with that ignatz. —Bernard Wolfe, *The Late Risers*, p. 130, 1954

I-guy *noun*
a member of a team who thinks of himself – the individual – more than the team *US*
Related to the sports addage: 'There is no "I" in "team"'.
- —Judi Sanders, *Da Bomb!*, p. 15, 1997

I hate it!
used for expressing solidarity with the misfortune just described by another *US*
- —Connie Eble (Editor), *UNC-CH Campus Slang*, p. 4, Fall 1984

I hate it when that happens
used for introducing humour, usually after someone else has described an extremely unlikely situation *US*
- —Connie Eble (Editor), *UNC-CH Campus Slang*, p. 4, Spring 1987
- —Pamela Munro, *U.C.L.A. Slang*, p. 35, 1989

- Into this delightfully revolting garbage heap steps Judd Nelson as a seriously untalented comic who, along with his buddy the accordion player (Bill Paxton), enjoys a brief career after growing a third arm. I hate it when that happens. — *Billboard*, p. 59, 22nd February 1992

I have nothing more to say about this that is either relevant or true
used as a humorous comment when there is nothing worthwhile to say *US*
Popularised by ESPN's Keith Olberman, paraphrasing Winston Churchill's claimed reaction when confronting an entrance essay at Eton.
- — Keith Olberman and Dan Patrick, *The Big Show*, p. 10–20, 1997

I heard it on the marl road
used for expressing rumour as the source of information *CAYMAN ISLANDS*
- — Aarona Booker Kohlman, *Wotcha Say*, p. 28, 1985

I heard that!
I agree with you! *US*
- — Judi Sanders, *Kickin' like Chicken with the Couch Commander*, p. 13, 1992

I heard ya
used for expressing assent *US*
- — William K. Bentley and James M. Corbett, *Prison Slang*, p. 46, 1992

ike *noun*
a feeling of displeasure, a bad mood *UK*
- [B]etter Tinky Winky than Old Ballsitch, as an uncle of mine was often referred to by my aunt whenever she had the ike with him. — Ray Puxley, *Fresh Rabbit*, p. 114, 1998

Ikey *noun*
1 a Jewish person *UK, 1835*
Derogatory; an abbreviation of the name Isaac.
- I'm buggered if she was a flamin' ikey!!! — Barry Humphries, *Bazza Pulls It Off!*, 1971

2 a student of the University of Cape Town, especially a member of one of the University's sports teams *SOUTH AFRICA, 1921*
- Vision 2000, an initiative devised by a group of University of Cape Town old boys, has breathed new life into Ikey rugby. — *Sunday Times (South Africa)*, 6th July 2003

Ikey Mo *noun*
a Jewish person *UK, 1922*
- — Barry Humphries, *A Nice Night's Entertainment*, p. 85, 1965
- Go back to Israel yourself you Ikey Mo! — Barry Humphries, *The Wonderful World of Barry McKenzie*, p. 39, 1968
- — Barry Humphries, *A Nice Night's Entertainment*, p. 207, 1981

I kid you not
used for humorously assuring the truth of the matter asserted *US*
The signature line of Jack Parr, host of the late-night *Jack Parr Show* (NBC, 1957–62). Repeated with referential humour.
- Next day, I kid you not, it snowed, — Sue Rhodes, *Now You'll Think I'm Awful*, p. 61, 1967
- RANDAL: Get out of here. SMOKER: I kid you not. — *Clerks*, 1994

Ilie Nastase *noun*
a lavatory *UK*
Rhyming slang for **KARZY**, formed from the name of the Romanian tennis player (b.1946).
- — Ray Puxley, *Fresh Rabbit*, 1998

I liiiiike it!
used for expressing approval *US*
A catchphrase from the film *The Rocketeer*, 1991.
- — Connie Eble (Editor), *UNC-CH Campus Slang*, p. 4, Fall 1991

ill *verb*
1 to perform excellently; to do anything superbly *US, 1992*
Originally black usage, generally 'to be illin'' rather than 'to ill'; widespread with hip-hop culture.

2 to undergo severe mental stress *US*
- — Terry Williams, *The Cocaine Kids*, p. 137, 1989

ill *adjective*
1 good, pleasing, desirable, admirable *US, 1991*
- His voice is what's so ill about him. — Q-Tip, *The Source*, p. 84, April 1994
- — Ethan Hilderbrant, *Prison Slang*, p. 68, 1998

2 wild or crazy *US, 1979*
Originally black usage, from the verb sense; spread through hip-hop culture.
- Get your ass up and let's get ill. — Crooklyn Clan *Let's Get Ill!*, 2000

3 wrong *US*
Originally black usage, probably a variation on 'sick'; widespread with hip-hop culture.

ill-ass *adjective*
excellent, superb *US*
- I finally made it. Not as a superstar rapper, not as an ill-ass white boy, but as a respected emcee. — Eminem (Marshall Mathers), *Angry Blonde*, p. 4, 2001

I'll be buggered!; I'm buggered!
used for registering surprise *UK, 1966*
- [W]ell I'll be buggered, young Richard's right!' — Will Self, *The Sweet Smell of Psychosis*, p. 23, 1996

I'll be damned!; well, I'm damned!
used as a general-purpose exclamation; also as an intensification of a personal opinion *UK, 1925*
- I thought I'd get clear on your involvement before I decided what to do." Well, I'll be damned. — Paula L Woods, *Inner City Blues*, p. 27, 1999
- Well, I'll be damned if it's a coincidence, a gas bomb, a violent robbery and an assault on the same day. — Paul Cornell, *'Human Nature', [a 'Doctor Who' story published on the BBC web site]*, August 2003

ill-behaved *adjective*
said of a computer program that becomes dysfunctional because of repeated error *US*
- — Eric S. Raymond, *The New Hacker's Dictionary*, p. 206, 1991

I'll bet!
▷ see: I BET!

I'll be there *noun*
a chair *UK*
Rhyming slang.
- — Julian Franklyn, *A Dictionary of Rhyming Slang*, 1961

I'll bet you a fat man
used for expressing supreme confidence *US, 1963*
- — Robert S. Gold, *A Jazz Lexicon*, p. 157, 1964

illegal tegel *noun*
any native or game bird taken illegally for food *NEW ZEALAND*
Tegel™ is a brand of dressed poultry.
- The kereru is sometimes called kuku in the north and sometimes by the name 'illegal Tegel'. — B. Parkinson, *The Traveling Naturalist Around New Zealand*, p. 28, 1989

illegit *noun*
a person or thing of questionable legality *US*
- It's the illegits, the ones you might call the semi-pros, who send house officers to the aspirin bottle. — Dev Collans with Stewart Sterling, *I was a House Detective*, p. 39, 1954

illegits *noun*
dice that have been altered for cheating *US*
- — Robert C. Prus and C.R.D. Sharper, *Road Hustler*, p. 170, 1977: 'Glossary of terms'

iller *adjective*
worse *US, 1979*
- Like I'm fond of saying, trust is even iller than you think. — Diran Adebayo, *My Once Upon A Time*, p. 35, 2000

illest *adjective*
best *US*
- [T]wo of the illest rappers in the world[.] — *The Source*, p. 44, March 2002

I'll holla
used as a farewell *US*
- — Connie Eble (Editor), *UNC-CH Campus Slang*, p. 5, Spring 1998

illies *noun*
marijuana *UK*
- — Mike Haskins, *Drugs*, p. 288, 2003

illin'; ill *verb*
to behave in a wild or crazy manner *US, 1986*
Originally black usage, generally 'to be illin'' rather than 'to ill'; widespread with hip-hop culture.

illing *noun*
marijuana *UK*
- —Mike Haskins, *Drugs*, p. 288, 2003

illing *adjective*
bad, troubling *US, 1980*
- —Connie Eble (Editor), *UNC-CH Campus Slang*, p. 3, October 1986
- —*Newsday*, p. B2, 11th October 1997

illo *noun*
an illustration *US*
- —*American Speech*, p. 27, Spring 1982: 'The langage of science fiction fan magazines'

ill piece *noun*
a male homosexual despised by his peers *US*
- —*American Speech*, p. 57, Spring-Summer 1970: 'Homosexual slang'

I'll tell you what I'm gonna do
used as a humorous, self-explanatory if nonce announcement of intent *US*
Popularised by Sid Stone, announcer on the *Texaco Star Theater*, hosted by Milton Berle (1948–1951). One of the very first television-spawned catchphrases to become part of the national vocabulary.

illy *noun*
1 a cigarette infused with embalming fluid *US*
- American buzz chasers are buying cigarettes dipped in embalming fluid in their search for a new high. The "wets" or "illys" are $20 (£13) and are said to induce a feeling of invincibility. —*Mixmag*, p. 37, December 2001

2 marijuana, especially sensimillia (a very potent marijuana from a plant with seedless buds) *US*
- —Bill Valentine, *Gang Intelligence Manual*, p. 110, 1995: 'Jamaican gang terminology'

illywhacker *noun*
a confidence trickster *AUSTRALIA, 1941*
Agent noun from the obsolete phrase 'whack the illy' (to swindle; to perform confidence tricks). 'Illy' may possibly be a variant of obsolete 'eelie' (a confidence trick) which in turn is possibly from 'eeler-spee', a pig Latin variant of **SPIELER**. This word was all but dead prior to gaining new life due to Peter Carey's 1985 novel *Illywhacker*.
- —Jim Ramsay, *Cop It Sweet!*, p. 48, 1977
- Con men, illywhackers and low-lifes hung around listening to Jesus. —Kel Richards, *The Aussie Bible*, p. 49, 2003

I'ma *verb*
used to preface an intention *US*
A slurred elision of 'I am going to', or 'I'm **LIKE**'.
- See, it's like every time someone disses me, I'ma talk about them. It's kind of like if you piss me off, I'ma respond in my songs. —Eminem (Marshall Mathers), *Angry Blonde*, p. 31, 2001

I'm about it!
I agree with your plan of action! *US*
- —Connie Eble (Editor), *UNC-CH Campus Slang*, p. 2, Spring 1999

imaginitis *noun*
an overactive imagination *AUSTRALIA, 1944*
- People like your old man, with all time on 'is ands, can afford to enjoy imaginitis. —Patrick White, *A Fringe Of Leaves*, p. 197, 1976

I'm all right, Jack!
a smug declaration of self-satisfaction *UK*
Used as the title of a 1959 film.
- There's an element of "I'm all right, Jack". Boards are conscious that other clubs might be up the creek financially, but they tell themselves: "If we've got more money and they've got less, then we're more likely to win." —*The Guardian*, 10th January 2002

I-man *noun*
an investigator from the Interstate Commerce Commission *US, 1938*
- —Montie Tak, *Truck Talk*, p. 89, 1971

I'm Audi; I'm Audi 5000
I'm leaving now *US*
- —Connie Eble (Editor), *UNC-CH Campus Slang*, p. 1, April 1995

imbo *noun*
a fool; an imbecile *AUSTRALIA, 1953*
- —Jim Ramsay, *Cop It Sweet!*, p. 48, 1977

I'm buggered!
▷ see: **I'LL BE BUGGERED!**

I'm deep enough
I quit, pay me *US*
- —Jerry Robertson, *Oil Slanguage*, p. 69, 1954

I mean
used for emphasis on that which follows *US*
- And I went up there, I said, "Shrink, I want to kill. I mean, I wanna, I wanna kill. Kill. I wanna." —Arlo Guthrie, *Alice's Restaurant*, 1967
- Instead of using Cockney or Liverpool slang for humorous effect, narked, knickers-job and all that, he began using American hip-lower-class slang, like, I mean, you know, baby, and a little late Madison Avenue. —Tom Wolfe, *The Pump House Gang*, p. 44, 1968
- "I mean," D.R. was saying, "I mean, like, if you take this tent down, you know, take the poles down, fold the whole thing up, and move it fifteen yards." —Gurney Norman, *Divine Right's Trip (Last Whole Earth Catalog)*, p. 29, 1971
- —David Claerbaut, *Black Jargon in White America*, p. 69, 1972
- Why did you want to come here? I mean, I can't imagine Ann painted a very flattering portrait of me. —*Sex, Lies and Videotape*, 1989
- This we had to have made special. I mean, sit in it. —*Goodfellos*, 1990

I mean that!
I agree with what you just said! *US*
- —Connie Eble (Editor), *UNC-CH Campus Slang*, April 1977

I mean to say!
used as an emphasis of the speaker's sincerity *UK, 1843*

I'm gone
used as a farewell *US*
- Nigga, I'm gone. —*Menace II Society*, 1993

I'm history
used as a farewell *US*
- —Connie Eble (Editor), *UNC-CH Campus Slang*, p. 4, Spring 1984

IMHO
*i*n *m*y *h*umble *o*pinion *US*
A ubiquitous piece of computer shorthand.
- —Eric S. Raymond, *The New Hacker's Dictionary*, p. 206, 1991

immo *adjective*
imitation *US*
Noted as 1940s–60s.
- —Clarence Major, *Juba to Jive*, 1994
- Judy was wearing a little black dress and some immo pearls. —John Milne, *Alive and Kicking*, p. 63, 1998

immortal *noun*
in stud poker, any hand that is certain to win; the best possible hand *US*
- —Oswald Jacoby, *Oswald Jacoby on Poker*, p. 142, 1947
- —Irwin Steig, *Common Sense in Poker*, p. 184, 1963

IMNSHO
used as Internet shorthand to mean '*i*n *m*y *n*ot *s*o *h*umble *o*pinion' *US*
- —Christian Crumlish, *The Internet Dictionary*, p. 94, 1995

IMO
used as Internet shorthand to mean '*i*n *m*y *o*pinion' *US*
- —Christian Crumlish, *The Internet Dictionary*, p. 94, 1995

Imp *noun*
a Chrysler Imperial car *US*
- You just goose that old Imp's accelerator and . . . No more Jag! —Robert Gover, *One Hundred Dollar Misunderstanding*, p. 143, 1961

impact zone *noun*
an area where the waves are breaking *SOUTH AFRICA*
Surfer usage.

import *noun*
a date who comes from out of town *US, 1926*
- And if a player, coach or manager should bring a girl with him to another city, she's called an import. —Jim Bouton, *Ball Four*, p. 252, 1970

impressionist *noun*
a person who is more interested in the impression they are making than they are in their substance *TRINIDAD AND TOBAGO, 1989*
- —Lise Winer, *Dictionary of the English/Creole of Trinidad & Tobago*, 2003

improve *noun*
▸ **on the improve**
improving *AUSTRALIA, 1959*
- We might be on the improve – we ran third in this race last year. —*Sunday Herald*, p. 51, 10th January 1989

Improved Scot *noun*
in Hudson Bay, a person of mixed Scottish and Indian blood *CANADA*
- A Metis of mixed Scottish and Indian parentage is an improved Scotsman. Another name, considerably kinder to the Scottish fathers, is Hudson Bay Scot.—Chris Thain, *Cold as a Bay Street Banker's Heart*, p. 88, 1987

imps file *noun*
a journalist's dossier on an important person or persons *UK*
- —John Gardner, *To Run a Little Faster*, 1976

I'm serious!
used for expressing strong agreement with what has just been said *US*
- —Connie Eble (Editor), *UNC-CH Campus Slang*, p. 6, March 1981

I'm sideways
used as a farewell *US*
- —*People Magazine*, p. 73, 19th July 1993
- —*Evening Sun (Baltimore)*, p. 12A, 19th January 1994

I'm sure!; I'm so sure!
used for expressing great doubt *US*
- I am SO SURE / He's like so GROSS.—Moon Unit and Frank Zappa, *Valley Girl*, 1982

I'm there!
I agree! I approve! *US*
- —Connie Eble (Editor), *UNC-CH Campus Slang*, April 1977

in *noun*
1 an inside connection *US, 1929*
- [T]he guy buys another TV set, another fur for his wife, and a couple of watches, everything at a discount because he's a big shot and has all kinds of ins.—Elmore Leonard, *The Big Bounce*, p. 113, 1969

2 an introduction *US*
- —Lou Shelly, *Hepcats Jive Talk Dictionary*, p. 13, 1945

3 in a casino, the amount of cash collected at a table in exchange for chips *US*
An abbreviation of 'buy-in'.
- —Lee Solkey, *Dummy Up and Deal*, p. 115, 1980

▸ **the in**
exclusive and positive access to something *UK*
- "I had 'The In'," says Richardson, but I think if anybody else had gone along and said, "Right, we're a rock 'n' roll band, give us a gig", the governor would have told them to fuck off.—Will Birch, *No Sleep Till Canvey Island*, p. 130, 2003

in *adjective*
1 fashionable *UK, 1960*
- In and Out: it was a new concept, and fascinating. From then on Carnaby Street was inevitable.—Nik Cohn, *Yellow Socks Are Out*, p. 21, 1989

2 socially accepted; popular *US, 1929*
- I'm in with the in crowd / I go where the in crowd goes / I'm in with the in crowd / And I know what the in crowd knows.—Bryan Ferry, *The In Crowd*, 1964
- There was always a big band from New York staying at the "Dunbar" Hotel and since I had money to buy drinks and hang out with the "In" people, everything was cool.—Babs Gonzales, *I Paid My Dues*, p. 20, 1967

3 assured of having amatory success *AUSTRALIA*
- Maybe she runs to a cobber. If she does you're in.—J.E. MacDonnell, *Don't Gimme the Ships*, p. 46, 1960
- Her lingering smile set his heart pumping. 'You're in Bertie-boy,' cooed Toggle, sucking noisily at his beer.—John Wynnum, *Tar Dust*, p. 28, 1962
- I'm *in* with her, he thought. You beaut.—Ray Slattery, *Mobbs' Mob*, p. 109, 1966
- You're in man, she'll give you a root.—Christos Tsiolkas, *Loaded*, p. 9, 1995

4 experiencing good luck or the like *AUSTRALIA*
- His eyes ran over the shining vehicle, and he recognised a Daimler. 'Struth!' Splinter corroborated his thoughts, 'are we in or are we!' —J.E. MacDonnell, *Don't Gimme the Ships*, p. 137, 1960

5 incarcerated *US, 1903*
- Guess what I've been in for?—S.E. Hinton, *The Outsiders*, p. 22, 1967

▸ **be in it**
to be actively and ethusiastically involved *AUSTRALIA, 1928*
- Reg is a certainty Kevin and he tells me you don't want to be in it. —Kevin Mackey, *The Cure*, p. 26, 1970

-in *suffix*
used in combination with a simple verb to create a communal activity as a means of protest *US, 1937*
- The "puff-in" calls for a large group to light up marijuana cigarettes in the police station, challenging the law.—*Los Angeles Free Press*, p. 5, 24th September 1964
- I'm goin' to a love-in / To sit and play my bongos in the dirt.—Frank Zappa, *Flower Punk*, 1968
- [T]he disruption of traffic by staging a mass stall-in of vintage cars on the express ways[.]—Richard Neville, *Play Power*, p. 54, 1970
- It is curious that whites have spoken thousands of times in the Vietnam teach-ins but have done so little to take the issue of the Panthers to the same audience.—*The Black Panther*, p. 18, 20th June 1970

in a minute
used as a farewell *US*
- —William K. Bentley and James M. Corbett, *Prison Slang*, p. 49, 1992

in-and-out *noun*
1 sex at its most basic *US*
- These shot-on-video features will now follow the usual formulas and should offer interesting alternatives to the usual in-and-out fare most companies are putting on tape.—*Adult Video*, p. 7, August/September 1986
- Just in town on business. Just in and out. Ha! A little of the old in-and-out.—*Fargo*, 1996
- After a minute of the ol' in-and-out, he yanks his dick out of her cunt, fumbles with his rubber (eventually snapping it off like a wet dishwashing glove), and releases tapioca onto Jasmin's belly. —Anthony Petkovich, *The X Factory*, p. 190, 1997

2 the nose *UK*
Rhyming slang for 'snout'.
- —Julian Franklyn, *A Dictionary of Rhyming Slang*, 1960
- —Ray Puxley, *Fresh Rabbit*, 1998

3 a tout; a ticket tout *UK*
Rhyming slang.
- —Ray Puxley, *Fresh Rabbit*, 1998

4 a cigarette; tobacco *UK*
Rhyming slang for **SNOUT**.
- —Ray Puxley, *Fresh Rabbit*, 1998

in-and-out-man *noun*
an opportunist thief or burglar *UK, 1957*
- —Angela Devlin, *Prison Patter*, p. 63, 1996

in a pig's valise!
used for expressing how very unlikely something is *US*
The title of a late 1990s play by Eric Overmyer.
- You think a built like that comes walking down the street every day in the week? In a pig's valise, buddy!—Max Shulman, *Rally Round the Flag, Boys!*, p. 12, 1957

in betweens *noun*
amphetamine tablets; depressant tablets; a mixture of amphetamines and barbiturates *US, 1975*
- —Richard A. Spears, *The Slang and Jargon of Drugs and Drink*, p. 271, 1986
- —Mike Haskins, *Drugs*, p. 279, 2003

inbred *noun*
a doctor with doctor parents *UK*
Medical slang.
- —Adam T. Fox, St Mary's Hospital, London, 10th October 2002

Inca message *noun*
cocaine *US, 1984*
A specific allusion to Peru, but generally a reference to South America as a source of cocaine.
- —Richard A. Spears, *The Slang and Jargon of Drugs and Drink*, p. 279, 1986
- —Mike Haskins, *Drugs*, p. 280, 2003

incandescent *adjective*
furiously angry *UK*
• They were incandescent when he skipped out of a challenge[.] — *The Guardian*, 21st March 2004

incantation *noun*
in computing, an esoteric command *US*
• This compiler normally locates initalized data in the data segment, but if you meter the right incantation they will be forced into text space. — Eric S. Raymond, *The New Hacker's Dictionary*, p. 207, 1991

incense *noun*
1 amyl nitrite or butyl nitrite *US*
The pungent vapours are inhaled, hence the term.
• — *Maledicta*, p. 227, Winter 1980: '"Lovely, blooming, fresh and gay": the onomastics of camp'
2 heroin *UK*
• — Mike Haskins, *Drugs*, p. 284, 2003

incest *noun*
sex between two similar homosexual types, such as two effeminate men *US*
• — Bruce Rodgers, *The Queens' Vernacular*, p. 113, 1972

inch-and-a-half *noun*
overtime pay at the standard overtime rate of one and a half the regular rate *US*
• — Ken Weaver, *Texas Crude*, p. 93, 1984

inch boy *noun*
a male who has or is thought to have a small penis *US*
• — Anna Scotti and Paul Young, *Buzzwords*, p. 23, 1997

include me out!
leave me out! *US, 1938*
A catchphrase coined by film mogul Samuel Goldwyn, 1882–1974.

include war *noun*
a prolonged inflammatory debate in an Internet discussion group in which the mass of former postings and counter-postings included make it impossible to follow who is saying what and when *US*
• — Christian Crumlish, *The Internet Dictionary*, p. 94, 1995

income tax *noun*
fines paid by prostitutes *UK*
• — New Statesman, 10th May 1947
• — Roger Blake, *The American Dictionary of Sexual Terms*, p. 107, 1964

incoming *noun*
enemy fire, especially artillery or mortar fire that is about to land *US*
• "This way," I said. " C'mon, move. We've got incoming." — Philip Caputo, *A Rumor of War*, p. 279, 1977
• This incredible fuckin' noise – I mean I've heard incoming, but that must have been the all-time prize. — Larry Heinemann, *Paco's Story*, p. 22, 1986

incoming!
used as a warning of impending enemy mortar or rocket fire *US*
• The scream went round the perimeter – "Incoming, hit it!" – and one hundred thirty-eight young filthy bodies scrambled for seventy foxholes. — Charles Anderson, *The Grunts*, p. 144, 1976
• Incoming! — *Apocalypse Now*, 1979
• And one of them soldiers squirting us shouts, "incoming," and he takes off running. — *Forrest Gump*, 1992

increase the peace!
used as a call for an end to violence *US*
• — *Boyz N The Hood*, 1990

indeedy *adverb*
indeed *US, 1856*
An intentionally folksy and intensifying addition of a syllable.
• Joe said, "Yes, indeedy. Just turn right on Fourteenth Place and go to Newberry, then turn left." — Iceberg Slim (Robert Beck), *Trick Baby*, p. 46, 1969

In Deep Shit *nickname*
Iain Duncan Smith, Conservative Party leader (elected 13th September 2001) *UK*
Back formation from Smith's initials: IDS.
• As for IDS, he may have been elected since the attack on New York, but it has not prevented some bright spark claiming that the initials stand for In Deep Shit. — *The Guardian*, 5th October 2001

index *noun*
the face *US*
• — Lou Shelly, *Hepcats Jive Talk Dictionary*, p. 13, 1945

India *noun*
marijuana *UK*
Variations of **INDIAN HAY** or **INDIAN HEMP**. Also known as 'Indian'.
• — Home Office, *Glossary of Terms and Slang Common in Penal Establishments*, July 1978
• — Richard A. Spears, *The Slang and Jargon of Drugs and Drink*, p. 278, 1986

Indian *noun*
1 an Indian meal, especially in, or prepared by, a restaurant *UK*
• "Going for an English"- [a satirical sketch] in which an Indian lout goes to an English restaurant in Bombay. — *The Sunday Times*, p. 7, 18th May 2003
2 an active firefighter, as distinguished from a Chief and other officers *US*
• — *American Speech*, p. 273, December 1954: 'Fire terms: additional words and definitions'

Indiana green *noun*
green marijuana claimed to have been grown in the state of Indiana *US*
• That afternoon they sold all the pot & we've had none since, save a little weak Indiana Green in chicago & some about as poor in Detroit. — Neal Cassady, *The First Third*, p. 216, 30th August 1965

Indiana pants *noun*
boots *US*
• — George Sullivan, *Harness Racing*, p. 104, 1964

Indian boy
marijuana *UK*
• — Mike Haskins, *Drugs*, p. 288, 2003

Indian charm *noun*
the arm *UK*
Rhyming slang.
• — Ray Puxley, *Fresh Rabbit*, 1998

Indian cocktail; Indian tea; Indian tonic *noun*
liquid poison as a means of suicide *TRINIDAD AND TOBAGO, 1985*
• — Lise Winer, *Dictionary of the English/Creole of Trinidad & Tobago*, 2003

Indian Country; Injun Country *noun*
during war, any area with a strong enemy presence *US, 1945*
• Area noted by reference A is definite Indian Country. — John Kerry, *The New Soldier*, p. 82, 1971
• In Vietnam, American officers liked to call the area outside GVN control "Indian country." — Frances Fitzgerald, *Fire in the Lake*, p. 368, 1972
• There is no front in this war, but we are aware that we have crossed an undefined line between the secure zone and what the troops call "Indian country." — Philip Caputo, *A Rumor of War*, p. 102, 1977
• It was in the heart of what Cunningham liked to call "Indian Country." There were MiG bases all around the area. — Robert K. Wilcox, *Scream of Eagles*, p. 255, 1990

Indian hand-rubbed *noun*
a powerful hashish from Himachel Pradesh in Northern India
• — Nick Jones, *Spliffs*, p. 82, 2003

Indian hay *noun*
marijuana *US, 1936*
• — Vincent J. Monteleone, *Criminal Slang*, p. 129, 1949
• — Richard A. Spears, *The Slang and Jargon of Drugs and Drink*, p. 278, 1986
• — Mike Haskins, *Drugs*, p. 288, 2003

Indian Heads *noun*
the Second Infantry Division, US Army *US*
So named because of the Division's insignia.
• — Linda Reinberg, *In the Field*, p. 113, 1991

Indian hemp *noun*
marijuana *US*
From 'East Indian hemp', the familiar name for *Cannabis indica*.
• — Richard A. Spears, *The Slang and Jargon of Drugs and Drink*, p. 278, 1986
• — Mike Haskins, *Drugs*, p. 288, 2003

Indian ice cream *noun*
a bitter confection made from soopolallie berries, water and white sugar *CANADA*
- To make "Indian ice cream," beat soopalallie berries and water in non-metal bowl until the foam forms. Gradually add the sugar. Beat till the foam is stiff. — Tom Parkin, *WetCoast Words*, p. 73, 1989

Indian Indian *noun*
an American Indian who has retained his indigenous culture and language *US*
- — *American Speech*, p. 272, December 1963: 'American Indian student slang'

Indian list *noun*
the Interdict list, a law forbidding a person from buying, selling or consuming alcohol; by extension any list of those who may not buy alcohol *CANADA*
- — *American Speech*, p. 272, December 1958: 'Ranching terms from eastern Washington'
- The Interdict list, also called the Indian list, prohibiting alcohol use and sale, could be applied to anyone. — Tom Parkin, *WetCoast Words*, p. 74, 1989

Indian rope *noun*
marijuana *US*
A play on 'hemp' as a material used in the making of ropes, **HEMP** (marijuana) and, perhaps, the Indian rope trick as a magical method of getting high.
- — Richard A. Spears, *The Slang and Jargon of Drugs and Drink*, p. 278, 1986

Indian steak *noun*
bologna *US*
- — *American Speech*, p. 272, December 1963: 'American Indian student slang'

Indian talk *noun*
in trucking, smoke rising from a diesel smoke stack *US*
An allusion to smoke signals used by American Indians to communicate over long distances.
- — Montie Tak, *Truck Talk*, p. 89, 1971

Indian tea; Indian tonic *noun*
▷ see: **INDIAN COCKTAIL**

Indian time *noun*
used for denoting a lack of punctuality *US*
- This is why he is not embarrassed when he is late for an appointment by white man's standards, for he kept that appointment by Indian time, which could be defined as some unspecified time following a specified time. — *American Speech*, p. 276, December 1963: 'American Indian student slang'

Indian weed *noun*
marijuana *US*
A variation of **INDIAN HAY** or **INDIAN HEMP**.
- — Richard A. Spears, *The Slang and Jargon of Drugs and Drink*, p. 278, 1986

indie *noun*
a vague categorisation within rock music, familiar since the 1980s and identified as 'serious' music that is marketed as independent and non-commercial, in its bid for commercial success *UK*
Also used as an adjective.
- Indie legends the Pixies set to reform. — *The Guardian*, 11th September 2003

Indie *noun*
▸ **the Indie**
the *Independent* (the youngest of the UK's national daily newspapers) first published in October 1986 *UK*
The Sunday edition is less well-known as 'the Sindie'.
- The Times, like the Indie, has seen its circulation slip over the past year. — *The Observer*, 1st June 2003

indie; indy *adjective*
independent *US, 1928*
- As soon as I find that Chevy I'm going indy. I'm going to buy myself a two truck, a couple of pitbulls, and run a yard. — *Repo Man*, 1984
- Based on how I worked my ass off to become one of the highest paid indie promoters in the industry, and to where I am now, with my own lable, NTL Records, Inc. — Elmore Leonard, *Be Cool*, p. 11, 1999

Indo *noun*
1 Indonesia *AUSTRALIA*
- — Trevor Cralle, *The Surfin'ary*, p. 57, 1991

2 an Indonesian *AUSTRALIA, 1966*
- The Indos don't take much notice of me – they think I'm a local. — C.J. Koch, *The Year Of Living Dangerously*, p. 36, 1978

3 marijuana cultivated in Indonesia *US*
- Rollin down the street, smokin indo, sippin' on gin and juice — Snoop Doggy Dogg, *Gin and Juice*, 1993
- — Mike Haskins, *Drugs*, p. 288, 2003

Indon *noun*
an Indonesian *AUSTRALIA, 1966*
This has for the most part died out in favour of **INDO**.
- We don't want the Indons to find out either. — Gerald Sweeney, *Invasion*, p. 44, 1982

Indonesian bud *noun*
1 marijuana cultivated in Indonesia *UK, 1998*
- — Mike Haskins, *Drugs*, p. 288, 2003

2 heroin *UK*
- — Mike Haskins, *Drugs*, p. 284, 2003

industrial language *noun*
swearing, profanity *US*
- That didn't seem to work so I used my industrial language, and told them if another ballcame over onto the field, we'd come over there with our sticks. — *Sports Illustrated*, p. 402, 18th July 1984
- McCarthy's tension was borne out by the industrial language aimed at his players. — *The Guardian*, 14th August 2003

Indy *noun*
the Indianapolis Speedway, home to a 500-mile race every May *US*
- — John Lawlor, *How to Talk Car*, p. 63, 1965

inexplicable mob *noun*
a large crowd that materialises in a public place to perform a scripted action for several minutes before dissolving *US*
- "There seems to be something inherently political about an inexplicable mob," he said. — *Wired.com*, 5th July 2003
- Well, many of us were milling around waiting for it to be exactly 7:27 and sort of steeling glances at each other and wondering who was there for this inexplicable mob[.] — *All Things Considered (National Public Radio)*, 20th June 2003

infant killer *noun*
a paedophile *UK*
Prison use, recorded August 2002.

infant mortality *noun*
the tendency of computer components to fail within the first few weeks of operation *US*
- — Eric S. Raymond, *The New Hacker's Dictionary*, p. 208, 1991

infernal *adjective*
execrable, detestable, annoying *UK, 1764*
- Even if he is not a "grave danger to our war effort" he is certainly an infernal nuisance. — *The Guardian*, 24th July 2003

infernally *adverb*
detestably, execrably, annoyingly *UK, 1638*
- It is easy to be stalwart on one side of the argument or another. It is infernally difficult to be where most voters find themselves: tacking irresolute in the middle. — *The Guardian*, 28th May 2001

infil *verb*
to *infil*trate (of military troops or spies) *UK*
Military.
- We could then infil (infiltrate) later without the bulk kit, because it was already cached. — Andy McNab, *Immediate Action*, p. 104, 1995

infinitely fine *adjective*
in computing, used as the ultimate praise *US*
- — Karla Jennings, *The Devouring Fungus*, p. 222, 1990

in flaggers *noun*
in *flagrante delicto* (in the commission of a crime; red-handed) *AUSTRALIA*
The first syllable elaborated by application of the Oxford **-ER**. Recorded in use in Australia by Alexander Buzo, 1973.

influence *noun*
▸ **under the influence**
drunk or drug-intoxicated *UK, 1937*
- — James Robert Milam and Katherine Ketcham, *Under the Influence*, 1981

info *noun*

information *US, 1907*

- Hi great mag but wot about some info on the main man Commander Tom?—*Muzik*, p. 9, February 2003

Ingersol Willie *noun*

in horse racing, the track's official timer of morning work-outs *US*

- —David W. Maurer, *Argot of the Racetrack*, p. 38, 1951

In Hock Constantly *noun*

the owner of an International Haverster Company truck *US*

A back formation from the company's initials: IHC.

- —Montie Tak, *Truck Talk*, p. 89, 1971

Injun Country *noun*

▷ see: INDIAN COUNTRY

ink *noun*

1 space or coverage in a newspaper *US, 1953*

- Got plenty of ink. Maybe we can brainwash us some famous white bitch.—Carl Hiaasen, *Tourist Season*, p. 106, 1986

2 oil *US*

- — Elementary Electronics, *Dictionary of CB Lingo*, p. 78, 1976

3 inexpensive wine *US, 1917*

- —Clarence Major, *Dictionary of Afro-American Slang*, p. 69, 1970

4 alcoholic drink *AUSTRALIA, 1977*

Probably a backformation from INKED which appears from C19.

- —Jim Ramsay, *Cop It Sweet!*, p. 48, 1977
- —Ryan Aven-Bray, *Ridgey Didge Oz Jack Lang*, p. 32, 1983
- We hopped into our police cars and broke up a brawl between a few rock apes who had filled themselves with ink over several hours.—Rex Hunt, *Tall Tales – and True*, p. 64, 1994

ink *verb*

in the production of comic books, to draw over pencil art with a pen *US*

- I ink it and I'm also the colorist. The guy next to me draws it.—*Chasing Amy*, 1997

ink-and-paper man *noun*

a counterfeiter who uses a printing press *US*

- You're an ink-and-paper man and you always have been.—Gerald Petievich, *The Quality of the Informant*, p. 6, 1985

inked; inked up *adjective*

drunk *AUSTRALIA, 1898*

- This may have been due to coming under her castigations himself, especially after arriving home so inked up that Ma had to put him to bed.—Norman Lindsay, *Halfway to Anywhere*, p. 72, 1947
- Driver [was] found well and truly inked and lying down to it.—Patsy Adam-Smith, *Folklore of the Australian Railwaymen*, p. 85, 1969

inked in *adjective*

planned *UK*

- [T]he Navy's down to the Royal Yacht and even that's inked in to be a theme park cruiser moored off Tower Bridge.—Andrew Nickolds, *Back to Basics*, p. 165, 1994

inkie *noun*

in the television and film industries, an incandescent light bulb *UK*

- —Oswald Skilbeck, *ABC of Film and TV Working Terms*, p. 69, 1960

inkie-dinkie *noun*

in the television and film industries, a 250 watt light source *UK*

- —Oswald Skilbeck, *ABC of Film and TV Working Terms*, p. 69, 1960

ink in the pen

the ability to achieve erection and to ejaculate *US*

- —Dale Gordon, *The Dominion Sex Dictionary*, p. 90, 1967

ink-slinger *noun*

a clerical employee *US, 1889*

- —Jerry Robertson, *Oil Slanguage*, p. 95, 1954

ink stick *noun*

a fountain pen *US, 1942*

- —Don Wilmeth, *The Language of American Popular Entertainment*, p. 140, 1981

inky *noun*

1 a newspaper, especially one dedicated to music journalism *UK*

- The tour was a huge success, propelling Ian to nationwide fame and on to the front cover of the inkies.—Jim Drury, *Ian Dury and the Blockheads – Song by Song*, p. 62, 2003

2 a felt-tipped pen *UK: SCOTLAND*

Used in Glasgow schools.

- Away an ask Mr Mackay for a packet of inkies and come right back with them... and don't run!—Michael Munro, *The Patter, Another Blast*, p. 35, 1988

inland squid *noun*

a surfer who does not live at or near the beach *US*

- —Mitch McKissick, *Surf Lingo*, 1987

inmate *noun*

used as a term of derision, applied to a prisoner who follows prison rules and curries favour with the prison admistration *US*

- —Inez Cardozo-Freeman, *The Joint*, p. 508, 1984

innards *noun*

1 the entrails, the stomach, the guts *UK, 1825*

A dialect and vulgar alteration of 'inwards'.

- [M]e dick spasming like artillery firing shells of what I know must just be spunk but which feels like me innards[.]—Niall Griffiths, *Kelly + Victor*, p. 91, 2002

2 the inner workings of a car's engine or transmission *US*

- —John Edwards, *Auto Dictionary*, p. 84, 1993

inner space *noun*

a person's deepest psychological being *US*

- —Joe David Brown (Editor), *The Hippies*, p. 218, 1967: 'Glossary of hippie terms'

innie *noun*

an inward-turned navel *US*

- —John D. Bell et al., *Loosely Speaking*, p. 11, 1966
- Erin's mother had paid a plastic surgeon $1,500 to transform her "outie" belly button to an "innie."—Carl Hiaasen, *Strip Tease*, p. 56, 1993

innit

isn't it?; also used as a general purpose tag regardless of grammatical context *UK, 1959*

Originally, and still, a lazily pronounced interrogative stressing the verb 'is' in the preceding sentence, e.g. 'It's raining, innit?'.

- Anyway, it turns out this house is being watched, innit[.]—Shaun Ryder, *Shaun Ryder... in His Own Words*, 1997
- It was in the newspapers, innit?—P. Watt and K. Stenson, *Cool Places*, p. 254, 1998
- [W]e are gonna 'ave a word or two about boys, wot are disgusting, innit.—Richard Topping, *Havin' It Large*, p. 40, 2000

in on *adjective*

being a part of something; participating in or sharing in something *UK, 1923*

- Are you in on the secret?—*The Guardian*, 28th October 2003

ins-and-outs *noun*

▸ **want to know the ins-and-outs of a cat's arse; want to know the ins-and -outs of a duck's arse**

to be very inquisitive *UK, 1984*

Generally in catchphrase form as 'you want to know', 'he'd want to know', etc. Variations include 'the ins-and-outs of a nag's arse', also 'of a duck's backside' and 'of a duck's bum'.

insane *adjective*

1 excellent *US, 1955*

- —Robert George Reisner, *The Jazz Titans*, p. 159, 1960
- —Trevor Cralle, *The Surfin'ary*, p. 59, 1991

2 fearless; willing to try anything for fun *US*

- —Vann Wesson, *Generation X Field Guide and Lexicon*, p. 96, 1997

3 ridiculous, in either a good or bad way *US*

- —Judi Sanders, *Da Bomb!*, p. 16, 1997

insanely great *adjective*

in computing, magnificent to a degree that can be fully grasped by only the most proficient practitioners *US*

- —Eric S. Raymond, *The New Hacker's Dictionary*, p. 209, 1991

insaniac *noun*
a lunatic *UK*
A compound of 'insane' and 'maniac'.
- They went for it like insaniacs, grimacing comically[.] —Kevin Sampson, *Powder*, p. 22–28, 1999

insanity stripe *noun*
in the US armed forces, the insignia designating a three-year enlistment *US*
- —*American Speech*, p. 238, October 1946: 'World War II slang of maladjustment'

insects and ants *noun*
men's under*pants* *UK*
Rhyming slang.
- —Julian Franklyn, *A Dictionary of Rhyming Slang*, 1960

insensitive care unit *noun*
a hospital's intensive care unit *US*
- —*Maledicta*, p. 32, 1988–1989: 'Medical maledicta from San Francisco'

inside *adverb*
imprisoned *UK, 1888*
- "He's goin inside," Dincher added, casually. —George Mandel, *Flee the Angry Strangers*, p. 89, 1952
- TICH: [indicating Grandpa] I bet he's never been inside. Have you, Grandpa? GRANDPA: Have I what? TICH: Been inside? GRANDPA: No, I haven't. I been in hospital[.] —Clive Exton, *No Fixed Abode [Six Granada Plays]*, p. 121, 1959
- Why I'd not recently seen him, is that he'd been away inside. —Colin MacInnes, *Absolute Beginners*, 1959
- Still think about geezing when you're inside? —Joseph Wambaugh, *The Blue Knight*, p. 29, 1973
- You were outside, I was inside, you were s'posed to keep in touch with the band. —*The Blues Brothers*, 1980
- I thought you were inside. —*48 Hours*, 1982
- —Angela Devlin, *Prison Patter*, p. 64, 1996

inside job *noun*
a crime committed by, or with the assistance of, someone who lives or works in the place where it occurs *UK, 1908*
- —Angela Devlin, *Prison Patter*, p. 65, 1996

inside man *noun*
in a big con swindle, a confederate to whom the victim is turned over once he has been lured into the enterprise *US, 1940*
- The inside man is the guts of a store. He makes one mistake and he's lost the mark and the score. —Iceberg Slim (Robert Beck), *Trick Baby*, p. 119, 1969

inside oil *noun*
inside information *AUSTRALIA*
- Each week hundreds of tipster letters are received in every State – generally from some other State. They inevitably declare the writer has the genuine 'inside oil'. —James Holledge, *The Great Australian Gamble*, p. 154, 1966

insider *noun*
a pocket *US*
- —Lou Shelly, *Hepcats Jive Talk Dictionary*, p. 13, 1945

inside the Beltway *noun*
literally, the area of Washington D.C. surrounded by a motorway known as the Capital Beltway; figuratively, the Washington political and journalistic establishment *US, 1977*
- "It's never good to be inside the Beltway," said Robert Squier, a political consult." "Inside the Beltway" is what one politican accuses another of being after he's just come back from a visit to his home state. —*New York Times*, p. A16, 29th May 1985
- It is that splendid region called Outside the Beltway. Why so wonderful? Because that's where the real people live. The place inhabited by the other kind of people is called Inside the Beltway. —*Seattle Post-Intelligencer*, p. E3, 20th May 1990
- I'm tired to talking to experts who never set foot outside the beltway. —*Traffic*, 2000

inside track *noun*
a position of advantage; information which provides such an advantage *US, 1857*
A figurative use of racing wisdom.
- Our correspondent Jon Henley gives you the inside track on the city [Paris]. —*The Guardian*, 12th January 2002

inside work *noun*
any internal alteration of dice for cheating *US*
- —John S. Salak, *Dictionary of Gambling*, p. 131, 1963

instaga; instagu *noun*
marijuana *UK*
- —Mike Haskins, *Drugs*, p. 288, 2003

Instamatic *noun*
a police radar unit used for measuring vehicle speed *US*
A brand name extrapolation from CAMERA (a generic term for radar).
- —*Complete CB Slang Dictionary*, p. 8, 1976

Instant Dictator Kit *noun*
in the Canadian military, items of brass and braid that transform an ordinary uniform into a ceremonial one *CANADA*
- Gold wire epaulettes, ceremonial belt, gold trouser stripes, and fancy embroidery on the sleeves – the Instant Dictator Kit could be used for bandsmen and officers. —Tom Langeste, *Words on the Wing*, p. 150, 1995

instant LZ *noun*
a 10,000 to 15,000 pound bomb used to clear jungle and create an instant landing zone in Vietnam *US*
The bomb was designed to create a wide but shallow crater in the jungle, literally creating an instant landing zone.
- —Gregory Clark, *Words of the Vietnam War*, p. 133, 133

instant zen *noun*
LSD *US*
- —Carl Chambers and Richard Heckman, *Employee Drug Abuse*, p. 206, 1972

insurance cheater *noun*
in oil drilling, a safety belt *US*
- —Jerry Robertson, *Oil Slanguage*, p. 70, 1954

intel *noun*
military intelligence *AUSTRALIA*
- Intel and Ops already know about it, but you'd better check with Chiefy Tanner to see that he's got his crews alerted. —W.R. Bennett, *Wingman*, p. 120, 1961
- —W.R. Bennett, *Night Intruder*, p. 42, 1962

intellectual *noun*
in the army, a member of the intelligence section *UK*
- At one of the lectures, one of the lance-corporal "intellectuals" of our intelligence section warned us not to carry any mail or personal photographs on to the [Falkland] Islands. —Ken Lukowiak, *A Soldier's Song*, p. 11, 1993

intellectual hour *noun*
all time spent watching cartoons on television *US*
- —Connie Eble (Editor), *UNC-CH Campus Slang*, p. 4, Fall 1980

intelligence center *noun*
a field latrine *US*
Gulf war usage.
- —*American Speech*, p. 392, Winter 1991: 'Among the new words'

intense *adjective*
extreme, wild *US*
A conventional adjective rendered slang by attitude and pronunciation; emphasis on the second syllable.
- —Douglas Simonson, *Pidgin to da Max Hana Hou*, 1982
- —Connie Eble (Editor), *UNC-CH Campus Slang*, p. 4, Fall 1984

Inter *nickname*
the intermediate examination taken after completing the first three years of secondary school in Ireland *IRELAND*
- Even if I told her I failed she wouldn't believe me seeing as how I did so well in my Inter. —Ardal O'Hanlon, *The Talk of the Town*, p. 27, 1998

Intercourse 80 *nickname*
Interstate 80, a major east–west motorway in the US *US*
- —Gwyneth A. "Dandalion" Seese, *Tijuana Bear in a Smoke 'Um Up Taxi*, p. 14, 1977

intercoursed *adjective*
exhausted *UK*
Archly euphemistic for FUCKED.
- "How was the office, darling?" "I feel utterly intercoursed." —*The Sunday Telegraph*, 11th March 1979

interesting *adjective*
in computing, annoying or difficult *US*
- —Eric S. Raymond, *The New Hacker's Dictionary*, p. 210, 1991

interesting, yes – provocative
used for expressing possible interest in what has just been said *US*
A catchphrase from the film *Tommy Boy*.
• —Connie Eble (Editor), *UNC-CH Campus Slang*, p. 5, April 1997

interior decorating *noun*
the act of having sex during the day *UK*
Upper-class society usage.
• —Ann Barr and Peter York, *The Official Sloane Ranger Handbook*, p. 158, 1982

Interlake potato *noun*
a rock *CANADA*
• The Interlake area of Manitoba was left strewn with rocks by the retreating glaciers of long ago. Rock picking is a way of life; people speak of their rock farms. This vision of rocks growing year after year is reflected in the name Interlake potato.—Chris Thain, *Cold as a Bay Street Banker's Heart*, p. 91, 1987

internal *noun*
a person who smuggles drugs inside their bodies *US*
• —Jim Crotty, *How to Talk American*, p. 89, 1997

internals *noun*
intrusive medical examinations as part of sexual role-play, especially when advertised as a service offered by a prostitute *UK*
• —Caroline Archer, *Tart Cards*, 2003

International House of Pancakes *noun*
a hospital ward for severe stroke victims, who lie in bed muttering in their own language *US*
• —*Maledicta*, p. 68, Summer/Winter 1978: 'Common patient-directed pejoratives used by medical personnel'

international milk thief *noun*
a petty thief *UK*
An example of police humour; heavily ironic.
• —David Powis, *The Signs of Crime*, 1977

interrogation by altitude *noun*
the reported practice by US troops of interrogating a group of suspected Viet Cong in a helicopter, throwing those who refused to answer to their death below and thus encouraging co-operation from those left *US*
• —Gregory Clark, *Words of the Vietnam War*, p. 249, 1990

in the nude *noun*
food *UK*
Rhyming slang.
• [T]hose who are taters in the mould [cold]; those without any in the nude at all[.]—Ronnie Barker, *Fletcher's Book of Rhyming Slang*, p. 39, 1979

in there; in thar *adjective*
excellent *US*
An allusion to surfing inside the hollow of a breaking wave.
• —Trevor Cralle, *The Surfin'ary*, p. 57, 1991

into *preposition*
1 in debt to *US, 1893*
• "Dupre lost his job," Pat said. "He's already into me for twenty dollars."—William Burroughs, *Junkie*, p. 78, 1953
• I was into him for over a hundred and he threatened to tell my boss I was usin' stuff.—Emmett Grogan, *Ringolevio*, p. 53, 1972
2 in organised crime, in control of *US*
• "The problem is, they also do business with us, indirectly. By that I mean by controlling some of our suppliers. I don't have to mention any names, I think you know what I'm talking about. Basic materials and services you need to run a hotel. Not to mention they're into a couple of unions.—Elmore Leonard, *Glitz*, p. 155, 1985
3 interested in; participating in *US, 1965*
• —Joe David Brown (Editor), *The Hippies*, p. 218, 1967: 'Glossary of hippie terms'
• Q: What are you into? LENORE: People and words, dreams and visions. But I'm not really into science and machines.—Leonard Wolfe (Editor), *Voices from the Love Generation*, p. 33, 1968
• Into: To be involved with.—*Screw*, p. 7, 12 October 1970
• I used to love jungle, but then I got much more into House and Happy Hardcore.—Macfarlane, Macfarlane and Robson, *The User*, p. 90, 1996

intro *noun*
an *intro*duction *UK, 1923*
• So it wasn't exactly like intros were needed that night in the garage when she was twelve and he was drunk and bent her over the Pontiac's front fender and went to town.—Seth Morgan, *Homeboy*, p. 3, 1990

intro *verb*
to *intro*duce *US, 1986*
• [H]e intros his latest flying visit to the world of populist archaeology.—James Hawes, *Dead Long Enough*, p. 10, 2000

invertebrated *adjective*
very drunk *US*
• —Connie Eble (Editor), *UNC-CH Campus Slang*, p. 3, Fall 1982

investment *noun*
a bet, especially on a horse race *NEW ZEALAND, 1944*
• —Harry Orsman, *A Dictionary of Modern New Zealand Slang*, p. 70, 1999

invitation *noun*
a speeding ticket *US*
A humorous euphemism.
• — "Slingo", *The Official CB Slang Dictionary Handbook*, p. 34, 1976

invite *noun*
an invitation *UK, 1659*
A verb-as-noun that began as standard English and then evolved into slang.
• Anyway, I got an invite to peace and rest.—Iceberg Slim (Robert Beck), *Airtight Willie and Me*, p. 116, 1979

in with *preposition*
in a friendly or social relationship with someone *UK, 1677*
• At night he hung around the estate's parade of shops and, as his mother says, "got in with the wrong people".—*The Guardian*, 20th April 2000

in you go, says Bob Munro
used as a toast *NEW ZEALAND*
If a real Bob Munro gave his name to this toast, he is lost in the alcohol fog of history.
• —Harry Orsman, *A Dictionary of Modern New Zealand Slang*, p. 14, 1999

in-your-chops *adjective*
direct, provocative *UK*
• [S]piky, in-your-chops pop music[.]—*The Guardian*, p. 4, 28th June 2004

in-your-face; in-yo-face *adjective*
aggressive, provocative *US*
• Yet its fast tempos [...], in-yo-face word, and down home flavor made it [...] the South's hottest rape record.—Nelson George (writing in 1988), *Hip Hop America*, p. 132, 1998

in your oils *adjective*
delighted; in your elemant *UK: WALES*
From Welsh *hwyl* (mood).
• —John Edwards, *Talk Tidy*, 1985

IOW
used as Internet shorthand to mean '*i*n *o*ther *w*ords' *US*
• —Andy Ihnatko, *Cyberspeak*, p. 102, 1997

I owe you money or what?
why are you looking at me that way? *US*
Hawaiian youth usage.
• —Douglas Simonson, *Pidgin to da Max*, 1981

IQ anniversary *noun*
the anniversary of a person's quitting smoking *US*
The 'IQ' stems from '*I Q*uit', punning on the more commonly understood sense of the abbreviation. Collected in San Francisco Bay Area, 1998.

IQ Charley *noun*
a half-wit *US*
Teen slang; unkind.
• —*American Weekly*, p. 2, 14th August 1955

irie; irey *adjective*

good, great, wonderful *JAMAICA*

- "FEELING IRIE" was the inscription on the front, with a photo of palm trees at sunset. The postcard from Jamaica was from his brother. —Donald Gorgon, *Cop Killer*, p. 49, 1994
- Oh man, it was mellow, strickly irie an' dem kinda vibes, y'know. —Donald Gorgon, *Cop Killer*, p. 98, 1994

iris *noun*

an Indian homosexual male *SOUTH AFRICA*

Gay slang, formed on the name Iris, probably elaborating the initial 'I' for 'Indian', and originating among Cape coloureds.

- —Bart Luirink (translated by Loes Nas), *Moffies*, p. 150, 2000

Irish *noun*

Irish imports, such as snuff, whisky, linen, tea, etc *UK*

Linen from 1784, snuff from 1834 and whisky from 1889.

- [T]he little shops on the corner where you got the three pennyworth of fine irish, the old snuff, and the twist of tobacco[.] —Alan Bleasdale, *Boys From the Blackstuff*, 1982

Irish *nickname*

any athletic team from Notre Dame University *US*

An abbreviation of the fuller **FIGHTING IRISH**.

- The Irish had a great team, with five all-Americans[.] —Jimmy Snyder, *Jimmy the Greek*, p. 35, 1975

Irish apple *noun*

a potato *UK, 1896*

- — *Maledicta*, p. 162, 1979: 'A glossary of ethnic slurs in American English'

Irish baby buggy *noun*

a wheelbarrow *US, 1919*

- — *Maledicta*, p. 162, 1979: 'A glossary of ethnic slurs in American English'

Irish banjo *noun*

a shovel *US, 1941*

- — *Maledicta*, p. 162, 1979: 'A glossary of ethnic slurs in American English'
- [T]he worst job aboard was "playing the Irish banjo" – that is, shoveling coal. — *Washington Post*, p. E2, 5th October 1997

Irish clubhouse *noun*

a police stationhouse *US, 1904*

- —Vincent J. Monteleone, *Criminal Slang*, p. 129, 1949

Irish confetti *noun*

1 semen spilled on a woman's body *US*

- — *Maledicta*, p. 57, 1986–1987: 'A continuation of a glossary of ethnic slurs in American English'

2 stones, bricks, etc, when used as offensive missiles *US, 1913*

- —John Ayto, *The Oxford Dictionary of Slang*, p. 176, 1998

3 small stones kept in a pocket for disciplining sheepdogs *NEW ZEALAND*

- Promptly Fred picked up a handful of gravel ... scattered the Irish confetti somewhere in its vicinity. —Ian Mackay, *Puborama*, p. 70, 1961

Irish curtain *noun*

on Prince Edward Island, a cobweb inside the house *CANADA*

- Mainers [people from the mainland] took part in the general laughter of the times about the Irish. Irish draperies and cobwebs, perhaps a bit of one-upmanship with "lace-curtain" Irish: hence "Irish curtains." —T.K. Pratt, *oral citation from Dictionary of Prince Edward Island English*, p. 80, 1988

Irisher *noun*

a person of Irish descent *US, 1807*

- We have seventy percent Jewish on the junkets, thirty percent Italian, and we bring along a couple of Irishers and Polocks to drink the booze. —Edward Lin, *Big Julie of Vegas*, p. 95, 1974
- An old man hands me a paper yarmulke, but I ask him is it all right I wear my crushed tweed hat. "You want you should look like an Irisher in a kosher house, so what difference is that to God?" he says sweetly. —Robert Campbell, *Junkyard Dog*, p. 34, 1986

Irish horse *noun*

1 salted beef *UK, 1748*

- —John Gould, *Maine Lingo*, p. 142, 1975
- — *Maledicta*, p. 162, 1979: 'A glossary of ethnic slurs in American English'

2 a flaccid or impotent penis *US*

- — *Maledicta*, p. 57, 1986–1987: 'A continuation of a glossary of ethnic slurs in American English'

Irish hurricane *noun*

a flat calm sea *US, 1803*

- —John Gould, *Maine Lingo*, p. 142, 1975

Irish jig; Irish *noun*

a wig *UK, 1972*

Rhyming slang.

- I will have to take this Irish into custody. Have you got a plastic bag or something? —Anthony Masters, *Minder*, p. 115, 1984

Irish lace; Irish lace curtains *noun*

a spider's cobweb *US, 1950*

- — *Maledicta*, p. 162, 1979: 'A glossary of ethnic slurs in American English'
- —Claudio R. Salvucci, *The Philadelphia Dialect Dictionary*, p. 45, 1996

Irish linen *noun*

in pool, the cloth used as a grip on the end of a cue stick *US*

- —Mike Shamos, *The Illustrated Encyclopedia of Billiards*, p. 124, 1993

Irishman's gate *noun*

any makeshift gate *NEW ZEALAND*

- I found my way blocked by an obstruction called in the north a 'Taranaki' gate, and in the south an Irishman's gate. —Spencer Westmacott, *The After-Breakfast Cigar*, p. 173, 1977

Irish pennant *noun*

a dangling thread on a recruit's uniform *US, 1941*

Marine humour, marine usage.

- —Linda Reinberg, *In the Field*, p. 115, 1991

Irish picnic wagon *noun*

a police van *US*

- —Claudio R. Salvucci, *The Philadelphia Dialect Dictionary*, p. 46, 1996

Irish pop *noun*

a shot of whisky and glass of beer *US*

- —Bill Reilly, *Big Al's Official Guide to Chicagoese*, p. 28, 1982

Irish rose *noun*

the nose *UK*

Rhyming slang.

- —Julian Franklyn, *A Dictionary of Rhyming Slang*, 1961

Irish shave *noun*

an act of defecation *US*

- — *Maledicta*, p. 163, 1979: 'A glossary of ethnic slurs in American English'

Irish steak *noun*

cheese *UK: SCOTLAND*

An allusion to Irish poverty.

- He grabs a big dod a the Irish Steak, slaps it between two outsiders[.] —Michael Munro, *The Patter, Another Blast*, p. 35, 1988

Irish sulk *noun*

a fit of depression after being spirited and happy *CANADA*

- — *oral informant in Dictionary of Newfoundland English*, p. 270, 1982

Irish toothache *noun*

1 an erection *UK, 1882*

- And in case you haven't heard, an Irish toothache is an erection. —Richard Farina, *Letter to Peter Tamony*, 24th August 1959

2 pregnancy *US*

- —Robert A. Wilson, *Playboy's Book of Forbidden Words*, p. 147, 1972

Irish turkey *noun*

corned beef *US, 1915*

- —Joseph E. Ragen and Charles Finston, *Inside the World's Toughest Prison*, p. 805, 1962: 'Penitentiary and underworld glossary'

Irish waterfall *noun*

a manner of cigarette smoking in which smoke is drawn into the mouth and then allowed to drift out and upwards for inhalation through the nose *UK*

- —Chris Lewis, *The Dictionary of Playground Slang*, p. 119, 2003

Irish wedding *noun*

masturbation *US*

- — *Maledicta*, p. 57, 1986–1987: 'A continuation of a glossary of ethnic slurs in American English'

Irish whip *noun*

in handball, a stroke hitting the ball close to the body *US*

- —Peter Tyson and Mort Leve, *Handball*, p. 68, 1972: 'Glossary of handball terms'

irk *noun*

▷ **see: ERK**

iron *noun*

1 a gun, especially a handgun *US, 1838*
- The town's full of old iron. —Raymond Chandler, *The Little Sister*, p. 19, 1949
- "I give you twenty dollars apiece for iron that costs you fucking nothing," Jackie Brown said. —George V. Higgins, *The Friends of Eddie Doyle*, p. 35, 1971
- Then he stood up, flicked his iron to rock and roll and gave the little zero a long burst through the Playboy mag. —*Apocalypse Now*, 1979
- I ain't gonna hassle you about the iron you carry even if it looks offensive. —Joseph Wambaugh, *The Secrets of Harry Bright*, p. 8, 1985
- We're hard on private Johnny Hams what come aroun' totin' iron. —Robert Campbell, *In La-La Land We Trust*, p. 173, 1986
- The Corcoran brothers, carrying heavy iron. —Gerald Petievich, *Shakedown*, p. 214, 1988
- He's packin' a rod. Iron. Fill you full of lead. BAM BAAM muthafucka. —Nick Barlay, *Curvy Lovebox*, p. 137, 1997

2 the penis *UK, 1706*
- —Lise Winer, *Dictionary of the English/Creole of Trinidad & Tobago*, 2003

3 money *UK, 1705*
- —*Washington Post Magazine*, p. 7, 20th September 1987

4 in the used car business, collectively the worst cars on the sales lot *US*
- —Peter Mann, *How to Buy a Used Car Without Getting Gypped*, p. 193, 1975
- Then he had a strange twinge of remorse for his cranky client because he knew the Ford wagon was tired iron. —Stephen Cannell, *Big Con*, p. 30, 1997

5 an old, dilapidated truck *US*
- —Montie Tak, *Truck Talk*, p. 90, 1971

6 in hot rodding, a custom-built chrome bumper *US*
- —*American Speech*, p. 305, December 1956: 'Hot-rodders' jargon again'

7 an older mainframe computer *US*
- —Eric S. Raymond, *The New Hacker's Dictionary*, p. 211, 1991

8 a railway track *US*
- —Ramon Adams, *The Language of the Railroader*, p. 85, 1977

▸ **push iron; bump iron; drive iron; pump iron**
to lift weights *US*
Prison use.
- "You best stick to rasslin', and – "He back-handed Cat's softening belly – "pushing iron." —Malcolm Braly, *On the Yard*, p. 342, 1967
- And sometimes I go to the weight-lifting area, strip down to a pair of trunks, and push a little iron for a while and soak up the sun. —Eldridge Cleaver, *Soul on Ice*, p. 44, 1968
- —*American Speech*, p. 201, Fall 1984: 'The language of bodybuilding'
- Gordon [Liddy] is gone now – he went off to prison and pumped iron for three years and gave them nothing but his name and his Social Security number. —Hunter S. Thompson, *Generation of Swine*, p. 104, 14 April 1986
- Let's bump some iron. —Seth Morgan, *Homeboy*, p. 224, 1990
- Only two other cons were mad enough to be driving iron on the weight pile beneath Tower Three. —Seth Morgan, *Homeboy*, p. 224, 1990
- I was pumping that iron at least three times a day. —*Boyz N The Hood*, 1990
- It was imperative that all members drive iron on a regular basis. —Bill Valentine, *Gangs and Their Tattoos*, p. 10, 2000

Iron Age *noun*
in computing, the period approximately between 1961 (the first PDP-1) and 1971 (the first commercial micro-processor) *US*
- —Eric S. Raymond, *The New Hacker's Dictionary*, p. 211, 1991

iron ass *noun*
a stern, demanding, unrelenting person *US, 1942*
- I was always the iron ass. —Leonard Shecter and William Phillips, *On the Pad*, p. 237, 1973

iron ben *noun*
a bullet-proof vest *US*
- —Vincent J. Monteleone, *Criminal Slang*, p. 130, 1949

ironbender *noun*
a severe foreman, a strict disciplinarian *CANADA*
- Dad was a good man, but a real ironbender. He was strict as a monk, and he thought of little else but work. —John Gowland, *Sinaska Trail*, p. 42, 1956

iron bomb *noun*
a conventional aerial bomb that is simply dropped from the sky without any targeting capability in the bomb *US, 1962*
- —Gareth Perry, *The Guardian*, 2nd July 1982
- The bombs that Bush knew firsthand over 40 years ago are what the military calls "iron" or "dumb" bombs, those used since World War 1 to terrify the enemy from the air by opening bomb bay doors and letting them loose. —*The Houston Chronicle*, 19th January 1991

iron box *noun*
a domestic iron *INDIA*
- —Paroo Nihalini, R.K. Tongue and Priya Hosali, *Indian and British English*, 1979

iron cure *noun*
the sudden and complete deprivation of a drug to an addict in jail who suffers intensely *US*
- —David Maurer and Victor Vogel, *Narcotics and Narcotic Addiction*, p. 418, 1973

iron curtain *noun*
a girdle *US*
- —Collin Baker et al., *College Undergraduate Slang Study Conducted at Brown University*, p. 142, 1968

iron dog *noun*
a snowmobile *US, 1961*
- —Russell Tabbert, *Dictionary of Alaskan English*, p. 231, 1991
- —Bernadette Hince, *The Antarctic Dictionary*, p. 191, 2000

iron door *noun*
▸ **behind the iron door**
in prison *US*
- —William K Bentley and James M. Corbett, *Prison Slang*, 1992

iron duke *noun*
in poker, a hand that is either certain to win or at least played as if it is certain to win *US*
- —Albert H. Morehead, *The Complete Guide to Winning Poker*, p. 266, 1967

iron girder *noun*
a murder *UK*
Rhyming slang.
- There'll be iron girders if the gaffer [boss] tumbles [discovers] what you're up to. —Ray Puxley, *Fresh Rabbit*, 1998

iron God *noun*
the Burroughs B-550 computer *US*
- —*Current Slang*, p. 1, Spring 1968

iron hat *noun*
a safety helmet *US*
Most commonly known as a 'hard hat'.
- —Jerry Robertson, *Oil Slanguage*, p. 71, 1954

iron hoof; iron *noun*
a male homosexual *UK, 1936*
Rhyming slang for **POOF**.
- The girl I'd tried to wive / was an iron call Harry Ashcroft[.] —Ronnie Barker, *Fletcher's Book of Rhyming Slang*, p. 22, 1979
- —*Maledicta*, p. 144, Summer/Winter 1986–1987: 'Sexual slang: prostitutes, pedophiles, flagellators, transvestites, and necrophiles'
- —Angela Devlin, *Prison Patter*, p. 65, 1996
- Get off yer fuckin arse and get to Brighton, and don't be getting to fuckin cosy with those fuckin irons down their either[.] —J.J. Connolly, *Layer Cake*, p. 203, 2000
- His name was Salih, but everyone called him Sal or Sally. As he was a raving iron, Sally suited him best. —Garry Bushell, *The Face*, p. 126, 2001

iron horse *noun*
a tank or other armoured vehicle *US, 1918*
- —Lou Shelly, *Hepcats Jive Talk Dictionary*, p. 46, 1945

iron idiot *noun*
an imprecise but easily manoeuvered manual sight on a tank's main gun *US, 1986*
- —Gregory Clark, *Words of the Vietnam War*, p. 150, 1990

Iron Lady *nickname*
British Prime Mininster (1979–90) Margaret Hilda Thatcher (b.1925)
Coined by the Soviet media for Thatcher's unyielding anti-communist sentiments; always used with 'the'.
- [T]hey grew up with Lech Walesa and Solidarity instead of Ronnie RayGun [Ronald Reagan] and the Iron Lady. —John King, *Human Punk*, p. 137, 2000

iron lot *noun*
a used car business specialising in old, inexpensive cars *US*
- —*American Speech*, p. 312, Autumn-Winter 1975: 'The jargon of car salesmen'

iron lung *noun*
a tip, a gratuity *UK*
Glasgow rhyming slang for **BUNG**.
- —Michael Munro, *The Original Patter*, 1985

iron man *noun*
one US silver dollar ($1) *US, 1908*
From the metal coin.
- —Lou Shelly, *Hepcats Jive Talk Dictionary*, p. 26, 1945
- —Don Wilmeth, *The Language of American Popular Entertainment*, p. 142, 1981

Iron Mike *noun*
1 a bicycle *UK*
Rhyming slang for 'bike', formed from the nickname of US boxer Mike Tyson (b.1966).
- —Ray Puxley, *Fresh Rabbit*, 1998

2 a pair of brass knuckles *US*
- —Vincent J. Monteleone, *Criminal Slang*, p. 130, 1949

Iron Mike *nickname*
US Army Major General John O'Daniel *US*
Commander of the Third Division, US Army, in World War 2, and a vocal supporter of US support for South Vietnamese President Diem.
- —Gregory Clark, *Words of the Vietnam War*, p. 250, 1990

iron mouth *noun*
any person with orthodontia *US*
- I would be in school, and notice that if a girl had braces on her teeth the other kids would call her 'tinsel-teeth' or 'iron mouth.'—*Washington Post*, p. D1, 24th November 1979

iron nose *noun*
in British Columbia, a steelhead trout *CANADA*
- I took a picture that day of Kamloops steelheader Doug Lyons holding a nineteen pound iron-nose.—*BC Digest*, p. 30, November-December 1963

iron out *verb*
1 to correct a misunderstanding, to negotiate differences and achieve agreement, to put right *UK, 1930*
- Soon those problems of payment will be ironed out. No one pretends it will be easy to start charging for something that previously came free.—*The Guardian*, 11th July 2002

2 to knock a person down; to flatten *AUSTRALIA, 1953*
- But that report did not deter two sides hellbent on grasping premiership honors, as evidenced by Darrin Pritchard being ironed out at the centre bounce of the third quarter—*Sunday Sun*, p. 9, 1st October 1989

iron pile *noun*
the area in a prison recreation yard where the weightlifting equipment is kept *US*
- —Frank Prewitt and Francis Schaeffer, *Vacaville Vocabulary*, 1961–1962
- —Paul Glover, *Words from the House of the Dead*, 1974
- They agreed to eat together in the culinary, to work out together on the iron pile or handball court, and to have a weapon within easy reach at all times.—Bill Valentine, *Gangs and Their Tattoos*, p. 27, 2000

iron pony *noun*
a motorcycle *US*
- —Lou Shelly, *Hepcats Jive Talk Dictionary*, p. 46, 1945

irons *noun*
1 handcuffs *US, 1929*
Also used in the singular.
- "Pull the sleeves down over the irons and put on that there overcoat," he directed.—Chester Himes, *The Real Cool Killers*, p. 48, 1959
- I want this bastard in irons so we can put a call in and have a car pick them up.—Donald Goines, *Daddy Cool*, p. 151, 1974
- Cat on a family dispute almost draws down on Francis when he tried to lay the iron on his wrists after the dude had went upside Momma's head.—Joseph Wambaugh, *The Choirboys*, p. 314, 1975

2 in horse racing, stirrups *US*
- —David W. Maurer, *Argot of the Racetrack*, p. 38, 1951
- I believe that this is partly because he rides with his irons ridiculously short[.]—*Daily Racing Form*, p. 4, 27th November 1959

3 tyre chains used for winter driving *US*
- —Montie Tak, *Truck Talk*, p. 125, 1971

iron skull *noun*
on the railways, a boilermaker *US*
- —Norman Carlisle, *The Modern Wonder Book of Trains and Railroading*, p. 265, 1946

iron tank *noun*
a bank *UK*
Rhyming slang.
- —Julian Franklyn, *A Dictionary of Rhyming Slang*, 1960

Iron Triangle *noun*
1 a major North Korean industrial complex between Pyongyang to the north, Chorwon to the west and Kumhwa to the east *US*
- A few days later, the ROK II Corps struck up the center of the peninsula, making for the industrial complex known as the Iron Triangle.—Robert Leckie, *The Wars of America, Vol. II*, p. 361, 1968

2 a dense jungle area near the Cu Chi District of South Vietnam, about 20 miles northwest of Saigon, dominated by the Viet Cong and the scene of heavy fighting *US*
- Did myself a tour with the 173rd Airborneski! Iron fucking Triangle, Hobo Woods, the Bo Loi Woods, Lai Khe, An Loc, Cu Chi – back in the days when Ben Suc was still a ville.—Larry Heinemann, *Paco's Story*, p. 152, 1986

iron undies *noun*
the notional underwear worn by a woman who is not willing to have sex *NEW ZEALAND*
- —Sonya Plowman, *Great Kiwi Slang*, p. 99, 2002

iron worker *noun*
a criminal who specialises in breaking in to safes *US*
- —Vincent J. Monteleone, *Criminal Slang*, p. 130, 1949
- —Hyman E. Goldin et al., *Dictionary of American Underworld Lingo*, p. 108, 1950

iron yard *noun*
the area where weight lifting equipment is left and used, especially in prison *US*
- They pulled up on each other in the Chino maximum security facility iron yard.—Odie Hawkins, *Midnight*, p. 16, 1995

I say!
used for attracting attention or for registering surprise or pleasure *UK, 1909*
- "Oooh, I say!" [Dan] Maskell would exclaim[.]—Stuart Jeffries, *Mrs Slocombe's Pussy*, p. 62, 2000

I say, I say, I say!
used as a catchphrase introduction to a corny joke *UK, 1927*
From music hall comedy routines.
- I say, I say, I say. Have you heard the one about the three kinds of people in the world? Those who can count and those that can't.—*The Guardian*, 20th December 2001

isda *noun*
heroin *US, 1977*
- —Richard A. Spears, *The Slang and Jargon of Drugs and Drink*, p. 281, 1986
- —Robert Ashton, *This Is Heroin*, p. 206, 2002
- —Mike Haskins, *Drugs*, p. 284, 2003

I see nothing.
used as a humorous expression of complicity *US*
A catchphrase from the unlikely wacky-Nazi-POW-camp-comedy television programme *Hogan's Heroes* (CBS, 1965–71). Uttered frequently by Sergeant Hans Schultz, the full phrase was 'I see nothing. I hear nothing. I know nothing!'. Repeated with referential humour.

I see, said the blind man (and he saw)
used for expressing sudden comprehension in a teasing and humorous way *US*
- The Liberian glanced around nervously. "Oh, it is nothing, I assure you. Just a few people letting off steam." "I see, said the blind man."—Odie Hawkins, *The Life and Times of Chester Simmons*, p. 194, 1991

ish *noun*
an *is*sue (of a magazine, especially a single-interest fan magazine) *US, 1967*
- —Patricia Byrd, *American Speech*, Spring 1978: 'Star trek lives: Trekker slang'
- —*American Speech*, p. 27, Spring 1982: 'The langage of science fiction fan magazines'

▸ **the ish**
a Royal Marine *is*sued with all possible kit; or a full complement of equipment *UK*
Derives from '*issue*'.
- Ping [see] the bootie [Marine] – the ish!—Nigel Foster, *The Making of a Royal Marine Commando*, 1987

-ish *suffix*

1 added to an adjective or phrase to form a less precise adjective, or to suggest a vaguer, often wider, interpretation of the preceeding adjective or phrase *UK, 1815*

- I'm quite agnostic on whether the great figure [in the Millennium Dome] is maleish, femaleish or nothingish at all. — Minister Without Portfolio Peter Mandelson, *BBC News*, 23rd February 1998

2 added to a proper name to form an adjective *UK, 1845*

- No, the Blair doctrine is not in the neo-conservative lexicon of the White House, though Bush sometimes borrows Blairish words as camouflage. — *The Guardian*, 16th April 2003

I shit them

I am superior *UK*

- Vegetarians. I shit 'em. — *Scum*, 1979

I shit you not

I am very serious *US*

- She looked like Gracie. I shit you not. — *Platoon*, 1986

I should cocoa!; I should coco!

I should say so *UK, 1936*

Rhyming slang, 'coffee and cocoa', unusually reduced to its second element. Derisive and sarcastic.

- "That is a fine philosophical point -" "I should cocoa!" said Arthur indignantly. — Anthony Masters, *Minder*, p. 175, 1984
- Do you think he'd be selling the car that cheap if there wasn't something wrong with it? I should cocoa. — Ray Puxley, *Cockney Rabbit*, 1992
- [H]e asked if there was any chance of me making it four. I should coco. — Ken Lukowiak, *Marijuana Time*, p. 171, 2000

I shouldn't wonder!

I should not be surprised *UK, 1836*

- They're probably the sort of people who Can't Believe It's Not Butter, I shouldn't wonder. — *The Guardian*, 24th December 2001

ishy *adjective*

disgusting, unappealing *US*

- — Collin Baker et al., *College Undergraduate Slang Study Conducted at Brown University*, p. 144, 1968

is it?

1 used for registering a mild disbelief *UK*

- "Yeah I'm sorry. I got pulled by the police up in Leytonstone." "Is it?" replied Millie, clearly disinterested in any excuses. — Donald Gorgon, *Cop Killer*, p. 41, 1994

2 used for indicating polite interest, astonishment, incredulity, etc *SOUTH AFRICA, 1970*

Used rhetorically without regard to gender, subject or number. Sometimes spelt 'izzit'.

- — Jean Branford, *A Dictionary of South African English*, 1978

Island *noun*

▸ **the Island**

the Isle of Wight, off the south coast of England; in particular the prisons: HMP Camp Hill, HMP Albany or HMP Parkhurst *UK*

- I had just finished a lagging on the Island[.] — Charles Raven, *Underworld Nights*, p. 126, 1956
- The Island. From the name of this nick most people think that it is a prison without bars but that is not the case — Frank Norman, *Bang To Rights*, p. 54, 1958
- — Angela Devlin, *Prison Patter*, p. 65, 1996
- [T]hose IRA geezers down on the Island. The Parkhurst Brigade of the Provisional IRA. — J.J. Connolly, *Layer Cake*, p. 39, 2000

Isle of Man *noun*

a pan *UK*

Rhyming slang, formed on the name of the island off the north west of England.

- Bung some bangers in the Isle of Man[.] — Ray Puxley, *Cockney Rabbit*, 1992

Isle of Wight *noun*

a light *UK*

Rhyming slang.

- — Ray Puxley, *Fresh Rabbit*, 1998

Isle of Wight *adjective*

1 right; both as an expression of approval and indicative of direction *UK*

Rhyming slang, formed from the name of the island off the south coast of England.

- — Julian Franklyn, *A Dictionary of Rhyming Slang*, 1960

2 tight (in a state of drunkenness or mean with money) *UK*

Rhyming slang.

- — Ray Puxley, *Cockney Rabbit*, 1992

I smell bacon!

there are police nearby! *US*

A catchphrase from *Wayne's World*, heard before but popularised by it.

- — Connie Eble (Editor), *UNC-CH Campus Slang*, p. 4, Fall 1993

ism *noun*

▷ see: **IZM**

isn't it?

used rhetorically, without regard to gender, subject or number: is that not so? *SOUTH AFRICA, 1956*

- — Jean Branford, *A Dictionary of South African English*, 1978

isn't that special?

used for expressing sarcastic disdain *US*

From Dana Carvey's 'Church Lady' skit on *Saturday Night Live*.

- — Connie Eble (Editor), *UNC-CH Campus Slang*, p. 5, Spring 1987

Israelite *noun*

1 a Jewish person *US*

- A little way down the street an Israelite with a thick coat collar, broad-brimmed hat and cigarette at the corner of his lips is just letting himself into his house. — Douglas Rutherford, *The Creeping Flesh*, p. 97, 1963

2 someone who is temporarily without money *JAMAICA*

- Whenever time you is down and out – busted – haven't got any bread – you call yourself an Israelite. — Desmond Decker, 1969

issue *noun*

a problem *US*

Often used in a mocking way, borrowing from the lexicon of self-improvement and popular psychotherapy. Most often heard in the plural.

- — Connie Eble (Editor), *UNC-CH Campus Slang*, p. 4, Spring 1999
- — Don R. McCreary (Editor), *Dawg Speak*, 2001

issues *noun*

crack cocaine *UK*

- — Mike Haskins, *Drugs*, p. 282, 2003

-ista *suffix*

when combined with a subject-noun, a follower or afficianado of something or someone *UK*

From Spanish. An example is **FASHIONISTA**.

- Blairista [for UK prime minister Tony Blair], Clintonista [for US president Bill Clinton], Portillista [for Conservative politician Michael Portillo], garagista [garage music], tequilista [tequila], sandalista [sandals], feminista [femininsm]. — Susie Dent, *The Language Report*, p. 17, 2003

Is the Pope (a) Catholic?

yes; a nonsense retort used as an affirmative answer to a silly question, often sarcastic *US*

Often mixed with the synonymous **DO BEARS SHIT IN THE WOODS?** to achieve **DOES THE POPE SHIT IN THE WOODS?**. Used in the UK since the 1970s.

- "Do you think we can find anything?" "Is the Pope Catholic?" — Stuart Browne, *Dangerous Parking*, p. 267, 2000

I suppose *noun*

a nose *UK, 1859*

Rhyming slang.

- He was a truly ugly man – his north and south drooped, his mince pies were watery, and he had a big red I suppose — Ronnie Barker, *A Sermon in Slang*, 1979

I swallow!

used as a cry of submission *UK*

- [H]e decided he'd had enough and shouted, "No more Eddie, I swallow, I swallow"[.] — Brian McDonald, *Elephant Boys*, p. 185, 2000

iswas *noun*

a contemptible, very much disliked person *UK*

This appears to be a compound of 'is' and 'was' and is therefore perhaps implying that the person so described is (soon to be) in the past tense. Noted in connection with a legal dispute over rap lyrics by *BBC News*, 6th June 2003.

Is your father a glass maker?
used to suggest that somebody in front of you at a public event sit down and stop blocking your view *TRINIDAD AND TOBAGO*
- — Lise Winer, *Dictionary of the English/Creole of Trinidad & Tobago*, 2003

it *noun*
1 sex *UK, 1599*
- It took us some time to figure out why there were so many pretty young girls whoring in Baltimore. If they left home to sell it, why didn't they go to New York? — Jack Lait and Lee Mortimer, *Washington Confidential*, p. 274, 1951
- Was there something – uh – wrong with me, perhaps? Didn't I like "it"? — Jim Thompson, *Roughneck*, p. 89, 1954
- Prostitutes; ten quid for it, a fiver for a hand job. — Irish Jack (writing of the 1960s), *History, The Sharper Word*, p. 31, 1998

2 the penis *US, 1846*
- MARY'S DAD: You got what stuck? TED: It. MARY'S DAD: It? Oh, it. — *Something About Mary*, 1998

3 a short-term sexual partner, a casual pick-up *UK*
- — Paul Baker, *Polari*, p. 178, 2002

4 in male homosexual usage, a heterosexual male or a homosexual male who is not part of the speaker's inner circle *US*
- — *Male Swinger Number 3*, p. 46, 1981: 'The complete gay dictionary'

It *noun*
sweet vermouth *UK, 1937*
Originally *It*alian vermouth as used in 'gin and it'.

it ain't over 'til the fat lady sings
used as a humorous aphorism meaning that something is not over until it is over *US*
The battle cry of those who are about to lose.
- Yeah, well, it ain't over til the fat lady sings. — *A Few Good Men*, 1992

ital *adjective*
natural, unadulterated; (of food) organic, salt-free; (of sex) without a condom *JAMAICA*
- Lloyd finished the last can of Tennants, turned up the music and rolled up an ital spliff without tobacco. — Donald Gorgon, *Cop Killer*, p. 23, 1994

Italian airlines *noun*
walking *US*
- — *Maledicta*, p. 57, 1986–1987: 'A continuation of a glossary of ethnic slurs in American English'

Italian mausoleum *noun*
a car boot (trunk) *US*
From the stereotype of the corpses of Mafia murder victims being stuffed in car boots.
- — Bill Reilly, *Big Al's Official Guide to Chicagoese*, p. 38, 1982

Italian shower *noun*
a liberal application of aftershave or scent *UK*
- A quick Italian shower, another look in the mirror and Russell was off[.] — Greg Williams, *Diamond Geezers*, p. 19, 1997

ITALY
written on an envelope, or at the foot of a lover's letter, as lovers' code for 'I trust and love you' *UK*
Widely-known, and well-used by servicemen but, apparently, has not transferred to the coded vocabulary of texting. Used by John Winton in *We Saw the Sea*, 1960.

itch *noun*
▸ **he (she) wouldn't give you the itch**
said of a person with a reputation for meanness *UK*
In Glasgow use.
- [H]e wouldny gie ye the itch. — Michael Munro, *The Patter, Another Blast*, 1988

itch *verb*
to have a desire to do something *UK, 1225*
- I was itching to know more about her mother. — Sue Monk Kidd, *The Secret Life of Bees*, p. 144, 2002

itch and scratch; itch *noun*
a match (a vesta) *UK, 1931*
- The cheapest form of ignition is a box of "itches". — Ray Puxley, *Cockney Rabbit*, 1992

itchy backside *noun*
said of a restless person *SINGAPORE*
- — Paik Choo, *The Coxford Singlish Dictionary*, p. 50, 2002

itchy feet *noun*
1 attributed to a person who is restless *UK, 1984*
- He landed a job working in radio in Quebec, but had itchy feet and one winter decided to visit Nicaragua[.] — *The Guardian*, 2nd December 2002

2 attributed to a prison inmate who is considered to be a potential absconder *UK*
A specialisation of 'have itchy feet' (to be restless).
- — Home Office, *Glossary of Terms and Slang Common in Penal Establishments*, July 1978

itchy pussy *noun*
a Mitsubishi car *US*
- — Lewis Poteet, *Car & Motorcyle Slang*, p. 112, 1992

ite
all right (as an adjective, or a greeting) *UK*
A shortening of 'all right'. Teen slang.
- — Susie Dent, *The Language Report*, p. 76, 2003

item *noun*
a romantically-linked couple *US, 1981*
Expressing a commitment that the two individuals be considered as a single item.
- Said he thought we were an item! We were but we hadn't ever talked. — Sally Cline, *Couples*, p. 136, 1998

Itie *noun*
an Italian *UK, 1941*
Variation of **EYETIE**.
- You don't look like an Itie ter me. — Nino Culotta (John O'Grady), *They're A Weird Mob*, 1957
- The boy was pale. Could have passed as an Itie or a Spic [Spaniard]. — Greg Williams, *Diamond Geezers*, p. 9, 1997

Itie *adjective*
Italian *AUSTRALIA*
- A larrikin smart-arse gambler, an Itie lair, plus a good mate of that Jazza and Guido, two no-goods who would finish up in the boob or worse. — Clive Galea, *Slipper*, p. 16, 1988

-itis *suffix*
used to create imaginary medical conditions, such as lazyitis (congenital laziness) and cobitis (an aversion to prison food) *US, 1912*
- Maybe the Premier was suffering from a bad case of electionitis. What is electionitis? I have never once suggested that the Premier suffered from a case of electionitis. I don't even know what it is. — *Hansard (British Columbia, Canada)*, 12th May 1982

it's all good
used for expressing optimism or a sense that all is well in the world *US*
- — Connie Eble (Editor), *UNC-CH Campus Slang*, p. 6, April 1995
- — Don R. McCreary (Editor), *Dawg Speak*, 2001

it's been great
used as a farewell *US*
- — John D. Bell et al., *Loosely Speaking*, p. Appendix, 1969

it's been real
used as a farewell, suggesting that the time spent together has been enjoyable *US*
- — Connie Eble (Editor), *UNC-CH Campus Slang*, p. 7, Spring 1982
- As they say in the movies, it's been real. — *The Guardian*, p. 56, 24th May 2003

it's better to give than receive
used as a declaration that it is better to be the active rather than passive partner in homosexual anal intercourse *UK*
A charitable philosophy.
- I bet he was one of the "It's better to give than receive" school as well, always had one of the waifs and strays in tow. — J.J. Connolly, *Layer Cake*, p. 194, 2000

it's breakfast!
used by firefighters in the woods to mean that the fire is out and their work is finished *US*
- — *American Speech*, p. 205–209, Summer 1991: 'The language of smokejumping – again'

it's dead
the issue being discussed need not be discussed any further *US*
- —Gary K. Farlow, *Prison-ese*, p. 33, 2002

it's hard to feel good about that
used as an intentionally laconic expression of sympathy or commiseration *US*
- —Connie Eble (Editor), *UNC-CH Campus Slang*, p. 4, Fall 1987

it's not my job
used for expressing a lack of interest in helping to do something *US*
A signature line of comedian Freddie Prinze on the television comedy *Chico and the Man* (NBC, 1974–78). Repeated with referential humour.

it's not the end of the world!
offered as consolation to someone who has suffered a mishap *UK, 1984*
- "Of course I am disappointed but this is not the end of the world," said [skier Stephan] Eberharter. "I have had good results all season and it should pay off here."—*The Guardian*, 11th February 2002

it's on!
used for announcing the start of hostilities between youth gangs *US*
- —Dale Kramer and Madeline Karr, *Teen-Age Gangs*, p. 175, 1953

it's the oil that counts
in oil drilling, used for expressing doubt about any new process, equipment or idea *US*
- —Jerry Robertson, *Oil Slanguage*, p. 71, 1954

it's there
used as a stock answer about something that is acceptable but not great *CANADA*
- —Jack Chambers (Editor), *Slang Bag 93 (University of Toronto)*, p. 4, Winter 1993

itsy bitsy *noun*
the vagina *US*
Childish euphemism.
- The name stuck. Yes, there it is, my Itsy Bitsy.—Eve Ensler, *The Vagina Monologues*, p. 88, 1998

itsy-bitsy *adjective*
tiny *US, 1938*
- Two, three, four, tell the people what she wore / It was an itsy-bitsy, teen-weeny yellow polka-dot bikini / That she wore for the first time today.—Brian Highland, *Itsy-Bitsy Teeny-Weeny Yellow Poka-Dot Bikini*, 1960
- He's shorter than me, and I'm only six! He was this little, itsy-bitsy man. He was a little, little man.—*Avalon*, 1990

it's you
used as a greeting *US*
- —Malachi Andrews and Paul T. Owens, *Black Language*, p. 86, 1973

it takes all sorts
an elliptical variation of the homespun philosophy: it takes all sorts to make a world (or a universe) *UK, 1951*
- [T]hat odd mixture of "it takes all sorts" tolerance with the social conservatism of the natural snob[.]—*The Guardian*, 13th September 2003

it takes one to know one
you are as bad as the person you are criticising *UK, 1984*
- It takes one to know one, and believe me, [Peter] Mandelson's behaviour has been recognisable.—*The Guardian*, 27th January 2001

itty *adjective*
tiny *UK, 1798*
A childish form of 'little'.
- "[H]ack it up into a zillion itty bits and – " "No, we don't chop down any trees," Sairy said.—Sharon Creech, *Ruby Holler*, p. 71, 2003

itty-bitty *adjective*
tiny *UK, 1938*
A reduplicated variation of **ITTY**, perhaps by combination with **BITTY**.
- Kitchen workers dole out itty-bitty portions of the organic meals[.] —*The Guardian*, 6th July 2004

Ivan *noun*
a Russian, especially a soldier; the nation of Russia; sometimes used in the plural to represent Russians in general *US, 1944*
Originally military; the popular male forename is the Russian equivalent to John.

ivories *noun*
1 the teeth *UK, 1782*
- The bastard jammed a shotgun in my mouth. Knocked out half my ivories and thought my brains were going to follow them.—Christopher Brookmyre, *Boiling a Frog*, p. 213–214, 2000

2 the keys of a piano or a similar instrument *UK, 1818*
- [T]hat was how we got Joe Sullivan on the ivories.—Mezz Mezzrow, *Really the Blue*, 1946

3 dice *US*
- —Frank Garcia, *Marked Cards and Loaded Dice*, p. 262, 1962

4 billiard balls *UK, 1888*
- —Steve Rushin, *Pool Cool*, p. 17, 1990

▸ **spank the ivories**
play the piano in a jazz-style *US*
- Eart Hines one of the cleverest piano players in the country... VOICE 1: sure spanks the ivories... VOICE 2: ... ain't that boy hot!—Frederic Ramsey Junior, *Chicago Documentary*, p. 31, 1944

▸ **tickle the ivories**
to play the piano *UK*
- They want someone to "tickle the ivories" during the afternoons and in return receive no pay, just free beer.—*Wanstead & Woodford Guardian*, 31st October 2002

ivory flake *noun*
cocaine *US*
- DEALER: Hey, man. You wanna cop some blow? / JUNKIE: Sure, watcha got? Dust, flakes or rocks? / DEALER: I got China White, Mother of Pearl, ivory flake. What you need?—Grandmaster Flash & The Furious Five featuring Melle Mel, *White Lines*, 1983

ivory soap *noun*
in dominoes, the double blank piece *US*
- —Dominic Armanino, *Dominoes*, p. 17, 1959

Ivory Tower *noun*
used as a metaphor for an attitude that is elitist, intellectual and removed from the real world *US, 1911*
- Nobody," said Pearl, "can accuse you of being an ivory-tower professor. Political science is a living, breathing subject, and the way you teach it is real and vital.—Max Shulman, *The Many Loves of Dobie Gillis*, 1951
- The piece was crutched and flawed by the usual contrived soul shit that white writers and Ivory Tower black scribes use when writing about street Niggers.—Iceberg Slim (Robert Beck), *The Naked Soul of Iceberg Slim*, p. 199, 1971

I wonder!
I doubt it!, I can't believe it!; I think it may be so *UK, 1922*

I wouldn't fuck her with your dick
used as a jocular disparagement of a woman's sexual attractiveness *US*
- "I wouldn't fuck her with your dick!" was the consensus.—Earl Thompson, *Tattoo*, p. 291, 1974

I wouldn't kick her out of bed; I wouldn't kick that out of bed
used as an expression of general sexual interest *UK, 1984*
Sometimes elaborated as 'I wouldn't kick her out of bed for farting' or '... for eating crackers'.
- RACHEL: Do you see what all the guys see in her? MONICA: Wouldn't kick her out of bed. No more vodka for me!—*Friends (Episode 12, Series 9)*, 2003

ixnay
no *US, 1929*
Pig Latin for 'nix'.
- Ixnay, solider. Or I'll have three guards on you before you can say Jesus.—Robert Edmond Alter, *Carny Kill*, p. 3, 1966
- I swear by the time he got around to askin me for it you could hear his brain sizzlin through his ears, and like a fool I told him ixnay[.]—Seth Morgan, *Homeboy*, p. 8, 1990
- Ixnay, dude, I tried that. She's out for the night.—*Airheads*, 1994
- Spade said, "Ixnay – Rock's a fruit."—James Ellroy, *Hollywood Nocturnes*, p. 34, 1994
- Ixnay on the big appetite.—*Something About Mary*, 1998

-iz- *infix*

used as an infix to hide the meaning of a word *US*
Used in prison and other fields with a tentative relationship to the law. 'Dope' becomes 'dizope'.

- —John R Armore and Joseph D. Wolfe, *Dictionary of Desperation*, 1976

-iz-i *infix*

an embellishment that adds no meaning to a word *US*
Popularised by Frankie Smith in the 1999 song 'Double Dutch Bus'.

IZM; ism; izm *noun*

marijuana *US*

- Spread the ism around until the ism reach each end—Redman *How To Roll A Blunt*, 1992
- —Mike Haskins, *Drugs*, p. 288, 2003

Izzy *noun*

any Jewish male *US*

- —Vincent J. Monteleone, *Criminal Slang*, p. 130, 1949